PUBLISHER'S PAGE

This is the second edition of the Global Directory.

Last year I wrote: "We look forward to compiling the second edition. Lawyers and clients, we hope, will then be familiar with the Chambers concept and will be more relaxed about commenting on law firms and practitioners."

Fortunately, this has proved to be true. Our researchers have had an excellent response. Both lawyers and clients knew what to expect, and understood our research methods.

For those who may still be uncertain about our methods, let me clarify.

One misunderstanding continues to come to our notice. Some people still assume that lawyers can 'buy their way in' to our directory. This is not so. Inclusion in our rankings, and in the accompanying text, is based solely on our market research. If the reputation of a lawyer or firm is high enough, they are included.

Then, having been included, their name is also included in the 'profile' sections. They either have a standard profile or, if they wish, they pay for an extended profile.

Please see page 7 for further explanation.

THIS YEAR, in addition to a new focus on IP we have added four new countries: Cuba, Moldova, Haiti and Puerto Rico. We have also extended our research in most of the other countries, covering more areas of practice and industry sectors.

As readers will see, we have divided the book by country this year, not by practice area (as last year).

Michael Chambers
Publisher.

CONTENTS

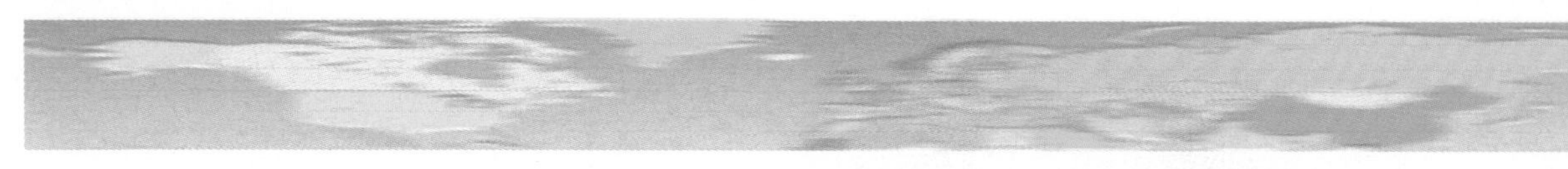

INTRODUCTION

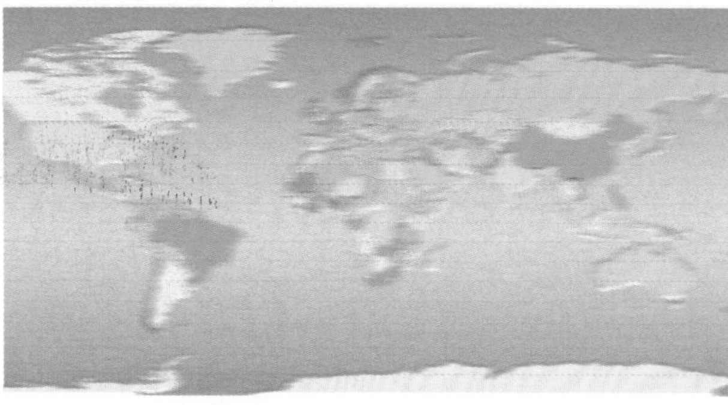

COUNTRIES

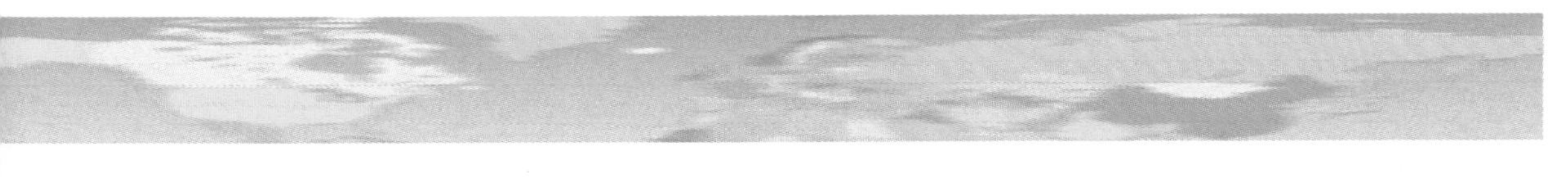

IN-HOUSE LAWYERS

FIRM PROFILES

A-Z OF LAW FIRMS

OTHER RECOMMENDED FIRMS

INDEXES

FIRM INDEX

CHAMBERS GLOBAL 4000

Chambers & Partners Legal Recruitment:
+44 20 7 606 8844

Published by **Chambers & Partners Publishing**
(a division of Orbach & Chambers Ltd)
Saville House, 23 Long Lane, London EC1A 9HL
Tel: +44 20 7 606 1300 **Fax:** +44 20 7 600 3191

Publisher: Michael Chambers
Editor: James Fairweather
Deputy Editor: Rieta Ghosh
Assistant Editor: Catherine Willberg
Editorial Assistant: Jo Morgans
Profiles Manager: Mark Lomelí
Profiles Assistants: Richard Pettet, Anna Quine, Laura Gladwin, Hayley Whiting, Charlotte Brown

Project Co-ordination: Fiona Boxall
Database Manager: Derek Wright
Production Manager: John Buck
Production Assistant: Paul Cummings
Business Development Manager: Brad Sirott
Distribution Manager: Tony Adams

Orders to: Chambers & Partners Publishing
Also available on CD-Rom

Printed in England by Polestar Wheatons Limited

ISBN: 0-85514-361-4

INTRODUCTION

ABOUT THIS GUIDE

This Guide is not like other Guides. It is independent. It is objective. It is research-based. It's not simply a collection of paid-for entries. No lawyers can get into this guide unless they have strong recommendations in the market. No-one can 'buy his way in.'

We have produced a similar guide to lawyers in the UK every year since 1990. It is used by clients to identify suitable lawyers in over sixty specialist areas of practice.

Other law firms use it to refer work. Individual lawyers use it when assessing the merits of their competitors. Candidates use it when deciding which law firm to join. It has an influence in the profession unequalled by any other guide or directory.

We now bring this tradition to bear on the global guide. Like the UK guide, it seeks to reflect the judgement of the market. Our team of researchers (see their biographies on the overleaf) interviewed thousands of leading practitioners and clients world-wide, canvassing their opinions on who they thought were the best lawyers and why.

Unlike the UK guide, this guide only covers global areas of practice. To cover all specialisms would be impossible. The areas chosen are Arbitration, Banking & Finance, Capital Markets, Communications, Competition/Anti-trust, Corporate/M&A, Energy & Natural Resources, Intellectual Property, Private Equity, Project Finance, Shipping and Tax.

For this second edition we have expanded our geographical coverage, adding Cuba, Haiti, Moldova and Puerto Rico. We have also added new specialist areas to many countries.

HOW TO USE THIS GUIDE

The guide is organised alphabetically by country – from Albania to Zimbabwe. Within each country we cover areas of practice where there is significant activity. In Greece, for example, we have covered Corporate/M&A and Shipping. In India we have covered Corporate/M&A and Project Finance. The focus is on areas of law which are international, such as Communications, Energy and Capital Markets.

In many countries we have simply covered Corporate/Commercial law. Here, we have pin-pointed the best general commercial practitioners in countries which do not have sophisticated legal systems. These lawyers tend to be those that have been used on a regular basis by instructing foreign firms or major multi-nationals.

Leaders in their field

The tables of individual lawyers are selective. Only those who have been strongly recommended are included. Unlike *Martindale-Hubbell*, this guide is not a comprehensive listing of every international lawyer. The names in our tables are at the very top of their profession, and have gained international recognition in the market.

Every lawyer recommended in our tables is given the opportunity to supply biographical details which we publish at the end of each country's editorial.

Firm Profiles

Firm Profiles provide factual details about the firms. This information has been supplied by the firms themselves.

All the law firms mentioned in the guide are listed here. However, some firms choose to buy extra space, and their details are included in 'Full Firm Profiles' beginning on page 955. Details of the other firms are contained in 'Other Recommended Firms' beginning on page 1483.

Best Business Lawyer Survey

We carried out a 'Best Business Lawyer' survey in 15 countries, which reflects the opinion of clients. The results can be found page 36.

Indexes

Full indexes to firms and individuals are at the back of the book.

CHAMBERS RESEARCH TEAM 2001

Chambers researchers work full-time for six months researching the legal profession. They conduct thousands of telephone interviews discussing the strengths of leading specialists and their rankings. This research provides an objective survey of the profession's leading practitioners throughout the world.

- **Rieta Ghosh (Deputy Editor)**

Read Ancient History at University of Durham. Former Client Information Manager with European market research agency. Previously worked as a recruitment consultant at a leading business advisory company.

- **Anna Williams**

Solicitor (1991) Read Human Sciences at St Anne's College, Oxford. Practised commercial property and social housing at a top West End firm for eight years.

- **Lloyd Pearson**

Read Politics at University of Leeds. Worked as a political researcher for a government minister. Subsequently took up graduate scheme in publishing and worked as researcher for a travel organisation.

- **Paula Wasley**

Read English at Princeton University and took Diploma in French at the Sorbonne. Subsequently a bi-lingual assistant at a top Paris Hotel and a research assistant to a correspondent at the Paris office of a major news agency.

- **Sheena Lee**

Solicitor. Read Chemistry at University of York. Trained with leading niche City practice specialising in environmental law and personal injury. Qualified in 1997 and practised personal injury at legal aid firm.

- **Ross Cogan**

Read Philosophy at Nottingham University. M.Phil at St. John's College, Cambridge. PhD in Logic from Bristol in 1998. Has taught at several universities and previously worked in underwriting.

- **Robert Wainwright**

Solicitor. Read Law and English at University of Queensland, Australia. Practised mainly litigation in Queensland and wrote for a national legal journal.

- **Ian McLachlan**

Read Classics at Brasenose College, Oxford. Worked in Italy for three years, first as an English teacher, then as a writer and translator for a computer software company. Has recently written a novel. Fluent in Italian.

- **Angela Woodruff**

Solicitor. Read Psychology/Criminology at Melbourne University followed by Law at Monash University. Trained in Melbourne in general commercial law before joining the banking and finance practice of a leading Australian law firm.

- **Michael Leigh**

Gained a First in Philosophy from Bristol University, where he also completed a doctorate in modern social contract theory. Has taught ethics and political philosophy, and undertaken freelance satire for local newspapers.

- **Helen Smith**

LLB Law and Spanish at Cardiff University and Universidad de Oviedo. Taught TEFL in Ecuador and has lived in Spain and the US. Bilingual. Future trainee solicitor with medium City firm.

- **Barbara Gruber**

Read Law at University of Munich, Germany. In-house lawyer at a German regional television station and then at an IT company. Last worked for a personal injury law firm in Miami, Florida. Bi-lingual.

- **Daniel Freed**

Read Politics and Modern History at the University of Manchester. Gained experience in broadcasting, journalism and youth work before travelling extensively.

- **John Doy**

Read English Literature and Language at Mansfield College, Oxford. Previous experience includes working for a local advertising publication and the National Opinion Poll.

- **Fleur Darkin**

Graduated from Bretton Hall with a First in Fine Art, and received a Masters with Distinction in Philosophy at Leeds. Has worked as a writer and an artist.

- **Petra Einwiller**

Member of the Berlin Bar. Read Law at University of Cologne. Practiced law in Potsdam and Berlin, specialing in employment law. Regularly represented clients at court.

- **James Cowdell**

Barrister. Read Modern History at The Queen's College, Oxford. Practised at the Criminal Bar for five years and was a fee-earner in the family department of a leading London law firm.

- **Caroline Murphy**

Graduated from Brasenose College, Oxford, with a First in Classics. Previously freelanced for The Independent newspaper.

- **Irena Sabic**

Read Law at University of Cambridge (New Hall College), specialising in international human rights. Bilingual.

- **Matthew Butt**

UCL Law graduate. Previously served full time as President of the University of London Union and has worked as a communications consultant. Member of British National Debate team 2000.

- **Vanessa Lyus**

Read Philosophy and Politics at Bristol. Has worked in international research for two years.

- **David Nicholls**

Read Theology at Keble College, Oxford, before working as a political researcher for an MP and the campaign Business for Sterling.

REGIONAL OVERVIEWS

Africa (Sub-Saharan)

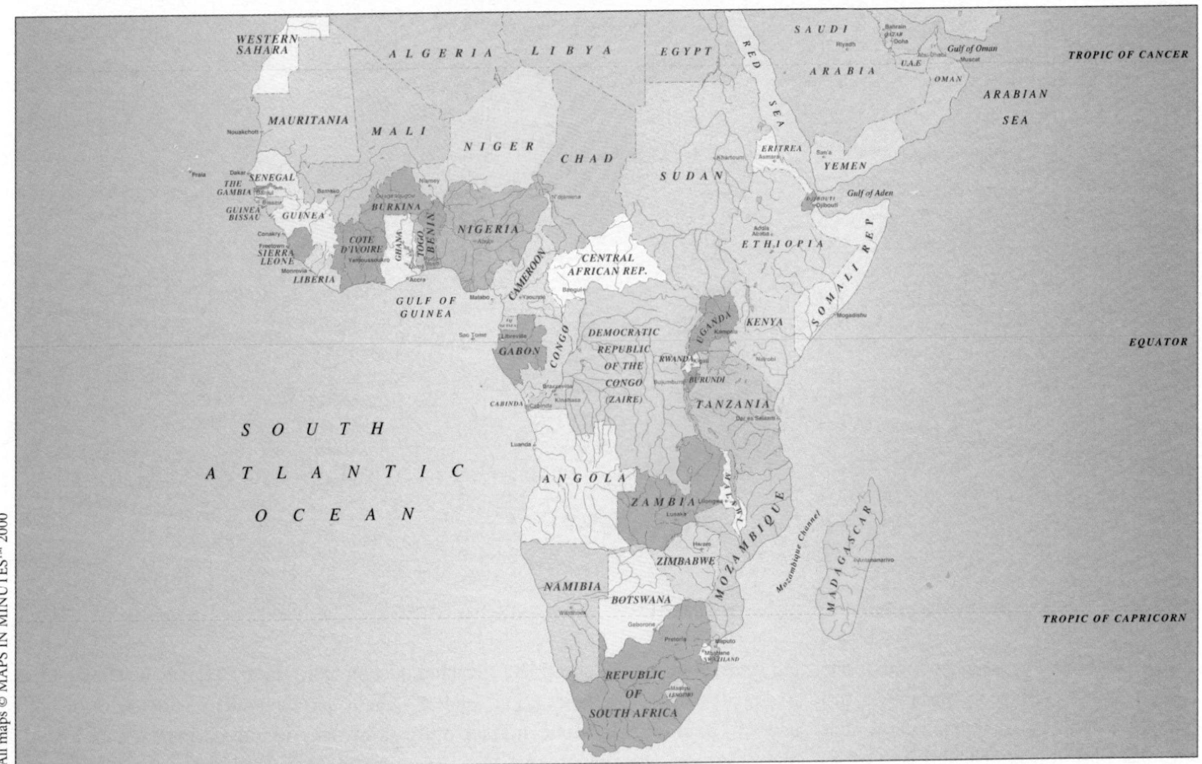

There is a great contrast between the North and South of this vast continent. While the *Maghreb* countries have some established law firms with western educated lawyers, the legal market in sub-Saharan Africa is shaped far more by the political situation in each individual country. Many of the firms have close links to the government or one of the national parties, and in some countries an election or *coup d'état* results in the search for a new lawyer.

The anomaly is, of course, South Africa. Six years after the end of apartheid and the transition to majority rule, black empowerment schemes, deregulation and the wider trend of privatisation are shaping the country's identity. That said, the success of black empowerment schemes remains under debate. With the continent's largest financial and banking institutions based in Johannesburg, there is no shortage of work for local lawyers who service the industry. Tony Behrmann of Werksmans remains South Africa's star. Combining intellect and experience, his commercial practice is internationally esteemed.

The final wave of privatisation seems to be now sweeping through Africa. The opening up of many African markets attracting foreign investment is occurring far more than ever before. Africa is a continent rich in natural resources and, as most countries have access to either oil and gas or mineral reserves, it is these sectors which are developing rapidly.

France has long been an important economic and political player throughout Francophone Africa with many of the best African legal experts based in Paris, such as esteemed practitioner Stéphane Brabant of Herbert Smith. Dealing with legal or commercial matters in many African countries requires an intimate knowledge of local custom, practice and language. The foundation of Lex Africa, the first truly pan-African network of leading law firms, has done much to boost intra African business.

Australasia

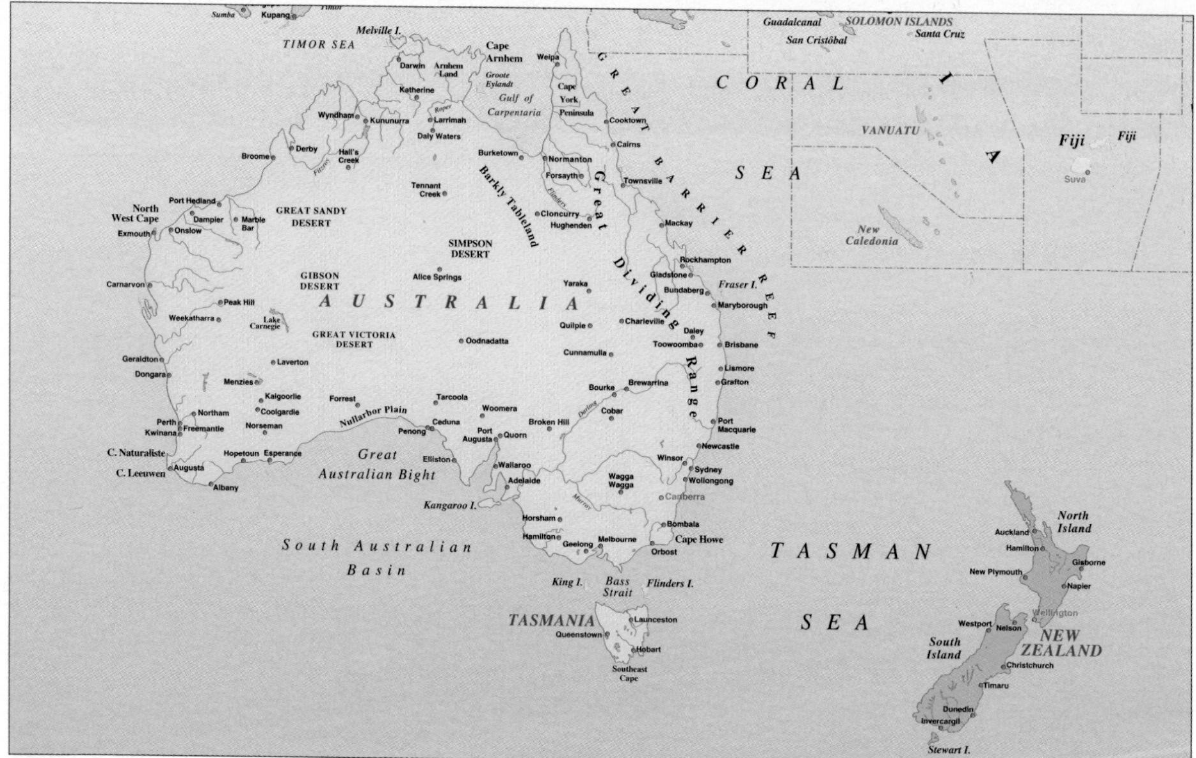

Australasia has seen a period of stability with consolidation and growth in banking, energy and communications. Firms such as Mallesons Stephen Jaques and the component firms of the Allens Arthur Robinson Group have spread their domestic dominance into the Asia Pacific region, changing the nature of the legal landscape. In New Zealand, Bell Gully remains the biggest national firm with a stellar international and domestic client base. Chapman Tripp has a premier reputation for banking work and Russell McVeagh is rated for its dominance of the syndicated loan market.

Consolidation in the corporate and financial markets has led to speculation over the future legal landscape. Mallesons' global aspirations were set back with the collapse of merger talks with Clifford Chance and subsequently Linklaters. However, global giants should be attracted to local firms for their high quality lawyers, booming domestic market and ambitions to access the rest of Asia.

Mallesons Stephen Jaques The firm has consolidated its leading status in the region. It is again ranked in the top band in all ten Australian sections including our new intellectual property section. Its strongest offices overall are in Sydney and Melbourne, although it is universally viewed as being "*strong across the board and across the nation*" with a "*treasure chest of stars and support acts*" in all of its offices.

Like other top Australian firms, it has continued its expansion into the Asia-Pacific region, although the recent fall-through of its merger talks with Clifford Chance and Linklaters has given it pause for thought in its aspirations to take a larger role on the world legal stage. Its client list reads like a who's who of both domestic and international giants, including Telstra and BHP, and National Australia Bank, for whom it has recently been appointed as principal legal counsel in Australia until October 2003.

CHAMBERS' TOP FIVE FIRMS

1. Mallesons Stephen Jaques
2. Allens Arthur Robinson Group
3. Freehills
4. Clayton Utz
5. Blake Dawson Waldron

Indeed, one practitioner was moved to comment that "*the other firms get work because Mallesons and Allens can't act for everyone.*" In light of the firm's consistently high reputation in recent years, it seems that the question is not whether the firm will put in a strong overall performance next year but just how strong that performance will be.

The Allens Arthur Robinson Group The Group has been hot on the heels of Mallesons this year, with top band ratings in nine of the ten Australian sections through the combined practice and personnel strengths of its member firms Allen Allen & Hemsley and Arthur Robinson & Hedderwicks. Like Mallesons, the Group is seen to have "*an impressive and extensive list of blue-chip clients, depth of expertise and truly national coverage,*" and also has increasing presence and respect throughout the Asia-Pacific region.

However, its Achilles' heel in this year's rankings is seen to be its telecommunications and IT practice. The Group is widely perceived to have suffered now that its lone telco sharpshooter, Ian McGill, has been made managing partner resulting in a "*significantly lower profile in the market.*" It is this lower rating which has put it marginally behind Mallesons this year. Having said that, the status of the Group as one of the country's strongest law firms (or, more accurately, strategic alliance of law firms) is well-established.

Freehills This firm has maintained its top band rating in the areas of corporate M&A, energy & natural resources and project finance. It also received premier rating for its intellectual property practice. Rated for capital markets work, John O'Sullivan is seen to have a "*golden reputation in acting for underwriters.*" Viewed as "*one of the best in the Sydney market for management buy-out work,*" the multi-faceted John O'Sullivan has risen in prominence since Peter Hay's elevation to become National Executive of the firm. In tax much of the firm's strength lies with its Sydney office.

The firm's project finance practice continues to be one of its strongest, having built on the reputation gained through advising the Victorian government on its privatisation programme. In this sphere, the "*ultra-commercial*" Nicholas Grambas acts for a number of blue-chip lending institutions. In the energy sector, Robert Nicholson is seen to be "*a national benchmark for energy transactions*" while Susan Taylor is an "*excellent regulatory lawyer*" who has been particularly active in the Victorian electricity and gas sectors. Undeniably a force to be reckoned with domestically, the firm has now set its sights firmly on expanding its operations in the Asia-Pacific market.

Clayton Utz Although perceived by the market to be slightly off the pace in comparison to our troika of leaders, it is nevertheless rated as "*the best of the rest by a considerable margin*" in the corporate field. Key to the firm's profile is Rod Halstead, perceived as being "*always on the ball technically*" with "*good corporate nous.*" The firm is also seen to have a "*first-class*" capital markets lawyer in Brian Salter, who "*leads the firm's securitisation team by example.*" Two tax practitioners, Allan Blaikie and David Cominos, are held in high regard by competitors and have "*thoroughly deserved*" national profiles. Still some way from the market leaders Mallesons, Allens and, to a lesser extent, Freehills, the firm has yet to enter the truly premier league of Australian law firms.

Blake Dawson Waldron A stable practice that has had a good showing in *Chambers Global.* The firm scored well for its tax and corporate activity. It is also highly rated for its banking & finance practice, where Melbourne-based John Field is seen to be "*a star all-purpose finance lawyer,*" and in its competition practice, where John Kench is a long-established and "*phenomenally efficient*" practitioner in Sydney. The firm has an active energy & natural resources practice, a healthy private sector client base in oil and gas, and a respectable public sector client base in the water market. However, while the firm has performed solidly overall, like Clayton Utz, it forms the second tier of the market at present.

Eastern Europe

Allen & Overy Across the region as a whole, A&O continues to lead the field by a long way. Ranked in thirteen of our tables, it secured the top slot in seven of them. The Bratislava office, opened just last year, jumps straight into the front rank of Slovakian firms. Warsaw and Prague remain the strongest offices and have been expanding as the firm takes advantage of healthy markets, while the Moscow outfit, over-dependent upon Russia's moribund international capital markets, has been reined back.

Considered *"one of the best for banking and finance,"* with a great referral network, it is seen to focus on the largest and most complex international transactions. Several clients commended the firm as the place to go for derivatives, securitisations or structured products – all nascent fields in eastern Europe. One of the best project finance practices in the region, it has recently been involved in the largest ever Polish power sector project, the $333 million financing of the Chorzów plant, where it advised Dresdner Kleinwort Benson.

White & Case LLP In an outstanding year for the firm, it increased its showing in our tables from eleven to thirteen sections, making the first band of five of them. Strong across the whole region in energy, communications and project finance, it is particularly recommended for capital markets work and cross-border M&A.

This year's merger with Feddersen has underlined its commitment to the region and improved its profile in the all-important German market. In the Czech Republic, despite the loss of a team of ex-Feddersen people to Altheimer & Gray, the firm now has the country's largest corporate team and, in Michal Dlouhý, arguably its leading lawyer.

CHAMBERS' TOP SIX FIRMS

1	Allen & Overy
2	White & Case LLP
3	Baker & McKenzie
4	Clifford Chance Pünder
5	Linklaters
6	Weil, Gotshal & Manges

Warsaw is also strong, while the superb privatisation practice of the Budapest office and its highly influential managing partner István Réczicza won repeated plaudits. Most impressive, however, is the near incredible turn-around of the Moscow office. New managing partner Hugh Verrier is credited with taking it from nothing last year to *"one of the strongest firms around"* with a lot of work for EBRD and IFC, including the $150 million loan to Lukoil, EBRD's largest loan to a Russian company since 1993.

Baker & McKenzie One of the region's largest firms, its full service strategy has had mixed results across the region. Rated in fourteen specialist areas in eight countries, more than any other firm, it manages only three top band rankings. These are in Azerbaijan, Kazakhstan and the Ukraine. The approach works well in the developing conditions of the Russian economy, where it is considered *"one of the most important players in the domestic market."*

The large, well-respected office in Warsaw was further affected by losses of high-profile personnel while Budapest remains the strongest link in its chain. The small but busy Czech office, unranked last year, emerged from the shadows, advising KBC Bank on the $1.1 billion privatisation of ČSOB. Many of the year's highlights have been on-going work on high-profile privatisations and project work, like the A2 Toll Motorway, the financing of which was announced in 1999 but completed late in 2000.

Clifford Chance Pünder With offices in central Europe's major commercial centres, where this firm appears it is frequently top. Nowhere is this more true than Moscow, where *"any discussion of the leading corporate firms has to start with them."* Weathering the bleak economic conditions better than most, it has been involved in some outstanding transactions including the London Club restructuring of Russia's $22 billion external debt and AT&T's $5 billion acquisition of IBM Russia's global network assets.

Across central Europe the benefits of the Pünder merger are witnessed as the firm's profile is raised amongst important German clients. In Hungary the corporate department has achieved *"premier league"* status, and it has one of the best telecoms practices in Budapest. However, its core finance practice was hit by the loss of a team to Linklaters. Warsaw had a good year representing the Ministry of the State Treasury on the $4.3 billion sale of 35% of TPSA, an agreement finally tied up on 25 July 2000.

Linklaters The region's most improved firm, this year it secured ten rankings, three in the top band. The Czech office has particularly impressed, achieving prominence with a series of loans and a high-profile international bond issue for the City of Prague. In Hungary it made a splash when Csaba Berecz set up the office with a team taken from Clifford Chance, catapulting it straight into the first band of our banking tables.

In a quiet market it has featured in some impressive transactions, including advising the lead managers on the HUF45 billion MTN programme for MATÁV. Elsewhere the firm's commitment to the region has been demonstrated by its recruitment of the bulk of the Burns Schwartz offices in Romania and Slovakia, and high profile appointments to the Warsaw office, previously an alliance firm. Only Russia has bucked the trend. In line with the moribund conditions, the firm has downsized in Moscow and closed its St Petersburg office.

Weil, Gotshal & Manges A highly focused operation, it concentrates on central Europe and its strengths in international capital markets, cross-border M&A, privatisation and real estate. With only three offices in the region, the firm attained seven rankings, with five in the top band. Competitors repeatedly praised the seamless nature of its property practice. The small Budapest office is recommended for general corporate work and private equity, while both the Polish and Czech offices have consolidated their superb reputations this year with high-profile transactions. These include the privatisation of PKN in Poland, and the CZK5 billion bond issue for the Czech Export Bank.

Latin America

Its well-established stability in all the major jurisdictions, and a lack of trans-border presence of any local firms, makes Baker & McKenzie *the* firm for regional coverage. Venezuela, Argentina and Brazil are by far the largest markets on the continent, and so our leaders have greatest activity in these countries. Cuba is a new addition to our Latin American coverage.

Baker & McKenzie This international network puts in a solid performance in all jurisdictions where it is present. The most notable office is in Venezuela, where it is outstanding, achieving top rankings in corporate and energy. Its strength lies in its breadth of coverage; with 12 regional offices and nine outstanding individual practitioners ranked in *Chambers Global*, no other firm comes close to challenging its extensive representation. Benefiting from referrals, these offices are often shielded from the vagaries of the local market while being kept somewhat apart from national legal circles.

All branches of the firm are among the best in their countries for corporate/M&A work, and represent an impressive array of big-ticket multi-national, largely US corporates, such as Procter & Gamble, Sony, AT&T, BAT. In Brazil and Venezuela, the firm also has strong domestic clientele. Admirable results are seen in office collaboration on cross-border M&A transactions, such as the series of acquisitions by AT&T and the establishment of AT&T Latin America. The firm also has extensive experience in acting for concessionaires in the privatised utilities and energy sector.

Pinheiro Neto The largest firm in Brazil and one of the strongest. It is top tier in four areas of practice (banking & finance, communications, competition/ anti-trust, corporate/commercial) with 14 practitioners ranked by *Chambers Global*. Clients enthuse about a "*proactive*" service.

The firm's banking and finance department is particularly outstanding. Overseen by Antonio Mendes, "*one of Brazil's leading finance gurus,*" it was involved in all three of the year's leading banking/M&A deals. In addition, the widely admired Esther Nunes is opening up a strong communications practice, while the project finance group is "*making a major effort out of its regional offices.*"

Tozzini Freire Teixeira e Silva This is a hi-tech, young firm that has rapidly become a market leader. It is top tier in four areas of practice (communications, competition/anti-trust, corporate/ commercial, project finance), with nine individuals ranked by *Chambers Global*. Such rapid growth has led to market accusations of "*variable quality*," but the firm is generally considered a model for up and coming Brazilian firms.

Much of the firm's current success can be attributed to star-ranked (in corporate/M&A) Syllas Tozzini. Other major names include Jose Emilio Nunes Pinto, a "*pioneer*," who heads up the firm's renowned project finance department. The firm is also noted for its "*conscientious, professional*" telecoms group.

Machado, Meyer, Sendacz e Opice Powerful all-round firm "*well-connected in the financial world*." Star-ranked Jose Roberto Opice described as "*the best finance lawyer in Brazil*," is the name to look for. His areas of expertise include banking & finance, corporate/ commercial and project finance. The firm was rated top-tier in all three of these categories this year with nine ranked practioners (including Opice.)

The M&A practice is particularly active, and has scored some notable deals in the telecoms sphere. On the project finance side, the firm's Rio office has recently been boosted by the arrival of a group of oil and gas lawyers from Veirano Advogados. The firm has also extended its influence internationally by forming an alliance with Spanish organisation Cuatrecasas, as well as firms in Portugal and Argentina.

Marval O'Farrell & Mairal The largest firm in the country enjoys an excellent reputation in an enviable spread of practice areas. It is ranked top in four of the five listed focus areas, and has seven individuals considered leaders in their fields. Despite rapid growth in recent years the consistency of its lawyers is praised, as is its international clientele, including many international banks. The firm started the current trend of international associations, by forming an alliance with Demarest & Almeida of Brazil and Uría y Menéndez of Spain. It also has an office in New York.

CHAMBERS' TOP FIVE FIRMS

1. **Baker & McKenzie**
2. **Pinhiero Neto**
3. **Tozzini Freire Tiexeira e Silva**
4. **Machado, Meyer, Sendacz e Opice**
5. **Marval O'Farrell & Mairal**

Famed for advising YPF on its takeover by Repsol last year, this year the firm acted on the acquisition of part of Grupo Clarín by a group of investment funds, led by Goldman Sachs. It has also established excellent practices in communications, where it represents a number of big name telecoms and IT corporates, and competition, to complement its strong M&A practice, where it has one of few acknowledged experts in the field.

Middle East & North Africa

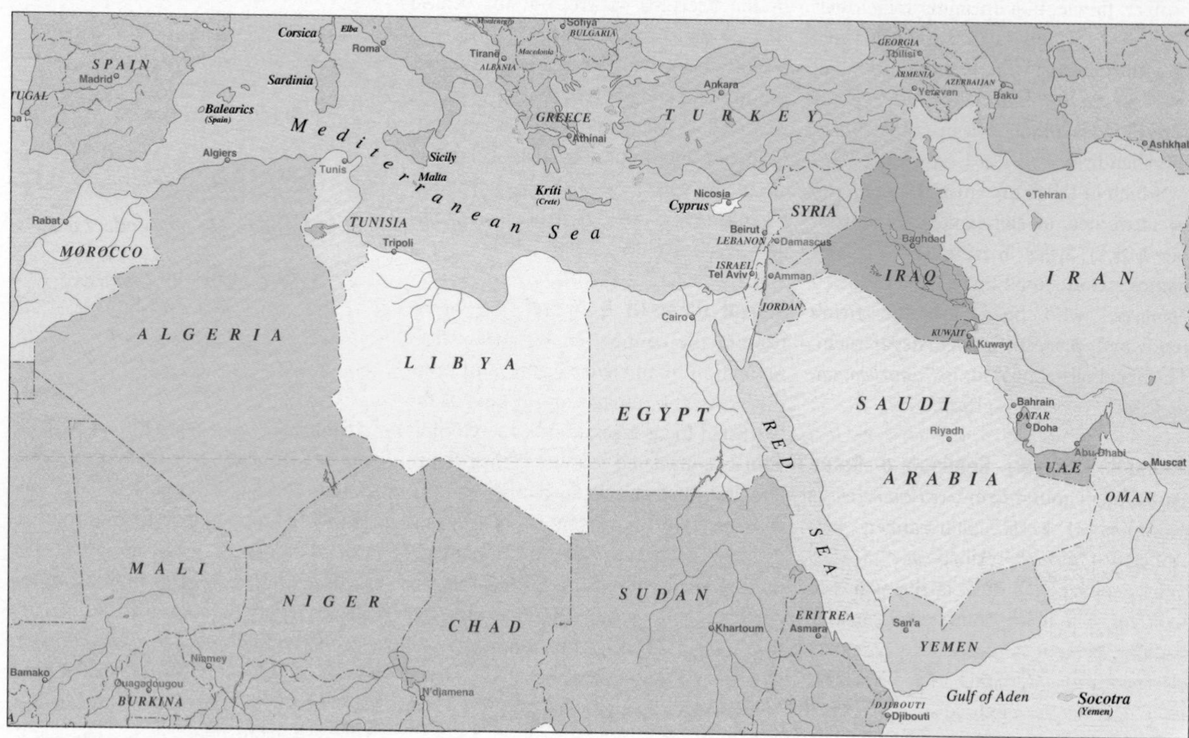

Many countries in the Middle East and North Africa are now enjoying burgeoning economic and social development following times of recession or political conflict. However, these countries are still led by their counterparts in other developing economies such as South East Asia and Latin America.

The Middle East's energy sector continues to play an integral role in the region's economy and political standing internationally. The dynamic new economy, embraces a broader revenue base that includes information and resources technology, privatisation and service industries such as tourism.

The shortages of investment funding and currency crises are among factors that have caused an ebb in energy related projects. However, as privatisation moves up the political agenda, independent power plants have been developed in countries such as Egypt, Oman, the United Arab Emirates and Morocco. Several countries including Egypt, Oman, Saudi Arabia, Qatar, Jordan and Morocco have wholly or partially privatised their telecom systems. Other sectors undergoing restructuring include electricity and water systems, postal services, construction and transport facilities.

This wealth of business opportunities presents *"a lot of high quality work for relatively few lawyers in a narrow market."* Practices distinguish themselves by virtue of their strong regional bases and pedigree. Arabic language skills and grounding in local custom and tradition are essential for successful interpretation of Islamic Shari'a law, the primary basis of regulations throughout the region.

UAE Abu Dhabi is the focus of federal government and large projects work.

CHAMBERS' TOP FOUR FIRMS IN THE MIDDLE EAST & NORTH AFRICA

1. **Trowers & Hamlins (Oman, UAE, Bahrain, Egypt)**
2. **Baker & McKenzie (Saudi Arabia, Egypt, Bahrain)**
3. **Richards Butler (Abu Dhabi, Oman, Qatar)**
4. **Denton Wilde Sapte (UAE, Egypt, Oman, Turkey)**

Middle East & North Africa

Corporatisation of its power and water industry provided the template for the Middle East's first privatisation law. Dubai's Internet City and its free port area at Jebel Ali, cement its reputation as the main trading point for the Gulf region. While **Trowers & Hamlins** and **Denton Wilde Sapte** have offices in both cities, Dubai's more liberal commercial environment makes it the preferred regional base for most foreign firms. **Allen & Overy** opened there in 1978 while Clifford Chance recently consolidated its operations there, after closing down its offices in Saudi Arabia and Bahrain.

Allen & Overy's strong government connections originate from its work on the Emirates' Airlines formation in 1985. Experts in high end complex financings, their recent work includes advising the arrangers led by ANZ Grindlays of the UAE's $1 billion Thuraya Satellite project. With its splendid regional practice and sector specialisms, Clifford Chance scored high profile transactions including privatisations of Saudi and Omani telecoms.

Saudi Arabia Riyadh is home to its banking sector, while shipping and commerce are concentrated in its port city, Jeddah. Amidst much speculation, the Middle East's biggest oil exporter is gradually opening out to foreign investment. With prospects of WTO membership in the offing, its laws are undergoing unprecedented evolution. Saudi's projects sector revival appears imminent in light of recent government negotiations with leading oil and gas companies. The stage is set for pioneering privatisation of its telecoms system with **Baker & McKenzie, White & Case** and **Clifford Chance** representing the key players.

Bahrain The Gulf's major financial hub, is one of the most liberal economies in the region with the highest rates of foreign investment. It recently achieved ratification of a bilateral investment treaty with the US. **Norton Rose**'s benchmark banking practice underlies its reputation in corporate work and project financings. The firm advised Bahrain Telecommunications Company (Batelco) on its multi-million dollar investment in the Kuwait-based Quality Net.

Qatar faces stellar economic prospects. Straddling the world's largest natural gas reserves, it has recently announced its co-operation on gas supply with Kuwait and plans are underway for the cross-border LNG Dolphin Project, a gas pipeline to neighbouring states. The Kuwaiti government has sought international participation in a $7 billion project to develop its Northern oil fields bordering Iraq.

Egypt A liquidity crisis has created a drain on local financing, although corporate work has reportedly been booming. Projects remain a struggling sector with few developments since the Sidi Krir private sector power project deal. The country's anticipated privatisation programme appears to have lost momentum. Meanwhile, the legal community awaits the ratification of privatisation-related legislation by the newly elected People's Assembly. **Baker & McKenzie, Trowers & Hamlins** and **Denton Wilde Sapte** are key examples of foreign firms with local affiliations, although there is a trend towards a more western style among domestic firms. The Shalakany Law Office remains the doyen of Egyptian firms. A top scorer in all three sector rankings, this firm's banking and finance expertise is second to none. Its recent work includes the first $500 million plus GSM Telecom Concession to MobiNil.

Turkey has witnessed the introduction of privatisation laws, a banking supervisory board, and a general swell in M&A work. That said, many foreign firms are forced to handle major project finance deals from abroad owing to ever-tightening practice restrictions. Established ahead of its competitors in 1985, **White & Case** has the edge in cross border transactions. The firm recently represented the sponsors in the $1.45 billion project financing of the 1210MW imported coal IPP in Southern Turkey. Scoring equally highly in all three sector ranks, **Hergüner Bilgen & Özeke** is distinguished among local firms for its government links and expertise in telecoms and energy.

Israel A booming high-tech based economy is the Middle East's showcase. Herzliyya or 'Silicon Wadi' is driving the market. Although opportunities abound, the legal market is reaching saturation levels and prospects of cross-border law firm mergers and multi-disciplinary practices loom in the horizon.

Trowers & Hamlins Active in the Middle East for over 40 years, it remains the number one international practice. Since first opening in Oman, the firm has rapidly gained momentum with further offices in the UAE in 1990 and Bahrain eight years later, culminating in the Cairo office from May last year. The firm also has associations in Jordan and Yemen. Working closely with its London-based International Projects team, its regional coverage is fortified by the Saudi Arabian and Kuwaiti client base of its Bahrain office.

Senior management moves have done little to deflect the firm's inexorable advance in Oman. It has worked on several key projects including the Sultanate's water and electricity privatisation programme. The pinnacle of the team's portfolio is for United Power Co, developers for the Gulf's first BOOT infrastructure power project at Manah.

The Manama office has made considerable progress in closing the gap with Norton Rose, particularly in banking and project finance. Stronger regional focus combined with its wider client representation appear to be key factors in the firm's success. A new Cairo office is already making headway in project finance and consolidating its regional expertise in IT, telecoms, power and oil and gas in pace with Egypt's changing economy.

Middle East & North Africa

Baker & McKenzie Lacking an office in the UAE, the global titan has focused its attentions westward to Saudi Arabia and Egypt, where it has operated since the early eighties under the names of its associate local firms. The Riyadh office remains the pre-eminent corporate and finance practice, tending a glittering client roster. Notably the team acted on the restructuring of the $850 million loan to the Arabian Industrial Fibres Company (Ibn Rushd.)

Advisors to the government in its tentative forays into economic reform, the firm has been involved in development of the stock market, water, electricity and telecoms privatisations. In emerging foreign investment, the firm has ongoing work with Saudi Telecom Company (STC) on two original BOOT projects. The market is tracking the development of its freshly opened office in Bahrain, as it competes against the stronghold of Norton Rose's banking practice.

Founded in 1985, the Cairo office represents the longest established formal international affiliation in the Egyptian legal market. Its domestic counterpart, Helmy & Hamza, is one of the local elite, with influential contacts in business and government circles. Often opposite the kingpin, Shalakany Law Office, the firm has been involved in Egypt's privatisation and debt conversion programmes from the outset, covering its first privatisation, Telecom Egypt's IPO.

Richards Butler With over 30 years' experience in the UAE, the firm has vindicated its atypical choice of Abu Dhabi as its first international base by building links with government bodies and the local business community. Its resources are strongly focused in commercial and projects related matters throughout Oman, Saudi Arabia, Kuwait and Egypt.

A ubiquitous presence, the firm has considerable expertise in deregulation and privatisation matters. Jointly with London, it recently advised the purchasing consortium in relation to the $508 million privatisation of Jordan Telecommunications Company. Affiliations with local practices in Oman and Qatar have boosted the firm's presence. Successfully converging its banking and privatisations expertise in the south, the Muscat office has gained a pivotal role advising the Oman Gas Company on the $410 million Oman LNG Project.

The firm's Doha office represents Qatar's first foreign legal affiliation. Acting for major Qatari financial institutions in relation to non-energy sector matters, its recent clients include Commercial Bank of Qatar in a £120 million private sector loan agreement and Qatar Industrial Development Bank.

Denton Wilde Sapte With a network of offices encompassing the GCC states, Egypt, Turkey and Gibraltar, the firm commands the widest regional spread among its peers. Its presence has mushroomed following its take-over of Fox Gibbons' veteran Middle Eastern practice and the 1999 merger with Wilde Sapte.

As a pioneering presence in several countries, much of the firm's kudos originates from its strong governmental links throughout the region. Making an impressive debut on the UAE's privatisation programme, the firm advised the Abu Dhabi government on the regulatory framework for privatisation of its water and electricity sectors.

The Muscat practice undertakes an analogous role for the government, having been involved in key projects including Oman's first IPPs, the 275MW Al Kamil power project and the $450 million Barka Power and Desalination IPP Project. The firm's Cairo office is also advising the Egyptian government on regulatory matters relating to its telecoms, IT and water sectors. It also boasts a unique presence in Turkey via its joint venture consultancy with Denton Güner Fox & Gibbons, a vibrant Istanbul practice. With its estimable corporate and commercial expertise, this office is the one to watch.

North America

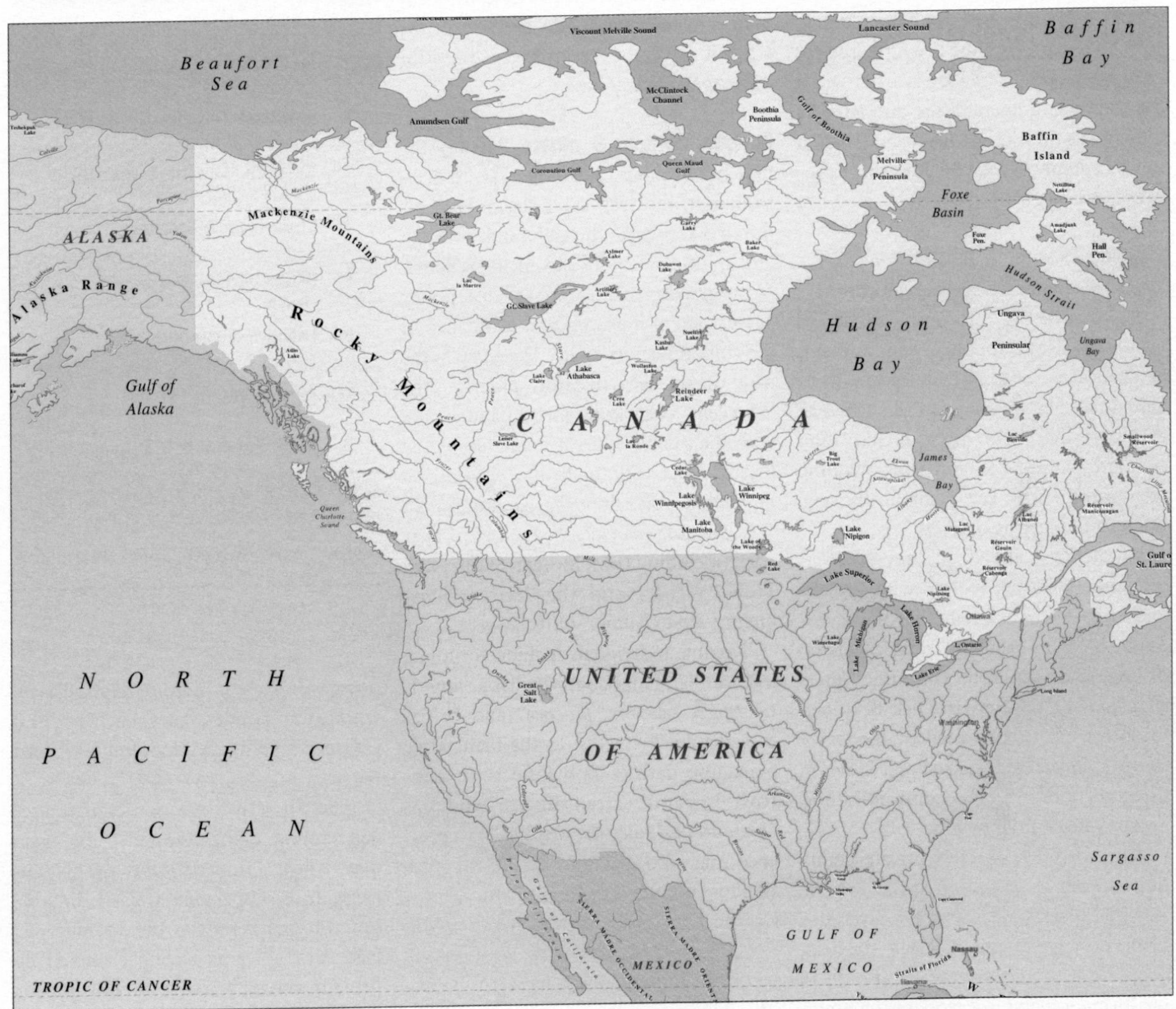

Skadden, Arps, Slate, Meagher & Flom
Memorably described as the "*giant that ate New York,*" Skadden has certainly not stopped there. Unrivalled in its national depth, the "*expansionist*" attitude of this successful full service practice has made it a familiar sight across many jurisdictions.

Big ticket M&A is the engine which drives this firm and there is no greater figure than the legendary Joe Flom. Although less seen at the battle-front this year, his tactical skills and supreme command of corporate America have promoted the firm world wide. The firm has twenty-one offices and is a major force in Europe. At home it has built up an expertise in corporate restructurings and financing in both Chicago and Palo Alto. The only firm to set up in LA in the early 80s, it is now a dominant force on the West coast.

Full service since the 70s, across the board levels of excellence were noted by our researchers. Capitalising on opportunities created by European convergence, anti-trust guru Barry Hawk continues to operate on both sides of the Atlantic and the tax team is involved in the more creative side of financial product structuring.

The banking practice is growing steadily, cultivating relationships with all investment banks rather than being tied to the fortunes of one. Producing big names in the capital markets (Tom Kunz and Matt Mallow for example,) it is at the cutting edge of creative developments. It dominates the equity markets acting for the issuer which can come as no surprise considering the firm's global corporate

North America

clients. Ranked as a leader in project finance, energy and communications, the firm has set out to dominate all industry sectors. Its rapid growth has garnered negative comment, with the firm critcised for its fielding of 'B-team' players. That said it has the pick of lateral hires, and with 54 individuals ranked in *Chambers Global*, it is has certainly developed powerful, innovative attorneys.

Simpson Thacher & Bartlett One of the largest law firms in New York, its attorneys are consistently recommended to *Chambers Global* for their commitment, excellence and integrity. Indeed 28 individuals receive a ranking. The success of the firm is due in part to the its cultivation of highly profitable and long-standing relationships with key clients in the corporate and banking market.

It attracts global players such as Seagram (tripartite merger with Vivendi and Canal+ this year) and has made corporate M&A its priority. Strong leadership distinguishes the firm with the "*broad shoulders*" of LBO doyen Dick Beattie at the helm. He is supported by the "*razor sharp*" Casey Cogut, ranked as a leader in three sections; M&A, comm-unications and private equity buyouts.

The fortunes of LBO private equity houses such as Kohlberg Kravis Roberts and The Blackstone Group has given this firm a powerful presence. It leads the field, adopting a 'cradle to grave' approach to the formation and exit work of the funds. As these clients go global so has the partnership with well-established offices in Asia and London.

This corporate powerhouse is more than matched by a superb banking team. In acquisition finance and the syndicated loan market its relationship with Chase Manhattan has the envy of the market. It provided much of the volume and cutting edge work for stars such as the "*constructive and personable*" Frank Huck. In project finance the firm has yet again landed one of the biggest clients with the innovative, expansionist attitude of Global Crossing.

Although the firm has well-established offices overseas, it has yet to follow the expansionist models of its rivals. Its dominance of the senior debt markets in the US will no doubt exacerbate the need for a European power base.

Cravath, Swaine & Moore Possibly the best brand name in the market. In controlling its relatively small size, it has produced excellence through and through and an associate pool which clients adore. Many credit this to the firm's policy against lateral hires and an avoidance of the cult of the personality. However, in the case of its securitisation practice, the "*excellent*" Greg Shaw, forms its mainstay, with the practice's focus being limited by its size. That said, the firm's "*pre-eminent reputation*" overall is based around an "*exceptional blue-chip client base*" in New York (including IBM, Morgan Stanley and Time Warner) and the "*extraordinary quality, top to bottom*" of its lawyers.

Notable individuals include corporate legend Allen Finkelson, who has a "*fantastic M&A telecoms practice*" and brings considerable "*gravitas*" to the firm, while managing partner Bob Joffe is an anti-trust litigator extraordinaire who has "*been around since the year dot.*" His presence may also explain Cravath's reputation for producing aggressive attorneys.

The firm has a significant focus on telecoms and hi-tech work, with a track record in public company M&A "*to end all others,*" having represented Time Warner in its $165 billion merger of equals with AOL. The firm's banking & finance practice is particularly highly rated by the market. The practice is dominated by a close and productive relationship with Chase Manhattan, the acquisition financing leviathan whose formidable presence in the lending market gives the firm a "*hugely effective*" LBO capacity. Allen Parker is widely seen to be the "*power player*" at the firm for leveraged acquisition finance. It also receives top band rating for its capital markets debt & equity practice, which possesses "*outstanding relationships*" with leading underwriters such as CSFB, Chase Securities and Salomon Smith Barney.

The derivatives practice secured a top band rating, being counsel to the "*marquee client*" International Swaps and Derivatives Association (ISDA). In addition, the market views the opening of a Palo Alto office as having bolstered the firm's merchant banking and private equity/LBO practices. All in all, a successful year for this highly professional, blue-chip firm.

Shearman & Sterling This global practice has secured a high profile in a number of practice areas, namely international arbitration, project finance and capital markets, debt & equity. It is a corporate powerhouse that has its sights firmly on the cross border market. Much of the firm's success is due to its broad banking relationships. In project finance, the firm scored well for its involvement in the restructuring of Latin American debt.

CHAMBERS' TOP TEN FIRMS

1. Skadden, Arps, Slate, Meagher & Flom
2. Simpson Thacher & Bartlett
3. Cravath, Swaine & Moore
4. Shearman & Sterling
5. Davis Polk & Wardwell
6. Latham & Watkins
7. Sullivan & Cromwell
8. Weil Gotshal & Manges
9. Mayer Brown & Platt
10. Cleary, Gottlieb, Steen & Hamilton

However there exists an impression in the market that the firm relies heavily on its international connections rather than tackling rivals on the domestic front. In the arbitration practice, the real heart of the practice remains in Paris under Emmanuel Gaillard, although he continues to dominate the New York market. Rated as one of the best for communications in the transactional sphere, researchers were informed that the firm's M&A practice has "*always had a keen eye for the tech market*" and that its "*effective cross border strategy*" has struck a chord with the global consolidation in this market.

John Madden is a key M&A force, described as a "*fine transactional lawyer*" and he guided British Telecom through its corporate transactions. In banking and finance Bill Hirschberg is said to bring a "*calming influence*" to this internationally active team which boasts relationships with Citibank and Morgan Stanley. Overall an ambitious and pragmatic player with aggressive recruitment strategies and an eye on the greater picture.

Davis Polk & Wardwell The firm has an impressive 29 individuals ranked this year. Its premier practice areas are banking & finance and capital markets: debt & equity in New York. Two recent events that have no doubt been of considerable interest to the banking & finance practice are the merger of CSFB with DLJ and the acquisition of JP Morgan by Chase Manhattan, as both DLJ and JP Morgan are well-established clients of the firm. While it is impossible to predict the full impact of these events, competitors are overwhelmingly of the view that the firm's "*old and deep*" roots in the community will see it continue to enjoy success in the banking field.

Its "*uniformly excellent*" banking & finance team contains the "*calm, co-operative, incredibly smart*" Brad Smith. As the stalwart head of the firm's Credit Transactions Group, he is particularly active in work for JP Morgan. The firm is seen to be "*a top notch operation*" in capital markets with an international coverage, recently highlighted by its work with the firm's Tokyo and Hong Kong offices in advising the Japanese Ministry on the $15.9 billion equity offering from NTT.

Frank Morrison is noted as a veteran in the market who maintains close links with Morgan Stanley and acts as underwriters' counsel for General Motors and GMAC on a regular basis. The firm also has a highly focused equity derivatives team and a project finance group that has relationships with the most active agencies.

Although considered to be more domestically focused, its corporate team are leaders in both public company M&A and private equity (buyouts and fund formation.) Here Dennis Hersch is described as "*one of the greats*" leading a "*pure old school*" corporate practice that benefits from a profitable relationship with Morgan Stanley. Providing support are the outstanding tax and anti-trust practices, rated as independently strong.

The firm's branding and first rate attorneys are known around the globe yet at present it offers US counsel only. Strategic 'best friends' relationships with Hengeler Mueller (Germany) and Slaughter and May (UK) fill any gaps in cross border service. That said, the increasing drive for consolidation on the European landscape might yet affect these firms and thus the prominence of Davis Polk.

Latham & Watkins At the beginning of 2000, the firm was in negotiations to merge with Ashurst Morris Crisp (UK), an attempt to create one of the largest law firms in the world. Although the proposal collapsed, it is an indication of how far the Los Angeles-based firm has come in the past ten years. Now a national giant with increasing aspirations of international expansion, the firm has followed the global expansion of its clients.

18 individuals are ranked in *Chambers Global* this year and the firm has been rated most highly for its corporate profile in its heartland, Los Angeles. Described as an expanding force, "*extremely successful on the West Coast and beyond.*" The firm is active in top notch M&A transactions and particularly prominent in venture capital, hi-tech transactions and real estate investment. Kit Kaufman in particular has impressed the market as being an "*incredibly hard working guy*" who "*covers a lot of ground.*"

The firm's truly international practice area is project finance in New York, where a "*huge*" practice derives largely from the energy markets, with a wide range of power projects. Two prominent leaders of the practice are the "*devastatingly effective star player*" Bill Voge and Dave Gordon, who has been described by peers as being "*one of the greatest project finance lawyers in the world.*"

A broadly successful practice, it has noted recommendations in banking & finance and capital markets, as well as the communications regulatory sphere. While the market overall has suffered with the downturn of the high yield debt markets, the New York based team continues to attract admiration in this field.

A highly visible team in London is leading the European charge and the firm's presence in Asia and Latin America is secured to an active financing team. This is a highly ambitious firm that has secured areas of specialism as a basis for growth.

Sullivan & Cromwell The firm has performed well in a number of practice areas this year, including tax, capital markets, and derivatives, all of which make appearances in the top band of *Chambers Global* rankings. The fact that 24 individuals make an appearance in this year's rankings bears further testament to the firm's strong performance this year.

The firm offers a "*phenomenally successful*" M&A practice that enjoys the cross border benefits of a well-established overseas network. Its blue-chip corporate client base includes Glaxo Wellcome, BP Amoco and Olivetti, while Goldman

North America

Sachs provides a high volume deal flow. Here the "*intellectual dancer*" Ben Stapleton promotes the corporate practice worldwide while corporate "*giant*" Rodgin Cohen is highly rated as a financial services guru.

In the area of tax, the firm is perceived to have "*enormous capacity*" with a "*hugely diverse*" although primarily M&A driven tax practice and acknowledged strengths in debt instrument advice and cross-border tax planning work. Its dream team of practitioners who display "*tremendous energy*" include the "*prolific*" and "*expert*" David Hariton, with his bias towards financial products.

In the capital markets sphere, the firm is respected for its experienced personnel and an impressive volume of work. Bill Williams is singled out as having a significant presence in the transactional field while also being "*a wonderful academic resource*" for the firm.

The derivatives practice is widely regarded as being "*one of the broadest*" in the market, balancing transactional ability with regulatory expertise. Ken Raisler is head of the Commodities, Futures and Derivatives Group, and is widely credited with "*putting the practice on the map.*" In anti-trust, the firm's representation of Microsoft in its ongoing trial has boosted the profile of this highly rated litigation team.

The firm's steady expansion and its excellence in the financial services markets have secured its place on the world stage.

Weil Gotshal & Manges A major presence in the US and overseas, where this practice is known for its major corporate client base. The firm has 22 individuals ranked in *Chambers Global* this year, and considerable strength in competition in New York and intellectual property on the West Coast, both of which attained top band rating. The firm is seen to have an "*active and visible presence on the west coast*" and is particularly noted for IP litigation, strategic patent counselling and licensing where Matt Powers is the undoubted star. Its IP litigators contest "*some of the biggest and best cases*" with "*intelligence and thoughtfulness*" as well as considerable tenacity.

In the anti-trust sphere, the firm has "*across the board strength*" with high regard amongst clients and competitors alike for its merger control practice and its litigation expertise before the FTC and DOJ. Helene Jaffe receives praise from the market for being "*an incredibly intelligent problem-solver*" and a "*good tactician.*"

Its key relationship in the private equity field with Hicks, Muse, Tate & Furst has driven both the New York and Dallas offices. Both in the area of buyouts and fund formations, this firm is an internationally known player. The banking & finance team benefits from a first rate insolvency practice and has cemented its international goals with the move of Ron Daitz to the London office. It has a solid reputation for asset based lending in New York and on the West coast.

A healthy presence across Europe has been supported by top tier activity in the capital markets and private equity. Although these offices stand on their own merits in many practice areas, the firm overall is developing a brand name for innovation and quality.

Mayer Brown & Platt This Chicago-based firm has made tremendous strides in establishing a national reputation for excellence in a variety of fields. The firm's "*flexible*" practice structure allows individual practitioners to act across a number of fields, fulfilling client's expectations of full-service capabilities. 21 such "*rounded*" individuals from the firm's Chicago and New York offices feature in the *Chambers Global* tables.

The firm's greatest reputation lies in finance where its has grown in both stature and scope under the aegis of mainstay client Bank of America. Mayer Brown & Platt undertakes major syndicated lending and acquisition finance work out of its Chicago, New York and London offices and has, in a related field, built up a leading practice in international project finance. Mayer Brown's distinction as the only non-New York firm to be rated within the New York banking and finance market testifies to the group's strength in the area.

In the field of securitisation, Jason Kravitt enjoys national recognition as a luminary and has done much to enhance the firm's image in cutting-edge finance transactions despite the departure of a number of securitisation specialists from the New York office. Although the group's profile in derivatives does not match its reputation for securitisation expertise, the firm has nonetheless been seen advising on complex new products relating to exchange traded instruments, credit and equity derivatives.

The firm also receives a top band rating in Chicago for its M&A capabilities. A stable blue chip client base includes a number of originally Midwestern clients such as Monsanto and Sears Roebuck who have grown into global conglomerates. Additionally, the firm is well known for handling corporate issues for a number of international banks and insurance companies.

In litigation, particularly in the field of tax controversy, the firm has been described as a "*heavyweight presence in Chicago and beyond.*" Within the communications market it is a major player for IT outsourcing. This broad based practice is a key figure on the domestic market and attempting to spread its financial savvy overseas.

Cleary, Gottlieb, Steen & Hamilton The firm has thirteen individuals ranked in *Chambers Global*, with a top band rating for its derivatives practice in New York. Here the firm is well regarded for its top notch OTC and structured finance practice in both the transactional and regulatory fields. Ed Rosen is particularly active in this area as primary derivatives counsel for Morgan Stanley and is also highly regarded for his innovative product development and his knowledge of US commodities law regulation.

The firm is also highly rated in debt and equity and securitisation where Alan Beller offers outstanding regulatory advice.

While the firm represents a powerful crop of US issuers and underwriters, the prevailing market comment is that the firm's robust international practice overshadows the work undertaken domestically. Viktor Lewkow is "*practical and intelligent*" in his leadership of the first rate global practice. Indeed the team advised Deutsche Telekom on its proposed $55.7 billion acquisition of VoiceStream Wireless. Its European presence has proved invaluable on multi-jurisdictional trans-actions.

Although not broad enough to secure its place in the *Chambers Global* top ten, the "*extraordinarily successful*" and "*laser-like focus*" of M&A stars, **Wachtell, Lipton, Rosen & Katz** cannot pass without mention. The specialist in hostile takeovers, this firm is noted for its top to bottom excellence with its associates "*groomed for excellence.*" Praised by clients for avoiding the full service route, the firm is dominated by the legendary presence of Marty Lipton, inventor of the poison pill defence and the most creative client magnet around. He is supported by senior partners of world renown, Dick Katcher and the "*battle-hardened*" Ed Herlihy. With a client roster to beat all others, this firm is the undoubted master of the M&A market.

Although the Canadian firms failed to break into the North American rankings, that belies a year of consolidation and involvement in the most important corporate deals. Leading corporate firm Davies Ward & Beck strengthened its already enviable muscle. Combining with Montréal tax powerhouse Phillips and Vineberg (formerly affiliated with Goodman & Goodman) to create **Davies Ward Phillips & Vineberg**, it now looks set to dominate Canada's business law arena.

North Asia

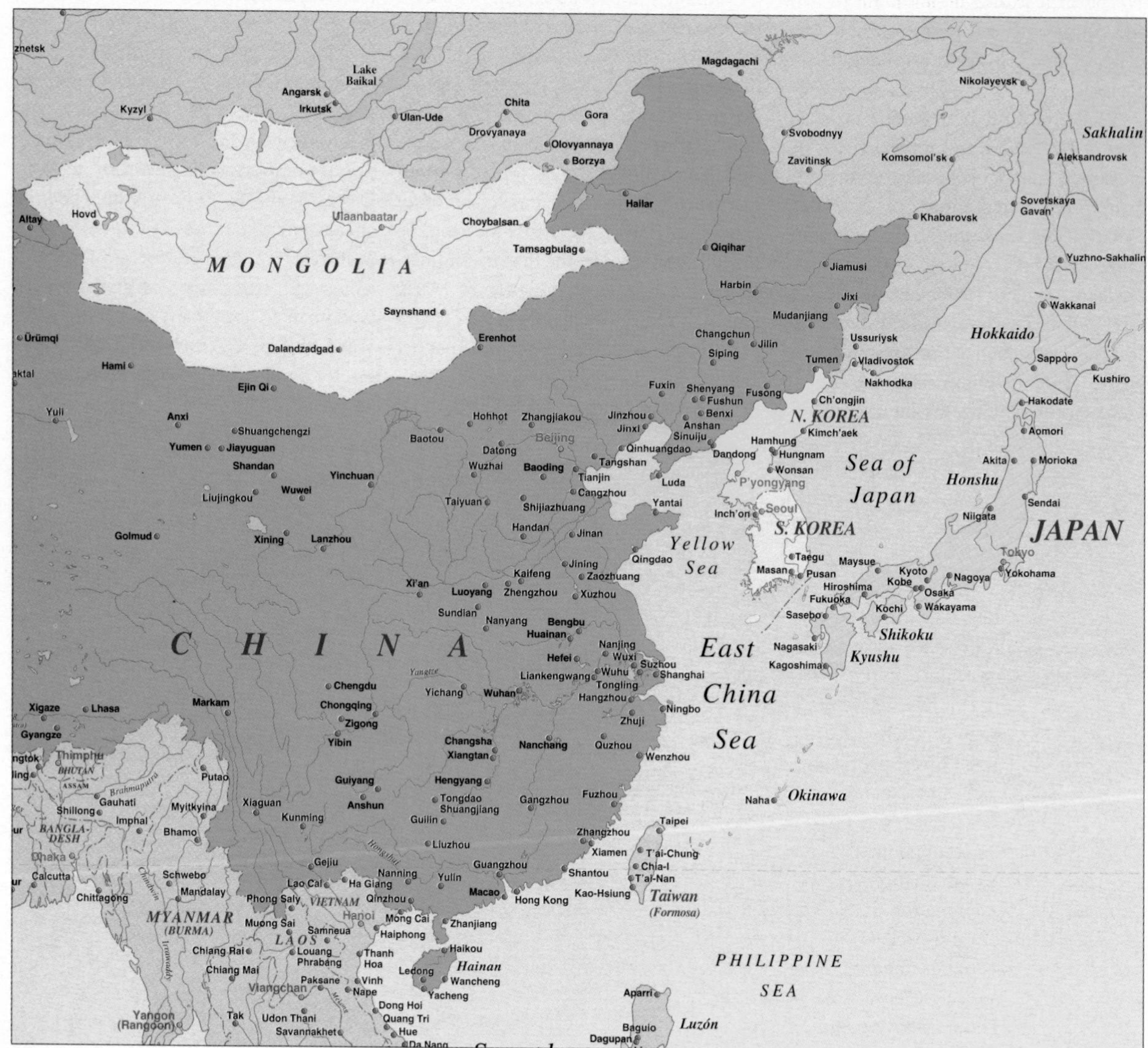

In the past year, some of Japan's best known companies have retrenched from their overseas concerns, or have been taken over by overseas rivals. Nissan has sold a controlling stake to Renault, Toho Mutual has been taken over by GE Capital and Nippon credit bank has been bought by Ripplewood, a US private equity group. In South Korea, a similar upsurge in M&A can be expected if government fails in its efforts to keep

CHAMBERS' TOP THREE FOREIGN FIRMS

1. Clifford Chance
2. White & Case LLP
3. Allen & Overy

CHAMBERS' TOP FOUR LOCAL FIRMS

1. Nagashima Ohno & Tsunematsu
2. Nishimura & Partners
3. Anderson Mori
4. Mitsui, Yasuda Wani & Maeda

domestic companies afloat. A cautious optimism reigns among major firms trying to break into the closed market of South Korea. Hard lobbying is taking place to persuade the government to end its continued prohibition on the establishment of foreign practices in the country.

Four main groups are emerging from the original ten commercial banks in Japan and entrants into the once-protected financial sector have created greater competition for domestic groups. In this climate, law firms are seeing a considerable increase in instructions from foreign financial institutions. Foreign law offices are benefiting through the increasing foreign investor interest, whilst the Japanese lawyers themselves are so sought after that "*the best are working around the clock.*"

Clifford Chance Continues to be one of the most active foreign law firms in Tokyo and has the largest presence amongst the London-based firms. Since its establishment in 1976, it has developed a broad-based practice. Regular clients include multinationals, foreign investment banks, securities companies, and Japanese and foreign corporates.

The firm's focus throughout the Asia region is international finance, and the firm enjoys a reputation for developing new financial products, as well as for project and asset financing. It stands alone at the top of the *Chambers Global* ranking. That said, the corporate/M&A practice in Tokyo is growing strongly and increasingly acts for foreign companies and financial institutions, particularly in connection with new economy investments in Japan. In South Korea, where the firm is at the forefront of the lobby for the liberalisation of the legal market, the corporate practice is also highly rated. The firm's five Asian offices are fully integrated.

White & Case LLP A sterling performance in both Tokyo and South Korea (acting out of Hong Kong) sees White & Case impressing itself upon our rankings. The first firm to establish a joint enterprise in Japan, it has proved itself to be the largest and the best, offering respected foreign and Japanese law advice to Japanese and international clients. Robert Grondine is widely credited with the success of the office – "*he's been here a long time, forged good connections and built a strong team.*"

Although strong in banking and project finance, it is in the corporate arena that the firm shines, receiving wholehearted endorsement from competitors and clients alike. In South Korea, where for more than 25 years White & Case has provided international legal services, the corporate practice also achieves top-band rating under the stewardship of Korean national, Eric Yoon.

Allen & Overy Enjoys success in South Korea, where its corporate team, acting out of Hong Kong, is seen to be challenging its stronger competitors. Meanwhile the Tokyo office maintains last year's strong showing in project finance, capital markets and banking and finance. Established, like the Hong Kong office, in 1988, it provides a comprehensive legal service with advice on English and European law. It is currently bulking up its staff, in response to the rapid increase in demand for international legal services in the Japanese markets.

Despite the negative influence of the Asian crisis on the project finance market in the region, the firm's top rated practice seems to have been largely unaffected, whilst its involvement in Latin American projects indicates a global capability. In addition, the firm entered into a joint enterprise with Akatsuki International Law Office intended in particular to bolster its financial strengths. Although too early to gauge the effects of this alliance, it is likely to support a firm that has "*the edge on a client basis and in terms of connections and know-how.*"

Nagashima Ohno & Tsunematsu This newly merged firm is a leviathan in the legal world. Although some have commented that the "*problem of bringing two different cultures together is even more pronounced in Japan,*" the firms have proved a "*good fit*" with Nagashima & Ohno's strength in M&A complementing Tsunematsu Yanase & Sekine's capital markets expertise.

Striding away from competitors, it achieves top tier rating in all three practice areas, and a roll of honour that boasts 11 individually ranked practitioners. Its pre-eminence is evident to competitors, who warmly recommended the firm to our researchers for its "*high concentration of outstanding individuals.*" Notably it advised the global coordinators (Goldman Sachs, Nomura Securities, Merrill Lynch and Nikko Salomon Smith Barney) on the first ever issuance by NTT of its own shares.

Nishimura & Partners Provides the hottest competition for Nagashima, Ohno & Tsunematsu, and only slips a band in our corporate rankings as its rival pulls ahead of the field. It boasts a formidable client base, and represented internet investor SOFTBANK Corporation on its acquisition of the failed Nippon Credit Bank (NCB).

Mr Toshiro Nishimura himself is still felt to be a significant presence at the firm, although as a "*figurehead*" rather than a practitioner. Highly rated in the banking field, this "*excellent firm*" enjoys an unrivalled relationship with the banks, representing twenty-one in their constitutional challenge to the government's New Enterprise Tax. It is likewise top tier for Capital Markets, a field in which many feel it has been "*involved from the first.*"

Anderson Mori Weighs in with eight practitioners ranked in three areas of practice. Banking and finance, the jewel in the firm's crown, scores a band one rating,

North Asia

and the practice represents an impressive array of Japanese banks and major US and European securities houses. The leading light in this practice area is regulatory expert Kunihiko Morishita, whose specialism reflects the firm's roots. Its corporate and capital markets practices both merit a good rating in *Chambers Global.*

Mitsui, Yasuda, Wani & Maeda Once again demonstrates remarkable consistency in all areas of practice, with each one of the name partners ranked in at least two disciplines. Among these, Mitsuhiro Yasuda, described by peers as "*the most innovative of the 3rd generation lawyers*" stands out, star-rated for his work in capital markets.

The firm's practice in this field is felt by many to be "*number one competition.*" Its broad banking practice is also band-one rated, and conducts project finance work as financial advisor to banks. Mitsui is held to be a "*good general commercial firm*" although less prominent on the M&A scene.

South & South East Asia

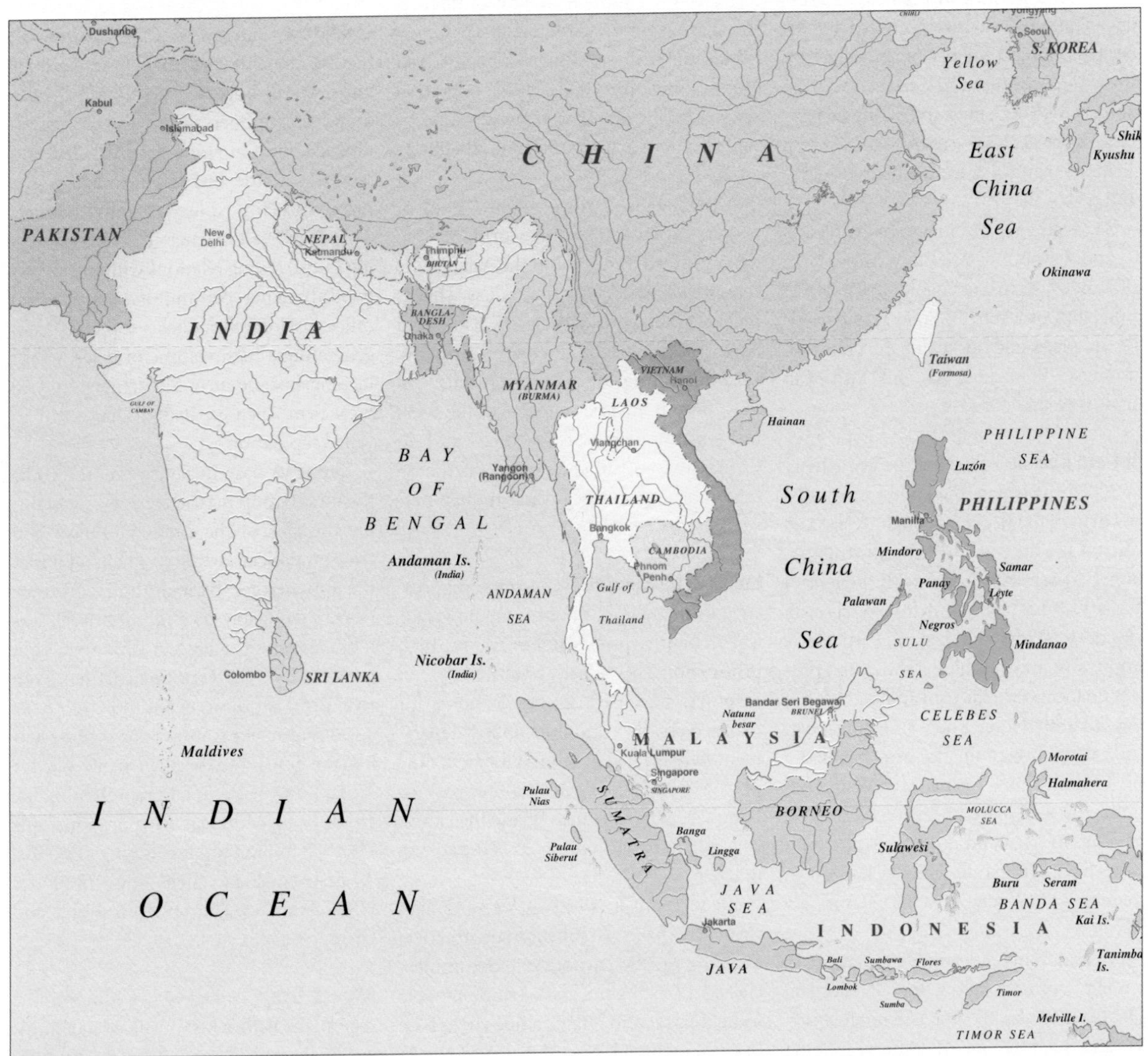

The spectre of the 1997 economic downturn continues to haunt the region. The apparent optimism of last year has been replaced by uncertainty in anticipation of credit crunches in many countries.

In the southern half of the region clear trends are detectable. National programmes spearheaded by the government shape much of the legal market. In Malaysia the government attempted to stimulate the market and restructure debt through bank mergers and the state backed Danaharta which has been purchasing all loans. In Indonesia privatisation work increases as IBRA begins to move state owned assets into the market. In response, firms are seeing their practices focus around restructuring work.

Countries such as Malaysia, Vietnam, Laos and Nepal continue to prohibit the establishment of foreign practices. In the interim, encroachment into regional markets such as Thailand, the Philippines and Indonesia continues apace, as firms establish associations and strategic alliances with local firms.

India's restrictions on foreign law firms remain, with foreign firms permitted to practice under a strict regulatory environment. Hostility to both foreign companies and legal firms resulting in protectionist measures have led to a decline in investor

South & South East Asia

interest in the country and in particular in the projects sector.

Poised to join the WTO, China is seeing an increase in direct inward investment and project finance remains healthy. Most high-profile work is centred on Hong Kong but Beijing and Shanghai have burgeoned as legal centres as Western clients demand a presence on the mainland.

Across the region, firms are expressing a cautious optimism. Whilst short-term difficulties seem inevitable there is no indication of a retreat. Solid foundations are in place and jockeying for position amongst the major US and European firms is well underway.

Clifford Chance Following merger activity in 2000, this is now the largest integrated law firm in the world. Through its size and reach it has attracted high profile transactions, whilst its merger with Rogers & Wells LLP has allowed it to capitalise on US deals across the region. Particularly impressive in corporate, banking, and project finance work, the firm attained the top tier in both Hong Kong and Singapore. Indeed its project finance arm has had a presence in China for many years and has built up a respected team of over 50 lawyers. In Thailand a joint venture with local firm Wirat International has led to increased M&A activity in the telecom sector.

It maintains a leading reputation as lenders' counsel acting for JP Morgan, Deutsche Bank and UBS, and notable corporates such as Gulf Resources, Deloitte Consulting and Volvo. It recently acted for Chase in connection with the HK$3.3 billion financing of the Hong Kong Disneyland project.

Freshfields Bruckhaus Deringer The corporate teams are respected in China, Singapore, Vietnam and Hong Kong for their depth and focus. The Singapore practice is engaged in a joint venture with local firm Drew & Napier whilst in India it has close ties with government entities.

Its premier base of operations is in Hong Kong, where the capital markets team shines. Excellent in project finance, the firm again enjoys the top *Chambers Global* ranking in China, Singapore and Hong Kong. In Thailand its operation relies heavily on ex-pat lawyers and is rated in banking and for its corporate work.

Drawing on a distinguished pool of lawyers from across the world, it is a dynamic force throughout the Asia Pacific region. A roster of first class clients includes Standard Chartered, Goldman Sachs, Ford, ICI, and Hewlett-Packard. Demonstrating these credentials, in Singapore it advised lenders on the $350 million financing of Petronas and in China advised China Telecom on the $6 billion acquisition of several mobile networks.

Baker & McKenzie A long-standing presence in the region, the firm is known for its competitive pricing policy and the high proportion of local practitioners it employs. Localised in Hong Kong for many years, its communications department here is rated as among the best. One of the best offices in the network is Bangkok, where the firm boasts the largest Thai office by far and an envied banking practice.

In Vietnam it is one of a few foreign firms to have a substantial practice, excelling on the corporate and commercial side. Despite the loss of some notable individuals it also retains a fine client base in China where it is in the second tier in both corporate and project finance. One cause for concern is its Singapore office where it has lost two partners to Sidley & Austin. It remains, however, active on the local side and has been especially visible in the Indonesian restructuring market.

Clients include Merrill Lynch, NPC Power, ING Barings and British Telecom. A strong showing in telecoms was illustrated by its representation of Telecom Asia in its $1.5 billion restructuring. It also advised Goldman Sachs regarding the $2.9 billion privatisation of PetroChina Company Ltd.

Linklaters Comprising six firms in total, this is an international practice that impresses through the depth and quality of its practitioners. One of the first to establish itself in Hong Kong, its desire to compete at the highest level across the region is being realised. Capital markets work is where Linklaters truly excels having forged strong relations with the investment banking community. Its flagship office in Hong Kong has a top class team generating a high volume of deals, whilst its Singapore branch, in partnership with local firm Allen & Gledhill, has an unrivalled reputation.

From its base in Singapore, the India Business Group is as active as ever, obtaining the pick of the country's power and telecom projects, whilst in Thailand it is in the top tier for banking and corporate work. Predictably, as a recent arrival, it is looking to consolidate in China where it has been actively recruiting partners from rival firm, Simmons & Simmons.

Recent major transactions include acting for Singapore Telecom in its bid for Hong Kong Telecom and representing the Hong Kong Mortgage Corporation in its HK$500 million public offering of bonds. A distinguished client base includes HSBC, Citicorp, Enron, Mitsubishi, and Groupe Casino.

Allen & Overy A relative newcomer in the region, the firm is now involved in a number of the larger transactions particularly in its core financial areas. A sound relationship with the top tier banks and an ability to handle complex matters, have led the Hong Kong practice to gain top marks for its banking, capital markets and project finance work. The Singapore office is respected for the quality of its practitioners and, in conjunction with London, it co-ordinates an Indian practice which is highly regarded for its project finance work.

Its visibility in China is less pro-

CHAMBERS' TOP TEN FIRMS

1	Clifford Chance
2	Freshfields Bruckhaus Deringer
3	Baker & McKenzie
4	Linklaters
5	Allen & Overy
6	Shearman & Sterling
7	White & Case
8	Herbert Smith
9	Johnson Stokes & Master
10	Slaughter and May

nounced and it scored a second band ranking for project finance. A merger with MP & Associates in Thailand has seen it translate its traditional strength in banking to this market.

The firm possesses a raft of leading clients of the calibre of HSBC, Dresdner Bank, Chase, ICICI, and Warburg Dillon Reed. It advised Cable & Wireless on its $38.1 billion takeover bid by PCCW and acted for ING Barings as lead arranger of the GEM listing of Timeless Software.

Shearman & Sterling's project finance practice has a global influence reflected in its healthy rankings in both Hong Kong, where it is one of the key US performers, and China, where the recruitment of David Platt from Linklaters is seen as a major coup. Its corporate team is becoming more prominent in Singapore from where it conducts operations in India, a market where it specialises in telecoms and power. Now prominent across the region, Thailand is the one area where the firm has not made its presence felt.

Its much-vaunted relationship with investment banks is reflected in its blue-chip client base, which includes Deutsche Bank, Citibank, and Goldman Sachs for whom it acted on the $1.6 billion offering, by Taiwan Semiconductor Manufacturing. In a further highlight, it represented TelecomAsia in its $1.5 billion restructuring.

White & Case This leading US firm followed its corporate and banking clients to Asia and is now a respected force across the region. The Singapore office, soon to be buttressed by a joint venture with Colin Ng & Ptrs (January 2001,) has strength in depth, gaining respectable rankings for its banking, corporate, and project finance arms. In India it is highly rated by lenders and has carved out a niche in the recently liberalised insurance market.

Progress has been slower in China, but the firm is still rated for its corporate and projects work as it follows a policy of pursuing high-end direct investment deals. Making swift progress in Thailand, it has expanded rapidly and is a respected advisor on debt restructuring and corporate reorganisation. It was seen to best effect here advising on the $1.2 billion restructuring of Thai Oil.

It has a collection long standing clients of high repute such as Salomon Smith Barney, Credit Suisse First Boston and US Exim Bank.

Herbert Smith An effective presence, this leading UK firm has received market approval in a number of areas across the region. Its Hong Kong office boasts Asia's largest dispute resolution team and enjoys a rewarding connection with mid tier banks. Rated on the equity side, it is renowned for its derivatives work and has acted for the HK Futures Exchange, while its corporate department features regularly on regulatory and contentious matters. Continuing to expand in China, it has a good reputation in IPO and projects work.

The Singapore practice, established six years ago, is successful in the restructuring and energy sectors. It is actively fortifying its banking practice where it acts mainly for lenders. In India the project finance team flourishes. It is seen as a safe pair of hands for the mid-sized deals, occasionally appearing in heftier transactions, for example its representation of Tata Tea on the $427 million acquisition of the entire shared issue capital of Tetley Group Ltd. A commitment to the region as a whole is evidenced by its presence in Thailand and the establishment of an associated office in Jakarta. It is also endeavouring to break into China where it recently acted for the issuer in the SINOPEC $3.4 billion privatisation.

Clients include ICICI Ltd, BNP, and ING Barings.

Johnson Stokes & Master The only firm in our top ten to be exclusively concerned with the Asia Pacific region. Extremely well known and with a long local tradition, it has a fine reputation on the financial side and excellent corporate clients. Principally deriving its power from an enviable relationship with HSBC, it is particularly strong in capital markets and has access to top restructuring deals. A loss of capacity following the dissolution of its relationship with Norton Rose and reservations concerning the move of the respected Patricia Shih to a consultancy role, have been offset by the recruitment of a number of partners from top UK firms.

The engine of its operations is the Hong Kong office, which gains approval in corporate, banking, capital markets, project finance and shipping. It is, however, also active in China doing work for lenders and strong in Thailand where its banking practice is viewed as amongst the best.

Recent highlights include its debt reconstruction work for TPI in Thailand and its representation of MLC Ltd on the HK$1.2 billion acquisition of a controlling interest in CEF Life. Clients include HSBC, The Swire Group and TBC.

Slaughter and May Known for the superior quality of its advice rather than the vol-

South & South East Asia

ume of its work. Its excellence in corporate and M&A work remains its strong suit. That said, it makes occasional forays into project finance, banking and capital markets, where it has appeared in a number of important equity offerings. Present in Hong Kong for a number of years it advises on high profile, complex transactions such as the global offering of shares in China Unicom Ltd.

Not known for a consistent presence in India, it nevertheless has had success operating a client driven strategy. Project finance has been another area of success with the firm advising, inter alia, on the Tirapur water project. In Singapore it again chooses to focus on a small number of high quality matters exemplified by its work on the debt restructuring of the Lion Group. From its platform here it has moved into Malaysia where it is one of a select band of UK firms who have carved out a reputation for excellence.

Its major clients include many of the top FTSE corporates, and a number of leading banks such as Morgan Stanley, Standard Chartered, and ANZ Bank.

Western Europe

CHAMBERS' TOP TWELVE FIRMS

1	Clifford Chance
2	Freshfields Bruckhaus Deringer
3=	Allen & Overy
3=	Linklaters
5	Baker & McKenzie
6	Cleary, Gottlieb, Steen & Hamilton
7	Hengeler Mueller Weitzel Wirtz
8	Stibbe
9	Lovells
10	Herbert Smith
11	Shearman & Sterling
12	Slaughter and May

Clifford Chance Is the highest rated Western European firm in *Chambers Global.* It beats off stiff competition from Freshfields because of the sheer breadth of its practice. However, it also has depth in key financial markets through strategic mergers with firms such as Pünder in Germany and Grimaldi in Italy. A year on, the merger with Pünder is settling down despite some partner losses. The firm is also strong in France, the Netherlands, Spain and naturally the UK office is still its key centre. At a lower level, the merger with Luxembourg's Faltz & Kremer (now Kremer & Associés) is felt to be paying dividends.

A top tier finance ranking is attained in every country, and most of the firm's top ranked lawyers are banking practitioners. A generous stable of British experts such as Stuart Popham and Michael Bray now includes European colleagues such as Dutch capital markets doyen Frank Graaf, Spanish star Jaime de San Roman and German based Caroline Jury. In project finance, the Italian and French offices stand out from the crowd.

The corporate practice is not as highly rated as its finance practice, and achieves second or third ranking in most countries. The only exception to this is in the Netherlands, where it achieves a first tier ranking. This was helped by the acquisition of two prominent lawyers from Stibbe, Hector de Beaufort and Tom de Waard.

While the firm has to be mindful of Freshfields, and increasingly Linklaters, its balanced mix of established offices allied with the experience to blood new acquisitions will ensure its future as one of the leading European firms.

Freshfields Bruckhaus Deringer 2000 was an unbelievably busy year for Freshfields who simultaneously pulled off the most respected merger in Europe as

Western Europe

well as laterally hiring top names throughout its practice. The gap between it and Clifford Chance in Western Europe has seriously narrowed. The firm stunned the market with the announcement of its merger with Bruckhaus in August 2000. This is now an Anglo-German firm with a global reach. It is the M&A leaders in Frankfurt and London, well able to advise on premium cross-border M&A work. The team advised Daimler Chrysler on its €18 billion merger with France's Aerospatiale-Matra and Spain's CASA into EADS. According to our rankings, the Paris office is the strongest foreign player in that market and will no doubt benefit from Patrick Bonvarlet's arrival from Stibbe. The Spanish office is also strong, although we rate it some distance behind the Clifford Chance operation. The newly acquired Austrian office is another asset.

While most of the firm's star names are competition and corporate lawyers, the number of finance experts it can call upon is increasing. The banking practice is developing and scored a first tier ranking in Brussels, Frankfurt and Paris.

The Dutch market is still reeling from the impact of Freshfields at its most aggressive. The Amsterdam office has now raised its partner count to 14 after cherry-picking some of the finest Dutch names. Competition stars Onno Brouwer and Winfred Knibbeler, and M&A lawyers Jan Willem van der Staay and Jeroen Thijssen have all added essential critical mass to a fast rising unit. Amsterdam, with London, forms the axis of the renowned international tax practice. High profile acquisitions from former tax specialists Loyens & Volkmaars have helped to assure its leading transactional status.

The competition practice is now the largest in Europe and represents one of the firm's strongest practice areas. In Brussels, a prodigious capacity and a perfectly balanced international cast of lawyers is rivalled only by Cleary Gottlieb. Germany and London provide additional expertise. A headline grabbing piece of work was the yearlong advice to EMI in view of its proposed merger with Time Warner.

Some local markets have proved tough nuts to crack. There is still work to do in the Italian offices, where despite good showings, the firm has yet to attract star names. However, these are mere quibbles, Freshfields has set a pace which others must follow.

Allen & Overy The only magic circle firm with clearly stated international aspirations which has NOT concluded a deal in Germany. Critics point to this gap as a serious flaw in the firm's international strategy. However, despite not having a German partner, *Chambers Global* rates the firm's Frankfurt office as the sixth leading practice in Germany overall. The firm may well pick up the fall-out from the other mergers or the dissolution of national German firms. It benefited from the break-up of Schilling Zutt Anschutz and acquired eight German partners in May 2000.

This opportunism has paid off best in the Lowlands. The final pieces of the firm's Benelux jigsaw were slotted into place with the acquisition of the remaining chunk of Loeff Claeys Verbeke in Belgium, and the merger with Beghin & Feider in Luxembourg. *Chambers Global* now rates A&O as the number one firm in the Netherlands. After successful integration with Loeff, it tops the corporate, banking and energy tables.

The link up with Brosio Casati points to a rosy future in Italy. The alliance has made steady ground and captured top project finance lawyer Franco Vigliano from rival firm Chiomenti. The opening of a small office in Madrid over 12 months ago signals the firm's intentions in southern Europe.

A clear UK powerhouse, it has a leading finance practice second only to Clifford Chance in Europe. Its corporate practice is gathering strength and achieves 4th place in the M&A league table of deals by value. However, as Linklaters move towards closer union with its partners and the Freshfields surge continues, A&O's own relationships will require further bolstering.

Linklaters The Linklaters Alliance still has the potential to become a European legal superpower. At present, however only the union with German firm Oppenhoff & Rädler has been fully consummated (January 2001.) The firm faces stiff competition from Freshfields and Clifford Chance who have been bedding down their German mergers over the past year. Oppenhoff enhances Linklaters' already impressive global finance and capital markets capability.

However, several of the alliance partnerships have some way to go before full merger, although many of the Alliance firms are forging closer ties to the UK giant. Italians Gianni Origoni are mounting a strong challenge for top honours in M&A. De Bandt in Belgium and De Brauw are already corporate powerhouses. The only weak link is the patchy relationship with Lagerlöf in Sweden. With consolidation in France and Germany, consistency in the UK and growth in Spain, Linklaters have turned in a fine performance.

The UK accounts for half of Linklaters' total *Chambers Global* ranking in Europe. The M&A team has topped every league table published, of cross-border European M&A deals completed in 2000. Lateral hire Thierry Vassogne has raised the game of the French M&A practice in an already strong Paris office which we rate second alongside Clifford Chance's.

The finance practice is also going from strength to strength. With particular expertise in equity issues, the London capital markets team is home to three of the four highest rated individual lawyers in the UK. Paris ranks equally highly, its debt work for bond issuers acknowledged by *Chambers* research. Several project finance lawyers are rated in the upper European tier.

Baker & McKenzie Rated by *Chambers Global* in eight different countries in

Western Europe, the firm exhibits the highest level of continental market penetration. It fares well across the region, but Germany is undoubtedly the trump card. Regarded as its best office in Europe, Döser Amereller Noack/Baker & McKenzie is rated in the top tier for private equity and project finance, and in the second band for banking, capital markets and communications. Possessing wide ranging expertise in buyouts and venture capital, the private equity practice has a valued client base and is home to leading practitioners, Christian Brodersen and Walter Henle. The projects team is a true world player, as is the banking practice expertly headed up by derivatives guru Rainer Magold. The Belgian and Dutch practices are also noted for their moderate finance practices, while the London capital markets team is well known for smaller European equity offerings.

The firm excels across Western Europe in the telecoms sector. It scores well in Germany, Italy, the UK and Belgium. Joachim Scherer spearheads the German telecoms regulatory practice, while the pre-eminent Italian practice is the domain of figurehead Rafaele Giarda. London is the focus of a fine communications practice, which incorporates wide-ranging strength across IT, IP and e-commerce.

For corporate work, Baker & McKenzie rarely hits the headline in any of its jurisdictions. The main exception is in Switzerland, where it is one of the few foreign firms to have made an impact. Urs Schenker lends the practice considerable transactional acumen. Tax is the dominant feature of Dutch partner firm Caron & Stevens, who with more than 50 specialist advisors maintain their traditional position as a key player in the market.

It has only limited impact in France, while the announcement of the merger with Briones Alonso y Martin (creating the largest international law firm in Spain,) may assist its comparatively low profile in Spain. Regardless, the firm has cemented its fifth position in our Western European rankings as a reliable and ever-present feature of the legal landscape.

Cleary, Gottlieb, Steen & Hamilton Having made great strides, most of the impact has been made in three key countries: France, Germany and Belgium. With a decent showing in Italy, only the lack of a broad, fully oiled London office is felt to hinder its overall European presence. Although it lags some way behind the top five firms in terms of coverage, it is a benchmark of quality in its chosen specialities.

The enormous anti-trust practice is the central plank of the firm's European operations. Based in Brussels, it has acquired a uniquely Belgian character, exploiting the talents of a universally acclaimed team to great effect. With Mario Siragusa now at the helm in Rome, the firm's European competition practice is matched only by Freshfields. The Paris office is another crown jewel. Antoine Winckler is the key anti-trust man, involved in Renault's sale of its truck business to Volvo. The corporate practice challenges Bredin Prat for pre-eminence, and is moving in on all the cutting edge deals. Pierre-Yves Chabert is the most prominent lawyer in a unit that excels in domestic and cross-border M&A. Decent French performances in project finance and tax round off a great year for the Paris office.

The backbone of its presence in Frankfurt is its banking and capital markets practice. Christof von Dryander is the notable partner in a small but focused office. In London, the small corporate practice lacks a star name, but is widely regarded as one of the leading US outposts.

Hengeler Mueller Weitzel Wirtz The firm ranks seventh in our overall European rankings through its dominance of the German market. It has 19 individuals ranked in 13 different areas of practice. Its only serious rival in Germany is Freshfields Bruckhaus. A modest Brussels competition office gives the firm an extra dimension in Belgium, but it clearly lacks the office spread and blanket coverage of other firms.

It leads in all the key German commercial sections. Pre-eminent in capital markets work, it has an unsurpassed reputation for muscling in on all the lucrative deals. An obvious highlight was €13.4 billion share issue of Deutsche Telekom DT3 that was simultaneously sold in fifteen European countries.

Other notable strengths are in acquisition finance, and straight M&A, where the 'best friends' policy with Slaughter and May (UK) help to keep it breathing down the neck of corporate rival Freshfields Bruckhaus Deringer. An elite practice, it has been instrumental in a raft of big ticket European M&A. The firm's standing in the tax and communications sectors is relatively low key, however its acclaimed competition practice is clearly a market front-runner.

A supreme performance from the German finance masters but it faces an increasingly tough challenge to oust Freshfields from their perch.

Stibbe This leading European corporate firm has endured a number of trials and tribulations this year. Partner losses have stemmed, in the main, from a reluctance to embrace the international mergers and alliances favoured by rivals in Belgium and the Netherlands. Involved in much publicised merger talks with UK firm Lovells (early 2000,) and still widely tipped by insiders as a prime European merger candidate, the firm has continued to follow a three-country strategy. Remarkably, it has managed to turn in creditable performances, particularly in Belgium and the Netherlands where their impact is greatest, and to a lesser degree, France.

While it is rarely a table topper, acknowledged strength in M&A is complemented by decent showings in banking, competition, telecoms and tax. The firm has a high reputation for quality and its somewhat academically inclined part-

Western Europe

ners. Banking and corporate finance expert André Bruyneel is the firm's highest ranked lawyer in Belgium. He, with the assistance of all three offices, played a key role in the Euronext merger, bringing together the Paris, Amsterdam and Brussels Stock Exchanges.

The loss of competition supremo Onno Brouwer and corporate partners Tom de Waard and Hector de Beaufort has stung the firm's best office in Amsterdam. That said, its corporate and banking practices are still ranked highly in *Chambers Global.* A key loss in France was that of senior corporate partner Patrick Bonvarlet, but its high corporate deal flow and related strengths in finance, tax and competition ensure a reasonable profile.

TOP TEN EUROPEAN M&A FIRMS

(By value of complete deals with a European target in 2000)

	Firm	Value
1.	Linklaters	€ 244615.02 bn
2.	Slaughter and May	€ 129483.47 bn
3.	Freshfields Bruckhaus Deringer	€ 96140.43 bn
4.	Allen & Overy	€ 89064.25 bn
5.	Norton Rose	€ 58956.63 bn
6.	Clifford Chance	€ 50505.24 bn
7.	Cleary, Gottlieb, Steen & Hamilton	€ 42158.74 bn
8.	Bredin Prat	€ 29755.72 bn
9.	Bonelli, Erede & Pappalardo	€ 24505.90 bn
10.	Herbert Smith	€ 24415.90 bn

Source: Commercial Lawyer

Lovells Only features in four countries in *Chambers Global* rankings but crucially these include the key economies of the UK and Germany. A modest French presence and an established Brussels office serve the EC needs of its clients. Seven individual lawyers register in twenty areas of practice in Europe. The merger with Boesebeck Droste has given this UK based firm access to the dynamic German mid-tier corporate market, and a spread of domestic offices. In Germany, Boesebecks scored well in corporate, banking, competition, IP and communications. Although not resting in the upper tier, the breadth and coverage of the practice is a feather in the cap for Lovells.

The German merger has also boosted the fortunes of the M&A and private equity practice, while the quality of the IT and banking departments is well known. A key deal was the advice to Merrill Lynch and Schroders on the £1.6 billion bid by Hicks Muse for United Biscuits. Anti-trust remains one of the firm's strongest suits with London, Brussels and German offices all highly rated. It has a particular reputation at the EC for its cartel and court work. In France, the small capital markets team received recognition.

With most commentators endorsing the Boesebeck Droste merger, Lovells has set out to further exploit the considerable synergy between its UK and German arms. With a small but growing Paris office, murmurings of good things to come from Milan and Rome, and a solid post in Brussels, the firm has the foundations on which to develop its European strategy.

Herbert Smith A leading corporate/M&A player, just a shade adrift of the City's magic circle giants, the firm is a quality UK practice. However, the lack of a coherent international strategy is felt to represent an obstacle to further progress, although it appears to be redressing this with its alliance in Germany with Southern M&A firm Gleiss Lutz Hootz Hirsch.

The firm's presence in Paris and Brussels supports its UK base. A fine competition practice is the thread that links all three offices. In London, the practice edged into the top band in *Chambers Global* rankings. With clients such as Coca-Cola and Air France (Paris,) and First Choice and BSkyB (London), the practice has been exposed to the regulatory battlefields. At EC level, the headline case was representing Time Warner in the mega-billion AOL merger, and the eventually aborted joint venture with EMI.

One of the leading UK energy practices, senior partner Richard Bond is an instrumental figure with expertise in oil, gas and water. The French law-oriented practice in Paris, home to African energy specialist Stéphane Brabant, is highly sought after for its experience on the subcontinent. The arbitration practice continues to be rated in both Paris and London. With 36 individual lawyers ranked in 17 different areas of practice, the firm has performed creditably in Western Europe.

Shearman & Sterling A long-time player in Western Europe, its international strategy is paying dividends. It is well represented in all the key countries of Western Europe and 14 of its lawyers feature in 14 different practice areas in *Chambers Global.* In Germany, it grabbed eight lawyers as a result of the demise of Schilling Zutt & Anschutz. Despite only opening in Frankfurt and Dusseldorf in 1991, an aggressive recruitment drive and the immense presence of Georg Thoma have helped to ensure seamless international quality.

Credit must be handed to the corporate finance team in London who secured a top tier position out of US firms there for its outstanding practice. The office handles M&A work for top US and European clients. The firm also scores well for its project finance presence running deals across the region.

Capital markets acumen is equally acclaimed, with Germany acknowledged for its strength in equity linked products, and the Paris office for its record of acting on behalf of French issuers into the US market. The practice handled the Air France $778 million privatisation and Thomson multi-media's $520 million privatisation. The firm's international project finance expertise is also highly rated.

Slaughter and May The leading corporate firm in London, it consciously eschews an expansionist international strategy in favour of its 'best friend' relationships with Hengeler Mueller in Germany, and its looser relationships with independent firms Bredin Prat in Paris, Nauta Dutilh in the Netherlands and Uría & Menéndez in Spain.

However, despite the lack of integrated offices, the firm still manages to win top quality cross-border M&A work from its City base. This is in part due to the sheer excellence of the firm's lawyers – men such as Nigel Boardman, William Underhill and Michael Pescod – an also to the firm's client base. A chunky deal list includes the likes of Glaxo Wellcome's £114 billion merger with SmithKline Beecham.

Naturally, the competition and tax practices also profit from their M&A expertise. Competition cases of note include the attempted mergers of Telia/Telenor and Airtours/FirstChoice, and for BOC on its joint acquisition by Air Liquide and Air Products. In all, Slaughter and May have 40 individual lawyers recommended in 16 different practice areas. An impressive tally, but the future holds some important questions concerning the direction of its European strategy.

BEST BUSINESS LAWYER SURVEY 2001 –

We contacted top corporations throughout the world and asked them to tell us who – from their own experience – were the best business lawyers and law firms in their jurisdiction. 'Best business lawyer', we said, means those who combine legal ability with a shrewd commercial awareness and an understanding of their client's business. It means all-round corporate and commercial lawyers to whom clients naturally turn when needing advice.

Unlike the research for the rest of the directory, this survey has focused entirely upon 'the client's choice'. In other words, it is simply a survey. And it focuses on just one particular type of lawyer. Unlike the other information found here, it is not based on in-depth research into the views of colleagues and clients. This year we present the client's choice in sixteen countries - the results of contacting 4016 of the world's leading commercial organisations.

John Atanaskovic, Atanaskovic Hartnell

Peter Cameron, Allen Allen & Hemsley

Xavier Dieux, Dieux Geens Cornelis

AUSTRALIA

Australian clients had difficulty coming to a consensus about their favourite business lawyer. **John Atanaskovic** of Atanaskovic Hartnell, admired for *"taking the interests of the client to heart,"* and "*transactional legend.*" **Peter Cameron** of Allen Allen & Hemsley, proved to be the ultimate winners.

The results were more clear-cut in the category of best business firm in which **The Allens Arthur Robinson Group** came out on top by a wide margin over second place Freehills.

BELGIUM

For a comparatively small firm, corporate specialists Dieux Geens Cornelis punched above their weight in the survey. Belgian clients backed original name partner **Xavier Dieux** as best Belgian business lawyer and voted the small niche firm third in the best law firm category. Up and coming M&A specialist Jan Meyers of Cleary Gottlieb Steen & Hamilton finished joint second along with Dieux's colleague Koen Geens.

It was noted Dieux *"had to be there in terms of quality alone."* He was described as "*a real niche corporate finance player.*"

Linklaters Alliance member and leading Belgian corporate firm, **De Bandt, van Hecke, Lagae & Loesch** performed well in the survey, emerging as the clear client choice for Belgium's best business law firm. Low Countries specialist Stibbe finished a strong second.

BRAZIL

Banking specialist, **Sergio Spinelli Silva** of Mattos Filho was selected by Brazilian businesses as their choice for best business lawyer. Silva was specifically praised for both his experience and his understanding of client's businesses.

The best law firm award was shared between **Machado Meyer Sendacz e Opice** and **Mattos Filho, Veiga Filho,** closely followed by Pinheiro Neto Advogados in third position.

CANADA

An exceptional response to the survey was received from Canadian businesses. Three corporate finance lawyers headed a fierce battle for best Canadian business lawyer. **J-P Bisnaire** of Davies, Ward, Phillips & Vineberg emerged as the client's choice. He was described as "*a master of strategy*". Bisnaire was closely followed by John Stransman of Stikeman Elliott with J David A Jackson of Blake Cassels & Graydon in third place.

THE CLIENT'S CHOICE

"Best business lawyers are those who combine legal ability with a shrewd sense of commercial awareness"

Sergio Spinelli Silva, Mattos Filho, Veiga Filho

J-P Bisnaire, Davies, Ward, Phillips and Vineberg

Davies, Ward, Phillips and Vineberg and **Stikeman Elliott** shared the spoils for best business law firm, just ahead of rivals Torys.

FRANCE

French clients highlighted four exceptional business lawyers in a tight contest for the top slot. **Jean-François Prat** of Bredin Prat narrowly beat Jean-Michel Darrois of Darrois Villey Maillot Brochier, Didier Martin, also of Bredin Prat and Thierry Vassogne of Linklaters.

Prat's extensive experience was referred to: "*Prat is older and more experienced than the rest*". Interestingly in our survey of French businesses, Linklaters was the only Anglo Saxon firm to have a partner contending for best business lawyer – former Gide Loyrette Nouel man Thierry Vassogne.

In the best business law firm category, **Bredin Prat** emerged as the clear winners.

GERMANY

An overwhelming response from German corporates placed **Dr. Michael Hoffmann-Becking** of Hengeler Mueller Weitzel Wirtz securely at the top of the tree. His reputation as being "*able to move mountains*" pervades the German market. Hans-Jörg Ziegenhain of Döser Amereller Noack finished second in the poll, followed closely by Rainer Bechtold at Gleiss Lutz Hootz Hirsch.

Despite foreign firms' valiant attempts to break into the German market, survey results show that German businesses still prefer local counsel. Indigenous firm **Hengeler Mueller Weitzel Wirtz** emerged slightly ahead of UK-German composite Freshfields Bruckhaus Deringer, with Linklaters Oppenhoff & Rädler placed some distance behind in third place.

GREECE

The contest in Greece boiled down to a fraternal run off between the original named partners of Kyriakides – Georgopoulos Law Firm, Leonidas Georgopoulos and **Constantine Kyriakides.** In a photo finish, Kyriakides edged victory over his colleague by the narrowest of margins.

Kyriakides was described as "*an exceptional commercial lawyer.*"

Leonidas Georgopoulos need not be too depressed, however, given that his firm, **Kyriakides – Georgopoulos Law Firm** was voted best business law firm by Greek clients, closely followed by competitors Karatzas & Partners.

Continued overleaf

Jean-François Prat, Bredin Prat

Dr. Michael Hoffmann-Becking, Hengeler Mueller Weitzel Wirtz

Constantine Kyriakides, Kyriakides – Georgopoulos Law Firm

Ram Caspi, Caspi & Co

Yasuharu Nagashima, Nagashima, Ohno & Tsunematsu

Akira Kawamura, Anderson Mori

Sjoerd Eisma, De Brauw Blackstone Westbroek

Tony Behrmann, Werksmans

ISRAEL

A tight race in Israel concluded with **Ram Caspi** of Caspi & Co defeating strong contenders Yigal Arnon of Yigal Arnon & Co and Oded Eran at Goldfarb, Levy, Eran & Co. "*A hard-nosed advocate,*" Caspi practices as both litigator and transactional lawyer and was reputed to be "*adept at brokering deals.*"

Yigal Arnon & Co was voted best business law firm, with Herzog, Fox & Neeman coming in second, followed by S Horowitz & Co and Goldfarb, Levy, Eran & Co inseparable in third place.

JAPAN

Yasuharu Nagashima and **Akira Kawamura**, of local law firms Nagashima, Ohno & Tsunematsu and Anderson Mori respectively, share the top slot in Japan, closely followed by Kenichi Fujinawa and Hisashi Hara.

Whilst Nagashima, now in his seventies, is "*no longer always hands on doing the deals*" his name still has considerable weight and he remains a major rainmaker for the firm. Kawamura was regarded by several Japanese businesses as a true leader in his field.

Mori Sogo Law Offices was the clear winner of the best business law firm survey.

NETHERLANDS

Corporate lawyer **Sjoerd Eisma** of De Brauw Blackstone Westbroek was voted best Dutch business lawyer in the client survey, finishing comfortably ahead of the field. De Brauw notary Martin Van Olffen proved as popular with clients as many senior partners, finishing a strong third in the survey.

Eisma's firm, **De Brauw Blackstone Westbroek**, dominated the response from Dutch clients. In addition to a strong showing for recommended individual lawyers, it collected the best business law firm award by a wide margin.

SOUTH AFRICA

Michael Katz topped the poll in South Africa but has not been included in the results as he left private practice last year. **Tony Behrmann** emerges therefore as the runaway winner in the country. Behrmann was praised for his "*incisive legal mind*".

Behrmann's firm **Werksmans** was the clear choice for best business law firm but many South African businesses also nominated Katz's former firm Edward Nathan Friedland. This firm would have finished a close second were it not for the fact that it ceased private practice last year and is now the in-house legal department of Nedcor Investment Bank.

SPAIN

A successful year for Spain's **Uría & Menéndez**. Spanish businesses clearly favoured this "*classy*" firm over Spanish and foreign alternatives. Uría & Menéndez was not only elected firm of the year, but also provided the top three choices for best lawyer. Survey results gave the "*instinctively commercial lawyer*" **Salvador Sánchez-Terán** a narrow victory. His strong performing colleagues were capital markets lawyer Luis de Carlos Bertrán, for one client "*one of the top business lawyers in Spain,*" and corporate specialist Juan Miguel Goenechea.

SWEDEN

White & Case partner **Claes Zettermarck** topped the best business lawyer poll in Sweden. He was considered "*well regarded not only as a transactional lawyer but as a litigator and arbitrator*".

Established leading firm **Mannheimer Swartling** emerged as the clients' favourite in a close contest, marginally ahead of relative newcomers Gernandt & Danielsson Advokatbyrå.

SWITZERLAND

Whilst the result for best business lawyer was tied in Switzerland, two lawyers and one firm emerged head and shoulders above the rest. **Peter Kurer** of Homburger Rechtsanwälte and **Peter Isler** of Niederer Kraft & Frey were inseparable at the top throughout the survey.

It was noted that Isler was "*the lawyer at the firm, calm and experienced,*" whilst Kurer was described as "*shining in the M&A sky.*"

Swiss businesses voted strongly for **Homburger Rechtsanwälte** as best business law firm. Homburger finished with almost twice as much support as its nearest rival, Niederer Kraft & Frey.

UNITED KINGDOM

Nigel Boardman of Slaughter and May picks up the United Kingdom award for best business lawyer. Boardman was described by a leading in house counsel as "*one of our heroes.*"

Boardman's firm, **Slaughter and May**, was the clear leader in the best firm category, polling almost twice as many nominations as its nearest rival.

USA

Clients from all corners of the USA agreed that for top legal advice New York is unquestionably 'the place to go.' Two corporate legends, **Martin Lipton** of Wachtell, Lipton, Rosen & Katz and **Rodgin Cohen** of Sullivan & Cromwell, tied in the polls for best business lawyer. Lipton, who has long been a household name both in the US and internationally as the "*inventor of the poison pill defence*" was praised for his "*tremendous creativity*" in M&A transactions. Rodgin Cohen, "*the king of banking lawyers,*" has a tremendous following within the financial services sector where his experience of bank mergers is unparalleled. Slightly behind these two giants, another banking specialist, Edward Herlihy, considered by many to be "*Lipton's heir apparent*" at Wachtell Lipton, came in third position in *Chambers'* client survey.

Again based on research across the USA, New York law firm, **Skadden, Arps, Slate, Meagher & Flom** was the clear leader for best US firm, overshadowing its closest rivals Sullivan & Cromwell and Wachtell, Lipton, Rosen & Katz.

Salvador Sánchez-Terán, Uría & Menéndez

Claes Zettermarck, White & Case

Peter Kurer, Homburger Rechtsanwälte

Peter Isler, Niederer Kraft & Frey

Rodgin Cohen, Sullivan & Cromwell

Martin Lipton, Wachtell Lipton

Nigel Boardman, Slaughter and May

INTERNATIONAL LAW FIRM MERGERS

The trend towards consolidation of national and international law firms persisted throughout 2000 with the majority of activity centring on Europe. As expected, penetration into the German market intensified with both US and UK giants following Clifford Chance's lead in establishing a presence whilst more modest incursions were made into France, Spain and Italy. The Nordic firms, however, continued to resist such absorption, choosing to limit their ambitions to mergers between domestic practices only. Outside Europe, the one notable arena has been Canada where merger mania has seen a number of firms coming together to offer larger, more centralised practices focused on Toronto. Whether this is a strategy to make themselves more attractive or merely an attempt to frustrate any potential takeovers remains to be seen. Whichever is the case, there seems no reason to doubt that consolidation internationally will continue throughout the next year especially if attempts to liberalise some of the closed legal markets prove successful in allowing the major firms to secure a foothold. Those mergers which have reached conclusion in the past year, or have been timetabled to do so in 2001, are listed below.

Merger	New Name	Total Number of Lawyers Worldwide	Date
Clifford Chance (UK) and Grimaldi (Italy)	Grimaldi Clifford Chance (in Italy)	3000	1st Jan 2001
Linklaters (UK) and Oppenhoff & Rädler (Germany)	Linklaters Oppenhoff & Rädler (in Germany)	2900	31st Jan 2001
Baker & McKenzie (USA) and Briones Alonso y Martin (Spain)	Baker & McKenzie (in Barcelona) Baker & McKenzie-Briones Alonso Martin (in Madrid)	2891	1st Jan 2001
Freshfields (UK) and Bruckhaus Westrick Heller Löber (Germany)	Freshfields Bruckhaus Deringer	1962	1st Aug 2000
Allen & Overy (UK) and Loeff Claeys Verbeke (Belgium)	Allen & Overy	1546	1st Jan 2001
White & Case LLP (USA) and Feddersen Laule Ewerwahn Scherzberg Finkelnburg Clemm (Germany)	White & Case, Feddersen	1300	Aug 2000
Lovells (UK) and Ekelmans Den Hollander (Netherlands)	Lovells	1200	1st May 2001
Akin, Gump, Strauss, Hauer & Feld LLP and Troop, Steuber, Pasich, Reddick & Tobey LLP (both USA)	Akin, Gump, Strauss, Hauer & Feld LLP	1050	1st Jan 2001
Foley & Lardner and Freedman, Levy, Kroll & Simonds and Hopkins & Sutter (all USA)	Foley & Lardner	900	1st Feb 2001

Merger	New Name	Total Number of Lawyers Worldwide	Date
Denton Wilde Sapte (UK) and Salès Vincent & Associés (France)	Denton Salès Vincent & Thomas (in France)	864	1st July 2000
Winthrop Stimson Putnam & Roberts and Pillsbury Madison & Sutro (both USA)	Pillsbury Winthrop	850	2nd Jan 2001
Coudert Brothers (USA) and Schürmann & Partner (Germany)	Coudert Schürmann (in Germany)	700	1st Jan 2000
Warner Cranston (UK) and Reed Smith (US)	Reed Smith Warner Cranston	670	1st Jan 2001
Borden & Elliott, Howard Mackie, McMaster Gervais, Scott & Aylen and Ladner Downs (all Canada)	Borden Ladner Gervais LLP	590	29th Feb 2000
Russell & DuMoulin and Fasken Campbell Godfrey and Martineau Walker (all Canada)	Fasken Martineau DuMoulin LLP	515	1st Feb 2000
Gowling Strathy & Henderson and Lafleur Brown (both Canada)	Gowlings	470	1st July 2000
Fraser Milner and Byers Casgrain (both Canada)	Fraser Milner Casgrain	465	1st June 2000
Howrey & Simon and Arnold White & Durkee (both USA)	Howrey Simon Arnold & White LLP	440	31st Jan 2000
Davies, Ward & Beck and Phillips & Vineberg (both Canada)	Davies Ward Phillips & Vineberg LLP	190	1st Jan 2001
Taft Stettinius & Hollister LLP and Kelley McCann & Livingstone LLP (both USA)	Taft Stettinius & Hollister LLP	180	2nd Jan 2001
Plesner & Grønborg and O. Bondo Svane (both Denmark)	Plesner Svane Grønborg	110	15th Sep 2000
Arntzen Underland & Co and de Besche & Co (both Norway)	Arntzen de Besche	60	1st Jan 2001

TOP 20 GLOBAL M&A DEALS

The commercial world is witnessing an increase in cross-border deals. Worldwide there has been a 5% increase in activity over the past year, with a total of 37,400 transactions valued at €3,801 billion ($3,495 billion) according to Thomson Financial Securities Data. Corporates have opted to let globalisation lead their strategic thinking. It is predominantly the financial, hi-tech/media/telecom and biochemical markets that have matured by means of consolidation. Market opinion is judging these deals on their 'pacemaker' effect. Visionary corporates are imposing industry standards with a strength borne from the fusion of these global plans.

The globalisation hitting the corporates is also affecting the legal market. The one stop international shops have fared well, catering to local and foreign jurisdictions alike. Local house firms are still found mostly on the sidelines, warding off unforeseen local legal problems.

Announcement Date	Target Full Name (Nationality)	Bid Value	Target Lead Lawyer(s) / Target Adviser(s)	Bidder Full Name (Nationality)	Bidder Lead Lawyer(s) / Bidder Adviser (s)	Divestor Full Name (Nationality)	Other Significant Lawyers
10 Oct 2000	Time Warner (US)	$181.5bn	Cravath, Swaine & Moore (US) Herbert Smith (Europe)	AOL (US)	Simpson Thacher & Bartlett (US) Skadden, Arps, Slate, Meagher & Flom (Europe)		Jones, Day, Reavis & Pogue (Bdr) Wilmer Cutler (Bdr)
17 Jan 2000	SmithKline Beecham plc (UK)	€76.2bn	Linklaters / Morgan Stanley Dean Witter	Glaxo Wellcome Plc (UK)	Slaughter and May / Goldman Sachs		Shearman & Sterling (Tgt) Sullivan & Cromwell (Bdr)
28 Jan 2000	Nortel Networks Corp (35%) (Canada)	€62.4bn (Cdn $89.3bn)	Ogilvy Renault / Morgan Stanley Dean Witter RBC Dominion Securities Inc Credit Suisse First Boston	BCE Shareholders (International)	Davies Ward Phillips & Vineberg	BCE Inc (Canada)	
24 Jul 2000 (Pending)	VoiceStream (US)	$54.7bn	Wachtell, Lipton, Rosen & Katz CMS Hasche / Goldman Sachs	Dt Telekom (Germany)	Cleary, Gottlieb Hengeler / Donaldson Lufkin & Jenrette Dredner Kleinwort Benson		Friedman Kaplan Seiler (Tgt) Jones, Day (Tgt) Wilmer Cutler (Bdr)
23 Oct 2000 (Pending)	Honeywell International Inc (US)	$50.1bn	Skadden, Arps, Slate, Meagher & Flom	General Electric Co (US)	Shearman & Sterling		
30 May 2000	Orange Plc (UK)	€49.9bn	Linklaters / UBS Warburg Goldman Sachs Donaldson, Lufkin & Jenrette Inc Dresdner Kleinwort Benson	France Telecom SA (France)	Norton Rose / Rothschild Credit Suisse First Boston Salomon Smith Barney Morgan Stanley Dean Witter	Vodafone Airtouch Plc (UK)	Shearman & Sterling (Bdr)
16 Oct 2000 (Pending)	Texaco Inc (US)	$43.3bn	Davis Polk & Wardwell	Chevron Corp (US)	Fried Frank Harris Shriver & Jacobson		Howrey, Simon, Arnold & White (Tgt) Weil Gotshal (Tgt) Pillsbury Madison (Bdr)
04 Oct 2000	China Mobile Communications Corp (7 Mobile Phone Networks) (China)	€37.3bn ($32.8bn)	Shearman & Sterling	China Mobile (Hong Kong) Ltd (Hong Kong)	Linklaters / Rothschild Goldman Sachs & Co China International Capital Corp (Hong Kong) Ltd	China Mobile Communications Corp (China)	Commerce & Finance Law Office Sullivan & Cromwell Baker & McKenzie

Announcement Date	Target Full Name / (Nationality)	Bid Value (Euro)	Target Lead Lawyer(s) / Target Adviser(s)	Bidder Full Name / (Nationality)	Bidder Lead Lawyer(s) / Bidder Adviser (s)	Divestor Full Name / (Nationality)	Other Significant Lawyers
13 Sep 2000	JP Morgan (US)	€34.2bn ($34bn)	Davis, Polk & Wardwell / JP Morgan Securities Inc	Chase Manhattan Corp (US)	Simpson, Thacher & Bartlett / Chase Securities Inc		Skadden Arps (Bdr)
06 Sep 2000	Associates First Capital Corp. (US)	€29.8bn ($31.1bn)	Simpson, Thacher & Bartlett / Goldman Sachs	Citigroup, Inc (US)	Skadden, Arps, Slate, Meagher & Flom / Salomon Smith Barney		
15 Feb 2000	Cable & Wireless HKT Ltd (Hong Kong)	€28.4bn ($38.1bn)	Allen & Overy / Merrill Lynch Greenhill & Co NG Barings Robert Fleming & Co Ltd	Pacific Century Cyberworks (Hong Kong)	Simmons & Simmons/ Warburg Dillon Read Bank of China International Credit Suisse First Boston Salomon Smith Barney Morgan Stanley Dean Witter	Cable & Wireless Plc (54%) (UK)	Cleary, Gottlieb (Tgt) Richards Butler (Tgt) Cravath (Tgt) Slaughter & May (Tgt) Herbert Smith (Tgt) Fried, Frank (Bdr) Lovells (Bdr)
20 Jun 2000	Seagram Co Ltd (Canada)	€25.2bn ($33.4bn)	Simpson, Thacher & Bartlett / Goldman Sachs Morgan Stanley Dean Witter	Vivendi SA (France)	Bredin Prat / Lazard Freres & Cie		Osler Hoskins (Tgt) Cleary, Gottlieb (Tgt) Gide Loyrette Nouel (Tgt) Cravath (Bdr) Blake Cassels(Bdr) Davies Ward (Tgt)
02 May 2000	Bestfoods (US)	€22.0bn ($24.3bn [incl.dept])	Fried, Frank, Harris, Shriver & Jacobson / Merrill Lynch Salomon Smith Barney	Unilever Plc (UK)	Cravath, Swaine & Moore, Slaughter & May / Goldman Sachs Warburg Dillon Read		Wilmer Cutler (Tgt)
25 Jun 2000	Nabisco Holdings, Inc. (US)	€19.8bn ($18.9bn [incl. dept])	Davis, Polk & Wardwell / UBS Warburg, Morgan Stanley Dean Witter	Philip Morris Cos. Inc. (US)	Wachtell, Lipton, Rosen & Katz / Chase Securities Inc Credit Suisse First Boston Wasserstein Perella	Nabisco Group Holdings, Inc (US)	Morris, Nichols, Arsht & Tunnell (Tgt) Hunton & Williams (Bdr)
15 Mar 2000	Tin.it SpA (Italy)	€17.5bn	Bonelli Erede Pappalardo / Morgan Stanley Dean Witter Chase Manhattan	Seat Pagine Gialle SpA (Italy)	Gianni Origoni and Partners / Lehman Brothers Credit Suisse First Boston	Olivetti SpA (Italy)	
17 Jan 2000	E-Tek Dynamics Inc. (US)	€17.1bn	Wilson, Sonsini, Goodrich & Rosati / Goldman Sachs	JDS Uniphase Corp (US)	Morrison & Foerster LLP / Thomas Weisel Partners LLC Bank of America Securities LLC		
07 Mar 2000	Network Solutions, Inc. (US)	€15.9bn ($21 bn)	Davis, Polk & Wardwell / JP Morgan Securities Inc Chase H&Q	Veri Sign, Inc. (US)	Fenwick & West / Morgan Stanley Dean Witter		
21 Feb 2000	Norwich Union plc (UK)	€15.7bn	Slaughter & May/ Kleinwort Benson Ltd	CGU Plc (UK)	Clifford Chance/ Goldman Sachs International		
30 Aug 2000	Donaldson, Lufkin & Jenrette, Inc. – DLJ (US)	€13.8bn	Wachtell, Lipton Davis, Polk & Wardwell / Donaldson, Lufkin & Jenrette Inc Goldman Sachs Wasserstein Perella Morgan Stanley Dean Witter	Credit Suisse Group, Credit Suisse First Boston Corp. (Switzerland)	Shearman & Sterling / Credit Suisse First Boston		Debevoise & Plimpton (Tgt) Cravath (Tgt) Richards, Layton & Finger (Tgt)
20 Jun 2000	Canal Plus SA (51%) (France)	€12.3bn	Cleary, Gottlieb, Steen & Hamilton / Merrill Lynch International	Vivendi SA (France)	Bredin Prat / Lazard Freres & Cie		Cravath (Bdr)

Tgt = Target Bdr = Bidder. Source: *Thomson Financial Securities Data; Computasoft Research / Commscan – M&A Data; with legal research by Chambers & Partners.*

Based upon deals announced and completed between 1st January 2000 and December 31st 2000. Based on full amount credit.

INTERNATIONAL ASSOCIATIONS OF LAW FIRMS

Below, we list the major associations of law firms. Some are continent-confined, while others are truly global in character. Some are stepping stones to full mergers, others are merely work referral clubs. All are fully functioning entities. Best friends arrangements and very informal associations have been excluded from the table.

Alliance name	Founded	Size	Contact details	Geographical reach of members
Association of European Lawyers	1989	36 firms in 32 countries.	Michael Scott (Secretary General) Tel. +44 20 7203 5000 Fax. +44 20 7203 0202 E-Mail: mikes@cr-law.co.uk Website: www.europeanlawyers.org	Austria, Belgium, Bulgaria, Cyprus, Denmark, Eire, England, Estonia, France, Germany, Gibraltar, Greece, Guernsey, Hungary, Iceland, Isle of Man, Italy, Jersey, Latvia, Liechtenstein, Netherlands, Northern Ireland, Norway, Poland, Portugal, Scotland, Spain, Sweden, Switzerland, Wales.
BBLP	1999	4 firms with 450 lawyers in 28 offices in 14 countries.	Any of the members. As yet, no central administration. Website: www.bblp.com	France, Germany, Italy, Switzerland.
Club Abogados-Iberoamerica	1966	21 firms in 20 countries.	Helio Nicoletti Tel. +55 11 237 8509 E-Mail: club@clubdeabogados.com Website: www.clubdeabogados-ibero.com	Argentina, Bolivia, Brazil, Chile, Colombia, Costa Rica, Ecuador, El Salvador, Guatemala, Honduras, Mexico, Nicaragua, Panama, Paraguay, Peru, Portugal, Puerto Rico, R. Dominicana, Spain, Uruguay, Venezuela.
CMS Alliance	1999	5 firms with 35 offices in 17 countries.	No central administration, CMS Cameron McKenna Tel. +44 20 7367 3000 Fax. +44 20 7367 2000	Austria, Belgium, Germany, Netherlands, Switzerland, United Kingdom.
Commercial Law Affiliates (CLA)	1990	192 firms with 5364 lawyers in 66 countries.	Wendy Horn (Executive Director) Tel. +1 612 339 8680 E-Mail: cla@claonline.org Website: www.claonline.org	over 50% of members are US firms. The remaining members are scattered throughout the rest of the world.

Alliance name	Founded	Size	Contact details	Geographical reach of members
Denton International Group of Law Firms	1991	6 firms with headquarters in 6 countries, with 1100 lawyers in 32 offices.	John Griffith-Jones, Denton Wilde Sapte, London Tel. +44 20 7242 1212 Website: www.dentonwildesapte.com	Asia, Austria, Denmark, France, Germany, Hungary, Middle East, Norway, Spain, UK.
European Law Group (ELG)	1983	9 firms with headquarters in 9 countries.	Any of the member firms. Website: www.elgroup.com	Austria, Belgium, Denmark, France, Germany, Italy, Netherlands, Norway, Spain, Sweden, Switzerland, UK.
Insurolaw	1995	16 firms in 16 countries, with 1000 lawyers in 27 offices.	Chris Blythe Tel. +44 20 7456 7600 Website: www.insurolaw.com	Belgium, Denmark, Eire, England, France, Finland, Greece, Italy, Netherlands, Norway, Portugal, Scotland, Spain, Sweden.
Interlaw	1981	59 firms with 4000 lawyers in 110 offices.	Beverly L. Weise Tel. +1 310 556 1667 E-Mail: bweise@interlaw.org Website: www.interlaw.org	Africa, Asia Pacific, Europe, Latin America, Middle East, North America.
Interlex	1973	35 firms in 30 countries.	Lawrence B. Swibel (Secretariat) E-Mail: lswibel@fhslc.com Website: www.inlex.com	Australia, Brazil, India, Israel, Japan, Korea, Nigeria, North America, Singapore, South Africa, Western Europe.
International Lawyers Network (ILN)	1988	73 law firms in 59 countries, with 4000 lawyers.	Jim Haggerty (Executive Director) Tel. +1 212 683 9363 E-Mail: jhaggerty@prcg.com Website: www.lawinternational.com	worldwide.
Lex Africa	1990	17 firms in 17 countries, with over 100 lawyers.	Vicky Bunyan, Werksmans Attorneys Tel. +27 11 488 0000 E-Mail: vbunyan@werksmans.co.za Website: www.werksmans.co.za	Botswana, Burkina Faso, Côte d'Ivoire, Ghana, Kenya, Lesotho, Malawi, Mauritius, Morocco, Namibia, Senegal, South Africa, Swaziland, Tanzania, Uganda, Zambia, Zimbabwe.
Lex Mundi	1989	158 firms with 14,000 lawyers in 375 offices.	Tel. +1 713 626 9393 Fax. +1 713 626 9933 E-Mail: lexmundi@lexmundi.org Website: www.lexmundi.org	global spread, with members concentrated in Western Europe and the USA.
Linklaters and Alliance	1998	6 firms in 14 countries and 2,200 lawyers in 36 offices.	Linklaters Tel. +44 20 7456 2000 Fax. +44 20 7456 2222 Website: www.linklaters-alliance.com	Belgium, Germany, Italy, Luxembourg, Netherlands, Sweden, UK.

Continued overleaf

INTERNATIONAL ASSOCIATIONS OF LAW FIRMS continued

Alliance name	Founded	Size	Contact details	Geographical reach of members
Multilaw	1990	52 firms in 41 countries with 4000 lawyers in 120 offices.	The Secretariat Tel. +44 20 7410 9269 E-Mail: secretariat@multilaw.com	Africa, Europe, South America, South-East Asia, USA.
Pacific Rim Advisory Council	1984	27 firms with 28 offices in 21 countries.	Website: www.prac.org/PRACalph.html	The entire Pacific Rim plus Brazil, Venezula, India, South Africa and The Netherlands.
Scandinavian Law Alliance	1991	3 firms with 800 lawyers in 15 offices.	Claes Enhörning Tel. +46 42 24 80 80	Denmark, Norway, Sweden.
Techlaw Group, Inc	1986	17 firms in 15 countries, with 4,000 lawyers in 96 offices.	Lawrence A. Heller Tel. +1 412 820 0670 E-Mail: lheller@techlaw.org Website: www.techlaw.org	Albania, Belgium, Canada, France, Germany, Italy, Mexico, Portugal, Peoples Republic of China, Republic of Ireland, Switzerland, The Netherlands, United Arab Emirates, United Kingdom, United States.
TerraLex	1990	140 member firms in 93 countries.	Jacqueline Kiviat (Executive Director) Tel. +1 305 858 8825 Fax. +1 305 858 8986 E-Mail: jkiviat@terralex.org Website: www.terralex.org	Angola, Anguilla, Antigua, Argentina, Aruba, Austria, Bahamas, Bangladesh, Barbados, Belarus, Belgium, Belize, Bermuda, Bolivia, Brazil, British Virgin Islands, Bulgaria, Cameroon, Canada, Cayman Islands, Channel Islands, Chile, China, Colombia, Costa Rica, Croatia, Cyprus, Denmark, Dominican Republic, Ecuador, Egypt, Estonia, El Salvador, France, Germany, Ghana, Gibraltar, Greece, Guatemala, Honduras, Iceland, India, Indonesia, Ireland, Isle of Man, Israel, Italy, Jamaica, Korea, Latvia, Lebanon, Liechtenstein, Luxembourg, Malaysia, Malta, Mauritius, Mexico, The Netherlands, Netherlands Antilles, Nicaragua, Nigeria, Norway, Pakistan, Panama, Paraguay, Peru, Philippines, Poland, Portugal, Puerto Rico, Romania, Russia, Saint Kitts & Nevis, Saint Lucia, Saint Vincent and the Grendadines, Singapore, Slovenia, South Africa, Spain, Sweden, Switzerland, Tanzania, Trinidad & Tobago, Turkey, Turks & Caicos Islands, Ukraine, United Kingdom, Uruguay, USA, Venezuela, Vietnam, Zimbabwe.
World Law Group	1988	44 firms with headquarters in 34 countries.	Jennifer P. Pinkerton Tel. + 1 312 245 2940 Fax. + 1 312 644 3381 E-Mail: jpinkerton@gcd.com Website: www.theworldlawgroup.com	Australia, North and South America, South-East Asia, Western Europe.

THE LAW FIRMS

ALBANIA

Corporate/Commercial: Local Firms

ALBANIA Leading firms (Corporate/Commercial)
1 Boga & Associates
Kalo & Associates
2 Loloçi & Associates
3 Vani & Associates

Firms are listed alphabetically in each band.

Leading individuals (Corporate/Commercial)
1 **BOGA Genc** *Boga & Associates*
KALO Perparim *Kalo & Associates*
2 **LOLOÇI Krenar** *Loloçi & Associates*
3 **VANI Gjergji** *Vani & Associates*

Individuals are listed alphabetically in each band.

Boga & Associates (3 ptrs, 5 asscs) This growing law firm with *"good international connections"* is *"still improving,"* and there are plans to open an office in Kosovo. Seen as a commercially oriented firm, it is adept in all areas of tax, aviation, mineral resources, investment and banking, acting for a diverse client base of local and international business. *"Competent"* managing partner **Genc Boga*** is the stand-out practitioner here. The firm advised on the tendering process for the privatisation of a beer factory in Albania, which was ultimately won by Peroni. **Clients:** Airlines; embassies; banks; hotels; oil companies; accountants.

Kalo & Associates (1 ptr, 8 asscs) The second of the 'big two' local firms is recommended as *"a good law firm for investment."* The majority of work is international company law, focusing on banking, privatisation, restructuring, M&A and telecommunications. **Perparim Kalo*** is *"a careful lawyer with excellent language skills."* The firm acted on behalf of Lafarge on the acquisition of a cement factory. **Clients:** Ericsson; Alfa Credit Bank; Shell; Agip; Commercial Bank of Greece.

Loloçi & Associates (1 ptr, 2 asscs) General corporate/commercial practice specialising in IP and contract law. *"Well prepared"* **Krenar Loloçi*** is *"a superb lawyer"* with *"some excellent clients."* The team acted on the privatisation of AMC, a deal worth $85 million. **Clients:** Embassies and telecommunications companies.

Vani & Associates (1 ptr, 2 asscs) A corporate finance and general commercial law specialist firm headed by *"experienced finance lawyer"* **Gjergji Vani***, who works on the process of establishing foreign and domestic banks in Albania. The firm is notably proficient on drafting regulatory frameworks and joint venture agreements. Instructed by Deloitte & Touche on a project concerning the liquidation of five permit schemes utilising a grant of $5 million issued by the World Bank. **Clients:** Deloitte & Touche; Inter Commercial Bank; Tirana Bank.

Corporate/Commercial: Foreign Firms

ALBANIA: Foreign Firms Leading firms (Corporate/Commercial)
1 Studio Legale Tonucci
2 Brosio Casati & Associati

Firms are listed alphabetically in each band.

Leading individuals (Corporate/Commercial)
1 **BALDISSONI Mauro** *Studio Legale Tonucci*
2 **CIGNA Gianpiero** *Studio Legale Tonucci*
SALLUSTIO Riccardo *Brosio Casati & Associati*
SHUKE Enyal *Brosio Casati & Associati*

Individuals are listed alphabetically in each band.

Studio Legale Tonucci (2 ptrs, 8 asscs) Italian firm with an established name in Albania since 1995. A full-service operation, it offers advice to the government on the privatisation of state-owned enterprises in telecoms, oil and gas. **Mauro Baldissoni*** is *"the leading Italian in Albania"* and **Gianpiero Cigna*** is also highly regarded. The team advised on the drafting of the new customs code in 1999. **Clients:** Ministry of Public Economy and Privatisation; Italian Embassy; European Commission; Occidental Petroleum; American Bank of Albania.

Brosio Casati & Associati (in Association with Allen & Overy) (1 ptr, 3 asscs) The firm represents international clients in Albania on all aspects of commercial law, including equity finance, banking and export finance. Italian **Riccardo Sallustio*** is the managing partner and **Enyal Shuke*** is described as *"one of the best lawyers in Albania."* The firm advised on the privatisation of a national commercial bank, and represented the German company BOT on its application for a concession to supply drinking and waste water in Albania. **Clients:** EBRD; IFC.

*See leaders' profiles on page 50

Leaders' profiles – Albania

A

BALDISSONI, Mauro
Studio Legale Tonucci, Tirana +355 42 507 11/2/4
mbaldissoni@tonucci.it
Specialisation: Legal advisor in privatisation of public and private companies. Advised privatisation of the holding Telecom Italia. Supervised project for privatisation of state-owned companies operating in strategic sectors of economy in Albania (telecommunications, energy, oil, gas). Expert in modification of company by-laws, introduction of golden-share, floatation procedures. Expert in corporate and commercial law, EU law, harmonisation of legislation. Team expert for law reform within the approximation and development of Albanian economic legislation.
Prof. Memberships: Rome and International Bar Association.
Personal: Born on April 14, 1970. Law Degree – University of Rome (1993). Lives in Tirana and Rome.

BOGA, Genc
Boga & Associates, Tirana +355 42 51050

CIGNA, GianPiero
Studio Legale Tonucci, Tirana +355 42 507 11/2/4
tonucci-al@icc.al.eu.org
Specialisation: Expert in privatisation, BOT and project finance. Advisor in the World Bank project for privatisation of state-owned companies operating in Albanian strategic sectors (telecommunications, energy, oil, gas, mines). Expert in EU law and harmonisation of national legislation. Advisor in the Phare program 'Approximation of Albanian legislation'. Advisor of EU Customs Assistance Mission, Delegation of European Commission and Italian Embassy, Tirana.
Prof. Memberships: Rome Bar Association.
Personal: Born on September 29, 1966 – Alassio (SV). Lives in Tirana.

KALO, Perparim
Kalo & Associates, Tirana +355 42 335 32

LOLOÇI, Krenar
Loloçi & Associates, Tirana +355 4250 736

SALLUSTIO, Ricardo
Brosio, Casati e Associati (in association with Allen & Overy), Tirana +355 42 28966

SHUKE, Enyal
Brosio, Casati e Associati (in association with Allen & Overy), Tirana +355 42 28966

VANI, Gjergji
Vani & Associates, Tirana +355 4250 719

ALGERIA

Corporate/Commercial

ALGERIA Leading firms (Corporate/Commercial)
1 Cabinet Sator
2 Aidoud Law Firm
Mustapha Hamdane

Firms are listed alphabetically in each band.

Leading individuals (Corporate/Commercial)
1 SATOR Mohamed *Cabinet Sator*
2 AIDOUD Mamoun *Aidoud Law Firm*
HAMDANE Mustapha *Mustapha Hamdane*
Individuals are listed alphabetically in each band.

Cabinet Sator (1 ptr, 5 asscs) The *"oldest and most important"* law firm in the country. A commercially oriented firm, it also focuses on the protection of industrial property. The *"experienced"* **Mohamed Sator** is instructed by international corporate clients to advise on local tax and business law. **Clients:** International banks; government agencies; energy and insurance companies.

Aidoud Law Firm (1 ptr, 4 asscs) An internationally recognised firm headed by **Mamoun Aidoud**, a former legal consultant to the ministry of finance and author of legal texts on investment in Algeria. Offers legal advice to foreign firms and companies and practices commercial law, IP law and foreign investment. **Clients:** International energy companies; banks; corporate investors.

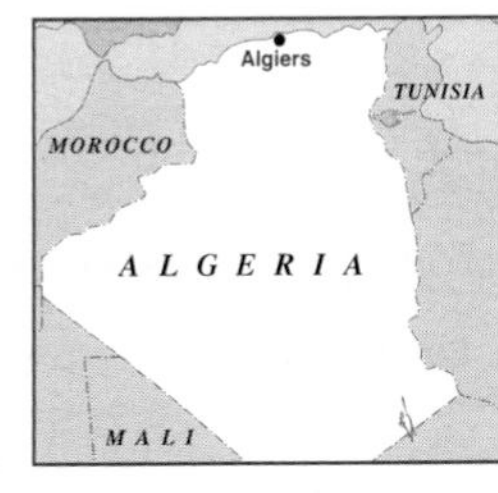

Mustapha Hamdane (1 ptr, 4 asscs) **Mustapha Hamdane** is an authority on the legislation and government regulation of the country's energy sector. He heads a commercial law firm which is strong in banking and finance in addition to oil and energy. **Clients:** Oil and energy corporate clients; international banks; local administration.

Leaders' profiles – Algeria

AIDOUD, Mamoun
Aidoud Law Firm, Algiers +213 21 719655/+213 21 719736

HAMDANE, Mustapha
Mustapha Hamdane, Algiers +213 21 714 803

SATOR, Mohamed
Cabinet Sator, Algiers +213 21 735 659

ANGOLA

Corporate/Commercial

ANGOLA Leading individuals (Corporate/Commercial)
1 DOS SANTOS Fernando *Sole Practitioner*
Individuals are listed alphabetically in each band.

Fernando Dos Santos Currently the director of the Legal Department of Sociedade Nacional de Combustíveis de Angola (SONANGOL). As the Chief Lawyer of SONANGOL he is involved in general legal and contractual issues for the oil and gas industry. His work ranges from concession agreements to joint ventures, new company formation and financings. Aside from his work with SONANGOL he is also an independent lawyer affiliated to the Angolan bar, representing clients in corporate and commercial matters.

Leaders' profiles – Angola

DOS SANTOS, Fernando
Fernando Dos Santos – Sole Practitioner, Luanda +2442 334 143

ARGENTINA

Index

A

OVERVIEW: The second wave of telecoms privatisations in November 2000 brought a stream of foreign investors interested in opportunities previously monopolised by Telefónica of Spain and Telecom Italia (jointly French and Italian owned). With the highest number of internet start-ups in Latin America, Argentina is enjoying the emergence of communications specialists. A change in government regulations means that most mergers are now subject to prior approval, ensuring that competition considerations are now a standard part of M&A activity. In response to the prevalence of cross-border investment, particularly in the energy sector, associations with Spanish, Brazilian or Portuguese firms are on the increase while the penetration of foreign firms remains low.

Banking & Finance

Bruchou, Fernandez Madero, Lombardi & Mitrani (8 ptrs, 62 asscs) *"Definitely top for banking,"* this *"terrific"* young firm acts as general counsel to a number of international banks, which comprise 90% of its clientele. The firm has acknowledged expertise in capital markets, although syndicated loans, banking M&A and project finance are also important elements of the workload. *"Aggressive, effective"* founding partner **Enrique Bruchou*** is well known in banking circles as a lawyer who *"fights for the deals,"* and is acclaimed as a market leader in securities. Younger partners **Javier Errecondo*** and **Jaime Madero*** are also well known for financial acumen.

The firm represented Deutsche Bank as arranger of the first trust programme to be approved by the Argentine Securities Commission. Its capital markets practice includes corporate bond offerings, MTN programmes, ASCPs, global equity offerings, IPOs, Yankee bonds, structured notes, high yield bonds, FRNs, and tender offers. The team advised on the first international exchange offer involving shares of an Argentine company.

In acquisition finance, the firm acted for Deutsche Bank on a loan to Bodegas Viñedos Andinos, while project finance expertise was exemplified by advice to CSFB and Citibank on the issue of $685 million of secured project bonds by Compañía Mega. **Clients:** Merrill Lynch; Solomon Brothers; Goldman Sachs; Morgan Stanley; CSFB; Citibank; Citicorp; Chase Manhattan; Deutsche Bank; BankBoston; Bank of America; HSBC; BBVA Banco Frances; Banco Santander/ Río de la Plata; First Boston; Bank of America; HSBC.

Hope Duggan & Silva (9 ptrs, 31 asscs) Our researchers have found that the firm has a reputation as *"one of the country's best for banking and finance advice,"* and is particularly known for its capital markets expertise. Financial clients include investment and retail banks, venture capital and private equity funds, investment funds and government agencies. The team handles derivatives, trade finance, bonds, security instruments, banking due diligence and securities regulations.

Many competitors and clients consider **Juan Duggan*** to be the country's leading finance practitioner. *"A serious player,"* he is said to be *"the man I'd go to if I had a conflict of interest."* Other name partners **Adrian Hope*** and the *"extremely smart"* **Roberto Silva*** also gain market recognition. **Clients:** Chase Manhattan; BBV; Bank of Montréal; Credit Suisse Financial Products; HSBC; Morgan Grenfell.

Marval, O'Farrell & Mairal (14 ptrs, 50 asscs) This giant of a firm is regarded as having *"a potent finance team,"* and is consistently recommended for its work on bonds and syndicated loans. Acting principally for large brokerage houses, the firm represents Goldman Sachs on derivatives transactions and Morgan Stanley on structured finance work, as well as representing the IFC on a variety of projects. **Juan Antonio Gallo*** has a first-rate name for finance, having been a member of the Argentine Steering Committee dealing with the country's foreign debt in the 1980s. Harvard-educated partner **Patricia Lopez Aufranc*** is also recognised as *"an active player,"* with acclaimed experience in privatisations, IPOs, derivatives and project finance.

The firm acted for Deutsche Bank and CSFB as underwriters to the issue of eurobonds in the Republic of Argentina. It also advised ABN Amro Argentina as trustee in the issue of $600 million debt securities by Banco Bansud, and for the same client in an issue of $500 million securities by Fideicomiso Financiero. **Clients:** CSFB; Goldman Sachs; DLJ; Morgan Stanley; Lehman Brothers; Societe Generale; UBS; IFC; World Bank; IDB; OPIC; Banco Santander; Bank Boston; JP Morgan; Bank Paribas; Citibank; Banco Hipotecario.

Perez Alati, Grondona, Benites, Arntsen & Martinez de Hoz (6 ptrs, 19 asscs) *"Aggressive"* young firm which has rapidly carved out a reputation in the banking world, and is especially highly regarded for syndicated loans and bond issues. Principally seen representing US lenders,

ARGENTINA Leading firms (Banking & Finance)
1 Bruchou, Fernandez Madero, Lombardi & Mitrani
Hope Duggan & Silva
Marval, O'Farrell & Mairal
Perez Alati, Grondona, Benites, Arntsen & Martinez de Hoz
2 Estudio Beccar Varela
Cárdenas Cassagne & Asociados
3 Allende & Brea
Baker & McKenzie
Muñoz de Toro
Estudio O'Farrell

Firms are listed alphabetically in each band.

Leading individuals (Banking & Finance)
1 **DUGGAN Juan** *Hope Duggan & Silva*
2 **BRUCHOU Enrique** *Bruchou, Fernandez Madero*
FORTUNATI Roberto *Estudio Beccar Varela*
GALLO Juan Antonio *Marval, O'Farrell & Mairal*
HOPE Adrian *Hope Duggan & Silva*
3 **DELL'ORO MAINI Atilio** *Cárdenas Cassagne*
ERRECONDO Javier *Bruchou, Fernandez Madero*
GRONDONA Mariano *Perez Alati, Grondona*
LA PORTA DRAGO Rafael *Allende & Brea*
LOPEZ AUFRANC Patricia *Marval, O'Farrell*
MADERO Jaime *Bruchou, Fernandez Madero*
SERRANO Diego *Perez Alati, Grondona*
SILVA Roberto *Hope Duggan & Silva*

Individuals are listed alphabetically in each band.

the firm also has a thoroughbred stable of issuer and borrower clients. **Diego Serrano***, head of the capital markets practice, is a noted name on international lending transactions, while **Mariano Grondona*** has also raised his profile for traditional bank lending work.

The firm advised on the Profertil project, acting for a group of banks and lending institutions led by Chase Manhattan on a $339 million complex security package. A national leader in IPOs, the group advised on the Transener IPO in 2000, and also represented the lead arrangers on the $200 million USCP program for HSBC Argentina. Other transactions include advising Metrogas on a $50 million loan from the European Investment Bank, and acting for Duke Energy in connection with two credit facilities obtained from West LB for debt refinancing of the company's Argentine subsidiaries. **Clients:** Banco Santander; Chase Manhatten; Morgan Stanley; CSFB; Banco Río; Barclays Bank.

Estudio Beccar Varela (23 ptrs, 70 asscs) "*Conservative*" firm with a sound reputation in capital markets, banking and finance and debt restructuring. A client base of international financial institutions is augmented by a number of Argentine provinces, for whom the firm has advised on several bond issues and structured finance transactions.

Our researchers discovered that **Roberto Fortunati***, formerly a name in the energy sector, has acquired great stature in the banking and finance world. He has advised on restructuring work for Citicorp, Banco Santander and ING, and has niche expertise in mining projects. He and his team acted on the financing of the Alumbrera mining project, representing the arrangers of a $542 million syndicated credit facility. The firm's debt restructuring practice comes in for market approval, and acted for the creditors (including Citibank and Dresdner) of Sociedad Comercial del Plata, a process involving debts of approximately $800 million. **Clients:** Citicorp; DKB; KFW; Banco Santander; Société Générale; UBS Warburg; Banco de Galicia y Buenos Aires; Banco de Itaú; Lloyds Bank; Barclays Bank; IDB; IFC; Chase Manhattan.

Cárdenas Cassagne & Asociados Acting for a number of large investment funds and international banks, the department has an especially fine reputation for project finance. Noted individual **Atilio Dell'Oro Maini*** is a "*multi-faceted, multi-talented*" lawyer. The firm has ample lending experience, and recognised capital markets and securitisation expertise. Restructuring work includes representing foreign and domestic banks in the reworking of public debt and the issuance of bonds by the Republic of Argentina throughout the 1990s. **Clients:** Banco Exterior; domestic banks; banks from Brazil, Chile and Uruguay; Bank of Nova Scotia; CSFB; Goldman Sachs; ING; IBD; Midland Bank.

Allende & Brea (18 ptrs, 63 asscs) The firm "*usually does a good job*" on banking matters, although it is better known for its corporate expertise. Instructed by a number of investment banks, the group advises on bank regulatory issues, equity placements, ADRs, bonds, and other debt instruments in the domestic and the international markets. It also has experience in syndicated loans, where it represents national borrowers. A key client is private equity house Hicks Muse Tate & Furst. Dual qualified (Spain and Argentina) partner **Rafael La Porta Drago*** is the firm's acclaimed head of banking. **Clients:** Bank of America; Banca Nazional del Lavoro; Deutsche Bank; Exim Bank; Federal Deposit Insurance Corporation; J Henry Schroder; Hicks Muse Tate & Furst; Chase Capital Partners; DKB; Fidelity Investments; Eagle Star.

Baker & McKenzie (8 ptrs, 60 asscs) The Buenos Aires branch of the international network has a reputation for containing "*good lawyers to refer to,*" and the banking team has experience of handling big-ticket financial transactions for international investment banks. Regulatory advice, syndicated loans, project finance, stock option plans, placement of securities, and global custody agreements are important areas in the group's workload.

The firm represented the arranger in a $1.2 billion syndicated loan to Cablevisión, and advised the Central Bank of the Argentine Republic on a contingent swap program worth $500 million. Acting for Lloyds Bank's Argentine retail subsidiaries and Chase Manhattan on regulatory matters, the firm also has experience in advising equity funds. Advised Chase Manhattan on the issue of the first affinity credit card in Argentina. **Clients:** ABN AMRO; ANZ Bank; Banco Central de Argentina; Société Générale; Dresdner; Lloyds Bank; Merrill International; Visa; Royal Bank of Scotland; Chase Manhattan.

Muñoz de Toro (2 ptrs, 3 asscs) A small firm that is said to be "*making noise*" in the finance sector, becoming particularly renowned for its work on the restructuring of Banco Río de la Plata. Capital markets advice and lending work, primarily for the borrower are key areas of the practice, and the team has pioneered the development of new financial products on the local market, advising banks on asset-backed securities, financial trusts and derivatives.

The group advised on the first credit-card receivable financial trust for Banco de Galicia, a transaction worth $35 million, and acted on a $170 million syndicated loan for Arcor. **Clients:** Banco Santander Central Hispano; Banco de Galicia; Banco Rió de la Plata; BankBoston; Chase Manhattan; Goldman Sachs; HSBC; Argentine Ministry of the Economy.

Estudio O'Farrell Argentina's second-largest firm is well regarded by competitors or its work in capital markets, where it is reputed to have "*a decent practice.*" The group represents national and international financial institutions on regulatory and transactional matters, and advises on the design and structure of financial products. Syndicated loans are another area of particular expertise. The team has acted on debt and equity transactions for Cablevisión, Merrill Lynch, Prudential Securities, and Telefónica de Argentina, including the placement of shares and ADRs, negotiable obligations, and other debt securities. **Clients:** Prudential Securities; Merrill Lynch; Ford Credit; IFC; IBD; John Deere Credit; Bozano Simonsen; KBC; Telefónica de Argentina.

*See leaders' profiles on pages 60-63

Communications

ARGENTINA
Leading firms (Communications)

Band	Firm
1	Allende & Brea
	Marval, O'Farrell & Mairal
	Sanchez Elia, Pinedo, Diaz Bobillo & Richard
2	Negri Teijeiro & Incera
	Oyhanarte & Fargosi
3	Altmark & Brenna
	Baker & McKenzie
	M&M Bomchil
	Estudio Millé
	Morrison & Foerster
	Estudio O'Farrell

Firms are listed alphabetically in each band.

Leading individuals (Communications)

Band	Individual	Firm
1	FARGOSI Alejandro	*Oyhanarte & Fargosi*
	MARSIGLIA Gabriela	*Gabriela Marsiglia*
	PINEDO Federico	*Sanchez Elia, Pinedo, Diaz*
	SANCHEZ ELIA José	*Sanchez Elia, Pinedo, Diaz*
2	AROCENA Juan Martín	*Allende & Brea*
	BUSSO Federico	*Negri Teijeiro & Incera*
	GARRIDO Gustavo	*Allende & Brea*
	MATARASSO Gabriel	*Marval, O'Farrell & Mairal*
3	GARRIDO Gustavo Enrique	*Allende & Brea*
	MILLÉ Antonio	*Estudio Millé*

Individuals are listed alphabetically in each band.

Allende & Brea (7 ptrs, 31 asscs) One of few firms in the country that is known to be *"devoted to internet start-ups,"* it counts among its clients over 200 nascent local net companies and 15 internet investment funds, and is involved in substantial M&A and investment activity in the local web market. Our researchers found that the firm's strategy of capitalising part of its fee for such clients and of being *"one of the most aggressive in the market,"* has led to its position as *"the most important lawyers in IT."* The firm acts for several traditional off-line companies starting on-line ventures, and negotiates contracts with investment funds. Although it is overshadowed by the IT practice, the firm handles regulatory and transactional telecoms issues.

Juan Martín Arocena* *"knows what he's talking about,"* and has expertise in structuring internet ventures. He forms an impressive team with **Gustavo Garrido***, *"a software expert,"* and younger partner **Gustavo Enrique Garrido*** *("also good for IT.")*

The firm acted for Chase Equity Associates on the acquisition of holdings in several local start-ups, including Patagon.com, and assisted Salutia.com in its round of financing with Merrill Lynch, and Agrositio on its financing by Morgan Stanley. **Clients:** Agrositio; America Online; Intel; Letsbuyit.com; Patagon.com; UOL Argentina; WebCom; Worldwide Wireless Communications.

Marval, O'Farrell & Mairal (4 ptrs, 9 asscs) Established leaders in most areas of convergence, the firm has an impressive client base of international and domestic entities. The telecoms department has been particularly busy advising foreign clients on their bids for telecoms concessions, as well as their acquisitions in Argentina. The firm advised Telmex on its acquisition of 60% of Techtel, a national network previously fully owned by Techint. It has also been counsel to Velecom in developing a wireless internet connection system.

In IT, **Gabriel Matarasso*** has impressed peers with his internet and e-commerce acumen. The internet practice group acts for a number of local start-ups, such as Musimundo.com, for whom it acted in the issuance of $10 million of convertible shares to Santander Central Hispano Trust & Banking Corporation. It also has experience as counsel for investors, acting for PuntoCom Holdings in the acquisition of $3.5 million shares in domestic web venture Autocompra.com. **Clients:** Chello broadband; Telmex; Velecom; Ambito Financiero; Educ.ar; Latinstocks.com; Net Partners; Paginar.Net; UBS Capital; StarMedia.

Sanchez Elia, Pinedo, Diaz Bobillo & Richard (3 ptrs, 11 asscs) *"A dynamic regulatory boutique,"* which has won widespread admiration for its telecoms practice, an area where it is *"important and well- connected."* Two high-calibre name partners, **José Sanchez Elia*** and **Federico Pinedo***, are considered to be the major reasons for the firm's pre-eminence. The two have government telecoms backgrounds, both having been Vice Chairman of the National Telecommunications Commission in the early 1990s. Sanchez Elia was Governor for Intelsat for Argentina, Chile and Paraguay, and Pinedo was Advisor to the Argentine Secretary of Communications and to the Caribbean Telecoms Union, and wrote the 'Blue Book' of telecoms policies for the Americas.

The firm acted on the acquisition of Keytech Ltd by AT&T Latin America, and represented Deutsche Aerospace on a satellite launch by Nahuelsat. It also advised on the start-up of Globalstar in Argentina, Chile and Paraguay. **Clients:** AT&T; Globalstar; Deutsche Aerospace; BT; MCI Worldcom; Diveo; IDT; OptiGlobe; Internet Argentina.

Negri Teijeiro & Incera Described by peers as *"One of the main names in e-commerce,"* the firm handles the whole range of legal work for internet start-ups, including organising corporate structures, tax planning, preparation for venture capital, software and product development, the establishment of strategic alliances with software companies and the development of stock option plans. It also has a practice in internet IP issues, such as protection from cyber-squatters and linking agreements. Clients include national start-ups and venture capital funds, and the firm also advises its clients on entrance into web-based distribution and marketing. **Federico Busso*** is considered an *"e-commerce guru."*

The firm acted on the sale of Patagon.com to Banco Santander Central Hispano, and has also advised on numerous investments in start-ups, such as Latinseguros.com, and on a strategic alliance between Mercosur.com and a Brazilian partner. **Clients:** Patagon.com; Mercosur.com; Small Enterprise Growth Fund; The Tower Fund; Antarctic Ventures Ltd.

Oyhanarte & Fargosi (8 ptrs, 5 asscs) Telecoms boutique, well-known for local regulatory advice, but which also carries out medium-ticket transactions. Clients include heavyweight international carriers, mainly US telecoms and satellite companies who are active in the local market. The firm also acts on the negotiation of contracts with customers, suppliers, partners and banks. Name partner **Alejandro Fargosi***, formerly director of legal affairs at Telefónica, is acknowledged by competitors to be *"one of the great telecoms specialists."* In IT, the firm advises a number of local start-up clients. **Clients:** MetroRed; AOL; Grupo Clarín; Movicom BellSouth; Comsat; PSINet; FirstMark; Tachyon Inc; Nextel Argentina; Techtel SA.

Altmark & Brenna An esteemed boutique with a focus on e-commerce. Rivals have commented that *"it's a pleasure to talk to them they know the issues."*

Baker & McKenzie (12 lawyers) *"One of the main players in e-commerce,"* and a respected player in telecoms, the Buenos Aires branch of the international network advises internet clients, including several local start-ups, on privacy rights, stock swaps, tax planning and finance negotiation. The team represented dot.com client Latinstocks on its recent $10 million restructuring, and Terramark, a Miami-based public company, on its acquisition of Spectrum Telecommunications' local branch. The telecoms group acted for Media One on its acquisition by AT&T, and advised Microsoft on reviewing its licensing agreements. The firm handles all Novel's local work, and advises on regulatory issues for clients such as Southern Cone, Teligen, and Terramark. **Clients:** Harris Corp; Telefónica de España; Nortel; Intel; DeRemate.com; Lucent Technologies; 3Com; Cisco; Compaq; Lycos; Yaonline.com.

M&M Bomchil (11 lawyers) The firm has extensive regulatory telecoms experience, and has handled corporate, tax and finance matters for an eclectic client base, which includes local TV, radio and cable providers. It handles all France Telecom's corporate interests, and advised on 360 Networks's project of installing a submarine cable from North America to Argentina and Brazil. The telecoms team includes a former manager of regulatory and legal affairs of the National Communications Commission. A two year old e-commerce practice advises local start-ups and internet investment funds on operational aspects, M&A, and IP issues. The firm acted for Liberty Media on its acquisition of a 51% interest in Cablevisión. **Clients:** Telecom Argentina; Nextel; 360 Networks; Alcatel Cable; Prime Television Ltd; Silicon Graphics; Winstar; Teledesic; iplan networks.

Estudio Millé (2 ptrs, 5 asscs) Our reseachers have found that this boutique is *"completely focused on the internet"* and has built its reputation in e-commerce from a history of working on IT-related IP issues. Noted for helping its clients to apply for licences and to form joint ventures, the firm has recently advised companies on developing internet-based voice communications. Managing partner **Antonio Millé*** has 20 years experience in e-commerce and has written widely on the subject. He is Chairman of the Latin American High Technology, Computers and Law Institute.

The firm is renowned for its advice to Microsoft, and it has been said that *"Microsoft's legal procedures in Argentina are developed by Millé."* The firm's clientele includes local start-ups, international blue-chip software companies and television and media corporates. **Clients:** 3Com; Business Software Alliance; AOL; Yahoo!; Microsoft; National Computer Software Chambers; CompuServe; Dell; EDS; Hewlett Packard; Siemens; 20th Century Fox.

Morrison & Foerster (9 lawyers) In the wake of Argentina's internet boom, the firm has used its international expertise to kick-start a thriving e-commerce practice, now acknowledged to be *"one of the big three."* It is supported by a lower profile telecoms capability. The firm advises internet clients on venture capital, IPOs, internet-related contracts, and regulatory matters. Acted for DeRemate.com on a $40 million Series B investment from Terra Networks, an investment and co-branding deal with Deautos.com and numerous IP issues. It has also represented Accor and eVision Partners on various venture capital investments in technology companies throughout the region. **Clients:** ViaX; Internet Argentina; DeRemate.com; Advertium.com; Amtec.net; Accor; 7por24.com; eVision Partners.

Estudio O'Farrell Well known for being counsel to Telefónica, this full-service firm's telecoms experience extends to acting for the company's internet and mobile phone subsidiaries. It is also building a reputation for itself in e-commerce and advises entertainment and mass communications clients, such as Cablevisión, on editing and artistic production contracts. **Clients:** Telefónica de Argentina; Cablevisión; Miniphone; Startel; Advance.

Other Notable Practitioner Sole practitioner **Gabriela Marsiglia*** is known in local legal circles as *"one of the best for telecoms."* Her practice concentrates on regulatory matters, including obtaining licences and representing clients before the national regulatory body. Current clients include telecoms big-hitters such as Movicom, Sprint Cellular, Grupo Clarín, SkyTel, Embratel, and Comsat.

A

Competition/Anti-trust

Alvarez Prado, Cabanellas & Kelly (5 ptrs, 17 asscs) Full-service firm with an acclaimed competition practice, which makes merger control applications for corporate clients from all industries, and has wide experience of anti-trust advocacy. **Guillermo Cabanellas*** is a competition law guru, widely regarded among the Buenos Aires étite as *"the paramount authority in Argentina,"* having written the standard anti-trust text book in South America. His expertise is not merely theoretical: he has defended a number of foreign companies before the national anti-dumping authority. The firm's most active clients are General Electric, United Technologies and Coto (national supermarket chain) for whom it undertakes a stream of merger control and associated anti-trust applications. **Clients:** General Electric; United Technologies; Coto.

Marval, O'Farrell & Mairal (2 ptrs, 9 asscs) With the largest corporate department in the country, the firm has developed a commensurably highly regarded competition practice, and has particular expertise on merger control work. **Fernando Aranovich***, head of the firm's anti-trust department, is a *"bright, serious lawyer."* A former adviser to the Secretary of State for Economic Planning and a professor of antitrust law, he has made frequent appearances before the anti-trust commission, and has advised a number of multinationals on anti-trust matters arising from their acquisitions in Argentina.

The firm acted as counsel to Philip Morris in a successful challenge before the anti-trust commission to a change to its distribution system, and advised on the purchase of Nabisco by Kraft. The team also advised on the merger between Carrefour and Promodès. **Clients:** Danone; Carrefour; Philip Morris; Kraft.

Allende & Brea According to market opinion this large general commercial firm has a strong M&A practice, and an increasing reputation for its merger control work. Active for the highly acquisitive Hicks, Muse, Tate & Furst, the firm has made several applications to the anti-trust commission, such as that over the acquisition of Cablevisión. The team also advised on the sale of Chase Equity's holding in Patagon.com to Banco Santander, and the acquisition of several cable companies by Teledigital Cable. **Clients:** Chase Equity Associates; Hicks, Muse, Tate & Furst; Teledigital Cable SA.

G Breuer (7 ptrs, 10 asscs) Our researchers found that this leading IP firm, has established a name

*See leaders' profiles on pages 60-63

A

ARGENTINA Leading firms (Competition/Anti-trust)
1 Alvarez Prado, Cabanellas & Kelly
Marval, O'Farrell & Mairal
2 Allende & Brea
G Breuer
Estudio Ramos Mejia
3 Harfouche, Graneros & Asociados
Klein & Franco

Firms are listed alphabetically in each band.

Leading individuals (Competition/Anti-trust)
1 ARANOVICH Fernando *Marval, O'Farrell*
CABANELLAS Guillermo *Alvarez Prado*
2 GOLDARACENA Fernando *Ramos Mejia*
OTAMENDI Jorge *G Breuer*
SPOLANSKY Norberto *Spolansky Bobbio*
3 FRANCO Carlos *Klein & Franco*
HARFOUCHE Pablo *Harfouche, Graneros*

Individuals are listed alphabetically in each band.

for anti-trust advice in the area of trademarks and patents. The firm is acknowledged as *"the best"* where competition and IP converge. **Jorge Otamendi*** commands universal market respect. Advising on a wide range of competition activity, the firm handles applications for prior approval of mergers and acquisitions, as well as complaints over anti-trust violations, and the defence of such complaints. The team has also been consulted by Argentinean corporates on the preparation of defences to US anti-dumping claims. **Clients:** Praxair; Walt Disney; Dow Chemical Co; PepsiCo; Levi Strauss; Mars; Reebok; Volkswagen; L'Oreal; Unilever.

Estudio Ramos Mejia (3 ptrs) Lacking the corporate clout of the market leaders, the firm is famed for its work on anti-cartel cases. The firm predominantly advises domestic corporates, although it has recently begun to represent a limited number of blue-chip international concerns. **Fernando Goldaracena*** is the outstanding name here, and one of the most well-respected anti-trust lawyers in the country. He was a member of the original anti-trust commission for five years in the early 1980s, and has a fine academic record. The firm advised YPF on its appeal against the largest anti-cartel fine in Argentine history ($250 million) and has also represented Nobleza Picaro and Lever in anti-cartel claims. **Clients:** YPF; Nobleza Picaro; Lever (with Procter & Gamble).

Harfouche, Granero & Asociados (8 lawyers) The firm owes its considerable anti-trust reputation to the esteemed **Pablo Harfouche***, whose practice entails work on merger control, anti-competitive practices, and state aids cases. He also has niche expertise in anti-dumping cases. The firm advised Ambito Financiero on an action against Clarín, which has reached the Supreme Court. **Clients:** Volvo; Parmalat; Banco Mercantil; TV Vision; Wal Mart; Unisys Argentina.

Klein & Franco (4 lawyers) Respected since its work on a series of anti-monopoly cases in the 1990s, the firm is now active on filing merger applications before the anti-trust commission, and has acknowledged anti-dumping expertise. The tobacco and paper industries are substantial contributors to the firm's client roster. **Carlos Franco*** is regarded in local legal circles as *"one of very few genuine competition law experts"* in Argentina. The firm advised on CNG's sale of its Argentinean gas and electricity interests to Sempra Energies, and the sale by Exxel of a controlling interest in Supermercados Norte to Promodès. **Clients:** Filimores; Tetrapak; CNG International;

Other Notable Practitioner Sole practitioner **Norberto Spolansky** is regarded as an *"effective litigator in the anti-trust sphere."*

Corporate/M&A

Marval, O'Farrell & Mairal (50 ptrs, 200 asscs) By far the largest Argentinian law firm, it is also widely regarded as the *"number one"* for general commercial work, notably cross-border M&A. Especially strong in financial services, the corporate group has a huge international client base and *"a tradition in the market"* which gives it an advantage over most of its rivals.

Considered by both peers and clients to possess *"a constellation of stars,"* the department has grown rapidly in the last decade, and includes the *"excellent"* **Héctor Mairal***, *"one of the best lawyers in the country,"* who is an expert in administrative law, as well as a corporate guru. *"Rainmaker"* **Juan Cambiaso*** has a similarly towering reputation, while **Alfredo O'Farrell*** also retains his share of market support.

The firm advised YPF on its takeover by Repsol, acted for a group of investment funds, led by Goldman Sachs, on the acquisition of part of Grupo Clarín, the Argentinian media group, and represented JP Morgan, underwriters of the sale of securities in Telecom Argentina. **Clients:** JP Morgan; international and domestic corporates and financial institutions.

Cárdenas Cassagne & Asociados (4 ptrs, 12 asscs) A well-established, *"prestigious"* firm, with a strong M&A reputation, notably in the energy industry. The department also advises a range of investment funds, banks and leading players in the food industry.

Respected name partner **Juan Carlos Cassagne*** has vast experience of work on behalf of utilities and telecoms clients, and remains a leading national figure, although his transactional profile is not as strong as formerly. His work on the privatised industries in the early 1990s has led to a client base which now includes top companies such as Edenor, Telefónica, Aguas Argentinas, and Metrogas. Rising name **Luis Lucero*** has built an enviable reputation amongst Buenos Aires lawyers for his advice on the acquisition of companies owning rights to mining projects. He co-headed the team acting for YPF in the acquisition of part of a Brazilian oil refinery, Manghinhos.

Highlight transactions include advising JP Morgan on the sale of shares in the holding company of Telecom Argentina. The firm also acted for BAT in connection with its tender offer for an interest in a local tobacco company, and NH Hoteles of Spain on their acquisition of several Buenos Aires hotels. **Clients:** British Gas; BAT; Bank of Nova Scotia; Christie's Inc; West LB Group; Banque Nationale de Paris; JP Morgan; NH Hoteles; Newmont Gold.

Hope Duggan & Silva (4 ptrs, 20 asscs) In spite of its historical reputation for capital markets advice, rivals informed our researchers that the firm is now equally recognised for its M&A work, acting for an international clientele which

ARGENTINA
Leading firms
(Corporate/Mergers & Acquisitions)

Band	Firm
1	Marval, O'Farrell & Mairal
2	Cárdenas Cassagne & Asociados
	Hope Duggan & Silva
	Estudio O'Farrell
	Perez Alati, Grondona, Benites, Arntsen & Martinez de Hoz
3	Estudio Alegria
	Allende & Brea
	Estudio Beccar Varela
	Bruchou, Fernandez Madero Lombardi & Mitrani
	M&M Bomchil
4	Baker & McKenzie
	Brons & Salas
	Klein & Franco
	Negri Teijeiro & Incera
	Quattrini, Laprida & Asociados
5	Abeledo Gottheil Abogados
	Alfaro Navarro
	Basilico Fernandez Madero & Duggan
	Muñoz de Toro

Firms are listed alphabetically in each band.

Leading individuals
(Corporate/Mergers & Acquisitions)

Band	Individual
1	**CAMBIASO Juan** *Marval, O'Farrell & Mairal*
	MAIRAL Héctor *Marval, O'Farrell & Mairal*
2	**ALEGRIA Hector** *Estudio Alegria*
	CASSAGNE Juan Carlos *Cárdenas Cassagne &*
	DUGGAN Juan *Hope Duggan & Silva*
	HOPE Adrian *Hope Duggan & Silva*
	KLEIN Guillermo Walter *Klein & Franco*
	O'FARRELL Juan Patricio *Estudio O'Farrell*
	QUATTRINI Sergio *Quattrini, Laprida*
	SILVA Roberto *Hope Duggan & Silva*
3	**BECCAR VARELA Damian** *Estudio Beccar Varela*
	BOMCHIL Maximo *M & M Bomchil*
	NEGRI Juan Javier *Negri Teijeiro & Incera*
	PEREZ ALATI Jorge Luis *Perez Alati, Grondona*
	ROVIRA Alfredo *Brons & Salas*
4	**BRUCHOU Enrique** *Bruchou, Fernandez Madero*
	BUEY FERNANDEZ Pablo *Estudio Alegria*
	LASHERAS Alberto *Estudio Beccar Varela*
	MUÑOZ DE TORO Fernando *Muñoz de Toro*
	O'FARRELL Alfredo *Marval, O'Farrell & Mairal*

Up-and-coming individuals

LUCERO Luis *Cárdenas Cassagne & Asociados*

Individuals are listed alphabetically in each band.

includes industrial names, investment and retail banks, public utilities, venture capital/private equity firms, investment funds and government agencies. The strength of the firm is considered to lie in its individual lawyers, of whom three enjoy especially strong reputations. The *"easy-going"* **Roberto Silva*** is a *"technically superb corporate lawyer,"* while **Juan Duggan*** *("a serious player")* and **Adrian Hope*** are felt to excel on both M&A and financing transactions.

The firm acted for Citicorp on the sale of its holding in Grupo Atlantida Comunicaciones, and has also represented PSINet on its acquisition of local internet companies, including Argentina On Line. **Clients:** Alcatel; BP; BBV; Citicorp Holdings; Chase Manhattan; Enron; HSBC; Morgan Grenfell; Siemens.

Estudio O'Farrell One of the oldest firms in the country, it is regarded as having maintained a high level of activity despite the loss of one of its main domestic clients, Telefónica de Argentina. A broad commercial practice encompasses a wide range of domestic and foreign clients from traditional industries, insurance, communications, energy and financial services. **Juan Patricio O'Farrell*** is the firm's leading practitioner. **Clients:** Ford.

Perez Alati, Grondona, Benites, Arnsten & Martinez de Hoz (12 ptrs, 64 asscs) *"Young and dynamic"* firm with a strong focus on M&A advice and an *"aggressive"* style. A heavyweight client base includes privatised public utilities, manufacturers, telecoms entities, insurance companies and banks. Joint ventures and leasing agreements form key elements of the caseload, but it is the firm's specialisation in the energy sector which provides the transactions with the greatest profile. **Jorge Luis Perez Alati*** is a respected commercial all-rounder. The firm represented the refiners Sol Petrolero in the spin-off of its fuel marketing business to ANCAP, the Uruguayan national oil company. It also advised on the acquisition by Banco Santander of a controlling interest in Banco Río de la Plata, one of the largest banks in Argentina. **Clients:** ING; Chase Manhattan; CSFB; Banco Santander; DKB; Motorola; Hewlett Packard; Proctor & Gamble; Time Warner; Western Union; Standard & Poor's.

Estudio Alegria Chambers researchers have found that this Small firm, acclaimed for its insolvency practice, which has also increased its general commercial profile. Advising a number of international and domestic corporates and financial institutions, the team is led by the *"king of bankruptcy"* **Hector Alegria***, who receives *"valuable support"* from **Pablo Buey Fernandez***.

Allende & Brea (18 ptrs, 63 asscs) One of the largest firms in Buenos Aires, it is well known for its sound M&A practice, which advises a client roster laden with blue-chip names, notably financial institutions. All associates trained at the firm spend a year working in the US, leading to a *"homogenous profile"* and a high level of bilingualism. The team has specific expertise in IT, where it has experienced marked transactional growth.

Chase Equity Associates were advised on the acquisition of a stake in Patagon.com and its subsequent sale to Banco Santander, and the group also represented Hicks, Muse, Tate & Furst on its acquisition of a controlling interest in CEI Citicorp Holdings SA. **Clients:** Microsoft; AOL; Universe on line; P&O; Chase Equity Associates; AETNA; Telecom Italia; Renault; STET-France Telecom; Bank of America; Eagle Star.

Estudio Beccar Varela (23 ptrs, 70 asscs) Traditional firm, characterised by competitors as *"good people with good clients,"* which has acknowledged expertise in acting for financial institutions. The beneficiary of numerous referrals, the firm has acquired a number of multi-national clients. **Damian Beccar Varela*** has an outstanding individual reputation, while **Alberto Lasheras*** was also strongly recommended to our researchers.

The firm represented Grupo Financiero SA and Banco de Galicia y Buenos Aires, the largest bank in Argentina, in the forging of a strategic alliance between Portugal Telecom, Unibanco and Banco Galicia. **Clients:** SmithKline Beecham; Glaxo Welocme; Beyer; ING; Citibank; Banco Galicia; Sigma; Ace; ABN AMRO; Dresdner Kleinwort Benson; KFW.

Bruchou, Fernandez Madero Lombardi & Mitrani (8 ptrs, 62 asscs) Formed from the banking department of Estudio Beccar Varela, the firm is gaining a reputation for general commercial work on the back of its top-class financial base. Eschewing day to day matters, the firm is noted for its involvement on big-ticket M&A transactions. As well as advising the lenders on major acquisitions, the firm also acts for a select group of industrial clients. Harvard-educated **Enrique Bruchou***, formerly of Shearman & Sterling, is considered by rivals as *"an excellent lawyer."*

The team advised Banco Bisel on the acquisition of the capital stock of Banco Suquía, and acted for the shareholders of Keytech LD, a local telecoms company, during its sale to AT&T Latin America. **Clients:** Perez Companc group; AT&T; Techint.

M&M Bomchil (8 ptrs, 48 asscs) *"Definitely a player,"* this is a traditional firm which advises on

*See leaders' profiles on pages 60-63

cross-border M&A, IPOs and joint ventures, and enjoys an especially secure reputation in the energy sector. Considered to have *"almost a monopoly on French clients in Argentina,"* the firm also boasts a strong domestic clientele. Managing partner **Maximo Bomchil*** is the outstanding name here, and is best known for his work on the Buenos Aires airport deal.

The firm recently acted for Promodès on its acquisition of a 49% interest in Supermercados Norte SA, and for Groupe Bongrain on its acquisition of Nestlé's cheese business. **Clients:** ADECCO; Aguas Argentinas; Alcatel Cable; Bloomberg; Endesa; France Telecom; Hasbro; Mango; PepsiCo; PSA Peugeot; Renault; TotalFinaElf; UPS.

A

Baker & McKenzie (2 ptrs, 10 asscs) Acting almost exclusively for international clients, the group thrives on referrals from the firm's international network. Cross-border M&A is considered to be the Buenos Aires office's forte, with much of the work coming from the telecoms, e-commerce and banking sectors.

A major recent coup saw the firm gain Telefónica as a client, while a raft of multi-jurisdictional transactions include representing Procter & Gamble on its acquisition of 50% of a company producing paper products in Chile and Argentina. The firm also represented an insurance company on the acquisition of competitors in Argentina and Uruguay. **Clients:** Adecco; Calvin Klein; Lloyd's Bank; Procter & Gamble; Sony; Intergen Energy.

Brons & Salas (15 ptrs, 70 asscs) Considered by competitors to be especially strong on corporate matters, the firm's client base is split between Argentinian companies and multi-nationals. E-commerce has provided an eye-catching series of transactions. The esteemed **Alfredo Rovira*** *("an academic with a commercial mind")* is professor of commercial law at Buenos Aires University and joint head of the firm's M&A department. He handles all varieties of commercial transactions, including debt restructuring work, and also supervises the firm's anti-trust department. The firm recently acted on the merger of 22 companies into RTC Argentina. **Clients:** Bacardi Martini Argentina; CBS; Citicorp; General Motors; Hitachi; HSBC; Mercedes Benz; Michelin; Revlon; Mitsui Taiyo Kobe Bank.

Klein & Franco (6 ptrs, 23 asscs) Market opinion suggests that this traditional, but small firm owes its continuing corporate status to the outstanding individual reputation of name partner **Guillermo Walter Klein***. Recognised as *"a major figure,"* he has been largely responsible for forging relationships with both Argentinean and US clients in the energy sector, banking and media.

Frequently acting for the seller, the firm represented Exxel on the sale of a controlling interest in Supermercados Norte to Logidis, a member of the Promodès Group. The group also represented Sideco Americana in the sale of the postal service in Argentina to International Mail Corporation. On the buy side, the team advised the Argentine subsidiary of Tabletop Acquisition on the acquisition of the sweetener business of Nutrasweet, Equal and Canderel from the local subsidiary of Monsanto. **Clients:** Aegis; Electrolux; American Express Bank; CNG; Ernst & Young; Banco Bansud; Coca-Cola (local subsidiary); Correo Argentino; Sideco; Exxel.

Negri Teijeiro & Incera (45 lawyers) Medium-sized firm known by peers and clients for its variety of cross-border M&A work on behalf of a number of household names. The corporate team's stand-out figure is **Juan Javier Negri***. The group acted for the sellers on the sale of Petrolera Argentina San Jorge to Chevron Canada, and represented internet financial services company, Patagon.com, on its sale to Banco Santander, a deal worth $585 million. Internet clients have made up the bulk of the firm's workload this year. **Clients:** ABN AMRO; Banque Nationale de Paris; Barclays Bank; Coca-Cola; CompuServe Argentina; CSFB; Enron; InterAmerican Investment Corporation; Mitsubishi; Patagon.com; Smithkline Beecham.

Quattrini, Laprida & Asociados (40 lawyers) The loss of major client, the Exxel Group, heralded a difficult year for a firm which had hitherto enjoyed almost unbroken success. However, the firm maintains a strong transactional reputation, and the Peruvian **Sergio Quattrini***, who started his career as Baker & McKenzie's point of contact in Argentina, is said to be *"a spectacular M&A lawyer."* **Clients:** Den Norske Bank; HJ Heinz.

Abeledo Gottheil Abogados (12 ptrs, 38 asscs) A general commercial firm that acts for a large number of multi-nationals and enjoys a particular reputation in energy. An active M&A profile is enhanced by an alliance with UK firm Allen & Overy, a link which brings it work for Morgan Grenfell. Recent transactions include acting for Morgan Grenfell on the acquisition of Worldwide Polymers from CIBA. The firm also advised Burlington Northern, a US rail company, on the sale of its shares in Argentinean train and metro companies to local groups. A key client is Microsoft, for whom the firm acted on the issue of software licences to the federal and provincial governments. **Clients:** Compagnie Nationale des Ors (Vivendi); PepsiCo; Andersen Consulting; Torneos y Competencias; Microsoft; Dupont; PWC; ING; Vodafone Airtouch; Shell.

Alfaro Navarro (5 ptrs, 35 asscs) Although a comparatively small organisation, the firm has offices in New York, London and Madrid. The firm is also a member of the World Law Group. Now one of the representatives of the Exxel Group, one of the largest buy-out companies in South America, the firm has advised them on several big-ticket transactions, as well as acting for clients in the commodities, energy and IT sectors. The firm advised on the sale of Supermercados Norte to Carrefour. **Clients:** Exxel; Sun Microsystems; OPIC; InterAmerican Investment Bank; Pirelli; J Aaron (of Goldman Sachs); Hess Trading Corporation; Georgia Pacific.

Basilico Fernandez Madero & Duggan Advising both local and international coporates, the firm is represented for its medium-ticket M&A work and has particular expertise in Telecoms, energy and e-commerce. It is also well known for its work on Argentina's recent round of privatisation. Among its clientele are a number of high profile US and western European companies. **Clients:** Agencies; pharmaceutical companies; financial institutions.

Muñoz de Toro (5 ptrs, 15 asscs) Relatively new, *"aggressive"* and expanding firm, with a rapidly growing reputation in the Argentine legal scene for M&A, capital markets and general corporate finance work. Commended for its international outlook, the firm principally advises big-name Argentinean corporates and financial institutions. Founding partner **Fernando Muñoz de Toro*** is said to be *"quite exceptional."* It started life representing the first international investment banks to venture into Argentina and branched into M&A work later.

The group represented the Argentinean Ministry of the Economy on its sale of holdings in various utility entities, and acted for the Arcor group on its sale of two companies to an offshore vehicle, controlled inter alia by JP Morgan. Also assisted Newbridge Latin America on its acquisition of a holding in local investment fund Diginet, and advised on the merger of Hoyts Cinemas Argentina with General Cinema de Argentina. **Clients:** Argentine Ministry of Economy; Arcor Group; Heller Financial; Galicia Capital Markets; Sociedad Comercial del Plata; Hoyts Cinemas.

Energy & Natural Resources

ARGENTINA
Leading firms
(Energy & Natural Resources)

Band	Firm
1	Bazan Cambré & Orts
	Maciel Norman & Asociados
	Perez Alati, Grondona, Benites, Arntsen & Martinez de Hoz
2	Cárdenas Cassagne & Asociados
	M&M Bomchil
	Martelli Abogados
	Marval, O'Farrell & Mairal
3	Abeledo Gottheil Abogados
	Allende & Brea
	Estudio Beccar Varela
	Estudio Bruzzon & Asociados
	Estudio O'Farrell

Firms are listed alphabetically in each band.

Leading individuals
(Energy & Natural Resources)

Band	Individual
1	**MARTINEZ DE HOZ José** *Perez Alati, Grondona*
	NORMAN Justo *Estudio Maciel Norman*
	ORTS Mario *Bazan Cambré & Orts*
2	**BOMCHIL Maximo** *M&M Bomchil*
	FORTUNATI Roberto *Estudio Beccar Varela*
	MARTELLI Hugo *Martelli Abogados*
3	**BIANCHI Daniel** *Allende & Brea*
	CASSAGNE Juan Carlos *Cárdenas Cassagne*
	ERIZE Luis *Abeledo Gottheil Abogados*
	MAIRAL Héctor *Marval, O'Farrell & Mairal*
	O'FARRELL Uriel *Estudio O'Farrell*
	TAWIL Guido *M&M Bomchil*
	VALIENTE-NOAILLES Carlos *Bazan Cambré*

Individuals are listed alphabetically in each band.

Bazan Cambré & Orts (12-15 lawyers) A specialised energy boutique, with a particular niche in oil and gas, which advises a strong client base of local and international entities. The group's Canadian clientele is especially strong. Our researchers found that the *"distinguished"* **Mario Orts*** is one of Argentina's leading energy lawyers, and receives valuable support from oil specialist **Carlos Valiente-Noailles***. **Clients:** Alberta Energy; Atomic Energy of Canada; Oil-Gener Argentina; ProPak; Reef Exploration; Canadian Airlines International.

Maciel Norman & Asociados (2 ptrs, 25 asscs) Although the firm has lost two younger partners, who left to establish Martelli Abogados, the energy group is still regarded by peers as among the leaders in Argentina. A *"traditional energy practice"* excels in upstream oil and gas advice, and receives substantial support from the firm's corporate department. Transactional work remains the forte, and the energy team advises a number of blue-chip US and Canadian companies. Founding partner **Justo Norman*** is renowned for his advice, both transactionally and as a *"leading academic resource."*

The firm advised Petrogas on its acquisition of a refinery and 700 gas stations from YPF/Repsol, and represented Santa Fe Energy in handling the first exploration block located in an area owned by two cities, in Neuquen (Southern Argentina). **Clients:** Petrobras; Santa Fe Energy; British Gas; Lasmo; Canadian Occidental Petroleum; Esso Argentina; Parker Drilling; Petronas; Rio Alto Explorations.

Perez Alati, Grondona, Benites, Arntsen & Martinez de Hoz (3 ptrs, 8 asscs) The firm's thriving energy practice attracts market commendation for both its oil and gas and electricity expertise. Energy projects, such as power plants, are other areas of strength, and the team has established a name for advising on pipeline gas exports to neighbouring countries.

The group is led by *"first-class specialist"* **José Martinez de Hoz***, who advises on regulatory matters, contracts and transactions, and was a leading player on the acquisition of TransCanada's assets in Brazil, Argentina and Chile by TotalFinaElf Argentina. Activity in the electricity sector includes power marketing and distribution agreements, and the team advised a syndicate of banks led by Chase Manhattan in financing the Profertil project.

Other transactions include the purchase by Duke Energy of all the energy assets of Dominion in the Southern Cone, and the acquisition for the same client of an Argentinian hydro-electric facility and thermal power plant. **Clients:** PanAmerican Energy (subsidiary of BPAmoco); Shell; Enron; Duke Energy; CNS Energy; GPU; Wintershal; Entergy Corporation; Enersis; TotalFinaElf.

Cárdenas Cassagne & Asociados (19 ptrs, 40 asscs) A fine reputation for oil and gas regulatory work has sprung from the firm's history of advising the foreign oil companies that invested in the country in the 1980s and 1990s. The team is consistently acknowledged by Buenos Aires lawyers for its work in the privatised utilities. Although not a specialist energy lawyer, **Juan Carlos Cassagne**'s* ability to win oil and gas clients and his all-round regulatory ability are beyond contest.

The department advised the successful consortium on the Peruvian gas transport and distribution concession, and acted on a joint venture, led by General Electric, concerning operations and maintenance agreements for several power plants in Argentina and Chile. **Clients:** MetroGas; Aguas Argentinas; YPF/ Repsol; Telefonica; Edenor; Shell; Endesa; GPU; ASTRA.

M&M Bomchil (1 ptr, 8 asscs) *Chambers'* researchers have found that the energy team has a first-class reputation for advice in the electricity sector, acting for utilities, electrical and thermoelectrical producers. Although best known for its regulatory work, the group also handles medium-ticket transactions, and has further expertise in oil and gas, water and general energy litigation. The team has acted against the federal government over tariffs in the privatised utilities.

Maximo Bomchil* *("a class A performer")* and **Guido Tawil*** form a respected spearhead of the practice. The latter has extensive experience of acting on gas pipeline projects. Cross-border work has included representing CEMSA in the first electricity export deal to Brazil, and the team has also advised on the privatisation of the Bolivian and Uruguayan water industries. Also represented Transelec on its bid for the national grid concession, and advised CMS Gas on the acquisition of a stake in Transportadora de Gas del Norte. **Clients:** Endesa; Total Raffinage; Elf; CMS Gas; Enron; CEMSA; Transelec; Aguas Argentinas; Aguas de Barcelona; Aeropuertos Argentina 2000.

Martelli Abogados (2 ptrs, 2 asscs) A spin-off from Maciel Norman, the firm has immediately established its reputation in the energy industry, from where 50% of its clients originate. The team principally handles regulatory aspects of energy work, including environmental and anti-trust regulations. The majority of the client base are US, Canadian or European concerns, principally associated with gas transportation systems and oil production. Name partner **Hugo Martelli***, who is highly recommended by rivals as an oil and gas expert, also handles the firm's mining work. The bulk of his practice revolves around oil and gas exploration and production pipeline construction and mining exploration.

The firm represented TransCanada on the sale of some of its assets in Argentina, Chile and Brazil

*See leaders' profiles on pages 60-63

to TotalFina, and advised the same company on the construction of a gas pipeline from Argentina to Concepcion (Chile) worth $350 million. Other recent work includes advising on the construction and operation of a gas pipeline from Bolivia to Brazil, and acting on distribution and transportation contracts and sale and purchase agreements. **Clients:** TransCanada; Pioneer Natural Resources; Petrobras; Petrona; Champion Technologies; Parker Drilling; British Gas; ExxonMobile; Phelps Dodge.

Marval O'Farrell & Mairal (3 ptrs, 12 asscs The largest Argentinian law firm offers a sizeable, *"top quality"* energy practice, with experience in gas and electricity. Transactional and regulatory matters are handled for a powerful clientele of domestic and international energy companies. Leading light **Héctor Mairal*** is described by counterparts as *"vastly experienced,"* and advised the government on the development of the regulatory framework for the gas industry.

The group assisted Tractabel (a subsidiary of French Suez Lyonnaise des Eaux) on its acquisitions in Argentina, and represented Compañía Mega (a joint venture) on its financing of the construction of a gas separation plant and pipeline, and storage and loading port facilities worth $472 million. **Clients:** Sempra Energy; British Gas; Tractabel (and its local subsidiaries).

Abeledo Gottheil Abogados (50 lawyers) Although this *"small and active"* team advises such oil and gas giants as Shell, its reputation lies principally in electricity. Power projects, regulatory advice and medium-ticket transactions are cornerstones of the practice. **Luis Erize*** is a familiar figure nationally, and is respected for his *"technical competence."*

The firm advised Tierra Nueva Resources on the acquisition of an interest in an oil exploration plant from a Perez Companc subsidiary, and has represented Black & Veatch on several power plant projects. On contentious matters, the firm assisted a well-known oil producer on an environmental dispute with surface owners. **Clients:** Shell; EMEC; Gemplus Argentina; Global Marine Drilling Co; Hidrovia; NRG Energy; Pluspetrol; Vivendi; Union Texas Petroleum; BOC.

Allende & Brea (18 ptrs, 63 asscs) The firm is respected for its activity in oil, gas, mining and environmental law. **Daniel Bianchi*** is well known as the head of the firm's natural resources department, and is the first Argentinian to be a trustee of the Rocky Mountain Mineral Law Foundation. The firm represents clients in electricity generation and gas transportation and distribution projects, as well as regulatory issues arising from electricity distribution.

The team advises several US and Canadian clients who successfully obtained concessions under the electricity privatisation in the 1990s. It also represents international concerns on the construction of oil and gas pipelines, and advised a US client on the construction of the first gas pipeline from Argentina to Brazil, and on the negotiation of a gas purchase agreement with YPF. **Clients:** RTC; Western Mining; Rio Algam; Felps Large; Mobil Argentina; Texaco; Coastal Corp (transport wing of El Paso Natural Gas); CVRD; Bechtel.

Estudio Beccar Varela Full-service firm with *"a long tradition of work in power,"* where it is particularly commended for project finance. The team handles regulatory matters, supply contracts, environmental issues, and litigation for clients such as EDS, whom it has assisted on several hydroelectric projects. Electricity clients include transmission, distribution and large consumer companies. **Roberto Fortunati***, former in-house counsel at Amoco Argentina, has a top-class name for project finance, and has also advised on a number of electricity transactions. The firm was counsel on the $1 billion Minera Alumbrera mining project. **Clients:** Lubrizol; Quintana Minerals; Sunshine Mining and Refining; EDS; ENEL; Amoco; PDVESA; Total; Global Natural Resources; Rio Tinto; Thyssen Mining.

Estudio Bruzzon & Asociados (3 ptrs, 17 asscs) Comparatively young firm which handles both regulatory and transactional matters in oil, gas, water and mining, and is said to *"dabble"* in electricity. The group recently sprang to prominence through its advice to Chevron on its acquisition of Petrolera San Jorge, the largest ever acquisition between private companies in Argentina. The firm has experience of both inbound and outbound investment in the energy sector, and has represented Argentinean conglomerates investing in the rest of Latin America and in the Middle East. **Clients:** Refinor; Oleoductos del Valle; Chevron; Amoco; Mobil; Perez Companc; Pioneer Natural Resources; Houston Industries.

Estudio O'Farrell For rivals and clients alike the firm's energy reputation lies mainly with its transactional advice in the electricity industry, although it also advises oil and gas clients on regulatory matters, marketing, and the expansion and operation of transportation facilities. **Uriel O'Farrell*** is the team's most recognisable name. The firm has advised on the export of gas to Chile, Uruguay and Brazil, and has represented domestic and foreign oil clients on the exploration and exploitation of hydrocarbons.

Leaders' profiles – Argentina

ALEGRIA, Hector
Estudio Alegria, Buenos Aires +54 11 4812 5500
Recommended in Corporate/M&A

ARANOVICH, Fernando
Marval, O'Farrell & Mairal, Buenos Aires +54 11 4310 0100
Recommended in Competition/Anti-trust

AROCENA, Juan Martín
Allende & Brea, Buenos Aires +54 11 4318 9900 jma@allendebrea.com.ar
Recommended in Communications
Specialisation: Partner of *Allende & Brea* since 1999. Main areas of work are M&A and transnational transactions in general, capital markets and other corporate matters including public and private combinations, spin-offs and securitisation.
Personal: Born in Montevideo, Uruguay on March 25 1964. Admitted to the bar in Argentina in 1988 and in New York in 1990. Legal education: Universidad Católica Argentina (LLB 1988). University of Illinois (LLM 1990).

BECCAR VARELA, Damian
Estudio Beccar Varela, Buenos Aires +54 11 4379 6800
Recommended in Corporate/M&A

BIANCHI, Daniel
Allende & Brea, Buenos Aires +54 11 4318 9900 dab@allendebrea.com.ar
Recommended in Energy & Natural Resources
Specialisation: Partner in charge of the Natural Resource Department. Main areas of work are Oil, Gas and Mining.
Prof. Memberships: Buenos Aires Bar Association; American Bar Association; Natural Resources Committee of the Buenos Aires Bar Association (Chairman 1996 to date); Trustee at Large of the Rocky Mountain Mineral Law Foundation (Denver, Colorado, July 2000 to date).
Personal: Born in Buenos Aires, Argentina, on May

7, 1945. Attended University of Buenos Aires Law School 1965-69, Juris Doctor (JD).

BOMCHIL, Maximo

M & M Bomchil, Buenos Aires +541 1 4321 7500
Recommended in Corporate/M&A, Energy & Natural Resources

BRUCHOU, Enrique

Bruchou, Fernandez Madero, Lombardi & Mitrani, Buenos Aires +54 11 5288 2300
eb@bfmyl.com.ar
Recommended in Banking & Finance, Corporate/M&A

Specialisation: Founder and Senior Partner of the firm. Main area of work is corporate finance, banking and mergers & acquisitions. Since the firm's set up in 1989, has represented many major investment banks and large corporations both in groundbreaking capital markets and mergers and acquisitions transactions in Argentina. Participated in, among others, the largest initial public offering of an Argentine Company of US$3 billion, YPF (1993), the acquisition of Banco Rio de la Plata S.A. (at the time, the largest Argentine commercial bank) by Banco Santander of Spain (1997), the acquisition of the largest Argentine food company, Molinos Rio de la Plata S.A. by the Perez Companc Family Group (1999) and the first hostile take over in Argentina, Repsol/YPF for over US$13 billion (1999).
Career: Graduated from the Argentine Catholic University Law School in 1979, and also taught Monetary and Banking Law. Obtained an LLM degree from Harvard Law School in 1982 and practised as foreign associate in *Shearman & Sterling* New York, for two years. Lectured on Corporate Finance and Capital Markets at seminars and served for several years as member and secretary of the Board of the Harvard Club of Argentina.
Personal: Born on February 24, 1956. Leisure interests include marathon running. Lives in Buenos Aires.

BUEY FERNANDEZ, Pablo Andres

Estudio Alegria, Buenos Aires +54 11 4812 5500
Recommended in Corporate/M&A

Specialisation: Partner in corporate department. Main area of work is mergers and acquisitions, direct foreign investments, new issues of equity and debt in related capital market transactions, financial restructurings and general corporate finance advice. Has handled acquisitions of local companies by foreign strategic purchasers, acting on behalf of sellers and buyers; lead role in the merger of two publicly listed companies, Juan Minetti SA and Corcemar SA, resulting in the country's second largest cement undertaking and in the acquisition of one of the leading local banks by a European financial group. Serves in several boards on behalf of foreign clients. Since 1981 teaches commercial law, international business transactions and comparative securities regulation at the University of Buenos Aires, Law School and in other Masters and Post raduate programs; lecturer in several international and local conferences, scientific meetings and training programs in Argentina, and Brazil. Reporting member of the Committee J of the IBA Conference in Buenos Aires, 1988.
Prof. Memberships: Buenos Aires Bar Association; City of Buenos Aires Bar Association; International Bar Association; American Bar Association and American Society of International Law.
Publications: Author of several articles in law journals and publications in Argentina and reports to national conferences of commercial and corporate law; co-author of the national report for the International Bar Association Biannual Conference 1988.
Career: Obtained law degree in 1979; Master of Laws degree at Harvard Law School in 1985. Joined *Estudio Alegria* in 1980, becoming partner in 1989. Practised as foreign lawyer in United States in 1985. Member of several committees of the City of Buenos Aires Bar Association and of the International and American Bar Associations.
Personal: Born August 8, 1957. Lives in the city of Buenos Aires.

BUSSO, Federico

Negri Teijeiro & Incera, Buenos Aires +54 11 4328 8008
Recommended in Communications

CABANELLAS, Guillermo

Alvarez Prado, Cabanellas & Kelly Abogados, Buenos Aires +54 11 4324 7600
Recommended in Competition/Anti-trust

CAMBIASO, Juan E.

Marval, O'Farrell & Mairal, Buenos Aires +54 11 4310 0100
marval@marval.com.ar
Recommended in Corporate/M&A

Specialisation: Specialises in financial, banking and corporate law.
Career: *Ince & Co.*, London 1971; *Estudio de los Dres. Pinedo* 1971-1976; joined *Marval, O'Farrell & Mairal* as a partner in 1976.
Personal: Law Degree, University of Buenos Aires, 1968.

CASSAGNE, Juan Carlos

Cárdenas Cassagne & Asociados, Buenos Aires +54 11 4321 8000
jcc@ccas.com.ar
Recommended in Corporate/M&A, Energy & Natural Resources

Specialisation: Founding partner of the firm, is a specialist in Administrative Law.
Prof. Memberships: National Academy of Law and Social Sciences in Buenos Aires, runs the Administrative Law Institute; Royal Academy of Moral al Political Sciences in Madrid; Inter-American Academy of International and Comparative Law.
Publications: Author of several books on administrative law. Has also written over two hundred articles published in local and foreign specialised law magazines.
Career: Lawyer and Doctor of Law and Social Sciences with a major in Administrative Law, Universidad de Buenos Aires. Has taken part in the drafting of important laws, such as the State Reform Law, the National Expropriation and Condemnation Law, and the Code of Administrative-Litigation Proceedings of the Province of Buenos Aires. Has served as Associate Justice of the Argentine Supereme Court of Justice, and of the National Court of Appeals for Federal Administrative Litigation Proceedings. Was Statutory Auditor or Chairman of the Board of Directors of electric power and gas distribution companies, respectively, in the City of Buenos Aires and the Greater Buenos Aires since 1992. Currently Chairman of the Board of Aguas Argentinas S.A., member of the Board of Directors of IDEA, and Secretary of ADESPA of the Argentine Chamber of Commerce. Has been full Professor in the Chair of Administrative Law at Universidad de Buenos Aires School of Law since 1974, a teaching position also in other local Universities. Has been visiting professor at many Universities abroad, and has been involved in a number of postgraduate and doctoral courses in different national and foreign universities.
Personal: Born 2 December, 1937.

DELL'ORO MAINI, Atilio

Cárdenas Cassagne & Asociados, Buenos Aires +5411 4326 5880
adom@ccas.com.ar
Recommended in Banking & Finance

Specialisation: Specialises in providing advice to clients on a wide range of financial issues. Has advised local and foreign banks on the establishment of branches in Argentina, on all legal aspects in connection with banking activities and on the representation of clients before the federal and provincial governmental authorities. In the area of capital markets, has represented corporate issuers, financial advisors, and federal and provincial governments in all matters related to the issuance of debt securities, equity and derivatives, including the creation of global short- and medium-term note programs, the issuance of common and preferred shares (convertible or not), convertible bonds, warrants, securitisations, and all kinds of derivatives. Has also actively worked in mergers & acquisitions, representing buyers, shareholders, investment banks, financial advisors, creditors and institutional investors in the purchase and sale of shares in private and public corporations and in the transfer of going concerns, including transnational acquisitions, acquisition of indebted companies, mergers and spin-offs, and tax-exempt reorganisations. Has also advised several consortia on corporate and regulatory matters related to the acquisition of state-owned companies during the privatisation process.
Prof. Memberships: Law Society, City of Buenos Aires.
Career: Qualified in 1984. Joined *Cárdenas, Cassagne & Asociados* in 1984, becoming a partner in 1990. Joined *White & Case*, a leading law firm based in New York, with offices in more than 20 countries in 1987 as a foreign associate. After practising law for a year, moved to *Simpson, Thacher & Bartlett*, a leading law firm with more than 400 lawyers, based in New York City, as a foreign associate until the end of 1989.
Personal: Born in Buenos Aires on February 13, 1956. Attended the school of law of the Universidad Católica Argentine (1980-84). Also obtained two other academic degrees: Licenciado en Ciencias Politicas (Bachelor of Political Sciences) from the

A

Universidad Católica Argentina School of Law and Political Sciences on June 17, 1981, and Ingeniero en Producción Agropecuaria (Farming Production Engineer) from the Universidad Católica Argentina School of Farming Science on November 17, 1980. Leisure interests include climbing, scubadiving, windsurfing and flyfishing. Lives in Pilar, Province of Buenos Aires.

DUGGAN, Juan
Hope Duggan & Silva, Buenos Aires
+54 11 4891 1000
Recommended in Banking & Finance, Corporate/M&A

A

ERIZE, Luis Alberto
Abeledo Gottheil Abogados, Buenos Aires
+54 11 4315 4721
erize@abeledogottheil.com.ar
Recommended in Energy & Natural Resources
Specialisation: Experience in the field of oil & gas law, and administrative law, with special emphasis on aspects of governmental regulations of environmental law, special system, and privatisation of public services in the hydrocarbon and electric energy sectors. Developed work in the following areas: Legal advice and counsel in aspects of auditing and control of internal legal systems, and other issues of corporate organisation with special emphasis on environmental law. Legal advice and counsel on negotiation and execution of contracts referring to major public and private works, energy, international finance, licenses of technology and industrial investments, joint ventures, mergers & acquisitions, and business matters in general. Legal advice and counsel to auditors on their role in businesses and in particular with regard to principles of auditing, environmental management, auditing and monitoring systems, regulations on financing and financial entities, customs regulations, and international arbitration. Litigation practice in the above mentioned areas.
Prof. Memberships: Argentina Association of Insurance Law; International Council of Environental Law, Bonn, Germany; International Bar Association; Natural Gas Committee.
Publications: 'Argentina's Exploration Plan: The Return of Exploration and Exploitation Concessions', published in Journal of Energy & Natural Resources Law (Vol 10). Co-author of 'Future Evolution of the Electric Energy Market towards more elaborate term contracts – Energy supply contracts with large customers', presented at the Seminar 'The Future of Electric Energy within the process of reconversion of the Electric Energy', organised by the Institute for International Research and co-author of 'Proposed Supplement to the regulatory framework of the Argentine Electric Energy Industry'. Author of 'Demythification of Project Finance: legal aspects to have in consideration for a successful structuring' with a particular view of the financing of natural gas and electric energy projects, presented in the Seminar on 'Development and Financing of Energy Projects', organised by the Institute for International Research. President of the seminar on 'Financement of Infrastructure Projects' and author of 'New Instruments of financing'. Professor of Constitutional law in the University of Buenos Aires, 1975-1986.
Career: Lawyer, 1975. Managing Partner of *Abeledo Gottheil Abogados SC – Gottheil – Garcia Cozzi – Erize* and Partner from 1978.
Personal: Born January 1, 1946. Education: School of Law, University of Buenos Aires.

ERRECONDO, Javier
Bruchou, Fernandez Madero, Lombardi & Mitrani, Buenos Aires +54 11 5288 2300
Recommended in Banking & Finance

FARGOSI, Alejandro
Oyhanarte & Fargosi, Buenos Aires
+54 11 4815 7650
Recommended in Communications

FORTUNATI, Roberto
Estudio Beccar Varela, Buenos Aires
+54 11 4379 6813
rfortunati@beccarv.com.ar
Recommended in Banking & Finance, Energy & Natural Resources
Specialisation: Partner of the law firm *Estudio Beccar Varela* in Buenos Aires, Argentina, and is currently a member of the firm's Management Committee. Main area of practice is project financing and corporate finance, particularly structured financing for private and public sector. Also deeply involved in out of courts debt restructurings representing mostly creditors. Practice in those fields has related to the energy sector and natural resources, including oil, gas and mining projects. Intensively participated in the start-up of the venture capital investments as well as privatisation of Argentine State owned companies, acting on behalf of buyers. Started practice as in-house counsel for Amoco Argentine Oil Company and has been closely involved advising companies related to the upstream sector of the oil and gas industry since then.
Prof. Memberships: Member to the Council of the Law School of Universidad Torcuato Di Tella (Buenos Aires), to the International Bar Association (Sections on Business Law and on Energy and Natural Resources Law), the Argentine Derivatives Association, the Argentine Petroleum Institute (Legal Section), and the Argentine Association of Energy and Mineral Resources Law.
Career: Graduated as a lawyer at the University of Buenos Aires, and has been a lecturer in postgraduate courses or seminars for lawyers on several oil and gas issues as well as corporate finance matters.

FRANCO, Carlos
Klein & Franco, Buenos Aires +54 11 4315 4000
Recommended in Competition/Anti-trust

GALLO, Juan Antonio
Marval, O'Farrell & Mairal, Buenos Aires
+54 11 4310 0100
Recommended in Banking & Finance

GARRIDO, Gustavo
Allende & Brea, Buenos Aires +54 11 4318 9900
Recommended in Communications

GARRIDO, Gustavo Enrique
Allende & Brea, Buenos Aires +54 11 4318 9900
geg@allendebrea.com.ar
Recommended in Communications
Specialisation: Partner of *Allende & Brea* since 1998. Main areas of work are mergers and acquisitions and transnational transactions in general.
Prof. Memberships: Buenos Aires Bar Association.
Career: *Sullivan & Cromwell* (New York), Foreign Associate (1993-1994).
Personal: Born in Buenos Aires, Argentina, on October 27, 1967. Admitted to the bar in Argentina in 1991. Legal education: Catholic University of Argentina (LLB, 1991); Duke University School of Law (LLM, 1993).

GOLDARACENA, Fernando
Estudio Ramos Mejía, Buenos Aires
+54 11 4371 9851
Recommended in Competition/Anti-trust

GRONDONA, Mariano
Perez Alati, Grondona, Benites, Arntsen & Martinez de Hoz, Buenos Aires +54 11 4114 3000
Recommended in Banking & Finance

HARFOUCHE, Pablo
Harfouche, Graneros & Asociados, Buenos Aires
+54 11 4371 0012
Recommended in Competition/Anti-trust

HOPE, Adrian
Hope Duggan & Silva, Buenos Aires
+54 11 4891 1000
Recommended in Banking & Finance, Corporate/M&A

KLEIN, Guillermo Walter
Klein & Franco, Buenos Aires +54 11 4315 4000
Recommended in Corporate/M&A

LA PORTA DRAGO, Rafael
Allende & Brea, Buenos Aires +54 11 4318 9900
rlp@allendebrea.com.ar
Recommended in Banking & Finance
Specialisation: Co-Managing Partner of *Allende & Brea*. Main areas of practice are banking & finance, mergers & acquisitions and transnational transactions in general. Has been outside local counsel for Bank of America NA since 1960.
Prof. Memberships: Buenos Aires Bar Association (Vice-Chairman 1997-99; Chairman 1999); International Bar Association.
Personal: Born in Buenos Aires, Argentina, on August 1, 1938. Admitted to the bar in Argentina in 1960. Legal education: University of Buenos Aires (LLB, 1960).

LASHERAS, Alberto
Estudio Beccar Varela, Buenos Aires
+54 11 4379 6800
Recommended in Corporate/M&A

LOPEZ AUFRANC, Patricia
Marval, O'Farrell & Mairal, Buenos Aires
+54 11 4310 0100
Recommended in Banking & Finance

LUCERO, Luis E
Cárdenas Cassagne & Asociados, Buenos Aires
+54 11 4321 8000
lel@ccas.com.ar
Recommended in Corporate/M&A
Specialisation: Practice includes almost all areas in

the mining business, including project finance, as well as Banking, Contracts, Corporate and Financial Law. Member of the Board of Directors and Statutory Auditor of several mining and financial services companies.
Prof. Memberships: Buenos Aires City Bar Association; International Bar Association; American Bar Association; Australian Mining and Petroleum Association.
Publications: Has written articles for Latin Law, The Buenos Aires Herald and Latin Lawyer Review. Contributor to 'Sweet & Maxwell'. Published 'An Overview of the Argentine Legal Mining System' in Mineral Resources Engineering, a publication of the Royal School of Mines, UK.
Career: Lawyer, Universidad de Buenos Aires. Became a partner with *Cardenas, Cassagne & Asociados* in 1994. Acted as Foreign Law Consultant for *Pillsbury, Madison & Sutro* (San Francisco, California). Trained at Harvard Law School (Program of Instruction for Lawyers, 1993) and at Columbia University Graduate School of Business (Fundamentals of Management, 2000). Has taught Commercial Law at the Universidad de Buenos Aires and teaches Natural Resources law at the Universidad del Salvador.
Personal: Born 30 June, 1960.

MADERO, Jaime
Bruchou, Fernandez Madero, Lombardi & Mitrani, Buenos Aires +54 11 5288 2300
Recommended in Banking & Finance

MAIRAL, Héctor A.
Marval, O'Farrell & Mairal, Buenos Aires +54 11 4310 0100
marval@marval.com.ar
Recommended in Corporate/M&A, Energy & Natural Resources
Specialisation: Specialises in administrative and business law, government contracts, mergers and acquisitions, project financing in natural resources and infrastructure projects, arbitration.
Career: Ministry of Economy, Promotion of Foreign Investment, 1968-69; *Klein & Mairal*, 1971-91; joined *Marval, O'Farrell & Mairal* as a partner in 1991.
Personal: Law Degree cum laude, University of Buenos Aires, 1961; LLM cum laude in Comparative Law, Southern Methodist University 1963; PhD, University of Buenos Aires 1973.

MARSIGLIA, Gabriela
Gabriela Marsiglia – Sole Practitioner, Buenos Aires +54 11 4325 5050
Recommended in Communications

MARTELLI, Hugo
Martelli Abogados, Buenos Aires +54 11 4328 7337
Recommended in Energy & Natural Resources

MARTINEZ DE HOZ, José
Perez Alati, Grondona, Benites, Arntsen & Martinez de Hoz, Buenos Aires +54 11 4114 3000
Recommended in Energy & Natural Resources

MATARASSO, Gabriel
Marval, O'Farrell & Mairal, Buenos Aires +54 11 4310 0100
Recommended in Communications

MILLÉ, Antonio
Estudio Millé, Buenos Aires +54 11 4331 8191
Recommended in Communications

MUÑOZ DE TORO, Fernando
Muñoz de Toro & Muñoz de Toro, Buenos Aires +54 11 43 43 34 88
Recommended in Corporate/M&A

NEGRI, Juan Javier
Negri Teijeiro & Incera, Buenos Aires +54 11 4328 8008
Recommended in Corporate/M&A

NORMAN, Justo
Maciel Norman & Asociados, Buenos Aires +54 11 4394 4535
Recommended in Energy & Natural Resources

O'FARRELL, Alfredo Miguel
Marval, O'Farrell & Mairal, Buenos Aires +54 11 4310 0100
marval@marval.com.ar
Recommended in Corporate/M&A
Specialisation: Specialises in corporate matters, mergers and acquisitions, joint ventures, privatisations, financings and other related matters.
Career: *Rosenman, Colin, Freund, Lewis, & Cohen*, Attorneys, New York, USA, 1977. Joined *Marval, O'Farrell, & Mairal* as a partner in 1978.
Personal: Law Degree, University of Buenos Aires 1975. LLM, New York University School of Law 1977.

O'FARRELL, Juan Patricio
Estudio O'Farrell, Buenos Aires +54 11 4346 1000
Recommended in Corporate/M&A

O'FARRELL, Uriel
Estudio O'Farrell, Buenos Aires +54 11 4346 1000
Recommended in Energy & Natural Resources

ORTS, Mario Jorge
Bazan Cambré & Orts, Buenos Aires +54 11 4326 7777
Recommended in Energy & Natural Resources

OTAMENDI, Jorge
G. Breuer, Buenos Aires +54 11 4312 5678
Recommended in Competition/Anti-trust

PEREZ ALATI, Jorge Luis
Perez Alati, Grondona, Benites, Arntsen & Martinez de Hoz, Buenos Aires +54 11 4114 3000
jpa@pagbam.com.ar
Recommended in Corporate/M&A
Prof. Memberships: Bar Association of the City of Buenos Aires; Committee of Bank Lawyers of the Republic of Argentina; Argentine Association of Comparative Law; Association of the Bar of the City of New York; American Bar Association, sections: Corporation & Business, International, Real Property, Probate and Trust. American Society of International Law; Inter-American Law Association; International Bar Association, section: Business Law.
Career: Bachelor of Law (Abogado), School of Law, Argentine Catholic University (1977). Academy of American and International Law, Southwestern Legal Foundation, Dallas, Texas, (1978). LLM, Master of Laws, School of Law, Columbia University, New York (1979). Fellowship: Southwestern Legal Foundation Scholarship. John N. Johnson Scholarship, Dallas, Texas. Assistant professor of: Consitutional Law, School of Law, University Buenos Aires (1984); Commercial Law, School of Law, Argentine Catholic University (1985); Capital Markets and Financial Entities at the ESEADE (1986). Lecturer at the 'Second Annual Legal Aspects of Doing Business in Latin America. New Rules and Future Trends 1989', Miami, (1989). Associated with *Dewey, Ballantine, Bushby, Palmer & Wood* (1979-1980). Member of *Klein & Mairal* (1981-1991).
Personal: *Languages: Spanish and English.*

PINEDO, Federico
Sanchez Elia, Pinedo, Diaz Bobillo & Richard, Buenos Aires +54 11 4312 4991
Recommended in Communications

QUATTRINI, Sergio
Quattrini, Laprida & Asociados, Buenos Aires +54 11 4814 1190
Recommended in Corporate/M&A

ROVIRA, Alfredo
Brons & Salas, Buenos Aires +54 11 4891 2700
Recommended in Corporate/M&A

SANCHEZ ELIA, José
Sanchez Elia, Pinedo, Diaz Bobillo & Richard, Buenos Aires +54 11 4312 4991
Recommended in Communications

SERRANO, Diego
Perez Alati, Grondona, Benites, Arntsen & Martinez de Hoz, Buenos Aires +54 11 4114 3000
Recommended in Banking & Finance

SILVA, Roberto
Hope Duggan & Silva, Buenos Aires +54 11 4891 1000
Recommended in Banking & Finance, Corporate/M&A

SPOLANSKY, Norberto
Estudio Spolansky Bobbio, Buenos Aires
Recommended in Competition/Anti-trust

TAWIL, Guido
M & M Bomchil, Buenos Aires +541 1 4321 7500
Recommended in Energy & Natural Resources

VALIENTE-NOAILLES, Carlos
Bazan Cambré & Orts, Buenos Aires +54 11 4326 7777
Recommended in Energy & Natural Resources

A

AUSTRALIA

Index

The clients' choice

BUSINESS LAWYER OF THE YEAR
JOHN ATANASKOVIC, *Atanskovic Hartnell*
PETER CAMERON,
Allens Arthur Robinson Group

BUSINESS LAW FIRM OF THE YEAR
ALLENS ARTHUR ROBINSON GROUP

***John Atanaskovic** and **Peter Cameron** tie for the award, with the **Allens Arthur Robinson Group** winning 'best firm' by a significant margin.*

For details see page 36.

OVERVIEW: Continued consolidation in the M&A, banking, energy and communications sectors has increased the lead by the top five firms. The recent overhaul of the country's taxation legislation, particularly the introduction of the goods and services tax (GST), continues to be a source of ongoing counselling. Mallesons Stephen Jaques remains the pre-eminent Australian firm, despite the failure of merger talks with Clifford Chance and Linklaters and together with the member firms of the Allens Arthur Robinson Group and the newly named Freehills it is pulling away from the chasing pack. Growth in telecoms and IT, M&A and tax has also supported the predominance of a number of boutiques.

Arbitration (International)

AUSTRALIA Leading individuals (Arbitration (International))
1 **DOWNES Garry** *Sole Practitioner* **PRYLES Michael** *Minter Ellison* **ROGERS Andrew** *Clayton Utz* **STOCKDALE Peter** *Mallesons Stephen Jaques*
2 **DAWSON Darryl** *Sole Practitioner* **DORTER John** *Allen Allen & Hemsley (Allens Arthur Robinson Group)* **STREET Laurence** *Commercial Mediator*
Individuals are listed alphabetically in each band.

Arbitration (International) There is a small but growing number of Australians who regularly sit as arbitrators in disputes of an international nature, the majority of whom are retired judges. Although the total number of Australians who sit as international arbitrators is relatively small when compared with their European or US counterparts, there are some who are regarded as eminent in the field. Most of these individuals are based in Sydney, reflecting the city's reputation as the commercial and financial centre of Australia and its increasing significance as a gateway into Asian markets.

Formerly Chief Judge of the Commercial Division of the New South Wales Supreme Court, **Andrew Rogers QC*** of Clayton Utz sits in international arbitrations arising from disputes in the financial, commercial or construction arena. A partner at Minter Ellison's Sydney office, **Michael Pryles QC*** comes from *"an esteemed academic background"* and is said to be a *"highly proficient and well-known arbitrator."* The *"outstanding"* **Garry Downes QC*** divides his time between Sydney and London, sitting as arbitrator on a variety of international disputes, including sale of goods, IP and maritime matters. He is the only Australian representative on the ICC Court and, unusually in this field, also remains a practising barrister. Formerly Chief Justice of the New South Wales Supreme Court, the *"amazingly energetic"* **Laurence Street*** is said to be *"the founding father of mediations and arbitrations in Australia."* However, he is seen to have continued to move towards mediations as his primary focus. **Darryl Dawson*** has become *"more prominent as an arbitrator"* in international disputes following his retirement from the High Court of Australia. **Peter Stockdale*** of Mallesons Stephen Jaques remains particularly active in *"arbitrations involving international insurance issues,"* which is closely linked to his thriving insurance litigation practice, while **John Dorter*** of the Allens Arthur Robinson Group is noted as a *"pre-eminent construction arbitration expert."*

Banking & Finance

AUSTRALIA Leading firms (Banking & Finance)
1 Allens Arthur Robinson Group
Mallesons Stephen Jaques
2 Blake Dawson Waldron
Clayton Utz
Freehills
3 Minter Ellison

Firms are listed alphabetically in each band.

Leading individuals (Banking & Finance)
1 **CORNWELL Phillip** *Allen Allen & Hemsley (Allens Arthur Robinson Group)*
FIELD John *Blake Dawson Waldron*
LOXTON Diccon *Allen Allen & Hemsley (Allens Arthur Robinson Group)*
STUMBLES John *Mallesons Stephen Jaques*
2 **ANGUS John** *Freehills*
HAMMOND Gregory *Mallesons Stephen Jaques*
WALLACE Ian *Allen Allen & Hemsley (Allens Arthur Robinson Group)*
3 **DUNSTAN Jim** *Allen Allen & Hemsley (Allens Arthur Robinson Group)*
LYNCH Simon *Arthur Robinson & Hedderwicks (Allens Arthur Robinson Group)*
MAXTON Alan *Allen Allen & Hemsley (Allens Arthur Robinson Group)*
ROBINSON Trevor *Clayton Utz*
RUSSELL Rowan *Mallesons Stephen Jaques*
ST JOHN Patrick *Clayton Utz*
TAYLOR Philip *Freehills*
4 **DANOS Trevor** *Blake Dawson Waldron*
DUNNE Ambrose *Minter Ellison*
FUZI Grant *Clayton Utz*
PEMBERTON Stephen *Arthur Robinson & Hedderwicks (Allens Arthur Robinson Group)*

Individuals are listed alphabetically in each band.

Allen Allen & Hemsley/Arthur Robinson & Hedderwicks (member firms of the Allens Arthur Robinson Group) (44 ptrs, 84 asscs) The group handles a diverse range of high-end financing work on behalf of an international banking clientele, and has advised on around 45% of all Australian syndicated loans over the past twelve months. Large acquisition finance transactions are another staple of the workload. *"An integrated team"* is said *"to eclipse most of its rivals through sheer size,"* and contains a number of top practitioners.

Phillip Cornwell* acts primarily for lenders, and is widely seen to be *"one of the best finance lawyers around,"* while **Diccon Loxton*** is *"rated top in just about anything in this area."* **Ian Wallace*** is seen to do *"a bit of everything,"* but is primarily associated with a strong structured finance practice, while the *"always impressive"* **Jim Dunstan*** is said to have *"played a major role on a number of acquisition financings." "Commercially aware"* **Simon Lynch*** and the *"realistic and pragmatic"* **Alan Maxton*** both continue to command substantial levels of market approval. Melbourne-based **Stephen Pemberton*** *"protects his clients well, but still moves forward through commercial realism and sensible dealings."*

The team acted for National Bank Australia Ltd on the acquisition of the financial services business MLC from Lend Lease Corporation for A$4.56 billion. Another important transaction was advising Principal Finance Group on the acquisition of Bankers Trust Australia Group for A$2.1 billion and the onward sale of the investment bank for A$100 million, one of the largest ever Rule 144A issues in Australia. Also advised on the debt finance acquisition of Transmission Pipelines Australia (TPA), the last step in the A$25 billion privatisation of gas assets in Victoria. **Clients:** ANZ; BNP; Deutsche Bank; Dresdner; Fuji; Merrill Lynch; Morgan Stanley; Rothschild; Royal Bank of Canada; Westpac.

Mallesons Stephen Jaques (37 ptrs, 117 asscs) An enormous team handles all aspects of financial law, including asset finance/equipment leasing, asset reconstruction, consumer financial services, e-banking and payment systems. Acting both for blue-chip corporate borrowers and global financial institutions, the group is also a fixture on big-ticket syndicated loans and acquisition financings. A major recent coup saw the firm appointed as the principal advisor to National Australia Bank Group in Australia until October 2003.

In a *"slick team with depth and cohesiveness,"* **John Stumbles*** stands out. *"A superb lawyer and a formidable opponent,"* he is also considered to be *"pleasant to deal with."* Sydney-based **Greg Hammond*** is *"a quick and practical lawyer,"* although his practice now also embraces a high proportion of capital markets advice. **Rowan Russell*** remains a respected practitioner, although his visibility is felt to have dropped since his move into management in the firm's Melbourne office.

The firm served as English legal advisors to a syndicate of banks including in relation to a US$60 million secured term financing for two Boeing 737 aircraft purchased by Air New Zealand. Also represented the joint borrowers on £1.6 billion of facilities provided to AMP Holdings Ltd and AMP UK Holdings Ltd by Barclays Capital, ABN AMRO, Warburg Dillon Read, and Deutsche Bank in the form of four bilateral facility agreements. The team advised on the development of Australia's first full-service supermarket banking business, a strategic alliance between Woolworths Ltd and the Commonwealth Bank of Australia. **Clients:** AES Corporation; BNP; Deutsche Bank; Industrial Bank of Japan; Lion Nathan; Morgan Stanley; Reserve Bank of Australia; Rothschild.

Blake Dawson Waldron (12 ptrs, 30 asscs) The firm's *"transactionally-driven"* Financial Services Group acts for both lenders and borrowers on a variety of domestic and international financing matters. Prominent domestic and overseas financial institutions rub shoulders with a number of Commonwealth and State authorities, government- sponsored entities and public listed companies on the firm's client roster.

John Field* in Melbourne is a *"star all-purpose finance lawyer,"* while the *"proactive"* **Trevor Danos*** is especially rated for packaging work. The team acted for the lenders on a A$1.1 billion syndicated debt facility for Publishing and Broadcasting Ltd, and advised US company GATX Capital on a A$800 million leasing transaction, involving two of the privatised rail franchises in Victoria. Other work includes acting for the Commonwealth of Australia on the lease financing and privatisation of the Federal Government's VIP air fleet, a transaction valued at A$500 million. **Clients:** ANZ Bank; GATX Capital; GE Capital; JP Morgan Australia; Qantas.

Clayton Utz (34 ptrs, 78 asscs) *"Innovative"* financing group with particular emphasis on project finance, securitisation, capital markets, leveraged leasing, derivatives, bank syndications, big-ticket property lending and structured finance. Acting for a number of major domestic banks as well as leading international financial institutions, the firm now focuses on the broader financial services market, and the convergence of financial products offered by banks, investment banks, insurers, funds and superannuation managers.

Trevor Robinson* has an accomplished reputation for his advice on consumer credit issues, while **Patrick St John*** is said to have *"made the cross-over successfully"* between banking and finance and project finance, prompting the comment that *"if you're as good as he is, people will come to you in both areas."* **Grant Fuzi*** *"works*

A

*See leaders' profiles on pages 82-101

closely with Patrick St John," and is also recommended for his mixed banking and project finance work.

The team advised Barclays Bank plc, HSBC Bank and Warburg Dillon Read, who provided the acquisition finance for the A$3.5 billion privatisation of ETSA Power and ETSA Utilities, where the assets were acquired by Cheung Kong and CKI. Origin Energy Ltd instructed the firm on a A$620 million syndicated facility arranged by National Australia Bank, and the group also represented the bank syndicate which is arranging a A$1 billion facility for a subsidiary of One-Tel, to finance the construction of a new mobile telephone network in Australia. **Clients:** ANZ; Bank of America; Chase Manhattan; Citibank; Commonwealth Bank of Australia; Merrill Lynch; Société Générale; UBS Warburg; West LB.

Freehills (20 ptrs, 40 asscs) *"Solid and versatile team,"* with expertise in syndications, security management arrangements, acquisition finance, cross-border and domestic leasing, structured property financing and leveraged buyouts. The firm advises a mixed clientele of borrowers and lenders, predominantly high-profile Australian institutions.

John Angus* is highly regarded for his cross-border leasing advice on behalf of state governments, as well as his expertise on tax-based structured finance work. *"Practical and popular,"* **Philip Taylor*** is also recommended for leasing cases.

The firm advised on a A$110 million domestic equipment leveraged lease for Foxtel and acted on the A$1 billion corporate refinancing of the Crown Casino in Melbourne. Additional key transactions saw the firm advise Westfield Trust on an acquisition financing for a stake in the St Luke's Group and A$500 million bilateral facilities, and represent the borrower on the A$252 million refinancing by Royal Bank of Canada of the TransAlta Group's investment in the Southern Cross Energy Partnership. **Clients:** Allco Finance Group; Babcock & Brown Pty Ltd; Bankers Trust; Chase Manhattan Bank; Coles Myer; Colonial State Bank; Commonwealth Bank of Australia; Diners Club; Dresdner Bank; Lend Lease; Macquarie Bank; Pasminco.

Minter Ellison (22 ptrs, 42 asscs) Considered to have a profile in consumer credit work, debt reconstruction, leveraged equities, banking regulation and leasing finance, the team is still thought to have *"a fair way to go before it's up with the big boys."* **Ambrose Dunne*** is *"a sound practitioner,"* credited with *"putting the banking group on the map."*

The firm recently advised AMP on the demutualisation and A$12 billion public listing of AMP Society, and also acted for ABN AMRO, ANZ, Macquarie and Bain on the A$364 million equity issue of stapled securities by Stadium Australia, comprising shares in the operating company, units in the Stadium Australia Trust and Olympic tickets. In addition, the team acted for Leighton Holdings on its equity investment in the Eastern Distributor project and subsequent sale of part of that interest. **Clients:** AMP; ANZ; Colonial State Bank; Westfield America Trust; Westpac.

Capital Markets

Allen Allen & Hemsley/Arthur Robinson & Hedderwicks (member firms of the Allens Arthur Robinson Group) (28 ptrs, 88 asscs) One of the two clear leaders in the sector, the group's strength is considered to lie in the breadth of its practice. It acts for issuers on IPOs, rights issues, placements and buybacks, as well as underwriters, lead managers and strategic investors. Euromarkets, kangaroo bonds, tier 1 capital raising, securitisation, retail property syndication, capital matched programmes and structured debt advice are other cornerstones of the workload. **Andrew Jinks*** is widely regarded as *"the leader of the pack"* for his securitisation expertise, while **Mark Wormell*** in Sydney and Melbourne-based **Ian Renard*** are also generally recommended in this area.

Significant work includes acting on the Exchangeable Eurobond issue by Foster's Securities Corporation, a US subsidiary of Foster's Brewing Group, and acting for Fuji International Finance (Australia) on the ECP / ECD programme guaranteed by the Fuji Bank Ltd, which was a US$800 million multi-currency global programme to fund Fuji's Australian operations. The group also represented Westpac on a A$1 billion e-bond issue by Telstra, sold over the internet through a dedicated website, and constituting the first issue of bonds over the internet in Australia. **Clients:** ABN AMRO; Bank of America; Deutsche Bank; General Electrics Capital; Merrill Lynch; New Corporation.

Mallesons Stephen Jaques (27 ptrs, 128 asscs) The firm's strength in capital markets is universally acclaimed. Now perceived to be balancing its traditional banking work with a beefed up structured securities practice, the firm has experienced notable growth in mortgage securitisation and income securities work. Prevailing market opinion considers the group to be *"strong across the spectrum"* of capital markets work, and to possess a *"team of unparalleled depth."*

Reg Barrett* has been described as *"a fantastic lawyer – I'd put him at the top of any capital markets list,"* while **Stuart Fuller*** is also recognised as *"one of the leading securitisation lawyers in Australia."* **Greg Golding*** is seen to best advantage on IPOs, and is said to do *"a lot of underwriting work for Macquarie Bank,"* and **Adrienne Showering*** is *"a fine securitisation lawyer"* who *"thoroughly deserves her good reputation."* **Greg Hammond*** is *"a solid performer,"* particularly on securities offerings, **Ted Kerr*** has *"ISDA expertise"* as his claim to fame, and is seen to have *"a superb niche in derivatives,"* while **Richard Mazzochi*** *"has a good relationship with a number of major banks,"* advising on securitisations and capital markets financings. The *"underrated"* **David Olsson*** has been particularly active in the kangaroo bond market.

The firm advised Telstra in connection with its A$18 billion second tranche sale of shares, and represented BHP on the establishment of its A$3 billion MTN Programme. In addition, the firm acted for ETSA Utilities in relation to the establishment of its A$1.6 billion MTN Programme and the simultaneous issue of A$1.1 billion of MTN notes, involving a credit wrap by Ambac Assurance Corporation and a further A$500 million issue of notes. **Clients:** ABN AMRO; Chase Manhattan; Colonial Ltd; Merrill Lynch; Morgan Stanley; Publishing & Broadcasting Ltd; Telstra Corporation Ltd.

Clayton Utz (11 ptrs, 22 asscs) The firm's capital markets practice undertakes a variety of work from complex structured transactions to debt issues in Australia's developing corporate bond market. International capital markets work is not neglected, and the firm advises Australian issuers and arrangers of offshore programmes in US and European markets, as well as arrangers of debt issues by offshore borrowers. Securitisation clients include leading issuers in the mortgage and asset-backed securities market in Australia.

Although the team's 'first division' of lawyers is considered to stand comparison with any of its rivals, it is felt to lack the strength in depth of the market leaders. The *"first-class"* **Brian Salter*** *"leads the firm's securitisation team by example,"* while **Matthew Allchurch*** is *"close to the top of the tree"* for his all-round capital markets expertise. The firm advised Coca-Cola Amatil in establishing and maintaining its US$1 billion Euro MTN programme, and also acted for Deutsche Bank AG in the establishment of a A$1 billion transferable deposit programme for its Sydney branch. Other matters include advising the Commonwealth Bank of Australia on its A$1.7 billion global mortgage-backed securities issue, and acting for the same bank on Australia's first credit derivative securitisation, with credit reference entity obligations of A$1.5 billion. **Clients:** Boral; Coca-Cola Amatil; Deutsche Bank; Merrill Lynch; UBS Warburg.

Freehills (22 ptrs, 43 asscs) The firm conducts capital markets and securitisation work from both its business group and its managed funds group. Growth areas for the team over the past twelve months have included property securitisation and e-commerce-related financing.

John O'Sullivan's* abilities have led some to describe him as *"the bee's knees."* He has advised the Victorian government on its privatisation programme, and one rival commented: *"If I were going to float my law firm, I would go to John O'Sullivan – he's the best for mega-floats."* Sydney-based **Richard Gray*** is *"an astute practitioner,"* best known for his work on securitisations and asset-based financings, while **Mark Rigotti*** is said to be *"starting to cut some mustard in the market,"* particularly in structured finance transactions. The *"switched-on"* **Phillipa Stone*** and the *"capable"* **Kathleen Farrell*** also continue to be well-regarded by the market.

The firm advised Caltex Australia on its A$1 billion group refinancing, and acted for the General Property Trust on a CPI-indexed bond issue to the value of A$200 million. Also acted for the eleven banks participating in the A$2 billion Commercial Paper standby facility for the Australian Wheat Board, and assisted on a A$1 billion global bond issue for the National Mutual Group. **Clients:** Caltex Australia; National Mutual Group; General Property Trust.

Blake Dawson Waldron (15 ptrs, 30 asscs) Acting principally for lead managers, issuers and trustee companies, the firm has been active on securitisation work, credit-linked structures and offshore issuance of Australian mortgage-based securities. Considered to be a *"respectable and versatile team,"* it contains Melbourne-based **Mark Breheny***, an *"on the ball"* practitioner, rated for his structured finance expertise. **Fred Pucci*** in Sydney has recently been made a partner, and is said to be a *"good operator,"* with particular expertise in advising on debt-based derivatives. **Bruce Whittaker*** is a respected securitisation lawyer.

Significant transactions include acting for Chase Capital Markets as Security trustee, guarantee trustee and paying agent on the A$1.6 billion program for ETSA Utilities Finance Pty Ltd, guaranteed by ETSA Utilities. The firm has also advised Lucent Technologies on a A$1.15 billion vendor financing for equipment supply to One.Tel. **Clients:** ANZ Bank; JP Morgan Australia; UBS Warburg.

Minter Ellison (29 ptrs, 44 asscs) Considered to have a stranglehold on mid-market work, the firm advises on derivatives, securitisation, capital raisings and debt reconstruction. Said to be *"a hugely active and respected all-purpose lawyer,"* **Leigh Brown*** is the team's shining light, but is felt by the market to lack support of a similar quality. The firm recently acted for National Australia Trustees in connection with the Salomon Smith Barney Amazon.com convertible note issue, raising up to A$1 billion. Also advised Westfield on a debt and equity issue into Australia which raised A$465 million, and Nestlé Australia on its US$250 million convertible Eurobond issue (listed on the Luxembourg Stock Exchange). **Clients:** AMP; GE Capital Finance; HIH Insurance; Westfield; Nestlé.

AUSTRALIA
Leading firms (Capital Markets)

Band	Firm
1	Allens Arthur Robinson Group
	Mallesons Stephen Jaques
2	Clayton Utz
	Freehills
3	Blake Dawson Waldron
	Minter Ellison

Firms are listed alphabetically in each band.

Leading individuals (Capital Markets)

Band	Individual	Individual
1	**BARRETT Reg** *Mallesons Stephen Jaques*	**FULLER Stuart** *Mallesons Stephen Jaques*
	JINKS Andrew *Allen Allen & Hemsley (Allens Arthur Robinson Group)*	
	O'SULLIVAN John *Freehills*	**SALTER Brian** *Clayton Utz*
2	**ALLCHURCH Matthew** *Clayton Utz*	**GOLDING Greg** *Mallesons Stephen Jaques*
	SHOWERING Adrienne *Mallesons Stephen Jaques*	
	WORMELL Mark *Allen Allen & Hemsley (Allens Arthur Robinson Group)*	
3	**BROWN Leigh** *Minter Ellison*	**GRAY Richard** *Freehills*
	HAMMOND Gregory *Mallesons Stephen Jaques*	**KERR Edward** *Mallesons Stephen Jaques*
	MAZZOCHI Richard *Mallesons Stephen Jaques*	**OLSSON David** *Mallesons Stephen Jaques*
	RIGOTTI Mark *Freehills*	**STONE Phillipa** *Freehills*
4	**BREHENY Mark** *Blake Dawson Waldron*	**FARRELL Kathleen** *Freehills*
	PUCCI Fred *Blake Dawson Waldron*	
	RENARD Ian *Arthur Robinson & Hedderwicks (Allens Arthur Robinson Group)*	
	WHITTAKER Bruce *Blake Dawson Waldron*	

Individuals are listed alphabetically in each band.

A

*See leaders' profiles on pages 82-101

Communications

AUSTRALIA Leading firms (Communications)
1 Gilbert & Tobin
Mallesons Stephen Jaques
2 Baker & McKenzie
Blake Dawson Waldron
Clayton Utz
Freehills
3 Allens Arthur Robinson Group
Corrs Chambers Westgarth
Minter Ellison

Firms are listed alphabetically in each band.

A

Gilbert & Tobin (9 ptrs, 35 asscs) **Telecoms:** Telecommunications and IT work is handled by the Communications and Technology Group, a group of commercial and regulatory lawyers which comprises approximately a third of the firm. The practice undertakes work across the telecommunications, internet, broadcasting and print media and IT industries, acting for a range of national and overseas operators. However, it is the firm's relationship with the nation's second-largest carrier, Optus, which is the jewel in its crown.

The team is headed by *"communications legends"* **Peter Leonard*** and **Peter Waters***, who are said to be *"the crux of a bloody good telco team."* Rivals have admitted that *"there's Leonard and Waters, and then there's the rest of us."* **Gina Cass-Gottlieb*** is a respected competition lawyer who has handled several complex transactions for the Kerry Packer-owned broadcasting company, PBL. *"Whatever she does, she does it pretty well,"* said peers. **Angus Henderson*** is said to be *"making his mark"* as the partner handling the telco work for Singapore Telecom and New Century InfoComm in Taiwan. A major growth area for the practice over the last twelve months has been in the building of telco infrastructure and the wholesale provision of capacity to telco providers.

The team advised Australian Fibre Networks on the construction of a new fibre optic between Sydney and Melbourne, as well as acting for the Australian Broadcasting Commission in respect of ongoing digital terrestrial TV transmission contracts.

IT: Although some have described the team as *"streets ahead for e-commerce and internet work,"* advising an impressive array of new economy clients, the departures of David Standen to an in-house position at Macquarie Bank, and Michael Reede to Paul Weiss Rifkind Wharton & Garrison, are thought to have left the team *"somewhat overstretched."* **John Gray*** *"knows what he's talking about"* and *"can grasp which points are worth pushing and which aren't."* The firm acted for Cisco Systems Inc on major contracts for the supply of internet equipment, including contracts with Powertel, Telstra and Alcatel Australia. **Clients:** Optus; Cisco Systems; Samsung; Vodafone; Allianz; Ampol/Caltex; Aristocrat Leisure.

Mallesons Stephen Jaques (31 ptrs, 120 asscs) **Telecoms:** The firm continues as the principal external lawyers of Telstra, Australia's largest telecommunications company. Advising on contractual work, regulatory work, litigation and M&A transactions, the team is said to be *"an ever-increasing presence, particularly on international M&As."*

A massive department includes the *"switched on"* **Neil Carabine***, described as *"the whole package – he's got regulatory knowledge, commercial acumen and he's a deal-doer."* Sydney-based **Roger Featherston*** is a *"pretty flash"* performer in telecoms-related competition work, while **Stephen Mead*** continues to be well-regarded in Melbourne, *"not just for competition work; he's got regulatory nous too."* **Michael Herring*** continues to lead the corporate advisory division of the practice, although his focus is seen to incline more to general corporate work than specific telecoms cases.

The firm recently acted for Telstra on the merger of Telstra New Zealand and Saturn Communications Ltd to form Telstra Saturn Ltd, and advised on the A$840 million rollout of a New Zealand broadband network.

IT: Specialising in IT, e-commerce and technology law, **Anthony Borgese*** is said to be *"a rising star in the new economy area – a bright young man, involved and keen,"* while newly-ranked **Philip Argy*** *"has a real passion for this area of law."* **Maurice Gonsalves*** has been commended for his *"commercial outlook,"* and **Cheng Lim*** is *"becoming a mover and shaker in IT circles,"* often acting for Telstra on its IT transactions. Connie Carnabuci has recently left to join the firm's Hong Kong office.

The firm recently acted for Microsoft on a range of IT contracts including software licence agreements and consulting services contracts, and represented both NRMA Ltd and NRMA Insurance Ltd on the restructuring of its IT operations in light of the proposed listing and demutualisation of NRMA Ltd. **Clients:** Telstra; SITA; Compaq.

Baker & McKenzie (6 ptrs, 26 asscs) **Telecoms:** The Australian arm of the worldwide network advises local and overseas carriers, service providers and equipment suppliers on a range of regulatory issues in the sector. The firm's global reach has brought the team into contact with a number of major international carriers, with the result that the team is said to have *"strengthened its commercial communications work over the last year, particularly in Sydney."* Formerly in-house counsel at Optus, **Rob Simpson*** is a *"powerhouse"* with a proven track record in communications. He is *"ably assisted"* by the respected **Penny Ward***. The team advised One.Tel Ltd in the rollout of GSM 1800 Network in Australia, and acted for the same company on its successful bid at the 1.8 Mhz spectrum auction.

IT: The firm's IT client base consists mainly of IT suppliers. In particular, the team continues to act for ninemsn, Australia's largest on-line network, on an exclusive basis, recently advising it on innovative on-line promotional deals with the Commonwealth Bank and the strategic acquisition of Ausbuy.com. Practice head **Anthony Foley*** is seen to be *"committed and sharp,"* and advises on a range of on-line transactions and the establishment of on-line services. The firm recently acted for Nortel in negotiating a five year A$1 billion contract with Telstra relating to the supply of equipment for Telstra's core data network using IP protocols. **Clients:** PowerTel; One.Tel; MCI Worldcom; Cisco Systems; Fujitsu; Unisys.

Blake Dawson Waldron (10 ptrs, 45 asscs) **Telecoms:** Along with rivals Mallesons, the firm continues to do *"a lot of work on the Telstra account, particularly on the funding side."* Through this relationship the department is said to have *"a significant presence in the communications arena in Australia."* Practice group leader **Chris Shine*** is said to be *"an integral part"* of the national telecoms market. Renowned for its transactional expertise, the firm recently advised AT&T on the sale of its subsidiary EasyLink to AAPT, and represented Lucent Technologies on the sale of CDMA networks in the Australian market, undertaking vendor financing and site acquisition work in this context. The team is currently acting for Telstra in relation to its A$515 million acquisition of equity in Keycorp, a public company manufacturing EFTPOS/point of sale terminals.

IT: Melbourne-based **Gordon Hughes*** has been described as *"Australia's most knowledgeable IT practitioner,"* with a *"highly innovative approach"* and the ability to *"explain technical*

AUSTRALIA
Leading individuals
(Communications: Telecoms)

Band	Individual
1	**LEONARD Peter** *Gilbert & Tobin*
	WATERS Peter *Gilbert & Tobin*
2	**CARABINE Neil** *Mallesons Stephen Jaques*
	CASS-GOTTLIEB Gina *Gilbert & Tobin*
	CREAN Mark *Freehills*
	FEATHERSTON Roger *Mallesons Stephen Jaques*
	McGREGOR Sheila *Freehills*
	MEAD Stephen *Mallesons Stephen Jaques*
	SHINE Christopher *Blake Dawson Waldron*
	SIMPSON Robert *Baker & McKenzie*
3	**HERRING Michael** *Mallesons Stephen Jaques*
	McGILL Ian *Allen Allen & Hemsley (Allens Arthur Robinson Group)*
4	**FERRARO Michael** *Freehills*
	FITZSIMONS James *Clayton Utz*
	HENDERSON Angus *Gilbert & Tobin*
	WARD Penny *Baker & McKenzie*

Individuals are listed alphabetically in each band.

Leading individuals (Communications: IT)

Band	Individual
1	**ARTHUR John** *Freehills*
	HUGHES Gordon *Blake Dawson Waldron*
2	**BORGESE Anthony** *Mallesons Stephen Jaques*
	FOLEY Anthony *Baker & McKenzie*
	PATTISON Michael *Arthur Robinson & Hedderwicks (Allens Arthur Robinson Group)*
	SAINTY Katherine *Allen Allen & Hemsley (Allens Arthur Robinson Group)*
3	**AHERN Chris** *Corrs Chambers Westgarth*
	ARGY Philip *Mallesons Stephen Jaques*
	BROOKS Tim *Corrs Chambers Westgarth*
	GONSALVES Maurice *Mallesons Stephen Jaques*
	HERRON Louise *Minter Ellison*
	KNIGHT Peter *Clayton Utz*
	RITSON Lisa *Blake Dawson Waldron*

Up-and-coming individuals

Individual
ARMITAGE Peter *Blake Dawson Waldron*
GRAY John *Gilbert & Tobin*
LIM Cheng *Mallesons Stephen Jaques*

Individuals are listed alphabetically in each band.

issues in a layperson's language." In Sydney, practice leader **Lisa Ritson*** is said to be a *"client-friendly"* practitioner, although her name is increasingly associated with IP work. **Peter Armitage*** is increasingly *"making his presence felt,"* particularly on IT outsourcing work. **Clients:** Lucent Technologies; Telstra Corporation Ltd; TVP (Hong Kong).

Clayton Utz (13 ptrs, 17 asscs) **Telecoms:** The firm remains the primary counsel to AAPT, Australia's third largest telecommunications carrier. Last year the team advised AAPT on four substantial transactions, including the rollout of its mobile CDMA network across Australia, the rollout of its LMDS network across Australia and a lease of fibre optic cable connecting all the major population centres of Australia. The team is also the primary outside lead counsel to Cable & Wireless plc, and advises the company on all aspects of its investment in Cable & Wireless Optus, in which it is the majority shareholder. The leading figure here is the *"commercially-minded"* **James Fitzsimons***, said to be *"at the epicentre of a number of client relationships."* In addition to its work for AAPT, the firm has advised the Olympic Co-ordination Authority on telecoms issues arising from the staging of the Olympic Games.

IT: The Technology and Intellectual Property Group provides advice across a range of IT transactions including procurement, outsourcing, joint ventures, acquisitions, capital raisings and disputes. **Peter Knight*** is the Group's best-known practitioner, and possesses a *"good grasp of a wide range of IT issues."* The Group acts for Sausage Software, one of Australia's premier new economy companies, which in the past 18 months has embarked on an ambitious program of business alliances and product launches. Advised on Skynet Global's worldwide undertaking to roll out a wireless internet connection, providing all the technology contracts including installation, hardware sourcing and fulfilment records for companies such as Unisys, ASA and Nortel. **Clients:** AAPT; Cable & Wireless Optus; Cable & Wireless Optus; Network Seven; Great Southern Energy; Sabre Pacific.

Freehills (23 ptrs, 50 asscs) **Telecoms:** The practice handles work across the converging areas of media, technology and communications, with **Mark Crean*** still highly regarded for his *"general media nous."* **Sheila McGregor*** is *"a thorough and tough negotiator,"* while **Michael Ferraro*** continues to be respected as *"a class act who's becoming classier,"* notably on telecoms services agreements. The group received a recent setback when it was dropped from Telstra's panel. However, the practice is perceived to be *"still active"* in the sector, recently advising Telecom New Zealand Australia (TNZA) on a range of telecommunications agreements with other carriers and advising Telecom Ventures Group (a Hong Kong-based investment/venture capital fund) on various IT investments and alliances in Australia. The firm advised Nextgen in an A$800 million financing project to build a fibre-optics network around Australia.

IT: Undertaking substantial IT outsourcing work over the past twelve months, the team's leading light is the *"proficient"* **John Arthur***, who has particular expertise in e-commerce work and has a strong relationship with the Commonwealth Bank. The firm recently acted for Comscraft (formerly known as Datacraft Technologies) on the acquisition of Scitel Ltd's communications equipment manufacturing business. The team also acted for Telstra in the sourcing of telephony products from Nortel and Alcatel, and in its negotiation with AMS Inc on the implementation of its credit management system. **Clients:** Nortel; Pacific Access; Stellar; Advantra Pty Ltd; Airservices; Network Design and Construction Ltd.

Allen Allen & Hemsley/Arthur Robinson & Hedderwicks (member firms of the Allens Arthur Robinson Group) (120 lawyers) **Telecoms: Ian McGill*** is widely seen to have been *"a pretty perceptive and solid operator in the media sector for many years, particularly with his work for Murdoch and Foxtel."* However, he has just been made Managing Partner of the Allens Arthur Robinson Group, and this is widely held to have *"lowered his profile in telecoms."* No individual of comparable stature has yet stepped into the breach. Nevertheless, a substantial client base still exists here, including such names as Telecom NZ, whom the firm advised on its successful bid for telecommunications work outsourced by the Commonwealth Bank. The team also acted for Southern Cross Cables Ltd on the Southern Cross Cable Project Financing, a joint venture between Telecom NZ, Optus Communications and MCI Worldcom, which involved the $US920 million project financing of a 28,200 kilometre fibre optic cable between Australia, New Zealand, Fiji and the USA.

IT: The practice undertakes a broad range of IT work including procurement issues, IT corporate work and litigation. **Michael Pattison*** is *"the big name"* in the Group's Melbourne office, and is particularly noted for his IT contracts work, while the Sydney-based **Katherine Sainty*** is *"always in control of transactions."* The firm recently acted for CSC on its successful bid for the acquisition of BHP IT and the provision of outsourced IT services back to BHP. **Clients:** News Corporation; Telecom NZ; United Energy; KeyCorp; Megadyne; Norwich Union; Tyco Australia Pty Ltd; Ansett.

Corrs Chambers Westgarth (7 ptrs, 27 asscs) **Telecoms:** The firm has national Communications and Information Technology Groups serving both domestic and international clients throughout the country. The telecommunica-

*See leaders' profiles on pages 82-101

tions team is focused around providing advice regarding commercial, regulatory and access issues, particularly in relation to interconnection, the roll out of networks and submissions to regulatory authorities including the ACCC and the ACA (Australian Communications Authority). The work is often carried out for entrants into the telecommunications industry, especially in regard to regulatory compliance, network building and access to declared services, and the team has particular experience in arbitrating on behalf of access seekers. The team has recently advised Walker Wireless, a fixed and wireless New Zealand telecommunications carrier, on its entry into the Australian telecommunications market. The firm also advised Nextel Inc, a major US wireless telecommunications adviser, on its potential entry into the Australian market through the acquisition of a large existing mobile network. In addition, the firm recently advised Macro Corporation, an Australian telecommunications consortium, on the establishment of a mobile telecommunications network.

IT: The firm acts for a mixture of both suppliers and consumers of communications and information technology services. The IT team are seen to be *"very keenly building their practice in this area"* and to be *"aggressively moving into the market."* Head of Communications Group **Chris Ahern*** and **Tim Brooks*** are said to be *"leading the charge"* for the firm with their *"impressive"* IT outsourcing work in particular. The firm is seen to have *"made significant inroads into the IT/IP market in the last twelve months, whereas it hasn't been a huge part of their practice before."* Further comment has been that *"reputation-wise it's not yet up with the big boys, but it's definitely on the rise."* The firm recently acted for Microsoft Inc in the establishment and proposed establishment of various internet portal joint ventures with major telecommunications carriers and content providers in both Australia and New Zealand. It also won the tender to act for SAP AG in Australia and SAP Australia Pty Limited generally, acting on a variety of matters including SAP's supply of software to a major electronic marketplace and other matters relating to software licensing, software implementation and general technology services. The firm also advised First Data, a provider of online transaction processing and settlement services to major Australian financial institutions, on the consolidation of all of First Data's outsourcing agreements with a major Australian financial institution. **Clients:** Bloomberg LP; BNP Australia Pty Ltd; GE Capital Finance Australia Pty Ltd; Manpower Services (Australia) Pty Ltd; Woolworths Ltd.

Minter Ellison (21 ptrs, 64 lawyers) **Telecoms:** Renowned for its transactional expertise in the sector, the firm is now perceived to be an emerging force, undertaking work such as telecommunications access and facilities sharing, supply and wholesale/selling, as well as infrastructure acquisition/sale, datacasting, licensing and broadcasting/transmission. The firm continues to undertake quality work for Optus Communications as its *"number two firm after Gilbert & Tobin."* Significant matters from the past 12 months include acting for Cable & Wireless Optus in relation to the acquisition of its C1 satellite, which involved contract negotiations with the Department of Defence to provide satellite capability and communications functions and support, a contract valued at $300 million. A further matter was acting for NTL Inc on its successful bid to acquire the national transmission network from the Commonwealth of Australia for A$650 million. The firm is currently acting for Asia Pacific Space Centre in relation to the establishment of the new space launch centre on the Australian teritory of Christmas Island, Indian Ocean.

IT: The firm undertakes a variety of IT work including outsourcing, copyright, infrastructure, dispute resolution, information services agreements, supply and distribution arrangements and hardware/software acquisitions and supply. It is seen to be *"starting to get some presence in the new economy venture capital area."* **Louise Herron*** is *"pretty clued up on e-commerce matters,"* although her profile has dipped this year. **Clients:** Optus Communications.

Competition/Anti-trust

Allen, Allen & Hemsley/Arthur Robinson & Hedderwicks (member firms of the Allens Arthur Robinson Group) (8 ptrs, 52 asscs) Renowned for its work across the spectrum of anti-trust law, the firm has advised on merger control issues, deregulation of government businesses, access issues, misuse of market power and price exploitation. Its formidable corporate client base sees it *"consistently involved in the top transactions and investigations."*

Melbourne-based **Robert Baxt*** is said to get *"the lion's share of the interesting work"* and *"seems to be everywhere,"* notably on behalf of key client National Australia Bank. **Gaire Blunt*** is on the Trade Practices Committee of the Law Council, and is *"a great stalwart of anti-trust law,"* although his transactional profile has diminished recently. **Pat Ryan*** has *"a wealth of experience,"* gained from his work as a litigator on behalf of the Trade Practices Commission, while Sydney name **Louise Castle*** is a *"committed, bright and able"* practitioner. **Tim Bednall*** is widely regarded as *"a superb operator,"* particularly in the energy and finance sectors. However, he now spends a substantial proportion of his time in-house at Southcorp. **Wendy Peter*** and **Craig Phillips*** are *"sound, sensible"* lawyers and **Timothy L'Estrange*** is a respected litigator. Of the younger generation, **David Brewster*** is a rising star *"with his wits about him."*

The firm advised National Australia Bank Limited on the trade practices and associated regulatory issues associated with its acquisition of the insurance business of Lend Lease Australia. Also represented PepsiCo before ACCC as the intervening party on the proposed merger between Coca-Cola and Schweppes, and advised the South Australian Government on the reform and privatisation of its electricity assets, which involved a number of complex trade practices issues. **Clients:** Amcor; Philip Morris; Rio Tinto; PepsiCo.

Mallesons Stephen Jaques (12 ptrs, 44 asscs) An enormous volume of cross-border M&A transactions guarantees the firm's anti-trust department a similar flow of merger control work. In addition, the group advises on access and price-fixing issues, particularly in the electricity and gas industries, while communications is another area of niche strength. This derives not only from the firm's relationship with Telstra, but a substantial increase in competition work relating to business to business e-commerce operations.

Roger Featherston* is said to be *"Telstra's number one competition litigator,"* and is acclaimed as one of Australia's leading anti-trust lawyers. **Peter Kelly*** *"certainly knows what he's doing,"* while **David Poddar*** is an *"intelligent* *young fellow with all the skills,"* who is seen as *"the future of the department."*

The team successfully defended Telstra in the Telstra Commercial Churn litigation, one of Australia's largest trade practices cases. This involved a series of legal moves against Telstra by the ACCC, alleging anti-competitive conduct and seeking pecuniary penalties, injunctions and damages against Telstra of over A$1 billion. Merger control work includes advising AMP in the A$3.2 billion hostile takeover of GIO. **Clients:** BHP; Macquarie Bank; Telstra Corporation Limited.

Blake Dawson Waldron (5 ptrs, 23 asscs) The Competition Law Group advises a range of corporate and government clients on both contentious and non-contentious matters, including mergers, horizontal and vertical restraints, access to infrastructure, misleading and deceptive conduct, consumer protection and product liability. The team has expanded significantly, and is now considered to produce *"interesting and good quality work."*

Long-established name **John Kench*** is a *"phenomenally efficient"* leader in Sydney, while **Aldo Nicotra*** has recently been *"at the forefront of an increasing number of transactions."* The firm advised Alcoa Inc in lodging a submission with the ACCC, addressing potential anti-trust issues arising from the merger in the US with Reynolds Metals Company. Also defended Boral Ltd against a predatory pricing prosecution brought by the ACCC. Further matters include advising Mobil in relation to the recent Mobil/Exxon merger, advising Shell on the privatisation of the Victorian Plantations Corporation, and acting for North Ltd in relation to the sale of the Warman International Pumps business to the Weir Group. **Clients:** BHP Limited; Boral Ltd; Goodman Fielder; Mayne Nickless; Qantas; Shell.

Clayton Utz (5 ptrs, 11 asscs) The firm's competition law practice group has three principal elements. Advice on merger control work, access to monopoly facilities (such as gas, rail, ports, freight operators) and enforcement investigations or litigation by the ACCC for misuse of market power constitute the main areas of the caseload. Particularly noted for its work in the energy and transport industries, the team now has Bob McComas working in a consultant role. However, **Linda Evans*** has arrived from Andersen Legal's Sydney office, and is reckoned to be a *"tenacious litigator."* Group head **Michael Corrigan*** is the firm's other remaining anti-trust heavyweight.

The firm advised Hope Downs in respect of rail access in the Robe/Hammersley region in Western Australia, represented Woolworths on a range of matters in front of the ACCC, and acted for Rothmans on competition aspects of its merger with British Tobacco. **Clients:** Alcoa; Alinta Gas; Western Power; WMC.

Gilbert & Tobin (7 ptrs, 20 asscs) A rising force in anti-trust matters, the firm's enormous strength in telecoms has led to a slew of transactional and regulatory competition advice in that industry. Energy is another area of expertise, and the group's litigation capacity draws widespread market approval. Considered to contain *"some sterling people,"* the team's stand-out practitioner is **Gina Cass-Gottlieb***, described by some as *"the best young trade practices lawyer in Australia."* **Liza Carver*** has *"a deservedly good reputation"* for her work in the field, while *"gamekeeper turned poacher"* **Luke Woodward*** has recently joined the firm from the ACCC, where he was general counsel and National Enforcement Director. *"Pretty good and getting better,"* he is considered to be *"making the transition well."*

The firm has advised on a number of mergers in the gas and electricity sectors, particularly for AGL, which has acquired a number of businesses and entered into joint ventures around Australia. Additionally, the team has acted for new economy clients such as e.com plc and keycorp on trade practice issues relating to e-commerce. **Clients:** AGL; CSR; PBL; Optus; Vodafone; Macquarie Bank; ACCC.

Freehills (10 ptrs, 30 asscs) The nature of the firm's competition practice varies from state to state, with the majority of the workload conducted from Victoria and New South Wales. In Victoria, the anti-trust group has advised extensively on access arrangements and other competition issues arising from privatised industries, while in New South Wales, the team's strength lies more in financial services. Although the firm is clearly a national anti-trust player, it is felt to lack the depth and case volume of the market leaders. **Don Robertson***, known for his work on behalf of VISA, and **Michael Gray*** are prominent and respected practitioners.

The firm acted for the Commonwealth Bank on its A$9 billion merger with Colonial Limited, and advised VISA on both the investigation by the ACCC of price-fixing allegations and the joint Reserve Bank of Australia/ACCC inquiry into payment cards. Other work includes advising VENCorp on the authorisation of Victorian gas

AUSTRALIA
Leading firms (Competition/Anti-trust)

Band	Firm
1	Allens Arthur Robinson Group
	Mallesons Stephen Jaques
2	Blake Dawson Waldron
	Clayton Utz
	Gilbert & Tobin
3	Freehills

Firms are listed alphabetically in each band.

Leading individuals (Competition/Anti-trust)

Band	Individual	Individual
1	**BAXT Robert** *Arthur Robinson & Hedderwicks (Allens Arthur Robinson Group)*	
	BLUNT Gaire *Allen Allen & Hemsley (Allens Arthur Robinson Group)*	
	FEATHERSTON Roger *Mallesons Stephen Jaques*	**KENCH John** *Blake Dawson Waldron*
2	**BEDNALL Timothy** *Allen Allen & Hemsley (Allens Arthur Robinson Group)*	
	CASS-GOTTLIEB Gina *Gilbert & Tobin*	
	CASTLE Louise *Allen Allen & Hemsley (Allens Arthur Robinson Group)*	
	KELLY Peter *Mallesons Stephen Jaques*	
	RYAN Patrick *Arthur Robinson & Hedderwicks (Allens Arthur Robinson Group)*	
3	**CARVER Liza** *Gilbert & Tobin*	**CORRIGAN Michael** *Clayton Utz*
	EVANS Linda *Clayton Utz*	**NICOTRA Aldo** *Blake Dawson Waldron*
	O'BRYAN Michael *Minter Ellison*	
	PETER Wendy *Arthur Robinson & Hedderwicks (Allens Arthur Robinson Group)*	
	PHILLIPS Craig *Arthur Robinson & Hedderwicks (Allens Arthur Robinson Group)*	
	ROBERTSON Don *Freehills*	
4	**GRAY Michael** *Freehills*	**HUGHES Paul** *Corrs Chambers Westgarth*
	L'ESTRANGE Timothy *Allen Allen & Hemsley (Allens Arthur Robinson Group)*	
	TAPPERELL Geoffrey *KPMG Legal*	
Up-and-coming individuals		
	BREWSTER David *Arthur Robinson & Hedderwicks (Allens Arthur Robinson Group)*	
	PODDAR Dave *Mallesons Stephen Jaques*	**WOODWARD Luke** *Gilbert & Tobin*

Individuals are listed alphabetically in each band.

*See leaders' profiles on pages 82-101

market rules, and the subsequent challenge by BHP Petroleum to that authorisation before the Australian Competition Tribunal. **Clients:** Cashcard; Lend Lease; MLC; Austar; Telecom New Zealand.

Other Notable Practitioners **Paul Hughes*** is the national co-ordinator of the competition law and policy practice group at Corrs Chambers Westgarth. He is felt to have *"a quality practice,"* with a recent emphasis on conducting trade practices audits and competition policy reviews of government enterprises. In Melbourne, **Michael O'Bryan*** heads Minter Ellison's anti-trust team, and advises a clientele which includes AMP Society, BHP Petroleum and WMC Ltd. At KPMG Legal, the *"well-travelled"* **Geoffrey Tapperell*** is felt to know *"all the tricks in the book."*

A

Corporate/M&A

Allen Allen & Hemsley/Arthur Robinson & Hedderwicks (member firms of the Allens Arthur Robinson Group) (40 ptrs, 104 asscs) Considered to have *"an impressive and extensive list of blue-chip clients, depth of expertise and truly national coverage,"* the group's M&A practice is part of the wider Corporate & Commercial divisions within the firm's various offices. In the past twelve months, world-wide and domestic takeover activity for the firm has continued to rise, with a trend towards consolidation in the financial, property trust and mining sectors in particular. The Group acted on twelve deals worth over A$10 billion for the six months up to June 30 2000, a 47% market share, with the mining industry accounting for 44% of the firm's M&A activity in the same period.

Peter Cameron* is said to be *"far and away the strongest M&A force at Allens, a practitioner with incredibly precise judgement."* **Tim Bednall*** also has a fine reputation, but he now spends a large proportion of his time in-house at Southcorp, and consequently has a reduced profile this year. **John Harry*** is recommended as *"a heavy hitter in Melbourne,"* while **Colin Galbraith*** possesses *"all the right moves when he's doing deals."* **Ian Renard*** is admired for his *"ability to fuse technical ability with commercial nous."* In Brisbane, **Ken Macdonald*** retains his share of market support, while Melbourne-based **Jon Webster*** is *"described as an emerging talent."* Such an array of talent cushions the blow of the loss of respected practitioners John Martin and Stephen Menzies to in-house positions at dot.com enterprises.

Significant recent matters for the group include acting for National Australia Bank Ltd in its A$4.56 billion acquisition of MLC Holdings Ltd. The Group also acted for Rio Tinto Ltd in its A$3.02 billion hostile takeover of North Ltd, which was Australia's biggest resources takeover under the post-CLERP regime (corporate law economic reform program legislation.) Instrumental in the privatisation of the South Australian electricity industry, the organisation acted for the South Australian Department of Treasury and Finance in the sell-off of seven stand-alone business units. **Clients:** Amcor; News Corporation; Southcorp.

Freehills (40 ptrs, 90 asscs) Clients regard the firm as an *"exemplary"* corporate operation, and it continues to rank as one of the country's leading M&A forces. The firm advised on five of the top seven M&A transactions in Australia in 1999-2000, and enjoyed notable success in the finance, energy, utility and telecommunications sectors. **John O'Sullivan*** has become *"more and more prominent since Peter Hay moved into management"* and is said to be *"one of the best in the Sydney market for management buy-out work."* **Peter Hay*** is widely seen to be *"still a class act but much less on the scene since taking the National Executive role."* Sydney-based **Braddon Jolley*** is *"as sharp as a tack"* and *"a lawyer with a reputation which he never fails to live up to,"* while **Robert Nicholson*** remains *"Freehills' main man in Melbourne"* for M&A work. The firm advised the Commonwealth Bank on its takeover of Colonial Mutual, the largest ever Australian takeover (valued at A$9.5 billion), Air New Zealand on the sale of the remaining 50% of its second airline, and Metalcorp on its A$3 billion hostile takeover by Smorgan Steel. **Clients:** Commonwealth Bank; Pacific Dunlop; Santos.

Mallesons Stephen Jaques (26 ptrs, 73 asscs) Leading firm on big-ticket transactions, increasingly seen on major cross-border deals, most obviously in the energy sector. The *"astute"* **Tony Bancroft*** is highly rated for his work with leading financial institutions, while **Greg Golding*** *("the man we see most often on the other side of transactions")* has a particularly strong relationship with Lion Nathan Limited. Long-term name **Reg Barrett*** has had a lower profile this year, but Melbourne-based **Stephen Minns*** has been prominent on a number of acquisitions involving listed companies. Joint head of the firm's national Corporate Advisory Clients practice group, **John Atkin*** is *"an experienced and versatile practitioner,"* and **Michael Lishman*** is *"just about the number one player in Perth."* The team advised Telstra on the second tranche of its privatisation, and is currently acting for NRMA on its A$4.5 billion demutualisation. Elsewhere, the firm represented Cheung Kong Infrastructure Holdings and Hong Kong Electric on the privatisation of the South Australian electricity businesses ETSA Utilities and ETSA Power, a transaction valued at A$3.5 billion. **Clients:** AXA; Glencore International AG; NRMA.

Clayton Utz (40 ptrs, 90 asscs) The firm undertakes a variety of corporate work, including big-ticket M&A transactions, private equity/venture capital matters, MBOs and capital raisings. Although felt to lack the depth and volume of work of the three market leaders, the corporate team is considered *"the best of the rest by a considerable margin."* Practice head **Rod Halstead*** has *"good corporate nous"* and is felt to be *"always on the ball technically,"* while Sydney-based **John Elliott*** is *"taking the driver's seat more and more on the bigger transactions."* The firm advised the Colonial Group in relation to its A$9.5 billion merger with the Commonwealth Bank, the largest takeover in Australian corporate history. Also represented Liberty Media on its US$2 billion reconstruction involving the sale of its 50% interest in Fox Sports to News Corp, and acted for Coca-Cola Beverages plc on the Australian aspects of its merger with the Hellenic Bottling Company SA. **Clients:** Coca-Cola Beverages plc; Sausage Software; Sydney Airports Corporation Limited.

Atanaskovic Hartnell (20 lawyers) The majority of the firm's work remains big-ticket M&A transactions, both on the acquisition and defence side. The firm is particularly active on contested bids, whether acting for the target or the acquirer. **John Atanaskovic*** is said to be *"a unique character"* who possesses *"exceptional business sense"* combined with *"a deep knowledge of the law." "When he's doing deals, he's large and he's in charge – don't get in his way."* **Tony Hartnell*** is *"a straight-talker"* and *"good at getting down to business – he knows his way around a big-ticket transaction and* *he works well in tandem with Atanaskovic.*" The firm has recently been acting for Broken Hill Proprietary (BHP) and, before it was recently spun out as a separate listed company, BHP's former wholly owned subsidiary, OneSteel, in relation to the joint A$815 million bid by Smorgon Steel and OneSteel for Email. The firm continues to act for BHP, one of Australia's largest listed companies, having this year been appointed BHP's preferred counsel for M&A work. The firm has also been appointed this year to a similar role by Cable & Wireless Optus (Australia's second largest telco) and Consolidated Press Holdings (Kerry Packer's main company), and recently took control of the A$500 million listed MTM Office Trust for CPH in a hotly contested transaction. The firm generally acts for Macquarie Bank on its own M&A activity, and continues to act for Rupert Murdoch's private companies and also his listed News Corporation, and is currently working exclusively working on the proposed approx US$40 billion Sky Global Network spin out by News Corporation. **Clients:** Goodman Fielder; Macquarie Bank; Cable & Wireless Optus.

AUSTRALIA Leading firms (Corporate/Mergers & Acquisitions)
1 Allens Arthur Robinson Group
Freehills
Mallesons Stephen Jaques
2 Clayton Utz
3 Atanaskovic Hartnell
Blake Dawson Waldron
Minter Ellison
4 Arnold Bloch Leibler
Baker & McKenzie
Corrs Chambers Westgarth
Gilbert & Tobin

Firms are listed alphabetically in each band.

Blake Dawson Waldron (57 ptrs, 190 asscs) This firm is seen to have had *"a perfectly respectable year"* for M&A work, having been particularly active in the resources and telecoms/IT sectors. Melbourne-based **David Williamson*** is acknowledged to be *"a top lawyer,"* although his profile has been reduced this year, while **David Somervaille*** is also recommended as *"a decent general corporate lawyer."* In the firm's Canberra office, **William Conley*** has a long-standing reputation. The team acted for ANZ Bank in the sale of Grindlays Bank (value A$3.1 billion), and represented BHP in the sale of Email Ltd, a transaction worth A$900 million. The firm is currently acting for Telecom New Zealand in its proposed acquisition of the balance of AAPT (in which Telecom New Zealand already holds a majority interest.) **Clients:** Acacia Resources; AMP Limited; BHP.

Minter Ellison (73 ptrs, 175 lawyers) Undertaking work *"mainly for smaller listed companies,"* the firm is felt to have *"a decent M&A practice in some of its offices,"* but it is not felt to have the depth of some of its leading competitors. **Leigh Brown*** is *"a fine lawyer,"* and is widely regarded as *"the only lawyer at the firm who immediately springs to mind"* for this type of work. Recent significant matters for the firm include advising on all Australian legal aspects of French company Cap Gemini's US$12.4 billion acquisition of Ernst & Young's consulting businesses world-wide. Another significant matter was acting for PBL on the A$1.8 billion acquisition of all the shares in the owner/operator of the Crown Casino in Melbourne, Crown Limited. The firm was also a lead adviser to CSR on its rationalisation program, which included the merger of CSR and Mobil's surfacing businesses and the merger of CSR's sugar refining interests with those of Mackay Refined Sugars, with the total value of the transactions in the sum of A$250 million. **Clients:** AMP; Cap Gemini; CSR; PBL.

Leading individuals (Corporate/Mergers & Acquisitions)	
1 **ATANASKOVIC John** *Atanaskovic Hartnell*	**BANCROFT Anthony** *Mallesons Stephen Jaques*
CAMERON Peter *Allen Allen & Hemsley (Allens Arthur Robinson Group)*	
GOLDING Greg *Mallesons Stephen Jaques*	**HALSTEAD Rod** *Clayton Utz*
O'SULLIVAN John *Freehills*	
2 **BARRETT Reg** *Mallesons Stephen Jaques*	**HARTNELL Anthony** *Atanaskovic Hartnell*
HAY Peter *Freehills*	**JOLLEY Braddon** *Freehills*
MINNS Stephen *Mallesons Stephen Jaques*	**WILLIAMSON David** *Blake Dawson Waldron*
3 **ATKIN John** *Mallesons Stephen Jaques*	
BEDNALL Timothy *Allen Allen & Hemsley (Allens Arthur Robinson Group)*	
BROWN Leigh *Minter Ellison*	
HARRY John *Arthur Robinson & Hedderwicks (Allens Arthur Robinson Group)*	
LISHMAN Michael *Mallesons Stephen Jaques*	**NICHOLSON Robert** *Freehills*
4 **BESSON Gary** *Gilbert & Tobin*	**CONLEY William** *Blake Dawson Waldron*
GALBRAITH Colin *Arthur Robinson & Hedderwicks (Allens Arthur Robinson Group)*	
GLANZ Steven *Baker & McKenzie*	**KOECK William** *Corrs Chambers Westgarth*
LAWLER Gary *Gilbert & Tobin*	
MACDONALD Ken *Allen Allen & Hemsley (Allens Arthur Robinson Group)*	
RENARD Ian *Arthur Robinson & Hedderwicks (Allens Arthur Robinson Group)*	
SHERIDAN Jane *Arnold Bloch Leibler*	**SLATTERY John** *Corrs Chambers Westgarth*
SOMERVAILLE David *Blake Dawson Waldron*	**STOREY John** *Corrs Chambers Westgarth*
Up-and-coming individuals	
ELLIOTT John *Clayton Utz*	
WEBSTER Jon *Arthur Robinson & Hedderwicks (Allens Arthur Robinson Group)*	

Individuals are listed alphabetically in each band.

Arnold Bloch Leibler (13 ptrs, 25 asscs) Still felt to be rebuilding in the wake of the departure of John Fast to an in-house position at BHP, the firm is nevertheless reckoned to retain the capacity to *"pull off a decent M&A deal."* **Jane Sheridan*** is the best-known practitioner left to the department. The firm recently acted on behalf of Trust Bank of Tasmania in the successful sale of its assets and business to Colonial Limited. In addition, the team advised Fernz Nufarm, a publicly listed New Zealand agribusiness company, in relation to a comprehensive corporate restructuring and its migration to Australia. **Clients:** Commonwealth Bank of Australia; Lend Lease; Toyota; Telecom NZ.

Baker & McKenzie (9 ptrs, 23 asscs) This firm undertakes M&A transactions out of its General Corporate Group, concentrating on major trade sales, public company takeovers and negotiated acquisitions. Key strengths include the power industry, IT/e-commerce, outsourcing, private equity/venture capital and financial services. Said to *"do a good job at the medium-ticket level"* the firm *"gets good references from its international network."* **Steven Glanz*** is warmly recommended by the market this year. The firm was the Australian Counsel for PacifiCorp on its A$12 billion acquisition by Scottish Power and acted for Opti-

A

*See leaders' profiles on pages 82-101

ma, which owns the largest gas-fired power station in Australia, in its acquisition by Texas Utilities from the South Australian Government to the value of A$300 million. **Clients:** Gresham Private Equity; Scottish Power; Texas Utilities.

Corrs Chambers Westgarth (18 ptrs, 26 asscs) This firm is seen to be *"less on the radar these days"* for large scale M&A work, although it continues to be *"quite prominent in the smaller matters."* There is further comment that the firm's *"main market remains Melbourne – it just doesn't have the extensive client base or national coverage of the bigger firms."* **William Koeck*** is widely regarded as being *"the highest profile Corrs lawyer for general corporate work – he's good across the board,"* while **John Slattery**'s* profile has dipped slightly this year. **John Storey*** is seen to be *"a real name in Brisbane"* for M&A work.

Gilbert & Tobin This firm undertakes corporate work out of its Corporate Commercial Department, and primarily advises listed companies and banks on public company takeovers. The firm is widely seen as having *"really bolstered its M&A practice in the last few years,"* with **Gary Lawler*** and **Gary Besson*** instrumental in *"whipping the department into shape."* Particularly active in the telecoms market, the firm acted for Cable & Wireless Optus in its acquisition of AAPT to the value of A$1.5 billion. The firm also acted for Consolidated Press Holdings in its acquisition of Hoyts Cinemas to the value of A$800 million and is currently acting for Dairy Farmers in defending a $A700 million takeover by Parmalat. **Clients:** Email Ltd; Open Telecommunications; Publishing & Broadcast Ltd.

A

Energy & Natural Resources

Allen Allen & Hemsley/Arthur Robinson & Hedderwicks (member firms of the Allens Arthur Robinson Group) (32 ptrs, 75 asscs) Undertaking the spectrum of energy and natural resources advice from all its member offices, the group is renowned both for transactional and regulatory expertise. A historical eminence in mining matters has been supplemented by a growing reputation for work on privatisations in the energy sector, often representing state governments. Blue-chip Australian concerns also feature strongly on the group's client roster.

Among an enormous team, **Anthony Wassaf*** is *"an exceptional lawyer with vast experience,"* who has *"a high profile in Sydney for projects work."* Resources specialist **Scott Langford*** has recently moved to the Sydney office from Perth, and is seen as *"the man for mining,"* while **Dale Nicholls*** is said to be *"one of the pre-eminent natural resources lawyers in the Melbourne market."* **Tim Bednall*** is still acknowledged as *"a superb regulatory and energy lawyer,"* having recently advised the South Australian government on the privatisation of its electricity industry. However, he now spends a large proportion of his time in-house at Southcorp, having moved to Adelaide from Sydney for this purpose, and as a result has a *"vastly diminished profile"* in the market. Respected senior figure **Kevin McCann*** maintains his transactional reputation in Sydney, while **John Greig*** is highly rated in the lower-profile Brisbane market. **David Maloney*** is *"highly proficient"* and has *"been around for ages in Sydney,"* and Perth-based **Angus Jones*** *"knows how to handle himself in a mining matter"* and is said to be *"coming through the ranks"* for his resources work.

The firm recently advised Rio Tinto on its A$3.5 billion takeover of the diversified resources company, North Limited, Australia's largest ever resources takeover. The team also represented the National Gas Pipelines Advisory Committee (NGPAC) on the amendment of the code that regulates third party access to natural gas pipelines in Australia. **Clients:** BHP Minerals; Hammersley Iron; United Energy.

Freehills (15 ptrs, 40 asscs) This practice breaks its energy and resources work into five main areas: hard rock, coal, oil and gas, power and gas transportation pipelines. The practice is said to be *"particularly strong on the government side,"* notably handling *"a number of the major privatisations in Victoria,"* and is also noted for advising distributors on national electricity projects. Additionally, the firm is widely considered to have *"the leading energy and resources practice in Perth."* During the past twelve months, the practice has been involved in the regulatory reforms and restructure of the South Korean electricity industry, and has also been involved in the electricity industry reforms in Malaysia and the Philippines.

Melbourne-based **Robert Nicholson*** is felt to be *"a national benchmark for energy transactions,"* while the *"thoroughly impressive"* **Susan Taylor*** is said to be an *"excellent regulatory lawyer,"* following her work in the Victorian electricity and gas sectors. The *"always proactive"* **Stuart Barrymore*** is *"a major player in Perth"* for his M&A advice in the Western Australian oil and gas sectors, while the respected **Peter Hay*** has recently been appointed National Chief Executive of the firm. As a result, while he is still regarded as an *"outstanding regulatory energy lawyer,"* there has been comment that he *"isn't at the coal-face nearly so much nowadays."* **Gary Maguire***, in the firm's Brisbane office, is *"always on the ball"* and has an *"innovative approach to problem-solving."* He practises almost exclusively in the electricity sector. Recently made up partner **Baden Furphy*** is primarily involved in energy structural work, advising governments on privatisation issues. He is currently working with the South Korean government on the privatisation of its electricity industry.

The firm recently acted on the BHP Petroleum sale of its Timor Sea interests to Philips Petroleum, which was the first sale of production under the Timor Treaty between Australia and Indonesia, and is now advising Philips as project operator on the development of Phase 1 of the project which is budgeted to cost in excess of A$2 billion. The firm also recently acted for Anglo American on the A$243 million acquisition of 23% of Anaconda Nickel. In addition, the firm acted for the Southern Cross Energy consortium (consisting of TransAlta Energy Corporation and The Australian Gas Light Company) on the purchase of four Western Mining power stations for A$230 million, a transaction which increased the presence of independent power producers in Western Australia by outsourcing to an independent power producer (Southern Cross Energy) the power requirements of WMC Ltd. **Clients:** AGL; Intergen; Shell.

Mallesons Stephen Jaques (20 ptrs, 51 asscs) The massive Project and Energy Resources Group has continued its focus on major core clients in the private enterprise non-government area, particularly in asset sales and reconstruction work. Now established as *"one of the premier energy and resources practices in Australia,"* the team is also renowned for its work in the minerals sector, where competitors *"invariably see Mallesons acting on one side or the other of a deal."* An enviable clientele is advised on big-ticket acquisitions and regulatory matters, not only throughout Australia, but increasingly in South East Asia.

Melbourne practice leader **Robert Milliner*** is said to be *"incredibly industrious,"* and *"one of the legendary names in the industry"* for his ability to *"cut to the main issues"* and his *"commercial approach to solving problems."* **Peter Doyle*** is said to be *"good at getting energy projects off the ground"* with his *"astute appraisal of a project's individual requirements on a case-by-case basis."* **Rowan Kennedy*** is *"still the principal transactional figure"* in the Melbourne energy market, while **Tony Snell*** is the main adviser to NEMMCO (National Electricity Market Management Company), the Australian electricity systems operator. **Martin James*** is *"an impressive negotiator,"* who is particularly active in the electricity derivatives market, Perth-based **Alan Murray*** has a strong reputation in oil and gas and **Richard Marshall*** is held to be *"thorough, hard-working and commercial."* Two up and coming names have been picked out this year. **Louis Chiam*** has been *"handling an increasing number of big transactions in Melbourne – in time he will do very well."* **Dominic Bortoluzzi*** is *"relatively young, but he's developed a good understanding of the gas industry – he's definitely on his way up."*

The firm recently acted for Cheung Kong Infrastructure/Hong Kong Electric Holdings on their successful bid for electricity distribution and retail businesses leased by the South Australian Government, and subsequent divestment of ETSA Power to AGL (value A$3.46 billion.) In addition, the team acted for the financiers to Texas Utilities Inc in connection with the company's A$1.6 billion acquisition of the Westar-Kinetik gas distribution/retailing business in Victoria. **Clients:** ABN AMRO Australia Limited; BHP Steel; ETSA Utilities.

AUSTRALIA Leading firms (Energy & Natural Resources)	
1	Allens Arthur Robinson Group
	Freehills
	Mallesons Stephen Jaques
2	Blake Dawson Waldron
	Clayton Utz
	Corrs Chambers Westgarth
3	Deacons
	Middletons Moore & Bevins
	Minter Ellison
	Phillips Fox

Firms are listed alphabetically in each band.

Leading individuals (Energy & Natural Resources)		
1	**KELLY John** *Corrs Chambers Westgarth*	**MILLINER Robert** *Mallesons Stephen Jaques*
	NICHOLSON Robert *Freehills*	**TAYLOR Susan** *Freehills*
	WASSAF Anthony *Allen Allen & Hemsley (Allens Arthur Robinson Group)*	
2	**BARRYMORE Stuart** *Freehills*	**DENNIS Graeme** *Corrs Chambers Westgarth*
	DOYLE Peter *Mallesons Stephen Jaques*	**HAY Peter** *Freehills*
	KENNEDY Rowan *Mallesons Stephen Jaques*	
	LANGFORD Scott *Arthur Robinson & Hedderwicks (Allens Arthur Robinson Group)*	
	MAGUIRE Gary *Freehills*	
	NICHOLLS Dale *Arthur Robinson & Hedderwicks (Allens Arthur Robinson Group)*	
	SNELL Tony *Mallesons Stephen Jaques*	**WIESE Peter** *Clayton Utz*
3	**BEDNALL Timothy** *Allen Allen & Hemsley (Allens Arthur Robinson Group)*	
	EVANS Bernard *Middletons Moore & Bevins*	**FRECKER David** *Blake Dawson Waldron*
	JAMES Martin *Mallesons Stephen Jaques*	**LIMBERS Peter** *Middletons Moore & Bevins*
	MARTIN Andrew *Deacons*	
	McCANN Kevin *Allen Allen & Hemsley (Allens Arthur Robinson Group)*	
	MURRAY Alan *Mallesons Stephen Jaques*	**OWEN Gail** *Blake Dawson Waldron*
4	**GATELY Denis** *Minter Ellison*	
	GREIG John *Allen Allen & Hemsley (Allens Arthur Robinson Group)*	
	MALONEY David *Allen Allen & Hemsley (Allens Arthur Robinson Group)*	
	MARSHALL Richard *Mallesons Stephen Jaques*	**RAINEY Paul** *Corrs Chambers Westgarth*
Up-and-coming individuals		
	BORTOLUZZI Dominic *Mallesons Stephen Jaques*	**CHIAM Louis** *Mallesons Stephen Jaques*
	FURPHY Baden *Freehills*	
	JONES Angus *Arthur Robinson & Hedderwicks (Allens Arthur Robinson Group)*	

Individuals are listed alphabetically in each band.

Blake Dawson Waldron (11 ptrs) The firm has a strong private sector client base for its oil and gas and electricity practices, to which it adds substantial public sector clients for its water practice. Best known for its work on National Electricity Market issues, the team has advised extensively on the National Electricity Code. Other work includes negotiating and drafting agreements associated with the supply and use of electricity and gas. In addition, the firm regularly advises the Australian Petroleum Production & Exploration Association Limited, the Minerals Council of Australia and the Queensland Mining Council. **David Frecker*** is *"an experienced player"* in the mining sector, while Melbourne-based **Gail Owen*** is commended for her ability to *"move deals along."* The firm recently acted on the Edison Mission Energy project in New Zealand, a project with a value of NZ$1.2 billion, and also advised on the Boral/Envestra merger, which had a value of A$1.67 billion. **Clients:** Alcoa; Lihir Gold; Mobil; Shell; WMC.

Clayton Utz (16 ptrs, 25 asscs) This firm is the only major Australian law firm with an office in Darwin, a city adjacent to the oil and gas-rich Timor Sea and also a centre for native title issues. Indeed, a substantial proportion of the firm's recent work in energy and natural resources has involved native title matters and local acquisitions or divestments. In particular, the firm has negotiated and settled agreements with native title claimants and advised mining companies on all aspects of native title which have bearing on their exploration and development activities.

Elsewhere, the firm's reputation is highest in Perth, where it has amassed an impressive client base comprising a number of leading Western Australia-based corporates. The *"exemplary"* **Peter Wiese*** is seen on *"most of the firm's big energy matters."*

One of only two firms selected to advise the Northern Territory Department of Mines and Energy, the firm also advised UtiliCorp United Inc on its consortium bid for the South Australian electricity distribution and retail business. The firm also acted for WMC on the sale of its interest in the Goldfields Gas Pipeline and four power stations, a deal valued at A$625 million. **Clients:** Alcoa; Consolidated Rutile; TransAlta.

Corrs Chambers Westgarth (25 lawyers) The firm's Energy and Natural Resources Group undertakes work form corporate structure and capital raising, to exploration, licensing and project development. Its experience includes open cut

*See leaders' profiles on pages 82-101

and underground mines, coal and gas fired power stations, oil and gas operations and the development of a wide range of resources including coal, gold, uranium, nickel, copper, mineral sands and industrial minerals. Although still respected as a *"competent operation,"* capable of handling a variety of transactions, the team is felt to lack the depth of its leading market rivals. **John Kelly*** has been described as *"an absolute legend"* in the Brisbane market and is *"at the top for project development in the resources sector."* With his *"superb attention to detail"* and *"extensive knowledge of the sector,"* he is regarded as the firm's principal asset in this area. Sydney-based **Graeme Dennis*** *"has been at the game a long time"* and is said to possess *"expertise that matches his experience"* in energy regulatory work. **Paul Rainey*** is *"a practitioner of note in the electricity sector"* in Melbourne, although his profile has dipped this year.

Deacons (11 ptrs, 14 asscs) Approximately 75% of the practice's work is transactional and the balance involves advising existing clients on regulatory issues. The practice's major source of energy work has traditionally been state governments, although that focus has shifted recently towards the private sector, notably investment banks, offshore utilities and infrastructure players. **Andrew Martin*** is the team's stand-out practitioner. The firm has played a substantial part in recent privatisations of both the electricity and gas industries, and DGJ Projects has advised on a wide variety of high-profile and complex projects throughout Australia. These have included the Gas Retail Project, where DGJ Projects has been engaged by the NSW Ministry of Energy and Utilities to project manage the gas industry's development of the rules, codes and procedures required to support the progressive introduction of retail competition in gas. Further projects include the ACTEW Corporation, where the team has been engaged to advise the ACT Government about options for future ownership and management of ACTEW, and for the design of a comprehensive utilities regulatory regime for the ACT covering electricity, water and sewerage. In addition, DGJ Projects has been the Project Manager responsible for the overall planning and implementation of the corporatisation of the Snowy Mountain Hydro-Electric Authority (SMHEA) which has assets of over $3 billion. This project involves complex commercial and regulatory issues arising out of the stakeholders' requirements, tax legislation, the emerging National Electricity Market and water rights. **Clients:** ACT Government; NSW Ministry of Energy and Utilities; Snowy Mountain Hydro-Electric Authority.

Middletons Moore & Bevins (3 ptrs, 6 asscs) Although it does undertake transactional work, the firm is mostly noted for its regulatory advice on behalf of major electricity utilities. Approximately 75% of the firm's work is in the energy sector, with the balance in the resources sector, particularly in the New South Wales coal industry, where the firm has a number of major clients. The experienced **Bernard Evans*** is said to have *"a healthy profile in Sydney,"* while **Peter Limbers*** is described as *"a master of electricity."* Although not felt to have the corporate clout of the market leaders, the firm has advised NorthPower on the Direct Link power project between New South Wales and Queensland, and Delta Electricity, a New South Wales generator, on a range of acquisitions. In its niche coal sector, the firm has acted for Exxon Coal on the divestment of its coal interests. **Clients:** BOC Gases; Caltex; Transgrid.

Minter Ellison (26 ptrs, 53 asscs) The resources and energy team at this firm advises a diverse range of clients, with expertise in commodity sales agreements, energy supply agreements, exploration agreements (farm-ins and farm-outs) and utility regulation, inter alia. Market comment is that the firm has *"a strong energy practice in Brisbane and Perth, but less so in Sydney and Melbourne."* **Denis Gately*** is said to be *"Minters' energy man in Brisbane,"* although there has been comment that he's really *"close to being a solo performer"* for its Brisbane energy practice. The firm recently acted for Korea Zinc, one of the world's largest zinc producers, in negotiating various state agreements and electricity supply arrangements for the Townsville Refinery Project in North Queensland, which is an A$1 billion project to construct the world's most modern zinc smelter. The firm also acted for Duke Energy International LLC, a subsidiary of Duke Energy Corporation, in its successful A$509 million bid for BHP's assets. The firm is currently advising Royal Dutch / Shell Group on the Callide Power Project, a 480MW green field base load power station being constructed near Biloela, central Queensland. The project has a three year construction period and its capital expenditure is in excess of A$800 million. **Clients:** Comalco Aluminium; Duke Energy; PowerGen; Shell Coal.

Phillips Fox (12 ptrs, 24 asscs) Newly ranked this year, this national firm is structured so that the Melbourne and Brisbane offices undertake gas and electricity work, while the Sydney and Perth offices advise on mining and natural resources issues. The focus of the caseload is regulatory, although the firm is capable of advising on big-ticket energy transactions. Advised BMS Energy on the sale of its 50% interest in the Loy Yang Power Station, the largest power station in Australia, and Centennial on the sale of its coal interests. In the past twelve months, a significant growth area for the practice has been acquisitions and developments of co-generators, particularly for Origin Energy. **Clients:** BMS Energy; China Light & Power; NECA.

Intellectual Property

Allen Allen & Hemsley/Arthur Robinson & Hedderwicks (member firms of the Allens Arthur Robinson Group) (47 ptrs, 123 asscs) Handling a huge range of IP advice, the firm is *"easily entitled to top-tier status,"* handling trademarks, patents, copyright, and registering of industrial designs. The group also advises on commercial exploitation of assets, such as due diligence in takeovers, formations and mergers. Also prominent in IT, the team's clientele includes leading players in pharmaceuticals, metallurgy, biotechnology and engineering.

Jim Dwyer*, from the group's Sydney office, is said to be *"always impressive, particularly for contentious work,"* while **Philip Kerr*** is also rated for his litigation, notably on patent infringement actions. *"If he turns up on the other side, you take him seriously."* In Melbourne, **Tim Golder*** *"has been around a long time"* and is highly-rated, and **Richard Hamer*** *"knows his stuff on IP licensing."* A recent recruit from Corrs Chambers Westgarth, **Carolyn Oddie*** *"takes a commercial and realistic view,"* and *"will do well there."* **Rosemary Addis*** is now head of Information Dynamics at the firm, and is considered to have great potential.

The firm advised Tyco Australia Pty Ltd on an action in the Federal Court involving confidential information and copyright, as well as acting for the Australian Grand Prix Corporation in

AUSTRALIA Leading firms (Intellectual Property)
1 Allens Arthur Robinson Group
Freehills
Mallesons Stephen Jaques
2 Baker & McKenzie
Blake Dawson Waldron
Clayton Utz
Gilbert & Tobin
Minter Ellison

Firms are listed alphabetically in each band.

Leading individuals (Intellectual Property)
1 **DWYER Jim** *Allen Allen & Hemsley (Allens Arthur Robinson Group)*
MURATORE Tony *Freehills*
2 **ARGY Philip** *Mallesons Stephen Jaques*
CONDON Wayne *Freehills*
KERR Philip *Allen Allen & Hemsley (Allens Arthur Robinson Group)*
LIM Cheng *Mallesons Stephen Jaques*
RITSON Lisa *Blake Dawson Waldron*
3 **BORGESE Anthony** *Mallesons Stephen Jaques*
CHERRY James *Freehills*
GONSALVES Maurice *Mallesons Stephen Jaques*
GOUGH Richard *Baker & McKenzie*
HARRISON Kate *Gilbert & Tobin*
ODDIE Carolyn *Allen Allen & Hemsley (Allens Arthur Robinson Group)*
4 **COLLINS John** *Clayton Utz*
FOLEY Anthony *Baker & McKenzie*
GOLDER Tim *Arthur Robinson & Hedderwicks (Allens Arthur Robinson Group)*
HAMER Richard *Arthur Robinson & Hedderwicks (Allens Arthur Robinson Group)*
KNIGHT Peter *Clayton Utz*
PASCARL Ian *Blake Dawson Waldron*
Up-and-coming individuals
ADDIS Rosemary *Arthur Robinson & Hedderwicks (Allens Arthur Robinson Group)*
EVERETT Kathryn *Freehills*

Individuals are listed alphabetically in each band.

connection with a variety of IP matters associated with the Qantas Association Grand Prix. The Sydney office represented Koninglijke Philips Electronics in an appeal to the full Federal Court of Australia over the alleged infringement of Philips' trademarks and design rights by Remington Electronics Australia Pty Ltd. This was the first Australian case to test the new provisions of the Trade Marks Act. **Clients:** Amcor Limited; Newscorp; Sony Corporation.

Freehills (9 ptrs, 30 asscs) Advising on registration and prosecution of patents and trademarks, in addition to the commercial aspects of IP and enforcement, the firm is particularly recommended for patent work. IT, pharmaceuticals, publishing and manufacturing are especially fruitful client areas.

Both **Tony Muratore*** and **Wayne Condon*** are on the IP Sub-Committee of the Law Council of Australia. The former is head of the firm's IP team in Sydney, and is *"thoroughly proficient across the board, whether on commercial work or litigation."* Condon is the firm's stand-out name in Melbourne. Said to be a *"bloody good litigator,"* he is renowned for his work on trademark and design infringement actions. In general patent work and trademark protection, **James Cherry*** is rated as *"a solid technician and someone you can negotiate with."* Prominent trademark litigator **Kathryn Everett*** is expected to be *"a real force in a few years."*

The firm advised FH Faulding & Co in a patent infringement and revocation action against Bristol-Myers Squibb Co, relating to a method of administering the anti-cancer agent Paclitaxel. Also acted for NRMA Insurance in developing and documenting strategies for the ownership and use of NRMA brands in the restructure of the NRMA Group, and represented Rosemount in trademark litigation against CA Henschke & Co, concerning the trademarks Hill of Grace and Hill of Gold. **Clients:** 3M; Pacific Dunlop; VISA; NRMA Insurance.

Mallesons Stephen Jaques (15 partners, 60 lawyers) The majority of the firm's IP practice is contentious, and relates particularly to trademark, patent and copyright disputes. Market opinion is that the firm is *"right up there for overall experience and general coverage of the field,"* with a *"number of high quality people who cover all the IP needs of their superb client base."* Telecoms giant Telstra is the leading name on the firm's client roster.

In Melbourne, **Cheng Lim*** has *"a good profile in the industry,"* and *"an outstanding knowledge of both technology and the law."* He is *"able to see the bigger picture without getting bogged down in minor details."* Sydney-based **Anthony Borgese*** is noted for his work on web development and computer agreements, and has a fine reputation for IT-related IP work. **Philip Argy*** is *"active in IP dispute resolution,"* and has a computer science and programming background which enables him *"to talk to technology clients in their own language."* **Maurice Gonsalves*** has *"a strong practice in protection and enforcement of IP rights,"* handling substantial work in trademark and copyright litigation.

The group successfully defended Alphapharm Pty Ltd (part of the Merck Generics Group) against a patent infringement claim involving a formulation of the world's largest selling prescription drug (Omeprazole). In addition, the team conducted Federal Court proceedings for Telstra against cybersquatters and obtained WIPO's third ruling under its Uniform Domain Name Dispute Resolution Policy against another cybersquatter. Also advised the Australian Stock Exchange in obtaining the first orders from the Federal Court of Australia to restrain the unauthorised use of the domain name asx.investor.com.au. **Clients:** Intel Corporation; Microsoft Corporation; Telstra Corporation Limited.

Baker & McKenzie (10 partners, 35 associates) The firm has a strong trademark practice, having advised US corporates and other multi-nationals in Australia since establishing offices in Australia in 1964. The firm's IP practice has a symbiotic relationship with its IT practice, and the explosion in IT-related work for dot.coms and telecommunications clients has led to a commensurate increase in trademark work. Copyright litigation and patent prosecution are other important elements of the caseload, although these are widely felt to be overshadowed by the trademark practice.

Head of the IT team in Sydney, **Anthony Foley*** is said to have *"a good client base in the new economy sector,"* which he advises on a range of IT and IP issues. Particularly prominent in on-line transactions, he acts for the on-line network ninemsn. **Richard Gough*** is the head of the IP practice, and a comparatively recent arrival from the UK. Said to be *"doing a lot of good quality work,"* he is *"someone to keep your eye on – he hasn't been in Australia long, but he's already making quite an impact."*

Major copyright client, the Australian Vice-Chancellors Committee, was recently advised on copyright litigation concerning student access to information. The firm was also involved in the first multi-jurisdictional action brought under new American anti-cybersquatting laws, acting for Tennis Australia. Notable patent litigation cases have included acting for Flexible Steel Lacing in the recently completed Federal Court matter concerning conveyor belt lagging technology. **Clients:** Estée Lauder Group; Harley-Davidson; Kelloggs.

Blake Dawson Waldron (14 partners, 72 lawyers) The departure of Mary Padbury, one of Australia's leading IP practitioners, to the firm's London office, is considered to leave a large gap at home. The firm has moved to fill the breach by

*See leaders' profiles on pages 82-101

poaching *"innovative and astute tactician"* **Ian Pascarl*** from Minter Ellison. The group advises on commercial IP issues and litigation, appearing in cases involving protection of trademarks, designs, copyrights, patents, and the registration and protection of business names.

Considered to contain *"genuine IP specialists, rather than a group of dabblers,"* the team's leading name in Sydney is now **Lisa Ritson***, *"a more than capable IP litigator,"* who has particular expertise in brand name and patent litigation. Significant matters from the past twelve months include acting for SOCOG in protecting the intellectual property associated with the Sydney 2000 Olympic Games, as well as doing all the registration and defence work for Meccano and advising Monsanto Australia in relation to patent protection of its Australian technology. The firm has also been acting for American Home Products Inc in a patent office opposition to an Amgen patent application relating to pharmaceutical compositions and treatments involving recombinant tumour necrosis factor inhibitors. **Clients:** Department of Finance & Administration; Southern Pacific Hotel Corp Ltd.

Clayton Utz (55 lawyers) Working from the Technology and Intellectual Property Group, the IP team advises leading Australian and international organisations such as Apple Computer Inc on trademark work, copyright issues in computer software, corporate transactions and litigation.

Respected litigator **John Collins*** is *"a tough negotiator, who also knows when to concede a point,"* while **Peter Knight***, leader of the IP group in Sydney, is commended for maintaining *"important relationships with a number of major clients."* The firm advised Apple Computer Inc with respect to the registration of trademarks and all aspects of domain name, copyright and trademark protection. Also advised AAPT's wholly owned internet service provider subsidiary, Connectr.com.Pty.Limited, in Federal Court proceedings against GoConnect, alleging breach of sections 52 and 53 of the Trade Practices Act. Other work includes advising Nintendo on its Pokémon intellectual property anti-piracy campaign in both Australia and New Zealand. **Clients:** AAPT; Cable & Wireless plc; Apple Computers; AT&T.

Gilbert & Tobin (5 ptrs, 12 asscs) Specialising in IP matters relating to communications, the internet, media and IT, the firm advises leading Australian entities such as Channel 9 and Optus. Copyright disputes, anti-piracy cases and distribution agreements are all areas of specific expertise.

Kate Harrison* is the firm's *"major IP lawyer in the media and entertainment industry,"* and has notable relationships with ARIA and Paramount Pictures. The firm represented ARIA (Australian Record Industry Association) in proceedings before the Copyright Tribunal to determine a new rate and method for calculating royalties payable by record companies to music publishers. Additionally, the team advised PPCA (Phonographic Performance Company of Australia) on attempts to establish the rate payable by television broadcasters for the use of sound recordings. Sky Channel have instructed the firm on remedies for piracy of Sky Channel signals, copyright issues and distribution agreements. **Clients:** Nickelodeon US; Sony Music Entertainment; Universal Music Australia.

Minter Ellison (21 ptrs, 64 asscs) Large team with an outstanding record for advising on IP issues arising from the print media industry, a specialism which is considered to overshadow the rest of the practice. The workload includes drafting agreements for the sale, transfer and licensing of IP rights, brand protection strategies and trade mark portfolio management, as well as patent, copyright, trade mark and design litigation. The team handles all IP matters for the Fairfax Group of newspapers, which includes the Melbourne Age.

Melbourne is where the firm's IP strength is chiefly held to lie. However, the loss of Ian Pascarl to Blake Dawson Waldron must be accounted a setback to the group. The firm advised on joint ventures and distribution arrangements aimed at commercialising intellectual property developed by CSIRO, Australia's national science agency. Other work includes advising Qantas on international brand portfolio management, and acting for Bristol-Myers Squibb Australia against FH Faulding in the landmark case concerning the patentability of methods of medical treatment. **Clients:** Cable & Wireless Optus; Fairfax Group; Nestlé; Qantas.

Project Finance

Allen Allen & Hemsley/Arthur Robinson & Hedderwicks (member firms of the Allens Arthur Robinson Group) (44 ptrs, 84 asscs) Over the past twelve months, the firm has been involved in a number of major project and infrastructure developments around the country, as well as advising on privatisations of existing infrastructure and energy assets. Growth areas have included acquisition financing and refinancing in the power telecommunications industries. The firm is perceived to have *"real strength in acting for sponsors"* and a *"hugely enviable blue-chip corporate client base."*

A *"massive team"* includes **Phillip Cornwell***, whose huge reputation encompasses both projects and banking work, and the similarly versatile and *"simply outstanding"* **Diccon Loxton***. *"User-friendly"* **Robert Cornish*** has an enviable name for his work on behalf of sponsors, and is *"always focused on getting the job done." "Superb"* **Steve Pemberton*** is another respected finance generalist, widely seen as the group's leader in Melbourne, while **Stephen Spargo*** is viewed as *"a pretty sharp operator."*

The firm acted for ANZ, NAB, CBA, Bank of America, ABN AMRO and BT Alex Brown on the A$1.46 billion project financing of Millmerran Power Station, the first base load coal-fired merchant power plant project to be financed in Australia. Also advised the lead arrangers, National Australia Bank Ltd, BNP Paribas and Bank of America on providing the finance for the acquisition by InterGen of a half interest in Callide C Power Station, a deal valued at A$600 million. Further work for lenders involved the financing of the acquisition of AGL's gas transmission pipelines throughout Australia. **Clients:** ANZ; Bank of America; Commonwealth Bank of Australia; JP Morgan; Merrill Lynch; Morgan Stanley; National Australia Bank; Westpac.

Freehills (23 ptrs, 60 asscs) One of the firm's acknowledged strong suits, the projects group covers all aspects of project financing, including planning and environmental issues, project management, design, construction and the operational requirements of major projects and infrastructure developments. The team advises governments, financial institutions, contractors, resource houses and sponsors on projects across a range of industries, including power and gas, mining and resources projects, construction, telecoms and IT and transport. Perceived to have *"a practice with a healthy balance between sponsors*

AUSTRALIA
Leading firms (Project Finance)

1	Allens Arthur Robinson Group
	Freehills
	Mallesons Stephen Jaques
2	Clayton Utz
3	Blake Dawson Waldron
	Minter Ellison

Firms are listed alphabetically in each band.

Leading individuals (Project Finance)

1	**CORNWELL Phillip** *Allen Allen & Hemsley (Allens Arthur Robinson Group)*
	DOYLE Peter *Mallesons Stephen Jaques*
	GRAMBAS Nicholas *Freehills*
	LOXTON Diccon *Allen Allen & Hemsley (Allens Arthur Robinson Group)*
2	**CLARK Jeff** *Mallesons Stephen Jaques*
	CORNISH Robert *Allen Allen & Hemsley (Allens Arthur Robinson Group)*
	CURTIS John *Freehills*
	FUZI Grant *Clayton Utz*
	HOLLAND Tony *Mallesons Stephen Jaques*
	JOHNSTON Campbell *Blake Dawson Waldron*
	ST JOHN Patrick *Clayton Utz*
3	**CRAVEN Clive** *Clayton Utz*
	DUNNE Ambrose *Minter Ellison*
	FIELD John *Blake Dawson Waldron*
	PEMBERTON Stephen *Arthur Robinson & Hedderwicks (Allens Arthur Robinson Group)*
	SHIRBIN John *Clayton Utz*
4	**MACHIN Peter** *Mallesons Stephen Jaques*
	MACLEAN Alan *Freehills*
	MILLINER Robert *Mallesons Stephen Jaques*
	OLSSON David *Mallesons Stephen Jaques*
	SPARGO Stephen *Arthur Robinson & Hedderwicks (Allens Arthur Robinson Group)*
	STORR David *Mallesons Stephen Jaques*
	TAYLOR Philip *Freehills*
	TRAHAIR Andrew *Clayton Utz*

Up-and-coming individuals

CHO Yuen-Yee *Mallesons Stephen Jaques*
CREED Nicholas *Mallesons Stephen Jaques*

Individuals are listed alphabetically in each band.

and lenders," the firm has gained a high profile through its advice to the Victorian Government on its privatisation programme.

Nicholas Grambas* has an established reputation as one of the country's leading projects experts. *"Ultra-commercial,"* he is generally seen acting for a range of blue-chip lending institutions. Vastly experienced **John Curtis*** has a respected infrastructure practice, while **Alan MacLean*** is recommended as a *"focused and methodical"* practitioner. In Sydney, **Philip Taylor*** also gains market recognition. The firm advised the Australian arrangers (National Australia Bank Ltd, Salomon Smith Barney, SocGen) and the Eurobond arrangers (WDR, HSBC, Barclays) on the A$1.6 billion capital markets programme to finance the CKI/HEI purchase of the South Australian power distribution company ETSA. Also advised InterGen (Australia) Pty Ltd on the Millmerran Power Project, and acted for the financers of Utilicorp's A$2.5 billion bid for ETSA. **Clients:** Citibank; InterGen; Lend Lease; National Australia Bank; NRG Asia-Pacific Ltd; Victorian Government.

Mallesons Stephen Jaques (10 ptrs, 24 asscs) Active on trade financing and international infrastructure project development, the projects team continues to be regarded as *"a lender-oriented practice,"* which also acts extensively for sponsors on energy projects. Hugely respected, the group is considered to be *"ahead by a country mile in terms of depth."*

Peter Doyle* is acknowledged to *"sit at the top of the tree"* in this field. Principally seen on the sponsor side, he has *"taken the lead on a number of serious projects"* for the firm. **Jeff Clark*** has *"some good relationships with banks in Melbourne,"* while the *"easy to deal with"* **Tony Holland*** is well regarded for his *"general infrastructure work." "First-class"* **Peter Machin*** is *"good on his feet,"* **Robert Milliner*** is head of the firm's Project and Energy Resources Group in Melbourne and has acknowledged expertise on energy projects, while the *"under-rated"* **David Olsson*** is said to be held in high regard by his banking clients. **David Storr*** is recommended for his advice on behalf of sponsors, with one rival commenting that *"if I were conflicted out, I'd say go to him."* Of the younger generation, **Nicholas Creed*** is *"a capable player"* with a focus on rail infrastructure projects, while **Yuen-Yee Cho*** is a *"super-bright hard worker,"* who is expected to rise through the ranks quickly.

The firm advised National Australia Bank Ltd on a US$1.03 billion facility to finance Texas Utilities' A$1.6 billion acquisition of the Westar/Kinetik energy distribution businesses from the Victorian State Government. Also advised GPU Inc on its successful bid for the US$768 million project financing of the acquisition of Transmission Pipelines of Australia, and represented Citibank NA on a A$400 million project financing facility for the development of a new mobile telephone network, to be built by the Hutchison Group. **Clients:** ABB Energy Ventures Inc; Banque Nationale de Paris; Barclays Capital; Commonwealth Bank of Australia; Deutsche Bank AG; Enron International; Macquarie Bank Limited; National Australia Bank Limited; Westpac.

Clayton Utz (23 ptrs) Over the past twelve months, the firm's infrastructure and project finance group has been involved in projects in telecoms, roads, transport, aviation and rail. Especially renowned for government infrastructure projects, the firm has acted for the Hydro-Electric Corporation of Tasmania on the A$2.5 billion Basslink electricity interconnector, the South Australian and Northern Territory governments on the AustralAsia Railway, and the New South Wales government on the Parramatta Rail Link.

Grant Fuzi* has *"performed extremely well this year,"* and is known for his close relationship with Deutsche Bank. **Patrick St John*** is a *"highly efficient finance lawyer; you know things are going to go smoothly when you've got him on the other side."* **Clive Craven*** is praised for his versatility in advising lenders and sponsors on various projects, while **John Shirban*** *"pops up quite a bit on the debt side"* and scored a great success with his advice on the Adelaide to Darwin Railway. **Andrew Trahair*** is another experienced and respected practitioner.

The firm advised Barclays, HSBC and Warburg Dillon Read on the financing of the A$3.5 billion acquisition of ETSA Utilities and ETSA Power, acted for ABN AMRO and Chase Manhattan Bank on the A$500 million acquisition of ADI Limited, and represented Deutsche Bank, Citibank, Barclays and Bank of Tokyo Mitsubishi on the financing of the Kogan Creek Power Project. **Clients:** ABN AMRO; Barclays; Chase Manhattan; Deutsche Bank; National Australia Bank; Toronto Dominion; Westpac.

Blake Dawson Waldron (12 ptrs, 33 asscs) Widely seen as *"more of a sponsor's practice than a borrower's practice,"* the projects team is considered to contain *"a number of capable people,"* although its overall profile still lags behind the market leaders. The team handles projects for toll-roads, airports, railways, water treatment plants, power stations, mining projects, hospitals and entertainment facilities.

Campbell Johnston* has *"an excellent profile in Melbourne,"* generally advising sponsors, while banking supremo **John Field*** is also felt to be *"on anyone's list of leading project finance lawyers."* He has played a leading role on a number of Qantas cross-border leasing projects. The firm advised on the A$1.67 billion financing of National Express' acquisition of three of the five passenger transport businesses offered for sale by the State of Victoria. Also represented the successful con-

A

*See leaders' profiles on pages 82-101

sortium on all financing aspects of the BOOT project for the construction and operation of the Alice Springs to Darwin Railway, and the acquisition of the existing line from Tarcoola to Alice Springs. **Clients:** ANZ Bank; JP Morgan Australia; UBS Warburg.

Minter Ellison (17 ptrs, 37 asscs) A player on a variety of infrastructure projects, the firm advises some lenders, as well as sponsors and borrowers. Although lacking the heavyweight clientele of some of its principal rivals, the team includes the versatile **Ambrose Dunne***, the firm's principal name for most financial transactions. The team advised Westpac and ANZ on a A$200 million syndicated facility to the Lend Lease/Mirvac Village Consortium for the construction of the Olympic Village. Also advised ANZ Bank, Commonwealth Bank of Australia and Westpac Banking Corporation on a syndicated limited recourse facility relating to the Jacksons Landing development at Pyrmont in Sydney, where the finance structure provides for the funding of multiple developments simultaneously. In addition, the group represented Multiple/Walker Corporation Joint Venture on all aspects of the joint venture's involvement in the King Street/Wharves 9 and 10 Darling Harbour project in Sydney. **Clients:** ANZ; Duke Energy; Multiplex Construction Group; Westpac.

A

Tax

AUSTRALIA Leading firms (Tax)
1 Allens Arthur Robinson Group
Mallesons Stephen Jaques
2 Blake Dawson Waldron
Clayton Utz
Freehills
3 Arnold Bloch Leibler
Minter Ellison

Firms are listed alphabetically in each band.

Allen Allen & Hemsley/Arthur Robinson & Hedderwicks (member firms of the Allens Arthur Robinson Group) (15 ptrs, 27 asscs) The group advises on all aspects of direct and indirect taxation including the tax implications of mergers and acquisitions, offshore borrowings and investment of funds, restructuring, employee share schemes structuring, and new financial products. Considered to have particular expertise in the areas of international tax, double tax treaties and transfer pricing, the group also acts on large-scale tax audits and tax litigation. Servicing an *"excellent blue-chip client base,"* the team is *"up in the top band for market presence and quality of advice,"* and has strong presence in Sydney and Melbourne.

Former Arthur Andersen man **Larry Magid*** is a *"superb"* lawyer, with a practice that focuses on financial products. He is renowned for his close relationship with Westpac. **Charles Armitage***, who has an accountancy background at KPMG, is recommended for his work on the tax aspects of aircraft leasing transactions. **Kevin Pose*** is *"one of the elder statesmen"* of tax in Australia, and now advises principally on income tax and capital gains tax. The *"outstanding"* **Cameron Rider*** is *"technically sound"* and advises extensively on tax structuring work arising from big-ticket M&A transactions. **Andrew Boxall***, a tax finance specialist, and **Sue Williamson***, a former consultant to the Ralph Committee on Tax Reform, both have a high profile for their expert Goods & Services Tax (GST) advice.

The firm advised NAB on its acquisition of MLC from Lend Lease, represented the South Australian Government on the sale/lease of its electricity assets, and acted for Australian Grand Prix Corporation Ltd on structures designed to minimise the impact of GST on international transactions. Other significant matters include advising Westpac Banking Corporation as sponsor and guarantor of US$322.5 million worth of Trust Originated Preferred Securities, issued in the US by Westpac Capital Trust, and representing the Queensland Investment Corporation on the restructuring of its A$23 billion property trust fund. **Clients:** ANZ Bank; BHP; NAB; Rio Tinto; Westpac.

Mallesons Stephen Jaques (19 ptrs, 53 asscs) Acknowledged to have *"incredible national depth of expertise,"* the firm's tax group has advised as GST legal advisers for major corporates in Australia, especially in financial services, insurance, property, construction and telecommunications. Other areas of expertise include income tax, sales tax, customs and stamp duty litigation, as well as cross-border M&A transactions, international debt capital and securitisations, and tax audits of listed companies.

The team has been bolstered by two high-profile arrivals from The Allens Arthur Robinson Group, both of whom have *"been around a long time"* and have *"excellent names."* **Peter Green*** is *"a first-class tax advisor,"* who is a stamp duty specialist, while the *"well-travelled"* **Ian Stanley*** is noted for his tax advice on structured finance transactions. **Andrew Clements*** is *"a sound operator"* with a reputation for capital gains tax work, **Michael Clough*** has *"good relationships with a number of banks,"* and **David Williams*** is an experienced campaigner with specific expertise in indirect tax. **John King*** is *"a solid performer"* who appears mainly on capital markets and general finance transactions. Rising star **David Temby*** is *"an impressive income tax lawyer"* who has established a name for advising on asset-based financing. Executive Partner of the Tax Group, **Eric Mayne*** is a former sales tax specialist who has become a leading GST specialist. The esteemed Michael Wiley retired from private practice in July 2000.

The firm acted for BHP on the income tax and stamp duty aspects of the restructure of BHP Minerals and BHP Coal, and provided similar advice to NRMA, Australia's largest general insurer, in relation to the demutualisation and listing proposal for the NRMA Insurance Group. Also advised Woolworths on securities and finance tax issues arising from A$600 million of Woolworths income note transactions, as well as obtaining an Australian Tax Office sign-off on Woolworths' off-market buyback of 10% of its issued shares. **Clients:** AMP; AXA; BHP; Colonial Mutual; Deutsche Bank; GE Capital; Lion Nathan; Macquarie Bank; Telstra; Unilever; Woolworths.

Blake Dawson Waldron (14 ptrs, 24 asscs) *"Far stronger in Sydney than Melbourne,"* the tax team has expertise in corporate, finance, GST, state and indirect taxes, employee remuneration and superannuation tax, advising a number of Australian and multi-national corporates and investment banks, as well as private organisations and individuals. Particularly accomplished on international tax issues, the group also handles domestic and cross-border M&A, and the development of innovative financing structures and instruments.

Robert Upfold* is said to do *"a fine job in project finance,"* and is *"the firm's main player in Sydney,"* while the *"respected"* **William Cannon*** is a leading name for GST work. The group has

Leading individuals (Tax)

Band	Individual
1	**BLAIKIE Allan** *Clayton Utz*
	COMINOS David *Clayton Utz*
	MAGID Larry *Allen Allen & Hemsley (Allens Arthur Robinson Group)*
2	**CLEMENTS Andrew** *Mallesons Stephen Jaques*
	CLOUGH Michael *Mallesons Stephen Jaques*
	GREEN Peter *Mallesons Stephen Jaques*
	LEIBLER Mark *Arnold Bloch Leibler*
	STANLEY Ian *Mallesons Stephen Jaques*
	UPFOLD Robert *Blake Dawson Waldron*
3	**ARMITAGE Charles** *Allen Allen & Hemsley (Allens Arthur Robinson Group)*
	POSE Kevin *Arthur Robinson & Hedderwicks (Allens Arthur Robinson Group)*
	WILLIAMS David *Mallesons Stephen Jaques*
4	**FULLER Jeff** *Minter Ellison*
	GATES Stephen *Clayton Utz*
	KING John *Mallesons Stephen Jaques*
	MANN Geoff *Freehills*
	NORRIS Brian *Freehills*
	RIDER Cameron *Arthur Robinson & Hedderwicks (Allens Arthur Robinson Group)*
	SHARP Jeff *Freehills*
	THOMPSON Bill *Minter Ellison*

Up-and-coming individuals

Individual
CHANG Ernest *Freehills*
TEMBY David *Mallesons Stephen Jaques*

Individuals are listed alphabetically in each band.

Leading individuals (Goods & Services Tax)

Band	Individual
1	**CANNON William** *Blake Dawson Waldron*
	MAYNE Eric *Mallesons Stephen Jaques*
2	**BOXALL Andrew** *Allen Allen & Hemsley (Allens Arthur Robinson Group)*
	CLARKE Simon *Freehills*
	WILLIAMSON Sue *Arthur Robinson & Hedderwicks (Allens Arthur Robinson Group)*

Individuals are listed alphabetically in each band.

advised on various complex floats and capital raisings, including Lihir Gold, Crown Casino, GIO Australia, ANZ Bank and Woolworths. Joint venture work has been highlighted by advice on Mission Energy/Loy Yang B, IBM/Telstra, Sony/Australis/Foxtel and BP/Mission Energy. In addition, the team has advised on the creation of the original converting preference share (CPS) concept and in many of the subsequent CPS issues, including those by Metway Bank Ltd, GWA International Ltd, Coles Myer Ltd and Green's Foods Ltd. **Clients:** Allco Finance Group Ltd; GIO Australia; Industrial Equity Ltd; Mobil; NRMA.

Clayton Utz (17ptrs) Offering advice on investment in Australia by foreign companies, corporate restructuring tax advice, employee share option plan advice and taxation audit advice, this is one of Australia's most respected tax groups. The firm has developed particular expertise in GST, reviewing leasing contracts, property trusts, IT and communications contracts and commercial credit contracts. Leading corporates, individuals and the Commonwealth Government have all been advised on the impact of reforms to capital gains tax and other business taxes on mergers and acquisitions.

Although it lacks the size of its leading rivals there is no doubt about the quality of the firm's leading players. Sydney-based **Allan Blaikie*** is *"held in the highest respect"* by peers, and is an expert on asset-based financing. **David Cominos***, although based in comparatively low-profile Brisbane, has a *"thoroughly deserved national reputation,"* while long-serving **Stephen Gates*** is a *"sensible and competent"* performer. The firm advised the Department of Defence on the GST aspects of its contracts, and has provided strategic advice to other Commonwealth Departments on how GST will affect policies and policy development. Acted on Sonic Healthcare's A$300 million acquisition of Sullivan and Nicolaides, advising the vendor in structuring a tax-effective sale to comply with the new capital gains tax regime. **Clients:** Department of Defence; Gandel Group; Northern Territory Treasury.

Freehills (20 ptrs, 55 asscs) This firm's Revenue Law Group advises existing clients on a variety of taxation issues, including income tax, GST, stamp duty and other state taxes. The firm has *"a superb tax practice in Sydney,"* courtesy of its affiliated office Greenwoods & Freehills, from where it draws on the expertise of a mixture of accountants and lawyers.

In Melbourne, **Geoff Mann*** has a fine name for M&A and corporate restructuring tax advice, while **Brian Norris*** has been described as *"one of the best tax practitioners in Sydney,"* although his work for Lend Lease is sometimes felt to overshadow the rest of his practice. **Jeff Sharp*** is *"highly regarded and highly able,"* the *"diligent"* **Ernest Chang*** is *"on his way up"* and **Simon Clarke*** *"flies the GST flag"* for the firm in Sydney. The firm advised GE Capital on tax issues relating to its acquisition of AVCO Australia Pty Ltd, and represented Anglo Gold on its acquisition of Acacia Resources. Further matters include advising on the tax restructuring for the Government of Singapore Investment Corporation following its acquisition of an interest in Rams Home Loans Pty Ltd. **Clients:** GE Capital; Anglo Gold; Government of Singapore Investment Corporation.

Arnold Bloch Leibler (22 lawyers) Melbourne-based firm which provides advice on tax, stamp duty and other revenue implications of commercial transactions, as well tax audits and negotiations with the Tax Office. The client base includes institutions and private clients, who are also represented on tax and estate planning, venture capital, research and development and overseas tax matters.

While **Mark Leibler*** is seen to be *"an exceptionally able lawyer"* and *"a great keeper of high-quality clients,"* he is seen to be *"a bit light on support,"* with the result that the firm's profile has dwindled in recent years. The team has acted on the tax audits of many of the largest public companies in Australia, with some of these audits involving amounts between A$50 million and A$1.3 billion. **Clients:** Private clients, institutions, public companies.

Minter Ellison The tax team's varied workload includes advice on the tax apects of corporate mergers, restructurings, GST contracts and implementation issues, capital gains tax efficiency, income tax, international tax and stamp duty.

The *"knowledgeable"* **Jeff Fuller*** in the firm's Melbourne office is considered to have *"consistently good judgement,"* and is a former Assistant Commissioner at the ATO. **Bill Thompson*** is *"well thought of in Brisbane"* and operates a mixed income tax and GST practice. The firm advised AUSTA Electric on a US$1 billion cross border lease of Units 1-3 of Stanwell Power Station, and acted for consortia led by Macquarie Bank and Serco Group on taxation issues involved in the purchase of the Australian Airports, where the total value has exceeded A$3.7 billion. Also advised New York Venture Capital Fund, Castle Harlan, on establishing the CHAMP Fund, a joint venture with Australian Mezzanine Investments which is the largest private equity fund in Australia. The team provided taxation and project financing advice on the A$2.5 billion Melbourne Docklands project, acting as principal advisor to the Docklands Authority. **Clients:** AMP; Bankers Trust; Cable & Wireless Optus; Qantas.

A

*See leaders' profiles on pages 82-101

Leaders' profiles – Australia

ADDIS, Rosemary
Allens Arthur Robinson Group (AAR Group), Melbourne +61 3 9613 8637
Recommended in Intellectual Property

AHERN, Chris
Corrs Chambers Westgarth, Sydney +61 2 9210 6500
Recommended in Communications: IT

ALLCHURCH, Matthew
Clayton Utz, Sydney +61 2 9353 4000
mallchurch@claytonutz.com
Recommended in Capital Markets
Specialisation: Partner in Financial Services Department. Practises in securitisation, capital markets and structured finance. Acts for a number of prominent securitisation issuers and arrangers, including SG Australia, Citibank, Australian Mortgage Securities Ltd (the wholly owned ABN AMRO mortgage securitisation vehicle) and State Street. Recent high profile transactions include Australia's first aircraft securitisation (Ansett Australia), Australia's first master trust revolving line of credit structure (Citibank's Compass program), the first issue by an Australian securitisation vehicle of Euro denominated asset backed securities (SG Australia's ACE Euro MTN program) and Australia's first securitisation of lease receivables (Sogelease ABF).
Prof. Memberships: Admitted to practice: 1985, United Kingdom, 1989, Supreme Court of New South Wales.
Career: Qualified in England in 1985 with *Watson Farley & Williams* in London. Came to Australia to join *Clayton Utz* in 1989, becoming a partner in 1992.
Personal: Married with 3 children. Leisure interests include surfing and golf.

ANGUS, John
Freehills, Sydney +61 2 9225 5000
Recommended in Banking & Finance

ARGY, Philip
Mallesons Stephen Jaques, Sydney +61 2 9296 2000
philip.argy@msj.com.au
web://www.msj.com.au/msj/opco/profiles/argp.htm
Recommended in Communications: IT, Intellectual Property
Specialisation: Intellectual property (patent, trademark, copyright and confidential information), science and high technology law and trade practices (anti-trust and fair trading). Main areas include dispute resolution strategies involving intellectual property, electronic commerce and digital certificates and signatures. Hybrid commercial and litigation practice.

ARMITAGE, Charles
Allen Allen & Hemsley, Sydney +61 2 9230 4000
charles.armitage@allens.com.au
Recommended in Tax
Specialisation: Corporate Tax and GST, specialising in project and infrastructure finance transactions, including asset financing, securitisation and infrastructure projects; as well as structured equities transactions, including Installment Warrants; and mergers and acquisitions. Recent major transactions include the David Jones' Infrastructure Yield Securities and the associated dual securitisation.
Publications: Various conference papers on the income tax and GST aspects of equipment leasing, securitisation and infrastructure investment.

ARMITAGE, Peter
Blake Dawson Waldron, Sydney +61 2 9258 6000
peter.armitage@bdw.com.au
Recommended in Communications: IT
Specialisation: A partner in the fields of intellectual property, information technology and competition law. Acting for a wide range of Australian and international corporations and governent bodies in a variety of industries including the manaufacturing, energy, insurance, entertainment and resources industries.
Prof. Memberships: President of the Intellectual Property Society of Australia and New Zealand and a member of the Trade Practices Committee of the Law Council of Australia.
Career: 1982-1985 – solicitor at *Dawson Waldron*; 1986-1989 – solicitor at *Clifford Chance* in London and Brussels; 1990 to date – solicitor then partner at *Blake Dawson Waldron*.
Personal: BA, and an LLB, from the University of Sydney.

ARTHUR, John
Freehills, Sydney +61 2 9225 5000
Recommended in Communications: IT

ATANASKOVIC, John
Atanaskovic Hartnell, Sydney +61 2 9777 7000
Recommended in Corporate/M&A

ATKIN, John
Mallesons Stephen Jaques, Sydney +61 2 9296 2000
john.atkin@msj.com.au
Recommended in Corporate/M&A
Specialisation: Senior partner in corporate/mergers and acquisitions team: lead partner advising BHP on OneSteel spinout; key member of *Mallesons Stephen Jaques* team advising on NRMA demutualisation.
Prof. Memberships: International Bar Association; Law Council of Australia.
Career: Joined *Mallesons Stephen Jaques* in 1982. Partner since 1987.
Personal: Bachelor of Arts (first class honours in pure mathematics), Australian National University; Bachelor of Law (first class honours), University of Sydney.

BANCROFT, Anthony
Mallesons Stephen Jaques, Sydney +61 2 9296 2000
anthony.bancroft@msj.com.au
Recommended in Corporate/M&A
Specialisation: Partner in the Sydney office of *Mallesons Stephen Jaques*; heads the M&A team. Wide experience in major corporate and commercial transactions. Regularly advises the boards of corporations and leads public acquisitions and capital raising transactions, often working in conjunction with leading financial advisors. Some of the major M&A transactions include: AMP take-over offer for GIO (AUS$1.9 billion); AMP/GIO scheme of arrangement (AUS$750 million); take-over of TNT Limited by KPN (AUS$2 billion); Walker Corporation/Australand merger by scheme of arrangement (AUS$350 million); contested take-over of Bridge Oil by Parker & Parsely (AUS$380 million); contested take-over by National Foods for Pauls Limited (AUS$350 million); contested take-over of Gasgoyne Gold Mines by Coeur d'Alene Mines Corporation (AUS$160 million); Coal & Allied take-over defence (AUS$500 million); acquisition by Advance Bank of Bank of South Australia (AUS$750 million) and associated capital raising (AUS$500 million); Lang Corporation contested take-over for Holyman (AUS$110 million). Major floats worked on include: Woolworths (AUS$2.4 billion); Commonwealth Bank (Stages 2 and 3) (AUS$1.7 billion and AUS$4 billion); GIO (AUS$1.2 billion). Other significant capital raisings include: David Jones Limited (AUS$750 million); Westpack Convertible Preference Share issue (AUS$600 million); TNT Convertible Preference Share issue (AUS$325 million); Walker Corporation float (AUS$350 million); AMP Income Securities (AUS$500 million); Woolworths Income Notes (AUS$600 million).
Career: 1972-1974 – Solicitor, *Mallesons Stephen Jaques*, Sydney. 1974 to present – Partner, *Mallesons Stephen Jaques*, Sydney. 1978 – Master of Laws degree, University of Sydney. 1981-1984 – Partner in Charge, *Mallesons Stephen Jaques*, New York. 1993-1999 – Head of M&A Group, Sydney.
Personal: 1969 – Bachelor of Laws degree, University of Sydney. 1970 – Bachelor of Arts degree, University of Sydney.

BARRETT, Reg
Mallesons Stephen Jaques, Sydney +61 2 9296 2000
reg.barrett@msj.com.au
Recommended in Capital Markets, Corporate/M&A
Specialisation: Partner in the Sydney office of *Mallesons Stephen Jaques*, specialising in corporate law with a long standing interest in the corporate form and corporate structures. Has practical experience in a range of corporate acquisitions and matters involving fundamental questions about the relationships between corporations and their members.
Career: 1967, admitted as a Solicitor of the Supreme Court of New South Wales. 1971, Master of Laws (first class honours), University of Sydney. 1964-1991, *Allen Allen & Hemsley* (Partner 1971-1991), specialising in corporation and securities law. 1973-1974, and 1976-1987, part-time Lecturer in Law, University of Sydney. 1987-1989, Resident Partner, *Allen Allen & Hemsley* London. 1983-1987, part-time member of the Companies and Securities Law Review Committee (appointed by the Ministerial

Council for Companies and Securities), contributing particularly to that body's publications and reports in response to the Ministerial Council's reference on 'the corporate form'. 1991-1995, Group Secretary and General Counsel, Westpac Banking Corporation. Since 1991, part-time member of the Companies and Securities Advisory Committee and Convenor of its Legal Committee (appointed by Commonwealth Government). Since May 1995, Partner *Mallesons Stephen Jaques*, Sydney. Since January 1998, Chairperson, Australian Stock Exchange Appeal Tribunal (Deputy Chairperson 1997).
Personal: 1964, Bachelor of Arts, University of Sydney. 1967, Bachelor of Laws, University of Sydney. Married with two sons.

BARRYMORE, Stuart
Freehills, Perth +61 8 9211 7777
Recommended in Energy & Natural Resources

BAXT, Robert
Allens Arthur Robinson Group (AAR Group), Melbourne +61 3 9613 8637
Recommended in Competition/Anti-trust

BEDNALL, Timothy
Allen Allen & Hemsley, Sydney +61 2 9230 4000
tim.bednall@allens.com.au
Recommended in Competition/Anti-trust, Corporate/M&A, Energy & Natural Resources
Specialisation: Partner in the Corporate department, specialising in competition law and corporate transactions. Recent major transactions include representing: the South Australian Government in its electricity industry reform and privatisation programme (lead partner); Transfield/Thomson-CSF in the acquisition of ADI Ltd; Southcorp Limited in the sale of its whitegoods division to Email Ltd; Owens-Illinois acquisition of BTR/ACI Packaging (Australian assets); Westpac Banking Corporation in its merger with Bank of Melbourne; Ampol in its merger with Caltex.
Prof. Memberships: Law Societies of New South Wales and South Australia; Deputy Chairman, Law Council BLS Trade Practices Committee.
Career: Admitted in 1984; Partner of *Finlaysons* 1988 to 1992; Partner of *Allen Allen & Hemsley* 1993 to present; Member of Companies and Securities Advisory Committee 1991 to 1995.

BESSON, Garry
Gilbert & Tobin, Sydney +61 2 9263 4000
gbesson@gtlaw.com.au
Recommended in Corporate/M&A
Specialisation: Has extensive corporate and M&A expertise and experience, acting for major Australian listed public companies, investment banks and overseas companies which hold Australian investments. This practice often requires close involvement with investment banks and corporate advisors in implementing significant transactions for sophisticated corporate clients and these transactions frequently include hostile takeovers and corporate reconstructions.
Prof. Memberships: Member, Law Society of NSW; Law council of Australia-Business Law Section.
Career: Admitted 1977. Partner – *Gilbert & Tobin* since July 1996. Director: Lumley Insurance Group.
Personal: Educated at the University of Sydney (LLB, LLM).

BLAIKIE, Allan
Clayton Utz, Sydney +61 2 9353 4000
ablaikie@claytonutz.com
Recommended in Tax
Specialisation: Practical expertise in taxation, international law, banking and finance law and public and private infrastructure financing. Principal clients include Australian and international companies in the financial services and property sectors as well as in manufacturing and distribution.
Prof. Memberships: Admitted to practice: 1991, Supreme Court of New South Wales; 1991, Supreme Court of Victoria; The Institute of Chartered Accountants in Australia; The International Fiscal Association and the International Tax Planning Association.
Career: Joined *Clayton Utz* in 1991. Previously a partner with *Arthur Andersen* between 1980 and 1986. As a member of the Taxation Institute of Australia, has served on numerous Institute and Government Committees.
Personal: Born 16 April 1950. Attended University of Queensland (BCom. LLB). Resides in Sydney.

BLUNT, Gaire
Allen Allen & Hemsley, Sydney +61 2 9230 4000
Recommended in Competition/Anti-trust

BORGESE, Anthony
Mallesons Stephen Jaques, Sydney +61 2 9296 2000
anthony.borgese@msj.com.au
Recommended in Communications: IT, Intellectual Property
Specialisation: Partner, Sydney. Technology, communications and intellectual property practice, specialising in the Internet, electronic commerce and technology law. The Internet and cyberspace represent the majority of work, dealing with online exchanges, Internet content agreements, web development and hosting agreements, linking and framing agreements and domain name disputes. Acting for Australia's largest telecommunications company (which includes Australia's largest and most successful ISP). Has extensive experience in online trading, providing advice on all areas of Internet operations and dealing with all manner of Internet and data services. Is also involved in the preparation and negotiation of all kinds of agreements involving computers and other technology, including technology joint ventures, ASP businesses, hardware and software licence agreements, technology development agreements, complex system integration and outsourcing agreements and telecommunications agreements.
Prof. Memberships: Law Society of NSW; Law Society of England and Wales; NSW Society for Computers and the Law (past President); Intellectual Property Society of Australia and New Zealand; Computer Law Association.
Career: Joined *Mallesons Stephen Jaques* in 1990, becoming a Partner in 1999.
Personal: University of Sydney, BEc., LLM. Born 10 November 1963, lives in Sydney and enjoys sailing.

BORTOLUZZI, Dominic
Mallesons Stephen Jaques, Melbourne +61 3 9643 4000
dominic.bortoluzzi@msj.com.au
Recommended in Energy & Natural Resources
Specialisation: Partner in Corporate Group. Has handled debt and equity arrangements for major energy and infrastructure acquisitions. Acts on power and gas sale arrangements. Has spoken at many conferences in Asia and Australia.
Publications: Has written numerous articles on energy projects.
Career: Qualified in 1991. Joined *Mallesons Stephen Jaques* in 1990, becoming a Partner in 2000. Worked for two years in Hong Kong with a leading UK law firm.
Personal: Born 8 February 1967. Attended Monash University (LLB/BA). Lives in Melbourne.

BOXALL, Andrew
Allen Allen & Hemsley, Sydney +61 2 9230 4000
andrew.boxall@allens.com.au
Recommended in Tax (Corporate): Goods & Services Tax
Specialisation: Indirect Taxes (GST and stamp duty); banking and finance; project and infrastructure finance; capital markets; property finance; asset and structured finance.
Career: Partner, *Allen Allen & Hemsley* since 1986. Resident Partner, Singapore 1988-1994. *Freshfields*, London 1980-1983. BA LLB (University of Sydney) DSU (University De Paris II).

BREHENY, Mark
Blake Dawson Waldron, Melbourne +61 3 9679 3000
mark.breheny@bdw.com.au
Recommended in Capital Markets
Specialisation: Partner in the Melbourne office specialising in banking and finance, covering the full range of banking and finance transactions. Particular expertise in the structured financing of assets including extensive experience in tax-based domestic and cross-border leasing transactions acting variously for arrangers, lessors and lessees, as well as in other tax effective financing arrangements. Recently acted on the financing aspects of a number of privatisations, as well as acting for the Commonwealth Government in the debt management aspects of the sale of Government owned enterprises. Recently acted for National Express Group in the acquisition and related AUS$800 million structured financing of new rolling stock for its newly acquired Victorian rail franchises, and for ANZ and Bank of America in the financing of the AUS$585 million acquisition by the Australian Railroad Group of Westrail Freight from the Western Australian Government.
Prof. Memberships: Member of the Banking Law Association, and represents the firm in its membership of the Australian Equipment Lessors Association.
Career: Bachelor of Law and Bachelor of Commerce, University of Melbourne 1976; 1976 articled clerk, *Blake & Riggall*, Melbourne; 1979 *Nabarro Nathanson*, London; 1983 to present, partner *Blake Dawson Waldron* based in Melbourne.
Personal: Born 2 November 1952. Married to Susan

A

A

with four children. Interests include snow skiing, cricket, swimming and films.

BREWSTER, David
Allens Arthur Robinson Group (AAR Group), Melbourne +61 3 9613 8637
Recommended in Competition/Anti-trust

BROOKS, Tim
Corrs Chambers Westgarth, Sydney +61 2 9210 6500
Recommended in Communications: IT

BROWN, Leigh
Minter Ellison, Sydney +61 2 9921 8888
Recommended in Capital Markets, Corporate/M&A

CAMERON, Peter
Allen Allen & Hemsley, Sydney +61 2 9230 4000
Recommended in Corporate/M&A

CANNON, William
Blake Dawson Waldron, Sydney +61 2 9258 6000 william.cannon@bdw.com.au
Recommended in Tax (Corporate): Goods & Services Tax

Specialisation: A partner in the taxation and revenue law group in the Sydney office of *Blake Dawson Waldron*, specialising in advising on the capital gains tax, goods and services tax and stamp duty aspects of the purchase, sale and leasing of assets and the formation of corporations, partnerships, trusts and joint ventures (including the purchase and sale of shares, units and other interests in them).
Prof. Memberships: A member of the Taxation Committee of the Business Law Section of the Law Council of Australia.
Publications: 'Hill – Duties Legislation': Assistant Editor. 'Australian Tax Review': Stamp Duty Editor.
Career: Joined *Blake Dawson Waldron* in 1974 and has practised in the revenue area of the firm since 1975.
Personal: Graduated from the University of Sydney with an LLB in 1973 and LLM in 1976.

CARABINE, Neil
Mallesons Stephen Jaques, Sydney +61 2 9296 2000 neil.carabine@msj.com.au
Recommended in Communications: Telecoms

Specialisation: Partner in the Sydney office of *Mallesons Stephen Jaques.* Specialises in communications law and mergers and acquisitions. Advises Telstra Corporation Limited (the largest carrier in Australia and the third largest in Asia) on many facets of the operations of a full service telecommunications service provider, including mergers and acquisitions (domestic and overseas), access agreements, regulatory change and compliance, marketing and competitive strategies and general commercial, competition and contractual advice. Has extensive experience in energy and resources projects in Australia and throughout the Asian region. Major transactions include advice on substantial merger and acquisition activities in Australia and in the US (e-commerce), Asia Pacific (including the Telstra PCCW alliance and the Telstra Saturn Joint Venture), Saudi Arabia (operating an exisitng network), Pakistan (installing a network) and Indonesia (installing a network); negotiation of key access agreements with major competitors; extensive advice concerning new telecommunications legislative regimes, including drafting detailed submissions to Government about proposed legislation and assisting in implementing the new legislation; extensive advice concerning distributorship arrangements with intermediaries; construction ownership and operation of two gas fired combined cycle power stations in Malaysia; among others.
Career: University of Melbourne, Bachelor of Commerce, (1984); Bachelor of Law (Honours) (1985); *Mallesons Stephen Jaques* Melbourne; Associate (1985-94), Melbourne and Sydney; Partner (1995-present); secondment as solicitor, *Slaughter and May*, London (1991-1993); Co-Editor, 'Communications Law and Policy in Australia' (Butterworths, 1998-present).

CARVER, Liza
Gilbert & Tobin, Sydney +61 2 9263 4000
Recommended in Competition/Anti-trust

Specialisation: Partner in Competition and Regulation Group. Practice areas include Antitrust, Competition, Economic Regulation Law. Has advised clients in telecommunication, gas, electricity, transport, media and manufacturing industries in relation to restrictive trade practices matters under Part IV of the Trade Practices Act. Expertise includes analysis of economic conditions of industries and markets, commercial transactions, mergers and acquisitions. Also advises public and private sector clients in respect of all aspects of National Competition Policy including restructuring public sector organisations, third-party access regulation, legislative review and pricing regulation. Has particular expertise in the operation of the National Gas Code, National Electricity Code and telecommunications regulation.
Prof. Memberships: Part-time member NSW Independent Pricing & Regulatory Tribunal which regulates the gas, electricity, water and rail industries in NSW; Law Society of New South Wales; Law Council of Australia – Trade Practices Committee; American Bar Association – Antitrust Division.
Career: Admitted 1986, New South Wales. Joined *Gilbert & Tobin* in 1996 and was made partner in 1998. Prior to joining the firm was senior lawyer at the Public Interest Advocacy Centre. Also an Associate Commissioner with the Trade Practices Commission and a part-time Associate Commissioner with the ACCC between 1994 and 1999. Also a Director of the Board of the NSW Rail Access Corporation.
Personal: Educated at the University of Sydney (BEc, LLB, LLM).

CASS-GOTTLIEB, Gina
Gilbert & Tobin, Sydney +61 2 9263 4000 gcass-gottlieb@gtlaw.com.au
Recommended in Communications: Telecoms, Competition/Anti-trust

Specialisation: Partner in Competition & Regulation group. Practice areas include Antitrust; Competition; Economic Regulation Law. Has advised clients in transport, mining, manufacturing, construction, telecommunications and media industries, and both domestic and international financial services in relation to anti-trust including corporate structuring of transactions taking account of the Act, preparation of submissions to the Australian Competition and Consumer Commission (ACCC) including obtaining informal clearances and authorisations for mergers, joint ventures, privatisations and corporate reconstructions, and representation of clients in inquiries and prosecutions by the ACCC. Recent matters include securing ACCC clearances to US$800 million building products transactions, US$1 billion defence asset acquisition, US$1 billion energy sector acquisitions, Australia and New Zealand clearance to merge Case Corp and New Holland International (US$12 billion worldwide transaction) and adviser to major bank in credit card interchange anti-trust investigation.
Prof. Memberships: Trade Practices Committee of Law Council; Law Society of New South Wales; Australian Academy of Forensic Science.
Career: Admitted 1986, New South Wales. Joined *Gilbert & Tobin* as a partner in 1995. Education: University of Sydney (BEc., Hons & Medal; LLB, Hons); Boalt Hall Law School, University of California at Berkeley (LLM), Fulbright Scholar.

CASTLE, Louise
Allen Allen & Hemsley, Sydney +61 2 9230 4000
Recommended in Competition/Anti-trust

CHANG, Ernest
Freehills, Sydney +61 2 9225 5000
Recommended in Tax

CHERRY, James
Freehills, Sydney +61 2 9225 5000
Recommended in Intellectual Property

CHIAM, Louis
Mallesons Stephen Jaques, Sydney +61 2 9296 2000 louis.chiam@msj.com.au
Recommended in Energy & Natural Resources

Specialisation: Senior Associate in Projects, Energy and Resources Group. Principal areas of work are in privatisations, mergers and acquisitions in energy and related industries, electricity and gas regulation and energy related contracts. In 2000, acted for Cheungkong Infrastructure/Hongkong Electric on acquisitions of ETSA Utilities and Powercor Australia; for GPU on sale of GPU PowerNet; and for ACTEW on merger of ACTEW's electricity business with AGL's gas business in the Australian Capital Territory.
Prof. Memberships: Victorian Lawyers RPA Limited.
Career: 1994, Articled Clerk, *Deacons Graham & James*, Melbourne. 1995-1997, Solicitor, *Deacons Graham & James*, Melbourne. 1996, Seconded to *Graham & James LLP*, San Francisco. 1997, Seconded to United Energy (6 months). 1997-present, Solicitor *Mallesons Stephen Jacques*, Melbourne.
Personal: 1993, Bachelor of Laws (Hons) and Bachelor of Science, University of Melbourne.

CHO, Yuen-Yee
Mallesons Stephen Jaques, Sydney +61 2 9296 2000 yuen-yee.cho@msj.com.au
Recommended in Project Finance

Specialisation: Senior Associate in Project Finance

Group. Acts for financiers and sponsors in major projects including energy, resources, water, transport and telecommunications. Recent transactions include privatisation of the South Australian electricity transmission and generation businesses, the Lihir Gold project (PNG), the M2 Motorway refinancing, Hutchinson's CDMA network financing and the Bulong nickel/cobalt project. Has delivered papers on banking, project finance and private international law.
Prof. Memberships: Law Society (NSW, England & Wales), Banking Law Association.
Career: Qualified in 1992. Joined *Mallesons Stephen Jaques* in 1992, returning as Senior Associate in 1998. Associate at *Allen & Overy*, London, in 1995-97.
Personal: Born 8 November 1969. Attended University of Sydney, 1991 (Bachelor of Economics, Bachelor of Laws) and Oxford University, 1995 (Bachelor of Civil Law).

CLARK, Jeff
Mallesons Stephen Jaques, Melbourne
+61 3 9643 4000
jeffrey.clark@msj.com.au
Recommended in Project Finance
Specialisation: Partner in the Melbourne office of *Mallesons Stephen Jaques*, practising in the Financial Services group. Acts for both financiers and borrowers specialising in corporate and project finance. Practice also includes property finance, financial restructures and workouts and general insolvency advice, finance leasing and domestic and international capital markets. Has been actively involved advising financiers to the purchasers of a number of recently privatised Victorian Government entities.
Prof. Memberships: Law Institute of Victoria.
Career: 1987, Solicitor, *Mallesons Stephen Jaques*, Melbourne gaining early legal experience in the areas of intellectual property law, corporate and commercial litigation and property development and leasing; 1988, Solicitor, Banking and Finance, *Mallesons Stephen Jaques*, Melbourne; 1996 to present, Partner, *Mallesons Stephen Jaques* Melbourne. Has presented a number of seminars and written a number of journal papers.
Personal: Born 1 March 1964. 1986, Bachelor of Law (Hons) and Science degrees, University of Melbourne. Leisure interests include golf, tennis and opera.

CLARKE, Simon
Freehills, Sydney +61 2 9225 5000
Recommended in Tax (Corporate): Goods & Services Tax

CLEMENTS, Andrew
Mallesons Stephen Jaques, Melbourne
+61 3 9643 4000
andrew.clements@msj.com.au.
Recommended in Tax
Specialisation: Partner in the Melbourne office of *Mallesons Stephen Jacques* specialising in income tax with an emphasis on capital gains tax, imputation and international tax work. Practice concentrates on corporate tax, capital gains, imputation and the foreign tax credit system and accruals tax together with the income tax consequences of dealing in intellectual property rights and with the taxation treatment of the funds management industry. Also has extensive experience in relation to both the tax and legal issues associated with employee share schemes. Major transactions include: First and Second Tranche of the privatisation of Telstra Corporation Ltd; establishment of employee share plan for numerous major public companies, including Telstra, National Australia Bank; the development of numerous products in the funds management industry.
Prof. Memberships: Taxation Institute of Australia; Law Council of Australia; Law Council Taxation Committee.
Career: 1986, Master of Law, University of Melbourne; 1982-1984, Solicitor, commercial law including banking and finance, take-overs and tax work; 1984-1989, Solicitor/Senior Associate, *Mallesons Stephen Jaques*, Melbourne; 1989 – present. Partner, *Mallesons Stephen Jaques*, Melbourne.
Personal: Born 3 August 1957. 1981, Bachelor of Commerce and Law degrees, University of Melbourne. Leisure activities include cricket. Lives in Melbourne, Victoria.

CLOUGH, Michael
Mallesons Stephen Jaques, Melbourne
+61 3 9643 4000
michael.clough@msj.com.au
Recommended in Tax
Specialisation: Partner in the Melbourne office of *Mallesons Stephen Jacques* and National Group Coordinator for the Tax group. Specialises in income tax issues which arise in the domestic and international capital and debt markets. Has also been closely involved in the development of financial instruments, tax based financing and capital market products. Works closely with Australian and international banks, financial intermediaries and corporations. Work also includes all aspect of tax audits and litigation such as negotiations and actions in relation to the collection of tax, access to premises, production of documents and tax appeals generally.
Prof. Memberships: Australian Institute of Chartered Accountants; Fellow, Taxation Institute of Australia.
Career: Bachelor of Economics and Law degrees, University of Sydney; Chartered Accountant advising on large finance related transactions in international and corporate taxation; Master of Law, University of Sydney; Managing director of an international food company. Has presented papers to universities, legal colleges, and professional bodies such as the Australian Society of Practising Accountants, the Taxation Institute of Australia and the Institute of Chartered Accountants. Is also a Visiting Fellow at the University of Melbourne lecturing in International Tax Law in the Masters of Law programme.

COLLINS, John
Clayton Utz, Sydney +61 2 9353 4000
jcollins@claytonutz.com
Recommended in Intellectual Property
Specialisation: Partner practising in information technology law with considerable experience in intellectual property and technology related litigation (including failed computer systems), telecommunications and trade practices advice and litigation, commercial division and equity litigation. Has also advised on alternative dispute resolution, the obtaining of interlocutory and ex parte injunction, Anton Piller and other orders. Major involvement in IT litigation/arbitration matters for key IT suppliers, major banks and financial institutions as well as telecommunications companies.
Prof. Memberships: BA. LLB. LLM. Admitted to practice: 1984, Supreme Court of New South Wales; 1988, High Court of Australia; 1988, Federal Court. Intellectual Property Committee, Law Council of Australia, NSW Society for Computers and the Law, Computer Law Association, Lawyers Engaged in Alternative Dispute Resolution (LEADR).
Career: Has been a lawyer with *Clayton Utz* for ten years.
Personal: Enjoys spending time with his family as a busy father of four, including the new addition.

COMINOS, David
Clayton Utz, Brisbane +61 7 3292 7000
dcominos@claytonutz.com
Recommended in Tax
Specialisation: Heads the highly regarded taxation practice in Brisbane. Combines expertise in income tax, stamp duty and other revenue laws with considerable experience in documenting and structuring corporate and commercial transactions. Has a keen interest in GST and has published articles dealing with certain constitutional aspects. As a member of the National Technical Committee of the Tax Institute of Australia has been involved in responding to various Government reform proposals including those which are the subject of the Ralph Committee. Has also conducted and advised upon several landmark pieces of litigation in the Constitutional and Revenue fields and negotiated the settlement of a number of tax disputes. Regularly invited to contribute as a speaker on revenue law matters and has published a number of articles.
Prof. Memberships: Admitted to practice in 1975. Member of Supreme Court of Queensland; Queensland Law Society; Revenue Law Committee of Queensland Law Society; Taxation Institute of Australia (Qld Branch) – (Member of the State Council and National Technical Committee); Advisory Board, Butterworths Australian Tax Practice; National CGT Liaison Committee.

CONDON, Wayne
Freehills, Sydney +61 2 9225 5000
Recommended in Intellectual Property

CONLEY, William
Blake Dawson Waldron, Canberra
+61 2 6234 4000
william.conley@bdw.com.au
Recommended in Corporate/M&A
Specialisation: Main areas of practice are corporate law, mergers and acquisitions and privatisations. Recent matters include: acting for the Australian government on the sale of ADI Limited (a former government-owned major defence manufacturer in Australia) advising the Australian government on its shareholding in the Australian Submarine Corporation; advising the government on major

A

defence equipment acquisition contracts, and representing a principal defendant in corporate law litigation involving claims of breaches of corporate law and conspiracy arising out of a takeover. Has also acted as a consultant to the Asian Development Bank on corporatisation and privatisation issues.
Prof. Memberships: Law Society of the ACT, Law Society of New South Wales.
Career: Joined *Blake Dawson Waldron* in 1973, becoming a Partner in 1981. In 1986 was seconded for a year to practise in London with *Morgan Grenfell & Co.* Appointed Convenor, Mergers and Acquisitions group Sydney in 1988, and in 1995 appointed Managing Partner, Canberra, responsible for the firm's leading Commonwealth government practice. Has been a contributor to various international publications on Australian corporate law, particularly mergers and acquisitions.
Personal: Born 24 January 1950. Attended UNSW (BA/LLB) and University of Sydney (LLM). Leisure interests include squash and body surfing.

A

CORNISH, Robert
Allen Allen & Hemsley, Sydney +61 2 9230 4000
Recommended in Project Finance

CORNWELL, Phillip
Allen Allen & Hemsley, Sydney +61 2 9230 4000
Recommended in Banking & Finance, Project Finance

CORRIGAN, Michael
Clayton Utz, Sydney +61 2 9353 4000
mcorrigan@claytonutz.com
Recommended in Competition/Anti-trust
Specialisation: Main experience is in Competition Law, Mergers and Litigation, Corporations Law and general commercial and marketing advice. Has acted for major public corporations in these areas and various Federal and State Government business authorities. Provided advice to Government task forces on implications of major law reform and Competition Law generally.
Career: Spent one year as Associate to Justice Deane of the High Court of Australia before joining *Clayton Utz* in 1984. Admitted to practice: 1983, High Court of Australia; 1983, Supreme Court of New South Wales; 1983, Supreme Court of ACT; 1990, Supreme Court of Victoria; 1995, Supreme Court of South Australia. Immediate Past Deputy Chairman, Trade Practices Committee Business Law Section of the Law Council of Australia. Past Consultant to the Australian Law Reform Commission.
Personal: Resides in Sydney.

CRAVEN, Clive
Clayton Utz, Sydney +61 2 9353 4000
ccraven@claytonutz.com
Recommended in Project Finance
Specialisation: Partner in Financial Services Department and key adviser to banks, arrangers, government, borrowers and investors in infrastructure financings and other large projects. Also acted for the Commonwealth of Australia on the sale of airports and the Olympic Co-ordination Authority on a number of olympic related projects.
Prof. Memberships: Admitted to practice, 1972, New South Wales; 1980, England; 1981, Hong Kong. Director, The Banking Law Association and member of the International Bar Association.
Career: Former partner at *Baker & McKenzie* before joining *Clayton Utz* in 1991.
Personal: Attended University of Sydney (LLB & LLM). Resides Sydney.

CREAN, Mark
Freehills, Sydney +61 2 9225 5000
Recommended in Communications: Telecoms

CREED, Nicholas
Mallesons Stephen Jaques, Melbourne
+61 3 9643 4000
nicholas.creed@msj.com.au
Recommended in Project Finance
Specialisation: Senior Associate in the Melbourne office practising in the Financial Services Group. Acts for both financiers and borrowers specialising in project and infrastructure finance. Experienced in acting for sponsors and financiers in energy and resources and infrastructure projects. Practice also includes structured finance, general corporate finance and privatisations.
Prof. Memberships: Law Institute of Victoria; Law Council of Australia; member of Financial Services Committee of the Law Council of Australia.
Career: 1992-1997 Articled Clerk and Solicitor, Banking and Finance, *Mallesons Stephen Jaques*, Melbourne; 1997-1998 Solicitor, Banking and Capital Markets, *Simmons & Simmons*, London; 1998 – present: Senior Associate, Financial Services, *Mallesons Stephen Jaques*, Melbourne. Has taught banking and finance subjects at postgraduate level.
Personal: Born 12 March 1969. Bachelor of Arts and Honours Degree of Bachelor of Laws, 1991 Monash University. Married to Mary O'Hanlon Creed. Member of Committee of Australian Financial Markets Foundation for Children. Leisure interests include swimming, theatre, classical studies and choral music.

CURTIS, John
Freehills, Melbourne +61 3 9288 1234
Recommended in Project Finance

DANOS, Trevor
Blake Dawson Waldron, Sydney +61 2 9258 6000
trevor.danos@bdw.com.au
Recommended in Banking & Finance
Specialisation: Specialises in domestic and international corporate finance; structured and asset-based finance including equity, leveraged and cross-border leasing; and property, development and project finance. Advises credit providers, borrowers and financial packagers in all sectors of industry and the public sector. Acts for a number of prominent domestic and overseas financial institutions including leading Australian banks and investment banks and a number of Commonwealth and State Government authorities and government sponsored entities. Recent major matters include: acting for the US investors in the Cross-border leases of generating assets at the Stanwell and MT Piper Power Stations and transmission assets in South Australian and Queensland; acting for the lead manager (ANZ and Westpac) in the A$1,500 million re-financing of Consolidated Press and for the agent and lead manager (ANZ) in the A$1,000 million re-financing of PBL (Nine Network); and acting for the Commonwealth Government in the financing of its VIP aircraft fleet.
Prof. Memberships: Chair of the task force on Banking Law at the Securities Institute.
Publications: Co-author of the chapter on 'Guarantees and Indemnities' in Butterworths Australian Encyclopaedia of Forms and Precedents (Fifth Edition).
Career: Partner of the firm since 1988, practising in the area of banking and finance law since 1981. Before joining the firm, practised in large commercial law firms and was General Counsel for 2 years for Chemical Australia International Limited, the Australian subsidiary of Chemical Bank of New York (now part of Chase Manhattan Bank).
Personal: University of Sydney with BEc. and an LLB.

DAWSON, Darryl
Darryl Dawson – Sole Practitioner, Melbourne
+61 3 9629 6799
Recommended in Arbitration (International)

DENNIS, Graeme
Corrs Chambers Westgarth, Sydney
+61 2 9210 6500
Recommended in Energy & Natural Resources

DORTER, John
Allen Allen & Hemsley, Sydney +61 2 9230 4865
john.dorter@allens.com.au
Recommended in Arbitration (International)
Specialisation: Construction and building, arbitration and contract disputes, specialises in both 'ends' of construction contract, V12. The negotiation and advice on the contract documentation and at the other end, claims and disputes in respect of the project, particular construction projects include freeways and other road contracts, dams, dredging, mining, power stations, smelters, nuclear reactors and high rise buildings. Project delivery (specialising in D&C and derivatives) for mines, gas, plants, smelters, mills and treatment plants.
Prof. Memberships: Law Council of Australia, Representative on OB/3 Construction Contracts, Committee of Standards Association of Australia, Member of Joint Building Standards Policy Board.
Publications: Co-author of 'Building and Construction Contracts in Australia – Law and Practice', 'Commercial and Arbitration in Australia – Law and Practice'. General Editor of 'Building and Construction Law Journal'.

DOWNES QC, Garry
Garry Downes QC – Sole Practitioner, Sydney
+61 2 8224 3004
downesqc@sevenwentworth.com.au
Recommended in Arbitration (International)
Specialisation: Queens' Counsel and barrister in Australia and England (Inner Temple) practising from Chambers in Sydney and London. Sits as arbitrator in international and domestic arbitrations as well as acting as counsel for parties in arbitrations and litigation. Specialises in commercial disputes, including international trade, maritime, intellectual property, insurance and reinsurance cases.

Experience in institutional and ad hoc arbitrations. Has particular experience in ICC Arbitrations and arbitrations under UNCITRAL Arbitration Rules and Model Law. Is the Australian member of the ICC International Court of Arbitration. Has written widely on arbitration including Australian Chapter in 'Arbitration Procedures in Asia' (Sweet & Maxwell).
Prof. Memberships: Australian Member ICC International Court of Arbitration; Chartered Arbitrator; Fellow of the Chartered Institute of Arbitrators; Chairman of the Australian Branch of the Chartered Institute of Arbitrators; member of the London Court of International Arbitration; member of panels of CIArb, LCIA, WIPO, Qingdao Arbitration Commission (China).
Personal: Born 7 January 1944. Educated Sydney University. After three years as associate to Chief Justice of Australia began practice as barrister in 1970. Was President Union Internationale des Avocats (UIA) (1994-1995) and is founding President of the Anglo-Australasian Lawyers Society (1998-). Appointed member in the Order of Australia in 1997.

DOYLE, Peter
Mallesons Stephen Jaques, Sydney +61 2 9296 2000
peter.doyle@msj.com.au
Recommended in Energy & Natural Resources, Project Finance
Specialisation: Partner in the Sydney office of *Mallesons Stephen Jaques* specialising in project and infrastructure finance. Has acted for both sponsors and financiers in relation to a number of major energy, resources and infrastructure project financings. Also has considerable experience in the areas of privatisation, banking and finance, tax and commercial law.
Prof. Memberships: Banking Law Association; Australian Mining & Petroleum Law Association; International Bar Association.
Career: 1976, Master of Laws and Bachelor of Commerce, University of Melbourne; 1977-78, Articled Clerk/Solicitor, *Coltmans*, Melbourne; 1979-1980, Tax Lawyer, *Wallace McMullin & Smail*, Melbourne; 1981, Solicitor, *Mallesons Stephen Jaques*, Sydney; 1981-1984, Solicitor, *Mallesons Stephen Jaques* New York; 1985, Partner, *Mallesons Stephen Jaques* Sydney; 1993-94, Managing Partner, *Mallesons Stephen Jaques* Sydney; 1995 Managing Partner, *Mallesons Stephen Jaques* Melbourne and Perth; 1997- present, Partner *Mallesons Stephen Jaques* Sydney. Has presented papers at the Rocky Mountain Mineral Law Foundation conference in Reno, Nevada. Delivered a range of papers at industry conferences and seminars on many banking topics.

DUNNE, Ambrose
Minter Ellison, Sydney +61 2 9921 8888
Recommended in Banking & Finance, Project Finance

DUNSTAN, Jim
Allen Allen & Hemsley, Sydney +61 2 9230 4000
Recommended in Banking & Finance

DWYER, Jim
Allen Allen & Hemsley, Sydney +61 2 9230 4000
jim.dwyer@allens.com.au
Recommended in Intellectual Property
Specialisation: Intellectual Property with particular emphasis on litigation. Acted over many years for large corporations (both international and Australian based) in trade mark, passing off, copyright, design, patent and confidential information disputes. Has considerable experience in the music and entertainment industry and acts for prominent figures and organisations in the sporting area.
Prof. Memberships: Law Council of Australia – Intellectual Property Committee.
Publications: Co-author – Lahore Gamsey Dwyer – 'Intellectual Property in Australia', Butterworths 1981. Co-editor – 'Intellectual Property Reports', Butterworths 1982. Appeared as an expert witness on Australian Copyright Law before U.S. Copyright Tribunal, Washington 1981.
Career: BA LLB (University of Sydney), 1970; Solicitor with *Allen Allen & Hemsley* 1971; Partner with *Allen Allen & Hemsley* 1977; Member of the Board of *Allen Allen & Hemsley* (1992-98); Commissioner of NSW Legal Aid Commission 1991-94; Chairman of *Allen Allen & Hemsley* Charity Committee (1998-present).
Personal: Educated St Aloysius' College, Sydney; married with three children.

ELLIOTT, John
Clayton Utz, Sydney +61 2 9353 4000
jelliott@claytonutz.com
Recommended in Corporate/M&A
Specialisation: Partner in the firm's Mergers and Acquisitions Practice Group with extensive experience in the securities industry concerning public company shares. Has acted in both bid and defence roles in some of Australia's largest takeover matters and in mergers and demergers by scheme of arrangement. Has had extensive dealings with Government and regulatory bodies including the Australian Securities and Investments Commission, the Foreign Investment Review Board and the Australian Stock Exchange.
Prof. Memberships: International Banks and Securities Association of Australia Companies and Securities Urgent Issues Committee; Corporations Law Committee of the Law Council of Australia.
Career: Admitted to practice in New South Wales (1983), Victoria (1990) and Western Australia (2000). Joined *Clayton Utz* in 1983 and became a partner in 1989.
Personal: Born 9 December 1959. Attended Sydney University (LLB (Hons); B.Ec) – captain of the Inter-Varsity Golf team; member of the Killara Golf CLub. Elder of Northside Christian Life Centre.

EVANS, Bernard
Middletons Moore & Bevins, Sydney +61 2 9390 8100
Recommended in Energy & Natural Resources
Specialisation: Partner in Commercial Department and Group Leader Energy and Resources Group. Main areas of work are energy and resources law and competition law. Has handled mine acquisitions, joint ventures and corporate reorganisations and mergers. Also well versed in all operational matters relating to mines and resources projects, acts for Exxon Corporation and other coal mining and resources companies. Resources practice includes oil and gas, coal, gold and base metals and includes all aspects of mine operation, trading and related corporate matters. Strong and growing energy law practice centred around the electricity industry with major clients in both the generation and distribution sectors (Delta Electricity and NorthPower). Competition law practice advising on the electricity markets and also for a range of manufacturing, industrial and chemical clients (Aventis, United Distillers, Carter Holt Harvey).
Prof. Memberships: Australian Mining and Petroleum Law Association
Career: Qualified in 1981. Legal Counsel for Esso Australia Ltd from 1981 to 1987. Solicitor at *Clayton Utz* and *Middletons Moore & Bevins* from 1987 to 1991. Appointed partner of *Middletons Moore & Bevins* in 1991.
Personal: Born 26 October 1957. Attended the University of Sydney (BA, LLB and LLM).

EVANS, Linda
Clayton Utz, Sydney +61 2 9353 4217
levans@claytonutz.com
Recommended in Competition/Anti-trust
Specialisation: Partner in the competition law group. Involved in all aspects of competition and anti-trust law. Has advised on regulatory approvals for major Australian mergers including the Commonwealth Bank takeover of Colonial Bank, the acquisition by SITA-BFI of the Australian assets of Waste Management Holdings Inc. Has acted for the National Competition Council in proceedings in the Australian Competition Tribunal concerning the declaration of certain freight handling facilities at Sydney International Airport and in relation to applications to regulate a major gas transmission pipeline serving the Sydney region. Advises on a wide range of essential facility access issues in network industries including telecommunications.
Prof. Memberships: Law Council of Australia. Law Society of New South Wales.
Publications: 'Access Under the Trade Practices Act', 2000 8 CCLJ 45.
Career: Qualified in 1987. Joined *Clayton Utz*, Perth (then known as *Robinson Cox*), becoming a partner in 1994. Joined *Andersen Legal*, Sydney in 1996 as a partner. Joined *Clayton Utz*, Sydney as a partner in 2000.
Personal: Born London, 1965. Educated St Hilda's Anglican School for Girls, Perth, Western Australia; B.Juris, LLB (University of Western Australia). Director, Network Economics Consulting Group Pty Ltd.

EVERETT, Kathryn
Freehills, Sydney +61 2 9225 5000
Recommended in Intellectual Property

FARRELL, Kathleen
Freehills, Sydney +61 2 9225 5000
Recommended in Capital Markets

A

FEATHERSTON, Roger

Mallesons Stephen Jaques, Sydney +61 2 9296 2000
roger.featherston@msj.com.au
Recommended in Communications: Telecoms, Competition/Anti-trust

Specialisation: Head of the National Competition Law Team of *Mallesons Stephen Jaques*, Sydney. Over twenty years experience in the practice of Competition Law, including four years as a solicitor acting for the former Trade Practices Commission. Practice encompasses corporate advice work, regulatory work and litigation for a wide range of clients. Particular emphasis on competition law aspects of mergers, price fixing, pricing strategies, banking and telecommunications.
Prof. Memberships: Former Chair, Business Law Section, Law Council of Australia and of its Trade Practices Committee; admitted in ACT, NSW, VIC, WA and NT.
Career: Solicitor, Attorney-General's Department, Canberra (Trade Practices Commission) (1974-79); *Mallesons Stephen Jaques* Solicitor (1980), Partner (1986-present).
Personal: Australian National University, LLB/BEc. (1974).

FERRARO, Michael

Freehills, Melbourne +61 3 9288 1234
Recommended in Communications: Telecoms

FIELD, John

Blake Dawson Waldron, Melbourne +61 3 9679 3000
john.field@bdw.com.au
Recommended in Banking & Finance, Project Finance

Specialisation: Project and structured finance; aircraft finance; capital markets. Telstra Corporation – AUS$2.25 billion global syndicated facility; Qantas Airways – US$700 million US cross-border leases.
Prof. Memberships: Financial Services Committee (former chairman), Law Council of Australia.
Publications: Speaker at many local and international conferences on project finance and aircraft finance.
Career: *Blake Dawson Waldron* partner since 1981, previously with *Davis Polk & Wardwell* (New York) and *Linklaters* (London).
Personal: LLB, (Hons) (Melbourne). Married, two daughters. Interests: golf, skiing, wine.

FITZSIMONS, James

Clayton Utz, Sydney +61 2 9353 4000
jfitzsimons@claytonutz.com
Recommended in Communications: Telecoms

Specialisation: Telecommunications, Information Technology and Intellectual Property. Main area of work in recent years is telecommunications law acting for AAPT Limited, Australia's third largest carrier as their principal external counsel. Advised on contracts for the rollout of a mobile CDMA network and an LMDS network including all the related transactions for those leading edge technologies. Also advised on inter-connection agreements, satellite services contracts, facilities access agreements, software acquisition and implementation and resale agreements. In addition acts for a number of large corporate clients acquiring technology. Outsourcing is another major part of the practice and is continually advising in this area. Managing editor of the Compulaw Newsletter, contributing editor to Computer Law and Security Report, and the World Computer Law Report. Continually speaking at conferences both domestically and internationally.
Prof. Memberships: New South Wales Law Society, New South Wales Society of Computers and the Law, Copyright Law Society, Inter-Pacific Bar Association, Computer Law Association.
Career: Graduated with degrees in computer science and law from University of Sydney, 1980. After working as a programmer/analyst in Ottawa, joined *Blake Dawson Waldron* in 1982. In 1985 moved to *Abbott Tout Russell Kennedy* becoming a partner in 1988. Joined *Clayton Utz* as a partner in 1991. President of the New South Wales Society for Computer and Law in 1987/1988; Vice Chair of Intellectual Property Committee of the IPBA 1996. Appointed Australian jurisdictional representative for IPBA 1997. Councillor-at-Large (responsible for website)

FOLEY, Anthony

Baker & McKenzie, Sydney +61 2 9225 0289
anthony.foley@bakernet.com
Recommended in Communications: IT, Intellectual Property

Specialisation: Specialises in information technology, electronic commerce, trade practices and intellectual property. Acts extensively for leading global information technology companies and has substantial experience in providing advice and documentation on a wide range of IT, ecom, outsourcing and online transactions. Has been lead partner on a number of the largest outsourcing projects undertaken in Australia in recent years. Has negotiated and drafted a broad range of documentation for complex IT transactions and for the establishment of online services. Has also extensive experience in dealing with competition law issues on behalf of IT companies and other IP owners.
Prof. Memberships: Copyright Society.

FRECKER, David

Blake Dawson Waldron, Sydney +61 2 9258 6000
Recommended in Energy & Natural Resources

FULLER, Jeff

Minter Ellison, Sydney +61 2 9921 8888
Recommended in Tax

FULLER, Stuart

Mallesons Stephen Jaques, Sydney +61 2 9296 2000
stuart.fuller@msj.com.au
Recommended in Capital Markets

Specialisation: Partner in the Sydney office of *Mallesons Stephen Jaques* specialising in securitisation and structured finance. Concentrates on securitisation and has acted for issuers or arrangers of programmes in the Australian, euro, and US bond and commercial paper markets. Primarily acts for the arrangers and issuers of asset backed, mortgage backed and repackaging transactions.
Prof. Memberships: Member of the Law Society of New South Wales. Member of the Australian Securitisation Forum.
Career: Achieved Bachelor of Commerce and Laws degrees, University of New South Wales (1990); solicitor, *Mallesons Stephen Jaques*, Sydney (1990); partner, *Mallesons Stephen Jaques*, Sydney (1997).
Personal: Married with three children.

FURPHY, Baden

Freehills, Sydney +61 2 9225 5000
Recommended in Energy & Natural Resources

FUZI, Grant

Clayton Utz, Sydney +61 2 9353 4000
gfuzi@claytonnutz.com
Recommended in Banking & Finance, Project Finance

Specialisation: Experience in all aspects of major projects, acting for banks and sponsors, and has also acted in many of the significant recent project finance projects in Australia. Experience spans gas, electricity, telecommunications, defence and MBS's/LBO's.
Prof. Memberships: Admitted to practice 1989, Supreme Court of New South Wales. Law Society of New South Wales.
Career: Solicitor at *Clayton Utz* 1990-1993. Seconded for two years to the project finance group of *Allen & Overy*. Returned to *Clayton Utz* and became a partner in 1998.

GALBRAITH, Colin

Allens Arthur Robinson Group (AAR Group), Melbourne +61 3 9613 8637
Recommended in Corporate/M&A

GATELY, Denis

Minter Ellison, Brisbane +61 7 3226 6333
Recommended in Energy & Natural Resources

GATES, Stephen

Clayton Utz, Sydney +61 2 9353 4000
sgates@claytonutz.com
Recommended in Tax

Specialisation: Tax practice ranges over the principal areas of domestic and international corporate taxation. In addition to Commonwealth and State taxation affecting inbound and outbound investment, has had extensive experience in connection with commercial structures, business reorganisations and asset acquisitions and disposals. Practice has focused on banking and finance, including securitisation, financial instruments and syndications. Has advised governments on a wide variety of questions and is also experienced in all aspects of the corporation imputation system, employee share schemes and corporate finance. The nature of this work has regularly involved approaches to the Australian Taxation Office for private rulings and advance opinions regarding the anticipated taxation treatment of proposed transactions. In addition to income and capital gains taxation, is an experienced adviser in relation to goods and services tax and other business taxes.
Prof. Memberships: Admitted to practice: 1970, Supreme Court of New South Wales; 1988, Supreme Court of Victoria; 1975, Supreme Court of ACT and any Federal Court. Fellow, Taxation Institute of Australia. Member, International Fiscal Association, Australian Taxation Research Foundation.
Publications: Author of two books: 'Tax Aspects of Corporate Restructuring' (1976) and 'Tax and

Insolvency' (1997) and for 12 years was a joint author of the 'Australian Tax Handbook', published annually. Has also published widely in journals and loose-leaf tax services.
Career: Began career with *Clayton Utz* in 1968. After a period as a lecturer and senior lecturer in taxation and corporations law with the Faculty of Law, Australian National University, returned to *Clayton Utz* as a tax partner in 1988 and has practised solely in taxation since that time.

GLANZ, Steven
Baker & McKenzie, Sydney +61 2 9225 0200
steven.glanz@bakernet.com
Recommended in Corporate/M&A
Specialisation: Principal areas of practice are capital markets and mergers and acquisitions. Has extensive experience in complex acquisitions and joint venture proposals. Acted for: MCI Corporation in its US$2 billion investment in News Corporation and related joint venture arrangements; BellSouth on its joint venture arrangements in respect of Optus Communications (Australia's second largest telecommunications carrier); Primary Industry Bank in connection with the sale of its $2 billion residential mortgage portfolio; Billiton plc in connection with the acquisition of CSR's and AMP's interests in the Gore alumina project, Hagemeyer NV in its acquisition of Pacific Dunlop's electical distribution business. Chairman of *Baker & McKenzie's* Regional M&A Committee and member of firm's Global M&A Steering Committee.
Prof. Memberships: Law Society; Governor of the American Chamber of Commerce in Australia.
Career: Qualified in 1978; joined *Baker & McKenzie* in 1979 becoming a partner in 1984. Practised with *Baker & McKenzie's* New York office. Managing Partner of the Australian offices of *Baker & McKenzie* 1991-95.
Personal: Born 24 February 1955. Attended University of New South Wales (BComm/LLB) and Columbia University (LLM). Interests include running and modern U.S. history.

GOLDER, Tim
Allens Arthur Robinson Group (AAR Group), Melbourne +61 3 9613 8637
Recommended in Intellectual Property

GOLDING, Greg
Mallesons Stephen Jaques, Sydney +61 2 9296 2000
greg.golding@msj.com.au
Recommended in Capital Markets, Corporate/M&A
Specialisation: Partner in the Sydney office of *Mallesons Stephen Jaques* specialising in the areas of contested public company take-overs, reconstructions, and capital raisings. In recent years has been involved in some of Australia's most significant mergers and acquisition transactions. Counts among clients many leading intermediaries.
Career: Solicitor, *Mallesons Stephen Jaques*, Sydney from 1984-86. Attorney, *Skadden Arps Slate Meagher & Flom*, New York (mergers and acquisitions). Partner of *Mallesons Stephen Jaques*, Sydney from 1990-present.
Personal: Achieved Bachelor of Commerce and Laws degrees, University of NSW, Sydney.

GONSALVES, Maurice
Mallesons Stephen Jaques, Sydney +61 2 9296 2000
maurice.gonsalves@msj.com.au
Recommended in Communications: IT, Intellectual Property
Specialisation: Partner in Technology Communications and Intellectual Property Group. Main areas of practice are intellectual property and information technology law, including the protection and enforcement of IP rights and the application of IP law to computers and the Internet. Has handled major trade mark and copyright litigation for leading international companies such as Intel Corporation and Microsoft Corporation. Has obtained favourable judgments in a number of test cases including Microsoft v Atifo, Microsoft v Auschina Polaris and Intel v Computer Touch. Represents the Business Software Alliance and its Australian affiliate the Business Software Association of Australia (BSA) comprising many of the world's leading software companies. Has advised BSA since the start of its campaign against software piracy in Australia in 1989. Regularly involved in high level government consultations and submissions on IP law reform issues, most recently in relation to the landmark Copyright Amendment (Digital Agenda) Act 2000. Also advises on the IP aspects of major corporate transactions such as the recent AUS$1.6 billion demutualisation and listing of NRMA Insurance, Australia's largest general insurer.
Prof. Memberships: Law Society; Intellectual Property Society of Australia and New Zealand; Copyright Society of Australia; NSW Society for Computers & the Law.
Publications: Contributor to the 'Encyclopaedia of International Commercial Litigation' (Intellectual Property).
Career: Qualified in 1985. Solicitor at *McKenna & Co.* in London from 1983 to 1988. Joined *Mallesons Stephen Jaques* Sydney in 1989, becoming a partner in 1992. Member *Mallesons Stephen Jaques* Pro Bono Committee 1998-2000. Group Coordinator Technology Communications and Intellectual Property (TCIP) 2000. Member of the Management Committee of the Copyright Society of Australia since 1996.
Personal: Attended Bristol University 1976-1980 (BA). College of Law Guildford 1980-1982. Leisure interests include opera, theatre, film, swimming and surfing.

GOUGH, Richard
Baker & McKenzie, Sydney +61 2 9225 0200
Recommended in Intellectual Property
Specialisation: Specialises in intellectual property disputes and litigation including anti-counterfeiting. Has particular expertise in Federal Court trade mark, copyright and patent litigation. Acts for Australian universities in relation to their participation in and litigation regarding statutory schemes for copyright licensing. Has a particular interest in devising and implementing strategies for the cost-effective protection and enforcement of intellectual property rights in Australia and the Asia Pacific region.
Prof. Memberships: International Trademarks Association, International Anti-Counterfeiting Coalition, Intellectual Property Society of Australia and New Zealand and the Copyright Society.
Publications: Author of the Australian chapter of the looseleaf 'Worldwide Trade Secrets' Law and editor of the quarterly publication Asia Pacific Legal Developments Bulletin
Career: Joined *Baker & McKenzie* in 1988, becoming partner in 1990.
Personal: Qualified UK 1985, Australia 1989.

GRAMBAS, Nicholas
Freehills, Melbourne +61 3 9288 1234
Recommended in Project Finance

GRAY, John
Gilbert & Tobin, Sydney +61 2 9263 4000
jgray@gtlaw.com.au
Recommended in Communications: IT
Specialisation: Main areas of work are technology transactions, including licensing and commercialisation of technology, outsourcing, systems integration and solution development; intellectual property, including IP audits and due diligence and IP contracting; commercial transactions for 'new economy' participants, including joint ventures, alliance agreements and venture capital funding arrangements; e-commerce; and regulatory work for corporations engaged in the IT&T market.
Prof. Memberships: Law Society of NSW. Australian Information Industry Association Legal Sub-Committee. NSW Society for Computers and the Law.
Publications: Has written and presented widely on IT&T project topics, including in relation to system integration agreements, service level agreements, strategic IT contract management and the protection and commercialisation of intellectual property.
Career: Admitted 1992. Joined *Gilbert & Tobin* in 1996.
Personal: University of Sydney (BA, LLB (Hons)).

GRAY, Michael
Freehills, Sydney +61 2 9225 5000
Recommended in Competition/Anti-trust

GRAY, Richard
Freehills, Sydney +61 2 9225 5000
Recommended in Capital Markets

GREEN, Peter
Mallesons Stephen Jaques, Sydney +61 2 9296 2000
peter.green@msj.com.au
Recommended in Tax
Specialisation: Partner of *Mallesons Stephen Jaques* practising in the Sydney office in all fields of revenue law. Began to specialise in revenue law in 1975. Chaired the IBC Annual Stamp Duty Symposium for a number of years.
Prof. Memberships: Member of the Office of State Revenue – NSW Law Society Stamp Duty Liaison Committee.
Publications: Over the years has presented papers and written articles for publication on topics including income tax; capital gains tax; stamp duty; financial institutions duty and, most recently, GST. Also joint author of the third edition of 'Principles of Income Taxation'. A number of those papers have been presented to the IBC Annual Stamp Duty Symposium.
Career: BA, and LLM, (Hons 1) from Sydney University.

A

A

GREIG, John
Allen Allen & Hemsley, Brisbane +61 7 3334 3000
Recommended in Energy & Natural Resources

HALSTEAD, Rod
Clayton Utz, Sydney +61 2 9353 4000
rhalstead@claytonutz.com
Recommended in Corporate/M&A
Specialisation: Partner who heads the firm's Mergers and Acquisitions Practice Group. Senior mergers and acquisitions lawyer with more than 20 years' experience in advising corporations and directors in relation to contested and negotiated takeovers, acquisitions, mergers, divestments and reconstructions.
Prof. Memberships: Admitted to practice, 1966, Supreme Court of New South Wales; 1966, High Court of Australia; 1974, Supreme Court of Australian Capital Territory (ACT); 1984, Supreme Court of Western Australia; 1986, Supreme Court of Victoria; Director Boral Limited; Director Cambooya Pty Limited (private investment company of Sir Vincent Fairfax family).
Career: Joined *Clayton Utz* in 1993 after more than two decades at *Mallesons Stephen Jaques.* In the 1970s practised as a general corporate lawyer demonstrating particular expertise in foreign investment and company and business acquisitions. Also advised on income tax and other revenue law advice. Also has considerable experience and expertise in dealing with government and regulatory bodies, including the Australian and Securities Investment Commission, the Australian Stock Exchange, the Australian Competition and Consumer Commission and the Foreign Investment Review Board.
Personal: Leisure interests include recreational golf and is a member of the Royal Sydney Golf Club.

HAMER, Richard
Allens Arthur Robinson Group (AAR Group), Melbourne +61 3 9613 8637
Recommended in Intellectual Property

HAMMOND, Gregory
Mallesons Stephen Jaques, Sydney +61 2 9296 2000
greg.hammond@msj.com.au
Recommended in Banking & Finance, Capital Markets
Specialisation: One of Australia's leading banking and capital market lawyers. Partner in the firm's Sydney office, specialises in capital markets, securities, payments and clearance and settlement systems and corporate finance. Was partner-in-charge of the firm's London office from 1995 to 1998 and has extensive experience in advising Australian and overseas financial institutions and corporations in these areas.
Prof. Memberships: Member of the Law Society of New South Wales; the International Bar Association (Sections on Business and Energy and Resources Law); the Banking Law Association and several other professional and industry associations. Admitted to practice in New South Wales, Victoria, Western Australia and the Australian Capital Territory and a Registered Foreign Lawyer with The Law Society of England and Wales.
Career: After graduating with honours in law, anthropology (prehistory) and theology from the University of Sydney and the Australian College of Theology, worked with *Stephen Jaques Stone James* in Sydney and *Allen & Overy* in London. Became a partner of *Mallesons Stephen Jaques* in 1987 and was President of Australian Business in Europe in 1998.
Personal: Born 10 September 1957. Lives in Sydney and is married to Beth with two children (Alison and Andrew). Actively involved in the Anglican Church, interests include golf, philately and history.

HARRISON, Kate
Gilbert & Tobin, Sydney +61 2 9263 4000
kharrison@gtlaw.com.au
Recommended in Intellectual Property
Specialisation: Currently heads the intellectual property group. Has a range of legal experience across a variety of areas of intellectual property, media and communications law, civil law and commercial law. Has been involved in drafting various agreements, including licensing agreements for record companies, manufacturers and industry associations, production and distribution agreements, advice and advocacy for pay TV channel providers, and technology and supply agreements. Experience in advising broadcasting clients, and has acted in litigation in various matters including communications cases. Advised and acted in IP and communications litigation for the Australian Record industry Association, the Australian Film Television and Radio School, the Phonographic Company of Australia, Lexmark Australia, RG Capital Radio and other IP holders and communications companies.
Prof. Memberships: Member, Law Society of NSW; Communications and Medical Law Association; Intellectual Property Society of Australia and New Zealand.
Career: 1986 – Barrister, NSW Supreme Court; 1988 – Solicitor, NSW Supreme Court; 1993 – New York, Court of Appeals; 1993 – S.D.N.Y., US Federal Court. Joined *Gilbert & Tobin* in April 1996.
Personal: Educated at University of Sydney (BA Hons); University of New South Wales (LLB); Columbia Law School (LLM); University of Sydney (PhD in Government).

HARRY, John
Allens Arthur Robinson Group (AAR Group), Melbourne +61 3 9613 8637
Recommended in Corporate/M&A

HARTNELL, Anthony
Atanaskovic Hartnell, Sydney +61 2 9777 7000
Recommended in Corporate/M&A

HAY, Peter
Freehills, Melbourne +61 3 9288 1234
Recommended in Corporate/M&A, Energy & Natural Resources

HENDERSON, Angus
Gilbert & Tobin, Sydney +61 2 9263 4000
ahenderson@gtlaw.com.au
Recommended in Communications: Telecoms
Specialisation: Partner in the Commercial, Communications & Technology group. Practice areas are Telecommunications Law; Corporate; Competition Law; Communications Law. Acts for clients such as Cable and Wireless Optus, Singapore Telcom and Sri Lanka Telecom. Practice is mainly devoted to interconnection and access issues and the development of regulatory models in the telecommunications and broadcasting industries. Provides advice and assistance to the Optus Interconnect and wholesale section. Has also advised Hongkong Telecom in the transition to open competition in the domestic services market and has assisted with the interconnection negotiations in Hong Kong. Advises Sri Lanka Telecom on all aspects of telecommunications regulation in that country. Also advises Singapore Telecom on their interconnection arrangements in Singapore. A regular speaker at communications, broadcasting and technology conferences in Australia. Has also recently presented papers in the Philippines, Indonesia, Malaysia and Singapore.
Prof. Memberships: Law Society of New South Wales.
Career: Admitted to the Bar in 1990, New South Wales. Joined *Gilbert & Tobin* in 1994, becoming a Partner in 1998. Education: University of New South Wales (BSc; LLB), Contributing Editor: 'Communications Law and Policy in Australia'.

HERRING, Michael
Mallesons Stephen Jaques, Sydney +61 2 9296 2000
michael.herring@msj.com.au
Recommended in Communications: Telecoms
Specialisation: Executive Partner of *Mallesons Stephen Jaques*'s Corporate Advisory practice. Practises corporate and commercial law specialising in cross-border corporate acquisitions and telecommunications law, particularly privatisation, regulatory, strategic joint ventures and major supply contracts.
Prof. Memberships: Sydney Chapter Chair, The Section of International Law and Practice of the New York State Bar Association; non-practising attorney of the State Bar of California; Governor, The American Chamber of Commerce; Member, The National and International Practice Committee, Law Society of New South Wales; President of the Australia Society of New York from 1993-94.
Career: Solicitor/Senior Associate, *RI Rosenblum and Partners*, Sydney (1981-85); Attorney, *Thelen Marrin Johnson & Bridges*, San Francisco (1985-87); Solicitor, *Mallesons Stephen Jaques*, Sydney (1987-88), Partner- Sydney (1989), Partner- New York (1990-94), Partner- Melbourne & Sydney (1994-1998), Managing Partner- Sydney Brisbane and Canberra (1998-1999), Executive Partner- Sydney (1999-present).
Personal: Bachelor of Commerce and Law, University of New South Wales (1980); Master of Law, University of Sydney (1989).

HERRON, Louise
Minter Ellison, Sydney +61 2 9921 8888
Recommended in Communications: IT

HOLLAND, Tony
Mallesons Stephen Jaques, Melbourne +61 3 9643 4000
tony.holland@msj.com.au
Recommended in Project Finance
Specialisation: Partner in the Melbourne office of

Mallesons Stephen Jaques, practising primarily in project and infrastructure finance, and also in energy, resources and infrastructure projects, domestic and international finance and acquisition finance.
Prof. Memberships: The Banking Association Limited; Australian Mining and Petroleum Law Association.
Career: After joining *Mallesons Stephen Jaques* in 1982, was seconded to the international banking section of a major London law firm in 1986. Became a Partner in 1987 and worked in the London office of *Mallesons Stephen Jaques*, returning to Melbourne in 1988. Was the head of Banking and Finance Practice Group in Melbourne between 1996 and 1998.
Personal: Completed a Bachelor of Laws (with Honours) degree and a Bachelor of Commerce degree from the University of Melbourne in 1977. Hobbies include golf, tennis, surfing and outdoor pursuits.

HUGHES, Gordon
Blake Dawson Waldron, Melbourne
+61 3 9679 3000
gordon.hughes@bdw.com.au
Recommended in Communications: IT
Specialisation: Partner in intellectual property and computer technology law. Experience extends to creation, interpretation and dispute resolution advice in design, development, licensing, distribution and franchising of IT products and technologies including e-commerce and joint ventures acquisitions and sale of businesses as well as litigation of all kinds. International aspects of practice encompass Australian companies wishing to expand overseas and international companies wishing to explore market opportunities in Australia and Asia Pacific. Clients include small and large businesses, government departments and financial institutions.
Prof. Memberships: Former president of the Victorian Society for Computers and the Law and an honorary life member of that society. Chairman of the LAWASIA Computers and Technology Group and Chairman of the Privacy Committee of the Law Council of Australia. Was president of the Law Institute of Victoria in 1992-1993. Elected vice president of LAWASIA in 1999, also became president of the Law Council of Australia.
Publications: Co-author of a leading text on IT law, 'Computer Contracts: Principles and Precedents', and is the author of another text, 'Data Protection in Australia'.
Career: Graduated from the University of Melbourne in 1971 with an LLB, (Hons), and completed Master of Laws at the same tertiary institution in 1973. Also completed a PhD at Monash University in 1989. Is Grade 1 Arbitrator with the Institute of Arbitrators and Mediators Australia.

HUGHES, Paul
Corrs Chambers Westgarth, Sydney
+61 2 9210 6500
Recommended in Competition/Anti-trust

JAMES, Martin
Mallesons Stephen Jaques, Sydney +61 2 9296 2000
martin.james@msj.com.au
Recommended in Energy & Natural Resources
Specialisation: Project finance, structured finance, structured derivatives, energy derivatives, syndicated lending and infrastructure finance. Lectures on a variety of derivatives related areas.
Publications: Australia OTC Guide, Chapters 20 and 29 (published by AFMA).
Career: 1980-1990: *Freehill Hollingdale & Page*; 1990-1994: *Mallesons Stephen Jaques*; 1994-1995: Barclays – Mining & Metals. 1995-present: *Mallesons Stephen Jaques*.
Personal: BJuris (Hons), LLB, (Hons), University of Western Australia. Leisure interest – sailing.

JINKS, Andrew
Allen Allen & Hemsley, Sydney +61 2 9230 4000
andrew.jinks@allens.com.au
Recommended in Capital Markets
Specialisation: Securitisation and debt capital markets (domestic and international). Transactions include Deutsche/David Jones IYS issue; Westpac's WST securitisations; St. George's crusade securitisations; Interstar's Millennium securitisations; SAFE Commercial Paper conduit structure.

JOHNSTON, Campbell
Blake Dawson Waldron, Melbourne
+61 3 9679 3000
cam.johnston@bdw.com.au
Recommended in Project Finance
Specialisation: Partner in the Melbourne office of *Blake Dawson Waldron* specialising in banking & finance, project and infrastructure finance, energy and major projects representing both financiers and sponsors.
Prof. Memberships: Law Institute of Victoria, The Banking Law Association of Australia, IBA Sections on Banking Law and Energy & Resources Law, Australian Institute of Company Directors.
Career: Joined *Blake Dawson Waldron* in 1973 and seconded to a major New York law firm in 1975 & 76. Partner since 1977 and Chairman of Partners 1995-98.
Personal: LLB, BCom., University of Melbourne. Married with three children. Member Council of Scotch College Melbourne and director of The Bell Shakespeare Company. Leisure interests include rowing, golf and theatre.

JOLLEY, Braddon
Freehills, Sydney +61 2 9225 5000
Recommended in Corporate/M&A

JONES, Angus
Allens Arthur Robinson Group (AAR Group), Perth
+61 8 9420 4222
Recommended in Energy & Natural Resources

KELLY, John
Corrs Chambers Westgarth, Brisbane
+61 7 3228 9333
Recommended in Energy & Natural Resources

KELLY, Peter
Mallesons Stephen Jaques, Melbourne
+61 3 9643 4000
peter.kelly@msj.com.au
Recommended in Competition/Anti-trust
Specialisation: Partner in the Melbourne office of *Mallesons Stephen Jaques*, in the corporate group specialising in competition law, corporate reconstructions and M&A transactions. Clients cover a number of important industry groups. Also the Deputy Chairman of the Board of *Mallesons Stephen Jaques* and Senior Partner. Approach to practice is to be accessible, practical, and effective while maintaining the highest standards of professionalism.
Prof. Memberships: Trade Practices Committee of the Business Law Section of the Australia Law Council; Law Institute of Victoria; Law Society of New South Wales.
Career: Solicitor, *Molomby & Molomby*, Melbourne (1962-65). Solicitor, *Malleson Stewart & Co* (1965). Partner *Mallesons Stephens Jaques*, Melbourne (1970-present). *Mallesons Stephen Jaques* Board (1991-present). Deputy Chairman and Senior Partner, *Mallesons Stephen Jaques* Board (1995-present).
Personal: Born 1939 in Melbourne. Bachelor of Laws (Hons), University of Melbourne (1961).

KENCH, John
Blake Dawson Waldron, Sydney +61 2 9258 6000
john.kench@bdw.com.au
Recommended in Competition/Anti-trust
Specialisation: A partner of the firm since 1983, practises predominantly in the anti-trust aspects of trade practices law, the law relating to economic regulation of business practices, intellectual property law and entertainment law. Specialises in mergers, horizontal and vertical business arrangements, prices surveillance, consumer protection and product safety, copyright and technology related matters, film production and distribution, and the exploitation of related rights. Also engaged in certain industry related matters, for example, copyright law reform. Currently acts for many of Australia's largest companies in both the public and private sectors in the manufacturing, media, resources, agricultural, transport, entertainment and film industries.
Prof. Memberships: Vice Chairman of the Entertainment Law Committee of the International Bar Association; Member of the Corporate Lawyers Association; Member of the International Association of Entertainment lawyers; Foreign member of the American Bar Association; Member of the Copyright Society; Member of the German-Australian, the Belgium-Australia, and the Switzerland-Australia Chamber of Commerce; and Member of Australian Business in Europe.
Career: Prior to commencing with the firm in 1980, was Senior Division Attorney for four years with the Australasia Division of The Coca-Cola Export Corporation, responsible for all that company's legal affairs in Australia, New Zealand, Papua New Guinea, Fiji, and American Western Samoa. Served articles of clerkship and practised trade practices and corporate law with a principal Australian law firm.

KENNEDY, Rowan
Mallesons Stephen Jaques, Melbourne
+61 3 9643 4000
rowan.kennedy@msj.com.au
Recommended in Energy & Natural Resources
Specialisation: Corporate and Commercial Partner in the Melbourne office of *Mallesons Stephen Jaques*. Has a wide-ranging background in energy law, company law and litigation, and is regarded as a transac-

A

tion lawyer specialising in energy related transactions, leveraged buy-outs, capital markets work, work-outs and insolvency related matters. Was joint National Managing Partner of the Firm during the period 1987-1989.
Career: Accountant, Deloitte Haskins & Sells, Melbourne; 1985-present, Partner, *Mallesons Stephen Jaques*, Melbourne; 1987-1989, National Managing Partner, *Mallesons Stephen Jaques*.
Personal: Bachelor of Commerce and Laws degrees, University of Melbourne. Married with two children. Leisure pursuits include farming, golf and bridge.

KERR, Edward
Mallesons Stephen Jaques, Sydney +61 2 9296 2000
edward.kerr@msj.com.au
Recommended in Capital Markets
Specialisation: Partner in the Sydney office of *Mallesons Stephen Jaques* specialising in derivatives, consumer credit law and standard bank documents. Acts for many institutions in Australia relating to their derivatives transactions. This includes advising on regulatory and netting issues as well as preparing documents for a wide range of derivatives. Has also been involved in numerous standard documents projects for leading financial institutions. In charge of the firm's Financial Services Precedents Group and Plain English Unit, and is one of Australia's leading experts on plain English drafting. Has spoken at numerous international conferences on plain English including in Cambridge, England and Vancouver, Canada.
Prof. Memberships: Legal advisor, AFMA Documentation Committee.
Career: Achieved Bachelor of Arts and Laws degrees, University of New South Wales (1975). Solicitor *Sly & Russell*, Sydney (1976). Solicitor, Commonwealth Bank's legal department (1979). Solicitor, *Mallesons Stephen Jaques*, Sydney (1985). Partner, *Mallesons Stephen Jaques*, Sydney (1986-present). Legal representative on industry-wide Australian Netting Working Group (Oct 1991). Part-time lecturer, Masters Course – Derivatives Regulation, University of New South Wales.

KERR, Philip
Allen Allen & Hemsley, Sydney +61 2 9230 4000
philip.kerr@allens.com.au
Recommended in Intellectual Property
Specialisation: All aspects of intellectual property litigation both in Court and before the Patent/Trade Mark Office. Acts for major international companies in the health care and life sciences in patent disputes. Trade mark advice to Tricon Global Restaurants (KFC, Pizza Hut, Taco Bell) Frito-Lay/Smith's Snackfood.
Prof. Memberships: Law Council of Australia – Past Chairman Intellectual Property Committee. International Trademark Association. Member Drafting Committee 1990 Australian Patents Act.
Career: Bachelor of Arts (Hons) 1971. Bachelor of Laws 1974. Articled Clerk *Allen Allen & Hemsley* 1973-1974. Partner *Allen Allen & Hemsley* 1981.
Personal: Married Elizabeth, three sons.

KING, John
Mallesons Stephen Jaques, Sydney +61 2 9296 2000
john.king@msj.com.au
Recommended in Tax
Specialisation: Partner in the Sydney office of *Mallesons Stephen Jaques* specialising in taxation. Practice concentrates on the taxation aspects of financial markets and capital markets transactions and products (including securities lending and repos, other equity, debt and hybrid products and aspects of global training), structured (ie. tax based) financings, and mergers and acquisitions work. These areas also involve capital gains tax, dividend, interest and royalty withholding taxes and CFC and FIF regimes. Has been closely involved in the tax audits of several major financial institutions. Also advises on the tax aspects of real estate transactions, trusts and partnerships.
Prof. Memberships: Taxation Institute of Australia; International Fiscal Association (Australian Chapter); International Bar Association (Taxes Committee); American Bar Association (Section of Taxation).
Career: Achieved Bachelor of Arts and Laws (Hons) degrees, Sydney University in 1970 and 1973. Articled clerk, solicitor (from 1974) and partner (since 1979), *Mallesons Stephen Jaques*, Sydney, except for periods overseas as follows: Master of Laws degree, University of London (1974-75); resident partner, *Mallesons Stephen Jaques*, New York (1986-88).
Personal: Married (in 1973, to Genevieve), with five children.

KNIGHT, Peter
Clayton Utz, Sydney +61 2 9353 4000
pknight@claytonutz.com
Recommended in Communications: IT, Intellectual Property
Specialisation: Partner in intellectual property and computer technology law. Experience extends to creation, interpretation and dispute resolution advice in design, development, licensing, distribution and franchising of IT products and technologies including e-commerce and joint ventures acquisitions and sale of businesses as well as litigation of all kinds. International aspects of practice encompass Australian companies wishing to expand overseas and international companies wishing to explore market opportunities in Australia and Asia Pacific. Clients include small and large businesses, government departments and financial institutions.
Prof. Memberships: Admitted to practice: 1978, Supreme Court of NSW; High Court of Australia; Federal Court of Australia; 1990, Supreme Court of Australian Capital Territory (ACT); 1991, Supreme Court of Victoria; Member of the Law Society of NSW, Copyright Society and United States Trade Mark Association Board Member, Computer Law Association.
Career: Before joining *Clayton Utz* held the position of Senior Counsel – Asia Pacific Operations for Apple Computer, Inc from 1986 to 1990. Experience with Apple's legal affairs gave valuable experience in managing legal issues in all non-communist countries in the region. Joined *Clayton Utz* in 1990.
Personal: Born 1953. Attended University of Sydney (BA; LLB), University of London (LLM). Interested in doing a good job of bringing up a family.

KOECK, William
Corrs Chambers Westgarth, Melbourne
+61 3 9672 3000
Recommended in Corporate/M&A

L'ESTRANGE, Timothy
Allen Allen & Hemsley, Sydney +61 2 9230 4000
Recommended in Competition/Anti-trust

LANGFORD, Scott
Allens Arthur Robinson Group (AAR Group), Perth
+61 8 9420 4222
Recommended in Energy & Natural Resources

LAWLER, Gary
Gilbert & Tobin, Sydney +61 2 9263 4000
glawler@gtlaw.com.au
Recommended in Corporate/M&A
Specialisation: Specialises in corporate and securities law generally with a particular emphasis on mergers and acquisitions including public company takeovers, public company takeover defences and corporate reconstructions, asset and share acquisitions, fund raisings and foreign investment. Confines practice exclusively to advising public companies, large private companies and investment banks on complex corporate transactions. Expertise extends to capital raisings and prospectuses, foreign investment, joint ventures, stock exchange regulation as well as the broad range of corporate and securities matters which commonly affect public companies and financial intermediaries. Has been involved in cross border transactions for a range of international companies.
Prof. Memberships: Member, Law Society of NSW; Commercial Law Association of Australia Directorships; Dominion Mining Limited.
Career: Admitted 1975. 1982-1989 Partner *Clayton Utz*; 1989-1996 Partner *Freehills*; With *Gilbert & Tobin* since July 1996.
Personal: Education: University of Sydney (BA, LLB., LLM); Securities Institute of Australia, ASIA.

LEIBLER, Mark
Arnold Bloch Leibler, Melbourne +61 3 9229 9999
mleibler@abl.com.au
Recommended in Tax
Specialisation: Senior Partner of the Firm and head of Taxation Team. One of Australia's leading tax lawyers and corporate strategists. With formidable knowledge of tax planning, has acted in the tax affairs of many of Australia's largest businesses. Has played a central role in the satisfactory resolution of numerous major Australian tax audits and provides a wide range of major clients with creative, individualised and strategic advice. Input into government taxation policy has been sought consistently under successive Australian Prime Ministers and Treasurers.
Prof. Memberships: Victorian Law Institute.
Publications: Frequent media commentator on taxation issues, and is much sought by industry groups as a keynote speaker on issues of taxation and revenue law reform.
Career: Deputy Chairman and Chairman of the

Law Council of Australia's Taxation Committee. Member of the Commissioner of Taxation's Advisory Panel. National Tax Liaison Group. Capital Gains Tax sub-committee of the National Tax Liaison Group. In 1987 was appointed an Officer in the General Division of the Order of Australia.
Personal: Holds an honours degree in law from the University of Melbourne and a Master of Law from Yale University.

LEONARD, Peter
Gilbert & Tobin, Sydney +61 2 9263 4000
pleonard@gtlaw.com.au
Recommended in Communications: Telecoms
Specialisation: Focus on commercial and corporate transactions and structuring for corporations active in the communications, technology, media and e-business fields. Experience includes e-business implementations, systems integration, outsourcing, development and hosting, applications service provider and portal and alliance arrangements in Australia and through the Asia Pacific region. Practice includes communications and competition regulation.
Prof. Memberships: Law Society of NSW; New Zealand Law Society's Electronic Commerce Committee; International Legal Experts of INTELSAT; Technology Law Committee of the International Bar Association; Internet Law Committee of the Antitrust Division of the American Bar Association.
Publications: Writes and lectures extensively in Australia and internationally. Also co-editor of 'Communications Law and Policy in Australia', the leading text in this area, and general editor of 'Telemedia'.
Career: Admitted 1980. Joined *Gilbert & Tobin* as third partner in 1989.
Personal: University of Sydney (BEc. (Hons), LLB, LLM).

LIM, Cheng
Mallesons Stephen Jaques, Melbourne
+61 3 9643 4000
cheng.lim@msj.com.au
Recommended in Communications: IT, Intellectual Property
Specialisation: Partner in Technology, Communications and IP (TCIP) Group. Main area of work is information technology (computer law), e-commerce and telecommunications. Has handled major information technology transactions including outsourcings (recently: the National Group's innovative global outsourcing to Equifax Card Services Inc. of the credit card processing for its banks in the United Kingdom, Republic of Ireland, Australia and New Zealand; GE Mortgage Solution Limited's outsourcing of the processing and management of a new line of mortgage products) and major IT and systems equipment acquisitions (recently: Telstra Corporation Limited's contract with Nortel Networks for the supply of new generation telecommunication products and platforms for use on its new IP network). Heads the firm's national e-Commerce Coordination Committee; acted on O2-e Limited's (a subsidiary of the National Australia Bank) equity and affiliate arrangements with Peakhour, an Australian applications service provider; acted for Orica in the establishment of Myspace.com.au; has acted in relation to a number of electronic procurement market places. Has a wide ranging telecommunications practice (recently advised Telstra on regulatory, commercial and related issues for the unbundling of the local loop). Has spoken at various conferences.
Prof. Memberships: Law Society (New South Wales), Law Institute (Vic), The Licensing Executives Society, The Intellectual Property Society of Australia and New Zealand, the Computer Law Association.
Publications: Author of Patent Exploitation Chapter, 'Halsbury's Laws of Australia' (to be published late 2000).
Career: Qualified in 1986. Joined *Mallesons Stephen Jaques* in 1985, becoming a partner in 1995. Is a member of the Advisory Board for the Centre for Media, Communications and Information Technology Law (University of Melbourne).
Personal: Born 16 September 1960. Attended University of Melbourne 1980-85. Science fiction fan.

LIMBERS, Peter
Middletons Moore & Bevins, Sydney
+61 2 9390 8100
Recommended in Energy & Natural Resources
Specialisation: Partner specialising in energy and utilities law in the Energy & Resources Group. Acted for the New South Wales Government as legal project manager for the restructure and corporatisation of the New South Wales generation and distribution businesses, as well as the introduction of wholesale spot market, retail competition and network access. Also acted on introduction of regulatory reforms for competition and access to Australian gas pipelines and the introduction of the National Electricity Market. Acts on major energy projects in electricity and gas transmission infrastructure, cogeneration power station joint ventures and renewable energy market development for major Australian and overseas utilities and investors. Also advises extensively on energy contracting and trading as well as network connection, interconnection, pricing and access.
Prof. Memberships: Australian Mining and Petroleum Law Association; Law Society of New South Wales.
Career: Qualified in 1987. Joined *Middletons Moore & Bevins* in 1988; appointed Senior Associate in 1992; appointed Partner in 1996.
Personal: Born 30 September 1963. Attended the University of Sydney (BCom, LLB).

LISHMAN, Michael
Mallesons Stephen Jaques, Perth +61 8 9269 7000
michael.lishman@msj.com.au
Recommended in Corporate/M&A
Specialisation: Currently Partner in Charge of *Mallesons Stephen Jaques* – Perth office, and partner in the Corporate Advisory Group. Main area of work is mergers and acquisitions, ASX Listings and privatisations. Has acted for a variety of Australian public companies and overseas investors into Australia. Has acted on privatisations in the insurance, banking, gas and railway industries. Has acted on major corporate reconstructions as well as on takeover defences for a variety of targets. Acted on the Austalian Stock Exchange listings of companies in the construction, ship building and casino industries.
Prof. Memberships: Australian Mining and Petroleum Law Association, Banking Law Asociation, Australian Institute of Company Directors and Securities Institute of Australia.
Career: Commenced Articles with *Mallesons Stephen Jaques* in 1983 and admitted to practice in Western Australia. Qualified in 1983. Worked at *Linklaters & Paines* 1987-1988 and is admitted as a solicitor in England and Wales. Became a partner of *Mallesons Stephen Jaques* in 1991. Completed 'Managing Critical Resources' at Darden Graduate School of Business Administration, University of Virginia in October 1997. Completed 'Leadership in Professional Service Firms' at Harvard Business School in July 1998. Appointed Partner in Charge of Perth office of *Mallesons Stephen Jaques* in November 1997.
Personal: Graduate of the University of Western Australia (degrees in law and economics). Married with two children. Foundation member of Conservatives for an Australian Head of State.

LOXTON, Diccon
Allen Allen & Hemsley, Sydney +61 2 9230 4000
Recommended in Banking & Finance, Project Finance

LYNCH, Simon
Allens Arthur Robinson Group (AAR Group), Melbourne +61 3 9613 8637
Recommended in Banking & Finance

MACDONALD, Ken
Allen Allen & Hemsley, Brisbane +61 7 3334 3000
ken.macdonald@allens.com.au
Recommended in Corporate/M&A
Specialisation: Corporate advisory, mergers and acquisitions, capital markets, with special emphasis on the energy and resources industry.
Career: National Practice Leader, Energy and Resources Practice Group, Queensland Practice Director, member of the *Allen Allen & Hemsley Board*; Deputy Chairman, Queensland Investment Corporation; Director, MIM Holdings Limited; former National President, Australian Mining & Petroleum Law Association; national chairman, Law Council of Australia Resource Committee; Chairman, Coal Committee, International Bar Association Section on Energy and Resources Law.

MACHIN, Peter
Mallesons Stephen Jaques, Sydney +61 2 9296 2000
peter.machin@msj.com.au
Recommended in Project Finance
Specialisation: Partner in developing and financing energy, resources and infrastructure projects. Represented Consolidated Natural Gas of Pittsburgh on Epic Gas Pipelines Trust restructure. Representing senior banks on Australian Magnesium project.
Prof. Memberships: Australian Mining and Petroleum Law Association, International Bar Association, Rocky Mountain Mineral Law Foundation.
Publications: Papers on major project structuring, acquisitions, financing and insolvency delivered in

A

Australia and internationally.
Career: Qualified 1973 in London. Joined *Mallesons* in 1980 – became a partner in 1982. Ran New York office 1988-1991.
Personal: Born 1949. Attended Oxford University (MA Jurisprudence and BCL). Leisure interests include travel, sports, food and wine. Married. Living in Sydney.

MACLEAN, Alan
Freehills, Melbourne +61 3 9288 1234
Recommended in Project Finance

MAGID, Larry
Allen Allen & Hemsley, Sydney +61 2 9230 4000
larry.magid@allens.com.au
Recommended in Tax
Specialisation: Corporate and International Income Taxation including, in particular, the taxation aspects of mergers and acquisitions, reorganisations and project, asset and other corporate financings. Advised RTZ Plc on its dual listed company arrangements with CRA limited (now both known as Rio Tinto) and advised Rio Tinto on its acquisitions during 2000 of Comalco Limited, North Limited and Ashton Mining Limited.
Prof. Memberships: Taxation Institute of Australia; Law Council of Australia (and the Taxation Committee of its Business Law section).
Career: Bachelor of Arts (Boston University, 1973); Juris Doctor (Boston University Law School, 1976); Master of Laws in Taxation (New York University School of Law, 1983). Partner, *Allen Allen & Hemsley*, 1984 to present.

MAGUIRE, Gary
Freehills, Brisbane +61 7 3258 6666
Recommended in Energy & Natural Resources

MALONEY, David
Allen Allen & Hemsley, Sydney +61 2 9230 4000
Recommended in Energy & Natural Resources

MANN, Geoff
Freehills, Melbourne +61 3 9288 1234
Recommended in Tax

MARSHALL, Richard
Mallesons Stephen Jaques, Sydney +61 2 9296 2000
richard.marshall@msj.co.au
Recommended in Energy & Natural Resources
Specialisation: Partner in Energy, Resources and Development Department in Sydney, main areas of which are corporate and resources law, principally mergers and acquisitions; specialises in major coal and mineral projects both within and outside Australia; has acted for Glancore International AG in its coal, nickel, copper and other base metal acquisitions in Australia as well as in Zambia and the Philippines; has also acted for Xstrata AG in its acqusition of its vanadium and coal interests in Australia; has acted for White Industries Australia Limited in its turnkey contract for Coal India Limited at Piparwar, Bahar State, Northern India; has acted on numerous coal developments in Australia, including Ulan, North Goonyella and Oaky Creek with respect to their general trading activities, such as coal sales contracts and environmental compliance issues.
Prof. Memberships: Law Society; Law Society of New South Wales, ACT and Victoria; Past President of Inter-Pacific Bar Association; Member of International Bar Association.
Publications: Editor and contributor to the IPBA Journal.
Career: Qualified in 1979; employed by *Amery Partners & Co.* (1977-1979); joined *Mallesons Stephen Jaques* (1979), becoming a Partner in 1984; worked in *Mallesons Stephen Jaques* New York office (1981-1982) and seconded to *Fulbright & Jaworski*, Houston (1982).
Personal: Born 28 August 1954; Office Bearer of Australian Red Cross (NSW) Division, Inc; interests involve cycling and other outdoor activities; lives in Sydney, New South Wales with four children.

MARTIN, Andrew
Deacons, Sydney +61 2 9330 8000
Recommended in Energy & Natural Resources

MAXTON, Alan
Allen Allen & Hemsley, Sydney +61 2 9230 4000
alan.maxton@allens.com.au
Recommended in Banking & Finance
Specialisation: Principal areas of specialisation are project and infrastructure finance, structured finance, including leveraged leases, corporate and property finance. Major matters on which has acted during the last twelve months include the Alice Springs to Darwin Rail Project, the privatisation of West Rail, the financings of Adelaide Airport, and Fox Studios Australia, the sale of Bankers Trust Australia Limited and Sonic Healthcare Limited's acquisition of the SGS Australia Medical Group.
Career: Bachelor of Economics, Sydney University 1981. Bachelor of Law (Hons), Sydney 1984. 1985-86 *Allen Allen & Hemsley* Sydney. 1987 Associate at *Allen Allen & Hemsley* Singapore. 1988-91 *Allen Allen & Hemsley* Sydney. 1992-93 Associate at *S. Horowitz & Co.*, Tel Aviv. 1994 to present Partner *Allen Allen & Hemsley*, Sydney.
Personal: Born 16 September 1961. Married with three children.

MAYNE, Eric
Mallesons Stephen Jaques, Sydney +61 2 9296 2000
eric.mayne@msj.com.au
Recommended in Tax (Corporate): Goods & Services Tax
Specialisation: Managing Partner of *Mallesons Stephen Jacques* since July 2000 and is responsible nationally for the firm's indirect taxation practice. Practice concentrates on the goods and services tax, sales tax, customs and excise duty and pay-roll tax. Also involved in advising clients in structuring their business to reduce exposure to customs duty and sales tax, maximising savings and the use of tariff concessions, antidumping inquiries and advising on the sales tax and customs duty implications which arise in relation to commercial contracts or agreements for the supply of goods and services. Has made submissions to the Commissioner of Taxation on proposed indirect tax rulings and has consulted to the Federal Government on proposed legislative amendments and sales tax reform. Was a member of the 'Cole Committee' which advised the Opposition Party in 1992/93 on the design features of a Goods and Services Tax. Currently a member of the GST Technical Committee which advised Treasury and the Australian Taxation Office on the GST legislation in the lead up to its implementation on 1st July 2000. Is also one of three external advisers on the GST Public Rulings Panel.
Prof. Memberships: Sales Tax Sub-Committee of the Legislative Committee; Taxation Institute of Australia; Customs and Indirect Tax Committee; Law Council of Australia; Taxation Committee; National Sales Tax Liaison Committee; Honary Consultant, Australian Law Reform Commission on Customs Duty.
Publications: Co-author of the Sales Tax chapter of the Laws of Australia publication and the Butterworths publication, 'GST Online'.
Career: 1972-1982, Australian Tax Office – specialising in sales tax, payroll tax and income tax; 1983, Bachelor of Laws (Hons) degree, Monash University, Melborne; 1984-present, Solicitor/Partner, *Mallesons Stephen Jacques* Melbourne; 1996-1997, Partner in Charge, Melbourne Office, *Mallesons Stephen Jaques*; 1997-1998, Member of Board of Partners *Mallesons Stephen Jaques*; 1999-2000, Executive Partner (Taxation), *Mallesons Stephen Jaques*. Has lectured in the Masters of Tax subject, Federal Indirect Taxes (Sales Tax and Customs Duty) at Melbourne University. Regularly speaks on indirect tax matters at the Law Institute of Victoria, the Leo Cussen Institute, the Institute of Chartered Accountants and the Television Education Network.

MAZZOCHI, Richard
Mallesons Stephen Jaques, Sydney +61 2 9296 2000
richard.mazzochi@msj.com.au
Recommended in Capital Markets
Specialisation: Partner in the Sydney office of *Mallesons Stephen Jaques* specialising in banking and finance. Has extensive experience in a broad range of significant matters including capital markets financing in the domestic, European, American and Asian markets, securitisation, project and infrastructure finance and derivatives. Has specialist domestic and international capital markets practice. Acts for arrangers, dealers and issuers including Merrill Lynch, The Chase Manhattan Bank, Westpac Banking Corporation, Macquarie Bank, Société Générale, Australia and New Zealand Banking Group Limited, Telstra, AMP, Goldman Sachs, Morgan Stanley, UBS Warburg and Deutsche Bank. Regularly named in international publications as one of the leading practitioners in capital markets.
Career: 1995-present, Partner, *Mallesons Stephen Jacques*, Sydney; 1992, Solicitor, *Mallesons Stephen Jacques*, Sydney; 1989-1992, returned to Sydney with former employer; 1987-1989, seconded to *Linklaters & Paines*, London working in the international finance section specialising in the issuance of listed and unlisted securities by mainly Australian issuers; 1985, Solicitor in Singapore working on a range of legal issues including eurocurrency lending; 1983, Bachelor of Laws degree, University of Sydney; 1981, Bachelor of Economics, University of Sydney.

McCANN, Kevin
Allen Allen & Hemsley, Sydney +61 2 9230 4000
Recommended in Energy & Natural Resources

McGILL, Ian
Allen Allen & Hemsley, Sydney +61 2 9230 4000
Recommended in Communications: Telecoms

McGREGOR, Sheila
Freehills, Sydney +61 2 9225 5000
Recommended in Communications: Telecoms

MEAD, Stephen
Mallesons Stephen Jaques, Melbourne
+61 3 9643 4000
stephen.mead@msj.com.au
Recommended in Communications: Telecoms
Specialisation: Corporate Advisory Partner in the Melbourne office of *Mallesons Stephen Jaques.* Specialises in telecommunications and competition law and mergers and acquisitions in the telecommunications sector. Acts for Australia's largest telecommunications company, Telstra Corporation Limited, in numerous acquisitions and divestitures including Telstra's pan-Asian alliance with Pacific Century Cyberworks Ltd., the sale of Telstra's Small Business Systems business and establishment of the PlesTel Joint Venture, the establishment of Telstra's wholly owned construction subsidiary, Network Design and Constructions Limited and Telstra's potential investment in the SkyBridge low earth orbit satellite venture. Also advises Telstra on the competition law aspects of mergers, acquisitions and divestitures and does some work in relation to the consumer protection trade practices law for Telstra. Acted for Telstra on the Wiring Repair Plan mass customer refund and negotiated the necessary undertakings with the Australian Competition and Consumer Commission. Also acted for Telstra in the establishment and introduction of its Wholesale Billing System and handled the contractual, regulatory and trade practices issues associated with that system. Has played a role in both the first and second tranches of Telstra's privatisation program and generally provides legal advice to Telstra on a broad range of general commercial legal issues.
Prof. Memberships: Law Institute of Victoria.
Career: Admitted as Solicitor (1989); Solicitor, *Mallesons Stephen Jaques* (1990), Senior Associate (1993), Partner (1996-present).
Personal: Bachelor of Law (Honours), Queensland University of Technology (1989).

MILLINER, Robert
Mallesons Stephen Jaques, Melbourne
+61 3 9643 4000
robert.milliner@msj.com.au
Recommended in Energy & Natural Resources, Project Finance
Specialisation: Partner at the Melbourne office of *Mallesons Stephen Jaques*, specialises in major projects with emphasis on electricity and gas industry mergers and acquisitions and restructuring, electricity and gas sales contracts, international project and domestic finance and other resource arrangements. Has extensive corporate, commercial and major project financing experience in all of Australia's major jurisdictions. Major matters in 2000 include acting for Cheungkong Infrastructure / Hongkong Electric on the acquisition of ETSA Utilities (AUS$3.5 billion) and refinancing (AUS$2.5 billion), the sale by GPU Inc. of GPU PowerNet and GPU GasNet and power industry restructuring proposals in China for the ADB.
Prof. Memberships: Chairman of the Electricity Committee of the International Bar Association's Section on Energy and Resources Law; Australian Mining and Petroleum Law Association; Law Asia; numerous State law societies.
Publications: Written extensively on a range of legal issues and presented papers at a wide range of forums in Australia and overseas conducted by the International Bar Association, Australian Mining and Petroleum Law Association and Law Societies and other industry seminars on financing and energy related topics.
Career: 1984 to present, Partner *Mallesons Stephen Jaques.* Lectured in the Master of Laws program at the University of Western Australia on international financing and energy law and in the Graduate Program at the University of Melbourne on energy law, regulation and policy.
Personal: Born 20 October 1956. 1976, Bachelor of Commerce, University of Queensland; 1980, Bachelor of Law (Hons), University of Queensland; 1985, Master of Business Administration, University of Western Australia. Married with three young daughters. Interests include architecture, modern art and sport.

MINNS, Stephen
Mallesons Stephen Jaques, Melbourne
+61 3 9643 4000
stephen.minns@msj.com.au
Recommended in Corporate/M&A
Specialisation: Partner in the Melbourne office of *Mallesons Stephen Jaques* specialising in public company acquisitions and equity issues as well as general corporate work. Brings to the corporate and commercial practice experience in merchant banking in both Australia and overseas.
Career: Investment Banker, 1981 Morgan Grenfell Australia, Sydney – working on corporate advisory matters such as take-overs, prospectuses, corporate restructuring, valuations and financial packaging; Investment Banker, 1984-1985, Morgan Grenfell & Co, London – working on international capital markets and later, further corporate advisory work on public company mergers and acquisitions and prospectuses; Solicitor, 1986 *Mallesons Stephen Jacques* Sydney; Partner, 1988-present, *Mallesons Stephen Jaques*, Sydney and Melbourne.
Personal: Born 25th February 1957 in Perth, Western Australia. Bachelor of Law and Commerce degrees, 1980 University of New South Wales.

MURATORE, Tony
Freehills, Sydney +61 2 9225 5000
Recommended in Intellectual Property

MURRAY, Alan
Mallesons Stephen Jaques, Perth +61 8 9269 7000
alan.murray@msj.com.au
Recommended in Energy & Natural Resources
Specialisation: Partner in corporate and resources area, focusing on resources clients in both the minerals and oil and gas sectors. Has handled joint ventures, sales and acquisitions, project development, State Agreements and a wide range of operational issues in both sectors. Amongst others, acts for Chevron concerning its oil and gas interests in Western Australia and a bid in China, and for Reynolds Metals Company and Worsley in relation to the Worsley Alumina Project.
Prof. Memberships: Director and President (WA Branch) of Australian Mining and Petroleum Law Association; Law Society of Western Australia.
Publications: Contributor to, and presenter at AMPLA publications and conferences.
Career: Qualified 1986. Articled at *Mallesons Stephen Jaques* in 1987. Seconded to *Mallesons* London office 1990-1994, and became Partner in 1998.
Personal: Scotch College, Perth; University of Western Australia 1982-1986. Leisure interests include outdoor activities.

NICHOLLS, Dale
Allens Arthur Robinson Group (AAR Group), Melbourne +61 3 9613 8637
Recommended in Energy & Natural Resources

NICHOLSON, Robert
Freehills, Melbourne +61 3 9288 1234
Recommended in Corporate/M&A, Energy & Natural Resources

NICOTRA, Aldo
Blake Dawson Waldron, Sydney +61 2 9258 6000
aldo.nicotra@bdw.com.au
Recommended in Competition/Anti-trust
Specialisation: A partner of *Blake Dawson Waldron* since 1993. Principal areas of practice include all aspects of contentious and non-contentious trade practices (access, competition law and unfair practices) and intellectual property. In the area of trade practices, has acted for both public and private companies, as well as advised government instrumentalities. Major clients include Goodman Fielder, Sydney Airport Corporation, Sydney Organising Committee for the Olympic Games (SOCOG), Sony/Columbia Tri Star, Australian Medical Association, Disney, Qantas, LEGO, Dunhill, and Dow Jones Inc. One of only a few Arbitrators appointed by the Premier to the New South Wales Prices and Regulatory Tribunal to hear access disputes.
Prof. Memberships: Law Council of Australia – Trade Practices.
Publications: Has written and presented numerous papers nationally and internationally on the areas of trade pratices, sales contracts, intellectual property and customs.
Personal: Degrees in Law and first class honours in Economics.

NORRIS, Brian
Freehills, Sydney +61 2 9225 5000
Recommended in Tax

O'BRYAN, Michael
Minter Ellison, Melbourne +61 3 9229 2000
Recommended in Competition/Anti-trust

O'SULLIVAN, John
Freehills, Sydney +61 2 9225 5000
Recommended in Capital Markets, Corporate/M&A

A

ODDIE, Carolyn
Allen Allen & Hemsley, Sydney +61 2 9230 4000
carolyn.oddie@allens.com.au
Recommended in Intellectual Property
Specialisation: An expert in intellectual property and trade practices. Provides advice and conducts litigation across a wide range of industries. Conducted actions on trade mark infringement, passing off, misleading and deceptive conduct for large brand owners, in a variety of industries including fast food and the internet. Advises on brand protection issues. Acted in a variety of copyright protection and infringement actions involving fabric designs, computer software, engineering drawings and literary works. Acted in cases involving infringement and validity of patents and lobbying for increased patent terms and effective patent life. Has particular knowledge of the pharmaceutical industry. Strong knowledge of advertising and marketing regulations. Represents clients in proceedings and dealings with the Australian Competition and Consumer Commission (ACCC) on restrictive trade practices such as anti-competitive arrangements, exclusive dealing, misuse of market power, resale price maintenance and consumer protection. Has strong working relationship with the ACCC. Regularly advises on merger regulation, prepares submissions and negotiates with the ACCC to enable acquisitions to proceed. Has been involved in contested merger proceedings. Advises on access issues in telecommunications, rail and gas industries. Strong expertise in trade practices compliance including conducting audits to identify trade practices risks and assisting business to implement compliance programs and associated education training.
Prof. Memberships: Alternate Chairperson of the Therapeutic Goods Advertising Code Complaints Panel which hears complaints about therapeutic goods advertising in mainstream media.
Publications: Publications include articles on comparative advertising and the law of trade libel, copyright, trade marks, designs, confidential information and passing off, accounting for profits in patent infringement actions and patent infringement.
Career: Bachelor of Law (Hons) and Bachelor of Arts, Sydney University 1987; Masters of Law, Sydney University 1999. Partner, *Allen Allen & Hemsley.*

OLSSON, David
Mallesons Stephen Jaques, Melbourne
+61 3 9643 4000
david.olsson@msj.com.au
Recommended in Capital Markets, Project Finance
Specialisation: Senior financial services Partner in the Melbourne office of *Mallesons Stephen Jaques.* Main area of work is capital markets and securitisation. Regularly acts for Australia's largest corporations (and their advisers) in accessing the domestic and international capital markets. Also has a leading practice in the areas of corporate and institutional finance and structured financing. Acted for Cheungkong Infrastructure and Hongkong Electric in relation to the acquisition of the SA electricity transmission network and the subsequent capital markets refinancing. Acted for Telstra in relation to the financing of its joint venture arrangements with Pacific Century Cyberworks Ltd in Hong Kong.
Prof. Memberships: Law Society of Victoria, Banking Law Australia (committee member), International Bar Association, Law Asia, Inter-Pacific Bar Association, Hong Kong Capital Markets Association.
Publications: Regular contributions to various professional journals.
Career: Qualified and joined *Mallesons Stephen Jaques* in 1979; worked on secondment in London and Bahrain (1983-1987); became Partner in 1990; Partner-in-Charge, Hong Kong office 1995-1996; currently national co-ordinator of Banking and Finance Services team.
Personal: Attended Australian National University 1974-1979 (LLB). Leisure interests include tennis, golf, sailing.

OWEN, Gail
Blake Dawson Waldron, Melbourne
+61 3 9679 3000
gail.owen@bdw.com.au
Recommended in Energy & Natural Resources
Specialisation: Joint ventures, mining agreements, electricity regulation.
Prof. Memberships: Law Institute of Victoria (honorary life member), International Bar Association Section on Energy and Resource Law; Australian Mining and Petroleum Law Association Limited (director and Victorian branch President).
Career: Legal counsel for two Australian mining companies before moving to *Blake Dawson Waldron* since 1987.
Personal: BA, LLB, (Hons) (Monash); LLM, (Melbourne).

PASCARL, Ian
Blake Dawson Waldron, Sydney +61 2 9258 6000
ian.pascarl@bdw.com.au
Recommended in Intellectual Property
Specialisation: Has extensive experience advising both private and public sector clients about a wide range of intellectual property and competition law issues. In particular, conducting major patent, trade mark, copyright, industrial design and competition law litigation, intellectual property and trade practices compliance work, the drafting of technology, commercialisation and other agreements, in devising, developing, implementing and applying legal, regulatory and marketing strategies for the protection of intellectual property and in relation to agricultural and veterinary chemicals issues, especially data protection and ECRP.
Prof. Memberships: Intellectual Property and Trade Practices Committee of the Law Institute of Victoria; Member of the Intellectual Property Committee of the Law Council of Australia; Member of the Licensing Executives Society of Australia and New Zealand; Member of the Intellectual Property Society of Australia and New Zealand; Vice-Chairman, Intellectual Property Committee, Inter Pacific Bar Association as well as various legal and civic committees. Accredited mediator (LEADR).
Publications: Author of various articles concerning intellectual property and competition law subjects, in publications such as Australian Intellectual Property, IP Asia and Patent World.
Career: Prior to *BDW*, head of the Intellectual Property Group at *Minter Ellison* Melbourne.
Personal: Married with three children. In spare time enjoys reading, cinema, keeping fit (including swimming, gymnasium and golf) and has a very casual interest in the fortunes of the Essendon Football Club.

PATTISON, Michael
Allens Arthur Robinson Group (AAR Group), Melbourne +61 3 9613 8637
Recommended in Communications: IT

PEMBERTON, Stephen
Allens Arthur Robinson Group (AAR Group), Melbourne +61 3 9613 8637
Recommended in Banking & Finance, Project Finance

PETER, Wendy
Allens Arthur Robinson Group (AAR Group), Melbourne +61 3 9613 8637
Recommended in Competition/Anti-trust

PHILLIPS, Craig
Allens Arthur Robinson Group (AAR Group), Melbourne +61 3 9613 8637
Recommended in Competition/Anti-trust

PODDAR, Dave
Mallesons Stephen Jaques, Sydney +61 2 9296 2000
dave.poddar@msj.com.au
Recommended in Competition/Anti-trust
Specialisation: Partner in the Sydney office of *Mallesons Stephen Jaques,* specialising in competition law, mergers and acquisitions and general corporate law. Regularly deals with Australia's anti-trust agency, the Australian Competition & Consumer Commission in relation to mergers, general competition issues and competition litigation. In recent years has acted in numerous high profile financial services mergers, acquisitions and joint ventures and has also been involved in providing advice to private parties in Australia's deregulating energy, rail and media sectors.
Prof. Memberships: Law Council of Australia – Business Law Section; Law Council of Australia – Trade Practices Committee; The American Bar Association Section of Anti-trust Law.
Publications: Presented various papers at internal and external seminars on mergers and acquisitions and the competition aspects of joint ventures and strategic alliances. Published a number of articles in journals including the European Competition Law Review, the Journal of International Banking Law and The National Australia Bank's, National Business Review.

POSE, Kevin
Allens Arthur Robinson Group (AAR Group), Melbourne +61 3 9613 8637
Recommended in Tax

PRYLES AM, Michael
Minter Ellison, Sydney +61 3 9229 2931 (Ellison, Melbourne)
michael.pryles@minters.com.au
Recommended in Arbitration (International)
Specialisation: Partner in Major Projects and

International. Main area of work is dispute resolution with an emphasis on international dispute resolution, particularly arbitration. Is one of Australia's most experienced international arbitrators and has sat as an arbitrator throughout Asia as well as in Europe and North America. Arbitration experience includes proceedings under the ICC, UNCITRAL and SIAC rules in disputes involving joint ventures, energy related projects and technology matters in disputes up to $1 billion. Has also led teams of lawyers involved in government corporisation and restructures and acting for bidders acquiring major energy facilities.
Prof. Memberships: President, Australian Centre for International Commercial Arbitration; Fellow, Chartered Institute of Arbitrators (UK); Fellow, Institute of Arbitrators and Mediators, Australia; Fellow, Arbitrators and Meditators Institute of New Zealand; Grade 1 Arbitrator, Institute of Arbitrators and Mediators, Australia; Member, American Law Institute; included on the following panels of arbitrators: ICSID; British Columbia; AAA; Hong Kong; ACICA; SIAC; CIETAC, Nanton; WIPO; Korean Commercial Arbitration Board; Mauritius.
Publications: Co-editor, 'Journal of International Arbitration'; Author of nine books on International Dispute Resolution, Private International Law and International Trade Law.
Career: Partner, *Minter Ellison* since 1989; Commissioner, United Nations Compensation Commission (since 1987); Commissioner, Australian Law Reform Commission, 1983-1987; Henry Bournes Higgins Professor of Law, Monash University 1985-1989.
Personal: Born 25 September 1945. Holds Doctorates from the Universities of Melbourne, Southern Methodist University, Texas, Bond University, Queensland. Leisure interests include reading history, playing tennis and listening to opera. Appointed member in the Order of Australia, 1989.

PUCCI, Fred
Blake Dawson Waldron, Sydney +61 2 9258 6000
fred.pucci@bdw.com.au
Recommended in Capital Markets
Specialisation: Practises in the area of capital markets (domestic and international), securitisation structured fianance, derivatives and financial markets. Acts for investment houses, banks, trustees, corporates and other financial markets participants. Has acted on euromarket, Australian and US mortgage-backed note issues, domestic short- and medium-term note programmes, advised on and documented single asset securitisations and advised on a range of swaps, credit derivatives and other derivative products. Recent highlight deals include credit derivative structures and varied securitisations involving a range of new asset types, and infrastructure deals.
Prof. Memberships: Member of Financial Services Committee of the Law Council of Australia.
Publications: Various articles in Corporate Finance, Euromoney and International Financial Law Review.
Career: Treasury and capital markets focus throughout the last 10 years; now focus on credit risk, and related credit derivatives, synthetic securitisations products and regulatory issues, as well as new asset classes. Prior to joining *Blake Dawson Waldron*, worked as a currency products price maker at Bain Capital Markets and as a securitisation manager at Westpac Group Treasury.
Personal: University of Sydney – Bachelor of Economics and Bachelor of laws; Georgetown University Law Center – Master of Laws (Sec Reg).

RAINEY, Paul
Corrs Chambers Westgarth, Melbourne
+61 3 9672 3000
Recommended in Energy & Natural Resources

RENARD, Ian
Allens Arthur Robinson Group (AAR Group), Melbourne +61 3 9613 8637
Recommended in Capital Markets, Corporate/M&A

RIDER, Cameron
Allens Arthur Robinson Group (AAR Group), Melbourne +61 3 9613 8637
Recommended in Tax

RIGOTTI, Mark
Freehills, Sydney +61 2 9225 5000
Recommended in Capital Markets

RITSON, Lisa
Blake Dawson Waldron, Sydney +61 2 9258 6000
lisa.ritson@bdw.com.au
Recommended in Communications: IT, Intellectual Property
Specialisation: Partner in the Intellectual Property and Communications group. Specialises in information technology and intellectual property, doing both the commercial and litigious work. Major matters include: Advising a number of companies on internet/e-commerce projects, including the establishment of an internet portal, a joint venture for a portal, on-line marketing agreements, web site terms and conditions and internet content agreements; advising a major computer games manufacturer in relation to a variety of issues including copyright and parallel importation issues and joint venture and distribution arrangements; advising on Internet intellectual property and associated issues, including software development, joint ventures, outsourcing, systems integration agreements and associated issues including disputes about information technology contracts; conducting intellectual property and information technology due diligence in connection with substantial acquisitions and floats in a variety of industries. Advising an international luxury goods company on trade mark registration, anti-counterfeiting, copyright and parallel importation issues in Australia; advising the Sydney Organising Committee for the Olympic Games on intellectual property issues associated with staging the event, including international trade mark protection, advice on copyright, design, trade mark and sponsorship issues and conducting intellectual property infringement proceedings; acting in patent infringement proceedings in the medical device field; advising on a number of domain name disputes and other intellectual property issues associated with the internet; advising a major film studio in relation to restructuring its distribution arrangements in Australia; advising on and executing Anton Pillar seizure orders in relation to counterfeit products.
Prof. Memberships: Copyright Society; Licensing Executives Society; NSW Society for Computers and the Law; Intellectual Property Society of Australian and New Zealand; International Trademark Association.
Career: BA (Hons)-Sydney University; LLB-Sydney University; joined *Blake Dawson Waldron* on graduation in 1985; Solicitor 1985-1988; Senior Associate 1988-1991; Partner 1991-present.
Personal: Family (2 children), opera, art, food.

ROBERTSON, Don
Freehills, Sydney +61 2 9225 5000
Recommended in Competition/Anti-trust

ROBINSON, Trevor
Clayton Utz, Sydney +61 2 9353 4000
trobinson@claytonutz.com
Recommended in Banking & Finance
Specialisation: Partner of the Financial Services Department of the Sydney office and practises in structured finance and retail credit. His structured finance practice is directed primarily to securitisation. Acts for banks, other financial institutions and participates in the securitisation industry. Retail credit practice provides an important link between the asset and liability aspects of client's securitisation arrangements.
Prof. Memberships: Admitted to practice, New South Wales 1981; Victoria 1985. Member of the Australian Securitisation Forum.
Career: Joined *Clayton Utz* Sydney in 1981. Seconded to an Australian Merchant Bank in 1983. Worked in *Clayton Utz* Melbourne in 1985-7.
Personal: Born 27 May 1957. Attended University of New South Wales (BCom, LLB). Lives in Sydney.

ROGERS QC, Andrew
Clayton Utz, Sydney +61 2 9353 4000
arogers@claytonutz.com
Recommended in Arbitration (International)
Specialisation: Australia's foremost expert on resolving commercial disputes, joined *Clayton Utz* in May 1993 as a consultant. Experienced in advising governments and corporations on dispute prevention including evaluation of existing processes, design and administration of dispute avoidance and resolution systems, management of disputes including litigation, risk assesment and management, international commercial arbitrator.
Prof. Memberships: Non-Executive Director, NSW Treasury Corporation; President, Securities Industry Research Centre of Asia Pacific; Director, The Garvan Institute of Medical Research.
Career: Previously chief Judge of the Commercial Division of the Supreme Court of New South Wales to speed up the litigation process and advocated cheaper and faster forms of dispute resolution.

RUSSELL, Rowan
Mallesons Stephen Jaques, Melbourne
+61 3 9643 4000
rowan.russell@msj.com.au
Recommended in Banking & Finance
Specialisation: Executive Partner with *Mallesons Stephen Jaques*. Banking, international and domestic

A

finance, project and infrastructure finance, workouts, capital markets, structured finance and consumer credit. Has undertaken major transactions for National Australian Bank including acquisition financings, project financings, structured financings, R&D syndications and retail credit work. Has a great deal of experience in eurobond uses and euronote programmes and other euro facilities for a range of Australian issuers including Alcoa of Australia Limited, National Australia Bank Limited and also on behalf of a number of arrangers; has also acted extensively for the Australian Bankers Association including assistance in the preparation of the Code of Banking Practice.
Prof. Memberships: Past Chairman, Banking Finance and Consumer Credit Committee, Business Law Section, Law Council of Australia; Banking Law Association; Advisory Board Graduate Diploma of Finance Law, University of Melbourne; Honorary Visiting Fellow, Centre for Studies in Money, Banking and Finance, Macquarie University.
Career: 1979 Articled Clerk, *Mallesons* Melbourne; 1983-1984 *Linklaters & Paines* London; 1986 to present Partner *Mallesons Stephen Jaques* based in Melbourne; 1991 to 1995 Member of the National *Mallesons Stephen Jaques* Board; 1996-1999 Managing Partner, *Mallesons Stephen Jaques* Melbourne; 1999-current Executive Partner, *Malleson Stephen Jaques.*
Personal: Born 5 October 1955. Bachelor of Law (Hons) Monash University 1979 and Bachelor of Arts, Monash University 1979. Married to Susan with two children. Interests include royal tennis, bridge and opera.

RYAN, Patrick
Allens Arthur Robinson Group (AAR Group), Melbourne +61 3 9613 8637
Recommended in Competition/Anti-trust

SAINTY, Katherine
Allen Allen & Hemsley, Sydney +61 2 9230 4000
Recommended in Communications: IT

SALTER, Brian
Clayton Utz, Sydney +61 2 9353 4000
bsalter@claytonutz.com
Recommended in Capital Markets
Specialisation: Partner in Financial Services Department. Practises in securitisation and structured capital markets products. Acts for a number of prominent securitisation issuers and arrangers, including PUMA (Australia's largest mortgage backed issuer), Commonwealth Bank of Australia (Australia's largest bank), UBS Warburg, Macquarie Bank, Suncorp, Metway Bank, Adelaide Bank, BankWest and Bank of Queensland. Recent high profile transactions include Australia's first bank securitisation in compliance with prudential requirements, first mortgage conduit program, first securitisation of commercial mortgages, first fully segregated multi-issuer and multi-rated securitisation vehicle, first credit derivative securitisation and first Australian 144A MBS issue.
Prof. Memberships: Law Society of NSW. Governing body of the Australian Securitisation Forum (and present Chairman).
Career: Qualifications: BA, LLB (Hons), LLM (Hons). Qualified in 1981, joined *Clayton Utz* 1982, becoming a partner in 1989. Part-time lecturer in the Law of Securitisation at Sydney Law School and the Securities Institute of Australia.
Personal: Married with one child. Leisure interests include swimming and biking.

SHARP, Jeff
Freehills, Sydney +61 2 9225 5000
Recommended in Tax

SHERIDAN, Jane
Arnold Bloch Leibler, Melbourne +61 3 9229 9999
jsheridan@abl.com.au
Recommended in Corporate/M&A
Specialisation: Partner in Corporate and Commercial. Practice centres around corporate and commercial transactions, with an emphasis on major projects and public listings. Acted for Commsoft Group Limited in relation to its migration from New Zealand and listing on the Australian Stock Exchange Limited. Has been heavily involved in the privatisation of the Victorian power industry, acting for the Australian partners in the acquisition of Hazelwood Power Station ($2.4 billion) and Loy Yang A Power Station ($4.7 billion). Acted for the equity underwriters in the $1.8 billion Melbourne City Link Project, the largest BOOT project in Australia since the Snowy Mountain Scheme. Acted in relation to the acquisition of Brisbane, Coolangatta and Adelaide airports. Provides general advice relating to commercial issues and regulatory requirements and acts for numerous managed investment schemes.
Prof. Memberships: Victorian Law Institute.
Career: Qualified in 1987, joined *Arnold Bloch Leibler* in 1993 becoming a partner in 1995.
Personal: Born in 1963. Attended Monash University 1980-85 (BSc LLB (Hons)). Leisure interests include sea kayaking, basketball and rock and roll.

SHINE, Christopher
Blake Dawson Waldron, Sydney +61 2 9258 6000
chris.shine@bdw.com.au
Recommended in Communications: Telecoms
Specialisation: Has a unique blend of international and Australian experience in telecoms, broadcasting, satellite technology and on-line services. Has extensive government and private sector experience. Acts as relationship partner to a major telco with extensive Australian and International operations.
Prof. Memberships: Communications and Media Law Association; Australian Information Industry Association; and Australian Telecommunications Users Group. Also appointed as a member of the Murdoch University Telecommunications Management MBA (HK) Board of Advisors and a member of the NSW Committee of the Hong Kong/Australia Business Association.
Publications: Paper on 'Telecommunications in Thailand', Winning Telecommunications Trade with Asia Conference, Sydney. Paper on 'Legal Hurdles in Telecommunications Reform', Telecommunication Deregulation in Hong Kong Conference. Paper entitled 'Integrating New Pan-Asia Regional Satellite Services into National Service Strategies', Pan Asia Mobile Communications Summit. Opening Address and Chairman for 'Mobile Comms' Conference, Hong Kong. Paper entitled 'Satellite National Policy and Planning for Telecommunications and Broadcasting in Asia', Pan Asian Telecommunications Summit. Article entitled 'Cable and Satellite Television: The Hong Kong Experience'. Published by International Cable. Paper entitled 'Hong Kong – The Fundamentals', Cathay Pacific China Trader Awards.
Career: Former legal and policy adviser to Hong Kong Government on telecoms and broadcasting and played significant roles in the development of Pan-Asian Satellite broadcasting, fixed and mobile network competition, moves to cost based accounting rates and bids for new service licences (PCS, GSM, fixed, cable and satellite). Spent 8 years offshore and regularly travels from Sydney base to serve regional clients. Has extensive contacts in the Asian regulatory community.

SHIRBIN, John
Clayton Utz, Sydney +61 2 9353 4000
jshirbin@claytonutz.com
Recommended in Project Finance
Specialisation: Partner in the Major Projects group. Advises on major projects in the water, power and health industries, telecommunications, and road and rail transport within Australia and internationally. Advises governments, financiers, equity investors, banks and investment banks. Has experience in debt and equity raisings, structured and tax-based finance, particularly infrastructure and project financing. The principal legal advisor to the Olympic Co-ordination Authority in relation to the development and private financing of new venues for the Sydney 2000 Olympics including Olympic Stadium and SuperDome.
Prof. Memberships: Law Society of New South Wales; Banking Law Association.
Publications: Correspondent to the Journal of International Banking Law.
Career: Qualified in 1975. Joined *Clayton Utz* in January 1975. Partner since 1979 and Managing Partner of the firm from 1987 to 1990. Currently Chairman of the Pacific Rim Advisory Council and Chair of the firm's Board of Directors.
Personal: Born 21 December 1950. Attended St Patrick's College Strathfield and Sydney University (BA; LLB). Married with three children.

SHOWERING, Adrienne
Mallesons Stephen Jaques, Sydney +61 2 9296 2000
adrienne.showering@msj.com.au
Recommended in Capital Markets
Specialisation: Partner in the Sydney office of *Mallesons Stephen Jaques* specialising in securitisation, structured finance, financing transactions, commercial documentation, trusts and securities law. One of the few lawyers with substantial practical experience in the complex area of securitisation. Has worked on matters involving issuing into the Australian, Euro and US bond and commercial paper markets. As a result, practice includes a large portion of work in the area of institutional and public offerings, from the perspective of issuers, advisors, underwriters, and board of directors of an issuer.

Career: 1978-80: College of Law and completion of two years articles with a leading London law firm. 1981: Joined *Freehill Hollingdale & Page* concentrating on corporate and finance work. 1985: Solicitor, *Mallesons Stephen Jaques*, working in the corporate area with emphasis on mergers and acquisitions as well as securitisation, trusts, underwriting and broadcasting law. 1999-00: Executive Partner, Financial Services Clients. 1987-present: Partner *Mallesons Stephen Jaques.*
Personal: 1977: Bachelor of Laws degree, Kings College, London.

SIMPSON, Robert
Baker & McKenzie, Sydney +61 2 9225 0200
robert.simpson@bakernet.com
Recommended in Communications: Telecoms
Specialisation: Telecommunications including advice and documentation of transactions regarding (fixed and mobile) network rollouts, satellite issues, regulatory advice to carriers and service providers, customer contracts and related issues, and liaison with regulators. Network rollout experience includes advising on carrier powers, negotiating supply agreements and other contracts for equipment, software and hardware and negotiating interconnect and facilities access agreements. Acts for several wireline carriers establishing operations and intercity and CBD fibre networks. Acts for a mobile carrier on the construction of a GSM 1800 network in five capital cities in Australia. Acts for other new entrants and service providers generally.
Prof. Memberships: Australian Communications Industry Forum; Australian Telecommunications Users Group; and Australian Corporate Lawyers Association. Qualified in Australia (1981) and England and Wales (1985).
Career: Following experience in major law firms in Sydney and London and as General Counsel of a substantial Australian listed group, joined Optus Communications (1992-1997), the second major carrier in Australia, as General Counsel and then Director, Legal and Regulatory. Board member of Telecommunications Industry Ombudsman Scheme (1993-1997). Board member of Australian Communications Industry Forum (1997). Joined *Baker & McKenzie* in 1998 as Partner.
Personal: Born 4 September 1957. Married with one child. Leisure interests include swimming.

SLATTERY, John
Corrs Chambers Westgarth, Sydney
+61 2 9210 6500
Recommended in Corporate/M&A

SNELL, Tony
Mallesons Stephen Jaques, Melbourne
+61 3 9643 4000
tony.snell@msj.com.au
Recommended in Energy & Natural Resources
Specialisation: Partner at the Melbourne office of *Mallesons Stephen Jaques* specialising in energy and telecommunications regulation and major projects and transactions. Recent projects include: implementation of national electricity market in Tasmania (client – State of Tasmania, 2000); implementation of national electricity market (client – National Electricity Market Management Company Limited, 1997-00); Western Australia electricity transmission and distribution access regimes (client – Western Power, 1996-97); advising the Queensland Electricity Reform Unit on aspects of the restructuring of the Queensland electricity industry, 1994-96; power purchase arrangements for the Bell Bay Smelter (client – State of Tasmania and the Hydro-Electric Commission, 1995-96); sale of Loy Yang B 1000 MW power station (client – State Electricity Commission of Victoria, 1991-92).
Prof. Memberships: Law Institute.
Career: Bachelor of Laws and Economics degrees, University of Adelaide in 1987. Joined *Mallesons Stephen Jaques*, Melbourne in 1987. Seconded to Telstra Corporation Limited's Legal Office in 1988. Partner *Mallesons Stephen Jaques*, Melbourne from 1996 to present.

SOMERVAILLE, David
Blake Dawson Waldron, Sydney +61 2 9258 6000
david.somervaille@bdw.com.au
Recommended in Corporate/M&A
Specialisation: Wide experience includes privatisation, corporate reconstruction, corporate governance, structuring of projects and new ventures, and private investment in infrastructure projects. Has acted recently as principal adviser and team leader on the demutualisation of the Commonwealth wool stockpile; on the privatisation of the rail freight and passenger operations of Australian National Railways Commission in South Australia and Tasmania; for the Commonwealth, NSW and Victoria on the current privatisation of National Rail Corporation Limited; and for Asia Pacific Transport Consortium, the preferred bidder for the construction, operation and maintenance of the A$1.2 billion Alice Springs to Darwin rail link.
Prof. Memberships: The business law section of the Law Council of Australia; the banking law committee of the International Bar Association.
Career: Commenced with *Blake Dawson Waldron* in 1972 and has been a partner of the firm since 1977.
Personal: University of Sydney with a BA and an LLM.

SONNENBERG, Michael
Freehills, Melbourne +61 3 9288 1234
Recommended in Corporate/Commercial: Bhutan Foreign

SPARGO, Stephen
Allens Arthur Robinson Group (AAR Group), Melbourne +61 3 9613 8637
Recommended in Project Finance

ST JOHN, Patrick
Clayton Utz, Sydney +61 2 9353 4000
pstjohn@claytonutz.com
Recommended in Banking & Finance, Project Finance
Specialisation: Partner in Banking & Finance Section with particular expertise in project finance and acquisition financing. Experienced in the use of capital markets debt to fund major projects. Expert in bullion lending and hedging products. Acted on financings of privatised electricity and gas assets, telecommunications projects, power stations and transport and infrastructure projects. Has worked on numerous resource financings in Australia, Asia and Pacific.
Prof. Memberships: Admitted to practice: 1988, New South Wales; 1993, England.
Career: Commenced with *Clayton Utz* 1988, became a partner 1996. Secondment to Macquarie Bank Limited 1990; Secondment to *Allen & Overy* London 1992-1994; Member of the Legal & Documentation Committee of the Australian Branch of the Asia Pacific Loan Market Association 1999 - 2000.
Personal: Born 4 November 1963. Attended University of NSW (BCom, LLB). Leisure interests include sailing and fishing. Resides in Sydney.

A

STANLEY, Ian
Mallesons Stephen Jaques, Sydney +61 2 9296 2000
Recommended in Tax

STOCKDALE, Peter
Mallesons Stephen Jaques, Sydney +61 2 9296 2000
peter.stockdale@msj.com.au
Recommended in Arbitration (International)
Specialisation: National Group Co-ordinator of Dispute Resolution with *Mallesons Stephen Jaques.* Specialises in Professional and Product liability, insurance law and reinsurance law. Has strong relationships with insurance underwriters throughout the world, giving valuable insight on the insurance and reinsurance market. Acts for GIO Reinsurance, brokers, valuers and accountants, as well as several of Australia's major law firms on both domestic and internationally-based disputes. Has a strong reputation for use of all forms of Alternative Dispute Resolution and for solution-based approach to commercial disputes.
Prof. Memberships: Australian Insurance Law Association; LEADR; 1998 and 1999 Euromoney Legal Group Guide to the World's Leading Litigation Lawyers.
Career: 1978-1980, *Dave Hope & Furniss* in Manchester; 1981-1984, Solicitor, *Stephen Jaques and Stephen*, Sydney specialising in litigation; 1984-1986, Solicitor *Herbert Smith*, London concentrating on insurance and reinsurance litigation; 1986, Solicitor, *Mallesons Stephen Jaques*, co-founder of the firm's Insurance Law Group; 1998 to present, Partner *Mallesons Stephen Jaques*, Sydney. 1999-2000, Executive Partner, *Mallesons Stephen Jaques.*
Personal: 1978, Bachelor of Arts and Laws (First Class Hons) degrees, Manchester Polytechnic.

STONE, Phillipa
Freehills, Sydney +61 2 9225 5000
Recommended in Capital Markets

STOREY, John
Corrs Chambers Westgarth, Brisbane
+61 7 3228 9333
Recommended in Corporate/M&A

STORR, David
Mallesons Stephen Jaques, Sydney +61 2 9296 2000
david.storr@msj.com.au
Recommended in Project Finance
Specialisation: Partner in the Sydney office of *Mallesons Stephen Jaques* specialising in project

finance, infrastructure consortium work and financial services industry restructuring. Current projects include: several financial sector acquisitions and alliances; disposal and restructuring of power, gas and other infrastructure projects; bid consortiums for the Cross City Tunnel (Sydney road BOOT) and Sydney/Canberra very fast train ('Speedrail' BOOT); a fibre optic cable project. Recent projects include Australia/Japan undersea cable (acted for the consortium) and various hospital/tollway projects; Olympic transport and other contracts.
Career: Australian taxation Office (Appeals branch); High Court and other litigation (both wins and losses). Joined *Mallesons Stephen Jaques* in 1981. Partner for 13 years.
Personal: Achieved BEc./LLB (Hons) from Australia National University.

STREET, Laurence
Sir Laurence Street
Commercial Mediator, Sydney +61 2 9258 0801
Recommended in Arbitration (International)

STUMBLES, John
Mallesons Stephen Jaques, Sydney +61 2 9296 2000
john.stumbles@msj.com.au
Recommended in Banking & Finance
Specialisation: Expertise in payment systems and insolvency, which was drawn upon by the Australian government and Reserve Bank in connection with the introduction into Australia of legislation relating to netting and real time gross settlement. Major transactions throughout career include advising foreign banks on setting up business in Australia. Has also advised on solvent and insolvent reconstructions. Recently acted as counsel for Australian and offshore financiers in settling standstill and override arrangements arising out of the collapse of a large Australian based multinational conglomerate. Currently Australian counsel for CLS Bank in relation to continuous linked settlement of foreign exchange transactions. Written and lectured on matters relating to the law of banking and finance, payment systems and insolvency law. Has been a speaker at recent international seminars organised by the International Bar Association and the American Bankruptcy Institute on cross-border insolvency.
Prof. Memberships: Former Chairman, Business Law Section, Law Council of Australia. Former member of the Law Council of Australia's Banking, Finance and Consumer Credit Committee (1985-90), made and assisted in the preparation of submissions to Federal and State Governments on the code of conduct for electronic funds transfer, cheque legislation, consumer credit, and amendments to the companies legislation in relation to banking and bankruptcy law. Companies and Securities Advisory Committee's Netting Sub-Committee which produced a report entitled 'Netting in Financial Markets Transactions' and resulted in legislative change. International Relations Co-ordinating Committee, Law Council of Australia. International Bar Association. Anglo-Australasian Lawyers Society.
Career: 1972-75 Articled Clerk and Solicitor employed by *Freehill Hollingdale & Page.* 1975-76 full time student, Master of Law programme, University of Pennsylvania, USA. 1977-78 Solicitor, *Freehill Hollingdale & Page,* Sydney. 1978-80 Lecturer, part-time, University of Sydney. 1979 joined *Mallesons Stephen Jaques,* Sydney, becoming a partner in 1984.
Personal: 1968-70 Bachelor of Arts, University of Sydney. 1970-74 Bachelor of Law (Honours), University of Sydney. 1975-76 Master of Law, University of Pennsylvania, USA.

TAPPERELL, Geoffrey
KLegal, Sydney +61 2 9335 7000
Recommended in Competition/Anti-trust

TAYLOR, Philip
Freehills, Sydney +61 2 9225 5000
Recommended in Banking & Finance, Project Finance

TAYLOR, Susan
Freehills, Melbourne +61 3 9288 1234
Recommended in Energy & Natural Resources

TEMBY, David
Mallesons Stephen Jaques, Sydney +61 2 9296 2000
david.temby@msj.com.au
Recommended in Tax
Specialisation: Australian taxation aspects of domestic and cross-border banking and finance transactions, particularly securitisation, leasing, debt capital markets issues and derivatives.
Prof. Memberships: Taxation Institute of Australia; International Fiscal Association.
Career: Qualified in 1985. Joined *Mallesons Stephen Jaques* in 1988, became a partner in 1996.

THOMPSON, Bill
Minter Ellison, Sydney +61 2 9921 8888
Recommended in Tax

TRAHAIR, Andrew
Clayton Utz, Sydney +61 2 9353 4000
atrahair@claytonutz.com
Recommended in Project Finance
Specialisation: Managing Partner, Financial Services Department with experience in all aspects of project finance. Acts for banks, financial institutions, sponsors, borrowers and multilateral organisations. Particular expertise in power, telecommunications, infrastructure, gas and transport projects.
Prof. Memberships: Admitted to practice, NSW 1987. Admitted to practice, England & Wales 1991.
Career: Joined *Clayton Utz,* Sydney, in 1987. Joined *Allen & Overy,* London, in 1989 becoming a Partner in 1994. Rejoined *Clayton Utz,* Sydney, as a Partner in 1998.
Personal: Born 7 September 1963. Attended University of New South Wales (BCom, LLB). Resides Sydney.

UPFOLD, Robert
Blake Dawson Waldron, Sydney +61 2 9258 6000
robert.upfold@bdw.com.au
Recommended in Tax
Specialisation: Specialises in corporate financing, structured and asset based finance, leveraged and cross-border leasing and structuring of project finance including infrastructure projects. Advises credit providers, borrowers, equity participants and financial packagers in all sectors of industry. Has advised on many significant domestic transactions concentrating principally on structured debt/equity hybrid transactions and infrastructure projects.
Career: Practised in the area of income tax law for over twenty years, the last fifteen years being principally involved in banking and finance matters. Before joining firm, practised with the accounting and advisory firm, KPMG in Sydney. Was a partner in the taxation practice of KPMG for nine years. Seconded full-time in 1988 and 1989 to the project and advisory group of Westpac Banking Corporation. Appointed to the Australian Taxation Office's Consultative Committee for detailed discussions on the policy and legislative problems arising from the Consultative Document 'Taxation of Financial Arrangements'.
Personal: University of New South Wales with a B.Juris., and an LL.B. Was also a chartered accountant.

WALLACE, Ian
Allen Allen & Hemsley, Sydney +61 2 9230 4000
Ian.Wallace@allens.com.au
Recommended in Banking & Finance
Specialisation: All aspects of aircraft acquisition, financing and leasing acting for airlines, lessors and financiers. Expert in domestic and international capital markets and securitisation.
Career: Partner since 1989.

WARD, Penny
Baker & McKenzie, Sydney +61 2 9225 0167
penny.j.ward@bakernet.com
Recommended in Communications: Telecoms
Specialisation: Communications and licensing commercial advice and transactions, with particular emphasis on the telecommunications and internet sectors; telecommunications regulatory advice; negotiation of supply and access agreements between Telcos and suppliers of software/hardware and services to them; IP and commercial licensing agreements.
Prof. Memberships: Australian Communications Industry Forum; Service Providers Industry Association; Communications and Media Law Association; and Australian Telecommunications User Group.
Career: Admitted in 1984. Has practised in Melbourne, Sydney and London.
Personal: BA (Hons) and LLB from Monash University; and LLM from the University of Sydney. Enjoys theatre, travel, sailing, art galleries, fine dining and pro bono work with theatre groups.

WASSAF, Anthony
Allen Allen & Hemsley, Sydney +61 2 9230 4000
Recommended in Energy & Natural Resources

WATERS, Peter
Gilbert & Tobin, Sydney +61 2 9263 4000
Recommended in Communications: Telecoms
Specialisation: Partner in Communications & Technology Group. Main area of work is communications regulation, including telecommunications, Internet and broadcasting. Also specialises in the negotiation of voice, data, mobile and Internet (peering) interconnection arrangements between operators. Has acted for Optus Communications, Australia's second carrier, since 1991. Also acts on

regulatory and interconnection matters for Hongkong Telcom, Singapore Telecom, Cable and Wireless plc and CLEAR Communications. Acts for a number of Internet service providers, in business-to-business and business-to-consumer applications, including online auctions, trading of shares and other intangibles online and providers of Internet authentication systems.
Prof. Memberships: Law Society of New South Wales, International Bar Association.
Career: Qualified in 1988. Joined *Gilbert & Tobin* in 1988 becoming a Partner in 1991. Seconded to Cable & Wireless plc London 1998-99 including as acting Director of Regulation. Previously a lawyer in a Washington, DC international tax practice.
Personal: Born 22 October 1957. Attended Australian National University 1976-82 (BA Asian Studies/LLB) and Harvard Law School (LLM). Previously Chair and currently Director of the Communications Law Centre, a public interest organisation in media and telecommunications.

WEBSTER, Jon
Allens Arthur Robinson Group (AAR Group), Melbourne +61 3 9613 8637
Recommended in Corporate/M&A

WHITTAKER, Bruce
Blake Dawson Waldron, Melbourne +61 3 9679 3000
bruce.whittaker@bdw.com.au
Recommended in Capital Markets
Specialisation: Specialises in securitisation, acting for issuers, arrangers, trustees and enhancement providers on both domestic and offshore MBS and ABS issues. Recent highlights include the inaugural global MBS issue by Members Equity and a securitised refinancing of indexed annuity project bonds, utilising one of the first credit-linked note structures in Australia.
Prof. Memberships: Member of the Australian Securitisation Forum, and a founding member of the Melbourne Securitisation Discussion Group.
Publications: Author of the chapter on Australia in 'Securitisation' (Kluwer Law International, 1998). Lectures on securitisation for the Securities Institute of Australia and the Australian Securitisation Forum.
Career: Admitted to practice in Australia in 1984. Worked overseas with law firms in New York and Germany for 2 1/2 years in the late 1980's. Speaks fluent German.
Personal: BA, (Hons) / LLB, (Hons). Admitted to the New York Bar. Married with three young children.

WIESE, Peter
Clayton Utz, Perth +61 8 9426 8000
pwiese@claytonutz.com
Recommended in Energy & Natural Resources
Specialisation: Partner in the Energy and Natural Resources Department. Main area of work relates to the development, acquisition and disposal of energy infrastructure and mining projects and assets.
Prof. Memberships: Law Society of Western Australia, International Bar Association.
Career: Joined *Robinson Cox* (now *Clayton Utz*) in 1972, qualified in 1974, became a partner in 1976.
Personal: Born 7 July 1950, attended St Peter's College (Adelaide) and the University of Western Australia, graduating LLB (Hons) in 1972.

WILLIAMS, David
Mallesons Stephen Jaques, Sydney +61 2 9296 2000
david.j.williams@msj.com.au
Recommended in Tax
Specialisation: Specialises in the impact of taxation laws on corporate taxpayers including corporate tax planning; contributions to and distributions by corporations and trusts, inward and outward international investment and financing transactions; tax audits; transfer pricing; taxation aspects of mining, oil and gas; tax shelters; film investment; taxation disputes and litigation; employee benefits.
Prof. Memberships: Taxation Institute; Law Society.
Publications: Author of text, 'Investigations by Administrative Agencies', as well as many articles.
Career: Partner at *Mallesons Stephen Jaques* since 1985.
Personal: BCom, LLB (NSW), LLM (Sydney). Interests include travel, family history, history.

WILLIAMSON, David
Blake Dawson Waldron, Melbourne +61 3 9679 3000
david.williamson@bdw.com.au
Recommended in Corporate/M&A
Specialisation: Mergers and Acquisitions, Corporate Finance and Company Law. Major transactions in the ten months to October 2000 include acting as lead partner in: ANZ's sale of Grindlays Bank to Standard Chartered (AUS$3.1 billion, including pre-acquisition dividends); and Advising North in relation to competing take-over bids by Rio Tinto and Anglo American (AUS$3.6 billion).
Career: Commenced at *BDW* in 1982. Secondment to *Linklaters & Paines* 1986-87. Partner, *BDW*, 1989. London Resident Partner, *BDW* 1993-95. Convenor, Sydney Corporate, *BDW* 1996-97. Convenor, Melbourne Corporate, *BDW* 1998-2000.

WILLIAMSON, Sue
Allens Arthur Robinson Group (AAR Group), Melbourne +61 3 9613 8637
Recommended in Tax (Corporate): Goods & Services Tax

WOODWARD, Luke
Gilbert & Tobin, Sydney +61 2 9263 4000
lwoodward@gtlaw.com.au
Recommended in Competition/Anti-trust
Specialisation: Partner in the firm's Competition and Regulation Group. Formerly General Counsel and National Enforcement Director of the Australian Competition and Consumer Commission, experience includes the conduct and oversight of major trade practices litigation involving price fixing, misuse of market power, mergers and joint venture agreements and also major ACCC investigations of international cartel arrangements, including liason with anti-trust law enforcement agencies in the USA, Canada, UK and New Zealand. As General counsel, responsibilities include in-house legal advisory team covering all ACCC regulatory issues. Formerly head of the ACCC mergers and asset sales branch and responsible for the ACCC reviews of the Ampol/Caltex, Foxtel/Australis, Watty/Taubmans, Coles/FAL, Amcor/APPM and Village/Austereo acquisitions.
Prof. Memberships: Law Society of NSW; Australian Corporate Lawyers Association.
Publications: Various publications and public seminar papers on merger clearance and regulatory issues and the operation of the Australian Trade Practices Act.
Career: Partner at *Gilbert & Tobin* since July 2000. Has principally advised private and public sector clients in relation to regulatory matters in the telecommunications (Vodafone, One-Tel), aviation (Virgin Blue) and electricity industries (Energy Australia and the Office of the Regulator-General) and has the carridge of ACCC and ASIC Investigations on behalf of major corporate clients. Admitted 1988, NSW; 1989, Northern Territory; 1990 ACT.
Personal: Educated at University of Sydney (BEc., LLB Hons); Harvard University (MPA).

WORMELL, Mark
Allen Allen & Hemsley, Sydney +61 2 9230 4000
mark.wormell@allens.com.au
Recommended in Capital Markets
Specialisation: Asset backed securitisation, mortgage backed securitisation, domestic and off shore capital markets, Banks Capital work. Has acted for the arranger of the first margin load, auto loan and auto lease backed securitisation in Australia. Was part of *Allens Allens & Hemsley's* team acting for Deutsche Bank on the David Jones commercial property securitisation. Acted for Westpac on its TOPrS and NZ Class share issues.
Publications: 'Securitisation and set-off' Journal of Banking Finance Law & Practice Volume 9 (1998).
Career: Worked in London 1984-86, Singapore 1987-88.

A

AUSTRIA

Index

A

OVERVIEW: The attempts of Austrian firms to follow in Germany's Anglo alliance fever stumbled when the Freshfields Bruckhaus Deringer merger ended the 'best friends' relationship with Wolf Theiss & Partners, although the latter keeps an eye on international opportunities. Interest in the Austrian market for global firms has been more restrictive than in neighbouring countries. That said, privatisation is finally catching up with the country, Telekom Austria having been floated in 2000 and it forms an attractive base into Eastern Europe. Research has pointed to the growing significance of international arbitration with Austria regarded in a similar vein to Switzerland for neutrality and the prevalence of Eastern European cases landing on its turf. Over the past year, the negotiation of settlement payments and the restitution of the properties and businesses seized from Austria's Jews at the time of World War II has precipitated much legal activity.

Arbitration (International)

AUSTRIA Leading individuals (Arbitration (International))
1
HELLER Kurt *Freshfields Bruckhaus Deringer*
HEMPEL Karl *Cerha Hempel & Spiegelfeld*
MELIS Werner *Baier Böhm Orator & Partners*
TORGGLER Hellwig *Schönherr Barfuss Torggler*
2
BAIER Anton *Baier Böhm Orator & Partners*
HAUSMANINGER Christian *Hausmaninger Herbst Wietrzyk*
HORVATH Günther *Freshfields Bruckhaus*
LIEBSCHER Christoph *Wolf Theiss & Partners*
REINER Andreas *Andreas Reiner*
Individuals are listed alphabetically in each band.

With long years of experience in the field working as an arbitrator and as counsel to parties at arbitral proceedings, **Kurt Heller*** *("calm and assertive")* of Freshfields Bruckhaus Deringer is also a widely published author. A member of the board of the International Arbitral Centre of the Federal Economic Chamber in Vienna, he works on international cases, most recently in Turkey and the Middle East, although he established his reputation in Eastern Europe. His colleague **Günther Horvath*** is said to be *"making his way in the sector."*

At Cerha Hempel & Spiegelfeld, **Karl Hempel*** was recommended to researchers as a *"skilled negotiator,"* who has particular experience of arbitrations in the telecoms and technology industries. Working exclusively on international cases, the *"direct"* **Werner Melis*** of Baier Böhm Orator & Partners, specialises in turnkey investment contract cases in the construction industry, and has recently advised on two big power plant construction cases. His colleague **Anton Baier*** was commended by peers as *"a shrewd psychologist,"* and handles a number of Eastern European countries as both arbitrator and counsel.

The versatile **Hellwig Torggler*** of Schönherr Barfuss Torggler & Partners is *"a US-style lawyer,"* who combines arbitration with his corporate practice. Relatively young, **Christian Hausmaninger*** is a *"somewhat brash"* lawyer, with niche expertise in banking and finance arbitrations.

Christoph Liebscher* of Wolf Theiss & Partners was recommended to researchers for his *"deep theoretical knowledge,"* while **Andreas Reiner*** is a sole practitioner with many years of experience as an arbitrator and a trial lawyer.

Banking & Finance

Cerha Hempel & Spiegelfeld (5 ptrs, 6 asscs) Recommended to researchers as a top-tier finance firm, it takes high rank for capital markets, investment funds and e-banking advice. **Edith Hlawati*** is acknowledged by competitors as a *"top lawyer,"* and complements her corporate expertise with a leading capital markets practice. Her colleague **Karl Hempel*** is seen as *"a prominent all-round commercial figurehead."*

The firm advised the Vienna Stock Exchange on developing the trading framework for NEWEX, the new exchange for Eastern securities. It also acted on the Telekom Austria IPO, worth ATS30 billion, and represented Kohlberg Kravis Roberts on the leveraged acquisition of Wassall by Zumtobel. **Clients:** Telekom Austria; ÖIAG; Kohlberg Kravis Roberts.

Ortner Pöch Foramitti (4 ptrs, 4 asscs) Niche banking and finance firm, commended by competitors for its *"international outlook,"* which handles an

AUSTRIA Leading firms (Banking & Finance)
1 Cerha Hempel & Spiegelfeld
Ortner Pöch Foramitti
2 Binder, Grösswang & Partner
Wolf Theiss & Partners
3 Dallmann & Partners
Doralt Seist & Csoklich
Dorda Brugger & Jordis
Freshfields Bruckhaus Deringer
Hausmaninger Herbst Wietrzyk
4 CMS Strommer Reich-Rohrwig Karasek Hainz
Preslmayr & Partners
Schönherr Barfuss Torggler & Partners

Firms are listed alphabetically in each band.

Leading individuals (Banking & Finance)
1 FORAMITTI Louis *Ortner Pöch Foramitti*
HLAWATI Edith *Cerha Hempel & Spiegelfeld*
2 BINDER Michael *Binder, Grösswang & Partner*
DALLMANN Armin *Dallmann & Partners*
DORALT Paul *Doralt Seist & Csoklich*
HAUSMANINGER Christian *Hausmaninger*
HEIDINGER Markus *Wolf Theiss & Partners*
3 DORDA Christian *Dorda Brugger & Jordis*
HEMPEL Karl *Cerha Hempel & Spiegelfeld*
HUBER Peter *CMS Strommer Reich-Rohrwig*
PRESLMAYR Karl *Preslmayr & Partners*
WOLF Richard *Wolf Theiss & Partners*

Individuals are listed alphabetically in each band.

eclectic workload, including securities, project and asset finance, regulatory issues and e-banking.

Louis Foramitti* is the leading figure here. A specialist on US leasing transactions, he was recommended to researchers for his *"incredible work ethic."* The firm has advised on the leasing of rolling stock and technical equipment, and has assisted both lenders and lessors on the financing of the acquisition of passenger aircraft. In capital markets, the team has advised on a number of debt issue programmes and acted on international and national netting arrangements and securities issues by Austrian banks. **Clients:** Österreichische Kontrollbank

Binder, Grösswang & Partner (5 ptrs, 5 asscs) Especially strong on international transactions, the team advises a number of English speaking clients. Researchers were especially impressed by the weight of market approval for its equity financing and asset finance expertise.

The leading light here is the *"outstanding"* **Michael Binder***, who is liked by clients for *"not being too hung up about theory."* The firm advised the lead bank (PSK) of the consortium financing the Voest Alpine Stahl plant in Brazil. It has also represented banks on syndicated loans, acting for Creditanstalt on the financing for the AMS plant expansion. Advised Merrill Lynch on the Telekom Austria IPO. **Clients:** Merrill Lynch; Creditanstalt; PSK; ÖBB; Julius Bär; Edison.

Wolf Theiss & Partners (3 ptrs, 10 asscs) Growing firm, which is now considered to be one of the front-runners in the banking and finance sector, and has niche expertise in acquisition finance. Considered by peers to adopt *"an aggressive approach"* with an *"American flair."*

"Meticulous and driven," **Richard Wolf*** is the team's leading light, although clients warn that **Markus Heidinger*** *"is not to be to be underestimated."* The firm advised UBS/Chase Manhattan on the financing of the take-over of Wassall by Zumtobel, and represented Citibank on the refinancing of the acquisition of Neste Chemicals OY for the takeover of Krems Chemie AG. Elsewhere, the team advised Erste Bank on setting up its asset-backed securities structure. **Clients:** Andersen Consulting; Citibank; Erste Bank; Neste Chemicals; GE Capital; DaimlerChrysler Reinsurance; Goldman Sachs; Barclays Capital.

Dallmann & Partners (1 ptr, 1 assc) Spin-off from former Hügel & Partners which, in spite of its diminutive size, was commended to researchers as *"a firm you should take seriously."* The expert here is **Armin Dallmann***, formerly in-house at Girocredit, who is admired for his *"tremendous negotiating skills."*

The firm acted as lead counsel to Erste Bank on nine real estate development project finance transactions in Hungary and the Czech Republic, including the financing of Shopping Center Budaörsi. It also advised a leading Austrian bank on its issue of a €3 billion Global Medium Term Note program. **Clients:** Chase Manhattan; Erste Bank; Österreichische Volksbanken; Bloomberg LP; Alchemy; C Quadrat.

Doralt Seist & Csoklich (2 ptrs, 1 assc) A small firm which is said to offer a *"high level of legal acumen,"* it specialises in banking litigation and cross-border leasing transactions. *"Old fox"* **Paul Doralt*** has a high profile in the domestic banking market, and is best known for his relationship with Creditanstalt AG. **Clients:** Creditanstalt AG.

Dorda Brugger & Jordis (6 ptrs, 10 asscs) A familiar figure in the sector, the firm has particular experience of advising on IPOs, notably representing the banks on the dual listing of Head NV on both the Vienna and the New York Stock Exchanges. **Christian Dorda*** is an *"analytical practitioner who knows how to reach his goal."* The firm has represented Austrian Electricity on numerous cross-border leasing transactions, most notably involving hydroelectric power plants. Also acted for Jungbunzlauer in establishing a credit facility for a new citric acid plant in Ontario, Canada, a deal worth CDN$89 million. **Clients:** Citibank; Merrill Lynch; Credit Suisse; BNP-Paribas; SocGen; Salomon Brothers; Templeton; Mercury; Fidelity.

Freshfields Bruckhaus Deringer (2 ptrs, 7 asscs) Although the firm's recent merger is expected to provide added resources and an expanded client base, it is not yet perceived to have banking strength to equal its corporate reputation. The firm advises its clientele of international financial institutions on acquisition financing, syndicated loans and capital market transactions. The team represented an Austrian producer of microchips on negotiations with banks to finance the extension of production facilities, and advised on the listing of Erste Bank on the Vienna Stock Exchange. **Clients:** Commerzbank; UBS.

Hausmaninger Herbst Wietrzyk (3 ptrs, 3 asscs) *"Upwardly mobile young firm,"* with a focus on banking and finance, and a name for capital markets advice. The banking and finance department is headed by **Christian Hausmaninger***, acknowledged by competitors as an *"agile and active brain."* The firm handled the IPOs for BETandWIN, an Austrian sports betting internet company, and JoWood Productions Software AG. **Clients:** BETandWIN; JoWood Productions Software AG.

CMS Strommer Reich-Rohrwig Karasek Hainz (8 ptrs, 12 asscs) Advising investment banks and investors on securities law, structured finance and regulatory issues, the firm has a solid name among peers for its banking and finance department. **Peter Huber*** is a *"tough negotiator,"* who focuses on capital markets issues and cross-border leasing arrangements.

The firm has assisted on a variety of listings on the Vienna Stock Exchange, and also advises on Austrian law as it applies to international securities offerings. A recent highlight involved advising the American Branch Banking and Trust Company on the cross-border leasing of OÖ Ferngas AG's gas network. Also represented Erste Bank on a secondary offering of CyberTron Telekom AG. **Clients:** Erste Bank AG; Wiener Städtische; RZB; Lloyds TSB; Morgan Stanley Dean Witter; HSBC; Kirch Gruppe.

Preslmayr & Partners (4 ptrs, 4 asscs) The firm's historic name in banking and insolvency is felt to

*See leaders' profiles on pages 105-107

owe much to the *"high quality"* **Karl Preslmayr***, a towering figure who is still active on financing and securities matters. The firm represents BAWAG on an on-going basis, most recently on the acquisition of PSK from ÖIAG (owned by the Republic of Austria). Also acted on behalf of Chase Manhattan on the refinancing of a multinational group from the paper industry, and for Citibank in connection with the refinancing of a leading international sports company. **Clients:** BAWAG; Citigroup; Chase Manhattan; Morgan Stanley.

Schönherr Barfuss Torggler & Partners (3 ptrs, 5 asscs) Although one of the major firms in Austria, its banking and finance department is not felt to match the profile of its corporate counterpart. However, the team covers bank privatisations and restructuring, as well as having niche expertise in bond issues.

The firm acted for ÖIAG on the ATS17.4 billion privatisation of PSK, and was counsel to the managers of a €200 million bond issue for Energie AG OÖ, and Bank Austria's ZYPS convertible bond. Also represents investors and lessors on cross-border infrastructure leases, and advised on the restructuring of Bank Burgenland. **Clients:** Bank Burgenland; ÖIAG; Gericom AG; Trigon Bank.

A

Corporate/M&A

AUSTRIA Leading firms (Corporate/Mergers & Acquisitions)
1 Freshfields Bruckhaus Deringer
Schönherr Barfuss Torggler & Partners
2 Cerha Hempel & Spiegelfeld
3 CMS Strommer Reich-Rohrwig Karasek Hainz
Dorda Brugger & Jordis
Wolf Theiss & Partners
4 Binder, Grösswang & Partner
Haarmann Hemmelrath Hügel
Preslmayr & Partners

Firms are listed alphabetically in each band.

Leading individuals (Corporate/ Mergers & Acquisitions)
1 **HERBST Christian** *Schönherr Barfuss Torggler*
HLAWATI Edith *Cerha Hempel & Spiegelfeld*
TORGGLER Hellwig *Schönherr Barfuss Torggler*
2 **DORDA Christian** *Dorda Brugger & Jordis*
HÜGEL Hanns *Haarmann Hemmelrath Hügel*
LÖBER Heinz *Freshfields Bruckhaus Deringer*
REICH-ROHRWIG Johannes *CMS Strommer*
WOLF Richard *Wolf Theiss & Partners*
3 **HEMPEL Karl** *Cerha Hempel & Spiegelfeld*
HORVATH Günther *Freshfields Bruckhaus*
JORDIS Teresa *Dorda Brugger & Jordis*
KUTSCHERA Michael *Binder, Grösswang*
4 **PLESSER Willibald** *Freshfields Bruckhaus*
PRESLMAYR Martin *Preslmayr & Partners*
Up-and-coming individuals
BRODEY Martin *Dorda Brugger & Jordis*
FROTZ Stephan *Schönherr Barfuss Torggler*
KÖCK Stefan *Freshfields Bruckhaus Deringer*
WENGER Thomas *Schönherr Barfuss Torggler*

Individuals are listed alphabetically in each band.

Freshfields Bruckhaus Deringer (8 ptrs, 24 asscs) Already a corporate leader in Austria, the firm's high-profile merger with Freshfields gives it huge international M&A strength and a matchless blue-chip clientele.

The corporate team includes a number of the country's leading lawyers. **Günther Horvath*** *"has a finger in every pie,"* and was mentioned to researchers as an *"excellent negotiator."* Although he is less active on transactions than formerly, **Heinz Löber*** is still regarded by clients as a *"doyen of Austrian law."* All-round commercial lawyer **Willibald Plesser*** has a respected transactional reputation, while **Stefan Köck*** is the team's rising star, and has an established new economy client base.

The firm advised on the public take-over of the pharmaceutical distributor Herba Chemosan by Gehe, and represented BP Austria on the dissolution of its joint venture with Mobil Oil Austria. **Clients:** BP Austria; Nomura; Apax; other private equity investors; Young & Rubicam; Gehe; SMS.

Schönherr Barfuss Torggler & Partners (6 ptrs, 7 asscs) Unanimously mentioned to researchers as one of the leading corporate firms in the country, the firm has an established reputation for corporate restructuring, big-ticket cross-border M&A and privatisation.

Competitors acknowledge that the corporate team contains *"quality through and through."* Leading the transactional charge is the *"forceful and goal-oriented"* **Christian Herbst***, who is noted for his relationships with leading American companies. Senior partner **Hellwig Torggler*** *"is a regular presence on the biggest deals,"* and is valued by clients for his *"intellectually forceful opinions."* The younger generation is represented by the *"energetic and client-friendly"* **Stephan Frotz***, and **Thomas Wenger***, who is especially noted for his expertise in the energy sector.

Substantial cases of the last year include representing ÖIAG on the ATS17.4 billion privatisation of PSK, and advising 3i Group plc on its ATS1 billion acquisition of the venture capital subsidiary of a leading Austrian bank. The team also advised on the corporate restructuring of two major Austrian banks. **Clients:** Red Bull; BBAG; ÖIAG; Microsoft; Reuters; DaimlerChrysler; Frantschach Group.

Cerha Hempel & Spiegelfeld (8 ptrs, 11 asscs) Renowned both for banking and corporate strength, the firm's chief reputation lies in its advice on IPOs and privatisations. Telecoms provide an area of specific expertise.

Researchers were left in no doubt that **Edith Hlawati**'s* *"incredible transactional output and negotiating talent"* put her among the country's leading corporate lawyers. **Karl Hempel*** also maintains his long-established reputation as an *"outstanding client-getter."* The firm represented Telekom Austria on its acquisition of Czech Online, and advised the Julius Meinl Group on the sale of part of its supermarket interests to Spar. Also handled the privatisation of Telekom Austria, and the dual listing of Dutch company, Head NV, on the New York Stock Exchange and the Vienna Stock Exchange. **Clients:** Telekom Austria; Julius Meinl Group; Head NV.

CMS Strommer Reich-Rohrwig Karasek Hainz (11 ptrs, 15 asscs) Known for advising national and international companies on their restructuring programmes, the firm also assists its domestic clientele on structuring investments in neighbouring Central European countries.

Although he speaks little English, **Johannes Reich-Rohrwig*** is regarded by competitors as a *"sharp and aggressive"* corporate lawyer. Market opinion suggests that he lacks support of a comparable calibre. The firm advised Österreichische Post on the disposal of Postbus. **Clients:**

*See leaders' profiles on pages 105-107

Mobilkom Austria; Österreichische Post; Gehe; HSBC; Kirch Gruppe.

Dorda Brugger & Jordis (10 ptrs, 18 asscs) The corporate team covers a broad caseload, but is best known for advising its predominantly international clientele on cross-border M&A. **Christian Dorda*** "knows how to get things done," according to clients, and has a powerful French client base. **Teresa Jordis*** was commended to researchers as a *"serious and well-connected foil."* Active in the telecoms sector, **Martin Brodey*** is a rising younger name, and is said to be *"dynamic and clever."*

The firm represented the Zumtobel-Gruppe on its merger with Thorn Lighting Group, advised Electricité de France on the proposed merger of ESTAG with Energie Oberösterreich. It also acted on the Austrian legal aspects of Glaxo Wellcome's merger with Smithkline Beecham. **Clients:** Telecom Italia; Glaxo Wellcome; Atomic Austria; Motorola; Getronics.

Wolf Theiss & Partners (5 ptrs, 25 asscs) *"Young and dynamic firm"* which has rapidly acquired a reputation for cross-border M&A and IPO work, notably in the hi-tech industries. The collapse of the firm's relationship with Freshfields Deringer, following the latter's merger with Bruckhaus Westrick Heller Löber, has been described by competitors as *"a temporary setback."* **Richard Wolf*** *("one of Austria's young lions")* is viewed as the team's leading light.

The firm advised CapVis Equity Partners on its bid for the acquisition of Chemson Group from Dynamit Nobel, and on the acquisition of a majority stake in Polytec Group. **Clients:** Analog Services Inc; CapVis Equity Partners; DaimlerChrysler; ICI; GE Capital, Novartis.

Binder, Grösswang & Partner (8 ptrs, 15 asscs) *"More and more visible,"* researchers were impressed by market approval of an *"old school firm"* with cross-border M&A expertise.

Michael Kutschera* is regarded as a *"persistent negotiator with an international outlook,"* and has notable connections with US clients. The firm advised Cap Gemini on its takeover of Ernst & Young's consulting business. **Clients:** HypoVereinsbank; Westvaco; Cap Gemini; SANDVIK; Bull SA; Black & Decker; MAN Roland; debis Systemhaus.

Haarmann Hemmelrath Hügel (7 ptrs, 15 asscs) The merger of Hügel & Partner with leading German firm Haarmann Hemmelrath has given the firm acknowledged tax expertise to set beside its existing cross-border M&A capacity. The corporate team also advises on corporate restructuring and privatisations for a mixture of domestic and international clients.

"Dynamic figure" **Hanns Hügel*** is the firm's spearhead, and, although he speaks little English he is acknowledged by competitors as one of Austria's *"leading academic practitioners."* The firm represented Shell Austria AG on the sale of a subsidiary, and handled the corporate restructuring for tele.ring Telekom Service. **Clients:** RWA Raiffeisen Ware Austria; VA Tech ELIN; Mobil; Shell Austria; BP Austria; RH1; Novartis.

Preslmayr & Partners (7 ptrs, 10 asscs) Traditionally known for its insolvency speciality, this small firm also has an acknowledged presence in M&A. The corporate team advises leading international companies such as Shell and Oracle, and is also strong in telecoms and the film industry. Clients praised **Martin Preslmayr*** as a *"versatile and effective practitioner."*

The firm acted for Linde/AGA Group on the sale of AGA GmbH to Air Liquide for €130 million. Other work includes representing BAWAG on its acquisition of PSK, and advising DII Group in Austria on its merger with Flextronic. **Clients:** BAWAG; Linde/AGA Group; Citigroup; Flextronics; Miele; Braun Electric; British Post Office; Saatchi & Saatchi; Shell; Oracle.

A

Leaders' profiles – Austria

BAIER, Anton
Baier Böhm Orator & Partners, Vienna +43 1 516 20
Recommended in Arbitration (International)

BINDER, Michael
Binder, Grösswang & Partner, Vienna +43 1 534 800
Recommended in Banking & Finance

BRODEY, Martin
Dorda Brugger & Jordis, Vienna +43 1 533 47 95-0
Recommended in Corporate/M&A

DALLMANN, Armin
Dallmann & Partners, Vienna +43 1 504 4142 office@dallmann.cc
Recommended in Banking & Finance
Specialisation: (www.dallmann.cc) Senior Partner. Main area of work is banking, capital markets law, and mergers and acquisitions. Recent matters: Acted as lead counsel in several large real estate development project finance transactions in Hungary and the Czech Republic; advised a large Austrian bank in connection with its first time issue of a Euro 3 billion Global Medium Term Note programme; advised a major foreign investment bank on insider trading regulations in connection with its trading activities in Austria; assisted a leading international financial news and information provider in setting up its new activities in the financial services sector.
Prof. Memberships: Rechtsanwaltskammer Wien, International Bar Association, Harvard Law School Association of Europe.
Career: Qualified in 1988. Assistant lecturer at the Department for Tax Law at the University of Vienna, Law School (1980). Foreign Associate at *Shearman & Sterling*, New York (1983). Special Counsel for a major Austrian bank (since 1986). Founding partner of *Hügel Dallmann & Partners* (1993-1999). Founding partner of *Dallmann & Partners* (2000).
Personal: Born 23 February 1956. Salzburg, Linz (economics) and Vienna Universities (Dr. jur. 1980). Georgetown University (1980). International Tax Programme as part of an LLM course at Harvard Law School (LLM 1982). Leisure interests include opera, travel. Lives in Vienna, Austria.

DORALT, Paul
Doralt Seist & Csoklich, Vienna +43 1 319 45 20
Recommended in Banking & Finance

DORDA, Christian
Dorda Brugger & Jordis, Vienna +43 1 533 47 95-0
Recommended in Banking & Finance, Corporate/M&A

FORAMITTI, Louis
Ortner Pöch Foramitti, Vienna +43 1 535 3721
Recommended in Banking & Finance

FROTZ, Stephan
Schönherr Barfuss Torggler & Partners, Vienna +43 1 534 37 0
Recommended in Corporate/M&A

HAUSMANINGER, Christian
Hausmaninger Herbst Wietrzyk, Vienna +43 1 513 9540
Recommended in Arbitration (International), Banking & Finance

HEIDINGER, Markus
Wolf Theiss & Partners, Vienna +43 1 51510 5060 mheidinger@wtp.at
Recommended in Banking & Finance
Specialisation: Corporate, M&A, banking, capital markets.
Prof. Memberships: Vienna Bar Association; Czech Bar Association; Vienna Juridical Society; federation of Austrian Industry; International Bar Association; SBL; Friends of the Institute of Advanced Legal Studies.
Publications: 'Tasks and responsibilities of the Board of Directors of a Limited Liability Company'

(Ueberreuter, 1989); 'Corporate Structure after the Tax Reform 1989' (Ueberreuter, 1989 and 1994); 'The Austrian Stock Corporation Act' (Manz, 3rd edition 1999), the Austrian Investment Funds Act (Linde, 1998), The Austrian Pension Funds Act (Linde, 1999); further publications in the fields of banking, corporate and tax law; Austrian country correspondent to the Journal of International Banking Law and to the Journal of International Financial Markets.
Career: Admitted in Austria since 1993; partner of *Wolf Theiss & Partners* since 1994; admitted in the Czech Republic since 1999.
Personal: Born 1963 in Graz; University of Graz Law School (Mag jur 1987, Dr jur 1989 with honours); University of London, King's College (LLM 1991 with honours).

HELLER, Kurt
Freshfields Bruckhaus Deringer, Vienna +43 1 515 150
kurt.heller@freshfieldsbruckhaus.com
Recommended in Arbitration (International)
Specialisation: Specialises in dispute resolution and environmental planning and regulation.

HEMPEL, Karl
Cerha Hempel & Spiegelfeld, Vienna +43 1 514 350
Recommended in Arbitration (International), Banking & Finance, Corporate/M&A

HERBST, Christian
Schönherr Barfuss Torggler & Partners, Vienna +43 1 534 37 0
ch.herbst@schoenherr.at
Recommended in Corporate/M&A
Specialisation: Partner specialising in M&A, privatisations, corporate, foreign investment and telecoms. Focuses on cross-border financial and corporate transactions including acquisitions and divestitures by way of open bids or otherwise, public tender offers, restructurings and joint ventures, thereby representing mostly foreign clients. Has been, and is, involved in highly publicised privatisations and M&A transactions representing and advising from time to time, the divesting entity, the target or the acquirer. With the firm's M&A team, covers a wide range of economic sectors and industries including financial services, energy, telecoms and IT, in transactional and corporate work. Author of articles on international transactions, M&A, and corporate law. A permanent correspondent to the EEIL-Merger Control Newsletter, London.
Prof. Memberships: IBA; UIA. Forum Kartellrecht.
Career: Admitted to the Bar in Austria in 1988. Partner at the Vienna based firm of *Schönherr Torggler, & Partners* since 1990. Lectures at seminars and conferences on corporate law and international transactions.
Personal: Born 1959. Attended the University of Salzburg (Dr.jur. 1982); School of Advanced International Studies; Johns Hopkins University, Bologna (Diploma 1983); Harvard University (LLM 1984). Foreign Associate with a New York City Law Firm (1984). Resides in Vienna.

HLAWATI, Edith
Cerha Hempel & Spiegelfeld, Vienna +43 1 514 350
Recommended in Banking & Finance, Corporate/M&A

HORVATH, Günther
Freshfields Bruckhaus Deringer, Vienna +43 1 515 150
guenther.horvath@freshfieldsbruckhaus.com
Recommended in Arbitration (International), Corporate/M&A
Specialisation: Specialises in dispute resolution and corporate work.

HUBER, Peter
CMS Strommer Reich-Rohrwig Karasek Hainz, Vienna +43 1 40 4430
Recommended in Banking & Finance

HÜGEL, Hanns F.
Haarmann, Hemmelrath & Partner, Vienna +43 1 503 77 80
Hanns_Huegel@hhp.de
Recommended in Corporate/Commercial
Specialisation: Specialises in Corporate Law, Company and Tax Law, Mergers & Acquisitions, Reorganisations, Copyright Law and Arbitration. Numerous publications on Austrian company and tax law.
Prof. Memberships: Bar Association of Lower Austria; Lawyers' Club Soupirium; International Bar Association; Tax Law Committee of the Austrian Chamber of Tax Advisers.
Career: Admitted in 1979; educated at University of Vienna (Dr. iur. 1974); Professor at University of Vienna, Faculty of Law, Department of Commercial Law.
Personal: Born 14 July 1951 in Vienna. Four children.

JORDIS, Teresa
Dorda Brugger & Jordis, Vienna +43 1 533 47 95-0
Recommended in Corporate/M&A

KÖCK, Stefan
Freshfields Bruckhaus Deringer, Vienna +43 1 515 150
stefan.koeck@freshfieldsbruckhaus.com
Recommended in Corporate/M&A
Specialisation: Specialises in corporate and employment law with particular focus on telecoms – regulatory and contracts, antitrust law, public takeovers and the Takeover Code and mergers and acquisitions.

KUTSCHERA, Michael
Binder, Grösswang & Partner, Vienna +43 1 534 800
Recommended in Corporate/M&A

LIEBSCHER, Christoph
Wolf Theiss & Partners, Vienna +43 1 51510 5110
cliebscher@wtp.at
Recommended in Arbitration (International)
Specialisation: Arbitration, international litigation, intellectual property, distribution, pharmaceuticals.
Prof. Memberships: Vienna Bar Association; Czech Bar Association; Austrian Franchise Association; Federation of Austrian Industry; International Bar Association, SBL; Association Internationale des Jeunes Avocats' ASA: Chartered Institute of Arbitrators; DIS; LCIA.
Publications: (Author or co-author): 'Patents and the European Biotechnology Lag' (Insead, 1987); 'European Coproduction in Film and Televisions' (Nomos, 1989); 'Franchising in Austria' (Orac, 1992; 2nd edition 2001); 'The Advertising Agency Agreement' (Orac, 1993); 'Corporations in the Czech and the Slovak Republics' (Linde, 1993); 'Courts and the European Integration' (Austrian Ministry of Justice, 1993); 'Distribution Agreements' (Orac, 1996; 2nd edition 2000); 'EEA-Almanach' (Signum, 1994); 'Corporate Acquisitions' (Service Fachverlag, 1994); 'Duties and Liabilities of Auditors' (MANZ, 1997); 'Austrian Legal Guide for Entrepreneurs' (WEKA, 1998); 'Licensing Agreements' (forthcoming) (Orac, 2001); 'Practitioner's Handbook of International Arbitration' (forthcoming) (Beck, 2001); 'International Arbitration in Central and Eastern Europe' (Juris Publishing) (forthcoming) (2001); 'The Healthy Award' (Kluwer) (forthcoming) (2001).
Career: Admitted in Austria, 1985; admitted in the Czech Republic, 1999; partner of *Liebscher Hübel & Heinrich*, Salzburg, 1985-1997; partner of *Wolf Theiss & Partners* since 1997; head of European co-operation, Kirch Group, Munich, 1987-1989; responsible for business development for two European multinational companies, 1987-1991; arbitrator under ICC Rules and other rules; member of the ICC Commission on International Arbitration; Austria correspondent of the International Arbitration Institute, 1999; member of the SECI.OSCE Expert Group on International Arbitration, 2000; delegate at the UNCITRAL working group on arbitration, 2000; listed as arbitrator with the International Court of Arbitration of the Austrian Economic Chamber, 2000; member of the expert group on the reform of the Austrian arbitration law, 2000; member of the expert committees of the ICC on franchising and on vertical restrictions, since 1994/97; member of the legal committee of the Federation of Austrian Industry; lecturer, University of Economics and Business Administration, Vienna, since 1995; lecturer (dispute resolution); INSEAD, Fontainebleau, since 1999; lecturer University Linz (business law) 2000.
Personal: Born 1957 in Salzburg, Austria; University of Vienna Law School, University of Salzburg Law School (Dr jur 1979); INSEAD, Fontainebleau (MBA 1986); research assistant, INSEAD, 1987; Fellow of the Chartered Institute of Arbitrators, 2000.

LÖBER, Heinz
Freshfields Bruckhaus Deringer, Vienna +43 1 515 150
heinz.loeber@freshfieldsbruckhaus.com
Recommended in Corporate/M&A
Specialisation: Core areas of practice are partnership, stock corporation and limited liability company law; the law regarding branches, groups of companies and transformation of companies, joint ventures; IPO's privatisations; public takeover and the takeover code; M&A; the law of security and guarantee, succession into enterprises/family owned companies; law of agency and distribution; and commercial law.

MELIS, Werner
Baier Böhm Orator & Partners, Vienna
+43 1 516 20
Recommended in Arbitration (International)

PLESSER, Willibald
Freshfields Bruckhaus Deringer, Vienna
+43 1 515 150
willibald.plesser@freshfieldsbruckhaus.com
Recommended in Corporate/M&A
Specialisation: Specialises in information technology and communications, and corporate law.

PRESLMAYR, Karl
Preslmayr & Partners, Vienna +43 1 533 16 95
karl@preslmayr.at
Recommended in Banking & Finance
Specialisation: M&A, copyright and advertising law, corporate law, banking and finance, antitrust, competition law, public procurement, arbitration.
Prof. Memberships: Austrian Bar Association; DACH; official arbitrator of the International Arbitral Center of the Austrian Federal Economic Chamber, the International Chamber of Commerce (ICC), International Court of Arbitration.
Career: Vienna University (Doctorate in Law) 1958.

PRESLMAYR, Martin
Preslmayr & Partners, Vienna +43 1 533 16 95
martin@preslmayr.at
Recommended in Corporate/M&A
Specialisation: M&A, due diligences, corporate, corporate finance, project finance, company law, contracts, product liability and torts.
Prof. Memberships: Austrian Bar Association; International Bar Association; Advisory Board of TAGLaw.
Career: Vienna University (Docorate in Law) 1992, Exeter University (Master of Law in European Legal Studies) 1994. Research Assistant at the Department of Private and Private International Law 1989-91. Research in EU and International Law, Cambridge, 1991. Partner of *Preslmayr & Partners* since 1996.

REICH-ROHRWIG, Johannes
CMS Strommer Reich-Rohrwig Karasek Hainz, Vienna +43 1 40 4430
Recommended in Corporate/M&A

REINER, Andreas
Andreas Reiner – Sole Practitioner, Vienna
+43 1 532 23 32 0
Recommended in Arbitration (International)

TORGGLER, Hellwig
Schönherr Barfuss Torggler & Partners, Vienna
+43 1 534 37 0
h.torggler@schoenherr.at
Recommended in Arbitration (International), Corporate/M&A
Specialisation: Partner specialising in corporate, M&A, tax law and arbitration. Concentrates on domestic and international corporate restructuring, joint ventures and M&A transactions. A highly regarded specialist on trusts and acts both as adviser to and member of the board of various trusts. The firm's M&A team covers a wide range of economic sectors and industries including financial services, energy, telecoms and IT. Author of numerous articles on tax, corporate and commercial law. Co-author of Commentary on the Austrian Commercial Code.
Prof. Memberships: Examining Board for the Austrian Bar Examination; Austrian Delegation to the Arbitration Court of the International Chamber of Commerce, Paris. IBA; ILA.
Career: Admitted to the Bar in Austria in 1969. Senior partner at the Vienna based firm of *Schoenherr Barfuss Torggler & Partners* since 1970. Professor for commercial law and taxation at the University of Graz, since 1993. Lecturer and Guest Professor, Vienna Business School 1985-95. Lecturer, University of Krems, Department for European Integration, Anwaltsakademie.
Personal: Born 1938. Attended the Universities of Vienna, St. Gallen, Switzerland, Berne, Switzerland, Graz (Dr.jur. 1961, Dr.rer.pol. 1962). Southern Methodist University, Dallas (LLM 1963). Resides in Vienna.

WENGER, Thomas
Schönherr Barfuss Torggler & Partners, Vienna
+43 1 534 37 0
th.wenger@schoenherr.at
Recommended in Corporate/M&A
Specialisation: Partner in Corporate, Commercial Law, Energy Management, Procurement Law, Construction Law, Antitrust, Municipalities and Trade Law. Author of articles on Corporate and Trade Law. Co-editor: 'Österreichische Zeitschrift für Recht und Rechnungswesen'.
Career: Admitted to Bar, Austria, 1992. University of Vienna (Dr.jur. 1983) and Vienna Business School (Mag.rer.soc.oec. 1987). Partner at the Vienna-based firm of *Schoenherr Barfuss Torggler & Partners* since 1994.
Personal: Born 1960. Attended the University of Vienna and the Vienna Business School. Resides in Vienna.

WOLF, Richard
Wolf Theiss & Partners, Vienna +43 1 51510 5080
rwolf@wtp.at
Recommended in Banking & Finance, Corporate/Commercial
Specialisation: M&A, banking and finance, capital markets, merger control, pharmaceuticals.
Prof. Memberships: Vienna Bar Association; Czech Bar Association; International Bar Association, SBL; Studienvereinigung Kartellrecht; Association of Austrian Fulbright Scholars.
Career: European Commission, DG IV, internship 1987; admitted in Austria since 1991; Second Vice President, M&A, Chase Manhattan Bank Austria, 1992-1993; Investment and Finance Manager, Crédit Lyonnais Austria, 1993-1994; partner of *Wolf Theiss & Partners* since 1994; admitted in the Czech Republic since 2000.
Personal: Born 1962 in Paris; University of Vienna Law School (Dr jur 1985); Harvard Law School (LLM 1986).

A

AZERBAIJAN

Energy & Natural Resources

AZERBAIJAN Leading firms (Energy & Natural Resources)
1 Baker Botts LLP
Baker & McKenzie
Ledingham Chalmers
Salans Hertzfeld & Heilbronn

Firms are listed alphabetically in each band.

Baker Botts LLP (1 ptr, 4 asscs) Perceived as *"players"* in the jurisdiction by its competitors, the firm has long experience of energy pipeline projects, and advises local oil and gas companies on their investments around the Caspian Sea. **Clients:** AIOC; Howard Energy International.

Baker & McKenzie (1 ptr, 5 asscs) General corporate and commercial law practice with a particular emphasis on oil, gas and major natural resources and infrastructure projects. The firm advised on an aircraft financing worth $130 million, supplying Boeing 757s to Azal, the national airline. Also acted on the privatisation of the Georgian electrical grid, and represented Halda Bank on the privatisation of Gradaga Cement Plant. **Clients:** Azal; Halda Bank; Mobil.

Ledingham Chalmers (6 asscs) The first foreign firm to establish an office in Azerbaijan, said by clients to have a *"broader base"* than some of its rivals. Inward investment has formed an integral part of the firm's work in the past year, although the group's core energy work has involved production sharing and joint operating agreements. **Clients:** BP Amoco; Ramco; Abbot Group.

Salans Hertzfeld & Heilbronn (1 ptr, 5 asscs) Clients told our researchers that they were *"more than happy"* with the service provided by this firm, which is especially known for its expertise in local law issues. The firm is currently advising major western companies on energy projects in

the jurisdiction, with an emphasis on due diligence, licensing, structuring, contracting and negotiations with the government. Specific matters include advising a western company on a project involving the upgrading of a petrochemical installation, and advising oil field operators and participators on the drafting of tax provisions in production sharing agreements. **Clients:** Arco; Lasmo; AGIP.

BAHAMAS

Corporate/Commercial

BAHAMAS Leading firms (Corporate/Commercial)
1 Graham Thompson & Co
Higgs & Johnson
McKinney, Bancroft & Hughes

Firms are listed alphabetically in each band.

Leading individuals (Corporate/Commercial)
1 DELANEY John *Higgs & Johnson*
McWEENEY Sean *Graham Thompson & Co*
PINDER Hartis *McKinney, Bancroft & Hughes*

Individuals are listed alphabetically in each band.

Graham Thompson & Co (14 ptrs, 12 asscs) Full service commercial firm, covering a broad spectrum of commercial services including trusts, probate, insurance and admiralty. However, its principal reputation lies in international banking, M&A and commercial litigation. Former Attorney-General **Sean McWeeney** is an expert on trusts and M&A advice, and has an *"excellent reputation."* The group advised on the merger of the two largest liquor wholesalers in the Bahamas, and has also dealt with a large number of bond issues. **Clients:** Credit Suisse First Boston; retail chains; wholesalers; hotels.

Higgs & Johnson (10 ptrs, 10 asscs) *"Excellent commercial firm,"* as renowned for litigation as for corporate work, which provides advice on trusts, banking and shipping. **John Delaney** is counsel to the Association of International Banks & Trust Companies of the Bahamas, and is perceived as a *"major player in M&A."* He has been involved in the restructuring of the legislative and regulatory framework of the financial services industry. In the past year, the firm has been engaged in the Oracle Fund liquidation (on behalf of the liquidators,) the Socimer liquidation (on behalf of a creditor) and the purchase by Commonwealth Breweries of Butler & Sands and Clifton Cay Development. **Clients:** Royal Bank of Canada; Citibank; United Bank of Switzerland; Credit Suisse (Bahamas) Ltd; SG Hambros Bank & Trust Co; Texaco Bahamas Ltd; Esso Standard Oil; Bacardi Co; Finance Corporation of The Bahamas; Commonwealth Brewery; KPMG; Microsoft; RBS.

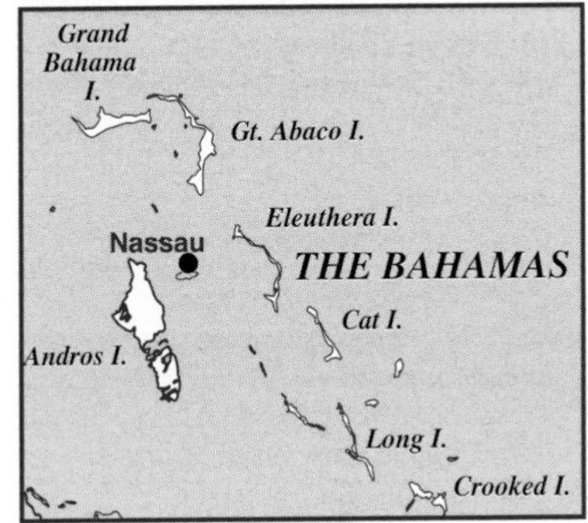

McKinney, Bancroft & Hughes (10 ptrs, 10 asscs) Large commercial firm, *"held in high regard"* on the islands. The Bahamas member of Lex Mundi, it has an established reputation for litigation and off-shore banking advice, and advises international financial institutions and insurance companies. **Hartis Pinder** is *"the M&A man at MBH."* **Clients:** Barclays; British America; Jerris Johnson (largest insurance brokers in the Bahamas); General Accident.

Leaders' profiles – Bahamas

DELANEY, John
Higgs & Johnson, Nassau +1 242 322 8571

McWEENEY, Sean
Graham Thompson & Co, Nassau +1 242 322 4130

PINDER, Hartis
McKinney, Bancroft & Hughes, Nassau +1 242 322 4195

BAHRAIN

Banking & Finance

BAHRAIN Leading firms (Banking & Finance)
1 Norton Rose
2 Towers & Hamlins
3 Al-Mahmood & Zu'bi
Hassan Radhi & Associates

Firms are listed alphabetically in each band.

Leading individuals (Banking & Finance)
1 INGLIS John *Norton Rose*
TROWER Christopher *Trowers & Hamlins*
2 RADHI Hassan *Hassan Radhi & Associates*
STOKES Hugh *Al-Mahmood & Zu'bi*

Individuals are listed alphabetically in each band.

Norton Rose (1 ptr, 6 asscs) The main focus of the firm's Manama office has traditionally been on finance-related matters, including asset and project finance, Islamic finance and corporate finance. It is still seen to be the *"clear leader"* in the region for general finance work, despite the recent departure of its former banking star Neil Miller back to London.

Managing partner **John Inglis*** is highly rated for his work, and is seen to have *"done an admirable job of stepping into the breach"* left by Miller's departure. Highlights from the past year include advising Shamil Bank of Bahrain, ABC Islamic Bank, The Arab Investment Company and Dubai Islamic Bank in respect of the rescheduling of four syndicated Morabaha financing facilities made available to public sector companies in Pakistan, with an aggregate value of $215 million. The firm also advised Saudi National Commercial Bank (SNCB) in relation to a $70 million oil import financing, and is currently advising Korea Development Bank (the lenders) in relation to a $100 million financing for oil purchasing. **Clients:** ANZ; Faysal Islamic Bank; Gulf International Bank; National Bank of Bahrain; Nomura; Saudi National Commercial Bank.

Trowers & Hamlins (1 ptr, 1 assc) The firm has consolidated its presence in the banking and finance sector over the past twelve months, particularly on the offshore lending side, although it still has *"some way to go"* before it reaches the *"status of Norton Rose"* in the region. The firm's primary focus has been on increasing its regional ability to provide a *"one-stop shop"* to banks and financial institutions based in Bahrain who are entering into transactions in foreign jurisdictions.

The firm has been increasingly visible on behalf of Saudi-based clients. Office head **Christopher Trower*** is recognised by peers for his general finance expertise. Recent significant matters include acting on a share purchase agreement by local shareholders of an international bank's stake in a Bahraini incorporated bank. **Clients:** Banks and financial institutions.

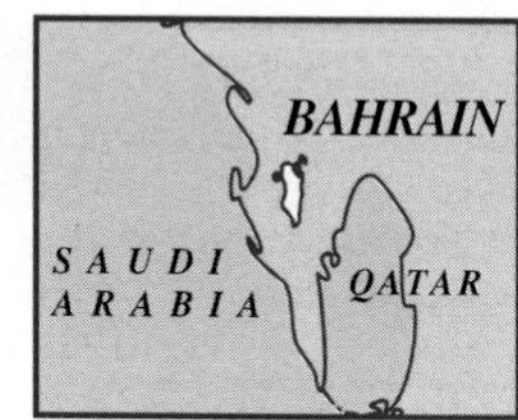

Al Mahmood & Zu'bi (6 ptrs, 4 asscs) The firm has a strong banking practice, acting on retainer for many of the top banks based in Bahrain, and also undertakes work by referral or association for a number of leading international banking and finance law firms, particularly White & Case, with which it maintains a close relationship. The *"well-established"* **Hugh Stokes*** is seen to be a *"crucial element"* in the strength of the firm's banking practice. **Clients:** Bahrain-based banks.

Hassan Radhi & Associates (3 ptrs, 4 asscs) The firm has acted for a large number of banks in the region including Bahraini-Saudi Bank, Paribas Bahrain and the Arab-Asia Bank. **Hassan Radhi*** is seen to have *"maintained good relationships with the banks over the years"* and has *"just as respectable a finance practice as he does a corporate practice."* **Clients:** Arab-Asia Bank; Bahraini-Saudi Bank; Paribas Bahrain.

Corporate/M&A

BAHRAIN Leading firms (Corporate/Mergers & Acquisitions)
1 Norton Rose
Trowers & Hamlins
2 Al-Mahmood & Zu'bi
Hassan Radhi & Associates

Firms are listed alphabetically in each band.

Norton Rose (1 ptr, 6 asscs) The firm undertakes a variety of corporate/commercial work, mergers and acquisitions and private equity work in the region. In the past twelve months, the firm has been very active in M&A work, as well as commercial contracts work, and corporate finance work (including investment funds and private placements). The respected **John Inglis*** is the new managing partner of the firm's Manama office, having recently relocated from London, and *"heads up all its major corporate transactions"* in the region.

Recent significant transactions include advising Bahrain Telecommunications Company on the multi-million dollar takeover of Quality Net, a company in Kuwait, and advising Bahrain Telecommunications Company on the US takeover of two Jordanian ISP companies. The firm also advised MAN-AHLI (a joint venture between ED&F Man Investment Products and Al-Ahli Commercial Bank) in connection with the launch of three investment funds, namely MAN-AHLI Prisma Guaranteed EC, MAN-AHLI Guaranteed 220 Plus EC and MAN-AHLI Converter Limited. **Clients:** Aluminium Bahrain; Batelco; CVRD; Gulf Finance House; MAN-AHLI Investment Bank.

Trowers & Hamlins (1 ptr, 1 assc) The firm's Bahrain office has seen the volume of its corporate and commercial work increase to the point where

*See leaders' profiles on pages 111

BAHRAIN Leading individuals (Corporate/Mergers & Acquisitions)	
1	**INGLIS John** *Norton Rose*
	TROWER Christopher *Trowers & Hamlins*
2	**RADHI Hassan** *Hassan Radhi & Associates*
	STOKES Hugh *Al-Mahmood & Zu'bi*

Individuals are listed alphabetically in each band.

it now accounts for almost half of its total activity. **Christopher Trower*** heads the firm's operations in Manama, covering all aspects of business law in the Gulf, including commercial and contract law, mergers, privatisations and initial public offerings, as well as banking and finance.

Known for its corporate restructuring activities, the firm advises a number of the larger foreign companies with activities in Bahrain in the insurance sector and the oil and gas sector. The firm has had an extensive advisory role in relation to the restructuring of an insurance company. **Clients:** Local, regional and international companies.

Al Mahmood & Zu'bi (6 ptrs, 4 asscs) This firm is seen to be *"probably the best-known local firm"* in Bahrain, and is also seen to provide *"good advice on specific aspects of Bahraini law,"* as well as being *"popular for local corporate and finance matters."* **Hugh Stokes*** has been in the region for two decades and has recognised expertise in both corporate and general finance matters and a particularly good relationship with the British Embassy. The firm has built up a strong relationship with regional powerhouse White & Case. **Clients:** Local and regional corporations.

Hassan Radhi & Associates (3 ptrs, 4 asscs)A well respected firm which does *"more of the local corporate work rather than the larger-scale transactions,"* advising corporate clients such as ALBA, the Arab Shipbuilding and Refitting Yard (ASRY) and Nissho Iwai. The *"high profile"* **Hassan Radhi*** is the former President of the Bar Association in Bahrain, and is respected as a *"versatile and effective commercial practitioner."* **Clients:** ALBA; ASRY; Nissho Iwai.

B

Project Finance

BAHRAIN Leading firms (Project Finance)	
1	Norton Rose
2	Trowers & Hamlins

Firms are listed alphabetically in each band.

Leading individuals (Project Finance)	
1	**INGLIS John** *Norton Rose*
2	**TROWER Christopher** *Trowers & Hamlins*

Individuals are listed alphabetically in each band.

Norton Rose (1 ptr, 2 asscs) The firm has maintained its status as the premier project finance practice in the region, with **John Inglis*** seen as having *"bolstered"* the office's project finance and privatisation capabilities. Highlights of project finance work from the past twelve months include advising the lead arranging banks on the construction and financing of a $2 billion motorway and bridge crossing at Izmit Bay in Turkey. The firm also advises a number of banking groups in relation to the $850 million upgrade to the Bapco Refinery in Bahrain, and is currently advising SACE, JBIC and EID/MITI on the $1.5 billion financing of the Bluestream Gas Pipeline from Russia to Turkey. **Clients:** QAFAC; Bahrain Petroleum Company (Bapco).

Trowers & Hamlins (1 ptr, 1 assc) Although still seen to lie *"a fair way behind"* Norton Rose, the firm has been increasingly acting at a local level for banks on projects, mainly in connection with the electricity and power sectors. **Christopher Trower*** is seen to have been *"instrumental"* in building the firm's profile in this area. **Clients:** Banks and financial institutions throughout the Gulf.

Leaders' profiles – Bahrain

INGLIS, John
Norton Rose, Manama +973 226 424
inglisjdc@nortonrose.com
Recommended in Banking & Finance, Corporate/M&A, Project Finance
Specialisation: International Managing Partner of *Norton Rose*'s Bahrain office. Specialises in banking and finance (including project finance and Islamic finance), and mergers and acquisitions. In relation to project financing, has acted for: Attiki Odos in relation to the Athens Ring Road Project; Qatar General Electricity and Water Corporation in relation to the Ras Abu Fontas 'B' 400 MW Expansion Project in Qatar; BNP Paribas and Citibank in relation to the Taweelah Al independent water and power project US$1,015 million financing in Abu Dhabi; Qatar Fertiliser Company in relation to the phase 1 QAFCO-4 Expansion in Qatar. In relation to mergers and acquisitions, has acted for: Companhia Vale do Rio Doce and Gulf Investment Corporation in relation to the US$183 million acquisition of 100% of the shares in Gulf Industrial Investment Corporation in Bahrain from Kuwait Petroleum Corporation; Bahrain Telecommunications Company in relation to the acquisition of 51% of the shares in two internet service providers in Jordan.
Prof. Memberships: Law Society; New Zealand Law Society.
Publications: Regular speaker on banking and project finance. Has also written a number of articles in respect of these areas.
Career: Qualified as a Barrister and Solicitor of the High Court of New Zealand in 1989; Judges' Clerk of the Court of Appeal of New Zealand 1989-90; awarded LLM with first class honours 1991; Associate *Buddle Findlay*, Wellington New Zealand 1992-95; Senior Associate *Baker & McKenzie*, Hong Kong 1995-96; Senior Associate *Norton Rose*, London 1997-99 then transfered to Bahrain office and became partner in 2000.
Personal: Born 28 July 1966.

RADHI, Hassan
Hassan Radhi & Associates, Manama +973 535 252
Recommended in Banking & Finance, Corporate/M&A

STOKES, Hugh
Al-Mahmood & Zu'bi, Manama +973 225 151
Recommended in Banking & Finance, Corporate/M&A

TROWER, Christopher
Trowers & Hamlins, Manama +973 530 082
Recommended in Banking & Finance, Corporate/M&A, Project Finance

BANGLADESH

Corporate/Commercial

BANGLADESH Leading firms (Corporate/Commercial)
1 Dr Kamal Hossain & Associates
2 Syed Ishtiaq Ahmed & Associates
The Law Associates

Firms are listed alphabetically in each band.

Leading individuals (Corporate/Commercial)
1 AHMED Syed Ishtiaq *Syed Ishtiaq Ahmed*
HOSSAIN Kamal *Dr Kamal Hossain*
2 HUQ Rafique-ul *Huq & Co*
MAHMUD Rokanuddin *Rokanuddin Mahmud*
UL-ISLAM Amir *The Law Associates*
ZAHIR Mohammed *Mohammed Zahir*

Individuals are listed alphabetically in each band.

Dr Kamal Hossain & Associates (1 ptr, 12 asscs) A well-known specialist corporate practice staffed by *"good young advocates with a lot of potential."* Although barely visible on the local scene due to his extensive travels, distinguished partner **Dr Kamal Hossain** continues to uphold the reputation of his firm. Competitors commend his internationally sought expertise in oil and energy sector work and leadership of UN delegations. A former government minister and retained counsel with Clifford Chance, he is noted for his *"fine legal mind."* Represented the Asian Development Bank (as one of the advisors in a consortia of international law firms) in relation to the takeover of the New England Power Co power plant by Coastal Power. **Clients:** New England Power Co; Mitsui Corporation; Coastal Power; Asian Development Bank; United Meridian; Wartsila; Enron.

Syed Ishtiaq Ahmed & Associates (1 ptr, 6 asscs) A respected practice handling a broad base of general corporate, commercial and banking work, specialising in telecommunications and power projects financing work. Researchers noted numerous accolades for named partner **Syed Ishtiaq Ahmed**. A former minister for Legal and Parliamentary Affairs and Attorney General, he enjoys a personal rapport with his judicial contemporaries and *"carries weight in the team."* Recent work includes representing US Exim Bank Finance on project financing and drafting of security agreements in relation to three power projects. The firm acts as local counsel to a consortium of CitiBank, SH&E and Clifford Chance advising on the commercialisation, restructuring and privatisation of Biman Bangladesh Airlines. **Clients:** Shell Bangladesh Exploration & Development BV; Cairn Energy; Teledesic LLC; GrameenPhone; WorldTel; AES; BRAC (NGO); HSBC; Holder Bank; KAFCO.

The Law Associates (1 ptr, 15 asscs) One of the key players in telecommunications and power projects deals, often seen representing senior lenders such as key client IFC World Bank. Active in political circles, **Amir Ul-Islam** is noted for his public law and litigation work. The firm is currently acting for investors in several infrastructure gas and power projects including one with the Rural Electrification Board and another at national level. Advised Cemex Cement in relation to set up of operations, land acquisition and ongoing matters. In litigation, the firm successfully acted for the Central Bank in respect of landmark regulatory actions against its defaulters, barring them from holding future directorships. **Clients:** Bangladesh Bank; Coca-Cola; Unilever (Lever Bangladesh); OPIC; IFC; Caltex Oil Corp.

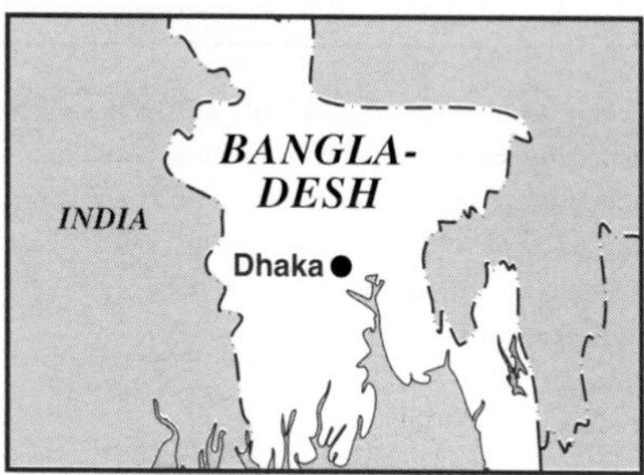

Other Notable Practitioners *"Clever and hard-working"* **Rafique-ul Huq** of Huq & Co attracts critical acclaim for his predominantly local commercial, banking and criminal practice. Notwithstanding his controversial image, the former Attorney General is credited as a *"thorough, dependable advocate who can represent his clients with good skill and ability." "Hands-on and dynamic"* **Rokanuddin Mahmud** of Rokanuddin Mahmud & Associates is *"on his way to the top."* An impressive figure, respected for his high volume commercial and corporate litigation and banking work. Advised Hoechst in its mergers with Rhone Poulenc and Marion Roussel. Projects work include the Khulna Power Project (private power barge.) On panel of advisors to the board of United Commercial Bank (UCBL.) Researchers received widespread recommendation for sole practitioner **Dr Mohammed Zahir**. He is a well known figure in high profile banking litigation, often seen representing the defaulting parties. Appointed to the panel of the ICC Court of Arbitration in Paris, he is described as *"thorough with excellent academic foundations."* A key advisor to the Securities & Exchange Commission, he is currently involved in its share market manipulation prosecutions.

Leaders' profiles – Bangladesh

AHMED, Syed Ishtiaq
Syed Ishtiaq Ahmed & Associates, Dhaka +880 2 9665354

HOSSAIN, Kamal
Dr Kamal Hossain & Associates, Dhaka +880 2 956 0655

HUQ, Rafique-ul
Huq & Co, Dhaka +880 2 955 2196

MAHMUD, Rokanuddin
Rokanuddin Mahmud & Associates, Dhaka +880 2 862 0078

UL-ISLAM, Amir
The Law Associates, Dhaka +880 2 933 0877/3253

ZAHIR, Mohammed
Mohammed Zahir - Sole Practitioner, Dhaka +880 2 911 4850

BARBADOS

Corporate/Commercial

BARBADOS Leading firms (Corporate/Commercial)
1 Chancery Chambers
2 Clarke & Co
Cottle Catford & Co
David King & Co

Firms are listed alphabetically in each band.

Leading individuals (Corporate/Commercial)
1 CARMICHAEL Trevor *Chancery Chambers*
2 CLARKE Gillian *Clarke & Co*
KING David *David King & Co*
NICHOLLS Philip *Cottle Catford & Co*

Individuals are listed alphabetically in each band.

Chancery Chambers (1 ptr, 4 asscs) The country's most respected corporate firm is said to get through *"a huge volume of work."* **Trevor Carmichael** is *"well versed in off-shore work,"* and has a fine reputation as a *"more than capable lawyer."* His team also offers advice on international banking, corporate organisation and private investment.

Clarke & Co (2 ptr, 1 assc) A *"serious, able and traditional firm"* with a respected commercial practice, which advises a series of Canadian and US companies on their investments in Barbados. The Barbados member of Lex Mundi, it boasts the services of **Gillian Clarke**, who has been *"instrumental in the firm's expansion into international work."* **Clients:** International Canadian and US corporates.

Cottle Catford & Co (3 ptrs, 2 asscs) One of the oldest firms in Barbados, generally associated with its high volume conveyancing and mortgages advice. An exception to this tradition is the respected **Philip Nicholls**, who represents a number of major financial companies on international transactions. The firm advised on the refinancing of The Hilton International in Barbados. **Clients:** Barclays; Life of Barbados Ltd; Barbados Mutual Life; Barbados Fire and General Insurance.

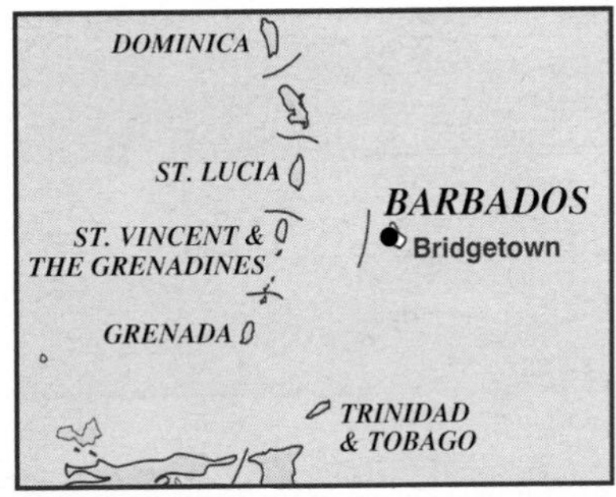

David King & Co (1 ptr, 2 asscs) Widely respected **David King** is the former in-house counsel at the Barbados Central Bank, and was a key player in constructing the legal framework for the country's offshore financial services industry. Respected for litigation, the bulk of the firm's work comes from international financial transactions. **Clients:** International corporates.

Leaders' profiles – Barbados

CARMICHAEL, Trevor A.
Chancery Chambers, Bridgetown +1 246 431 0070

CLARKE, Gillian
Clarke & Co, St Michael +1 246 436 6287

KING, David
David King & Co, Bridgetown +1 246 427 3174

NICHOLLS, Philip
Cottle Catford & Co, Bridgetown +1 246 426 3298

BELARUS

Corporate/Commercial

BELARUS Leading firms (Corporate/Commercial)
1 Borovtsov & Salei
BusinessConsult
Vlasova & Partners
2 Apices Juris
Trust

Firms are listed alphabetically in each band.

Leading individuals (Corporate/Commercial)
1 LAZARENKOV Eugene *Trust*
SYSUEV Timur *BusinessConsult*
VERKHOVODKO Igor *BusinessConsult*
2 ERCH Andrei *Trust*
SALEI Vassili *Borovtsov & Salei*
TONKACHEVA Elena *Vlasova & Partners*
·VASHKEVICH Andrei *Vashkevich Sapego*
VLASOVA Lilia *Vlasova & Partners*

Individuals are listed alphabetically in each band.

Borovtsov & Salei (3 ptrs, 3 asscs) Judged by peers as *"one of the best,"* this strong commercial firm is the *"most focused of all on international companies."* Its broad coverage includes IP, real estate, insurance and banking cases, as well as litigation capabilities. The team advised on the opening of new plants for MAN, and acted for Ford on land and contractual issues surrounding the construction of a plant. Rivals aver that **Vassili Salei*** *"takes a lot of care with his clients."'* **Clients:** Coca-Cola Beverages; Ford Motor Company; McDonald's; MAN; EBRD; Maersk Medical JVC.

BusinessConsult This *"highly professional"* team is said to have expertise in commercial litigation and arbitration matters. **Timur Sysuev*** teaches commercial law at the University and is praised for his courtroom abilities. Likewise, the widely recommended **Igor Verkhovodko*** is *"famous for his successes in court."*

Vlasova & Partners (3 ptrs, 7 asscs) A *"good corporate firm"* recommended as *"representing big clients,"* both international and Belarusian. The team acted on the $1 million acquisition of a hotel in Minsk for a Turkish company and advised Reynolds Tobacco International on its takeover by Japan Tobacco International. Key to the firm's success is **Lilia Vlasova***, admired as a *"good specialist,"* while **Elena Tonkacheva*** is also recommended. Active in construction, trade and hotel matters, the firm has opened a branch in Warsaw. **Clients:** JTL; L'Oreal; UPS.

Apices Juris (10 lawyers) A *"rather young team"* focused on commercial matters pertaining to Russia, Belarus and the Ukraine. Telecommunications is the backbone of the practice and the *"aggressive"* team is known to *"get good results."*

Clients: Philip Morris; Cosmos TV; BelCel; textile companies.

Trust (10 lawyers) Headed by the *"perfect lawyer"* **Eugene Lazarenkov***, the firm undertakes a range of commercial and arbitration matters. The team has seen a growth in new, smaller clients often attracted by *"good banking lawyer"* **Andrei Erch***. **Clients:** Philips; Moulinex; British American Tobacco; International Paper; Metromedia International; Teledezik; Itera.

Other Notable Practitioner Recommended for a *"detailed approach"* and his *"deep knowledge,"* former Trust lawyer **Andrei Vashkevich*** has established the Group Codex Partnership, focused on developing links with Germany.

*See leaders' profiles on pages 115

Leaders' profiles – Belarus

ERCH, Andrei N.
Trust, Minsk +375 1 7239 4708
pb8603@belsonet.net
Specialisation: Main areas of work are Corporation and Business Law (creation of companies, mergers and supervising trading operations). Participated in the sell-off by Ford Union of its subsidiary company Ford in Belarus and in the creation of a subsidiary of the company CENTRA S.A. Was consultant to Colgate-Palmolive and Moulinex and to IRIDIUM during the creation of the network in Belarus.
Prof. Memberships: City of Minsk Law Society. American Bar Association.
Publications: Commentaries to the Civil Code of Belarus.
Career: Qualified in 1994. Joined *Trust* in 1996, becoming a partner in 1998. Arbiter of the International Arbitration Court of the ICC 1999-2000.
Personal: Born February 13 1972. Attended Belarus University 1989-1994, post-graduate course at Belarus University 1994-1997. Leisure interests include swimming. Lives in Minsk, Belarus.

LAZARENKOV, Eugene V.
Trust, Minsk +375 172 101 750
trust@belsonet.net
Specialisation: Main areas of work are Corporation and Business Law (creation of companies, mergers and supervising trading operations). From 1993 - Philips country consultant, legal consultant of companies Metromedia IT, International Paper, The Church of Jesus Christ of Latter-Day Saints.
Prof. Memberships: City of Minsk Law Society; American Bar Association.
Publications: Author of the commentaries to the Civil Code of Belarus.
Career: Qualified in 1990. Joined *TRUST* in 1992, becoming Partner in 1992; an Arbiter of the International Arbitration Court of the ICC.
Personal: Born December 24, 1965. Attended State Belarus University 1983-1990, post-graduate course of European Humanitarian University, 1998-2000. Teaches Antimonopoly Law in European Humanitarian University. Leisure interests include tennis. Lives in Minsk, Belarus.

SALEI, Vassili
Borovtsov & Salei, Minsk +375 17 239 44 18

SYSUEV, Timur
Businessconsult, Minsk +375 1 7229 1633

TONKACHEVA, Elena
Vlasova & Partners, Minsk +375 17 211 8142

VASHKEVICH, Andrei
Vashkevich Sapego & Kaznacheev, Minsk +375 1 7222 4433
codex@infonet.by
Specialisation: Corporate, tax, merchant law. Main area of work is conducting legal consultations on corporation activities, especially on the problems of privatisation, reorganisation and analysing of the abovementioned matters from the point of view of tax legislation. Besides, advising in the fields of accounting legislation and realty. Acted on a stock capital and privatisation project development of Belarusian state enterprise Beltransgas with the investments of Russian company Gasprom. At present gives consultations to a number of investment projects concerned with free economic zones in Belarus.
Prof. Memberships: A Member of the Belarusian Association of Lawyers in the Sphere of Economics.
Publications: Contributor to a specialised collection of articles in judiciary under the title of 'Law in the Sphere of Economics'. Having been published since 1998 it is still recognised and supported by Supreme Economic Court of the Republic of Belarus.
Career: Qualified in 1992. Licensed in 1997 on rendering legal aid. In 1997 founded Group Codex Partnership (a new name *Vashkevich Sapego & Kaznacheev*). A Member of the Public Council of Lawyers under the supervision of Ministry of Justice of the Republic of Belarus, a Member of the Board of Directors of the Belarusian Association of Lawyers in the Sphere of Economics.
Personal: Born 1 August 1968. Attended Belarusian State University 1985-1992 (Jurisprudence). Married.

VERKHOVODKO, Igor
Businessconsult, Minsk +375 1 7229 1633

VLASOVA, Lilia
Vlasova & Partners, Minsk +375 17 211 8142

B

BELGIUM

Index

The clients' choice

BUSINESS LAWYER OF THE YEAR
XAVIER DIEUX, *Dieux Geens Cornelis*

BUSINESS LAW FIRM OF THE YEAR
DE BANDT, VAN HECKE, LAGAE & LOESCH

*Intellectual heavyweight **Xavier Dieux** wins in Belgium some way ahead of his contemporaries. His comparatively small niche practice **Dieux Geens Cornelis** finished third in the law firm award.*

For details see page 36.

OVERVIEW: The Anglo-Saxon onslaught continues. Allen & Overy's merger with Loeff Claeys Verbeke is set to create a Benelux powerhouse, adding the former's international brand name to the latter's formidable corporate clientele. Linklaters is cementing its link up with corporate leaders De Bandt, while Freshfields continues to strengthen its financial muscle complementing its premier European competition team. Domestically minded firms such as Stibbe have faced a battle to retain their best lawyers while niche firms like Dieux Geens Cornelis have prospered. The thriving anti-trust market was dominated by mega-mergers, such as EMI/Time Warner and subsequent AOL/Time Warner alliance. The most notable individual move was that of competition guru Jim Venit from Wilmer Cutler & Pickering to Skadden, Arps, Slate, Meagher & Flom.

Arbitration (International)

BELGIUM Leading individuals (Arbitration (International))	
1	**FAURÈS André** *Coudert Brothers*
	HANOTIAU Bernard *Derks Star Busmann Hanotiau*
	SIMONT Lucien *Stibbe*
	VAN HOUTTE Hans *Sole Practitioner*

Individuals are listed alphabetically in each band.

Belgium is home to a clutch of acclaimed international arbitrators. Leading light **André Faurès*** of Coudert Brothers Coppens van Ommeslaghe & Faurès, is described as a *"specialist with vast experience and a lot of common sense."* He is often appointed in important international cases as arbitrator, chairman, expert or counsel. **Bernard Hanotiau*** of CMS Derks Star Busman Hanotiau enjoys *"great repute"* as a legal writer on arbitration and is *"always present on the international scene."* His time is spent counselling and arbitrating in Europe, America and the Middle East, on, amongst others, construction projects, telecommunications and aviation. **Hans van Houtte***, a sole practitioner, is warmly recommended for his depth of experience. He acts mostly as Chairman, and has recently handled arbitrations in North Africa and Eastern Europe. *"Strong practitioner,"* **Lucien Simont*** of Stibbe was commended for his mixed practice comprising arbitration, financial law and appeals before the Supreme Court.

Banking & Finance

Clifford Chance Pünder (1 ptr, 4 asscs) Chambers research reveals a practice that is universally commended for its ability across the financial spectrum, and which acts for a number of leading international investment banks. Core areas of specialisation are securitisation, funds, banking regulation, acquisition and asset/aircraft finance, with a fee earner generally devoted to each. At the top of the tree sits *"obvious player"* and *"hugely impressive"* **Yves Herinckx*** who is, say clients and rivals, *"on everyone's leading list."* A lawyer who *"speaks with authority,"* he *"presents in a measured but humorous manner."* He is credited with building a good team, pulling in attractive work from elsewhere in the Clifford Chance empire (often London) and for generating a high caseload himself. His niche expertise in securitisation and debt capital markets are acknowledged by the market. Big-ticket property financing is an increasingly prominent feature of the practice. The team acted for Credit Suisse First Boston in the financing of the acquisition by Cofinimmo, a listed Belgian property fund, of the Primaedis portfolio of office properties. In the aviation sector, the practice continues to act for a number of airlines, including the national flag carrier, Sabena. Acted for ABN AMRO in numerous

BELGIUM
Leading firms (Banking & Finance)

Band	Firm
1	Clifford Chance Pünder
	De Bandt, van Hecke, Lagae & Loesch
	Freshfields Bruckhaus Deringer
2	Allen & Overy
	Baker & McKenzie
	Liedekerke Wolters Waelbroeck Kirkpatrick & Cerfontaine
	Stibbe

Firms are listed alphabetically in each band.

Leading individuals (Banking & Finance)

Band	Individual
1	**HERINCKX Yves** *Clifford Chance Pünder*
	PEETERS Ivan *Freshfields Bruckhaus*
	SUNT Chris *De Bandt*
	VAN DER HAEGEN Marc *Liedekerke Wolters*
2	**BIENENSTOCK Peter** *Allen & Overy*
	BRUYNEEL André *Stibbe*
	FORIERS Paul Alain *Stibbe*
	HAELTERMAN Axel *Freshfields Bruckhaus*
	LECHIEN Dominique *Baker & McKenzie*
	MAES Ignace *Baker & McKenzie*
	NELISSEN GRADE Jean-Marie *De Bandt*

Individuals are listed alphabetically in each band.

securitisations of international pools of trade receivables. **Clients:** Salomon Smith Barney; Lehman Brothers; ABN AMRO; Sabena; Dexia.

De Bandt, van Hecke, Lagae & Loesch (9 ptrs, 22 asscs - corporate, banking and finance combined) Research suggests the practice *"continues to play a lively role"* and is *"definitely top tier."* This established corporate heavyweight has a fused corporate finance and banking structure, whose fluidity allows the full weight of its practice resources to be deployed on international financings. Pure banking, capital markets, securitisation and asset finance are other notable areas of expertise. The firm continues to act for a portfolio of domestic banks on syndicated loans and project financings, increasingly in cross-border deals.

Peers believe **Chris Sunt*** is *"great for finance work – the number one."* His input into transactions is frequently praised, as is his structured finance, capital markets and securitisation expertise. Felt to be *"stoical and low-key,"* he is however, *"a damn good lawyer."* In the more traditional mould, **Jean-Marie Nelissen Grade*** leans towards corporate finance transactions and equity securities/IPO work. He is considered *"shrewd and intelligent"* in his capacity as advisor to a number of domestic banks. Now primarily a corporate lawyer and litigator, his experience has seen him act on a number of banking merger cases and consolidations, and more recently on asset and portfolio management matters. The firm played a leading role on the IPO of Interbrew, one of the largest offerings in Belgium. Also handled a minority participation and revolving credit agreement for the Belgian subsidiary of the American Shurgard Group. **Clients:** Interbrew; Agfa-Gevaert; Shurgard Group; Cobepa; KBC Group.

Freshfields Bruckhaus Deringer (3 ptrs, 5 asscs) Our researchers found the firm continuing to power ahead in the financial sectors, its efforts in Brussels eclipsing those of its more traditional corporate team. A vast range of international expertise embraces capital markets, securitisation, asset and project finance. The team boasts a core team of highly regarded lawyers. Regarded by interviewees as *"extremely able technically,"* **Ivan Peeters'*** securitisation and capital markets practice regularly gains plaudits. He was joined in April 2000 by former head of tax at Loeff Claeys Verbeke, **Axel Haelterman***, who is considered to have substantially boosted the unit. In securitisation matters, the practice acted for Dexia and Deutsche Bank in respect of a proposed securitisation of Belgian residential mortgage loans. The team also represented EuropeLoan Bank in designing a permanent funding structure for cross-border mortgage origination using securitisation of mortgage loans. Capital markets highlights include acting for Belgacom in its $1 billion EMTN programme and for ENI on its €1 billion commercial paper programme. **Clients:** Lehman Brothers; Citibank; Deutsche Bank; Banque Bruxelles Lambert; CIBC; Dexia; Bank One; Merrill Lynch; De Nationale Investeringsbank; KBC Bank. Clients in the aircraft financing sector include Airbus and Crédit Agricole Indosuez.

Allen & Overy (1 ptr, 9 asscs) The banking and finance arms of Loeff Claeys Verbeke suffered painful recent blows, including the departure of tax and finance partner Axel Haelterman to Freshfields Bruckhaus Deringer. However, the merger with Allen & Overy, and accompanying vast banking firepower should ensure a rosy future. Although the banking practice of the former Loeff was not felt to compare to its top-flight corporate team, **Peter Bienenstock*** remains *"excellent for international transactional finance"* and *"always has both feet on the ground."*

Cross-border structural finance, bank lending, property and acquisition finance are prominent features of the practice, with a particular strength in the capital markets/IPO domain. Helped by its close connections to investment banks and small-medium sized Flemish businesses, the firm has overseen a number of equity buyouts. Acting on behalf of issuers, the practice has been involved in over 50% of all IPOs in Belgium, including Keyware Technologies on the EASDAQ. It acted for Commerzbank in launching several warrant programmes on the Brussels Stock Exchange, for ABN-AMRO/NM Rothschild in conjunction with the Belgian Government and the Belgian Institute for postal services (BIPT) in organising the first Belgian UMTS auction, and for KBC Securities and Crédit Suisse First Boston on the secondary €600 million public offering of GIMV. **Clients:** ABN-AMRO/NM Rothschild; Keyware Technologies; Commerzbank; Ackermans van Haaren; KBC Securities; Crédit Suisse First Boston.

Baker & McKenzie (2 ptrs, 6 asscs) Our researchers found the practice retains a body of support for its advice in specific finance areas, chiefly aircraft financing, property financings, projects and capital markets. Within these fields, the firm is felt to compete well, although it still lacks the stature of its leading competitors. **Dominique Lechien*** (*"a secure commercial lawyer with a fund of knowledge"*) continues to be recognised for his asset and property finance practice, and has advised AXA in the disposal of a Belgian investment property company.

Recommended by leading peers, **Ignace Maes*** is seen as a classical banking lawyer, and has attracted favourable comment for his work on behalf of a number of domestic banks. He recently acted as counsel to the borrower in a BEF12 billion refinancing of a fixed line telecommunication cable network. The firm advises several banks (KBC, Fortis) as underwriters, and acted for one in a €250 million trade receivables securitisation. **Clients:** AXA; Fortis Bank; KBC. IPO/SPOs include Real Software; Bricsnet; VMS.Keytrade; Arinso; Vasco; FLV Fund.

Liedekerke Wolters Waelbroeck, Kirkpatrick & Cerfontaine (3 ptrs, 5 asscs) **Marc van der Haegen*** maintains his unquestioned status as one of the leading practitioners – *"his quality, stability and judgement are first class."* The face of the firm's financial practice, his joint corporate/banking role embraces restructuring, bank regulation, public offerings and privatisations. However, he is best known as lead advisor to Euroclear, the international clearance and settlement system for internationally traded securities. His eminent reputation is felt to have stemmed from this position, which has expanded to include advice to a series of other banks and financial institutions.

A renowned tax capability and a solid string of domestic clients also enable the firm to remain a serious player in the local market. Nevertheless, the lack of a substantial international clientele and the continued absence of an obvious succes-

B

*See leaders' profiles on pages 127-133

sor to van der Haegen are thought by the market to prevent a genuine challenge to the top firms in the sector. **Clients:** Euroclear; domestic banks and financial institutions.

Stibbe (2 ptrs, 6 asscs) Traditional banking and finance practice which continues to be renowned by other lawyers for its *"high level of legal quality"* and *"strength of principle,"* although it is occasionally accused of being slightly old-fashioned and academic in style. The *"eminent"* **André Bruyneel*** and widely-published **Paul Alain Foriers*** are both still regarded as *"big names well respected by the market."* Bruyneel was the first person to publish the Euro-code, a bi-lingual French/Flemish text outlining the legal and financial implications of the Euro. Public take-overs, banking litigation and capital markets work are the most visible strands of a practice that acts for a number of local banks and corporates. The team played a leading role in the EURONEXT merger between the Paris, Amsterdam and Brussels Stock Exchanges. **Clients:** Belgian banks and other European financial institutions.

B

Communications

BELGIUM
Leading firms (Communications)

Band	Firm
1	Jones, Day, Reavis & Pogue
	Squire, Sanders & Dempsey
	Weil, Gotshal & Manges
2	Allen & Overy
	Cleary, Gottlieb, Steen & Hamilton
	Coudert Brothers – Coppens van Ommeslaghe & Faurès
	Freshfields Bruckhaus Deringer
	Olswang
3	Baker & McKenzie
	White & Case
	Wilmer, Cutler & Pickering
4	Bird & Bird
	De Bandt, van Hecke, Lagae & Loesch
	Liedekerke Wolters Waelbroeck Kirkpatrick & Cerfontaine
	Stibbe

Firms are listed alphabetically in each band.

Leading individuals (Communications)

Band	Individual
★	**AMORY Bernard** *Jones, Day*
	CANTOR David *Weil, Gotshal & Manges*
1	**ALEXIADIS Peter** *Squire, Sanders & Dempsey*
	DOLMANS Maurits *Cleary, Gottlieb, Steen*
	GLAS Geert *Allen & Overy*
	METAXAS George *Weil, Gotshal & Manges*
	VAN LIEDEKERKE Dirk *Olswang*
2	**BRANDENBURGER Rachel** *Freshfields Bruckhaus*
	SPINKS Stephen *Coudert Brothers*
3	**DUVERNOY Christian** *Wilmer, Cutler & Pickering*
	GUTERMANN Arne *Baker & McKenzie*
	POWELL Mark *White & Case LLP*
	RAMSEY Thomas *Squire, Sanders & Dempsey*
	STEENBERGEN Jacques *Allen & Overy*
	TOPPING Simon *Bird & Bird*
	VENIT James *Skadden, Arps, Slate, Meagher*
	VERHEYDEN Alexandre *Jones, Day*

Individuals are listed alphabetically in each band.

Jones, Day, Reavis & Pogue (2 ptrs, 10 asscs) Widely revealed by our researchers to be a leader on competition-related telecoms matters, and respected by the European Commission, the firm has expertise in cross-border EU matters, but retains a core Belgian domestic capability and large numbers of native lawyers. *"Five star lawyer"* **Bernard Amory*** has *"been there from day one,"* and is still regarded as the *"master"* by a large number of market interviewees. His regulatory expertise and knowledge of domestic legislation gives him a unique breadth of practice. He is described by peers as a *"trustworthy, dependable"* practitioner, whose understanding of the issues rarely falters. The firm is far from a one-man show. **Alexandre Verheyden*** also receives a clutch of endorsements for his work on behalf of a number of Belgian clients.

With less of an IT focus, the group is primarily renowned for its pure telecoms expertise, typically for new domestic market entrants. Competition issues have been dominated by third party interventions on big-ticket mergers. The firm acted for AT&T and BT in helping to block the MCI/Worldcom/Sprint merger, for BT against Vodafone/Mannesmann, Tele Denmark in the Telia/Telenor case, and for Bouygues Telecom in an EU procedure against the French State. Other work has involved assisting a number of foreign governments, including Mali, in the preparation of new telecommunications laws. **Clients:** BT; AT&T; Tele Denmark; SES (Société Européenne des Satellites); Mobistar; KPN Belgium; Telenet; Versatel; WorldBank; Moroccan government.

Squire, Sanders & Dempsey (3 ptrs, 9 asscs) The practice is becoming a leader in the ultra-competitive anti-trust aspects of the sector, but allies this expertise to the provision of regulatory advice to international telecoms operators. **Peter Alexiadis*** is a familiar and visible figurehead, popular with prominent EU officials. A *"strong character,"* he *"fights hard for his clients."* The team is renowned for its international composition, and US lawyer **Thomas Ramsey*** *("vastly experienced")* is another to gain market commendation.

E-commerce has been a recent growth area for the firm, which has also advised foreign governments such as Hungary, Greece and Cyprus on the redrafting of domestic telecommunications legislation. The team represented MCI Worldcom before the EC on its proposed merger with Sprint. **Clients:** MCI Worldcom; GRAPES; ECCO; Worldcell; major American and European telecoms companies.

Weil, Gotshal & Manges (2 ptrs, 10 asscs) The firm continues to be a top tier choice for telecoms regulatory work. Steeped in the industry, our research pointed to a team who have *"developed a lot of related expertise."* Although not felt to possess comparable anti-trust-related expertise, such is the reputation of the firm's partners that *"you can never discount them."* **David Cantor*** *("a force of nature")* is an *"energetic and brash"* regulatory lawyer, who acts for a raft of major US and European operators. His colleague **George Metaxas*** is commended by rival lawyers as *"calm, impressive and congenial,"* and has carved out a formidable reputation of his own. He is closely associated with his advice on behalf of France Telecom and is an acknowledged expert in the field of mobile licences.

The firm increasingly advises on data protection and internet/e-commerce issues and boasts an international client roster. The firm continues to advise KPN on its bid to acquire BTC, the Bulgarian national phone company, in a $600 million JV with OTE of Greece. Also represented Mobistar in its litigation against Belgacom (the Belgian incumbent) in a dispute regarding leased lines, the first case to make use of new Belgian telecoms dispute procedures. **Clients:** Bell Atlantic; France Telecom; KPN; Mobistar.

Allen & Over (3 ptrs, 17 asscs) The former Loeff Claeys Verbeke team's reputation as a leading light for domestic regulatory and related competition matters is expected to be enhanced by the firm's merger with Allen & Overy.

The department boasts widely respected strength in depth. Originally an IP lawyer, **Geert Glas*** *("bright and committed")* is an esteemed name for his domestic work. His practice, incorporating telecoms, media and IT, marks him down as one of Belgium's leading regulatory practitioners *("he's well versed in the language of telecoms.")* Complementing him is the *"eminent and patrician"* **Jacques Steenbergen***, who boasts years of experience in competition matters affecting the sector. The department has a strong litigation dimension, frequently appearing before the Belgian regulators and courts, and also acts on the telecoms aspects of the firm's corporate transactions. Internet, inter-connection and access issues are particular areas of focus. A recent highlight was the team's selection to advise the Belgian Government, the Belgian Institute for postal services (BIPT) and ABN-AMRO/NM Rothschild in organising the first Belgian UMTS auction for the third generation of mobile licences. The firm has also advised the ISPA (Internet Service Provider Association) and the Belgian authority responsible for administering domain names.

Famed more for its competition prowess, the original Allen & Overy team was renowned for its *"business generation"* power, regularly *"popping up on the big deals."* Major client Sprint has been advised on a variety of matters, including as intervener in the BT/AT&T merger, and on its withdrawal from Global One. The team represented Sun Microsystems on its intervention before the European Commission over Microsoft's acquisition of joint control of Telewest. Also on the competition front, the firm advised a consortium of major telecoms providers in an Article 81 matter relating to the provision of undersea cable repair and maintenance services. **Clients:** Cable & Wireless; Sprint; Dolphin; GTS.; France Telecom; KPN; Sun Microsystems.

Cleary, Gottlieb, Steen & Hamilton (2 ptrs, 5 asscs) Although the telecoms and IT practices act largely as an adjunct to the firm's mighty competition department, Chambers' extensive research views the practice as a *"stalwart department"* with a *"phalanx of skills and legal specialities."* Not felt to be as strong on regulatory matters, the team is nevertheless considered to *"know its stuff."* At the forefront of the department is **Maurits Dolmans***, rated by clients as *"fantastic"*. A superb competition lawyer with profound IT/IP knowledge, even peers praise him as *"an unsung genius who is thorough, serious and gets his nose to the grindstone."*

The firm is recognised for its media and cable TV work which form part of the over-arching communications practice. In the last year, it acted for IBM on the sale of its global network to AT&T. Reflecting an expanding IT and internet capability, it was also involved in the anti-trust aspects of the myaircraft.com case, the first B2B e-commerce market to be approved by the Commission. **Clients:** IBM; Disney; Compaq; Texas Instruments; Telecom Italia; UPC.

Coudert Brothers – Coppens van Ommeslaghe & Faurès (5 ptrs, 6 asscs) Through Chambers' market research, the practice is regarded as a bona fide player *("a good, solid mainstay of the market.")* The firm's recent merger is considered to signal an end to its recent period of tribulation, and a reinforcement of its position as a substantial competition-oriented telecoms entity. Core client AT&T is perhaps the jewel in the crown, and the focus of much of the team's caseload. Despite a succession of partner departures, **Stephen Spinks*** has remained. Felt by interviewees to be a *"definite force,"* he is regularly recommended for his breadth of experience, which has built upon a traditional EU/competition base to include other transactional and regulatory skills. *"In a sense, he is a complete telecoms lawyer."* The firm handles the gamut of telecoms work, including telephone, satellite and cable ventures on behalf of TV channels and e-commerce companies. The team advised a financial investor on the acquisition of a controlling interest in a French cable TV network operator. Also represented a US-based telecommunications manufacturer on the acquisition of a data networking product manufacturer. **Clients:** AT&T; Disney; Intelsat; Canal +.

Freshfields Bruckhaus Deringer (2 ptrs, 6-10 asscs) The expanded communications department has demonstrated its ability through involvement in some of the biggest sector mergers. Lacking the regulatory profile of some of its market rivals, the firm's competition lawyers have *"undoubtedly learnt a lot"* and have raised the department's profile. Featuring prominently is leading competition lawyer **Rachel Brandenburger***, a *"real terrier"* who *"knows the detail and works very hard on it."*

The firm advises a wide spread of major telecoms and media clients, and has recently represented Pearson plc on a number of competition-related matters, including the merger of Pearson Television with CLT-UFA and its acquisition of Dorling Kindersley. It represented EMI on the Phase II European Commission investigation into its proposed joint venture with Time Warner, and acted for Tyco in a number of matters including the EU notifications of a joint venture with Telefónica. **Clients:** EMI; Pearson plc; Tyco; MCI Worldcom.

Olswang (1 ptr, 4 asscs) The small Brussels office of this progressive telecoms, IT and media firm received special attention from interviewees this year. Spanning both the EU competition and regulatory spheres, and possessing Belgian law capability, the team has an embryonic *"boutique-like"* character but has *"certainly become a player."* Ex-Coudert Brothers **Dirk Van Liedekerke*** has *"blossomed since arriving"* and combines a *"deep scholarly legal understanding"* with *"increasingly tough and fine-tuned negotiating skills."* He is most closely associated with a strong domestic practice, in particular his role as principal advisor to incumbent state operator Belgacom. Recent involvement for the firm has centred around internet access pricing issues, while the group has also advised on lease lines, high speed data transmission and interconnection matters. **Clients:** Belgacom; domestic new market entrants; major international operators.

Baker & McKenzie (1 ptr, 1 assc) The small practice exhibits a strong Belgian character and is active in domestic corporate and regulatory matters while simultaneously profiting from the firm's global network of supporting offices. Although our research suggests the practice is not considered to be challenging for top honours, the team is noted for the consistency of its deal-flow. Experienced, **Arne Gutermann*** retains his position as one of *"the better Belgian regulatory lawyers."*

The group has niche strengths in areas such as UMTS licences, wireless loop, mobile telephony and broadband. Advised Telenet and its shareholders on the proposed participation of a new shareholder, and acted for a consortium of companies on its intended bid for a fixed wireless access licence in Belgium. **Clients:** Telenet; BIPT (national regulatory agency); numerous mobile operators and fixed telephone and data communication service providers.

White & Case (4 ptrs, 5 asscs) Research points to an *"active practice on the rise"* which maintains some *"interesting client relationships."* **Mark Powell***, characterised as *"a player who seems to pull in the work,"* is an experienced Brussels competition lawyer with a high level of telecoms expertise. The teams caseload centres around advice to leading foreign telecoms companies on merger regulation matters, with the added ability to handle pan-European regulatory matters. In the latter field, the firm advised Finnish operator Sonera on the EU law aspects of its privatisation, IPO and subsequent share offer. The team acted for Deutsche Telekom on its acquisition of the UK mobile telephony operator One2One and the Westel companies (Hungarian mobile telecoms

B

*See leaders' profiles on pages 127-133

operator.) Also advised Deutsche on its acquisition of @Entertainment, a company operating in Poland via its subsidiary Polska Telewizja Kablowa, the largest Polish cable network. **Clients:** Deutsche Telekom; UPC; Sonera.

Wilmer, Cutler & Pickering (4 ptrs, 6 asscs handle a mixture of competition and regulatory. 2 ptrs, 3 asscs on specifically communications regulatory matters.) Traditionally regarded for its competition-driven expertise, the practice is equally adept at providing regulatory advice to a clutch of top sector names. Although it has had to weather the loss of star competition lawyer Jim Venit, the firm has retained much of the work for AOL, representing the company before the commission in connection with its merger with Time Warner. A respected regulatory lawyer, **Christian Duvernoy*** again received endorsement for his *"modest but smooth and quietly effective manner."* Praised for his *"cordiality, thoroughness and tenacity,"* his practice includes mobile telephony, access disputes, digital TV, UMTS licences and internet issues. The firm represented German telecoms operator VIAG as a third-party complainant in the Vodafone Airtouch/Mannesmann merger, and for Concert in relation to the AT&T/BT joint venture. On the regulatory side, the team acted for Connect Austria in preparing a strategy to handle the UMTS licensing process. **Clients:** AOL; VIAG; Concert; Connect Austria.

Bird & Bird (7 ptrs, 33 asscs all handle media, IT and telecoms matters) Researchers discovered a *"quality firm!"* This expanding media, communications and IT office is increasingly thought to be making an impact in the premium EU/Competition market. It allies this to a proven track record on regulatory matters, where it offers domestic Belgian law capability. The firm has acquired a number of top media and IT lawyers, and is felt to be poised to add further competition to the market. Well-established in Brussels, **Simon Topping*** is the *"quintessentially English"* practitioner, and is noted for his fused competition and regulatory practice. The practice has niche specialisations in broadcasting and cable networks access issues, as well as wireless local loop and high-speed data issues. The team acts in tandem with its highly-rated London counterpart to service a client base of major European media and telecoms companies. **Clients:** Eurosports; BBC; Canal+; BT Belgium; Broadnet Belgium; Mercury One2One; Concert Communications; TF1.

De Bandt, van Hecke, Lagae & Loesch (3 ptrs, 14 asscs) Corporate heavyweight with an extensive roster of domestic corporate clients, although researchers found it was felt to lack the profile of market rivals. An IT/IP department formed in late 1999 hints at an intention to expand the scope of the practice, as it spans the range of internet, e-commerce, media and broadcasting cases. However, major telecoms clients are often seen to be handled by the firm's corporate fee-earners. The firm offers regulatory advice on a range of matters including mobile telephony, UMTS matters and increasing numbers of internet start-ups. Recent activity has included a number of M&A and joint venture arrangements for multi-national telecoms operators, assistance for the granting of a third generation mobile licence, and e-commerce projects in auction sales, industrial platforms and e-banking. **Clients:** Belgian and international telecoms companies; mobile phone operators; broadcasting and cable TV companies; internet start-ups.

Liedekerke Wolters Waelbroeck Kirkpatrick & Cerfontaine (3 ptrs, 3 asscs) Like other leading corporate and competition-led firms, the department oversees a consistent supply of EC and regulatory activity for telecoms clients. Specific regulatory expertise is not yet felt to match its abilities in other areas. A trio of competition and corporate partners recently represented the European satellite organisation Eutelsat before the commission, in respect of its ongoing privatisation process. The firm also advised French company 9Telecom (a subsidiary of Olivetti/Telecom Italia) against France Telecom in a case before the French Competition Council involving a local loop and high speed internet access matter. Recently notified the European Commission Merger Task Force on a joint venture between Telenor Media and VIAG Interkom, which was cleared after a first-phase investigation. **Clients:** Eutelsat; 9Telecom; Newbridge Networks Corporation; Deutsche Telekom; Global Crossing; Mobistar.

Stibbe The practice remains a player, but the loss of competition lawyer Onno Brouwer to Freshfields in Amsterdam and Marco Bronckers' role as more of an EC and trade generalist leaves the team short of big-hitters. It does work in close tandem with its Dutch and French offices, and offers competition and regulatory advice to both incumbents and challengers on sizeable pan-European cases. A highlight involved advice on competition issues consequent from France Telecom's acquisition of Orange. **Clients:** France Telecom; Libertel; Vertel.

Other Notable Practitioner **Jim Venit*** left Wilmer, Cutler & Pickering to join Skadden, Arps, Slate, Meagher & Flom. *"Top of the heap"* for his competition expertise, he has directed this advice to major communications clients such as AOL and Ericsson. A *"sharp-minded lethal practitioner,"* he lacks the regulatory breadth to be judged a complete all-rounder, but is expected to maintain a degree of sector involvement at his new firm.

Competition/Anti-trust

Cleary, Gottlieb, Steen & Hamilton (7 ptrs, 25 asscs) According to the findings of our research, the practice has become the *"stable giant"* of the Brussels competition market. Long-established and with *"rock solid"* links to Belgian corporate clients, this has become a *"hybrid quasi-Belgian firm,"* which exploits a first-class reputation in the US and Europe. The team is considered to have successfully ridden the recent wave of M&A activity, and has matured into a cohesive, tight-knit unit, if sometimes felt by observers to be *"a touch on the robust side."*

The departure of Mario Siragusa to head the firm's Rome office has had no discernible effect in Brussels. A team with depth includes universally rated young British partner **Nick Levy***, regarded by economists and clients as a *"bright guy with a real future." "Urbane and charming,"* he is said to be *"driven and technically brilliant,"* and handles merger control cases with *"great facility."* He, like the rest of the team, is felt to possess a high standard of economic, as well as legal, literacy. **Romano Subiotto*** also continues to be recommended. His caseload primarily comprises pharmaceuticals, sports and transport sector work. Commuting between the Paris and Brussels offices, *"charismatic"* **Antoine Winckler*** is

BELGIUM
Leading firms (Competition/Anti-trust)

Band	Firm
1	Cleary, Gottlieb, Steen & Hamilton
	Freshfields Bruckhaus Deringer
2	Linklaters & Alliance
3	Allen & Overy
	Lovells
	Skadden, Arps, Slate, Meagher & Flom
	Slaughter and May
	Wilmer, Cutler & Pickering
4	Ashurst Morris Crisp
	Clifford Chance Pünder
	Herbert Smith
	Liedekerke Siméon Wessing Houthoff
	Norton Rose
	Van Bael & Bellis
	White & Case
5	Coudert Brothers – Coppens van Ommeslaghe & Faurès
	Hengeler Mueller Weitzel Wirtz
	Stanbrook & Hooper

Firms are listed alphabetically in each band.

"pleasant to work with," and is known for his merger control work. **Maurits Dolmans*** continues to win support for his mixed anti-trust and IT/telecoms practice. He is *"decent, honest and forthcoming"* and has *"great technical knowledge of the IT and computer market."*

Beyond merger control issues, the team has seen increased anti-cartel, article 82 and B2B internet matters. Notable merger control cases from the last year include acting for Coca Cola in its acquisition of brands from Cadbury Schweppes. Also represented Lagardère SCA and Aérospatiale-Matra on its merger with Daimler-Chrysler AG and Casa to form EADS, the third largest aerospace defence company in the world. Other matters include advising Group Danone in connection with a beer cartel investigation, and acting in Volvo's acquisition of the truck business of Renault. **Clients:** DuPont; British Airways; Exxon Mobil; Goodyear; Coca-Cola; Group Danone; Volvo; Lagardère SCA; Aérospatiale-Matra.

Freshfields Bruckhaus Deringer (9 ptrs, 42 asscs) *"Undoubtedly still on the up."* Freshfields Deringer's merger with German firm Bruckhaus Westrick Heller Löber has created a competition practice with real critical mass, as well as an entry into the premium German corporate market. Merger control work represents the pivotal feature of the new firm's workload, which is divided among an array of respected practitioners.

A *"well-seasoned"* Brussels operator, **John Davies*** is the *"archetypal ambassadorial partner."* He is *"fair, modest and doesn't put people's backs up – not far off being the complete lawyer."* Hard working ex-Deringer German lawyer **Frank Montag*** *("exceptionally good")* is consistently recommended by the market for his competition and trade expertise. *"Popular, straightforward and client-friendly,"* his eminent reputation has lead to him being dubbed *"Germany's most able competition lawyer."* The existing triumvirate of leading partners is completed by **Rachel Brandenburger***, known for her mixed competition and telecoms practice. Experienced in the merger field, she is *"active, organised and frighteningly hard-working."* As a result of the merger, new Bruckhaus recruits include **Cornelis Canenbley***, known for his mobility between Brussels and Düsseldorf. Felt to be the most notable German addition, his *"elaborate and charming manner"* results in a *"winning way with both clients and commission officials."* On the trade side, **Michael Schütte**'s* arrival offers a distinctive boost to that arm of the practice. Hans-Joachim Priess moves in the other direction to assume a permanent role in Germany. Among a vast supply of merger control work, highlights include advice to EMI in its proposed 50-50 joint venture with Time Warner to create Warner EMI Music (Phase II ECMR.) The group also acted for DaimlerChrysler/DASA on its proposed merger with Aérospatiale-Matra and Casa to form EADS. Represented Pepsi in a series of actions against Coca Cola's market practices. Other work includes advice to Westdeutsche Landesbank before the EC in a prominent state aids case, and cartel investigations in the banking, newsprint, steel pipes and vitamins sectors. Advised Eurofer in anti-dumping proceedings concerning imports of hot-rolled coils from nine Eastern European and Asian countries. **Clients:** Degussa-HUls; UPM Kymmene; Mexican government.

Linklaters & Alliance (11 ptrs, 26 asscs) The practice is frequently mentioned by Chambers interviewees in the same breath as the two leading firms, particularly for merger control work, with the Alliance profiting more than most from the recent M&A boom. Seen frequently on deals by competitors, the practice is felt to be edging ahead of most other UK rivals. By common consent, both parties have benefited from the Alliance, with high end domestic corporate firm De Bandt gaining access to previously untapped markets, and the Linklaters brand welcoming a clutch of top-quality European lawyers. Ambitious partner **Alec Burnside*** has, in the view of opposing solicitors, an *"assertive and forceful personality"* and a *"high level of technical ability." "Undoubtedly a talented lawyer,"* he has *"really grown into the job."* Widely commended Belgian lawyer **Gerwin van Gerven*** is *"perfect for Linklaters – he works like an Anglo Saxon lawyer."* He is regarded as *"perhaps the best Belgian lawyer in town."* Practice head **Bernard van de Walle***, prominent in cartel investigations, *"knows what he's talking about"* and *"looks for solutions not problems."* He is *"serious but agreeable to work with – absolutely first class."* Aside from large chunks of merger work (the firm as a whole advised on more than a quarter of all EC merger regulation decisions in first half of 2000), the team is increasingly involved in cartel work and state aids cases, and has a substantial court practice. The firm advised on the GlaxoWellcome/SmithKline Beecham, VodafoneAirTouch/Mannesmann and BPAmoco/Castrol mergers, and represented the complainant in the Formula One case before the European Commission. Also advised on cases such as Deutsche Post v GZS and Citicorp in the European Court. Increasingly involved in internet-related work, representing B2B websites on anti-trust matters. **Clients:** Ahold; Allied Domecq; Alcatel; Alpharma; Anglo American; Bass; BG Group; BICC; BT; BAT; Billiton; BP Amoco; British Aerospace; CGNU; Centrica; Decaux; Deutsche Post; DHL; Dow Chemical; Enron; Europay International; Hewlett Packard; Interbrew; IPC; KLM; Lattice; Microsoft; National Power; PSA Peugeot Citroën; Reckitt/Benckiser; Sabena; Scottish & Newcastle; SmithKline Beecham; Suez Lyonnaise des Eaux; VNU; Vodafone.

Allen & Overy (4 ptrs, 17 asscs) Considered a slick and efficient practice which acts for quality clients on high profile cases, although not quite positioned at the level of Brussels' weightier corporate-driven outfits. The completion of a full merger with Loeff Clays Verbeke is set to provide a substantial Belgian domestic corporate dimension to an already impressive array of clients. The practice is able to draw substantial work from the impeccable *"client-getting"* abilities of **Michael Reynolds***, whose connections and individual reputation alone is enough to ensure *"fantastic levels of work."* He is a *"real door opener."* Not felt to *"get into the trenches that much"* (his commitments include active involvement at the IBA), his vast experience and expertise are nevertheless universally praised. He tends to act on the weightier behavioural cases, notably on telecoms matters. *"Perennially hard-working"* **David Harrison*** is routinely applauded for his involvement on large merger transactions. New recruit **Tom Ottervanger*** arrived from Loeff Claeys Verbeke in January 2000, and his presence is said to represent a *"real bonus"* for the unit. He has acknowledged expertise in state aids work, and has appeared numerous times before the Euro-

B

*See leaders' profiles on pages 127-133

B

BELGIUM Leading individuals (Competition/Anti-trust)	
1 **COLLINS Philip** *Lovells*	**DAVIES John** *Freshfields Bruckhaus Deringer*
FORRESTER Ian *White & Case*	**LEVY Nicholas** *Cleary, Gottlieb, Steen & Hamilton*
MONTAG Frank *Freshfields Bruckhaus Deringer*	**REYNOLDS Michael** *Allen & Overy*
VENIT James *Skadden, Arps, Slate, Meagher*	
2 **BOYCE John** *Slaughter and May*	**BRANDENBURGER Rachel** *Freshfields Bruckhaus*
BURNSIDE Alec *Linklaters & Alliance*	**CANENBLEY Cornelis** *Freshfields Bruckhaus*
SOAMES Trevor *Norton Rose*	**SUBIOTTO Romano** *Cleary, Gottlieb, Steen*
VAN GERVEN Gerwin *Linklaters & Alliance*	**WINCKLER Antoine** *Cleary, Gottlieb, Steen*
3 **BROMFIELD Nick** *Lovells*	**HARRISON David** *Allen & Overy*
HUSER Henry *Skadden, Arps, Slate, Meagher*	**KINSELLA Stephen** *Herbert Smith*
RATLIFF John *Wilmer, Cutler & Pickering*	**SIBREE William** *Slaughter and May*
VAN BAEL Ivo *Van Bael & Bellis*	**VAN DE WALLE Bernard** *Linklaters & Alliance*
WAELBROECK Denis *Liedekerke Siméon*	
4 **BAXTER Simon** *Clifford Chance Pünder*	**BELLIS Jean-François** *Van Bael & Bellis*
BURRICHTER Jochen *Hengeler Mueller Weitzel*	**CELLI Riccardo** *Norton Rose*
CLOUGH Mark *Ashurst Morris Crisp*	**DOLMANS Maurits** *Cleary, Gottlieb, Steen*
ELLISON Julian *Ashurst Morris Crisp*	**NORALL Christopher** *Morrison & Foerster*
OTTERVANGER Tom *Allen & Overy*	**SCHÜTTE Michael** *Freshfields Bruckhaus*
SPINKS Stephen *Coudert Brothers*	**STANBROOK Clive** *Stanbrook & Hooper*
STEENBERGEN Jacques *Allen & Overy*	**VANDENCASTEELE Alexandre** *Liedekerke Siméon*
Up-and-coming individuals	
ART Jean-Yves *Coudert Brothers*	**McQUAIL Tom** *Lovells*
MUELLER Thomas *Wilmer, Cutler & Pickering*	**VAN KERCKHOVE Marleen** *Clifford Chance Pünder*

Individuals are listed alphabetically in each band.

pean courts on cartel matters. Also from Loeff, **Jacques Steenbergen***, a professor at the University of Leuven, is *"extremely good on his feet, a great talker."* The team handles merger control cases and joint ventures, cartel work, telecoms and other EC law and regulatory issues. Major merger activity includes advice to General Electric on the acquisition of Alstom's heavy duty gas turbines business. In conjunction with the Italian and London offices, advised Finmeccanica on its proposed joint venture with Westland Helicopters, and also acted for Singapore Airlines on its acquisition of a 49% interest in Virgin Atlantic. Represented Sun Microsystems over its complaint to the Commission against Microsoft for alleged abuses of a dominant position in relation to the world group server markets. The former Loeff team advised the Belgian Government, the Belgian Institute for postal services (BIPT) and ABN-AMRO/NM Rothschild in organising the first Belgian UMTS auction. **Clients:** Borden Chemical; Crompton; Cable & Wireless; Chevron; Coca-Cola; Delta Airlines; EVC; France Telecom; General Electric Company; GE Capital; Global One; Halliburton; Heineken; Inco; KPN; Lonmin; Rexam; RMC; Santa Cruz Operation; Sega; Shiseido; Singapore Airlines; Sprint; Sun Microsystems; Time Warner; Toshiba; 3Com; Micron; Honeywell.

Lovells (4 ptrs, 12 asscs) The practice has long enjoyed a healthy reputation in Brussels for its stand-alone expertise, notably on behavioural issues. Research by Chambers has discovered that it continues to occupy a leading position for cartel work *("great on the adversarial cases,")* but has been eclipsed in mainstream merger control work by firms with greater corporate punch. **Philip Collins*** continues to enjoy peer approval, and is characterised as *"capable, co-operative, easy to work with."* Brussels managing partner **Nick Bromfield*** combines pure competition with trade work, and retains his share of market support. Made up in 1999, new partner **Tom McQuail*** was acknowledged this year by market commentators as a rising name to watch. He has been active in a series of cartel and whistle-blowing cases.

Major transactional work has seen Lovells acting for Telia, the Swedish telephone operator in the ECMR merger clearance process of its abortive merger with Telenor from Norway. Also acted for ALSTOM to secure ECMR clearance for its sale of its heavy duty gas turbine business to General Electric. In the contentious sphere, represented the liner shipping industry in multiple proceedings before the European Court relating to agreements which govern maritime container traffic between Europe and North America. Continues to represent Mars on competition issues and proceedings regarding access to ice cream markets. **Clients:** British Steel; Cho Yang (Korean shipping line.)

Skadden, Arps, Slate, Meagher & Flom (3 ptrs, 15 asscs) The cross-town move of *"star performer"* **Jim Venit*** from Wilmer Cutler & Pickering was the year's most significant lateral hire in Brussels. Well-known to the firm's New York-based eminence grise Barry Hawk (who is still a frequent visitor to Brussels) and an expert on merger control cases, Venit's arrival is considered *"a real catch for Skaddens."*

Boasting high levels of profitability and a premium US corporate client base, the practice has taken advantage of the unprecedented wave of recent cross-border mergers. The firm is now viewed by many as the next most credible US presence in Brussels after Cleary Gottlieb. Venit himself is considered one of Brussels' elite competition lawyers: *"He's hard-working and has tremendous intellectual capacity."* Although occasionally *"demanding to work with,"* he has that *"certain something – real stand-out qualities."* The practice is also boosted by the continued industry of *"thoroughly reliable merger man"* **Henry Huser***, who completes a *"formidable team of ferocious personalities."* The vast majority of the team's case-load is merger-related, and the client roster includes both US and European clients. The team represented AOL in the Time Warner deal, Warner Lambert against Pfizer, Mannesmann against Vodafone, US Air against UAL and Covisint in a B2B joint venture of automotive equipment manufacturers. **Clients:** Anheuser-Busch; Bechtel; Ford; NTL.

Slaughter and May (2 ptrs, 5 asscs) Chambers researchers have revealed the practice has become a byword for transactional quality, despite a comparatively small Brussels office. Seen to act in close harmony with the formidable London operation, the team also benefits from the firm's 'best friends' arrangement with German powerhouse Hengeler Mueller Weitzel Wirtz. Merger control work is widely acknowledged to be first-rate.

From both clients and peers, *"top player"* **John Boyce*** is *"congenial, intelligent and wonderful to work with."* His *"measured and cautious approach"* complements *"likeable"* **William Sibree**'s* *"more theatrical style."* Both partners *"will always do a good job."* Acted for BOC on its joint acquisition by Air Liquide and Air Products, and advised on the creation of a joint venture by Reuters and Equant to provide extranet services to major financial businesses. Other major merger control cases include the merger of British Steel and Koninklijke Hoogovens to form Corus, Norwich Union and CGU to form CGNU and a public offer by Lafarge for Blue Circle. **Clients:** SAS; BOC; Corus ; Unilever; Gillette.

Wilmer, Cutler & Pickering (5 ptrs, 20 asscs) The loss of esteemed practitioner Jim Venit to fellow US firm Skadden Arps should have stung badly. While it has obviously been a blow, the practice has weathered the storm better than might have been expected. This has much to do with their representation of AOL in its high-profile merger with Time Warner. In addition, a solid corps of *"promising younger lawyers"* and a steady flow of work from the US are felt to have insulated the firm against the setback. The well-regarded **John Ratliff*** *("quiet, but good fun to work with")* becomes the main name in a unit which is expected to temper its formerly robust approach.

Prominent among the new young team is US-trained **Thomas Mueller*** *("really coming through")* who led the AOL deal. Merger work forms half the workload, with the rest comprising cartel defence, article 82 and state aids matters. A string of notable mergers saw the practice acting for Bestfoods in its merger with Unilever, and Volvo as it fused with Scania. Represented one of eight Austrian banks in a cartel case, and acted for ABB (pre-insulated pipes industry) before the Court of First Instance. Transport is an area of notable niche strength, and the team has acted for Deutsche Lufthansa AG in several alliance proceedings. **Clients:** AOL; Allied Signal; RAG; Coca Cola Beverages.

Ashurst Morris Crisp (2 ptrs, 8 asscs) The results of our research indicate the practice has become a permanent fixture on the Brussels scene, albeit lacking the profile of its competitors. An active participant in a clutch of merger cases, the firm is also respected for its expertise in cartel and European court work. Considered by peers, *"extrovert"* and *"barristerial,"* **Mark Clough QC*** is now based in London again, but divides his time evenly between there and Brussels. Rated for his court performances, he is *"flamboyant, flowery and full of humour"* and adds a potent dimension to the contentious aspect of the practice. Recently appeared in cartel hearings connected with the cement and shipping industries. Resident managing partner **Julian Ellison*** is also recommended for his across the board competition experience, embracing merger control, state aids and public procurement.

Notable merger clearances have included Case/New Holland, BellSouth/KPN, Nabisco/United Biscuits and WPD/Hyder. Contentious involvement has spanned the ECJ Cewal abusive pricing case, and representing Cembureau, the trade association at the centre of the cement cartel case. **Clients:** Bell South; P&O; ITW; Mitsubishi; Metso; Cembureau; FGV; Kingdom of Spain.

Clifford Chance Pünder (5 ptrs, 16 asscs) The firm has embarked in recent times on a well-publicised and sustained campaign to raise its game in Brussels. Some observers believe it is finally paying off. Seen increasingly on the other side of transactions, a *"revamped Brussels operation"* has resulted in a more visible profile *("they've come out of the doldrums,")* although it remains some way short of the City's corporate heavyweights.

Simon Baxter* has become increasingly well-known on the local circuit. He has made a *"significant contribution,"* and is active in joint ventures, mergers, distribution systems and licensing. New Belgian partner **Marleen Van Kerckhove*** *("smart and straightforward")* also received commendation. With her, there is *"no game playing. When the chips are down, she doesn't blink."* She acts for clients in the media, telecoms and pharmaceuticals industries.

The firm recently acted for CGU on the Norwich Union merger, for CVC on the acquisition of Acordis (large fibre producer) and for UPC on the acquisition of Greater Rotterdam Cable Network from Eneco. However, it is trade law which is felt to represent the Brussels office's true forte. The team has advised Korean manufacturer Toray Saehan Inc as a defendant exporter in EC anti-dumping proceedings against imports of polyethylene. Also acted for General Electric Lighting Services over imports of electronic fluorescent lamps originating in China. **Clients:** GEC; Shell; Burlington Industries Inc; EMI.

Herbert Smith (2 ptrs, 9 asscs) A succession of chunky cases has lead observers to suggest that the firm *"are definitely on the up."* Acting on behalf of Time Warner in both the €173 billion AOL merger and the now aborted joint venture with EMI was one obvious highlight of a productive year. A relatively small office has given rise to suggestions that the team can seem *"overstretched,"* but expertise is widely acclaimed in a number of areas, notably trade law.

Now becoming a well-known Brussels resident, Chambers' researchers received warm recommendations for **Stephen Kinsella***. A *"bright young man about town,"* he is *"on everyone's list of lawyers to refer work to."* Felt to *"understand the system well,"* his practice is slanted towards the behavioural aspects of competition law such as Article 81 and 82 work and other contentious matters. However, other merger notification activity has arisen in sectors as diverse as steel, publishing, alcoholic drinks, postal services and aircraft parts. **Clients:** Time-Warner; foreign governments; FIA; newspaper groups.

Liedekerke Siméon Wessing Houthoff (15 ptrs, 15 asscs) The EU/Competition arm of Belgian firm Liedekerke Wolters Waelbroeck Kirkpatrick & Cerfontaine has a tough battle to retain its share of the market, but the team is felt to be holding its own. A large group, it has had a busy year competing on merger notifications, anti-dumping and regulatory work, notably in the telecoms sector. The firm is felt to be at its best in proceedings before the European Court, where the impeccably connected **Denis Waelbroeck*** continues to carve out his own reputation. He is considered to have a commanding knowledge of case law, a *"good instinct for what are attractive points"* and a *"style of pleading which suits the European Commission."* The experienced **Alexandre Vandencasteele*** is a name synonymous with high profile cartel and state aids cases. Recent examples include investigations in the cement (representing Belgian company CBR), steel beams and banking sectors. A highlight of the year was a Court of Justice victory on behalf of IECC, a world-wide association of express carriers including TNT, Fedex and UPS. On the merger side, the firm recently notified the purchase by Electrabel of EPON, the largest cross-border merger in the European electricity market to date. **Clients:** Kawasaki Steel Corporation; Newbridge Networks Corporation; De Telegraaf; 9Telecom.

Norton Rose (2 ptrs, 6 asscs) The practice remains a solid mid-tier fixture in Brussels. Responses to Chambers suggest they *"don't seem to grow much, but are always active,"* albeit generally within the confines of certain industry sectors. The office is felt to function with a greater degree of independence from London than a number of its City of London rivals. The leading partners, who have carved out their own realms of interest, are well-known names in their key specialisms. Personified by the enthusiasm of **Trevor Soames***, who is *"great on transport,"* the practice has considerable expertise in the aviation and shipping markets acting for a number of major airlines such as United and British Midland, shipping group Sea-Land and airport operator TBI Group. Soames is said to *"know how to play the game in Brussels"* by leading rival lawyers. A key transport success was the defence of United's transatlantic alliance with Lufthansa and SAS in the face of a commission investigation. The

B

*See leaders' profiles on pages 127-133

practice scored another success in obtaining EC clearance for United's proposed $4.3 billion acquisition of US Airways, the world's largest airline merger.

The other leading name here is the *"promising"* **Riccardo Celli*** who is praised for his work on cartel and state aids investigations. He acts for a number of southern European clients, such as Italian oil company ENI on its takeover of UK firm British Borneo. The firm scored a notable merger success in obtaining clearance for UK tour operator Thomson's takeover by Preussag. In late 2000, the practice assisted the Hellenic Republic in amending a commission decision for state aid to Olympic Airways, in particular the relocation to the new airport at Spata. Advice on public procurement, trade law, and regulatory matters complete a well-balanced picture. **Clients:** EMTV; Primark Corporation; HSBC Bank plc; TXU Europe.

B

Van Bael & Bellis (4 ptrs, 10 asscs) Remains a well-known independent force, despite some market suggestion that their *"glory days are behind them."* With a reputation that *"extends way back,"* the omnipresent **Ivo van Bael*** is a *"tough cookie"* who *"tells people what he thinks."* His *"firebrand methods"* polarise opinion, but he maintains a healthy body of admirers, who consider him to be *"a convincing advocate."* The *"charming"* **Jean-François Bellis***, while not arousing the same level of comment, is seen to be a successful operator *"doing just fine."*

Traditionally renowned for high volume trade and anti-dumping advice, where *"they know as much as anyone,"* recent workload has involved large cartel cases, Article 82 work and merger filing. The firm represented Boeing before the EC's merger task force on its acquisition of the satellite business of Hughes Electronics Corporation. Also acted for Cable & Wireless plc before the UK Competition Commission on its sale to NTL of its UK cable network and its associated pay-TV and telecommunications businesses. Acting in a number of cartel cases such as that for Nippon Steel, challenging a commission decision in the seamless tubes market. **Clients:** Daesang (Korea); Cable & Wireless; Nippon Steel; Boeing Company.

White & Case (7 ptrs, 25 asscs) The practice is large, well-respected and can call upon some fine individual experts, although its acknowledged expertise in trade, litigation, lobbying and anti-dumping is not felt to extend deeply into the merger and transactional sphere. The personification of the practice is still felt by interviewees to be **Ian Forrester QC*** *("outstanding and humorous")* who has been *"canny enough"* to retain the essence of his former boutique practice, while simultaneously exploiting the resources and branding of the White & Case empire. Widely admired, he is *"one of the last of a dying breed – a real EC generalist"* who spans the contentious and non-contentious divide with an *"all-round and superb knowledge"* of competition and trade law.

One of the firm's highest-profile pieces of litigation was on behalf of Pfizer, an appeal to the European Court of First Instance concerning the banning of an antibiotic feedstuff additive. The team advises a number of pharmaceutical companies on the implications of national rules on price controls and their relationship with competition rules. Another sizeable litigation involved DuPont and other European PET film manufacturers, over the granting of EC duty preferences to imports from countries which offer subsidies to their exporters. **Clients:** ABB; Nordik Satellite; UEFA; Lyondell; Mitsubishi; Otto; DuPont; Pfizer.

Coudert Brothers – Coppens Van Ommeslaghe & Faurès (6 ptrs, 11 asscs) The firm have overcome some of its recent difficulties, *("it's a lot calmer now")* and by common consent, the merger with Coppens Van Ommeslaghe & Faurès has helped to raise its domestic corporate capability. The Brussels office is still felt to be a bit overshadowed by Paris, although its profile is increasing with the help of a crop of emerging younger lawyers. Experienced *"main man"* **Stephen Spinks*** is *"quietly effective"* and a *"really level-headed performer."* He is recognised for his combined competition and telecoms/internet-driven practice. **Jean-Yves Art*** was also recommended this year, particularly for his contribution to the merger between client Total Fina and Elf. He *"speaks clearly and gets his points across well."* Although merger control has been the major focus of the last 12 months, article 82 and vertical restraints cases have also been prominent. Several telecoms clients feature on the roster. The practice advised Arianespace, a consortium involved in satellite launch programmes, in challenging Boeing's acquisition of Hughes, both in the US and Europe. It was also involved in the merger filing between two large Finnish paper producers Metsä and Serla. In state aids matters, it advised a German steel company on possible actions against a grant of state aid to a competitor. **Clients:** Arianespace; Total Fina; Canal Plus; Disney; Intelsat.

Hengeler Mueller Weitzel Wirtz Our researchers found the relationship with Slaughter and May is increasingly proving its worth in the market as the Germans apply their corporate expertise to a steady stream of competition work. Some way off being a definitive Brussels competition practice, the team's appearances in Brussels are somewhat sporadic, but *"when they occasionally muscle in,"* interviewees believe them to be a *"wonderfully good firm."* Based primarily in Düsseldorf, **Jochen Burrichter*** is still a regular visitor to Brussels and continues to be positively endorsed by the market. The firm handles the spectrum of anti-trust work, advising on merger control cases, state aids, cartel inquiries and public procurement. The clientele is naturally dominated by large German corporations, banks and financial institutions but also includes some notable international names. **Clients:** Kraft Foods; Philip Morris; RWE; VAW Aluminium.

Stanbrook & Hooper (2 ptrs, 14 asscs) A *"heterogeneous practice"* which has experimented with *"several kinds of imaginative, creative and courageous structures"* to achieve success. With over twenty years to its name in Brussels, this small regulatory firm is easily the longest surviving competition boutique of any stature. *"Irrepressible"* **Clive Stanbrook*** maintains enviable contacts with sizeable European corporate entities, and his lobbying and co-ordination skills are regarded with admiration. *("He's brilliant at getting clients.")* The merger with Cannart Andre-Dumont Erkelens Goethals has refocused the firm more towards the domestic Belgian market but is also expected to boost the firm's already acknowledged trade practice. Merger filings, WTO and cartel work also remain integral features of the caseload. The firm's clientele largely comprises companies with head offices in North and South America, and the Far East. Major second-phase MCR filings of note have included MCI/BT, MCI/WorldCom, Boeing McDonnell Douglas and KPMG/Ernst & Young. It is currently representing Indian exporters of PET film in anti-subsidy proceedings, EC importers of ring-binder mechanisms in an anti-absorption case, and has recently conducted a review of anti-dumping duties on behalf of Hong Kong exporters of leather bags made in China. **Clients:** MCI; Leatherhead (food research); companies in the banking, express packaging, food and telecommunications sector; national governments.

Other Notable Practitioner Former White & Case lawyer **Christopher Norall*** is a *"highly likeable"* practitioner who has joined Morrison & Foerster's Brussels office, and is charged with the task of building an anti-trust practice there.

Corporate/M&A

BELGIUM
Leading firms
(Corporate/Mergers & Acquisitions)

Band	Firm
1	De Bandt, van Hecke, Lagae & Loesch
2	Allen & Overy
	Liedekerke Wolters Waelbroeck Kirkpatrick & Cerfontaine
	Stibbe
3	Baker & McKenzie
	Cleary, Gottlieb, Steen & Hamilton
	Clifford Chance Pünder
	Dieux Geens Cornelis
	Freshfields Bruckhaus Deringer
4	Coudert Brothers – Coppens van Ommeslaghe & Faurès

Firms are listed alphabetically in each band.

Leading individuals
(Corporate/Mergers & Acquisitions)

Band	Individual
1	**BIENENSTOCK Peter** *Allen & Overy*
	MILLER Axel *Clifford Chance Pünder*
	SUNT Chris *De Bandt*
	VAN DER HAEGEN Marc *Liedekerke Wolters*
	VERBEKE Louis *Allen & Overy*
2	**BLUMBERG Jean-Pierre** *De Bandt*
	BRUYNEEL André *Stibbe*
	CORNELIS Ludo *Dieux Geens Cornelis*
	DIEUX Xavier *Dieux Geens Cornelis*
	GEENS Koen *Dieux Geens Cornelis*
	MEYERS Jan *Cleary, Gottlieb, Steen*
	PEETERS Jan *Stibbe*
	VANHAERENTS Koen *Baker & McKenzie*
3	**JORIS Jean-Louis** *Cleary, Gottlieb, Steen*
	LECHIEN Dominique *Baker & McKenzie*
	MEEUS Dirk *Allen & Overy*
	NELISSEN GRADE Jean-Marie *De Bandt*
	NIEUWDORP Roel *De Bandt*
	REDING Jacques *Cleary, Gottlieb, Steen*
	VAN HOOGHTEN Paul *De Bandt*

Individuals are listed alphabetically in each band.

De Bandt van Hecke Lagae & Loesch (Brussels 9 ptrs, 22 asscs; Antwerp 2 ptrs, 12 asscs) Our research concluded the firm is a *"clear leader for corporate work."* Prodigious M&A activity for an array of local and pan-European clients edges the firm ahead of its domestic 'club' rivals to assume a pre-eminent position. Market commentary points to a firm filled with quality practitioners *("ranging from big deal-makers to specialist technicians")* who have exploited the increasingly close co-operation with the Alliance to best advantage. Culturally *"as Belgian as they come,"* the firm's *"increasing use of Anglo-Saxon methods,"* has allowed it to *"retain its Belgian character and flexibility"* within the broader international framework. *"Phlegmatic"* and active, **Chris Sunt*** is primarily regarded by market commentators as a leading finance figure, but his mixed practice, spanning M&A, banking, capital markets and structured finance continues to win him the approval of his peers. Helping to service the industrial north, Antwerp-based corporate partner **Jean-Pierre Blumberg*** is *"really focused on transactions"* and *"a fixture on the national scene."* Head of the company/M&A Group, **Jean-Marie Nelissen Grade*** continues to be recommended. His eclectic practice touches upon traditional M&A in addition to litigation and banking finance. Experienced managing partner **Roel Nieuwdorp*** *("one of the best there")* and younger M&A practitioner **Paul van Hooghten*** *("we always see him around")* complete an imposing phalanx of ranked individuals.

The firm has acted for SAIT RadioHolland on its merger with Stento (Norway) and for IPSO-ILG on its union with Jensen Group (Denmark.) Advised major client Agfa-Gevaert on the sale of its digital printing division to Xeikon, a NASDAQ listed company, and represented Copeba in its take-over by BNP-Paribas. **Clients:** Ford Motor Company (Belgium); Van Hool; GIB; CMB; CERA Holding.

Allen & Overy (7 ptrs, 30 asscs spread across Brussels and Antwerp.) The solidity of Loeff Claeys Verbeke's primary client base of Flanders-based medium-sized enterprises has been greatly reinforced by the merger with Allen & Overy and consequent addition of pan-European corporate and financial muscle.

Client-getter in chief, **Louis Verbeke*** *("a real dynamo")* rarely ventures to the coal-face, but is impeccably well-connected in the Flemish industrial north where he has *"close ties to the economic fibre of the region."* American lawyer **Peter Bienenstock*** *("very much the New Yorker")* fuses his corporate practice with finance and private equity buyout work. A *"pragmatic, no-nonsense dealmaker"* he is frequently involved in the international financing aspects of major cross-border deals and is *"excellent at documentation."* The newer breed of lawyer is epitomised by **Dirk Meeus***, a young partner with an academic style who is *"good at the legal substance."*

Especially active in the IT sector, a major chunk of the firm's caseload has been devoted to equity buyouts where it has acted for large numbers of technology companies on public issuances, start-ups and IPOs. The practice assisted EASDAQ listed Keyware Technologies in their acquisitions including Newton Online Business Solutions, Alacarte Engineering, Riverland Next Generation, Tech Talk and LEX Solutions. It acted for UBS on its partially debt-financed acquisition of Kipling, a retail group, worth – 140 million, for Candover Partners on its acquisition of Diamant Boart, a Belgian industrial group and for Omega Pharma in their recent acquisition of Netherlands based Chefaro International BV from Akzo Nobel, with subsidiaries in eight European jurisdictions. **Clients:** UBS; Candover Partners; Omega Pharma; Borealis; Keyware Technologies; Cera Holding.

Liedekerke Wolters Waelbroeck Kirkpatrick & Cerfontaine (7 ptrs, 15 asscs) As a result of Chambers' research, widely regarded as a leading Belgian figure for both corporate and banking matters, **Marc van der Haegen*** *("the key hope for them")* continues to personify the firm's corporate department. Although he has cemented his own top tier reputation, questions are still raised about the firm's strength in depth. In spite of this, the firm remains a leading corporate name, and exerts a *"solid domestic grip"* on its client base. Van der Haegen is *"well connected with public institutions – a top name."* He is a *"gentlemanly lawyer," "well appreciated by colleagues"* and is *"focused and driven,"* if at times *"slightly inflexible."* The firm has a fine reputation for domestic public–privatisations, take-overs and restructurings, where it *"appears a lot on major transactions,"* notably on behalf of leading Belgian banks. **Clients:** Euroclear; Belgian publicly listed companies; credit and mortgage institutions.

Stibbe (6 ptrs, 19 asscs) Although it has lost some key figures lately, most notably Axel Miller to Clifford Chance and Ludo Cornelis to Dieux Geens, the firm has successfully retained its local reputation for a high standard of legal quality. *"Eminence grise"* **André Bruyneel*** is still a leading name in a full service practice that is structurally broad, fusing corporate, tax, banking and finance practices into one. A leading professorial finance figure, he is also active on the M&A front, having been a key player in a number of major public take-overs in early 2000, as well as some acquisitions in the real estate sector. While *"he is a real authority in public transactions,"* the future is felt to lie with **Jan Peeters*** who embodies the younger generation and *"is a fine manager of a*

*See leaders' profiles on pages 127-133

transaction." He has a split M&A/capital markets practice.

The firm advised on the successful public takeover bid ('OPA') launched by Suez Lyonnaise des Eaux (and Société Générale de Belgique) on the shares of Tractebel – a leading Belgian energy and engineering firm. Also acted in the acquisition by Cofinimmo (Belgian real estate investments company) of a major real estate company of the AXA Royale Belge group, and in the squeeze-out bid by German cement group Heidelberger for the minority shareholders of the Belgian company CBR. **Clients:** A series of Belgian and foreign corporate entities, banks and financial institutions.

Baker & McKenzie (4 ptrs, 15 asscs) Regarded by numerous interviewees as a dependable mid-tier corporate department which *"has really got moving recently."* Flemish lawyer **Koen Vanhaerents*** was singled out by the market as foremost amongst a clutch of younger partners increasingly seen on sizeable corporate transactions. Running a corporate and a securities/IPO practice, he is well known for his work for Telenet, and assisted in the recent sale of a majority stake, as well as in a substantial part of the Flemish cable assets. **Dominique Lechien*** was again recommended as a *"good consistent performer"* although his eclectic general commercial practice touches upon a varied mixture of asset and property financing in addition to M&A work. The firm advised AXA on the disposal of the Belgian property portfolio company Primaedis. **Clients:** AXA; BARCO; Unilever; Telenet.

Cleary, Gottlieb, Steen & Hamilton (4 ptrs, 20 asscs) *"A big player with a lot of M&A strength."* Rated highly by many, the firm is felt to be the best placed to challenge the pre-eminence of the traditional Belgian corporate firms. Complementing its core leading EU/competition practice, a flood of international transactions has allowed the firm to raise its game in pure M&A matters at the *"high end,"* where it increasingly features on big-ticket cross-border deals.

Widely recommended for his input into domestic transactions, **Jan Meyers*** has progressed from understudy to become a *"definite player."* Highly regarded by, and closely connected to the Belgian government, he is retained by them to advise on privatisations. Internationally focused **Jacques Reding*** does not possess such a high profile, but is still consistently mentioned for his involvement in a number of transactions of US origin. **Jean-Louis Joris*** also retains market support for his broader corporate, finance and restructuring practice. Activity in the advertising/media industry has seen the group represent the Interpublic Group on a number of transactions averaging €10 million, and Canal+ on its Belgian joint venture proposals. **Clients:** Owens Corning; TPG; Canal+; Interpublic Group; Belgian government; European Stock Exchanges.

Clifford Chance Pünder (3 ptrs, 14 asscs) By the common consent of our research respondents, *"good buy"* **Axel Miller**'s* increased profile and work-rate have breathed life into a formerly insubstantial practice. Widely commended by peers, he gives them a *"real credibility"* adding a *"great depth in corporate finance knowledge"* with his *"excellent drafting ability."* The upshot is now a practice with more clout – a *"force with experience."* While still lacking the depth of resources to challenge the established leaders, practice expertise in M&A, securities and some litigation has seen involvement on an increasingly big-ticket scale. Acting for Dexia Belgium, the firm advised on the €2.3 billion equity offering on all outstanding shares of Dexia France to form a unified unit. It also represented the Belgian lime and quarrying operator Carmeuse in its acquisition of a string of Eastern European entities including the large Slovakian ceramics group VSZ Keramika. Also represented Calcipar in the sale of Carfide Re, a captive reinsurance company, to Zurich. **Clients:** Dexia Belgium; Artel; CDM; Paribas; Sony Entertainment

Dieux Geens Cornelis : *"For quality alone"* this much-admired small niche corporate finance firm is felt to compete adequately in a market of far larger players. Size obviously limits the practice to small and medium-ticket involvement, but the firm is respected for its advice on M&A, IPOs and other commercial undertakings. Original name partners **Xavier Dieux*** and **Koen Geens*** display *"enormous quality."* They have been recently joined by litigator and corporate expert **Ludo Cornelis*** from Stibbe, an acquisition which has met with widespread approval. Among a raft of surprisingly weighty clients, the practice acted for FICS Group in connection with an acquisition by Security First Technologies, for Eurodisney in connection with a public bond offering in a number of European countries and for Xeikon in connection with the acquisition of the digital printing systems division of Agfa Gevaert. It handles a range of corporate, commercial and litigation matters for state telecoms operator Belgacom, and has a transactional record involving a number of international banks. **Clients:** Clients include Belgian and international banks, venture capital funds, manufacturing, leisure, telecoms and retail companies.

Freshfields Bruckhaus Deringer : (4 ptrs, 22 asscs in the Belgian and international commercial practice; 2 ptrs, 7 asscs in M&A) Our research this year revealed that despite a heavyweight M&A reputation to its name, and an aggressive assault on the European market, some observers noted that the firm's corporate impact in Brussels has been comparatively muted. With Ivan Peeters now concentrating almost exclusively on banking, finance and capital markets advice, the team is felt to lack an individual big-hitter.

The firm's expertise lies in local and cross-border corporate advice, particularly on joint ventures, corporate restructurings and public M&A transactions involving Belgian listed companies. Highlights include advice to Heller International on the sale of its stake in Belgofactors to Fortis Bank, and to Kingfisher in its acquisition of a Belgian market leader in electrical household products. **Clients:** Solvay; Hewlett Packard; Merrill Lynch; Deutsche Bank; Morgan Stanley.

Coudert Brothers – Coppens van Ommeslaghe & Faurès: The merger with local firm Coppens van Ommeslaghe & Faurès has rejuvenated the corporate team, which is now better equipped to handle domestic work in tandem with its acknowledged international and EU expertise. Competitors acknowledge that the firm is *"certainly making inroads."* The practice handles the full gamut of corporate work from public and private take-overs to corporate joint venture agreements and contentious matters such as post-acquisition shareholder disputes. The practice acted for French retailing group Carrefour in its acquisition of a stake in Belgian supermarket chain GB Group. Following its merger with Elf Group, the practice acted for Total Fina in divesting a number of its assets, such as a series of highway petrol stations in France, and also on its proposed merger and joint venture arrangements in the UK and Germany. It also assisted BNP Paribas in a fierce public take-over bid to acquire a 100% stake in Copeba. **Clients:** Carrefour; Total Fina; BNP Paribas.

*See leaders' profiles on pages 127-133

Leaders' profiles – Belgium

ALEXIADIS, Peter
Squire, Sanders & Dempsey LLP, Brussels
+32 2 627 1111
Recommended in Communications

AMORY, Bernard E.
Jones, Day, Reavis & Pogue, Brussels
+32 2 645 1511
bamory@jonesday.com
Recommended in Communications
Specialisation: Practices in the areas of European Union competition law and telecommunications regulations. Has extensive experience in dealing with joint ventures and mergers and acquisitions before the European Commission and abuse of dominant position cases. Represents leading wireline and wireless communications operators and manufacturers in relation to strategic alliances, licence applications, privatisations and a range of regulatory issues. Advises a number of European telecommunications operators before the European Commission. Also represents some EU Governments in relation to the implementation of EU regulations. Also represented a French oil company before the European Commission in a major acquisition and an airline in an attempted merger.
Prof. Memberships: Co-chairman of the Communications Committee of the International Bar Association.
Career: Brussels Partner, admitted in Brussels in 1984. Joined the firm in 1996. Educated at the Law Faculty of Namur, Belgium (BA 1978); University of Louvain, Belgium (Licence en Droit, 1981); University of Exeter , England (LLM,1983).

ART, Jean-Yves
Coudert Brothers - Coppens Van Ommeslaghe & Faurès, Brussels +32 2 542 8888
jart@belgium.coudert.com
Recommended in Competition/Anti-trust
Specialisation: Concentrates on EC Competition Law. Has handled a number of EC merger review filings, including several Phase II cases, in various sectors. Has also represented private companies as well as the European Commission in antitrust litigation before the European Courts.
Publications: Author of the annual review of EC competition law published by the Common Market Law Review from 1994 through 1999.
Career: Partner at *Coudert Brothers* since 1996, residents in Brussels. Professor at the College of Europe, Bruges, since 1999 (EC Merger Control). Legal secretary at the EC Court of Justice form 1989 to 1992.
Personal: Born 4 November 1959. Law degree, University of Liège 1982 (Magna cum laude). LLM Economic Law, University of Liège 1983 (Summa cum laude). Graduate Institute of International Studies, Geneva 1985 (International law, economics and politics).

BAXTER, Simon
Clifford Chance, Brussels +32 2 533 59 11
baxter.simon@cliffordchance.com
Recommended in Competition/Anti-trust
Specialisation: Partner specialising in competition law. Advises at both EU and national levels across a range of industries, particularly in relation to joint ventures, mergers, dstribution systems and licensing.
Career: Qualified 1987; made partner *Clifford Chance* Brussels 1998.
Personal: Studied law at University of Sussex; graduated in 1985. Resides Brussels.

BELLIS, Jean-François
Van Bael & Bellis, Brussels +32 2 647 7350
vbb@vanbaelbellis.com
Recommended in Competition/Anti-trust
Specialisation: Managing partner of *Van Bael & Bellis.* Two main areas of practice are EC competition and EC trade law. Has been involved since the mid 1970s in some of the major EC competition cases to have reached the Court of Justice - United Brands, BP, BMW Belgium, Hugin, Michelin and Akzo. Has an extensive experience in advising clients in complex competition cases including merger clearances, cartels and abuses of dominant positions, as well as EC anti-dumping and anti-subsidy cases.
Prof. Memberships: Member of the Brussels Bar since 1972.
Career: Law, University of Brussels (1972). LLM University of Michigan Law School (1974). Served as Legal Secretary to Lord McKenzie Stuart, Judge of the Court of Justice of the European Communities in 1979-1980. Co-founded *Van Bael & Bellis* in 1986. Has written numerous books and articles in the field of competition and trade law. Teaches EC competition law at the University of Brussels and EC trade law at the University of Liège.

BIENENSTOCK, Peter
Allen & Overy, Brussels +32 2 778 2434
Recommended in Banking & Finance, Corporate/M&A

BLUMBERG, Jean-Pierre
De Bandt, van Hecke, Lagae & Loesch (a member firm of Linklaters & Alliance), Antwerp
+32 3 203 6315
Recommended in Corporate/M&A
Specialisation: Partner in the Antwerp office of *De Bandt, van Hecke, Lagae & Loesch* and a senior member of the Corporate and M&A Practice Group. Specialises in corporate matters, particularly private and public mergers and acquisitions, take-over bids, reorganisations and joint ventures as well as equity offerings (IPO's and secondary transactions).
Prof. Memberships: Member of the Antwerp Bar.
Publications: Published a series of articles on selected topics relating to company law, mergers and acquisitions as well as financial law.
Career: Graduate of the University of Antwerp (1977), Louvain (1980) and Cambridge (1981). Lecturer at the University of Antwerp (UFSIA) in comparative law. Joined *De Bandt, van Hecke, Lagae & Loesch* in 1982 and became a partner in 1990. Member of various editorial boards.
Personal: Born 1957. Married to Anne Mathen, four children.

BOYCE, John
Slaughter and May, Brussels +32 2 737 94 00
john.boyce@slaughterandmay.com
Recommended in Competition/Anti-trust
Specialisation: Specialises in EU and UK Competition law for a broad range of clients. Includes merger control notifications, competition investigations of agreements and practices by the European Commission, the UK Office of Fair Trading and Competition Commission, as well as state aid rules and European Court proceedings.
Career: Qualified 1987 with *Slaughter and May.* Partner in Competition Group. Based in Brussels Office.
Personal: Born 30 July 1961. Educated at the Edinburgh Academy, King's College London (LLB) and Panthéon-Sorbonne, Paris (Maîtrise en Droit).

BRANDENBURGER, Rachel
Freshfields Bruckhaus Deringer, Brussels
+32 2 504 7000
rachel.brandenburger@freshfields.com
Recommended in Communications, Competition/Anti-trust
Specialisation: Specialises in EU and UK competition and regulatory law within the telecoms, media and technology sectors. Has experience of mergers and strategic alliances and privatisations, as well as licensing, interconnection and other regulatory issues in the communications sector. Has led many cases in front of the European Commission and the UK regulators.

BROMFIELD, Nick
Lovells, Brussels +32 2 647 06 60
nick.bromfield@lovells.com
Recommended in Competition/Anti-trust
Specialisation: Partner in the Brussels office, practising principally in the competition law area. Wide experience of notifications under EC Merger Regulation, Reg 17/62 and similar. Representation of a wide range of clients in proceedings before the European Commission, the Court of First Instance and the European Court of Justice.
Prof. Memberships: Law Society. Law Society's European Group.
Career: Educated at King's College School, Wimbledon. Read Jurisprudence at Corpus Christi College, Oxford University (1977-1980). Articled at *Lovells* (1981-1983), qualified in 1983. Resident in Brussels since 1985. Partner since 1989. Currently managing partner of Brussels office of *Lovells.*
Personal: Married with three children. Interests include sports and classic cars.

BRUYNEEL, André
Stibbe, Brussels +32 2 533 52 53
andre.bruyneel@stibbe.be
Recommended in Banking & Finance, Corporate/M&A
Specialisation: Banking and financial law, including arbitration; mergers and acquisitions.
Prof. Memberships: President of the Commission 'Mergers and Acquisitions' of the Union Internationale des Avocats. Formerly treasurer of the Brussels Bar.

B

Publications: About 140 studies, papers and reports, mainly in banking and financial law.
Career: D. Juris (Univ. of Brussels); LLM (Harvard University). Professor University of Brussels (Law School; Solvay Business School).

BURNSIDE, Alec
Linklaters (a member firm of Linklaters & Alliance), Brussels +32 2 505 0211
alec.burnside@linklaters.com
Recommended in Competition/Anti-trust
Specialisation: Partner specialising in EC law, competition law and WTO matters. Substantial experience in both commercial and contentious cases involving anti-trust, merger control, state aid and trade issues. Advises particularly on deal structures and regulatory implications; campaigns for reform of competition law and procedures. Major deals include the BP/Mobil joint venture, Deutsche Post/DHL, Nedlloyd and ASG deals, and mergers between Commercial Union/General Accident, BAe/Marconi, BAT/Rothmans and SmithKline Beecham/Glaxo Wellcome. Foreign member of the Brussels Bar.
Prof. Memberships: Associate of the Institute of Linguists, London (French and German).
Publications: Editor of Sweet & Maxwell's 'In Competition'.

BURRICHTER, Jochen
Hengeler Mueller Weitzel Wirtz, Brussels +32 2 737 1530
jochen.burrichter@hengeler.com
Recommended in Competition/Anti-trust
Specialisation: EU and German competition law, merger control, unfair competition, intellectual property and arbitration. Advises foreign and domestic clients from a variety of industries.
Prof. Memberships: Member of the Board ('Vorstand') of the Studienvereinigung Kartellrecht e. V. (Association for Competition Law Studies); co-founder of the European Competition Lawyers Forum and member of its Committee; Senior Vice chairman of Committee C (Anti-trust) of the Section of Business Law on the International Bar Association.
Publications: Co-author of 'Immenga/Mestmäcker: EC Competition Law'; various publications in the field of competition law.
Career: Joined *Hengeler Mueller Weitzel Wirtz* in 1973; partner since 1977. Resident in the Düsseldorf and Brussels offices.
Personal: Born September 23, 1941. Attended universities of Freiburg and Münster. Qualified 1973.

CANENBLEY, Cornelis
Freshfields Bruckhaus Deringer, Brussels +49 211 49 79 0
cornelis.canenbley@freshfieldsbruckhaus.com
Recommended in Competition/Anti-trust
Specialisation: Partner in the Competition and Trade group.

CANTOR, David
Weil, Gotshal & Manges, Brussels +32 2 543 7460
david.cantor@weil.com
Recommended in Communications
Specialisation: Leading telecommunications lawyer based in Brussels and the partner co-ordinating the international telecommunications practice of *Weil, Gotshal & Manges*. Counsel on telecommunications regulatory affairs to major international companies in the telecommunications and mass media industries. Regularly engaged by new entrants into deregulated European telecommunications markets, both as strategic regulatory adviser and to handle pioneering litigation. Current practice focuses substantially on high-profile telecommunications merger cases before the EU Commission, and also on major telecommunications transactions, including telecommunications privatisations in the emerging markets of Central and Eastern Europe. In the past frequently advised the European Commission on its programme for the progressive liberalisation of European telecommunications markets. Led the outside legal team that counselled the Commission on its strategy for implementing the deregulatory 'big bang' in European basic telecommunications which occurred on January 1, 1998. Also advised the Commission on the development of new licensing regimes for European mobile and satellite communications networks, and on bilateral EU-US telecommunications issues.
Prof. Memberships: California and New Jersey Bars.
Personal: Born 30 December 1948. Education: University of California, Boalt Hall (J., 1980), Institute on International and Comparative Law, University of San Diego School of Law, Paris (Diplome, 1978), Brandeis University (MA 1974), Wesleyan University BA, 1970).

CELLI, Riccardo
Norton Rose, Brussels +32 22 37 6111
cellirx@nortonrose.com
Recommended in Competition/Anti-trust
Specialisation: Managing Partner of the Brussels Office of *Norton Rose*. Specialises in EC, UK and Italian competition law, as well as regulatory and general EU law. Has extensive experience in mergers and acquisitions as well as cartel investigation, anti-competitive behaviour, abuse of monopoly positions, state aids and the public procurement directives. Has particular expertise in advising oil, gas and electricity companies and governmental agencies in the application of competition and regulatory legislation to the energy sector.
Publications: Has contributed to various publications on energy and anti-trust and has spoken at many conferences on this area of law. Author of the chapter titled 'Liberalisation in the Electricity and Gas sectors: regulation and competition' for the book 'Antitrust Between EC Law and National Law' published by Giuffrè and Bruylant; the chapter on 'Energy and natural resources' for the report 'The European Antitrust Review 2000' published by Global Competition Review, and the chapter on 'EC Merger Regulation' for the new edition of Kluwer's 'Corporate Acquisitions & Mergers'. Also co-author of a book on 'Merger Control in the UK and European Union' published by Kluwer.
Career: Qualified 1994 as English solicitor. Qualified 1986 as Avvocato, member of Rome Bar.
Personal: Law degree from the University of Rome (1983). Speaks Italian, English and French.

CLOUGH QC, Mark
Ashurst Morris Crisp, Brussels +32 2 628 1900
mark.clough@ashursts.com
Recommended in Competition/Anti-trust
Specialisation: Solicitor Advocate (partner 1995) specialising in European law, WTO, UK competition law and related sectoral regulation including telecommunications, broadcasting, energy, transport, pharmaceuticals and financial services. Advocacy practice before European and National Courts. Head of WTO Group. Established author (including books on EU competition, mergers and international trade). Member Editorial Board 'International Trade Law and Regulation' (Sweet & Maxwell). Expert ECOSOC, Brussels (telecommunications convergence policy numbering UMTS).
Career: Bar 1978 (Gray's Inn). Solicitor Advocate (All Courts), 1996. Queens Counsel, 1999.

COLLINS, Philip
Lovells, Brussels +32 2 647 06 60
philip.collins@lovells.com
Recommended in Competition/Anti-trust
Specialisation: Head of the Competition and EU Law Practice. EC and UK competition law; advises mainly multinational corporations on business practices, pricing and discount issues, commercial agreements and corporate alliances, joint ventures and transactions; handles complaints, investigations and administrative and judicial proceedings on competition issues. Also advises on other areas of EU law and legal developments affecting businesses including the four freedoms, public procurement and the development of European legislation and its implementation in the Member States.
Prof. Memberships: Competition Law Sub-Committee, City of London Solicitors Company; Anti-trust Section, American Bar Association; Competition Law Committee, International Bar Association.
Career: Qualified *Lovell White & King* in 1973; partner 1978. Following secondment to industry, established the firm's specialist competition group. Based in Brussels since 1993.

CORNELIS, Ludo
Dieux Geens Cornelis, Brussels +32 2 538 68 69
Recommended in Corporate/M&A

DAVIES, John
Freshfields Bruckhaus Deringer, Brussels +32 2 504 7000
john.davies@freshfields.com
Recommended in Competition/Anti-trust
Specialisation: Main areas of practice are competition and regulatory law at both EU and national levels (including the co-ordination of cases before several European competition authorities). Has broad experience across a wide range of industries ñ acting for notifying parties, defendants and complainants. Also has a number of clients in regulated industries, notably in the telecommunications and gas sectors.

DIEUX, Xavier
Dieux Geens Cornelis, Brussels +32 2 538 68 69
Recommended in Corporate/M&A

DOLMANS, Maurits
Cleary, Gottlieb, Steen & Hamilton, Brussels
+32 2 287 20 00
Recommended in Communications, Competition/Anti-trust

DUVERNOY, Christian
Wilmer, Cutler & Pickering, Brussels
+32 2 285 4900
Recommended in Communications

ELLISON, Julian
Ashurst Morris Crisp, Brussels +32 2 626 1900
julian.ellison@ashursts.com
Recommended in Competition/Anti-trust
Specialisation: Specialises in UK and EU competition and regulatory matters (including public procurement and state aid) with a particular emphasis on mergers and anti-competitive practices. Transactions include a number of leading Phase II Merger Regulation enquiries and leading Phase I Merger cases settled with undertakings.
Prof. Memberships: International Bar Association.
Career: Joined *Ashursts* in 1980, qualified in 1982 and has been the resident partner in the firm's Brussels office since 1989.

FAURÈS, André
Coudert Brothers, Brussels +32 2 542 8888
Recommended in Arbitration (International)

FORIERS, Paul Alain
Stibbe, Brussels +32 2 533 5211
Recommended in Banking & Finance

FORRESTER QC, Ian S.
White & Case LLP, Brussels +32 2 219 1620
iforrester@whitecase.com
Recommended in Competition/Anti-trust
Specialisation: One of the world's leading competition law advisers and has been in practice in Brussels since 1972. Advises on matters involving EC competition law, EU trade law, sport and litigation. Has represented governments, leading corporations and the European Commission in cases before the European Courts. Heads the 30-strong Brussels office of International law firm *White & Case.*
Career: Co-founded *Forrester, Norall & Sutton* which merged with *White & Case* in 1998. Visiting professor in European Law at Glasgow University.

GEENS, Koen
Dieux Geens Cornelis, Brussels +32 2 538 68 69
Recommended in Corporate/M&A

GLAS, Geert
Allen & Overy, Brussels +32 2 778 2561
Recommended in Communications

GUTERMANN, Arne
Baker & McKenzie, Brussels +32 2 639 36 11
arne.gutermann@bakernet.com
Recommended in Communications
Specialisation: Partner in Brussels office. Main areas of work include M&A and telecoms, principally telecoms regulatory and licence work and telcoms litigation. Part-time judge in Commercial Courts, Brussels.
Prof. Memberships: American Chamber of Commerce (telecoms); Belgian Telecommunications Users Group.
Career: Qualified 1988. Joined *Baker and McKenzie* in 1988; becoming a partner in 1998. University of Leuven (Licentiate) 1987; University of Virginia (LLM) 1988.
Personal: Speaks Dutch, French, English and German.

HAELTERMAN, Axel
Freshfields Bruckhaus Deringer, Brussels
+32 2 504 7000
axel.haelterman@freshfields.com
Recommended in Banking & Finance
Specialisation: Specialises in corporate tax, bank taxation, taxation of financial instruments, derivatives, stock options and tax transparent entities.

HANOTIAU, Bernard
CMS Derks Star Busmann Hanotiau, Brussels
+32 2 626 2200
Recommended in Arbitration (International)

HARRISON, David
Allen & Overy, Brussels +32 2 739 5000
Recommended in Competition/Anti-trust

HERINCKX, Yves
Clifford Chance, Brussels +32 2 533 59 11
yves.herinckx@cliffordchance.com
Recommended in Banking & Finance
Specialisation: Partner specialising in banking, capital markets, funds and real estate.
Career: Université Libre de Bruxelles (1982); Hitotsubashi University, Tokyo (1984). Admitted Brussels 1984; admitted England and Wales 1992. Partner *Cliffird Chance* Brussels 1992.
Personal: Born 1959; resides Brussels.

HUSER, Henry L.
Skadden, Arps, Slate, Meagher & Flom LLP, Brussels +32 2 639 0300
hhuser@skadden.com
Recommended in Competition/Anti-trust
Specialisation: Partner, Brussels. U.S. and International Anti-trust and European Union Law. Counsels clients on world-wide anti-trust and other regulatory issues arising in mergers, acquisitions and joint ventures between multinational corporations. Has represented clients in numerous reviews by the European Commission of transactions subject to review under the EC Merger Regulation or Articles 81/82 of the EC Treaty including Anheuser-Busch, Citigroup, Deere, EMC, Gucci, Huntsman, NTL, Visteon and Warner-Lambert. Also focuses on European Union competition and related issues arising in non-M&A areas, including cartel investigations, state aids and trade-related matters. Has received several distinctions, including election to The International Who's Who of Competition Lawyers (2d ed.) and being selected by Global Competition Review as one of '45 under 45,' a survey listing the leading competition lawyers under the age of 45. Has participated in a variety of seminars on European Union competition law and is a guest lecturer at the European Pallas Programme on European Business Law for graduate law and business students.
Prof. Memberships: Admitted in District of Columbia and Wisconsin.
Publications: Authored several articles on EU competition law and is co-author of a leading treatise on the EC Merger Regulation.
Career: JD, University of Wisconsin, 1984; BA, 1981. Joined *Skadden, Arps, Slate, Meagher & Flom*, 1986.

JORIS, Jean-Louis
Cleary, Gottlieb, Steen & Hamilton, Brussels
+32 2 287 20 00
Recommended in Corporate/M&A

KINSELLA, Stephen
Herbert Smith, Brussels +32 2 511 7450
stephen.kinsella@herbertsmith.com
Recommended in Competition/Anti-trust
Specialisation: Partner specialising in EC and UK competition law, trade law, intellectual property and media. Provides legal advice to major public and private companies seeking to defend their interests before the European Commission and the European Courts. Was instructed by the European Commission in 1999 defending the Commission in an appeal against its prohibition of a merger between the Finnish retailers Kesko and Tuko. Advised FIA and FOA on agreements relating to Formula One and other professional motor sport, and obtained a public apology from the Commission for leaking documents and making prejudicial statements. Advised BSkyB on its participation in the British Interactive Broadcasting Venture and Time Warner on its proposed mergers with AOL and EMI.
Prof. Memberships: President of British Chamber of Commerce in Belgium; advisory board of the European Law Students' Association; the Society of European Affairs Practitioners; Solicitors' European Group; Cercle Royal Gaulois Artistique et Literaire.
Career: Trinity Hall, Cambridge. Qualified in 1985; partner *Herbert Smith* 1991; head of Brussels office, based since 1989; editor 'Merger Control Reporter' (Kluwer); IBA Committee C (Antitrust and Trade Law) Newsletter; author of a book on EU Technology Licensing, published by Palladian.
Personal: Theatre (past president of Brussels Shakespeare Society), cinema, football, skiing.

LECHIEN, Dominique
Baker & McKenzie, Brussels +32 2 639 36 11
dominique.lechien@bakernet.com
Recommended in Banking & Finance, Corporate/M&A
Specialisation: Partner working in commercial and company matters with an emphasis on M&A, including IPO's. Also working on banking and finance matters. Has handled various acquisitions and disposals of companies and businesses for domestic and international clients. Handled the creation of Belgian joint venture between a major card issuer and a major Belgian bank. Assisted a major US/German institution in their inventory financing business in Belgium. Acting for two Belgian airlines in connection with their fleet leasing. Assisted AXA in their disposal of a Belgian property portfolio company and of a Belgian property investment company.
Prof. Memberships: Member of the Brussels Bar.
Career: Admitted to the Brussels Bar in 1980. Joined *Baker & McKenzie* in 1980, becoming a partner in 1991. Received law degree from the University of Brussels, 1980 also obtaining a special degree in busi-

B

ness law, 1982. Obtained LLM degree from University of Michigan, 1987. Has served as assistant in charge of liens, security interest and mortgage at the Law Faculty, University of Brussels. Research assistant at the Centre for private and economic law, University of Brussels.
Personal: Born 1957. Leisure interests include reading, music and outdoor activities. Two children.

LEVY, Nicholas
Cleary, Gottlieb, Steen & Hamilton, Brussels +32 2 287 20 00
Recommended in Competition/Anti-trust

MAES, Ignace
Baker & McKenzie, Brussels +32 2 639 36 11 ignace.maes@Bakernet.com
Recommended in Banking & Finance
Specialisation: Banking & Finance. Responsible for a large number of financial institutions, including Belgium's most important banks. Recent transactions include negotiation of and advice on: limited recourse facilities for the financing of cable telecommunications network; multiple seller cross-border trade receivables securitisation programme; limited recourse financing of take-over bids on companies listed on Paris and London stock exchanges. Reorganisation of the institutional portfolio management of a major Belgian bank.
Prof. Memberships: Brussels Bar.
Career: Gent Bar, 1969. Associate *Baker & McKenzie*, 1975. Partner, 1980.
Personal: Born 28 April 1946. FUNDP, Namur and KUL, Leuven (Doctor juris) and Northwestern University Chicago (LLM).

McQUAIL, Tom
Lovells, Brussels +32 2 647 06 60 tom.mcquail@lovells.com
Recommended in Competition/Anti-trust
Specialisation: Partner specialising in EU and UK competition law, in particular ECMR filings, investigations by the European Commission and proceedings before the European Courts. Represents clients in a wide range of sectors including telecommunications, paper and packaging, steel, consumer goods and energy.
Prof. Memberships: Member of Law Society.
Career: Articles *Lovells*, qualified 1992, partner 1999.
Personal: Born in Leeds in 1965. Education: European School, Bergen, The Netherlands; Pembroke College, Oxford (1988 Jurisprudence). Languages: English, Dutch and French. Married with two children. Resides Brussels.

MEEUS, Dirk
Allen & Overy, Brussels +32 2 778 24 63
Recommended in Corporate/M&A

METAXAS, George
Weil, Gotshal & Manges, Brussels +32 2 543 7460 george.metaxas@weil.com
Recommended in Communications
Specialisation: Partner in the Brussels office of *Weil, Gotshal & Manges LLP*, specialising in telecommunications regulation and transactions. Advises, on an ongoing basis, fixed and mobile affiliates of major operators on a broad range of telecommunications issues, representing them in private party negotiations, litigation and dealings with the European Commission and national regulators. Extensive experience in interconnection negotiations. Has spearheaded landmark complaints and notifications before the European Commission in cases involving fixed/mobile convergence, abuses of dominant position in the media industry and the antitrust clearance of strategic telecommunications alliances. Has spoken at various telecommunications conferences.
Prof. Memberships: Athens Bar, Brussels Bar (List 'E').
Career: Qualified in 1984. Worked in the European Patent Office (International Legal Affairs) between 1987-1989. Joined *Stanbrook and Hooper*, Brussels in 1987. Moved to *Weil, Gotshal & Manges*, Brussels in 1995, becoming a partner in 1998.
Personal: Married, four children. Fluent in English, German, French, Dutch, Spanish and Greek.

MEYERS, Jan
Cleary, Gottlieb, Steen & Hamilton, Brussels +32 2 287 20 00
Recommended in Corporate/M&A

MILLER, Axel
Clifford Chance, Brussels +32 2 533 59 11 axel.miller@cliffordchance.com
Recommended in Corporate/M&A
Specialisation: Partner specialising in M&A, securities offerings, IPOs, international joint ventures and corporate law.
Career: Qualified 1987; admitted Brussels Bar 1987; joined *Clifford Chance* as a partner in May 1999.
Personal: Born and resides in Brussels. Université Libre de Bruxelles, Magna cum laude, 1987.

MONTAG, Frank
Freshfields Bruckhaus Deringer, Brussels +32 2 504 7000 frank.montag@freshfields.com
Recommended in Competition/Anti-trust
Specialisation: Main areas of practice are EU and German competition law, trade and general EU law, in particular merger control, joint ventures, cartel investigations, state aid, antidumping and general trade law matters and litigation before the European Courts.

MUELLER, Thomas
Wilmer, Cutler & Pickering, Brussels +32 2 285 4900
Recommended in Competition/Anti-trust

NELISSEN GRADE, Jean-Marie
De Bandt, van Hecke, Lagae & Loesch (a member firm of Linklaters & Alliance), Brussels +32 2 501 94 11 jmnelissengrade@debandt.com
Recommended in Banking & Finance, Corporate/M&A
Specialisation: Partner in the Corporate Department of *De Bandt, van Hecke, Lagae & Loesch* (Company Law ñ M&A Group) of *De Bandt, van Hecke, Lagae & Loesch* Brussels office. Admitted to the Brussels Bar in 1969; Supreme Court of Belgium in 1982. Experience in private and public mergers and acquisitions, takeover bids, reorganisations and joint ventures, especially in the area of banking and financial institutions, and equity offerings. Litigation in takeover disputes, especially actions brought by minority shareholders and disputes concerning liability of directors, auditors and banks. Domestic and international arbitration in the fields of company law (joint ventures, post acquisition claims) and financial law.
Prof. Memberships: Interuniversitair centrum voor rechtsvergelijking, Financiewezen nu en morgen (association for the study of financial law).
Career: Studied Law at KU Leuven University (Lic. Jur., 1967), Applied Economics at UCL University (Lic. 1968), Ph.D. Law at KU Leuven (1976). Assistant Professor at KU Leuven University (1969-1976). Part-time lecturer at KU Leuven University (1976-1986). Part-time Professor in Company Law at KU Leuven University (1986 to date). Head of the Bar of the Supreme Court of Belguim (2000 to date). Chairman of the partnership *De Bandt, van Hecke, Lagae & Loesh* (1999 to date). Head of Company law - M&A Practice Group (2000 to date). Editor of 'Tijdschrift voor Handelsrecht/Revue de droit commercial' (section company law). Joined *De Bandt, van Hecke, Lagae & Loesch* in 1976, becoming a partner in 1978.
Personal: Born 28 September 1945.

NIEUWDORP, Roel
De Bandt, van Hecke, Lagae & Loesch (a member firm of Linklaters & Alliance), Brussels +32 2 501 94 11
Recommended in Corporate/M&A

NORALL, Christopher
Morrison & Foerster, Brussels +32 2 347 0400 cnorall@mofo.com
Recommended in Competition/Anti-trust
Specialisation: Partner concentrating on EU law, especially competition and trade issues. In the competition law area, has represented clients seeking EU approval for joint ventures, mergers and acquisitions and distribution and licensing agreements. Has also handled a variety of anti-dumping and anti-subsidy investigations involving exporters from Asia, Eastern Europe and the US. Has particular experience of the WTO, customs law and public procurement rules.
Career: Admitted to New York State Bar in 1970. Practised corporate and commercial law in New York and Brussels offices of a US law firm. Became partner with *White & Case* in 1998 when the specialist law firm he co-founded (*Forrester Norall*) merged with *White & Case*.
Personal: BA History, Cambridge University, 1967; JD, University of Pennsylvania Law School, 1970. Has Italian citizenship.

OTTERVANGER, Tom
Allen & Overy, Brussels +32 2 739 5000
Recommended in Competition/Anti-trust

PEETERS, Ivan
Freshfields Bruckhaus Deringer, Brussels +32 2 504 7000 ivan.peeters@freshfields.com
Recommended in Banking & Finance
Specialisation: Main area of work is banking, finance law and capital markets. Has a broad experience of financial and commercial transactions, including leasing, securitisation, other types of asset financing, defeasance, investment vehicles, mergers &

acquisitions and corporate restructuring, both in a Belgian and an international context.

PEETERS, Jan
Stibbe, Brussels +32 2 533 5211
jan.peeters@stibbe.be
Recommended in Corporate/M&A
Specialisation: Corporate law, mergers and acquisitions and related capital market operations (including initial public offerings, public takeover bids and privitisations). Financial Services Regulations.
Publications: Various publications in the area of corporate law and financial services regulations.
Career: Admitted to the Brussels Bar in 1982 and became a partner in 1996.
Personal: University of Antwerp (Lis. jur. 1986); School of Law Boult Hall University of California in Berkeley (LLM 1987).

POWELL, Mark
White & Case LLP, Brussels +32 2 219 1620
mpowell@whitecase.com
Recommended in Communications
Specialisation: UK-qualified partner based in the Brussels office of *White & Case.* Has a broad-based European trade and competition law practice, with a particular focus on information technology, media and intellectual property. Regularly represents a number of major players in the international communications sector.
Career: Was a partner of *Forrester Norall & Sutton* until its merger with *White & Case* in 1998.
Personal: Speaks fluent English, French and Portuguese.

RAMSEY, Thomas J
Squire, Sanders & Dempsey LLP, Brussels +32 2 627 1111
Recommended in Communications

RATLIFF, John
Wilmer, Cutler & Pickering, Brussels +32 2 285 4900
Recommended in Competition/Anti-trust

REDING, Jacques
Cleary, Gottlieb, Steen & Hamilton, Brussels +32 2 287 20 00
Recommended in Corporate/M&A

REYNOLDS, Michael
Allen & Overy, Brussels +32 2 739 5000
Recommended in Competition/Anti-trust

SCHÜTTE, Michael
Freshfields Bruckhaus Deringer, Brussels +32 2 287 2611
michael.schuette@freshfields.com
Recommended in Competition/Anti-trust
Specialisation: Specialises in banking and finance law, information technology and communications, antitrust/European law and corporate law. Main focus is state guarantees, state aid and international trade, as well as partnership and limited liability law, M&A and privatisations.

SIBREE, William
Slaughter and May, Brussels +32 2 737 94 00
william.sibree@slaughterandmay.com
Recommended in Competition/Anti-trust
Specialisation: All areas of UK and EU Competition Law, both contentious and non-contentious. Cases have involved representing Unilever in the UK monopoly inquiry into ice cream; Cadbury Schweppes in the disposal of its non-US beverages businesses to Coca-Cola; and British Steel in its merger with Hoogovens. Full civil rights of audience.
Prof. Memberships: Law Society.
Career: Queens' College, Cambridge and Inner Temple. Qualifed at the Bar 1984. Pupillage Monckton Chambers. Joined *Slaughter and May* 1986, Partner in 1993.
Personal: Born 1 March 1961. Leisure interests include bridge, painting and skiing.

SIMONT, Lucien
Stibbe, Brussels +32 2 533 5211
Recommended in Arbitration (International)

SOAMES, Trevor
Norton Rose, Brussels +32 22 37 6111
soamest@nortonrose.com
Recommended in Competition/Anti-trust
Specialisation: Main area of practice is all aspects of EC and UK competition, trade and regulatory law. Has substantial experience in handling major merger and joint venture cases under the EC Merger Regulation (most recently representing United Airlines in its merger with US Airways, opposing the hostile takeover of Air Canada by Onex/AirCo and the merger of Sea-Land with Maersk) as well as under Article 81. Has handled a number of important multi-national cartel cases (such as Cement where, together with John Cook , the *Norton Rose* team was successful in quashing the fine imposed on Castle Cement and reducing the fines imposed on other clients). Cases include major recent decisions of the European Commission under Articles 81, 82 and 86 in a number of economic sectors. Has handled a number of high-profile state aid cases before the European Commission and the European Court on behalf of complainants as well as for donor Governments and recipients. Represents and advises a substantial number of major US and EU corporations in a wide variety of economic sectors, on all matters relating to competition law, including Article 81 and 82 investigations as well as the implementation of compliance programmes. Recent clients include: Honeywell, Monsanto, British Midland, United Airlines, the Greek Government, Stena AB, Stena Line AB, Olympic Airways, Sea-Land, CSX, P&O Stena Line, Bombardier and Castle Cement. Is an experienced litigator and proficient advocate, representing clients before the European Commission and European Court, as well as before the UK competition authorities.
Publications: Author of many articles on competition and regulatory law as well as being editor of, or contributor to, a number of books including: 'Corporate Mergers and Acquisitions', 'Air Transport and the European Community: Recent Developments', 'Airline Mergers and Co-operation and State Aids to Airlines'. Also an Associate editor of 'Butterworths Competition Law Encyclopaedia'.
Career: Member of IBA, ABA, EALA, EMLO and others.

SPINKS, Stephen
Coudert Brothers - Coppens Van Ommeslaghe & Faurès, Brussels +32 2 542 8888
spinks@belgium.coudert.com
Recommended in Communications, Competition/Anti-trust
Specialisation: Partner of *Coudert Brothers* - Brussels. Specialises in EC competition, trade and telecommunications law. Has twenty years experience handling competition and merger control filings and advising on proceedings and notifications involving a number of the world's largest multinational companies in a number of major industries. A regular speaker and writer on EC competiton law topics.
Prof. Memberships: New York and Georgia Bars and an associate member of the Brussels Bar. Registered in the UK as a foreign lawyer.

STANBROOK, Clive
Stanbrook & Hooper, Brussels +32 2 230 50 59
stanbrook.hooper@stanbrook.com
Recommended in Competition/Anti-trust
Specialisation: Known for defending and co-ordinating the defence in leading EU cartel cases. Extensive experience in MCR filings. Has been involved in major second-phase MCR filings before the Commission: MCI/BT; MCI/WorldCom, Boeing McDonell Douglas and KPMG/Ernst & Young. Has organised and co-ordinated numerous filings in multiple jurisdictions for mergers below the EU thresholds. Other main areas of international practice: telecommunication sector (Outside EU Regulatory Counsel to MCI 1993 to 1999), experienced practitioner in Trade and Anti-dumping.
Career: Called Bar in London (1972); Turks and Caicos Islands (BWI) (1984); New York (1988). Early career as an advocate in extradition, white collar crime, licensing and EC law. Moved to Brussels and founded *Stanbrook and Hooper* in 1978. Advocacy remains the central theme of work, has appeared in many tribunals, including the European Court, courts in various Member States, the People's Revolutionary Tribunal in Angola, 1975, and the Supreme Court in Malawi (successful defence of Former President), 1995. Awarded OBE January 1988; Queen's Counsel 1989.
Publications: Author of 'Dumping and Subsidies'. 1970; co-author, 'Dumping and Subsidies', 3rd edition 1996; 'Extradition: law and practice', 2nd edition 2000

STEENBERGEN, Jacques
Allen & Overy, Brussels +32 2 778 2508
Recommended in Communications, Competition/Anti-trust

SUBIOTTO, Romano
Cleary, Gottlieb, Steen & Hamilton, Brussels +32 2 287 20 00
Recommended in Competition/Anti-trust

SUNT, Chris
De Bandt, van Hecke, Lagae & Loesch (a member firm of Linklaters & Alliance), Brussels +32 2 501 94 11
csunt@debandt.com
Recommended in Banking & Finance, Corporate/M&A

B

Specialisation: Partner in the Corporate Department (Finance Group) of *De Bandt, van Hecke, Lagae & Loesch*'s Brussels office. Areas of practice include capital markets, corporate finance, M&A and banking. Member of the management teams of the Capital Markets and Banking Practice Groups of *Linklaters & Alliance.*
Prof. Memberships: IBA (International Bar Association-Section on Business Law, Committees E&Q), Vereeniging Handelsrecht (Holland), AEDBF (Association Européenne pour le Droit Bancaire et Financier).
Career: Joined *De Bandt, van Hecke, Lagae & Loesch* as a partner in 1992.
Personal: Born 5 February 1955. Studied Law at University of Antwerp (Cand. Jur., 1975) and Ghent (Lic. Jur., 1978) and at Harvard Law School (LLM, 1980). Assistant Professor University of Ghent (1978-1982).

TOPPING, Simon
Bird & Bird, Brussels +32 2 282 6000
simon.ropping@twobirds.com
Recommended in Communications
Specialisation: UK and EC competition law in telecoms/IT/e-commerce/new media sectors, and in its application to intellectual property. Experience includes advising on all aspects of competition law from the provision of detailed competition advice concerning IP licensing, franchising and distribution strategies, pricing, advising clients in respect of allegations of abuse of a dominant market position through to advising on complex monopoly investigations under the Fair Trading Act, and acting in Merger Cases and competition law disputes before the EC Commission, and the notification of joint ventures and mergers to national and EC competition authorities. Frequent speaker on UK and EC competition law issues and has written extensively on this subject.
Career: Called to the Bar of England and Wales 1988; pupillage in Francis Taylor Builidng specialising in EC law 1988-89; Brussels office of French law firm SG Archibald 1990 and 1991-92; stage in Directorate General IV (Competition) of the European Commission 1991; *Bird & Bird* 1992; seconded to Brussels office OCtober 1992; qualified as solicitor 1995; partner *Bird & Bird* 1995.
Personal: Oxon (1985 BA Hons Politics, Philosophy, Economics); Polytechnic of Central London (1986 Diploma in Law); Trier, 1988 Magister luris (masters degree in German law); Universite Libre de Bruxelles, 1991 Licence Speciale en Droit European (masters degree in European law).

VAN BAEL, Ivo
Van Bael & Bellis, Brussels +32 2 647 7350
vbb@vanbaelbellis.com
Recommended in Competition/Anti-trust
Specialisation: Has acted in a number of landmark EC anti-trust and trade cases before the European Commission and the EC courts. Major anti-trust cases handled include United Brands, BP, Hugin, Pioneer, Michelin, IBM, John Deere, Woodpulp, Akzo, and more recently, Boeing/McDonnell Douglas, Enso and Benetton. Has lectured at the University of Tokyo and is currently teaching at the College of Europe in Bruges and at the University of Amsterdam.
Prof. Memberships: Member of the Brussels Bar. Has been active in both the American Bar Association (ABA) and the International Bar Association (IBA). Has been Chairman of the Anti-trust and Trade Law Committee of the IBA's Section on Business Law.
Publications: Written several books and numerous articles in the field of competition and trade law.
Career: Born 15th February 1939 in Antwerp. Obtained law degree at the University of Louvain in 1961. Also studied at the University of Bologna Law School at the Bologna Centre of John Hopkins University, and at the University of Michigan Law School, and received the degree of Master in Comparative Law. Started the practice of law in New York in 1963 with a Wall Street firm, subsequently worked in their offices in Paris and Brussels. Co-founded *Van Bael & Bellis* in 1986.

VAN DE WALLE DE GHELCKE, Bernard
De Bandt, van Hecke, Lagae & Loesch (a member firm of Linklaters & Alliance), Brussels
+32 2 501 94 11
bvandewalle@alliancebrussels.com
Recommended in Competition/Anti-trust
Specialisation: Partner in the EU/Competition Law Practice Group. Areas of practice include EC and Belgian competition law, including merger control and state aid, and free movement. Has represented clients active in amongst others the following industries: chemicals, glass, cement, construction materials, steel, air transport, banking, payment systems, automotive, food retail, beer. Has been involved in numerous EC merger control proceedings since the EMCR came into force, in merger control proceedings before the Belgian authorities, in anti-trust cases before the Commission and the European Courts as well as state aid cases. Represents the Belgian Government before the ECJ in preliminary ruling cases concerning taxation issues.
Prof. Memberships: Member of the Brussels Bar (admitted 1977); Board Member and past chairman of the Belgian Association for European law; Member of the Belgian Association for the Study of Competition Law; Professor at the College of Europe (Bruges) since 1994.
Career: Joined *Van Ryn, Van Ommeslaghe, Faurès and Flagey* in 1974, becoming partner in 1979. Joined *De Bandt, van Hecke, Lagae & Loesch* in 1988. Practising EU/competition law with the Brussels Office of *Linklaters & Alliance*, of which *De Bandt, van Hecke, Lagae & Loesch* is a member. Head of the EU Competition Law Practice Group of *Linklaters & Alliance.*
Personal: Born 23rd May 1947. Studied Law (Doctor in de rechten, 1970 and Licenciaat Europees recht, 1973) at Leuven University (Belgium) and Brussels University (LLB) (Licence spéciale en droit économique, 1972). Languages: Dutch, French, English.

VAN DER HAEGEN, Marc
Liedekerke Wolters Waelbroeck Kirkpatrick & Cerfontaine SC, Brussels +32 2 551 1541
Recommended in Banking & Finance, Corporate/M&A

VAN GERVEN, Gerwin
De Bandt, van Hecke, Lagae & Loesch (a member firm of Linklaters & Alliance), Brussels
+32 2 501 94 11
gerwin.vangerven@linklaters.com
Recommended in Competition/Anti-trust
Specialisation: Partner in the EU/Competition Law Practice Group. Areas of practice include merger control, Articles 81 & 82, state aid. Has represented clients before the European Commission, the European Courts and national competition authorities, active in amongst others the following industries: IT, telecommunications, computers, energy, air transport, aerospace, medical devices, pharmaceuticals, consumer goods, retail distribution, chemicals. Has been involved in seven 2nd phase merge control proceedings before the European Commission in the last several years. Editor-in-Chief of the 'EC Merger Control Reporter' (Kluwer International) and many more EU filings and multi-jurisdictional filings. Member of the Executive Committee and Vice-Chairman of the Competition Policy Subcommittee, of the EU Committee of the American Chamber of Commerce, Belgian Member of the Executive Committee of the European Air Transport Law Association.
Prof. Memberships: Member of the Brussels Bar; Member of the International Bar Association and the American Bar Association.
Career: Associate with US law firm in Washington D.C ., 1984/85. Joined the Brussels Bar in 1985. Joined *De Bandt, van Hecke, Lagae & Loesch* in 1985, becoming a partner in 1991. Practising EU/competition law with the Brussels Office of *Linklaters & Alliance*, of which *De Bandt, van Hecke, Lagae & Loesch* is a member.
Personal: Born 23 February 1960. Studied Law (Lic. Law, 1982) and Economics (Lic. Econ. Sc., 1983) at Leuven University (Belgium) and Harvard Law School (LLM, 1984).

VAN HOOGHTEN, Paul
De Bandt, van Hecke, Lagae & Loesch (a member firm of Linklaters & Alliance), Brussels
+32 2 501 94 11
pvanhooghten@debandt.com
Recommended in Corporate/M&A
Specialisation: Partner in the Corporate Department (Company Law - M&A Group) of *De Bandt, van Hecke, Lagae & Loesch*'s, Brussels office; Direct Investment Law Practice Group of *De Bandt, van Hecke, Lagae & Loesch*; Corporate, Mergers & Acquisitions Practice Group of *Linklaters & Alliance.* Has extensive experience in international and domestic mergers and acquisitions. Main areas of practice include mergers and acquisitions, joint ventures, management buy-outs, general corporate advice and privatisations.
Prof. Memberships: ABA (American Bar Association ñ associated member), IBA (International Bar Association ñ Section G), University of Illinois alumni. Vice-chair of ABA (American Bar Association ñ Committee International Business Transactions 1996-1999).
Career: Studied Law at Catholic University of Louvain KUL (Lic. Jur., 1983); Master of Comparative Law at University of Illinois at Urbana

Champaign College of Law (USA) (M.C.L, 1984); Assistant at the College of Law of the University of Louvain KUL; Department of International and Foreign Law (1984-1985). Advisor for Foreign Trade (Royal Decree of December 15 1995). Joined *De Bandt, van Hecke, Lagae & Loesch* in 1988, becoming Partner in 1994. Managing Partner of the *De Bandt, van Hecke, Lagae & Loesch* New York office (1992-1996).
Personal: Born 11 September 1960.

VAN HOUTTE, Hans
Hans van Houtte - Sole Practitioner, Brussels +32 1 6489 464
Recommended in Arbitration (International)

VAN KERCKHOVE, Marleen
Clifford Chance, Brussels +32 2 533 59 11
marleen.vankerckhove@cliffordchance.com
Recommended in Competition/Anti-trust
Specialisation: Specialises in competition law (EC and Belgian), including intellectual property related issues.
Prof. Memberships: Member of the Brussels Bar, Licensing Executives Society.
Career: Partner *Clifford Chance* since 1999.
Personal: Attended University of Leuven, Belgium (1982); University of Nancy, France (1983); and the London School of Economics, UK (1987).

VAN LIEDEKERKE, Dirk
Olswang, Brussels +32 2 647 4772
dvl@olswang.com
Recommended in Communications
Specialisation: Specialised in telecommunications and competition law matters at European and Belgian level. Handling various litigations (national courts, NRA and NCA and European Commission) and transactional matters.
Prof. Memberships: Member of Brussels Bar, IBA.
Publications: Various publications on telecommunications, access and competition law.
Career: Teaching assistant at College of Europe (Bruges). Associate with *Coudert Brothers.* Partner at *Olswang.*

VANDENCASTEELE, Alexandre
Liedekerke Siméon Wessing Houthoff, Brussels +32 2 551 16 13
A.Vandencasteele@lswh.be
Recommended in Competition/Anti-trust
Specialisation: EC Law, with a special emphasis on competition related issues (merger control, regulations, rules applicable to cooperative agreements and abuses of a dominant position, state aids rules, privatisation, deregulations). Specialises in European law; regularly represents clients before the European Court of Justice, as well as in administrative proceedings before the European Commission. Extensive client base; has special expertise in a wide range of economic sectors, such as the steel, oil, chemical and manufacturing industries, consumer goods, utilities, telecommunication, media and financial services.
Prof. Memberships: Association Belge de Droit Européen, International Bar Association.
Publications: Author of several articles in the Journal des Tribunaux, the Cahiers de Droit Européen, and the Revue Trimestrielle de Droit Européen.
Career: 1980 to 1982, legal secretary to Lord McKenzie Stuart, Judge at the Court of Justice of the European Communities. 1996 to 1999, visiting professor in EC Competition Law at the Université Catholique de Louvain. Currently senior partner with *Liedekerke Siméon Wessing Houthoff,* working with a team of some 30 competition law specialists.
Personal: Speaks French, English and Dutch. Married, two children.

VANHAERENTS, Koen
Baker & McKenzie, Brussels +32 2 639 36 11
koen.vanhaerents@bakernet.com
Recommended in Corporate/M&A
Specialisation: Head of the Corporate Finance Group handling mergers & acquisitions, capital markets and venture capital. Has handled several M&A transactions in several industries (telecommunications, food, electronics, e-commerce) and advised, as counsel to issuers and underwriters, on many IPOs and SPOs on EASDAQ, Euronext and NASDAQ. In addition, advises several venture capital funds in their investment and buy-out business.
Publications: Several articles in the corporate finance area.
Career: Advokaat, Member of the Brussels Bar since September 1987; Associate *Baker & McKenzie* August 1987 - June 1994; International Partner *Baker & McKenzie* since July 1994; Co-Managing Partner of Brussels office since December 1999; Member of the Steering Committee of the European Venture Capital Group of *Baker & McKenzie.*
Personal: Born on July 6, 1963; LLM, Boalt Hall, UC Berkeley (1986-1987); Law degree, KU Leuven (1981-1986); Baccalaureus in Philosophy, KU Leuven (1983-1984).

VENIT, James S.
Skadden, Arps, Slate, Meagher & Flom LLP, Brussels +32 2 639 0300
jvenit@skadden.com
Recommended in Communications, Competition/Anti-trust
Specialisation: Senior partner in the Brussels office of *Skadden, Arps, Slate, Meagher & Flom* LLP and co-chairs the firm's European competition law practice. Has had extensive experience representing multinational companies before the European Commission in proceedings under Articles 81, 82, and the Merger Regulation involving a wide range of economic sectors and industries, including air transport, pharmaceuticals and telecommunications. Also advises on telecommunications and intellectual property issues that affect hardware manufacturers, network operators, service providers, and cntent suppliers active in the development of the Information Society.
Prof. Memberships: Member of the American Bar Association Section on Anti-trust and of the International Bar Association.
Career: Qualified in 1979. 1967 B.A., Yale University; Phi Beta Kappa, Summa Cum Laude. 1971 M.A., Columbia University. 1976 Ph.D., Columbia University. 1979 J.D., New York University; Law Review, Order of the Coif. Has practised EC competition law in Brussels since 1980, and has ben a partner in the Brussels office of [Wilmer, Cutler & Pickering since 1989. A frequent lecturer on EC competition law at conferences and seminars both in Europe and the United States, and has written extensively on various subjects of EC competition law, including intellectual property, joint ventures, mergers, essential facilities and compliance programs.

VERBEKE, Louis
Allen & Overy, Brussels +32 2 778 24 43
Recommended in Corporate/M&A

VERHEYDEN, Alexandre
Jones, Day, Reavis & Pogue, Brussels +32 2 645 1509
averheyden@jonesday.com
Recommended in Communications
Specialisation: Practices in the area of competition law with a particular emphasis in the telecommunications sector and of telecommunications regulations (both at the EU and national levels). Has extensive experience in relation to notifications to the European Commission, abuse of dominant position cases before competition authorities and litigation cases before national courts and national telecommunications regulatory authorities involving competition matters. Assists operators in obtaining all necessary telecommunications licenses / authorisations in the EU. Represents various governments in the preparation of their telecommunications regulatory frameworks. Also represents various Internet start up companies and governments for the preparation of their E-Commerce regulations.
Career: Antitrust partner based in Brussels, admitted in Belgium in 1990 and New York in 1995. Joined the firm in 1996. Educated at the Law Faculty of the University of Louvain (Licence en droit, 1990) and at the University of Chicago Law School (LLM 1992)

WAELBROECK, Denis
Liedekerke Siméon Wessing Houthoff, Brussels +32 2 551 16 15
D.Waelbroeck@lswh.be
Recommended in Competition/Anti-trust
Specialisation: EC Law, in particular competition law (merger control, co-operative agreements, control of dominance). Advises on various aspects of EC legislation including competition, mergers, State aids, trade law and regulatory affairs. Regularly represents major EC and US clients in a wide range of economic sectors and industries, including energy, telecommunication, media, transport, pharmaceuticals, consumer goods, steel, chemical products, cement, cartonboard and others. Has been involved in several dozen proceedings before the Court of Justice and the Court of First Instance of the European Communities.
Prof. Memberships: Union des Avocats Européens, Association Belge de Droit Européen.
Publications: Author of numerous books and/or articles on Community Law and regularly lectures in EC competition law at conferences and seminars.
Career: Partner with *Liederkerke Siméon Wessing Houthoff,* working with some other 30 competition law specialists. Also professor of European Competition Law at the College of Europe in Bruges and the Université Libre de Bruzelles. 1983-85, référendaire of the EC Court of Justice.
Personal: Married, two children.

WINCKLER, Antoine
Cleary, Gottlieb, Steen & Hamilton, Brussels +32 2 287 20 00
Recommended in Competition/Anti-trust

BELIZE

Corporate/Commercial

BELIZE Leading firms (Corporate/Commercial)
1 Barrow & Co
Barrow & Williams
WH Courtenay & Co
2 Lois Young Barrow & Co
Mussa & Valderamos
Young's Law Firm

Firms are listed alphabetically in each band.

Leading individuals (Corporate/Commercial)
1 **BARROW Denys** *Barrow & Co*
COURTENAY Derek *WH Courtenay & Co*
WILLIAMS Rodwell *Barrow & Williams*
YOUNG Michael *Young's Law Firm*
YOUNG BARROW Lois *Lois Young Barrow & Co*
2 **BARROW Dean** *Barrow & Williams*
LUMOR Fred *Mussa & Valderamos*

Individuals are listed alphabetically in each band.

Barrow & Co (3 lawyers) Considered by some to be *"a league above its competitors,"* the firm has a strong reputation in banking, insurance, offshore work and real estate. Former director of Atlantic Bank, **Denys Barrow** is a *"charismatic and competent lawyer,"* commended for his commercial acumen. **Clients:** Atlantic Bank; Regent Insurance Co.

Barrow & Williams (2 ptrs, 1 assc) The Belize member of Lexmundi operates an almost exclusively commercial practice, consisting of corporate, maritime, banking and insurance law as well as some litigation. The firm also enjoys a thriving off-shore practice under the eye of **Rodwell Williams**, who is President of the Off-shore Practitioners Association. *"Quiet but strong,"* he is considered to be a top-class corporate deal manager. Former Attorney-General **Dean Barrow** is also highly recommended. **Clients:** Multi-national companies; insurance companies; Belize Bank.

WH Courtenay & Co (2 ptrs, 5 asscs) The oldest and largest law firm in Belize enjoys a high reputation amongst its competitors. Its commercial practice includes banking, real estate and company organisation. **Derek Courtenay** is a senior practitioner who is *"analytical and first-class."* Involved in preparation of documents relating to the flotation of bond issues carried out by Citicorp Merchant Bank of Trinidad and the Royal Merchant Bank of Trinidad. Represented TECO in their unsuccessful bid for the purchase of shares in Belize Electricity Co Ltd. **Clients:** TECO; Barclays; CDC; IFC.

Lois Young Barrow & Co (1 ptr, 1 assc) **Lois Young Barrow** presides over a *"substantial civil and business practice."* The country's only female senior counsel, she is a *"passionate, intelligent and assertive"* lawyer, who can be relied on to deliver *"a first class product."* She recently represented one of the parties in a multi-million dollar property dispute between two Mennonite communities, and has also represented the interests of the Belize Telecommunications Authority for many years. **Clients:** Castile Group; Belize Telecommunications Authority.

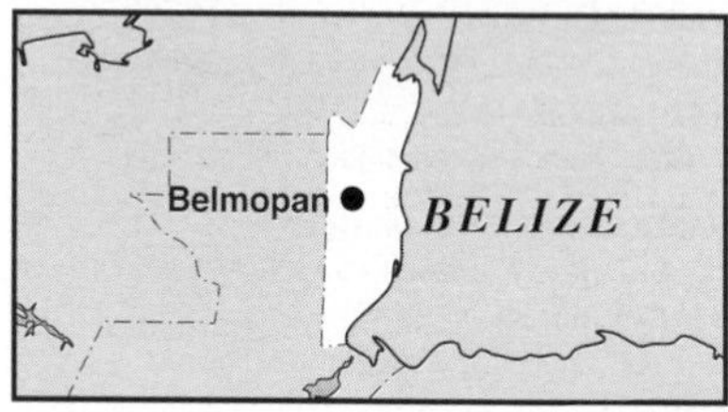

Mussa and Valderamos (2 ptrs, 1 assc) Reputable law firm whose partners include the Prime Minister and Solicitor-General. The practice is now in the hands of **Fred Lumor**, *"an aggressive, tenacious work-horse."* The firm's workload generally comprises banking, real estate and civil litigation. **Clients:** Bank of Nova Scotia; Belize Waste Control Ltd; Citrus Growers Association; Belize Airports Authority; LAAD.

Young's Law Firm (1 ptr, 2 asscs) Specialising in corporate and property work, as well as undertaking civil litigation and IP cases, the firm has a sound reputation. **Michael Young** is a senior lawyer with *"tremendous ability,"* who provides a *"professional and meticulous"* service. **Clients:** Exxon; Shell; Belize Sugar Industries Ltd; Belize Electricity Ltd.

Leaders' profiles – Belize

BARROW, Dean
Barrow & Williams, Belize City +501 275 280

BARROW, Denys
Barrow & Co, Belize City +501 277 410
barroweo@btl.net
Specialisation: Admiralty, banking, civil litigation, corporate, commercial, insurance, offshore, real property.
Prof. Memberships: Member, Bar Association of Belize. Member, General Legal Council. Member, Attorney General's Advisory group.
Career: Qualified in 1977. Partner of *Staine & Barrow* until dissolved in 1994, then formed *Barrow & Co.* Elevated to Senior council in 1990. Appointed Acting Judge of High Court of the Organisation of Eastern Caribbean States, January to April, 2001. Director of one of the three locally established commercial banks.
Personal: Born 8 July 1952. Attended University of the West Indies 1972 - 1975, (LLB, upper second). Attended Norman Manley Law School 1975 - 1977 (Legal Education Certificate), most outstanding final year student. Leisure interests include cycling and scuba diving.

COURTENAY, Derek
WH Courtenay & Co, Belize City +501 2 72037

LUMOR, Fred
Mussa & Valderamos, Belize City +501 232 940

WILLIAMS, Rodwell
Barrow & Williams, Belize City +501 275 280

YOUNG, Michael
Young's Law Firm, Belize City +501 277 406

YOUNG BARROW, Lois
Lois Young Barrow & Co, Belize City +501 235 924

BENIN

Corporate/Commercial

BENIN Leading firms (Corporate/Commercial)
1 Cabinet Edgar Yves Monnou
Cabinet Hounnou
Cabinet Robert M Dossou

Firms are listed alphabetically in each band.

Leading individuals (Corporate/Commercial)
1 **DOSSOU Robert** *Cabinet Robert M Dossou*
HOUNNOU Severin *Cabinet Hounnou*
MONNOU Edgar *Cabinet Edgar Yves Monnou*

Individuals are listed alphabetically in each band.

Cabinet Edgar Yves Monnou (1 ptr, 3 asscs) The firm handles a variety of work, and often acts as legal advisor to foreign companies. Strengths are banking, project finance and the establishment and incorporation of foreign companies. **Edgar Monnou** is highly regarded, and worked on the establishment of the International Bank of Benin. **Clients:** Banks; insurance companies.

Cabinet Hounnou (1 ptr, 2 asscs) Highly recommended for commercial law and banking, the firm also handles contract, insurance and maritime law. **Severin Hounnou** has a sound national reputation. **Clients:** Banks; insurance companies.

Cabinet Robert M Dossou (1 ptr, 4 asscs) A strong commercial law firm which *"has now established itself in the market."* The firm advises on international commercial law, banking, investment, contracts, joint venture agreements, maritime and aviation law. **Robert Dossou** is an excellent lawyer with *"good political connections."* **Clients:** Banks; African, American, Asian and European industrial and commercial companies; shipping companies; road transport trade unions.

Leaders' profiles – Benin

DOSSOU, Robert
Cabinet Robert M Dossou, Cotonou
+229 314 411

HOUNNOU, Severin
Cabinet Hounnou, Cotonou
+229 321 995

MONNOU, Edgar
Cabinet Edgar Yves Monnou, Cotonou
+229 310 856

BERMUDA

Corporate/Commercial

BERMUDA Leading firms (Corporate/Commercial)
1 Conyers Dill & Pearman
2 Appleby Spurling & Kempe
3 Cox Hallet Wilkinson
Mello Jones & Martin
Wakefield Quin

Firms are listed alphabetically in each band.

Leading individuals (Corporate/Commercial)
1 COLLIS John *Conyers Dill & Pearman*
MARTIN Peter *Mello Jones & Martin*
2 BUBENZER Peter *Appleby Spurling & Kempe*
CABRAL Warren *Appleby Spurling & Kempe*
COOKE David *Conyers Dill & Pearman*
DOYLE David *Conyers Dill & Pearman*
HOLLIS Wendell *Hollis & Co*
LINES David *Appleby Spurling & Kempe*
MORRISON Ernest *Cox Hallet Wilkinson*
QUIN Max *Wakefield Quin*

Individuals are listed alphabetically in each band.

Conyers Dill & Pearman (14 ptrs, 35 asscs) *"The leading firm on the island"* offers a full range of corporate and commercial services, from asset financing and securities to mutual funds and e-commerce. Internationally known for its *"high quality work and lawyers,"* its clients include the big insurance companies, *"the cream of Bermudan business." "Driving force"* **John Collis** is the island's *"leading commercial attorney."* **David Cooke** has *"huge potential for the future"* and **David Doyle** is also recommended. The firm acted on the cross-border restructuring of an offshore multi-billion dollar development stage communications company and its subsidiaries. **Clients:** Banks; Fortune 500 companies; investment, oil, manufacturing and trading companies.

Appleby Spurling & Kempe (17 ptrs, 48 asscs) Established, broad-based firm which covers insurance, professional liability, insolvency, offshore finance, mutual funds, international joint ventures and telecommunications. **Peter Bubenzer** is *"one of the country's leading lights,"* **Warren Cabral** has great *"legal acumen"* and **David Lines** *("working with him is a pleasure")* is also highly regarded. The firm acted on behalf of a large telecommunications company in connection with its $2 billion IPO and its listing on the New York stock exchange and the Bermuda Stock Exchange. **Clients:** Insurance and industrial companies; mutual funds; telecommunications companies.

Cox Hallett Wilkinson (7 ptrs, 7 asscs) Known to attract referrals from a number of other firms, the team maintains a respected general commercial practice. Areas of expertise include offshore finance, insurance, share purchases, mutual funds, unit trusts, M&A, e-commerce and telecommunications. The team is led by *"steady"* **Ernest Morrison**, and acted on the restructuring of Cable & Wireless. **Clients:** Cable & Wireless; Sabre Fund Management.

Mello Jones & Martin (6 ptrs, 12 asscs) Although best known for its emphasis on litigation, the firm nevertheless has some *"first-class"* corporate clients, whom it advises on mutual funds, aircraft

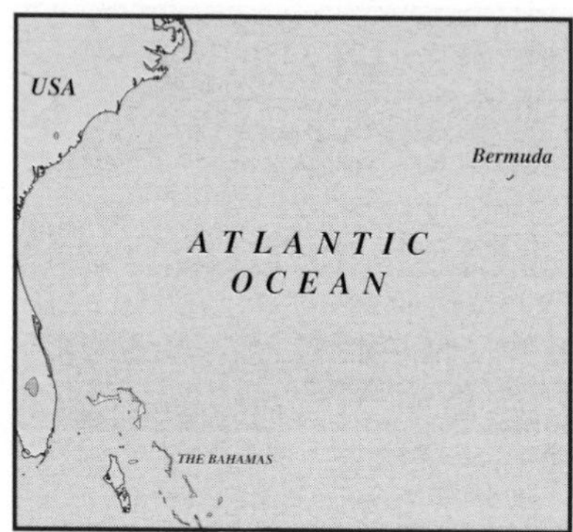

leasing, banking and internet-related business. *"First-class"* **Peter Martin** is the key lawyer here. **Clients:** Financial institutions; new telecom companies.

Wakefield Quin (1 ptr, 3 asscs) A niche commercial practice with an emphasis on mutual fund work, which also provides advice on all transactions of a corporate and commercial nature, trusts, banking and finance, partnerships, insurance, shipping and aviation. **Max Quin** has built up a firm with an *"excellent and loyal client base."* **Clients:** Top mutual funds; mining and pharmaceutical companies.

Other Notable Practitioner **Wendell Hollis**, in association with Ernst & Young, has set up a boutique firm dealing exclusively with corporate/commercial matters, including insurance, mutual funds, e-commerce, restructuring and M&A. He recently acted on behalf of Destination Villages in the acquisition of two overseas hotels.

Leaders' profiles – Bermuda

BUBENZER, Peter
Appleby Spurling & Kempe, Hamilton HM 12
+1 441 295 2244

CABRAL, Warren
Appleby Spurling & Kempe, Hamilton HM 12
+1 441 295 2244

COLLIS, John C.R.
Conyers Dill & Pearman, Hamilton HM CX
+1 441 295 1422
jccollis@cdp.bm
Specialisation: Partner in the Bermuda law firm *Conyers Dill & Pearman.* Specialises in commercial and corporate law with particular emphasis on mutual funds and complex corporate structures as they relate to the offshore industry. Frequently advises on the development of, and proposals for, company and related laws in offshore jurisdictions.
Prof. Memberships: Bar of England and Wales; Bar of Bermuda.
Career: 1983 to present: Barrister and Attorney, *Conyers Dill & Pearman,* Bermuda. Partner since 1987. 1981 to 1983: Barrister and Attorney/Associate

with *Linklaters & Paines, London*; 1979 to 1981: Bachelor of Arts (Jurisprudence) Oxford University; Rhodes Scholarship. 1976 to 1979: Bachelor of Commerce Degree McGill University, Canada. Several committees of the Bermuda International Business Association; 1993-1994 Commission on Competitiveness - Chairman of Sub-committee on Future Opportunities; Secretary of the Bermuda Rhodes Scholarship Selection Committee and of The McGill Bermuda Scholarship and The Dudley & Deborah Butterfield Scholarship Selection Committee.
Personal: Born 9 June 1958 in Bermuda. Married with three children.

COOKE, David W.P.
Conyers Dill & Pearman, Hamilton HM CX
+1 441 295 1422
dwcooke@cdp.bm
Specialisation: Partner in the corporate department of the Bermuda law firm of *Conyers Dill & Pearman*. Involved in many areas of corporate and commercial law, with particular emphasis on asset financing, widely-held/public companies, mergers and acquisitions. Has advised a number of public companies that have moved their jurisdiction of incorporation to Bermuda. Has acted for companies and lenders in a range of financings and restructurings.
Prof. Memberships: Memberships: Bar of England and Wales; Bermuda Bar.
Career: 1994 to present: Barrister and Attorney *Conyers Dill & Pearman*. Partner since 1998. University of Kent (BA Hons); Inns of Court School of Law; Cambridge University (LLM). Called to Bar of England and Wales in 1987 and the Bermuda Bar in 1989.
Personal: Born 17 February 1962 in Bermuda. Married with two children.

DOYLE, David
Conyers Dill & Pearman, Hamilton HM CX
+1 441 295 1422

HOLLIS, Wendell
Hollis & Co, Hamilton +1 441 295 2208
wendell_hollis@ey.bm
Specialisation: Managing Partner of the firm. Main area of work is corporate law on behalf of both local and international clients. The firm is affiliated with *Ernst & Young* in Bermuda and is part of the international group of *EY Law*. Incorporated Kloster Cruise Limited in 1995 and has acted for the company and its successor entitled the Norwegian Cruise Line Limited since that time. Generally represents a number of Bermuda's larger trading companies including D&J Construction Company Limited, the Holmes Williams & Purvey Group of companies, the MEF group of companies. Incorporated and established in 1998 Bermuda's only new hotel development in the last 25 years, Destination Villages Daniel's Head Bermuda Limited. Has handled acquisitions of companies and undertakings of various sorts by Bermudian and overseas clients. Acted for the purchasers of the Harmony Club from the Forte Group and for the subsequent sale of the property to overseas purchasers. Acted for the purchasers of the Surfside Club, another well known Bermuda hotel property, and has acted generally for the aforementioned hotel properties and their dealings with the Bermuda government.
Prof. Memberships: Memberships: Lincoln's Inn; Bermuda Bar Association; International Tax Planning Association and the International Fiscal Association.
Publications: Author of numerous articles on Bermuda's laws generally, particularly questions involving Bermuda's immigration laws, Bermuda correspondent for Tax Notes International.
Career: Qualified as a Barrister in the United Kingdom in July of 1975. Joined *Cartwright & Hollis* in 1976, left to form *Hollis & Co.* in 1985 as managing partner. *Hollis & Co.* merged with *Mello & Jones* in 1990, served as managing partner of the merged *Mello Hollis Jones & Martin* from 1990 to 1998, served as chairman of *Mello Hollis Jones & Martin from 1998 to 2000. Left Mello Hollis Jones & Martin* to form *Hollis & Co.* in conjunction with *Ernst & Young* and *EY Law* in February 2000. Presently serves as managing partner of *Hollis & Co.* Government Appointments: Board of Education 1978-1982; Fishery Advisory Council 1979; Public Service Vehicle Licencing Board 1989-2000; Human Rights Tribunal 1986; Acting Magistrate 1981-1991; Air Advisory Committee 1991-1992; Member of Senate 1992-1993; Parlimentary Secretary for Finance and the Environment 1992-1993; Chairman of the Exemption Tribunal 1998-2000; Board of Governors Bermuda College 1998-1999; Deputy Chairman Board of Trustees Bermuda Golf Courses 1998-2000.
Personal: Born in Bermuda, 9 January 1953. Attended Bristol University 1971-1974 (LLB Hons); Inns of Court School of Law (Hons) 1975; Commissioned Officer Bermuda Regiment 1977-1988; Chairman of Board of Trustees Saltus Grammar School. Leisure interests include: Golf, swimming, gardening and architecture.

LINES, David
Appleby Spurling & Kempe, Hamilton HM 12
+1 441 295 2244

MARTIN, Peter
Mello Jones & Martin, Hamilton HM FX
+1 441 292 1345

MORRISON, Ernest
Cox Hallet Wilkinson, Hamilton HM FX
+1 441 295 4630

QUIN, Max
Wakefield Quin, Hamilton +1 441 292 7070

B

BHUTAN

Corporate/Commercial

BHUTAN
Leading individuals
(Corporate/Commercial)

1 **SONNENBERG Michael** *Freehills*

Individuals are listed alphabetically in each band.

A key figure in the development of a legal framework for the power sector, **Michael Sonnenberg** of Freehills has *"done considerable work in Asia,"* and is thought to be *"highly regarded by the Asian Development Bank."* His *"positive participation is always welcome"* and he advised the Bhutanese Government on the reform and restructuring of the electricity industry resulting in the authorship of a new Electricity Industry Act. The undeveloped legal system meant that it was *"no easy task to locate the law"* and Sonnenberg is praised for his hands-on involvement.

Leaders' profiles – Bhutan

SONNENBERG, Michael
Freehills, Melbourne +61 3 9288 1234

BOLIVIA

Corporate/Commercial

B

BOLIVIA Leading firms (Corporate/Commercial)
1 Bufete Aguirre
Carlos Gerke Mendieta Estudio Jurídico
CR & F Rojas Abogados
Indacochea & Asociados
Miranda Gutierrez & Guevara Servicios Legales
Quintanilla & Soria

Firms are listed alphabetically in each band.

Leading individuals (Corporate/Commercial)
1 AGUIRRE Fernando *Bufete Aguirre*
GERKE MENDIETA Carlos *Carlos Gerke Mendieta*
GUEVARA Ramiro *Miranda Gutierrez & Guevara*
NISHIZAWA TAKANO Santiago *Quintanilla*
QUINTANILLA BALLIVIÁN Eduardo *Quintanilla*
ROJAS Fernando *CR & F Rojas Abogados*
2 AGUIRRE Ignacio *Bufete Aguirre*
INDACOCHEA Ricardo *Indacochea & Asociados*
MENDIETA Gonzalo *Carlos Gerke Mendieta*

Individuals are listed alphabetically in each band.

Bufete Aguirre (3 ptrs, 2 asscs) Described by some as *"the best in the country,"* this commercially oriented firm is seen by its competitors to consist of *"serious guys"* who *"never mislead you."* Acting largely for foreign investor clients from the natural resources, energy, telecoms and banking sectors, the team is led by corporate guru **Fernando Aguirre***, who has *"experience, ability and intelligence."* **Ignacio Aguirre*** has quickly made a name for himself, and is perceived by peers to be *"extremely capable."*

The firm advised on negotiations over a gas pipeline from Bolivia to Brazil, and represented ABN AMRO on the financing of the Bolivian activities of a Western Wireless subsidiary. The team was also active on the $90 million hydroelectric project in La Paz for a local subsidiary of energy company Tenasca, and advised AES on the acquisition of a stake in a domestic telecoms company. **Clients:** OPIC; KFW; Grupo Iberdrola; YPF/Repsol; Unocal; Bank of America; Embol; Balfour Williamson; Novartis; Tetrapak; ADECCO; AES; Intelsat; American Express; Battle Mountain Gold.

Carlos Gerke Mendieta Estudio Jurídico (3 ptrs, 4 asscs) Leading commercial firm with a clientele which is 70% composed of domestic corporates in utilities, telecoms, oil and gas. Elsewhere, it is particularly active in debt restructuring, securities, and privatisation, and has advised private banks, concessionaires and US investors. *"Fantastic"* senior partner **Carlos Gerke Mendieta*** is a *"phenomenally intelligent"* leader, who divides his time between his practice and his duties as rector of the catholic university. His nephew **Gonzalo Mendieta*** is a rising star, unanimously considered by rivals to be a *"distinguished"* practitioner. The firm acted for Incesa on its high-profile acquisition of the national brewery. **Clients:** Petrobras; Incesa; Corporación Andina de Fomento.

CR & F Rojas Abogados (3 ptrs, 7 asscs) The oldest firm in the Bolivian market is regarded by peers an *"extremely well-connected"* operation, which advises national and international corporates and banks on syndicated loans and general corporate matters. The leading figure here is the *"popular and experienced"* **Fernando Rojas***. Energy is a key area of the workload, and the firm advised on a second gas pipeline to Brazil. **Clients:** Domestic and international corporates; international banks; oil and gas companies; foreign embassies.

Indacochea & Asociados (4 ptrs, 3 asscs) Based in the oil and gas centre Santa Cruz, our research shows that this rapidly expanding firm is seen as undoubtedly *"THE firm to recommend there,"* and is seen as a *"sophisticated international business organisation."* The firm advises a number of international blue-chips, and has niche expertise in the energy sector. *"Careful craftsman"* **Ricardo Indacochea*** has vast transactional experience in the natural resources industry.

The firm advised Enron and Shell on the Cuyaba international gas pipeline project, and represented a transport company involved in negotiations with the Environment Ministry over a petrol spill. **Clients:** Enron; Shell; Canadian cement company.

Miranda Gutierrez & Guevara (3 ptrs, 9 asscs) Respected for its internationally-focused corporate practice, the firm concentrates on the energy and natural resources industries. Highly regarded **Ramiro Guevara*** has an impressive academic track record, and has become *"a dominant national figure."*

A predominantly North American and European clientele is advised on general corporate, banking, M&A, capital markets and project finance transactions.

The firm has a loose association with Maciel Norman of Buenos Aires, and receives regular referrals from Linklaters. Among its most recent activity is work on the ongoing Bulo Bulo power plant, for clients NRG and Vattenfall, and the Puerto Suarez power export project for Enron. **Clients:** Enron; Exxon; Mobil; Vattenfall; NRG; International Water; Lyonnaise des Eaux; Citibank; Repsol; BHP.

Quintanilla & Soria (4 ptrs, 4 asscs) A thriving *"top-notch"* general practice firm that benefits enormously from the outstanding reputations of its two younger partners **Santiago Nishizawa Takano*** and **Eduardo Quintanilla Ballivián***. Both are regarded as *"among the best lawyers in the country."*

The firm's client base comprises international investors in the natural resources, electricity and telecoms sectors, as well as some local banking and mining entities. A fine reputation in project

* See leaders' profiles on pages 139

finance was further enhanced by the firm's advice on the San Cristobal silver mine, owned by the US corporate Apex Silver. The team also advised a domestic pension fund on financing a new project through a local bond issue. **Clients:** Coca-Cola; Rio Tinto; Enron; Pennzoil-Quaker State Company; West LB; AT&T; Telecom Italia; Entel; BancoSol; Ford; Toyota; Daihatsu.

Leaders' profiles – Bolivia

AGUIRRE, Fernando
Bufete Aguirre, La Paz +591 2 440937
faguirre@caoba.entelnet.bo
Specialisation: Senior Partner. Main areas: general commercial, corporate, business, banking, mining, hydrocarbons and tax law: incorporation of companies, mergers and acquisitions, general legal aspects of companies and corporations, securities and stock transactions, international commercial contracts involving foreign investments in Bolivia, banking and project finance, privatisation, joint ventures. Has represented several international companies in the privatisation process of Bolivian State companies. Currently Chairman of the Board of Directors of EMBOL S.A., the main Coca Cola bottler in Bolivia. Has represented Overseas Private Investment Corporation (OPIC) and KFW as lenders for the construction and operation of a pipeline to Brazil; Tenaska International for the financing of a new generation facility in Bolivia; various acquisitions of stocks in Bolivian corporations, and the establishment of various foreign companies and ventures in Bolivia.
Prof. Memberships: La Paz and Santa Cruz Bar Associations; Country representative of the International Bar Association, Bolivian member of GLOBALAW and the International Business Law Consortium; American Society of International Law; Honorary Member of the Association of Fellows and Legal Scholars of the Centre for International Legal Studies, Austria.
Career: Licentiate in Law, Political and Social Sciences and Lawyer, University of La Paz, Bolivia, 1968; Diploma in Law, University of Oxford, England, 1971.
Personal: Born in La Paz, Bolivia, November 24, 1943. Past-President of the International Movement of Apostolate in the Independent Social Milieus (MIAMSI). Past-Minister of the Presidency of the Republic (1979). Past-Director of the Bolivian Central Bank (1993/1996).

AGUIRRE, Ignacio
Bufete Aguirre, La Paz +591 2 440937

GERKE MENDIETA, Carlos
Carlos Gerke Mendieta Estudio Jurídico, La Paz +591 2 441 351

GUEVARA, Ramiro
Miranda Gutierrez & Guevara Servicios Legales, La Paz +591 231 6868

INDACOCHEA, Ricardo
Indacochea & Asociados, Santa Cruz +591 353 5356

MENDIETA, Gonzalo
Carlos Gerke Mendieta Estudio Jurídico, La Paz +591 2 441 351

NISHIZAWA TAKANO, Santiago
Quintanilla & Soria, La Paz +591 2 201 015

QUINTANILLA BALLIVIÁN, Eduardo
Quintanilla & Soria, La Paz +591 2 201 015

ROJAS, Fernando
CR & F Rojas Abogados, La Paz +591 2 313 737

BOTSWANA

Corporate/Commercial

BOTSWANA Leading firms (Corporate/Commercial)
1 Armstrongs
Collins Newman & Co
2 Minchin & Kelly

Firms are listed alphabetically in each band.

Leading individuals (Corporate/Commercial)
1 ARMSTRONG Neill *Armstrongs*
2 WILLIAMS David *Minchin & Kelly*
Up-and-coming individuals
BOOKBINDER Jeffrey *Collins Newman & Co*
DESAI Rizwan *Collins Newman & Co*

Individuals are listed alphabetically in each band.

Armstrongs (3 ptrs, 4 asscs) The firm remains one of Botswana's leaders for corporate and commercial work and enjoys a *"good reputation for international matters."* Key partner **Neill Armstrong** remains the *"first stop for major firms"* wishing to undertake complex business here. He has been involved in 15 out of the 16 listings of firms on the Botswana Stock Exchange. The firm advised on the privatisation of Air Botswana, and acted on the certification and listing process for the first international financial services centre company in Botswana. **Clients:** Barclays Bank; Standard Chartered Bank; First National Bank; Botswana Telecommunications Corp; Botswana Development Corp.

Collins Newman & Co (4 ptrs, 3 asscs) The main drive of the firm is corporate and commercial work, and it is seen to be an effective competitor for Armstrongs. Considered a *"slick organisation,"* the firm's range of work includes commercial property and inward investment. UK-trained **Rizwan Desai** has made a name for himself this year, while **Jeffrey Bookbinder** is known for his abilities in arbitration. **Clients:** Barclays Bank; First National Bank; International Financial Services Centre.

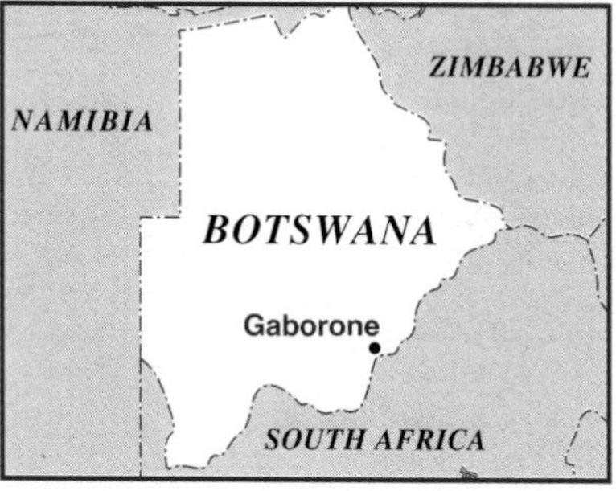

Minchin & Kelly (4 ptrs, 2 asscs) Undertaking a wide range of corporate work, the firm is, however, seen to have a lower profile than the two market leaders. **David Williams** is the senior partner, and reckoned to be *"the most effective worker"* at the firm. The team has advised on a number of takeovers and public flotations, and has niche strength in the real estate sector. **Clients:** Government-owned corporations; several multi-national companies.

Leaders' profiles – Botswana

ARMSTRONG, Neill
Armstrongs, Gabarone +267 353 481

BOOKBINDER, Jeffrey
Collins Newman & Co, Gaborone +267 352 702
jeff.bookbinder@collinsnewman.bw
Specialisation: Partner. Main areas of work are corporate finance and banking law, international financial services law, mergers and acquisitions, securities and bankruptcy/insolvency. Acted for the provisional liquidator of Swedish Motor Corporation in the sale, as a going concern, of the truck and bus assembly plant from an insolvent franchisee to Volvo AB. In addition acts for a number of major financial institutions, such as First National Bank of Botswana, Barclays Bank of Botswana, Stanbic Bank Botswana, Bank of Botswana, African Alliance, Botswana Development Corporation and National Development Bank, on a wide variety of corporate and commercial matters.
Prof. Memberships: Law Society of Ontario, Canada; Law Society of England and Wales; and Law Society of Botswana.
Publications: Chapter on Botswana in 'Trade Marks – World Law and Practice Journal'.
Career: Qualified Ontario 1989; England and Wales 1993; and Botswana 1993. Joined *Day Wilson Campbell*, Toronto, Ontario 1986. Lecturer in Law, University of Botswana 1990. Joined *Collins Newman & Co* in 1993, becoming a partner in 1996.
Personal: Born 19 March 1959. Attended University of Winnipeg 1979 – 1983 (BA); York University – Osgoode Hall 1983 – 1986; University of London 1986 – 1987 (LLM). Leisure interests include reading and collecting rare books. Lives in Gaborone, Botswana.

DESAI, Rizwan
Collins Newman & Co, Gaborone +267 352 702
rizwan.desai@collinsnewman.bw
Specialisation: Partner. Main areas of work are corporate finance and banking law, international financial services law, mergers and acquisitions, securities and bankruptcy/insolvency. Acted for the sellers, Acumen, in the RPC Data deal, one of the largest share for share transactions in Botswana during 2000 and has advised founding committee members on aspects of the proposed International Financial Services Centre. Acts for a number of major financial institutions, such as First National Bank of Botswana, Barclays Bank of Botswana, Stanbic Bank Botswana, Bank of Botswana, African Alliance, Botswana Development Corporation and National Development Bank, on a wide variety of corporate and commercial matters. Is principal legal adviser to Mascom Wireless, Botswana's leading cellular communications provider.
Prof. Memberships: Law Society of Scotland, Law Society of England and Wales, New York Bar and Law Society of Botswana.
Career: Qualified Scotland 1995; New York 1995; Botswana 1997; and England and Wales 1998. Joined *McGrigor Donald* Scotland in 1993. Joined *Collins Newman & Co* in 1999, becoming a partner in 2000. Member of the Finance Committee of the Botswana Democratic Party.
Personal: Born 16 January 1968. Attended University of Edinburgh 1986 – 1990 (LLB (Hons)) and 1990 – 1991 (Post-Graduate Diploma in Legal Practice); Harvard University 1991 – 1992 (LLM). Leisure interests include cinema and outdoor activities. Lives in Gaborone.

WILLIAMS, David
Minchin & Kelly, Gabarone +267 312 734

BRAZIL

Index

The clients' choice

BUSINESS LAWYER OF THE YEAR

SERGIO SPINELLI SILVA, *Mattos Filho, Veiga Filho, Marrey Jr, Moherdaui e Quiroga*

BUSINESS LAW FIRM OF THE YEAR

MATTOS FILHO, VEIGA FILHO, MARREY JR, MOHERDAUI E QUIROGA

MACHADO MEYER SENDACZ E OPICE

A banking lawyer, ***Sergio Spinelli Silva*** *tops this year's poll.* ***Machado Meyer Sendacz e Opice*** *and* ***Mattos Filho, Veiga Filho, Marrey Jr, Moherdaui e Quiroga*** *were equal as best firm.*

For details see page 36.

B

OVERVIEW: The prohibition of Anglo-American firms from practising Brazilian law continues to keep the global threat at bay. That said, the auditors and their affiliated firms have started to win a foothold, capital markets transactions are dominated by international firms and Anglo-American appetites have been further whetted by the announced privatisation of water and sewage utilities. As a result of the flourishing market, domestic firms are exploding in size, and Spanish and Portuguese alliances have been forged. On the regulatory front, competition law's major body, CADE, is set to be transformed, while much needed tax reforms are under discussion in a tax market that has moved away from litigation towards consultancy and planning.

Banking & Finance

Machado, Meyer, Sendacz e Opice (5 ptrs, 18 asscs) "*Well-connected in the financial world,*" with *"an especially fine capital markets team,"* the firm has advised on a number of local offerings and Eurobond offers, is regularly instructed on Brazilian banking regulatory issues, and has done substantial work in the local capital markets. Regional heavyweight **José Roberto Opice*** *("the leading guy")* is the stand-out player here. He has been particularly active in banking work with an M&A slant this year. His colleague, **Nei Zelmanovits***, has also retained his share of market support. Other major cases include advising on a global offering for Grupo Ultra on the NY Stock Exchange, and carrying out several structured financings in the telecoms sector. Strong in project finance, especially in electricity, oil and toll roads, the team has also been involved in a project finance for Autoban financed by IFC, IDB and the Brazilian Development Bank. **Clients:** Brazilian Government; investment banks; blue-chip corporates such as Shell.

Mattos Filho, Veiga Filho, Marrey Jr, Moherdaui e Quiroga (5 ptrs) Having participated in some of the largest securities deals of recent years, the firm is universally considered to rank among the leading finance advisors in Brazil. Renowned for its work on behalf of investment banks, the department's client base includes Merrill Lynch & Co, CSFB Garantia, Morgan Stanley Dean Witter and ABN AMRO Rothschild. The firm is also noted for its equity work. It played a major role in all three international public equity offerings conducted by Brazilian companies in 2000, with the aggregate of these SEC-registered, NYSE-listed offerings totalling over $4.8 billion. In addition, the team advised the underwriters on the international public offering of shares held by the Brazilian federal government in Petrobras, the largest corporation in Brazil. This global offering was the largest South American international equity offering ever at $4.3 billion, and resulted in the greatest dispersion of share ownership of any public company in South America, with over 300,000 Brazilian investors. Big-hitters at the firm include **Ary Oswaldo Mattos Filho***, a former President of the Brazilian Securities and Exchange Commission, and **Sergio Spinelli Silva***, *"an experienced practitioner who knows the needs of foreign clients."* The latter is personally conducting the department's international transactions. Debt transactions have constituted a substantial part of his caseload. A prominent example was the firm's advice on the international offering of fixed rate notes of SABESP, one of the largest water and sewerage companies in Brazil. **Clients:** Bandeirante Energia SA; Telesp Celular Participações SA; Construtora Sultepa SA; Brazil Realty SA; Empreendimentos e Participações; Lucent Technologies Inc; Embratel; Light.

Pinheiro Neto Advogados (11 ptrs, 35 asscs) Possessing the largest banking/finance department in Brazil, the firm enjoys notably high status among international corporates and financial institutions. Particularly prominent in structured financing and project finance, the team boasts an unparalleled clutch of recommended practitioners. **Antonio Mendes*** has an enviable reputation as *"one of Brazil's leading finance gurus."* **Alexandre Bertoldi*** *("extremely proactive on behalf of his clients")*, **Irene Dias da Silva*** *("thorough and easy to work with")*, **Ricardo Becker***, who has a reputable name for pure banking and securities advice, **Ricardo Coelho***, and **Fernando de Almeida Prado*** complete an imposing line-up. The team advised BBV on its acquisition of

* See leaders' profiles on pages 152-159

BRAZIL Leading firms (Banking & Finance)
1 Machado, Meyer, Sendacz e Opice
Mattos Filho, Veiga Filho, Marrey Jr, Moherdaui e Quiroga
Pinheiro Neto Advogados
2 Barbosa, Müssnich & Aragão
Levy & Salomão
Pinheiro Guimaraes Advogados
Tozzini Freire Teixeira e Silva
3 Demarest e Almeida
Trench Rossi e Watanabe (Baker & McKenzie)
Ulhôa Canto, Rezende e Guerra Advogados
Wald e Associados

Firms are listed alphabetically in each band.

Leading individuals (Banking & Finance)
★ MENDES Antonio *Pinheiro Neto*
OPICE José Roberto *Machado, Meyer, Sendacz*
1 SPINELLI SILVA Sergio *Mattos Filho*
2 ARAGÃO Paulo *Barbosa, Müssnich*
MÜSSNICH Francisco *Barbosa, Müssnich*
PINHEIRO GUIMARAES Francisco *Pinheiro Guimaraes*
PORTELLA Roberto *Demarest e Almeida*
SALOMÃO Eduardo *Levy & Salomão*
WALD Arnoldo *Wald e Associados*
3 BERTOLDI Alexandre *Pinheiro Neto*
DE ARAUJO CINTRA Antonio Felix *Tozzini Freire*
DE SALLES FREIRE José Luis *Tozzini Freire*
NUNES PINTO José Emilio *Tozzini Freire*
PINHEIRO GUIMARAES Plinio *Pinheiro Guimaraes*
ZELMANOVITS Nei *Machado, Meyer, Sendacz*
4 BARBOSA Plinio *Barbosa, Müssnich*
BECKER Ricardo *Pinheiro Neto*
COELHO Ricardo *Pinheiro Neto*
DE ALMEIDA PRADO Fernando *Pinheiro Neto*
DE ANDRADE Mario Cezar *Ulhôa Canto*
DIAS DA SILVA Irene *Pinheiro Neto*
GOMES DE SOUZA Renato *Ulhôa Canto*
MATTOS FILHO Ary Oswaldo *Mattos Filho*
SALLES Ricardo *Trench Rossi e Watanabe*
ULHÔA CANTO Carlos Alberto *Ulhôa Canto*
WALD Alexandre *Wald e Associados*

Individuals are listed alphabetically in each band.

Banco Excel, and acted for the issuer on Bozano Simonsen's management of a €50 million bonds deal for Bombril SA. **Clients:** BBV; BASF; Philip Morris; Shell; Lloyd's; Rolls Royce.

Barbosa, Müssnich & Aragão (15 lawyers) Although best known for its heavyweight corporate presence, the firm's finance team is also acknowledged by rivals for its expertise on *"more sophisticated transactions,"* notably in structured finance and capital markets. The team is felt to owe much to the *"versatile and brilliant"* **Paulo Aragão***, and to **Francisco Müssnich***, whose ability is said to be *"beyond question."* They receive capable support from **Plinio Barbosa***. In 2000, the firm was involved in the structuring and implementation of the $200 million private equity offering carried out by Sul America Private Equity Fund, LP. It also acted as legal adviser on the public offering by Brasil Telecom S/A of domestic commercial paper to the value of R$900 million, and advised on the public offering by Brasil Telecom Participacoes SA of domestic debentures worth around R$1 billion. **Clients:** Credit Suisse Financial Products.

Levy & Salomão (15 lawyers) *"An excellent firm,"* considered by its competitors to function *"more like a boutique,"* that has acquired an outstanding reputation for its local capital markets work. Having opened a Brasília office at the end of 1999, and a Rio de Janeiro office in the middle of this year, the group is beginning to establish itself as a serious national presence. Notable activity this year has been in the issue of securities, debentures and internal bonds in general. The firm possesses a number of experienced lawyers, including **Eduardo Salomão***, a *"bright, diligent guy,"* who has advised on the full range of banking and finance matters, including the issue of debentures for Iberdrola Group electricity distributorship companies in Brazil, and the issue of debentures for Editora Abril, the largest publishing company in Latin America. Frequently instructed by a number of blue-chip overseas financial institutions, the firm also acted for Deutsche Bank on the internet sale of banking and brokerage products, and advised JP Morgan on the structuring and development of new credit derivative products. Bank regulatory work has involved advice to financial institutions on compliance with Brazilian law. **Clients:** Deutsche Bank; Banco Santander Central Hispano; JP Morgan; Banco Espírito Santo; Globo; Chase Manhattan; Telemig/Telenorte.

Pinheiro Guimaraes Advogados (6 ptrs, 10 asscs) A firm with *"a successful strategy,"* and one that has been involved on a number of interesting transactions for a range of high-profile clients this year. Prominent among these is Citibank, with whom the firm has had a long-term relationship. Structured finance transactions are an area of niche expertise. **Francisco Pinheiro Guimaraes*** and **Plinio Pinheiro Guimaraes*** (formerly of Shearman & Sterling in New York) are the standout figures in a department which advised on the establishment of an MTN programme for Banco Safra SA to the value of $1 billion, and the issuance of $100 million worth of guaranteed notes by Bahia Sul Celulose SA. The team also represented Banque Indosuez on the issuance by Bombril SA of $150 million worth of notes with equity warrants, and acted on the issuance by the state of Minas Gerais of its $100 million series B bonds with covered warrants to purchase shares of preferred stock of Companhia Energética de Minas Gerais. These two transactions are the only transactions involving the issuance of convertible securities by Brazilian issuers in the international market to date. **Clients:** Citibank; Banco Safra SA; Banque Indosuez; Santista Alimentos SA.

Tozzini Freire Teixeira e Silva (5 ptrs, 19 asscs) Renowned for its project finance expertise, the firm also enjoys a respected position in the pure banking sphere, acting for a strong international clientele, normally on behalf of lenders. **Antonio Felix de Araujo Cintra***, **José Emilio Nunes Pinto*** and **José Luis de Salles Freire*** are all well respected members of the field. This year, the firm has been involved in the issue of Eurobonds by Banco Real ABN AMRO SA and Banco Santander under their respective Medium Term Note Programs. It has also assisted a syndicate of banks in Brazil, led by Banco Real ABN AMRO SA, on the underwriting of an issuance of local debentures by BCP SA, one of the largest cellular phone operators in Brazil. Lastly, the group advised the lenders, led by ABN AMRO, on a $1.75 billion syndicated loan to BCP SA, and advised ABN AMRO on the issuance of Eurobonds by the government of Brazil. **Clients:** ABN AMRO Bank; Banco Santander; Banco Sudameris; Bear Stearns; BankBoston; Mitsui & Co; United States Eximbank.

Demarest e Almeida (25 lawyers) Under the *"experienced eye"* of **Roberto Portella***, the department has grown by more than twenty per cent in the last year, and recently acquired two new lawyers from in-house positions at Citibank and BankBoston. The firm's client roster principally comprises European and multi-national banks. Important activities of the year include acting on Mediocredito Centrale SpA's bridging loan facility (value $25 million) to design, operate and maintain a major autoroad system in the state of São Paulo. The team also advised on the amendment to an export prepayment transaction (value $450 million) granted by Ford Brasil Trading Ltd to Ford Brasil Ltda. The funds were raised in the international market by a syndicate led by Chase Manhattan. **Clients:** Banco Icatu; Banco Pactual; Banco Santander.

Trench Rossi e Watanabe (Baker & McKenzie) (3 ptrs, 12 asscs) Often consulted by overseas financial institutions on their investments in Brazil, the firm maintains *"a definite involvement"* in structured finance, project finance, direct loans and securitisation, although it is thought to be assisted significantly by its international network. The respected **Ricardo Salles*** looks after both banking and insurance departments, and the firm has a strong specialisation in insurance products, regulatory work, joint ventures and acquisitions, representing both banks and large borrowers such as Petrobras. **Clients:** AIG; Nationwide; Nations Bank; Bank of America; Citibank; European Investment Bank.

Ulhôa Canto, Rezende e Guerra Advogados (10 lawyers) Although best known as a top-class tax litigation firm, it is widely considered to be *"making an effort to expand into new fields."* **Renato Gomes de Souza*** *("a senior figure and a fine lawyer")* is respected for his *"banking advice with a tax slant,"* while **Mario Cezar de Andrade*** *"has excellent relationships with investment banks,"* and **Carlos Alberto de Ulhôa Canto*** is a former member of the board of the Rio Stock Exchange. Transaction-wise, the firm assisted Bank of America LLC, Chase Securities Inc (arrangers) and Bank of America NA (administrative agent) in connection with a $300 million Note Purchase Agreement, and advised the borrower on a $200 million bridge loan agreement with BNDES and other financial institutions. The team also represented Kreditanstalt für Wiederaufbau (KfW) in connection with two import financing facilities worth $100 million. **Clients:** Nissho Iwai; Galva-Sud SA; ABN AMRO; Previ; Banco do Brasil SA.

Wald e Associados (5 ptrs, 26 asscs) A *"high-quality"* family firm with a reputation for banking litigation and corporate work. **Arnoldo Wald*** *("one of the cleverest men I've ever met")* worked for a time at the Brazilian Securities Commission. His son, *"bright"* **Alexandre Wald*** is also a well-known banking lawyer. The firm possesses offices in Rio de Janeiro, São Paulo and Brasília, and represents numerous financial institutions. It has advised several banks in connection with litigation over the indexation of financing agreements following the devaluation of the Brazilian Real, assisted foreign banks with the enforcement of creditors' rights, and acted as counsel to banks that are the subject of class action law suits. **Clients:** Gas de São Paulo; Lehman Brothers; Esso.

B

Communications

BRAZIL
Leading firms (Communications)

1. Mundie e Advogados
   Pinheiro Neto Advogados
   Tozzini Freire Teixeira e Silva
2. Fischer & Forster Advogados
   Machado, Meyer, Sendacz e Opice
   Trench Rossi e Watanabe (Baker & McKenzie)
3. Carvalho de Freitas e Ferreira Advogados Associados
   Demarest e Almeida
   Ulhôa Canto, Rezende e Guerra Advogados

Firms are listed alphabetically in each band.

Leading individuals (Communications)

1. **MUNDIE Kevin** *Mundie e Advogados*
   NUNES Esther *Pinheiro Neto*
   VALLE Regina *Tozzini Freire Teixeira e Silva*
   VIEGAS Juliana *Trench Rossi e Watanabe*
2. **BARRETTO Ricardo** *Carvalho de Freitas e Ferreira*
   CELLI Umberto *Fischer & Forster*
   COTAIT Elinor *Mundie e Advogados*
   FISCHER George *Fischer & Forster*
   ROSSI Mariza *Ulhôa Canto, Rezende e Guerra*
   SENDACZ Moshe *Machado, Meyer, Sendacz*
   SUNDFELD Carlos *Porto & Sundfeld*
3. **BASSO Maristela** *Tozzini Freire Teixeira e Silva*
   DE CUNTO Rafael *Pinheiro Neto*

Individuals are listed alphabetically in each band.

Mundie e Advogados (2 ptrs, 10 asscs) *"Clearly one of the main telecoms firms,"* this highly respected boutique is also active in internet-related work. One of the major players in the B-Band tender, it has been an active contributor to proposed rule-making for the regulation of telecommunication services. **Kevin Mundie*** is *"perhaps the most renowned telecoms lawyer in Brazil,"* while *"outstanding practitioner"* **Elinor Cotait*** is a former state attorney of São Paulo. The firm advises many clients in the mobile and satellite sectors, and is extensively involved in public consultations and the issuing of regulations. **Clients:** Large foreign and Brazilian corporations.

Pinheiro Neto Advogados (5 ptrs, 20 asscs) A major communications player ever since initial attempts to privatise Brazilian telecoms services in 1989, the firm advises extensively on both telecoms and IT matters in the transactional and regulatory spheres. *"Heavily involved"* **Esther Nunes*** *("I'd recommend her without question")* is chairman of the Brazilian Association for Information Technology and Telecommunications Law, and head of its Telecommunications Studies Commission. Her colleague **Rafael de Cunto*** also maintains his share of market approval. Since 1993, the firm has represented one of the first US-based groups to operate SMR services in Brazil, and for the past three years has advised on public bidding procedures for MMDS licensing. The group acted as Brazilian legal counsel for the NASDAQ-listed, high-yield IPO of Multicanal. In the internet sector, the firm has advised on a number of financings for service providers. **Clients:** Major telecoms companies.

Tozzini Freire Teixeira e Silva *"Conscientious, professional"* group with a name across the telecoms sector. The firm's caseload includes privatisations, restructuring and licensing for a client base which covers mobile and fixed telephony, cable and satellite companies. Familiar faces **Regina Valle*** and **Maristela Basso*** have been singled out by the market for their regulatory expertise. Key activities of the year include representing RBS, a member of the successful consortium in the sale of shares of Companhia Riograndense de Telecomunicações, and advising IFC on the provision of financial support to Lightel/CTBC group. The firm also advised on the bidding for B-Band cellular phones, represented AirTouch Communications, Inc. on the privatisation of the Telebras System, and advised on seven public bids involving the concession of licences for the development of cable TV services. **Clients:** Alcatel; Ericsson; Sky; Adelphia Group.

Fischer & Forster Advogados Renowned in the convergence areas of practice, the firm advises across the spectrum of telecoms and IT, handling M&A, joint ventures, litigation, anti-trust issues and IP matters. *"Intelligent and well-prepared"* IT man **George Fischer*** and satellite expert **Umberto Celli Jr*** are regularly recommended by the market. The group's caseload has included the filing of applications for foreign satellite landing rights in Brazil, advising on the first tender for

* See leaders' profiles on pages 152-159

Brazilian orbital slots, and acting on the tender for fixed telephony for the State of São Paulo and 17 other states. The firm has also advised e-business clients on contractual, IP and foreign exchange matters. On contentious matters, the team represented an Argentinean satellite company on an arbitration proceeding against a Brazilian long distance company. **Clients:** Qualcomm; international corporates.

Machado, Meyer, Sendacz e Opice (12 lawyers) Broad-based department with expertise in both IT and telecoms, which advises on financing in the industry, as well as regulatory matters. **Moshe Sendacz*** heads the telecommunications and IT department, and is noted for his transactional acumen. In the IT field, the firm represented Telefónica Interactiva S.A. in connection with its acquisition of Nutec Informática S.A, acted for Terra on the launch of the Terra Livre program, and advised on the structuring and negotiation of the exclusivity agreement for the supply of news content between Terra Networks and Grupo Estado. The group has also assisted a number of clients in connection with private equity investments in Internet companies, notably UOL, Hipernet and Zoyd. The telecoms team has assisted Bell Canada International in the acquisition of an equity interest in Cambras, a cable TV operator in the State of São Paulo, and advised Chase Manhattan on its acquisition of an equity interest in TVA. The firm also advises clients from beyond the Americas, representing Korea Telecom on its bid to acquire minority equity interest in CRT. **Clients:** Chase Manhattan Bank; Telefónica Interactiva SA; UOL; Hipernet; Zoyd; Bell Canada International.

Trench Rossi e Watanabe (Baker & McKenzie) (2 ptrs, 5 asscs) A leading communications firm with a particular reputation in the fast-growing IT sector, and niche expertise in e-commerce, which accounts for more than half the department's workload. Former president of the Brazilian Association of Intellectual Property **Juliana Viegas*** is largely responsible for building up the IT practice. *"Knowledgeable, competent and respected,"* she is considered one of Brazil's leading communications lights. Typical activities include domain name registrations, infringements, problems with privacy, opinions on agreements closed over the internet, revision and correction of terms of site. All aspects of the organisation and arrangement of dot.com companies are also regularly undertaken. **Clients:** Brazilian and international dot.coms; service providers.

Carvalho de Freitas e Ferreira Advogados Associados (8 lawyers) Used by major players such as Embratel for telecoms regulatory work, the firm has a strong reputation in this field. Respected by peers for its advice on interconnection agreements and bidding for high frequency band slots, the team also has recognised litigation prowess. In IT, the firm deals with web-hosting, framing, linking contracting and ethics codes for communication through the net. Head of department, *"excellent technician"* **Ricardo Barretto***, is a former president of ABDI (Brazilian Computer and Telecommunications Law Association) and a prolific writer. The firm assisted a major European player on the B-Band bidding process, and a US concern on the privatisation of Telebràs. **Clients:** Embratel; international telecoms companies.

Demarest e Almeida (8 ptrs, approx 35 asscs) Considered by rivals to have *"developing practices"* in both IT and telecoms law, the firm has advised on mergers between internet companies and telecom companies, the acquisition of start-up companies, hosting and content agreements, the registering of domain names and domain name disputes. In addition, it offers legal consultations on such areas as webpage copyright protection, personal data protection, cybercrimes and online contests and games. In telecoms, the firm advises one of the leading telecom investors in Brazil, assisting on both regulatory and transactional matters. The team advised one of the participating bidders in the country's recent cable auction. **Clients:** Internet and telecoms companies.

Ulhôa Canto, Rezende e Guerra (5 lawyers) **Mariza Rossi*** *("a strong lawyer")* heads a department that is noted for its involvement in a wide range of telecoms and IT work. This year, it has been involved in the incorporation of telecoms companies in Brazil, due diligence on telecoms contracts, and advising companies on bids in licence auctions. The firm has advised on the formation of numerous internet venture companies, such as Submarino Ltd, and the formation of the first Brazilian mutual fund focused on internet companies (IP.Com Fundo de Aoes.) **Clients:** Telemar; Telmex; SES/Astra.

Other Notable Practitioner **Carlos Sundfeld*** of Porto & Sundfeld Advogados leads *"a small practice with top quality clients."* Consultant, professor of administrative law, and president of the Brazilian Society of Public Law, he was involved in drafting the Brazilian Telecommunications Act.

Competition/Anti-trust

Franceschini e Miranda (2 ptrs, 15 asscs) Located in São Paulo, but with offices in Brasília, Rio de Janeiro and Lisbon, this is a firm of increasing scope, with *"a genuine focus on anti-trust work."* Merger control work constitutes a substantial proportion of the caseload. The stand-out player here is **José Ignacio Franceschini***, a member of the commission appointed by CADE to draft the Brazilian anti-trust law. *"One of the best in the business,"* he is considered to be *"absolutely dedicated to this area of law."* The firm advised CVRD as a third party to the Unilever/Bestfoods case, and acted on the global Dow Chemical/Union Carbide merger. **Clients:** Gessy Lever; DEL; Unilever; Schindler; Volvo; Akzo; ICI; AstraZeneca .

Advocacia José del Chiaro (2 ptrs, 7 asscs) **José del Chiaro***, according to clients *"a real technical expert,"* heads a small firm with *"excellent connections"* and *"a specialisation in economic law in general."* The organisation handles a choice number of complex cases each year for a client roster of international blue-chip corporates. This year, the firm has been involved in proceedings filed by Philip Morris Brasil SA against Souza Cruz SA for anti-competitive behaviour, and is currently representing the Philip Morris Group before the Brazilian competition authorities in a world-wide transaction covering the acquisition of Nabisco Holdings Corp. It has also represented Fiat in the merger of Case Corporation and New Holland NV. **Clients:** Philip Morris Group; Fiat Group; Volkswagen; LM Ericsson Telecom Group.

Magalhães, Ferraz, Prado, Lino e Bruna (3 ptrs, 9 asscs) Renowned both for big-ticket merger control work and anti-cartel advice, the firm is seen by rivals as *"one of the pioneers of competition law in Brazil."* **Carlos Magalhães*** is considered *"a man of real substance,"* while **Tercio Sampaio Ferraz Jr*** is *"a brilliant academic,"* and **Sergio**

BRAZIL Leading firms (Competition/Anti-trust)
1 Franceschini e Miranda
Advocacia José del Chiaro
Magalhães, Ferraz, Prado, Lino e Bruna
Advocacia Pedro Dutra
Pinheiro Neto Advogados
Tozzini Freire Teixeira e Silva
2 Machado, Meyer, Sendacz e Opice
Trench Rossi e Watanabe (Baker & McKenzie)
3 Demarest e Almeida
Levy & Salomão Advogados
Mattos Filho, Veiga Filho, Marrey Jr, Moherdaui e Quiroga
Piquet Carneiro & Associados

Firms are listed alphabetically in each band.

Leading individuals (Competition/Anti-trust)
1 DUTRA Pedro *Advocacia Pedro Dutra*
FRANCESCHINI José Ignácio *Franceschini*
2 DEL CHIARO José *Advocacia José Del Chiaro*
COELHO Tulio *Trench Rossi*
MAGALHÃES Carlos *Magalhães, Ferraz*
MATTOS Ubiratan *Pinheiro Neto*
3 CELEDONIO Lauro *Mattos Filho, Veiga Filho*
FERRAZ Tercio Sampaio *Magalhães, Ferraz*
MOURA ROCHA Bolivar *Levy & Salomão*
NOGUEIRA Mario *Demarest e Almeida*
PIQUET CARNEIRO João Geraldo *Piquet Carneiro*
REGAZZINI José Augusto *Tozzini Freire Teixeira*
SALOMÃO FILHO Calixto *Levy & Salomão*
SILVA Eugenio *Machado, Meyer, Sendacz*
Up-and-coming individuals
BRUNA Sergio *Magalhães, Ferraz*
FERRAZ Helena *Mattos Filho, Veiga Filho*
SACCAB ZARZUR Cristianne *Pinheiro Neto*

Individuals are listed alphabetically in each band.

Bruna* *"a young, open-minded guy"* with *"a bright future ahead of him."* The department also includes two in-house economists. Important cases of the year include acting in the General Motors/Fiat Auto case and advising on the long-running MCI/Sprint affair. **Clients:** Ambev; Brazil Alcool SA.

Advocacia Pedro Dutra (1 ptr, 2 asscs) A boutique firm, specialising in competition and regulatory law, which is noted for handling important merger filings (albeit in restricted numbers), and for its growing international practice. The reputation of the firm centres on that of **Pedro Dutra***. *"Brilliant, aggressive and well-prepared,"* he possesses *"an encyclopaedic knowledge of anti-trust law."* The firm has been involved in a number of important cases, including the merger between Petrobras and OPP this year. Among its clientele is a clutch of around 25 major American companies in Brazil. **Clients:** Total Elf; IBM; Embraer; Nordisk.

Pinheiro Neto Advogados (7 ptrs, 15 asscs) *"If I couldn't do a case, I'd give it to them. They have a fine structure and they train their lawyers well."* A highly rated corporate department provides the firm's anti-trust department with an imposing list of big-ticket merger control cases. Head of the department **Ubiratan Mattos*** *("a wonderful technician")* is the current president of the Brazilian Institute of Anti-trust and Consumer Relations (IBRAC). He is ably supported by new name **Cristianne Saccab Zarzur***, a *"brilliant lawyer."* This year, the firm advised on Microsoft's joint venture with Andersen Consulting (Avanade), and acted on the sale of Fletcher Challenge Ltd's paper division to Norske Skog. Other merger control work included advising on BASF SA's acquisition of the agrochemical division of Cynamid, the acquisition of Daimler Chrysler Rail Systems (Brasil) Ltda. by Balfour Beatty, and Andarko Petroleum Corporation's merger with Union Pacific Resources Group Inc. **Clients:** Anheuser-Busch.

Tozzini Freire Texeira e Silva (2 ptrs, 5 asscs) Generally acknowledged to be performing a very high volume of merger filings, the firm is considered to have *"a good position in the market, on the back of an excellent brand name."* The principal focus of the caseload is on merger reviews, but there is an increasing involvement in the anti-trust aspects of major European transactions. **José Augusto Regazzini***, according to peers *"a charismatic lawyer who knows how to deal with complex cases"* heads up a department which has grown continuously over the last four years and has recently been strengthened by the arrival of a former Cade commissioner. **Clients:** Colgate Palmolive.

Machado, Meyer, Sendacz e Opice (1 ptr, 4 asscs) The past year's caseload has been characterised by *"an impressive volume of merger control work,"* with the IT sector proving an area of niche expertise. **Eugenio Silva*** *("serious and technically proficient")* heads up an able team which has advised on the creation of Avanade, a joint venture between Microsoft and Andersen Consulting for IT consulting and services. The team also advised on the merger of Novartis Crop Protection and Seeds and AstraZeneca's agro-chemicals division to form Syngenta, and on the global sale of coal by Shell to an Anglo-American group. **Clients:** Usinor.

Trench Rossi e Watanabe (Baker & McKenzie) (2 ptrs, 7 asscs) Acting largely for multi-national blue-chips, the firm *"does a lot of this kind of work."* A balanced caseload includes work on big and medium-ticket merger filings and a number of anti-cartel investigations. **Tulio Coelho***, who heads up the practice, is *"an active and familiar"* name on the circuit. This year, the firm has acted for Kaiser, one of the major players in the opposition to the merger between the two major Brazilian brewery companies, Brahma and Antarctica, which resulted in the incorporation of AmBev. Other major cases include acting on the Exxon/Mobil merger control case, representing BASF Brasil in the vitamins cartel investigation, and representing Archer Daniels Midland in the lysine cartel investigation. **Clients:** Proctor & Gamble; Ericsson; Motorola.

Demarest e Almeida (1 ptr, 2 asscs) Small but expanding department, which now has a competition presence both in merger control cases and in contentious matters. Leading light **Mario Nogueira*** *("doing a fine job")* is a respected figure. This year, his department has been involved in a number of important cases, including the purchase of Land Rover by the Ford Motor Company, Telecom Italia's purchase of part of the Brazilian Internet portal Global.Com for R$1 billion, and the merger of Honeywell and AlliedSignal. The team also represented Klabin in the purchase of the Brazilian branch of the American paper company Riverwood, and advised on a case where three laboratories were sued by the government in relation to the price of medicines in Brazil. **Clients:** Ford; BMW; Telecom Italia; Honeywell; AlliedSignal; Klabin; WPP; Bank of New York.

Levy & Salomão (2 ptrs, 8 asscs) *"They're looking to become a big law firm and they're growing rapidly."* The anti-trust group has increased its market profile with the return of **Bolivar Moura Rocha*** to active practice, following his period as Secretary of Economic Monitoring of the Ministry of Finance. Complex issues are handled by **Calixto Salomão Filho***, professor of commercial and competition Law at São Paulo University, who is acknowledged by peers for his *"considerable intellect."* This year, the firm represented TAM Airlines in the negotiations for a possible merger with TransBrasil, advised the National Association of Car Dealerships (Fena-brave) against Ford, General Motors, Fiat and Volkswagen in connection with alleged anti-competitive behaviour, and represented Consórcio Rodobens in an abuse of a dominant position case against Mercedes-Benz

* See leaders' profiles on pages 152-159

and DaimlerChrysler. **Clients:** Petrobras; Coca-Cola; TAM Airlines; Consórcio Rodobens.

Mattos, Filho Veiga Filho, Marrey Jr, Moherdaui e Quiroga (2 ptrs, 4 asscs) *"Well-structured"* group which offers extensive advice on merger control cases involving foreign companies with activities in Brazil. **Lauro Celedonio*** is a *"serious practitioner,"* while **Helena Ferraz*** *("a very smart lawyer")* is regarded as a rising star. Recent transactions filed with CADE include the acquisition of Fletcher Challenge Ltd's paper division by Norske Skogindustrier ASA, the acquisition of Patagon.com International Inc by Banco Santander Central Hispano SA, and the acquisition of Vitopel SA and Koppol Ltda by BOPP Holdings. A number of important joint ventures between both Brazilian and foreign companies were also filed this year. **Clients:** Lucent; Henkel; Lugold.

Piquet Carneiro & Associados (3 ptrs, 3 asscs) *"If a case requires more than just legal production, I'd hire them."* The firm's anti-trust reputation is thought to hinge on that of **João Geraldo Piquet Carneiro***, *"an influential negotiator,"* who has a long experience of regulatory issues and their competition implications. **Clients:** Major domestic companies.

B

Corporate/M&A

Barbosa, Müssnich & Aragão (12 ptrs, 32 asscs) *"May be the best firm in Brazil for corporate law."* Medium-sized, but fast-growing, it is *"aggressive, active, and has found its niche with Brazilian investment banks."* The firm was founded in Rio de Janeiro, where **Francisco Müssnich*** *("an excellent technician")* is primarily based. *"Vastly experienced"* **Paulo Cezar Aragão*** *("undoubtedly one of the best lawyers in Brazil"*according to our research*)* heads up the São Paulo office, which has a matchless reputation for transactional ability. Major activities of the year include assisting the Arbed Group and Companhia Siderúrgica Belgo-Mineira in the transfer of their iron ore controlling interests in SA Mineração Trindade and Samarco Mineração SA to Companhia Vale do Rio Doce. The team also advised Companhia Cervejaria Brahma in structuring and implementing the Brahma and Antarctica Paulista transaction, which resulted in the creation of Companhia de Bebidas das Americas – Ambev, currently one of the top brewery companies in the world. **Clients:** Arbed Group; Companhia Siderúrgica Belgo-Mineira; Companhia Cervejaria Brahma.

Demarest e Almeida (7 ptrs, 50 asscs) The firm made its name in labour law, and derives substantial corporate work from an industrial client base. Noted by rivals for representing *"major multi-nationals,"* it has grown substantially, more than doubling in the last four years. *"Creative"* **Altamiro Boscoli*** *("a superb negotiator and deal-closer")* and the respected **Rogerio Lessa*** are the key players here. Highlights of the year include advising Indústrias Klabin SA on the purchase of Igaras Papéis e Embalagens SA, a deal worth $500 million, advising Petroquímica Española on the acquisition of Deten Química SA, and representing Telecom Italia on the acquisition of 30% of Globo.com, one of the largest Brazilian dot.com ventures. **Clients:** Olivetti; BSCH; Ford; Monsanto; Goldman Sachs.

Machado, Meyer, Sendacz e Opice (4 ptrs, 30 asscs) *"An excellent department"* producing *"top-quality corporate work."* The firm is particularly noted for its connections with leading financial institutions, and possesses a roster of top lawyers, including the *"outstanding"* **Antonio Meyer***and **José Roberto Opice*** *("the best finance lawyer in Brazil.")* That said, a group of the firm's lawyers has recently broken away to set up an independent practice, thus weakening capacity somewhat. Globally, the firm has formed an alliance with Spanish organisation Cuatrecasas, as well as firms in Portugal and Argentina. Transactionally, the team acted as counsel for Citibank NA in the sale of Banco Crefisul SA by Citibank NA, and acted for a group of investors in the acquisition of the minority interest of UOL Inc SA. Recognised, too, as a major telecoms player, the firm acted on the merger of Telesp, Telesp Participações SA and CTBC SA, and represented the controlling shareholder, Telefónica International SA, in a follow-up share-swap. **Clients:** AstraZeneca Do Brasil Ltda; Citibank; BankBoston Capital; Deloitte & Touche Consulting Group.

Mattos Filho, Veiga Filho, Marrey Jr, Moherdaui e Quiroga (4 ptrs, 15 asscs) *"A young partnership with a hands-on approach"* which has rapidly gained critical mass and now has offices in São Paulo, Rio de Janeiro and Brasília. Among a respected team, **Ary Oswaldo Mattos Filho***, **João Ricardo de Azevedo Ribeiro*** and **Moacir Zilbovicius*** were most frequently mentioned by the market. The firm is particularly noted for its private equity work, one commentator observing that *"they do more equity deals out of Brazil than anyone else."* Strong, too, in the hi-tech sector, the team recently acted as counsel to the controlling shareholder of ZipNet SA, one of the major Brazilian Internet Portals, in its recent sale of control to Portugal Telecom SA. This was the largest M&A transaction on the Internet to date. In addition, the firm can count on a constant stream of work from a number of international blue-chip corporates. This year, it advised Fiat Automóveis SA on its joint venture with General Motors do Brasil Ltd concerning the development of the power train operations of the Fiat and GM groups in Brazil. **Clients:** Motorola; Ericsson Sweden; Lucent.

Pinheiro Neto Advogados (25 ptrs, 85 asscs) The largest firm in Brazil, it has a conservative but widely-admired character, and is specifically recognised for its *"client-oriented approach."* The corporate team boasts an array of ranked practitioners. **Antonio Mendes*** *("knows how to negotiate and reach an agreement; he's something special")* is generally recognised to be *"one of the finest lawyers in São Paulo."* **Irene Dias da Silva***, telecoms expert **Esther Nunes*** and **Hélio Nicoletti*** have also received widespread commendation. And **Alexandre Bertoldi*** is considered an *"outstanding"* transactional force, notably in the financial sphere. Over the last twelve months, the firm has been involved in all three of the year's leading banking M&A deals, including advising Banco Bradesco SA on its $600 million acquisition of Banco Boavista SA, and advising Caixa Geral de Depósitos on the sale of its subsidiary Banco Bandeirantes to Unibanco SA. In addition, the firm possesses a top-flight stable of blue-chip international clients, and is a regular player in retail and telecoms transactions. Substantial recent deals of this kind include representing Royal Ahold on the acquisition of Supermercados Bompreço. **Clients:** Philip Morris; Shell; Lloyd's; Rolls-Royce; Telefónica.

Tozzini Freire Teixeira e Silva (17 ptrs, 62 asscs) A massive recruitment drive has seen the firm expand rapidly over the last few years. While this has led to the occasional comment about *"variable quality,"* most commentators believe that the firm is *"aggressive, organised, and knows what it's doing."* The *"excellent and well-connected"* **Syllas Tozzini*** is renowned for his international work, while the *"conscientious"* **José Luis de Salles Freire*** also commands general market respect. Noted for its advice on complex, multi-jurisdictional transactions, the firm's areas of strength include the hi-tech industries and electricity. Among recent highlights, the firm advised on the acquisition by Principal Financial Group of 50% of the shares of a Brazilian private pension company. The team also acted on the acquisition of Brazilian filing and data and imaging processing companies by Recall Corporation. **Clients:** Alcatel; Ericsson; Macri Group; Invensys (BTR Siebe).

BRAZIL Leading firms (Corporate/Mergers & Acquisitions)	
1	Barbosa, Müssnich & Aragão
	Demarest e Almeida
	Machado, Meyer, Sendacz e Opice
	Mattos Filho, Veiga Filho, Marrey Jr, Moherdaui e Quiroga
	Pinheiro Neto Advogados
	Tozzini Freire Teixeira e Silva
2	Goulart Penteado, Iervolino & Lefosse Advogados
	Lobo & Ibeas
	Trench Rossi & Watanabe (Baker & McKenzie)
	Ulhôa Canto, Rezende e Guerra Advogados
	Veirano Advogados Associados
3	Azevedo Sette Advogados
	Motta Fernandes Rocha Advogados
	Vieira, Rezende, Barbosa e Guerreiro
	Xavier Bernardes e Bragança
4	Amaro, Stuber e Advogados Associados
	Carvalhosa Eizirik & Motta Veiga
	Escritorio de Advocacia Gouvea Vieira
	Pinheiro Guimaraes Advogados

Firms are listed alphabetically in each band.

Goulart Penteado, Iervolino & Lefosse Advogados (6 ptrs, 23 asscs) *"A small, prestigious boutique"* that *"concentrates on quality,"* and possesses *"excellent clients."* The bulk of its work is done on behalf of industrial clients, particularly those drawn from the automobile industries. The firm's *"mastermind,"* **João Caio Goulart Penteado***, formerly at Pinheiro Neto, *"has an outstanding reputation,"* and *"combines technical expertise with originality."* **Geraldo Lefosse*** is *"thoroughly efficient"* and has *"a tremendous following amongst foreign companies."* The team acted on the acquisition of the leading independent Brazilian stamping company, and on the acquisition of the leading local company in the ink-printing sector. **Clients:** Mercedes-Benz; Volkswagen; Audi; Coca-Cola; Compaq.

Lobo & Ibeas (Approx 10 lawyers) *"A talented group"* according to our research which, although originally known for its expertise in the mining sector, is now felt to be *"increasing its market share across the transactional board."* *"Experienced"* **Carlos Alberto Da Silveira Lobo*** is the key figure here. His knowledge of the M&A market is hard to match. The firm recently worked on the sale of a company belonging to Souza Cruz (the Brazilian subsidiary of British American Tobacco) and advised on a joint venture between the Swedish Group Stora Enso and Odebrecht. **Clients:** Deutsche Bank.

Leading individuals (Corporate/Mergers & Acquisitions)		
★	**ARAGÃO Paulo Cezar** *Barbosa, Müssnich*	**TOZZINI Syllas** *Tozzini Freire Teixeira e Silva*
1	**BOSCOLI Altamiro** *Demarest e Almeida*	**BULHÕES PEDREIRA José Luiz** *Bulhões Pedreira*
	CANTIDIANO Luiz Leonardo *Motta Fernandes*	**GOULART PENTEADO João Caio** *Goulart Penteado*
	MENDES Antonio *Pinheiro Neto*	**MEYER Antonio** *Machado, Meyer*
	OPICE José Roberto *Machado, Meyer*	
2	**AZEVEDO SETTE Ordelio** *Azevedo Sette*	**BERTOLDI Alexandre** *Pinheiro Neto*
	CESCON AVEDISSIAN Maria Cristina *Souza, Cescon*	**RIBEIRO João Ricardo de Azevedo** *Mattos Filho*
	DE SALLES FREIRE José Luis *Tozzini Freire*	**DIAS DA SILVA Irene** *Pinheiro Neto*
	EIZIRIK Nelson *Carvalhosa Eizirik & Motta Veiga*	**LEFOSSE Geraldo** *Goulart Penteado, Iervolino*
	MÜSSNICH Francisco *Barbosa, Müssnich*	**VEIRANO Ronaldo** *Veirano Advogados Associados*
	VIEIRA Paulo *Vieira, Rezende, Barbosa*	**ZILBOVICIUS Moacir** *Mattos Filho, Veiga Filho*
3	**BARRETO Robson** *Veirano Advogados Associados*	**BERNARDES-NETO Horacio** *Xavier Bernardes*
	DA SILVEIRA LOBO Carlos Alberto *Lobo & Ibeas*	**REZENDE Fabio de** *Vieira, Rezende, Barbosa*
	FISCHER George Charles *Fischer & Forster*	**LESSA Rogerio** *Demarest & Almeida*
	MATTOS FILHO Ary Oswaldo *Mattos Filho, Veiga Filho*	**MEIRELLES DE MIRANDA Aloysio** *Ulhôa Canto*
	NICOLETTI Hélio *Pinheiro Neto*	**NUNES Esther** *Pinheiro Neto*
	PRADO Claudia *Trench Rossi*	**ROSSI Carlos Alberto de Souza** *Trench Rossi*
	STUBER Walter Douglas *Amaro, Stuber*	**ULHÔA CANTO Carlos Alberto** *Ulhôa Canto*
	VEIRANO Ricardo *Veirano Advogados Associados*	**VIEGAS Juliana** *Trench Rossi*

Individuals are listed alphabetically in each band.

Trench Rossi e Watanabe (Baker & McKenzie) (Approx 35 lawyers) A *"successful"* and *"well-organised"* firm, which not only takes advantage of the obvious benefits of the Baker & McKenzie international network, but is also acknowledged for its *"powerful"* domestic client base. **Juliana Viegas***, **Carlos Alberto de Souza Rossi*** and **Claudia Prado*** currently enjoy the highest corporate profile at the firm. *"Particularly strong on oil and gas issues,"* the Rio office advised Petrobras on a pair of oil and gas deals worth an estimated £2 billion this year. Other major transactions include acting for Apax Partners & Co on the acquisition of Wangner Itelpa Ltda, and advising Companhia Siderúrgica Belgo-Mineira on the sale of 63% of the shares of Samitri-SA Mineração da Trindade held by ARBED group. **Clients:** Cabletron Systems do Brasil Ltda; Emerson Eletric do Brasil Ltda; Archer Daniels Midland Company; Manpower Brasil Ltda.

Ulhôa Canto, Rezende & Guerra Advogados (Approx 45 lawyers) *"Active and hungry,"* the firm's superb tax tradition has been a substantial factor in its developing corporate profile, given the substantially tax-driven nature of Brazilian M&A work. Major transactions of the year include representing CVRD in connection with the $525 million acquisition of SA Minerao da Trindade (SAMITRI). Also well known for its involvement in transactions throughout the energy sector, the corporate team represented Gas Natural SDG SA on the acquisition of the concession for the distribution of natural gas in southern São Paulo. The leading lights at the firm are acknowledged by the market to be **Aloysio Meirelles de Miranda*** and **Carlos Alberto Ulhôa Canto***. **Clients:** Elektro-Eletricidade e Servicos SA; Sithe energies; CSFB; Electrobras; Enron; Société Générale; OPP Petroquimica; Tractabel; Iberdrola; Banco do Brasil Investimentos; ENEL.

Veirano Advogados Associados (11 ptrs, 52 asscs) National firm praised by the market for its *"proactive"* nature, it has an enviably deep client roster, notably among energy companies and financial institutions. Its lawyers are *"first-class"*

* See leaders' profiles on pages 152-159

too. **Ronaldo Veirano*** is described as *"an able practitioner,"* **Ricardo Veirano*** *"makes any type of transaction feasible,"* and **Robson Barreto*** also maintains his share of market support. Significant activities of the year include representing Aracruz Celulose on the acquisition of 40% of the capital stock of Veracel Celulose SA, and representing the issuer on the refinancing of the $125 million Series A Eurobond issuance of MRS Logística SA. The team has also represented a number of private equity funds on their acquisitions and strategic investments. **Clients:** AES; Amerada Hess; America Online; Andersen Consulting; AT&T; Azurix; BAT Industries; BHP; British-Borneo; British Gas; Chevron; De La Rue; Dell Computers; Enron; Eximbank; ExxonMobil; Ford Motors; Glaxo Wellcome; Marriott; Nokia; Nortel; Petrobras; Pharmacia & Upjohn; Philip Morris; PSiNet; Shell; Telecom Italia; World Bank.

Azevedo Sette (17 ptrs, 55 asscs) The largest firm in the state of Minas Gerais has consolidated its reputation as a sound choice for cross-border M&A transactions, as well as gaining plaudits for its advice to the government on several privatisations. **Ordelio Azevedo Sette*** is, according to rivals, an *"experienced and smart"* lawyer with *"excellent local connections."* The firm handles a number of big-ticket transactions for international blue-chips and local heavyweights. Chief among these was the corporate team's advice to Brasil Telecom on its $800 million acquisition of the equity interest of CRT from TBS Participações SA. **Clients:** GE Capital; Xerox; Exxon; Microsoft; MAPFRE; Labinal; Pinault-Printemps; Citibank; Banco Santander; Unibanco; CVRD; FCA; Global Environment Fund.

Motta Fernandes Rocha (6 ptrs, 6 asscs) *"A traditional Rio firm"* which is home to one of the *"big players,"* the *"supremely competent"* **Luiz Leonardo Cantidiano***, around whom much of the firm's corporate work revolves. Financial institutions form an important constituent of the firm's client base. An eclectic caseload includes acting on the sale of a bank, working on a joint venture involving a television company, representing a foreign group in its acquisition of part of the capital of a holding company in Brazil, and advising a foreign company on its presentation of proposals for the auction of new licences for mobile phones in Brazil. **Clients:** Dresdner Kleinwort Benson; Inepar; Banco Espírito Santo; Banco Pactual.

Vieira, Rezende, Barbosa e Guerreiro (7 ptrs, 20 asscs) *"Distinctive and attentive"* firm beloved of clients, who praise the corporate team for its *"responsiveness, US-style aggression and precision."* **Paulo Vieira*** is *"superbly equipped to deal with any situation that arises,"* and receives reliable support from **Fabio de Rezende***. The department calls on the expertise of partners from a number of areas of practice, and is further commended for its *"flexibility."* Generally recognised to assist front-rank domestic companies, it advised the consortium formed by Previ, BB Banco De Investimentos SA and Iberdrola on the acquisition of the corporate control of Celpe, the energy distributor of the state of Pernambuco. Also represented Latinvest Online on the acquisition of a minority interest in Conectiva SA, a software company that has the exclusive representation of Linux in Brazil. **Clients:** National Grid; Iberdrola; Bradesco; Camargo Corrêa; LatinTech Capital.

Xavier Bernardes e Bragança (7 ptrs, 40 asscs in firm) Boutique tax firm with a strong niche in corporate work. A young firm too, which has expanded rapidly, and now possesses offices in São Paulo, Rio de Janeiro, Joinville, Lisbon and Funchal. Active in the electrical, telecommunications, chemical and internet industries, the firm primarily advises household name clients from Europe. **Horacio Bernardes-Neto*** *("a fine lawyer building an international reputation")* is the stand-out partner here. This year, the firm advised on the acquisition by Southwestern Bell Corporation of part of the shares of Algar Telecom Lest, and represented IFX Group on the acquisition of companies belonging to the Conex Group. **Clients:** Lloyds Bank; Alcatel; Crédit Agricole Indosuez; Amanco Holding Inc.

Amaro, Stuber e Advogados Associados (3 ptrs, 20 asscs) Founded in 1992 by a pair of former Mattos Filho partners, the firm is considered *"a hard-working market presence"* with a particular niche in acting for financial institutions, notably on bond issues. Transactionally, the firm advised on the acquisition of a factory in Brazil, and on the acquisition of an Internet business in Brazil, which subsequently led to an IPO. **Walter Douglas Stuber*** retains his status among his peers as a *"trustworthy and capable"* practitioner. **Clients:** JP Morgan Securities Inc; Banco Santander; Stryker Corporation; Citibank NV; Dow Corning Corporation; Continental Grain Company.

Carvalhosa Eizirik & Motta Veiga (3 ptrs, 9 asscs) *"A name to be watched,"* the firm has been noted as a rising presence in the market due to its participation in a number of complex recent multi-jurisdictional transactions. **Nelson Eizirik***, a former Commissioner to the Brazilian Securities Commission, is recommended both for his securities work and for corporate expertise. Over the past year, the firm has been involved in numerous mergers, listings and delistings of public corporations, as well as administrative proceedings before the Central Bank and the Brazilian Securities Commission. **Clients:** Bradesco; Credit Suisse; Warburg Bank; Companhia Vale do Rio Doce; Bolsa de Valores de São Paulo; USIMINAS.

Escritorio de Advocacia Gouvea Vieira (9 ptrs, 15 asscs) Established firm with *"excellent clients,"* a notable involvement in insurance work, and a stable position in the market. This year, the firm has been involved in the acquisition of a bank, a cement company, a telephone company, and several electrical companies. Most recently, the corporate team advised Spain's Endesa on its tender offer for Brazilian distribution company CERJ. **Clients:** EDP; Endesa.

Pinheiro Guimaraes Advogados (6 ptrs, 10 asscs) One of Brazil's oldest firms, it possesses a historic link with Citibank, and *"can never be ruled out when it comes to corporate finance."* Transactional activities of the year include negotiating the shareholders' agreement of Espírito Santo Centrais Eléctricas SA (ESCELSA) on behalf of a consortium of local pension funds, and representing Bell Canada International in the negotiations of the shareholders' agreements for Telet SA and Americel SA. The team also represented Mellon Bank, NA on the acquisition of 40% of the voting shares of Banco Brascan SA, and acted for Banco Liberal SA on the acquisition of 50% of its voting shares by Nations Bank. **Clients:** Bell Canada; CSFB; Goldman Sachs.

Other Notable Practitioners **José Luiz Bulhões Pedreira*** of Bulhões Pedreira, Bulhões Carvalho & Advogados Associados is, according to a number of good judges, *"perhaps the most important corporate finance lawyer in Brazil." "Creative business-like"* **Maria Cristina Cescon Avedissian*** has just left Machado, Meyer, Sendacz e Opice to form her own firm, Souza, Cescon Avedissian, Barrieu e Flesch. **George Charles Fischer*** of Fischer & Forster Advogados was also strongly recommended by the market.

Project Finance

BRAZIL Leading firms (Project Finance)
1 Machado, Meyer, Sendacz e Opice
Tozzini Freire Teixeira e Silva
2 Mattos Filho, Veiga Filho, Marrey Jr, Moherdaui e Quiroga
Pinheiro Neto Advogados
Ulhôa Canto, Rezende e Guerra Advogados
Veirano Advogados Associados
3 Barbosa, Müssnich & Aragão
Demarest e Almeida
Lacaz Martins, Halembeck, Pereira Neto, Gurevich & Schoueri
Trench Rossi e Watanabe (Baker & McKenzie)

Firms are listed alphabetically in each band.

Leading individuals (Project Finance)
★ NUNES PINTO José Emilio *Tozzini Freire*
1 DE SOUSA Luis Antonio *Machado, Meyer*
2 MEYER Antonio *Machado, Meyer*
OPICE José Roberto *Machado, Meyer*
VIEIRA COELHO Ricardo *Pinheiro Neto*
3 ARAGÃO Paulo Cezar *Barbosa, Müssnich*
BARBOSA Plinio *Barbosa, Müssnich*
DE ARAUJO CINTRA Antonio Felix *Tozzini Freire*
DE AZEVEDO RIBEIRO João Ricardo *Mattos Filho*
FLESCH Cristiane *Souza Cescon*
SPINELLI SILVA Sergio *Mattos Filho*

Individuals are listed alphabetically in each band.

Machado, Meyer, Sendacz e Opice (2 ptrs, 5 asscs) Clearly one of the market leaders, the firm advises on projects involving ports, hydro and thermo plants, fibre optics, oil and gas, toll roads, water and sanitation, and the financing and leasing of equipment, typically acting for the lenders. A vastly experienced team includes **Luis Antonio de Sousa*** *("a brilliant and smart performer,")* the *"ever-present"* **Antonio Meyer***, and **José Roberto Opice***, a leading figure for around 30 years. The Rio office has further been strengthened by the arrival of a group of oil and gas lawyers from Veirano Advogados. This year, the firm advised on a US$80 million bond issue designed to finance the sale of scanners, ultrasound devices and other medical equipment to Brazil, and acted on Petrolífera Marlim's debut offering of a US$200 million five-year bond. It was also involved in the second half of the Marlim project, in which Marlim will be raising US$500 million in the market, thus completing 50% of its expected capitalisation of $1.5 billion. **Clients:** Petrolífera Marlim; Petrobras.

Tozzini Freire Teixeira e Silva (1 ptr, 15 asscs) Aggressive department with a peerless client base of domestic and international financial institutions, and an involvement in the majority of the nation's leading recent projects. Energy and infrastructure are two specific areas of expertise. **José Emilio Nunes Pinto*** *("a pioneer and a great client man")* and **Antonio Felix de Araujo Cintra*** are the group's key figures. Recent instructions have included the Dutra Toll Road (São Paulo-Rio de Janeiro Highway), the AutoBan Toll Road, the Bolivia-Brazil Gas Pipeline, where the firm represented Petrobras, and the Uruguaiana-Porto Alegre Gas Pipeline, where the firm represented the project company jointly owned by Gaspetro, TotalFinaElf, Techint, YPF Repsol and Ipiranga. The firm also advised Equity Investors on the Cabiunas project financing for the development of a gas field and the construction of a pipe line, valued at around $800 million. **Clients:** ABN AMRO Bank; Banco Santander; Banco Sudameris; Bear Stearns; BankBoston; Mitsui & Co Ltd; United States Eximbank.

Mattos Filho, Veiga Filho, Marrey Jr, Moherdaui e Quiroga Perceived to have had *"a quieter year,"* but still recognised for its advice on behalf of banks, often in energy projects. **Sergio Spinelli Silva*** is acknowledged to do *"a substantial amount of this kind of work,"* while **João Ricardo de Azevedo Ribeiro*** has *"a good working knowledge of the area."* In 2000, the department participated in a variety of high-profile structured financings and vendor financings, to the value of $1.7 billion, representing clients such as Lucent Technologies Inc. **Clients:** Lucent Technologies Inc; Embratel; Light.

Pinheiro Neto Advogados (9 ptrs, 28 asscs) Although *"making a major effort out of its regional offices,"* the department is still considered to lack the volume of the two market leaders. It nevertheless maintains a considerable reputation for its work with banks, and is noted for its connections with JP Morgan and Morgan Stanley. **Ricardo Vieira Coelho*** *"has a fine track record,"* and was involved in the largest project financing in Brazilian history, acting for a group of lenders. The firm also represented Gaspetro in the project financing of a thermal power plant in the southern state of Paraná. **Clients:** Duke Energy; Petrobras/ Gaspetro; Endesa; Duke Energy; GE Capital; Marubeni; Mitsubishi; Mitsui.

Ulhôa Canto, Rezende e Guerra Advogados (8 ptrs) *"Definitely a player,"* the firm has shed its 'tax boutique' image, and is noted for its involvement on a number of high-profile energy projects. Although lacking star individuals, the department is felt to function as an effective unit. This year, it assisted ABN AMRO on a project financing for Itapebi Geracao de Energia SA, concerning the generation of hydroelectric power (450 MW) in Rio Jequitinhonha, sponsored by Companhia de Electridade do Estado da Bahia SA, Iberdrola, Banco do Brasil SA and Previ. It also advised GalvaSud SA in connection with a $250 million project financing for a steel galvanisation plant in the State of Rio de Janeiro, and was involved in the development of the Frade, Albacora, Bijupira-Salema and Pescada-Arabaiana oil and gas fields. Further energy projects include advising Sithe Energies and Marubeni in connection with an electric power and steam co-generation project in Cubato, and acting on the construction and operation of the Cuiaba pipeline and power plant. **Clients:** Petrobras; GalvaSud SA; ABN AMRO.

Veirano Advogados Associados (10 ptrs, 38 asscs) *"One of the leading firms for oil and gas projects,"* the group has also been active on a number of hi-tech projects, often acting on behalf of the borrowers. Major activities of the year include representing the borrower in a $1 billion project for the expansion of plant facilities and the creation of port and road infrastructure. The group has also represented borrowers and lenders on oil and gas field exploration projects. **Clients:** Dell; Telecom Italia; AT&T.

Barbosa, Müssnich & Aragão *"Always involved in large transactions,"* the firm is, however, better known for its corporate prowess. M&A experts **Plinio Barbosa*** and the ubiquitous **Paolo Cezar Aragão*** head a department which is increasingly active on behalf of sponsors and borrowers. This year, the firm acted as legal advisor for the Brazilian investors in a 400 MW thermo-electric power plant in the state of Rondonia, implemented in association with El Paso Energy International do Brasil Ltda. **Clients:** LAIF; domestic and international corporates.

Demarest e Almeida (2 ptrs, 2 asscs) Although not possessing a separate projects department, the firm is viewed by rivals as an increasingly powerful presence on energy matters, advising a number of international corporates and financial institutions. The group advised on a project financing for a thermal plant in Rio, where the co-ordinator was Dresdner Kleinwort Benson.

* See leaders' profiles on pages 152-159

Several oil and gas projects are currently under negotiation. **Clients:** Industrial companies; financial institutions.

Lacaz Martins, Halembeck, Pereira Neto, Gurevich & Schoueri (2 ptrs, 6 asscs) *"Young, dynamic"* firm with expertise in infrastructure projects, notably in water and sanitation. The group advised on a pair of toll road projects with a combined value of R$500 million, and has also acted on waste treatment and power plant projects. **Clients:** Odebrecht Group.

Trench Rossi e Watanabe (4 ptrs, 12 asscs) Experienced in the negotiation of PPAs and EPCs, and on projects involving IPPs, the firm recently represented Petrobas in the Barracuda and Caratinga (Oil Platform) Project, valued at $2.5 billion. It also advised a sponsor on the financing, building and operation of the natural gas-fired thermo-electric power plant DUNAS I, and was involved in the public bid for the grant of a concession to distribute piped gas in the southern area of the state of São Paulo. **Clients:** Petrobas; Comgás; CESP.

Other Notable Practitioner **Cristiane Flesche***, whose PF profile has increased dramatically over the past year, recently left Machado, Meyer, Sendacz e Opice to form her own firm, Souza, Cescon Avedissian, Barrieu e Flesche.

B

Tax

BRAZIL
Leading firms (Tax)

Band	Firm
1	Ulhôa Canto, Rezende e Guerra Advogados
2	Lacaz Martins, Halembeck, Pereira Neto, Gurevich & Schoueri
	Machado, Meyer, Sendacz e Opice
	Mattos Filho, Veiga Filho, Marrey Jr, Moherdaui e Quiroga
	Pinheiro Neto Advogados
	Tozzini Freire Teixeira e Silva
	Xavier Bernardes e Bragança
3	Bulhões Pedreira, Bulhões Carvalho & Advogados Associados
	Demarest e Almeida
	Dias de Souza Advogados Associados SC
	Trench Rossi e Watanabe (Baker & McKenzie)
4	Barbosa, Müssnich & Aragão
	Gaia, Silva, Rolim & Associados SC
	Mariz de Oliveira, Siqueira Campos e Bianco Advogados SC

Firms are listed alphabetically in each band.

Leading individuals (Tax)

Band		
★	**BULHÕES PEDREIRA José Luiz** *Bulhões Pedreira*	
1	**DIAS DE SOUZA Hamilton** *Dias de Souza*	**MARIZ OLIVEIRA Ricardo** *Mariz de Oliveira*
	XAVIER Alberto *Xavier Bernardes e Bragança*	
2	**APOCALYPSE Sydney** *Tozzini Freire*	**GANDRA MARTINS Ives** *Gandra Martins*
	MARREY Pedro Luciano *Mattos Filho*	**QUIROGA MOSQUERA Roberto** *Mattos Filho*
	SCHOUERI Luis Eduardo *Lacaz Martins*	
3	**ANDREZANI Luis Carlos** *Andrezani Advocacia Impresareial*	**CONSENTINO Arion** *Demarest e Almeida*
	GRECO Marco Aurelio *Dias de Souza*	**GUERRA JD Cordeiro** *Ulhôa Canto*
	LACAZ MARTINS Ricardo *Lacaz Martins*	**PASQUALIN Roberto** *Demarest e Almeida*
	PISANI Jose Roberto *Pinheiro Neto*	
4	**CARVALHO Paulo Barros** *Sole Practitioner*	**FARROCO JR Antonio Carlos** *Trench Rossi*
	GALHARDO Luciana Rosanova *Pinheiro Neto*	**MEIRELLES DE MIRANDA Aloysio** *Ulhôa Canto*
	MEYER Antonio *Machado, Meyer, Sendacz*	**NOVAIS Raquel** *Machado, Meyer, Sendacz*
	REZENDE Condorcet *Ulhôa Canto*	**ROMANELI Mario Antonio** *Tozzini Freire*
	ULHÔA CANTO Carlos Alberto *Ulhôa Canto*	**ZANCAN Leandro Luiz** *Barbosa, Müssnich*

Individuals are listed alphabetically in each band.

Ulhôa Canto, Rezende e Guerra Advogados (35 lawyers) *"Still the best,"* the firm's reputation for tax expertise has been re-emphasised this year. Possessing a wealth of acclaimed practitioners, the group is frequently asked to serve as tax advisors to American banks, and has represented a number of recently privatised companies before the tax authorities in contentious matters. **JD Cordeiro Guerra*** is *"a superb litigator,"* **Aloysio Meirelles de Miranda*** has an excellent reputation for advising on the tax aspects of big-ticket M&A transactions, and **Condorcet Rezende*** is a *"strong ideas man."* **Carlos Alberto Ulhôa Canto*** is also recommended by clients for his all-round expertise. The firm acted for the State of Ceara in discussions with the Federal Government, Congress and the other States on the reform of the tax chapter of the Federal Constitution. It also advised ONIP in connection with a special tax regime (known as 'Repetro') for the import/export of equipment for the exploration and production of oil and natural gas. **Clients:** IBM; Citibank; Coca-Cola Bottling; Exxon; Petrobras; Telemar.

Lacaz Martins, Halembeck, Pereira Neto, Gurevich & Schoueri (2 ptrs, 12 asscs) Rapidly expanding firm with a young team which wins market approval for its tax specialisation. The department is divided into tax consulting and tax litigation teams, and includes the *"excellent"* **Ricardo Lacaz Martins*** and **Luis Eduardo Schoueri*** *("a scholar, well-known for tax planning.")* A growing international workload, notably transfer pricing and tax planning, is undertaken for a varied clientele, among which leading pharmaceutical companies stand out. The firm has also increased its influence in public regulated sectors, such as communications, energy and toll roads. **Clients:** Nova Dutra; DuPont do Brasil; AES Corporation; Siemens.

Machado, Meyer, Sendacz e Opice (3 ptrs, 18 asscs) Leading corporate firm with an exemplary record in M&A-related tax work, and additional strength in tax litigation. **Antonio Meyer*** and **Raquel Novais*** are regarded as distinguished national figures in corporate tax. Highlight work includes the $500 million acquisition of a public Brazilian company by a Swiss company, advising a European purchaser on an international transaction in the mining sector, and restructuring assets after privatisation in the telecommunications industry (value approx $2 billion), the oil and gas industry (value approx $16 billion), and the electrical sector. **Clients:** Shell; Texaco; Telefónica.

Mattos Filho, Veiga Filho, Marrey Jr, Moherdaui e Quiroga (5 ptrs, 45 asscs) A huge department covers a correspondingly large volume of tax litigation and transactional cases. The *"top-class"* **Pedro Luciano Marrey***, a former administrative judge, supervises the litigation group, while **Roberto Quiroga Mosquera*** *("one of the best tax lawyers among the younger guys")* is a prolific author and specialist in the tax aspects of financial products. The firm advised ZipNet SA on the sale of control of Portugal Telecom SA, and has been involved in extensive litigation against the federal government. **Clients:** ZipNet SA; Portugal Telecom SA.

Pinheiro Neto Advogados (10 ptrs, 50 asscs) "*Immensely strong*" team which advises numerous multi-nationals and financial institutions on tax structuring and tax incentive negotiating for start-up businesses. **José Roberto Pisani*** *("excellent on indirect tax issues")* and **Luciana Rosanova Galhardo***, a respected figure with a corporate background, are the key players in a department which sub-divides into tax consultancy/planning and tax litigation (administrative and judicial) teams. **Clients:** Financial institutions; multi-nationals.

Tozzini Freire Teixeira & Silva (2 ptrs, 12 asscs) "*Excellent*" department, dealing with oil and gas joint ventures, structurings, and the preparation of alternatives to avoid double taxation. Top tax planning name **Sydney Apocalypse***, known for his presence on big-ticket corporate transactions, is *"building a strong team,"* which includes rising name **Mario Antonio Romaneli***. The firm has advised the American power company Enron, and was involved in a $20 million tax administration case. **Clients:** Petrobras; Enron.

Xavier Bernardes e Bragança (7 ptrs, 30 asscs) Specialists in international taxation, the department is headed by *"creative"* **Alberto Xavier***, a professor of international tax law and a practitioner of global standing. The firm advised on the tax aspects of Southwestern Bell Corporation's acquisition of part of the shares of Algar Telecom Lest, and on the IFX Group's acquisition of companies belonging to the Conex Group. **Clients:** Lloyds Bank; Brasil Telecom; Bradespar SA; Alcatel.

Bulhões Pedreira, Bulhões Carvalho & Advogados Associados **José Luiz Bulhões Pedreira***, according to one client *"the father of all corporate lawyers,"* heads a *"small, brilliant law firm"* with niche expertise in tax. Operating out of both Rio de Janeiro and São Paulo, the firm is active in both consultation and litigation, advising banks and large industrial and commercial corporations. **Clients:** Banks; industrial/commercial corporations.

Demarest e Almeida (7 ptrs, 19 asscs) The lateral hire of the respected **Roberto Pasqualin*** from Tess Pasqualin is considered to have given the department a fillip. He joins indirect tax expert **Arion Consentino*** at a team with a high reputation for both tax consultancy and planning. The group has advised on the tax structuring of several acquisitions and investments in Brazil, acted on a number of internet transactions, and advised clients on the tax consequences of international trade disputes. Litigation matters have included questions relating to the taxable basis of the PIS contribution, criteria for the restatement of tax debts, and the use of net operating losses. The team has also worked on several complex administrative procedures derived from notices of deficiency. **Clients:** Mainly industrial corporates; some individuals.

Dias de Souza Advogados Associados SC (18 lawyers) Founded by éminence grise and major rainmaker **Hamilton Dias de Souza***, the firm focuses on advisory and litigation matters, and is commended for public law advice, especially in the tax, administrative and economic law areas. **Marco Aurelio Greco*** (according to clients *"a genuine tax expert")* provides much of the department's day to day transactional expertise. The team advises on civil liability issues involving losses related to government policy, such as economic plans, price policies and restrictions on foreign trade. Other work includes tax planning and taxation reduction suits. **Clients:** Akzo Nobel; Bradesco; Copersucar; Ford; Mercedes-Benz; Pirelli; Volkswagen; Scania; Siemens; Souza Cruz; Banco Sudameris; Suzano; Telemar.

Trench Rossi e Watanabe (Baker & McKenzie) (7 ptrs, 42 asscs) Occasionally regarded as *"overcautious,"* the firm is still acknowledged to possess a *"thoroughly respectable"* tax department, which benefits from its access to Baker & McKenzie's international network. The group has advised on tax minimisation structures for bidders in the telecommunication and energy industries, and on tax-efficient structures for a number of multinational clients. Although **Antonio Carlos Farroco Jr's*** practice extends beyond pure tax matters, it is accepted that *"when he does tax, he does it really well."* The firm advised on the analysis and implementation of tax-efficient structures for the largest project finance deal ever concluded in the Latin American oil industry, (value over $2 billion.) **Clients:** AGIP; AIG.

Barbosa, Müssnich & Aragão (1 ptr, 10 asscs) Better known for its corporate work, the firm retains its reputation for advising on the tax implications of M&A transactions and corporate reorganisations. **Leandro Luiz Zancan*** *("a smart person and a great litigator")* is involved in both tax and IPO work. The firm recently advised on the merger between the two major Brazilian brewery companies, Brahma and Antarctica, which resulted in the incorporation of AmBev, and is currently offering tax efficiency advice to companies in the energy sector. **Clients:** Companhia Siderúrgica Belgo-Mineira; Companhia Cervejaria Brahma.

Gaia, Silva, Rolim & Associados SC (10 ptrs, 80 asscs) Tax specialists with a powerful presence nation-wide, encompassing offices in São Paulo, Rio de Janeiro, Belo Horizonte, Curitiba and Brasília. Niche expertise exists in tax planning, the review of tax-related procedures, the treatment of tax contingencies in corporate diversification, the analysis and wording of articles of incorporation (by-laws), and general corporate restructuring. The firm recently handled all the corporate and tax advising in the restructuring of the Alstom Group. **Clients:** Wal-Mart; Ericsson; Alstom Group; Ajinomoto Interamericana; Oracle Corporation; Byk Química; OptiGlobe Inc (internet data centre); Fiat Automóveis.

Mariz de Oliveira, Siqueira Campos e Bianco Advogados SC Founded in 1972, this is a *"high-profile, quality boutique firm,"* with *"a niche specialisation in tax."* **Ricardo Mariz Oliveira*** *("one of the best"* according to our research*)* specialises in administrative defences, and is the author of several books and numerous articles on tax law. The team assists on both litigation and consultancy work. **Clients:** Domestic and international corporates.

Other Notable Practitioners A number of other individuals in Brazil win great acclaim for their tax work. **Ives Gandra Martins*** of Gandra Martins law firm specialises in the constitutional aspects of tax legislation, while former PwC man **Luis Carlos Andrezani*** of Andrezani Advocacia Impresareial is considered a *"really knowledgeable guy."* The *"scholarly"* **Paulo Barros Carvalho*** was also strongly recommended by the market.

* See leaders' profiles on pages 152-159

Leaders' profiles – Brazil

ANDREZANI, Luis Carlos
Luis Carlos Andrezani – Sole Practitioner, São Paulo +55 11 3078 5344
Recommended in Tax

APOCALYPSE, Sidney
Tozzini Freire Teixeira e Silva, São Paulo
+55 11 232 2100
sap@tozzini.com.br
Recommended in Tax
Specialisation: Partner in charge of Tax Department. Provides tax advice to Brazilian and foreign clients engaged in commercial and financial business in Brazil and abroad. Legal counselling services, particularly in capital markets, mergers and acquisitions, banking transactions and tax planning.
Prof. Memberships: Brazilian Bar Association, since 1974.
Publications: 'Revista de Direito Tributário' : 'Sistema Constitucional Tributário Brasileiro', 'Planejamento Tributário no Brasil'.
Career: Joined *Tozzini, Freire, Teixeira e Silva* in 1999. Member of the São Paulo Institute of Lawyers (IASP). Member of the Brazilian Academy of Tax Law (ABDT). Lecturer, Tax Law specialisation courses promoted by the Brazilian Institutes of Law.
Personal: Born October 14, 1947. Graduated from the Mackenzie University Law School in 1973. Specialisation in Tax Law from the Catholic University of São Paulo School of Law in 1974.

ARAGÃO, Paulo Cezar
Barbosa, Müssnich & Aragão, Rio de Janeiro
+55 21 3824 5833
pca@bmalaw.com.br
Recommended in Banking & Finance, Corporate/M&A, Project Finance
Specialisation: Senior Partner. Corporate and securities law, principally mergers, acquisitions, privatizations, new issues of securities in Brazil and abroad and other corporate finance matters, private equity, securitization and arbitration related thereto. Handled the legal structuring of the largest privatization in Latin American and worked in some of the largest M&A transactions in Brazil. Former General Counsel of the Brazilian Securities and Exchange Commission.
Prof. Memberships: Brazilian Bar Association (Rio de Janeiro and São Paulo chapters), Brazilian Law Institute, Brazilian Fiscal Association (affiliated with the International Fiscal Association). Director and former Chairman of the Legal Committee of the Brazilian Association of Public Companies. Legislation Committee appointed by the Brazilian Securities and Exchange Commission (1987-). Commission on International Arbitration, International Chamber of Commerce, Paris. Former General Counsel and Director of the American Chamber of Commerce.
Career: Admitted in 1973. Trained at *Cezar G. Aragão* (1968-1972) and member (1973-78). Joined the Brazilian Securities and Exchange Commission in 1978 as Associate General Counsel (1978-79) and General Counsel (1978-81). Joined *Escritório de Advocacia Gouvêa Vieira* in 1982. Managing Director of GP Investimentos, a private equity firm (1994-1997). Senior Partner *Barbosa, Müssnich & Aragão.* Heads the São Paulo branch of *Barbosa, Müssnich & Aragão.*
Personal: Born 19 November 1950 in Rio de Janeiro.

AZEVEDO SETTE, Ordelio
Azevedo Sette Advogados, Belo Horizonte
+55 31 3261 6656
Recommended in Corporate/M&A

BARBOSA, Plinio
Barbosa, Müssnich & Aragão, Rio de Janeiro
+55 21 3824 5800
Recommended in Banking & Finance, Project Finance

BARRETO, Robson
Veirano Advogados Associados, Rio de Janeiro
+55 21 824 4747
Recommended in Corporate/M&A

BARRETTO, Ricardo
Carvalho de Freitas e Ferreira Advogados Associados, São Paulo +55 11 3066 5999
Recommended in Communications

BASSO, Maristela
Tozzini Freire Teixeira e Silva, São Paulo
+55 11 232 2100
mbasso@tozzini.com.br
Recommended in Communications
Specialisation: Partner in charge of the International Trade, Intellectual Property and E-Commerce Department.
Prof. Memberships: Brazilian Bar Association, since 1982.
Publications: 'Contratos Internacionais do Comércio' (International Business Contracts), 2nd edition, Porto Alegre; Livraria do Advogado-Editora, 1998; 'Mercosul – Seus Efeitos Jurídicos, Econômicos e Políticos nos Estados Membros' (Mercosur – Its Juridical, Economical and Political Effects in member States), 2nd edition, Porto Alegre; Livraria do Advogado – Editora, 1997; 'Joint Venture – Manual Prático das Associações Empresariais' (Joint Venture – the Practical Manual of Corporate Associations), 2nd edition, Porto Alegre; Livraria do Advogado Editora, 1998; 'O Direito da Propriedade Intelectual' (The International Intellectual Property Law), Porto Alegre; Livraria do Advogado, 2000.
Career: Joined *Tozzini, Freire, Teixeira e Silva Advogados* in 1999. Professor of International Law at the University of São Paulo School of Law in graduation and post-Graduation levels (Master and PhD). Member of 'Associação Brasileira de Direito de Informática e Telecomunicações – ABDI', "Associação Brasileira da Propriedade Intelectual – ABPI," and International Trademark Association – INTA.
Personal: Born 28 May, 1960. PhD in International Law from the University of São Paulo School of Law, with the thesis 'International Intellectual Property Law and the OMC – TRIPS'.

BECKER, Ricardo
Pinheiro Neto Avogados, São Paulo
+55 11 237 8400
Recommended in Banking & Finance

BERNARDES-NETO, Horacio
Xavier Bernardes e Bragança, São Paulo SP
+55 11 3069 4300
horaciobernardes@xbb.com.br
Recommended in Corporate/M&A
Specialisation: Banking law and capital markets, foreign investments, telecommunications, privatisation, international financial transactions, mergers and acquisitions.
Prof. Memberships: Brazilian Bar Association, São Paulo (1978) and Rio de Janeiro (1984) and Joinville (1999). Portuguese Bar Association (1988), DAV, president of the Association Internationale des Jeunes Avocats – AIJA (1998), vice president of CESA.
Publications: 'Brazilian Telecommunications – Privatisation' (August 14, 1995); 'Investitionen Auslandischer Firmen in Brasilien nach der Verfassungsreform – Voraussetzungen, Bedingungen, Entwicklungsmoglichkeiten' (September 1995); 'Die Neuen Trands in der Internationalen Besteuerung in Brasilien' (November 1995); 'Mercosul – Trade and Opportunities in the Common Markets (February, 1996), 'Infrastructure Outsourcing Services in Brazil' (February 1996); 'Professional Ethics in Law Firms' (September 1996); 'Privatisierung in Brasilien – Eine Einfuhrung' (November 1998).
Career: Resident Partner at *Bomchil, Castro, Goodrich, Claro, Arosemena and Associates* with Dr Graf von der Goltz, Dr Wessing & Partners in Dusseldorf, Germany (1980-1983) and in London (1983).
Personal: Law degree from the São Paulo University Law School (1977); Bachelor in Education at the Oswaldo Cruz University of São Paulo (1977); Postgraduate degree at the International Commercial Law Institute of the University of Cologne, Germany (1980-1982).

BERTOLDI, Alexandre
Pinheiro Neto Avogados, São Paulo
+55 11 237 8400
alexbertoldi@pinheironeto.com.br
Recommended in Banking & Finance, Corporate/M&A
Specialisation: Partner in *Pinheiro Neto – Advogados* and member of the corporate/banking sector of the São Paulo office. Specialised in the corporate/finance area, carries out activities related to financial operations, capital markets, projects finance, mergers & acquisitions and privatisations.
Publications: Articles published in specialised journals on financial and banking law, especially in the Journal of International Banking Law.
Career: Member of the Brazilian Bar Association and of the Deutsche-Brasilianische Juristenvereinigung (Brazi-Germany Jurists Association). Has been with *Pinheiro Neto – Advogados* since 1982, and became a partner in 1993.

Participated in a number of merger & Acquisition and fund-raising transactions for Brazilian companies on the foreign market; in the structuring of the first global offering of shares for a Brazilian company in June 1992 as well as various ADRs transactions; in transactions involving companies specialised in the generation and distribution of power. Structured the spin-off and the sale of Lojas Renner S.A. to J.C. Penny – 1998. Advised Banco Bilbao Viscaya in the aquiring of Excell Economico S.A. in 1998 and Banco Braqdesco in acquiring Banco Boavista in 2000.

BOSCOLI, Altamiro
Demarest & Almeida, São Paulo +55 11 888 1800
Recommended in Corporate/M&A

BRUNA, Sergio
Magalhães, Ferraz, Prado, Lino e Bruna, São Paulo +55 11 3826 4411
Recommended in Competition/Anti-trust

BULHÕES PEDREIRA, José Luiz
Bulhões Pedreira, Bulhões Carvalho & Advogados Associados, Rio de Janeiro + 55 21 531 2414 jlbp@bpbc.com.br
Recommended in Corporate/M&A, Tax
Specialisation: Practises mainly in tax and corporate laws, financial institutions and capital markets regulation; M&A and corporate acquisitions; has as clients mostly banks and large industrial and commercial corporations.
Prof. Memberships: Member of the Institute of Brazilian Lawyers (IAB) since 1958.
Publications: Published the following books: 'Draft Bill of an Income Tax Code'; 'Income Tax'; 'Monetary Correction of Financial Statements'; co-author with Manoel Ribeiro da Cruz Filho; 'Corporate Income Tax'; 'Corporate Finance and Financial Statements and Corporate Law', co-author with Alfredo Lamy Filho.
Career: Held several public offices in the Federal Administration such as Legal Counselor of the National Bank of Economic Development (BNDES), Central Eletrica de Furnas SA, Ministry of Transportation and Public Works, Federal Railroad Company; Member of commissions that drafted bills on the Capital Market, Corporate Law and Reorganisation of Financial Institutions.
Personal: Born 1 July 1925, Rio de Janeiro. Attended National Law School of the University of Brazil (1947).

CANTIDIANO, Luiz Leonardo
Motta Fernandes Rocha Advogados, Rio de Janeiro +55 215 332 200 lcantidiano@mfra.com.br
Recommended in Corporate/M&A
Specialisation: Acts in Corporate Law, principally mergers, acquisitions, joint venture agreements, business organisation, restructuring of companies and privatisations. Acted as private Counsel of the Brazilian Government on the drafting of the chapter of the Brazilian Telecommunications General Law that established the rules about the restructuring and privatisation of Telebrás. Acted as private Counsel of the Brazilian government in the definition of the model of the restructuring and privatisation of Telebrás and in the restructuring of 26 companies controlled by Telebrás, in order to separate the mobile service from the existing companies. Acted in the organisation of Telet S.A. and Americel S.A., both companies incorporated in order to acquire licenses to operate in the mobile service. Acted in the acquisition of Tele Centro Sul Participações S.A., Telemig Celular Participações S.A. and Tele Norte Celular Participações S.A. Acted in the acquisition of Perdigão S.A. by the major Brazilian Pensions Funds. Acted in the sale of Frangosul S.A. to a French company (Doux S.A.).
Prof. Memberships: Member of the Board of Brazilian Institute of Capital Market (IBMEC).
Career: Qualified in 1972. Partner of *Motta Fernandes Rocha Advogados.* Former Member of the Board of Rio de Janeiro Stock Exchange, former Commissioner of the Brazilian Securities and Exchange Commission, former Member of the Court of Appeal of the National Financial System.

CARVALHO, Paulo Barros
Paulo Barros Carvalho – Sole Practitioner, São Paulo +55 11 3263 6400
Recommended in Tax

CELEDONIO, Lauro
Mattos Filho, Veiga Filho, Marrey Jr, Moherdaui e Quiroga, São Paulo +55 11 3170 7600
Recommended in Competition/Anti-trust

CELLI JR, Umberto
Fischer & Forster Advogados, São Paulo +55 11 3168 1799 ucj@fischerforster.com.br
Recommended in Communications
Specialisation: Specialises in administrative law, with emphasis on telecommunications regulatory matters, public tenders and antitrust. Has handled substantial work in the area of telecommunications for leading multinational operators.
Prof. Memberships: Brazilian Computer and Telecommunciation Law Association – ABDI (Board Member).
Publications: Author of the book 'Competition Rules in Modern International Law' Has published extensively in Brazil and abroad in area of expertise.
Career: Admitted in 1982. Partner at *Fischer & Forster.* Holds a Master in International Law degree form the University of Nottingham, England, and a Phd in International Law from the University of São Paulo. Speaker, several seminars, in Brazil and abroad especially on Brazilian Telecommunications Law and Mercosur.
Personal: Born October 11, 1958.

CESCON AVEDISSIAN, Maria Cristina
Souza, Cescon Avedissian, Barrieu e Flesch, São Paulo +55 11 3089 6503
Recommended in Corporate/M&A

COELHO, Ricardo
Pinheiro Neto Avogados, São Paulo +55 11 237 8400
Recommended in Banking & Finance

COELHO, Tulio
Trench Rossi e Watanabe, Brasilia, DF + 55 61 327 3273
Recommended in Competition/Anti-trust
Career: Former General Counsel of the Ministry of Science and Technology (1987-88). Has been practising law before the High Federal Courts since 1981. Specifically in antitrust, has been practising before the Brazilian antitrust agency (CADE) since 1989, representing several multinational clients. Since 1995 has been giving lectures about Antitrust and Antidumping Laws for two post-graduation programs for Economic Law, at Fundação Getúlio Vargas, Rio de Janeiro. Became international partner of *Baker & McKenzie* in 1997.
Prof. Memberships: Instituto Brasileiro de Estudo das Relaçoes de Consumo e da Concorrência – IBRAC, Associação Brasileira de Direito de Informática e das Telecomunicaçoes – ABDI, Ordem dos Advogados do Brasil, Federal District Chapter. Member of the Ethics Tribunal of the Ordem dos Advogados do Brasil, Federal District Chapter.
Personal: Born in Rio de Janeiro on May 11, 1959. Graduated at the Universidade de Brasília in 1981 and post-graduated in Economic Law in 1982 at the same University. Lives in Brasilia, Federal District, since 1971.

CONSENTINO, Arion
Demarest & Almeida, São Paulo +55 11 888 1800
Recommended in Tax

COTAIT, Elinor
Mundie e Advogados, São Paulo +55 11 3040 2900 ecc@mundie.com.br
Recommended in Communications
Specialisation: Main areas of work are telecommunications and administrative law. Possesses recognised expertise in public bids, governmental contracts and telecommunications, including licensing application and auctions, fixed and cellular telephone services, cable TV, broadcasting, private networks, internet, satellites, submarine cables, SMR, MMDS, infrastructure, rights of way, and the like. Has been involved in almost every relevant telecommunication project in Brazil and has substantial experience in dealing with the Brazilian regulatory authorities, having actively contributed to proposed rule-makings for the regulation of telecommunication services.
Prof. Memberships: Consultative Council of the Brazilian Society of Public Law (SBDP); São Paulo Association of Attorneys-at-Law (AASP); Brazilian Association of Informatics and Telecommunications Law (ABDI).
Career: São Paulo State Attorney (1985-1995); partner in *Mundie e Advogados* (since 1996). Admitted in Brazil (São Paulo and Rio de Janeiro Bar Sections).
Personal: Born São Paulo, Brazil, April 1, 1962. Attended Universidade de São Paulo (JD, 1984).

DA SILVEIRA LOBO, Carlos Alberto
Lobo & Ibeas, Rio de Janeiro +55 21 509 4818
Recommended in Corporate/M&A

DE ALMEIDA PRADO, Fernando
Pinheiro Neto Avogados, São Paulo +55 11 237 8609 faprado@pinheironeto.com.br
Recommended in Banking & Finance
Specialisation: Legal counseling on corporate and financing transactions, capital markets, securities regulations, loans and financing, debt securities offers to international markets, aircraft leasing trans-

B

actions, derivative transactions, company formation in Brazil, including joint ventures and consortia. Mergers and acquisitions, due dilligence performance, public bids in connection with the privatisation process in Brazil, general consulting on the matters incidental thereon, such as exchange control regulations, banking laws and regulations, corporate and tax laws, civil and civil procedure legislation and principles of international private law applicable in Brazil.
Prof. Memberships: Admitted as a trainee in 1986; Associate with the firm in 1988; Partner of the firm in 1998; Foreign Associate in 1996.
Publications: Author of several articles on exchange controls, foreign loans and financing, derivative transactions in Brazil in domestic and foreign publications such as the 'Journal of International Taxation', 'Journal of International Banking Law' and 'IBDF Publications, Inc', in New York. Speaker in various conferences on the above matters, as well as on power related matters in Brazil.
Career: Education: Mackenzie University; Law School (LLB). Graduated in 1988. Specialisation in corporate law in 1992.
Personal: Languages: Portuguese and English. Spanish and French (reasonable).

DE ANDRADE, Mario Cezar
Ulhôa Canto, Rezende e Guerra Avogados, Rio de Janeiro +55 21 824 3265
Recommended in Banking & Finance

DE ARAUJO CINTRA, Antonio Felix
Tozzini Freire Teixeira e Silva, São Paulo
+55 11 232 2100
afac@tozzini.com.br
Recommended in Banking & Finance, Project Finance
Specialisation: Head of Capital Markets Department. Work in domestic and international capital markets transactions; domestic and international financings, including syndicated loans and structured finance; securitisation; project finance; foreign investments in the Brazilian capital markets.
Prof. Memberships: Brazilian Bar Association, since 1988.
Career: Joined *Tozzini, Freire, Teixeira e Silva* in 1988, becoming a partner in 1997. Worked at *Cleary, Gottlieb, Steen and Hamilton*, in New York, in 1990.
Personal: Born April 3, 1961. Graduated from the Law School of the University of São Paulo in 1986. LLM from University of Notre Dame, in 1990.

DE CUNTO, Rafael
Pinheiro Neto Avogados, São Paulo
+55 11 237 8400
Recommended in Communications

DE SALLES FREIRE, Jose Luis
Tozzini Freire Teixeira e Silva, São Paulo
+55 11 232 2100
jlfreire@tozzini.com.br
Recommended in Banking & Finance, Corporate/M&A
Specialisation: Founding partner of *Tozzini, Freire, Teixeira e Silva Advogados.* In addition to overseeing the Firm's Corporate Practice, specialises in Banking and Corporate Finance, with special focus on mergers and acquisitions. Extremely involved in international business transactions.
Prof. Memberships: Member of the Brazilian Bar Association, São Paulo Lawyers' Institute, São Paulo Lawyers' Association, the Board of the São Paulo Stock Exchange, the New York Foreign Lawyers' Association, the Legislation Committee of the American Chamber of Commerce for Brazil, the Executive Board of International and Comparative Law Center of Southwestern Legal Foundation, the International Bar Association, the Inter-Pacific Bar Association and the former President of the World Law Group.
Publications: Co-author of 'Business Operations in Brazil', published by Tax Management International; 'Privatisation in Brazil', published by Hastings International and Comparative Law Review, University of California, in 1994 and 'International Business Acquisitions – Major Legal Issues & Due Diligence', published by Kluwer Law International in 1996.
Personal: Born 3 October, 1948. In 1971, he graduated from the University of São Paulo School of Law and was admitted to the São Paulo Bar in 1971 and the Rio de Janeiro Bar in 1997. Received the Specialisation Degree on Business Administration from Fundação Getúlio Vargas, School of Business Administration in 1974. In 1976, was granted the MCJ degree from the New York University School of Law.

DE SOUSA, Luis Antonio
Machado, Meyer, Sendacz e Opice, São Paulo
+55 11 3150 7000
Recommended in Project Finance

DEL CHIARO, José
Advocacia José Del Chiaro, São Paulo
+55 11 3816 2066
ajdc@vol.com.br/jdchiaro@vol.com.br
Recommended in Competition/Anti-trust
Specialisation: Works specifically in the Economic Corporate Law area, including privatisations, consumers' rights, administrative agreements, bids, anti-dumping and also those issues related to regulation and to competition law. Has been operating with and for companies of significant economic power, governed by said competition law.
Publications: Published articles in the Journal of the Administrative Council of Economic Defense – 'CADE', Industry Journal, edited by 'FIESP', in the Journal of Commercial, Industrial, Economic and Financial Law, collaborating, from time to time, on articles for newspapers.
Career: Director of the Governmental Relationships of 'IBRAC' – Brazilian Institute for the Study of Competition and Consumption Relationships, an entity engaged in the disclosure of politics for the free competition defense, as well as of loyal practices in relation to consumers. Member of 'IASP' – Institute of the Attorneys of São Paulo, and took an active part in studies regarding the constitutional revision, supervising the work related to the chapter of economic and financial order, the results of which gave rise to the publication of the book entitled 'Estudos Para a Revisão Constitucional de 1993' (Studies for the Revision of 1993), published by the Official Press of the State 'IMESP'.
Personal: Attorney, born in São Paulo, on February 23, 1956. Higher education: College of Law of the University of São Paulo (1979). Worked as a legal adviser for the Federation of Industries of the State of São Paulo – 'FIESP', from 1981 to 1990. Was also Secretary of Economic Law of the Ministry of Justice, leading the implementation of the Economic Law Department during the period referred to as 'the Brazilian economic opening'.

DIAS DA SILVA, Irene
Pinheiro Neto Avogados, São Paulo
+55 11 237 8400
Recommended in Banking & Finance, Corporate/M&A

DIAS DE SOUZA, Hamilton
Dias de Souza Advogados Associados SC, São Paulo
+55 11 3083 4277
Recommended in Tax

DUTRA, Pedro
Advocacia Pedro Dutra, São Paulo
+55 11 3085 9033
pdutra@pedrodutra.com.br
Recommended in Competition/Anti-trust
Specialisation: Senior partner in a boutique firm specialising in competition and regulatory law. Cases include telecommunications, electric energy, oil, gas, the pharmaceutical industry and transport. Acts as a legal adviser and is frequently requested to issue legal opinions on regulatory, competition and administrative law. Frequently publishes and lectures on competition and regulatory law.
Prof. Memberships: Brazilian Bar Association.
Publications: Author of 'Literatura Juridica do Imperio' (Brazilian legal literature of the 19th century) and 'A Concentracao do Poder Economico' (Mergers and Acquisitions: main cases in Brazilian anti-trust law). Published various papers on competition, regulatory and administrative law in legal journals and the main newspapers of Rio de Janeiro and São Paulo.
Career: Qualified in 1974. Until 1977 was assistant to the president of the financial system at the State Bank of Rio de Janeiro. Trained at *Clifford Chance* Law Firm, London in 1978. Attorney for the INB (Brazilian Nuclear Industry) 1981-1991. Own practice since 1988, transferring to São Paulo in 1992. Director of the Brazilian Institute of Competition and Consumer Relations Studies (IBRAC) and Editor of its Monthly Review.
Personal: Attended Rio de Janeiro State University. Lives in São Paulo, Brazil.

EIZIRIK, Nelson
Carvalhosa Eizirik & Motta Veiga, Rio de Janiero
+55 21 240 4724
Recommended in Corporate/M&A

FARROCO JR, Antonio Carlos
Trench Rossi e Watanabe, São Paulo, SP
+55 11 3048 6800
Recommended in Tax
Specialisation: Partner of the Brazilian office of *Baker & McKenzie* and member of the Mergers & Acquisition Practice Group. Practice includes corporate tax planning, mergers & acquisitions, joint ven-

tures and general corporate law. Has co-ordinated several M&A deals in Brazil, representing major companies, such as GE Capital and Belgo-Mineira.
Prof. Memberships: Brazilian Bar Association (1986), American Chamber of Commerce (São Paulo Chapter) legislative committee.
Career: Joined *Baker & McKenzie*, São Paulo in 1988 and worked in 1991-92 in their Chicago office.
Personal: Born on 23 November 1960. Graduated in 1985 from the University of São Paulo School of Law. Fluent in Portuguese and English. Leisure interests include travelling and reading.

FERRAZ, Helena
Mattos Filho, Veiga Filho, Marrey Jr, Moherdaui e Quiroga, São Paulo +55 11 3170 7600
Recommended in Competition/Anti-trust

FERRAZ JR, Tercio Sampaio
Magalhães, Ferraz, Prado, Lino e Bruna, São Paulo +55 11 3826 4411
Recommended in Competition/Anti-trust

FISCHER, George Charles
Fischer & Forster Advogados, São Paulo +55 11 3168 1799
Recommended in Communications, Corporate/M&A

FLESCH, Cristiane
Souza, Cescon Avedissian, Barrieu e Flesch, São Paulo +55 11 3089 6500
cflesch@mmso.com.br
Recommended in Project Finance
Specialisation: Partner in Project Finance Department. Main area of work is corporate finance and especially project financing, principally representation of lenders, developers and investors in connection with the development, financing, construction, and operation of a wide range of capital-intensive projects in Brazil, including hydro and thermo plants, oil & gas, toll roads, water & sanitation and ports. Has handled structuring and financing of several infrastructure projects in Brazil in those areas. Acted for the Inter-American Development Bank in the financing of hydro plants in the south of Brazil and toll roads in the State of São Paulo. Acted for the project company in the financing of a hydro plant in the State of Tocantins, a thermo plant in the State of São Paulo and is currently advising clients in the development, construction, operation and financing of thermo plants included in the Priority Program of the Brazilian Government. Acted on the structuring and financing of the Marlim Oil Project (Campos Basin, Rio de Janeiro) and of secondary recovery oil fields in the State of Rio de Janeiro.
Prof. Memberships: Brazilian Bar Association.
Career: Admitted to Bar, 1991, São Paulo, Brazil. Joined *Machado, Meyer, Sendacz e Opice* in 1991, becoming a Partner in 2000. Foreign Associate at *Clifford Chance*, NY (1995) and at *Mayer, Brown & Platt*, NY (1996-1997). Masters of International Law at Cornell University Law School, Ithaca, NY (LL.M., 1996).
Personal: Born 29 August 1969. Attended Pontifical Catholic University Law School (LLB, 1991) and Cornell University Law School, Ithaca, NY (LLM, 1996). Married to Marcos Flesch.

FRANCESCHINI, José Inácio
Franceschini e Miranda – Advogados, São Paulo +55 11 3814 2566
Recommended in Competition/Anti-trust

GALHARDO, Luciana Rosanova
Pinheiro Neto Avogados, São Paulo +55 11 237 8400
Recommended in Tax

GANDRA MARTINEZ, Ives
Ives Gandra Martinez – Sole Practitioner, São Paulo +55 11 3085 4544
Recommended in Tax

GOMES DE SOUZA, Renato
Ulhôa Canto, Rezende e Guerra Avogados, Rio de Janeiro +55 21 824 3265
Recommended in Banking & Finance

GOULART PENTEADO, João Caio
Goulart Penteado, Iervolino e Lefosse Advogados, São Paulo SP +55 11 3816 7399
goulart.penteado@gpilbra.com.br/gpilbra@gpilbra.com.br
Recommended in Corporate/M&A
Specialisation: Main areas of practice are Corporate and Tax Law, Mergers & Acquisitions, Litigation and Arbitration.
Prof. Memberships: Member of the Brazilian Bar Association. Former Chairman of the Legislation Committee and former Member of the Board of the American Chamber of Commerce. Founder and Former Chairman of the Arbitration Commission of the Brazil-Canada Chamber of Commerce.
Publications: Contributor to the Brazilian chapter of Matthew Bender's 'Enforcement of Money Judgments Abroad' and to the 'Avoidance and Tax Evasion' volume of the Tax Research series (Caderno de Pesquisas Tributárias).
Career: Associate and partner of *Pinheiro Neto-Advogados* (1966-1986). Trainingship at *Kirkland & Ellis*, Chicago (1969). Founding partner of *Goulart Penteado, Iervolino e Lefosse Advogados.*
Personal: Attended University of São Paulo Law School (LLB). Degree in Economic Law from Getúlio Vargas Foundation (FGV).

GRECO, Marco Aurelio
Dias de Souza Advogados Associados SC, São Paulo +55 11 3083 4277
Recommended in Tax

GUERRA, JD Cordeiro
Ulhôa Canto, Rezende e Guerra Avogados, Rio de Janeiro +55 21 824 3265
Recommended in Tax

LACAZ MARTINS, Ricardo
Lacaz Martins, Halembeck, Pereira Neto, Gurevich & Schoueri, São Paulo +55 11 3068 8373
Recommended in Tax

LEFOSSE JR., Geraldo Roberto
Goulart Penteado, Iervolino e Lefosse Advogados, São Paulo SP +55 11 3816 7399
geraldo.lefosse@gpilbra.com.br/gpilbra@gbilbra.com.br
Recommended in Corporate/M&A
Specialisation: Business Organisation, Mergers & Acquisitions, Corporate and Contract Law. Extensive experience in dealing with shareholders issues and reorganisation matters, as well as in developing and negotiating business structures. Has been heavily involved in assisting the major companies of the Brazilian automotive sector in the last years.
Prof. Memberships: Brazilian Bar Association. Former Chairman of the Legislation Committee of the Brazil-Canada Chamber of Commerce.
Career: Trainee, associate and partner of *Pinheiro Neto-Advogados* (1973-1986). Founding partner of *Goulart Penteado, Iervolino e Lefosse Advogados.*
Personal: University of São Paulo Law School (LL.B) and University of Illinois (MCL).

LESSA, Rogerio
Demarest & Almeida, São Paulo +55 11 888 1800
Recommended in Corporate/M&A

MAGALHÃES, Carlos
Magalhães, Ferraz, Prado, Lino e Bruna, São Paulo +55 11 3826 4411
Recommended in Competition/Anti-trust

MARIZ OLIVEIRA, Ricardo
Mariz de Oliveira, Siqueira Campos e Bianco Advogados SC, São Paulo + 55 11 257 7600
Recommended in Tax

MARREY JR, Pedro Luciano
Mattos Filho, Veiga Filho, Marrey Jr, Moherdaui e Quiroga, São Paulo +55 11 3170 7600
Recommended in Tax

MATTOS, Ubiratan
Pinheiro Neto Avogados, São Paulo +55 11 237 8400
Recommended in Competition/Anti-trust

MATTOS FILHO, Ary Oswaldo
Mattos Filho, Veiga Filho, Marrey Jr, Moherdaui e Quiroga, São Paulo +55 11 3170 7600
Recommended in Banking & Finance, Corporate/M&A

MEIRELLES DE MIRANDA, Aloysio
Ulhôa Canto, Rezende e Guerra Avogados, Rio de Janeiro +55 21 824 3265
Recommended in Corporate/M&A, Tax

MENDES, Antonio
Pinheiro Neto Avogados, São Paulo +55 11 237 8400
Recommended in Banking & Finance, Corporate/M&A

MEYER, Antonio
Machado, Meyer, Sendacz e Opice, São Paulo +55 11 3150 7030
ameyer@mmso.com.br
Recommended in Corporate/M&A, Project Finance, Tax
Specialisation: Senior Partner in Corporate, Tax and Energy, Oil & Gas Department with particular expertise in merger and acquisitions, corporate tax, project finance and regulatory matters. Has extensive experience in corporate transactions of any nature, consolidations, mergers, spin-offs and liquidations, advising both international and national sponsors and lenders in structuring acquisition transactions

B

and rendering advice on the acquisition or disposal of controlling interests, minority interests (venture capital). Also has broad experience in tax planning structure of foreign investments in Brazil, including tax consulting on investments in infra-structure activities, electric power and oil & gas. Has recently taken a leadership position participating in some of the most significant infra-structure transactions in Brazil (ie, electric energy, transport, public sanitation, oil & gas and telecommunication), developing particular expertise on negotiating, structuring and financing of electric and oil & gas transactions with project developers, investment companies, gas suppliers and financial institutions.
Prof. Memberships: Admitted to bar, 1969, São Paulo, Brazil, Member: Inter American Bar Association; Brazilian Bar Association; São Paulo Lawyers Institute, Vice-President of The International Institute of Association and Foundation Lawyers, Inc. (Virginia, USA). Was invited to participate and present several conferences related to natural gas and electric energy issues: 'The natural gas expansion in 1988' (promoted by International Business Communications (IBC), April 28 to 30, 1998), 'The Impact of Law 9.478 in the Concession Agreements for Petroleum Exploitation' ('Financing Oil & Gas Projects in Brazil', promoted by IBC from September 28 to 30, 1998) and 'Managing and Moulding Risks in Energy Project Finance' (promoted by IBC on February 15, 2000).
Career: Founder Partner of *Machado, Meyer, Sendacz and Opice Advogados* (1972); Vice-President of the Brazilian Law Firm Association (CESA) (1987 – 1988); Legal Counsel and Chairman of the Legislation Committee of the American Chamber of Commerce for Brazil (1987-1989); Member of the Board of the American Chamber of Commerce of Brazil (1987-1990/1997-2000); Member of the Legal Committee of Associação Brasileira das Companhias Abertas (ABRASCA) (1987-1990); Vice-President of the São Paulo Lawyers Association (AASP) (1990); President of the São Paulo Lawyers Association (AASP) (1991-1992); Member of the Board of the Brazilian Bar Association (OAB) (1999-2000); Member of the Board of the Brazilian Law Firm Association (CESA); Member of the Board of the São Paulo Medical Foundation; Member of the Board of Examination for State Judges of São Paulo State Justice (2000); Member of the Board of Examination for Federal Judges of Brazilian Federal Justice (2001).
Personal: Born São Paulo, Brazil; Preparatory education, Mackenzie College, São Paulo (BA, 1964); Legal Education, University of São Paulo Law School (LLB, 1969); Lecturer at the 43rd and 48th Congresses of the International Fiscal Association (IFA); Secretary of Justice of the State of São Paulo (1993-1994); Secretary of Public Security of the State of São Paulo (1994).

MOURA ROCHA, Bolivar
Levy & Salomão Advogados, São Paulo
+55 11 3030 0500
Recommended in Competition/Anti-trust

MUNDIE, Kevin Louis
Mundie e Advogados, São Paulo +55 11 3040 2900
klm@mundie.com.br
Recommended in Communications
Specialisation: Main area of work is telecommunications. Possesses recognised expertise in the telecommunications area, assisting and advising on matters covering all aspects of the industry: licensing application and auctions, fixed and cellular telephone services, cable TV, broadcasting, private networks, internet, satellites, submarine cables, SMR, MMDS, infrastructure, rights of way, service agreements and the like. Has been involved in almost every relevant telecommunication project in Brazil and has substantial experience in dealing with the Brazilian regulatory authorities, having also actively contributed to proposed rule-makings for the regulation of telecommunication services.
Prof. Memberships: Member of American Bar Association; New York State Bar Association; Bar Association of the City of New York; Brazilian Association of Informatics and Telecommunications Law – ABDI.
Career: Joined *Baker & McKenzie* in 1979, becoming a partner in 1987 until 1996; senior partner in *Mundie e Advogados* since 1997. Admitted in New York, New York and Brazil (São Paulo and Rio de Janeiro Bar Sections).
Personal: Born July 23, 1950. Attended Loyola University at Louisiana (BA, summa cum laude, 1973); Harvard University (JD, 1980); Universidade do Estado do Rio de Janeiro (Revalidation 1996).

MÜSSNICH, Francisco
Barbosa, Müssnich & Aragão, Rio de Janeiro
+55 21 3824 5800
Recommended in Banking & Finance, Corporate/M&A

NICOLETTI, Hélio
Pinheiro Neto Avogados, São Paulo
+55 11 237 8400
Recommended in Corporate/M&A

NOGUEIRA, Mario
Demarest & Almeida, São Paulo +55 11 888 1800
Recommended in Competition/Anti-trust

NOVAIS, Raquel
Machado, Meyer, Sendacz e Opice, São Paulo
+55 11 3150 7032
rnovais@mmso.com.br
Recommended in Tax
Specialisation: Partner in Tax Corporate Department with particular expertise in corporate tax law, tax planning and foreign investments, mainly in relation to regulated industries (namely petroleum and natural gas, power and telecommunications). Consultant to investors which participate in the privatisation process providing tax advice on corporate restructuring processes. Active in tax planning in significant merger and acquisition transactions. Was invited to participate in and present several conferences and workshops – International Business Communications ('IBC'): 'The Natural Gas Sector Expansion in 1998' (1998) and 'The Impact of Law 9.478 in the Concession Agreements for Petroleum Exploitation' (1998) – Brazilian Association of Computer and Telecommunication Law ('ABDI'): 'XIII International Congress on Computer and Telecommunciation Law' (1999), 'Telecommunication, Electric Energy, Oil and Other Public Rendering Services Companies' (1999), 'Infra-structure Share – Revenue Tax System' (1999) and 'XIV International Tax Law Congress – Taxation on Internet' (2000). Invited to perform lectures in Masters Courses sponsored by Brazilian Institute of Tax Researches ('IBET'), over the years of 1999 and 2000.
Prof. Memberships: Brazilian Bar Association, São Paulo's Law Association, International Fiscal Association ('IFA').
Publications: Author of 'Analysis of Tax Event Rules over Credit, Exchange, Insurance or Security Operations', 1992.
Career: Admitted to the Bar in 1985, São Paulo, Brazil. Joined *Machado, Meyer, Sendacz e Opice Advogados* in 1987, becoming a partner in 1990. Masters of Law at Pontificial Catholic University Law School (LLM, 1992).
Personal: Born on December 9, 1961 – Franca, S.P., Brazil. Attended Faculdade de Direito de Franca, São Paulo (LLB, 1983). Escola Auto Padrão – Instituto Francano de Ensino São Paulo (BA, 1979).

NUNES, Esther
Pinheiro Neto Avogados, São Paulo
+55 11 237 8400
Recommended in Communications, Corporate/M&A

NUNES PINTO, Jose Emilio
Tozzini Freire Teixeira e Silva, São Paulo
+55 11 232 2100
jenp@tozzini.com.br
Recommended in Banking & Finance, Project Finance
Specialisation: Head of the Project Finance and Infrastructure Practice Groups at *Tozzini, Freire, Teixeira e Silva Advogados*, and extremely involved in International Business Transactions. Extensive experience advising infrastructure projects, such as power, oil and gas and toll roads, among others, and the related project financing issues.
Prof. Memberships: Brazilian Bar Association, since 1974.
Publications: Author of the Brazil chapter 'Brazil – a journey into the world of project finance', published in 'Latin Lawyer Review Project Finance 2001', a Law Business Research Ltd's publication. Author of the Brazil chapter 'Brazil benchmarks', published in the 'Project Finance Legal Guide: the devil's in the details', a publication of Euromoney Institutional Investor Publications plc, March 2000 Edition.
Career: Joined the firm in 1985. Member: Former Brazilian alternate representative of the International Court of Arbitration of the International Chamber of Commerce, Paris, France (1989-1992). Arbitrator of the Arbitration Committee of the Brazilian Canadian Chamber of Commerce.
Personal: Born 1 January, 1949. Admitted to the Rio de Janeiro Bar in 1974 and the São Paulo Bar in 1989, after having received the LLB degree in 1972 from the University of the State of Guanabara School of Law in Rio de Janeiro. Further attended the

Programme Internacionale de Gestion Générale – PIGG in Fountainebleau, France.

OPICE, Jose Roberto
Machado, Meyer, Sendacz e Opice, São Paulo +55 11 3150 7000
Recommended in Banking & Finance, Corporate/M&A, Project Finance

PASQUALIN, Roberto
Demarest & Almeida, São Paulo +55 11 888 1800
Recommended in Tax

PINHEIRO GUIMARAES, Francisco
Pinheiro Guimaraes Advogados, Rio de Janeiro +55 21 533 3006
fpgn@pgadv.com
Recommended in Banking & Finance
Specialisation: Domestic and international debt and equity offerings, syndicated loans, trade finance, project finance, cross-border lease transactions, structured finance, securitisation of exports and other receivables and derivatives. Acts for a number of large international banks and financial institutions. Senior partner of the firm.
Prof. Memberships: Rio de Janeiro Bar Association, São Paulo Bar Association.
Publications: 'Debt Renegotiation-Capitalisation Programmes', International Financial Law Review, January, 1988; 'Global Derivatives Study-Enforceability Survey-Brazil', published by the Group of Thirty, Washington DC, July, 1993.
Career: Qualified 1963 in Rio de Janeiro, and 1990 in São Paulo. Joined the firm as an intern in 1960, becoming partner in 1970.
Personal: Born September 7, 1938. Attended Colegio Padre Antonio Vieira, Rio de Janeiro (BA); University of Brazil Law School, Rio de Janeiro, (LLB), 1963. Lives in Rio de Janeiro, RJ.

PINHEIRO GUIMARAES, Plinio
Pinheiro Guimaraes Advogados, Rio de Janeiro +55 21 533 3006
ppgn@pgadv.com
Recommended in Banking & Finance
Specialisation: Domestic and international debt and equity offerings, syndicated loans, trade finance, project finance, cross-border lease transactions, structured finance, securitisation of exports and other receivables and derivatives. Acts for a number of large international banks and financial institutions.
Prof. Memberships: Rio de Janeiro Bar Association, São Paulo Bar Association, New York Bar.
Publications: 'Liberalizing the Law, Part II': Project Finance in Latin America, Latin Finance, June 1994.
Career: Qualified 1990 in Rio de Janeiro, 1995 in New York and 1996 in São Paulo. Joined the firm as an intern in 1986, becoming a partner in 1996.
Personal: Born March 5, 1967. Attended Colegio Padre Antonio Vicira, Rio de Janeiro (BA); Candido Mendes Law School, Rio de Janeiro, (LLB), 1990. Columbia Law School, New York (LL.M., 1994). Parker School Recognition of Achievement with Honours in International Law, 1994. Foreign Associate, *Shearman & Sterling*, New York, 1993-1995. Lives in Rio de Janeiro, RJ.

PIQUET CARNEIRO, João Geraldo
Piquet Carneiro, Brasilia +55 61 2232 402
Recommended in Competition/Anti-trust

PISANI, Jose Roberto
Pinheiro Neto Avogados, São Paulo +55 11 237 8400
Recommended in Tax

PORTELLA, Roberto
Demarest & Almeida, São Paulo +55 11 888 1800
Recommended in Banking & Finance

PRADO, Claudia
Trench Rossi e Watanabe, São Paulo, SP +55 11 3048 6800
claudia.f.prado@bakernet.com
Recommended in Corporate/M&A
Specialisation: Partner of the Brazilian office of *Baker & McKenzie* and head of the Mergers & Acquisition Practice Group. Practice includes Mergers & Acquisitions, Joint Ventures and general corporate law. Co-ordinated several acquisition deals in Brazil, representing major companies, such as Motorola and ADM.
Prof. Memberships: Brazilian Bar Association (1985), Portuguese Bar Association (1990).
Career: Graduated in 1984 from the University of São Paulo Law School. Obtained an MCL degree in 1986 from the Southern Methodist University School of Law, Dallas, Texas, USA Joined *Baker & McKenzie* – São Paulo in 1983 and worked in 1986-1987 in the Chicago office of *Baker & McKenzie.*
Personal: Born May 3, 1962, is fluent in Portuguese and English and speaks Spanish. Leisure interests include travelling and cooking.

QUIROGA MOSQUERA, Roberto
Mattos Filho, Veiga Filho, Marrey Jr, Moherdaui e Quiroga, São Paulo +55 11 3170 7600
Recommended in Tax

REGAZZINI, Jose Augusto
Tozzini Freire Teixeira e Silva, São Paulo +55 11 232 2100
joreg@tozzini.com.br
Recommended in Competition/Anti-trust
Specialisation: Head of the Antitrust department. Main areas of work are Antitrust and Mergers and Acquisitions. Has handled merger reviews by the Brazilian antitrust authorities of cases for both Brazilian and overseas clients. In charge of the firm's Retailing Department, having acted in several acquisitions of supermarket chains in Brazil. Responsible for a number of merger reviews related to transnational transactions referred by US and European law firms.
Prof. Memberships: Member, Brazilian Bar Association. Vice President, IBRAC – Brazilian Institute of Studies Related to Competition and Consumers.
Publications: Author of the Brazil chapter published in the 1999-2000 edition of the 'European Counsel – Competition Handbook', entitled 'From Notification to Approval'.
Career: Joined *Tozzini, Freire, Teixeira e Silva Advogados* in 1996.
Personal: Law School of the University of São Paulo, Brazil MCJ – New York University, NY.

REZENDE, Condorcet
Ulhôa Canto, Rezende e Guerra Avogados, Rio de Janeiro +55 21 824 3265
Recommended in Tax

REZENDE, Fabio de
Vieira, Rezende, Barbosa e Guerreiro, Rio de Janeiro +55 21 533 6240
frezende@vrbg.com.br
Recommended in Corporate/M&A
Specialisation: Partner. Main area of practice is Corporate Law and Telecom, principally general corporate matters, mergers, acquisitions, privatisations, foreign investments and regulatory issues. Has handled acquisitions of companies and undertakings of varying sorts by domestic and overseas clients. Selected projects include the sale of the controlling interest in Acesita to Usinor, the acquisition of long distance license by National Grid and related joint-venture with France Telecom and Sprint.
Prof. Memberships: Ordem dos Advogados do Brasil, Rio de Janeiro State Section. International Bar Association, Section on Business Law.
Publications: Author of 'A Convenção de Varsóvia de 1929 e a Responsabilidade Civil no Transporte Aéreo Internacional' (Revista de Direito Aeroespacial, vol. 63). Co-author of 'The Brazilian Privatization Program' (Supp. 34 to the World Reports, by Lex Mundi).
Career: Qualified in 1992. Joined *Castro, Barros, Sobral e Xavier* in 1991, became an associate in 1992. Founding partner of *Vieira, Rezende, Barbosa e Guerreiro Advogados* (since 1995). Member of the Brazilian Code of Aeronautics' Revision Commission, a project sponsored by the Ministry of Aviation (1994-95). Legal consultant to the Inter-American Investment Corporation (1996-98).
Personal: Born Jan 19, 1969. Attended the School of Law of the Pontifical Catholic University of Rio de Janeiro, Brazil (LLB '91) and the School of Law of the University of Virginia, USA (LLM '96).

RIBEIRO, João Ricardo de Azevedo
Mattos Filho, Veiga Filho, Marrey Jr, Moherdaui e Quiroga, São Paulo +55 11 3147 7643
Recommended in Corporate/M&A, Project Finance

ROMANELI, Mario Antonio
Tozzini Freire Teixeira e Silva, São Paulo +55 11 232 2100
romaneli@tozzini.com.br
Recommended in Tax
Specialisation: Partner in charge of Tax Department. Provides Tax advice to Brazilian and foreign clients engaged in commercial and financial business in Brazil and abroad, with special focus on litigation matters.
Prof. Memberships: Brazilian Bar Association, since 1971.
Career: Joined the firm in 1979, becoming a partner in 1995. Member of Tax Law Studies Center in São Paulo.
Personal: Born 30 May, 1942. Graduated from the University of São Paulo School of Law in 1971 and the Southwestern Legal Foundation – Academy of American and International Law, Dallas, Texas in 1996. Admitted to the São Paulo Bar in 1971 and to the Rio de Janeiro Bar in 1997.

B

ROSSI, Carlos Alberto de Souza
Trench Rossi e Watanabe, São Paulo, SP
+55 11 3048 6800
CARLOS.ALBERTO.S.ROSSI@BAKERNET.COM
Recommended in Corporate/M&A
Specialisation: Senior Partner and Chairman of the Brazilian offices of *Baker & McKenzie.* Practice includes M&A, joint ventures, financing and tax planning. Has spoken at various conferences.
Prof. Memberships: Brazilian Bar Association (1967); Portuguese Bar Association (1989).
Career: Qualified in 1965 from the Catholic University of São Paulo, School of Law. Received the degree of Master in Comparative Law in 1967 from the Southern Methodist University School of Law, Dallas, Texas. Initiated legal career as a member of the Legal Department (tax area) of the Union of Industries of the State of São Paulo – FIESP and joined *Baker & McKenzie* in 1967.
Personal: Born 19 April 1942. Acted as a member, among others, of the finance, policy, executive and nominating Committees of *Baker & McKenzie* and as Director of the Commercial Association of the State of São Paulo. In addition to native Portuguese, is fluent in English, Spanish, and French.

ROSSI, Mariza
Ulhôa Canto, Rezende e Guerra Avogados, Rio de Janeiro +55 21 824 3265
Recommended in Communications

SACCAB ZARZUR, Cristianne
Pinheiro Neto Avogados, São Paulo
+55 11 237 8400
Recommended in Competition/Anti-trust

SALLES, Ricardo
Trench Rossi e Watanabe, Rio de Janeiro, RJ
+55 21 516 4941
Recommended in Banking & Finance
Specialisation: Partner in Corporate, Insurance, Banking & Finance. Member of the Project Finance Group of *Baker & McKenzie.*
Prof. Memberships: Member of the Brazilian Bar Association in 1971 (Section of the State of Rio de Janeiro); International Chamber of Commerce (Director, Brazilian Committee 1985); Inter-American Bar Association; Asociación Argentina de Derecho Comparado.
Publications: Published Article: 'What is a Performance Bond' – Gazeta Mercantil – March 2, 1999 – Gazeta do Rio – Page 2. 'What does Bancassurance mean?' – Gazeta Mercantil – January 20, 2000 – Gazeta do Rio – Page 2.
Career: Qualified in 1971; joined *Baker & McKenzie* in 1988; becoming a Partner in 1989. Participation in Seminars as Speaker: 'Securitisation of Receivables', São Paulo, Brazil – 1999; 'Financial Globalisation', São Paulo, Brazil – 1998.
Personal: Born in Rio de Janeiro, Brazil, January 27, 1948. Attended the University of the State of Guanabara Law School (LLB, 1970); the Federal University of Rio de Janeiro Law School (LLM, 1980). Languages: Portuguese, English, German, Italian, French, Spanish and Russian.

SALOMÃO, Eduardo
Levy & Salomão Advogados, São Paulo
+55 11 3030 0500
Recommended in Banking & Finance

SALOMÃO FILHO, Calixto
Levy & Salomão Advogados, São Paulo
+55 11 3030 0500
Recommended in Competition/Anti-trust

SCHOUERI, Luis Eduardo
Lacaz Martins, Halembeck, Pereira Neto, Gurevich & Schoueri, São Paulo +55 11 3068 8373
Recommended in Tax

SENDACZ, Moshe
Machado, Meyer, Sendacz e Opice, São Paulo
+55 11 3150 7000
Recommended in Communications

SILVA, Eugenio
Machado, Meyer, Sendacz e Opice, São Paulo
+55 11 3150 7000
Recommended in Competition/Anti-trust

SPINELLI SILVA, Sergio
Mattos Filho, Veiga Filho, Marrey Jr, Moherdaui e Quiroga, São Paulo +55 11 3170 7600
Recommended in Banking & Finance, Project Finance

STUBER, Walter Douglas
Amaro, Stuber e Advogados Associados, São Paulo, SP +55 11 284 9911
walter@amarostuber.com.br
Recommended in Corporate/M&A
Specialisation: Partner responsible for international investment and corporate development. Main area of work in banking, corporate law, mergers and acquisitions. Specialist in structuring international project finance transactions.
Publications: Contributor to several domestic and international legal magazines and journals of law. Has spoken at various conferences.

SUNDFELD, Carlos
Porto & Sundfeld Advogados, São Paulo
+55 11 3079 4244
Recommended in Communications

TOZZINI, Syllas
Tozzini Freire Teixeira e Silva, São Paulo
+55 11 232 2100
syllas@tozzini.com.br
Recommended in Corporate/M&A
Specialisation: Founding partner of *Tozzini, Freire, Teixeira e Silva Advogados.* In addition to overseeing the Firm's Corporate Practice, specialises in Mergers and Acquisitions and transnational contracts. Extremely involved in international business transactions.
Prof. Memberships: Brazilian Bar Association, since 1972.
Publications: Co-author of 'Business Operations in Brazil' published by Tax Management International.
Career: Special Consultant in Brazil to the Tax Management International Journal, Washington D.C. Member of the International Bar Association and the Inter-American Bar Association.
Personal: Born 20 June, 1949. Graduated from the University of São Paulo School of Law in 1972 and Parker School of Foreign and Comparative Law, Columbia University, in 1987. Admitted to the São Paulo Bar in 1972 and the Rio de Janeiro Bar in 1997.

ULHÔA CANTO, Carlos Alberto
Ulhôa Canto, Rezende e Guerra Avogados, Rio de Janeiro +55 21 824 3265
Recommended in Banking & Finance, Corporate/M&A, Tax

VALLE, Regina
Tozzini Freire Teixeira e Silva, São Paulo
+55 11 232 2100
rvalle@tozzini.com.br
Recommended in Communications
Specialisation: Practising Corporate Law for more than 20 years, joined *Tozzini, Freire, Teixeira e Silva Advogados* in 1998. Focuses activities on telecommunications and Internet transactions, assisting clients in M&A transactions, privatisation and public auctions, besides providing full contract statutory and regulatory consulting.
Publications: Author of the chapter on 'Telecommunications in Brazil' published in 'Telecommunications in the Present World', a Pacific Rim Association in Australia's publication.
Personal: Born 17 December, 1952. Graduated from University of São Paulo Law School, PhD in International Law and Corporate Law from the University of São Paulo Law School. Associated to CLA – Computer Law Association, to the International Law Association – ILA, to the Brazilian Association for Computer Law and Telecommunication- ADBI, to the French – Brazilian Commerce Chamber and to the Brazilian Institute for the Consumer Defense – IDEC. Member of the Telecommunication Committee of the American Chamber of Commerce.

VEIRANO, Ricardo
Veirano Advogados Associados, Rio de Janeiro
+55 21 824 4747
Recommended in Corporate/M&A

VEIRANO, Ronaldo
Veirano Advogados Associados, Rio de Janeiro
+55 21 824 4747
Recommended in Corporate/M&A

VIEGAS, Juliana
Trench Rossi e Watanabe, São Paulo, SP
+55 11 3048 6800
Juliana.Viegas@BakerNet.com
Recommended in Corporate/M&A
Specialisation: Senior partner and coordinator of the Intellectual Property Practice Area in the São Paulo office. Main area of work includes trademarks, patents, transfer of technology, licensing and franchising. Has handled substantial work in the area of software protection, licensing and distribution arrangements, and has rendered advice to clients in the internet, domain name protection and e-commerce area.
Prof. Memberships: Prior president of the Brazilian Association of Intellectual Property (ABPI – Associacão Brasileira da Propriedade Intelectual);

Brazilian Group of AIPPI – Association Internationale pour la Protection de la Propriete Industrielle; LES – Licensing Executives Society; ASIPI – Interamerican Association of Industrial Property; and of LIDC – Ligue Internationale pour la Defense de la Concurrence, for the period 1996/1999; Executive Vice-President of the Brazilian Information Technology and Telecommunications Association (ABDI – Associacão Brasileira de Direito de Informatica e Telecomunicacoes) for the period 1999/2000.
Career: Graduated in 1969 from the University of São Paulo Law School. Became a partner of *Baker & McKenzie* in 1981. Is a member of *Baker & McKenzie* Policy Committee and the Managing Partner in the São Paulo Office.
Personal: Born on Jan 18, 1945. Married, three daughters. Leisure interests: good literature.

VIEIRA, Paulo
Vieira, Rezende, Barbosa e Guerreiro, Rio de Janeiro +55 21 533 6240
pvieira@vrbg.com.br
Recommended in Corporate/M&A
Specialisation: Partner in Commercial Law, in general. Focuses: (i) corporate law: acquisitions and takeovers financing; (ii) banking and corporate finance; (iii) project finance in infrastructure areas: telecommunications, electric power, gas; (iv) regulatory matters. Highlights: has handled privatisation and project finance ventures in infrastructure areas, and the restructuring of the financial sector in Brazil. Electric power generation, transmission, distribution: TermoRio, Bandeirantes, mining: Companhia Vale do Rio Doce; telecommunications: Intelig; bank restructurings and privatisations: Banco Bamerindus, Banco Excel Economico, BEMGE, Credireal. Selected projects in 2000 include the incorporation and negotiation of all financing and commercial contracts of TermoRio, as well as the restructuring of the corporate control of Companhia Vale do Rio Doce and Companhia Sideurgica Nacional.
Prof. Memberships: Ordem dos Advogados do Brasil, Rio de Janeiro State Bar Association; International Bar Association; Cambridge University Law Society; British Chamber, Legal Committee.
Career: Qualified in 1989. 1989-1995: associate at *Castro, Barros, Sobral e Xavier Advogados S/C*; March-August 1990 interstice: *Bomchil Castro Goodrich Claro Arosemena e Associados*, London; Since 1995: founding partner of *Vieira, Rezende, Barbosa e Guerreiro Advogados.*
Personal: Born October 5, 1966. Attended the School of Law of the Pontifical Catholic University of Rio de Janeiro, Brazil (Bachelor of Laws) and Cambridge University, England (Master of Laws). Professor of Commercial and Banking Law at the School of Law of the Catholic University of Rio de Janeiro.

VIEIRA COELHO, Ricardo E.
Pinheiro Neto Avogados, São Paulo
+55 11 237 8400
Recommended in Project Finance

WALD, Alexandre
Wald e Associados Advogados, São Paulo
+55 11 3048 0600
Recommended in Banking & Finance

WALD, Arnoldo
Wald e Associados Advogados, São Paulo
+55 11 3048 0600
Recommended in Banking & Finance

XAVIER, Alberto
Xavier Bernardes e Bragança, São Paulo SP
+55 11 3069 4300
albertoxavier@xbb.com.br
Recommended in Tax
Specialisation: Taxation, International Taxation, International Tax Planning, Foreign Investments, International Financial Transactions.
Prof. Memberships: Portuguese Bar Association (1975), Brazilian Bar Association, São Paulo and Rio de Janeiro Chapters (1975), Brazilian Lawyers Institute.
Publications: Published in Brazil: 'Tax Law Subjects' (1991), 'The Tax Act, Procedure and Process – A General Theory' (1998) among others. Published in Portugal: 'International Tax Law' (1993), among others. Published abroad: 'The Taxation of Foreign Invesments in Brazil' (Kluwer, Boston, London 1980), 'L'imposition des Investissements Etrangers au Brésil' (Paris 1983). Published articles in the main international tax magazines (International Tax Review, Revista de Derecho Financiero y Hacienda Publica, Revista di Diritto, Finanziario e Scienza delle Finanze, Italy, Steur um Wintschaft). Intertax: Fiscalité Européenne, Cahiers de Droit Fiscal International.
Career: Professor of Tax Law and Corporate Law at Lisbon University (1972-1975), Professor of Tax Law, LLM Course at São Paulo Catholic University (Doctorate and Specialization Course), Secretary of State for Economic Planning of the Portuguese Government (1974).
Personal: Law degree from the University of Lisbon (1964), Supplemental Course in Juridical-Economic Sciences (1965).

ZANCAN, Leandro Luiz
Barbosa, Müssnich & Aragão, Rio de Janeiro
+55 21 3824 5800
llzancan@bmalaw.com.br
Recommended in Tax
Specialisation: Partner in corporate department. Main area of work is corporate tax planning, especially in connection with M&A transactions, both for foreign clients and enterprises investing and doing business in Brazil. Extensive experience in advising and implementing transnational operation of cross-border joint ventures. Notable recent work includes (1) creation of a joint venture between a Brazilian company and an American textile export company, (2) structuring and acquisition of various outdoor advertising companies through investment by a private equity fund managed by one of the largest international financial institutions, (3) capitalisation of the principle textile export company in Brazil, (4) capitalisation of Globo Cabo and structuring of the entry of major new shareholders, such as Microsoft and Bndespar, (5) structuring and acquisition of one information technology company through investment by a private equity fund.
Prof. Memberships: Brazilian Bar Association, Rio de Janeiro and São Paulo, the International Fiscal Association.
Career: Former partner of *Coopers & Lybrand* Auditores/Consultores. Partner of *Barbosa, Müssnich & Aragão Advogados* since late 1997. Professor of Securities at Funação Getúlio Vargas, 1988-94, and Professor of Corporate Law at Moraes Junior University, 1995. Professor of Tax Laws and Securities at IBMEC, Rio de Janeiro, 1998.
Personal: Born on 13 December 1955, in Frederico Westphalen, RS. Brazil. Graduate of Candido Mendes University School of Law (JD, 1985) and Catholic University of Rio Grande do Sul (Certified Public Accountant, 1978). Postgraduate work in securities at Funação Getúlio Vargas, 1979.

ZELMANOVITS, Nei
Machado, Meyer, Sendacz e Opice, São Paulo
+55 11 3150 7000
Recommended in Banking & Finance

ZILBOVICIUS, Moacir
Mattos Filho, Veiga Filho, Marrey Jr, Moherdaui e Quiroga, São Paulo +55 11 3147 7643
Recommended in Corporate/M&A

B

BRITISH VIRGIN ISLANDS

Corporate/Commercial

B

BRITISH VIRGIN ISLANDS Leading firms (Corporate/Commercial)	
1	Harney Westwood & Riegels
2	Smith-Hughes, Raworth & McKenzie
3	Farara George-Creque & Kerins
	O'Neal Webster O'Neal Myers Fletcher & Gordon

Firms are listed alphabetically in each band.

Leading individuals (Corporate/Commercial)	
1	**PARSONS Richard** *Harney Westwood & Riegels*
2	**KERINS Charles** *Farara George-Creque & Kerins*
	McINTYRE Rob *Smith-Hughes, Raworth*
	McKENZIE Christopher *Smith-Hughes, Raworth*
	O'ROURKE Kieron *Harney Westwood & Riegels*
	PETERS Richard *Harney Westwood & Riegels*
	TARN Peter *Harney Westwood & Riegels*
	WEBSTER Paul *O'Neal Webster O'Neal Myers*

Individuals are listed alphabetically in each band.

Harney Westwood & Riegels (8 ptrs, 19 asscs) *"Well-known internationally,"* and by far the largest firm in the islands, it offers a full range of company and commercial services, including mutual funds, insurance and trusts. **Richard Parsons*** *"turns things around very quickly,"* as does the *"long-serving"* **Richard Peters***. **Kieron O'Rourke** and **Peter Tarn*** have also established excellent reputations. The firm advised the Chodiev Group on a dispute with Trans-World Group over a joint venture for the management and assets of certain smelting plants and energy providers in Kazakhstan, worth over $200 million. **Clients:** Barclays Bank; Cable & Wireless.

Smith-Hughes, Raworth & McKenzie (4 ptrs, 5 asscs) The *"number two firm"* on BVI has made *"huge strides"* in improving its profile. Strong in the spheres of mutual funds, trust, finance, commercial litigation, e-commerce and aviation law, the firm often acts on the instructions of overseas law firms. **Rob McIntyre*** and **Christopher McKenzie*** are its recommended lawyers. The firm advised Canadian telecommunications company Bell Canada International in its recent joint venture with América-Móvil and SBC International. **Clients:** Banks; investment funds.

Farara George-Creque & Kerins (3 ptrs, 4 asscs) The firm largely concentrates on commercial and corporate litigation, but is also active in legal opinion work, trusts, insolvency, mutual funds, IP, admiralty and ship registration, regularly acting on instruction from major law firms. The *"highly competent"* **Charles Kerins*** is the firm's stand-out commercial practitioner. The firm acted as legal counsel for a BVI company used as the financing vehicle in the production of a major Hollywood film and was involved in the US listing of a BVI company bidding for a Russian cellular licence. **Clients:** Banks; hotel owners; trust companies.

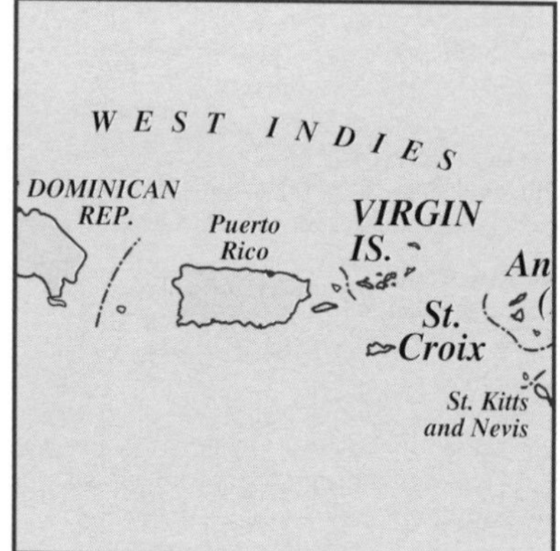

O'Neal Webster O'Neal Myers Fletcher & Gordon (5 ptrs, 5 asscs) *"One of the major litigation firms,"* it also provides corporate and commercial advice for an international clientele, often acting on referrals from international law firms. **Paul Webster*** is highly recommended. **Clients:** AT&T; HSBC.

* See leaders' profiles on pages 161

Leaders' profiles – British Virgin Islands

KERINS, Charles
Farara George-Creque & Kerins, Tortola
+1 284 494 2717

McINTYRE, Rob
Smith-Hughes, Raworth & McKenzie, Tortola
+1 284 494 3384

McKENZIE, Christopher
Smith-Hughes, Raworth & McKenzie, Tortola
+1 284 494 3384

O'ROURKE, Kieron J.
Harney Westwood & Riegels, Tortola
+1 284 494 2233
kieron.orourke@harneys.com.
Specialisation: Mutual Funds/Regulatory. Trained as a Corporate Finance lawyer at *S J Berwin & Co.*, London between 1989-1994. Head of the Mutual Funds and Regulatory Department at *Harney Westwood & Riegels* and specialises in all aspects of the formation of collective investment schemes under the laws of the British Virgin Islands. Member of the Mutual Funds Advisory Committee of the British Virgin Islands.
Career: Admitted in England & Wales 1990. Admitted in New York 1991. Admitted in the British Virgin Islands 1996. Admitted in Anguilla 2000. Partner since 1998.
Personal: Central Lancs (LLB (Hons)). Queens University, Belfast (CPLS).

PARSONS, Richard
Harney Westwood & Riegels, Tortola
+1 284 494 2233
richard.parsons@harneys.com
Specialisation: Corporate Law. Before joining *Harney Westwood & Riegels* in 1984, practised in a major central London law firm and subsequently for six years in Doha, Qatar. Experience includes a wide variety of corporate and commercial matters, banking, commercial property and conveyancing. Current primary responsibility is for company secretarial work undertaken by HWR Services Limited, the firm's associated corporate services company, which handles the establishment of, and provides on-going support for, BVI companies, partnerships and trusts.
Career: Admitted as solicitor in England 1972. Admitted as solicitor in the British Virgin Islands 1984. Admitted as solicitor in Anguilla 1999. Partner since 1986.
Personal: Christ's College, Cambridge (MA Hons) 1969. Speaks French and German and is a Notary Public.

PETERS, Richard A.
Harney Westwood & Riegels, Tortola
+1 284 494 2233

TARN, Peter R.N.
Harney Westwood & Riegels, Tortola
+1 284 494 8137
peter.tarn@harneys.com
Specialisation: Banking and Finance. Trainee and subsequently an associate in the London offices of *Allen & Overy* from 1990 to 1997, where specialised in emerging market debt. Joined *Harney Westwood & Riegels* in 1997 and is now Head of the Banking and Finance department. Client base comprises major financial institutions and corporates throughout the world. Team advises on all aspects of syndicated and bilateral lending, project and structured finance, bond issues, derivatives and workouts.
Career: Admitted in England & Wales 1992. Admitted in the British Virgin Islands 1997. Admitted in Anguilla 1999.
Personal: Bristol University (LLB) 1989. College of Law Guildford 1990.

WEBSTER, Paul
O'Neal Webster O'Neal Myers Fletcher & Gordon, Tortola +1 284 494 5808

BRUNEI

Corporate/Commercial

BRUNEI Leading firms (Corporate/Commercial)
1 Abrahams, Davidson & Co
CCW Partnership
Dr Colin Ong Legal Services
DF Abang Zen
Pengiran Izad & Lee
YC Lee & Company

Firms are listed alphabetically in each band.

Leading individuals (Corporate/Commercial)
1 **ABANG ZEN Dayang Feridahanam** *Abang Zen*
CHIEW James *Abrahams, Davidson & Co*
LEE Yew Choh *YC Lee & Company*
LEE Ronnie *Pengiran Izad & Lee*
ONG Andrew *CCW Partnership*
ONG Colin *Dr Colin Ong Legal Services*

Individuals are listed alphabetically in each band.

Abrahams, Davidson & Co (5 lawyers) The *"main corporate firm"* which also has an office in Kuala Lumpur, Malaysia. It has recently been involved in the merger of two banks, a satellite project, the conversion from conventional banking to Islamic based banking and bullion transaction agreements. **James Chiew*** is *"building up the firm"* and copes well with the firm's *"large volume"* of work. **Clients:** Denton Wilde Sapte; Khattar Wong; Datastream; GEC Marconi; HSBC; StanChart Bank; Baiduri Bank; other Islamic banks.

CCW Partnership (2 ptrs, 1 snr assc) A *"strong firm"* that is said to be feeling the loss of TC Chan. The firm has a broad client base covering both domestic and foreign companies. Its main focus lies in banking, securities, documents and debt matters. Recommended by competitors, **Andrew Ong*** is a *"thorough and competent lawyer."* **Clients:** Local and international clients.

Dr Colin Ong Legal Services (1 ptr, 3 asscs) An *"ambitious"* firm that has been in Brunei for two years. It has been involved in the creation of offshore financial centres made possible by new legislation as part of an ongoing bid to establish Brunei as a tax haven. Other work includes an advisory role for Société Générale on structured products. Acts for Singapore Airlines in Warsaw convention cases. The firm is also involved in international joint venture agreements between Brunei entities and offshore companies such as US Filter and Johnson Screens. **Colin Ong*** *"knows his law."* **Clients:** Société Générale; Singapore Airlines; Standard Charter Bank.

DF Abang Zen **Dayang Feridahanam Abang Zen** is a *"formidable lawyer"* with a reputation in Islamic banking, currently a *"lucrative growth area."* Market reaction suggests that the firm has felt the loss of a partner and two very able legal assistants, perhaps more keenly than anticipated. **Clients:** Brunei Shell; Development Bank of Brunei; StanChart Bank; Baiduri Bank; Malayan Banking; Freshfields; Rajah & Tann; RHB (the major state-owned investment vehicle.)

Pengiran Izad & Lee (2 ptrs, 2 asscs) This is a firm built on *"good connections"* in Brunei with partners who are said to have *"eminent backgrounds."* Senior partner **Ronnie Lee*** is *"the main force"* behind the firm and is *"responsible for corporate work."* Acts for local banks, insurance companies and some local construction companies **Clients:** MNSC in Brunei; leading Singaporean law firm.

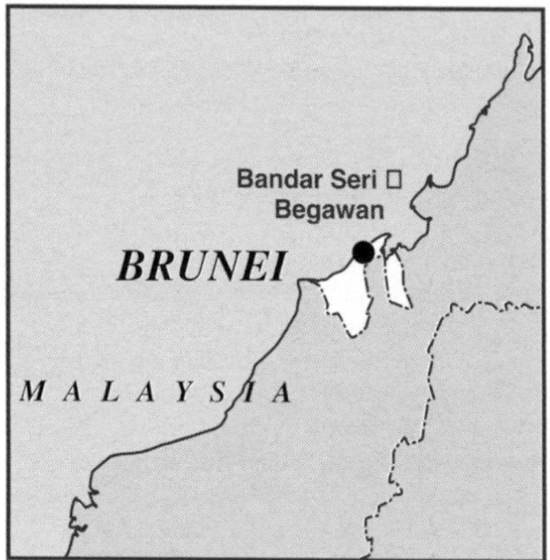

YC Lee & Company (3 ptrs, 2 asscs) Although considered to have a greater reputation for litigation, the firm has been active in a number of transactions involving the acquisition of Brunei companies in construction, cement and the industrial sectors. Also acted in an abortive attempt to set up a joint venture operating an internet service provider. The firm is legal advisor to the British High Commissioner and German and French ambassadors. It receives referrals from B&M and Simmons & Simmons. Capitalising on legislation passed in July to make Brunei a tax haven, it acted in setting up a specialist trust company – the first law firm in the jurisdiction to undertake this. **Yew Choh Lee*** is *"calm, easy-going and well-liked"* by fellow lawyers and clients alike. **Clients:** Bank of Brunei; HSBC; IRB Finance; Institute Marine; Standard Insurance; foreign law firms such as Rajah & Tann; Slaughter and May; Linklaters; Islamic Development Bank of Brunei; Royal Brunei Airlines.

* See leaders' profiles on pages 163

Leaders' profiles – Brunei

ABANG ZEN, Dayang Feridahanam
DF Abang Zen, Bandar Seri Begawan
+673 2 22 1877/236681/236680
dfabangzen @brunet.bn
Specialisation: Broad-based corporate and commercial lawyer with a wide range of practice in both advisory and substantial court work encompassing all fields of commerce and trade, corporate matters, acquisitions and mergers, banking, industries, joint-ventures, intellectual property, franchising, building contracts disputes, arbitration, insolvency, conveyancing, landed property disputes, estate matters, insurance and shariah matters. Has been instructed by the Government of Brunei Darussalam through various ministries in both major corporate matters and even death penalty cases. Has also been instructed by a large number of major commercial mercantile banks, financial institutions, major corporations, quasi-governmental corporate bodies, property owners & developers, and intellectual property owners locally and from abroad.
Prof. Memberships: INTA (International Trademark Association).
Career: Called to the English Bar in 1977, and the Borneo Bar in 1978. Was an associate in one of the law firms in Brunei Darussalam from 1978 to 1981. In January 1981 set up the firm *D F Abang Zen* as a sole practitioner. In January 1987 set up a branch office in Miri, Sarawak, Malaysia. On 1 June 1995, took in a partner in each of the main practice, Bandar Seri Begawan and the Associate office, in Miri.
Personal: Born 4 January 1954. Educated at St Columba's School (1959-70) and Kolej Tun Dato Tuanku Haji Bujang (1970-1972) in Miri, Sarawak, Malaysia. Studied law at Manchester Polytechnic, United Kingdom (1973-1976), and did the Bar Finals at the Council of Legal Education, London, in 1977.

CHIEW, James
Abrahams, Davidson & Co, Bandar Seri Begawan
+673 2 242 819
adco@brunet.bn
Specialisation: Senior Partner in Company and Commercial Department. Principal areas are corporate law and commercial law subjects. Has experience in bank mergers. Set up legal documentation for a new bank and an Islamic financial institution. Dealt with legal issues relating to set up of factories and plants. Advised on matters relating to various telecommunication areas and a satellite project.
Career: University College, Cardiff, from 1976 to 1979 (law faculty). Qualified in 1980. Joined Brunei Government as Counsel and Deputy Public Prosecutor (1980) and in 1988 appointed as Deputy Chief Registrar of the High Court, Brunei Darussalam. Joined M/s *Yu & Chiew, Advocates & Solicitors* as a partner (1989). Joined *Abrahams, Davidson & Co* as Senior Partner (1990).
Personal: Born 18 October 1955. Enjoys swimming. Resides in Bandar Seri Begawan, Brunei Darussalam.

LEE, Ronnie
Pengiran Izad & Lee, Bandar Seri Begawan
+673 2 232 945

LEE, Yew Choh
YC Lee & Company, Bandar Seri Begawan
+673 2 228 725
ycleelaw@brunet.bn
Specialisation: Managing Partner. Main area of work is commercial corporate and Intellectual Property related works. Has frequently advised on sales restrictions in Brunei of shares issues, bonds and employee share schemes for various UK and overseas clients. Acts as a legal advisor to the French and German Embassies as well as the British High Commissioner in Brunei. Practice also geared towards litigation and has acted as lead Counsel in recent high profile cases such as Yaohan winding up, invocation of diplomatic immunity defences against Standard Chartered Bank and Chinese Chamber of Commerce members' disputes. Experienced in and was involved in most of the recent significant Intellectual Property infringement suits. Invited speaker at APEC Intellectual Property Rights Business Conference in 1997 and Japan-ASEAN Symposiums on Intellectual Property in 1998-1999.
Prof. Memberships: Barrister of Lincoln's Inn, Advocate & Solicitor of the Supreme Court of Brunei. Fellow of the Chartered Institute of Arbitrators.
Career: Qualified in 1986. Brunei Correspondent, Singapore Journal of Legal Studies; Lecturer, Principles of Law, Banking Law Course organised by the Brunei Association of Banks 1991-93; Lecturer, Business Law, Department of Management and Business Administration, University of Brunei Darussalam 1995 semester; Member of the Working Committee on Law Revision – Legal Profession Act – 1999; Council Member of ASEAN Intellectual Property Association since 1998; Brunei correspondent member of ICC – Counterfeiting Intelligence Bureau since 1999.
Personal: Born 30 November, 1961 in Brunei. Bristol University 1982-1985 (LLB). Lived and Studied in Hong Kong 1974-79. Lives and works in Brunei since 1986.

ONG, Andrew
CCW Partnership, Bandar Seri Begawan
+673 2 451 606

ONG, Colin
Dr Colin Ong Legal Services, Bandar Seri Begawan
+673 2 420 913
Specialisation: Managing Partner. Broad-based international commercial lawyer with extensive court, advisory practice and commercial deals experience. Has been instructed directly and has also provided indirect advisory support, in a large number of major commercial deals and high profile disputes within Brunei, Singapore and Malaysia. Main areas of practice include arbitration, banking, company law, conflict of laws, oil and gas, shipping, aircraft, mergers & acquisitions, swaps, project finance and syndicated loans, insolvency and business reconstructions. Also acts in Intellectual Property enforcement matters as well as trademark oppositions. Frequently advises English and International Law firms on matters concerning Brunei and English law on securities and structured financial products, IPOs, due dilligence and in drafting joint ventures. Has acted for and against several major multinationals in several commercial matters. Also advises on commercial transactions for certain foreign quasi-government bodies within the ASEAN region and for several major global banks, and has assisted in setting up the first Offshore Bank in the new Brunei International Financial Centre regime. Also provides offshore trust services. Legal Advisor to the Australian and British High Commissions as well as the US Embassy in Brunei.
Prof. Memberships: British Institute of International and Comparative Law, London Court of International Arbitration, MCIArb (London), IBA, ASEAN Intellectual Property Association, ITPA and STEP.
Publications: Author of 'Cross Border Litigation within ASEAN' (Kluwer 1997) and the forthcoming 'Civil and Commercial Laws of Brunei' (MLJ/ Butterworths 2001). Occasional law lecturer and Secretary of the Brunei Toastmasters/Speaker's Club.
Career: Qualified as Barrister of England & Wales (1991). Essex Court Chambers (1992 - ongoing practising door tenant); appointed as Visiting Fellow of Faculty of Law, QMW College,University of London (1996 - ongoing); 3 Verulam Buildings (1996 - ongoing door tenant). Advocate & Solicitor of Brunei Supreme Court; Managing Partner at *Dr Colin Ong Legal Services*, Brunei (1997).
Personal: Sheffield University (LLB Hons); University of London (LLM, PhD).

B

BULGARIA

Corporate/Commercial

BULGARIA Leading firms (Corporate/Commercial)
1 Borislav Boyanov & Co
Braykov Law Office
Djingov, Gouginski, Kyutchukov & Velichkov
Lega Interconsult Penkov, Markov & Partners
2 Chernev, Komitova & Partners
Georgiev, Todorov & Co
Legacom Antov & Partners

Firms are listed alphabetically in each band.

Leading individuals (Corporate/Commercial)
1 **BOYANOV Borislav** *Borislav Boyanov & Co*
BRAYKOV Valentin *Braykov Law Office*
2 **KYUTCHUKOV Stephan** *Djingov, Gouginski*
PENKOV Vladimir *Lega Interconsult Penkov, Markov*

Individuals are listed alphabetically in each band.

Borislav Boyanov & Co (4 ptrs, 11 asscs) Interviewees admired the *"high reputation"* of this broad practice involved in foreign investment, privatisations, M&A and with a focus on aircraft financing and telecommunications. The firm advised on the privatisation of Chelopech, a Bulgarian company working the biggest operational gold-copper-pyrites mine in Europe.

It also advised American Life Insurance Company in the establishment and licensing of a subsidiary in Bulgaria, assisted in the privatisation process of the Bulgarian Telecommunications Company, and acted on the acquisition of the second GSM License in the jurisdiction. Clients describe the team as *"thorough"* and **Borislav Boyanov*** as *"just brilliant."* **Clients:** American Life Insurance Company; Chelopech; United Bulgarian Bank; Podem; Bulgartabac Holding; KPN/OTE Consortium.

Braykov Law Office (4 lawyers) *"One of the best"* offices in Sofia specialising in commercial law, arbitration, contract, copyright and trademark issues. With its offices in Bourgas and Varna, the firm advised General Electric on two lease agreements for Balkan Bulgarian airlines. *"Excellent"* **Valentin Braykov*** is considered to be the firm's leading light. **Clients:** Xerox; IBM; Kodak; British American Tobacco; HBO Warner Bros; Johnson & Johnson.

Djingov, Gouginski, Kyutchukov & Velichkov (5 ptrs, 10 asscs) *"Reputable practitioners in the country"* who operate *"on a highly professional basis."* An extensive commercial practice, it concentrates on privatisation, large-scale infrastructure projects, securities, energy and communications. The firm represented Deutsche Bank on the privatisation of the Bulgarian Telecommunications Company, and acted for CAIB-Dresdner Kleinwort Benson on the privatisation of Bulgartabac Holding.

As counsel to EBRD and IFC, the firm is involved in the financing of projects, such as the structuring and securitisation of the Sofia water supply and sewerage system. The *"broadly educated"* **Stephan Kyutchukov*** is *"a brilliant lawyer."* **Clients:** Deutsche Bank; CAIB-Dresdner Kleinwort Benson; EBRD; IFC; AIRO Catering; KBC Bank; Anglian Water; Marriott Worldwide Corporation; Zoom Television.

Lega Interconsult Penkov, Markov & Partners Historically one of the biggest firms in the country, this practice has broad corporate and commercial coverage. Vice president of the chamber of commerce **Vladimir Penkov*** has *"many years of practice in the country."* **Clients:** Leading domestic corporates and financial institutions.

Chernev, Komitova & Partners (4 ptrs in Sofia) A *"well known practice"* with offices in Sofia, Varna, Bourgas, Plovdiv, Smolyan and Yambol. The corporate team advises pharmaceutical group Balkanpharma and offers general counsel for Abela-International catering group. It represented Voluyak (fresh produce refrigeration) in its privatisation and advised on a major piece of international arbitration concerning the protection of investment and privatisation. **Clients:** Balkanpharma; Abela-International; Voluyak

Georgiev, Todorov & Co (7 ptrs, 20 asscs in Sofia) A *"young team, doing very well,"* its strengths lie in litigation, arbitration, telecoms and tax. With offices in Sofia Plovdiv, Varna, Bourgas, Rousse, Stara Zagora and Velikovo, the firm also enjoys close ties with Eversheds. It is advising on the privatisation of the Bulgarian Telecommunications Company and acted on behalf of Balkan Bulgarian Airlines in a court case regarding taxation for over $10 million. **Clients:** EBRD; Balkan Bulgarian Airlines; ABN AMRO; AT&T; Bulgarian National Bank

Legacom Antov and Partners (3 ptrs, 6 asscs) Established in Sofia in 1990, this expanding firm works primarily in corporate, investment, privatisation, banking and finance law, commercial, maritime and transport law, real estate and property law, litigation and arbitration. The team advised on the privatisation of the corn processing plant, Tzarevichni Produkti-Razgrad, the first privatisation transaction in Bulgaria involving foreign capital.

More recently the team acted for Oiltanking Bulgaria, on a joint venture between Oiltanking Ijmond, Union Miniere Pirdop Copper, and the Port of Varna, established for the construction and operation of a new terminal for liquid bulk products at the Port of Varna West. **Clients:** CA-IB; Arthur Andersen; NCH Corporation; Pfizer International; Solvay Belgium and Solvay-Sodi; Union Miniere; Oriflame Bulgaria; The Bulgarian Telegraph Agency.

* See leaders' profiles on pages 165

Leaders' profiles – Bulgaria

BOYANOV, Borislav
Borislav Boyanov & Co, Sofia +359 2 981 3007

BRAYKOV, Valentin
Braykov Law Office, Sofia +359 2 951 6040

KYUTCHUKOV, Stephan
Djingov, Gouginski, Kyutchukov & Velichkov, 1000 Sofia +359 2980 1358
Specialisation: Privatisation, Securities, Project Finance, Secured Transactions, Telecommunications, Energy and Infrastructure.
Prof. Memberships: International Bar Association, Legal Initiative for Training and Development, Institute for Market Economics.
Publications: 'Liability for Pecuniary Damages', Annual Book of the Sofia University School of Law; 'Law on Economic Activity of Foreign Persons and on Protection of Foreign Investment'.
Career: Academy of American and International Law, Dallas, Texas (1992); Law clerk, Sofia City Court (1992); Foreign attorney, *Hutchinson Black & Cook, L.L.C.*, Boulder, Colorado (1993); General Counsel, Bulgarian American Enterprise Fund (1994-); Principal drafter: Draft Law on Non-Profit Organisations, Regulation on Registries Maintained by the Securities Commission; Lecturer, University of Colorado at Boulder and Denver University (1994); Chairman, Collateral Law Reform Drafting Group (1995); Lecturer, Salzburg Seminar, Austria (1995).
Personal: Fluent in English, Bulgarian, Russian.

PENKOV, Vladimir
Lega Interconsult Penkov, Markov & Partners, Sofia +359 2 732 936
penkov@legainterconsult.com
Specialisation: Commercial and company law, foreign investments, licenses and know-how, privatisation, mergers & acquisitions, taxation and customs law, international commercial arbitration. Handled numerous acquisitions and joint-venture establishment in breweries, banking, insurance, electronics, telecommunications, soft-beverages, etc. Recently represented Domaine Boyar AD for debt and equity financing by EBRD and Baring Central European Investments; Allianz AG, Germany for acquisition of shares of Bulgaria Holding AD; subsidiary of TBT Holding for acquisition of shares of BULSTRAD insurance and re-insurance.
Career: Qualified in 1977. Legal Counsel and Senior Legal Counsel Bulgarian Ministry of Foreign Economic Relations 1977-1987, 1989-1990 Chief Legal Counsel Technica Foreign Trade Organisation 1987-1989. Founder of *Lega InterConsult* in 1990, Managing Partner ever since. Vice President of the Bulgarian Chamber of Commerce and Industry (BCCI). Member of the Managing Board of Bulgarian International Business Association Arbitrator with the Arbitration Court at BCCI. Member of the Consultative Committee of the Agency on Foreign Investments, Sofia, Bulgaria. Member of the Bulgarian National Group in the International Association for Industrial Property Protection (AIPPI). Member of the Board and Executive Director of Zagorka AD Stara Zagora.
Personal: Born 28 September 1952. Attended Economy University in Berlin 1970-1972 and Sofia University St Clement Ohridsky 1972-1976 Master in Law. Chartered member and former President of the first Lions Club in Bulgaria.

BURKINA FASO

Corporate/Commercial

BURKINA FASO Leading firms (Corporate/Commercial)
1 Cabinet Baadhio
Cabinet Benoît Joseph Sawadogo
Cabinet d'Avocats Barthélémy Keré

Firms are listed alphabetically in each band.

Leading individuals (Corporate/Commercial)
1 **BAADHIO Issous** *Cabinet Baadhio*
KERÉ Barthélémy *Barthélémy Keré*
SAWADOGO Benoît *Benoît Joseph Sawadogo*

Individuals are listed alphabetically in each band.

Cabinet Baadhio (1 ptr, 3 asscs) An internationally well-connected firm, which handles all corporate and commercial work, including mining and business law, privatisation, banking and aircraft leasing. **Issous Baadhio** is known for his offshore work. The firm advised on a gold mining project in Niger out of its Niamey office, and acted on an investment project for a petroleum prospector in Burkina Faso. **Clients:** Air France; American and Canadian mining companies; BNP Paribas; Cogema; Niger and Burkina Faso governments.

Cabinet Benoît Joseph Sawadogo (1 ptr, 4 asscs) An *"established"* firm with a strong general commercial practice active in joint ventures, consultations, incorporations and foreign investment. **Benoît Sawadogo** *"knows the mining sector well."* **Clients:** Insurance companies; Air Burkina; Air Afrique; Central West African Bank.

Cabinet d'Avocats Barthélémy Keré (1 ptr, 2 asscs) *"A strong firm with excellent clients,"* which specialises in company law, joint ventures, foreign

investment, commercial contracts and mining law. **Barthélémy Keré** is *"internationally-oriented,"* and is reputed to have good connections. The firm has negotiated joint venture agreements between the government and several foreign mining companies. **Clients:** State of Burkina Faso; mining companies; insurance companies.

Leaders' profiles – Burkina Faso

BAADHIO, Issous
Cabinet Baadhio, Ouagadougou 01 +226 312 101

KERÉ, Barthélémy
Cabinet d'Avocats Barthélémy Keré, Ouagadougou 01 +226 310 860

SAWADOGO, Benoît
Cabinet Benoît Joseph Sawadogo, Ouagadougou 01 +226 306 975

BURUNDI

Corporate/Commercial

BURUNDI Leading firms (Corporate/Commercial)
1 Cabinet Augustin Mabushi
Cabinet Sylvestre Banzubaze
Cabinet Tharcisse Ntakiyica
2 Cabinet Astère Bapfunya

Firms are listed alphabetically in each band.

Leading individuals (Corporate/Commercial)
1 **BANZUBAZE Sylvestre** *Sylvestre Banzubaze*
MABUSHI Augustin *Augustin Mabushi*
NTAKIYICA Tharcisse *Tharcisse Ntakiyica*
2 **BAPFUNYA Astère** *Cabinet Astère Bapfunya*
MUBIRIGI Gédéon *Tharcisse Ntakiyica*

Individuals are listed alphabetically in each band.

Cabinet Augustin Mabushi (1 ptr, 1 assc) In a country where specialisation is rare, French-trained **Augustin Mabushi**, *"a good young lawyer,"* has gained a reputation for commercial work, particularly arbitration, banking and M&A. The firm advised on a transaction involving BBL, a Belgian bank and SFOM, a Swiss bank. **Clients:** Bank Commerciale de Burundi (subsidiary of BBI/ING); SDV Burundi; Burundi Insurance Corporation; Compagnie de Gerance du Coton (Cogerco); Malta Forest.

Cabinet Sylvestre Banzubaze (1 ptr, 2 asscs) One of the oldest firms in Burundi, Interviewees told our researchers that it has established a name for *"mixing the old with the new."* **Sylvestre Banzubaze** is a respected practitioner. The firm covers banking, insurance and international law, and has links with clients in Belgium, Greece, Switzerland and France.**Clients:** Local and international manufacturing clients; local concessions to international corporations.

Cabinet Tharcisse Ntakiyica (1 ptr, 1 assc) A former chairman of the Bar Association, **Tharcisse Ntakiyica** is according to our researchers, findings *"one of the best lawyers in Burundi."* He deals with a high volume of cases, and has a reputation as a *"serious man."* His practice involves company formations and restructurings for local businesses. **Gédéon Mubirigi** is also recommended. **Clients:** Banks; SOCABU (insurance company); local businesses.

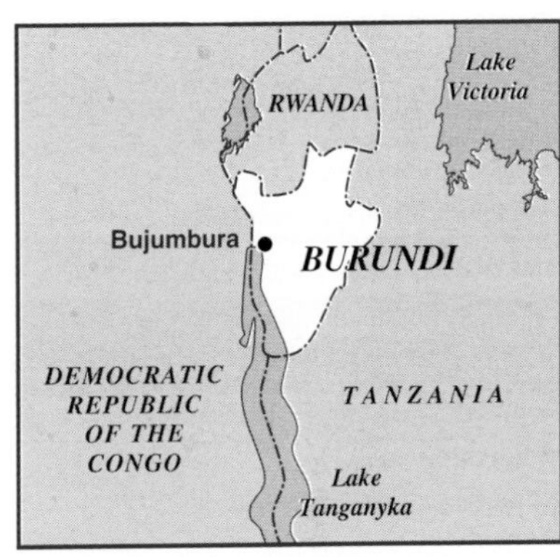

Cabinet Astère Bapfunya (2 ptrs) The firm has a *"sound reputation"* for dealing with civil and commercial law. Name partner **Astère Bapfunya** has substantial experience and is a former judge. The firm advises both local and foreign companies, as well a number of banks and insurance companies. **Clients:** MBB; BGS; Dicor.

Leaders' profiles – Burundi

BANZUBAZE, Sylvestre
Cabinet Sylvestre Banzubaze, Bujumbura
+257 226 427

BAPFUNYA, Astère
Cabinet Astère Bapfunya, Bujumbura
+257 222 475

MABUSHI, Augustin
Cabinet Augustin Mabushi, Bujumbura
+257 217 475

MUBIRIGI, Gédéon
Cabinet Tharcisse Ntakiyica, Bujumbura
+257 223 871

NTAKIYICA, Tharcisse
Cabinet Tharcisse Ntakiyica, Bujumbura
+257 223 871

CAMBODIA

Corporate/Commercial

CAMBODIA Leading firms (Corporate/Commercial)
1 Dirksen Flipse Doran & Lê
2 Tilleke & Gibbins and Associates

Firms are listed alphabetically in each band.

Leading individuals (Corporate/Commercial)
1 DORAN David *Dirksen Flipse Doran & Lê*
2 SCIARONI Bretton *Tilleke & Gibbins and Associates*

Individuals are listed alphabetically in each band.

Dirksen Flipse Doran & Lê (1 ptr, 6 asscs) An *"international class"* firm recommended for its quality work. Focusing on, infrastructure projects, the energy sector, M&A and commercial contracts, the firm represented the foreign lenders and equity partners in the $25 million financing of a local commercial bank. It is currently advising on a legal reform project for the World Bank. Founding partner **David Doran** *"knows the Cambodian scene very well."* **Clients:** Dumez GTM; Nestlé; IFC; First Commercial Bank; Mobitel; Caterpillar.

Tilleke & Gibbins and Associates (1 ptr, 4 asscs) The firm has a strong bias towards corporate and commercial work and peers agree that it handles *"a lot of local business."* A Thai firm with an office in Phnom Penh, the team is active in joint venture agreements, property transactions, contract agreements and government relations and it acted on several major IPP projects. The *"excellent"* **Brett Sciaroni** is a *"well regarded"* practitioner. **Clients:** Foreign and domestic companies.

Leaders' profiles – Cambodia

DORAN, David
Dirksen Flipse Doran & Lê, Phnom Penh
+855 23 428 726

SCIARONI, Bretton
Tilleke & Gibbins and Associates, Phnom Penh
+855 23 362 670

CAMEROON

Corporate/Commercial

CAMEROON Leading firms (Corporate/Commercial)
1 Etah-Nan & Co
Henri Job Law Firm
Cabinet Marie-Andrée Ngwe
2 Nico Halle Law Firm

Firms are listed alphabetically in each band.

Leading individuals (Corporate/Commercial)
1 ETAH Akoh *Etah-Nan & Co*
JOB Henri Pierre *Henri Job Law Firm*
NGWE Marie-Andrée *Cabinet Marie-Andrée Ngwe*
2 EKOBO Emmanuel *Sole Practitioner*
HALLE Nico *Nico Halle Law Firm*
JING Paul *Henri Job Law Firm*

Individuals are listed alphabetically in each band.

Etah-Nan & Co (4 ptrs, 3 asscs) *"Competent and hard-working,"* the firm is noted for its client roster of high-profile international corporate clients. The firm specialises in banking, commercial and corporate law and has completed the due diligence for several foreign holding companies interested in local businesses. Our researchers received recommendations for **Akoh Etah** as a *"tenacious and reliable"* practitioner. The firm advised on the privatisation of Cameroon Airlines. **Clients:** Commercial Bank of Cameroon; BICET; Société Générale; World Bank; Arthur Andersen; Deloitte & Touche; PricewaterhouseCoopers.

Henri Job Law Firm (1 ptr, 5 asscs) *"Thorough and diligent,"* **Henri Pierre Job** enjoys a position of great respect among his peers. A former president of African Lawyers in France, he is also a noted commercial arbitrator with alternative disputes body GICAM. **Paul Jing** also retains his share of market support. The firm advises on banking, finance, corporate, maritime and trademark law, and acted for MTN (Mobile Telephones Network) on its successful application for its licence in Cameroon. **Clients:** Société Générale; GMC; MTN; Matix France.

Cabinet Marie-Andrée Ngwe (1 ptr, 5 asscs) As a French national and member of Consulegis EEIG, the European organisation of lawyers, **Marie-Andrée Ngwe** attracts a high volume of French clients as well as many others from elsewhere in Europe. Described to our researchers as *"Personable, dynamic, hard-working and professional,"* she is considered to run a *"well-structured organisation"* which advises a number of international clients on trademarks, corporate restructuring, debt recovery and business law matters. A recent highlight was the firm's involvement in the Chad-Cameroon pipeline project. **Clients:** Exxon Mobil; Air France; Texaco; Mercedes-Benz; Mobil France; Guinness Cameroon; Ibis; Amity Bank; Commercial Bank of Cameroon.

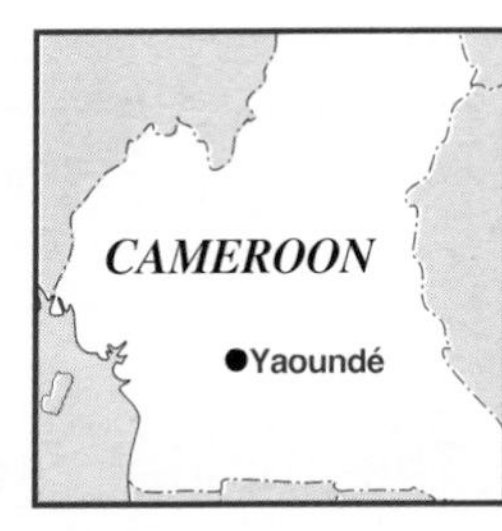

Nico Halle Law Firm (3 ptrs, 6 asscs) The firm has major clients in corporate, banking, tax and financial sectors, and specialises in joint ventures, insurance and patent law. **Nico Halle** is a familiar face in Cameroon legal circles. The firm handled the restructuring of Pamol, a subsidiary of Unilever, and oversaw the leasing of GECAS' aeroplanes to Cameroon Airlines. **Clients:** Unilever; Delmonte; Cameroon Airlines; TMOA; American Express.

Other Notable Practitioner Described as *"very talented,"* and *"one of Cameroon's leading lawyers,"* **Emmanuel Ekobo** has the highest profile of Cameroon's numerous sole practitioners.

Leaders' profiles – Cameroon

EKOBO, Emmanuel
Maître Emmanuel Ekobo - Sole Practitioner, Douala +237 422 053
cabekoba@camnet.cm
Specialisation: Main areas of practice: corporate law, banking law, insurance law, maritime law, foreign investment.
Prof. Memberships: Cameroon Bar Association, International Association of Young Lawyers (AIJA), International Association of Lawyers (UIA).
Career: Qualified in 1975, training 1976-78. Practice at the Bar since 1978. Member of the Bar Council 1994-1996.
Personal: Born 18 July 1949. Attended Yaounde University 1971-1975 (Business Law). Leisure interests include tennis and swimming.

ETAH, Akoh
Etah-Nan & Co, Douala +237 42 56 09

HALLE, Nico
Nico Halle Law Firm, Douala +237 42 6479
hallelaw1@aol.com
Specialisation: Corporate law, finance law, banking law, arbitration, natural resources, real estate, commercial law, merger, conveyancing, succession and wills, family counselling, civil aviation law, intellectual property protection and privatisation.
Prof. Memberships: Member of Commercial law affiliates, Member of Terralex International, Member of American Bar (Foster-long Inc.), Member of American Bank Attorneys, Member of the London Court of Arbitration, Member of International Bar Association.
Publications: Author of many articles published in International legal updates such as Privatisation International, World Law Business, Impact, Regional Airlines World, AIMET, Global telecoms Business, International projects 500, International Telecom Review 99 and Banking and the Law 1997.
Career: Qualified 1985, established *Nico Halle Law Firm* same year.

JING, Paul T.
Henri Job Law Firm, Douala +237 424 802

JOB, Henri Pierre
Henri Job Law Firm, Douala +237 424 802

NGWE, Marie-Andrée
Cabinet Marie-Andrée Ngwe, Douala +237 425 362

CANADA

Index

C

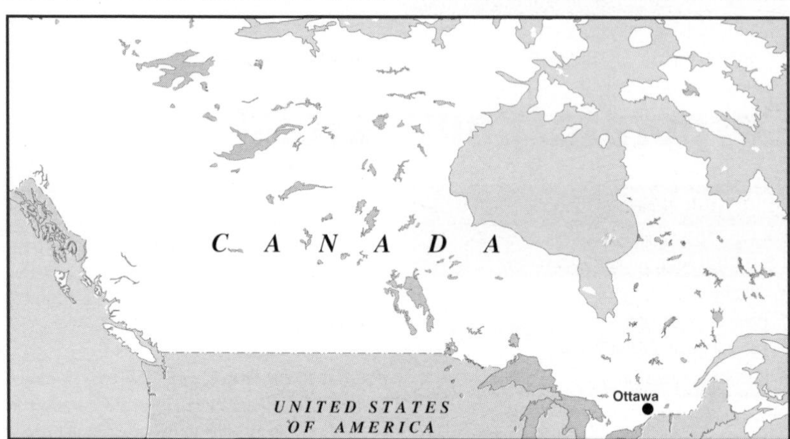

The clients' choice

BUSINESS LAWYER OF THE YEAR
JP BISNAIRE,
Davies Ward Phillips & Vineberg

BUSINESS LAW FIRM OF THE YEAR
DAVIES WARD PHILLIPS & VINEBERG

*A huge response from Canadian clients saw **JP Bisnaire** win by the narrowest of margins. **Davies Ward Phillips & Vineberg** and **Stikeman Elliott** came in equal as best firm.*

For details see page 36.

OVERVIEW: A year of consolidation in the legal market culminated in the merger between Davis Ward & Beck and the Montréal office of Goodman Phillips & Vineberg, creating a corporate powerhouse that dominates the market (Davis Ward Phillips & Vineberg.) Firms struggle to establish a presence across the country's multiple jurisdictions, enticing international clients who view Canada as a single market. Toronto, as financial capital, overshadows Calgary while Montréal, has witnessed a dramatic growth in the hi-tech and biotech sectors. Cross-border activity is booming, with many international investors attracted by the low Canadian dollar. Competition from US firms is high in the banking and insurance sector, where legislation has created a new ownership regime for many federally regulated financial institutions. In the tax arena, law firms are beginning to see the encroachment of the international accountancy firms, with practitioners of the ilk of Jim Wilson joining PwC.

Banking & Finance

CANADA Leading firms (Banking & Finance)
1 Blake, Cassels & Graydon LLP
2 Davies Ward Phillips & Vineberg
McCarthy Tétrault
Osler, Hoskin & Harcourt LLP
3 Fasken Martineau DuMoulin
Fraser Milner Casgrain
Ogilvy Renault
Stikeman Elliott
Torys
4 McMillan Binch
5 Bennett Jones LLP
Goodmans
Meighen Demers
Smith Lyons

Firms are listed alphabetically in each band.

Blake, Cassels & Graydon LLP (35 lawyers nationwide) Pulling away from its competitors, Canada's *"foremost banking firm"* is admired for its unrivalled *"breadth of practitioner."* Renowned for its work on behalf of the Canadian Imperial Bank of Commerce, the team generally acts for institutional clients on the lender side. The firm's western province offices handle energy-related financings, while the Toronto office has a growing reputation for acquisition finance in the telecoms sector.

Despite being the firm's managing partner, **James Christie***, *"a great business lawyer,"* is still regarded as a *"star with huge experience and a measured approach."* Securities specialist **Martin Fingerhut*** is regarded as *"a leader in his field,"* **David Kee*** is a *"technically superb finance practitioner"* and **John Teolis*** is highly regarded both for syndicated loans and bank regulatory advice. The firm advised CIBC on the financing of GT Group Telecom's acquisition of the fibre optic assets of Shaw Communications, and has advised Clearnet Communications on a number of debt financings over the past year. Also represented a syndicate of banks, led by Chase Manhattan, on the financing for Norigen Communications. **Clients:** CIBC; Newcourt Credit; Citicorp; Fuji Bank; Deutsche Bank; ABN Amro; Chase Manhattan.

Davies Ward Phillips & Vineberg (20 ptrs, 10 asscs) Focusing principally on complex big-ticket structured finance transactions, the firm advises all the 'big five' banks in this area. Historically associated with its work for the Canadian subsidiaries of foreign banks, the firm's international transactions still constitute a substantial element of the overall caseload. Generally acting for lenders, the firm also includes a number of borrowers among its clientele. The addition of the

CANADA
Leading individuals (Banking & Finance)

Band	Individual
1	**BAILLIE James** *Torys*
	CHRISTIE James *Blake, Cassels & Graydon*
	DEMERS Jacques *Meighen Demers*
	LEVIN Jonathan *Fasken Martineau DuMoulin LLP*
	RILEY James *Ogilvy Renault*
	SWARTZ Jay *Davies Ward Phillips & Vineberg*
	ZIMMERMAN Alec *Osler, Hoskin & Harcourt LLP*
2	**BARRETT Roderick** *Stikeman Elliott*
	BRANDS Andrew *Smith Lyons*
	CARFAGNINI Jay *Goodmans*
	FINGERHUT Martin *Blake, Cassels & Graydon*
	KEE David *Blake, Cassels & Graydon*
	KENT Andrew *McMillan Binch*
	LISSON James *Osler, Hoskin & Harcourt LLP*
	MURPHY Peter *Fraser Milner Casgrain*
	SAIBIL Norman *Borden Ladner Gervais LLP*
	TEOLIS John *Blake, Cassels & Graydon*
3	**BOIVIN Charles** *Ogilvy Renault*
	DESCHAMPS Michel *McCarthy Tétrault*
	MARTIS Xeno *Fasken Martineau DuMoulin LLP*
	PENNYCOOK Carol *Davies Ward Phillips & Vineberg*
	RYAN Barry *McCarthy Tétrault*
	WOLOSHYN William *McMillan Binch*
4	**ANDERSON Jean** *Davies Ward Phillips & Vineberg*
	BACKMAN Philip *Bennett Jones LLP*
	BARKER Bruce *Bennett Jones LLP*
	JASON John *Osler, Hoskin & Harcourt LLP*
	KEEFE Blair *Torys*
	WALKER Ross *Fraser Milner Casgrain*
	WIERCINSKI Henry *McCarthy Tétrault*

Up-and-coming individuals

Individual
KELLY Mary *Ogilvy Renault*
ROBERTSON Holly *McMillan Binch*

Individuals are listed alphabetically in each band.

Montréal office of Goodman Phillips & Vineberg is expected to be of added benefit to the firm.

"Fantastic and versatile" **Jay Swartz*** is said by the market to be *"one of Canada's premier banking lawyers."* Especially strong on derivatives, he also takes high rank for his banking regulatory work. Securities expert **Carol Pennycook*** is considered to be a *"bright, excellent"* practitioner. The respected **Jean Anderson*** has also arrived from Macmillan Binch. The firm advised on the leveraged acquisition financing for the Onex Corporation's acquisition of Celestica from IBM, and acted for McCain Foods in establishing a global credit facility for its operations in Canada, the United States, Europe, Australia, New Zealand and South America. **Clients:** McCain Foods; Celestica; Cadillac Fairview Corporation, Foothills Capital; domestic and international banks.

McCarthy Tétrault (50 ptrs, 50 asscs) A *"clear leader both in Montréal and Toronto,"* the firm's banking and finance reputation is assured. Advising on the spectrum of financial matters, the group acted for Merrill Lynch on the first four public offerings of commercial-backed securities in Canada, worth CDN$800 million. Additionally, the team handles securitisation, syndicated loans and big-ticket acquisition finance. Such is the firm's strength in depth that it is expected to weather the retirement of long-time leader Alan Peters.

The *"capable and skilled"* **Barry Ryan*** is an emerging name, known for his work on behalf of TD Bank. **Henry Wiercinski***, *"a strong technician,"* and Montréal-based **Michel Deschamps***, *"a banking authority with an academic inclination,"* are also warmly recommended. The firm advised TD Waterhouse on its CDN$1.5 billion IPO in the US and Canada. **Clients:** Bank of Nova Scotia; TD Bank; Bank of America (Canada); Hong Kong Bank of Canada; National Bank of Canada.

Osler, Hoskin & Harcourt LLP (10 ptrs, 10 asscs) A leading banking practice, seen on *"many of the deals,"* which offers advice on syndicated lending, structured finance and securitisation for an enviable client roster. This includes international banks, trust companies, insurance companies, mutual and hedge funds, pension funds and securities dealers. The firm has strong links with Chase Manhattan and is principal counsel in Canada for Morgan Stanley Dean Witter and Goldman Sachs.

Although principally renowned for his insolvency work, *"technical wizard"* **Alec Zimmerman*** is also *"terrific for straight banking transactions."* The strong team also includes regulatory expert **John Jason*** and *"fine lawyer"* **James Lisson***. The firm acted for CanWest on the financing of its CDN$3.5 billion acquisition of most of Hollinger's Canadian newspaper, magazine and news media interests, and advised Metronet Communications Corp (prior to its merger with AT&T) on a number of high-yield issues. **Clients:** Bank of Montréal; Chase Manhattan: TD Bank (insolvency matters); CanWest Global Communications; Morgan Stanley Dean Witter; Goldman Sachs.

Fasken Martineau DuMoulin (75 lawyers nationwide) A *"leading player,"* the firm's most recent merger has generated increasingly high-profile work, best exemplified by its role as counsel to JP Morgan and TD Securities on the CDN$7.7 billion syndicated financing of the Telus takeover of Clearnet. The group advises Canada's largest banks, as well as foreign bank subsidiaries, trust companies, mutual savings banks, insurance companies and financial leasing companies. The Toronto office is fronted by *"stellar, old school public lawyer"* **Jonathan Levin***, as much respected by his peers for banking matters as for his corporate expertise. In Montréal, **Xeno Martis*** remains a familiar and popular name. **Clients:** TD Bank; Royal Bank of Canada; CIBC; Bank of Montréal; Scotia McLeod; ING; JP Morgan; AT&T Canada.

Fraser Milner Casgrain (27 ptrs, 27 asscs nationwide) The banking department is seen to be one of the firm's strongest weapons. The group acts for both lenders and borrowers on equipment leasing and finance transactions (notably in film financing), synthetic leases, asset-based securitisations, and bank regulatory issues.

"True gentleman, and fabulous lawyer" **Peter Murphy*** has *"a wonderfully varied practice,"* and his work for Bank of Montréal received special commendation. Newly rated **Ross Walker*** is considered to be an underrated performer. The firm advised Chase Manhattan, as Canadian Bank Act regulatory counsel, in connection with its US$11 billion global acquisition of the businesses of Robert Fleming. Also provided Bank Act regulatory advice to CIT in connection with its US$3 billion acquisition of Newcourt Financial in Canada. **Clients:** Bank of Montréal; Chase Manhattan; HSBC Bank Canada; Lloyds TSB; ABN AMRO; ING Bank; Deutsche Bank Canada; Fleet Bank; Royal Bank Of Canada; State Street Canada; National Bank of Canada; Société Générale.

Ogilvy Renault (23 ptrs, 10 asscs) Relatively new to Toronto, the firm is *"growing a good franchise"* after its expansion from Montréal. High-end acquisition finance and syndicated loans are key elements of the workload for a team which is expected to become *"a Toronto player of the first rank."*

Star individual **James Riley*** is a *"multi-faceted, tenacious and commercial lawyer, who looks for creative solutions."* Rising star **Mary Kelly***, also in Toronto, is *"a terrific talent."* In Montréal, **Charles Boivin*** has a respected practice, which includes a close relationship with the Royal Bank of Canada. The firm advised Citibank and Royal Bank of Canada, the lead lenders, on the syndicated financing of the Alcan Aluminium merger with Alusuisse Lonza Group. Also represented Bombardier on a syndicated financing valued in excess of CDN$1 billion, and advised a

C

*See leaders' profiles on pages 183-202

syndicate of banks on the attempted three-way financing of CanWest's acquisition of the newspaper and publishing assets of Hollinger. **Clients:** CIBC; Bank of Montréal; Royal Bank of Canada; Société Générale; CSFB.

Stikeman Elliott (15 ptrs, 16 asscs) Powerful firm which, in addition to core expertise in syndicated loans, advises on unsecured and secured lending, project finance, acquisition and lender offer financings, securitisations and derivatives. The firm's client base includes Canadian and other financial institutions, investment funds, governments and their agencies and corporations from a wide range of industries.

Roderick Barrett* is a *"bright and aggressive lawyer, loved by his clients."* However, market perception is that the group's weakness lies in a lack of support for his *"energetic, deal-doing"* style. The team has acted for both buyers and sellers on numerous asset and share purchases, and advised Nova Bancorp Group (Canada) on a recent share acquisition. **Clients:** CIBC; Bankers Trust; Royal Bank of Canada.

Torys (15 ptrs, 30 asscs) Not a traditional banking practice, and one that is seen to its greatest effect on regulatory matters, the firm is frequently retained to act on special projects, merchant banking, secured transactions, institutional lending and investment funds and management matters. Its client base embraces all types of domestic and international financial institutions. The team includes legendary *"polished performer"* and regulatory expert **Jim Baillie*** and **Blair Keefe***, the *"young and respected"* head of the firm's financial institutions group. Acted in the $2.5 billion leveraged buy-out of Shoppers Drug Mart by a group of investors led by Kohlberg Kravis Roberts, from British American Tobacco, acting for the borrower, Shoppers Drug Mart, on two facilities to finance the acquisition. The first, led by CIBC World Markets, was a senior credit facility of $1.55 billion that was secured by shares of Shoppers Drug Mart and its subisidiaries and certain real property. The other was a $525 million unsecured loan facility led by CIBC World Markets and Scotia Capital. **Clients:** TD Bank; Deutsche Bank Canada; Bank of Nova Scotia; CIBC World Markets; Citibank Canada; Thomson Corporation; Brascan Corporation.

McMillan Binch (12 ptrs, 13 asscs) A difficult year for the firm has left the banking practice, *"traditionally a powerhouse,"* bereft of Bruce Barker and Jean Anderson, who have left for Bennett Jones and Goodman Phillips & Vineberg respectively. However, the firm continues to work for both Schedule I and Schedule II banks, and has specific expertise in asset-based lending work (in which area the group does substantial work for GE Capital), derivatives, and structured financings.

Bill Woloshyn* remains a *"senior and influential banking man,"* while **Andrew Kent*** is admired for his corporate restructuring work, especially on behalf of the Royal Bank of Canada. **Holly Robertson*** is considered to be a practitioner with potential. The firm advised on the cross-border offerings by Canadian issuers of Liquid Yield Option Notes, worth in excess of US$1.3 billion at maturity. Also represented a US credit corporation and its Canadian subsidiaries on a US$100 million secured loan to complete the privatisation of a Quebec steel manufacturer. **Clients:** Royal Bank of Canada; Congress Financial; GE Capital.

Bennett Jones LLP (14 ptrs, 8 asscs) Still said to dominate the Calgary market, the firm maintains a respected name for acquisition financing in the energy sector, project finance and aircraft finance. *"Great lawyer"* **Philip Backman*** is a popular figure in Calgary, while the Toronto office's recruitment of **Bruce Barker*** from McMillan Binch has divided the market. *"The challenge for him will be to get the people to build the practice."* Barker represented Deutsche Bank Canada in connection with its CDN$200 million investment in convertible debentures issued by Sherritt International Corporation. The firm also advised Shell Canada Ltd on the CDN$4 billion Athabasca Oil Sands Project, in which Shell has a 60% interest, and represented the Maritimes & Northeast Pipleline partnership on a US$1.1 billion cross-border bank and bond financing. **Clients:** Royal Bank of Canada; Bank of Montreal; CIBC.

Goodmans (15 ptrs, 10 asscs) An *"iconoclastic"* practice, acting both for and against most of Canada's leading banks, which is seen almost exclusively on complex syndicated transactions. An exception is asset-based lending, where the finance group undertakes more traditional work, acting for both borrowers and lenders. However, the loss of the firm's Montréal office to Davies Ward & Beck has cast doubt on the firm's pan-national capabilities.

Head of the firm's financial services group is **Jay Carfagnini***, *"a charismatic client developer,"* who is also considered one of the country's leading insolvency lawyers. The firm represented the Toronto-Dominion Bank on the Senior Credit Facilities of ISPCO, a transaction valued at US$250 million, and advised Bank of Nova Scotia, the Toronto-Dominion Bank and Bank One on the acquisition financing (CDN$300 million) for Slater Steel's takeover of Atlas Steels. **Clients:** National Bank of Canada; GE Capital (Montréal Office); Bank of Montréal; Congress Financial; Wells Fargo; TD Bank; GMAC.

Meighen Demers (6 ptrs, 4 asscs) A *"really nice boutique that packs a pretty good punch,"* the firm is thought to be a national force in certain financial areas, most notably project finance and asset-based lending transactions. Recent work encompasses public offerings and private placements on behalf of Canadian and US issuers, including offerings of special warrants, common and preferred shares and debt instruments.

Most agree that **Jacques Demers***, *"a no-nonsense man with good business sense,"* is *"right in the top league"* for securities and capital markets advice. The firm represented the banks underwriting the financing of the acquisition by Aur Resources Inc of a 76.5% stake in a Chilean copper mine, Quebrada Blanca. **Clients:** Barclays Bank; ABN Amro; Deutsche Bank; Royal Bank of Canada; Dresdner Bank.

Smith Lyons (29 ptrs, 10 asscs) The firm advises a variety of domestic and foreign clients including Schedule I and Schedule II banks, trust companies, asset-based lenders and venture capitalists on the design, structuring and implementation of innovative financing packages.

According to the findings of our researchers, **Andrew Brands*** is thought to have a *"serious practice,"* and has been involved in financings and reorganisations for a range of corporate borrowers. The firm is noted for its advice on behalf of the Bank of Nova Scotia, and has niche expertise in real estate finance. Represented CIBC Capital on the acquisition (valued at CDN$2.5 billion) of Shoppers Drug Mart by an investor group led by KKR. **Clients:** CIBC; Bank of Nova Scotia; TD Bank; Congress Financial.

Other Notable Practitioner The *"excellent and practical"* **Norman Saibil*** at Borden Ladner Gervais in Montréal continues to win market commendation for his mixed international and domestic banking practice.

Communications

CANADA Leading firms (Communications)
1 Johnston & Buchan
McCarthy Tétrault
2 Osler, Hoskin & Harcourt LLP
3 Goodmans
Stikeman Elliott
Torys
4 Bennett Jones LLP
Gowling Lafleur Henderson
5 Nelligan O'Brien Payne
6 Blake, Cassels & Graydon LLP

Firms are listed alphabetically in each band.

Leading individuals (Communications)
1 ABUGOV Lorne *Osler, Hoskin & Harcourt LLP*
DUNBAR Laurence *Johnston & Buchan*
INTVEN Hank *McCarthy Tétrault*
2 BUCHAN Robert *Johnston & Buchan*
DALFEN Charles *Torys*
JOHNSTON Chris *Johnston & Buchan*
KANE Gregory *Stikeman Elliott*
KEENLEYSIDE Anthony *McCarthy Tétrault*
ROBINSON Kathryn *Goodmans*
ROGERS Phil *Gowling Lafleur Henderson*
WHITEHEAD Stephen *Johnston & Buchan*
3 KOCH Michael *Goodmans*
LOWE John *Bennett Jones LLP*
SALZMAN Lorne *McCarthy Tétrault*
4 CAMPBELL Dan *Cox Hanson O'Reilly Matheson*
EMBREE Kirsten *Osler, Hoskin & Harcourt LLP*
GRANT Peter *McCarthy Tétrault*
TACIT Christian *Nelligan O'Brien Payne*
ZOLF Stephen *Heenan Blaikie*

Individuals are listed alphabetically in each band.

Johnston & Buchan (8 ptrs, 2 asscs) Although a boutique firm, lacking the ability of its full-service competitors to handle the big-ticket telecoms transactions, the firm is considered by many to be *"the foremost communications practice in Canada."* Said to possess *"unrivalled practical expertise,"* the team is often brought in by other firms to advise on regulatory aspects of a deal.

The firm has enviable strength in depth, but its star player remains **Laurence Dunbar***, who *"would be head counsel on any dream team,"* and is rated for his work in both wired and wireless telecoms, where he is *"superb on the vital detail."* **Bob Buchan*** and **Chris Johnston*** are both *"great old-school lawyers with excellent contacts at the Communications Commission and fantastic clients."* Buchan has a broad practice, with a particular niche in cable TV and satellite to cable services, whilst Johnston is rated for his traditional broadcasting and satellite to cable expertise. The *"knowledgeable"* **Stephen Whitehead***, who comes from a corporate and securities background, specialises in satellite and ownership work. The firm advised Rogers Communications on its takeover of Vidéotron, and Shaw Cable Systems on its takeover of Cancom. **Clients:** Shaw Cable Systems; Rogers Communications Inc.

McCarthy Tétrault (6 ptrs, 7 asscs) Fielding the largest telecoms group in Canada, the firm spreads its communications team through four offices. Toronto is the centre of operations, and brings together three layers of expertise – domestic telecommunications regulatory work, domestic broadcasting regulatory work, and international regulatory and transactional work. The team advises a number of competitive entrant telecoms and broadcasting companies, as well as CLECs (competitive local exchange carriers) and satellite suppliers.

The international arm of the practice, under the leadership of *"absolutely first-rate"* **Hank Intven***, has advised more than 20 governments on restructuring their telecoms networks, facilitating privatisation and preparing new law. The group has also represented both governments and bidders on the licensing of cellular operators. Other key members of the group are **Lorne Salzman*** and newly ranked broadcasting expert **Peter Grant***. Ottawa-based **Tony Keenleyside*** is deemed to be *"one of the most knowledgeable lawyers on satellite communications."* The firm advised the Government of Jordan when it sold a 40% share of Jordan Telephone Company to France Telecom, a deal worth around US$600 million. **Clients:** Craig Broadcasting Systems; Standard Broadcasting Corp; Government of Jordan; AT&T Canada; ClearNet Communications; Alliance Atlantis.

Osler, Hoskin & Harcourt LLP (6 ptrs, 5 asscs) Admired for its balance of corporate and regulatory work, the team advises American and other international clients on Canadian telecommunications and broadcasting industry issues, as well as appearing on regulatory proceedings before the CRTC and Industry Canada. Nevertheless, the department is felt to be fractionally off the pace of the leaders in the field, principally because of its comparative lack of star practitioners. Such a criticism cannot apply to **Lorne Abugov***, however, who handles both telecoms and broadcasting issues, and is considered *"an intelligent and clear thinker with an international outlook."* **Kirsten Embree*** is regarded as *"a talented all-rounder."*

The firm represented Newbridge on its acquisition by Alcatel, advised JDS Fitel on its merger with Uniphase and acted for Nextlink on its joint bid with Wispra during Canada's first spectrum auction. **Clients:** JDS Fitel; Nextlink; CanWest.

Goodmans (3 ptrs, 4 asscs) The firm is widely considered to have *"come on more strongly than any other recently"* and is now *"in the ascendant,"* having broadened its focus from its traditional strength in broadcasting to incorporate a strong telecoms practice. The broadcasting caseload includes acting for broadcasting licensees before the CRTC, and representing them on licence applications, renewals and transfers of ownership. In telecoms matters, the group advises on policy proceedings before the CRTC, as well as M&A advisory work. In addition, the team has expertise in IP, competition and international trade law as they affect the broadcasting and telecoms industries.

Chair of the Broadcasting, Telecoms & New Media Group, and veteran of numerous cases on behalf of CTV, **Kathy Robinson*** is *"an exceptional leader, right at the top for TV broadcasting work."* For telecoms advice, **Michael Koch*** is considered an *"emerging player you can rely on."* The firm represented GT Group Telecom in a series of acquisitions relating to fibre-optic networks owned by Shaw Communications, and acted for CTV on its acquisition by BCE. **Clients:** CTV; Look Communications; GT Group Telecom; British Telecom.

Stikeman Elliott (4 ptrs, 2 asscs) The firm acts for a number of domestic and international carriers and operators on the spectrum of communications activities. Primarily, the team has advised on significant regulatory matters, ranging from rate and service proceedings through to applications for entry and the provision of competitive telecommunication services.

Managing partner of the Ottawa office and head of telecoms, **Greg Kane*** is *"a fine lawyer, a real player."* Although his own practice focuses on telecoms, he has also developed expertise in new media through his work, inter alia, for AOL, and has carved out a further niche in competitive cable systems. The firm advised CAPE (Canadian Association of Internet Providers) in proceedings before the regulatory bodies, and represented

*See leaders' profiles on pages 183-202

BCE on its proposed CTV TV network. **Clients:** CAPE; AOL Canada; BCE; Teleglobe; ICO.

Torys (3 ptrs, 5 asscs) Transactionally focused department, which provides strategic and regulatory advice on communications deals. The team is considered to owe much to **Charles Dalfen***, *"clearly one of Canada's most experienced and knowledgeable practitioners." "Idiosyncratic, but a high-flier,"* he has a leading name for domestic and international telecoms advice, as well as developing a notable new media practice.

The firm acted for CanWest Global Communications on its CDN$792 million take-over bid for WIC (Western International Communications) and the subsequent agreement with Shaw Communications to reorganise WIC's assets. Also advised Rogers Communications on its CDN$5.6 billion purchase of Vidéotron, and represented GlobeNet Communications during its US$600 million take-over by Worldwide Fibre. **Clients:** BCE; Uniphase Corp; CanWest Global Communications; MaxLink Corporation; Norigen Communications; Wispra Networks; North Point Communications; TD Capital.

Bennett Jones LLP (7 ptrs, 5 asscs) Although the firm's franchise in Calgary and the Western provinces is seen as an *"awesome"* operation, in this, as in other areas of practice, its profile is somewhat unfairly dismissed by some of the Toronto élite as a *"regional"* firm. In truth, the firm provides a full regulatory and corporate/commercial service for a clientele which includes both domestic and international names.

The highly rated **John Lowe*** is renowned for his work on behalf of Telus, and is a respected force in both telecoms and broadcasting. He represents telecoms service providers in price cap implementation proceedings, industry restructuring hearings (including contribution reform), competition and commercial matters. The firm advised Telus on the regulatory matters concerning its CDN$6.5 billion acquisition of Clearnet, and continues to represent that company on a number of CRTC proceedings. **Clients:** Telus.

Gowling Lafleur Henderson (3 ptrs, 2 asscs) A well-rounded practice, which advises clients on government policy, government relations, regulatory procedures, litigation and international law in relation to both broadcasting and telecommunications. Headed by the experienced **Phil Rogers***, former Assistant General Counsel at Bell Canada, and an established name in the international arena, the group has been involved in satellite and DTH policy and enhanced services both at home and abroad. The team has acted on numerous CRTC and Information Highway hearings, and recently conducted substantial public regulatory work for a leading Canadian service provider. **Clients:** BCE and related companies (Bell Canada; Telesat Canada; NorthWest Tel.)

Nelligan O'Brien Payne (2 ptrs, 2 asscs) Small but respected Ottawa firm *("they know what they're doing")* with a presence in the domestic telecoms market. Acknowledged as *"a minor player"* on M&A transactions, the team has less of a regulatory profile, but maintains a niche in acting for competitive entrants into the telecoms market.

Stand-out practitioner **Christian Tacit*** is *"a tenacious advocate for his clients,"* and has also been described as a *"bulldog who will fight tooth and nail."* The firm represented the Federation of Canadian Municipalities in regulatory proceedings concerning the use of municipal rights of way by communications carriers. **Clients:** RSL Com Canada; ON Tel; Federation of Canadian Municipalities.

Blake, Cassels & Graydon LLP (2 ptrs, 4 asscs) Low-key department, known almost exclusively for its transactional expertise, unsurprising for a firm with such an outstanding corporate reputation. However, the telecommunications and broadcasting team also provides a full range of legal services on all issues relating to the regulation of telecoms, broadcasting, satellite and radio. The firm advises a number of US broadcasting companies on regulatory matters in Canada. Advised a Christian Broadcaster in its unsuccessful bid to obtain a radio frequency to broadcast in Toronto, and represented the National Hockey League on the formulation of a new broadcasting entity. **Clients:** Worldcom; Stratos Global; Bell Canada; CNAC; National Hockey League.

Other Notable Practitioners Two practitioners at comparatively low-profile firms stand out as individuals of unusual merit. Based in Halifax, Nova Scotia, **Dan Campbell*** of Cox, Hanson, O'Reilly, Matheson has been commended as *"the best communications lawyer east of Montréal."* In Toronto, **Stephen Zolf***, of Heenan Blaikie is adjudged *"a fine counsel for broadcasting and entertainment issues."*

Competition/Anti-trust

Davies Ward Phillips & Vineberg (8 ptrs, 4 asscs) The firm fields a *"vigorous team and a large bunch of quality players who tend to drive harder than all the rest."* Advises an array of blue-chip clients on the gamut of competition matters, including merger control, joint ventures, trade practices, pricing policies, relationships with customers and competitors, and marketing, distribution and licensing arrangements. The team represents both plaintiffs and defendants on antitrust litigation in various Canadian courts and before the Competition Tribunal, and defends individuals and corporations in criminal antitrust prosecutions. The clientele encompasses a wide range of industries, and includes IT and telecommunications companies, financial institutions and energy concerns.

Ex-commissioner **Calvin Goldman*** is thought by many to be Canada's *"top competition lawyer,"* and *"a no less talented rainmaker."* He *"is surrounded by a bevy of good players."* The *"impressive"* **Paul Crampton*** is *"a prolific writer,"* while **John Bodrug**'s* *"grasp of the technicalities,"* is also felt to make an important contribution to the department's success. Newly-ranked **Neil Finkelstein*** is considered to be a *"litigation whiz"* with competition expertise. A strong lobby believes that *"great lawyer"* **Milos Barutciski**'s* name *"shouldn't be left off any list."* The firm represented Superior Propane in litigation against the Commissioner of the Competition Bureau. Also advised RBC Dominion Securities on its acquisition of a leading competitor, a transaction which created the largest retail brokerage firm in Canada. **Clients:** Major domestic and international corporations, trade associations and individuals.

Osler, Hoskin & Harcourt LLP (6 ptrs, 6 asscs) Praised for its strength in depth and its *"co-operative approach,"* the firm's competition group is widely acknowledged as a national leader. The *"experienced and first-class"* **Tim Kennish*** remains at the helm, a former Commissioner who is held to be a *"master strategist."* Behind him there is an impressive array of names. High-profile litigator **John Rook*** is *"a rounded performer with sound knowledge, who flourishes in court."* He

CANADA Leading firms (Competition/Anti-trust)
1 Davies Ward Phillips & Vineberg
Osler, Hoskin & Harcourt LLP
Stikeman Elliott
2 Blake, Cassels & Graydon LLP
McCarthy Tétrault
McMillan Binch
3 Davis & Co
Fraser Milner Casgrain
Smith Lyons
4 Bennett Jones LLP
Lang Michener
Ogilvy Renault
Torys
5 Kelly Affleck Greene

Firms are listed alphabetically in each band.

Leading individuals (Competition/Anti-trust)
1 **BÉRIAULT Yves** *McCarthy Tétrault*
GOLDMAN Calvin *Davies Ward Phillips*
HUNTER Lawson *Stikeman Elliott*
KENNISH Tim *Osler, Hoskin & Harcourt LLP*
2 **AFFLECK Donald** *Kelly Affleck Greene*
CAMPBELL Neil *McMillan Binch*
CRAMPTON Paul *Davies Ward Phillips*
GRAHAM Bruce *Smith Lyons*
HUGHES Randal *Fraser Milner Casgrain*
ROOK John *Osler, Hoskin & Harcourt LLP*
ROWLEY William *McMillan Binch*
WONG Stanley *Davis & Co*
3 **FINKELSTEIN Neil** *Davies Ward Phillips*
FRANKLYN Peter *Osler, Hoskin & Harcourt LLP*
HOUSTON Donald *Kelly Affleck Greene*
MUSGROVE James *Lang Michener*
QUINN Jack *Blake, Cassels & Graydon LLP*
STREKAF Jo'Anne *Bennett Jones LLP*
ZALMANOWITZ Barry *Fraser Milner Casgrain*
4 **BARUTCISKI Milos** *Davies Ward Phillips*
BODRUG John *Davies Ward Phillips*
CLIFFORD John *McMillan Binch*
COLLINS Paul *Stikeman Elliott*
GASCON Denis *Ogilvy Renault*
HOLSTEN Jay *Torys*
RENAUD Madeleine *McCarthy Tétrault*
THOMSON Kent *Torys*

Up-and-coming individuals
COMTOIS Yves *McCarthy Tétrault*
LALLY Michelle *Osler, Hoskin & Harcourt LLP*

Individuals are listed alphabetically in each band.

has recently been retained by the Commissioner of Competition to act on the Superior Propane appeal. *"Hard-working"* **Peter Franklyn*** is *"a very strong individual in all fields of competition law"* and is particularly admired for his advice on misleading advertising. Newcomer **Michelle Lally*** is said to *"stand out among all juniors across Canada; she's young, promising, active in the CBA and doing great work."* The firm's expertise in the convergence areas of law has been emphasised by its recent recruitment of another former Commissioner from an in-house position at Telus. Advised Time Warner in its proposed merger with AOL, and Warner Music (Time Warner) in its proposed merger with EMI. Represented Seagram in its merger with Vivendi. **Clients:** American Express; Bank of Montréal; Cadbury; General Motors; Goldman Sachs; Imperial Tobacco; OMERS; Proctor & Gamble; Telus Corp.

Stikeman Elliott (10 ptrs, 14 asscs) A *"significant"* nationwide competition group, said by rivals to be *"developing fast."* The department advises on anti-trust issues arising from big-ticket transactions in a range of industrial sectors, most notably communications, financial services, e-commerce and transport. The firm is the only one in Canada to have an anti-trust practice in Ottawa, the national capital, and is thus seen to be one of the most influential in Government circles. Practice head, **Lawson Hunter***, an ex-Commissioner of the Competition Bureau, is said to have *"top-class government connections." "An energetic, brilliant lawyer,"* he is regarded by many as *"Canada's pre-eminent competition practitioner,"* and is widely regarded as a *"good negotiator and a benchmark for policy and strategy."* The quality of the team below him is felt by some commentators to be *"variable,"* and the team lacks a litigator of senior status, but there is unanimous acclaim for the *"fabulous"* **Paul Collins*** *("young, hard-working and extremely knowledgeable.")*

The firm represented Hoechst in class action suits arising from food additive price-fixing accusations. Also advised on the Canadian anti-trust aspects of the attempted AOL/Time Warner merger, acted for Alcatel on its acquisition of Newbridge and represented BCE on its acquisition of CTV. **Clients:** AOL; Hoechst; McCaine Foods; Hollinger Corporation; Air Canada; BAT.

Blake, Cassels & Graydon LLP (6 ptrs, 6 asscs) The historical transactional bias of this respected competition practice reflects the firm's large corporate client base. However, while merger control work is still the focus of the workload, the team also represents clients before the Competition Tribunal and before civil and criminal courts in cases involving alleged violations of competition law. **Jack Quinn*** is *"high-profile and thoroughly capable."*

The firm acted as Canadian counsel for Vivendi in its merger with Seagram, was retained by Billiton in its CDN$1.7 billion acquisition of Rio Algom, and advised Clearnet, the mobile wireless firm acquired by Telus for US$6.6 billion. **Clients:** Union Carbide Corp; Interac Association; Philips; Interbrew/Labatts; Visa Canada; Carmeuse; Vivendi; Weyerhaeuser Company.

McCarthy Tétrault (7 ptrs, 8 asscs nationwide) Unusually for a Toronto-dominated market, it is the firm's anti-trust team in Montréal which is regarded as *"among Canada's foremost,"* while the Toronto office languishes in relative obscurity. The firm is noted for making representations before the Competition Bureau in response to amendments to the Competition Act, as well as conducting anti-trust litigation and advising on the competition aspects of a number of cross-border transactions.

The Montréal team is headed by *"first-class competition lawyer and litigator,"* **Yves Bériault***. Described by peers as *"excellent and full of flair,"* he is said to be *"one of the first lawyers to come to mind for high-level referrals."* He is supported by **Madeleine Renaud*** who *"runs transactions skilfully,"* while rising practitioner **Yves Comtois***, is recognised for his *"reliable"* contribution to the practice. The department acted for Groupe Vidéotron on its merger with Rogers Communications, and represented The Dow Chemical Company in its US$11.6 billion merger with Union Carbide. **Clients:** Groupe CGI; Groupe Vidéotron; The Dow Chemical Company; Lafarge Canada; Bank of Nova Scotia; American Airlines.

McMillan Binch (4 ptrs, 7asscs) The firm's competition practice remains highly respected and focuses on three principal areas: merger clearances, anti-cartel cases and reviewable practices, such as abuse of a dominant position. The team is also considered to have a niche in public policy work as it relates to competition law.

Head of the practice and firm chairman, the *"flamboyant"* **Bill Rowley*** enjoys a *"super high profile through his IBA work,"* and his practice is now assuming an increasingly international dimension. While he is held to be *"fantastic at client-development,"* **Neil Campbell***, *"a really first class practitioner of an academic bent,"* is widely regarded as the team's intellectual *"eminence grise."* **John Clifford*** also maintains his share of market endorsement.

Merger control work has included advising Alcan Aluminium on the attempted three-way

C

*See leaders' profiles on pages 183-202

merger of Alcan, Pechiney and Alusuisse group. The team also represented Coca-Cola in its acquisition of the soft drinks business of Cadbury Schweppes, acted for Daimler Chrysler on its acquisition of Detroit Diesel and advised Freight Liner on its acquisition of Western Star Trucking. **Clients:** Royal Bank of Canada; Coca-Cola; American Home Products Corporation; IBM; Nortel Networks; Dupont; Xerox.

C

Davis & Co (5 ptrs, 4 asscs) Vancouver firm whose high profile in this area owes almost everything to the presence of the inimitable **Stan Wong***, *"a super guy who can turn his hand to anything."* Rated both as a litigator and as a transactional lawyer, he is regarded as *"the top solicitor out west,"* although he now divides his time between Vancouver and Toronto.

Much of the team's caseload is on behalf of private companies, such as the Jim Pattison Group, Canada's largest privately owned group of companies, and the firm also advises a substantial number of Japanese clients across a range of industries. The firm acted for the Commissioner of Competition in his review of the Financial Post and Sun Media transactions, and was recently involved in the criminal investigation of an international cartel. **Clients:** West Coast Energy; Jim Pattison Group; Competition Bureau.

Fraser Milner Casgrain (6 ptrs, 4 asscs) Post-merger, the firm offers a larger team, with members working across Canada. The team offers the full spectrum of competition-related expertise, developing compliance programs for Canadian and international businesses, obtaining Competition Act and Investment Canada approval for corporate transactions and litigating before the Competition Tribunal. In addition to this, the group advises on international trade regulations, export and import controls, anti-dumping and customs matters.

"*Classy individual*" **Randy Hughes*** *("astute and easy to get on with")* is said to be *"well-versed in all aspects of competition law."* He is national chairman of the competition law group, and it is felt that the firm's profile in this area is largely dependent on him. His colleague, the *"talented"* **Barry Zalmanowitz***, works out of the lower-profile Edmonton office.

The firm represented Petro-Canada in proceedings before the Competition Tribunal related to the sale of its ICG Propane business to Superior Propane. Acted for BP in its acquisitions of Amoco, Arco and Burmah Castrol and advised Volvo on its acquisition of Renault's truck business. **Clients:** Petro-Canada; Bowater; KPMG; Bayer; BP; Bank of Montréal; Volvo; Sprint Canada.

Smith Lyons (3 ptrs, 1 assc) With a client base that includes a wide range of corporations, trade associations, and non-profit organisations, both domestic and foreign, the competition, marketing and advertising group is an active one. It handles merger filings and clearances, labelling and advertising compliance advice and represents clients both in civil actions and criminal proceedings.

The *"academically inclined,"* **Bruce Graham*** is *"a talented practitioner, full of good ideas,"* and is renowned in the market place for his advice on behalf of Canadian brewing giant Molson. However, the competition team is not considered to have access to the level of big-ticket corporate transaction of some of its principal market rivals. The firm acted for British Energy on the acquisition of the Bruce Nuclear Power Generation Stations from the Ontario government. **Clients:** Molson; British Energy.

Bennett Jones LLP (3 ptrs, 4 asscs) Calgary's premier competition practice provides assistance in relation to all aspects of the Competition Act and offers advice on the full spectrum of anti-trust issues, with notable expertise in the oil and gas industry. Noted for her work as counsel to the Commissioner of Competition in the Superior Propane proceedings before the Competition Tribunal, **Jo'Anne Strekaf*** is clearly, *"the person to go to in Calgary; she's efficient, knowledgeable and has important connections."* Although primarily known as a litigator, she also has experience of big-ticket merger control cases. **Clients:** Competition Bureau; Inland Cement.

Lang Michener (3 ptrs, 1 assc) The practice advises on all aspects of competition and marketing law including merger notification, distribution strategies and practices and pricing, advertising and marketing matters. The team has a particular niche in the advertising industry, where the *"scholarly and thorough"* **James Musgrove*** is thought to be *"a strong litigator, especially on pricing issues."* Although lacking the corporate muscle of the leading anti-trust firms, the firm is still felt to be a sound merger control operation, and has advised Rogers Communications on a number of its acquisitions during the past year. The team acted on two matters before the Competition Bureau (NutraSweet and Interac) and recently succeeded in an appeal on behalf of Polaroid in a civil action relating to the Competition Act. **Clients:** Rogers Communications; Shell Canada/Shell International; MasterCard International; Nabisco; Ikea; Polaroid.

Ogilvy Renault (7 ptrs, 4 asscs) Although the majority of the anti-trust team is located in Quebec, the firm has the capability to handle mandates across the country. Cross-border merger control work forms a substantial part of the practice, although all anti-trust matters are handled. The stand-out practitioner here is *"terrific litigator"* **Denis Gascon***. He has appeared before the courts of Quebec and the Federal Court as well as before the Canadian International Trade Tribunal in dumping and tariff relief matters. The firm acted for Québecor on its merger with Vidéotron, and represented Donohue on its merger with Abitibi-Consolidated. **Clients:** Bombardier; SGL; Nortel Networks.

Torys (4 ptrs, 4 asscs nationwide) The firm's anti-trust practice is seen to be based almost entirely on the back of an outstanding M&A department, and is still felt to lack a stand-alone profile commensurate with the organisation's overall influence. However, the firm's US merger is expected to provide increased opportunity to advise on big-ticket merger control work across North America. **Kent Thomson*** is a respected competition litigator, with experience in defending clients in anti-trust criminal prosecutions and class actions. **Jay Holsten*** is the name that *"springs to mind on the M&A side,"* and has established his name nationally, in spite of his relative youth.

The team advised JDS Uniphase Corporation on its US$41 billion merger with SDL, and acted for CanWest on its acquisition of the WIC television broadcasting business. **Clients:** JDS Uniphase Corporation; Petro-Canada; Toronto Dominion Bank; Mitsubishi (Canada & International); Thomson Group: West Coast Energy; CanWest Global Communications.

Kelly Affleck Greene (2 ptrs, 3 asscs) A litigation boutique with substantial competition expertise, its quality is highly rated by the rest of the market, although its size dictates that it cannot often compete on the high-value international transactions. However, the firm often profits from conflicts, and boasts two highly-rated partners. **Donald Affleck*** is *"an old-school competition lawyer with masses of experience,"* while **Donald Houston*** is regarded as a *"sophisticated anti-trust litigator."* The firm represented a number of European-based chemical companies who were the subject of civil and criminal actions over the price-fixing of vitamins. Also acted as lead Canadian counsel for Pepsi-Cola on its third party opposition to the merger of Coca-Cola and Cadbury Schweppes. **Clients:** Pepsi-Cola; Competition Bureau.

Corporate/M&A

CANADA Leading firms (Corporate/M&A)
1 Davies Ward Phillips & Vineberg
Goodmans
Osler, Hoskin & Harcourt LLP
Stikeman Elliott
Torys
2 Blake, Cassels & Graydon LLP
McCarthy Tétrault
3 Fasken Martineau DuMoulin LLP
Fraser Milner Casgrain
Ogilvy Renault
4 Bennett Jones LLP
Borden Ladner Gervais LLP
Meighen Demers
5 Aird & Berlis
Goodman and Carr LLP
McMillan Binch
Smith Lyons

Firms are listed alphabetically in each band.

Leading individuals (Corporate/M&A)	
★ BAILLIE James *Torys*	BISNAIRE JP *Davies Ward Phillips & Vineberg*
HALPERIN Stephen *Goodmans*	JACKSON David *Blake, Cassels & Graydon LLP*
STRANSMAN John *Stikeman Elliott*	
1 AINLEY William *Davies Ward Phillips & Vineberg*	BRAITHWAITE William *Stikeman Elliott*
GIRVAN Garth *McCarthy Tétrault*	JEWETT Peter *Torys*
LAMPE Jonathan *Goodmans*	LEVIN Jonathan *Fasken Martineau DuMoulin*
RILEY James *Ogilvy Renault*	
2 ALEXANDER Deborah *Osler, Hoskin & Harcourt*	BARNES Jeffery *Fraser Milner Casgrain*
BELL Alan *Blake, Cassels & Graydon LLP*	HORNER Clay *Osler, Hoskin & Harcourt*
LASTMAN Dale *Goodmans*	PORTNER Christopher *Osler, Hoskin & Harcourt*
SCARLETT James *Torys*	SORELL René *McCarthy Tétrault*
3 ALLEN Francis *Borden Ladner Gervais LLP*	DEMERS Jacques *Meighen Demers*
FRASER Jean *Osler, Hoskin & Harcourt*	OLASKER Patricia *Davies Ward Phillips & Vineberg*
ROSS Donald *Osler, Hoskin & Harcourt*	
4 CURRIE Gordon *Blake, Cassels & Graydon LLP*	DAVIDGE Marlene *Torys*
FINNERTY Patrick *Blake, Cassels & Graydon LLP*	GOW Graham *McCarthy Tétrault*
KAZANJIAN John *Osler, Hoskin & Harcourt*	LAMBERT Martin *Bennett Jones LLP*
McDERMOTT Robert *McMillan Binch*	McREYNOLDS Shawn *Davies Ward Phillips & Vineberg*
NIXON Christopher *Stikeman Elliott*	PETCH Jack *Osler, Hoskin & Harcourt*
RAYMOND Pierre *Stikeman Elliott*	ROBOTTOM David *Fraser Milner Casgrain*
ROMANO Simon *Stikeman Elliott*	STEINBERG Norman *Ogilvy Renault*
SUGIYAMA Connie *Fasken Martineau DuMoulin*	SWARTZ Jay *Davies Ward Phillips & Vineberg*
YONTEF Marvin *Stikeman Elliott*	

Individuals are listed alphabetically in each band.

Davies Ward Phillips & Vineberg (65+ ptrs & asscs) "*Wonderful*" transactional boutique which is applauded by its rivals for "*having a concept from the beginning and sticking to it.*" With the ability to manage the largest, most complex, cross-border M&A deals, the team participates in transactions on behalf of every conceivable client, among them buyers and sellers, individuals, Canadian and international investment banks. The addition of the Montréal office gives the firm genuine national strength.

"*Absolute superstar*" **JP Bisnaire*** is "*a master of strategy*" and clearly rated as one of the country's leading players. **Bill Ainley*** also maintains a first-class name and "*gets through a lot of work.*" Although better known for his banking practice, **Jay Swartz*** is also commended for his "*high quality*" M&A work, notably for financial institutions. "*Exemplary underwriters' lawyer*" **Patricia Olasker*** wins market plaudits, as does **Shawn McReynolds***. Such is the team's strength in depth that one commentator observed: "*If you put any four partners in a rotating door and took out one at random, you'd be able to guarantee the same degree of quality.*"

The firm represented BCE on its spin-out to its common shareholders of a 35% interest in Nortel Networks, and on its pending acquisition of Teleglobe Inc (CDN$9.65 billion). **Clients:** Goldman Sachs; Scotia McLeod; BCE; Nesbitt Burns; RBC Dominions Securities.

Goodmans (40 ptrs, 40 asscs worldwide) Acknowledged to have great presence in Toronto, the firm has again enjoyed a high-profile year. However, the loss of the Montréal office to Davies Ward & Beck has been considered a setback, despite the firm's great strength in Toronto. Overwhelmingly a transactional practice, it represents a range of domestic and overseas clients, often in the telecoms and media sectors.

Steve Halperin*, considered to be "*undoubtedly a star,*" is "*quite simply in a different class from most other lawyers.*" "*Almost as accomplished*" is **Jonathan Lampe***, who advises a number of international clients and is admired for his technical proficiency. "*Well-connected*" **Dale Lastman*** is considered "*a forceful and magnetic character whose leading attribute is flair.*" The firm represented BT on two major strategic deals in Canada to secure a share in both AT&T Canada and in Rogers Cantel, Canada's largest mobile carrier. Also advised (alongside Osler, Hoskin & Harcourt) Seagram on its acquisition by Vivendi, and was Canadian counsel to Pechiney on its unsuccessful attempt to merge with Alcan and Alusuisse. **Clients:** CTV; CIBC Worldmarkets; Seagram Corporation; British Telecom; FourSeasons Hotels; Abitibi Consolidated.

Osler, Hoskin & Harcourt LLP (145 lawyers in business law group, of whom approx 45 are M&A specialists) "*A large but focused team. They're well managed and they know what to do.*" A popular destination for referrals, the firm boasts enviable strength in depth, although it is currently felt to lack the single outstanding practitioner of some of its rivals. **Chris Portner*** is "*strong on financial matters, M&A and real estate work,*" and "*is terrific to deal with.*" "*Rising star*" **Clay Horner*** is "*showing up clearly on the radar,*" while **Donald Ross*** and **John Kazanjian*** also add weight to the department. **Debbie Alexander*** is "*a popular option*" for corporate finance referrals, and the experienced **Jack Petch*** is considered a "*great sounding-board*" for junior lawyers. Although principally recognised for her corporate finance work, **Jean Fraser*** is also recommended as a

*See leaders' profiles on pages 183-202

"first class lawyer." The pre-eminence of the firm's tax practice allows it to handle all aspects of complicated cross-border corporate work. Advised Imasco on the acquisition by British American Tobacco of the public shareholders' majority interest, the largest ever cash acquisition of a Canadian company. Acted for CanWest in its US$3.5 billion acquisition of Hollinger's Canadian newspaper, magazine and news media interests. The team also represented The Seagram Company Ltd in its three-way merger with Vivendi and Canal+ to create Vivendi Universal (CDN$100 billion). **Clients:** Imasco; Alusuisse Lonza Group; JDS Fitel; CanWest Global Communications Corporation; Time Warner.

Stikeman Elliott (140 lawyers in business law group, of whom approx 45 are M&A specialists) Almost universally considered *"one of the market leaders,"* the firm has consolidated its share of the public M&A market, typically acting for corporations and lenders based in Canada, the US and the UK. On the corporate finance side, the team is active in both public and private debt and equity financings, and in policy and compliance matters.

Many consider **John Stransman*** *"the hottest name in M&A."* Considered to have *"a wonderful rapport with his clients,"* he can count on the support of **Bill Braithwaite***, also said by competitors to be *"a top pick."* Both lawyers are said to be *"above posturing and petty point scoring."* *"Now really emerging,"* **Simon Romano*** is described as *"technically very good – if a little excitable,"* while **Marvin Yontef*** is a *"versatile, practical and experienced"* corporate lawyer. *"First rate"* **Pierre Raymond*** is regarded as the firm's leading player in Calgary. Respected all-rounder **Christopher Nixon*** has joined the firm from Osler, Hoskin & Harcourt, although Calvin Rovinescu has departed to an in-house position at Air Canada. The firm acted for Nortel Networks in its acquisition of all the issued shares of Architel. The value of the transaction was approximately CDN$600 million. The team also advised Alcatel on its acquisition of Newbridge Networks. **Clients:** British American Tobacco; Alcatel; Nortel Networks.

Torys (86 ptrs; 109 asscs) The firm is felt to have emerged strongly from its US merger last year. An *"outstanding"* department handles the full spectrum of corporate/commercial work for a client base which includes public, private and non-profit organisations, governments, and Crown corporations. *"Second to none as a rain-maker,"* **James Baillie*** now has a less transactional role, although he still appears on a number of major deals. The *"first class"* **Peter Jewett*** has taken up the transactional baton, while **Marlene Davidge*** maintains an enviable reputation for securities work. **Jamie Scarlett***, recently hired from McMillan Binch, is considered to be *"an excellent acquisition"* for the team. Recent transactions include the CDN$3 billion financing of NAV Canada in connection with the privatisation of Canada's air navigation system, and acting for Hollinger in its acquisition by CanWest. **Clients:** CanWest Global Communications Corporation; Hollinger; Petro-Canada; EdperBrascan; Fairfax Financial Holdings; Manulife Financial; Sun Life; The Thomson Corporation.

Blake, Cassels & Graydon LLP (Toronto 100 lawyers; Calgary 20 lawyers; Vancouver 20 lawyers; Ottawa 5 lawyers) Felt to be *"slightly off the pace set by those in the top tier,"* the firm nevertheless remains a force to be reckoned with. The corporate team handles all aspects of private and public M&A work across a range of industry sectors including financial services, traditional manufacturing and hi-tech industry. Most major transactions here involve a cross-border element. **David Jackson*** is widely regarded as an *"outstanding lawyer"* and is the firm's major player. Co-head of the Securities Group, **Alan Bell***, is *"another leading light"* and is acknowledged for his work on big-ticket transactions such as advising Vivendi on its merger with Seagram (a deal valued at US$34 billion). **Gordon Currie*** is *"coming along nicely"* and is considered *"terrific"* for public finance M&A. **Patrick Finnerty*** is a *"strong player in Calgary,"* to whom peers *"refer work with confidence."* The firm represented Clearnet on its acquisition by Telus, and Weyerhaeuser on its takeover of MacMillan Bloedel. **Clients:** Vivendi; Clearnet Communications; British American Tobacco; Biliton; Citibank; Canadian Imperial Bank of Commerce; Hunt Oil Tobacco.

McCarthy Tétrault (Toronto 60 ptrs, 80 asscs in corporate group) The firm has one of Canada's largest corporate finance and capital markets practices, and is expected to be strengthened by its new alliance with US firm Fried, Frank, Harris, Shriver & Jacobson. Although occasionally accused of *"uneven quality,"* the team has a triumvirate of leaders who inspire nothing but respect. **Garth Girvan*** is widely praised for his transactional flair, while **René Sorell*** is *"bright and an excellent strategist."* **Graham Gow*** is *"a visible and reliable practitioner."* It is too early to assess the effect on the Montréal office of the departure of Hubert Lacroix. The firm acted as Canadian Counsel for Gold Fields Limited in its attempted merger with Franco-Nevada Mining Corporation (CDN$5.4 Billion). **Clients:** Merrill Lynch Mortgage Loans; Toronto Stock Exchange; Toronto Dominion Bank; Noranda; Canadian Pacific; Bank of Nova Scotia; Trans-Canada Pipelines.

Fasken Martineau DuMoulin LLP (67 ptrs, 51 asscs internationallly) The firm's most recent merger, this time with Russell & DuMoulin, has transformed it into a truly national entity, with offices in Vancouver to add to those in Toronto, Montréal and Quebec City. Considered to be strongest in Toronto, the corporate department is admired for its breadth of transaction, covering a variety of financial institutions and traditional industries. The team's *"shining light"* is **Jonathan Levin***, *"an excellent corporate all-rounder of the old school."* He is equally renowned for his banking and finance practice. While it is widely held that Levin *"doesn't have the bench strength behind him that he deserves,"* **Connie Sugiyama*** is now seen to be *"establishing herself in her own right."* The firm acted for the principal shareholder of Newbridge in connection with its acquisition by Alcatel. **Clients:** AT&T Canada; TD Securities; JP Morgan.

Fraser Milner Casgrain (Approx 200 corporate/M&A lawyers nationwide) Created from the recent merger of Fraser Milner with Byers Casgrain in Quebec, the new firm boasts offices in six cities and an overall resource of approximately 500 lawyers. This consolidation has divided market opinion; the acknowledged benefits of increased critical mass are set against suggestions that the team has become *"unwieldy."*

The department advises national and multinational companies in a variety of industries including financial services, automotive, manufacturing, leasing, energy and resources, petrochemicals, manufacturing, pharmaceutical, food processing and distribution. Hi-tech has been an area of growth, with the team involved in a large number of acquisitions in the sector. Key player here is the universally admired *"deal-doer"* **Jeff Barnes***, whose profile eclipses that of his colleagues. Also recommended is **David Robottom***. The firm advised the independent committee of the Board of Canoxy (Canadian Occidental) in a series of negotiations with their major shareholder, Occidental Petroleum, and acted for Cambridge on its acquisition by Ivanhoe. **Clients:** Cisco Systems; Redback; Call-Net Enterprises; TD Securities; Nesbitt Burns; Bank of Montréal; Alliance Pipeline; Onex Corporation and Shaw Enterprises.

Ogilvy Renault (100 lawyers in business law group, of whom 25 ptrs & 22 asscs are M&A specialists) Seen as a firm on the upgrade, its Toronto office has now firmly established itself and is beginning to push for a place among the big players. Boasting a strong portfolio of domestic and international clients, the corporate team has been active on a variety of cross-border transactions. **James Riley*** *"is a great guy of high calibre,"* and is credited with building a successful team. *"He's adopted a strategy of aggressive expansion, he's doing a terrific job and is pushing them into the top tier. In a few years they'll be up there with the very best if they continue in their current vein."* He has a notably strong relationship with the Royal Bank of Canada. In the Montréal office, **Norman Steinberg*** is a recommended practitioner. The firm represented Québecor on its acquisition of Vidéotron, and LGI in connection with its acquisition by IBM. **Clients:** Royal Bank of Canada; Nortel; Québecor; Bombardier.

Bennett Jones LLP (35 ptrs, 55 asscs in corporate/commercial group) Universally acknowledged to *"dominate"* the Calgary marketplace, the firm is felt to marshal *"real transactional strength on the back of big-ticket oil and gas deals."* It is commended for its *"high calibre operations"* in both Alberta and Saskatchewan. Although still not a major player in Toronto, the firm has nevertheless participated in a number of substantial domestic transactions, typically acting for the buyer. **Martin Lambert*** is a leading name in the Alberta market. He played a lead role in representing Burlington Resources on its US$3.7 billion acquisition of Poco Petroleums. The firm also advised Anderson Exploration on its CDN$1 billion white knight bid for Ulster Petroleums, trumping a Hunt Oil bid, and Hunt Oil on its CDN$800 million acquisition of Newport Petroleums. **Clients:** Burlington Resources; Gulf Canada; Devon Energy/Northstar; TELUS Corp; RBC Dominion Securities; Canadian Utilities.

Borden Ladner Gervais LLP (40 ptrs, 35 asscs in securities and capital markets group, of whom 15-20 ptrs are M&A specialists) The five-way merger of Borden & Elliott in Toronto, Howard Mackie in Calgary, Ladner Downs in Vancouver, McMaster Gervais in Montréal and Scott & Aylen in Ottawa, has created a 590-lawyer firm. While the mergers give the organisation a strong national platform from which to operate, it is felt to be far too early to assess the effectiveness of such a mammoth undertaking. One immediate benefit has been the luring of the respected **Francis Allen*** from Osler's Calgary office to head the new firm's corporate department. Generally noted for a strong portfolio of domestic clients, the firm advised Calgary-based Husky Energy on its CDN$3.1 billion merger with Renaissance and for Precision Drilling in connection with its successful CDN$250 million acquisition of Plains Energy. **Clients:** Bank of Nova Scotia; BMO Nesbitt Burnes; HSBC Bank; Husky Energy; Scotia Capital; Mackenzie Financial; TransCanada Pipelines.

Meighen, Demers (11 ptrs, 8 asscs M&A; 3 ptrs corporate finance) *"Utterly reliable,"* if smaller than most of its competitors, the firm has a respected position in the domestic market, and also *"punches above its weight internationally."* Although the firm's quality is beyond question, *"it just doesn't have the numbers to do the genuinely big-ticket stuff."* Sustaining an excellent reputation among financial services clients and in the hi-tech sphere, the team is widely regarded as *"technically precise."* Name partner, the *"practical, creative and persuasive"* **Jacques Demers*** remains the firm's stand-out practitioner. The team acted as special counsel to the Independent Director's Committee of Centre Fund, the object of a hostile take-over bid (to the value of CDN$170 million). **Clients:** Scotia Capital; Cashway; UBS.

Aird & Berlis (24 ptrs, 6 asscs) *"Historically entrepreneurial firm"* doing *"solid middle-ticket work,"* which is still felt by competitors to lack *"heavyweight individual players in this area of practice."* Strong in the hi-tech market, the firm's client roster also includes financial institutions, energy companies and biopharmaceutical concerns. The team offers advice on the spectrum of corporate matters, and is especially regarded for its work in obtaining and maintaining listings on all Canadian Stock Exchanges, as well as the New York Stock Exchange and the Nasdaq. Represented California-based Autodesk, the world's leading supplier of PC-design software, in the acquisition of Discreet Logistics in a share exchange transaction valued at approximately CDN$600 million. Recent corporate finance highlights in cross-border transactions include acting for US corporations such as Autodesk, Peregrine Systems, JD Edwards, Wind River Systems, Polycom, Photon Dynamics and Numerical Technologies in the acquisition of publicly and privately-held Canadian corporations with transaction values ranging from CDN$50 million to $600 million. **Clients:** Bank of Montréal and Nesbitt Burns; Bank of Nova Scotia and Scotia Capital; Royal Bank of Canada; Ontario Teachers' Pension Plan Board; Ontario Municipal Employees Saving Plan; HSBC Canada; Wells Fargo.

Goodman and Carr LLP (30 ptrs & asscs in business law group, of whom approx 15 are M&A specialists) Although the firm is considered to have *"done really well"* during the past year, the majority of market opinion has specifically linked this to the *"amazing practice"* of Jeff Blidner. In the wake of his August 2000 departure to an in-house role at Trilon, difficult times are forecast for the corporate department. *"The implications of his leaving are profound, as there is no-one of his standing to take over the practice."* The firm has attempted to plug the gap through active recruitment – five new partners have arrived recently. A notably strong financial institution client base was highlighted by the firm's advice to the National Bank of Canada in connection with its acquisition of Browning Ferris, a large waste-management company. The team also acted for a Canadian purchaser on its acquisition of France's largest forest products company. **Clients:** Royal Bank Equity Partners; Nesbitt Burnes; Scotia Merchant Capital; Ontario Teachers Pension Fund; Schroders.

McMillan Binch (15 ptrs, 20 asscs) *"A firm facing challenging times."* The departure of James Scarlett to Torys is felt to leave the corporate/M&A team *"under extra strain,"* while **Robert McDermott*** is regarded as *"the only player of real stature"* left at the department. The firm retains a respected client base, acting for a number of foreign companies in Canada, including several pharmaceutical organisations. Advised a large Canadian bank in the sale of the profile buildings in its real-estate portfolio, and in the outsourcing of the management of its remaining buildings. The corporate team also acted as external counsel for Alcan Aluminum in connection with its proposed three-way merger with Alusuisse and Pecheney. **Clients:** Boliden; Royal Bank of Canada.

Smith Lyons (80+ ptrs & asscs in corporate group, of whom 4 ptrs & 4 asscs are M&A specialists) Lower-profile, though highly respected firm which includes amongst it clients two of the three largest pension funds in Canada, as well as two of the 'big five' schedule one Canadian banks. The firm acted for Rothmans in connection with the disposition by British American Tobacco of its 71.2% share interest in Rothmans. Also advised Franco-Nevada Mining Corporation on its abortive merger with Gold Fields. **Clients:** Ontario Municipal Employees Retirement System; BLP Group; Flowserve Corp; Rothmans.

C

*See leaders' profiles on pages 183-202

Energy & Natural Resources

C

CANADA Leading firms (Energy & Natural Resources)
1 Bennett Jones LLP
2 Macleod Dixon LLP
3 Burnet, Duckworth & Palmer LLP
4 Fraser Milner Casgrain McCarthy Tétrault Stikeman Elliott
5 Ballem MacInnes LLP Osler, Hoskin & Harcourt LLP

Firms are listed alphabetically in each band.

Leading individuals (Energy & Natural Resources)
★ **DESBARATS Robert** *Bennett Jones LLP*
1 **BOOTH Robert** *Bennett Jones LLP* **PARK Jay** *Macleod Dixon LLP* **STICKLAND Kenneth** *Burnet Duckworth* **YATES Kemm** *Stikeman Elliott*
2 **CURRAN John** *Bennett Jones LLP* **DAVIES Don** *Macleod Dixon LLP* **HIRST Tom** *Macleod Dixon LLP* **HOLGATE David** *Stikeman Elliott* **MILLAR Timothy** *Fraser Milner Casgrain* **SAVILLE Francis** *Fraser Milner Casgrain* **SMITH Laurie** *Bennett Jones LLP* **THRASHER Jack** *Osler, Hoskin & Harcourt LLP*
3 **CUTHBERTSON John** *Burnet Duckworth* **JOHNSON Clifford** *McCarthy Tétrault* **KEOUGH Loyola** *Bennett Jones LLP* **McLARTY Allan** *Fraser Milner Casgrain*

Individuals are listed alphabetically in each band.

Bennett Jones LLP (10 ptrs, 12 asscs) The *"cream of the crop"* in Canada, this *"pre-eminent, cutting-edge"* energy team is considered to have no rival to its strength in depth, client base and quality of domestic work. Principally involved in asset acquisition and divestiture, the firm handles both power and oil and gas work, and has acknowledged expertise in co-generation issues and pipeline projects. Although primarily known for its Canadian clientele, the firm has an international reputation for upstream oil and gas advice.

In spite of the departure of Gordon Brown, the team retains a potent appearance. *"Star of the transactional scene"* is **Robert Desbarats***, praised as a superb client developer, and now rated *"the best practitioner in this sphere."* **Bob Booth*** is *"a pleasure to work with on a deal,"* while the venerable **John Curran*** is regarded as *"energy royalty."* On regulatory matters, **Laurie Smith*** is seen to provide *"formidable competition,"* while **Loyola Keough*** provides sound support. The firm advised Shell Canada on its involvement in the CDN$6 billion Athabasca Oil Sands project, acted for The Williams Companies on its purchase of the natural gas liquids portion of TransCanada's midstream operations, and represented Burlington Resources on its US$3.7 billion acquisition of Poco Petroleums. **Clients:** Shell Canada; Pan-Canadian Petroleum; Gulf Canada; Petro-Canada; Canadian Occidental Petroleum; The Williams Companies; Westcoast Power; Burlington Petroleum.

Macleod Dixon LLP (23 lawyers) A *"dominant force for a long time,"* the firm clearly ranks as the leading competitor to Bennett Jones' domestic supremacy. The group has often been viewed as the strongest international operation, with involvement in transactions across the globe and offices in Russia, Venezuela and Kazakhstan. Specialists in oil and gas, the firm advises on exploration, development, production and transportation, assists clients on structuring joint ventures and partnerships, and has a leading reputation for major projects such as processing plants, pipelines and co-generation facilities.

Jay Park* is *"the outstanding name here,"* and is felt to be *"a distinguished and knowledgeable practitioner,"* while **Tom Hirst*** wins plaudits for his *"strong transactional work."* **Don Davies*** has a first-class reputation for regulatory advice. The team advised on Keyspan Energy Development Company's acquisition of the midstream assets of Gulf Canada Resources and acted on Calpine Corporation's acquisition of Quintana Minerals Canada Corporation and TriGas Exploration. Abroad, the group has advised the World Bank and the Government of Vietnam on revisions to Vietnam's Petroleum Law and Petroleum Decree. In conjunction with PricewaterhouseCoopers, the firm represented Kuwait Petroleum Company and Kuwait Oil Company in connection with the proposed operating service agreement for four fields in northern Kuwait. **Clients:** Pan-Canadian Petroleum; Government of Vietnam; World Bank; Kuwait Petroleum Company; Kuwait Oil Company.

Burnet, Duckworth & Palmer LLP (10 ptrs, 10 asscs) A strong team respected for its domestic regulatory advice, which has also acted on projects in Alberta and Newfoundland. Internationally, it has worked on a deal in Argentina, and regularly advises clients on cross-border energy transactions. The caseload includes public and private energy financing, oil exploration, the development of business structures and the advice on energy legislation. A niche area of expertise is pipeline work, including construction, tolls and tariffs and access rights.

Admired by competitors for his *"commercial sense and negotiating skills,"* **Ken Stickland*** is a popular client man, while **John Cuthbertson*** is a leading transactional figure. The firm advised Poco Petroleums on all aspects of its acquisition by Burlington Resources, and represented Utilicorp on its acquisition of the distribution facilities of Transalta Utilities. **Clients:** Chevron Canada Resources; Mobil Oil Canada; Poco Petroleums; Westcoast Energy.

Fraser Milner Casgrain (10 ptrs, 10 asscs) *"Always a strong player,"* the firm advises a number of leading names in the Canadian oil and gas industry, as well as representing domestic and international clients in the mining industry. In the power industry, the team has worked on the development and operation of co-generation projects and the deregulation of electrical energy. Also advises on regulatory approval hearings, energy export applications and rates and tolls proceedings.

Vice-chairman of the firm, **Francis Saville*** is deemed a *"notable regulatory lawyer,"* while **Allan McLarty*** provides noteworthy support. **Timothy Millar*** is considered *"a sound transactional lawyer."* A highlight of the past year was the team's advice on the Alliance Pipeline project. The firm also represented BP Amoco on the sale of its heavy oil assets (a transaction valued at CDN$900 million), and advised Enbridge on its acquisition of a part of TransCanada Pipelines's interest in a Columbian pipeline. **Clients:** Syncrude Canada; Suncor; Enbridge; BP Energy Canada; Petro-Canada.

McCarthy Tétrault (24 ptrs, 15 asscs worldwide) A varied energy practice advises on both transactional and regulatory matters in mining, oil and gas, power and water. The group has been prominent in advising on the deregulation of the electricity industry in a number of countries, while a predominantly transactional oil and gas practice handles both domestic and international energy transactions.

Cliff Johnson* is rated for his work on the East Coast, but overall, the group is felt to lack the depth of its principal competitors. The firm represented one of the companies involved in the

Syncrude Project. **Clients:** TransAlta Utilities; Hydro Quebec; Enwave District Energy; Zimbabwe Electricity Supply Authority; Upper Canada Alliance.

Stikeman Elliott (20 ptrs, 15 asscs nationwide) Focused in Calgary, the firm's energy practice is principally admired for its regulatory work. The oil and gas group has experience in all aspects of the industry, representing clients on exploration, development, production and processing, pipeline construction and downstream marketing. The firm has developed a niche in advising on the transportation of oil and gas and related environmental issues.

Peers consider **Kemm Yates*** *"one of Canada's top regulatory lawyers,"* notably in dispute resolution, while **David Holgate*** also has an established reputation for his advice on the transactional and regulatory sides of both the oil and gas and the electricity industry. The firm acted as lead regulatory counsel on the Alliance Pipeline, and advised BP Energy Canada on its transactions with several midstream companies. **Clients:** Alliance Pipeline; Imperial Oil Resources; Pacific Gas & Electric Company; BP Energy Canada; TransCanada Pipelines; Electricity Supply Board of Ireland-Alberta Ltd.

Ballem MacInnes LLP (10 ptrs, 6 asscs) Perceived to be in a process of *"generational change,"* heralded by the retirement of name partner Wallace MacInnes, the firm continues to advise on regulatory and transactional matters for national and multi-national oil and gas corporations. **Clients:** Shepco; Husky Oil; Imperial Oil Ltd; Pan-Alberta Gas Ltd; Petro-Canada.

Osler, Hoskin & Harcourt LLP Although this major corporate firm advises Canadian and foreign oil and gas companies on their transactions, the team clearly lacks the profile of the leading energy players. Said to owe *"almost everything"* to the *"tremendously reputable"* transactional leader **Jack Thrasher***, the firm does have experience of energy regulatory issues, and has appeared frequently before the National Energy Board, Ontario Energy Board and other provincial regulators. The international element to the practice has seen it advising on projects in Dubai and Qatar. The firm represented the consortium behind the Hibernia Development project, and was lead counsel for the consortium on the Terra Nova offshore development. **Clients:** Shell Canada; Chevron Canada Resources; Mobil Oil Canada; Murphy Oil; Petro-Canada.

C

Tax

CANADA Leading firms (Tax)
1 Davies Ward Phillips & Vineberg
Osler, Hoskin & Harcourt LLP
2 Fasken Martineau DuMoulin
McCarthy Tétrault
3 Blake, Cassels & Graydon LLP
Goodmans
Thorsteinssons
Torys
4 Felesky Flynn
Fraser Milner Casgrain
Stikeman Elliott

Firms are listed alphabetically in each band.

Davies Ward Phillips & Vineberg (14 ptrs, 2 asscs) Unanimously seen as a *"top-tier"* operation, the tax team is admired for *"the sheer brilliance"* of its practitioners. *"Huge and enduring,"* the group carries out cross-border and domestic transactional work both for private clients and high-profile public companies, with notable recent growth in IT and e-commerce instructions. Peers also commend the firm for its *"always respected"* opinion work. The recent addition of the Montréal office of Goodman Phillips & Vineberg has given the tax team a further huge shot in the arm. Two practitioners, in particular, are of such calibre that they show up on all Toronto radar screens. Their *"markedly different personalities and capabilities"* are felt to *"make a strong combination."* **Nathan Boidman*** is noted for his writing, and his *"specialised knowledge of international tax issues."* In contrast, **Robert Raizenne*** is considered the *"best commercial tax practitioner in Montréal."*

The plaudits come in thick and fast for *"out and out star"* **David Smith***, dubbed by many *"Canada's premier corporate tax adviser."* A *"smart, controlled, meticulous"* individual, he combines a *"creative, business-oriented approach"* with *"unrivalled depth of knowledge and experience."* His colleagues also garner their share of acclaim. The *"tremendously gifted"* **John Ulmer*** is *"valued for his intelligent and creative planning in an international context,"* while **David Ward***, *"one of the icons of the tax community,"* although less visible on transactional work, is considered *"as formidable as ever."* Up and coming name **Siobhan Monaghan*** is commended as *"a bright, hard-working lawyer."*

The firm acted for Celestica on its acquisition from IBM of printed circuit board assembly and test services operations in Minnesota and printed circuit board system assembly operations in Italy. Also represented Cadillac Fairview Corporation during its CDN$2.3 billion acquisition by Ontario Teachers' Pension Plan Board and advised Mozaic Venture Partners on the establishment of its venture capital fund. **Clients:** Celestica; Onex Corporation; Polo Ralph Lauren Corporation.

Osler, Hoskin & Harcourt LLP (19 ptrs, 17 asscs) Acknowledged for its fabulous strength in depth, the tax team is regarded as one of the pre-eminent forces in Canada. The group's forte lies mainly in big-ticket corporate tax work; this is not considered a team for mundane, day to day tax advice.

Richard Tremblay's* reputation continues to flourish. *"He is now a top-tier international tax specialist."* **Norman Loveland*** is seen as *"an experienced leader in the field,"* and has a predominantly domestic tax focus, while *"intelligent and theoretical"* **Scott Wilkie*** is highly rated for his international work and transfer pricing expertise. **Firoz Ahmed***, whose M&A tax work has drawn market approval, is esteemed as *"a young star,"* while **David Tetreault*** is a *"highly talented"* rising name. The firm acted for BCE on the tax and structuring aspects of the CDN$85 billion spin-off of Nortel Networks Corporation. **Clients:** BCE; Canadian corporates; Canadian subsidiaries of foreign multi-nationals.

Fasken Martineau DuMoulin (8 ptrs, 4 asscs) Respected tax team which many feel *"does not get the recognition it deserves,"* in view of the calibre and variety of its caseload. The firm handles all types of tax work, including M&A, corporate reorganisations, financial products, international tax and deferred compensation, and is said to be *"exceptionally strong"* on commodity tax advice.

Stephen Ruby* is a *"class one practitioner with a well-rounded practice,"* who advises on major

*See leaders' profiles on pages 183-202

Leading individuals (Tax)		
★	**SMITH David** *Davies Ward Phillips & Vineberg*	**WILSON James** *PricewaterhouseCoopers*
1	**RICHARDSON Stephen** *Torys*	**RUBY Stephen** *Fasken Martineau DuMoulin LLP*
	TREMBLAY Richard *Osler, Hoskin & Harcourt LLP*	
2	**BOIDMAN Nathan** *Goodmans*	**CARR Brian** *Fraser Milner Casgrain*
	DURAND Ronald *Stikeman Elliott*	**HARRIS Neil** *Goodmans*
	LOVELAND Norman *Osler, Hoskin & Harcourt LLP*	**O'KEEFE Michael** *Thorsteinssons*
	RAIZENNE Robert *Goodmans*	**ULMER John** *Davies Ward Phillips & Vineberg*
	WILKIE Scott *Osler, Hoskin & Harcourt LLP*	
3	**AHMED Firoz** *Osler, Hoskin & Harcourt LLP*	**COULOMBE Gérard** *Desjardins Ducharme Stein*
	EWENS Douglas *McCarthy Tétrault*	**FELESKY Brian** *Felesky Flynn*
	HAUSMAN James *Blake, Cassels & Graydon LLP*	**KELLOUGH Howard** *Fraser Milner Casgrain*
	MITCHELL Warren *Thorsteinssons*	**RICHARDSON Elinore** *Stikeman Elliott*
	WOODS Judith *McCarthy Tétrault*	
4	**BIES Bill** *Fasken Martineau DuMoulin LLP*	**MORGAN Leslie** *Blake, Cassels & Graydon LLP*
	QUIGLEY Michael *McCarthy Tétrault*	**RICHARDS Gabrielle** *McCarthy Tétrault*
	TAMAKI Paul *Blake, Cassels & Graydon LLP*	**TETREAULT David** *Osler, Hoskin & Harcourt LLP*
	WARD David *Davies Ward Phillips & Vineberg*	**WELKOFF Jim** *Torys*
Up-and-coming individuals		
	MONAGHAN Siobhan *Davies Ward Phillips & Vineberg*	
Individuals are listed alphabetically in each band.		

transactions, and is a renowned litigator. His lower-profile colleague, **Bill Bies***, whose practice is more domestic in its focus, is commended for his *"attention to detail."* The team represented O&Y Properties on its takeover of First Place Tower, advised a bank on the financing of the Telus takeover of Clearnet and acted for Architel on its acquisition by Nortel. **Clients:** O&Y Properties; TD Bank; Scotia McLeod; DaimlerChrysler Corporation; Upper Lake Shipping.

McCarthy Tétrault (23 ptrs, 15 asscs) Said to be *"without a star"* since the *"startling loss"* of Jim Wilson to PricewaterhouseCoopers, the firm is still considered to retain *"a deep, talented group of tax partners,"* and is rated a *"substantial enough team"* to withstand his loss. A large part of the practice's workload involves M&A and financial products-related tax advice, but the team also has a solid name for tax litigation.

Despite his location in Calgary, **Douglas Ewens*** is reckoned to be *"the best-known player in the firm now, and just about the best tax lawyer west of Toronto."* Toronto is home to a *"young, developing team,"* among whom **Judith Woods*** is singled out as *"a damned good lawyer."* **Gabrielle Richards*** is noted for her tax litigation practice, while **Michael Quigley*** is said to *"get the work done effectively."* The team advised Gold Fields on the proposed merger of Canadian and South African companies. **Clients:** Gold Fields; corporates; financial institutions.

Blake, Cassels & Graydon LLP (8 ptrs, 5 asscs) *"Competent"* team thought to have been left *"slightly weaker"* by the retirement of long-time linchpin Joel Shafer, and to lack the depth and breadth of the market leaders. The group advises Canadian, US & European clients on work that includes M&A and corporate finance-related tax work, tax planning and tax dispute resolution.

"By far the most prominent there," seasoned partner **James Hausman*** is considered to be *"a player in the international tax arena that is the focus of his practice."* **Leslie Morgan*** is *"terrifically smart and great to have on any team,"* while **Paul Tamaki*** is thought to be *"a reliable, if conservative performer."* The team advised Vivendi on the tax aspects of its takeover of Seagram, Billiton on its takeover bid for Rio Algom and Clearnet on its acquisition by Telus. **Clients:** Coca-Cola; CIBC; Interbrew; Citigroup; Weyerhaeuser; Hudson's Bay Company; the National Hockey League.

Goodmans (6 ptrs, 8 asscs) The loss of the firm's Montréal office to Davies Ward & Beck has come as a crippling blow to the tax department. The departure of such respected names as Nathan Boidman and Robert Raizenne leaves a hole which will be difficult to fill. This has come at a time when the Toronto team is felt to be *"well on its way to great things."* The *"knowledgeable and practical"* **Neil Harris*** is now faced with a massive task.

The team had acted for Seagram on its acquisition by Vivendi, and advised Caisse de Depot as co-purchaser with Québecor, on the contested acquisition of Vidéotron, a transaction valued at CDN$4.9 billion. Also represented Teleglobe and its shareholders on its acquisition by BCE, a CDN$6 billion transaction. **Clients:** Seagram; BCE; GT Telecom.

Thorsteinssons A tax boutique, principally seen in Vancouver, where it is perceived to have a *"lock"* on the tax work and is unquestionably the dominant practice. In the more competitive market of Toronto, the firm is seen to be doing *"very different"* work to the full-service firms, and is acknowledged for its private corporate tax work. Around 80% of the team's caseload is corporate tax advice, although the firm also has a reputation for tax litigation expertise. The *"experienced, smart and capable"* **Michael O'Keefe*** is thought to be *"a highly credible corporate tax lawyer,"* while **Warren Mitchell*** is an *"excellent tax litigator,"* felt by some to be *"the best in the country."* **Clients:** Domestic and foreign corporates; private clients; governments; non-profit organisations.

Torys (7 ptrs, 3 asscs) The team handles domestic and international tax work as it relates to public and private M&A, capital markets, structured finance and project finance. Tax planning advice for its international client roster is an area of outstanding niche expertise.

The market has nothing but praise for *"the clever and innovative"* **Stephen Richardson***, who *"sees all the issues at the cutting-edge of tax law."* Newcomer to the list **Jim Welkoff*** is *"a sound technician"* with the capacity to handle big-ticket transactions. The firm acted for SBC Communications on its acquisition of a privately owned web-hosting company. Also represented Thomson Corp on the sale of its US Newspaper assets. **Clients:** Sun Life Insurance; Rogers Communications; SBC Communications; The Thomson Corp.

Felesky Flynn (19 ptrs, 4 asscs) Seen to *"dominate the Calgary market in the same way that Thorsteinssons dominates Vancouver,"* this niche firm is considered to field a *"a first-rate team."* The team acts for a range of corporates and private individuals on all aspects of corporate tax planning. Particular expertise exists in energy and natural resources taxation, and a number of lawyers here have served on the Board of Directors of the Canadian Petroleum Tax Society. Name partner **Brian Felesky*** is a prominent national name, and is seen as a *"good client man who has great technical back-up."*

*See leaders' profiles on pages 183-202

Fraser Milner Casgrain The firm's tax department is felt to have *"held its own"* despite the organisation's perceived lack of a big-hitting corporate department. In Vancouver, the team is led by **Howard Kellough***, renowned for his private client practice, while the Toronto tax capacity rests on the shoulders of the *"impressive"* **Brian Carr***, whose niche in natural resources taxation is felt to mark him out from other Toronto practitioners. Advice on public corporate reorganisations and financings also feature strongly in Toronto, while the Vancouver and Edmonton offices focus on tax litigation and private corporate instructions.

The firm represented TD Bank on the proposed privatisation of Mississanga Hydro, and acted for the principal debtor on the public restructuring of Royal Oak Mines. **Clients:** Bank of Montréal; Nesbitt Burns; Bowater; RBC Dominion Securities; Canadian Council of Christian Charities; BP Amoco.

Stikeman Elliott (16 ptrs, 19 asscs) Some have seen the firm to be *"coasting"* on the back of its marvellous corporate department, but a majority acknowledges a team with *"a solid presence"* in the corporate tax market. Most agree that **Ronald Durand*** is *"a talented guy,"* while in the Montréal office, **Elinore Richardson*** maintains her reputation for international tax work. The firm represented BAT Tobacco on its acquisition of Imasco in Canada, Canadian National Railway during its proposed merger with Burlington Northern Santa Fe Railroad, Amec on its acquisition of Agra and Tekologix on its acquisition by Psion. **Clients:** BAT Tobacco; Canadian National Railway; Alcatel; Amec; Tekologix.

Other Notable Practitioners The most discussed move of the year has seen **Jim Wilson*** leave McCarthy Tétrault for PricewaterhouseCoopers, a transfer with obvious implications for the Canadian market. It is too early to assess PwC's position, but no-one is in any doubt about Wilson's *"stellar calibre."* Peers consider him one of *"the finest tax lawyers of his generation."* **Gérard Coulombe*** of Desjardins Ducharme Stein Monast is also recommended as a *"fine, commercially-minded"* practitioner.

C

Leaders' profiles – Canada

ABUGOV, Lorne

Osler, Hoskin & Harcourt LLP, Ottawa,
+1 613 787 1019
labugov@osler.com
Recommended in Communications

Specialisation: Partner in Ottawa office of *Osler, Hoskin & Harcourt LLP*. Practice centres on all legal and regulatory/policy and business transactional aspects of Canada's telecommunications, broadcasting, cable, satellite, radiocommunications and Internet based communications industries. Represents major Canadian and international broadcasting and telecommunications companies. One of the founders of the National Capital Association of Communications Lawyers.
Prof. Memberships: Canadian Bar Association, National Capital Association of Communications Lawyers (co-founder), American Bar Association, Information Technology Law Association, Computer Law Institute.
Career: Has been involved in communications law for nineteen years as corporate counsel, senior legal counsel to Canada's regulatory body - the CRTC - and now as head of the firm's communication law practice group. Articled with Canada's telephone companies (formerly Stentor) in 1980-81. Called to the Bar (Ontario) in 1982, beginning communications law practice as Legal Counsel to the Department of Communications, Ottawa. Served as Legal Counsel to Bell Canada within the company's Regulatory Law Branch in Hull, Quebec from 1986 to 1988, before joining the CRTC and then *Osler, Hoskin & Harcourt* in 1994.

AFFLECK, Donald S.

Kelly Affleck Greene, Toronto +1 416 360 2800
dsaffleck@kag.net
Recommended in Competition/Anti-trust

Specialisation: Specialises in competition and trade practice law as well as estate, environmental and products liability litigation. Practice involves appearances at both the trial and appellate levels as well as before specialised tribunals such as the Competition Tribunal. Represents a number of major Canadian corporations. During the year 2000, represented Pepsi-Cola in its successful opposition to the proposed merger of Cadbury Schweppes and Coca-Cola.
Prof. Memberships: Member of Executive of National Competition Law section, Canadian Bar Association, The Law Society of Upper Canada (certified as a specialist in Civil Litigation), the Advocate's Society (1968 to date), American Bar Association (Anti-trust Law Section).
Publications: Publications include 'Canadian Competition Law', a two volume service on the competition law of Canada that was first published in 1989, as well as numerous articles for professional publications.
Career: Called to the Bar of Ontario in 1966. Associate and senior partner from 1966 to 1992 with *Fasken Martineau DuMoulin* in Toronto. Senior partner and founder of the law firm of *Kelly Affleck Greene* in 1992. Appointed Queen's counsel in 1979.
Personal: University of Toronto - Honours BA, (1961), LLB, (1964). Senior Chair of Disciplinary Tribunal, University of Toronto (1990-1999). Recipient of Arbor Award (1994).

AHMED, Firoz

Osler, Hoskin & Harcourt LLP, Toronto
+1 416 862 6696
fahmed@osler.com
Recommended in Tax

Specialisation: Partner in Taxation Department of *Osler, Hoskin & Harcourt LLP*. Practice focuses on the taxation of mergers and acquisitions, restructurings, other corporate reorganisations and international taxation. Acted for BCE in spin-off of Nortel Networks Corporation; acted for Imasco in BAT Imasco/Canada Trust acquisition; acted for Bell Canada on Ameritech 20% investment in Bell Canada.
Prof. Memberships: Law Society of Upper Canada; Canadian Tax Foundation.
Publications: Has presented papers on a number of income tax subjects for the 'International Tax Review', 'Journal of International Taxation', Canadian Tax Foundation and the Tax Executives Institute.
Career: Joined the firm in 1986, was called to the Ontario Bar that same year and became a partner in 1992. Seconded to the Rulings Directorate of Revenue Canada, as a senior rulings officer in 1989.
Personal: Born 26 April 1960. Attended Carleton University (B.Comm. 1981), Queen's University (LLB, 1984).

AINLEY, William M.

Davies Ward Phillips & Vineberg LLP, Toronto
+1 416 863 5509
wainley@dwpv.com
Recommended in Corporate/M&A

Specialisation: Securities law, with an emphasis on mergers and acquisitions and corporate finance. Lead counsel to Onex Corporation in take-over bid for Air Canada and Canadian Airlines; to Polo Ralph Lauren in take-over bid for Club Monaco Inc.; to Nortel Networks' acquisition of Cambrian Systems; and to Celestica Inc. in its initial public offering.
Prof. Memberships: Canadian Bar Association.
Career: Articled at the firm. Qualified in 1981. Partner since 1983. Seconded, 1984, to Ontario Securities Commission as legal advisor to Chairman. Member, Securities Advisory Committee to OSC, 1986-90 and Chairman 1989-90. Frequent lecturer in M&A and corporate finance.
Personal: Born 9 June 1954. Attended Cambridge University 1973-77 and McGill University 1977-79. Married with three children.

C

ALEXANDER, Deborah M.
Osler, Hoskin & Harcourt LLP, Toronto
+1 416 862 6573
dalexander@osler.com
Recommended in Corporate/M&A
Specialisation: Senior partner in the Business Law department of *Osler, Hoskin & Harcourt LLP* since 1977. Specialises in corporate finance and merger and acquisition transactions in the Canadian, U.S. and international capital markets. Responsible for managing large, complex and high profile transactions for Canadian and international investment dealers and for large Canadian public corporations. Transaction experience includes participating and advising in innovative financing structures, such as Deutsche Telekom equity-linked notes, British privatisations, international financings involving multiple jurisdictions, the proposed merger of the Royal Bank of Canada and the Bank of Montréal and the merger of JDS Fitel Inc. and Uniphase Corporation. Acts as corporate finance counsel for the Bank of Montréal with respect to all of its financing activities and is securities counsel to Ontario Hydro Services Company, a successor company to Ontario Hydro.
Prof. Memberships: American Bar Association, Canadian Bar Association, Law Society of Upper Canada.
Career: Called to the Bar of Ontario in 1977. Joined *Osler, Hoskin & Harcourt LLP* in 1977, becoming a Partner in 1982. Former head of the Corporate Commercial Department and is on the firm's Executive Committee. Has been a member of the Securities Advisory Committee to the Ontario Securities Commission and has lectured in various areas of securities law including lectures in the United States and Canada, with respect to multijurisdictional financings and innovative financing structures.
Personal: Attended University of Toronto, LLB 1975, Queen's University at Kingston, BA (Economics) 1972. Lives in Toronto, Ontario, Canada.

ALLEN, Francis
Borden Ladner Gervais LLP, Calgary, Alberta
+1 403 260 7010
Recommended in Corporate/M&A

ANDERSON, Jean E.
Goodmans LLP, Toronto +1 416 597 4297
jeanderson@GoodmansLaw.com
Recommended in Banking & Finance
Specialisation: Member of the Financial Services Group of *Goodmans* . Practice is focused on financing and corporate transactions. With more than 20 years of legal experience, has developed extensive expertise in the areas of project finance, structured finance, asset-based lending, debt restructuring and complex domestic and cross-border financings. Clients represented include Bank of Montreal, Congress Financial Corporation (Canada), First Union Corporation, GE Capital Corporation, Reservoir Capital and Royal Bank of Canada.
Career: Graduated from Osgoode Hall Law School in 1979. Called to Bar of Ontario in 1981 and also served as a law clerk to the Chief Justice of the Ontario Court of Appeal. Prior to joining *Goodmans* in 2000, was a partner at another major Toronto law firm.

BACKMAN, Philip
Bennett Jones LLP, Calgary +1 403 298 3100
backmanp@bennettjones.ca
Recommended in Banking & Finance
Specialisation: Partner in the corporate department and head of the firm's financial services team. Practice is focused on financing and commercial transactions. Has acted for major North American corporations and financial institutions, project financings and public and private debt issues involving oil and gas, forestry, telecommunications, independent power and other industries. Recent transactions have included acting as counsel for: Anderson Exploration Ltd. on syndicated credit facilites aggregating Cdn. $1.4 billion and a $200 million Canadian bond issue in connection with its recent take-over of Ulster Petroleum Ltd; Shell Canada Limited in connection with various financial matters relating to the Cdn. $4 billion Athabasca Oil Sands Project; and Canadian Occidental Petroleum Ltd. on a $1.0 billion syndicated bank financing and on public debt issues in the United States of US $800 million.
Prof. Memberships: Professional memberships: Law Society of Alberta, Canadian Bar Association.
Career: Admitted to the Alberta Bar in 1977. Graduated from University of Manitoba Law School in 1976 on the Dean's honour list. Joined *Benett Jones* in 1976 and became a partner in 1983.
Personal: Born 2 August, 1951. Married with three children.

BAILLIE Q.C., James C.
Torys, Toronto +1 416 865 0040
jbaillie@torys.com
Recommended in Banking & Finance, Corporate/M&A
Specialisation: Advises on strategic and policy issues for clients in the private, public and NGO sectors. Has acted as counsel to independent directors of public corporations, including NOVA Systems (predecessor of TransCanada Pipeline) and Air Canada.
Career: Former Chair of the Ontario Securities Commission December, 1996 to June, 1997. Chair of the Independent Electricity Market Operator (IMO), the not-for-profit entity which will operate Ontario's wholesale electricity grid and will administer the competitive market pricing for electricity to begin during the year 2000. Chair of Corel Corp., and a member of the boards of directors of Sun Life Financial and of FPI Inc.
Personal: Born 6 August, 1938. Attended University of Toronto, 1958 (BA), 1961 (LLB), and Harvard University, 1964 (LLM)

BARKER, Bruce
Bennett Jones LLP, Toronto +1 416 777 4818
barkerb@bennettjones.ca
Recommended in Banking & Finance
Specialisation: Practised banking law for over twenty years, representing institutional creditors and investors of all types, including major Canadian banks, many of the United States money centre banks and an American global financial services company. Also represents some of the traditional investment banks in complex or specialised structured finance transactions, including asset based financing, leveraged leasing, synthetic leasing, securitisations and other types of innovative off balance sheet financing, both domestic and offshore. Has participated as investors' counsel in numerous restructurings during the recessions of the 1980s and 1990s.
Personal: Graduated from Dartmouth College, N.H. (summa cum laude, 1971) and the University of Toronto Law School (1975). Member of the editorial board of the 'Banking and Finance Law Journal', and is an instructor in the Master of Laws programe at Osgoode Hall Law School, as well as teaching the 'International Banking and Finance Law' course. Member of the Advisory Board of the Institute for Entrepreneurship, Innovation and Growth, Richard Ivey School of Business, University of Western Ontario.

BARNES, Jeffery A.
Fraser Milner Casgrain, Toronto +1 416 863 4644
jeff.barnes@fmc-law.com
Recommended in Corporate/M&A
Specialisation: Mergers and acquisitions, debt and equity financings, restructurings, privatisations, project finance and corporate governance. Advises financial intermediaries and securities dealers on underwriting, valuations and fairness opinions. Counsel to: 407 International on privatisation and financing of toll highway; independent committee of Canadian Occidental Petroleum; Toronto Waterfront Revitalisation Task Force.
Prof. Memberships: Law Society of Upper Canada; Canadian Bar Association.
Career: Year of call to the Bar: 1976. Joined *Fraser Milner Casgrain* in 1990. Past Chair, Partnership Board. Past member, Securities Advisory Committee, Ontario Securities Commission.
Personal: Born 1951. Attended University of Toronto. Married with four children.

BARRETT, Roderick
Stikeman Elliott, Toronto +1 416 869 5500
Recommended in Banking & Finance

BARUTCISKI, Milos
Davies Ward Phillips & Vineberg LLP, Toronto
+1 416 367 6906
mbarutciski@dwpv.com
Recommended in Competition/Anti-trust
Specialisation: Competition law and international trade law. Represented clients in mergers, criminal cartel cases, distribution and pricing practices and cross-border enforcement matters, as well as in anti-dumping, countervailing duty and government procurement cases, foreign investment review, WTO and NAFTA issues, foreign corrupt practices and other international business matters.
Prof. Memberships: Chair, International Law Section, Canadian Bar Association; Chair, International Affairs Committee, Canadian Chamber of Commerce.
Career: Qualified in 1987. Special Advisor to the Director of the Canadian Competition Bureau (1991-93).
Personal: Born: June 10, 1956. LLB, University of Ottawa.

BELL, Alan
Blake, Cassels & Graydon LLP, Toronto
+1 416 863 2662
ab@blakes.com
Recommended in Corporate/M&A
Specialisation: Practises securities and business law in the Toronto Office and specialises in mergers and acquisitions, corporate reorganisations and private and public financing. Acts for public companies, independent committees of directors of public companies, investment dealers and financial advisors. Head of the *Blakes* project team in respect of its 1995/2000 retainer from the Ontario Securities Commission for the Reformulation Project of its Policies. Acted for Ontario Power Generation Inc., on its $8.5 billion acquisition in March 1999 of the electricity generating business of Ontario Hydro, and acted as Canadian Counsel to Weyerhaeuser Company on its $3.6 billion acquisition in November 1999 of MacMillan Bloedel Limited and to United Airlines Corporation and Deutsche Lufthansa A6 of the sector allowance on their strategic allowance with and investment in Air Canada in the context of the Ones Bid for Air Canada and as Canadian Counsel to Vivendi SA on its 2000 US$34 billion acquisition of Seagram and for Clearnet Communication Inc. on Telus Corporation's $6billion acquistion of Clearnet in 2000.
Prof. Memberships: Member of the Law Society of Upper Canada, associate member of the American Bar Association.
Career: Qualified in 1975. Joined *Blake, Cassels & Graydon* and became a partner in 1986. Lectures securities law at Queen's University Law School, was a member of the Securities Advisory Committee to the Ontario Securities Commission for 1991-1993 and has participated in conferences and seminars on securities and corporate law.
Personal: Born August 27, 1948. Attended York University 1967-1970 (BA summa cum laude) and Osgoode Hall Law School 1970-1973.

BÉRIAULT, Yves
McCarthy Tétrault, Montréal, Québec
+1 514 397 4120
yberiault@mccarthy.ca
Recommended in Competition/Anti-trust
Specialisation: Partner and head of the Montréal Competition Law Group. Experienced antitrust lawyer. Advises Canadian and international clients on all aspects of competition law. Involved in many landmark cases before all courts and the Competition Tribunal. Past lecturer on competition law, University of Montréal.
Prof. Memberships: Past Chairman of the Competition Law Section of the CBA.
Publications: Co-authored 'Le droit de la concurrence au Canada' (with Madeleine Renaud and Yves Comtois), Carswell, 1999. Contributed to numerous books on competition law.
Career: Admitted to the Québec bar in 1968.

BIES, Bill
Fasken Martineau DuMoulin LLP, Toronto, Ontario +1 416 366 8381
wbies@tor.fasken.com
Recommended in Tax
Specialisation: Partner in corporate taxation with a concentration on domestic and international mergers and acquisitions work, corporate finance and reorganisations. Extensively involved in advising both non-residents who wish to do business in Canada and Canadian companies which wish to do business abroad. Currently the Chair of the firm's Tax Department. Recent significant matters: Acted for such clients as Allied Domecq, American International Group, Anglo American, Auditor General of Canada, Boart Longyear, Canada Deposit Insurance Corporation, Colgate-Palmolive, DeBeers, DuPont, ESPN, InfoSpace Inc., LodgeNet Entertainment Corporation, PricewaterhouseCoopers, Province of Ontario, Rio Algom Limited, Standard Life.
Prof. Memberships: Canadian Bar Association, Canadian Tax Foundation, International Fiscal Association, former member of the Joint Committee on Taxation of the Canadian Bar Association and Canadian Institute of Chartered Accountants.
Publications: Most recent papers were on the topics of international transfer pricing, interest deductibility and financing costs, and hybrid instruments.
Career: Admitted to the Ontario Bar in 1976. Joined *Fasken & Calvin* (now *Fasken Martineau DuMoulin* LLP) in 1976, becoming a Partner in 1982. Was an Assistant Professor, Faculty of Law, Laval University, Quebec City, 1972-1974. Taught the corporate income tax course in the Graduate Law Program (LLM) at Osgoode Hall Law School in 1998. From 1979 to 1999, a Special Lecturer, Corporate Income Taxation, Faculty of Law, University of Toronto. Frequent speaker at conferences and seminars.
Personal: Graduated with a law degree (LLB) in 1971, from the University of Windsor, and obtained graduate law degree (LLM) from the University of London, London (England) in 1972.

BISNAIRE, J-P
Davies Ward Phillips & Vineberg LLP, Toronto
+1 416 863 5539
jbisnaire@dwpv.com
Recommended in Corporate/M&A
Specialisation: Mergers and acquisitions and corporate finance, including divestitures, take-over bids, corporate reorganisations, going private transactions, spin-offs, and corporate governance matters.
Prof. Memberships: Canadian Bar Association; International Bar Association; Canadian Tax Foundation.
Career: Qualified in 1978. Partner since 1980. Taught Securities Regulation at University of Ottawa Law School, 1985-87.
Personal: Born 27 April 1951. Attended Wilfrid Laurier University (BA, 1973) and University of Ottawa Law School (LLB, 1976).

BODRUG, John D.
Davies Ward Phillips & Vineberg LLP, Toronto
+1 416 863 5576
jbodrug@dwpv.com
Recommended in Competition/Anti-trust
Specialisation: Competition law, including mergers, price fixing investigations and other pricing and distribution matters. Represented Canadian and US-based corporations, including energy and resources, transportation, agricultural, manufacturing, financial services and consumer products.
Career: Qualified in 1987. Special counsel for Director of Competition Bureau in 1996 Competition Tribunal proceedings in Interac abuse of dominance case. Wrote numerous articles on competition and trade practice law. Lecturer in Competition Law at University of Western Ontario, 1998-present.
Personal: Born 15 March 1962. Attended University of Western Ontario (LLB, 1985).

BOIDMAN, Nathan
Davies Ward Phillips & Vineberg LLP, Montréal
+1 514 841 6409
nboidman@dwpv.com
Recommended in Tax
Specialisation: Tax Partner. Exclusive practice in tax, principally respecting international M&A and other corporate transactions and matters (including a recognised expertise in intercompany transfer pricing). Lead or co-lead counsel on over $35 bn of cross-border mergers and acquisitions since 1995, as well as involvement in $10 to $15 bn in other M&A deals.
Prof. Memberships: Council and Past President, Canadian Branch of the International Fiscal Association (I.F.A.); Current Member, Executive Committee, International Fiscal Association (Amsterdam) since 1998. Past Member, Joint Committee on Taxation, Canadian Bar Association and Canadian Institute of Chartered Accountants; past Member, Board of Governors, Canadian Tax Foundation; Tax Management Advisory Board on Foreign Income; Tax Management Inc., 1981.
Publications: Frequent author and lecturer on international taxation, including authorship or co-authorship of four books, Canadian chapters for several services and numerous articles and papers presented at seminars, conferences, etc. and past or present contributory or editorial functions for prominent tax journals.
Career: Admitted to the Order of Chartered Accountants of Quebec, 1964; admitted to the Order of Chartered Accountants of Ontario, 1977; called to the Bar of Quebec, 1981. Appointed, Nov 1999, fellow of The Order of Chartered Accountants of Quebec (FCA). Public practice in accountancy, 1964-1974; Tax Consultant to *Verchere, Noel & Eddy*, Montreal 1974-1979; Tax Consultant to and then partner *Clarkson, Tetrault, Attorneys*, Montreal, 1980-1982; Partner of the firm since 1982.
Personal: McGill University, B.Com. 1962. McGill University, Bachelor of Civil Law (B.C.L.) 1980; McGill University, Bachelor of Common Law (LLB.) 1980.

BOIVIN, Charles J.
Ogilvy Renault, Montréal +1 514 847 4402
cboivin@ogilvyrenault.com
Recommended in Banking & Finance
Specialisation: Senior partner in the Business Law Group and co-ordinator of the firm's Financing and Financial Services team. Specialises in commercial and bank financing of corporations and regulatory matters, including syndicated credit agreements and security, project finance, export financing, structured

C

finance and securitisation, derivatives, letters of credit, payment systems and financial leasing. Regularly advises Canadian and foreign financial institutions and has acted for both syndicate lenders and large corporations in structuring local and cross-border financings in America and Europe.
Prof. Memberships: Quebec Bar, Ontario Bar and Canadian Bar Association.
Career: Graduated from McGill University, qualified in 1973, worked intensively as outside counsel for Canada's export credit agency, spent five years as in-house counsel to Royal Bank of Canada and joined *Ogilvy Renault* in 1986. Has written many articles and chaired or participated in several seminars and conferences dealing with various aspects of financial services and bank financing.
Personal: Born August 6, 1946. Married with three children. Leisure interests include downhill skiing and hiking. Lives in Westmount, Quebec.

C

BOOTH, Robert
Bennett Jones LLP, Calgary +1 403 298 3100
boothb@bennettjones.ca
Recommended in Energy & Natural Resources
Specialisation: Partner in the energy and natural resources department with a broad commercial practice in many areas of the domestic and international energy and resources business. Has represented clients in oil and gas exploration, production and marketing activities; major oil and gas pipeline transportation projects; uranium mining and production projects; electric power generation and transmission projects; and energy utility businesses. Experience includes acting in the puchase and sale of businesses, establishment of new businesses, structuring joint ventures and partnerships and advising management in strategic decision making, both for Canadian and foreign corporations. Has spoken and authored several articles on Canadian oil and gas law and Canadian natural gas deregulation for the Canadian Petroleum Law Foundation, the Alberta Law Review and various professional and business seminars.
Prof. Memberships: Law Society of Alberta, Canadian Bar Association including CBA's Natural Resources Subsection.
Career: Member of the Law Society of Alberta and the Canadian Bar Association and is a director of both public and privately held corporations. Is recognised as one of the leading Canadian lawyers in energy law. Called to the Alberta Bar in 1978. Joined *Bennett Jones* in 1977, became partner in 1984.
Personal: Born 26 November, 1952. Attended the Royal Military College of Canada 1970-74 (B. Engineering) and Dalhousie Law School 1974-77 (LLB).

BRAITHWAITE, William J.
Stikeman Elliott, Toronto +1 416 869 5500
Recommended in Corporate/M&A

BRANDS, Andrew D.
Smith Lyons, Toronto +1 416 369 4644
ADBrands@SmithLyons.ca
Recommended in Banking & Finance
Specialisation: Senior partner of the firm's banking and creditors' rights group and has earned a distinguished reputation for comprehensive counsel to domestic and foreign financial institutions, in the area of policy matters impacting on the industry, as well as in specific transactions. Mr Brands has extensive experience with major financings, mergers, and acquisitions, financial reorganisations, and insolvencies. Has assembled teams for significant cross-border financings, multi-currency transactions, as well as providing advice in the management, restructuring, and securing of loans. Has been invited to give numerous presentations including: Techniques in Merchant Banking, Recent trends in Mezzanine Finance, Negotiating Loan Agreements, Creative Structures and Srategies for Reorganisations, Credit Analysis, Risk Capital in Canada, and Cross Border Financings.
Prof. Memberships: Association of Canadian Venture Capital Companies, Canadian Bar Association, Business Law Section of the Canadian Bar Association – Ontario, Executive member of the Insolvency Section of the Canadian Bar Association – Ontario, and of the Independent Power Producers' Society.
Career: Called to the Ontario bar in 1981. Graduated in 1976 with honours with a Bachelor in History and Philosophy from the University of Guelph. Received LLB from Dalhousie University in 1979.

BUCHAN, Robert
Johnston & Buchan, Ottawa +1 613 236 3882
Recommended in Communications

CAMPBELL, Dan
Cox Hanson O'Reilly Matheson, Halifax
+1 902 421 6262
Recommended in Communications

CAMPBELL, Neil
McMillan Binch, Toronto +1 416 865 7025
Recommended in Competition/Anti-trust

CARFAGNINI, Jay A.
Goodmans LLP, Toronto +1 416 597 4107
jcarfagnini@GoodmansLaw.com
Recommended in Banking & Finance
Specialisation: Partner in the Financial Services Group of *Goodmans*; practises exclusively in the areas of banking law, corporate reorganisations, bankruptcies and insolvency law, with particular emphasis and expertise in cross-border and international transactions. Has been an active participant and advisor in most of the largest restructurings in Canada in recent years, including Dome Petroleum Limited, Olympia & York Developments Limited, Campeau Corporation, Dylex Limited, The Eaton Co. Ltd, the Tee-Comm Electronics and AlphaStar digital home TV Group, Air Atlantic, PWA Corporation Group and the Sammi Atlas Steel Group.
Prof. Memberships: Member of the Ontario and Alberta Bars; International Bar Association; the Law Society of Upper Canada; the Canadian Bar Association; the Insolvency Institute of Canada and the American Bar Association, and is a participant in INSOL International.
Publications: Author of numerous articles for Canadian and international publications.
Career: Is an occasional lecturer at the University of Western Ontario, Osgoode Hall and McGill University Faculties of Law and writes and speaks extensively on banking and insolvency law matters.

CARR, Brian
Fraser Milner Casgrain, Toronto +1 416 863 4366
brian.carr@fmc-law.com
Recommended in Tax
Specialisation: Practice is restricted to income tax matters with special emphasis on corporate reorganisations, resource taxation and income tax litigation. Participated in numerous acquisitions and divestitures of shares and assets and issues of securities, including numerous issues of flow-through shares, and the development of a number of mining projects.
Prof. Memberships: Board of Governors, Canadian Tax Foundation; Editorial Board, Canadian Tax Journal; CICA/CBA Joint Committee on Taxation; Member and Past Chair, legislative subcommittee of the Taxation Section of the Canadian Bar Association (Ontario).
Publications: 'Taxation of Resource Industries', Carswell, 1987; Author, 'Canadian Resource Taxation', Carswell, 1996; Contributing editor, 'Ward's Tax Law and Planning' (1983-1995); Assistant editor, Canadian Petroleum Tax Journal (1988-1996); 1996 co-winner of the Canadian Tax Foundation's Douglas J. Sherbaniuk Distinguished Writing Award.
Career: Year of call to the Bar: 1975 (Ontario), 2000 (Alberta).
Personal: University of Toronto, LLB,1970-1973; University of Toronto, BSc. (Mathematics, Physics and Chemistry), 1966-1970.

CHRISTIE, James
Blake, Cassels & Graydon LLP, Toronto
+1 416 863 2546
Recommended in Banking & Finance
Specialisation: Partner in the Financial Services Group in Toronto and Managing Partner of *Blake, Cassels & Graydon.* Acts primarily for lenders and has extensive experience in all aspects of bank regulation, secured and unsecured debt financing, project financing, debt restructuring, and insolvency law. For a number of years, acted as senior counsel to Canadian Imperial Bank of Commerce and CIBC World Markets on many of their largest transactions. Member of the Board of Directors of the National Foundation for Family Research and Education. Also lectured and written on a broad range of topics in the financial services area as well as law firm management and the changing environment in the legal profession.
Prof. Memberships: Canadian Bar Association, Ontario; Law Society of Upper Canada.
Career: Admitted to the Ontario Bar in 1978. Joined *Blake, Cassels & Graydon* 1976, becoming a Partner in 1984 and appointed firm managing partner in 1995.
Personal: Born 31 July 1953. Attended University of Toronto 1976, (LLB). Lives in Toronto, Ontario with wife and two children.

CLIFFORD, John Frederick
McMillan Binch, Toronto, Ontario
+1 416 865 7188
Recommended in Competition/Anti-trust

COLLINS, Paul
Stikeman Elliott, Toronto +1 416 869 5500
Recommended in Competition/Anti-trust

COMTOIS, Yves
McCarthy Tétrault, Montréal, Québec
+1 514 397 4282
ycomtois@mccarthy.ca
Recommended in Competition/Anti-trust
Specialisation: Associate in the Montréal Business Law Section. Practice focuses on competition law, foreign investments and mergers and acquisitions.
Prof. Memberships: Called to the Québec bar in 1995.
Publications: Co-authored 'Le droit de la concurrence au Canada' (with Yves Bériault and Madeleine Renaud), Carswell, 1999.
Career: Practised competition law in a Belgian law firm before joining *McCarthy Tétrault*. Member of the National Competition Law Section of the CBA.
Personal: Received a Diploma of Advanced European Legal Studies from the College of Europe in Bruges (Belgium).

COULOMBE, Gérard
Desjardins Ducharme Stein Monast, Montréal
+1 514 878 5526
Recommended in Tax

CRAMPTON, Paul S.
Davies Ward Phillips & Vineberg LLP, Toronto
+1 416 367 6902
pcrampton@dwpv.com
Recommended in Competition/Anti-trust
Specialisation: Counsels clients on competition law aspects of mergers, joint ventures, strategic alliances, pricing policies and other distribution practices. Navigates matters through and prepares submissions to the Competition Bureau. Advises clients regarding application of Investment Canada Act.
Prof. Memberships: Chair, Canadian Chamber of Commerce, Task Force on Competition Law and Policy. Immediate Past-Chair, Mergers Committee, National Competition Law Section of Canadian Bar Association. Co-Chair, International Anti-trust Committee, International Section of American Bar Association.
Career: Qualified in 1988. Former Special Advisor to Director of Investigation & Research. Principal drafter of Bureau's 1991 Merger Enforcement Guidelines and contributor to other Bureau Guidelines.
Personal: B.Phil. (Quebec), 1981. LLB/MBA (Ottawa), 1985. LLM (Toronto), 1987.

CURRAN, John
Bennett Jones LLP, Calgary +1 403 298 3244
curranj@bennettjones.ca
Recommended in Energy & Natural Resources
Specialisation: Partner in the energy and natural resources department. Has practised oil and gas and corporate law in Canada for more than 30 years. Practice is focused on representing Canadian and American companies in the oil and gas industry, including advising on Canada's foreign investment laws applicable to Americans, negotiating, structuring and financing of oil and gas transactions (such as acquisitions and dispositions of companies and/or assets) and preparing contracts relating to exploration, production, development and merging activities. Serves as a director on the Canadian boards of a number of Canadian and American private and public companies as well as the boards of the Canadian subsidiaries of Tokyo-based Japan National Oil Corporation and Beijing-based China National Overseas Exploration and Development Corporation. Taught oil and gas law at the University of Alberta and University of Calgary.
Prof. Memberships: Law Society of Alberta; Canadian Bar Association; Calgary Bar Association; Past Director and officer of the Canadian Petroleum Foundation.
Career: Called to the Alberta Bar in 1967. Appointed Q.C. in 1994.
Personal: Born 19 December, 1934. Attended the University of Texas (BSc in Geology, 1959) and the University of Alberta (LLB, 1963). Former chairman of the Calgary Board of Education.

CURRIE, Gordon
Blake, Cassels & Graydon LLP, Toronto
+1 416 863 2718
Recommended in Corporate/M&A

CUTHBERTSON, John
Burnet Duckworth & Palmer LLP, Calgary, Alberta
+1 403 260 0305
Jhc@bdlaw.com
Recommended in Energy & Natural Resources
Specialisation: Partner in Energy and Corporate & Commercial departments. Member of *BD&P's* Executive Committee. Main area of focus is corporate work primarily for junior, intermediate and multinational energy clients. Includes the negotiation and drafting of a variety of energy contracts relating to energy projects (pipelines, oilsands, heavy oil), royalty trusts, partnerships, joint ventures, construction and ownership agreements, international operating agreements and joint acquisition, facilities, processing, marketing and transportation agreements and has been retained as an arbitrator for an energy dispute. Representations include public companies, financial, insurance and pension corporations in an extensive number of acquisition, divestiture, swap and royalty trust transactions. Counsel to many U.S./Canadian energy corporations with cross-border implications and transactions.
Prof. Memberships: Member of Law Society of Alberta, Canadian Law Foundation, Petroleum Joint Ventures Association and SEAPAC (Small Explorers and Producers Association of Canada). Director and Member of Executive Committee of Calgary Legal Guidance (a not for profit organisation providing legal service to Calgary's disaffected). Awarded the Canadian Bar Association's and the Law Society of Alberta's Distinguished Service Award in 1999 for distinguished service to the community.
Career: Admitted to the Alberta Bar in 1980 and Nova Scotia Bar in 1983. Joined *Burnet, Duckworth & Palmer* in 1979, partner since 1987. Member of Executive Committee since 1993.
Personal: Graduated from University of Alberta with a Bachelor of Science degree, zoology major in 1973 and a Bachelor of Commerce (with Distinction) in 1975. Graduated from Dalhousie University with a joint LLB and an MBA (International Business and Marketing concentration) in 1979. Leisure pursuits include running, reading and volunteer activities.

DALFEN, Charles
Torys, Toronto +1 416 865 8131
cdalfen@torys.com
Recommended in Communications
Specialisation: Chairman of the firm's Communications Group. Advises Canadian and foreign clients on domestic and international telecommunications and broadcasting laws. Has managed regulatory and licensing matters for clients involved in the radio, television, cable TV, satellite, mobile and fixed wireless business throughout the world. Clients include governments and private sector clients seeking to establish, review or alter regulatory policies and regimes. Formerly Vice-Chairman of the Canadian Radio-television and Telecommunications Commission.
Personal: University of Ottawa, 1969 (LLB); Oxford University, 1966 (B.Phil.); McGill University, 1964 (BA).

DAVIDGE, Marlene
Torys, Toronto +1 416 865 7322
mdavidge@torys.com
Recommended in Corporate/M&A
Specialisation: Practice is transaction oriented and focuses on mergers and acquisitions, public offerings, financings, advising boards and their committees, and all other aspects of securities law. Well known for work in connection with public and private managed products, both domestically and internationally, including mutual, pooled and segregated funds, wrap accounts and pension vehicles and the myriad of issues surrounding portfolio management. Recent transactions include the merger of Abitibi-Stone, Stericycle's takeover bid for Med-Tech, Merrill Lynch's realisation on Reichmann's First Canadian Place and major transactions relating to AGF, Perigee, Nike Securities and Primerica. Member of the Securities Advisory Committee, Ontario Securities Commission from 1984-89.
Prof. Memberships: Law Society of Upper Canada (Ontario).
Career: Admitted to the Ontario Bar in 1979. Joined *Torys* in 1979, becoming a Partner in 1985.
Personal: Attended University of Toronto (Honours BA, 1974); Osgoode Hall Law School (LLB, 1977). Lives in Toronto.

DAVIES, Don
Macleod Dixon LLP, Calgary +1 403 267 8230
daviesd@macleoddixon.com
Recommended in Energy & Natural Resources
Specialisation: Partner and Chair of the Regulatory Law Department. Represents oil and gas producers, marketers and pipelines in proceedings before the National Energy Board and the Alberta Energy &

C

Utilities Board. Has acted for proponents of various energy projects, including pipelines, oil sands developments, and well and field facilities. Has also acted for shippers in proceedings involving the tolls and tariffs on pipelines, and for producers and purchasers in applications to export natural gas to the United States.
Prof. Memberships: Law Society of Alberta. Canadian Bar Association.
Career: Bachelor of Laws Degree from the University of Alberta in 1978. Admitted to Alberta Bar in 1979. Partner at *Macleod Dixon* since 1985.
Personal: Born August 25, 1954. Married with 3 children.

C

DEMERS, Jacques
Meighen Demers, Toronto +1 416 340 6000
jdemers@meighen.com
Recommended in Banking & Finance, Corporate/M&A
Specialisation: Corporate, Banking and Structured Finance with emphasis on project finance, syndicated corporate and government financings and infrastructure development. Recent matters and financing in which has been involved in a lead role include: Senior triple-project secured financing of Aur's US$265 purchase of Quebrada Blanca, Chile (Counsel to Senior Lenders), $100 million structured lease financing of co-generation assets of Suncor Oil Sands Facility, Alberta (Counsel to senior, secured boundholders), NATO Flying Training Program ($720 million bond issue), Fredericton-Moncton Highway Project (Counsel to successful private sector consortium BOT/negotiated conversion to shadow tolling) Borealis Infrastructure Trust ($160 million bond-issue), Ferihegy Airport, Budapest (Counsel to private sector developer/operator-BOT), BHP and DIAVIK Diamond Projects, Northwest Territories (Counsel to Canadian government), The Toronto Hospital ($281 secured bond issue), Andacollo Project, Chile (Counsel to Senior Project Lenders). Currently active in a number of projects for private/public sector projects involving airports, ports, health and education services as well as certain structured and project financings in oil and gas and mining sectors both in Canada and abroad.
Prof. Memberships: Member of Law Society of Upper Canada, Montreal and Quebec Bars and Canadian Bar Association.
Career: Graduated 1973 McGill University (D.C.S.) and 1976 Laval University LLB. 24 Years of practice, eight with *McMaster Meighen* (Montreal) from 1977-1984 and 16 with *Meighen Demers* (1984 to date). Director of several business corporations.
Personal: Born February 28, 1954. Married with three children. Member of Board of Governors, Crescent School. Leisure interests: golf, swimming, skiing, badminton, history, and music. Fluent in French and English.

DESBARATS, Robert
Bennett Jones LLP, Calgary +1 403 298 3100
desbaratsr@bennettjones.ca
Recommended in Energy & Natural Resources
Specialisation: Head of energy and natural resources department, with considerable experience in commercial transactions related to the oil and gas industry, including transactions involving the buying and selling of oil and gas properties and companies, joint ventures, corporate financing, preparation and interpretation of contracts, natural gas marketing arrangements and property title opinions. Lecturer at the Alberta Bar Admission Course, Mount Royal College, Southern Alberta Institute of Technology and the Canadian Bar Association.
Prof. Memberships: Canadian Petroleum Foundation (Past President 1991-1992), Law Society of Upper Canada, Law Society of Alberta, Canadian Bar Association.
Publications: Authored and co-authored numerous papers for the Canadian Petroleum Law Foundation, among other publications.
Career: Joined *Bennett Jones* in 1976, became a partner in 1983.
Personal: Born 17 November, 1950. Attended the University of Ottawa (BS, 1971; LLB, 1974).

DESCHAMPS, J. Michel
McCarthy Tétrault, Montréal, Québec
+1 514 397 4138
jmdeschamps@mccarthy.ca
Recommended in Banking & Finance
Specialisation: Partner in the Montréal Business Law Section. Practises in banking, commercial and bankruptcy law.
Prof. Memberships: Admitted to the Québec bar in 1970.
Publications: Author of numerous articles.
Career: Currently serves on the Canadian Delegations for the UNCITRAL Convention on Assignment of Receivables in International Trade and for the UNIDROIT-ICAO Convention on International Interests in Mobile Equipment. Lecturer at the Law Faculty of the Université de Montréal in banking law, company law and corporate finance. Frequent speaker at conferences for legal practitioners and business people.

DUNBAR, Laurence
Johnston & Buchan, Ottawa +1 613 236 3882
Recommended in Communications

DURAND, Ronald
Stikeman Elliott, Toronto +1 416 869 5500
Recommended in Tax

EMBREE, Kirsten
Osler, Hoskin & Harcourt LLP, Ottawa
+1 613 787 1051
kembree@osler.com
Recommended in Communications
Specialisation: Partner in the Ottawa office of *Osler, Hoskin & Harcourt LLP.* Practises telecommunications and broadcast law as a member of the Communications Law Practice Group. Extensive involvement in high profile telecommunications mergers and financings. Governor-in-Counsel appointee to Canada's Sector Advisory Group on International Trade (SAGIT) for the Information and Communications Technologies sectors.
Prof. Memberships: Law Society of Upper Canada, Canadian Bar Association, National Capital Association of Communications Lawyers, Canadian Women in Communications.
Career: Joined *Osler, Hoskins & Harcourt* 's Communications Law Practice Group in 1996. Formerly Director of Regulatory Matters and Legal Counsel at AT&T Canada. Also worked for the former federal Department of Communications, Telesat Canada, the Canadian Independent Telephone Association and the Canadian Film Institute. Recipient of the Jeanne Sauvé Award in Communications.
Personal: BA (Mass Communications), Carleston University; LLB, McGill University; MA (Communications Management), University of Southern California.

EWENS QC, Douglas S.
McCarthy Tétrault, Calgary,
+1 403 260 3616
dewens@mccarthy.ca
Recommended in Tax
Specialisation: Partner in the Calgary Tax Section. Advises on structuring of Canadian business operations, financings and reorganisations of public and private business enterprises.
Prof. Memberships: Called to the Ontario bar in 1971; Alberta bar in 1981; appointed Q.C. in 1990.
Publications: Co-editor of the 'Corporate Reorganizations' feature of the Canadian Tax Journal.
Career: Frequent speaker at conferences of the Canadian Tax Foundation, Canadian Petroleum Tax Society and American Bar Association. Recognised as one of Canada's leading tax lawyers by LEXPERT, Chambers Global and International Tax Review.

FELESKY, Brian Q.C.
Felesky Flynn, Calgary +1 403 260 3301
bfelesky@felesky.com
Recommended in Tax
Specialisation: Senior Partner, *Felesky Flynn* Barristers and Solicitors, Tax Counsel (Calgary & Edmonton, Alberta, Canada).
Prof. Memberships: Past president of the Canadian Bar Association (Alberta); past president of the Calgary Bar Association; past governor of the Canadian Tax Foundation; past chairman of the Joint Committee on Taxation (the Canadian Bar Association and the Canadian Institute of Chartered Accountants); Distinguished Service Award 1998 of the Law Society of Alberta; Distinguished Citizen Award 1990 – JAC.
Career: Director, TransCanada Power Corporation, L.P.; past-chairman, University Technologies International Inc. ('ITI'); director, World Track and Field (2001 -Edmonton); co-chair, Calgary Justice Working Committee on Domestic Violence; director of The Council for Canadian Unity; member of the Board of Regents of Athol Murray College of Notre Dame; past governor University of Calgary; past governor of The International Development Research Centre; past director, Calgary Olympic Development Association.
Personal: Lecturer: Canadian Petroleum Tax Society, 'Judicial Anti-Avoidance - Where Are We?'; Canadian Tax Journal (50th Anniversary Issue) - 'The New Rules on Debt Forgiveness and

Foreclosures'; Canada-Mexico Conference - 'Canada-Mexico Tax Issues'; Tax Executive Institute, International Conference, Washington DC - 'Foreign Affiliates'; Canadian Tax Foundation - 'Substance Over Form'; Legal Education Society of Alberta 'Major Acquisitions and Divestitures in the Resource Industry'; 'Advance Course in Oil and Gas Taxation' CICA - Instructor.

FINGERHUT, Martin
Blake, Cassels & Graydon LLP, Toronto
+1 416 863 2638
martin.fingerhut@blakes.com
Recommended in Banking & Finance
Specialisation: Partner in Financial Services Group specialising in securitisation and structured finance. Represents sellers, purchasers, investment bankers, conduits, credit enhancers, trustees and rating agencies in domestic and cross-border transactions involving trade receivables, credit card receivables, corporate loans, franchise loans, floor plan loans, conditional sale contracts, leases, residential and commercial mortgages, natural resources and other assets. Advises domestic and international financial institutions on electronic banking matters. Chair of *Blakes'* Structured Finance Group. Chaired and spoke at numerous International Bar Association, Canadian Bar Association, American Bar Association and other conferences on these topics. Past instructor in Bar Admission Course and taught course on secured transactions at Osgoode Hall Law School.
Prof. Memberships: Canadian Bar Association, American Bar Association, International Bar Association.
Career: Joined *Blakes*, 1971. Partner since 1978. Vice-chair (1998) Securitisation Subcommittee of IBA Banking Committee. Fellow of American College of Commercial Finance Lawyers.
Personal: Born Toronto 1945. LLM, (Osgoode Hall Law School) 1980.

FINKELSTEIN, Neil
Davies Ward Phillips & Vineberg LLP, Toronto
+1 416 863 5566
nfinkelstein@dwpv.com
Recommended in Competition/Anti-trust
Specialisation: Litigated corporate, commercial, securities and public law cases at every level of court up to and including appeals in Supreme Court of Canada. Advised federal and provincial governments on constitutional reform.
Prof. Memberships: Bencher, Law Society of Upper Canada. Fellow, American College of Trial Lawyers. Member, Institute of Chartered Accountants of Ontario. Order of Chartered Accountants of Quebec. Canadian Institute of Chartered Accountants.
Publications: Laskin's Canadian Constitutional Law (5th ed.); 'Constitutional Rights in the Investigative Process'.
Career: Qualified in 1982. Law Clerk to Rt. Hon. Bora Laskin, Chief Justice of Canada, 1980-81. Senior Policy Advisor to Hon. Ian Scott, Attorney General of Ontario, 1985-86.
Personal: B., (McGill); LLB, (McGill), 1979; LLM, (Harvard), 1980.

FINNERTY, Patrick
Blake, Cassels & Graydon LLP, Calgary
+1 403 260 9608
pcf@blakes.com
Recommended in Corporate/M&A
Specialisation: Practice focuses on commercial and corporate transactions, with an emphasis on public offerings, private placements and public company mergers and acquisitions for both issuers and investment bankers. Substantial experience in domestic and cross-border financings, advising special committees and in related party transactions and independent valuations.
Prof. Memberships: Presently a member of the Alberta Securities Commission Oil & Gas Securities Task Force; past member of the OSC Securities Advisory Committee and of the Legal Advisory Committee to the ASC. Called to the Ontario Bar in 1981 and to the Alberta Bar in 1985.
Career: BA, University of Washington in 1973, LLB, University of Toronto in 1976, LLM from Harvard University in 1977, MBA from University of Chicago in 1979. Member, *Blake, Cassels & Graydon*, 1979 to present.

FRANKLYN, Peter
Osler, Hoskin & Harcourt LLP, Toronto
+1 416 862 6494
pfranklyn@osler.com
Recommended in Competition/Anti-trust
Specialisation: Partner in the Business Law Department of *Osler, Hoskin & Harcourt LLP*. Practises business law with particular emphasis on competition law matters (including mergers and acquisitions, pricing, trade practices and distribution matters), Canadian/foreign investment and entertainment/cultural industry matters.
Prof. Memberships: American Bar Association (Section of Antitrust Law and Business Law Section), Canadian Bar Association (Competition Law Section - vice-chairman Mergers Committee, and Media and Entertainment Law Section).
Career: Called to the Bar in 1984 and has practised with *Osler, Hoskin & Harcourt LLP* since that time. Became partner in 1990. Has represented clients before the Competition Bureau in connection with numerous competition law matters, and has also acted as counsel to the Competition Bureau in the preparation of the pre-merger notification regulations under the Competition Act (1986-87).

FRASER, Jean
Osler, Hoskin & Harcourt LLP, Toronto
+1 416 862 6537
jfraser@osler.com
Recommended in Corporate/M&A
Specialisation: Managing partner and senior partner in the Business Law Department of *Osler, Hoskin & Harcourt LLP*. Acts for public and private companies, investment dealers, governments and other public institutions on a wide range of corporate and financing matters. With the principal focus of practice being on securities and corporate finance, experience encompasses domestic and international public and private offerings of debt and equity, project and infrastructure financing, privatisations, financial restructurings and mergers and acquisitions.
Prof. Memberships: Canadian Bar Association, Law Society of Upper Canada.
Career: Called to the Bar in 1977. Has written and lectured on both securities and corporate law matters in various forums and is a past member of the Ontario Securities Commission Policy Advisory Committee.
Personal: Received LLB from University of Toronto in 1975.

GASCON, Denis
Ogilvy Renault, Montréal +1 514 847 4435
dgascon@ogilvyrenault.com
Recommended in Competition/Anti-trust
Specialisation: Partner in the firm's Litigation Group. Areas of expertise are international trade law and competition law. Heads the Competition and Trade Law Team of the firm. Has represented Canadian and foreign-based clients before the Competition Bureau and the Competition Tribunal in merger transactions reviewed by the Commissioner of Competition and advises clients on a regular basis with respect to restrictive trade practices and price fixing investigations under the Competition Act; industries covered include pulp and paper, transportation, telecommunications, media and entertainment, financial services, food services, real estate, home hardware and consumer products. Has appeared on numerous occasions before the Federal Court of Canada as well as before the Canadian International Trade Tribunal. Has also appeared in several trade disputes which have given rise to review panel decisions in disputes relating to anti-dumping duties pursuant to the provisions of Chapter 19 of the Canada-U.S. Free Trade Agreement. Has taught at the Quebec Bar School and has lectured on economics at Université Laval and Université du Québec à Montréal. Has authored and co-authored several papers and given several conferences on various topics dealing with competition and international trade law.
Prof. Memberships: Member of the Canadian Bar Association, the Anti-trust Law and International Law Sections of the American Bar Association and the International Bar Association (Committee C). Past Chairman of the Enforcement Practices and Procedures Committee of the Competition Law Section of the Canadian Bar Association.

GIRVAN, Garth M.
McCarthy Tétrault, Toronto, Ontario
+1 416 601 7574
ggirvan@mccarthy.ca
Recommended in Corporate/M&A
Specialisation: Partner in the Toronto Business Law Section and member of Ontario Executive Committee and National Management Committee. Extensive experience in mergers and acquisitions and corporate finance. Advises major corporate, financial institution and investment banking clients. Frequent speaker and writer on securities law topics.
Prof. Memberships: Called to the Ontario bar in 1978; Alberta bar in 1982; New York bar in 1986.
Career: Spent 1985 with the firm of *Cleary, Gottlieb, Steen & Hamilton* in New York and has since had active involvement in cross-border financing and acquisitions transactions.

C

C

GOLDMAN, Calvin S.
Davies Ward Phillips & Vineberg LLP, Toronto
+1 416 863 5561
cgoldman@dwpv.com
Recommended in Competition/Anti-trust
Specialisation: Competition law. Strategic advice and representation before Competition Bureau regarding mergers, acquisitions, joint ventures, abuse of dominance and other trade practice matters and on criminal matters under the Competition Act.
Prof. Memberships: Canadian Bar Association; American Bar Association; International Bar Association.
Career: Qualified in 1976. Appointed Queen's Counsel in 1987. Co-Chair, ABA Anti-trust Section's International Anti-trust and Foreign Competition Law Committee. Chair, International Chamber of Commerce's Joint Working Party on Competition and International Trade. Chair, Competition Policy Committee, Canadian Council for International Business. Past Chair, Canadian Bar Association National Competition Law Section. Former Director (since renamed 'Commissioner'), Canadian Competition Bureau. Former Vice-Chair, OECD Committee on Competition Law and Policy.
Personal: Born 4th November 1949. Attended Osgoode Hall Law School (LLB, 1973) and Harvard Law School (LLM, 1974).

GOW, Graham P.C.
McCarthy Tétrault, Toronto, Ontario
+1 416 601 7677
ggow@mccarthy.ca
Recommended in Corporate/M&A
Specialisation: Partner in the Toronto Business Law Section. Practice focuses on mergers and acquisitions. Also acts for clients on corporate finance and capital market transactions. Recent M&A assignments include: the bid by Noranda Inc. and Billiton PLC for Rio Algom; the purchase by Siemens AG of Milltronics Inc.; the bids by CREIT and Summit REIT for Avista REIT; the bids by Canwest Global Communications and Shaw Communications for WIC Western International Communications; and many others.
Prof. Memberships: Called to the Ontario bar in 1982.

GRAHAM, Bruce M.
Smith Lyons, Toronto, Ontario +1 416 369 7302
BMGraham@SmithLyons.ca
Recommended in Competition/Anti-trust
Specialisation: Senior Partner whose practice involves all competition/antitrust areas including advising a wide range of corporations, trade associations and non-profit organisations, both domestic and foreign, on the implications of competition law for their business activities including advising and assisting corporations with merger filings and clearances; advising and representing firms which become involved in an investigation by the Competition Bureau; assisting organisations to develop internal compliance programs; and representing firms in civil and criminal competition/antitrust proceedings before the Courts and Competition Tribunal.
Prof. Memberships: Executive, Economics and Law, Mergers and Regulatory Policy Committees of the Canadian Bar Association Competition Law Section, and the Canadian Law and Economics Association.
Career: Qualified in 1978 and joined *Smith Lyons* in 1980. Two year secondment as Commerce Officer at Competition Bureau, Industry Canada, Ottawa, 1978-1980. 1998 Chair of the CBA Annual Fall Conference on Competition Law. Panellist at CBA conferences, various commercial conferences and the University of Toronto Law and Economics Symposium.
Personal: University of Chicago Law School, LLM (Antitrust and Regulated Industries) 1976: Dalhousie University Law School, LLB, 1975: Acadia University, Honours B.B.A. (Business and Economics Majors), 1972.

GRANT, Peter S.
McCarthy Tétrault, Toronto
+1 416 601 7620
pgrant@mccarthy.ca
Recommended in Communications
Specialisation: Partner and head of the Toronto Communications and Entertainment Law Group. Practice includes broadcasting and cable television regulation, satellite services, copyright collectives, new media, cultural industries and trade law, and telecommunications regulation.
Publications: Author of numerous articles and publications, including 'Canadian Broadcasting Regulatory Handbook', the standard reference on CRTC regulations and policies, now in its fifth edition.
Career: Special Counsel to the CRTC (1974-78). Member of the Canadian delegation to the G7 Ministerial Conference on the Information Society in Brussels, 1995. Admitted to the Ontario bar in 1969.

HALPERIN, Stephen H.
Goodmans LLP, Toronto +1 416 597 4115
shalperin@GoodmansLaw.com
Recommended in Corporate/M&A
Specialisation: Partner and member of the executive committee of *Goodmans*, and chairs the corporate/securities practice group. Has practised transactional corporate and securities law, focusing primarily on domestic and international corporate finance and M&A, both negotiated and unsolicited, involving both publicly and privately-held entities for more than 20 years. Has represented numerous Canadian and multi-national corporations, financial institutions, and investment banks in connection with their M&A and other corporate activities and has been involved in many of the high profile Canadian transactions in recent years.
Prof. Memberships: Bars of the Canadian provinces of Ontario, Quebec, and Alberta.
Career: An adjunct professor of law at the University of Toronto from 1993-99, teaching advanced corporate law and securities regulation. Serves on the editorial board of Corporate Financing Quarterly, and the CCH Corporate Law Advisory Committee. A past member of the Securities Advisory Committee of the Ontario Securities Commission. Has written and spoken extensively on corporate securities law matters for various publications, seminar organisations, and professional associations in Canada, the US, and abroad. Holds degrees in both civil and common law from McGill University. Serves on Faculty Advisory Board of McGill Law School, and as a director of several public corporations and community organisations.

HARRIS, Neil
Goodmans LLP, Toronto +1 416 597 4117
nharris@GoodmansLaw.com
Recommended in Tax
Specialisation: Senior Tax Partner. Specialises in Canadian and International tax matters with particular emphasis on cross-border mergers and acquisitions and taxation aspects of corporate finance, transfer pricing and e-commerce. Has represented domestic and foreign corporations before Canada Customs and Revenue Agency, federal and provincial Departments of Finance and the Courts.
Career: Has written and lectured extensively on domestic and international taxation issues for the International Fiscal Association, the Canadian Tax Foundation and other Canadian and International tax organisations and has also lectured at the Faculty of Law, University of Western Ontario on Advanced Tax Planning. Admitted to the Ontario Bar in 1972.

HAUSMAN, James
Blake, Cassels & Graydon LLP, Toronto
+1 416 863 2492
james.hausman@blakes.com
Recommended in Tax
Specialisation: Partner in the tax group dealing with all aspects of taxation with special emphasis on international tax matters and in the planning and implementation of major international mergers and reorganisations.
Prof. Memberships: Law Society of Upper Canada, Canadian Bar Association, International Bar Association, International Fiscal Association, Canadian Tax Foundation.
Career: Called to the Bar of Ontario in 1963. Lecturer at the Faculty of Law of the University of Toronto on International Tax Planning. Member of the Permanent Scientific Committee of the International Fiscal Association.
Personal: Born 24 March 1937 in Toronto, Canada. Attended University of Toronto (BA, 1958; LLB, 1961).

HIRST, Tom
Macleod Dixon LLP, Calgary +1 403 267 8211
hirstt@macleoddixon.com
Recommended in Energy & Natural Resources
Specialisation: Oil and gas, banking, project financing and commercial matters. Has extensive experience in petro-chemical and mining joint ventures. In the oil and gas area, represents numerous junior and large oil companies in respect of acquisitions and dispositions of property, property exchanges, the creation of joint ventures and strategic alliances, and structuring projects for exploration and development of reserves. Has extensive experience in international energy-related transactions, including projects located in Australia, New Zealand, Great Britain, Indonesia, Papua-New Guinea, the Netherlands, and more recently in the Sudan and Norway.

Prof. Memberships: Law Society of Alberta and the Calgary Bar Association.
Career: Received BA in economics from the University of Calgary in 1966, bachelor of laws degree from the University of Alberta in 1968 and was admitted to the Alberta Bar in 1969. Has been a partner with *Macleod Dixon* since 1976 and is a senior partner in its corporate business unit. Appointed as Queen's Counsel in 1996. Has also spent two years in the capacity of vice president and general counsel of a small oil company with extensive North American and international holdings.
Personal: Born October 28, 1945. Married with two children. Leisure interests include flyfishing and hunting.

HOLGATE, David
Stikeman Elliott, Montréal +1 514 397 3000
Recommended in Energy & Natural Resources

HOLSTEN, R. Jay
Torys, Toronto +1 416 865 7523
jholsten@torys.com
Recommended in Competition/Anti-trust
Specialisation: Chair of the Anti-trust and Competition Law Group at *Torys.* A partner in the firm's corporate department with significant experience in mergers and acquisitions. Practice focuses on merger review and the regulatory aspects of other business arrangements. Also regularly advises clients on the structuring of joint ventures, reviewable trade practices, marketing and distribution arrangements, and regulatory compliance issues. Advised The Toronto Dominion Bank on its proposed 1998 merger with Canadian Imperial Bank of Commerce and its 1999 acquisition of Canada Trust. Canadian anti-trust counsel to JDS Uniphase Corporation, The Thomson Corporation, CanWest, Global Communications, Brascan Corporation and Abbott Laboratories.
Prof. Memberships: Member of the Merger Committee of the Competition Law Section of the Canadian Bar Association and the American Bar Association, Anti-trust section. Has written a number of papers discussing recent developments in Canadian competition law.
Career: Admitted to the Ontario Bar, 1985. Joined *Torys* in 1985 becoming a partner in 1992.
Personal: Born Toronto December 9, 1957. Attended Carleton University 1976-79 (BA, Political Science). Attended University of Ottawa 1980-83 (LLB). Gold Medallist. Leisure interests include skiing/snowboarding and rock climbing. Lives in Toronto.

HORNER, Clay
Osler, Hoskin & Harcourt LLP, Toronto
+1 416 862 6590
chorner@osler.com
Recommended in Corporate/M&A
Specialisation: Business law partner and Chair of the Business Law Department at *Osler, Hoskin & Harcourt LLP.* Recent transaction involvements include acting for BCE Inc. in connection with the formation of a new multimedia company (including CTV Inc., Sympatico-Lycos Inc. and The Globe & Mail) with The Thomson Corporation and The Woodbridge Company Limited, for the Seagram Company Limited in connection with its proposed business combination with Vivendi and Canal Plus (largest merger transaction involving a Canadian company in Canadian history), for Imasco Limited in connection with the acquisition of the public shareholders' interest by British American Tobacco and the related sales of Canada Trust and Shoppers Drug Mart (largest cash transaction in Canadian history), acting for Newbridge Networks Corporation in connection with its acquisition by Alcatel S.A., for CTV Inc. in connection with its acquisition of a controlling interest in Netstar Communications (TSN), and for Placer Dome Inc. in connection with its South African Joint Venture with Western Areas Limited and its acquisition of Getchell Gold Corporation.
Career: Established and practised in the New York office of *Osler, Hoskin & Harcourt* from 1990 to 1995.
Personal: BA from Queen's University, LLB from the University of Toronto and an LLM from Harvard Law School.

HOUSTON, Donald B.
Kelly Affleck Greene, Toronto
+1 416 360 2800
DHouston@kag.net
Recommended in Competition/Anti-trust
Specialisation: Competition Law and Commercial Litigation. Counsel to the Competition Bureau (Canada) 1991-1994. Has since acted in numerous competition matters, including criminal prosecutions, civil cases before the Competition Tribunal, and private actions in the Courts. Advises clients on mergers and competition aspects of business transactions. Notable competition cases include Canada v. Air Canada (1993), Canada v. Southam Inc. (1995), Canada v. D & B Companies of Canada Ltd. (1996), Canada v. Law Society of Upper Canada (1996), Boehringer Ingleheim v. Bristol Myers (1998). Publications include 'Private Remedies For Anti-Competitive Conduct', CBA 1998, with R. Bell et al, 'The Trial Of An Action' (2nd), 1998, with the late Mr. Justice John Sopinka. Further information available at www.kag.net.
Prof. Memberships: Canadian Bar Association; American Bar Association; Advocates' Society, Chair of CBA 2000 Competition Law Conference.
Career: Called to the Ontario Bar in 1981; Associate *Stikeman Elliott,* 1981-1986; Partner *Stikeman Elliott,* 1986-1991 and 1994-1998; counsel to Competition Bureau (Canada), 1991-1994; Partner *Kelly Affleck Greene,* 1998 – present.
Personal: Born 20 March 1955. Attended University of Manitoba, BA (1975), LLB (1979). Married with four children. Lives in Toronto, Canada.

HUGHES, Randal T.
Fraser Milner Casgrain, Toronto +1 416 863 4446
randy.hughes@fmc-law.com
Recommended in Competition/Anti-trust
Specialisation: National Chair of the Competition Law Practice Group specialising in all aspects of competition law and other regulatory matters. Successfully handled the competition law aspects of numerous mergers and acquisitions. Acted for the Commissioner of Competition and for private sector clients in leading merger cases and other proceedings before the Competition Tribunal. Represents clients in international conspiracy investigations and prosecutions involving competition authorities in Canada, the United States and Europe. Acts for clients in substantial civil actions, including class actions, in competition law matters. Senior Editor of the Canadian Competition Record.
Prof. Memberships: Competition Law Section - Canadian Bar Association; Antitrust Section/Committee - ABA and IBA.
Career: Year of call to the Bar: 1982
Personal: University of Toronto, LLB, 1980; University of Toronto, B. Comm., 1977.

C

HUNTER, Lawson
Stikeman Elliott, Toronto +1 416 869 5500
Recommended in Competition/Anti-trust

INTVEN, Hank
McCarthy Tétrault, Toronto, Ontario
+1 416 601 7878
hintven@mccarthy.ca
Recommended in Communications
Specialisation: Partner in the Toronto Business Law Section. Practice focuses on the telecommunications industry and related fields. Advises companies in the telecommunications sector, investors, regulators, governments, financial institutions, and other clients with an interest in telecommunications. Has worked on telecom projects in more than 20 countries in North, Central and South America, Europe, the Middle East, Africa, South and East Asia. These projects include the establishment of new telecom businesses, privatisations, joint ventures, licensing and other forms of concession agreements.
Prof. Memberships: Called to the Ontario bar in 1976.
Career: Former Executive Director of Telecommunications at the CRTC.

JACKSON, J. David A.
Blake, Cassels & Graydon LLP, Toronto
+1 416 863 2636
david.jackson@blakes.com
Recommended in Corporate/M&A
Specialisation: Practises primarily in the area of securities law, advising public corporations and investment dealers. Practice includes private and public financings, take-over bids, issuer bids, and other merger, acquisition and disposition transactions, and has advised in respect of many major Canadian and international transactions. Led the *Blake* team in the 1997 acquisition of London Insurance Group Inc. by Great-West Lifeco Inc., the 1999 combination of the four Atlantic province telephone companies to form Aliant Inc. and the 2000 acquisition of Rio Algom Limited by Billiton plc. Involved in the preparation and review of the draft bills leading up to the current Ontario Securities Act. Participated as one of three practitioners who reviewed the take-over bid provisions of the Ontario Securities Act and provided recommendations to the Ontario Securities Commission which led to the current uniform Canadian take-over bid code. Has taught at the Ontario Bar Admission Course and lec-

tured at Osgoode Hall Law School on matters of securities and corporate law. Has participated in numerous panels on Ontario, Quebec, Alberta, and British Columbia securities legislation and the Canada Business Corporations Act.
Prof. Memberships: Law Society of Upper Canada and Canadian Bar Association; Ontario Bar.
Career: Associate *Blake Cassels & Graydon*, Toronto, Ontario, March 1974 to February 1980; Partner from February 1980-present. Chair, Partnership Committee, 1995-present, Executive Committee, 1997-present, Co-chair, Securities Law Practice Group, *Blake Cassels & Graydon*.
Personal: Born 29 January 1947 in Chatham, Ontario. Educated, University of Windsor, B.Comm. 1969; Osgoode Hall Law School LLB, 1972. Leisure interests include golf, fishing and reading.

JASON, John
Osler, Hoskin & Harcourt LLP, Toronto
+1 416 862 4702
jjason@osler.com
Recommended in Banking & Finance
Specialisation: Partner in the Financial Services Group, specialising in matters relating to the regulation of financial institutions. Has recently acted for two insurance companies as regulatory counsel in respect of their demutualisations.
Career: Called to the Ontario Bar in 1988. Chief of Policy Development and Implementation (1990-1992) for the Legislative Reform Task Force of the Department of Finance, responsible for the general revision of the federal financial institutions legislation that came into force in June 1992. Currently acting for the Department in respect of the implementation of the June 1999 Policy Paper released by the Minister of Finance, announcing reforms for Canada's financial sector. Frequent speaker on topics relating to the regulation of financial institutions. Also a steering committee member for the Forum on the Insurance Industry, an annual industry and government think tank on issues relating to the insurance industry.
Personal: LLB from Osgoode Hall Law School of York University, MBA from Ohio University and a Bachelor of Commerce degree from McGill University.

JEWETT, Peter E. S.
Torys, Toronto +1 416 865 7364
pjewett@torys.com
Recommended in Corporate/M&A
Specialisation: Practice consists of a wide range of corporate and securities law matters including many major Canadian and international corporate finance and merger and acquisition transactions. Has participated in many of the largest acquisitions and divestitures in Canada in recent years and many of the largest public privatisations by the federal and provincial governments. Recent transactions include Fishery Products International in its defence against a hostile takeover bid by Neos, CanWest Global in its acquisition of WIC, National Bank of Canada's merger with First Marathon and Uniphase's merger with JDS Fitel.
Career: Qualified in 1974. Has been a member of a number of Ontario Securities Commission and Canadian Bar Association committees. Has participated in and written papers for a number of conferences on securities law, corporate law and legal opinions. Has also taught securities regulation at the University of Toronto's Faculty of Law.
Personal: Born 12 August 1951. Attended Queen's University (BA, 1969); University of Toronto (LLB, 1972 Gold Medallist).

JOHNSON, Clifford D.
McCarthy Tétrault, Calgary
+1 403 260 3544
cjohnson@mccarthy.ca
Recommended in Energy & Natural Resources
Specialisation: Senior partner and head of the Calgary Energy, Resources and Environment Section. Energy, oil and gas (including offshore), environment and corporate/commercial (including directors and officers) practice includes contract negotiations, joint ventures, asset and share, gas, mineral leasing and other related transactions. Environmental practice includes commercial matters, environmental compliance and contaminated sites. Frequent speaker and writer.
Prof. Memberships: Called to the Alberta Bar in 1982.
Career: President and a director of the Canadian Petroleum Law Foundation. Firm representative to several industry associations.

JOHNSTON, Chris
Johnston & Buchan, Ottawa +1 613 236 3882
Recommended in Communications

KANE, Gregory T.
Stikeman Elliott, Ottawa +1 613 566 0524
Recommended in Communications

KAZANJIAN, John
Osler, Hoskin & Harcourt LLP, Toronto
+1 416 862 6763
jkazanjian@osler.com
Recommended in Corporate/M&A
Specialisation: Senior partner in the Business Law Department of *Osler, Hoskin & Harcourt LLP* providing corporate commercial, competition and related strategic advice in connection with mergers and acquisitions, joint ventures and strategic alliances, outsourcing agreements and a range of cross-border and international business transactions. Also provides ongoing corporate governance advice and is involved in representing private sector interests on various government relations and corporate and competition law reform initiatives.
Prof. Memberships: American Bar Association, member of Negotiated Acquisitions Task Force, Canadian Bar Association, past Chairman of the Mergers Committee, Competition Law Section, Coalition for Canada Business Corporations Act Reform - Counsel, Public Policy Forum - Counsel.
Publications: Regularly publishes articles and gives speeches on a range of business law topics, including mergers and acquisitions, corporate governance, joint ventures, outsourcing agreements and competition law. Contributing editor to several publications and is a member of the Queen's Business Law Symposium Permanent Advisory Board.
Personal: Born 8 April 1948. Osgoode Hall Law School, LLB (1973); Harvard Law School, LLM (1975). Lives in Toronto, Canada.

KEE, David
Blake, Cassels & Graydon LLP, Toronto
+1 416 863 2514
Recommended in Banking & Finance
Specialisation: Member of the Financial Services Group of *Blake Cassels & Graydon* in Toronto. Has substantial experience in acting for lendors and investors, both Canadian and American, in financial transactions, including large projects, and in debt restructuring and other insolvency matters. Has for many years acted in a senior capacity for Canadian Imperial Bank of Commerce.
Prof. Memberships: Member of the Law Society of Upper Canada and the Canadian Bar Association.
Career: B. Com – Queen's University, 1963; LLB – University of Toronto, 1966; qualified in 1968; LLM – Osgoode Hall Law School, 1978.

KEEFE, Blair
Torys, Toronto +1 416 865 8164
bkeefe@torys.com
Recommended in Banking & Finance
Specialisation: Head of the firm's Financial Institutions Group. Practice focuses on corporate and regulatory issues relating to financial institutions, including mergers and acquisitions, and corporate finance. While on secondment to the Canadian Bankers' Association, testified before Parliamentary committees, drafted amendments to the legislation and advised the Canadian Bankers' Association on the 1991 revisions to the legislation affecting federal financial institutions. Currently providing advice to the Canadian life insurance industry on the upcoming reform to the federal financial institution legislation.
Prof. Memberships: Co-Chair Canadian Bar Association's Federal Financial Legislative Reform Committee.
Publications: Co-editor of Carswell's Consolidated *Bank Act* and Consolidated *Trust and Loan Companies Act*. Written several papers and made numerous presentations on the laws affecting financial institutions.
Personal: Dalhousie University (MBA/LLB); Osgoode Hall Law School (LLM).

KEENLEYSIDE, Anthony H.A.
McCarthy Tétrault, Ottawa
+1 613 238 2112
akeenley@mccarthy.ca
Recommended in Communications
Specialisation: Partner in the Ottawa Business Law Section. Practice focuses on telecommunications, radiocommunication, broadcasting and copyright-related areas, before the CRTC, Industry Canada and the Copyright Board.
Prof. Memberships: Member of the Federal Communications Bar Association. Called to the Ontario bar in 1975.
Publications: Co-edited the '2000 Canadian Broadcasting Regulatory Handbook' (fifth edition).
Career: Legal Counsel to the Canadian Radio-television and Telecommunications Commission (CRTC), 1976 - 1978. Was outside regulatory counsel to Canada's domestic satellite company for 15 years.

KELLOUGH, Howard J.
Fraser Milner Casgrain, Vancouver
+1 604 443 7102
howard.kellough@fmc-law.com
Recommended in Tax
Specialisation: Practises tax law and advises local, national and international clients on corporate and related tax matters; deals with Revenue authorities regarding reassessments and litigation.
Prof. Memberships: British Columbia Law Society; Canadian Bar Association; B.C. Institute of Chartered Accountants; Quebec Order of CAs; Canadian Institute of Chartered Accountants.
Publications: Co-Author, Kellough & McQuillan, 'The Taxation of Private Corporations and Their Shareholders' (CTF - third ed.); numerous articles.
Career: Year of call to the Bar: 1967 (Sask.), 1972 (B.C.) partner *Ladner Downs*; Founding Partner *Mawhinney & Kellough* (1980-1990); merged with *Fraser & Beatty* 1990, now *Fraser Milner Casgrain.*
Personal: University of Denver (1963); University of Saskatchewan, LLB; McGill University (CA designation).

KELLY, Mary
Ogilvy Renault, Toronto +1 416 216 4010
mkelly@ogilvyrenault.com
Recommended in Banking & Finance
Specialisation: Partner in the Business Law Group. Main area of expertise is cross-border financings, regulatory work, restructurings and private mergers and acquisitions. Has acted for major Canadian financial institutions with respect to loans to the telecom industry, the mining industry and the general manufacturing industry. Has provided regulatory advice on the proposed merger of two Canadian banks. Has acted as legal advisor on restructurings in the commercial real estate/condominium business and the environmental waste management business. Has spoken at various conferences and has taught banking law at Queen's University, Canada.
Prof. Memberships: Law Society of Upper Canada, Canadian Bar Association.
Career: Graduated University of Toronto Law School, 1986. Called to the Bar, 1988. Practiced at *Stikeman Elliott* (Toronto) until 1999 (as associate and partner). Joined *Ogilvy Renault* (Toronto), 1999.
Personal: Born 1960. Graduated Queen's University with Bachelor of Commerce, 1983. Married with 3 children. Leisure interests include travelling and hiking.

KENNISH, Tim
Osler, Hoskin & Harcourt LLP, Toronto
+1 416 862 6432
tkennish@osler.com
Recommended in Competition/Anti-trust
Specialisation: Main practice emphasis is in the areas of competition law and foreign investment. Principal activities in the area of mergers and competition law counselling generally. Represents client dealings with the Competition Bureau.
Prof. Memberships: Member of the Law Society of Upper Canada (Ontario). Member of the American Bar Association (Anti-Trust Law section). Vice-Chairman (Policy) of the National Competition Law Committee of the Canadian Bar Association.
Career: Called to the Bar in 1966 in the Province of Ontario. Joined *Osler, Hoskin & Harcourt LLP* (Toronto) in 1966. Became a partner in 1972. Chairman of the firm since January 1999, and Chairman of its Competition and Trade Law Practice Group. Prior to 1999 was Co-Managing Partner of the firm. Frequent writer and speaker on competition law subjects.
Personal: Born March 26, 1939. Graduate of Harvard College (1961) and Osgoode Hall Law School (1964). Resides in Toronto, Ontario with his wife, dog, and cats. Has four children and two grandchildren.

KENT, Andrew J. F.
McMillan Binch, Toronto, Ontario
+1 416 865 7160
Recommended in Banking & Finance

KEOUGH, Loyola
Bennett Jones LLP, Calgary +1 403 298 3429
keoughl@bennettjones.ca
Recommended in Energy & Natural Resources
Specialisation: Partner in the regulatory/environmental department. Acts primarily for project developers, pipelines, industry associations, utility companies, gas buyers, producers and banks, with particular experience in oil, gas and electricity proceedings on tolls, facilities, including environmental implications, and exports. Practises before the National Energy Board and Alberta Energy and Utilities Board, and has participated in proceedings before the British Columbia Utilities Commission and the public utilities boards of the Yukon and Northwest Territories. Former counsel to the National Energy Board and spent several years with the Federal Department of Energy, Mines and Resources. Frequent speaker and presenter on the subject of procedures, approvals and necessary applications involved in exporting gas to the U.S. and on recent legislative and regulatory developments in the oil, gas and electricity fields, including competition in the provision of pipeline transportation services, deregulation of electricity and performance based regulation.
Prof. Memberships: Law Society of Alberta, Law Society of Upper Canada, Law Society of the Northwest Territories and the Calgary Bar Association.
Publications: Co-author of chapter on the NEB for 'Energy Law and Transaction', by Matthew Bender.
Career: Called to the Ontario Bar in 1982, the Alberta Bar in 1991 and the Northwest Territories Bar in 1994.
Personal: Born 20 October 1955. Attended Memorial University of Newfoundland (B.Comm., 1977) and University of Ottawa (LLB, 1980).

KOCH, Michael Steven
Goodmans LLP, Toronto +1 416 597 5156
mkoch@GoodmansLaw.com
Recommended in Communications
Specialisation: Counsel in the Broadcasting Telecommunications and New Media Group. Practice focused on regulatory, strategic and intellectual property advice regarding the communications industries. Served on secondment to the CRTC as Legal Counsel in 1993/94. Since returning to private practice has played a role in each of the major proceedings to establish the competitive framework for the Canadian telecommunications industry. Has also drawn on expertise in the communications and copyright fields to provide strategic, industry specific advice to communications companies and Internet and Application service providers, as well as to investors and other clients interacting with the communications and Internet industries. Recently advised British telecom regarding its investment, together with AT&T, in Canadian wireline and wireless businesses and structured a joint venture between a competitive local exchange carrier and leading U.S. DSI provider. Has written and spoken on the subject of communications regulation both nationally and internationally, with a particular emphasis on issues affecting the Internet.
Prof. Memberships: Law Society of Upper Canada; Canadian Bar Association; International Bar Association; International Telecommunications Society.
Career: Called to the Bar in 1988. Engaged in private practice at another major Canadian law firm since 1986. Seconded to the Canadian Radio-television and Telecommunications Commission in 1993-94. Joined *Goodmans* in 1999.
Personal: Born 17 May 1961. Attended University of Western Ontario and University of Toronto Faculty of Law 1980-86 (LLB). Leisure interests include skiing, cycling, hiking and canoeing.

LALLY, Michelle
Osler, Hoskin & Harcourt LLP, Toronto
+1 416 362 2111
Recommended in Competition/Anti-trust

LAMBERT, Martin A.
Bennett Jones LLP, Calgary +1 403 298 3100
lambertm@bennettjones.ca
Recommended in Corporate/M&A
Specialisation: Partner in the corporate/commercial department and member of mergers and acquisitions group. Practises principally in area of mergers and acquisitions. Acted as a lead counsel in many 'Canadian firsts': the first major 'permitted bid' transaction (Anderson Exploration's acquisition of Home Oil), the first (and only) triggering of a shareholder rights plan (Alberta and Manitoba Wheat Pool's bid for United Grain Growers), the first (and only) bid for a public company prior to the commencement date of its listing (Precision Drilling's successful bid for Kenting Energy Services), the first (and only) successful 'just say no' defence in the retail sector (defending Dylex's hostile bid for Mark's Work Warehouse) and the then largest cross-border oil and gas stock merger ever (Pioneer's acquisition of Chauvco). Most recently, acted for Burlington Resources in its US$3.7 billion acquisition of Poco Petroleums and acting for Canadian Airlines in the restructuring of the Canadian airline industry. Served as CEO of firm 1996-1999.
Prof. Memberships: Law Society of Alberta; Canadian Bar Association.
Career: Called to the Alberta Bar in 1980. Joined *Bennett Jones* in 1979, became a partner in 1987.
Personal: Born 31 October 1955. Attended the University of Calgary (mathematics and philosophy, 1976-78) and the University of Alberta (LLB, 1979).

C

C

LAMPE, Jonathan
Goodmans LLP, Toronto +1 416 597 4128
jlampe@GoodmansLaw.com
Recommended in Corporate/M&A
Specialisation: Partner. Practice focuses on corporate and securities law, with an emphasis on M&A and structured financings, in both domestic and cross-border transactions and corporate governance. Former General Counsel to the Ontario Securities Commission. Engaged frequently as special counsel in connection with M&A, and has provided expert evidence in connection with related court proceedings. Has represented the staff of the Commission and market participants in regulatory proceedings before the Commission as General Counsel and in private practice.
Career: Chair of the Securities Advisory Committee, which is comprised of senior securities practitioners and provides policy advice to the Ontario Securities Commission on an ongoing basis. In addition to lecturing extensively on topics including emerging issues in corporate governance and alternative acquisition and financing structures, has taught Advanced Corporate Law and Securities Regulation at University of Toronto Law School. Identified regularly in publications including Chambers Global, Euromoney and Law Business Research as a leading practitioner in corporate, capital markets, corporate finance and M&A.

LASTMAN, Dale H.
Goodmans LLP, Toronto +1 416 597 4129
dlastman@GoodmansLaw.com
Recommended in Corporate/M&A
Specialisation: Co-Chair of *Goodmans* practising corporate, commercial, and securities law since 1984. Counsel in connection with public offerings, M&A, and business restructurings. Has acted in a number of high profile mergers and acquisitions, including the highly contested take-over bids of John Labatt Ltd, Ault Foods Ltd, and Sun Media Corporation.
Career: On the Advisory Board of XDL and Intervest Capital Corporation. Director of MLG Hodings Limited, Maple Leaf Sports & Entertainment Ltd., Patriot Equities Group, Roots Canada Ltd., The Second Cup Ltd., Sun Media Corporation, Trimark Trust Company and Young Peoples Theatre. A recipient, and now director, of Canada's Top 40 Under 40. Member of the Executive Committee and director of the Toronto 2008 Olympic Bid Corporation. Director and member of the Board of Governors of Mount Sinai Hospital. Chairman of the Board of York University Alumni Association and member of the Board of Governors of York University. Director of the Toronto Community Foundation, Bayerest Centre for Geriatric Care, member of the Patrons Council of the Metropolitan Toronto Association for Community Living and member of the Toronto Zoo Campaign Advisory Cabinet. Lecturer in securities law at Osgoode Hall Law School.

LEVIN, Jonathan A.
Fasken Martineau DuMoulin LLP, Toronto
+1 416 366 8381
jlevin@tor.fasken.com
Recommended in Banking & Finance, Corporate/M&A
Specialisation: Partner in Business Law and Corporate Financings. Practice also includes mergers and acquisitions, and securities regulation. Chairman of the Finance Committee. Recent significant matters. Lenders' counsel, Cdn.$7.7 billion Telus Corporation syndicated credit facilities; Canadian counsel to Chapter 11 Creditors' Committee of The Loewen Group Inc. in connection with its cross-border insolvency; Canadian counsel to the largest creditor group of Livent Inc. in connection with its cross border insolvency; counsel to Strategic Value Corporation, a Cdn.$3.5 billion mutual fund company in connection with regulatory proceedings, the renegotiation of overdue credit facilities and a public takeover of the company; counsel to the founder and major shareholder of Newbridge Networks in connection with negotiating takeover and lock-up terms on the US$8 billion acquisition of that company by Alcatel; and counsel to the underwriters on the demutualization of Canada Life and its initial public offering.
Prof. Memberships: Canadian Bar Association - Ontario; Corporate Opinions Committee.
Publications: Author of numerous articles including 'Security Offerings - How to Manage Your Risk', 'Making the Offer', 'Survey of Cross Border Merger and Acquisition Issues', 'Multi-Bank Financings', 'Debt Financing and related Matters' and 'Financial Assistance'.
Career: Admitted to the Ontario Bar in 1975. Joined *Fasken & Calvin* (now *Fasken Martineau DuMoulin* LLP) in 1975, becoming a Partner in 1981. Member of the Executive, Business Law Section, Canadian Bar Association - Ontario (1978-1988). Chairman, Business Law Section, Canadian Bar Association - Ontario (1986-1988). Member, Canadian Bar Association Advisory Committee for the Ontario Business Corporation Act (1978 to date). Vice-Chairman, International Sales Committee, International Bar Association (1988-1990). Member, Canadian Bar Association - Ontario Subcommittee on Legal Opinions (1991 to date). Member of the Specialist Advisory Board, Queen's Business Law Symposium (1995 and 1996). Frequent panelist and lecturer before various programs and conferences. Recipient, Dedicated Service Award, Canadian Bar Association.
Personal: Graduated with a Bachelor of Arts degree in 1970, and obtained a law degree in 1973, both from the University of Toronto.

LISSON, James
Osler, Hoskin & Harcourt LLP, Toronto
+1 416 862 7682
jlisson@osler.com
Recommended in Banking & Finance
Specialisation: Partner in the Business Law Department of *Osler, Hoskin & Harcourt LLP.* Practice emphasis is on financial institutions. Practises in the areas of mergers and acquisitions, corporate finance, regulation and banking. Assists various clients with respect to acquisitions, business alliances and restructurings, and the development and offering of innovative and traditional services and products.
Prof. Memberships: Law Society of Upper Canada, Canadian Bar Association, American Bar Association.
Career: Called to Ontario Bar in 1978 when joined *Osler, Hoskin & Harcourt* and has been a partner since 1983. During 1985-1986 served on secondment as Special Counsel for financial institution matters to the Federal Department of Finance. Co-Chairman CBA/Canadian Institute of Chartered Accountants Committee concerning Audit Inquiries (1993-1997). Former Chairman of The Cadillac Fairview Corporation Limited during 1993-1994 and a director from 1987-94. Canadian Nominee to the Financial Services Dispute Resolution Panel under the North American Free Trade Act.
Personal: Graduate of McGill University (B.Comm) (Hon.Econ & Acc. '72), Dalhousie University (LLB '75) and Yale University (LLM '76). Married with two children. Director of the Centre for Addiction and Mental Health Foundation.

LOVELAND, Norman
Osler, Hoskin & Harcourt LLP, Toronto
+1 416 862 6463
nloveland@osler.com
Recommended in Tax
Specialisation: Co-Chair and Senior Partner in the Taxation Department of *Osler, Hoskin & Harcourt LLP.* Practice is restricted to taxation with a particular emphasis on mergers and acquisitions, reorganisations, financing, tax audits and dispute resolution. Has extensive experience in advising in a wide variety of major business transactions.
Prof. Memberships: Canadian Bar Association (former Chair of the National Taxation Section and of the Ontario Taxation Section), Canadian Tax Foundation (former Governor), former Co-Chair of the Canadian Bar Association/Canadian Institute of Chartered Accountants Joint Committee on Taxation, Association of Professional Engineers of Ontario, International Fiscal Association.
Career: Called to the Ontario Bar in 1974.
Personal: Graduate of University of Toronto Law School and Queens University (Civil Engineering). Married with two children.

LOWE, John
Bennett Jones LLP, Calgary +1 403 298 3100
lowej@bennettjones.ca
Recommended in Communications
Specialisation: Partner in the regulatory/environment department. Has appeared before the Federal Court of Canada and all court levels in Alberta, as well as the Canadian Radio-television and Telecommunications Commission (CRTC), the National Energy Board and the Alberta Energy and Utilities Board. Practice emphasises telecommunications proceedings before the CRTC, including economic regulation, ownership and control and competition issues and, with Industry Canada, spectrum licensing matters. Has taken part in various telecommunications conferences.

Prof. Memberships: Calgary Bar Association, Law Society of Alberta and the Canadian Bar Association.
Publications: Co-authored a chapter on 'Canadian Communications Law' in the recently published book 'International Telecommunications Law', Centre for International Legal Studies.
Career: Joined *Bennett Jones* in 1986. Called to the Alberta Bar in 1987.
Personal: Born 3 October, 1961. Attended the University of Alberta (BA, 1983) and Dalhousie University (LLB, 1986).

MARTIS, Xeno C.
Fasken Martineau DuMoulin LLP, Montréal
+1 514 397 7400
xmartis@mtl.fasken.com
Recommended in Banking & Finance
Specialisation: Specialises in the area of corporate financing. Chairman of the Banking Section of the Quebec office of *Fasken Martineau DuMoulin* LLP. Has lead teams of lawyers acting on behalf of lending syndicates and investors in the areas of project financing, public and private takeovers, asset acquisitions, structured leverage and synthetic lease financings, debt restructuring and workouts. Is a frequent panelist and lecturer before various continuing legal education programs sponsored by McGill University (Meredith Memorial Lectures), Insight Professional Conferences, Canadian Institute and private clients. Through the World Bank, has advised a foreign government on its banking legislation and on legalisation providing for the creation of security interests on personal and real property.
Prof. Memberships: Member of the Bar of the Province of Quebec, Canadian Bar Association, International Bar Association and Associate Member of the American Bar Association.
Career: Graduated from McGill University with a Bachelor of Arts degree in 1971. Graduated from the Law Faculty of McGill University in 1975 under the National Program after having been granted the degrees of Bachelor of Civil Law and Bachelor of Common Law. In 1976, entered practice with the firm of *Martineau Walker*, one of the legacy firms of *Fasken Martineau DuMoulin*, and was admitted as a partner in 1983.

McDERMOTT, Robert K.
McMillan Binch, Toronto, Ontario
+1 416 865 7085
Recommended in Corporate/M&A

McLARTY, Allan Lawrence
Fraser Milner Casgrain, Calgary +1 403 268 7022
al.mclarty@fmc-law.com
Recommended in Energy & Natural Resources
Specialisation: Partner in Energy Law Group. Practice devoted principally to energy and resources law including project developments, conflict resolution and regulation. Has represented a broad range of industry clients with respect to oil and gas projects, including pipeline developments, electric generation, transmission and coal developments as well as with respect to related matters of environmental and rate regulation.
Prof. Memberships: L.S.A., Cal B.A. and C.B.A.
Career: Year of call to the Bar: 1972 (Alberta), practised with the former Alberta Energy Resources Conservation Board to 1980, when joined a predecessor firm. Was invited to join the partnership in 1982, and was appointed a Q.C. in Alberta in 2000. Currently a member of the FMC National Partnership Board, and is a director of the Private Sector Sponsors of the Canadian Energy Research Institute.

McREYNOLDS, Shawn
Davies Ward Phillips & Vineberg LLP, Toronto
+1 416 863 0900
smcreynolds@dwpv.com
Recommended in Corporate/M&A
Specialisation: Corporate finance, securities, mergers and acquisitions, with an emphasis on financings, including IPOs, mergers and acquisitions involving public companies.
Career: Articled at the firm. Qualified in 1984. Partner since 1986. Former Chairman, Securities Advisory Committee to Ontario Securities Commission, 1994-96. Lecturer in Securities Regulation, McGill University, 1999-present.
Personal: Born 22 July 1955. Attended Royal Roads, 1971-73, Royal Military College of Canada, 1973-75 (BA) and McGill University, 1979-82 (LLB).

MILLAR, Timothy G.
Fraser Milner Casgrain, Calgary +1 403 268 3048
tim.millar@fmc-law.com
Recommended in Energy & Natural Resources
Specialisation: Manager of the Commercial Practice Section, with significant experience in the commercial area of Resources Law. Practises principally in oil and gas, including matters involving acquisitions and dispositions of oil and gas assets, mergers and acquisitions, corporate share transactions, production related matters such as facilities and ownership and operating agreements, joint venture matters, co-generation projects and gas marketing issues. Represented major corporations and government in respect of oil and gas matters. Regularly acts as general counsel to a number of junior oil and gas companies. Involved in commercial arbitration matters.
Prof. Memberships: LSA, CalBA, Natural Resources Subsection of the CBA, and PJVA. Extensively involved in the Canadian Petroleum Law Foundation, having been President and on its Board of Directors for six years.
Career: Year of call to the Bar: 1971 (Alberta).
Personal: University of Alberta, BA, LLB, 1970.

MITCHELL, Warren J. A., Q.C.
Thorsteinssons, Toronto +1 416 864 0829
Recommended in Tax
Specialisation: Vancouver (+1 604 689 1261). Practises exclusively in the field of large case tax litigation. Has appeared often as counsel in the Tax Court of Canada, the Federal Court, and the Supreme Court of Canada, as well as in the Trial and Appellate Divisions of the British Columbia and Ontario courts. Former counsel for the Department of National Revenue. Admitted to the bar of Alberta in 1963, British Columbia in 1966 and Ontario in 1990.

MONAGHAN, K. A. Siobhan
Davies Ward Phillips & Vineberg LLP, Toronto
+1 416 863 5558
smonaghan@dwpv.com
Recommended in Tax
Specialisation: Income tax issues regarding commercial transactions, reorganisations, cross-border financings, acquisitions, divestitures, spin-offs and financial products.
Publications: Contributed to 'International Stock Options'; contributing editor to 'Corporate Structures and Groups'.
Career: Qualified in 1985 (Alberta); 1988 (Ontario). Partner since 1990.
Personal: B.Comm., (Memorial University), 1981; LLB, (Osgoode Hall), 1984; LLM, (Osgoode Hall), 1994.

MORGAN, Leslie
Blake, Cassels & Graydon LLP, Toronto
+1 416 863 2696
leslie.morgan@blakes.com
Recommended in Tax
Specialisation: Corporate taxation, focusing on corporation reorganisations. Has been Canadian tax counsel to Weyerhauser Company, over the last 12 months, in connection with their take over of MacMillan Bloedel Limited, to Vinvendi S.A. in connection with their proposed acquisition of Seagram Company Ltd., and to Billiton plc. in connection with their take over of Rio Algom.
Prof. Memberships: Canadian Bar Association. Canadian Tax Foundation.
Publications: Author of numerous articles for Federated Press and contributor to North American Free Trade & Investment Report.
Career: B.Arch., University of British Columbia - 1973; LLB, University of Toronto - 1977; Admitted to the Ontario Bar - 1979. Has practised in the area of income taxation since 1979 and is currently a partner at *Blake, Cassels & Graydon LLP*.
Personal: Married with one son. Practises law and lives in Toronto.

MURPHY, Peter Eugene
Fraser Milner Casgrain, Toronto +1 416 863 4503
peter.murphy@fmc-law.com
Recommended in Banking & Finance
Specialisation: Partner in the Financial Services Group of the Toronto office. Main area of work is banking and corporate debt financing including cross-border transactions, project finance, aircraft financing, equipment leasing, syndicated financings, LBO financings, structured financings, financial institutions regulatory advice to domestic and foreign clients, trade finance and letter of credit transactions, debt restructuring and loan workouts. Clients include Bank of Montreal, HSBC Bank Canada, Chase Manhattan Bank of Canada, Sanwa Bank Canada and Fleet Bank Canada.
Prof. Memberships: Law Society of Upper Canada, International Insolvency Association, Canadian Bar Association.
Publications: Lectured and written materials for various groups including the Institute of Canadian Bankers, the Canadian Bar Association and Insight Educational Services and from 1990 to 1998 was an

C

Adjunct Professor at University of Toronto Law School, teaching a course in Debt Financing and Debt Restructuring.
Career: Year of call to the Bar: 1980 (Ontario). Joined *Fraser Milner Casgrain* (then known as *Fraser & Beatty*) in 1981 becoming a partner in 1985.
Personal: Queen's University, BA (Honours), 1975; LLB, 1978.

MUSGROVE, James
Lang Michener, Toronto +1 416 307 4078
jmusgrove@langmichener.ca
Recommended in Competition/Anti-trust
Specialisation: Chair of *Lang Michener's* Competition and Marketing Law Group. Work includes merger review and challenges; distribution arrangements; advertising and marketing review and litigation. Recent work has included advising Nabisco respecting its merger with Philip Morris; advising MasterCard in relation to the merger of Toronto Dominion Bank and Canada Trust; and advising Rogers Communications in relation to the Vidéotron transaction.
Prof. Memberships: Chair of the Canadian Bar Association Competition Law section Marketing Committee, and has served in various capacities with the Competition Law section of the CBA. Member of various professional organizations.
Publications: Writes and speaks frequently with respect to competition and advertising law issues. Contributor to 'Canadian Advertising and Marketing Law' (Carswell), and a member of the Editorial Board of the Canadian Competition Record.
Personal: Born March 8, 1960. University of Toronto Faculty of Law (LLB 1984). Director and Secretary of the National Advertising Benevolent Society.

NIXON, Christopher
Stikeman Elliott, Calgary +1 403 266 9017
Recommended in Corporate/M&A

O'KEEFE, Michael J., Q.C.
Thorsteinssons, Toronto +1 416 864 0829
mjokeefe@thor.ca
Recommended in Tax
Specialisation: Vancouver (+1 604 689 1261). Taxation. Regularly advises Canadian multinationals and foreign multinationals with Canadian interests on Canadian and international tax matters, and works extensively in the area of cross-border transactions.
Prof. Memberships: Bars of British Columbia, Alberta and Ontario.
Career: Graduate of the University of British Columbia in Commerce (1964) and Law (1965); Masters of Law degree (1967) from the University of California, Berkeley. Partner of *Thorsteinssons* and practises in both its Vancouver and Toronto offices. Served as a Special Assistant to the Minister of Finance, Government of Canada; was a member of the Joint Taxation Committee of the Canadian Bar Association and the Canadian Institute of Chartered Accountants, and of the board of Governors of the Canadian Tax Foundation. Speaks and writes frequently on subjects relating to Canadian and international tax planning matters.

OLASKER, Patricia L.
Davies Ward Phillips & Vineberg LLP, Toronto
+1 416 863 5551
polasker@dwpv.com
Recommended in Corporate/M&A
Specialisation: Corporate and securities law, with an emphasis on cross-border and international corporate finance transactions, public company mergers and acquisitions and development of structured debt and equity products.
Prof. Memberships: Canadian Bar Association; International Bar Association.
Career: LLB, (Osgoode Hall), 1977. Qualified in 1979. Boalt Hall School of Law, University of California at Berkeley (LLM Program, 1981). Seconded to Ontario Securities Commission as legal advisor to Chairman (1984-85). Served on Advisory Committee to Senate Banking Committee. Chair, Securities Advisory Committee, Ontario Securities Commission (2000).
Personal: Born 17 September 1954. Married with one child. Avid skier and runner.

PARK, Jay
Macleod Dixon LLP, Calgary +1 403 267 8354
parkj@macleddixon.com
Recommended in Energy & Natural Resources
Prof. Memberships: Law Society of Alberta, the Canadian Bar Association and the International Bar Association. Petroleum Joint Venture Association (President, 1991), the Petroleum Accounts Society of Canada (Director, 1997-present), the Canadian Petroleum Law Foundation and the Association of International Petroleum Negotiators.
Career: Received undergraduate degree at the Faculty of Business at the University of Calgary, and LLB (1980) from Osgoode Hall Law School, York University. Has practised exclusively in the area of oil and gas law in Calgary since being called to the Alberta Bar in 1981. Practice includes oil and gas, property and pipeline acquisitions, joint ventures and marketing. International oil and gas experience includes work in Russia, Kazakhstan, Kuwait, Thailand, Nigeria and Sudan.

PENNYCOOK, Carol D.
Davies Ward Phillips & Vineberg LLP, Toronto
+1 416 863 5546
cpennycook@dwpv.com
Recommended in Banking & Finance
Specialisation: Corporate finance, securities and general corporate and commercial law. Financing transactions, including syndicated loan transactions, off-balance sheet and structured financings, infrastructure financings, corporate reorganisations and arrangements, public issues, mergers and acquisitions and derivative product transactions.
Prof. Memberships: Canadian Bar Association; Commodity Futures Advisory Board; Law Society of Upper Canada (Ontario); Law Society of Alberta.
Career: Qualified in 1981. Seconded 1984, Corporate Finance Branch of Ontario Securities Commission. Co-ordinator, Advanced Business Law Workshop, Osgoode Hall Law School. Chair, Commodity Futures Advisory Board.
Personal: Born 19 July 1952. BSc, (University of Calgary), 1972; LLB, (University of Calgary), 1980.

PETCH, Jack
Osler, Hoskin & Harcourt LLP, Toronto
+1 416 862 6581
jpetch@osler.com
Recommended in Corporate/M&A
Specialisation: Practises business law with an emphasis on mergers and acquisitions, securities law, fiduciary law and corporate governance matters, representing public and private clients in various business sectors including financial services, consumer products and real estate. Personal advisor to senior members of the business community and director/officer of public, private and pension fund corporations.
Prof. Memberships: Member of the Canadian Bar Association, Law Society of Upper Canada, American Bar Association and the Canadian Corporate Counsel Association.
Career: Called to the Ontario Bar in 1965. Appointed Q.C. in 1982. Senior partner and Vice-Chair of *Osler, Hoskin & Harcourt.* Former member of the firm's Executive Committee and Chair of its Business Law Department. Special lecturer on business law at the Universities of Toronto and Western Ontario, and at Queen's School of Business.
Personal: LLM from Osgoode Hall in 1980.

PORTNER, Christopher
Osler, Hoskin & Harcourt LLP, Toronto
+1 416 862 6412
Recommended in Corporate/M&A

QUIGLEY, Michael G.
McCarthy Tétrault, Toronto
+1 416 601 7920
mquigley@mccarthy.ca
Recommended in Tax
Specialisation: Partner in the Toronto Tax Section. Practises Canadian taxation law with emphasis on advising financial institutions, structuring domestic and international corporate finance, and capital markets and commercial transactions. Also focuses on tax disputes resolution and has appeared before federal and provincial courts in tax litigation matters. Founding partner of the firm's London, England office. Has written and spoken extensively on tax matters.
Prof. Memberships: Member of the IBA and the Canadian Tax Foundation. Called to the Ontario bar in 1980.

QUINN, John Joseph
Blake, Cassels & Graydon LLP, Toronto
+1 416 863 2648
jack.quinn@blakes.com
Recommended in Competition/Anti-trust
Specialisation: Partner practising Competition and International Trade Law. Works on a wide variety of competition and international trade law matters involving the obtaining of regulatory clearance for acquisition, mergers and joint venture transactions, the representation of participants in federal tribunals with jurisdiction over competition and trade law matters and general counselling and compliance planning. Due to the specialised nature of practice, has worked with clients in a wide variety of industries including food and beverage, transportation,

multi-media/publishing, financial services, energy and a wide variety of manufacturing, resource harvesting and processing industries. Has been closely involved in many of the major cases before the federal Compassion Tribunal since its creation in 1986.
Prof. Memberships: Competition Law Section of the Canadian Bar Association. Anti-trust and International Trade Law Sections of the American Bar Association.
Career: Began career as a professor teaching law full-time at Osgoode Hall Law School. Was also a visiting professor at Georgetown Law Centre in Washington D.C. in 1984 prior to joining *Blakes*. Taught courses in competition law, international trade law and investment law, business associations and corporate finance. Served as a consultant to federal government ministries and departments with respect to competition and international trade law matters. Past appointments include Canadian Director of the Canada-US Law Institute (1979-81) and a consultant on legal issues for Canada's Royal Commission on the Economic Union and Canada's Development Prospects (i.e. McDonald Commission (1982-85).
Personal: Born 11 October 1948. Degrees obtained include LLM, from Yale University 1976; JD, from Indiana University; 1974; BA, from Georgetown University, 1971. Academic Honours and Scholarships include: Yale Law School Graduate Fellowship, 1975-76; Indiana University Foundation Scholarship, 1971-74; Articles Editor, Indiana L.J., 1973-74; BA, with Honours, 1971.

RAIZENNE, Robert
Davies Ward Phillips & Vineberg LLP, Montréal
+1 514 841 6440
rraizenne@dwpv.com
Recommended in Tax
Specialisation: Tax partner.
Prof. Memberships: Canadian Tax Foundation; International Fiscal Association; Canadian Bar Association; Association de Planification Fiscale et Financière, Canadian Association of Law Teachers; American Bar Association.
Publications: Author of various publications and frequent speaker.
Career: Called to Quebec Bar, 1981 and Ontario Bar, 1997. Sessional lecturer in International Taxation, Faculty of Law, McGill University (1990-1997); Sessional lecturer in Tax Policy and Practice, Faculty of Law, McGill University (1998 to present).
Personal: Concordia University, Faculty of Arts, Montreal (BA, Double Honours – Political Science and Economics, 1976); University of Toronto, School of Graduate Studies, Department of Political Economy, Toronto (MA, 1977); McGill University, Faculty of Law, Montreal (B.C.L., 1980); Quebec Bar School, Montreal (Bar Admission Course, 1980 to 1981). Speaks English and French.

RAYMOND, Pierre A.
Stikeman Elliott, Montréal +1 514 397 3000
Recommended in Corporate/M&A

RENAUD, Madeleine
McCarthy Tétrault, Montréal
+1 514 397 4252
mrenaud@mccarthy.ca
Recommended in Competition/Anti-trust
Specialisation: Partner in the Montréal Litigation Section. Practises general litigation, including competition law, constitutional, administrative and human rights law.
Prof. Memberships: Called to the Québec bar in 1988; Ontario bar in 1989.
Publications: Published numerous papers on competition and administrative law. Co-authored the first French-language book on Canadian competition law (Carswell, 1999).
Career: Clerked with the Right Honourable Mr. Justice Antonio Lamer of the Supreme Court of Canada. Participated in major cases involving constitutional, administrative and competition law issues.

RICHARDS, Gabrielle M.R.
McCarthy Tétrault, Toronto
+1 416 601 7766
grichard@mccarthy.ca
Recommended in Tax
Specialisation: Partner in the Toronto Tax Section. Practice focuses on tax implications of corporate reorganisations and corporate finance including securitisation. Represents clients dealing with income tax audits and reassessments at all levels of courts, including the Supreme Court of Canada. Frequent speaker on taxation matters. Contributing editor for 'Canadian Current Tax' and for 'Corporate Structures and Groups'.
Prof. Memberships: Admitted to the Ontario bar in 1982.

RICHARDSON, Elinore
Stikeman Elliott, Montréal +1 514 397 3030
Recommended in Tax

RICHARDSON, Stephen R.
Torys, Toronto +1 416 865 7302
srichardson@torys.com
Recommended in Tax
Specialisation: Head of the firm's Tax Department. Specialises in the tax aspects of mergers and acquisitions, corporate finance and reorganisations with a significant emphasis on international transactions. Clients include EdperBrascan Corporation, Sun Life Assurance Company, Rogers Communications Inc., Moore Corporation, Petro-Canada, Westcoast Energy and Canadian Tire Corporation. U.S. clients (cross-border investment transactions) have included SBC Corporation, NIKE Inc., Homestake Mining Corp. and Boeing Corporation.
Prof. Memberships: Past governor of the Canadian Tax Foundation; member of Council of the International Fiscal Association - Canadian Branch.
Career: Former visiting professor at the Faculty of Law, University of Toronto and taught tax courses as an Adjunct Faculty member. Has conducted courses for the International Tax programme of Harvard University. Qualified 1975. Director of Tax Policy Legislation in the Department of Finance, Canada, 1983-1985, counsel to the House of Commons Standing Committee on Finance in 1994. Served as a member of the Technical Committee on Business Taxation (Mintz Committee) which presented its report to the Honourable Paul Martin, Minister of Finance, in 1998.
Personal: Born 4 November, 1946. Attended Wayne State University, 1968 (BA); University of Michigan, 1970 (MA); University of Toronto, 1973 (LLB).

RILEY, James A.
Ogilvy Renault, Toronto +1 416 216 3912
jriley@ogilvyrenault.com
Recommended in Banking & Finance, Corporate/M&A
Specialisation: Head of the Business Law Practice in Toronto. Main area of practice is corporate law - mergers, acquisitions, bank lending and insolvency. Has handled a wide variety of acquisitions and dispositions. Acted as lead partner advising in insolvency matters in connection with Olympia & York Developments, Central Guaranty Trust, Curragh Inc. and Cadillac-Fairview. Acted as counsel to Royal Bank of Canada on the acquisition of their interest in AOL Canada, their proposed acquisition of London Life, and proposed merger with Bank of Montreal. Has acted on behalf of various domestic and foreign lending syndicates in connection with credit facilities to, among others, Abitibi-Consolidated, Canadian Pacific and Quebecor. Has participated as chairperson, panellist and speaker at numerous conferences on the reform of financial institutions, banking regulation and practice and public and private derivative products.
Prof. Memberships: The Law Society of Upper Canada, Canadian Bar Association.
Career: Qualified in 1979.
Personal: Born 18 April 1952. Attended University of Toronto Law School, LLB (gold medallist), Harvard University LLM

ROBERTSON, Holly
McMillan Binch, Toronto
+1 416 865 7147
Recommended in Banking & Finance

ROBINSON, Kathryn
Goodmans LLP, Toronto +1 416 597 4143
krobinson@GoodmansLaw.com
Recommended in Communications
Specialisation: Senior partner of *Goodmans*, and chairs the firm's Broadcasting, Telecommunications & New Media Group. The Group represents a broad range of clients including small, medium and major radio and television broadcasters, speciality and pay programming services, cable companies, direct-to-home and wireless distribution systems, telecommunications carriers and resellers, internet service providers, new media companies, investors, financial institutions, utilities, entertainment companies, trade associations and entrepreneurs, as well as government agencies and task forces. Assists clients on an ongoing basis with the preparaton of licence applications, licence renewals, transfers of ownership, interventions and policy submissions to, and appearances before, the Canadian Radio-television and Telecommunications commission (the CRTC). Acted over the past year as regulatory counsel to BCE and CTV in BCE's acquisition of CTV, and in CTV's acquisition of NetStar Communications.

C

Prof. Memberships: Serves as a Director and member of the Executive Committee of Canadian Women in Communications, and sits as a member of the Cultural Industries SAGIT which advises the Minister of International Trade.
Publications: Has presented papers to various conferences on Communications Law and Broadcasting Law, and taught the Communications Law Course at the Faculty of Law, University of Toronto.
Career: Graduated from Trent University, Peterborough with a BA in Political Science and Economics in 1971, and received LLB from Osgoode Hall Law School, York University in 1974. Called to the Bar in 1976 and joined *Goodmans* (then *Goodman & Goodman*) the same year.

C

ROBOTTOM, David T.
Fraser Milner Casgrain, Calgary +1 403 268 7150
david.robottom@fmc-law.com
Recommended in Corporate/M&A
Specialisation: Chief Executive Officer of the firm and member of the firm's corporate transactions group. Primary areas of practice are corporate and securities law, with an emphasis on mergers and acquisitions, corporate reorganisations and public financing. Advises companies and financial advisors in structuring and effecting corporate and capital markets transactions, as well as in private equity fund and merchant banking matters. Acts as regular and special counsel to buyers, sellers, boards of directors and special board committees in corporate transactions, as well as acting as general counsel to a number of business groups.
Prof. Memberships: Canadian Bar Association, CalBA and LSA.
Career: Year of call to the Bar: 1980.
Personal: University of Alberta, B.Comm. (with distinction), 1976; MBA, 1979, LLB, 1979.

ROGERS, Phil
Gowlings, Toronto +1 416 862 7525
Recommended in Communications

ROMANO, Simon A.
Stikeman Elliott, Toronto +1 416 869 5500
Recommended in Corporate/M&A

ROOK, John
Osler, Hoskin & Harcourt LLP, Toronto
+1 416 862 4280
Recommended in Competition/Anti-trust

ROSS, Donald
Osler, Hoskin & Harcourt LLP, Toronto
+1 416 862 4288
dross@osler.com
Recommended in Corporate/M&A
Specialisation: Former chair of the firm's Business Law Department and current chair of its Mergers and Acquisitions Practice Group. Practice focuses on corporate and securities law including mergers and acquisitions, public offerings and private placements of securities, restructurings, and the provision of general corporate advice on various matters including corporate governance.
Prof. Memberships: Law Society of Upper Canada (Ontario).
Career: Experience includes various Canadian financings, various Canadian domestic acquisitions and divestitures, the purchase of several Canadian public companies by British public companies, the combination of Alcan and Alusuisse Lonza and corporate advice on governance issues to public companies.
Personal: Graduate of Osgoode Hall Law School at York University, LLB, London School of Economics, University of London and University of Toronto.

ROWLEY QC, J. William F.
McMillan Binch, Toronto
+1 416 865 7008
Recommended in Competition/Anti-trust

RUBY, Stephen
Fasken Martineau DuMoulin LLP, Toronto
+1 416 366 8381
sruby@tor.fasken.com
Recommended in Tax
Specialisation: Broad range of corporate taxation matters, including corporate acquisitions and reorganisations, financings, international tax and tax litigation.
Prof. Memberships: Law Society of Upper Canada; International Fiscal Association: Canadian Bar Association.
Publications: Frequent speaker and author of published articles on corporate taxation matters for the Canadian Tax Foundation, the Canadian Bar Association, Infonex, The International Fiscal Association, The Canadian Institute and the Federated Press.
Career: Former Special Adviser to the Senior Assistant Deputy Minister Tax Policy and Legislation Branch, Department Finance (1990-1991); Vice-President of the Canadian Branch of the International Fiscal Association: Co-Chairman of the Canadian Bar Association/Canadian Institute of Chartered Accountants Joint Committee on Taxation; Chairman of the National Tax Subsection of the Canadian Bar Association.
Personal: Hons. BA (1966) The University of Western Ontario; LLB (1971) Osgoode Hall Law School. Leisure interests include music, tennis and skiing.

RYAN, Barry J.
McCarthy Tétrault, Toronto
+1 416 601 7799
bryan@mccarthy.ca
Recommended in Banking & Finance
Specialisation: Partner in the Toronto Business Law Section. Practice focuses on corporate finance, banking, project finance and the regulation of financial institutions. Extensive corporate finance and banking experience. Acts for large Canadian banks, major non-Canadian financial institutions and institutional investors in their capital market activities, regulatory affairs and credit and financial restructuring matters. Frequent speaker on banking and corporate finance topics.
Prof. Memberships: Called to the Ontario bar in 1983.

SAIBIL, Norman
Borden Ladner Gervais LLP, Calgary
+1 403 232 9500
Recommended in Banking & Finance

SALZMAN, Lorne P.
McCarthy Tétrault, Toronto, Ontario
+1 416 601 7867
lsalzman@mccarthy.ca
Recommended in Communications
Specialisation: Partner in the Toronto Business Law Section. Practice focuses on telecommunications regulation and on competition law. Represents clients in telecommunications proceedings involving local and international competition, interconnection, licensing, universal service, and unbundling. Advises governments and regulators on contemporary issues of market opening and regulatory reform, including competitive radio-spectrum licensing, local interconnection, mobile interconnection, reforming legislation and build-operate-transfer arrangements. Also participates in telecommunications-related mediations, including acting as a mediator in an interconnection dispute.
Prof. Memberships: Admitted to the Ontario bar in 1975.

SAVILLE, Francis M. Q.C.
Fraser Milner Casgrain, Calgary +1 403 268 7020
francis.saville@fmc-law.com
Recommended in Energy & Natural Resources
Specialisation: A Vice-Chairman of the firm and a member of the firm's Regulatory and Litigation Practice Section. Served as the firm's Executive Chairman from 1987 to 1991. Extensive practice in the areas of Energy and Environmental Law, Municipal Law and Land-Use. Represents energy and other corporations respecting major applications before a number of regulatory tribunals. Projects include acting as senior counsel on successful applications for expansion of Syncrude Canada Ltd. and on the Alliance PipeLine project.
Prof. Memberships: LSA, CalBA, CBA, ABA and IBA.
Career: Year of call to the Bar: 1966 (Alberta). Former Director, Chairman of the Canadian Institute of Resources Law, Director of the Alberta Chamber of Resource and a Director of a number of publicly-traded corporations. Former Director of the Alberta Environmental Law Centre.
Personal: Appointed Q.C. in 1984; University of Alberta, BA, 1962; University of Alberta, LLB, 1965.

SCARLETT, James
Torys, Toronto +1 416 865 8199
jscarlett@torys.com
Recommended in Corporate/M&A
Specialisation: Partner in corporate department. Main area of work is corporate and securities law for public companies, principally mergers and acquisitions, public finance and capital markets regulation. Has handled wide range of public financing transactions acting for both corporate issuers and underwriters. Acts on mergers and acquisitions involving public companies, both negotiated and hostile. Advises new entrants to Canadian capital markets on structure and regulatory issues.
Prof. Memberships: Law Society of Upper Canada, Canadian Bar Association.
Career: Qualified in 1983. Joined *McMillan Binch* in 1981 becoming partner in 1988. Seconded to the Ontario Securities Commission, November 1986

until March 1990 working as a solicitor in the Corporate Finance Branch, counsel to the Chairman and Executive Director and Director, Capital Markets Branch from June 1 1988. Joined *Torys* in March, 2000.
Personal: Born 24 August 1953. Attended McGill University 1972 to 1975 (Bachelor of Commerce) and University of Toronto 1978 to 1981 (Bachelor of Laws).

SMITH, David W.
Davies Ward Phillips & Vineberg LLP, Toronto
+1 416 863 5542
dsmith@dwpv.com
Recommended in Tax
Specialisation: Income tax matters, with emphasis on international tax, mergers and acquisitions, corporate reorganisations and restructurings, corporate finance and trusts.
Prof. Memberships: Canadian Bar Association; Canadian Tax Foundation; International Fiscal Association; International Bar Association.
Career: Qualified in 1968. Appointed Queen's Counsel in 1984. Former Co-Chairman, Joint Committee on Taxation, Canadian Bar Association and Canadian Institute of Chartered Accountants. Former Chair, Board of Governors, Canadian Tax Foundation.
Personal: BA, (University of Manitoba), 1963; LLB, (University of Toronto), 1966 Gold Medal.

SMITH, Laurie
Bennett Jones LLP, Calgary +1 403 298 3100
smithl@bennettjones.ca
Recommended in Energy & Natural Resources
Specialisation: Vice Chairman, Partner and Head of the regulatory/environmental department. Former counsel to National Energy Board of Canada. Practice restricted to regulatory and related corporate/commercial, litigation and arbitration matters, focusing on major international pipeline and power projects. Recently acted as lead regulatory counsel to the Sable Offshore Energy project, Maritimes & Northeast Pipeline, the PanCanadian Deep Panuke Offshore project amongst many other international facilites and exports projects. Lead regulatory counsel to the major gas distribution companies within Alberta.
Prof. Memberships: Law Society of Alberta, Law Society of Upper Canada, Canadian Bar Association and the U.S. Federal Energy Bar Association.
Publications: Co-author of a chapter of the National Energy Board and the Canada/U.S. Free Trade Agreement for 'Energy Law and Transactions' by Matthew Bender.
Career: Articled with *Herridge Tolmie* (Ottawa) in 1980. Called to the Ontario Bar in 1981 and the Alberta Bar in 1984. Joined *Bennett Jones* in 1984, became partner in 1987. Counsel, National Energy Board of Canada, 1981-84. Served as a policy advisor to a minister of the Government of Canada (1978-79), participated in the Deputy Prime Minister's Task Force on regulatory reform.
Personal: Born 10 June, 1953. Attended St. Patrick's College (BA, 1974), University of Ottawa (LLB, 1977) and University of Oxford (MA, 1990).

SORELL, René R.
McCarthy Tétrault, Toronto
+1 416 601 7947
rsorell@mccarthy.ca
Recommended in Corporate/M&A
Specialisation: Partner in the Toronto Business Law Section and head of the Mergers and Acquisitions Group. Practice focuses on contested and uncontested take-over bids, public company reorganisations, the adoption of shareholder rights plans and advice to investment dealers. Acts for special committees of public company boards of directors and undertakes many other mergers and acquisitions assignments often involving litigation before securities regulators.
Prof. Memberships: Called to the Ontario bar in 1978.

STEINBERG, Norman
Ogilvy Renault, Montréal +1 514 847 4521
nsteinberg@ogilvyrenault.com
Recommended in Corporate/M&A
Specialisation: Partner in Business Group. Specialises in Corporate Finance, both private placements and public financings, international financing, mergers and acquisitions, privatisation and Corporate Governance. Acted for Quebecor Inc. and Donohue Inc. in the merger of Donohue and Abitibi-Consolidated Inc. Acted for Quebecor Printing Inc. in its merger with World Color Press Inc., thereby creating the world's largest printing company. Acted as Canadian Counsel to the Underwriting syndicate in the Canadian distribution of common shares of The Seagram Company Ltd. Acted as Special counsel to the board of directors of Alcan in its proposed merger with Pechiney SA of France and Alusuisse Lonza Group. Acted as Counsel to BCE Mobile Communications Inc., in its privatisation by its controlling shareholder Bell Canada. Acted as Counsel for both issuers and underwriting syndicates in IPOs and other capital market financings during the year including the Canadian/US IPO of Exfo Electro-Optical Engineering Inc. Member of the Advisory Committee to the Quebec Securities Commission.
Prof. Memberships: Québec Bar Association.
Career: Admitted to the Québec Bar in 1976 and joined *Ogilvy Renault* the same year, becoming partner in January 1986. Member of the Firm's Executive Committee. Director of various Public and Private Company boards and Philanthropic boards; past-President of The Canadian Club of Montreal.
Personal: Born February 10, 1950 in Montreal, Québec, Canada. Attended McGill University, Bachelor of Science (1971) and Bachelor of Civil Law (1975). Leisure interests include reading, photography and music. Lives in Montreal, Québec, Canada.

STICKLAND, Kenneth
Burnet Duckworth & Palmer LLP, Calgary
+1 403 260 0100
KSS@bdplaw.com
Recommended in Energy & Natural Resources
Specialisation: Partner in Energy, Corporate & Commercial and International Law business units. Main area of focus is high level corporate work primarily for junior, intermediate and multinational energy clients concerning all aspects of their activities and operations - domestically and internationally. Practice emphasises acquisitions and divestitures, business combinations, strategic alliances, joint operations, project and structured financings of assets and the negotiation of leasing, licensing, operation and royalty agreements and international concessions. Has counseled on the marketing of petroleum, natural gas, liquids and related projects. Has acted on behalf of production and exploration companies, producers/marketers, brokers, aggregators, distributors and end users in all commercial aspects of energy product marketing activities. Presents numerous papers and seminars on energy related matters on an ongoing basis.
Prof. Memberships: Member, Law Society of Alberta, and both the Natural Resources and Corporate Counsel Subsections of the Canadian Bar Association. Former member of the Independent Petroleum Association of Canada and a legislative review subcommittee which provided input on natural gas deregulation legislation in Canada. Past Director of the Canadian Petroleum Law Foundation.
Career: Admitted to the Alberta Bar in 1981. Joined *Burnet, Duckworth & Palmer* in 1980, partner since 1987. Graduated from the University of British Columbia with a Bachelor of Commerce degree in 1977, and in 1980 with an LLB.

STRANSMAN, John M.
Stikeman Elliott, Toronto +1 416 869 5500
Recommended in Corporate/M&A

STREKAF, Jo'Anne
Bennett Jones LLP, Calgary +1 403 298 3100
strekafj@bennettjones.ca
Recommended in Competition/Anti-trust
Specialisation: Partner in litigation department and a member of the competition law and research groups. Has appeared before the Court of the Queen's Bench of Alberta, the Alberta Court of Appeal, the Federal Court of Appeal, the Supreme Court of Canada and various administrative tribunals including the Public Utilities Board, the Surface Rights Board, the Energy Resources Compensation Board, the National Transportation Agency, the Competition Tribunal and the National Energy Board. Has participated in numerous arbitration proceedings and has acted in all aspects of competition law. Represented the Commissioner of Competition in the Superior/ICG Propane merger proceedings.
Prof. Memberships: Law Society of Alberta, Canadian Bar Association, Calgary Bar Association, American Bar Association, Association of Women Lawyers.
Publications: Author of numerous articles on various aspects of competition law.
Career: Called to the Alberta Bar in 1981. Joined *Bennett Jones* in 1980, became a partner in 1989.
Personal: Born 8 November, 1957. Attended the University of Regina (B.Admin., 1979) Queen's University (LLB, 1980) and Cambridge University (LLM).

C

SUGIYAMA, Constance L.
Fasken Martineau DuMoulin LLP, Toronto
+1 416 366 8381
csugiyama@tor.fasken.com
Recommended in Corporate/M&A
Specialisation: Partner in the Business Law Department. Practice group leader in Securities and Mergers and Acquisitions Law Group. Advises public and private issuers and financial institution clients on a variety of corporate finance, mergers and acquisitions, governance and regulatory compliance issues, as well as on general business law matters. Clients include securities firms, public and private companies (including those in the technology, resource and automotive sectors), and many charitable and non-profit organisations. Acted as legal counsel for De Beers Canada, in connection with its successful take-over bid for Winspear Diamonds Inc., for Select Technology Group Inc. in connection with its acquisition by Amdocs Limited, for Hummingbird Communications Ltd. in connection with its successful take-over bid for PC DOCS Group International Inc. and its acquisition of Andyne Computing Limited, for Architel Systems in connection with various transactions, for The Toronto Hospital in connection with its innovative $281 million public offering of amortizing secured bonds; and for ING Canada Holdings in its acquisition of Canadian Property and casualty business of Guardian Insurance.
Prof. Memberships: Member of the Canadian Bar Association, the International Bar Association, the American Bar Association and the Inter-Pacific Bar Association.
Publications: Contributor to 'The Guide to World Equity Markets', an annual publication, and to various magazines and law reviews.
Career: Admitted to the Ontario Bar in 1979. Joined *Fasken & Calvin* (a predecessor firm) in 1979, and became a partner in 1985. Member of the Securities Advisory Committee of the Ontario Securities Commission (1999-present). Advisor and Legal Counsel, Women in Capital Markets (1998-present), a non-profit organisation sponsored by 11 major investment banking firms and fund managers and currently comprised of more than 400 senior capital markets professionals. Frequent chair and speaker before various programs and conferences.
Personal: Graduated from the University of Toronto with a BA in 1974, and with a law degree in 1977. Director, Toronto Olympic Bid Corporation, appointed by Toronto City Counsel (1998-present). Budget and Administration Committee (1998-present). Director, The Hummingbird Centre for the Performing Arts, appointed by Toronto City Council (1996-present). Founder and Chair of WCM's Heather L. Main Memorial Scholarship Fund (1996-present). Director, The Japan Society (1994-present). Program Committee (1991-present). Special Advisor, Japanese Canadian Cultural Centre (1997-present). Honorary Co-Chair JCCC Capital Campaign (1998-present). Special Advisor to the board of directors of the Japanese Canadian Redress Foundation (1993-present).

SWARTZ, Jay A.
Davies Ward Phillips & Vineberg LLP, Toronto
+1 416 863 5520
jswartz@dwpv.com
Recommended in Banking & Finance, Corporate/M&A
Specialisation: Banking, debt financing, financial product development, structured finance, corporate restructurings and private equity funds, and private company acquisitions. Instrumental in developing asset-backed securities and derivatives business in Canada. Worked with bankers and investment dealers to develop numerous financial products.
Prof. Memberships: Canadian Bar Association; Fellow, American College of Commercial Finance Lawyers; Member, Insolvency Institute of Canada, Insol International.
Career: Qualified in 1975. Instructor, Advanced Business Law Workshop, Osgoode Hall Law School. Guest Lecturer, Osgoode Hall, University of Western Ontario Law School and York University Faculty of Business Administration.
Personal: Born 11 March 1949. Attended York University (BA, Economics, 1970) and Osgoode Hall Law School (LLB, 1973). Married to Linda Shumaker (1970), two daughters. Member, Donalda Club, Ontario Club.

TACIT, Christian
Nelligan O'Brien Payne, Ottawa +1 613 238 8080
Recommended in Communications

TAMAKI, Paul
Blake, Cassels & Graydon LLP, Toronto
+1 416 863 2697
paul.tamaki@blakes.com
Recommended in Tax
Specialisation: Partner in tax group. Main area of practice is corporate income tax including reorganisations, joint ventures, corporate finance, leasing, restructurings, intercompany transfer pricing and other international transactions. Acted on take-over of Newcourt Credit Group Inc. by The CIT Group, Inc. and the subsequent reorganisation of Newcourt's international foreign affiliate network; acted for Clearnet Communications Inc. on the take-over by TELUS Corporation; for Transamerica Corp. on the acquisition of NN Life Insurance Company of Canada from ING Group. Advises several foreign banks on the conversion of their Canadian bank subsidiaries into branch operations. Also represents clients on administrative tax appeals and other representations to governments.
Prof. Memberships: Law Society of Upper Canada, Professional Engineers (Ontario), Canadian Tax Foundation, International Fiscal Association, Canadian Bar Association.
Publications: Contributing editor of Federal Press 'Business Vehicles' and 'Corporate Finance' quarterly publications. Recently presented a paper at the Annual Conference of the Canadian Tax Foundation on 'Recent Developments in Transfer Pricing'.
Career: Joined *Blake, Cassels & Graydon LLP* in 1977, became a partner in 1983. Member of the Tax Committee of the Board of Trade of Metropolitan Toronto.
Personal: Born May 11th, 1947. Attended McGill University (B.Eng., 1969). Professional Engineer (Ontario) 1972. University of Toronto (LL.B., 1975) Admitted to the Ontario Bar, 1977. Leisure activities include golf. Lives in Toronto, Ontario, Canada.

TEOLIS, John
Blake, Cassels & Graydon LLP, Toronto
+1 416 863 2548
john.teolis@blakes.com
Recommended in Banking & Finance
Specialisation: Partner in Financial Services Group. Involved in legal and regulatory issues involving various types of financial institutions. Has been legal counsel to several Canadian and foreign entities in the establishment of their Canadian operation and acquisitions of Canadian companies. Canadian general counsel for a number of financial institutions. Member of the international Advisory Committee for 'Journal of International Banking and Financial Law'.
Prof. Memberships: Chairman of The Arthritis & Autoimmunity Research Centre Foundation and a director of several Canadian corporations. Member of the American Bar Association - Banking and Commercial Finance Committees; International Bar Association - Vice Chairman Banking Law Committee. Admitted to Ontario Bar in 1976.
Publications: Co-authored loose-leaf publications on the Canadian Bank Act. Canadian contributor to the book, 'Regulation of Foreign Banks'.

TETREAULT, David
Osler, Hoskin & Harcourt LLP, Toronto
+1 416 362 2111
dtetreault@osler.com
Recommended in Tax
Specialisation: Specialises in corporate tax with particular emphasis on mergers, acquisitions and divestitures, corporate reorganisations and corporate finance.
Prof. Memberships: Member of the Canadian Tax Foundation and the Canadian Bar Association.
Publications: Author of several papers on Canadian corporate taxation.
Career: Partner of *Osler, Hoskin & Harcourt* since 1990.
Personal: University of Toronto (LLB), McGill University (B.Com).

THOMSON, Kent
Torys, Toronto +1 416 865 7507
kthomson@torys.com
Recommended in Competition/Anti-trust
Specialisation: Litigation partner. Focuses on competition law, tax, sports and commercial disputes. Appeared at all levels of court in Ontario, including the Court of Appeal, as well as the Federal Court of Canada and the Supreme Court of Canada. Has also appeared before courts in other provinces and been involved in litigation in the United States and Europe. Acted in a number of civil and criminal matters involving international price fixing and market allocation conspiracies, and cases involving price maintenance, bid-rigging, misleading advertising, predatory pricing, price discrimination, reviewable trade practices and mergers. Appeared as counsel before the Competition Tribunal.

Publications: 'The Aftermath of Thomson Newspapers: Compelled Testimony Under the Competition Act', Canadian Institute, Toronto, May, 1996; 'The Private Enforcement of Rights Under the Competition Act', Insight Conference, Toronto, June, 1996.
Career: Qualified in 1984, Ontario Bar.
Personal: Attended Queen's University (LLB 1982).

THRASHER, Jack
Osler, Hoskin & Harcourt LLP, Calgary
+1 403 260 7019
Recommended in Energy & Natural Resources

TREMBLAY, Richard
Osler, Hoskin & Harcourt LLP, Toronto
+1 416 862 6441
Recommended in Tax

ULMER, John M.
Davies Ward Phillips & Vineberg LLP, Toronto
+1 416 863 5505
julmer@dwpv.com
Recommended in Tax
Specialisation: Income tax-related matters, tax aspects of international business ventures, corporate finance and real estate transactions.
Prof. Memberships: Canadian Bar Association; Canadian Tax Foundation; International Fiscal Association.
Career: Qualified in 1980. Speaks widely on tax matters. Appointed Canadian National Reporter for 2000 Congress of International Fiscal Association. Contributing editor of Corporate Finance (Federated Press).
Personal: Born 29 October 1954. LLB, (Osgoode Hall); LLM, (Harvard).

WALKER, Ross
Fraser Milner Casgrain, Toronto +1 416 863 4742
ross.walker@fmc-law.com
Recommended in Banking & Finance
Specialisation: Partner with *Fraser Milner Casgrain*'s Financial Services Group. Has over 24 years of practice in the financial services area. Areas of expertise include financing, insolvency and restructuring transactions. Provides general legal advice to financial institutions, receivers, bankruptcy trustees and corporate borrowers. Occasional lecturer and author for various groups, including the Law Society of Upper Canada, the Canadian Bar Association, the Institute of Canadian Bankers and Insight Educational Services.
Prof. Memberships: Canadian Bar Association
Career: Year of call to the Bar: 1976
Personal: Osgoode Hall, LLB, 1974; York University, MBA, 1971; York University, BA, 1970.

WARD, David A.
Davies Ward Phillips & Vineberg LLP, Toronto
+1 416 863 5504
dward@dwpv.com
Recommended in Tax
Specialisation: Taxation, concentrating on Canadian and international tax advice, planning and tax dispute resolution, including tax litigation.
Prof. Memberships: Canadian Bar Association; International Bar Association; Canadian Tax Foundation; International Fiscal Association.
Career: Qualified in 1958. Founding partner of the firm. Former President, Canadian Branch, International Fiscal Association. Former Governor, Canadian Tax Foundation. Lectured at Osgoode Hall Law School. Former member, Advisory Committee to Minister of National Revenue.

WELKOFF, Jim
Torys, Toronto +1 416 865 0040
jwelkoff@torys.com
Recommended in Tax
Specialisation: Senior partner in Tax Department. Specialises in corporate taxation, with emphasis on corporate finance and financial transactions, mergers and acquisitions, financial institutions and international transactions and structuring.
Prof. Memberships: Canadian Bar Association, Canadian Tax Foundation, International Fiscal Association and ISDA Canadian Tax Subcommittee.
Publications: Author of a number of articles, including co-author of 'The Interpretation of Tax Conventions in Canada' Canadian Tax Journal 50th Anniversary Edition.
Career: Called to the Ontario Bar in 1983. Attended University of Toronto (BA), Osgoode Hall Law School (LLB) and New York University (LLM Taxation). With Department of Finance, Tax Policy from 1983-1985.
Personal: Born 28 June 1955.

WHITEHEAD, Stephen
Johnston & Buchan, Ottawa +1 613 236 3882
Recommended in Communications

WIERCINSKI, Henry J.P.
McCarthy Tétrault, Toronto, Ontario
+1 416 601 7842
hwiercin@mccarthy.ca
Recommended in Banking & Finance
Specialisation: Partner in the Toronto Business Law Section. Practice focuses on asset securitisation, banking, creditors' rights, corporate reorganisations, equipment leasing (domestic, cross-border, leveraged and synthetic), financial institution capital markets activities, financial institution regulation, public-private partnership, project finance, secured transactions and structured finance.
Prof. Memberships: Called to the Ontario bar in 1975.

WILKIE, Scott
Osler, Hoskin & Harcourt LLP, Toronto
+1 416 862 4252
Recommended in Tax

WILSON, James
PricewaterhouseCoopers, Toronto +1 416 869 1130
Recommended in Tax

WOLOSHYN, William
McMillan Binch, Toronto
+1 416 865 7063
Recommended in Banking & Finance

WONG, Stanley
Davis & Co, Toronto +1 416 365 3525
stan_wong@davis.ca
Recommended in Competition/Anti-trust
Specialisation: Partner and head of firm's National Competition Law Practice. Administrative Partner of Toronto office. Lead counsel for Canadian Bureau of Competition in 'Southam' newspaper merger case, the first contested case under the 1986 merger laws. Significant engagements in 2000 include: private actions under the Competition Act; international cartel investigation; arbitration under NAFTA regarding competition law; mergers in fisheries, forestry, construction materials and technology industries; counselling on compliance in a broad range of industries.
Prof. Memberships: Chair, of Canadian Bar Association National Competition Law Section.
Career: Admitted as Barrister and Solicitor in Ontario (1984) and British Columbia (1987) and as Solicitor in England and Wales (1992). BA Honours in Economics (Simon Fraser, 1969); PhD in Economics (Cambridge, 1976); LLB (Toronto, 1982). Lecturer to Associate Professor of Economics, Carleton University, Ottawa (1973-84). Contributing Editor – Competition Law, Rapporteur on Canadian competition law for Antitrust and Trade Law Newsletter, Section on Business Law, International Bar Association.

WOODS, Judith M.
McCarthy Tétrault, Toronto
+1 416 601 7957
jwoods@mccarthy.ca
Recommended in Tax
Specialisation: Partner and head of the Toronto Tax Section. Practises income tax law with emphasis on mergers and acquisitions, corporate reorganisations and international tax. Editor of 'Focus on Current Cases'. Frequent speaker on tax topics at professional seminars.
Prof. Memberships: Member of the Executive Committee of Board of Governors of Canadian Tax Foundation and the CICA/CBA Joint Committee on Taxation. Admitted to the Ontario bar in 1976.

YATES, Kemm
Stikeman Elliott, Calgary +1 403 266 9000
Recommended in Energy & Natural Resources

YONTEF, Marvin
Stikeman Elliott, Montréal +1 514 397 3000
Recommended in Corporate/M&A

ZALMANOWITZ, Barry
Fraser Milner Casgrain, Edmonton
+1 780 423 7344
barry.zalmanowitz@fmc-law.com
Recommended in Competition/Anti-trust
Specialisation: Member of national competition law group. Advises and represents clients in all aspects of the Competition Act, including mergers and notifiable transactions, conspiracy and other criminal provisions, private damage actions, reviewable practices and misleading advertising. Has been competition law counsel in many large transactions providing pre-transaction advice, compliance with pre-notification filings and obtaining clearances from Commissioner of Competition. Experience includes representing clients in contested merger proceedings before the Competition Tribunal, and defence of clients in complex conspiracy prosecu-

C

tions. Lecturer, Faculty of Law, University of Alberta (competition law). Clients include large oil and gas, energy, oil and gas service and pipeline companies. Numerous panels, presentations and papers on competition law. Testified on behalf of Canadian Bar Association before Parliamentary committee on amendments to the Competition Act. Chair of CBA National Competition Law Annual Conference to be held September 20-21, 2001.
Prof. Memberships: Law Society of Alberta, Canadian Bar Association National Competition Law Section.
Career: Year of call to Bar: 1980 (Alberta); partner of firm since 1985.
Personal: University of Alberta, BA, 1973; MA (Economics), 1975; LLB, 1979; employed Competition Bureau Ottawa 1975, 1976.

C

ZIMMERMAN, H. Alec
Osler, Hoskin & Harcourt LLP, Toronto
+1 416 862 5955
azimmerman@osler.com
Recommended in Banking & Finance
Specialisation: Partner in the Financial Institutions and Insolvency and Restructuring Practice Groups. Practice centres on acting for banks, near-banks and other financial institutions, intermediaries and syndicates in connection with structured finance, insolvencies and restructurings, and regulatory compliance. Member of the Board of Directors of The Chase Manhattan Bank of Canada, Castrol Canada Inc., Masterfile Canada Inc. and CanadaHelps.com. Acted for Chase and Chemical on their merger in Canada, for MBNA in incorporating a Canadian chartered bank, and for Chase and J.P. Morgan on their merger in Canada. Lead counsel to court-appointed liquidator of Confederation Trust Company, to Bank of Montreal and to Chase in connection with numerous insolvencies, and acting for Trust Company of Bank of Montreal in respect of the Loewen insolvency. Acting for CanWest in financing its $3.5 billion purchase of Hollinger publishing assets in Canada.
Prof. Memberships: Member of Insolvency Institute of Canada, ABA (Bankruptcy section), INSOL International, IBA (Committees E and J).
Publications: Author of several published papers relating to structured and project finance, letters of credit, trends and developments in the use of the Companies' Creditors Arrangement Act, the liquidation of financial institutions, debt restructuring and debtor in possession financing. Developed and taught advanced debtor-creditor course at University of Toronto Law School 1983 to 1987.
Career: Called to Ontario Bar 1978. Joined *Osler, Hoskin & Harcourt LLP* as partner in 1997. Concurrently recognised in various national and international directories as one of Canada's leading banking lawyers and leading insolvency lawyers.
Personal: University of Toronto Law School (1976). Board of Governors, Canadian Olympic Foundation.

ZOLF, Stephen
Heenan Blaikie, Toronto +1 416 643 681
szolf@heenan.ca
Recommended in Communications
Specialisation: Specialises in communications law, regulation and policy. In the broadcasting area, acts for various pay and speciality programming services, industry associations and other cultural sector organisations. In the telecom area, provides ongoing advice to clients in the telecommunications and broadcasting sectors, acting for competitive local exchange carriers, long distance resellers and other providers of telecommunications services.
Prof. Memberships: Past Chair of the Entertainment, Media and Communications Section of the Canadian Bar Association (Ontario), having served on the Executive of the Bar Association since 1993.
Publications: Has published in the area of international telecommunications regulation and has written numerous commentaries on legal and public policy issues in the broadcasting and telecommunications sectors.
Career: Called to the Ontario Bar in 1989. Prior to commencing legal studies, acted as an economist and policy advisor with the Canadian Government, in the area of regulatory reform. Served as an economist in the telecommunications branch of the Canadian Radio-television and Telecommunications Commission (CRTC).
Personal: Law degree from the University of Toronto in 1987. Completed a masters degree in Economics from the London School of Economics, England in 1983 and received a BA in Economics from the University of British Columbia in 1981.

CAYMAN ISLANDS

Corporate/Commercial

CAYMAN ISLANDS Leading firms (Corporate/Commercial)
1 Maples and Calder
Walkers
2 Boxalls
Hunter & Hunter
3 Solomon Harris

Firms are listed alphabetically in each band.

Leading individuals (Corporate/Commercial)
1 BAGNALL James *Boxalls*
HARFORD Henry *Maples and Calder*
LEWIS Mark *Walkers*
POPE Gus *Maples and Calder*
PUTTERILL Bruce *Hunter & Hunter*
2 ASHMAN Ian *Walkers*
JENNINGS Charles *Maples and Calder*
SCRIVENER Paul *Solomon Harris*
TODD Rory *Hunter & Hunter*

Individuals are listed alphabetically in each band.

Maples and Calder (16 ptrs, 30 asscs) Our researchers found that the largest firm in the Cayman Islands enjoys *"a total dominance of the market in some areas."* IPOs, cross-border mergers, reorganisations, joint ventures and infrastructure development are all important elements of the workload. Offices in Europe and Hong Kong add to rivals' perception of a group with a *"City of London attitude."*

Henry Harford heads the corporate department, and is known for his *"common sense"* and *"technical knowledge,"* while **Gus Pope** and **Charles Jennings** have particular expertise in mutual funds and insurance respectively. *"Founding father"* Anthony Travers is no longer based in the Cayman Islands, although he still exerts great influence from his new London base. **Clients:** Major financial institutions and wealthy individuals.

Walkers (10 ptrs, 20 asscs) The firm is associated by rivals with a *"roll your sleeves up and get down to work"* image. Also renowned for litigation expertise, the firm's international finance work still forms the bulk of the caseload, principally in capital markets, asset finance and mutual and investment funds. The retirement of Bill Roberts does leave a gap, but **Mark Lewis**, described by opponents as a *"big personality,"* and **Ian Ashman**, an *"expert in funds and capital markets,"* continue to receive market plaudits. **Clients:** Leading banks, investors and law firms.

Boxalls (4 ptrs, 7 asscs) An expanding firm which has its principal reputation in the commercial areas, notably in mutual funds, although it also deals with asset and structured finance, banking, corporate and insurance work. The firm also serves as listing agents to the Cayman Stock Exchange. **James Bagnall** was commended to researchers as a *"user-friendly and familiar name."* **Clients:** Public companies; commercial and merchant banks; airlines; financial institutions; ship owners; insurance companies; investment managers; mutual insurance associations.

Hunter & Hunter (6 ptrs, 15 asscs) The biggest litigation firm in the islands, it is equally recognised for asset finance and mutual funds, as well as private equity, an area which has seen considerable expansion in the last year. **Bruce Putterill**, known as a *"strong all round technical lawyer,"* is a specialist in corporate/commercial law and is recognised for his expertise in shipping. **Rory Todd** was also recommended to our researchers. The firm was recently involved in a major reorganisation of satellite telecoms group ICO to accommodate a new investor, as well as advising on a substantial fund for Munda. **Clients:** International corporates and financial institutions.

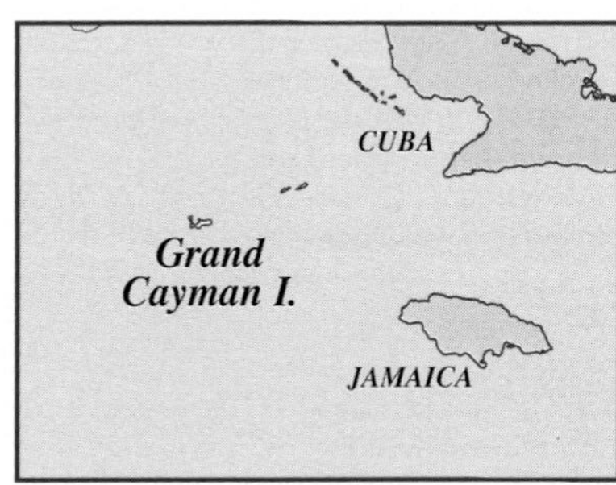

Solomon Harris (2 ptrs, 2 asscs) A small firm, mentioned to our researchers as a *"highly ambitious"* operation, with a broad range of expertise in corporate and commercial work. **Paul Scrivener** is considered to be the outstanding practitioner here. Particular focus lies in offshore work, mutual funds, capital markets and trust banking. The firm advised on the restructuring of Fortis/MeesPierson Group. **Clients:** Bank of Bermuda (Cayman) Ltd; Barclays Bank; Cayman National Bank; Scotiabank (Cayman Islands) Ltd; Deloitte & Touche; Ernst & Young; KPMG; PricewaterhouseCoopers.

Leaders' profiles – Cayman Islands

ASHMAN, Ian
Walkers, Grand Cayman +1 345 949 0100
iashman@walkers.com.ky
Specialisation: Partner in Corporate & International Finance Department, specialising in capital markets and structured finance products including securitisations, repackagings, note programmes, CBOs/CLOs and project bonds as well as asset finance and investment banks and corporates establishing various commercial paper and note programmes and other structured products, and also has extensive experience in aircraft finance transactions acting for a number of major investment banks, airlines and operating lessors on an ongoing basis. Has acted for major international companies in the sale, cross-border lease and financing of various assets. Joint Head of the Hyperlink 'capi.htm' Capital Markets & Structured Finance team of *Walkers.*
Prof. Memberships: Law Society of England & Wales, Cayman Islands Law Society.

Publications: Has published a number of articles, including 'Using Cayman Islands Special Purpose Vehicles' IFLR International Financial Law Review.
Career: Trained as a solicitor with *Denton Hall* in London. After qualifying in 1991, moved to the corporate department of *Theodore Goddard*; acted for mainstream corporate clients in the UK and also worked extensively in central and Eastern Europe. In 1993 moved to the role of UK and International Counsel to a large multinational company. Was principally involved in advising a major UK subsidiary and the Asia Pacific operation of the company on all aspects of corporate and commercial law. Admitted as an attorney in the Cayman Islands and joined *Walkers* in 1995. Became a partner in 2000.
Personal: Born 15 February 1967. Law degree form Newcastle University, England. Leisure interests include tennis, golf and fishing. Lives in Grand Cayman, Cayman Islands.

C

BAGNALL, James

Boxalls, Grand Cayman +1 345 949 9876
jbagnall@boxalls.com.ky
Specialisation: Partner in Corporate and Finance Department. Principal areas of work are corporate, commercial banking and finance law.
Prof. Memberships: Law Society, Cayman Islands Law Society.
Career: Qualified as a solicitor in England and Wales in 1983 and admitted as an attorney-at-law in the Cayman Islands in 1985. Joined *Boxalls* in 1993, becoming a Partner in 1995.
Personal: Born London, 1956, graduated from Oxford University (MA) in 1978. Lives in George Town, Grand Cayman.

HARFORD, Henry

Maples and Calder, Grand Cayman
Specialisation: Corporate law including mergers and acquisitions and a wide range of general corporate transactions. Also advises on a wide range of capital markets and structured finance vehicles and mutual funds transactions. Is a regular speaker at conferences.
Prof. Memberships: The Cayman Islands Law Society; The Law Society of England and Wales.
Career: Qualified as a solicitor in England and Wales (1989) and was admitted as an attorney at law in the Cayman Islands in 1991. Joined *Maples and Calder* from *Travers Smith Braithwaite* in 1991, becoming a Partner in 1996.
Personal: Born Bristol, England, 19 July 1963. Graduated from Oxford University in 1985. Lives in Pease Bay, Grand Cayman.

JENNINGS, Charles

Maples and Calder, Grand Cayman
csj@maples_candw.ky
Specialisation: Corporate commercial, particularly cross-border joint ventures, and collective investment schemes, specialising in limited partnerships.
Prof. Memberships: The Cayman Islands Law Society (Vice President and Secretary 1994-to date).
Career: Qualified as a Solicitor in England and Wales 1982 and admitted as an attorney at law in the Cayman Islands in 1986. Joined *Maples and Calder* from Baker & McKenzie in 1986, becoming a Partner in 1992.
Personal: Born United Kingdom, 15 September 1957. Graduated from Oxford University in 1979. Lives in George Town, Grand Cayman.

LEWIS, Mark Phillip

Walkers, Grand Cayman +1 345 949 0100
mlewis@walker.com.ky
Specialisation: Partner in the Corporate & International Finance Department and joint head of the Investment Funds Group. Main practice area is corporate law, particularly hedge funds, private equity funds and asset securitisation. Has handled investment fund projects for major American, European, Australian and Japanese law firms, investment fund managers and major institutions, including Chase Manhattan Bank, American Express Bank, Merrill Lynch, Morgan Stanley, ABN AMRO, CIBC, AXA Global, Soros Fund Management, Long Term Capital Management L.P. (now JWM Partners L.P.), CITCO, and Fortis/MeesPierson. Has also acted in numerous securitisations for Citibank and major capital markets transactions for Petróleos Mexicanos and Petróleos de Venezuela, the State oil companies of Mexico and Venezuela. Has spoken at several conferences on various aspects of both private equity and hedge funds.
Prof. Memberships: Law Society of England & Wales, Cayman Islands Law Society.
Publications: 'Legal Aspects of Doing Business in Hungary' (Longmans) and contributor of the Cayman Islands Digest entry to the Martindale-Hubbell International Digest.
Career: Graduated University of Western Australia in 1981. Admitted to practice as a barrister and solicitor in western Australia in December 1982. Prior to joining *Walkers* worked with *Freehill, Hollingdale & Page*, Australia, gained extensive international experience with *Denton Hall* (now *Denton Wilde Sapte*) in London and Japan (Banking, Corporate Finance and Entertainment Law Departments) and with *Theodore Goddard* working on international asset finance and capital markets transactions in Russia, Poland and Hungary. Joined *Walkers* after graduating with a Master of Laws degree (LLM) in corporate finance and international taxation from Cambridge University (Jesus College) England in 1993.
Personal: Born 26 January 1959. Leisure interests include triathlon - represented Cayman Islands at the 1996 and 1998 World Triathlon Championships.

POPE, Gus

Maples and Calder, Grand Cayman
Specialisation: A wide range of corporate transactions with a particular emphasis on mutual funds (corporate, limited partnerships and unit trusts), special purpose vehicles and general corporate law.
Prof. Memberships: The Cayman Islands Law Society; The Honourable Society of the Middle Temple.
Career: Called to the bar in England (1987) and was admitted as an attorney at law in the Cayman Islands in 1987. Joined *Maples and Calder* in 1987 becoming a Partner in 1992.
Personal: Born Belfast, Northern Ireland, 9 December 1962. Graduated from Cambridge University 1985, University of Pennsylvannia 1986. Lives in George Town, Grand Cayman.

PUTTERILL, Bruce

Hunter & Hunter, Grand Cayman
+1 345 949 4900
bputterill@huntlaw.com.ky
Specialisation: Head of the Commercial Department. Specialising in shipping and aviation law, mutual funds, bank and insurance company licensing, joint ventures and structured and project finance.
Prof. Memberships: Law Society, Cayman Islands Law Society.
Career: Qualified as a Solicitor in England in 1978. Practised with *Norton Rose* in London prior to being admitted as a Cayman Islands attorney in 1982. Senior Partner of *Hunter & Hunter* since 1997.
Personal: Born 18 November 1953, Zimbabwe. Educated at Churchill School, Harare, Zimbabwe; University of Zimbabwe; College of Law, London, England.

SCRIVENER, Paul

Solomon Harris, Grand Cayman +1 345 949 0488
Pscrivener@solomonharris.com
Specialisation: Partner specialising in corporate and commercial law, principally mergers and acquisitions, investment funds, banking, capital markets and securitisations. Clients include international financial institutions, investment banks and major onshore law firms. In 2000 acted on the acquisition by Fortis of ABN Amro's fund administration business and the Cayman aspects of the worldwide restructuring of a major international financial institution. Whilst at *Eversheds*, led a team which acted for Du Pont in its US$3 billion acquisition of ICI heavy chemicals business. Has spoken at various conferences.
Prof. Memberships: Law Society of England and Wales; Cayman Islands Law Society; admitted to Cayman Islands Bar.
Publications: Contributor to various publications including Offshore World and Fund Forum.
Career: Qualified in 1986. Partner with *Eversheds* 1991 - 1998.
Personal: Born 1962. Downing College, Cambridge University 1980-83 (MA Law). Leisure interests: golf and swimming.

TODD, Rory

Hunter & Hunter, Grand Cayman
+1 345 949 4900
rtodd@huntlaw.com.ky
Specialisation: Partner in the commercial department. Specialising in mutual funds, joint ventures and structured and project finance.
Prof. Memberships: Member of the Law Society and the Cayman Islands Law Society.
Career: Qualified as a Solicitor in England in 1984. Practised with *Richards Butler* in London and Tokyo prior to being admitted as a Cayman Islands attorney in 1994. Became a Partner in *Hunter & Hunter* in 1997.
Personal: Born 14 April, 1959. Educated at Durham School and Cambridge University.

CENTRAL AFRICAN REPUBLIC

Corporate/Commercial

CENTRAL AFRICAN REPUBLIC Leading firms (Corporate/Commercial)
1 Cabinet Nicolas Tiangaye
Cabinet Zarambaud Assingambi
2 Cabinet Konjbeto

Firms are listed alphabetically in each band.

Leading individuals (Corporate/Commercial)
1 **TIANGAYE Nicolas** *Cabinet Nicolas Tiangaye*
ZARAMBAUD Assingambi *Cabinet Zarambaud*
2 **KONJBETO Martin** *Cabinet Konjbeto*

Individuals are listed alphabetically in each band.

Cabinet Nicolas Tiangaye (1 ptr, 2 asscs) **Nicolas Tiangaye** has a *"good full service law practice"* which is strong in commercial law. Clients are drawn from sectors such as transportation and distribution. **Clients:** International companies; charities.

Cabinet Zarambaud Assingambi (1 ptr, 2 asscs) *"The best lawyer in the country,"* according to some, and the chairman of the national bar association, **Assingambi Zarambaud** heads a firm practising commercial law for international clients, particularly from the banking and telecommunications sectors. **Clients:** Telesel; transport companies; banks; UBAC (Groupe Crédit Lyonnais).

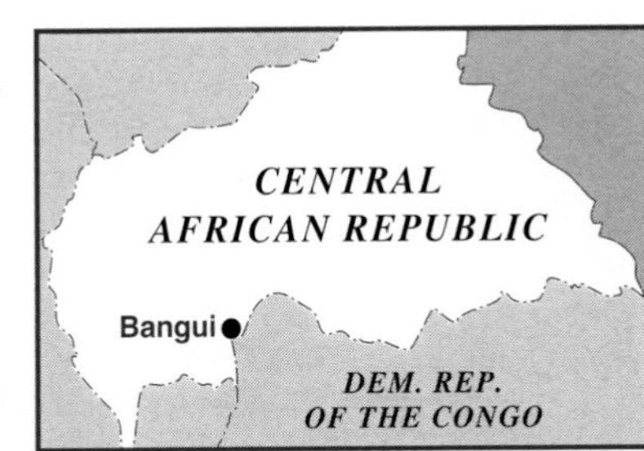

Cabinet Konjbeto (1 ptr, 2 asscs) **Martin Konjbeto** has *"a good name"* for commercial work, especially in the provision of legal advice and the drafting of commercial contracts. **Clients:** CES; domestic companies.

Leaders' profiles – Central African Republic

KONJBETO, Martin
Cabinet Konjbeto, Bangui +236 611 762

TIANGAYE, Nicolas
Cabinet Nicolas Tiangaye, Bangui +236 612 571

ZARAMBAUD, Assingambi
Cabinet Zarambaud Assingambi, Bangui +236 612 416

CHAD

Corporate/Commercial

CHAD Leading firms (Corporate/Commercial)
1 Cabinet Thomas Dingamgoto

Firms are listed alphabetically in each band.

Leading individuals (Corporate/Commercial)
1 **DINGAMGOTO Thomas** *Thomas Dingamgoto*

Individuals are listed alphabetically in each band.

Cabinet Thomas Dingamgoto (1 ptr, 2 asscs) *"The name for Chad,"* **Thomas Dingamgoto** is a *"technically superb and hard-working"* lawyer. Capable of handling all corporate and commercial work, his firm is notably strong in banking and finance. The team is the regular beneficiary of referrals from French law firms. **Clients:** Esso; Air Afrique; Biao; Sogea; Coton-Chad.

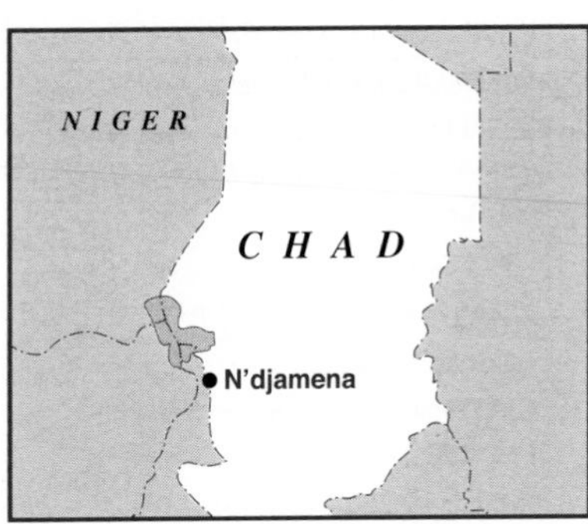

Leaders' profiles – Chad

DINGAMGOTO, Thomas
Cabinet Thomas Dingamgoto, N'Djamena +235 515 588

CHILE

Index

OVERVIEW: In a conservative market, populated by members of the same family, the Santiago legal scene was shaken by the departure of corporate guru Arturo Yrarrazaval from Philippi to form his own rapidly expanding firm. Privatisation in the water sector and toll roads and telecoms activity has led to increased foreign investment. The lack of international firms is striking, with only Baker & McKenzie having a meaningful presence.

C

Banking & Finance

CHILE Leading firms (Banking & Finance)
1 Carey y Cia
Claro y Cia
Guerrero, Olivos, Novoa y Errazuriz
Philippi, Yrarrazaval, Pulido & Brunner
2 Barros & Errazuriz
Cariola Diez Perez-Cotapos y Cia
3 Larrain y Asociados
Morales Noguera Valdivieso & Besa
Urenda Rencoret Orrego & Dörr

Firms are listed alphabetically in each band.

Leading individuals (Banking & Finance)
1 EYZAGUIRRE José María *Claro y Cia*
LEVIN Juan Guillermo *Carey y Cia*
PERALTA Diego *Carey y Cia*
PULIDO Alberto *Philippi, Yrarrazaval, Pulido*
2 BRONFMAN Jimena *Guerrero, Olivos, Novoa*
GUERRERO Roberto *Guerrero, Olivos, Novoa*
ILLANES Francisco *Cariola Diez Perez-Cotapos*
MARTÍNEZ Jaime *Carey y Cia*
OLIVOS Carlos *Guerrero, Olivos, Novoa*
ORREGO Alberto *Urenda Rencoret Orrego & Dörr*
3 BARROS Cristián *Barros & Errazuriz*
BESA Eugenio *Morales Noguera Valdivieso*
DEL PIANO Jorge *Guerrero, Olivos, Novoa*
GRANICH Jorge *Larrain y Asociados*
OBACH Sebastian *Cariola Diez Perez-Cotapos*
Up-and-coming individuals
LARRAIN Paulo *Morales Noguera Valdivieso*

Individuals are listed alphabetically in each band.

Carey y Cia (4 ptrs, 16 asscs) The firm has a *"high level"* practice in banking and finance, advising on syndicated loans, bond issues, project finance and banking M&A for both international and domestic financial institutions.

Juan Guillermo Levin* is regarded by peers as one of the leading project finance practitioners in Chile, and is *"a real leader."* He often works in collaboration with the equally esteemed **Diego Peralta***, while **Jaime Martínez***, former in-house counsel at an international bank, also maintains his share of market support.

Recent project finance activity has focused on toll-road concessions, including the $211 million road to Concepción where the firm acted for a Mexican concessionaire and the governmental Mexican bank, Bancomext. The firm was counsel to a subsidiary of Groupe GTM on a projected local bond issue for the refinancing of the $250 million Chillán-Collipulli toll road. Well-known as general counsel to Bank of America, the firm advised it on the sale of its Chilean insurance business to Ohio National, as well as representing the underwriters on the issue of $1 billion of eurobonds by Enersis and Endesa. **Clients:** Bank of America; First Chicago; Bancomext; Banco Santander; InvestAmérica.

Claro y Cia (5 ptrs, 10 asscs) It is evident from our research that the finance department of this traditional firm is known for performing *"top quality"* work for an enviable array of international investment banks. The team is highly rated for its capital markets expertise, and handles transactions financed by Yankee and local bonds, acting for the guarantors and underwriters on issues by MBIA and Exxel Capital. Project finance is another speciality, which has been highlighted by the team's involvement on the privatisation of toll roads and of Santiago airport. The firm acted for the IDB on the financing of the toll road from Santiago to Valparaíso. The outstanding name here is **José María Eyzaguirre Jnr***, who is said to *"perform on most of the banking deals in Chile."* The group represented Internet Holdings, a local start-up incubation fund, which is now in its third round of financing, and advised Citibank on its acquisition of Atlas, a local consumer credit company. The firm was also counsel to Citibank in a $1.1 billion syndicated loan to Hydro-Quebec and local subsidiary to finance the acquisition of Transelec. **Clients:** JP Morgan; Bank of America.

Guerrero, Olivos, Novoa y Errazuriz (4 ptrs, 7 asscs) *"One of the best for banking,"* the firm is recognised as one of the few specialists in Chile, acting for investment banks, syndicates and blue-chip corporates on syndicated loans, capital markets, securities, project finance and refinancing.

The department can call on an impressively deep pool of rated practitioners, many of whom have served on the boards of local branches of international banks. The experienced **Jimena Bronfman*** has *"a good pedigree in financing deals and banking arrangements,"* and frequently advises on cross-border transactions. **Roberto Guerrero Jnr*** is a familiar face on a range of financing matters, as is **Carlos Olivos***, chairman of Banco Santander in Chile. LSE-educated **Jorge del Piano*** is known by competitors as a *"technically skilled lawyer"* who has recently raised his profile in the domestic market. Said to be an *"innovative"* team on financial structuring, it advised Banco Edwards on an equity issue in the US, and acted for Banco Santander as underwriter to a project finance deal. The firm also represented Banco Edwards CSFB on a public offering of pre-emptive rights worth around $150 million. **Clients:** Goldman Sachs; Salomon Brothers; Merrill Lynch; CSFB; Morgan Stanley; Nomura; Banco de Chile; Banco Edwards; Banco de Santiago; Deutsche Bank.

Philippi, Yrarrazaval, Pulido & Brunner (2 ptrs, 4 asscs) The banking team's experience of working for international banks on cross-border transactions has propelled it to the ranks of leading firms in Chile. Renowned for its banking M&A work, the group also advises on syndicated loans, securitisation and asset finance.

Head of the banking department is the highly recommended **Alberto Pulido Snr***, described by rivals as *"a technical wizard, who is a good negotiator and has thorough knowledge of banking regulations."* The firm acted for a syndicate, led by Crédit Lyonnais, on a $1.3 billion loan to LanChile for the purchase of 27 planes. As sole Chilean counsel to JP Morgan, the firm also acted on a $550 million syndicated loan to Grupo Angelini, Chile's second largest conglomerate, to acquire a holding in a foreign company. **Clients:** Chase Manhattan; JP Morgan; Union Bank of Switzerland; Goldman Sachs; Morgan Stanley; Citibank; BBVA.

Barros & Errazuriz (2 ptrs, 5 asscs) Research has shown that this small team maintains high visibility in the financial areas, notably on local capital markets, where it is well known for representing domestic corporates. Project and acquisition finance are other specific areas of expertise.

"Capable" **Cristián Barros*** has long experience of acting for borrowers. The firm handled the renegotiation of five syndicated loans on behalf of Colbún, worth $600 million, and advised the same client on a $150 million local bond issue.

Other matters include advising Morgan Stanley and others on a toll road financing, involving credit facilities and a bond offering, and was counsel to a subsidiary of Banco Santander on a $100 million domestic bond placement for CAP, the largest Chilean steel company. **Clients:** Morgan Stanley; Bank of America; DKB; BBVA; CABC; Salomon Smith Barney.

Cariola Diez Perez-Cotapos y Cia (2 ptrs, 6 asscs) A financial practice that has *"blossomed"* in recent years is known for its international experience in securities, local bond offerings, project finance, and acquisition financing. The firm acts for lenders, borrowers and issuers, and is renowned for work on renegotiating foreign loans and export finance.

An *"inventive"* department is headed by **Francisco Illanes***, who has a Central Bank background, while **Sebastian Obach*** has a sound reputation for his mixed finance and M&A practice. In project finance, the firm advised the lenders on the financing of Puerto Mejillones, and has acted for ABN AMRO on the development of various derivative-based financial products. **Clients:** Rabobank; ABN AMRO; Bank One; American Express; Corp Banca; Chase Manhattan; Banco Santander; BNP; Goldman Sachs; Morgan Stanley; IDB.

Larrain y Asociados (2 ptrs, 2 asscs) Counsel to a number of Spanish and US investment banks, the firm is respected for its finance advice, notably in project finance. **Jorge Granich*** enjoys the approval of his peers. The team has acted as general counsel to Barclays in Chile, acting on project finance and a number of local acquisitions. It acted for Citibank in a $400 million loan to the concessionaires of a toll road running from the North to the South of Chile, and represented ESSAL, domestic water company, in the negotiation of a $70 million syndicated loan. **Clients:** BBVA; Citibank; Barclays.

Morales Noguera Valdivieso & Besa (3 ptrs, 12 asscs) Full service firm with a *"high level"* of experience in the banking sector, normally acting for borrowers, especially Spanish investors, on infrastructure projects, securities transactions and syndicated loans. Our researchers have found that the *"reliable"* **Eugenio Besa*** is known for having *"an eye for detail,"* and leads a financial team which also includes **Paulo Larrain***, for whom a bright future is predicted.

The firm acted on the $700 million issue of local bonds and syndicated loans to finance the Pan-American highway construction from Santiago to the South of Chile. Securities experience includes acting for Quiñenco, listed on the Santiago and New York Stock Exchanges, on its $177 million issuance of debt securities. Also represented the Republic of Chile on a $500 million global bond offering. **Clients:** Quiñenco; Merrill Lynch; Republic of Chile; DLJ; Madeco SA; Deutsche Bank; Terranova; VTR.

Urenda Rencoret Orrego & Dörr A strong finance practice with a *"good profile,"* acting for a mixture of domestic borrowers and international banks. Banking activity includes lending, capital markets, securities and innovative financial instruments advice, while the firm's experience in project finance was highlighted by its advice on the Minera Escondida project. Leading name **Alberto Orrego Snr** has an acknowledged reputation in mining finance, acting for both project companies and financiers.

The firm acted on the first Chilean ADR transaction, and has since acquired wider expertise in advising on ADR offerings by Chilean companies. **Clients:** Banco Español de Crédito; Bank of New York.

Corporate/M&A

Carey y Cia (4 ptrs, 16 asscs) The largest in the Chilean market, the firm is considered to be *"well set up,"* has good international connections and enjoys universal admiration in its home market for its *"extensive experience in M&A."* Generally acting for multi-nationals, the firm has enjoyed particular recent success in the fishing and telecoms industries.

Said to contain *"audacious, aggressive"* lawyers, the corporate team is led by the Carey brothers. **Jaime Carey*** *"knows the law from a technical aspect"* and has a *"reasoned and sound approach,"* while managing partner **Jorge Carey*** is a respected client-getter who has *"a lot of commercial clout."* The *"thoughtful"* **Jaime Martínez*** is also recommended for the first time this year.

The firm advised Swedish and Spanish companies on a successful bid for a $500 million toll road and its subsequent international financing, and acted on the merger of two Chilean health service providers, a deal valued at $300 million. **Clients:** Aur Resources; National Grid; Skanska; Dragados; Danisco; Statkorn Holding; Massai Agricultural Services; Celfor.

Cariola Diez Perez-Cotapos y Cia Market opinion suggests that this expanding and relatively young firm, is now considered to have one of the foremost corporate departments in Chile. Handling a range of work for multi-national clients

*See leaders' profiles on pages 209-210

C

CHILE Leading firms (Corporate/Mergers & Acquisitions)
1 Carey y Cia
Cariola Diez Perez-Cotapos y Cia
Claro y Cia
Philippi, Yrarrazaval, Pulido & Brunner
2 Guerrero, Olivos, Novoa y Errazuriz
Morales Noguera Valdivieso & Besa
Prieto y Cia
3 Barros & Errazuriz
Larrain y Asociados
Urenda Rencoret Orrego & Dörr
Yrrarazaval, Ruiz Tagle, Lagos & Silva
4 Cruzat, Ortuzar & McKenna (Baker & McKenzie)
Vial & Palma

Firms are listed alphabetically in each band.

Leading individuals (Corporate/Mergers & Acquisitions)
★ EYZAGUIRRE JNR José María *Claro y Cia*
1 CAREY Jorge *Carey y Cia*
CAREY Jaime *Carey y Cia*
EYZAGUIRRE Cristián *Claro y Cia*
MORALES Guillermo *Morales Noguera Valdivieso*
2 ERRAZURIZ José Thomas *Barros & Errazuriz*
GUERRERO JNR Roberto *Guerrero, Olivos*
HERRERA Luis Oscar *Cariola Diez Perez-Cotapos*
PRIETO Patricio *Prieto y Cia*
UNDURRAGA Claudio *Prieto y Cia*
YRARRAZAVAL Jaime *Philippi, Yrarrazaval*
YRARRAZAVAL Arturo *Yrarrazaval, Ruiz Tagle*
3 BARROS Fernando *Barros & Errazuriz*
CONCHA Carlos *Prieto y Cia*
DÖRR Juan Carlos *Urenda Rencoret Orrego*
EYZAGUIRRE SNR José María *Claro y Cia*
GUERRERO SNR Roberto *Guerrero, Olivos*
LARRAIN Carlos *Larrain y Asociados*
MARTÍNEZ Jaime *Carey y Cia*
OBACH Sebastian *Cariola Diez Perez-Cotapos*
ORREGO Alberto *Urenda Rencoret Orrego*
PALMA Juan Eduardo *Vial & Palma*

Individuals are listed alphabetically in each band.

such as Siemens, Coca-Cola, Rio Tinto and Walt Disney, the firm has extensive cross-border M&A experience in industries such as energy and food. A niche speciality in mining was highlighted by the team's advice on the restructuring of foreign investment contracts for the Minera Escondida project. **Luis Oscar Herrera*** and **Sebastian Obach*** are the firm's key corporate players.

The group advised Endesa on its sale of Transelec, the largest Chilean electricity company, a $1.1 billion deal. It also represented Kimberly-Clark on the purchase of local company Mimo, and Unilever on the sale of its Chilean food division. **Clients:** Endesa; Royal Dutch Shell; Unilever; Kimberly-Clark; Teledesic; Moranda.

Claro y Cia (5 ptrs, 30 asscs) A big-name corporate firm, with a proportionately strong litigation reputation, which numbers several North American clients among its international roster. Active in most industries, the firm has advised on the privatisations of toll roads, water and sewage companies and Santiago airport, as well as representing both buyers and sellers on cross-border M&A deals.

The *"excellent"* **José María Eyzaguirre Jnr*** is one of the most renowned lawyers in South America. Described by competitors as *"a young star, bright and energetic,"* he is *"just so gifted,"* and is rated in a category of his own in Chile. He receives strong support from the *"intelligent"* **Cristián Eyzaguirre***, a renowned transactional player, while paterfamilias **José María Eyzaguirre Snr*** remains an active and respected presence at the firm.

The team handled the $850 million acquisition of Enerquinta for PSCG, and the disposal by TransCanada of its Chilean assets. It also acted for AES in its prospective $1 billion takeover of Gener, domestic electricity provider. **Clients:** Citibank; American Airlines; TransCanada; PSCG.

Philippi, Yrarrazaval, Pulido & Brunner (4 ptrs, 10 asscs) *Chambers'* research indicates that the firm possesses an outstanding reputation for corporate work with an international focus, and maintains a traditional image, offering a service that is said to be *"serious and personalised."* The corporate group advises multi-nationals on their investments in Chile, as well as handling the international business of leading Chilean companies. Mining and natural resources are key specialist areas.

Undergoing rapid expansion, the team is considered to provide a uniformly high standard, although **Jaime Yrarrazaval*** stands out for his transactional expertise. The firm acted for Bank of Nova Scotia on its acquisition of Banco Suramericano, and for Gines (the second largest Chilean electric company) on its association with TotalFinaElf. Also advised on the acquisition by BBVA of the first Chilean pension fund, Provida. **Clients:** AT&T; Baff; Ford Motors; Patagon.com; Phelps Dodge; Aur Resources.

Guerrero, Olivos, Novoa y Errazuriz (5 ptrs, 10 asscs) An *"excellent"* smaller firm that is commended for *"quality"* M&A and financial work on behalf of international and national telecoms and utilities clients. Particularly regarded for its expertise in electricity, the team advised Hydro Quebec on its $1.1 billion acquisition of Transelec. This deal was led by **Roberto Guerrero Jnr***, who is respected for his transactional acumen. His father, **Roberto Guerrero Snr***, is known amongst rival firms as the *"driving force"* of the firm's recent expansion.

Recent transactional work includes the acquisition by Norske Skogg of a pulp plant from Fletcher Challenge, and the sale by Telefónica CTC Chile of a 40% holding in a major Chilean cable TV provider. **Clients:** Endesa; Zurich Financial Services; Accor; BAT; CSFB; Hilton; IFC; Siemens; Telefónica de España; Enron; Energis; Telefónica CTC Chile; Coca-Cola.

Morales Noguera Valdivieso & Besa (5 ptrs, 20 asscs) *"Aggressive"* new firm that is growing *"vigorously,"* and has been active on M&A and restructuring work, particularly in the telecoms sector. It advises both international purchasers and Chilean targets, and advised on the takeover by Iron Mountain of Chilean data management companies. The firm's informal relationship with White & Case provides it with a number of referrals from US-based entities, and the team acts as counsel to the Luksic Group, the major Chilean multi-national. Dynamic name partner **Guillermo Morales*** is seen by peers as an *"energetic and forceful"* practitioner.

The firm advised on Chilean aspects of the SmithKline Beecham/Glaxo Wellcome merger, advised a subsidiary of Quiñenco on the acquisition of Brazil's largest copper manufacturer and represented TotalFinaElf on the takeover of the Argentinean assets of Gener. **Clients:** British Embassy; Republic of Chile; Bechtel; Georgia-Pacific Corporation; Optiglobe; SmithKline Beecham; StarMedia; TotalFinaElf; Banco Edwards.

Prieto y Cia (7 ptrs, 11 asscs) Well known by peers for its transactional advice on behalf of Spanish clients, the corporate team continues to enjoy a sound reputation. Clients are both international and domestic, and include pension and insurance funds, local investment banks, and utilities.

"First-class" senior partner **Patricio Prieto*** heads the firm, with the assistance of M&A specialist **Claudio Undurraga***, and the *"more academic"* **Carlos Concha***, who is also acclaimed for anti-trust and tax matters. The three advised as counsel to two US rail freight clients on their acquisition of a controlling stake in Bolivian and Chilean rail cargo companies. Other transaction-

*See leaders' profiles on pages 209-210

al activity includes acting for Cadbury Schweppes on the purchase of a Chilean chocolate producer, and for Tractabel on acquiring interests in local power generating companies. **Clients:** Telefónica de España; Coface; Mapfre; Royal & SunAlliance; Larrain Vial; Electroandina; Grupo Santa Carolina; Grupo Malls Plaza; El Mercurio On-line.

Barros & Errazuriz (4 ptrs, 6 asscs) Although its size leads some in the market to consider the firm a corporate boutique, the group offers a full service to a mix of national and international clients, and has niche strength in financial services. Other areas of expertise include forestry, telecoms and internet start-ups. The *"thrusting"* **José Thomas Errazuriz*** and the well-connected **Fernando Barros*** are both recommended for M&A.

The firm advised Colgate-Palmolive on the acquisition of Cosméticos Bárbara Lee, and Patagon.com on the acquisition of Santander Direkt Bank from Banco Santander. Also represented Salomon Smith Barney, advisors to the Rabat family, on the sale of a stake in Telefónica Manquhue to Metrocom. **Clients:** Coca-Cola; Marriott; Southern Cross Private Equity Fund; Sky Latin America; Inter-American Investment Corporation; Telefónica Móvil; Viña Santa Carolina.

Larrain y Asociados (7 ptrs, 11 asscs) Name partner **Carlos Larrain*** now combines his legal practice with a career in local politics, a move which has affected the firm's overall profile, as this *"smart lawyer"* is *"the outstanding figure at the firm."* The firm is known for its advice on public works and electricity transactions, and advises its predominantly domestic client base on day-to-day corporate matters and commercial contracts. **Clients:** BBV; Chilequinta; Royal & Sunalliance; The Southern Company; Locktite; Iberdrola; Cristofel; Coninental; Glencore; W. Grace.

Urenda Rencoret Orrego & Dörr A small, full-service firm that is principally recognised for its expertise with mining clients and its general M&A work. The firm also advises Mercurio, the leading local media group owned by the Edwards family. Experienced **Juan Carlos Dörr*** is respected for transactional work, while his partner **Alberto Orrego Snr*** is a *"good technician"* with a track record of cross-border advice. **Clients:** El Mercurio; Minera Escondida; General Electric; General Motors; Hewlett Packard; IFC; 3M; Reuters; Sony; Dow Chemicals.

Yrarrazaval, Ruiz Tagle, Lagos & Silva (4 ptrs, 6 asscs) A March 2000 spin-off from Philippi Yrarrazaval, this new firm has gained an enviable reputation in a short time. Considered by rivals to have an *"interesting"* future, the corporate team advises a blue-chip international clientele, and is strongly transactionally inclined.

The *"outstanding"* **Arturo Yrarrazaval*** has a superb reputation for corporate work, and heads a team which advised on the acquisition by Industri Kapital of Dyno Nobel's activities in Chile. The firm's transactional activity includes representing Bahco in the Chilean leq of acquisition of a holding in Swedish multinational, Sandrik, and acting for the largest sugar producer IANSA on a joint venture with Cargill. **Clients:** Mitsubishi; Etna; BOC; Cemex; CIBA; Compaq; Continental Airlines; Generali; Levi-Strauss; M&M/Mars; McDonalds; Procter & Gamble; Whirlpool.

Cruzat, Ortuzar & McKenna (Baker & McKenzie) (5 ptrs, 17 asscs) The Santiago office of the international network concentrates on cross-border M&A work, but our researchers have found that it is not considered to have had a major impact on the domestic transactional scene.

The corporate department recently acted for the Williams companies on the acquisition of 50% of Telefónica Manquehue, and advised on the formation of AT&T Latin America, the product of the $1 billion merger between AT&T and FirstCom. **Clients:** Viña Concha de Toro; SouthWestern Bell; AT&T; Henry Walker Mining; Nortel; Vivendi; Willis Insurance; Fomento de Construcciones y Contratos.

Vial & Palma (6 ptrs, 11asscs) A small firm with a long history of transactional involvement in the telecoms, retail and banking sectors. Market consensus is that the firm owes much to the respected **Juan Eduardo Palma***, who *"clearly stands out."* The group is a familiar player on cross-border transactions within Latin America, and represented Chilean/Peruvian Farmacias Ahumada on the purchase of a Brazilian pharmacy chain. It also acted for Viña Carta Vieja on the distribution of wines in Ecuador. Elsewhere, the team advised the Luksic Group on the sale of Banco Santiago to Banco Santander Central Hispano. **Clients:** Liberty Media; BP; Inchcape; Lloyds TSB; Toronto Dominion Bank; Williamson Balfour.

C

Leaders' profiles – Chile

BARROS, Cristián
Barros & Errazuriz Abogados, Santiago +56 2 378 9777
Recommended in Banking & Finance

BARROS, Fernando
Barros & Errazuriz Abogados, Santiago +56 2 378 9777
Recommended in Corporate/M&A

BESA, Eugenio
Morales Noguera Valdivieso & Besa, Santiago +56 2 750 2900
Recommended in Banking & Finance

BRONFMAN, Jimena
Guerrero, Olivos, Novoa y Errazuriz, Santiago +56 2 639 0169
Recommended in Banking & Finance

CAREY, Jaime
Carey y Cia, Santiago +56 2 365 7200
Recommended in Corporate/M&A

CAREY, Jorge
Carey y Cia, Santiago +56 2 365 7200
Recommended in Corporate/M&A

CONCHA, Carlos
Prieto y Cia, Santiago +562 280 5000
Recommended in Corporate/M&A

DEL PIANO, Jorge
Guerrero, Olivos, Novoa y Errazuriz, Santiago +56 2 639 0169
Recommended in Banking & Finance

DÖRR, Juan Carlos
Urenda Rencoret Orrego & Dörr, Santiago +56 2 655 9090
Recommended in Corporate/M&A

ERRAZURIZ, José Thomas
Barros & Errazuriz Abogados, Santiago +56 2 378 9777
Recommended in Corporate/M&A

EYZAGUIRRE, Cristián
Claro y Cia, Santiago +56 2 367 3000
ceyzaguirre@claro.cl
Recommended in Corporate/M&A
Specialisation: Corporate law, securities, banking and finance law, international transactions, mergers and acquisitions and project finance.
Prof. Memberships: International and Inter-American Bar Associations, British Chamber of Commerce, US Chamber of Commerce.
Publications: 'International Survey of Investment Adviser Regulation' Graham & Trotman (1994). 'International Franchising Law' Matthew Bender (1994). 'Aircraft Liens & Detention Rights' Sweet &

Maxwell (to be published in 2001). 'Aircraft Finance: Registration, Security & Enforcement – Release 23' Sweet & Maxwell (2000).
Career: Admitted 1976, Chile. Professor of Commercial Law, University of Chile.

EYZAGUIRRE JNR, José María
Claro y Cia, Santiago +56 2 367 3000
Recommended in Banking & Finance, Corporate/M&A

EYZAGUIRRE SNR, José María
Claro y Cia, Santiago +56 2 367 3000
Recommended in Corporate/M&A

GRANICH, Jorge
Larrain y Asociados, Santiago +56 2 203 1241
Recommended in Banking & Finance

GUERRERO JNR, Roberto
Guerrero, Olivos, Novoa y Errazuriz, Santiago +56 2 639 0169
Recommended in Banking & Finance, Corporate/M&A

GUERRERO SNR, Roberto
Guerrero, Olivos, Novoa y Errazuriz, Santiago +56 2 639 0169
Recommended in Corporate/M&A

HERRERA, Luis Oscar
Cariola Diez Perez-Cotapos y Cia Ltda, Santiago +56 2 360 4000
Recommended in Corporate/M&A

ILLANES, Francisco Javier
Cariola Diez Perez-Cotapos y Cia Ltda, Santiago +56 2 360 4000
Recommended in Banking & Finance

LARRAIN, Carlos
Larrain y Asociados, Santiago +56 2 203 1241
Recommended in Corporate/M&A

LARRAIN, Paulo
Morales Noguera Valdivieso & Besa, Santiago +56 2 750 2900
Recommended in Banking & Finance

LEVIN, Juan Guillermo
Carey y Cia, Santiago +56 2 365 7200
Recommended in Banking & Finance

MARTÍNEZ, Jaime
Carey y Cia, Santiago +56 2 365 7200
Recommended in Banking & Finance, Corporate/M&A

MORALES, Guillermo
Morales Noguera Valdivieso & Besa, Santiago +56 2 750 2907 (mobile +56 9 333 4398)
Recommended in Corporate/M&A

OBACH, Sebastian
Cariola Diez Perez-Cotapos y Cia Ltda, Santiago +56 2 360 4000
Recommended in Banking & Finance, Corporate/M&A

OLIVOS, Carlos
Guerrero, Olivos, Novoa y Errazuriz, Santiago +56 2 639 0169
Recommended in Banking & Finance

ORREGO, Alberto
Urenda Rencoret Orrego & Dörr, Santiago +56 2 655 9090
Recommended in Banking & Finance, Corporate/M&A

PALMA, Juan Eduardo
Vial & Palma, Santiago +56 2 240 6500 jpalma@vialpa.cl
Recommended in Corporate/M&A
Specialisation: Main area of work is corporate law, principally mergers, acquisitions, joint ventures and project finance in Chile and overseas. Has handled acquisitions of companies and undertakings of varying sorts by international clients. Acted for lenders and investors, project finance Nittetsu Mining Co., Ltd. in a joint venture for the construction and development of a copper concentrate flotation plant and new copper mine in the North of Chile. Acted for British Petroleum (now British Petroleum Amoco) in the incorporation in Chile of BP Chile Petrolera Limitada, a 100% subsidary of British Petroleum Amoco. Acted as a member of the advising team, for the Luksic Group in the sale of Banco Santiago (Chile) to Banco Santander Central Hispano (España) as a result of the merger in Spain of Banco Santander and Banco Central Hispano.
Prof. Memberships: Member, Arbitration Commission of the Chilean/North American Chamber of Commerce of the Chilean, Chilean Bar Association (Former Council Member), IBA and UIA.
Career: Awarded the Montenegro award for highest academic performance, 1973. Professor, Commercial Law, Universidad de Chile School of Law. Director: Standard Wool Chile, Canon Chile. Former Director Chilean/British Chamber of Commerce; Banco BHIF BBV.
Personal: Born April 11, 1952. Attended James B. Conant High School, Hoffman Estates, Illinois, 1968-69. Attended Universidad de Chile School of Law.

PERALTA, Diego
Carey y Cia, Santiago +56 2 365 7200
Recommended in Banking & Finance

PRIETO, Patricio
Prieto y Cia, Santiago +562 280 5000
Recommended in Corporate/M&A

PULIDO SNR, Alberto
Philippi, Yrarrazaval, Pulido & Brunner, Santiago +56 2 364 3700
Recommended in Banking & Finance

UNDURRAGA, Claudio
Prieto y Cia, Santiago +562 280 5000
Recommended in Corporate/M&A

YRARRAZAVAL, Arturo
Yrarrázaval, Ruiz Tagle, Lagos & Silva, Santiago +56 2 750 0200 ayrarrazaval@yrls.cl
Recommended in Corporate/M&A
Specialisation: Senior Partner. Main areas of work include General Corporate and Commercial Law, Foreign Investments and Financing, Mergers and Acquisitions, Antitrust and Commercial Arbitration.
Prof. Memberships: Chilean Bar Association, International Bar Association and Inter-American Bar Association.
Career: Admitted in 1970 in Chile. New York University Law School – Master in Comparative Jurisprudence. Yale Law School – Juris Science Doctor. Partner *Philippi, Yrarrázaval, Pulido & Brunner* 1973-1999. Member Antitrust Committee 1979-1989, 1995-1997. Professor of Law and Post Graduate Programs at Catholic University and University of Los Andes. Founding Partner *Yrarrázaval, Ruiz-Tagle, Lagos & Silva*, 2000.
Personal: Born Santiago, 7 July 1946.

YRARRAZAVAL, Jaime
Philippi, Yrarrazaval, Pulido & Brunner, Santiago +56 2 364 3700
Recommended in Corporate/M&A

CHINA

Index

OVERVIEW: Poised to join the WTO, western firms are currently cementing their presence on the mainland (one office per firm and permission required from the Ministry of Justice) in response to client demand for local expertise. Shanghai, traditionally the commercial focus, has now joined Beijing in assisting state-owned entities raise cash on the capital markets. A further relaxation in the market is anticipated as demand for sophisticated legal services outstrips the capacity at the domestic bar. The widespread perception persists that China is set to be one of the great legal honey-pots.

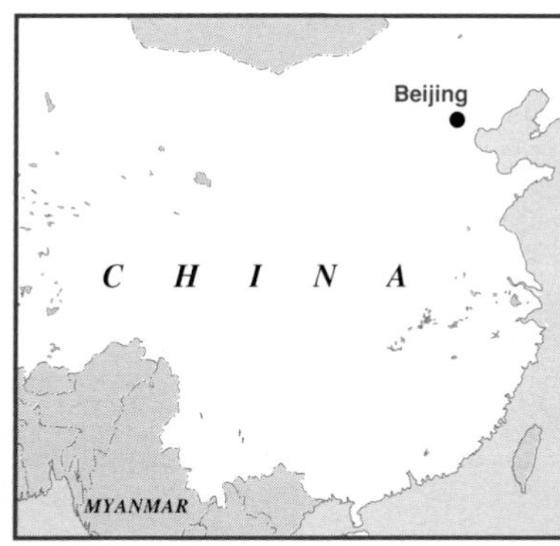

C

Corporate/M&A: Local Firms

CHINA Leading firms (Corporate/Mergers & Acquisitions)
1 Commerce & Finance Law Offices
Haiwen & Partners
Jingtian & Gongcheng
Jun He Law Offices
2 King & Wood
3 Fangda Partners
Llinks Law Office
Summit Law Office
4 Shanghai Pu Dong Law Office
Zheng Liu Yuan & Zhou Law Office

Firms are listed alphabetically in each band.

Leading individuals (Corporate/Mergers & Acquisitions)	
1 **HE Fei**	*Haiwen & Partners*
JI Jianfeng	*Summit Law Office*
2 **LIU Gang**	*Commerce & Finance Law Offices*
WANG Ling	*King & Wood*
XIAO Wei	*Jun He Law Offices*
ZHANG Xusheng	*Jingtian & Gongcheng*
3 **HAN Xiaojing**	*Commerce & Finance Law Offices*
LIU Linfei	*Jun He Law Offices*
LIU David Dali	*Llinks Law Office*
MAO Baigen	*Shanghai Pu Dong Law Office*
ZHENG Shujun	*Zheng Liu Yuan & Zhou Law Office*

Individuals are listed alphabetically in each band.

Commerce & Finance Law Offices (9 ptrs, 31 asscs) A leader in the market with a major share of big ticket telecoms deals, the team also scores well with a long track record for IPOs. A strong group of individuals is led by the *"particularly good"* **Gang Liu*** while **Xiaojing Han*** receives market commendation. The team acted in China Mobile's $6 billion acquisition of the mobile telephone networks of Fulian, Henan and Hainan provinces in the PRC and advised Morgan Stanley as lead arranger in the $5 billion dual listed IPO of China Unicom. **Clients:** Morgan Stanley; Goldman Sachs; Fiat; China Telecom.

Haiwen & Partners (8 ptrs, 20 asscs) With a strong focus on corporate finance and IPO work, this strong team is recommended for its depth of experience in quality transactions. Instrumental in the success of the practice is US-trained **He Fei***, judged to *"really know what he is doing."* He has earned a reputation as *"the most prestigious securities lawyer in China,"* when he speaks *"everyone listens."* The team acted as PRC counsel to Chase Securities, the arranger in a $234 million securitisation of freight receivables generated by China Ocean Shipping (Group) Company and as PRC counsel to China Unicom in its $5 billion IPO. **Clients:** China corporates; arrangers; underwriters.

Jingtian & Gongcheng The merger of the two quality firms Jingtian Associates and Gong Cheng Associates has been warmly welcomed as a positive move. Competitors view the firm as strong in securities and IPO work. In a team of fine individuals, **Xusheng Zhang*** is well regarded for producing a *"high volume"* deal flow with *"impressive quality."* **Clients:** Corporates; arrangers; underwriters.

Jun He Law Offices (15 ptrs, 30 asscs) A blend of local and foreign lawyers have combined to produce particular strengths in direct investment and finance. In this arena the high profile **Wei Xiao*** is considered *"knowledgeable"* while **Linfei Liu*** is recommended as a *"good technical lawyer."*

The team represented Colgate-Palmolive in its $30 million acquisition of Jiangsu Sanxia Group, advised the main shareholder of the target company in China Huawen Enterprise Development Corporation's $120 million acquisition of Hainan Minsheng Gas Corporation, and represented China Cinda in its $3.2 million acquisition of 11 large companies in Shanxi and Inner-Mogolia. **Clients:** Dow Jones; Eastman Kodak; Nippon Steel; Mitsubishi.

King & Wood (7 ptrs, 20 asscs) A large Beijing-based practice with a broad coverage and strength in litigation. Although senior partner Yaoliang Gu has left to form his own practice, **Ling Wang*** maintains the team's senior profile in corporate and banking law. The team acted as Chinese counsel to the issuer in SINA.com's Nasdaq offering and advised China National Petroleum Corporation on its IPO. In M&A it advised Huaneng Power International on the merger by absorption of Shandong Huaneng Power Development Co.

*See leaders' profiles on pages 216-218

Clients: Multi-national corporations; financial institutions; major domestic companies; private investors.

Fangda Partners (5 ptrs, 13 asscs) A Shanghai based practice with a fine reputation for direct investments and IPOs, acting on six domestic public offerings in the past year. The team represented CICC as lead underwriter and sponsor in the public offering of Baosteel and was involved in four IPOs listed in the GEM market including SIIC MedTech and Qianlong Technologies. Active in private equity work, the firm represents investors and start-ups in the telecoms, media and internet industries. **Clients:** CICC; Merrill Lynch; Salomon Smith Barney; Guotai Securities; DBS Capital; ING Baring; NewMargin; IDG; Morningside.

Llinks Law Office (5 ptrs, 6 asscs) A relatively recent entrant to the market, this Shanghai based team is renowned for the quality of its work with a focus on foreign investment. It is also one of the firms authorised to advise on Chinese securities law. **David Dali Liu*** is *"well-known"* in the Shanghai market.

The team assists Hong Kong and Singaporean entities wishing to list in China and recently represented the first insurance company in the world to do so. It advised Fosters in a joint venture to merge its FIEs into a fully-owned enterprise and advised Unilever in its merger of its 4 FIE entities into one company. **Clients:** Morgan Stanley; JP Morgan; Peregrine; international corporates; PRC-listed companies.

Summit Law Office Although thought to be overshadowed by its projects prowess, the team is well respected for finance-related corporate work where **Jianfeng Ji***, whose *"name means Summit"*, is particularly noted. The firm advised Bright World Enterprise in relation to its acquisition of a 2x300MW unit thermal power plant in Shanxi Province and acted for Compagnie Generale des Eaux of France in its acquisition of water treatment projects and waste water treatment projects in China. **Clients:** Lenders; local banks; Chinese corporates.

Shanghai Pu Dong Law Office A powerful relationship with the state and a strong track record continues to drive this firm's profile. Thought to have suffered with the loss of individuals recently, *"senior player"* **Baigen Mao*** maintains the firm's strong reputation for corporate and litigation matters. **Clients:** GM; Barclays Bank; Intel; Shanghai Petro-Chemical; China Eastern Airlines.

Zheng Liu Yuan & Zhou Law Office (A small office with an outstanding reputation for commercial work particularly on the projects side. **Shujun Zheng*** is a senior lawyer with a depth of experience who *"keeps well on top of market developments."* **Clients:** Chinese corporates; lenders.

Corporate/M&A: Foreign Firms

CHINA: Foreign firms Leading firms (Corporate/Mergers and Acquisitions)	
1	Freshfields Bruckhaus Deringer
2	Baker & McKenzie
	Clifford Chance
3	Allen & Overy
	Paul, Weiss, Rifkind, Wharton & Garrison
	Shearman & Sterling
4	Coudert Brothers
	Denton Wilde Sapte
	Linklaters
	White & Case LLP
5	Herbert Smith
	Lovells
	O'Melveny & Myers LLP

Firms are listed alphabetically in each band.

Freshfields Bruckhaus Deringer A clear leader in the field due to its depth, ever expanding work load and a set of lawyers with strong market knowledge and Chinese language skills. It has a following of governments and top-drawer corporations. Steeped in Chinese deal experience, **Michael Moser*** brings impeccable language skills to his international arbitration general commercial work where rivals acknowledge that *"he's the man."* The *"superb"* **Norman Givant*** is another *"old China hand,"* focused on direct investment in Shanghai, while **Thomas Jones*** is *"calm and steady"* bringing *"good technique and historical perspective"* to his listing of China companies. **Lucille Barale*** is a *"quiet achiever."*

The team acted for China Mobile on the $60 billion acquisition of the mobile telephone networks of Fujian, Henan and Hainan provinces in the PRC, financed by a $2 billion international equity offering and a $600 million debt offering. It also advised China Telecom on its $6.4 billion acquisition of mobile networks in China, financed through a $1.65 billion equity offering and a $500 million debt offering, and advised Nokia on the development of a world-class telecoms industrial park in Beijing. **Clients:** Multinational and local corporates.

Baker & McKenzie (6 ptrs, 10 asscs) Bouncing back after the departure of some notable individuals, the practice still has a healthy band of names. Tightly knit, the group is seen to take full advantage of a great client base and concrete know-how systems. High profile and long established, the *"excellent"* **Stephen Nelson*** has a low-key attitude and really *"knows his stuff"* on the structuring side of transactions. **Clients:** Multinational corporates and lenders.

Clifford Chance (9 ptrs, 30 asscs) A wonderful broad-based practice which benefits from the support of a world-wide network. Philip Rapp has relocated to Singapore leaving the group in the capable hands of the *"calm, collected and steady"* **Gao Peiji***, who *"understands the concerns of Western business"*, and **Stuart Valentine*** with his *"good length of experience."*

The team acted for a major multi-national in setting up a hi-tech R&D centre and assisted two foreign insurance companies with approval to establish and operate joint ventures. In M&A it advised a major pharmaceutical company in a proposed merger of its manufacturing joint ventures in Shanghai and represented ING on the acquisition of Aetna's business in China, Hong Kong and several other Asian jurisdictions. **Clients:** Multi-national corporates and major financial institutions.

Allen & Overy Strong in finance and banking, the team has a great client base and is active on big ticket deals. It advised Morgan Grenfell Private Equity on the Chinese aspects of the billion dollar acquisition by a European investment bank of a global manufacturing business (Performance Polymers) spreading over 15 countries. **Mitchell Silk*** is *"a solid practitioner"* considered by peers to be China's leading environmental lawyer, and **Kenneth Chan*** is a *"steady hand"* whose indus-

CHINA: Foreign firms Leading individuals (Corporate/Mergers & Acquisitions)
1 **GAO Peiji** *Clifford Chance*
GIVANT Norman *Freshfields Bruckhaus Deringer*
HARPOLE Sally *Morrison & Foerster LLP*
JONES Thomas *Freshfields Bruckhaus Deringer*
MOSER Michael *Freshfields Bruckhaus Deringer*
2 **BARALE Lucille** *Freshfields Bruckhaus Deringer*
BERSANI Matthew *Shearman & Sterling*
CHAO Howard *O'Melveny & Myers LLP*
KAY David Ben *Denton Wilde Sapte*
KUZMIK John *White & Case LLP*
NEE Owen *Coudert Brothers*
NELSON Stephen *Baker & McKenzie*
VALENTINE Stuart *Clifford Chance*
3 **BATH Vivienne** *Coudert Brothers*
CHAN Kenneth *Allen & Overy*
CHAN Jeanette *Paul, Weiss, Rifkind, Wharton*
HOWSON Nicholas *Paul, Weiss, Rifkind, Wharton*
SILK Mitchell *Allen & Overy*
YOUNG Jack *Herbert Smith*
Individuals are listed alphabetically in each band.

try experience allows him *"a business perspective"* on deals.

The team advised China Insurance HK (Holdings) Co Ltd, the Hong Kong subsidary of one of the PRC's largest insurance companies on its listing in Hong Kong. Acted for Daewoo in the unwinding of its arrangements of China Unicom in the GSM network involving the negotiation of a multi hundred million dollar compensation package. **Clients:** Daewoo; Morgan Greenfell; Private Equity; China Insurance HK (Holdings) Co; ING Baring; Miler Freeman.

Paul, Weiss, Rifkind, Wharton & Garrison (4 ptrs, 15 asscs) Although it is occasionally thought of as *"conservative,"* researchers were impressed by the firm's reputation for high quality work notably in the telecommunications sector. **Jeanette Chan*** is considered a *"telecoms specialist"* and **Nicholas Howson*** is respected on the commercial side. The famed Jerome Cohen is now based in New York. The team represented CSFB and Merrill Lynch in the NYSE listing of Shangdong Huaneng Power Generation, advised George Soros on the acquisition of a 25% stake in Hainan Airlines and represented Metromedia Corporation in the China Unicom CCF unwind. **Clients:** Soros Funds Management; ExxonMobil; Credit Agricole Indosuez; IFC; Heinz; McDonald's Corporation; News Corp; Monsanto Corporation; Metromedia; General Motors.

Shearman & Sterling (3 ptrs, 15 asscs) Heavily weighted towards capital markets and securities, the firm is also recommended for its work in privatisations. Speaking fluent Mandarin **Matthew Bersani*** has a number of large Beijing deals under his belt. The team represented PetroChina and China National Petroleum Corporation in the $3 billion dual listing and IPO of PetroChina and acted for the underwriters, led by Bear Stearns, in the $270 million dual listing and IPO of Yanzhou Coal Mining Company. It also advised the underwriters in the $4 billion dual listing of China Telecom and its subsequent $2 billion 1999 follow-on equity offering. **Clients:** Multi-national corporates; leading underwriters.

Coudert Brothers A practice with a long history in China, it has retained the respect of the market despite recent defections and subsequent instability. *"Old hand"* **Owen Nee*** is a high profile player with *"good political skills"* and the *"superb"* **Vivienne Bath*** is *"well-recognised"* for GEM listings. The practice is focused on direct investment work and has represented clients accross a broad range of industries and includes acting as counsel to international oil companies; representing multi-national automobile companies investing in China and advising NEC in its television venture in China. **Clients:** Underwriters; arrangers; international corporates.

Denton Wilde Sapte (2 ptrs, 5 asscs) A long-standing presence in the Chinese market, this team has a good reputation for direct investment work. Much of this profile is attributed to the success of the *"superb"* **David Ben Kay*** who enjoys a *"wonderful reputation"* in direct investment. **Clients:** Multi-national corporates; investment banks.

Linklaters (2 ptrs, 15 asscs) A relatively recent arrival in China, the practice continues to grow after recruiting two of the Simmons & Simmons Shanghai partners. Heavily involved in the hi-tech and telecoms market, the team acted for China Telecom (Hong Kong) Ltd in its acquisition of mobile networks in Fujian, Henan and Hainan provinces worth about $6.4 billion, and advised a leading US electronics group in the acquisition of a $325 million stake in a manufacturing business in the PRC. The firm also advised a Hong Kong-based private equity fund in the acquisition of a manufacturing business in the PRC and represented Softbank on its e-commerce investments. **Clients:** Multi-national corporates; investment banks.

White & Case LLP This developing practice has followed its corporate and banking clients over to Asia and is focused on big-ticket direct investment and projects work. **John Kuzmik*** has a broad coverage on the corporate side and is active in direct investment where peers have judged him *"a great lawyer with good commercial skills."* Recent deals include the documentation and negotiation of several oil and gas exploration and development contracts for multinational and independent petroleum companies; the establishment of an automobile manufacturing joint venture in central China and the establishment of several petrochemical and speciality chemical joint ventures. **Clients:** International investment banks.

Herbert Smith (3 ptrs, 8 asscs) Interviewees recommended this practice to our researchers for its business-like approach and strength in share listings and IPO work. *"Strong commercial lawyer"* **Jack Young*** is active in direct investment work and a key player in the firm's success. The team acted for the issuer in the SINOPEC $3.4 billion privatisation and triple listed IPO and advised Beijing Beida Jade Bird Universal Sci-Tech Company on its GEM listing. It also advised Expressway Company on a secondary listing in London and represented the investment banks in the IPO of Phoenix Satellite Television Holdings. **Clients:** ABN (Overseas); British Sugar; Amway; Metro Holdings; Grünenthal; BAA Pacific; HSBC.

Lovells (2 ptrs, 7 asscs) Since receiving a licence in 1992 this small practice has been run out in Hong Kong and Beijing. This active team is thought to contain solid, commercial lawyers yet run a low profile operation. Advised a major American metals company on land use rights issues relating to the building of a $45 million metals fabrication plant at a Chinese coastal city; advised a major Japanese telecommunications network company in establishing its first formal presence in the PRC; advised a Hong Kong investment company on its joint venture turn key project in iron and steel processing and acted for a British water company in structuring its technology-intensive joint venture project with a Chinese municipal government. **Clients:** International investment banks; corporates.

O'Melveny & Myers LLP (2 ptrs, 8 asscs) A recent entrant to the scene with a small operation in Shanghai. This growing team has a solid base of corporate and finance clients in Asia and is focused on direct investment and finance related work. Well established **Howard Chao*** is a *"smart lawyer"* recommended for his investment work. The firm advised private equity fund ASIMCO in the sale of stakes in two beer ventures to Qingdao,

C

*See leaders' profiles on pages 216-218

and advised renren.com and an investor group on the acquisition of a controlling stake in Ankor Group. It also advised China Southern Airlines in its acquisition of domestic Chinese carriers and Softbank AIG in its investment in Good Baby. **Clients:** Pillsbury Foods; Chengwei Ventures; China Southern Airlines; Ford Motors.

Other Notable Practitioner **Sally Harpole*** has recently departed Deacons to head up the Chinese practice of Morrison & Foerster LLP. Recommended for her depth of experience and knowledge of the technology market, she has an outstanding reputation for corporate matters and international arbitration.

Project Finance: Local Firms

CHINA Leading firms (Project Finance)
1 Summit Law Office
East Associates
Zheng Liu Yuan & Zhou Law Office
2 Jingtian & Gongcheng
Jun He Law Offices
King & Wood
3 Commerce & Finance Law Offices
Llinks Law Office
Shanghai Pu Dong Law Office

Firms are listed alphabetically in each band.

Leading individuals (Project Finance)
1 CHEN Ji Yuan *Xin Ji Yuan Law Office*
JI Jianfeng *Summit Law Office*
ZHENG Shujun *Zheng Liu Yuan & Zhou Law Office*
2 WANG Ling *King & Wood*

Individuals are listed alphabetically in each band.

Summit Law Office (3 ptrs, 2 asscs) A highly focused practice regarded by peers as a local leader on the finance side. With his *"considerable experience"* **Jianfeng Ji*** is a key player at the firm who takes the time to deal with issues *"thoroughly and carefully."* The team acted for the international syndicated lenders on the $530 million project financing of the Changsha BOT Power Project in the Hunan Province and advised the lenders in relation to the $502 million financing of the BOT Laibin B Power Project in Guangxi Zhuang Autonomous Region. **Clients:** Crédit Agricole Indosuez; Barclays de Zoete Wedd Limited; HSBC Investment Bank; National Westminster Bank.

East Associates (6 ptrs, 7 asscs) A new firm resulting from a merger between Xin Ji Yuan Law Office, East Capital Law Offices and Tianda Law Firm. A key player in the projects domain largely due to the presence of **Ji Yuan Chen***, who has played a major role in recent large projects. A *"real market leader,"* she is admired as an analytical lawyer who can deal with complex transactions and has a good grasp of English law concepts. The team acted for China Power Technology Import and Export Corporation, the investor on the Cambodia Hydro-power Plant Rehabilitation BOT Project. It advised the China Water Company (Changchun) on the Changchun Waste Water Plant and Singapore investors on the Jilin Panshi Water Treatment Project. **Clients:** Compagnie Generale des Eaux; China Power Technology Import and Export Corporation; China Water Company (Changchun).

Zheng Liu Yuan & Zhou Law Office A niche practice, with a broad experience, reputed to have a good degree of consistency on major projects. *"Sensible and focused,"* **Shujun Zheng*** is a senior lawyer who is regarded by peers as experienced in the market place. **Clients:** Leading lenders.

Jingtian & Gongcheng Well regarded by peers locally and in the international market, this team has a strong client base and is a regular player in the projects market. The firm is heavily involved in telecoms, energy and natural resources. **Clients:** Leading international investment banks.

Jun He Law Offices (6 ptrs, 20 asscs) Known in the market for doing projects work and assisting-foreign companies with investment projects in China. Acts as local counsel in advising clients about their China investments in a range of industries including power, telecomunications, pharmaceuticals, mining and electronics. Work over the past year includes working on the Enron International power plant project and the Placer Dome gold mine project. **Clients:** Investment banks; local corporates; foreign corporates.

King & Wood (7 ptrs, 20 asscs) Chambers' researchers were told that this broad-based practice is an important part of the local market where **Ling Wang*** has enjoyed *"a good deal of success"* over past years. The team acted for the syndicated lenders and ECGD on the financing for the Shandong Zhonghua Power Company project including a 2x30MW coal-fired Shiheng I Power Station, a 2x30MW coal-fired Shiheng II Power Station, a 2x30MW coal-fired Heze II Power Station and a 2x60MW coal-fired Liaocheng Power Station. **Clients:** Multi-national corporations; financial institutions; major domestic companies; private investors.

Commerce & Finance Law Offices (2 ptrs, 2 asscs) A good name for finance generally and highly regarded for project work. Acted for the lender in the in the $755 million 2x360MW Meizhou Wan Power Project. **Clients:** Bank of America; CSFB; Paribas; Tokai Bank; Bear Sterns; US industrial and infrastructure investors

Llinks Law Office (2 ptrs, 4 asscs) One of the best known practices in Shanghai, strong in finance work encompassing banking and projects. The team is active in power projects and restructuring transactions. **Clients:** Financial institutions.

Shanghai Pu Dong Law Office Known for its projects work in Shanghai, the team represents clients in negotiations between Chinese and foreign parties with a focus on the industrial, manufacturing and real estate sectors. **Clients:** Financial institutions.

Project Finance: Foreign Firms

CHINA: Foreign firms Leading firms (Project Finance)
1 Clifford Chance
Freshfields Bruckhaus Deringer
2 Allen & Overy
Baker & McKenzie
Shearman & Sterling
3 Coudert Brothers
Herbert Smith
Linklaters
Paul, Weiss, Rifkind, Wharton & Garrison
White & Case LLP
4 Denton Wilde Sapte
Johnson Stokes & Master

Firms are listed alphabetically in each band.

Leading individuals (Project Finance)
1 HARDER Stephen *Clifford Chance*
JENKINS Huw *Clifford Chance*
PLATT David *Shearman & Sterling*
YOUNG Jack *Herbert Smith*
2 BARALE Lucille *Freshfields Bruckhaus Deringer*
CROZER George *White & Case LLP*
GAO Peiji *Clifford Chance*
JONES Thomas *Freshfields Bruckhaus Deringer*
KUZMIK John *White & Case LLP*
NELSON Stephen *Baker & McKenzie*
SILK Mitchell *Allen & Overy*
3 GIVANT Norman *Freshfields Bruckhaus Deringer*
NEE Owen *Coudert Brothers*
SHAO Zili *Linklaters*

Individuals are listed alphabetically in each band.

Clifford Chance Well-established in the market, the practice garnered the admiration of the market for its work with lenders and sponsors alike. A consistently high-quality team is driven by its enviable client base. **Stephen Harder*** is perceived to be heavily involved and is described by his peers as a lawyer who *"knows how to get things done"* in China and can *"build a consensus in meetings."* **Huw Jenkins*** is *"highly skilled and well-rounded,"* while **Gao Peiji** * is a senior PRC-generalist who brings good local perspective to a transaction. Advised the preferred bidder on the Changsha BOT power project in Hunan Province; advised the investor group in relation to the development of a Greenfield 2x660 MW class coal-fired plant in Taishan, Guangdong province, and advised one of the potential bidders to the Bejing No. 10 Water Treatment BOT project. Also acted for a consortium in relation to an LNG project in Guangdong Province with an estimated total investment of $550 million and advised the commercial lenders on the $4.2 billion Integrated Petrochemical Site financing for Sinopec Yangzi Petrochemical Company and Germany's BASF in Nanjing, PRC. **Clients:** Leading financial institutions; multi-national corporates.

Freshfields Bruckhaus Deringer The firm's good internal structure is seen as an important element of its success, with a broad client base of governments, sponsors and banks. With a number of complex deals under her belt **Lucille Barale*** is *"gifted"* in Chinese matters. **Norman Givant*** has a *"formidable reputation"* for project financing and **Thomas Jones***'s *"broad China experience"* and *"good connections"* add value to US transactions.

The team acted for TotalFina and Gaz de France on its proposed bid for the foreign investor stake in the Guangdong LNG receiving terminal project in the PRC and advised US EXIM on the Changshu Power Project. **Clients:** International financial institutions and sponsors.

Allen & Overy (6 ptrs, 15 asscs) Drawing on a strong banking reputation, the project finance practice is judged to be one of the best in the market. Leading light **Mitchell Silk*** is respected for his depth of experience and fluent language skills. The team advised the Asian Development Bank and EIB as lead lenders on the Chengdu No. 6 Water Plant Project in the Sichuan Province and advised Thames Water International, Mitsui & Co and Bovis in a bid for the development of the $300 million Beijing No. 10 Water Treatment Plant 'A' Project. It acted for the lead financiers on the $528 million 750MW Meizhouwan Power Project and as part of the large-scale restructuring of Guangdong Enterprises, the group has advised on the financing of a $600 million renovation for the Dongshen Water Project. **Clients:** A consortium of major international water developers.

Baker & McKenzie (4 ptrs, 8 asscs) Supported by a strong Chinese presence and broad general practice, **Stephen Nelson*** continues to be a major presence on project financings. The firm acted for BP Amoco on the $2.5-3 billion Jinshan petrochemical project, one of the two major approved Ethylene Cracker Projects in China, and advised the European Investment Bank on the $75 million Chengdu BOT Water Treatment Plant. Also active on infrastructure projects in Taiwan including three out of four IPP power projects and the CKS Airport Rail project. **Clients:** BP Amoco; European Investment Bank.

Shearman & Sterling (2 ptrs, 7 asscs) A strong practice recently boosted by the recruitment of the respected **David Platt*** from Linklaters. With an *"excellent market reputation,"* and a *"good grasp"* of Chinese matters, he adds a valuable English law capability to the team. The firm advised the banks in both the Changsha and Puqi power projects. On the sponsor side, the team acted for InterGen in the $755 million 2x360MW Meizhou Wan Power Project and advised BASF on a potential petrochemical project. **Clients:** World Bank; InterGen; BASF.

Coudert Brothers On the scene for a number of years, the team has a strong reputation for acting on the financing side of projects. Head of the office, **Owen Nee*** has a good depth of experience in Chinese projects. Recent matters include acting as counsel to international oil companies, assisting them in documenting their Chinese oil concessions or other petroleum-related projects; advising clients with downstream development projects, including refineries, petrochemical production facilities and chemical plants. Have also assisted various oil industry sub-contractors to establish themselves in China and comply with government formalities. **Clients:** International financial institutions; major sponsors.

Herbert Smith A practice which specialises in energy and infrastructure projects development, it is thought to have strong, diplomatic lawyers who have good connections. The team benefits from the presence of **Jack Young*** with his long experience, language skills and in-house energy experience bringing *"good perspective"* to a deal. Recent deals include advising HP Bulmer on the establishment of a cider joint venture in northern China; advising Metro Holdings on establishing an entertainment centre in Shanghai; assisting the German pharmaceutical company Grünenthal in the financing and equity increase for its wholly-owned enterprise in Zhongshan, PRC and advising Armstrong Group on the capital increase of its joint venture in Panyu, PRC. **Clients:** YTL Corporation Berhad and China Power International; China Travel Holdings; Hopewell Holdings; Okabe ; Wah Kwong.

*See leaders' profiles on pages 216-218

Linklaters (1 ptr, 8 asscs) This strong team has maintained its standing in the market despite the loss of star player David Platt. Interviewees recommended **Zili Shao*** for work on the development side with the ability to *"flip in and out of the two cultures better than anyone."* The firm acted for the lenders on the Puqi and Changsha power projects, represented a major American developer on the purchase of a 284MW CHP station in Sichuan and acted for a major petrochemical refinery on the restructuring and sale of a 150MW gas fired station and the development of the captive power plant and gasification facility. **Clients:** International financial institutions.

Paul, Weiss, Rifkind, Wharton & Garrison (4 ptrs, 7 asscs) Considered to be a strong player in the development and governmental side of projects, with an excellent reputation in the telecoms field. The team represented Metromedia Corporation in the financing of telecoms network buildouts in China. Elsewhere in the energy market, the firm advised the consortium (led by ExxonMobil) on the Trunkline and South China LNG Terminal. Also advised on upstream production sharing contracts (onshore, offshore and coal bed methane) for companies including ExxonMobil, Exxon Exploration, Phillips Petroleum, BP Amoco and Husky Oil. **Clients:** ExxonMobil; China Light & Power; Nissho Iwai; Chubu Electric Power Company; Mitsubishi Corporation; Metromedia; ADB; BP Amoco; Phillips Petroleum; Husky Oil; Plantation Timber Products; ING Real Estate; Emerging Markets Funds; Ogden Energy; AES; ADB; General Motors.

White & Case LLP (6 ptrs, 20 asscs) A strong team of lawyers based in Hong Kong with a newly opened office in Shanghai. Known for producing quality work it draws on a strong projects team globally and is seen to be active particularly in telecoms and regional projects. **George Crozer*** is *"a first-class lawyer who knows what he is doing."* **John Kuzmik*** was also recommended for his practice. Advised on the project financing of an LNG terminal facility in Eastern China and on the establishment and financing of several coal and LNG-fired power plot projects. Represented the Indonesian Government on the Paiton I project in Indonesia. **Clients:** Developers; government entities; lenders.

Denton Wilde Sapte (3 ptrs, 6 asscs) A solid practice, known for its advice to the Chengdu Government on the high profile Chengdu No. 6 Water Plant B BOT Project. The team has strong relationships in the sponsor market and represented China National Offshore Oil Corporation and the Chinese sponsors in the Guangdong LNG Terminal & Trunk Pipeline Project. Also advised FINAME on the financing of five regional jet aircraft ordered by Sichuan Airlines. **Clients:** Chengdu Government; IBM; Asian Infrastructure Development; China Construction Bank; China National Offshore Oil Corporation; FINAME; Ishii Ironworks Co.

Johnson Stokes & Master (1 ptr, 1 assc) Focused on South East Asia, the practice derives an advantage from its strong relationship with HSBC. The team advised a syndicate of banks on the $150 million development of the satellite town 'Taipinqiao' in the Lu Wan District of Shanghai. It also acted for the lender on a $20 million letter of credit facility for joint venture companies operating the Hefei-Yejei Highway in Anhui Province and represented the World Bank sponsored Phu My 2x2 715MW power project in Vietnam. **Clients:** Investment banks.

Leaders' profiles – China

BARALE, Lucille
Freshfields Bruckhaus Deringer, Hong Kong
+852 2846 3400
lucille.barale@freshfields.com
Recommended in Corporate/Mergers & Acquisitions: China Foreign, Project Finance: China Foreign
Specialisation: Specialises in the establishment of joint ventures, wholly-owned subsidiaries and holding companies in the PRC, as well as in the financing of foreign investment projects in China.

BATH, Vivienne
Coudert Brothers, Beijing 100020
+ 86 10 6597 3851
Recommended in Corporate/Mergers & Acquisitions: China Foreign

BERSANI, Matthew D.
Shearman & Sterling, Beijing +86 10 6505 3399
mbersani@shearman.com
Recommended in Corporate/Mergers & Acquisitions: China Foreign
Specialisation: Partner in *Shearman & Sterling*'s Hong Kong office. Specialises in corporate finance and securities transactions. Typical matters handled include: advising PetroChina and China Mobile on their recent offerings, advising the Hong Kong Government on the establishment of the Tracker Fund, advising the Siam Commercial Bank in a $1.5 billion recapitalisation and Rule 144A/Regulation S offering; and advising Korea Thrunet, a Korean internet company, on a US IPO.
Prof. Memberships: Admitted to the Bar of the State of New York.
Career: Qualified in 1988. Practised with *Paul, Weiss* from 1988 to 1994. Joined *Shearman & Sterling* in 1994, becoming a Partner in 1997. Featured speaker at many conferences addressing the issue of access to US capital markets by Asian issuers.
Personal: Born in 1958. Obtained an undergraduate degree (BA) from Princeton University in 1982 and has law degree (JD) from Columbia University 1988. Fluent reader and speaker of Mandarin Chinese.

CHAN, Jeanette K.
Paul, Weiss, Rifkind, Wharton & Garrison, Beijing
+86 10 6505 6822
Recommended in Corporate/Mergers & Acquisitions: China Foreign

CHAN, Kenneth D.C.
Allen & Overy, Beijing +86 10 6510 2368
Recommended in Corporate/Mergers & Acquisitions: China Foreign

CHAO, Howard
O'Melveny & Myers LLP, Shanghai
+86 21 5298 5600
hchao@omm.com
Recommended in Corporate/Mergers & Acquisitions: China Foreign
Specialisation: Partner in charge of China practice and Vice-chair of the International Practice Group. Expertise in corporate work with a strong focus on Chinese and East Asian matters. Frequently advises multinational clients on their business in China and has experience handling transactions in China such as joint ventures, wholly foreign-owned enterprises, project financings, technology transfers, and many other matters. Has advised clients in China in a variety of industries, including electric power and other infrastructure, food products, alcoholic beverages, bio-products, pharmaceuticals, medical products, and animal by-products. Represents clients in securities offerings, business acquisitions, investment funds, and lending transactions including project financings. Advised Japanese clients on their international investment and financing activities.
Personal: Native of Taiwan. Educated in the US. University of California at Berkeley, JD (1980); Purdue University, BS (1976). Fluent in Mandarin and French.

CHEN, Ji Yuan
East Associates, Beijing +86 10 6590 6639
Recommended in Project Finance

CROZER, George K.
White & Case Solicitors, Hong Kong
+852 2822 8700
gcrozer@whitecase.com
Recommended in Project Finance, Project Finance: China Foreign
Specialisation: Executive Partner of *White & Case's* Hong Kong office and is responsible for the firm's overall activity in Asia. Has over 30 years' experience in corporate finance, project and related financings, mergers and acquisitions and joint ventures. Has worked on greenfield LNG projects and electric power projects in Indonesia, oil and gas and telecoms projects in the Philippines, an IPP project in Thailand and a proposed major refinery and petrochemical plant joint venture in China. In the area of M&A, was involved in the purchase by GE Capital of a substantial interest in the finance subsidiary of PT Astra International and the Bakrie Group's purchase of a substantial minority interest in PT Freeport Indonesia. Also has experience of securities offerings such as when advised the Electricity Generating Authority of Thailand on its inaugural global bond offering in 1998 and the Kingdom of Thailand on a series of yankee bond and MTN offerings.
Career: Admitted to the New York State Bar in 1969 and as a Solicitor of the High Court of the Hong Kong Special Administrative Region in 1997.
Personal: US citizen. Graduated from Princeton University in 1965 and Michigan Law School in 1968.

GAO, Peiji
Clifford Chance, Shanghai +86 21 6279 8461
Recommended in Corporate/Mergers & Acquisitions: China Foreign, Project Finance: China Foreign

GIVANT, Norman
Freshfields Bruckhaus Deringer, Beijing
+86 10 6410 6338
norman.givant@freshfields.com
Recommended in Corporate/Mergers & Acquisitions: China Foreign, Project Finance: China Foreign
Specialisation: Specialises in corporate, corporate finance, banking and direct investment in China and represents a broad spectrum of US and European multinational corporations in their investment in China.

HAN, Xiaojing
Commerce & Finance Law Offices, Beijing
+8610 6599 2255
Recommended in Corporate/M&A

HARDER, Stephen
Clifford Chance, Shanghai +86 21 6279 8461
Recommended in Project Finance: China Foreign

HARPOLE, Sally A.
Morrison & Foerster, Beijing +86 10 6526 9798
sharpole@mofo.com
Recommended in Corporate/Mergers & Acquisitions: China Foreign
Specialisation: Legal pioneer in the China law field. Specialises in handling strategic planning, negotiation, dispute resolution, documentation and legal compliance relating to the full scope of matters in which foreign entities engage in China. This includes joint ventures and wholly owned subsidiaries, direct investment in Chinese companies, restructuring, merger and acquisition, technology licensing, intellectual property protection, arbitration and others. Is a CIETAC arbitrator and on arbitrator panels of other major arbitration institutions.
Career: Admitted to practice in the State of California. Was with *Graham & James* until 1990, seconded to *Deacons Graham & James* in Hong Kong, joining *Morrison & Foerster* in 2000. Was President of the American Chamber of Commerce in Beijing in 1985 and 1986, and also served four terms as AmCham Vice President in Hong Kong. Has published numerous articles and is a frequent speaker on topics related to legal issues in China.
Personal: A.B., Phi Beta Kappa, University of California, Berkeley, 1972; J.D., University of Washington Law School of Law, Asian Law Program, 1978. Fluent in Mandarin and Spanish.

HE, Fei
Haiwen & Partners, Beijing +86 10 8642 1166
Recommended in Corporate/M&A

HOWSON, Nicholas C.
Paul, Weiss, Rifkind, Wharton & Garrison, Beijing
+86 10 6505 6822
Recommended in Corporate/Mergers & Acquisitions: China Foreign

JENKINS, Huw
Clifford Chance, Shanghai +86 21 6279 8461
Recommended in Project Finance: China Foreign

JI, Jianfeng
Summit Law Office, Beijing +86 10 6804 6255
Recommended in Corporate/M&A, Project Finance

JONES, Thomas
Freshfields Bruckhaus Deringer, Hong Kong
+852 2846 3400
thomas.jones@freshfields.com
Recommended in Corporate/Mergers & Acquisitions: China Foreign, Project Finance: China Foreign
Specialisation: Specialises in direct investment and project financing transactions in China.
Prof. Memberships: State Bar of California; Law Society of Hong Kong.

KAY, David Ben
Denton Wilde Sapte, Beijing +86 10 6505 4891/2
dbkay@dentonwildesapte.com.cn
Recommended in Corporate/Mergers & Acquisitions: China Foreign
Specialisation: Head of the firm's China practice and Managing Partner of the Beijing Office. Over fifteen years of experience in Hong Kong and Beijing advising multinational corporations on legal and commercial aspects of investing and doing business in China, including direct investment, technology licensing, intellectual property and regulatory matters.
Prof. Memberships: California State Bar Association, American Bar Association.
Personal: Brown University, A.B. Magna cum laude; AGSIM, Masters in International Management; UCLA, J.D. Lives in Beijing with wife, Gabrielle Harris, and two children.

KUZMIK, John T.
White & Case Solicitors, Hong Kong
+852 2822 8700
Recommended in Corporate/Mergers & Acquisitions: China Foreign, Project Finance: China Foreign

LIU, David Dali
Llinks Law Office, Shanghai +86 21 6881 8100
Recommended in Corporate/M&A
Specialisation: Main areas of practice are banking and finance, project finance and corporate commercial. Career highlights include being involved in the first B-share listing in PRC; being involved in a number of important project finance transactions including Shanghai Bovis Thames Da-Chang Water Treatment Plant, Zhadian Power Plant and Shanghai Yanan City Elevated Road; representing a number of PRC and foreign banks. Highlights of the last year include advising merger of Unilever's invested enterprises in China; advising acquisition of Chinese investment by Foster Brewing Group Ltd; being involved in the first RMB syndication led by a foreign bank; acting for 45 banks in the Asian deal of 1998 – Shanghai General Motors Project Finance; being appointed as the PRC legal counsel to Shanghai Banking Association.
Prof. Memberships: All China Bar Association; Shanghai Bar Association; Arbitrator, Shanghai Arbitration Commission.
Career: 1982-89, attended East China Institute of Politics and Law (LLB, LLM); 1993-94, attended a practical training scheme for young Chinese lawyers in the UK and Hong Kong. Previous employers: Pu Dong Law Office, Shanghai Foreign Economic Law Office.
Personal: Born 3 June 1965. Leisure interests include music, swimming, basketball, boxing and reading.

LIU, Gang
Commerce & Finance Law Offices, Beijing
+8610 6599 2255
Recommended in Corporate/M&A

LIU, Linfei
Jun He Law Offices, Beijing +86 10 8519 1300
Recommended in Corporate/M&A

MAO, Baigen
Shanghai Pu Dong Law Office, Shanghai
+86 21 5820 4822
Recommended in Corporate/M&A

MOSER, Michael
Freshfields Bruckhaus Deringer, Hong Kong
+852 2846 3400
michael.moser@freshfields.com
Recommended in Corporate/Mergers & Acquisitions: China Foreign
Specialisation: Expertise includes advising on direct investment, technology licensing, corporate restructuring and the settlement of business disputes between Chinese and international entities.

NEE, Owen
Coudert Brothers, Shanghai +86 200 120
neeo@coudert.com
Recommended in Corporate/Mergers & Acquisitions: China Foreign, Project Finance: China Foreign
Specialisation: China foreign investment and dispute resolutions in China. Various matters for international petroleum companies, onshore and offshore.
Prof. Memberships: New York Bar; Solicitor – England & Wales; Solicitor – Hong Kong. Member New York City Bar Association, Law Society, Law Society of Hong Kong.
Publications: Oceana: 'Laws of the People's Republic of China'. Bureau of National Affairs: 'Tax Portfolio on the People's Republic of China'.
Career: Partner *Coudert Brothers.*
Personal: Princeton University, 1965, A.B., Columbia University, 1973, Juris Doctorate.

NELSON, Stephen
Baker & McKenzie, Hong Kong +852 2846 1888
stephen.nelson@bakernet.com
Recommended in Corporate/Mergers & Acquisitions: China Foreign, Project Finance: China Foreign
Specialisation: International partner of *Baker & McKenzie* and co-head of the China Practice Group based in the Hong Kong office. Practice focuses on trade with and investment in the People's Republic of China, with a particular specialisation in PRC infrastructure, telecommunications and information technology projects and Chinese taxation.
Publications: Has published numerous articles on Chinese investment and taxation in various publications and is a frequent participant in seminars and presentations focusing on PRC tax and investment.
Career: Admitted in California (1986). Joined *Baker & McKenzie's* Hong Kong office in 1986 and became a partner in 1992.
Personal: University of Pennsylvania (B.A., 1980); Columbia University (J.D., 1986). Interests include backgammon and wine.

PLATT, David
Shearman & Sterling, Hong Kong +852 2978 8000
dplatt@shearman.com
Recommended in Project Finance, Project Finance: China Foreign
Specialisation: Specialises in project finance, energy and construction law. Has acted for developers and financiers on power, rail and other infrastructure projects throughout the Asia Pacific region. Major transactions worked on include Sajiao C, Shandong Rizhao, Hebei Hanfeng, Anhui Hefei, Guangdong Zhuhai, Laibin B and Wuhu power plants in China, the Bangkok Mass Transit System and Independent Power (Thailand) power project in Thailand, the Melaka power project in Malaysia and the North Luzon Expressway in the Philippines. Currently working for sponsors and financiers on power, petrochemical and industrial projects in the PRC and the Philippines.
Prof. Memberships: Law Society of England & Wales; Law Society of Hong Kong SAR.
Career: Education: St Paul's School, London, University of Cambridge. Career: 2000, Partner, *Shearman & Sterling* Hong Kong; 1995, Partner, *Linklaters*, Hong Kong; 1991-95, Solicitor, *Linklaters*, Hong Kong; 1989-91, Solicitor, *Linklaters*, London; 1987-88, Articled Clerk, *Linklaters* (London and New York).
Personal: Born 1963. Resides Hong Kong.

SHAO, Zili
Linklaters (a member firm of Linklaters & Alliance), Shanghai +8621 6841 5858
zili.shao@linklaters.com
Recommended in Project Finance: China Foreign
Specialisation: Specialist, primarily in PRC direct investments and regional resources, projects with a particular interest in joint ventures and project finance in the natural resources and project field in the PRC.

SILK, Mitchell
Allen & Overy, Beijing +86 10 6510 2368
Recommended in Corporate/Mergers & Acquisitions: China Foreign, Project Finance: China Foreign

VALENTINE, Stuart
Clifford Chance, Shanghai +86 21 6279 8461
Recommended in Corporate/Mergers & Acquisitions: China Foreign

WANG, Ling
King & Wood, Beijing +86 10 65612299
Recommended in Corporate/M&A, Project Finance

XIAO, Wei
Jun He Law Offices, Beijing +86 10 8519 1300
Recommended in Corporate/M&A

YOUNG, Jack
Herbert Smith, Beijing +86 10 6505 6512
Recommended in Corporate/Mergers & Acquisitions: China Foreign, Project Finance: China Foreign

ZHANG, Xusheng
Jingtian & Gongcheng, Beijing +86 10 6588 2200
Recommended in Corporate/M&A

ZHENG, Shujun
Zheng Liu Yuan & Zhou Law Office, Beijing +86 10 6510 1250
Recommended in Corporate/M&A, Project Finance

COLOMBIA

Index

OVERVIEW: The Colombian legal market lost two of its most respected practitioners this year as Enrique Gomez Pinzon and Eduardo Cárdenas relocated to the States. Beyond this, corporate hot shot Eduardo Zuleta has departed Baker & McKenzie to establish an arbitration focused firm. Telecoms and e-commerce provided a constant deal flow, whilst the privatisation of municipal assets and the energy sector has increased financial activity. Despite a distinct lack of international firms, Bogotá lawyers report interest from US and Spanish entities. National firms are increasingly shedding the traditional family structure to create corporate organisations peopled by largely US-educated lawyers.

C

Banking & Finance

COLOMBIA
Leading firms (Banking & Finance)

Band	Firm
1	Cardenas & Cardenas
2	Brigard & Urrutia
	Gomez Pinzon & Asociados
	Prieto Gutierrez Carrizosa & Asociados
	Raisbeck Lara Rodriguez & Rueda (Baker & McKenzie)
	Silva & Piñeros
3	Parra Rodriguez & Cavelier
	Posse Herrera & Ruiz

Firms are listed alphabetically in each band.

Leading individuals (Banking & Finance)

Band	Individual
1	**CARDENAS NAVAS Dario** *Cardenas & Cardenas*
	URRUTIA-VALENZUELA Carlos *Brigard & Urrutia*
2	**CARDENAS Bernardo** *Cardenas & Cardenas*
	SILVA Alejandro *Silva & Piñeros*
3	**GUTIERREZ Gonzalo** *Prieto Gutierrez Carrizosa*
	LARA Jorge *Raisbeck Lara Rodriguez & Rueda*
	LINARES-CANTILLO Alejandro *Gomez Pinzon*
	MICHELSEN Sergio *Brigard & Urrutia*
	ROCHA Juan Carlos *Prieto Gutierrez Carrizosa*
	RODRIGUEZ Bernardo *Parra Rodriguez*

Individuals are listed alphabetically in each band.

Cardenas & Cardenas Described by rivals as *"traditionally, the banks' lawyers,"* the firm has a long-standing reputation in banking and has niche expertise in structured and project finance. *"Strongman"* **Dario Cardenas Navas*** is the firm's leader in financial and corporate matters, and is backed up by the equally well regarded **Bernardo Cardenas*** who is a *"particularly effective operator."* The firm has recently been involved in a number of high-profile banking mergers in Colombia. **Clients:** Investment banks; other international and domestic financial institutions.

Brigard & Urrutia (2 ptrs, 5 asscs) A top finance firm, it was constantly mentioned by competitors as *"a group we see on most of the important transactions."* The team has acknowledged expertise in syndicated loans, debt restructuring and project finance, and a growing niche in aircraft financing. Here, it has advised lessees such as Ansett Worldwide, and lessors like Crédit Lyonnais, whom the team represented on the financing for the lease of three planes to a local operator. **Carlos Urrutia-Valenzuela*** is an all-rounder whose financial work has won recognition locally, while **Sergio Michelsen*** was also recommended to our researchers.

The firm advised Citibank on a syndicated loan to Orbitel, the domestic telecoms entity, and acted for ABN AMRO on a syndicated bridging loan to Celumovil, and on the restructuring of the company's debt, including a local bond placement. Other restructuring work includes assisting BBVA in the refinancing of a major generation company. **Clients:** Citibank; ABN AMRO; BBVA; local corporates.

Gomez Pinzon & Asociados The firm remains respected for its advice to a number of blue-chip international lenders, as well as representing domestic borrowers on syndicated loans. The finance team's reputation is at its highest on complex capital markets transactions. Senior partner **Alejandro Linares-Cantillo*** was recommended to researchers for his *"technical expertise and client-friendly attitude."*

The firm acted for Goldman Sachs and Chase Securities as underwriters in two sovereign debt offerings by the Republic of Colombia, of $250 million and $500 million. It also assisted Morgan Stanley as managers of European MTN issues by the government worth a total of €450 million. Elsewhere, the group counselled RCN Televisión as borrower on an international bridging loan. **Clients:** Société Générale; The Tokai Bank; Goldman Sachs; Banco Santander Investment; ABN AMRO; Standard Chartered Bank; Bank of America; JP Morgan; Lehman Brothers; Merrill Lynch.

Prieto Gutierrez Carrizosa & Asociados (2 ptrs, 5 asscs) The firm enjoys a fine reputation for project finance, and has acknowledged banking and capital markets expertise, where clients include several important international banks. **Gonzalo Gutierrez*** is an admired senior figure, while **Juan Carlos Rocha***, who studied in the US and France, is known as *"the person for project finance deals."*

Recent projects work has centred on road privatisations; the firm acted for Banco Santander Central Hispano on the structuring of a $500 million roads concession. Other project finance work involved the $92 million financing of the La Sierra thermo-electric plant. The team acted for Citibank on a $250 million credit facility on behalf of the national government, and was also counsel to US investors on the acquisition of a 15% holding in Bancolombia. **Clients:** Société Générale; Merrill Lynch; Citibank; NM Rothschild & Sons; Banco Santander Central Hispano; Robert Fleming.

*See leaders' profiles on pages 222-223

Raisbeck Lara Rodriguez & Rueda (Baker & McKenzie) (2 ptrs, 4 asscs) Known to be *"particularly strong in this area,"* the banking team was commended to researchers for its *"shrewd"* use of the firm's international network. It acts for a mixture of local corporates and international banks in lending, restructuring and some local capital markets transactions. As Baker & McKenzie's regional co-ordinator of banking and finance, **Jorge Lara**'s* expertise is widely acknowledged by rivals.

Restructuring experience includes representing Celumovil in the refinancing of a $750 million debt, through bridge and syndicated loans and local bond issues, and assisting Bank of America on the restructuring of a local power generator. The firm also acted for Cessna Finance in the lease of four aircraft to national airline Avianca, and for the Standard Bank of London on a note issue by the airline. Project finance work has seen the firm advise the lenders on the $600 million public transport project in the city of Cali, while privatisation work includes the sell-off of Bancafé, a domestic bank. **Clients:** Schroders Salomon Smith Barney; Cessna Finance Corporation; Bank of America; Standard Bank London; ING; Dresdner Bank.

Silva & Piñeros (3 ptrs, 5 asscs) Fronted by respected financial player **Alejandro Silva***, who worked for the IFC in Washington for two years, the firm is recognised by local financial institutions as *"a strong banking force."* It has long experience of advising multilateral lenders, acting for the IFC on loans in Jamaica and Ecuador. Other IFC work includes a $30 million loan to a Panamanian subsidiary of a Colombian leasing company, and a $10 million loan to a Colombian-owned Peruvian venture. The firm also regularly acts for the CAF, representing it and Citibank on the $100 million financing of a publicly owned power plant, via an international leasing agreement. Non-agency work includes advising an international syndicate on equity investment and a loan worth $60 million to Avantel, a domestic telecoms corporate. **Clients:** IFC; IDB; Corporación Andina de Fomento; Citibank; international banks.

Parra Rodriguez & Cavelier Especially prominent in its niche areas of asset and mining finance, the firm assists a variety of Colombian and foreign financial institutions on their domestic transactions, and is counsel to the large domestic conglomerate Grupo Aval, which controls 25% of the Colombian financial system.

Bernardo Rodriguez* is a renowned asset finance expert, and has overseen a number of leverage-leased transactions for planes and equipment. Restructuring and capital markets have been other key elements of the firm's recent caseload. **Clients:** Major US and Japanese banks; domestic financial institutions; Grupo Aval.

Posse Herrera & Ruiz (6 lawyers) The firm has a growing finance department, which is said by competitors to be *"making its presence felt."* Active in project finance in the energy and telecoms sectors, the firm also advises an international lending clientele on syndicated loans.

The team acted for a US bank on a $100 million loan to a soft drinks company and for the same client as agent on a loan to a domestic telecoms company. Other financial work includes assisting a US bank in structuring a lease finance deal for another telecoms entity. On the borrower side, the firm represented a Colombian bank on a $60 million facility granted by a syndicate of German banks, while capital markets work has included acting for the Colombian subsidiary of a UK corporate in the placement of preferred stock. **Clients:** Chase Manhattan; international banks; national corporates.

Corporate/M&A

Brigard & Urrutia (4 ptrs, 29 asscs) Described by competitors as a *"dominant corporate player,"* the firm acts for a largely multi-national clientele, and has notable experience in telecoms and utilities transactions. The corporate team includes **Carlos Urrutia-Valenzuela***, who was recommended to researchers as a leading corporate figure in Colombia. **Sergio Michelsen*** is a respected all-round commercial lawyer, while *"gentlemanly"* **Carlos Umana*** is head of the recently opened IP practice, and is noted for his IT/telecoms expertise.

The firm advised on the purchase of a large domestic retail company for French client Casino, and the acquisition of a pension fund management company for a Spanish group. **Clients:** Multi-national corporates in utilities, telecoms and retail.

Cardenas & Cardenas (4 ptrs, 15 asscs) A family firm that is well regarded by Bogotá lawyers for its high levels of *"professionalism and dedication"* and the *"consistent quality of its lawyers."* The group generally advises international corporates on their Colombian investments, and has niche expertise in banking, energy and insurance. **Dario Cardenas Navas*** is a leading figure in domestic corporate circles, and a bright future is predicted for the *"promising"* **Bernardo Cardenas***. **Clients:** International and domestic corporates.

José Lloreda Camacho & Co (7 ptrs, 17 asscs) *"Sound corporate firm,"* praised by competitors for its ability to modernise while remaining a family operation. Traditionally strong in IP, the firm is said to have *"enhanced its general corporate practice"* and has particular expertise in telecoms. Clients emphasised to researchers the firm's *"attentive service."*

Possessing an IP background and good European connections, **José Antonio Lloreda*** is a well known corporate name who *"does fine work"* under the guidance of *"natural leader"* **José Lloreda Camacho***. **Gustavo Tamayo*** is also well known for his corporate and IP experience.

Recent transactional experience includes acting on the purchase of a soap factory by a UK multi-national, and advising on the merger of two large IT companies. The firm's clients are principally international corporates, for whom it also undertakes projects work, such as the extension of a mining project in the north of the country. **Clients:** Unilever; Nestlé; BBV.

Prieto Gutierrez Carrizosa & Asociados (25 lawyers) *"Aggressive and well-connected firm"* with a predominantly international clientele, and an acknowledged reputation for cross-border M&A and privatisation advice. The *"capable"* **Juan Manuel Prieto*** is a rainmaker who *"successfully attracts business,"* while **Martin Carrizosa*** was commended to researchers as *"the leading transactional figure among the younger generation."*

The firm advised the government on the Cali airport privatisation, and acted for the government and Rothschild's on the privatisation of 14 energy distribution companies. In M&A, the team represented Spanish group Union Fenosa on the acquisition of three domestic electricity distributors, and advised AT&T on the acquisition of FirstCom Colombia. **Clients:** Philip Mor-

COLOMBIA Leading firms (Corporate/Mergers & Acquisitions)
1 Brigard & Urrutia
Cardenas & Cardenas
Jose Lloreda Camacho & Co
Prieto Gutierrez Carrizosa & Asociados
2 Parra Rodriguez & Cavelier
Posse Herrera & Ruiz
Raisbeck Lara Rodriguez & Rueda (Baker & McKenzie)
Silva & Piñeros
3 Cavelier Abogados
Gomez Pinzon & Asociados
Zuleta Garrido Araque & Jaramillo
4 Muñoz Tamayo & Asociados

Firms are listed alphabetically in each band.

Leading individuals (Corporate/Commercial)
1 CARDENAS NAVAS Dario *Cardenas & Cardenas*
PRIETO Juan Manuel *Prieto Gutierrez Carrizosa*
URRUTIA-VALENZUELA Carlos *Brigard & Urrutia*
2 CARDENAS Bernardo *Cardenas & Cardenas*
LINARES-CANTILLO Alejandro *Gomez Pinzon*
LLOREDA José Antonio *Jose Lloreda*
MICHELSEN Sergio *Brigard & Urrutia*
PIÑEROS Mauricio *Silva & Piñeros*
SILVA Alejandro *Silva & Piñeros*
UMANA Carlos *Brigard & Urrutia*
ZULETA Eduardo *Zuleta Garrido Araque*
3 CARRIZOSA Martin *Prieto Gutierrez Carrizosa*
CAVELIER Ernesto *Parra Rodriguez & Cavelier*
CAVELIER Germán *Cavelier Abogados*
HERRERA Jaime *Posse Herrera & Ruiz*
LARA Jorge *Raisbeck Lara Rodriguez & Rueda*
LLOREDA CAMACHO José *José Lloreda*
MUÑOZ TAMAYO Diego *Muñoz Tamayo*
RODRIGUEZ Bernardo *Parra Rodriguez*
TAMAYO Gustavo *José Lloreda*

Individuals are listed alphabetically in each band.

ris; Mitsubishi; PwC; UPS; Exxon Mobil; TransCanada; AT&T.

Parra Rodriguez & Cavelier (5 ptrs, 19 asscs) A full service firm that enjoys particular repute for general corporate work and privatisations. **Ernesto Cavelier*** and **Bernardo Rodriguez*** are regarded as the firm's leading lights. 70% of the firm's clientele is composed of international corporates, and it has traditional areas of focus in aviation, IP, IT and energy. M&A activity includes acting for the buyers of a large domestic coal exporter, while the team has also assisted in the reorganisation of Grupo Aval, the largest Colombian financial group. **Clients:** International and national corporates; supermarkets; Grupo Aval.

Posse Herrera & Ruiz (8 lawyers) A *"young and buoyant"* firm, which has created a good impression locally, and was recommended to researchers for its work on behalf of both buyers and sellers on cross-border M&A transactions. Energy, manufacturing, IT and banking are all areas of notable activity. **Jaime Herrera*** is the firm's outstanding figure.

The team represented an international insurance company on the merger of its two Colombian subsidiaries, and acted for a US/Spanish telecoms and construction company on the acquisition of a domestic corporate. It also advised a US energy client on the acquisition of 50% of its Colombian interests by a European entity. Work for domestic clients includes assisting a group of investors on the sale of their business to a German car manufacturer, and advising on the sale of a stake in a mobile phone company. **Clients:** Multinational and domestic corporates.

Raisbeck Lara Rodriguez & Rueda (Baker & McKenzie) (5 ptrs, 13 asscs) Despite a split, which resulted in the departure of a number of lawyers, headed by Eduardo Zuleta, this is still regarded by peers as *"an important corporate player."* The team is a familiar sight on medium-ticket cross-border transactions, and acts for an array of international companies, most notably in the telecoms industry. Senior partner **Jorge Lara*** is respected by local lawyers, who describe him as *"an internationally significant figure."*

The team advised on the privatisation of Nicaragua's power distribution network, worth $115 million. M&A work has included advising BellSouth on the $400 million acquisition of domestic mobile phone company, Celumovil. The firm also acted for Enbridge on the $100 million acquisition of TransCanada's interests in an oil pipeline, and for Cyanamid on the sale of its Colombian operations to BASF. **Clients:** American Home Products; BellSouth; Cabot; Frito-Lay; Enbridge International; Pfizer; Cyanamid; Celumovil; Cementos Caribe.

Silva & Piñeros (3 ptrs, 5 asscs) A young firm that has established itself firmly in the Colombian corporate market and is predicted to have *"a promising future."* It is respected for its *"unaggressive, user-friendly"* approach, and is said to *"give sound, common sense advice."* Notable for its telecoms work, the firm acts for flagship client Telefónica on its local acquisitions, recently assisting on the privatisation of the national telecoms company, and the purchase of two local telecoms operators and their subsequent merger. **Mauricio Piñeros*** and **Alejandro Silva*** are highly respected by clients for their all-round corporate expertise.

The firm acted for TotalFina Elf on the privatisation of Carbocol, and advised Newbridge on the merger of two local retail companies. **Clients:** Telefónica de España; Parmalat; IFC; Cinemark; IDB; El Tiempo; TotalFina Elf.

Cavelier Abogados (7 ptrs, 20 asscs) The firm is now better known as an IP specialist and is said to *"have 40% of the market."* However, a number of recent splits have robbed the firm of its former corporate profile. **Germán Cavelier*** is still regarded as *"an aggressive, commercial and talented lawyer,"* and leads a firm with long experience of M&A advice on behalf of companies from the pharmaceutical, food, health and IT sectors. E-commerce has been a recent growth area here. **Clients:** International and domestic corporates.

Gomez Pinzon & Asociados (5 ptrs, 25 asscs) Now under the aegis of **Alejandro Linares-Cantillo***, *"a well-connected and prominent commercial lawyer,"* the firm is renowned for its transactional work for utilities, energy and IT companies, and its privatisation expertise. The latter includes counselling the bidder on the privatisation of the Cerrejon Zona Norte coal mine.

In M&A, the team has acted for the sellers of Electrocosta and Electricaribe, the electricity distribution companies, and acted for McCain on the acquisition of a food company. The firm also has a thriving IT practice which recently assisted the successful bidder for an on-line lottery system. **Clients:** TransCanada; Avianca; Suez Lyonnaise des Eaux; BASF; Dragados; BP Amoco; AES; AT&T; Bristol-Myers Squibb; Daimler-Chrysler; Sun Microsystems; Whirlpool.

Zuleta Garrido Araque & Jaramillo (5 ptrs, 6 asscs) A *"fine group of attorneys,"* which split in April 2000 from Raisbeck Lara Rodriguez & Rueda. Peers spoke to researchers of a firm *"rapidly finding its feet"* in the local market. Although the firm is especially highly rated for its litigation and arbitration practice, it is led by corporate law guru **Eduardo Zuleta***, described by competitors as *"a serious brain."* He heads up a team containing a number of former in-house counsel from leading multi-nationals. Advising a largely international corporate clientele drawn from telecoms, consumer products and the pharmaceutical industry, the firm represented a Japanese consortium in a dispute with a Spanish company over payments under a supply contract.

*See leaders' profiles on pages 222-223

The team also acted for Frito-Lay on its acquisition of Margarita, a local snack producer. **Clients:** Nortel Networks; BP Amoco; Frito-Lay; Nissho Iwai Corporation; Revlon.

Muñoz Tamayo & Asociados (3 ptrs, 7 asscs) Although it has lost a number of lawyers over the past few years, the firm is still regarded as a *"good quality"* domestic corporate player. Name partner **Diego Muñoz Tamayo*** is a *"clearly influential"* local figure. **Clients:** Domestic corporates.

Leaders' profiles – Colombia

C

CARDENAS, Bernardo
Cardenas & Cardenas, Bogotá +57 1 312 3600
Recommended in Banking & Finance, Corporate/M&A

CARDENAS NAVAS, Dario
Cardenas & Cardenas, Bogotá +57 1 312 3600
Recommended in Banking & Finance, Corporate/M&A

CARRIZOSA, Martin
Prieto Gutierrez Carrizosa & Asociados, Bogotá +57 1 326 8600
Recommended in Corporate/M&A

CAVELIER, Ernesto
Parra Rodriguez & Cavelier, Bogotá +57 1 376 4200
Recommended in Corporate/M&A

CAVELIER, Germán
Cavelier Abogados, Bogotá +57 1 347 3611
cavelier@colomsat.net.co
Recommended in Corporate/M&A
Specialisation: Founded *Cavelier Abogados* in 1953. In charge of International Law area, however advises all areas of the firm.
Prof. Memberships: ABA; FICPI; ITMA: CAMYP; INTA; ASIL, Academia Colombiana de Jurisprudencia e Historia.
Publications: Several books on International Law, Industrial Property and Business Law.
Career: LL.D Rosario University, Bogota, cloister founded in 1664. Former Secretary General Foreign Ministry.
Personal: Born Chicago, Illinois, USA, 1922 (Colombian and American citizen). Admitted 1946, Colombia.

GUTIERREZ, Gonzalo
Prieto Gutierrez Carrizosa & Asociados, Bogotá +57 1 326 8600
Recommended in Banking & Finance

HERRERA, Jaime
Posse Herrera & Ruiz, Bogotá +571 312 3157
Recommended in Corporate/M&A
Specialisation: Partner in the Corporate Department, specialising in M&As, energy, utilities and privatisations. Practice includes development and financing of infrastructure projects, international lending, and competition related matters. Has participated in a number of mergers and acquisitions and related matters, representing both acquirers and sellers, and advises clients in corporate governance matters.
Prof. Memberships: International Bar Association, American Bar Association, LES Colombia, Ecuador Peru (Past President).
Career: Lawyer, Pontificia Universidad Javeriana (1985); Diploma in Intellectual Property Law, Queen Mary College, University of London (1987). Member of the Governmental Commission for the Modification of the Company Law Section of the Code of Commerce (1994). Director of private companies.

LARA, Jorge
Raisbeck Lara Rodriguez & Rueda (Baker & McKenzie), Bogotá +57 1 332 2600
jorge.lara@bakernet.com
Recommended in Banking & Finance, Corporate/M&A
Specialisation: Partner in the Corporate and Finance Department. Main areas of work are corporate, commercial, banking and finance law, principally foreign finance, privatisation, infrastructure, project finance, capital market transactions and securities, M&A. Has handled complex finance transactions representing US and European banks as lenders and advisers. Has represented large multinational companies in acquisition of local companies; large local companies in international placement of securities. Currently represents SalomanSmith Barney, Dresdner Bank, BNP Paribas, Bank Boston, Bank of America, ING, Standard Bank London and other major finance institutions in large projects in Columbia and other Latin American jurisdictions. Also, represents General Motors and its Columbian subsidiary concerning their participation in the massive transportation system being implemented in Bogotá.
Career: Qualified in 1967, working at *Raisbeck & Raisbeck* since 1963, formed *Lara & Lara* in 1973, joined *Baker & McKenzie* (acting locally under the name *Raisbeck Lara Rodriguez & Rueda*) in 1979, becoming a partner in 1980. Director of the Banking, Finance and Major Projects of the firm in Colombia. Co-ordinator of the Latin American Banking and Finance Practice Group of *Baker & McKenzie.* Member for Latin America of the Professional Responsibility and Practice Committee of *Baker & McKenzie.*
Personal: Born on 9 July 1944. Attended Universidad del Rosario in Bogotá (Doctor in Jurisprudence). Postgraduate studies at Kenk Law School and Kellogg School at Northwestern University, Chicago, Illinois. Board member of the Council of American Companies and the Colombia Venezuela Chamber of Commerce. Leisure interest include golf, ski and card games. Lives in Bogotá, Colombia with second homes in Caracas, Venezuela and Miami, Florida, US.

LINARES-CANTILLO, Alejandro
Gomez Pinzon & Asociados, Bogotá +57 1 310 5066
alinares@gomezpinzon.com
Recommended in Banking & Finance, Corporate/M&A
Specialisation: Project Finance, Securities Regulation, Energy Law and Foreign Investment.
Prof. Memberships: Asociacion de Derecho Economico; International Fiscal Association (IFA); ABA, International Law & Practice; LES Colombia-Ecuador; International Bar Association (IBA).
Career: Admitted 1984, Colombia. Education: Universidad de los Andes, Law School (J.D., 1984), Graduate Studies in Finance. 1989, Harvard University Law School (LLM, 1985: ITP, 1995: P.I.L., 1997). Georgetown University Law Center and International Law Institute (Orientation in the U.S. Legal System, 1984). Presidency of the Republic of Colombia. Director of the National Rehabilitation Program, and Executive Director of the Solidarity and Social Emergency Fund, 1993-1994: Advisor to the President of Colombia on Social Policy, 1992-1993; Vice-Minister of Agriculture, 1992; Colombian Embassy in Paris. Plenipotentiary Minister, 1991-1992; National Planning Department, Director of the Foreign Investments Division, 1989-1991: Colombian negotiator before GATT in matters related to Intellectual Property Rights and Trade Related Investment Measures, 1990; IBM of Colombia. Manager of the Legal and External Relationships Department, 1989, and Legal Counsel, 1986-1989; Ministry of Finance and Public Credit, Director of Legal Division, Public Credit Office, 1986; *Sidley Austin*, New York, Foreign attorney, 1985-1986.
Personal: Languages: Spanish, English, and French.

LLOREDA, José Antonio
José Lloreda Camacho & Co, Bogotá +57 1 3264270
Recommended in Corporate/M&A

LLOREDA CAMACHO, José
José Lloreda Camacho & Co, Bogotá +57 1 3264270
Recommended in Corporate/M&A

MICHELSEN, Sergio
Brigard & Urrutia, Santa Fe de Bogotá, +57 1 346 2011
Recommended in Banking & Finance, Corporate/M&A

MUÑOZ TAMAYO, Diego
Muñoz Tamayo & Asociados, Bogotá
+57 1 621 2855
Recommended in Corporate/M&A

PIÑEROS, Mauricio
Silva & Piñeros, Bogotá +57 1 345 5066
Recommended in Corporate/M&A

PRIETO, Juan Manuel
Prieto Gutierrez Carrizosa & Asociados, Bogotá
+571 326 8600
Recommended in Corporate/M&A

ROCHA, Juan Carlos
Prieto Gutierrez Carrizosa & Asociados, Bogotá
+571 326 8600
Recommended in Banking & Finance

RODRIGUEZ, Bernardo
Parra Rodriguez & Cavelier, Bogotá
+57 1 376 4200
Recommended in Banking & Finance, Corporate/M&A

SILVA, Alejandro
Silva & Piñeros, Bogotá +57 1 345 5066
Recommended in Banking & Finance, Corporate/M&A

TAMAYO, Gustavo
José Lloreda Camacho & Co, Bogotá +57 1 3264270
Recommended in Corporate/M&A

UMANA, Carlos
Brigard & Urrutia, Santa Fe de Bogotá
+57 1 346 2011
Recommended in Corporate/M&A

URRUTIA-VALENZUELA, Carlos
Brigard & Urrutia, Bogotá
+57 1 346 2011
Recommended in Banking & Finance, Corporate/M&A

ZULETA, Eduardo
Zuleta Garrido Araque & Jaramillo, Bogotá
+57 1 3106614
ezuleta@zulga.com
Recommended in Corporate/M&A

Specialisation: International Partner in Corporate, Banking and Finance and Arbitration. Areas of work include foreign finance and project finance, anti-trust, e-commerce, M&A and international commercial arbitration. Acted for Bank of America in the financing of cellular phone licenses and energy projects; for Royal Bank of Canada in project financings; for Nortel Networks in association agreements and has represented ICI, Frito-Lay, PepsiCo, Cyanamid (BASF), General Motors Acceptance, Abbott Laboratories and other multinational companies in M&A projects.
Career: Qualified in 1980. Worked for the Banking Association and for Banco de Colombia. Joined *Baker & McKenzie* in 1982 becoming an international partner in 1989. Professor of principles of law at Universidad del Rosario (Bogotá); member panel of arbitrators for the Center of Arbitration of the Chamber of Commerce of Bogotá; member LCIA; arbitrator ICC; tutor in international arbitration.
Personal: Born in Bogotá, Colombia, July 30, 1955. Universidad del Rosario (Doctor in jurisprudence). Postgraduate studies in Universidad del Rosario. Leisure interests include golf, music and medieval history. Lives in Bogotá, Colombia.

C

CONGO

Corporate/Commercial

CONGO Leading firms (Corporate/Commercial)
1 Etude Alexis Vincent Gomes
2 Cabinet D'Advocats Fernand Carle

Firms are listed alphabetically in each band.

Leading individuals (Corporate/Commercial)
1 **GOMES Vincent** *Etude Alexis Vincent Gomes*
2 **CARLE Fernand** *Cabinet D'Advocats Fernand Carle*

Individuals are listed alphabetically in each band.

Etude Alexis Vincent Gomes (1 ptr, 3 asscs) *"A firm with good associates,"* competent in all areas of commercial law, which is considered to be particularly *"good for oil matters."* **Vincent Gomes** is a renowned practitioner who has *"a good relationship with the political authorities."* The firm acts as legal counsel to Stolt Offshore oil and gas company on financial regulation and tax work. **Clients:** Schlumberger; Elf; Agip.

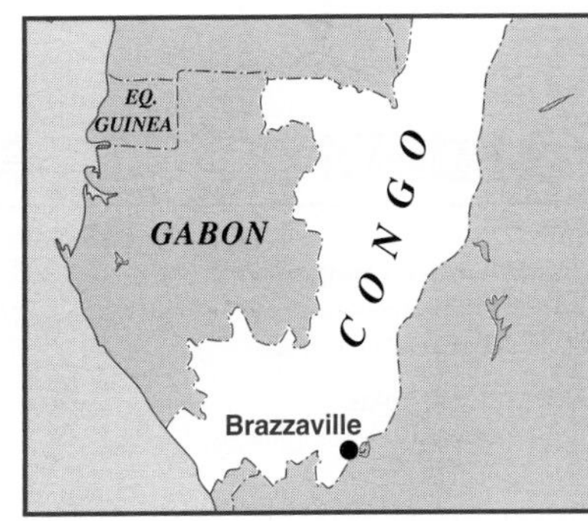

Cabinet D'Avocats Fernand Carle (4 ptrs, 4 asscs) The firm's commercial practice focuses on the creation, transfer and fusion of foreign companies in Congo. **Fernand Carle** has great experience, and is said to be *"well-connected."* In the past year, the firm has worked on the establishment of an American wheat company and one Malaysian and one German logging company in the Congo. **Clients:** Shell; SDV; Hydro Congo; BIDC; SFI.

Leaders' profiles – Congo

CARLE, Fernand
Cabinet D'Avocats Fernand Carle, Ponte-Noire
+242 940 293/940 195

GOMES, Vincent
Etude Alexis Vincent Gomes, Pointe-Noire
+242 942 104/944 550

DEMOCRATIC REPUBLIC OF CONGO

Corporate/Commercial

C

DEMOCRATIC REPUBLIC OF CONGO Leading firms (Corporate/Commercial)
1 Cabinet Kisimba
Turlot & Associates
2 Cabinet Mabeka
Cabinet Matadiwamba

Firms are listed alphabetically in each band.

Leading individuals (Corporate/Commercial)
1 **KISIMBA-NGOY Honorius** *Cabinet Kisimba*
TURLOT Jean-Michel *Turlot & Associates*
2 **MABEKA Nicholas** *Cabinet Mabeka*
MATADIWAMBA Tharcisse *Cabinet Matadiwamba*
Individuals are listed alphabetically in each band.

Cabinet Kisimba (1 ptr, 7 asscs) A *"political and important"* firm with a strong commercial practice, focusing on banking, mining, transport, aviation and maritime law. The name to follow here is **Honorius Kisimba-Ngoy**, a former deputy prime minister and chairman of the national bar association, who has a wealth of experience and a *"strong personality."* **Clients:** Transport companies; seafaring companies; mining companies.

Turlot & Associates (1 ptr, 6 asscs) A *"strong firm,"* particularly in matters relating to the petroleum industry, with an international reputation for patent and trademarks work. **Jean-Michel Turlot** is *"an excellent lawyer,"* and comes highly recommended. **Clients:** Petroleum companies; banks; insurance companies; textile manufacturers.

Cabinet Mabeka (1 ptr, 4 asscs) French-trained **Nicholas Mabeka** heads a firm which has advised on a number of transactions involving commercial, mining, banking, trademarks, telecommunications and petroleum law. The firm's caseload includes advice on international finance contracts and the establishment of local companies for international corporates. **Clients:** International Credit Bank; Total; Elf; Mobil; SOFIDE; SEPCongo.

Cabinet Matadiwamba (1 ptr, 4 asscs) A full-service law firm which also has a good reputation in the petroleum sector. Former minister **Tharcisse Matadiwamba** is the current chairman of the national bar association and has an established name. **Clients:** Transport and distribution companies.

Leaders' profiles – Democratic Republic of Congo

KISIMBA-NGOY, Honorius
Cabinet Kisimba, Kinshasa Gombe
+243 12 41869/+243 12 25586

MABEKA, Nicholas
Cabinet Mabeka, Kinshasa Gombe
+243 12 40980

MATADIWAMBA, Tharcisse
Cabinet Matadiwamba, Kinshasa Gombe
+243 12 43279

TURLOT, Jean-Michel
Turlot & Associates, Kinshasa Gombe
+243 88 44578

COSTA RICA

Corporate/Commercial

COSTA RICA Leading firms (Corporate/Commercial)
1 Facio & Cañas
Zürcher, Montoya & Zürcher
2 Bufete Odio y Raven
Pacheco Coto
3 Vargas Jimenez & Peralta
4 Lara Lopez Matamoros Rodriguez & Tinoco

Firms are listed alphabetically in each band.

Leading individuals (Corporate/Commercial)
1 **CHACON Francisco** *Bufete Odio y Raven*
OREAMUNO Rodrigo *Facio & Cañas*
ZÜRCHER Edgar *Zürcher, Montoya & Zürcher*
2 **FACHLER Freddy** *Pacheco Coto*
GARITA Victor *Facio & Cañas*
LOPEZ Arnoldo *Lara Lopez Matamoros*
PACHECO Humberto *Pacheco Coto*
PACHECO Mario *Zürcher, Montoya & Zürcher*
RAVEN-RAMIREZ Alberto *Bufete Odio y Raven*
ZÜRCHER Harry *Zürcher, Montoya & Zürcher*
3 **RAVEN-ODIO JR Alberto** *Bufete Odio y Raven*
VARGAS Fernando *Bufete Odio y Raven*
VARGAS Fernan *Vargas Jimenez & Peralta*

Individuals are listed alphabetically in each band.

Facio & Cañas (15 ptrs, 18 asscs) A *"long-established firm with a good roster of clients"* which regularly provides legal advice to corporations, focusing on M&A, foreign investment and tourism. Viewed by clients and competitors as a *"well organised"* firm, its *"strong, reliable team"* is a *"good blend of youth and experience."* Renowned for its work on behalf of international clients, the firm represented McDonald's on the buy-back of the local restaurant franchise, and Cargill Corp on the acquisition of Cinta Azul, a local food industry group.

Former vice-president of Costa Rica **Rodrigo Oreamuno*** is an *"excellent and honourable commercial attorney, diplomatic and gentlemanly."* Commended to our researchers as *"the driving force of the firm,"* **Victor Garita*** has *"expertise in corporate affairs"* and is *"likeable and responsible."* The firm recently acted as local counsel to Rabobank Nederland on the restructuring of a $600 million credit facility granted to a multinational fruit company with local interests. **Clients:** Intel; Compaq; American Airlines; Marriott Corp; McDonald's; Harken Corp.

Zürcher, Montoya & Zürcher (8 ptrs, 5 asscs) Praised by competitors as *"a family firm with a good reputation in the commercial law field,"* the firm's two major assets are perceived to be *"strong team work"* and the fact that the lawyers are *"recognised as honest, straightforward people."* The firm handles general commercial work, including corporate law, foreign investment and M&A, and has particular expertise in the oil industry.

"Leader of the firm" **Edgar Zürcher*** is a *"businessman and client-getter,"* while brother **Harry Zürcher Jr*** is recommended to researchers for his *"excellent connections."* **Mario Pacheco*** *"pays attention to detail"* and is *"devoted to his subject."* The firm represented Procter & Gamble on the establishment of a Global Business Services Branch in Costa Rica. **Clients:** Merrill Lynch; BBV; SBC; Citibank; Seagram; Chrysler; P&G; Microsoft; Hewlett-Packard; Otis; Sbarro; Kmart.

Bufete Odio y Raven (6 ptrs, 10 asscs) Although the firm is a respected commercial presence in Costa Rica, researchers noted the widespread market perception that it *"lacks strength in depth."* The firm acts as general counsel to corporations and is active in M&A, corporate law, public law, infrastructure and telecommunications projects. The group has also developed a niche in private investment for public works.

Francisco Chacon Jr* is a *"prominent business lawyer, building up an excellent professional name,"* **Alberto Raven-Ramirez*** is a *"meticulous old school lawyer,"* and **Alberto Raven-Odio*** is *"a young guy doing well."* **Fernando Vargas*** is regarded by opponents as *"a pleasure to work with."* The firm handled the acquisition of a commercial concern in Honduras in a $11.7 million transaction. **Clients:** Browing-Ferris Industries; Global Energy Inc; Neworld Network; Sarah Lee Corp; Shell; Siemens; The Economist Intelligence Unit.

Pacheco Coto (4 ptrs, 6 asscs) Considered *"an interesting firm to watch,"* by both peers and clients, the firm has *"good young associates, clients and international connections."* The group is active in M&A transactions, joint venture agreements, commercial contracts, and international trade. **Humberto Pacheco*** is *"extremely efficient at promoting Costa Rican companies abroad"* and **Freddy Fachler*** is regarded as *"a corporate strong man."* The team acted on a corporate reorganisation and estate planning in Italy. **Clients:** Motorola; Dole Fresh Fruit; BMW; Sheraton; Mattel; Scotiabank; Starwood Hotels; Pillsbury.

Vargas Jiminez & Peralta (5 ptrs, 12 asscs) Traditionally an *"important and respectable"* firm, the departure of a number of key lawyers is felt by the market to have *"left them weaker."* However, the team still acts as legal counsel to a range of foreign companies operating in Costa Rica and is handling the financing of a new airport in San José and the privatisation of state-owned entities. **Fernan Vargas*** is a *"highly-qualified and popular business lawyer."* **Clients:** Novartis; JP Morgan; Texaco; Sony; Taco Bell; Pfizer.

Lara Lopez Matamoros Rodriguez & Tinoco (5 ptrs, 15 asscs) A firm with a long history which is felt to have suffered, following the untimely death of Manuel Rodriguez. The firm is generally viewed as a force in banking and finance, often advising international corporates. *"Tough negotiator"* **Arnoldo Lopez*** is *"an excellent and pragmatic corporate attorney."* **Clients:** BTC; Coca-Cola; Lacsa.

*See leaders' profiles on page 226

Leaders' profiles – Costa Rica

CHACON, Francisco
Bufete Odio & Raven, San José +50 6 234 9710
francisco.chacon@odioraven.com
Specialisation: Partner in Administrative Law. Heads Administrative Law Dept. Main area of work: foreign trade regulations and investment (private and public projects). Has handled major public bidding projects and was involved in the International Airport concession. Has spoken at several conferences and seminars.
Prof. Memberships: Costa Rica Bar Association.
Publications: Author of several articles and reports on foreign trade and investment issues. Writes regularly in various newspapers and periodicals.
Career: Qualified in 1985. Partner at firm in 1988. Served as Viceminister of Foreign Trade (1994-1997).
Personal: Born 27 October 1961. Attended Georgetown University Law Center (LLM 1998); University of Costa Rica (JD 1985).

FACHLER, Freddy
Pacheco Coto, San José +50 6 258 1619
ffachler@racsa.co.cr
Specialisation: Corporate and financial law.
Prof. Memberships: IBA, ABA.
Publications: Most recent: 'Non-National Passports', co-authored with Humberto Pacheco.
Career: Harvard MCL. Largest Costa Rican real estate fund offering.
Personal: Long distance running. Wife and daughter and son.

GARITA, Victor
Facio & Cañas, San José +50 6 256 5555

LOPEZ, Arnoldo
Lara Lopez Matamoros Rodriguez & Tinoco, San José +50 6 223 1628

OREAMUNO, Rodrigo
Facio & Cañas, San José +50 6 256 5555

PACHECO, Humberto
Pacheco Coto, San José +50 6 258 1619

PACHECO, Mario
Zürcher, Montoya & Zürcher, San José +50 6 222 6633

RAVEN-ODIO, Alberto
Bufete Odio & Raven, San José +50 6 234 9710
alberto.raven@odioraven.com
Specialisation: Partner in Corporate Law Department. Main area of work is foreign investment, telecommunications and energy. In the past year has represented foreign corporations in the development of hydroelectric plants, telecommunications infrastructure, and a hospital products production plant. Acts for a number of major corporations dedicated mainly to industrial/export business.
Prof. Memberships: Costa Rica Bar Association.
Career: Qualified 1984. Joined firm as partner in 1986. Member of the Board of Directors of Banco Nacional de Costa Rica (1997-1998), Banco de Costa Rica (1998 – present).
Personal: Born 1962. Attended Universidad de Costa Rica (JD 1983).

RAVEN-RAMIREZ, Alberto
Bufete Odio & Raven, San José +50 6 234 9710
araven@racsa.co.cr
Specialisation: Senior Partner. Main area of work: corporate, constitutional and administrative law, with emphasis on government procurement. During past year has participated in diverse projects such as the bid of a new public hospital, of the new cellular phone network, and development of gasoline stations.
Prof. Memberships: Costa Rica Bar Association.
Career: Qualified in 1958. Founded firm in 1960. Member of Board of Directors of Bar Association (1978), Union Costarricense de Abogados (1974), National Theater (1964-1990), President, Asociación Nacional de Fomento Económico (1973).
Personal: Born 1934. Attended Universidad de Costa Rica (JD 1958).

VARGAS, Fernan
Vargas Jimenez & Peralta, San José +50 6 222 8622

VARGAS, Fernando
Bufete Odio & Raven, San José +50 6 234 9710

ZÜRCHER, Edgar
Zürcher, Montoya & Zürcher, San José +50 6 222 6633

ZÜRCHER JR, Harry
Zürcher, Montoya & Zürcher, San José +50 6 222 6633

COTE D'IVOIRE

Corporate/Commercial

COTE D'IVOIRE Leading firms (Corporate/Commercial)	
1	Cabinet Dougé et Abbé Yao
	FDKA
2	Cabinet Chauveau
	Elisha & Associés
	N'Goan Asman & Associés
3	SCPA Konate, Moise-Bazie & Koyo

Firms are listed alphabetically in each band.

Leading individuals (Corporate/Commercial)	
1	ABBÉ YAO Vincent *Cabinet Dougé et Abbé Yao*
	FADIKA Karim *FDKA*
2	CHAUVEAU Jean-François *Cabinet Chauveau*
	DOUGÉ Charles *Cabinet Dougé et Abbé Yao*
	ELISHA Jean-Pierre *Elisha & Associés*

Individuals are listed alphabetically in each band.

Cabinet Dougé et Abbé Yao (2 ptrs, 8 asscs) One of the oldest firms in Abidjan, it *"deserves its excellent reputation"* as an *"efficient firm carrying out high quality work,"* particularly in the corporate arena. Strong in banking, finance, investment and general commercial law, the firm boasts two high-calibre partners. **Vincent Abbé Yao** is transactionally active, and is viewed by other practitioners as a *"professional, busy and hard-working young lawyer."* *"Senior figure"* **Charles Dougé** is also highly respected. The firm advised on a project on behalf of Bouyges to build the third bridge in Abidjan. **Clients:** Bouyges; Apache; IPS; IFC.

FDKA (4 ptrs, 4 asscs) A *"thorough and professional"* firm of young lawyers, which is gaining a first-class reputation for commercial and public law work. **Karim Fadika** is viewed as an *"excellent and ethical lawyer."* The firm has expertise in M&A, contracts and foreign investment, and advised on the merger between Sisca and Jag, and on the privatisation of Côte d'Ivoire Telecom and SOGB. **Clients:** Shell; World Bank; SOGB; SIR; Côte d'Ivoire Telecom.

Cabinet Chauveau (1 ptr, 5 asscs) A *"strong commercial practice"* with close links to French firms is also recognised for its international public law work. The team advises on privatisations, contracts, concessions for public services and banking. Leading light **Jean-François Chauveau** is an experienced lawyer, who has advised on a merger between a Belgian bank and an Ivorian bank. **Clients:** Local and foreign banks and corporates.

Elisha & Associés (1 ptr, 3 asscs) Our researchers found that this is a *"strong, smaller firm"* which advises both local and international companies on all areas of corporate, mining, transportation, banking, tax and labour law. **Jean-Pierre Elisha** is highly regarded. The firm represented two multi-national investment funds on the investment of $1.5 million in a battery manufacturing company in Mali, and $2.5 million in an offshore

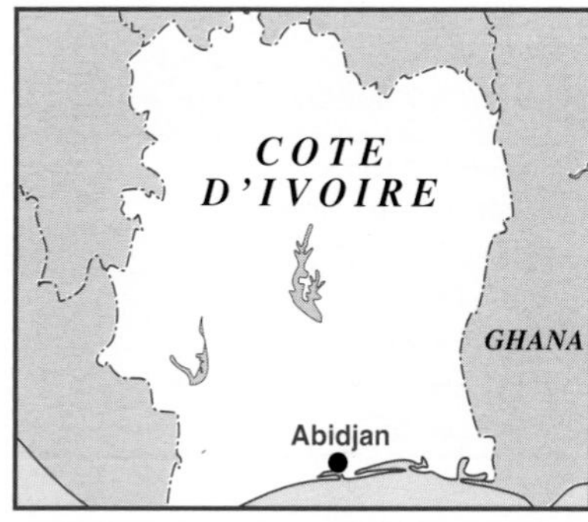

gas and oil production facility in Côte d'Ivoire. **Clients:** Banks; international companies; airlines.

N'Goan Asman & Associés (2 ptrs, 6 asscs) Commercially inclined firm which advises companies on stock offerings, incorporations, regulatory work and foreign investment, and has worked with governmental organisations on project finance transactions. The firm has American lawyers as legal counsel in Côte d'Ivoire. **Clients:** Government organisations; international companies.

SCPA Konate, Moise-Bazie & Koyo (4 ptrs, 4 asscs) A *"thrusting young firm"* which is *"always willing to learn."* A full-service commercial law firm, it has been active on the liberalisation of the cocoa and coffee sectors. **Clients:** State companies; banks; construction companies.

Leaders' profiles – Côte D'Ivoire

ABBÉ YAO, Vincent
Cabinet Dougé et Abbé Yao, Abidjan +225 202 22 127

CHAUVEAU, Jean-François
Cabinet Chauveau, Abidjan +225 202 12 852

DOUGÉ, Charles
Cabinet Dougé et Abbé Yao, Abidjan +225 202 22 127

ELISHA, Jean Pierre
Elisha & Associés, Abidjan +225 202 11 880

FADIKA, Karim
FDKA, Abidjan +225 202 12 031

CROATIA

Corporate/Commercial

CROATIA Leading firms (Corporate/Commercial)
1 Bogdanovic & Dolicki
Hanzekovic & Radakovic
Porobija & Porobija
Zuric & Partners
2 Markovic & Pliso
Vukić, Jelušić, Sulina & Stanković
Vukmir Law Office

Firms are listed alphabetically in each band.

Leading individuals (Corporate/Commercial)
1 BOGDANOVIC Mirko *Bogdanovic & Dolicki*
HANZEKOVIC Marijan *Hanzekovic & Radakovic*
POROBIJA Boris *Porobija & Porobija*
VUKMIR Mladen *Vukmir Law Office*
ZURIC Ratko *Zuric & Partners*

Individuals are listed alphabetically in each band.

Bogdanovic & Dolicki (in association with Lovells Boesebeck Droste) (2 ptrs, 7 asscs) Said to be *"doing well,"* the firm has a particular reputation for capital markets expertise, but also handles cross-border M&A, banking and finance and litigation. Competition told our researchers that the *"gentlemanly and professional"* **Mirko Bogdanovic*** *"runs a tight ship."* Recent transactions include advising Deutsche Telecom on its acquisition of a stake in Croatian Telecom and representing Dresdner Kleinwort Benson on its investment in the first independent Croatian internet provider, Iskon. **Clients:** EBRD; HEP; IFC; World Bank; Deutsche Bank ; ABN AMRO; Credit Suisse First Boston.

Hanzekovic & Radakovic (2 ptrs, 7 asscs) Described to our researchers as a large and *"well-connected"* firm which advises on corporate, commercial and trade law as well as infrastructure projects such as motorways and electricity. Senior partner **Marijan Hanzekovic*** is a former president of the Croatian bar and a figure of national repute. The firm advised on the privatisation of state-owned banks and the telecoms system, and represented Merrill Lynch, lead managers of the first US$ Eurobond issue in Croatia. **Clients:** Enron; Buick; Danone; UBS; Lafarge; Creditanstalt.

Porobija & Porobija (2 ptrs, 11 asscs) *"Steadily expanding firm"* whose caseload typically involves advice to foreign clients on their investments in Croatia. It has carried out due diligence for international concerns in a variety of industries, and acted on some 70 privatisations. Our researchers were told that leading light **Boris Porobija*** *"displays an interesting balance of restraint and aggression."* The firm has been involved in four motorway projects for Italian, German and French clients. **Clients:** Foreign construction companies; banks; agricultural and industrial enterprises.

Zuric & Partners (4 ptrs, 11 asscs) A recent alliance with UK firm Stephenson Harwood has *"brought them a lot of English work."* Its corporate workload consists mainly of reorganisation and M&A, which the team conducts alongside an active banking and finance practice. **Ratko Zuric*** *"has been on the scene for a number of years now"* and is *"the strategic mind of the firm."* The firm advised on the takeover of a local Croatian tobacco factory for BAT and, in collaboration with Stephenson Harwood, advised on the financing of a new fleet for Croatia Airlines. **Clients:** British American Tobacco; Croatia Airlines.

Markovic & Pliso (2 ptrs, 4 asscs) Active on corporate and commercial law, the firm is also known for its involvement in securities, banking and finance, privatisation and project finance. Represented a leading western bank on the financing both of Croatian companies and the Croatian government, and acts for a mix of Croatian and international companies. **Clients:** Zagrebačka banka; Privredna banka Zagreb; PBZ American Express; McDonald's Croatia; Schneider Group; Renault; Rank Xerox Ltd; Air France; Shell; Agip.

Vukić, Jelušić, Sulina & Stanković (5 ptrs, 5 asscs) The biggest firm outside of Zagreb, this Rijeka-based organisation has a particular reputation for shipping. Other elements of the caseload include commercial, foreign investment, M&A and finance advice. The team advised a port company on obtaining a priority concession. **Clients:** WestLB, Morgan Stanley Dean Witter; Bank Austria; Olivetti; Mobil; Sumitomo; American Express Bank Ltd; Bayerische Landesbank.

Vukmir Law Office (2 ptrs, 6 asscs) The *"reliable and modern-thinking"* **Mladen Vukmir**'s* Silicon Valley experience helps to explain his firm's growing focus on IP and both transactional and regulatory IT advice. The firm acts for a number of blue-chip multi-nationals on their Croatian business, including Coca-Cola and McDonalds, often advising on compliance and IP issues. **Clients:** Hewlett-Packard; Amazon.com; Yahoo!; Gillette; Mars; Microsoft.

*See leaders' profiles on page 229

Leaders' profiles – Croatia

BOGDANOVIC, Mirko
Bogdanovic & Dolicki, Zagreb +385 1 615 9595

HANZEKOVIC, Marijan
Hanzekovic & Radakovic, Zagreb +385 1 618 4611

POROBIJA, Boris
Porobija & Porobija, Zagreb +385 1 455 1325

VUKMIR, Mladen
Vukmir Law Office, Zagreb +385 1 376 0511
vukmir@vukmir.net
Specialisation: Partner. All work in commercial law including the drafting and reviewing of licensing, franchising and distribution contracts as well as general commercial contracts. Experience in acquisitions, contract negotiation and debt collection. Qualified in litigation and arbitration work. Familiar with securing trade agreements (Italy in particular), litigation, copyright and patent infringement and copyright issues in the entertainment and software industries. An appointed arbitrator for domestic disputes under the Permanent Arbitration Court of the Croatian Chamber of Commerce.
Prof. Memberships: International Bar Association, Computer Law Association, International Association for the Protection of Industrial Property, International Trademark Association, Licensing Executives Society.
Career: Law degree from the University of Zagreb, Croatia. Master of Intellectual Property degree from Franklin Pierce Law Center, United States. Worked at law firms in France, Italy and the United States as a visiting attorney. Worked as advisor to the United Nations Industrial Development Organisation and as a liaison to the Licensing Executives Society ad hoc committee for the Manual on Technology Transfer for the U.N. Speaks Croatian, English, French, German, Italian, Slovene. Court interpreter for the English language in Croatia. Contributor to 'International Franchising Law' and 'International Licensing'. Appointed Honorary Royal Danish Consul General in Zagreb, Croatia (June 1999).

ZURIC, Ratko
Zuric & Partners, Zagreb +385 1 488 1333

C

CUBA

Corporate/Commercial

CUBA Leading firms (Corporate/Commercial)
1 Balsanyda & Asociados
Business Strategies International Inc
Rado & Asociados

Firms are listed alphabetically in each band.

Leading individuals (Corporate/Commercial)
1 **CHAO Chukin** *Balsanyda & Asociados*
EDWARDS Alina *Rado & Asociados*
KIM John *Business Strategies International Inc*

Individuals are listed alphabetically in each band.

Balsanyda & Asociados (3 ptrs, 5 asscs) One of the *"leading maritime firms"* in the country is also said by competitors to be *"highly recommended for foreign investment work."* Moving more into the corporate/commercial sphere, the firm is developing a general practice covering inward investment and banking. *"Accurate and focused"* **Chukin Chao** is *"honest and trustworthy"* and was commended to our researchers as a lawyer experienced beyond his years. The firm regularly advises foreign banks on loans and financing to Cuban companies. **Clients:** Lloyds TSB; Société Générale.

Business Strategies International Inc (2 ptrs) Specialising in corporate law, this is *"an excellent firm to come to for an opinion."* Active in M&A, foreign investment, joint ventures, contracts and strategic entries, the firm has connections with a number of international law firms. Canadian **John Kim** is recommended by peers as an *"excellent and keen lawyer."* **Clients:** Mining companies; manufacturing companies; insurance companies.

Rado & Asociados (3 ptrs, 8 asscs) A firm which offers *"high quality service from good lawyers."*

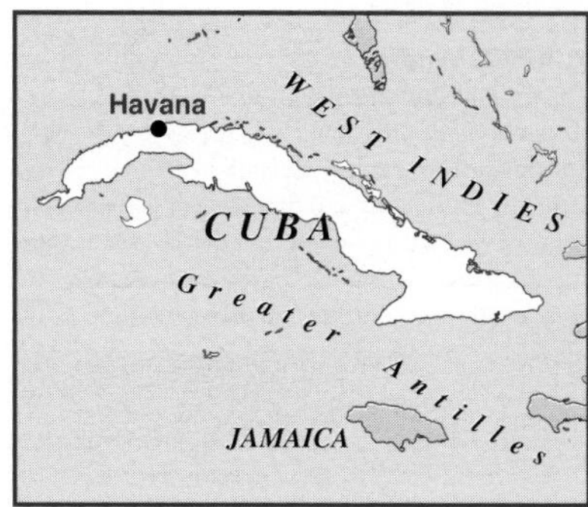

Traditionally a maritime and company law firm, it is now handling foreign investment, legal counsel, banking, finance and tax work. *"Efficient"* **Alina Edwards** is reckoned by rivals to be *"the smartest young lawyer in Cuba."* **Clients:** P&I Clubs.

Leaders' profiles – Cuba

CHAO, Chukin
Balsanyda & Asociados, Havana +537 240 672
chukin.balsanyda@compunet.com.cu
Specialisation: Maritime Law. Main areas of work are Charterparties, Sale & Purchase (Finance), Joint Ventures and Arrests. Acted for many Shipowners, Cargo Owners and P&I Clubs around the world in Charterparties, Casualties and General Average matters. Acted for major shipping companies in negotiations, discussions and implementing of loan agreements, joint ventures schemes and ships sale and purchase transactions. Also given many Legal Opinions on Cuban law on different kinds of contracts to important Banks and Financing Institutions, eg. ING Bank (Holland), Société Générale (France), Lloyds TSB Plc. (UK), Netherlands Caribbean Bank (NA).
Prof. Memberships: Cuban National Jurisconsult Union (Unión Nacional de Juristas de Cuba).
Career: Graduated (qualified) at the Law School of Havana University in July 1995. Judge (Criminal Prosecution and Civil Actions) at the Municipal Court of Boyeros, Havana City Sept 1995 – March 1996. Joined *Balsanyda y Asociados* in April 1996 becoming an associate in 1998.
Personal: Born 11 January 1972. Attended Havana University 1990-1995 (Law School – Title: Licensed in Law (qualified lawyer)). Attended courses: Chartering (1997); Ships and Purchase (1998) and Maritime Arbitration (1999) UNTACD Latin American Program. 3 months work experience in the English law firm Clyde & Co. (London).

EDWARDS, Alina
Rado & Asociados, Havana +537 338 186

KIM, John
Business Strategies International Inc, Havana +537 805 780

CYPRUS

Corporate/Commercial

CYPRUS Leading firms (Corporate/Commercial)
1 Antis Triantafyllides & Sons
Chrysses Demetriades & Co
2 Andreas Neocleous & Co

Firms are listed alphabetically in each band.

Leading individuals (Corporate/Commercial)
1 **PSILLAKI Efti** *Chrysses Demetriades & Co*
TRIANTAFYLLIDES Stelios *Antis Triantafyllides*
2 **TRIANTAFYLLIDES George** *Antis Triantafyllides*
Individuals are listed alphabetically in each band.

Antis Triantafyllides & Sons (10 lawyers) A *"good, serious"* smaller firm admired as *"competent in complex matters"* covering commercial, banking and litigation. It acts for Russian companies using Cypriot entities for investment purposes, benefiting from a Russo-Cypriot treaty on tax. **Stelios Triantafyllides** is a *"promising lawyer who knows what he is doing"* and his brother, **George Triantafyllides**, is key player for litigation, supporting an international commercial arbitration practice. **Clients:** British American Tobacco; Morgan Stanley Trust Company; Chase Manhattan Bank.

Chrysses Demetriades & Co (10 ptrs, 22 asscs) The focus of this firm is split between shipping and a strong general corporate practice. This includes foreign investment issues and flotations for a range of international companies. The team acted on the acquisition of a Nasdaq listed company by a Cypriot company and the listing of a Cypriot company on the Greek Stock Exchange. *"Leading maritime lawyer"* **Efti Psillaki** heads the shipping department and is widely recommended by peers. **Clients:** Multinational companies; local and international banks; major companies listed on the Cyprus Stock Exchange.

Andreas Neocleous & Co (8 ptrs, 42 asscs) Focusing on international commercial work, the

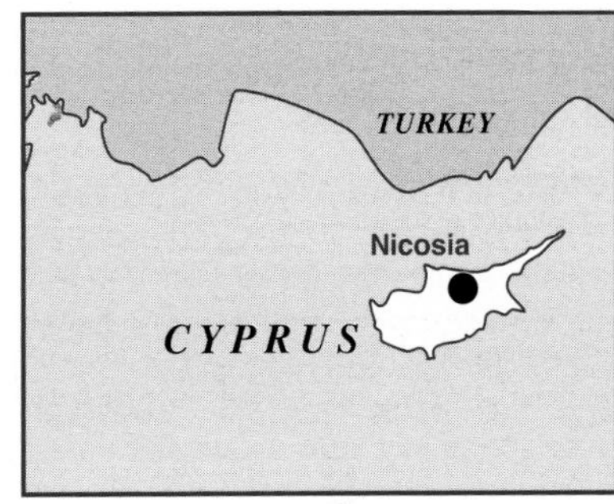

firm's strength lies in its network of offices in Eastern Europe supporting cross border corporate transactions and international litigation. Admired as *"leading in commercial transactions,"* it acted for Bass plc on the construction of a new inter-continental hotel in Cyprus, advised on the construction of a water desalination plant and provides ongoing support for DLJ in securitisation deals and netting advice. **Clients:** Credit Agricole Indo-Suez; Unitemp; Ericsson; CSFB.

Leaders' profiles – Cyprus

PSILLAKI, Efti
Chrysses Demetriades & Co, Limassol 3601
+357 5 582 484

TRIANTAFYLLIDES, George
Antis Triantafyllides & Sons, Nicosia
+357 267 8888

TRIANTAFYLLIDES, Stelios
Antis Triantafyllides & Sons, Nicosia
+357 267 8888

CZECH REPUBLIC

Index

C

OVERVIEW: With the successful privatisation of the banking sector drawing to a close, attention is turning to energy and the amendments to the Securities and Bonds acts following EU directives. Liberalisation of the communications sector promises high-speed, low-cost internet access and the market anticipates growth in the energy sector. Amendments to the commercial code offering clarification of the law are welcomed, although clients still complain of uncertainty, particularly in contract enforcement.

Firms have avoided the consolidation occurring elsewhere in the region, the most important merger was between White & Case and Feddersen, though the subsequent defection of 14 ex-Feddersen lawyers to Altheimer & Gray provoked much speculation. 2000 also saw the departure of some familiar figures, with Graham Donnell, Robert Bata and Joe Tortorici all relocating.

Banking & Finance

CZECH REPUBLIC Leading firms (Banking & Finance)
1 Allen & Overy
Clifford Chance Pünder
Weil, Gotshal & Manges
White & Case, Feddersen
2 Linklaters
Procházka Randl Kubr
3 Kocian Solc Balastik
Squire, Sanders & Dempsey LLP

Firms are listed alphabetically in each band.

Leading individuals (Banking & Finance)
1 **DLOUHÝ Michal** *White & Case, Feddersen*
HORÁKOVÁ Karolina *Weil, Gotshal & Manges*
PETRUS Vladimir *Clifford Chance Pünder*
TOUŠKA Mikuláš *Allen & Overy*
2 **ASCHENBRENNER Martin** *Procházka Randl Kubr*
CESTR Ivan *White & Case, Feddersen*
KUČERA Francis *Linklaters*
MATĚJČEK Jan *White & Case, Feddersen*

Individuals are listed alphabetically in each band.

Allen & Overy (2 ptrs, 8 asscs) *"Always in the running for any finance work,"* the market recommends the firm for high-profile capital markets transactions, large domestic issues and loans. Especially strong in export finance, where it performs substantial work for the Czech Export bank, this expanding department works for a range of international and domestic clients, primarily on behalf of lenders. Active on substantial syndicated lending, the team has also featured on many of the year's largest project finance and capital markets transactions, and is at the forefront of the nascent derivatives and structured finance market. Our researchers were impressed by the weight of recommendation for *"one of the best lawyers in town,"* **Mikuláš Touška*** who *"has a detailed understanding of Czech law and a sense of how international banking transactions work."* The firm advised the Czech Export Bank on a $212 million export credit facility and a $32 million commercial facility for the financing of the Turkish Afsin Albistan power project. Also assisted Chase Manhattan and CIBC World Markets as arrangers of a €480 million credit facility for Český mobil. **Clients:** Czech Export Bank; Westdeutsche Landesbank; Deutsche Bank Prague; Chase Manhattan.

Clifford Chance Pünder (2 ptrs, 4 asscs) Led by the *"experienced and commercial"* **Vlad Petrus*** *("his thought is original, and he always tries to find a way out of intractable problems,")* the banking department is considered by the market to have had a good year. The merger with Pünder has raised the firm's profile in the lucrative German market, and the team advises a high-powered international clientele on a number of transactions, notably in syndicated lending and more complex financial deals, where it benefits from its international network. The team advised HSBC as arranger of a CZK5 billion syndicated loan, and acted for ČSOB on a CZK4.3 billion state-guaranteed loan to Czech Railways. **Clients:** HSBC; Citibank; ČSOB; Komerčni banka; Fuji Bank; Siemens.

Weil, Gotshal & Manges LLP (1 ptr, 4 asscs) A strong presence in local capital markets transactions and a *"forceful approach"* are the principal characteristics of this highly rated banking and finance team. Increasingly focused on derivatives, the firm generally represents foreign investment banks on a variety of complex matters, including hedging and swaps. The *"impressive"* **Karolina Horáková*** is felt by competitors to be a *"calm, experienced and efficient"* capital markets lawyer. The firm acted for the Czech Export Bank on a CZK5 billion bond issue, raised domestically and swapped into dollars. **Clients:** GE Capital; Citibank; Česká Spořitelna.

White & Case, Feddersen (3 ptrs, 9 asscs) Although possessing an *"experienced straight banking team,"* the firm's primary focus is on capital markets, and it is acknowledged as a market leader for derivatives and structured finance transactions. Notably visible in the domestic bond market, the group has also been involved in Eurobond and Yankee bond arrangements, and has represented some of the largest local and international banks on syndicated lending and regulatory work. *"Brilliant individual"* **Michal Dlouhý*** is acknowledged by clients and competitors to be *"an outstanding capital markets lawyer,"* while a strong department also includes *"big picture man"* **Jan Matějček***, recommended for his managerial ability, and **Ivan Cestr*** who has a leading reputation in the market for project finance. The firm advised the Republic of Hungary on the establishment of a $1 billion shelf registration with the US SEC, and the issue of $750 million of global bonds. The team has also represented ČEZ on domestic bond issues totalling CZK7 billion. **Clients:** ČEZ; Republic of Hungary; Czech Railway; Citibank; Interbanka; CSFB; JP Morgan Securities.

Linklaters (2 ptrs, 5 asscs) Recent rapid expansion has made this one of Prague's largest firms, and it has dramatically increased its finance profile. Presided over by "*polished*" **Francis Kučera***, the team has generated market approval for domestic bond issues and syndicated lending, and has represented the City of Prague on a high-profile international bond issue and a series of loans. Experienced in all aspects of capital markets work, the firm also has expertise in project finance and bank regulatory work. The team advised Komerční banka on a CZK8 billion fraud. **Clients:** BNP Paribas; CSFB; Chase Manhattan; Goldman Sachs; Merrill Lynch; City of Prague.

Procházka Randl Kubr (4 ptrs, 12 asscs) "*Invited to bid on every capital markets deal,*" this high-quality domestic finance boutique has "*more or less cornered the market on local bond issues.*" Experienced in all aspects of securities work, mostly for lead underwriters, the firm also possesses a respected track record in straight and syndicated lending and bank regulatory work. A "*talented*" team of Czech lawyers, many of them Swiss or German educated, includes the "*smart and effective*" **Martin Aschenbrenner***, considered by some competitors "*the driving force behind the capital market practice.*" The team represented ING Barings as lead manager of a CZK3.75 billion structured multi-tranche note offering, used to fund a loan to the City of Prague. **Clients:** ING Barings; Crédit Lyonnais Bank Praha; JP Morgan; ABN AMRO; Commerzbank.

Kocian Solc Balastik (6 lawyers) Seen in the market representing Czech domestic banks, the firm also acts for major foreign financial organisations on syndicated lending, credit facilities, securities issues and private placements. Strong on documentation and regulatory advice, the firm has assisted on major project finance transactions in the electricity generation and brewing sectors. **Clients:** Czech National Bank; Prague Stock Exchange.

Squire Sanders & Dempsey LLP (1 ptr, 4 asscs) Although not considered to be financial specialists, the firm does appear on complex export finance transactions, usually representing the borrower. High profile transactions disclosed to our researchers include acting for the City of Prague on a CZK3.7 billion refinancing, and assisting Ceská rafinérská in obtaining a CZK5 billion syndicated loan. **Clients:** Ceská rafinérská; City of Prague; Vítkovice; OB Heller; Czech Export Bank.

C

Communications

CZECH REPUBLIC
Leading firms (Communications)

Band	Firm
1	Linklaters
	Squire, Sanders & Dempsey LLP
	Weil, Gotshal & Manges
2	Allen & Overy
	Kocian Solc Balastik

Firms are listed alphabetically in each band.

Leading individuals (Communications)

Band	Individual
1	**BALAŠTÍK Jiří** *Kocian Solc Balastik*
	KINES Stephen *Linklaters*
	McGEHEE Jeffrey *Squire, Sanders & Dempsey*

Up-and-coming individuals

Individual
SLACH Petr *Squire, Sanders & Dempsey*

Individuals are listed alphabetically in each band.

Linklaters (1 ptr, 9 asscs) The firm has shown growing interest in central Europe, and a profusion of talent in the Prague office includes the "*professional*" **Stephen Kines***. Representing major players such as Vivendi, and assisting new entrants on all aspects of regulatory and corporate work, our researchers confirmed that the group's profile has continued to rise. Advised DBG on the $220 million sale of Czech On Line to Telecom Austria, the largest central European IT transaction to date. **Clients:** BT; Vivendi; Zephyr; CE Com; UPC.

Squire Sanders & Dempsey LLP (1 ptr, 4 asscs) Clients have praised a "*great telecoms team,*" pointing out that while many firms lack specialist regulatory knowledge, the firm is "*a real exception in the Czech Republic.*" **Jeffrey McGehee*** is "*impressively knowledgeable,*" while the "*wonderful*" **Petr Slach*** is considered to be a rising star. Experienced in all aspects of communications work, the team is well known for having advised the National Property Fund on the privatisation of Český Telecom, and also represented Callahan Broadband Wireless in connection with its tender for fixed wireless access licences. **Clients:** Callahan Broadband Wireless; MCI WorldCom; Teleglobe; Telia International Carriers; KPNQwest.

Weil, Gotshal & Manges LLP (1 ptr, 4 asscs) According to one competitor "*If you concentrate on the purely regulatory side, this is the strongest firm in Prague.*" Its regulatory expertise stems from its work for incumbent operator Český Telecom, most recently representing it on its $1 billion privatisation. Also responsible for much of Český Telecom's corporate work, the firm is skilled in licensing, authorisations, M&A and litigation. A strong IT department is experienced in areas such as supply agreements and software licensing, and the department is considered capable of withstanding the loss of Joe Tortorici to Frankfurt. **Clients:** Český Telecom; KPN.

Allen & Overy (1 ptr, 4 asscs) A superb firm on all aspects of telecommunications and IT law, its primary focus is seen to be in telecoms financing. The department is best known for representing Český Telecom on a series of bonds, syndicated loans and acquisitions, such as its recent purchases of ISP Spinet and MIA. **Clients:** Český Telecom; Spray Ventures; Telekom Austria.

Kocian Solc Balastik (5 lawyers) A respected Czech firm, visible in the telecoms market, where "*it plays the role of experienced local counsel*" to a mixture of domestic and international clients. Widely experienced on tenders for mobile networks, compliance and corporate work within the telecoms sector, the firm is also active on IT litigation and contractual issues. **Jiří Balaštík*** is "*highly regarded for his transactional experience.*" **Clients:** IT providers and customers; telecommunications operators.

*See leaders' profiles on pages 235-236

Corporate/M&A

CZECH REPUBLIC Leading firms (Corporate/Mergers & Acquisitions)
1 Allen & Overy
Weil, Gotshal & Manges
White & Case, Feddersen
2 CMS Cameron McKenna
3 Altheimer & Gray
Kocian Solc Balastik
Squire, Sanders & Dempsey LLP
4 Baker & McKenzie
Clifford Chance Pünder
Linklaters
Lovells

Firms are listed alphabetically in each band.

Leading individuals (Corporate/Mergers & Acquisitions)
1 **DLOUHÝ Michal** *White & Case, Feddersen*
ŠOLC Martin *Kocian Solc Balastik*
2 **DŘEVÍNEK Karel** *Weil, Gotshal & Manges*
MATĚJČEK Jan *White & Case, Feddersen*
McDAID Ray *CMS Cameron McKenna*
SCHIFF Kenneth *Weil, Gotshal & Manges*
3 **BÁNYAIOVÁ Alena** *Altheimer & Gray*
HEWKO John *Baker & McKenzie*
JOHNSON Nick *Allen & Overy*
KOTÁB Petr *Altheimer & Gray*
McGEHEE Jeffrey *Squire, Sanders & Dempsey*
MYŠKA Jan *Allen & Overy*
PAPIRNIK Vladimira *Squire, Sanders & Dempsey*

Individuals are listed alphabetically in each band.

Allen & Overy (1 ptr, 11 asscs) A talented collection of Czech lawyers forms the backbone of a department commended by clients and competitors for its experience and consistency. A sizeable chunk of the workload involves assisting Czech clients and government agencies, but the firm also services its international blue-chip client base on cross-border acquisitions and multi-jurisdictional transactions with a Czech element.

Although Graham Donnell has relocated to it's Madrid office, the firm still includes **Jan Myška***, *"a smart lawyer who deals well with people,"* and **Nick Johnson***, who is considered to be *"solid and hard-working."* The team has advised the National Property Fund on two large privatisation projects in the telecommunications and water industries, *"high profile work which has enhanced their reputation greatly."* **Clients:** Nomura International; Český Telecom; Czech Export Bank; Chase Manhattan; National Property Fund.

Weil, Gotshal & Manges LLP (2 ptrs, 13 asscs) A leading force in the Czech Republic, the firm *"has a strong balance of international and Czech lawyers."* Experienced in all aspects of corporate work, the team combines a high profile among domestic institutions with *"a great referral business from New York and London."*

Ken Schiff* is *"international and commercial and runs a good team,"* and forms an admired combination with **Karel Dřevínek***, seen by many competitors as *"definitely one of the stars of the future."* The firm represented Česká Spořitelna on its recent privatisation, and acted for the US Steel group on its acquisition of Slovak steel company VSZ, involving an initial price of $60 million and the assumption of $325 million of debt. **Clients:** Česká Spořitelna; US Steel; Česky Telecom; ARGUS Capital; GE Capital; Bancroft Eastern Europe Fund.

White & Case, Feddersen (3 ptrs, 27 asscs) The August 2000 merger with Feddersen is expected to provide White & Case with improved access to German business, thereby strengthening an already formidable corporate offering. With first-class privatisation experience and particular strength in large, complex cross-border transactions, the firm represents an impressive mixture of foreign investors and Czech target companies. The country's largest corporate team is renowned for the strength of its Czech lawyers, of whom none receives more recommendation than *"successful business lawyer"* **Jan Matějcěk***, who *"has to be on any list"* for his managerial and rainmaking skills. The group also includes *"key figure"* **Michal Dlouhý*** who impressed our researchers by his weight of market recommendation. A fluent Czech speaker with *"a true-blue New York background,"* he *"sometimes seems to act on every deal they get."* The firm represented the National Property Fund on the restructuring and privatisation of Česká Spořitelna, the Czech savings bank, involving the sale of a controlling interest to Erste Bank. **Clients:** National Property Fund; Ford Europe; Eastman Chemicals; Credit Suisse First Boston; Novus Holding; Riverside; Komerčni banka.

CMS Cameron McKenna (1 ptr, 7 asscs) Known for its excellent referral network, the firm has *"a decent and growing corporate practice"* and a reputation for consistent transactional ability. Although the department is not considered to have quite recovered from the departure of Duncan Weston, the *"solid"* **Ray McDaid*** continues to win the respect of the market. Historically seen as a more UK-focused firm, with a strong group of expatriate lawyers, its multi-national client base has recently been bolstered by closer ties with Czech companies. The group has been active in the privatisation process, has core expertise in real estate and energy, and has been at the forefront of the expanding private equity sector. Acted for Erste bank on the $1 billion purchase of the Czech savings Bank, and also advised the Czech Government on the privitisation of IPB Bank. **Clients:** Erste Bank; The Czech Government; BNP Paribas; Bancroft Eastern European Fund.

Altheimer & Gray (2 ptrs, 6 asscs) A *"competent group of Czech attorneys"* lies at the heart of this expanding office, which has taken a team of ex-Feddersen lawyers from White & Case. According to one competitor *"the numbers and oomph this gives the firm will be important."* Visible on mid-sized domestic business, the firm also advises western investors on general corporate matters, regulatory work, private equity and financing. **Alena Bányaiová*** is *"a driven attorney,"* while the *"clever"* **Petr Kotáb*** is a respected M&A practitioner, whose tax expertise makes this, in the opinion of some, *"the only firm to trust on local tax issues."* The group represented Thrall on the acquisition of a railcar manufacturer and BorsodChem Rt on the acquisition of a chemical company. **Clients:** Motorola; BP; Monsanto; Gillette; Best Foods; Thrall.

Kocian Solc Balastik (12 lawyers) The most respected purely domestic operation owes its position to *"the most international approach of all the Czech firms."* The firm advises on all aspects of M&A, including due diligence and the creation of tax-efficient structures, and generally represents local companies on big-ticket transactions. Although many market authorities stressed the uniform competence of the team, the *"proactive"* **Martin Šolc***, *"a senior practitioner, who can talk to international clients,"* stands out. He *"understands Czech law well and can apply it creatively,"* and is regarded as the doyen of Czech lawyers. The firm acted for an oil consortium in connection with an investment in the Czech petrochemical industry, and assisted in amending the country's recently adopted Commercial Code. **Clients:** Telecoms companies; an oil consortium; cement and lime producers; a Czech retail chain.

*See leaders' profiles on pages 235-236

Squire Sanders & Dempsey LLP (1 ptr, asscs) M&A remains an important part of this firm's caseload, and April 2000's merger with local firm Šturm Mottl has considerably boosted the corporate team's domestic expertise. Sound privatisation experience is supplemented by expertise in asset and share interest acquisitions and joint ventures for a client base that has a strong technological flavour. Managing partner and *"fine transactional lawyer"* **Vladimira Papirnik*** is *"an important organisational figure,"* while **Jeffrey McGehee*** is, according to one competitor, *"a street-fighting lawyer with a good commercial feel."* The firm represented the Czech Direct Equity Fund in relation to its investment in DITEC, and advised GTC in a share swap involving Dattelkabel and Dattel. **Clients:** Czech Direct Equity Fund; GTS; Duncan Aviation; Callino; Callahan Broadband Wireless.

Baker & McKenzie (2 ptrs, 4 asscs) The firm has come to prominence this year, advising KBC Bank NV on its $1.1 billion acquisition of ČSOB from the Czech National Bank and the Czech National Property Fund, and acting on the further acquisition by ČSOB of Investicni and Postovni Banka. A small but busy office advises on classic M&A transactions for a largely foreign client base, although the group is now also acknowledged to have a foothold in the domestic market. **John Hewko*** stands out, and is viewed in the market as *"a cautious and experienced lawyer with good judgement."* The firm represented Pepsi-Cola on the acquisition of a Czech soft drink producer. **Clients:** ČSOB ; Česká Spořitelna; Deutsche Morgan Grenfell; CSFB; Sun Microsystems; Dell Computers.

Clifford Chance Pünder (1 ptr, 7 asscs) Despite its top-class banking department and acknowledged strength in real estate, the firm's M&A practice continues to lack market visibility. However, the firm does advise its blue-chip clientele on a range of acquisitions and restructurings, and wins market plaudits for the quality of its documentation and its local knowledge. The team represented Tiscali SpA on its acquisition of ČD Telekomunikace, and acted for Pliva DD on its acquisition of a majority stake in Lachema. **Clients:** Pliva; Tiscali; ZPS; ThyssenKrupp Stahl Baulemente.

Linklaters (3 ptrs, 12 asscs) *"A new arrival with a fantastic brand"* and a rapidly expanding office, the firm is acknowledged by rivals to be *"definitely on the way up."* Active on a number of M&A transactions, much of the corporate team's multi-jurisdictional work is on behalf of leading international companies. The group has experience of company formation, joint ventures, general trading agreements and the purchase of equity interests in a range of sectors including manufacturing, utilities, financial services, telecoms and energy. A highlight was the firm's advice to Frantschach on its purchase of a paper production factory from ASSI Domän. **Clients:** Frantschach; Ruhrgas; Rodamco Continental Europe.

Lovells (2 ptrs, 6 asscs) Despite *"a good reputation and some good UK clients,"* the firm's profile is perceived to have declined with the retirement of Chris Smith. The corporate team's principal strength lies in public company work, including public offers for shares, buying out minority shareholders and the cancellation of public trade ability. The firm also advises inward investors on transactions, joint ventures, private equity and restructuring. Have acted for Tesco throughout its ongoing hypermarket development programme. **Clients:** National Power; Tesco; Bass.

C

Leaders' profiles – Czech Republic

ASCHENBRENNER, Martin
Procházka Randl Kubr, Prague
+420 2 2143 0111
aschema@prkadvo.cz
Recommended in Banking & Finance
Specialisation: Main area of practice is securities and capital markets, mainly debt offerings and banking. Has acted for underwriters on a number of bond issues in the Czech market, including bond offerings by Skoda Auto, Koninklijke Ahold, Glaverbel Czech, ING Bank, etc. Has acted for the arranger of the first rated securitisation of a Czech asset placed in the Czech capital market. Has advised leading banks in a number of securities-based structured products. Has spoken at various conferences.
Prof. Memberships: Czech Bar Association, New York Bar Association, Harvard Club of Prague (Board Member).
Career: 1991-1995 law clerk at *White & Case*, 1995-1998 associate at *White & Case*, 1998-present partner at *Prochazka Randl Kubr*. Member of the Prague Stock Exchange Listing Committee. Member of the Czech Securities Commission Appellate Board.
Personal: Charles University, Prague (JD 1995, PhD 1998). Harvard Law School, Cambridge (LLM 1996).

BALAŠTÍK, Jiří
Kocian Solc Balastík, Prague +420 2 2410 3316
Recommended in Communications

BÁNYAIOVÁ, Alena
Altheimer & Gray, Prague +420 2 2481 2782
banyaiovaa@altheimer.cz
Recommended in Corporate/M&A
Specialisation: Partner. Specialises in corporate law, mergers, acquisitions, privatisations, joint ventures, commercial litigation and arbitration. Represented Motorola in acquisition of semiconductor producers in Czech Republic and Slovak Republic, acted for Aero Vodochody with the sale of equity interest to Boeing Corporation. Contributor to 'Global Competition Review'. Frequent lecturer.
Prof. Memberships: Czech Chamber of Advocates, International Bar Association.
Career: Arbitrator at Czechoslovak Federal Arbitration Agency. Member of Administrative Law Commission of Legislative Council of the Government of the Czech Republic, Appellate Commission of the Czech Securities Commission.
Personal: Charles University School of Law (Master and Doctor of Law, CSc, PhD).

CESTR, Ivan
White & Case, Feddersen, Prague
+420 2 2481 0808
icestr@whitecase.com
Recommended in Banking & Finance
Specialisation: Partner based in *White & Case* Prague office. Practice focuses on energy, bank finance and securities, real estate and projects. Extensive knowledge of Czech energy sector in particular.
Prof. Memberships: Member of Czech Bar.
Personal: Speaks Czech, English and Russian.

DLOUHÝ, Michal
White & Case, Feddersen, Prague
+420 2 2481 1796
mdlouhy@whitecase.com
Recommended in Banking & Finance, Corporate/M&A
Specialisation: Partner of *White & Case*, based in the firm's Prague office. Head of Capital Markets, Central & Eastern Europe. Strong reputation for corporate finance, M&A and securities law advice working with leading domestic and international financial institutions in the Czech Republic and abroad.
Prof. Memberships: Member of New York State Bar, Chamber of Czech Advocates and chairman of the Board of Appeals of Czech Securities Commission.
Personal: Fluent in English, Czech, French and Spanish.

DŘEVÍNEK, Karel
Weil, Gotshal & Manges, Prague
+420 2 2140 7300
karel.drevinek@weil.com
Recommended in Corporate/M&A
Specialisation: Associate in the firm's Prague office. Regularly represents local and international corpo-

rate, banking and securities law clients in connection with their mergers and acquisitions, bank privatisation work and debt and equity offerings in Central Europe. Member of the Appellate Committee of the Czech Securities Commission.
Personal: Fluent in Czech, English and Russian. Graduate of Charles University School of Law, Prague School of Economics and Columbia University School of Law.

HEWKO, John
Baker & McKenzie, Prague +420 2 2185 5001
john.hewko@bakernet.com
Recommended in Corporate/M&A
Specialisation: Managing partner of the Prague office. Principal area of work is mergers and acquisitions, corporate law and privatisations. Over the past ten years has handled some of the largest acquisitions and privatisations in Ukraine and the Czech Republic, including representing KBC Bank in 1999 in its acquisition of Ceskoslovenska obchodni banka (CSOB) (at the time one of the two largest privatisations in the history of the Czech Republic) and representing CSOB in 2000 in its subsequent acquisition of Investicni a postovni banka (IPB) (thereby creating the largest bank in Central and Eastern Europe). Has spoken at numerous conferences on doing business in Central and Eastern Europe.
Prof. Memberships: Admitted in Washington DC, Pennsylvania and the Czech Republic (foreign advocate).
Publications: Numerous op-ed pieces in the Wall Street Journal, Los Angeles Times, Christian Science Monitor and other US and South American publications on Latin America and Central and Eastern Europe.
Career: 1985 – foreign associate *Klein & Mairal*, Buenos Aires, Argentina. 1986 – foreign associate *Pinheiro Neto Advogados*, Sao Paulo, Brazil. 1987-89 – associate *Gibson Dunn & Crutcher* Washington, DC. 1990 joined *Baker & McKenzie* in Moscow, becoming partner in 1992. 1991 to 1995 established and managed the *Baker & McKenzie* Kiev office. 1996 to present managed the *Baker & McKenzie* Prague office.
Personal: Born 18 November 1957. Attended Hamilton College 1975-79 (AB), Oxford University 1979-1981 (Marshal Scholar; MLitt) and Harvard Law School 1982-1985 (JD). Leisure interests include triathalons, ice hockey and skiing. Lives in Prague, Czech Republic.

HORÁKOVÁ, Karolina
Weil, Gotshal & Manges, Prague
+420 2 2140 7310
karolina.horokova@weil.com
Recommended in Banking & Finance
Specialisation: Specialises in international finance and frequently advises on corporate matters, particularly mergers and acquisitions, including competition aspects thereof. Also a well-respected advisor on local and international banking, capital markets and derivative transactions.
Career: Joined *Weil, Gotshal & Manges'* Prague office in 1993 and has been a partner since 1999.
Personal: Visiting lecturer of financial law at Charles University Law School. Graduate of Charles University in Prague and Pace University. Fluent in English and Czech.

JOHNSON, Nick
Allen & Overy, Prague +420 2 2210 7111
Recommended in Corporate/M&A

KINES, Stephen
Linklaters (a member firm of Linklaters & Alliance), Prague +420 2 2162 2111
stephen.kines@linklaters.com
Recommended in Communications
Specialisation: Partner and head of information technology, communication, and intellectual property. Also practising corporate and M&A. Represents some of the largest global telcos (BT, Vivendi Telecom, Telia, UPC) in their investment into the Czech Republic and throughout Central Europe, as well as local ISPs (World On Line, Czech On Line), microwave, satellite, fixed line, cable, and software/hardware clients. Largest dedicated team of communication lawyers in the Czech Republic, supported by the global *Linklaters & Alliance* communication team.

KOTÁB, Petr
Altheimer & Gray, Prague +420 2 2481 2782
kotabp@altheimer.cz
Recommended in Corporate/M&A
Specialisation: Partner. Member of the Department of Financial Law of Charles University School of Law. Specialises in taxation and has published extensively on the subjects of financial law, banking and foreign investment. Was previously a member of expert commissions on privatisation at the Ministry of Industry and the Ministry of Finance.
Prof. Memberships: Member, Chamber of Advocates of the Czech Republic.
Personal: Charles University School of Law (Master and Doctor of Law).

KUČERA, Francis
Linklaters (a member firm of Linklaters & Alliance), Prague +420 2 2162 2111
francis.kucera@linklaters.com
Recommended in Banking & Finance
Specialisation: International capital markets, international finance, especially issues of debt, equity and equity-linked securities in the capital markets. Recent significant transactions include advising: Paribas, Natwest and SBC as the manager to the Lukoil Convertible Bond issue (the first convertible bond to be issued by a Russian company); Global Securities as lead manager to the GDR issue by Banca Turco Romana A.S. (the first GDR issue by a Romanian company); Daiwa as financial adviser to the State on the privatisation of the Romanian Development Bank (the first Romanian bank to be privatised); the City of Prague on its fiduciary issue of EURO 200,000,000 Notes due 2009; CSFB as lead manager on the issue by CEZ a.s. of EURO 200,000,000 Notes due 2006; and the City of Prague on its EURO 50,000,000 syndicated guarantee facility.

MATĚJČEK, Jan
White & Case, Feddersen, Prague
+420 2 2481 1796
jmatejcek@whitecase.com
Recommended in Banking & Finance, Corporate/M&A
Specialisation: Head of firm's Prague office since 1995. Wide range of transactional experience. Is familiar with strategic as well as legal issues faced by domestic and international investors on their financing and corporate transactions in the Czech and Slovak Republics.
Career: Qualified to practise in Canada and in the Czech Republic. Fluent Czech, English, French and German.

McDAID, Ray
CMS Cameron McKenna Vos, Prague
+420 2 2109 8888
Recommended in Corporate/M&A

McGEHEE, Jeffrey A
Squire, Sanders & Dempsey LLP, Prague
+420 2 2166 2111
Recommended in Communications, Corporate/M&A

MYŠKA, Jan
Allen & Overy, Prague +420 2 2210 7111
Recommended in Corporate/M&A

PAPIRNIK, Vladimira N
Squire, Sanders & Dempsey LLP, Prague
+420 2 2166 2111
Recommended in Corporate/M&A

PETRUS, Vladimir
Clifford Chance, Prague +420 2 2409 7410
Recommended in Banking & Finance

SCHIFF, Kenneth E.
Weil, Gotshal & Manges, Prague
+420 2 2140 7300
ken.schiff@weil.com
Recommended in Corporate/M&A
Specialisation: Managing Partner of the firm's Prague Office. In Corporate Department. Practice areas include general corporate law, banking and financial services, business and securities, capital markets, debt and equity offerings, international law, joint ventures, mergers and acquisitions and private equity. Has extensive experience in establishment of investment funds, private equity and venture capital investments and acquisitions, financing, privatisations, capital markets, domestic and international debt and equity offerings and commercial leasing.
Prof. Memberships: New York, New Jersey and Czech bar associations.
Career: Managing Partner of the firm's Prague office. Practised seven years in the firm's New York office before joining the Prague office in 1994.
Personal: Brooklyn Law School (JD, 1987). New York University School of Business and Public Administration (BS, 1984).

SLACH, Petr
Squire, Sanders & Dempsey LLP, Prague
+420 2 2166 2111
Recommended in Communications

ŠOLC, Martin
Kocian Solc Balastík, Prague +420 2 2410 3316
Recommended in Corporate/M&A

TOUŠKA, Mikuláš
Allen & Overy, Prague +420 2 2210 7111
Recommended in Banking & Finance

DENMARK

Index

OVERVIEW: The trend towards consolidation in the Danish legal market continues unabated with Aarhus firm Løber & Lauritsen swallowed by Gorrissen Federspiel Kierkegaard and Plesner & Grønborg merging with O. Bondo Svane creating Denmark's fourth largest firm. Market response has been positive: the complementary strengths of the two firms make this a 'sensible merger.' Meanwhile Kromann Reumert has emerged as Denmark's leading firm, and one of the first where the younger generation is coming to the fore. M&A continues to expand supported by the 270% increase in private equity funds. Though most banking work is still done by large in-house departments, enough is now outsourced to warrant a new banking section. October 2000's amendments to the competition regulations introduce national merger control for the first time, and our competition section tracks developments in this sector.

D

Banking & Finance

DENMARK Leading firms (Banking & Finance)
1 Gorrissen Federspiel Kierkegaard
Kromann Reumert
Plesner Svane Grønborg
2 Bech-Bruun & Trolle

Firms are listed alphabetically in each band.

Leading individuals (Banking & Finance)
1 **BIER Jacob** *Plesner Svane Grønborg*
FEDERSPIEL Herman *Gorrissen Federspiel*
MADSEN Jørgen Kjegaard *Kromann Reumert*
PERMIN Jørgen *Plesner Svane Grønborg*
SØGAARD Klaus *Gorrissen Federspiel*
2 **HANSEN Poul Flemming** *Plesner Svane Grønborg*
JACOBSEN Ulrik *Kromann Reumert*
JENSEN Jørgen Reimer *Bech-Bruun & Trolle*
LIND Henrik *Gorrissen Federspiel Kierkegaard*
Individuals are listed alphabetically in each band.

Gorrissen Federspiel Kierkegaard (12 ptrs, 15 asscs) *"The strongest firm for non-equity lending advice,"* competitors acknowledged that it has *"good banking contacts"* and *"any number of well-qualified lawyers."* Active in listings, bonds, MTN programmes, notes and derivatives, the team has advised on a number of securitisations and regulatory matters, especially for foreign banks on cross-border transactions. Asset and project finance transactions round off a varied workload.

Herman Federspiel* is *"as solid as a rock,"* and is said to have *"sound connections with the UK banking market." "Bankers' favourite"* **Klaus Søgaard*** is *"probably the most experienced capital markets lawyer in Denmark,"* and a first choice for banks on verifications, while **Henrik Lind***, although increasingly involved in M&A, remains *"a financing expert par excellence."* The firm advised MeritaNordbanken on its $4.5 billion merger with Unidanmark. **Clients:** Citibank; Deutsche Bank; ABN AMRO.

Kromann Reumert (7 ptrs, 18 asscs) Denmark's largest law firm has grafted the former Reumert & Partners' outstanding shipping finance practice onto a first-class capital markets capacity, to make itself one of the country's leading all-round finance operations. The group has advised on IPOs, hostile banking takeovers and asset finance, and, although less visible on classical regulatory banking, it has also helped to establish several internet banking operations.

Some *"excellent banking people"* include *"eminent"* capital markets expert **Jørgen Kjegaard Madsen***, described by one competitor as *"technically good and a joy to work with,"* and **Ulrik Jacobsen***, consistently recommended for his ship financing expertise. The firm represented International Service System on a new offering of $450 million to fund the acquisition of a large Dutch company. **Clients:** Danish and international companies including ISS, Genmab and Maconomy.

Plesner Svane Grønborg (4 ptrs, 9 asscs) Inheriting capital markets strength from the O. Bondo Svane side of the merger, the firm has advised on a number of IPOs and equity issues, including representing the joint lead underwriters on the $450 million offering on the Copenhagen and London Stock Exchanges of shares in International Service System. Also visible in derivatives, bonds and traded debt work, the team has a notably strong asset finance capability.

Among a team renowned in the market for its *"consistent quality,"* vastly experienced asset finance specialist **Jørgen Permin*** stands out, while *"you will always get a good result"* from *"skilled capital markets lawyer"* **Jacob Bier***. *"A classical banking man,"* **Poul Flemming Hansen*** mixes his respected corporate practice with loan documentation expertise. The firm represented Unidanmark on its merger with MeritaNordbanken, and advised on the $200 million share offer on the Copenhagen Stock Exchange by Coden. **Clients:** Goldman Sachs; Morgan Stanley; JP Morgan; Danske Securities; Enskilda Securities; Unidanmark.

Bech-Bruun & Trolle (2 ptrs, 2 asscs) *"Probably the purest M&A firm in Copenhagen,"* its banking department is nevertheless perceived to be doing *"high quality work."* Active for banks, borrowers and issuers on IPOs and syndicated loans, the firm is one of the few in Denmark with substantial derivatives expertise. An enviable client base includes a large number of foreign investment

*See leaders' profiles on pages 240-242

banks. *"Knowledgeable and experienced"* **Jørgen Reimer Jensen*** is considered by clients to be *"a good draftsman."* The firm advised on the demerger of Novozymes from Novo Nordisk and its separate listing on the Copenhagen Stock Exchange. **Clients:** Goldman Sachs; Chase Manhattan; Merrill Lynch; Lehman Brothers.

Competition/Anti-trust

D

DENMARK Leading firms (Competition/Anti-trust)
1 Kromann Reumert
2 Bech-Bruun & Trolle
Gorrissen Federspiel Kierkegaard
Plesner Svane Grønborg
3 Jonas Bruun
Nielsen & Nørager

Firms are listed alphabetically in each band.

Leading individuals (Competition/Anti-trust)
1 DYEKJÆR-HANSEN Karen *Plesner Svane*
KOFMANN Morten *Bech-Bruun & Trolle*
MERSING Erik Mohr *Kromann Reumert*
SVENSSON Jan-Erik *Gorrissen Federspiel*
2 PEYTZ Henrik *Nielsen & Nørager*
3 PLUM Jens Munk *Kromann Reumert*
SKADHAUGE Jeppe *Jonas Bruun*
Up-and-coming individuals
BERTELSEN Erik *Kromann Reumert*

Individuals are listed alphabetically in each band.

Kromann Reumert (7 ptrs, 5 asscs) Active in all areas of competition work for international concerns and dominant domestic players in agriculture and telecoms, the firm is increasingly assisting large clients on compliance programmes. Merger filing is another area of growth, in line with the firm's superb corporate practice, and our researchers learned that it was involved in the merger control aspects of around half of the largest mergers and acquisitions in Denmark last year.

Erik Mohr Mersing* is *"a leading character in more ways than one."* The *"intellectual"* **Jens Munk Plum*** is *"a fine legal analyst,"* while **Erik Bertelsen*** is *"a notable young competition specialist."* **Clients:** TeleDanmark.

Bech-Bruun & Trolle (1 ptr, 5 asscs) Transactionally driven, the firm has strength in domestic merger control and multi-jurisdictional filings, which it co-ordinates from its Brussels office. The firm advises on franchise agreements and compliance programmes for a blue-chip international client base, and has made frequent appearances before the domestic and European competition authorities.

The *"energetic"* **Morten Kofmann*** is considered by competitors *"a clever fellow,"* with *"a good understanding of business,"* and remains a familiar figure in front of the Danish competition authorities, in spite of being based in Brussels. During the past year, the team has acted on article 81 representations, performed merger filings in the aviation and shipping sectors and advised on several cartel investigations. **Clients:** Blue-chip international and Danish companies.

Gorrissen Federspiel Kierkegaard (1 ptr, 4 asscs) Representing a number of leading Danish and other Scandinavian clients, the anti-trust team is reputed to have *"a strong international profile."* Merger notifications, especially under Article 81 of EU law, are a growing area, and the team has advised extensively on filings in Brussels and Copenhagen.

Leading practitioner **Jan-Erik Svensson*** is *"focused, reliable and has a good understanding of the problems,"* and has raised the profile of the practice through his work with the Danish Bar Association's special competition committee. Work this year has included advising clients on complaints against anti-competitive behaviour. **Clients:** Leading Danish and international companies.

Plesner Svane Grønborg (1 ptr, 5 asscs) Renowned for its work on the contentious aspects of competition law, the firm advises a predominantly Danish client base on multiple merger notifications, free movement of goods and parallel imports, particularly in the pharmaceutical industry.

"Strong character" **Karen Dyekjær-Hansen*** has a long-established anti-trust reputation, and according to one authority *"probably attends more pleadings in Luxembourg than anyone else in Denmark."* The firm advised on an appeal to the EU Court of Justice on behalf of Aalborg Portland, and was a leading player on the insulated pipes cartel case. **Clients:** Danish and international clients including Aalborg Portland.

Jonas Bruun (2 ptrs, 1 assc) A force in the Danish public sector, the firm advises on all areas of competition law, and has particular expertise in public procurement and state aids issues. An increase in M&A has recently seen the team more active in merger control and multi-jurisdictional filings for a principally domestic client base. *"Prudent"* **Jeppe Skadhauge*** *"has a light touch."* **Clients:** Domestic and international blue-chips.

Nielsen & Nørager (1 ptr, 3 asscs) Small firm, specialising in competition, which handles a variety of behavioural competition issues, including state aids, public procurement and appeals before the competition commission and European Court of Justice.

Previously with Kromann Reumert, **Henrik Peytz*** is carving out a rapidly growing profile. The firm has niche expertise in telecoms and media issues, and represented TV Danmark on a series of competition disputes with public broadcasters. Also represented shipping concern Easyline on the principle of access to ports. **Clients:** Easyline; TeleDanmark; TV Danmark; Løgstør Rør.

Corporate/M&A

DENMARK
Leading firms
(Corporate/Mergers & Acquisitions)

Band	Firm
1	Kromann Reumert
2	Gorrissen Federspiel Kierkegaard
3	Bech-Bruun & Trolle
4	Dragsted Schlüter Aros
	Plesner Svane Grønborg
5	Hjejle Gersted & Morgensen
	Jonas Bruun
6	Lind & Cadovius

Firms are listed alphabetically in each band.

Leading individuals
(Corporate/Mergers & Acquisitions)

Band	Individual
1	**CHRISTENSEN Jan Schans** *Bech-Bruun & Trolle*
	LIND Henrik *Gorrissen Federspiel Kierkegaard*
	NIELSEN Niels Erik *Dragsted Schlüter Aros*
	STENBJERRE Henrik *Kromann Reumert*
2	**ENGELL Oluf** *Hjejle Gersted & Morgensen*
	HANSEN Poul Flemming *Plesner Svane*
	HEERING Niels *Gorrissen Federspiel Kierkegaard*
	MEISLING Soren *Bech-Bruun & Trolle*
	PHILIP Marianne *Kromann Reumert*
	SKIPPER-PEDERSEN Mogens *Kromann Reumert*
3	**AASMUL-OLSEN Henning** *Jonas Bruun*
	BOE Jørgen *Kromann Reumert*
	EBELING Mogens *Jonas Bruun*
	KJØLBYE Christian *Plesner Svane Grønborg*
	KROGSTRUP Sven *Bech-Bruun & Trolle*
	LAVESEN Anders *Kromann Reumert*
	LERNØ Finn *Plesner Svane Grønborg*
	MØGELMOSE Henrik *Kromann Reumert*
	STOKHOLM Jon *Lind & Cadovius*
	SVANHOLM Michael *Hjejle Gersted & Morgensen*
Up-and-coming individuals	
	KETELSEN Peter *Kromann Reumert*

Individuals are listed alphabetically in each band.

Kromann Reumert (15 ptrs, 50 asscs) Following its merger last year, the biggest firm in Denmark is now also considered to be the best. *"A huge number of top lawyers"* are making substantial inroads in the IT, biotech and telecoms markets, while the firm retains its usual share of work in the traditional economy. Our researchers were impressed by the strength of market recommendations for a number of individuals.

"Top rainmaker" **Henrik Stenbjerre*** is considered *"a particularly skilful corporate lawyer,"* **Mogens Skipper-Pedersen*** is *"still an important part of the team,"* and **Marianne Philip*** is *"sharp, quick and able to handle a variety of cases at once."* The *"technically adept"* **Henrik Møgelmose*** is *"easy to work with,"* while **Jørgen Boe*** is *"a conscientious and sound draftsman."* From an impressive younger generation, **Anders Lavesen*** is *"potentially something special"* and rising star **Peter Ketelsen*** is *"energetic and professional."* The firm represented Falck Securities in its DKK18 billion merger with Group 4. **Clients:** Falck Securities; ISS; J Lauritzen-group; EQT; Schneider Electric.

Gorrissen Federspiel Kierkegaard (15 ptrs, 35 asscs) *"Traditionally a shipping and banking firm,"* the group now has strength in all areas of corporate law, notably in transport, insurance and cross-border M&A, often acting on referrals from investment banks. One of the leading firms in Denmark *"in terms of volume of deals and professionalism,"* it is increasingly active in the launching and listing of biotech and IT firms.

An impressive team includes *"practical solutions man"* **Henrik Lind***, who is *"well-organised, hard-working and a good communicator,"* and **Niels Heering***, commended by competitors and clients for his commercial acumen. The firm advised Sonofon on its $1.89 billion sale of a 53.5% stake to Telenor, and American company Asland on its purchase of Superfos and subsequent sale of a majority of the assets. **Clients:** Morgan Stanley; the AP Møller Group; Citibank; TeleDanmark.

Bech-Bruun & Trolle (9 ptrs, 25 asscs) A *"traditional leader in the old economy,"* the firm still *"has a fine client list,"* but is felt by the market to lack depth among its younger practitioners. Particular strength in traditional Danish industry is complemented by the team's increased transactional activity in IT, biotechnology and telecommunications.

The *"academic"* **Jan Schans Christensen*** *"stands out – he's extremely knowledgeable."* *"Excellent"* **Soren Meisling*** is *"commercial, bright and has the ability to work around the clock,"* while **Sven Krogstrup*** is *"a solid practitioner."* The firm represents a client base split between major Danish and international clients, and has recently acted on a number of transactions in the aviation industry. **Clients:** FLS; SCA; NKT; Ameritech.

Dragsted Schlüter Aros (7 ptrs, 28 asscs) Transactionally oriented firm, focusing on the communications and biotech industries, which is considered by competitors to have enviable critical mass and *"a clearly-defined strategy."* The firm is generally acknowledged to have emerged strongly from its series of mergers in 1999, and is *"making a difference in the market."*

Much is owed to the industry and determination of **Niels Erik Nielsen***, *"a prominent figure in corporate law,"* who has, according to one source, *"great expertise at putting deals together."* In addition to its excellent connections with Danish pension funds, the firm retains a strong following among domestic corporates, while increasing its base of foreign clients, especially investment banks. The group represented Intel on its acquisition of a subsidiary of NKT for around DKK10 billion, and advised Group 4 on its DKK18 billion merger with Falck. **Clients:** Group 4; Icopal; Intel.

Plesner Svane Grønborg (9 ptrs, 19 asscs) Although it is still too early to judge the September 2000 union of Plesner & Grønborg and O. Bondo Svane, the *"sensible merger"* of Plesner's corporate muscle with Bondo Svane's traditional banking strength is almost universally reckoned to be *"a recipe for success."* A versatile team represents a blue-chip clientele of Danish and international entities on cross-border and domestic M&A.

"Skilled and cautious," **Poul Flemming Hansen*** is particularly recommended for M&A within the finance sector. *"When you have a complex transaction, he's your man."* **Finn Lernø*** is *"a competent practitioner, who advises top clients,"* while *"versatile and pragmatic"* **Christian Kjølbye*** is a respected younger lawyer with an especially strong following in the telecoms industry. The firm was one of the advisors to Unidanmark on its merger with MeritaNordbanken, which created an organisation with a market capitalisation of €15.6 billion. Also represented Telenor on its acquisition of a $1.89 billion stake in Sonofon from GN Great Nordic. **Clients:** GE Capital; Telenor; Ford; Glaxo Wellcome.

Hjejle Gersted & Morgensen (8 ptrs, 20 asscs) *"A brass and mahogany law firm,"* it has a traditional style and a predominantly domestic client base, showing strength in banking, industry, retail and agriculture. *"Conservative in the best sense of the word,"* the corporate team is noted by competitors for its versatility, and is considered *"to do what it does really well."* The *"brilliant"* **Oluf**

D

*See leaders' profiles on pages 240-242

Engell* *"can handle just about anything,"* while **Michael Svanholm*** is recommended by his peers as *"a fine general commercial and tax lawyer."* Among an increasing number of mergers and acquisitions over the past year, the firm advised Danske Bank on its offer to purchase shares in RealKredit Denmark. **Clients:** Danish Steel Mills; Carlsberg; Danske Bank.

Jonas Bruun (5 ptrs, 12 asscs) Established 'old school' firm with a name for representing clients from traditional Danish industries. Although comparatively small, the department has been involved in a number of the year's largest transactions, has strong relationships with banking, insurance, telecoms and energy clients, and possesses niche expertise in the pharmaceuticals industry. **Henning Aasmul-Olsen*** and **Mogens Ebeling*** are both respected as *"straightforward, far-sighted"* lawyers. The firm advised Unidanmark on their huge merger with MeritaNordbanken, a transaction valued at approximately DKK110 billion. **Clients:** Unidanmark; Tryg-Baltica; Sonofon; Sjaellanske Kraftdaerker.

Lind & Cadovius (5 ptrs, 5 asscs) Respected for M&A, capital markets and insolvency advice, the firm *"has a slightly higher profile now,"* largely owing to the efforts of the chairman of the Danish bar association, **Jon Stokholm***. *"A towering figure,"* according to one authority, he is said to be *"likeable and direct in negotiations."*

The firm advises sellers and purchasers on M&A in all sectors, acting for a clientele which is beginning to assume a more international appearance. Telecommunications is a notable area of expertise. The group represented a consortium of venture companies on the £90 million acquisition of Aalborg Industries from the J Lauritzen Group, and advised a Canadian company as part of the 'white knight consortium' involved in the takeover of Icopal. **Clients:** Goldman Sachs; Danske Bank.

Leaders' profiles – Denmark

AASMUL-OLSEN, Henning
Jonas Bruun, Copenhagen +45 33 47 88 00
Recommended in Corporate/M&A

BERTELSEN, Erik
Kromann Reumert, Copenhagen +45 33 11 11 10
Recommended in Competition/Anti-trust

BIER, Jacob
Plesner Svane Grønborg, Copenhagen
+45 33 12 11 33
jbi@psglaw.dk
Recommended in Banking & Finance
Specialisation: Partner in the Corporate Finance Department. Main area of work is corporate finance including M&A, securities, equity capital markets, private equity and venture capital. Has handled major transactions for Scandinavian and international investment banks, private equity funds and corporations, including telecoms, high tech/high growth companies and media companies. Transactional experience includes some of the largest corporate transactions and equity issues in Denmark. Clients include ArosMaizel, Danske Securities, Goldman Sachs, Morgan Stanley Dean Witter, numerous private equity funds and corporations. Member of the European Association of Securities Dealers Tax and Legal Commitee.
Prof. Memberships: Danish Bar Association, International Bar Association, Union International d'Avocats and other law societies.
Publications: Editor of 'Danish Corporate Finance Laws'. Contributor to 'Mergers and acquisitions in Europe'. Contributor of various articles on corporate law. Currently in charge of a pan-european survey on the use of legal opinions in public offerings, due to be published during 2001.
Career: Qualified 1989. Joined *Plesner Svane Grønborg* in 1986, becomming partner in 1993. Lecturer contract law 1986-1990 University of Copenhagen. Chairman of the board of Case Technology A/S 1994-1997, Zebra A/S 2000-, member of the board of directors of Refshaleøens Ejendomsselskab A/S 1996-1998, Bema A/S 1999-, Speednames, Inc. 2000-, chang2day.com A/S 2000-.
Personal: Born 18 June 1961.

BOE, Jørgen
Kromann Reumert, Copenhagen +45 33 11 11 10
Recommended in Corporate/M&A

CHRISTENSEN, Jan Schans
Bech-Bruun & Trolle, Copenhagen
+45 33 12 12 33
jsc@bbtlaw.dk
Recommended in Corporate/M&A
Specialisation: Company Law; Mergers & Acquisitions; Natural Resources; Energy Law.
Prof. Memberships: Danish Bar Association; Copenhagen Bar Association; International Bar Association; Danish Corporate Law Association (Co-Founder and Secretary and Director).
Publications: 'Hostile Takeovers in the USA' Copenhagen, 1989; 'Contested Takeovers in Danish Law; A Comparative Analysis based on a Law and Economics Approach', Copenhagen 1992; 'Cross-Border Corporate Transactions,' Copenhagen 1998.
Career: University of Copenhagen (Law Degree, 1981); Columbia University School of Law, New York (Research Assistant, 1987-1988; LLM, 1988); *Debevoise & Plimpton*, New York, 1988-1989; University of Copenhagen (Dr. jur., 1991). Admitted, 1984, Denmark; 1986, High Court of Denmark.
Personal: Born August 15, 1957 in Bennekom, The Netherlands.

DYEKJÆR-HANSEN, Karen
Plesner Svane Grønborg, Copenhagen
+45 33 12 11 33
Recommended in Competition/Anti-trust

EBELING, Mogens
Jonas Bruun, Copenhagen +45 33 47 88 00
Recommended in Corporate/M&A

ENGELL, Oluf
Hjejle Gersted & Morgensen, Copenhagen
+45 33 134 262
Recommended in Corporate/M&A

FEDERSPIEL, Herman
Gorrissen Federspiel Kierkegaard, Copenhagen
+45 33 41 41 41
Recommended in Banking & Finance

HANSEN, Poul Flemming
Plesner Svane Grønborg, Copenhagen
+45 33 12 11 33
pfh@psglaw.dk
Recommended in Banking & Finance, Corporate/Commercial
Specialisation: Company law; commercial law; mergers & acquisitions; banking and financing. Advisor to Unidanmark A/S in the merger of Unidanmark A/S and Tryg-Baltica Insurance in 1999 and the merger of Unidanmark A/S and Nordic Baltic Holding AB in 2000; advisor to Mols Ferry Lines in the merger with Scandlines in 1999. Represents a number of major listed companies including Danish and international banks and other financing institutions. Member of *Plesner Svane Grønborg*'s managing committee.
Prof. Memberships: Danish Bar Association and other national and international legal societies.
Career: University of Copenhagen (Cand. Jur 1974), admitted 1979, Copenhagen. Assistant Professor in Administrative Law, University of Copenhagen (1976-1981), Secretary at the Ministry of Justice (1974-1976), admitted to the Supreme Court of Denmark (1993), Substitute Judge in the Danish Labour Court.
Personal: Born 5 September 1947.

HEERING, Niels
Gorrissen Federspiel Kierkegaard, Copenhagen
+45 33 41 41 41
Recommended in Corporate/M&A

JACOBSEN, Ulrik
Kromann Reumert, Copenhagen +45 3393 3960
Recommended in Banking & Finance

JENSEN, Jørgen Reimer
Bech-Bruun & Trolle, Copenhagen
+45 33 12 12 33
jrj@bbtlaw.dk
Recommended in Banking & Finance
Specialisation: Banking; capital markets; mergers and acquisitions.
Prof. Memberships: Danish Bar Association; Copenhagen Bar Association; International Bar Association.
Career: University of Copenhagen (law degree, 1982); University of Michigan Law School (LLM, 1986). *Sullivan & Cromwell*, New York, 1986-1987.
Personal: Born January 17, 1958 in Copenhagen, Denmark. Admitted, 1985, Denmark and High Court of Denmark; 1990, Supreme Court of Denmark.

KETELSEN, Peter
Kromann Reumert, Copenhagen +45 33 11 11 10
Recommended in Corporate/M&A

KJØLBYE, Christian Th.
Plesner Svane Grønborg, Copenhagen
+45 33 12 11 33
Recommended in Corporate/Commercial
Specialisation: Partner, corporate law and corporate finance. Specialises in company and commercial law, stock exchange regulations, telecommunications, mergers and acquisitions, trademark law. Advisor to a number of major Danish and foreign companies, investment banks and private equity investors. Acted for Telenor AS in its acquisition of a majority stake in Danish telecommunications company Sonofon in June 2000.
Prof. Memberships: International Bar Organisation and various national legal societies. Board member in various Danish companies.
Career: Joined *Plesner Svane Grønborg* in 1987. Assistant professor in property law at the University of Copenhagen 1987-88. Supreme Court admission 1991. Reporter on company law matters to the Danish Law Society since 1995.
Personal: University of Copenhagen (degree 1976). LLM New York University 1987.

KOFMANN, Morten
Bech-Bruun & Trolle, Brussels +32 2 736 05 23
kof@bbtlaw.dk
Recommended in Competition/Anti-trust
Specialisation: Partner of *Bech-Bruun & Trolle* and heads the firm's Brussels office. Provides specialist advice on EU and Danish competition law and on EU law more generally, specialising in EU and national merger control, joint ventures, cartel investigations, state aid, public procurement and litigation before the European courts.
Prof. Memberships: Member of The Law Society's Solicitors' European Group and the Board of Directors of the Danish Competition Law Society.
Publications: Author of various articles on competition law published in Danish and foreign periodicals, and a contributor to the Competition Law of the European Community.
Career: Admitted to the Bar and to the High Court of Denmark in 1989. Graduate of the University of Copenhagen (1986) and the London School of Economics and Political Science (LLM 1990). Has spent time with the European Commission, with the Directorate General for Competition (1990-91) and part-time lecturing EC Law at the Copenhagen Business School (1991-93) and Competition Law at the University of Copenhagen (1992-96).
Personal: Born 10 October 1962 in Copenhagen, Denmark.

KROGSTRUP, Sven
Bech-Bruun & Trolle, Copenhagen
+45 33 12 12 33
sk@bbtlaw.dk
Recommended in Corporate/M&A
Specialisation: Mergers & Acquisitions; Aviation; Company Law.
Prof. Memberships: Danish Bar Association.
Career: University of Copenhagen (Law Degree, 1970). Admitted, 1973, Denmark Université de Grenoble. Practice in Jeddah, Saudi Arabia, 1978-1980. High Court of Denmark.
Personal: Born September 10, 1943 in Aarhus, Denmark.

LAVESEN, Anders
Kromann Reumert, Copenhagen +45 33 11 11 10
Recommended in Corporate/M&A

LERNØ, Finn J.
Plesner Svane Grønborg, Copenhagen
+45 33 12 11 33
fjl@psglaw.dk
Recommended in Corporate/Commercial
Specialisation: Partner in the Corporate Finance and M&A Department of *PSG*, specialising in international and Danish acquisitions and derivatives. Lead counsel to NCC AB, Sweden, in the acquisition of the largest Danish construction company, Rasmussen & Schiøtz A/S, the largest Danish asphalt company, Superfos Construction A/S, and of the inter-nordic Roads-division from Rieber ASA, Norway. Head counsel to Girobank A/S in the merger with Sparekassen Bikuben A/S, now BG Bank A/S.
Prof. Memberships: Danish Bar Association, International Bar Association.
Publications: Co-author of 'The Commentaries to the Stamp Duty Act', 2nd edition 1994. National correspondent to international publication on the distributorships and agencies and to Committee S of IBA/SBL.
Career: Associate, the law offices of Poul Schmith (the Danish Queen's Counsel), 1979-1985. Associate, the law offices of Erik Münter (now *Kromann Reumert*), 1985-1988. Associate, the law offices of *Bornstein & Grønborg* (now *Plesner Svane Grønborg*), 1988-1990. Publication officer of Committee S, 1998-present.
Personal: Born 27 April 1953. University of Copenhagen (Master of Laws), 1979. California State University, Northridge.

LIND, Henrik
Gorrissen Federspiel Kierkegaard, Copenhagen
+45 33 41 41 41
Recommended in Banking & Finance, Corporate/M&A

MADSEN, Jørgen Kjegaard
Kromann Reumert, Copenhagen +45 33 11 11 10
Recommended in Banking & Finance

MEISLING, Soren
Bech-Bruun & Trolle, Copenhagen
+45 33 12 12 33
sm@bbtlaw.dk
Recommended in Corporate/M&A
Specialisation: Mergers & Acquisitions; Company Law; Natural Resources.
Prof. Memberships: Danish Bar Association; Copenhagen Bar Association; International Bar Association; Danish Corporate Law Association.
Publications: 'Going Concern' in Danish Corporate Law, 1992. Co-Author of chapter on Danish Law in 'A Practitioner's Guide to Takeover Regulation and Practice in the European Union' 1999.
Career: University of Copenhagen (Law Degree, 1972). Joined *Bech-Bruun & Trolle* Law Firm 1972. Partner since 1981. Admitted, 1976 High Court of Denmark; 1981 Supreme Court of Denmark.
Personal: Born October 17, 1947 on Frederiksberg, Denmark. Married with four children.

MERSING, Erik Mohr
Kromann Reumert, Copenhagen +45 33 11 11 10
Recommended in Competition/Anti-trust

MØGELMOSE, Henrik
Kromann Reumert, Copenhagen +45 33 11 11 10
Recommended in Corporate/M&A

NIELSEN, Niels Erik
Dragsted Schlüter Aros, Copenhagen
+45 77 33 77 33
nen@dragsted.com
Recommended in Corporate/M&A
Specialisation: Specialises in M&A, stock exchange regulations and banking. Has acted as legal advisor to Danish and international undertakings as well as venture funds in connection with many major acquisitions, restructurings and mergers as well as cross-border transactions. Chairman of the boards of various listed Danish companies. Sits on committees and councils set up by the Danish Government.
Career: University of Copenhagen 1972; qualified 1975; Partner 1978; Chairman of the board of *Dragsted Schlüter Aros* 1999.
Personal: Sailing and golf.

PERMIN, Jørgen
Plesner Svane Grønborg, Copenhagen
+45 33 12 11 33
jpe@psglaw.dk
Recommended in Banking & Finance
Specialisation: Partner in the banking and finance department of *Plesner Svane Grønborg*, specialising in lending, project and asset based financing – with particular emphasis on ship and aircraft financing and derivatives. Advisor to Danish and foreign financial institutions and airlines.
Prof. Memberships: Danish Bar Association. IBA. UIA.
Publications: 'International banking Law & Regulation' (Oceana), chapter on Denmark, articles in Danish periodicals on derivatives.
Career: Danish Department of Justice (assistant dis-

D

trict attorney) 1982. Attorney-at-law, *O. Bondo Svane*, Copenhagen 1986. *Haight, Gardner, Poor & Havens* 1991. Partner at *O. Bondo Svane* (now *Plesner Svane Grønborg*) 1992, member of the executive committee of *Plesner Svane Grønborg*, teacher at the Danish Bar Association courses on derivatives.
Personal: Born 1956. Copenhagen University Law School 1983. Studies (international law) in the US 1979. Resides in Copenhagen.

PEYTZ, Henrik
Nielsen & Nørager, Copenhagen +45 33 11 45 45
Recommended in Competition/Anti-trust

PHILIP, Marianne
Kromann Reumert, Copenhagen +45 33 93 3960
Recommended in Corporate/M&A

PLUM, Jens Munk
Kromann Reumert, Copenhagen +45 33 11 11 10
Recommended in Competition/Anti-trust

SKADHAUGE, Jeppe
Jonas Bruun, Copenhagen +45 33 47 88 00
Recommended in Competition/Anti-trust

SKIPPER-PEDERSEN, Mogens
Kromann Reumert, Copenhagen +45 33 11 11 10
Recommended in Corporate/M&A

STENBJERRE, Henrik
Kromann Reumert, Copenhagen +45 33 11 11 10
Recommended in Corporate/M&A

STOKHOLM, Jon
Lind & Cadovius, Copenhagen +45 33 338100
Recommended in Corporate/M&A

SVANHOLM, Michael
Hjejle Gersted & Morgensen, Copenhagen +45 33 134 262
MS@HGMLAW.DK
Recommended in Corporate/M&A
Specialisation: Corporate law, mergers and acquisitions, tax law, legal advice to corporations within the agricultural sector, and litigation.
Prof. Memberships: The Danish Bar Association, Member of the Board of The Danish Bar Association, Copenhagen Department, admission to practice for the Supreme Court in 1991.
Career: Bachelor of Law (University of Copenhagen) 1983, qualified as a solicitor 1986, joined *Hjejle, Gersted & Mogensen* 1983 and became a partner in 1989, member of the Board of Directors in several companies and institutions, legal counsel to The Danish Medical Association.
Publications: Author of a number of tax law articles in legal magazines.
Personal: Born 28 September 1959, living in Copenhagen.

SVENSSON, Jan-Erik
Gorrissen Federspiel Kierkegaard, Copenhagen +45 33 41 41 41
Recommended in Competition/Anti-trust

SØGAARD, Klaus
Gorrissen Federspiel Kierkegaard, Copenhagen +45 33 41 41 41
Recommended in Banking & Finance

DJIBOUTI

Corporate/Commercial

DJIBOUTI Leading firms (Corporate/Commercial)
1 Martinet & Martinet
2 Cabinet Wabat Daoud

Firms are listed alphabetically in each band.

Leading individuals (Corporate/Commercial)
1 **MARTINET Alain** *Martinet & Martinet*
2 **DAOUD Wabat** *Cabinet Wabat Daoud*
MARTINET Marie-Paule *Martinet & Martinet*

Individuals are listed alphabetically in each band.

Martinet & Martinet (2 ptrs, 1 assc) The firm is said to provide *"a similar standard to a Paris firm,"* and advises multi-national clients on establishing and reorganising their local corporate presence. Strong in banking, trademark and maritime law, the firm is recognised for its *"promptness of response."* **Alain Martinet** *"is an excellent lawyer by any reckoning,"* while his wife **Marie-Paule Martinet** is also highly regarded. The firm acted for the Djibouti government in an arbitration against Cotenca in Paris. **Clients:** Bank Indosuez; Inchape Shipping Services; Mobil; Shell; Sheraton.

Cabinet Wabat Daoud (1 ptr, 1 assc) President of the Djibouti Bar Association **Wabat Daoud** is *"a sound lawyer"* who is highly regarded for his international trade law expertise. French trained and qualified, he has particular strength in shipping, IP and foreign investment. **Clients:** BNP; IBB; shipping companies.

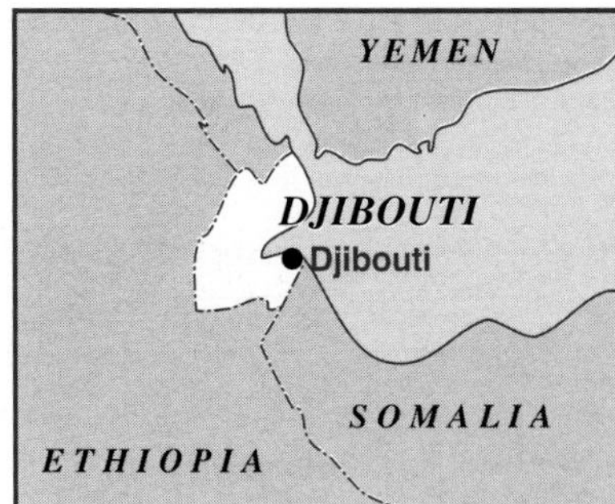

Leaders' profiles – Djibouti

DAOUD, Wabat
Cabinet Wabat Daoud, Djibouti +253 35 47 02

MARTINET, Alain
Martinet & Martinet, Djibouti +253 35 28 79

MARTINET, Marie-Paule
Martinet & Martinet, Djibouti +253 35 28 79

DOMINICAN REPUBLIC

Corporate/Commercial

DOMINICAN REPUBLIC Leading firms (Corporate/Commercial)
1 Headrick Rizik Alvarez & Fernandez
Pellerano & Herrera
Russin, Vecchi & Heredia Bonetti
Troncoso y Caceres

Firms are listed alphabetically in each band.

Leading individuals (Corporate/Commercial)
1 **BONETTI Luis** *Russin Vecchi & Heredia*
HEADRICK William *Headrick Rizik Alvarez*
PELLERANO Juan Manuel *Pellerano & Herrera*
SANTONI George *Russin Vecchi & Heredia*
TRONCOSO Marcos *Troncoso y Caceres*

Individuals are listed alphabetically in each band.

Headrick Rizik Alvarez & Fernandez (5 ptrs, 12 asscs) Relatively new firm, formed from a number of lawyers formerly with Russin Vecchi & Heredia Bonetti. *"Hard-working, with a sensible and conscientious approach to their work,"* the firm has quickly forged a strong reputation in banking, foreign investment, international loans and the sale of stock. US lawyer **William Headrick** was recommended to our researchers as a *"particularly active"* corporate practitioner. The firm recently represented Occidental Hotels on the purchase of a majority stake in Allegro Resorts. **Clients:** Citibank; Banco BHD; Quotatel; Merck & Co; IATA; Unilever; Texaco.

Pellerano & Herrera (5 ptrs, 3 asscs) Having grown rapidly in recent times, the firm has a strong reputation among its competitors for corporate and financial advice. **Juan Manuel Pellerano** enjoys an admired name for his *"willingness to take risks."* The firm advised on an electrical power generation issue, as well as acting on the acquisition of one part of a local company by Unilever. **Clients:** International Corporations.

Russin, Vecchi & Heredia Bonetti (2 ptrs, 5 asscs) *"One of the old pioneers,"* with a large international client base and a *"sound number of English-speaking attorneys."* **George Santoni** is *"a capable commercial lawyer,"* while the experienced **Luis Bonetti** was recognised for his expertise in foreign investment. **Clients:** Aerovías Venezolanas; Agentes y Estibadores Portuarios; American Airlines; Bacardi International; Bristol-Myers Squibb Dominicana; Chevron; AB Electrolux; Mobil Oil Corporation; SmithKline Beecham; Unilever Export.

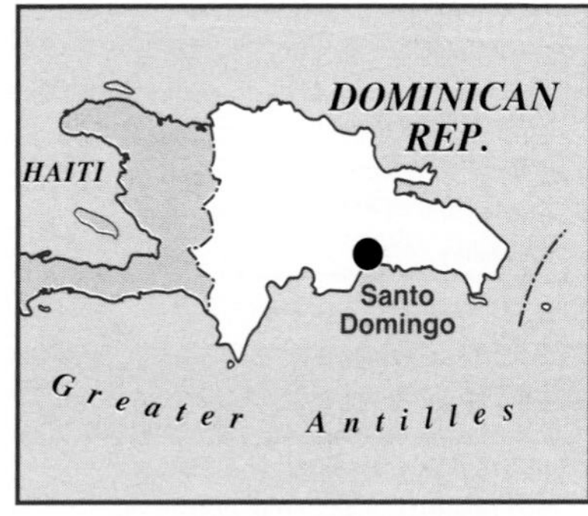

Troncoso y Caceres (5 ptrs, 3 asscs) *"Traditional"* firm with a particular reputation in international commercial law. Niche areas of expertise lie in banking, mining and IP. **Marcos Troncoso** was recommended as a *"co-operative and friendly"* trademarks specialist. The firm advised Nabisco on the purchase of new warehouses and advised a new client from Costa Rica on the purchase of Palé Supermarkets. **Clients:** Texaco; IBM; American Express; Merck; Nova Scotia; Falcon Bridge.

Leaders' profiles – Dominican Republic

BONETTI, Luis
Russin, Vecchi & Heredia Bonetti, Santo Domingo
+1 809 535 6649

HEADRICK, William
Headrick Rizik Alvarez & Fernandez, Santo Domingo +1 809 685 4137

PELLERANO, Juan Manuel
Pellerano & Herrera, Santo Domingo
+1 809 541 5200

SANTONI, George
Russin, Vecchi & Heredia Bonetti, Santo Domingo
+1 809 535 6649

TRONCOSO, Marcos
Troncoso y Caceres, Santo Domingo
+1 809 689 2158

ECUADOR

Corporate/Commercial

ECUADOR Leading firms (Corporate/Commercial)
1 Bustamante & Bustamante
Coronel & Perez
Esudio Jurídico Perez Bustamante & Ponce
Quevedo y Ponce

Firms are listed alphabetically in each band.

Leading individuals (Corporate/Commercial)
1 BUSTAMANTE José Rafael *Bustamante*
BUSTAMANTE Juan Carlos *Bustamante*
CORONEL César *Coronel & Perez*
JIJON Rodrigo *Perez Bustamante*
PEREZ José Maria *Perez Bustamante*
PONCE Alejandro *Quevedo y Ponce*
RUMANZO-ARCOS José *Perez Bustamante*

Individuals are listed alphabetically in each band.

Bustamante & Bustamante (13 ptrs, 25 asscs) Respected by the Quito elite, the firm is a *"serious, prestigious"* outfit, boasting an international office in Alicante, which has grown from an IP leader to gain an increasingly strong reputation for general commercial work. The corporate team advises a predominantly multi-national client base, drawn principally from the energy and finance industries.

Juan Carlos Bustamante* is one of the most respected lawyers in Ecuador, widely regarded by his peers as *"of great importance, both nationally and internationally,"* while younger partner and ex-Fulbright scholar **José Rafael Bustamante*** has a leading transactional reputation in his own right.

The firm's workload covers cross-border M&A and establishing Ecuadorean branches of multinational companies. A highlight was the team's advice on the merger of three local Coca-Cola bottling companies. **Clients:** ABN AMRO; Alcatel; Alitalia; AT&T; IBD; BellSouth; BAT; Citibank; Chase Manhattan; Duke Energy; Enron; IBM; ING; Lloyds; PepsiCo; Repsol; Warner Bros.

Coronel & Perez (2 ptrs, 8 asscs) Our research has shown that this Guayaquil-based firm is *"easily the most important firm in that city,"* and is known for its referral relationship with Quito firm Estudio Jurídico Perez Bustamante & Ponce. Often acting for American and European clients, the group specialises in advising on the establishment of foreign companies in Ecuador. **César Coronel*** creates *"a great impression"* with peers and clients. The firm represented International Waters on the privatisation of the state water company, advised Bass on an environmental dispute with local shrimp farmers, and acted for Unilever and Toyota on their local acquisitions. **Clients:** Shell; International Waters; Bass; Grupo Weng; Unilever; Toyota.

Estudio Jurídico Perez Bustamante & Ponce (14 ptrs, 24 asscs) The largest firm in the country was recently formed from the merger of two respected local operations, Perez Bustamante & Perez and Fabian Ponce. The new entity is anticipated to be *"a good combination"* of the corporate and IP strength of the former and the litigation prowess of the latter. The firm represents international corporate and banking clients, and is acknowledged for its expertise in oil and telecoms.

A powerful team includes **José Rumanzo-Arcos*** *("one of the best in the country")*, chairman of the US/Ecuadorean chamber of commerce. The esteemed **Rodrigo Jijon*** is the new firm's managing partner, while the *"outstanding"* **José Maria Perez*** also gains widespread acclaim from competitors. The firm's recent activity includes assisting on a $25 million banana port construction, and acting on the sale of an Ecuadorean

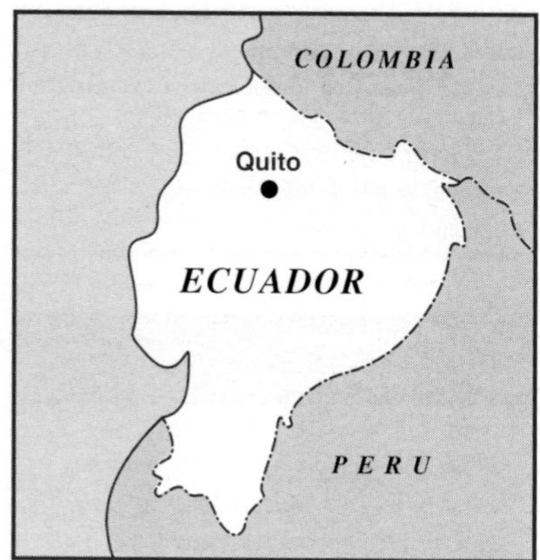

petrol company at a value of $180 million. The firm was also active on the negotiation of a strategic alliance with an aviation company. **Clients:** BellSouth; Hilton; Goldman Sachs; Merrill Lynch; Citibank; British Gas Services.

Quevedo y Ponce (16 ptrs) With a reputation as an *"aggressive and influential"* firm, it is accepted as an *"effective"* corporate player. However, some competitors have described the operation as *"more like a union of sole practitioners"* than a cohesive modern law firm. The firm is felt to owe much to **Alejandro Ponce***, *"an excellent lawyer,"* whose corporate expertise is supplemented with IP and litigation experience.

Advising a mixed client base of foreign investors, domestic exporters and retail banks, the group is considered to have a stranglehold on the local insurance market. Recent activity includes acting for multinationals such as Texaco and Pfizer in the defense of their IP rights against local companies. **Clients:** Procter & Gamble; Microsoft; Pfizer; Glaxo Wellcome; Novartis; McDonald's; Ericsson; Johnson & Johnson; Toshiba; ABN AMRO.

*See leaders' profiles on pages 245

Leaders' profiles – Ecuador

BUSTAMANTE, José Rafael
Bustamante & Bustamante, Quito +593 2 564 068
jrbustamante@bustamante.com.ec
Specialisation: Main areas of work are Commercial; Corporation; Civil; Foreign Investment; Intellectual Property; Licensing Agreements; Distribution and Agency Agreements; Oil and Gas; Mining; Taxation; Insurance; Labor; Banking Law.
Prof. Memberships: Ecuadorian Bar; Inter-American Bar Associations; Multilaw (Chairman, 1995-1999); American Society of International Law; International Bar Association (Ecuador Representative); United States Trademark Association (INTA); AIPPI; ECTA; LES.
Publications: Patents and Trademarks in the Andean Pact, Transference of Technology to Ecuador, Amendments to Companies Law Affecting Foreign Investment, Trial and Court Procedures in Ecuador, Trademark Practice in Ecuador.
Career: Admitted in 1978, became partner of *Bustamante & Bustamante* in 1987.
Personal: Born in Quito, on November 29, 1953. Graduated from the Catholic University of Ecuador in 1978 (Juris Doctor). Georgetown University, Master of Comparative Law, 1979. Leisure interests include horseback riding, motorcycle riding. Lives in Quito, Ecuador.

BUSTAMANTE, Juan Carlos
Bustamante & Bustamante, Quito +593 2 564 064
jcbustamante@accessinter.net
Specialisation: Main areas of work are private international law, oil law, tax law, corporate and administrative law. Has handled acquisitions of companies, such as Otecel for BellSouth, Electroquil for Duke Energy, Duragas for Repsol, and Omnibus BB Transportes for General Motors Corporation. Currently acting as counsel to Alberta Energy, Repsol YPF, Kerr-McGee, Agip Petroli and Occidental Exploration and Production Co. in the construction and operation of a main private oil pipeline in Ecuador.
Prof. Memberships: Law Society, City of Quito; International Academy of Trial Lawyers; Inter-American Bar Association; Lawyers Committee for Human Rights.
Publications: 'Foreign Investment in Ecuador'.
Career: Admitted in 1985. Became a Partner of *Bustamante & Bustamante* in 1968; Professor of Private International Law; Arbitrator of the National Mediation and Arbitration Center of the Chamber of Construction; Arbitrator of the Ecuadorian-American Chamber of Commerce; Member of the Tax Reform Commission.
Personal: Born November 14, 1943. Graduated from the Catholic University of Ecuador (Doctorate). Leisure interests include antique collection, horseback riding, antique cars. Lives in Quito, Ecuador.

CORONEL, César
Coronel y Perez, Guayaquil +59 34 519 900
ccoronel@cypaboga.com.ec
Specialisation: Senior Partner. Main area of work is corporate law, principally commercial, mergers and acquisitions, litigation and arbitration. Has handled litigation in intellectual property (Colgate vs. Ecuadorian company), environmental (BASF vs. Ecuadorian shrimp farmers), oil distribution (Shell vs. Ecuadorian oil state company). Has been advisor for some of the most important industrial companies with foreign investment in Ecuador and clients include: Industrias Rocacem (Cement Factory subsidiary of Holderbank), Cridesa (Glass Factory subsidiary of Owen-Illinois), BASF (USA), Colgate-Palmolive (Ecuadorian subsidiary), Starkist (Ecuadorian subsidiary), Shell (Ecuadorian subsidiary), International Water Limited, Compañia de Cervezas Nacionales (Brewery subsidiary of Bavaria, Colombia).
Publications: Writes for 'Hoy,' a well-known Ecuadorian newspaper. Wrote the book 'La Simulación de los Actos Juridicos' (The Simulation of the Legal Acts).
Career: Registered Lawyer in 1975. Doctor in Law in 1980. Member of the Advisory Council of Foreign Relations in Ecuador. Dean and Professor of the Law School at the Catholic University of Guayaquil. Member of the Conciliation Board of the International Centre for the Solution of Investments Related Differences (Washington DC). Founder Partner of *Coronel & Perez.* Arbiter of the Guayaquil Chamber of Commerce. Founder member of the LCIA's Latin American User's Council (London Court of International Arbitration). Former Delegate in Guayaquil of the Superintendent of Companies of Ecuador. Promoted and led the creation of the 'Ley de Concurso Preventivo' (Bankruptcy Law in Ecuador) and Casation Law. At the moment, Alternate Executive Director for Ecuador and Chile at the Inter-American Development Bank.
Personal: Born 24 April 1952. Attended Law School at Catholic University of Guayaquil (Lawyer 1975, Doctor in Law 1980). Member of the Civic Board of Guayaquil. Lives in Guayaquil, Ecuador.

JIJON, Rodrigo
Perez Bustamante & Ponce, Quito +593 225 4323

PEREZ, José Maria
Perez Bustamante & Ponce, Quito +593 2 561 710

PONCE, Alejandro
Quevedo y Ponce, Quito +593 2 986 570

RUMANZO-ARCOS, José
Perez Bustamante & Ponce, Quito +593 2 561 710

E

E

EGYPT

Banking & Finance

EGYPT Leading firms (Banking & Finance)
1 Shalakany Law Office
2 Baker & McKenzie (Helmy & Hamza)
3 Kamel Law Office
Zaki Hashem & Partners

Firms are listed alphabetically in each band.

Leading individuals (Banking & Finance)
★ ZULFICAR Mona *Shalakany Law Office*
1 HAMZA Samir *Baker & McKenzie (Helmy & Hamza)*
2 HELMY Taher *Baker & McKenzie (Helmy & Hamza)*
SAFWAT Mahmoud *Shalakany Law Office*

Individuals are listed alphabetically in each band.

Shalakany Law Office (15 ptrs; 45+ asscs) *"Undoubtedly the best,"* with a client base and experience dating from the country's 1974 'open door' foreign investment policy providing an advantage over the rest. With all round capability and expertise in aircraft financing and securities offerings, the team has handled major transactions including the first six GDR issues offered by Egyptian entities.

"Super smart" **Mona Zulficar*** is the star of an *"excellent"* team which includes senior founding member, *"inspiring"* **Mahmoud Safwat*** (now 'of counsel.') The firm acted on the first GSM telecom concession to MobiNil (subsidiary of France Telecom, Motorola, Orascom) in a deal exceeding $500 million, and the $200 million Orascom Telecom financing. **Clients:** Citibank; American Express; HSBC Egypt.

Baker & McKenzie (Helmy & Hamza) (2-3 ptrs, 3 asscs) Since its headline work on the Sidi Krir project syndicated loan, the firm has maintained its reputation as a *"quality"* banking practice. Providing *"excellent service,"* **Taher Helmy**'s* government connections are a key aspect of the firm's strength in this sector and *"first class lawyer"* **Samir Hamza*** has a good grounding in UK and Egyptian law.

The group acted for ABN AMRO Rothschild in the Telecom Egypt IPO and advised Merrill Lynch in an electricity privatisation. Other recent key transactions include work on the Ain Shokhna Port/Container Handling Facility, Sharm El Sheikh Airport and Cairo Airport. **Clients:** Banque du Caire; African Development Bank; BNP; Merrill Lynch; Morgan Stanley.

Kamel Law Office (3 ptrs, 30 asscs) With a client base dominated by major US banks and subsidiaries of foreign banks, the firm was unsurprisingly perceived to have a lower profile in the local market than on the international scene. Typical work includes handling share purchases and acquisitions, liquidation and regulatory authority approvals. **Clients:** Chase Manhattan; National Bank; CSFB; Crédit Agricole Indosuez.

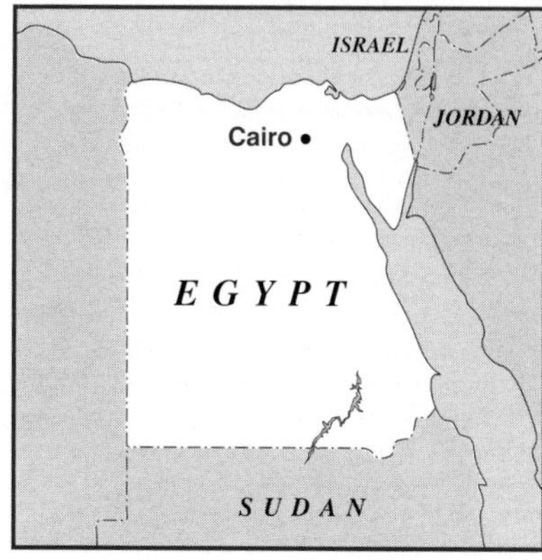

Zaki Hashem & Partners (9 ptrs, 25 asscs) Although experienced and highly rated for its work, peers agreed that the firm's sterling reputation in corporate and project finance work eclipses its profile in this area, particularly since Nagla Nassar has taken up post as Chief Strategic Planning Officer to construction company AIC. The group advised on the €2.4 billion transaction for Misr Phone (a Vodafone subsidiary) and acted in an ongoing international securitisation, the first of its kind in Egypt. **Clients:** Bank of Tokyo; Deutsche Bank; Banca Commerciale Italiana; Arab Bank; Bank of Tokyo-Mitsubishi; EGCD (UK).

Corporate/M&A

EGYPT Leading firms (Corporate/Mergers & Acquisitions)
1 Baker & McKenzie (Helmy & Hamza)
Shalakany Law Office
Zaki Hashem & Partners
2 Kamel Law Office

Firms are listed alphabetically in each band.

Baker & McKenzie (Helmy & Hamza) (4 ptrs, 7 asscs) *"Involved in many high profile deals,"* this *"sound"* full service practice is noted for its political connections. Interviewees claim it has *"the strongest reputation for consistency and quality of advice."* The *"backbone"* of the practice on technical aspects, **Samir Hamza*** is a *"hardworking problem-solver,"* who works in successful tandem with *"charmer"* **Taher Helmy***, a *"strong presence"* on the western aspects of deals. The firm acted for Egypt's largest steel manufacturer, EZZ, in its acquisitions of public sector companies and the establishment of greenfield operations. **Clients:** Cemex; Blue Circle; Al Ahram Beverages; Fiat Auto; Daewoo Motors; EZZ Group; PepsiCo; Oracle; Cisco; NCR; Sun Microsystems; Lockheed Martin; General Dynamics; Boeing; Raytheon.

Shalakany Law Office (15 ptrs, 45+ asscs) Operating *"like a finely tuned machine,"* researchers

EGYPT Leading individuals (Corporate/Mergers & Acquisitions)
1 HAMZA Samir *Baker & McKenzie (Helmy & Hamza)*
HASHEM Yasser *Zaki Hashem & Partners*
2 HELMY Taher *Baker & McKenzie (Helmy & Hamza)*
ZULFICAR Mona *Shalakany Law Office*

Individuals are listed alphabetically in each band.

received strong commendation for this outfit's integrated forward-thinking advice. The largest firm in Egypt with branches in Alexandria and Dubai, it has links with correspondent firms throughout the surrounding region. Sectors within its *"fully diversified"* practice include tourism, entertainment, manufacturing, IP and industrial property, construction and project management.

"*Clever lawyer*" **Mona Zulficar*** produces *"lots of good ideas"* and leads meetings with her *"strong personality."* The team acted for Amoun Pharmaceuticals in its acquisition by Glaxo Wellcome and advised Orascom Telecom in its recent acquisitions in Egypt and the surrounding region. **Clients:** MobiNil (France Telecom); EDF; General Motors; Orascom Telecom.

Zaki Hashem & Partners (9 ptrs, 35 asscs) *"One of the best firms in Cairo,"* a presence in Egypt for 50 years, this highly experienced practice *"has the advantage over the rest"* on government related matters and mature relationships with blue chip clients. A clear leader in telecoms work, the firm represents key players in the field, acting exclusively for Clic, a subsidiary of Vodafone.

"*Excellent*" **Yasser Hashem*** is recommended for his successful development of the practice. The team advised Sainsbury's on its establishment of 150 outlets in Egypt, the country's largest acquisition. **Clients:** General Electric; PepsiCo; Rothmans; American Home Products; Pfizer; Heinz.

Kamel Law Office (3 ptrs, 30 asscs) Despite the recent loss of senior players, researchers received commendations for the firm's *"professional"* approach. The practice handles a mixture of mining, petroleum, maritime, IP and licensing matters. The firm advises foreign investors on tax, shares transfers and reorganisation. It acted for Agyptco in ICC and local administrative courts, and was involved in the country's two largest investment arbitrations. **Clients:** LG Electronics; France Telecom; Alstom; ABB; American Standard; Ritz Carlton; Marriott; Microsoft.

E

Project Finance

EGYPT Leading firms (Project Finance)
1 Shalakany Law Office
Zaki Hashem & Partners
2 Baker & McKenzie (Helmy & Hamza)
3 Denton Wilde Sapte (in association with El Oteifi Law Office)
Kamel Law Office
Trowers & Hamlins (in association with Nour Law Office)

Firms are listed alphabetically in each band.

Leading individuals (Project Finance)
1 ZULFICAR Mona *Shalakany Law Office*
2 HAMZA Samir *Baker & McKenzie (Helmy & Hamza)*
HASHEM Yasser *Zaki Hashem & Partners*
HELMY Taher *Baker & McKenzie (Helmy & Hamza)*

Individuals are listed alphabetically in each band.

Shalakany Law Office (15 ptrs, 45+ asscs) Predictably, the team's size and unrivalled expertise in securities and capital markets gives it a major advantage in projects work. Since handling Intergen's interests in the seminal Sidi Krir BOOT power project, it has been involved in several other BOOT and privatisation projects in the water, roads and telecoms sectors.

Highly rated for her *"good logic and negotiation skills,"* **Mona Zulficar*** "*understands her clients' objectives.*" The team acted for EDF in the Port Said project and new economic zone Suez project. Also acted for Lavalla (Canadian water company) on new BOT water project. **Clients:** InterGen, EDF; Bechtel Power.

Zaki Hashem & Partners (9 ptrs, 35 asscs) Researchers received resounding recognition for the firm's broad coverage work and its focus in telecommunications, oil and gas and petrochemicals. A leader in the telecoms sphere, **Yasser Hashem*** is judged to be the most prominent practitioner within a *"strong"* team. It acted for Maersk on a unique BOT project, (largest to date) the private harbour container terminal for the East Port Said project. Also acted for the government in relation to AIG's acquisition of Alexandria Portland Cement. **Clients:** Vodafone AirTouch; France Telecom; Apache; British Gas; Phillips Petroleum.

Baker & McKenzie (Helmy & Hamza) (2-3 ptrs, 4 asscs) Despite a relatively low profile, the firm has considerable strength in set up and advisory work in the local and international arena. Handling referrals from its US offices, typical activity includes advising bidding consortia on infrastructure and utilities projects in the petrochemicals, power, water, airports and seaports sectors.

"*Brains of the operation*" **Samir Hamza*** is *"quiet and thoughtful,"* while international lenders seek **Taher Helmy*** for project financings on account of his strong government connections and rapid turnaround of instructions. The group acted for the Oriental Weavers' Group on a greenfield operation for an ammonia plant and advised leading Dutch company Vopak on a port bunkering project. **Clients:** Egyptian Basic Industries Corp; Halliburton; Kellogg; British Gas; Exxon/Esso/Mobil; Total; Enron; Pennzoil.

Denton Wilde Sapte (in association with El Oteifi Law Office) (1 ptr, 15 asscs) With its predominantly expatriate staff and local representation at associate level, researchers received greater recommendation for this young practice outside the local legal market. The main source of work comes from government advisory work and international and direct investment entities in Europe and the United States.

The team is supported by the telecoms expertise of the London office and it advises the Ministry of Telecommunications and Information Technology on its regulatory reform project. The firm acted for Blue Circle in completing the largest privatisation and acquisition of a majority stake in public sector company Alexandria Portland Cement. **Clients:** Legal & General; Blue Circle; Shell.

Kamel Law Office (3 ptrs, 30 asscs) Interviewees saw the firm as a key player in the local arena act-

*See leaders' profiles on page 248

ing for multinational clients. Typically providing advice relating to financing agreements, it acted for EDF in several matters including the Power Generation Plant on a BOOT basis from initial bidding to negotiations and establishment of project. The firm also advised foreign clients on the negotiation of joint ventures including a mineral mining project and an IT infrastructure project. **Clients:** EDF; International Finance Corporation; Visa International; Elkem.

Trowers & Hamlins (in association with Nour Law Office) (2 ptrs, 8 local lawyers) Strong in Oman and the UAE, researchers received recommendations for the firm's Cairo office as *"making some noise"* since opening in September 1999. A broadly based corporate and commercial outfit, its international expertise in projects has spawned from its banking, capital markets and M&A practice. IT and telecoms work are additional specialisms.

The firm advised on a major petrochemicals project and advised Foster Wheeler (UK) on the maintenance and operations contract for the MIDOR Oil Refinery. It also advised the promoters of a new telecoms investment fund focusing on the Middle East. **Clients:** Leading international financial institutions.

E

Leaders' profiles – Egypt

HAMZA, Samir
Helmy & Hamza, Cairo +202 579 1801
Recommended in Banking & Finance, Corporate/M&A, Project Finance
Specialisation: Partner in *Baker & McKenzie.* Main areas of specialisation are: Company/commercial/mergers & acquisitions. Worked on privatisation of several government owned companies. Intellectual Property – worked for foreign companies combating privacy. Project finance – worked on the first BOOT power plant project in Egypt representing all the lenders.
Prof. Memberships: Egyptian Bar Association (since 1961); Egyptian Association for Protection of Industrial Property (Board); Egyptian Internet Society (Head of Legal Section).
Career: Worked as a lawyer in the legal departments of Egyptian public sector companies and in the Shuaiba Area Authority in Kuwait. Joined *Baker & McKenzie,* as associate, in January 1977. In 1983, became partner of *Baker & McKenzie,* and still a partner in the Cairo office of *Baker & McKenzie (Helmy & Hamza).*

HASHEM, Yasser
Zaki Hashem & Partners, Cairo +202 393 3766
Recommended in Corporate/M&A, Project Finance

HELMY, Taher
Helmy & Hamza, Cairo +202 579 1801
Recommended in Banking & Finance, Corporate/M&A, Project Finance
Specialisation: Partner, M&A, Banking and Finance, and Securities Practice Groups. Recent transactions include acting for bidding consortium (GPU International/ABB) in Sidi Krir 2x235MW BOOT Power Plant bid; acting as counsel for Ezz Stell Rebars, Almereyah Cement, Al Ahram Beverages' IPOs; currently acting as underwriters' counsel for electricity and telecom privatisation.
Prof. Memberships: Member of the Illinois Bar Association; the Chicago Bar Association and the Egyptian Bar Association.
Career: Received BA degree and JD degree from St Louis University in 1972 and 1974 respectively. First Arab lawyer admitted before the US Supreme Court. In 1974, joined *Cahill, Gordon, & Reindel.* In May 1975, joined *Baker & McKenzie* and was elected full partner in 1981. Co-founder of *Baker & McKenzie's* offices in Riyadh and Cairo. Participated in drafting key legislation in Egypt, such as the Privatisation Law. Founder and Chairman of the Egyptian Centre for Economic Studies. Member of the US-Egypt Presidents' Council. Founder and Board member of the British Egyptian Businessmen Association, Former Vice President and currently member of the American Chamber of Commerce in Egypt.
Personal: Born 14 December 1949.

SAFWAT, Mahmoud
Shalakany Law Office, Cairo +202 735 3331
Recommended in Banking & Finance

ZULFICAR, Mona
Shalakany Law Office, Cairo +202 735 3331
Recommended in Banking & Finance, Corporate/M&A, Project Finance

EL SALVADOR

Corporate/Commercial

EL SALVADOR Leading firms (Corporate/Commercial)
1 Espino Nieto Umaña & Asociados
Bufete FA Arias
Guandique Segovia Quintanilla

Firms are listed alphabetically in each band.

Leading individuals (Corporate/Commercial)
1 ARIAS Francisco Armando *Bufete FA Arias*
GUANDIQUE MEJIA Luis Ernesto *Guandique*
UMAÑA Felipe Francisco *Espino Nieto Umaña*

Individuals are listed alphabetically in each band.

Espino Nieto Umaña & Asociados (2 ptrs, 10 asscs) Typically representing foreign corporations in industries such as pharmaceuticals, cleaning products, chemicals and processed foods, the firm was recommended to researchers as *"among the country's leaders."* **Felipe Francisco Umaña** is rated as the group's outstanding practitioner. The firm advised Duke Energy Corporation on the privatisation of El Salvador's energy industry, and assisted Citibank on the first domestic syndicated credit to a national company, worth $100 million. **Clients:** Duke Energy Corporation; Citibank; Telmex.

Bufete FA Arias (4 ptrs, 12 asscs) *"Strong in banking,"* the firm also has a considerable corporate practice, dealing with a number of multi-national and local companies, particularly in the telecoms, energy, aeronautics, petroleum, textiles, banking and finance sectors. **Francisco Armando Arias** has a reputation as an *"aggressive"* practitioner. The firm advised on a senior term loan agreement of $65 million, granted to AES Clesa y Compañia. Also advised Dresdner Bank on a $100 million bridging loan to AES El Salvador Distribution Ventures, Ltd. **Clients:** 3M; Telefónica; Texaco Caribbean Inc; United Airlines; IFC.

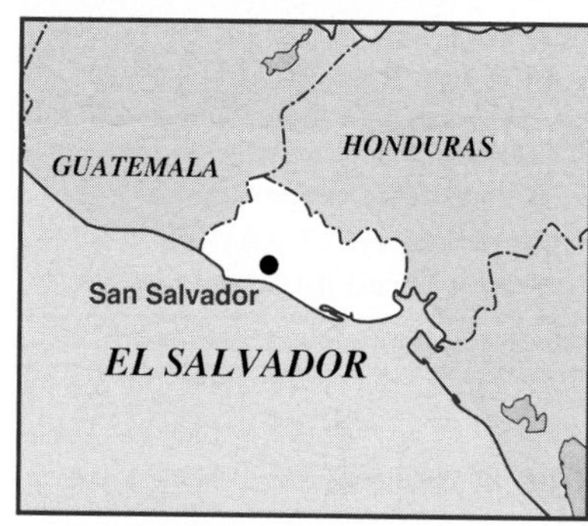

Guandique Segovia Quintanilla (3 ptrs, 9 asscs) Competitors regard this as a *"thoroughly honest firm,"* which advises a raft of domestic clients on commercial matters, notably in the banking sector. **Luis Ernesto Guandique Mejia** *"has been practising for a long time,"* and has long-standing government connections.

Leaders' profiles – El Salvador

ARIAS, Francisco Armando
Bufete F.A. Arias, San Salvador +503 257 0900
faarias@ariaslaw.com
Specialisation: Partner in Corporate Department. Main area of work is corporate law, mergers, acquisitions, privatisations, tax planning, international trade and contracts, banking law and financial projects. Has undertakings of varying sorts by Salvadoran and overseas clients (1978 to date).
Prof. Memberships: Founding member and chairman of the Salvadoran Association of Banking Law (1997 to date). Admitted as a higher member by the International Bar Association (1995). Member of the Centre for Legal Studies (1982 to date).
Personal: Born 12 May 1950, Doctorate Degree in Law, Law School, Universidad de El Salvador in 1978 and studies in Economy at Universidad Centroamericana Jose Simeon Canas.

GUANDIQUE MEJIA, Luis Ernesto
Guandique Segovia Quintanilla, San Salavador
+503 245 3444

UMAÑA, Felipe Francisco
Espino Nieto Umaña & Asociados, San Salvador
+503 263 7522

ERITREA

Corporate/Commercial

ERITREA Leading individuals (Corporate/Commercial)
1 **BERHANE Teferi** *Sole Practitioner*
BERHANE Yohannes *Sole Practitioner*
HABTE Fessehaye *Sole Practitioner*
MICHAEL Kebreab Habte *Sole Practitioner*
Individuals are listed alphabetically in each band.

Teferi Berhane Served as in-house lawyer for four years at Kriendler & Kriendler in Manhattan. Our researchers were impressed by his reputation in Eritrea as a *"good, experienced lawyer."* He has recently been involved in the registration of BAT Rothmans and the privatisation and IPOs for the state-owned brewery. **Clients:** Coca-Cola; British American Tobacco Rothmans; Government of Eritrea.

Yohannes Berhane A former judge who is said to have *"considerable experience."* He is an expert in company and partnership law, investment, intellectual property and maritime law. Most of his clients are high-profile foreign corporations needing advice in establishing or maintaining their businesses in Eritrea. He has had particular involvement with, and is retained by, a number of international oil companies. **Clients:** Shell; Mobil Oil; foreign embassies.

Fessehaye Habte Described to our researchers by competitors as a *"well-schooled"* man, he was presiding judge for 25 years in the Supreme and High Court, and deals mostly with commercial cases for business organisations. He is legal counsel to the Insurance Corporation of Eritrea, and advised on a partnership agreement between Eritrean Telecom and a Greek company. **Clients:** Falcon International; Eritrean Telecom.

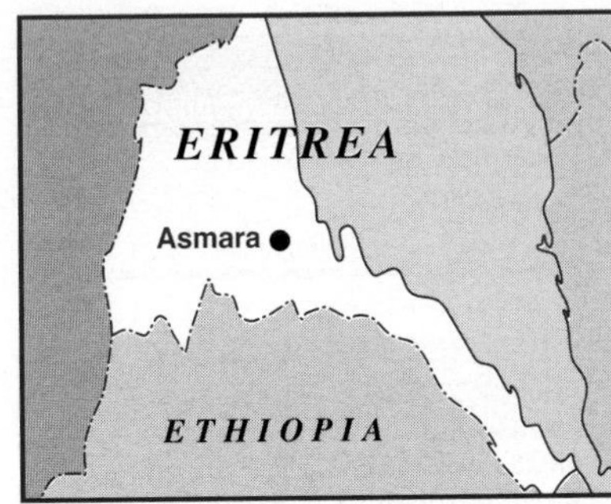

Kebreab Habte Michael A relatively young practitioner who is said to have *"a fine intellect,"* and divides his time between lecturing at the local university and advising international companies on their Eritrean investments. He advised a local construction company on a joint venture, and has acted as local counsel to Alcatel Italia. **Clients:** Alcatel Italia; foreign and domestic companies.

Leaders' profiles – Eritrea

BERHANE, Teferi
Teferi Berhane - Sole Practitioner, Asmara
+291 1 123 337

BERHANE, Yohannes
Dr Yohannes Berhane – Sole Practitioner, Asmara
+291 1 114 306

HABTE, Fessehaye
Fessehaye Habte – Sole Practitioner, Asmara
+291 1 124 444

MICHAEL, Kebreab Habte
Mr Kebreab Habte Michael – Sole Practitioner, Asmara +291 1 202 689

ESTONIA

Corporate/Commercial

ESTONIA Leading firms (Corporate/Commercial)
1 Lepik & Luhaäär
Raidla & Partners
2 Heta Law Offices
Law Office Tark & Co
V Kaasik & Co

Firms are listed alphabetically in each band.

Leading individuals (Corporate/Commercial)
1 **KAASIK Viktor** *V Kaasik & Co*
LEPIK Peeter *Lepik & Luhaäär*
LUHAÄÄR Toomas *Lepik & Luhaäär*
PAPP Sven *Raidla & Partners*
RAIDLA Juri *Raidla & Partners*
TALVISTE Üllar *Heta Law Offices*
TARK Aare *Law Office Tark & Co*

Individuals are listed alphabetically in each band.

Lepik & Luhaäär (12 ptrs, 15 asscs) Large firm, a member of both LAWW and Lex Mundi, which is considered to have *"excellent legal expertise,"* and has close ties with Baker & McKenzie. The firm also has an office in Riga, Latvia under the name Stanislavska, Lepik & Luhaäär. The two partners, **Peeter Lepik*** and **Toomas Luhaäär***, have a *"solid reputation"* and concentrate on inward investment, privatisation, IP and corporate recovery advice. Among the firm's client roster are multi-national corporations and major international banks. The team was involved on the privatisation of Estonia Railways. **Clients:** International banks and corporates.

Raidla & Partners (3 ptrs, 17 asscs) This is *"one of the best law firms in Estonia, with an excellent reputation, a big staff and skilled lawyers in most fields."* The firm has thriving M&A, corporate, energy and telecommunications departments under the supervision of partner **Sven Papp*** *("an excellent lawyer.")* Managing partner and former Justice Minister **Juri Raidla*** specialises in privatisation and government relations, is *"vastly experienced"* and for many, is *"in a league of his own."* The firm advised AS Eesti Telekom on its IPO, and represented a leading European consumer goods manufacturer on the acquisition of the Estonian distributorship network of a US tobacco company. **Clients:** AS Eesti Telekom; IFC; AS Hansapank; AS ERA Pank; AS Starman; AB Elukindlustuse AS.

Heta Law Offices (19 lawyers) *"Big players"* in the commercial market, the firm has a number of branches across Estonia in Parnu, Tartu, Narva and Tallinn. The firm advises US and European companies on their investments in Estonia, notably in pharmaceuticals and telecoms. **Üllar Talviste*** is said to be a *"good negotiator."* **Clients:** Nissan Baltics; Philip Morris; Netcom; Tele2 (Tallinn cable operator).

Law Office Tark & Co (4 ptrs, 12 asscs) Known to have *"good political contacts,"* the firm boasts a number of US and European-educated attorneys, and specialises in corporate and business law with a particular focus on banking and M&A. Telecoms is an area of notable expertise. The workload has included the privatisations of Narva Power Plants, Estonia Telecom and Estonian Railways, and the team has also acted on a number of debt investment cases for a wide range of international banks. **Aare Tark***, current chairman of the Estonian Bar Association is considered *"a talented lawyer."* The firm advised on drafting legislation for the Central Bank of Estonia and the Tallinn Stock Exchange. **Clients:** Hansapank; Credit Suisse First Boston; Nomura Bank; Eesti Ühispank; Hypo Vereinsbank; Skandinaviska Enskilada Banken; Estonia Telecom Group; Microlink; Starman; Levicom.

V Kaasik & Co (1 ptr, 3 asscs) Small but high-profile firm which owes much to the reputation of leading light **Viktor Kaasik***. He is *"held in the highest regard"* by peers, who admire his *"excellent marketing ability."* The team has advised on the widely-reported 'property form' cases, restoring estates to Estonians that were nationalised during the Soviet occupation. Other elements of the caseload include M&A, direct investment and licensing arrangements. **Clients:** International corporates and financial institutions.

*See leaders' profiles on page 252

Leaders' profiles – Estonia

KAASIK, Viktor
V Kaasik & Co, Tallinn +372 6 106 000

LEPIK, Peeter
Law Office of Lepik & Luhaäär, Tallinn +372 6 306 460

LUHAÄÄR, Toomas
Law Office of Lepik & Luhaäär, Tallinn +372 6 306 460

PAPP, Sven
Raidla & Partners Law Office, Tallinn +372 6 407 170
sven@raidla.ee
Specialisation: Partner in charge of the Corporate practice group. Main area of work is corporate law, principally mergers & acquisitions, restructuring of corporations and industry sectoral restructurings. Has been advising Estonian Telecom Ltd and the Estonian Government on IPO (the first ever IPO in Estonia) and the restructuring of the Estonian Telecom Group; renegotiating the exclusive concession on the fixed line telephony on behalf of Estonian Telephone Company; advising the national Energy Company and the Estonian Government on the restructuring of the energy sector, privatisation of the power generation assets of Energy Company Group; advising the Estonian Government on the restructuring of Estonian Railways Ltd and preparation of the privatisation plan for the company. Has also been advising domestic and foreign investors on acquisitions of businesses in Estonia, incl. advising the major Estonian commercial banks on their acquisitions of banks in Latvia and Russia. Serves as a member of the Supervisory Boards of several companies in Estonia. Has spoken at various conferences. Has advised on the preparation of the Commercial Code, Law on Investment Funds and Telecommunications Act.
Prof. Memberships: Member of the Estonian Bar Association since 1987.
Publications: Translation of Swedish Companies' Act into Estonian, Contributor to Sweet & Maxwell 'Journal of International Financial Markets: Law and Regulation'.
Career: Practicing as an attorney in Estonia since 1987, in 1989 at *Height Gardner Poor & Heavens* (New York), 1990-1991 *White & Case* (New York and Stockholm), 1992-1994 *Law Office Sven Papp* and associated legal counsel of SIAR Bossard Management Consultants (Stockholm), 1995-1998 General Counsel of Swedish Match East Europe (Stockholm), since 1994 partner of *Raidla & Partners* Law Office.
Personal: Born on 5 January 1963. Graduated from Tartu University Law School 1986. LLM from Stockholm University in private international law. Leisure interest includes alpine skiing. Lives in Tallinn, Estonia and Stockholm, Sweden.

RAIDLA, Juri
Raidla & Partners Law Office, Tallinn +372 6 407 170
raidla@raidla.ee
Specialisation: International Partner at *BBLP Moquet Borde* and head of the firm's Tallinn office *Raidla & Partners.*
Prof. Memberships: Estonian Bar Association (Board Member, 1995).
Career: Minister of Justice of the Republic of Estonia, 1990-1992. Head of Expert Commission on Elaborating the Constitution of the Republic of Estonia, 1992. Managing Director, Estonia Banking Association.
Personal: Born Parnu, Estonia, July 2 1957. University of Tartu, Estonia (Master of Law, 1980). University of St Petersburg (PhD, 1987). Speaks Estonian, English and Russian.

TALVISTE, Üllar
Heta Law Offices, Tallinn +372 6 996 611

TARK, Aare
Law Office Tark & Co, Tallinn +372 6 11 0900
tarkco@tarkco.ee
Specialisation: Partner. Main area of work is corporate law and taxation. Handled number of acquisitions of local companies by multinationals, such as Autoliv, Falck, NRGEnergy, Swedbank, etc acting as local counsel for the latter. Has advised major bank mergers in Estonia; counsel for the central bank of Estonia. Expert in privatisation (Estonian Telecom, Estonian Railways, Estonian Energy, Tallinn Water etc.). Led *Tark & Co.* team in several greenfield projects, such as building hotel SAS Radisson, department store Stockmann, metal galvanisation facility Ruma-Galvex, etc.
Prof. Memberships: Chairman of the council of Estonian Telecom. President of the Estonian Bar Association. International Bar Association: 1998-2000 professional ethics committee; 2000- Council.
Publications: Several articles on legal profession and on other legal issues. Has spoken at various conferences.

ETHIOPIA

Corporate/Commercial

ETHIOPIA Leading firms (Corporate/Commercial)
1 Teshome Gabre-Mariam Bokan Law Office

Firms are listed alphabetically in each band.

Leading individuals (Corporate/Commercial)
1 BOKAN Teshome Gabre-Mariam *Teshome*

Individuals are listed alphabetically in each band.

Teshome Gabre-Mariam Bokan Law Office (1 ptr, 5 asscs) The *"well-connected"* **Teshome Gabre-Mariam Bokan** is *"tuned in to international practices"* and has *"a good understanding of what the larger corporations need."* He is a former government minister who has worked with the IFC and the World Bank, and has experience in IP, contract negotiations and the granting of concession documents for natural resources, mining and petroleum. Advised the Commercial Bank of Ethiopia on the granting of a loan by Citibank. **Clients:** BP Amoco; BHP; IPC; mineral companies.

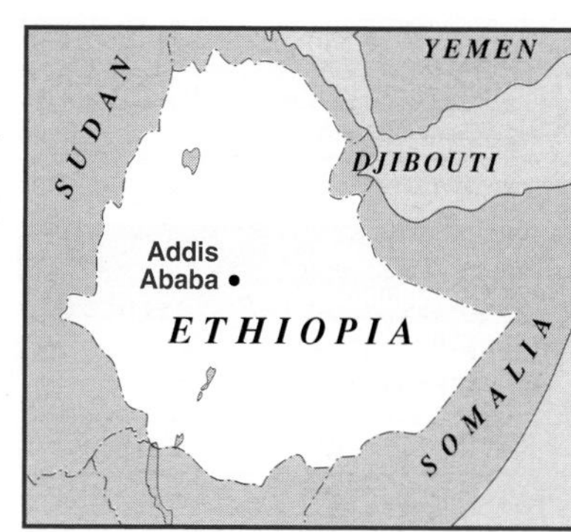

Leaders' profiles – Ethiopia

BOKAN, Teshome Gabre-Mariam
Teshome Gabre-Mariam Bokan Law Office, Addis Ababa +251 1 518 484
tgmb@telecom.net.et
Specialisation: With *Mitchell, Friedlander, Gittleman, and Teshome* worked in various areas including: international finance, joint ventures, energy and natural resource development, commercial transactions (including the international sale of goods), investment, third world debt, trade arbitration and litigation.
Prof. Memberships: 1957-1958 Institute of Air and Space Law, McGill University; Fellow,1963-1964 Economic Development Institute, I.B.R.D; 1963, Drafting Committee of the OAU Charter; Addis Ababa Bar Association; Interjurist Ltd.; International Bar Association (Section Energy and Natural Resources Law); Consultant to the Mineral Resources and Energy Division, United Nations; Vice President, African International Law Association.
Career: University College of Addis Ababa, BA ; McGill University, B.C.L; International University of Comparative Sciences, Luxembourg, Diplome de Droit compare; 1958, Legal Advisor at the Ministry of Public Works and Communications; 1958, Ethiopian Airlines as Executive Assistant to the General Manager and Principal Legal Advisor; 1961, Director General, Ministry of Public Works and Communications; 1962, Principal Legal Advisor and Secretary to the Board of Directors of the Development Bank of Ethiopia; 1965, Attorney General of Ethiopia; 1967-74, Vice Minister and later Minister of State at the Ministry of Mines and Energy, Government of Ethiopia; 1974-82, A political detainee; 1983, Principal Advisor to the department of Labour and Social Affairs, Government of Ethiopia; 1989, Partner *Mitchell, Friedlander, Gittleman, and Teshome.*
Personal: Born 15 December 1931, Adama, Ethiopia. Married with one daughter and other dependents. Speaks Amharic, English, French and Italian. Enjoys reading, swimming, gardening and playing chess.

FALKLAND ISLANDS

Corporate/Commercial

FALKLAND ISLANDS Leading firms (Corporate/Commercial)
1 Ledingham Chalmers

Firms are listed alphabetically in each band.

Leading individuals (Corporate/Commercial)
1 **FERGUSON Hugh** *Ledingham Chalmers*
KILMARTIN Kevin *Sole Practitioner*

Individuals are listed alphabetically in each band.

Ledingham Chalmers (1 ptr, 1 assc) **Hugh Ferguson** is said to offer *"excellent advice,"* and was recommended to researchers as a *"master of all trades."* He undertakes most commercial work, but is best known for commercial property, fishing and maritime law. **Clients:** Oil companies; fishing companies.

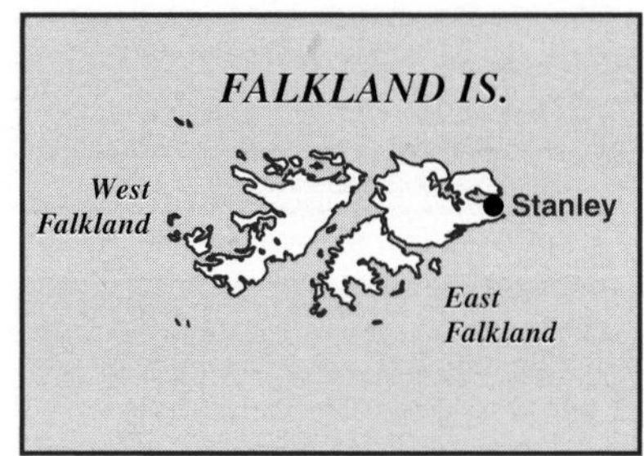

Other Notable Practitioner Kevin Kilmartin is a sole practitioner who advises on a full range of commercial work, as well as having a particular speciality in marine advice. With the decline of oil exploration in the islands, the fishing industry has become an area of particular focus. He has undertaken admiralty proceedings against the Queen of Vevey, a vessel which was abandoned by its owners in Stanley after the company collapsed, leaving the crew destitute, and acted on the case of the Suderhavid, which sank off South Georgia with considerable loss of life. Clients include fishing companies and shipping owners.

Leaders' profiles – Falkland Islands

FERGUSON, Hugh
Ledingham Chalmers, Stanley +500 22690

KILMARTIN, Kevin
Kevin Kilmartin – Sole Practitioner, Stanley +500 22765

FINLAND

Index

OVERVIEW: Roschier-Holmberg & Waselius, Finland's largest law firm, is consolidating its position. Already the clear leader in communications, the market perceives that it has pulled away from its closest rivals in corporate law too. Finland continues to be a centre for technology firms, reflected by the emergence this year of IT specialists like Fennica Attorneys at Law. Research indicated the growing importance of competition law to the corporate market, hence the new section.

F

Communications

FINLAND
Leading firms (Communications)

Band	Firm
1	Roschier-Holmberg & Waselius, Attorneys Ltd
2	Borenius & Kemppinen
	Castrén & Snellman
	Fennica Attorneys at Law Ltd

Firms are listed alphabetically in each band.

Leading individuals (Communications)

Band	Individual	Firm
1	REKOLA Kimmo	*Castrén & Snellman*
	TAKKI Pekka	*Fennica Attorneys at Law Ltd*
	TARKELA Pekka	*Borenius & Kemppinen*
	THOMPSON Craig	*Roschier-Holmberg & Waselius*
Up-and-coming individuals		
	KORPIOLA Eki	*Roschier-Holmberg & Waselius*

Individuals are listed alphabetically in each band.

Roschier-Holmberg & Waselius, Attorneys Ltd (4 ptrs, 10 asscs) *"It has the resources, it has experienced lawyers and it stands in a class of its own for size."* Our researchers learned that, while other firms can approach this organisation in IT, for pure telecoms work it is still well out in front. Active on the full range of communications, the team advises operators on regulation, lobbying, interconnections, alternative access, satellite issues and submarine cable build-out. Encryption and network management are two of several growing areas for this large and expanding department. IT strengths include software distribution agreements, licensing, and ASP solutions.

"Telecoms expert" **Craig Thompson** is recognised by competitors as a knowledgeable IT practitioner, while *"brilliant"* IT associate **Eki Korpiola*** *"has brains and asks all the right questions."* The firm recently acted on the Finnish aspects of Solid Information's €55 million second round venture deal, and was part of a team advising Pangea on the construction and financing of a £272.5 million fibre optic network. **Clients:** Nokia; Solid Information Technology.

Borenius & Kemppinen (2 ptrs, 5 asscs) With particular strength in venture capital and IP, the firm ranks as one of the leading Finnish IT players. The group advises a mixture of international clients, typically US, and Scandinavian blue-chips, on issues such as financing and licensing agreements, research and development agreements, portal solutions and IT-specific company overviews.

The most prominent practitioner here is **Pekka Tarkela***, who *"really attends to the detail."* Active on behalf of start-up software providers, the team represented More Magic Software, a company which has developed technology for e-commerce transactions over mobile phones, on its $8 million venture capital financing. **Clients:** More Magic Software; Finpro; Mediaclick; Suomen Matkatoimisto Oy.

Castrén & Snellman (3 ptrs, 5 asscs) Led by the *"outstanding"* **Kimmo Rekola*** *("the person to go to for Finnish IT,")* Finland's third largest firm *"has grown fast and has the resources to serve demanding IT clients"* according to one competitor. The firm advises emerging companies on outsourcing, distribution and licence agreements and other contractual issues. On telecoms matters, the team represents companies providing software solutions to the mobile sector, as well as domestic and foreign telecommunications companies. Recently assisted Telia on the Finnish aspects of its IPO and advised 3i Finland on its hi-tech investment portfolio. **Clients:** Telia; 3i Finland.

Fennica Attorneys at Law Ltd (4 ptrs, 4 asscs) Established in 1999, the meteoric rise of this technology boutique has impressed our researchers and the market. Known for its new media work, it is active in IT-related contractual issues, outsourcing and software procurement for well-known international companies on both an established and one-off basis. Increasingly involved in the telecommunications sector, the team has particular expertise in such areas as application service provision and location-based services. The well-known **Pekka Takki*** is *"like a bulldog on behalf of his clients."*

The firm acted on the share exchange arrangement and public offering of the Oulu Telephone Company. **Clients:** International household names and major Finnish companies.

*See leaders' profiles on pages 257-260

Competition/Anti-trust

FINLAND	
Leading firms (Competition/Anti-trust)	
1	Hannes Snellman
	Roschier-Holmberg & Waselius, Attorneys Ltd
2	Castrén & Snellman
3	Attorneys' House ANPR Ltd

Firms are listed alphabetically in each band.

Leading individuals (Competition/Anti-trust)	
1	**POKELA Hannu** *Attorneys' House ANPR Ltd*
	WALLIN Carl-Henrik *Hannes Snellman*
2	**LEIVO Kirsi** *Hannes Snellman*
	WJK Christian *Roschier-Holmberg*
3	**AALTO-SETÄLÄ Ilkka** *Roschier-Holmberg*
Up and coming individuals	
	HILTUNEN Sari *Castrén & Snellman*
	MENTULA Arttu *Castrén & Snellman*

Individuals are listed alphabetically in each band.

Hannes Snellman (2 ptrs, 5 asscs) One of the dominant firms in this area, it has an excellent reputation in the market for merger control and applications for exemption, has participated in numerous proceedings before the national competition authority and the EU, and has been involved in public procurement and compliance programmes.

A *"professional team"* is headed by the *"intelligent and experienced"* **Carl-Henrik Wallin***, recognised by competitors as *"a good negotiator."* He is well supported by *"skilful newcomer"* **Kirsi Leivo*** who is renowned for her Commission background and is a prolific writer. The firm advised on a recent anti-cartel case at European level, and acted on the competition dispute between Pepsi Cola and Coca-Cola. **Clients:** Large Finnish and international companies.

Roschier-Holmberg & Waselius, Attorneys Ltd. (1 ptr, 7 asscs) *"If you have a large transaction in Finland you see Roschier-Holmberg all the time,"* and on the back of its superb corporate practice, it has built a strong competition team with *"an aggressive US style."* Especially active in merger control cases, the team has particular expertise in the media and telecoms sectors, often representing clients seeking access to networks. State aid, public procurement, compliance programmes and competition audits all form increased elements of the caseload.

The respected **Christian Wik*** *"doesn't make mistakes"* according to one source, while **Ilkka Aalto-Setälä*** is *"capable and professional."* The firm has advised on merger control issues involving Sempo Leonia, and acted on a merger filing in connection with the merger of IVO and Neste. **Clients:** Sempo Leonia; Fortum; YLE.

Castrén & Snellman (1 ptr, 5 asscs) *"Able to handle this type of work well,"* the firm has expanded its highly rated anti-trust team. Active across the board, the group has experience in merger notifications and pre-notification agreements, horizontal and vertical restraints, and abuse of a dominant position cases.

"Experienced" **Arttu Mentula*** and **Sari Hiltunen*** are the leading practitioners here. The latter has an administrative background and *"has been involved in a lot of legislative work."* The firm recently advised on a major anti-cartel case. **Clients:** Listed Finnish and international companies.

Attorneys' House ANPR Ltd (1 ptr, 2 asscs) A niche competition boutique, which although it lacks the capacity of the full-service firms, does have *"one of the very few senior lawyers in this area in Finland."* **Hannu Pokela*** is highly respected by competitors as a litigation expert with long experience of proceedings before the Finnish competition authorities, especially in cases involving abuse of a dominant position. The firm regularly represents large Finnish companies holding monopolistic positions, and also advises on merger filings and compliance programmes. Acted on the first merger regulation case in the Finnish competition court. **Clients:** Leading Finnish incumbents.

Corporate/M&A

Roschier-Holmberg & Waselius, Attorneys Ltd (8 ptrs, 22 asscs) *"Traditionally the market leader,"* opinion sees the firm *"slightly out in front"* this year. This slim lead is attributed to *"a most comprehensive all-round practice,"* an enviable network of international contacts and what one client described as *"an efficient and professional manner."* Transactionally focused, with particular strength in cross-border mergers, capital markets, take-overs, share swaps and structured sales, the firm has an impressive overseas client base and a reputation in such areas as telecoms, forestry, energy, banking and finance and insurance.

"Skilful, experienced and high profile," **Tomas Lindholm*** continues to stand out. Not merely *"the key figure in the market,"* he is also seen by competitors as *"a fine technician and a good negotiator"* as well as *"an effective client lawyer."* The *"efficient"* **Carita Wallgren*** continues to attract market recommendation, while *"hard-working and pleasant"* **Lennart Simonsen*** *"would be a good lawyer in any team."* **Ulf-Henrik Kull*** is *"the rising M&A man,"* especially rated for his drafting skills. The firm advised Cultor Oyi on its public take-over bid by Danisco A/S, and Neste on the Finnish law aspects of its £147 million high yield debt offering. **Clients:** Nokia; Fortum; Metsä-Serla; the Finnish government; Sampo-Leonia.

Hannes Snellman (10 ptrs, 12 asscs) *"It always used to be the law firm for the old Finnish money in Helsinki,"* but our researchers discovered that it has modernised dramatically, developing a first-class practice in cross-border M&A, and visibility in industries like insurance, energy, pharmaceuticals, financial services and pulp and paper. An excellent tax practice lends further support.

Among *"an excellent team," "knowledgeable, pragmatic business lawyer"* **Juhani Mäkinen*** is *"a hard-nosed M&A type who serves his clients well."* His colleague, the *"gentlemanly"* **Johan Aalto***, is a well-known and reliable practitioner. The firm is active on capital markets work, restructurings and divestitures, and works extensively for venture capital companies. Advised on the IPO of BiotieTherapies and acted on the division of Finvest and Aspo into separate listed companies. **Clients:** Warburg Dillon Reed; Merita Corporate Finance; Merrill Lynch; Carnegie Alfred Berg.

Castrén & Snellman (6 ptrs, 14 asscs) *"An old-school organisation with good international con-*

*See leaders' profiles on pages 257-260

FINLAND Leading firms (Corporate/Mergers & Acquisitions)
1 Roschier-Holmberg & Waselius, Attorneys Ltd
2 Hannes Snellman
3 Castrén & Snellman
Dittmar & Indrenius
White & Case
4 Borenius & Kemppinen
Merilampi Marttila Laitasalo Law Offices

Firms are listed alphabetically in each band.

Leading individuals (Corporate/Mergers & Acquisitions)
★ **LINDHOLM Tomas** *Roschier-Holmberg*
1 **HAUSSILA Petri** *White & Case*
MÄKINEN Juhani *Hannes Snellman*
SIMONSEN Lennart *Roschier-Holmberg*
TROBERG Markus *Dittmar & Indrenius*
2 **AALTO Johan** *Hannes Snellman*
KULL Ulf-Henrik *Roschier-Holmberg*
KUUSIMÄKI Antti *Dittmar & Indrenius*
MERILAMPI Pekka *Merilampi Marttila Laitasalo*
WALLGREN Carita *Roschier-Holmberg*
3 **ASPELIN Mikael** *Castrén & Snellman*
JAATINEN Pekka *Castrén & Snellman*
LEHTINEN Pekka *Castrén & Snellman*
TÄHTINEN Jyrki *Borenius & Kemppinen*

Individuals are listed alphabetically in each band.

tacts," Finland's third largest law firm is still recovering from last year's loss of Lennart Simonsen, but retains an enviable client base and a wealth of individual experience. With a client base spread evenly between domestic and international companies and expertise in financial services, IT, telecoms and energy, the firm is involved in a number of cross-border acquisitions. It also advises western investors in Russia through its St Petersburg office.

Respected technician **Pekka Lehtinen*** stands out for his capital markets work, in company with the more experienced **Mikael Aspelin***. Former insolvency lawyer **Pekka Jaatinen*** wins respect from rivals for *"successfully reshaping his practice"* and is now a *"top M&A guy."* A record year for IPOs has seen the firm acting on the listings of HPY Holdings and Sanitec Corp. **Clients:** Scandinavia Online; Telia.

Dittmar & Indrenius (5 ptrs, 12 asscs) *"Good lawyers with good skills and good clients."* This corporate and M&A boutique's reputation for quality has helped it to develop a first-class client list of international and large Finnish listed companies, which it represents in big-ticket cross-border transactions.

"Well known figure" **Markus Troberg*** remains one of Finland's market leaders, while *"likeable, knowledgeable and practical"* **Antti Kuusimäki*** *"handles clients well."* Strong in financial services, transport and pharmaceuticals, the firm has advised a number of blue-chip international companies on their Finnish investments. **Clients:** General Electric; General Motors; Cisco; Hewlet-Packard; Cap Gemini; Compaq; Glaxo Wellcome; Bank of America; Ikea.

White & Case (1 ptr, 10 asscs) The Helsinki office of this American giant *"has successfully gained a large share of the capital markets work."* Cross-border M&A transactions form an increasingly important element of the caseload, and the firm is also making inroads into the smaller domestic venture capital market.

The *"pragmatic and energetic"* **Petri Haussila*** is respected by competitors for the skill and *"tough, American-style approach,"* which makes him arguably *"the number one man in the capital markets sector in Finland."* Clients appreciate his ability to advise on both US and UK capital markets transactions, especially when *"he can draw on the international strength of White & Case."* The firm acted on the €3.4 billion second stage of the privatisation of Sonera, the largest Nordic equity offering registered with the SEC and listed on a US exchange. Also advised Swedish biotechnology company Pyrosequencing AB on its IPO. **Clients:** Sonera; UPM-Kymmene Corporation; Metso Corporation; Proha Oyj.

Borenius & Kemppinen (4 ptrs, 9 asscs) *"A firm that wants to grow,"* it is known in the market for its *"aggressive"* approach, its far-sighted, new economy focus and its *"good market share of middle-sized domestic clients."* Becoming more international and gaining foreign clients, the firm is increasingly visible on cross-border M&A, along with restructurings and contract negotiations, although its great strengths remain in venture capital and private equity.

Largely responsible for the team's progress is **Jyrki Tähtinen***, who is particularly respected for his venture capital work. The group has advised on a number of HEX listings, including Satama Interactive, and acted on the FIM 3.6 billion multi-jurisdictional sale of Timberjack by Metso Oyj to Deere & Co. **Clients:** Capman; MeritaNordbanken.

Merilampi Marttila Laitasalo Law Offices (4 ptrs, 4 asscs) *"A well known local firm acting for well known local companies,"* it may be domestically focused, but a *"five star"* array of Finnish clients testifies to the quality of its work. Active on IPOs, the team also has a respectable market share of M&A work, notably in forestry, media and investment banking.

The firm's highest profile partner is **Pekka Merilampi***, said by competitors to be *"the leading Companies Act specialist in Finland."* The firm advised on the restructuring of Helsinki telephone company Elisa Communications and on its development from a co-operative to a listed company. **Clients:** MeritaNordbanken; Elisa Communications.

Leaders' profiles – Finland

AALTO, Johan
Hannes Snellman, Helsinki +358 9 228 841
johan.aalto@snellman-law.fi
Recommended in Corporate/M&A
Specialisation: Head of the firm's Corporate Finance Department. Main areas of work are corporate finance, banking, mergers and acquisitions. Acted as counsel to managers in the IPO of Fortum, and as counsel to Perlos and Rapala in their IPOs. Acted as counsel to Danisco in public tender offer for Cultor and as counsel to EQT in acquisition of Vaasan Banking Division from Cultor and Salcomp from Nokia. Acted as counsel to Biotie Therapies in the first biotech IPO in Finland.
Prof. Memberships: Finnish Bar Association, The Association of Finnish Lawyers, International Bar Association.
Career: Graduated from Helsinki University in 1987. Partner 1994.
Personal: Family includes wife and four kids.

AALTO-SETÄLÄ, Ilkka
Roschier-Holmberg & Waselius, Attorneys Ltd, Helsinki +358 9 228 551
ilkka.aalto-setala@rhw.fi
Recommended in Competition/Anti-trust
Specialisation: EU and Competition Law. Has acted for a number of Finnish and foreign companies on matters ranging from notifications and cartel procedures at the European Commission to general competition law issues.

Prof. Memberships: Finnish Society for European Law; AIJA; Finnish Association for Competition Law.
Career: Became a member of the Bar in 1999. Joined *Roschier-Holmberg & Waselius* in 1997. Worked for The Finnish Competition Authority as a research officer (1995-97) and for The European Commission, Merger Task Force, as a national expert (1996).
Personal: Born 1969. Attended the University of Turku (LLM, 1994).

ASPELIN, Mikael
Castrén & Snellman, Helsinki +358 9 228 581
mikael.aspelin@castren.fi
Recommended in Corporate/M&A
Specialisation: Mergers and acquisitions; company law; contract law; marketing law; IP law. Has been responsible as project leader for various M & A projects and as general counsel for numerous foreign companies in Finland. Has also been co-ordinator for a Tacis project in Russia and partner for the firm's St. Petersburg office 1995-98.
Prof. Memberships: International Bar Association; Finnish Bar Association; Union of Finnish Lawyers; Juridiska Föreningen i Finland; Nordiska Juristmötena National Secretary; Suomen Teollisoikeudellinen yhdistys – Finnish IP Association; Finnish Anti-Counterfeiting Group.
Career: University of Helsinki (LLM 1980); Court Practice 1981; Vrije Universiteit of Brussels (LLM 1986); *Castrén & Snellman* 1979-present, partner 1983-present.
Personal: Leisure interests include outdoor life and sports. Married with three children.

HAUSSILA, Petri Y J
White & Case, Helsinki +358 9 228 641
phaussila@whitecase.com
Recommended in Corporate/M&A
Specialisation: Co-Head of the firm's international securities practice. Specialises in domestic and international M&A, in addition is an experienced securities and capital markets law adviser. Heads the firm's office in Helsinki, which advises on a wide range of international corporate and finance law transactions.
Career: Qualified to practice under both US and Finnish law.

HILTUNEN, Sari
Castrén & Snellman, Helsinki +358 9 228 581
sari.hiltunen@castren.fi
Recommended in Competition/Anti-trust
Specialisation: Associate, EU- and Competition Law Group and Intellectual Property and Information Technology Group of *Castren & Snellman.* Core area of work is legal advice on Finnish and EU competition law and merger control. Has drafted reports and notifications in connection with mergers and acquisitions and has represented companies before competition authorities. Has spoken at various conferences and seminars on EC law, competition law and merger control.
Prof. Memberships: Union of Finnish lawyers, Finnish Association of EC Law, Finnish Association of Competition Law.
Publications: Co-author of 'Merger Control' (WSOY, 1998). Written several articles on competition law and merger control.
Career: LLM 1991 (University of Helsinki), has worked as a lawyer in *Nystén* 1993-1994, Research Officer, Lawyer and Senior Research Officer in the Finnish Competition Authority 1994-1996 and Senior Advisor and Government Secretary in the Ministry of Trade and Industry 1996-2000. Has acted as Secretary of the Competition Court Committee 1998-1998 and was a member of the OECD Committee on Competition Law Policy 1996-1999. Joined *Castrén & Snellman* in 2000.
Personal: Born May, 8 1967. Attended University of Helsinki 1987-1991 (LLM). Lives in Helsinki.

JAATINEN, Pekka
Castrén & Snellman, Helsinki +358 9 228 581
pekka.jaatinen@castren.fi
Recommended in Corporate/M&A
Specialisation: Managing Director and in charge of the insolvency department of the firm. Corporate, Securities and Insolvency Law.
Prof. Memberships: Finnish Bar Association, AIJA and its Executive Committee, The Scientific Coordinator of AIJA Working Commissions, IBA and International Insolvency Institute.
Publications: Has been a co-author to several books, Rescue of Companies, Directors' Liabilities in Case of Insolvency (Kluwer Law)
Career: In recent years has been deeply involved in the major insurance transactions both in Finland and abroad. Has acted as the trustee and administrator of several major Ginnish bankruptcy estates and restructuring proceedings.
Personal: Born in 1956 (44). University of Helsinki, (LLM 1983).

KORPIOLA, Eki
Roschier-Holmberg & Waselius, Attorneys Ltd, Tampere +358 3 316 7444
eki.korpiola@rhw.fi
Recommended in Communications
Specialisation: IT-law, e-commerce, intellectual property rights and media law. Special emphasis on data protection and computer law. Has acted as counsel in several international and domestic data protection and e-commerce compliance programs as well as complex software licensing arrangements. Has acted as IT and IPR expert in major transactions, IPOs and private placements.
Prof. Memberships: Computer Law Association, Inc.; Finnish Computer Law Association.
Career: Joined *Roschier-Holmberg & Waselius* in 1998. Worked for Sonera Corporation (a major Finnish telecommunications operator) in 2000 (6-month-secondment).
Personal: Born 1973. Attended the University of Helsinki (LLM, 1998).

KULL, Ulf-Henrik
Roschier-Holmberg & Waselius, Attorneys Ltd., Helsinki +358 9 228 551
ulf-henrik.kull@rhw.fi
Recommended in Corporate/M&A
Specialisation: M&A including New Economy Transactions. Has been involved in a great number of mergers and acquisitions, especially cross-border merger transactions.
Prof. Memberships: Many international and domestic professional organisations.
Career: Became a member of the Bar in 1995. Joined *Roschier-Holmberg & Waselius* in 1991; partner 1998. Commercial Law Assistant at Abo Academy University (1989-90). Worked for *Clifford Chance*, London, as a visiting lawyer (1993).
Personal: Born 1964. Attended the University of Turku (LLM 1990) and Abo University (MSc (Pol.) 1987).

KUUSIMÄKI, Antti
Dittmar & Indrenius, Helsinki +35 8968 1700
Recommended in Corporate/M&A

LEHTINEN, Pekka
Castrén & Snellman, Helsinki +358 9 228 581
pekka.lehtinen@castren.fi
Recommended in Corporate/M&A
Specialisation: Partner and the head of *Castrén & Snellman's* Banking, Finance and Securities Department. Main area of work is M&A, finance and capital markets. Has been in charge of a wide range of international projects including the largest ever acquisition financing transaction in Finland and the preparation of the financing documentation for the first PFI deal in Finland. Is a legal advisor to a number of investment and commercial banks and other financial institutions, corporations and private equity investors operating in Finland and internationally. Is a regular speaker in seminars on M&A, finance and capital markets topics including IPOs, international equity offerings and Public Private Partnerships in Finland.
Prof. Memberships: Finnish Bar Association, Uion of Finnish Layers, International Bar Association.
Career: 1988-1989, Associate, *O'Callaghan,Saunders & Stumm*, Atlanta; 1989-1992, in-house counsel, Kansallis-Osake-Pankki (now Marita Nordbanken), Helsinki and New York; 1991, visiting lawyer, *Arent, Fox, Kintner, Plotkin & Kahn*, Washington DC; 1992-1995, associate, *White & Case*; 1995 to present, *Castrén & Snellman*, partner 1999-.

LEIVO, Kirsi
Hannes Snellman, Helsinki +358 9 228 841
kirsi.leivo@snellman-law.fi
Recommended in Competition/Anti-trust
Specialisation: EC and national competition law. Highlights of the last year include acting as counsel to the Finnish Bankers' Association before the European Commission in an alleged cartel case relating to bank charges for the exchange of euro-zone currencies; notification of a full function joint venture between Sonera and ICL to the European Commission. Gives frequent lectures on competition law in seminars and conferences.
Prof. Memberships: Memberships: The Association of Finnish Lawyers; The Finnish Competition Law Association.
Publications: Co-author of Leivo-Leivo: 'Competition Law of the European Communities' (Helsinki 1997, 723p., university textbook); other publications in the field of EC and Competition Law.
Career: LLM Helsinki 1992, LLM College of Europe 1994. Joined the firm in 1995. In 1997-1999, member of the Legal Service of the European Commission

F

(Competition Team). Returned to the firm in 2000.
Personal: Married, one child.

LINDHOLM, Tomas
Roschier-Holmberg & Waselius, Attorneys Ltd, Helsinki +358 9 228 551
tomas.lindholm@rhw.fi
Recommended in Corporate/M&A
Specialisation: M&A, capital markets, litigation and arbitration, industrial property rights. Has been involved in a great number of domestic and cross-border mergers and acquisitions and capital markets transactions, including some of the largest transactions undertaken by Finnish companies.
Prof. Memberships: Member and officer of many international and domestic professional and civic organisations including the IBA; LES Scandinavia (President 1989-90); Finnish Bar Association (Board 1990-95, Chairman of the International Committee 1995-98, President 1998-); the Auditors' Board of the Central Chamber of Commerce of Finland (1992-95); Invest in Finland Bureau (Board 1996-); board member of several foreign-owned subsidiaries in Finland; permanent expert to the study group at the Ministry of Justice for the revision of the Companies' Act (1998-2000).
Career: Trained at the Bench in 1978 and became a member of the Bar in 1983. Joined *Roschier-Holmberg & Waselius* in 1983; partner 1984 and Managing Partner 1996-. President of the Finnish Bar Association (1998-). Former general counsel of Outokumpu Oy (1978-82), a major industrial enterprise in Finland. Worked for *Arent, Fox, Kinter, Plotkin & Kahn*, Washington DC, as a visiting lawyer (1980).
Personal: Born 1953. Attended the University of Helsinki (LLM 1975) and Swedish School of Economics in Helsinki (BSc (Econ.) 1977).

MÄKINEN, Juhani
Hannes Snellman, Helsinki +358 9 228 841
juhani.makinen@snellman-law.fi
Recommended in Corporate/M&A
Specialisation: Mergers & Acquisitions, capital markets and finance. Advised the companies in the first two demergers of public companies Aspo Oyj and Finvest Oyj respectively in Finland.
Prof. Memberships: Finnish Bar Association; International Bar Association; The Association of Finnish Lawyers.
Career: Chairman, Managing Partner 1994-2000, partner since 1985, resident lawyer in Scandinavian Law Office, Rotterdam 1982-1984, associate 1979-1982.
Personal: Graduated Helsinki University 1979.

MENTULA, Arttu
Castrén & Snellman, Helsinki +358 9 228 581
arttu.mentula@castren.fi
Recommended in Competition/Anti-trust
Specialisation: Specialised in EU and competition law. Advises corporations on matters relating to merger control, abuse of dominant position, cartels and restrictive agreements. In addition, advises corporations in various mergers & acquisitions and represents clients in civil proceedings.
Prof. Memberships: Finnish Bar Association, Finnish Competition Law Association (Chairman), Association for European Law and ICC's Commission on Competition Law and Practice in Finland.
Publications: Written a number of articles relating to EU and competition law, Co-author of 'Abuse of a Dominant Position in Competition Law'.
Career: Prior to joining *Castrén & Snellman*, worked at *Kari Kuitunen*, Attorneys at Law 1990-1995. Thereafter, worked as in-house counsel at Valio Ltd, 1995-1998 as corporate counsel and 1998-1999 as joint general counsel.
Personal: Leisure interests include hunting, golf and jogging. Lives in Espoo, Finland.

MERILAMPI, Pekka
Merilampi Marttila Laitasalo Law Offices, Tampere +358 3 260 1600
Recommended in Corporate/M&A

POKELA, Hannu
Attorneys' House ANPR Ltd, Helsinki +358 9 474 21
Recommended in Competition/Anti-trust

REKOLA, Kimmo
Castrén & Snellman, Helsinki +358 9 228 581
kimmo.rekola@castren.fi
Recommended in Communications
Specialisation: Partner, heads the firm's competence group on Intellectual Property and Information Technology Law. Main area of work is information technology law, private equity and venture capital, mergers and acquisitions, internet and e- and m-commerce. Has been responsible for several domestic international M&A projects and represented institutional investors in a number of venture capital and private equity transactions and related exit projects especially in the IT and m-commerce sector. Has also participated in several listing projects. Has participated in domestic and international contract negotiations for complex IT projects, and drafted related contract documentation. Has acted as an expert member of IT 2000 Conditions committee and been responsible for the drafting of the terms (the general terms and conditions for IT contracts in Finland). Acts on permanent basis for a number of international and Finnish IT companies. Has spoken at various conferences on information technology law, private equity and venture capital transactions, contracts law, data protection and electronic commerce.
Prof. Memberships: Finnish Bar Association, International Bar Association, Committee on Electronic Commerce at the Central Chamber of Commerce of Finland, Finnish Computer Law Association (Chairman 1998-2000, Board member 1995-1997, 2000-), Computer Law Association, Finnish Information Processing Association.
Publications: Written numerous articles on information technology law, contract law, data protection and electronic commerce. Author of 'Mergers and Acquisitions – Finland' (Jordans Publishing).
Career: University of Helsinki, (LLM 1983). Joined *Castrén & Snellman* as partner in 2000. Prior to joining *Castrén & Snellman*, partner and head of IT and Telecommunications law group at another law firm and a founding partner of the law firm *Bardy, Engstöm & Rekola*. From 1989 to 1994 served as subsidiary legal counsel for Oy Unisys Ab and from 1983-1989 as general legal counsel and Vice President for Finnish Corporate Finance Plc (presentely Merita Finance Ltd.). Has been a member of the Finnish Bar Association since 1995.
Personal: Born 2 July 1958. Attended University of Helsinki 1973-83 (LLM). Leisure interest include sports, chess, stamps and R&B music. Lives in Helsinki.

SIMONSEN, Lennart
Roschier-Holmberg & Waselius, Attorneys Ltd, Helsinki +358 9 228 551
lennart.simonsen@rhw.fi
Recommended in Corporate/M&A
Specialisation: M&A, including New Economy Transactions, and capital markets. Has been involved in a great number of domestic and cross-border mergers and acquisitions as well as capital markets transactions.
Prof. Memberships: Many international and domestic professional organisations.
Career: Trained at the Bench in 1987 and became a member of the Bar in 1995. Joined *Roschier-Holmberg & Waselius* in 1999; Partner 1999. Former Director of Pietarsaari tax district (1986-91). Former associate (1992-96), Partner and Managing Partner (1997-99) at *Castrén & Snellman* Attorneys at Law.
Personal: Born 1960. Attended the University of Helsinki (LLM 1985).

TÄHTINEN, Jyrki
Borenius & Kemppinen, Helsinki +358 9 615 333
jyrki.tahtinen@borenius.fi
Recommended in Corporate/M&A
Specialisation: Managing partner. Main areas of work include private equity and venture capital, M&A, capital markets, corporate restructuring and corporate governance. Acts for a number of private equity and venture capital firms in drafting fund documentation, making investments (from seed finance to MBO/MBIs) and exits. Acted for the Finnish Ministry of Transport in the division of PT Finland into Post and Telecom (Sonera). Advised in the PK Cables and PMJ Automec IPOs to Helsinki Stock Exchange, private equity investors in the PI-Consulting de-listing and Suunto's board in the hostile take-over by Amer. During the recession in the early 1990s was the trustee for the Eka and Diamond Cruise corporate restructurings (Finnish equivalent of Chapter 11). Acts frequently for numerous lenders and borrowers in senior and mezzanine finance transactions (Sonera MDEM1000 revolving credit facility). Serves in a number of domestic and foreign boards of directors including listed companies. A frequent lecturer and author in the areas of private equity, M&A, capital markets and corporate governance.
Prof. Memberships: Finnish Bar Association.
Career: Law degree from the University of Helsinki 1985; admitted to Bar 1990; MBA (Master of Business Administration) Helsinki School of Economics and American Graduate School of International Management (Thunderbird) Phoenix, Arizona 1989; joined *Borenius & Kemppinen* as

F

Partner 1991 from a competing firm. Managing Partner since 1997; Member of Board of the Helsinki Bar Association since 1995.
Personal: Born 16 November 1961.

TAKKI, Pekka
Fennica Attorneys at Law Ltd, Helsinki
+358 9 622 6670
pekka.takki@fennicalaw.fi
Recommended in Communications
Specialisation: Information technology, communications. Acts for a number of domestic and international IT-companies. Speaks and lectures regularly on IT-law and communication.
Prof. Memberships: Membership: AIPPI, Licensing Executive Society, Finnish Association for Protection of Intellectual Property Rights, Finnish Information Technology Law Society (vice chairman 2000), Finnish Bar Association, Finnish Lawyers Association
Publications: Author of 'IT-Contracts A Practical Guide' (Finnish Lawyer's Union Publishing House 1999)
Career: Associate at *Pello & Tiivola Attorneys-at-law* 1991 - 1992; Qualified for the bench 1993; Legal Counsel for Xerox Nordic 1993 - 1995; Associate and Junior Partner at *Heikki Haapaniemi Attorneys-at-law* 1996 - 1999; Managing Partner at Fennica Attorneys-at-law Ltd 1999 to date.
Personal: Born January 1, 1966, attended Helsinki University 1987 - 1991 (Candidate at Law). Leisure interests include music and sailing.

TARKELA, Pekka
Borenius & Kemppinen, Helsinki +358 9 615 333
pekka.tarkela@borenius.fi
Recommended in Communications
Specialisation: Partner, intellectual property and IT. Main practice areas: IP, communications, media and entertainment, IT, electronic commerce and internet regulation. Acts for a number of companies on intellectual property and information technology related contract, strategic planning and M&A matters and IP Litigation. Advises major Finnish media and publishers' organisations and domestic and international companies in the field of digital content production and infocom projects. Has acted as IP advisor in several IT and communications related M&A, venture capital and private equity transactions in Finland and for arrangers and IT and infocom companies in several IPOs in the Helsinki Stock Exchange, most recently Saunalahti (telecoms, 2000) and Iocore (internet applications, 2000). Frequent lecturer and author in the area of IP and IT.
Prof. Memberships: Finnish Bar Association, Association of Finnish Lawyers, Finnish Copyright Society, Finnish Industrial Property Society.
Career: LLM 1992, University of Helsinki; admitted to Bar 1999; General Secretary of the Finnish State Copyright Commission 1992 - 1997; governmental expert in WTO, WIPO and EU preparatory bodies 1992 - 1997 (copyrights, IP); member of the editorial board of the NIR magazine (Nordic Intellectual Property Review); member of the International Chamber of Commerce ICC Commission on Intellectual Property Rights (national expert); joined *Borenius & Kemppinen* in 1997, Partner since 2000.
Personal: Born 3 May 1965.

THOMPSON, Craig
Roschier-Holmberg & Waselius, Attorneys Ltd, Oulu +358 8 551 3300
craig.thompson@rhw.fi
Recommended in Communications
Specialisation: Telecommunications, broadcasting, IPR, technology transfers and licensing, e-commerce, data protection, electricity and competition laws. Has been involved in numerous domestic and international assignments relating to telecommunications and broadcast regulatory matters, interconnection and network access agreements, network infrastructure financing, telecommunications e-commerce, as well as IPR driven M&A transactions, private placements and public listings, data protection, and R&D and licensing agreements.
Prof. Memberships: LES.
Career: Telecommunications analyst for the U.S. government (1983-87). Joined *Roschier-Holmberg & Waselius* in 1994; partner 1999.
Personal: Born 1961. Attended the University of Helsinki (LLM 1994), Columbia Law School, New York (LLM 1997).

TROBERG, Markus
Dittmar & Indrenius, Helsinki +358 9 681 700
Recommended in Corporate/M&A

WALLGREN, Carita
Roschier-Holmberg & Waselius, Attorneys Ltd, Helsinki +358 9 228 551
carita.wallgren@rhw.fi
Recommended in Corporate/M&A
Specialisation: M&A and international arbitration. Has been involved in a great number of major domestic and cross-border mergers and acquisitions. Acts as counsel and arbitrator, mainly in international arbitration.
Prof. Memberships: Member and officer of many international and domestic professional and civic organisations including the IBA; Board of Arbitration of the Central Chamber of Commerce of Finland (Board 1996-); Commission of International Arbitration of the ICC; Finnish Arbitration Association (Board 1996-); Legislative Committee for Contracts Act (1987-90); the Spanish-Finnish Trade Association (Board 1993-96); Lex Mundi (Board 1996-2000).
Career: Trained at the Bench in 1983 and became a member of the Bar in 1983. Joined *Roschier-Holmberg & Waselius* in 1984; partner 1989. Associate lawyer of *S.G. Archibald*, Paris (1981-82). Trainee at *Surrey & Morse* (now *Jones, Day, Reavis & Pogue*), Paris 1980. Various research related assignments at the University of Helsinki, Department of Comparative Law (1979, -80, -81).
Personal: Born 1953. Attended the University of Helsinki (LLM 1979). Studies in the United States; undergraduate diploma in languages from University of Helsinki.

WALLIN, Carl-Henrik
Hannes Snellman, Helsinki +358 9 228 841
carl-henrik.wallin@snellman-law.fi
Recommended in Competition/Anti-trust
Specialisation: Head of firm's Competition Law Department. Main areas of work are competition and mergers & acquisitions.
Prof. Memberships: Finnish Bar Association; The Association of Finnish Lawyers; International Bar Association.
Publications: Textbook on Finnish Merger Control and a number of articles on various competition law subjects.
Career: Master of Laws Helsinki University 1991, researcher Institute for International Economic Law 1991, LLM University of Amsterdam 1993, partner at *Hannes Snellman 1998.*

WIK, Christian
Roschier-Holmberg & Waselius, Attorneys Ltd, Helsinki +358 9 228 551
christian.wik@rhw.fi
Recommended in Competition/Anti-trust
Specialisation: Competition and EU, M&A. Has frequently been involved in large joint ventures, mergers and take-overs with competition law and merger control considerations, as well as assignments relating to telecommunications and the energy market.
Prof. Memberships: IBA; Legal Society of Finland (Treasurer 1989-95); Finnish Society for European Law; International League of Competition Law (Board member, the Nordic Group 1998-); European Association of Lawyers; Deutsch-Nordische Juristenvereinigung.
Career: Trained at the Bench in 1985 and became a member of the Bar in 1989. Joined *Roschier-Holmberg & Waselius* in 1986; partner 1993. Worked for *Cleary, Gottlieb, Steen & Hamilton*, Brussels, as a visiting lawyer (1990).
Personal: Born 1960. Attended the University of Helsinki (LLM, 1984) and the Southern Methodist University, Dallas, Texas (LLM, 1985).

FRANCE

Index

The clients' choice

BUSINESS LAWYER OF THE YEAR
JEAN-FRANÇOIS PRAT, *Bredin Prat*

BUSINESS LAW FIRM OF THE YEAR
BREDIN PRAT

Domestic firms dominated the survey, ***Jean-François Prat*** *wins a tight four way race with his firm* ***Bredin Prat*** *finishing well ahead of the field.*

For details see page 36.

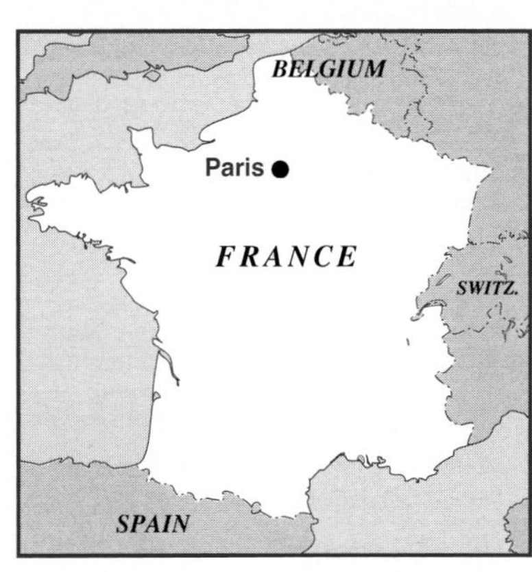

F

OVERVIEW: The French legal market has been characterised by the concurrent rise of the Anglo-Saxon firm and decline of the traditional Franco-French firm. Domestic firms watched as senior partners in all departments defected to their Anglo-Saxon counterparts. Jeantet suffered losses across the board with leading tax partners Patrick Dibout and Pascale Coudin departing for HSD Ernst & Young and Sullivan & Cromwell respectively. While Jean-Pierre LeGall and esteemed corporate player Gérard Mazet joined the Cleary Gottlieb ranks. Finally, competition guru Claude Lazarus left for Herbert Smith. This trend was echoed many times over with Stibbe losing Patrick Bonvarlet to Freshfields, which also claimed Gide's Antoine Colonna D'Istria. As a result, most of the medium sized French firms have been plunged into restructuring or are struggling to keep afloat.

High profile boutiques Bredin Prat and Darrois Villey maintained their position in the premier league working on nearly all the top M&A deals for the year, although the market questioned how long this will last. Their reputation rests with a handful of senior partners, many nearing retirement. Although these firms have a number of impressive younger lawyers, it is apparent that the French model firm comprised of "individuals" is unable to compete with the aggressive Anglo-Saxon model with its emphasis on a tight organisational structure and team work.

Similarly, foreign firms tend to dominate the Paris banking scene with Gide Loyrette Nouel and De Pardieu Brocas the only indigenous firms to retain a substantial market share. Financial specialists report a resurgence in the number of CLOs and CBOs flooding the French market while acquisition finance is becoming an increasingly complex affair as more mixed debt and equity funding is required to meet rising values. While fewer individuals focus exclusively on securitisation in France (as compared with the US or UK), the recent institution of mortgage-backed bonds (obligations fonciers) has provided new opportunities for structured finance lawyers.

Armed with the domestic expertise of lateral hires, international giants such as Cleary Gottlieb lead the high-end transactions. In competition, the market is dominated by larger firms, with Cleary Gottlieb closely followed by Herbert Smith and Freshfields. Similarly in tax, Allen & Overy has moved swiftly to become a leading practice. The Anglo-Saxon firms excel in cross border work where they are able to draw on the resources of offices around the globe. With depth in numbers, it is the international firms which are meeting client demand for an integrated service.

Arbitration (International)

FRANCE Leading firms (Arbitration (International))
1 Freshfields Bruckhaus Deringer
2 Shearman & Sterling
White & Case LLP
3 Coudert Frères
4 Herbert Smith
Jones, Day, Reavis & Pogue
Norton Rose
Salans Hertzfeld & Heilbronn

Firms are listed alphabetically in each band.

Freshfields Bruckhaus Deringer (5 ptrs, 12 asscs) The premier practice in Paris for international arbitration is perceived to have *"more arrows in its quiver"* than its leading competitors. The group's reputation rests largely on the presence of **Jan Paulsson***, commended to researchers as *"one of the top arbitration figures in the world."* He acts as both counsel and arbitrator across a variety of fields, including energy, mining and investment disputes, and specialises in conflicts relating to international treaties for the promotion of investments. He leads a *"gifted and enormous team,"* known for handling *"show case arbitrations."*

Former ICC secretary general, **Eric Schwartz*** is rated as a *"steady operator,"* with a *"great knowledge of the inner workings of ICC and arbitration procedure."* A *"successful generator of work,"* he has particular expertise in construction disputes.

The firm acted on a long-running natural gas price determination dispute, resulting in four distinct ICC arbitrations, and defended a leading gas company on a gas-related ICC arbitration conducted in Stockholm under Norwegian law.

Active all over the world, the team advised an investment bank against the Czech Republic over allegations of a breach of the Dutch/Czech bilateral investment treaty, defended a Chilean soft

*See leaders' profiles on pages 282-295

FRANCE Leading individuals (Arbitration (International))
★ **PAULSSON Jan** *Freshfields Bruckhaus Deringer*
1 **GAILLARD Emmanuel** *Shearman & Sterling*
2 **BOND Stephen** *White & Case LLP*
CRAIG William Laurence *Coudert Frères*
DERAINS Yves *Derains & Associés*
MAYER Pierre *Sole Practitioner*
SCHWARTZ Eric *Freshfields Bruckhaus Deringer*
3 **BAUM Axel** *Hughes Hubbard & Reed*
JARVIN Sigvard *Lagerlöf & Leman Advokatbyrå*
LAZAREFF Serge *Cabinet d'Avocats Lazareff*
SEPPALA Christopher *White & Case LLP*
4 **BÜHLER Michael** *Jones, Day, Reavis & Pogue*
DE BOISSÉSON Matthieu *Darrois Villey Maillot*
DELVOLVÉ Jean-Louis *Delvolvé Rouche*
KAPLAN Charles *Herbert Smith*
KIRRY Antoine *Debevoise & Plimpton*
LEE Michael *Norton Rose*
MOREAU Bertrand *Moreau-Bernard-Amigues*
Individuals are listed alphabetically in each band.

drink bottler in proceedings brought by a multinational arising from the transfer of brands to a competing multi-national, and represented an African state on an ICC arbitration brought by an Italian company, concerning a dam construction contract.

In the Middle East, the firm represented a country in ICSID proceedings brought by a UK company for recovery of alleged losses due to expropriation and failure to protect its investments, and advised the State of Bahrain on its border dispute with Qatar before the International Court of Justice.

Shearman & Sterling (3 ptrs, 23 asscs) The Paris office is considered by competitors to dominate the firm's international arbitration offering, with *"charismatic"* **Emmanuel Gaillard*** at the pinnacle of the firm's *"hierarchical structure."* Known to have *"a long list of devoted clients,"* he is recognised both in France and internationally as a *"first class arbitrator."* His scholarly articles on arbitration and competition matters reflect a *"great academic mind."*

He is supported by a *"well-organised army"* of *"able young associates."* The group's structure has been described to researchers as *"one big chief and lots of Indians,"* but rates highly for the sheer manpower at its disposal. Handling a huge volume of arbitrations for clients all over the world, the team is particularly visible representing French and American parties. A focus on energy disputes is supplemented by additional expertise in construction, engineering, cross-border M&A, international investment and environmental cases. Many are multi-claim arbitrations, valued at around $100 million.

The team represented a US construction contractor against a US sub-contractor on a $50 million contract dispute, which was subject to AAA arbitration in New York, and advised a European energy group on an ICC arbitration against an African state and a local oil company over a transportation dispute.

Highly visible on behalf of French companies, the firm advised on a Brussels ICC arbitration for a construction contractor against a Portuguese customer in a power dispute, represented a French technology group on a $30 million dispute against a Franco-Italian customer, subject to AFA arbitration in Paris, and served as counsel to a French defence manufacturer against a Norwegian shipbuilder in a $30 million joint venture dispute.

High-premium disputes have included advising a US construction contractor against an African owner on a $100 million power dispute, and representing NBC on an ICC arbitration in Mexico involving $150 million worth of claims, relating to the broadcasting giant's alliance with Mexican television station, TV Azteca.

White & Case LLP (3 ptrs, 5 asscs) Although the Paris team is said to have *"a strong American flavour,"* the firm's renowned arbitration practices in New York, Washington DC, Stockholm, Johannesburg and Hong Kong are the *"tentacles which bring in work from all areas of the world."* The firm has expertise in banking, insolvency, international construction and joint venture arbitrations, and was recommended to researchers for its international coverage and *"depth of experience."* However, it is perceived by some to be *"partner heavy and thin on associates."*

"Knowledgeable" **Christopher Seppala*** has earned a reputation as *"a leading figure in construction arbitration."* As legal advisor to FIDIC, he has played a pivotal role in the drafting of standardised construction contract forms. Possessing extensive experience of BOT disputes, he is frequently called upon to advise on disagreements relating to infrastructure in Europe, the Middle East and developing countries.

Former secretary general of the ICC, **Stephen Bond*** is rated as an *"all purpose lawyer with good forensic skills."* Most of his arbitrations involve joint venture or collaboration agreements in areas as diverse as manufacturing, mineral exploitation, military supply contracts and industrial co-operation. He has recently been involved in arbitrations with total claims of several hundred million dollars, arising from joint venture relationships in India, Scandinavia and Africa, in transportation, military supply and mineral exploitation.

The firm served as lead counsel for an oil-producing state in an arbitration relating to a production-sharing contract dispute with foreign oil companies. Also advised a contractor in relation to a dispute with an Asian group, involving claims of $50 million, arising from a power project built on a BOT basis in Asia.

Other work includes advising a syndicate of international banks, led by BAII, on court proceedings in France and Jordan, concerning the recognition and enforcement of an arbitration award obtained against The Inter-Arab Investment Guarantee Corporation, an international corporation based in Kuwait and owned by 22 Arab states.

Coudert Frères (2 ptrs, 4 asscs) Although he is seen by some to lack support, the presence of the *"distinguished"* **William Laurence Craig***, the *"elder statesman of the arbitration community,"* enables the firm to advise on *"some huge arbitrations."* This *"able and knowledgeable figure"* serves both as counsel and ICC arbitrator, and specialises in representing state enterprises from developing countries. His team has been strengthened by the arrival of a partner from the firm's Bangkok office, while the high-profile sole practitioner Pierre Mayer acts as a consultant to the firm.

The group has recently acted in a dispute concerning asset value of capital contribution to a multi-national venture with a disputed amount of $500 million, and an arbitration concerning a procurement contract (defence materials) with the Federal Republic of Germany.

Other commercial disputes include an arbitration between two large French conglomerates and their Indian JV partners in a power project in Northern India and a dispute involving European motor vehicle distributors and a Korean manufacturer. Active in construction disputes, the firm was chosen as counsel in a European Development Fund arbitration in Mauritania and acted in a dispute concerning a large French conglomerate and the Korean vendors of a Philippine industrial company.

Herbert Smith (2 ptrs, 8 asscs) Combining arbitration and litigation in one practice, the firm is noted for acting on both French and English language disputes, and has a superb reputation for advising on energy-related disputes in Africa and the rest of the developing world.

Aided by a team of *"sound young lawyers,"* **Charles Kaplan*** is reportedly *"beginning to make his talent known."* Trained in marine law, he specialises in insurance litigation, and has developed a respected niche in international commodity disputes. He has also conducted arbitrations over oil production-sharing agreements, long-term commodity supply agreements, construction and engineering projects and political risk insurance.

The firm represented an oil company in an ICC arbitration concerning cost recovery provisions in a joint operating agreement, and prepared a claim on behalf of a French contractor against a Dutch operator in relation to a refinery revamping project. Also advised on an ICSID arbitration claim on behalf of an international consortium against an African State, in relation to an electricity concession.

Jones, Day, Reavis & Pogue (2 ptrs, 4 asscs) The firm is involved in commercial disputes throughout Europe, Eastern Europe and the Middle East. In addition to arbitration advocacy, the team is active in negotiating settlements or arranging adjudication for the firm's global base of corporate clients. The lion's share of the caseload consists of representing construction and engineering companies in contract arbitrations before the ICC or other institutional or ad hoc bodies. Particularly recommended to our researchers for its skill in negotiating turnkey construction contracts, the team also has extensive experience of drafting multi-party arbitration clauses. Other work encompasses general commercial disputes arising from joint ventures.

"Keen" **Michael Bühler*** is recommended as the firm's leading arbitration practitioner. As the German alternate member of the ICC court of arbitration, he is a high-profile representative of German clients on arbitrations in Zurich, Geneva, Vienna, Paris and London. Bühler acted as lead counsel to a European manufacturer of industrial equipment with a non-European factory over a supply and services agreement in a Paris arbitration and acted for a European consortium for the refurbishment of cement factories in a dispute with a Middle Eastern contractor.

Other recent work includes acting in a Geneva arbitration as lead counsel to a multi-national mining company in a dispute with a consulting engineer over professional malpractice claims relating to inadequate design review of mining equipment.

Norton Rose (2 ptrs, 4 asscs) Working closely with the London group, the firm's Paris office is considered by peers to have an excellent presence in international arbitration. While the firm is best known for its activities in maritime and insurance matters, the arbitration team handles a diverse range of contractual disputes in areas including defence technology, airline services and construction and engineering projects.

Michael Lee* is a popular arbitrator both in ad hoc and institutional arbitrations. He deals with English language disputes in Paris, has been particularly active in ICC reinsurance disputes and serves as alternate UK member on the ICC International Court of Arbitration.

The firm advised on a dispute between a European airline and European service provider involving a contract for provision of services. Also represented Australian reinsurer QBE in a FF1 million dispute against Lafayette RE under French law. Other work includes acting on an arbitration between a North American corporation and a French corporation, involving a contract for defence technology, and advising on a dispute between an Indian and a Swiss corporation over a contract for the supply and running of an industrial plant.

Salans Hertzfeld & Heilbronn (7 ptrs, 3 asscs) Arbitration has historically been one of the firm's core areas, and the team is still praised to *Chambers'* researchers as a *"serious contender"* in the field.

The group has a strong presence in East-West arbitrations, acting on a number of disputes in the former Soviet Union. The group includes Russian-qualified lawyers, and can call on practitioners from offices in Moscow, Kyiv, Almaty and Warsaw. Partners have acted on Eurotunnel disputes and the US-Iran tribunals in the Hague.

The firm advised an African bank on a multi-jurisdictional dispute over recognition and enforcement of an ICC award. Also served as counsel to French and Spanish companies in an ad hoc arbitration in Paris against a Scandinavian company, concerning distribution contracts. In Eastern Europe, the group took the leading role in an UNCITRAL dispute involving Western investment in a Russian mining venture, and advised the Russian Central Bank on a successful defence of attachment proceedings in France, based on an award rendered against the Russian government.

Other Notable Practitioners Our research confirmed the presence of a number of other first-class arbitration figures in Paris. **Yves Derains*** of Derains & Associés heads a boutique practice which has an association with US firm Weil, Gotshal & Manges. Former secretary general of the ICC, Derains is *"as knowledgeable about French arbitration as anyone,"* and splits his time between acting as counsel and arbitrator.

Sole practitioner **Pierre Mayer*** is considered the *"leading professor in international law in France of his generation."* This *"first class arbitrator"* is frequently consulted as an expert on legal questions, and acts as consultant to Coudert Frères. Although rarely acting as counsel, he is internationally recognised as an *"approachable and intelligent arbitrator."*

Axel Baum* at Hughes Hubbard & Reed is also far better known in his capacity as arbitrator, but occasionally acts as counsel in disputes across a range of industries. Peers and clients appreciate his *"pragmatic, realistic approach."*

Sigvard Jarvin* of Swedish firm Lagerlöf & Leman has extensive experience of the main international arbitration institutions and is regularly involved as both counsel and arbitrator in disputes relating to energy and the sale and distribution of goods. Currently acting as co-head of Linklaters & Alliance's international arbitration group, he advised on a dispute between an Indian mining company and a French manufacturer of mining equipment, following the collapse of a mine in India.

Serge Lazareff* of Cabinet d'Avocats Lazareff & Associés is a leading Paris arbitrator, particularly active in construction, joint venture and financial co-operation disputes. As member of the World Council of the ICC and chairman of the ICC Institute of World Business Law, he is highly respected as a *"senior figure"* in the community. Although predominantly an arbitrator, he has acted as counsel to a US-Scandinavian group on the reactivation of a French shipyard, and advised a Japanese construction group investing in France.

Matthieu de Boisséson* at Darrois Villey Maillot Brochier acts primarily in French language arbitrations as both arbitrator and advocate. He maintains close relations with NY firm Wachtell, Lipton, Rosen & Katz and advises on arbitrations relating to M&A, company restructurings, telecoms, and armaments disputes. He advised Publicis on its FF7 billion dispute with True North.

Jean-Louis Delvolvé* at Delvolvé Rouche is an *"international figurehead,"* operating a boutique practice specialising in French arbitration, while **Antoine Kirry*** of Debevoise & Plimpton maintains a mixed practice focusing on transactional M&A and M&A-related arbitrations. He is recommended as a *"meticulous and convincing advocate,"* involved as both counsel and arbitrator.

Bertrand Moreau* of Moreau Bernard Amigueset-Darmon is considered *"one of the top figures in France"* but rarely acts on English language matters. As president of the French Arbitration Association, he exerts considerable influence throughout the French arbitration community, and is acknowledged for his expertise on the enforcement and setting aside of awards.

*See leaders' profiles on pages 282-295

Banking & Finance

FRANCE Leading firms (Banking & Finance)	
1	Clifford Chance
	Freshfields Bruckhaus Deringer
	Gide Loyrette Nouel
2	Allen & Overy
	Ashurst Morris Crisp
	De Pardieu Brocas Maffei & Leygonie
	Linklaters
	White & Case LLP
3	Norton Rose
	Watson, Farley & Williams
	Willkie Farr & Gallagher
4	Jones, Day, Reavis & Pogue
	Shearman & Sterling
	Simmons & Simmons
	Slaughter and May
	Stibbe

Firms are listed alphabetically in each band.

Clifford Chance (4 ptrs, 30 asscs) *"A top name in financial services,"* this strong team is considerably bolstered by the reputation of the London office. Following a period of rapid firm-wide expansion, the group has a *"whole army of people"* to draw upon and a widened jurisdiction throughout the world's major financial centres. Clifford Chance now boasts of one of the biggest finance teams in Paris and many interviewees agreed that the firm merited its top band position *"for size reasons alone."* The group covers all areas of syndicated loans, acquisition and asset-backed finance but is particularly distinguished in the market for its securitisation and structured finance expertise.

Head of Finance, **Olivier Bertin-Mourot*** has a considerable pure banking and regulatory practice but is also highly rated for his capital markets expertise.

On the regulatory side, the firm is seen to have made *"fantastic inroads to French government"* and advises major financial institutions Lazard, the French Treasury and CIC on the provision of banking and investment services in France. The banking team has been particularly active in advising businesses on disposals and portfolio management through the internet. In acquisition finance, the group acted for Citibank in connection with the €150 million acquisition finance extended to Financier Dufort, and represented Société Générale in connection with the $5 billion facility to finance the AXA tender offer on AXA Financial Inc.

The team is also heavily involved in various aspects of real estate finance and recently advised Crédit Lyonnais on the financing of Hines towers PB6 and CB16. Other real estate transactions include the FF12 billion disposal by Carrefour of its shopping centres in France to the Klepierre group. The group also advised Deutsche Bank on a structured umbrella facility for a property fund acquiring a warehouse and other industrial properties. **Clients:** Morgan Stanley; UBS; Société Générale; BNP-Paribas; Crédit Lyonnais; Natexis; Citibank; Merrill Lynch.

Freshfields Bruckhaus Deringer (9 ptrs, 30 asscs) An integrated finance group which undertakes lending, acquisition and asset finance work, as well as a heavy share of capital markets work and structured finance. The group's reputation for the latter is gradually overtaking its renown for more traditional financing, as the changing market has brought the firm into more sophisticated structured finance and securitisation transactions.

Senior partner **Jean-Luc Michaud*** was recommended to our researchers as an *"outgoing"* banking generalist, covering all areas of banking law such as letters of credit, loans and guarantees, as well as asset finance and structured finance.

Freshfields has a strong real estate finance practice, with two dedicated partners advising on real estate loan portfolios. The group recently acted for Bouygues on the sale of four buildings to SimCo for €250 million, and advised Crédit Agricole Indosuez on an acquisition finance of the takeover by SimCo of property group Société des Immeubles de France for €275 million.

Head of finance **Michel Quéré*** is *"top of the hit list"* for his *"all round expertise,"* and has particular experience of defeasance restructuring and securitisation work. Referred to by some clients as *"the best French banking lawyer in Paris,"* he is *"highly spoken of on the largest transactions,"* and is frequently seen acting for Société Générale on structured finance matters, such as the refinancing of Remy Cointreau. He recently advised COFACE insurance company on an e-factoring b2b transaction involving factoring agreements, banking and insurance regulation and tax issues in 30 countries. Quéré was particularly recommended for his role in the precedent-setting debt recycling/restructuring of Comptoir des Entrepreneurs and of Consortium de Réalisation (set up to redeem the bad assets of Crédit Lyonnais) and the purchase by Bred Banques Populaires of the Crédit Martiniquais.

The firm has also acquired **Patrick Bonvarlet*** from Stibbe. Considered by peers to be an *"excellent IPO, bonds, capital market and banking lawyer,"* his practice defies categorisation. Known as a *"tough character,"* this *"outstanding lawyer"* has a range of experience in acquisition finance and mezzanine debt and was recommended for *"table thumping transactions."* **Jean L'Homme*** maintains a varied banking and regulatory practice and received widespread commendation as a *"highly professional"* lawyer, with the skills to tackle *"anything sophisticated in French law."* The firm's historic niche in aviation finance is upheld by **Glenn Matheson***, who is seen as *"the number one name for aircraft securitisations."* **Clients:** Bayerische Landesbank; UBS; Crédit Agricole Indosuez; ABN AMRO; Société Générale; Lazard Frères; Air Liquide; West LB; Goldman Sachs; GE Capital; Morgan Stanley; Chase Manhattan; Citibank; Coface; Commerzbank; BNP Paribas; Crédit Lyonnais; Fortis Bank; Despa.

Gide Loyrette Nouel (6 ptrs, 40 asscs) With strong ties to all the major French banks, Gide Loyrette Nouel was consistently mentioned to our researchers as the French firm most visible in representing lenders and investors. Although predominantly focused on the domestic market, the group boasts a number of Canadian and UK-qualified practitioners. By comparison with a number of other departments, the firm's banking practice has remained relatively untouched by the recent wave of poaching, and maintains consistent strength in general banking, asset, structured and acquisition finance, and regulatory matters.

"Mr. French Banking" **Jacques Terray*** works for both French and American banks, and has recently been active on the takeover of unlisted banks. He remains the firm's banking *"figurehead"* and although less visible on transactions, *"pilots a successful banking practice."*

The practice's transactional mantle has effectively been handed over to *"first-class operator"* **Eric Cartier-Millon***, a *"technically great"* general banking lawyer, who *"dabbles in everything."* Clients *"take their hats off"* to his extensive experience in LBO financing. One of the few who *"did not succumb to the siren song of the Anglo-Saxon firms,"* he is praised by opponents as *"an excellent lawyer who gets the job done."*

He works in tandem with *"rainmaker"* **Kamel Ben Salah***, whose *"flamboyant personality reels in the business."* Ben Salah led the group's advice to Eurohypo AG in financing the acquisition of approximately 30 real estate assets by subsidiaries of the Whitehall funds (managed by Goldman Sachs.)

The group works closely with the property

FRANCE Leading individuals (Banking & Finance)	
1	**CARTIER-MILLON Eric** *Gide Loyrette Nouel*
	PEIGNEY Gilles *White & Case LLP*
	TERRAY Jacques *Gide Loyrette Nouel*
2	**ANDRIANI Bertrand** *Linklaters*
	BERTIN-MOUROT Olivier *Clifford Chance*
	BILLOT Philippe *Jones, Day, Reavis & Pogue*
	MAFFEI Antoine *De Pardieu Brocas Maffei*
	QUÉRÉ Michel *Freshfields Bruckhaus*
	VILANOVA Richard *Sullivan & Cromwell*
3	**BEN SALAH Kamel** *Gide Loyrette Nouel*
	BONVARLET Patrick *Freshfields Bruckhaus*
	CORK Rod *Allen & Overy*
	GDANSKI Martin *Norton Rose*
	KETT Peter *Slaughter and May*
	L'HOMME Jean *Freshfields Bruckhaus*
	MICHAUD Jean-Luc *Freshfields Bruckhaus*
	NABARRO Jonathan *Ashurst Morris Crisp*
	PAYAN Daniel *Willkie Farr & Gallagher*
	SYED David *Watson, Farley & Williams*
4	**BESSE Eryl** *Linklaters*
	DE MOÜY Diane *De Pardieu Brocas Maffei*
	DE VARAX Matthieu *Simmons & Simmons*
	DIRANI Georges *Herbert Smith*
	LEBEUF Martin *De Pardieu Brocas Maffei*
	MATHESON Glenn *Freshfields Bruckhausr*
	MCDONALD Thomas *White & Case LLP*
	RENTMEESTERS Luc *Allen & Overy*
	TORDJMAN Olivier *Cabinet Tordjman*
Up-and-coming individuals	
	JAUFFRET Olivier *Linklaters*

Individuals are listed alphabetically in each band.

finance department, and undertakes a substantial amount of real estate work on behalf of investment banks Morgan Stanley and Goldman Sachs. Recent property transactions include advising CCF on the financing of the acquisition of Aventis tower in La Défense by MSREF funds (managed by Morgan Stanley Dean Witter) and the Hines group. Also represented Société Générale in the financing of the acquisition of real estate assets in Poland and France. On the asset finance side, the group advised CCF in relation to a car-ferry leasing in favour of Seafrance (an SNCF subsidiary), while the group also advised Crédit Lyonnais on a synthetic leasing transaction for the English TDG group. **Clients:** Société Générale; Crédit Lyonnais; BNP Paribas; Caisse de Dépôt et Consignation (CDC); CIC; JP Morgan; Deutsche Bank; Goldman Sachs; Merrill Lynch; Crédit Commercial de France; Eurohypo AG.

Allen & Overy (4 ptrs, 22 asscs) This fast growing firm has reportedly *"tripled its size in eighteen months"* and receives market recommendation for the calibre of its banking practice and commercial savvy in *"recruiting a number of excellent individuals."* Although the new group undoubtedly *"will need some time to get its act together,"* the banking team is already seen as *"strong competition"* and has been tipped as most likely to join the top band through its quality and depth of resources.

The group handles the range of general banking, securitisation, acquisition finance, project finance, syndicated loans and real estate finance under both French and English law, although the firm's strength lies far more in UK-governed transactions.

Interviewees report that the practice has *"taken a good market share in heavy corporate syndicated lending transactions."*

Thanks to the presence of former CCF lawyer **Rod Cork***, a *"major player in telecoms finance,"* the group has particularly distinguished itself in the field of communications.

His practice spans acquisition and project finance, and this *"versatile"* practitioner earns much of the credit from rivals for the development of the firm's banking practice. Cork advised Société Générale, ABN AMRO and Chase Manhattan on a dual currency loan to an Egyptian mobile phone network, and represented ABN AMRO on the financing of a $1.1 billion GSM phone licence in Morocco for a consortium led by Telefónica of Spain.

Former in-house counsel at Citibank, **Luc Rentmeesters*** undertakes structured finance, defeasance and credit enhancement work, and has an acknowledged niche in aircraft and asset finance. Reputed to possess a *"flair for marketing,"* he maintains close ties with clients Crédit Agricole Indosuez, Aig and CIT. He has advised on complex transactions such as the securitisation and credit-enhancement of three trade receivables by AGF.

Other highlights of the past year include acting for Goldman Sachs International, Banque Nationale de Paris, Morgan Stanley Dean Witter and Crédit Agricole Indosuez as arrangers of a €18 billion loan facility for Elf Aquitaine to establish the cash portion of Elf's counter bid for TotalFina. **Clients:** Société Générale; Crédit Lyonnais; Goldman Sachs; BNP Paribas; Crédit Agricole Indosuez; Chase Manhattan; ABN AMRO; Citibank; Deutsche Bank.

Ashurst Morris Crisp (4 ptrs, 11 asscs) While the Paris office is generally better known for its corporate work, the banking group has developed a considerable niche in acquisition finance, in which it is said to have a *"stranglehold on the market."* Much of the workload involves corporate support, and a number of practitioners straddle the corporate and banking departments. The firm was highly rated for its LBO capabilities, perceived by some to be *"the leading practice for financing management buyouts."*

"Precise" **Jonathan Nabarro*** leads the acquisition finance team, and was recommended for drafting *"sophisticated documents."* His background in shipping and aviation finance is felt by the market to complement the firm's developing project finance practice. Recent highlights include representing Goldman Sachs and BNP Paribas on the FF7.5 billion acquisition of Finelist. The firm also acted for BNP Paribas and ICG on the €750 million purchase of power supply device producer MGE, advised Crédit Agricole Indosuez and ICG on the €243 million purchase of Frans Bonhomme (PVC piping), and assisted Crédit Agricole Indosuez on the €289 million purchase of Groupe Salins.

On the non-leveraged side, the group acted in a French overseas territories tax financing of several Airbus A330 and A320 aircraft for Air Calédonie International, and represented Lyonnaise des Banques on the financing of joint venture Matussière & Forest and Arjo Wiggins' acquisition and rehabilitation of a paper mill in France. **Clients:** Crédit Agricole Indosuez; BNP Paribas; Lyonnaise des Banques; Goldman Sachs; Barclays Capital; ICG; Natexis Banques Populaires; Deutsche Bank.

De Pardieu Brocas Maffei & Leygonie (6 ptrs, 15 asscs) The firm's banking department covers a mix of traditional lending, capital markets, regulatory work, bankruptcy and workout litigation. Considered by the market to have a less international focus than many of its leading rivals. The group has a solid reputation for French syndicated lending, trade financing and letters of credit. The firm advises a number of leading French banks, but also takes instructions from a growing number of foreign banks.

Antoine Maffei* splits his practice between capital markets work and export financing. He was consistently recommended to researchers for his skill in building up the practice. He is renowned for negotiating export credit for insurance client COFACE, and advised Deutsche Bank and ABN AMRO on a $270 million power generation project in Mexico.

Diane de Moüy* maintains a mixed practice in derivatives and international banking, she has a reputation for being *"tenacious in negotiations,"* and is widely respected for her *"driven"* style. **Martin Lebeuf*** focuses on acquisition finance and is reputed to have a loyal client following. He

*See leaders' profiles on pages 282-295

acted for Rheinhyp Rheinische Hypothekenbank on a €925 million financing of a property acquisition by Commerzbank Gründbesitz Investment.

The group has a strong reputation for e-banking, and advised on the creation of first-e, the first cross-border electronic bank. **Clients:** BNP Paribas; Société Générale; Crédit Agricole Industriel; Crédit Lyonnais; Caisse de Dépôt; ABN AMRO; Deutsche Bank.

F

Linklaters (3 ptrs, 7 asscs) The firm still maintains a stronger reputation for capital markets transactions, but is reported by competitors to be developing a creditable mainstream banking practice. The group suffered a setback with the loss of Georges Dirani to Herbert Smith, but is still seen to have a stable of excellent practitioners. Also ranked in project finance, *"pragmatic"* **Bertrand Andriani*** is highly esteemed for his asset finance expertise. He acts chiefly on domestic matters, and led the team in advising Paribas Affaires Industrielles and Frans Bonhomme as equity investor and borrower on a FF2.5 billion leveraged buy-out acquisition financing.

Eryl Besse* handles both capital markets and general banking on UK law-governed transactions, and led the group's advice to Lafarge on the jumbo financing of its £3.95 billion hostile bid for Blue Circle Industries in the form of a term loan and revolving credit facility. **Olivier Jauffret*** was recommended to our researchers as a practitioner *"at the forefront of the next generation of Linklaters banking stars."*

The team advised Chase Manhattan and Dresdner Bank Luxembourg SA on French aspects of a €2.1 billion syndicated loan facility for Tele-Invest SA to acquire 10% of the issued share capital of Polish telecoms company Telekomunkacja Polska Akcyjna from the State Treasury of the Republic of Poland. The group acts equally for borrowers, and recently represented Rémy Cointreau Group on the secured refinancing of existing short and medium term bilateral loans valued at FF3.5 billion and again on the FF400 million refinancing of this facility. **Clients:** Crédit Lyonnais; Lafarge; Paribas Affaires Industrielles; Rémy Cointreau; Bayerische Landesbank; Crédit Agricole Indosuez; Compagnie Générale de Géophysique; CSFB; Eutelsat; J.C. Decaux.

White & Case LLP (5 ptrs, 5 asscs) The group is rated highly for transactional banking and the quality of its small but *"cohesive"* team. It represents investment banks on public deals, IPOs and follow-up offerings, usually acting on the debt side of MBOs and acquisition finance transactions. The firm advised Crédit Lyonnais and Crédit Agricole Indosuez in connection with aggregate loans of €1 billion made to Fimalac to finance its tender offer for Duff & Phelps. Department head **Gilles Peigney**'s* practice is oriented mostly toward acquisition finance and financing of tender offers. *"A good legal mind,"* according to opponents, he is said to be *"utterly trustworthy for complicated transactions."* His personal reputation is considered to overshadow that of the firm, and it is *"his name that keeps the clients."*

Thomas McDonald* is a *"big name in asset finance,"* and has particular expertise in financing of aircraft and railway stock. He recently advised US operating lessor, the CIT Group in connection with the negotiation of an export loan/lease facility supported by COFACE, HERMES and ECGD for up to 30 Airbus aircraft with a total value of $1.5 billion. Other notable work includes the representation of Decaux SA in connection with the refinancing of its banking indebtedness in view of the listing of Decaux SA on the Paris Stock Exchange market with Goldman Sachs as the arranger. The group also undertakes occasional sovereign financing and represented the fiscal agent in connection with the default by the Republic of Côte d'Ivoire with respect to its Brady bonds issued in 1998 in connection with the restructuring of the London Club debt of the Republic. **Clients:** BNP Paribas; Crédit Lyonnais; Crédit Agricole Indosuez; The Royal Bank of Scotland; Eximbank; Société Générale; ING Bank.

Norton Rose (5 ptrs, 15 asscs) Possessing outstanding strength in project and asset finance, the firm was commended to our researchers as the leaders in Paris for aviation finance and a close second to Watson Farley & Williams for shipping finance. A dedicated team of eight aviation finance lawyers is active in cross-border tax-based leasing and debt products, often enhanced by export credit finance for clients such as Crédit Agricole Indosuez, BNP Paribas, Crédit Lyonnais and several airlines. The group acted for the banks on the ECA financing of four Airbus A319 aircraft for TAM-Transportes Aereos Regionais SA. Major clients include Société Générale, Natexis Banque, and SA Louis Dreyfus.

"Precise" **Martin Gdanski*** heads the group's telecoms practice and was recommended for his *"good all-round skills."* He has led telecoms network financings for the UPC Group, CompleTél, Dolphin Telecom and UAB Bité GSM.

Regular advisors on financing deals for railway rolling stock, the firm recently represented the banks on a cross-border financing for rolling stock produced by high speed rail manufacturer Alstom. Developing strength on the debt side of management buy-outs was highlighted by advice on the financing of Le Figaro newspaper. **Clients:** Société Générale; Royal Bank of Scotland; Crédit Industriel et Commercial; HSBC Equator Bank; Crédit Agricole Indosuez; BNP Paribas; Crédit Lyonnais; SA Louis Dreyfus; Coflexip; ING Bank; Bank of Scotland.

Watson, Farley & Williams (7 ptrs, 17 asscs) Researchers found that the firm's shipping finance practice is considered to be without equal. The group acts for an even mix of corporate and banking clients, and is also visible on structured finance and asset finance transactions. Corporate giants Vivendi and Renault are key names on the client roster.

The group has worked in co-operation with the firm's US offices in the arranging and refinancing of $7.2 billion of debt in Vivendi's acquisition of Seagram, and on a number of bridge financings for Vivendi. It also represents a number of US equity investors in cross-border tax leasing of aircraft, railcars, equipment and real estate.

"Commercial" **David Syed*** *"can sell snow to an Eskimo,"* and maintains a high profile in transport-related lease financings. He and his team acted for US equity investors in two tranches of a US/France cross-border leasehold financing of railcars for the national French rail operator. In shipping finance, the firm advised the operator of a COFACE export credit for two 700 passenger vessels, and acted as counsel to the arranger for the French lease financing of a roll-on roll-off passenger ferry. **Clients:** Crédit Agricole Indoseuz; Crédit Lyonnais; BNP Paribas; CCF; Vivendi; Renault; Rothschild; Babcock & Brown.

Willkie Farr & Gallagher (10 lawyers) Acting almost exclusively on the side of the borrower, the firm's acquisition finance practice is grouped within the larger M&A department. Competitors acknowledge the team's substantial share of the LBO financing market, and the team has been seen acting for institutions such as Goldman Sachs in mezzanine finance.

Corporate legend **Daniel Payan*** was commended to researchers as a *"shrewd lawyer"* with extensive expertise in representing venture capital funds on the equity side of buyout transactions. The group acted for CDC on the acquisition of Danone's glass business in a blended finance arrangement. **Clients:** BNP Paribas; Lazards; CVC; Bank of Scotland; DCI; Warburgs; BC Partners; UBS.

Jones, Day, Reavis & Pogue (3 ptrs, 12 asscs) Former in-house counsel at CCF, **Philippe Billot*** co-chairs the firm's lending and structured finance practice. A banking generalist, his individual reputation is said by peers to outshine the firm. The mainstay of the workload is cross-border asset finance, supported by substantial real estate finance expertise. A strong M&A team contributes to acquisition finance activity.

Generally seen on complex transactions, the team is noted for its presence on deals with multi-jurisdictional elements. Recent activity includes representing Winterthur, acting as credit enhancer, in connection with the securitisation by the Chargeurs SA group of its interlining equipment for €60 million. The firm also advised on a structured finance transaction for Toyota, entailing FF1.78 billion of tax leases on its new plant in Valenciennes (Société Générale as arrangers and underwriters). **Clients:** HSBC-CCF; Société Générale; JP Morgan; Goldman Sachs.

Shearman & Sterling (5 ptrs, 5 asscs) Although better known for capital markets transactions, the group does perform its share of banking and finance work, generally in tandem with its M&A and project finance departments. The group receives particular recommendation from clients for its US capital raising work under SEC regulations. Acting chiefly on behalf of the borrower, the firm is strong on multi-jurisdictional transactions, and served as US and French counsel to Trianon Industries, Inc on obtaining a credit facility and bridging loan valued at $200 million. **Clients:** Trianon.

Simmons & Simmons (2 ptrs, 4 asscs) The group covers a broad range of banking, regulatory, financial services and acquisition finance, but researchers noted greatest recognition for its strength in leveraged leasing and asset finance.

Matthieu De Varax* has built up a respected niche in domestic aircraft and ship finance, and has recently been active in the financing of jet aircraft. Other areas of expertise include the financing of IT and telecoms equipment, real estate and export credit finance. The group acted on the cross border financing of a train in Australia, and represented a German bank on the acquisition and financing of a property portfolio. Additional instructions come from debt providers on LBO and MBO transactions. **Clients:** BNP Paribas; Société Générale; Royal Bank of Scotland; CDC.

Slaughter and May (5 ptrs, 9 asscs) The banking group is said to produce *"top quality work,"* but researchers continually met the market perception that the firm has not committed its resources to Paris in the manner of the market leaders.

"Class act" **Peter Kett*** created and continues to run a respected banking practice, which has considerable expertise in syndicated lending. The firm has additionally been involved in acquisition finance, debt restructurings, and project finance.

Recent work includes vendor financings to Kosovo authorities and Satelindo, and secured financings for Oberthru and Butachimie. The group also acted on the LBO of Flender, and has completed a number of loans to Aventis, Essilor, Gensec, Rexel and Société Foncière Lyonnaise. **Clients:** Abbey National Group; Alcatel Group; BNP Paribas; Commerzbank; Crédit Lyonnais; Essilor; JP Morgan; Rexel; Société Foncière Lyonnaise; Société Générale.

Stibbe (4 ptrs, 6 asscs) The practice has been hard hit by the recent departures of both Patrick Bonvarlet and Richard Vilanova, and is considered to have a drastically reduced profile. However, the group still has strong asset finance capabilities and an international team of aviation specialists. Other primary areas of activity include synthetic leasing, defeasance work, non-recourse and structured finance.

The firm represented CCF as lender in connection with a French lease financing of high speed trains manufactured by Alstom for Amtrak, and also acted for TAT Group and a bank syndicate, led by Crédit Agricole Indosuez, on the lease-financing of a fleet of ATR 72 aircraft for Jet Airways (India). **Clients:** Ingepar/Group Caisses d'Epargne; CCF; Eurofirma.

Other Notable Practitioners **Richard Vilanova**, a *"prominent asset finance lawyer, notably on railway rolling stock,"* joined Sullivan & Cromwell in January of 2001 from Stibbe, and is expected to galvanise the firm's banking practice. **Georges Dirani*** has left Linklaters to develop an international banking and finance group at Herbert Smith, where he will build on his strengths in syndicated and structured finance. **Olivier Tordjman***, formerly of Wilde Sapte, has a fine reputation for advice on MBO financing, and now operates at his own firm, Cabinet Tordjman & Associés.

Capital Markets

Allen & Overy (6 ptrs, 16 asscs) The group's stature has risen dramatically over the past few years following the acquisition of a number of highly respected practitioners both from the firm's London office and competing firms in Paris. A young team still has *"a few wrinkles to iron out,"* but is seen to have *"the right experience"* and was commended to our researchers for *"working in everyone's best interests."* Typically, the workload consists of advising on debt issues (both stand-alone and tranches under EMTN programs) and assisting on warrants and other derivative securities offerings under French and English law. The group has been involved in establishing and updating EMTN programs for French banks Société Générale, BNP-Paribas, Crédit Lyonnais and CCF, and has set up similar programs for corporate giants France Telecom, Lafarge and AXA.

"Calm" **Pierre Gissinger*** is known throughout the market as a *"derivatives guru."* He is also involved in the firm's capital markets regulatory work and has advised on the statutory framework for 'obligations foncières', the new French bond backed by mortgage debt. Formerly in-house counsel at BNP, **François Poudelet*** rates highly for a broad capital markets and securities practice in the primary market. The firm advised Bull SA on an issue of convertible and exchangeable bonds.

A developing niche in e-commerce has seen the group advise Bear Stearns, CSFB, Deutsche Bank, JP Morgan, Salomon Smith Barney and Société Générale on offering and trading securities over the internet. The group is also active in documenting Employee Share Ownership plans for international financial institutions and can draw on the expertise of a number of tax lawyers who specialise in capital markets tax matters. **Clients:** ABN AMRO; AGF; AXA; BNP-Paribas; Chase Manhattan; ISDA; Citibank; Crédit Agricole Indosuez; Infineon Technologies; Merrill Lynch; Parisbourse (SBF); Siemens AG; CDC Marchés; Deutsche Bank; Goldman Sachs; Crédit Foncier de France; Société Générale; CSFB; Crédit Lyonnais; Lehman Brothers.

Gide Loyrette Nouel (3 ptrs, 8 asscs) Consistently recommended to our researchers for securitisation and structured finance capabilities, the firm is a powerful force within the domestic market. The capital markets group works in co-operation with the banking and corporate teams to cover a range of debt and equity offerings, securi-

*See leaders' profiles on pages 282-295

FRANCE Leading firms (Capital Markets)	
1	Allen & Overy
	Gide Loyrette Nouel
	Linklaters
2	Freshfields Bruckhaus Deringer
	Shearman & Sterling
3	Cleary, Gottlieb, Steen & Hamilton
	Clifford Chance
	De Pardieu Brocas Maffei & Leygonie
4	Jeantet & Associés
	Jones, Day, Reavis & Pogue
	Lovells
	Stibbe
	Willkie Farr & Gallagher

Firms are listed alphabetically in each band.

Leading individuals (Capital Markets)	
1	**CHABERT Pierre-Yves** *Cleary, Gottlieb, Steen*
	DE KERGOMMEAUX Xavier *Gide Loyrette Nouel*
	ENDRÉO Gilles *Linklaters*
	GISSINGER Pierre *Allen & Overy*
	TREUHOLD Robert *Shearman & Sterling*
2	**ANDRIANI Bertrand** *Linklaters*
	BERTIN-MOUROT Olivier *Clifford Chance*
	BESSE Antonin *Freshfields Bruckhaus*
	BILLOT Philippe *Jones, Day, Reavis & Pogue*
	BONVARLET Patrick *Freshfields Bruckhaus*
	MAFFEI Antoine *De Pardieu Brocas Maffei*
	POUDELET François *Allen & Overy*
3	**FAUGÉROLAS Laurent** *Willkie Farr & Gallagher*
	PAROLAI Richard *Clifford Chance*
	TOURAINE Hervé *Freshfields Bruckhaus*
4	**D'HÉROUVILLE Jean-Guillaume** *Gide Loyrette Nouel*
	LETRÉGUILLY Hervé *Shearman & Sterling*
	MICHAUD Jean-Luc *Freshfields Bruckhaus*
	MINOR Pierre *De Pardieu Brocas Maffei*
	PORTIER Philippe *Jeantet & Associés*
Up-and-coming individuals	
	HERBELIN Philippe *Linklaters*
	LE GRIS Ines *Willkie Farr & Gallagher*
	LEWIS Jonathan *Clifford Chance*

Individuals are listed alphabetically in each band.

tisation and derivatives. The team has niche expertise in synthetic products using derivatives and capital markets instruments.

Xavier de Kergommeaux* *"made his name in pure French securitisation"* and is rated by peers as an *"immensely likeable practitioner."* The firm assisted Merrill Lynch on the securitisation of Chantiers de l'Atlantique (shipyard) future receivables for $600 million.

Jean-Guillaume d'Hérouville* is seen more on IPO and regulatory issues, and acted for Euromarket Paris on the substitution of the Rolling Settlement System of the French Bourse with the new Delayed Settlement Service.

The group was involved in the formation of Compagnie de Financement Foncier, the first French issuer of mortgage-backed securities under the 1999 legislation, and advised on CCF's investment in mortgage-backed securities issued in the European Economic Area.

Work on a number of listings on the Nouveau Marché of the Paris Bourse includes a combined public offering and private placement for Business Interactif, lead managed by ABN-AMRO Rothschild and Natexis Capital Marchés Primaires, and advising NET2S on the international placement of shares to institutional investors. The group also advised on the offering of new shares to individuals in France, from a listing managed by Robertson Stephens International and Oddo Pinatton Corporate. **Clients:** Crédit Lyonnais; Kazibao; Wavecom; Business Interactif; JP Morgan Securities Ltd; Crédit Agricole Indosuez; Lazards; BancBoston; Robertson Stephens; ABN-AMRO Rothschild.

Linklaters (7 ptrs, 14 asscs) The firm's historical work on behalf of bond issuers has given it the reputation as *"one of the leading practices in Paris for debt capital markets."*

Long considered by peers and clients to be one of the Paris office's strongest suits, the capital markets group advises both French and international investment and commercial banks and multi-national companies on equity, equity-related debt and derivative transactions.

Despite noting some market observation that the group is *"cautious about going into new products,"* our researchers established that the firm has been closely involved in the development of the first covered warrants in the French market and the first issue of exchangeable bonds governed by French law to be exchangeable for UK shares. The group advised Lafarge on its offering of €1,726,593,453 bonds, redeemable in Lafarge shares or cash, each with a warrant attached to subscribe for Lafarge shares, in connection with Lafarge's hostile bid for Blue Circle Industries plc.

In securities, the team advises banks and corporates on both debt and equity offerings, including high yield bonds, convertible and exchangeable bonds, IPOs and privatisations.

Interviewees praised the firm's investments in sophisticated software. *"They have built their collective experience into templates so that they can rapidly and efficiently produce a good set of first papers for capital market transactions."* International finance specialist **Gilles Endréo*** *"works well in a cross-cultural setting,"* advising on debt and equity issues in primary markets. Considered to have *"one of the leading capital markets practices in Europe,"* Endreo advised Deutsche Bank on the French law Euro MTN Programmes for Dexia Municipal Agency (obligations foncières), LVMH, Compagnie de Financement Foncier, Casino and La Poste.

Bertrand Andriani* *"does a bit of everything"* and was rated highly for project finance, banking and capital markets. *"Intellectually fabulous,"* he is most visible on securitisation transactions, and advised AXA IM as originator and collateral arranger on its Concerto I 'arbitrage' CDO issue of £477 million floating rate notes. This is due in five tranches in 2012, secured on a portfolio of European high yield bonds and leveraged loans.

Newly made up partner **Philippe Herbelin*** rates as an up-and-coming capital markets practitioner. He recently advised Warburg Dillon Read and Crédit Lyonnais on the global offering of up to 138,800,000 existing shares of Vinci, valued at €464 million. **Clients:** BNP Paribas; CDC Marchés; Deutsche Bank; Merrill Lynch; JP Morgan; Société Générale; ABN Amro; Banque Internationale à Luxembourg; Lehman Brothers; UBS Warburg.

Freshfields Bruckhaus Deringer (9 ptrs, 28 asscs) A combined finance and capital markets team lays particular emphasis on securitisation and structured finance. Although considered by some in the market to be narrower in scope than some of its competitors, the firm was universally commended to researchers for its capabilities in whole business securitisations and trade receivable transactions. The group concentrates on tailor-made financial products such as certificates and warrant programmes, rather than plain vanilla transactions.

Involvement in a number of innovative transactions was highlighted by the team's work on behalf of Marne & Champagne on the first champagne securitisation, a €396 million secured Euro MTN programme. This was led by respected M&A and structured finance generalist **Jean-Luc Michaud***. **Hervé Touraine*** is well known as a securitisation specialist, active in transactions utilising both French and offshore structures. He advised BNP Paribas as arranger and liquidity provider on a €92 million securitisation of both inventories and trade receivables, arising from the sale of wines and spirits originated by various entities of the Grands Chais Group. Other recent successes include the team's work in advising EDF and Bayerische Landesbank Girozentale on the securitisation of future receivables from day to day electricity consumption by French corporates.

Antonin Besse* handles a number of synthetic CLO and CBO deals. He recently acted for Citibank, N.A on the establishment of a second synthetic CBO for Bank of Austria, worth approximately $650 million.

The team has received a boost from the arrival of *"maverick"* **Patrick Bonvarlet*** from Stibbe. He focuses on equity-linked debt work, and has particular expertise in IPO equity transactions. **Clients:** BNP Paribas; Bayerische Landesbank Girozentrale; Citibank; Lazard Frères; Marne et Champagne; Electricité de France.

Shearman & Sterling (4 ptrs, 25 asscs) Rated by clients and peers as *"a good Franco-American practice,"* the group generally acts on behalf of French issuers on the US market. Including three US partners, the Paris capital markets team advises on both debt and equity offerings and debt convertibles. Researchers were impressed by market approval for the firm's expertise in multi-jurisdictional transactions, which capitalises on the firm's ability to combine US and local law expertise.

A regular feature as issuer's counsel on IPOs, the team acted on the Wanadoo and Orange flotations, and also represented NicOx on its $31 million IPO, listed on the Nouveau Marché of the Paris Bourse.

Robert Treuhold* is an acknowledged leader for privatisations, representing large French corporates in international transactions. He served as counsel on both the Air France $778 million privatisation, and on Thomson Multimedia's $520 million privatisation.

French partner **Hervé Letréguilly*** has extensive experience of IPOs and convertible bond offerings. As counsel to Giraudy SA and its parent company Go Outdoor Systems, he led the team advising on Giraudy's $102 million high-yield note offering.

Notable debt transactions include acting as counsel to the underwriters in Pinault-Printemps-Redoute's $1,040 million convertible share offering, and representing Rhône-Poulenc and Rhodia in Rhône-Poulenc's offering of notes exchangeable into shares of Rhodia valued at $1,120 million. **Clients:** Crédit Lyonnais; Lafarge; Air France; Pinault-Printemps-Redoute; Unibail; France Telecom; NicOx; Equant N.V.

Cleary, Gottlieb, Steen & Hamilton (6 ptrs, 16 asscs) *"Visible on the equity side,"* the group focuses on complex international equity offerings for French companies and underwriters. Most matters contain some US component, and are either 144A or SEC-registered transactions, while the team also handles a large volume of IPOs for French companies listed on the Premier Marché. The group acted as counsel to the managers on Wanadoo's IPO, which included a Premier Marché listing and 144A placement in the US. Other activity in this area includes advising the underwriters on the second stage of the Thomson Multi-media privatisation, entailing a secondary offering of €1.3 billion worth of shares by the French government and a €860 million primary offering of shares by Thomson Multimedia, with an accompanying offering of convertible/exchangeable bonds. The firm has also advised leading companies on their equity offerings, including JC Decaux, Canal+ Technologies and Direct Finance.

The practice's chief luminary is *"knowledgeable"* **Pierre-Yves Chabert***, reckoned to be *"absolutely top notch for big tender offers."*

Renowned for its expertise on tier 1 preferred securities transactions, the group represented Natexis Banques Populaires in connection with a $200 million issue of Tier 1 preferred securities by a US trust established by the bank. Also represented BNP Paribas on its issue of $500 million of Tier 1 preferred securities by a US trust established by the bank. **Clients:** JC Decaux; Canal+ Technologies; Direct Finance; Morgan Stanley; Goldman Sachs; Deutsche Bank; CSFB; BNP Paribas.

Clifford Chance (3 ptrs, 3 asscs) *"Active on all types of finance,"* the firm specialises in cross-border transactions and was particularly recommended to researchers for its experience of bond issues. The group handles a large deal flow of trade receivables on a pan-European basis and advises locally on setting up multi-seller conduits. It recently advised UBS in connection with the establishment of Aventis' EMTN Programme, and acted for Lehman Bros International in connection with the creation of Alcatel's Global Euro commercial paper programme.

"Widely respected" by opponents, **Olivier Bertin-Mourot*** maintains a broad-based practice in banking, regulatory and capital markets work. He has been active in setting up international shareholder employee schemes for major French corporates Suez Lyonnais des Eaux, PPR and Sodaxo.

Richard Parolai*, an international securitisation and structured finance specialist, is esteemed by clients for *"doing an awful lot to bring Clifford Chance up in the world of securitisation."* He regularly advises on more esoteric matters, such as sophisticated synthetic CLOs, and acted for BNP Paribas in the innovative synthetic CLO involving a credit default swap transaction, which resulted in the creation of Olan Enterprises plc.

He is assisted by junior partner **Jonathan Lewis***, who handles UK securitisation and structured finance transactions, and has increasingly caught the eye of clients this year. **Clients:** Morgan Stanley; UBS; Société Générale; BNP Paribas; Crédit Lyonnais; Suez Lyonnais des Eaux.

De Pardieu Brocas Maffei & Leygonie (4 ptrs, 10 asscs) Visible in plain vanilla capital markets and derivatives work, the practice is generally associated with purely French work. At a domestic level, the team was recommended to researchers for its activity in representing major French issuers on derivative products. The market also commented approvingly on the versatility of practitioners, who handle a mix of traditional banking, securities and capital markets transactions.

"Old war horse of the Paris market" **Antoine Maffei*** has extensive capital markets' experience through years as legal advisor to the World Bank and Banque Française du Commerce Extérieur and is reputed to be *"well-liked by clients."* His expertise spans derivative products, structured finance and equity issues, and he advised Morgan Stanley Dean Witter and Davis Polk & Wardwell on French matters relating to the Dexia SA equity issuance (13.9 million ordinary shares) and acted for Bred Banques Populaires and Natexis Banques Populaires on a securities portfolio repackaging.

Pierre Minor*, former head of structured finance at BNP, sustains a mixed practice in banking, structured finance and derivatives. He acted on both the restructuring of Lazard group and the creation of the first cross-border electronic bank, 'first-e.'.

The group also has a developed employee benefits practice, acting for Crédit Agricole Indosuez on employee stock programmes for Suez Lyonnaise des Eaux and Pinault Printemps Redoute. **Clients:** Alcatel; Caisse Nationale des Caisses d'Epargne et de Prévoyance; Danone; Dexia Municipal Agency; Caisse d'Amortissement de la Dette Sociale; BNP Paribas; Société Générale; CDC Marché; European Banking Federation.

Jeantet & Associés (9 lawyers) Strongly focused on the domestic market, the firm has no dedicated capital markets team, instead handling IPO transactions through its M&A and restructuring departments. Our researchers were told by the market that the firm's profile in this area is generally considered to be declining. Despite this, *"sophisticated"* **Philippe Portier*** garners extensive commendation as a *"bright young lawyer,"* who has experience in derivatives, securitisation and equity matters. In the past year, he has acted

F

*See leaders' profiles on pages 282-295

for seller Sopartech in the €1 billion reorganisation of Labinal and cash takeover by SNECMA, and has also advised on a number of cash takeover bids on behalf of ABN AMRO and C3D.

On IPOs, the firm represented the corporate issuer on the listings of Aufeminin.com and 3A-Trade. Other notable work includes acting for Crédit Mutuel (BFCM) and BNP Paribas on the creation of a €3 billion MTN programme. The group has particular expertise in the area of insurance securitsation and recently completed trade receivable securitisation schemes for arrangers BankOne and Rabobank. **Clients:** Framatome; BFCM (Crédit Mutuel); CDC Group; Suez-Lyonnaise des Eaux; Telecom Italia; 9 Telecom.

Jones, Day, Reavis & Pogue (3 ptrs, 3 asscs) Predominantly a debt capital markets team, it has a strong reputation for advising on derivatives under French law. The team rarely acts on plain vanilla transactions, but serves as issuer's counsel in convertible bond and Euromarket offerings. Frequently seen on the US side of commercial paper and MTN transactions, the firm is also visible representing French institutions such as Société Générale and Banque Bruxelle Lambert under both English and US law. The team also advises offshore investment entities on their issues of CLOs and CBOs.

Formerly general counsel at CCF, **Philippe Billot*** is *"a respected name in capital markets and securities."* As co-chair of the firm's lending and structured finance practice, he has represented a number of private companies in securitisation transactions. The group acted for Total Fina in its issue of $49 billion shares and ADSs of Total Fina in exchange offers, registered in the United States and France, for shares and ADSs of Elf Aquitaine. Also represented arranger UBS Warburg on a $1.4 billion senior zero coupon convertible bond issue by ST Microelectronic in a global public offering. This included a 144A offering in the US and related listing on the Paris Bourse. **Clients:** UBS Warburg; Total Fina; Société Générale; Banque Bruxelle Lambert.

Lovells (2 ptrs, 5 asscs) Small capital markets team, which works closely with the firm's banking department and London office. Partners specialise in representing equity interests in IPOs and exchangeable bond issues, as well as securitisation and repackaging deals. The group represented Alstom on the $580 million securitisation for European shipyard Chantiers de l'Atlantique. Other notable work includes acting for JP Morgan Securities Ltd and Banque Nationale de Paris on the Laurent-Perrier €53 million IPO on the Second Marché of the Paris Bourse. A developed practice in debt issuance programmes was highlighted by work for EDF in a $1.5 billion Commercial Paper Programme. **Clients:** JP Morgan Securities Ltd; Alstom; Continental; Citibank; Merrill Lynch; Crédit Agricole Indosuez; Crédit Commercial de France; EDF.

Stibbe (4 ptrs, 6 asscs) Although the capital markets team suffered a setback with the departure of Patrick Bonvarlet to Freshfields Bruckhaus Deringer, researchers still detected plenty of market respect for the firm's bond issue work. The bulk of the workload consists of IPOs and domestic and international equity-linked transactions. The group advised Emme on its IPO on the Nouveau Marché. Team members are particularly active in real estate securitisation, and recently completed several for a Canadian institution, while the firm also regularly acts for institutional issuers Dexia, CNCA, LVMH and CADES on bond issues, complex securities and EMTN programmes. **Clients:** Emme; Bankgesellschaft Berlin; Dexia; CNCA; LVMH; Réseau Ferré de France.

Willkie Farr & Gallagher (3 ptrs, 3 asscs) A combined M&A and IPO practice is led by the highly regarded **Laurent Faugérolas***. He acted as underwriter counsel in Alcatel's issue of tracking stocks to its Optronics division for €1.4 billion, involving a dual listing on the Premier Marché of the Paris Bourse and Nasdaq. He is assisted by rising star **Ines Le Gris***, who served as underwriter's counsel in the primary offering of Guillemot Corporation. The group has a niche in new economy IPOs and has advised on e-business private placements and global offerings. **Clients:** Morgan Stanley; Crédit Agricole Indosuez; Lazard Frères.

Communications

FRANCE Leading firms (Communications)
1 Bird & Bird
2 De Pardieu Brocas Maffei & Leygonie
Gide Loyrette Nouel
Serra Michaud & Associés
3 Alain Bensoussan
August & Debouzy
Coudert Frères
Kahn Associés
Nomos
Willkie Farr & Gallagher
4 Bureau Francis Lefèbvre
Clifford Chance
Salans Hertzfeld & Heilbronn

Firms are listed alphabetically in each band.

Bird & Bird (8 ptrs, 30 asscs) Home to the star of the communications field, **Frédérique Dupuis-Toubol***, who is regarded by her peers as *"a reference in France."* Researchers found the firm to be the *"main competitor,"* appearing in *"one third of all disputes and deals."* Organised and efficient, this team is the market *"number one."* Covers a broad spectrum including network and service agreements, outsourcing, dispute resolution and other regulatory issues.

Equally experienced in IT law, the group worked on one of the first internet domain name disputes in France. Its international reach, supported by a respected London office, attracts banks, insurers and industrial organisations. The firm adopts a full service approach and has been strengthened by recent arrivals. **Clients:** Telecoms operators; financial institutions; industrial concerns, ISP, IT suppliers, software publishers, start-ups.

De Pardieu Brocas Maffei & Leygonie (2 ptrs, 2 asscs) **Martine Georges***, formerly of Moquet Borde, has developed an impressive telecoms practice. Described by competitors as a *"regulatory leader,"* the team is boosted by her background as head of the Direction Generale des Postes et Telecommunications and in-house counsel for the French National Telecommunications regulatory board. Active in both regulatory and corporate matters the group advises major domestic telephone operators (fixed, cable, mobile) and foreign operators interested in expanding their business into France. **Clients:** Leading international and domestic corporates.

Gide Loyrette Nouel (2 ptrs, 10 asscs) Established in the market *"with a strong regulatory practice,"* the group is led by the *"highly active"* **Olivier Cousi***. A traditional force in the audiovisual field, convergence in the hi-tech and internet sec-

FRANCE Leading individuals (Communications: Telecoms)
1 **DUPUIS-TOUBOL Frédérique** *Bird & Bird*
2 **BREBAN Yann** *Alain Bensoussan*
COUSI Olivier *Gide Loyrette Nouel*
RAPP Lucien *Serra Michaud & Associés*
3 **BLOCH François** *Willkie Farr & Gallagher*
DE LA TAILLE Benoît *Coudert Frères*
DEBOUZY Olivier *August & Debouzy*
GEORGES Martine *De Pardieu Brocas Maffei*
SERRA Claude *Serra Michaud & Associés*
Individuals are listed alphabetically in each band.

Leading individuals (Communications: IT)
1 **DUPUIS-TOUBOL Frédérique** *Bird & Bird*
2 **BENSOUSSAN Alain** *Alain Bensoussan*
FÉRAL-SCHUHL Christiane *Salans Hertzfeld*
3 **DE LA TAILLE Benoît** *Coudert Frères*
FREGET Olivier *Andersen Legal*
KAHN Daniel *Kahn Associés*
Individuals are listed alphabetically in each band.

tor is a growth area resulting in the establishment of an integrated internet and e-commerce group with an additional ten partners from M&A, competition, IP, tax, and banking. Heavyweight clients include Wanadoo. The team advised the World Bank on the implementation of new telecoms regulation in Mauritania and Algeria. **Clients:** The World Bank; Wanadoo.

Serra Michaud & Associés (1 ptr, 4 asscs) Focusing on transactional elements, interviewees agreed that the firm is traditionally focused in the telecommunications sector. The *"competent"* **Lucien Rapp*** is described as a *"key regulatory player"* while **Claude Serra*** *"handles the transactions with ease."* Clients include 200 corporates, from international blue chips to internet start-ups, TV and newspapers. The group has displayed growth in satellite and space operators and equipment manufacturers. **Clients:** Multi-national corporates.

Alain Bensoussan (1 ptr, 19 asscs) Founding partner **Alain Bensoussan*** is considered by rivals to be *"one of the first"* in the IT field having established this hi-tech boutique in 1978. **Yann Breban*** is an *"active"* player on the telecoms side and the firm's strong internet practice now accounts for over 30% of its deal flow. Involved in regulation, project management and litigation, the group is noted for its expertise in contract drafting for a client base of new entrants to the market. **Clients:** Hi-tech French companies.

August & Debouzy (3 ptrs, 7 asscs) A smaller practice whose *"reputation has grown."* Focusing on regulatory and licensing issues, the team led by the distinguished **Olivier Debouzy*** works closely with a strong corporate department. A full service approach has attracted US and European multi-nationals such as Microsoft. The IT strength lies in encryption and broad band internet matters. **Clients:** Microsoft.

Coudert Frères (2 ptrs, 4 asscs) A balanced IT and telecoms practice, where the technically astute **Benoît de la Taille*** is key to the firm's success. Supported by a strong Brussels office, a seasoned group acts mainly for new entrants. It advised Fujitsu on the establishment of a joint company with Alcatel in relation to third generation mobile phones, and represented Cable & Wireless on regulatory issues concerning stock options. It also advised Outrade.com on the provision of server architecture enabling it to provide an e-mail outsourcing service dedicated to ISP and other businesses. Advised Lucent Technologies on litigation with one of its French operator customers. Advised Neustar on the regulatory regime of pooling and profitability in France and Belgium. Worked with Covad on a range of telecommunications issues including the terms of a joint venture for the application of several wireless local loop licenses in France. **Clients:** Sprint; Lucent Technologies; Neustar; Covad.

Kahn Associés (7 ptrs, 17 asscs) Founded in 1988 this practice headed by the *"extremely focused"* **Daniel Kahn*** has become *"ever present in the IT field."* Acting primarily for e-commerce and IT companies, the firm advises on incorporation, setting-up and development as well as subsequent transactions and the development of international contracts. Working for both domestic and international clients, the firm has close ties with leading firms in America Europe and Israel. **Clients:** E-commerce and IT companies.

Nomos (2 ptrs, 9 asscs) Touted as a multi-niche practice, it is active in three areas: communications, distribution and private equity. The communications team handles clients in the entertainment, IT, telecoms, and cable fields. A growth in its internet practice has seen the team working for market leaders, AOL. **Clients:** AOL; Giroux; multi-national communications groups.

Willkie Farr & Gallagher (1 ptr, 6 asscs) Competitors and clients acknowledge that the practice is well-developed, offering expertise in internet, e-commerce, public procurement matters and power management. Previously at Clifford Chance, recent arrival **François Bloch*** brings extensive experience to the telecoms sector.

The group is also heavily involved in broadcasting, IPOs and privatisation. It is recommended for the development of an integrated corporate approach. **Clients:** Multi-national telecoms companies.

Bureau Francis Lefèbvre (1 ptr, 4 asscs) A smaller telecoms practice where the backbone lies with corporate, regulatory and competition advice to deregulated industries in France and the EU. The practice has a solid client base with major domestic players such as Tele2. **Clients:** Tele2; Canal+; Bouygues Telecom; Cegetel.

Clifford Chance (2 ptrs, 5 asscs) The Media, Computer, Communications group devotes 50% of its time to telecoms. Despite the loss of François Bloch, its *"strong brand name"* around the globe continues to attract a high proportion of overseas clients, although peers have pointed to capacity issues. Clients include start-ups, incumbents and network operators who value the team *"because of their global network."* Advised Société Generale, BNP Paribas and Crédit Agricole in the setting up of a joint venture with Cap Gemini to operate a market place on the internet providing e-procurement services. **Clients:** Nokia Mobile Phones; Amazon; Société Genérale; BNP Paribas; Credit Agricole; Carrefour.

Salans Hertzfeld & Heilbronn (4 ptrs, 8 asscs) Regarded as experts in IT, **Christiane Féral-Schuhl*** is a key player in the internet sector where competitors view her as *"one of the best."* Concentrated on the convergence between IT and telecommunications, the team is active in satellite, internet, and e-commerce transactions and regulatory issues. Telecoms accounts for around 40% of the workload, and the team is experienced in multi-jurisdictional mergers, joint ventures and satellite projects. Telecoms outsourcing transactions have been a growth area for the firm. The group represents a number of new and international operators, systems providers and investors, both in French and international transactions. Provide French regulatory advice to Teleglobe, Cignal Global Communications, Advanced Fiber Communications. **Clients:** Level Three; Teleglobe; Alcatel; SITA; GTS; Omnicom; IDT; Advanced Fiber Communications; Cignal Global Communications.

Other Notable Practitioner Rivals concede that IT practioner **Olivier Freget*** of Andersen Legal Association d'Avocats *"must be in the list,"* handling both domestic and international clients including start-ups, incumbents and e-businesses.

F

*See leaders' profiles on pages 282-295

Competition/Anti-trust

Bredin Prat (1 ptr, 2 asscs) Setting the standard, it captures the *"cream of the crop"* of cases on behalf of *"splendid corporate clients like Vivendi."* With expertise in both litigation and advisory issues, the practice is one of the few able to provide a full domestic competition capability. Unsurpassed in the opinions of interviewees, **Robert Saint-Esteben***, is regarded as a *"brilliant role model"* with *"experience in every area of competition law"* and well known for practising contentions before the competition council.

Strong on EU law, the group has a partner based in Brussels and acted before the EC on the mergers between of Vivendi, Canal+ and Seagram. Capitalising on a growth in merger compliance activity, it acted for Ernst & Young in connection with its acquisition of Cap Gemini. **Clients:** Accor; Vivendi; Cap Gemini; Bolloré; Danone; Philips; Unilever.

FRANCE Leading firms (Competition/Anti-trust)	
1	Bredin Prat
	Cleary, Gottlieb, Steen & Hamilton
2	Herbert Smith
	Vogel & Vogel
3	Freshfields Bruckhaus Deringer
	Rambaud Martel
	Stibbe
4	Clifford Chance
	Gide Loyrette Nouel
	Jeantet & Associés
	Linklaters
	Siméon & Associés
5	Coudert Frères
	Coutrelis & Associés
	DS Avocats
	Fourgoux et Associés
	Meffre & Grall

Firms are listed alphabetically in each band.

Leading individuals (Competition/Anti-trust)		
★	**SAINT-ESTEBEN Robert** *Bredin Prat*	
1	**DE LA LAURENCIE Jean-Patrice** *Norton Rose*	**LAZARUS Claude** *Herbert Smith*
	VOGEL Louis *Vogel & Vogel*	**WINCKLER Antoine** *Cleary, Gottlieb, Steen*
2	**CALVET Hugues** *Stibbe*	**COT Jean-Mathieu** *Clifford Chance*
	D'ORMESSON Olivier *Linklaters*	**GEORGES Alain** *Stibbe*
	GUNTHER Jacques-Philippe *Freshfields Bruckhaus Deringer*	
	LUCAS DE LEYSSAC Claude *DS Avocats*	**MORGAN DE RIVERY Eric** *Siméon & Associés*
3	**DONNEDIEU DE VABRES Loraine** *Jeantet*	**MAÎTRE-DEVALLON Claudine** *Rambaud Martel*
	SALZMANN Joëlle *Gide Loyrette Nouel*	**VOGEL Joseph** *Vogel & Vogel*
4	**BRUNET François** *Cleary, Gottlieb, Steen*	**COHEN-TANUGI Laurent** *Cleary, Gottlieb, Steen*
	COUTRELIS André *Coutrelis & Associés*	**DANY Mireille** *Clifford Chance*
	DE JUVIGNY Olivier *Rambaud Martel*	**DE ROUX Xavier** *Gide Loyrette Nouel*
	DEBROUX Michel *Herbert Smith*	**FOURGOUX Jean-Louis** *Fourgoux et Associés*
	PARLEANI Gilbert *Gilbert Parleani*	

Individuals are listed alphabetically in each band.

Cleary, Gottlieb, Steen & Hamilton (3 ptrs, 5 asscs) Peers acknowledge that the firm has cultivated a strong stand-alone practice active at the French and EU levels. Predictably, given the strength of its Brussels practice, much of the work is multi-jurisdictional with the *"highly respected and authoritative"* **Antoine Winckler*** moving between the two offices. Its capacity for cross border work attracts multinationals and medium sized domestic firms seeking advice on expansion abroad.

On the domestic front, the *"brilliant"* **François Brunet*** focuses on M&A and the respected **Laurent Cohen-Tanugi's*** expertise lies in telecoms and IT. The firm advised Renault on the proposed sale of its worldwide truck business to Volvo, acted for Coca-Cola on its acquisition of Orangina, and acted for Elf Acquitaine on its merger with TotalFina. Acted for Canal+ in the EU notification of the Vivendi/Seagram/Canal+ merger. **Clients:** Canal+; Coca-Cola; Renault; Vivendi; Elf Acquitaine; HSBC; DuPont; Valeo; DuPont.

Herbert Smith (1 ptr, 4 asscs) Led by *"one of the brightest competition lawyers in Paris,"* **Claude Lazarus***, the team is considered by competitors to be *"perfect, strong in counselling and litigation."* Lazarus developed a strong deregulation practice while at Jeantet and has an increasing presence on high profile cases for globally known corporates. Much of its workload involves deregulation in liberalising industries where **Michel Debroux*** is highly rated. Growth areas for the practice include sports, telecommunications and energy, currently 80% of its work. **Clients:** EDF Vivendi; CGTel; GEMS; Air France; Group Jean Claude Darmond; Coca-Cola.

Vogel & Vogel (2 ptrs, 26 asscs) Rapidly expanding, it is considered by rivals and clients to provide first rate *"regulatory and competition watch advice"* at EU and French levels. The firm advises both corporate clients and those firms seeking a second opinion. Celebrated academic **Louis Vogel*** adds to his excellent knowledge of competition law with expertise in car distribution agreements, and he is supported by his brother **Joseph Vogel***, who has a *"good reputation in EC law."* Growth is seen in e-business and in the reorganisation of distribution contracts, agriculture, machinery, boats and motor vehicles. **Clients:** VW Group; D Boug Telecom.

Freshfields Bruckhaus Deringer (1 ptr, 11 asscs) Former Gide partner **Jacques-Philippe Gunther*** (*"a future star,"*) is credited with the development of what is considered *"a young practice but high in quality."* Its reputation in the field has been strengthened by the merger with leading anti-trust operation Bruckhaus, and much of the caseload comes from international financial institutions.

The practice has diversified, undertaking anti-cartel, state aid and merger control cases and rapidly expanded into the hi-tech and telecoms sector where Gunther is noted for his expertise in deregulation. **Clients:** Gaz de France; Thomson CSF, France Télévision.

Rambaud Martel (2 ptrs, 7 asscs) Involved in a broad spectrum of competition and merger cases, it operates a balance of EU and French law. Researchers were told that the practice is *"highly specialised"* in litigation and counselling. Heading this tight-knit team is **Claudine Maître-Devallon***, with her *"good reputation in distribution."* She is supported by the young but *"extremely clever"* **Olivier de Juvigny***. The firm is active in a wide range of sectors including pharmaceutical, telecoms, agriculture, the electrical and computer industries. **Clients:** Leading international and domestic corporates.

Stibbe (3 ptrs, 10 asscs) With the *"brilliant"* **Alain Georges*** in its ranks, the firm has a sound competition practice with expertise in French privatisation and deregulatory issues. The team acted on the privatisation of Paris Airport, First Telecom, La Poste and other utilities. It is balanced by a substantial M&A practice, advising big-ticket corporates such as Accor, Value and Apple.

Distinctly international in outlook, it has a pan-European team of 30 lawyers spread across Brussels, Paris and Amsterdam. **Hugues Calvet*** is rated in the domestic market. **Clients:** La Poste; First Telecom; Paris Airport; Accor; Value; Apple.

Clifford Chance (1-2 ptrs, 6-7 asscs) A small yet high profile team focused on M&A compliance cases. The highly respected **Jean-Mathieu Cot*** who *"wrote one of the bibles of competition law,"* leads the group and a key player. **Mireille Dany*** has a *"good reputation in EC competition law."* The firm has an impressive client portfolio of both domestic and international companies. **Clients:** US financial institutions.

Gide Loyrette Nouel (4 ptrs, 15 asscs) Until recently considered to be the *"most powerful player"* on the French market, it, like many others, has suffered significant losses in the past year. Weathering *"management crises,"* the firm retains its impressive client base and a high visibility both at home and abroad. The respected, if *"underestimated,"* **Xavier De Roux*** (former member of the French Parliament) and the dynamic **Joëlle Salzmann*** are considered key to the firm's success. The group has experience in a broad range of sectors including agriculture, insurance and motor transport. **Clients:** Financial institutions.

Jeantet & Associés (1 ptr, 2 asscs) Over the last year the firm has been hit by several high profile departures including the loss of Lazarus to Herbert Smith. Researchers found that much of the work load is merger control activity led by **Loraine Donnedieu de Vabres***, a *"promising young lawyer"* with a *"good reputation for M&A."* The group concentrates on high value activity for international and French corporates with industrial groups forming a substantial part of its portfolio. Its EU competition practice is less prominent following an office closure and its departure from the Alliance of European Lawyers. **Clients:** Domestic and international corporates.

Linklaters (1 ptr, 3 asscs) Traditionally considered support for a *"splendid M&A practice,"* the team focuses on merger control, state aid and the regulation of subsidies. Supported by a strong Brussels offering, it has a European focus and handles both merger control issues at EU level and multi-jurisdictional filings outside the scope of the Commission. The market rates **Olivier D'Ormesson***, who does *"more true competition work before the council"* than many contemporaries. On the domestic front, the team has been active in deregulation in the energy sector and the internet. **Clients:** Multi-nationals and domestic corporates.

Siméon & Associés (2 ptrs, 2 asscs) The practice is split between Paris and Brussels with a combined competition department of over 30 lawyers and strength on a pan-European level. On the domestic front, the team is active in distribution, vertical agreements and litigation. Team leader **Eric Morgan de Rivery*** is described by clients as *"a US type lawyer, thorough and yet sympathetic"* and is *"especially well known in Brussels"* for his regulatory work. **Clients:** Domestic corporates.

Coudert Frères (1 assc) Rivals and clients believe that the firm is in danger of losing its *"reputation as someone significant"* with a continued loss of partners in 2000, most notably Jean-Patrice De La Laurencie's move to Norton Rose. The department is active in unfair competition (dumping, advertising) and merger control work and works closely with the Brussels office on large notifications. Clients include large industrial organisations in the food, telecoms, IT, insurance and banking sectors. **Clients:** Domestic corporates.

Coutrelis & Associés (2 ptrs, 8-9 asscs) A niche firm practicing both EU and French competition law, lead partner **André Coutrelis*** divides his time between Paris and Luxembourg. Although EC matters currently form only 5% of the practice, it remains the most high profile element. The firm has expanded its involvement in GMO work representing manufacturers, VAT cases, litigation and regulatory work for French, EU and International (WTO) food law. It acted for Haladjian in litigation against manufacturing company Caterpillar. **Clients:** BNP Paribas; Haladjian; international and domestic food and pharmaceuticals corporations.

DS Advocats **Claude Lucas de Leyssac*** heads this medium sized corporate firm with an established EU competition practice. A respected academic, he is recommended by peers as a counsellor, litigator and arbitrator, noted for his work in distribution agreements. The group has scored well with its involvement in OTC pharmaceuticals, advertising, and parallel imports. **Clients:** Domestic corporates.

Fourgoux et Associés (3 ptrs, 7 asscs) Considered to be a *"highly specialised"* practice, it focuses on distribution and the franchising side of competition law. Active in the retail of cars and the distribution of any elementary products, **Jean-Louis Fourgoux*** is the public face of the firm, rated as a *"specialist in consumer issues."* The firm is undergoing expansion into the M&A market. **Clients:** Casino; ABN AMRO.

Meffre & Grall (2 ptrs, 1 assc) Recommended for its work in consumer goods and communications issues (advertising, publishing and television) as well as information technology, construction, and electricity. Although rivals consider the firm to be more focused on distribution than competition, any imbalance should be rectified by the merger with Le Pen, Le Goff & Associés, a small competition boutique. **Clients:** Domestic corporates.

Other Notable Practitioners *"Highly experienced"* **Jean-Patrice De La Laurencie**'s* move to Norton Rose is viewed as *"a great catch"* by the market. His focus on merger compliance issues is anticipated to develop the team. As professor of law, **Gilbert Parleani*** divides his time between academia and practice where his *"extensive experience in competition law"* is offered to clients such as Gucci. Although considered to be *"theoretical rather than practical,"* his legal opinions are widely sought after.

F

*See leaders' profiles on pages 282-295

Corporate/M&A

FRANCE Leading firms (Corporate/Mergers & Acquisitions)
1 Bredin Prat
Cleary, Gottlieb, Steen & Hamilton
Darrois Villey Maillot Brochier
2 Freshfields Bruckhaus Deringer
Linklaters
Rambaud Martel
Willkie Farr & Gallagher
3 Clifford Chance
De Pardieu Brocas Maffei & Leygonie
4 Gide Loyrette Nouel
Jones, Day, Reavis & Pogue
Shearman & Sterling
Sullivan & Cromwell
Veil Armfelt Jourde La Garanderie
5 BBLP Moquet Borde & Associés
Coudert Frères
Jeantet & Associés
Skadden, Arps, Slate, Meagher & Flom LLP
Stibbe
6 Allen & Overy
Ashurst Morris Crisp
August & Debouzy
Denton Salès Vincent & Thomas
Salans Hertzfeld & Heilbronn
Siméon & Associés
Slaughter and May
White & Case LLP

Firms are listed alphabetically in each band.

Bredin Prat (14 ptrs, 18 asscs) Perceived to have *"maintained the edge"* with its depth of experience and the expertise of its *"brilliant individuals,"* who provide *"excellent structural and theoretical advice."* The *"outstanding"* **Jean-Francois Prat*** heads the practice focusing on M&A, privatisations and securities law and is supported by **Didier Martin*** (head of corporate finance) who advises investment banks including Morgan Stanley and Lazard.

Recent recruit **Sebastien Prat***, regarded as *"a legitimate rising star"* has moved to his father's firm from Jeantet where he developed clients such as Rothschilds. **Philippe Beurier***, viewed by clients as *"professional,"* the *"bright"* **Elena Baxter***, and the trusted **Dominique Bompoint*** add weight to the team.

An indisputable name for quality, the firm has a blue-chip international client base and has been active in major privatisations. It advised Vivendi on its acquisition of Seagram and its merger with Canal+ and acted as French counsel for Saatchi & Saatchi in the acquisition by Publicis. It also represented Aerospatiale-Matra in the creation of the European Aeronautic Defense and Space company (EADS). **Clients:** BNP Paribas; Cap Gemini; Danone; Fiat; Lagadère; Péchiney; Vivendi; Lazard Brothers; Morgan Stanley; Rothschilds; Aerospatiale-Matra; Saatchi & Saatchi.

Cleary, Gottlieb, Steen & Hamilton (5 ptrs, 35 asscs) Market leaders consider it to be *"one of the finest firms in Paris."* It has established a reputation for consistency and quality, present on *"all the cutting edge deals in France in the last couple of years."* Excelling in the domestic M&A market, the team advised Canal+ on the acquisition of Seagram and the reorganisation of Canal+ and Vivendi.

Leading light **Pierre-Yves Chabert*** is commonly regarded as *"one of the most high profile M&A lawyers"* in Paris with clients involved in the Elf Total merger. He is accompanied by a strong team including **Jean-Michel Tron***, thought to be *"both an M&A and tax expert,"* and the respected **Robert Bordeaux-Grouelt***.

The resources of a global network support cross border transactions. The team acted for Coca-Cola on its proposed acquisition of Orangina from Pernod Ricard, and advised Forte in its acquisition of the Meridien Hotel chain from Air France. **Clients:** HSBC Holdings; Coca-Cola Company; Nortel Networks; La Rochette; Forte.

Darrois Villey Maillot Brochier (7 ptrs, 12 asscs) Researchers found the practice to be *"high profile and specialised"* advising on the top deals in France, often in conjunction with a larger Anglo-Saxon firm. Its domestic client base is a balance of industry and banking with international corporates, predominantly from the US and Italy. The firm represented Total in the $55.34 billion Fina-Elf merger, advised France Telecom in its $35 billion bid for Orange and represented Publicis in its acquisition of Saatchi & Saatchi.

Led by the charismatic **Jean-Michel Darrois***, this impressive team includes **Alain Maillot*** *("handles clients very well")* and **Philippe Villey***, who together are considered by peers to be *"both absolutely superb, equally stars."* The *"exceptional and discreet"* **François Sureau*** is advisor to the French state on privatisation, **Olivier Diaz*** is predicted to have a *"good future,"* and M&A player **Emmanuel Brochier*** also received market approval. **Clients:** TotalFina; France Telecom; La Poste; Renault; Alcatel; Lagadère; Zannier; Monoprix; CCF Publicis.

Freshfields Bruckhaus Deringer (11 ptrs, 40 asscs) A leading player, its reputation for cross border transactions has been strengthened by its advice to DaimlerChrysler on an agreed €18 billion merger with France's Aerospatiale-Matra and Spain's CASA creating EADS, the world's third largest aerospace and defence company. Senior partner **Yves Huyghé de Mahenge*** is considered by competitors to be *"equipped to deal with complex cross border deals."*

On the domestic front, the team has seen a growth in public company M&A supported by the arrival of the *"outstanding"* **Patrick Bonvarlet*** (formerly at Stibbe) who carries a wealth of local expertise. The team also boasts the well respected **Jean-Claude Cotoni***. **Clients:** DaimlerChrysler Aerospace; Lafarge; Group Danone; Thomson CSF; CDR; Coface.

Linklaters (8 ptrs, 30 asscs) **Thierry Vassogne*** (formerly of Gide) has done much to raise the profile of this practice with a wealth of M&A experience in the domestic market. Interviewees agreed that the firm *"churns out"* big ticket transactions in Paris. Its well established cross border capacity drawing on the resources of the Alliance firms, provides M&A and restructuring advice to multi-national corporates. It advised Vizzavi (a Vodafone and Vivendi Net joint venture) on its acquisition from Libertal of its internet portal business in the Netherlands. **Jean-Marc Lefèvre*** is respected for his grasp of complex transactions. **Clients:** Vizzavi.

Rambaud Martel (6 ptrs, 12-15 asscs) Regarded by peers as the *"oldest star"* in the corporate market, managing partner **Jean-Pierre Martel*** is an M&A expert, specialising in privatisations and restructurings. **Jean-Michel Lepretre*** is well respected for his work on MBOs, and this solid team is short-listed for most of the major public and private bids in France particularly in banking. It represented Galeries Lafayette in the establishment of a partnership with INTEL, acted for Gallimard in its restructuring and the development of Gallimard Numerique, and advised Nord Est in the acquisition of Raffypack. **Clients:** BNP Paribas; Galeries Lafayette; Crédit Lyonnais; Vinci; Casino; PriceWaterhouseCoopers.

Willkie Farr & Gallagher (10 ptrs, 55 asscs) The arrival of the *"highly educated"* **Laurent Faugérolas*** (previously Jones Day) has helped to consolidate its reputation as a growing M&A firm. Although its focus remains on private equity transactions with major clients such as Goldman

FRANCE
Leading individuals (Corporate/Mergers & Acquisitions)

Band		
1	**DARROIS Jean-Michel** *Darrois Villey Maillot Brochier*	
	MARTEL Jean-Pierre *Rambaud Martel*	**MARTIN Didier** *Bredin Prat*
	PRAT Jean-Francois *Bredin Prat*	**VASSOGNE Thierry** *Linklaters*
2	**BAXTER Elena** *Bredin Prat*	**BONVARLET Patrick** *Freshfields Bruckhaus*
	BRANDFORD GRIFFITH Henri *Veil Armfelt Jourde*	**CHABERT Pierre-Yves** *Cleary, Gottlieb, Steen*
	FAUGÉROLAS Laurent *Willkie Farr & Gallagher*	**MAILLOT Alain** *Darrois Villey Maillot Brochier*
	PAYAN Daniel *Willkie Farr & Gallagher*	**SERVAN-SCHREIBER Pierre** *Skadden, Arps, Slate*
	TRON Jean-Michel *Cleary, Gottlieb, Steen & Hamilton*	
3	**BORDE Dominique** *BBLP Moquet Borde*	**BROCAS Thierry** *De Pardieu Brocas*
	DE PARDIEU Charles-Henri *De Pardieu Brocas*	**DIDIER Edouard** *Allen & Overy*
	FORSCHBACH Thomas *Ashurst Morris Crisp*	**HURSTEL Daniel** *Willkie Farr & Gallagher*
	LEYGONIE Jean *De Pardieu Brocas Maffei*	**MAZET Gérard** *Sullivan & Cromwell*
	PRAT Sebastien *Bredin Prat*	**SCHOEN Thierry** *Clifford Chance*
	VEIL Jean *Veil Armfelt Jourde La Garanderie*	**VILLEY Philippe** *Darrois Villey Maillot Brochier*
4	**AUGUST Gilles** *August & Debouzy*	**BEAUVISAGE Patrick** *Stibbe*
	BEURIER Philippe *Bredin Prat*	**BOMPOINT Dominique** *Bredin Prat*
	BONNASSE Antoine *Gide Loyrette Nouel*	**BORDEAUX-GROUELT Robert** *Cleary, Gottlieb, Steen*
	BROCHIER Emmanuel *Darrois Villey Maillot*	**BUHART Jacques** *Coudert Frères*
	COTONI Jean-Claude *Freshfields Bruckhaus*	**DIAZ Olivier** *Darrois Villey Maillot Brochier*
	DJEHANE Youssef *Gide Loyrette Nouel*	**EPSTEIN Jacques** *Shearman & Sterling*
	FOLLIE Robert *Lovells*	**HUYGHÉ DE MAHENGE Yves** *Freshfields Bruckhaus*
	LEBEUF Martin *De Pardieu Brocas Maffei*	**LEFÈVRE Jean-Marc** *Linklaters*
	LEPRETRE Jean-Michel *Rambaud Martel*	**SALÈS Jacques** *Denton Salès Vincent & Thomas*
	SARRAILHÉ Philippe *Ashurst Morris Crisp*	**SUREAU François** *Darrois Villey Maillot Brochier*
	TERRIER Georges *Jeantet & Associés*	**TREUHOLD Robert** *Shearman & Sterling*
	VERKHOVSKOY Pierre *Clifford Chance*	**WEHRLI Yves** *Clifford Chance*

Individuals are listed alphabetically in each band.

Sachs and Lazards, the firm has *"aggressively"* captured a share of public company M&A.

The formidable team is led by **Daniel Hurstel*** who represented Lehman Brothers in its purchase of the real estate portfolio of Vivendi. *"One of the best"* **Daniel Payan***, rated for both M&A and LBOs, advised Cinven and BNP Paribas in their acquisition of United Biscuits. The team acted for TotalElfFina on its FF18 billion buyout tender offer on the remaining 5% of Elf Acquitane's capital. **Clients:** TotalFinaElf; Deutsche Bank; UBS Capital; Bols; Bridgepoint Capital; Lycos Europe; Lehman Brothers; Cinven; BNP Paribas.

Clifford Chance (2 ptrs, 40 asscs) A *"good M&A practice,"* the merger with Rogers & Wells and Pünder has increased its capacity for cross border transactions. It is advising British Airways on the sale of its 86% of Participation Aeronautique to Taitbout Antibes. **Thierry Schoen*** acted on the Premier Marché listing of EADS shares. The market also recommended **Yves Wehrli*** and **Pierre Verkhovskoy***, the latter advised GE Capital on

its investment in Travelprice.com. The arrival of two partners from Darrois Villey has enabled the firm to develop a domestic client base that includes BNP Paribas and Société Générale. **Clients:** Duke Street Capital; Société Générale; BNP Paribas; Crédit Agricole; Cap Gemini; Chase Capital Partners; Wartsila; Deutsche Telekom/Online.

De Pardieu Brocas Maffei & Leygonie (7 ptrs, 18 asscs) Described as the *"most successful of the Franco-French firms"* it has developed a strong corporate department focused on the finance and banking sides of M&A. Senior partner **Charles-Henri De Pardieu*** has worked extensively in acquisitions and restructurings for major French and foreign industrial and financial groups. **Jean Leygonie***, formerly at Moquet Borde, has a wealth of experience in M&A, **Thierry Brocas*** is well regarded for his finance and banking expertise and **Martin LeBeuf*** is recommended for structured finance and M&A. The team advises issuers and investment banks. Represented Crédit Lyonnais in their joint venture with CCF

with respect to certain leasing activities. **Clients:** AGF; Crédit Lyonnais; Pechiney; Rentokil.

Gide Loyrette Nouel (15 ptrs, 40 asscs) One of the oldest corporate firms, it is judged to be *"back on track"* after the loss of partners to Linklaters. Strength lies in three areas; listed companies, privatisations and restructurings, and M&A. The firm has witnessed a growth in the size of its transactions.

"Excellent in quality and productivity" **Youssef Djehane*** is said to be *"leading the way."* He acted on the Vivendi and Seagram merger, one of the largest transactions of the year. The well-respected **Antoine Bonnasse*** negotiated a complex squeeze out procedure for the Bank of International Settlement in its attempt to remove all minority shareholders from the bank's share capital. **Clients:** Seagrams; Bank of International Settlement; Swissair; Lycos Multi-Media.

Jones, Day, Reavis & Pogue (12 ptrs, 43 asscs) Highly rated for its negotiated-deals practice boasting clients such as La Poste and Avantis, it draws on the resources of the network attracting high profile multi-nationals. It advised Ernst & Young on the $13 billion sale of their consulting business to Cap Gemini. Despite such high profile successes, it suffered the loss of Laurent Fugerolas, creating a gap in the corporate team which has yet to be filled. **Clients:** TotalFina; Ernst & Young; Aventis; Rodhia; La Poste; Hachette; Société Générale.

Shearman & Sterling (9 ptrs, 35 asscs) Renowned for his expertise in IPOs, **Bob Treuhold*** is key to the firm's high profile. The team advised Rhodea in its acquisition of Chirex pharmaceutical company and advised France Telecom in its negotiations with Orange. The practice has been strengthened by the arrival of **Jacques Epstein*** and his team from Siméon & Associés providing extensive experience in corporate M&A. **Clients:** Rhodea; France Telecom; Alcatel.

Sullivan & Cromwell (4 ptrs, 17 asscs) With offices in New York and across Europe, this firm is well placed for cross border merger work. The team advised Cap Gemini on its acquisition by Ernst & Young and represented Olivetti in its acquisition of Telecom Italia. It also advised Vodafone AirTouch in its acquisition of Mannesman and the subsequent sale of Orange to France Telecom. The arrival of former Jeantet partner **Gérard Mazet***, regarded by rivals as *"one of the most intelligent lawyers in Paris,"* completes the corporate team after Pierre Servan-Scheiber's move to Skadden Arps. **Clients:** Cap Gemini;

*See leaders' profiles on pages 282-295

Olivetti; Société Générale; Elf Acquitaine; Vodafone AirTouch.

Veil Armfelt Jourde La Garanderie (5 ptrs, 20 asscs) Considered to be a *"nice practice"* dealing with *"high profile deals."* Experts in hostile take-overs, managing partner **Jean Veil*** is renowned as a corporate litigator with a *"good list of contacts."* The team acted as French counsel to Publicis on its $4 billion merger with Saatchi & Saatchi. The *"smart and aggressive"* **Henri Brandford Griffith*** is highly recommended for his work on large scale M&A. The firm advised BNP Paribas and Allianz on the public takeover bid for AGF. **Clients:** Publicis; Bull; Aérospatiale; Crédit Lyonnais; BNP Paribas.

F

BBLP Moquet Borde & Associés (5 ptrs, 28 asscs) A traditional firm, currently undergoing a major restructure following the move of several partners (including Jean Leygonie to De Pardieu Brocas.) It retains a strong reputation for corporate work. **Dominique Borde*** heads a practice active in all industrial areas and part of the BBLP international partnership. The practice has increased its capacity to deal with complex transactions. **Clients:** Leading domestic and international corporates.

Coudert Frères (12 ptrs, 10 asscs) Founded in 1853, its long-established domestic reputation is complemented by an international outlook, with offices in 16 countries and over 80% of the client base originating overseas. Noted for cross border transactions, the backbone of the firm lies in the telecoms sector including French giant Bouygues Telecom. It acts for foreign banks, large credit institutions and French issuers with a corporate team which doubled in size over the last year. **Jacques Buhart*** is the team's leading light. **Clients:** Leading international corporates and financials.

Jeantet & Associés (5 ptrs, 15 asscs) An *"excellent name"* in the French market currently undergoing reorganisation after the departure of several senior partners and the failed merger negotiations with White & Case. The market awaits the outcome, although the team continues to be active with **Georges Terrier*** known for *"important EADS transactions."*

Over two thirds of its client base is overseas and its strength lies in cross border work particularly between France and Germany. The firm advised Suez-Lyonnaise des Eaux in the merger of its cable activities with France Telecom and Noos and acted for BSCH in its joint ventures with Société Générale. **Clients:** Coca-Cola Enterprise; BNP Parisbas; Suez-Lyonnaise des Eaux; Vivendi Enviroment; Eastman Kodak.

Skadden, Arps, Slate, Meagher & Flom LLP (3 ptrs, 15 asscs) **Pierre Servan-Schreiber*** heads a corporate department that focuses almost exclusively on international acquisition and corporate finance. The team advised Gucci in its acquisition of Boucheron and acted for NTL on its acquisition of a majority stake in Noos, the largest cable advisor in France. With an outstanding global network, it has strength in cross border transactions. The firm acted as counsel to ABN AMRO Rothschilds and Deutsche Bank as lead underwriters in the IPO of EADS. **Clients:** Gucci; ABN AMRO; Rothschilds; Deutsche Bank; NTL.

Stibbe (15 ptrs, 35 asscs) Recovering from the departure of senior partner Patrick Bonvarlet for Freshfields, the firm is a leading M&A light with an international outlook. It works closely with offices in the Netherlands and Belgium. The practice has seen an increase in both the size and number of transactions over the last year. Interviewees noted **Patrick Beauvisage*** as the key player at the firm. The team is advising Atlas Venture, BarTech, and Goldman Sachs in their investment in Ebazaar. **Clients:** Atlas Venture; Bartech; Goldman Sachs.

Allen & Overy (4 ptrs, 14 asscs) A *"serious competitor"* of the top firms in Paris with offices in Germany, the Netherlands and the United Kingdom. All-rounder **Edouard Didier*** is part of a strong domestic practice that has worked big ticket deals in France. It represented Cable & Wireless on its acquisition of the Softway group and advised Goldman Sachs International on the corporate aspects of Elf's merger with TotalFina. **Clients:** Cable & Wireless; Barclays Bank; Goldman Sachs International; Sdage Group; Exxon Mobil; Mobil Oil Francais.

Ashurst Morris Crisp (8 ptrs, 48 asscs) Private M&A transactions are the mainstay of this practice led by solid legal players, **Thomas Forschbach*** and **Philippe Sarrailhé***. Considered by competitors to be *"active but still young,"* the firm is anticipated to grow across the board. The firm advised Goldman Sachs on the FF7.3 billion financing of Autodistribution's public bid for Finelist in the UK. On the domestic front it assisted Intermediate Capital Group in the FF3.2 billion bid led by ABN AMRO for De Dietrich, the French electricals group, and acted for Crédit Lyonnais in the IPO of Hubwoo.com on the Nouveau Marché. **Clients:** Goldman Sachs; BNP Paribas; Giruady; Affelou (optical retail chain); Capital Group.

August & Debouzy (2 ptrs, 36 asscs) A young firm striving *"to reach the first league."* Competitors view founding partner **Gilles August*** to be the driving force behind the team. Clients are found in all sectors including industry, IT, telecommunications, entertainment, tourism and banking. Operating at the highest level, the firm represented Morgan Stanley Dean Witter on NTL's €1.5 billion acquisition of 49% of Noos' stock held by French Telecom. It also acted in the restructuring of the French newspaper, Libération and the sale of stock to outside investors. **Clients:** Morgan Stanley Dean Witter; Deutsche Bank; Libération; Nexity; Microsoft; Vivendi; Twentieth Century Fox.

Denton Salès Vincent & Thomas (5 ptrs, 11 asscs) The recent merger between partners from Salés Vincent, Denton Wilde Sapte and Thomas & Associés is hoped to bring together sound corporate expertise with Denton's international client base. Competitors have voiced concerns over the compatibility of the respective firms. Trained at Cleary Gottlieb, **Jacques Salès*** has the highest profile and recently acted on Bausch & Lomb's FF1.6 billion acquisition of French Chauvin pharmaceuticals group. It has a balanced domestic and overseas client base covering the pharmaceuticals, energy and advertising sectors. **Clients:** Bausch & Lomb; Havas Advertising; France Telecom; EDF.

Salans Hertzfeld & Heilbronn (12 ptrs, 40 asscs) Reaping the benefits of its recent merger with Christy & Viener (New York) and IT boutique FG & Associés, the firm is judged by competitors as a *"highly competent operator."* In addition to classic M&A transactions, it has expanded into the IT and the internet field. Offices in New York, London and Eastern Europe give it an excellent cross border capacity. It represented Lycos Europe in its acquisition as a stock deal of Multimania and advised on the French aspects of the merger between Pfizer and Warner-Lambert. **Clients:** Lycos Europe; Pfizer; Laird Group.

Siméon & Associés (7 ptrs, 43 asscs) A *"traditional"* firm with a long-standing reputation in Paris for M&A. The loss of several corporate partners has been judged by peers to be a *"knock but not a drama."* The firm retains its solid reputation for M&A and restructurings. **Clients:** Leading domestic corporates.

Slaughter and May (6 ptrs, 30 asscs) A small but *"high quality"* practice that is active with its domestic and foreign blue-chip client base. The London office feeds through a steady deal flow and the team is active in traditional M&A, restructuring and joint ventures. **Clients:** Vivendi Enviroment; Ernst & Young; Société Foncière Lyonnaise; CGIP; SNECMA.

White & Case LLP (10 ptrs, 30 asscs) Although the real focus of the firm is financing, it has a small but respected M&A practice. The arrival of a partner from Moquet Borde, dedicated solely to M&A should see the practice increase. The majority of its clients remain financial institutions. **Clients:** Domestic and international financial institutions.

Other Notable Practitioner Robert Follie* of Lovells is recommended for his work in acquisitions and joint ventures.

Project Finance

FRANCE
Leading firms (Project Finance)

Band	Firm
1	Clifford Chance
	Freshfields Bruckhaus Deringer
	Gide Loyrette Nouel
	White & Case LLP
2	Herbert Smith
	Linklaters
3	Bureau Francis Lefèbvre
	Cleary, Gottlieb, Steen & Hamilton
	Coudert Frères
	Stibbe

Firms are listed alphabetically in each band.

Leading individuals (Project Finance)

Band	Individual
1	**ANDRIANI Bertrand** *Linklaters*
	ELLAND-GOLDSMITH Michael *Clifford Chance*
	FONTAINE Emmanuel *Gide Loyrette Nouel*
	GIUSTINI Anthony *White & Case LLP*
2	**BONVARLET Patrick** *Freshfields Bruckhaus*
	BRIMSON Neil *Herbert Smith*
	RIGGS John *White & Case LLP*
	VILANOVA Richard *Sullivan & Cromwell*
3	**BASDEVANT Dominique** *Stibbe*
	CROTHERS John *Gide Loyrette Nouel*
	HUSE Joseph *Freshfields Bruckhaus*
	LECAT Jean-Jacques *Bureau Francis Lefèbvre*
	SALBAING Christian *Freshfields Bruckhaus*

Individuals are listed alphabetically in each band.

Clifford Chance (1 ptr, 7 asscs) The retirement of a senior practitioner and the loss of another partner to a position in industry have left the project finance team a little short of experience. Nevertheless, many still perceive the practice to have the necessary *"critical mass"* to keep it in its top band position. The group is seen to benefit greatly from the reputation and resources of the *"powerhouse"* London office, and is renowned for handling many major French infrastructure projects, often financed by complex securitisations.

"Fabulous lawyer" **Michael Elland-Goldsmith*** heads the group and was recommended to researchers as *"the name that attracts the business."* Said to *"know everything about financing anything on rails,"* his *"reputation is gold-plated."* He and his team handle most aspects of projects, from documentation to arranging financing for banks and sponsor institutions, with particular emphasis on rail and road infrastructure and transport projects.

The group has been appointed by the Franco-Spanish inter-governmental commission, which is charged with preparing a concession for the international section of the high-speed train link between Madrid and Paris. Other infrastructure projects include preliminary work on the Franco-Italian rail link between Lyon and Torino, and continued work on a buried Franco-Spanish aqueduct, designed to bring water from the Rhone Valley to Barcelona. Further afield, the group has acted on an IPP in Oman for French lenders, a telecoms project financing in East Africa for development banks, and a hotel financing in Warsaw for the Caisse des Dépôt's new commercial bank subsidiary.

Described as *"a creative force on municipality projects,"* the firm also undertakes a substantial number of French domestic projects, financed by French banks and involving administrative contract law. The team is currently advising the French Ministry of Transport on a motorway project at Millau. **Clients:** Franco-Spanish inter-governmental commission; French Ministry of Transport; ABN-AMRO; BNP Paribas; CDC Finance.

Freshfields Bruckhaus Deringer (5 ptrs, 11 asscs) A mixed team of French, US and UK qualified lawyers acts principally for sponsors, although it is seeing increased work on behalf of lenders. The group undertakes a substantial volume of project finance for large French utilities EDF, GDF, Lyonnaise des Eaux and Vivendi. Recent French domestic work includes two electricity projects with financing on a non-recourse basis. Particularly active in Francophone Africa, the firm has also advised on major projects in Asia, Latin America and Eastern Europe.

Christian Salbaing* *"takes French sponsors all around the world"* and has a solid reputation for telecoms, oil, gas and water projects. He has been particularly visible on projects in China, working alongside the firm's Hong Kong and Beijing offices.

Practice head **Joseph Huse*** has extensive expertise in construction law, and specialises in international and French infrastructure projects. The recent acquisition of former Stibbe partner **Patrick Bonvarlet***, a corporate practitioner who made his name in the field through his work on EuroDisney, is expected by competitors to reinforce the group's strength in the area.

The team has been chosen to advise on the KEDO nuclear project in North Korea, and has completed a number of energy projects in Brazil and Mexico. Other notable work includes a regasification project in India and a variety of energy projects in the Czech and Slovak Republics. **Clients:** EDF; GDF; COFACE; Lyonnaise des Eaux; Vivendi.

Gide Loyrette Nouel (6 ptrs, 9 asscs) An expanding mixed Anglo-French team with transactional capabilities under both civil and common law, which was recommended to our researchers as *"the French firm that does more than anyone else in project finance."* Although Paris-based, approximately two-thirds of the group's activity is derived from projects outside of France. The firm is well known for energy work in China and the arrival of a practitioner from the firm's Beijing office is predicted by rivals to enhance the group's reputation in this area. The team is led by *"versatile"* **Emmanuel Fontaine***, who specialises in water and power projects, and is known for his relationship with French and American banks. His team has built up a substantial electricity practice, and recently advised the sponsors of a 600MW combined cycle power plant in Dunkirk France, the first IPP under the new French electricity legislation. Other IPP projects include acting on behalf of the sponsors of a 500MW combined cycle power plant in Iran, a BOT project financed on a limited recourse basis.

John Crothers* (formerly counsel to the EBRD) has considerable experience of project financing in Eastern Europe and former Soviet

*See leaders' profiles on pages 282-295

FRANCE
Leading individuals
(Project Finance: Francophone Africa)

1
ANDRIANI Bertrand *Linklaters*
ANDRIEUX Jean-Pierre *Bureau Francis Lefèbvre*
BRABANT Stéphane *Herbert Smith*
GIUSTINI Anthony *White & Case LLP*
KROTOFF François *Gide Loyrette Nouel*
LAURIOL Thierry *Jeantet & Associés*
PETILON Jean-Claude *Coudert Frères*
VIGNAUD Jean-Pierre *Cleary, Gottlieb*

Individuals are listed alphabetically in each band.

Union countries. He regularly advises UNIDO on structuring concession and BOT laws, most recently in relation to public/private partnerships in Eastern Europe and the Balkans. **François Krotoff***, *"an old Africa hand,"* has comprehensive experience of African oil and mining projects.

The group has recently been active on a number of outsourcing and privatisation projects in Africa in water, energy and telecoms. These include advising the Lagos State government on a private sector participation in the water sector, and counselling Agence Nationale de Régulation de Télécommunications du Maroc on the review of the telecommunications licences of Maroc Telecom following privatisation. On infrastructure financings, the group has been active in toll motorway projects in areas as widespread as Poland (A2 Motorway), Philippines (North Luzon Expressway), South Korea (Taejon Riverside Expressway) and France (A26). **Clients:** Vivendi; ABB; Bouygues; IFC; EBRD; Suez Lyonnais des Eaux.

White & Case LLP (3 ptrs, 7 asscs) An internationally-oriented project finance practice works closely with the firm's London and New York teams, providing both public and private law coverage in energy, telecoms, and privatisation projects. Many projects involve co-financing structures on behalf of a variety of lenders. The team handles all aspects of project finance documentation, including security package and financing documentation.

Anthony Giustini* was recommended to our researchers as *"one of the principal lawyers in France for energy and natural resources,"* and acts as co-head of the firm's project finance group for Europe, Middle East and Africa. Said by clients to combine an Anglo-American approach with civil law expertise, his projects experience includes commercial bank finance, export credit finance, insurance guarantees and multi-lateral organisation financing, often in high political risk areas. He is widely acclaimed as a Francophone Africa specialist, advised one of the lenders for the financing of the Chad-Cameroon oil pipeline, and represented a consortium in its bids for the development and financing of a second GSM network in Morocco. The team draws also upon the vast experience of *"éminence grise"* **John Riggs***, a highly respected project finance practitioner who now occupies a largely managerial position within the group.

The firm acted as lender's counsel on the financing of an Abidjan toll bridge in Côte d'Ivoire, advised a consortium bidding to develop and finance toll roads in Portugal, and represented the project company on the financing of the public waterworks in Manila. **Clients:** Société Générale; International Finance Group; Exim-Bank; CDC; Crédit Lyonnais; BNP Paribas; Proparco; Suez Lyonnais des Eaux.

Herbert Smith (2 ptrs, 10 asscs) A largely French law-oriented practice, which is felt by competitors to complement the common law strength of the firm's London office. The team receives recognition for its formidable expertise in Africa, which comprises approximately 60-70% of the project finance team's activity. Advising throughout Northern, Central and West Africa, the firm has experience of oil and gas, mining, water, electricity, infrastructure and construction projects.

Neil Brimson*, managing partner of the Paris office, has wide experience of cross-border corporate and finance work, with particular emphasis on the oil and gas industry. His practice has a slightly more European focus, although he is also active in many of the firm's large African transactions. He has served as advisor to the Eurotunnel project since its inception in 1987, both on the original financings and the re-engineering of part of Eurotunnel's debt. Peers praised him to researchers for the *"tremendous project finance experience and know-how,"* which makes him *"a driving force in France."* His work on other European-based transactions include advising EDF on the creation and operation of EDF Trading, the company's energy trading joint venture with Louis Dreyfus.

Stéphane Brabant*, *"a specialist in African energy and natural resources,"* has done much to develop the practice since arriving with a team of African specialists from PwC in 1998. The group has a high profile in projects relating to extractive industries and handles the tax and legal aspects of project finance, as well as contract negotiations. The firm acted for the banks, led by Rothschild, on the financing of a gold project in Mali, valued at $100 million, and recently closed an oil agreement between the Moroccan national company ONAREP and Enterprise Oil and its partners Kerr McGuee and Energy Africa. On the infrastructure side, the firm was appointed to advise the banks on the FF310 million financing of a mining industrial project in Gabon. **Clients:** AEF; EDF.

Linklaters (2 ptrs, 8 asscs) A comprehensive projects practice, covering all aspects of project development and finance, works in close co-operation with the firm's London headquarters. The Paris group undertakes a number of projects in France and Francophone Africa that are sponsored by French institutions.

The team is said to be dominated by *"major project finance presence"* **Bertrand Andriani***, extolled to researchers as *"one of the smartest lawyers in Paris."* Although also a noted presence on structured finance deals, he receives widespread commendation for his expertise in the mining and hydrocarbon sectors.

The firm has continued to advise on the Transnational Cameroon-Chad Pipeline Project, acting for a consortium of three major oil companies (Exxon, Petronas and Chevron.) Other African work includes representing the Anglo American Corporation of South Africa on the negotiation of a joint venture agreement with a Moroccan mining company for the development of a copper mine in Morocco. In France, the group acted for Dolphin Telecom on the financing of its French ESMR network, and continues to represent the Agent Banks on the Eurotunnel project financing.

In Eastern Europe, the firm frequently acts on behalf of the EBRD, advising them on the concession-based project financing of the water and waste services of the Municipality of Sofia in Bulgaria, and on the financing of the construction of industrial warehouses in Irde, Romania. **Clients:** Exxon; Anglo American Corporation of South Africa; EBRD.

Bureau Francis Lefèbvre (3 ptrs, 3 asscs) A domestic firm with *"small offices in every city,"* it is seen by the market to have limited scope for international transactions, but was consistently recommended to researchers for its high volume of small-ticket financing throughout France. The firm does not possess a dedicated project finance practice, instead drawing on practitioners from construction and administrative law departments who handle projects through a framework of contracts rather than loan agreements. **Jean-Jacques Lecat***, well known for his projects work in Eastern Europe, advises on multi-utility municipal services contracts, and has acted on telecom privatisations in Macedonia and the Balkans, assisted by the firm's small outposts in Romania and Moscow. **Jean-Pierre Andrieux*** specialises in domestic and African projects, and is seen to contribute considerable tax expertise to the department. The group was appointed as consultants to the French government on the Galileo satellite project. **Clients:** French government.

Cleary, Gottlieb, Steen & Hamilton (2 ptrs, 4 asscs) Specialising in privatisation and emerging country government work, the projects group is led by respected Francophone Africa specialist **Jean-Pierre Vignaud***. Most of the group's project finance work falls within the mining, oil and utilities sectors, and shows particular emphasis on Africa.

The firm recently represented the Republic of Congo on a number of matters, including its privatisation of the water and electricity sectors, a eucalyptus forest reorganisation and restructuring, and several large structured finance projects based on oil production. Also acted for the governments of Cameroon and Romania on the privatisation of their respective electricity distribution sectors.

Other work saw the firm continue its representation of Air Afrique, owned by 11 Central and West African governments, on its privatisation process. **Clients:** National governments; Air Afrique.

Coudert Frères (2 ptrs, 4 asscs) Frequently seen acting on energy and natural resources projects throughout Africa and North Africa, the group has the advantage of calling on the services of three New York bar qualified lawyers from Togo, Chad and the Ivory Coast.

Jean-Claude Petilon* was recommended to researchers as a *"four star"* lawyer by clients and peers, and has long experience of African project finance. A Washington DC qualified lawyer, he spent several years as legal advisor to the President of the Republic of Zaire. He leads a team that has been involved in a number of telecoms privatisations in Africa, most recently in Togo and Chad.

In the mining sector, the group represented private mining clients in Niger and Burkina Faso on a project financing for the creation of gold mines, and advised the African Development Bank on the financing of iron ore extraction projects in Mauritania. **Clients:** African Development Bank.

Stibbe (3 ptrs, 4 asscs) The practice has had a shaky year, following the departure of leading lights Patrick Bonvarlet and Richard Vilanova. A historic reputation in projects, which dates back to the EuroDisney and Eurotunnel projects is now considered by the market to be under threat. However, the group remains rated for its experience in structured recourse and non-recourse financing applied to cross-border projects work.

Dominique Basdevant* was recommended to researchers for *"keeping the practice alive,"* with his work on non-recourse infrastructure finance and real estate finance. He recently advised bank syndicates on a wind-powered electrical project in Morocco, and a co-generation project in France. The firm also acted on the refinancing of a real estate acquisition for the Caisse de Dépôt et Classement de Quebec. **Clients:** Crédit Agricole Indo-Suez; Caisse de Dépôt et Classement de Quebec; ELF; Eurofima.

Other Notable Practitioners The latest defection from Stibbe is finance specialist **Richard Vilanova***, who moved to the Paris office of Sullivan & Cromwell in early 2001. He is well known for his work on the project financing of Eurotunnel, and interviewees expect his new firm to gain a greatly improved profile for project finance as a result of his move.

Thierry Lauriol* of Jeantet et Associés was rated for his energy and natural resources projects work for OHADA treaty countries in Africa. He has been involved in a number of gas and electricity liberalisation projects in both Europe and Africa.

F

Tax

Bureau Francis Lefèbvre (32 ptrs, 82 asscs) Considered by competitors to be *"almost the tax administration,"* the firm acts as a *"reference"* for many clients with its *"concentration of tax lawyers."* Half the firm is devoted to domestic and international tax issues and it has strong links with Madrid-based Briones Alonso, and a further network of international offices. It has close ties to the tax authority with partners formerly part of the French administration.

The firm's key strength is its wealth of first rate players. **Bruno Gouthière*** *"has a strong background"* in the civil service while **Jean-Claude Bouchard*** is a noted *"VAT specialist."* **Renaud Streichenberger*** is *"recognised as one of, if not the, leading lawyer in France,"* the *"expert,"* **Henri Bardet*** is *"technically good"* and *"excellent"* **Jean-Pierre Andrieux*** finds his niche in francophone countries. The market also rated the expertise of **Pierre-Sebastien Thill*** and **Pierre-Jean Douvier***. Lacking the corporate clout of Anglo-French competitors, it has *"difficulties being in the whole transaction,"* and yet dominates the specialism. **Clients:** Leading domestic and international corporates.

Andersen Legal Association d'Avocats (23 ptrs, 230 asscs) *"One of the top boutiques"* for tax in France, researchers found that competitors and clients admired its *"great capacity."* Although the offering is occasionally thought to take a *"standardised approach,"* it has developed an integrated tax and corporate team.

Dedicated teams focus on individual areas such as banking, insurance and telecoms covering VAT, transfer pricing, customs and litigation. The *"professional and dynamic"* **Claire Acard*** is a *"specialist on tax reorganisation in France,"* while **Marie-Hélène Raffin*** is described as *"excellent"* and the respected **Yann de Kergos*** focuses on pharmaceuticals. **Clients:** Domestic and international corporates.

Cleary, Gottlieb, Steen & Hamilton (3 ptrs, 8 asscs) A smaller *"excellent"* practice that has *"succeeded in being involved in major transactions."* Peers agreed that the team undertakes *"sophisticated tax work."* Closely tied to the corporate department, its key players, *"creative"* **Jean-Michel Tron*** and **Arnaud de Brosses***, bridge the gap.

Viewed as deal focused, it is increasingly involved in restructuring and general counsel. The team is supported by a global network of offices and enjoys a strong international client base that accounts for around 50% of the workload. **Pascal Coudin*** (formerly Jeantet) has consolidated a department that already boasts the *"excellent"* **Gilles Entraygues***. **Clients:** Multinational corporates.

Allen & Overy (1 ptr, 4 asscs) Considered *"a new player"* on the tax market, it has been boosted by the arrival of the *"creative"* **Siamak Mostafavi*** (formerly Gide.) *"One of the best in his field,"* he has shaped the focus of the team with his *"specialism in financial products"* and the area now accounts for 55-75% of the workload. Concentrating on corporate and finance related tax mat-

*See leaders' profiles on pages 282-295

FRANCE Leading firms (Tax)
1 Bureau Francis Lefèbvre
2 Andersen Legal Association d'Avocats
Cleary, Gottlieb, Steen & Hamilton
3 Allen & Overy
Baker & McKenzie
Clifford Chance
Freshfields Bruckhaus Deringer
HSD Ernst & Young
Jeantet & Associés
Jones, Day, Reavis & Pogue
KPMG Fidal
Linklaters
Cabinet Turot
Veil Armfelt Jourde La Garanderie
4 BBLP Moquet Borde & Associés
Coudert Frères
Landwell
Mesny et Associés
Slaughter and May
Stibbe
Tirard Naudin
Willkie Farr & Gallagher
5 Denton Salès Vincent & Thomas
Gide Loyrette Nouel
Ginestié Paley-Vincent & Associés
Shearman & Sterling
Watson, Farley & Williams
White & Case LLP

Firms are listed alphabetically in each band.

ters, the majority of clients are banks and also large domestic firms. **Clients:** Financial institutions; banks; domestic firms.

Baker & McKenzie (2 ptrs, 12 asscs) Former lecturer, **Pierre-Yves Bourtourault*** is regarded by peers as an *"excellent tax lawyer,"* and a key player in the development of the firm. Strong in M&A and cross border transactions, the team can draw on the global and regional experience of the firm's international network. The heart of the firm is in financial transactions, restructurings, transfer pricing and stock option plans, and it has seen a growth in environmentally focused tax relief. **Clients:** Leading international corporates.

Clifford Chance (2 ptrs, 12 asscs) The highly regarded **Eric Davoudet*** heads a department reputed for its *"specialised financial work."* It has become *"larger and more visible,"* and acted on most of the major employee share schemes launched in 2000. Structured finance tax work includes tax driven products developed for major investment banks and the team has been involved in tax deductible Tier One capital issues by French banks. It is also active in international tax planning, restructurings, M&A and public offers. **Clients:** JP Morgan; Merill Lynch; Schroders; Lasalle Investment Management; Carrefour; Société Générale.

Freshfields Bruckhaus Deringer (3 ptrs, 7 asscs) Researchers found it to be a *"busy and expanding tax department."* The team plays an essential support role for the M&A and finance practice with a strong client base of financial institutions. **Eric Thomas*** is regarded by competitors as an *"expert in securitisation work"* which forms over half of the practice. **James Vaudoyer*** is seen to be *"heavily involved in management"* and works closely with the firm's foreign offices. Recent acquisition from Gide, **Antoine Colonna D'Istria***, is *"a first rate tax lawyer"* and *"should be a positive move,"* as the firm attempts to increase its domestic client base. **Clients:** Pechiney (Luxembourg); France Télévision; NRJ; GDF; BNP Paribas; BLB (German Bank.)

HSD Ernst & Young (50 ptrs, 400 asscs) The *"excellent"* **Patrick Dibout*** is valued as *"a brain,"* and a key player in the market. The team advises on a broad range of VAT and customs services, and on M&A structuring and transfer pricing. As head of department, **Robert Tarika*** is developing the international tax capability with a foreign 'desk policy' placing French tax experts throughout the network and a US transfer pricing desk in Paris. **Clients:** Balanced domestic and international corporates.

Jeantet & Associés (3 ptrs, 2 asscs) An established tax department, it is undergoing *"structural problems"* following the loss of three leading players (Coudin's move to Cleary Gottlieb, Dibout to Ernst & Young and Le Gall to Sullivan & Cromwell.) The *"brilliant"* **Gauthier Blanluet*** holds the fort, respected by his peers as *"one of the best,"* and the arrival of the *"professional"* **Dominique Godet*** from Bureau Francis Lefèbvre has signalled a recovery to the market. The tax team has a large stand alone practice, accounting for over 50% of its turnover, working for mainly international clients. **Clients:** Domestic corporates; international concerns.

Jones, Day, Reavis & Pogue (1 ptr, 3 asscs) This small team draws on the resources of 94 tax lawyers worldwide, over a third based in Europe. The *"well regarded"* **Pierre Ullmann*** has a pivotal role in coordinating the European tax practice. The Paris office is active in four main sectors: M&A, real estate, public offerings and new financial products. Adding weight to the team is the *"brilliant"* **Vincent Agulhon*** who peers acknowledge is *"on the fast track."* **Clients:** Cap Gemini.

KPMG Fidal (40 ptrs, 360 asscs) Like other members of the 'Big Five,' this tax practice benefits from its worldwide network of offices. The focus is with M&A and employee shareholding. *"Well regarded technician"* **Yann de Givré*** is *"an active tax lawyer in Paris."* Peers agree that his *"high profile and visibility"* boosts the firm. **Clients:** International corporates.

Linklaters (2 ptrs, 6 asscs) Researchers were told that **Philippe Derouin*** is *"one of the most well known tax lawyers"* in Paris. The team has successfully consolidated its position in the market with a 60-40% split between corporate transactions and litigation.

Derouin advised Peugeot and Faurecia on the tax aspects of the acquisition of SIT (a controlling shareholder of Sommer Allibert) and advised Scottish & Newcastle on the tax aspects of its FF18 billion acquisition of Kronenberg. **Clients:** International corporates.

Cabinet Turot (1 ptr) *"A special animal,"* the firm's reputation rests with its named partner, former member of the supreme court, **Jérôme Turot***. Researchers were told that *"all the practitioners in Paris have a high opinion of him,"* and his *"intellectual skills are outstanding."* He now divides his time between litigation and counsel, where his opinions are highly valued. Clients include multi-national corporations seeking advice on the most complex of tax matters. **Clients:** Multi-national corporates.

Veil Armfelt Jourde La Garanderie (3 ptrs, 5 asscs) *"A top boutique"* with a *"rising team."* The majority of the practice is devoted to independent tax cases, although the team does work with partners on corporate deals. It is known for its IT based techniques which integrate financial and accounting issues into its legal advice. Respected practitioner, **Alain Frenkel*** *"has a high visibility"* and **Neils Dejean*** is considered by rivals to have won *"a lot of good clients."* **Clients:** Domestic and international corporates.

BBLP Moquet Borde & Associés (2 ptrs, 2 asscs) Clients and opponents view leading practitioner **Henri de Feydeau*** as *"a professional who knows his work."* Around 30% of the group's work load is finance, the remainder is M&A, litigation and individual clients counsel. It retains a good reputation in France, however losses in the corporate team have had a knock-on effect. **Clients:** Domestic corporates.

FRANCE Leading individuals (Tax)	
1	
BARDET Henri *Bureau Francis Lefèbvre*	**ENTRAYGUES Gilles** *Cleary, Gottlieb, Steen*
STREICHENBERGER Renaud *Bureau Francis Lefèbvre*	
TUROT Jérôme *Cabinet Turot*	**ULLMANN Pierre** *Jones, Day, Reavis & Pogue*
2	
ACARD Claire *Andersen Legal Association d'Avocats*	
ANDRIEUX Jean-Pierre *Bureau Francis Lefèbvre*	**BEAUVAIS Richard** *Gide Loyrette Nouel*
BOUCHARD Jean-Claude *Bureau Francis Lefèbvre*	**COUDIN Pascal** *Cleary, Gottlieb, Steen*
DE WAAL Allard *Willkie Farr & Gallagher*	**DEROUIN Philippe** *Linklaters*
DIBOUT Patrick *HSD Ernst & Young*	**GOUTHIÈRE Bruno** *Bureau Francis Lefèbvre*
LE GALL Jean-Pierre *Sullivan & Cromwell*	**MESNY Jean-Paul** *Mesny et Associés*
MOSTAFAVI Siamak *Allen & Overy*	
3	
AGULHON Vincent *Jones, Day, Reavis & Pogue*	**BLANLUET Gauthier** *Jeantet & Associés*
BOURTOURAULT Pierre-Yves *Baker & McKenzie*	**BRUNEAU Pierre-Pascal** *Slaughter and May*
COLONNA D'ISTRIA Antoine *Freshfields Bruckhaus*	**DAVOUDET Eric** *Clifford Chance*
DE GIVRÉ Yann *KPMG Fidal*	**DEJEAN Neils** *Veil Armfelt Jourde La Garanderie*
DELATTRE Olivier *Stibbe*	**FRENKEL Alain** *Veil Armfelt Jourde La Garanderie*
GODET Dominique *Jeantet & Associés*	**TIRARD Jean-Marc** *Tirard Naudin*
TRON Jean-Michel *Cleary, Gottlieb, Steen*	
4	
CHARPENTIER Catherine *Coudert Frères*	
DE BROSSES Arnaud *Cleary, Gottlieb, Steen*	**DE FEYDEAU Henri** *BBLP Moquet Borde*
DE KERGOS Yann *Andersen Legal Association d'Avocats*	
DERVEAUX Dominique *Denton Salès Vincent*	**DOUVIER Pierre-Jean** *Bureau Francis Lefèbvre*
GINESTIÉ Philippe *Ginestié Paley-Vincent*	**MAJERHOLC Norbert** *White & Case LLP*
RAFFIN Marie-Hélène *Andersen Legal Association d'Avocats*	
TARIKA Robert *HSD Ernst & Young*	**THILL Pierre-Sebastien** *Bureau Francis Lefèbvre*
THOMAS Eric *Freshfields Bruckhaus*	**VAUDOYER James** *Freshfields Bruckhaus*

Individuals are listed alphabetically in each band.

Coudert Frères (1 ptr, 3 asscs) The practice works closely with the New York and German teams. Although transactional M&A continues to be the mainstay of its activity, it has developed a significant stand alone practice led by senior partner **Catherine Charpentier***. Specialising in financial products, the team has an impressive client portfolio and a wealth of experience in hi-tech transactions and cross border work. The team has also advised both the French and US tax departments. **Clients:** Financial institutions; blue chip companies.

Landwell (40 ptrs, 300 asscs) With the benefits of a large team the firm is *"capable of producing good work,"* and considered by competitors to be developing well. The focus of the practice is pure tax counselling and each team has a specialised focus. **Clients:** Leading corporates.

Mesny et Associés (3 ptrs) A boutique that deals more with *"individuals than with corporations,"* it undertakes predominantly tax litigation. Founding partner **Jean-Paul Mesny*** is "*a good technician*" who works on *"complicated structurings and investments."* Reputed to be *"highly creative,"* he is key to the firm's prominence. **Clients:** Leading corporates.

Slaughter and May (1 ptr, 4 asscs) The Paris practice boasts the *"professional"* **Pierre-Pascal Bruneau*** regarded by clients as *"a clever guy."* Acting in tandem with the corporate department, the team advises on tax-efficient structures for both corporate and project finance transactions and new capital market instruments. It is supported by overseas offices on multi-jurisdictional transactions. **Clients:** Primarily international corporates.

Stibbe (5 ptrs, 12 asscs) M&A, restructurings and IPOs form the backbone of this tax practice. The majority of clients are corporate although it does act for individuals. Head of department **Olivier Delattre*** is *"especially good at estate planning,"* and he has developed a broad practice incorporating litigation, consulting and transactional services. **Clients:** Domestic corporates.

Tirard Naudin (2 ptrs, 2 asscs) A niche practice focusing on international tax planning. Founding partner **Jean-Marc Tirard*** is rated for his advice to high net worth individuals and first port of call for those seeking a second opinion. Active on transfer pricing issues, the team represented several major US firms. **Clients:** US firms; international corporates.

Willkie Farr & Gallagher (3 ptrs, 4 asscs) A *"well established"* practice boosted by the *"young and talented"* **Allard de Waal***. Famed for his *"excellent analysis,"* peers describe him as *"more of a theoretician"* than a practitioner. Deal orientated, the team spends about 50% of its time on M&A work with a *"specialism in LBOs."* **Clients:** Investment banks; private equity investors.

Denton Salès Vincent & Thomas (1 ptr, 3 asscs) The market awaits the results of the merger between Salès Vincent & Associés, international firm Denton Wilde Sapte and tax boutique Thomas et Associés. The respected **Dominique Derveaux*** (of Salès Vincent) has built up a strong profile on the domestic scene and the team has witnessed an increase in instructions from overseas entities, particularly financial institutions seeking advice on stock option plans. **Clients:** Domestic and international corporates.

Gide Loyrette Nouel (3 ptrs, 10 asscs) Described to researchers as a troubled firm after the loss of Antoine Colonna D'Istria (to Freshfields.) **Richard Beauvais*** is respected and acts for individuals as well as large corporations. The team advised on the restructuring Swissair's French business and the restructuring of France Télévision and acted on the acquisition of Nostrum by Facconable. **Clients:** Vivendi Seagram; Swissair; France Télévision.

Ginestié Paley-Vincent & Associés Founding partner, the *"sharp"* **Philippe Ginestié*** displays *"lots of imagination"* in his leadership of this practice. A broad based corporate firm, the practice has a solid reputation for M&A and tax planning. **Clients:** Domestic corporates.

Shearman & Sterling (1 ptr, 2 asscs) The Paris team works closely with the firm's cross border network providing international tax planning advice for M&A, equity and debt issues, and real estate transactions. Clients are both multi-national corporations and large French industrial groups. **Clients:** Domestic industrial operators; multi-nationals.

Watson, Farley & Williams (1 ptr, 2 asscs)A *"well established"* department with a focus on cross border transactions, it draws on offices in London, New York and Moscow. Renowned for its exper-

F

*See leaders' profiles on pages 282-295

tise in financial taxation including asset based financing and leasing with the development of new financial products. The team is also active in litigation, representing clients in disputes before the fiscal authorities. **Clients:** Domestic financial institutions and international corporates.

White & Case LLP (2 ptrs, 2 asscs) A growing practice led by the respected **Norbert Majerholc***. The team advises domestic and foreign corporations on international acquisitions and divestitures, and corporate restructuring. It also assists on ruling applications, tax audits and litigation. A high proportion of the client base is financial institutions. **Clients:** Mainly financial institutes.

Other Notable Practitioner "*Guru*" **Jean-Pierre Le Gall**, recommended for his scholarly tax knowledge, has recently moved from Jeantet & Associés to Sullivan & Cromwell.

F

Leaders' profiles – France

ACARD, Claire
Andersen Legal Association d'Avocats, Neuilly-sur-Seine +33 1 55 61 10 10
Recommended in Tax

AGULHON, Vincent
Jones, Day, Reavis & Pogue, Paris +33 1 5659 3939
vagulhon@jonesday.com
Recommended in Tax
Specialisation: Specialises first in international and then in French direct taxes matters. Has substantial experience in cross-border investments, including foreign investors in French real estate, as well as in reorganisations, tax aspects of mergers and acquisitions, including for listed companies, financial products and structured financing.
Career: Paris Associate. Admitted Nanterre Bar as Avocat in 1995; then Paris Bar in 1999. Educated at the University of Paris XI (DESS de Fiscalité Internationale 1991); Ecole des Hautes Etudes Commerciales (Graduate Business School – 1991); University of Paris I (Maîtrise de Droit 1993). Joined the firm in 1999. Practiced with *Bureau Francis Lefèbvre*, a leading French tax law firm, from 1992-99. Also worked as a foreign associate with the New York firm *Cravath, Swaine & Moore*. Was an associate professor at the Ecole des Hautes Etudes Commerciales. Has also been a lecturer at various seminars on the taxation of holding companies in Europe, harmful tax competition in Europe, taxation of investment funds and their management companies.

ANDRIANI, Bertrand
Linklaters (a member firm of Linklaters & Alliance), Paris +33 1 56 43 56 43
bertrand.andriani@linklaters.com
Recommended in Banking & Finance, Capital Markets, Project Finance, Project Finance: Francophone Africa
Specialisation: Principal areas of practice are major project financings, structured finance, banking, secured and unsecured syndicated loans, international securities offerings, derivatives products, insolvency and corporate restructuring. French adviser to the Agents on the Eurotunnel Project; the sponsors on the Morocco Meditel telecom project finance; the Coface lenders on the Mauritius CTBV Power Project; the sponsors on the Mali Sadiola gold mine project; French legal adviser and civil law consultant to a consortium of three major oil companies on the financing of a proposed transnational oil pipeline across Chad and Cameroon.

ANDRIEUX, Jean-Pierre
Bureau Francis Lefèbvre, Neuilly-sur-Seine Cedex +33 1 47 38 55 00
Recommended in Project Finance: Francophone Africa, Tax

AUGUST, Gilles
August & Debouzy, Paris +33 1 45 61 51 80
Recommended in Corporate/M&A

BARDET, Henri
Bureau Francis Lefèbvre, Neuilly-sur-Seine Cedex +33 1 47 38 55 00
Recommended in Tax

BASDEVANT, Dominique
Stibbe, Paris +33 1 40 62 20 00
dominique.basdevant@stibbe.fr
Recommended in Project Finance
Specialisation: Advising on project documentation, with a particular emphasis on infrastructure and industrial projects and the administrative law aspects involved, advised the lenders in connection with the restructuring of the Euro Disney project and various industrial non recourse financing.
Career: Admitted in Paris 1968, Partner *Stibbe Simont Monahan Duhot.*

BAUM, Axel H.
Hughes Hubbard & Reed, Paris +33 1 44 05 80 00
baum@hugheshubbard.com
Recommended in Arbitration (International)
Specialisation: Partner of *Hughes Hubbard & Reed* LLP, based in the firm's Paris office, which has headed for many years. American lawyer, admitted in New York, Connecticut, and before the U.S. Supreme Court, and an Avocat à la Cour in France. Familiar with common and civil law principles.
Career: Long experience in international business transactions and international arbitration. Has participated in more than 60 international arbitrations, serving as Counsel to Parties, Chairman of Tribunals, party-nominated or sole arbitrator, or expert witness. Acted as Counsel in obtaining the first contested award before the Iran-U.S. Claims Tribunal, and as counsel to the prevailing party in the landmark Dutco case. Alternate U.S. Member on the ICC's International Court of Arbitration, and chairs a key forum of the ICC Commission on Arbitration. On the panels of arbitrators maintained by leading institutions, including CPR's Panel of Distinguished International Mediators, and is a frequent speaker at arbitration conferences. Has acted in cases covering a wide range of industries (e.g., pharmaceutical, chemical, automotive, high technology) and commercial transactions (e.g., joint ventures, acquisitions, turnkey projects, licenses, government concessions). They have involved many different countries and Rules, including ICC, LCIA, AAA, UNCITRAL, Stockholm Chamber, Vienna Center, and others.
Personal: Graduated from Amherst College and Yale Law School, where was Managing Editor of the Yale Law Journal. Fluent in English, German and French.

BAXTER, Elena
Bredin Prat, Paris +33 1 44 35 35 35
elenabaxter@bredinprat.com
Recommended in Corporate/M&A
Specialisation: Main area of work is corporate law, principally mergers and acquisitions with particular focus on multi-jurisdictional transactions for European and American clients.
Career: Admitted to New York Bar in 1983, joined *Coudert Brothers* as an associate in New York and then in Paris until 1990. Admitted to Paris Bar in 1989 and joined *Bredin Prat* as partner in 1990, with co-responsibility for developing the firm's international practice. Legal work is in English and French languages.
Personal: Awarded Juris Doctor degree from the University of Virginia School of Law in 1982. Order of the Coif and Phi Beta Kappa.

BEAUVAIS, Richard
Gide Loyrette Nouel, Paris +33 1 40 75 61 20
beauvais@gide.fr
Recommended in Tax
Specialisation: Partner at *Gide Loyrette Nouel* since 1981. Leads the firm's Tax Department and has 27 years of experience in advising on corporate taxation, domestic and international tax planning and personal taxation for high net worth individuals.
Prof. Memberships: Founding member of the board of the Association Française des Avocats Fiscalistes.
Career: Graduated from the Universities of Caen (1969) and Paris (1971) and admitted to the Paris Bar in 1974. Joined the firm in 1973. Has written and spoken frequently on tax matters including as a French reporter on non-discrimination in interna-

tional taxation to the 1993 congress of the International Fiscal Association. Has lectured for many years on tax matters at the leading business school, HEC.
Personal: Born 27 April, 1946. Married, two children.

BEAUVISAGE, Patrick
Stibbe, Paris +33 1 40 62 20 00
patrick.beauvisage@stibbe.fr
Recommended in Corporate/M&A
Specialisation: Practises in general corporate, mergers and acquisitions, stock exchange, leveraged buyouts and public offers. Has acted in the privatisation of Banque Hervet. Exchange public offer Suez Lyonnaise des Eaux/Tractebel.
Prof. Memberships: A.B.A. Association des Anciens Secretaires de la Conference.
Career: Managing Partner 1989-1999.
Personal: DES Droit Public, Paris. DES Droit Prive, Paris.

BEN SALAH, Kamel
Gide Loyrette Nouel, Paris +33 1 40 75 61 54
bensalah@gide.fr
Recommended in Banking & Finance
Specialisation: Partner of the Finance/Project Finance department, in charge of the structured and acquisition finance group which assists clients in structuring, documenting, and negotiating sophisticated transactions in this area. Expertise includes asset financing (including leasing, leveraged leasing, and lease receivables securitisations), real estate financing and refinancing, off-balance sheet financing transactions, receivables financing.
Prof. Memberships: Member of the working group for the last revision of the International Chamber of Commerce (ICC) rules on Arbitration. Former member of the International Court of Arbitration of the ICC.
Career: Joined the firm in 1982 and became a partner in 1993. A graduate of the University of Tunis. Obtained DEA (advanced studies degree) in Private Law and Criminal Law from the university of Paris II in 1979 and 1980. Admitted to the Tunis Bar in 1985 and to the Paris Bar in 1992.
Personal: Fluent in French and English.

BENSOUSSAN, Alain
Alain Bensoussan, Paris +33 1 4133 3535
Recommended in Communications: IT

BERTIN-MOUROT, Olivier
Clifford Chance, Paris Cedex 16 +33 1 44 05 52 52
Recommended in Banking & Finance, Capital Markets

BESSE, Antonin
Freshfields Bruckhaus Deringer, Paris
+33 1 44 56 44 56
antonin.besse@freshfields.com
Recommended in Capital Markets
Specialisation: Partner in Finance Department. Practice covers international financing transactions, with particular focus on structured securities transactions, securitisations, derivatives (including credit derivatives), capital markets transactions and regulatory work.

BESSE, Eryl
Linklaters (a member firm of Linklaters & Alliance), Paris +33 1 56 43 56 43
eryl.besse@linklaters.com
Recommended in Banking & Finance
Specialisation: Specialist with 16 years' experience in international finance, including debt and equity issues (including privatisations); structured financings and secured and unsecured international credit facilities. Recent matters include advising Unibail on its hostile bid for Blue Circle Industries; advising Merrill Lynch in connection with the establishment of Unibail's Euro1,000,000,000 EMTN Programme.
Career: Since May 1990, partner in London and Paris offices.

BEURIER, Philippe
Bredin Prat, Paris +33 1 44 35 35 35
philippebeurier@bredinprat.com
Recommended in Corporate/M&A
Specialisation: Partner in Corporate Department. Main area of work is corporate law, mergers and acquisitions, and securities law. Has handled acquisitions of companies and undertakings of varying sorts by French and foreign clients.
Career: Worked as an Associate with an Avocat à la Cour de Cassation et au Conseil d'Etat (French Supreme Court). Qualified in 1985, joined *Gide Loyrette Nouel* the same year, working for the Brussels, New York and Paris offices. Joined *Bredin Prat* in 1989, becoming a partner in 1992.
Personal: Born 6 April 1959. Attended Rennes and Paris University 1978-1983 (Maîtrise de Droit des Affaires, troisième cycle de Droit Privé). Lives in Paris.

BILLOT, Philippe
Jones, Day, Reavis & Pogue, Paris +33 1 5659 3939
pbillot@jonesday.com
Recommended in Banking & Finance, Capital Markets
Specialisation: Co-chairs the Firm's Structured Finance / Financial Products Practice and has extensive experience in French and international bank finance, with particular emphasis in the areas of structured finance, acquisition finance, banking regulations, restructurings, and workouts. In addition, has experience in M&A and real estate transactions. Recently advised GE Capital in the acquisition of UIS and regularly advises French clients such as Crédit Commercial de France and Société Générale in structured finance and real estate transactions.
Career: Paris Partner. Joined the firm in 1994. Qualified Paris in 1980 as Notaire and Avocat; admitted 1991 Paris Bar as Avocat. Educated at University of Paris (Ma"trise in Private Law 1976); Centre for Advanced Notarial Studies, Paris (Diploma 1976). Has served with several Paris law firms, including *Jeantet & Associés*, where practised from 1991-94 as a partner and headed their financial institutions practice. At the Crédit Commercial de France from 1985-91, where he served as the head of international business affairs in the legal department and then as general counsel. Was an associate professor at the University of Paris, Dauphine from 1991-93. Has written numerous articles for legal and financial publications and is a frequent lecturer at banking or financial seminars.

Personal: Fluent in French and English, has a working knowledge of Spanish and a basic knowledge of Italian.

BLANLUET, Gauthier
Jeantet & Associés, Paris +33 1 45 05 80 08
Recommended in Tax

BLOCH, François
Willkie Farr & Gallagher, Paris +33 1 53 43 45 00
francois.bloch@cliffordchance.com
Recommended in Communications: Telecoms
Specialisation: Partner in telecommunications, Internet, Media and Entertainment (T.I.M.E.) Group in Paris. Practice focus is on commercial, transactional, privatisations, cross-border, joint-ventures, IP, regulatory as well as litigation/arbitration issues for Telecommunications (including equipment, networks and services providers), Internet and E-commerce (including market places and auction/reverse auction sites and portals), Media (TV, radio and film), biotech, IT, sports and entertainment businesses. Advises major global Asian, American and European companies, investors and institutions in all sectors. Frequently speaks at specialised conferences in Europe and presides or is a member of several specialised work groups and associations. Contributes regularly to legal and specialised publications and was also associated to reports to the French Government on Internet and new Media related existing and potential regulations. Finally, is a lecturer on 'New economy law' at the Sorbonne law school.
Career: Bull HN Information System Inc., Boston (1990-1991); *Baker and McKenzie*, Paris (1991-1993). *Clifford Chance* Paris and London (1993-2000). Partner with *Willkie Farr & Gallagher*, Paris.
Personal: Born 1964; resides France; married with three children. Business law school ('Magistère'), University of Paris II (1990), LLM in business and tax law ('DESS'), University of Paris II (1990); PIL Harvard Law School (1991); Paris Bar (CAPA) (1990).

BOMPOINT, Dominique
Bredin Prat, Paris +33 1 44 35 35 35
Recommended in Corporate/M&A

BOND, Stephen
White & Case LLP, Paris +33 1 55 04 15 10
sbond@whitecase.com
Recommended in Arbitration (International)
Specialisation: International commercial law practice specialising in international arbitration and dispute resolution. Counsel or arbitrator in a number of international arbitrations under various arbitration rules involving disputes under a variety of civil and common law legal systems in such fields as oil and gas, construction, computer and international sales, joint ventures and distribution. Counsel in international mediations. US member of ICC International Court of Arbitration (1994-1999) and Vice-President of ICC Working Group which revised the ICC Rules of Arbitration.
Prof. Memberships: Member New York (since 1969) and Paris (since 1992) Bars. Chartered Institute of Arbitrators (Fellow), Panel of Arbitrators of: AAA (International Panel), Arbitral Centre of the

F

Federal Economic Chamber (Vienna, Austria), Centre for Public Resources International Panel of Distinguished Neutrals, Court of Arbitration at the Polish Chamber of Commerce, Hong Kong International Arbitration Centre, Korea Commercial Arbitration Board, London Court of International Arbitration, Singapore International Arbitrators Centre, US Council for International Business (ICC Committee in US), World Industrial Property Organisation and others.
Career: Law Clerk, Federal District Court (EDNY) 1968-69; associate lawyer in New York and Paris, 1969-1973; Office of the Legal Adviser, US Department of State, Washington & Geneva, 1974-85; Secretary General ICC International Court of Arbitration, Paris, 1985-91; *White & Case*, Paris, 1991-present.
Personal: Born 5 July 1943; Brown University (BA 1965), Columbia University Law School (JD 1968).

F

BONNASSE, Antoine
Gide Loyrette Nouel, Paris +33 1 40 75 36 17
bonnasse@gide.fr
Recommended in Corporate/Commercial
Specialisation: Specialises in corporate reorganisations, privatisations, mergers & acquisitions, LBO and domestic and international transactions and corporate law. Coordinating partner of *Gide Loyrette Nouel*'s M&A department. Has acted as counsel in a number of privatisations including those of the BNP, GAN, CIC, Crédit Lyonnais and Crédit Foncier – all major French banks. Was also involved in numerous transnational operations such as the Autodistribution-Finelist deal and the Vivendi Canal+/Seagram merger.
Career: Admitted to the Paris Bar in 1987. Partner of the firm since 1996. DESS (postgraduate degree) in Corporate Taxation from Paris University, 1986. Maîtrise in Business Law and Taxation from Paris University, 1985.
Personal: Speaks both French and English.

BONVARLET, Patrick
Freshfields Bruckhaus Deringer, Paris
+33 1 44 56 44 56
patrick.bonvarlet@freshfields.com
Recommended in Banking & Finance, Capital Markets, Corporate/M&A, Project Finance
Specialisation: Partner in the corporate practice group specialising in securities and M&A.

BORDE, Dominique
BBLP Moquet Borde & Associés, Paris
+33 1 42 99 04 50
d.borde@bblp-fr.com
Recommended in Corporate/M&A
Specialisation: Founding Partner of *BBLP Moquet Borde*, specialising in mergers and acquisitions, securities law and privatisations with a significant litigation practice. Has an international outlook with nearly half of the firm's practice being internationally based. One of the driving forces behind *BBLP*, the Continental Law Firm, which provides world-wide legal services from the major economies in the Eurozone and Continental Europe's leading stock markets.
Prof. Memberships: Permanent member of the International Chamber of Commerce (Registered Arbitrator). Member of the Law Committee of the French National Federation of Industries and Services (MEDEF). Member of the Board of Visitors of Columbia University Law School and of the Pedagogical Committee of the Law and Tax Studies Department of the Ecole des Hautes Etudes Commerciales (HEC). Member of the Board of Directors of Médecins sans Frontières.
Career: Joined *Cleary, Gottlieb, Steen & Hamilton* in 1966 where he became a partner. Founded *Moquet Borde & Associés* in 1976. Member of the Paris and Brussels Bars.
Personal: Law degrees from the University of Paris (Maîtrise en Droit 1963) and Colombia University (LLM 1966).

BORDEAUX-GROUELT, Robert
Cleary, Gottlieb, Steen & Hamilton, Paris
+33 1 40 74 68 00
Recommended in Corporate/M&A

BOUCHARD, Jean-Claude
Bureau Francis Lefèbvre, Neuilly-sur-Seine Cedex
+33 1 47 38 55 00
Recommended in Tax

BOURTOURAULT, Pierre-Yves
Baker & McKenzie, Paris +33 1 44 17 53 00
pierre-yves.bourtourault@bakernet.com
Recommended in Tax
Specialisation: International tax planning and structures; M&A; cross-border restructuring; asset financing and refinancing; large projects; electronic commerce; transfer pricing.
Prof. Memberships: Association Nationale des Docteurs en Droit; IFA; IACF.
Career: Partner of *Baker & McKenzie*, Paris, since 1983; Faculté de Droit Dijon, France 1974, Doctorate in Law; Lecturer in Law at Dijon Law School 1974-1975; taught tax and commercial law from 1972 to 1975 at Dakar and Dijon; before joining *Baker & McKenzie* in 1979 worked as assistant to the tax manager of *SNECMA* (an aircraft engine manufacturer) and as head of the tax department of *ENTREPOSE GTM* (offshore oil works). Recent articles and conferences on telecommunications and e-commerce, international joint ventures, cross-border restructuring, transfer pricing, tax controversies, partnerships.
Personal: Leisure interests include reading and cycling. Married with three children.

BRABANT, Stéphane
Herbert Smith, Paris +33 1 53 57 70 70
Recommended in Project Finance: Francophone Africa

BRANDFORD GRIFFITH, Henri
Veil Armfelt Jourde La Garanderie, Paris
+33 1 56 69 56 62
Recommended in Corporate/M&A

BREBAN, Yann
Alain Bensoussan, Paris +33 1 4133 3535
Recommended in Communications: Telecoms

BRIMSON, Neil
Herbert Smith, Paris +33 1 53 57 70 70
Recommended in Project Finance

BROCAS, Thierry
De Pardieu Brocas Maffei & Leygonie, Paris
+33 1 53 57 71 71
Recommended in Corporate/M&A

BROCHIER, Emmanuel
Darrois Villey Maillot Brochier, Paris
+33 1 45 02 19 19
Recommended in Corporate/M&A

BRUNEAU, Pierre-Pascal
Slaughter and May, Paris +33 1 44 05 60 00
pierre-pascal.bruneau@slaughterandmay.com
Recommended in Tax
Specialisation: Partner in the Tax Department since 1995. Practice consists principally of international tax planning, advising on a number of group reorganisations, tax-related financial instruments, share-stapling arrangements and structured financings.
Prof. Memberships: IACF (Institut des Avocats Conseils Fiscaux, Paris); IBA (Illinois Bar Association); IFA (Institut Fiscal des Avocats); The Law Society, London; Paris Bar; Illinois Bar.
Career: Joined *Slaughter and May* in 1994, having commenced his career with a leading French tax firm and subsequently worked with an American law firm, in Paris, New York, and Chicago. Qualified as an avocat in 1981 and spent five years in the USA, where he obtained an LLM at Georgetown University and a JD at Chicago-Kent University.

BRUNET, François
Cleary, Gottlieb, Steen & Hamilton, Paris
+33 1 40 74 68 00
Recommended in Competition/Anti-trust

BUHART, Jacques
Coudert Frères, Paris +33 1 53 83 60 00
buhartj@paris.coudert.com
Recommended in Corporate/M&A
Specialisation: Mergers & Acquisitions, EU Competition, Telecoms, Electricity.
Prof. Memberships: IBA Vice-Chairman SBL.
Career: Joined *Coudert Frères* 1976.

BÜHLER, Michael
Jones, Day, Reavis & Pogue, Paris +33 1 5659 3939
mbuhler@jonesday.com
Recommended in Arbitration (International)
Specialisation: Partner in international commercial arbitration and international business transactions. Main areas of work advising clients in dispute resolution under, amongst others, the Rules of the ICC, AAA, German Arbitration Association, Vienna Arbitration Centre and ad hoc arbitrations. These disputes arise principally in the fields of supply of industrial or power generation plants, or of industrial machinery and equipment and civil construction works (in various countries such as Germany, France, Spain, the U.K, India, Iran, Sri Lanka, Jordan, Turkey, Bulgaria, Egypt, Turkmenistan, Guinea, Tunisia, Libya, Algeria Czech Republic, and the U.A.E.), project finance transactions, hotel development projects and distribution agreements, in particular in the food industries, and have involved the application of the laws of Austria, France, Germany, Switzerland, New York, Pennsylvania, Hungary, Japan, the U.A.E. and Singapore. Dr Bühler also reg-

ularly serves as chairman, sole arbitrator and party appointed arbitrator.
Prof. Memberships: German (alternate) member of the International Court of Arbitration of the ICC (1997 -); ICC Commission on International Arbitration (1988 -); International Bar Association: German, French and Swiss Arbitration Associations; Admitted to Bars of Düsseldorf, New York and Paris.
Career: Counsel at ICC Court of Arbitration (1985-1988); joined *Frere Cholmeley Bischoff* (Paris) in 1988, becoming partner in 1992; joined *White & Case* (Paris) 1995; joined *Jones Day* (Paris) in 1999.
Publications: The German Arbitration Act 1997: Text and Notes, The Hague 1998 (A tri-lingual publication , Kluwer Law International) Co-author of GLOSSNER, Das Schiedsgericht in der Praxis, Heidelberg, 3rd edition 1990 (4th edition in preparation). Technical Expertise: 'An Additional Means for Preventing or Settling Commercial Disputes' in 'J. of Int. Arb'. vol. 6 (1989), pp. 135-157; 'Costs in ICC arbitration: A practicioner's view', in: 'The American View of International Arbitration', Vol 3 (1992), Nos 1-4, 'Essays in Honour of Hans Smit', pp. 117-152; 'Witness Testimony pursuant to the 1999 IBA Rules of Evidence in International Commercial Arbitration-Novel or tested standards?' (Co-author) in 'J. of Int. Arb'., vol. 17 no. 1 (2000), pp. 3-30.
Personal: Born in 1956, in Munich: Received German law degrees (1st and 2nd state exams) in Bonn and Düsseldorf (1979, 1984); Dr. jur. University of Geneva School of Law, 1983; LLM, Columbia University School of Law, 1985.

CALVET, Hugues
Stibbe, Paris +33 1 40 62 20 00
Recommended in Competition/Anti-trust
Specialisation: Partner at *Stibbe Simont Monahan Duhot*, active in both the Paris and Brussels offices of the firm. Covers the range of French and EU antitrust work. Appears regularly before the European Commission, the French antitrust Authority (Conseil de la concurrence) and the French and the European Courts. Has specific expertise in the regulated sectors, such as air transport, telecommunications and energy, having participated in many high profile cases. Also handles numerous competition cases in the fields of media and entertainment. Teaches European competition law at the University of Paris 1 Panthéon Sorbonne (DESS de droit Européen).
Prof. Memberships: Admitted, 1992, Paris.
Career: University of Toulouse Law School (DEA de droit privé fondamental, 1979). Ecole Nationale de la Magistrature (1981-1983). French judiciary (1983-1987). Law clerk (référendaire) at the European Court of Justice in Luxembourg (1987-1992). Joined French law firm *Salès Vincent Georges* (1994) Paris and Brussels. Joined the EU/WTO Department of *Stibbe Simont Monahan Duhot* (1994).
Personal: Born 13 April, 1958.

CARTIER-MILLON, Eric
Gide Loyrette Nouel, Paris +33 1 40 75 36 17
bonnasse@gide.fr
Recommended in Banking & Finance
Specialisation: Specialises in structured and project financing.
Career: Joined the firm in 1990, and has been a partner since 1998. Admitted to the Paris Bar in 1990. Magistère de Juriste d'Affaires (postgraduate degree) from Paris University, 1989. DESS (postgraduate degree) in Business Law and taxation from Paris University, 1989. Maîtrise in Private Law from Paris University, 1988.
Personal: Speaks both French and English.

CHABERT, Pierre-Yves
Cleary, Gottlieb, Steen & Hamilton, Paris
+33 1 40 74 68 00
Recommended in Capital Markets, Corporate/M&A

CHARPENTIER, Catherine
Coudert Frères, Paris +33 1 53 83 60 00
charpentierc@paris.coudert.com
Recommended in Tax
Specialisation: Partner in charge, tax department. Practice concentrates on corporate tax matters, including M&A, IPO, joint ventures and reorganisations, tax-advantaged international financing and derivative transactions, international investment funds, international stock option plans, and international tax planning for high net wealth individuals. Has represented major financial services clients including JP Morgan, Crédit Lyonnais and major corporate clients including American Airlines, Packard Bell, and Laurrent-Perrier. Has spoken at many tax conferences on topics including the tax treatment of mergers under EU Directives, cross-border acquisitions and international financing, international investment funds, dividend access plans in cross-border acquisitions, treasury management. Regularly has articles published in tax and finance journals.
Prof. Memberships: American Bar Association; International Bar Association (committee N Tax); International Fiscal Association; IACF (French Institute of Tax Counsel) and ACE (French Association of Business Lawyers). Paris Bar.
Career: Qualified in 1981. Joined *Coudert Frères* in 1993.
Personal: Born 17 April 1957. Attended the Sorbonne University (DESS Conseil Juridique et Fiscal, 1981, honours; DEA in Anglo-Saxon Law, 1984, honours). Speaks English and French. Board member of various charities. Leisure interests include singing in a choir.

COHEN-TANUGI, Laurent
Cleary, Gottlieb, Steen & Hamilton, Paris
+33 1 40 74 68 00
Recommended in Competition/Anti-trust

COLONNA D'ISTRIA, Antoine
Freshfields Bruckhaus Deringer, Paris
+33 1 44 56 44 56
antoine.colonna@freshfields.com
Recommended in Tax
Specialisation: Partner in the tax group with a particular focus on banking clients, investment funds and various types of financial products; as well as real estate tax.

CORK, Rod
Allen & Overy, 75009 Paris +33 1 40 06 54 00
Recommended in Banking & Finance

COT, Jean-Mathieu
Clifford Chance, Paris Cedex 16 +33 1 44 05 52 52
Recommended in Competition/Anti-trust

COTONI, Jean-Claude
Freshfields Bruckhaus Deringer, Paris
+33 1 44 56 44 56
jean-claude.cotoni@freshfields.com
Recommended in Corporate/M&A
Specialisation: Partner in Corporate Practice. Main area of work is mergers and acquisitions, joint ventures, privatisations, venture capital work and commercial law and co-operative arrangements. Sector specialisations include the media and automotive industries

COUDIN, Pascal
Cleary, Gottlieb, Steen & Hamilton, Paris
+33 1 40 74 68 00
Recommended in Tax

COUSI, Olivier
Gide Loyrette Nouel, Paris +33 1 40 75 61 73
cousi@gide.fr
Recommended in Communications: Telecoms
Specialisation: Offers extensive experience in intellectual property law, audiovisual regulations and telecommunications law, regularly advising governments and leading private communications groups worldwide. The development of Internet and new technology has also prompted him to offer advice to French and foreign telecommunications operators regarding on-line services, access provider services and data exchange on the Internet.
Prof. Memberships: Former secretary of the Paris Bar debating society (1987). Member of the Comité Français de Normalisation of the AFNOR, responsible for setting norms for multimedia products.
Publications: Has written numerous articles in the areas of multimedia, telecommunications and Internet.
Career: Admitted to the Paris Bar since 1985. Partner in the firm since 1993. Has been teaching multimedia law at the École Nationale Supérieure des Télécommunications since 1996.
Personal: Graduated from the Paris Institute of Political Science (1983) and from the Institut Français de Presse (1980). Obtained an advanced studies degree (DEA) in Public Law, Paris University, 1983. Speaks both French and English.

COUTRELIS, André
Coutrelis & Associés, Paris +33 1 53 57 47 95
Recommended in Competition/Anti-trust

CRAIG, William Laurence
Coudert Frères, Paris +33 1 53 83 60 00
craigw@paris.coudert.com
Recommended in Arbitration (International)
Specialisation: Head of *Coudert Brothers* International Arbitration Practice in Europe. Acted as counsel in over 150 International Chamber of Commerce arbitrations, including numerous disputes involving states and state agencies (also arbitration involving states before the International Centre

F

for the Settlement of Investment Disputes). Acted as arbitrator (party-appointed, sole arbitrator or chairman) in 20 ICC arbitrations and in numerous AAA, LCIA, CIETAC and ad hoc arbitrations. Acting as counsel in current arbitration matters which include: ICC arbitration involving major public works contract in North African country; European Development Fund arbitration concerning public works project in African country; ICC arbitration regarding termination of automobile distribution contract between Asian automobile manufacturer and European distributor; UNCITRAL Rules arbitration concerning long term power purchase agreement (PPA).
Prof. Memberships: Member of the Bars of New York, District of Colombia and the US Supreme Court; Qualified in France as Avocat, member of the Paris Bar; Fellow Chartered Institute of Arbitrators.
Career: Harvard Law School, Juris Doctor cum laude (1957). University of Paris, Docteur en droit de l'Université. Partner, *Coudert Frères* Paris 1967 to date, specialising in International Commercial arbitration. US member – Court of Arbitration, International Chamber of Commerce (1976-84).
Personal: Visiting Lecturer, Yale Law School (1999) (International Arbitration). Publications: 'International Chamber of Commerce Arbitration' (with W.W. Park and J. Paulsson) (Oceana Publications/ICC Publishing, 3rd ed. 2000). 'Annotated Guide to the 1998 ICC Arbitration Rules' (with W.W. Park and J. Paulsson) (Oceana Publications/ICC Publishing 1998). 'International Commercial Arbitration Cases, Materials and Notes on the Resolution of International Business Disputes' (with M. Reisman, W.W. Park and J. Paulsson) (Foundation Press 1997).

CROTHERS, John
Gide Loyrette Nouel, Paris +33 1 40 75 29 84
crothers@gide.fr
Recommended in Project Finance
Specialisation: Practice concentrates on project finance, banking and privatisation in both the developing and developed world. Has advised international financial institutions, concession companies, operators, contractors and bidding consortia in infrastructure projects ranging from toll roads to IPPs, water treatment facilities and mobile telephony.
Career: Admitted to the New York Bar (1987) and the Paris Bar (1992). Partner in the firm since 1999. Speaks regularly at international conferences on project finance. Member of UNCITRAL expert group advising on the drafting of a model law on BOTs. Has advised the government of India on its road and ports concession laws as an expert for UNIDO and has advised the government of Romania on its toll motorway laws and an EBRD expert.
Personal: Obtained a Common Law Degree in 1984 and a Civil Law Degree in 1985 from McGill University (Montreal, Canada), and an advanced degree in International Law, Strasbourg University, in 1986. Speaks both French and English.

D'HÉROUVILLE, Jean-Guillaume
Gide Loyrette Nouel, Paris +33 1 40 75 61 72
herouville@gide.fr
Recommended in Capital Markets
Specialisation: Specialises in banking/financial corporate and regulatory matters, and in financial markets regulations and litigation. Also does lobbying work in the same matters with the European Union and French authorities. Has been involved in cross-border and domestic acquisitions and restructurings of regulated entities, and in the privatisation of French and foreign credit institutions.
Prof. Memberships: Paris Bar (1985); New York Bar (1990).
Personal: Born 16 March 1958. Institute of Political Sciences (1980); DEA in Business Law (1982); LLM, Georgetown University (1984).

D'ORMESSON, Olivier
Linklaters (a member firm of Linklaters & Alliance), Paris +33 1 56 43 56 43
olivier.dormesson@linklaters.com
Recommended in Competition/Anti-trust
Specialisation: EC and French competition law, with substantial experience in EC and French merger control, State aid and other areas of European law including deregulation of former monopolies, free movement of goods and services, public procurement, etc.
Publications: Prolific publisher of numerous articles and contributions to journals and textbooks in field.
Career: Since June 1999 has been partner in Brussels and Paris.

DANY, Mireille
Clifford Chance, Paris Cedex 16 +33 1 44 05 52 52
Recommended in Competition/Anti-trust

DARROIS, Jean-Michel
Darrois Villey Maillot Brochier, Paris
+33 1 4502 1919
Recommended in Corporate/M&A

DAVOUDET, Eric
Clifford Chance, Paris Cedex 16 +33 1 44 05 52 52
Recommended in Tax

DE BOISSÉSON, Matthieu
Darrois Villey Maillot Brochier, Paris
+33 1 4502 1919
Recommended in Arbitration (International)

DE BROSSES, Arnaud
Cleary, Gottlieb, Steen & Hamilton, Paris
+33 1 40 74 68 00
Recommended in Tax

DE FEYDEAU, Henri
BBLP Moquet Borde & Associés, Paris
+33 1 42 99 04 50
Recommended in Tax
Specialisation: Partner in charge of the Tax Department. Main areas of work are: real estate, mergers and acquisitions (tax aspects) international and national tax planning, taxation of perpetual bonds, leverage buy out, financial engineering. Written and spoken widely on various matters related to French taxation, both domestic and international.
Prof. Memberships: International Fiscal Association, Director of the Institut des Avocats Conseils Fiscaux, International Bar Association, International Tax Planning Association (ITPA).
Publications: Co-author: 'Optimisation Fiscale et Abus de Droit' (Tax Planning and Abuse of Law) (1990). French correspondent of the 'Tax Management International' review, published by the Bureau of National Affaires, Inc. Washington DC, USA.
Career: Qualified in 1971. Head of the international tax department at Compagnie Saint-Gobain in 1974. Joined *Coopers & Lybrand*, Paris in 1982 as a tax partner and *Moquet Borde & Associés* in 1990.
Personal: Born 21 May 1947, registered as Conseil Juridique 1985; admitted 1990, Paris. Education: Institut d'Etudes Politiques de Paris (1969), University of Paris DES ès Sciences Economiques (1971). Leisure interests include sylviculture, restoration of listed historical monuments. Resides in Paris. Married with four children.

DE GIVRÉ, Yann
KPMG Fidal, Neuilly-sur-Seine +33 1 46 39 46 39
Recommended in Tax

DE JUVIGNY, Olivier
Rambaud Martel, 75782 Paris Cedex
16 +33 1 40 67 17 00
o.dejuvigny@rambaud-martel.com
Recommended in Competition/Anti-trust
Specialisation: Partner specialising in EC and French competition law, litigation and distribution law; has handled numerous merger control and antitrust cases both on the EU and French levels. Also involved in a number of high profile abuse of dominance cases. Has advised French, US and British major companies on the EC and French competition aspects of joint ventures and other agreements. Has specific expertise in a number of industries including air transport, banking, construction, chemistry, distribution, electronic, entertainment, financial services, insurance, IT services and pharmaceuticals.
Publications: Contributor to 'Encyclopédie DALLOZ droit communautaire'.
Career: Qualified in 1991. Joined the Competition Department of *Salès Vincent Georges* (Paris and Brussels) in 1991. Joined the EU & Competition Department of *Stibbe Simont Monahan Duhot* in 1994. Joined *RAMBAUD MARTEL* in 1996, and became a partner in 1998.
Personal: Ecole Supérieure des Sciences Economiques et Commerciales (ESSEC). Paris 2 Panthéon – Assas University (Magistère de Juriste d'Affaires ; DESS).

DE KERGOMMEAUX, Xavier
Gide Loyrette Nouel, Paris +33 1 40 75 36 52
kergommeaux@gide.fr
Recommended in Capital Markets
Specialisation: Structuring of securitisation programs and transactions, both for national and cross-border arrangements. Extensive experience in the areas of defeasance and structured financing.
Prof. Memberships: A former Secretary of the Paris Bar debating society (1993).
Publications: Regularly writes for French and Anglo-Saxon specialist publications on the subject of securitisation.
Career: Became a partner in the firm in 1998.

Previously employed in the major corporate client division of a French bank before joining the firm in 1990.
Personal: Graduated from France's leading business school, HEC, in 1985 and has two additional degrees in Business Law and Taxation, and in Public Law.

DE KERGOS, Yann
Andersen Legal Association d'Avocats, Neuilly-sur-Seine +33 1 55 61 10 10
Recommended in Tax

DE LA LAURENCIE, Jean-Patrice
Norton Rose, Paris +33 1 53 89 56 00
Recommended in Competition/Anti-trust

DE LA TAILLE, Benoît
Coudert Frères, Paris +33 1 53 83 60 00
delatailleb@paris.coudert.com
Recommended in Communications: IT, Communications: Telecoms
Specialisation: Associate with *Coudert Brothers*' Telecommunications Practice group. Advises new French or foreign operators which intervene in all the activity sectors (local, national and international), all customer segments (company, SME or individual), and regardless of the transmission technology used (cable, hertzian, terrestrial or satellite), on the legal framework for establishing their network. In addition, advises operators, ISP and vendors on IT structure finance and negotiates technology refresh lease, pay-per-use or revenue sharing model contracts.
Prof. Memberships: Member of the Paris Bar since March 17, 1999.
Career: Prior to joining *Coudert Brothers* in 1999, was General Counsel for regulatory and legal affairs for the French subsidiary of Belgacom. Previously, was responsible for regulatory and legal aspects of the corporate market of France Telecom, and spent four months with the regulatory team at Nynex to study the introduction of competition in the local loop.
Personal: One-year postgraduate degree in law and finance.

DE MOÜY, Diane
De Pardieu Brocas Maffei & Leygonie, Paris +33 1 53 57 71 71
Recommended in Banking & Finance

DE PARDIEU, Charles-Henri
De Pardieu Brocas Maffei & Leygonie, Paris +33 1 53 57 71 71
Recommended in Corporate/M&A

DE ROUX, Xavier
Gide Loyrette Nouel, Paris +33 1 40 75 61 04
roux@gide.fr
Recommended in Competition/Anti-trust
Specialisation: Competition and consumer law, and white collar crime. Represents interests of private French and international companies, either before the European Commission and the European Court of Justice, or before the French jurisdictions, on various aspects of competition law, antidumping law, and agri-food processing regulations.
Prof. Memberships: IBA and IFRI. Former First Secretary of the Paris Bar debating society.
Career: Partner in the firm since 1968. Admitted to the Paris Bar in 1962. In addition to career as a lawyer, was a member of the French Parliament from 1993 to 1997.
Personal: Maîtrise in Law from Paris University, 1961. Speaks both French and English.

DE VARAX, Matthieu
Simmons & Simmons, Paris +33 1 53 05 31 31
matthieu.de.varax@simmons-simmons.com
Recommended in Banking & Finance
Specialisation: Advises French and international arrangers, financiers and lessors in relation to cross-border big ticket asset finance transactions with a particular emphasis on aviation finance. Also advises international leasing companies and arrangers in connection with pan-European vendor programmes and equipment finance structures. Regular contributor to leasing and asset finance publications.
Prof. Memberships: Ordre des Avocats à la Cour d'Appel de Paris; European Air Law Association.
Career: Qualifed as an *Avocat* in January 1993 and joined *Simmons & Simmons* from *Wilde Sapte*, as a partner in 1998.
Personal: Born 27 July 1963. Educated at the Faculté de Droit de Malakoff, Université Paris V. Member Automobile Club de France.

DE WAAL, Allard
Willkie Farr & Gallagher, Paris +33 1 53 43 45 00
adewaal@willkie.com
Recommended in Tax
Specialisation: Partner in the Paris office tax department, specialised in international taxation. Has been acting as counsel on major LBO assignments, reorganisations and structuring of in- and out-bound investments with extensive experience in multi-jurisdictional networking and integrated tax and legal advice. Is frequently appointed as speaker at seminars and has authored a series of publications in practice area.
Career: HEC (MBA) and Master in international taxation. Joined *Wilkie Farr & Gallagher* in 1993, becoming a partner in 2000.

DEBOUZY, Olivier
August & Debouzy, Paris +33 1 45 61 51 80
Recommended in Communications: Telecoms

DEBROUX, Michel
Herbert Smith, Paris +33 1 53 57 70 70
michel.debroux@herbertsmith.com
Recommended in Competition/Anti-trust
Specialisation: Senior associate in EC and Competition Law Department. Main area of work is French and EC competition law, with a particular focus on deregulated industries (mainly telecommunications, air transport and electricity). Has handled various antitrust cases and merger filings before French and EC authorities, including: clearance of the TPS agreements, creating France's second largest digital pay-TV operator, clearance of the CEGETEL agreements, creating France's largest telecom new entrant; acted on various antitrust complaints against France Télécom ('essential-facility' cases, pricing issues); advised two air carriers (US and UK) on a slot transfer deal; advises EDF on a number of competition, pricing and regulatory issues; has handled various merger filings (French and EC) in the field of electricity. Has spoken at various conferences, in French, English and Dutch.
Prof. Memberships: Former Executive Secretary, European Law Moot Court Society.
Career: Qualified in 1993 (Brussels Bar); Trainee at the EC Commission Legal Service (1991-92); awarded various leading prizes (1993-95); joined the Brussels office of *Lafleur Brown*, Canadian Law Firm, in 1992; joined *Jeantet & Associés* (Paris) in 1995. Joined *Herbert Smith* in January 2000.
Personal: Born July 9, 1966; 'Licence en droit' (LLM), University of Louvain, 1992; Postgraduate Diploma in EC Competition Law, King's College London (2000). Leisure interests include outdoor activities and theatre.

DEJEAN, Neils
Veil Armfelt Jourde La Garanderie, Paris +33 1 56 69 56 62
Recommended in Tax

DELATTRE, Olivier
Stibbe, Paris +33 1 40 62 20 00
olivier.delattre@stibbe.fr
Recommended in Tax
Specialisation: Partner at *Stibbe* in Tax Department. Practice consists mainly in international tax planning for corporations and high net worth individuals, including mergers and acquisitions, reorganisation and financial products. Also very active in tax litigation.
Prof. Memberships: IFA, ABA, IACF, Paris Bar.
Career: Master of Law and DESS of University of Paris Law School. Attended Boston University Law School. *Davis Polk & Wardwell* in 1981/1982. *Bureau Francis Lefebvre* from 1983 to 1994. Joined *Stibbe* in 1994.
Personal: Born March 12, 1955.

DELVOLVÉ, Jean-Louis
Delvolvé Rouche, Paris +33 1 42 27 70 68
Recommended in Arbitration (International)

DERAINS, Yves
Derains & Associés, Paris +33 1 45 53 38 38
Recommended in Arbitration (International)

DEROUIN, Philippe
Linklaters (a member firm of Linklaters & Alliance), Paris +33 1 56 43 56 43
phillipe.derouin@linklaters.com
Recommended in Tax
Specialisation: Specialist in taxation, providing general tax advice to business, particularly in relation to mergers and acquisitions, financial instruments, project and asset financing, both domestic and international; also tax litigation, including liability relating to taxation. Further specialisation in administrative law, providing advice relating to utilities projects (concessions and BOT) and privatisations. Also experienced in inheritance and estate planning and litigation.

DERVEAUX, Dominique
Denton Salès Vincent & Thomas, Paris +33 1 53 05 16 00
Recommended in Tax

F

DIAZ, Olivier
Darrois Villey Maillot Brochier, Paris
+33 1 45 02 19 19
Recommended in Corporate/M&A

DIBOUT, Patrick
HSD Ernst & Young, 92037 Paris-la-Défense
+33 1 46 93 60 33
Recommended in Tax

DIDIER, Edouard
Allen & Overy, 75009 Paris +33 1 40 06 54 00
Recommended in Corporate/M&A

DIRANI, Georges
Herbert Smith, Paris +33 1 53 57 70 70
gdirani@herbertsmith.com
Recommended in Banking & Finance
Specialisation: All types of financings, in particular banking, secured and unsecured syndicated loans, acquisition finance, structured finance (including securitisation), OTC derivatives products.
Career: 1987-92, Legal Advisor, Banque Nationale de Paris, in Paris and London. 1991-93, Lecturer in International Financial Law at CERAM Université de Nice. 1992-97, Legal director, Deutsche Bank/ Deutsche Morgan Grenfell, France. 1997-00 Partner, *Linklaters*, Paris. From 2000, has been Partner, *Herbert Smith*, Paris.
Personal: Born 19 September 1959. Published 'AFB Swap Master Agreement', Revue Banque 1988.

DJEHANE, Youssef
Gide Loyrette Nouel, Paris +33 1 40 75 61 87
djehane@gide.fr
Recommended in Corporate/Commercial
Specialisation: M&A, public listed corporations, take-overs and joint ventures. Advised on a number of cross-border transactions and has acted as counsel in several privatisations, both in France and internationally. Was involved in numerous transnational operations such as the Vivendi Canal+/Seagram merger.
Career: Partner in the firm since 1994. Admitted to the Paris Bar in 1987.
Personal: DESS (postgraduate degree) in Private Law, Paris University, 1985. Maîtrise in Law, Paris University, 1984. Speaks both French and English.

DONNEDIEU DE VABRES, Loraine
Jeantet & Associés, Paris +33 1 45 05 80 08
Recommended in Competition/Anti-trust

DOUVIER, Pierre-Jean
Bureau Francis Lefèbvre, Neuilly-sur-Seine Cedex
+33 1 47 38 55 00
Recommended in Tax

DUPUIS-TOUBOL, Frédérique
Bird & Bird, Paris +33 1 42 68 60 00
frederique.dupois-toubol@twobirds.com
Recommended in Communications: IT, Communications: Telecoms
Specialisation: Managing partner of *Bird & Bird* in Paris. Specialises in the Communications and Information Technology sectors. Main areas of work include: e-commerce contracts, litigation in IT, advice to telecommunications operators on licensing procedures with the French regulatory authorities, assisting cable operators to obtain transmission and broadcasting frequencies, advice to operators in commercial agreements, negotiation and dispute regulation relating to interconnection agreements (both for mobile and fixed line operators), advising many operators in commercial disputes with France Telecom.
Prof. Memberships: IBA Vice-president Committee Cm.
Career: Qualified in 1983. Joined *Jeantet & Associés* in 1983, becoming a partner in 1990. Joined *Bird & Bird* in 2000 as Managing Partner of the Paris Office. On the editorial board of 'Computer and Telecommunications Law Review'.
Personal: Born 24 March 1959. Studied at Paris X Nanterre for a PhD in Private Law (thesis: 'Software, a Legal Analysis', published by LGDJ).

ELLAND-GOLDSMITH, Michael
Clifford Chance, Paris Cedex 16 +33 1 44 05 52 52
Recommended in Project Finance

ENDRÉO, Gilles
Linklaters (a member firm of Linklaters & Alliance), Paris +33 1 56 43 56 43
gilles.endreo@linklaters.com
Recommended in Capital Markets
Specialisation: Specialist in international finance, in particular French securities and derivatives. Experience includes international and multinational offers of securities (including offers of securities denominated or capable of being denominated into Euros) and French privatisations, for example the tobacco company SEITA. Recent matters include acting for Deutsche Bank and Morgan Stanley on the establishment of the first ever EMTN Programme for the issue of obligations foncières; acting for Deutsche Bank on the first ever EMTN Programme for a corporate (LVMH); acting for Deutsche Bank on the establishment of French law EMTN Programmmes for Caisse Nationale des Caisses d'Epargne; La Poste; Casino and Suez Lyonnaise des Eaux.

ENTRAYGUES, Gilles
Cleary, Gottlieb, Steen & Hamilton, Paris
+33 1 40 74 68 00
Recommended in Tax

EPSTEIN, Jacques Henri
Shearman & Sterling, Paris +33 1 53 89 70 00
jacquesepstein@shearman.com
Recommended in Corporate/M&A
Specialisation: Partner in the Mergers & Acquisitions Group. Developed a strong corporate, merger and acquisition practice over the last twenty years. Represented major European telecommunications and aerospace companies, both privately and government owned, in their international acquisitions and alliances. Advises institutional investors and industrial companies in the creation of the corporate structure and the negotiations of the governance arrangements applicable to major projects. Frequently represents investors in private equity transactions.
Prof. Memberships: Paris Bar since 1977 and Brussels Bar since 1985.
Personal: Columbia University School of Law (LLM 1976) and University of Paris I, DES in private law (1975) and in European Community Law (1975).

FAUGÉROLAS, Laurent
Willkie Farr & Gallagher, Paris +33 1 53 43 45 00
Recommended in Capital Markets, Corporate/M&A

FÉRAL-SCHUHL, Christiane
Salans Hertzfeld & Heilbronn, Paris
+33 1 42 68 48 00
Recommended in Communications: IT

FOLLIE, Robert
Lovells, Paris +33 1 53 67 47 47
Recommended in Corporate/M&A

FONTAINE, Emmanuel
Gide Loyrette Nouel, Paris +33 1 40 75 61 16
fontaine@gide.fr
Recommended in Project Finance
Specialisation: Joint ventures, project and asset financing, transactions, civil engineering, and construction contracts. Clients include governments, banks, contractors, and concession companies in major infrastructure projects in France and abroad.
Prof. Memberships: Paris Bar (1973).
Career: Partner in the firm since 1979.
Personal: Institute of Political Science, 1968. DESS in Law, 1968. LLM, University of Berkeley, 1971.

FORSCHBACH, Thomas
Ashurst Morris Crisp, Paris +33 1 53 53 53 53
Recommended in Corporate/M&A

FOURGOUX, Jean-Louis
Fourgoux et Associés, Paris +33 1 55 65 16 65
Recommended in Competition/Anti-trust

FREGET, Olivier
Andersen Legal Association d'Avocats, Neuilly-sur-Seine +33 1 55 61 10 10
Recommended in Communications: IT

FRENKEL, Alain
Veil Armfelt Jourde La Garanderie, Paris
+33 1 56 69 56 62
Recommended in Tax

GAILLARD, Emmanuel
Shearman & Sterling, Paris +33 1 53 89 70 00
egaillard@shearman.com
Recommended in Arbitration (International)
Specialisation: Partner, Head of firm's International Arbitration Group and Managing Partner in *Shearman & Sterling's* Paris Office. Has acted as Counsel in more than 150 and as Arbitrator in more than 30 international arbitrations around the world, conducted in English and French. Co-author (with Professors Fouchard and Goldman) of 'Traité de l'Arbitrage Commercial International' (Litec 1996) and 'Fouchard Gaillard Goldman on International Commercial Arbitration' (Kluwer 1999), as well as numerous other publications on international arbitration and private international law.
Prof. Memberships: International Arbitration Institute (Chairman); Association Française de l'Arbitrage; Association Suisse de l'Arbitrage; IBA; ICC Institute ñ Corresponding Member; London Court of International Arbitration.
Career: Member of Paris Bar. Professor of Law, University of Paris XII (Private International Law,

International Commercial Arbitration). Visiting Professor of Law, Harvard Law School, 1984 (International Commercial Treaties, Comparative Private International Law). Chairman, International Arbitration Committee, International Law Association (1989-98). Member, Comité Français de Droit International Privé.
Personal: Born 1952. Educated Agrégé des Facultés de Droit, 1982, University of Paris II, PhD 1981. Fluent English.

GDANSKI, Martin
Norton Rose, Paris +33 1 53 89 56 00
gdanskimi@nortonrose.com
Recommended in Banking & Finance
Specialisation: French-qualified avocat dealing with mergers and acquisitions, acquisition finance, banking, structured finance. Main area of practice is international corporate and structured finance, including cross-border acquisitions and acquisition finance, management buy-outs/buy-ins, secured lending, and cable and telecommunications finance in France and in French-speaking Africa. Has advised French and foreign purchasers and sellers in several major acquisitions of French companies, has advised arrangers, agent banks or participating banks in a significant number of financings for cable and telecommunications companies following opening of sector to private companies.
Career: New York University (BA, 1973); Yale Law School (JD, 1976). Associate *Cleary, Gottlieb, Steen & Hamilton* (New York, 1976-78; Paris 1978-88); *Baudel, Salès, Vincent & Georges* (now *Salès Vincent & Associés*) partner Paris 1988-1994; *Norton Rose* 1993, Partner 1994, resident in Paris office.

GEORGES, Alain
Stibbe, Paris +33 1 40 62 20 00
Recommended in Competition/Anti-trust
Specialisation: Active in French and EU competition law, representing major companies and organisations before the European Commission, the French Conseil de la concurrence and the French and European Courts. Expertise in banking, payment systems and interbank settlement systems, in telecommunications and new technologies and in distribution. Involved in a number of high-profile cases in all of these areas.
Prof. Memberships: Admitted, 1974, as Conseil Juridique, Paris; 1981 (Paris Bar); 1993 (Brussels Bar)
Publications: Author of 'L'ultilisation en bourse d'informations privilégiées dans le droit des Etats-Unis' (Editions Economica, 1976).
Career: Ecole Supérieure des Sciences Economiques et Commerciales, Paris (1968); Paris 1 University (Doctorate of law, 1974). Practised from 1974 through 1981 at *Cleary Gottlieb Steen & Hamilton* (Paris and New York). Partner of Salès Vincent Georges from 1981 through 1994 (Paris and Brussels).
Personal: Born May 23, 1946.

GEORGES, Martine
De Pardieu Brocas Maffei & Leygonie, Paris
+33 1 53 57 71 71
Recommended in Communications: Telecoms

GINESTIÉ, Philippe
Ginestié Paley-Vincent & Associés, Paris
+33 1 5323 4012
ginestie@ginestie.com
Recommended in Tax
Specialisation: Founder of *Ginestié-Paley Vincent & Associés* and uses experience in law, tax and business for an original approach to the service offered to clients. Main areas of work are negotiation, mergers and acquisitions, tax and arbitration. Has acted for a number of companies on matters concerning the legal organisation of corporate power control. Is responsible for the renewed interest in France in the sociétés en commandite par action (Limited partnerships), a type of company which had almost fallen into disuse. Showed how the great flexibility of this type of company was particularly well suited for a number of purposes (anti-takeover devices, family control organisation, professional team management co-optation, organisation of relationships between capital and management and any type of reallocation of power and profits within a corporation). Has developed the scope of firms' activities in arbitration both as a litigator and as an arbitrator, thus gaining an insider view of the arbitration process.
Prof. Memberships: Supervisory board of Castorama Dubois Investissment S.C.A. (a listed company in DIY).
Career: Ecole des Hautes Etudes Commerciales (HEC), DES in Law, MBA at Harvard Business School, ITP at Harvard Law School. Joined Peat Marwick Mitchel until 1973 setting up own firm. Director of Société Rochefortaise Communication (a listed French Industrial group).
Personal: Born 1 January 1943, leisure interest include playing the flute and the piano. Lives in Paris.

GISSINGER, Pierre
Allen & Overy, 75009 Paris +33 1 40 06 54 00
Recommended in Capital Markets

GIUSTINI, Anthony
White & Case LLP, Paris +33 1 55 04 15 33
agiustini@whitecase.com
Recommended in Project Finance, Project Finance: Francophone Africa
Specialisation: Partner, currently based in the firm's Paris office. Leading commercial lawyer whose diverse expertise ranges from finance (particularly project finance) and M&A to restructuring and licensing. Co-heads the firm's projects, energy and infrastructure group in Europe, Middle East and Africa as well as the firm's Italian practice.
Prof. Memberships: A member of the New York State Bar, the DC and Paris Bars.
Personal: Speaks fluent English, Italian and French.

GODET, Dominique
Jeantet & Associés, Paris +33 1 45 05 80 08
Recommended in Tax

GOUTHIÈRE, Bruno
Bureau Francis Lefebvre, Neuilly-sur-Seine Cedex
+33 1 47 38 55 00
Recommended in Tax

GUNTHER, Jacques-Philippe
Freshfields Bruckhaus Deringer, Paris
+33 1 44 56 44 56
jacques.gunther@freshfields.com
Recommended in Competition/Anti-trust
Specialisation: Partner in corporate group. Main areas of competence are French and EC merger control, restrictive practices, state aids and distribution law for a wide range of corporate clients, in particular in the media, telecoms and energy sectors.

HERBELIN, Philippe
Linklaters (a member firm of Linklaters & Alliance), Paris +33 1 56 43 56 43
philippe.herbelin@linklaters.com
Recommended in Capital Markets
Specialisation: Specialises in international finance, French securities and bourse matters. Experience includes acting as French advisor on primary and secondary offerings of shares (including privatisations) and other equity-linked securities, primarily in France and in relation to the listing of French and foreign companies on the Paris Bourse; and advising on a wide variety of other euro and French capital markets, bourse and derivative matters including French law MTN programmes, CP and CD programmes, bond issues, and covered warrants.

HURSTEL, Daniel
Willkie Farr & Gallagher, Paris +33 1 53 43 45 00
Recommended in Corporate/M&A

HUSE, Joseph
Freshfields Bruckhaus Deringer, Paris
+33 1 44 56 44 56
joseph.huse@freshfields.com
Recommended in Project Finance
Specialisation: Mains areas of work are project finance, construction, enviromental law and international arbitration. Sector experience includes the energy, telecoms and water industries.

HUYGHÉ DE MAHENGE, Yves
Freshfields Bruckhaus Deringer, Paris
+33 1 44 56 44 56
yhm@freshfields.com
Recommended in Corporate/M&A
Specialisation: Head of the Corporate and M&A department of the Paris office. Principal practice areas cover mergers and acquisitions, privatisations and stock exchange litigation. Professional experience includes diverse sectors of industry, such as telecommunications, automotive, and large scale distribution.
Personal: Native language is French, but speaks fluent English and Italian.

JARVIN, Sigvard
Lagerlöf & Leman Advokatbyrå (A member firm of Linklaters & Alliance), Paris +33 1 56 43 56 86
sigvard.jarvin@lol.se
Recommended in Arbitration (International)
Specialisation: Partner, co-head of *Linklaters & Alliance* International Arbitration Group in Paris. General Counsel of the ICC International Court of Arbitration (1982-1987). Member of the same Court (1988-1995). Has been involved in some 150 international arbitrations as arbitrator or counsel.

F

Arbitration experience includes various fields of industry and commerce such as large and complex disputes relating to oil and geothermal energy, the supply of industrial plants, reinsurance claims, construction claims, licensing of know-how in the telecommunications sector, sale of armaments and maritime transport.
Prof. Memberships: Swedish Bar Association, Paris Bar Association.
Publications: General editor of Stockholm Arbitration Report and in charge of the arbitration chronicle of Lamy Contrats Internationaux. Rapporteur at the 1998 ICCA Congress. Author of a number of articles.
Career: Qualified in 1966 at the University of Stockholm. Associate of Law Offices of *S G Archibald*, Paris (1987-1991), joined *Lagerlöf & Leman* in 1991.
Personal: Born 30 August, 1942. Speaks English, French, German and Swedish.

JAUFFRET, Olivier
Linklaters (a member firm of Linklaters & Alliance), Paris +33 1 56 43 56 43
olivier.jauffret@linklaters.com
Recommended in Banking & Finance
Specialisation: Experienced in all types of financings, secured and unsecured syndicated loans, LBO acquisition financings, property financings, structured capital market products (including securitisation), OTC derivatives and international securities offerings. Recent significant transactions include advising the arrangers of the senior debt and the mezzanine debt on the financing of the LBO of the Eurogestion Group; advising the equity investor on the financing of the LBO of Michel Thierry (through a public takeover) and of its clothing division; advising the arranger on the property financing of the Hyatt Regency Charles de Gaulle; and advising AXA on the financing of the exchange offer on Axa Financial.

KAHN, Daniel
Kahn Associés, Paris +33 1 45 01 45 01
Recommended in Communications: IT

KAPLAN, Charles
Herbert Smith, Paris +33 1 53 57 70 70
ckaplan@brownwoodlaw.com
Recommended in Arbitration (International)
Specialisation: Head of the Litigation/Arbitration Group in the Paris Office of *Herbert Smith.* Specialises in international commercial litigation and arbitration. Has appeared in a large number of commercial proceedings before the French Courts as well as in arbitrations under ICC, ICSID, UNCITRAL, and AFA (French Arbitration Association) and other rules. Principal areas of specialisation are international sale contracts, insurance litigation (both marine and non-marine, including hull and cargo claims, liability insurance, fine arts insurance and broker's liability), commodity trading, and international commercial disputes, generally. Also acts in disputes involving large-scale projects in the fields of energy and natural resources. Editor of the section on French Arbitration Law of the International Law Office website.
Prof. Memberships: Comité Français de l'Arbitrage; Association Française de Droit Maritime.
Career: Qualified in England and Wales in 1980 and in 1992 as a member of the Paris bar; *Coudert Frères* Paris, Arbitration and Litigation, 1984-96 (Partner 1994-96); Litigation Partner *Herbert Smith*, Paris, from 1996 to the present.
Personal: Born 26 December 1958. Attended Cambridge University 1976-79 (MA Philosophy and Law). Lives in Paris.

KETT, Peter
Slaughter and May, Paris +33 1 44 05 60 00
peter.kett@slaughterandmay.com
Recommended in Banking & Finance
Specialisation: Practice consists principally of general company, commercial and banking work in both English and French law. In the banking field has been heavily involved in sovereign foreign debt reschedulings, asset financings, acquisition financings and loan transactions generally. Company and commercial experience relates particularly to foreign corporate investments into France, with particular emphasis on mergers and acquisitions.
Prof. Memberships: The Law Society, Paris Bar.
Career: Joined *Slaughter & May* in 1970, qualified as a solicitor in 1972 and became a partner in 1978. Has been in Paris since 1974.
Personal: Speaks English, French and German.

KIRRY, Antoine
Debevoise & Plimpton, Paris +33 1 40 73 12 12
Recommended in Arbitration (International)

KROTOFF, François
Gide Loyrette Nouel, Paris +33 1 40 75 61 26
krotoff@gide.fr
Recommended in Project Finance: Francophone Africa
Specialisation: Project financing with a particular emphasis on mining projects and infrastructure projects (fixed and cellular telephone networks, water distribution, road infrastructures, etc.). Wide experience in the restructuring and privatisation of companies, mainly in Eastern Europe and Africa.
Publications: Co-author of a book published in 1992: 'Investing in Central and Eastern Europe' (Joly Editions).
Career: Partner in the firm since 1984. Admitted to the Paris Bar in 1978.
Personal: Maîtrise in Private Law, Aix-en-Provence University, 1976. Graduated from the Institute of Political Science, Paris, 1975. Speaks both French and English.

L'HOMME, Jean
Freshfields Bruckhaus Deringer, Paris +33 1 44 56 44 56
jean.l'homme@freshfields.com
Recommended in Banking & Finance
Specialisation: Specialises in Paris Banking and Finance work including structured and asset-based financing and cross-border leasing.

LAURIOL, Thierry
Jeantet & Associés, Paris +33 1 45 05 80 08
tlauriol@jeantet.fr
Recommended in Project Finance: Francophone Africa
Specialisation: Partner in charge of the Energy and Natural Resources Department. Specialises in energy and mining law (including the whole process to valorise natural resources i.e. exploration, prospecting, development, production, transportation, refining, fining and distribution), liberalisation of electricity and natural gas in Europe the drafting of legal opinions and contracts having incidences in transportation law, environmental law, insurance law, private international law, public international law, project financing and arbitration. These activities cover counsel to governments and private investors in privatisation operations regarding the energy and natural resources sector, especially in Europe and Africa.
Prof. Memberships: Paris Bar (President of the Africa Commission), IBA (member of the section 'Energy and Natural Resources Law', I.D.E.F. (Institut internatonal de droit d'expression et d'inspiration francaise). Listed arbitrator for the Court Commune de Justice et d'Arbitrage (Abidjan) and Comite Francais de la Chambre de Commerce Internationale (ICC).
Career: Admitted 1991, Paris Bar certificate in Droit Economique and Droit des relations internationale. November 1987 – October 1992 *Coudert Frères*, January 1993 to present *Jeantet & Associés.*
Personal: Born 16 May 1958 in Algiers. Attended University of Paris Pantheon/Sorbonne (DEA International Private Law and International Trade Law, 1981, DESS in comparative law on energey, 1982), Institut de Droit compare (Diploma 1983), University of California at Berkeley (visiting scholar 1983-1985), University of Paris-Sceaux (doctorat d'Etat, 1989 with distinction 'trés honorable', award Henri Capitant. 'The contracts relative to the exploitation of natural resources').

LAZAREFF, Serge
Cabinet d'Avocats Lazareff & Associés, Paris +33 1 44 29 32 53
Recommended in Arbitration (International)

LAZARUS, Claude
Herbert Smith, Paris +33 1 53 57 70 70
Recommended in Competition/Anti-trust

LE GALL, Jean-Pierre
Sullivan & Cromwell, Paris +33 1 44 50 60 00
legallj@sullcrom.com
Recommended in Tax
Specialisation: Corporate and tax law in French and English, including French company tax. Practises international and domestic tax law, focusing in particular on M&A, financial instruments, and estate tax planning.
Prof. Memberships: Chairman of the Permanent Scientific Committee of the International Fiscal Association.
Career: Joined *Sullivan & Cromwell* as partner in 2001. Previously a partner at *Jeantet & Associés.*
Personal: Graduated from Grenoble Law University in 1957 and took doctor's degree in 1961 at the University of Paris. Was admitted as a professor of law in 1963 (agrégation de droit privé). Now teaches tax and corporate law at the Paris II University. Actively participates in conferences and congresses. Author of many books and articles.

LE GRIS, Ines
Willkie Farr & Gallagher, Paris +33 1 53 43 45 00
Recommended in Capital Markets

LEBEUF, Martin
De Pardieu Brocas Maffei & Leygonie, Paris +33 1 53 57 71 71
Recommended in Banking & Finance, Corporate/M&A

LECAT, Jean-Jacques
Bureau Francis Lefèbvre, Neuilly-sur-Seine Cedex +33 1 47 38 55 00
Recommended in Project Finance

LEE, Michael
Norton Rose, Paris +33 1 53 89 56 00
leemja@nortonrose.com; porterk@nortonrose.com
Recommended in Arbitration (International)
Specialisation: Head of *Norton Rose*'s International Arbitration Group. Main areas of practice are international arbitration and commercial banking litigation in which he has had over twenty five years experience. Acts as counsel for clients worldwide involved in international commercial arbitration and also sits as an arbitrator in both ad hoc and institutional arbitrations. Also sits on professional disciplinary tribunals. Joint editor of the IBA publication 'Obtaining Evidence in Another Jurisdiction in Business Disputes'. Has also written various articles and spoken at seminars worldwide principally on international arbitration and banking dispute resolution.
Prof. Memberships: Member Law Society of England and Wales; International Bar Association; American Bar Association; UK Member ICC Court of International Arbitration; Member of ICC Commission on International Arbitration; Fellow Chartered Institute of Arbitrators; Director City Disputes Panel; CEDR Accredited Mediator.
Career: Qualified 1996; joined *Norton Rose* in 1970, becoming a partner in 1973; Managing Partner of Commercial Litigation Department 1989-1996; Managing Partner Paris office 1997 to date.
Personal: Born 1942. Graduated in law from Durham University in 1963. Leisure interests include sailing and skiing. Resides in Paris.

LEFÈVRE, Jean-Marc
Linklaters (a member firm of Linklaters & Alliance), Paris +33 1 56 43 56 43
jean-marc.lefevre@linklaters.com
Recommended in Corporate/M&A
Specialisation: Extensive experience in a broad range of corporate work with main areas being mergers and acquisitions, joint ventures and project financing (eg Channel Tunnel). Recent major transactions include advising Lafarge SA in relation to the LBO of its speciality products business, Allied Domecq on its acquisition of the Mumm and Perrier-Jouët champagnes and Philips on the merger of Atos S.A. and Origin.
Career: Co-head of *Linklaters* Paris.

LEPRETRE, Jean-Michel
Rambaud Martel, 75782 Paris Cedex 16
+33 1 40 67 17 00
secret.jpm@rambaud-martel.com
Recommended in Corporate/M&A
Specialisation: Has jointly led the corporate, M & A and securities practice of *Rambaud Martel* since 1978. Represents clients in regulatory matters, transactions and disputes involving acquisitions, financing, restructuring and divestitures. Also advises capital equity and MBOs. Acts as counsel to several of France's leading corporations, commercial and investment banks, and other state-owned or private-sector firms in the industrial, financial and services areas. Through representation of both French and foreign clients, has been involved in several highly publicised transactions, court litigations and arbitration matters in recent years.
Publications: Author of a number of publications and speeches relating to corporate reorganisation, MBOs and other corporate law issues.
Career: Member of the Paris Bar since 1978. Co-Managing partner of *RAMBAUD MARTEL*, a firm which comprises 80 attorneys, including 28 partners.
Personal: Born 18 December 1952, former student of the Institut d'Etudes Judiciaires in Paris and received degrees from the University of Paris Law School in 1977.

LETRÉGUILLY, Hervé
Shearman & Sterling, Paris +33 1 53 89 71 30
hletreguilly@shearman.com
Recommended in Capital Markets
Specialisation: Partner in the Capital Markets and Mergers and Acquisitions Groups. Specialises in French and international corporate, capital markets and mergers and acquisitions transactions. Extensive experience in initial public offerings, privatisations, securities, specialised financial products and mergers and acquisitions.
Prof. Memberships: Avocat at the Paris Bar.
Publications: 'Record breaking growth in the French securities market in 1999 as the euro market asserts itself', in 2000 International Investment review published by Euromoney in Revue des Sociétés – Dalloz; 'France', in the Issuing Securities Supplement published by Corporate Finance, September 1999; 'Tender Offer Regulations in France', in the Global M&A Yearbook published by Corporate Finance, May 1999; 'Corporate Governance in France', published by International Financial Law Review and 'Offres publiques d'acquisition: les réformes apportées par le nouveau règlement général du Conseil des Marchés Financiers', published by La Revue des Sociétés, October 1999.
Career: Joined *Shearman & Sterling* in July 1987.
Personal: Attended Université of Paris I-Panthéon Sorbonne, DEA (1986).

LEWIS, Jonathan
Clifford Chance, Paris Cedex 16 +33 1 44 05 52 52
Recommended in Capital Markets

LEYGONIE, Jean
De Pardieu Brocas Maffei & Leygonie, Paris +33 1 53 57 71 71
Recommended in Corporate/M&A

LUCAS DE LEYSSAC, Claude
DS Avocats, Paris +33 1 53 67 50 00
Recommended in Competition/Anti-trust

MAFFEI, Antoine
De Pardieu Brocas Maffei & Leygonie, Paris +33 1 53 57 71 71
Recommended in Banking & Finance, Capital Markets

MAILLOT, Alain
Darrois Villey Maillot Brochier, Paris +33 1 45 02 19 19
Recommended in Corporate/M&A

MAÎTRE-DEVALLON, Claudine
Rambaud Martel, 75782 Paris Cedex 16
+33 1 40 67 17 00
c.maitredevallon@rambaud-martel.com
Recommended in Competition/Anti-trust
Specialisation: Head of EC and French competition law department, represents major companies and organisations before the French competition authorities (Conseil de la Concurrence, Ministère de l'Economie) and the European Commission. Covers the whole spectrum of distribution and competition law, including antitrust, merger controls and state aids cases. Has handled numerous high profile antitrust and merger control cases, in particular in the construction, concrete, cement, electricity, advertising, transport, distribution, and paper sectors. Has extensive experience in cartel investigations. Has also specific expertise in advertising law and in white-collar crime cases connected with antitrust law.
Publications: Articles and commentaries on competition law issues.
Career: Qualified in 1969. Joined *RAMBAUD MARTEL* in 1976, and became a partner in 1977. Head of EC/competition law Department since 1986.
Personal: Born 27 March, 1945. University of Paris (Law, Sociology); Center for European Communities; Institut d'Etudes Judiciaires (Paris).

MAJERHOLC, Norbert
White & Case LLP, Paris +33 1 55 04 15 15
nmajerholc@whitecase.com
Recommended in Tax
Specialisation: Partner in *White & Case* Paris office. Registered as a specialist in tax law, corporate law and international transactions. Has extensive experience in structuring M&A transactions, especially LBOs, structured financings and applications for tax rulings with the French Ministry, undertaking tax audits and court representations in tax litigation matters.
Prof. Memberships: Member of the Paris Court.
Career: Joined *White & Case* in 1997. Fluent French and English.

MARTEL, Jean-Pierre
Rambaud Martel, 75782 Paris Cedex 16
+33 1 40 67 17 00
secret.jpm@rambaud-martel.com
Recommended in Corporate/M&A
Specialisation: Has led the corporate, M & A and securities practice of *RAMBAUD MARTEL* since 1967. Represents his clients in regulatory matters, transactions and disputes involving acquisitions,

F

financing, restructuring and divestitures. Also advises the French stock exchange authorities on issues relating to securities regulations and take-overs of listed companies. Acts as counsel to several of France's leading corporations, commercial and investment banks, as well as major companies in the industrial, financial and services areas. Through representation of both French and foreign clients, has been involved in several highly publicised transactions, court litigations and arbitration matters in recent years, including some of the most sharply contested acquisitions in the country.
Prof. Memberships: Paris Bar, IAI Member.
Publications: Author of a number of publications and speeches relating to stock exchange and securities laws, bankruptcy and reorganisation, and other corporate law issues.
Career: Member of the Paris Bar since 1967. Founding member of *RAMBAUD MARTEL*, a firm which comprises 80 attorneys, including 28 partners.
Personal: Born 6 January 1944, former student of the Institute of Political Studies in Paris and received degrees from the University of Nancy and the University of Paris Law School in 1967.

MARTIN, Didier
Bredin Prat, Paris +33 1 44 35 35 35
didiermartin@bredinprat.com
Recommended in Corporate/M&A
Specialisation: Advice on both non-contentious and contentious commercial matters and in penal matters. In 1999, instructed in respect of the privatisations of Air France, Aérospatiale Matra and Crédit Lyonnais, advised on the Lagardère/Canal+ agreement, on the Sanofi/Synthélabo merger, on the combination project between Pechiney, Alcan and Algroup and the takeover regarding Promodès (launched by Carrefour). In 2000, advised on the merger of Aérospatiale Matra and Dasa into EADS. Instructed in respect of numerous mergers, acquisitions, takeovers and litigations arising from them, over several years.
Prof. Memberships: Member of the Financial Market Committee of the MEDEF (Confédération of Medium and Large Enterprises).
Publications: Author of various works on company law and on takeovers and privatisations.
Career: Admitted to the Paris Bar in 1978. Partner of *Gide Loyrette Nouel* law firm from 1985 to 1991. Partner of *Bredin Prat* law firm since 1992.

MATHESON, Glenn
Freshfields Bruckhaus Deringer, Paris
+33 1 44 56 44 56
glenn.matheson@freshfields.com
Recommended in Banking & Finance
Specialisation: Specialises in asset finance and banking. Sector experience includes banking, aircraft, ships and rolling stock.

MAYER, Pierre
Pierre Mayer – Sole Practitioner, Paris
+33 1 4020 9622
Recommended in Arbitration (International)

MAZET, Gérard
Sullivan & Cromwell, Paris +33 1 4450 6000
mazetg@sullcrom.com
Recommended in Corporate/M&A
Specialisation: Partner, specialising in domestic and cross border mergers and acquisitions, corporate reorganisations and strategic alliances. Has covered many aspects of corporate and tax law with progressive specialisation in cross border acquisitions. Regularly involved in major transactions representing purchasers, sellers and joint venture partners of both listed and private companies and, in the case of some privatisations, as advisor to the French State. In recent years has been particularly involved in transnational mergers and similar transactions. With respect to non-listed companies, has extensive experience in open bid procedures. Acts as arbitrator in acquisition related disputes.
Prof. Memberships: Paris Bar; currently chairs the International Committee of the French National Bar Council (CNB).
Career: Joined *Sullivan & Cromwell* as partner in 2001. Previously a partner at *Jeantet & Associés*.
Personal: Educated in England to university level before combining studies in Law (graduated from Universities of Paris and Montpellier) and business (MBA of the Ecole des Hautes Etudes Commerciales – HEC).

MCDONALD, Thomas J.
White & Case LLP, Paris +33 1 55 04 15 15
tmcdonald@whitecase.com
Recommended in Banking & Finance
Specialisation: Senior partner working in firm's Paris office. Extensive experience in international financial transactions, with emphasis on asset and equipment finance. Acts for banks, lessors and equity participants in cross-border transactions involving aircraft, vessels and other equipment. Skilled in adapting range of US and UK finance techniques to the French legal environment.
Prof. Memberships: Member New York State Bar, Louisiana State Bar, Avocat au Barreau de Paris.
Personal: Fluent English and French.

MESNY, Jean-Paul
Mesny et Associés, Paris +33 1 43 80 71 94
Recommended in Tax

MICHAUD, Jean-Luc
Freshfields Bruckhaus Deringer, Paris
+33 1 44 56 44 56
jean-luc.michaud@freshfields.com
Recommended in Banking & Finance, Capital Markets
Specialisation: Partner in Finance Department. Has a wide range of experience including banking, structured finance and asset finance.

MINOR, Pierre
De Pardieu Brocas Maffei & Leygonie, Paris
+33 1 53 57 71 71
Recommended in Capital Markets

MOREAU, Bertrand
Moreau Bernard Amigues et Darmon, Paris
+33 1 42 66 10 11
Recommended in Arbitration (International)

MORGAN DE RIVERY, Eric
Siméon & Associés, Paris +33 1 40 75 08 08
Recommended in Competition/Anti-trust

MOSTAFAVI, Siamak
Allen & Overy, 75009 Paris +33 1 40 06 54 00
Recommended in Tax

NABARRO, Jonathan
Ashurst Morris Crisp, Paris +33 1 53 53 53 53
Recommended in Banking & Finance

PARLEANI, Gilbert
Gilbert Parleani, Paris +33 1 44 76 83 78
Recommended in Competition/Anti-trust

PAROLAI, Richard
Clifford Chance, Paris Cedex 16 +33 1 44 05 52 52
Recommended in Capital Markets

PAULSSON, Jan
Freshfields Bruckhaus Deringer, Paris
+33 1 44 56 44 56
jan.paulsson@freshfields.com
Recommended in Arbitration (International)
Specialisation: Partner in the dispute resolution group, specialising in international arbitration and public international law.

PAYAN, Daniel
Willkie Farr & Gallagher, Paris +33 1 53 43 45 00
Recommended in Banking & Finance, Corporate/M&A

PEIGNEY, Gilles
White & Case LLP, Paris +33 1 55 04 15 15
gpeigney@whitecase.com
Recommended in Banking & Finance
Specialisation: One of the most well-respected French finance lawyers. Executive Partner of the *White & Case* Paris office. Range of bank finance and corporate law expertise. Regularly represents major borrowers, senior and junior lenders in financings involving the acquisition of companies in Europe and in the United States. Has also advised huge range of sovereign borrowers.
Prof. Memberships: Member of Paris Bar.
Personal: Fluent French and English.

PETILON, Jean-Claude
Coudert Frères, Paris +33 1 53 83 60 00
petilonjc@paris.coudert.com
Recommended in Project Finance: Francophone Africa
Specialisation: Of Counsel, heads the African department of *Coudert Frères*. Primary specialist areas are Energy (petroleum and mining, and the restructuring of the electricity/water sectors) and Privatisation (both as an advisor to governments on private operations and as a contributor to preparing and drafting privatisation laws and regulations). Has acted for African governments and has assisted in the reorganisation of various sectors such as power and telecommunications, has drafted legislation and regulations, assisted major mining and petroleum companies in negotiating contracts and special tax regimes, and private operators in obtaining investment code privileges and financing for the implementation of their projects. Negotiates and drafts in both French and English.

Career: Admitted to District of Columbia Bar in 1975; admitted as French Conseil Juridique in 1981; admitted to Paris Bar in 1992. Before joining *Coudert Frères* in 1981, practised with *Duncan Allen and Mitchell* in Kinshasa, Zaîre (now known as République Democratique du Congo).

PORTIER, Philippe, Paul
Jeantet & Associés, Paris +33 1 45 05 80 08
Recommended in Capital Markets

POUDELET, François
Allen & Overy, 75009 Paris +33 1 40 06 54 00
Recommended in Capital Markets

PRAT, Jean-Francois
Bredin Prat, Paris +33 1 44 35 35 35
Recommended in Corporate/M&A

PRAT, Sebastien
Bredin Prat, Paris +33 1 44 35 35 35
sprat@jeantet.fr
Recommended in Corporate/M&A
Specialisation: Partner dealing with securitites and stock market regulating, corporate law, bankruptcy and litigation. Contributor to various working groups with French Government related to the evolution of corporate and stock market law.
Prof. Memberships: Paris Bar.
Publications: Author of 'Pactes relatifs aux transferts de valeurs mobilere' and various articles 'Le Rachat d'Entreprise par les Salaries (LMBO)', 'Les apports du project Marini au droit des societes francais').
Career: Qualified 1992 (Paris).
Personal: Born 31 May 1965. Attended Paris II University DEA, Paris V University Doctorat en droit.

QUÉRÉ, Michel
Freshfields Bruckhaus Deringer, Paris
+33 1 44 56 44 56
michel.quere@freshfields.com
Recommended in Banking & Finance
Specialisation: Specialist finance (including syndicated loans, refinancing, securitisation, defeasances, restructurisations), mergers and acquisitions.

RAFFIN, Marie-Hélène
Andersen Legal Association d'Avocats, Neuilly-sur-Seine +33 1 55 61 10 10
Recommended in Tax

RAPP, Lucien
Serra Michaud & Associés, 75008 Paris
+33 1 44 21 97 97
Recommended in Communications: Telecoms

RENTMEESTERS, Luc
Allen & Overy, 75009 Paris +33 1 40 06 54 00
Recommended in Banking & Finance

RIGGS, John
White & Case LLP, Paris +33 1 55 04 15 15
jriggs@whitecase.com
Recommended in Project Finance
Specialisation: Well-respected international finance partner based in *White & Case* Paris office. Leading reputation for work in areas of project finance, equipment finance, capital markets and structured finance as well as international mergers and acquisitions.
Career: Qualified to practice in the United States and in France.
Personal: Fluent English and French.

SAINT-ESTEBEN, Robert
Bredin Prat, Paris +33 1 44 35 35 35
Recommended in Competition/Anti-trust

SALBAING, Christian
Freshfields Bruckhaus Deringer, Paris
+33 1 44 56 44 56
christian.salbaing@freshfields.com
Recommended in Project Finance
Specialisation: Specialises in international joint ventures, project work (particularly in emerging markets) and cross-border M&A.
Prof. Memberships: Avocat á la Cour, Paris Bar (1979); also admitted to the State Bar of California (1974); U.S. District Court for Northern District of California (1974) and the Bar of the Province of Quebec (1971). American Bar Association, the International Bar Association.

SALÈS, Jacques
Denton Salès Vincent & Thomas, Paris
+33 1 53 05 16 00
Recommended in Corporate/M&A

SALZMANN, Joëlle
Gide Loyrette Nouel, Paris +33 1 40 75 61 67
salzmann@gide.fr
Recommended in Competition/Anti-trust
Specialisation: Has acquired extensive knowledge and experience in all areas of French and EC competition law. Has developed a particular know-how in the field of French merger control, advising major clients such as Eurosucres (sugar production and commercialisation), Casino (retail distribution) and Fort James (household and health products). Also handles numerous antitrust cases before the French Competition authorities (among others, important recent cases concerned anti-competitive practices of the main French advertising operators and abuse of dominant position on the couponing market).
Prof. Memberships: Paris Bar (1987).
Publications: Is the author of one of the most consulted books on French merger control ('Le Contrôle National des Concentrations,' July, 1996) and regularly publishes in a French competition newsletter ('Concurrence Actualité Express'). Also spoken at numerous conferences.
Career: Joined *Gide Loyrette Nouel* in 1989, partner since 1999.
Personal: Holds a postgraduate degree in EC Law (University of Paris I).

SARRAILHÉ, Philippe
Ashurst Morris Crisp, Paris +33 1 53 53 53 53
Recommended in Corporate/M&A

SCHOEN, Thierry
Clifford Chance, Paris Cedex 16 +33 1 44 05 52 52
Recommended in Corporate/M&A

SCHWARTZ, Eric
Freshfields Bruckhaus Deringer, Paris
+33 1 44 56 44 56
eric.schwartz@freshfields.com
Recommended in Arbitration (International)
Specialisation: Has extensive experience in international arbitration, in particular of disputes relating to civil engineering and construction contracts.

SEPPALA, Christopher
White & Case LLP, Paris +33 1 55 04 15 15
cseppala@whitecase.com
Recommended in Arbitration (International)
Specialisation: Partner based in the firm's Paris office with a reputation for excellence across broad-ranging commercial arbitration and litigation practice. Acts on a wide variety of disputes for both corporate and sovereign entities. Legal Adviser to FIDIC Contracts Committee.
Prof. Memberships: Member of New York and Paris Bars.
Career: Joined *White & Case* as a partner in 1988.
Personal: Fluent English and French.

SERRA, Claude
Serra Michaud & Associés, 75008 Paris
+33 1 44 21 97 97
Recommended in Communications: Telecoms

SERVAN-SCHREIBER, Pierre
Skadden, Arps, Slate, Meagher & Flom LLP, Paris
+33 1 55 27 11 00
Recommended in Corporate/M&A

STREICHENBERGER, Renaud
Bureau Francis Lefèbvre, Neuilly-sur-Seine Cedex
+33 1 47 38 55 00
Recommended in Tax

SUREAU, François
Darrois Villey Maillot Brochier, Paris
+33 1 45 02 19 19
Recommended in Corporate/M&A

SYED, David
Watson, Farley & Williams, Paris +33 1 5383 1212
dsyed@wfw.com
Recommended in Banking & Finance
Specialisation: Head of Paris office. Major work: Specialises in banking, domestic and cross-border tax leasing (aircraft, railcars, equipment and real estate) and structured finance. Also handles project agreements and financings. Has spoken recently at various US/ European cross-border leasing and asset finance conferences.
Prof. Memberships: Ordre des Avocats, International Bar Association, Association des Avocats Conseils d'Enterprise.
Career: Four years as in-house lawyer in the Legal Department at Renault in Paris, followed by two years as an associate and local partner at *Baker & McKenzie* Paris. Joined *Watson, Farley & Williams* in 1992 as a partner.
Personal: Born 1 March 1964. Married. Attended Université de Reims (1985 LLB Hons), University of Exeter (1987, LLM Hons).

F

TARIKA, Robert
HSD Ernst & Young, 92037 Paris-la-Défense
+33 1 46 93 60 33
Recommended in Tax

TERRAY, Jacques
Gide Loyrette Nouel, Paris +33 1 40 75 61 07
terray@gide.fr
Recommended in Banking & Finance
Specialisation: Senior Partner in the Finance/Project Finance department. Assists bank clients, French and foreign, in their establishment, their lending and other credit activities, their funding, as well as in regulatory matters. Expertise in letters of comfort and other guarantees, and more recently on the setting up of project finance (Eurotunnel, 1986), and rescheduling of project finance (Eurodisney, 1994). Played a decisive role in the launching of securitisation in France (1989), advising arrangers and originators in domestic and offshore transactions. Addressed the issues raised by the introduction of the single European currency in January 1999.
Prof. Memberships: Member of the Association for the European Monetary Union and of the American Arbitration Association.
Career: Joined the firm in 1965, and became a partner in 1971.
Personal: Obtained a Master's degree from the University of Paris in 1961, was admitted to the Paris Bar in 1962 and obtained an LLM at Colombia Law School (USA) in 1965.

TERRIER, Georges
Jeantet & Associés, Paris +33 1 4505 8008
Recommended in Corporate/M&A

THILL, Pierre-Sebastien
Bureau Francis Lefèbvre, Neuilly-sur-Seine Cedex
+33 1 47 38 55 00
Recommended in Tax

THOMAS, Eric
Freshfields Bruckhaus Deringer, Paris
+33 1 44 56 44 56
eric.thomas@freshfields.com
Recommended in Tax
Specialisation: Specialises in domestic and international tax, capital markets, securitisations, asset and structured finance.

TIRARD, Jean-Marc
Tirard Naudin, Paris +33 1 53 57 36 00
tirard.naudin@online.fr
Recommended in Tax
Specialisation: French and international tax. Has considerable experience advising major French and foreign companies and financial institutions on domestic and international corporate tax issues as well as negotiating with the French tax authorities and handling tax litigation. Has been associated with numerous high-profile corporate transactions, including major international acquisitions and cross-border mergers. Firm also practises extensively in the international transfer pricing area with a particular emphasis on the consensual resolution of transfer pricing issues through advance pricing agreements (APA). It is involved in several of the few APA applications introduced by major multinational firms further to the recent introduction of this procedure in France. Also has extensive experience in tax and estate planning for high net worth individuals. Has published many articles and books in French and English including 'Corporate Taxation in EU Countries' (Longmans).
Prof. Memberships: International Fiscal Association (IFA), Union International des Avocats (UIA), Licensing Executives Society (LES), Society of Trust and Estate Practitioners (STEP).
Career: Co-founded present firm in 1997. Began career in tax administration (DVNI) before becoming partner in charge of the Paris tax department of Ernst and Whinney. Partner with *Clifford Chance* and established the tax department in France (1989-97). Chairman of the Tax Commission of the French Committee of the International Chamber of Commerce (ICC) and co-chairman of the International Tax Committee. Arbitrator with the International Court of Arbitration of ICC. Teaches comparative European corporate tax law at the University of Burgundy and is visiting professor at the Brussels School for Tax Sciences. Member of the European Commission panel of independent experts for the qualitative analysis of the taxation of companies in the European Union.
Personal: Born 10 August 1948. Attended University of Dijon and École Nationale des Impôts 1967-71.

TORDJMAN, Olivier
Cabinet Tordjman & Associés, Paris
+33 1 58 36 20 20
Recommended in Banking & Finance

TOURAINE, Hervé
Freshfields Bruckhaus Deringer, Paris
+33 1 44 56 44 56
herve.touraine@freshfields.com
Recommended in Capital Markets
Specialisation: Partner in Finance Department. Practice covers banking, finance, structured finance, securities law and capital markets.

TREUHOLD, Robert C.
Shearman & Sterling, Paris +33 1 53 89 70 00
rtreuhold@shearman.com
Recommended in Capital Markets, Corporate/M&A
Specialisation: Partner in the Capital Markets and M&A Groups. Specialises in U.S. and international corporate and financial transactions. Has extensive experience in privatisations, public offerings, international joint ventures, project financings, and mergers and acquisitions. Joined the firm in New York in 1984 and has practised in the firm's London and Abu Dhabi offices. Deputy Managing Partner of the firm's Paris office where resident since 1990. Experience includes representation of: Aerospatiale, Air France, Crédit Lyonnais, France Telecom, Pechiney, Thomson Multimedia, Usinor and Rhone-Poulenc in their privatisations; the underwriters in the privatisations of ENEL, Banca di Roma, BNP and UAP, and to the French State in the privatisation of Elf Aquitaine; French and other European issuers, including Alcatel, Transgene, Groupe Danone, Louis Dreyfus Citrus, AGF, Euler, Gemplus, Devoteam, Usinor, Genset, Technip, Lafarge and Legrand in numerous IPOs, secondaries and debt offerings.
Prof. Memberships: New York; Avocat at the Paris Bar; American Bar Association; International Bar Association; American Society of International Law.
Personal: New York University Law School, JD, 1983; Georgetown University, BS, 1978; Université de Montpellier, Diplome, 1975. Languages: English and French.

TRON, Jean-Michel
Cleary, Gottlieb, Steen & Hamilton, Paris
+33 1 40 74 68 00
Recommended in Corporate/M&A, Tax

TUROT, Jérôme
Cabinet Turot, Paris +33 1 45 48 55 96
Recommended in Tax

ULLMANN, Pierre
Jones, Day, Reavis & Pogue, Paris +33 1 56 59 39 39
pullmann@jonesday.com
Recommended in Tax
Specialisation: Extensive experience in areas such as the structuring of cross-border investments, mergers and acquisitions, joint ventures between companies in different jurisdictions, corporate finance, and restructurings. Also has experience in the organisation of French and international investment funds. In the last five years, has been involved in the acquisition and structuring of major real estate projects in France, essentially for the benefit of foreign investors.
Prof. Memberships: International Fiscal Association, the International Bar Association, and the American Tax Institute in Europe.
Career: Paris partner. Admitted at the Paris Bar as Avocat in 1975. Educated at the Institut d'Etudes Politiques de Paris (Graduate in Economics and Finance, 1971); University of Paris X (Maîtrise, 1973, DES 1974). Joined the firm in 1990 in which he is now coordinator of the European Tax Group. From 1983-90, practiced as a partner and co-manager of the international tax department with *Bureau Francis Lefèbvre*, a leading French tax law firm. From 1977-83, was an avocat and partner at another Paris law firm. A frequent speaker in tax seminars and an associate professor at the University of Paris. Cited every year as one of the best tax lawyers in France in the Guide to the US World Leading Tax Lawyers published by Euromoney.

VASSOGNE, Thierry
Linklaters (a member firm of Linklaters & Alliance), Paris +33 1 56 43 56 43
thierry.vassogne@linklaters.com
Recommended in Corporate/M&A
Specialisation: Main areas of specialisation, within a broad range of corporate work, are public takeovers, mergers and acquisitions, joint ventures, litigation and arbitration. Recent significant transactions include advising France Telecom in relation to the Equant acquisition, advising Peugeot and Faurecia on the acquisition of SIT and EL.Fi on its merger with Moulinex S.A.
Career: Co-head of the Paris office 1998 to date.

VAUDOYER, James
Freshfields Bruckhaus Deringer, Paris
+33 1 44 56 44 56
james.vaudoyer@freshfields.com
Recommended in Tax
Specialisation: Partner in the Tax Department. Practises in the areas of corporate and international taxation, particularly in the fields of mergers and acquisitions, structured finance and real property.

VEIL, Jean
Veil Armfelt Jourde La Garanderie, Paris
+33 1 56 69 56 62
Recommended in Corporate/M&A

VERKHOVSKOY, Pierre
Clifford Chance, Paris Cedex 16 +33 1 44 05 52 52
Recommended in Corporate/M&A

VIGNAUD, Jean-Pierre
Cleary, Gottlieb, Steen & Hamilton, Paris
+33 1 40 74 68 00
Recommended in Project Finance: Francophone Africa

VILANOVA, Richard
Sullivan & Cromwell, Paris +33 1 44 50 60 00
vilanovar@sullcrom.com
Recommended in Banking & Finance, Project Finance
Specialisation: Partner in *Sullivan & Cromwell's* General Practice Group. Main areas of practice are project finance, cross-border assets financings and securities. Acted as counsel to the syndicate of lenders or to equity investors in a number of transportation infrastructures, industrial and energy project financings within and outside France. Represented as French counsel the banks acting as equity underwriters of the Eurotunnel project (1985-1994) and the institutional investors and subordinated lenders of Phase 1A and the senior lenders of Phase IB of the Euro Disney project. Has most recently been involved in energy and co-generation projects.
Career: Joined *Sullivan & Cromwell* as partner in 2001. Previously a partner of *Monahan & Duhot* (now *Stibbe Simont Monahan Duhot*). Admitted to Paris bar in 1979.
Personal: Born 1950. Attended University of Paris (DES, 1973) and Harvard Law School (LLM, 1975).

VILLEY, Philippe
Darrois Villey Maillot Brochier, Paris
+33 1 4502 1919
Recommended in Corporate/M&A

VOGEL, Joseph
Vogel & Vogel, Paris +33 1 53 67 76 20
info@vogel-vogel.com
Recommended in Competition/Anti-trust
Specialisation: Main areas of work are French and EU competition law, distribution law, and in particular automobile law. Advises undertakings in the field of competition law at European and French level. Handles actions based on article 81 or 82 of the treaty, merger notifications to the Merger Task Force, competition cases before the Commission, the Court of First Instance and the Court of Justice of the European Communities and advises on all issues linked to the validity and performance of exclusive distribution contracts, selective distribution agreements, franchise or agency contracts including where necessary all subsequent litigation.
Prof. Memberships: American Bar Association; Deutscher Anwaltverein; Association des Juristes Franco-Allemands.
Career: University of Paris, DEA in business law (1983); Ecole des Hautes Etudes Commerciales (1982); Diplômé d'Etudes Comptables Supérieures (1982), Institut d'Etudes Politiques de Paris (1980). Admitted to the Paris Bar in 1985, and New York Bar in 1990. Worked for Banque Paribas in 1984-85. Joined *Tomasi & Partners* in 1985. Created the Firm *Vogel & Vogel* with brother in 1990.
Personal: Speaks French, English, and German.

VOGEL, Louis
Vogel & Vogel, Paris +33 1 53 67 76 20
info@vogel-vogel.com
Recommended in Competition/Anti-trust
Specialisation: Leading competition lawyer. Has published widely on the topics of competition and distribution rules and has developed an expertise as well for clients as for non-specialised lawyers who consult him in the fields of merger control and competition law.
Prof. Memberships: American Bar Association; Deutscher Antwaltverein; French Arbitration Committee; International Chamber of Commerce; Association des juristes franco-allemands; Association Française d'Etudes de la Concurrence; Commission pour l'Etude des Communautés Européennes; International Law Association; Union des Avocats Européenns.
Publications: The author of several books on French commercial law, French and EU competition law and editor of several legal journals.
Career: Admitted to the Bar of Paris in 1981, and of New York in 1990. Created the firm *Vogel & Vogel* with brother in 1990. Professor of Law at the University of Paris Panthéon-Assas and Director of the Institute of Comparative Law of the University of Paris. Also lectures in European and Comparative Competition Law.
Personal: Agrégé des Facultés de Droit (1989); University of Paris, Doctor of Law (1985), Yale Law School (LLM, 1982), Institut d'Etudes Politiques de Paris (1976). Speaks French, German and English.

WEHRLI, Yves
Clifford Chance, Paris Cedex 16 +33 1 44 05 52 52
Recommended in Corporate/M&A

WINCKLER, Antoine
Cleary, Gottlieb, Steen & Hamilton, Paris
+33 1 40 74 68 00
Recommended in Competition/Anti-trust

FRENCH GUIANA

Corporate/Commercial

FRENCH GUIANA Leading firms (Corporate/Commercial)
1 Cabinet Marcault-Derouard
Cabinet Prevot

Firms are listed alphabetically in each band.

Leading individuals (Corporate/Commercial)
1 **MARCAULT-DEROUARD Jean** *Marcault-Derouard*
PREVOT Thérèse-Murielle *Cabinet Prevot*

Individuals are listed alphabetically in each band.

Cabinet Marcault-Derouard (1 ptr, 5 asscs) *"The best firm in the country, with excellent lawyers."* It carries out classic commercial law work, covering sale and purchase and joint venture agreements, admiralty, banking, insurance and commercial contracts. **Jean Marcault-Derouard** was recommended to our researchers as an obvious choice for commercial work. **Clients:** Texaco; AGF; banks; insurance companies.

Cabinet Prevot (1 ptr, 2 asscs) Specialised commercial law firm, considered to be *"strong and active."* Areas of work include M&A, contracts and company law. **Thérèse-Murielle Prevot** is the outstanding practitioner here. **Clients:** Crédit Agricole; BNP-Paribas.

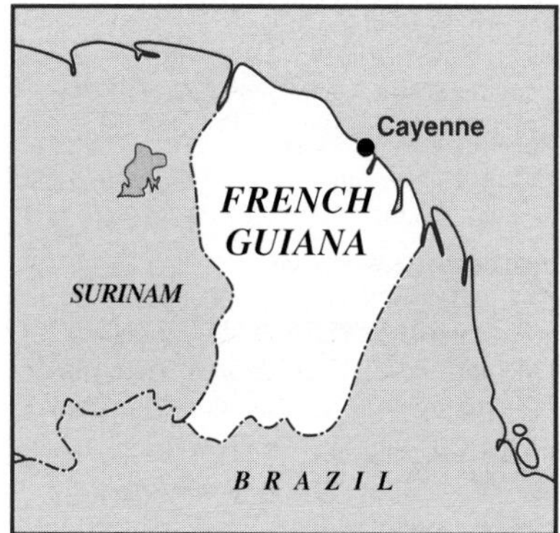

Leaders' profiles – French Guiana

MARCAULT-DEROUARD, Jean
Cabinet Marcault-Derouard, Cayenne +594 255 100

PREVOT, Thérèse-Murielle
Cabinet Prevot, Cayenne +594 282 121

GABON

Corporate/Commercial

GABON Leading firms (Corporate/Commercial)
1 FFA Ernst & Young
Fidafrica
2 Cabinet Laurelli

Firms are listed alphabetically in each band.

Leading individuals (Corporate/Commercial)
1 **CHAREYRE Jacques** *Fidafrica*
ESTEVE Bernard *FFA Ernst & Young*
LAURELLI Philippe *Cabinet Laurelli*
MBOZA Gaëtan *FFA Ernst & Young*
RELONGOUE Christophe *Fidafrica*

Individuals are listed alphabetically in each band.

FFA Ernst & Young (2 ptrs, 6 asscs) *"Serious competitors offering a high quality service"* in corporate law, energy, banking and finance, tax and restructuring. **Bernard Esteve** has a reputation for being a *"good professional lawyer"* and **Gaëtan Mboza** is considered to be *"commercially aware."* The firm's clientele largely comprises heavyweight international names. **Clients:** Arco; Elf; Marathon; Mobil; Citibank; DHL; Veritas; Swissair.

Fidafrica (2 ptrs, 7 asscs) Influential firm, linked to PWC, which practices company law and contract law and advises on tax matters for a diverse range of international clients. **Jacques Chareyre** is a *"famous lawyer in Gabon,"* while the *"experienced"* **Christophe Relongoue** is also recommended. The team has worked on the privatisation of state-owned sectors including telecommunications and transport. **Clients:** Airlines; forestry companies; petroleum companies; local banks; retailers.

Cabinet Laurelli (1 ptnr, 1 assc) *"The number three firm in Gabon"* is said to have considerable *"expertise in fiscal law."* **Philippe Laurelli** is a *"fine lawyer"* with a strong commercial practice. **Clients:** Groupe SOGAFRIC; Aventis; Ipedex; Getma.

Leaders' profiles – Gabon

CHAREYRE, Jacques
Fidafrica, Libreville +241 762 508

ESTEVE, Bernard
FFA Ernst & Young, Libreville +241 742 168

LAURELLI, Philippe
Cabinet Laurelli, Libreville +241 7721 42/43

MBOZA, Gaëtan
FFA Ernst & Young, Libreville +241 742 168

RELONGOUE, Christophe
Fidafrica, Libreville +241 762 508

THE GAMBIA

Corporate/Commercial

THE GAMBIA Leading individuals (Corporate/Commercial)
1 BENSOUDA Amie *Sole Practitioner*
DABO Ousainou *Basangsang Chambers*
DRAMMEH Ida *Barrister at Law*
GEYE Antouman *Sole Practitioner*
SEMEGA-JANNEH Suharata *Barrister at Law*
Individuals are listed alphabetically in each band.

Amie Bensouda A "*Hard-working and dedicated*" former attorney and solicitor-general. Characterised to our researchers as an *"aggressive"* practitioner, she represents a number of high-profile international companies on their Gambian investments. Among these have been a UK textile company and a Belgian insurance company. **Clients:** Domestic and international corporates.

Ousainou Dabo Trained in Nigeria and Canada, he specialises in commercial, land and admiralty law and advises a number of German and Swedish clients. He also handles the affairs of Forth International and Continent Bank and is regarded by many as *"one of the best lawyers here."* However, he is currently the Leader of the Opposition in The Gambia, a position which limits his involvement in day-to-day affairs. **Clients:** Forth International Bank; Continent Bank.

Ida Drammeh Described by competitors as "*strong, well organised*" and "*popular*", this Cambridge educated lawyer is renowned for the international depth of her client base. She advised on proposed amendments to national company legislation, and negotiated the partnership agreement between an electricity company and Eskom of South Africa. **Clients:** Standard Chartered Bank; Shell; Elf; Banjul Breweries Ltd.

Antouman Geye Although better known as a litigator, *("one of the first lawyers that comes to mind in the Gambia")* has also been involved in constitutional work and has a growing reputation for cross-border M&A, often on behalf of financial institutions. **Clients:** Forth International Bank.

Suharata Semega-Janneh Admired throughout the country for his *"outstanding, calm advice,"* a generalist with niche expertise in commercial and land law. Among his clientele are a number of international and domestic banks. **Clients:** International Bank for Commerce; Continent Bank; CMI Trading (UK) Ltd.

Leaders' profiles – The Gambia

BENSOUDA, Amie
Amie N.D. Bensouda - Sole Practitioner, Banjul
+220 223 256
amieben@qanet.gm
Specialisation: Commercial litigation, legislative drafting, corporate law, administrative law, industrial property law.
Prof. Memberships: Gambia Bar Association, African Society of International Law and Comparative Law, Gambia Chapter.
Publications: 'Law and Media in The Gambia'. 'Arbitration Practice in The Gambia'. Co-editor, Gambia Monthly Law Report.
Career: State Counsel (1981-1983), Legal Draftsperson (1983-1987), Chief Parliamentary Draftsperson. Solicitor-General and Legal Secretary (1990-1995). Consultant to the World Bank on the creation of GAMWORKS (March 1993). Consultant to UNDP on governance (August - November 1995). Private Legal Practitioner since 1995.
Personal: Qualified in 1981 in both Nigeria and The Gambia. Attended Kenya School of Law and obtained a certificate in Legislative Drafting (1982). Attended various medium and short term training programmes at the International Development Law Institute, Rome, International Law Institute in Washington DC and other. Partook in various Government related activities including privatisation of public enterprises, public enterprises reform, petroleum agreements, loan negotiations and human issues. Married with four children.

DABO, Ousainou
Basangsang Chambers, Banjul +220 227 442

DRAMEH, Ida D.
Miss Ida Drameh, Barrister at Law, Banjul
+220 228 882
hemard@qanet.gm
Specialisation: Partner in Corporate Department. Main area of work is corporate law, principally company banking, insurance, securities, litigation. Holds retainer for local bank and other companies. Acts for Shipping Agents in The Gambia. Handles Admirality work and acts for P&I Clubs. Consulted about proposed amendment to Company Legislation and amendments of Local Legislation. Acts for International Finance Corporation in The Gambia.
Prof. Memberships: Vice President – Gambia Bar Association 1998-2000.
Career: Qualified in 1980, worked in private practice until 1983, acted as Personal Assistant to Special Adviser of The Gambia Government on Constitutional and International Law 1981-1982. Formed partnership *Macauley and Drameh* 1984-1998. Law Research Officer with Law Reform Commission of The Gambia 1985-1996. Member of Committee appointed to enquire into functioning of District Tribunals in The Gambia 1990-1991. Managing Partner (*Ida D. Drameh*) with three other lawyers presently.

Personal: Born 23 July, 1958. Attended University of Lagos 1976-1979 LLB, Nigeria Law School 1979-1980, Cambridge University, England (LLM) 1983-1984. Governor Methodist Academy The Gambia; Governor Saint Joseph's High School, The Gambia 1993-2000.

GEYE, Antouman
AAB Geye – Sole Practitioner, Banjul +220 229 941

SEMEGA-JANNEH, Surahata
S B S Janneh, Barrister at Law, Banjul
+220 228 174
sbsjanneh@qanet.gm
Specialisation: Corporate work, company formation and acquisition, banking law, import/export and shipping. Has held retainers with banks, insurance companies, parastatals and private manufacturing and trading companies. Handles conveyances.
Prof. Memberships: Hon. Society of Grays Inn Barrister and Solicitor of Supreme Court of Gambia.
Career: Qualified in 1970, Registrar and Master of High Court 1971-1973. Private practice 1974 to date. Member of the Law Reform Commission and African Commission on Human and People's Rights 1992-93. Past President Gambia Bar Association.
Personal: Born 6 November 1942. Attended Hull University LLB Chairman Kombo Beach Hotel 1978 to date. Member National Consultative Committee 1995. Married with seven children.

G

GEORGIA

Corporate/Commercial

GEORGIA Leading firms (Corporate/Commercial)
1 Georgian Consulting Group
2 Begiashvili & Co
Okruashvili & Partners

Firms are listed alphabetically in each band.

Leading individuals (Corporate/Commercial)
1 RIZHINASHVILI Constantin *Georgian Consulting Group*

Individuals are listed alphabetically in each band.

Georgian Consulting Group A *"pre-eminent"* firm, known as *"extremely good for international commercial work"* and *"the number one for its major investing clients,"* representing both foreign and domestic companies clients. Its focus lies on energy and power matters, including pipeline construction. The team advises on joint ventures, corporate structurings, project finance and litigation matters. *"Smart"* **Constantin Rizhinashvili** was recommended to researchers as *"leading a good practice."* **Clients:** Shell; Arco; Ramco; British American Tobacco.

Begiashvili & Co (1 ptr, 7 asscs) With a considerable commercial deal flow, this *"good law firm"* undertakes contract, liability and construction matters, as well as property and IP cases. The firm has good experience in oil and gas including privatisation work in Georgia's growing energy industry. **Clients:** Philip Morris; international power companies.

Okruashvili & Partners (7 ptrs) The firm represents foreign clients on general commercial matters with a niche specialism in telecoms. Known for its *"good commercial team,"* it acted on the privatisation of Tbilisi power station and has seen a growth in aviation matters. It has a strong litigation department with three dedicated lawyers. **Clients:** Ericsson; Procter & Gamble; international airline companies.

Leaders' profiles – Georgia

RIZHINASHVILI, Constantin
Georgian Consulting Group, Trisili
+995 32 93 64 22

GERMANY

Index

The clients' choice

BUSINESS LAWYER OF THE YEAR
DR. MICHAEL HOFFMAN-BECKING,
Hengeler Mueller Weitzel Wirtz

BUSINESS LAW FIRM OF THE YEAR
HENGELER MUELLER WEITZEL WIRTZ

*Winners **Michael Hoffmann Becking** and **Hengeler Mueller Weitzel Wirtz** were a good way clear of their rivals.*

For details see page 36.

OVERVIEW: The most prominent development in the German legal market over the last year has been the further entrance of UK/US firms by way of mergers and new offices, the latter witnessing the arrival of Willkie Farr & Gallagher and Brobeck Hale and Dorr. Following in the wake of the Clifford Chance Pünder merger (January 2000), the next major symbiosis has been the Freshfields Bruckhaus Deringer merger of August 2000 and on a smaller scale, the merger between Lovells Boesebeck Droste. Linklaters Oppenhoff & Rädler cemented its alliance membership, while US firm White & Case merged with Feddersen Laule Ewerwahn Scherzberg Finkelnburg Clemm and Schilling Zutt Anschütz split to join, in parts (eight partners each), Allen & Overy and Shearman & Sterling.

Amid this consolidation frenzy, the collaboration of 'best friends' relationships has satisfied Hengeler Müeller Weitzel Wirtz with its ties to Slaughter and May (UK) and Davis Polk & Wardwell (US), and also Gleiss Lutz Hootz Hirsch linked to Herbert Smith (UK.) Pan-European expansion has fired the interests of Haarmann Hemmelrath, having opened offices in London, Moscow, Brussels and Vienna this past year.

Although one-stop global consultation remains the holy grail for these firms, the downside has been a cluster of conflicts of interests (the Mannesmann/Vodafone transaction for the Oppenhoff & Rädler, Linklaters Alliance, benefited Haarmann Hemmelrath), a departure of some key players, and the marginalising of less lucrative legal areas.

The technology sector has been setting foot in Bavaria, promoting Munich as an industry landmark. Frankfurt is unquestionably the centre of all matters financial, with private equity, IPOs and M&A transactions escalating here in the last year. Berlin remains the natural port of call for all government-related issues. Düsseldorf also attracts a great deal of business for corporate lawyers, particularly in the heavy industries and is also the centre for competition matters. German competition lawyers are proficient in both German and EU matters. In this sector there is a perceived distancing from the employment of smaller boutique firms due to the organisational benefits and the international coverage ability of the big names. That said, the IP sector, particular patent law, is still in the hands of niche firms.

In August 2000 the European Energy Exchange started trading in Frankfurt. The main tax sector topic in the past year being yet another intricate 'Steuerreform 2001.' The explosion resulting from the convergence between IT and telecoms has been highlighted by the process of acquisition of the entire cable-TV network from the DTAG. Along with the other momentous event in the industry this past year in Germany (the UMTS auctioning) the all-round digitalisation of the network will be perfected and ripe for further investor activity.

Banking & Finance

Clifford Chance Pünder (5 ptrs, 18 asscs) Acting for a heavyweight client base in all areas of banking and finance, the firm specialises in syndicated loans, acquisition finance and asset finance, and is said by admiring clients to be able to *"perform complex transactions with its eyes closed."*

Researchers were convinced by the weight of market opinion that the firm has recovered from departures from the banking team, which followed the announcement of the merger last year. The group contains a number of the most eminent finance practitioners in Germany. **Riko Vanezis*** heads the financing group, and focuses on cross-border transactions, where he has a notable reputation for aircraft financing. The *"intelligent, convincing"* **Caroline Jury*** is admired by competitors as *"a serious player in acquisition finance,"* while top-rated **Manfred Heemann*** is *"greatly appreciated for his professionalism and efficiency."* The team advised Commerzbank on the take-private of Honsel AG, and on the financing of CNN's unsuccessful bid for Thomas Travel, and acted for Deutsche Bank on the £8 billion syndicated loan to Mannesmann for its bid for Orange.

An *"outstanding"* asset finance capability is most apparent in aircraft financing. Clients view **Martin Schödermeier*** as *"a hard and fair negotiator,"* while **Patrick Biagosch*** is known for his work on US leases in tandem with the New York office. The firm acted for Deutsche Structure Finance (DSF) on the leasing of 11 aircraft by Air Littoral, and acted for Bayerische Landesbank as lead arranger on the financing of five aircraft for Aero Lloyd. Other matters have included advising a consortium of banks on the DM2.5 billion financing of the German airline manufacturer Fairchild Dornier.

In banking M&A, a highlight transaction was the firm's advice to SSB on the acquisition of BfG Bank. **Clients:** Royal Bank of Scotland; BNP-Paribas; Deutsche Bank; Commerzbank; Dresdner Bank; HypoVereinsbank.

GERMANY Leading firms (Banking & Finance)	
1	Clifford Chance Pünder
	Freshfields Bruckhaus Deringer
	Hengeler Mueller Weitzel Wirtz
2	Allen & Overy
	Döser Amereller Noack/Baker & McKenzie
	Linklaters Oppenhoff & Rädler
3	Ashurst Morris Crisp
	Cleary, Gottlieb, Steen & Hamilton
4	CMS Hasche Sigle Eschenlohr Peltzer Schäfer
	Haarmann, Hemmelrath & Partner
	Lovells Boesebeck Droste

Firms are listed alphabetically in each band.

Leading individuals (Banking & Finance)		
1	**HAAG Hendrik** *Hengeler Mueller Weitzel Wirtz*	**HEEMANN Manfred** *Clifford Chance Pünder*
	HEIN Peter *Allen & Overy*	**JURY Caroline** *Clifford Chance Pünder*
	MAGOLD Rainer *Döser Amereller Noack/Baker*	**NORDHUES Hans-Günther** *Ashurst Morris Crisp*
	SCHMALENBACH Dirk *Freshfields Bruckhaus*	**SCHNEIDER Hannes** *Hengeler Mueller Weitzel Wirtz*
	SCHÖDERMEIER Martin *Clifford Chance Pünder*	
2	**BRUSKI Johannes** *Allen & Overy*	**EMDE Thomas** *Freshfields Bruckhaus Deringer*
	FEICK Carl-Peter *Linklaters Oppenhoff & Rädler*	**LÜDICKE Jochen** *Freshfields Bruckhaus*
3	**BIAGOSCH Patrick** *Clifford Chance Pünder*	**FEICK Hans-Georg** *Döser Amereller Noack/Baker*
	FEURING Wolfgang *Freshfields Bruckhaus*	**OPITZ Peter** *Freshfields Bruckhaus Deringer*
	STENZ Peter *Allen & Overy*	**VANEZIS Riko** *Clifford Chance Pünder*
	VON DRYANDER Christof *Cleary, Gottlieb, Steen*	
4	**KULLMANN Walburga** *Freshfields Bruckhaus*	**REUDELHUBER Eva** *Linklaters Oppenhoff & Rädler*
	WENSERSKI Markus *Haarmann, Hemmelrath*	**WEYLAND Peter** *Hengeler Mueller Weitzel Wirtz*

Individuals are listed alphabetically in each band.

Freshfields Bruckhaus Deringer (17 ptrs, 34 asscs) The merger of the two giant firms has produced the largest banking team in the country, with an enormous client base of blue-chip corporates and financial institutions. Acquisition finance, bank regulatory advice, syndicated loans, asset finance and real estate finance are all recognised areas of strength. Capable of handling massive transactions both at home and abroad, the firm is home to a number of lawyers with international reputations.

"Strong technical individual" **Peter Opitz*** is a senior banking lawyer who receives consistent market plaudits, while **Wolfgang Feuring*** is said to have *"really established his name now"* for acquisition finance and syndicated loans. The team acted for Infineon Technologies ERG on a €750 million multi-currency revolving credit facility, and represented Mannesmann on the German legal aspects of its syndicated loan for the purchase of Orange. It also advised EMTV on the financing of the $750 million acquisition of Formula 1.

Bank regulatory law is one of the firm's traditional strong suits, and it has advised leading financial institutions such as Dresdner Bank, DG Bank and Bank of New York on a range of regulatory matters. Although the *"experienced"* **Thomas Emde*** is considered to have a greater focus these days on capital markets, researchers received consistently promising reports of **Walburga Kullmann*** who is regarded by peers as *"a serious new talent."*

As well as aircraft financing, the firm has substantial experience of advising both lessors and borrowers on a wide range of asset finance transactions, involving rolling stock, water pipes, purification plants and incinerators. Clients regularly praise the *"superb"* **Dirk Schmalenbach*** and the *"remarkable"* **Jochen Lüdicke*** for their expertise in this area. The team represented Bank of America on the financing of a sewage treatment plant and acted for Chrysler Capital on two service contracts for sewage treatment plants in Nürnberg and Stuttgart. **Clients:** Dresdner Bank; KfW; Chase Manhattan, Bank of America; Bank of New York; DG Bank; Helaba.

Hengeler Mueller Weitzel Wirtz (9 ptrs, 15 asscs) Admired for its work on high-premium transactions, the firm is acknowledged for a strong acquisition finance practice and its knowledge of bank supervisory law, which *"leaves its competitors behind."* A world-class M&A capability has yielded a number of acquisition finance transactions for the team, acting on behalf of both lenders and borrowers.

"Precise and controlled," **Hendrik Haag*** is viewed as *"a generalist who is able to think his way around different transactions,"* while clients regard **Hannes Schneider*** as *"one of Germany's pre-eminent finance lawyers."* **Peter Weyland*** also retains his share of market support. The team advised Deutsche Telekom on the financial structuring of the sale of its entire cable business, and acted for Deutsche Bank on a €480 million loan

G

*See leaders' profiles on pages 320-335

to Firstmark Group for the financing of the roll-out of a wireless local loop network.

Well known for its advice on the regulatory aspects of internet banking, the team also advised Credit Suisse on the formation of a new private bank. **Clients:** CVC; ABN AMRO; Bayerische Landesbank; Citibank; Deutsche Bank; Merrill Lynch; Deutsche Telekom.

Allen & Overy (6 ptrs, 19 asscs) A major force in asset finance and leasing, the firm's massive international network of financial institution clients also gives it a prominent place for syndicated loans and real estate finance.

Peter Stenz* is the team's most visible practitioner on syndicated loans, and is perceived to possess *"a safe pair of hands."* The team advised a syndicate of eleven banks in connection with the €30 billion syndicated loan to Vodafone AirTouch for its hostile bid for Mannesmann. It also acted for KPN on a €13 billion syndicated loan for the acquisition of E-Plus Mobilfunk.

The asset finance team contains a pair of practitioners who were commended to researchers as *"outstanding by any standards."* **Peter Hein*** heads the team and, together with the esteemed **Johannes Bruski***, is praised for his *"superb commercial aptitude."* Focused on cross-border aircraft leasing, notably in the US, the firm advised Lufthansa Cargo on the leasing of a number of aircraft, a transaction worth $600 million.

The firm's acquisition of a property finance lawyer from an in-house position at Deutsche Bank serves to underline its emphasis on real estate finance. The team advised Citibank on the financing of a new Manhattan office building. **Clients:** Bank of America; Barclays; Citibank; Goldman Sachs; KPN; Deutsche Bank; Lufthansa; Sachsen LB; Nord LB.

Döser Amereller Noack/Baker & McKenzie (3 ptrs, 7 asscs) Although this is not perceived as a classical banking and finance firm, researchers discovered that the team is regarded as a leading international player in acquisition finance. Its track record shows an impressive volume of deals for an array of German and international financial institutions. *"Quick, competent and experienced,"* **Rainer Magold*** is universally respected by his peers. His colleague **Hans-Georg Feick*** is acclaimed for *"his ability to focus on the crucial point."*

The firm acted for Dresdner Bank on the financing of the public to private transformation of Grohe AG, and advised Allianz Capital and Clayton, Dubilier & Rice on the financing for the acquisition of the Fairchild Dornier Group. Renowned for its expertise on mezzanine financings, the team advised Intermediate Capital Group on a DM200 million mezzanine financing for the purchase of the Takko Group.

Not regarded as a market leader for bank regulatory work, the firm nevertheless acted for the Chicago Board of Trade on the regulatory aspects of its Eurex alliance. **Clients:** Dresdner Bank; Bank of Scotland; CDR; Allianz Capital; Apax; 3i; Chicago Board of Trade; Clariant; Vivendi; Intermediate Capital Group.

Linklaters Oppenhoff & Rädler (4 ptrs, 10 asscs) Recommended to researchers for its *"classical"* finance practice, the firm is a consistent presence on cross-border acquisition finance transactions, syndicated loans and bank regulatory advice. The formalisation of the firm's merger is seen by competitors as an *"important step for the future."*

Carl-Peter Feick* is regarded by clients as part of Germany's acquisition finance *"upper class,"* while **Eva Reudelhuber*** is commended for her versatile practice, which encompasses syndicated loans and project finance. The team advised Commerzbank on a €250 million syndicated loan to Epcos AG, and acted for Barclays and Commerzbank on a €750 million multi-currency revolving credit facility to Infineon Technologies.

Regulatory advice is given to a range of US and UK investment banks on e-commerce and internet banking issues, and the team acted for five foreign internet banks and brokerage units on setting up their German business. **Clients:** HypoVereinsbank; Commerzbank; Barclays.

Ashurst Morris Crisp (2 ptrs, 5 asscs) Comparatively recent addition to the German market which is felt to have *"almost unlimited potential."* Known for acquisition finance and regulatory advice, the team is considered to have built on last year's gain of *"superb acquisition finance man"* **Hans-Günther Nordhues*** from Clifford Chance Pünder. He impresses clients for his ability *"to read the market in the right way."*

The firm has advised Dresdner Kleinwort Wasserstein on a wide range of regulatory issues, and acted for companies on establishing virtual banks. Other work includes advising on leasing structures and real estate investments. **Clients:** Dresdner Bank; Bank of Scotland; HypoVereinsbank; Bayerische Landesbank; Merrill Lynch; Lehman Brothers; Goldman Sachs; Dresdner Kleinwort Wasserstein.

Cleary, Gottlieb, Steen & Hamilton (3 ptrs, 6 asscs) Although better known for capital markets and corporate advice, the firm is still respected for its advice on banking regulatory issues. The esteemed **Christof von Dryander*** acts for an array of domestic and international financial institutions on regulatory aspects of bank mergers, electronic banking and hybrid capital instruments. His team advised Eurex on regulatory issues arising from its alliance with the Chicago Board of Trade. **Clients:** Deutsche Bank; HypoVereinsbank; DG Bank; Salomon Brothers; Morgan Stanley; Eurex.

CMS Hasche Sigle Eschenlohr Peltzer Schäfer (7 ptrs, 4 asscs) Respected for its all-round expertise in banking and finance, the firm advises on a range of medium-ticket acquisition finance transactions, as well as asset finance, real estate finance and regulatory matters. In spite of the absence of a recognised individual heavyweight, competitors acknowledge that the team has *"plenty of promise."* It has advised a number of US banks on the financing of acquisitions by German Mittelstand companies and foreign companies with German subsidiaries.

The team's association with US firm Thacher Proffitt & Wood has reinforced its capacity for US leasing advice. It acted for a German bank on the financing of nine aircraft for Delta Airlines, and advised a US arranger in connection with two US tax leases for utilities in Germany. The firm has niche expertise in financing the acquisition of container vessels, and acted for a multinational consortium of banks in connection with a €500 million financing of nine container vessels.

Real estate finance has seen the firm act for a US arranger on a tax lease for property in Germany, while in banking regulatory matters, the team's connections with the Federal Banking Supervisory Authority gives it acknowledged prominence. **Clients:** International and German banks and corporates.

Haarmann, Hemmelrath & Partner (18 ptrs, 45 asscs)Far from a classical banking firm, but its expertise on the tax aspects of cross-border leasing deals is acknowledged by all competitors. In Frankfurt, **Markus Wenserski*** is respected for his work as local counsel on US leasing transactions, often involving products such as water facilities and purification plants, including pipes. Clients are mainly US investors, although the firm also acts for some German lenders. The team advised on a US leasing transaction worth DM2.1 billion in connection with equipment for a wastewater project. **Clients:** Sachsen LB.

Lovells Boesebeck Droste (6 ptrs, 9 asscs) The former Boesebeck Droste's strong clientele of German financial institutions and overseas investment banks has been added to Lovells' acclaimed acquisition finance practice to form a respected department. The team advises on the German legal aspects of cross-border acquisition finance transactions. The firm acted for Dresdner

Bank in connection with the acquisition of the Flaberg Gruppe, and for Deutsche Bank on the acquisition of the Pipetronics Group.

Bank regulatory experience includes advising on banking licences, group consolidations, outsourcing and repeat exemptions. The team advised a US corporate on the formation of its banking operations in Germany, and acted for a syndicate of banks on the regulatory aspects of the privatisation of Berlin Airport. **Clients:** ING; Dresdner Kleinwort Benson; Deutsche Bank.

G

Capital Markets

GERMANY
Leading firms
(Capital Markets: Debt)

Band	Firm
1	Hengeler Mueller Weitzel Wirtz
2	Cleary, Gottlieb, Steen & Hamilton
	Freshfields Bruckhaus Deringer
3	Clifford Chance Pünder
	Linklaters Oppenhoff & Rädler
4	Allen & Overy
	Shearman & Sterling
	Sullivan & Cromwell

Firms are listed alphabetically in each band.

Leading individuals
(Capital Markets: Debt)

Band	Individual
1	**HAAG Hendrik** *Hengeler Mueller Weitzel*
	KÖNIG Andreas *Freshfields Bruckhaus Deringer*
	KUSSEROW Berthold *Linklaters Oppenhoff*
	MORRISON David *Sullivan & Cromwell*
	SCHNEIDER Hannes *Hengeler Mueller Weitzel*
	VON DRYANDER Christof *Cleary, Gottlieb*
2	**JACKSON Ian** *Clifford Chance Pünder*
	MÜHLMANN Johann Georg *Shearman & Sterling*
3	**CRON Thomas** *Hengeler Mueller Weitzel*
	WELLING Mark *Allen & Overy*

Individuals are listed alphabetically in each band.

Hengeler Mueller Weitzel Wirtz (15 ptrs, 23 asscs) Beyond question the leading capital markets firm in Germany, the firm sweeps the board in international debt and equity, securitisation and derivatives. Said to *"target the lucrative, high-profile deals,"* the team has been involved in a high proportion of the largest IPOs in Germany, such as the €13.4 billion share issue of Deutsche Telekom, "DT3", which was simultaneously offered in fifteen European countries, the United States, Canada, and Japan.

Acting for household names both on the traditional stock exchange and the Neuer Markt, the firm represents both underwriters and issuers, and has enviable relationships with leading investment banks. The team's close relationship with US firm Davis Polk & Wardwell is an obvious benefit for dual listings. It also has an outstanding track record on Eurobond offerings, both stand-alone issues and MTN programmes for heavyweights such as Deutsche Bank, Merrill Lynch and Goldman Sachs. The team acted on a huge convertible bond offering (€2.3 billion) for Mannesmann Finance.

A debt and equity team of unparalleled depth includes **Hannes Schneider***, a rainmaker of *"the greatest importance,"* and the ubiquitous **Hendrik Haag***, recommended to researchers for his expertise on both debt and equity issues. For equity transactions, however, it is **Torsten Busch*** who receives the clients' vote as the *"most prominent practitioner in Germany."* He led the team on the DT3 transaction. Debt specialist **Thomas Cron*** has also left an impression of *"supreme competence"* with competitors.

The team advised the banks on the €5.3 billion IPO of Infineon Technology, and acted on the €2.7 billion IPO of T-Online International. It also represented Goldman Sachs on a €2.5 billion bond issue by Siemens.

In securitisation, the team is also considered to head the field, largely through the efforts of the *"cool-headed, commercially astute"* **Stefan Krauss***. The team acted for Deutsche Bank on the leveraged synthetic CLO transactions Cast 2000-1, worth €4.5 billion, and GLOBE-R 2000-1, worth €2 billion. Other highlights include advising Euro Hypo on a €500 million synthetic RMBS (Residential Mortgage-Backed Securities) transaction, and acting for IKB Deutsche Industriebank on a credit-linked note structure to securitise a portfolio of US assets.

On derivatives transactions, both **Hannes Schneider*** and **Stefan Krauss*** help the team to retain its pre-eminence. The firm acted for Deutsche Bank on a programme to issue securitised and exchange-listed derivatives, and advised Deutsche Hypothekenbank on its issue of public sector credit-linked notes. **Clients:** Deutsche Bank; Merrill Lynch; Goldman Sachs; Chase Manhattan; Morgan Stanley Dean Witter; IKB.

Cleary, Gottlieb, Steen & Hamilton (6 ptrs, 11 asscs) Acclaimed for its expertise on international debt and equity issues and derivatives, the firm offers both US and German legal advice, and is praised by competitors for its *"steady organic growth."* The firm has wide experience of acting on Neuer Markt IPOs, and concentrates almost exclusively on high-end transactions. Bond issues have included global 'Pfandbrief' issues, such as that for Rheinhyp, a subsidiary of Commerzbank, and acting for Callahan Nordrhein-Westfalen, a German cable television network operator, on a $939 million high yield bond offering.

Clients agree that **Christof von Dryander*** is a *"reassuring figure of immense stature."* Respected both for debt and equity advice, he led the team acting for Deutsche Telekom on its global bond offering. **John Palenberg*** is also considered to offer *"superb"* advice on equity transactions, and is known for his close relationship with FSA, a US financial insurance company. The team advised the underwriters on the IPO of Deutsche Post, and acted for T-Online International and T-Mobil on their IPOs.

The derivatives team is said to have *"a good market share and good clients,"* advising investment banks on credit derivatives, and increasingly structuring derivatives for German insurance companies. **Clients:** Deutsche Telekom; Salomon Brothers; Lehman Brothers; UBS Warburg; Rheinhyp; Rabobank; Merrill Lynch; Credit Suisse; FSA.

Freshfields Bruckhaus Deringer (12 ptrs, 15 asscs) Seen as *"serious competition in all areas of capital markets,"* the newly merged firm advises extensively on IPOs, notably advising US and European companies on their flotations on the Neuer Markt. The firm was counsel to Software AG on its IPO, which included a 144A placement. Although debt offerings are not felt to constitute the team's core business, the firm has caught the eye of a number of heavyweight clients, advising Goldman Sachs on the issue of Siemens bonds (€2.5 billion) exchangeable into Infineon Technology shares.

Thomas Emde* is a senior and respected national figure on equity deals, while **Andreas König*** recommended to researchers as *"one of Germany's leaders for debt issues,"* also has a strong

*See leaders' profiles on pages 320-335

G

GERMANY Leading firms (Capital Markets: Equity)
1 Hengeler Mueller Weitzel Wirtz
2 Freshfields Bruckhaus Deringer
Shearman & Sterling
3 Cleary, Gottlieb, Steen & Hamilton
Clifford Chance Pünder
Linklaters Oppenhoff & Rädler
4 Davis Polk & Wardwell
Sullivan & Cromwell
5 Allen & Overy
Döser Amereller Noack/Baker & McKenzie

Firms are listed alphabetically in each band.

Leading individuals (Capital Markets: Equity)
★ **BUSCH Torsten** *Hengeler Mueller Weitzel Wirtz*
KENADJIAN Patrick *Davis Polk & Wardwell*
1 **FEURING Wolfgang** *Freshfields Bruckhaus*
HAAG Hendrik *Hengeler Mueller Weitzel Wirtz*
HUTTER Stephan *Shearman & Sterling*
MORRISON David *Sullivan & Cromwell*
VON DRYANDER Christof *Cleary, Gottlieb*
2 **EMDE Thomas** *Freshfields Bruckhaus*
HARRER Herbert *Linklaters Oppenhoff*
KÖNIG Andreas *Freshfields Bruckhaus*
MÜHLMANN Johann Georg *Shearman & Sterling*
PALENBERG John *Cleary, Gottlieb*
PFÜLLER Markus *Clifford Chance Pünder*
3 **BANES John** *Davis Polk & Wardwell*
KRÄMER Lutz *Freshfields Bruckhaus*
VAUPEL Christoph *Linklaters Oppenhoff*
4 **IHRIG Hans-Christoph** *Allen & Overy*
MARTIN Eckhard *Freshfields Bruckhaus*
SCHLITT Michael *Allen & Overy*

Individuals are listed alphabetically in each band.

GERMANY Leading firms (Capital Markets: Securitisation)
1 Hengeler Mueller Weitzel Wirtz
2 Clifford Chance Pünder
3 Allen & Overy
Freshfields Bruckhaus Deringer

Firms are listed alphabetically in each band.

Leading individuals (Capital Markets: Securitisation)
1 **KRAUSS Stefan** *Hengeler Mueller Weitzel Wirtz*
2 **VASU Kirti** *Clifford Chance Pünder*
3 **BARTSCH Andreas** *Freshfields Bruckhaus*
KAISER Bernhard *Freshfields Bruckhaus*
SCHAAR Bodo *Allen & Overy*

Individuals are listed alphabetically in each band.

GERMANY Leading firms (Capital Markets: Derivatives)
1 Hengeler Mueller Weitzel Wirtz
2 Clifford Chance Pünder
Döser Amereller Noack/Baker & McKenzie
3 Allen & Overy
Cleary, Gottlieb, Steen & Hamilton
Freshfields Bruckhaus Deringer

Firms are listed alphabetically in each band.

Leading individuals (Capital Markets: Derivatives)
1 **KRAUSS Stefan** *Hengeler Mueller Weitzel*
MAGOLD Rainer *Döser Amereller Noack/Baker*
SCHNEIDER Hannes *Hengeler Mueller Weitzel*
2 **SCHERER Peter** *Clifford Chance Pünder*
3 **SCHAAR Bodo** *Allen & Overy*
STENZ Peter *Allen & Overy*

Individuals are listed alphabetically in each band.

profile for advising on IPOs. Competitors have picked out **Wolfgang Feuring*** as the firm's *"chief asset"* on the equity side. He is supported, amongst others, by the *"academically top-flight"* **Lutz Krämer***, formerly in-house at Dresdner Bank, and **Eckhard Martin***, another to have caught the eye of commentators this year.

The team advised Dialog Semiconductor plc on its IPO on the Neuer Markt and ESDAQ, and its secondary placement six months later, and acted for ABN AMRO and Deutsche Bank on the IPO of EADS NV, a deal worth €2,7 million. Other IPOs include those of CargoLifter, where the firm advised the banks, and Infonet Services Corporation, combined with a 144A placement, where the team represented Merrill Lynch.

The firm's derivatives workload includes standard index, share or currency options, currency swaps and certificates of deposit. It advised Dresdner Bank on developing a vehicle for private equity investments.

Although not considered a major force in securitisation, the firm advises a range of leading financial institutions on multi-seller conduit structures and ABS structures. **Andreas Bartsch*** and fast rising **Bernhard Kaiser*** are highly respected by their peers. **Clients:** Goldman Sachs; WestLB; Deutsche Bank; UBS Warburg; Merrill Lynch; Dresdner Bank; Software AG.

Clifford Chance Pünder (7 ptrs, 29 asscs) *"Cultural differences have been solved"* at this significant all-round capital markets team, according to competitors. A superb financial client base underpins the team's high standing in international debt and equity, securitisation and derivatives. In equity transactions, the team acts for underwriters on Neuer Markt listings, as well as blue-chip issuers such as Siemens and Deutsche Telekom on their IPOs. The debt workload largely consists of high-yield bond issues.

"Hard-working and experienced," **Markus Pfüller*** is highly respected for equity issues, while UK lawyer **Ian Jackson*** has acquired a solid name for his work at the head of the firm's German debt practice.

The firm advised Deutsche Telekom on German law aspects of its third global issue, and acted for the European Aeronautic Defence and Space Company on its IPO in Germany, France, and Spain. It also advised HypoVereinsbank in connection with the convertible bond issue of a Neuer Markt listed company, Augusta Technologie AG.

Derivatives remain a key element of the overall capital markets practice. Researchers had their attention drawn to the *"redoubtable"* **Peter Scherer*** and his team's expertise on OTC derivatives. The group advised a Frankfurt and London subsidiary of one of the world's biggest energy trading companies on its first German weather derivatives swap with a local energy supplier, and acted for RWE on German agreements concerning energy derivatives.

Securitisation still shows emphasis on private transactions, usually acting on behalf of German banks. The firm advised DWS Finanz-Service, a subsidiary of Deutsche Star, on the EuroStar I collective debt obligation. **Kirti Vasu*** has gained a strong client following in this area. **Clients:** Barclays Capital; Morgan Stanley Dean Witter; Merrill Lynch; HypoVereinsbank; Siemens; Deutsche Telekom.

Linklaters Oppenhoff & Rädler (4 ptrs, 13 asscs) Known mainly for advising on international debt and equity issues, the firm is felt to have gained increased referrals from the London office since the formalisation of the merger. High-yield bonds and structured products such as credit-linked notes and MTN programmes are areas of niche strength, and the team advises a strong German and international financial client base. The firm advised the government in connection with the Deutsche Telekom 3 issue, and has acted on a number of Neuer Markt IPOs.

A *"solid team"* includes **Herbert Harrer***, who is acknowledged by clients for his *"diligence."* **Christoph Vaupel*** is also seen to be establishing his name in the market, but the firm's driving force is considered to be the *"shrewd and organised"* debt specialist **Berthold Kusserow***.

The firm acted for Trintech on its IPO and capital increase, acted for Carrier 1 on its IPO on the Neuer Markt and represented Commerzbank on a €25 billion MTN programme. **Clients:** Commerzbank; Merrill Lynch; HypoVereinsbank; WestLB; UBS Warburg.

Allen & Overy (5 ptrs, 15 asscs) Active in all areas of capital markets advice, the firm focuses on cross-border work for its renowned banking clientele. The recent acquisition of two partners and two associates from Schilling, Zutt & Anschütz is considered by competitors to have added *"real weight"* to the team's equity capacity. **Hans-Christoph Ihrig*** and **Michael Schlitt*** add long experience of domestic IPOs to the team's international expertise. Debt matters rest in the hands of the *"battle-hardened"* **Mark Welling***, who typically advises German issuers and underwriters.

The firm advised Deutsche Bank on the issue by Vodafone AirTouch of its €5 billion EMTN programme. Also advised KPN Mobile on an abortive IPO in Germany and the Netherlands, and acted on the IPO of MVV Energy, which was the first IPO in Germany of a municipal corporation.

The securitisation team, under the aegis of the respected, if *"somewhat confrontational"* **Bodo Schaar***, is known for its advice on commercial paper conduits, while the derivatives group, although considered to have been *"more quiet recently,"* also retains the services of *"jack of all trades"* **Peter Stenz***. **Clients:** SAP AG; Dresdner Bank; Deutsche Bank; West LB.

Shearman & Sterling (3 ptrs, 8 asscs) Although the firm is also active on the debt side, by far its greatest profile is for international equity transactions, notably big-ticket IPOs. The team is another to have benefited from the split of Schilling, Zutt & Anschütz, and is now commended to researchers for its *"focus on transactions and excellent client service." "Highly successful"* equity lawyer **Stephan Hutter*** is rated among the market leaders in Germany, while clients warm to the *"professional and hard-working"* **Johann Georg Mühlmann*** who splits his practice between equity and debt.

The team advised Mannesmann on securities law aspects of its capital increase in connection with the Orange offer, and on its convertible bond offering, worth €2.3 billion. It also acted for Morgan Stanley Dean Witter on the biggest Neuer Markt IPO, Carrier 1. **Clients:** Mannesmann; Merrill Lynch; Morgan Stanley Dean Witter.

Sullivan & Cromwell (5 ptrs, 8 asscs) Respected for its experience of both the debt and equity markets, the team is considered by some commentators to be *"a little limited"* by opting to advise solely on US offerings or 144a placements in transactions with a German element. Together with Hengeler Mueller, it advised the underwriters Dresdner Bank and Goldman Sachs on share issues by Deutsche Telekom (DT3) and Deutsche Post. The team has improved its volume of Neuer Markt IPOs for non-German companies.

Researchers were impressed by the weight of recommendation for the firm's capital markets wizard **David Morrison***, who heads the Frankfurt office and advises on both debt and equity issues. His team has had a busy year of big-ticket public debt issues, including those for KfW and Deutsche Ausgleichsbank. On the equity side, the firm advised the underwriters on the IPOs of T-Online and T-Mobile. **Clients:** Dresdner Bank; Goldman Sachs; KfW; Deutsche Ausgleichsbank.

Davis Polk & Wardwell (2 ptrs, 6 asscs) Peers regard the firm as *"a similar animal to Sullivan & Cromwell,"* although it lacks the latter's profile in Germany on debt issues. However, the firm's 'best friends' alliance with Hengeler Mueller provides it with a high volume of work on the equity side to add to the transactions that are self-generated.

The power at the firm is *"star lawyer"* **Patrick Kenadjian***, commended to researchers for his *"infallible understanding of the market."* Although slightly overshadowed by his illustrious colleague, **John Banes*** is acclaimed by his peers as a *"decent and hard-working professional."* The firm acted with Freshfields Bruckhaus Deringer as underwriters' counsel for the IPO of Comdirekt, and the team has also advised the underwriters on the IPOs of ThyssenKrupp Steel, EPCOS and Tele Atlas. **Clients:** Investment banks; international and German corporates.

Döser Amereller Noack / Baker & McKenzie (8 ptrs, 13 asscs) Although not a force on debt issues, the firm has developed a respected equity practice from its outstanding contacts with venture capital and private equity funds. The team's expertise lies in advising smaller companies on IPOs on the Neuer Markt, and acting for underwriting banks such as Deutsche Bank, Dresdner Bank and HypoVereinsbank. The team advised Dresdner Bank on the IPO of Dicom on the Neuer Markt, with an accompanying 144A placement.

Headed by **Rainer Magold***, the firm's derivatives team retains its status among peers and clients. Magold himself is seen as a *"superlative commercial lawyer,"* and is considered by competitors to be the principal factor behind the group's eminence. The team's strengths include advising on credit derivatives and programmes for German and foreign investment banks based on financial or commodity derivatives. **Clients:** Deutsche Bank; Dresdner Bank; HypoVereinsbank.

*See leaders' profiles on pages 320-335

Communications

GERMANY Leading firms (Communications: Telecoms)
1 Freshfields Bruckhaus Deringer
2 Döser Amereller Noack/Baker & McKenzie
Redeker Sellner Dahs & Widmaier
3 Clifford Chance Pünder
Linklaters Oppenhoff & Rädler
PricewaterhouseCoopers Veltins
4 Hengeler Mueller Weitzel Wirtz
Piepenbrock & Schuster
Wilkinson Barker Knauer, LLP
5 Haarmann, Hemmelrath & Partner
White & Case, Feddersen
6 Gleiss Lutz Hootz Hirsch
Wilmer, Cutler & Pickering

Firms are listed alphabetically in each band.

Leading individuals (Communications: Telecoms (Regulatory))
1 **MAYEN Thomas** *Redeker Schön Dahs & Sellner*
NOLTE Norbert *Freshfields Bruckhaus*
SCHERER Joachim *Baker & McKenzie*
TSCHENTSCHER Thomas *Freshfields Bruckhaus*
2 **ESSER-WELLIÉ Michael** *Freshfields Bruckhaus*
HEUN Sven-Erik *Willkie Farr & Gallagher*
SCHMITTMANN Michael *PricewaterhouseCoopers Veltins*
3 **HOENIKE Mark** *White & Case LLP*
LEITERMANN Richard *Wilkinson Barker Knauer*
PIEPENBROCK Hermann-Josef *Piepenbrock & Schuster*
SCHÜTZ Raimund *Freshfields Bruckhaus*
WISSMANN Martin *Clifford Chance Pünder*

Individuals are listed alphabetically in each band.

Leading individuals (Communications: Telecoms (Transactional))
1 **HAIDINGER Michael** *Freshfields Bruckhaus*
LEYENDECKER Ludwig *Freshfields Bruckhaus*
2 **FOULKES Hilary** *Skadden, Arps, Slate*
HENTZEN Matthias *Hengeler Mueller Weitzel*
JÄCKLE Christof *Hengeler Mueller Weitzel*
3 **HEY Christian** *Linklaters Oppenhoff*
RIEHMER Klaus *Haarmann, Hemmelrath*
SCHÄFER Helge *White & Case LLP*

Individuals are listed alphabetically in each band.

Freshfields Bruckhaus Deringer (Telecoms: 15 ptrs, 20 asscs; IT: 6 ptrs, 9 asscs) The newly merged firm has pooled the established strengths of both constituents to form a new TMT (Telecom Media Technology) team. The firm has emerged as the clear leader in both telecoms and IT, acting for a broad range of high-calibre international clients, as well as domestic blue-chips.

Top-flight regulatory telecoms man, the *"greatly respected"* **Thomas Tschentscher*** is renowned for his regulatory expertise on behalf of Mannesmann Arcor/o.tel.o. Together with his new regulatory colleague **Norbert Nolte*** *("has an agile brain")* he has played a leading role in the UMTS licence application process. Other notable figures include versatile telecoms/competition lawyer **Michael Esser-Wellié***, *("an energetic fighter for his clients' rights")* and **Raimund Schütz***, a regular visitor to the administrative courts.

Transactionally, the firm boasts the two national leaders. **Michael Haidinger*** has a formidable reputation for his knowledge of international company law, and now teams up with **Ludwig Leyendecker***, considered to be a *"confident negotiator."* The TMT team has been involved in the acquisition of the entire cable-TV network from Deutsche Telekom for various clients in different regions, acting inter alia for Goldman Sachs in Hessia and Deutsche Bank in Bavaria.

The firm's presence in the IT sector owes much to the *"enthusiastic"* **Peter Chrocziel*** *("one of the leaders in the field.")* The team advises on a broad spectrum of new media areas, including distribution agreements, data protection, e-commerce, new frequencies, outsourcing and domain name disputes. Microsoft is one of the firm's key clients for matters including OEM (original equipment manufacturer) issues. **Clients:** Mannesmann Arcor/o.tel.o; Bertelsmann; Deutsche Bank; France Telecom; BT; Microsoft; Global Crossing (European Network); Viatel (German Network); Star One; Intel; Andersen Consulting.

Döser Amereller Noack/Baker & McKenzie (Telecoms: 5 ptrs, 10 asscs; IT: 3 ptrs, 9 asscs) A primarily regulatory telecoms firm whose reputation relies substantially on its 'flagship' **Joachim Scherer***, *"the grand seigneur of telecoms, and undoubtedly the most experienced telecoms lawyer in Germany"*, formerly advisor to the German post and telecommunications ministry.

His latest coup was to advise E-Plus in its successful bid in the UMTS auction process. The firm is also active at an international level, lately representing the Saudi Arabian government on the country's telecoms privatisation, having completed a similar task for the Croatian government.

"Superb draftsman" **Wolfgang Fritzemeyer*** heads the IT team from Munich, advising companies on outsourcing and data protection issues, copyright and licensing, in addition to dealing with e-commerce and internet-access issues. The firm acts for Compaq, most recently on the integration of its digital equipment company, as well as handling its distribution issues. **Clients:** Cisco; Compaq; Primakom; E-Plus; Virtual Telecoms Group.

Redeker Sellner Dahs & Widmaier (Telecoms: 1 ptr, 4 asscs; IT: 1 ptr, 3 asscs) Boutique firm with an outstanding reputation in the regulatory aspects of the telecoms sector. The team is particularly noted for its strong administrative law capability, an essential component of telecoms law in Germany. **Thomas Mayen*** *("a key man in the industry, who knows his subject intimately and possesses great integrity")* and his team have represented key client Deutsche Telekom at the German Regulatory Authority, the Administrative Court and the European Commission on questions of rate regulations, open network provisions, interconnection agreements and competition/misuse proceedings.

Led by well-known name **Gernot Lehr***, the IT team is also respected for its regulatory work, which it approaches from an IP/anti-trust angle. He and his team handle issues ranging from data protection and software protection to domain name and copyright on behalf of international and German clients. The firm represented a major television client on the installation of its IT portal, and advised on the set-up of an internet lottery. **Clients:** Deutsche Telekom; Microsoft (software licensing); Radio RPR (internet related consultation); National Association of German Industries; German private TV and broadcast companies.

Clifford Chance Pünder (Telecoms: 8 ptrs, 23 asscs; IT: 8 ptrs, 12 asscs) The past twelve months have seen some upheaval for the firm's communications department, with notable departures including Sven-Erik Heun and IT guru Thomas Heymann to American firm Willkie Farr & Gallagher. The firm's focus is felt to have shifted to its IT sector team in Frankfurt, where **Joachim Schrey*** *("quick and accurate")* and *"outsourcing king"* **Klaus Sommerlad*** stand out. Recent work has involved advising international banks and insurance companies on the installation of their businesses on the internet, licensing and data pro-

GERMANY Leading firms (Communications: IT)
1 Freshfields Bruckhaus Deringer
2 Linklaters Oppenhoff & Rädler
PricewaterhouseCoopers Veltins
Schneider & Schiffer
3 Clifford Chance Pünder
Graf von Westphalen Fritze & Modest
Nörr Stiefenhofer Lutz
4 Döser Amereller Noack/Baker & McKenzie
CMS Hasche Sigle Eschenlohr Peltzer Schäfer
Hengeler Mueller Weitzel Wirtz
Lovells Boesebeck Droste
Redeker Sellner Dahs & Widmaier
Wessing

Firms are listed alphabetically in each band.

Leading individuals (Communications: IT)
★ CHROCZIEL Peter *Freshfields Bruckhaus*
HEYMANN Thomas *Willkie Farr & Gallagher*
SCHNEIDER Jochen *Schneider & Schiffer*
1 HEUSSEN Benno *PricewaterhouseCoopers*
2 ABELS Michael *Linklaters Oppenhoff*
MORITZ Hans-Werner *Graf von Westphalen*
3 FRITZEMEYER Wolfgang *Baker & McKenzie*
HOENE Thomas *CMS Hasche Sigle Eschenlohr*
SCHREY Joachim *Clifford Chance Pünder*
SOMMERLAD Klaus *Clifford Chance Pünder*
4 BRÄUTIGAM Peter *Nörr Stiefenhofer Lutz*
HARTE-BAVENDAMM Henning *Lovells*
LEHR Gernot *Redeker Schön Dahs & Sellner*
SCHEJA Katharina *Graf von Westphalen*
WUERMELING Ulrich *Wessing*
Up-and-coming individuals
SCHUPPERT Stefan *Lovells Boesebeck Droste*

Individuals are listed alphabetically in each band.

tection issues. Out-sourcing, systems integration and project contracts representation are other notable areas of strength. The firm advised a major German bank on the launch of its SAP R/3, a leading software package.

The firm's telecoms centre is now to be found in the Düsseldorf office. **Martin Wissmann*** heads a team which remains proficient in both the regulatory and transactional aspects of the telecom sector. The firm has handled anti-trust and telecoms issues for a number of clients, including Deutsche Telekom, and advised on various IPOs on behalf of DTAG and its subsidiaries. **Clients:** Deutsche Telekom; Facilion; Sun Microsystems.

Linklaters Oppenhoff & Rädler (Telecoms: 3 ptrs, 6 asscs; IT: 3 ptrs, 7 asscs) The firm's reputation in telecoms has historically been in the regulatory sphere, dealing with obtaining permits and licences, subscriber-lease connections and interconnection issues. However, the advent of the full merger between Oppenhoff & Rädler and Linklaters has heralded a greater concentration on transactional matters, where **Christian Hey*** carries weight in the market having consulted VodafoneAir-Touch on merger aspects.

The *"dynamic"* **Michael Abels*** heads an IT team which advises on ISP/ASP, internet and e-commerce issues, as well as traditional IT software matters for their international clients, notably in the defence industry. Niche strength lies in data protection. **Clients:** Sony; EDS; TNT; Comdisco; Sema Group; Sonera; ICO; Vodafone AirTouch; CompleTel; Arcor; Telefonica; First-Mark; Alcatel; CETECOM; Israel Aircraft Industries.

PricewaterhouseCoopers Veltins (Telecoms: 1 ptr, 3 asscs; IT: 4 ptrs, 14 asscs) The legal arm of the accountancy giant has sprung to life in the communications sector with the acquisition of the former Heuking Kühn Lüer Heussen Wojtek team. The *"versatile"* **Michael Schmittmann***, originally a media lawyer, heads the telecoms team. He is now known for his work on the regulatory telecoms industry, with particular expertise on satellite issues. The firm also advises on interconnection agreements, frequency applications and disputes before the regulatory authorities. Transactional matters have seen work on the privatisation of the cable sector.

The IT team has gained credibility through the addition of **Benno Heussen*** *("one of the old guard, but a diligent and strong negotiator")* in Munich, the heart of new technology projects in Germany. The firm's strength lies in the legal management of software projects, involving transactional work, company and contract law and licensing. The team has acted for a number of banks and insurance companies on data protection issues. **Clients:** Hutchinson Whampoa; BroadNet; TNT & CNN; Deutsche Bundespost; Oracle Deutschland; Real Names; Ericsson.

Hengeler Mueller Weitzel Wirtz (Telecoms: 11 ptrs, 8 asscs; IT: 8 ptrs, 8 asscs) Almost exclusively known for its acclaimed transactional strength, the firm advises a number of leading German telecoms clients. **Matthias Hentzen*** *("a sharp mind and a pleasant man")* and **Christof Jäckle*** *("has a deep knowledge of the law")* are the main transactional players. The firm advised Deutsche Telekom on the acquisition of Voice Stream Wireless, as well as on the sale of its broad band cable business.

On the IT front, the firm is prominent on the booming industry start-ups and IPOs, and also handles e-commerce b2b and b2c projects involving company law, trademark and competition issues and data protection. The firm acted on the 'global-e' project on behalf of Deutsche Bank. **Clients:** Deutsche Telekom; Deutsche Bank; Deutsche Post; Bertelsmann; T-Online; freenet.de; Infineon; Ebay; American Express; Saatchi & Saatchi.

Piepenbrock & Schuster (Telecoms: 2 ptrs, 3 asscs) Although a boutique telecoms firm, it has competed successfully in the national market with much larger organisations, and is active on both regulatory and transactional matters.

Hermann-Josef Piepenbrock* has had an enviable name in the industry for the past decade. A former in-house telecoms lawyer, he is especially singled out for his work on interconnection agreements. The firm represented 01051 Telecom on the element based cost order proceedings to define future IC-tarif codes, as well as advising on this year's round of UMTS licence auctioning. **Clients:** ID-Switch GmbH; MobilCom; 01051 Telecom; ISIS; DOKOM; Talkline; Callino; GTS; Elisa; Mox Telecom; QSC.

Wilkinson Barker Knauer LLP (Telecoms: 1 ptr, 5 asscs) Based in Frankfurt, the German office of this US telecoms boutique maintains a strong reputation for its regulatory work. **Richard Leitermann*** *("knows his field")* heads a team which acts for a predominantly international clientele on interconnection issues, and has also handled a number of IPOs. The firm recently advised a multi-national telecoms company on a government procurement case.

The team's IT portfolio has also expanded during the past year, notably representing internet start-ups on their IPOs. **Clients:** Telegate AG; national governments; leading US mobile phone company.

Haarmann, Hemmelrath & Partner (Telecoms: 8 ptrs, 22 asscs) Known for its tax expertise, the firm has developed a sound reputation as a transactional force in the telecoms industry.

Klaus Riehmer* *("excellent transactional lawyer")* sprang to wider prominence through his advice to Vodafone during the Mannesmann take-over. His team has also represented investment banks on private equity deals in the telecoms industry, and is considered to have niche strength in broadband access. The firm has taken a leading role in the recent round of UMTS auctioning. Regulatory matters are also handled,

*See leaders' profiles on pages 320-335

most typically frequency questions and interconnection agreements. **Clients:** Swisscom AG; Vodafone; Star Telecom GmbH.

White & Case Feddersen (Telecoms: 3 ptrs, 4 asscs) The recent merger of the two firms, both possessing established telecoms expertise, is expected to form a well-balanced unit with international scope. The communications team is headed by **Helge Schäfer*** *("quick and analytical")* who provides the firm's transactional strength. He is renowned for M&A and joint venture telecoms work, and advised on the broadband cable sale of the Deutsche Telekom cable net. Regulatory issues are the domain of the *"tenacious"* **Mark Hoenike***, praised for his work on interconnection/intercarrier agreements. **Clients:** Versatel International NV; France Telecom; Telenor Nextel AS.

Gleiss Lutz Hootz Hirsch (Telecoms: 3 ptrs, 4 asscs) The recent announcement of a formal relationship with City of London heavyweight Herbert Smith is expected to boost the firm's emerging reputation in the telecoms sector. Best-known for regulatory advice to an expanding roster of domestic and international clients, the team also offers anti-trust and transactional advice. Involved in the abortive Deutsche Telekom/Telecom Italia merger, the team acted for NTL on the broadband cable sale of the Deutsche Telekom cable network. **Clients:** NTL; various multinational telecommunications providers.

Wilmer, Cutler & Pickering (Telecoms: 2 ptrs, 5 asscs) Benefiting from a strong Brussels competition and telecoms presence, the firm maintains a respected presence in Germany, both for regulatory and transactional matters. Acting for a range of international clients, the firm's strength lies chiefly in advice to American telecoms companies entering the German market. The team has acted for Viag on a number of projects in Germany, including the negotiating of the first national roaming agreement with a German cellular network operator. It also represented Genuity (formerly BBN Corp,) a US Internet backbone operator, before the German regulatory authority. **Clients:** Genuity; major US companies; Iridium; a major German telecommunications operator.

Schneider & Schiffer (IT: 4 ptrs, 1 assc) This IT boutique firm is known primarily through the reputation of its leading lawyer, **Jochen Schneider***. Described as a *"consistently impressive performer,"* his book 'Handbuch des EDV-Rechts' is a standard work in the industry. He and his team advise on traditional software matters for leading software companies, as well as internet presence issues, ISP/ASP queries, industry-contractual expertise and data protection issues. Receiving referrals from major firms due to its specialist IT practice, it is considered first port of call for legal opinions on user issues and service provision. **Clients:** International software houses; technology companies; service provider and out-sourcing companies.

Graf von Westphalen Fritze & Modest (IT: 7 ptrs, 8 asscs) This new media-oriented firm covers traditional software legal matters, internet/e-commerce and industry start-ups, advising on a number of recent IPOs. **Hans-Werner Moritz***, former in-house counsel at IBM Germany, is renowned for his work on behalf of CompuServe. He heads a team with expertise in IT contractual matters, employment law, company law and anti-trust issues. **Katharina Scheja*** *("a fierce litigator,")* former in-house counsel for Microsoft GmbH, is best known for her work on IT piracy, trademark and software copyright infringement issues. The firm has negotiated out-sourcing agreements for Sage KHK and a major German bank, and has been consulted by several start-ups in software licensing and distribution agreements. **Clients:** Microsoft (piracy, trademark and software IP); Sage KHK; Concord Eracom; start-up companies.

Nörr Stiefenhofer Lutz (IT: 2 ptrs, 18 asscs) This firm has made a name for itself in the IT sector, with especially rapid growth in the e-commerce sector. **Peter Bräutigam*** *("an IT big shot")* leads the team, covering legal queries related to project contracts for software related cases, internet platform establishing, ISP/ASP enabling, and related anti-trust matters. On e-commerce matters, the firm advises its international and national clientele on b2b and b2c issues. The team has also acted on a number of IPOs in the industry. **Clients:** e-bay; Kirch New Media AG; Consors Discount Broker AG; Philip Morris GmbH.

CMS Hasche Sigle Eschenlohr Peltzer Schäfer (IT: 3 ptrs, 7 asscs) The firm has established a reputation for expertise in the IT field, and is best known for advice on project contracts and licensing/trademark issues. **Thomas Hoene*** *("has an extensive practice")* is the resident expert, having specialised in this industry for ten years, and is backed by a group of young lawyers. He and his team cover software implementation, out-sourcing and company law and IPOs, as well as developing an e-commerce capability.

Recently represented a federal ministry on the distribution of IT project services. **Clients:** German and international software houses.

Lovells Boesebeck Droste (IT: 6 ptrs, 15 asscs) The firm has established its 'Computer Communication and Media' group to cover both IT and telecoms matters, although the market perceives the department's forte to lie in IT. The caseload covers traditional software advice, domain name disputes and e-commerce b2b queries.

In the Hamburg office **Henning Harte-Bavendamm***, who comes from an IP background, covers more the traditional software issues from the data-protection and copyright side, but also drafts project and systems contracts in the industry. In Munich, **Stefan Schuppert*** *("a rising genius")* has been working on internet software cases involving cryptography and electronic signature. **Clients:** SAP AG; Compaq Computer GmbH; Reuters; Deutsche Telekom.

Wessing (IT: 6 ptrs, 12 asscs) The firm's IT department, headed by **Ulrich Wuermeling*** *("well on his way to top status,")* is best known for data protection expertise. All aspects are covered, from traditional IT/software advice to distribution of domain name issues, e-commerce matters such as the bol.de project on behalf of Bertelsmann, and anti-trust law. The firm represented Sun Microsystems in their acquisitions of Star Division Corp and Gridware Inc. **Clients:** Motorola; Denic; Bertelsmann; Sun Microsystems; Deutsche Telekom.

Other Notable Practitioners At Skadden, Arps, Slate, Meagher & Flom, **Hilary Foulkes*** *("a full-blooded transactional lawyer")* has been active in the telecoms industry this year. He was a leading figure on the broadband cable sale of the Deutsche Telekom cable-net. American firm Willkie Farr & Gallagher are recent arrivals in Germany, but caused raised eyebrows with their hire of two leading lawyers from Clifford Chance Pünder. Although it is too early to rank the firm, such high-profile names are expected to make their presence felt in the near future. **Sven-Erik Heun*** *("a star")* is renowned for his regulatory expertise, advising on licensing, and cable infrastructure. Among a host of blue-chip clients, his work on behalf of MCI WorldCom has taken a particularly high profile. **Thomas Heymann***, the *"inventor"* of IT law in Germany, is regarded as another tremendous acquisition. He deals with issues such as systems integration, outsourcing, IT project contracts, data protection, protection of industrial property and international company structure.

Competition/Anti-trust

GERMANY Leading firms (Competition/Anti-trust)
1 Freshfields Bruckhaus Deringer
2 Gleiss Lutz Hootz Hirsch
Hengeler Mueller Weitzel Wirtz
3 Clifford Chance Pünder
Linklaters Oppenhoff & Rädler
4 Gaedertz Rechtsanwälte
Lovells Boesebeck Droste
Oppenländer Rechtsanwälte
Shearman & Sterling

Firms are listed alphabetically in each band.

Leading individuals (Competition/Anti-trust)
★ **BECHTOLD Rainer** *Gleiss Lutz Hootz Hirsch*
1 **BURRICHTER Jochen** *Hengeler Mueller Weitzel*
CANENBLEY Cornelis *Freshfields Bruckhaus*
MOOSECKER Karlheinz *Freshfields Bruckhaus*
SEDEMUND Jochim *Freshfields Bruckhaus*
WIEDEMANN Gerhard *Freshfields Bruckhaus*
2 **ESSER-WELLIÉ Michael** *Freshfields Bruckhaus*
KLUSMANN Martin *Freshfields Bruckhaus*
SCHROEDER Dirk *Linklaters Oppenhoff*
STADLER Christoph *Hengeler Mueller Weitzel*
3 **HELLMANN Hans** *Sole Practitioner*
HERMANNS Ferdinand *Sole Practitioner*
QUACK Karlheinz *Gaedertz Rechtsanwälte*
RÖHLING Andreas *Freshfields Bruckhaus*
SATZKY Horst *Hengeler Mueller Weitzel*
4 **BACH Albrecht** *Oppenländer Rechtsanwälte*
BOSCH Wolfgang *Gleiss Lutz Hootz Hirsch*
JESTAEDT Thomas *Lovells*
SCHÜTZE Joachim *Clifford Chance Pünder*

Individuals are listed alphabetically in each band.

Freshfields Bruckhaus Deringer (13 ptrs, 17 asscs) Acclaimed by the entire market as the firm at the top, the recent merger of the two biggest competition teams in Germany is considered to provide not merely the largest anti-trust force in the country, but the one with the greatest quality. The team of experts covers a comprehensive range of competition matters both from Düsseldorf and the firm's nearby Brussels office, where practitioners spend a proportion of their time. A power on multi-jurisdictional merger filings, the firm also advises on Article 81 and 82 cases and anti-cartel proceedings in industries such as pharmaceuticals, energy and telecoms. Public procurement is another key area of strength.

Leading figure **Cornelis Canenbley*** is *"capable of dealing with both the legal and political aspects of a case,"* and was recommended to our researchers as a *"flamboyant strategist and a great communicator."* He operates in both Düsseldorf and Brussels *"with great finesse."* **Karlheinz Moosecker*** *("pragmatic and practical")* is prominent on anti-cartel cases, while the *"brilliant"* **Gerhard Wiedemann*** is regarded by clients as an *"outstanding solver of complex competition problems,"* although his *"strong-minded approach"* is not to everyone's taste.

Renowned for his expertise in the regulatory telecoms industry, **Michael Esser-Wellié*** is a *"colourful and energetic lawyer."* **Martin Klusmann*** is a *"convincing client man,"* who acted on behalf of Sumitomo Chemical on the vitamin price-fixing case before the EC Commission.

In Berlin, **Jochim Sedemund*** is seen as *"a doyen of competition law in Germany."* He has niche expertise in the pharmaceuticals industry, advising Hoffman-La Roche and Bayer AG on numerous anti-trust matters.

Slightly overshadowed by his colleagues, **Andreas Röhling*** is nevertheless *"a thoroughly diligent lawyer,"* who defended Esso against an alleged restrictive practices complaint by small and medium-sized petrol station owners. **Clients:** VEBA; Deutsche Bahn; SAir Group; RWE Energie; Iberdrola; DEA Mineraloel; BP Amoco; Esso; Air Liquide; Mannesmann; PSK; Sumitomo Chemical.

Gleiss Lutz Hootz Hirsch (6 ptrs, 7 asscs) Originally founded with a focus on competition law, the firm is still perceived by the market to have a leading name in this area. Stuttgart-based **Rainer Bechtold*** is the department's outstanding name. *"Academically top-notch and a creative thinker,"* he was unanimously commended to researchers as the top competition lawyer in Germany. He has advised on a number of contentious matters for Volkswagen, as well as acting on merger control cases for DaimlerChrysler, Novartis and Adtranz.

In Frankfurt, **Wolfgang Bosch*** is said to be *"at the head of the next generation of competition lawyers at the firm,"* and has advised on the anti-competitive fuel pricing inquiry. He is best known, however, for his competition work in the telecoms industry. **Clients:** DaimlerChrysler; Volkswagen; Porsche; General Electric; Lufthansa; Dresdner Bank; German Banking Association; European Banking Association; Siemens.

Hengeler Mueller Weitzel Wirtz (8 ptrs, 9 asscs) Renowned for its transactional strength, the firm's competition department receives high praise from peers and clients for its merger control work across the spectrum of industry.

Dividing his time between Brussels and Düsseldorf, **Jochen Burrichter*** is *"an old war-horse and an outstanding tactician,"* who has maintained his excellent reputation through his work on alleged price-fixing in the petroleum industry. He also advises on merger control cases for his blue-chip clientele, mainly in banking and energy. His colleague **Christoph Stadler*** *"knows how to handle clients and officials,"* and advised on the RWE-VEW merger.

In Frankfurt, the *"precise"* **Horst Satzky*** does not have the profile of his Düsseldorf counterparts, but has advised on some huge cases, most notably the abortive merger between the German and London Stock Exchanges. **Clients:** RWE; Frankfurt Airport; Deutsche Bank; German Stock Exchange; German Unilever; Allianz.

Clifford Chance Pünder (6 ptrs, 10 asscs) A top-flight competition firm since the days of one of the founders of modern EU/competition law, Oliver Axster, who still works for the firm on an of-counsel basis, it is still considered to have substantial strength in this area. This is considered by the market to have been accentuated since the firm's merger with Clifford Chance became official at the start of 2000.

A member of the firm's new generation of competition lawyers, **Joachim Schütze*** is *"a sound litigator,"* who has particular expertise in telecoms. He also advises clients from the pharmaceutical and energy industries, handling multi-jurisdictional merger control cases, co-operation issues and exemption proceedings. His work on the liberalisation of the German electricity and gas sector, particularly in Article 82 cases, has kept him in the public eye.

The firm defended clients on a compensation litigation suit over allegedly unfair pricing in the telecoms industry and advised the German federal government on the WestLB state aid case. Also acted on a Phase II merger control case in connection with the acquisition of one of the largest IT suppliers in Germany. **Clients:** Pfizer Group; ENRON; Rüttgers; Sulzer; Deutsche Telekom Group; German Federal Government; GE; Melitta; Hilton Group.

Linklaters Oppenhoff & Rädler (1 ptr, 5 asscs) The firm's recent merger with Linklaters is expected by the market to have a particularly gal-

*See leaders' profiles on pages 320-335

vanising effect in Brussels, but in Germany, the firm has still been commended to researchers for its *"firm grasp of competition law."* **Dirk Schroeder*** is a *"meticulous competition lawyer,"* who represents clients on a wide range of merger control and contentious matters cases in the chemical, healthcare, postal, energy, transport, media and sports industries. He successfully represented Deutsche Post on an Article 82 case against GZS and Citicorp Kartenservice.

Other important elements of the firm's caseload include merger control, Article 81 and state aids cases. **Clients:** Hoechst Roussel Vet; Babcock Borsig; Ültje; Carlyle Europe; Deutsche Post; Dow Chemical; MIBRAG; Enron.

Gaedertz Rechtsanwälte (20 lawyers) Researchers were particularly impressed by the weight of recommendation for the firm's leading practitioner, **Karlheinz Quack***. "*One of the old guard,*" he remains transactionally active. At the time of press the Cologne office announced its merger plans with Norton Rose.

The team advised on Preussag's $2.7 billion acquisition of Thomson Travel, and represented engineering group Linde on its bid for the Swedish industrial concern AGA. **Clients:** Preussag; Linde AG; BASF.

Lovells Boesebeck Droste (4 ptrs, 6 asscs) Since the consummation of the firms' merger at the beginning of 2000, the competition group has suffered a setback, with the departure of Ferdinand Hermanns to establish his own practice. However, **Thomas Jestaedt***, considered by opponents to be *"a pleasant and affable lawyer,"* has cemented his reputation both at home and in Brussels. Particularly renowned for state aid cases in Brussels, he has also represented SAP on all its German and European competition cases.

The firm also advises on merger notifications, notably in the hi-tech sphere, and advised on the acquisition of the German cable network business of Deutsche Telekom subsidiaries. **Clients:** SAP; Texaco; WestLB.

Oppenländer Rechtsanwälte (1 ptr) Boutique firm, whose reputation depends almost entirely on the abilities of competition expert **Albrecht Bach***. *"Enthusiastic and experienced,"* he handles merger control cases at German and EU level for his international clients, and has a specialism in the energy industry.

The firm advised on the take-over of the largest Austrian pharmaceutical distributors. **Clients:** Pharmaceutical, consumer health and energy companies.

Shearman & Sterling (3 ptrs, 6 asscs) Perceived as a transactional force, the firm was recommended to researchers for its merger control expertise. The firm advises on merger control proceedings, anti-cartel cases and Article 82 matters. Especially renowned in banking and the energy industry, the firm has represented international clients such as Viacom and Morgan Stanley on Article 81 and 82 cases. The firm acted in the Visio/Microsoft merger in matters of domestic competition law. Another case, on which the firm was consulted, involved negotiations in the Alcoa/Reynolds case, resulting in obtaining a refinery in Australia for its client. The competition team also represented Wal-Mart in its case regarding the matter of predatory pricing. **Clients:** Lonza; CSFB; Bayerische Hypo-und; Vereinsbank; Georgia Pacific; DaimlerChrysler; Campell Soup; Morgan Stanley; Viacom; Wal-Mart; Leitz.

Other Notable Practitioners **Ferdinand Hermanns*** and **Hans Hellmann*** are sole practitioners with long-established reputations in the competition field. Hellmann is best known for his work on behalf of Hoechst, while Hermanns *("an old fox")* has left Lovells Boesebeck Droste after a short stint, to set up on his own again.

Corporate/M&A

GERMANY
Leading firms (Corporate/Mergers & Acquisitions)

Band	Firm
1	Freshfields Bruckhaus Deringer
2	Hengeler Mueller Weitzel Wirtz
3	Clifford Chance Pünder
	Döser Amereller Noack/Baker & McKenzie
	Gleiss Lutz Hootz Hirsch
	Linklaters Oppenhoff & Rädler
	Shearman & Sterling
4	Cleary, Gottlieb, Steen & Hamilton
	CMS Hasche Sigle Eschenlohr Peltzer Schäfer
5	Allen & Overy
	Haarmann, Hemmelrath & Partner
	Lovells Boesebeck Droste
	P+P Pöllath + Partners
	Wessing
6	BBLP Beiten Burkhardt Mittl & Wegener
	Nörr Stiefenhofer Lutz
	White & Case, Feddersen

Firms are listed alphabetically in each band

Freshfields Bruckhaus Deringer (78 ptrs, 118 asscs) Already a *"mighty force in M&A in Germany,"* Bruckhaus Westrick Heller Löber's merger with UK giant Freshfields Deringer is considered to have given the firm unparalleled cross-border strength. The largest team in Germany, it is invariably to be found on the largest transactions, whether M&A, privatisations or IPOs. A huge client base covers most areas of industry, although telecoms, energy and banking are particularly well represented.

Harald Voss* is one of the stars of the German legal scene, and *"has the entrepreneurial sense to translate theory perfectly into practice."* A fixture on the biggest deals, he advised on the DaimlerChrysler merger. **Christian Wilde*** was equally recommended to our researchers. Based in Hamburg, he has niche expertise in representing big family-run businesses in northern Germany. He was lead counsel to Mannesmann on its hostile take-over by Vodafone AirTouch. Admired by both clients and competitors, **Ralph Wollburg*** is an *"intense and intellectually gifted corporate lawyer,"* while **Axel Epe*** is *"the top man in Düsseldorf,"* and is well known for his German industrial client base. *"A tough negotiator,"* **Andreas Fabritius*** has renowned relationships with US corporates, while **Günther Stratmann*** is a transactional lawyer who is said by rivals to have *"nerves of steel."* **Norbert Meister**'s* practice is a "*superb combination*" of tax and M&A advice, while **Burkhard Bastuck*** is another eminent transactional lawyer, who advised France Telecom on the German implications of the acquisition of Orange. Best known for his work on behalf of new economy companies, prolific author **Gerhard Picot*** is an *"academic"* practitioner, who was singled out to researchers for his distinguished corporate track record. **Christoph von Bülow*** and **Andreas von Werder*** are other lawyers to receive consistent market approval.

The firm advised MobilCom on a joint venture with France Telecom in connection with the bidding for a UMTS licence, assisted Deutsche Bank on the spin-off of its retail banking activities into Bank 24 and advised VIAG on its merg-

GERMANY Leading individuals (Corporate/Mergers & Acquisitions)		
★	**HOFFMANN-BECKING Michael** *Hengeler Mueller Weitzel*	
	VOSS Harald *Freshfields Bruckhaus*	**WILDE Christian** *Freshfields Bruckhaus*
	WOLLBURG Ralph *Freshfields Bruckhaus*	
1	**PICOT Gerhard** *Freshfields Bruckhaus*	**SCHIESSL Maximilian** *Hengeler Mueller Weitzel*
	THOMA Georg *Shearman & Sterling*	
2	**FABRITIUS Andreas** *Freshfields Bruckhaus*	**KOERFER Hans Rolf** *Shearman & Sterling*
	MAIER-REIMER Georg *Linklaters Oppenhoff*	**PÖLLATH Reinhard** *P+P Pöllath + Partners*
	WEGEN Gerhard *Gleiss Lutz Hootz Hirsch*	
3	**AUSTMANN Andreas** *Hengeler Mueller Weitzel*	**BLUMERS Wolfgang** *Gleiss Lutz Hootz Hirsch*
	BRUSE Matthias *P+P Pöllath + Partners*	**DE LOUSANOFF Oleg** *Hengeler Mueller Weitzel*
	EPE Axel *Freshfields Bruckhaus*	**KELLET Christopher** *Clifford Chance Pünder*
	KÖNIG Stephan *Linklaters Oppenhoff*	**MEISTER Burkhardt** *Hengeler Mueller Weitzel*
	MEISTER Norbert *Freshfields Bruckhaus*	**OPPENHOFF Michael** *Linklaters Oppenhoff*
	STRATMANN Günther *Freshfields Bruckhaus*	**WINTER Martin** *Shearman & Sterling*
	ZIEGENHAIN Hans-Jörg *Döser Amereller*	
4	**BASTUCK Burkhard** *Freshfields Bruckhaus*	**BUHL Thomas** *Cleary, Gottlieb, Steen & Hamilton*
	GASTEYER Thomas *Clifford Chance Pünder*	**GROSSMANN Klaus** *Clifford Chance Pünder*
	HAARMANN Wilhelm *Haarmann, Hemmelrath*	**HÖNIG Klaus** *Linklaters Oppenhoff*
	JUNG Harald *CMS Hasche Sigle Eschenlohr*	**LANGE Gustav** *Wessing*
	MAX Dietrich *Wessing*	**OVERLACK Arndt** *Allen & Overy*
	SCHMEDING Jörg *White & Case LLP*	**SCHMIDT Gerhard** *BBLP Beiten Burkhardt Mittl*
	STERZINGER Richard *Lovells Boesebeck Droste*	**VON BÜLOW Christoph** *Freshfields Bruckhaus*
	VON SCHENCK Kersten *Clifford Chance Pünder*	**VON WERDER Andreas** *Freshfields Bruckhaus*
	WEBER-REY Daniela *Clifford Chance Pünder*	

Individuals are listed alphabetically in each band.

er with VEBA. Other significant work includes advising Deutsche Bank on the acquisition of the entire broadband cable business of Deutsche Telekom, and acting for Hewlett-Packard on its worldwide split into HP and Agilent. **Clients:** Deutsche Bank; Hewlett-Packard; France Telecom; Tyco.

Hengeler Mueller Weitzel Wirtz (45 ptrs, 60 asscs) Competitors draw a picture of an *"elite transactional firm"* with the ability to handle complex deals of the highest value. Although lacking the international network of Freshfields Bruckhaus Deringer, the firm is still renowned for its expertise on cross-border M&A, fortified by its 'best friends' relationship with Slaughter and May in London.

Although the corporate team has had to cope with the untimely death of Axel Schmidt-Hern, it still contains some of Germany's leading lawyers. **Michael Hoffmann-Becking***, a particular favourite with leading German companies, is described by many as *"the first port of call"* for corporate law. **Maximilian Schiessl*** has gained a strong reputation for advising on IPOs, such as those for Deutsche Post and ThyssenKrupp Stahl, while **Burkhardt Meister*** is said to be *"a versatile corporate lawyer of the old school."* **Andreas Austmann*** is well known for advising a number of blue-chip utilities, and **Oleg de Lousanoff***, *"a practitioner with his own style,"* looks after French companies such as Vivendi.

The team acted for Cap Gemini on the acquisition of the consulting activities of Ernst & Young in Germany, Austria, and Poland, advised E.on on the sale of VEBA Electronix and advised Deutsche Telekom subsidiary T-Online on the acquisition of Freeserve. **Clients:** RWE; Vivendi; Deutsche Telekom; Cap Gemini; E.on.

Clifford Chance Pünder (19 ptrs, 32 asscs) Generally better known for its finance practices, the firm is also a force on cross-border M&A. The merger is considered by rivals to have *"settled down satisfactorily,"* and the team is acclaimed for its high volume of big-ticket deals. Financial institutions, energy companies and traditional industry leaders feature prominently on the firm's client roster.

"Elder statesman" **Kersten von Schenck*** was commended to researchers as the firm's most substantial figure, and advised the London Stock Exchange on the abortive merger with the Deutsche Börse. **Klaus Grossmann*** is noted for his relationships with leading names in heavy industry, and acted for Imperial Gruppe on the acquisition of ThyssenKrupp's logistics division. UK lawyer **Christopher Kellet*** is *"bright and well-schooled,"* and has co-ordinated a number of large international transactions in fields such as insurance and healthcare. He advised Kimberly-Clark on the purchase of Hakle from Attisholz in Germany, Switzerland and Austria. *"Tough cookie"* **Daniela Weber-Rey*** is said by peers to have *"real transactional flair,"* and acted for Electricité de France in connection with its acquisition of an interest in Energy Baden-Württemberg. **Thomas Gasteyer*** was also praised as a *"sound corporate practitioner."* **Clients:** Kimberly-Clark; Electricité de France; Imperial Gruppe; London Stock Exchange.

Döser Amereller Noack / Baker & McKenzie (18 ptrs, 35 asscs) Renowned for M&A and private equity, the firm now has a strong presence in Düsseldorf, as well as Frankfurt, and advises a number of key industrial clients in the Rhine-Ruhr area on their acquisitions. Pharmaceuticals and banking are areas of particular strength. Clients respect **Hans-Jörg Ziegenhain*** as someone who *"thinks commercially and offers consistently sound advice."* He heads a team that acted for Degussa-Hüls on the sale of Vestolit and advised BfG Bank on its proposed acquisition by SE Banken. Other matters include advising Bewag on its acquisition of a stake in HEW Hamburger Elektrizitäts-Werke, and acting for Metro on the purchase of a trading chain in South America and Asia. **Clients:** Degussa-Hüls AG; Bewag AG; Metro AG; BfG Bank.

Gleiss Lutz Hootz Hirsch (8 ptrs, 20 asscs) Long known for its strong domestic corporate practice, the firm put itself firmly on the international map this year through its alliance with UK firm Herbert Smith. Stuttgart-based, the group compensates for a perceived lack of presence in Frankfurt by its strong contacts with industry in southern Germany. The *"internationally oriented"* **Gerhard Wegen*** was acclaimed by his peers as *"an excellent technician,"* while **Wolfgang Blumers*** is said to be *"a sound M&A and tax practitioner."*

The team advised Dresdner Bank on its abortive merger with Deutsche Bank, and acted for Hewlett-Packard on the German legal aspects of the spin-off of its measurement technique unit. **Clients:** Dresdner Bank; Hewlett-Packard.

Linklaters Oppenhoff & Rädler (12 ptrs, 24 asscs) The consolidation of the alliance between the two firms into a full-blown merger has met with general market approval. Rivals consider

*See leaders' profiles on pages 320-335

that the firm now has a range *"which shouldn't be underestimated."* The team has strong connections with the European defence industry, and has special expertise in transactions for the European aeronautical industry. It advised the Spanish concern Casa on the merger of French, German, and Spanish aerospace companies to form EASDF.

Although Hans Jörg Koerfer left for Shearman & Sterling at the beginning of 2000, the firm still boasts a number of strong corporate practitioners. **Michael Oppenhoff*** is *"a feisty eminence grise,"* who is seen as the firm's strategic driving force, while the *"thorough"* **Stephan König*** is head of corporate, and has established a name for advising clients from the automobile and traditional engineering industries. **Georg Maier-Reimer*** was commended to researchers as *"the firm's best transactional M&A lawyer,"* and is also known for his tax expertise. **Klaus Hönig*** also maintains his share of market support.

The team advised Vodafone AirTouch on the sale of its stake in E-Plus, and acted for BSkyB on the purchase of a stake in Kirch, a German media group. **Clients:** Vodafone AirTouch; BSkyB; Casa.

Shearman & Sterling (11 ptrs, 15 asscs) Having opened offices in Frankfurt and Düsseldorf in 1991, this US firm is now felt to have taken giant strides in the corporate sector. Having initially acquired the services of *"deal machine"* **Hans Rolf Koerfer*** from Linklaters Oppenhoff at the beginning of 2000, the team took advantage of the disintegration of Schilling, Zutt & Anschütz to gain four partners and three associates. Among the new arrivals was **Martin Winter***, commended to researchers as *"an outstanding brain."* Competitors continue to admire **Georg Thoma*** as a lawyer who *"combines all the talents needed for a top M&A practitioner."*

Renowned for a powerful international client base, the firm has specific expertise in banking, insurance and heavy industry. Generally advising on German law in high-end cross-border deals, the team acted for VEBA on its $14 billion merger with VIAG. The team also advised Daimler-Chrysler Aerospace in connection with its merger with Matra Aero Spatiale and Casa to form the European Aeronautic Defence and Space Company (EADS). **Clients:** Süd-Zucker; Daimler-Chrysler; VEBA.

Cleary, Gottlieb, Steen & Hamilton (3 ptrs, 7 asscs) Researchers were impressed by the weight of recommendation for the firm, which was described as a *"rising star in Germany."* Over 90% of the corporate team's caseload are cross-border transactions for a blue-chip international client base. The respected **Thomas Buhl*** is a German and French-qualified lawyer, who is renowned for his relationships with leading French corporates.

The team acted for Bank Austria on its acquisition of a majority stake in Creditanstalt, advised Goldman Sachs on Vodafone AirTouch's takeover of Mannesmann, and represented Valeo, the French car component producer, on the sale of its 50% stake in LuK, the German clutch producer. **Clients:** Valeo; Bank Austria; Goldman Sachs.

CMS Hasche Sigle Eschenlohr Peltzer Schäfer (30 ptrs, 30 asscs) Although the firm merged with smaller Düsseldorf player Schäfer Wipprecht Schickert, it is still best known for its work on domestic M&A transactions, and has its chief strength in southern Germany. Renowned for its extensive clientele of German Mittelstand companies, the firm is acknowledged by peers for its expertise in life sciences and publishing, and has seen an increased deal flow on behalf of US clients. Leading light **Harald Jung*** is recognised by clients as *"one of the best of the new generation of emerging German lawyers."* The firm advised a US company producing electronic components on their European transactions. **Clients:** German companies; US electrical company.

Allen & Overy (5 ptrs, 14 asscs) Highly respected for its banking and finance prowess, the firm's corporate profile is less marked, and is felt by many commentators to owe much to referrals from the London office. Generally known for its strong international clientele, the firm has increased its standing among German Mittelstand companies, largely as a result of its acquisition of three partners and four associates from the now defunct Schilling Zutt & Anschütz. **Arndt Overlack***, recommended to researchers as *"a guy who knows what he's doing,"* is the firm's most recognised practitioner.

Acting for a strong private equity and telecoms clientele, the team, in concert with the Amsterdam and London offices, advised Dutch telecoms group KPN on a joint venture with Hutchison Whampoa and NTT DoCoMo, concerning a joint bid for the German UMTS licence. The firm also represented UPC on the $1 billion acquisition of the German EWT/TSS Group. **Clients:** Morgan Grenfell Private Equity; KPN; UPC; Lufthansa.

Haarmann, Hemmelrath & Partner (28 ptrs, 27 asscs) A top tax firm, it is now expanding its corporate activities, with a growing international network assisting its profile on cross-border deals. A number of clients come from the new economy, although the firm also has experience of media, insurance and the automobile industry.

Wilhelm Haarmann*, one of the firm's founders, earns high marks from competitors for his M&A and tax structuring expertise. Amongst other high calibre transactions, he advised on the sale of Atecs Mannesmann to Siemens/Bosch and represented Swisscom in connection with the acquisition of Debitel AG. **Clients:** Swisscom; Vodafone AirTouch.

Lovells Boesebeck Droste (25 ptrs, 35 asscs) Now firmly ensconced as a merged entity, the firm is a respected mid-tier player, typically seen on domestic transactions. A strong German client base includes a number of hi-tech companies. The *"central figure"* is considered to be **Richard Sterzinger***, head of the corporate department.

The firm acted for Ernst & Young on the sale of its consulting business to Cap Gemini, and advised a consortium of bidders on the privatisation of Berlin airport. Other work includes advising on the sale of Kabel Hessen to a consortium led by NTL. **Clients:** Grundig; Quelle; Ernst & Young; Georgsmarienhütte.

P+P Pöllath + Partners (10 ptrs, 15 asscs) Small firm, noted for its tax expertise, which is said by competitors to have made *"astonishing progress"* in corporate matters. Clients include investment banks and hi-tech companies, and the team has advised on a number of medium-ticket cross-border deals. Clients consider that *"workaholic"* **Reinhard Pöllath*** *"delivers work of the highest quality."* He receives able support from the esteemed **Matthias Bruse***. The firm acted for Carlyle on its acquisition of Andritz, and advised on the sale of a major German cable-net company to UPC. **Clients:** Carlyle.

Wessing (9 ptrs, 5 asscs) Market opinion suggests that the firm's corporate profile has fallen over the past year, although it remains respected for its privatisation expertise, as well as cross-border M&A from its Düsseldorf office. Pharmaceuticals, telecoms/IT and the aviation industry are said to be areas of niche strength, and the firm's American client base has been boosted by the corporate team's close relationship with US firm Mayer Brown & Platt.

The *"impressive"* **Dietrich Max*** was part of the team which advised Alpharma on the purchase of the Isis Pharma Group and acted for a major German bank on the sale of LTU to SAir-Group. **Gustav Lange*** is also strongly recommended by his peers. The firm advised a bidder on the privatisation of Hamburg Airport. **Clients:** Lufthansa; Alpharma.

BBLP Beiten Burkhardt Mittl & Wegener (19 ptrs, 55 asscs) Munich-based firm which is respected for its corporate expertise, and is often the beneficiary of referrals arising from conflicts of interests. Frequent advisors to US and UK clients, the corporate team has experience of a variety of industries, including telecoms, media and leisure.

Gerhard Schmidt* has *"an aggressive style,"* and is the group's leading figure. The firm advised a European consortium on the acquisition of a stake in the Kirch Gruppe, and acted for another consortium on the acquisition of the entire cable business of Deutsche Telekom. **Clients:** Vodafone AirTouch.

Nörr Stiefenhofer Lutz (10 ptrs, 35 asscs) *"Very German in character,"* the team is best known for advising German Mittelstand clients from both the old and new economy on IPOs, M&A and corporate restructuring. Areas of specific expertise include pharmaceuticals, IT, mechanical engineering and media.

The team advises the German media giant, the Kirch Gruppe, on various investment matters, having also acted on its behalf in Lehman Brothers' acquisition of a stake of its company. Acting also for foreign investors on the privatisation of the public utilities in Kiel. **Clients:** Kirch Gruppe.

White & Case, Feddersen (11 ptrs, 30 asscs) The first merger between a German and a US firm has resulted in the union of Feddersen's prolific domestic M&A and privatisation practice *("certainly worth mentioning,"* according to peers,) with White & Case's powerful global network. Key industries are expected to include energy, telecoms, IT, retail and biotechnology.

In Hamburg, **Jörg Schmeding*** was recommended to researchers as a *"prominent local practitioner."* The firm advised on the privatisation of Stadtwerke Bremen and Hamburg, and acted for Motorola in connection with its acquisition of a stake in a German trunk radio network. **Clients:** Textron; Vasa Gruppe; Motorola.

G

Intellectual Property

GERMANY Leading firms (Intellectual Property: Patent)
1 Boehmert & Boehmert
Eisenführ, Speiser & Partner
Hoffmann Eitle
2 Grünecker, Kinkeldey, Stockmaier & Schwanhäuser
von Kreisler Selting Werner
Vossius & Partner
3 Bardehle Pagenberg Dost Altenburg Geissler Isenbruck
Meissner, Bolte & Partner
4 Uexküll & Stolberg

Firms are listed alphabetically in each band.

Leading individuals (Intellectual Property: Patent)
1 GODDAR Heinz *Boehmert & Boehmert*
HANSEN Bernd *Hoffmann Eitle*
SPEISER Dieter *Eisenführ, Speiser & Partner*
2 GEISSLER Bernhard *Bardehle Pagenberg Dost*
SELTING Günther *von Kreisler Selting Werner*
TAUCHNER Paul *Vossius & Partner*
3 JAENICHEN Hans-Rainer *Vossius & Partner*
POPP Eugen *Meissner, Bolte & Partner*
SCHUSTER Thomas *Grünecker, Kinkeldey,*

Individuals are listed alphabetically in each band.

Boehmert & Boehmert (24 patent attys, 23 general lawyers) One of the biggest specialised IP firms in Germany, it is perceived to have its greatest reputation for patent prosecutions. The firm's workload includes defending and enforcing patents, utility models and registered designs in Germany and Europe, as well as advising on licensing issues. The team's client base covers a number of industries, including engineering sciences, biochemistry, microbiology, and software technology.

Renowned patent attorney **Heinz Goddar*** is considered by clients to be *"a technical wizard with absolute mastery of his subject."* Possessing a degree in physics, he specialises in the chemical and bio-chemical industries, and is regarded as an *"expert prosecutor."*

Other elements of the caseload here are German and international copyright law, competition and trademark law for an international client base, filing applications at the German Patent and Trademark Office, and international trademark applications to the World Intellectual Property Organisation. **Clients:** Hewlett-Packard; Huntsman; Lucasfilm; Matsushita Electric Works; Mars; Novo Nordisk; Rohm; SABIC; Saudi Aramco; Sony; Sun Microsystems; Texaco Development; Time Warner; Tokyo Electron.

Eisenführ, Speiser & Partner (14 ptrs, 16 asscs) Originally from Bremen, the firm focuses on the patent side of IP, handling both prosecution and litigation in all fields of industry, with particular emphasis on the electronics and communication industries. Outstanding patent attorney **Dieter Speiser*** was recommended to researchers for his *"highly dedicated and flexible style"* and his *"familiarity with the latest developments."*

The firm advises both domestic clients and major international corporates on obtaining, defending, litigating and licensing protective rights under national and European law. It represented the Società Italiana per lo Sviluppo dell' Electtronica against 200 companies involved in the television receiver industry, including Siemens, Pioneer, Grundig and Samsung. The team has also advised on a variety of patent infringement cases for Philips. **Clients:** Philips; Samsung; Hyundai; Rambus; SISVEL.

Hoffmann Eitle (22 patent attys, 4 general lawyers) A long-established IP firm with its headquarters in Munich, it has a strong reputation for patent prosecution, in industries such as mechanical engineering, electrical engineering and the pharmaceutical industry. Competitors regard leading light **Bernd Hansen*** as a *"reliable practitioner, full of common sense."* He is especially noted for his expertise in the chemical industry.

The firm has appeared on patent, copyright and trademark cases, for international and domestic clients before the European Patent Office, the German Patent Office and the German Federal Patents Court. **Clients:** German pharmaceutical, electronics and engineering companies.

Grünecker, Kinkeldey, Stockmaier & Schwanhäuser (22 ptrs, 33 asscs) One of the country's largest IP firms, it handles a huge volume of German and European patent prosecution cases in Germany. This is where the firm's reputation is greatest, although it also handles patent infringement cases and trademark issues.

The firm has offices in both IP centres of Germany, Munich for patent prosecution and Cologne for patent litigation, and boasts the services of **Thomas Schuster***, respected by peers for his expertise in software patents. The client

*See leaders' profiles on pages 320-335

GERMANY Leading firms (Intellectual Property: General)
1 Klaka Rechtsanwälte
Krieger Gentz Mes & Graf von der Groeben
Seelig & Preu, Bohlig
Von Rospatt, von der Osten, Pross
Wildanger & Kehrwald
2 Bardehle Pagenberg Dost Altenburg Geissler Isenbruck
Harmsen & Utescher
3 Freshfields Bruckhaus Deringer
Lovells Boesebeck Droste
Wessing
4 Clifford Chance Pünder
Linklaters Oppenhoff & Rädler

Firms are listed alphabetically in each band.

Leading individuals (Intellectual Property: General)
1 **MES Peter** *Krieger Gentz Mes*
NIEDER Michael *Klaka Rechtsanwälte*
PROSS Ulrich *Von Rospatt, von der Osten*
WILDANGER Günther *Wildanger & Kehrwald*
2 **BRANDI-DOHRN Matthias** *Seelig & Preu, Bohlig*
CHROCZIEL Peter *Freshfields Bruckhaus*
GIEBE Olaf *Klaka Rechtsanwälte*
HARTE-BAVENDAMM Henning *Lovells*
3 **INGERL Reinhard** *Lorenz Seidler Gossel*
REIMANN Thomas *Clifford Chance Pünder*
ROJAHN Sabine *Wessing*
SCHILLING Tilman *Sole Practitioner*
SCHULZ-SÜCHTIG Rolf *Sole Practitioner*
4 **JONAS Kay-Uwe** *Linklaters*
PAGENBERG Jochen *Bardehle Pagenberg Dost*
SCHAEFFER Michael *Harmsen & Utescher*
VON MEIBOM Wolfgang *Wessing*

Individuals are listed alphabetically in each band.

base comprises a number of hi-tech companies, generally of international origin. **Clients:** US and Japanese hi-tech clients.

von Kreisler Selting Werner (11 patent attys) One of the oldest patent firms on the German market has its base in Cologne, and although comparatively small, was recommended to researchers for its *"absolute quality."* The team's patent attorneys work for both domestic and European clients, concentrating on all areas of the chemical industry, and handling prosecution, appeals, infringement litigation and licensing. The *"knowledgeable"* **Günther Selting*** received consistent market plaudits.

Other matters handled here include trademarks, utility models, design patents, plant species protection, topography law, and software protection. **Clients:** Asahi Kasei Kogyo Kabushiki; Bayer; Braun Melsungen; Henkel; Hitachi Chemical Co; Minnesota Mining and Manufacturing Company; Thermomax.

Vossius & Partner (13 ptrs) Regarded by peers as one of the top patent firms in Munich, it specialises in pan-European patent prosecution, and has niche expertise in the biochemistry sphere. With this prosecution focus they are especially renowned for handling biochemistry cases. **Paul Tauchner***, commended to researchers as *"a clear and logical thinker,"* has a prominent profile in the pharmaceutical industry, advising on the Terfenadine patent infringement case, the Diltiazem manufacturing case and the Paclitaxel (Taxol) and Viagra patent cases. Specialising in gene technology, **Hans-Rainer Jaenichen*** also receives widespread praise as *"a dynamic thinker."*

The firm usually operates for European clients and often acts as an intermediary in filing applications in eastern European countries, but also represents a growing number of American and Japanese clients. **Clients:** Biogen; Genetics Institute; Hoffmann-La Roche; Human Genome Sciences; Max Planck Institute; MorphoSys.

Bardehle Pagenberg Dost Altenburg Geissler Isenbruck (22 patent attys, 22 general lawyers) The firm's caseload is evenly split between patent litigation and more general matters. A respected team of patent attorneys works both on prosecution and litigation, while the rest of the group handles trademark, copyright, design protection and due diligence matters in industries such as biotechnology, pharmaceuticals and the chemical industry. **Bernhard Geissler*** is said to be a *"top notch patents man,"* while **Jochen Pagenberg*** *("dedicated and aggressive")* has a strong American clientele, and advises on patent, trademark, and copyright matters, as well as licensing issues.

The firm recently represented Samsung on a patent litigation case worth $23 million, and advised Boston Scientific on a patent matter worth $32.5 million. **Clients:** BASF; Philips; Petroleum; Hitachi; Samsung.

Meissner, Bolte & Partner (16 lawyers) Boutique patent firm, with offices in Bremen and Munich, which generally handles prosecutions in the mechanical engineering and electronics sectors. A small general IP team also offers advice on trademarks, copyright, design, and licensing cases.

Eugen Popp* is the firm's stand-out practitioner, and leads a team which has become increasingly prominent in IP cases in the telecoms industry. **Clients:** German and European corporates.

Uexküll & Stolberg (15 lawyers) Researchers found that the firm is considered to be one of the leading operations for patent cases in the chemical industry although, as yet, it is felt to lack an outstanding individual practitioner. Other areas of strength include biotechnology and IT. Working from offices in Hamburg and Munich, the firm makes frequent appearances before the German and European Patent Offices.

The team also advises on copyright and trademarks, industrial design filing and litigation and licensing, and it caters for an international clientele, with a high proportion of names coming from the US. **Clients:** Amgen; Black & Decker; Colgate; Exxon Mobil; Johnson & Johnson.

Klaka Rechtsanwälte (6 ptrs, 4 asscs) Another boutique firm based in Munich, it is highly rated for its patent and trademark specialisations. The team represents an international client base before the courts and authorities on a variety of patent litigation and copyright cases. Among a team that is respected for its *"modern attitude,"* the *"well-connected"* **Michael Nieder*** stands out to competitors for his *"sheer technical brilliance."* His junior colleague **Olaf Giebe*** is also commended as *"flexible and quick thinking."* **Clients:** International corporates.

Krieger Gentz Mes & Graf von der Groeben (6 ptrs, 4 asscs) Based in Düsseldorf, the firm is renowned for its experience of patent infringement cases, and is also frequently consulted on licensing contracts, distribution agreements, trademark and copyright cases. Key areas of expertise include gene technology, pharmaceuticals and the hi-tech industry.

Regarded by competitors as the firm's *"flagship,"* **Peter Mes*** is an *"outstandingly eloquent advocate who lives for the law."* The firm advises extensively on cross-border injunctions, as well as on the seizure and destruction of IP counterfeiting material. **Clients:** German and foreign chemical and pharmaceutical companies.

Seelig & Preu, Bohlig (30 lawyers) Covering an even mix of patent, trademark and copyright cases, the team advises clients from the electronics, automotive, pharmaceutical and biochemical industries. Although characterised by some commentators as *"slightly conservative,"* **Matthias Brandi-Dohrn*** is said to *"be a genuine patent expert, who knows all the tricks of the litigation trade."*

On trademark and copyright matters, the firm has niche expertise in advising on seizure of counterfeit goods, and has acted extensively on copyright issues involving protected software. **Clients:** German and international companies.

Von Rospatt, von der Osten, Pross (7 ptrs, 2 asscs) Another long-established niche IP firm, which has offices in Düsseldorf and Mannheim, and is known for its *"meticulous"* work on patent litigation. The team also advises on trademarks, copyright, licensing, design and passing off. **Ulrich Pross*** is respected by peers as a *"diligent draftsman,"* and handles patent infringements for an international client base. Areas of activity include biotechnology and gene technology. **Clients:** US, Europe, Far Eastern and Canadian companies.

Wildanger & Kehrwald (2 ptrs, 1 assc) A *"small but excellent firm,"* specialising in IP, notably on patent infringement cases. *"Impressive"* **Günther Wildanger*** was recommended to researchers for his *"clear presentation of cases."* **Clients:** German companies.

Harmsen & Utescher (14 ptrs, 20 asscs) Hamburg-based IP firm, which has its highest profile for trademark and copyright advice, although it also conducts patent litigation cases.

Clients consider **Michael Schaeffer*** to be an *"expert litigator."* He led the first product-by-process patent claim in Germany, as well as advising on a number of cases connected with CD technology.

The firm represented Bristol-Myers Squibb on the 'Catopril' patent invalidity case, and has advised on a number of copyright issues for leading names in the music business. **Clients:** Allergan; Allied Domecq; Bahlsen; Bristol-Myers Squibb; Douglas; Ferrero; Intersnack; LEO; Matsushita; Premiere TV; Procter & Gamble; SPAR; United Distillers.

Freshfields Bruckhaus Deringer (11 ptrs, 16 asscs) The IP team of this newly merged international firm is perceived to be particularly prominent on trademark and copyright cases, especially where they overlap anti-trust issues. However, patent law is also catered for, and the firm advised Esteve SA on the introduction of its product Omeprazol.

Competitors view **Peter Chrocziel*** as an *"exceptional presence"* on IT-related trademark and copyright cases. He and his team have handled substantial licensing and piracy issues for Epson and Valspar, and the firm is also *"a popular choice"* for passing-off and comparative advertising advice. **Clients:** Hoechst; Aventis; Intel; Motorola; ST Microelectronics; Heinz; Becks; UPS; Bayer; Glaxo Wellcome; Pfizer; SmithKline Beecham; Mannesmann Mobilfunk.

Lovells Boesebeck Droste (12 ptrs, 22 asscs) Possessing several offices throughout Germany, and one in the Spanish IP centre of Alicante, the firm's major IP focus is on its Hamburg team, which was particularly commended to researchers for its expertise on trademark and copyright matters.

Henning Harte-Bavendamm* is a *"high quality"* trademark and copyright specialist, whose practice encompasses product replication, piracy and know-how protection. The firm advises Levi Strauss & Co on enforcing its trademarks, and has also conducted litigation against unauthorised imports from non-EEA countries. **Clients:** Anheuser-Busch; Levi-Strauss & Co; Unilever; Estée Lauder; LEGO; Citibank; Exxon Mobil; Karstadt; Pro Sieben; Beiersdorf; Pelikan.

Wessing (20 ptrs, 20 asscs) Considered by peers to be an important department for the firm, the IP team has established itself as a national player in Munich and Düsseldorf.

Wolfgang von Meibom* *("a skilled tactician")* was commended to researchers for his work on cross-border injunctions, while in Munich, the *"conscientious"* **Sabine Rojahn*** is said to *"get straight to the point."*

In copyright matters, the firm represents MP3-players and mobile phone production companies, in addition to content providers such as Real Networks. On the patent front, the firm enforced a Unilever patent for pregnancy tests, and won a case for Meissen against Tchibo, forcing the latter to obtain an appropriate licence. Other areas of expertise include IT and pharmaceuticals. **Clients:** Real Networks; Unilever; Glaxo Wellcome; Hilfiger; Deutsche Telekom; DaimlerChrysler.

Clifford Chance Pünder (5 ptrs, 12 asscs) Viewed by rivals as an IP team *"to be taken seriously,"* it is led from Düsseldorf by **Thomas Reimann***, who is said to *"know the game inside out."* The firm covers the full range of IP advice, but is considered to specialise in patent law, notably in the electronics and automotive industries. A growing international and domestic client base is regularly represented on litigation before the national authorities in cases concerning patent infringement, trademark and copyright. **Clients:** International and domestic companies.

G

Linklaters Oppenhoff & Rädler (4 ptrs, 3 asscs) Perceived by the market to concentrate on trademark cases, the Cologne office traditionally forms the heart of this IP group. One of the bigger names, it claims a broad-range IP practice, including litigation, which covers not only trademark, patent law, copyright, licensing and unfair advertising cases. The trademark specialist here is the *"young but conscientious"* **Kay-Uwe Jonas***. Admired for his *"emphasis on quality"* he acts for a great number of US clients. The firm acted for Cologne publisher, DuMont Schauberg, against the distribution of a complimentary newspaper by the foreign publisher, Schibsted. The IP team also represented Tupperware Deutschland GmbH/Dart Industries against Liefheit AG over the imitation of various products. In cross border matters the firm represented the Czech Budweiser Budvar National Corp against the US Anheuser-Busch company in the long anticipated defence of its name. In matters of trademark infringement, the firm also acted for Universal City Studios. **Clients:** Johnson & Johnson; Dow Chemical Company; Procter & Gamble; Reebok International; Viacom International; Deutsche Post.

Other Notable Practitioners Our researchers were told that the *"aggressive"* trademark lawyer **Reinhard Ingerl*** is a key element in Lorenz Seidler Gossel's success, admired for his commentary on German IP law. Sole practitioner **Tilman Schilling*** is *"thorough and critical, not easy to convince."* Formerly part of the dissolved Schilling Zutt & Anschütz office, peers acknowledge that *"there is no-one better."* The *"meticulous"* **Rolf Schulz-Süchtig***, formerly at Lovells Boesebeck Droste, a *"top notch"* player, maintains his senior profile in the market as a sole practitioner.

*See leaders' profiles on pages 320-335

Private Equity

GERMANY Leading firms (Private Equity)
1 Döser Amereller Noack/Baker & McKenzie
2 Clifford Chance Pünder
Freshfields Bruckhaus Deringer
Hengeler Mueller Weitzel Wirtz
P+P Pöllath + Partners
3 CMS Hasche Sigle Eschenlohr Peltzer Schäfer
Haarmann, Hemmelrath & Partner
Linklaters Oppenhoff & Rädler
4 Ashurst Morris Crisp
White & Case, Feddersen

Firms are listed alphabetically in each band.

GERMANY Leading individuals (Private Equity)
1 **BRODERSEN Christian** *Döser Amereller*
HENLE Walter *Döser Amereller*
RODIN Andreas *P+P Pöllath + Partners*
2 **BRUSE Matthias** *P+P Pöllath + Partners*
HOLZAPFEL Hans-Joachim *Linklaters Oppenhoff*
KELLET Christopher *Clifford Chance Pünder*
PÖLLATH Reinhard *P+P Pöllath + Partners*
SCHIESSL Maximilian *Hengeler Mueller*
SCHÜCKING Christoph *CMS Hasche Sigle*
3 **HAARMANN Wilhelm** *Haarmann, Hemmelrath*
JALETZKE Matthias *Döser Amereller*
NUSSBAUM Peter *Freshfields Bruckhaus*
SCHÄFER Helge *White & Case LLP*
WEYLAND Peter *Hengeler Mueller*
4 **EINEM Christoph von** *Haarmann, Hemmelrath*
ERNST Reinhold *Hengeler Mueller*
SIMMAT Udo *CMS Hasche Sigle Eschenlohr*
STRELOW Markus *Ashurst Morris Crisp*
VON METTENHEIM Heinrich *Clifford Chance*
WEBER-REY Daniela *Clifford Chance*

Individuals are listed alphabetically in each band.

Döser Amereller Noack/Baker & McKenzie (7 ptrs, 17 asscs) Clients consider that the firm is a market leader as a result of its versatility. *"Where other firms tend to specialise, they advise on the whole private equity spectrum."* An international network, top-quality lawyers, and a reputation for advising on *"the most complex transactions"* lend weight to this view. Advising both investment banks and venture capital funds, the team was recommended to researchers as *"an obvious choice for cross-border transactions,"* notably in the hi-tech and biotechnology spheres.

Walter Henle* and **Christian Brodersen*** are considered to be *"experts on fund structuring,"* and are *"right at the top of the legal ladder,"* while **Matthias Jaletzke*** has an acknowledged relationship with venture capital giant Apax. The firm advised Allianz Capital Partners and CD&R on a $400 million investment in Fairchild/Dornier, and acted for Advent on its acquisition of a Hoechst subsidiary. **Clients:** Allianz Capital Partners; Advent; GE Capital; Apax.

Clifford Chance Pünder (8 ptrs, 17 asscs) Benefiting from the London office's reputation for fund structuring, the firm in Germany is said to be *"flourishing"* in high-end cross-border acquisitions. Now possessing *"a more homogeneous team,"* the firm advises a powerful range of UK and German funds and blue-chip corporates.

Christopher Kellet* is said by rivals to have *"the necessary drive"* to advise on international transactions, while **Heinrich von Mettenheim*** (*"well connected"*) and the *"versatile"* **Daniela Weber-Rey*** are acknowledged for their advice on private equity investments.

The firm advised Chase Capital Partners on its acquisition of the container glass division of Gerresheimer Glas from VIAG Group, and acted for Grohe on its buy out by BC Capital. **Clients:** Goldman Sachs; Deutsche Beteiligungs; Industrie Kapital; Schroders; Advent; Gilde; JP Morgan.

Freshfields Bruckhaus Deringer (12 ptrs, 18 asscs) Although sometimes branded as *"purely an M&A firm"* by competitors, clients are in no doubt of the value of the private equity team's advice on big-ticket deals. The opening of a new office in Munich paid dividends with the acquisition of Apax as a client to set beside a host of foreign private equity groups, venture capitalists and start-up companies.

Peter Nussbaum* is regarded as *"an ideal private equity lawyer, both deal-oriented and able to focus on the essentials."* The team acted for Softbank on its internet venture capital investments, advised Clayton Dubilier & Rice on the purchase of Thyssen Schulte Bautechnik, and represented Schroders in its defence of Banca San Geminiano against the hostile takeover bid by Banca Popolare di Verona. **Clients:** Softbank; Schroders; Clayton Dubilier & Rice.

Hengeler Mueller Weitzel Wirtz (10 ptrs, 7 asscs) Primarily a transaction-focused team, it features a number of corporate and banking lawyers with experience of IPOs and acquisition finance. The firm is admired by competitors for its presence on *"quality big-ticket deals"* and its high-profile client base, which includes leading international corporates and private equity groups. Niche expertise exists in LBOs, and the firm has regularly assisted in taking listed companies private.

Maximilian Schiessl*, who made his reputation in M&A, is now viewed as *"a private equity guru,"* who has a close relationship with KKR. **Reinhold Ernst*** was strongly commended to researchers as *"a fine technician,"* while **Peter Weyland*** is praised for *"his commercial sense and reasonable negotiating style."* The firm advised KKR on the acquisition of Bosch Private Networks and acted for Gerresheimer Glas, which was acquired by Investcorp. **Clients:** Cinven; Schroders; KKR; Goldman Sachs.

P+P Pöllath + Partners Described as *"a jewel in the firm's crown,"* the private equity team is not typically seen on the biggest acquisitions, instead earning a reputation among its competitors as *"the dominant name in fund structuring."* The firm creates fund-of-funds in the US market, pools for Venture Capital Management (VCM) and venture funds for wealthy individuals. Clients range from household names to smaller venture capitalists.

"Structuring king" **Andreas Rodin*** is said to have *"his own distinctive style,"* **Matthias Bruse*** is admired by clients for *"the entrepreneurial perspective which he brings to tax-complicated venture deals,"* and legendary rainmaker **Reinhard Pöllath*** is renowned for his transactional work on behalf of Apax. The firm advised Schroders on the setting up of all its funds, Goldman Sachs on its new fund GSCP2000, and Prudential on the acquisition of Hoffmann Menue. **Clients:** Carlyle; Prudential; Schroders; Apax.

CMS Hasche Sigle Eschenlohr Peltzer Schäfer (7 ptrs, 7 asscs) Concentrated in Frankfurt and offices in the south of Germany, the team has made its name in venture capital transactions, often with German hi-tech companies as targets. Researchers were told that *"they have a talented team,"* which is built around **Christoph Schücking***, who has an established relationship with 3i. Often used as counsel to BC Partners, **Udo Simmat*** is also strongly recommended.

The firm advises medium-sized foreign funds, high net-worth individuals and start-up companies, and advised on the acquisition of Technologieholding, now a subsidiary of 3i. Also acted for BC Partners on the take-private of Grohe AG. **Clients:** 3i; BC Partners.

Haarmann, Hemmelrath & Partner (12 ptrs, 13 asscs) Renowned tax firm, whose Munich office has a strong reputation for venture capital advice, acting for clients from early stages through to mezzanine financing. Clients include German private investors, domestic and foreign venture capital and private equity funds, and hi-tech start-ups.

In Munich, transactional lawyer **Christoph von Einem*** is perceived by competitors as *"efficient, if not the easiest to deal with."* Éminence grise **Wilhelm Haarmann*** also maintains his reputation for dealing with cases involving complex tax elements. The firm acted on the structuring of the Dutch fund Parcom, as well as advising on structuring funds for Bayerische Landesbank and WestLB, with ensuing acquisitions. Other notable work includes advising on the founding of Go Industry AG, and acting for the company on the sale of a 25% stake to Atlas Venture, and the sale of a further 25% to a consortium. **Clients:** BC Partners; Quadriga; GoIndustry AG.

Linklaters Oppenhoff & Rädler (7 ptrs, 14 asscs) Still said by competitors to be getting *"its share of the cake,"* the firm lacks the domestic presence of the market leaders, although it retains a strong clientele of UK and US funds. The team advises on the formation of cross-border funds for clients such as Rabobank, and acts for hi-tech start-up companies, their investors and private equity funds on acquisitions.

Hans-Joachim Holzapfel* was widely mentioned to researchers as a lawyer with *"invaluable experience"* in this area. The firm advised Triton on the DM240 million buyout of Weru AG, and acted for a consortium of venture funds on the €72 million venture capital funding of Star One AG. **Clients:** Triton; Tax Specific; GE Capital; Dresdner Kleinwort Benson; Rabobank.

Ashurst Morris Crisp (1 ptr, 5 asscs) Appreciated by clients as *"a useful conduit for German-UK cross-border deals,"* this relatively young German office has also left competitors with a *"vivid impression."* Able to capitalise on the London office's peerless buyout expertise, the Frankfurt team advises a powerful venture capital and private equity fund clientele. **Markus Strelow*** was commended to researchers as *"a lawyer with an academic bent, who really understands the legal niceties."*

The team acted for Gilde (backed by Gilde Investment Management and CVC Capital Partners) on the acquisition of the insulation products division of Armstrong World Industries Group, and advised Morgan Grenfell Private Equity on the sale of its stake in Formula 1 to EMTV. **Clients:** Morgan Grenfell Private Equity; Deutsche Bank Capital; Gilde; Cinven.

White & Case, Feddersen (7 ptrs, 14 asscs) Newly merged firm, which has added White & Case's strong portfolio of high-growth new economy clients to Feddersen's acknowledged domestic private equity skills. Vastly experienced **Helge Schäfer*** is said to have *"the right commercial attitude for the job."*

The team advised 3i on its acquisition of the yellout AG, and acted for Triton on acquiring Datentechnik from Siemens. W&C Frankfurt's interest is high-growth companies from the new economy. In conjunction with White & Case's Stockholm office, the firm represented Nordic Capital on a 95% acquisition of the paper pulp business of Henkel KGaA, one of the largest buyouts in Scandinavia. **Clients:** BdW; Legal & General Ventures; Nordic Capital; 3i; Triton; First Atlantic Capital.

G

Project Finance

Döser Amereller Noack/Baker & McKenzie (4 ptrs, 7 asscs) The firm is seen as a truly international player, and researchers were told that *"the world is the projects team's oyster."* Domestically, the team is involved in a variety of infrastructure, water and power projects for a clientele ranging from leading banks and corporates to the German Federal Government. Abroad, the firm's international network has assisted the German office to work on projects throughout Europe and beyond.

Clients have recommended **Stephen Hodgson***, a dual qualified German and UK lawyer, as someone *"who is at home with major cross-border projects,"* while **Rainer Magold*** also wins market approval for his project finance expertise. The team advised KfW on a waste water treatment plant in Croatia, worth $400 million and governed by both English and German law, and acted for Vivendi on its joint venture with RWE in connection with the privatisation of the Berliner water utility. **Clients:** Dresdner Bank; KfW; German Federal Government; Vivendi.

GERMANY Leading firms (Project Finance)	
1	Döser Amereller Noack/Baker & McKenzie
	Freshfields Bruckhaus Deringer
2	Allen & Overy
	Clifford Chance Pünder
3	Hengeler Mueller Weitzel Wirtz
4	Linklaters Oppenhoff & Rädler
	Shearman & Sterling

Firms are listed alphabetically in each band.

Leading individuals (Project Finance)	
1	**MANNSFELDT Ulrich** *Freshfields Bruckhaus*
	STILLER Dietrich *Clifford Chance Pünder*
2	**HAAG Hendrik** *Hengeler Mueller*
	HODGSON Stephen *Döser Amereller*
3	**HUTTER Stephan** *Shearman & Sterling*
	MAGOLD Rainer *Döser Amereller*
	REUDELHUBER Eva *Linklaters Oppenhoff*
	STENZ Peter *Allen & Overy*
	VANEZIS Riko *Clifford Chance Pünder*
	VON SCHLABRENDORFF Fabian *Clifford*

Individuals are listed alphabetically in each band.

Freshfields Bruckhaus Deringer (2 ptrs, 4 asscs) Seen by competitors as a *"superb projects team, both at home and abroad,"* the firm is noted for its expertise on high-premium energy and infrastructure projects. Advising both lenders and sponsors, this small team is said to *"consist of nothing but specialists."* **Ulrich Mannsfeldt*** is felt by some commentators to *"stand out, not only at the firm, but in Germany."* Opponents compliment him for *"devoting himself entirely to the sector in a manner that is unusual for a German lawyer."*

The firm acted for a consortium comprising KfW, WestLB, Bayerische Landesbank and Com-

*See leaders' profiles on pages 320-335

merzbank on the DM1.6 billion financing of a Thyssen-Krupp coking plant. It also advised German utility group RWE on the privatisation of the Berlin water utility. **Clients:** West LB; RWE; Commerzbank; KfW; Bayerische Landesbank.

Allen & Overy (3 ptrs) Renowned for the project finance expertise of the London office, the firm's profile in Germany almost inevitably suffers by comparison. However, the team is still respected for its work both on domestic telecoms projects and infrastructure, construction and energy projects in Eastern Europe, notably advising lenders. **Peter Stenz*** is regarded by competitors as the group's leading light.

The firm advised WestLB on a €60 million financing for the Intercontinental Hotel Group in Prague, and acted for Nokia on the financing of its equipment supplies to a German start-up telecoms service provider. **Clients:** WestLB; Nokia; Deutsche Bank; Rabobank.

Clifford Chance Pünder (4 ptrs, 13 asscs) Often instructed by German clients (notably financial institutions) on cross-border projects, the team is acknowledged for its work in South East Asia, and has specific experience in Indonesia. *"Versatile"* finance lawyer **Riko Vanezis*** heads the team, while **Dietrich Stiller*** was unanimously acclaimed to researchers as *"an intense and tough negotiator."* The latter generally represents German clients in South East Asia, and was involved in the restructuring of a leading Indonesian cement producer. **Fabian von Schlabrendorff*** splits his practice between project finance and arbitration, and is respected by peers in both spheres.

Domestically, the firm advised the European Investment Fund on the financing of the high-profile 'Warnequerung' project in eastern Germany, and acted for Helaba as lead arranger of the financing of the world's first recycling plant, Polyamid, in Premitz. Elsewhere, the team acted for Dresdner Bank, KfW and WestLB on the $1.4 billion financing of a coal-fired plant in Southern Turkey. **Clients:** Hoch Tief; Siemens; Helaba; Dresdner Bank; European Investment Fund.

Hengeler Mueller Weitzel Wirtz (3 ptrs, 12 asscs) Focusing on complex, high premium projects, rather than volume work, the firm is best known for its work on telecoms projects at home and abroad, acting for lenders, sponsors and borrowers. Pan-European projects are also a feature, often arriving through the firm's relationship with Slaughter and May in London.

Researchers were left in no doubt that the bulk of the team's reputation lies with the *"genius"* of **Hendrik Haag***. Both clients and rivals queued up to salute a practitioner who is seen as *"a man of many parts."* The firm advised Deutsche Bank on a wireless local loop project in Germany, and represents utilities giant RWE on a number of domestic projects. **Clients:** KfW; RWE; Deutsche Bank.

Linklaters Oppenhoff & Rädler (2 ptrs, 4 asscs) Beginning to expand its project finance department in the wake of the formalisation of the merger, the firm is expected by competitors *"to be a real threat in the future, with Linklaters' expertise permanently available."* The team's speciality currently lies in financing start-up projects, and it advised a major foreign telecom company on the €240 million financing of a German start-up.

Partner in charge **Eva Reudelhuber*** is described as *"a young, capable project finance lawyer, who is going from strength to strength."* Her team has acted recently for KfW on domestic and foreign projects, such as a power station and a cement plant in Poland. **Clients:** KfW; domestic and international banks and corporates.

Shearman & Sterling (2 ptrs, 3 asscs) Dual qualified in German and US law, the respected **Stephan Hutter***, known as the firm's capital markets specialist, devotes part of his practice to international project finance work for banks and existing corporate clients. Normally found on big-ticket transactions, the team has been active on projects from South America to eastern Europe, and advised Dresdner Bank and KfW on a satellite financing in Argentina, governed by US law. **Clients:** Dresdner Bank; KfW.

Tax

Flick Gocke Schaumburg (15 ptrs, 40 asscs) Boutique tax firm, universally commended to researchers as the leader in the field. A top-quality team of lawyers and tax consultants advises an overwhelming percentage of DAX listed companies on the tax aspects of corporate and financial transactions, as well as offering tax planning advice.

The group's leading lawyers are said to *"complement each other superbly."* **Detlev Piltz*** has an academic style, and is renowned for his connections at government level. The *"dynamic"* **Harald Schaumburg*** is a *"real tornado,"* and is regarded by peers as the firm's leading transactional exponent. The team advises on domestic and international taxation, inbound and outbound investment, reorganisations, estate planning, due diligence and special audits. Researchers' attention was pointed to the firm's non-lawyer, expert tax consultants, of which the *"worldclass"* Thomas Rödder (*"at the top of the guild"*) clearly stands out, being involved in all of the firms important cases. **Clients:** German European and US blue-chip companies from such industries as pharmaceuticals, communications, automobiles and the airline industry.

Haarmann, Hemmelrath & Partner (48 ptrs, 69 asscs) Although the firm is now recognised in other areas of practice as well, its tax department remains its chief asset. The team handles a wide range of domestic and international tax matters, including M&A tax advice, cross-border leasing, corporate re-organisations, company successions, real estate transactions and company pension schemes.

"Omnipresent" **Wilhelm Haarmann*** is considered by clients to be a *"jack of all trades,"* and led the tax team representing Vodafone AirTouch on the hostile take-over of Mannesmann. His team also advised on the establishment of a German-Dutch investment bank and in litigation acted in a dividend-stripping trial. The support of their non-lawyer tax consultant team, foremost that of *"strong minded"* Eugen Bogenschütz (*"great transactional strength with format"*) is not to be undermined. **Clients:** Banks; insurance companies; hi-tech, pharmaceutical and engineering enterprises.

Freshfields Bruckhaus Deringer (18 ptrs, 26 asscs) The merger is felt to have increased the tax team's strength, notably on corporate transactional work and structured tax advice. As well as key investment banks, the firm advises an array of blue-chip corporate clients, and has a renowned international presence.

The firm's global co-head of tax is **Stephan Eilers***, recommended to our researchers as an *"outstandingly creative lawyer."* He advised on the

GERMANY Leading firms (Tax)
1 Flick Gocke Schaumburg
2 Haarmann, Hemmelrath & Partner
3 Freshfields Bruckhaus Deringer
P+P Pöllath + Partners
4 Linklaters Oppenhoff & Rädler
Raupach & Wollert-Elmendorff
5 Clifford Chance Pünder
Hengeler Mueller Weitzel Wirtz
Streck Mack Schwedhelm

Firms are listed alphabetically in each band.

Leading individuals (Tax)
1 **BREUNINGER Gottfried** *Cleary, Gottlieb, Steen*
HAARMANN Wilhelm *Haarmann, Hemmelrath*
PILTZ Detlev *Flick Gocke Schaumburg*
PÖLLATH Reinhard *P+P Pöllath + Partners*
SCHAUMBURG Harald *Flick Gocke Schaumburg*
2 **RAUPACH Arndt** *Raupach & Wollert-Elmendorff*
RODIN Andreas *P+P Pöllath + Partners*
3 **EILERS Stephan** *Freshfields Bruckhaus*
LÜDICKE Jochen *Freshfields Bruckhausr*
4 **BENKERT Manfred** *Clifford Chance Pünder*
HARITZ Detlef *Clifford Chance Pünder*
JACOB Friedhelm *Hengeler Mueller*
MÜLLER Welf *Linklaters Oppenhoff*
STRECK Michael *Streck Mack Schwedhelm*
Up-and-coming individuals
VON WALLIS Georg *Linklaters Oppenhoff*

Individuals are listed alphabetically in each band.

Rhone-Poulenc/Hoechst merger, dealing particularly with the tax aspects of holding location and restructuring. Part of his newly merged team is **Jochen Lüdicke***, *"a precise, if reserved"* leasing specialist, who was involved in the sale of Aral to Mobil. In contentious matters, the firm appeared before the Federal Tax Court in connection with multi-parent tax integration. **Clients:** Goldman Sachs; Hoechst; Daimler Chrysler; Siemens; Deutsche Bank; Dresdner Bank.

P+P Pöllath + Partners (9 ptrs, 15 asscs) Founded by former Oppenhoff & Rädler tax star, **Reinhard Pöllath***, said by competitors to be *"a pragmatic workaholic, who is dedicated to the profession,"* the firm's reputation continues to grow. He and the similarly diligent **Andreas Rodin*** handle a number of private equity cases from a tax-structuring perspective, as well as M&A and real estate cases. Asset management tax advice is another key element of the workload.

The team has acted on several private equity matters for Apax and Carlyle, has advised financial institutions such as Allianz, and has represented Infineon in M&A-related tax issues. **Clients:** Apax; Carlyle; Alchemy; Earlybird; Star; Allianz; Infineon; Quandt; EIM.

Linklaters Oppenhoff & Rädler (24 ptrs, 30 asscs) Recovering from the loss of a number of tax stars, the firm has been recommended to our researchers as a *"young team with new ideas."*

Welf Müller* is an *"experienced all-rounder,"* who runs a mixed tax and corporate practice, while rising star **Georg von Wallis*** is an *"outstanding young tax lawyer"* with a specialism in the tax aspects of the media industry. He has acted for a number of US film studios.

The firm has advised on tax structuring arising from cross-border M&A transactions in telecommunications, media and the defence industry. In the contentious sphere, the firm has been involved on several precedent-setting matters, including the Saint-Gobain case, involving EU law interpretation of taxation on industrial premises. **Clients:** American multi-nationals; media companies; international investment banks; German banks and insurance companies.

Raupach & Wollert-Elmendorff (9 ptrs, 11 asscs) Although smaller than the market leaders, the firm's link with Deloitte & Touche, and its consistent presence on both contentious and transactional matters, is considered by peers to make it one of the market leaders in Germany. The team advises an array of domestic and international clients on the tax implications of cross-border leasings, estate planning and holding structures, and has acknowledged expertise in tax litigation.

Our researchers were impressed by the weight of recommendation for **Arndt Raupach***. *"A star in the German tax sky,"* he is considered by opponents to dominate his team. The group advised a subsidiary of an international insurance group on the tax implications of a joint venture with a leading American insurance group. Also co-ordinated and led court proceedings on the subject of the acceptance of IFSC-companies on the Dublin docks. **Clients:** Multi-national blue-chips.

Clifford Chance Pünder (17 ptrs, 30 asscs) Since losing key players two years ago, the firm is considered by the market to have settled into a *"solid if unspectacular"* unit. The tax team covers tax restructuring, M&A transactions, cross-border real estate tax issues and corporate investment tax matters for a clientele with a strong financial institution flavour.

Manfred Benkert* is a multi-talented individual, and was recommended to researchers for his abilities as a tax lawyer, consultant, and certified accountant. **Detlef Haritz*** is an *"extremely intelligent"* lawyer and a prolific writer.

The firm advised the London Stock Exchange on its abortive merger with the Deutsche Börse, and represented Philipp Holzmann on the sell-off of real estate projects and shareholdings. **Clients:** Deutsche Bank; London Stock Exchange; Philipp Holzmann.

Hengler Mueller Weitzel Wirtz (3 ptrs, 6 asscs)The firm's small tax department is perceived to act as a support to its powerful corporate team. However, ambitions to expand have been underlined by the acquisition of a number of new personnel from KPMG. The outstanding practitioner here is **Friedhelm Jacob***, who is noted for his extensive contacts with US industry.

The firm has been involved in numerous asset-backed securitisations for German financial institutions. It represented Deutsche Bank on the tax aspects of its acquisition of Bankers Trust, and acted for Cap Gemini on its acquisition of the worldwide Ernst & Young business consultancy division. Also advised on the merger between RWE and VEW. **Clients:** Deutsche Bank; Commerzbank; SmithKline Beecham; BASF; RWE; Goldman Sachs; Cap Gemini.

Streck Mack Schwedhelm (8 ptrs, 1 assc) Partner-heavy tax boutique firm with a niche speciality in criminal tax law. The group also advises on the tax aspects of company re-structuring, corporate succession, M&A, inheritance cases and tax litigation.

Leading figure **Michael Streck*** was recommended to researchers as an *"excellent litigator."* The firm has advised on a number of tax inspections on behalf of wealthy individuals, medium-sized German companies and international concerns. **Clients:** German companies; international corporates; private clients.

Other Notable Practitioner Now at Cleary, Gottlieb, Steen & Hamilton, **Gottfried Breuninger*** is perceived by clients and competitors to be *"a first-class man with all-round tax expertise."* The market is still monitoring his progress in building a tax department at his new firm.

G

*See leaders' profiles on pages 320-335

Leaders' profiles – Germany

ABELS, Michael
Linklaters Oppenhoff & Rädler, Berlin
+49 30 21 49 60
Recommended in Communications: IT

AUSTMANN, Andreas
Hengeler Mueller Weitzel Wirtz, Düsseldorf
+49 211 830 40 211 83040
andreas.austmann@hengeler.com
Recommended in Corporate/M&A
Specialisation: Cross-border mergers, international mergers and acquisitions, company restructurings. Advises major listed companies from a variety of industries.
Publications: Author of various articles on corporate law.
Career: Qualified in 1990 (Germany) and 1992 (New York). Joined *Hengeler Mueller* in 1990, becoming a partner in 1995.
Personal: Born 31st March 1959. Attended Universities of Heidelberg and Muenster (Dr.jur. 1989), Harvard Law School (LLM 1990).

BACH, Albrecht
Oppenländer Rechtsanwälte, Stuttgart
+49 711 601 870
bach@oppenlaender.de
Recommended in Competition/Anti-trust
Specialisation: Partner specialising in EC and German competition law and M&A work. Has led a substantial number of cases in front of the European Commission and the German Bundeskartellamt. Has handled acquisition of companies of varying sorts namely in the health care sector. Acts for a major German electricity provider and a leading pharmaceutical wholesaler. Has published and spoken on various aspects of EC and German competition law.
Prof. Memberships: IBA, Studienvereinigung Kartellrecht.
Publications: Author of 'Anti-competitive State Measures under EC Law' (in German).
Career: Qualified in 1989. Partner of *Oppenländer* in 1994.
Personal: Born 1959. Attended universities of Tübingen and Aix-en-Provence.

BANES, John
Davis Polk & Wardwell, Frankfurt am Main
+49 69 97 57 030
Recommended in Capital Markets: Equity

BARTSCH, Andreas
Freshfields Bruckhaus Deringer, Frankfurt am Main +49 69 17 09 90
andreas.bartsch@freshfields.com
Recommended in Capital Markets: Securitisation
Specialisation: Specialises in tax and corporate law, in particular, mergers and acquisitions, domestic, EU and international tax and capital markets.

BASTUCK, Burkhard
Freshfields Bruckhaus Deringer, Frankfurt am Main +49 69 27 30 80
burkhard.bastuck@freshfieldsbruckhaus.com
Recommended in Corporate/M&A
Specialisation: Specialises in Corporate Law, including partnership law, limited liability company law, stock corporation law, law regarding groups of companies, law regarding transformation of companies, law of security and guarantee, employee and management stock option plans, mergers and acquisitions, joint ventures, privatisations, public takeovers and commercial law.

BECHTOLD, Rainer
Gleiss Lutz Hootz Hirsch, Stuttgart +49 711 89 97 0
rainer.bechtold@gleiss-law.com
Recommended in Competition/Anti-trust
Specialisation: Partner in competition/anti-trust department of *Gleiss Lutz.* Main area of work is European and German competition law, principally European and German merger control, in addition, also focuses on general EC and German competition law and state aids. Has handled a great number of notifications, both on the European and national level. These comprise the clearance of the following transactions: Varta / Bosch, Daimler / Chrysler, Ciba-Geigy / Sandoz (Novartis), UBS (Schweizerische Bankgesellschaft / Schweizerischer Bankverein), Siemens / Elektrowatt and other cases on behalf of Siemens, numerous transactions on behalf of Daimler Chrysler, Volkswagen and Robert Bosch GmbH. Represented a significant number of companies before the EU Commission, the EU Court of Justice, the German Federal Cartel Office and the Higher Court of Appeals in Berlin as well as the German Federal Supreme Court, inter alia John Deere, DaimlerChrysler, Volkswagen, Heidelberger Zement, Pronuptia, Holtzbrinck Group and others.
Prof. Memberships: German Bar Association, Studienvereinigung Kartellrecht.
Publications: Author of a commentary on German Act Against Restraints of Competition as well as of books and numerous articles. Frequent speaker at conferences.
Career: Qualified in 1970. Joined *Gleiss Lutz* in 1972, becoming a partner in 1974. Born 21 September 1941. Attended Universities of Freiburg i.Brg, Besançon / France and Berlin.

BENKERT, Manfred
Clifford Chance Pünder, Frankfurt am Main
+49 69 71 99 01
manfred.benkert@cliffordchance.com
Recommended in Tax
Specialisation: Senior Partner of *Clifford Chance Pünder* and managing director of PVW Treuhandgesellschaft mbH Steuerberatungsgesellschaft as well as PVW Gmb Wirtschaftsprüfungsgesellchaft. Advises international corporations, institutional investors and financial institutions on all questions of international and German tax law, especially in connection with tax structures, corporate take-overs and restructurings as well as real estate transactions. Advises high net worth individuals on estate planning domestically and internationally including inheritance tax.
Prof. Memberships: German Bar Association, International Bar Association, German and International Fiscal Association.
Publications: Co-editor and co-author of the commentary Haritz/Benkert Umwandlungssteuergesetz and the bi-lingual edition (German/English) of Benkert/Bürkle Umwandlungsgesetz/ Umwandlungssteuergesetz as well as co-author of the books Real Property in Germany.
Career: Studied law and economics at universities in Berlin, Münster and Würzburg; works as lawyer, certified public accountant and tax adviser.
Personal: Born 1942.

BIAGOSCH, Patrick
Clifford Chance Pünder, Munich +49 89 216 320
patrick.biagosch@cliffordchance.com
Recommended in Banking & Finance
Specialisation: Lawyer and Tax Advisor, Partner in the Tax Department and managing director of PVW tax consulting company. Main areas of work are national and international tax law, structured finance (asset finance and leasing), mergers & acquisitions and private equity. Has handled national and international structured finance transactions, national and international leasing transactions as well as acquisitions of companies and undertakings of varying sorts by national and overseas clients. Heads the Munich Tax Department.
Prof. Memberships: International Fiscal Association, Union International des Avocats.
Career: Studied law and economics at the Universities in Tübingen and Munich. Obtained a doctorate in law from the University in Cologne. Partner since 1997.

BLUMERS, Wolfgang
Gleiss Lutz Hootz Hirsch, Stuttgart +49 711 89 97 0
Recommended in Corporate/M&A

BOSCH, Wolfgang
Gleiss Lutz Hootz Hirsch, Frankfurt am Main
+49 69 955 140
wolfgang.bosch@gleiss-law.com
Recommended in Competition/Anti-trust
Specialisation: Partner specialising in competition/anti-trust, mergers and acquisitions and telecommunications law. Main areas of work are transactions and complex anti-trust and merger control cases. Has been active in a number of major telecommunications M&A transactions over the last years.
Prof. Memberships: German Bar Association, International Bar Association, Studienvereinigung Kartellrecht.
Publications: Co-author on a commentary on the German Act against Restraints of Competition regarding merger control procedures and has published a number of articles. Is also co-author on a commentary to the German Telecommunication Act.
Career: Qualified in 1987, joined *Gleiss Lutz Hootz Hirsch* in 1990, becoming a partner in 1994.
Personal: Born November 24, 1961. Universities of Konstanz and Bern (CH).

BRANDI-DOHRN, Matthias
Seelig & Preu, Bohlig, Munich +49 89 3838 700
Recommended in Intellectual Property: General

BRÄUTIGAM, Peter
Nörr Stiefenhofer Lutz, Munich +49 89 28 6280
Recommended in Communications: IT

BREUNINGER, Gottfried
Cleary, Gottlieb, Steen & Hamilton, Frankfurt am Main +49 69 97 1030
Recommended in Tax

BRODERSEN, Christian
Döser Amereller Noack, Frankfurt am Main +49 69 29 90 80
christian.brodersen@bakernet.com
Recommended in Private Equity
Specialisation: Partner in Corporate and Tax Department. Main area of work is corporate law, acquisitions, group reorganisations, with special focus on accounting and tax issues. Advice is rendered both to German and overseas clients. Acted on the privatisation of Deutsche Waggonbau AG and the spin-off by Stadtwerke Frankfurt of its electricity branch. Acted for Kuwait Petroleum as largest shareholder in merger of Hoechst with Rhone-Poulenc, acted for Compaq Computer in tax restructuring, Bellsouth in e-plus restructuring and UMTS auction. Regularly writes on tax issues and speaks at legal and tax conferences.
Prof. Memberships: Chamber of Tax Consultants; Chamber of Chartered Public Accountants; International Fiscal Association.
Career: Qualified in 1975. Joined Coopers & Lybrand in 1976, qualifying as a tax consultant and CPA. Joined *Baker & McKenzie* in 1981, becoming a partner in 1987.
Personal: Born 21 September 1948. Attended Geneva University, Frankfurt University, Edinburgh University, and London School of Economics (LLM). Leisure interests include golf and tennis. Lives in Frankfurt, Germany.

BRUSE, Matthias
P+P Pöllath + Partners, Munich +49 89 2424 00
matthias.bruse@pplaw.de
Recommended in Corporate/M&A, Private Equity
Specialisation: Legal and tax advise for corporate acquisitions, participations, joint-ventures, corporate restructurings, IPOs and privatisations. Numerous speeches and papers (IBA, ABA), current contributor to M&A Review.
Prof. Memberships: IBA, ABA.
Career: 1984 admitted to the Munich Bar; 1985 Dr. jur., (University of Bonn); 1988 LLM, (University of Miami); 1990-1997 partner of a major German law firm. Founding partner of *P+P Pöllath + Partners.*
Personal: Born September 1956, lives in Munich.

BRUSKI, Johannes
Allen & Overy, Frankfurt am Main +49 69 2648 5000
Recommended in Banking & Finance

BUHL, Thomas
Cleary, Gottlieb, Steen & Hamilton, Frankfurt am Main +49 69 97 1030
Recommended in Corporate/M&A

BURRICHTER, Jochen
Hengeler Mueller Weitzel Wirtz, Düsseldorf +49 211 830 40 211 83040
jochen.burrichter@hengeler.com
Recommended in Competition/Anti-trust
Specialisation: EU and German competition law, merger control, unfair competition, intellectual property and arbitration. Advises foreign and domestic clients from a variety of industries.
Prof. Memberships: Member of the Board ('Vorstand') of the Studienvereinigung Kartellrecht e. V. (Association for Competition Law Studies); co-founder of the European Competition Lawyers Forum and member of its Committee; Senior Vice chairman of Committee C (Anti-trust) of the Section of Business Law on the International Bar Association.
Publications: Co-author of 'Immenga/Mestmäcker: EC Competition Law'; various publications in the field of competition law.
Career: Joined *Hengeler Mueller Weitzel Wirtz* in 1973; partner since 1977. Resident in the Düsseldorf and Brussels offices.
Personal: Born September 23, 1941. Attended universities of Freiburg and Münster. Qualified 1973.

BUSCH, Torsten
Hengeler Mueller Weitzel Wirtz, Frankfurt am Main +49 69 170 950
torsten.busch@hengeler.com
Recommended in Capital Markets: Equity
Specialisation: Concentrates on equity capital markets and corporate law.
Career: Qualified in 1991 (Germany). Joined *Hengeler Mueller* in 1991, becoming a partner in 1996 (Brussels office 1992, New York office 1993; foreign associate at New York law firm 1993/1994).
Personal: Born 1960. Attended University of Hamburg (Dr.jur.).

CANENBLEY, Cornelis
Freshfields Bruckhaus Deringer, Düsseldorf +49 211 49790
cornelis.canenbley@bruckhaus.com
Recommended in Competition/Anti-trust
Specialisation: Partner in the Competition and Trade Group.

CHROCZIEL, Peter
Freshfields Bruckhaus Deringer, Frankfurt am Main +49 69 273080
peter.chrocziel@freshfieldsbruckhaus.com
Recommended in Communications: IT, Intellectual Property: General
Specialisation: Specialises in intellectual property, IT and telecoms. Core activities are trademarks, patents and know-how, competition and advertising, software, internet/multimedia and outsourcing.

CRON, Thomas
Hengeler Mueller Weitzel Wirtz, Frankfurt am Main +49 69 170 950
thomas.cron@hengeler.com
Recommended in Capital Markets: Debt
Specialisation: Main area of work comprises debt capital markets and equity related products. Also advises on bank lending and acquisition finance.
Career: Qualified in 1993. Joined *Hengeler Mueller Weitzel Wirtz* in 1993, becoming a patner in 1999. Foreign associate *Davis Polk & Wardwell* (New York) 1996/97.
Personal: Born July 6th, 1963. Attended University of Tuebingen 1983-89 (Dr.jur.).

DE LOUSANOFF, Oleg
Hengeler Mueller Weitzel Wirtz, Frankfurt am Main +49 69 170 950
oleg.delousanoff@Hengeler.com
Recommended in Corporate/M&A
Specialisation: Cross-border mergers, international mergers and acquisitions, corporate and commercial.
Prof. Memberships: Union Internationale des Avocats.
Career: Assistant Professor, Law Faculty, University of Freiburg im Breisgau, 1976 to 1980; associate of *Hengeler Mueller Weitzel Wirtz* between 1981 and 1984, then becoming a partner from 1984 to the present time.
Personal: Born 1952. Attended University of Freiburg (Dr. jur.), London School of Economics, Keio University Tokyo, University of California at Berkeley (LLM).

EILERS, Stephan
Freshfields Bruckhaus Deringer, Cologne +49 221 20 50 70
stephan.eilers@freshfields.com
Recommended in Tax
Specialisation: Specialises in national and international tax law in particular relating to the planning for corporate succession and capital markets (IPO's, derivatives, bonds and options).

EINEM, Christoph von
Haarmann, Hemmelrath & Partner, Munich +49 89 216 36 70 5
christoph_von_einem@hhp.de
Recommended in Private Equity
Specialisation: Focuses on private equity and venture capital transactions; Co-Chairman of the HHP-Venture Capital Group. Responsible for legal questions surrounding the establishment of venture capital funds and their investments, the structuring and set-up of biotech start-ups and other hightech companies, their financing, the negotiations of strategic alliances and Employee Stock Option Plans throughout Europe, and Initial Public Offerings.
Prof. Memberships: Advises numerous US, German, and other Venture Capital Funds, including more than 40 Biotech and Life Science Companies and some of the most successful IT start-ups. Chairs the Munich Venture Capital Club.
Publications: Most recent include Schäffer-Poeschel Verlag Stuttgart (Achleitner/Wollmert): Stock Options, VDI Nachrichten (Feb, April and July 2000): Venture Capital Panel, Capital: Stockoptions für alle, Time E-Europe: Venture Capital.
Career: Joined *Bruckhaus Kreifels Winkhaus & Lieberknecht* in Dusseldorf 1987. Moved to *Haarmann, Hemmelrath & Partner* in 1989, becoming a partner in 1990.
Personal: Born 6 April 1955. Received legal degree from the University of Göttingen School of Law in 1982, and Master of Laws from University of California at Berkeley in 1986. Admitted to the Bar in Germany in 1986.

G

EMDE, Thomas
Freshfields Bruckhaus Deringer, Frankfurt am Main +49 69 27 30 80
thomas.emde@freshfieldsbruckhaus.com
Recommended in Banking & Finance, Capital Markets: Equity
Specialisation: Partner in the finance group, specialising in securities, investment law, IPO's, the Banking Act and the Prospectus Sales Act.

EPE, Axel
Freshfields Bruckhaus Deringer, Düsseldorf +49 211 49 79 0
axel.epe@freshfieldsbruckhaus.com
Recommended in Corporate/M&A
Specialisation: Partner in the Corporate group specialising in partnership law, limited liability company law, stock corporation law, law regarding groups of companies, succession into enterprises/family-owned companies, mergers and acquisitions, joint ventures, privatisations, initial public offerings and public takeovers.

G

ERNST, Reinhold
Hengeler Mueller Weitzel Wirtz, Düsseldorf +49 211 830 40 211 83040
reinhold.ernst@hengeler.com
Recommended in Private Equity
Specialisation: Main areas of work are corporate law, mergers & acquisitions and capital markets (IPOs) and private equity.
Career: Foreign associate London law firm 1993; foreign associate New York law firm 1995-96; *Hengeler Mueller* since 1991; Partner since 1999.
Personal: Born 14th January 1963. Universities of Passau and Cologne (Dr. jur.).

ESSER-WELLIÉ, Michael
Freshfields Bruckhaus Deringer, Düsseldorf +49 211 49790
michael.esser@freshfieldsbruckhaus.com
Recommended in Communications: Regulatory, Competition/Anti-trust
Specialisation: Specialises in IT and Communications and Antitrust/European law. Core activities are data protection, internet/multimedia, broadcasting and telecoms.

FABRITIUS, Andreas
Freshfields Bruckhaus Deringer, Frankfurt am Main +49 69 27 30 80
andreas.fabritius@freshfieldsbruckhaus.com
Recommended in Corporate/M&A
Specialisation: Partner in the corporate group specialising in company law, mergers and acquisitions, joint ventures, privatisations, and public takeovers.

FEICK, Carl-Peter
Linklaters Oppenhoff & Rädler, Frankfurt am Main +49 69 71 00 30
Recommended in Banking & Finance

FEICK, Hans-Georg
Baker & McKenzie, Frankfurt am Main +49 69 29 90 80
hans-georg.feick@bakernet.com
Recommended in Banking & Finance
Specialisation: Principal areas of work include all aspects of commercial bank lending, including project finance, structured finance, asset finance, and acquisition finance. Additional interest in M&A.
Prof. Memberships: Frankfurter Anwaltskammer; Illinois Bar Association; American Bar Association.
Career: Admitted in Illinois, USA, since 1970 and in Germany since 1972. Joined *Baker & McKenzie* in 1969, became partner in 1975.
Personal: Born 24th February 1940. Attended Universities of Frankfurt 1959; Freiburg 1960-61; Munich 1961-63; University of California Law School at Berkeley, California, USA, 1964-65 (LLM); Illinois Institute of Technology Kent Law School, Chicago, USA, 1969-70 (JD).

FEURING, Wolfgang
Freshfields Bruckhaus Deringer, Frankfurt am Main +49 69 170990
wolfgang.feuring@freshfields.com
Recommended in Banking & Finance, Capital Markets: Equity
Specialisation: Specialises in banking and finance, capital markets, securities, corporate law, and cross border mergers.

FOULKES, Hilary
Skadden, Arps, Slate, Meagher & Flom LLP, Frankfurt am Main +49 69 742 200
hfoulkes@skadden.com
Recommended in Communications: Transactional
Specialisation: Cross-border, mergers & acquisitions and corporate finance transactions.

FRITZEMEYER, Wolfgang
Döser Amereller Noack, Munich +49 89 55 23 8 0
wolfgang.fritzemeyer@bakernet.com
Recommended in Communications: IT
Specialisation: Partner in the Munich office of *Baker & McKenzie*, Co-Chairman of German offices' IT Group. Also Co-Chairman of the Steering Committee pertaining to the European IP/IT Practice Group. Main areas of work include IT law; software; hardware and Internet contracts; franchising; and technology transfer. Member of the Ad-hoc Group for the development of the German EDI (Electronic Data Interchange) Contract (under auspices of the Arbeitsgemeinschaft für wirstschaftliche Verwaltung). Author and Co-author of various publications relating to computer and franchising law.
Career: Qualified New York, USA, 1979; Germany 1980; New South Wales, Australia, 1990. Joined *Baker & McKenzie* in 1983, becoming a partner in 1988.
Personal: University of Freiburg; University of Heidelberg (Ref.), 1973; Assessor Exam, 1976; Cornell Law School (LLM), 1977; University of Konstanz (Dr.jur.), 1983.

GASTEYER, Thomas
Clifford Chance Pünder, Frankfurt am Main +49 69 71 99 01
Thomas.Gasteyer@cliffordchance.com
Recommended in Corporate/M&A
Specialisation: Practice is concentrated in the area of mergers and acquisitions, private equity and corporate real estate including finance.
Prof. Memberships: German and International Bar Associations.
Career: Studied law in Frankfurt am Main; admitted to the Bar of Frankfurt in 1979 and New York in 1982; tax department of major accounting firm, 1979; Master of Laws (Columbia University) 1981; certified tax attorney; partner at *Pünder* since 1983; managing partner at *Pünder, Volhard, Weber & Axster* until the end of 1999; deputy chairman of *Clifford Chance* since January 2000.
Personal: Born 1952.

GEISSLER, Bernhard
Bardehle Pagenberg Dost Altenburg Geissler Isenbruck, Munich +49 89 92 80 50
Recommended in Intellectual Property: Patent
Career: Professional Experience: 1963-1965, research physicist at the Technical University in Munich in the Field of low temperature irradiation of solids in nuclear reactors. 1964-1968, Patent Attorney clerkship in two German patent law firms, the German Patent Office, German Federal Patent Court and the District Court Munich. 1968-1971, Legal Research Fellow at the Max-Planck-Institute for Foreign and International Patent, Copyright and Competition Law in Munich. 1971-1973, Patent Attorney at Kalle AG (Farbwerke Hoechst). 1973-1985, Patent Division of Phillips Petroleum Company, Associate General Patent Counsel, the work included supervision of patent prosecution and licensing and other contracts, work as a Liason Attorney in major litigation in the field of high polymers and managing a section of twelve people including seven professionals. Since 1985, private practice; Partner of the firm *Patent-und Rechtsanwälte Bardehle, Pagenberg, Dost, Altenburg, Geissler, Isenbruck*, Munich. Various publications and lectures.
Personal: Education: 1957-1963, Study of Physics at the Technical University of Munich. 1963, Examination as Diplom-Physiker. 1963-1967, Law School at the University of Munich. 1969, German Patent Attorney Examination. 1971, Admission as a German Attorney-at-law at the District Court of Wiesbaden. 1971, Degree of Dr. jur., of the University of Munich (scope of patent protection for chemical products). 1974, US Patent Bar Examination. 1979-1981, Law School at the George Washington University in Washington DC. 1980, graduated from George Washington University with a Master of Comparative Law (MCL) degree. 1981, DC Bar Examination and Admission to Bar of the District of Columbia.

GIEBE, Olaf
Klaka Rechtsanwälte, Munich +49 89 99 89 190
Recommended in Intellectual Property: General

GODDAR, Heinz
Boehmert & Boehmert, München +49 89 384 07 20
goddar@boehmert.de
Recommended in Intellectual Property: Patent
Specialisation: Patent consultation, licensing and litigation.
Prof. Memberships: AIPPI – Association Internationale pour la Protection de la Propriete Industrielle; CIPA – The Chartered Institute of Patent Agents; ECTA – European Communities Trademark Association; EPI – European Patent Institute; FICPI – Federation Internationales des Conseils en Propriete Industries; GPI – German

Patent Institute (Deutsche Patentanwaltskammer); LESI – Licensing Executives Society International; NZIPA – New Zealand Institute of Patent Attorneys.
Publications: 'European Patent Stategies for the Internet' in 'Intellectual Property Statergies for Internet Technologies' published 1997, 'International Exhaustion: The European Dimension' in 'European Community Trade Mark' published 1997, and others.
Career: Ph.D. in physics 1968. German patent attorney 1972, European patent attorney 1978, lecturer for intellectual property at Bremen University since 1996, Honorary judge at the senate for patent attorney matters of the German Federal Supreme Court 1993.
Personal: Born July 23rd, 1939, high school at Monchengladbach, studies at Tubingen and Mainz, Germany, lives in Munich. Leisure interests: golf, sailing and skiing.

GROSSMANN, Klaus
Clifford Chance Pünder, Düsseldorf
+49 211 43 550
klaus.grossmann@cliffordchance.com
Recommended in Corporate/M&A
Specialisation: M&A, Private Equity, corporate and commercial cross-border transactions.
Prof. Memberships: IBA, AIJA.
Career: University of Cologne (Dr. jur. 1990); admitted 1988; 1988/89 *Arnold & Partner* and 1989/90 *Dow, Lohnes & Albertson*, both Washington, DC, USA, 1990-1997 *Wessing*; partner with *Wessing* since 1993, Partner with *Clifford Chance* since 1997.
Personal: Born 1960, Philadelphia, Pennsylvania, USA.

HAAG, Hendrik
Hengeler Mueller Weitzel Wirtz, Frankfurt am Main +49 69 170 950
Recommended in Banking & Finance, Capital Markets: Debt, Capital Markets: Equity, Project Finance

HAARMANN, Wilhelm
Haarmann, Hemmelrath & Partner, Frankfurt am Main +49 69 9 20 59 0
Wilhelm_Haarmann@hhp.de
Recommended in Corporate/M&A, Private Equity, Tax
Specialisation: Rechtsanwalt (Attorney-at-law), Wirtschaftsprüfer (Certified public auditor) and Steuerberater (Certified tax adviser). The practice focuses on international and national tax law, company law, corporate reorganisations, mergers and acquisitions, going public, fund structuring, leasing, including cross-border-leasing, and venture capital.
Prof. Memberships: Member of International Bar Association; International Fiscal Association (German board); Institute of German Chartered Accountants (IDW; Chairman of Tax Experts Committee); Deutscher Anwaltsverein; German British Lawyers Association; Chairman or member of the supervisory board of leading companies of the IT and telecommunications industry as well as in the real estate field.
Publications: Author of several articles on international tax, accounting and company law matters. Has spoken at conferences and seminars, and is Professor of taxation at the University of Bamberg.
Career: From 1977 to 1979 worked at *Arthur Young & Co.* in Frankfurt. Subsequently joined *Peat Marwick, Mitchell & Co.* and became a partner in 1983. One of the founding partners of *Haarmann, Hemmelrath & Partner* in 1987, a leading multidisciplinary partnership comprising (October 2000) approx. 560 fee-earners (total staff approx. 925), thereof approx. 345 lawyers, tax advisers and certified public auditors with offices in Frankfurt, Munich, Dusseldorf, Berlin, Leipzig, Hamburg, Cologne, Paris, Milan, London, Brussels, Vienna, Prague, Warsaw, Bucharest, Budapest, Moscow, Tokyo, Shanghai and Singapore. Based in Frankfurt office.
Personal: Born 24th May 1950. Studied law and economics at the Universities of Münster and Freiburg, then gained J.D. in 1979 from the University of Münster.

HAIDINGER, Michael
Freshfields Bruckhaus Deringer, Hamburg
+49 40 369 060
michael.haidinger@freshfieldsbruckhaus.com
Recommended in Communications: Transactional
Specialisation: Joint head of international TMT (Telecommunications, Media and Technology) Group. Specialises in information technology and communications and corporate law, where core activities are mergers and acquisitions and joint ventures.

HANSEN, Bernd
Hoffmann Eitle, München +49 89 92 40 90
Bhansen@hetnet.de
Recommended in Intellectual Property: Patent
Specialisation: Main area of work revolves around patents in the chemical field, principally litigation, both cross-border and national, opinion work, Opposition and Appeal Proceedings before the European and German Patent Offices, as well as patent prosecution. Special experience in fine chemicals, pharmaceuticals, polymers and fibres, photochemistry, electrochemical sciences. Litigation experience with pharmaceutical patents relating to, inter alia, Diltiazem, Consensus Interferon, Nifedipine, Omeprazole, Pantoprazole, Pro-urokinase, Ranitidine, Salinomycin, as well as with protective rights covering, e.g., high tenacity polymer filaments, textile fabrics and alkaline batteries.
Prof. Memberships: AIPPI, FICPI, LES, EPI, VPP and Deutsch-Japanische Juristische Vereinigung.
Publications: Author of Hansen/Hirsch 'Protecting Inventions in Chemistry' (Wiley VCH 1997); more than one hundred publications on questions of German, European and East European patent law in GRUR, GRUR Int., Mitt., AIPPI and FICPI journals, IIC, Patent & Licensing and other professional gazettes.
Career: Diploma in Chemistry 1969, Ph.D. in 1971. German Patentanwalt (1975), European Patent Attorney since 1978. Senior partner in *Hoffmann. Eitle* heading its Chemical Department. European correspondent of Patents & Licensing, Tokyo, Japan (since 1976). Frequent speaker.
Personal: Born January 26, 1943. Student of chemistry at Munich's Technical University (1962-1970). Leisure interests include tennis and other outdoor sports, literature.

HARITZ, Detlef
Clifford Chance Pünder, Berlin +49 302 54 657 800
detlef.haritz@cliffordchance.com
Recommended in Tax
Specialisation: Partner in the Tax Department. Concentrates on tax law and associated questions of company law.
Prof. Memberships: German Bar Association.
Publications: Author of the commentary on transformation tax law published in the Beck-Verlag; published articles regarding financial statements for tax purposes and tax problems in connection with real property investments; co-author of 'Rechtshandbuch Vermögen und Investitionen in der ehemaligen DDR' and 'Immobilien
Recht und Steuern'.
Career: Universities of Kiel and Berlin (Dr. rer. pol., 1984); admitted 1985; Tax Advisor 1986; Auditor 1991; Partner since 1994.

HARRER, Herbert
Linklaters Oppenhoff & Rädler, Frankfurt am Main +49 69 71 00 30
Recommended in Capital Markets: Equity

HARTE-BAVENDAMM, Henning
Lovells Boesebeck Droste, Hamburg
+49 40 419 93 0
Henning.hartebavendamm@lovells.com
Recommended in Communications: IT, Intellectual Property: General
Specialisation: Intellectual property, competition law and information technology.
Prof. Memberships: German Association for Intellectual Property (GRUR) – Chairman of Committee on Unfair Competition Law and Trademark Law; International Trademark Association (INTA); European Community Trademark Association (ETCA) – Anti-Counterfeiting Committee; German Association for Law and Information (DGR).
Publications: Editor/Author: Handbuch der Markenpiraterie in Europa (Anti-Counterfeiting in Europe), Munich 2000. Co-author: Handbuch des Wettbewerbsrechts (Handbook on Unfair-Competition Law); 2nd edition 1997; Munchner Vertragshandbuch (Munich Handbook of Contracts) 4th edition 1998; Computerrechts-Handbuch (Computer Law Handbook) 1990 et seq (looseleaf); World Intellectual Property Guidebook (Germany), New York 1990; Articles on trademark, competition and computer law.
Career: Admitted to the bar of Hamburg in 1976. Partner of the Hamburg law firm of DROSTE since 1981, Doctorate (Dr. jur.) University of Hamburg 1977. Lectures Intellectual Property Law at University of Hamburg.
Personal: Born 1950, resides Hamburg. Interests include music, art, sport.

HEEMANN, Manfred
Clifford Chance Pünder, Frankfurt am Main
+49 69 71 99 01
Manfred.Heemann@cliffordchance.com
Recommended in Banking & Finance
Specialisation: Predominantly works within the field of finance law. Advises especially on bank lending and acquisition financing.

G

Prof. Memberships: Member of International Association of Young Lawyers.
Career: Studied law at the University of Münster (Dr.) and the University of Chicago (LL.M., 1993). Admitted 1993 in Frankfurt am Main (Rechtsanwalt) and 1994 in New York (attorney at law). Partner since 1999.
Personal: Born 1963.

HEIN, Peter E.
Allen & Overy, Frankfurt am Main
+49 69 2648 5000
Recommended in Banking & Finance

HELLMANN, Hans
Hans Hellmann – Sole Practitioner, Cologne
+49 221 494 058
Recommended in Competition/Anti-trust

HENLE, Walter
Döser Amereller Noack, Frankfurt am Main
+49 69 29 90 80
Recommended in Private Equity
Specialisation: Partner at the Munich office of *Baker & McKenzie.* Areas of practice include transactional work, in particular M&A. Private Equity and Capital Markets, with an emphasis on IPO work.
Prof. Memberships: Member of the board of the German Venture Capital Association ('BVK').
Publications: Author of numerous publications and presentations on topics relating to D&O Liabilities, Venture Capital, M&A and Capital Markets.
Career: Qualified 1983. Joined *Baker & McKenzie* in 1986 becoming partner in 1992. Transferred from the firm's Frankfurt office in 1997 to open *Baker & McKenzie's* Munich office.
Personal: Languages; German; English and French. University of Munich (ref.), 1979; (Assessor Exam), 1983; University of Munich (Dr jur.), 1984; New York University (LLM) 1986, Fulbright Scholar.

HENTZEN, Matthias
Hengeler Mueller Weitzel Wirtz, Düsseldorf
+49 211 830 40 211 83040
matthias.hentzen@hengeler.com
Recommended in Communications: Transactional
Specialisation: Cross-border mergers and acquisitions often in the context of large international joint ventures and other business combinations.
Publications: Corporate, M&A and arbitration.
Career: *De Bandt, van Hecke,* Brussels, (1989). Qualified 1990, joined *Hengeler Mueller* in 1990, Partner since 1995.
Personal: Universities of Saarbrucken and Muenster (Dr.jur. 1987), Georgetown University (LLM. 1986).

HERMANNS, Ferdinand
Ferdinand Hermanns – Sole Practitioner, Meerbusch +49 2132 5835
f.hermanns@dr-hermanns.de
Recommended in Competition/Anti-trust
fax +49 2132 5450
Specialisation: German and European competition and anti-trust law. Acting as an arbitrator for the ICC, Paris.
Career: Dr. jur. in Cologne and Paris; Attorney at law since 1966. Bundesverband der Deutschen Industrie (Federation of German Industries) Competition Department (1963-72); Director of the Brussels Liaison Office of the Federation of German Industries to the EC Commission (1973-77); Acting chair of the ICC Commission on law and practices relating to competition; Attorney at law, admitted to the Court of Appeal in Dusseldorf (1977).
Personal: Born 1934.

HEUN, Sven-Erik
Willkie Farr & Gallagher, Frankfurt am Main
+49 69 79 30 20
Recommended in Communications: Regulatory

HEUSSEN, Benno
PricewaterhouseCoopers Veltins, München
+49 89 2909 70
benno.heussen@de.pwcglobal.com
Recommended in Communications: IT
Specialisation: Partner of *Pricewaterhouse Coopers Veltins.* Chairman of the German Law Society's (DAV) Information Technology working party, a group of lawyers specialising in information technology multimedia and telecommunications law. Member of the board of the German Law Society (DAV) and responsible for all questions in this field in the legal community in Germany. Lecturer on law at University of Hanover. Clients include hardware- and software-houses and service companies, including manufacturers of chips and PCBS Companies developing and marketing databases, Internet-Serviceproviders, E-Commerce-Businesses and medium to large industrial companies using (and in some cases, developing) their own computer systems.
Prof. Memberships: Law Society, German-American Lawyers Association, German-Japanese Lawyers Association.
Publications: Co-editor and co-author of 'Computerrechts-Handbuch' (C.H.Beck Verlag), of the 'Lawyers Handbook' (C.H. Beck Verlag), of the 'Handbook Negotiation and Management of contracts' (Otto Schmidt Verlag) and of numerous other publications (for further information see www.cybercourt.de).
Career: Qualified in 1970, admitted to the bar 1973. Founded *Heussen Braun von Kessel* in 1973, specialised in IT-law since 1985. Founded *Heussen Braun von Kessel's* Berlin office 1991. Has lectured on law in Berlin and now in Hanover. Leads *Pricewaterhouse Coopers Veltins* Information Technology Committee since 2000.
Personal: Born 18 May 1944. Attended Universities in Berlin, Munich and Freiburg 1965 - 1969, J.D. 1972 (Munich) Lives in Munich.

HEY, Christian
Linklaters Oppenhoff & Rädler, Berlin
+49 30 21 49 60
Recommended in Communications: Telecoms (transactional)

HEYMANN, Thomas
Willkie Farr & Gallagher, Frankfurt am Main
+49 69 79 30 20
thomas.heymann@cliffordchance.com
Recommended in Communications: IT
Specialisation: Partner specialising in private equity, computer law, outsourcing arrangements, corporate and corporate transactions of technology-driven companies.
Prof. Memberships: President of the International Federation of Computer Law Associations. Board Member, formerly President (1995-1999) Vice President (1991-1995) of the German Computer Law Association.
Publications: A frequent speaker at conferences and author of many articles on IT-related issues. Is co-editor of 'Computer and Recht International' and 'Computer and Recht'.
Career: Universities of Frankfurt, Paris, Hamburg. Qualified in 1985 as Rechtsanwalt; joined *Willkie Farr & Gallagher* as resident partner, previously being partner in *Clifford Chance Pünder* and before that in *Koch, von Braunschweig & von Mettenheim,* which later became *Wessing Berenberg-Gossler Zimmermann Lange.*
Personal: Born 1952; resides Frankfurt.

HODGSON, Stephen
Döser Amereller Noack, Frankfurt am Main
+49 69 29 90 80
stephen.hodgson@bakernet.com
Recommended in Project Finance
Specialisation: Partner in banking and finance department. Main focus of practice is structured finance, in particular, acquisition finance, project finance and trade finance but including general banking advisory work, banking regulation and derivatives. Acts on behalf of lenders and borrowers, both domestic and overseas. Clients include Dresdner Bank, Deutsche Bank AG, London, Kreditanstalt für Wiederaufbau, Bank of Scotland, DG Bank, Intermediate Capital Group and Advent.
Prof. Memberships: UK Law Society; local Bar of Hessen; admitted to practise in England, Hong Kong and Germany, member British German Jurists Association.
Publications: Englisches Handels- und Wirtschaftsrecht (1995); Contributor to Butterworths Journal of International Banking and Financial Law.
Career: Qualified 1985; admission as German Rechtsanwalt 1998; solicitor at *Slaughter and May,* London and Hong Kong; joined *Baker & McKenzie* 1995, becoming partner in 1998.
Personal: Born 28 January 1956; Queens' College Cambridge (1975-80) (MA); University of Tübingen 1981.

HOENE, Thomas
CMS Hasche Sigle Eschenlohr Peltzer Schäfer, Stuttgart +49 711 97 133
thomas.hoene@cmslegal.de
Recommended in Communications: IT
Specialisation: Main areas of work are information technology and telecommunications law, especially the structuring, negotiating and development of IT project contracts, outsourcing contracts and litigation relating to IT, the structuring and negotiating of transactions involving IT companies, and acting as arbitrator or mediator in IT law disputes. Clients: Siemens AG, IBM Deutschland Informationssysteme GmbH, debis Systemhaus GmbH, INTEGRATA Unternehmensberantung GmbH, TDS

Informationstechnologie AG, CENIT AG, Deutsche Perot Systems GmbH, Land Baden-Württemberg Finanzministerium.
Prof. Memberships: German Bar Association; German Association of Electronic Data Processing and Law (Chairman of the Advisory Board); German-Australian Chamber of Commerce, Melbourne.
Publications: 'Software und das Jahr-2000-Problem' in: Computer und Recht 1999. S.281ff.; 'Stellungnahme der DGRI zu den Entwürfen für neue EVB-IT' in: Computer und Recht 1998, 567ff.
Career: University of Münster, admitted to bar in 1981; joined the firm (formerly *Sigle Loose Schmidt-Diemitz*) in 1981; partner since 1985; lecturer on the structure and content of contracts in connection with IT projects at several occasions.
Personal: Born 1952 in Hann-Münden. Speaks German and English.

HOENIKE, Mark
White & Case, Feddersen, Hamburg
+49 40 350 05 0
mhoenike@whitecase.com
Recommended in Communications: Regulatory
Specialisation: Leading communications law adviser basd in the Hamburg office. Wide-ranging corporate and regulatory law experience is focused on the communications, media and technology sectors. Is a regular adviser on major interconnection, infrastructure and licensing agreements.
Prof. Memberships: Member of Hamburg Bar.
Personal: Speaks fluent German and English.

HOFFMANN-BECKING, Michael
Hengeler Mueller Weitzel Wirtz, Düsseldorf
+49 211 830 40 211 83040
michael.hoffmann-becking@hengeler.com
Recommended in Corporate/M&A
Specialisation: Corporate Law. Regularly advises on large scale merger and acquisitions as well as complex transformations and reorganisations of companies and groups.
Prof. Memberships: Past member of the Board of the German law Society (Standige Deputation des Deutxchen Juristentags) 1988-2000. Chairman of the Committee on Corporate Law of the German Bar Association (Handelsrechtsausschuss des Deutschen Anwaltvereins).
Publications: Editor and co-author of Munich handbook of Corporate Law Vol. IV: Stock Corporation, 2nd edition 1999. Some other books on corporate law and a great number of law review articles.
Career: Qualified in 1971. Joined *Hengeler Mueller* 1971, partner since 1975. Assistant Professor at the University of Bonn since 1999.
Personal: Born February 8th, 1943. Attended Universities of Freiburg, Munich, Muenster (Dr. Jur.).

HOLZAPFEL, Hans-Joachim
Linklaters Oppenhoff & Rädler, Munich
+49 89 41808 0
Recommended in Private Equity

HÖNIG, Klaus
Linklaters Oppenhoff & Rädler, Cologne
+49 221 2091 0
Recommended in Corporate/M&A

HUTTER, Stephan
Shearman & Sterling, Frankfurt am Main
+49 69 9711 1230
shutter@shearman.com
Recommended in Capital Markets: Equity, Project Finance
Specialisation: A partner of *Shearman & Sterling* since 1995. Practiced in the New York and Frankfurt offices, specialising in M&A, corporate finance, and project finance transactions. Extensive experience in international equity offerings of German, Austrian, and Swiss companies, including public offerings and private placements of securities in the US. Frequently lectures at seminars on international equity offerings as well as Neuer Markt and dual listings by German companies.
Prof. Memberships: Chairman of the International Bar Association's Subcommittee E-1 (Legal Opinions) of Committee E (Banking Law). New York Bar since 1987.
Publications: Co-author of Legal Opinions in International Transactions (Kluwer, 3rd edition, 1997), Acquisitions of Shares in a Foreign country (Graham & Trotman, 1993), an author of 'Übernahmerecht in den USA' (DAI Schriften zum Kapitalmarkt, volume 2, 1999), 'Obligations of German Issuers in connection with Public Securities Offerings and Stock Exchange Listings in the United States' (DAI Schriften zum Kapitalmarkt, volume 1, 1998) and 'The Corporate Opinion in International Transactions' (Columbia Business Law Review 427, 1989).
Career: Graduate of the University of Vienna Law School (Dr. jur., 1984) and the University of Illinois (Champaign-Urbana) Law School (LLM, 1986, Fulbright Scholar).

IHRIG, Hans-Christoph
Allen & Overy, Frankfurt am Main
+49 69 2648 5000
Recommended in Capital Markets: Equity

INGERL, Reinhard
Lorenz Seidler Gossel, Munich +49 89 290 100
Recommended in Intellectual Property: General

JÄCKLE, Christof
Hengeler Mueller Weitzel Wirtz, Düsseldorf
+49 211 830 40 211 83040
Recommended in Communications: Transactional

JACKSON, Ian
Clifford Chance Pünder, Frankfurt am Main
+49 69 71 99 01
ian.jackson@cliffordchance.com
Recommended in Capital Markets: Debt
Specialisation: Partner active in securities and securitisation, representing issuers, lead managers and trustees in the field of debt and equity.
Prof. Memberships: The Law Society, England; Deutsche Anwaltskammer, Frankfurt.
Career: University of Cambridge, Pembroke College, B.A., (Law)1979, M.A., 1983. Joined *Clifford Chance* 1980; qualified as a Solicitor, England 1983 and as a Solicitor, Hong Kong 1985; seconded to *C&C Law Office* Beijing 1988; moved to Securities Group, *Clifford Chance* London 1989; transferred to Frankfurt office 1998; made partner 1991.
Personal: Born 1958 in Bristol, England; resides in Kronenberg, Germany with his wife and two children.

JACOB, Friedhelm
Hengeler Mueller Weitzel Wirtz, Frankfurt am Main +49 69 170 950
friedhelm.jacob@hengeler.com
Recommended in Tax
Specialisation: Partner in the tax department. Advises on domestic and treaty law issues of cross-border and domestic tax planning; acquisitions and transactions of large corporate groups; structuring of innovative financial products, with particular focus on tax treaties and CFC legislation.
Prof. Memberships: International Fiscal Association (National reporter for 2000 congress).
Publications: US German Tax Treaty Handbook (IBFD); numerous articles on international treaties.
Career: 1983 – Visiting Administrator with Fiscal Affairs Department of International Monetary Fund, Washington DC. 1980-1986 Associate International Tax Counsel, Ministry of Finance, Bonn. 1986-1991 Fiscal Counselor German Embassy, Washington DC. Joined *Hengeler* in 1991.
Personal: Born in 1948. Attended Universities of Marburg, Bidefeld and Geneva (Switzerland).

JAENICHEN, Hans-Rainer
Vossius & Partner, München +49 89 41 30 40
jaenichen@vossiusandpartner.com
Recommended in Intellectual Property: Patent
Specialisation: Patent prosecution, opposition proceedings and litigation (patent infringement and compulsory licences) in the field of biotech intellectual property. HSA, BGH, insulin, IFN-α, IFN-β, IFN-γ, IL-2, G-CSF, EPO, tPA, recombinant viruses, Ti plasmid technology and other systems for the production of recombinant plants, transgenic animals, how to patent plants and animals in the EPO, bacterial, yeast and mammalian expression systems, methods for the purification of recombinantly produced proteins, antibody technology (monoclonals, single chain, humanised, ect.), PCR, Taq polymerase and other thermostable enzymes, NASBA, antisense technology, ribozymes, etc.
Prof. Memberships: Member of the German Patent Attorney Bar Association, EPI, FICPI, AIPPI and GRUR. Member of the Board of Editors of 'Biotechnology Law Report'.
Publications: Numerous lectures and articles about patenting biotech inventions in the European Patent Office and enforcing such patents. Has published a book entitled 'The European Patent Office's Case Law on the Patentability of Biotechnology Inventions', Heymanns, 1993 (first edition) and, together with two co-authors from the United States, 1997 (second edition, with annotations on corresponding US case law and practice).
Career: PhD in molecular biology, 1984; German Patent Attorney, 1987; European Patent Attorney, 1988; European Trademark Attorney, 1995.

G

G

JALETZKE, Matthias
Döser Amereller Noack, Frankfurt am Main
+49 69 29 90 80
matthias.jaletzke@bakernet.com
Recommended in Private Equity
Specialisation: Partner in the Mergers & Acquisitions and Corporate Department; member of the *Baker & McKenzie* Global Mergers & Acquisitions Steering Committee. Main area of work is mergers & acquisitions, in particular, leveraged buy-outs for private equity firms and major strategic acquisitions and ventures for large corporate clients. Has handled a variety of national and multinational transactions for domestic and foreign clients. Acted on the privatisation of all German highway rest stops (Tank&Rast) for a private equity fund, the first attempted takeover by KKR in Germany (Herberts), the acquisition by various investment funds of the BTR Paper Technology group. Frequently holds seminars on issues such as M&A documentation, due diligence and company valuation matters.
Prof. Memberships: Frankfurt bar; Association of Antitrust Lawyers (Studienvereinigung Kartellrecht).
Career: Qualified in 1987. Joined *Baker & McKenzie* in 1987, becoming a partner in 1993; worked in the Chicago office of *Baker & McKenzie* 1990-91; member of the firm's Finance Committee.
Personal: Born 1960. Attended Mannheim University (1st state exam 1983), 2nd state exam 1987, Dr. jur. 1988.

JESTAEDT, Thomas
Lovells Boesebeck Droste, Düsseldorf
+49 211 13 68 0
thomas.jestaedt@lovells.com
Recommended in Competition/Anti-trust
Specialisation: Partner in, and joint head of, Competition and EU-Law Department. Main area of work is anti-trust law, merger clearance, cartels, state aid, and public procurement. Has acted for parties in the Cartonboard, Pre-isolated Pipes, and Austrian Banks cartel cases before the European Commission and before the European courts. Has successfully challenged privatisation of Berlin Airport before German courts. Acts for a variety of German and international clients in competition and EU law matters. Contributor to Lange/Bunte (German language commentary on German and EU antitrust law), 'Merger Control in the EU' and Matthew Bender 'Antitrust Laws and Trade Regulation', numerous articles on competition, state aids, and public procurement law.
Prof. Memberships: Düsseldorf Bar, German Academic Association for Competition Law, European Competition Lawyers Forum, European Lawyers Association.
Career: Attended Universities of Bonn and Munich to qualify as German solicitor in 1981. Obtained Dr. jur. degree of University of Munich and LLM of University of Michigan Law School in 1985. Worked for US firm in Washington and London 1985/1986 and in Brussels 1989/1991. Joined *Lovells* in 1986 to become Partner in 1992.
Personal: Born 1 July 1956. Married, three daughters. Lives in Brussels.

JONAS, Kay-Uwe
Linklaters Oppenhoff & Rädler, Cologne
+49 221 20910
Recommended in Intellectual Property: General

JUNG, Harald
CMS Hasche Sigle Eschenlohr Peltzer Schäfer, Frankfurt am Main +49 69 71 70 10
harald.jung@cmslegal.de
Recommended in Corporate/M&A
Specialisation: After having specialised for many years in advising banks and financial institutions the main area of work is now in M&A transactions, venture capital and corporate work for international and German clients. A special expertise exists in transactions in the life sciences, chemical industries, electronic components and banking areas. In these branches also extensive professional experience in joint ventures, joint development agreements and in licensing is given.
Prof. Memberships: German Bar Association; Gesellschaft für Rechtsvergleichung; Chairman of the Legal and Company Law Committee of the American Chamber of Commerce in Germany e.V.
Career: 1975 assistant lecturer at the law faculty of the University of Frankfurt am Main; admitted to Bar in 1978; Dr. jur. 1976; joined the firm (formerly *Peltzer & Riesenkampff*) in 1978; 1981/1982 foreign associate with law firms in New York and Houston; partner since 1982; admitted as Notary Public 1996.
Personal: Born 1948 in Dusseldorf. Universities of Marburg and Munich.

JURY, Caroline
Clifford Chance Pünder, Frankfurt am Main
+49 69 71 99 01
caroline.jury@cliffordchance.com
Recommended in Banking & Finance
Specialisation: Partner specialising in corporate banking and structured finance, concentrating on leverage acquisition finance and secured and unsecured lending. Principally advises leading financial institutions and private equity houses on transactions ranging from pure German domestic deals to multi-layered, multi-jurisdictional cross-border transactions, including those with mezzanine finance and high-yield elements. Is also active in the development of financing structures for the newly developing public to private market in Germany.
Prof. Memberships: Law Society of England and Wales.
Career: Qualified in 1990; *Clifford Chance* London, Amsterdam and Frankfurt since 1991; partner since 1998.
Personal: Born 1965.

KAISER, Bernhard
Freshfields Bruckhaus Deringer, Frankfurt am Main +49 69 27 30 80
bernhard.kaiser@freshfieldsbruckhaus.com
Recommended in Capital Markets: Securitisation
Specialisation: Partner in the finance group specialising in bonds, asset backed securities, derivatives, stock exchange listings, indexation, warranties, certificates of indebtedness, loan contracts, and the Selling Prospectus Act.

KELLET, Christopher
Clifford Chance Pünder, Frankfurt am Main
+49 69 71 99 01
christopher.kellett@cliffordchance.com
Recommended in Corporate/M&A, Private Equity
Specialisation: Co-head of German Corporate Practice. Main area of work is M&A, in particular private equity and leveraged acquistions in Germany. Regularly handles multi-jurisdictional acquistions for financial and private equity investors as well as industrial groups. Also advises lenders to private equity transactions with regard to structuring and equity-related issues. Examples of transactions include advising on PPMV's buy-out of Suspa and NWEP's buy-out of Erftcarbon, Telefonica's acquisition of mediaWays and Kimberly Clark's acquisition of Hakle.
Prof. Memberships: Law Society; Rechtsanwaltskammer Frankfurt am Main.
Career: Oxford University (Balliol College) 1982-85. Partner since 1996.
Personal: Born 1963; Interests include cycling, classic cars and golf.

KENADJIAN, Patrick S.
Davis Polk & Wardwell, Frankfurt am Main
+49 69 97 57 030
Recommended in Capital Markets: Equity

KLUSMANN, Martin
Freshfields Bruckhaus Deringer, Düsseldorf
+49 211 49 79 0
martin.klusmann@freshfieldsbruckhaus.com
Recommended in Competition/Anti-trust
Specialisation: Partner in the Competition and Trade group.

KOERFER, Hans Rolf
Shearman & Sterling, Düsseldorf +49 21 11 78 880
rkoerfer@shearman.com
Recommended in Corporate/M&A
Specialisation: Partner in the M&A/Corporate Department of *Shearman & Sterling*. Specialised in mergers and acquisitions and corporate re-organisations, in particular, in the primary and reinsurance business, inter alia the acquisition of Aachen Reinsurance and Frankona Reinsurance by ERC International Reinsurance, disposal of Veritas Reinsurance (Switzerland) by VHV V.a.G, acquisition of Constitution Reinsurance (USA) by Gerling; acquisition of the AXA Life Insurance Business, AXA Financial Services (Austria) and AXA Fondsmanagement Company by Gerling, disposal of AXA Fondsmanagement by Gerling, acquisition of General Accident Versicherungs-AG by Gerling, acquisition of a variety of smaller primary and reinsurance companies (including joint ventures) and insurance agents/brokers in England, Russia, Poland, Singapore and Greece and the development of strategies for the demutualisation of mutual insurance funds. Recently advised the INA-Schaeffler Group in its acquisition of 100% of the shareholding in Luk Lamellen und Kupplungsbau GmbH and Siemens AG in its joint acquisition with Robert Bosch GmbH of Atecs Mannesmann AG.
Prof. Memberships: Member of the Corporate

Law Committee of the German Federal Bar Association.
Career: 1978-1979 University of Tübingen (Law), 1979-1984 University of Cologne (Law), 1985, First State Examination, 1985-1988 legal trainee (1986 foreign trainee with a London City law firm), 1988, Second State Examination (admission to the bar), 1988-1991 associate with *Oppenhoff & Rädler* and from 1991 to January 2000 Partner in *Oppenhoff & Rädler*. Since February 2000, has been a Partner of *Shearman & Sterling.*
Personal: Born 26 September 1957, married, three children. Lives in the countryside of Cologne.

KÖNIG, Andreas
Freshfields Bruckhaus Deringer, Frankfurt am Main +49 69 273080
andreas.koenig@freshfieldsbruckhaus.com
Recommended in Capital Markets: Debt, Capital Markets: Equity
Specialisation: Partner in the finance group. Core practice area is in IPOs, stock exchange listings, asset backed securities, the Banking Act and the selling Prospectus Act.

KÖNIG, Stephan
Linklaters Oppenhoff & Rädler, Cologne +49 221 2091 0
Recommended in Corporate/M&A

KRÄMER, Lutz
Freshfields Bruckhaus Deringer, Frankfurt am Main +49 69 27 30 80
lutz.kraemer@freshfieldsbruckhaus.com
Recommended in Capital Markets: Equity
Specialisation: Partner in the Corporate Group specialising in equity capital markets (IPO's, secondary offerings, equity linked products such as convertibles and exchangeables, OTC – derivatives, the law of stock corporations and corporate governance).

KRAUSS, Stefan
Hengeler Mueller Weitzel Wirtz, Düsseldorf +49 211 830 40 211 83040
Recommended in Capital Markets: Derivatives, Capital Markets: Securitisation

KULLMANN, Walburga
Freshfields Bruckhaus Deringer, Frankfurt am Main +49 69 27 30 80
walburga.kullmann@freshfieldsbruckhaus.com
Recommended in Banking & Finance
Specialisation: Partner in the finance group specialising in derivatives (including warrants, options, swaps, repos); debt (including bonds, note programmes, loans); equity capital market transactions, listing of securities on the stock exchange, take-overs, insider rules and disclosure rules.

KUSSEROW, Berthold
Linklaters Oppenhoff & Rädler, Frankfurt am Main +49 69 71 00 30
Recommended in Capital Markets: Debt

LANGE, Gustav
Wessing, Frankfurt am Main +49 69 97 1300
g.lange@wessing.com
Recommended in Corporate/M&A
Specialisation: Head of corporate and mergers & acquisitions division as well as corporate civil law, notary services of the Frankfurt office of Wessing. Advises corporate restructuring, domestic and cross-border mergers & acquisitions, privatisation activities and capital markets transactions.
Prof. Memberships: Member of the supervisory board of national and multinational companies.
Career: Graduated from Munich Law School, J.D., 1961, Doctor's degree for international and comparative law 1963. Admitted to the bar in 1967, admitted as civil law notary in 1971.
Personal: Born in Berlin. Legal education at the Universities of Frankfurt, Munich and Paris. Languages: English, German, French. Resident in Frankfurt.

LEHR, Gernot
Redeker Schön Dahs & Sellner, Bonn +49 228 726 250
Recommended in Communications: IT

LEITERMANN, Richard
Wilkinson Barker Knauer, LLP, Frankfurt am Main +49 69 20876
Recommended in Communications: Regulatory

LEYENDECKER, Ludwig
Freshfields Bruckhaus Deringer, Cologne +49 221 205070
ludwig.leyendecker@freshfields.com
Recommended in Communications: Transactional
Specialisation: Main practice areas are mergers and acquisitions, joint ventures, establishment of new businesses and issues of media & telecommunications and general corporate law. Has advised on numerous transactions, particularly in the areas of telecommunications, television, new media and film as well as in the aviation and pharmaceutical industries.

LÜDICKE, Jochen
Freshfields Bruckhaus Deringer, Düsseldorf +49 211 49790
jochen.luedicke@freshfieldsbruckhaus.com
Recommended in Banking & Finance, Tax
Specialisation: Specialises in banking and finance, tax and corporate law. Core activities are tax planning and leasing.

MAGOLD, Rainer
Döser Amereller Noack, Frankfurt am Main +49 69 29 90 80
rainer.magold@bakernet.com
Recommended in Banking & Finance, Capital Markets: Derivatives, Project Finance
Specialisation: Partner in Banking and Finance Department. Main area of work is acquisition finance and project finance. Has handled financing transactions for German and foreign banks, equity funds, borrowers and sponsors. Acted for Apax/Allianz/Lufthansa consortium on privatisation of Autobahn Tank & Rast AG, for Dresdner Bank AG on financing of 'public to private' acquisition of Friedrich Grohe AG for Bayerische Hypo- und Vereinsbank on financing of Kiekert AG acquisition, and for Vivendi on financing of various property and water privatisation transactions. Represented the Chicago Board of Trade in its alliance with EUREX. Heads the German offices' finance group. Steering committee member of B&M Global Finance Group. Regularly speaks at conferences. Publishes frequently in his area of speciality.
Career: Qualified in 1986. Joined *Baker & McKenzie's* Frankfurt office the same year. Practised in the Firm's Paris office in 1989 and 1990. Became partner in 1992.
Personal: Born 7 September 1955. Attended Heidelberg, Mannheim and Geneva universities 1975-1981. LLM (Tulane) 1982. Doctorate (Mannheim University) 1986. Leisure interest include hiking, scuba diving, fine wines and food.

MAIER-REIMER, Georg
Linklaters Oppenhoff & Rädler, Cologne +49 221 2091 0
Recommended in Corporate/M&A

MANNSFELDT, Ulrich
Freshfields Bruckhaus Deringer, Frankfurt am Main +49 69 273080
ulrich.mannsfeldt@freshfieldsbruckhaus.com
Recommended in Project Finance
Specialisation: Specialises in banking and finance law. Specialist focus is loan contracts.

MARTIN, Eckhard
Freshfields Bruckhaus Deringer, Frankfurt am Main +49 69 170990
eckhard.martin@freshfieldsbruckhaus.com
Recommended in Capital Markets: Equity
Specialisation: Specialises in capital markets, securities, bank regulatory, corporate. Has taken responsibility for various capital market transactions, advising issuers, and underwriters in the context of going publics, block trades, and advising banks in connection with debt instrument of all kinds.
Career: Admitted 1991 in Germany and New York.

MAX, Dietrich
Wessing, Dusseldorf +49 211 83 870
duesseldorf@wessing.com
Recommended in Corporate/M&A
Specialisation: Areas of practice: contract Law, commercial law, corporate law, mergers and acquisitions, litigation and arbitration.
Prof. Memberships: Member of the Management Board of the Chamber of Lawyers, Duesseldorf, member of the Advisory Board of the Faculty of Law of the University of Duesseldorf and member of the Board of 'Verband freier Berufe'.
Career: Born 1947 in Detmold. Studied law at the University of Gottingen. In 1975 took a degree as Dr. jur. in intellectual property law. Between 1974 and 1976 worked as academic assistant with the faculty of the University of Gottingen. Admitted to the Duesseldorf Bar in 1977 and started working at *Wessing*. Became a partner of the firm in 1980, specialising in tax matters. Managing Partner of the firms office at Duesseldorf.

MAYEN, Thomas
Redeker Schön Dahs & Sellner, Bonn +49 228 726 250
Recommended in Communications: Regulatory

G

G

MEISTER, Burkhardt
Hengeler Mueller Weitzel Wirtz, Düsseldorf +49 211 830 40 211 83040
Recommended in Corporate/M&A

MEISTER, Norbert
Freshfields Bruckhaus Deringer, Frankfurt am Main +49 69 27 30 80 norbert.meister@freshfieldsbruckhaus.com
Recommended in Corporate/M&A
Specialisation: Specialises in tax and corporate law, with particular focus on taxation of earnings, international tax law, restructuring/reorganisation, corporate acquisitions, law regarding groups of companies, law regarding transformation of companies, mergers and acquisitions and joint ventures.

MES, Peter
Krieger Gentz Mes & Graf von der Groeben, Düsseldorf +49 211 450711
Recommended in Intellectual Property: General

MOOSECKER, Karlheinz
Freshfields Bruckhaus Deringer, Düsseldorf +49 211 49 79 0 karlheinz.moosecker@freshfieldsbruckhaus.com
Recommended in Competition/Anti-trust
Specialisation: Partner in the Competition and Trade group. Specialisation includes competition and antitrust law.

MORRISON, David F.
Sullivan & Cromwell, Paris +33 1 4450 6000 morrisond@sullcrom.com
Recommended in Capital Markets: Debt, Capital Markets: Equity
Specialisation: Conducts pan-European work out of *Sullivan & Cromwell's* offices in Frankfurt and Paris, with a focus on international financial transactions (including privatisations) as well as mergers & acquisitions. Specialises in U.S. and international equity and debt offerings for major European industrial companies and financial institutions. In Germany, represented the underwriters for Deutsche Telekom in its privatisation, involving three offerings in 1996, 1999 and 2000, and its global debt offering in 2000; and the underwriters for T-Online in its IPO (Rule 144A) and German listing. Advised Deutsche Post in its recent privatisation by global equity offering, and was responsible for the overall relationship with Siemens in the IPO spin-offs of EPCOS and Infineon in 1999 and 2000, and in Siemens' own U.S. listing planned for early 2001. From 1997 to 1999 was responsible for the firm's work on the international equity offerings of debitel, Hawesko, Jenoptik, Lufthansa, Pfleiderer, and Volkswagen. Active in debt financings for German issuers, most notably for Kreditanstalt für Wiederaufbau and Deutsche Ausgleichsbank, and a director of KfW's international finance company. In France, work includes representing the underwriters for ATOS in connection with the CDR's disposition of its interest, and acting for UAP and Renault in their respective privatisations. Other work in Europe includes the representations Swisscom in its privatisation and NYSE listing, Cimentos de Portugal in its privatisation, Banco Espírito Santo in connection with its NYSE listing and international equity offerings, and the Portuguese State and Hellenic Republic in connection with international debt offerings. In the M&A area, European activity has included representation of Swiss Re in its acquisition of SAFR (France), among other transactions.
Prof. Memberships: International Bar Association.
Career: Joined *Sullivan & Cromwell* in 1979. Elected a Partner of the firm in 1986.
Personal: Born 1952. Attended Yale University (BA, 1974) and the UCLA Law School (JD, 1978). Fulbright Scholar at the University of Frankfurt, 1978-1979. Admitted to the Bar in California, Frankfurt am Main, New York and Paris. Fluent in French and German.

MORITZ, Hans-Werner
Graf von Westphalen Fritze & Modest, Frankfurt +49 69 959 570
Recommended in Communications: IT

MÜHLMANN, Johann Georg
Shearman & Sterling, Frankfurt am Main +49 69 9711 1642 jmuhlmann@shearman.com
Recommended in Capital Markets: Debt, Capital Markets: Equity
Specialisation: International corporate finance and capital markets. Advises financial institutions and companies in corporate finance transactions, with a special emphasis on cross-border transactions. Current work includes international securities transactions relating to both equity and debt, in particular initial public offerings and Neuer Market listings in Germany as well as convertible bond, global bond, euro bond and Pfandbrief offerings.
Prof. Memberships: Frankfurt Bar, New York Bar.
Career: Qualified 1992. Joined *Shearman and Sterling* in 1992, moved to the Frankfurt office in 1993 and became a partner in 1997.
Personal: Received legal education in Germany (University of Heidelberg and University of Bonn) and New York (New York University). Received a degree MCJ from New York University.

MÜLLER, Welf
Linklaters Oppenhoff & Rädler, Frankfurt am Main +49 69 71 00 30
Recommended in Tax

NIEDER, Michael
Klaka Rechtsanwälte, Munich +49 89 99 89 190
Recommended in Intellectual Property: General

NOLTE, Norbert
Freshfields Bruckhaus Deringer, Cologne +49 221 205070 norbert.nolte@freshfields.com
Recommended in Communications: Regulatory
Specialisation: Telecommunications (regulatory and operational); Information Technology; Data protection; Broadband Cable. Cases: interconnection agreements; local loop access disputes; representation of clients before the Regulatory Authority and the administrative courts in all kinds of proceedings; strategic alliances; acquisition of internet service providers; software agreements; content provider agreements.

NORDHUES, Hans-Günther
Ashurst Morris Crisp, Frankfurt am Main +49 69 97 11 26 hans-guenther.nordhues@ashursts.com.
Recommended in Banking & Finance
Specialisation: Head of banking/finance in Frankfurt. Focuses on leveraged, structured and project finance, derivatives and supervisory work. Participated in creation of a Master Netting Agreement for the FOA and delivered German opinion on effectiveness of netting provisions.
Career: Involved in the LCHSwapClear project and advises on mergers in the finance, clearing and settlement industries. Advises German and foreign credit institutions on regulatory, compliance and capital adequacy requirements. Lecturer at Bonn University. Admitted to Court of Appeal (Oberlandesgericht) 1996.

NUSSBAUM, Peter
Freshfields Bruckhaus Deringer, Frankfurt am Main +49 89 24 21 82 22 peter.nussbaum@freshfieldsbruckhaus.com
Recommended in Private Equity
Specialisation: Partner specialising in mergers and acquisitions, equity capital markets, public takeovers and corporate restructurings with particular experience in working on private equity and venture capital transactions. Joint head of the international private equity group.

OPITZ, Peter
Freshfields Bruckhaus Deringer, Frankfurt am Main +49 69 170990 peter.opitz@freshfields.com
Recommended in Banking & Finance
Specialisation: Main areas of specialisation are banking, capital markets and securities laws, mergers and acquisitions, demergers, joint ventures, company law. Acts for a wide range of corporate clients, banks and financial institutions.

OPPENHOFF, Michael
Linklaters Oppenhoff & Rädler, Cologne +49 221 2091 0
Recommended in Corporate/M&A

OVERLACK, Arndt
Allen & Overy, Frankfurt am Main +49 69 2648 5000
Recommended in Corporate/M&A

PAGENBERG, Jochen
Bardehle Pagenberg Dost Altenburg Geissler Isenbruck, Munich +49 89 92 80 50
Recommended in Intellectual Property: General
Specialisation: Attorney-at-Law, Munich.
Prof. Memberships: AIPLA, AIPPI, ALAI, ECTA, IBA, INTA, LES, Marques, German-American Chamber of Commerce, Computer Law Association, ATRIP, PTMG.
Publications: Author of four books on patent, trademark and computer law, e.g. License Agreements, (English-German Licensing Handbook for Patents, know-how and computer software), 4th Edition, Cologne 1997, Manual on the European Community Trademark, Heymanns, Köln 1996, and more than 50 articles in all fields of industrial prop-

erty law, among them Opposition based on unregistered Rights under the future Community Trademark System, 20 IIC 595 (1989); Protection of Famous Trademarks, International Intellectual Property Law Vol. 2, Hansen, ed., Fordham University School of Law, 1998, Vol. 2, p.44-1; The Community Trademark – Pros and Cons of the System Revisited, INTA 1997 Bulletin Annual Meeting p. 498; The Scope of Article 69 European Patent Convention: Should Sub-Combinations be protected?, 24 IIC 314 (1993); More Refined Rules of Claim Interpretation in Germany, 26 IIC 228 (1995); The WIPO Patent Harmonization Treaty, 19 AIPLA Quarterly Journal 1 (1991); The Opposition Procedure of the Community Trademark – New Trademark Law Strategies, 29 IIC (1998).
Career: Fellow, Max Planck Institute for International Patent, Copyright and Competition Law, Munich since 1973. Admitted to Munich Bar in 1973, Partner of *Bardehle, Pagenberg et al* since 1979, a firm of lawyers and patent agents who have offices in Munich, Düsseldorf, Mannheim, Paris, Alicante and a liaison office in Shanghai and who exclusively specialises in intellectual and industrial property law, especially Patent, Trademark and Copyright Litigation. Executive Editor of the International Review of Industrial Property and Copyright Law (IIC) since 1973; Lecturer at the Universities of Strasbourg (France), Pierce Law Centre (Concord, NH-USA) and Alicante (Spain), numerous other lectures.
Personal: Dr. jur., University of Munich (1974); LLM, Harvard Law School (1973).

PALENBERG, John
Cleary, Gottlieb, Steen & Hamilton, Frankfurt am Main +49 69 97 1030
Recommended in Capital Markets: Equity

PFÜLLER, Markus
Clifford Chance Pünder, Frankfurt am Main
+49 69 71 99 01
markus.pfueller@cliffordchance.com
Recommended in Capital Markets: Equity
Specialisation: Head of the *Clifford Chance* German Equity Capital Markets Group. Practice concentrates on banking and capital markets law and has specialised in advising securities offerings, stock exchange listings and securities trading; advised underwriters and underwriters and issuers on domestic and international securities offerings; also specialises in the areas of internet banking and banking regulatory law. In 2000, inter alia advised on Deutsche Telekom's secondary offering and on the IPOs of T-Online, Infineon and EADS.
Prof. Memberships: British-German Lawyers Association, IBA, American Chamber of Commerce – Financial Services Committee.
Career: University of Freiburg; admitted 1992; Partner since 1999
Personal: Married, two children.

PICOT, Gerhard
Freshfields Bruckhaus Deringer, Cologne
+49 211 20 50 70
gerhard.picot@freshfields.com
Recommended in Corporate/M&A
Specialisation: Partner in the Corporate Law practice group specialising in the areas of mergers and acquisitions, restructuring, corporate security and succession as well as co-operations.

PIEPENBROCK, Hermann-Josef
Piepenbrock & Schuster, Düsseldorf
+49 211 6878 880
Recommended in Communications: Regulatory

PILTZ, Detlev
Flick Gocke Schaumburg, Bonn +49 228 95 94 0
djpiltz@fgs.de
Recommended in Tax
Specialisation: Main area of work is tax and legal consultation for companies, entrepreneurs and high net-worth individuals in the fields of national and international tax law, inheritance law, and estate tax law, as well as national and international fiscal planning. Clients are mainly from Germany but also from the EU and North America.
Prof. Memberships: International Fiscal Association; International Bar Association; Deutsche Steuerjuristische Gesellschaft (German Tax Law Society); Fachinstitut der Steuerberater (Institute of Tax Consultants). Honorary Professor of Tax Law, University of Mannheim.
Publications: Has written numerous books and articles on fiscal and civil law e.g. 'German Civil Law', 1975; Arndt/Piltz, 'Fundamentals of Tax Law: Taxation of Earnings and Taxation of Enterprises', 1996; 'The International Guide to Partnerships, Portfolio: Germany', 1999 (website http://www.fgs.de), Flick/Piltz, 'Cross-border Cases of Inheritance', 1999; General Reporter of the International Fiscal Association on the subject 'International Aspects of Thin Capitalisation' 1996. Lecturer at the Federal Academy of Finance. Numerous lectures on these subject areas.
Career: Studied law at Freiburg and Bonn Universities. State examinations 1972 and 1975. Admitted to the bar 1975. Partner with *Flick Gocke Schaumburg* since 1991.
Personal: Born 10th December 1944; lives in Königswinter near Bonn.

PÖLLATH, Reinhard
P+P Pöllath + Partners, Munich +49 89 2424 00
reinhard.poellath@pplaw.de
Recommended in Corporate/M&A, Private Equity, Tax
Specialisation: All legal and tax aspects of mergers and acquisitions, private equity funds, institutional investors and family offices, including real estate and East German issues.
Prof. Memberships: IBA, IFA.
Publications: Author of many contributions on the above subjects including a handbook of German M&A (9th ed., 1999), foundations and trusts (2nd ed., 1999), etc.
Career: Studied in Germany and U.S.A. (LLM, Harv. 1974); partner of major German law firm, 1980-1993; of counsel of major international law firm, 1993-1997; member of management board of hotel and real estate group, 1993-1996; *P+P Pöllath + Partners*, founded in 1997.
Personal: Born January 1948, extensive charitable activities (third world mini-loan programs, etc.); two nice children.

POPP, Eugen
Meissner, Bolte & Partner, Bremen
+49 421 34 87 40
Recommended in Intellectual Property: Patent

PROSS, Ulrich
Von Rospatt, von der Osten, Pross, Düsseldorf
+49 211 577 2450
Recommended in Intellectual Property: General

QUACK, Karlheinz
Gaedertz Rechtsanwälte, Berlin +49 30 88 02 50
Recommended in Competition/Anti-trust

RAUPACH, Arndt
Raupach & Wollert-Elmendorff, Munich
+49 89 29 03 69 01
Recommended in Tax

REIMANN, Thomas
Clifford Chance Pünder, Düsseldorf
+49 211 43 550
thomas.reimann@cliffordchance.com
Recommended in Intellectual Property: General
Specialisation: Practises litigation, advisory and transactional work in relation to all intellectual property rights with a particular emphasis on patents and multijurisdictional litigation
Prof. Memberships: International Bar Association; German and International Association for the Protection of Industrial Property and Copyright; L.E.S. Germany; German and International Association for the Protection of Industrial Property and Copyright, Chairman of Patent and Utility Patent Law Committee; Experts Committee advising German Federal Minister of Justice on IP problems.
Career: Universities of Munich and Bonn (Dr. jur.); Partner since 1974.

REUDELHUBER, Eva
Linklaters Oppenhoff & Rädler, Frankfurt am Main +49 69 71 00 30
Recommended in Banking & Finance, Project Finance

RIEHMER, Klaus
Haarmann, Hemmelrath & Partner, Frankfurt am Main +49 69 920 59 605
klaus_riehmer@hhp.de
Recommended in Communications: Transactional
Specialisation: Acts for multinational and national companies operating on the telcommunications, IT and multimedia markets, as well as for investment banks and financial institutions. Advises particularly in the following three areas: (i) Transactions in the field of telecommunications, IT and internet (combines a high degree of specialisation in German telecommunications law with a substantial M&A experience in the same sector). (ii) Regulatory proceedings. (iii) Telecom operation and internet contracts such as service provider or outsourcing contracts.
Prof. Memberships: International Bar Association. German Bar Association.
Publications: The German Draft Takeover Act in Light of Vodafone/Mannesmann.

G

Career: Joined *Hengeler Mueller Weitzel Wirtz* in 1994. Changed to *Haarmann, Hemmelrath & Partner* in 1997 as a Partner.
Personal: Born 17 November 1962. Attended Universities in Freiburg, Munich, Kiel (Dr. jur) and Austin, Texas (USA, LLM). Research fellow at Max-Planck-Institute, Hamburg.

RODIN, Andreas
P+P Pöllath + Partners, Berlin +49 30 2233 2233
andreas.rodin@pplaw.de
Recommended in Private Equity, Tax
Specialisation: Practice focuses on M&A (representing sellers and buyers of German and international businesses), post acquisition restructurings and reorganisations of business with an emphasis on tax aspects, structuring of inbound and outbound investment funds, corporate finance and financial products, negotiations of German tax rulings and tax litigation.
Publications: Publications include the tax section of two partnership handbooks, articles on taxation of investments, speeches and papers to national and international conferences and seminars on M&A, financial products and privatisation.
Career: Graduated from Munich Law School in 1983 where also obtained a Dr. Juris degree in 1987. Practised tax and corporate law since 1986, for many of those years, with P+P partners, as a partner in a leading German law firm, and as a partner in a major international law firm. Founding partner of *P+P Pöllath + Partners.*
Personal: Lives in Berlin.

RÖHLING, Andreas
Freshfields Bruckhaus Deringer, Cologne
+49 221 205070
andreas.roehling@freshfields.com
Recommended in Competition/Anti-trust
Specialisation: Main areas of work are antitrust and competition law, energy and EU law and trade mark law.

ROJAHN, Sabine
Wessing, Dusseldorf +49 (0) 89 2 10 38-0
s.rojahn@wessing.com
Recommended in Intellectual Property: General
[SPEC] Litigation, EU Law, Anti Trust Law, Patents
Career: Became Partner of *Wessing* in 1979 and established the department for intellectual property rights in Munich. In 1995 was appointed Honorary Judge of the Lawyer's Court Munich by the Free State of Bavaria and she is speaker of the German-Japanese Lawyer's Association in Bavaria. She was appointed Minister of the Committee of Experts on Intellectual Property with the Federal Ministry of Justice.
Personal: Was born in Remscheid in 1950.

SATZKY, Horst
Hengeler Mueller Weitzel Wirtz, Frankfurt am Main +49 69 170 950
horst.satzky@hengeler.com
Recommended in Competition/Anti-trust
Brussels: 0032 2 737 1530
Specialisation: Main area of work is European and German competition and anti-trust law, principally merger control and litigation. Advises foreign and domestic clients from a variety of industries.
Prof. Memberships: Studienvereinigung Kartellrecht.
Publications: German Anti-Trust Law (5th ed., together with Heidenhain and Stadler).
Career: Worked at the Federal Cartel Office and the Federal Economics Ministry. Joined *Hengeler Mueller* in 1988 and became partner in 1993.
Personal: Born 1954. Universities of Berlin and Kiel (Dr. jur.), foreign temporary associate with *Davis Polk & Wardwell.*

SCHAAR, Bodo
Allen & Overy, Frankfurt am Main
+49 69 2648 5000
Recommended in Capital Markets: Derivatives, Capital Markets: Securitisation

SCHAEFFER, Michael
Harmsen & Utescher, Hamburg +49 40 376 909 0
Recommended in Intellectual Property: General

SCHÄFER, Helge
White & Case, Feddersen, Hamburg
+49 40 350 05 0
hschafer@whitecase.com
Recommended in Communications: Transactional, Private Equity
Specialisation: Leading corporate law adviser based in the firm's Hamburg office. Has extensive experience of acting on domestic and cross-border commercial transactions, mergers and acquisitions, venture capital transactions, joint ventures, management buyouts and international corporate restructurings. Particular experience of acting for the communications sector.
Prof. Memberships: Member of the Hamburg Bar.
Personal: Speaks fluent German and English.

SCHAUMBURG, Harald
Flick Gocke Schaumburg, Bonn +49 228 95 94 0
Recommended in Tax
Specialisation: Work encompasses consultation for entrepreneurs and companies in the fields of German and international tax law and includes related company law issues, mergers and acquisitions, reorganisation, financing, transfer pricing and tax planning. Clients are mainly from Germany but also from the EU and North America.
Prof. Memberships: International Fiscal Association.
Publications: Has written numerous books and articles on his specialist areas, e.g. 'Reorganisation Tax Law', 1995/1999, 'Fiscal and Legal Aspects of Company Acquisitions', 1997, 'International Taxation', 1998, 'Schaumburg/Jesse, National and International Holding Companies from a Fiscal Point of View', 1998, 'Affiliated Group Financing in International Tax Law', 1998, 'International Joint Ventures', 1999. Lecturer at the Federal Academy of Finance. Numerous lectures on these subject areas.
Career: Studied law at Cologne University, Doctor of Law 1973, legal internship (Referendardienst), State examination 1975, admitted to the bar in 1976. Partner with *Flick Gocke Schaumburg* since 1976 (www.fgs.de). Honorary Professor University Cologne 1994.
Personal: Born 16 April 1944. Lives in Bad Godesberg near Bonn.

SCHEJA, Katharina
Graf von Westphalen Fritze & Modest, Frankfurt
+49 69 959 570
Recommended in Communications: IT

SCHERER, Joachim
Döser Amereller Noack, Frankfurt am Main
+49 69 29 90 80
Joachim.Scherer@Bakernet.com
Recommended in Communications: Regulatory
Specialisation: Head of Telecommunications Law Department of *Baker & McKenzie's* German offices and of *Baker & McKenzie's* European and Global Telecommunications Practices Groups. Also a member of the firm's European Law Centre, Brussels. Specialises in national, European and international telecommunications law. Advises national, European and international telecommunications enterprises and governmental entries. Head of the firm's regulatory team, assisting the government of Saudi Arabia in its privatisation of the telecommunications company (1999). Has assisted clients in international telecommunications projects, licensing and interconnection procedures, and telecommunications privatisations in Germany, eastern Europe, Africa, and Latin America. Editor and Co-author of 'Telecommunications Laws in Europe', 4th ed., Butterworths, 1998.
Prof. Memberships: Rechtsanwaltkammer Frankfurt, Brussels Bar (B-list).
Career: Joined *Baker & McKenzie* in 1987, becoming a partner in 1989. Professor of law at University of the Armed Forces, Münich, 1990; Professor at Frankfurt University; member and vice-chairman of Advisory Committee on Regulation and Competition of the Federal Minister of Post and Telecommunications, 1990-95; advisor to the Directorate General XII of the European Commission, 1987-1993.
Personal: Born 14 March 1953. Married with three children.

SCHERER, Peter
Clifford Chance Pünder, Frankfurt am Main
+49 69 71 99 01
Peter.Scherer@CliffordChance.com
Recommended in Capital Markets: Derivatives
Specialisation: Main areas of work are derivatives (including engineering, documentation and regulatory matters), debt instruments and regulatory matters. Also advises on German and international safe custody law (clearing, settlement and collateralisation). Has handled convertibles, bonds and silent participation notes issues for leading German banks and international investment banks as well as for issuers. Acted for leading energy trading companies and banks on numerous OTC energy derivatives transactions on the German market. Advised international credit institutions on the capital treatment and other regulatory matters in connection with credit derivatives, securitisations and other innovative financial structures and instruments. Heads the firm's Derivatives & Regulatory product groups.
Prof. Memberships: German and International Bar Associations, German Banking Law Association.
Publications: Author of several publications in 'Journal of International Banking Law', 'Euromoney

Derivatives Handbook 1999' and 'IFLR Securitisation Yearbook 1999'. Has spoken at numerous, and chaired some, conferences.
Career: Universities of Frankfurt and Indiana University (LLM). Partner since 1995. Before studying law, in the late 1970s and early 1980s worked in the securities trading department and the back office of international banks in Frankfurt and London.
Personal: Born 1958. Leisure interests include 18th and 19th century European and Japanese arts history.

SCHIESSL, Maximilian
Hengeler Mueller Weitzel Wirtz, Düsseldorf
+49 211 830 40 211 83040
Recommended in Corporate/M&A, Private Equity
Specialisation: Corporate finance with a focus on public takeovers, cross-borders, M&A, private equity and equity offerings.
Prof. Memberships: Chairman of Committee G Corporate and M&A of IBA.
Career: Joined *Hengeler Mueller* in 1989 after practising in New York law firm (partner since 1991).
Personal: Munich Law School (J.D., 1982); Doctorate in Corporate Law (1985). Harvard Law School (LLM, 1986). Born October 28th 1960.

SCHILLING, Tilman
Tilman Schilling – Sole Practitioner, Mannheim
+49 621 32 85 631
Recommended in Intellectual Property: General

SCHLITT, Michael
Allen & Overy, Frankfurt am Main
+49 69 2648 5000
Recommended in Capital Markets: Equity

SCHMALENBACH, Dirk
Freshfields Bruckhaus Deringer, Frankfurt am Main +49 69 273080
dirk.schmalenbach@freshfieldsbruckhaus.com
Recommended in Banking & Finance
Specialisation: Specialises in banking and finance law, tax law and corporate law focusing particularly on asset-backed securities, loan contracts, leasing and project finance.

SCHMEDING, Jörg
White & Case, Feddersen, Hamburg
+49 40 350 05 0
jschmeding@feddersen.com
Recommended in Corporate/M&A
Specialisation: Partner of *White & Case, Feddersen* based in the firm's Hamburg office. Is a well-respected corporate law adviser with experience of advising on mergers & acquisitions, anti-trust matters and international commercial arbitrations.
Prof. Memberships: Member of the Hamburg and New York State Bars.
Personal: Fluent in German and English, has good working knowledge of French and Italian.

SCHMIDT, Gerhard
BBLP Beiten Burkhardt Mittl & Wegener, Munich
+49 89 3 50 65 00
Recommended in Corporate/M&A

SCHMITTMANN, Michael
PricewaterhouseCoopers Veltins, Düsseldorf
+49 211 8289 380
michael.schmittmann@de.pwcglobal.com
Recommended in Communications: Regulatory
Specialisation: Leading telecommunications lawyer and partner. Areas of practice include German and European telecommunications and media law with a special emphasis on regulatory matters including national and European competition law, cable, satellite and broadcasting. Major part of client base is satellite operators, broadcasters, private service providers, network operators and equipment manufacturers. Instructions have included work for the German Federal Government in connection with the governmental intranet Bonn/Berlin (1998). Delivered a study on 'Intellectual Property Rights and Space Activities in Europe' to the ESA in Paris (1997). Core activities in 1999 were frequency applications, interconnection agreements, privatisation of German cable networks of DTAG, complaints against tariffs and prices to the National Regulatory Authority in Bonn, advice on article 81/82 issues, international transactions in the internet area, developments of a new digital TV-project, advice in connection with IPOs of IT, media and telecom companies. In summer 2000, successfully coordinated the UNTS License auction for a bidder consortium. Head of the e-business group of *PricewaterhouseCoopers Veltins* and member of the Landwell e-business leaders team.
Prof. Memberships: International Bar Association, Chairman of Committee 7 SLP (Constitutional and Administrative Law).
Career: Internship in a Paris law firm, legal clerkship in Konstanz and at the European Commission. Second state examination in 1987. Consultant to the Commission in Brussels, with an emphasis on broadcasting law. Professional practice in Düsseldorf since 1989, partner in *Heuking Kühn* 1992 and 2000, opening office in Brussels in 1995. Partner in *PricewaterhouseCoopers Veltins* since April 2000.
Publications: Publishes regularly on EU-Telecom policy and law.
Personal: Born 21 August 1958. Studied law at the universities of Cologne and Geneva. Leisure interests include golf. Lives in Düsseldorf.

SCHNEIDER, Hannes
Hengeler Mueller Weitzel Wirtz, Frankfurt am Main +49 69 170 950
hannes.schneider@hengeler.com
Recommended in Banking & Finance, Capital Markets: Debt, Capital Markets: Derivatives
Specialisation: Senior member of the firm's banking and capital markets group. Legal advisor to a large number of German, foreign and international banks, trade associations, international financial institutions, central bank and governmental agencies.
Publications: Author of various books and articles in the field of banking, finance and capital markets.
Prof. Memberships: Chairman of the Banking Law Committee of the Internal Bar Association, a Co-Chairman of the Capital Markets Forum of the International Bar Association and on the Board of Governors of the International Capital Markets Group.
Career: Partner at *Hengeler Mueller* since 1971.
Personal: Attended Universities of Heidelberg, Goettingen, Freiburg and Bonn (Dr.jur., 1967).

SCHNEIDER, Jochen
Schneider & Schiffer, Munich +49 89 5434 9100
schneider_schiffer@compuserve.com
Recommended in Communications: IT
Specialisation: Specialises in IT law, especially computer law (including the law on data protection and outsourcing and internet law). Particularly concerned with the drafting and examination of contracts and standard terms regarding to software development, software distribution, licensing and maintenance of software and hardware systems as well as with copyright (especially in relation to software, databases and domain names) and with outsourcing, telecommunications law and data protection law.
Prof. Memberships: Co-founder and member Deutsche Gesellschaft für Informatik und Recht (DGRI, 'German Association for Information Studies'). Co-founder and member Contract Law Committee of the DGRI. Member of the legislation committee 'information law' of the DAV (German Lawyer's Association). Member of the managing committee of the Information Technology Association of the DAV. Cooperation in the field of EDP-experts. Seminars with several JHK, Deutsche Richterakademie, Deutsche Anwaltsakademie and other institutions (Forum, Verlag Dr. Otto Schmidt).
Publications: 'Handbuch des EDV-Rechts' ('Handbook of EDP-Law'), 2nd Edition. 'Rechtsfragen zu Hard- und Software' ('Legal Issues of Hard- and Software'), 2nd Edition. Co-author 'Recht im Internet' ('Law in the Internet'), edited by Prof. Dr. Matthias Schwarz. Co-author 'Handbuch des Informationsmanagements des Unternehmens' ('Handbook of an Undertakings's Information-Mangement'), edited by Prof. Bullinger. 'Handbuch der IT-Verträge' ('Handbook of IT Contracts'), edited by Dr. Helmut Redeker. Editor of 'Praktische Internet-Nutzung fur Juristen, 2nd ed. and of 'JT-Rechtsberater' (journal); member of the editorial staff of 'Computer und Recht'.
Career: Law School in Munich, 1st State Exam 1970, Dr. jur 1977; 2nd State Exam 1980, In-House Counsel 1980-1982, Admission to the Bar 1982, Attorney at Law in Munich since 1982, appointment to Honorary Professor, Ludwig-Maximilian University, Munich 1992.

SCHÖDERMEIER, Martin
Clifford Chance Pünder, Frankfurt am Main
+49 69 71 99 01
Martin.Schödermeier@cliffordchance.com
Recommended in Banking & Finance
Specialisation: Practises in the areas of banking and finance law. Specialises in structured loans, project finance, asset finance (especially aircraft financing) and securitisations. Extensive experience in the areas of securities custody and collateralisation. Also advises in the field of private banking.
Prof. Memberships: German-American Lawyers' Association; International Bar Association (Aeronautical Law Committee, Banking Law Committee, Securities Law Committee).

G

Career: Studied Law at Cologne University, received doctorate in 1989; Harvard University Law School (LLM); University of Paris, Sorbonne (DEA European Community Law); practised with the Belgian law firm of *DeBandt, van Hecke & Lagae* in Brussels, 1985-1991; joined *Pünder* in 1992, and became partner in 1996.

SCHREY, Joachim
Clifford Chance Pünder, Frankfurt am Main +49 69 71 99 01
joachim.schrey@cliffordchance.com
Recommended in Communications: IT
Specialisation: Practice is concentrated in the area of IT law, especially in major projects on software development, system integration and outsourcing; new media and Internet; and distribution law and competition. Advises domestic and foreign companies active nationally and internationally on both supplier/licenser and customer/licensee sides. Lectures at the University Frankfurt am Main.
Prof. Memberships: German Bar Association, German Association for Industrial Property Rights and Copyright.
Career: University of Mannheim; was awarded the Cusanuswerk scholarship; worked as an assistant to the Chair for Public Law and Tax Law 1983-1990; partner since 1995.
Personal: Born 1961.

SCHROEDER, Dirk
Linklaters Oppenhoff & Rädler, Berlin
+49 30 21 49 60
Recommended in Competition/Anti-trust

SCHÜCKING, Christoph
CMS Hasche Sigle Eschenlohr Peltzer Schäfer, Frankfurt am Main +49 69 71 70 10
Christoph.Schucking@cmslegal.de
Recommended in Private Equity
Specialisation: Partner in the banking department specialising in banking, capital markets, and corporate law. Main areas of work include private equity transactions and public offerings. Acts for German and mostly international clients. Recent transactions include a multi-billion telecom financing and several IPO's and secondary offerings on Neuer Markt.
Prof. Memberships: IBA; Gesellschaft für Rechtsvergleichung; Deutscher Juristentag; Rechtsanwaltskammer Frankfurt am Main.
Career: Bank apprenticeship 1970-72; Universities of Freiburg im Breisgau (1972-76) and Geneva (1977-78); admitted to Bar 1981; joined *Peltzer & Riesenkampff* 1981; became a partner in 1984; foreign associate with *Cahill, Gordon, & Reindel*, New York, and with *Latham & Watkins*, Los Angeles, 1983; admitted as Notary Public, 2000; member of several Boards.
Personal: Born 5 November 1951. Speaks German, English, and French. Lives in Frankfurt am Main.

SCHULZ-SÜCHTIG, Rolf
Rolf Schulz-Süchtig – Sole Practitioner, Hamburg +49 40 309 6760
Recommended in Intellectual Property: General

SCHUPPERT, Stefan
Lovells Boesebeck Droste, Munich +49 89 290 12 0
stefan.schuppert@lovells.com
Recommended in Communications: IT
Specialisation: Information technology law, intellectual property rights, international licensing.
Prof. Memberships: GRUR, DGRI, NYSBA, IBA, AMMV.
Publications: Categories of provider contracts, Website-Hosting, Domain Agreements, Content-Purchase, Advertising Banner Agreements, Linking Agreements, in Spindler (ed.), 'Vertragsrecht der Internet Provider' (Law of Internet Provider Contracts), Cologne 2000.
Career: Associate since 1996, partner since 2000, qualified 1994 (State of New York, USA) and 1996 (Germany).
Personal: Born 1963, resides Munich. Speaks English, German and French. Law studies at University of Munster, Germany, Geneva, Switzerland and Kiel, Germany (Doctor's degree 1997), Harvard Law School (Master's degree, LLM 1993).

SCHUSTER, Thomas
Grünecker, Kinkeldey, Stockmaier & Schwanhäuser, München +49 89 212 350
Recommended in Intellectual Property: Patent

SCHÜTZ, Raimund
Freshfields Bruckhaus Deringer, Düsseldorf +49 211 49790
raimund.schuetz@freshfieldsbruckhaus.com
Recommended in Communications: Regulatory
Specialisation: Main areas of practice are information technologies and communications and environmental /planning/regulation. Core activities are internet/multimedia, media and broadcasting telecoms-regulatory aspects, and environmental law.

SCHÜTZE, Joachim
Clifford Chance Pünder, Düsseldorf
+49 211 43 550
joachim.schuetze@cliffordchance.com
Recommended in Competition/Anti-trust
Specialisation: Main area of practice is anti-trust law, including German and European merger control proceedings and other notification procedures vis-à-vis German and European anti-trust authorities. Counsel to pharmaceutical, medical advice and telecommunication companies. Focuses on online and Internet business and other types of media distribution. Deals regularly with anti-trust questions regarding the energy sector. Specialised in the core contractual configurations for the distribution of products and services.
Prof. Memberships: Studienvereinigung Kartellrecht, IBA.
Career: Universities of Tübingen and Münster (Dr. jur.). Joined *Pünder, Volhard, Weber & Axster* in 1991, became a partner in 1996.
Personal: Born 18th August 1960.

SEDEMUND, Jochim
Freshfields Bruckhaus Deringer, Berlin
+49 30 20 28 36
jochim.sedemund@freshfields.com
Recommended in Competition/Anti-trust
Specialisation: Partner in the Corporate Group specialising in competition and EU Law. Advises a wide range of German and multinational clients, trade associations, and governmental authorities, particularly from the chemical, steel, and food sectors.

SELTING, Günther
von Kreisler Selting Werner, Cologne
+49 221 91 65 20
Recommended in Intellectual Property: Patent

SIMMAT, Udo
CMS Hasche Sigle Eschenlohr Peltzer Schäfer, Frankfurt am Main +49 69 71 70 10
udo.simmat@cmslegal.de
Recommended in Private Equity
Specialisation: Private equity, mergers & acquisitions; public to private; capital markets (IPO). Acted 1999/2000 for BC Partner Funds on the largest German LBO to date, the acquisition of Grohe AG including public tender, public to private, high yield offering; IPOs (Techem, ad pepper). [PRO] IBA; Chamber of Industry and Commerce Tokyo.
Career: Bank apprenticeships in Geneva and Paris 1972; University of Augsburg; state exam Munich; admitted to Bar in 1979; Dr. jur. 1980; joined the firm (formerly *Sigle Loose Schmidt-Diemitz*) in 1979; partner since 1983.
Personal: Born 1951; interests include golf, skiing, mountain biking, art. Speaks German, English and French.

SOMMERLAD, Klaus
Clifford Chance Pünder, Frankfurt am Main +49 69 71 99 01
Klaus.Sommerlad@cliffordchance.com
Recommended in Communications: IT
Specialisation: Practice areas are industrial property rights, licensing, distribution agreements and product liability, as well as information technology, media and telecommunications. Advises national and international companies with regard to development, distribution and maintenance of software. Legal adviser in a large number of IT-outsourcing and system-integration projects in Germany and abroad. Regularly publishes articles and gives talks on subjects of this nature.
Prof. Memberships: German Bar Association; AIPPI; German Association for the Protection of Industrial Property and Copyright; Association for Anti-trust Law Studies; Licensing Executive Society.
Career: Studied law at the Universities of Marburg (Dr. jur.) and Freiburg; partner since 1978; was appointed notary public in 1990.
Personal: Born 1944.

SPEISER, Dieter
Eisenführ, Speiser & Partner, München
+49 89 54 90 75 0
Recommended in Intellectual Property: Patent

STADLER, Christoph
Hengeler Mueller Weitzel Wirtz, Düsseldorf
+49 211 830 40 211 83040
christoph.stadler@hengeler.com
Recommended in Competition/Anti-trust
Specialisation: EU and German competition law, merger control. Advises foreign and domestic clients

from a variety of industries. Based in Duesseldorf and Brussels.
Prof. Memberships: Studienvereinigung Kartellrecht.
Publications: Publications in the field of competition law.
Career: Qualified in 1990 (New York) and 1994 (Germany). Joined *Hengeler Mueller* in 1993, becoming a partner in 1998.
Personal: Born 25th May 1962. Attended Universities of Bonn, Geneva, Konstanz (Dr. Jur.) and Michigan Law School (LLM ,1990).

STENZ, Peter
Allen & Overy, Frankfurt am Main
+49 69 2648 5000
Recommended in Banking & Finance, Capital Markets: Derivatives, Project Finance

STERZINGER, Richard
Lovells Boesebeck Droste, Frankfurt am Main
+49 69 962 36 0
richard.sterzinger@lovells.com
Recommended in Corporate/M&A
Specialisation: Contracts, company law, M&A, building law and notary public.
Career: Attorney at law since 1974. Notary since 1991. Partner.
Personal: Born 1945, resides Frankfurt. Languages: German & English. Education: Study of law (Dr.rer. Pol) in Marburg and Darmstadt, study of US law (M.C.J.) at the University of Miami.

STILLER, Dietrich
Clifford Chance Pünder, Frankfurt am Main
+49 69 71 99 01
dietrich.stiller@cliffordchance.com
Recommended in Project Finance
Specialisation: Practice is concentrated in the area of banking and capital markets (including domestic and international project financing), as well as corporate law, cross-border investment law (with a regional focus on Indonesia, other ASEAN jurisdictions and Korea) and privatisation law. Author of several publications on Korean and Indonesian law.
Prof. Memberships: International Bar Association; Inter-Pacific Bar Association; Korean Commercial Arbitration Board (Panel of Arbitrators, 1997-present).
Career: Bonn University, and Yonsei University (Seoul, Korea); in-house lawyer in an enterprise of the automotive industry 1988-90; partner since 1995; registered as a Foreign Lawyer in Hong Kong, 1997.
Personal: Born 1960. Fluent in German , English, Korean and Bahasa Indonesia, Leisure intersets include travel, music and reading.

STRATMANN, Günther
Freshfields Bruckhaus Deringer, Düsseldorf
+49 211 49 79 0
guenther.stratmann@freshfieldsbruckhaus.com
Recommended in Corporate/M&A
Specialisation: Specialises in corporate, intellectual property and information technology law.

STRECK, Michael
Streck Mack Schwedhelm, Köln +49 2234 94 6660
Recommended in Tax

STRELOW, Markus
Ashurst Morris Crisp, Frankfurt am Main
+49 69 97 11 26
markus.strelow@ashursts.com
Recommended in Private Equity
Specialisation: Private Equity, Venture Capital, Acquisition Finance.
Career: Head of Buy-Out Group, partner 1998. Qualified 1993.
Personal: Married. Leisure interests include wandering and swimming.

TAUCHNER, Paul
Vossius & Partner, München +49 89 41 30 40
tauchner@vossiusandpartner.com
Recommended in Intellectual Property: Patent
Specialisation: General patent, industrial design patent, trademark prosecution and advisory work. Representing clients from the pharmaceutical and chemical industry. Participating in opposition proceedings, patent and trademark litigation cases, nullity proceedings and cross-border injunction cases (e.g. the terfenadine prodrug infringement case, the diltiazem manufacturing case, the paclitacel (Taxol® and Viagra® patent opposition matters).
Prof. Memberships: Member of German Patent Attorney Bar Association, EPI, FICPI, AIPPI, GRUR, LES, IBA, INTA, MARQUES, PTMG, ECTA and the German-Japanese Lawyer's Association.
Publications: Various papers concerning patents in chemistry and the patentability of pharmaceutical substances, litigation proceedings and patent invalidation proceedings in Germany and aspects of German trademark law; e.g. 'The Principles of the Doctrine of Equivalence in Germany' (2000), 'Reflections on the German TERFENADINE Prodrug Case' (1999), 'Preliminary Injunctions for Patent Infringement' (1999).
Career: Doctor of Natural Science degree from the Institute of Organic Chemistry of the University of Munich. German Patent Attorney since 1977, European Patent Attorney since 1978 and European Trademark Attorney since the establishment of OHIM. Lecturer of various patent and trademark topics in US, Japan, the UK and Germany.

THOMA, Georg F.
Shearman & Sterling, Düsseldorf
+49 211 17888 819
gthoma@shearman.com
Recommended in Corporate/M&A
Specialisation: Capital market and M&A Department. Managing Partner of the German offices in Düsseldorf, Frankfurt and Mannheim and a member in the Mergers & Acquisitions Group since 1991, the Managing European Partner from 1994 until 2000 and from 2000 a member of the firm's Executive Group. Practices primarily in the areas of corporate law, mergers and acquisitions, corporate restructuring and privatisations. Acts as counsel for German and international corporations, as well as investment banks in national and cross-border mergers and acquisitions and other transactions.
Publications: Published articles on legal topics in various publications. Co-publisher of The 'Corporate Finance Handbuch'.
Career: Practiced in London with *Linklaters & Paines* in 1977 and New York with *Shearman & Sterling* in 1978. Remainder of career was with the Düsseldorf law firm *Galler, Meyer-Landrut and Thoma* until the 1991 merger between former partnership and *Shearman & Sterling*.
Personal: Languages: German, English. Education: University of Freiburg, University of Bonn.

TSCHENTSCHER, Thomas
Freshfields Bruckhaus Deringer, Frankfurt am Main +49 69 273080
thomas.tschentscher@freshfieldsbruckhaus.com
Recommended in Communications: Regulatory
Specialisation: Specialises in IT and communications and environmental planning regulation. Core practice areas are media and broadcasting, telecoms (regulatory aspects and contracts), trade law, aviation law, environmental law, general adminstrative law, EC law and constitutional court and adminstrative procedure.

VANEZIS, Riko
Clifford Chance Pünder, Frankfurt am Main
+49 69 71 99 01
riko.vanezis@cliffordchance.com
Recommended in Banking & Finance, Project Finance
Specialisation: Partner acting for financial institutions on a wide range of projects, including infrastructure, telecommunications, and energy as well as other structuring financings.
Prof. Memberships: Law Society of England and Wales.
Career: Graduated from the University of Sussex and the University of Konstanz, Germany. Joined *Clifford Chance* in 1984; qualified as solicitor in finance and banking in 1986; seconded to *Clifford Chance* Tokyo in 1988; Frankfurt since 1990, was made partner in 1994; Head of Finance Practice in Germany; member of steering committee of *Clifford Chance* Worldwide Projects Group.
Personal: Born 1960 in London; resides in Frankfurt with wife and two children.

VASU, Kirti
Clifford Chance Pünder, Frankfurt am Main
+49 69 71 99 01
kirti.vasu@cliffordchance.com
Recommended in Capital Markets: Securitisation
Specialisation: Partner specialising in international structured finance, with a particular focus on multi-seller conduit programmes, securitisation and arbitrage vehicles, CLOs, CDOs and synthetic structures for the securitisation or repackaging of a wide range of bank and corporate assets originated in Germany, UK and other European jurisdictions.
Prof. Memberships: The Law Society of England and Wales; International Bar Association; German Bar Association.
Career: University of Keele, Staffordshire, England (B Soc. Sci. in Law and Politics): admitted as solicitor in England and Wales in 1987; partner since 1998.

VAUPEL, Christoph
Linklaters Oppenhoff & Rädler, Frankfurt am Main +49 69 71 00 30
Recommended in Capital Markets: Equity

G

VON BÜLOW, Christoph
Freshfields Bruckhaus Deringer, Frankfurt am Main +49 69 17 09 90
christoph.vonbuelow@freshfields.com
Recommended in Corporate/M&A
Specialisation: Specialises in corporate law and mergers and acquisitions.

VON DRYANDER, Christof
Cleary, Gottlieb, Steen & Hamilton, Frankfurt am Main +49 69 97 1030
Recommended in Banking & Finance, Capital Markets: Debt, Capital Markets: Equity

VON MEIBOM, Wolfgang
Wessing, Dusseldorf +49 211 83 870
duesseldorf@wessing.com
Recommended in Intellectual Property: General
Specialisation: Advises major multinational firms as well as the 'Mittelstand' in all aspects of intellectual property law. Amongst others he frequently represents major life science and pharmaceutical companies. Has made important decisions for clients with an impact on case law in Germany. Furthermore, handled several of the crucial pan-European cases developing German jurisdiction for cross-border injunctions. Areas of practice: Patents, trademarks & design, anti-trust-law, EU law and telecommunications.
Prof. Memberships: Member of German and International IP associations.
Career: Head of *Wessing's* department for patents, technology transfer, anti-trust and telecommunication in Dusseldorf and the firm's EU-law department in Brussels. Since 1990 has been member of the Board of *Wessing* and since 1998 its chairman.
Personal: Born in 1944.

VON METTENHEIM, Heinrich
Clifford Chance Pünder, Frankfurt am Main +49 69 71 99 01
heinrich.von.mettenheim@cliffordchance.com
Recommended in Private Equity
Specialisation: Partner specialising in mergers and acquisitions, corporate restructuring and management buyouts for private equity clients.
Career: Universities of Heidelberg, Paris (faculté de droit) and graduated from the Johann-Wolfgang-Goethe University in Frankfurt. Qualified as Rechtsanwalt 1968 and as a civil law notary in 1978 after joining *Wessing Berenberg-Gossler Zimmerman Lange*; partner in the *Clifford Chance* Corporate Practice Frankfurt since 1996.

VON SCHENCK, Kersten
Clifford Chance Pünder, Frankfurt am Main +49 69 71 99 01
kersten.schenck@cliffordchance.com
Recommended in Corporate/M&A
Specialisation: Specialises in banking regulatory law and mergers and acquisitions, in each case with an international connection.
Prof. Memberships: German and International Bar Associations.
Career: Studied law at Freiburg and Munster (Dr. jur.) as well as at New York University (MCJ); worked as foreign associate in a Washington, DC law firm. Afterwards for approximately four years as a junior notary in Hamburg. Admitted to the bar in Germany in 1986; licensed to practice as notary public in 1996; partner since 1987.
Personal: Born 1951.

VON SCHLABRENDORFF, Fabian
Clifford Chance Pünder, Frankfurt am Main +49 69 71 99 01
fabian.schlabrendorff@cliffordchance.com
Recommended in Project Finance
Specialisation: Practice is concentrated in the area of take-overs and acquisitions, and international litigation and arbitration with a foreign investment background. Clients include major European and Asian companies, commercial and investment banks and other financial institutions.
Prof. Memberships: Member ICC International Court of Arbitration.
Career: Universities of Tübingen, Berlin, Frankfurt (Dr. jur.) and Geneva; MA, in Political Science at the University of Chicago. Partner since 1986.
Personal: Born 1944.

VON WALLIS, Georg
Linklaters Oppenhoff & Rädler, Frankfurt am Main +49 69 71 00 30
Recommended in Tax

VON WERDER, Andreas
Freshfields Bruckhaus Deringer, Frankfurt am Main +49 69 273080
andreas.vonwerder@freshfieldsbruckhaus.com
Recommended in Corporate/M&A
Specialisation: Partner in the Corporate Group. Specialises in limited liability company and stock corporation law, the law regarding branches and transformation of companies, employee and management stock option plans, mergers and acquisitions and joint ventures.

VOSS, Harald
Freshfields Bruckhaus Deringer, Frankfurt am Main +49 69 273080
harald.voss@freshfields.com
Recommended in Corporate/M&A
Specialisation: Member of the corporate practice.

WEBER-REY, Daniela
Clifford Chance Pünder, Frankfurt am Main +49 69 71 99 01
daniela.weber-rey@cliffordchance.com
Recommended in Corporate/M&A, Private Equity
Specialisation: Specialises in corporate law, principally mergers and acquisitions, including private equity transactions and public take-overs. Has handled acquisitions of companies and undertakings in different industries by UK, US, French and domestic clients. Acted on a number of major M&A and private equity transactions. Has written many publications and has spoken at many conferences and seminars.
Prof. Memberships: American and International Bar Associations; French-German Lawyers' Association.
Career: Universities of Frankfurt am Main and Geneva; admitted to the bar in Frankfurt am Main and joined *Pünder* in 1984; Columbia University, 1985 (LLM), New York bar (1986); partner at *Pünder* in 1989; lecturer at the JW Goethe University, Frankfurt am Main, for Mergers and Acquisitions since 1996.
Personal: Born 1957. Leisure interests include music, reading and horseback riding. Married, three children.

WEGEN, Gerhard
Gleiss Lutz Hootz Hirsch, Stuttgart +49 711 89 97 0
gerhard.wegen@gleiss-law.com
Recommended in Corporate/M&A
Specialisation: Concentrates on company law, corporate finance, private equity, financial services, mergers and acquisitions, securities work, joint venture. M&A practice includes the acquisition, structuring and disposal of quoted and privately-held companies and partnerships and all aspects of corporate finance work, insider trading, disclosure requirements and public take-overs. Works particularly in the EDP and software, food and food processing, automotive, financial services, media, manufacturing, telecommunications, and machine tool industries.
Prof. Memberships: German, NY City, NY State, American, Inter-Pacific and International Bar Associations (member of IBA-SBL Council); American Society of International Law; International Law Association, (American and German branches); German Banking Law Association; German and Swiss Arbitration Associations.
Publications: Author of 'The Law Applicable to Corporate Securities Transactions' (1999), 'Indian Company Law' (1997), 'Litigation Issues in the Distribution of Securities: An International *Prospective*' (1997). Corresponding editor of 'International Legal Materials', member of the advisory board of 'World Securities Law Report' and country editor, 'International Securities Regulation' (Rosen, gen. ed.). Professor of Law, University of Tübingen Law School.
Career: Worked with a major US Wall Street law firm (1982). Banking trainee with Deutsche Bank AG (1968-70). Practising since 1981 in Germany, 1983 in New York, and 1987 in Brussels.
Personal: Born March 13, 1950. PhD, University of Tübingen, 1985; LLM, Harvard Law School, 1981.

WELLING, Mark
Allen & Overy, Frankfurt am Main +49 69 2648 5000
Recommended in Capital Markets: Debt

WENSERSKI, Markus
Haarmann, Hemmelrath & Partner, Frankfurt am Main +49 69 9 20 59 0
Recommended in Banking & Finance
Specialisation: Partner in banking department. Main areas of work are IPOs, in particular at the Neue Markt in Frankfurt, private equity and venture capital projects as well as cross-border leasing transactions both from a legal and tax point of view.
Prof. Memberships: Bar Association (Rechtsanwaltskammer) Frankfurt am Main; Tax Chamber (Steuerberaterkammer) Hessen.
Career: Qualified in 1989. Joined KPMG Peat Marwick in Frankfurt in 1989. Changed to *Baker & McKenzie* in 1992 after further qualification as tax

adviser (Steuerberater). Joined *Haarmann, Hemmelrath & Partner* in 1994, becoming a partner in 1995.
Personal: Born 1st July 1963. Attended Frankfurt and Munich Universities.

WEYLAND, Peter
Hengeler Mueller Weitzel Wirtz, Frankfurt am Main +49 69 170 950
peter.weyland@hengeler.com
Recommended in Banking & Finance, Private Equity
Specialisation: M&A and acquisition finance in connection with leveraged buy-outs.
Career: Qualified in 1989. Worked as foreign associate for *Kilpatrick Stockton*, Atlanta, joined *Hengeler Mueller Weitzel Wirtz* in 1991, became a partner in 1995.
Personal: Born 7 August 1960. Attended Freiburg im Breisgau University 1980-85 (Dr.jur. 1986).

WIEDEMANN, Gerhard
Freshfields Bruckhaus Deringer, Düsseldorf +49 211 49 79 0
gerhard.wiedemann@freshfieldsbruckhaus.com
Recommended in Competition/Anti-trust
Specialisation: Partner in the competition and trade practice group specialising in competition law and antitrust.

WILDANGER, Günther
Wildanger & Kehrwald, Düsseldorf +49 211 498 2911
Recommended in Intellectual Property: General

WILDE, Christian
Freshfields Bruckhaus Deringer, Hamburg +49 40 369 060
christian.wilde@freshfieldsbruckhaus.com
Recommended in Corporate/M&A
Specialisation: Senior partner of *Freshfields Bruckhaus Deringer*. Practises real estate and corporate law, specialising in limited liability company law.

WINTER, Martin
Shearman & Sterling, Mannheim +49 62 1425 70
Recommended in Corporate/M&A

WISSMANN, Martin
Clifford Chance Pünder, Frankfurt am Main +49 69 71 99 01
Martin.Wissmann@CliffordChance.com
Recommended in Communications: Regulatory
Specialisation: Main areas of practice are German and European competition and telecommunications law, EC law. Recent experiences includes: merger notification proceedings in the telecommunications sectors, Article 81 (3) EC Treaty exemption proceedings; various proceedings under Article 82/86 EC Treaty regarding predatory pricing and discrimination by telecommunications operators vis-à-vis the European Commission, the German regulator and civil courts (damage litigation); compliance advice; Article 81 (3) EC Treaty litigation; advice and representation in interconnection and rate regulation vis-à-vis the German regulator; stategic advice on regulatory framework and specifies on licensing, interconnection, pricing etc. in various European countries in conjunction with acquisitions or bidding proceedings, IPO's and other financial tools; advising service providers and network operators on a broad scale of telecommunications issues and drafting negotiating of all kinds of contracts in the telecommunications and IT sectors.
Prof. Memberships: IBA, Studienvereinigung Kartellrecht, LES, GRUR, DAJV.
Career: University of Frankfurt/Main and Georgetown University, Washington, D.C. (LLM). Admitted to Bar in 1991. Partner since 1996.
Personal: Born 1961.

WOLLBURG, Ralph
Freshfields Bruckhaus Deringer, Düsseldorf +49 211 49 79 0
ralph.wollburg@freshfieldsbruckhaus.com
Recommended in Corporate/M&A
Specialisation: Partner in the Corporate Group, specialising in limited liability company law, mergers and acquisitions, law of securities and law regarding groups of companies.

WUERMELING, Ulrich
Wessing, Frankfurt am Main +49 69 97 130 190
u.wuermeling@wessing.de
Recommended in Communications: IT
Specialisation: Head of the Multimedia-Group at the Frankfurt office of *Wessing]IT-]. The group comprises of specialists in the area of telecommunications, e-commerce, information technology and digital media.*
Publications: Several articles and conference speeches on multimedia law issues. Since 1991, co-editor of the data protection journal Datenschutz-Berater (Handelsblatt) and since 2000, a correspondent of the Computer Law and Security Report (Elsevier). Publication of the book 'Handelshemmnis Datenschutz' (Trade Barrier Data Protection) in July 2000.
Career: Universities Bayreuth, Southampton, London, Wurzburg, New York; Master of International Business Law (LLM) at the University of London; Doctorate at the University of Wuerzburg. Attorney in Frankfurt since 1996.

ZIEGENHAIN, Hans-Jörg
Döser Amereller Noack, Frankfurt am Main +49 69 29 90 80
hans-joerg.ziegenhain@bakernet.com
Recommended in Corporate/M&A
Specialisation: Partner in M&A and Securities departments. Main areas of work are corporate law, venture capital and securities, in particular mergers and acquisitions, privatisations and initial public offerings in Germany. Has advised on various domestic and multijurisdictional offerings. Has also handled various acquisitions and dispositions of companies and undertakings both domestically and internationally. Acts for a number of venture capital companies, including Advent International, 3I, ABN Amro Capital. Also acts for large German publicly traded stock corporations in connection with their M&A related activities. Industry focus is on telecoms, IT, automobile and chemistry. Member of the firm's European M&A group and its international securities group. Has spoken at various conferences. Opened *Baker & McKenzie*'s Düsseldorf office in April 1999.
Prof. Memberships: German Tax Attorneys Association.
Career: Qualified in 1990. Joined *Baker & McKenzie* in 1991, becoming a Partner in 1997. Qualified as a Tax Attorney in 1994.
Personal: Born 9 August 1961. Attended Law School at the University of Regensburg (1981-1983) and Law School at Maximilians Universität München (1984-1987). Attended Tulane Law School, New Orleans (1983-1984). Attended Law School of the University of Michigan and earned LLM Degree (1991). Obtained PhD from Maximilians Universität München (1991).

GHANA

Corporate/Commercial

GHANA Leading firms (Corporate/Commercial)
1 Bentsi-Enchill & Letsa
Fugar & Company
Sey & Co
2 Awoonor Law Consultancy
Kudjawu & Co
Tetteh & Co

Firms are listed alphabetically in each band.

Leading individuals (Corporate/Commercial)
1 **FUGAR William** *Fugar & Company*
KUDJAWU Norbert *Kudjawu & Co*
2 **BENTSI-ENCHILL Kojo** *Bentsi-Enchill & Letsa*
TETTEH Kwami *Tetteh & Co*
3 **AWOONOR Ekow** *Awoonor Law Consultancy*
SEY Kweku *Sey & Co*

Individuals are listed alphabetically in each band.

Bentsi-Enchill & Letsa (2 ptrs, 11 asscs) *"Major competitors"* who have *"grown rapidly"* and cover all aspects of corporate law, including international loan and equity investment, corporate restructuring, IT, telecommunications, mining, tax, planning and project finance. **Kojo Bentsi-Enchill** is said to *"have a thorough grasp of the details."* The firm acted on a $100 million loan from the IFC to Ghana Telecom and a $160 million non-recourse project financing for Samsung Corp for the expansion of the Tema oil refinery. Also advised on a $12.5 million loan from Overseas Private Investment Corp to Phyto-Riker Pharmaceuticals. **Clients:** IFC; Chevron; Samsung; Heinz.

Fugar & Company (1 ptr, 13 asscs) A firm with *"good government connections,"* which is active in cross-border M&A and banking and finance, often serving as local counsel to international financial institutions. The *"discreet"* **William Fugar** *"has the ability to get things done"* and has *"used his political contacts brilliantly."* He and his team have advised on regulations governing the telecoms industry, and were instructed on the expansion of a thermal plant and the West African pipeline project. **Clients:** IFC; OPEC; HSBC; Goldman Sachs; Morgan Stanley Dean Witter; Merrill Lynch; Marubeni.

Sey & Co (2 ptrs, 5 asscs) Commended for its *"excellent client service,"* the firm is often to be found advising on work with an international dimension. Focusing on corporate law, the group has niche expertise in the mining sector, as well as advising on cross-border M&A and financing. Leading light **Kweku Sey** is reputed to be *"a safe pair of hands."* The firm represented SIPH on its US$8 million acquisition of Ghana Rubber Estates. **Clients:** Abosso Gold Fields; Bogoso Gold; Obenemase Gold Mines; Westel.

Awoonor Law Consultancy (1 ptr, 4 asscs) Advising on corporate finance, trademark infringement and investment funds, the firm has particular knowledge of the telecoms sector. Top name here is the *"sharp and ambitious"* **Ekow Awoonor**. The majority of the team's caseload is carried out on behalf of the Modern Africa Fund, a US fund dedicated to investment in Africa. **Clients:** Modern Africa Fund.

Kudjawu & Co (4 ptrs) One of the oldest law firms in Ghana is best known for its trademark and patent work, but also handles banking, shipping, corporate and mining work. The *"towering figure"* of **Norbert Kudjawu***, our researchers were informed, has been *"at the top of the profession for a long time"* and is universally viewed as *"an extremely experienced and able lawyer."* The firm advised PwC on the liquidation of two banks. **Clients:** Ashanti Goldfields; Standard Bank; Shell; BAT.

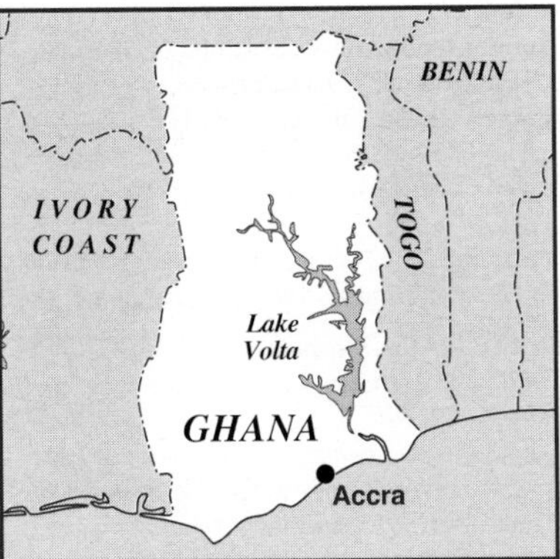

Tetteh & Co (2 ptrs, 4 asscs) Commercial firm with a *"broad scope"* which has been involved in the formation in Ghana of such companies as Millicom Ghana, Volta Investments Ghana and Ghana Agro-Food. Paterfamilias **Kwami Tetteh** is *"an excellent senior lawyer"* who has a reputation for bringing on younger lawyers. The firm was instructed by a consortium of international banks to work on a $270 million revolving credit facility for Ashanti. **Clients:** Ashanti; Social Security Bank; Millicom Ghana; foreign construction firms.

Leaders' profiles – Ghana

AWOONOR, Ekow
Awoonor Law Consultancy, Accra +233 21 227 307

BENTSI-ENCHILL, Kojo
Bentsi-Enchill & Letsa, Accra +233 21 229 396

FUGAR, William
Fugar & Company, Accra +233 21 228 988

KUDJAWU, Norbert
Kudjawu & Co, Accra +233 21 664 552

SEY, Kweku
Sey & Co, Accra +233 21 220 624

TETTEH, Kwami
Tetteh & Co, Accra +233 21 221 433

GIBRALTAR

Corporate/Commercial

GIBRALTAR Leading firms (Corporate/Commercial)	
1	Hassans
2	Louis W Triay & Partners
	Triay & Triay
3	Isola & Isola
	Marrache & Co
	Massias & Partners

Firms are listed alphabetically in each band.

Leading individuals (Corporate/Commercial)	
1	**CASTIEL Michael** *Hassans*
	LEVY James *Hassans*
	TRIAY Joseph *Triay & Triay*
2	**MASSIAS Isaac** *Massias & Partners*
	NEISH James *Louis W Triay & Partners*
	PROVASOLI Anthony *Hassans*
	TRIAY Louis *Louis W Triay & Partners*
	VAZQUEZ Robert *Triay & Triay*
3	**FEETHAM Nigel** *Hassans*
	ISOLA Peter *Isola & Isola*
	MARRACHE Benjamin *Marrache & Co*
	MARRACHE Isaac *Marrache & Co*
	SERFATY Abraham *Triay & Triay*

Individuals are listed alphabetically in each band.

Hassans (11 ptrs, 14 asscs) This *"pioneering"* and *"well-connected"* firm is the largest on the Rock, with a strong corporate practice. It excels in the fields of corporate restructuring, tax, securitisation and telecommunications. With specialist teams working in each area, it recently completed a $30 billion restructuring for an American multi-national. *"Sharp and creative thinker"* **James Levy** is *"a leading brain"* and a major force on tax-related work. Known for his ability to deal with cross-border issues, **Michael Castiel** has *"a diplomat's touch on transactions"* and is *"a force to be reckoned with."* **Anthony Provasoli** has an international reputation as a telecoms specialist, while **Nigel Feetham** is also recommended for investment, insurance and banking work. **Clients:** Shell Gibraltar; Deutsche Bank; Credit Suisse.

Louis W Triay & Partners (4 ptrs, 1 assc) Our researchers found this to be an *"efficient and respectable"* partner-driven firm which is *"growing both in size and client base."* The team handles a variety of offshore work including M&A, trusts and tax planning. **Louis Triay** is an experienced commercial lawyer, while the *"hard-working"* **James Neish QC** is *"quiet but effective."* The firm completed a £20 million arbitration involving an incinerator. **Clients:** BP; Mobil; Nestlé; Gibtel.

Triay & Triay (10 ptrs, 6 asscs) Established firm, known for its *"professionalism,"* and a niche specialism in shipping. *"In a class of his own,"* **Joseph Triay QC** is universally recognised as the *"one of the most able lawyers in Gibraltar."* The *"admirable"* **Robert Vazquez** is *"able to grasp problems quickly."* **Abraham Serfaty QC** is also recommended. The firm advised on the sale of Europort for a reported £17 million. **Clients:** A broad range of international and offshore clients.

Isola & Isola (4 ptrs, 6 asscs) A *"commercially-minded firm"* with a large corporate department which advises an array of financial institutions, and has developed its client base in the increasingly lucrative offshore gambling industry. The team handles all aspects of commercial law, from company formation and trust management, and has particular strength in e-commerce and telecommunications. **Peter Isola Sr** has *"a tremendous track record."* The team advised on the establishment of GibNet, the first internet service providers in Gibraltar. **Clients:** Eurobet.com; banks; Gibraltar Treasury; insurance companies.

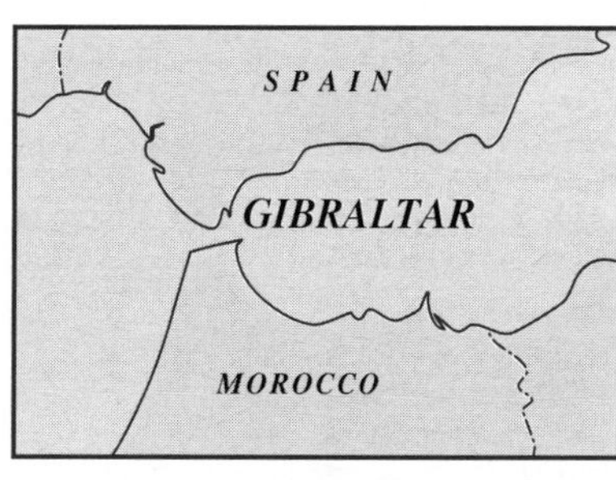

Marrache & Co (2 ptrs, 9 asscs) The firm is said to have a *"fine pool of institutional clients,"* and the vast majority of its workload is international. Key elements of the practice are tax, shipping, e-commerce and internet law, and this is the only Gibraltarian firm to have opened an office in London. **Isaac Marrache** and **Benjamin Marrache** are both acknowledged as *"influential businessmen and lawyers."* The firm advised on the $300 million establishment of Satfonico in Morocco. **Clients:** Multi-nationals and wealthy individuals.

Massias & Partners (2 ptrs, 1 assc) Primarily involved in banking, finance and commercial trust work, the firm has acted on several multi-million pound property transactions this year. **Isaac Massias** is *"a noted banking lawyer"* who has long experience in Gibraltar. The firm acted on behalf of a consortium of banks in a $75 million securitisation transaction involving telecommunications in Morocco. **Clients:** Citibank; Deutsche Bank.

Leaders' profiles – Gibraltar

CASTIEL, Michael
Hassans International Law Firm, Gibraltar
+350 79000
castiel@gibnynex.gi

Specialisation: Leading partner in the firm and the head of the Corporate and Commercial Team, specialising in international tax, corporate and business law. Regularly advises major US and European based multinationals on the establishment of offshore structures and operations, as well as on the structuring of cross-border transactions and has developed a reputation for innovative solutions to achieve client's

aims. Other areas of expertise include corporate restructuring, joint venture work, mergers and acquisitions as well as franchising law and insolvency, advising both receivers and liquidators in high profile cases. In recognition of business and marketing expertise, has recently been appointed the firm's Business Development Partner.
Publications: Has written numerous articles on various aspects of Gibraltar corporate and commercial law.
Career: Studied law at London University and the Inns of Court School of Law and was called to the English and Gibraltar Bar in 1993. Legal training is complemented by qualifications in management and business administration, and eight years of industry experience in the UK. Speaks English, Spanish. French and Portuguese.

FEETHAM, Nigel
Hassans International Law Firm, Gibraltar +350 79000
nfeetham@gibnynex.gi
Specialisation: Partner in the International and Finance and Banking Team and specialises in financial services licensing, regulation and structuring. Is a recognised expert on the implementation of structures, such as Protected Cell Companies and Special Purpose Vehicles, for repackaging and securitisation and has written and lectured extensively on these matters. As a member of the Government of Gibraltar Legislation Committee, contributes fully to innovative legislative programmes. Also recognised as having the market for bond issues in Gibraltar. Has advised Deutsche Bank, UBS AG, Goldman Sachs, Barclays Capital and Credit Suisse.
Career: Graduated with First Class Honours degree from Manchester Metropolitan University, and was awarded a Masters degree in law with Distinction at Manchester Victoria University. Recipient of numerous academic prizes from both Universities.

ISOLA SR, Peter
Isola & Isola, Gibraltar +350 78363

LEVY, James
Hassans International Law Firm, Gibraltar +350 79000
jlevyjahp@gibnynex.gi
Specialisation: Senior Partner of the firm. Specialises in corporate and international tax work, and has earned a reputation in Gibraltar for innovation in these areas. For example, was involved in setting up one of the first substantial unit trusts in Gibraltar and recently advised on the drafting and piloting of a bill through the Gibraltar House of Assembly relating to a bank's conversion from a subsidiary to a branch. Also progressed the use of Alternative Dispute Resolution in Gibraltar. Has been involved in trust legislation, advising the Government of Gibraltar on relevant legislation and drafting a standard form of discretionary trust clause which has been used widely in Gibraltar.
Publications: Is a contributing author to Tolleys Tax Planning International and joint editor of Tolleys Taxation in Gibraltar, and frequently lectures on various aspects of financial services legislation.
Career: After graduating with Honours from Manchester University, attended the Council of Legal Education in London. Qualified in 1972 and became a partner of *Hassans* in 1974. Speaks English, Spanish, French and Hebrew.

MARRACHE, Benjamin John Samuel
Marrache & Co, Gibraltar +(350) 79918
marrache@marrache.com
Specialisation: Managing partner at *Marrache & Co*, Gibraltar.
Prof. Memberships: Memberships: International Tax Planning Association; International Bar Association; Institute of Directors; Society of Trust and Estate Practitioners, Association of Young Lawyers, (AIJA).
Publications: Achievement/writings: International Business Lawyer, IBA (1991) 'Offshore Opportunities in Gibraltar'; International Banking Yearbook 1992 and 1994; Euromoney Publication 'Gibraltar, a developing offshore oppertunity'; the journal of Asset Protection and Financial Crime – Henry Stewart Publication (1994); 'Asset Protection Trust and Gibraltar's Legislation', Trademark yearbook (1994); Euromoney 'Trademark Law in Gibraltar'; author of 'Asset Protection Trusts and Gibraltar's Legislation' (1994); Author of 'Gibraltar – High Net Worth Individuals' (1994); Law digest Martindale Hubbell jurisdiction author for Gibraltar section; Sweet & Maxwell International Banking Secrecy Gibraltar section; contributor to The New Law Journal (Butterworths); The Offshore Financial Review (Financial Times); The International Financial Law Review (Euromoney); The Journal of International Banking Law (Sweet & Maxwell); Resident Abroad Magazine (Financial Times); and Insurance International (Mitre House Published). 'Gibraltar: An Overview', (1998) Institute of Advanced Legal Studies; author of Gibraltar chapter of the 'Law of International on-line Business' (Sweet & Maxwell), (1999).
Career: Education: Brympton School, Gibraltar; Colegio Santa Rita, Cadiz, Spain; L'ecole Francaise, Malaga, Spain; Bayside Comprehensive School, Gibraltar; University of London (LLM); Council of Legal Education; Commissioner-for-Oaths; Special Examiner of the Supreme Court of Gibraltar (1994); Country Representative for the London School of Economics Alumni Association.
Personal: Born in Gibraltar, 18 October 1963. Son of Samuel Abraham Marrache and Reina Massias. Married to Anjette Nadine Jones, 12 August 1996, two children Samuel Abraham and Jonathan Isaac. Clubs: Calpe Rowing Club. Religion: Jewish.

MARRACHE, Isaac Samuel
Marrache & Co, Gibraltar +(350) 79918
marrache@marrache.com
Prof. Memberships: Gibraltar Lawyers Association, International Tax Planners Association, STEP, American Bar Association, Honourable Society of the Inner Temple.
Publications: Author and Consultant: International Tracing of Assets, FT Law and Tax, International Bar Society (Sweet & Maxwell), Enforcement of Foreign Judgements (Kinnear Law International), International Tax Planning (Kinnear Law International), International Succession (Kinnear Law International), Martindale Hubbell section on Gibraltar and various legal journals.
Career: Barrister-at-Law, Commissioner for Oaths, Notary Public of Gibraltar, Sub-Lieutenant R.N.R. Brympton Primary School (1960-1967); Carmel College Preparatory School, Gibraltar; Clifton College, Bristol. John Mackintosh Educational Trust Scholarship, Gibraltar, Government Scholarship, University of London, School of Oriental & African Studies. London School of Economics and Political Science, Convenor (Senator Law). President of London University Law Students. London University Representative Council. Reported to the Royal Commission on Legal Services. Founder member of Editorial Board (Wig & Gavel). Council of Legal Education. Called to Bar, Inner Temple, pupil John Alliots, Chambers, 1 Crown Office Row, Temple, and Anthony Evans, Chambers, 4 Essex Court Temple. Founder and Senior Partner Marrache & Co. Freeman and Livery-man of the City of London 1985.
Personal: Born Gibraltar, 24 November 1955.

MASSIAS, Isaac
Massias & Partners, Gibraltar +350 40888

NEISH QC, James
Louis W Triay & Partners, Gibraltar +350 79423

PROVASOLI, Anthony
Hassans International Law Firm, Gibraltar +350 79000
provasoli@gibnynex.gi
Specialisation: Specialises in telecommunications and financial services. Work in recent years has focused on developments in international telecoms, advising several governments and multinational corporations. Experience in acting on international banking matters.
Prof. Memberships: Member of Gibraltar's Financial Services Commission (regulatory body and independent supervisor of the financial sector, since 1991).
Publications: Contributed various articles to Butterworths; Journal of International Banking and Financial Law as well as numerous articles in the professional press.
Career: Graduated from University College Cardiff with Honours degree. Attended College of Law in London. Called to the Bar in London in 1975 and in Gibraltar in 1976. Currently serves as Vice Chairman of the Council of Gibraltar. Partner of *Hassans* in 1982, serves as firms Managing Partner.
Personal: Speaks English and Spanish.

SERFATY QC, Abraham
Triay & Triay, Gibraltar +350 72020

TRIAY QC, Joseph Emanuel
Triay & Triay, Gibraltar +350 72020

TRIAY QC, Louis W.
Louis W Triay & Partners, Gibraltar +350 79423

VAZQUEZ, Robert
Triay & Triay, Gibraltar +350 72020

GREECE

Index

The clients' choice

BUSINESS LAWYER OF THE YEAR
CONSTANTINE KYRIAKIDES,
Kyriakides – Georgopoulos Law Firm

BUSINESS LAW FIRM OF THE YEAR
KYRIAKIDES – GEORGOPOULOS LAW FIRM

A hat trick for ***Kyriakides – Georgopoulos Law Firm****, not only winning as best firm but also with named partners* ***Constantine Kyriakides*** *and* ***Leonidas Georgopoulos*** *first and second in the lawyer poll.*

For details see page 36.

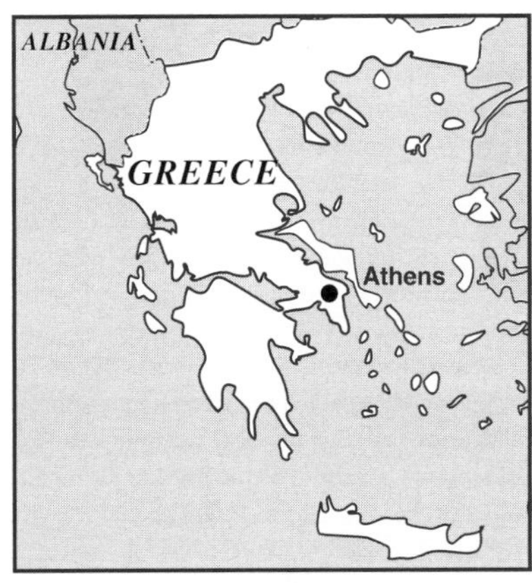

OVERVIEW: Several major infrastructure projects are underway and the prospect of hosting the Olympic Games 2004 is generating a substantial amount of work. Currently the market produces general commercial lawyers, however, research indicated that certain firms and individuals are gaining a reputation as experts in specialist fields from telecommunications to competition law. A few foreign firms operate in Athens with the majority registered in Piraeus where they focus primarily on maritime matters. Recently, some of the traditional Greek shipping firms have established themselves in the capital and are undertaking more general corporate and financial work.

Corporate/M&A

GREECE
Leading firms (Corporate/Commercial)

Band	Firm
1	Kyriakides – Georgopoulos Law Firm
2	Law Firm Karatzas & Partners
	Law Office TJ Koutalidis
	M&P Bernitsas Law Offices
	Zepos & Zepos
3	Dryllerakis & Associates

Firms are listed alphabetically in each band.

Leading individuals (Corporate/Commercial)

Band	Individual
1	**BERNITSAS Panayotis** *M & P Bernitsas*
	GEORGOPOULOS Leonidas *Kyriakides – Georgopoulos*
	KARATZAS Katarina *Karatzas & Partners*
	KOUTALIDIS Tryfon *Law Office TJ Koutalidis*
2	**DRYLLERAKIS John** *Dryllerakis & Associates*
	KYRIAKIDES Constantine *Kyriakides – Georgopoulos*
	ZEPOS Dimitrios *Zepos & Zepos*
Up-and-coming individuals	
	KORITSAS Nikos *Law Office TJ Koutalidis*
	METALLINOS Alexander *Karatzas & Partners*
	VOUTERAKOS Costas *Kyriakides – Georgopoulos*

Individuals are listed alphabetically in each band.

Kyriakides – Georgopoulos Law Firm (9 ptrs, 17 asscs) Rivals view this as a *"well respected and organised law firm,"* which is *"always working towards a realistic solution."* Renowned for its powerful domestic client base, the corporate team also represents a variety of overseas blue-chips on their investments in Greece. The firm recently confirmed an alliance with PwC on certain matters of common interest.

"Collaborative, flexible and trustworthy" **Leonidas Georgopoulos*** is *"a good rainmaker"* who *"establishes and holds good relationships with his clients."* **Constantine Kyriakides*** is *"a fine commercial lawyer"* and **Costas Vouterakos*** is a *"young, promising lawyer"* with a growing reputation. The group acted on behalf of Alpha Bank on the acquisition of Ionian Bank, and represented the Greek State on the privatisation of the Corinth Canal and the Public Power Corporation. **Clients:** IBM; McDonald's; Aegean Airlines; Alpha Bank; Colgate; Hellenic Bottling Co.

Law Firm Karatzas & Partners (5 ptrs, 10 asscs) This firm pocesses a *"huge potential"* and *"major clients"* and is commended by clients being there for you and never letting you down. Strong in cross-border M&A and corporate finance work, the firm takes a prominent role in the financial services sphere.

Katarina Karatzas* is *"quick, thorough and well-schooled,"* while **Alexander Metallinos*** *"covers all the bases."* The firm represented Ergo Bank on the defence of a hostile take-over bid by CEH, the controlling shareholder of EFG Eurobank. In creating the strategy for a white knight defence, the team helped to force CEH to increase its offer by more than $500 million. The group also represented foreign banks on the financing of the Athens ring road. **Clients:** EFG Eurobank Ergasias; Hellenic Petroleum; Alpha Bank; Unilever.

Law Office TJ Koutalidis (4 ptrs, 2 asscs) An *"excellent firm with a strong pool of clients,"* which advises on all corporate matters and was recommended to researchers for its expertise on privatisation and financing advice.

Dominated by **Tryfon Koutalidis***, said to be *"a leading figure in Greek law,"* the corporate department also includes **Nikos Koritsas***, a *"successful and business- oriented M&A lawyer."* The firm advised Bachtell on the building of the Athens Metro and represented EIB on the financing of the Salonica Metro. Other work includes acting for the Greek government on the partial privatisation of the Post Office. **Clients:** Aramco;

*See leaders' profiles on pages 342-343

Dassault; Deutsche Bank; Alpha Credit Bank; Lambrakis Press; Mega Channel; Intracom; General Electric.

M&P Bernitsas Law Offices (2 ptrs, 4 asscs) *"Serious players,"* with a sound corporate reputation and acknowledged expertise in telecoms. However, market opinion spoke to our researchers of the firm's heavy reliance on managing partner **Panayotis Bernitsas***. He has *"wide experience in a variety of fields"* and *"grasps issues quickly."*

The firm acted as legal counsel to BP on the implementation of the BP-Mobil joint venture in Greece, and advised on the merger of Coca-Cola Beverages with the Hellenic Bottling Company. **Clients:** BP Greece Oil International; easyJet; UPS; Astra Hellas; AT&T; British Telecom; Citibank; Salomon Brothers; Chase Manhattan; Airbus Industrie.

Zepos & Zepos (10 ptrs, 10 asscs) The oldest corporate firm in Greece is said by competitors to have *"a fine tradition and a client base to match."* Perceived to have *"a new generation of lawyers full of potential,"* the team has a notably strong hi-tech client base. **Dimitrios Zepos*** is *"a pleasure to work with"* and is unquestionably the firm's leading light.

The team advised Caisse Nationale de Crédit Agricole on the acquisition of a 6.7% stake in Commercial Bank of Greece, acted for Scandinavian Broadcasting Systems in the acquisition of one of Greece's major radio stations, and represented Shell International on the acquisition of Texaco Hellas' fuel interests in Greece. **Clients:** Nokia; Compaq; Merrill Lynch; Salomon Smith Barney; Arla Foods, Cisco Systems.

Dryllerakis & Associates (6 ptrs, 6 asscs) Researchers found a firm that is *"definitely on its way up,"* and that is now seen by rivals *"on a number of the important transactions."* The group deals almost exclusively with cross-border M&A and the formation of new companies in Greece. *"Distinguished"* **John Dryllerakis*** is considered to be *"a tough but fair negotiator."*

The firm acted on the purchase of a majority shareholding in Kronos by the Irish company Glencork, and advised on the sale of Bimcom Services Greece by Cable & Wireless to GN Comtext. **Clients:** Barclays; Hitachi; Hyatt; Marconi; Raytheon; Shell; Nintendo.

G

Shipping: Local Firms

GREECE Leading firms (Shipping)
1 GJ Timagenis Law Office
Sarantitis & Partners
Theo V Sioufas, Law Offices
2 Deucalion Rediadis & Sons
Law Offices N Goyios – A Nassikas
Scorinis Law Offices
Vgenopoulos & Partners

Firms are listed alphabetically in each band.

Leading individuals (Shipping)	
1 SIOUFAS Theo	*Theo V Sioufas, Law Offices*
TIMAGENIS Gregory	*GJ Timagenis Law Office*
2 PAPANGELIS Miltos	*Vgenopoulos & Partners*
SARANTITIS Vassilis	*Sarantitis & Partners*
SCORINIS Nicholas	*Scorinis Law Offices*
3 GOYIOS Nicholas	*N Goyios – A Nassikas*
IATRIDIS George	*Vgenopoulos & Partners*
NASSIKAS Andreas	*N Goyios – A Nassikas*
REDIADIS Deucalion	*Deucalion Rediadis & Sons*

Individuals are listed alphabetically in each band.

GJ Timagenis Law Office (8 ptrs, 4 asscs) A *"serious, reliable and co-operative"* firm with a strong ship finance practice, it regularly handles sale and purchase agreements, stock exchange listings and M&A and foreign investment work. The litigation department is particularly active in collision, cargo claims and charter party disputes. Peers speak highly of the *"well connected"* **Gregory Timagenis***, said to be *"an excellent lawyer with an established personal track record, who is capable of handling difficult issues."* The firm acted on the merger between Louis Cruises and Royal Olympic Cruises. **Clients:** Stringesline; Royal Olympic Cruises; Hellenic War Risk Association; Attica Enterprises.

Sarantitis & Partners (4 ptrs, 10 asscs) A *"well organised"* full service law firm with *"deep roots in the Piraeus shipping market,"* its workload includes litigation, sale and purchase agreements, shipping finance, incorporation of companies and ship registration. *"Ambitious"* **Vassilis Sarantitis*** is *"an established figure in Piraeus"* and is successfully expanding the practice into the Athens market. The firm is acting on behalf of the Russian Navy in a dispute regarding the return of two vessels to the state and is assisting the owners of M/V Marieva after its sinking off Benghazi. **Clients:** Zim Israel Navigation; Volga Shipping Co; Hellastir Maritime SA; Chase Manhattan; Nordisk Skibsrederforening.

Theo V Sioufas, Law Offices (9 ptrs, 7 asscs) One of the largest shipping teams in Greece is acknowledged by rivals to have *"a fine tradition"* in all areas of the industry. The firm features prominently in ship finance, litigation and enforcement. *"Extremely busy"* **Theo Sioufas*** *"knows his business"* and has been at *"the forefront in Piraeus for the past twenty-five years."*

The firm is handling the Express Samina Ferry Disaster on behalf of the owners, and is representing the Lloyd's Register of Shipping and the Hellenic Register of Shipping in litigation. **Clients:** Deutsche Bank; EFG Eurobank; Scotiabank; ABN AMRO; Banque Agricole Indosuez; Alpha Credit Bank; Greek Owners.

Deucalion Rediadis & Sons (4 ptrs, 4 asscs) The oldest shipping practice in Piraeus was established in 1892 and is still *"involved in many serious cases."* Its *"highly respected, strong team"* has a traditional shipping practice focusing on both wet and dry litigation. The bulk of the workload revolves around handling P&I claims. **Deucalion Rediadis*** is *"an exceptional young man,"* recommended to our researchers as *"one of the most promising lawyers around."* **Clients:** The West of England P&I club; Gard Services; The Britannia P&I Club; Societe de Gestion Evge; Piraeus Prime Bank.

Law Offices N Goyios – A Nassikas (3 ptrs, 3 asscs) Smaller firm, known primarily for its work on behalf of P&I Clubs. The majority of the work is on the wet side, and the team handles a variety of claims, including cargo, personal damage and pollution. **Nicholas Goyios*** and **Andreas Nassikas*** are both regarded by opponents as *"experienced and able lawyers."* **Clients:** North of England P&I; Steamship Mutual; Standard.

Scorinis Law Offices (6 ptrs, 5 asscs) Researchers were repeatedly informed that this is *"definitely one of the leading shipping firms in Piraeus."* The shipping group handles litigation *("its major strength,")* banking, M&A and sale and purchase agreements. Former Master Mariner **Nicholas Scorinis*** is an *"excellent man"* with a *"good approach to legal problems."* The firm represented GA Ferries on the sale of 46% of its fleet to Minoan. **Clients:** GA Ferries; Good Faith Shipping Co SA; Clifford Chance; Bank of New York; Seward & Kissel; National Bank of Greece; Ionian and Popular Bank of Greece; Elinoil SA; European Navigation Inc.

Vgenopoulos & Partners (7 ptrs, 7 asscs) Rivals view this as an *"aggressive"* firm, which is *"involved in many fields"* and is *"gaining ground."* The caseload includes ship finance deals, joint ventures, sale and purchase agreements, litigation and advice on IPOs. **Miltos Papangelis*** is a *"knowledgeable and professional litigator"* and **George Iatridis*** is *"modest, diligent and careful in handling his clients' needs."* **Clients:** Matsas; P&I clubs; charterers/owners; international banks.

G

Shipping: Foreign Firms

GREECE: Foreign Firms Leading firms (Shipping)
1 Ince & Co Consultants OE
Law Office Howard in Association with Norton Rose
Watson, Farley & Williams
2 Clyde & Co (Greece)
Hill Taylor Dickinson OE
Holman Fenwick & Willan (Consultants) OE
3 Stephenson Harwood Consultants OE

Firms are listed alphabetically in each band.

Leading individuals (Shipping)
1 ELVEY Jonathan *Ince & Co Consultants OE*
2 HOWARD Tim *Law Office Howard*
KRZYWKOWSKI John *Watson, Farley & Williams*
RICE Tony *Watson, Farley & Williams*
WATSON Jeremy *Watson, Farley & Williams*
3 BAKER David *Law Office Howard*
HAWKINS Patrick *Hill Taylor Dickinson OE*
LOWE Charles *Holman Fenwick & Willan*
PITLARGE David *Holman Fenwick & Willan*
REECE John *Law Office Howard*
SLADE David *Stephenson Harwood*

Individuals are listed alphabetically in each band.

Ince & Co Consultants OE (2 ptrs, 4 asscs) One of the strongest litigation firms is, according to its clients, *"always there when you need them."* The group is considered by most to be a *"major rival,"* and is acknowledged to have secured a *"stronghold in the insurance market."* Active in both wet and dry litigation and contracts, the firm acts on casualty work, shipping and insurance. *"Its main face in Greece"* is the *"well-liked and versatile"* **Jonathan Elvey***. **Clients:** Ship operators; P&I clubs; insurers; cargo owners.

Law Office Howard in Association with Norton Rose (3 ptrs, 10 asscs) A mixed shipping finance and litigation practice which is currently expanding its operations in Greece, and advises on big-ticket M&A, new building finance and all areas of litigation. A strong team includes **Tim Howard***, *"a well-known figure locally."* **David Baker*** has *"an excellent reputation for finance,"* while **John Reece*** is an *"extremely competent litigator."* The firm advised on 'The Aconcagua' container ship fire off South America. **Clients:** Owners; banks; insurers.

Watson, Farley & Williams (4 ptrs, 6 asscs) *"At the forefront of the ship finance market for some time now,"* the firm is considered by rivals to be *"well organised and well-resourced."* The team is best known for advising lenders on structured finance transactions, although its client base of ship owners is also growing.

Head of the practice, the *"meticulous"* **Tony Rice***, has been joined from Holman Fenwick & Willan by **Jeremy Watson***, who is rated by peers as one of the leading ship finance practitioners in the market. The further acquisition from HF&W of **John Krzywkowski*** has signalled the firm's intention to develop its litigation capacity. The team represented ABN on the equity financing of the acquisition of stock capital from AS Torm of Denmark. **Clients:** Banks; owners; shipyards; P&I clubs; insurance companies; finance packages.

Clyde & Co (Greece) (1 ptr, 1 assc) A *"high quality small practice"* which is *"traditionally a cargo insurance firm"* and is now *"trying to broaden its range."* Active in both wet and dry work, the firm advises on salvage, collision, and sinking cases, and was instructed on the sinking of 'The Treasure' off South Africa. **Clients:** A. Bilborough & Co; Golden Union Shipping; Tsavliris Group of Companies.

Hill Taylor Dickinson OE (2 ptrs, 4 asscs) Acknowledged by the market as a *"good dry firm,"* it deals exclusively with shipping and marine insurance and litigation, for which it is *"usefully connected."* **Patrick Hawkins*** *"has been there a long time"* and *"knows his way around."* The group has been involved in a number of casualties and arbitration cases, including the loss of the 'Didyomi' yacht. **Clients:** Owners/charterers; hull insurers; P&I clubs.

Holman Fenwick & Willan (Consultants) OE (3 ptrs, 3 asscs) An established litigation firm, which has undergone recent difficulties in Greece with the loss of several senior practitioners. However, researchers were left in little doubt that the team *"remains a major force"* in the contentious sphere, both in shipping and related insurance cases. *"Senior wet man"* **Charles Lowe*** has arrived from the London office, and is *"carrying the torch forward"* while **David Pitlarge*** has maintained his share of market support. **Clients:** Owners; P&I clubs; insurers.

Stephenson Harwood Consultants OE (2 ptrs, 3 asscs) Our research has found a firm with *"a toehold in the ship finance market,"* which is also attempting to develop the litigation side of the practice. **David Slade*** has been *"a name in ship finance forever."* The group reviews ship-building contracts for owners, advises on new building work for Greek owners and performs due diligence for corporate acquisitions. Litigation includes the Skopje oil refinery case in Macedonia, a matter worth $50 million. **Clients:** Royal Bank of Scotland; ship owners; brokers.

*See leaders' profiles on pages 342-343

Leaders' profiles – Greece

BAKER, David
Law Office Howard in Association with Norton Rose, Athens +30 1 721 7111
bakerd@lawofficehoward.com
Recommended in Shipping: Foreign Firms
Specialisation: Partner in the Shipping Finance Department of *Norton Rose.* Head of the Shipping Finance Section of *Law Office Howard*, the associated office of *Norton Rose* in Greece. Main areas of work are shipping finance and banking.
Prof. Memberships: The Law Society and Athens Bar Association.
Career: Qualified in 1985. Joined *Norton Rose* in 1985 becoming a partner in 1997. Worked in *Norton Rose* London office from 1985 to 1989, *Norton Rose* Singapore office from 1989 to 1991 and for *Norton Rose* Consultants O.E. from 1991 to 2000.
Personal: Born 15 May 1958. Attended Oxford Brookes University 1978 to 1982. Married with 3 children. Lives in Agia Marina, Athens, Greece.

BERNITSAS, Panayotis M
M & P Bernitsas Law Offices, Athens +301 361 5395
bernlaw@otenet.gr
Recommended in Corporate/M&A
Specialisation: Managing Partner. Main areas of specialisation are international transactions, mergers, acquisitions and privatisations, banking and finance, project finance, public procurement, EU Law and telecommunications. Has acted on the merger of Marinopoulos and Carrefour and on the merger of Coca Cola Beverages and the Hellenic Bottling Company. Has acted as legal counsel to the Hellenic Republic in relation to the restructuring of "EYDAP SA" and the listing of its shares on the Athens Stock Exchange. Currently involved in the privatisation and restructuring of Olympic Airways SA and the Hellenic Posts (ELTA) and in the restructuring of the Organisation of Prognostics of Football Games (OPAP) and the listing of its shares on the Athens Stock Exchange. Has regularly spoken at various international conferences on European Union and project finance matters.
Publications: Author of numerous articles and publications on European Union Law and banking and finance.
Career: Admitted, 1974, Athens Bar; Athens Court of Appeal and Supreme Court of Greece. Associate Professor of International Economic Law and Law of International Business Transactions and European Community Law, University of Thrace. Arbitrator in various arbitrations of the International Chamber of Commerce (ICC).
Personal: Born Athens, 16 October, 1948. Attended University of Athens Law School (Law Degree), University of Paris (DES in Public Law, 1973), Hague International Law Academy (1973), Institute of Advanced Legal Studies, London (Research, 1975) and University of Thessaloniki (PhD, 1979). Leisure interests include theatre and reading.

DRYLLERAKIS, John
Dryllerakis & Associates, Athens +301 362 8159
Recommended in Corporate/M&A

ELVEY, Jonathan
Ince & Co Consultants OE, Piraeus +30 1429 2543
Recommended in Shipping: Foreign Firms

GEORGOPOULOS, Leonidas
Kyriakides – Georgopoulos Law Firm, Athens +30 1 683 7520
Recommended in Corporate/M&A

GOYIOS, Nicholas
Law Offices N Goyios – A Nassikas, Piraeus +30 1 429 2904
Recommended in Shipping

HAWKINS, Patrick
Hill Taylor Dickinson OE, Pireaus +30 1 4220330
Recommended in Shipping: Foreign Firms

HOWARD, Tim
Law Office Howard in Association with Norton Rose, Athens +30 1 721 7111
howardtcm@lawofficehoward.com
Recommended in Shipping: Foreign Firms
Specialisation: Partner in the Litigation Department of *Norton Rose.* Head of *Law Office Howard*, the associated law office of *Norton Rose* in Greece. Main areas of work are shipping arbitration and litigation.
Prof. Memberships: Law Society, Athens Bar Association, City of London Law Society.
Publications: Numerous articles in trade journals.
Career: Qualified in 1973. Joined *Norton Rose* in 1970 becoming a partner in 1978. Member of the Management Committee of *Norton Rose* 1988-1991. Senior Consultant of *Norton Rose* Consultants OE in Greece 1995-2000. Joint President of British Hellenic Chamber of Commerce 1998 – Editorial Board of Journal of Maritime Law and Transport.
Personal: Born 29 July 1947. Attended St Andrew's University (Dundee Queens College) 1966-70. Married with 3 children. Lives in Greece and Curdridge, Hants.

IATRIDIS, George
Vgenopoulos & Partners, Athens +301 7220 150
Recommended in Shipping

KARATZAS, Katarina
Law Firm Karatzas & Partners, Athens +30 1 371 3600
Recommended in Corporate/M&A

KORITSAS, Nikos
Law Office TJ Koutalidis, Athens +30 1 360 7811
Recommended in Corporate/M&A

KOUTALIDIS, Tryfon
Law Office TJ Koutalidis, Athens +30 1 360 7811
Recommended in Corporate/M&A

KRZYWKOWSKI, John
Watson, Farley & Williams, Piraeus +30 1 422 3660
jkrzywkowski@wfw.com
Recommended in Shipping: Foreign Firms
Specialisation: Marine litigator, having practised in the world's leading maritime legal services centres – London, Hong Kong, and Piraeus. Specialises in hull claims and dry shipping work (P&I and FD&D), and also handles salvage and war risks insurance claims. Experiences in maritime criminal matters, having successfully defended an accused master against charges of manslaughter at sea ("Man Loy" – Hong Kong 1992). Last year, successfully handled a number of constructive total losses for Piraeus-based shipowners.
Prof. Memberships: Law Society.
Career: Previously senior partner of *Holman Fenwick & Willan*'s offices in Hong Kong and Piraeus.
Personal: Born in 1955. BA(Juris) at St Catherine's College, Oxford University. Interests: rugby, classic cars, fine wines, woodworking and renovating medieval properties in Umbria.

KYRIAKIDES, Constantine
Kyriakides – Georgopoulos Law Firm, Athens +30 1 683 7520
Recommended in Corporate/M&A

LOWE, Charles
Holman Fenwick & Willan (Consultants) OE, Piraeus +30 1 429 3978
Charles.Lowe@hfw.co.uk
Recommended in Shipping: Foreign Firms
Specialisation: Partner in Admiralty Department. Admiralty law. 29 years specialisation in collision, salvage, total loss, wreck removal, fixed and floating installation damage, oil pollution claims, disputed claims on H & M underwriters and the whole ambit of admiralty (wet) practice on a 100% specialisation basis. Numerous salvage and collision casualties handled last year.
Career: Malvern College (1958-1964), Christs College Cambridge (1964-1967) MA Cantab. Admitted 1971. Joined *Holman, Fenwick & Willan* 1971. Joined partnership 1978. Opened Hong Kong office as first resident partner 1978-82. Appointed Managing Partner Greek office August 2000.
Personal: Born 1945. Divorced. Two children. Resident Athens. Leisure activities: sailing, scuba diving, fly-fishing & tying, horse riding worldwide and wildlife.

METALLINOS, Alexander
Law Firm Karatzas & Partners, Athens +30 1 371 3600
Recommended in Corporate/M&A

NASSIKAS, Andreas
Law Offices N Goyios – A Nassikas, Piraeus +30 1 429 2904
Recommended in Shipping

PAPANGELIS, Miltos
Vgenopoulos & Partners, Athens +301 7220 150
Recommended in Shipping

PITLARGE, David
Holman Fenwick & Willan (Consultants) OE, Piraeus +30 1 429 3989
David.Pitlarge@hfw.co.uk
Recommended in Shipping: Foreign Firms
Specialisation: Commercial and marine litigation and arbitration: advising on disputes involving bills of lading, charterparties, insurance coverage (both Hull and P&I), ship sale/construction contracts and ship management agreements. Also general commercial litigation and advice.
Prof. Memberships: Law Society; LMAA (supporting members).
Career: Articled *Titmus Sainer & Webb* 1987-89; admitted 1989; joined *Holman Fenwick & Willan* in 1989. Made partner in 1997. A resident partner in the Greek office since 1998.
Personal: Nottingham University (BA Hons 1984). Resident in Athens. Leisure interests include reading, tennis, travel, cricket and skiing.

REDIADIS, Deucalion
Deucalion Rediadis & Sons, Piraeus +301 429 4900
Recommended in Shipping

REECE, John
Law Office Howard in Association with Norton Rose, Athens +30 1 721 7111
reecejl@lawofficehoward.com
Recommended in Shipping: Foreign Firms
Specialisation: Partner in the Litigation Department of *Norton Rose.* Head of the Litigation Section of *Law Office Howard,* the associated office of *Norton Rose* in Greece. Main areas of work are shipping litigation and admiralty.
Prof. Memberships: The Law Society and Athens Bar Association.
Publications: Contributed to the book 'The Mariner's Role in Collecting Evidence', published by the Nautical Institute.
Career: Qualified in 1979. Joined *Norton Rose* in 1990 becoming a partner in 1996. Worked for *Norton Rose* Consultants OE from its foundation in 1990 until 2000. Visiting lecturer in Marine Insurance at City University London.
Personal: Born 7 August 1954. Attended Cambridge University (Fitzwilliam College) 1973-1976. Married with two children. Lives in Dionysos, Athens, Greece.

RICE, Tony
Watson, Farley & Williams, Piraeus +30 1 422 3660
Recommended in Shipping: Foreign Firms

SARANTITIS, Vassilis
Sarantitis & Partners, Athens Piraeus +301 42 907 80
Recommended in Shipping

SCORINIS, Nicholas
Scorinis Law Offices, Piraeus +301 418 1818
scorinis@ath.forthnet.gr
Recommended in Shipping
Specialisation: Main area of work is all legal aspects relating to the shipping industry, including shipping finance. Also, corporate law and acquisitions. Acts for a number of clients among which are several leading banks, financial institutions, chambers and unions, governmental agencies, foreign and international law firms as well as a great number of international and Greek shipowners, shipyards, underwriters, brokers, ship suppliers and agents. Litigator before all Greek courts and, very often, before the European Court of Human Rights in Strasbourg.
Prof. Memberships: Vice-President of the Hellenic Association of Maritime Law, Titulary Member of the Comité Maritime International (CMI), Vice-President of the Hellenic Society of Maritime Lawyers, Member of the Permanent Drafting Laws Committee of the Greek Ministry of Justice, Member of the Legal Committee of the Union of Greek Shipowners, Member of the Legal Committee of the Greek Chamber of Shipping, Arbitrator at the Greek Chamber of Shipping, Arbitrator at the Mediterranean Maritime Arbitration Association.
Publications: Author of various articles in Shipping Law. Speaker in many conferences worldwide.
Career: Sea service as a deck hand and deck officer in dry cargo and tanker vessels (1955-1966). Qualified Master Mariner in ocean going vessels (1968). Qualified as a lawyer (1969). Established *Scorinis Law Offices* (1969).
Personal: Born 17 September 1936.

SIOUFAS, Theo V
Theo V Sioufas, Law Offices, 185 35 Piraeus +30 1 422 12 10
Recommended in Shipping

SLADE, David
Stephenson Harwood Consultants OE, Piraeus +30 1 429 5160
david.slade@stephensonharwood.com
Recommended in Shipping: Foreign Firms
Specialisation: Partner. Main area of practice is shipping finance, shipbuilding contracts and sale and purchase of ships, acting mainly for banks, shipowners, shipbuilders and shipbrokers. Also deals with disputes under shipbuilding contracts and sale and purchase contracts. Based at *Stephenson Harwood Consultants OE* in Piraeus office developing the firm's expanding practice in and about the countries bordering the Eastern Mediterranean and also providing continuing support in our International Shipping work. Has lectured on syndicated loans, ship finance, sale and purchase and construction of ships.
Prof. Memberships: Law Society, Worshipful Company of Shipwrights.
Career: Qualified in 1966. *Smiles & Co* 1963-66; *Constant & Constant* 1966, became a partner in 1972. Joined *Stephenson Harwood* as Partner in 1985. Head of Shipping Department 1985-96. Became Senior Partner in 1966-April 1999. Based at *Stephenson Harwood* Consultants OE, Piraeus.
Personal: Born on 3 July 1941. Educated at St. Peter's, York 1954-64; Emmanuel College, Cambridge. Was Head of School, Captain of Rugby and Boats, President of Debating Society, 1960-63 and 1966 (MA, LLM 1966). Married. Leisure interests include collecting paintings (on a relatively small scale) and antique furniture. Formerly member of the Territorial Army (Airborne Artillery); holder of T.D. Resides: Greece and London.

TIMAGENIS, Gregory J
G.J. Timagenis Law Office, Piraeus +30 1 422 0001
Recommended in Shipping

VOUTERAKOS, Costas
Kyriakides – Georgopoulos Law Firm, Athens +30 1 683 7520
Recommended in Corporate/M&A

WATSON, Jeremy
Watson, Farley & Williams, Piraeus +30 1 422 3660
jwatson@wfw.co
Recommended in Shipping: Foreign Firms
Specialisation: Ship finance partner based at *Watson, Farley & Williams'* Piraeus office. Acts for most of the major ship finance banks lending into the Greek market, whether based inside or outside Greece, as well as borrowers.
Prof. Memberships: Law Society.
Career: Articled *Norton Rose* 1990-1992. Qualified 1992. Joined *Watson, Farley & Williams* as a partner in 2000.
Personal: Born 1965. Educated Friary Grange School, Lichfield. University of Wales, Cardiff 1984-1987 (LLB Hons 2:1). Law Society Finals Chester. Lives in Athens. Enjoys tennis, skiing, scuba diving and cinema.

ZEPOS, Dimitrios
Zepos & Zepos, Athens +301 775 3341
Recommended in Corporate/M&A

GREENLAND

Corporate/Commercial

GREENLAND Leading firms (Corporate/Commercial)
1 Advokatfirma Henrik Hey
Nuna Advokater I/S
Advokatfirma Wilhelm Malling & Co

Firms are listed alphabetically in each band.

Leading individuals (Corporate/Commercial)
1 DICKMEISS Vilhelm *Nuna Advokater I/S*
HEY Henrik *Advokatfirma Henrik Hey*
MALLING Wilhelm *Advokatfirma Wilhelm Malling & Co*
SYMES Nicholas *Advokatfirma Henrik Hey*

Individuals are listed alphabetically in each band.

Advokatfirma Henrik Hey (2 ptrs) **Nicholas Symes** is regarded by peers as the key to the firm's expanding presence in the market. With an international focus, the firm undertakes general commercial work with a niche in employment issues and has represented companies of the Home Rule Government. The well-established **Henrik Hey** has considerable local knowledge and is able to *"serve his clients well."* **Clients:** Real Kredit Danmark; BG Bank; Polar Seafood; Great Greenland.

Nuna Advokater I/S (2 ptrs, 1 assc) Originally two Danish firms, the merged entity continues links with its parents by providing support on cross border deals. That said, the turnover of staff on secondment from Denmark is considered a hindrance. Well regarded by competitors and clients as *"legally well-founded"* it has been *"successful for many years,"* in M&A and general commercial and financial matters. Acting on the establishment of businesses in Greenland, the practice is led by **Vilhelm Dickmeiss**. **Clients:** Fishing and enterprise industries; state companies.

Advokatfirma Wilhelm Malling & Co (5 lawyers) This firm, led by **Wilhelm Malling**, undertakes a

wide range of work which includes acting for the Home Rule Government and major companies in the fishing and mining industries. The largest Greenlandic firm, it also has links with other Danish and international law firms. **Clients:** Fishing and mining companies; the Home Rule Government.

Leaders' profiles – Greenland

DICKMEISS, Vilhelm
Nuna Advokater I/S, Nuuk +299 321 370

HEY, Henrik
Advokatfirma Henrik Hey, Nuuk +299 321 252

MALLING, Wilhelm
Advokatfirma Wilhelm Malling & Co, Nuuk +299 323 400

SYMES, Nicholas
Advokatfirma Henrik Hey, Nuuk +299 321 252

GUATEMALA

Corporate/Commercial

GUATEMALA Leading firms (Corporate/Commercial)
1 Mayora y Mayora
2 Bonilla Montano & Toriello
Carrillo y Asociados
Saravia y Muñoz
Viteri & Viteri

Firms are listed alphabetically in each band.

Leading individuals (Corporate/Commercial)
1 **MAYORA ALVARADO Eduardo** *Mayora y Mayora*
SARAVIA CASTILLO Salvador *Saravia y Muñoz*
VITERI ARRIOLA Ernesto *Viteri & Viteri*
2 **CARRILLO Alfonso** *Carrillo y Asociados*
MAYORA DAWE Eduardo *Mayora y Mayora*
VITERI ECHEVERRIA Ernesto *Viteri & Viteri*
3 **BONILLA Guillermo** *Bonilla Montano & Toriello*
TORIELLO Rodrigo *Bonilla Montano & Toriello*

Individuals are listed alphabetically in each band.

Mayora y Mayora (2 ptrs, 7 asscs) The country's *"largest competitor"* enjoys a first class reputation for its *"strong corporate practice."* M&A is a growth area, and the firm recently acted for Coca-Cola on the sale of a bottling plant. **Eduardo Mayora Alvarado** is *"a ubiquitous corporate lawyer,"* and his father **Eduardo Mayora Dawe** has *"a wealth of experience."* The firm advised on the concession for the first privatised tolled highway in the country and acted for Curacao in their withdrawal from Guatemala. **Clients:** Texaco; Securities Exchange; Bank of Central America; Biersdorf.

Bonilla Montano & Toriello (5 ptrs, 9 asscs) The firm is prominent in M&A transactions, distribution agreements, incorporation of companies and foreign investment work. Researchers were impressed by the weight of commendation for a *"serious and reputable group."* Acted in the $20 million financing for a hydro-electric power project and is advising Duke Energy of Texas in its entry into Guatemala. **Rodrigo Toriello** is an *"internationally-oriented and dedicated corporate lawyer,"* and **Guillermo Bonilla** is also recommended. The firm represented Marsk on its acquisition of Sealand in Guatemala, and is advising Vitro of Mexico on its distribution agreements in Central America. **Clients:** Microsoft; IDB; CDC; JC Penney; Kimberly Clark; Dial Corp; Textron Financial Corp; Asgrow Seed Corp.

Carrillo y Asociados (4 ptrs, 9 asscs) *"A complete and hard-working firm,"* which is *"strengthening its corporate practice,"* and has particular expertise in telecoms and energy. Participated in the joint venture of Royal Ahold with La Fragua and represented Gas Silza in acquiring operations in Guatemala and Honduras. *"Capable and hard working"* **Alfonso Carrillo Jr** is the firm's leading light. The firm recently acted on the acquisition of Cybernet by Convergence Communications. **Clients:** Lloyds TSB; Unilever; BAT; UPS; Sol Melia; Itochu; Rabobank; Curacao; Global One; Novell; AES Americas; IFC; United Airlines; France Telecom.

Saravia y Muñoz (2 ptrs, 6 asscs) Well-known for its work on behalf of international business,

researchers had their attention drawn to this team above all for its *"strong teamwork."* The group handles banking, legal advice, commercial transactions, incorporation of companies and M&A work. **Salvador Saravia Castillo** is an *"excellent and experienced lawyer,"* well known in the banking community. The firm represented a Central American Group acquiring local companies and worked on the financing for a local telephone company. **Clients:** Banque National de Paris; UBS; Proctor & Gamble; SmithKline Beecham; Swiss Embassy.

Viteri & Viteri (2 ptrs, 4 asscs) A *"respected and honourable"* firm with a *"strong trademark practice."* On the corporate side, the firm is involved in the organisation of corporations and accompanying tax work. Regularly works on foreign loans to local companies. **Ernesto Viteri Arriola** is extremely well regarded and his father **Ernesto Viteri Echeverria** is *"intelligent and hard-working."* **Clients:** Colgate Palmolive; Nabisco; Pharmacia & Upjohn; Galderma; Allergan; Exxon; Pfizer.

Leaders' profiles – Guatemala

BONILLA, Guillermo
Bonilla Montano & Toriello, Guatemala City +502 334 8155

CARRILLO, Alfonso
Carrillo y Asociados, Guatemala City +502 331 5441

MAYORA ALVARADO, Eduardo
Mayora y Mayora, Ciudad de Guatemala +502 366 2531

MAYORA DAWE, Eduardo
Mayora y Mayora, Ciudad de Guatemala +502 366 2531

SARAVIA CASTILLO, Salvador
Saravia y Muñoz, Guatemala City +502 333 6576

TORIELLO, Rodrigo
Bonilla Montano & Toriello, Guatemala City +502 334 8155

VITERI ARRIOLA, Ernesto Jose
Viteri & Viteri, Guatemala City +502 331 1707

VITERI ECHEVERRIA, Ernesto Ricardo
Viteri & Viteri, Guatemala City +502 331 1707

GUERNSEY

Corporate/Commercial

GUERNSEY Leading firms (Corporate/Commercial)
1 Carey Langlois
Ozannes
2 Collas Day
3 Babbe Le Pelley Tostevin

Firms are listed alphabetically in each band.

Leading individuals (Corporate/Commercial)
1 **CAREY Nigel** *Carey Langlois*
HALL Graham *Carey Langlois*
HARWOOD Peter *Ozannes*
SIMPSON William *Ozannes*
2 **HOWITT Simon** *Babbe Le Pelley Tostevin*
KIRK Ian *Collas Day*
LANGLOIS John *Carey Langlois*

Individuals are listed alphabetically in each band.

Carey Langlois (7 ptrs, 12 asscs) One of the *"big two,"* the firm is well known for its investment fund and trusts advice. *"Highly regarded"* **Nigel Carey** and **Graham Hall** are the two leading lawyers on commercial matters, while **John Langlois** is also held in high esteem. The firm acted on the rights issue for the Channel Islands Stock Exchange. **Clients:** Guernsey Stock Exchange; Princess Group; Schroeder Ventures; Alchemy Partners.

Ozannes (10 ptrs, 7 asscs) *"One of the leading firms on the island,"* competitors informed our researchers is expanding, and has an established name for buy-outs and securitisation work. **Peter Harwood** has *"wide commercial knowledge,"* while the *"competent and personable"* **William Simpson** also comes highly recommended. Acted on the Aurigny Air Services management buyout, as well as securitisations for BUPA and Citibank. **Clients:** Lloyds TSB; Rothschild.

Collas Day (8 ptrs, 7 asscs) Although felt to lack the punch of the two market leaders, the firm retains a sound reputation for general corporate and financial work, particularly in lending and structured finance. The experienced **Ian Kirk** is *"a significant player in the corporate field."* The firm acted on the sale of the trust and corporate administration businesses of Ernst & Young to Royal Bank of Canada. **Clients:** Clearing banks and international financial institutions.

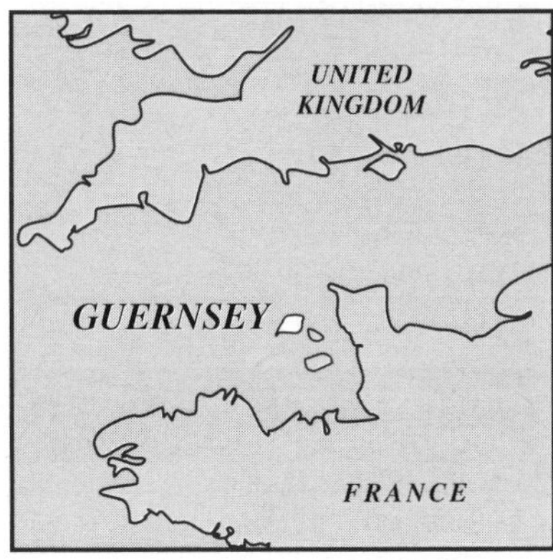

Babbe Le Pelley Tostevin (8 ptrs, 5 asscs) A recent merger has formed a large team with *"a decent balance of expertise."* The firm has increased its workload in banking, trusts and funds, and has its strongest reputation in the insurance industry. **Simon Howitt** has been referred to as *"the main man,"* for the firm, which advised on the Columbus plc sale of assets. **Clients:** HSBC; Credit Suisse Trust; Walbrook Trustees.

Leaders' profiles – Guernsey

CAREY, Nigel
Carey Langlois, St. Peter Port +44 1481 727272
nigel.carey@careylanglois.com
Specialisation: Partner in the Corporate Department. Acts for many of the banks and financial institutions in Guernsey. Main area of work is collective investment schemes. Is a Director of a number of the Guernsey companies involved in banking, insurance and investment business.
Prof. Memberships: Former Chairman of the Guernsey Bar Council; currently a member of Guernsey Financial Services Commission.
Personal: Born 29 May 1948.

HALL, Graham
Carey Langlois, St. Peter Port +44 1481 727272

HARWOOD, Peter
Ozannes, St Peter Port +44 1481 723466

HOWITT, Simon
Babbe Le Pelley Tostevin, St Peter Port
+44 1481 713 371
s.howitt@bltguernsey.com
Specialisation: Partner in Financial Services Group. Main areas of work involve advising banks and fiduciaries and general company/commercial work. Acts for a clearing bank (and a number of smaller banks) on general matters, including loan documentation and security, and for one of Guernsey's largest corporate fiduciaries. A frequent speaker at professional conferences, principally on company law, obligations of trustees and anti-money laundering legislation.
Prof. Memberships: Vice President of the Guernsey Chamber of Commerce. Guernsey Bar Council. Guernsey International Legal Association.
Publications: 'The Disclosure of Confidential Information under Guernsey Law' – The Guernsey Law Journal 1990. 'Taking Security over Personal Intangible Property under Guernsey Law' – Sweet & Maxwell's Journal of International Banking Law (Vol 10 Issue 1).
Career: Qualified as a Barrister in 1987 and as an Advocate in 1988. Joined *Le Pelley & Tostevin* in 1987, becoming a Partner in 1991. *Le Pelley & Tostevin* merged with *Babbe Le Poidevin Allez* in 2000 to form the new partnership of *Babbe Le Pelley Tostevin.* Member of the Council of the Guernsey International Business Association 1996 - 1999; secretary to the Guernsey Bar Council 1997 - 1999;

member of the Council of the Guernsey Chamber of Commerce, 1998 to date (vice-president 1999 to date).
Personal: Born on 27 February, 1965. Educated at Elizabeth College, Guernsey. Attended de Montfort University 1983 to 1986 (LLB Hons). Leisure interests include playing the guitar. Lives in St Peter Port, Guernsey.

KIRK, Ian
Collas Day, St Peter Port +44 1481 723191
irnkirk@collasday.com
Specialisation: An advocate of the Royal Court of Guernsey and an English solicitor. Partner in the corporate and commercial department of *Collas Day*. Main areas of work are corporate and commercial law and banking. Has handled numerous acquisitions both locally and as adviser on Guernsey legal and regulatory issues in connection with international transactions. Advises a number of banks and financial institutions on lending, security and regulatory issues and holds a number of directorships. Writes on, and is a regular lecturer on, company law, trusts and financial services in Guernsey.
Prof. Memberships: Law Society; The Society of Trust and Estate Practitioners; Guernsey International Legal Association; The Institute of Directors.
Publications: Writer of the chapter on Guernsey in: 'Asset Protection Domestic and International Law and Tactics' published by Clark Boardman & Callaghan. 'International Taxation of Low Transactions'. Has contributed to a number of publications on Guernsey company, trust and financial services law including the Channel Islands Financial Services Guide and the Offshore Trust Year Book.
Career: Joined *Freshfields* in 1982. Qualified in 1984 and worked in their company commercial department. 1987 to 1994 – Partner with *Edwin Coe* specialising in corporate, banking and insolvency matters. 1994 to date – *Collas Day*, specialising in banking, commercial and corporate trust matters.
Personal: Born 3 April 1959 in Liverpool. Attended Oxford University 1977 to 1980 (MA Jurisprudence); Cambridge University 1980 to 1981 (LLM). Leisure interests include football. Lives with wife, Allison in St Peters, Guernsey, Channel Islands.

LANGLOIS, John
Carey Langlois, St. Peter Port +44 1481 727272
John.@Langlois.com
Specialisation: Senior Partner. Main area of work: corporate and trust law and e-commerce, extensive experience in captive insurance.
Prof. Memberships: Called to the English Bar (1970) and Guernsey Bar (1971); Fellow, Chartered Institutute of Arbitrators, 1993. Extensive political career in Guernsey: Vice President, States Advisory & Financial Committee, President: States Housing Authority, President: Island Development Committee, Chairman: States Review Board, (Ombudscommittee).
Publications: Contributing author; 'Guidelines for Guernsey Directors' (1992), contributing author 'The Guernsey Financial Services Director', 'Trident Practical Guide to Offshore Trusts'.
Career: Sole practitioner 1971 - 1973, merged practice and re-named firm *Carey Langlois* in 1973, Senior partner since 1977 .
Personal: Born 31 October 1942. University of London (LLB (Hons) 1970. University of Caen, France 1971. Speaks French. Leisure interests include charitable work for human rights organisations, boating, gardening and travel.

SIMPSON, William
Ozannes, St Peter Port +44 1481 723466

G

GUINEA

Corporate/Commercial

GUINEA Leading firms (Corporate/Commercial)
1 Etude Diallo et Chalhoub

Firms are listed alphabetically in each band.

Leading individuals (Corporate/Commercial)
1 DIALLO Alpha-Abdoulaye *Diallo et Chalhoub*

Individuals are listed alphabetically in each band.

Etude Diallo et Chalhoub (2 ptrs, 3 asscs) A *"well-connected"* firm capable of handling all corporate matters as well as banking and maritime issues. Our researchers discovered that former vice-president of the country and vice-president of the United Nations General Assembly, **Alpha-Abdoulaye Diallo** is *"an honest and intelligent gentleman who works for the good of the country."*
Clients: Airlines; commercial and industrial businesses; banks.

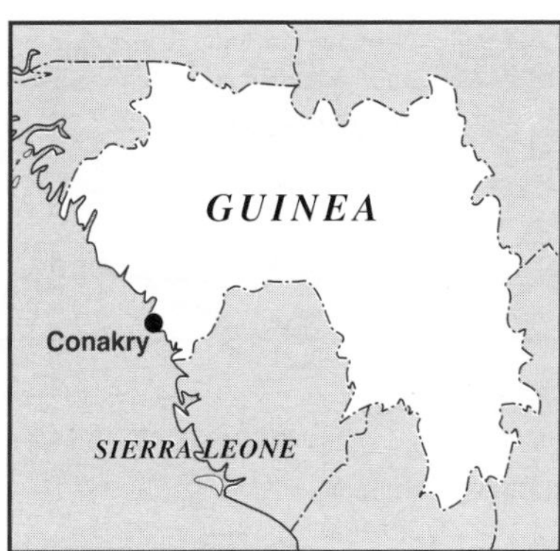

Leaders' profiles – Guinea

DIALLO, Alpha-Abdoulaye
Etude Diallo et Chalhoub, Conakry +224 411 948

GUYANA

Corporate/Commercial

GUYANA Leading firms (Corporate/Commercial)
1 Cameron & Shepherd
De Caires, Fitzpatrick & Karran
Hughes, Fields & Stoby
Luckhoo & Luckhoo
Rex McKay & Partners

Firms are listed alphabetically in each band.

GUYANA Leading individuals
1 **FITZPATRICK Miles** *De Caires, Fitzpatrick*
MCKAY Rex *Rex McKay & Partners*
2 **FIELDS Richard** *Hughes, Fields & Stoby*
HUGHES Clarence *Hughes, Fields & Stoby*
LUCKHOO Edward *Luckhoo & Luckhoo*
RAMKARRAN Hari *Cameron & Shepherd*
STOBY Robin *Hughes, Fields & Stoby*

Individuals are listed alphabetically in each band.

Cameron & Shepherd (4 ptrs, 1 assc) The oldest firm in the country has an *"excellent reputation"* for corporate work, and a name for *"stability and dependability."* The only exclusively commercial firm in Guyana, it services clients from all areas of the business community including banking, mining, insurance and manufacturing. IP is another key area of expertise. Senior partner **Hari Ramkarran** is regarded as the *"star of the firm."* **Clients:** University of Guyana; Guyana Oil Company; DIH; NBIC.

De Caires, Fitzpatrick & Karran (3 ptrs, 2 asscs) The commercial department in this firm is acclaimed by clients and opponents as *"one of the best in the country."* The key player is the respected **Miles Fitzpatrick**, a *"leading practitioner"* with *"great experience and a sound grasp of commercial issues."* The firm handles securities and mortgages work for Demerara Bank Ltd, and has handled corporate work for GLP and GTT. Other areas of expertise include shipping and insurance. **Clients:** Trust Company Guyana Ltd; Demerara Bank Ltd; ESSO; Vinelli Industries Ltd.

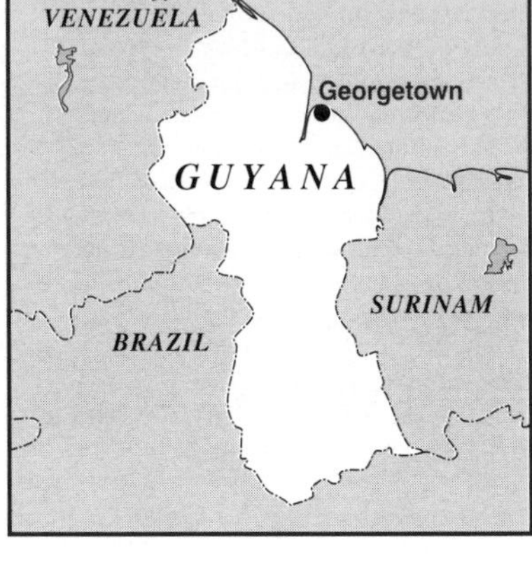

Hughes, Fields & Stoby (3 ptrs, 4 asscs) Formed by three ex-barristers, the firm is considered to be a *"solid legal player."* **Clarence Hughes**, **Richard Fields** and **Robin Stoby** are all rated as *"exceptional lawyers"* and are members of the Senior Counsel. They bring to the commercial practice a wealth of experience in international corporate work, and niche expertise in the banking sector. **Clients:** Bank of Novia Scotia; Guyana Bank of Trade and Industry.

Luckhoo & Luckhoo (2 ptrs) Established by a distinguished Guyanese family, the firm is now considered to be a *"a one man show,"* in the form of the *"extremely able"* **Edward Luckhoo**. Over 50% of the firm's work is commercial, with a focus on mining, insurance and trademarks on behalf of both foreign and domestic clients. **Clients:** Reynolds Metal Company; Omai.

Rex McKay & Partners (8 ptrs) Specialisng in public law, the firm also has a strong commercial department. The outstanding partner here is **Rex McKay** who possesses a *"thorough knowledge of commercial law."* The firm advises the Guyanese Revenue Authority on many commercial matters, as well as advising large foreign entities working in Guyana. **Clients:** Nagafar Saw Ltd; Mazaruli Granite ltd.

Leaders' profiles – Guyana

FIELDS, Richard
Hughes, Fields & Stoby, Georgetown +592 258 914

FITZPATRICK, Miles
De Caires, Fitzpatrick & Karran, Georgetown +592 261 126

HUGHES, Clarence
Hughes, Fields & Stoby, Georgetown +592 258 914

LUCKHOO, Edward
Luckhoo & Luckhoo, Georgetown +592 259 232

McKAY, Rex
Rex McKay & Partners, Georgetown +592 272 317

RAMKARRAN, Hari
Cameron & Shepherd, Georgetown +592 262 671

STOBY, Robin
Hughes, Fields & Stoby, Georgetown +592 258 914

HAITI

Corporate/Commercial

HAITI Leading firms (Corporate/Commercial)
1 Cabinet Hudicourt-Woolley
Mayard-Paul Law Firm
Pasquet & Gousse
Cabinet Sales

Firms are listed alphabetically in each band.

Leading individuals (Corporate/Commercial)
1 BRUN Alexandra *Cabinet Sales*
HUDICOURT EWALD Chantal *Cabinet Hudicourt-Woolley*
MAYARD-PAUL Constantin *Mayard-Paul*
PASQUET Gerds *Pasquet & Gousse*

Individuals are listed alphabetically in each band.

Cabinet Hudicourt-Woolley (4 ptrs, 5 asscs) The largest firm in Haiti has an enviable international client base, as well as a *"straight and ethical"* reputation. The firm provides a general service to Shell, legal opinions for Citibank and handles all the legal work for Seaboard Marine Corp. Debt recovery and document drafting are other key areas of the workload. **Chantal Hudicourt Ewald** is *"an experienced international corporate lawyer."* **Clients:** Shell; Citibank; IFC; Seaboard Marine.

Mayard-Paul Law Firm (3 ptrs, 3 asscs) Recommended by competitors as *"a decent corporate law firm,"* the firm is led by **Constantin Mayard-Paul**, a lawyer of vast experience, who *"remains transactionally active."* The team represented BUH on its merger with Soca Bank, and was involved in contract work for Ferrovial Agroman on a road construction project in Haiti. **Clients:** BUH; Ferrovial Agroman; Antillas Air.

Pasquet & Gousse (1 ptr, 1 assc) *"One of the best"* firms in the country, it recently did all the legal work involved in the merger between Soca Bank and the International Bank of Commerce. The firm has a number of major clients in Port-au-Prince for which it provides general commercial advice. **Gerds Pasquet** was recommended to researchers as a recognised corporate specialist.

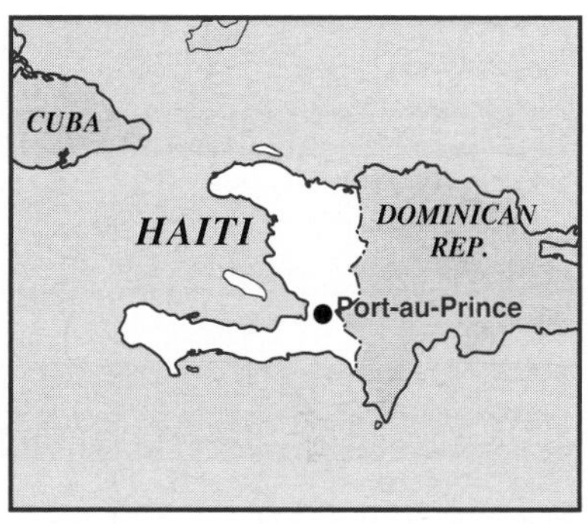

Clients: Soca Bank; Central Bank; Bank of Development; Esso; Tropical Airlines

Cabinet Sales (6 lawyers) *"Prominent for trademark work,"* the firm also has an acknowledged corporate practice and a substantial client base of financial institutions. **Alexandra Brun** is regarded as a *"rising local star."* The firm represented Scotia Bank on its sale to Capital Bank. **Clients:** PromoBank SR; Scotia Bank.

Leaders' profiles – Haiti

BRUN, Alexandra
Cabinet Sales, Port-au-Prince +509 222 2818

HUDICOURT EWALD, Chantal
Cabinet Hudicourt-Woolley, Port-au-Prince +509 223 9555 / +509 223 9666

MAYARD-PAUL, Constantin
Mayard-Paul Law Firm, Port-au-Prince +509 222 2343

PASQUET, Gerds
Pasquet & Gousse, Port-au-Prince +509 222 5621

HONDURAS

Corporate/Commercial

HONDURAS Leading firms (Corporate/Commercial)
1 Batres y Asociados
Bufete Gutierrez Falla
Lopez Rodezno & Asociados

Firms are listed alphabetically in each band.

Leading individuals (Corporate/Commercial)
1 BATRES Cesar *Batres y Asociados*
GUTIERREZ FALLA Laureano *Bufete Gutierrez*
LÓPEZ RODEZNO René *Lopez Rodezno*

Individuals are listed alphabetically in each band.

Batres y Asociados (8 lawyers) *"Prestigious, large law firm"* in Tegucigalpa, specialising in corporate law and advising a number of blue-chip multinationals. Like many of its lawyers, **Cesar Batres** has been involved in government, as minister for foreign affairs and as substitute justice for the supreme court. He is recognised by peers as *"one of the top attorneys in the country."* **Clients:** International corporates.

Bufete Gutierrez Falla (3 ptrs, 5 asscs) Renowned for its international banking practice, the firm advises several financial institutions in Honduras. It has represented the IFC in lending to local banks, and is effectively in-house attorney for the Seaboard Corp. Harvard graduate **Laureano Gutierrez Falla** is *"an experienced and highly reputed local lawyer,"* according to contemporaries. **Clients:** GBM; Seaboard Corp; IFC; Lucent Technologies; Chiquita.

Lopez Rodezno & Asociados (2 ptrs, 2 asscs) Recommended to researchers as a *"highly competitive corporate practice"* with an *"excellent reputation nationally and internationally."* US-trained lawyer **René López Rodezno** is a respected and *"well-prepared"* lawyer. The firm

has advised on the incorporation of new companies in Honduras, as well as franchise and commercial law. Conducted due diligence for Unilever on the acquisition of the Cressida group, and represented Maduro, a Central American group, on the acquisition of certain enterprises from the Dutch group Ceteco. **Clients:** Maduro & Curiel's Bank; Unilever.

Leaders' profiles – Honduras

BATRES, Cesar A.
Batres y Asociados, Tegucigalpa +504 236 9200

GUTIERREZ FALLA, Laureano
Bufete Gutierrez Falla, Tegucigalpa +504 236 5455

LÓPEZ RODEZNO, René
Lopez Rodezno & Asociados, Tegucigalpa MDC +504 232 8114
rlopez@david.intertel.hn
Specialisation: Head of Corporate Department. Main area of work is corporate law, principally incorporation of companies, mergers, acquisitions, privatisations and foreign investment. Has incorporated thousands of companies. Prepared many due diligences of local companies and participated in their merger or acquisition by local or foreign companies. Acted on the merger of several companies, creating the largest shrimp culture operation in Latin America. Prepared the due diligence of Grupo Crosside that lead to its acquisition by Unilever. Represented IFC and DEG in several important lending operations in Honduras.
Prof. Memberships: Honduran Bar Association, Honduran Notarial Law Association, Club de Abogados Ibero América, International Business Law Consortium.
Career: Attended the University of Honduras Law School 1957-1963, New York University Law School (MCJ Program) 1964-1965. Delegate to the United Nations General Assembly 1965 and 1967, and delegate to the United Nations Law of the Sea Meetings. An Eisenhower Exchange fellow in 1968. Alternate member of the Supreme Court of Justice for four years. Joined *López Rodezno & Asociados* in 1966 and now Senior Partner.
Personal: Member of Rotary Club, Chancellor of Honduras Malta Order Association. Leisure interests include outdoor activities, opera and classical music. Lives in Tegucigalpa, Honduras.

HONG KONG

Index

OVERVIEW: Despite the PRC's efforts to promote Beijing and Shanghai, Hong Kong is still at the forefront economically and legally. Recovered fully from the economic downturn of the 1990s, firms are enjoying an upswing in corporate work whilst restructuring and insolvency practices continue to flourish. Salary hikes across the board have followed increased competition and the exodus of young legal talent to the burgeoning e-commerce sector.

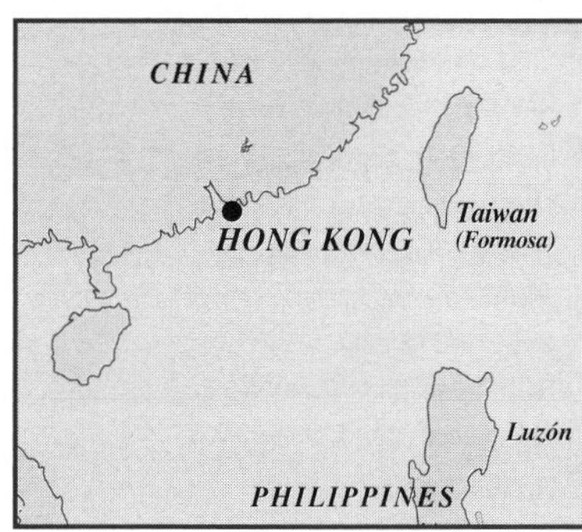

H

Banking & Finance

HONG KONG Leading firms (Banking & Finance)
1 Allen & Overy
Clifford Chance
2 Baker & McKenzie
Linklaters
3 Freshfields Bruckhaus Deringer
Johnson Stokes & Master
4 Deacons
Herbert Smith
Richards Butler
Shearman & Sterling
Slaughter and May
5 Koo and Partners
Simmons & Simmons

Firms are listed alphabetically in each band.

Allen & Overy (4 ptrs, 11 asscs) A strong domestic and regional practice with a reputation for quality, depth and a strong relationship with top-tier banks. An ability to advise on complex deals and involvement in innovative big-ticket syndicated loan transactions places the firm in the top category. Restructuring work is also a forte, and has included acting for the steering committee of lenders to KDLC (Hong Kong) on the cross-border restructuring of the company's debts.

Head of department **Alan Rae Smith*** is known for being *"practical and extremely commercial,"* while **Joseph Tse*** *"knows what he is doing"* and is *"a tough negotiator."*

The firm advised Société Générale Asia as the lead co-ordinating arranger in the HK$4 billion secured facility to Zenuna for the refinancing of the construction facility for Times Square in Hong Kong. Also advised Citibank on a $120 million revolving financing for Universal Scientific Industrial Co, and represented Standard Chartered Bank on a $45 million standby letter of credit facility for Ingram Micro International Trading (Shanghai) Co. **Clients:** Bank of America; Chase Manhattan; HSBC; SocGen; Citibank; Sanwa; Sumitomo; ABN AMRO; Standard Chartered.

Clifford Chance (7 ptrs, 16 asscs) Competing on both the domestic and international stage, the Hong Kong office is considered to benefit from the firm's massive world-wide banking reputation. Generally seen acting for the lenders, the group has a superb reputation for acquisition finance, and is acknowledged to have beefed up its US banking law capability. **Huw Jenkins*** is a *"competent practitioner with some great clients,"* while head of department **Patrick O' Connor**'s* profile continues to rise through his restructuring expertise.

The firm advised Chase Manhattan Asia as arranger on the $700 million multi-tranche, multi-currency acquisition financing and working capital facility for Yageo Corporation. Other transactions include representing Standard Chartered Bank and others in connection with a HK$600 million revolving credit facility for SME-Loan Hong Kong. **Clients:** Dai-Ichi Kangyo Bank; Citibank; ABN AMRO; Chase Manhattan; UBS; Goldman Sachs; JP Morgan.

Baker & McKenzie (6 ptrs, 13 asscs) A high volume of big-ticket deals, most notably in debt restructuring and litigation, has maintained the firm's high banking profile. Aircraft financing represents another area of solid achievement. **Stephen Eno*** is a *"familiar name in the market,"* although his *"aggressive style"* does not meet with unanimous approval. **Patrick Fontaine*** acted for Disney on its joint venture with the Hong Kong government for the proposed development of a theme park, and is described as *"a super lawyer."*

The firm advised GZITIC on legal action against Guangzhou Finance Company and the restructuring of the GZITIC Group and represented Telecom Asia on its $1.5 billion restructuring. **Clients:** Citibank NA; The Walt Disney Co; ING Barings.

Linklaters (2 ptrs, 12 asscs) Respected for its traditional banking expertise, the firm is recognised for the quality, rather than quantity of its deals. The trend for banks to form global panels has resulted in consolidating relationships with key banking clients such as Chase Manhattan, HSBC and Citicorp. **Steven Christopher*** is *"competent, reasonable and a nice opponent."*

Recent restructurings have included the Celcom/TRI restructuring in Malaysia, Piltel/PLOT in the Philippines and the Alphatec buyout. The firm also handled the transfer of Bankers Trust to Deutsche Bank and the Schroders business to

*See leaders' profiles on pages 362-371

HONG KONG Leading individuals (Banking & Finance)
1
CHAPMAN Ian *Johnson Stokes & Master*
RAE SMITH Alan *Allen & Overy*
2
CHRISTOPHER Steven *Linklaters*
ENO Stephen *Baker & McKenzie*
JENKINS Huw *Clifford Chance*
JOHNSTON Nic *Freshfields Bruckhaus Deringer*
McGUINNESS John *Richards Butler*
MOULT Jonathan *Herbert Smith*
TSE Joseph *Allen & Overy*
3
FAIRBAIRN Mark *Deacons*
FLAHERTY St John *Slaughter and May*
FONTAINE Patrick *Baker & McKenzie*
MACKINNON Robert *Shearman & Sterling*
O'CONNOR Patrick *Clifford Chance*
4
DEANE Simon *Deacons*
KOO Donald *Koo and Partners*
LEE Paul *Herbert Smith*
Individuals are listed alphabetically in each band.

Citicorp/Salomon Smith Barney. **Clients:** CSFB; HSBC; Chase Manhattan; Citicorp.

Freshfields Bruckhaus Deringer (4 ptrs, 10 asscs) Historically strong on securitisation, structured finance and aircraft finance, the group also has expertise in more mainstream banking work. **Nic Johnston** is a respected and popular all-round finance lawyer.

The team has acted for IFC on a number of matters, including its proposed establishment of a credit guarantee fund for enterprises in Sichuan, its purchase of an equity interest in the Bank of Shanghai, and a number of limited recourse financings for industrial projects. On the restructuring front, the firm represented Mitsui & Co on the debt restructuring of the Telecom Asia Group. **Clients:** Goldman Sachs; Morgan Stanley; Chase Manhattan; ING; Bank of America; Standard Chartered; ABN AMRO.

Johnson Stokes & Master (12 ptrs, 20 asscs) Although this Hong Kong player has a reputation for acting on behalf of lenders, it also boasts an enviable client list of local corporates. Renowned for its relationship with Hong Kong Bank, the firm is consequently seen on a number of leading restructuring deals. **Ian Chapman*** commands universal respect from clients and peers. He is *"extremely commercially aware, grasps the issues quickly"* and is said to know Hong Kong Bank *"better than it knows itself."* As well as doing a range of ongoing matters such as restructuring and specialised finance for HSBC, the practice acted for the foreign lead adviser to the Liquidation Committee of Guangdong International Trust and Investment Corporation and acted for the creditors in the restructuring of Thai Petrochemical. **Clients:** HSBC; Heng Seng; Bank of America; Fleet Bank; BNP Paribas; Credit Agricole Indosuez.

Deacons (8 ptrs, 9 asscs) Respected local group with a varied caseload including restructuring, insolvency and banking litigation. Asset finance work is another key element of the practice. **Mark Fairbairn**'s* strength lies in insolvency and workouts, while **Simon Deane*** has moved away from shipping finance, and is now considered to be an accomplished all-purpose finance lawyer. Advised the liquidators of the Peregrine Group on its local and regional asset disposal programmes, acted on a $155 million and HK $600 million vendor and bank financing for a local telecommunications company and acted for a bank syndicate in relation to a HK $400 million receivables financing of a major Hong Kong construction company. **Clients:** BNP Paribas Peregrine; shipping and aviation companies; Standard Chartered; American Express; Bank of Tokyo-Mitsubishi; Agricultural Bank of China; Kerry Properties; Sino Land; HKATL and MTRC.

Herbert Smith (2 ptrs, 7 asscs) Working hard to build its banking practice, the firm is acknowledged to have enjoyed success on behalf of a number of financial institutions, although relationships with leading investment banks continue to prove elusive. Structured finance and restructuring are cornerstones of the team's workload.

Jonathan Moult* is a *"no-nonsense lawyer"* and a respected business-getter. He is ably supported by *"sound technician"* **Paul Lee***. The firm has advised on structured finance transactions for Standard Chartered Bank and HSBC, and has acted on a number of local and regional restructurings, including several in Indonesia. **Clients:** ING; ABN AMRO; BNP; Agricultural Bank of China; ICBC; Standard Chartered Bank; Citic Ka Wah Bank.

Richards Butler (2 ptrs, 5 asscs) *"Aggressive"* group, said to offer competitive prices, and to have a particular reputation for asset finance advice. In addition to representing international banks, the firm has flourishing connections with local corporates, and advises them on a range of acquisition financings. **John McGuinness*** is a *"senior player"* with an outstanding name in asset finance. In 2000, the firm acted as Hong Kong legal adviser to the People's Government of Guangdong Province in the restructuring of the foreign debt of its wholly-owned conglomerate, Guangdong Enterprises (Holdings). Also acted for the companies in the HK$700 million debt restructuring of Easyknit International Holdings and Easy Concepts and Easy Concepts Group, and acted for Philippine Long Distance Telephone Company as major shareholder in the $810 million debt restructuring of Pilipino Telephone Corporation. **Clients:** Japanese, European and American banks.

Shearman & Sterling A newcomer to this year's rankings, the firm has perceptibly developed its relationships with major clients, and has been visible on a number of leading restructurings in Hong Kong over the past year. **Robert MacKinnon*** has a tremendous reputation in this area, and was described by one rival as *"a phenomenon."* Recent deals include acting for the Steering Committee of Foreign Bank Lenders to the Daewoo Group of companies with about $7 billion of foreign debt, acting for the Guandong Provincial Government as the beneficial owner of Guangdong Enterprises Group, the Hong Kong window company and Nam Yue Group in Macau in its corporate and financial restructure of $6 billion of debt, and advising the Steering Committee of Secured Creditors for the restructuring of TelecomAsia in Thailand involving approximately $2 billion in debt. **Clients:** Investment banks; creditors' committees.

Slaughter and May (5 ptrs, 22 asscs) Although generally to be found advising its blue-chip international corporate clientele rather than lenders, the firm's presence on a number of big-ticket acquisition finance deals makes its banking and finance group dangerous to ignore. *"Jack of all trades"* **St John Flaherty*** is a renowned figure in Hong Kong and popular with his clients. Acted for Chase Asia Equity Partners in the ASAT leveraged buy-out. **Clients:** ABN AMRO; BNP; DBS; Standard Chartered.

Koo and Partners (6 ptrs, 5 asscs) One of the best local practices, which maintains high visibility through its relationship with Bank of China. Syndicated loans are an area of niche expertise. **Donald Koo*** is the department's mastermind, and is said to combine *"technical ability with good business skills."* Highlight matters include acting for a syndicate of lenders on a HK$705 million term loan to a consortium for the development of a residential complex in Taipo. The firm also represented a loan syndicate on a HK$1.87 billion term loan to finance a toll road from Guangzhou to Pangyu. **Clients:** Bank of China; other local banks.

Simmons & Simmons (2 ptrs, 5 asscs) Generally acting for borrowers, and still establishing itself, the firm moved into the spotlight this year following its appointment to advise PCCW on its restructuring. Telecoms financing is a noted strength of the banking department. The firm advised on a $350 million convertible bond issue for New World Capital Finance guaranteed by New World Development Company. Restructuring work has included advising a consortium of Japanese and Singaporean investors on an 18 month restructuring of the Daido Group, and acting on the $2.5 billion purchase of the Dongshen Water Supply Project as part of the restructuring of Guangdong Enterprises and its subsidiaries. **Clients:** UBS Warburg; Crédit Lyonnais; LG Investment & Securities; Maquarie Equities (Asia).

H

Capital Markets

HONG KONG Leading firms (Capital Markets: Debt & Equity)	
1	Freshfields Bruckhaus Deringer
	Linklaters
	Sullivan & Cromwell
2	Allen & Overy
	Clifford Chance
	Shearman & Sterling
3	Davis Polk & Wardwell
4	Baker & McKenzie
	Herbert Smith
	Milbank, Tweed, Hadley & McCloy
	Simpson Thacher & Bartlett
	Skadden, Arps, Slate, Meagher & Flom LLP
	Woo, Kwan, Lee & Lo
5	Cleary, Gottlieb, Steen & Hamilton
	Cravath, Swaine & Moore
	Deacons
	Johnson Stokes & Master
	Richards Butler
	Simmons & Simmons
	Slaughter and May

Firms are listed alphabetically in each band.

Leading individuals (Capital Markets: Debt & Equity)		
1	**BERSANI Matthew** *Shearman & Sterling*	**CARMICHAEL Andrew** *Linklaters*
	DELAMATER Robert *Sullivan & Cromwell*	**KO Teresa** *Freshfields Bruckhaus Deringer*
2	**BAIRD Jim** *Clifford Chance*	**BARRON Bill** *Davis Polk & Wardwell*
	BRIEN Peter *Slaughter and May*	**HARDEE Ian** *Clifford Chance*
	JOHNSON Clayton *Cravath, Swaine & Moore*	**LAM Celia** *Linklaters*
	LEUNG Cheuk Yan *Baker & McKenzie*	**LIU Michael** *Allen & Overy*
	MALCOLM Andrew *Linklaters*	**PEDERSEN Jonathan** *Skadden, Arps, Slate*
	ROOT Anthony *Milbank, Tweed, Hadley*	**TANNER Douglas** *Milbank, Tweed, Hadley*
	YOUNG John *Sullivan & Cromwell*	
3	**DENNY Roger** *Clifford Chance*	**FLAHERTY St John** *Slaughter and May*
	LEE Angelina *Woo, Kwan, Lee & Lo*	**NEUVILLE David** *Baker & McKenzie*
	NICHOLSON Robin *Richards Butler*	**NORMAN David** *Richards Butler*
	SZE Beryl *Linklaters*	**TORTOISHELL Andrew** *Herbert Smith*

Individuals are listed alphabetically in each band.

Freshfields Bruckhaus Deringer (7 ptrs, 39 asscs) **Debt & Equity:** The highly visible practice is packed with strong lawyers and seen to dominate the IPO market. **Teresa Ko** is rated by interviewees as *"capable, experienced and hard-working,"* and she *"takes charge of the situation."* The team acted for China Telecom on a $1.65 billion equity offering and a $500 million debt offering with the US SEC and advised i-CABLE on the global offering of 360 million shares, a dual HKX, Nasdaq listing. It also acted for China Brilliance on its new issue (HKX) and international placing of shares.
Securitisation: Much of the firm's profile lies with **Clive Rough*** who has *"the ability to get the deal done."* The firm acted for SocGen on the securitisation of the US$ denominated Korean lease and loan receivables originated by Sogeko, acted for the HKMC on the arrangement of its mortgage backed securitisation programme and acted for Hong Kong bank on a securitisation via an issue of credit-linked notes as of part of its residential mortgage portfolio.
Derivatives: The team is focused on derivatives embedded in securitisation work where **Patrick Lines*** brings his expertise. Recent deals include a warrant program for Morgan Stanley listed on Cayman Stock Exchange and a synthetic securitisation for the HK branch of ABN AMRO, which involved a credit default swap in respect of a pool of residential mortgages held by ABN AMRO. **Clients:** China Telecom; leading international banks.

Linklaters (7 ptrs, 22 asscs) **Debt & Equity:** A long established practice considered technically excellent on the debt side and involved in the biggest deals. *"Reliable"* **Andrew Carmichael***, rated for his structured products work, is *"bright and thinks outside the box"* while **Andrew Malcolm*** is acknowledged as *"right up there."* Younger partners are also recommended with **Celia Lam***, *"competent and trusted by clients,"* and *"bright"* **Beryl Sze*** noted as leaders. The team represented the Hong Kong Mortgage Corp in the HK$500 million offering of bonds, advised Jardine Fleming as sponsor and underwriter in the HK$1.06 billion IPO of Pacific Century Insurance Holdings and represented HSBC Investment Bank in the HK$900 million global offer for Henderson Cyber.
Securitisation: This likeable, experienced team acted for American Express Bank on its $200 million consumer loan receivables securitisation and on the HK$630 million mortgage backed securitisation, which involved AMEX selling into the Hong Kong Mortgage Corporation securitisation vehicle.
Derivatives: Strong regulatory side where key player **Pauline Ashall*** is *"highly regarded"* and *"extremely experienced."* The team advised on the structuring and marketing of derivatives and other financial products including warrant issues. **Clients:** Leading international financial institutions.

Sullivan & Cromwell (3 ptrs, 12 asscs) A high profile US securities practice with a sterling image and technically skilled and commercial lawyers. **John Young*** is commended as *"versatile and confident"* while **Bob DeLaMater*** is *"the complete package,"*

*See leaders' profiles on pages 362-371

HONG KONG Leading firms (Capital Markets: Securitisation)
1 Clifford Chance
Freshfields Bruckhaus Deringer
2 Linklaters
3 Baker & McKenzie
Simmons & Simmons

Firms are listed alphabetically in each band.

Leading individuals (Capital Markets: Securitisation)
1 **KRUGER Paul** *Clifford Chance*
2 **CARMICHAEL Andrew** *Linklaters*
ROUGH Clive *Freshfields Bruckhaus Deringer*
3 **KONII Junri** *Baker & McKenzie*

Individuals are listed alphabetically in each band.

H

a solid lawyer with *"good judgement."* The team acted in a number of high-profile US IPOs by non-US issuers including the $81.2 million of common stock in Asiacontent.com, $274 million of ordinary shares in GigaMedia and $2.89 billion of ADRs in PetroChina. **Clients:** Sohu.com; SingTel; China Mobile; China Unicom.

Allen & Overy (5 ptrs, 19 asscs) **Debt & Equity:** Driven by *"technically good lawyers"* with a strong sense of direction, it is a key player in the market with a strong Korean focus. Head of department **Michael Liu*** *"really stands out."* The firm advised Deutsche Bank and HSBC (joint lead arrangers) on the €500 million guaranteed bond issue by Hutchison Whampoa and acted for ING Barings as lead arranger of the GEM listing of Timeless Software. A growing US team advised Nomura Securities Co on the US aspects of the Rule 144A equity offering by Benesse Corporation and is advising the Singapore Government on issuance of guaranteed notes by Finlayson Global Corporation.
Derivatives: Enjoying a steady deal flow as South East Asian counsel to ISDA, this quality team is promoted by the *"great reputation"* of its head, **Catherine Husted***, and the *"high activity levels"* of **Chin-Chong Liew***. The firm advised ISDA on their submissions to banks and regulatory authorities on matters affecting OTC Derivatives; advised foreign financial institutions in relation to their swap claims against GITIC; advised creditors in relation to OTC transactions including creditors of the Peregrine Group and advised on 200 listed derivative warrant transactions representing a large number of Hong Kong Exchange approved issuers. **Clients:** HSBC; Lehman Brothers; KBC Financial Products; BNP Paribas; Sociéte Géneralé; Morgan Stanley Dean Witter; Salomon Smith Barney; JP Morgan; Chase Manhattan; ING Barings; Deutsche Bank; Merrill Lynch; Sanwa International; UBS Warburg.

Clifford Chance (14 ptrs, 53 asscs) **Debt & Equital:** *Chambers'* researchers were told that the Rogers & Wells merger has assisted the team on a recent increase in US deals. Key players **Roger Denny*** and **Jim Baird*** maintain a high standing in the market, whilst **Ian Hardee*** has a good length of experience. The team acted for HSBC and Morgan Stanley Dean Witter in the Kowloon-Canton Railway Corporation $1.5 billion MTN programme and advised the LG Chemical $75 million Floating Rate Notes due 2002.
Securitisation: Noted as one of the big two, strong on commercial mortgage backed securitisation where " guru" **Paul Kruger*** is *"effective and gets the deals done."* The firm acted for SocGen on an issue of commercial mortgage backed securities by Commercial Plaza Securitisation Ltd (involving Hong Kong commercial properties owned by the Paliburg Group) and acted for Citicorp on an issue of asset backed securities by AEON Funding Corporation, involving credit card receivables originated by Aeon Funding Corporation.
Derivatives: Known for OTC derivatives, stock loans and recalls and collateral issues, **Jeremy Walter*** is *"well-established in the market."* The firm advised Soc Gen on the derivatives aspects of the Windsor House securitisation and advised Merrill Lynch on the derivatives aspects of the Harbour City Funding. **Clients:** Morgan Stanley; Merrill Lynch; Goldman Sachs.

Shearman & Sterling (3 ptrs, 15 asscs) Interviewees felt that this bullish practice has achieved great things in a short space of time. Mandarin speaker **Matthew Bersani*** is both *"pleasant to work with"* and effective in *"getting the deal done."* The firm represented PetroChina in its privatisation and represented Goldman Sachs on the $1 billion offering by Taiwan Semiconductor Manufacturing. Elsewhere in the telecoms sector the team represented Hutchinson Telecom in its $3 billion dollar convertible note program and China Mobile in its $7 billion public offering. **Clients:** Goldman Sachs; China Mobile; Merrill Lynch; PetroChina.

Davis Polk & Wardwell (4 ptrs, 14 asscs) Advising on the US aspects of transactions, the firm has a focus in Korea and acts for the underwriters on big-ticket Chinese deals. Key securities lawyer **Bill Barron*** has a *"careful and thorough"* approach. The firm represented Morgan Stanley and China International Capital Corporation in connection with China Unicom's dual HK, NYSE $5.7 billion IPO and the Sinopec $3.4 billion IPO. It represented Advanced Semiconductor Engineering and Industrial Credit and Investment Corporation of India in NYSE listings. **Clients:** Morgan Stanley; JP Morgan; DBS; ACER; ACE; Far Eastern; ICICI; Industrial Development Bank of India; Reliance Corporation; Bangkok Bank; Ayala Corporation.

Baker & McKenzie (10 ptrs, 24 asscs) **Debt & Equity:** Peers acknowledge that the firm runs a fine local operation combined with a steady flow of US work. The *"highly competent"* **Cheuk Yan Leung*** is rated for work in Hong Kong and China and **David Neuville*** is active on the US aspects of transactions. The team represented Goldman Sachs in the $2.9 billion privatisation and listing of PetroChina and represented ABN AMRO Rothschilds on the $355 million Beijing Capital International Airport listing. It also advised Shangdong International Power Development Co in its $290 million listing.
Securitisation: Much of the firm's presence in the structured finance market is based on the quality work of **Junri Konii***. Recent work has mostly been of a private nature with a focus on trade and consumer credit receivables both in Hong Kong and throughout the region. Represented a number of financial institutions looking to issue in Asian markets and represented an originator in relation to PRC hard currency receivables.
Derivatives: The practice is recommended for its strengh in Chinese derivatives products. **Andrew Lockhart*** is *"technically impressive and has been in Hong Kong a long time."* **Clients:** Goldman Sachs; ABN AMRO; Merrill Lynch; Crédit Lyonnais; Sino Land.

Herbert Smith (4 ptrs, 20 asscs) **Debt & Equity:** Active in both debt and equity transactions, where **Andrew Tortoishell*** is *"pleasant to work with."* The team advised BNP Prime Peregrine on the GEM flotation of techpacific.com and on the $60 million international HKX offering of China Insurance International Holdings.

It represented China Merchants Co in its $100 million synthetic exchangeable bond issue and advised BP Amoco in its acquisition of PetroChina Co as part of its IPO and dual listing.
Derivatives: Peers agree that the team has a good level of experience in acting for the Hong Kong Futures Exchange and has developed a fine exchange traded practice. **Clients:** YTL corporation Berhad and China Power International; China Travel Service Holdings Ltd; Hopewell Holdings; Okabe Ltd; Wah Kwong.

HONG KONG Leading firms (Capital Markets: Derivatives)
1 Allen & Overy
Clifford Chance
Linklaters
2 Baker & McKenzie
Freshfields Bruckhaus Deringer
Herbert Smith

Firms are listed alphabetically in each band.

Leading individuals (Capital Markets: Derivatives)
1 ASHALL Pauline *Linklaters*
WALTER Jeremy *Clifford Chance*
2 HUSTED Catherine *Allen & Overy*
LINES Patrick *Freshfields Bruckhaus Deringer*
3 LIEW Chin-Chong *Allen & Overy*
LOCKHART Andrew *Baker & McKenzie*

Individuals are listed alphabetically in each band.

Milbank, Tweed, Hadley & McCloy (4 ptrs, 9 asscs) A quality unit with a strong track record among US investment banks where the *"competent"* **Anthony Root*** is respected and **Doug Tanner*** exudes *"good judgement and experience."* The firm advised Kowloon-Canton Railway Corporation in its $1 billion offering of notes due 2010, advised Sunday Communications on the $300 million global offering and acted for Morgan Stanley Dean Witter in the $1.29 billion ADR IPO of United Microelectronics Corporation on the New York Stock Exchange. **Clients:** Morgan Stanley; CSFB; Salomon Brothers; Lehman Brothers; Merrill Lynch; Barings; KCRC; NTT; Globe Telecommunications; Bayantel; PLDT; Sunday Communications; Asia Pacific Resources Holdings; Pacific Internet.

Simpson Thacher & Bartlett (3 ptrs, 11 asscs) An important presence in the market which belies this relatively small team's size. The firm is rated for its advice to issuers and underwriters on US aspects of deals and is felt to score well in the technology and internet field. Its regional coverage includes particular strengths in Korea and Taiwan. Recent deals include the UMC ADR offering, Chunghwa Telecom's equity offerings, Yageo's asset acquisition from Philips Group and Asia Global Crossing's various joint venture investments. **Clients:** Multi-national corporates; leading financial institutions.

Skadden, Arps, Slate, Meagher & Flom LLP (4 ptrs, 15 asscs) The office serves as a base for the firm's activities throughout Asia, covering US-registered public offerings, Euro-offerings, Rule 144A and traditional US private and institutional placements. A team of *"fair and likeable"* lawyers is led by Head of Asian Operations **Jonathan Pedersen***. Often seen acting for issuers and underwriters, he is popular amongst fellow lawyers who describe him as *"able, reasonable and easy to work with."* **Clients:** Leading multi-national corporations.

Woo, Kwan, Lee & Lo (8 ptrs, 21 asscs) The most high profile local practice, it has a long track record in capital markets work, often acting for issuers. The seasoned team is led by **Angelina Lee***, a *"well-known figure-head"* in the market. It advised on the SUNeVision and Henderson Cyber IPOs with market capitalisation at listing of over HK$21 billion and HK$6 billion respectively and acted on the listing of H shares of Beijing Capital Airport. **Clients:** Issuers; underwriters.

Cleary, Gottlieb, Steen & Hamilton (3 ptrs, 7 asscs) A small active practice that also houses a strong Korean securities team. It represents Asian and non-Asian clients in international securities offerings and assists the firm's clients worldwide with investment and trade projects in Southeast Asia and China. **Clients:** Major Asian corporates; financial institutions in Korea, Thailand, the Philippines, Malaysia, Indonesia and China.

Cravath, Swaine & Moore Developing a fine team despite coming to the market relatively late, it has been involved in big-ticket transactions although interviewees believe its small size prevents it from enjoying a higher profile. Key player at the firm **Clayton Johnson*** is recognised as *"capable and strong."* **Clients:** Leading financial institutions.

Deacons (5 ptrs, 10 asscs) A traditional player in local securities work. Seen to score well in the hi-tech and communications sector, the team advised BNP Prime Peregrine in the GEM listing of high-profile technology companies (including iMerchants and AcrossAsia Multimedia), and acted for SUNDAY Communications in a $90 million pre-IPO convertible note issue and its $300 million dual listing on HKX and NASDAQ. It also advised on various local share and warrant placements including major fund raising for Pacific Century CyberWorks and TVB. **Clients:** HSBC Investment Bank Asia; Kerry Properties.

Johnson Stokes & Master (5 ptrs, 14 asscs) Active in capital markets, the team has been bolstered by the recruitment of partners from top UK firms. The team advised on the HK$70 million listing of Quality Food International and the HK$765.9 million listing of Shenyang Public Utility Holdings, and on the GEM listings of China Data Broadcasting Holdings and Fortune Tele.com Holdings. **Clients:** Local and international corporates; listed and private companies; financial institutions and other intermediaries.

Richards Butler (9 ptrs, 32 asscs) Peers admire this effective and efficient team, said to be a major player for issuers and investors in the mid tier market where **Robin Nicholson*** *"can solve problems"* and *"knows his way around the deals"* and **David Norman*** is *"capable and experienced."* The team acted as local counsel to the underwriters in the HK$876 million IPO by tom.com and acted for AcrossAsia Multimedia, the broadband network and internet technology company, on its GEM listing and regional IPR protection. It also advised the Stock Exchange of Hong Kong on the formation of the Growth Enterprise Market and on the applicable listing rules. **Clients:** ING Barings; BNP Paribas Peregrine; UBS Warburg; Vickers Ballas; Yuanta; Tai Fook.

Simmons & Simmons (6 ptrs, 18 asscs) A broad based practice, developing with the experience of some major deals. It advised the lead manager on a $350 million guaranteed convertible bond issue for New World Capital Finance and acted for Crédit Lyonnais Securities (Asia) and CSFB Securities on the $334 million global offering of SUNDAY Communications (HKX and Nasdaq listing).

Securitisation: An active player, the team advised KAMCO on its first international securitisation transaction of non-performing loans and is involved in the issuance of credit-linked asset-backed notes. **Clients:** UBS Warburg; Crédit Lyonnais; LG Investment & Securities; Macquarie Equities (Asia).

Slaughter and May (5 ptrs, 22 asscs) A strong team seen to act for both issuers and investment banks on top quality equity offerings. The knowledgeable **Peter Brien*** *"handles a deal practically and efficiently,"* while all-rounder **St John Flaherty*** is *"well trusted in the market."* The practice acted as Hong Kong counsel to Morgan Stanley and as underwriters on the $5 billion IPO of China Unicom, the second largest telecommunications provider in China, and acted for the underwriters for the IPO of Sinopec. It also advised Mass Transit Railway Corporation on its HK$ 9 billion privatisation share offer. **Clients:** Morgan Stanley; MTR Corporation; investment banks.

*See leaders' profiles on pages 362-371

H

Communications

HONG KONG Leading firms (Communications)
1 Baker & McKenzie
Bird & Bird
Paul, Weiss, Rifkind, Wharton & Garrison
2 Clifford Chance
Johnson Stokes & Master
Mallesons Stephen Jaques
Masons

Firms are listed alphabetically in each band.

Leading individuals (Communications)
1 CROOK Vivien *Bird & Bird*
REEDE Michael *Paul, Weiss, Rifkind, Wharton*
TAN Poh Lee *Baker & McKenzie*
2 CANHAM Janine *CMS Cameron McKenna*
CARNABUCI Connie *Mallesons Stephen Jaques*
LAIGHT Matthew *Bird & Bird*

Individuals are listed alphabetically in each band.

Baker & McKenzie (6 ptrs, 12 asscs) A strong telecoms practice, particularly on the M&A side, it is also acknowledged for regulatory ability in both telecoms and IT. Acting for large telecoms companies and IT clients, the firm serves as regional counsel for a number of US vendors. **Poh Lee Tan*** is the team's best-known name, comes from an M&A background and is *"highly respected in the market."*

The firm acted for Commerce One in negotiations with SUNeVision, Jardines, iCable, Beijing Enterprises, WI Harper, Swires and New World in setting up a B2B exchange. Other work includes advising Hutchison in joint venture negotiations with Priceline to set up a reverse auction portal for the Asia Pacific region, and advising Pacific Century Convergence on setting up its interactive broadband Now service. **Clients:** Hutchison; British Telecom; AT&T; Level 3 Communications; Commerce One; Pacific Century CyberWorks; Star TV/Newscorp; Cisco.

Bird & Bird (4 ptrs, 4 asscs) A specialised IT practice which has grown dramatically over the past two years. **Vivien Crook*** has an established name for her IT work, while **Matthew Laight*** has a reputation for his e-commerce work, and is described as *"trustworthy and pleasant."*

Paul, Weiss, Rifkind, Wharton & Garrison (4 ptrs, 18 asscs) A regional leader in telecoms, the firm has a huge team and a substantial reputation for telecoms projects. **Michael Reede***, who recently joined from niche Australian firm Gilbert & Tobin, is a respected telecoms practitioner. Represented Hutchison Telecommunications in the sale of 50% of Hutchison's fixed line telephone business and certain Hong Kong internet-related assets to Global Crossing. Also represented News Digital Ventures, a subsidiary of News Corporation, in connection with a large number of internet investments in India, and represented STAR TV in connection with with the formation of a joint venture with Cable & Wireless. Advised PCCW and tom.com on a range of communications and regulatory matters. **Clients:** America Online; Verizon (GTE); Cable & Wireless HKT; Hutchison Telecom; SITA; CCT Telecom; Motorola; CNK Telecom; MIH Asia; Metromedia; tom.com; Star Digitel; Asia Satellite; News Corporation.

Clifford Chance (4 ptrs, 4 asscs) Active in both IT and telecoms, the firm's principal reputation lies in financing and privatisation work. Acted for Telstra as joint venture partner in the $1.5 billion pooling of telecommunication assets of Telstra, Pacific Century Cyberworks and Cable & Wireless. Advised the Hong Kong Government in relation to a judicial review application instigated by Hong Kong Telecom on OFTA and advised America Online and China Internet Corp in relation to their cooperation in the provision of the AOL Internet service in Hong Kong. **Clients:** Telstra; America Online; China Internet Corp; NEC.

Johnson Stokes & Master (2 ptrs, 4 asscs) Seen as an *"innovative"* e-commerce-focused group, the firm is noted for a strong relationship with Hong Kong Bank. The firm also has a reputation for advising on domestic regulatory telecoms matters. Advised internet services and web development company Lemon-Asia in its bank financing and standard documentations and acted for DLJ Direct, an online securities business, in setting up its Hong Kong operations. Also acted for Li & Fung in the acquisition of B2B sourcing company Colby Group. **Clients:** Lemon (Asia); Hitari; debtdomain.com

Mallesons Stephen Jaques (4 ptrs, 3 asscs) Renowned for its relationship with Telstra, the team is considered to show *"distinct signs of promise for the future."* **Connie Carnabuci** has arrived from the firm's Sydney office with a reputation as a *"very useful technology lawyer."* The firm advised Telstra in relation to its proposed $3 billion alliance with Pacific Century Cyberworks and has acted for Microsoft on a range of e-commerce and IT consulting initiatives in the region. Also advised Et-china.com Holdings in relation to an on-line airline ticketing service. **Clients:** Airport Authority of Hong Kong; Telstra Corporation Limited; GE; Microsoft; Siemens.

Masons (1 ptr, 3 asscs) A practice which opened in 1997, with a focus on IT from a construction angle. Work over the past year has concentrated on project-oriented IT deals. The firm was instructed on the first major dot.com insolvency, involving a Chinese on-line book store, and has also advised on a number of M&A transactions. Acted for the Hong Kong & China Gas Company in relation to the IT law aspects of its launch of the iCare.com portal and for Dream Asia in relation to the IT systems contracts for the launch of a cosmetics superstore. Advised EDS (UK) in relation to the public inquiries into the opening of the new Hong Kong International Airport. **Clients:** EDS; Marconi; Hewlett-Packard; Hong Kong & China Gas Company; Microsoft; Dream Asia; CyberCity Holdings; Scott-Wilson.

Other Notable Practitioner **Janine Canham** of CMS Cameron McKenna is making a name for herself with her mixed IT and telecoms practice. Recent deals include advising on the disposal of a stake in a mobile telecommunications company in Pakistan, advising a satellite television equipment supplier on joint ventures and representing a leading internet portal on acquisition of rights for its use.

Corporate/M&A

HONG KONG Leading firms (Corporate/Mergers & Acquisitions)
1 Clifford Chance
Freshfields Bruckhaus Deringer
Linklaters
Richards Butler
2 Allen & Overy
3 Baker & McKenzie
Herbert Smith
Simmons & Simmons
Slaughter and May
4 Chao and Chung
Deacons
Johnson Stokes & Master
Woo, Kwan, Lee & Lo
5 Gallant YT Ho & Co
Iu, Lai & Li
Kwok & Yih
Stephenson Harwood & Lo
Victor Chu & Co

Firms are listed alphabetically in each band.

Leading individuals (Corporate/Mergers & Acquisitions)
1 **BAIRD Jim** *Clifford Chance*
KO Teresa *Freshfields Bruckhaus Deringer*
NICHOLSON Robin *Richards Butler*
NORMAN David *Richards Butler*
2 **DENNY Roger** *Clifford Chance*
FLAHERTY St John *Slaughter and May*
LEE Angelina *Woo, Kwan, Lee & Lo*
LEE Lawrence *Baker & McKenzie*
LIU Michael *Allen & Overy*
REES Nick *Linklaters*
3 **ALDER Ashley** *Herbert Smith*
CARMICHAEL Andrew *Linklaters*
CHAO Tien-yo *Chao and Chung*
CHEUNG Yuk Tong *Baker & McKenzie*
LEE Carmelo *Woo, Kwan, Lee & Lo*
LIE Sue *Linklaters*
NORRIS Nicholas *Simmons & Simmons*
THORNHILL Richard *Slaughter and May*
TORTOISHELL Andrew *Herbert Smith*
4 **CHUNG Julian** *Chao and Chung*
GALE John *Stephenson Harwood & Lo*
KWOK Larry *Kwok & Yih*
YIH Dieter *Kwok & Yih*

Individuals are listed alphabetically in each band.

Clifford Chance (12 ptrs, 38 asscs) An established name in the market, the firm is considered by its peers to provide *"experienced opposition,"* and to be growing in strength. The past year has seen the group involved on high-profile deals including the Tracker Fund, on which **Roger Denny*** has proved himself to be *"bright and extremely diligent."* **Jim Baird*** has been in Hong Kong for a long time and combines long-term experience in Hong Kong with a reputation for *"inspiring confidence in clients."* Advised Chase Manhattan and JP Morgan on the Hong Kong and China aspects of their recently announced merger and advised Chase Manhattan globally on its acquisition of Robert Fleming. Acted for New World Capital on a variety of acquisitions including its acquisition from First Group and advised Unilever in its acquisition of an ice-cream business from Watsons. **Clients:** Deutsche Bank; New World Capital.

Freshfields Bruckhaus Deringer (4 ptrs, 25 asscs) A *"truly international"* corporate practice with an *"aggressive"* approach and a presence on big-ticket transactions in most industries. Well-known personality **Teresa Ko*** continues to be the group's most high-profile lawyer, and has strong connections with Chinese business and a reputation for being *"good with clients."* The firm represented China Mobile on in its $6 billion acquisition of the mobile telephone networks of Fulian, Henan and Hainan provinces in the PRC, and acted for Jinro on its $170 million share sale and joint venture with Allied Domecq. Other significant matters include advising Hewlett-Packard on the Asian aspects of its global demerger and listing of its world-wide measurements business, and acting for Merrill Lynch on the Hong Kong Futures Exchange and Hong Kong Stock Exchange merger. **Clients:** NTT Mobile Telecommunication Networks; Merrill Lynch; Jinro; Hewlett-Packard; China Mobile.

Linklaters (4 ptrs, 15 asscs) A practice which boasts established corporate relationships and lawyers who *"conduct themselves with composure."* In addition to assisting foreign companies to acquire a stake in regional listed entities, the firm has advised on a number of internet/e-commerce listings, including hongkong.com and Sunevision. The team is noted for its relations with US investment banks.

Managing partner of the office, having recently arrived from Moscow, **Nick Rees*** is hugely respected, and possesses a style that is *"gentlemanly and friendly."* **Andrew Carmichael*** and **Sue Lie*** both retain a name for their regional corporate expertise. The firm advised Singapore Telecom on its bid for Hong Kong Telecom, and advised China Merchant on the sale of its controlling stake in Hong Kong Bank. **Clients:** China Merchant; Singapore Telecom; hongkong.com; SUNeVision.

Richards Butler (9 ptrs, 32 asscs) A rising force in Hong Kong, the group has a growing reputation as a highly efficient outfit, capable of discharging deals *"with high speed and high quality."* Sheer volume of transaction in a wide range of industries has pushed the team to the top of the lists. **Robin Nicholson***, who is *"bright, commercial and gets the deal done,"* and **David Norman***, an *"effective and experienced"* practitioner, are both held in high regard by peers and clients.

The firm represented First Pacific Company on its acquisition of further voting rights in Philippine Long Distance Telephone Company, and advised on the merger of Philippine Long Distance Telephone Company with SMART communications. Other matters have involved advising Hong Kong Telecom on its mooted acquisition by the Pacific Century Cyberworks Group, and acting for First Pacific Company in respect of is acquisition of a 40% interest in PT Indofood Sukses Makmur Tbk for $650 million. **Clients:** First Pacific; Hong Kong Telecom; Pacific Century Cyberworks; GDI; China Internet Global Alliance.

Allen & Overy (13 ptrs, 26 asscs) The corporate team has been involved in a substantial number of large transactions, particularly in its core financial areas, but is still felt to lack the regional profile of its leading rivals. Head of department **Michael Liu*** is *"a big name"* who successfully *"blends international and local knowledge."*

The firm advised Cable & Wireless on the $38.1 billion take-over bid by PCCW, and acted for the Department of Justice on the merger of the Stock Exchange, futures exchange and three clearing houses into HKEx, a deal valued at HK$4.1 billion. In other financial matters, the group advised Chase Manhattan on the sale of a wholly-owned subsidiary and its retail banking operations in Hong Kong for an aggregate consideration of $1.32 billion. **Clients:** Cable & Wireless; HK Exchanges and Clearing; Union Bank; Chase; CTI.

Baker & McKenzie (7 ptrs, 22 asscs) *"Savvy and competent"* group which has developed strong client relationships, and has its principal strength

*See leaders' profiles on pages 362-371

in the new economy. **Lawrence Lee*** is *"steady and wise,"* and is commended for his marketing and business development abilities. The more junior **Yuk Tong Cheung*** is said to be *"one smart lawyer."*

The firm advised the Walt Disney Company on the HK$20 billion project to build a theme park, and acted for Next Media on its reverse take-over of Paramount, worth HK$523 million. Other transactions include acting for the Bank of America in the $1.3 billion disposal to ABN Bank of retail banking businesses in Taiwan, India and Singapore and credit card businesses in Taiwan. **Clients:** Bank of America; Bear Stearns; British Telecom; Cheung Kong Holdings; Crédit Lyonnais; Disney; Goldman Sachs; Hutchison Whampoa; Merrill Lynch; Pacific Century Cyberworks; Warburg Pincus.

Herbert Smith (4 ptrs, 19 asscs) Said to be operating *"at a different level"* to the market leaders, the firm is nevertheless a regular feature on 'red-chip' listings and on regulatory and contentious matters. **Ashley Alder*** has a *"relaxed approach,"* and is *"technically and commercially sound,"* while **Andrew Tortoishell*** is both *"likeable and effective."* Recent deals include advising Wah Kwong on the offer by Oxaca for Wah Kwong; advising China Resources Enterprise Limited on the offer by its wholly-owned subsidiary for Ng Fung Hong Limited and advising e-Lux and Mr Yamada on the acquisition of a major stake in Mansion Holdings Limited, a company listed on the Hong Kong Stock Exchange for HIL $118 million. **Clients:** ABN AMRO; Arthur Anderson; Bank of China; BNP Paribas Peregrine; Deutsche Bank; Stagecoach Holdings; UBS Warburg.

Simmons & Simmons (4 ptrs, 18 asscs) The team is seen as an increasingly prominent force in Hong Kong, a view that was underscored by the firm's advice to PCCW on its high-profile $35.9 billion merger with Cable & Wireless HKT. This deal was led by **Nicholas Norris***, who with his *"calm and measured approach"* has created a favourable impression this year.

The group also advised on PCCW's proposed multi-billion dollar strategic alliance with Telstra Corporation, represented Next Media Group on the absorption of its internet and magazine publishing business into Paramount Publishing Group, and acted for Kin Wing Chinney (Investments) on its acquisition of Quality Healthcare Technologies and Services for $255 million by way of issue of new shares. **Clients:** PCCW; Next Media Group; New World Development; Crédit Lyonnais; China.com.

Slaughter and May (5 ptrs, 22 asscs) A profitable practice, renowned for its quality, which advises its established clientele on *"high-profile, complex"* transactions. Although it lacks the transactional volume of its rivals, it is a respected opponent on big-ticket matters, such as advising sponsors, retail managers and institutional managers on the listing of the Tracker Fund of Hong Kong.

Much of the high-profile work is done by **St John Flaherty***, *"a charming and constructive"* all-rounder. **Richard Thornhill*** combines his management responsibilities with transactional work on behalf of MTR Corporation, notably on its privatisation and global share offering. The firm acted for the underwriters on the global offering of shares in China Unicom, and advised the independent board of Cable & Wireless HKT on the merger with Pacific Century Cyberworks. **Clients:** Mass Transit Railway.

Chao and Chung (2 ptrs, 8 asscs) A boutique practice with experienced partners and *"the ability to produce good quality work."* The firm is said to have *"got out of the blocks nicely,"* and is said to have built up excellent contacts with Hong Kong corporates and banks. Leading individuals here are **Julian Chung***, who is particularly active in mainland China, and **Tien-yo Chao***.

The firm advised TCC International on its $200 million acquisition of a 10% shareholding in KG Telecom of Taiwan and the related $150 million share placement by TCC International. Also advised Hong Kong-listed Founder Holdings of Mainland China in its reverse take-over of another Hong Kong Listed company by way of the transfer of Founder's e-commerce businesses. **Clients:** TCC International; Founder Holdings.

Deacons (5 ptrs, 10 asscs) Undergoing a period of regrouping, following its severance from Graham & James, the firm is still seen as a player on medium-ticket domestic M&A, but has also had to come to terms with the decision of William Mackesy to become a part-time consultant. The group acted for Li & Fung on its HK$450 million purchase of assets from the trading division of Swire Pacific, and advised Nam Tai Electronics in its HK$255 million purchase of the JIC group from JIC Holdings. **Clients:** Li & Fung; Nam Tai Electronics.

Johnson Stokes & Master (5 ptrs, 14 asscs) A firm with a long local tradition and a loyal client base, which has successfully survived the dissolution of its relationship with UK firm Norton Rose. The corporate group is especially known for its work in the financial services sector. The respected Patricia Shih has become a consultant, and in consequence the team lacks a heavyweight individual, but the firm still appears on high-end M&A transactions. It acted for MLC on the HK$1.2 billion acquisition of a controlling interest in CEF Life, and advised Li & Fung on its HK$450 million purchase of assets from the trading division of Swire Pacific and its HK$2.2 billion acquisition of Colby Group Holdings. **Clients:** HSBC; The Swire Group; Li & Fung; BNP Prime Peregrine.

Woo, Kwan, Lee & Lo (8 ptrs, 21 asscs) Known for its high-class Hong Kong and Chinese clientele, the corporate team is considered to provide *"a broad-based offering."* **Angelina Lee*** is *"bright and highly regarded,"* while **Carmelo Lee*** is *"a pleasant and reasonable negotiator."* The firm advised Miramar Hotel on a general offer for its shares, and represented Hong Kong Holdings on its acquisition of interest in Shenzhen CyberCity. **Clients:** Miramar Hotel; Hong Kong Holdings.

Gallant YT Ho & Co (1 ptr, 2 asscs) A traditional Chinese practice doing traditional local business, which has worked hard to build up a reputation for M&A work and corporate finance. The team is acknowledged to have had particular success in advising PRC issuers. Represented the Hong Kong Special Administrative Regional Government on its negotiation with the Disney Group. **Clients:** Large local underwriters and corporates.

Iu, Lai & Li A *"well-connected"* practice with substantial local clients, which is perceived to have had an active year. The corporate team has a reputation for doing small-ticket deals in an *"economical and efficient manner."* Work over the past year includes takeovers and merger transactions involving listed companies, securities transactions, acquisition and disposal of private companies and joint ventures. **Clients:** Publicly listed companies; private companies; financial institutions.

Kwok & Yih One of the oldest Hong Kong firms is acknowledged to have important local ties. It *"markets aggressively,"* and *"does a more than adequate job of executing the deals."* **Larry Kwok*** is well-known in the market, while **Dieter Yih*** is *"very practical."* The firm represented Tricom on its HK$2.7 billion reverse take-over by the Pacific Century Group, advised Fung Cheung Kee Holdings on its HK$250 million take-over by a Taiwan-based conglomerate, and acted for Harbour Ring on its HK$1.1 billion take-over by Internet Capital Group and Hutchison Whampoa. **Clients:** Tricom; Harbour Ring; Quality Healthcare Asia; Golik Holdings.

Stephenson Harwood & Lo (6 ptrs, 13 asscs) Although seen comparatively infrequently, the corporate team is acknowledged to be *"competent and pleasant,"* and has a niche speciality in advising high-tech companies on corporate matters. **John Gale** is an *"experienced and senior"* name in Hong Kong. Recent transactions include acting for Regent Pacific Group in conection with its acquisition of an internet investment vehicle, and advising techpacific.com on its GEM listing. Also represented Cheung Wah Development in relation to a 61% investment by Softbank, a Japanese internet investor. **Clients:** China Light & Power; Regent Pacific Group; techpacific.com.

Victor Chu & Co (3 ptrs, 10 asscs) A niche practice with strong mainland China connections, which has had a lower profile in Hong Kong this year. Said to be an *"entrepreneurial"* group, the firm still maintains a respectable small-ticket transactional flow.

Project Finance

HONG KONG Leading firms (Project Finance)
1 Allen & Overy
Clifford Chance
Freshfields Bruckhaus Deringer
Linklaters
2 Shearman & Sterling
White & Case LLP
3 Baker & McKenzie
Slaughter and May
4 Paul, Weiss, Rifkind, Wharton & Garrison
5 CMS Cameron McKenna
Hunton & Williams
Johnson Stokes & Master
Latham & Watkins
Lovells

Firms are listed alphabetically in each band.

Leading individuals (Project Finance)
1 CLEARY Peter *Freshfields Bruckhaus Deringer*
CROZER George *White & Case LLP*
JENKINS Huw *Clifford Chance*
RAE SMITH Alan *Allen & Overy*
2 COHEN Evan *Clifford Chance*
EAST John *Clifford Chance*
FLAHERTY St John *Slaughter and May*
PLATT David *Shearman & Sterling*
TREACY Peter *Linklaters*
3 JOHNSTON Nic *Freshfields Bruckhaus Deringer*
LANGE John *Paul, Weiss, Rifkind, Wharton*

Individuals are listed alphabetically in each band.

Allen & Overy (3 ptrs, 13 asscs) Top quality, competitive practice whose *"well-schooled"* lawyers are active locally and regionally, and are particularly strong on the financing of water and power projects. **Alan Rae Smith*** has had a busy year, and was particularly impressive in acting for the seven arrangers of Asia Container Terminals' share of the Container 9 deal, where he was considered to be *"thorough, commercial and controlled."* The firm advised the lenders on the 250MW Neyveli lignite-fired power project in Tamil Nadu, India, represented Vivendi on its acquisition of the water treatment plants owned by Hyndai Petrochemical co in Daesan, South Korea, and acted for ADB on the financing of the 450MW gas-fired Meghnaghat Independent Power Project in Bangladesh. **Clients:** ADB; Vivendi; international financial institutions.

Clifford Chance (8 ptrs, 17 asscs) Top-tier firm with a number of high-profile lawyers and strength acting for both sponsors and lenders. The projects team benefits from the firm's regional presence, and has notable influence on transactions in China. **Huw Jenkins***, an *"impressive character,"* is the group's leading light, and has a long-established name for his work in China, Hong Kong and the Philippines. **John East***, as well as managing the office, still *"rolls his sleeves up"* on the more complex cases. **Evan Cohen***, who combines his practice with banking work, has a great reputation as a *"solid technician."*

The firm advised the arrangers of the PolyMirae deal, concerning the acquisition and operation of polypropylene manufacturing and related facilities in Korea. This involved both US$ and Korean Won financing tranches. Additionally, the team acted for the arranging banks of the HK$4 billion limited recourse financing of Hutchinson Telephone's mobile networks in Hong Kong, and represented the Hong Kong Government on establishing a Project Agreement, following which Kowloon-Canton Railway would construct West Rail. **Clients:** Citibank; HK China Light & Power; Chase Manhattan; Disney; SocGen; Mitsubishi; Anglian Water; Woodside Petroleum; HSBC.

Freshfields Bruckhaus Deringer (3 ptrs) A heavy hitting group, considered to be strong across the board, and *"an especially serious competitor"* on the sponsor side. The firm has a notable client base of financial institutions, government bodies and blue-chip corporate clients. **Peter Cleary*** has long-term Asia experience and the ability to *"win the confidence of his clients."* **Nic Johnston*** also enjoys high standing for his all-round finance practice.

The firm advised ADB on the limited recourse financing of the Manila North Tollway, and acted for ADB, JBIC and KfW on the limited recourse financing of the Ninoy Aquino International Airport Passenger Terminal Project. On the sponsor side, the team acted for Taiwan High Speed Rail Corporation on the $18 billion Taiwan High Speed Rail Project, and advised the DBE consortium on the development of a combined LNG receiving terminal, regasification facility and 1,800MW power plant at Ennore, Tamil Nadu, India. **Clients:** Taiwan High Speed Rail Consortium; ADB; JBIC; KfW.

Linklaters (3 ptrs, 9 asscs) A strong projects team, which acts for both lenders and sponsors. Despite the loss of the well-regarded David Platt, the firm has maintained a strong position in the market and a busy workload. **Peter Treacy*** has a fine track record acting for sponsors, and *"does a good job for his clients."* In Hong Kong, the firm advised the developers on the Container Terminal 9 project, and represented the lenders in connection with the Eastern Harbour Crossing refinancing and the restructuring of the Tates Cairn Tunnel financing. Regionally, the firm acted on telecommunications projects in India, the refurbishment of the North Luzon Expressway in the Philippines and a high-speed rail link in Korea. **Clients:** International banks and sponsors.

Shearman & Sterling (2 ptrs, 6 asscs) Considered to be the hottest US competitor, with capability on both the sponsor and financing side of transactions. A strong push in the local market has been highlighted by the arrival of **David Platt*** from Linklaters. He is seen as a *"fine catch,"* possesses solid Asia experience, and adds *"increased*

*See leaders' profiles on pages 362-371

depth and English law capability" to an already strong team. The past year has seen the firm active on major infrastructure projects in China and the Philippines, including acting for InterGen as a project sponsor in the development, construction and financing of the $755 million Meizhou Wan Power Project in Fujian Province, China. The firm also acted for the lenders on the San Lorenzo power project in the Philippines and for the borrower on the Ilijan Power Plant Project, also in the Philippines. **Clients:** InterGen; international banks and corporates.

H

White & Case LLP (4 ptrs, 20 asscs) Active throughout Asia, particularly in India and the Philippines, the firm's reputation for projects, notably power and infrastructure, remains secure. Senior lawyer **George Crozer*** has been in Hong Kong for a long time and is *"practical and a pleasure to deal with."* The firm represented the Indonesian government on the Paiton I project; the lenders on the Regco Rayong project; the lenders on the Pagbilao project and the Export Import Bank of Japan on the Cilacap IPP project in Indonesia. **Clients:** Export Import Bank of Japan; international corporates.

Baker & McKenzie (4 ptrs, 8 asscs) A respected team has retained its market position through a number of high-profile projects, notably in China, although it will miss the presence of Neil Donoghue, who has returned to the London office. Major deals include acting for BP Amoco on the $3 billion Jinshan petrochemical project, and acting for a major US theme park operator on the $275 million Hong Kong Disneyland project. In addition, the team advised Hong Kong International Terminals on the $1 billion Terminal 9 Hong Kong Container Port, and represented the European Investment Bank on the Chengdu BOT Water Project in China valued at $75 million. **Clients:** BP Amoco; HK Disneyland; EIB; HK International Terminals; Thai Airlines.

Slaughter and May (5 ptrs, 22 asscs) Although enjoying a wonderful reputation for project work, the firm tends only to be seen on specific big-ticket deals on behalf of its blue-blooded corporate clientele. The versatile **St John Flaherty*** has experience in major projects and retains the admiration of his peers for his *"technically sound"* advice. **Clients:** Large banks and corporates.

Paul, Weiss, Rifkind, Wharton & Garrison (4 ptrs, 7 asscs) The firm's projects team has a long-standing reputation in Hong Kong, and an outstanding record in telecoms projects. **John Lange*** is the firm's stand-out practitioner here. The firm enjoyed a major success with its advice to the Hong Kong government on the $725 million Hong Kong Disneyland project. Other deals included representing a consortium of lenders in connection with the $303 million Bontang LNG Reliability Enhancement (BLRE) project financing in relation to the Botang LNG plant in Indonesia; representing the Sumitomo corporation in connection with a project finance transaction for the construction and operation of two 2x 660 MW coal fired power plants in Indonesia and acting as counsel to the Electric Power Company in connection with various projects in China.

CMS Cameron McKenna (3 ptrs, 3 asscs) Although primarily known for its work on construction projects, the firm has also been active on both energy and airport work. Currently going through a period of reorganisation, with several recent departures and new arrivals, however the firm retains its strength in privatisation and regulatory work. Recently appointed for the second phase of the restructuring of the Thai electricity market. Also acted for the turnkey contractor Takanaka Corporation of Japan in the $350 million project financing of the new international passenger terminal project at Manila Airport and advised one of the bidders for the privatisation of Chennai Port in India. **Clients:** ADB; Asian energy commissions including the Energy Commission (Taiwan);Takanaka Corporation of Japan; major international port operator.

Hunton & Williams A small office, renowned for advising on power projects, which is active on behalf of developers and governments, and enjoys an especially strong profile in Thailand and Taiwan.

Johnson Stokes & Master (2 ptrs, 3 asscs) *"Technically adept"* firm, primarily active on local projects. A strong real estate practice and good Chinese connections has led to increased activity on behalf of sponsors. Represented the Hong Kong Government in the negotiation of arrangements for the development of the Cyberport projects in Hong Kong and represented AsiaSat in the $250 million financing of AsiaSat 4. Has been active in the power industry including acting in conjunction with K&M Engineering on The World Bank sponsored 700 MW Phu My 2.2 power facility in Vietnam and acting for Electricity of Vietnam in the negotiation of power purchase agreement relating to the 715 MW Phu My 3 power project. **Clients:** Wartsila NSD Corporation; CLP Power International Limited; Asia Satellite Telecommunications Co Ltd; K&M Engineering & Consulting Corporation; Electricity of Vietnam; Government of Vietnam; Government of Hong Kong; HSBC Investment Bank Asia Ltd; Hong Kong Electric International Ltd.

Latham & Watkins (2 ptrs, 5 asscs) The firm is enjoying an increasingly good reputation for work on behalf of both lenders and sponsors throughout the region. It represented Chase Manhattan Asia and Industrial Bank of Japan, the lead co-ordinating banks to the $2.56 billion financing for the 1230 MW Paiton coal-fired power plant to be built in Java, Indonesia. Also advised ADB, Bank of America, Paribas, CSFB and The Tokai Bank in connection with the negotiating and financing of 2 x 362 MW Meizhou Wan coal-fired power plant in Fujian Province. **Clients:** ABN Amro; Bear Stearns; Chase Manhattan Bank; Citibank; McDermott; Merck & Co; Morgan Guaranty Trust Company of New York; Salomon Smith Barney.

Lovells (2 ptrs, 4 asscs) A strong corporate base has given the firm muscle on the sponsor side of regional projects, notably in construction and infrastructure. The firm has advised sponsors of a Philippines toll road, a Turkish bridge project, power projects in the US and Australia, and a nickel mine and refinery in the Philippines. Construction-related work includes acting on behalf of Pacific Energy in connection with the acquisition of Kvaerner plc's infrastructure and project assets, and acting for the Airport Authority of Hong Kong on all construction disputes on the new airport. **Clients:** Pacific Energy; Airport Authority of Hong Kong.

Shipping

HONG KONG Leading firms (Shipping)
1 Clyde & Co
Holman Fenwick & Willan
Ince & Co
2 Richards Butler
3 DLA
Johnson Stokes & Master
Sinclair Roche & Temperley
4 Deacons
Healey & Baillie LLP

Firms are listed alphabetically in each band.

Leading individuals (Shipping)
1 **BEESLEY Clive** *Ince & Co*
HATZER Paul *Holman Fenwick & Willan*
HEATH Martin *Clyde & Co*
LATHAM Simon *Ince & Co*
REES SMITH Peter *Holman Fenwick & Willan*
SHELFORD Peter *Clyde & Co*
2 **CRESSWELL Corinna** *Clyde & Co*
HOWSE Chris *Richards Butler*
3 **BENNETT Jeremy** *Johnson Stokes & Master*
DILLON John *Holman Fenwick & Willan*
MALLARD Nicholas *DLA*
THOMSON Mary *Koo and Partners*
ZINKE Jon *Keesal, Young & Logan LLP*
4 **COOGANS David** *Richards Butler*
CUTLER Andrew *Holman Fenwick & Willan*
DARTON Robin *Deacons*
MO Philip *Holman Fenwick & Willan*
POTTS Chris *Crump & Co*
ROSTRON Jonathan *Sinclair Roche & Temperley*

Individuals are listed alphabetically in each band.

Clyde & Co (7 ptrs, 10 asscs) Although involved in some owner work, this market leader's reputation lies principally in cargo work, where it is perceived to have *"a stranglehold."* Elder statesman **Martin Heath*** is a *"pleasant and knowledgeable"* lawyer with excellent regional contacts, while **Peter Shelford***, *"one of the more experienced lawyers in Hong Kong,"* has an enviable clientele of owners. He is also noted for his expertise in the Korean market and his advice on international trade. **Corinna Cresswell*** draws praise for being *"a sensible negotiator."* The firm advised NYK on the 'OOCL AMERICA' case, involving damage to over 500 containers while on a voyage from the USA to the Far East, and represented Lloyd's underwriters in a piracy case, 'TENYU,' involving the shipment of aluminium ingots from Indonesia to Korea. **Clients:** Glencore Singapore; Thomas R Miller; NYK; Lloyd's underwriters.

Holman Fenwick & Willan (10 ptrs, 15 asscs) Versatile group, where a solid wet practice has been augmented by successful work on behalf of owners and P&I clubs. The firm is considered to contain *"good technicians who are not afraid of fighting a case to the very end."* Senior partner **Peter Rees Smith*** is a lawyer boasting *"a big name and a long-term reputation,"* and **Paul Hatzer*** continues to be recognised as one of the most influential figures in Hong Kong. *"Brains, energy, hard work and an aggressive litigation style"* have earned **Andrew Cutler*** the respect of his peers for dry work, while **Philip Mo*** is *"a well-connected and popular client man."* The arrival of **John Dillon*** from Ince & Co, *"well-respected on the wet side"*, enhances the shipping team considerably.

Admiralty work includes regular instructions from P&I Clubs, hull underwriters and shipowners on collision, salvage, total loss, groundings, wreck removal and oil pollution matters. Dry work includes acting for P&I Clubs, major shipping companies and large container lines in matters including cargo claims, bills of lading and charterparty disputes and various related contractual disputes. Finance work has included ship sale and purchase, ship finance and P&I compliance issues. **Clients:** P&I clubs; hull underwriters; owners in Hong Kong, South Korea, Japan, Taiwan and China.

Ince & Co (4 ptrs, 18 asscs) *"Practical and commercial"* firm, which is said to *"combine legal aptitude with an attractive, co-operative culture."* Clearly at the top for collision and salvage advice, the team also has respected dry capability. *"Straight-talking individual"* **Clive Beesley*** is the firm's heavyweight on the wet side, while **Simon Latham*** is a senior player who represents owners, charterers and P&I Clubs, and is *"succinct and pragmatic."*

During the past year, the firm has advised on large-scale cargo claims and cargo losses, as well as delivery disputes, bills of lading and trading disputes arising from the steel, grain and copper industries. **Clients:** Owners; P&I club; insurers; charterers; trading companies; commodity traders.

Richards Butler (5 ptrs, 15 asscs) A strong team, snapping at the heels of the 'big three,' which has both wet and dry capability, and a focus on contentious maritime and international trade matters. Typically, the firm advises P&I clubs, owners, charterers and insurers. **Chris Howse***, who has been in Hong Kong for 20 years, is increasingly seen in a managerial role, but also remains transactionally active. The wet practice has benefited from the return of the *"bright and energetic"* **David Coogans***.

The firm advised on the 'TIAN SHENG 8' case and acted for the owners of the cruise ship 'WORLD DISCOVERER,' following a running aground in the Solomon Islands. Also represented the owners and underwriters of the 'HANDY HUMANITY,' following a collision with the 'NEW ARGOSY,' and advised the cargo insurers and owners in a loss and damage case involving the 'OOCL AMERICA.' **Clients:** P&I clubs; cargo interests; owners/charterers.

DLA (3 ptrs, 7 asscs) Still perceived to be building up its Hong Kong shipping practice, the firm is principally known for its dry and transport club work. **Nicholas Mallard*** is a *"lawyer of the old school,"* renowned for bringing in clients and being *"a real fighter"* for their interests. Over the past year, the firm has acted on a broad range of club work, insurance advice and casualty cases, and advised on a marine construction arbitration in Brunei. **Clients:** P&I clubs; owners; insurers; underwriters; insurance brokers; banks.

Johnson Stokes & Master (3 ptrs, 6 asscs) Local firm which is best known for its shipping finance advice, where it is considered to be *"streets ahead"* of its rivals. Its clients include a series of blue-chip financial institutions. Other elements of the caseload include wet work, arrest cases and mortgage enforcement matters. **Jeremy Bennett*** has notable experience of arrest cases and is held in high regard for his *"good technical skills."* Represented a number of leading ship finance banks in several repossession and ship mortgage enforcement proceedings to recover outstanding loans, together with related handling of bunker, crew and charterer claims. Represented the owners and insurers of the vessel 'Brij' in the successful defence of proceedings brought by cargo interests alleging mis-delivery of cargo, and advised a Greek commodity trading firm in relation to a $17 million dispute with PRC buyers and various banks following non-payment for a number of liquid petroleum gas cargoes. **Clients:** Banks; owners; insurers; P&I clubs; commodity trading firms.

*See leaders' profiles on pages 362-371

Sinclair Roche & Temperley (4 ptrs, 9 asscs) Although smaller than the market leaders, the firm retains high status in the local market, and is considered to have broadened its shipping practice successfully. **Jonathan Rostron*** is an *"energetic and able lawyer"* with a predominantly dry practice, who is popular with clients due to his willingness to *"go the extra mile."* A fluent German speaker, he has been instrumental in the firm's work on behalf of owners, charterers and container line operators in Hamburg and Bremen. The group's recent workload has included cases for Nordiske and other Scandinavian P&I clubs, acting for Korean and mainland Chinese charterers, cargo smuggling and explosion advice, and commodities work for a large US trading house. **Clients:** P&I clubs; owners; underwriters.

H

Deacons (3 ptrs, 3 asscs) A Hong Kong institution with a long history, best known for cargo recovery work and shipping finance advice. The versatile **Robin Darton*** is a shipping generalist described as a *"strong technician."* The firm advises leading Indian traders and is increasingly involved in international trade commodities work. Finance work has included loan documentation for two syndicates led by Credit Agricole Indosuez, increasing to $248 million the 16 car carrier financing for the CIDO Group of Japan. In addition, the group has acted on mis-delivery claims worth tens of millions of dollars. **Clients:** Recovery agents; Hong Kong and Japanese banks; owners.

Healy & Baillie LLP (3 ptrs, 4 asscs) A branch of the US firm which has had a degree of success acting in multi-jurisdictional matters. The practice has wet capacity and recently acted in some collision cases, but the majority of work is dry and includes bill of lading and charter-party disputes and finance work including sale of ships and mortgage enforcement matters. Has also acted for insurance companies and P&I Clubs. The three partners cover four jurisdictions between them being variously qualified in Hong Kong, UK, China and New York. **Clients:** P&I Clubs; shipowners; commercial companies.

Other Notable Practitioners **Chris Potts*** of Crump & Co is an *"experienced China hand"* and a *"thoroughly good lawyer."* He has a broad practice, but primarily concentrates on contentious work including collisions, loss and damage and cargo claims, in which he represents both claimants and defendants. Newly arrived at Koo and Partners is **Mary Thomson***, commended as *"a tenacious litigator."* She recently represented the owner in the 'Tian Sheng No.8' case, a dispute over entitlement to arrest. With 15 years of experience in Asia, **Jon Zinke*** of Keesal, Young & Logan is the lawyer that clients turn to for specialised advice on the US aspects of transactions.

Leaders' profiles – Hong Kong

ALDER, Ashley
Herbert Smith, Hong Kong +852 2845 6639
ashley.alder@herbertsmith.com
Recommended in Corporate/M&A
Specialisation: Partner in Corporate Department. Main area of work is corporate law, concentrating on public and private mergers and acquisitions, management buy-outs, investment funds, IPOs, and regulatory/compliance work. Clients include leading investment banks and corporates as well as a range of private equity, venture capital and investment vehicles. Recent work includes IPO of China National Aviation Company, the acquisition by Stagecoach Holdings of Citybus (a leading bus operator in Hong Kong and China), the acquisition of the Asia-wide distribution operations in Inchcape, acting for the Hong Kong Futures Exchange in its merger with the Hong Kong Stock Exchange and the IPO of China Reinsurance International Holdings Ltd.
Prof. Memberships: Law Society. Law Society of Hong Kong.
Career: Qualified with *Herbert Smith* in 1986. Moved to the firm's Hong Kong office in 1990, becoming a partner in 1994. Member, working party, Hong Kong Government Company Law Review project (1997). Consultant to the Hong Kong Securities Institute.
Personal: Born 30 June 1959. LLB (London) 1982. LLM (Cambridge) 1993. Elected the Title Scholar, Downing College, Cambridge, 1994. Leisure interests include flying, riding, outdoor activities. Married (Dr Lucy Lord), two children, eight years and two years.

ASHALL, Pauline
Linklaters (a member firm of Linklaters & Alliance), Hong Kong +852 2842 4888
pauline.ashall@linklaters.com
Recommended in Capital Markets: Derivatives
Specialisation: Partner in Financial Markets Group, which provides a focus for specialised services to clients in the financial markets industry. Involved in the development of the current regulatory framework in the United Kingdom at the time the Financial Services Act was enacted in 1986 and worked on the implementation of the Investment Services Directive throughout the EU. Expertise includes optimal structuring of financial markets businesses with regard to legal, regulatory and taxation constraints, structuring and marketing of derivatives, stocklending, repo, global custody and fund management products and services, corporate and commercial transactions for financial markets participants including joint ventures and acquisitions, advising on regulations, exchange rules and industry standard documentation, including for derivatives and collateral management, advice and support on customer and counterparty disputes, regulatory investigations and disciplinary proceedings.
Career: Located in Hong Kong since 1996.

BAIRD, Jim
Clifford Chance, Hong Kong +852 2825 3488
jim.baird@cliffordchance.com
Recommended in Capital Markets: Debt & Equity, Corporate/M&A
Specialisation: Senior partner in the Corporate Securities and Financial Markets Group based in Hong Kong. With over 20 years experience in corporate and securities law in the United Kingdom, Hong Kong and the PRC. Advising merchant banks and companies on IPOs on the Hong Kong and PRC stock exchanges, as well as in-depth experience of mergers and acquisitions, takeovers and debt and equity investment transactions.
Career: Admitted Scotland 1981, England and Wales 1988, Hong Kong 1990, became partner in 1989.

BARRON, Bill
Davis Polk & Wardwell, Hong Kong
+852 2533 3300
Recommended in Capital Markets: Debt & Equity

BEESLEY, Clive
Ince & Co, Hong Kong +852 2877 3221
clive.beesley@ince.com.hk
Recommended in Shipping
Specialisation: Specialises in the investigation and conduct of marine casualty cases of a varied nature.
Career: Joined *Ince & Co.*, Hong Kong, in 1991, and is one of the Hong Kong Emergency Response team members. Has wide-ranging experience in resolving casualty related disputes.
Personal: Hong Kong resident since 1984.

BENNETT, Jeremy
Johnson Stokes & Master, Hong Kong
+852 2843 2211
Recommended in Shipping

BERSANI, Matthew D.
Shearman & Sterling, Hong Kong +852 2978 8000
mbersani@shearman.com
Recommended in Capital Markets: Debt & Equity
Specialisation: Partner in *Shearman & Sterling's* Hong Kong office. Specialises in corporate finance and securities transactions. Typical matters handled include: advising PetroChina and China Mobile on their recent offerings, advising the Hong Kong Government on the establishment of the Tracker Fund, advising the Siam Commercial Bank in a $1.5 billion recapitalisation and Rule 144A/Regulation S offering; and advising Korea Thrunet, a Korean internet company, on a US IPO.
Prof. Memberships: Admitted to the Bar of the State of New York.
Career: Qualified in 1988. Practised with *Paul, Weiss* from 1988 to 1994. Joined *Shearman & Sterling* in 1994, becoming a Partner in 1997. Featured speaker at many conferences addressing the issue of access to U.S. capital markets by Asian issuers.
Personal: Born in 1958. Obtained an undergraduate degree (BA) from Princeton University in 1982 and has law degree (JD) from Columbia University 1988. Fluent reader and speaker of Mandarin Chinese.

BRIEN, Peter
Slaughter and May, Hong Kong +852 2521 0551
peter.brien@slaughterandmay.com
Recommended in Capital Markets: Debt & Equity
Specialisation: Capital markets, corporate finance, M&A, and general corporate.
Career: King's College School, Wimbledon; University of Birmingham (LLB); qualified 1987, partner at *Slaughter and May* in 1995.

CANHAM, Janine
CMS Cameron McKenna, Hong Kong
+852 2846 9100
Recommended in Communications

CARMICHAEL, Andrew
Linklaters (a member firm of Linklaters & Alliance), Hong Kong +852 2842 4888
andrew.carmichael@linklaters.com
Recommended in Capital Markets: Debt & Equity, Capital Markets: Securitisation, Corporate/M&A
Specialisation: Head of the International Finance Department, based in Hong Kong since 1996. Specialist with over 15 years' experience in international securities issues. Typical matters include repackagings, structured financings, convertible bonds by Asian companies, medium term notes, derivatives warrants, volume eurobonds and property finance transactions.

CARNABUCI, Connie
Mallesons Stephen Jaques, Hong Kong
+852 2848 4600
connie.carnabuci@msj.com.au
Recommended in Communications
Specialisation: Australian Partner in the Technology Communications and Intellectual Property group of *Mallesons Stephen Jaques.* As of January 2000, practises out of the firm's Hong Kong office specialising in the intellectual property and information technology aspects of corporate deals involving mergers, acquisitions, strategic alliances and joint ventures. Also undertakes specialist commercial work in the area of information technology outsourcing, electronic commerce and Internet. Has worked with *Mallesons Stephen Jaques* in the United States (New York) and is now resident in Hong Kong. Major transactions 2000: acting in relation to the strategic alliance Telstra Corporation and Pacific Century Cyberworks in respect of the formation of 2 pan-Asian joint ventures for the delivery of international voice and data services and mobile telephony services respectively; advising a Hong Kong company, Et-China.com Holdings Limited, in relation to the formation of a JV with a PRC company to establish and operate a travel website in China; advising a Hong Kong company, iSwitch HK Limited, in relation to the provision of an e-commerce transaction platform for the distribution of content to a variety of terminal types including PDA, mobile phone and desktop computers; advising Palm in relation to content arrangements for the web clipping application and the establishment of the Palm mobile Internet kit; advising GE ECXpress (HK) Limited in relation to the establishment of various B2B e-commerce platforms for use as trading exchanges.
Prof. Memberships: New South Wales Society for Computers and The Law, Past President; Copyright Society, Member; Intellectual Property Society of Australia and New Zealand, Member; International Bar Association, Member; Information Technology (Committee Representative); Computer Law Association, Member.
Career: 1986: Bachelor of Commerce (Marketing) (Merit) and Laws degrees, UNSW; 1987: Associate to the Honourable Justice Wilcox, Federal Court of Australia; 1988-1993: Solicitor, *Mallesons Stephen Jaques*, Sydney; 1994-1995: Senior Associate, *Mallesons Stephen Jaques*, New York; 1995-1997: Senior Associate, *Mallesons Stephen Jaques*, Sydney; 1997-1999: Partner *Mallesons Stephen Jaques*, Sydney; 2000 to date: Foreign Legal Consultant, *Mallesons Stephen Jaques*, Hong Kong.

CHAO, Tien-yo
Chao and Chung, Hong Kong +852 2820 7555
Recommended in Corporate/M&A

CHAPMAN, Ian
Johnson Stokes & Master, Hong Kong
+852 2843 2211
Recommended in Banking & Finance

CHEUNG, Yuk Tong
Baker & McKenzie, Hong Kong +852 2846 1916
yt.cheung@bakernet.com
Recommended in Corporate/M&A
Specialisation: Main area of work is corporate finance, principally mergers and acquisitions, fund raisings and other corporate transactions by listed companies. Major M&A transactions handled recently: acted for Paramount Publishing in its reverse takeover by the Next Media Group; acted for Citybus in its takeover by Stagecoach; acted for Core Pacific Securities in its acquisition of Yamaichi's securities business in Hong Kong; handled the very substantial group restructuring among Cheung Kong, Hutchison, Cheung Kong Infrastructure and Hongkong Electric. Handled major international share offerings and listings on Hong Kong, New York and PRC stock exchanges: China National Aviation Company, Cheung Kong Infrastructure, Huaneng Power International, and Tsingtao Brewery.
Prof. Memberships: Hong Kong Law Society; Law Society of England and Wales; New York State Bar.
Career: Joined *Baker & McKenzie* in 1982. From 1985 to 1986, worked in Beijing and Shanghai and from 1986 to 1988 in the Chicago office of *Baker & McKenzie.* Currently head of the Commercial & Securities Group in *Baker & McKenzie's* Hong Kong office.
Personal: LLB (1980) and PCLL (1981) from the University of Hong Kong and LLM (1982) from the London School of Economics. Hobbies include golf, reading and music. Married with two children.

CHRISTOPHER, Steven
Linklaters (a member firm of Linklaters & Alliance), Hong Kong +852 2842 4888
steven.christopher@linklaters.com
Recommended in Banking & Finance
Specialisation: Partner and Head of the Banking Department in Hong Kong. Specialises in transactional financings and general banking but has also focused for several years on insolvencies and restructurings. In the Hong Kong office since 1991. In Asia, has developed a broad debt financing practice. Expertise includes Asian and Australasian structured and project financings, secured and unsecured syndicated lending, MTN and other straight and structured capital markets issues. Also covers asset backed and lease financings, L/C backed issues and trade financing. Particular experience in telecoms financing and restructurings. Closely involved in the HK dollar capital market and advises on CD transactions and local banking supervision issues. Recent experience includes Japan Leasing (HK) (acting for the liquidator); Thai Petrochemical Industries (Thai debt restructuring); Celcom/TRI (Malaysian telecoms debt restructuring); Piltel (Philippine telecoms debt restructuring); Paliburg/Century City (Hong Kong debt restructuring); HK Airport financings.
Prof. Memberships: Committee member of Hong Kong Capital Markets Association.

CHUNG, Julian
Chao and Chung, Hong Kong +852 2820 7555
Recommended in Corporate/M&A

CLEARY, Peter
Freshfields Bruckhaus Deringer, Hong Kong
+852 2846 3400
peter.cleary@freshfields.com
Recommended in Project Finance
Specialisation: Specialises in project finance and infrastructure.

COHEN, Evan
Clifford Chance, Hong Kong +852 2825 8888
Recommended in Project Finance

COOGANS, David
Richards Butler, Hong Kong +852 2810 8008
davidcoogans@richardsbutler.com.hk
Recommended in Shipping
Specialisation: Practice covers a wide range of maritime and international trade disputes including

H

collision cases, charterparty and bill of lading disputes. Acts predominantly for shipowners and their insurers.
Prof. Memberships: Law Societies of Hong Kong, England & Wales and New South Wales.
Career: Deck apprentice Cunard Steamship Company, 1977-1980; British Second Officer's Licence 1980; BA hons law 1984; qualified in England & Wales 1987, Hong Kong 1989, ACT 1990, NSW and Victoria 1997. Articles *Sinclair, Roche & Temperley* 1985-1987 joined *Richards Butler*, Hong Kong 1989, Partner 1994.
Personal: Born Glasgow 1960. Leisure interests include golf, running and scuba diving. Lives in Hong Kong.

H

CRESSWELL, Corinna
Clyde & Co, Hong Kong +852 2878 8600
Corinna.Cresswell@clyde.com.hk
Recommended in Shipping
Specialisation: Insurance and maritime litigation and arbitration with particular emphasis on cargo recoveries, charterparty disputes and policy claims, international trade and bunkering disputes, writes and lectures extensively in these areas.
Prof. Memberships: Law Society (Hong Kong and England and Wales), Council Member, International Bunker Industry Association.
Career: Qualified as a solicitor in England and Wales in 1978 and joined *Clyde & Co* in 1980, becoming a partner in 1984. Admitted to practise in Hong Kong in 1991. Based in Hong Kong from 1991 to 1995, returning to Hong Kong from England once again in 1999.
Personal: BA (Honours), Cambridge University England.

CROOK, Vivien
Bird & Bird, Hong Kong +852 2248 6000
vivien.crook@twobirds.com
Recommended in Communications
Specialisation: Consultant for *Bird & Bird* in Hong Kong. Specialises in information technology, digital media and e-commerce. Main areas of work include media and entertainment, sport and information technology. Has worked for numerous telecommunications clients primarily in respect of outsourcing projects.
Prof. Memberships: Hong Kong Information Technology Management Association: Hong Kong Telecoms User Group: Hong Kong Chamber of Commerce.
Publications: Has written articles for 'Asian Lawyer', 'Asian Commercial Law Review' and 'Banker's Journal Malaysia'.
Career: Qualified in UK in 1990. Worked for *Baker & McKenzie* 1990-1991. Joined *Bird & Bird* in 1991, becoming a partner in 1995.
Personal: Born 1966. Studied at Sheffield University (1987 LLB First Class Hons), resides Hong Kong.

CROZER, George K.
White & Case Solicitors, Hong Kong
+852 2822 8700
gcrozer@whitecase.com
Recommended in Project Finance, Project Finance: China Foreign
Specialisation: Executive Partner of *White & Case's* Hong Kong office and is responsible for the firm's overall activity in Asia. Has over 30 years' experience in corporate finance, project and related financings, mergers and acquisitions and joint ventures. Has worked on greenfield LNG projects and electric power projects in Indonesia, oil and gas and telecoms projects in the Philippines, an IPP project in Thailand and a proposed major refinery and petrochemical plant joint venture in China. In the area of M&A, was involved in the purchase by GE Capital of a substantial interest in the finance subsidiary of PT Astra International and the Bakrie Group's purchase of a substantial minority interest in PT Freeport Indonesia. Also has experience of securities offerings such as when advised the Electricity Generating Authority of Thailand on its inaugural global bond offering in 1998 and the Kingdom of Thailand on a series of yankee bond and MTN offerings.
Career: Admitted to the New York State Bar in 1969 and as a Solicitor of the High Court of the Hong Kong Special Administrative Region in 1997.
Personal: US citizen. Graduated from Princeton University in 1965 and Michigan Law School in 1968.

CUTLER, Andrew
Holman Fenwick & Willan, Hong Kong
+852 2522 3006
Andrew.Cutler@hfw.com.hk
Recommended in Shipping
Specialisation: International shipping litigation and arbitration (Hong Kong, England & Wales, PRC, including CIETAC), in particular charterparty disputes, bills of lading claims and related insurance claims. Recent cases include acting for two major container lines following a casualty resulting in 500(+) containers being lost/damaged; acting for owners/their P&I Club on the total loss of a cargo of frozen fish.
Prof. Memberships: Law Society of England and Wales. Law Society of Hong Kong. Hong Kong Maritime Law Association. Hong Kong Admiralty Court Users Committee.
Publications: Speaker at numerous seminars on arrest of vessels in Hong Kong; carriage of goods by sea; letters of credit; former editor HLT Publications 'Equity & Trusts'.
Career: October 1990 called to Lincoln's Inn as a Barrister of England and Wales; pupillage with 11, Stone Buildings and 12, New Square, Lincoln's Inn; October 1991 in-house counsel with International Group P&I Club; November 1992 joined *Holman Fenwick & Willan*, London; April 1994 admitted as a Solicitor of England and Wales; January 1995 transferred to Hong Kong office; July 1995 qualified as a Solicitor of Hong Kong; May 1999 made a partner.
Personal: Born July 1966. Brunel University (1988 LLB Hons). Leisure interests include Formula One GPs and trail running.

DARTON, Robin
Deacons, Hong Kong +852 2825 9211
Recommended in Shipping

DEANE, Simon
Deacons, Hong Kong +852 2825 9211
Recommended in Banking & Finance

DELAMATER, Robert G.
Sullivan & Cromwell, Hong Kong +852 2826 8664
delamaterr@sullcrom.com
Recommended in Capital Markets: Debt & Equity
Specialisation: Partner in the Corporate and Financial, Mergers & Acquisitions and General Practice groups. Has served as the Managing Partner of the firm's Hong Kong office since 1997 and of its Tokyo office since 1993. Extensive experience advising non-U.S. issuers and their financial advisors in public offerings and private placements of equity and debt securities in the United States or as part of a global offering. Has led *Sullivan & Cromwell's* work on various matters for clients in Hong Kong and the mainland of China, including the representation of MTR Corporation Limited in SEC-registered debt offerings and its US$3.3 billion privatisation by global equity offering, and China Mobile in its US$ 4.2 billion SEC-registered international IPO and NYSE listing. Has also been active in most of the firm's recent work on equity and debt offerings by Japanese issuers, including NTT in its recent SEC-registered US$15 billion secondary offering, NTT DoCoMo in its US$18.1 billion IPO and Internet Initiative Japan in its US$187 million SEC-registered IPO and NASDAQ listing. In addition to capital markets expertise, has been involved in some of the most significant M&A and joint venture transactions involving Asian companies including the firm's representation of Singapore Telecom in its proposal to acquire Cable & Wireless HKT; Interbrew in its US$250 million joint venture with Oriental Brewery; and Neptune Orient in its US$825 million acquisition of APL Ltd.
Prof. Memberships: American Bar Association; Association of the Bar of the City of New York; Inter-Pacific Bar Association; International Bar Association.
Publications: 'Target Defensive Tactics as Manipulative under Section 14(e)', 84 Colum. L. Rev. 228 (1984).
Career: Judicial Clerk to the Honorable James M. Sprouse, U.S. Court of Appeals (4th Circuit) 1984-1985. Joined *Sullivan & Cromwell* in 1985. Became a Partner of the firm in 1992.
Personal: Born 1959. Attended Harvard College (AB, 1981) and Columbia University Law School (JD, 1984; Columbia Law Review).

DENNY, Roger
Clifford Chance, Hong Kong +852 2825 8888
roger.denny@cliffordchance.com
Recommended in Capital Markets: Debt & Equity, Corporate/M&A
Specialisation: A partner in the Corporate and Securities Group and based in Hong Kong since 1990. Advises European, US and Asian companies on business development in Asia and advises principally on mergers, acquisitions, takeovers, joint ventures and strategic alliances. Also advises international investment banks on IPOs, share issues, convertible bond and warrant issues.
Prof. Memberships: Law Society of England and Wales, Law Society of Hong Kong.
Career: Qualified (1987). Moved to Hong Kong (1990), became partner (1994).
Personal: Born 22 April 1962.

DILLON, John
Holman Fenwick & Willan, Hong Kong +852 2522 3006 John.Dillon@hfw.com.hk
Recommended in Shipping
Specialisation: Served for several years as a Deck Officer with BP Tanker Co. and Ocean fleets. Subsequently qualified as a solicitor in England and is also admitted in Hong Kong. Spent five years in Hong Kong office managing an admiralty practice as a legal executive, before returning to London to qualify. Transferred to Singapore in 1996. Joined *Holman Fenwick & Willan* as a partner on 1 December 2000; specialises in casualty work and apart from regular practice has been involved in various major headline cases including 'Eleni V/Roseline, Aegen Sea/Atlantic Empress', Sea Empress and most recently the loss of the 'Sun Vista'.
Career: BP Tanker Company 1967-76; BSc in Maritime Studies 1976; Metropolitan Police 1976/78; *Ince & Co.* 1979-2000; CPE 1994; qualified as a solicitor in 1996; admitted in Hong Kong 1998.
Personal: Born October 1948. Married with two grown up children. A keen rugby player for 28 years. Now concentrates on golf.

EAST, John
Clifford Chance, Hong Kong +852 2825 8888
Recommended in Project Finance

ENO, Stephen
Baker & McKenzie, Hong Kong +852 2846 1888 eno@bakernet.com
Recommended in Banking & Finance
Specialisation: International partner of *Baker & McKenzie's* Hong Kong office and head of the office's Finance Group, also head of *Baker & McKenzie's* Asia-Pacific Corporate and Debt Restructuring Group. Has extensive experience in Hong Kong and cross-border debt restructuring gained over the past twelve years, advising both financial institutions and troubled companies. In addition to debt restructuring, is also involved in general commercial, banking and finance law. Has advised on and acted in numerous debt restructuring matters in Hong Kong and, in particular, has represented several Steering Committees representing groups of banks and financial institutions with exposure to troubled companies with assets in China, Hong Kong and elsewhere in the region; various financially troubled Hong Kong listed groups in negotiating and documenting standstill arrangements with banks and financial institutions; and third party investors wishing to invest in troubled companies in their negotiation with the relevant banking group.
Prof. Memberships: Admitted to practice in England & Wales (1980) and Hong Kong (1984).
Career: University of Kent (LLB, 1977) and Chester College of Law (1978). Joined *Baker & McKenzie* as an associate (1983) and became a partner in 1987.
Personal: Enjoys rugby, golf, squash, bridge and water-skiing.

FAIRBAIRN, Mark
Deacons, Hong Kong +852 2825 9211
Recommended in Banking & Finance

FLAHERTY, St John
Slaughter and May, Hong Kong +852 2521 0551 stjohn.flaherty@slaughterandmay.com
Recommended in Banking & Finance, Capital Markets: Debt & Equity, Corporate/M&A, Project Finance
Specialisation: Banking, project finance.
Prof. Memberships: The Law Societies of England and Hong Kong.

FONTAINE, Patrick B.
Baker & McKenzie, Hong Kong +852 2846 1888 patrick.fontaine@bakernet.com
Recommended in Banking & Finance
Specialisation: International partner in the Finance Practice Group of the Hong Kong office of *Baker & McKenzie* and a member of the Firm's Global Securities Practice. International finance and debt securities/capital markets practice includes structured, acquisition-related and non-recourse/project financings for numerous arrangers, lead managers, borrowers and issuers. Was a member of the consultative committee to the Securities and Futures Commission on banks' securities businesses; has lobbied the Bills Committee of the Legislative Council on foreign exchange and banking laws; and was a member of a consultative group to the State Administration for Foreign Exchange of the PRC in respect of swaps and derivatives undertaken by PRC entities.
Prof. Memberships: Admitted to practice in England & Wales (1985) and Hong Kong (1987).
Career: University College, London (LLB, 1981); College of Law, Guildford (1982). Joined *Baker & McKenzie* as an associate (1987) and became a partner in 1991.
Personal: Married with two children.

GALE, John
Stephenson Harwood & Lo, Hong Kong +852 2868 0789
Recommended in Corporate/M&A
Specialisation: Partner in the Corporate and Commercial Department, *Stephenson Harwood & Lo*, Hong Kong. Head of Corporate and Commercial Department and Head of Financial Services Group. While in Hong Kong, has handled a broad range of corporate, commercial, banking, insolvency and financial services related work. Principal corporate work includes fund raising through private or public offers, as well as acquisitions, disposals and joint ventures, both domestic and cross-border. Financial services work has included the establishment of mutual funds, unit trusts and closed-ended investment companies, whether publicly or privately offered fund mergers and reconstructions, and associated regulatory work applicable to funds and fund managers.
Prof. Memberships: Law Society; Law Society of Hong Kong.
Career: Joined *Stephenson Harwood*, London in 1980 and qualified in 1982. Seconded to *Stephenson Harwood & Lo* in Hong Kong in 1983 and has practised in Hong Kong since then. Became a Partner in both *Stephenson Harwood* and *Stephenson Harwood & Lo* in 1988.
Personal: Born 1 February 1958. Trinity Hall, Cambridge 1976-79 (MA in Law).

HARDEE, Ian
Clifford Chance, Hong Kong +852 2825 8888
Recommended in Capital Markets: Debt & Equity

HATZER, Paul
Holman Fenwick & Willan, Hong Kong +852 2522 3006 Paul.Hatzer@hfw.com.hk
Recommended in Shipping
Specialisation: Maritime and commercial litigation in the fields of shipping, international trade and commodities, and general commerce. Particular experience of shipping disputes (charterparty problems, S&P disputes, bill of lading and cargo claims, personal injuries and P&I insurance matters generally), international trade and commodity disputes (including arbitrations in London, Hong Kong, Singapore, Vietnam, Japan and CIETAC Beijing), ship finance and sale and purchase, together with insurance and insolvency matters within the maritime and trading sphere.
Prof. Memberships: Law Society of England and Wales, Law Society of Hong Kong. Hong Kong Maritime Law Association. RAC, London. Naval & Military Club, London.
Career: Articled *Robert Blackford & Co.* (London); qualified in England in 1984; *Braby & Waller* (London) 1984-1985; practised with *Cridlands* in Darwin, Australia 1985-1987; admitted as both barrister and solicitor in Australia 1985; *Holman Fenwick & Willan*, London 1988 and Hong Kong office 1991; admitted Hong Kong 1991. Partner 1993; delivered papers at numerous international seminars and articles in newspapers, magazines and periodicals within the maritime industry. Major cases include 'Super Servant II' (UK Court of Appeal, 1989), 'Pioneer Container'/'K.H. Enterprise' (Privy Council, 1994) and CIETAC Arbitrations Beijing 1995-2000 (various).
Personal: Born 1956. Resides in Stanley, Hong Kong. Thornleigh College, Bolton, Lancashire; University of Hull (1978 LLB Hons); College of Law, Lancaster Gate. Leisure: water sports.

HEATH, Martin
Clyde & Co, Hong Kong +852 2 878 8600
Recommended in Shipping
Specialisation: Hong Kong Admiralty and Commercial Court practice; some arbitration. Mainly handling a range of insurance and maritime litigation (hull, P&I and cargo) and trading disputes, with some emphasis on representation of cargo in collision, salvage and general average casualties and cargo insurers in policy disputes. Regional client base, in particular, over 20 years experience acting for Japanese insurers and trading companies. Developing mainland PRC and Vietnamese related work.
Prof. Memberships: The Law Society of Hong Kong; The Law Society of England and Wales; Hong Kong Maritime Law Association (Deputy Chairman, Executive Committee; Member Casualty Sub-committee).
Career: LLB University College, London 1962. Qualified as a Solicitor in England and Wales and joined *Clyde & Co*, London in 1965, becoming a partner in 1968. Admitted as a solicitor in Hong

H

Kong and transferred to *Clyde & Co's* Hong Kong office in 1988.
Personal: Children and grandchildren; sailing; travel; hill walking (4,000m max!); reading; eating out.

HOWSE, Chris
Richards Butler, Hong Kong +852 2507 9888
chrishowse@richardsbutler.com.hk
Recommended in Shipping
Specialisation: Maritime litigation, charterparty and bill of lading problems and all aspects of P&I and Defence Club work, particular expertise in maritime and international trade disputes in the PRC. Conducts CMAC and CIETAC arbitrations in Beijing. Undertakes work in connection with international trade disputes, commodities and sale of goods, insurance litigation, and professional negligence work for solicitors, barristers, doctors, dentists and accountants.
Career: Qualified England and Wales 1978 and Hong Kong 1981. Senior partner, Hong Kong office, since 1983.

HUSTED, Catherine
Allen & Overy, Hong Kong +852 2974 7000
Recommended in Capital Markets: Derivatives

JENKINS, Huw
Clifford Chance, Hong Kong +852 2825 8888
Recommended in Banking & Finance, Project Finance

JOHNSON, Clayton
Cravath, Swaine & Moore, Hong Kong +852 2509 7200
Recommended in Capital Markets: Debt & Equity

JOHNSTON, Nic
Freshfields Bruckhaus Deringer, Hong Kong +852 2846 3400
nic.johnston@freshfields.com
Recommended in Banking & Finance, Project Finance
Specialisation: Has a broad range of experience in banking, asset finance, project finance and non-contentious aspects of insolvency and corporate recovery.

KO, Teresa
Freshfields Bruckhaus Deringer, Hong Kong +852 2846 3400
teresa.ko@freshfields.com
Recommended in Capital Markets: Debt & Equity, Corporate/M&A
Specialisation: Specialises in corporate finance and securities and investment and has wide experience in international public offerings. Practice also involves private and public acquisitions and disposals, and corporate reorganisations, the establishment of investment funds and joint ventures in the PRC.

KONII, Junri
Baker & McKenzie, Hong Kong +852 2846 1888
junri.konii@bakernet.com
Recommended in Capital Markets: Securitisation
Specialisation: Practice encompasses asset-backed and structured financings, including securitisation and project financings, as well as general banking and finance, derivatives and regulatory advice. Has led the team acting for the originator in some of the landmark securitisations in Hong Kong and the PRC, and has advised the arranger/lead manager in numerous other transactions involving a wide range of asset classes in various Asian jurisdictions.
Prof. Memberships: Law Society of England & Wales; Law Society of Hong Kong. Also a member of various related organisations. Regular speaker at conferences and seminars in the Asian region and is mentioned in a number of legal directories and listings featuring specialists lawyers.
Career: BA and MA from the University of Cambridge, England (Churchill College). Joined *Baker & McKenzie's* London office in 1983 and moved to the Hong Kong office in 1989. Has been a partner of the Hong Kong office since 1993.
Personal: Leisure activities include playing chamber music (violin and piano), reading and dance. Married with two children. Japanese national and, in addition to English, speaks fluent Japanese.

KOO, Donald
Koo and Partners, Hong Kong +852 2867 9988
dk@kooandpartners.com
Recommended in Banking & Finance
Specialisation: During many years of practice as a solicitor, has represented a variety of banks and other institutional clients. Experience spans the areas of banking and finance, insolvency law, commercial law, property and conveyancing and commercial litigation. Has overseen the growth of the firm to over 200 staff.
Prof. Memberships: Law Societies of Hong Kong and England and Wales, ACIArb, Notary Public, China Appointed Attesting Officer.
Career: Qualified in 1982. Legal consultant to Bank of China, Hong Kong Branch since 1986. Established *Koo and Partners* in 1993 and currently senior partner.
Personal: Graduate, University of Hong Kong.

KRUGER, Paul
Clifford Chance, Hong Kong +852 2825 8888
Recommended in Capital Markets: Securitisation

KWOK, Larry
Kwok & Yih, Hong Kong +852 2523 1000
LKwok@KnY.com
Recommended in Corporate/M&A
Specialisation: Substantial experience in a wide range of capital market, corporate finance and commercial transactions both in Hong Kong and regionally. Areas of engagement include: listings, take-over mergers and acquisitions, corporate reorganisations, corporate rescue, rights issues, convertible bonds and direct investments. Also regularly advises multinational Chinese and Hong Kong corporations on their business and legal affairs. Author of several publications and was co-author of 'Kwok & Amour's Corporate Securities Law' published by Butterworths.
Prof. Memberships: Law Society of Hong Kong, Law Society of Singapore, Law Society of England and Wales, Law Society of New South Wales, Australia, Australian Society of Certified Practising Accountants, Hong Kong Society of Accountants, Macau Society of Certified Practising Accountants.
Career: Senior partner of the firm. Qualified as a solicitor in Hong Kong, Australia, England and Singapore. Is also a qualified accountant in Australia and Hong Kong. Fluent in Mandarin, Cantonese and English. Before founding the firm, worked for *Baker & McKenzie* and was partner of *Simmons & Simmons*. Member of the Political Consultative Committee of Guangxi of the People's Republic of China. Serves on a number of government advisory boards and committees of the Hong Kong Government, and the board of directors of several listed companies in Hong Kong, including a number of influential Chinese corporations.
Personal: Graduated from the University of Sydney, Australia with bachelor degrees in economics and law respectively as well as a masters degree in law.

LAIGHT, Matthew
Bird & Bird, Hong Kong +852 2248 6000
matthew.laight@twobirds.com
Recommended in Communications
Specialisation: Partner and head of intellectual property in Hong Kong. Has advised leading multinational corporations, locally listed companies and individuals on all aspects of IP, both contentious and non-contentious, Internet and IT matters. Conducted patent litigation on Hong Kong and China (with local lawyers).
Prof. Memberships: Treasurer and Council Member of the Hong Kong Institute of Trademark Practitioners; Intellectual Property and Information Technology Committees of the American Chamber of Commerce in Hong Kong; International Trademark Association; Asian Patent Attorneys Association; Overseas Member Institute of Trademark Agents (UK).
Publications: Numerous articles in legal publications.
Career: Qualified in UK in 1991 and Hong Kong in 1993. Joined *Bird & Bird* as a partner in 1999.
Personal: Born 1966. Studied at London School of Economics, University of London (1987); City of London Polytechnic (1989); University of Bristol (external 1993). Resides Hong Kong.

LAM, Celia
Linklaters (a member firm of Linklaters & Alliance), Hong Kong +852 2842 4888
celia.lam@linklaters.com
Recommended in Capital Markets: Debt & Equity
Specialisation: Specialist in corporate finance matters, with extensive experience in securities offerings (both domestic and international), joint ventures, unit trusts and mutual funds.

LANGE, John E.
Paul, Weiss, Rifkind, Wharton & Garrison, Hong Kong
Recommended in Project Finance

LATHAM, Simon
Ince & Co, Hong Kong +852 2877 3221
Recommended in Shipping
Specialisation: Resident senior partner of *Ince & Co, Hong Kong* since 1991. Oversees a growing firm which represents many major ship owners, salvors, charterers, hull/cargo underwriters, P&I Clubs and trading companies in all kinds of shipping and trade

disputes. Has worked on many major casulties, including bulk carrier total losses, and has particular experience of hull and machinery and cargo insurance cases.
Personal: Graduate of Exeter University, UK. Has lectured and spoken at seminars in Hong Kong and China on a wide variety of shipping subjects, including documentary credits, charterparty and insurance matters. Leisure interests include sailing.

LEE, Angelina
Woo, Kwan, Lee & Lo, Hong Kong +852 2847 7955
angelina.lee@wkll.com
Recommended in Capital Markets: Debt & Equity, Corporate/M&A
Specialisation: Main area of practice is corporate and commercial work, principally corporate finance, including initial public offerings, mergers and acquisitions (public and private), reorganisations.
Prof. Memberships: Fellow of the Institute of Chartered Accountants in England and Wales. Takeovers and Mergers Panel, Standing Committee on Company Law Reform, Banking Advisory Committee of the Hong Kong Monetary Authority, Listing Committee of the Growth Enterprise Market of the Hong Kong Stock Exchange, Town Planning Board, Mandatory Provident Fund Schemes Appeal Board, Securities Law Subcommittee and Company and Financial Law Subcommittee of the Law Society of Hong Kong.
Career: Deloitte & Co. London 1971-1974. Qualified as Chartered Accountant in 1974. *Woo, Kwan, Lee & Lo* from 1976. Qualified as solicitor in 1978. Partner from 1981.
Personal: Graduated from University College London in 1970.

LEE, Carmelo
Woo, Kwan, Lee & Lo, Hong Kong +852 2847 7999
Recommended in Corporate/M&A
Specialisation: Partner in Corporate and Commercial Department. Main area of practice is corporate and commercial work, principally corporate finance including mergers and acquisitions (public and private), initial public offerings (including H-shares), reorganisation and securities law generally. Has spoken at numerous conferences and seminars.
Prof. Memberships: The Law Society of Hong Kong. Listing Committee Member of the Main Board of the Hong Kong Stock Exchange.
Career: Joined *Woo, Kwan, Lee & Lo* in 1983. Qualified in 1985. Partner of *Woo, Kwan, Lee & Lo* from 1989. Non-executive director of several listed public companies in Hong Kong, namely China Everbright International Limited, Yugang International Limited, Pak Fah Yeow International Limited, China Pharmaceutical Enterprise & Investment Corporation Limited, Yunnan Enterprise Holdings Limited, Termbray Industries International (Holdings) Limited and Tern Properties Company Limited. SIIC Medical Science and Technology (Group) Limited, Safety Godown Company Limited and Prestige Properties Holdings Limited.
Personal: Born 3 May 1960. Received Bachelor of Laws degree and the Post-graduate Certificate in Laws from Hong Kong University in 1982 and 1983 respectively. Admitted to practise law in Hong Kong, England, Singapore and the Australian Capital Territory.

LEE, Lawrence
Baker & McKenzie, Hong Kong +852 2846 1888
lawrence.lee@bakernet.com
Recommended in Corporate/M&A
Specialisation: Chairman of *Baker & McKenzie's* Hong Kong, China and Vietnam offices. Principally engaged in the Commercial and Securities Group of the Firm's Hong Kong office. Focus is on corporate finance, including the flotation of new companies; merger and acquisition of public companies; establishment of investment funds; and other securities related matters. This includes both Hong Kong and China-related securities issues such as the issuance of B shares and H shares.
Prof. Memberships: Hong Kong Law Society; Law Society of New South Wales; Law Institute of Victoria; and Law Society of England & Wales.
Career: LLB. (1978) and PCLL (1979) from the University of Hong Kong. Started career with *Baker & McKenzie's* Hong Kong office in 1979. From 1982 to 1999, was based in the Firm's Sydney office before being transferred back to Hong Kong. Became a partner in 1986.

LEE, Paul
Herbert Smith, Hong Kong +852 2845 6639
Recommended in Banking & Finance
Specialisation: Partner in the International Banking and Finance Department at *Herbert Smith.* Has extensive experience acting for banks and borrowers on a wide range of general banking matters including syndicated and bilateral loans (secured and unsecured), project finance and cash pooling arrangements. Has also advised on standstill arrangements, rescheduling and restructuring of debt, creditors' schemes of arrangement, appointment of receivers and enforcing securing. Specialises in syndicated loans and acquisition finance. Clients include a number of leading international financial institutions and banks such as HSBC Investment Bank Asia Limited, ABN AMRO Bank and BNP Paribas.
Prof. Memberships: Law Society of England and Wales; Law Society of Hong Kong.
Career: Trained and worked at a leading City of London law firm prior to being transferred to its Hong Kong office in 1993. Admitted as a solicitor in England in 1991 and in Hong Kong in 1994. Joined *Herbert Smith* in July 1988. Co-editor of Butterworths' 'Hong Kong Banking Law and Practice' and has spoken at various conferences.
Personal: Born 15 May 1965. Speaks fluent English and Cantonese.

LEUNG, Cheuk Yan
Baker & McKenzie, Hong Kong +852 2846 1888
cy.leung@bakernet.com
Recommended in Capital Markets: Debt & Equity
Specialisation: Partner of the Hong Kong office of *Baker & McKenzie* and member of the office's Commercial & Securities Group. Since the early 1990's, practice focus has been the privatisations of, and capital raisings by, major state-owned corporations in the People's Republic of China. Most of the companies has worked for, either as issuer's or as underwriters' counsel, were listed on stock exchanges in Hong Kong and the United States. These include PetroChina Company Limited, which raised close to US$3 billion in April 2000, China Mobile (Hong Kong) Limited, which raised US$7.6 billion in November 2000, and a great majority of the China-related IPOs completed by Baker & McKenzie in recent years. Has also advised the Hong Kong Government on Hong Kong's first privatisation project, the IPO of MTR Corporation completed in October 2000.
Prof. Memberships: Law Society of Hong Kong; Law Society of England & Wales; Law Institute of Victoria.
Publications: Frequent contributor of articles on company and securities law for journals such as the International Financial Law Review and China Law and Practice. Also regularly gives public lectures and seminars on securities matters in Hong Kong, the PRC and overseas.
Career: Chinese University of Hong Kong (BSocSc, 1976); University of Oxford (MPhil, 1981); College of Law, Lancaster Gate (1982). Joined *Baker & McKenzie's* Hong Kong office in 1987 and became a partner in 1990. During 1989 to 1991, worked in the firm's Melbourne office.
Personal: Senior Associate Member of St. Anthony's College, Oxford.

LIE, Sue
Linklaters (a member firm of Linklaters & Alliance), Hong Kong +852 2842 4888
slie@linklaters.com
Recommended in Corporate/M&A
Specialisation: Corporate finance and general corporate experience, in particular in securities offerings, mergers and acquisitions, securities regulation and compliance, joint ventures and reorganisations. Acted on a number of domestic and international mergers and acquisitions, public equity offerings and stock exchange listings, joint ventures, corporate reorganisations and investment funds work. Acted in the UK and in Hong Kong including advising both listed and unlisted corporations and underwriters on Hong Kong IPOs, H share issues, demergers, spin-offs, rights issues, joint ventures, private placements, company acquisitions and disposals, and PRC investment projects.

LIEW, Chin-Chong
Allen & Overy, Hong Kong +852 2974 7000
Recommended in Capital Markets: Derivatives

LINES, Patrick
Freshfields Bruckhaus Deringer, Hong Kong +852 2846 3400
patrick.lines@freshfields.com
Recommended in Capital Markets: Derivatives
Specialisation: Specialises in capital markets and derivatives work and has advised in connection with securitisations and other structured products, a wide range of Eurobond issues, including convertible and exchangeable bonds, as well as MTN programmes, warrant issues, swaps, stock lending and repo agreements and related regulatory matters.

H

H

LIU, Michael S.L.
Allen & Overy, Hong Kong +852 2974 7000
Recommended in Capital Markets: Debt & Equity, Corporate/M&A

LOCKHART, Andrew
Baker & McKenzie, Hong Kong +852 2846 1912
andrew.lockhart@bakernet.com
Recommended in Capital Markets: Derivatives
Specialisation: Partner of the Hong Kong office of *Baker & McKenzie* and a member of the office's Finance Practice Group. Leads the aviation and structured finance team within the Finance Practice Group and regularly advises airlines, banks, arrangers and equity participants on a wide variety of asset financing and structured finance transactions.
Prof. Memberships: Law Society of Hong Kong; Law Society of England & Wales.
Career: Auckland University (LLB, 1986); Cambridge University (LLM, 1988). Joined the Hong Kong office of *Baker & McKenzie* in 1988 and became a partner in 1996.

MACKINNON, Robert
Shearman & Sterling, Hong Kong +852 2978 8005
rmackinnon@shearman.com
Recommended in Banking & Finance
Specialisation: Singapore (+65 230 3828). Senior partner of the firm, who served as a member of the firm's Policy Committee for nine years through April 1997, and headed the firm's Private Finance Practice consisting of more than 160 lawyers. Is the firm's 'relationship partner' for Citicorp and Citibank work. Previously, beginning in 1972, headed the firm's Corporate Reorganisation Practice Group, comprised of both bank and corporate finance, bankruptcy, litigation and tax practitioners handling private sector workouts, both within the United States and abroad. Continues as an active practitioner in this area in addition to broader responsibilities.
Prof. Memberships: Member, New York Bar and Practicing Law Institute's Securities Law Advisory Committee.
Career: Joined *Shearman & Sterling* in 1961 and has been a partner since 1969. Spent two years in the Paris office (1964-1966), headed the Brussels office (1967) and is now based in both Hong Kong and Singapore. Lecturer, Workouts and Restructurings at Euromoney Conferences in Hong Kong. Lecturer, Bankruptcy and Restructuring, the American Law Institute, the Practising Law Institute and Robert Morris Associates. Lecturer, Bankruptcy and Workout Techniques, Citibank's Global Banking Institute and the Consumer Banking Group of Citibank. Faculty, Citibank's Senior Risk Seminar in Switzerland. Requested to be a mediator by Bank of Thailand under its CDRAC restructuring process.
Personal: Attended Harvard Law School (LLB, cum laude, 1960) and Yale University (AB, magna cum laude, 1957).

MALCOLM, Andrew
Linklaters (a member firm of Linklaters & Alliance), Hong Kong +852 2842 4888
andrew.malcolm@linklaters.com
Recommended in Capital Markets: Debt & Equity
Specialisation: International finance transactions such as equity and equity-linked securities issues in the Asian and Euro capital markets. Privatisations and strategic investments, debt restructurings and workouts, banking and derivatives transactions (both listed and OTC in Hong Kong).

MALLARD, Nicholas H.
DLA, Hong Kong +852 2 524 2003
Recommended in Shipping

McGUINNESS, John D.
Richards Butler, Hong Kong +852 2810 8008
johnmcguinness@richardsbutler.com.hk
Recommended in Banking & Finance
Specialisation: Partner in the Finance Department since 1990. Specialises in debt capital markets and in particular aircraft finance and structured finance transactions including export credit supported financings; tax based leasing; off-balance and securitised transactions. Chaired conferences in Hong Kong on PRC aircraft and project financing.
Career: Qualified in England and Wales in 1980 and in Hong Kong in 1990. Joined *Richards Butler* in January 1988 and became a partner in 1990.
Personal: Born August 1955. Attended Birmingham University (LLB Honours). Lives in Hong Kong.

MO, Philip
Holman Fenwick & Willan, Hong Kong +852 2522 3006
Philip.Mo@hfw.com.hk
Recommended in Shipping
Specialisation: Admitted in England as a solicitor having spent a number of years in the U.K. where he navigated successfully through the education system there. Returned to Hong Kong with *Holman Fenwick & Willan* in 1983, given that the early 80's were the breakthrough years of Hong Kong as an emerging market and an entreport in Asia, with improving economic fundamentals particularly mired in intense trades between the People's Republic of China and the rest of the globe. Principal areas of practice are shipping litigation including bill of lading claims, cargo claims, total loss, charterparty disputes, general average, total loss, collision related matters, MOA and insurance disputes, as well as general commercial litigations in Hong Kong. Also has extensive experience in shadowing the conduct of litigation and arbitration in the PRC, Singapore and Taiwan. Has developed an amicable relationship with local lawyers in those jurisdictions. Practice has grown since 1983 with *Holman Fenwick & Willan*'s Hong Kong office to the present which has a complement of over sixty personnel including partners, fee earners and support staff.
Prof. Memberships: Member of the Hong Kong Maritime Law Association, the Law Society in England and Wales, and the Hong Kong Law Society.
Career: Also admitted in Singapore and Victoria, Australia as an advocate and solicitor.

MOULT, Jonathan
Herbert Smith, Hong Kong +852 2845 6639
jonathan.moult@herbertsmith.com
Recommended in Banking & Finance
Specialisation: Partner in the Banking Department in Hong Kong and head of Debt Finance for the firm in Asia. Has handled numerous transactions in international banking and capital markets, as well as general banking advisory work for a number of financial institutions, banks, corporates and government agencies. Experience gained from both a legal perspective (within private practice in London, Germany – worked for 1 year in Frankfurt with the leading European law firm *Bruckhaus Westrick Heller Löber* – and in Hong Kong), and from a commercial perspective, with Bankers Trust International (worked in the transaction management group in London). Has experience in acting for both banks and borrowers/issuers in banking transactions, as well as the full range of international capital markets deals, with particular emphasis on convertible/exchangeable bonds. Acted on the banking aspects of the demerger of the financial and tobacco interests of BAT, in the emerging debt markets in Eastern Europe and while in Asia has undertaken a number of exchangeable and convertible bond issues for leading 'red chips' and lead managers and, latterly, bank mergers.
Prof. Memberships: Law Society of England and Wales, Law Society of Hong Kong and the City of London Law Society.
Career: Qualified October 1987. Served articles with *Norton Rose* and worked there for six years after qualification, before joining *Herbert Smith's* International Finance & Banking Department in 1993. Became a partner in April 1995. Resident in Asia since September 1997.
Personal: Born 4 September 1961. Attended Leicester University 1980-1983. Harrogate Grammar School. Interests include playing and collecting percussion instruments and gongs.

NEUVILLE, David E.
Baker & McKenzie, Hong Kong +852 2846 1888
david.neuville@bakernet.com
Recommended in Capital Markets: Debt & Equity
Specialisation: Regional co-ordinator of *Baker & McKenzie*'s International Securities Practice for the Asia Pacific region, and a partner in the Hong Kong office's Commercial & Securities Group. Also a member of *Baker & McKenzie*'s Mergers and Acquisitions Practice, as well as the international Firm's Global Securities Steering Committee. Practice emphasises public and private securities offerings, mergers and acquisitions, and debt restructurings. Securities offerings have included both debt and equity offerings and the representation of issuers, underwriters and selling shareholders in the U.S. and abroad. Has been active in transactions in the PRC, Hong Kong, Taiwan, Thailand, Indonesia, Korea, India, Australia and the Philippines. Has developed special expertise in New York/Hong Kong dual listing transactions.
Prof. Memberships: Admitted to the New York Bar (1986).
Career: Swarthmore College (BA, 1982); Harvard University (JD, 1985). Joined *Baker & McKenzie*, Hong Kong in 1994 and became a partner in 1995.

NICHOLSON, Robin
Richards Butler, Hong Kong +852 2810 8008
robinnicholson@richardsbutler.com.hk
Recommended in Capital Markets: Debt & Equity, Corporate/M&A

Specialisation: 19 years of experience as a corporate finance lawyer and in particular specialises in cross-border mergers and acquisitions, Hong Kong takeover transactions and PRC privatisations and capital raising. Chief representative of the firm's Beijing office with extensive experience in relation to transactional work undertaken within the PRC and countries in the South East Asian Region.
Prof. Memberships: The Law Society of Hong Kong and The Law Society of England & Wales.
Career: Qualified in England and Wales in 1980 and in Hong Kong in 1982. Joined *Richards Butler* in January 1985 and became a partner in May 1986.
Personal: Born in December 1955. BA (Law) from The University of Kent. Enjoys walking, boating and reading. Lives in Hong Kong.

NORMAN, David
Richards Butler, Hong Kong +852 2810 8008
davidnorman@richardsbutler.com.hk
Recommended in Capital Markets: Debt & Equity, Corporate/M&A
Specialisation: Partner in the Corporate Finance/Company Department. Specialises in mergers and acquisitions, corporate finance, direct investment and joint ventures and general commercial law, especially in the internet and hospitality industries.
Prof. Memberships: The Law Society of Hong Kong.
Publications: Contributing editor, 'Hong Kong Securities Law', contributor: 'Hong Kong Company Secretarial Manual'.
Career: Qualified in 1981 in England and Wales and in Hong Kong in 1984. Joined *Richards Butler* in November 1986, becoming a partner in May, 1988.
Personal: Born April 1956. Scholar of Balliol College, Oxford. BA (Oxford University) in philosophy and psychology 1978. Leisure interests include opera, good food and skiing. Lives in Hong Kong.

NORRIS, Nicholas
Simmons & Simmons, Hong Kong +852 2868 1131
nicholas.norris@simmons-simmons.com
Recommended in Corporate/M&A
Specialisation: Main areas of practice are corporate finance, mergers and acquisitions and international capital markets. Leads the equity capital markets and mergers and acquisitions practices. Advises major corporates and investment banks on a wide range of corporate finance and capital market transactions, including international securities offerings, capital raising exercises and derivative warrant programmes. Also advises on broad range of corporate matters, including mergers & acquisitions, joint ventures, restructuring and work-outs.
Prof. Memberships: The Law Society of England and Wales. The Law Society of Hong Kong.
Career: Bachelor of Laws (LLB) Law Society's Final Examinations. Admitted as a solicitor in 1988 in England and Wales. Admitted as a solicitor in 1992 in Hong Kong. Joined *Simmons & Simmons* in1986 as a trainee. Upon qualification in 1988, became an assistant solicitor in the Banking and Capital Markets department. Joined *Simmons & Simmons* Hong Kong in March, 1992 and was made a partner in 1995. Became Head of the Corporate Group in Hong Kong in 1998.
Personal: Born 16 July 1964. Educated at St Mary's Grammar School, Kent (1975 to 1982) and Warwick University (1982 to 1985).

O'CONNOR, Patrick
Clifford Chance, Hong Kong +852 2825 8888
Recommended in Banking & Finance

PEDERSEN, Jonathan
Skadden, Arps, Slate, Meagher & Flom LLP, Hong Kong +852 2820 0700
Recommended in Capital Markets: Debt & Equity

PLATT, David
Shearman & Sterling, Hong Kong +852 2978 8000
dplatt@shearman.com
Recommended in Project Finance, Project Finance: China Foreign
Specialisation: Specialises in project finance, energy and construction law. Has acted for developers and financiers on power, rail and other infrastructure projects throughout the Asia Pacific region. Major transactions worked on include Sajiao C, Shandong Rizhao, Hebei Hanfeng, Anhui Hefei, Guangdong Zhuhai, Laibin B and Wuhu power plants in China, the Bangkok Mass Transit System and Independent Power (Thailand) power project in Thailand, the Melaka power project in Malaysia and the North Luzon Expressway in the Philippines. Currently working for sponsors and financiers on power, petrochemical and industrial projects in the PRC and the Philippines.
Prof. Memberships: Law Society of England & Wales; Law Society of Hong Kong SAR.
Career: Education: St Paul's School, London, University of Cambridge. Career: 2000, Partner, *Shearman & Sterling* Hong Kong; 1995, Partner, *Linklaters*, Hong Kong; 1991-95, Solicitor, *Linklaters*, Hong Kong; 1989-91, Solicitor, *Linklaters*, London; 1987-88, Articled Clerk, *Linklaters* (London and New York).
Personal: Born 1963. Resides Hong Kong.

POTTS, Chris
Crump & Co, Hong Kong +852 2537 7000
crumps@hk.super.net
Recommended in Shipping
Specialisation: 28 years' experience focusing on all aspects of maritime, transport and insurance law, especially: Collision, fire/explosion, total loss, salvage, P&I, charterparty, carriage of goods by road and air, product liability, commodities, letters of credit, personal injury, insolvency, and pleasure craft, including numerous headline cases.
Prof. Memberships: Memberships: Solicitor, Chartered Institue of Arbitrators.
Publications: Hong Kong Correspondent Lloyd's Maritime & Commercial Law Quarterly.
Career: Practised with *Norton Rose*, London and Hong Kong; set up *Crump&Co.*, Hong Kong 1981; headed *Crump&Co* 1981-present; resolving complex, often high profile, shipping and insurance cases on behalf of a broad range of clients.
Personal: Educated at Sedbergh School, Cumbria, Manchester University, and College of Law Lancaster Gate. Hobbies: Admiralty Practice; boating; walking; scuba diving; motor cycling; Hong Kong; English Lake District.

RAE SMITH, Alan
Allen & Overy, Hong Kong +852 2974 7000
Recommended in Banking & Finance, Project Finance

REEDE, Michael
Paul, Weiss, Rifkind, Wharton & Garrison, Hong Kong
Recommended in Communications

REES, Nick
Linklaters (a member firm of Linklaters & Alliance), Hong Kong +852 2842 4888
nick.rees@linklaters.com
Recommended in Corporate/M&A
Specialisation: International corporate and commercial lawyer specialising in cross-border work including mergers and acquisitions, privatisations and IPOs, joint ventures, financings, infrastructure projects and financial markets.
Career: Managing Partner, Moscow 1996-99. Managing Partner, Hong Kong 1999 to date.

REES SMITH, Peter
Holman Fenwick & Willan, Hong Kong +852 2522 3006
PeterReesSmith@hfw.com.hk
Recommended in Shipping
Specialisation: All areas of shipping litigation in particular charterparty disputes, bill of lading claims, cargo claims, fire and explosion claims, general average, MOA disputes and ship building disputes. Major cases include success in Aliakmon Progress in Court of Appeal in London, and in Antonis P. Lemos in House of Lords in London. Recent highlights include acting for the arresting party in the Halla Liberty litigation in Hong Kong, and acting for a major UAE shipping company in connection with a series of cargo misdelivery cases in China.
Prof. Memberships: Law Society of England and Wales; Hong Kong Law Society; Hong Kong Maritime Law Association, and Supporting Member of London Maritime Arbitrators Association.
Career: Articled *Herbert Smith & Co.* and qualified as a solicitor in 1975. Joined *Holman Fenwick & Willan* in 1975 and became a partner in 1979. Admitted as a solicitor in Hong Kong in 1980. Managing partner of the Hong Kong office from 1981-84, and 1994 to date.
Personal: Born February 1950. Bristol University (1971 LLB Hons). Leisure interests include mountaineering, sailing, skiing, and rugby. Born February 1950.

ROOT, Anthony
Milbank, Tweed, Hadley & McCloy, Hong Kong +852 2971 4888
Recommended in Capital Markets: Debt & Equity

ROSTRON, Jonathan E.S.
Sinclair Roche & Temperley, Hong Kong +852 2820 0200
jonathan.rostron@srtlaw.com.hk
Recommended in Shipping
Specialisation: Partner in Hong Kong office. Heads Litigation Department. Specialises in charterparty and bill of lading disputes, commodity trading, insurance and reinsurance disputes. Acts for a num-

H

ber of German shipowners, freight forwarders and underwriters. Speaks fluent German.
Prof. Memberships: Memberships: Law Society; Hong Kong Law Society; Hong Kong Maritime Law Association.
Publications: Contributor to various shipping and insurance publications and has spoken at conferences in Hong Kong, Seoul, Taipei, Vietnam and Singapore.
Career: Qualified in 1985. Joined *Holman Fenwick and Willan* in 1985 in London and subsequently worked for *Holman Fenwick and Willan* in Hong Kong. In 1990 joined *More Fisher Brown*. In 1992 joined *Sinclair Roche & Temperley*, Hong Kong. Became a partner in 1994. Member of the Hong Kong Maritime Law Association Arbitration Sub-Committee, Member of Solicitors' Disciplinary Panel, Hong Kong.
Personal: Born 20 July 1960. Attended Bolton School and Sheffield University (1979-1982). Leisure interests include golf, tennis and horse racing.

ROUGH, Clive
Freshfields Bruckhaus Deringer, Hong Kong +852 2846 3400
clive.rough@freshfields.com
Recommended in Capital Markets: Securitisation
Specialisation: Specialises in finance work and has wide experience of capital markets, securitisations, derivatives, international banking and international finance matters both in Europe and Asia.

SHELFORD, Peter
Clyde & Co, Hong Kong +8522 878 8600
Peter.Shelford@clyde.com.hk
Recommended in Shipping
Specialisation: Partner in litigation department specialising in shipping and marine insurance, principally charterparties, cargo claims, and insurance policy advice. Substantial experience of English and Hong Kong Court procedure and arbitrations. Has worked extensively for Far Eastern clients and in particular, has established a substantial Korean client based practice. Has written papers and delivered talks at seminars on many topics, including 'Charterers' liability for loss and damage to cargo', 'Associated ship arrest', 'Liability for cargo claims – Clause 8 NYPE and the NYPE interclub agreement', 'Time charters – off hire issues', and 'Recent developments on hull insurance.' Has also acted for a major bank in a substantial banking dispute, and was heavily involved in acting for one of the parties in the judicial inquiry into the opening of the new Hong Kong airport
Prof. Memberships: Law Societies of England and Wales and Hong Kong, Panel Member of Hong Kong International Arbitration Centre, Chairman of the HKMLA Arbitration and ADR Sub-committee, and secretary of the Hong Kong Maritime Arbitration Group.
Career: Law degree at Southampton University, 1972. Joined *Clyde & Co* in September 1973. Qualified 1975. Became a partner in November 1979. Transferred to *Clyde & Co*'s Hong Kong office, July 1996.
Personal: Born 20 February 1951. Married July 1977. Three children. Leisure interests include tennis, golf and bridge.

SZE, Beryl
Linklaters (a member firm of Linklaters & Alliance), Hong Kong +852 2842 4888
beryl.sze@linklaters.com
Recommended in Capital Markets: Debt & Equity
Specialisation: Structured finance and capital market financings, including (particularly in Asia) full scale securitisations, collateralised loan obligations, collateralised bond obligations, repackagings, off balance sheet financings, credit refinancings, structured funds and deals structured to overcome regulatory or accounting or tax constraints/problems. Also equity and equity-linked issues and debt capital market offerings, banking transactions and derivatives.

TAN, Poh Lee
Baker & McKenzie, Hong Kong +852 2846 1888
pohlee.tan@bakernet.com
Recommended in Communications
Specialisation: International partner of *Baker & McKenzie* and heads the ITC Group in *Baker & McKenzie*, Hong Kong and is the practice group leader for *Baker & McKenzie*'s ITC practice in the Asia Pacific region. Practice consists of advising on projects in the communications, IT and e-commerce sectors in Hong Kong and throughout the Asia Pacific region. Has advised on and structured transactions in Thailand, Philippines, Malaysia, Indonesia, Hong Kong and Korea.
Prof. Memberships: Admitted in England, Hong Kong, Australia and Singapore.
Career: London School of Economics (LLB, 1980); Inns of Court Law School (Barrister, 1981); Queen's College, Cambridge (LLM, 1982). Joined *Baker & McKenzie*'s Hong Kong office in 1985 and became a partner in 1989.
Personal: Married with two children.

TANNER, Douglas
Milbank, Tweed, Hadley & McCloy, Hong Kong +852 2971 4888
Recommended in Capital Markets: Debt & Equity

THOMSON, Mary B.L.
Koo and Partners, Hong Kong +852 2867 9988
Recommended in Shipping

THORNHILL, Richard
Slaughter and May, Hong Kong +852 2521 0551
richard.thornhill@slaughterandmay.com
Recommended in Corporate/M&A
Specialisation: Corporate Finance, Corporate and Commercial and financings.
Prof. Memberships: Law Society. Hong Kong Law Society. Member of Standing Committee on Company Law Reform.
Career: Qualified in 1979 with *Slaughter & May*. Partner 1986. Hong Kong Office since 1990.

TORTOISHELL, Andrew
Herbert Smith, Hong Hong +852 2845 6639
andrew.tortoishell@herbertsmith.com
Recommended in Capital Markets: Debt & Equity, Corporate/M&A
Specialisation: Partner in the company department of *Herbert Smith* in Hong Kong. Joined the firm in England in 1984, transferring to the Hong Kong office in 1990. Has a wide-ranging corporate practice encompassing equity corporate finance and initial public offerings, mergers and acquisitions, corporate rescues and restructurings. Clients range from Hong Kong, UK and US listed companies, financial institutions and investment banks, to direct investment and financial services groups. Has worked on a significant number of initial public offerings in Hong Kong including Morgan Stanley and Peregrine on the initial public offering of Beijing Enterprises and Merrill Lynch, CSFB and Salomon Smith and Barney, and BOCI on the initial public offering of CNOOC.
Prof. Memberships: Law Society of Hong Kong; Law Society of England and Wales.
Career: Sheffield University (LLB). Admitted in England and Wales in 1986 and in Hong Kong in 1991. Partner in 1994.
Personal: Born on the 19 September 1961. Leisure interests include sailing and golf.

TREACY, Peter
Linklaters (a member firm of Linklaters & Alliance), Hong Kong +852 2842 4888
peter.treacy@linklaters.com
Recommended in Project Finance
Specialisation: Specialist in banking, structured finance and project finance. Prior to moving to the Hong Kong office in 1994, practised in the Banking Department in London, particularly in the areas of syndicated lending, corporate recovery and acquisition financing. Since moving to Hong Kong, has concentrated on project financing, structured financing and corporate recovery.

TSE, Joseph L.B.
Allen & Overy, Hong Kong +852 2974 7000
Recommended in Banking & Finance

WALTER, Jeremy
Clifford Chance, Hong Kong +852 2825 8888
Recommended in Capital Markets: Derivatives

YIH, Dieter
Kwok & Yih, Hong Kong +852 2523 1000
DYih@KnY.com
Recommended in Corporate/M&A
Specialisation: Has extensive experience in mergers and acquisitions and listed company takeovers, IPOs and secondary fund-raisings, and corporate restructuring. Frequently advises multinational and Hong Kong corporations on direct investments, joint ventures, regulatory compliance and investigation and Stock Exchange disciplinary proceedings.
Prof. Memberships: Law Society of Hong Kong; Law Society of Singapore; Law Society of England and Wales; Law Society of Australian Capital Territory, Australia.
Career: Co-founding partner of the firm. Qualified as a solicitor in Hong Kong, Australia, England and Singapore. Prior to founding the firm worked for many years in the corporate departments of *Woo, Kwan, Lee & Lo* and of *Slaughter and May*, focusing on capital market and corporate finance work. Serves on the board of directors of several listed companies in Hong Kong.

Personal: Graduated from King's College, University of London with a bachelor degree in law. Fluent in English, Cantonese and Mandarin.

YOUNG JR., John D.
Sullivan & Cromwell, Hong Kong +852 2826 8688
youngj@sullcrom.com
Recommended in Capital Markets: Debt & Equity
Specialisation: Partner actively involved in the firm's international corporate practice. Presently leads an exclusively Asian-focused practice in *S&C*'s Hong Kong office that includes securities offerings and exchange listings, privatisations, merger and acquisition work, joint ventures, debt restructuring, project finance, and general corporate advice. Partner in charge of China Unicom's restructuring and IPO. Involved in dozens of international securities offerings by Asian issuers, including Rediff.com, Ranbaxy Laboratories and Tata Engineering and Locomotive Company in India; Tenaga Nasional Berhad in Malaysia; San Miguel Corporation, National Power Corporation and Philippine Long Distance Telephone Company in the Philippines; Hong Kong Index Tracker Fund, Hutchison Whampoa Limited, Mass Transit Railway Corporation and National Mutual Asia Limited in Hong Kong; Taiwan Semiconductor Manufacturing Company and ASE Test Limited in Taiwan; PTTEP and Thai Farmers Bank in Thailand; and Ek Chor China Motorcycle Company Limited, which operates motorcycle and automotive component manufacturing joint ventures in China. Also has coordinated transactions involving several multinational companies, including Philips Electronics N.V., Sumitomo Corporation, Inco Limited, Doncasters PLC (formerly a subsidiary of Inco Limited), Service Corporation International, and Quiñenco S.A., VTR S.A., Compañía Cervecerías Unidas S.A. and other companies in the Luksic Group of Chile. These transactions included registered public offerings of debt and equity securities, Rule 144A and other non-registered securities offerings, establishment of international joint ventures, and advising on structured corporate financing transactions.
Prof. Memberships: American Bar Association; New York State Bar Association.
Career: Joined *Sullivan & Cromwell* in 1990. Became a Partner of the firm in 1998.
Personal: Born 1961. Graduated from Wake Forest University (BS, 1982), the University of Southwestern Louisiana (MBA, 1989) and Wake Forest University School of Law (JD, cum laude, 1990).

ZINKE, Jon
Keesal, Young & Logan LLP, Hong Kong
+852 2854 1718
Recommended in Shipping

H

HUNGARY

Index

H

OVERVIEW: The Hungarian commercial firms are facing a trying time as the privatisation process draws to a close, the promised internet revolution has not taken hold, and the capital markets are flat. Corporate growth is witnessed in consolidations, most obviously in the financial sector as ABN AMRO Hungary is merging with K&H Bank, and HypoVereinsbank is acquiring Bank Austria. In January 2000 it was further shaken up when Csaba Berecz and a finance team left Clifford Chance to set up the Linklaters office propelling the firm to the top of the banking market. Consolidation amongst law firms saw Squire Sanders and Dempsey take over teams from Strook & Strook, and Arent Fox, including high profile 'fixer' Ivan Szasz, leaving it well placed to play a greater role in the region.

Banking & Finance

HUNGARY Leading firms (Banking & Finance)
1 Allen & Overy
Berecz & Andrékó Linklaters
CMS Cameron McKenna Ormai
2 Köves & Partners Clifford Chance
3 Mártonyi és Kajtár/Baker & McKenzie
4 Gárdos, Benke, Mosonyi, Tomori
Réczicza Law Firm White & Case LLP
5 Nagy és Trócsányi

Firms are listed alphabetically in each band.

Leading individuals (Banking & Finance)
1 BERECZ Csaba *Berecz & Andrékó Linklaters*
DANKÓ Péter *Allen & Overy*
DOUGHTY Alex *CMS Cameron McKenna Ormai*
KÖVES Péter *Köves & Partners Clifford Chance*
SIEGLER Konrád *Mártonyi és Kajtár*
2 GÁRDOS Istvan *Gárdos, Benke, Mosonyi, Tomori*
ORMAI Gabriella *CMS Cameron McKenna Ormai*
3 HEGEDÛS Éva *Allen & Overy*
IRVING Robert *Réczicza Law Firm White & Case*

Individuals are listed alphabetically in each band.

Allen & Overy (1 ptr, 8 asscs) *"A traditional banking firm"* which has weathered the slump in financial work in Budapest by concentrating on areas such as debt refinancing. Transactions here have involved innovative capital markets structures designed to minimise risk exposure. The firm's superb international network and financial experience have seen it advise on major cross-border financings and foreign bond issues for its clientele of leading financial institutions.

Péter Dankó* is praised by competitors for being *"knowledgeable, skilled and thorough,"* while **Éva Hegedûs*** attracts recommendation for her project finance work. The group advised a syndicate of banks on a €100 million loan to BorsodChem Rt. **Clients:** Deutsche Bank; CSFB; ING Bank; CIB Bank.

Berecz & Andrékó Linklaters (1 ptr, 8 asscs) One of the year's major events has been the move of a team of finance lawyers from Clifford Chance to Linklaters. The *"aggressive"* approach of *"ambitious and experienced"* **Csaba Berecz*** has quickly established it as, in the words of one authority *"one of the market leaders in terms of volume of transactions."*

Involved for either the bank or the borrower on most of the major transactions of 2000, the team has strength in all areas of banking and finance advice and a powerful international client roster. The firm represented MKB Hungarian Foreign Trade Bank on the financing of the Meder real estate project, and advised ABN AMRO, Bank Austria Creditanstalt & CIB Bank as lead managers of the HUF45 billion MTN programme issued by MATÁV. **Clients:** MKB; ABN AMRO; Bank Austria Creditanstalt; CIB Bank; Chase Manhattan.

CMS Cameron McKenna Ormai (2 ptrs, 12 asscs) *"Eager and aggressive,"* this versatile banking group advises on project finance, syndicated lending, derivatives and regulatory work for a clientele that is weighted more towards lenders.

Alex Doughty* is *"technically good, thorough and helpful,"* while, in addition to her M&A and managerial roles, **Gabriella Ormai*** is *"a reputable banking lawyer"* with a good name in the market for regulatory work. The firm acted for Citibank in negotiating a HUF13.5 billion loan facility to MATÁV Rt, and advised a syndicate including DG Bank, ING Bank, Fuji Bank and RZB on granting a $350 million syndicated facility to MOL Rt. **Clients:** DG Bank; ING Bank; Citibank; ABN AMRO.

Köves & Partners Clifford Chance (1 ptr, 7 asscs) While the loss of much of the banking department to Linklaters has clearly had a profound short-term effect, the market views it as a temporary setback. The resources and experience of the Clifford Chance network ensure that the office *"still has the power to pull off high-profile coups."* The team also retains the services of the *"incomparable"* **Péter Köves***, *"a devoted lawyer with a superb reputation."*

Experience in public take-overs, project financing and refinancing has been reinforced by an increase in derivatives and structured finance transactions. The firm advised Citibank and ABN AMRO on a €350 million facility relating to the VRAM loan, and acted for HTCC on obtaining a €130 million refinancing facility. **Clients:** Citibank; ABN AMRO; Budapest Bank; HTCC.

Mártonyi és Kajtár/Baker & McKenzie (1 ptr, 6 asscs) Led by **Konrád Siegler***, who received an impressive degree of market approval as *"a precise, sharp, clever negotiator,"* the firm *"has the expertise locally"* and a universally acclaimed capital markets practice. International project finance is another area of strength, as is M&A within the banking sector. The firm advised on the HUF45 billion MTN programme and first public offering of MATÁV, representing the issuer, and represented Bank Austria and KPC on their respective mergers. **Clients:** KPC; Bank Austria; MATÁV.

Gárdos, Benke, Mosonyi, Tomori (3 ptrs, 6 asscs) Renowned for advising on banking and regulatory matters, Hungary's leading finance boutique is considered by competitors *"a good home-grown law firm with good banking lawyers."* Though lacking an international network, the firm advises on a number of smaller transactions, and assists its clients on regulatory compliance. Growth areas include assisting banks to establish themselves as 'universal banks' offering securities and state banking, and establishing companies as 'financial enterprises' operating under the supervision of the banking authority.

"Knowledgeable and precise," **Istvan Gárdos*** is *"a good technician with lots of experience."* The firm advised EBRD in assisting the Ministry of Justice on its project of modernising the Hungarian law on collaterals. **Clients:** EBRD; European Commercial Bank Ltd; Budapest Bank; Hypo-Vereinsbank; State Banking Supervisory Authority.

Réczicza Law Firm White & Case LLP (2 ptrs, 5 asscs) *"Strong on capital markets,"* the firm is less visible in classical banking matters, but *"the potential is there; they have good people."* Respected for its high-profile privatisation work, the firm also represents underwriters on offerings and advises on project finance, derivatives and bank lending work. Though better known for his M&A practice, **Rob Irving*** is also recommended for his project finance expertise.

The firm advised CA IB Securities and ÁPV Rt in connection with the auction sale on the Budapest Stock Exchange of HUF4.5 billion worth of shares in BorsodChem Rt, the first such auction based on modified trading rules. Also advised CIB Bank, Raiffeisen Bank and Crédit Lyonnais on the granting of a $30 million revolving loan facility to IKARUSBUS. **Clients:** HSBC; CA IB; Crédit Lyonnais; CIB Bank; Raiffeisen Bank; European Bank for Reconstruction and Development.

Nagy és Trócsányi (2 ptrs, 3 asscs) Visible in the market on traditional banking, structured finance and aircraft finance, the firm is active on a range of smaller and medium-sized transactions. A skilled team of Hungarian lawyers attracts market plaudits for its *"knowledge and energy."* Strong in all areas of financing, it has been active on regulatory work for its domestic & international client base. **Clients:** ABN AMRO; Bank of America; EBRD; BCI Bank.

H

Communications

HUNGARY Leading firms (Communications)
1 Köves & Partners Clifford Chance
Réczicza Law Firm White & Case LLP
2 Allen & Overy
Komáromi és Erös Squire, Sanders & Dempsey LLP
3 Bán, S Szabó & Partners in Co-operation with Altheimer & Gray
CMS Cameron McKenna Ormai
Mártonyi és Kajtár/Baker & McKenzie

Firms are listed alphabetically in each band.

Leading individuals (Communications)
1 LAKATOS Péter *Köves & Ptnrs Clifford Chance*
RÉCZICZA István *Réczicza White & Case LLP*
2 RIESZ Tamás *Allen & Overy*
Up-and-coming individuals
RAUSCH János *Bán, S Szabó/Altheimer & Gray*

Individuals are listed alphabetically in each band.

Köves & Partners Clifford Chance (1 ptr, 6 asscs) *"Probably the best known telecoms lawyer in Budapest,"* regulatory expert **Péter Lakatos*** is acknowledged by competitors to be *"a high quality man, who knows all aspects of the industry."* As well as representing the association of local telephone companies on interconnection and regulatory issues, the firm *"does all the telecommunications work for Vivendi and several other international operators,"* and has been active on telecoms acquisitions, licensing, tenders, contracts and financing.

Strong in IT, the group represented Unisys on its successful bid to supply hardware and software to the national postal operator. Also acted for local telephone concession group HTCC on the restructuring and refinancing of its $200 million debt. **Clients:** Association of Local Telephone Operators; Vivendi; UPC; Alcotel; Unisys; BKV; Deutsche Telekom.

Réczicza Law Firm White & Case LLP (1 ptr, 3 asscs) Undeniably one of the leading telecommunications and technology practices in Hungary, our researchers noted its superb reputation for *"advising the government all the time."* However, it also assists an extraordinary range of international high-tech clients and *"no one can argue that its anything less than superb."* Especially strong in cable television and the internet, the firm is commended for its understanding of regulatory matters.

István Réczicza* is *"a real expert,"* praised both as a rainmaker, and for his legal skills and experience. The firm acted for Deutsche Telekom on its proposed acquisition of SBC Communication's equity stake in MATÁV Rt. Also advised the government on certain aspects of the creation of a new regulatory communications framework. **Clients:** Deutsche Telekom; ARGUS Capital; ProNet; PSINet; Nokia; Ministry of Telecommunications; Antenna Hungária.

Allen & Overy (1 ptr, 3 asscs) *"Very professional"* team, which *"has been dealing with telecoms from the start."* Although it gives both regulatory and transactional telecoms advice, the firm's greatest visibility comes in telecoms financing. E-commerce is an expanding sector, where the team conducts M&A, licensing and regulatory advice. **Tamás Riesz*** is praised by clients as *"a young and capable specialist."*

The firm advised Swisscom Ltd and KPN Telecoms BV on the disposal of shares in Jász-Tel Rt to Magyar Telecom BV/CG-SAT. **Clients:** BT; KPN Telecom; PanTel.

Komáromi és Erős Squire Sanders & Dempsey LLP (6 asscs) Seen in the market representing LTOs and mobile operators, the firm *"has a reputation for telecoms work"* and advises a high-powered clientele. Active on both regulatory and transactional matters, the firm represents domestic and international telecoms operators (fixed line and mobile), satellite operators, cable television companies, broadcast media and government agencies. Represented the Hungarian Communication Authority in connection with preparing the terms and conditions of the 3,5 GHz frequency auction, the first such auction in the region. **Clients:** Teleglobe; MK International; Vodafone; Callahan; Interware; Sláger Rádió.

*See leaders' profiles on pages 376-377

Bán, S. Szabó & Partners in co-operation with Altheimer & Gray (2 ptrs, 2 asscs) Having changed its association from Shearman & Sterling to Altheimer & Gray, our researchers have discovered that this respected local firm has been flourishing. Strongly focused on telecommunications, the team has set up joint ventures, advised on licensing and telecoms-related M&A and also has experience of MMDS.

A strong department includes the *"skilled"* **János Rausch***, who *"represents his clients' interests firmly but flexibly."* The firm advised Antenna Hungária as minority shareholder in the establishment of Vodafone Hungary, the third incumbent DCS 1800 licence-holder. **Clients:** Antenna Hungária.

Cameron McKenna Ormai (1 ptr, 3 asscs) The firm has been especially visible in IT this year, representing suppliers and large users such as Postabank on IT procurement. Telecoms experience includes concessions, tenders, negotiating general terms and conditions and transactional work within the sector. E-commerce is an expanding area of focus, and the firm advised on a series of internet transactions for banks, as well as providing a telecoms sector study for Telenor. **Clients:** Westel 900; ICL; OTP; Postabank; Danubius Radio.

Mártonyi és Kajtár/Baker & McKenzie (1 ptr, 4 asscs) With its broad international communications expertise and first-rate client base, *"you couldn't ignore Baker & McKenzie."* Having acted on all three stages of the MATÁV privatisation, much of the group's traditional strength lies in financing and corporate work. However, it also provides substantial licensing and regulatory advice, working on contract drafting and reviewing and representing some leading IT companies. The firm acted for Orange on its DCS 1800 application, and represented Panon GSM on its international offering of high-yield notes. **Clients:** MATÁV; Orange; Panon GSM.

H

Corporate/M&A

Köves & Partners Clifford Chance (3 ptrs, 18 asscs) *"In the premier league in terms of deals done and number of lawyers,"* market opinion suggests that this is the corporate team to beat in Budapest. *"A strong corporate client base, hard-working lawyers, good connections and sheer quality"* were the reasons cited to our researchers that keep the department at the top. Strong in telecoms, energy and financial services, the firm has been active on big-ticket M&A for a range of international and domestic blue-chip concerns.

"Calm and correct" **Richard Lock*** stands out as a *"knowledgeable, creative, diligent and precise"* practitioner, while **Éva Talmácsi*** is *"painstaking and diligent."* The firm advised the State Privatisation Agency on the ongoing privatisation of MALÉV, and represented Frantschach Packaging on its successful public offer for Cofinec NV and subsequent disposal of assets. **Clients:** Frantschach AG; Kékkúti Ásványvíz; Borsod-Chem Rt; State Privatisation Agency (ÁPV Rt).

Allen & Overy (2 ptrs, 10 asscs) A large and expanding office, it *"has a balanced European client base and an excellent transactional record in Hungary."* The department's focus is on cross-border M&A for an international clientele, often in conjunction with the firm's first-rate finance department. However, it also acts on smaller domestic deals, particularly in the telecoms sector.

"Good negotiator" **Jonathan Porteous*** *"takes a sensible, practical approach"* and is *"focused on results,"* while **Éva Hegedûs*** is *"skilled and professional."* The firm acted for MOL Rt on its proposed merger with INA, and for Schroder Salomon Smith Barney on the acquisition of shares by MOL in TVK. **Clients:** KPN Telecom; MOL Rt; ICN Pharmaceuticals Inc; ING Bank Rt.

CMS Cameron McKenna Ormai (3 ptrs, 11 asscs) *"An effective firm with a large, well-organised office,"* it is highly visible in the Hungarian market. Although finance is the firm's particular forte in Budapest, the corporate team has recruited shrewdly and, according to one competitor, *"adapted well to local conditions,"* advising on an increasing volume of acquisitions and disposals. The department is particularly commended for its work in the energy industry.

"Switched on" **Gabriella Ormai*** is *"impressive, practical and sensible,"* and receives high praise for her building of the corporate practice, and **Istvan Kovari*** is held to have *"a good balance of international and local knowledge."* The firm represented Metsä-Serla on its $40 million acquisition of Cofinek, and acted for Citibank in acquiring the consumer banking business of ING. **Clients:** Citibank; ICL; Fortum; Metsä-Serla.

Mártonyi és Kajtár/Baker & McKenzie (4 ptrs, 12 asscs) *"It has always emphasised M&A, it's always had good people and it has interesting cases."* Our researchers noted that its strong group of Hungarian lawyers combined with the firm's international network gives the corporate team the best of both worlds. Only recent personnel departures are considered to darken an otherwise rosy picture. The team has corporate strength in industries ranging from telecoms to food, and has developed a strong purely domestic practice to complement its extensive cross-border work.

Ines Radmilovic* is *"the one pulling the practice in the right direction,"* while *"polite and professional"* **Zoltán Barakonyi*** is *"a good, well-prepared lawyer,"* visible on the competition aspects of transactions, most notably in the energy sector. The firm advised Compaq on the acquisition of a controlling stake in Digital Equipment Corporation and Wallis Investments Ltd on the acquisition of a majority holding in Hajdú Bét Rt. **Clients:** Ford Motor Company; Compaq; MATÁV; AT&T; Orange.

Réczicza Law Firm White & Case LLP (3 ptrs, 10 asscs) *"A good quality firm that's always in the frame,"* its real strength is its people; *"it has been successful in combining good US lawyers with talented Hungarians who help to develop business."* Chief among them is *"big picture guy"* **István Réczicza***, universally acknowledged by clients and competitors to be *"a good negotiator with excellent connections"* to the current government. *"Solid and experienced"* **Rob Irving*** *"keeps clients happy,"* and has *"a balanced combination of skills,"* and **Zsuzsanna Kovács*** is respected both for her corporate and capital markets expertise.

2000's merger with German firm Feddersen has improved the group's profile among important German clients, bolstering a client base which already included leading American and French concerns. Renowned for its ability on privatisations, the firm advises a number of venture capital companies on cross-border transactions, and is especially strong in the regulated industries. The team represented Perrier Vittel on its acquisition of a majority stake in Hungarian mineral water company Kékkúti Ásványvíz Rt, the

HUNGARY
Leading firms (Corporate/M&A)

Band	Firm
1	Köves & Partners Clifford Chance
2	Allen & Overy
	CMS Cameron McKenna Ormai
	Mártonyi és Kajtár/Baker & McKenzie
	Réczicza Law Firm White & Case LLP
3	BBLP Moquet Borde & Associés
	Komáromi és Erös Squire, Sanders & Dempsey LLP
	Nagy és Trócsányi
	Weil, Gotshal & Manges
4	Dewey Ballantine LLP
	Freshfields Bruckhaus Deringer

Firms are listed alphabetically in each band.

Leading individuals (Corporate/M&A)

Band	Individual	Firm
1	**LOCK Richard**	*Köves & Partners Clifford Chance*
	RÉCZICZA István	*Réczicza White & Case LLP*
	SZASZ Ivan	*Komáromi, Sanders & Dempsey*
	SZECSKAY András	*BBLP Moquet Borde*
2	**IRVING Robert**	*Réczicza White & Case LLP*
	ORMAI Gabriella	*CMS Cameron McKenna Ormai*
	PORTEOUS Jonathan	*Allen & Overy*
	RADMILOVIC Ines	*Mártonyi/Baker & McKenzie*
	TALMÁCSI Éva	*Köves & Partners Clifford Chance*
3	**BARAKONYI Zoltán**	*Mártonyi/Baker & McKenzie*
	DEDERICK David	*Weil, Gotshal & Manges*
	DERI Bela	*Deri & Lovrecz*
	ERÖS Ákos	*Komáromi, Sanders & Dempsey*
	HANÁK András	*Dewey Ballantine LLP*
	HEGEDÛS Éva	*Allen & Overy*
	KOVÁCS Zsuzsanna	*Réczicza White & Case LLP*
	KOVARI Istvan	*CMS Cameron McKenna Ormai*
	PASZTORY Blaise	*Komáromi, Sanders & Dempsey*
	REIN Ulrike	*Freshfields Bruckhaus Deringer*
	VARGA Ildiko	*Nagy és Trócsányi*

Individuals are listed alphabetically in each band.

first contested public tender offer for a Hungarian listed company. **Clients:** Perrier Vittel; AIG New Europe Fund; ARGUS Capital; Electricité de France.

BBLP Moquet Borde & Associés (1 ptr, 7 asscs) *"Client friendly, mature and experienced,"* **András Szecskay*** continues to keep this French firm's Hungarian office above the problems afflicting the firm elsewhere. Competitors agree that he has built *"quite a team of solid lawyers with a good sensible approach."*

The firm has developed all round corporate expertise in areas including pharmaceuticals and energy, while financial services and private equity work also form a substantial proportion of the caseload. The clientele now extends far beyond the firm's French heartland. The team advised on the demerger into six companies of the printing and packaging company Cofinec. **Clients:** Cofinec Group; Zwack Unicum Rt; Richter; BNP; Dresdner; CV Online.

Komáromi és Erös, Squire Sanders & Dempsey LLP (2 ptrs, 11 asscs) The acquisition of teams from Arent Fox Kinter Plotkin & Kahn and Stroock & Stroock & Lavan to boost the Budapest office of Squire Sanders & Dempsey was one of last year's most discussed developments in Hungary. Although it is still considered too early to judge the effect on the firm, the corporate team is especially commended for its telecoms and e-commerce expertise. Additional strength lies in private equity, while cross-border transactions are conducted for a range of multi-national and domestic clients.

The highest profile among the team's new recruits belongs to *"well-connected and shrewd client-getter"* **Ivan Szasz***, regarded by many as *"the father of modern Hungarian corporate law."* *"Gentlemanly and experienced"* **Blaise Pasztory*** and *"calm and commercially minded"* younger lawyer **Akos Erös*** also come warmly recommended. The firm has advised GE on numerous Hungarian investments, including the purchase of Tungsram. **Clients:** Audi; Bouygues; Cooper Industries; GE; Procter & Gamble; SPB Securities; Templeton Funds.

Nagy és Trócsányi (4 ptrs, 9 asscs) *"The strongest of the basically independent Hungarian firms"* is said to have *"good government relations"* and picks up substantial work from foreign investors. *"Taken very seriously"* by competitors, the firm's association with Coudert Brothers has assisted in building *"good contacts and a solid profile."* Experience in traditional industry, utilities and telecoms, a strong aviation practice and increasing instructions from property companies have led to high-profile work on major privatisations.

"Outstanding transactional lawyer" **Ildiko Varga*** is *"able to organise a case so everything runs smoothly."* The firm advised on the creation of one of the top five industrial developments in Hungary. **Clients:** Coca-Cola; ABN AMRO; MALÉV; Lexmark.

Weil, Gotshal & Manges (1 ptr, 5 asscs) *"Picking up some good work"* from local clients, as well as advising some high-profile global concerns, the firm is considered to be one of the leaders for private equity. M&A expertise has been used for transactions in energy, real estate and the high-tech market.

Sole partner **David Dederick*** is considered by competitors to be *"professional, persuasive, thoughtful and client-friendly."* His team represented the board of TVK on its successful defence against a hostile takeover by MOL, and advised GE Equity, Raiffeisen Private Equity and ABN AMRO Capital on a $20 million private equity transaction with InterCom. **Clients:** TVK; GE Equity; Raiffeisen Private Equity; ABN AMRO; PRICOA.

Dewey Ballantine LLP (1 ptr, 7 asscs) *"Respectable"* corporate team, which advises a client base that is evenly split between American, western European and domestic entities. The firm acts on large and medium-sized cross-border transactions, provides general corporate and contractual advice, and focuses on energy and telecoms.

"Pleasant to deal with," but *"a formidable opponent,"* **András Hanák*** led the team who advised a potential purchaser of the Csepel powerplant. The firm also represented the minority shareholder on the acquisition of a real estate holding company with retail assets. **Clients:** Disney; GE Capital; Electrolux; El Paso International; MCI WorldCom.

Freshfields Bruckhaus Deringer (3 ptrs, 12 asscs) Although the August 2000 merger gives the firm's Budapest office access to a formidable network of clients and corporate expertise, our researchers discovered that its visibility in Hungary remains comparatively low.

Active on cross-border M&A, restructuring and consolidation, especially in energy, chemicals, media and IT, the team advises a number of leading German companies. *"Highly professional"* **Ulrike Rein*** is considered to be the office's leading light. The group represented VNU on the acquisition of the largest publishing house in Hungary, and acted for Nutreco in an asset purchase involving new nutrition technology. **Clients:** VNU; Nutreco; Lufthansa Techknik.

Other Notable Practitioner *"Definitely a presence in the market,"* **Bela Deri***, the highest profile lawyer at KPMG-associated firm Deri & Lovrecz, is *"capable and well prepared."* A flamboyant character, *"some clients clearly love him."*

H

*See leaders' profiles on pages 376-377

Leaders' profiles – Hungary

BARAKONYI, Zoltán
Mártonyi És Kajtár/Baker & McKenzie, Budapest +36 1 302 3330
zoltan.barakonyi@bakernet.com
Recommended in Corporate/M&A
Specialisation: Partner in charge of the Competition, Trade and European Law Practice Group at the Budapest Office. Specialises in competition law and trade regulations, commercial transactions and litigation including public procurement matters. Leads the competition practice of the Budapest Office representing major international companies in competition law cases. Advised Hungarian and international companies on their merger control notifications to the Hungarian Competition Office. Published a number of articles on competition law and merger control.
Prof. Memberships: Hungarian Bar Association; Vice-President of the Hungarian Competition Law Association. Frequent speaker at internal and external conferences and lecturer in competition law in the MBA Program of the Technical University of Budapest.
Career: Admitted in 1996. Worked for the Hungarian Competition Office in 1992. Completed an internship at the Federal Trade Commission and the Antitrust Division of the US Department of Justice in 1993. Joined the Budapest Office of *Baker & McKenzie[TT-] in 1994. Became a partner in 1999.*
Personal: Born 9 March 1967. Attended the Law School of Janus Pannonius University, Pécs, Hungary 1986-92 (Juris Doctor); Indiana University of Pennsylvania, Indiana, PA, USA 1992-93 (Master of Arts in Political Sciences); the College of William & Mary in Virginia, Williamsburg, VA, USA 1993-94 (Master of Laws). Lives in Budapest. Speaks fluent Hungarian and English.

BERECZ, Csaba
Berecz & Andrékó Linklaters, Budapest +36 1 428 4400
csaba.berecz@linklaters.com
Recommended in Banking & Finance
Specialisation: Head of Budapest office. Specialist in domestic and international finance and capital market transactions, with specific experience in syndicated lending, project finance, structured trade finance, ISDA derivatives, MTN programmes, FRN/bond issues and general banking regulation.
Prof. Memberships: Budapest Bar.

DANKÓ, Péter
Allen & Overy, Budapest +36 1 483 2200
Recommended in Banking & Finance

DEDERICK, David
Weil, Gotshal & Manges, Budapest +36 1 302 9100
david.dederick@weil.com
Recommended in Corporate/M&A
Specialisation: Partner in the Corporate Department. Practice involves a broad range of transactional matters, including M&A, corporate, securities, capital markets, venture capital and private equity. Has particular expertise in the media, telecoms and internet areas. Served as lead counsel in major transactions in Hungary, Poland, the Czech Republic, Austria, Slovakia and Romania.
Prof. Memberships: Washington, D.C. Bar. New Jersey Bar. Foreign Legal Advisor, Budapest Bar Association. International Bar Association.
Career: Managing Partner of the Firm's Budapest Office. From 1996 to 1998, Deputy General Manager and General Counsel of Compagnie Financière pour l'Europe Centrale – S.A., Vienna, Austria. From 1991 to 1993, seconded as Counsel, Hungarian-American Enterprise Fund, Budapest, Hungary.
Personal: George Washington University Law School (JD 1988); Cornell University (BS 1985). Guest Lecturer, Eötvös Loránd University Law School, Budapest. Guest Lecturer, Central European University Legal Studies Program, Budapest.

DERI, Bela
Deri & Lovrecz, Budapest +361 270 7430
Recommended in Corporate/M&A

DOUGHTY, Alex
CMS Cameron McKenna Ormai, Budapest +36 1 302 9302
Recommended in Banking & Finance

ERÖS, Ákos
Komáromi & Erös Squire, Sanders & Dempsey LLP, Budapest +36 1 428 7111
Recommended in Corporate/M&A

GÁRDOS, Istvan
Gárdos, Benke, Mosonyi, Tomori, H-1056 Budapest +36 1 235 74 60
Recommended in Banking & Finance

HANÁK, András I.
Dewey Ballantine LLP, Budapest +36 1 374 2660
ahanak@deweyballantine.com
Recommended in Corporate/M&A
Specialisation: Managing lawyer in *Dewey Ballantine's* Budapest Office. Main areas of specialiasation include mergers and acquisitions, telecommunications and power projects. Represents Hachette Distribution Services in connection with acquistions and corporate matters. Active in the power generation sector, representing EL Paso Energy and NRG Energy in connection with Hungarian power projects.
Prof. Memberships: Hungarian Bar Association, Pennsylvania Bar Association.
Career: Commenced international corporate and commercial practice in Washington D.C. in 1987 and returned to Budapest, Hungary in 1991.
Personal: Born 30 August 1951. Acquired JD degree in Budapest, Hungary (1975), left Hungary and acquired an LLM degree (1982- Columbia University School of Law) and a JD degree (1987 – University of Pennsylvania Law School). Lecturer at Budapest University School of Law, Central European University.

HEGEDÛS, Éva
Allen & Overy, Budapest +36 1 483 2200
Recommended in Banking & Finance, Corporate/M&A

IRVING, Robert
Réczizca Law Firm White & Case LLP, Budapest +36 1 488 5200
rirving@budapest.whitecase.com
Recommended in Banking & Finance, Corporate/M&A
Specialisation: Leading corporate and finance law partner based in the firm's Budapest office. Regularly represents major domestic and international corporates and financial institutions on many of the most high profile transactions in the Hungarian market. Recent work includes financings, projects and M&A transactions involving the telecoms, energy, highway, water, and oil industry sectors.
Career: US-qualified.

KOVÁCS, Zsuzsanna
Réczizca Law Firm White & Case LLP, Budapest +36 1 488 5200
zkovacs@whitecase.com
Recommended in Corporate/M&A
Specialisation: Leading corporate finance and securities lawyer based in *White & Case* Budapest office. Specialises in domestic and international capital markets transactions. Most recently has acted for oil and gas, electricity, banking, food & drink and telecommunications sectors in Hungary.
Career: Has worked previously for *Baker & McKenzie, Debevoise & Plimpton* and the Hungarian State Property Authority. Joined *White & Case* in 1999.
Personal: Fluent English and Hungarian. Qualified under Hungarian law.

KOVARI, Istvan
CMS Cameron McKenna Ormai, Budapest +36 1 302 9302
Recommended in Corporate/M&A

KÖVES, Péter
Köves & Partners Clifford Chance, Budapest +36 1 429 1300
Recommended in Banking & Finance

LAKATOS, Péter
Köves & Partners Clifford Chance, Budapest +36 1 429 1300
Recommended in Communications

LOCK, Richard
Köves & Partners Clifford Chance, Budapest +36 1 429 1300
Recommended in Corporate/M&A

ORMAI, Gabriella
CMS Cameron McKenna Ormai, Budapest +36 1 302 9302
Recommended in Banking & Finance, Corporate/M&A

PASZTORY, Blaise G A
Komáromi & Erös Squire, Sanders & Dempsey LLP, Budapest +36 1 428 7111
Recommended in Corporate/M&A

PORTEOUS, Jonathan
Allen & Overy, Budapest +36 1 483 2200
Recommended in Corporate/M&A

RADMILOVIC, Ines
Mártonyi És Kajtár/Baker & McKenzie, Budapest +36 1 302 3330
ines.radmilovic@bakernet.com
Recommended in Corporate/M&A
Specialisation: Partner and Head of the M&A Practice Group, advising domestic and international clients principally on mergers, acquisitions, corporate group reorganisations, venture capital, private equity and privatisations. Member of the firm's M&A and Venture Capital Practice Groups.
Prof. Memberships: Illinois State Bar Association, registered 'Foreign Adviser' in Hungary. Representative to American Chamber in Budapest. Founding member of the Professional Women's Association of Budapest.
Career: Qualified 1988. Joined *Baker & McKenzie's* Chicago office and transferred to Budapest office in 1992, becoming a partner in 1996. Speaks at various conferences on M&A issues. Contributes to various firm and third party publications; including the Hungarian chapter of the European Counsel's international M&A supplement.
Personal: Born 5 January 1964. Georgetown law graduate. Lives in Budapest with husband and son. Speaks intermediate Hungarian, fluent in English, Croatian, French.

RAUSCH, János
Bán, S. Szabó & Partners in Co-operation with Altheimer & Gray, Budapest +36 1 266 3522
Recommended in Communications

RÉCZICZA, István
Réczizca Law Firm White & Case LLP, Budapest +36 1 488 5200
ireczicza@whitecase.com
Recommended in Communications, Corporate/M&A
Specialisation: Co-head of the firm's Budapest office and has been the senior Hungarian lawyer in the office since joining the firm in June 1997. Practice focuses primarily on transactions involving foreign investment in regulated industries, particularly in the telecoms, energy, media and financial services sectors. Has become one of Hungary's leading figures in the analysis of industry regulation and the drafting of proposed amendments in connection with such legislation.
Career: Admitted to Hungarian Bar.
Personal: Fluent Hungarian and English.

REIN, Ulrike
Freshfields Bruckhaus Deringer, Budapest +36 1 487 4040
ulrike.rein@freshfieldsbruckhaus.com
Recommended in Corporate/M&A
Specialisation: Specialises in environmental, planning and regulatory work.

RIESZ, Tamás
Allen & Overy, Budapest +36 1 483 2200
Recommended in Communications

SIEGLER, Konrád
Mártonyi És Kajtár/Baker & McKenzie, Budapest +36 1 302 3330
konrad.siegler@bakernet.com
Recommended in Banking & Finance
Specialisation: Partner and Head of the Securities and Finance Practice Group. Specialises in securities and finance transactions, international public offerings and private placements of equity securities, offering of debt securities, project financing, general and syndicated lending. Lecturer of securities law at the ELTE University in Budapest. Author of various articles in the field of capital markets and finance. Contributes to European Legal Developments Bulletin and Central European and CIS Legal Update, concerning Hungarian law. Has been published in various firm and third party publications. Has spoken at various firm and third-party organised conferences on securities and project finance related matters.
Prof. Memberships: Hungarian Bar Association (1994); Issuers Committee of the Budapest Stock Exchange.
Career: Qualified in Budapest, Hungary in 1993; joined *Baker and McKenzie's* Budapest Office in 1991, becoming a partner in 1998.
Personal: Born 1 October 1966. Attended ELTE University in Budapest (Faculty of Law 1991); lives in Budapest and is married with two sons Áron (5) and Márk (2).

SZASZ, Ivan
Komáromi & Erös Squire, Sanders & Dempsey LLP, Budapest +36 1 428 7111
Recommended in Corporate/M&A

SZECSKAY, András
BBLP Moquet Borde & Associés, Budapest +36 1 353 1255
moquet_borde_paris@compuserve.com
Recommended in Corporate/M&A
Specialisation: Counsel at *BBLP Moquet Borde* and Head of the Firm's Budapest office. Has a broad experience of mergers and acquisitions/corporate law practice with special expertise in privatisation and intellectual property. Has been advisor to several major international companies in the preparation and implementation of privatisation projects and was counsel to the state-owned enterprises for restructuring and privatisation activities. In addition, advises on domestic and international share offerings and listings on the Budapest Stock Exchange.
Prof. Memberships: President of the Budapest Bar; Hungarian Association for the Protection of Industrial Property; International Licensing Executives Society (LES); International Bar Association.
Career: Frequent speaker at international conferences on legal and business issues in Hungary and other Central and Eastern European Countries and was the author for the Hungary section of 'The Digest of Commercial Laws of the World' (L. Nelson, editor). Before joining *BBLP Moquet Borde* in 1992, was a Partner with *SBG&K Patent Law Office.*
Personal: Masters of Law graduate of the University of Szeged Law School (1973- summa cum laude) and was selected to participate in the Canada-Eastern European Lawyers Internship Program in Canada in 1990.

TALMÁCSI, Éva
Köves & Partners Clifford Chance, Budapest +36 1 429 1300
Recommended in Corporate/M&A

VARGA, Ildiko
Nagy és Trócsányi, Budapest +36 1 487 8700
varga.ildiko@nagyestrocsanyi.hu
Recommended in Corporate/M&A
Specialisation: Executive partner, head of corporate and M&A group. Main area of work includes corporate law, privatisation, media, industrial developments. Advised the Hungarian Privatisation Agency on the privatisation of the regional gas companies, also advised the National Radio and Television Board on the privatisation of the national commercial radio channels. Advised on the creation of one of the top five Hungarian industrial developments.
Prof. Memberships: New York Bar, Budapest Bar.
Publications: Author of 'Comparative Study of Constitutional Courts of Europe and the USA I-II', published by the Legal Institute of the Hungarian Academy of Sciences, 1988.
Career: Joined *White & Case*, New York in 1990 as foreign attorney, moved to *Arent Fox*, Washington in 1991. Joined *Nagy és Trócsányi* as partner in 1993.
Personal: Graduated Eötvös Loránd Tudományegyetem Faculty of Law in 1988, Faculty of Arts in 1980. Obtained PhD in Philosophy and Jurisprudence in 1984. Studied comparative law at Université de Strasbourg in 1987. Studied law and philosophy at NYU, Graduate School of Arts and Sciences in New York in 1989-1990.

ICELAND

Corporate/Commercial

ICELAND Leading firms (Corporate/Commercial)
1 Logos Legal Services
2 Jonsson & Hall
Lex
3 AM Praxis

Firms are listed alphabetically in each band.

Leading individuals (Corporate/Commercial)
1 **ÁRNASON Hákon** *Logos Legal Services*
JONSSON Gunnar *Jonsson & Hall*
JONSSON Gestur *Jonsson & Hall*
MÖLLER Jakob *Logos Legal Services*
VILHJÁLMSSON Árni *Logos Legal Services*
2 **ADALSTEINSSON Jónas** *Lex*
ADALSTEINSSON Ragnar *Sole Practitioner*
JONATANSSON Hrobjartur *AM Praxis*
SIGURDSSON Jóhannes *Logos Legal Services*

Individuals are listed alphabetically in each band.

Logos Legal Services (9 ptrs, 12 asscs) The merger of two of Iceland's premier firms has produced an organisation of a size hitherto unseen in Iceland. Our researchers were informed that this is a *"reputable firm with honest, hard-working lawyers"* offering the full range of corporate and commercial services, including insurance, shipping, investment, IP, business and company law. *"Ambitious"* **Jakob Möller*** has *"the ability to provide solutions,"* while litigator **Hákon Árnason*** *"does a good job away from the spotlight."* *"Dedicated"* **Árni Vilhjálmsson*** and **Jóhannes Sigurdsson***, who teaches corporate law at university, complete a formidable group of recommended practitioners. The firm worked on the merger between Landsbanki and Bundarbanki and is handling the financing and construction contracts for a new mall on behalf of Smaralint. **Clients:** Eimskip; Iceland Air; Landsbanki; Smaralint.

Jonsson & Hall (3 ptrs, 2 asscs) Smaller *"family firm"* which is highly regarded for business law, banking, M&A, communications, IP, shipping, competition and labour law. *"Main man"* **Gestur Jonsson*** is considered to be *"a leading authority,"* while **Gunnar Jonsson*** is respected for his international experience. The firm acted on the merger and refinancing of Channel 2 multimedia company and on behalf of a consortium which acquired 25-30% of the Iceland Investment Bank. **Clients:** Northern Lights Communications; Shell; Samskip; Islandsflug; Morgonbladid.

Lex (11 ptrs, 4 asscs) A merger with KPMG has formed *"a large firm which as yet lacks really big name individuals."* Particularly noted for expertise in cross-border M&A and contract law, the team has a strong clientele in shipping and insurance. The most senior figure here is **Jónas Adalsteinsson***, who has an established name for international work. The firm recently acted as Icelandic legal advisor for Bank Paribas on a $170 million refinance and finance for an expansion of the Nordural aluminiu smelter. It also represented S.R Mjöl in an acquisition and the restructuring of Atlantic Coast Seafood, an American fisheries company. **Clients:** Domestic and foreign banks; financial institutions; merchants and ship owners.

AM Praxis (4 ptrs, 4 asscs) Each lawyer has their own area of expertise at a firm which covers commercial law, telecommunications, biotechnology agreements, contracts, finance, maritime law and investment banking. **Hrobjartur Jonatansson*** has a US law degree and a name which carries domestic weight. The firm acts as legal counsel to lina.net and represented them in a deal with Motorola regarding the installation of a Tetra telecommunications system. **Clients:** A major US software company; BSA members; insurance companies; Icelandic banks; investment banks.

Other Notable Practitioner **Ragnar Adalsteinsson**'s decision to establish himself as a sole practitioner came as a surprise to some, but others view it as *"a return to his roots."* Chairman of the Board of Human Rights in Iceland, he focuses almost exclusively on human rights and telecommunications, and represents TAL, the mobile telephone operator.

*See leaders' profiles on pages 379

Leaders' profiles – Iceland

ADALSTEINSSON, Jónas A.
Lex, Reykjavik +354 590 2600
lex@lex.is
Specialisation: Partner in *Lex* Law Offices. Main area of work is corporate law, principally mergers, acquisitions, privatisation, banking and finance as well as shipping law. Acted as legal advisor in a merger of four Icelandic banks into Icebank, which recently merged with the Icelandic Investment Bank; acted as legal advisor for Spölur Ltd, in the first major project finance an Iceland, which took place in the years of 1994-1998, and concerned a building of a tunnel under the bay of Hvalfjöröur; acted as legal advisor to SR-mjöl in their acquisition of a fisheries factory in USA; has acted as legal advisor for various foreign investors and foreign banks investing in Iceland, as a recent example is work undertaken as Icelandic legal advisors with *Allen & Overy* acting for the investors, for the finance of an aluminium plant in Iceland. Has handled acquisition of companies and legal counseling of various sorts for Icelandic and overseas clients.
Prof. Memberships: Member of the Icelandic Bar Association, the International Chamber of Commerce, the Icelandic Lawyers Association, and the Icelandic Maritime Society.
Career: Deputy Judge at the City Court of Reykjavik during 1963. Legal counsel at the Central Bank of Iceland during 1964/1965, after which started own legal practice in affiliation with other lawyers, later to form *Lex* Law Offices.
Personal: Born 25 of May 1934. Graduated from the University of Iceland, Faculty of Law 1962. Admitted to the Bar 1963. Admitted to practice before the Supreme Court 1968.

ADALSTEINSSON, Ragnar
Ragnar Adalsteinsson – Sole Practitioner, Reykjavik +354 511 1206

ÁRNASON, Hákon
Logos, 105 Reykjavik +354 540 0300

JONATANSSON, Hrobjartur
AM Praxis, Reykjavik +354 533 3333

JONSSON, Gestur
Jonsson & Hall, 108 Reykjavik +354 581 2122

JONSSON, Gunnar
Jonsson & Hall, 108 Reykjavik +354 581 2122

MÖLLER, Jakob R.
Logos, 105 Reykjavik +354 540 0300

SIGURDSSON, Jóhannes
Logos, 105 Reykjavik +354 540 0300

VILHJÁLMSSON, Árni
Logos, 105 Reykjavik +354 540 0300

I

INDIA

Index

OVERVIEW: There is increasingly overt domestic hostility against the foreign invader and The Bombay Lawyers' Collective action in the High Court (against Ashurst Morris Crisp, White & Case, and Chadbourne & Parke) continues. Chadbourne & Parke has pulled out altogether and firms remain "resigned to a long haul." Under the present 'protectionist' measures India has witnessed a dramatic decline in investor-interest. Power and Infrastructure projects have ground to a halt, and in many cases have become embroiled in expensive arbitration. That said, domestic firms are thriving in this area although issues arise over scale and resources. Hopes of a liberalisation rest with the friend of the WTO, Arun Jaitley, who has taken over the government's law portfolio. Optimism in India's success story, telecoms media and technology companies remains high with a highly educated and skilled workforce. Almost 80% of deals in the first half of 2000 were IT related and there is an increase in lucrative associations between Indian and offshore firms in this sector. There have been profound changes in the habits and structure of domestic firms, with talented junior lawyers quitting the more traditional firms for dynamic firms such as Nishith Desai Associates and Dua Associates.

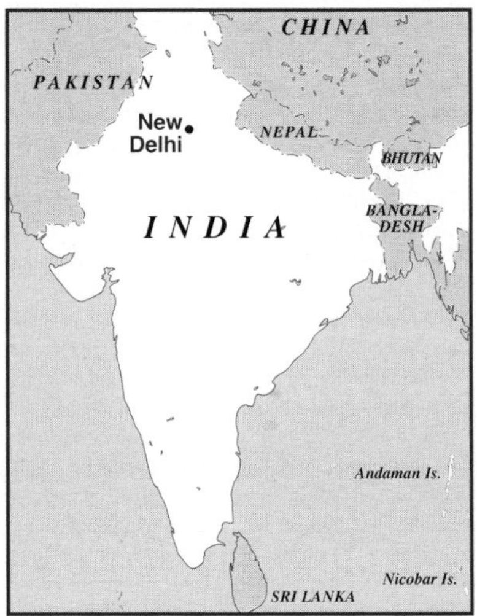

Corporate/M&A: Local Firms

Amarchand & Mangaldas & Suresh A Shroff & Co (5 ptrs, up to 65 fee earners) This *"absolutely excellent"* and *"enterprising"* firm stands unopposed at the pinnacle of corporate and projects work in India, and has an especially enviable reputation in the telecoms sector. The team acts on cross-border M&A transactions for a clientele which includes a host of blue-chip international names. Mumbai-based **Cyril Shroff*** is regarded as one of India's finest lawyers and is considered *"a joy to work with or against."* His New Delhi-based brother, **Shardul Shroff***, retains his reputation as a *"superb technician,"* and the *"competent"* **MP Bharucha*** is also recommended. The firm acted as transaction counsel (to issuer and backer) in the $350 million (rupee funded) IPO of Hughes Telecom; for the backers and for HCL Technologies in its $300 million IPO; for Goldman Sachs on the completed ADR offering of rediff.com; for all parties in the amalgamation of the e-cellular businesses of Birla, Tata and AT&T. **Clients:** Tata Group; Birla Group; Housing Development Finance Corporation; The Coca-Cola Company; General Electric; EM Warburg Pincus; Kotak Mahindra; Goldman Sachs; Credit Suisse First Boston; Capital Group International; Standard Chartered Bank; Great Eastern Shipping.

Crawford Bayley & Co (5 ptrs, 15 fee-earners) Market opinion is that the firm, one of India's oldest, is not quite the force of previous years. The departure of star partner Darius Udwadia is perceived to have been a setback, although the firm remains highly regarded for its bespoke services, both in corporate/M&A and trademark law. An impressive international client roster includes banks, pharmaceuticals, aviation and petrochemicals companies. The two top lawyers here are the IP and corporate specialist **Rajendra Shah***, who has a *"prodigious deal flow"* and is director of more than 30 commercial concerns, and *"star name"* **Suresh Talwar***, renowned for his connections with financial institutions.

Recent highlights for the department include advising on the mergers of SmithKline Beecham with Glaxo India Ltd, and Warner Lambert and Parke Davis with Pfizer Ltd. **Clients:** BASF; Abbott Laboratories; Bayer AG; Glaxo Wellcome; Hoechst AG; Procter & Gamble; Siemens AG; Alfa Laval; Ingersoll-Rand; Boeing Co; Ford; Mercedes Benz; Alcatel; Exxon.

Little & Co (18 ptrs, 27 fee-earners) Another *"old school"* firm which has seen a general increase in transactional work, thanks to a general growth in M&A work, notably in energy, telecoms, pharmaceuticals and the automobile industry. Managing partner **Ravindra Kulkarni*** is universally admired for his *"commercial instincts,"* while *"corporate specialists"* **Dara Mehta*** and **Dina Wadia*** also remain respected nationally. Notable transactions include acting for Bank of America in the arrangement of a $100 million loan for ICICI; for the State Bank of India in the arrangemenmy of a loan to Telcon. **Clients:** Kotak Mahindra; Godrej Group; British Gas.

Dua Associates (16 ptrs, 74 asscs) This New Delhi-based firm is seen as a success story, and is now adjudged to hold a position of *"great prominence"* in the market. *"Certainly well-established with multi-nationals,"* the firm acts for a range of domestic and international clients, with particular strength among financial institutions and IT concerns. Name partner **Ranji Dua***, a former protégé of the legendary J.B. Dadachanji, continues to receive high praise from peers and clients. Recent work has included advice on joint ventures, corporate reorganisations, exchange controls and regulatory issues, securities, M&A transactions and technology licensing agreements. **Clients:** Privately owned and publicly listed companies; investment banks; government agencies.

INDIA Leading firms (Corporate/Mergers & Acquisitions)
1 Amarchand & Mangaldas & Suresh A Shroff & Co
2 Crawford Bayley & Co
Little & Co
3 Dua Associates
4 Kanga & Co
Mulla & Mulla & Craigie Blunt & Caroe
Nishith Desai Associates
5 Ajay Bahl & Co Advocates & Solicitors
Chambers of Zia Mody, Advocate
Fox Mandal & Co
Jyoti Sagar & Associates
Khaitan & Co
Pathak & Associates
6 Desai & Diwanji
Gagrat & Co
Rajinder Narain & Co
Surana & Surana International Attorneys
Udwadia Udeshi & Berjis

Firms are listed alphabetically in each band.

Leading individuals (Corporate/Mergers & Acquisitions)
1 **BHAKTA ML** *Kanga & Co*
KULKARNI Ravindra *Little & Co*
SHAH Rajendra *Crawford Bayley & Co*
SHROFF Shardul *Amarchand & Mangaldas*
SHROFF Cyril *Amarchand & Mangaldas*
2 **MEHTA Dara** *Little & Co*
MODY Zia *Chambers of Zia Mody, Advocate*
TALWAR Suresh *Crawford Bayley & Co*
3 **BAHL Ajay** *Ajay Bahl & Co*
DESAI EB *Mulla & Mulla & Craigie Blunt*
DUA Ranji *Dua Associates*
KHAITAN OP *Khaitan & Co*
NATH Ravindra *Rajinder Narain & Co*
PATHAK Jai *Pathak & Associates*
THACKER Shardul *Mulla & Mulla & Craigie Blunt*
4 **BHARUCHA MP** *Amarchand & Mangaldas*
DADACHANJI JB *JB Dadachanji & Co*
MANDAL Som *Fox Mandal & Co*
MERCHANT Kalpana *Kanga & Co*
SAGAR Jyoti *Jyoti Sagar & Associates*
WADIA Dina *Little & Co*
Individuals are listed alphabetically in each band.

Kanga & Co (4 ptrs, 8 asscs) Long-established Mumbai firm with a respected corporate/commercial department. Specialising in cross-border M&A, the firm acts for a number of heavyweight domestic and international corporates, and is also acknowledged for its expertise in IP. **ML Bhakta*** *"has a wonderful intellect,"* and continues to command widespread market respect, while projects expert **Kalpana Merchant*** also enjoys high status for her corporate advice. The firm acted for Dutch giant Philips Limited on a recent high-profile transaction and advised Mitsu Industries Limited, one of India's largest agrochemical concerns, on its joint venture with Hoechst Schering AgrEvo. **Clients:** Pirelli Cavi; Pillsbury Company; Pacific Century; Reliance Group; British American Tobacco; Thyssen-Krupp; Gujarat Ambuja Cement Limited.

Mulla & Mulla & Craigie Blunt & Caroe (20 ptrs, 80 fee-earners) The largest law firm in India now has offices in Mumbai and Bangalore, and is regarded as a corporate specialist. Areas of expertise include aviation, shipping, privatisation, infrastructure and IP issues arising from the IT sector. The firm works closely with UK City firm Norton Rose, notably on shipping and aviation matters, and represents a number of big-name international investors on acquisitions and joint ventures. The firm represents a number of blue-chip companies and has a large and lucrative practice. **Shardul Thacker*** and **EB Desai*** are the firm's stand-out practitioners. Notable transactions include acting for Hindalco Industries Limited in acquisitions of shares in Indian Aluminium Comapany limited from Alcan Aluminium Limited; for the Birla Group in its joint venture with Sun Life Assurance Company of Canada; acting for Birla AT&T Communications Limited in its merger with Tata Cellular Limited. **Clients:** International corporates and financial institutions.

Nishith Desai Associates (11 lawyers) Praised for its *"modern, client-driven style,"* this is an *"exceptionally capable firm,"* which has enjoyed a highly successful year. Specialising in cross-border M&A, the firm has niche expertise in the IT sector, to which it adds a respected tax department. The team is only felt to lack an individual big-hitter.

The firm advised on the merger between BFL and MphasiS, acting as Indian counsel to both parties, and has also represented various clients, including Bennett Coleman & Co Limited, in on-line domain name dispute resolutions. Acted for WorldTel and Navin.Com on international and Indian telecommunication laws, especially with respect to the internet, satellite and telephony. **Clients:** Bechtel Corporation; ABN AMRO Asia Securities Ltd.; Prudential Corporation plc; Barclays plc; Bear Stearns Inc; GE Capital; Prudential Corp; HSBC Private Equity Mgt Ltd.

Ajay Bahl & Co Advocates & Solicitors (4 ptrs, 7 asscs) Primarily advising overseas corporates on their Indian investments, the firm is also respected for its tax and litigation capacities. The team is involved in M&A, divestments and corporate restructuring for a wide-ranging clientele from such diverse sectors as travel, broadcasting, communications, heavy industry and energy. Managing partner **Ajay Bahl*** is also a qualified chartered accountant and comes highly recommended by the market. The firm recently assisted a major food conglomerate in a spate of brand acquisitions; acted for a major international media group in its reorganisation and numerous acquisitions. **Clients:** Domestic and international corporates.

Chambers of Zia Mody, Advocate Highly respected boutique firm which has developed an *"aggressive"* M&A and joint ventures practice. The past year has seen the firm become a specialist in (mostly offshore) venture capital funds, while other specialisms include the structuring of joint ventures, telecoms and computer transactions, and entertainment and advertising law. *"Astute lawyer"* **Zia Mody*** is universally regarded as *"worthy of admiration"* for her *"innovative, yet reliable style."*

The firm advised a leading French cement manufacturer on various acquisitions in India, was instructed by Alcan on its recent divestment of equity in an Indian listed company, and represents Telstra, the Australian national carrier, on its operations in India. **Clients:** Alcan; Telstra.

Fox Mandal & Co (8 ptrs, 14 asscs) The firm's *"especially strong ties with Slaughter and May"* bear testimony to the high regard in which its corporate/commercial work is widely held, especially among offshore firms. The *"dynamic"* **Som Mandal*** presides over a team with solid experience in M&A and joint ventures, and is an established name in the IT and telecoms sectors. The firm advised Invensys on its investments in India, and Pioneer International Ltd on its acquisition of Fletcher Challenge Concrete Industries (I) Private Limited. **Clients:** AXA Insurance; Trinity Inc; Invensys; Ion Bean Appliances; ITW Inc; Ingram Micro Asia Ltd; Pioneer International Ltd; Symbol Technologies Inc.

Jyoti Sagar & Associates (7 ptrs, 27 asscs) One of the newer operations in the market, the firm rises in the rankings on the back of a fast-growing corporate practice specialising in joint ventures and M&A. The firm is considered to have *"seized its opportunities"* in the hi-tech sector, where helping international concerns to acquire Indian software companies is an area of niche

*See leaders' profiles on pages 387-390

expertise. **Jyoti Sagar*** is a familiar name nationally, and presides over a team which has handled recent acquisitions for such heavyweight names as Gillette and LG Chemical. **Clients:** Gillette; LG Chemical; PepsiCo; Enron; Novell; Adobi Systems.

Khaitan & Co (22 lawyers) This New Delhi firm has a flourishing project finance practice, but is best known for its advice on M&A and joint ventures. In common with a number of its rivals, the firm has experienced an increase in IT work, notably acting for internet start-ups. Name partner **OP Khaitan*** is an experienced and respected member of the New Delhi legal market. The practice acted for UK based Grand Prix plc in establishing a Formula 1 race track in West Bengal, and for the Usha Martin Group in relation to its mobile telephone project, where it assisted in the privatisation process, license agreements and regulatory issues. Overseas clients include Phoenix, a German company which was represented in the privatisation of the Andrew Yule Belting Division in West Bengal. The team is also actively involved in a major merger in the coffee sector, the amalgamation of Consolidated Coffee with Coffee Lands and Asian Coffee. **Clients:** Aketa; Bharat Sugar Mills;Convest; Display Associates; Eveready; Govind Sugar Mills; Hindustan Motors; Indo Rama Synthetics; Jindal Strips; Kilburn Engineering; NRC; Quantas Airways; RPG; Seagrams; UTI Bank; Zenith.

Pathak & Associates (2 ptrs, 14 asscs) Offering a broad range of commercial and financial services from offices in New Delhi and Mumbai, name partner **Jai Pathak*** and his firm crowned an excellent year by acting on the Air India privatisation. The firm's main strength is considered to lie in M&A, privatisations and corporate finance, although recent activities have seen a marked rise in IT work and arbitration. A close 'cross-referral' relationship with US firm Jones, Day, Reavis & Pogue continues to pay dividends through the firm's *"considerable foreign clientele,"* which includes a number of Fortune 500 companies. The client roster is enhanced by large domestic conglomerates and banks, as well as Indian governmental organisations. On the finance side, the firm's securitisation experience has included transactions on behalf of Nations Bank and Hikal Chemical, while the team also handled a syndicated loan for the refinancing of Reliance Industries. **Clients:** Abbott Laboratories; Alcan Aluminium Limited; Caltex; Dana Corporation; Bharti Telecom; Indian Government; Mitsubishi Corporation; Reliance Industries; Warburg Pincus.

Desai & Diwanji (2 ptrs, 11 asscs) Acknowledged to have *"come on a lot in the last year,"* the firm advises a blue-chip client base on acquisitions in India. Areas of strength include IT software, financial services and pharmaceuticals. Highlight deals include advising adventis on the restructuring of its interests in India following its creation; TotalFinaElf on the indian aspects of the merger; Glaxo Wellcome on the Indian aspects of its merger with SmithKline Beecham; international Indian Counsel to China Light & Power in its purchase of the Asia-Pacific energy assests PowerGen plc. **Clients:** DaimlerChrysler; Volkswagen AG; Mitsui; General Signal Corporation Inc; Elf Lubrifiants; Louis Vuitton Moet Hennessy SA; Henkel KGaA; BG; Rothschild.

Gagrat & Co (19 ptrs, 41 asscs nationally) Mumbai firm which remains *"one of the most staunchly conservative in India."* Upholding a history of close trading links with the Middle East, the firm also maintains a small office in Dubai. The team is considered to be *"low-key, but with satisfied customers,"* and advises on anti-trust law, arbitration, banking and capital markets, as well as M&A transactions. Niche expertise exists in the aviation industry. **Clients:** Domestic and international corporates.

Rajinder Narain & Co (5 ptrs, 17 fee-earners) One of the oldest in New Delhi, the firm includes two Chief Justices and a president of the Bar Association among its practitioners. *"First-rate"* **Ravindra Nath*** has a long-standing name for aviation work, and is experienced in leasing and securitisation. The firm also has specialist experience in IP and international arbitration, and advises a largely international clientele. Highlight transactions include acting for US Exim Bank in the $400 million cross border financing of Jet Airways of India's ten new Boeing 737s; for Alcatel in its withdrawl from a joint venture in the telecoms sector for Bechtel in negotiating EPC contracts for a major water facility in southern India. **Clients:** Alcan; BMW; Boeing; Sony; Imperial Tobacco; BG; Airbus Industrie AG; Degussa AG; Alcatel; Entergy; New York Life; Bechtel.

Surana & Surana International Attorneys (4 ptrs corporate, 28 assts all sectors) This *"forward-looking"* firm is clearly the pre-eminent operation in Chennai (Madras). Over 40% of the firm's caseload is corporate/ commercial-based. Although some have commented that the firm is *"rather restricted to Chennai,"* this has proved no obstacle to acting on high prestige transactions, much of it referred from Delhi and Mumbai firms. Sole advisor for Chennai-based Hyundai Motors India Limited, the firm has been closely involved with the company's $1.8 billion investment in India. Geographically situated to take advantage of India's IT boom, the firm has a growing IP and IT practice, with one lawyer currently on secondment to Cysphere.com. The firm acted as legal consultant to the state-sponsored Tidel Park Project in Tamil Nadu, intended to be India's largest cyberpark. **Clients:** Hyundai Motors India Limited; General Motors Acceptance Corporation; Tidel Park Project; Cysphere.com; Videocon Power; Mitsui & Co; Abloy.

Udwadia Udeshi & Berjis Relatively young outfit, regarded as *"big growers"* in both corporate/M&A and project finance. The firm has an enviably consistent reputation for *"top-quality work."* Its Corporate services are mostly offered to foreign multinationals investing in India, in all aspects of their business, and backed up litigation and arbitration services as necessary. Recent transactions include ongoing representation of the Indian subsidiary of Enron in matters relating to the second phase of the Dahol power plant. **Clients:** Mostly foreign multinationals investing in India.

Other Notable Practitioner The firm of JB Dadachanji Ravindra Narain Mathur & Co has ceased to function in its former guise. However, founding partner **JB Dadachanji*** is, by the reckoning of most, one of the foremost legal minds in the country, and the *"grand old man of Indian law."*

Corporate/M&A: Foreign Firms

INDIA: Foreign Firms Leading firms (Corporate/Mergers & Acquisitions)
1 Clifford Chance
Freshfields Bruckhaus Deringer
Linklaters
2 Allen & Overy
Ashurst Morris Crisp
Slaughter and May
3 Jones, Day, Reavis & Pogue
Shearman & Sterling
4 Davis Polk & Wardwell
Herbert Smith
White & Case LLP

Firms are listed alphabetically in each band.

Leading individuals (Corporate/Mergers & Acquisitions)
1 AMIN Pratap *Freshfields Bruckhaus Deringer*
2 BRADLEY Edward *Clifford Chance*
MEHTA Nikhil *Linklaters*
3 PANDE Raj *White & Case LLP*
SINGH Arun *KLegal*

Individuals are listed alphabetically in each band.

Clifford Chance (3 ptrs, 9 asscs) The firm is considered to have had *"an excellent year."* Corporate work has increased since the merger with Rogers & Wells LLP and Pünder, Volhard, Weber & Axster in January 2000, a timely growth given the general malaise in Indian projects, the firm's usual bastion. Work has included advising on various GDR issues by Indian corporates, advising foreign corporates on the acquisition of Indian holdings, and advising on the roll out of a new internet service. **Edward Bradley**'s* name continues to carry weight on the sub-continent. Sample activities of the firm include advising Merrill Lynch on the $87 million GDR issue by a leading Indian IT company; advising NewellRubbermaid on the acquisition of the Indian branch of Gillette's stationery business; advising ABN AMRO on its acquisition of Bank of America's retail banking business in India, Singapore and Taiwan. **Clients:** Deloitte Consulting; Merrill Lynch; NewellRubbermaid; ABN AMRO.

Freshfields Bruckhaus Deringer (5 ptrs) The firm's corporate practice retains its high profile. Close ties with various government entities help to ensure a flourishing and lucrative practice which is inundated with new deals. Heading the firm's dedicated India Group is the *"redoubtable"* **Pratap Amin***, who specialises in M&A and joint ventures and has extensive experience of advising international banks and other financial institutions on their investments in India. His familiarity with the local market is considered to *"give him quite an edge."* The firm has acted for a range of international financial institutions on hteir activities in India, and for diverse corporates, domestic and foreign, from computers to energy. **Clients:** Cazenove; NatWest; Hewlett-Packard; ICI; The Walt Disney Company; Morgan Crucible; Cinven; Pillsbury.

Linklaters (2 ptrs, 6 asscs) The firm's India Business Group is *"as active as ever"* and its reputation for excellence is said to be *"unassailable."* **Nikhil Mehta*** is a qualified Indian advocate who specialises in corporate taxation, with particular emphasis on international finance, derivatives, cross-border structures, M&A and litigation. The firm acted for TD Waterhouse in connection with a joint venture with Tata Finance Limited. **Clients:** BG; Enron; TD Waterhouse.

Allen & Overy (10 ptrs) The firm's focus inclines more towards banking, but it is also known for high-end corporate work, notably in the power industry. Much of the Indian corporate practice, co-ordinated from London and Singapore, lies in servicing international clients doing business in India. Highlight transactions include advising the Indian subsidiary of a European energy company on the development of gas transmission facilities in Western India, and advising British Gas on the development of an LNG receiving terminal project in Gujarat. The firm also represented Utkal Alumina International Limited on the development and financing of an aluminium-refining project in Orissa. **Clients:** Utkal Alumina International Limited; BG; UBS Warburg.

Ashurst Morris Crisp (4 ptrs, 8 asscs) Despite persistent problems with the Bombay Lawyers' Collective, the firm is felt to have enjoyed a successful transactional year. A steady flow of inward investment-related work has included advising BUPA on a joint venture with the Piramal Group in the health sector, and acting for Voith Bespannungstechnik GmbH on its acquisition of a 59% shareholding in Porritts & Spencer (Asia) Limited. The team also advised Unocal on the acquisition of a 26% stake in the 300 MW Bidadi power project in Karnataka. **Clients:** BUPA; Voith Bespannungstechnik; Unocal.

Slaughter and May (5 ptrs, 13 asscs) The firm is not known for a consistent presence in India, although it is known for work that is *"head and shoulders above everyone"* when it does get involved. Considered to operate a *"client-driven"* strategy in India, the team has represented its traditional blue-chip clientele on a number of major acquisitions. Advised on GDR work for the Gas Authority of India Ltd, acted for a major Indian building group on the proposed acquisition of various companies' cement assets, and represented a leading UK corporate on the disposal of its majority interest in a healthcare business in India. **Clients:** Gas Authority of India Ltd; leading international corporates.

Jones, Day, Reavis & Pogue Specialising in M&A, privatisations, joint ventures and securitisations, the firm's profile in India has been greatly enhanced by its complex 'cross-referral' relationship with local firm Pathak & Associates. Advised HealthScribe Inc in connection with its $8.5 million sale of a 71.4% stake in wholly-owned subsidiary HealthScribe India Private Ltd to Max India Ltd. **Clients:** HealthScribe Inc.

Shearman & Sterling (4 ptrs) Better known for its projects work, the firm nevertheless has long experience in corporate/commercial transactions. In particular the team is known for representing the underwriters of the GDR offerings of such heavyweights as ICICI and Tata Electric Companies. **Clients:** BPL Cellular Holdings; Modi Group; Tamilnadu Petroproducts Limited.

Davis Polk & Wardwell (6 ptrs, 19 asscs) In India, the firm is known for work in capital markets and the technology industries, typically on big-ticket deals. Corporate-driven, the firm has handled the IPOs of Indian companies on the New York stock exchange and US companies in India, especially in the IT sector. Worked closely with 'best friend' Slaughter and May on the restructuring of Indian cement businesses. **Clients:** ICICI Limited; ICICI Bank; Reliance Industries; CONCOR.

Herbert Smith (7 ptrs) Operating principally out of London, Singapore and Hong Kong, the firm's reputation was forged in projects work, but is now also in the ascendant in the corporate sphere after a vigorous year. Highlight of the year was advising Tata Tea (GB) Ltd on the $427 million acquisition of the entire issued share capital of Tetley Group Limited. **Clients:** Tata Tea (GB) Ltd; international power companies.

*See leaders' profiles on pages 387-390

White & Case LLP Advising principally on capital markets and M&A transactions, the firm has niche strengths in the recently liberalised insurance market and hi-tech industry. Most work is carried out through the influence of the respected **Raj Pande***. Highlight deals include acting for Singapore Telecommunications Ltd on its acquisition of a 15% stake in Bharti Televentures Ltd. **Clients:** Singapore Telecom; domestic and international corporates.

Other Notable Practitioner The *"well-connected"* **Arun Singh** of KLegal is still considered to be a commercial lawyer of unusual merit. Focusing on M&A, joint ventures and foreign investment, he advises a number of European companies on their Indian operations. Clients include multinational oil and gas companies and Rugby Cement. He recently advised on the $75 million acquisition of an Indian telecoms company, and the acquisition of a major Indian tobacco company.

Project Finance: Local Firms

INDIA
Leading firms (Project Finance)

Band	Firm
1	Amarchand & Mangaldas & Suresh A Shroff & Co
2	Dua Associates
	Jyoti Sagar & Associates
	Little & Co
3	Desai & Diwanji
	Fox Mandal & Co
	Kanga & Co
	Luthra & Luthra Law Offices
	Mulla & Mulla & Craigie Blunt & Caroe
	Rajinder Narain & Co
	Udwadia Udeshi & Berjis
4	Crawford Bayley & Co
	Dave & Girish & Co
	Pathak & Associates

Firms are listed alphabetically in each band.

Leading individuals (Project Finance)

Band	Individual	Firm
★	**SHROFF Cyril**	*Amarchand & Mangaldas*
1	**KULKARNI Ravindra**	*Little & Co*
	NATH Ravindra	*Rajinder Narain & Co*
	SHROFF Shardul	*Amarchand & Mangaldas*
	UDWADIA Darius	*Udwadia Udeshi & Berjis*
2	**DESAI Vishwang**	*Desai & Diwanji*
	DUA Ranji	*Dua Associates*
	MANDAL Som	*Fox Mandal & Co*
	MERCHANT Kalpana	*Kanga & Co*
3	**BHAKTA ML**	*Kanga & Co*
	LUTHRA Rajiv	*Luthra & Luthra Law Offices*
	PATHAK Jai	*Pathak & Associates*
	THACKER Shardul	*Mulla & Mulla & Craigie Blunt*
	THAKORE Shoban	*Baishankar Kanga & Girdharlal*
	TITUS Diljeet	*Titus & Co*
	VISWANATHAN L	*Amarchand & Mangaldas*

Individuals are listed alphabetically in each band.

Amarchand & Mangaldas & Suresh A Shroff & Co (4 ptrs, 61 asscs) This remains India's pre-eminent firm in project finance, acting for both developers and lenders and maintaining a *"vigorous"* consultancy practice. Notably proficient in infrastructure projects, the team is said to *"stand alone in this area."* The *"excellent"* **L Viswanathan*** is regarded as a genuine project finance specialist, while **Shardul Shroff*** has an excellent all-round reputation, which extends beyond India. However, the firm's superstar remains **Cyril Shroff*** (*"there is nobody to touch him,"*) who is the unquestioned leader of this sector, and whose hand is felt in virtually every deal of consequence in India.

Representing both domestic and foreign companies, the firm has acted for the developers on several power and telecom infrastructure projects, road projects and water projects, and for the lenders on a number of power projects such as the Vizag, Korba, Ramagundam and Balagarh projects. **Clients:** ICICI; IDBI; PFC; IFC; ADB; ANZ; Enron; Alstom; ABB; China Light; Eastern Generation; Ogden Energy Group; Reliance Industries; Birla Group; IOC; Dabhol Power Company.

Dua Associates (16 ptrs) Although most project finance deals are handled from Mumbai, this New Delhi-based firm is still respected for its advice on infrastructure and oil and gas transactions. Led by the respected **Ranji Dua***, this *"aggressive"* operation is highly rated for its drafting ability, and advises both domestic and international corporates on both upstream and downstream oil and gas matters, including exploration and construction of refineries and pipelines. **Clients:** Energy and telecoms corporates.

Jyoti Sagar & Associates (2 ptrs, 3 asscs) This *"ever-popular firm"* is particularly well known for advising state electricity boards on restructuring and privatisation of state-owned utilities and roads. Clearly regarded as one of the leading players in India, the firm is only felt to lack a high-profile individual name. The team's principal experience lies in infrastructure and power projects, and has had notable success in completing gas transmission projects for state and private entities. Foreign lenders, especially German banks, comprise the bulk of the team's client base.

The team advised a Japanese corporation on a $130 million limited recourse project financing involving credit facilities from different Japanese banks and financial institutions. Also represented a German bank on a Rs30 million full recourse loan facility for a cellular mobile phone network. **Clients:** International corporates and financial institutions.

Little & Co (18 ptrs, 27 asscs) Regarded as a *"prominent and stable"* firm, the group is a renowned player on power projects, typically representing leading domestic concerns. Star lawyer **Ravindra Kulkarni***, an all-round finance expert, is seen as *"a good guy and a good lawyer."* Notable transactions of the firm include acting for Videocon in the arrangement of security and finance documentation; for Tata Electric in its acquisition of Powergens's Indian assets, and handling its investments in Cogentrix; for Korea Heavy Industries in connection with the Goindwal power project in the state of Punjab. **Clients:** Mahrashtra State Electricity Board; Essar Power.

Desai & Diwanji (3 ptrs, 16 asscs) This *"young and enthusiastic"* firm has a solid reputation in project finance, acting for sponsors, lenders and borrowers. The team has experience of advising on projects in power, pipelines, petrochemicals, telecoms, water, infrastructure and mining. Name partner **Vishwang Desai*** is regarded as one of the best project finance lawyers in India. The firm advised Daewoo Power India Ltd on the development and financing of the 3960 MW coal-fired power plant at Hirma, Orissa. **Clients:** DaimlerChrysler; Thyssen-Krupp; Henkel; Volkswagen; Siemens; Mitsui; Mitsubishi; Chase Manhattan Bank; Daewoo; Schroeders; NM Rothschild; BASF.

Fox Mandal & Co (4 ptrs, 6 asscs) A year of aggressive expansion has seen the firm take over venerable competitor Eastley Lamb, giving it a strong Mumbai presence, and bringing to seven the number of offices throughout India. **Som Mandal*** is a *"credible projects lawyer,"* and the firm has an excellent reputation for power projects. The firm advised on the fuel supply agreement for the IB Valley Power Project in West Bengal and also acted for SI-AL SBEC Bioenergy Limited on a co-generation power plant in Uttar Pradesh. **Clients:** Alcatel; SI AL SBEC Bioenergy Limited; EPC Contractor; Spice Telecom; Invensys.

Kanga & Co (2 ptrs, 3 asscs) Better known for its corporate expertise, the firm retains a respected name for advice on telecoms projects, often acting on behalf of financial institutions. *"Young and aggressive"* **Kalpana Merchant*** is an *"excellent and responsive lawyer,"* who is well complemented by the experienced **ML Bhakta***. The firm acted for the lenders on a 200MW naphtha based combined cycle power project in Andhra Pradesh; for Fleet National Bank in structuring a transaction, and drafting documents, for a secured guaranteed revolving credit facility, involving the creation of both onshore and offshore securities. **Clients:** State Bank of India; Deutsche Bank AG; HFDC Bank; Citibank; Larsen & Toubro Limited; Krupp (India) Limited.

Luthra & Luthra Law Offices (3 ptrs, 12 asscs) *"Highly professional"* firm with a sound projects reputation. Unusually for an Indian firm, the firm has a presence on foreign projects, having advised on deals in Bangladesh, Sri Lanka and China. Acting for offshore corporates and banks, the firm has niche expertise in infrastructure projects, having advised on more than 30 separate pieces of work during the past year. **Rajiv Luthra*** is the stand-out practitioner here. **Clients:** ABN AMRO; ExxonMobil Corporation; British Aerospace; AXA Insurance; Commerzbank; Enron; HSBC Group; Intel; Lockheed Martin; Monsanto; Rolls Royce; Schroders; Yamaha Group.

Mulla & Mulla & Craigie Blunt & Caroe (20 ptrs, 80 asscs) Although better known for corporate work, the firm regularly figures on some of the biggest transactions. Key areas of involvement are telecommunications and energy, and the team has acted as Indian legal counsel to international banks and overseas lenders on major bilateral projects. **Shardul Thacker*** continues to gain substantial market commendation.

The firm advised a consortium of foreign and domestic corporations on the establishment of an international airport at Bangalore and acted on the privatisation of the Pipavav port. **Clients:** Domestic and international corporates.

Rajinder Narain & Co (5 ptrs, 17 asscs) Projects are *"something of a speciality"* for this old New Delhi firm. The group has expertise in structuring power, telecoms, road, water and other infrastructure projects. Star partner **Ravindra Nath*** is generally agreed to be *"a superb practitioner."* **Clients:** Alcan, Degussa AG, Alcatel.

Udwadia Udeshi & Berjis Newly ranked group with a superb reputation for projects work. The *"experienced and tough"* name partner **Darius Udwadia*** commands universal respect at home and abroad. Much of the firm's business in this area consists of rendering opinions and vetting documents for entities engaging in large infrastructure projects, especially on matters concerning enforcibility. Main recent transactions consist of ongoing representation of Enron's Indian subsidiary in matters concerning the second phase of the Dabhol power project. **Clients:** Domestic and international corporates.

Crawford Bayley & Co (2 ptrs, 5 asscs) Traditional firm with a greater reputation for corporate work, but which has been involved in several infrastructure projects, including power, telecommunications, roads and water. The group's client base comprises an even mix of lenders and developers. **Clients:** Boots Pharmaceuticals; BASF; Novartis; Glaxo Wellcome; General Electric; World Bank; Asian Development Bank; IBRD; IMF; Cable & Wireless; Marubeni Corp; Morgan Stanley.

Dave & Girish & Co (4 ptrs) As well as its excellent reputation for litigation, the firm's project finance practice has a reputation for *"excellent service."* The firm advised on the structuring of documentation for the Bangalore-Mysore corridor power project, and acted on the financing of the Pune-Bombay Express Highway. **Clients:** ANZ Grindleys Bank; International Finance Corporation; Bharti Cellular Limited.

Pathak & Associates (2 ptrs, 14 asscs) The firm is building a creditable reputation in project finance, and is considered to have *"grown in stature."* Financing advice on power and telecoms projects has provided a notable recent growth area. **Jai Pathak*** is a familiar name in the sector.

The firm acted for ABN AMRO on a $65 million financing to the Indian government, represented Videocon Power Company on a 1050 MW power project in Tamil Nadu, and advised Goetze on a wind power project in Madhya Pradesh. **Clients:** ABN AMRO; Dodsal; Escorts; JP Morgan; Reliance Industries; Hikal Chemical.

Other Notable Practitioners **Shoban Thakore** of Mumbai firm Bhaishankar Kanga & Girdharlal is regarded by many as an éminence grise of Indian projects advice. At Titus & Co, **Diljeet Titus***, has a sound reputation for work on power and telecommunications projects.

Project Finance: Foreign Firms

Allen & Overy (10 ptrs) The firm's reputation in India is founded on its work on behalf of lenders, who describe the team as *"first-class for volume and quality."* **Graham Vinter*** and **Bimal Desai*** in London and **Chris Rushton*** in Singapore have a fine track record in India. The firm advised ANZ and HSBC on the 1000 MW coal-fired power station at Vishakhspatnam, Andhra Pradesh, and acted for National Grid International on the bid documentation for an electricity evacuation project between India and Bhutan. The firm also represented ICICI on the financing of the Jindal captive power plant. **Clients:** The National Grid Company; BG plc; Dresdner Bank; ANZ; HSBC; Standard Chartered Bank; ICICI.

Clifford Chance (4 ptrs, 16 asscs) The firm maintains a pre-eminent reputation for infrastructure and power projects acting for lenders, developers and sponsors. The respected **Chris Wyman*** is said to *"understand India,"* while colleague **Russell Wells*** also has a sound reputation. The firm advised the developers on the construction of fast-track power stations in Andhra Pradesh, Maharashtra and Orissa. **Clients:** AES; International Power; Alstom; Intergen.

Linklaters (7 ptrs, 12 asscs) Continuing involvement on the cream of power and telecoms projects in India ensures the firm's place among the

*See leaders' profiles on pages 387-390

INDIA: Foreign Firms Leading firms (Project Finance)
1 Allen & Overy
Clifford Chance
Linklaters
White & Case LLP
2 Freshfields Bruckhaus Deringer
Herbert Smith
3 Skadden, Arps, Slate, Meagher & Flom LLP
Slaughter and May
4 Ashurst Morris Crisp
CMS Cameron McKenna
Denton Wilde Sapte
Jones, Day, Reavis & Pogue
Milbank, Tweed, Hadley & McCloy
Norton Rose
Shearman & Sterling
5 Masons
Thelen Reid & Priest LLP

Firms are listed alphabetically in each band.

Leading individuals (Project Finance)
1 **AMIN Pratap** *Freshfields Bruckhaus Deringer*
STACEY Paul *Slaughter and May*
VINTER Graham *Allen & Overy*
WYMAN Chris *Clifford Chance*
2 **DESAI Bimal** *Allen & Overy*
GOODWILLIE Eugene *White & Case LLP*
INMAN Jonathan *Linklaters*
KLEPPER Martin *Skadden, Arps*
WELLS Russell *Clifford Chance*
3 **NEWBERY Mark** *Herbert Smith*
PANDE Raj *White & Case LLP*
RUSHTON Chris *Allen & Overy*

Individuals are listed alphabetically in each band.

market leaders. Tokyo-based **John Inman*** has maintained his reputation among his peers, notably in connection with the Balagarth and Hirma power projects. Other important deals include the Metgas LNG procurement and the Ircon fibre-optic cable project. The firm continues to work closely with Enron on matters connected with the Dabhol project. **Clients:** Enron; BG plc; ABB Alstom Power; Modicom; ECGD; Mitsubishi; Reliance Petroleum Limited; CEPA.

White & Case LLP "*Stable*" team with "*substantial market penetration,*" generally acting for the lenders. The esteemed **Raj Pande***, who has particular expertise in power projects, operates from the Singapore office, while in the US, the venerable **Eugene Goodwillie*** continues to wield enormous influence over the firm's strategy in the sub-continent. The firm has been involved on a number of power, telecommunications and other infrastructure projects, including Balagarh and Bina (for the lenders) and Cuddalore, Costal and the Bangalore-Mysore Corridor Project (for the developers.) **Clients:** International power, telecoms and petrochemical companies.

Freshfields Bruckhaus Deringer (15 ptrs, 20 asscs) Fielding an experienced international team drawn from around the world, the firm continues to enjoy a strong presence in the projects sector. **Pratap Amin*** is rated amongst the foremost experts on India. The firm's forte lies in infrastructure projects, which have included a light rail transit system in Bangalore and a power barge at Kakinada Port, Andhra Pradesh. **Clients:** CMS Energy Corp; UNOCAL; NationsBank; Siemens; Birla AT&T; Statkraft.

Herbert Smith (7 ptrs) Operating principally out of London, Singapore and Hong Kong, the firm's reputation for project finance has continued to improve, and it is regarded as "*a good choice for mid-sized deals.*" Specialising in power projects and litigation, the India group is headed by Singapore office managing partner, the "*outstanding*" **Mark Newbery***. The firm advised ICICI Limited, lead arranger for the Ramagundam and Samayunallur power projects, and represented the Karnataka Electricity Board on the Cogentrix power project and the Chamundi hydro project. **Clients:** ICICI Limited; ICICI Consulting; Tractabel; Karnataka Electricity Board; Karnataka Power Transmission Corporation.

Skadden, Arps, Slate, Meagher & Flom LLP (5 ptrs, 8 asscs) Respected projects group, which is said to do "*good and interesting work,*" largely on behalf of US clients doing business in India. The major client here continues to be Enron, on whose behalf the firm has engaged in 'aftercare' work in the wake of the Dabhol project. **Martin Klepper*** is an outstanding energy and projects lawyer who, according to some, is "*single-handedly responsible for the firm's reputation in India.*" **Clients:** Enron.

Slaughter and May (5 ptrs, 13 asscs) The firm's reputation for top-quality projects advice remains, largely through the efforts of the "*absolutely fantastic*" **Paul Stacey***, who is "*good for any project, and simply gets things done.*" Highlight work includes advising the project company on the new Tirapur water project, a groundbreaking public/private sewage treatment and water project. The firm also advised a leading European telecoms client on the supply of telecommunications equipment and services in Maharashtra and Goa, and the same client on a satellite project. **Clients:** Leading international corporates.

Ashurst Morris Crisp (4 ptrs, 7 asscs) Known for its work on energy projects, the firm advised Sumitomo, the consortium leaders, and Mitsubishi Heavy Industries and Hitachi, the turnkey contractors, on the Vizag project. Also represented Marubeni Corp (sponsor and EPC contractor) on the 300 MW Pillaiperumalannut IPP in Tamil Nadu, and on the Ramagundam 2x256 MW IPP. **Clients:** Unocal Bharat Ltd; Gujarat State Petroleum Corporation; Videocon.

CMS Cameron McKenna (6 ptrs) Acknowledged experts in the electricity market, the firm has been extensively instructed by state authorities and development agencies on energy and restructuring projects. However, the group has seen a decline in projects activity since the completion of the electricity privatisation in Orissa. **Clients:** Government of Orissa; Gridco; Orissa Electricity Regulatory Commission; World Bank; Asian Development Bank; Andhra Pradesh Regulatory Commission.

Denton Wilde Sapte (10 ptrs, 10 asscs) Involved in several power projects, especially on the financing side, the firm has also suffered from the general slowing of the projects market in India. However, its extensive contacts in the Middle East has enabled the group to advise on LNG supply, especially from Oman and Abu Dhabi. The firm advised on the Ennore LNG project, represented Gujarat State Energy Co on the new 156 MW Hazira IPP and acted for Venkatesh Coke & Power Ltd, the sponsors of a project to construct and operate a plant in southern India to produce metallurgical coke and co-generate power. **Clients:** Tata Electric; Indigas; Larsen & Toubro Information Technology Limited; WIPRO; Gujarat State Energy Co; BG Transco; Reliance Industries; Deutsche Morgan Grenfell.

Jones Day Reavis & Pogue The firm's complex 'cross-referral' relationship with Pathak & Associates in Delhi and Mumbai is considered to give it a "*distinct advantage*" in India. Particular areas of expertise include telecoms and power projects. **Clients:** International corporates.

Milbank Tweed Hadley & McCloy LLP (5 ptrs, 15-20 asscs) Drawing on partners and associates from its London, Hong Kong and Singapore offices, the firm has been involved on a number

*See leaders' profiles on pages 387-390

of recent projects, including the mammoth Videocon power project, where the group acted for the lenders. Highlight deals include acting for Consolidated Electric Power of Asia in connection with its planned investment in the Belagarh Power Company Ltd and representing SPIC Electric Power Corporation Ltd in the construction, operation and financing of a 500 MW coal-fired power plant in Tuticorin. **Clients:** Cogentrix Inc; China Light and Power; CVK Group; Ogden Projects Asia Pte; ABN AMRO; PowerGen/Birla Consortium; Siemens AG.

Norton Rose (3 ptrs) Fortified by its close ties with local firm Mulla & Mulla, the firm advises on a variety of projects in India. Leading transactions include acting for ANZ Investment Bank on its financing of LNG shipments to the Dabhol power plant; advising on a new satellite financing and representing the UK's Export Credit Guarantee Department on the financing and refinancing of offshore drilling rigs in India. **Clients:** ANZ Investment Bank; Royal Bank of Scotland.

Shearman & Sterling (4 ptrs) The firm has maintained its reputation for *"good people and good work,"* notably in the telecoms and power sectors. Projects experience includes representing PowerGen plc/Birla Group consortium as developer of the proposed coal-fired power station at Bina, Madhya Pradesh, as well as the Maharashtra State Electricity Board on the 1000 MW Bhadravati Power Project. **Clients:** PowerGen plc/Birla Group consortium; ANZ Investment Bank; KEPCO.

Masons (3 ptrs, 4-5 asscs) Best known on the sub-continent for projects work, the firm has a number of Indian corporates among its client roster. The firm's expertise is especially marked in infrastructure projects. The group was involved in establishing the corporate structure for the building of a 1000 MW power station at Visakhapatnam, Andhra Pradesh, and advised a European construction and engineering consortium on a hydro-electric project in Kashmir. **Clients:** Crompton Greaves; Bangalore Mass Rapid Transit Ltd; International Seaports Ltd; Jindal Steel & Power Ltd.

Thelen Reid & Priest (20 ptrs, 15 asscs) Operating out of the US, the firm has 20 years of experience in dealing with Indian projects, and has an association with Titus & Co in New Delhi. A large group has been involved in several recent power projects in India, including the concluded Dabhol Power Project, acting on behalf of Bechtel. The firm has also advised on infrastructure and telecoms projects. **Clients:** Bechtel; Loral; ARB Inc; MCN Corporation; Chubb; Indec; Fibro Energy; ICICI; Tata Infotech; Kaashyap Radiant Systems Ltd; Bank of India.

Leaders' profiles – India

AMIN, Pratap
Freshfields Bruckhaus Deringer, London
+44 20 7936 4000
pratap.amin@freshfields.com
Recommended in Corporate/Mergers & Acquisitions: India Foreign, Project Finance: India Foreign
Specialisation: Partner in Corporate Department and Head of India Group. Main areas of work include mergers and acquisitions, privatisations, international securities, banking, offshore funds and project finance.

BAHL, Ajay
Ajay Bahl & Co Advocates & Solicitors, New Delhi
+91 11 461 7697
Recommended in Corporate/M&A

BHAKTA, M.L.
Kanga & Co, Mumbai +91 22 288 6541
Recommended in Corporate/M&A, Project Finance
Specialisation: Main area of work is corporate law, pricipally mergers, acquisitions, project finance, taxation and public issues, including offshore issues. Has assisted and advised multi-national companies on acquisition of undertakings and companies in various fields. Assisted a number of foreign companies including British American Tobacco Company, JC Bamford Excavators Limited and SKF GmbH, Germany; Indian clients including Reliance Industries Limited and SKF Bearings India; Banks including Bank of America, NTSA, The Hongkong and Shanghai Banking Corporation Limited, Citibank NA, Deutsche Bank AG, Syndicate Bank and Bank of Baroda.
Career: Qualified in 1953. Joined *Kanga and Company* in 1954. Is a senior partner of the firm. Was the Chairman of Taxation Law Standing Committee of LAWASIA. Has been a member of the Advisory Committee, Life Insurance Corporation of India Limited for over six years, a Committee Member of the Bombay Incorporated Law Society for over ten years, the Chairman of the Taxation Committee, Indian Merchant's Chamber, and a member of Advisory Board of Deutsche Bank. Served on the Committee appointed by the Reserve Bank of India on legal aspects, relating to operations for banking and financial systems and is also a member of the Governing Board of the India Council of Arbitration.
Personal: Born 3 December 1931. Leisure interests include travelling.

BHARUCHA, M.P.
Amarchand & Mangaldas & Suresh A Shroff & Co, Mumbai +91 22 2650500
mp.bharucha@amarchand.com
Recommended in Corporate/M&A
Specialisation: Partner in corporate, commercial, litigation department.
Prof. Memberships: Bar Council of India, Incorporated Law Society Bombay.
Career: Qualified in 1972 in India. Advocate, High Court of Bombay. Solicitor, High Court of Bombay in 1973. Solicitor, Supreme Court of England in 1981. Solicitor, High Court of Hong Kong in 1995, becoming a partner in 1995.
Personal: Born 29 October 1948. Attended St Xavier's College (BA); Bombay University (LLB).

BRADLEY, Edward
Clifford Chance, London +44 20 7600 1000
edward.bradley@cliffordchance.com
Recommended in Corporate/Mergers & Acquisitions: India Foreign
Specialisation: Partner specialising in corporate finance, Stock Exchange matters and international capital markets.
Career: Magdalene College, Cambridge (MA). Articled *Slaughter and May*; qualified 1983; partner *Clifford Chance* since 1990.
Personal: Enjoys vintage motor racing and old cars generally. Born 1957; resides London.

DADACHANJI, J.B.
J.B. Dadachanji & Co, New Delhi +91 11 334 2628
Recommended in Corporate/M&A

DESAI, Bimal
Allen & Overy, London +44 20 7330 3000
Recommended in Project Finance: India Foreign

DESAI, Eruch B.
Mulla & Mulla & Craigie Blunt & Caroe, Mumbai
+91 22 204 4960
mullas@vsnl.com
Recommended in Corporate/M&A
Specialisation: Corporate field including privatisations, acquisitions, mergers, GDR/ADR issues, collaborations, etc. Recent and current transactions include Hindalco takeover of Alcan Aluminium shares in Indian Aluminium, Birla's ventures with Sun Life in Mutual Funds & Insurance, Merger of Birla AT&T and Tata Cellular, Indian Rayon's purchase of Madura Coats, Essar's disinvestment of

Energy Division, Lubrizol's venture with Indian Oil, Tata's venture with Systems Integrated Telemarketing, Netherlands, Hindalco's Bid for Balco's Shares, Videocon International Foreign Loan Transaction with American Express Bank.
Prof. Memberships: Bombay incorporated Law Society, The Law Society – England, The Law Society – Hong Kong.
Career: Director of several reputed Companies. Lecturer at several legal seminars, Ex-Member of Legal Committee of Bombay Chamber of Commerce. Appeared before Select Committee of Parliament to suggest amendments to the Companies Act and the Monopolies and Restrictive Trade Practices Act.

DESAI, Vishwang
Desai & Diwanji, Mumbai +91 22 2651 682
Recommended in Project Finance

DUA, Ranji
Dua Associates, New Delhi +91 11 371 4408
ranji@duaassociates.com
Recommended in Corporate/M&A, Project Finance
Specialisation: Founding partner of *Dua Associates.* Has vast breadth of experience in the fields of corporate law, mergers and acquisitions, privatisations, project finance, new issues, entry strategies, foreign investment, infrastructure projects and commercial aspects of doing business in India. Has advised clients ranging from Fortune 500 companies to privately owned companies, both Indian and foreign, public sector undertakings and listed companies in India. Amongst the transactional clients represented this year are General Motors, AT&T, Lucent Technologies, Dow Chemical, DuPont, AIG, Indian Airlines (privatisation), Petronet LNG, Texaco, Chevron, International Finance Corporation, Bank of America, Deutsche Bank, Citibank, Warburg Pincus and McDonald's.
Career: Commenced career as an individual practitioner in the mid 70's, which has since transformed into a national practice with the firm having over eighty professionals and a total strength in excess of one hundred and forty people and offices at Mumbai, New Delhi, Bangalore and Pune.
Personal: Born 3 November, 1951. Obtained Bachelor of Laws Degree from Delhi University after obtaining a Masters in Economics from the Delhi School of Economics. Interests include tennis and classical music. Resides in New Delhi.

GOODWILLIE, Eugene
White & Case LLP, New York +1 212 819 8432
egoodwillie@whitecase.com
Recommended in Project Finance: India Foreign
Specialisation: Main area of work is international and U.S. corporate and financial transactions, with significant experience in foreign investment projects, international and domestic natural resource projects, international joint venture transactions and domestic and international securities transactions. Represented investors in a broad range of transactions, including venture capital investments in the high technology area. Preeminent project finance lawyer with particular experience in the field of representing hydrocarbon and hydrocarbon related industries in connection with the full range of legal issues relevant to such industries. Select client list includes: IFC; U.S. Eximbank; Japan Eximbank; Asian Development Bank; CalEnergy Company; the Arabian American Oil Company and its successor, the Saudi Arabian Oil Company, in the restructuring of Aramco and the formation of Saudi Aramco, among other deals.
Prof. Memberships: New York State Bar, admitted 1967.
Career: Partner of *White & Case* since 1975. Currently serves as Chairman of *White & Case*'s Management Board. In charge of all *White & Case* overseas offices (1980-83); served on Management Committee (1983-91, 1998-2000). Named partner in charge of the firm's worldwide energy and project finance practice group (1991).
Personal: B.A., cum laude, Williams College, 1963, Phi Beta Kappa; J.D., cum laude, Columbia Law School, 1966, Stone Scholar.

INMAN, Jonathan
Linklaters (a member firm of Linklaters & Alliance), Tokyo +81 3 3568 3800
jonathan.inman@linklaters.com
Recommended in Project Finance: India Foreign
Specialisation: All aspects of major projects, including the structuring and documentation of the financing and security arrangements, and including expertise in the construction and electricity industries. Led the team working on the Dabhol Power project, advising in particular on the power purchase agreements, construction contracts and government contracts and guarantees. Advised in connection with the construction and financing of various independent power station projects in the UK, India and Pakistan, as well as the Indian Ministries of Finance and Power on power purchase agreements and currently advising sponsors on the largest of the Indian 'mega-projects'. Recent assignments include advising sponsors on a project to set up a utility complex to supply a large petrochemical plant in China, and advising foreign lenders to a major new toll road in Korea.
Career: Currently head of Project Finance Practice, Tokyo.

KHAITAN, O.P.
OP Khaitan & Co, New Delhi +91 11 464 6516
opkhaitan@opkhaitan.com
Recommended in Corporate/M&A
Specialisation: Heads the law firm *O.P. Khaitan & Co.* founded in 1990 and having 20 advocates and solicitors. Main areas of practice are corporate laws, mergers & acquisitions, arbitration, insurance laws, conveyancing, foreign collaborations, joint venture, litigation.
Prof. Memberships: International Bar Association; Bar Council of West Bengal; Bar Council of India; Bar Council of Delhi High Court; LAWASIA.
Career: Practising as Solicitor & Advocate since 1967. Earlier Partner in law firms *Khaitan & Co.* and *Khaitan & Partners.* Advocate-on-Record of Supreme Court of India, Attorney-at-Law (Solicitor).
Personal: Born November 21, 1943. Qualification-BCom, LLB Received Bell-Chambers Gold Medal from Calcutta High Court. Director in many Indian companies. Leisure interests include Golf. Lives in New Delhi, India.

KLEPPER, Martin
Skadden, Arps, Slate, Meagher & Flom LLP, Washington DC +1 202 371 7000
mklepper@skadden.com
Recommended in Project Finance: India Foreign
Specialisation: Development, financing and acquisition of energy, transportation and other large infrastructure projects throughout the world. Has also handled major transactions related to privatisation and restructurings within the electric and gas industry, and has extensive experience in financing sports stadiums and arenas. Has been the lead lawyer representing: developers and owners of power plants and gas pipelines, and contractors, banks, underwriters and equity investors in connection with acquisitions, joint ventures and project financings (over 100 major transactions) totalling more than $10 billion and including some of the most complex transactions in recent years, such as the Dabhol Power Project in India. Has helped develop and finance projects in more than two dozen countries throughout Africa, Asia, Europe, the Indian subcontinent, Latin America and the Middle East. Often serves as a guest speaker, chairman of programs, and lecturer at project and international financing conferences across the country. Has written and edited numerous publications, including ten books and more than twenty articles.
Prof. Memberships: Board of Directors, National Independent Energy Producers (1993-1995); Member, Co-ordinating Group on Energy Law, American Bar Association (1985-1989); Chairman, Energy Law Committee, Real Property Probate and Trust Section, American Bar Association (1980-1986).
Career: J.D., Rutgers Law School, 1973 (Articles Editor, Rutgers Law Review); B.A., University of Pennsylvania, Wharton School, 1969.

KULKARNI, Ravindra
Little & Co, Mumbai +91 22 265 9625
Recommended in Corporate/M&A, Project Finance

LUTHRA, Rajiv
Luthra & Luthra Law Offices, New Delhi +91 11 335 0633
Recommended in Project Finance

MANDAL, Som
Fox Mandal, New Delhi +91 11693 4401, +91 98110 51323 (Mobile)
som@foxmandal.com
Recommended in Corporate/M&A, Project Finance
Specialisation: Major areas of practice include Public and Private Mergers & Acquisitions, Establishment and restructuring of companies, Corporate Finance as well as General Corporate laws. Has extensive experience in Power Projects, Telecom and Foreign direct investments. During 12 years of practice has been a frequent speaker at national and international conferences.
Prof. Memberships: Member of International Bar Association, Law Asia, Union International Des Avocats, Commission on International Arbitration of ICC, Supreme Court Bar Association of India, Inter Pacific Bar Association, Secretary of Committee Q (Securities & Derivatives) and Committee 12 (litigation) of International Bar Association, International

Law Association, American Bar Association (International Section).
Publications: Written in several legal journals. Has presented papers at various conferences and International Seminars. Is presently preparing a chapter on application of FIDIC contracts under Indian law.
Career: A graduate of the University of Calcutta and has been practising law for over 12 years
Personal: Born on September 22, 1961. Belongs to a family of lawyers (4th generation of lawyers and the great grandson of one of the founding partners of the firm). Leisure interests include travelling, golf, cricket and table tennis.

MEHTA, Dara
Little & Co, Mumbai +91 22 265 2739
Recommended in Corporate/M&A

MEHTA, Nikhil
Linklaters (a member firm of Linklaters & Alliance), London +44 20 7456 2000
nikhil.mehta@linklaters.com
Recommended in Corporate/Mergers & Acquisitions: India Foreign
Specialisation: Corporate taxation with particular emphasis on international and structured finance, derivatives, cross-border structures, joint ventures, M&A structures, warrants and hedging instruments, preference share issues, US/UK and other cross-border offerings (public and private), bank finance.
Career: Practised as tax advocate in Bombay, 1977-80. Head of the India Business Group. Head of Contentious Tax Group since 2000. Qualified Indian Advocate and Solicitor of the Supreme Court of England and Wales.

MERCHANT, Kalpana
Kanga & Co, Mumbai +91 22 288 6542
km29@vsnl.com
Recommended in Corporate/M&A, Project Finance
Specialisation: Partner in Corporate Department. Main area of work is corporate law, principally mergers, acquisitions, project finance, telecom, ISP projects and infrastructure projects. Handled mergers and acquisitions of companies and undertakings by Indian and overseas clients. Assisted in acquisition of undertakings by Thyssen Krupp AG, The Pillsbury Company, Pirelli Cavi SpA.; also handles banking finance, investment projects, real estate matters and intellectual property matters. Advised on merger/joint venture of Hoechst Schering AgrEvo GmbH with Mitsu Group and also of Carnegie Mellon University/IUNet Inc with Department of Telecommunications of India. Represented Schindler Aufzuge AG, Pacific Century Regional Developments Limited (Hongkong), Bank of America, Fleet National Bank, Deutsche Bank and West LB. Also acts as legal counsel for a number of multi national companies and foreign banks.
Prof. Memberships: Bombay Incorporated Law Society and Bar Council of Maharashtra and Goa.
Career: Qualified as a Solicitor in 1981. Joined *Kanga & Company* in 1981. Became a Partner in 1985. Member of the Panel of Arbitrators of The Bombay Incorporated Law Society.

MODY, Zia
Chambers of Zia Mody, Advocate, Mumbai +912 2 265 4340
Recommended in Corporate/M&A

NATH, Ravindra
Rajinder Narain & Co, New Delhi +91 11 331 3232 /335 2831
Recommended in Corporate/M&A, Project Finance

NEWBERY, Mark
Herbert Smith, Singapore +65 536 7990
mark.newbery@herbertsmith.com
Recommended in Project Finance: India Foreign
Specialisation: Managing partner of the firm's Singapore office, with experience of a wide range of corporate matters including major M&A, energy and project finance transactions. Heads the firm's electricity practice. Has acted on over 50 energy related assignments and independent power generation projects in over 20 jurisdictions. Many of these have been India related and elsewhere in Asia. Works closely with the Indonesia firm, *Hiswara Bunjamin & Tandjung*, which is associated with *Herbert Smith*.
Prof. Memberships: Law Society, City of London Law Society, International Bar Association (SERL Electricity Committee Member).
Career: Qualified 1982. Joined *Herbert Smith* in 1980, becoming a partner in 1989.
Personal: Born 28 March 1957. Attended Nottingham University 1976-1979.

PANDE, Raj
White & Case LLP, Singapore +65 225 6000
rpande@whitecase.com
Recommended in Corporate/Mergers & Acquisitions: India Foreign, Project Finance: India Foreign
Specialisation: Partner of *White & Case* in Singapore. Practice involves mergers and acquisitions, project finance and development, banking and corporate financing, capital markets and investments. Experience includes representation of principals in both US and international mergers and acquisitions and of banks, multilateral agencies and corporate borrowers in US and cross-border corporate financings. Has represented large multinational companies and investment vehicles in connection with their joint venture and direct investment activities in India. Has substantial experience in project development and finance, representing both international lenders and developers in connection with infrastructure (power, telecommunications and road) projects and greenfield industrial and refinery projects. Has particularly strong experience in power projects and has advised lenders and developers in power generation projects in India aggregating over 3,000 MW. Has substantial experience representing the firm's clients on telecommunications financing projects in India. Also counsels Indian corporations in connection with their activities outside India.
Prof. Memberships: Admitted to New York State Bar in 1988.
Career: Prior to moving to *White & Case LLP*'s Singapore office, was based in the firm's New York office and worked in the firm's Tokyo office for two years.
Personal: BEng, McGill University, 1979; MBA, McGill University, 1987; LLB and BCL, McGill University, 1987. Canadian citizen. Speaks English and French.

PATHAK, Jai
Pathak & Associates, New Delhi +91 11 373 8793
Recommended in Corporate/M&A, Project Finance

RUSHTON, Chris
Allen & Overy, Singapore +65 535 1944
Recommended in Project Finance: India Foreign

SAGAR, Jyoti
Jyoti Sagar & Associates, New Delhi +91 11 651 8714
Recommended in Corporate/M&A

SHAH, Rajendra
Crawford Bayley & Co, Mumbai +91 22 266 3713
Recommended in Corporate/M&A

SHROFF, Cyril
Amarchand & Mangaldas & Suresh A Shroff & Co, Mumbai +91 22 432 4455
cyril.shroff@amarchand.com
Recommended in Corporate/M&A, Project Finance
Specialisation: Managing Partner, Bombay. Partner in company, commercial, mergers & acquisitions and project finance department.
Prof. Memberships: Bar Council of India, incorporated Law Society Bombay.
Career: Qualified in 1982 in India. Solicitor for High Court of Bombay in 1983. Advocate-on-record for the Supreme Court of India in 1984.
Personal: Born 7 November 1959. Attended Sydenham College, Bombay University and Government Law College Bombay (LLB).

SHROFF, Shardul
Amarchand & Mangaldas & Suresh A Shroff & Co, New Delhi +91 11 335 5147
shardul.shroff@amarchand.com
Recommended in Corporate/M&A, Project Finance
Specialisation: Managing Partner, New Delhi. Partner in Corporate and Project Finance Department.
Prof. Memberships: Bar Council of India, Delhi Bar Association, International Bar Association and Supreme Court Bar Association.
Career: Qualified in 1980. 1985, Advocate-on-record, Supreme Court, India.
Personal: Born 1 October 1955. Attended Sydenham College, Bombay University (BCom) and Government Law College Bombay (LLB).

SINGH OBE, Arun
KLegal, London +44 20 7694 2500
Recommended in Corporate/Mergers & Acquisitions: India Foreign
Specialisation: Partner in Corporate and Commercial Department. Main area of work is commercial and corporate law, both domestic and cross-border including joint ventures, transfer of technology, entry strategy into a range of emerging markets for manufacturers, service providers, IT companies and utilities. Also advises foreign companies upon inward investment into the UK. Advised a number of multi nationals and medium sized companies upon

legal, regulatory, strategic and commercial issues impacting upon their international investments.
Prof. Memberships: Law Society of England and Wales; Incorporated Law Society of Bombay; International Bar Association.
Career: Qualified in 1986. Joined *Masons* London in 1984, worked in the Hong Kong office in 1986 and 1987, becoming a Partner in 1992. Joined *KLegal* in 1999. Specialist Advisor to the House of Commons Trade and Industry Select Committee 1996-97; Board Member DTI and Foreign Office's Indo British Partnership Area Advisory Group 1993 to date; Member CBI International Committee 1996 to date; Chairman British Indian Law Association 1997-99; Member of the UK Government's British Trade International Markets Group 1997 to date; North American Task Force, London First Inward Investment Agency; appointed an O.B.E. for services to exports and international investment in New Years Honours List 1999. Contributing Editor to Euromoney's Practice Manual on Investment. Editorial Board of Global Law and Business. Written for the Financial Times. Has spoken at conferences in the UK and abroad. Leads courses at Business Schools in UK and abroad. Visiting fellow to Leeds University Business School. Adviser to Help the Aged International.
Personal: Born 27 January 1957. Sussex University 1976-79. Member, Board of Advisors of the Shrimati P W Loomba Memorial Trust to educate children of widows. Leisure interests include walking, cinema, modern art, swimming and architecture. Lives in Hampstead, London.

STACEY, Paul
Slaughter and May, London +44 20 7600 1200
paul.stacey@slaughterandmay.com
Recommended in Project Finance: India Foreign
Specialisation: Partner in the Commercial Department. Principal areas of practice include energy-related work, banking and project finance.
Prof. Memberships: The Law Society.
Career: With *Slaughter and May* throughout. Articles 1981, qualified 1983, Partner 1990. Hong Kong Office 1986-88.
Personal: Born 9 May 1959. Educated at Dulwich College and Trinity College, Cambridge.

TALWAR, Suresh
Crawford Bayley & Co, Mumbai +91 22 266 5186
suresh.talwar@crawfordbayley.com
Recommended in Corporate/M&A
Specialisation: Partner specialising in corporate law, principally joint ventures, acquisitions, mergers, restructuring, taxation and foreign collaborations. Advised several blue chip Indian companies regarding international issue of securities.
Prof. Memberships: Incorporated Law Society, Bombay (1966). Bar Council Of Maharashtra and Goa (1961).
Publications: A paper on Double Taxation Treatise for the Bombay Chartered Accountant Society.
Career: Qualified as a Solicitor (1966). Joined *Crawford Bayley & Co.* (1961) and became a partner (1976).
Personal: Born November 21, 1938. Educated at University Of Bombay (Bachelor of Commerce 1959; LLB 1961). Leisure interests include golf and horseracing.

THACKER, Shardul
Mulla & Mulla & Craigie Blunt & Caroe, Mumbai +91 22 204 4960
mmsit@bom2.vsnl.net.in
Recommended in Corporate/M&A, Project Finance
Specialisation: Extensive experience of project finance. Involved in a number of projects in the energy, power, telecon and port sectors. Has dealt with diverse issues including the financing of investment in joint venture companies. Recently advised project lenders in connection with power purchase agreements and fuel supply agreements. Extensively rendered advice and participated in negotiations and conducted due-diligence in projects relating to LNG, Power and Petrochemicals. Acted as Indian legal counsel to international banks and overseas lenders for major bilateral and syndicated facilities of all types including acquisition finance – Project & Ship Finance. Has presented several papers on various Indian law issues at International and National law conferences in London, Hong Kong, Cannes, Cyprus, Bombay, New Delhi and Madras. Also has extensive experience of corporate law including finance, cross-border transactions, mergers, acquisitions, joint ventures and demergers. Has conducted legal due diligence, negotiations, drafted and reviewed documentation, issued opinions, etc. Indian Legal Counsel to foreign investors in joint ventures with Indian companies. Participating and rendering advice in all aspects involving (i) the establishment of a new company, inter alia, through the hiving-off of existing manufacturing unit of the Indian investor; (ii) participation in the equity of the existing Indian company and (iii) advising on matters relating to tax, stamp duty, corporate law, etc. Has presented several papers on various Indian law issues at International and National law conferences in London, Hong Kong, Cannes, Cyprus, Bombay, New Delhi and Madras.

THAKORE, Shoban
Baishankar Kanga & Girdharlal, Mumbai +91 22 267 3861
Recommended in Project Finance

TITUS, Diljeet
Titus & Co, New Delhi +91 11 6470 700
Recommended in Project Finance

UDWADIA, Darius
Udwadia Udeshi & Berjis, Mumbai +91 22 288 3341
Recommended in Project Finance

VINTER, Graham
Allen & Overy, London +44 20 7330 3000
Recommended in Project Finance: India Foreign

VISWANATHAN, L
Amarchand & Mangaldas & Suresh A Shroff & Co, Mumbai +91 22 432 4455
L.Viswanathan@amarchand.com
Recommended in Project Finance
Specialisation: Partner in Project Finance Department.
Prof. Memberships: Bar Council of India.
Career: Qualified in 1994.
Personal: Born 4 May 1972. Attended National Law School of India University Bangalore (1989-94).

WADIA, Dina
Little & Co, Mumbai +91 22 265 5473
Recommended in Corporate/M&A

WELLS, Russell
Clifford Chance, London +44 20 7600 1000
russell.wells@cliffordchance.com
Recommended in Project Finance: India Foreign
Specialisation: Partner in the Projects Group at *Clifford Chance*. Specialises in power projects, with a particular emphasis on projects in the Indian sub-continent. Also experienced in oil and gas and infrastructure projects throughout Europe and the Middle East. Recent transactions include acting for the sponsors of three of the eight 'fast track' Indian Power Projects.
Career: University of London (Queen Mary's College) bachelor of Law 1987. Joined *Clifford Chance* in 1988; qualified as a solicitor in the Project Finance Group of *Clifford Chance* in 1990; made partner in the Projects Group of Clifford Chance 1997.

WYMAN, Chris
Clifford Chance, London +44 20 7600 1000
chris.wyman@cliffordchance.com
Recommended in Project Finance: India Foreign
Specialisation: Partner specialising in project finance, banking and energy, oil, gas, natural resources.
Career: Epsom College; Cambridge University. Articled *Coward Chance/Clifford Chance*; qualified 1981; partner *Clifford Chance* since 1986.

INDONESIA

Corporate/Commercial

INDONESIA Leading firms (Corporate/Commercial)	
1	Hadiputranto, Hadinoto & Partners
	Mochtar, Karuwin & Komar
2	Ali Budiardjo, Nugroho, Reksodiputro
3	Lubis Ganie Surowidjojo
	Soemadipradja & Taher
	Soewito, Suhardiman, Eddymurthy & Kardono
	Wiriadinata & Widyawan
4	Kartini Muljadi & Rekan
	Makarim & Taira S
	Soebagjo Roosdiono Jatim & Djarot
	Tumbuan Pane Counsellors at Law
5	Makes & Partners

Firms are listed alphabetically in each band.

Leading individuals (Corporate/Commercial)	
1	**HADIPUTRANTO Sri Indrastuti** *Hadiputranto*
	MULJADI Kartini *Kartini Muljadi & Rekan*
	TUMBUAN Fred *Tumbuan Pane*
2	**CHURCHILL Greg** *Ali Budiardjo, Nugroho*
	MANRING Tim *Hadiputranto*
	MORGAN Frank *Mochtar, Karuwin & Komar*
	SOEMADIPRADJA Rahmat *Soemadipradja & Taher*
	SUROWIDJOJO Arief *Lubis Ganie Surowidjojo*
3	**GOIN Thomas** *Mochtar, Karuwin & Komar*
	ISKANDAR Ratna *Makarim & Taira S*
	JOHNSON Darrell *Soewito, Suhardiman*
	WIRIADINATA Hoesein *Wiriadinata & Widyawan*
4	**MAKES Yozua** *Makes & Partners*
	SOEWITO Dyah *Soewito, Suhardiman*
Up-and-coming individuals	
	NURMAMSYAH Emir *Ali Budiardjo, Nugroho*

Individuals are listed alphabetically in each band.

Hadiputranto, Hadinoto & Partners (7 ptrs, 26 asscs) Benefiting from its association with Baker & McKenzie, the firm boasts an impressive foreign and domestic client base. Its connections in the public sector have afforded it involvement in the country's root and branch restructuring of state-owned entities.

"Running the show on many important deals," **Sri Indrastuti Hadiputranto*** is *"a fine lawyer with sound business instincts."* She is supported by **Tim Manring***, recommended to researchers as *"a seasoned professional."* The firm advised on IBRO's recapitalisation of Bank Central Asia, and represented Cycle and Carriage on the acquisition of $538 million worth of shares in Astra International Motors. **Clients:** Lippo Group; Bank Danamon; Chase Manhattan; American Express; Cemex Corp; IBRA; Ministry of Finance.

Mochtar, Karuwin & Komar (5 ptrs, 28 asscs) The changing financial landscape has led this long established firm to switch its focus from direct foreign investment to restructuring. **Frank Morgan*** *"knows his turf"* having used his corporate skills and fluency in Indonesian to make a name for himself in the oil and gas sector. Clients admire **Tom Goin*** as *"an active and effective corporate practitioner."* A strong relationship with IBRA has seen the firm acting on the $400 million sale of PT Astra, the disposal of shares in First Pacific, and the first sale of syndicated loans to an offshore party. **Clients:** IBRA; Exxon Mobil; Chase Manhattan; Cemex Corp; IBM.

Ali Budiardjo Nugroho Reksodiputro (8 ptrs, 15 asscs) One of the oldest firms in the country whose profile has increased this year, largely due to a newly established association with White & Case. The team, which includes a large contingent of Dutch-qualified lawyers, is renowned in the sphere of international finance, where it has advised extensively on the acquisition of distressed debt.

Greg Churchill* was approved to our researchers as *"a senior and gifted expatriate lawyer,"* while **Emir Nurmamsyah*** is held to be *"the country's leading young practitioner."* Predominantly engaged in restructuring work, the firm acted for the creditors' committee on the reorganisation of Astra International, and also advised on the restructuring of Satelindo. **Clients:** IFC; Rabobank; Coca-Cola; Dowell Schlumberger.

Lubis Ganie Surowidjojo (4 ptrs, 30 asscs) *"A versatile commercial firm,"* which has pursued an assiduous recruitment policy, and was recommended to researchers for its *"international approach."* **Arief Surowidjojo***, a *"skilful and reliable lawyer,"* was singled out by competitors.

The majority of the client base comprises Indonesian government bodies and foreign enterprises, although an affiliation with English firm Norton Rose and relationships with other US and Australian firms also gives the firm access to a powerful network of overseas clients. The team acted as counsel to PT Astra International on the group's restructuring, and has been active on behalf of IBRA on its reorganisation of the banking sector. **Clients:** Indonesian Government; IBRA; Goldman Sachs; Standard Chartered Indonesia.

Soemadipradja & Taher (4 ptrs, 26 asscs) Originally a breakaway from Makarim & Taira, the firm has developed into *"a secure and independent firm with a substantial foreign client base."* The team concentrates on corporate restructuring, and has a recognised specialisation in the mining sector, while increasing its profile in telecoms, project finance and IP. **Rahmat Soemadipradja*** is a *"level-headed man, possessing sound commercial sense."* The firm has advised extensively on the IBRA restructuring. **Clients:** Newmont Mining Corp; Microsoft; Bank Danamon; Mulia Group; Daya Mitra Telekomunikasi.

Soewito, Suhardiman, Eddymurthy & Kardono (4 ptrs, 32 asscs) *"Busy young firm,"* with a strong expatriate contingent, which features regularly on standard corporate deals and is especially strong in the oil, gas and mining sectors. Principal areas of experience are cross-border M&A and debt restructuring. The pivotal figure of the practice is

*See leaders' profiles on pages 392

the *"pleasant but tough"* **Darrell Johnson***, an expert in finance and M&A, who is ably supported by *"the outstanding talent"* of **Dyah Soewito***. **Clients:** Fortune 500 multi-national corporations.

Wiriadinata & Widyawan (5 ptrs, 15 asscs) Despite the breakaway of a number of partners to form a new firm in alliance with UK giant Herbert Smith, the firm has so far retained its sound reputation and enviable international client base. The team focuses on foreign investment, M&A, infrastructure projects and the power industry. Its formal association with Australia's Allens Arthur Robinson Group provides exposure to a number of high-profile regional cross-border transactions.

Hoesein Wiriadinata* is seen by clients as *"one of Indonesia's most senior and well respected lawyers,"* and has a practice that is divided between corporate work in the energy industry and capital markets advice. The firm acted for Dairy Foods on the purchase of Hero supermarkets, and advised Philip Morris on the takeover of Tresno. **Clients:** Rio Tinto; Cable & Wireless; Johnson & Johnson; Morgan Stanley; Philip Morris.

Kartini Muljadi & Rekan (5 ptrs, 25 asscs) Respected corporate firm, which competitors consider owes its reputation entirely to **Kartini Muljadi***, *"an extremely fine lawyer and an excellent businesswoman."* Her intermittent role as an advisor to the government results in limited availability for private practice, but she remains *"a redoubtable presence on major transactions."* Although also active in banking, capital markets and IP, the firm primarily endures for its transactional M&A expertise. **Clients:** Indonesian government.

Makarim & Taira S (3 ptrs, 25 asscs) Concentrating on corporate and finance law, the firm serves domestic clients doing business both in Indonesia and abroad, as well as conducting a number of relationships with overseas concerns, forged through an international network of correspondent offices in London, New York and Hong Kong. Traditionally linked to the public sector, where it remains strong, much of the team's reputation derives from its involvement in the two largest debt restructurings in Indonesia in the 1990s. Competitors acknowledge managing partner **Ratna Iskandar*** as *"a sound and technically proficient lawyer."* **Clients:** American Embassy; Lippo Group; Mitsubishi; Procter & Gamble; Ford; ICI; Glaxo Wellcome.

Soebagjo Roosdiono Jatim & Djarot (6 ptrs, 9 asscs) Chiefly associated with corporate work, the firm has a *"dependable, if unspectacular"* domestic presence in corporate and debt restructuring, M&A, and joint ventures, and a particular specialisation in the energy and mining sectors. It has become more internationally visible through a close working relationship with Australian firm Blake Dawson Waldron, and has substantially increased its client base of foreign inward investors. Our researchers encountered widespread approval for the firm's advice on the recent round of privatisations in Indonesia. **Clients:** Leading domestic and foreign corporates.

Tumbuan Pane Counsellors at Law (2 ptrs, 10 asscs) Small full-service firm, which was recommended to researchers for its *"quality and reliability,"* and specialises in joint venture and capital markets transactions. The whole operation revolves around **Fred Tumbuan***, seen by some commentators as *"the greatest company lawyer in Indonesia."* Such is his reputation that he is regularly retained by the government as an advisor, and has been involved, inter alia, in the revision of Indonesia's company and bankruptcy law. **Clients:** Astra; BDNI.

Makes & Partners (3 ptrs, 20 asscs) A force in the commercial areas of law, the firm's client base includes multi-nationals, major financial institutions and larger Indonesian corporates. At the hub of the firm is **Yozua Makes***, *"a switched on, younger member of the Indonesian legal fraternity,"* according to clients.

The firm represents the government of Indonesia on privatisation and divestments, having acted for the Office of Investment and Development of State Enterprises of the Republic of Indonesia since its inception. Recent highlights include acting for Astra International on the divestment of its semi-conductor subsidiary, and involvement in the privatisation of PT Semen Gresik Tbk. In the financial sector, the firm has acted on global offerings on the New York and London Stock Exchanges. **Clients:** IBRA; Lippo Group; Indonesian Capital Investment Board; Merrill Lynch; Samsung.

Leaders' profiles – Indonesia

CHURCHILL, Greg
Ali Budiardjo, Nugroho, Reksodiputro, Jakarta +62 21 250 5125

GOIN, Thomas
Mochtar, Karuwin & Komar, Jakarta +62 21 571 1130

HADIPUTRANTO, Sri Indrastuti
Hadiputranto, Hadinoto & Partners, Jakarta +62 21 515 5090

ISKANDAR, Ratna
Makarim & Taira S, Jakarta +62 21 252 1272 / 520 0001

JOHNSON, Darrell
Soewito, Suhardiman, Eddymurthy & Kardono, Jakarta +62 21 521 2038

MAKES, Yozua
Makes & Partners, Jakarta +62 21 574 7181

MANRING, Tim
Hadiputranto, Hadinoto & Partners, Jakarta +62 21 515 5090

MORGAN, Frank
Mochtar, Karuwin & Komar, Jakarta +62 21 571 1130

MULJADI, Kartini
Kartini Muljadi & Rekan, Jakarta +62 21 525 6968

NURMAMSYAH, Emir
Ali Budiardjo, Nugroho, Reksodiputro, Jakarta +62 21 250 5125

SOEMADIPRADJA, Rahmat
Soemadipradja & Taher, Jakarta +62 21 574 0088

SOEWITO, Dyah
Soewito, Suhardiman, Eddymurthy & Kardono, Jakarta +62 21 521 2038

SUROWIDJOJO, Arief
Lubis Ganie Surowidjojo, Jakarta +62 21 831 5005

TUMBUAN, Fred B G
Tumbuan Pane Counsellors at Law, Jakarta +62 21 720 8172

WIRIADINATA, Hoesein
Wiriadinata & Widyawan, Jakarta +62 21 250 5175

IRAN

Corporate/Commercial

IRAN Leading firms (Corporate/Commercial)
1 International Law Office Dr Behrooz Akhlaghi & Associates
Tavakoli & Shahabi
Torossian, Avanessian & Associates

Firms are listed alphabetically in each band.

Leading individuals (Corporate/Commercial)
1 AKHLAGHI Behrooz *Dr Behrooz Akhlaghi*

Individuals are listed alphabetically in each band.

International Law Office Dr Behrooz Akhlaghi & Associates (3 ptrs, 3 asscs) A multi-lingual, full-service firm particularly active in corporate and commercial matters. Active in foreign investment, international commercial contracts, banking, trade, arbitration and joint venture agreements. Involved in a construction project concerning the transfer of water to the UAE. **Dr Behrooz Akhlaghi** was described to our researchers as *"a sage"* and he has a *"good broad team underneath him."* The firm is retained as legal counsel by several embassies in Tehran and has close links with many international law firms. **Clients:** World Bank; IFC; Lloyds TSB; HSBC; Toshiba; Hyundai; Casio; UNHCR; Samsung; Sony; Marconi; Totalfina; BP Amoco; British Airways.

Tavakoli & Shahabi (4 ptrs, 3 asscs) *"A strong corporate practice which is doing well."* Across the board services are provided to foreign investors. Competitors recommend the firm for *"its impressive roster"* of international clients. Provides advice in the energy market and drafts contracts and joint venture agreements. **Clients:** Coca-Cola; DaimlerChrysler.

Torossian, Avanessian & Associates (2 ptrs, 1 assc) A smaller ethnic Armenian firm known for

"the quality of its legal advice" and commended for its trustworthiness. Involved in many transactions across the corporate sphere of work and benefits from an international client base. Regularly advises on energy projects. **Clients:** Sumitomo; Mitsubishi; Mannesmann; Nestlé; Peugeot; Alcatel; Italtel.

Leaders' profiles – Iran

AKHLAGHI, Behrooz
International Law Office Dr Behrooz Akhlaghi & Associates, Tehran +98 21 873 2138
bakhlaghi@kanoon.net
Specialisation: Main area of work: Civil and Commercial, International Trade, Foreign Investment, International Contracts, Banking Affairs, Labour, Corporate, Trademark, Patent, Immigration Law, Arbitration Law, and Tax Law. Acted as local lawyer for the Iran-Kuwait Water Transfer Project. Acted as local counsel for Waterloo-BR Amoco project involving reorganisation structuring and transfer of shares of a multinational chemical company to a subsidiary company. Formed a joint venture company for Union Capital Limited, an international mining company and has acted as their legal advisor. Acted for Shell on the operation of its Shell Global Share Plan in Iran. Advised International Finance Corporation (IFC), a member of the World Bank Group, in its investment objectives in Iran.
Prof. Memberships: Iranian Bar Association. American Bar Association. International Bar Association. The Law Association for Asia and the Pacific (Lawasia). Centre for International Studies. International Business Law Consortium (IBLC).
Publications: Author of 'Commercial Law: Negotiable Instruments – Commercial Contracts'. Contributed to International Trade Law. Translations: 'Schmitthoff's Export Trade Law & Practice of International Trade Law', Clive M. Schmitthoff, London Stevens & Sons, 1995, with the cooperation of the Iranian lawyers; 'Principles of International Commercial Contracts', Institute International pour L'Unification Du Droit Prive, Unidroit, Rome, 1994, with the cooperation of Mr Farhad Emam; 'European Union Law', Nutschells by Mike Cuthbert, London Sweet & Maxwell, 2001, with the cooperation of Dr Parviz Parvizian.
Career: Founded the firm in 1979 to provide advice to corporate and individual clients located in the region and around the world. Since then, has supervised all legal work carried out in the firm. Also conducts various eductional activities as an associate professor at Tehran University.
Personal: Born December 1, 1937. Tehran University, Faculty of Law (Bachelor and Doctorate Degree); Law faculty of Aix-en-Provence (France: Doctorat d'Etat-Ph.D.); Oxford University, Faculty of Law.

IRELAND

Index

OVERVIEW: The leading club of corporate firms is this year joined by Mathseon Ormsby Prentice, who, with renewed vigour and aggressive hiring, has successfully imposed itself in the upper tier. The buoyant Irish market has been dominated by the privatisations of state entities, public-private partnerships (PFI/PPP) and major transactions in the telecoms sector.

Premier blue-chip corporate firm Arthur Cox lead the way in acting for former state operator Telecom Eireann, now Eircom, who were floated for €8 billion in the biggest ever Irish offering. This was followed by BT's purchase of Esat for $2.5 billion, handled by hi-tech kings William Fry. The technology sector continues to move at frenetic pace and venture capital experts Matheson Ormsby Prentice and dynamic smaller firms such as LK Shields have made their mark here. Set in motion by the establishment of the International Financial Service Centre, our newly introduced banking and finance section reflects those firms who have actively courted this thriving market. Additionally, many firms have dedicated units catering to the lucrative investment funds market.

Banking & Finance

IRELAND Leading firms (Banking & Finance)
1 A&L Goodbody
Arthur Cox
McCann FitzGerald
2 Matheson Ormsby Prentice
William Fry
3 Dillon Eustace

Firms are listed alphabetically in each band.

Leading individuals (Banking & Finance)
1 HAUGHEY Stephen *A&L Goodbody*
HEALY Nathaniel *A&L Goodbody*
HENNESSY Grainne *Arthur Cox*
JOHNSTON William *Arthur Cox*
MOLONY Ronan *McCann FitzGerald*
2 DOBBYN Paul *A&L Goodbody*
MORRISSEY Daniel *William Fry*
PRENTICE William *Matheson Ormsby Prentice*

Individuals are listed alphabetically in each band.

A&L Goodbody (10 ptrs, 22 asscs) The firm's banking and financial services section is one of the two largest in Ireland and equipped with vast resources across the spread of financial disciplines. Newly housed in the International Financial Services Centre, it has signalled its intention to compete on the same footing as chief rival McCann Fitzgerald. Its cross-border capabilities are enhanced by a spread of international offices including London and New York. No stone is left unturned as specialist units knit together to offer expertise in asset financing, funds, financial services regulation, tax based leasing, structured finance, securitisations and derivatives. The watchword of the day in Ireland is PPP, and the practice has advised on the majority of major projecty finance deals to have taken place – with particular expertise in energy and telecoms. The highlight deal for Bank Of Scotland (Ireland) in relation to project finance for Drumglass High School, the first education PFI project in Northern Ireland, valued at £6.8 million. Department head **Stephen Haughey*** is rated highly by clients in the banking sector – *"he's vastly experienced and an excellent operator."* He has a particular focus on corporate banking and tax based finance and leasing. Likewise, **Nathaniel Healy*** is another senior partner recommended for his *"extensive track record on major transactions."* Reflecting the buoyancy of the Irish investment funds and financial services sector, mutual funds expert **Paul Dobbyn*** is singled out as one of the key names. He also advises on money laundering, financial services regulation and compliance. The clientele of the practice comprises a selection of banks and financial institutions, both domestic and foreign, corporate borrowers and lending companies. A highlight was acting as joint adviser to Irish Permanent on securitisation of a £600 million mortgage porfolio, the largest domestic mortgage to date. It advised Banco Bilbao Vizcaya Argentaria (BBVA) and Terra Networks on the proposed joint venture with enba – owner of First-e Group – to create UnoFirst, a global internet financial services provider. Capital markets activity saw the practice represent Trintech on its secondary offering on the Nasdaq and the Neuer Markt which raised $135 million. It advised Bank of Ireland on a £75 million syndicated loan to Mercia Limited, and on its City Link telecoms project to the tune of £335 million. **Clients:** Irish Life & Permanent; Banco Bilbao Vizcaya Argentaria (BBVA); GE Capital Woodchester; Bank of Scotland; Anglo Irish Bank; GECAS; KBC (KredietBank); Bank Of Ireland; Trinity Venture Capital.

Arthur Cox (6 ptrs, 20 asscs) The firm has a strong presence in domestic lending, advising an assortment of well-known Irish financial institutions. Although not possessing the international clout and experience of its nearest competitors, *"they represent the first choice for us in terms of experience, expertise and team spirit,"* according to one leading Irish client. Syndicated lending, project finance, PPP, securitisation, big-ticket acquisition finance and debt restructuring are cornerstones of the workload.

Head of the department, **William Johnston*** is an acknowledged leading light and has extensive experience of debt finance transactions, syndicated loans and leasing. **Grainne Hennessy*** is younger but has an established transactional record. She advises financial institutions and borrowers on project finance and syndications, and played a key role in the innovative EBBS Building Society mortgages securitisation – the first time an Irish law firm had assumed a lead role in such a securitisation. The firm also advised enba plc on its merger with BBVA (Banco Bilbao Vizcaya Argentaria) to form Unofirst, represented the Minister for Finance on the sale of TSB Bank, and acted for Anglo-American on the financing of the Lisheen lead and zinc mine. **Clients:** Bank of Ireland; Anglo Irish Bank; IIB Bank Limited; AIB Capital Markets; enba; Ulster Bank Markets; Barclays Bank; Scotiabank; Bank of Scotland (Ireland); Bank of Scotland; First Active; financing divisions of Aer Lingus, Eircom and Irish National Petroleum Corporation.

McCann FitzGerald (10 ptrs, 20 asscs) Considered by many to possess the strongest financial services practice, the firm's large banking team, international offices and unrivalled reputation for technical precision put it clearly at the top of the tree. *"We are always impressed,"* confirmed one satisfied client. Advice on domestic syndicated loans is offered in tandem with recognised expertise in cross-border structured finance, securitisation, derivatives, asset finance and project finance.

The spearhead of the practice is the *"superb"* **Ronan Molony***, *"a great thinker with an incisive mind,"* who is one of the most respected lawyers in Ireland and the firm's senior partner. His team advised global co-ordinators Merrill Lynch and AIB Capital Markets on the Eircom flotation, Ireland's largest ever equity offering, which raised over $5 billion. The firm's asset finance team is among the largest in Ireland, and handles work for a range of banks and leasing companies. Securitisations include an innovative $200 million Catastrophe Bond on behalf of SCOR and Goldman Sachs, while in project finance, the group advised ABN AMRO and Barclays on the Minorco Lisheen mine in Co Tipperary, and has acted on 12 major road projects for the National Roads Authority. **Clients:** Bank of Ireland; Citicorp; Ulster Bank; AIB Corporate Banking; AerFi Group (formerly GPA); Pembroke Capital; Orix Aviation; Anglo Irish Bank; Shannon Engine Support; Lombard Global Finance; Bank of America; Exim Bank; Babcock & Brown; De Lage Landen Leasing; ACC Bank; ABN AMRO; De Lage Landen International; Merrill Lynch; SCOR; Goldman Sachs; Barclays.

Matheson Ormsby Prentice (8 ptrs, 20 asscs) The firm's finance group is split into specialised units handling syndicated loans, structured finance and the booming investment funds industry. Although it is felt to lack the big-ticket deal visibility of the market leaders, the team is a respected force in international structured finance and securitisations.

William Prentice* is rated highly by peers, and heads a group which advises international financial institutions, financial services providers and corporate borrowers located at the IFSC. The firm advised ABN AMRO in connection with a $56 million standby letter of credit facility to Vroon Shipping Group, and the Korean Development Bank on a $400 million re-packaging of Korean debt. The investment services group advised INVESCO on the integration and consolidation of its $5 billion funds range, and acted for Charles Schwab on the establishment of its Asian fund platform. An active asset finance team performs extensive work for Korean Airlines, which structures most of its aircraft financing through Ireland. **Clients:** BNP; KBC Bank; Natexis Banque Populaires; Credit Lyonnais; Hypoverinsbank; IKB; Banco Santander; Deutsche Bank; GLG Partners LP; Irish Life; Hiscox; HFC; PMPA; Korean Airlines; Flightlease; Engine Lease Finance Corporation; Nichimen Corporation; CIT Leasing Corporation.

William Fry (3 ptrs, 3 asscs in banking, 3 ptrs and additional asscs in investment funds) The banking team is comparatively small, but has a reputation for competence in areas ranging from acquisition finance to bond issues, PFI, property and lease finance. Considered one of the market front-runners for financial services, the team is headed by the esteemed **Daniel Morrissey***, and advises international companies seeking to establish operations in the IFSC, including custodians, administrators and investment funds themselves. Highlights include advice to Allied Irish Bank on the development of an infrastructural fund, in conjunction with the European Investment Bank, to provide finance to PPP SPV's. It is also advising the financiers to one of the bidders in the first school bundling/Cork School of Music PPP projects. The practice also advised a US multinational on the establishment of a European vendor financing vehicle, a number of European banking institutions in commercial paper/euro note programmes, and for Euro Capital Structures, set up recently to structure securitisation for Unicredito Italiano and Fiat. **Clients:** Ulster Bank; NIB; AIB Bank; Irish Life & Permanent; Deutsche Bank; Irish Stock Exchange; Royal & Sun Alliance.

Dillon Eustace (5 ptrs, 15 asscs) Niche financial services firm, founded in 1992, and rated as *"great for mutual funds."* Acknowledged to be a leader for investment products advice, the firm lacks the resources and transactional muscle of its larger rivals, but has managed to tap into overseas markets such as Japan, where it became the first Irish law firm to open an office in Tokyo, Korea (it has advised over 70% of all Korean funds established in Dublin) and South Africa. It recently formed an alliance with Luxembourg based funds practice Arendt & Medernach. The firm also advises offshore centres in drafting their mutual funds laws. Other areas of expertise include collective investment schemes, aircraft finance, structured finance, leasing, securitisation and derivatives. Since its inception, the firm has advised on the formation of more than 320 mutual funds with assets totalling around $25 billion. It currently acts for around 550 Dublin administered funds. In the corporate sphere, it is acting for Royal Bank of Scotland regarding Irish regulatory issues in the take-over of Natwest's Irish operations, and for Monte dei Paschi di Siena in the purchase of Banca del Salento. A major securitisation highlight was the KDB Capital transaction involving the issue of $150 million of notes backed by a portfolio of Korean lease receivables. **Clients:** Royal Bank of Scotland; Monte dei Paschi di Siena; Arca Vita International; KDB Capital; Buy4Now; Formus Communications; Irish Life and Permanent.

*See leaders' profiles on pages 399-405

Competition/Anti-trust

IRELAND Leading firms (Competition/Anti-trust)
1 A&L Goodbody
Arthur Cox
McCann FitzGerald
William Fry

Firms are listed alphabetically in each band.

Leading individuals (Competition/Anti-trust)
1 COLLINS Damian *McCann FitzGerald*
FITZGERALD Gerald *McCann FitzGerald*
HANDOLL John *William Fry*
MEADE John *Arthur Cox*
POWER Vincent *A&L Goodbody*
2 O'BRIEN Patrick *Arthur Cox*
Up-and-coming individuals
CASEY Denise *A&L Goodbody*
McCARTHY Alan *A&L Goodbody*

Individuals are listed alphabetically in each band.

A&L Goodbody (1 ptr, 5 asscs) The largest anti-trust team in Ireland handles all aspects of competition law, including merger filings, state aids cases, cartel investigations in the oil, drinks, banking and transport industries, and public procurement, notably advising the Irish government in relation to its deal with Global Crossing. The firm has operated a Brussels office since 1988, but does not staff it with a resident partner, instead sending a lawyer there on a rotating basis.

Vincent Power* is the group's high-profile leader. An academic by background, he is said to be *"great at bringing in clients"* and *"effectively communicating his point."* He has niche expertise in shipping cases. Two senior associates, **Denise Casey***, formerly of Simmons & Simmons and **Alan McCarthy***, with UK experience at Slaughter and May, also receive market plaudits. The firm defended the Irish telecoms regulator, ODTR, in the Supreme Court appeal by Orange over the director's decision to award the 3G mobile licence to Meteor Communications. It also assisted Ryanair in complaints to the Irish Competition Authority and European Commission, concerning a High Court injunction against Aer Rianta. M&A related activity included representing Coca-Cola on its purchase of Cadbury Schweppes, and advising on the competition aspects of the Natwest/Bank of Ireland merger. **Clients:** ODTR (Irish Telecoms Regulator); AIB; ACC Bank; TV3; Coca-Cola; Ryanair; Trinity Mirror Group; Department of Enterprise, Trade & Employment; Irish government; Cityjet; Servisair; Ulster Bank.

Arthur Cox (2 ptrs, 2 asscs) A powerful array of corporate clients generates a constant transactional flow for the competition practice. Merger filings, litigation and state aids are the principal components of the caseload.

With a track record including time at Clifford Chance in Brussels, **John Meade*** *("pleasant and easy to work with")* has extensive experience, and is *"technically impressive."* Younger partner **Patrick O'Brien*** is another important element in a *"strong and convincing team."* He has been a key adviser to Eircom, successfully defending a complaint for alleged abuse of a dominant position brought by Esat Telecom at the EC. The firm also acted for the Bank of Ireland in a case brought by the European Commission relating to bank charges, and advised Glanbia in proceedings brought by the Irish Competition Authority, following the Authority's investigation of the liquid milk market. Transactionally, the group is to advise on Eircell's proposed takeover by Vodafone. **Clients:** Eircom; Eircell; Aer Lingus; Bank Of Ireland; Glanbia.

McCann FitzGerald (1 ptr, 3 asscs in Dublin) The only Irish firm to have maintained a Brussels office staffed by a resident partner is consequently considered to have *"a real edge when you need quick contact with officials."* The team handles the complete range of Irish and EC competition law with specific expertise in energy, broadcasting and above all, telecoms. Our researchers found that, typically, the group advises new telecoms entrants all the way to full market operation. It also represents state, quasi-state and local authority clients on public procurement issues.

Resident Brussels partner **Damian Collins*** spends a proportion of his time in Ireland, and is considered *"great for heavy duty regulatory work."* He is respected for operating in a *"practical and workmanlike fashion."* Vastly experienced **Gerald Fitzgerald*** has *"been around since the Domesday Book,"* and is *"hands-on, thoughtful and capable."* He was recently asked by the Irish government to sit on the competition review group, the only solicitor to receive the invitation. The practice acted for commercial broadcaster TV3 in a state aids complaint to the EC concerning funding of state broadcaster RTE. It has also acted for Guinness on a series of matters including its acquisition of United Beverages, and against a court challenge to aspects of its distribution system. Also advised on a third party challenge to the abortive Airtours/First Choice link, represented Ladbrokes on its acquisition of a chain of betting shops, and oversaw NTL's purchase of Cablelink. **Clients:** Guinness; Ladbrokes; Department of Public Enterprise; National Grid; Esat Digiphone (controlled by BT); NTL; Voluntary Health Insurance Board (VHI); TV3; MCI Worldcom; McCook Metals; Compagnie de Saint-Gobain.

William Fry (1 ptr, 2 asscs) A broad competition practice embraces merger control, Article 81 and 82 matters, public procurement and extensive telecoms regulation, an area in which the firm is an acknowledged market leader. *"For analytical understanding and identification of the issues, it's the most thorough team in Dublin."*

Highly rated British lawyer **John Handoll*** is *"a regular fixture"* on the circuit. Twenty years of competition experience includes a stint at Clifford Chance in Brussels, and he is considered to be *"a thorough and careful guy, who will read a document and spot all the issues."* The firm has defended its banking clients from the EU-wide allegations of currency exchange price-fixing, and has advised a number of IT companies on competition issues, including acting for Esat Telecom on its recent acquisition by BT. **Clients:** E-power; Esat Telecom; Waterford Wedgwood; Tesco; Horizon Technologies; National Newspapers of Ireland; Bord Gais; Jefferson Smurfit Group.

Corporate/M&A

A&L Goodbody (20 ptrs, 50 asscs) The country's largest firm is considered to offer a consistently high quality corporate service to an impressive multi-national client base, which appreciates the firm's *"perfectly documented files."* Although a number of the IT/IP team have departed to PwC/Evans & Co, the firm's vast resources and strength in traditional industry keep it among the market leaders. Financial services are an area of notable expertise.

Leading light **Jack O'Farrell*** is *"a technically accomplished businessman"* with extensive public company experience, while managing partner **Frank O'Riordan*** *"leads well and keeps clients happy."* **John Olden*** is recommended for his transactional involvement, and is said to *"zone in on the key issues."* At the younger end, **Paul Carroll*** is rated as an *"energetic, hands-on lawyer,"* as is the *"brilliant"* **Eithne Fitzgerald***. The firm advised Steepleview on the acquisition of Jones Group, a rare public to private transaction valued at £12.7 million. In the telecoms sector, the team represented European strategic partners KPN and Telia on the flotation of state operator Eircom. Other activity has included advising Terex and Partek on the disposal of Moffett Engineering, and Unigate on its part-disposal to Dairycrest and Trintech, an Irish electronic credit card payments company, which took a unique joint listing on the Nasdaq and Neuer Markt. **Clients:** KPN; Telia; Irish Permanent; Elan; Terex Corporation; Partek; Unigate; Steepleview; Trintech; Heiton Holdings; European Leisure; ACT Venture Capital; Boston & Vision Capital; Ulster Bank Investment Managers; GE Capital Woodchester; Bank of Scotland; Anglo Irish Bank; Dungarvan Power Station/Rolls Royce Power Ventures; Dept of Public Enterprise; Hypo Vereins Bank.

IRELAND Leading firms (Corporate/Mergers & Acquisitions)	
1	A&L Goodbody
	Arthur Cox
	Matheson Ormsby Prentice
	McCann FitzGerald
	William Fry
2	LK Shields, Solicitors
	Mason Hayes & Curran
3	O'Donnell Sweeney
4	Eugene F Collins
5	Ivor Fitzpatrick & Co

Firms are listed alphabetically in each band.

Arthur Cox (22 ptrs, 21 asscs) A *"class act,"* rated by many as the best in the country, the corporate team has a history of advising Irish quasi-state companies. Advice on such key matters as the IPOs of Eircom and state airline Aer Lingus keeps the group at the top of the list. The firm is said to be *"brilliantly managed,"* and has *"a buoyantly confident culture,"* an ethos which encourages the development of strong personalities.

A leading figure in Dublin, senior partner **James O'Dwyer*** is *"a terrific character"* who applies a famously tough negotiating style *("he rules the roost")* to big-ticket transactions. Having *"slotted in well"* after taking over the managerial reigns, **Eugene McCague*** is popular with clients and peers alike, has *"a pleasant and easy-going manner"* and is the team's key deal-smoother. **Michael Meghen*** is a *"great technician"* who always *"tries to get the deal done."* **Ciarán Bolger*** is *"client-oriented and knows how to get on with people,"* and advised Ulster Bank on the sale of two of its subsidiaries, while **Colm Duggan*** is an *"aggressive and dynamic younger lawyer,"* who was instrumental in the deal for BT that saw them purchase telecoms giant Esat.

In addition to the flotation of Eircom (formerly Telecom Eireann), the biggest in Irish history at €8 billion, the firm advised the company on the proposed sale of its mobile phone subsidiary Eircell to Vodafone. The team also acted for Adare Printing on its MBO, and advised the Irish National Petroleum Corporation on the disposal of the Whitegate refinery and the Bantry Bay terminal facilities for $100 million. Other work includes representing UTV on its purchase of Cork FM for IR£31.5 million and Power Leisure Group (Paddy Power bookmakers) on its listing on the Dublin and London Stock Exchanges. **Clients:** Eircom; Eircell; Aer Lingus; Fyffes; Greencore; Adare Printing; Irish National Petroleum; Irish Life; Enba; Viridian (formerly Northern Ireland Electricity); Independent Newspapers; Irish Multichannel; Golden Vale; IAWS Group; Clondalkin; Jurys/Doyle; Kingspan; Green Properties; Lucent Technologies; UTV; Power Leisure Group.

Leading individuals (Corporate/Mergers & Acquisitions)		
1	**EGAN Paul** *Mason Hayes & Curran*	**O'CONNELL Owen** *William Fry*
	O'DWYER James *Arthur Cox*	**O'FARRELL Jack** *A&L Goodbody*
2	**DEVEREUX Barry** *McCann FitzGerald*	**DOYLE Andrew** *Matheson Ormsby Prentice*
	EARLEY William *McCann FitzGerald*	**FRY Houghton** *William Fry*
	McCAGUE Eugene *Arthur Cox*	**MEGHEN Michael** *Arthur Cox*
	O'RIORDAN Frank *A&L Goodbody*	**SCANLON Tim** *Matheson Ormsby Prentice*
	SHIELDS Laurence *LK Shields, Solicitors*	
3	**ARMSTRONG Fergus** *McCann FitzGerald*	**BEATTIE David** *O'Donnell Sweeney*
	BOLGER Ciarán *Arthur Cox*	**CAHILL Brendan** *William Fry*
	DUGGAN Colm *Arthur Cox*	**HENEGHAN Brendan** *William Fry*
	O'BEIRNE David *O'Donnell Sweeney*	**PRICE Alvin** *William Fry*
4	**COLL Gerard** *Eugene F Collins*	**COLLINS Anthony** *Eugene F Collins*
	HALPENNY Gerard *LK Shields, Solicitors*	**McEVOY Bernard** *Ivor Fitzpatrick & Co*
	McGOVERN Patricia *LK Shields, Solicitors*	**McKENNA Justin** *LK Shields, Solicitors*
	OLDEN John *A & L Goodbody*	**ROCHE Donal** *Matheson Ormsby Prentice*
	SWEENEY Joseph *O'Donnell Sweeney*	
Up-and-coming individuals		
	CARROLL Paul *A & L Goodbody*	**FITZGERALD Eithne** *A & L Goodbody*

Individuals are listed alphabetically in each band.

Matheson Ormsby Prentice (11 ptrs, 21 asscs) *"Definitely competing with the big boys,"* the firm has made its predicted advance to the top echelon, its credibility enhanced through the creation of dedicated groups of specialists. An aggressive recruitment campaign has reinvigorated the firm's profile, particularly in the technology sector, where it is a market leader, although its client roster is not yet perceived to have the big-name volume of its principal rivals.

The firm's number one practitioner is *"forceful negotiator"* and private equity expert **Andrew Doyle***. He *"understands the venture capital market inside out,"* and has *"built the best high-tech team in town."* The arrival of the *"superb"* **Tim**

*See leaders' profiles on pages 399-405

Scanlon*, like Doyle, a capture from A&L Goodbody, is considered to be a major coup. Managing partner **Donal Roche*** is less of a regular on the transactional front line, but won market plaudits for his advice on the proposed merger between ACC Bank and TSB Bank, and the mooted subsequent flotation. Involved on a number of domestic IPOs, the firm advised iTOUCH on its IPO, and acted for Apion as it was sold to phone.com for over $250 million. Also represented KBC Bank on the acquisition of Ulster Bank Investment Managers from Ulster Bank for over €100 million, and advised the Irish state in connection with the privatisation of the Irish National Petroleum Corporation. **Clients:** KBC Bank; ICC Bank; iTOUCH; Apion; Baltimore Technologies; Independent News and Media; Massana; Ebeon; Microsoft; Hewlett Packard; EMC; Amdahl; Computer Associates; Lehman Brothers; Morgan Stanley; JP Morgan.

McCann FitzGerald (16 ptrs, 21 asscs) The firm's corporate department rarely hogs the headlines, eschewing the limelight for a *"genteel, low-key and gentlemanly approach."* The firm is consistently recommended for its technical expertise, although it can be seen as *"excessively legalistic."* However, such is the group's reputation that clients believe *"you can never fail there."*

A number of the corporate team win the approval of the market. **Barry Devereux*** heads the public companies and corporate finance team and is frequently sighted on major transactions. **William Earley*** has *"a wealth of experience"* and is a TMT sector specialist, while *"old school intellectual"* **Fergus Armstrong*** also has an established corporate reputation.

The firm advised Tyco on its acquisition of Irish Building Services, acted for American Standard on its purchase of AEMAC Engineering, and represented AerFi on its takeover by Debis (part of the Daimler Benz Group). It was also involved in the MBO and venture capital financing of Clondalkin Paper Mills and ntl's acquisition of Cablelink. **Clients:** Tyco; American Standard; Clondalkin Paper Mills; ICC Bank; Readymix; Saville Systems; ntl; Kylemore Bakeries; C&C; Investec Bank UK; Sherry FitzGerald; Esat Digifone; AerFi Group; phone.com; Warner Chilcott; Ernst & Young Management Consultancy.

William Fry (13 ptrs, 28 asscs) Revealed by Chambers' research as a *"brilliant corporate finance boutique which gets bigger and bigger,"* the firm has a leading reputation in the technology sector and for venture capital work, where it is known as one of *the* IPO players.

Managerial commitments have not prevented **Owen O'Connell*** (*"a real leader"*) from playing an instrumental role in key transactions. He *"really grasps all aspects of a deal,"* and is rated as *"the best corporate negotiator in Dublin, bar none."* Such is his reputation, that *"everyone stutters a bit when they see him on the other side. He's not a bully but he is extremely strong in the challenge."* **Houghton Fry*** is chairman of the firm and applies an *"incredible intellect"* to transactions. **Brendan Cahill*** retains his share of admirers for his public M&A practice, as does *"technically superb"* **Brendan Heneghan***, a *"magnificent lateral thinker"* who is *"able to run hugely complex transactions."* He has acknowledged expertise in yellow book and takeover work. **Alvin Price*** has *"always maintained a consistently high standard."* He *"negotiates hard, but it's not the third world war every time you meet."*

The firm represented Esat on its $2.5 billion sale to BT, advised on the IPO of Riverdeep and its admission to the Irish Stock Exchange, and acted on the IPO of Horizon Technology and the Nasdaq listing of Baltimore Technologies. M&A activity includes acting for Hibernian Group on its merger with CGU, for IONA Technologies on the investment into it by the Intel 64 fund, and for James Crean on the demerger of its print and packaging division from Oakhill Group. **Clients:** Esat; Oriflame International; Jefferson Smurfit; James Crean; Hibernian Group; Baltimore Technologies; Horizon Technology; Riverdeep; IONA Technologies; IBM; Waterford Wedgwood; Global Crossing; E*Trade; Getty Images; NOVA Corporation; Federal Express; Boots; Porsche; Doubleclick International; Associates First Capital; DCC; Nintendo; Irish Stock Exchange; Sky Broadcasting; FIAT; Ardagh Group; Statoil; Arnotts.

LK Shields, Solicitors (6 ptrs, 12 asscs) Relatively youthful and aggressive firm which has *"really gunned for the corporate market"* and *"pursued an expansive growth drive"* with acknowledged success. They have been likened to UK firm Herbert Smith, not yet possessing the resources of the top five, but confidently pitching for premium business, notably on technology IPOs.

The corporate practice appears in the image of leading man **Laurence Shields***, said to *"run a tight ship."* He is a *"strong, persistent personality"* and *"unforgiving negotiator,"* who had the *"foresight to get into the technology boom early,"* thereby giving the group a leading reputation in that sector. **Gerard Halpenny*** remains a respected lawyer, but has spent much of the past year on secondment at mobile internet company Parthus, whose IPO the firm had previously handled. **Patricia McGovern*** is recommended for her *"established and sizeable practice,"* particularly in the venture capital and technology sphere. **Justin McKenna*** has a similar focus, with the lion's share of his practice devoted to advising high-tech companies.

The firm advised on Adare Printing Group's acquisition by NAPG, a special purpose MBO vehicle backed by venture capital funds, and acted for Conduit on its €55 million IPO on the Neuer Markt and subsequent joint venture with Sonera. The team also represented IAWS Group on its acquisition of Pierre's Food Service Business from Green Isle, a transaction valued at IR£22 million. **Clients:** Parthus; Conduit; IAWS Group; Adare Printing Group; Kilkenny People; Ireland on Sunday; Ovoca Resources; Trend Technologies; Gradient Solutions; Torc Telecom; Oniva; Accelerated Encryption Processing; Macalla Software; E-Smart.

Mason Hayes & Curran (4 ptrs, 17 asscs) A progressive firm, *"showing lots of vigour,"* which is home to a corporate team with the habit of *"pitching up on deals with a surprisingly large client."* Sound management is credited with *"repackaging the group from a steady and solid unit to a pushy and dynamic force."* An extensive record of public and private M&A, is bolstered by acclaimed work on capital markets, private equity and venture capital transactions.

The recipient of universal praise, the *"exceptional"* **Paul Egan*** is synonymous with the firm. A veteran of numerous high-profile transactions, he is *"extraordinarily hard-working, user-friendly and has an incredible grasp of business issues."* Peers describe him as *"the perfect person to refer work to."* Such is his profile that questions have been raised over the firm's strength in depth.

The firm represented DCC SerCom on its $25 million sale of ITP, advised Lake Communications in its sale of Topology Systems to Cable & Wireless, and assisted Air Foyle on its acquisition and later disposal of a controlling interest in CityJet. Also advised Shandwick International on its acquisition of FCC Communications. **Clients:** British Midland; Christian Salvesen; Davis Services; Granada Group; Iceland Frozen Foods; Orange; P&O; International Woolmark; Kelloggs; Royal Liver; Volex Group; Dunloe Ewart; Knowledgewell; Shandwick International; Radio Telifis Eireann (RTE); Bank of Scotland (Ireland); Unidare; Allied Foods; Bank of Ireland; Biotrin Holdings; Cambridge Diagnostics Ireland; Dragon Oil; INET; Norish; Bodycote International.

O'Donnell Sweeney (9 ptrs, 8 asscs,) The firm has been especially commended for its *"vigorously applied"* efforts in the emerging economy, where it has a *"great focus on small-cap companies."* Although not possessing the weighty client base of the market leaders, the group still advises a range of small and medium-sized Irish companies, banks, financial services providers and union organisations.

David Beattie* is frequently recommended as *"an active corporate man,"* who is *"great for complex yellow and blue book work."* He advises extensively on employee share scheme matters, as well as running a mixed practice comprising M&A, banking, financial services, IT, IPOs and tax. Managing partner **David O'Beirne*** is *"likeable and pragmatic"* and is especially noted for his corporate advice in the energy industry. *"Top deal maker"* **Joseph Sweeney*** has cemented his entrepreneurial, client-getting reputation.

Recent deal highlights include the sale of System Dynamics to Anna Technologies and the IFG Group acquisition of Barclay Jacobs. The practice also advised Dunloe Ewart on a scheme of arrangement, Celtic Resources Holdings on a acquisition in Kazakhstan and Transware's sale to Gladstone.0 **Clients:** Woodchester Investment; Kenmare Resources; Goodman International; IFG Securities; Credit Lyonnais; Minmet; Trinity Biotech; Pharma Patch; Aminex; Celtic Resources Holdings; Ormonde Mining; Seafield; SMF Technologies.

Eugene F Collins (5 ptrs, 7 asscs) Considered to be a first port of call for referrals, this *"thoroughly reliable"* firm maintains its reputation as a superb training ground for young lawyers and a place where client relationships are well managed. Market suggestion that the firm lacks the ambition of its larger rivals has been answered by the recent recruitment of two additional corporate partners, raising the total to five. The corporate team advises both medium-sized Irish companies and overseas concerns, and has experience in IT and e-commerce, pharmaceuticals, publishing, banking and manufacturing.

"Charming" **Anthony Collins*** has forged his reputation as a leading practitioner over the past decade. He is considered to be a *"gentlemanly proprietor who runs a good shop."* Similarly, **Gerard Coll*** is *"able, appealing and effective."* The firm advised Dublin-based PR firm Drury Communications on its recent sale to a foreign buyer, acted for Finnish mobile operator Sonera on its investment in telephone services provider Conduit, and represented VNU World Directories on its joint venture with Golden Pages. **Clients:** Drury Communications; Sonera; Maxell; E-bid; AIB; BNP Paribas; VNU World Directories; Worldspan; Johnson & Johnson.

Ivor Fitzpatrick & Co (9 ptrs, 12 asscs in firm) Small firm, which is acknowledged to possess an expanding and increasingly prolific corporate department. It services a broad range of domestic clients in areas as diverse as IT, professional services, media, entertainment and international trade. **Bernard McEvoy*** was singled out for special attention, after a year in which he has featured on some notable transactions. *"He's an impressive operator, who is clued up on the key points of a deal."* **Clients:** African Gold; Petrel Resources.

Leaders' profiles – Ireland

ARMSTRONG, Fergus
McCann FitzGerald, Dublin +353 1 829 0000
fergus.armstrong@mccann-fitzgerald.ie
Recommended in Corporate/M&A
Specialisation: Partner in Corporate and Commercial Department. Main area of work is corporate law, share acquisitions and disposals, capital raising and joint ventures, advising both international companies and domestic concerns. Clients include both major companies and emerging businesses in the telecoms and related sectors. Major assignments include advising NTL & ESAT Digifone on a range of corporate and regulatory matters and funding transactions for new economy clients such as the global email company and Mobile Aware.
Prof. Memberships: Law Society of Ireland, Dublin Solicitors Bar Association and The Irish Italian Business Association.
Career: Qualified 1968. Employed for four years as corporate counsel with Aer Lingus, before joining *McCann FitzGerald* as a partner in 1974. Served terms both as managing partner and chairman of the firm.
Personal: Graduate of University College Dublin (BCL & LLB) and Harvard Law School (LLM). Writes occasionally on philosophical and related topics.

BEATTIE, David
O'Donnell Sweeney, Dublin +353 1 662 5222
Recommended in Corporate/M&A

BOLGER, Ciarán
Arthur Cox, Dublin +353 1 618 0000
cbolger@arthurcox.ie
Recommended in Corporate/M&A
Specialisation: Partner in Company and Commercial Department. Specialises in mergers and acquisitions for both private and public companies with emphasis on IT, telecommunications and financial services.
Prof. Memberships: Institute of Taxation in Ireland.
Career: Admitted as a solicitor in 1990, partner at *Arthur Cox* since 1996.
Personal: Born 1964; BA mod (1985) Trinity College Dublin. Lives in Dublin, interests include golf and tennis.

CAHILL, Brendan
William Fry, Dublin +353 1 639 5000
Recommended in Corporate/M&A

CARROLL, Paul
A & L Goodbody, Dublin +353 1 649 2000
Recommended in Corporate/M&A
Specialisation: Senior partner in the Commercial Department of *A & L Goodbody.* Advises a range of international and Irish companies on corporate law including money laundering, inward investment, mergers and acquisitions, commercial and financial contracts.
Career: Graduated from Trinity College, Dublin in 1980 with a law degree and has been with *A & L Goodbody* until this time.

CASEY, Denise
A & L Goodbody, Dublin +353 1 649 2000
Recommended in Competition/Anti-trust
Specialisation: An Associate in the Commercial Department. Main areas of work include advising on numerous European, competition and regulatory law issues. In particular, advises on the competition law aspects of commercial transactions, the submission of notifications and complaints to both the Irish Competition Authority and the European Commission and the submission of merger filings to the Department of Enterprise, Trade and Employment and the European Commission. Also advises clients in the context of investigations by the Competition Authority and the European Commission, and advises generally on state aid, public procurement and transport, telecommunications and energy regulation.
Prof. Memberships: Incorporated Law Society of Ireland.
Career: Trained with the European Commission and practised with a British law firm in both London and Brussels, before joining *A & L Goodbody.*
Personal: Graduate of Trinity College, Dublin (LLB Hons), with a Master's Degree in European Law from the Université Libre de Bruxelles.

COLL, Gerard
Eugene F Collins, Dublin +353 1 202 6400
gcoll@efc.ie
Recommended in Corporate/M&A
Specialisation: Partner and head of the Corporate and Banking Department, dealing principally with

mergers and acquisitions and corporate reconstructions.
Prof. Memberships: Law Society of Ireland and the Association Internationale de Jeunes Avocats (former National Vice President for Ireland).
Career: Qualified in 1982 and became a partner in *Eugene F Collins* in 1986, former member of the Company & Commercial Law Committee of the Law Society of Ireland.
Personal: Born 1957. Attended University College, Dublin 1975/77 and the University of Amsterdam 1981/82. Interests include sports and family.

COLLINS, Anthony E.
Eugene F Collins, Dublin +353 1 202 6400
aecollins@efc.ic
Recommended in Corporate/M&A
Specialisation: Business lawyer who is partner in the Corporate and Banking Department with particular expertise and experience in mergers and acquisitions, venture capital, MBOs, start-up, corporate development situations and inward investment into Ireland. Clients include large and medium-sized companies, both Irish and international, particularly from the United States and the United Kingdom.
Prof. Memberships: Law Society of Ireland (former President); Dublin Solicitors Bar Association; Institute of Taxation; Canadian Bar Association (Honorary Member); Institute of Directors, International Bar Association.
Career: Partner in *Eugene F Collins* since the 1960s. For many years was an insolvency specialist and was a founder member of Committee J of the IBA. In the 1980s moved full time into corporate work.
Personal: Attended Trinity College, Dublin (MA and BComm), Chairman of Automobile Association in Ireland and Deputy Chairman of Grafton Group plc and Leinster Leader Limited.

COLLINS, Damian
McCann FitzGerald, Brussels +32 2 740 0370
damian.collins@mccann-fitzgerald.ie
Recommended in Competition/Anti-trust
Specialisation: Partner resident in Brussels, *McCann FitzGerald* is the only Dublin based law firm with a fully staffed Brussels office. Main areas of work: competition/antitrust and regulated sectors; advises clients on compliance with EU and Irish competition law, defends clients subject to cartel and dominance abuse investigations by the European Commission and the Irish Competition Authority; advises on merger filings and complaints under the EC Merger Control Regulation and the Irish Mergers and Take-overs (Control) Act; advises non-dominant operators in the Irish telecommunications sector, including East Digifone, the second Irish mobile operator, (including advice on the award of 3G mobile licences) and MCI Worldcom's Irish subsidiary; advises new entrants in recently liberalised sectors, including TV3, a commercial television operator, (including advice on a State aid complaint concerning the State-controlled broadcaster); advises on trade and WTO issues, including advice to IMRO on its complaint under the EC Trade Barriers Regulation which led to a WTO Panel finding of a TRIPs violation by the United States.
Prof. Memberships: Law Society of Ireland, International Bar Association and the American Bar Association (Vice Chair, International Anti Trust Law Committee).
Career: *Clifford Chance*, London and Brussels, 1986-1990; partner *McCann FitzGerald*, Brussels since 1990.
Publications: Contributor to 'Merger Control in the EU', 'Getting the Deal Through', 'Getting the Fine Down', 'Commercial Agency and Distribution Agreements' and 'International Legal Developments in Review – 1999'.
Personal: Qualified 1984. Graduate of Trinity College, Dublin (BA (Mod), Legal Science) and European University Institute, Florence (LLM).

DEVEREUX, Barry
McCann FitzGerald, Dublin +353 1 829 0000
barry.devereux@mccann-fitzgerald.ie
Recommended in Corporate/M&A
Specialisation: Partner in Corporate & Commercial Department. Main area of work is corporate law, particularly mergers and acquisitions, corporate finance, Stock Exchange-related matters and privatisations. Heads the firm's Corporate Finance Group.
Prof. Memberships: Law Society of Ireland and Dublin Solicitors Bar Association.
Career: Qualified in Ireland in 1988 and in England and Wales in 1995. Joined *Clifford Chance* in London in 1989. Became a partner and head of Corporate Finance for South East Asia with *Clifford Chance* in Singapore (1995 - 1998). Joined *McCann FitzGerald* in 1998 as a partner.
Personal: Attended University College, Dublin 1980 - 1983 (Bachelor of Civil Law). Interests: Golf, rugby and football.

DOBBYN, Paul
A & L Goodbody, Dublin +353 1 649 2000
Recommended in Banking & Finance
Specialisation: Partner in the Banking and Financial Services Group. Joined *A & L Goodbody* in 1981 and was admitted as a partner to the firm in 1986. Was responsible for the opening of the firm's London office and was the partner in charge of the office in 1988/1989.
Prof. Memberships: Has been actively involved in the promotion of the Financial Services Centre in Dublin particularly in the area of mutual funds. Acts for many of the leading fund managers and has advised on various aspects of domiciling and listing funds in Ireland.
Publications: Has written various articles and given many presentations at national and international conferences on the subject of financial services, with particular emphasis on mutual funds and is a contributor to the Journal of International Banking Law.
Career: Sitting member of the Irish Prime Minister's Committee on the regulation of mutual funds in ireland and has been heavily involved in the drafting of Irish domestic legislation in this area.
Personal: Born 7 November 1954. Admitted 1978, Ireland. Married with 2 children.

DOYLE, Andrew
Matheson Ormsby Prentice, Dublin
+353 1 619 9000
andrew.doyle@mop.ie
Recommended in Corporate/M&A
Specialisation: Partner Corporate Finance and Commercial Law Group. Specialises in corporate finance law, particularly for IT companies. Substantial experience in mergers and acquisitions, venture capital, inward investment, management buy-outs, management buy-ins and other private equity fund-raisings. Has represented institutional investors and companies in many of Ireland's largest equity financings and mergers and acquisition transactions in the last decade.
Prof. Memberships: Law Society of Ireland.
Career: Qualified in 1988. Joined *MOP* from *A&L Goodbody* in March 1999. Vice chairman and council member of the Irish Software Association ('ISA'). Has played a leading part in a number of the ISA's initiatives in the areas of legal reform and other areas such as the skills shortage currently facing the Irish technology sector. Council member of the Irish branch of the Licensing Executives Society of Britain and the Republic of Ireland. Has lectured extensively on information technology and corporate law matters.
Personal: Born 1962. Attended University College Dublin 1980-1984 (Bachelor of Civil Law).

DUGGAN, Colm
Arthur Cox, Dublin +353 1 618 0000
cduggan@arthurcox.ie
Recommended in Corporate/M&A
Specialisation: Mergers and acquisitions, corporate finance. Involved in the disposal of Cablelink Limited to NTL, the disposal of Irish Express Cargo Limited to Flextronics Inc. and the acquisition by the Anglo American Group of a 50% interest in Lisheenmine.
Prof. Memberships: Law Society of Ireland.
Publications: 'Company and Partnership Law in Ireland'.
Career: Admitted as a solicitor 1985; partner in *Arthur Cox* 1992.
Personal: Born 1960. BA (Mod) 1982, Trinity College Dublin, LLM 1983, University of London, (LSE).

EARLEY, William
McCann FitzGerald, Dublin +353 1 829 0000
william.earley@mccann-fitzgerald.ie
Recommended in Corporate/M&A
Specialisation: Partner in Corporate & Commercial Department. Main areas of work: e-commerce & information technology, dealing both with emerging technology companies and mergers/acquisitions by established companies, banks and other institutions. Heads the firm's E-commerce & Information Technology Group. Major cases in 2000 include the preparation of the legal framework and documentation for a proposed major e-banking operation, the recent Dalatex plc IPO and the sale of Exceptis Technologies to Trintech Group plc. Also led the firm's team which prepared the report on 'E-Commerce Legislation: Facilitating Requirements for Export Expansion' on behalf of the

Institute for International Trade of Ireland.
Prof. Memberships: Law Society of Ireland. Dublin Solicitors Bar Association. Institute of Taxation in Ireland.
Career: Qualified in 1973. Joined *McCann FitzGerald* as a partner in 1979. Founded and ran firm's London office 1986-1990. Managing Partner of firm 1993 to 1997.
Personal: Attended University College, Dublin 1967-1970 (BA, Economics and Politics). Interests: music (especially opera), tennis, golf. Lives in Dalkey, Co. Dublin. Member of Irish Software Association, Irish Internet Association.

EGAN, Paul
Mason Hayes & Curran, Dublin +353 1 614 5000
pegan@mhc.ie
Recommended in Corporate/M&A
Specialisation: Partner in Corporate Department. Main area of work is company law and securities law, principally mergers, acquisitions and new issues in Ireland. Acting for the Minister for Public Enterprise in connection with the Irish retail offer of Aer Lingus Group plc. Correspondent for Ireland for 'World Securities Law Report'.
Prof. Memberships: Law Society of Ireland.
Publications: Author of 'Companies Acts of Ireland and the UK: Comparative Tables' (Jordans 1991, 1995), co-author of 'The Acquisition of Public Companies in Ireland' (2000).
Career: Qualified in 1981, becoming a partner in *Mason Hayes & Curran* in 1987, on the Company Committee, Law Society of Ireland 1987-99 and on the CII/IAIM working group which devised current guidelines on insider dealing legislation for securities industry participants.
Personal: Born 24 March 1956. Attended Trinity College, Dublin 1973-77 (BA, (Mod) History and Politics), University of Paris 1978 (Dip. L .Fr). Leisure interests include music. Lives in Dublin.

FITZGERALD, Eithne
A & L Goodbody, Dublin +353 1 649 2000
Recommended in Corporate/M&A
Specialisation: Partner in Commercial Department of *A & L Goodbody*. Became a partner with *A & L Goodbody* in 1991 and managed the firm's London office for three years, ending February 1995. Areas of practice include mergers and acquisitions, joint ventures, corporate finance and capital markets and securities law, all aspects of non-contentious insurance law and regulatory matters relating to insurers, including establishment of insurers with head offices in Ireland or by way of a branch or the provision of services, transfers of policies and mergers and acquisitions of insurers, inward investment, commercial contract negotiation and general corporate law. Acts as lead adviser in a wide range of complex and sophisticated commercial transactions.
Publications: Regularly writes on legal topics and has contributed the Irish chapter of a book entitled 'A Practitioner's Guide to Take-over Regulation and Practice in the European Union'.
Career: Qualified as a solicitor with the Law Society of Ireland in 1986.
Personal: Born 22 June 1960. Holds a law degree from Trinity College, Dublin, and a diploma in European Law from University College, Dublin. Admitted 1986 in Ireland. Married with 2 children.

FITZGERALD, Gerald
McCann FitzGerald, Dublin +353 1 829 0000
gerald.fitzgerald@mccann-fitzgerald.ie
Recommended in Competition/Anti-trust
Specialisation: Head of the firm's EU & Competition Law group in Dublin. Practice covers Irish and EU competition and merger law, as well as market regulation in areas such as telecommunications, energy and postal services. Work over the last year has involved sectors such as the drinks industry; the automobile sector; the travel trade; wholesale and retail distribution; e-commerce; banking; health insurance; telecommunications; energy and postal services. Major cases dealt with include advising the National Grid in relation to the liberalisation of the Irish electricity market; assisting the Department of Public Enterprise in relation to new telecommunications legislation; assisting one of the retail banking groups in defending proceedings initiated by the European Commission in relation to alleged price fixing of euro-currency exchange charges; advising two of the major banks in relation to the merger control implications of two separate significant merger proposals. Member of the Government-appointed Competition and Mergers Review Group, which published its final report on the reform of Irish competition and merger control law in March 2000.
Prof. Memberships: Law Society of Ireland and the International Bar Association.
Publications: Contributor, Rowley and Baker: 'International Mergers: the Anti Trust Process' (Sweet and Maxwell), and 'Competition law in the EU, its Member States and Switzerland' (Kluwer). Member, Editorial Board of 'Global Competition Review'.
Career: Qualified in 1971. Partner in *McCann FitzGerald* 1977. Member of the Law Society's Business Law Committee (Chairman 1995 - 1998); member of the Board of the Irish Centre for European Law and Chairman Irish Society for European Law (1999).
Personal: Attended University College Dublin and the Centre Européen Universitaire, Nancy, France. Interests: History, theatre and tennis.

FRY, Houghton
William Fry, Dublin +353 1 639 5000
houghton.fry@williamfry.ie
Recommended in Corporate/M&A
Specialisation: Senior Partner in Commercial Department. Specialises in international corporate and financial law and has extensive transaction experience in Ireland and abroad. Has been involved in a significant number of cross border mergers and acquisitions and joint ventures, particularly in the United States and Europe. In Ireland, in addition to transaction work, advises many of the larger Irish companies (both public and private) as well as a range of financial institutions and multinational corporations.
Prof. Memberships: Law Society of Ireland. Institutute of Taxation in Ireland.
Career: Joined *William Fry* as an apprentice in 1962. Qualifed as a solicitor in 1967. Now Chairman of *William Fry*.
Personal: Born 1945. Attended Trinity College, Dublin (BA; LLB Hons) from 1962-1967.

HALPENNY, Gerard
LK Shields, Solicitors, Dublin +353 1 661 0866
Recommended in Corporate/M&A
Specialisation: Partner in Commercial Department. Extensive experience in all areas of corporate and commercial law, in particular mergers and acquisitions, venture capital, joint ventures, public offerings and corporate finance. Has handled many significant transactions involving Irish companies in recent years including international transactions undertaken by Irish companies. In particular has acted in connection with a number of recent initial public offerings by Irish Companies and several other public offering transactions. Has also acted on behalf of numerous international companies establishing businesses in Ireland whether by way of acquisition or start up.
Prof. Memberships: Law Society of Ireland, Dublin Solicitors Bar Association.
Career: Qualified in 1981. Admitted as a solicitor in England and Wales in 1992. Joined *LK Shields*, Solicitors as a partner in July 1998.
Personal: Born 1957. Attended University College Dublin 1975 -1978. Married with two children.

HANDOLL, John
William Fry, Dublin +353 1 639 5000
john.handoll@williamfry.ie
Recommended in Competition/Anti-trust
Specialisation: Partner in Commercial Department. Heads EU/Competition Unit, specialising in EU, competition and regulatory matters. Advises and represents companies in all areas of EU and national competition law. Extensively involved in national and EU merger filings.
Prof. Memberships: Law Society of Ireland.
Publications: 'Free Movement of Persons in the EU' (1995).
Career: Joined *William Fry* in 1996 after practice in Brussels and London. Member and currently chairman, of the Law Society's EU and International Affairs Committee.
Personal: Born 1957. Manchester University and University of Amsterdam.

HAUGHEY, Stephen
A & L Goodbody, Dublin +353 1 649 2000
Recommended in Banking & Finance
Specialisation: Partner specialising in banking and financial services with particular reference to aircraft finance, corporate banking, structured finance and asset financing.
Prof. Memberships: Head of Banking Group, which is the largest group in any Dublin firm devoted to banking and financial services work. The Group has developed a high degree of specialisation in asset financing, funds management, treasury operations work, as well as general banking work and structured finance.
Career: Joined *A & L Goodbody* as a solicitor in 1982 and became a partner in 1986. After qualifying as a solicitor in 1978, spent 4 years with the

I

Industrial Development Authority. Director of Airbus Industrie Financial Services and other companies in the IFSC.
Personal: Born 10 November 1953.

HEALY, Nathaniel
A & L Goodbody, Dublin +353 1 649 2000
Recommended in Banking & Finance
Specialisation: Partner specialising in banking and financial services with particular reference to aircraft finance, corporate banking, structured finance and asset financing.
Publications: Author of the Irish chapter in 'Aircraft Finance', ed. Haimes & McBain and has written various articles on aspects of asset financing in Ireland.
Career: Joined the firm as an apprentice in 1972, qualified in 1975 and became a partner in 1981.
Personal: Born 2 September 1949.

HENEGHAN, Brendan
William Fry, Dublin +353 1 639 5000
Recommended in Corporate/M&A

HENNESSY, Grainne
Arthur Cox, Dublin +353 1 618 0000
ghennessy@arthurcox.ie
Recommended in Banking & Finance
Specialisation: Partner in the Banking Department. Specialises in asset and project finance, syndications and securitisation. Acted for EBS Building Society in its first securitisation of domestic mortgages. The EBS securitisation saw *Arthur Cox* taking the lead legal role. Has also acted for lenders to the Princes Holdings telecommunications Group, to Ocean Communications Limited and to Meteor Mobile Communications Limited.
Prof. Memberships: Law Society of Ireland, Institute of Taxation in Ireland.
Publications: Co-author Irish Section, 'Digest of Commercial Laws of the World'.
Career: Admitted as a solicitor, 1990, became Partner in *Arthur Cox* 1995.
Personal: Born 1965. BLL, LLB, University College Cork.

JOHNSTON, William
Arthur Cox, Dublin +353 1 618 0000
wjohnston@arthurcox.ie
Recommended in Banking & Finance
Specialisation: Banking and financial services including syndications, acquisition financing, secured lending, restructuring, cross border leasing (aircraft, telecommunications and other big ticket), securitisation documentary credits, e-banking, consumer lending, banking regulation, money laundering, insurance and re-insurance, capital markets.
Publications: 'Banking and Security Law in Ireland' (Butterworths).
Career: Partner in *Arthur Cox* since 1986, member of Company Law Review Group (nominee of deputy Prime Minister), Banking and Security Law Correspondent: 'Commercial Law Practitioner' (Roundhall Sweet & Maxwell).

McCAGUE, Eugene
Arthur Cox, Dublin +353 1 618 0000
emccague@arthurcox.ie
Recommended in Corporate/M&A
Specialisation: Company and commercial law, corporate recovery and restructuring.
Prof. Memberships: Law Society of Ireland.
Career: Admitted as a solicitor 1982, partner at *Arthur Cox* since 1988.
Personal: Born 1958. BCL 1978; Dip E.L, 1980; University College, Dublin. Married with three children.

McCARTHY, Alan
A & L Goodbody, Dublin +353 1 649 2000
Recommended in Competition/Anti-trust
Specialisation: A Senior Associate in the Commercial Department. Has acquired a wide range of EC and Irish competition law and general regulatory law experience. In particular, has advised on the relevant EC and Irish competition law implications of large-scale mergers and acquisitions in the course of which has submitted filings to the European Commission and the Department of Enterprise, Trade and Employment. In addition, has advised a wide range of corporate clients on the EC and Irish competition law implications of their agreements and has notified the European Commission and Irish Competition Authority of certain arrangements. Has also given advice to the firm's clients on State aid issues, public procurement, regulatory matters (including telecommunications), the Irish Groceries Order, etc. Has assisted and advised clients in relation to investigations by the Competition Authority into possible cartel activities.
Career: Qualified in 1993. Worked for over three and a half years at a London City law firm in the firm's EC/Competition Department.

McEVOY, Bernard
Ivor Fitzpatrick & Co, Dublin +353 1 6787000
Recommended in Corporate/M&A

McGOVERN, Patricia
LK Shields, Solicitors, Dublin +353 1 661 0866
Recommended in Corporate/M&A
Specialisation: Partner in Commercial Department. Main areas of specialisation include corporate and commercial law, to include mergers and acquisitions, public and private capital raising exercises and compliance, general commercial transactions, competition law, pensions and all aspects of intellectual property law (contentious and non-contentious) including advice on and prosecution of trade marks, advice on copyright and patents, passing off, counterfeiting, distribution arrangements, franchising, competition aspects of intellectual property, e-commerce and trading on the Internet.
Prof. Memberships: Law Society of Ireland, Dublin Solicitors Bar Association. Also a member of many intellectual property law associations namely, INTA (Member of Projects Editorial Board); Marques; ECTA; The American Intellectual Property Law Association; Anti-Counterfeiting Group, and Counterfeiting Intelligence Bureau.
Publications: Contributor to several publications in areas of intellectual property, including Irish chapters in the Oceana Publications Inc., publication 'World Intellectual Property Rights & Remedies', the FT Law and Tax publication. The Sweet and Maxwell publication 'Trade Marks, Trade Names and Unfair Competition: World Law and Practice', 'European Trade Mark Litigation Handbook' and the BNA publication 'International Licensing'. Irish reporter for Sweet & Maxwell publications 'European Trade Mark Reports' and 'European Copyright and Design Reports'. Regular speaker at seminars on these and related subjects.
Career: Admitted as a solicitor in 1987. Also an Irish trademark agent and a community trademark attorney. Recipient of Guinness & Mahon Taxation Prize 1984. One of the founding partners of *LK Shields*, Solicitors. Chairman of the Business Law Committee of the Law Society of Ireland.
Personal: Born 1961. Attended Trinity College Dublin 1979 - 1983 (BA (Mod) Legal Science).

McKENNA, Justin
LK Shields, Solicitors, Dublin 2 +353 1 661 0866
Recommended in Corporate/M&A
Specialisation: Partner in Commercial Department. Main areas of specialisation include acquisitions of public companies, public IPO's and fundraisings, public offers of debt securities, private company mergers and acquisitions, tax based private company investments, building society law, venture capital investments and management buy-outs, corporate and commercial law, corporate finance and building society law. Has been involved in a number of high profile corporate deals in 2000 to include Conduit plc IPO listing on Neuer Markt, acquisition of 10% of Conduit plc by Sonera Media Holding BV, acquisition of Green Isle Foods Limited by IAWS and disposal of Ireland on Sunday.
Prof. Memberships: Law Society of Ireland, Dublin Solicitors Bar Association.
Career: Qualified in 1989. Joined *L.K. Shields*, Solicitors as a partner in 1998.
Personal: Born 1965. Attended University College Dublin 1982 - 1985. Married with three children. Leisure interests include sailing.

MEADE, John
Arthur Cox, Dublin +353 1 618 0000
jmeade@arthurcox.ie
Recommended in Competition/Anti-trust
Specialisation: EC and Competition Law, and EC and Irish merger control. Represented Eircom in unsuccessful ESAT Telecom complaint to European Commission; Glanbia in Competition Authority investigation; Bank of Ireland in European Commission Investigation.
Prof. Memberships: Law Society of Ireland, Law Society of Northern Ireland.
Career: Admitted as solicitor 1993, Northern Ireland and Ireland, Partner at *Arthur Cox* since 1993.
Personal: Born 1960, BA Mod (Legal Science) 1982, Trinity College Dublin; LLM, 1983, Cambridge University.

MEGHEN, Michael
Arthur Cox, Dublin +353 1 618 0000
mmeghen@arthurcox.ie
Recommended in Corporate/M&A
Specialisation: Partner in Corporate and Commercial Department; principal areas of practice, mergers and acquistions, joint ventures, corporate restructuring and company law.

Prof. Memberships: Law Society of Ireland.
Career: Admitted as solicitor 1980, Partner at *Arthur Cox* since 1985.
Personal: BBS, 1976, LLB 1978, Trinity College, Dublin. Lives in Dublin

MOLONY, Ronan
McCann FitzGerald, Dublin +353 1 829 0000
robert.molony@mccann-fitzgerald.ie
Recommended in Banking & Finance
Specialisation: Partner in the firm's Banking & Financial Services Department and has wide experience of financial transactions generally, including debt securities and securitisations, structured finance, tax-based financing, asset finance and derivatives.
Prof. Memberships: Law Society of Ireland, Law Society of England and Wales, Dublin Solicitors Bar Association and The American Chamber of Commerce.
Career: Qualified in Ireland in 1983 as a solicitor and in England and Wales in 1991. Qualified as an Associate of the Institute of Taxation in Ireland in 1982. Became a partner in 1984 and the firm's chairman in 1997.
Personal: Education: University College, Dublin (BCL).

MORRISSEY, Daniel
William Fry, Dublin +353 1 639 5000
Recommended in Banking & Finance

O'BEIRNE, David
O'Donnell Sweeney, Dublin 2 +353 1 662 5222
Recommended in Corporate/M&A

O'BRIEN, Patrick
Arthur Cox, Dublin +353 1 618 0000
pobrien@arthurcox.ie
Recommended in Competition/Anti-trust
Specialisation: EC and Competition Law and the review of mergers and acquisitions before Irish and EC regulatory authorities. Advising Aer Lingus in relation to strategic alliance with British Airways and American Airlines, advising Eircell in relation to competition law proceedings in Irish courts.
Prof. Memberships: Law Society of Ireland, Irish Centre for European Law.
Career: Admitted as a solicitor, 1993. Partner in *Arthur Cox* since July 2000.
Personal: Born 1965; married with two children. Graduate of University College Cork and The College of Europe Bruges 1988.

O'CONNELL, Owen
William Fry, Dublin +353 1 639 5000
owen.oconnell@williamfry.ie
Recommended in Corporate/M&A
Specialisation: Partner in Commercial Department. Advises large and medium-sized companies on corporate and commercial law, including acquisitions, disposals and venture capital transactions, distribution arrangements and competition, and with an emphasis on telecoms. Throughout career, has worked in the firm's commercial department, and has amassed extensive international experience, having acted in large, sometimes controversial or difficult transactions.
Prof. Memberships: Law Society of Ireland. Irish Centre for Commerical Law Studies (Director).
Career: Managing Partner of *William Fry*. After qualifying as a solicitor in 1978, joined *William Fry* in 1979 and was appointed a partner in 1985.
Personal: Born 1955. Studied University College, Dublin (BCL) from 1972 to 1976.

O'DWYER, James
Arthur Cox, Dublin +353 1 618 0000
jod@arthurcox.ie
Recommended in Corporate/M&A
Specialisation: Mergers and acquisitions, privatisations and public offers. Represented eircom plc in relation to its Global Public Offering, Aer Lingus Group plc in relation to its strategic alliance with British Airways and American Airlines, Adare Printing Group plc in relation to its recent management buy-out and Power Leisure plc in relation to its recent Initial Public Offering. Currently representing eircom plc in relation to the proposed Euro 4.5 billion sale of its mobile subsidiary to Vodafone plc, Aer Lingus plc in relation to its proposed Initial Public Offering and the Irish State Oil Company, Irish National Petroleum Corporation, in relation to the proposed sale of its Refinery and Terminal operations to Tosco Corporation.
Prof. Memberships: Law Society of Ireland, New York State and American Bar Associations.
Career: Chairman and Senior Partner of *Arthur Cox*. Admitted as a solicitor, 1969, New York Bar, 1986.
Personal: Born 1947; BCL 1968, LLB 1971 University College Dublin.

O'FARRELL, Jack
A & L Goodbody, Dublin +353 1 649 2000
jofarrell@algoodbody.ie
Recommended in Corporate/M&A
Specialisation: Partner in *A & L Goodbody*, specialising in Company and Commerical Law. Currently chairman of the firm's specialist Securities Unit, the members of which advise domestic and foreign clients on listed and unlisted share and debt offerings by Irish and foreign issuers, including those seeking listings on the Irish Stock Exchange, Nasdaq and other regulated markets. Part of the legal team which advised the Minister for Finance in relation to the privatisation and flotation of Irish Life plc in 1991. Was also involved in the conversion of Irish Permanent Building Society to a public limited company and its subsequent floation on the Stock Exchanges in Dublin and London, as well as the recent merger of that company with Irish Life plc. In addition to advising on privatisation and intial public offering, regularly advises on Irish legal aspects of domestic and foreign mergers and acquisitions, including those regulated by the Irish Takeover Panel Act 1997, as well as on shareholder disputes and joint ventures.
Career: Qualified in 1985 and holds a degree in Legal Science from Trinity College Dublin and a Master's deegree in law from Cambridge University. Has been a Partner in *A & L Goodbody* since 1991.
Personal: Born 28 November 1958.

O'RIORDAN, Frank
A & L Goodbody, Dublin +353 1 649 2000
Recommended in Corporate/M&A

OLDEN, John
A & L Goodbody, Dublin +353 1 649 2000
Recommended in Corporate/M&A
Specialisation: Specialises in the areas of corporate finance and capital markets work. Also a member of the Techlaw Unit. Has advised on Irish equity offerings both in Ireland and the United Kingdom and by means of public offering on Nasdaq. Has extensive experience of capital markets debt financing work including euro commercial paper programmes, euro note programmes, private placement of Tier-Two regulatory capital and stand alone bond issues. Was involved in the conversion and flotation of Irish Permanent Building Society in 1994.
Personal: Born 20 March 1962. Graduated as a solicitor in 1987 having studied at University College, Cork.

POWER, Vincent
A & L Goodbody, Dublin +353 1 649 2000
Recommended in Competition/Anti-trust
Specialisation: Partner practising European Union Law, Competition/Anti-Trust Law and Transport Law (particularly Shipping Law) at *A & L Goodbody*. Director of the firm's EU and Competition Law Unit. Advises both public and private bodies on EU, public procurement, energy, maritime and competition law matters. Has advised governments on competition and State Aid issues and has dealt with the competition law issues for national and multinational companies. Has argued cases before the European Commission and national competition authorities. An Expert of the ECU Institute at Lyon.
Prof. Memberships: A member of the Irish Government's Commission of Inquiry on the Newspaper Industry. Chairman of the Irish Government's Review Group on the Investigation of Marine Accidents. A member of the Editorial Advisory Board of the 'International Company and Commercial Law Review. A director of the Irish Centre for European Law at Trinity College.
Publications: Editor of 'Setting up a Business' (Sweet and Maxwell) as well as author of 'EC Shipping Law' (Lloyd's of London) and 'European Union and Irish Competition Law' (to be published shortly by Butterworths). Book on 'EC Shipping Law' won the prestigious Albert Lilar Prize from the Comité Maritime International. The Irish contributor to 'Corporate Acquisitions and Mergers', 'Mergers and Acquisitions in Europe', 'Corporate Finance Law in Europe' and 'International M&A Law'.
Career: Graduate of University College Cork (a College School) (BCL) and the University of Cambridge (an Evan Lewis-Thomas Law Student at Sidney Sussex College) (LLM). Former College Lecturer at University College, Cork. Visiting Professor of European Union Business Law at the Universiteit Nyenrode in The Netherlands.
Personal: Born 23 July, 1963.

PRENTICE, William
Matheson Ormsby Prentice, Dublin
+353 1 619 9000
william.prentice@mop.ie
Recommended in Banking & Finance
Specialisation: Partner, Head of Banking Law Group. Specialises in banking and structured international finance transactions. Acts for many of the worlds leading banks, financial institutions and other financial services companies carrying on business in Ireland. Provides legal advice for corporate borrowers and special purpose companies established at the International Financial Services Centre, Dublin.
Prof. Memberships: Law Society of Ireland.
Career: Qualified in 1982.
Personal: Born 1958. Attended Trinity College Dublin (Bachelor of Arts in Legal Science).

PRICE, Alvin
William Fry, Dublin +353 1 639 5000
alvin.price@williamfry.ie
Recommended in Corporate/M&A
Specialisation: Partner in Commercial Department. For many years has specialised in corporate and commercial law with a particular emphasis on venture capital, mergers and acquisitions, public company and stock exchange related work.
Prof. Memberships: Law Society of Ireland; Institute of Taxation in Ireland (Associate).
Career: Qualified as a solicitor in 1973. Joined *William Fry* in 1974. Became a Partner in 1979. Former Chairman of the Company and of the Commercial Law Committee of the Incorporated Law Society of Ireland 1993-95.
Personal: Born 1950. Studied at University College, Dublin (BCL) from 1970 to 1973. Leisure interests include current affairs, sport and gardening.

ROCHE, Donal
Matheson Ormsby Prentice, Dublin
+353 1 619 9000
donal.roche@mop.ie
Recommended in Corporate/M&A
Specialisation: Managing Partner and Head of the firm's Corporate Finance Group. Specialises in corporate law, corporate finance, mergers and acquisitions, management buy-outs, joint ventures, corporate re-construction, securities, debt and equity finance and general legal corporate advice.
Prof. Memberships: Law Society, Ireland. Institute of Directors; Dublin Chamber of Commerce.
Career: Qualified in 1980. Joined *Matheson Ormsby Prentice* in 1985 and was appointed Managing Partner in 1995. Has been involved in most of the major mergers and acquisitions that have occurred in Ireland in the last 10 years. Has also been retained by some of Ireland's largest corporates to provide ongoing general legal corporate advice.
Personal: Born in 1954. Attended Trinity College, Dublin 1971-75 (MA Legal Science).

SCANLON, Tim
Matheson Ormsby Prentice, Dublin
+353 1 619 9000
tim.scanlon@mop.ie
Recommended in Corporate/M&A
Specialisation: Partner Corporate Finance and Commercial Law Group. Specialises in corporate finance law and has extensive experience in mergers and acquisitions, securities law, venture capital, management buyouts, management buy-ins and corporate re-organisations. Has acted for many of Ireland's leading institutional investors and has advised both companies and investors on a large number of significant transactions in the last decade. Has advised both companies and underwriters on a number of IPOs and other transactions involving public companies. Has advised on a number of takeovers of Irish quoted companies. Has advised a large number of clients in the high-tech sector ranging from start-ups to established entities seeking to IPO.
Prof. Memberships: Law Society of Ireland.
Career: Qualified in 1989. Joined *MOP* from *A&L Goodbody* in May 2000. Has lectured extensively on corporate finance and securities law.
Personal: Attended Trinity College Dublin (LLB).

SHIELDS, Laurence K.
LK Shields, Solicitors, Dublin +353 1 661 0866
email@lkshields.ie
Recommended in Corporate/M&A
Specialisation: Managing Partner of the firm. Combines role of Managing Partner with an active professional role in the Commercial Department. Main areas of specialisation include company and commercial law; mergers and acquisitions; management buyouts; shareholders agreements; building society law; employment law; computer software law, corporate finance, venture capital.
Prof. Memberships: Law Society of Ireland (Council Member 1977 to date); Dublin Solicitors Bar Association (Council Member 1973 to date); International Bar Association; Chartered Institute of Arbitrators (Fellow, Irish Branch); Associate Member of the Institute of Taxation in Ireland.
Career: Qualified in 1972. In 1988 formed and became Managing Partner of *LK Shields*, Solicitors (formerly *LK Shields & Partners*). Lecturer and Examiner in Company Law and Partnership, Law Society of Ireland, 1972-1978. Former member of the Judging Panel for the Leinster Society of Chartered Accountants Published Accounts Awards. and a former member of the Disciplinary Scheme Appeal Board of the Society of Actuaries in Ireland and a former member of the Court Services Transitional Board. Member of the UCD Faculty of Law Development Council. Admitted as a solicitor in Northern Ireland and England and Wales in 1998. Director of a number of companies and an alternate director of the Irish Take-over Panel.
Personal: Born 1950. Attended University College Dublin 1967-1970. Leisure interests include golf and swimming. Married with two children.

SWEENEY, Joseph
O'Donnell Sweeney, Dublin +353 1 662 5222
Recommended in Corporate/M&A

ISLE OF MAN

Corporate/Commercial

ISLE OF MAN Leading firms (Corporate/Commercial)
1 Cains
Dickinson Cruickshank & Co
2 Maitland & Co

Firms are listed alphabetically in each band.

Leading individuals (Corporate/Commercial)
1 **CORLETT Andrew** *Cains*
DOYLE David *Dickinson Cruickshank & Co*
VANDERPLANK Richard *Cains*
2 **DOUGHERTY Paul** *Dougherty & Associates*
3 **WENTZEL Peter** *Maitland & Co*
Up and coming individuals
RIMMER John *Dickinson Cruickshank & Co*
SHERLOCK David *Cains*

Individuals are listed alphabetically in each band.

Cains (6 ptrs, 18 asscs) *"One can only have glowing comments"* for this large Manx firm, which has a strong bias towards commercial work. E-commerce and mutual fund advice have constituted growing elements of the practice. **Andy Corlett**, head of corporate, is, competitors commented to our researchers *"a practical individual, full of common sense,"* whose name extends beyond the island, and **Richard Vanderplank** is *"an excellent corporate lawyer."* **David Sherlock** is respected for his e-commerce expertise. The firm advised the Isle of Man government on its first foray into the capital bonds market, borrowing £75 million to fund infrastructure projects. **Clients:** Cathay Pacific; Bank of Bermuda; major shipping companies.

Dickinson Cruickshank & Co (11 ptrs, 5 asscs) Clearly one of the two leaders on the island, the firm has seen substantial work in IT transactional and regulatory matters, as well as advising on the potential impact of human rights legislation on the commercial arena. The *"likeable"* **David Doyle** is held in high esteem, while **John Rimmer** has experience in the City. The firm acted for KPMG when its trust and fiduciary services division was acquired by Singer & Friedlander. **Clients:** Financial Institutions; domestic and foreign corporates; private clients.

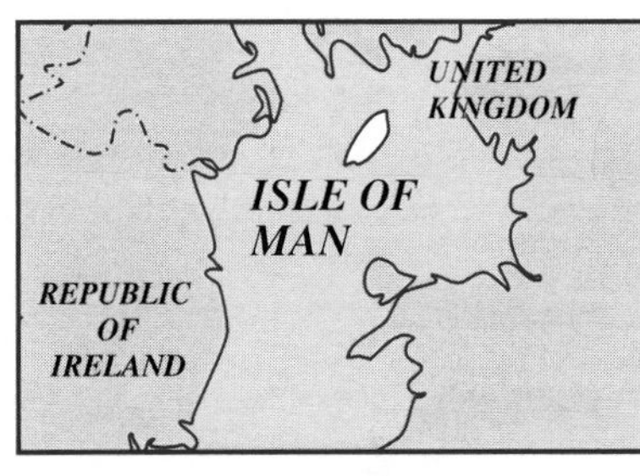

Maitland & Co (2 ptrs, 3 asscs) Part of a partnership covering several countries, the firm has been operating on the island for ten years. It has a niche in international tax and corporate structuring, typically servicing South African clients. **Peter Wentzel** is the leading name here. The team acted on the establishment of BIDVest plc which acquired Booker plc. **Clients:** South African mining and banking groups.

Other Notable Practitioner The *"extremely able"* **Paul Dougherty** heads a niche firm dealing exclusively in corporate, commercial and trusts advice. Clients include Royal Bank of Scotland; Anglo Irish Bank and Royal Scandia Life Assurance Ltd.

Leaders' profiles – Isle of Man

CORLETT, Andrew
Cains, Douglas +44 1624 638 300

DOUGHERTY, Paul
Dougherty & Associates, Douglas +44 1624 671 155

DOYLE, David
Dickinson Cruickshank & Co, Douglas +44 1624 647 647

RIMMER, John
Dickinson Cruickshank & Co, Douglas +44 1624 647 647

SHERLOCK, David
Cains, Douglas +44 1624 638 300

VANDERPLANK, Richard
Cains, Douglas +44 1624 638 300

WENTZEL, Peter
Maitland & Co, Douglas +44 1624 630 000
pwentzel.m@itland.com

Specialisation: Partner in international consulting. Has spoken at a number of conferences on computer related legal issues and tax. Main areas of work are international tax planning and corporate structuring as well as company, commercial and trust law. Also has a general commercial law background. Advises a number of South African owned companies and financial institutions in connection with their international tax strategy and advises a number of wealthy international families on aspects of personal financial and estate planning.

Prof. Memberships: The Isle of Man Law Society, The Law Society of the Transvaal, The Law Society of the Cape of Good Hope, The Society of Trust and Estate Practitioners.

Career: Qualified as a South African attorney in 1975 and as a notary public of the Transvaal Province. Served articles with *Webber Wentzel Bowens*, Johannesburg becoming a partner in March 1979. In 1986 joined the Luxembourg office of *Maitland & Co.* while continuing to be a partner of *Webber Wentzel Bowens.* September 1997 relocated to the Isle of Man office of *Maitland & Co.*

Personal: Born 15 October 1949. Attended the University of Witwatersrand 1968-1970 (BA) and 1972-1974 (LLB). Attended University of Cambridge 1975-1976 (Diploma in Comparative Legal Studies). Leisure interests include golf and African wildlife. Lives in Onchan, Isle of Man.

ISRAEL

Index

The clients' choice

BUSINESS LAWYER OF THE YEAR
RAM CASPI, *Caspi & Co*

BUSINESS LAW FIRM OF THE YEAR
YIGAL ARNON & CO

In a tight contest, ***Ram Caspi*** *tops the best lawyer survey with* ***Yigal Arnon & Co*** *some way clear as best law firm.*

For details see page 36.

OVERVIEW: A boom in new technology has brought about a greater internationalism to the legal market. Crucial to the future success of Israeli law firms will be the alliances reached with foreign law firms, and as ever, culture gaps are beginning to appear. Many younger firms are adopting the English and American style, targeting western trained lawyers and the hi-tech sector. Research has indicated the potential for mergers and a possible overhaul of the legal practice as the venerated and ageing lawyers retire. Firms have been seen to be restructuring, investing in the future.

Banking & Finance

ISRAEL Leading firms (Banking & Finance)
1 Kantor, Elhanani, Tal & Co
2 Herzog, Fox & Neeman
Horowitz & Co
3 I Gornitzky & Co
4 Yigal Arnon & Co
Zellermayer, Pelossof & Co

Firms are listed alphabetically in each band.

Leading individuals (Banking & Finance)
1 TAL Dalia *Kantor, Elhanani, Tal & Co*
2 NEEMAN Yaakov *Herzog, Fox & Neeman*
3 FOX Michael *Herzog, Fox & Neeman*
HERTMAN Alex *Horowitz & Co*

Individuals are listed alphabetically in each band.

Kantor, Elhanani, Tal & Co (2 ptrs, 4 asscs) Counsel to a wide range of financial institutions in Israel and abroad, the firm is accepted as the pre-eminent force in banking, notably for regulatory advice. The team also has a strong reputation for banking M&A, litigation and syndicated loans.

Researchers encountered no argument with the proposition that **Dalia Tal*** is *"the best banking lawyer in the country."* Deputy legal advisor to the Bank of Israel for thirteen years, she is now responsible for the firm's relationship with its principal client, Bank Leumi. The firm advised the Shlomo Eliahu Group on the government tender for the sale of control in Israel Discount Bank Ltd and was lead counsel on the sale of a controlling stake in Maritime Bank of Israel Ltd. Also acted for Otzar Hashilton Hamekomi Bank on its privatisation. **Clients:** Bank Leumi; Michael Steinhardt; Sir Bernard Schreier.

Herzog, Fox & Neeman (3 ptrs, 2 asscs) *"Excellent finance practice,"* which has its principal reputation in advising on project finance deals in Israel. The firm represents an impressive selection of American and European banks on syndicated loans to domestic corporates, and is also respected by peers for its strong banking litigation practice. **Yaakov Neeman*** is said to have *"an impeccable track record at the highest level,"* while **Michael Fox*** also remains a respected local figure. **Clients:** American and European banks.

Horowitz & Co (5 ptrs, 4 asscs) The firm has an established banking reputation in Israel, advising on litigation, domestic and international syndicated loans and trade finance. **Alex Hertman*** is a respected name among his peers.

The firm advised the syndicate of banks responsible for a $750 million loan facility to Partner Communications, and acted for the banks on a syndicated loan of $650 million to Zeevi Communications for the purchase of a 20% stake in Bezeq. Also acted for a syndicate lending over $400 million to a leading Israeli broadcasting and media company. **Clients:** United Mizrahi Bank; Israeli Discount Bank; Banque Privée Edmond de Rothschild; HSBC Republic Bank (Switzerland).

I Gornitzky & Co (5 ptrs, 4 asscs) Better known for its corporate practice, the firm was also commended to researchers for its project finance advice. The banking team represents leading Israeli banks on transactional and regulatory matters, and advised Arison Holdings Ltd on the purchase of a controlling stake in Bank Hapoalim. **Clients:** Bank Hapoalim; Bank Mizrahi; First International Bank.

Yigal Arnon & Co (4 ptrs, 6 asscs) Renowned for its project finance practice, the firm also advises foreign banks on their loans to Israeli companies. The firm acted for Tower Semiconductor Ltd on a $1.5 billion deal to construct a fabrication plant for wafer semi-conductors, and advised on the Ashkelon desalination plant and Jerusalem Light Railway projects. **Clients:** Discount Bank; Safra Group; UBS (Switzerland); Bank of New York.

Zellermayer, Pelossof & Co (3 ptrs, 4 asscs) Heavily involved in project finance and structured finance transactions, the firm was also recommended to researchers for its real estate finance practice. The team's client base includes overseas financial institutions and domestic corporates.

Highlight transactions include advising HSBC Investment Bank on a $102 million hedging of shares, and representing overseas and domestic real estate developers on a BOT bid for Israel's first light railway. Also advised Benchmark Capital on the arrangement of a $200 million venture capital fund, focusing on the Israeli hi-tech market. **Clients:** HSBC Investment Bank; Warburg Dillon Read; Siemens; Benchmark Capital; Mivtachim Group.

Communications

ISRAEL Leading firms (Communications)	
1	Eitan, Pearl, Latzer & Cohen-Zedek
	Goldfarb, Levy, Eran & Co
	Naschitz, Brandes & Co
	Yigal Arnon & Co
2	Herzog, Fox & Neeman
	Meitar, Liquornik, Geva & Co
3	Danziger, Klagsbald, Rosen & Co
	Fischer, Behar, Chen & Co
	Gross, Kleinhendler, Hodak, Halevy, Greenberg & Co
4	Avital Dromi & Co

Firms are listed alphabetically in each band.

Leading individuals (Communications)	
1	**COHEN Shlomo** *Dr Shlomo Cohen & Co*
	EITAN Tally *Eitan, Pearl, Latzer & Cohen-Zedek*
	FELIG Clifford *Meitar, Liquornik, Geva & Co*
	ROSEN Ori *Danziger, Klagsbald, Rosen & Co*
2	**AVITAL Gideon** *Avital Dromi & Co*
	BEHAR Reuven *Fischer, Behar, Chen & Co*
	BRANDES Hanina *Naschitz, Brandes & Co*
	GEVA Dan *Meitar, Liquornik, Geva & Co*
	LAMPERT Aaron *Naschitz, Brandes & Co*
	LEVENFELD Barry *Yigal Arnon & Co*

Individuals are listed alphabetically in each band.

Eitan, Pearl, Latzer & Cohen-Zedek (6 ptrs, 50 asscs) Undoubtedly a premier IT player, this specialist firm was recommended to researchers as *"unique in its field."* Clients waxed lyrical about a firm that offers *"a one-stop shop, combining all aspects of getting an idea to market."* A strong IP department also has a leading reputation for advice on patents in the IT sector.

Tally Eitan* is the driving force of the firm and has an international reputation. Opponents admire her for her *"client-friendly and commercial advice."* The firm represented Scitex Corporation on the $500 million sale of its pre-press division to Creo Technologies, and acted for Siemens Data Communication on its sale and merger with Seabridge Technologies. **Clients:** McDonald's; Siemens; 3Com; Elron; CreoScitex; Virata; Checkpoint; HMR; Hewlett-Packard; ECI; Amdocs; Comverse; Seiko.

Goldfarb, Levy, Eran & Co (14 ptrs, 42 asscs) Respected for its strong corporate profile, the team has a growing reputation in both telecoms and IT. As well as advising on internet start-ups, the firm's telecoms team acts for an enviable range of international clients on tenders, regulation, M&A and litigation. The firm acted on the IPOs of Radavision ($76 million), Metalink ($135 million) and Orckit Communications ($150 million). **Clients:** Scitex Corporation; ECI Telecom; Formula Systems; Rockwell International Corporation; TTI Team Telecom; Kardan Technologies; Applicom Software Industries.

Naschitz, Brandes & Co (11 ptrs, 27 asscs) Another corporate success story in the hi-tech sphere is regarded by competitors as *"one of the most experienced firms on the block."* Active on cross-border M&A and IPOs in the sector, the firm has a strong international clientele. **Hanina Brandes*** was recommended to our researchers as a *"pioneer of hi-tech,"* and **Aaron Lampert*** is considered to be a *"versatile and creative lawyer."* The firm acted for Geo Interactive Media on its $36 million acquisition of Orca Computers, and advised Back Web on its $16 million acquisition of Mobix Communications. **Clients:** AT&T Wireless; AudioCodes; BackWeb; BRM Technologies; Check Point Software Technologies; EZchip; GEO Interactive; Commtouch Software; LanOptics; RTImage; STEAG Electronic Systems.

Yigal Arnon & Co (4 ptrs, 5 asscs) Known as a *"corporate firm with hi-tech clients,"* the group was recommended to researchers for its advice to an international clientele. It advises on start-ups, venture capital funds (both formation and portfolio investment), M&A and IPOs, especially on Nasdaq. Other work includes IT licensing issues, while the team has also established a niche in advising leading cable companies. The firm recently opened a Jerusalem office, dedicated to the hi-tech sector. Peers regard **Barry Levenfeld*** to be *"near the top of anyone's list"* of communications lawyers.

The firm advised on the IPO of Compugen (listed on Nasdaq), acted on the acquisition of Gadline by Com21, and represented ADC Telecommunications on its $240 million acquisition of Teledata. **Clients:** Texas Instruments; Sun Microsystems; 3Com; Xerox; Phillips; Apax; UPC; ADC Telecommunications.

Herzog, Fox & Neeman (3 ptrs, 4 asscs) One of Israel's corporate leaders, the firm specialises in M&A and IPOs of hi-tech companies, often representing foreign buyers. The loss of senior lawyers, including Clifford Felig to Meitar Liquornik, has been a setback, but market opinion expects this to represent *"a temporary difficulty."* The firm advised Virata Corp on its $60 million acquisition of Inverness Systems, advised Comverse Technology Inc on its $26 million acquisition of Gaya Software Industries, and represented Microsoft on its equity investment in Itran Communications. **Clients:** Creo Products Inc; Virata Corp; GEO Interactive Media Group; BMC Software; SAFT; Converse Technology Inc; Microsoft Corporation; Nortel Networks; Siemens Medical Systems Inc; EZchip.

Meitar, Liquornik, Geva & Co (12 ptrs, 28 asscs) In no field has the rise of this young firm been more noticeable than in hi-tech. Primarily noted for its corporate muscle, the team has advised an international clientele on some major acquisitions. The arrival of the *"gifted"* **Clifford Felig*** from Herzog, Fox & Neeman, has been viewed by competitors as a step forward for the firm, while **Dan Geva*** is admired for his *"lucid advice."* The firm acted for Lucent on the $4.8 billion acquisition of Chromatis Networks, and for Amdocs on the $1 billion acquisition of a Canadian company. **Clients:** Amdocs; VocalTec; VeraNet; Lucent Technologies.

*See leaders' profiles on pages 410-412

Danziger, Klagsbald, Rosen & Co (5 ptrs, 23 asscs) Established IT team, specialising in venture capital funds and start-ups, which also represents small domestic hi-tech companies on their mergers with larger concerns. The *"excellent"* **Ori Rosen*** is a respected corporate lawyer with a *"high-powered intellect."* **Clients:** AbirNet; NCC; Mofet Technology Fund.

Fischer, Behar, Chen & Co (4 ptrs, 14 asscs) Despite losing lawyers to Meitar Liquornik, the firm is said to be *"definitely on the IT map."* It specialises in the IP aspects of IT, as well as handling anti-trust work, M&A and start-ups. Researchers also found a respected regulatory telecoms capacity here. **Reuven Behar*** is recommended for his versatility, and heads a team that advised on the acquisition of DSPC by Intel. **Clients:** Bezeq; TTI Team Telecom; Nogatech Inc; Intel; Servotronix Ltd.

Gross, Kleinhendler, Hodak, Halevy, Greenberg & Co (4 ptrs, 21 asscs) Newly merged firm with experience in the corporate aspects of telecommunications, IT and biotechnology. It is particularly well-known for venture capital advice and M&A. The former Kleinhendler & Halevy's expertise in these areas has been given *"added corporate weight"* by the addition of respected medium-sized firm Professor Joseph Gross, Hodak, Greenberg & Co.

The team has advised Gilat Satellite Networks on a joint venture with Microsoft and EchoStar. **Clients:** Comverse Technology Inc; Gilat Satellite Networks; Better Online Solutions; Merrill Lynch; Advanced Research Technologies; Comsys Communications; Trellis Photonics.

Avital Dromi & Co (5 ptrs, 8 asscs) One of the leading telecoms firms in Israel, this small group has earned a reputation among clients for its *"professionalism and experience."* The firm offers a full range of corporate services and handles regulatory matters for a range of telecoms, broadcasting, and cellular companies.

The firm's leading light is **Gideon Avital***, a *"senior telecoms lawyer,"* who is said to have *"good government connections."* The firm has advised domestic cable companies on an unbundling agreement with the DBS operator, and represented Exent on a $20 million equity investment in it by a US consortium led by AOL. **Clients:** MATÁV; Tevel; Zahav; Exent; ICP; Orange; Non-Stop; Giltek.

Other Notable Practitioner **Shlomo Cohen*** heads a small eponymous firm. *"A respected professional,"* he was consistently recommended to researchers for his expertise on IP/IT matters, notably in the contentious sphere.

Corporate/M&A

ISRAEL Leading firms (Corporate/Mergers & Acquisitions)	
1	Goldfarb, Levy, Eran & Co
	Herzog, Fox & Neeman
	Yigal Arnon & Co
2	Gross, Kleinhendler, Hodak, Halevy, Greenberg & Co
	Naschitz, Brandes & Co
	Horowitz & Co
3	Danziger, Klagsbald, Rosen & Co
	I Gornitzky & Co
	Meitar, Liquornik, Geva & Co
	Zellermayer, Pelossof & Co
4	Eitan, Pearl, Latzer & Cohen-Zedek
	Kantor, Elhanani, Tal & Co
5	Fischer, Behar, Chen & Co
	Shiboleth, Yisraeli, Roberts, Zisman & Co

Firms are listed alphabetically in each band.

Goldfarb, Levy, Eran & Co (16 ptrs, 42 asscs) *"Absolutely top league,"* the firm is known by competitors for its *"robust"* corporate advice, and handles IPOs, normally on behalf of the issuer, and cross-border M&A, often in the hi-tech industries. The *"superb"* **Oded Eran*** is one of Israel's most respected corporate lawyers, while his colleague **Yehuda Levy*** was recommended to researchers as *"a pleasure to work with."* **Shirin Halpern-Herzog*** also maintains her share of market support.

The team acted for IDB Corporation on its merger with Clal (Israel), represented Sungard Data Systems on its merger with Oshap Technologies, and advised Opal Inc on its acquisition by Applied Minerals. Elsewhere, the group represented the issuer on the IPO of Kardan Technologies. **Clients:** Scitex Corporation; Elco Holdings; ECI Telecom; Body Shop International; Figgie International; McDonnell Douglas Corporation; Häagen-Dazs Brands; Southwestern Bell Corporation; ABN AMRO.

Herzog, Fox & Neeman (6 ptrs, 19 asscs) One of Israel's most prestigious firms, it has *"impressive depth and competence,"* and is especially known for its *"superb M&A and tax capability."* The firm acts for a number of hi-tech companies and focuses particularly on international transactions. In spite of the departure of Clifford Felig to Meitar Liquornik, the corporate team is considered by the market to remain in safe hands. Co-founder **Yaakov Neeman*** is an *"outstanding corporate lawyer"* with *"excellent connections,"* while the highly respected **Alan Sacks*** was consistently mentioned to researchers for his *"technical accuracy."* Although less visible this year, **Michael Fox*** continues to receive recommendations from his peers.

The group acted for Creo Products on its $500 million acquisition of Scitex Corp's pre-print and print business, and advised Marvell Technology Group on its $2.7 billion acquisition of Galileo Technology. Other matters include acting for BMC Software on its $70 million of OptiSystems Solutions and for Microsoft on its $70 million acquisition of all shares in Peach Networks. **Clients:** Creo Products; Virata Corp; GEO Interactive Media Group; BMC Software; Saft SA; Converse Technology; Microsoft; Koor Industries; Nortel Networks; Siemens Medical Systems.

Yigal Arnon & Co (14 ptrs, 26 asscs) This *"strong"* firm has a reputation for *"a first-rate corporate practice,"* notably in the communications and hi-tech sectors. In addition to cross-border M&A and high-profile IPOs, the firm is known for VC fund formation and internet start-ups, and is commended by rivals for its real estate and litigation prowess. A number of the corporate team were either trained or have practised in the US, and much of the firm's workload is conducted on behalf of US clients investing in Israel, or Israeli clients seeking business opportunities in the US.

Yigal Arnon* is an elder statesman of the local legal community. Renowned for his international experience, he is admired by opponents for his combination of transactional and litigation skills. **Paul Baris*** and the *"outstanding"* **Barry Levenfeld*** are ubiquitous on big-ticket deals, while **David Schapiro*** focuses on Nasdaq IPOs and M&A.

Highlight transactions include handling multiple investments in the Tower Semiconductor fabrication plant, the IPO of Compugen on Nasdaq

Leading individuals (Corporate/Mergers & Acquisitions)
1
ARNON Yigal *Yigal Arnon & Co*
ERAN Oded *Goldfarb, Levy, Eran & Co*
NEEMAN Yaakov *Herzog, Fox & Neeman*
2
FELIG Clifford *Meitar, Liquornik, Geva & Co*
GROSS Joseph *Gross, Kleinhendler, Hodak*
LAMPERT Aaron *Naschitz, Brandes & Co*
LEVY Yehuda *Goldfarb, Levy, Eran & Co*
OREN Ruth *Horowitz & Co*
RUBIN Pinhas *I Gornitzky & Co*
SACKS Alan *Herzog, Fox & Neeman*
3
BARIS Paul *Yigal Arnon & Co*
BEHAR Reuven *Fischer, Behar, Chen & Co*
BRANDES Hanina *Naschitz, Brandes & Co*
CASPI Ram *Ram Caspi & Co*
GOLDENBERG Amnon *Horowitz & Co*
LEVENFELD Barry *Yigal Arnon & Co*
TAL Dalia *Kantor, Elhanani, Tal & Co*
4
DANZIGER Yoram *Danziger, Klagsbald, Rosen*
EITAN Tally *Eitan, Pearl, Latzer & Cohen-Zedek*
FOX Michael *Herzog, Fox & Neeman*
HALPERN-HERZOG Shirin *Goldfarb, Levy, Eran*
KANTOR Israel *Kantor, Elhanani, Tal & Co*
ROSENSWEIG Joshua *I Gornitzky & Co*
SCHAPIRO David *Yigal Arnon & Co*
Up-and-coming individuals
HACOHEN Itay *Zellermayer, Pelossof & Co*
Individuals are listed alphabetically in each band.

and the acquisition of Gadline by Com21. The firm also represented ADC Telecommunications on its $240 million acquisition of Teledata and handled the Israeli aspects of Unilever's $24 billion acquisition of Bestfoods. **Clients:** Sun Microsystems; Tower Semiconductor; 3com; Philips; Xerox; General Motors; ADC; Broadcom; Gemini Fund; Texas Instruments; Pegasus; Challenge Fund; Cimatron; Unilever; Rolls Royce; UPC; Cellcom.

Gross, Kleinhendler, Hodak, Halevy, Greenberg & Co (6 ptrs, 15 asscs) The result of a *"strategically sound merger,"* the new firm combines the IT-based expertise of the former Kleinhendler & Halevy firm with the enormous corporate reputation of **Joseph Gross***. The latter is regarded as *"a great scholar and a lawyer with real commercial savvy."* Researchers were left in no doubt that this is a firm with *"an interesting client base and huge potential."* The erstwhile Prof. Joseph Gross, Hodak, Greenberg & Co had advised Elbit on its restructuring and demerger into three separate companies. **Clients:** Koor; Blue Square; Tadiran; Elron; Elbit; Tempo; Bank Leumi; Israel Discount Bank; United Mizrahi; Union Bank; Motorola; Netvision; Intel.

Naschitz, Brandes & Co (11 ptrs, 27 asscs) *"Impressive"* firm, which is said by rivals to have found itself *"in the right place at the right time with the right clients."* An early beneficiary of the country's IT boom, the firm specialises in related corporate work, and has a healthy workload of IPOs and big-ticket acquisitions. The team also undertakes substantial work on behalf of issuers and underwriters in connection with the listing of Israeli firms overseas.

Stars at the firm include the *"outstanding"* **Aaron Lampert***, whose *"international knowledge,"* especially of US law, is highly respected by clients, and *"one of a kind"* **Hanina Brandes***, acknowledged by peers as *"an excellent commercial lawyer."* The firm acted for Terayon Communications Systems on its $150 million acquisition of Telegate and its $60 million acquisition of RadWiz, advised the purchaser on the $150 million acquisition of Tadiram Com, and represented the underwriters on the $112 million IPO of Magic Software Enterprises. **Clients:** Agrexco Agricultural Export Company; Citibank; Chase Manhattan Bank; Disney; El Al Israel Airline Pilots' Association; Pillsbury.

Horowitz & Co (6 ptrs, 8 asscs) Old style firm, which, in spite of the lack of a serious profile in the new economy, maintains relationships with an impressive array of traditional blue-chip companies from home and abroad. Acknowledged by peers as a pre-eminent commercial litigation operation, the team includes **Amnon Goldenberg***, recommended to researchers both as a litigator and for his corporate practice. The venerable **Ruth Oren*** *"has seen it all,"* and heads a corporate team which advises a number of international companies on their investments in Israel, and has notable strength in aviation, banking and pharmaceuticals.

The firm advised Bear Stearns on the sale of its holdings in TLC Finance and Management and the Alliance Tyre Company, and acted for Hewlett-Packard on its acquisition of a stake in Indigo. Also advised SAFT on its acquisition of Tadiran Batteries, and Starbucks on its establishment of a franchise network in Israel. **Clients:** HSBC; PepsiCo; Lego; BellSouth; Bear Stearns; ICI; Heinz; Benetton; Motorola; Citibank; Pfizer; Bank Hapoalim; Bank Leumi; British Airways; Air Canada; Delta Airlines; Citroen; Hilton; Israel Electric Corporation; Paz; Sonol.

Danziger, Klagsbald, Rosen & Co *"Small but high-quality firm,"* which, in addition to its high-profile reputation as a leader in litigation, advises a mainly domestic clientele on IPOs and M&A transactions in Israel. The team was commended to researchers as an *"excellent referral option,"* and specialises in hi-tech industry. **Yoram Danziger*** is regarded by peers as the firm's outstanding practitioner. **Clients:** Clal Industries and Investments; M-Systems Flash Disk Pioneers; Dovrat Shrem DS Polaris funds; Chase Capital Partners.

I Gornitzky & Co (8 ptrs, 22 asscs) Domestically oriented firm which, although acknowledged by peers for its work on medium-ticket M&A transactions, has its primary reputation as one of Israel's leading tax operations. *"A1 tax man"* **Pinhas Rubin*** is regarded by clients as *"a credit to the firm,"* while **Joshua Rosensweig*** is seen as an *"accomplished corporate lawyer."* The firm acted for Arison Holdings on its acquisition of a controlling stake in Bank Hapoalim. **Clients:** A range of corporate and banking clients.

Meitar, Liquornik, Geva & Co (12 ptrs, 28 asscs) One of Israel's *"bright young firms"* was repeatedly mentioned to our researchers for its *"aggressive and proactive style."* A number of American lawyers give the team a *"distinctly transatlantic style,"* and it has made *"giant strides"* in cross-border M&A and venture capital transactions. The hi-tech market sees the firm's primary focus, and the clientele includes high-profile software and hardware names.

Top corporate lawyer **Clifford Felig***, acquired from Herzog, Fox & Neeman, is universally regarded as a *"first-rate lawyer and a first-rate guy."* The firm acted for Lucent on its $4.8 billion acquisition of Chromatis Networks, and for Amdocs on its $1 billion acquisition of a Canadian company. **Clients:** Amdocs; VocalTec; VeraNet; Lucent Technologies.

Zellermayer, Pelossof & Co (6 ptrs, 18 asscs) *"Top flight corporate firm,"* which specialises in M&A, especially on behalf of organisations acquiring companies in Israel, and the flotation of Israeli companies on EU stock exchanges. Sometimes considered by clients to have a *"higher profile abroad than at home,"* the firm acts for a number of IT and telecoms clients, and recently opened an office in the hi-tech centre of Herzliyya. Recently arrived from Horowitz & Co, **Itay Hacohen*** received widespread recommendation for his tax expertise.

The firm represented Cable & Wireless on the $643 million sale of a 20% stake in Bezeq, and the subsequent sale of $16 million of Bezeq bonds. It also advised Shamrock on its $600 million bid to acquire a 50% stake in Pelephone from Motorola, and Cisco on its $118 million acquisition of Pentacom. **Clients:** Rafael Armament Develop-

*See leaders' profiles on pages 410-412

ment Authority; RDC; Cisco Systems; MCI WorldCom; Cable & Wireless; Cellcom; Tadiran Communications; Enron; Mashav; Kellogg's; Colgate Palmolive; Hoechst; Shamrock.

Eitan, Pearl, Latzer & Cohen-Zedek (3 ptrs, 12 asscs) Almost exclusively concerned with hi-tech industry, and possessing a respected IP department, the firm approaches the corporate sector from a different angle to its major competitors. The firm advises on joint ventures, M&A and venture capital investments for a powerful international hi-tech clientele. **Tally Eitan*** is considered by peers and clients to be one of Israel's leading technology lawyers, and is developing a *"sound corporate reputation."*

The firm acted for Siemens Data Communication on its merger with Seabridge Technologies, and advised Scitex Corporation on the $500 million sale of its pre-press division to Creo Technologies. **Clients:** McDonald's; Siemens; 3Com; Elron; CreoScitex; Virata; Checkpoint; HMR Inc; Hewlett-Packard; ECI Telecom; Amdocs; Comverse; Medinol; Seiko.

Kantor, Elhanani, Tal & Co (3 ptrs, 9 asscs) Although generally regarded as a banking firm, it has also been recommended to researchers for its increased corporate activity in the telecoms and IT spheres. The team generally advises a range of Israeli companies on their transactions at home and abroad.

Peers hold **Dalia Tal*** and **Israel Kantor*** in high esteem for their *"experience and competence."* The firm advised Bank Leumi on the sale of holdings in Israel Credit Cards, valued at $140 million, and represented Bezeq on the purchase of 50% of the shares of Pelephone Communications, a deal worth $1.2 billion. **Clients:** Infineon Technologies; Bank Leumi ; Philip Morris; Siemens Group; Ericsson Group; Bezeq; Israel Telecommunications Corp; Paz Oil Company; Israel Lands Authority.

Fischer, Behar, Chen & Co (4 ptrs, 11 asscs) Assiduous recruitment has netted the firm *"some good new partners,"* and in spite of a market reputation for *"doing things their own way,"* it is said to be *"a growing force in hi-tech,"* specialising in M&A and start-ups.

Reuven Behar* was mentioned to researchers as *"an admirable corporate lawyer,"* and also won plaudits for his anti-trust practice. The firm represented DSP Communications on its acquisition by Intel, acted for Pica Plast on the sale of its assets to Superior Cables and advised Nogatech on its merger with Zoran Corporation. **Clients:** Applied Materials; Bank Hapoalim; Bezeq; CIBC World Markets; Crédit Lyonnais; Credit Suisse; Intel; Kenwood Corp; Nogatech Inc; Mehadrin-Pri Or Group.

Shiboleth, Yisraeli, Roberts, Zisman & Co (8 ptrs, 22 asscs) Tel Aviv firm, which focuses on general corporate work, and advises a predominantly hi-tech client base on M&A, joint ventures and venture capital transactions. Highlight transactions include acting for Novanet Semiconductors on its acquisition by Conexant, and advising Telecom Italia on its involvement in the Nautilus undersea fibre optic cable project, which involved the acquisition of a controlling stake in Med-1. **Clients:** Conexant; Telecom Italia; Israel Military Industries; Israel Chemicals.

Other Notable Practitioner Legendary *"deal fixer"* **Ram Caspi*** is the choice of some clients as *"the best attorney in Israel."* He is *"certainly the Alpha and Omega of Caspi & Co."* Famously well connected, his practice combines classic M&A and litigation, and he is *"the man you turn to when you need to fight."*

Leaders' profiles – Israel

ARNON, Yigal
Yigal Arnon & Co, Tel Aviv +972 3 608 7777
Recommended in Corporate/M&A

AVITAL, Gideon
Avital Dromi & Co, Tel Aviv +972 3 575 5755
Recommended in Communications

BARIS, Paul
Yigal Arnon & Co, Tel Aviv +972 3 608 7777
paul@arnon.co.il
Recommended in Corporate/M&A
Specialisation: Country Chair, Committee on Creditor's Rights, Insolvency, Liquidation and Reorganisations.
Prof. Memberships: New York State and American Bar Associations; Israel Bar Association; International Bar Association.
Publications: Co-author 'Creditors' Rights against Business Debtors in Israel-International Loan Workouts and Bankruptcies,' Butterworth Legal Publishers 1989. Author: chapter on Israel securities law in 'International Capital Markets and Securities Regulation,' Multi Volume Treatise, Clark Boardman Callaghan, 1994. Contributing Editor 'Journal of International Financial Markets – Law and Regulations.' Reporter for Israel Committee on Issues and Trading Securities (section on Business law).
Career: Admitted 1958, New York; 1972, District of Columbia; 1973 US Supreme Court; 1974, Israel. Cornell University (AB with Honours 1955) Harvard Law School (JD, cum laude 1958). Associate 1960-1964 and member 1965-1973, *Berlack Israels & Liberman*, New York. Visiting Professor of Law, Bar Ilan University 1971-1972. Professor of Law 1973 to present.
Personal: Born New York 1934. Speaks English and Hebrew.

BEHAR, Reuven
Fischer, Behar, Chen & Co, Tel Aviv
+972 3 694 4111
Recommended in Communications, Corporate/M&A

BRANDES, Hanina
Naschitz, Brandes & Co, Tel Aviv +972 3 623 5000
Recommended in Communications, Corporate/M&A

CASPI, Ram
Ram Caspi & Co, Tel Aviv +972 3 796 1000
Recommended in Corporate/M&A

COHEN, Shlomo
Dr Shlomo Cohen & Co Law Office, Tel Aviv
+972 3 527 1919
Recommended in Communications

DANZIGER, Yoram
Danziger, Klagsbald, Rosen & Co, Tel Aviv
+972 3 611 0700
Recommended in Corporate/M&A

EITAN, Tally
Eitan, Pearl, Latzer & Cohen-Zedek, Herzlia
+972 9 970 9000
Recommended in Communications, Corporate/M&A

ERAN, Oded
Goldfarb, Levy, Eran & Co, Tel Aviv
+972 3 608 9999
Recommended in Corporate/M&A

FELIG, Clifford
Meitar, Liquornik, Geva & Co, Ramat Gan
+972 3 610 3100
Recommended in Communications, Corporate/M&A

FOX, Michael
Herzog, Fox & Neeman, Tel Aviv +972 3 692 2033
fox@hfn.co.il
Recommended in Banking & Finance, Corporate/M&A
Specialisation: Founding partner of the firm in 1972, starting its corporate department. Specialises in mergers and acquisitions and has been active in act-

ing for multinational acquirers of Israeli technology companies including General Electric, Microsoft and 3Com. In project finance, acted for the main lenders on the billion dollar Cross Israel Highway project. In energy projects, acts for British Gas in Israel.
Prof. Memberships: Israel Bar Association; Law Society of England and Wales; International Bar Association (country representative); World Law Group.
Career: Qualified in England as a solicitor in 1958. Founding partner of London law firm formerly known as *Fox & Gibbons*. After emigrating to Israel in 1968, founded the Tel-Aviv firm of *Herzog, Fox & Neeman* in 1972 together with Chaim Herzog and Yaakov Neeman.
Personal: Born in London in 1934. Educated at City of London School and London University. Emigrated with wife to Israel in 1968. Chairman of the Israel Britain and the Commonwealth Association. Leisure pursuits include reading and music.

GEVA, Dan
Meitar, Liquornik, Geva & Co, Ramat Gan
+972 3 610 3100
Recommended in Communications

GOLDENBERG, Amnon
Horowitz & Co, Tel Aviv
+972 3 567 0666/0604
Recommended in Corporate/M&A

GROSS, Joseph
Gross, Kleinhendler, Hodak, Halevy, Greenberg & Co, Tel Aviv +972 3 608 3333
Recommended in Corporate/M&A

HACOHEN, Itay
Zellermayer, Pelossof & Co, Tel Aviv
+972 3 625 5555
Recommended in Corporate/M&A

HALPERN-HERZOG, Shirin
Goldfarb, Levy, Eran & Co, Tel Aviv
+972 3 608 9816
Recommended in Corporate/M&A

HERTMAN, Alex
Horowitz & Co, Tel Aviv
+972 3 567 0666/0604
Recommended in Banking & Finance

KANTOR, Israel
Kantor, Elhanani, Tal & Co, Tel Aviv
+972 3 714 0400
Recommended in Corporate/M&A

LAMPERT, Aaron
Naschitz, Brandes & Co, Tel Aviv +972 3 623 5000
Recommended in Communications, Corporate/M&A

LEVENFELD, Barry
Yigal Arnon & Co, Tel Aviv +972 3 608 7777
barry@arnon.co.il
Recommended in Communications, Corporate/M&A
Prof. Memberships: Israel Bar Association.
Publications: Author 'Copyright Protection for Computer Software in Israel' – The Computer Lawyer, Vol 4, No 8, August 1987; 'Israel Considers Comprehensive Computer Law' – Computer Law Advisor, Vol 2, No 6, March 1988; 'Look and Feel New Law of the Land: This and Other Recent Developments in Israel' – The International Computer Lawyer, Vol 1, No 4, March 1993.
Career: Admitted 1981 New York and Southern and Eastern districts of New York; 1983 US Court of Appeals, Second Circuit; 1985 Israel. Harvard College (AB with honours, 1976); Fletcher School of Law and Diplomacy; Harvard Law School (JD with honours 1980).
Personal: Born Chicago 1954. Languages: English and Hebrew.

LEVY, Yehuda
Goldfarb, Levy, Eran & Co, Tel Aviv
+972 3 608 9999
Recommended in Corporate/M&A

NEEMAN, Yaakov
Herzog, Fox & Neeman, Tel Aviv +972 3 692 2020
neeman@hfn.co.il
Recommended in Banking & Finance, Corporate/M&A
Specialisation: Founding partner of *Herzog, Fox & Neeman*, specialising in banking and finance, corporate/mergers and acquisitions, as well as multinational transactions and tax law. Has been involved in a significant number of the most noteworthy transactions that have occurred in Israel in recent years.
Prof. Memberships: Israel Bar Association.
Publications: The author of several academic texts and numerous articles in professional publications both in Israel and overseas.
Career: Qualified in 1966. Practised law at *I. Gornitzky & Co.* between 1965-1968. Held numerous academic positions at several law faculties both in Israel and overseas in the fields of Corporate Law, Tax Law and Contracts Law. Founded *Herzog, Fox & Neeman* in 1972 together with Chaim Herzog and Michael Fox. On several occasions during his legal career held public office at the highest level in a number of different capacities and has served as a member or chairman of several public committees.
Personal: Born 16 September 1939. Attended the Hebrew University of Jerusalem 1961-1964 (LLB Hons); New York University, Law School, 1965 (LLM Hons); New York University, Law School, 1968 (JSD Hons). Lives in Jerusalem. Interests include skiing and swimming.

OREN, Ruth
Horowitz & Co, Tel Aviv
+972 3 567 0666/0604
Recommended in Corporate/M&A

ROSEN, Ori
Danziger, Klagsbald, Rosen & Co, Tel Aviv
+972 3 611 0700
Recommended in Communications

ROSENSWEIG, Joshua
I Gornitzky & Co, Tel Aviv 61291 +972 3 710 9191
rosensweig@gornitzky.co.il
Recommended in Corporate/M&A
Specialisation: Partner, main areas of work: corporate law and taxation, including mergers, acquisitions, restructurings and international commercial transactions and taxation. Has handled acquisitions and sales of Israeli and foreign companies for Israeli and foreign clients. Acted on behalf of shareholders in the sale of Mirabilis (today ICQ) to AOL for close to US$400 million; acted for sellers in sale of shares of Paz (Israel's largest energy company) as part of a change-of-control transaction valued at approximately US$400 million; together with partner Moriel Matalon acted on behalf of Marconi Communications in the acquisition of RDC (today Marconi Communications Israel), an Israeli start-up.
Career: Qualified 1978. Founded and managed speciality firm providing advice on international transactions and taxation until 1999 merger with *I. Gornitzky & Co.* Legal Advisor to the Israeli Parliament Finance Committee (1983-1985). Member, Rafael Committee on Reform of International Taxation (1990). Member Somekh Committee on Mergers & Spin-Offs (Taxation) of Listed Companies (1993-1994).
Personal: Bar-Ilan University (Israel) – LLB 1976. New York University – LLM in Taxation (1979) and JSD in International Taxation (1981). Born Canada 1952.

RUBIN, Pinhas
I Gornitzky & Co, Tel Aviv 61291 +972 3 710 9191
rubin@gornitzky.co.il
Recommended in Corporate/M&A
Specialisation: Senior Partner, main areas of work and representative activities are M&A and restructuring, securities, taxation, litigation, banking, insurance and general corporate. In the field of M&A and restructurings: Recently advised the Paz Group (Israel's largest energy company) on its restructuring; advised Sonol (one of Israels' largest energy companies) on its restructuring; advised Ampal (one of Israel's holding companies) on its restructuring; represented all three entities in a three-way merger of Hadar, Noga and Dolev (all publicly-traded Israeli insurers); representation of Osem and Strauss two of Israel's largest food processing groups and of Yediot Aharonot (publisher of Israel's most widely circulated newspaper); representation of Israel's largest banks and their shareholders in merger and acquisitions; representation of American shareholders in sale of control of large Israeli industrial company (see also under banking below). In the field of securities: Recent representation of Bank Hapoalim (Israel's largest bank) in its offering of shares to foreign accredited investors by prospectus; representation of many other Israeli companies in their offerings of shares to the public; representation of a major Israeli traded company in respect of alleged securities law violations regarding a tender offer; representation of three former finance ministers and the former Commissioner of Insurance and Capital Markets before the Baskey Committee (Israel's largest ever governmental investigative committee) regarding alleged illegal actions concerning shares in several Israeli banks over a period of time (a large 'scandal' of its time). In the field of taxation: Representation of numerous clients including many of Israel's largest corporate groups in tax planning and in civil and criminal disputes; representation of the CEO (then and now) of Teva Pharmaceuticals

Industries Ltd. (Israel's largest pharmaceuticals company) in the ProMedico Affair which resulted in a landmark international taxation ruling (favourable to Teva's CEO) from the Israeli Supreme Court; representation of the former Israeli ambassador to the US in successful proceedings to prevent criminal charges; occasional representation of Bezek International (one of Israel's three international telephone carriers), Microsoft Israel, ATT, GE, Bloomberg, Citigroup. In the field of litigation: Representation of defendants in securities and commercial class actions including representation of Bezek (a government controlled company, Israel's largest telecommunications services provider and formerly Israel's domestic telephone monopoly) in class action suits on a regular basis; representation of Eurocom, another leading Israeli telecommunications group in class action suits; representation of foreign reinsurers in class action suits; representation of the Tel Aviv Stock Exchange in class action suits; representation of Israel's largest banks, insurers and energy companies in class action suits; representation of DBS (Israel's first licensed provider of digital broadcast satellite television) before the Israeli Supreme Court in various matters; representation of Bezek International (one of Israel's three international telephone carriers); representation of Israeli Educational TV company; representation of a foreign multi-millionaire in Israeli police investigation regarding claims of bribery involving the former President of Israel, Mr Ezer Weizman, which did not result in prosecution. In the field of banking: Acted on behalf of the buyers (a consortium of US and Israeli investors) in the acquisition of control of Israel's largest bank – Bank Hapoalim; acted on behalf of a group participating in the tender offer to buy control of Bank Mizrachi (one of Israel's five largest banks) from the Israeli state; currently represents Bank Hapoalim, Bank Mizrachi and other banks on a regular basis on various corporate and tax issues. In the field of insurance: Representations of the Phoenix and the Harel Group (both large publicly-traded Israeli insurers) and former Zion and Hasneh insurance companies on a variety of commercial, tax and corporate matters including litigation; provision of advice to AIG; acted as court appointed liquidator of IsraelRe (historically, Israel's only local reinsurer) involving numerous US and European creditors. In the field of estates: Though estates are outside field of practice, did represent the estate of the late Mr Theodore Arison (known to have been among the wealthiest persons in the world); and was appointed by the Israeli courts to represent the estate of the late Mr Shaul Eisenberg (known to have been among Israel's wealthiest persons as a result of extensive international business dealings).

Career: Qualified 1974. Chairman, Israel Bar Association Tax Committee (1985-1995); served as a member of the Advisory Committee on Reform of the Israeli Court System (the Orr Committee) based upon appointment by the Minister of Justice and the Chief Justice of the Israeli Supreme Court; representative in the past of the Israel Bar Association to the Israeli parliament in respect of proposed financial legislation; member various tax-related committees including participating in the drafting of recent Israeli tax legislation on mergers and spin-offs; lecturer, tax, corporate and commercial law – Tel Aviv University; lecturer: Training Institute for Judges; lecturer: Israel Bar Continuing Legal Education courses; lecturer: Annual Conference of Israeli Accountants.

Personal: LLB Tel Aviv University. Born Israel 1949.

SACKS, Alan

Herzog, Fox & Neeman, Tel Aviv +972 3 692 2020
sacks@hfn.co.il

Recommended in Corporate/M&A

Specialisation: Corporate – Mergers and Acquisitions; Banking. On the corporate side of the practice, has represented some of the world's leading corporations in connection with their activities in Israel and advised on a wide variety of corporate acquisitions, including government privatisations and the acquisition of banks in Israel. Has for many years represented the Claridge Group, one of the largest foreign investors in Israel, and has more recently represented the Koor Group, one of Israel's largest industrial conglomerates. Was one of the first in Israel to advise on the establishment of venture capital funds, and continues to be active in the venture capital field, representing both venture capitalists and Israeli start-up companies. In the banking and finance sector, advises many Israeli and international banks and financial institutions on a variety of commercial and regulatory issues encompassing syndicated loans, insolvency 'work outs', aircraft finance and project and asset financing.

Prof. Memberships: Israel Bar Association; Law Society of England and Wales; World Law Group.

Career: Qualified in England as a solicitor in 1981. As an advocate in Israel in 1985. Partner in *Herzog, Fox & Neeman* specialising in corporate, banking and finance.

Personal: Cambridge University (MA Law); University of London (LLM). Leisure interests include reading and sport.

SCHAPIRO, David H.

Yigal Arnon & Co, Tel Aviv +972 3 608 7856
davids@arnon.co.il

Recommended in Corporate/M&A

Prof. Memberships: American and Israel Bar Associations.

Career: Admitted 1988 New York, US District Court, Southern and Eastern Districts of New York and US Tax Court; 1991 Israel. Yeshiva University (BA cum laude 1984); Benjamin N. Cardozo School of Law, Yeshiva University (JD, magna cum laude 1987). Member Cardozo Law Review 1985-1987. Belkin Scholar, Alexander Fellow. Law Clerk, Judge Charles P Sifton, US District Court, Eastern District of New York, 1986. Corporate Dept. *Fried Frank Harris Shriver & Jacobson* 1987-1990.

Personal: Born New York 1962. Languages: English and Hebrew.

TAL, Dalia

Kantor, Elhanani, Tal & Co, Tel Aviv
+972 3 714 0400

Recommended in Banking & Finance, Corporate/M&A

ITALY

Index

OVERVIEW: With one eye on globalisation and another on the growing economy, Italian firms have become convinced that big is beautiful. Those firms that have yet to find an Anglo-American partner are under increasing pressure to do so, with the example of Grimaldi Clifford Chance pointing the way. Nevertheless, there has also been a revival in the development of independent firms doing sophisticated, high-quality work, with Bonelli Erede Pappalardo leading the M&A market and Chiomenti dominating the banking sphere. The telecoms sphere has been particularly active, with the acquisition of Telecom Italia by Olivetti and the tender process for UMTS third generation mobile network licences proving major sources of work. The market anticipates the full liberalisation of the telecoms market (in January 2001) to herald a further M&A wave. Elsewhere, the level of project finance activity in Italy has not lived up to market expectations, largely as a result of obstructive laws.

Banking & Finance

Chiomenti Studio Legale (7 ptrs, 20 asscs) Competitors acknowledge that the firm *"has a strong grip on the banking market,"* advising its blue-chip lender client base on syndicated loans, acquisition finance and securitisation. Regarded as pre-eminent for capital markets advice, the team is noted for its excellent relationship with bank regulatory authorities. **Francesco Ago*** receives widespread praise for his structured finance practice, and is *"one of the best finance lawyers in Italy."* **Michele Carpinelli***, *"a star of the firm,"* is *"strong on any financial transaction with a tax element in it,"* and **Roberto Ghio*** is another respected member of the group. The firm was involved in the acquisition of Autostrade by the Benetton Group, acting for Credito Italiano as lender. It also advised on a €500 million financing for Luxottica and a €13,500 million financing for the Telecom group, arranged by Chase Manhattan. On the capital markets side, the firm has advised on the securitisation of non-performing claims, originated by INPS, and of non-performing mortgage claims originated by BNL. **Clients:** Credito Italiano; Chase Manhattan; Deutsche Bank.

Grimaldi Clifford Chance (6 ptrs, 30 asscs) An *"integrated firm,"* with *"really solid roots in banking,"* that *"can handle both sides of an offering."* The firm has advised on a number of bond issues and securitisations, and is very well respected for its advice on syndicated loans and acquisition finance. A team of great depth can call on the services of **Nick Wrigley*** *("manages transactions with great efficiency,")* though his recent appointment to head of the firm's European Equity Practice may make him a little less available than before. **Alberta Figari*** is another *"extremely able"* banking and M&A lawyer, while **Vittorio Grimaldi*** is an eminence grise in most areas of commercial law, and is seen as *"one of Italy's top men."* **Luigi Chessa*** continues to create a fine impression for securitisations and structured finance advice, **Roberto Cappelli*** is *"unquestionably a major player,"* and **Francesco Novelli*** has begun to catch the market's attention. The firm acted on the first Italian project bond, on behalf of the arranger, Greenwich Natwest, for the construction of the Guardia di Finanza training academy in Bari, a deal which used the new securitisation law in Italy, known as 'Law 130'. It has also been involved in a number of syndicated loans, advising the arrangers on large loans to Prada and Mediocredito Centroitalia. Acquisition finance work includes acting for Banca Commerciale Italiana on financing the takeover of Netherlands based Parinvest Group by Euralcom. **Clients:** Luxottica; Benetton; Banca Commerciale Italiana; Morgan Stanley Dean Witter; Caboto; Deutsche Bank; BNP Paribas.

Freshfields Bruckhaus Deringer (6 ptrs, 35 asscs) A high quality department, with particular expertise in structured finance and securitisations, that is acknowledged for advising both borrowers and lenders on acquisition financing, asset financing and traditional lending. **Enrico Castellani***, *"a great guy with great skills,"* **Alan Newton*** *("an excellent lawyer")* and **Carlo Kostka***, who specialises in international debt and equity securities offerings, all draw substantial market commendation. The firm was involved on the second Banca di Roma Trevi securitisation, the Caesar Finance CBOs, arranged by Donaldson Lufkin & Jenrette, and the Perseo (CARIFI) and SCC (Leasinvest) securitisations. Debt securities issues have included advising Banca Intesa's debut €750 million FRN, and the establishment of the ENI Group's €2 billion MTN programme. **Clients:** AIG Europe; Chase Manhattan; ABN AMRO; Banca di Roma; IMI; UBS Warburg; Mediobanca; Goldman Sachs; BNP Paribas; Société Générale; Centre Solutions; Air One.

Bonelli-Erede-Pappalardo (6 ptrs, 20 asscs) *"Thoroughly committed team,"* renowned for its IPO work, and increasingly active on bond/convertibles issues. Securitisations and big-ticket acquisition finance are other key elements of the group's caseload, and it is normally seen acting on behalf of borrowers. **Roberto Cera*** is, according to the market, *"one of the leading names in Italy,"* and receives valuable support from **Alberto Saravalle*** and **Fabio Capelletti***. The firm advised on a Lit 1.66 billion bond issue by Finmeccanica, a bond issued by Tecnost, exchangeable for Telecom Italia shares, and an MTN programme, extended to US investors, of $10 billion. It has also worked on an innovative securitisation, and advised on numerous public offerings, including those of Thomson CSF, Axa, Rhodia, Aventis and Technip. **Clients:** Thomson CSF; Axa; Rhodia; Aventis; Thomson multi-media; Technip.

Brosio, Casati e Associati (in association with Allen & Overy) (9 ptrs, 11 asscs) *"Historically strong finance group"* which continues to expand and advises heavyweight international financial institutions on acquisition finance, asset finance, syndicated loans and a variety of capital markets transactions. **Roberto Casati*** is a *"big-time player of the old school,"* while US-qualified capital markets specialist **Max Aaron*** and the versatile, Rome-based commercial lawyer **Massimiliano Danusso*** are other leading names here. The firm acted for GE Capital Services (EEF) on the financing granted to Helitalia for its acquisition of a fleet of helicopters, and advised Fuji Bank, arranger of the financing for the acquisition of Piaggio by Texas Pacific Group. **Clients:** GE Capital Services; The Fuji Bank; Morgan Grenfell Development Capital.

Gianni Origoni & Partners (4 ptrs, 11 asscs) *"Comparatively new to the structured finance markets,"* the firm is already establishing a reputation as *"one of the big players,"* to add to its established name for banking M&A and acquisition finance. **Francesco Gianni*** is *"a fantastic rain-maker"* for the firm, while **Alberto Giampieri*** and **Antonio Segni*** *"know how to close a deal out."* The firm advised on the acquisition financing of the purchase of 50% of Costa Crociere by Carnival Corporation, valued at £350 million, and acted on the €215 million syndicated facility to finance the acquisition of the largest cruise ship operating in Europe. Capital markets work has involved advice on the securitisation of SEAT Pagine Gialle. **Clients:** Omnitel; RAI; Finnmechanica; Crédit Local de France; Lazard Brothers.

Simmons & Simmons & Grippo (2 ptrs, 3 asscs) *"A very aggressive competitor in capital markets"* and, according to our research, *"starting to show up on IPOs"* as well, the firm has a superb reputation for asset finance. **Filippo Pingue*** continues to attract market recognition. The firm has worked on a synthetic securitisation for one of the leading Italian banking groups, and is currently involved in three other securitisations, one on behalf of Diner's Club Italia, and another in the pharmaceuticals industry. It has also advised on credit derivatives and four acquisition finance deals since the start of 2000. **Clients:** Diner's Club Italia.

Studio Legale Ughi e Nunziante (8 lawyers) A *"traditionally powerful firm,"* which has recently seen the departure of a number of lawyers but remains respected for across the board financial expertise, notably in derivatives. In a *"rough year,"* **Marcello Gioscia***, *"a senior and active figure,"* has held the department together. Well known for advising ISDA on the Italian aspects of the derivatives market, he has also overseen a number of other operations, including the second tranche of the privatisation of Enel. The firm regularly advises IMI on its merchant banking operations in Italy, and advised the lenders (Dresdner Bank and Medio Credito Centrale) on a project finance operation in Southern Italy for the construction of a manufacturing plant. **Clients:** Enel; General Electric; JP Morgan; BBVA; IMI; Dresdner Bank; Medio Credito Centrale.

BBLP Pavia e Ansaldo (5 ptrs, 25 asscs) Our research seemed to suggest a firm more focused on corporate matters, but one that nevertheless maintains a reputation for some banking M&A and acquisition finance work. Recent transactions have included advising on the acquisition and financing of Italtel, and on the purchase of a stake in a bank by Morgan Stanley Dean Witter. **Roberto Zanchi*** and rising name **Francesco Manara*** are both respected transactional lawyers. The firm has also been active on the project finance front, advising on the metropolitan project that will link Monza and Milan. **Clients:** Morgan Stanley Dean Witter.

Macchi di Cellere e Gangemi (4 ptrs, 10 asscs) Headed by the popular **Claudio Visco***, the group has broad experience of export credits, syndicated loans and related security arrangements, refinancing transactions, leasing, securitisations and asset-backed transactions. It also advises banking clients on compliance issues, and has assisted several banks in opening branches and subsidiaries in Italy. The team advised the lenders on the financing of a pan-European optical fibre network, and assisted the sponsors on the expansion, operation and bond refinancing of a waste-to-energy plant. **Clients:** Banks and other financial institutions.

NCTM Studio Legale Associato (4 ptrs, 14 asscs) *"Increasing its market share"* on bank regulatory

ITALY
Leading firms (Banking & Finance)

Band	Firm
1	Chiomenti Studio Legale
	Grimaldi Clifford Chance
2	Freshfields Bruckhaus Deringer
3	Bonelli-Erede-Pappalardo
	Brosio, Casati e Associati (in association with Allen & Overy)
	Gianni Origoni & Partners
4	Simmons & Simmons & Grippo
	Studio Legale Ughi e Nunziante
5	BBLP Pavia e Ansaldo
	Macchi di Cellere e Gangemi
	NCTM Studio Legale Associato

Firms are listed alphabetically in each band.

Leading individuals (Banking & Finance)

Band	Individual	Individual
1	**AGO Francesco** *Chiomenti Studio Legale*	**CARPINELLI Michele** *Chiomenti Studio Legale*
	CASATI Roberto *Brosio, Casati e Associati*	**CASTELLANI Enrico** *Freshfields Bruckhaus*
	WRIGLEY Nicholas *Grimaldi Clifford Chance*	
2	**CAPPELLI Roberto** *Grimaldi Clifford Chance*	**CERA Roberto** *Bonelli-Erede-Pappalardo*
	CHESSA Luigi *Grimaldi Clifford Chance*	**GIANNI Francesco** *Gianni Origoni & Partners*
	GIOSCIA Marcello *Ughi e Nunziante*	**GRIMALDI Vittorio** *Grimaldi Clifford Chance*
3	**BELTRAMO Susanna** *Studio Legale Beltramo*	**DANUSSO Massimiliano** *Brosio, Casati*
	GIAMPIERI Alberto *Gianni Origoni & Partners*	**MANARA Francesco** *BBLP Pavia e Ansaldo*
	NEWTON Alan *Freshfields Bruckhaus*	**PINGUE Filippo** *Simmons & Simmons*
	RAYNAUD Daniele *Ashurst Morris Crisp*	**SARAVALLE Alberto** *Bonelli-Erede-Pappalardo*
	SEGNI Antonio *Gianni Origoni & Partners*	**VISCO Claudio** *Macchi di Cellere e Gangemi*
4	**AARON Max** *Brosio, Casati e Associati*	**CAPELLETTI Fabio** *Bonelli-Erede-Pappalardo*
	FIGARI Alberta *Grimaldi Clifford Chance*	**GHIO Roberto** *Chiomenti Studio Legale*
	KOSTKA Carlo *Freshfields Bruckhaus Deringer*	**NOVELLI Francesco** *Grimaldi Clifford Chance*
	PADOVANI Stefano *NCTM*	
	SCASSELLATI-SFORZOLINI Giuseppe *Cleary, Gottlieb, Steen & Hamilton*	
	ZANCHI Roberto *BBLP Pavia e Ansaldo*	

Individuals are listed alphabetically in each band.

matters, the firm is gaining a number of admirers in the financial sectors. *"We'll hear more of them in the future,"* said one commentator. **Stefano Padovani*** is the outstanding practitioner in a team that regularly advises Credit Italiano on litigation, acquisition and regulatory matters. The firm advised Credit Italiano on its acquisition of Bank Pekao (the second largest Polish bank), represented both Credit Italiano and Banca Commerciale Italiana on the disposal of the Fonspa bank to Morgan Stanley, and advised Banca Popolare di Lodi on the recent Henderson deal. **Clients:** Tecnodiffusione; Cairo Communications; Credit Italiano; JP Morgan.

Other Notable Practitioners **Giuseppe Scassellati-Sforzolini*** of Cleary, Gottlieb, Steen & Hamilton receives extensive commendation for his mixed capital markets/corporate finance practice. **Daniele Raynaud***, formerly of BBLP Pavia e Ansaldo, is a respected general finance lawyer, now helping to open Ashurst Morris Crisp's new office in Milan. And **Susanna Beltramo*** of Studio Legale Beltramo is acknowledged to have great experience of domestic banking issues.

I

Communications

ITALY Leading firms (Communications)	
1	Baker & McKenzie
2	Bonelli-Erede-Pappalardo
	Dalla Vedova
3	BBLP Pavia e Ansaldo
	Brosio, Casati e Associati (in association with Allen & Overy)
	Chiomenti Studio Legale
	Clarich, Libertini, Macaluso & Valli
	Gianni Origoni & Partners
	Simmons & Simmons & Grippo
4	Grimaldi Clifford Chance
	Macchi di Cellere e Gangemi
	Studio Legale Tonucci
	Studio Legale Ughi e Nunziante

Firms are listed alphabetically in each band.

Leading individuals (Communications)	
1	**GIARDA Raffaele** *Baker & McKenzie*
2	**D'ANGELO Davide** *Brosio, Casati e Associati*
	DALLA VEDOVA Marco *Dalla Vedova*
	LODIGIANI Francesca *BBLP Pavia e Ansaldo*
	LOMBARDO Nino *Simmons & Simmons & Grippo*
	RADICATI DI BROZOLO Luca *Chiomenti*
3	**BREMBATI Fabio** *Baker & McKenzie*
	CAIAZZO Rino *Studio Legale Ughi e Nunziante*
	GUARINO Giuseppe *Studio Legale Guarino*
	MACALUSO Fabio *Clarich, Libertini, Macaluso*
4	**CUGIA DI SANT'ORSOLA Fabrizio** *Tonucci*
	MACCHI DI CELLERE Stefano *Macchi di Cellere*
	OSTI Cristoforo *Grimaldi Clifford Chance*
	VENTO Cesare *Gianni Origoni & Partners*

Individuals are listed alphabetically in each band.

Baker & McKenzie (4 ptrs, 8 asscs) A *"well-staffed"* department with a *"heavy turnover"* and a historical strength in telecoms, which is perceived by its rivals to have *"a better position in the market than anyone else."* Competitors have also noted an increased emphasis on TV and broadcasting-related activities. **Raffaele Giarda*** *"possesses tremendous expertise,"* according to clients, and is the team's leading player. **Fabio Brembati's*** reputation lies in the competition aspects of telecoms cases. The firm participated in the public consultations with TLC operators, organised by the Regulatory Authority for the Ministry of Communications. It has also been advising one of the bidders for the UMTS licence, and assisting one of the bidders on the company which is the result of the spin-off of RAI. **Clients:** International telecom and internet companies.

Bonelli-Erede-Pappalardo (10 lawyers) A strong relationship with Telecom Italia is the basis of the firm's telecoms reputation. Particularly active on M&A matters, the firm has also begun to increase its regulatory capacity, where a strong competition department adds credibility. The firm has advised Telecom Italia on several regulatory issues such as reverse interconnection and unbundling of local loop, and has assisted it on several proceedings before the Italian communications authority. **Clients:** Telecom Italia.

Dalla Vedova (2 ptrs, 5 asscs) **Marco Dalla Vedova*** heads *"one of the main firms for telecoms work,"* which has a particularly strong reputation for its regulatory work. Noted for representing satellite and TV clients, the firm advised on a satellite and underwater cable project finance, and represented Vodafone on the Vodafone/Mannesmann deal. The group frequently advises on mobile and fixed interconnections, roaming agreements, spectrum allocation, unbundling of local loop, number allocation and DSL management. **Clients:** Vodafone Mannesmann.

BBLP Pavia e Ansaldo Possesses more of a reputation for *"high profile litigation and commercial law,"* but maintains a respectable communications clientele nonetheless. Key telecoms involvements this year include acting on the acquisition and financing of Italtel, and assisting Autostrade in its Blu-related activities. Rival firms consider **Francesca Lodigiani*** to be *"thoroughly capable."* **Clients:** Italtel; Autostrade.

Brosio, Casati e Associati (in association with Allen & Overy) (2 ptrs, 7 asscs) Offices in Milan, Rome and Turin all have telecoms capacity, but it is the Milan office which spearheads operations. *"A major competitor"* in the telecoms field, the firm has had a high profile on telecoms litigation this year, representing France Telecom in the dispute over the implementation of the shareholders' agreement between France Telecom, Deutsche Telekom and ENEL. The firm has also been involved in a number of regional joint ventures for the provision of telecoms services. Milan-based **Davide d'Angelo*** heads the department. A *"respected all-rounder,"* he has substantial experience of advising on the privatisation of the telecoms industry. **Clients:** France Telecom.

Chiomenti Studio Legale **Luca Radicati di Brozolo***, *"a first-class counsel,"* and *"a frequent writer on regulatory matters"* heads a small practice with a specialisation in Euro-telecoms. Acknowledged by clients as a *"superb"* competition lawyer, he is one of the most experienced regulatory lawyers in Italy. The firm's corporate telecoms practice is especially strong – the department advised TIM in connection with the conversion of its savings shares into ordinary shares, a deal valued at €10 billion. Also advised on the sale of 49% of ACEA Telefonica to Telefonica InterContinental, a transaction valued at Lit120 billion. In regulatory matters, the team advised ACEA Telefonica on its successful bid for a UMTS licence. **Clients:** ACEA Telefonica; TIM.

Clarich, Libertini, Macaluso & Valli (4 ptrs, 3 asscs) *"Emerging firm"* with a niche specialisation in communications, particularly e-commerce, where it has advised on a number of e-banking cases. The department is run by *"extremely knowledgeable and client friendly"* **Fabio Macaluso***, a former legal counsel to Omnitel and Wind. Major cases of the year include acting for ENEL and Omnitel on anti-trust proceedings, assisting Infostrada and AIIP against Telecom Italia, and defending RAI before the Communications Authority in a proceeding relating to its alleged dominant position. **Clients:** ENEL; Wind; Omnitel; RAI; Medusa Film; Lega Nazionale Calcio; e.Biscom.

Gianni Origoni & Partners (2 ptrs, 6 asscs) *"Heavily involved,"* the firm was recommended as a respected player, best known for advising its international telecoms clients on corporate matters. The firm also acts on IRUs, licensing procedures and interconnection agreements. **Cesare Vento*** has a corporate background, and leads a team which has advised on the Infostrada sale, the joint venture between Viatel and Finmeccanica, the merger between Tiscali and WOL, and the Wind joint venture. **Clients:** AT&T.

Simmons & Simmons & Grippo (2 ptrs, 4 asscs) Specialises in international transactions, in particular, assisting Telecom Italia on its international ventures. The firm also works with TIM and Telespazio, advising Telespazio on the Astrolink venture last year. **Nino Lombardo***, a *"versatile"* telecoms specialist in the eyes of his competitors, heads the department. Associated for a number of years with Stet International, he has recently been involved in advising Telecom Italia on its investments in India. **Clients:** Telespazio; Telecom Italia international; TIM.

Grimaldi Clifford Chance (2 ptrs, 8 asscs) *"High quality"* department, headed by *"well-known"* **Cristoforo Osti***, a competition/anti-trust specialist with expertise in telecoms who is recognised by peers and clients. The firm carries out facilities agreements and network building contracts for such long-standing clients as GTS, and regulatory work for Deutsche Telekom, Omnitel, and Telefónica. It has also acted for Enron on setting up a trading band width venture on the internet, and for IT service providers. The firm has recently been appointed by Blu (a UMTS contender) to conduct its financing and regulatory work. **Clients:** GTS; Blu; Deutsche Telekom; Telefónica; Enron; Omnitel.

Macchi di Cellere e Gangemi (2 ptrs, 5 asscs) **Stefano Macchi di Cellere*** heads a department that has been involved in a number of telecoms and IT matters, advising on both transactional and regulatory apects of the industries. The group has advised on the establishment of a multi-national group based in the UK for the installation and management of a fibre-based national telecoms network. Also acted on the establishment of an Italian joint venture in the pharmaceutical sector for the provision of services through the internet. Elsewhere, the group acted for a high-tech company in negotiations for the provision of WAP services to Italian mobile communications companies. **Clients:** MCI WorldCom; BellSouth; Fibernet; InterXion.

Studio Legale Tonucci (1 ptr, 7 asscs) Known for its focus on privatisations within the sector, the firm's telecoms department includes lawyers who have held in-house positions at major telecoms companies. As a result, the group advises an impressive range of national and international operators. **Fabrizio Cugia di Sant'Orsola***, *"a well-known writer on telecoms issues,"* heads the department. He has worked for a number of operators requesting national licences for fixed telephone services. The firm has acted extensively on the UMTS bidding process, and advised on wireless local loop issues in Italy and Greece. **Clients:** TAS; Grapes Communications; Wind.

Studio Legale Ughi e Nunziante (2 ptrs, 7 asscs) As well as offering regulatory advice to telecoms companies such as Albacom, the firm is a frequent advisor to the Italian government. It has advised on compliance issues in the sector, most recently with regard to a new statute on general authorisations and private networks. A familiar sight before the Italian competition authority, the respected **Rino Caiazzo*** has advised on proceedings concerning access conditions to the public telecoms networks, discriminatory practices and predatory prices by the incumbent operator in the IT sector. **Clients:** Italian Government; Albacom.

Other Notable Practitioner **Giuseppe Guarino*** of Studio Legale Guarino is renowned as *"Telecom Italia's favourite lawyer,"* and acknowledged by peers to possess a *"brilliant mind"* and *"great litigation skills."*

Competition/Anti-trust

Bonelli-Erede-Pappalardo (4 ptrs, 20 asscs) Clearly a market leader, the department has capitalised on the matchless reputation of the firm's corporate department to act on numerous high-profile merger control cases. These have involved a wide range of industries, including telecoms, IT, media and insurance. In addition, the team has appeared before the national and European competition authorities on various contentious matters, and has a notable reputation for advising on state aid and anti-cartel matters. The group's leading name is *"competition guru"* **Aurelio Pappalardo***, who specialises in anti-cartel cases and advises a number of important Italian companies and government bodies. An honorary Director General of the European Commission and a Professor of EC Competition Law at the University of Liège, he is widely recognised to be *"the best on the market."* He is ably assisted by **Massimo Merola***, who is a state aids expert, and the *"experienced"* and *"increasingly active"* **Claudio Tesauro***. The firm acted on Telecom Italia's acquisition of Seat Yellow Pages, advised on Seat's acquisition of Tele Monte Carlo, and represented Generali on its acquisition of INA. **Clients:** Telecom Italia; Seat; Alitalia; Stream; Generali; Finmeccanica; Benetton.

Cleary, Gottlieb, Steen & Hamilton (2 ptrs, 13 asscs) Historically strong in regulatory and anti-trust work throughout Europe, the firm has a strong brand which owes much to its superb Brussels office. The firm's original star there is now successfully building a notable anti-trust department in Rome. **Mario Siragusa*** is one of the world's great names in competition. An *"outstanding"* lawyer, he *"possesses an exceptionally high number of blue-chip clients,"* and is one of the founding fathers of modern European anti-trust law. He remains transactionally active, and rivals *"see him on almost every deal."* The team's workload encompasses big-ticket merger control advice, Article 81 and 82 matters and anti-cartel investigations. It represented Exxon Mobil before the European Commission in connection with the proposed $80 billion merger, and advised Fiat and General Motors in connection with their automobile operations. In contentious issues, the

ITALY Leading firms (Competition/Anti-trust)
1 Bonelli-Erede-Pappalardo
Cleary, Gottlieb, Steen & Hamilton
2 Chiomenti Studio Legale
Grimaldi Clifford Chance
Studio Legale Ughi e Nunziante
3 BBLP Pavia e Ansaldo
Brosio, Casati e Associati (in association with Allen & Overy)
Freshfields Bruckhaus Deringer
NCTM Studio Legale Associato
4 Clarich, Libertini, Macaluso & Valli
Rucellai & Raffaelli

Firms are listed alphabetically in each band.

Leading individuals (Competition/Anti-trust)
1 **PAPPALARDO Aurelio** *Bonelli-Erede-Pappalardo*
SIRAGUSA Mario *Cleary, Gottlieb*
2 **CAIAZZO Rino** *Studio Legale Ughi e Nunziante*
OSTI Cristoforo *Grimaldi Clifford Chance*
RADICATI DI BROZOLO Luca *Chiomenti*
3 **D'ALBERTI Silvia** *Brosio, Casati e Associati*
DENOZZA Francesco *Libonati Jaeger*
FRIGNANI Aldo *Frignani e Associati*
LIBERTINI Mario *Clarich, Libertini, Macaluso*
RAFFAELLI Enrico *Rucellai & Raffaelli*
ROSSI Guido *Studio Rossi*
TESAURO Claudio *Bonelli-Erede-Pappalardo*
4 **AROSSA Fabrizio** *Freshfields Bruckhaus*
GRASSANI Stefano *BBLP Pavia e Ansaldo*
MEROLA Massimo *Bonelli-Erede-Pappalardo*
PAVESIO Carlo *Brosio, Casati e Associati*
TOFFOLETTO Alberto *NCTM*

Individuals are listed alphabetically in each band.

team acted for Abbott Laboratories, Agip Petroli, United International Pictures and Robert Bosch before the Italian Anti-trust Authority in connection with alleged anti-competitive agreements and concerted practices. Before the European Court of First Instance, the department advised Alitalia on state aid proceedings. **Clients:** The Coca-Cola Company; Telecom Italia; SNAM; Telepiù; Otis.

Chiomenti Studio Legale (2 ptrs, 9 asscs) Best known for its merger control work, the firm has advised on filings in industries such as insurance, telecoms, energy and manufacturing. The team has also acted on appeals before the administrative courts against decisions of the Italian anti-trust authority, and assisted on the competition and state aid aspects of the privatisation of local municipal companies. Public procurement is another area of specific expertise. **Luca Radicati di Brozolo*** lectures on competition law at the University of Milan, and is, according to peers and clients, *"a first-class anti-trust lawyer."* An expert on merger filings, he has particular experience in the telecoms sector. This year, the firm acted on four state aids cases before the European Commission. **Clients:** Omnitel; Alitalia; Comune di Roma.

Grimaldi Clifford Chance (1 ptr, 6 asscs) An increasingly reputable department has advised on numerous recent merger filings, acting for clients in telecoms, energy, pharmaceuticals and IT. It has also advised on compliance programmes for large IT, fashion and appliances companies. **Cristoforo Osti*** is *"one of Italy's principal anti-trust lawyers,"* and heads a team which acted for Luxottica on its purchase of Bausch & Lomb. The firm has also advised on cartel cases, acting on behalf of Exxon, cement companies, and the Italian Association of Dentists. **Clients:** GTS; Omnitel; Exxon; Luxottica; Apple; Agip.

Studio Legale Ughi e Nunziante (2 ptrs, 4 asscs) Involved in a substantial number of filings, pre-merger notifications and anti-competition agreements. The firm has a particular specialisation in the communications sector, but is also noted for its work in banking, food and heavy metals. **Rino Caiazzo*** is an acknowledged expert in the telecoms sector. **Clients:** Albacom; Tiscali; Warner Brothers; Twentieth Century Fox; Omnitel.

BBLP Pavia e Ansaldo (1 ptr, 4 asscs) Respected competition department, which has overcome market doubts over the future of its alliance to advise on a variety of merger filings. Acting at both the national and EC level, it represented Commercial Union in a joint venture with Banca Popolare di Lodi, Montedison in its joint venture with Fuji, and L'Oréal in its acquisition of Matrix. The firm was also involved, on behalf of Universal Music, in the administrative procedures linked to the 'music cartel case', as well as those related to the 'hollow glass cartel case' (on behalf of the Saint Gobain company.) In addition, the department has acted as antitrust consultants in Italy for a number of multi-national groups such as Safilo, Alcoa Co, Schroeders, Union Banque Suisse, Corning Inc, and Aventis Corp. **Stefano Grassani*** is a highly respected practitioner. **Clients:** Universal Music; Commercial Union; Montedison; L'Oréal; Safilo; Alcoa Co; Schroeders; Union Banque Suisse; Corning Inc; Aventis Corp.

Brosio, Casati e Associati (in association with Allen & Overy) (4 ptrs, 4 asscs) Broad-based department, which advises its international and domestic clients on big-ticket merger control cases. Acted for Shell Italia on an investigation into the market for raw sulphur distribution, and for Comital on a similar investigation into the cling film and aluminium foil market. **Silvia d'Alberti*** is in charge of the anti-trust team in Rome. She worked with the Italian Anti-trust Authority for five years, where she established a reputation for expertise in the energy sector. In Turin, **Carlo Pavesio*** also comes warmly recommended. The firm drafted briefing papers to the Commission, relating to alleged unfair competition in the defence and advertising industries, and represented Sibeg on anti-trust proceedings concerning the soft drink distribution market. **Clients:** Swissair; MTS; Europ Assistance; Chrysler; Mayr; Shell Italia; Comital.

Freshfields Bruckhaus Deringer (1 ptr, 6 asscs) Principally associated with high-end merger control work, the firm's small anti-trust department is beginning to expand, recently acquiring a former Competition Authority lawyer. **Fabrizio Arossa*** is, according to market opinion, *"a versatile lawyer,"* who has particular expertise in transactions within regulated industries such as utilities and media. Major projects handled by the team include acting for Italian utility ENEL on the acquisition of a 30% interest in leading pay-TV operator Telepiù. The firm also advised a leading film distribution company on proceedings initiated by the Italian competition authority in relation to alleged anti-competitive practices, and was involved on an EU cartel investigation in the steel tubes sector. **Clients:** GEC; Ericsson; Hoffmann La Roche; ENEL.

NCTM Studio Legale Associato (2 ptrs, 4 asscs) *"Sound technician"* **Alberto Toffoletto*** is the leading name at a department which specialises in contentious cases, often challenging decisions of the anti-trust authorities. The firm advised on an anti-competitive proceeding concerning the auditing profession, appearing before the anti-trust authorities on behalf of the National Association of Auditors. **Clients:** Leading Italian corporates.

Clarich, Libertini, Macaluso & Valli (4 ptrs, 4 asscs) *"Firmly on the map,"* the firm's anti-trust department has *"an especially impressive reputation in the telecoms sector."* **Mario Libertini*** is singled out as *"a well-regarded lawyer"* with *"a fine legal mind."* A professor of Industrial Law at the University of Rome Law School, he is a regular speaker at anti-trust conferences. The firm has acted for ENEL and Omnitel in anti-trust pro-

*See leaders' profiles on pages 423-430

ceedings, advised Infostrada and AIIP on an alleged anti-competitive case against Telecom Italia, and defended broadcasting giant RAI before the Communications Authority in proceedings relating to its alleged dominant position. **Clients:** ENEL; Wind; Omnitel; RAI; Medusa Film; Lega Nazionale Calcio; e.Biscom.

Rucellai & Raffaelli (1 ptr, 6 asscs) Although lacking the corporate strength of the market leaders, this small firm is acknowledged to perform *"a respectable amount of competition work,"* both on merger filings and Article 81 and 82 cases. **Enrico Raffaelli*** is the leading player here. Possessing *"a strong IP background,"* he *"has some good clients, speaks frequently at seminars"* and is *"involved in a number of cases."* The firm advised on Cattolica Assicurazioni's purchase of the Duomo Group and Le Mans Vita, valued at Lit 430 million, and notified the authorities of an agreement between producers of single-use cameras. **Clients:** Kodak; IBM; Johnson and Johnson.

Other Notable Practitioners **Guido Rossi** is *"a famous name"* and, according to one commentator, *"the best academic involved in this field."* **Francesco Denozza*** of Studio Legale Libonati Jaeger *"has studied anti-trust law for 20 years,"* and is *"regularly involved in major cases,"* while Turin-based **Aldo Frignani*** is another sole practitioner to be favourably received by the market.

Corporate/M&A

Bonelli-Erede-Pappalardo (9 ptrs) *"Probably the number one firm in Italy for M&A,"* it is considered to have grown successfully, and to have dealt with the foreign invasion better than its Italian counterparts. This is partly due to its *"old connections with the establishment in Italy."* Much of the firm's current success is attributed to **Sergio Erede***. Vice-president of Telecom Italia, and a universally acknowledged *"star,"* he is *"all the rage at the moment, antagonistic, brilliant, well-connected"* and possessed of *"a ruthless killer instinct."* Stylistically different, but almost as renowned, **Franco Bonelli*** is another of the firm's major players. *"More conciliatory than Erede,"* he hails from *"a respectable academic background,"* and is *"an icon of the legal community."* Other leading lawyers in the department include *"top-quality"* **Umberto Nicodano*** and corporate/capital markets experts **Roberto Cera*** and **Alberto Saravalle***. The firm has been particularly active on behalf of Telecom Italia, advising on the disposal of the company's majority interest in Sirti and Italtel. Retained by a number of Italian blue-chips, the corporate team also represented Seat Pagine Gialle on its acquisition of TDL Infomedia for £308 million, and acted for Prada and LVMH on the acquisition of a majority interest in the Fendi Group. **Clients:** Advent International; Alitalia; Armani; ENEL; JP Morgan; Telecom Italia; TIM; Prada; Seat Pagine Gialle.

Chiomenti Studio Legale (6 ptrs, 15 asscs) *"Traditionally first-class,"* the firm has a reputation for *"aloofness and self-sufficiency,"* but has nonetheless been linked with a number of overseas suitors in its quest for an international alliance. Particularly noted for its work in telecoms, the group has conducted numerous transactions for investment banks and other financial institutions. The corporate team is generally recognised to contain some *"extraordinarily capable people."* **Michele Carpinelli*** *"does a unique blend of M&A and tax,"* and is *"a terrific structurer of deals"* with *"a huge client base."* **Francesco Ago*** has a versatile reputation for corporate and banking work, while **Francesco Tedeschini*** and **Carlo Croff*** also maintain their share of market approval. The group advised on the sale of 49% of ACEA Telefonica from ACEA to Telefonica InterContinental, a deal valued at around Lit 120 billion, and assisted TIM on the conversion of its savings shares into ordinary shares, a transaction worth €10 billion. Other work includes advising JP Morgan in connection with the privatisation and disposal by the Milan Municipality of Centrale del Latte di Milano to Granarolo, and acting for Chase Manhattan and Morgan Stanley International on the SEAT/Tin.it merger. Also advised Acqua Italia on the acquisition of the entire share capital of Acquedotto De Ferrari and Acquedotto Nicolay, a Lit 420 billion deal, and acted for AEM in connection with the sale by ENEL of the power grid of the municipality of Milan. **Clients:** Acqua Italia; ACEA Telefonica; AEM; Atlanet; Banca Antoniana Popolare Veneta; BNP Paribas; JP Morgan; Mediaset.

Gianni Origoni & Partners (12 ptrs, 90 asscs) *"Strongly challenging for the number one spot,"* the firm has prospered since its absorption into the Alliance, and is said to be *"particularly strong in Rome."* An impressive client base includes domestic and international corporates and a strong portfolio of financial institutions. **Francesco Gianni*** is still the key figure at the firm. His *"considerable expertise"* was frequently cited by the market as a reason for the firm's success. **Alberto Giampieri*** is also an active and respected practitioner. Major transactional activities of the year include acting on the merger between Seat and TIN.it, advising on the public sale of IRI's majority stake in Finmeccanica, assisting on Tiscali's bid for WOL and acting on the privatisation of Aeroporti di Roma. **Clients:** Philip Morris; Omnitel; Rai; Finnmeccanica; Deutschepost; Crédit Local de France; Lazard Brothers.

Grimaldi Clifford Chance (3 ptrs, 35 asscs) Active and important firm which has *"set the trend for mergers between English and Italian firms"* and possesses *"a superb reputation in the finance areas."* **Vittorio Grimaldi*** *("a super lawyer") "stands out for financial work"* and has been *"in the game a long time."* He is given much of the credit for the firm's continued progress. A corporate team with depth also includes **Roberto Cappelli*** *("absolutely outstanding,")* who receives rave reviews from clients, **Luigi Chessa*** *("very reasonable to deal with")* and **Nick Wrigley***, who has just been appointed head of Clifford Chance's European equity practice but maintains his transactional involvement. The firm has advised on a number of takeovers, including BPL's bid for the Banca Popolare di Crema. It has also acted on ERG Petroli's acquisition of around 200 petrol stations, and assisted on MPS' acquisition of 51% of Banca di Salento. Substantial IPO and private equity transactions have also been important elements of the caseload. The firm acted on Dresdner Kleinwort Benson's acquisition of a 46% stake in Sinterim, a leading Italian employment agency. **Clients:** Cantagirone; Ferretti; Ibiscom; Inet.

BBLP Pavia e Ansaldo (5 ptrs, 25 asscs) *"Undergoing a period of transition at the moment,"* but the firm is still a respected M&A force that *"gets a good amount of business"* and is particularly strong in Milan. A number of partner departures has cast a shadow over the firm however, and the BBLP alliance has failed to convince the market. The team's client base nevertheless includes leading Italian corporates and a range of international financial institutions. The firm has retained the services of **Marcello Agnoli***, **Maurizio Bernardi*** and **Roberto Zanchi***, all highly respected in the local market. Key transactions have included the privatisation of the Aeroporti di Roma, the acquisition and financing of Italtel, and a number of private equity deals, among them B&S Electra's commitment of €9 million in start-up finance to Invesmart, an asset management firm. Also acted on FinTech's acquisition of a 22.5% stake in Terasystem and UBS Capital's commitment of around €100 million in replacement capital to Campari, in return for an undisclosed minority stake. **Clients:** San Paolo-IMI; Parmalat; BNP Paribas; UBS; ABN AMRO; Walt Disney; Universal Studios; Italian Private Equity Fund; Lazard.

ITALY Leading firms (Corporate/Mergers & Acquisitions)	
1	Bonelli-Erede-Pappalardo
2	Chiomenti Studio Legale
	Gianni Origoni & Partners
	Grimaldi Clifford Chance
3	BBLP Pavia e Ansaldo
	Brosio, Casati e Associati (in association with Allen & Overy)
	Freshfields Bruckhaus Deringer
4	Giliberti & Associati
	Grande Stevens & Pedersoli
	NCTM Studio Legale Associato
	Simmons & Simmons & Grippo
	Studio Legale Ughi e Nunziante
5	Baker & McKenzie
	Studio Legale Carnelutti
	Macchi di Cellere e Gangemi
	Studio Legale Tonucci

Firms are listed alphabetically in each band.

Leading individuals (Corporate/Mergers & Acquisitions)		
★	**EREDE Sergio** *Bonelli-Erede-Pappalardo*	
1	**CARPINELLI Michele** *Chiomenti Studio Legale*	**GIANNI Francesco** *Gianni Origoni & Partners*
2	**BONELLI Franco** *Bonelli-Erede-Pappalardo*	**CASATI Roberto** *Brosio, Casati*
	GRIMALDI Vittorio *Grimaldi Clifford Chance*	**NICODANO Umberto** *Bonelli-Erede-Pappalardo*
	ROSSI Guido *Studio Rossi*	
3	**AGNOLI Marcello** *BBLP Pavia e Ansaldo*	**AGO Francesco** *Chiomenti Studio Legale*
	BASTIANINI Marino *Carnelutti Studio Legale*	**BRESCIA Marco** *Studio Legale Ughi e Nunziante*
	CAPPELLI Roberto *Grimaldi Clifford Chance*	**CROFF Carlo** *Chiomenti Studio Legale*
	DANUSSO Massimiliano *Brosio, Casati*	**GILIBERTI Enrico** *Giliberti & Associati*
	GIOSCIA Marcello *Ughi e Nunziante*	**GRANDE STEVENS Franzo** *Grande Stevens-Pedersoli*
	GRIPPO Eugenio *Simmons & Simmons & Grippo*	**MACCHI DI CELLERE Luigi** *Macchi di Cellere e Gangemi*
	MONTIRONI Paolo *NCTM*	**NEGRI-CLEMENTI Gianfranco** *NCTM*
	NUNZIANTE Gianni *Ughi e Nunziante*	**PAPPALETTERA Carlo** *Giliberti & Associati*
	PEDERSOLI Alessandro *Grande Stevens-Pedersoli*	**TRISCORNIA Alessandro** *Giliberti & Associati*
4	**ARNABOLDI Luca** *Carnelutti Studio Legale*	**BASTIANINI Nicolo** *Carnelutti Studio Legale*
	BERGER Julian *Linklaters*	**BERNARDI Maurizio** *BBLP Pavia e Ansaldo*
	BREMBATI Fabio *Baker & McKenzie*	**CERA Roberto** *Bonelli-Erede-Pappalardo*
	CHESSA Luigi *Grimaldi Clifford Chance*	**GIAMPIERI Alberto** *Gianni Origoni & Partners*
	GRANDI Giorgio *Carnelutti Studio Legale*	**LEGA Giovanni** *Freshfields Bruckhaus Deringer*
	McFADDEN Laurie *Freshfields Bruckhaus*	**NOBILI Rafaele** *Studio Biscozzi Nobili*
	SARAVALLE Alberto *Bonelli-Erede-Pappalardo*	**TEDESCHINI Francesco** *Chiomenti Studio Legale*
	TONUCCI Mario *Studio Legale Tonucci*	**WRIGLEY Nicholas** *Grimaldi Clifford Chance*
	ZANCHI Roberto *BBLP Pavia e Ansaldo*	

Individuals are listed alphabetically in each band.

Brosio, Casati e Associati (in association with Allen & Overy) (14 ptrs) *"A quality firm, every bit as good since the merger,"* which generally advises foreign investors in Italy looking to expand and restructure their business. Areas of expertise include telecoms and IT, military equipment and energy. The corporate team has acknowledged expertise in advising on privatisations. In Milan, the firm is headed by **Roberto Casati***, *"a tough but fair negotiator,"* while **Massimiliano Danusso***, a corporate finance lawyer with a tax background, is the principal figure in Rome. The team advised Tiscali on its integration with World Online, acted for helicopter builder Agusta on its proposed merger with GKN Westland Helicopters, and represented Mobil Oil Italiana on a number of major transactions, including its acquisition of Lasmo Mineraria Sud and the recent Mobil-Exxon merger. Also advised Fresenius on the acquisition of the entire capital of SIFRA, and on the subsequent divestiture of the subsidiary IPRA. **Clients:** Mobil Oil Italiana; WPP Group plc; Browing-Ferris Industries Inc; CARNAUDMETALBOX Group; TI Group plc.

Freshfields Bruckhaus Deringer (8 ptrs, 45 asscs) *"Capable of shifting a lot of work,"* this *"fully integrated business"* is said to *"produce a great product,"* and is considered *"a serious threat"* by market leaders. Big-ticket M&A work for a host of blue-chip national and international names continues to be the corporate department's forte. Only a *"lack of serious Italian individuals"* is considered to stand in the way of further progress. **Giovanni Lega*** is an exception to this general rule and, together with the esteemed **Laurie McFadden***, retains a substantial market following.

Generally recognised to have strong investment bank connections, the firm has advised Generali on its unsolicited takeover offer for INA, and assisted Crédit Agricole on the Banca Intesa merger. The team also represented General Motors on its strategic alliance with Fiat. Private acquisitions and disposals include advising Celestica on its acquisition of IBM's manufacturing operations in Italy, representing Airtours on the disposal of its 50% stake in Costa Crociere, and acting for ENEL on its proposed acquisition of a 30% stake in Telepiù. **Clients:** General Motors; Hewlett-Packard; ENEL; Marconi; BNP; Rolls Royce; UBS Warburg.

Giliberti & Associati (15-20 lawyers) Despite its demerger from the former Biscozzi Giliberti Nobili, this is regarded as *"a fine young boutique,"* with *"a specialisation in M&A"* and a key relationship with Italian banking giant Mediobanca. The team's reputation rests with *"three excellent international lawyers."* **Enrico Giliberti*** has vast experience, and is supported by the equally respected **Carlo Pappalettera*** and **Alessandro Triscornia***. The firm advised on the privatisation of Rome airport, represented the banks on the financing of the bid launched by Milano Central for Unim, and acted for Compart on its bid for Montedison. **Clients:** Mediobanca; Compart.

Grande Stevens & Pedersoli (8 ptrs, 16 asscs) Renowned for its relationship with the Fiat Group, this *"excellent firm,"* the result of a merger between two small, traditional players, is considered to be *"growing and heading in the right direction."* Heavily involved in the automobile industry, the firm has advised on a number of IPOs and M&A transactions over the past year. The *"classy"* **Franzo Grande Stevens*** *"has had*

*See leaders' profiles on pages 423-430

an enormous impact" on the firm, while **Alessandro Pedersoli*** is *"a serious lawyer"* who commands universal respect. In addition to advising on the bulk of the Fiat Group's transactions, the team advised on the IPO of Autogrille. **Clients:** Fiat Group.

NCTM Studio Legale Associato (6 ptrs, 25 asscs) In spite of the failure of its association with UK firm Ashurst Morris Crisp, the firm is a respected and expanding domestic player, with offices in Rome, Milan and Verona, to be joined by one in Vicenza. Known for its privatisation and private equity expertise, the corporate team has developed a reputation in the technology sectors, advising I.Net on its IPO on the Italian Nuovo Mercato, and acting for Arca Investment Funds on an e-offering of financial instruments. **Gianfranco Negri-Clementi*** is *"one of the old guard, but still one of the best,"* while **Paolo Montironi***, a private equity and M&A specialist, also receives widespread approval. This year, the firm has been involved in the global offering of the shares of Aeroporti di Roma, the second offering of the shares of Autostrade, and the privatisation of the Istituto Bancario San Paulo. It also advised TDL Infomedia on its sale to Seat Pagine Gialle for £308 million. Private equity work has included advising on Barclays Private Equity's investment of an undisclosed amount of development capital in Bluvacanze in return for a 42% stake in the company. **Clients:** UniCredito Italiano; NatWest Equity Partners; JP Morgan; British Telecom; Riva; TDL Infomedia.

Simmons & Simmons & Grippo (6 ptrs, 52 asscs) *"Increasingly visible,"* the firm is now *"a considerable presence"* in the market, advising Italian companies from a wide variety of industries on their corporate interests. **Eugenio Grippo***, *"a good name"* according to our research, heads a department with a particular specialisation in telecoms work. The firm has offered extensive advice to Telespazio, a subsidiary of the Telecom Italia Group, including advising several of its affiliated companies, such as Damos and Tiscom, on developing and commercialising satellite telecommunications services in Latin America. The team also acted on the leveraged buy-out of Finfaber, and advised on Interbanca SpA and private equity vehicle Interbanca Investimenti's buy-out of Pramak, a Siena-based manufacturer. **Clients:** Telespazio; Stet International; Mediobanca.

Studio Legale Ughi e Nunziante (10-15 lawyers) *"One of the top two firms during the 70s and 80s,"* and it still retains some *"respectable and important clients,"* but has lost the profile of its glory years. Nevertheless, *"the brand remains good,"* and the corporate team is especially active in the energy, telecoms and banking sectors. **Gianni Nunziante*** is a popular and respected practitioner, **Marco Brescia*** *"will always do a deal well,"* and **Marcello Gioscia*** is *"an old tiger, whom you should never underestimate."* The firm represented JP Morgan on a substantial transaction in the new economy sector, acted for the Soros Group on a real estate acquisition, and advised Enel on the second tranche of its privatisation. **Clients:** General Electric; Tiscali Andala; JP Morgan; BBVA; Enel; Soros Group.

Baker & McKenzie (4 ptrs, 25 asscs) Possessing a *"good M&A practice in Milan,"* and *"a solid involvement in general corporate activity,"* the firm *"continues its steady course."* Around half of the corporate department's work comes in the telecoms industry, and the firm advises on both M&A and IPOs. Complex venture capital transactions are another area of expertise. **Fabio Brembati*** is, according to a number of peers and clients questioned, *"a fine lawyer"* with *"a productive and aggressive telecoms-focused practice."* **Clients:** Alitalia.

Carnelutti Studio Legalė The firm *"has a name, a tradition and good connections with the establishment,"* as well as a new office in Milan, but is still felt to lack the cohesion of some of its principal rivals. Despite this, the market acknowledges *"a consistent level of quality"* and a corporate team of *"surprising depth."* **Marino Bastianini***, **Giorgio Grandi*** and **Luca Arnaboldi*** are all respected names in the profession, while **Nicolo Bastianini*** has a great reputation in the communications sector. This year, he advised on the acquisition by NewsCorp International of a shareholding in the Italian Pay TV Stream, and the acquisition of the Italian Football League broadcasting rights. The firm also acted on the sale of Moto Guzzi to Aprilia, and the IPO and listing on the Nuovo Mercato of Direct.it, Postalmarket, Netfraternity, Cairo Communications, and Freedomland ITN. **Clients:** Moto Guzzi; San Paulo IMI; Netfraternity; Cairo Communications.

Macchi di Cellere e Gangemi (7 ptrs, 30 asscs) The firm's corporate team is felt to benefit from the support of its highly rated tax group, and advises domestic, European and American clients both from traditional industries and the new economy. **Luigi Macchi di Cellere*** is *"an excellent lawyer"* and *"a reasonable person,"* who sits on the board of a number of leading Italian companies. Cross-border M&A and private equity deals are the team's specialities. **Clients:** BTicino; Legrand; Computer Sciences Corporation; Deutsche Post; Equifax Inc; Kohlberg Kravis Roberts; MCI WorldCom; Nortek Inc; Pfizer; Rohm & Haas Company.

Studio Legale Tonucci (10 ptrs, 30 asscs) Possessing *"good relations at a local level,"* the firm now has offices in Rome and Milan, as well as overseas outposts in New York, Paris and Tirana. The team has strong links with the Italian Treasury, and has assisted it on the privatisations of Telecom Italia and ENAV. Niche expertise in the high-tech sector was highlighted by advice on the IPO of TAS (an Italian software house), and representing Integra, a French IT company, on the acquisition of two Italian companies. **Mario Tonucci***, a former partner of Gianni Origoni, is *"well-versed in litigation, administrative and corporate law,"* and an *"indefatigable publicist"* for the firm. The corporate department advised Benckiser on the sale of the Italian subsidiary of its oleochemical division. **Clients:** Italian Treasury; TAS; Integra; Benckiser; World Bank.

Other Notable Practitioners Following his departure from Simmons & Simmons, the *"extremely able"* **Julian Berger*** has moved to Linklaters, and is operating from Gianni Origoni's Milan office, advising on cross-border transactions for increasingly acquisitive Italian corporates. Sole practitioner **Guido Rossi*** is *"an absolutely unbeatable reference for corporate law."* Dubbed *"Mr Corporate Law"* by one commentator, *"when there is a significant, complex case, he comes in to sort it out."* A professor of law at L Bocconi University in Milan, *"he knows all the corporate models,"* and advised on the privatisation of the Banca S Paulo di Torino. The *"professorial"* **Rafaele Nobili*** of Studio Biscozzi Nobili is *"a poised, effective"* corporate lawyer, who has just split from Biscozzi Giliberti Nobili to strike out on his own.

Project Finance

ITALY Leading firms (Project Finance)
1 Brosio, Casati e Associati (in association with Allen & Overy)
Grimaldi Clifford Chance
2 Chiomenti Studio Legale
Gianni Origoni & Partners
Macchi di Cellere e Gangemi
3 Freshfields Bruckhaus Deringer

Firms are listed alphabetically in each band.

Leading individuals (Project Finance)
1 **NOVELLI Francesco** *Grimaldi Clifford Chance*
TAYLOR Michael *Norton Rose*
VIGLIANO Franco *Brosio, Casati e Associati*
2 **VISCO Claudio** *Macchi di Cellere e Gangemi*
3 **CASATI Roberto** *Brosio, Casati e Associati*
ESPOSITO Paolo *Brosio, Casati e Associati*
INSTANCE Mark *Grimaldi Clifford Chance*
NOVO Massimo *Grimaldi Clifford Chance*

Individuals are listed alphabetically in each band.

Brosio, Casati e Associati (in association with Allen & Overy) (2 ptrs, 7 asscs) *"One of the main firms out there,"* with a particularly vigorous energy and telecommunications projects practice. Through its Rome office, the firm is especially active in Albania, recently acting on a project financing for the construction of a bottling plant there. **Roberto Casati*** and **Paolo Esposito*** are two of the firm's main specialists in this area. They have both been active on a number of waste-to-energy projects in Southern Italy, and a pair of integrated gasification combined cycle power station project financings in Sicily and on the mainland. In a notable recent coup, the firm acquired the services of **Franco Vigliano*** from rival firm Chiomenti Studio Legale, thereby gaining a lawyer described by some as *"head and shoulders above any other Italian"* for project finance work. The firm advised a global debt markets investment banking business on its bid to arrange the financing for a waste water project in Milan. It also acted for a large government-owned bank on the financing for a wind power project in Southern Italy. **Clients:** Barclays Capital; Greenwich NatWest; Riva Wind Power; Sarlux; ACIES (Gruppo Busi).

Grimaldi Clifford Chance (4 ptrs, 10 asscs) *"A major competitor,"* with both Italian and English wings of the firm said to contribute *"real expertise."* Active on behalf of lenders and sponsors, the firm has assisted on energy, iron and steel, and telecoms projects. A strong team includes **Francesco Novelli***, *"a senior lawyer with enormous experience in the field,"* **Massimo Novo*** and **Mark Instance***. The firm advised on the construction of the largest project-financed wind farm in the world, acted for the arrangers on the financing of the 180 MW power plant to be developed by ISE in Piombino, and represented the sponsors of a waste to energy plant in Trezzo, northern Italy. Overseas, the group acted for Danieli, a leading Italian steel producer, on its involvement in a $740 million hot rolled coil complex at Adabiya, Egypt. **Clients:** Greenwich NatWest; Falck; Ogden; Danieli.

Chiomenti Studio Legale (1 ptr, 5 asscs) Active predominantly from its Milan office, the firm can also call on the expertise of partners in London and Rome. The recent loss of Franco Vigliano to Brosio Casati/Allen & Overy has dealt the group a severe blow, though. Nevertheless, the firm has been involved in a number of high-profile projects in the energy sector. It advised on a waste to energy project, where the arranger was the Kamine Group, and acted on the completion of a thermos-valorisation plant in Rovato. **Clients:** Lone Star Fund.

Gianni Origoni & Partners (4 ptrs, 10 asscs) *"Involved in a significant way,"* especially on behalf of lenders, the firm's link with the Alliance is considered to have enhanced its project finance offering. Energy is a key area of expertise. Major deals of the year include acting for Enron in a joint venture development for wind power projects, and representing the arranger on a €400 million project for the construction of a car manufacturing plant. The firm also represented Kamine in a waste-to-energy project development and financing. **Clients:** Enron; Kamine.

Macchi di Cellere e Gangemi (2 ptrs, 8 asscs) **Claudio Visco***, *"a fine lawyer with a great reputation,"* heads a department that has assisted sponsors and banks on several major energy and waste projects. The firm represented the sponsors in connection with the financing of two co-generation plants and on the first waste-to-energy plant to be financed in Italy. The group also has expertise in structured financing for energy, transport and infrastructure projects. **Clients:** GE Capital.

Freshfields Bruckhaus Deringer (2 ptrs, 5 asscs) An increasing force on projects in Italy, the firm has advised sponsors and lenders on energy and telecoms projects. It advised ENEL on the sale and development of some of its power plants, and acted for AIG Europe on the project financing of a military academy in Bari. The firm's telecoms expertise was exemplified by its advice to Wind on the €2.4 billion financing of its fixed and mobile network. Other activities include acting for Rabobank, Hypovereinsbank and ABN AMRO in connection with the financing of hospital projects in Naples and Trento. **Clients:** ENEL; Rabobank; ABM AMRO; Wind; Hutchison Telecoms.

Other Notable Practitioner Michael Taylor* has just moved to Italy to head up Norton Rose's new Milan office. He brings with him a superb project finance reputation, notably in the energy sector.

*See leaders' profiles on pages 423-430

Tax

ITALY Leading firms (Tax)	
1	Maisto e Associati
	Studio Tremonti
2	Di Tanno e Associati
	Macchi di Cellere e Gangemi
3	Adonnino Ascoli & Cavasola Scamoni
	Studio Biscozzi Nobili
	Chiomenti Studio Legale
	Studio Uckmar Magnani Marongiu
4	Baker & McKenzie
	Freshfields Bruckhaus Deringer
	Haarmann, Hemmelrath & Partner
	Studio Legale Tributario F Gallo e Associati

Firms are listed alphabetically in each band.

Leading individuals (Tax)	
1	**GANGEMI Bruno** *Macchi di Cellere e Gangemi*
	MAISTO Guglielmo *Maisto e Associati*
	TREMONTI Giulio *Studio Tremonti*
2	**ADONNINO Pietro** *Adonnino Ascoli & Cavasola*
	BISCOZZI Luigi *Studio Biscozzi Nobili*
	CARPINELLI Michele *Chiomenti*
	DI TANNO Tommaso *Di Tanno e Associati*
	FANTOZZI Augusto *Fantozzi e Associati*
	UCKMAR Victor *Studio Uckmar Magnani*
3	**GALLO Francesco** *Tributario F Gallo*
	MANGANELLI Andrea *Haarmann, Hemmelrath*
	MANZITTI Andrea *Maisto e Associati*
	PATERNOLLO Renato *Chiomenti*
	PICCARDI Lorenzo *Studio Tremonti*
	VITALI Enrico *Studio Tremonti*
4	**DANUSSO Massimiliano** *Brosio, Casati*
	MICHELUTTI Riccardo *Maisto e Associati*
	RITTATORE VONWILLER Andrea *Carnelutti*
	ROMAGNOLI Dario *Studio Tremonti*
	VECCHIO Cesare *Freshfields Bruckhaus Deringer*
	ZULLI Claudio *– Studio Tributario*

Individuals are listed alphabetically in each band.

Maisto e Associati (3 ptrs, 17 asscs) *"One of the most important fiscal law firms in Italy," "frequently present on big transactions,"* and staffed by a mix of lawyers and accountants who are considered by clients *"a pleasure to work with."* The firm is widely perceived to be *"active internationally."* This year, it was involved in the structuring of four venture capital funds, managed by Italian and foreign leading banks. **Guglielmo Maisto*** (*"one of the best international tax lawyers in Italy"*) is a member of the board of statutory auditors of Omnitel, the leading mobile telecom operator controlled by Vodafone Airtouch. He heads up a practice with a particular expertise in telecoms, and advised the largest telecom company in Italy on the acquisition of the major telephone directory provider. Other notable practitioners include *"top quality"* **Andrea Manzitti***, who was appointed advisor to the Italian Ministry of Treasury for tax matters, and the *"promising"* **Riccardo Michelutti***. The firm was retained by a large Italian car manufacturer for a major joint venture with a US car manufacturer. **Clients:** Domestic and international blue-chips.

Studio Tremonti (6 ptrs, 18 asscs) A *"truly global"* firm, generally acknowledged to be *"right at the top"* for its tax advice on behalf of a powerful, domestic-led client base. Expert in the new economy, the firm has been involved in structuring IT and biotech companies such as Biosearch. Also present in the increasingly active real estate market, the firm advised US real estate investment funds on a number of transactions in Italy. Key practitioners at the firm include *"brilliant"* **Giulio Tremonti***, a former minister of finance, **Enrico Vitali***, *"rising star"* **Lorenzo Piccardi***, and the *"ever-present"* **Dario Romagnoli***. The firm has an unofficial relationship with Grimaldi Clifford Chance, and acts frequently with it on securities transactions. In addition, it has advised on tax aspects of the structuring of several venture capital funds. **Clients:** Convergenza; Biosearch.

Di Tanno e Associati (6 ptrs, 20 asscs) A boutique firm, with offices in Rome and Milan, which specialises in tax and the creation of collective investment vehicles. Noted by rivals for its *"excellent connections with newly privatised companies,"* the firm is composed of lawyers and accountants, and is perceived to be *"a growing force."* **Tommaso di Tanno*** oversees operations. Unquestionably *"one of the top guys"* and *"a model professional,"* he has been tax manager at Arthur Andersen's tax department in Rome, tax advisor to the Minister of Finance, and a tax professor at numerous universities. The firm assisted Omnitel and Infostrada in implementing stock option plans this year, as well as advising Autogrill on the acquisition of Host Marriott Int, and assisting S Paolo-IMI in setting up its first closed-end investment fund. **Clients:** Alitalia; Assicurazioni Generali; Barclays Private Equity; Enel; Interbanca; Omnitel; S Paolo IMI; UBS Capital; Unicredit.

Macchi di Cellere e Gangemi (15 lawyers) **Bruno Gangemi*** (*"one of the best tax lawyers I've ever met,"*) heads up an *"outstanding"* tax practice, which is noted for its work on behalf of international clients. The group has been particularly active on tax planning, carrying out company structurings and restructurings for Japanese, US and French multi-nationals. Regularly called on to support the M&A department on due diligence and tax structuring work, the tax team has advised on the Deutsche Post acquisition. The team also assisted a large US retail company on the restructuring of its Italian distribution, advised a US fund on restructuring the shareholdings of its Italian investment, and acted for a large insurance company in devising tax planning for the launch of an innovative policy targeted at high-income earners. **Clients:** Foreign and local multi-nationals.

Adonnino Ascoli & Cavasola Scamoni (4 ptrs, 7 asscs) A recently merged firm with offices in Rome and Milan that frequently advises leading US companies and possesses an *"international reputation."* The department is staffed by lawyers and business consultants, and carries out domestic and international tax work, including tax restructuring and litigation. It is particularly commended for its M&A work, recently acting on the acquisition of a listed company.

Pietro Adonnino* is *"one of the most important tax lawyers in Italy,"* a former President of the International Fiscal Association, and professor of tax law at the University of Rome. **Clients:** Foreign and local multi-nationals.

Studio Biscozzi Nobili (18 lawyers) Recently split from its partnership with Giliberti, this is now a corporate boutique with a niche specialisation in tax. **Luigi Biscozzi***, seen by rivals as *"a great professional,"* heads up the department. The firm's caseload has included the tax aspects of M&A transactions, due diligence reports related to operations of purchase and sale of shareholdings, the privatisation of state companies, international tax plannng and company reorganisations. **Clients:** Financial and industrial companies.

Chiomenti Studio Legale (3 ptrs, 7 asscs) *"Increasingly interested in tax,"* the firm's Rome, Milan and London offices work frequently on cross-border transactions. Much work is also done on securitisations and financial transactions, with the firm's powerful M&A and banking departments providing a steady stream of work. Clients include major investment banks and other financial institutions. Big hitters here include **Michele Carpinelli***, a *"smart guy,"* who

*See leaders' profiles on pages 423-430

is renowned for his mixed tax and corporate practice, and **Renato Paternollo***, an *"aggressive, high-level lawyer,"* with *"particular expertise in financial products."* The firm is currently involved in the corporate and tax issues relating to an investment bank following a merger between three separate entities. **Clients:** Goldman Sachs; Citibank; Morgan Stanley Dean Witter; Chase.

Studio Uckmar Magnani Marongiu (3 ptrs) Founded in 1920, the firm possesses offices in Genoa and Milan. Respected by its rivals for its *"strength in domestic transactions,"* the firm is *"strong on fiscal litigation,"* and heavily involved in privatisation consultancy work. Clients include primary companies that are quoted on the major stock exchanges. **Victor Uckmar*** again received high praise from the market. **Clients:** Fiat; Eni; Bank of Rome.

Baker & McKenzie (1 ptr, 2 asscs) Regarded by clients as a *"small, energetic department,"* its activity revolves around three principal areas: tax planning and restructuring for Italian clients with international aspirations; consultation work, involving giving second opinions to international clients with regard to more sophisticated tax planning structures; and general international tax planning advice. In the latter category, the firm has just completed the restructuring of two major groups, the result of a year-long operation. **Clients:** Telecom Italia.

Freshfields Bruckhaus Deringer (6 lawyers) A small tax department largely involved in supporting the corporate group, which focuses on offering advice on M&A, finance structured transactions, asset management and hybrid financial instruments. **Cesare Vecchio*** is the stand-out practitioner here. Primarily a securities specialist, he acquired tax expertise while working at the tax boutique Tremonti. The department advised Goldman Sachs/Westmount on the acquisition of the Italian Agip Hotels business, and the Orion fund on the cross-border corporate structure for real estate acquisitions. It also represented Deutsche Bank on the corporate structure for a joint venture with SEI (ENEL), and Merrill Lynch/Fortress on the tax structuring of the securitisation of non-performing mortgage loans. **Clients:** Goldman Sachs; Deutsche Bank; Merrill Lynch; ABN AMRO; ENEL; Hewlett-Packard.

Haarmann, Hemmelrath & Partner (1 ptr, 14 asscs) An international partnership of lawyers, accountants and tax advisors, which assists industrial, commercial and service-providing organisations, including banks and insurance companies. The typical caseload is divided between tax structuring work, particularly for funds investing in Italy, advising Italian multinationals on international tax planning, M&A-related work deriving from foreign groups investing in Italy, and advising Italian companies on corporate income tax. **Andrea Manganelli*** (on the management committee of the Italian branch of the International Fiscal Association) received high praise from peers. Major work this year includes advising on the Vodafone-Mannesmann deal, the acquisition of a major airport, and the setting up of private equity funds for two big UK investors. The firm also follows various large multi-national banks based in Holland, the UK and the USA. **Clients:** Italian multi-nationals; domestic and foreign banks.

Studio Legale Tributario F Gallo e Associati (4 ptrs, 12 asscs) *"Important"* tax boutique with a notable reputation for tax litigation, and offices in Rome and Milan. **Franco Gallo***, rated *"an excellent tax lawyer"* by both peers and clients, worked on the tax aspects of the Telecom Italia/Olivetti deal. About half the firm's workload consists of tax litigation cases for large companies, but it has also been involved in securitisation cases this year. Telecoms and energy are industries where the firm is acknowledged by competitors to have specific expertise. An impressive client base includes national and international industrial corporations, banks, insurance companies and other financial institutions. **Clients:** RAI; Olivetti; Telecom Italia Mobile.

Other Notable Practitioners **Augusto Fantozzi***, a former minister of finance, a tax professor and a famous name, has a small firm with offices in Rome and Milan. Peers respect his experience and versatility. **Massimiliano Danusso*** of Brosio Casati/Allen & Overy, **Andrea Rittatore Vonwiller*** of Carnelutti, and **Claudio Zulli*** of Studio Tributario e Societario were also recommended by the market for expertise which transcends that of their firms' tax departments.

Leaders' profiles – Italy

AARON, Max D.
Brosio, Casati e Associati (in association with Allen & Overy), Milan +39 02 290 491
Recommended in Banking & Finance

ADONNINO, Pietro
Adonnino Ascoli & Cavasola Scamoni, Rome +39 06 322 0662
Recommended in Tax

AGNOLI, Marcello
BBLP Pavia e Ansaldo, Milan +39 02 63381
Recommended in Corporate/M&A

AGO, Francesco
Chiomenti Studio Legale, Rome +39 06 809 701
Recommended in Banking & Finance, Corporate/M&A

ARNABOLDI, Luca
Carnelutti Studio Legale, Milan +39 02 655 851
Recommended in Corporate/M&A

AROSSA, Fabrizio
Freshfields Bruckhaus Deringer, Rome +39 06 695 331
fabrizio.arossa@freshfields.com
Recommended in Competition/Anti-trust
Specialisation: Specialises in competition/regulatory and corporate (transactional and contentious) matters, with a particular emphasis on M&A transactions in regulated industries including energy, utility and media and assistance in antitrust investigations.

BASTIANINI, Marino
Carnelutti Studio Legale, Milan +39 02 655 851
Recommended in Corporate/M&A

BASTIANINI, Nicolo
Carnelutti Studio Legale, Milan +39 02 655 851
Recommended in Corporate/M&A

BELTRAMO, Susanna
Studio Legale Beltramo, Rome +39 06 481 7747
slblex@tin.it
Recommended in Banking & Finance
Specialisation: Principal areas of practice comprise banking and capital markets, corporate and corporate finance, financial regulation, corporate law, mergers and acquisitions, securities. Has worked on different financing transactions such as Region of Lazio US$ 1,500,000,000 Global Medium Term Note Program, Banca Agrileasing S.p.A. Euro 1,000,000,000 Euro Medium Note Progamme, Region of Liguria Euro 300,000,000 Euro Medium Term Note Programme, Cassa di Risparmio in Bologna S.p.A Euro 3,000,000,000 Debt Issuance Programme, Region of Sicily Euro 1,700,000,000 Global Medium Term Note Program, ENEL Euro 10,000,000,000 Facility Agreement and is currently involved in various securitisation transactions.
Prof. Memberships: Rome Bar.

Publications: Contributor to 'International Financial Law Review' and 'Corporate Finance'.
Career: Partner of *Studio Legale Ercole Graziadei* until 1993 and then partner of *Studio Legale Beltramo.*

BERGER, Julian
Linklaters (a member firm of Linklaters & Alliance), London +39 06 478 751
julian.berger@linklaters.com
Recommended in Corporate/M&A
Specialisation: Partner in the Corporate Department seconded to the Milan office of *Gianni Origoni & Partners.* Spearheads the firm's cross-border M&A practice. Represents, in particular, foreign corporations doing business in Italy as well as Italian companies involved in international transactions. Practice areas include M&A, international joint ventures, acquisition finance, venture capital, financial services and international securities offerings. Recent deals include acting for GKN Westland on its joint venture with the Agusta division of Finmeccanica, BTR plc (now Invensys) on its Italian acquisitions and disposals, Bass plc and Lloyds TSB.

BERNARDI, Maurizio
BBLP Pavia e Ansaldo, Milan +39 02 63381
Recommended in Corporate/M&A

BISCOZZI, Luigi
Studio Biscozzi Nobili, Milan +39 02 76 36931
Recommended in Tax

BONELLI, Franco
Bonelli-Erede-Pappalardo, Milan +39 02 771 131
Recommended in Corporate/M&A

BREMBATI, Fabio
Baker & McKenzie, Rome +39 06 328 38-1
fabio.m.brembati@bakernet.com
Recommended in Communications, Corporate/M&A
Specialisation: Main areas of work include information technology, telecommunications, broadcasting and relevant project financing as well as corporate acquisitions and joint ventures in general. Advises the main Italian telecommunications and cable TV companies in connection with international alliances and privatisations. Has spoken at various conferences and seminars focusing on telecoms and IT subjects.
Career: Qualified in 1980 (JD, University of Rome). LLM, at University of California, Berkeley in 1982. Worked in 1985-86 with IBM Italy legal department. Joined *Baker & McKenzie* in 1982, becoming a partner in 1990. Apprenticeship at the European Community in 1991. Professor of International Contracts at the Pontificia Universitas Lateranensis of Rome (1986-97). Bi-lingual Italian and French. Fluent English.
Personal: Born 1957. Lives in Rome and Milan, Italy.

BRESCIA, Marco
Studio Legale Ughi e Nunziante, Milan
+39 02 762 171
mgbrescia@unlaw.it
Recommended in Corporate/M&A
Specialisation: Main area of work is corporate law, principally mergers, acquisitions and privatisations. Has handled acquisitions of companies and undertakings of various types by Italian and overseas clients.
Prof. Memberships: Admitted to the Milan Bar in 1968; member of Committee G (business organisations) of IBA-Section on Business Law.
Career: Member of the firm since 1976. Author of various articles and contributions to books in the field of corporate law.
Personal: Law Degree from Genoa University 1962; MCJ from New York University, New York, 1974.

CAIAZZO, Rino
Studio Legale Ughi e Nunziante, Rome
+39 06 474 831
r.caiazzo@unlaw.it
Recommended in Communications, Competition/Anti-trust
Specialisation: Competition law and telecommunications.
Prof. Memberships: Admitted to the Rome Bar in 1981; Past Vice-Chairman of Committee C (antitrust and trade law); International Bar Association Section on Business Law.
Publications: Has published several articles on telecommunications law, antitrust law, banking, and financial law in various Italian and international magazines including: 'The New Italian Antitrust Law' (International Merger Law, 1991); 'International Mergers-the Antitrust Process-Chapter on Italy' (Sweet & Maxwell, 1995); 'TLC Legal and Regulatory Development in Italy' (Sweet & Maxwell, Computer and Telecommunications Law Review, 1996).
Career: Partner of the firm since 1991. Educated at the University of Rome (Doctor of Jurisprudence, 1981) and University of London, School of Economics and Political Science (Master of Law, LLM, 1986). Chairman of the Italian Alumni Association of the London School of Economics and Political Science.
Personal: Born in Rome, 7 April 1958.

CAPELLETTI, Fabio
Bonelli-Erede-Pappalardo, Milan +39 02 771 131
Recommended in Banking & Finance

CAPPELLI, Roberto
Grimaldi Clifford Chance, Milan +39 02 806 341
Recommended in Banking & Finance, Corporate/M&A

CARPINELLI, Michele
Chiomenti Studio Legale, Milan +39 02 721 571
Recommended in Banking & Finance, Corporate/M&A, Tax
Specialisation: Partner in corporate, banking and tax department. Main areas of work are general assistance in corporate matters, company laws, banking laws and regulations, M&A, tender offer and taxation of companies and corporate reorganisations.
Prof. Memberships: Albo degli Avvocati di Roma, Albo dei Dottori Commercialisti di Roma.
Career: Joined *Chiomenti Studio Legale* in 1971. Partner in 1979. Admitted to the bar and to the representation before the Supreme Courts.
Personal: Born 22 November 1948. Attended 'Università La Sapienza' in Rome, degree cum laude in 1971 in Economics, degree cum laude in Law in 1980. Lives in Rome.

CASATI, Roberto
Brosio, Casati e Associati (in association with Allen & Overy), Rome +39 06 684271
Recommended in Banking & Finance, Corporate/M&A, Project Finance

CASTELLANI, Enrico
Freshfields Bruckhaus Deringer, Milan
+39 02 625 301
enrico.castellani@freshfields.com
Recommended in Banking & Finance
Specialisation: Specialises in banking and financial law and capital markets (including securitisation and securities offerings), litigation and bankruptcy and rescheduling.

CERA, Roberto
Bonelli-Erede-Pappalardo, Milan +39 02 771 131
Recommended in Banking & Finance, Corporate/M&A

CHESSA, Luigi
Grimaldi Clifford Chance, Rome +39 06 844 651
Recommended in Banking & Finance, Corporate/M&A

CROFF, Carlo
Chiomenti Studio Legale, Milan +39 02 721 571
Recommended in Corporate/M&A
Specialisation: Mergers and acquisitions, corporate law.
Prof. Memberships: Admitted to practice law in Italy in 1982 and in New York in 1985.
Career: Worked at *Crowell & Moring,* Washington DC in 1982, and at *Debevoise & Plimpton* in New York from 1982 to 1984. Joined *Chiomenti Studio Legale* in 1984 and became a partner at the Milan office in 1989.
Personal: Born in Auronzo di Cadore (Belluno), Italy on 24 August 1955. Received a JD from the University of Padua in 1979, an LLB from Cambridge University in the UK in 1980, and an LLM from Harvard University in 1981.

CUGIA DI SANT'ORSOLA, Fabrizio
Studio Legale Tonucci, Rome +39 06 362 271
Recommended in Communications

D'ALBERTI, Silvia
Brosio, Casati e Associati (in association with Allen & Overy), Rome +39 06 684271
Recommended in Competition/Anti-trust

D'ANGELO, Davide
Brosio, Casati e Associati (in association with Allen & Overy), Rome +39 06 684271
Recommended in Communications

DALLA VEDOVA, Marco
Dalla Vedova, Rome +39 06 444 0821
Recommended in Communications

DANUSSO, Massimiliano
Brosio, Casati e Associati (in association with Allen & Overy), Rome +39 06 684271
Recommended in Banking & Finance, Corporate/M&A, Tax

DENOZZA, Francesco
Studio Legale Libonati Jaeger, Milan +39 02 762 3271
Recommended in Competition/Anti-trust

DI TANNO, Tommaso
Di Tanno e Associati, Rome +39 06 845 661
Recommended in Tax

EREDE, Sergio
Bonelli-Erede-Pappalardo, Milan +39 02 771 131
Recommended in Corporate/M&A

ESPOSITO, Paolo
Brosio, Casati e Associati (in association with Allen & Overy), Rome +39 06 684271
Recommended in Project Finance

FANTOZZI, Augusto
Fantozzi e Associati, Rome +39 06 4200 611 studio@fantozzieassociati.it
Recommended in Tax
Specialisation: Head of *Fantozzi & Associates*, one of the top Italian tax advisory law firms. Actively involved in domestic and international taxation, M&A and tax-structured finance, and works on behalf of several major domestic and multinational companies. Frequently consulted by government officials and representatives on various aspects of tax legislation, and frequently lectures at tax seminars and conferences.
Prof. Memberships: Has been the Vice President of the Higher Council of Finance, President of the National Association of Tax Collection Service Licensee, a member of the Council of State of the Vatican City State, as well as Chairman of the Scientific Committee of the International Fiscal Association. Currently, a Member of the Executive Committee of international magazines, such as EC Taxation, Tax Notes International and major Italian reviews.
Publications: Author of many publications on the subject of taxation, including several books.
Career: Professor of tax law for a long time at the University of Rome 'La Sapienza', now a Professor of tax law at the LUISS (Private University of Rome). Is an attorney at the Court of Cassation, and practises in Rome and Milan. In 1995, Minister of Finance in the government Dini, interim Budget Minister and Minister for the Coordination of EU policies. In 1996, became a member of the Chamber of Deputies. In the Prodi government, was appointed the Minister of Foreign Trade and is, at present, the Chairman of the Fifth Budget and Treasury Committee of the Chamber of Deputies.
Personal: Born in Rome, married with two daughters.

FIGARI, Alberta
Grimaldi Clifford Chance, Milan +39 02 806 341
Recommended in Banking & Finance

FRIGNANI, Aldo
Frignani e Associati, Turin +39 0116 604 257
Recommended in Competition/Anti-trust

GALLO, Francesco
Studio Legale Tributario F Gallo e Associati, Rome +39 063 600 1069
Recommended in Tax

GANGEMI, Bruno
Macchi di Cellere e Gangemi, Rome +39 06 362 141 b.gangemi@macchi-gangemi.com
Recommended in Tax
Specialisation: Senior partner in the tax department: main area of work is the domestic and international corporate tax laws, principally tax planning connected with corporate reorganisations, mergers and acquisitions. Assists Italian and foreign companies belonging to international groups; significant experience in tax litigation, especially on transfer pricing issues. Handled, inter alia, the Chevron spin-off, the international distributorships, spin-off and mergers of Pfizer, LeGrand SA acquisitions, structuring the stock option plans of major international companies, structuring the activities of a multinational real estate company, tax planning of securitisation projects, assisting US Fund in restructuring its Italian investments, Rohm & Haas reorganisation; acted for Ford, Hertz, Foster Wheeler and Cabot Corp regarding corporate tax and transfer pricing litigation; assisted Deutsche Telekom with proposed merger with Telecom Italia.
Prof. Memberships: Italian Bar Association, International Bar Association, International Fiscal Association, American Bar Association (International Associate).
Career: Law Degree University of Rome (La Sapienza); Assistant Professor at La Sapienza (1962/1966); admitted to Bar 1971; admitted to practice before the Court of Cassation; Scholarship of Fritz Thyssen Stiftung (University of Cologne and Bonn Institute 'Finanzen und Steuern'); Seminar on American Law at the Salzburg Seminar; founder with Luigi Macchi di Cellere of the Law Firm *Studio Legale Macchi di Cellere e Gangemi* (1986). Chairman of the IBA Tax Committee 1992-1996, International Fiscal Association (Member of the Permanent Scientific Committee and Secretary of the Italian Branch); Reporter at the Buenos Aires Congress, 1984; General Reporter at the Stockholm Congress, 1990; Discussion Leader at the Geneva Congress, 1996; Conféderation Fiscale Européenne (Chairman of the Technical Committee); Lectures at La Sapienza and at LUISS Guido Carli (Rome). Author of several articles on international tax issues.
Personal: Born 8 November, 1938; married and two sons; interests: tennis, bridge. Languages: English, French and German.

GHIO, Roberto
Chiomenti Studio Legale, Milan +39 02 721 571
Recommended in Banking & Finance
Specialisation: Securitisation and Structured Finance.
Prof. Memberships: Admitted to practise law in May 1986.
Career: Joined *Chiomenti* in 1992. Became a partner on January 1, 1999.

GIAMPIERI, Alberto
Gianni Origoni & Partners (A member firm of Linklaters & Alliance), Rome +39 06 478 751 AGiampieri@gop.it
Recommended in Banking & Finance, Corporate/M&A
Specialisation: Partner in the Rome office. His practice concentrates on M&A, corporate finance and structured finance. Has advised a number of multinational corporations and global financial institutions in connection with acquisitions, financing of acquisitions, and structured finance transactions. His practice covers the entire field of M&A, banking and finance, including structured finance. Has been involved in the acquisition of the second largest Italian telephone fixed operator as well as in some significant M&A financings.
Prof. Memberships: Admitted to the Italian Bar and member of the International Bar Association.
Publications: Author of several publications and lectured extensively to bar and other organisations in Europe on banking and finance and M&A topics.
Personal: Educated at the University of Rome law school, JD, Maxima Cum Laude (1986); City of London Polytechnic (1990); Yale University, Visiting Scholar (1991/1993).

GIANNI, Francesco
Gianni Origoni & Partners (A member firm of Linklaters & Alliance), Rome +39 06 478 751 FGianni@gop.it
Recommended in Banking & Finance, Corporate/M&A
Specialisation: Managing partner of *Gianni, Origoni & Partners* (residing in the Rome office). Has practiced abroad in New York and Chicago. Practice concentrates on M&A, Capital Markets, Competition Law, Joint Ventures and Structured Finance. Has advised a number of domestic and multinational corporations in significant acquisition transactions and relating to acquisition financing, as well as in take-overs of listed corporations. Has advised investment banks and companies in connection with IPO's and other stock exchange transactions. Current projects include, the privatisation of two state-owned companies and the acquisition of companies located in Italy and abroad.
Prof. Memberships: Admitted to the Italian, New York State, American, Inter-Pacific and International Bar Associations; European Society for Banking and Financial Law; Southwestern Legal Foundation (Advisory Board); American Foreign Law Association (Vice President, 1988-93); Italian Fulbright Association; American Society of International Law; Honorary member, Association of Fellows and Legal Scholars of the Center for International Legal Studies.
Publications: Author of various works, including books, magazines and journals and has given speeches on a worldwide basis on various subjects.
Career: Educated at the University of Rome law school, JD, Maxima Cum Laude (1973); Academy of International Law, The Hague (1975); University of London, King's College (LLM, 1976); University of Michigan Law School (LLM, 1977). Is Corresponding Editor of International Legal Materials.

GIARDA, Raffaele
Baker & McKenzie, Rome +39 06 328 38-1 raffaele.giarda@bakernet.com
Recommended in Communications
Specialisation: Partner in telecommunication department. Main areas of work include voice tele-

phony, mobile and personal communication services (including all legal aspects of public bids), interconnection negotiations and agreements, network provision and access, sale, leasing and acquisitions of alternative networks, satellite networks, and communications services, as well as outsourcing and Internet scenarios. Has handled mergers and acquisitions of companies and businesses by foreign corporate clients. On behalf of major new entrants and upon invitation of the Italian Ministry of Communications, has participated in public consultations organised by the Ministry in connection with the enactment of laws and regulations related to the Italian liberalisation process. Co-author of the Italian chapter of 'Telecommunication Laws in Europe' edited by Butterworths in 1998. Has spoken at various conferences and seminars both in Italy and abroad.
Prof. Memberships: Italian Bar; ANUIT (Associazione Nazionale Utenti Italiani di Telecomunicazione – National Association of Italian Telecommunications Users). Honorary member of ANFOV (Associazione per la convergenza nei servizi di communicazione – Association for the convergence of communications services).
Career: University of Rome JD 1989. Joined *Baker & McKenzie* in 1989. Qualified in 1992. New York University graduate (Master of Comparative Jurisprudence 1994). Became a partner in 1999.
Personal: Born 6 July 1966.

GILIBERTI, Enrico
Giliberti & Associati, Milan +39 02 7600 1585
Recommended in Corporate/M&A

GIOSCIA, Marcello
Studio Legale Ughi e Nunziante, Rome
+39 06 474 831
Recommended in Banking & Finance, Corporate/M&A
Specialisation: Has developed a corporate, M&A, banking and financial law practice. Senior member of the firm in the banking and capital markets area and is a legal advisor to Italian and international banks and investment banks. Current work includes security transactions, structured finance, banking and security regulation, derivatives, privatisation, joint ventures and M&A.
Prof. Memberships: Ex Co-Chairman of the Banking Law Committee of the section on business law of the International Bar Association (1990-1994); member of the arbitration panel of the American Arbitration Association of New York; member of the advisory board for the secured transactions project of the European Bank for Reconstruction and Development (London) liaison for the International Bar Association with UNITROIT.
Publications: Author of various articles and contributions to books in the field of banking and finance.
Career: Qualified in 1964. Member of *Studio Ughi e Nunziante* since its formation in 1968.
Personal: Degree in Law from University of Genoa, 1961; LLM from Columbia University Law School, New York, 1971.

GRANDE STEVENS, Franzo
Grande Stevens & Pedersoli, Milan +39 02 76 03 31
Recommended in Corporate/M&A

GRANDI, Giorgio
Carnelutti Studio Legale, Milan +39 02 655 851
Recommended in Corporate/M&A

GRASSANI, Stefano
BBLP Pavia e Ansaldo, Milan +39 02 63381
Recommended in Competition/Anti-trust

GRIMALDI, Vittorio
Grimaldi Clifford Chance, Rome +39 06 844 651
Recommended in Banking & Finance, Corporate/M&A

GRIPPO, Eugenio
Simmons & Simmons & Grippo, Rome
+39 06 80955 1
eugenio.grippo@simmons-simmons.com
Recommended in Corporate/M&A
Specialisation: Specialises in corporate and financial law (currently advising Enel with respect to the flotation of the second tranche of capital) as well as in 'on-line' services and trading law. Involved in a leading advisory role in Joint Venture Agreements (recently Finmeccanica-Augusta/GKN-Westland) and project financing (recently Nosedo Water Treatment for the Municipality of Milan) and has particular experience in the electricity liberalisation process and in the gas sector (experience in this field started in the early eighties, when advised SNAM in connection with the Algeri-Italy gas pipeline).
Prof. Memberships: Consiglio dell'Ordine degli Avvocati di Roma.
Career: Admitted to Rome Bar. 1972 – Qualified to act before the Supreme Court. (1991) – Partner in the Law Firm *Avv Ercole Graziadei* (1974/5). Co-founder of *Studio Graziadei, Associazione Professionale.* (1978). Founder of *Studio AW. E. Grippo* (1985). Senior partner of *Studio Grippo Associati e Simmons e Simmons* since 1993. Senior partner and founder of the Italian offices.
Personal: Married. Two children. Educated in classics at the Rome Liceo Giulio Cesare and in law at the Rome University La Sapienza.

GUARINO, Giuseppe
Studio Legale Guarino, Rome +39 06 687 3391
Recommended in Communications

INSTANCE, Mark
Grimaldi Clifford Chance, Milan +39 02 806 341
Recommended in Project Finance

KOSTKA, Carlo
Freshfields Bruckhaus Deringer, Milan
+39 02 625 301
carlo.kostka@freshfields.com
Recommended in Banking & Finance
Specialisation: Main practice areas are international securities offerings, both equity and debt, mergers and acquisitions and joint ventures (including as to US aspects).
Prof. Memberships: Admitted to the Bar of the State of New York in 1991.

LEGA, Giovanni
Freshfields Bruckhaus Deringer, Milan
+39 02 625 301
giovanni.lega@freshfields.com
Recommended in Corporate/M&A
Specialisation: Partner in the Corporate Group, specialising in M&A, joint ventures, international business law, corporate finance work and property.

LIBERTINI, Mario
Clarich, Libertini, Macaluso & Valli, Rome
+39 06 4782 3746
Recommended in Competition/Anti-trust

LODIGIANI, Francesca
BBLP Pavia e Ansaldo, Milan +39 02 63381
Recommended in Communications

LOMBARDO, Nino (Antonio)
Simmons & Simmons & Grippo, Milan
+39 02 7250 51
Recommended in Communications

MACALUSO, Fabio
Clarich, Libertini, Macaluso & Valli, Rome
+39 06 4782 3746
Recommended in Communications

MACCHI DI CELLERE, Luigi
Macchi di Cellere e Gangemi, Rome +39 02 763 281
(m) +39 335 628 6095
l.macchi@macchi-gangemi.com
Recommended in Corporate/M&A
Specialisation: Specialises in corporate governance, mergers and acquisitions, joint ventures and international transactions, also dealing with financial and antitrust matters. Major clients assisted during 2000 include BTicino S.p.A. and its French parent Legrand SA. Deutsche Post AG (the giant German corporation going private), Equifax Inc, Kohlberg Kravis Roberts (the world's largest leveraged buy-out specialist), MCI WorldCom, Nortek Inc., Pfizer Corporation. Has been involved as leading lawyer in over 10 acquisition transactions, for Italian, French, German and US clients, operating both in traditional sectors and in the new economy. At present sitting on the Board of major Italian corporations (eg: BTicino S.p.A., Ferfina S.p.A.).
Prof. Memberships: Rome Bar; Italian Arbitration Association; American Arbitration Association; International Bar Association; Union Internationale des Avocats; Inter-Pacific Bar Association; American Bar Association; International Law Association; American Society of International Law; American Foreign Law Association; Association of the Bar of the City of New York; American Bar Foundation; Southwestern Legal Foundation; Rome Bar.
Career: Jurisprudence Law (maxima cum laude), University of Rome (1961); Masters, University of Michigan Law School (1965). Foreign Legal Consultant, New York; (1980 - 1986); Established *Studio Legale Macchi di Cellere e Gangemi* (1986).

MACCHI DI CELLERE, Stefano
Macchi di Cellere e Gangemi, Milan
+39 02 763 281
s.macchi@macchi-gangemi.com
Recommended in Communications
Specialisation: Partner in the Corporate Department of the firm in Milan. Particular areas are telecommunications, media and industrial law, also with regard to EU and Italian anti-trust issues. Assisted in acquisitions, joint-ventures, commercial transactions and contractual matters with companies such as BellSouth, BTicino, ENEL, Melitta, Pfizer,

Turner Broadcasting, Vebacom, Vobis Microcomputer. Currently assists groups such as Metro and MCI WorldCom.
Prof. Memberships: Chairman of the Aerospace Committee of the Inter-Pacific Bar Association 1998-2000; Vice Chairman 1996-1998; International Bar Association (Communications Law Committee); American-Italian Law Association; Institute of Lawyers in Europe; Alumni Association of the Academy of American and International Law; Rome Bar; Milan Bar.
Publications: Contributed to the journal 'Legal Media Monitor and Global Law & Business'. Published the study 'Telecommunications – The Role of the Regulator in the European Union and in Italy'. Co-author of the EU Study Report on 'Legal and Liability Issues of Market Introduction of Telematics Applications for Transport', 1998. Co-author of the EU Study Report 'Legal and Consumer Aspects of Advanced Driver Assistance Systems', 2000.
Career: Started legal practice in Milan 1990. Trained in USA and practised in 1991 as foreign attorney with *Arent Fox Kintner Plotkin & Kahn* of Washington, DC.
Personal: Born in Rome 4 April 1963, married with three children. Law degree 1990 at the University of Rome. Courses of the Academy of American and International Law, at the International and Comparative Law Centre of the Southwestern Legal Foundation in Dallas,1990. Program on US law for foreign lawyers at the Georgetown University Law School, Washington, DC, 1991. Seminar on EC law at University of Rome, 1992.

MAISTO, Guglielmo
Maisto e Associati, Milan +39 02 776 931
g.maisto@maisto.it
Recommended in Tax
Specialisation: Partner in a firm specialising in Italian corporate tax law. Work includes international and domestic tax and business law. Advises on mergers and acquisitions, corporate restructuring and international taxation. Also frequently retained for tax litigation.
Prof. Memberships: The Law Society, American Bar Association, International Bar Association, Ordine degli Avvocati di Milano, Istituto de Fiscalidad Internacional, Union Internationale des Avocats and the International Fiscal Association.
Publications: Has authored, edited and contributed to numerous books and articles. Publications include 'Business Law Guide to Italy', (CCH, 1992) and 'Il transfer price nel diritto tributario italiano e comparato' (Cedam, 1985), 'La tassazione dei dividendi nei rapporti tra società madri e figlie nella Comunità Europea' (Giuffrè 1996). Also edited 'Tax Treatment of Cost Contribution Arrangements' (Kluwer 1988). Currently at work on a new book planned for 2001.
Career: Partner and Founder of *Maisto e Associati.* Professor of Tax Law at The Catholic University of Piacenza and previously Professor of Tax Law at Bocconi University for six years. Sits on the editorial boards of various Italian and foreign tax and legal journals. Has been General and National Reporter at congresses of the International Fiscal Association. Sits on numerous committees, including the OECD Business Industry Advisory Committee in Paris. Member of the Board of Directors of the American Chamber of Commerce in Italy and delegated member of the Board of Trustees of the International Bureau of Fiscal Documentation in Amsterdam. Has acted as consultant to the Ministry for European Community Affairs. Frequent speaker at conferences.
Personal: Born 13 September 1952. Graduated in law at the University of Genoa in 1976 (cum laude). Trained at the EEC commission, Directorate General IV in 1977. Received a Masters from the University of Amsterdam in 1978.

MANARA, Francesco
BBLP Pavia e Ansaldo, Milan +39 02 63381
Recommended in Banking & Finance

MANGANELLI, Andrea
Haarmann, Hemmelrath & Partner, Milan
+39 02 7 71 94 111
Andrea_Manganelli@hhp.de
Recommended in Tax
Specialisation: International Tax Law – Domestic Tax Law – M&A – Corporate reorganisations – Transfer Pricing – Corporate Law – Financial Law – Private Equity funds.
Prof. Memberships: Italian Tax Advisers' Association – Italian Tax Lawyers' Association – Certified Public Accountants' Association. Member of the Management Committee of the International Fiscal Association (Italian Branch). Member of the Management Committee of the Association of Ex-Alumni of the International Bureau of Fiscal Documentation. President of the Board of Statutory Auditors of many Italian companies, listed or not listed on the Stock Exchange.
Publications: Italian report on application of Tax Treaties at the 1998 Annual Conference of the International Fiscal Association. Many chapters and articles in Italian and International tax guides and tax magazines.
Career: 1990: Awarded 'Researcher of the year 1990' of the International Fiscal Association. 1991-1993: Research Associate – International Bureau of Fiscal Documentation. 1993-1997: Partner of *Studio Fantozzi & Associati*, Rome. 1998 to present: Partner of *Haarmann, Hemmelrath & Partner*, Milan. 1990 to present: Lecturer in Tax Law – University of Rome 'La Sapienza'.
Personal: Married, 1 daughter. Leisure interests: vineyard cultivation and wine production at countryside house in Tuscany. Collection and production of funky music such as the one first invented in the seventies.

MANZITTI, Andrea
Maisto e Associati, Milan +39 02 776 931
a.manzitti@tin.it
Recommended in Tax
Specialisation: A founding partner in a firm dealing in Italian corporate tax law, specialising in the international sector. Main area of practice is with banks and financial institutions. Works with structured finance and financial products. Involved in tax work related to capital market transactions as well as in mergers and acquisitions and group restructuring. In 1999, was retained in the largest takeover in Italy.
Prof. Memberships: Milan Bar Association, International Bar Association, American Bar Association, International Fiscal Association.
Publications: Has authored and contributed to many publications and is a regular speaker at tax seminars and conferences.
Career: Founding Partner of *Maisto e Associati.* Lecturer in International Taxation at the Business Post Graduate Programme of Bocconi University in Milan. Now a consultant on tax affairs to the Italian Treasury.
Personal: Born 24 June, 1961. Graduated in Law (cum laude) at Genoa University in 1985 and received Masters in Business Tax Law from Bocconi University the same year. Later studied International Contracts at Kings College, London.

McFADDEN, Laurie
Freshfields Bruckhaus Deringer, Milan
+39 02 625 301
laurie.mcfadden@freshfields.com
Recommended in Corporate/M&A
Specialisation: Main areas of practice are mergers and acquisitions, joint ventures and securities offerings. Has extensive experience of cross-border mergers and acquisitions (including considerable public takeover experience).

MEROLA, Massimo
Bonelli-Erede-Pappalardo, Milan +39 02 771 131
Recommended in Competition/Anti-trust

MICHELUTTI, Riccardo
Maisto e Associati, Milan +39 02 776 931
r.michelutti@maisto.it
Recommended in Tax
Specialisation: Senior associate in a firm dealing in Italian corporate tax law, specialising in the international sector. Main area of practice is with mergers and acquisitions, corporate restructurings and financial products.
Prof. Memberships: Milan Bar Association; Milan Chartered Accountants Association; International Fiscal Association.
Publications: Has authored and contributed to many publications and is a regular speaker at tax seminars and conferences.
Career: Spent two years in the tax department of Arthur Andersen, Milan. Joined *Maisto e Associati* in 1996. Currently in charge of the London office of *Maisto e Associati.*
Personal: Born 18 December, 1968. Graduated in Economics (cum laude) at Bocconi University, Milan in 1992. Masters in Corporate Tax Law at Bocconi University, Milan in 1993. Graduated in Law (cum laude) at Milan University in 1997. Speaks Italian, English and French.

MONTIRONI, Paolo
NCTM Studio Legale Associato, Milan
+39 02 541 641
p.montironi@nctm.it
Recommended in Corporate/M&A
Specialisation: Partner of *Negri-Clementi Toffoletto Montironi & Soci.* Main area of work is commercial and corporate law, M&A, private equity and acquisition finance. Involved in major acquisitions and privatisations, both domestic and international. Acted, amongst other things, on the merger of Credito Italiano with Cassa di Risparmio di Verona, Cassa di

I

Risparmio di Torino and Cassamarca, one of the biggest transaction in the banking sector in Italy; acted on the acquisition of Cassa di Risparmio di Trento e Rovereto. Acted in the interest of the buyer on the privatisation of ILVA (Italy's main and one of the world's biggest steel producers); acted in the interest of the buyer in the privatisation of AST (Italy's main stainless steel producer); acted on the acquisition of Société des Acier d'Armature pour le Béton. Represented TMW Group, one of the preeminent international real estate investors, in a number of property acquisition deals. Handled a large number of LBOs on behalf of Bridgepoint Capital S.p.A. and other investment banks such as JP Morgan, Sofipa, IMI, ABN AMRO, Barclay's Private Equity, Rhône Capital LLC. Acted in the interest of the sponsors in the establishment of Opera, the private equity fund specialised in the Italian fine products sector, established by Bulgari and other managers.
Career: Admitted – JD, Catholic University of Milan, Italy. Joined the firm of *Negri-Clementi & Soci* in 1988; became a partner in 1990. Partner of *Negri-Clementi Toffoletto Montironi & Soci.*
Personal: Born 15 February 1962 in Senigallia, Italy. Lives in Milan, Italy.

NEGRI-CLEMENTI, Gianfranco
NCTM Studio Legale Associato, Milan
+39 02 541 641
g.negri-clementi@nctm.it
Recommended in Corporate/M&A
Specialisation: Founding Partner of *Negri-Clementi & Soci* in 1955 and Senior Partner of *Negri-Clementi Toffoletto Montironi & Soci.* Represented Italian and overseas clients in all the firm's areas of practice. Acted, amongst other things, on the merger between Credito Italiano and Cassa di Risparmio di Verona, Cassa di Risparmio di Torino and Cassamarca, one of the biggest transactions in the banking sector in Italy; acted on the acquisition of Bank Pekao in Poland and of Cassa di Risparmio di Trento e Rovereto and Cassa di Risparmio di Trieste; acted on the privatisation of ILVA (Italy's main and one of the world's biggest steel producers); acted on the privatisation of Corporacion Siderurgica integral in Spain. Handled a large number of LBOs on behalf of NatWest Equity Partners and other investment banks. Acted for Cagiva Group in the sale of Ducati Motor Holding to Texas Pacific Group.
Prof. Memberships: Has served on the boards of directors in numerous corporations, mainly in the insurance, banking and financial services sectors; College of Arbitrators to which was appointed by the National and International Chamber of Commerce.
Career: Admitted – 1953 JD, cum laude, University of Milan, Italy.
Personal: Born 12 June 1931 in Rome, Italy. Lives in Milan, Italy.

NEWTON, Alan
Freshfields Bruckhaus Deringer, Milan
+39 02 625 301
alan.newton@freshfields.com
Recommended in Banking & Finance
Specialisation: Main area of practice is capital markets work, including public and private debt and equity issues, structured placements, public and private securitisations, the development of OTC derivative products and related regulatory work.

NICODANO, Umberto
Bonelli-Erede-Pappalardo, Milan +39 02 771 131
Recommended in Corporate/M&A

NOBILI, Rafaele
Studio Biscozzi Nobili, Milan +39 02 86 03 88
Recommended in Corporate/M&A

NOVELLI, Francesco
Grimaldi Clifford Chance, Rome +39 06 844 651
Francesco.Novelli@cliffordchance.com
Recommended in Banking & Finance, Project Finance
Specialisation: Specialises in project and asset finance, privatisations and export credit.
Career: Rome University (LLB, magna cum laude 1981); Qualified 1984; *Davis Polk & Wardwell* 1985; Associate Studio Graziadei 1981-83/1986-88, Partner since 1989; Founding partner *Grimaldi e Clifford Chance* 1993; Partner Clifford Chance 1997.
Personal: Married with two children. Sports and reading. Languages: Italian, English.

NOVO, Massimo
Grimaldi Clifford Chance, Milan +39 02 806 341
Recommended in Project Finance

NUNZIANTE, Gianni
Studio Legale Ughi e Nunziante, Rome
+39 06 474 831
ughi.e.nunziante@unlaw.it
Recommended in Corporate/M&A
Specialisation: Advises on legal aspects and co-ordinates the teams doing the legal work on behalf of Italian and foreign clients in major acquisitions and other projects in the corporate/financial areas of practice. Contributor to legal publications and speaker at several events.
Career: Qualified in 1954. Columbia University, MCL 1962. Founding partner of *Ughi e Nunziante* in 1969. Salzburg Seminar in American studies. Board of Advisors, 1978-1988. Harkness Foundation Fellow. Southwestern Legal Foundation Advisory Board.

OSTI, Cristoforo
Grimaldi Clifford Chance, Milan +39 02 806 341
Cristoforo.Osti@cliffordchance.com
Recommended in Communications, Competition/Anti-trust
Specialisation: Specialises in European and Italian competition law, and in Telecommunications Law.
Prof. Memberships: American Bar Association.
Publications: A book on anti-trust and oligopoly, the merger section of the main commentary on Italian competition law and several articles on competition law and on contract law.
Career: Trainee: European Commission – General Directorate for Competition, Brussels, 1981-1982; *Olwine, Connelly, Chase, O'Donnell & Weyher,* New York, 1985-1986; *Feddersen Laule Scherzberg und Ohle Hansen Ewerwahn Finckelburg & Clemm,* Berlin, 1992; Qualified, Italy, 1986. Admitted to the Bar, New York, 1987. Professor of Law and Economics, LUISS University, Rome. Fluent in Italian, English, German and French.
Personal: University of Rome (LLB, magna cum laude, 1981) University of Michigan Law School (LLM, 1985).

PADOVANI, Stefano
NCTM Studio Legale Associato, Milan
+39 02 541 641
Recommended in Banking & Finance

PAPPALARDO, Aurelio
Bonelli-Erede-Pappalardo, Milan +39 02 771 131
Recommended in Competition/Anti-trust

PAPPALETTERA, Carlo
Giliberti & Associati, Milan +39 02 7600 1585
Recommended in Corporate/M&A

PATERNOLLO, Renato
Chiomenti Studio Legale, Milan +39 02 721 571
Recommended in Tax
Specialisation: Partner in tax department. Main area of work is taxation of financial transactions, corporate reorganisations, M&A, private equity funds. Assists many UK and US based investment banks in the analysis of the tax treatment applicable in Italy to various structured finance transactions. Has been involved in tax analysis of many of the major securitisation transactions carried out in Italy. Regular speaker at seminars and conferences on the above matters.
Prof. Memberships: Albo dei Dottori Commercialisti Milano (ie admitted to practice in front of tax courts in 1989).
Career: Qualified to practise in front of tax courts in 1989. Joined *Chiomenti Studio Legale* in 1988. Partner in 1998.
Personal: Born 15 December 1962. Attended Università Commerciale Luigi Bocconi in Milan, degree cum laude 1987. Lives in Milan.

PAVESIO, Carlo
Brosio, Casati e Associati (in association with Allen & Overy), Rome +39 06 684271
Recommended in Competition/Anti-trust

PEDERSOLI, Alessandro
Grande Stevens & Pedersoli, Milan +39 02 76 03 31
Recommended in Corporate/M&A

PICCARDI, Lorenzo
Studio Tremonti, Milan +39 02 5831 3708
piccardi@studiotremonti.it
Recommended in Tax
Specialisation: Main areas of work are international tax planning, mergers & acquisitions and transfer pricing. Director and statutory auditor in mid-sized Italian companies.
Prof. Memberships: Certified as 'Dottore Commercialista' and 'Revisore Contabile'.
Publications: Regular contributor to domestic and international tax magazines.
Career: Since 1989 with *Studio Tremonti ed Associati.* Since 1998, Partner of *Studio Tremonti ed Associati.*
Personal: Born 16 September 1964. Graduated with full legal marks, University L Bocconi of Milan. Panelist at several domestic and international workshops and seminars on international tax planning issues. Lives in Milan.

PINGUE, Filippo
Simmons & Simmons & Grippo, Rome
+39 06 80955 1
filippo.pingue@simmons-simmons.com

Recommended in Banking & Finance
Specialisation: Main areas of practice are corporate law and banking and capital market. Acts for national and international corporations, banks and securities houses. Areas of particular emphasis include securitisations and structured finance. Author of numerous articles in the professional press. Regular speaker at conferences.
Prof. Memberships: Rome Bar.
Career: Qualified in 1988. Became partner at *Studio Associato Prof. Aw. Franco Di Sabato* in 1989. Joined *Studio Aw. Eugenio Grippo* as Managing Partner of the Rome office in 1991. The firm merged with *Simmons & Simmons* in 1997.
Personal: Born 24 June 1961. Attended Naples University and graduated in law in 1983 with magna cum laude.

RADICATI DI BROZOLO, Luca
Chiomenti Studio Legale, Milan +39 02 721 571
Recommended in Communications, Competition/Anti-trust

RAFFAELLI, Enrico Adriano
Rucellai & Raffaelli, Milan +39 02 783 341
Recommended in Competition/Anti-trust

RAYNAUD, Daniele
Ashurst Morris Crisp, Milan +39 02 620 227 225
daniele.raynaud@ashursts.com
Recommended in Banking & Finance
Specialisation: Banking, structured finance, leveraged finance, acquisition financing, project financing, syndicated lending, debt restructuring; investment services, corporate finance, IPO; corporate deal structures, acquisitions, private equity investments, buy-outs.
Publications: Co-author of two books edited by Giuffre: 'Societa in accomandita per azioni' (1990) and 'Societa a responsabilita limitata' (1992).
Career: Admitted to the bar in 1986. Vice president, Head of Legal Department at Citibank, N.A. Milan (1990), Partner at *BBLP Pavia e Ansaldo*, Milan (1995-2000), Managing Partner of *Ashursts*', Milan (2000).

RITTATORE VONWILLER, Andrea
Carnelutti Studio Legale, Milan +39 02 655 851
Recommended in Tax

ROMAGNOLI, Dario
Studio Tremonti, Milan +390 2 5831 3707
milano@studiotremonti.it
Recommended in Tax
Specialisation: Main area of work is domestic tax, VAT, indirect taxes and tax litigation. Legal and tax consultant of several large Italian and multinational groups. Advised on several industrial acquisitions and reorganisations. Also advising several leading companies and domestic and cross-border lease transactions.
Prof. Memberships: Law Society of Bergamo from 1992.
Career: From 1983 to 1990 Official at the Guardia di Finanza with the degree of captain in Milan, he carried on inspection activities for the check of administrative, fiscal and accounting aspects of business administration. Since 1994, partner of *Studio Tremonti ed Associati.*
Personal: Born 14 August, 1962. Graduated cum laude, University of Pavia. Advanced level certificate on technical and commercial subjects with full marks. Four year course at the Fiscal Authority Police Academy for the training of officials in permanent regular service. Course of auditing at the Fiscal Police Superior School. Lives in Treviglio (Bergamo).

ROSSI, Guido
Studio Rossi, Milan +39 02 76 02 2012
Recommended in Competition/Anti-trust, Corporate/M&A

SARAVALLE, Alberto
Bonelli-Erede-Pappalardo, Milan +39 02 771 131
Recommended in Banking & Finance, Corporate/M&A

SCASSELLATI-SFORZOLINI, Giuseppe
Cleary, Gottlieb, Steen & Hamilton, Rome +39 06 69 52 22 1
Recommended in Banking & Finance

SEGNI, Antonio
Gianni Origoni & Partners (A member firm of Linklaters & Alliance), Rome +39 06 478 751
ASegni@gop.it
Recommended in Banking & Finance
Specialisation: Partner in the Rome office of *Gianni, Origoni & Partners.* Practice concentrates on financial markets. Has advised domestic and international clients on capital markets deals, IPOs, secondary offerings, privatisations, friendly and hostile acquisitions, mergers and spin-off, and in general in corporate reorganisations and compliance with respect to market regulations. Also advises banks and financial intermediaries with respect to regulatory compliance, structured finance, including derivatives and repackaging transactions. In the asset management field he advises multinational groups in the distribution of UCITS in Italy, and has advised clients in the structuring and organisation of private equity funds. Author of publications and has lectured in seminars on financial markets and corporate law matters.
Career: Served from 1989 to 1994 as an officer of the legal department of CONSOB, the Italian regulator of the securities market. Admitted to practice in Italy and the State of New York in 1993. From 1994 to date, has practised in the Rome office of *Gianni, Origoni & Partners.*
Personal: Graduated in law in 1988, maxima cum laude, at the University of Rome. Attended, as a Fulbright fellow, a master programme at the Harvard Law School, obtaining the LLM in 1992.

SIRAGUSA, Mario
Cleary, Gottlieb, Steen & Hamilton, Rome +39 06 69 52 22 1
Recommended in Competition/Anti-trust

TAYLOR, Michael
Norton Rose, Milan +39 02 799 144
taylormpg@nortonrose.com
Recommended in Project Finance
Specialisation: Partner, Projects Group, *Norton Rose.* Project finance and energy and natural resources. Based in *Norton Rose's* Milan office since November 2000. Has specialised in the development and financing of projects in the energy and natural resources fields since joining *Norton Rose* in 1974. Became a partner in 1979. A member of the editorial board of 'International Energy Law and Taxation Review'.
Publications: Co-author of a book on oil and gas joint ventures.

TEDESCHINI, Francesco
Chiomenti Studio Legale, Rome +39 06 809 701
Recommended in Corporate/M&A
Specialisation: Partner in Corporate Department. Main area of work is corporate law, principally mergers, acquisitions, privatisations and new equity and bond issues in Italy and abroad. Has handled acquisition of companies and undertakings in various sectors by Italian and foreign clients. Acted on the privatisation of INA; acted for INA in the acquisition of the controlling stake in Banco di Napoli and of a qualified minority in BNL; acted in the spin-off of INA in favour of UNIM and in the spin-off of Sanpaolo IMI in favour of Beni Stabili; acted for Sanpaolo IMI in the sale of CREDIOP to Dexia International; acted in the privatisation of ACEA and in the joint-venture between ACEA and Telefonica InterContinental; acted in the joint venture between ACEA, Telefonica Data, FIAT and IFIL; acted for Chase Manhattan Bank and Morgan Stanley in the SEAT-TIN.IT merger transaction; acted for INA in the spin-off of STET INTERNATIONAL'S activities and in the conversion of saving shares into ordinary shares; acted for ACEA Telefonica and IPSE in the successful UMTS Bidding Auction Member of the board of Directors of Poligrafico dello Stato. Speaker at various conferences.
Prof. Memberships: Qualified 1989.
Career: Joined *Chiomenti Studio Legale* in 1989, became Partner in 1998.
Personal: Born 18 March 1961. Attended Perugia University (JD). Master with LUISS of Rome 1987. Foreign Intern with *Skadden, Arps, Slate, Meagher & Flom*, New York in 1990-1991. Lives in Rome.

TESAURO, Claudio
Bonelli-Erede-Pappalardo, Rome +39 06 84 55 11
Recommended in Competition/Anti-trust

TOFFOLETTO, Alberto
NCTM Studio Legale Associato, Milan +39 02 541 641
a.toffoletto@nctm.it
Recommended in Competition/Anti-trust
Specialisation: Main areas of work are M&A, corporate finance and antitrust law. Involvement in many acquisitions and joint venture contracts, both domestic and international. Acted in 1999 for Telecom Italia in the negotiation for the merger with Deutsche Telekom. Acting as advisor concerning the newborn Italian Legislation to major international investment funds on takeover bids and financial services; to Italian-listed companies concerning corporate governance and financial regulation; to companies listed abroad concerning financial regulation for private placement and public offer. Regarding Antitrust law, acting for major clients (oil and gas industry, entertainment, telecommunication, computer, data bank, financial and auditor services) in some of the most relevant antitrust procedures before the Italian Antitrust Authority and, concern-

I

ing damage action, before the Civil Courts.
Career: Admitted 1998. *Jaeger* Associate 1987-91, Partner 1992-94. *Toffoletto e Associati*: Partner 1995-1999, when the firm merged with *Negri-Clementi Montironi & Soci*. Lecturer of Commercial & Company Law at LIUC (Castellanza) 1992-98, at Politecnico of Milan 1995-98. Professor of International Commercial Law at University of Milan-Bicocca since 1998 and Company Law in the Faculty of Law at LIUC since 1999.
Personal: Born 6 May 1960 and lives in Milan. JD University of Milan (Magna cum laude) 1983. LLM University of London 1988.

TONUCCI, Mario
Studio Legale Tonucci, Rome +39 06 362 271
mtonucci@tonucci.it
Recommended in Corporate/M&A
Specialisation: Privatisation and finance expert. Acted as legal advisor for Italian Treasury in several privatisation procedures. Legal advisor on financial issues concerning acqusitions and mergers. Advised in listing of foreign companies on the Italian Stock Exchange and of Italian companies on foreign Stock Exchanges. Provides legal assistance to foreign governments on legislative matters. Assists companies on anti-trust aspects of acquisition and merger transactions before Italian Anti-trust Authority.
Prof. Memberships: Rome and International Bar Association.
Personal: Born June 25, 1947. University of Rome 1967-71. Lives in Rome.

TREMONTI, Giulio
Studio Tremonti, Milan +390 2 5831 3707
milano@studiotremonti.it
Recommended in Tax
Specialisation: IPOs and Privatisations.
Prof. Memberships: Professor of Tax Law in the University of Pavia.
Publications: Author of numerous articles in various scientific and technical publications; author of two scientific books on tax law; editor of the 'Rivista di Diritto finanziario e Scienza dell finanze'; author of five books on tax policy and policy in general.
Career: Founder and Senior Partner of *Studio Tremonti ed Associati*.
Personal: Born on 18 August 1947. Law degree, cum laude, University of Pavia in 1970. Lives in Pavia. Member of the Italian Parliament, member of the special Committee charged with the reform of the Italian Constitution, Minister of Finance (from May 1994 until January 1995), member of the Executive Committee of the 'Aspen Institute Italia'.

TRISCORNIA, Alessandro
Giliberti & Associati, Milan +39 02 7600 1585
Recommended in Corporate/M&A

UCKMAR, Victor
Studio Uckmar Magnani Marongiu, Genoa +390 10 831 8871
Recommended in Tax

VECCHIO, Cesare
Freshfields Bruckhaus Deringer, Milan +39 02 625 301
cesare.vecchio@freshfields.com
Recommended in Tax
Specialisation: Specialises in securities, tax, banking and finance law. Has considerable experience in securities offerings, structured financial products and the relevant tax issues and has acted for the underwriters in a number of securitisations and structured finance transactions. Practice includes capital markets work, structured finance transactions and securitisations, international and national equities and securities issues.

VENTO, Cesare
Gianni Origoni & Partners (A member firm of Linklaters & Alliance), Rome +39 06 478 751
CVento@gop.it
Recommended in Communications
Specialisation: Partner in the Rome office of *Gianni, Origoni & Partners*. Current practice concentrates on general corporate, M&A and antitrust, with focus on the telecommunications and energy industries. Experience includes advising on several acquisitions, joint ventures and start-ups, established to operate in the Italian telecommunications market, (Western Europe's fastest growing telecoms market), as well as advising on acquisitions in other more traditional industries. Also involved acting for international operators in the privatisation of Telecom Italia. Other significant projects include advising on an unprecedentedly large TLC outsourcing transaction, involving Italy's energy utility company, and representing independent power producers in connection with the development of several waste-to-energy plants throughout the country. Is a frequent lecturer to professional organisations both in Italy and other countries on acquisitions and telecom and energy regulation topics.
Prof. Memberships: Admitted to the Italian Bar; International Bar Association; American Bar Association; New York Bar Association (heads the Rome chapter).
Personal: Received a JD, with the highest vote from the law school of the University of Rome in 1979; holds an LLM, degree from the University of Michigan Law School, 1980.

VIGLIANO, Franco
Brosio, Casati e Associati (in association with Allen & Overy), Milan +39 02 290 491
Recommended in Project Finance

VISCO, Claudio
Macchi di Cellere e Gangemi, Rome +39 06 362 141
Recommended in Banking & Finance, Project Finance

VITALI, Enrico
Studio Tremonti, Milan +390 2 5831 3707
vitali@studiotremonti.it
Recommended in Tax
Specialisation: Main area of work is structured finance, merger and acquisition, securitisation, real estate acquisition. Has taken part in relevant operations of cross-border acquisition, take-over, IPOs in Italy and the US, group reorganisation, financial product structuring, securitisation, issue of banking hybrid securities.
Prof. Memberships: Certified as 'Dottore commercialista' and 'Revisore contabile'.
Publications: Contributor to national and international technical magazines. International correspondant for Italy of 'The Journal of International Taxation'. Co-author of 'Pianificazione fiscale e investimenti all'estero', 1989, IPSOA.
Career: From 1985 to 1987, senior auditor in tax department, for Deloitte Haskins & Sells. Since 1990, partner of *Studio Tremonti ed Associati*, repsonsible for the international practice.
Personal: Born 3 March 1961. Graduated 'cum laude' in Political Sciences, International Law, University of Florence, 1985. Lives in Milan.

WRIGLEY, Nicholas
Grimaldi Clifford Chance, Milan +39 02 806 341
Recommended in Banking & Finance, Corporate/M&A

ZANCHI, Roberto
BBLP Pavia e Ansaldo, Milan +39 02 63381
Recommended in Banking & Finance, Corporate/M&A

ZULLI, Claudio
Studio Tributario e Societario, Milan +39 02 29 51 08 09
stsmilano@libero.it
Recommended in Tax
Specialisation: Partner in Mergers & Acquisitions Department. Main area of work is merger & acquisition transactions, new issues on the Italian Stock Exchange, as well as international taxation. Has handled mergers between listed companies, acquisitions and undertakings of different types by Italian and foreign clients. Acts for a number of major companies (including Hopa S.p.A. and Bell S.A. – Olivetti's holding companies – and the listed company Vemer-Siber Group S.p.A.) on matters ranging from international aspects to company shareholding restructuring. Acted on the Initial Public Offering (IPO) of Marcolin S.p.A. (fashion eyewear), acted on the merger of Vemer S.p.A. (electrical components – listed company) and Siber S.p.A.(electrical components). Has spoken at various conferences on international tax aspects.
Prof. Memberships: CERTI's (Bocconi University Tax Research Department) International Technical Committee; International Fiscal Association; lecturer at the University Centre of Business Organisation in Vicenza.
Publications: Has written a number of articles, published in tax and economics magazines as well as newspapers reaching the qualification of 'Pubblicista'. Acts as consultant for the international magazine 'Trust & Trustees'.
Career: Qualified in 1993. Joined *Pernigotto, Vavassori & Rivetti* in 1991, becoming partner in 1993. Founded *Studio Tributario Societario* in 1997 where he is currently in charge for the Milan and Brescia offices. *Studio Tributario Societario* has a close relationship in Italy with *Freshfields* for tax related matters.
Personal: Born 23 October 1965. Attended Brescia University and graduated in economics in 1991. Lives in Brescia with wife Daniela and son Matteo.

JAMAICA

Corporate/Commercial

JAMAICA Leading firms (Corporate/Commercial)
1 Dunn, Cox, Orrett & Ashenheim
Livingston, Alexander & Levy
Myers, Fletcher & Gordon
2 Nunes, Scholefield, DeLeon & Co

Firms are listed alphabetically in each band.

Leading individuals (Corporate/Commercial)
1 **HART Hugh** *Hart Muirhead Fatta*
HENRIQUES RNA *Livingston, Alexander & Levy*
HILTON Michael *Myers, Fletcher & Gordon*
LEVY Noel *Myers, Fletcher & Gordon*
2 **BOVELL Christopher** *Dunn, Cox*
GOLDSON Peter *Myers, Fletcher & Gordon*
JENKINSON Tony *Nunes, Scholefield*
LAZARUS Afeef *Livingston, Alexander & Levy*

Individuals are listed alphabetically in each band.

Dunn, Cox, Orrett & Ashenheim (21 ptrs, 8 asscs) *"An old established firm with a mixed bag of work"* it has one of Jamaica's leading commercial departments boasting three Queen's Counsel. With a focus on M&A and banking, the team has worked with large multi-nationals and the World Bank and is experiencing growth in IT and shipping. Although tax expert Richard Ashenheim has retired, the team can rely on the senior commercial partner **Christopher Bovell***, rated by the market for his depth of experience. **Clients:** Large multinationals; World Bank; financial institutions; tourism organisations.

Livingston, Alexander & Levy (14 ptrs, 7 asscs) A *"trusted, traditional firm"* thought by peers to have a formidable if *"conservative"* commercial team. The *"capable and experienced"* **RNA Henriques*** is widely considered to be Jamaica's leading commercial advocate, and **Afeef Lazarus*** adds weight as a *"sound"* lawyer who handles M&A, joint ventures and securities.

Most of the major banks in Jamaica and many international companies are clients. It advised Air Jamaica on a pension funds case and acted for BAT in their move to buy out Rothmans. It has a rapidly expanding IP department, advising Microsoft and leaders in the entertainment field. **Clients:** Xerox; Bank of Nova Scotia; Jamaican Public Service Company; Enron; Disney; Paramount; Cable & Wireless.

Myers, Fletcher & Gordon (17 ptrs, 12 asscs) The *"astute"* **Noel Levy*** is said to be *"in a league above the rest"* in his financial services and corporate work. His colleague **Michael Hilton*** is respected as a *"leader in his field"* and a *"strong corporate preparation lawyer"* with a high profile in insolvency, banking and security matters. This *"creative"* pair are not afraid to be original while **Peter Goldson*** is judged by the market to be *"up and coming"* with *"vast potential."* The team provided the principal lawyers for the government agency FINSAC, responsible for the reconstruction of the country's financial services industry. **Clients:** International banks; tourist operators;

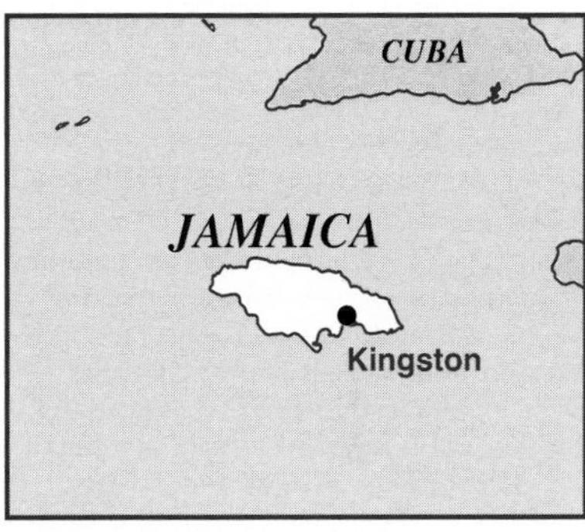

hotel/leisure chains; manufacturing companies; Jamaican government.

Nunes, Scholefield, DeLeon & Co (11 ptrs, 12 asscs) Although lacking the weight of the big three, it is *"a pro-active firm"* thought to be *"currently in a growth mode."* A strong commercial department handles high profile foreign investors from within the Caribbean and the UK and has expanded its telecoms and e-commerce department. British-born **Tony Jenkinson** brings a *"detailed approach coupled with vast knowledge"* and is *"prepared to go the extra mile."* The practice represented Mossel (UK) in its bids in the telecoms market. **Clients:** Goodyear; Gillette; British Airways; large overseas investors.

Other Notable Practitioner Considered one of the country's outstanding practitioners, **Hugh Hart*** of Hart Muirhead Fatta is described as a *"first class commercial lawyer. If I wanted to put a deal together, I would go straight to him."*

*See leaders' profiles on page 432

Leaders' profiles – Jamaica

BOVELL, Christopher
Dunn, Cox, Orrett & Ashenheim, Kingston
+1 876 922 1500
christopher.bovell@dunncox.com
Specialisation: Head of Corporate/Commercial Department. Works in areas of corporate law, mergers, acquisitions, privatisations and new issues/offers for sale. Also advises on foreign investment into Jamaica, banking law, and advising overseas lenders to the Government of Jamaica and Government corporations. Acted for Bear, Sterns & Co. Inc. in Government of Jamaica issue of Notes listed on Luxembourg Stock Exchange; also for J.P. Morgan Securities Inc. in offer and placing of notes secured by alumina sales from Government company to Glencore AG. Acted for Toyota Tsusho Corporation in acquisition of Jamaican distributor and local investment; acts for Guardian Holdings Limited of Trindidad and its Jamaican subsidiary, Guardian Life Limited in acquisition of Jamaican life insurance businesses from FINSAC Ltd., acquisition of Hotels and Royal & Sun Alliance Insurance (Jamaica) Ltd., acts for Grace, Kennedy & Company Limited, CIBC Jamaica Limited, Alcoa Minerals of Jamaica LLC, Kingston Wharves Ltd. and other Jamaican public companies, KBC Bank in loans to Agricultural Credit Bank Limited and Air Jamaica Limited. Chairman of Grace, Kennedy & Company Limited and Kingston Wharves Limited Corporate Governance committees.
Prof. Memberships: Jamaican Bar Association, Commonwealth Lawyers Association.
Career: Qualified as a barrister-at-law in 1961 in private practice, became a solicitor in 1964, joined *Dunn, Cox & Orrett* in 1964, became a partner in 1965. Member of the General Legal Council from 1976, member of the Disciplinary Committee of the General Legal Council from 1976, former Chairman of the Disciplinary Committee. Part-time tutor at Norman Manley Law School, University of the West Indies 1972-80. Government Senator (1983-89).
Personal: Born 7 October 1938. Attended Munro College, Jamaica (1950-55), attended St John's College, Cambridge University 1957-61 (MA Law and LLM Law), Barrister-at-Law, Middle Temple 1961.

GOLDSON, Peter
Myers, Fletcher & Gordon, Kingston
+1 876 922 5860

HART, Hugh
Hart Muirhead Fatta, Kingston +1 876 929 9677

HENRIQUES, RNA
Livingston, Alexander & Levy, Kingston
+1 876 922 6310

HILTON, Michael
Myers, Fletcher & Gordon, Kingston
+1 876 922 5860

JENKINSON, Tony
Nunes, Scholefield & Deleon, Kingston
+1 876 960 8995

LAZARUS, Afeef
Livingston, Alexander & Levy, Kingston
+1 876 922 6310

LEVY, Noel
Myers, Fletcher & Gordon, Kingston
+1 876 922 5860

JAPAN

Index

The clients' choice

BUSINESS LAWYER OF THE YEAR
YASUHARU NAGASHIMA,
Nagashima, Ohno, Tsunematsu
AKIRA KAWAMURA, *Anderson Mori*

BUSINESS LAW FIRM OF THE YEAR
MORI SOGO LAW OFFICES

The extensive experience of ***Yasuharu Nagashima*** *saw him share the best lawyer award with* ***Akira Kawamura. Mori Sogo Law Offices*** *finished comfortably ahead as best firm.*

For details see page 36.

OVERVIEW: Amid a wave of corporate restructuring, Japan's capital markets are becoming more powerful as relations between banks and favoured companies break down. The banking sector itself has been encouraged by government reforms to consolidate and there is a move underway from bank lending towards financing from capital markets. Firms have witnessed a considerable increase in instruction from foreign financial institutions, whilst deregulation and legal reform provides opportunities, particularly for foreign law firms, to employ advanced techniques and products.

The central issue for the foreign firms remains whether to enter into a joint enterprise, offering clients the services of Japanese lawyers (bengoshi.) Those in favour of joint enterprises believe that integrated local law advice is the only way forward, although those against question the quality produced by these alliances. On the domestic front, the market is dominated by the recently merged Nagashima Ohno & Tsunematsu, although as yet no other firms have followed suit and mergers between domestic firms remain unusual.

Banking & Finance: Local Firms

Anderson Mori (12 ptrs, 25 asscs) The firm's most active area of practice is acting for the Japanese banks – as well as the major US and European banks, securities and asset-management houses that have branches in Tokyo. Traditionally a leading regulatory practice, it provides clients with a variety of advice on the legality and distribution of new products. While it handles little project finance work, the firm has strong relations with Development Bank of Japan especially on Private Finance Initiative work. Regulatory expert and *"great all-rounder"* **Kunihiko Morishita*** was commended to researchers as a *"seriously knowledgeable"* practitioner. His colleagues **Tatsu Katayama***, **Masaakira Kitazawa*** are also *"greatly admired,"* while senior practitioner **Tsuyoshi Nagahama*** is seen as an *"invaluable client contact."* **Clients:** Mizuho Holdings Inc; Fuji Bank; DBJ; Goldman Sachs; Merrill Lynch; Morgan Stanley; JP Morgan; Deutsche Bank; Dresdner Bank; BNP Paribas; Barclays Bank; NatWest Bank.

Mitsui Yasuda Wani & Maeda (4 ptrs, 15 asscs) Acknowledged as a force for syndicated or

JAPAN · Leading firms (Banking & Finance)
1 Anderson Mori
Mitsui Yasuda Wani & Maeda
Nagashima, Ohno & Tsunematsu
Nishimura & Partners
2 Atsumi & Usui
Hamada & Matsumoto
Tanaka & Takahashi
3 Freshfields Law Office
Mori Sogo Law Offices

Firms are listed alphabetically in each band.

Leading individuals (Banking & Finance)	
1 ATSUMI Hiroo *Atsumi & Usui*	MIHARA Hidetaka *Nagashima, Ohno*
MORISHITA Kunihiko *Anderson Mori*	SENGOKU Katsu *Nishimura & Partners*
WANI Akihiro *Mitsui Yasuda Wani & Maeda*	YOSHIDA Masayuki *Nagashima, Ohno*
2 GOTO Izuru *Tanaka & Takahashi*	ISHIGURO Toru *Hamada & Matsumoto*
KATAYAMA Tatsu *Anderson Mori*	KINAMI Naoki *Freshfields Bruckhaus Deringer*
KOSUGI Akira *Nishimura & Partners*	MAEDA Hiroshi *Mitsui Yasuda Wani & Maeda*
SUGIMOTO Fumihide *Nagashima, Ohno*	
3 INOUE Satoshi *Nagashima, Ohno*	KITAZAWA Masaakira *Anderson Mori*
NAGAHAMA Tsuyoshi *Anderson Mori*	YASUDA Mitsuhiro *Mitsui Yasuda Wani & Maeda*

Individuals are listed alphabetically in each band.

*See leaders' profiles on pages 443-447

straight loan work, the firm advises on both cross-border and domestic matters, and also conducts substantial compliance work. **Akihiro Wani*** is said to be *"well connected in government circles"* and has a strong relationship with the Bank of Japan. His colleague, **Hiroshi Maeda***, is an *"adept technician,"* while **Mitsuhiro Yasuda*** also garners his share of market praise. The firm advised Sanwa on its merger with Tokai Bank and Toyo Trust Bank, and acted for Bank of Tokyo-Mitsubishi and Mitsubishi Trust Bank on the establishment of Mitsubishi-Tokyo Group. **Clients:** Daiwa; ING Barings; MITI; Bank of Tokyo-Mitsubishi; Chase; HSBC; IBJ; Sanwa; Tokai.

Nagashima, Ohno & Tsunematsu (9 ptrs, 11 asscs) A *"terrific firm"* which works for Japanese and foreign banks, both commercial and investment. Considered *"one of the few firms with a strong regulatory practice,"* it boasts *"stand-out"* regulatory *"expert,"* **Masayuki Yoshida***. The firm carries out substantial loan and syndicated loan work, securitisations arranged by banks, and continues to advise on the reorganisation of Japanese banks and formation of new entities.

Hidetaka Mihara* remains well-regarded by peers, while *"young star,"* **Satoshi Inoue*** is *"especially prominent." "Talented"* **Fumihide Sugimoto*** is hailed as *"one of the younger generation who takes a mature view of the market and is persuasive in his arguments."* The firm advised on the second stage of the reorganisation of Mizuho Holdings, to form three separate banking divisions from the umbrella holding company of IBJ, Fuji Bank and DKB. Acted on the reorganisation of Sanwa Bank, Tokai Bank and Toyo Trust Bank into a single holding company. **Clients:** Mizuho Holdings Inc; Bank of Tokyo-Mitsubishi; Sanwa; GE Capital Corp.

Nishimura & Partners (5 ptrs, 10 asscs) Researchers constantly had their attention drawn to this *"leading banking practice that can handle almost every aspect of a financial transaction and has great clients."* The firm continues to be especially strong in asset finance, notably aircraft financing, the domain of **Katsu Sengoku***. He is considered to be *"user-friendly and extremely able at everything he turns his hand to." "Big name"* **Akira Kosugi*** – a general finance practitioner – is likewise thought to be *"extremely strong."*

The firm has been appointed as the insolvency receiver in three significant work-outs (Toho Life Insurance, Daihyaku Life Insurance and Taisho Life Insurance) and in this capacity, acts as administrator for the bankruptcy, deals with lenders, assists with reorganisation plans and finds purchasers of assets. It represented 21 domestic banks on their constitutional challenge to the new enterprise tax put in place by the Government. **Clients:** Life Insurance Association of Japan; JBIC; IBJ; Sanwa Bank; Fuji Bank; Bank of Tokyo-Mitsubishi; ANA; NTT.

Atsumi & Usui (4 ptrs, 8 asscs) Considered to be *"an obvious port of call for syndicated loans advice,"* the firm is felt by competitors to owe much of its profile to *"powerful"* name partner, **Hiroo Atsumi.*** Generally working on cross-border transactions, he advises a clientele which includes major Japanese, US and European banks. The team advises on all types of traditional banking transactions as well as asset finance and structured finance, and is developing a niche in e-banking. **Clients:** Bank of Tokyo-Mitsubishi; DKB.

Hamada & Matsumoto (5 ptrs, 4 asscs) Formerly *"a clear leader"* in the sector, market opinion now suggests that the firm's profile has diminished recently. However, it continues to advise on a variety of regulatory matters, including regulations affecting the restructuring of internal divisions in banks. The team is also known for its acquisition finance capability, and is acknowledged as a pioneer of the disposition of bad debts. Among a respected team, **Toru Ishiguro*** was recommended to researchers as an *"outstanding practitioner."* **Clients:** Japan Tobacco; Mitsubishi Corp; Sumitomo Chemical; Nissan; Bank of Tokyo-Mitsubishi; Deutsche Bank; Société Générale; Crédit Lyonnais; Yasuda Trust & Banking; Nippon Trust & Banking; Dresdner; Sakura Bank.

Tanaka & Takahashi (2 ptrs, 2 asscs) Traditionally strong banking practice, which continues to be *"especially active in this area."* Perceived to be particularly *"expert at syndicated loans and leveraged finance,"* the firm also advises on issues of various types of debt and equity and has strong ties to Japanese banks. *"Really active on banking transactions,"* **Izuru Goto*** is highly recommended by his peers. **Clients:** Mainly Japanese banks and companies

Freshfields Law Office (2 ptrs, 5 asscs) The local firm of this highly respected legal joint venture offers niche strength in banking regulatory advice in relation to the conduct of FSA audits. Syndicated loans are another specialism, where **Naoki Kinami*** is rated by clients as *"a talented and experienced performer."*

The firm represented an international financial institution during an audit by the Financial Supervisory Authority of Japan of its bank and securities branch in Japan. **Clients:** Banque AIG; Daiwa SBCM; Bank of Tokyo-Mitsubishi; Sakura Bank; Lehman Brothers; Westdeutsche Landesbank Girozentrale; Morgan Stanley.

Mori Sogo Law Offices (3 ptrs) Perceived to be a *"solid"* domestic practice, the firm is outside counsel to ten Japanese banks. Known for its niche in electronic banking, the team has advised as counsel to the Electronic Money Project, being pursued by Sanwa Bank and the Industrial Bank of Japan. Also advised Monex on a similar project sponsored by Sanwa and the Japan Credit Bureau, and assisted on the establishment of NASDAQ Japan. **Clients:** IBJ; Citibank; Sakura Bank; Sumitomo Bank.

Banking & Finance: Foreign Firms

Clifford Chance (2 ptrs, 6 asscs) Widely acknowledged as *"the best"* for banking and asset finance, the firm is admired by Japanese clients for *"its ability to provide us in Tokyo with whatever advice we need."* Commended to researchers for its *"well-organised"* structure, the group includes *"smooth operator,"* **Rob Burley***, universally acclaimed as a *"good guy to deal with"* and especially strong on cross-border leasing work. **Malcolm Turner*** is also respected by peers.

In the past year, the firm has acted on debt and equity transactions in domestic Japanese leveraged leases, and has advised lessors, financiers and airlines on a number of cross-border Japanese operating lease transactions involving major airlines. **Clients:** Bank of Tokyo-Mitsubishi, Barclays; Bear Stearns; Chase Manhattan; Citibank; Dai-Ichi Kangyo Bank; ING Group; JBIC; Nomura Babcock & Brown; SB Leasing; Sumitomo Bank.

JAPAN: Foreign Firms Leading firms (Banking & Finance)
1 Clifford Chance
2 Allen & Overy
Freshfields Foreign Law Office
Sullivan & Cromwell
White & Case LLP
3 Davis Polk & Wardwell
Denton Wilde Sapte
Tokyo Aoyama Law Office – Baker & McKenzie

Firms are listed alphabetically in each band.

Leading individuals (Banking & Finance)
1 **BURLEY Rob** *Clifford Chance*
2 **AKAI Izumi** *Sullivan & Cromwell*
PARADISE Theodore *Davis Polk & Wardwell*
TURNER Malcolm *Clifford Chance*

Individuals are listed alphabetically in each band.

Allen & Overy (1 ptr, 4 asscs) *"Particularly focused on the banking area,"* the team has become increasingly involved in bank lending, as banking products and syndications in Japan become more complex. Its market position is anticipated to be strengthened by the recent joint venture with Akatsuki International Law Office, with the addition of Japanese law expertise.

JBIC is one of the firm's major clients, providing instructions for a number of loan and lease transactions. Other work has included advising Sanwa Bank on a complex structured financing made available to a special purpose company subsidiary of a Japanese trading company. The firm also acted for Chase Manhattan on a $700 million loan facility to the Bank of Tokyo-Mitsubishi. **Clients:** Chase Manhattan; Bear Stearns; JBIC; Bank of Tokyo-Mitsubishi; ABN AMRO; Barclays; CSFB; Citibank NA; Sakura Bank; Fuji Bank; Sanwa Bank; Nissho Iwai Corp; Marubeni Corp; Sumitomo Corp.

Freshfields Foreign Law Office (1 ptrs, 6 asscs) *"Good for banking,"* the firm undertakes the spectrum of banking work. This encompasses standard loan work for Japanese banks and insurance companies, structured finance (including a number of tax finance leases) acquisition of loan portfolios and venture capital financing. Regulatory work is also an important element of the caseload.

The team represented WestLB during an audit by the Financial Supervisory Authority of Japan of its bank and securities branch in Japan, and advised on all aspects of the move by Banque AIG of its existing operations in Asia to Tokyo. **Clients:** Banque AIG; Mizuho International (formerly DKB International); Lehman Brothers; Crédit Lyonnais; Morgan Stanley; Westdeutsche Landesbank Girozentrale; Goldman Sachs; Financial Security Assurance Inc.

Sullivan & Cromwell (3 asscs) Researchers were impressed by the weight of recommendation for a firm which *"stands out for general finance, in spite of opting to stay small."* The bulk of the work consists of assisting on the US law aspects of the reorganisations and mergers of Japanese banks. The firm's profile relies heavily on *"impressive individual,"* **Izumi Akai***, reputed to be *"exceptionally knowledgeable, and not given to histrionics."* **Clients:** Goldman Sachs; Nomura; Bank of Tokyo-Mitsubishi; Sumitomo; IBJ; Sakura Bank; Fuji Bank.

White & Case LLP (6 ptrs, 10 asscs) A broad-based *"active financing practice,"* that encompasses syndicated loan work, structured finance, acquisition finance, aircraft and equipment financing. Perceived to be *"strong in the Japanese operating lease area,"* the firm has a niche in aircraft and ship financing through complex cross-border lease structures. The firm has advised JBIC and Japanese trading companies on rescheduling Russian debt, and acted on Citibank's global credit facility to Nissan Motors. **Clients:** Citibank; WestLB; Bank of Tokyo-Mitsubishi; Bank of America; Diamond Leasing.

Tokyo Aoyama Law Office – Baker & McKenzie (3 ptrs, 8 asscs) *"Well known in the domestic banking sector,"* the firm's ability to combine international and local law skills, and its strong clientele of overseas financial institutions ensures its solid reputation. The team advised ComIto (a subsidiary of Comdisco) on the domestic lease financing of chip making equipment for NEC (¥30 billion.) Acted for the Japanese bank arrangers (led by Sumitomo Bank and the Japan Development Bank) on the financing of the Universal Studios Theme Park in Osaka (¥125 billion.) **Clients:** Citibank; Deutsche Bank; CSFB; Merrill Lynch; Nikko Salomon Smith Barney; Sumitomo Bank.

Davis Polk & Wardwell (1 ptr, 1 assc) Although the Tokyo office's main focus is on capital markets transactions and joint ventures it is also said to have a *"strong reputation for acquisition finance."* Seen *"to have admirable expertise in dealing with Japanese clients,"* peers opine that this success *"reflects the firm's high profile worldwide for banking."*

"Active on banking transactions," counsel **Theodore Paradise*** *"has great knowledge of Japanese banking clients."* The team represented Nikko Securities in connection with its groundbreaking Japanese and international investment banking joint ventures with Salomon Smith Barney, a multi-year transaction that was completed in March 2000. Also advised Fuji Xerox on a $1 billion multicurrency international syndicated loan agreement for which Chase Manhattan is the agent bank. **Clients:** JP Morgan; JBIC; Fuji Xerox.

Denton Wilde Sapte (2 ptrs, 5 asscs) Despite the defection of some partners, the merged firm maintains links with a large number of financial institutions, and is *"traditionally concentrated on structured finance."* The team has acted on large scale structured finance portfolio reviews, and is also known for aviation financing, usually on behalf of banks and trading houses.

The firm handled a comprehensive review and analysis of Morgan Stanley Dean Witter's structured finance portfolio in Japan, and has advised Commerz Securities (Japan) on a wide range of matters throughout the year, including regulatory matters and structured note placements. **Clients:** Crédit Agricole; Mitsubishi Trust & Banking Corp; Morgan Stanley Dean Witter; Bank of Tokyo-Mitsubishi; Citibank; Barclays Capital; JBIC.

*See leaders' profiles on pages 443-447

Capital Markets: Local Firms

JAPAN Leading firms (Capital Markets)
1 Hamada & Matsumoto
Mitsui Yasuda Wani & Maeda
Nagashima, Ohno & Tsunematsu
Nishimura & Partners
2 Anderson Mori
Mori Sogo Law Offices
Tomotsune Kimura & Mitomi
3 Atsumi & Usui
4 Freshfields Law Office
Matsuo & Kosugi

Firms are listed alphabetically in each band.

Leading individuals (Capital Markets)
★ **ISHIGURO Toru** *Hamada & Matsumoto*
KIMURA Akiko *Tomotsune Kimura & Mitomi*
SATO Masanori *Mori Sogo Law Offices*
YASUDA Mitsuhiro *Mitsui Yasuda Wani & Maeda*
1 **HAMADA Kunio** *Hamada & Matsumoto*
MIHARA Hidetaka *Nagashima, Ohno*
MITOMI Fuyuo *Tomotsune Kimura & Mitomi*
ONO Masaru *Nishimura & Partners*
TSUNEMATSU Ken *Nagashima, Ohno*
WANI Akihiro *Mitsui Yasuda Wani & Maeda*
2 **AOKI Kunio** *Aoki & Partners*
ATSUMI Hiroo *Atsumi & Usui*
KITAZAWA Masaakira *Anderson Mori*
SHINDO Isao *Anderson Mori*
3 **KATAYAMA Tatsu** *Anderson Mori*
KOSUGI Takeo *Matsuo & Kosugi*
KUWABARA Satoko *Mori Sogo Law Offices*
SUGIMOTO Fumihide *Nagashima, Ohno*
4 **KINAMI Naoki** *Freshfields Law Office*
KITANOSONO Masayuki *Matsuo & Kosugi*
MAEDA Toshihiro *Nishimura & Partners*
MITSUI Takuhide *Mitsui Yasuda Wani & Maeda*
SEKINE Osamu *Nagashima, Ohno*
YONEDA Takashi *Nishimura & Partners*
YOSHIDA Masayuki *Nagashima, Ohno*

Individuals are listed alphabetically in each band.

Hamada & Matsumoto (13 ptrs, 10 asscs) Respected commercial firm, whose main strength is considered by peers to lie in general capital markets work. Active in debt financings, the team also advises on Eurobond, Samurai bond, MTN and equity issues, and investment trusts. It offers its clients a combination of Japanese and foreign legal expertise.

The *"formidable"* **Kunio Hamada*** has now resumed private practice and is reckoned by clients to be *"clearly among the most talented lawyers in Japan."* The *"excellent"* **Toru Ishiguro*** is also respected as an *"active and strong player."* The firm advised Crayfish on its global offering, involving a fully SEC registered public offering in the US and a dual listing on the New York and Tokyo stock exchange. Represented JSAT Corp on its global offering, including a 144A offering in US, and acted for SKY PerfectTV on a similar offering. **Clients:** Mitsubishi Corp; Nissan; NTT DoCoMo; Toyota; Bank of Tokyo-Mitsubishi; Nomura; Morgan Stanley; Deutsche Securities; Société Générale; Crédit Lyonnais; Nikko; Merrill Lynch; Daiwa; DaimlerChrysler; Crayfish; JSAT.

Mitsui Yasuda Wani & Maeda (8 ptrs, 12 asscs) *"Particularly strong in capital markets and corporate finance,"* the firm is viewed by clients as one of a few which *"regularly represent the underwriters,"* in a market which *"historically tends to see things from the issuers' point of view."* Experts in repackaging and securitisation, the firm offers compliance advice and has developed a niche in e-commerce related transactions.

Recommended to researchers as *"the most innovative of the third generation of lawyers working in this area,"* **Mitsuhiro Yasuda*** is *"an outstanding securities lawyer,"* and is particularly esteemed by the investment banks for *"his understanding of the underwriters' perspective."* Respected derivatives practitioner **Akihiro Wani*** and **Takuhide Mitsui***, a prominent IPO specialist, complete a strong team. The firm advised the ISDA on credit derivative transactions. **Clients:** JBIC; Nomura; Nikko Salomon Smith Barney; Daiwa; Goldman Sachs; ING Barings; ISDA; Chase; JP Morgan; ABN AMRO; Société Générale; Merrill Lynch; Deutsche Bank.

Nagashima, Ohno & Tsunematsu Undoubtedly a *"market leader,"* the firm boasts a *"high concentration of outstanding individuals,"* and advises a wide range of investment banks on debt issues and securitisations.

Ken Tsunematsu* is the firm's *"most famous and experienced"* individual, although he is now perceived to be less active than his *"protegé and successor"* **Hidetaka Mihara***, said to be *"an extremely strong"* securities practitioner. **Fumihide Sugimoto*** is a *"great structured finance lawyer,"* while the *"versatile"* **Osamu Sekine*** and **Masayuki Yoshida***, *"an intimidating opponent on securities transactions"* – also win market plaudits.

The firm advised the global co-ordinators, Goldman Sachs, Nomura Securities, Merrill Lynch and Nikko Salomon Smith Barney, on the first ever issue by NTT of its own shares, and represented Toyoda Loom on its global share offering, worth around ¥70 billion. **Clients:** Sanwa; Morgan Stanley Dean Witter; Goldman Sachs; Nikko Salomon Smith Barney; Warburg Dillon Read; NTT.

Nishimura & Partners (10 ptrs, 25 asscs) Securitisation experts, with particular expertise on the securitisation of consumer loan receivables and auto loan receivables, and a strong underwriter client base. The team includes **Masaru Ono***, who *"may well be the most prominent securities practitioner in Japan."* **Toshihiro Maeda*** is another securities specialist with a fine national reputation, while the *"distinguished"* **Takashi Yoneda*** has a more generalised capital markets practice.

Active in advising venture capital funds, the team assisted on the formation of the ¥30 billion Kyocera Goldman Sachs Venture Fund, designed to provide venture capital for private hi-tech firms in Japan. Involved in the formation of private equity and buyout funds for foreign investors. It has also advised on 100 Samurai and Uridashi debt issues by sovereign clients such as the Republic of Croatia and the Philippines. **Clients:** Morgan Stanley Dean Witter; Goldman Sachs; Merrill Lynch; Daiwa SBCM; Mizuho Securities; Credit Suisse; Deutsche Securities; Lehman Brothers.

Anderson Mori (6 ptrs, 30 asscs) *"Always strong,"* the firm is said to *"specialise in structured transactions,"* and represents a notable client base, which includes most major European and US investment banks as well as many Japanese banks. The group was particularly recommended to researchers as *"market leaders for securitisation."* The team has advised on the IPOs of Japanese companies, often for the issuers, and also acts on public offerings of straight or exchangeable bonds.

Peers consider the *"excellent,"* **Masaakira Kitazawa*** and his colleague **Tatsu Katayama*** to be *"leaders for derivatives work,"* while **Isao Shindo*** is a *"rising star,"* who is *"seen almost everywhere these days."* The firm represented sponsors on the establishment of JREITs (Japanese Real Estate Investment Trusts,) and advised a Japanese company on its simultaneous IPO in Japan and the US. **Clients:** Foreign and domestic financial institutions.

Mori Sogo Law Offices (5 ptrs, 10 asscs) Best known for its securities expertise, the firm has advised on numerous structured finance and private equity transactions. Said to be the *"first port of call for the investment banks,"* **Masanori Sato** * *"understands the fundamentals of securitisation better than anyone else,"* according to competitors, and *"can handle almost any deal you throw at him."* **Satoko Kuwabara*** was also recommended to researchers in this area. The team represented Orient Credit on its ¥7.5 billion issue of junk bonds, and advised on the formation of Unison Capital, one of the country's most active private equity funds. **Clients:** Morgan Stanley; Merrill Lynch; Nomura Securities; Deutsche Securities; Sakura Bank.

Tomotsune Kimura & Mitomi (8 ptrs, 8 asscs) Advising both foreign entities in the Japanese market, and Japanese companies on overseas transactions, the firm has an excellent reputation for securitisation. The team has also acted on a number of IPOs by domestic and international clients, especially in the IT sphere, and assisted on several Samurai bond issues.

Highly recommended to researchers for her knowledge of securities law, **Akiko Kimura*** is *"a huge favourite with clients,"* including Nomura & Merrill Lynch. **Fuyuo Mitomi*** also comes warmly recommended. The firm acted for Deutsche Post on its global offering, and also advised on a Samurai bond issue by GMAC and a public offering by Fiat. **Clients:** Merrill Lynch; Morgan Stanley Dean Witter; Nikko Salomon Smith Barney; Goldman Sachs; Nomura; Daiwa; Bank Of Tokyo-Mitsubishi, NTT.

Atsumi & Usui (6 ptrs) With a developed niche in securitisation and an avowed focus on structured finance, the firm has had a strong year: some commentators even say that it is now *"among the leaders,"* for securitisation. Tends to act for the arrangers, but does occasionally handle work for the originators. Handles various asset-backed transactions, such as consumer receivables, property and lease payment securities, but has particular expertise in dealing with housing loan securitisations and consumer loan securitisation. **Hiroo Atsumi*** is *"absolutely first class for securities and has a great individual reputation."* **Clients:** Foreign investment banks and domestic commercial banks; foreign and domestic securities houses and financial institutions.

Freshfields Law Office (2 ptrs, 5 asscs) Acting for both Japanese and foreign financial institutions, including banks, securities companies and insurance companies, the firm provides a range of advice on securitisations, derivatives, capital enhancement and regulatory advice, including FSA audits. The firm's joint venture with the UK law firm of the same name enables it to offer English and US law capability, and it is consequently viewed as *"direct competition"* by both domestic and foreign firms.

Naoki Kinami* wins praise for his *"broad practice,"* and heads a team which advised the Bank of Tokyo-Mitsubishi on Japanese law in connection to a Universal Shelf Filing with the Securities and Exchange Commission. **Clients:** Banque AIG; Daiwa SBCM; Bank of Tokyo-Mitsubishi; Sakura Bank; Lehman Brothers; Westdeutsche Landesbank Girozentrale; Morgan Stanley.

Matsuo & Kosugi (2 ptrs, 2 assc) Well known for securitisation, the firm advises an array of Japanese banks on big-ticket transactions. **Takeo Kosugi*** is *"senior and excellent, especially for aircraft securitisation,"* while his colleague, **Masayuki Kitanosono*** is also regarded as an *"able"* practitioner by competitors. **Clients:** Sakura Bank, Tokai Bank, Norinchukin Bank.

Other Notable Practitioner Described as *"pre-eminent in this field,"* name partner, **Kunio Aoki***, of Aoki & Partners is said to have *"good judgement and knowledge of cross-border requirements."*

J

Capital Markets: Foreign Firms

Allen & Overy (2 ptrs, 7 asscs) Although the return to London of Angus Duncan means that the team boasts no established individual player, it is nonetheless perceived as made up of *"specialised capital markets lawyers,"* and is *"popular in Tokyo." "Traditionally very active in this field,"* it is regarded as the *"real competition"* by foreign legal firms, and by domestic firms as having *"the edge on a client basis and in terms of connections and know-how."* The joint venture with Akatsuki International Law Office of April 2000 is considered to have strengthened the firm's capital markets practice in particular, and allows clients access to Japanese law expertise in this and other financial practice areas.

The capital markets practice already encompasses securitisation, structured products, equity, and Eurobonds/MTNs. Has wide experience in securitisation, and work on a broad range of credit and equity-linked notes, repackagings and derivative products, typically involving issues under programmes. The team advised the underwriters on the Japan Tobacco Eurobond issue and the jumbo floating rate notes for Fuji Bank. Equity transactions include working on the IPO of Benesse Corporation arranged by Nomura. **Clients:** ABN AMRO; CIBC; Nomura International; Nikko Salomon Smith Barney; Goldman Sachs; Daiwa SBCM; Sumitomo; Toshiba; Hiroshima Bank; Honda; Merrill Lynch.

JAPAN: Foreign Firms Leading firms (Capital Markets)
1 Allen & Overy
Linklaters
Simpson Thacher & Bartlett
2 Freshfields Foreign Law Office
Sullivan & Cromwell
3 Clifford Chance
Davis Polk & Wardwell
Orrick, Herrington
4 White & Case LLP
5 Shearman & Sterling
Skadden, Arps, Slate, Meagher & Flom LLP

Firms are listed alphabetically in each band.

Leading individuals (Capital Markets)
★ **SNEIDER David** *Simpson Thacher & Bartlett*
1 **AKAI Izumi** *Sullivan & Cromwell*
2 **KEELER Mark** *Freshfields Foreign Lw Office*
PARADISE Theodore *Davis Polk & Wardwell*
3 **BURLEY Rob** *Clifford Chance*
DECK David *Shearman & Sterling*
GRUNDY Tony *Linklaters*
LEWIS Christopher *Orrick, Herrington*
Up-and-coming individuals
CAHILL Matthew *Clifford Chance*
HUNSAKER Mark *Sullivan & Cromwell*

Individuals are listed alphabetically in each band.

*See leaders' profiles on pages 443-447

Linklaters (4 ptrs, 21 asscs) Also thought to be *"traditionally active in this field,"* the firm is acknowledged by rivals as the *"leading firm for convertible bond work."* The return of the *"vastly experienced"* **Tony Grundy*** to manage the Tokyo office has been greeted with widespread enthusiasm in the market.

The firm has an increased profile on secondary listings by Japanese corporates on the London Stock Exchange. It is also active on advising on the international aspects of IPOs, especially for internet companies seeking listings on NASDAQ. Commentators were quick to point to the firm's work for Nomura International and Warburg Dillon Read on the international IPO of Lawson Inc. The team worked on a securitisation for Unimat, arranged by Nomura, as well as two transactions involving repackaging of assets for the arranger, Merrill Lynch. **Clients:** Nomura; Warburg Dillon Read; Nikko Salomon Smith Barney; Daiwa Securities; Goldman Sachs; Merrill Lynch; ING Barings.

Simpson Thacher & Bartlett (1 ptr, 5 asscs) Potent capital markets team that is *"involved in all the major transactions"* and is led by the *"only stellar foreign individual in Tokyo,"* **David Sneider***. He is *"an excellent lawyer, fully bilingual and long-established: he combines all the elements that you would want to see in a foreign lawyer in Tokyo."* Said by Japanese lawyers to have *"a wonderful insight into our culture,"* his peers of all nationalities are agreed that *"because of him the firm has the foremost IPO practice."* Particularly active in the telecommunications and technology sectors, the firm has a strong relationship with the investment banks. It represented the underwriters on a $2 billion subordinated note offering in the US market by the Bank of Tokyo-Mitsubishi, and acted for Oracle Corporation Japan on its $8 billion global offering. Also acted on the Japanese IPOs of Toys R Us Japan, JSAT Corp, Crosswave Communications and SKYPerfect Communications. **Clients:** Goldman Sachs; Nikko Salomon Smith Barney; Nomura; SKYPerfect Communications; Toys R Us Japan.

Freshfields Foreign Law Office (1 ptr 6 asscs) A respected finance team advises on securitisations, receivables acquisitions, structured finance and debt capital markets transactions. Has a bias towards the securitisation and purchase of Japanese assets, including consumer and leasing receivables. Other niche strengths include structured finance and derivatives work. Other leaders in the field acknowledge the team as *"major players."*

Popular with his clients, **Mark Keeler*** is described to our researchers as *"strong for securitisation."* The firm acted for DE Shaw as lead manager and Bankers Trustee Company Ltd as trustee on a ¥12 billion convertible bond issue by César Co. It also advised ING Barings as lead manager on the securitisation of a portfolio of Japanese small business loans originated by Shinko Co. **Clients:** Banque AIG; Mizuho International (formerly DKB International); Lehman Brothers; Crédit Lyonnais; Morgan Stanley; Westdeutsche Landesbank Girozentrale; Goldman Sachs; Financial Security Assurance Inc.

Sullivan & Cromwell (6 asscs) Active on IPOs, equity offerings and debt offerings, the firm advises some multi-national corporates, but principally represents US investment banks and Japanese securities houses. The mainstay of the firm's work is equity offerings.

Considered by competitors to be the *"second best of the US law firms in Tokyo,"* in this field, the firm is seen on *"almost all significant transactions."* **Izumi Akai***, qualified in both US and Japanese law, was recommended to researchers as a lawyer who is *"au fait with the legal details, and loved by his clients."* He is ably assisted by up and coming **Mark Hunsaker***, described as an *"emerging star,"* who impressed pundits with his work for the underwriters of the recent $11 billion global equity offering by NTT, a complex transaction which involved the first simultaneous sale of shares by a primary and secondary issuer. Also represented Nomura, the Japanese underwriter, on a global offering of equity securities by Toyoda Automatic Loom Works Ltd. **Clients:** Goldman Sachs; Nikko Salomon Smith Barney; Nomura; Merrill Lynch.

Clifford Chance (3 ptrs, 12 asscs) Handling a broad spectrum of capital markets work, the firm is almost invariably seen acting for arrangers and underwriters, on plain vanilla, structured and equity-linked MTN issues. Acknowledged as securitisation experts, the team has advised on a number of complex and innovative consumer finance transactions for European and US investment banks. **Rob Burley***, based in Tokyo for six years, is recommended for his all-round transactional ability, while *"talented"* **Matthew Cahill*** wins plaudits for his *"willingness to go the extra mile for his clients."*

The firm acted on the largest non-performing real estate securitisation transaction completed in Japan to date, the Morgan Stanley Dean Witter-arranged ¥31 billion International Credit Recovery Japan II issue, which closed in August 2000. Also advised Morgan Stanley, Goldman Sachs and Merrill Lynch on the update of MTN programmes for Japanese issuers. **Clients:** Bear Stearns; BNP Paribas; Chase; Goldman Sachs; IBJ International; JP Morgan; Lehman Brothers; Merrill Lynch; Morgan Stanley; UBS.

Davis Polk & Wardwell (1 ptr, 4 asscs) The office's principal focus is on capital markets transactions, notably US or global offerings of securities by Japanese firms. The firm has a balanced practice, acting for both underwriters and issuers, and has been involved in a significant number of the major international offerings by Japanese issuers in the last few years, including Oracle Corporation Japan, ORIX, Initiative Japan, and Sumitomo Bank. Advising on transactions involving the rapidly developing hi-tech sector, it has strong niche expertise in the area of wireless internet.

Well-established counsel, **Theodore Paradise*** is the most high-profile member of the firm and is praised as a *"great lawyer with solid Japanese."* The team represented Oracle Corporation Japan on an international common stock offering ($7.5 billion) that closed in April 2000. The offering was Japan's largest non-privatization stock sale. Also represented the underwriters in connection with the Japanese government's sale of 25% of the shares of JR East, the largest passenger railway company a transaction valued at $6 billion. **Clients:** JBIC; the Japanese government; JP Morgan; Merrill Lynch; Morgan Stanley Dean Witter; Nikko Salomon Smith Barney.

Orrick, Herrington & Sutcliffe (1 ptr, 3 asscs) Thought to be *"increasing their profile,"* the firm is increasingly perceived as the *"emerging competition."* Akin to the UK firms in its focus on securitisation and derivative linked structured finance – rather than IPOs – the team is perceived to do *"more volume work than other US leaders."* **Chris Lewis*** is perceived to be *"very active in securitisation and a good lawyer."*

The firm has acted on several auto loan receivables transactions, equipment lease receivables deals and consumer finance deals, and has worked on some commercial mortgage-backed securities. Acted on the Sanwa housing loan deal for Bear Stearns. **Clients:** Bank of America; Bear Stearns; Daiwa; Deutsche Securities; Lehman Brothers; ING Barings; Mizuho Holdings Inc; Nikko Salomon Smith Barney.

White & Case LLP (2 ptrs, 6 asscs) Although not as visible for capital markets work as for other areas, the firm's established expertise in both US and Japanese law guarantees a quality client base. The team works on real estate investment funds (JREITs,) and has been involved in the strongly emerging market for venture capital companies in the hi-tech industries. **Clients:** ING Barings; Lehman Brothers; Morgan Stanley; AIG; Fidelity Investment.

Shearman & Sterling (1 ptr) Active on securitisations and structured finance, the firm is led by the respected **David Deck***, who has long experience of advising arrangers and underwriters. It has acted on real estate loans for Morgan Stanley and Citibank, has handled consumer finance receivables for ING Barings. **Clients:** Morgan Stanley Dean Witter; Merrill Lynch; Sanwa; Toyota Motors.

Skadden, Arps, Slate, Meagher & Flom LLP (2 ptrs, 5 asscs) Perceived to be *"building up in Tokyo,"* the firm advises on a broad spectrum of capital markets work, including inbound and outbound global offerings and private placements, IPOs, hybrid securities and structured products. The firm has represented Japanese banks and investment banks on the securitisation of yen-denominated assets, including trade receivables and longer-term assets held by finance companies. Other financing transactions have involved secured and unsecured loan agreements and commercial paper programs. **Clients:** Goldman Sachs; Merrill Lynch; NKK; Toray; Asahi Glass; NEC; CFSB; Shinsei Bank.

J

Corporate/M&A: Local Firms

JAPAN
Leading firms
(Corporate/Mergers & Acquisitions)

Band	Firm
1	Nagashima, Ohno & Tsunematsu
2	Anderson Mori
	Mori Sogo Law Offices
	Nishimura & Partners
3	Mitsui Yasuda Wani & Maeda
4	Hamada & Matsumoto
	Hibiya Park Law Offices
	Tokyo Aoyama – Baker & McKenzie
5	TMI Associates

Firms are listed alphabetically in each band.

Leading individuals
(Corporate/Mergers & Acquisitions)

Band	Individual
1	**FUJINAWA Kenichi** *Nagashima, Ohno*
	HARA Hisashi *Nagashima, Ohno*
2	**KAWAMURA Akira** *Anderson Mori*
	KUSANO Koichi *Nishimura & Partners*
	MITSUI Takuhide *Mitsui Yasuda Wani & Maeda*
	NAGAHAMA Tsuyoshi *Anderson Mori*
	NAGASHIMA Yasuharu *Nagashima, Ohno*
	NISHIMURA Toshiro *Nishimura & Partners*
3	**EJIRI Takashi** *Asahi*
	FUJIEDA Atsushi *Nagashima, Ohno*
	HIRAKAWA Osamu *Anderson Mori*
	KUWABARA Satoko *Mori Sogo Law Offices*
	NAKAJIMA Tohru *Nagashima, Ohno*
4	**HASHIDATE Kenji** *Hashidate Law Office*
	KAKUYAMA Kazutoshi *Anderson Mori*
	NAMEKATA Kunio *TMI Associates*
	TANAKA Hideaki *Hamada & Matsumoto*
	UCHIDA Harumichi *Mori Sogo Law Offices*

Individuals are listed alphabetically in each band.

Nagashima, Ohno & Tsunematsu (10 ptrs, 40 asscs) Described by the market as the *"number one firm in Japan,"* it has emerged from last year's union with a top quality cross-border M&A capacity and enviable strength in depth. Foreign law firms in Japan were especially insistent about the *"tremendous degree of success"* achieved by the corporate team. The firm has expertise in a variety of industries, including finance, IT, telecoms and pharmaceuticals.

Peers consider *"top rank"* **Kenichi Fujinawa*** to be *"one of Tokyo's leading M&A lawyers,"* while *"leading light"* **Hisashi Hara*** also maintains his position at the top of the corporate tree. Although less transactionally active, *"famous name"* **Yasuharu Nagashima*** is experienced and *"brilliant with clients."* Clients recommend **Atsushi Fujieda*** as *"a strong negotiator,"* while **Tohru Nakajima*** is *"a talented representative of the younger brigade."*

The firm represented Sumitomo Corp in relation to the sale of one of its divisions to a foreign company, and Komatsu Corp on its sale of a subsidiary to another Japanese company. It has also represented a number of Japanese banks on their mergers. **Clients:** GE Capital; Manulife; AT&T; AIG; ORIX; Sumitomo Bank; Mitsubishi Trust Bank; Sumitomo Marine Insurance.

Anderson Mori (8 ptrs, 12 asscs) Universally acknowledged by competitors as *"one of the top firms,"* it advises a number of Japanese subsidiaries, branch offices and joint ventures of multi-national companies. The team has a strong investment bank clientele, and particular experience of cross-border M&A in pharmaceuticals, the automobile industry and the hi-tech sector.

Senior practitioner **Tsuyoshi Nagahama*** was recommended to researchers as an *"important client contact,"* while **Akira Kawamura*** is a *"visible and forceful commercial practitioner." "Busy and popular with clients,"* **Kazutoshi Kakuyama*** is *"an excellent younger partner,"* while opponents admire **Osamu Hirakawa*** for his *"critical role"* on more complex deals. He acted on the Ripplewood Holdings acquisition of Long Term Credit Bank of Japan (LTCB), and the firm now advises the subsequently formed Shinsei Bank. **Clients:** Mitsui Trust; IBM; Shinsei Bank; Goldman Sachs; JP Morgan

Mori Sogo Law Offices (10 ptrs, 15 asscs) Perceived by the market as *"a high-calibre, if rather conservative"* corporate team, it has been involved on a number of the year's biggest deals. Active on both domestic and cross-border transactions, the firm's clientele consists of an even mix of foreign and domestic corporates, as well as a selection of powerful financial institutions.

In addition to her reputation in securitisation, **Satoko Kuwabara*** was recommended to researchers for her corporate practice, while **Harumichi Uchida*** is characterised as *"a great general corporate practitioner of senior vintage."* The firm represented NTT DoCoMo on its alliance with AOL and acted as outside counsel on the merger of Sumitomo bank with Sakura bank. Also represented Mitsubishi Motors on its joint ventures with DaimlerChrysler. **Clients:** Morgan Stanley; Merrill Lynch; Tokyo Marine & Fire Insurance; NTT; NTT DoCoMo; Bloomberg.

Nishimura & Partners (10 ptrs, 25 asscs) Servicing a variety of multi-national and domestic clients, the firm's corporate team focuses on big-ticket transactions involving foreign entities. Active in the new media market, the firm enjoys long-standing relationships with Japanese financial institutions.

Clients raved about the *"cerebral qualities"* which **Koichi Kusano*** brings to the negotiating table. He is the firm's outstanding transactional lawyer, although senior partner **Toshiro Nishimura*** remains as an eminence grise and *"outstanding client getter."* The firm advised DDI

*See leaders' profiles on pages 443-447

Corp on its merger with KDD Corp, and represented internet investor SOFTBANK Corp on its acquisition of the failed Nippon Credit Bank (NCB). **Clients:** Motorola; SOFTBANK; DaimlerChrysler; Amazon.com; NTT; Glaxo Wellcome; Hitachi; Toshiba; DDI.

Mitsui Yasuda Wani & Maeda (4 ptrs, 10 asscs) Although best known for its capital markets prowess, the corporate practice at Mitsui Yasuda Wani & Maeda still wins its share of market support as a *"strong, mid-sized general commercial firm."* Known for its advice on joint ventures, the team has strong ties to a number of investment banks. All-rounder **Takuhide Mitsui*** was recommended to researchers as the firm's leading corporate practitioner. His team recently handled the acquisition by Osaka Gas of the liquid petroleum gas department from Nissho Iwai. **Clients:** Nomura; Merrill Lynch; Daiwa; Goldman Sachs; ING Barings; HSBC; Mitsubishi; Osaka Gas.

Hamada & Matsumoto (10 ptrs, 10 asscs) Although rivals maintain that the strength of the firm lies in its capital markets work, it is still regarded as a sound second-tier corporate player. Among a *"uniformly competent team,"* **Hideaki Tanaka*** is considered to stand out. The firm advises on corporate restructuring, joint venture agreements, incorporation, licensing and distributorship. The firm's client base generally inclines towards leading domestic corporates. **Clients:** Japanese companies and financial institutions.

Hibiya Park Law Offices (3 ptrs, 1 assc) According to peers at both domestic and foreign firms, this is the *"top notch corporate governance M&A boutique."* Acting largely for Japanese public companies on domestic transactions, the team specialises in M&A, restructurings, and defences to hostile takeover bids. The firm worked on the defence of the first hostile takeover bid in Japan, and advised IBJ on the establishment of its holding company, Mizoho. **Clients:** NTT DoCoMo; NTT Data; East Japan Railroad; Japan Tobacco; Nomura Securities.

Tokyo Aoyama Law Office/ Baker & McKenzie Attorney Foreign Law Office (5 ptrs, 12 asscs) A *"good firm with Japanese law strength"* is perceived by rivals as *"a strong and profitable operation,"* which has developed a niche in cross-border M&A in telecommunications, insurance and pharmaceuticals. The firm also boasts dedicated MBO and private equity investment teams.

The firm advised British Telecom on its strategic partnership with AT&T and Japan Telecom, and acted as Japanese counsel to Pacific Century CyberWorks on a $1 billion share swap deal between PCCW and Hikari Tsushin Inc. **Clients:** British Telecom; GE Capital; JAFCO Co Ltd; Kanematsu Corp; Pacific Century CyberWorks Ltd; Proudfoot Plc; Samsung Electronics; Sony Corporation; Sumitomo Electric Industries.

TMI Associates (6 ptrs, 15 asscs) *"An up and coming firm, full of bright people,"* it received especially glowing recommendations from foreign firms, who were keen to emphasise the group's expansion from its IP roots. The firm's expertise in hi-tech and telecommunications M&A has now been supplemented by important relationships in the financial sector. **Kunio Namekata*** is regarded as the team's star performer.

The firm advised Fuji Heavy Industries (Subaru) on its global strategic alliance with General Motors, and has represented VALEO – the French maker of automotive parts – on its Japanese M&A activities. It also advised Sanyo on its acquisition of Toshiba's Nickel Hydrogen Battery business, and L'Oréal on its acquisition of Shu Uemura cosmetics. **Clients:** Nomura Securities; SOFTBANK Corp; Sony Music; Subaru; VALEO; Sanyo; Sega; L'Oréal.

Other Notable Practitioners **Takashi Ejiri** of Asahi Law Office is recommended to our researchers as *"a seasoned and respected lawyer,"* while **Kenji Hashidate*** of Hashidate Law Office also possesses a sound commercial reputation, and is said to *"run a tight ship."*

Corporate/M&A: Foreign Firms

White & Case LLP (4 ptrs, 12 asscs) Perceived by competitors to be *"doing the most work in this field,"* the firm *"is involved in large local deals and is politically well connected."* Although best known for inbound M&A, the success of the firm's joint venture with local firm Kandabashi is acknowledged to have secured *"quality work for Japanese companies as well."*

Peers give much of the credit for the firm's leading position to *"great commercial lawyer"* **Robert Grondine***, who has *"been here a long time, forged good connections, and built a strong team."* The firm represented Sony Corp on the sale of its consumer product manufacturing plant to Solectron Corp, the US based electronics equipment maker. Also acted for General Motors Corp on the conclusion of a strategic alliance with Fuji Heavy Industries, and represented Cable & Wireless on its acquisition of 98% of the ownership of Digital Communications. **Clients:** Morgan Stanley; AIG; Lehman Brothers; GE Capital; General Motors.

Clifford Chance (2 ptrs, 4 asscs) Although *"mostly known for its finance work,"* the Tokyo office does *"quite a bit of corporate work which comes naturally through their international network."* The team handles a broad spectrum of corporate work, generally advising both domestic and international companies on their acquisitions. Regional joint ventures are another area of niche expertise.

Head of the office **Rob Burley*** is best known as a finance lawyer, but researchers discovered that his *"client-getting qualities"* are also felt to boost the office's profile in this area.

The firm advised Fujitsu in connection with its worldwide alliance with Siemens, and represented the Luxottica Group in connection with the acquisition of the eyewear division of Bausch & Lomb. **Clients:** China.com; Fujitsu; Grosvenor Ltd; Merill Lynch; Nikon; NTT DoCoMo; Olympus; Rodamco; Siemens; Whitney & Co.

Freshfields Foreign Law Office (3 ptrs, 10 asscs) The firm's *"pretty successful joint enterprise"* with Freshfields Law Office, which advises on Japanese law, enables it to act as a one-stop shop for its international and local clientele's cross-border transactions. Acknowledged by competitors to be *"expanding enormously,"* the corporate team is regarded as one of the *"big guns"* in Japan, flourishing under the guidance of *"old hand"* **Charles Stevens***, whose name stands out amid a *"talented"* department.

The team advises foreign companies on buyouts of Japanese joint venture partners and represents vibrant Japanese companies on foreign law issues as they affect overseas transactions. Advised Henkel Japan on its de-merger in Japan,

JAPAN: Foreign Firms Leading firms (Corporate/M&A)
1 White & Case LLP
2 Clifford Chance
Freshfields Foreign Law Office
Simpson Thacher & Bartlett
3 Ashurst Morris Crisp
Denton Wilde Sapte
Linklaters
Morrison & Foerster
4 Davis Polk & Wardwell
5 Sullivan & Cromwell

Firms are listed alphabetically in each band.

Leading individuals (Corporate/M&A)
1 GRONDINE Robert *White & Case LLP*
SNEIDER David *Simpson Thacher & Bartlett*
2 BURLEY Rob *Clifford Chance*
KITCHIN Alan *Ashurst Morris Crisp*
STEVENS Charles *Freshfields Foreign Law Office*
3 LEVINE Robert *Davis Polk & Wardwell*
LEWIS Steve *Herbert Smith*

Individuals are listed alphabetically in each band.

and acted for MetalSite Inc on its joint venture with three major Japanese trading companies to establish a website with a trading of metals in Japan. **Clients:** MetalSite Inc; NTT DoCoMo; KDD; Titus Communications (Microsoft); Japan Airlines; Bank of America Equity Partners; Eaton Corp; Sakura Bank; Kokusai Motorcars; Warburg Pincus.

Simpson, Thacher & Bartlett (1 ptr, 5 asscs) A *"strong"* firm, with an emphasis on capital markets work in Japan, is also acknowledged to have *"capitalised on a fantastic client base"* to bolster its corporate profile as well. The team conducts the full range of work, including strategic minority investment in public companies, domestic & international acquisitions and joint ventures.

"One of the best international lawyers," the *"fantastic"* **David Sneider*** wins universal acclaim. Researchers were impressed by his level of market support, which overshadows that of the firm itself. The corporate team represented Fuji Heavy Industries (Subaru) on its sale of a 20% interest to General Motors, worth $1 billion. Also represented Ripplewood on its acquisition of Long Term Credit Bank (now Shinsei Bank) from the Japanese Government, and advised AOL Japan in its joint venture with NTT DoCoMo. **Clients:** Japan Telecom; Goldman Sachs; Nomura; Merrill Lynch; Fuji Heavy Industries; Lehman Brothers; Ripplewood; GE Capital Corp.

Ashurst Morris Crisp (1 ptr, 8 asscs) More focused on M&A than many other foreign organisations, the firm is said to have put in a *"good performance"* this year. The corporate team advises on both inbound and outbound corporate/M&A work, and also handles joint ventures, private equity and corporate restructuring. It is particularly renowned for external investment work on behalf of Japanese corporate clients and trading companies.

Alan Kitchin*, who has been in Japan for nine years and speaks fluent Japanese, is adjudged by clients to be the firm's *"true strength."* He advised Morgan Grenfell Private Equity on the Asian aspects of the purchase of a 12.5 % stake in the holding company of Formula One Administration, valued at $325 million. The team also advised Takata Corporation on the purchase by its Singapore subsidiary of a 30% stake in an Indian private company that manufactures components for the automotive industry. Other work includes advising Nippon Electric Glass Ltd on the acquisition of Videotron, and acting for Marubeni on its acquisition of an interest in Chengdu Generale in China for $160 million. **Clients:** Mitsui & Co; Sumitomo; Marubeni; Royal & Sun Alliance; Cinven; Nippon Electric Glass Ltd.

Denton Wilde Sapte (1 ptr, 4 asscs) The departure of Steve Lewis and others to set up the new Herbert Smith office is seen by competitors to leave the Denton Wilde Sapte corporate practice as *"pretty much the Wilde Sapte practice pre-merger."* In spite of retaining a number of clients, researchers discovered that the department's profile has diminished over the past year.

The firm advises Japanese clients on joint ventures in Asia and offshore acquisitions, and represents European concerns on their investments in the Japanese market. The team advised MediaOne Group on its entire shareholding in three Japanese telephone/cable companies. Also represented BBC Worldwide on the establishment of a subsidiary distribution company in Japan, and acted for ITOCHU Corp in relation to its acquisition of an Italian luxury goods manufacturer. **Clients:** MediaOne Group Inc; BBC Worldwide Ltd; ITOCHU Corp; Tomen Corp; Sumitomo Corp.

Linklaters (4 ptrs, 25 asscs) An *"interesting"* corporate practice, recently established, and said by clients to be *"gaining in strength."* The firm's workload includes joint ventures and big-ticket M&A advice, and it is developing a niche in the IT sector. The office provides both UK and US law capabilities and frequently carries out a 'quarter-backing' role, to ensure that a transaction carried out under Japanese law is completed to international standards.

The firm has acted for a US manufacturer of consumer products in relation to its acquisition of a distribution network in Japan, and advised the majority shareholder in a leading retail chain on the disposal of part of its interests. **Clients:** Allied Domecq; Toyota Motor Corp.

Morrison & Foerster (2 ptrs, 15 asscs) Acknowledged by peers as *"an active team with a hi-tech focus,"* it is considered to *"deserve a lot of credit."* The firm works on outbound M&A transactions for Japanese companies and on inbound M&A for US companies, and has niche expertise in the structuring of joint ventures in Japan.

Highlights include acting for Verio, the world's largest operator of web sites for businesses, in NTT's $5 billion acquisition of the company. The team also represented Toshiba on its formation of a $600 million joint venture with General Electric for the development and sale of large scale industrial drive systems. Other work has included acting for Vodafone AirTouch on its joint venture with Japan Telecom and BT. **Clients:** Toshiba; Fujitsu; Asahi Breweries; SOFTBANK Corp; NTT; Toyota Automatic Loom.

Davis Polk & Wardwell (1 ptr, 4 asscs) Another New York capital markets oriented practice, which is perceived by the market to be *"a force on big-ticket M&A transactions."* The team maintains its strong financial services niche, having worked on a raft of cross-border joint ventures in that sector. **Robert Levine*** was recommended to researchers as *"a seasoned lawyer, focused on M&A."* The firm advised Morgan Stanley Dean Witter on its mutual fund alliance with Sanwa Bank, and represented Deutsche Securities on its joint marketing arrangement with Sakura Securities. Also acted for DLJ Direct on its joint venture with Hutchinson Whampoa. **Clients:** Nikko Salomon Smith Barney; Morgan Stanley Dean Witter; UBS Warburg; Oracle Japan.

Sullivan & Cromwell (7 asscs) Among the first US law firms to open an office in Tokyo, the firm maintains a registered joint enterprise with a Japanese bengoshi and a New York lawyer who spent five years practising US law in the firm's New York office. This allows the Tokyo office to advise on certain matters of Japanese law and combine Sullivan & Cromwell's global expertise with the typical services offered by a Japanese law firm.

*See leaders' profiles on pages 443-447

Although principally recognised as a force in capital markets, the firm is seen by competitors as *"active"* in M&A, joint ventures and private equity investment. It represented US firm on a Japanese joint venture in the hi-tech sector, and advised on the setting up of a joint venture between a Japanese firm and a foreign firm in the steel industry. **Clients:** SOFTBANK Corp; US and Japanese corporates.

Other Notable Practitioner Steve Lewis* has left the former Denton Hall to lead Herbert Smith's new corporate team in Tokyo. Respected by peers as an *"intelligent, experienced figure,"* he is regarded as a useful acquisition by his new firm.

J

Project Finance

JAPAN Leading firms (Project Finance)
1 Allen & Overy
Ashurst Morris Crisp
Milbank, Tweed, Hadley
2 Clifford Chance
Linklaters
Morrison & Foerster
White & Case LLP
3 Lovells
Tokyo Aoyama Law Office – Baker & McKenzie
4 Denton Wilde Sapte
Freshfields Foreign Law Office
Orrick, Herrington & Sutcliffe

Firms are listed alphabetically in each band.

Leading individuals (Project Finance)
1 **KITCHIN Alan** *Ashurst Morris Crisp*
2 **GRONDINE Robert** *White & Case LLP*
INMAN Jonathan *Linklaters*
McCLENAHAN John *Ashurst Morris Crisp*
TURNER Malcolm *Clifford Chance*
3 **BURLEY Rob** *Clifford Chance*
KEELER Mark *Freshfields Foreign Law Office*
KIM Young Joon *Milbank, Tweed, Hadley*
LEWI Rupert *Lovells*

Individuals are listed alphabetically in each band.

Allen & Overy (1 ptr, 2 asscs) A clear market leader, thought by many rivals to be *"our main competition,"* despite lacking a leading individual since Andrew Castle's return to London. Principally involved in project finance transactions in which Japanese investment is involved, the firm has handled work for the Japan Bank For International Cooperation. In the past 12 months, has acted for JBIC on infrastructure projects worth in excess of $2.4 billion.

Through the combination of its Japanese joint venture and its international project finance expertise, the firm is actively developing a domestic project financing capability, particularly in the property, electricity, telecommunications and PFI sectors. The team acted for JBIC on its participation in the $850 million financing by Petrobras of the Cabiunas Pipeline project in Brazil. Also advised the project company Global Telecom SA and its sponsors, Motorola, DDI, Nissho Iwai; Suzano and Inepa, on its $1.25 billion mobile telecom project in Brazil. **Clients:** JBIC; Bank of Tokyo-Mitsubishi; Mitsubishi Materials Corp; Sanwa Bank; Sumitomo Corp; Marubeni Corp; Mitsui; Itochu; Citibank.

Ashurst Morris Crisp (3 ptrs, 8 asscs) *"Star practice,"* that is seen to have *"good relationships with the trading houses" "superb relationships with government funding entities"* and *"traditional relations with the banking houses."* Many rivals attribute this to the *"great contacts"* of *"well-known practitioner and terrific rainmaker"* **Alan Kitchin***, who is ably supported by his *"point man,"* the *" highly regarded"* **John McClenahan***. Some commentators say that they *"make the best team on the Tokyo market for project finance."*

The team advised Marubeni on its borrowing of $60 million to develop the PPN power project in Tamil Nadu. On the lending side, the team advised on the $131 million financing of the Yetagun gas field in Myanmar, and represented JBIC in regard to the new airport project in Manila, the only airport project in Asia this year. **Clients:** Marubeni Corp; Mitsui; JBIC; Asian Development Bank; Bank of Tokyo-Mitsubishi.

Milbank, Tweed, Hadley & McCloy (2 ptrs, 3 asscs) Regarded by many competitors as the *"strongest practice in this field,"* it is especially rated for its global involvement which *"sets it apart."* Working for an even balance of foreign and domestic clients, the team is a respected force in power, energy (oil and gas) and, increasingly, telecoms projects.

Young Joon Kim* is seen *"on many transactions"* and is particularly noted for his Korean work. The firm represented JBIC on various power projects located outside Japan, including the Philippines and Latin America. Also assisted a major multi-national oil and gas company in exploring project development in Japan, and represented a major Thai telecommunications operator in its successful restructuring of project finance loans. **Clients:** JBIC; Sithe Energies; Enron; Marubeni; Mitsubishi Corp; Fuji Bank, Sanwa Bank; IBJ; Texaco; Exxon-Mobil.

Clifford Chance (2 ptrs, 8 asscs) Traditionally a lending practice, which although *"well-known in the past,"* is perceived by peers to be *"far less active on new projects"* in the past year. Instead, it has concentrated on restructuring work on old projects in Thailand and Pakistan.

It was impressed upon researchers that **Malcolm Turner*** has *"a strong, well-rounded practice,"* while his *"well-established"* colleague, **Rob Burley***, a general finance wizard, is thought to be a valuable rainmaker. The firm acted for the lead arrangers of the restructuring of over $500 million of project finance debt for the Aromatics Thailand Public Company. Also acted for the steering committee in relation to the restructuring of Thai Olefins Company's $328 million project finance debt. **Clients:** Industrial Bank of Japan; Itochu; JBIC; Mitsubishi Corp; Nissho Iwai, Sanwa Bank.

Linklaters (1 ptr, 1 assc) Considered by some interviewees to be *"one of the big players"* in this area. Although *"not a large team,"* it has continued to work on a variety of domestic and overseas deals this year and has seen a growth in transport infrastructure work.

The market maintains that **Jonathan Inman*** *"has a strong reputation for technical expertise, notably in India."* The team advised the LTCB on the disposal of numerous project finance assets and acted for them in relation to the restructuring of a LNG Tanker financing. The team continues to provide advice to a syndicate of Japanese and western banks on their interests in a Pakistani power project. **Clients:** Japanese and western banks; US companies; trading clients.

Morrison & Foerster (2 ptrs, 5 asscs) Commended by the competition as *"generally very active,"*

*See leaders' profiles on pages 443-447

Morrison & Foerster's *"strong established practice"* is thought to be *"terrific in this field."* A *"big presence"* in the market, it advises on power, transportation, oil and gas, petrochemical, telecommunications, water and PFI projects in Japan and throughout the Asia Pacific region. As in all areas of practice, the firm has its principal focus on technology and finance-related transactions.

The firm acts for a range of clients, including project sponsors, contractors and suppliers, commercial lenders and export credit agencies. The team advised JBIC in connection with the financing of the Ilijan Power Project, a 1200MW gas fired combined cycle power plant under development in the Philippines. Also represented the Taiwan Shikansen Consortium, a group of major Japanese companies in connection with the development of the High Speed Rail Project between Taipei and Kaohsiung in Taiwan. **Clients:** JBIC; Mitsubishi Heavy Industries; Mitsui; Itochu.

White & Case LLP (5 ptrs, 10 asscs) The practice represents sponsors, developers, lenders, equity investors and multilateral agencies. Held to be *"increasingly strong, notably on the borrower side,"* the majority of its work is conducted on behalf of Japanese corporations, both developers and constructors. The team has recently advised on projects in the Philippines, Thailand, Mexico and Indonesia.

Robert Grondine* is once again recommended by peers as the firm's leading light. He heads a team which acted for JBIC in relation to a number of loans in South America and on the restructuring of projects in Asia. It also represented Mitsubishi Materials Corp on a copper smelting project in Indonesia. **Clients:** Mitsubishi Corp; international banks; JBIC.

Tokyo Aoyama Law Office – Baker & McKenzie (3 ptrs, 4 asscs) Rivals acknowledge that the firm is *"doing quite a bit"* of projects work, *"due in no small part"* to the Aoyama connection. The team boasts a strong client base of Japanese utilities and sponsors, and is renowned for advising on investment by foreign entrants in the newly liberalised Japan electricity industry.

The team represented the Tokyo Electric Power Co on its New South Wales forestry investment, the first major carbon rights investment made by a Japanese company overseas. It has also acted on a number of other projects in concert with other Asian offices, including the Sumitomo Heavy Industries Manjung Project, the EPDC Malaysia Project and the EPDC Biomass office. **Clients:** Sumitomo Heavy Industries; Enron; Mitsubishi Materials Corp; Exxon; Electric Power Development; Itochu; Toshiba.

Lovells (2 ptrs, 2 asscs) Perceived to be *"executing an increasing amount of work for sponsors,"* the firm specialises in JBIC/MITI-backed financing and infrastructure projects. Among the team's *"energetic partners"* **Rupert Lewi*** stands out, recommended by a rival firm for *"absolutely excellent work on a big deal."*

The firm advised the Government of Sri Lanka, the Board of Investment of Sri Lanka, the Ceylon Electricity Board and the Ceylon Petroleum Corp in respect to the development of a 163.15MW combined-cycle power generation facility in Colombo by AES Corp of America. Also acted for Nissho Iwai Corp in relation to the 541MW Rosarito power project in Mexico (total project cost of $345 million). **Clients:** Mizuho Holdings; Sumitomo; JBIC; Nissho Iwai; Mitsubishi, Government of Sri Lanka.

Denton Wilde Sapte (1 ptr, 5 asscs) The key strength of this project finance practice is energy expertise, in which sector the firm maintains a solid reputation for advising trading houses. The team represented ITOCHU Corporation in regard to the restructuring of the Ras Laffan project financing, and acted for Tomen Corp in relation to some confidential project financing work. It was sole international adviser on a $3 billion oilfield development in Japan. **Clients:** Tomen; Sumitomo; ITOCHU; Marubeni.

Freshfields Foreign Law Office (1 ptr, 2 asscs) The firm's global network is considered by peers to provide great strength to the team in Tokyo. Advisory work and reviewing documentation accounts for a significant portion of the office's workload, while PFI is a growing area of focus. **Mark Keeler*** is admired for his skills in this area. **Clients:** Bank of Tokyo-Mitsubishi; Marubeni; JBIC.

Orrick, Herrington & Sutcliffe (1 ptr, 2 asscs) The firm has represented clients in the international project finance market in Asia and around the globe, working with them in all phases of infrastructure projects. These include the development, construction, financing and operation of power stations, telecommunications facilities, pipelines, roadways, petrochemical facilities, airports and other major public facilities. The Tokyo team advised on two Spanish wind power projects, and assisted on the establishment and financing of one of Japan's largest broadband and interactive cable television operating companies. **Clients:** Tomen; US banks.

Leaders' profiles – Japan

AKAI, Izumi
Sullivan & Cromwell, Tokyo +813 3213 6145
akaii@sullcrom.com
Recommended in Banking & Finance: Japan Foreign, Capital Markets: Japan Foreign
Specialisation: Counsel at *Sullivan & Cromwell's* Tokyo office since 1996. Actively participates in the U.S. law practices of the firm and is also available to render advice on certain matters of Japanese law. Has been involved in securities, mergers and acquisitions, project finance and other corporate work for a number of prominent Japanese and non-Japanese clients. Has extensively advised issuers and underwriters in securities offerings in the United States by a number of Japanese industrial issuers, Japanese financial institutions and non-Japanese issuers. Also very active in cross-border joint ventures, strategic investments, alliances and other merger and acquisition work. Has also been involved in a number of investments in Japanese real estate and bank loan portfolios by foreign investors.
Prof. Memberships: American Bar Association; Association of the Bar of the City of New York; Dai-Ichi Tokyo Bar Association; Japan Federation of Bar Associations.
Career: Began career as a lawyer in 1982. Joined *Sullivan & Cromwell* in New York from 1987 to 1992. Became Counsel (affiliated foreign lawyer in a registered joint enterprise with *Sullivan & Cromwell's* Tokyo office) in 1996.
Personal: Born 1955. Attended the University of Tokyo (LLB, 1980) and the University of Chicago (LLM, 1987). Admitted to the Bars of New York and Japan.

AOKI, Kunio
Aoki & Partners, Tokyo +81 3 3211 8871
Recommended in Capital Markets

ATSUMI, Hiroo
Atsumi & Usui, Tokyo 102-0083 +813 5276 6131
Recommended in Banking & Finance, Capital Markets

J

BURLEY, Rob
Clifford Chance Law Office, Tokyo +81 3 5561 6600
Recommended in Banking & Finance: Japan Foreign, Capital Markets: Japan Foreign, Corporate/Mergers & Acquisitions: Japan Foreign, Project Finance

CAHILL, Matthew
Clifford Chance Law Office, Tokyo +81 3 5561 6600
Recommended in Capital Markets: Japan Foreign

DECK, David D.
Shearman & Sterling, Tokyo +81 3 5251 1601
ddeck@shearman.com
Recommended in Capital Markets: Japan Foreign
Specialisation: Managing partner of *Shearman and Sterling*'s Tokyo office, representing major US, foreign and Japanese companies and financial institutions in cross-border mergers and acquisitions, venture capital and private equity transactions, securitisation transactions, public and private placement offerings, project financings and leveraged lease financings. Recent experience includes representation of: Morgan Stanley Dean Witter Principal Funding Inc. in Japan's first securitisation of non-performing loan portfolios; Merrill Lynch in its real estate conduit loan programme in Japan; Citibank, N.A in the structuring of a real estate securitisation for Mazda Motor Corporation; and ING Baring Securities (Japan) Limited in a consumer finance receivables securitisation.
Prof. Memberships: Member of Japan-America Society of New York and the American Chamber of Commerce in Japan.
Career: Admitted to New York Bar and in Japan as *Gaikokuho Jimu Bengoshi* (Foreign Legal Consultant).
Personal: Graduate of UCLA Law School (JD 1988); Columbia University (MA, East Asian Languages and Cultures, 1983); Bates College (BA, 1978); and Waseda University, International Division (1977).

EJIRI, Takashi
Asahi, Tokyo 107-8485 +813 35 050 003
Recommended in Corporate/M&A

FUJIEDA, Atsushi
Nagashima, Ohno & Tsunematsu, Tokyo +813 3288 7000
Recommended in Corporate/M&A

FUJINAWA, Kenichi
Nagashima, Ohno & Tsunematsu, Tokyo +813 3288 7000
Recommended in Corporate/M&A

GOTO, Izuru
Tanaka & Takahashi, Tokyo 107-0062 +813 3475 1631
goto@ttlaw.gr.jp
Recommended in Banking & Finance
Specialisation: Partner. Main area of practice is banking and securities law, particularly securitisation, project finance, and capital placement of bank issued debt. Advises banks and securities firms in derivative transactions and in general banking transactions.
Prof. Memberships: First Tokyo Bar Association; New York State Bar.
Publications: 'Credit Enhancement for Asset Backed CP Programs', NBL, 1994 538, 540.
Career: Admitted to Japanese bar in 1986, New York State bar in 1993.
Personal: Born in Aichi, Japan in 1957. LL.B from Tokyo University, 1981; LL.M from Duke University School of Law, 1992; attended Legal Research and Training Institute of the Supreme Court of Japan, 1984 to 1986. Native language Japanese; fluent in English.

GRONDINE, Robert
White & Case LLP, Tokyo +81 3 3259 0200
rgrondine@whitecase.com
Recommended in Corporate/Mergers & Acquisitions: Japan Foreign, Project Finance
Specialisation: Partner in the Tokyo office. Focuses on corporate, commercial and financial transactions involving Japan. Emphasis on mergers and acquisitions, asset-based structured finance and tax-effective finance transactions; an authority on Japanese cross-border equipment leasing (leveraged lease and aircraft financing); assists arrangers in developing some of the most innovative and sophisticated leasing structures used in Japan; assists non-Japanese companies in large and small acquisitions and joint ventures in Japan, and Japanese companies in acquiring plants and companies in various countries around the world, as well as setting up distribution and licensing networks, establishing subsidiaries and reorganising corporate operating structures in Japan and the US; advises on project financings involving Japanese parties as sponsors and lenders throughout Asia (restructurings and refinancings); has lectured in English and Japanese.
Prof. Memberships: American Bar Association, Section of International Law & Practice; New York State Bar Association (1981), International Law Section; Tokyo Chapter Chairman Association of the Bar of New York City, Co-Chair Committee on Bar Relations in Asia; California State Bar Association (1990), International Law Section; District of Columbia Bar Association (1991); Tokyo Second Bar Association; American Chamber of Commerce in Japan; Chair of Legal Services Committee, Board of Governors, Chair of 50th Anniversary Committee, Vice President, President 2000-2001.
Career: Southern District and Eastern Federal District Courts of New York, 1981; Registered as Gaikokuho Jimu Bengoshi in Japan, 1993.
Personal: Born 29 January, 1952. Dartmouth College, 1974, AB magna cum laude; Boston University Law School, 1980, JD magna cum laude; Cornell University Graduate School of Arts & Sciences, 1974-75, FALCON Program for Japanese language; Harvard Law School, 1979-80, East Asian Legal Studies Program. Lives in Tokyo.

GRUNDY, Tony
Linklaters (a member firm of Linklaters & Alliance), Tokyo +81 3 3568 3800
tony.grundy@linklaters.com
Recommended in Capital Markets: Japan Foreign
Specialisation: Specialist in international finance with experience in capital markets, banking, structured finance, securitisations and corporate recovery, advising investment banks and borrowers located in most parts of the world. Established the firm's Tokyo office in 1987 and has also worked in *Linklaters'* offices in London, Hong Kong and Singapore.

HAMADA, Kunio
Hamada & Matsumoto, Tokyo +813 3580 3377
Recommended in Capital Markets

HARA, Hisashi
Nagashima, Ohno & Tsunematsu, Tokyo +813 3288 7000
Recommended in Corporate/M&A

HASHIDATE, Kenji
Hashidate Law Office, Tokyo 100-0011 +81 3 3504 3800 / 1007
Recommended in Corporate/M&A

HIRAKAWA, Osamu
Anderson Mori, Tokyo +813 3214 1371
Recommended in Corporate/M&A

HUNSAKER, Mark
Sullivan & Cromwell, Tokyo +81 3 3213 6140
Recommended in Capital Markets: Japan Foreign

INMAN, Jonathan
Linklaters (a member firm of Linklaters & Alliance), Tokyo +81 3 3568 3800
jonathan.inman@linklaters.com
Recommended in Project Finance, Project Finance: India Foreign
Specialisation: All aspects of major projects, including the structuring and documentation of the financing and security arrangements, and including expertise in the construction and electricity industries. Led the team working on the Dabhol Power project, advising in particular on the power purchase agreements, construction contracts and government contracts and guarantees. Advised in connection with the construction and financing of various independent power station projects in the UK, India and Pakistan, as well as the Indian Ministries of Finance and Power on power purchase agreements and currently advising sponsors on the largest of the Indian 'mega-projects'. Recent assignments include advising sponsors on a project to set up a utility complex to supply a large petrochemical plant in China, and advising foreign lenders to a major new toll road in Korea.
Career: Currently head of Project Finance Practice, Tokyo.

INOUE, Satoshi
Nagashima, Ohno & Tsunematsu, Tokyo +813 3288 7000
Recommended in Banking & Finance

ISHIGURO, Toru
Hamada & Matsumoto, Tokyo +813 3580 3377
Recommended in Banking & Finance, Capital Markets

KAKUYAMA, Kazutoshi
Anderson Mori, Tokyo +813 3214 1371
Recommended in Corporate/M&A

KATAYAMA, Tatsu
Anderson Mori, Tokyo +813 3214 1371
Recommended in Banking & Finance, Capital Markets

KAWAMURA, Akira
Anderson Mori, Tokyo +813 3214 1371
Recommended in Corporate/M&A

KEELER, Mark
Freshfields Law Office, Tokyo +81 3 3584 8500
mark.keeler@freshfields.com
Recommended in Capital Markets: Japan Foreign, Project Finance
Specialisation: Principle area of practice is finance related including securitisations, international debt, equity and equity-related issues and structured financings.

KIM, Young Joon
Milbank, Tweed, Hadley & McCloy, Tokyo +813 3504 1050
Recommended in Corporate/Commercial: South Korea Foreign, Project Finance

KIMURA, Akiko
Tomotsune Kimura & Mitomi, Tokyo +813 3580 0800
Recommended in Capital Markets

KINAMI, Naoki
Freshfields Law Office, Tokyo +81 3 3584 8500
naoki.kinami@freshfields.com
Recommended in Banking & Finance, Capital Markets
Specialisation: Practice has focused primarily on international finance, corporate mergers and acquisitions and regulatory matters.

KITANOSONO, Masayuki
Matsuo & Kosugi, Tokyo +813 3542 9141
Recommended in Capital Markets

KITAZAWA, Masaakira
Anderson Mori, Tokyo +813 3214 1371
Recommended in Banking & Finance, Capital Markets

KITCHIN, Alan
Ashurst Morris Crisp, Tokyo +813 5276 5900
Recommended in Corporate/Mergers & Acquisitions: Japan Foreign, Project Finance

KOSUGI, Akira
Nishimura & Partners, Tokyo +813 5562 8500
Recommended in Banking & Finance

KOSUGI, Takeo
Matsuo & Kosugi, Tokyo +813 3542 9141
Recommended in Capital Markets

KUSANO, Koichi
Nishimura & Partners, Tokyo +813 5562 8500
Recommended in Corporate/M&A

KUWABARA, Satoko
Mori Sogo Law Offices, Tokyo +813 5223 7700
skuwabara@morisogo.com
Recommended in Capital Markets, Corporate/M&A
Specialisation: Partner. Main areas of work are mergers, acquisitions, corporate finance, structured finance as well as general corporate law. Has handled various mergers and acquisitions for both Japanese and overseas clients. Acted on sale of a collapsed bank, a merger between Japanese leading banks, acquisition and resolution by overseas investor of distressed loan assets held by various Japanese banks and other financial institutions. Acted for issuer of 'mezzanine bonds' in transaction described by The Asian Wall Street Journal as the first 'junk bond' offering by a Japanese issuer. Acts for a number of private equity funds on establishment and actual investment activities and a number of structured finance transactions involving real property. Contributor to 'Structuring International Transactions' (Kluwer 1997).
Prof. Memberships: Daini Tokyo Bar Association. Inter Pacific Bar Association.
Career: Qualified in 1990. Joined *Mori Sogo* in 1990, becoming partner in 1998. Seconded to *Freshfields* in London 1994-1996.
Personal: Born November 1964. Graduated from Tokyo University in 1988 (LLB). Attended Legal Research & Training Institute 1988-1990. Attended Oxford University 1993-1994 (M. Juris). Fluent in English. Lives in Tokyo.

LEVINE, Robert
Davis Polk & Wardwell, Tokyo +813 5561 4421
Recommended in Corporate/Mergers & Acquisitions: Japan Foreign

LEWI, Rupert
Lovells, Tokyo +81 3 3221 8511
rupert.lewi@lovells.com
Recommended in Project Finance
Specialisation: Partner specialising in: (1) the commercial and financial aspects of plant projects and energy and resources projects, involving limited recourse financing and export credit agency financing. Experience also extends to joint ventures and corporate and business acquisitions. Transactions include two power projects in Mexico, a coal mine project in Indonesia and petrochemical refinery projects in two CIS countries and an LNG receiving terminal project in China; and (2) mergers and acquisitions including JPY 170 billion Lawson convenience store acquisition in Japan and NT 17 billion telecommunications company acquisition in Taiwan.
Prof. Memberships: Law Society.
Career: Qualified in Western Australia in 1984; admitted in New South Wales in 1988 and in England & Wales in 1999; partner *Lovell White Durrant* in 1998.
Personal: Born 1961. Resides in Tokyo.

LEWIS, Christopher
Orrick, Herrington & Sutcliffe, Tokyo +813 3224 2922
clewis@orrick.com
Recommended in Capital Markets: Japan Foreign
Specialisation: Specialises in securitisation and other forms of structured finance, particularly asset repackaging and derivative-linked transactions. Many years of experience in Japan, Korea and other Asian jurisdictions. Recent Japanese securitisation experience includes consumer finance receivables, auto loan receivables, lease receivables, residential mortgages, commercial property and promissory notes.
Publications: 'Asset Repackaging Wins Further Followers' (IFLR, November 1996), 'Securitisation of Consumer Finance Receivables in Japan' (Asian Securitisation and Structured Finance Guide 2000) and many other articles.
Career: Partner, *Orrick*. Previously Partner with *Simmons & Simmons* in London and Hong Kong and investment banker in Tokyo and London. Frequent speaker at Japan-related securitisation conferences.
Personal: BA, BCL, Hertford College, Oxford. Speaks and reads Japanese fluently.

LEWIS, Steve
Herbert Smith, Tokyo +81 3 3508 4508
Steve.lewis@herbertsmith.com
Recommended in Corporate/Mergers & Acquisitions: Japan Foreign
Specialisation: Extensive experience of mergers, acquisitions and joint ventures in numerous industries including telecoms, media, publishing, energy, pharmaceuticals and heavy industry. International clients include AT&T, Gulfstream Aerospace, Pacific Century CyberWorks, Pearson and Premier Oil.
Prof. Memberships: Licensed to practise English law in Japan as a 'Gaikokuho Jimu Bengoshi'.
Career: Managing partner of *Herbert Smith*'s Tokyo Office.
Personal: St. Catharine's College, Cambridge University.

MAEDA, Hiroshi
Mitsui Yasuda Wani & Maeda, Tokyo +813 3224 0020
Recommended in Banking & Finance

MAEDA, Toshihiro
Nishimura & Partners, Tokyo +813 5562 8500
Recommended in Capital Markets

McCLENAHAN, John H.
Ashurst Morris Crisp, Tokyo +81 3 5276 5900
Recommended in Project Finance

MIHARA, Hidetaka
Nagashima, Ohno & Tsunematsu, Tokyo +813 3288 7000
Recommended in Banking & Finance, Capital Markets

MITOMI, Fuyuo
Tomotsune Kimura & Mitomi, Tokyo +81 3 3580 0800
Recommended in Capital Markets

MITSUI, Takuhide
Mitsui Yasuda Wani & Maeda, Tokyo +813 3224 0020
Recommended in Capital Markets, Corporate/M&A

MORISHITA, Kunihiko
Anderson Mori, Tokyo +813 3214 1371
Recommended in Banking & Finance

J

NAGAHAMA, Tsuyoshi
Anderson Mori, Tokyo +813 3214 1371
Recommended in Banking & Finance, Corporate/M&A

NAGASHIMA, Yasuharu
Nagashima, Ohno & Tsunematsu, Tokyo +813 3288 7000
Recommended in Corporate/M&A

NAKAJIMA, Tohru
Nagashima, Ohno & Tsunematsu, Tokyo +813 3288 7000
Recommended in Corporate/M&A

J

NAMEKATA, Kunio
TMI Associates, Tokyo +813 5472 8511
knamekata@tmi.gr.jp
Recommended in Corporate/M&A
Specialisation: Practice centres on mergers & acquisitions, joint ventures, corporate finance and investment funds. Also advises on all aspects of commercial contract law and on regulatory issues. Represents clients from diverse industries such as securities, e-commerce, manufacturing, retail, import/export, pharmaceutical, telecommunications and media. Clients include The Nomura Securities Co., Ltd. and the Softbank group of companies.
Prof. Memberships: Dai-ni Tokyo Bar Association (1979 - present). Disciplinary Maintenance Committee, Dai-ni Tokyo Bar Association (1999 - present). New York State Bar Association (1995 - present).
Career: Admitted to Japanese bar in 1979. Admitted to New York State bar in 1995. Tokyo Fuji Law Office (1979 - 1991). Joined *TMI Associates* as Partner in 1991. *De Bandt, van Hecke & Lagae*, Brussels, Belgium (1994 - 1995). *Stephenson Harwood & Lo*, Hong Kong (1995).
Personal: Born 15 May 1954. Graduated University of Tokyo (LLB 1977); Legal Training and Research Institute of Japan (1979); University of Michigan Law School (LLM 1994); Katholieke University Leuven (1995). Lives in Tokyo, Japan.

NISHIMURA, Toshiro
Nishimura & Partners, Tokyo +813 5562 8500
Recommended in Corporate/M&A

ONO, Masaru
Nishimura & Partners, Tokyo +813 5562 8500
Recommended in Capital Markets

PARADISE, Theodore
Davis Polk & Wardwell, Tokyo +813 5561 4421
Recommended in Banking & Finance: Japan Foreign, Capital Markets: Japan Foreign

SATO, Masanori
Mori Sogo Law Offices, Tokyo +81 3 5223 7700
msato@morisogo.com
Recommended in Capital Markets
Specialisation: Partner. Main areas of work are securitisation and other structured finance, corporate finance, M&A and general corporate law practice. Has handled various structured and corporate finance transactions for both Japanese and overseas clients. Acted on various innovative finance transactions, including the first publicly offered CMBS deal in Japan. Acts for a number of banks, securities companies, insurance companies and other financial institutions.
Prof. Memberships: Daini Tokyo Bar Association. New York State Bar Association.
Publications: Author 'Practical Issues Associated with Securitisation of Financial Assets' (NBL, 1995); 'Restoring the Trust – Japanese version of RTC' (1996); 'Problems Regarding Issuance of Corporate Bonds' (JICPA Journal, 1996); 'Forefront of Financial Transactions' (Co-author with Professor Shindo) (1996); 'Securitisation in Japan – Legal and Regulatory Updates' (ISR, 1998); 'Recent Trends in Japanese Securitisation' (ISR, 1999); 'New Developments in Japanese ABS, CMBS and J-REIT' (ISR, 2000).
Career: Qualified in Japan (1990) and in New York (1994). Joined *Mori Sogo* in 1990, becoming partner in 1997. Seconded to *Cleary, Gottlieb, Steen & Hamilton*, New York (1993-1994) and *Linklaters & Paines*, London (1994-1995). Lecturer in the summer program held by Duke University School of Law and the University of Hong Kong Faculty of Law regarding 'Securitisation in Japan' (1997). Member of Research Committee of the Structured Finance Institute of Japan (1997-1998). Member of the Financial Law Board of Japan from 1998.
Personal: Born November 1965. Graduated from the University of Tokyo (LLB, 1988) and University of Chicago Law School (LLM, 1993). Fluent in English. Lives in Tokyo.

SEKINE, Osamu
Nagashima, Ohno & Tsunematsu, Tokyo +813 3288 7000
Recommended in Capital Markets

SENGOKU, Katsu
Nishimura & Partners, Tokyo +813 5562 8500
Recommended in Banking & Finance

SHINDO, Isao
Anderson Mori, Tokyo +813 3214 1371
Recommended in Capital Markets

SNEIDER, David
Simpson Thacher & Bartlett, Tokyo +81 3 5562 8601
d_sneider@stblaw.com
Recommended in Capital Markets: Japan Foreign, Corporate/Mergers & Acquisitions: Japan Foreign
Specialisation: Member of *Simpson Thacher & Bartlett*'s Corporate Department and head of its Tokyo office since 1994. Has lived in Japan for more than 17 years, including ten years as a professional, and is proficient in Japanese. Advises both Japanese and multinational clients in cross-border corporate finance transactions involving Japan, including capital markets and M&A transactions. In 2000, transactions included acting for Toys "R" Us Japan in its $480 million global initial public offering, SKY Perfect Communications in its $1.4 billion global initial public offering, for the underwriters in Oracle Japan Corporation's $7.6 billion global equity offering, and for Fuji Heavy Industries in its sale of a 20% stake to General Motors. In 1999, transactions included acting for East Japan Railway Company in $5.6 US billion global privatisation transaction, for the underwriters in a $1.45 US billion global offering by Toyota Motor Corporation and for Japan Telecom in sale of 30% stake to British Telecom and AT&T.
Prof. Memberships: American Bar Association; New York State Bar Association, Inter-Pacific Bar Association.
Career: Qualified in 1985. 1988-91 responsible for legal affairs in Asia at Salomon Brothers Asia Limited based in Tokyo. Joined *Simpson Thacher & Bartlett* in 1992. Yale University 1975-79, BA summa cum laude; Harvard Law School 1980-84, JD cum laude; and Tokyo University, 1979-80 as a research student.
Personal: Born 25 July, 1957.

STEVENS, Charles
Freshfields Foreign Law Office, Tokyo +813 3584 8500
charles.stevens@freshfields.com
Recommended in Corporate/Mergers & Acquisitions: Japan Foreign
Specialisation: Specialisations include mergers and acquisitions, demergers, alliances, restructuring, arbitration and litigation and inward and outward investment.

SUGIMOTO, Fumihide
Nagashima, Ohno & Tsunematsu, Tokyo +813 3288 7000
Recommended in Banking & Finance, Capital Markets

TANAKA, Hideaki
Hamada & Matsumoto, Tokyo +813 3580 3377
Recommended in Corporate/M&A

TSUNEMATSU, Ken
Nagashima, Ohno & Tsunematsu, Tokyo +813 3288 7000
Recommended in Capital Markets

TURNER, Malcolm
Clifford Chance Law Office, Tokyo +81 3 5561 6600
Recommended in Banking & Finance: Japan Foreign, Project Finance

UCHIDA, Harumichi
Mori Sogo Law Offices, Tokyo +81 3 5223 7700
Recommended in Corporate/M&A
Specialisation: Partner. Main areas of work are mergers & acquisitions as well as general corporate law, information technology (IT) related transactions, competition law, and dispute resolution. Has handled numerous mergers and acquisitions, corporate restructurings and global alliances between leading multi-national companies. Advises major Japanese and non-Japanese clients on anti-trust law issues in mergers & acquisitions and transactions, and has defended clients in anti-trust investigations and proceedings. Counsels high-tech, internet and telecommunication businesses. Acts for clients in negotiations, dispute resolutions and litigations of a complex nature.
Prof. Memberships: Daini-Tokyo Bar Association (Chairman of International Committee 2000); Inter-Pacific Bar Association (Secretary General 1999-2001); IBA; ABA; ICC; LES; Fair Trade Institute.

Publications: Chief-editor 'Internet Laws' (1997); co-author 'Investment in US and Antitrust Law' (1982); co-author 'Legal Strategy in Mergers & Acquisitions' (1987) and other articles; frequent lecturer at professional seminars.
Career: Admitted to bar in Japan, 1973, in New York, 1980; Joined *Mori Sogo Law Offices* in 1973; worked for *Donovan, Leisure, Newton & Irvine* (N.Y., L.A.) 1979-1980; Visiting Professor of Hitotsubashi University Graduate School on International Legal Strategy (2000 -).
Personal: Tokyo University (LLB 1970). New York University School of Law (LLM 1979).

WANI, Akihiro
Mitsui Yasuda Wani & Maeda, Tokyo +813 3224 0020
Recommended in Banking & Finance, Capital Markets

YASUDA, Mitsuhiro
Mitsui Yasuda Wani & Maeda, Tokyo +813 3224 0020
Recommended in Banking & Finance, Capital Markets

YONEDA, Takashi
Nishimura & Partners, Tokyo +813 5562 8500
Recommended in Capital Markets

YOSHIDA, Masayuki
Nagashima, Ohno & Tsunematsu, Tokyo +813 3288 7000
Recommended in Banking & Finance, Capital Markets

J

JERSEY

Corporate/Commercial

JERSEY Leading firms (Corporate/Commercial)
1 Mourant du Feu & Jeune
Ogier & Le Masurier
2 Bedell Cristin
3 Olsens

Firms are listed alphabetically in each band.

Leading individuals (Corporate/Commercial)
1 **BYRNE Chris** *Ogier & Le Masurier*
HOWARD Simon *Bedell Cristin*
JAMES Ian *Mourant du Feu & Jeune*
LOMBARDI Michael *Ogier & Le Masurier*
RICHOMME Jacqueline *Mourant du Feu & Jeune*
THOMAS Richard *Ogier & Le Masurier*
2 **CHAPLIN Clive** *Ogier & Le Masurier*
HERBERT Tim *Mourant du Feu & Jeune*
KERSHAW Nick *Ogier & Le Masurier*
Up and coming individuals
GERWAT Richard *Bedell Cristin*
OHLSSON Alex *Olsens*

Individuals are listed alphabetically in each band.

Mourant du Feu & Jeune (17 ptrs, 9 asscs) The oldest firm on the island, it has *"traditionally secured some of the better work"* in international finance and commerce. **Ian James** has for years been *"well regarded as a finance practitioner"* and **Jacqueline Richomme** *"does difficult transactions well."* **Tim Herbert** is another corporate partner of high standing. The team advised on Arran One Ltd, a $1.6 billion credit card securitisation for the Royal Bank of Scotland. **Clients:** Goldman Sachs; Deutsche Bank; Morgan Stanley; easyJet.

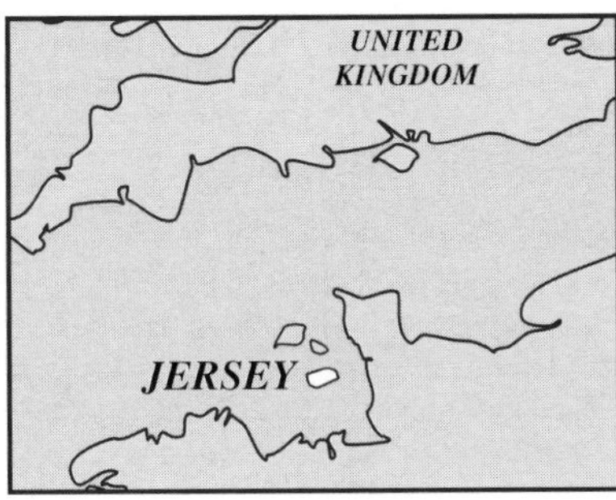

Ogier & Le Masurier (7 ptrs, 25 asscs) The firm has expanded significantly, adding twelve new lawyers to its ranks during the past year. Banking, securitisation, structured finance and capital markets are growth areas. **Michael Lombardi** and **Richard Thomas** have a *"high profile and presence,"* while the *"first-class"* **Chris Byrne**, **Clive Chaplin** and **Nick Kershaw** are also recommended. The firm advised Bank of America on the disposal of its EMEA private bank business to UBS, and Morgan Stanley on a $1.4 billion acquisition financing to Punch Taverns in connection with the Allied Domecq bid. **Clients:** ANZ; BNP; Flemings; Merrill Lynch.

Bedell Cristin (12 ptrs, 15 asscs) Regarded as *"the third firm in Jersey,"* it offers advice on structured finance, investment funds and trusts. Considered to field a number of *"able partners,"* the team includes **Simon Howard**, who has an excellent name for funds advice, and **Richard Gerwat**, a younger lawyer who our researchers found is *"making his mark in structured finance."* The team acted on the European Monthly Income Trust Ltd, listed in London and on the CISX, which raised gross assets of £195 million managed by Aberdeen Asset Managers. **Clients:** Deutsche Bank; Aberdeen Asset Managers.

Olsens (9 ptrs, 17 asscs) A growing firm with a growing reputation, and formerly known as Olsen, Backhurst & Dorey, it re-launched under its new name in April 2000. The firm specialises in sophisticated offshore corporate finance, and in **Alex Ohlsson**, it has a *"go-getting young lawyer"* who is held in high esteem. The team advised Morgan Stanley on the securitisation of Sainsbury's properties for £335 million. **Clients:** Investment banks and large local banks.

Leaders' profiles – Jersey

BYRNE, Chris
Ogier & Le Masurier, St. Helier +44 1534 504000
chris.byrne@ogier.com
Specialisation: Partner. Specialises in banking law, structured finance, investment funds, corporate law, commercial law, trusts and employee benefits.
Prof. Memberships: The Honourable Society of the Middle Temple; The English Law Society; The Law Society of Jersey; The International Bar Association.
Career: Trained *Allen & Overy*; qualified 1988; associate *Allen & Overy*; secondment from *Allen & Overy* to a London bank acting as bank's commercial in-house lawyer; posted to Asia to open *Allen & Overy's* Singapore office, 1992; admitted Jersey Bar, 1996; partner *Ogier & Le Masurier*, 1997.
Personal: Born 1965; resides St Clement, Jersey.

CHAPLIN, Clive
Ogier & Le Masurier, St. Helier +44 1534 504000
clive.chaplin@ogier.com
Specialisation: Partner Business Law Group; specialises in employee benefits, collective investment funds, limited partnerships, general commercial matters and trust law.
Prof. Memberships: The Law Society of England and Wales; The Law Society of Jersey; Member of the Jersey Law Commission.
Career: Admitted as an English solicitor 1977, Jersey solicitor 1986; became a partner at *Ogier & Le Masurier* 1994.
Personal: Born 1951. Resides in Trinity, Jersey. Leisure interests include tennis, choral singing and music. Language: English.

GERWAT, Richard
Bedell Cristin, St Helier +44 1534 814 814
richard.gerwat@bedellcristin.com
Specialisation: Partner and head of the structured finance practice area of the financial services law group. Extensive experience in banking and capital markets work with particular experience in securitisation. Has considerable experience in asset backed financing having acted as Jersey counsel in some of the most innovative securitisation transactions. *Bedell Cristin* is rated as a market leader in securitisation. Is frequently asked to write and speak on matters relating to the use of Jersey SPVs and regularly participates in initiatives with the Jersey regulatory authorities concerning matters relating to new legislation / codes of practice in this field.
Prof. Memberships: Memberships: The Law Society of Jersey; The Law Society of England and Wales; Member of the Finance Industry Sub-Committee of the Law Society of Jersey.
Career: Became a partner of *Bedell Cristin* in 1994 after joining the firm in 1989. 1986/89 employed by *Clifford Chance*, London.
Personal: Born London, January 1965. 1992 Advocate of the Royal Court of Jersey. 1988 Solicitor of the Supreme Court of England and Wales. 1985 University of Buckingham (LLB(Hons)) 1985.

HERBERT, Tim
Mourant du Feu & Jeune, St Helier
+44 1534 609000
tim.herbert@mourant.com
Specialisation: Partner of *Mourant du Feu & Jeune* in the Commercial Department. Specialises in corporate commercial, M&A and investment fund work.
Prof. Memberships: International Bar Association, Institute of Directors, Jersey Law Society, Jersey Offshore Insurance Association.
Career: Born and educated in Jersey. Bachelor of Arts and Master of Arts in Jurisprudence of Trinity College, Oxford. Called to the Bar in England in 1982, worked briefly in Chambers in the Middle Temple in London and then returned to Jersey. Called to the Bar in Jersey as an Advocate of the Royal Court in 1985. In October 1988 appointed Honorary Consul for Finland in Jersey.
Personal: Born 1959.

HOWARD, Simon
Bedell Cristin, St Helier +44 1534 814 814
simon.howard@bedellcristin.com
Specialisation: Partner and head of the investment funds and pension schemes practice area of the financial services law group. Over a decade of experience in Jersey specialising in investment fund structures and general compliance law matters for corporate and institutional clients. Main area of work involves advising asset managers based around the world on the launch, restructuring and termination of funds and on other legal and regulatory issues relevant to the industry. In the past twelve months has been involved with the establishment of four split capital investment funds for Aberdeen Asset Management in Jersey, a similar vehicle in Guernsey for Edinburgh Fund Managers and a closed ended fund for Legg Mason Investors which is the first Channel Islands fund to settle share dealings through CREST. Significant training role with frequent participation as a speaker at conferences and seminars.
Prof. Memberships: Memberships: The Law Society of Jersey, STEP, IBA.
Career: Became a partner of *Bedell Cristin* in 1994 after joining the firm in 1987. 1985 - 1987 employed by *Macfarlanes* in London.
Personal: Born 7th October, 1961 in Jersey. 1989 University of Oxford, Pembroke College (MA); 1985 Inns of Court School of Law London; 1984 University of Oxford, Pembroke College (BA Jurisprudence, First Class).

JAMES, Ian
Mourant du Feu & Jeune, St Helier
+44 1534 609000
ian.james@mourant.com
Specialisation: Partner in the International Finance Department. Specialises in wide range of finance transactions, with particular emphasis on securitisation and corporate finance matters.
Prof. Memberships: Jersey Law Society, Law Society of England and Wales.
Career: Educated at Queen's College, Oxford University. Admitted as an English solicitor in 1976. Became a solicitor of the Royal Court of Jersey in 1986. Articled with *Charles Russell & Co* London and worked for a period in the Middle East following qualification.
Personal: Born 1950.

KERSHAW, Nick
Ogier & Le Masurier, St. Helier +44 1534 504000

LOMBARDI, Michael
Ogier & Le Masurier, St. Helier +44 1534 504000
michael.lombardi@ogier.com
Specialisation: Partner in *Ogier & Le Masurier* in the Business Law Group and heads up the firm's securitisation practice. Has been engaged in structured finance work since the mid 1980's and has wide experience of international capital markets transactions with particular emphasis on asset-backed securities, collateralised bond offerings, structured debt instruments, securitisations and repackagings. Previous transactions in which has been involved include the US$10 billion ROSE CLO transactions for NatWest Bank, the US$6 billion Oasis programme and a US$24 billion CP and MTN programme for a leading German banking institution. Currently engaged on a proposed US$50 billion alternative trade credit settlement system utilising advanced internet technology and structured financing techniques being promoted by a syndicate of leading institutions.
Prof. Memberships: Law Society of Jersey; Law Society of England & Wales; Law Society of Scotland; Society of Writers to Her Majesty's Signet; The International Bar Association; Director of the Channel Islands Stock Exchange and an Executive Member of the European Securitisation Forum.
Career: Initially qualified as a solicitor in Scotland. Trained with *Dundas & Wilson* (now part of *Arthur Andersen*) in Edinburgh. Also qualified as a lawyer in England, Hong Kong, Bermuda and Jersey.
Personal: Attended University of Dundee (LLB) and University of Exeter (LLM). Leisure interests include golf, skiing and field hockey.

OHLSSON, Alex
Olsens, St Helier +44 1534 888 900

RICHOMME, Jacqueline
Mourant du Feu & Jeune, St Helier
+44 1534 609000
jacqueline.richomme@mourant.com
Specialisation: Partner in the International Finance Department. Specialises in capital markets and structured finance work, particularly private equity and venture capital funds, securitisation, and structured financing. Highlight of 2000 CVC Asia – a US$750 million private equity pool for joint investment in the Asia Pacific region by CVC Capital Partners Asia Pacific LP (a limited partnership controlled by a Jersey company and administrated by *Mourant & Co.*) and Citigroup.
Prof. Memberships: International Bar Association; Institute of Directors.
Career: Educated at the University of Durham and the College of Law, Chester. Admitted as an English Solicitor in 1982. Worked for four years with *Farrer & Co* London. Admitted as a solicitor of the Royal Court of Jersey in 1988.
Personal: Born in 1957.

THOMAS, Richard
Ogier & Le Masurier, St. Helier +44 1534 504000
richard.thomas@ogier.com
Specialisation: Business law group *Ogier & Le Masurier*, St Helier. Partner and head of group; offshore funds, banking law, trust law and general commerical lawyer.
Prof. Memberships: Trained College of Law, London; enrolled as English Solicitor 1976; *Slaughter & May* 1974-78; in industry 1979-84; assistant commercial relations officer, financial regulation (mutual fund and banking supervisor) 1984-86; joined *Ogier & Le Cornu* in 1986; became partner in 1990.
Personal: Born 1950; resides St Mary, Jersey. Education: Oundle School; St John's College, Oxford (MA Literae Humaniores). Leisure: Jersey Symphony Orchestra and cycling.

J

JORDAN

Corporate/Commercial

JORDAN Leading firms (Corporate/Commercial)
1 Ali Sharif Zu'bi & Sharif Ali Zu'bi Law Office
2 Nabulsi & Associates
3 Dallal & Associates Rajai KW Dajani & Associates

Firms are listed alphabetically in each band.

Leading individuals (Corporate/Commercial)
1 **ZU'BI Sharif Ali** *Ali Sharif Zu'bi & Sharif Ali Zu'bi*
2 **DALLAL Mubadda** *Dallal & Associates* **KHALILIEH Yousef** *Rajai KW Dajani* **NABULSI Omar** *Nabulsi & Associates*

Individuals are listed alphabetically in each band.

Ali Sharif Zu'bi & Sharif Ali Zu'bi Law Office (4 ptrs, 11 asscs, 2 of counsel) *"One of a kind."* This *"top notch"* commercial firm has a pedigree stretching back to the British courts mandated in 1948. *"Bright and intelligent"* **Sharif Ali Zu'bi** is credited for his modern management of a multi-faceted team *"committed to providing a good service."* Well known for their privatisation expertise, they are key advisors to the government and continue to advise its Executive Privatisation Unit on the privatisation of the state telecom JTC. The firm is currently acting jointly with Clifford Chance in relation to privatisation of state owned airline Royal Jordanian. Active on all public offerings of securities out of Jordan including advising the lead managers in Telecommunications Corporation's $50 million Eurobond and for the issuer in Jordan Phosphate Mines Company's $100 million Eurobond. Represented Tractabel and Amoco in negotiations with the Government of Jordan for the transfer and distribution of natural gas from Egypt to Jordan. **Clients:** Citibank; Jordan Export Finance Bank; Arab Banking Corp; BNP Paribas; Merrill Lynch; Nomura International; Crédit Lyonnais; ING Barings; Jordan Phosphate Mines Company; Sumitomo Corporation; Tractabel; BP Amoco; France Telecom; Siemens; Philip Morris; Royal Jordanian Airlines; General Electric.

Nabulsi & Associates (10 lawyers in total) A traditional established firm, prominent in the commercial and investment banking sector, although the findings of *Chambers'* researchers indicate a lowering in profile this year. Its *"skilled"* team of lawyers specialises in telecommunications, construction and contract law. Ex-minister **Omar Nabulsi** is well known in Jordan for his excellent connections. The firm acts as legal counsel to the only cellular operator and to one of the two payphone operators in Jordan in tendering, licensing procedures and litigation. Recently advised the Jordanian Government on the telecoms sector restructuring programme involving the privatisation of the Telecommunications Corporation. Has acted on BOT infrastructure projects for the World Bank and Jordanian Chamber of Industry, and advised international clients in relation to their bids for the Samra Power Project and Aqaba Railway. Other projects include financing and construction of the first phosphoric acid plant in Jordan. **Clients:** BP Amoco; Motorola; Lockheed Corporation; McDonald's International; Jordan Phosphate Mines Co; ANZ Grindlays Bank; Cairo Amman Bank; Union Investment Corp; Swiss Embassy.

Dallal & Associates (2 ptrs, 5 asscs) *"Professional people who provide good value for money."* Offering a comprehensive corporate and commercial service, the firm specialises in IP, franchising, agency, shipping, e-commerce and e-trade related work. Key partner **Mubadda Dallal** enjoys a good reputation. Recent work

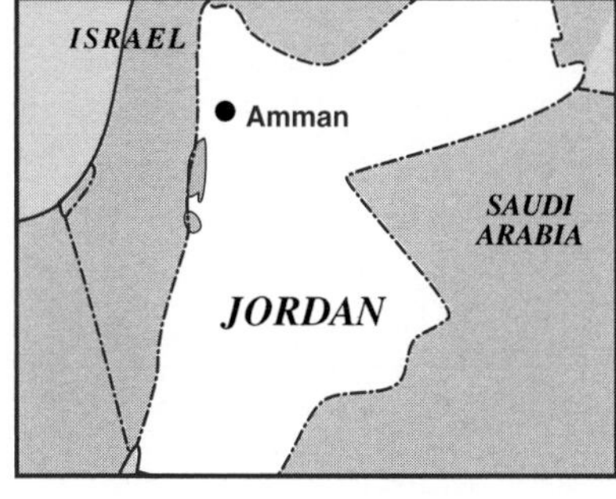

includes advising one of the world's largest multinational banks on its virtual internet banking operation due to be launched in Jordan, and in relation to a merger between two owning companies of the Sheraton and Marriott hotels. **Clients:** Gillette; Airbus Industrie Financial Services; France Telecom; Tradigrain SA.

Rajai KW Dajani & Associates (2 ptrs, 5 asscs) Researchers were impressed by the portfolio of this small but well regarded outfit. With the named partner now appointed judge to the Paris Court of Arbitration and the ICC, there is little doubt that *"hardworking and ambitious"* **Yousef Khalilieh** will increase the firm's profile with his *"practical approach."* Recent work includes representing Japanese contractors (Dai Nippon Construction, Hitachi Plant Engineering and the Ebara Corporation) in the Zay Water Supply project and acted for Amman Resources in a government agreement on a BOT basis. The firm advised the Jordan Gateway Project in negotiations with IFC regarding the set up of a free trade zone. **Clients:** The Danish Embassy; Mitsui & Co; Oneworld Software Solutions; Maktoob.com; Tella Terra Software Solutions; Saudi Aramco Lubricating Oil Refining Co; Kikkoman; Fuji Photofilm; Bridgestone.

Leaders' profiles – Jordan

DALLAL, Mubadda
Dallal & Associates, Amman +962 6464 2468

KHALILIEH, Yousef S
Rajai KW Dajani & Associates, Amman +962 6461 7417

NABULSI, Omar
Nabulsi & Associates, Amman +962 6465 4411

ZU'BI, Sharif Ali
Ali Sharif Zu'bi & Sharif Ali Zu'bi Law Office, Amman +962 6464 2908

KAZAKHSTAN

Energy & Natural Resources

KAZAKHSTAN Leading firms (Energy & Natural Resources)
1 Coudert Brothers
Denton Wilde Sapte
LeBoeuf, Lamb, Greene & MacRae LLP
Salans Hertzfeld & Heilbronn
2 Baker & McKenzie
White & Case LLP
3 Michael Wilson & Partners

Firms are listed alphabetically in each band.

Leading individuals (Energy & Natural Resources)
1 CAHN Jonathan *Coudert Brothers*
KENJEBAYEVA Aigoul *Salans Hertzfeld & Heilbronn*
VALDEZ Marla *Denton Wilde Sapte*
VARANESE James *LeBoeuf, Lamb, Greene*
2 MALTSEV Yuriy *White & Case LLP*
WILSON Michael *Michael Wilson & Partners*

Individuals are listed alphabetically in each band.

Coudert Brothers (2 ptrs, 10 asscs) A *"successful"* practice, which is acknowledged by rivals for its work on acquisitions of oil and gas companies. The team also advises on offshore exploration and production, and has experience of acting on energy financing transactions. The *"hard driving"* **Jonathan Cahn*** is an *"experienced guy"* who *"easily establishes contacts and develops trust with clients."* **Clients:** Chevron.

Denton Wilde Sapte (1 ptr, 5 asscs) Having acquired the CMS Cameron McKenna office in November 2000, the firm now has the presence on the ground to expand its *"already substantial slice"* of oil and gas work. *"Oil and gas specialist"* **Marla Valdez*** heads the office, and was commended to researchers for her *"sound commercial instincts."*

The firm recently represented the government on the privatisation of Mangistaumunaigaz, and advised Kazakhstan Petroleum on new legislation. **Clients:** Mangistaumunaigaz; Kazakhstan Petroleum

LeBoeuf, Lamb, Greene & MacRae LLP (1 ptr, 10 asscs) *"High pedigree firm with high pedigree clients,"* which has specific expertise on pipeline projects. **James Varanese*** has six years experience in the jurisdiction and comes highly recommended by his peers. The firm recently represented the Republic of Kazakhstan in selling a 5% stake in Tengiz Chevroil to Chevron, a deal valued at $500 million. Also represented Kaztransgaz on the acquisition of the pipeline assets of Intergas Central Asia, including the Bukhara-Uralsk pipeline system. **Clients:** Kaztransgaz; Republic of Kazakhstan.

Salans Hertzfeld & Heilbronn (1 ptr, 8 asscs) A strong oil and gas team was especially recommended to researchers for its work on behalf of agencies and leading international energy companies. Recent work includes advice on a tax dispute between British Gas and AGIP, as well as representing the EBRD and the IFC on the financing of AES. **Aigoul Kenjebayeva*** is a *"highly considered local oil specialist."* **Clients:** EBRD; Oryx; IFC.

Baker & McKenzie (2 ptrs, 7 asscs) A *"first rate name"* in the jurisdiction, which advises extensively on M&A, energy projects and debt restructuring in the region, often acting in concert with the highly rated Moscow office. The firm acted for AES in connection with the purchase of a 600MW thermal power plant, importing gas from Russia into Georgia. This transaction also involved the rescheduling of debts owed to the

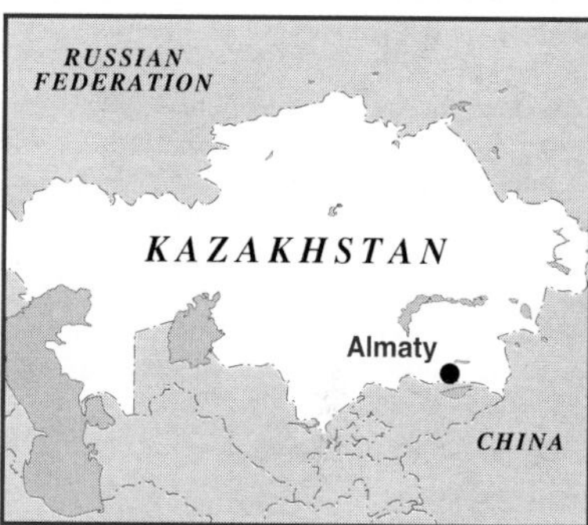

state of Georgia, funded by the World Bank, the EBRD and KFW. The team also acting for the purchasers of a distribution company in North Kazakhstan. **Clients:** AES.

White & Case LLP (1 ptr, 6 asscs) Entirely staffed by local lawyers, the office is known as a *"capital markets specialist,"* which also advises on M&A transactions in the energy sector. **Yuriy Maltsev*** has a fine reputation among his peers as a commercial lawyer. The firm represented Shimkent on its merger with Hurricane Hydrocarbons. **Clients:** Shimkent; Tractabel.

Michael Wilson & Partners (1 ptr, 4 asscs) An *"unusual entrepreneurial solicitor,"* with extensive experience in the region from his days at Baker & McKenzie, **Michael Wilson*** occupies a unique niche in the market. His firm represented JCI of South Africa on its bid to acquire 17 local enterprises which account for more than 20% of GDP, and advised Enterprise Oil in relation to the Baiganinsky Block license area. **Clients:** Tractabel; JCI; Enterprise Oil; Anglo Gold; Ormat Industries; BP Amoco Arco; Anglian Water International; Reuters; CJSC Air Kazakhstan.

*See leaders' profiles on page 452

Leaders' profiles – Kazakhstan

K

CAHN, Jonathan
Coudert Brothers, Almaty +7 3272 533 370

KENJEBAYEVA, Aigoul
Salans Hertzfeld & Heilbronn, Almaty +7 3272 324 841

MALTSEV, Yuriy
White & Case LLP, Almaty +7 3272 507 491
ymaltsev@whitecase.com
Specialisation: Head of Almaty office of *White & Case*. Range of high level corporate and securities law expertise with particular experience of acting as an adviser to the energy sector. Regularly represents wide range of major domestic and international corporates and financial institutions in Kazakhstan.
Career: Awarded Diploma of Honour of Kazakhstan for service in drafting the Constitution. Joined *White & Case* 1995 from *Clifford Chance*.
Personal: Citizen of Kazakhstan.

VALDEZ, Marla
Denton Wilde Sapte, Almaty +7 3272 581 950
almaty@dentonwildesapte.kz
Specialisation: Has been practising in natural resource law since 1988 and has worked full-time in Central Asia since 1993, primarily representing clients in the petroleum and mining industries. Most recent experience includes: participating in negotiations and advising clients on numerous energy projects in the Republics of Kazakhstan and Uzbekistan primarily in petroleum, hard minerals and uranium. Lead negotiator for one of the largest privatisation projects in the Republic of Kazakhstan (project worth 4.2 billion); advising clients on a broad range of commercial transactions in Kazakhstan and Uzbekistan including international and private financing, security arrangements, guarantees, commodity purchase and sale agreements, off-take sales and export arrangements; advising clients regarding corporate structures, privatisation, acquisitions, farm-outs, due diligence; advising clients on all aspects of investments in Kazakhstan and Uzbekistan from creation of joint ventures, registration of a legal presence, labour, operational licensing, ownership and leasing, importing and exporting, foreign investment law and civil transactions.
Prof. Memberships: Rocky Mountain Mineral Law Foundation. Colorado Bar Association.
Career: Qualified in 1988. In 1993 joined Welborn Sullivan Meck & Tooley, P.C. as a Shareholder and Director with postings in Almaty (Kazakhstan), Tashkent (Uzbeckistan) and Kiev (Ukraine). In 1998 joined *Denton Hall* as a Partner and Managing Partner of Central Asia practice group.
Personal: Born 17 April 1961 in Santa Fe, NM, USA. Attended Amherst College, Amherst, MA, USA. BA in Russian Studies *cum laude*, 1979-1984, and University of New Mexico, Alburquerque, NM, USA, *Juris Doctorate*, 1985-1988. Interests include outdoor activities. Resident in Almaty, Kazakhstan.

VARANESE, James
LeBoeuf, Lamb, Greene & MacRae, LLP, Almaty + 7 3272 507 575
jvaranes@llgm.com
Specialisation: Managing Partner in the Almaty Office. Since 1992, has advised clients active in Central Asia and the Caspian – the countries of Kazakhstan, Uzbekistan, Kyrgyzstan, Tajikistan, Turkmenistan, and Azerbaijan – on a broad range of legal matters critical in these emerging markets. Has advised foreign investors active in Central Asia and the Caspian in the following sectors: finance (project, trade/pre-export, and syndicated lending), telecommunications, natural resources (oil and gas, and hard minerals), privatisation, real estate, securities, and others. In addition to transactions in Central Asia, has also advised investors in the Czech Republic (where was resident in Prague for two years), the Slovak Republic, Poland, Hungary and the Russian Federation.
Career: Admitted to the bar in 1987 (Ohio), 1988 (District of Columbia). Partner with *LeBoeuf* since 1995.
Personal: Born November 22, 1958. Graduate of Harvard Law School, the Kennedy School of Government, and Harvard College.

WILSON, Michael E.
Michael Wilson & Partners, Almaty +7 3272 501 570
michael.wilson@mwp.kz
Specialisation: Power and heat energy generation, distribution and transmission; oil, gas, mining and natural resources; power and water, tariff and regulatory issues; corporate, commercial and joint ventures. Activities include: Tractebel SA; Ormat Industries Inc./International Power plc; power, water and gas distribution projects in Almaty, Astana, Atyrav, Aktobe and Karaganda; major international water and water treatment companies throughout Central Asia and the Caucasus; development of supplies of natural gas from Central Asia to the Caucasus, Ukraine and Central and Eastern Europe; Oil and gas field development in the Caspian region.
Prof. Memberships: Business Lawyers Association of Kazakhstan (founding member); Chairman and founding member of the European Business Association of Kazakhstan; Director, Kazakhstan Equestrian Federation; Law Society of England and Wales; Major Projects Association; Law Society of New South Wales, Law Society of Victoria, Australia.
Career: LLB (Hons) Manchester University, 1980; qualified, Chester Law School, 1980; admitted as Solicitor of the Supreme Court of England and Wales, 1984; Barrister and Solicitor of the Supreme Court, Victoria, Australia, 1988; Solicitor, Proctor and Attorney, Supreme Court of New South Wales, Australia, 1988; Partner, *Baker & McKenzie*, 1992-98.
Personal: Enjoys skiing, tennis, horse-riding, flying, running. Married with three children.

KENYA

Corporate/Commercial

KENYA Leading firms (Corporate/Commercial)
1 Kaplan & Stratton
2 Daly & Figgis
Hamilton Harrison & Matthews
3 Kapila Anjarwalla & Khanna

Firms are listed alphabetically in each band.

Leading individuals (Corporate/Commercial)
1 **FOWLER Oliver** *Kaplan & Stratton*
KEITH Hamish *Daly & Figgis*
2 **ALIBHAI Zul** *Daly & Figgis*
ANJARWALLA Atiq *Kapila Anjarwalla & Khanna*
WAYAIKI Peter *Hamilton Harrison & Matthews*

Individuals are listed alphabetically in each band.

Kaplan & Stratton (13 ptrs, 12 asscs) In spite of last year's loss of Hamish Keithh to Daly & Figgis and more recently Zul Alibhai, by common consent this firm is *"out in front."* A strong corporate department advises on joint ventures, cross-border M&A and project finance for a substantially international client base. Several lawyers here have City of London experience, including the esteemed **Oliver Fowler** *("astute and sharp")* who rivals describe as *"the leading technician in Kenya."* The firm has advised on the privatisation of Telecom Kenya and on independent power projects. **Clients:** CDC; IFC; Kenya Breweries Ltd/Guinness; BAT Kenya Ltd; Barclays Bank of Kenya Ltd.

Daly & Figgis (5 ptrs, 6 asscs) *"Making a big splash"* in the corporate pool, **Hamish Keith** has *"unquestionably strengthened the firm."* Primary activity is in M&A and banking and finance, with substantial work in mining, estate development and regulatory advice. The recent arrival of **Zul Alibhai*** a *"proactive lawyer who works exceptionally hard"* from leading competitors Kaplan & Stratton provides Keith with much needed support. The firm advises an impressive portfolio of big-name clients from Africa and beyond. Recent transactions include acting for Vodafone on its acquisition of a stake in Kenya's first mobile telecommunications licence. **Clients:** IFC; DFI; CDC; DEG; Citibank; Coca-Cola; Vodafone Airtouch; Mobil Oil; Lonrho Africa.

Hamilton Harrison & Matthews (8 ptrs, 12 asscs) Historically one of the market leaders, the firm is considered to have lost some of its lustre with the respected Michael Somen (*"their leading lawyer"*) increasingly taking a backseat role as a consultant. The corporate department is now headed by the *"acute"* **Peter Wayaiki** (*"a safe pair of hands"*) who is noted for his expertise on complex securities arrangements. The firm advises on foreign investment, privatisation, M&A, joint ventures and banking, and acted on the privatisation of Telecom Kenya. **Clients:** Domestic companies; domestic and foreign financial institutions; foreign embassies; international aid agencies.

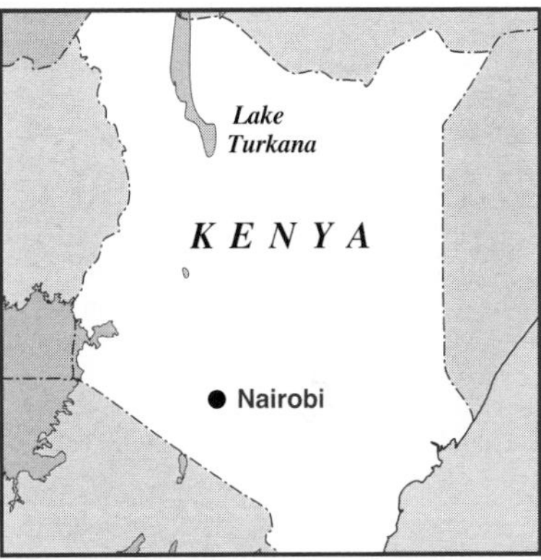

Kapila Anjarwalla & Khanna (7 ptrs, 7 asscs) The firm offers a predominantly corporate and commercial service from offices in Nairobi and Mombasa, with particular aptitude for finance and shipping advice. Maintains a strong link with UK firm Denton Wilde Sapte, with whom it has acted on privatisations. **Atiq Anjarwalla** is viewed by clients and competitors as a *"thoroughly competent"* practitioner. The firm advised on the drafting of standard terms and conditions for the largest grain and fertiliser handling terminal in Sub-Saharan Africa. **Clients:** Barclays Bank of Kenya Ltd; World Bank; Homegrown Limited; ABN AMRO; Citibank; Crédit Agricole Indosuez.

Leaders' profiles – Kenya

ALIBHAI, Zul

Daly & Figgis, Nairobi +254 2 310 304
zula@daly-figgis.co.ke

Specialisation: Partner in Corporate/Commercial Department. Specialises in mergers & acquisitions, privatisations, capital markets, joint ventures, banking and corporate financing, complex commercial litigation. Most recently has acted on the successful take-over of East African Cables Limited (listed on the Nairobi Stock Exchange), acted for Seaboard Corp's acquisition of stake in the Unga Group, for project sponsors in major Independent Power Project, and two bank mergers. Also handles large corporate financing transactions for Barclays Bank of Kenya. Previously handled IPOs, privatisation and issues of commercial instruments.

Prof. Memberships: Barrister-at-law(Lincoln's Inn), Law Society of Kenya, Law Society of Alberta, Canada.

Publications: Author of Kenya chapter in 'Tracing of Assets'. Joint author of 'A Lender's Guide to Receverships in Kenya'.

Career: Qualified as Barrister in 1980, as Kenya Advocate in 1982. Joined *Kaplan & Stratton* in 1982, Partner in 1987. Practised in Canada from 1990 onwards and rejoined *Kaplan & Stratton* in 1996 as partner. Partner of *Daly & Figgis* from February 2001. Member of the Capital Markets Authority Disclosure Standards Panel.

Personal: Born 1957. LLB, (Hons) King's College, London (1978) and LLM, London School of Economics.(1980).

ANJARWALLA, Atiq

Kapila Anjarwalla & Khanna, Mombasa
+254 11 312 848
asa@ka-legal.com

Specialisation: Partner and Head of Commercial Department. Main areas of work include company

commercial and banking law principally mergers, acquisitions, secured and unsecured loan facilities, refinancing and projects and offshore financing. Acts for most major international banks including Barclays Bank of Kenya Limited, Citibank, N.A., ABN AMRO Bank and Credit Agricole Indosuez. Has undertaken work for many City firms whose clients are involved in transactions in Kenya including *Slaughter and May, Allen & Overy, Cameron McKenna, Denton Wilde Sapte, Hill Taylor Dickinson, Macfarlanes, Nicholson Graham & Jones* and *Norton Rose.*
Prof. Memberships: Law Society of Kenya and Law Society (England).
Publications: Contributed to 'The Analyst', a business magazine in Kenya.
Career: University of Hull, England, 1982; Masters of Law at Jesus College, Cambridge, 1984; Qualified as Solicitor of England and Wales in 1986; articled with *Beale and Company; Slaughter and May*, 1987-90; *Cameron Markby Hewitt*, 1991-92; admitted as an Advocate of the High court of Kenya, 1993; partner of *Anjarwalla Abdulhusein & Co.*, 1993.
Personal: Born 20 October, 1960. Member of the Rotary Club. Leisure interests include fishing, jogging, tennis and sea sports.

FOWLER, Oliver
Kaplan & Stratton, Nairobi +254 2 335 333

KEITH, Hamish
Daly & Figgis, Nairobi +254 2 310 304
KeithH@daly-figgis.co.ke.
Specialisation: Partner in Corporate/Commercial Department. Main area of work is corporate and commercial law, principally joint ventures, mergers and acquisitions, regulatory advice in banking, insurance and capital markets. Has handled acquisition of companies and undertakings of various sorts for both Kenyan and foreign investors. Recent transactions include acting for African Lakes Corporation plc on its Nairobi Stock Exchange listing and various acquisitions; Lonrho Africa plc on various acquisitions and disposals; Vodafone Airtouch on its joint venture investment in the first Kenyan mobile telecommunications licence; IFC, CDC and DEG in respect of various Kenyan equity and loan investments, including their investment into Kenyan's first project financed independent power producer; IFC and other DFIs on the establishment of K-Rep Bank, Kenya's first commercialised micro-finance bank; and Tiomin Resources on the mining of Kenya's titanium based mineral resources.
Prof. Memberships: Law Society of Kenya, Law Society of England, International Bar Association, Kenya Association of Financial Analysts. Institute of Certified Public Secretaries of Kenya.
Career: Admitted English Solicitor 1973, Kenyan Advocate 1975. Joined *Kaplan & Stratton*, Head of its Commercial Department 1991-97. Joined *Daly & Figgis* as a partner in 1997. Chairman of the Nairobi Stock Exchange committe on mergers and takeovers, member of the Capital Markets Authority advisory committee, chairman of the Law Society sub-committee to establish a compulsory PI and Compensation Scheme, Chairman 1998 and 1999 British Business Association of Kenya.
Personal: Born 7 October 1948. Schooled in England 1962-67. Articled 1968-73. *Bower Cotton & Bower*, Chancery Lane, London. Enjoys the outdoors.

WAYAIKI, Peter
Hamilton Harrison & Matthews, Nairobi +254 2 330 870

KUWAIT

Corporate/Commercial

KUWAIT Leading firms (Corporate/Commercial)
1 Al-Sarraf & Al-Ruwayeh (in association with Stephenson Harwood)
2 Law Office of Al-Essa, Al-Bader & Partners
Mishare M Al-Ghazali & Partners

Firms are listed alphabetically in each band.

Al-Sarraf & Al-Ruwayeh (in association with Stephenson Harwood) (5 ptrs, 20 asscs) Noted for its integrity and efficiency, the market response to researchers confirmed that it is undoubtedly the leading firm in Kuwait in terms of size and reputation. With expertise in international and domestic law, it provides a full range of services to an equal mix of local and foreign clients. It is retained by major international law firms including Norton Rose, Trowers & Hamlins and Baker & McKenzie. Typical clients include Islamic and conventional banking institutions, telecommunications, oil and construction sector entities. The firm is currently acting for the foreign partner in the consortium of the Suaibiya Waste Water Plant, advising on the concession and relations between the partners. Advised the foreign promoter and operator on Kuwaiti legal issues concerning a water pipeline from Iran to Kuwait and advising Teledesic/ICO on Kuwaiti law in connection with its set up, licence acquisitions and authorisations. **Clients:** Arab Banking Corporation; HSBC; Deutsche Morgan Grenfell; Racal Group Services Ltd; Mitsui Engineering & Shipbuilding; Iridium Technologies.

Law Office of Al-Essa, Al-Bader & Partners (15 lawyers) Although not attracting much distinctive comment, researchers' findings confirmed that the practice is generally acknowledged to *"put out a good product."* It has a good reputation in corporate and commercial arbitration work. Other areas handled include general banking work, synchronised and secured lending, project finance, BOT work and some privatisations work. The firm recently acted in Kuwait's first major BOT project. **Clients:** Major local and foreign companies.

Mishare M Al-Ghazali & Partners (3 ptrs, 3 asscs) A full service firm with expertise in IP, banking and finance, privatisaton and petrochemical and gas related work. Typically involved in agency, franchise and software licensing agreements, partnerships, joint ventures, corporate entity formation and acquisitions work. The firm is no longer affiliated with Graham & James since the latter's acquisition by Squires Sanders & Dempsey. Highlights include advising the Kuwaiti Government in relation to the preliminary stages of setting up the Kuwait Free Trade Zone. **Clients:** Equate; Spic; Burgan Bank.

KYRGYZ REPUBLIC

Corporate/Commercial

KYRGYZ REPUBLIC Leading firms (Corporate/Commercial)
1 Chadbourne & Parke LLP
LeBoeuf, Lamb, Greene & MacRae, LLP

Firms are listed alphabetically in each band.

Leading individuals (Corporate/Commercial)
1 **SHEA Tony** *LegExp*
2 **ALDASHEV Niyaz** *LeBoeuf, Lamb, Greene*
KALIKOVA Gulnara *Chadbourne & Parke LLP*

Individuals are listed alphabetically in each band.

Chadbourne & Parke LLP (1 assc) Formerly of Mayer Brown & Platt since 1995, Kyrgyz lawyer **Gulnara Kalikova** works in close association with her Tashkent and London colleagues. *"One of the best local lawyers in town,"* she advises on a wide range of matters and is said to interact well with the foreign investors. Work includes corporate law, bankruptcy, banking, mining, labour and environmental law. Kalikova continues to advise Kumtor, the largest gold mining project in Central Asia. **Clients:** Hyatt International Corporation; Reemtsma Cigaretten Fabricen.

LeBoeuf, Lamb, Greene & MacRae, LLP (1 ptr, 2 asscs) Established in 1998, this office has a small but distinct presence in Bishkek. The practice undertakes general corporate work predominantly for foreign service and manufacturing companies. It also handles government and development/donor contracts. Researchers received strong recommendations for local partner **Niyaz Aldashev**. The firm is currently acting for a major tobacco multinational corporation on a range of commercial matters including $1 million real estate deal. Also represented the government in an arbitration concerning a contractual dispute with an investment advisory consultancy (value exceeding $16 million) and acted for national airline on a breach of lease agreement (value exceeding $20 million.) **Clients:** Local and foreign companies.

Other Notable Practitioner Researchers were impressed by the portfolio of former Clifford Chance banking partner, **Tony Shea** of LegExp. With at least eight years' experience of the local scene, he uniquely undertakes the lion's share of foreign investment and development projects in the Kyrgyz Republic for key clients such as EBRD, IFC, IMF and Central Asian American Enterprise Fund. Represented Kyrgyz Petroleum Company (KPC) in conjunction with the World Bank on a liquidation development project and currently advising on the formation of a new bank involving government participation.

Leaders' profiles – Kyrgyz Republic

ALDASHEV, Niyaz
LeBoeuf, Lamb, Greene & MacRae, LLP, Bishkek +996 312 22 2994

KALIKOVA, Gulnara
Chadbourne & Parke LLP, Bishkek +996 312 65 0256

SHEA, Tony
LegExp, Bishkek +996 312 21 3278

LAOS

Corporate/Commercial

LAOS Leading firms (Corporate/Commercial)
1 Dirksen Flipse Doran & Lê

Firms are listed alphabetically in each band.

Leading individuals (Corporate/Commercial)
1 **DIRKSEN Todd** *Dirksen Flipse Doran & Lê*
FLIPSE Mary *Dirksen Flipse Doran & Lê*

Individuals are listed alphabetically in each band.

Dirksen Flipse Doran & Lê (2 ptrs, 5 asscs) The only international law firm in Laos continues to cover a broad range of corporate and commercial work. It is enjoying an increase in corporate restructuring/reorganisation work, commercial mediation and arbitration. Represented Electricité de France, the major investor in the Nam Theun 2 Hydropower Project. Completed a major mediation and an ICC arbitration regarding contract disputes over infrastructure projects in Laos. American partners **Todd Dirksen*** and **Mary Flipse*** came highly recommended to our researchers. **Clients:** World Bank; IFC; ADB; Theun-Hinboun Power Company; Unilever; Nestlé; Crédit Agricole; Dyno-Nobel; HK Jardine; Nam Theun 2 Electricity Consortium.

***Todd Dirksen** and **Mary Flipse** are both partners at *Dirksen Flipse Doran & Lê, Vientiane +856 21 216 928*

LATVIA

Corporate/Commercial

LATVIA Leading firms (Corporate/Commercial)
1 Grunte & Cers, Law Office
Klavins, Slaidins & Loze
Lejins, Edzins, Torgans & Vonsovics
2 Blueger & Plaude
Blukis, Elksne & Rozenfelds
CB & M Law Offices

Firms are listed alphabetically in each band.

Leading individuals (Corporate/Commercial)
1 **CERS Gundars** *Grunte & Cers, Law Office*
GRUNTE Ivars *Grunte & Cers, Law Office*
KLAVINS Filip *Klavins, Slaidins & Loze*
LEJINS Girts *Lejins, Edzins, Torgans*
2 **LOZE Janis** *Klavins, Slaidins & Loze*
SLAIDINS Raymond *Klavins, Slaidins & Loze*
VONSOVICS Romualds *Lejins, Edzins, Torgans*

Individuals are listed alphabetically in each band.

Grunte & Cers, Law Office (3 ptrs, 3 asscs) Established in 1991, this firm was operating before Latvia gained its independence, and is noted for its *"aggressive"* approach. The group covers all areas of business law, advising international financial institutions and corporates. Name partners **Ivars Grunte*** and **Gundars Cers*** are *"well-known and well-connected"* practitioners. Our research team was impressed by its reputation for privatisation advice, the team has worked on the privatisation of a number of state enterprises such as Rigas Manufaktura, Rigas Audums and Rigas Motorupnica. The team has also worked extensively on the drafting of foundation documents and registrations of multi-nationals such as McDonald's and Telia. **Clients:** McDonald's; Telia; NCH Corp; Hewlett-Packard; Ford; Oriflamme; Michelin; Barclays Bank; Credit Suisse First Boston; Chase Manhattan Bank.

Klavins, Slaidins & Loze (5 ptrs, 7 asscs) The firm offers a comprehensive cross-border M&A service, which is said to *"combine knowledge of foreign law with local expertise."* **Filip Klavins*** and **Raymond Slaidins***, both members of the New York Bar, are *"serious lawyers, recognised in the international community."* **Janis Loze*** is newly recommended for his knowledge of the local market. Recent work has included representing two German companies during the privatisation of Latvian Gas. The team has also advised a number of foreign financial institutions on share offerings in Latvia. **Clients:** Coca-Cola; EBRD; Skanska; SAS; Sonera.

Lejins, Edzins, Torgans & Vonsovics (5 ptrs, 5 asscs) The firm has a thriving commercial practice working for both local and international clients. Considered to possess a *"strong commercial awareness,"* the firm is also felt by some to have *"cornered the privatisation market."* Niche areas of strength include aviation, food processing, consumer goods production and telecoms. The firm recently represented the interests of a local subsidiary of Procter & Gamble in a case brought on the grounds of the protection of consumer rights. **Girts Lejins***, a *"genuine corporate specialist,"* is the leading light of an effective team which also includes **Romualds Vonsovics***, commended to our researchers for his *"attention to detail."* **Clients:** Latvian Privatisation Agency; Latvian Development Agency; Kraft Jacobs Suchard; Pepsi-Cola; Philip Morris; Procter & Gamble.

Blueger & Plaude (4 ptrs, 4 asscs) Internationally experienced firm with expertise in company, business, banking and tax law, and a clientele which mixes domestic and foreign entities. The team advised on the privatisation of Latvia's state-owned shipping companies. **Clients:** Kuusakoski; Teito; EBRD; Greek shipping companies.

Blukis, Elksne & Rozenfelds (3 ptrs, 5 asscs) Respected corporate-oriented firm, whose client base is overwhelmingly foreign dominated. A close relationship with UK firm CMS Cameron McKenna has assisted the team's cross-border transactional volume. The firm represented Metromedia on the acquisition of stakes in Baltcom GSM (mobile phone service), Baltcom TV and SKONTO Radio, and advised Linstow on the acquisition of a number of hotels in the Baltic States. **Clients:** EBRD; IFC; Metromedia; Linstow; Electrolux; Shell.

CB & M Law Offices (5 ptrs, 3 asscs) Enjoying an enviable reputation overseas, the firm employs a number of foreign-qualified lawyers. The caseload generally involves representing foreign companies on their investments in Latvia. The firm is representing an international consortium of banks in relation to a SEK1.5 billion SEK financing facility for the acquisition of the national wireless telephone operator company – Baltkom GSM. It is also advising Morgan Stanley Dean Witter on foreign investment and securities law matters in Latvia and TotalFinaElf in relation to operations of its joint venture in Latvia. **Clients:** Nike; Lufthansa; Hydro Texaco; Lattelekom.

*See leaders' profiles on pages 457

Leaders' profiles – Latvia

CERS, Gundars
Grunte & Cers, Law Office, Riga +371 782 1315

GRUNTE, Ivars
Grunte & Cers, Law Office, Riga +371 782 1315

KLAVINS, Filip
Klavins, Slaidins & Loze, Riga +371 783 0000

LEJINS, Girts
Lejins, Edzins, Torgans & Vonsovics, Riga
+371 782 1525
girts@latnet.lv
Specialisation: Company, commercial and M&A. Acted for Latvia Privatisation Agency in legal audit of umbrella agreement with foreign investors for privatisation and modernisation of Latvian monopoly telecommunications company; for First Latvian Commercial Bank in its £30 million re-structuring and re-financing transaction; for Latvian State Forestry Service in negotiations with foreign investors on the project of construction of pulp mill plant with the planned total worth of US$1billion; for As Creati in acquisition of Banku Servisa Centrs, the biggest Latvian Center for card payment processing.
Prof. Memberships: Latvia Bar Association, Latvia Lawyers Association and International Bar Association.
Career: Before going into private practice worked for a number of years for the public prosecutors office specialising in white collar crimes. Full time Executive Director (1989-91), Vice President, and Board member (1989-93) of Latvia Lawyers Association. Founding partner of *CB&M (Carroll, Burdick, & McDonough*, 1992-94). Founding partner of *Lejins, Edzins, Torgans, & Vonsovics* in 1994. Member of Soros Foundation Latvia Committee on Law.
Personal: Born 4 June 1959. Graduated Latvia University Faculty of Law (1982). Leisure interests include tennis and skiing.

LOZE, Janis
Klavins, Slaidins & Loze, Riga +371 783 0000

SLAIDINS, Raymond
Klavins, Slaidins & Loze, Riga +371 783 0000

VONSOVICS, Romualds
Lejins, Edzins, Torgans & Vonsovics, Riga
+371 782 1525
romualdi@latnet.lv
Specialisation: Commercial and litigation. Acted for Central Bank of Latvia in a number of litigation matters and in negotiations for construction of new treasury premises, for Latvian Ministry of Economics in negotiations with AMOCO and Oljesprospektering AB on the License Agreement for drilling oil in the Baltic Sea. Acts on commercial and litigation matters for a number of Latvian subsidiaries of major multinational companies (Procter & Gamble Marketing Latvia, Philip Morris Latvia, etc.).
Prof. Memberships: Latvia Bar Association, Latvia Lawyers Association, International Bar Association, Latvia Judges Association (1991-92), Registered Patent Attorney with the Latvian Patent Office.
Career: Served as a Judge of Riga City Central District Court (1985-87), Associate Judge of the Supreme Court of Latvia (1987-92). In-house counsel of Arthur Andersen Riga office (1992). Founding partner of *CB&M (Carroll, Burdick & McDonough* 1992-94). Founding partner of *Lejins, Edzins, Torgans, & Vonsovics* in 1994.
Personal: Born 27 April 1958. Graduated Latvia University Faculty of Law (1981). Leisure interests include tennis, travelling.

L

LEBANON

Corporate/Commercial

LEBANON Leading firms (Corporate/Commercial)
1 Abouhamad, Merheb, Nohra, Chamoun, Chedid
Raphaël & Associés
2 Moghaizel Law Offices
Tyan & Associés
3 Abousleiman & Partners
Khattar Associates
Lyan & Associés
Nabil Abdel-Malek Law Offices
Étude Badri et Salim El Meouchi

Firms are listed alphabetically in each band.

Leading individuals (Corporate/Commercial)
1 CHEDID Nassib *Abouhamad, Merheb, Nohra*
MOGHAIZEL Fadi *Moghaizel Law Offices*
RAPHAEL Moussa *Raphaël & Associés*
TYAN Nady *Tyan & Associés*

Individuals are listed alphabetically in each band.

Abouhamad, Merheb, Nohra, Chamoun, Chedid (6 ptrs, 9 asscs) Widely acknowledged as one of the *"most credible"* firms in Lebanon, this *"well rounded"* outfit boasts a diverse client base ranging from local businesses to major international organisations in the UK, France and the US. Leaders in corporate and commercial work, they also have *"good know-how in the banking sector."* **Nassib Chedid*** attracts recognition for his involvement in international work and corporate transactions. Co-participators with Linklaters in the first issue of GDR in Lebanon and advisors in subsequent ones, the firm advised Société des Grands Hotels du Liban in a hotel project structuring deal. **Clients:** Société Générale Libano-Européenne de Banque; Biblos Bank; Banque du Liban et D'Outre-Mer; Société Bancaire du Liban; Middle East & Africa Bank; Lebanese Bank Association; Holcom Group; Pharaon Group; CCC.

Raphaël & Associés (6 ptrs, 14 asscs, 1 counsel) An *"extremely professional"* firm based in Antelias. Its team of *"talented"* lawyers provide an integrated multilingual service to clients by virtue of their foreign and domestic experience. Researchers noted an impressive client base including major groups of Saudi investors and Arab and Lebanese businesses. It has a particular focus in banking and construction work. The firm's recent affiliation with Ernst & Young looks set to expand its international dimension. With his substantial experience in international negotiation and drafting of contracts, **Moussa Raphael*** is a prominent figure in the legal community. A leader in arbitration work, the firm advised a telecommunications provider on a high profile action in the ICC against the Lebanese government. **Clients:** Al Mabani; Banque Libano Française; Libancell.

Moghaizel Law Offices (6 ptrs, 14 asscs) *"A clean firm with a clean reputation."* The firm's impressive image is widely attributed to its *"young and dynamic"* managing partner and successor to his founding parents, **Fadi Moghaizel***. Recently appointed as Chair of the Arab Regional Forum of the IBA. *"A clear presence"* in the international arena, the firm's foreign clients include major UK and US law firms (Cleary Gottlieb, Clifford Chance, Cameron McKenna, Baker & McKenzie). It is also a member of Lebanese Lex Mundi and the Alliance of Arab Lawyers and known for its work in human rights and public law, tax and real estate. **Clients:** Alico (member of AIG Insurance Group); Microsoft; Citibank; Goldman Sachs International; Hutchison Telecommunications International Ltd.

Tyan & Associés (1 ptr, 11 asscs) An *"extremely reputable"* outfit handling mainly corporate, banking and investment work. With an exclusively foreign client base, it is particularly well known for its enviable French clientele (which includes Air France, Banque National de Paris and France Telecoms). **Nady Tyan**'s* eclipsing reputation leads some to comment that it is *"rather a one man show."* Negotiated a $100 million loan on behalf of France Telecom from World Bank (IFC). **Clients:** Subsidiaries of Coca-Cola Middle East and Coca-Cola Bottling Co of Lebanon; Sensomatic Electronics Co; Maersk Shipping; Kone Corporation; ING Barings; Canon Europa NV; Air France.

Abousleiman & Partners (4 ptrs, 7 asscs) Researchers received impressive recommendations for this new entrant to the tables. A specialist practice, it is highly regarded for its capital markets work in the international corporate and finance arena. It represents corporate and bank issuers, placement agents, trustees and depositories in the private and public sector. Frequently acting as local counterparts of major international players such as Dewey Ballantine and Norton Rose, the firm has been involved in most of Lebanon's Eurobonds transactions. It worked with JP Morgan and CSFB on three of the four latest Eurobonds issues for the Government including the issuance of €250 million 7.25% notes due 2004 and acted in the establishment by Banque Audi SAL of its $500 million global deposit programme and subsequent issuance of $100 million series 1 deposit certificates. **Clients:** Solidere; Merrill Lynch International; Banque Paribas; CSFB; Banque Audi SAL; Banque de La Mediterranée SAL; Warburg Dillon Read; Schindler Management Ltd; Morgan Stanley.

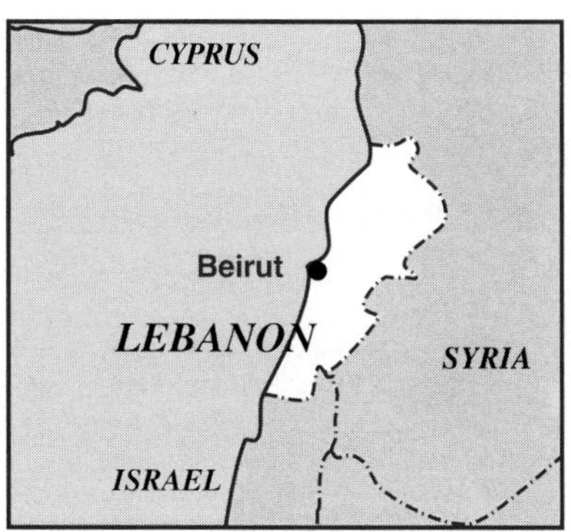

Khattar Associates (25 lawyers) The largest firm in Beirut, best known for its founding partner's post as former president of the Beirut Bar. Generally considered to have a stronger presence in commercial litigation and arbitration work. Clients are a mix of local and foreign corporates, banks and private individuals. Represented one of the Saade brothers in relation to long-running litigation concerning the family's shipping empire, and acted for TV cable station, Showtime, in relation to country-wide anti-piracy litigation totalling over $90 million. **Clients:** Saçonnable; Banque Paribas; Salomon Brothers; General Elec-

*See leaders' profiles on pages 459

tric Aviation Company; Showtime; Virgin Cola; Dollar Rent A Car; various national institutions eg. ITD (International Tourism & Development).

Lyan & Associés (5 ptrs, 6 asscs) Well regarded for its corporate and litigation work with both a solid local client base and good foreign contacts. Telecoms continues to be a major focus of work, supported by an in-house business and finance expert and telecom engineer. Competitors noted other specialisms including intellectual property rights, arbitration and trusts. The firm is involved in the negotiation, structuring and implementation of the Lebanese Telecom Operators Association and structuring the expansion of SkyBridge (Alcatel project for low orbit satellites) in the Middle East. Acted for PSINet Inc, a US telecom operator and fibre owner, in the acquisition of a local telecom operator in Lebanon. **Clients:** PSI Net Inc; Ministry of Telecoms; AT&T; Telechoice Inc; Radian International; CH2M Hill; Christian Dior; Daikon International; Tenecco; Gulf International Bank; Arab Banking Corporation; Hochtief.

Nabil Abdel-Malek Law Offices (6-8 lawyers) Researchers were impressed by the portfolio of this small but high quality practice. Handling corporate, M&A and trade law with a major focus in investment and commercial banking. Its predominantly foreign client base is mostly US and UK in origin. Active in derivatives transactions for Lebanese clients, it is often seen representing the Government. The firm dealt with Lebanon's first Eurobond issue in 1994 and recently acted for the Ministry of Finance in two latest Eurobond issues undertaken by the Lebanese Republic. **Clients:** Linklaters; Allen & Overy; Dewey Ballantine; Freshfields; Merrill Lynch; Deutsche Bank; CSFB; Commerce Bank; Banque Paribas; Standard Chartered.

Étude Badri et Salim El Meouchi (24 lawyers) *"Highly professional and ethical."* Researchers received strong recommendation for this well known firm's banking and finance work. The firm benefits from strong contacts in the local banking sector, representing a broad range of leading local, industrial and international banks. Members of the Central Bank's closed consultative committee on financial regulatory matters, it handled Standard Chartered Bank's acquisition of Metropolitan Bank. Acted for Fransa Bank in its acquisition of Universal Bank and issuance of certificates of deposit (value $300 million.) **Clients:** Banque Saradar SAL; Banque Saradar France; Banque Misr-Liban; Fransabank; Banque Nationale du Canada; Bank of Abu Dhabi.

L

Leaders' profiles – Lebanon

CHEDID, Nassib
Abouhamad, Merheb, Nohra, Chamoun, Chedid, Beirut +961 1331 737

MOGHAIZEL, Fadi
Moghaizel Law Offices, Beirut +961 1333 753

RAPHAEL, Moussa
Raphaël & Associés (formerly Raphaël Ziadé Abirached Rifaat et Associés), Beirut +961 401 5401
rzar@intracom.net.lb
Specialisation: Managing Partner overseeing the firm's Banking, Corporate and Litigation/Arbitration Departments. Main areas of work include banking, construction, telecommunications and international transactions. Acts for major Lebanese and European banks on matters ranging from litigation to insurance of financial instruments. Advises multinational construction companies in general construction issues as well as litigation/arbitration. Acts as outside counsel to leading telecommunications operator.
Prof. Memberships: International Bar Association and American Bar Association
Career: Admitted to the Beirut Bar in 1957. Founded the law firm of *Raphaël & Associés* (formerly known as *Raphaël, Ziadé Abirached, Rifaat & associés*). Continues to be managing Partner of *Raphaël & Associés*, a law firm currently composed of twenty-two lawyers. Has worked extensively in Arab countries, most notably in Saudi Arabia. Has served as arbitrator in several ICC arbitrations.
Personal: Born in Lebanon in 1932. Attended Saint Joseph University and obtained a French Master of Laws (1956) and a Lebanese Master of Laws (1957). Fluent in Arabic, French and English with a working knowledge of Italian. Married with three children, one of whom is a partner of *Raphaël & Associés*.

TYAN, Nady
Tyan & Associés, Beirut +961 1561 673
tyanasso@dm.net.lb
Specialisation: Senior Partner of the law firm *Tyan & Associés*. Has substantive expertise in corporate, financial and commercial matters. Prepared all the legal documents for Coca-Cola's acquisition of the Coca-Cola Bottling Company of Lebanon. Prepared and carried out all the legal documents needed for the establishment of ING Bank (Beirut Branch). Acted on the revision and the execution of the Loan Agreement signed between a major Lebanese company and IFC (International Finance Corporation). Legal advisor for various major international and local clients.
Prof. Memberships: Member of the Committee of revision of Lebanese laws, which is linked to the Lebanese Ministry of Justice. Member of TerraLex international network. President, Lebanese National Association of Political Sciences, Beirut.
Publications: Author of 'The Executive Power in Lebanon' and 'Legal Guide to Investments in Lebanon'.
Career: Admitted to the Beirut Bar, 1962, Lebanon; admitted to the Paris Bar, 1979, France; Arbitrator, ICC; Professor of Law (PhD) at Lebanese University; Legal advisor to the World Bank on issues related to investments in Lebanon.
Personal: Born 9 January 1938. Attended Saint Joseph University, Beirut, Lebanon; Université de Lyon, France (PhD in Law).

LESOTHO

Corporate/Commercial

LESOTHO Leading firms (Corporate/Commercial)
1 Harley & Morris
Webber Newdigate

Firms are listed alphabetically in each band.

Leading individuals (Corporate/Commercial)
1 HARLEY Seymour *Harley & Morris*

Individuals are listed alphabetically in each band.

Harley & Morris (1 ptr, 1 assc) Well-known for its commercial advice, the firm advises a range of domestic and international banks and corporations and specialises in liquidations, notably that of the Lesotho Airways Corporation. Financial services, energy and privatisation are other areas of the caseload, and **Seymour Harley*** has a fine local reputation. **Clients:** Acres International; Barclays Bank plc; John Laing International; Seaboard Corporation.

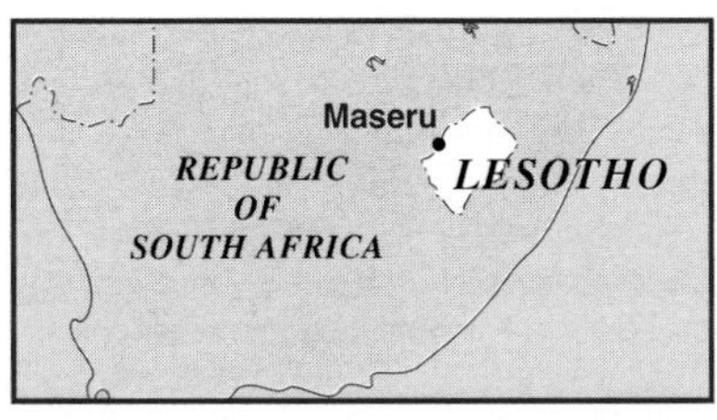

Webber Newdigate (4 ptrs, 3 asscs) The largest firm in the country has an excellent corporate reputation, often advising development agencies and blue-chip international concerns. Niche expertise exists in aviation and insurance. The firm advised the Lesotho Highlands Development Authority on the Lesotho Water Project, a concept designed to bring water from the Lesotho Highlands to Johannesburg and Pretoria in South Africa. **Clients:** Lesotho Highlands Development Authority; Lesotho Bank; Lesotho Telecommunications Corporation.

***Seymour Harley** is a partner at *Harley & Morris, Masem +266 313 840*

LIBERIA

Corporate/Commercial

LIBERIA Leading firms (Corporate/Commercial)
1 The David AB Jallah Law Firm
Dunbar & Dunbar Law Offices
Pierre Tweh & Associates
Sherman & Sherman Inc

Firms are listed alphabetically in each band.

Leading individuals (Corporate/Commercial)
1 DUNBAR Steven *Dunbar & Dunbar*
JALLAH David *The David AB Jallah Law Firm*
SHERMAN Vaney *Sherman & Sherman Inc*
TWEH Oswald *Pierre Tweh & Associates*
WUREH Emanuel *Dunbar & Dunbar*

Individuals are listed alphabetically in each band.

The David A B Jallah Law Firm (1 ptr, 6 asscs) One of the leading firms in Liberia is recognised for its *"strength and reliability"* in cross-border M&A. Noted for its work on behalf of humanitarian organisations, the group also advises leading insurance companies on work relating to the country's civil war. Dean of the law school **David Jallah** has a widely respected name. **Clients:** CIGNA Worldwide Insurance Company; Animata & Sons; DHL International Liberia; Save the Children Fund (UK) Liberia; Oxfam.

Dunbar & Dunbar Law Offices (3 ptrs, 3 asscs) *"A highly reputable firm with good clients,"* it handles general corporate matters, banking, tax and shipping work. **Emanuel Wureh** is president of the national bar association and a *"good commercial lawyer,"* while **Steven Dunbar** also comes warmly recommended. The firm advised IFC and Proparco on a loan to a Liberian rubber company. **Clients:** Banks; IFC; international companies.

Pierre Tweh & Associates (2 ptrs, 3 asscs) A strong commercial practice, offering legal guidance for subsidiaries and affiliates of foreign companies in Liberia. The organisation has experience in the formation of companies, corporations, partnerships, joint ventures, foreign investment and M&A work. Managing partner **Oswald Tweh** is highly regarded locally. **Clients:** Banks; shipping companies; logging industry.

Sherman & Sherman Inc (8 lawyers) The firm provides a legal consultancy service advising foreign clients on their investments in Liberia, and handling corporate formation and large insurance matters. *"One of the best known lawyers in Liberia"* is **Vaney Sherman**, a Harvard graduate with *"an international reputation."* **Clients:** Banks; Firestone Plantations; rubber industry; logging companies.

Leaders' profiles – Liberia

DUNBAR, Steven
Dunbar & Dunbar Law Offices, Monrovia +231 227 746

JALLAH, David A.B.
The David AB Jallah Law Firm, Monrovia +231 226 285

SHERMAN, H.Vaney G.
Sherman & Sherman Inc, Monrovia +231 226 927

TWEH, Oswald
Pierre Tweh & Associates, Monrovia +231 226 577

WUREH, Emanuel
Dunbar & Dunbar Law Offices, Monrovia +231 227 746

LIBYA

Corporate/Commercial

LIBYA Leading firms (Corporate/Commercial)
1 MTL Law Office
Rajab Bakhnug Attorney at Law
Tumi Law Firm

Firms are listed alphabetically in each band.

Leading individuals (Corporate/Commercial)
1 BAKHNUG Rajab *Rajab Bakhnug*
MARGHANI Salah *MTL Law Office*
TUMI Mohamed *Tumi Law Firm*

Individuals are listed alphabetically in each band.

MTL Law Office (3 ptrs, 2 asscs) A *"well-organised"* firm with a strong commercial practice. It provides advice on foreign investment and Libyan law and acts on the establishment of Libyan branches for foreign companies. Also strong in transport and shipping law and the oil industry, the firm includes the *"highly-qualified"* **Salah Marghani**. **Clients:** European, Middle Eastern and Japanese shipping and airline companies.

Rajab Bakhnug Attorney at Law (1 ptr, 2 asscs) The firm services foreign construction, trading and oil companies which have business in Libya. *"Easy to deal with"* **Rajab Bakhnug** is a *"professional and prudent lawyer."* **Clients:** Daewoo Corp; Hyundai Corp; Sumitomo Corp; GTME; oil service companies.

Tumi Law Firm (3 ptrs, 6 asscs) This well-known firm boasts Western-educated lawyers and an enviable international clientele. A full-service

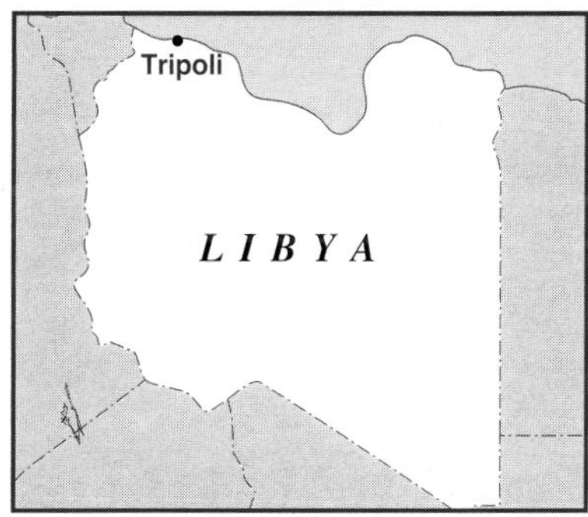

firm, it has a name for registering foreign companies in Libya. **Mohamed Tumi** is the stand-out practitioner here. **Clients:** Bilfinger & Berger; AMEC Group; ABB; Samsung; Merloni Progetti; British Airways; Austrian Airlines; Swiss Air; Mercedes-Benz.

Leaders' profiles – Libya

BAKHNUG, Rajab
Rajab Bakhnug Attorney at Law, Tripoli +218 21 444 0886
Career: 1969-1975 Prosecutor in Tripoli City. 1977-1979 Judge in Zawia Primary Court. 1979-1982 Legal advisor with the Libyan Army. 1985-1988 General Inspector, Judiciary Inspection Department, Ministry of Justice, Tripoli. 1989 to date, Attorney at Law, Private Profession in Private Office.
Personal: LLB (1969) University of Benghazi Faculty of Law. Diploma (1983) Polytechnic of Central London. Master Degree (MA) (1985) Salford University, UK. Speaks Arabic and English, a little Italian and French.

MARGHANI, Salah
MTL Law Office, Tripoli +218 21 444 0571

TUMI, Mohamed
Tumi and Associates, Tripoli +218 21 333 9024

LIECHTENSTEIN

Corporate/Commercial

L

LIECHTENSTEIN Leading firms (Corporate/Commercial)
1 Marxer & Partners
2 Batliner & Partners
Walch & Schurti
Wanger

Firms are listed alphabetically in each band.

Leading individuals (Corporate/Commercial)
1 **BATLINER Herbert** *Batliner & Partners*
MARXER Peter *Marxer & Partners*
SCHURTI Andreas *Walch & Schurti*
WANGER Markus *Wanger*

Individuals are listed alphabetically in each band.

Marxer & Partners (9 ptrs, 8 asscs) This extremely well-established law firm with *"the best reputation"* celebrated its 75th anniversary last year. **Peter Marxer** has *"helped shape and form the jurisdiction"* and consequently enjoys a high standing in Liechtenstein's legal community. **Clients:** Banks; insurance companies; asset fund managers; trust companies.

Batliner & Partners (3 ptrs, 2 asscs) A *"good, serious office"* advises on the establishment of Liechtenstein foundations, trusts and limited companies. As institutional advisers to European (particularly Swiss) fiduciaries, trusts and asset managers, the team is focused on the domestic market. The team and key senior partner **Herbert Batliner** continues to be highly rated by compatriot lawyers and international clients. **Clients:** LGT Bank; VP Bank; Trust Company Prokurations Anstalt.

Walch & Schurti (2 ptrs, 8 asscs) In this well regarded, seasoned team, both partners are admitted to the New York bar. Working with corporate entities and foundations, the team undertakes trustee, corporate, banking and insurance work. Partner **Andreas Schurti** is *"an expert"* with an *"international outlook"* and a *"good knowledge of common law."* **Clients:** Banks and finance houses; trust company Walpart.

Wanger (3 ptrs, 9 asscs) Formed by a merger with other financial service providers, this general commercial firm is acknowledged by rivals to offer *"a comprehensive counselling service."* The firm covers a range of specialisations including trusts, banking, IP and IT and arbitration. With offices in Switzerland, Austria, Spain and Belgium, the firm has also formed strategic alliances in Israel, Brazil and Canada. Senior partner **Markus Wanger,** a specialist in arbitration, is a member of the court of arbitration for the IOC. **Clients:** Leading financial institutions.

Leaders' profiles – Liechtenstein

BATLINER, Herbert
Batliner & Partners, Vaduz +423 236 0404

MARXER, Peter
Marxer & Partners, Vaduz +423 235 8181

SCHURTI, Andreas
Walch & Schurti, Vaduz +423 237 2000

WANGER, Markus
Wanger, Vaduz +423 237 5252

LITHUANIA

Corporate/Commercial

LITHUANIA Leading firms (Corporate/Commercial)
1 Lideika, Petrauskas, Valiūnas & Partners
2 Foresta Business Law Group
Lawfirm Glimstedt
UAB McDermott, Will & Emery

Firms are listed alphabetically in each band.

Leading individuals (Corporate/Commercial)
1 **SUTKIENE Eugenija** *UAB McDermott, Will & Emery*
VALIUNAS Rolandas *Lideika, Petrauskas*
2 **BERNOTAS Egidijus** *Advokatfirman Glimstedt*
DOMINAS Gediminas *Advokatfirman Glimstedt*
JAKUTIS Remigijus *Foresta Business Law Group*

Individuals are listed alphabetically in each band.

Lideika, Petrauskas, Valiūnas & Partners (7 ptrs, 20 asscs) This is the largest law firm in Lithuania, and has *"a decent reputation and high-quality lawyers."* The firm offers general company and commercial advice, with a particular emphasis on M&A, foreign investment and privatisation. Multi-national blue-chips constitute a substantial proportion of the firm's client base. **Rolandas Valiunas*** has a fine corporate reputation, and advised on Williams International's acquisition of one of Eastern Europe's biggest refineries. The firm advised on Danisco's acquisition of four sugar factories in Lithuania. **Clients:** McDonald's; Coca-Cola; Credit Suisse First Boston; Reuters; DHL Worldwide Express; JP Morgan; Unilever; Williams International; Statoil.

Foresta Business Law Group (3 ptrs, 8 asscs) Respected organisation with expertise in all aspects of foreign investment in Lithuania, and a proven track record in international finance and cross-border M&A. Said by competitors to *"combine youth and experience successfully,"* the firm includes the recommended **Remigijus Jakutis***. The firm has advised various foreign investors on the legal aspects of business start-ups and expansion in Lithuania as well as undertaking various assignments on behalf of the Lithuanian Government. The firm has participated as legal advisors in a number of international support and investment programmes sponsored by the EBRD, EU PHARE and other international agencies and institutions. **Clients:** EBRD; IFC; World Bank.

Lawfirm Glimstedt (3 ptrs, 7 asscs) The Vilnius office of this Swedish firm has a fine reputation for cross-border M&A, banking and tax, with niche strength in advising on privatisations. Access to a high-powered Swedish client base has provided a discernible increase in transactions during the past year. The firm is led by two *"shrewd guys,"* **Egidijus Bernotas*** and **Gediminas Dominas***. Recent deals include acting for

Vattenfall on a bid for Lithuanian Energy and representing the Lithuanian government on the privatisation of Lithuanian Gas. **Clients:** Lithuanian Government; Vattenfall; Hansa Bank Trust; Carlsberg.

UAB McDermott, Will & Emery (3 ptrs, 4 asscs) The first US law firm to establish itself in Lithuania, the team is said to combine *"local lawyers with an American aggression."* The workload includes privatisation, corporate M&A, project finance and real estate for a substantially international client base. *"Experienced and hard-working"* **Eugenija Sutkiene*** is described as the *"driving force behind the firm's success."* The team represented shareholders on the privatisation of the state-owned Lithuanian telecoms company. **Clients:** ABN AMRO; Philip Morris; Shell; Skanska.

*See leaders' profiles on page 464

Leaders' profiles – Lithuania

BERNOTAS, Egidijus
Lawfirm Glimstedt, Vilnius +370 2 683 700
Specialisation: Partner in firm. Main area of work is corporate law, principally mergers, acquisitions and privatisations. Has handled acquisitions and undertakings of various sorts by multinational companies. Acted on the privatisation of the State Agricultural Bank of Lithuania; acted for one of the world's largest breweries in its acquisition of the largest brewery in Lithuania; for a global UK-based bank on financing the upgrading of petrochemical installations; for both local and foreign investors regarding the agricultural industry in Lithuania and on the biggest sugar factory projects. Has been advising on several important acquisitions and reorganisations in the Lithuanian banking sector.
Prof. Memberships: Lithuanian Bar Association.
Career: Attorney, Legal and International Treaties Department, Ministry of Foreign Affairs 1993. Associate, *McDermott, Will & Emery*, Vilnius, 1993-96. Joined *Glimstedt* in 1996, becoming a Partner in 1999.
Personal: Born in 1971. Leisure interests include fishing and family (wife and son).

DOMINAS, Gediminas
Lawfirm Glimstedt, Vilnius +370 2 683 700
dominas@glimstedt.lt
Specialisation: Partner in firm. Main area of work is corporate law as well as banking and financial law. Has been involved in, inter alia, the following projects in Lithuania: advising investors on the acquisition of Sovereign Eurobonds; advising issuers and investors on questions relating to Corporate Eurobonds; advising large multinational utility and energy supply companies on business acquisitions in Lithuania; advising the Government of Lithuania on one of the largest acquisition transactions in the oil industry. Acts as a legal counsel for a number of major multinational companies in their activities in Lithuania. Has spoken at various conferences.
Prof. Memberships: Lithuanian Bar Association, European Society for Banking and Financial Law.
Career: Associate Professor, University of Vilnius, Faculty of Law, International Financial Transactions, Banking Law, Mergers and Acquisitions. Joined *Glimstedt* in 1998.
Personal: Born in 1971. Post-graduate studies at the University of London, 1996-97 (LLM, banking and financial law).

JAKUTIS, Remigijus
Foresta Business Law Group, Vilnius
+370 2 224 564

SUTKIENE, Eugenija
McDermott, Will & Emery, Vilnius +370 2 629 824
esutkiene@mwe.lt
Specialisation: Corporate practice. Main area of work is corporate law, principally mergers, acquisitions, privatisations, bankruptcy cases, real estate transactions (purchase, sale, development and building) as well as media and telecommunication law and representation of media and telecommunication companies. In the consortium with Union Bank of Switzerland acted as advisor to Lithuanian government on privatisation of Lithuania Telecom and represents Lithuania Telecom in IPO of its shares. Worked for the Bank CAIBC Wood Gundy on reorganisation and privatisation of Lithuanian electricity sector, acted for Lietuvos Telekomas on the disposal of its shares in mobile operator company, represented foreign investor in acquisition of Lithuanian shipping company, represented Philip Morris on acquisition of tobacco factory and Kraft General Foods on acquisition of confectionary factory. Represented Vattenfall on the transaction of the heating district facilities. Acts as a legal adviser to a large number of international corporations and joint ventures.
Prof. Memberships: Law Society; Member of Lithuanian Bar Association.
Publications: Worked on the drafting of the 'Law on Privatisation and implementing regulations'. 'Electricity Law', 'Law on Stock Companies'.
Career: Qualified in 1984. Joined *McDermott, Will & Emery* in 1991.
Personal: Born 3 February, 1956. Attended Vilnius University (1978 - 1984). Worked in the Court of Law and the Ministry of Trade as a head of legal department and commercial arbitration.

VALIUNAS, Rolandas
Lideika, Petrauskas, Valiûnas & Partners, Vilnius
+370 2 681 832
RValiunas@LPVP.LT
Specialisation: Managing Partner. Main areas of practice: corporate and commercial law, mergers and acquisitions, foreign investments. Acted for: McDonald's Restaurants – investments in Lithuania; SAS – general corporate consulting; Williams International – investments in oil sector of Lithuania; TeleDenmark – privatisation bidding of Lithuanian Telecom.
Prof. Memberships: Member of the Council of Lithuanian Bar Association; Member AIJA; Vice-President of UIA; Vice-Chairman of Eastern European Forum, IBA; Member of the Board of Investors' Forum, Lithuania.
Career: In 1992 founded *Lideika, Petrauskas, Valiunas & Partners*; Representative of International Chamber of Commerce (ICC) – Lithuania within ICC Commission of Arbitration.
Personal: Born 13 January 1965. Attended Vilnius University 1982-1989 (Law Faculty). Master's Degree in Business Administration, Vytautas Magnus University (Kaunas) 2000. Leisure interests: sailing, skiing. Married, three children.

LUXEMBOURG

Corporate/Commercial

LUXEMBOURG Leading firms (Corporate/Commercial)
1 Arendt & Medernach
De Bandt, van Hecke, Lagae & Loesch
Elvinger, Hoss & Prussen
2 Allen & Overy Beghin & Feider Avocats Associés
Kremer Associés & Clifford Chance

Firms are listed alphabetically in each band.

Leading individuals (Corporate/Commercial)	
1 **ELVINGER André**	*Elvinger, Hoss & Prussen*
FEIDER Marc	*Allen & Overy Beghin & Feider*
HOSS Philippe	*Elvinger, Hoss & Prussen*
LOESCH Tom	*De Bandt, van Hecke*
MOUSEL Paul	*Arendt & Medernach*
2 **BRAUSCH Freddie**	*De Bandt, van Hecke*
HARLES Guy	*Arendt & Medernach*
KREMER Christian	*Kremer Associés*

Individuals are listed alphabetically in each band.

Arendt & Medernach (7 ptrs, 3 asscs) This is the largest firm in Luxembourg, with an *"excellent"* reputation, among its competitors, and a high-profile for M&A advice. Said to be staffed by *"aggressive and intelligent"* lawyers, the firm's leading practitioner is **Paul Mousel***, commended to researchers as an *"intelligent and thorough lawyer."* **Guy Harles*** maintains his position as a leading corporate practitioner. The firm recently advised on two mergers between large media entities. **Clients:** Local banks; international banks; fund management companies; insurance companies.

De Bandt, van Hecke, Lagae & Loesch (4 ptrs, 8 asscs) Part of the Linklaters Alliance, the firm is said to have *"a sound international footing."* Commended by rivals for its *"impeccable quality,"* the firm advises extensively on M&A transactions either in Luxembourg or chanelled through Luxembourg, via bespoke SPVs. It also has experience in reorganisations of international corporations, listings and public takeover bids. The *"acute"* **Tom Loesch*** is the team's outstanding practitioner, while **Freddie Brausch*** is recommended for his investment funds practice. **Clients:** Multi-national corporations.

Elvinger, Hoss & Prussen (9 ptrs, 13 asscs) *"Long-term members of the top league,"* the team advises both buyers and sellers on M&A, drafting contracts, and due diligence. The team also acts on listings, and advises banks on financing acquisitions. **André Elvinger*** *"has an unsurpassed overview"* while **Philippe Hoss*** is a *"highly competent corporate lawyer."* **Clients:** Local and international corporates; banks.

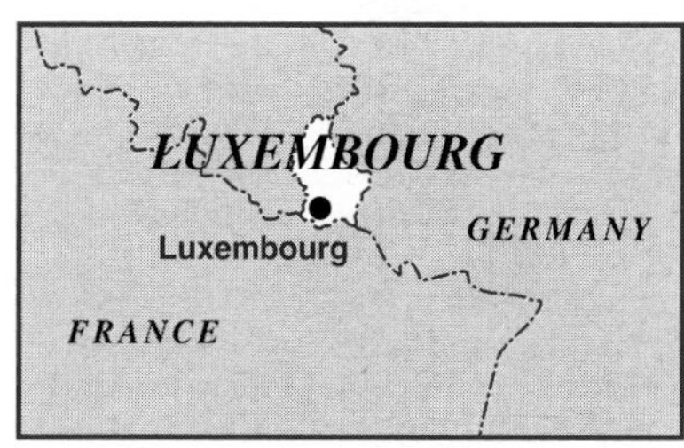

Allen & Overy Beghin & Feider Avocats Associés (4 ptrs, 12 asscs) Now bedding down its merger, the firm has capitalised on its international connections, to advise on joint ventures, mergers and acquisitions, restructurings, tax-driven finance structures, securitisations, listings and ICM work. **Marc Feider*** is said by opponents to play a *"big part in corporate work,"* and has an *"aggressive style."* **Clients:** International corporations; German banks.

Kremer Associés & Clifford Chance (3 ptrs, 18 asscs) A firm that is *"still getting up and running,"* has been described by competitors as *"one you can't ignore."* M&A and restructuring for leading international corporates form the core of the team's caseload, and it has attracted a number of new US clients. **Christian Kremer*** is the firm's leading light, and heads both the corporate and investment funds practices. **Clients:** European and US clients.

*See leaders' profiles on page 466

Leaders' profiles – Luxembourg

L

BRAUSCH, Freddie
De Bandt, van Hecke, Lagae & Loesch (a member firm of Linklaters & Alliance), Luxembourg
+352 26081
FBrausch@debandt.com
Specialisation: Partner in the Corporate Department of *De Bandt, van Hecke, Lagae & Loesch*, Luxembourg office. Areas of practice include investment funds; bank regulation; securities law; custody and settlement. Has represented clients active in, amongst others, the following industries: investment & commercial banking, global custody, asset management and securities settlement.
Prof. Memberships: Past Board and Executive Committee member of ALFI (Luxembourg Investment Fund Association, Luxembourg), EU Directive Committee of FEFSI (European Investment Fund Federation), International Committee of NICSA (US Investment Fund Association), Advisory Committees CSSF (Commission du Secteur Financier). IBA (International Bar Association); UIA (Union Internationale des Avocats).
Career: Studied Law at University of Aix-en-Provence, France (Maîtrise en Droit, 1978), and at University of London, London School of Economics (LLM, 1980). Joined *De Bandt, van Hecke, Lagae & Van Bael*, Brussels in 1980. Joined *Loesch & Wolter*, Luxembourg in 1985, becoming a partner in 1988.
Personal: Born 20 February 1955.

ELVINGER, André
Elvinger, Hoss & Prussen, Luxembourg
+352 44 66 440

FEIDER, Marc
Allen & Overy Beghin & Feider Avocats Associés, Luxembourg +352 44 44 551

HARLES, Guy
Arendt & Medernach, Luxembourg +352 40 78 78

HOSS, Philippe
Elvinger, Hoss & Prussen, Luxembourg
+352 44 66 440

KREMER, Christian
Kremer Associés & Clifford Chance, Luxembourg
+352 48 50 501

LOESCH, Tom
De Bandt, van Hecke, Lagae & Loesch (a member firm of Linklaters & Alliance), Luxembourg
+352 26081
TLoesch@debandt.com
Specialisation: Partner in the Corporate, M&A and Corporate Finance Department specialising in mergers, acquisitions, tender offers, listings and equity issues.
Prof. Memberships: Luxembourg Bar.
Publications: Articles on EC Competition Law applied in Luxembourg, the setting-up of a business in Luxembourg, Luxembourg telecommunications law, 'Luxembourg Guide on Company Law', 'Luxembourg Handbook on Contract Law'.
Career: Qualified in 1982. Joined *Loesch & Wolter* in 1982, becoming Partner in 1988. Since July 1, 1999 Partner of *De Bandt, van Hecke, Lagae & Loesch.* Member IBA and IFA.
Personal: Born April 20, 1956. Law Faculty Aix-Marseille III 1975-1979, Law Faculty Paris I 1979-1980 (DESS), London University – London School of Economics 1980-1991 (LLM).

MOUSEL, Paul
Arendt & Medernach, Luxembourg +352 40 78 78

MACAU

Corporate/Commercial

MACAU Leading firms (Corporate/Commercial)
1 C&C Law Firm
Leonel Alves
Neto Valente

Firms are listed alphabetically in each band.

Leading individuals (Corporate/Commercial)
1 **ALVES Leonel** *Leonel Alves*
CUNHA Rui *C&C Law Firm*
VALENTE Neto *Neto Valente*

Individuals are listed alphabetically in each band.

C&C Law Firm (4 ptrs, 12 asscs) This is a relatively large firm that shares good working relationships with major law firms such as Linklaters, Deacons and Woo Kwan Lee and Lo. Recommended to researchers for its work with international banks regarding their various acquisitions. It further provides corporate services to major local companies. Former judge **Rui Cunha** is a well known figure on the local scene. **Clients:** China Insurance; Espirit; StanChart; International Bank of Taipei.

Leonel Alves (1 ptr, 5 asscs) A *"capable and important"* office that is currently in the process of restructuring, gaining two new lawyers. A strong player in the financial services market, the firm is assisting Bank of China in an ongoing capacity. It is known as a *"small but high quality"* firm and **Leonel Alves** himself is *"bright, smart and qualified."* **Clients:** Bank of China and other Chinese banks; Tai Fung Bank; BCM.

Neto Valente (2 ptrs, 6 asscs) **Neto Valente** is a *"great lawyer, capable person and key personality."*

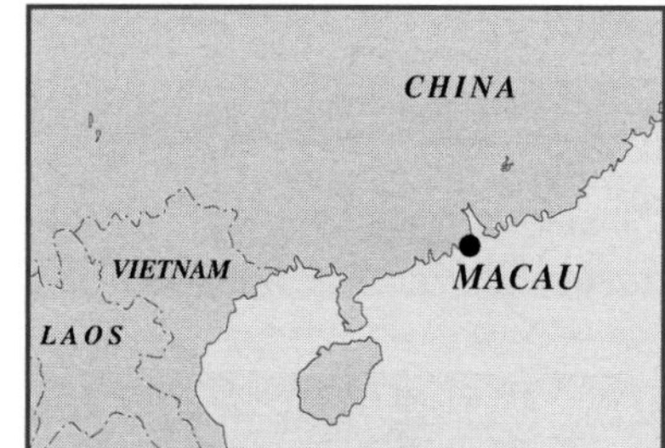

His firm specialises in civil law, commercial law, company, banking and finance. The firm is currently advising the steering committee involved in the restructuring of the GDE-state enterprise, dealing with major investments on mainland China. Also advising in the telecoms business. **Clients:** BNU; BES; Delta Asia; Nolasco.

Leaders' profiles – Macau

ALVES, Leonel
Leonel Alves, Macau +853 378 579

CUNHA, Rui
C & C Law Firm, Macau +853 372 623

VALENTE, Neto
Neto Valente, Macau +853 382 222

MADAGASCAR

Corporate/Commercial

MADAGASCAR Leading firms (Corporate/Commercial)
1 Madagascar Conseil International
2 Cabinet Radilofe
Cabinet Rakotoarivony

Firms are listed alphabetically in each band.

Leading individuals (Corporate/Commercial)
1 **JAKOBA Raphaël** *Madagascar Conseil*
2 **RADILOFE José** *Cabinet Radilofe*
RAKOTOARIVONY Hary Ratsimba *Rakotoarivony*

Individuals are listed alphabetically in each band.

Madagascar Conseil International (1 ptr, 3 asscs) Market-leading firm which provides day to day advice to foreign companies operating in Madagascar. The firm specialises in the preparation of joint ventures and the establishment of corporations in the country, and is also moving into telecommunications and computing. Senior partner **Raphaël Jakoba** established a centre for arbitration in Madagascar and is an *"excellent practitioner."* **Clients:** USAid; international oil companies; textiles companies; international retailing groups; local business groups.

Cabinet Radilofe (1 ptr, 1 assc) A generalist firm which handles corporate/commercial for a mixed client base of French and local concerns. The team has experience in maritime and insurance law and establishing companies in Madagascar. **José Radilofe** is recommended. **Clients:** French and local enterprises.

Cabinet Rakotoarivony (1 ptr, 3 asscs) Handling all areas of commercial law, the firm is particularly noted for its advice on maritime, banking and insurance law. **Hary Ratsimba Rakotoarivony** is a highly regarded lawyer. **Clients:** International energy companies; local businesses.

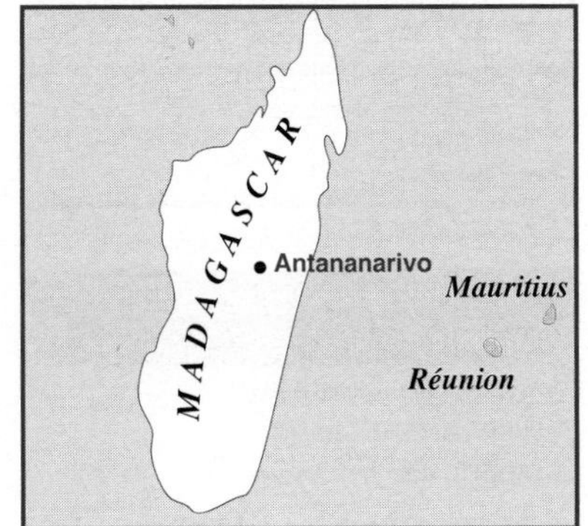

Leaders' profiles – Madagascar

JAKOBA, Raphaël
Madagascar Conseil International, Antananarivo
+261 2 0222 9525

RADILOFE, José
Cabinet Radilofe, Antananarivo
+261 2 0222 1228

RAKOTOARIVONY, Hary Ratsimba
Cabinet Rakotoarivony, Antananarivo
+261 2 0223 3360

MALAWI

Corporate/Commercial

MALAWI Leading firms (Corporate/Commercial)
1 Savjani & Co
2 Sacranie, Gow & Co
Wilson & Morgan

Firms are listed alphabetically in each band.

Leading individuals (Corporate/Commercial)
1 SAVJANI Krishna *Savjani & Co*
2 LATIF Shabir *Sacranie, Gow & Co*
RAVAL Dinker *Wilson & Morgan*

Individuals are listed alphabetically in each band.

Savjani & Co (1 ptr, 12 asscs) *"The leading firm in the country"* handles the whole range of corporate work in Malawi, typically for an international client base. Chairman of the Malawi Stock Exchange, **Krishna Savjani** is *"a hard-working corporate lawyer with a strong personality."* The firm advised on the acquisition of a controlling interest by BP in Oil Company of Malawi Ltd, and acted for IFC on a share subscription in and loan transaction with a mobile telephone company. **Clients:** CGU International Insurance plc; BAT (Malawi) Ltd; Carlsberg Malawi Brewery Ltd; Lever Brothers (Malawi) Ltd.

Sacranie, Gow & Co (3 ptrs, 7 asscs) A *"well connected firm"* which is part of the Lex Africa network. Specialising in international corporate finance, the group has niche strength in electronic banking. **Shabir Latif** is a *"bright and with-it lawyer."* The firm advised on the restructuring of Cargill plc in Malawi. **Clients:** International banks.

Wilson & Morgan (2 ptrs, 4 asscs) An *"established conservative firm"* which our researchers found to be a *"serious contender for corporate work."* Handles all types of corporate work, flotations, acquisitions and disposals. **Dinker Raval** is a *"professional corporate lawyer."* The firm advised Old Mutual when it demutualised and subsequently floated on the Malawi Stock Exchange. **Clients:** Old Mutual; Citibank; Philip Morris; Smallholder Farmers Fertiliser Revolving Fund of Malawi.

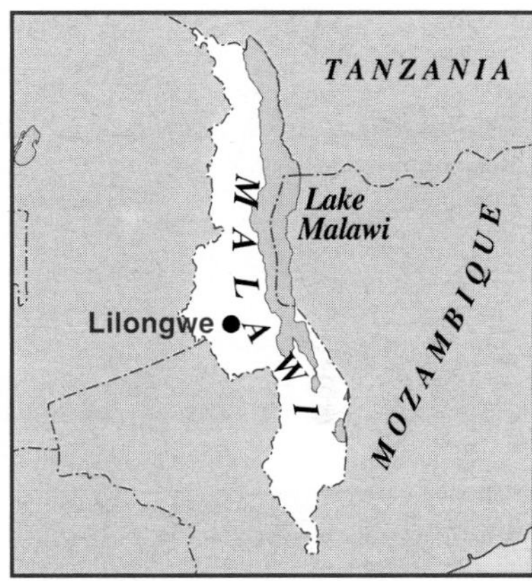

M

Leaders' profiles – Malawi

LATIF, Shabir
Sacranie, Gow & Co, Limbe +265 640 311

RAVAL, Dinker
Wilson & Morgan, Blantyre +265 620 988
Specialisation: Main area of work is corporate, commercial, intellectual property and conveyancing. Represented Old Mutual in recent listing on the Malawi Stock Exchange. Advised Citibank (Nairobi) and Philip Morris Inc. (America).
Career: Qualified in 1961, joined *Wilson & Morgan* in 1962. Became Partner in 1988.
Personal: Born 5 December 1935, called to the Bar from Middle Temple in 1961. Leisure interests include football and outdoor activities.

SAVJANI, Krishna
Savjani & Co, Blantyre +265 624 555
savjani&co@malawi.net
Specialisation: Corporate, commercial, mergers and acquisitions and finance. Main area of work includes acquisitions of private companies; takeovers of listed companies; flotations; placings; privatisation; shareholder agreements, joint venture agreements, project agreements, loan agreements; and restructuring. Has acted in the flotation of most of the listed companies in Malawi. Acted in the issue of depository receipts in the UK and the US by Malawi's biggest conglomerate and assisted with the listing of the global depository receipts on the London Stock Exchange. Acts for major banking and insurance companies in Malawi and many of the major corporates both Malawi-owned and foreign-owned, operating in key sectors of the Malawi economy.
Prof. Memberships: Barrister-at-Law of Gray's Inn, London. Malawi Law Society.
Career: Called to the Bar in 1969. Admitted as legal practitioner in Malawi in 1970. Appointed Senior Counsel by the President of Malawi. Chairman of the Malawi Stock Exchange.
Personal: Born 2 March 1947. British Honorary Consul. Honorary legal advisor to the British High Commission, Malawi. Chairman of a secondary and primary school, and trustee of a primary school. Chairman of a service club.

MALAYSIA

Index

OVERVIEW: On the corporate front, firms are witnessing an increase in M&A work and continued buoyancy in corporate restructuring, although a downturn in the market is anticipated. Whilst local lending remains healthy, direct foreign investment has dipped dramatically leading to a slowdown in many banking led practices. The government, however, has taken remedial steps through the institution of national programmes to restructure debt and stimulate the local capital markets. Infrastructure projects put on the backburner, following the crisis of 1997 have been re-instituted and commentators remain optimistic for the long term.

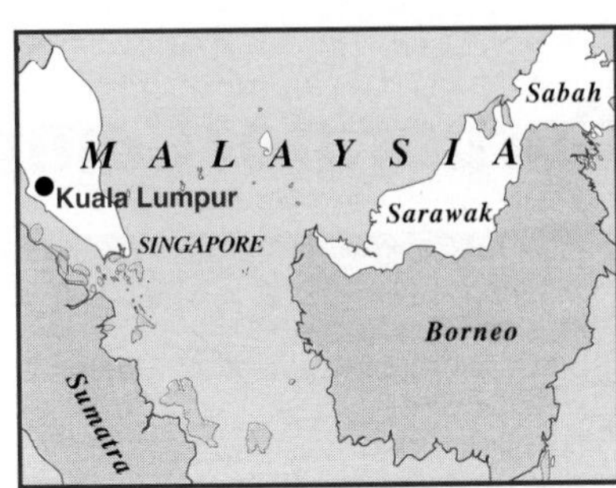

M

Banking & Finance

MALAYSIA
Leading firms (Banking & Finance)

Band	Firm
1	Shearn Delamore & Co
	Shook Lin & Bok
	Zaid Ibrahim & Co
2	Adnan, Sundra & Low
	Chooi & Co
	Skrine & Co
	Zul Rafique & Partners
3	Cheong Kee Fong & Co
	Kadir, Andri Aidham & Partners
	Zain & Co

Firms are listed alphabetically in each band.

Leading individuals (Banking & Finance)

Band	Individual	Firm
1	CHEONG Kee Fong	*Cheong Kee Fong & Co*
	DAVID Patricia	*Shook Lin & Bok*
	KASSIM Kadir	*Kadir, Andri Aidham & Partners*
	LIM Teong Sit	*Shearn Delamore & Co*
2	LAI Wing Yong	*Shook Lin & Bok*
	LOW Chee Choon	*Adnan, Sundra & Low*
	MUN SOU Chooi	*Chooi & Co*
3	KOK Che Kheong	*Skrine & Co*

Individuals are listed alphabetically in each band.

Shearn Delamore & Co (6 ptrs, 10 asscs) *"An integral part of the legal establishment,"* the firm continues to inspire a high degree of confidence among local banking clients. The workload encompasses loan syndication, retail banking and debt restructuring.

Head of banking **Teong Sit Lim*** is *"a name synonymous with excellence,"* and is particularly noted for his proficiency in capital markets work. Leading banks value his *"thorough and painstaking approach."* The firm represented Malaysian financial institutions on two major debt restructuring schemes to the value of RM1,200 million. **Clients:** Domestic and international financial institutions.

Shook Lin & Bok (3 ptrs, 18 asscs) One of the oldest and largest firms in Malaysia, it was recommended to researchers as *"a group of talented individuals one can turn to without hesitation."* Renowned for banking M&A, the firm has a sound reputation both for transactional work and litigation. Prominent members of the team are the *"unflappable and forthright"* **Wing Yong Lai*** and *"active and thorough"* **Patricia David***. **Clients:** Domestic and foreign financial institutions.

Zaid Ibrahim & Co (6 ptrs, 21 asscs) The firm's renowned corporate department is supported by an increasingly active banking team, recommended to researchers as *"an effective group with a high volume of work."* It is particularly visible on restructuring and bond issue work. A good relationship with government departments *"helps to oil the wheels on deals requiring regulatory approval."* The firm advised on the restructuring of the Lion Group. **Clients:** Bank of Commerce.

Adnan, Sundra & Low (3 ptrs, 3 asscs) Described by merchant banks as *"one of the firms we would turn to first,"* it specialises in international capital markets, project finance and securitisation. Acting on a number of big-ticket deals, the firm benefits from useful political connections and close relationships with large Malaysian corporates such as HICOM.

Chee Choon Low* is *"a superior lawyer, with an excellent bedside manner,"* whose *"vast experience allows him to understand the market fully."* The firm acted for CIMB on the MR4.3 billion Linkedua bond issue, and advised UOB on a MR1.5 billion bond issue. **Clients:** CIMB; UOB; Salomon Smith Barney.

Chooi & Co (3 ptrs, 6 asscs) A long-established firm, known by commentators for its adherence to *"the traditional ingrained values of the old-school practitioner."* The personification of this ethos is **Chooi Mun Sou***, a *"highly respected senior lawyer,"* whose connections with the Chinese business community provide a fertile source of work. The team generally advises foreign institutions on syndicated loan and acquisition finance transactions. **Clients:** Domestic and foreign financial institutions.

Skrine & Co (2 ptrs, 5 asscs) Established in 1963, the firm is known for its commercial approach and *"collection of esteemed practitioners."* Focusing on the more complex end of finance and banking, the firm has advised on a number of recent banking mergers. The team of *"first rate lawyers"* includes the regarded **Che Kheong Kok***, who is *"technically gifted"* and *"a man to turn to if you require the solution to a knotty problem."* **Clients:** Domestic and foreign financial institutions.

Zul Rafique & Partners (2 ptrs, 8 asscs) Although in its infancy, having emerged from the ashes of Albar Zulkifly & Yap a year ago, this firm is already seen as *"a major competitor."* Its close links with PwC have given the firm access to a clientele of international merchant banks, and clients suggest that *"many established names are now looking over their shoulders."* The firm advised a consortium of banks on the financing of Binariang Satellite Systems. **Clients:** International and domestic banks.

Cheong Kee Fong & Co (3 ptrs, 2 asscs) An *"excellent boutique firm"* with *"a quality client base which belies its size."* The firm advises on local law issues arising from offshore transactions, and has niche expertise on bond issues. Directing operations is **Kee Fong Cheong***, recommended to researchers as *"one of the best banking lawyers in Malaysia."* His *"knowledge and technical skills"* are said to allow him to *"pick and choose the more heavyweight clients."* A securities expert, he serves as an advisor to the Kuala Lumpur Stock Exchange. **Clients:** KLSE; international banks.

Kadir, Andri Aidham & Partners (2 ptrs, 4 asscs) *"Impressive full service firm,"* which advises on the spectrum of financial matters, including retail banking and syndicated structured finance. The team revolves around **Kadir Kassim***, *"a charming old school practitioner"* and member of the Malaysian securities commission, who is said by peers to have *"an excellent grasp of the law, derived from thirty years of experience."* The firm acted for the financiers on the MR1.2 billion Putrajaya Holdings bond issue, and advised on Punchak Niaga's MR2.1 billion bond issue. **Clients:** RHB Group; Malayan Banking.

Zain & Co (2 ptrs, 2 asscs) *"A good young practice"* with an emphasis on corporate banking, bond issues and syndicated loans. This *"enthusiastic and committed"* team has received market plaudits for its work with Deutsche Bank and recently acted on a bond issue on behalf of the holding company of a large hotel. **Clients:** Malaysian Industrial Development Finance; Oriental Bank.

M

Corporate/M&A

Shearn Delamore & Co (3 ptrs, 5 asscs) *"A traditional big-hitter with years of experience,"* the firm retains a long-standing, enviable client base. One of the largest firms in the country, it handles big-ticket corporate transactions, while also maintaining a reputation in project finance.

Although perceived to be a less active transactional figure, **Michael Lim*** was still mentioned to researchers as the firm's *"top corporate lawyer,"* and is said to have *"an excellent commercial mind."* Market suggestions of an ageing partnership have been answered by the rise to prominence of the *"young, knowledgeable and effective"* **Michael Tang***. The firm recently acted for a leading cement company on the acquisition of a RM696 million stake in a rival concern, and represented a major automobile distribution company on its de-merger proceedings. **Clients:** RHB Capital Berhad.

Skrine & Co (3 ptrs, 5 asscs) Established for nearly 40 years, this is *"a major firm with excellent corporate credentials."* The firm advises on M&A, joint ventures, corporate restructuring and public listings for a client base of leading Malaysian companies and foreign multinationals. *"A uniformly talented and industrious"* team is led by **Che Kheong Kok*** whose *"unassuming manner hides real talent."* Also highly regarded is **Kah Leng Chen***, recommended to researchers as *"an old school practitioner with a safe pair of hands."* **Clients:** Foreign and domestic corporates.

Zaid Ibrahim & Co (8 ptrs, 30 asscs) A member of the Arthur Andersen Worldwide legal network, the firm's *"aggressive expansion drive"* has resulted in a doubling in size. Concentrating mainly on foreign investment and domestic M&A, the firm was praised to researchers for its *"progressive approach."* The team also capitalises on its *"excellent political connections,"* advising government institutions on privatisation and restructuring.

"The driving force within the firm" is **Seng Kok Chew***, a former partner of Baker & McKenzie, acknowledged by peers as *"an excellent negotiator."* A *"distinguished team"* also includes the *"reliable and affable"* **Charon Wardini bin Mokhzani***. The firm advised on the restructuring of the Lion Group of companies. **Clients:** Government institutions; domestic and international corporates.

Cheong Kee Fong & Co (3 ptrs, 2 asscs) Researchers discovered that the firm is generally regarded as a showcase for the universally recognised talents of **Kee Fong Cheong***. His *"cautious, clever style"* and *"incisive sense of reasoning"* attracts a blue-chip international clientele. *"A pioneer of Malaysian corporate law,"* his personal reputation enables the firm to punch far above its weight. The firm's caseload consists largely of assisting foreign parties wishing to invest in Malaysia. **Clients:** International corporates.

MALAYSIA Leading firms (Corporate/Mergers & Acquisitions)	
1	Shearn Delamore & Co
	Skrine & Co
	Zaid Ibrahim & Co
2	Cheong Kee Fong & Co
	Shook Lin & Bok
	Zul Rafique & Partners
3	Cheang & Ariff
	Rashid & Lee
	Raslan Loong
4	Lee Hishamuddin
5	Adnan, Sundra & Low
	Wong & Partners

Firms are listed alphabetically in each band.

Leading individuals (Corporate/Mergers & Acquisitions)	
1	**CHEONG Kee Fong** *Cheong Kee Fong & Co*
2	**CHEW Seng Kok** *Zaid Ibrahim & Co*
	LO Siew Cheang *Cheang & Ariff*
	ZULKIFLY Rafique *Zul Rafique & Partners*
3	**CHEN Kah Leng** *Skrine & Co*
	DASS David *Rashid & Lee*
	LEE Christopher *Wong & Partners*
	LIM Michael *Shearn Delamore & Co*
	LOONG Caesar *Raslan Loong*
4	**ELIATHAMBY Sreesanthan** *Zain & Co*
	KOK Che Kheong *Skrine & Co*
	LEE Peter *Rashid & Lee*
	MOKHZANI Charon Wardini bin *Zaid Ibrahim*
Up-and-coming individuals	
	TANG Michael *Shearn Delamore & Co*

Individuals are listed alphabetically in each band.

*Profiles of leading lawyers mentioned here are on pages 472-473

Shook Lin & Bok (5 ptrs, 17 asscs) A commercial presence for over eighty years, the firm's market reputation as *"one of Malaysia's leading firms"* continues. Sought after by local clients for its domestic M&A expertise, the firm has a strong connection with the Singapore market where it has maintained an associated office since 1965. Also respected for its litigation and banking capacity, the firm advises leading local corporates and financial institutions. **Clients:** Malaysian banks and corporates.

Zul Rafique & Partners (6 ptrs, 20 asscs) Emerging from the split of Albar Zulkifly & Yap, this new firm has already gained the respect of clients and peers. An active recruitment policy has seen the firm grow in size to challenge its more established competitors. **'Dato' Rafique Zulkifly*** is viewed as *"a high-calibre and practical lawyer,"* while the firm's close links with PricewaterhouseCoopers have led one commentator to label the team as *"potentially the future of law in Malaysia."* The firm is principally involved in infrastructure work, and has a key client in Petronas, for whom it advised on the acquisitions of Premium Oil and Proton. **Clients:** Petronas; Tagana.

Cheang & Ariff (7 ptrs, 19 asscs) While civil litigation is the firm's forte, interviewees also mentioned the large corporate group with approval. Noted for a *"tenacious approach"* and a respectable foreign client base, the team specialises in M&A and corporate restructuring. **Siew Cheang Lo*** was commended to researchers as an *"imaginative lawyer, combining academic ability with practical application."* The firm was the first in Malaysia to gain an ISO accreditation. **Clients:** International corporates.

Rashid & Lee (3 ptrs, 20 asscs) Full service firm, especially commended for its niche in restructuring advice. In spite of the loss of Christopher Lee to Wong & Partners, the firm's work for major corporate client, Renong Group, and its connections with quasi-governmental companies were consistently impressed upon our researchers. **David Dass*** is credited as being *"a sound lawyer driving the practice forward,"* whilst elder statesman **Peter Lee*** is *"a highly respected figure regularly acting for the major companies."* **Clients:** Construction companies; telecom companies; development companies.

Raslan Loong (4 ptrs, 23 asscs) Fronted by **Caesar Loong***, said to be *"an accomplished marketeer with a good understanding of the law,"* the firm has increased its corporate profile, advising an international client base on big-ticket M&A.

The firm acted on NTT's MR5.5 billion proposed purchase of a stake in Malaysia Telecom. Respected for its expertise in the new technology market, the team has acted on the funding of start-up businesses and has drafted legislation for the Multimedia Commission. **Clients:** Lion Corporation Berhad; PwC; Salomon Smith Barney; AIG; Ministry of Finance; Merrill Lynch.

Lee Hishammuddin (4 ptrs, 12 asscs) A breakaway from Skrine & Co, the firm has built on its foundations as a litigation practice to achieve a reputation among competitors as *"a growing, purposeful corporate operator with a bright future."* The team handles all corporate areas including M&A, corporate restructuring, joint ventures and leveraged buyouts. With a client base stretching from multi-nationals to small domestic concerns, researchers were impressed by the weight of recommendation for a firm whose *"transactional visibility is increasingly high."*

The team advised on the sale of MBf by Danamodal, and acted on the disposal of assets by Danaharta, worth in excess of MR100 million. It is also a corporate group legal advisor to the Kuala Lumpur Stock Exchange. **Clients:** Petronas; HSBC; Danaharta; Danamodal; Mayban; Bank of America.

Adnan Sundra & Low (5 ptrs, 11 asscs) Although the firm is more renowned for banking, competitors recognise that it is *"quite capable of attracting the bigger corporate clients."* A broad workload covers M&A, joint ventures and corporate restructuring. The firm has advised on the restructuring of public companies such as Red Box, Faber Group, and Arab Malaysian Corporation, and acted for Proton on its acquisition of 80% of the shares of Lotus Group International Ltd. **Clients:** HICOM; Arab Malaysian Corp.

Wong & Partners (3 ptrs, 11 asscs) Possessing strong links with Baker & McKenzie, the firm eschews purely domestic transactions, generally representing international clients on their investments in Malaysia. Advice on M&A, direct foreign investment and corporate restructuring is supplemented by an increased reputation in the e-commerce sector.

The firm has acquired **Christopher Lee*** from Rashid & Lee, thereby gaining the services of *"a highly intelligent and effective lawyer."* Recent highlights include acting for foreign buyers on the takeover of two major public companies, and advising on the corporate restructuring of a leading Malaysian power plant. **Clients:** Japan Tobacco.

Other Notable Practitioner **Sreesanthan Eliathamby*** of Zain & Co has impressed competitors through his work for key client Tigana National, and is praised as *"a good lawyer who has made a name for himself in the power industry."*

Leaders' profiles – Malaysia

CHEN, Kah Leng
Skrine & Co, 50490 Kuala Lumpur +60 3 254 8111
Recommended in Corporate/M&A

CHEONG, Kee Fong
Cheong Kee Fong & Co, 50300 Kuala Lumpur +60 3 460 9906
Recommended in Banking & Finance, Corporate/M&A

CHEW, Seng Kok
Zaid Ibrahim & Co, Kuala Lumpur +60 3 257 9999
Recommended in Corporate/M&A

DASS, George Anthony David
Rashid & Lee, 50490 Kuala Lumpur
+60 3 2710 5555
rnl@rashidnlee.com.my
Recommended in Corporate/M&A
Specialisation: Senior Partner in Corporate Department. Main area of work is corporate law, primarily mergers and acquisitions, privatisations, debt rescheduling and restructuring, corporate insolvency and restructuring. Has been involved with project and corporate finance work in United Kingdom, India, China, Uzbekistan, Pakistan and Australia.

DAVID, Patricia
Shook Lin & Bok, Kuala Lumpur +60 3 2011 788
Recommended in Banking & Finance

ELIATHAMBY, Sreesanthan
Zain & Co, Kuala Lumpur +60 3 2698 6255
Recommended in Corporate/M&A

KASSIM, Kadir
Kadir, Andri Aidham & Partners, Kuala Lumpur +60 3 238 2888
Recommended in Banking & Finance

KOK, Che Kheong
Skrine & Co, 50490 Kuala Lumpur +60 3 254 8111
Recommended in Banking & Finance, Corporate/M&A

LAI, Wing Yong
Shook Lin & Bok, Kuala Lumpur +60 3 2011 788
Recommended in Banking & Finance

LEE, Christopher
Wong & Partners, 5088 Kuala Lumpur +60 3 2055 1888
Recommended in Corporate/M&A

LEE, Siew Choong Peter
Rashid & Lee, 50490 Kuala Lumpur +60 3 2710 5555
rnl@rashidnlee.com.my
Recommended in Corporate/M&A
Specialisation: Senior Partner in Corporate Department. Main areas of work include mergers, acquisitions, corporate restructurings and corporate and project finance. Has been involved recently in restructuring of various public companies and advising on various offerings in Malaysia. Handled project and corporate finance work in South Africa, Phillipines, United Kingdom, India, China and Australia.

LIM, Michael
Shearn Delamore & Co, 50100 Kuala Lumpur +60 3 2300644
Recommended in Corporate/M&A

LIM, Teong Sit
Shearn Delamore & Co, 50100 Kuala Lumpur +60 3 2300644
Recommended in Banking & Finance

LO, Siew Cheang
Cheang & Ariff, 50450 Kuala Lumpur +60 3 2161 0803
Recommended in Corporate/M&A

LOONG, Caesar
Raslan Loong, Kuala Lumpur + 60 3 253 3939
Recommended in Corporate/M&A

LOW, Chee Choon
Adnan, Sundra & Low, Kuala Lumpur +603 230 0466
Recommended in Banking & Finance

MOKHZANI, Charon Wardini bin
Zaid Ibrahim & Co, Kuala Lumpur +60 3 257 9999
Recommended in Corporate/M&A

MUN SOU, Chooi
Chooi & Co, 50250 Kuala Lumpur +60 3 2055 3888
Recommended in Banking & Finance

TANG, Michael
Shearn Delamore & Co, 50100 Kuala Lumpur +60 3 2300644
Recommended in Corporate/M&A

ZULKIFLY, Rafique
Zul Rafique & Partners, 50250 Kuala Lumpur +603 237 3500
zul@zulrafique.com.my
Recommended in Corporate/M&A
Specialisation: Managing Partner of the firm. Heads the Commercial, Corporate & Banking Department. Main areas of work are corporate finance and mergers and acquisitions. Has handled the acquisitions of companies and undertakings in both Malaysia and overseas, mergers and restructuring of major business entities in Malaysia, whilst also advising the private and public sectors in strategic planning and structuring of transactions. Industry experience ranges from acting on behalf of PETRONAS (Malaysian state oil company) on the purchase of Proton (the Malaysian national automobile company); acted for Petronas Carigali in its subscription of shares in Premier Oil Limited in the United Kingdom in 1999; advised ASEAMBANKERS in the issuance of Midciti Resources Sdn Bhd. CP/MTN bonds based on Islamic and conventional principles worth RM2.5 Billion; acted for Sapura Holdings Sendirian Berhad for the sale of its debt equity in Time dot com to Khazanah Nasional. Also acted for TELEKOM MALAYSIA BERHAD in the purchase of a cellular communications provider, EMARTEL from Malaysian Resources Corporation Berhad. Plays a major role in advising TENAGA NASIONAL BERHAD, the Malaysian electricity giant in its restructuring of itself. Advised PUTRAJAYA HOLDINGS BERHAD in issues concerning land concessions in the new Malaysian Federal Administrative Capital of Putrajaya.
Prof. Memberships: Barrister-At-Law of Lincoln's Inn; Advocate & Solicitor, High Court of Malaya; the International Bar Association.
Career: Qualified as a Barrister in 1978. Joined the Malaysian Legal and Judicial Service as a Magistrate in the same year. Between 1984 and until its dissolution in November 1999, headed the Corporate and Commercial Department of *Messrs. Albar, Zulkifly & Yap*, Kuala Lumpur. Is also a current member of the Malaysian Bar Corporate & Banking Committee which provides input on various aspects of corporate and commercial law to the governing body of lawyers in Peninsular Malaysia.
Personal: Born 1953. Graduated from University of London (LLB, Hons.) in 1977. Was awarded the royal honour of Darjah Sultan Salahuddin Abdul Aziz Shah which carries the title Dato' in 1998. Leisure interests include travelling and reading. Lives in Kuala Lumpur.

M

MALI

Corporate/Commercial

MALI Leading firms (Corporate/Commercial)
1 Cabinet Dongar et Modibo Kone
Cabinet Toureh et Associés

Firms are listed alphabetically in each band.

Leading individuals (Corporate/Commercial)
1 **KONE Modibo** *Cabinet Dongar et Modibo Kone*
TOUREH Harouna *Cabinet Toureh*

Individuals are listed alphabetically in each band.

Cabinet Dongar et Modibo Kone (2 lawyers) Primarily associated with its work on debt recovery, the firm is affiliated to La Ligne Internationale pour la Protection des Créances. Commercial contracts, trade marks, and the creation of commercial entities also account for a large proportion of the caseload. The clientele largely comprises foreign companies seeking to set up in Mali. **Modibo Kone** is a highly respected local practitioner.

The firm advised on a revolving credit facility of €4.5 million between the African Export-Import Bank and Mali company Etablissment Zoumana Traore Sarl. **Clients:** Foreign corporations.

Cabinet Toureh et Associés (5 lawyers) Interviews with foreign experts identified this firm as *"A good local name."* The firm counsels its international clientele on all aspects of business law, including registration, M&A and liquidation. Niche strength lies in the oil and gas industry. **Harouna Toureh** has a fine reputation among his clients. **Clients:** Total Texico Elf; Mobil Oil; SATOM; SOMAFREC; MAERSK; CNAR.

Leaders' profiles – Mali

KONE, Modibo
Cabinet Dongar et Modibo Kone, Bamako +223 225 240

TOUREH, Harouna
Cabinet Toureh et Associés, Bamako +223 214 578

MALTA

Corporate/Commercial

MALTA Leading firms (Corporate/Commercial)
1 Fenech & Fenech Advocates
JM Ganado & Associates
2 Camilleri Preziosi
3 Mamo TCV – Advocates

Firms are listed alphabetically in each band.

Leading individuals (Corporate/Commercial)
1 **GANADO Max** *JM Ganado & Associates*
MUSCAT Andrew *Mamo TCV – Advocates*
REFALO Iain *Buttigieg & Refalo Advocates*
2 **DE GABRIELE Louis** *Camilleri Preziosi*
MIZZI Henri *Camilleri Preziosi*
3 **CAMILLERI Richard** *Mamo TCV – Advocates*
CAMILLERI PREZIOSI Louis *Camilleri Preziosi*
FENECH Tonio *Fenech & Fenech Advocates*

Individuals are listed alphabetically in each band.

Fenech & Fenech Advocates (12 lawyers) The firm enjoys a reputation as *"prime for shipping"* on both litigation and registration, and has witnessed a growth in the financial services industry, including M&A work and listings. Involved in the establishment of an off-shore betting industry on the island, the team has assisted the Ministry of Finance in drawing up new regulations. Partner **Tonio Fenech** is a *"driving force in the firm"* undertaking international business transactions. **Clients:** Barclays plc; Air Malta; P&I Clubs; ship owners and agents; major banks and providers of financial services.

JM Ganado & Associates (7 ptrs, 7 asscs) Researchers were told that the firm is *"exceptionally strong"* in shipping and banking. It has witnessed growth in its financial services practice as investment fund companies are attracted to the island. The team recently acted for Maltese banks and in the listing of fund management companies on the Valletta Stock Exchange. Key arbitration partner, the *"thorough and efficient"* **Max Ganado,** *"pushes the firm forward."* He was recently appointed head of the government's Arbitration Centre. **Clients:** International banks and investment management companies.

Camilleri Preziosi (3 ptrs, 2 assts) This *"prestigious"* firm undertakes a range of company work including telecoms, construction, banking and capital markets transactions. Said to *"stand out consistently,"* it has acted on the privatisation of Malta Freeport and is involved in the island's largest commercial property programme. Senior figure **Louis Camilleri Preziosi** is *"the doyen of commercial lawyers"* and he is ably supported by *"intelligent"* **Henri Mizzi.** The *"fantastic, proactive and hard-working"* **Louis De Gabriele** was highly rated by clients and lawyers alike, and is known as *"the capital markets man of Malta."* **Clients:** International and domestic companies.

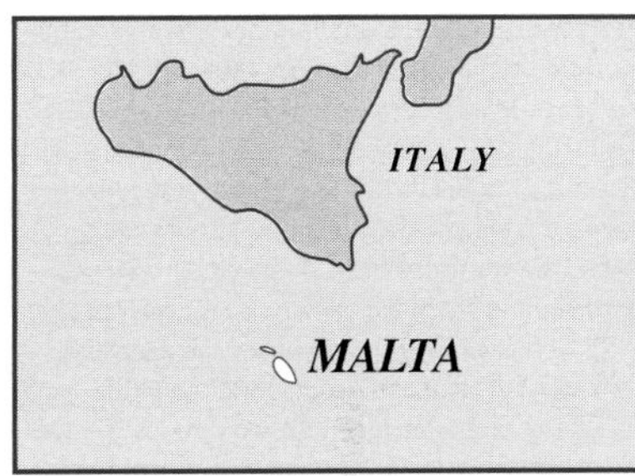

Mamo TCV – Advocates (7 ptrs, 10 asscs) The merger between John Mamo & Associates and Tonna, Camilleri, Vassallo & Co has been warmly welcomed by the market for its *"synergy."* Within a broad corporate practice, the firm focuses on telecommunications, property, insurance and commercial litigation. The TVC side of the practice brings strength in IP and maritime matters and it advised on the first public bond issue by a Maltese company. *"One of the best for company work,"* **Andrew Muscat** (of the John Mamo side) is widely praised as *"thorough and sees all the angles"* while **Richard Camilleri** (TVC) *"stands out for his legal expertise."* **Clients:** Middle Sea Insurance; international and domestic financial and telecoms companies.

Other Notable Practitioner Considered *"Malta's leading lawyer"* **Iain Refalo** of Buttigieg & Refalo Advocates is a *"man with a first rate brain and an enormous reputation."*

Leaders' profiles – Malta

CAMILLERI PREZIOSI, Louis
Camilleri Preziosi, Valetta +356 238 989

CAMILLERI, Richard
Mamo TCV – Advocates, Valletta +356 232 271

DE GABRIELE, Louis
Camilleri Preziosi, Valetta +356 238 989
louis.degabriele@camilleripreziosi.com
Specialisation: Partner responsible for banking and finance, investment services and capital markets. Main area of work is banking and corporate law. Acts for one of Malta's major banking groups – Bank of Valletta – and for a number of other banks and financial institutions. Has played a leading role in the development of Malta's investment services sector and its capital markets. Acted for the promoters of the first fund management company, in the launch of Malta's first investment funds and in several IPOs, including Malta's first privatisation by share sale and Malta's first convertible bond issue. Is currently advising the Government of Malta on the privatisation of the Malta International Airport. Is a lecturer in Banking and Finance at the University of Malta and has spoken at various conferences.
Prof. Memberships: Chamber of Advocates, Malta.
Career: Qualified 1989. Joined *Camilleri Preziosi* in 1993, becoming a partner in 1995.
Personal: Born 29 February. 1964. Attended University of Malta 1983-1988 (LLB) and University of London (LSE) 1988-1989 (LLM). Leisure interests include football and tennis. Lives in Balzan, Malta, is married and has two children.

FENECH, Tonio
Fenech & Fenech Advocates, Valletta
+356 2599 0641
tonio.fenech@fenlex.com
Specialisation: Handled major ship finance transactions for banking as well as ship owning interests and most aircraft leasing, sale and purchase transactions for Air Malta Co. Ltd. as their legal advisor. Has also been particularly active in the field of corporate finance, mergers, acquisitions and internal business transactions.
Prof. Memberships: International Bar Association (Section on Business Law) since 1988, and the European Maritime Law Organisation since 1992 and AIJA.
Career: Awarded warrant to practise at the Maltese Bar by the Malta Government in October 1987. Joined the law firm *Fenech & Fenech Advocates* as partner and practised ever since, particularly in the fields of maritime law, aviation law, company law, international tax planning, corporate and asset finance, as well as mergers and acquisitions. Elected Head of International/Corporate practice of the firm, as well as Managing Partner of the Firm as from 1995. March 1993, managing director of two companies specialising in servicing Maltese offshore companies, as well as ship registration services and corporate services. In 1998, was nominated director of Global Funds SICAV plc, a collective investment scheme regulated by the Malta Financial Services Centre. In 1999, became joint managing director of Malta Dispute Management Ltd, a joint venture between *Fenech & Fenech* and another law firm, with the object of promoting the use of alternative dispute resolution methods in and through Malta.
Personal: Born 13 October 1963. Attended University of Malta 1981-1986 (LLD); University of London 1986-1987 (LLM). Married to Anna Fenech; three children.

GANADO, Max
Professor JM Ganado & Associates, Valletta
+356 235 406

MIZZI, Henri
Camilleri Preziosi, Valetta +356 238 989
henri.mizzi@camilleripreziosi.com
Specialisation: Partner responsible for corporate and commercial law, litigation, EU and competition law, shipping and telecommunications. Has handled acquisitions of companies and undertakings of varying sorts by Maltese and overseas clients. Is acting in the privatisation of Malta Freeport; acted for Port Cottonera Ltd in the acquisition from Government of a major development site; acts for Melita Cable plc, an associate company of United Pan-Europe Communications N.V., in all telecommunications issues, including guiding the company in negotiations with the Government in the liberalisation of the telecommunications sector. Handles major litigation, mainly in the areas of company law, shipping and telecommunications.
Prof. Memberships: Chamber of Advocates, Malta.
Career: Qualified 1989. Joined *Camilleri Preziosi* in 1989, becoming a partner in 1995.
Personal: Born 3 February, 1965. Attended University of Malta 1983-1988 (LLB) and University of Cambridge (Trinity Hall) 1988 (LLM). Leisure interests include reading and sports. Lives in Swieqi, Malta, is married and has two sons.

MUSCAT, Andrew
Mamo TCV – Advocates, Valletta +356 232 271

REFALO, Iain
Buttigieg & Refalo Advocates, Valleta +356 223 515

MAURITANIA

Corporate/Commercial

MAURITANIA Leading firms (Corporate/Commercial)
1 Etude Bettah & Salah
Etude Mine Ould Abdoullah
2 Etude Bal Ahmedou Tidjane
Etude Brahim Ould Ebety
Etude Maroufa Diabira

Firms are listed alphabetically in each band.

Leading individuals (Corporate/Commercial)
1 **BETTAH Mahfoud Ould** *Bettah & Salah*
MINE Abdoullah Ould *Mine Ould Abdoullah*
MOHAMED SALAH Mohamed Mahmoud Ould *Bettah & Salah*
2 **DIABIRA Maroufa** *Maroufa Diabira*
EBETY Brahim Ould *Brahim Ould Ebety*
TIDJANE Ahmedou Bal *Bal Ahmedou Tidjane*

Individuals are listed alphabetically in each band.

Etude Bettah & Salah (2 ptrs, 3 asscs) A *"well-connected firm, capable of handling major work for international clients,"* which represents a diverse range of clients in the areas of banking and finance, telecommunications, shipping and insurance. Professor **Mohamed Mahmoud Ould Mohamed Salah** teaches at the University of Nouakchott and at a French university in Nice. He drafted the new Mauritanian Commercial Code and is described as a *"legal scholar with a sense of reality."* **Mahfoud Ould Bettah** is a *"professional lawyer"* with an *"impeccable reputation."* **Clients:** World Bank; national banks; private businesses.

Etude Mine Ould Abdoullah (1 ptr, 2 asscs) Our researchers found this to be one of the leading firms in the country, renowned for international commerce and business and foreign investment. President of the Mauritanian Board of Human Rights, **Abdoullah Ould Mine** is a *"commercial law expert"* with *"useful international connections."* **Clients:** World Bank; Citibank; SFI.

Etude Bal Ahmedou Tidjane (1 ptr, 2 asscs) One of the first lawyers in Mauritania was **Ahmedou Bal Tidjane.** He is highly regarded on a national level for his work in commercial law, business law and banking. His firm successfully negotiated a settlement over the closure of a fish factory.

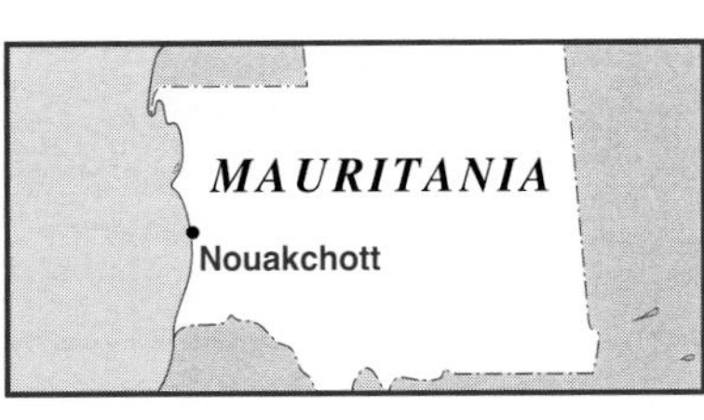

Clients: Mauritanian Bank of Commerce; BNCI; Amextip; Almar Fish.

Etude Brahim Ould Ebety (1 ptr, 3 asscs) Undertakes almost exclusively corporate/commercial work for international clients, particularly French, German and mining companies. The respected **Brahim Ould Ebety** represented a French client purchasing a hotel in Mauritania for $400 million. **Clients:** French Agency for Development; Morak; Nestlé; mining companies.

Etude Maroufa Diabira (1 ptr, 2 asscs) **Maroufa Diabira** is a *"well known player"* in Mauritanian law and has *"long-standing political connections."* He does some commercial law, particularly for banks, but he specialises in human rights, and has worked extensively in Rwanda and Burundi in recent years. **Clients:** Foreign and domestic banks.

Leaders' profiles – Mauritania

BETTAH, Mahfoud Ould
Etude Bettah & Salah, Nouakchott +222 251 540

DIABIRA, Maroufa
Etude Maître Maroufa Diabira, Nouakchott +222 251 502 / 222 252 894

EBETY, Brahim Ould
Etude Brahim Ould Ebety, Nouakchott +222 251 607

MINE, Abdoullah Ould
Etude Mine Ould Abdoullah, Nouakchott +222 255 954 mine_abdoullah@toptechnology.mr
Specialisation: Specialises in business law (droits des affaires), mergers and advising overseas clients on local privatisation work. The experience has helped to build a corporate commercial, financial and various laws practice with clients from a wide area (mining, banks, transport, fishing, insurance, labour conflicts, etc.). Clients include (in Mauritania): BMCI, UNCACEM, BAMIS, SOGECO, SONELEC, Atlantic Londongate Insurances. (Outside Mauritania): Telefónica (Spain), CFD, ELF (France), Woodside (Australia), Royal Air Maroc (Morocco), SFI, PNUD, World Bank, Citibank.
Prof. Memberships: President of Mauritanian Human Rights League, Rotarian, Former membership of Mauritanian Lawyers' Bar.
Publications: Joint author (with Foreign Office) of 'Juridical and Judicial Business Environment in Mauritania' (1994/1995); study on 'Bank Guarantees'; study on the Mauritanian Ratification of 'Vienna and La Haye Conventions'; study on 'Arbitration'; study on 'Investments Law "Problematic" in Mauritania'; 'Juridical, fiscal and accounts study for Projects executions in Mauritania'; articles on 'Juridical and judical reform', 'Judicial Organisation', 'Independance of Justice', 'Women and the Law'; author of 'The Citizen, his Rights and Liberties in Mauritania'.
Career: Member of Diplomatic from 1970 to 1980; General Manager of a fishing society (VOTRA-SA) from 1980 to 1985; legal and financial consultant for CGEM (Confération Générale des Employeurs de Mauritanie) from 1985 to 1987; lawyer from 1987; full Professor of Law at the University of Nouakchott, teaching Commercial Law, Obligations Law, Civil and International Private Law.
Personal: Born 10 Sept 1949 – attended the Universities of Mohamed V (Morocco) and Paris II (France).

MOHAMED SALAH, Mohamed Mahmoud Ould
Etude Bettah & Salah, Nouakchott +222 251 540

TIDJANE, Ahmedou Bal
Etude Bal Ahmedou Tidjane, Nouakchott +222 252 133

MAURITIUS

Corporate/Commercial

MAURITIUS Leading firms (Corporate/Commercial)
1 Chambers of Sir Hamid Moollan
De Comarmond & Koenig
2 Juristconsult Chambers

Firms are listed alphabetically in each band.

Leading individuals (Corporate/Commercial)
1 **KOENIG Thierry** *De Comarmond & Koenig*
MOOLLAN Hamid *Chambers of Sir Hamid Moollan*
ROBERT Georges *Georges Robert*

Individuals are listed alphabetically in each band.

Chambers of Sir Hamid Moollan (20 lawyers) According to the findings of our researchers, this is an *"excellent chambers,"* particularly strong for corporate work and known for acting on behalf of parastatal bodies. It services all the legal requirements for banking, insurance, commerce and industry and is competent in contract law. Also seen to be advising on strategy partnerships and joint venture agreements. Acted on the strategy partnership deal between Nedbank of South Africa and State Commercial Bank of Mauritius. **Sir Hamid Moollan** *"dominates"* the chambers and is considered to be *"the best barrister in Mauritius."* **Clients:** Banks; insurance companies; trade and industry.

De Comarmond & Koenig (4 ptrs, 2 asscs) *"One of the most important firms in Mauritius"* which *"advises major companies."* A *"strong corporate practice,"* it is rated for being *"established and well organised."* Handles corporate law, banking, insurance, legal advice, shipping, IP, joint venture agreements, project finance and company formations. *"Popular"* **Thierry Koenig** is an *"enterprising young lawyer."* The firm advised France Telecom in its bid for the upcoming privatised Mauritius Telecom and acted on the financing of a new hotel in the Seychelles. The firm completed the project finance for the rehabilitation of a sugar factory in Mozambique and one in Tanzania. **Clients:** The Mauritius Commercial Bank; Barclays Bank Offshore; sugar factories; Swan Insurance; financing corporations; Goldman Sachs; JP Morgan.

Juristconsult Chambers (10 lawyers) A *"good team of young barristers"* is expanding the corporate/commercial side of the practice. Handles offshore work, company law, international tax planning, foreign investment into and using Mauritius and the incorporation of companies. Acting as local counsel in the privatisation of the state telecommunications. **Clients:** Multinationals; banks; e-commerce.

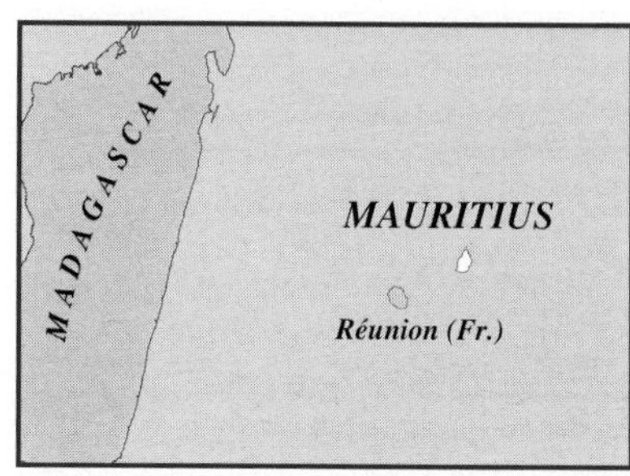

Other Notable Practitioner *"Excellent and honest"* **Georges Robert** is a *"top class commercial lawyer,"* providing offshore legal advice in banking, insurance and foreign investment. He worked with Clifford Chance in an electric power project.

Leaders' profiles – Mauritius

KOENIG, Thierry
De Comarmond & Koenig, Port Louis
+230 212 2215

MOOLLAN, Hamid
Chambers of Sir Hamid Moollan, Port Louis
+230 212 6913

ROBERT, Georges
Georges Robert – Sole Practitioner, Port Louis
+230 212 0862

MEXICO

Index

OVERVIEW: Transition in the market has seen large, older firms losing market share to mid-sized, more specialised outfits. International firms live somewhat in the shadow of their more prominent local counterparts although the international connections are envied. Ritch Heather y Mueller continues to dominate the banking sector although successful attempts to diversify may result in changes to the market place. Jose Raz-Gusman's departure from Ritch Heather y Mueller to join Mijares Angoitia Cortés y Fuentes confirmed that young, dynamic boutiques like the latter are making an impact in Mexico.

M

Banking & Finance

MEXICO
Leading firms (Banking & Finance)

Band	Firm
1	Ritch, Heather y Mueller, SC
2	Franck, Galicia, Duclaud y Robles, SC
	Jáuregui, Navarrete, Nader y Rojas SC
	Martinez, Algaba, Estrella, de Haro y Galvan Duque, SC
	Mijares, Angoitia, Cortés y Fuentes, SC
	White & Case LLP

Firms are listed alphabetically in each band.

Leading individuals (Banking & Finance)

Band	Individual
1	**HEATHER Thomas** *Ritch, Heather*
	NICOLAU Luis *Ritch, Heather*
2	**FRANCK Antonio** *Franck, Galica, Duclaud*
	GALVAN Carlos *Martinez Algaba*
	MUELLER-GASTELL Thomas *Ritch, Heather*
	RAZ-GUZMÁN José *Mijares, Angoitia SC*
	SEPÚLVEDA COSÍO Alberto *White & Case LLP*

Individuals are listed alphabetically in each band.

Ritch, Heather y Mueller SC (8 ptrs, 24 asscs) A firm that makes no secret of its *"focus on finance"* is universally acknowledged by competitors and clients as being *"in a league of its own."* **Luis Nicolau*** is *"conscientious and looks after the details,"* while **Thomas Heather*** is also a *"key player, savvy, practical and understanding of what a client needs."* **Thomas Mueller-Gastell*** is another *"serious, dedicated, hands-on lawyer."* Dominant on cross-border financial transactions, the firm advises a number of powerful US investment banks and covers all areas of finance law. The team represented Citibank on its acquisition of Confia, and advised Bancomer on Mexico's first unsolicited offer by two competing bidders, BDV and Banamex. Also acted for Merrill Lynch as arranger of the first issue of capital notes in Mexico. **Clients:** Anheuser-Busch; MCI WorldCom; Bancomer; Merrill Lynch; Citibank.

Franck, Galicia, Duclaud y Robles, SC (7 ptrs, 18 asscs) Although the firm is better known for its corporate work, its banking department was also commended to researchers as a *"young team with a solid presence."* The *"knowledgeable"* **Antonio Franck*** is known as an *"excellent lawyer"* in this field. Dynamic and forward looking, this department is considered to have strength in depth and expertise in a wide variety of financial transactions. **Clients:** Telmex; ING Barings.

Jáuregui, Navarrete, Nader y Rojas SC (5 ptrs, 15 asscs) *"Beginning to get active in this field,"* the firm has its highest profile for project finance and capital markets advice, acting for a number of Mexican concerns. The team represented EXIM Bank on the financing of the Baijo project, a 600 MW energy plant, and advised the bank steering committee on a workout for AHMSA, the largest Mexican steel producer. Also advised on a number of securitisations, worth in excess of $500 million. **Clients:** Flemings; Casa Autrey; Metropolitan Life; Unefon.

Martinez, Algaba, Estrella, de Haro y Galvan Duque, SC (8 ptrs, 22 asscs) Established firm, said by clients to have a *"real presence in local and international banking."* It acts as counsel to prestigious domestic and international banks, credit institutions and securities firms, notably on complex structured finance transactions, debt renegotiations and public and private placements. **Carlos Galvan*** is a recommended name, and is said to be *"right up there for local banking."* The firm enjoys working relationships with almost twenty international law firms in the UK and the US such as Clifford Chance and Latham & Watkins. **Clients:** Citibank; Bankers Trust Company; Société Générale; Bancomer; Banco Nacional de México; Banco Bilbao Vizcaya-México; GE Capital.

Mijares, Angoitia, Cortés y Fuentes, SC (4 ptrs, 7 asscs) Respected domestic banking practice, a frequent advisor on banking M&A, which recently received a boost with the arrival of the *"talented and experienced"* **José Raz-Guzmán***, formerly of Ritch Heather y Mueller. The firm acted on behalf of Grupo Financiero Serfin, one of Mexico's largest financial groups, on its sale for $1.4 billion to Santander-Mexicano Bank. **Clients:** Banamex; Televisa; Grupo Financiero Serfin.

White & Case LLP (2 ptrs, 13 asscs) The firm represents Mexican and non-Mexican commercial banks and other institutional lenders on all types of financing transactions, from traditional bank lending to the development and use of innovative financial products. It also acts for foreign banks establishing operations in Mexico and Mexican banks establishing offices outside the country.

A strong restructuring practice has seen advice on debt-for-equity swaps, and exchange offers involving Euronotes, Eurocommercial paper and pre-packaged bankruptcy plans. **Alberto Sepúlveda Cosío*** is a versatile commercial practitioner, and, according to peers, *"easily the firm's most significant lawyer."* **Clients:** Mexican and overseas financial institutions.

*See leaders' profiles on pages 481-482

M

Corporate/M&A

MEXICO
Leading firms (Corporate/Mergers & Acquisitions)

Band	Firm
1	Franck, Galica, Duclaud y Robles, SC
	Jáuregui, Navarrete, Nader y Rojas SC
	Mijares, Angoitia, Cortés y Fuentes, SC
	Santamarina y Steta, SC
2	Basham, Ringe y Correa, SC
	Creel García-Cuéllar y Müggengburg
	Kuri Breña, Sánchez Ugarte, Corcuera y Aznar
	White & Case LLP
3	Baker & McKenzie
	Goodrich, Riquelme y Asociados
	Ritch, Heather y Mueller, SC
	Von Wobeser y Sierra, SC

Firms are listed alphabetically in each band.

Leading individuals (Corporate/Mergers & Acquisitions)

Band	Individual
1	**GALICIA Manuel** *Franck, Galica, Duclaud*
	GARCÍA-CUÉLLAR Samuel *Creel García-Cuéllar*
	JÁUREGUI-ROJAS Miguel *Jáuregui, Navarrete*
	MIJARES DAVALOS Juan *Mijares, Angoitia*
	ROBLES Rafael *Franck, Galica, Duclaud*
	SANTAMARINA Augustin *Santamarina*
	VON WOBESER Claus *Von Wobeser y Sierra*
2	**BECERRA Javier** *Basham, Ringe*
	CORTES-ROCHA Jaime *Mijares, Angoitia*
	KURI BREÑA Daniel *Kuri Breña, Sánchez Ugarte*
	NADER Michell *Jáuregui, Navarrete*
3	**DELGADO Alejandro** *Santamarina*
	DUCLAUD Alejandro *Franck, Galica, Duclaud*
	LEVET Aaron *Santamarina*
	ROJAS Héctor *Jáuregui, Navarrete*
	SEPÚLVEDA COSÍO Alberto *White & Case LLP*

Individuals are listed alphabetically in each band.

Franck, Galicia, Duclaud y Robles, SC (7 ptrs, 18 asscs) *"Young team,"* containing *"top quality, seasoned"* individuals, which is considered to have an *"aggressive style,"* and to *"fight hard for clients."* The firm has an outstanding reputation for private equity work, and is acknowledged for its expertise in the financial services industry.

Our researchers were impressed with reports of **Manuel Galicia***, described as *"one of the best lawyers in Mexico,"* who has a *"hands-on, hard-working attitude."* The *"outstanding"* and relatively young **Rafael Robles*** is regarded by clients as a *"superstar in the making."* **Alejandro Duclaud*** was also recommended for his *"sane"* approach to transactions. The firm has represented ING Barings on a number of acquisitions of insurance and pension companies. **Clients:** Telmex; ING Barings.

Jáuregui, Navarrete, Nader y Rojas SC (5 ptrs, 15 asscs) Rapidly expanding firm, which advises on cross-border M&A and corporate restructuring for a mixed domestic and international clientele. Insurance and telecoms are notable areas of strength. *"Rainmaker and excellent PR man"* **Miguel Jáuregui-Rojas*** is characterised by some as *"Mexico's greatest promoter."* He is supported by the *"meticulous"* **Michell Nader***, and **Héctor Rojas***, seen by rivals as a *"sound corporate man."* The firm represented Metropolitan Life, a New York based insurance company, in its efforts to purchase a 49% share of Asegurodora Hidalgo, one of the largest government owned life companies in Mexico. **Clients:** Flemings; Casa Autrey; Metropolitan Life; Unefon.

Mijares, Angoitia, Cortés y Fuentes, SC (4 ptrs, 9 asscs) A *"top boutique firm,"* with *"big clients and talented people,"* which is generally seen on high-profile domestic transactions. *"The Don"* **Juan Mijares Davalos*** is a *"legendary tough guy,"* while the *"excellent"* **Jaime Cortes-Rocha***, a former partner with Santamarina y Steta, provides notable support. The firm acted on behalf of Grupo Televisa during its acquisition of Grupo Acir, and advised the sellers on the $100 million disposal of ABA Seguros. **Clients:** Banamex; Televisa.

Santamarina y Steta, SC (12 ptrs, 40 asscs) Highly respected corporate firm that maintains *"a talented stable of lawyers"* and an *"excellent client base."* A regular feature on privatisations, the firm has a strong following among pharmaceuticals companies, and is headed by **Augustin Santamarina***, a *"top-notch elder statesman."* The *"talented"* **Alejandro Delgado*** and **Aaron Levet*** were both recommended to our researchers for their *"commercial acumen."* The firm acted on the acquisition of ASARCO Incorporated by Grupo México, and advised on the privatisation of the Mexican airports. **Clients:** Banco Bilbao Vizcaya; Monsanto; Novartis; AstraZeneca.

Basham, Ringe y Correa, SC (4 ptrs, 10 asscs) *"Old-fashioned and gentlemanly"* firm with a firmly entrenched industrial client base. The corporate team has been involved in a number of substantial transactions in the chemical, pharmaceutical and food industries, and has acknowledged expertise in anti-trust law. **Javier Becerra*** is *"a resourceful lawyer, well-versed in common law."* **Clients:** International corporates and financial institutions.

Creel García-Cuéllar y Müggenburg (4 ptrs, 8 asscs) *"Decent commercial firm"* with a *"solid all-round reputation"* in the domestic M&A market. **Samuel García-Cuéllar*** is *"in every respect the head of the firm,"* and was commended to researchers for his *"responsiveness to clients."* The firm was counsel to Credit Suisse First Boston, as financial advisor to Grupo Financiero Bancomer in its merger with Grupo Financiero BBVA for an amount in excess of $1.2 billion, and advised Microsoft Corporation in its joint venture with Teléfonos de México for the creation of the Spanish language portal T1MSN.com. **Clients:** Anheuser-Busch Companies; BAT Industries; Credit Suisse First Boston; JP Mogan Capital Corporation; The Peabody Group; MCI Communications Corporation; Microsoft Corporation.

Kuri Breña, Sánchez Ugarte, Corcuera y Aznar (5 ptrs, 9 asscs) Researchers were impressed by the market approval for this rising corporate firm. Considered by rivals to possess *"an active group of strong partners,"* the corporate team is said to be able to *"attract Mexican and foreign clients at will."* **Daniel Kuri Breña*** has *"enormous experience in acquisitions and workouts,"* and the firm often represents foreign entities on their investments in Mexico. The team represented American Tower Corp on their purchase of telecom towers from Mexican companies, and has advised some of the bidders for Pemex, the Mexican state-owned petroleum company. **Clients:** American Tower Corp; Banamex.

White & Case LLP (2 ptrs, 16 asscs) Achieving *"high quality without necessarily having a high profile,"* this office has enjoyed success in acting as corporate counsel to both Mexican and non-Mexican clients on the structuring, operations and governance of Mexican corporations. The firm assists non-Mexican investors in obtaining approvals and licences and developing tax-efficient structures for investment. The *"dedicated"* **Alberto Sepúlveda Cosío*** is regarded by clients as a *"superb lawyer."* The firm represented a leading Mexican financial group in a joint venture with US telecommunications companies and advised a major US investment fund on its private equity investments in a number of Mexican companies. **Clients:** Mexican and overseas companies and financial institutions.

*See leaders' profiles on pages 481-482

Baker & McKenzie (20 ptrs, 43 asscs) The firm has offices all over Mexico, and is acknowledged by peers for *"making the most of its international network and blue-chip client base."* Appearing on a select number of high-premium deals, the team represented Telefonica de España on the acquisition of Infosel, and advised BAT on the acquisition of Cigarrere la Moderna, a deal worth $1.71 billion. **Clients:** Telefonica de España; BAT.

Goodrich, Riquelme y Asociados (2 ptrs, 8 asscs) Although not considered to be the force of former years, the firm is still regarded as an *"effective"* operation, which typically advises foreign private investors in Mexico. The team has recently been involved in the privatisation of the energy industry, airports and rail system. **Clients:** International investors.

Ritch, Heather y Mueller, SC (8 ptrs, 24 asscs) Best known for its unrivalled banking department, the firm has made well-received efforts to diversify into the corporate sector. Researchers were told that the corporate team has *"successfully built on the firm's general reputation for quality."* The team represented Anheuser-Busch on its $1.6 billion investment in Mexico, and advised MCI WorldCom on a joint venture with Banamex, valued at over $3 billion. **Clients:** Anheuser-Busch; MCI WorldCom.

Von Wobeser y Sierra, SC (3 ptrs, 12 asscs) Although this small firm has *"yet to acquire the profile of the market leaders,"* it maintains an active corporate presence in Mexico, advising an enviable range of American corporate heavyweights. This is principally ascribed to the efforts of the *"extraordinary"* **Claus Von Wobeser***, regarded by many competitors as *"a one-man band."* The firm represented Motorola on the sale of its cellular companies to Spanish giant Telefónica, a deal worth $300 million. Also advised Bancomer on its merger with Spanish bank BBV, and Grand Metropolitan on its merger with Guinness. **Clients:** Motorola; Nabisco; The Pillsbury Company; Burger King Co; US Tobacco.

M

Leaders' profiles – Mexico

BECERRA, Javier
Basham, Ringe y Correa, SC, Mexico City +525 261 0400
Recommended in Corporate/M&A

CORTES-ROCHA, Jaime
Mijares, Angoitia, Cortés y Fuentes, S.C., Mexico City +525 201 7400
jcortesr@macf.com.mx
Recommended in Corporate/M&A
Specialisation: Main area of work: acquisitions, mergers and privatisations in Mexico, as well as securities, banking and financial entities' affairs. Has handled incorporation, qualification, acquisition, merger and sale of Mexican banks, financial groups, brokerage firms, insurance companies, investment fund managers and Afores. Has acted as counsel for Mexican issuers and underwriters in a number of global and domestic IPOs. Acts for a number of major housing developers in Mexico on general constitutional matters. Has acted as arbitrator or as counsel in more than 150 arbitration proceedings on corporate finance matters.
Prof. Memberships: Barra Mexicana, Colegio de Abogados (Mexican Bar Association) and Ilustre y Nacional Colegio de Abogados. (At present, Member of the Directive Council and Chairman of the Practice Management Commission of the MBA.)
Publications: Author of a number of articles and contributions on corporate and finance matters for EL FORO, (Mexican Bar Review) and other specialised legal reviews.
Career: Qualified in 1969. Joined *Santamarina & Steta* in 1968, becoming a partner in 1975. Private practice from 1985 to 1992. Joined GBM Atlantico Financial Group as General Counsel and Secretary from 1992 through 1995. Joined *Mijares, Angoitia, Cortés & Fuentes* in 1996. Member of the Legal and Trust Committees of the Mexican Bankers Association (1992-1995). Member of the Mexican Delegation for the NAFTA Cross-border Legal Practice Committee (1995-2000). Member of the Board of Trustees of the Mexican Mediation Institute (2000).
Personal: Born February 25, 1947. Attended Universidad Nacional de Mexico 1964-1968 (Law Degree). Graduate Law Studies at University of Mississippi, USA (1969-1970). MBA from ITESM, Mexico (1977-1981). Leisure interests include jogging (22 marathon races) and other outdoor activities. Married and father of four children. Lives in Mexico City.

DELGADO, Alejandro
Santamarina y Steta, SC, Mexico City +525 279 5400
Recommended in Corporate/M&A

DUCLAUD, Alejandro
Franck, Galicia, Duclaud y Robles, S.C., Mexico City +525 540 9200
Recommended in Corporate/M&A

FRANCK, Antonio
Franck, Galicia, Duclaud y Robles, S.C., Mexico City +525 540 9200
Recommended in Banking & Finance

GALICIA, Manuel
Franck, Galicia, Duclaud y Robles, S.C., Mexico City +525 540 9200
Recommended in Corporate/M&A

GALVAN, Carlos
Martinez Algaba Estrella de Haro y Galvan-Duque SC, Mexico City +525 25 80 202
Recommended in Banking & Finance

GARCÍA-CUÉLLAR, Samuel
Creel García-Cuéllar y Müggenburg, Mexico City +525 246 0600
Recommended in Corporate/M&A

HEATHER, Thomas
Ritch, Heather y Mueller, S.C., Mexico City +525 207 6533
Recommended in Banking & Finance

JÁUREGUI-ROJAS, Miguel
Jáuregui, Navarrete, Nader y Rojas S.C., Mexico City +525 267 4500
Recommended in Corporate/M&A

KURI BREÑA, Daniel
Kuri Breña, Sánchez Ugarte, Corcuera y Aznar, Mexico City +525 251 7220
Recommended in Corporate/M&A

LEVET, Aaron
Santamarina y Steta, SC, Mexico City +525 279 54 00
Recommended in Corporate/M&A

MIJARES DAVALOS, Juan G
Mijares, Angoitia, Cortés y Fuentes, S.C., Mexico City +525 201 7400
Recommended in Corporate/M&A

MUELLER-GASTELL, Thomas
Ritch, Heather y Mueller, S.C., Mexico City +525 207 6533
Recommended in Banking & Finance

NADER, Michell
Jáuregui, Navarrete, Nader y Rojas S.C., Mexico City +525 267 4500
Recommended in Corporate/M&A

NICOLAU, Luis
Ritch, Heather y Mueller, S.C., Mexico City +525 207 6533
Recommended in Banking & Finance

RAZ-GUZMÁN, José
Mijares, Angoitia, Cortés y Fuentes, S.C., Mexico City +525 201 7400
jrazguzman@macf.com.mx
Recommended in Banking & Finance
Specialisation: Banking law and securities. Mergers and joint ventures. Aircraft Finance and Leasing. Acts for a number of international banks. Acted on the secondary offering by Grupo Televisa on behalf of the international underwriters. Acted on behalf of the board of Grupo Financiero Bancomer in connection with the unsolicited offer by Grupo Financiero Banamex. Acts for a number of aircraft lessors and lenders.
Publications: Contributor to Sweet & Maxwell's 'Aircraft Finance. Registration, Security and Enforcement' and 'Aircraft Liens & Detention Rights'.
Career: Qualified in 1988. *Shearman & Sterling*, New York office, Foreign Associate Program (1988-1990). Joined *Ritch, Heather y Mueller*, S.C. in 1984, becoming a partner in 1992. Joined *Mijares, Angoitia, Cortés y Fuentes*, S.C. as partner in 2000.
Personal: Born 23 August 1963. Attended the National University of Mexico 1982-1987 (Law degree), University of Virginia School of Law (LLM, 1988).

ROBLES, Rafael
Franck, Galicia, Duclaud y Robles, S.C., Mexico City +525 540 9200
Recommended in Corporate/M&A

ROJAS, Héctor
Jáuregui, Navarrete, Nader y Rojas S.C., Mexico City +525 267 4500
Recommended in Corporate/M&A

SANTAMARINA, Augustin
Santamarina y Steta, SC, Mexico City +525 279 54 00
Recommended in Corporate/M&A

SEPÚLVEDA COSÍO, Alberto
White & Case LLP, Mexico City +525 540 9600
Recommended in Banking & Finance, Corporate/M&A

VON WOBESER, Claus
Von Wobeser y Sierra, SC, Mexico City +525 258 1000
Recommended in Corporate/M&A

MOLDOVA

Corporate/Commercial

MOLDOVA Leading firms (Corporate/Commercial)
1 Turcan & Turcan

Firms are listed alphabetically in each band.

Leading individuals (Corporate/Commercial)
1 TURCAN Alexander *Turcan & Turcan*

Individuals are listed alphabetically in each band.

Turcan & Turcan (2 ptrs, 2 asscs) Admired for its *"western approach"* this small team is the first port of call for international companies entering Moldova. **Alexander Turcan*** is *"able to adapt the legal concepts of Moldova to a western mentality"* and heads the practice, which deals in general corporate, energy, banking and investments. In conjunction with US firm, Squire, Sanders & Dempsey, the team acted on the privatisation of the electricity distribution services. **Clients:** London based financial institutions; international corporations.

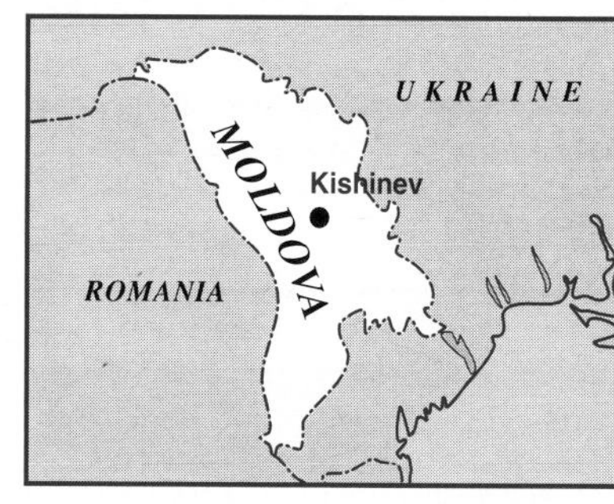

***Alexander Turcan** is a partner at *Turcan & Turcan, Chisinau +373 221 2031*

MONACO

Corporate/Commercial

MONACO Leading firms (Corporate/Commercial)
1 Eversheds

Firms are listed alphabetically in each band.

Leading individuals (Corporate/Commercial)
1 EASUN William *Eversheds*
WALFORD Peter *Eversheds*

Individuals are listed alphabetically in each band.

Eversheds (2 ptrs, 8 asscs) Recognised as the *"number one choice,"* it is the only international law firm in Monaco with French and English qualified lawyers. International and local work is undertaken for both private individual and corporate clients. Considered to offer *"heavyweight financial advice,"* it focuses on tax, inward investment and employment law and has a strength in franchising.

William Easun is a *"knowledgeable lawyer"* who is *"well able to guide clients"* and **Peter Walford** produces *"excellent work."* With its outstanding cross border capability, interviewees declared that *"nobody else does what they do."*

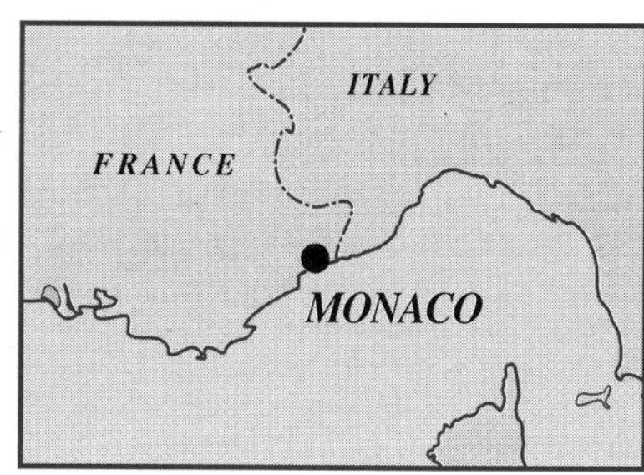

Clients: Christie's; asset management companies; banks; high-profile individuals.

Leaders' profiles – Monaco

EASUN, William
Eversheds, Monte Carlo +377 93 10 55 10
evershed@monaco.mc
Specialisation: Banking and Financial Services, Art Law, Tax and Estate Planning, Corporate Structuring, Relocation to the Principality of Monaco.
Prof. Memberships: Law Society, IBA, STEP, ITPA, IOD (Chairman Monaco), Institute of Art and Law.
Publications: 'Capital Taxes and Estate Planning in Europe'.
Career: *Frere Cholmeley* (Paris) 1980. *Frere Cholmeley Bishoas/Eversheds* (Monaco) 1981 to date.
Personal: Haileybury College, Aix en Provence University (Law). Family interests: Bringing up small children.

WALFORD, Peter
Eversheds, Monte Carlo +377 93 10 55 10

MONGOLIA

Corporate/Commercial

MONGOLIA Leading firms (Corporate/Commercial)
1 Brand Farrar Buxbaum LLP
Lynch, Idesh & Mahoney

Firms are listed alphabetically in each band.

Leading individuals (Corporate/Commercial)
1 **LYNCH Maurice** *Lynch, Idesh & Mahoney*
Up-and-coming individuals
TREGUBENKO Yevgeniy *Brand Farrar Buxbaum*

Individuals are listed alphabetically in each band.

Brand Farrar Buxbaum LLP (1 ptr, 3 asscs) A partnership with a presence in the USA, India and China, it also has an office in Ulaanbaatar. Recommended to researchers for its banking and finance work, including loans to local businesses and security agreements. The firm advised the IFC on its investments in local industries and Marubeni on its Mongolian corporate and financial deals. **Yevgeniy Tregubenko** is a young Russian lawyer with a growing reputation. **Clients:** IFC; World Bank; Marubeni; Crédit Lyonnais; Mees Pierson; American and British financial institutions.

Lynch, Idesh & Mahoney (3 ptrs, 2 asscs) The primary focus of this full-service law firm is the representation of western companies seeking to establish or acquire businesses or enter into joint ventures. Also advises agencies of the Government of Mongolia with respect to privatisation issues and is considered to do *"very good work for their clients."* Represented MIAT Mongolian Airlines in its purchase of an Airbus commercial aircraft and Boroo Gold Company in connection

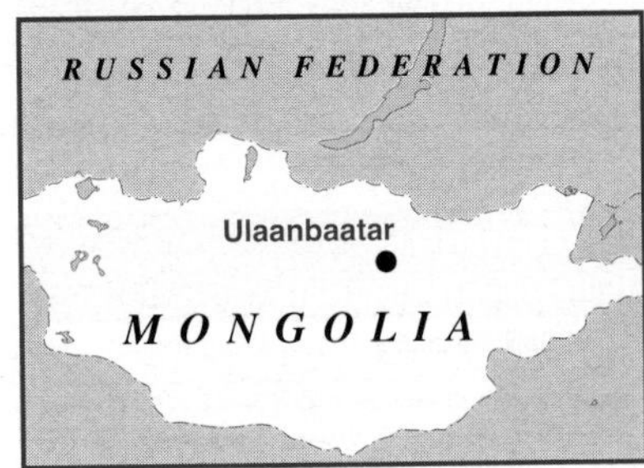

with the development of a gold mine. Also advised Philip Morris in the establishment of a representative office in Mongolia. American **Maurice Lynch** is acknowledged as *"the dean of foreign lawyers."* **Clients:** Arthur Andersen; BHP Minerals; Boroo Gold Company; Energy Authority of Mongolia; IFC; Philip Morris; Procter & Gamble; Reuters Asia.

Leaders' profiles – Mongolia

LYNCH, Maurice M.
Lynch, Idesh & Mahoney, Ulaanbaatar
+976 11 325344
lynch@mongolialaw.com
Specialisation: Corporate transactions,including joint venture, establishment and acquisition of companies, advising mining companies with respect to the development of mineral properties, and private and public offerings of securities. Experienced in arranging for the listing of publicly traded securities on major stock exchanges such as the New York Stock Exchange and the Nasdaq Stock Market.
Prof. Memberships: Bars of New York State; District of Columbia; Commonwealth of Virginia (USA). Member International Law, Business Law and Natural Resources Law Sections of the American and International Bar Associations, and the Rocky Mountain Mineral Law Foundation.
Career: Received AB degree with honours from Harvard University and JD degree from Harvard University Law School. Served for more than three years on board Destroyers as an officer in the US Navy. Admitted to practice in New York in 1959. Formerly a partner in the New York City law firm of *Dunnington, Bartholow & Miller* and of Counsel in the Washington office of the Denver-based firm of *Davis, Graham & Stubbs.* Co-founder of present firm in 1997. Admitted to practice in Mongolia as a solicitor.
Personal: Now lives in Mongolia as a long-term resident.

TREGUBENKO, Yevgeniy
Brand Farrar Buxbaum LLP, Ulaanbaatar
+976 11 310711

MOROCCO

Corporate/Commercial

MOROCCO Leading firms (Corporate/Commercial)
1 Amin Hajji Law Office
Kettani Law Firm
2 Cabinet Naciri & Associés

Firms are listed alphabetically in each band.

Leading individuals (Corporate/Commercial)
1 **HAJJI Amin** *Amin Hajji Law Office*
KETTANI Azzedine *Kettani Law Firm*
2 **NACIRI Mohamed** *Cabinet Naciri & Associés*
Up-and-coming individuals
KETTANI Nadia *Kettani Law Firm*
NACIRI Hicham *Cabinet Naciri & Associés*

Individuals are listed alphabetically in each band.

Amin Hajji Law Office (1 ptr, 2 asscs) Highly regarded firm with an impressive international client base. Competent in all aspects of business, corporate and tax law, the firm specialises in project finance, joint ventures and IP. An *"excellent service"* is provided by **Amin Hajji**, a *"fine young lawyer"* with a growing reputation. The firm acted on the financial restructuring for a holding company in Morocco. **Clients:** International law firms; Deutsche Bank; TWA.

Kettani Law Firm (1 ptr, 21 asscs) An established firm which has expanded significantly over the past few years. It has a first-class reputation in commercial law, banking, investment and international contracts. Professor **Azzedine Kettani** is an *"extremely able"* lawyer who is *"knowledgeable on international projects."* **Nadia Kettani** is recommended as a rising star. The firm advised France Telecom on the purchase of Maroc Telecom. It was also involved in the privatisation of Morocco's two oil refineries. **Clients:** Petroleum companies; state agencies; finance companies.

Cabinet Naciri & Associés (2 ptrs, 5 asscs) A reputable local firm which is making inroads into the international market. Strengths on the commercial side lie in maritime law, project finance and

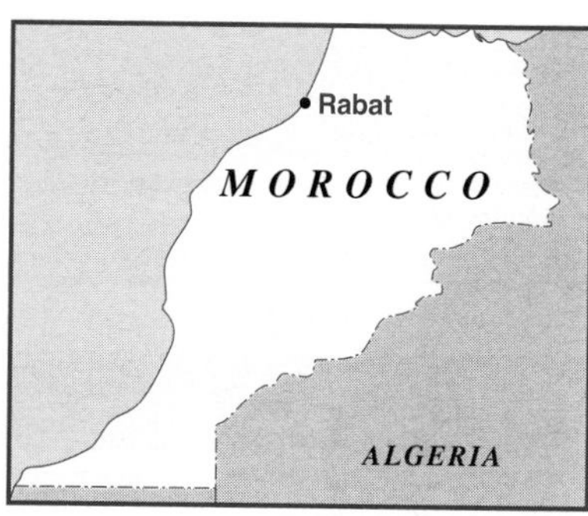

cross-border M&A. Former judge **Mohamed Naciri** is *"one of the best"* lawyers in Morocco, while his son **Hicham Naciri** *("switched on to the international market")* has returned from Norton Rose in Paris to practice in Casablanca. The firm acted as legal counsel for ABN AMRO on a bridge facility loan of $350 million to the second Moroccan GSM operator and has been involved in the largest Moroccan privatisation, advising a potential buyer of 35% of Maroc Telecom for $2 billion. **Clients:** Moroccan banks; ministries; international commercial banks; CIH; BMCE.

Leaders' profiles – Morocco

HAJJI, Amin
Amin Hajji Law Office, Casablanca +212 2 248 7474

KETTANI, Azzedine
Kettani Law Firm, Casablanca +212 2 220 1898

KETTANI, Nadia
Kettani Law Firm, Casablanca +212 2 220 1898

NACIRI, Hicham
Cabinet Naciri & Associés, Casablanca +212 2 227 4628

NACIRI, Mohamed
Cabinet Naciri & Associés, Casablanca +212 2 227 4628

MOZAMBIQUE

Corporate/Commercial

MOZAMBIQUE Leading firms (Corporate/Commercial)
1 Couto, Gonçalves Pereira, Castelo Branco & Associados
MGA (Monteiro, Graça & Associados)

Firms are listed alphabetically in each band.

Leading individuals (Corporate/Commercial)
1 **CARVALHO Alexandra** *Couto, Gonçalves Pereira*
DA SILVA Daniel *Sole Practitioner*
GRAÇA Georges *MGA (Monteiro, Graça & Assoc.)*

Individuals are listed alphabetically in each band.

MGA (Monteiro, Graça & Associados) (3 ptrs, 6 asscs) A firm which works *"mostly in the public sector,"* where our researchers were led to believe the *"partners have good connections with government authorities."* Especially active in foreign investment, incorporation of companies, commercial contracts and banking. **Georges Graça** is *"extremely competent and a pleasure to deal with."* The team has advised on concession agreements for the port of Maputo. **Clients:** IFC; CDC; International Bank of Mozambique; Commercial Bank of Mozambique; Bank Austral.

Other Notable Practitioner **Alexander Carvalho**, although *"new to Mozambique,"* the market informed our researchers that she is regarded as one of the leading figures in the country. During her time with Couto, Gonçalves Pereira, Castelo Branco & Associados she gained experience in a variety of corporate and comercial work including the incorporation of banks and companies, foreign investment, oil contracts, privatisation and project finance. She advised on the Mozal aluminium smelting project, representing the lenders. **Daniel da Silva** is a commercial and tax lawyer who provides legal advice to local and foreign businesses. He has *"vast experience on mega-projects,"* among which were the Mozal aluminum smelting project (worth $1.3 billion) and the Mozal aluminium smelting project and the Mineral Titanium project. His *"knowledge of commercial and maritime law is second to none"* and his work is considered to be of *"the highest quality."*

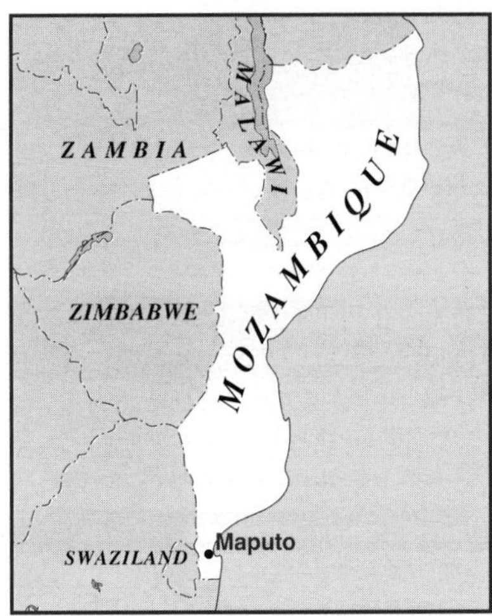

Leaders' profiles – Mozambique

CARVALHO, Alexandra
Alexandra Carvalho – Sole Practitioner, Maputo
+258 82 310 900
p>monjar@mail.tropical.co.mz
Specialisation: Commercial, corporate, banking, project finance, foreign investment. Counsel to the lenders on the Mozal Project.
Prof. Memberships: Portugese Bar Association. Mozambican Bar Association.
Career: Former member of *Couto, Gonçalves Pereira, Castelo Branco & Associados*; presently a sole practitioner.

DA SILVA, Daniel
Daniel da Silva – Sole Practitioner, Maputo
+258 1 780 225

GRAÇA, Georges
MGA (Monteiro, Graça & Associados), Maputo
+258 1 302 336

MYANMAR

Corporate/Commercial: Local Firms

MYANMAR Leading firms (Corporate/Commercial)
1 Maung Maung Gyi
Maw Htoon & Partners
2 Myanmar Legal Services Limited
Mya Thein & Associates

Firms are listed alphabetically in each band.

Leading individuals (Corporate/Commercial)
1 **HTOON Ye** *Maw Htoon & Partners*
KYI Khin Cho *Myanmar Legal Services Limited*
MAUNG MAUNG GYI Henry *Maung Maung Gyi*
THEIN Mya *Mya Thein & Associates*

Individuals are listed alphabetically in each band.

Maung Maung Gyi (1 ptr, 4 asscs) **Henry Maung Maung Gyi** is arguably *"the most senior lawyer in the country"* and is retained as legal counsel by several embassies in Yangon. He is described as *"experienced, honest, reliable and practical."* The firm is recommended for general corporate and commercial work. Currently working on a credit agreement and trademark registrations. **Clients:** Thai EXIM Bank; Gold Mining Co; embassies; Japanese and Swiss companies.

Maw Htoon & Partners (1 ptr, 6 asscs) The firm has *"a great reputation around town"* and much of its work comes on referral from international law firms. Involved in joint venture agreements, M&A work, it is prominent in the energy sector. *"Everybody thinks highly"* of **Ye Htoon. Clients:** Total Fina; Daewoo.

Myanmar Legal Services Limited (1 ptr, 2 asscs) *"Among the leading local firms"* for corporate work and has *"good international connections."* Affiliated to Thai firm Chandler & Thong-ek, it handles contracts and joint ventures, particularly in the mining and petroleum sectors. **Khin Cho Kyi** is *"a real good pick."* Described as *"educated, careful, pleasant to deal with"* she has *"a real presence."* She acts as legal counsel for Myanmar Ivanhoe Copper. **Clients:** Myanmar Ivanhoe Copper; construction and trading companies.

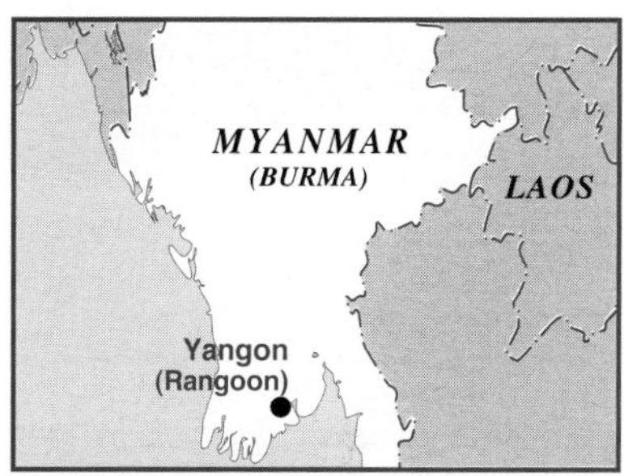

Mya Thein & Associates (1 ptr, 11 asscs) The firm has *"a good international reputation"* but is, like the others, suffering from the lack of investment into Myanmar at present. Provides some legal advice to foreign companies and handles general commercial law work. Recommended to Chambers' researchers, **Mya Thein** *"pays attention to detail."* **Clients:** Foreign companies.

Corporate/Commercial: Foreign Firms

MYANMAR: Foreign Firms Leading firms (Corporate/Commercial)
1 LWA Consultants Ltd
Russin & Vecchi Ltd

Firms are listed alphabetically in each band.

Leading individuals (Corporate/Commercial)
1 **CHRISTIE Alec** *LWA Consultants Limited*
FINCH James *Russin & Vecchi Ltd*

Individuals are listed alphabetically in each band.

LWA Consultants Ltd (2 ptrs, 3 asscs) Arguably the *"firm of choice for foreign companies"* working on the incorporation of companies and matters of investment. **Alec Christie** comes highly recommended to researchers. Currently active in the hotel and tourism sector assisting a number of multinational owners and managers. **Clients:** Total; Mitsui; Daishowa; Marubeni; Crédit Agricole.

Russin & Vecchi Ltd (1 ptr, 4 asscs) The firm works on projects related to trade finance and development finance, as well as carrying out general corporate and banking work. Provided advice to foreign companies interested in offering a telecommunications service to the government and active in agricultural, mining, hotel and infrastructure projects. **James Finch** is *"well liked"* and *"easy to deal with."* **Clients:** Canadian Metals Exploration; international hotel operator; banks.

Leaders' profiles – Myanmar

CHRISTIE, Alec
LWA Consultants Limited, Yangon +95 1 254 816

FINCH, James
Russin & Vecchi Ltd, Yangon +95 1 541 794

HTOON, Ye
Maw Htoon & Partners, Yangon +95 1 545 5378

KYI, Khin Cho
Myanmar Legal Services Limited, Yangon +95 1 650 740

MAUNG MAUNG GYI, Henry
Maung Maung Gyi, Yangon +95 1 533 720

THEIN, Mya
Mya Thein & Associates, Yangon +95 1 245 968

NAMIBIA

Corporate/Commercial

NAMIBIA Leading firms (Corporate/Commercial)
1 Lorentz & Bone
2 Engling, Stritter & Partners
PF Koep & Co
3 Weder Kruger & Hartmann

Firms are listed alphabetically in each band.

Leading individuals (Corporate/Commercial)
1 BOSSAU Hanno *Lorentz & Bone*
GERDES Hans-Bruno *Engling, Stritter & Partners*
KOEP Peter *PF Koep & Co*

Individuals are listed alphabetically in each band.

Lorentz & Bone (6 ptrs, 5 asscs) This is one of the oldest and biggest firms in Namibia. Described as *"highly competent"* by rivals, the commercial practice consists of company and tax law, patents and trade marks, notably for German blue-chip clients. Partner **Hanno Bossau** *"knows his stuff"* and is a *"solid"* operator in the commercial field. **Clients:** International and domestic corporates.

Engling, Stritter & Partners (4 ptrs, 3 asscs) Acting across the spectrum of commercial law, the firm has a sound reputation for its M&A advice. Partner **Hans-Bruno Gerdes** is said by competitors to be *"one of the best commercial lawyers in the country."* The team advised Brauerei Beck & Co of Bremen on its acquisition of a substantial stake in Namibia Brewery Investment Holdings Ltd, and was instructed on the merger between Namibia Fishing Industries and Sea Harvest Corporation of Namibia. **Clients:** BP Namibia; Shell Namibia; Siemens; Standard Bank Namibia; Commercial Bank Namibia; IFC; Berliner Wasser Betriebe.

PF Koep & Co (3 ptrs, 5 asscs) Respected firm with a first-class domestic client base. Headed by *"well-known lawyer and businessman"* **Peter Koep**, the firm advised an international oil company on its right to transport gas in Namibia, and acted on the sale of shares in a UK firm to a South African firm. **Clients:** First National Bank of Namibia Ltd (Barclays Bank); Murray & Roberts Construction (Namibia); Shell Exploration & Production Namibia; Commercial Bank Namibia Ltd; Fedsure Insurance.

Weder Kruger & Hartmann (7 ptrs) Predominantly a strong conveyancing practice, the firm is still considered to have a solid commercial practice. Although not as high-profile as the market leaders, it advises on contracts, incorporation of companies and the transfer of shares. **Clients:** Bank Windhoek; Agricultural Bank of Namibia; Santam Insurance; Coca-Cola Southern Africa.

Leaders' profiles – Namibia

BOSSAU, Hanno
Lorentz & Bone, Windhoek +264 61 273 600

GERDES, Hans-Bruno
Engling, Stritter & Partners, Windhoek +264 61 235031

KOEP, Peter
PF Koep & Co, Windhoek +264 61 224 591
pfk@koep.com.na
Specialisation: Specialises in corporate work, advising companies, invited to address directors of companies on their corporate responsibility. Main area of work is corporate agreements, review applications and advising clients in the fishing and mining industry, has given advice to oil exploration companies regarding their offshore rights, as well as rights to lay pipelines on the seabed where the right to mine offshore diamonds belongs to third parties, is representing fishing companies in a dispute regarding major claims for the delivery of defective cans for the canning of pilchards, has advised the Namibian Bankers Association on amendments to the laws governing insolvency, acts for and advises major companies in the building industry.
Prof. Memberships: Member of the Law Society of Namibia, previous Councillor of the Law Society of Namibia, member of the Institute of Mediation of South Africa, convenor of the Committee on Human Rights, member of the Board for Legal Education, member of the Committee of the University of Namibia to interview and appoint lectures to the Faculty of Law, Member of the International Bar Association.
Career: Qualified in 1980, commenced own practice in 1982, member of the Law Society's Human Rights and Rules Committee, founder member and subsequently President of Namibia Peace Plan 435, working for the implementation of Resolution 435 leading to the independence of Namibia, member of the President's Advisory Committee on Economic Affairs, assist in drawing Rules for the Namibian Stock Exchange and Vice-President of the Namibian Stock Exchange from its inception to date.
Personal: Born 2 December 1951, attended University of Cape Town. Leisure interests include outdoor activities, flying and relaxing with family.

NEPAL

Corporate/Commercial

NEPAL Leading firms (Corporate/Commercial)
1 Anup & Associates
Kusum Law Firm
Pioneer Law

Firms are listed alphabetically in each band.

Leading individuals (Corporate/Commercial)
1 **SHARMA Anup Raj** *Anup & Associates*
SHRESTHA Kusum *Kusum Law Firm*
UPRETI Bharat Raj *Pioneer Law*

Individuals are listed alphabetically in each band.

Anup & Associates (1 ptr, 5 asscs) The firm is *"good for corporate and other matters"* ranging from foreign investment and banking to the incorporation of companies and corporate tax. It has advised the government over the privatisation of tea plantations, manufacturing industries and hydro-electric power. Managing partner **Anup Raj Sharma** is recommended by competitors as a *"good banking lawyer."* **Clients:** Nepal Bank; Bank of India; Nepal Bank of Ceylon; Jyodi Spinning Mill; Hotel Everest; Hotel Summit.

Kusum Law Firm (1 ptr, 5 asscs) *"One of the oldest and most renowned firms in Kathmandu"* focuses on corporate law. Researchers noted its strength in aircraft finance and infrastructure projects. Honorary legal advisor to the British Embassy in Nepal is **Kusum Shrestha**, *"the most senior corporate lawyer in all of Nepal."* **Clients:** Nepal Indosuez Bank; Swiss Agency for Development and Co-operation.

Pioneer Law (2 ptrs, 10 asscs) A firm with an *"excellent reputation"* which is particularly *"strong in arbitration and commercial disputes."* The firm works for the IFC on power projects and its focus on corporate law also covers infrastructure projects, hydro-electric power, joint venture agreements and foreign investment. *"Leading corporate lawyer"* **Bharat Raj Upreti** is *"careful, thorough and accurate."* **Clients:** IFC; Asian Development Bank; Nabil Bank.

Leaders' profiles – Nepal

SHARMA, Anup Raj
Anup & Associates, Kathmandu
+977 1258 445

SHRESTHA, Kusum
Kusum Law Firm, Kathmandu
+977 1417 236

UPRETI, Bharat Raj
Pioneer Law, Kathmandu
+977 1221 340

THE NETHERLANDS

Index

The clients' choice

BUSINESS LAWYER OF THE YEAR
SJOERD EISMA, *De Brauw Blackstone Westbroek*

BUSINESS LAW FIRM OF THE YEAR
DE BRAUW BLACKSTONE WESTBROEK

***Sjoerd Eisma** was the clear winner as best lawyer with the Linklaters Alliance member **De Brauw Blackstone Westbroek** as best firm. Interestingly, Civil Law Notary **Martin Van Olffen** was popular with Dutch clients, finishing a strong third.*

For details see page 36.

OVERVIEW: The Netherlands is growing accustomed to its role as the battleground for warring parties of foreign and domestic law firm, desperate for a piece of its lucrative turf. Undoubtedly the year of Freshfields, who roared into Amsterdam, quickly established an office staffed by the highest calibre lawyers, nearly all poached from leading rivals. Native Dutch firms have experienced mixed fortunes. Backed by Linklaters, corporate heavyweight De Brauw is ensured a rosy future, as are telecoms innovators Houthoff Buruma. By contrast, leading independent firm Nauta Dutilh has suffered several senior partner departures despite a premier banking practice. Over-manned Trenité Van Doorne decided to split into two halves, and closed its office in The Hague in an effort to increase merger potential. Likewise, corporate stalwart Stibbe has eschewed a merger, consequently suffering partner exits and low morale.
Research indicated the need for a tax section, to reflect the growing importance of the Netherlands as a key international jurisdiction and prime location for holding company operations. Although dominated by the big five accountancy giants, the leading law firms have displayed a level of sophisticated transactional expertise.

Banking & Finance

Allen & Overy (8 ptrs, 25 asscs) With the development of the international Allen & Overy finance brand in the Netherlands, the practice has acquired a new breadth. It has built on the strengths of the former Loeff firm in acquisition and corporate finance, where it frequently acts for corporate borrowers. Traditionally, the firm's domestic banking and lender practice has been its weaker arm, but this is expected to change with added UK impetus and resources. The department has acknowledged expertise in several branches of finance, from capital markets and securitisation to asset and project finance. The latter is the preserve of **Bart Meesters***, who *"battles hard and closes the deals."* Clients here include energy giants Essent and NUON, and airlines Air Holland and Martinair. **Victor de Serière***, newly returned from London, was also highly recommended for his wide-ranging finance practice which touches upon structured and acquisition finance, bank lending and regulatory advice. Despite his relative youth, **Niels van de Vijver*** is an experienced transactional lawyer, noted for his debt and capital markets acumen.

In syndicated lending, the firm represented PWC in a NLG100 million stand-by roll-over loan agreement, and VNU in relation to a $500 million bridge facility arranged by ABN AMRO and Merrill Lynch. In acquisition finance matters, the team acted for UBS Capital in relation to the NLG485 million financing of the HIS Group and Fortis Bank, in connection with the financing of the acquisition of ARM Stokvis. Capital markets transactions include acting for the dealers of the $15 billion debt issuance programme of ABN AMRO Bank, and for UBS Warburg on the IPO of IsoTis. In addition, the firm has represented Société Générale on multi-jurisdictional securitisations including Unisys, Canal+ and Paragon. **Clients:** KPN; Maersk Benelux; Rabobank; VNU; Vedior; Bols International; UBS Capital; Fortis Bank; Unisys; Gaz de France; Canal+; Paragon; Deutsche Bank; Chase Manhattan; Magex (subsidiary of NatWest); Indover Bank; UBS Warburg; ABN AMRO; Devote; Equant; AEGON; ASR Bank; BAT International Finance; Dresdner Finance.

Clifford Chance (6 ptrs, 39 asscs) Our researchers have discovered a *"quick and slick"* finance team which is considered by many to be *"the team to beat"* for transactional productivity and logistical efficiency. With a fine bank lending, debt financing and capital markets pedigree, a large team and enviable international resources, the department is now reckoned to function as a fully-rounded unit.

One of the most respected finance lawyers in Holland is *"outstanding"* derivatives and capital markets expert **Frank Graaf***, a *"real forward thinker"* who *"handles people and relationships well."* Multi-faceted, he devotes a lot of time to writing and publishing as well as organising deals and running the department. **René Citroen*** has a large structured finance practice and *"manages a lot of work."* An *"artistic and influential rain-*

THE NETHERLANDS Leading firms (Banking & Finance)
1 Allen & Overy
Clifford Chance
De Brauw Blackstone Westbroek
Nauta Dutilh
2 Houthoff Buruma
Stibbe
3 Caron & Stevens/Baker & McKenzie
Van Doorne
4 Boekel de Nerée

Firms are listed alphabetically in each band.

Leading individuals (Banking & Finance)
1 **GRAAF Frank** *Clifford Chance*
MEERBURG Dirk *De Brauw Blackstone*
2 **BLOM Marc** *NautaDutilh*
MEESTERS Bart *Allen & Overy*
3 **BOELE Bas** *Houthoff Buruma*
CITROEN René *Clifford Chance*
DE SERIÈRE Victor *Allen & Overy*
KELLERMAN Joanne *NautaDutilh*
RUYS Willem *NautaDutilh*
SACHSE Hans *Boekel de Nerée*
VAN EVERDINGEN Huib *NautaDutilh*
WILLEUMIER Jaap *Stibbe*
4 **DE BOUTER Eduard** *De Brauw Blackstone*
KOTHE Tineke *Clifford Chance*
RANK Pim *NautaDutilh*
SCHLINGMANN Francine *De Brauw Blackstone*
SCHROEDER Piet *Caron & Stevens*
VAN DE VIJVER Niels *Allen & Overy*
VAN LEEUWEN Gijs *Houthoff Buruma*

Individuals are listed alphabetically in each band.

maker," he's the "*dean of the practice.*" Younger partner **Tineke Kothe*** won notable praise for her debt/equity capital markets and securitisation-based practice. The securities team made the headlines when it acted for Telefonica Europe on its $10 billion US shelf registration. The firm also acted for ABN AMRO Bank in the Amstel Consumer Loan Securitisation Company's €400 million securitisation of mortgaged-backed consumer loans. The firm also handled ABN AMRO's $6 billion financing of Interbrew's purchase of the brewing divisions of Bass and Whitbread – the largest syndicated loan arranged from the Netherlands in 2000. **Clients:** ABN AMRO Bank; UBS Warburg; Morgan Stanley; ING; Citibank; Fortis; Bear Stearns; GIMV.

De Brauw Blackstone Westbroek (15 ptrs, 25 asscs) This corporate giant has always run a broad finance practice, where notable strengths include debt/equity capital markets and domestic bank lending and regulation. The alliance with Linklaters is felt to have propelled the practice into the upper echelons of the international league. Strong on the equity side of the balance sheet, the firm can also hold its own against the debt transactional might of its principal rivals.

Universally respected, **Dirk Meerburg*** has progressively scaled down his M&A practice to focus on complex structured financings (many tier 1 transactions), bank lending and IPOs. One of the major names in the sector, he "*consistently outperforms most of his peers.*" **Eduard De Bouter*** retains his spot in the rankings, and is noted for advising a number of Spanish clients in equity financing matters. Since being made partner three years ago, **Francine Schlingmann**'s* profile has risen rapidly. She is routinely identified for her high quality equity capital markets and IPO practice. Other areas of the department's expertise include asset and project finance and litigation.

The team was involved in the IPO (AEX listing) of PinkRoccade, a Dutch IT services provider, and the IPO of KPNQwest, where it acted for the underwriting syndicate led by Morgan Stanley Dean Witter. Also advised VNU on its accelerated global tenders of common shares, a deal worth €610 million, and represented Ahold on its global offering of common shares (raising €2.4 billion) and convertible subordinated notes. **Clients:** Rabobank; Fortis; ING; Ahold; PinkRoccade; Morgan Stanley Dean Witter; VNU.

NautaDutilh (11 ptrs, 29 asscs) Banking has always represented one of the core areas for the firm, and continues to do so. Bolstered by rock-solid links with the Dutch banking community – the firm is adored by ABN AMRO – there is no question over its continuing status as one of the market leaders. Excelling in domestic bank lending and regulatory advice, the unit is considered to take an "*academic*" approach to its caseload. This was the first Dutch firm to handle securitisations, and it is still regarded as the market leader in this area. Banking litigation is another key feature of the practice. With a focus on domestic clients, some have questioned the firm's international strategy, but for intellectual rigour, it has few equals.

Among a team with real depth, **Marc Blom*** is "*indisputably a leading player.*" A master technician, he frequently advises major investment banks on Tier 1 matters and is an active litigator. He is "*bright and legally exact,*" and defended ABN AMRO in a headline-hitting case involving investors suing over the World Online prospectus. Banking and securities litigator **Huib van Everdingen*** is another whose technical abilities are held in high esteem. He defended the AEX on a recent NLG1.2 billion action. Younger partners **Joanne Kellerman*** and **Willem Ruys*** are securitisation experts, who have grown with this area of law – "*they've made it their own.*" **Pim Rank***, a well-known professor of securities law at Nijmegen university, was recognised for his expertise in derivatives and e-banking.

The firm assisted Rabobank in the creation of an innovative and complicated €650 million tier 1 structure for the issuance of 'hybrid' non-cumulative guaranteed trust preferred securities. Also advised the Amsterdam Stock Exchange in a full revision and new set-up of its Listing Rules. **Clients:** ABN AMRO; Rabobank; AEX; CLS Bank; Necigef; NIB Capital Bank; Banc One NA; HSBC; Deutsche Bank; Dresdner Bank.

Houthoff Buruma (5 ptrs, 10 asscs) Although it lacks the big-ticket transactional volume of its leading competitors, the firm is felt to provide a consistent and reliable service to a clientele comprising domestic banks and smaller financial institutions. The firm has particular strength in telecoms, IT and media, and has been active on a number of IPOs and bond offerings in these sectors.

Bas Boele* ("*quietly impressive*") is primarily a banking litigator. Acknowledged for his Supreme Court practice, he has a "*precise, technical and barristerial*" style. He has been representing Goldman Sachs in the high profile World Online internet litigation – a case concerning allegations of false promises made in the IPO prospectus. Also acted for ABN AMRO in the DAF litigation. **Gijs Van Leeuwen*** handles many of the firm's securities transactions and IPOs. He has advised Extra Clearing, the clearing entity of ING, and Achmea Bank on derivatives. **Clients:** Goldman Sachs; BNG; AEX Extra Clearing; Achmea Bank; Theodoor Gilissen (subsidiary of Fortis); Bloomberg.

Stibbe (10 ptrs, 20 asscs) The firm's finance practice lags some way behind its more widely acclaimed forte in M&A. This has not been helped by the loss of key corporate partners with a role to play on equity offerings and IPOs. However, the team retains a reputation for strength in acquisition finance, project finance and equity capital markets, although debt work does not feature heavily. **Jaap Willeumier*** has a broad finance practice which has included bank lending for ING and ABN AMRO. Exploiting the firm's pan-European capabilities, he is best known for his recent work on the Euronext merger – the new exchange fusing together the Paris, Brussels and Amsterdam Stock Exchanges. **Clients:** Euronext; ABN AMRO; ING; Goldman Sachs.

N

*See leaders' profiles on pages 501-506

Caron & Stevens/Baker & McKenzie (2 ptrs, 8 asscs) The firm has built on its respected corporate and tax foundations to sustain a small but well-regarded finance practice. It has witnessed a change of emphasis in the last year from straightforward bank lending and syndicated loans to greater numbers of complex structured finance, securities and derivatives transactions.

Regarded as the face of the practice, **Piet Schroeder*** is a *"dedicated banking lawyer with a focused practice."* He maintains a high reputation for his advice on acquisition and project finance. Drawing on its international network of offices, the firm acts for a range of medium to large sized financial institutions. Advised Citibank in connection with the transfer of the custody of a securities portfolio of €35 billion by Robeco, and is advising Rabobank on assignments ranging from structured finance and debt transactions to derivatives. Project finance work has included representing a Dutch SPV in a $3 billion oil and gas fields development project involving the Barracuda and Caratinga oil and natural gas fields. **Clients:** ING; Citibank; Fortis Bank; Rabobank.

Van Doorne (7 ptrs, 20 asscs) The firm is currently in a state of flux after splitting into two discrete halves, with the banking and finance department located in Amsterdam. Despite extensive resources, the group has lacked a profile to match and is seen less frequently than rivals on the bigger structured finance transactions. However, the team is considered to fare well on bank lending and syndicated credits advice. Acquisition finance and IPOs are also a prominent feature of the caseload.

Acted as Dutch counsel to Chase Manhattan in connection with a €512 million facility to finance the leveraged buy-out of Acordis by CVC Capital Partners from Akzo Nobel. Also advised Kappa Packaging in connection with the issue and Luxembourg listing of its NLG3.7 billion high-yield note, and Globaldrive on its $5 billion asset-backed note program for FCE Bank. In addition, represented Feyenoord football club on its private placement issue of NLG100 million worth of premium bonds. **Clients:** FC Feyenoord; Gorilla Park; Kappa Packaging; Globaldrive; Imperial Tobacco; Chase Manhattan; Seagull Holding.

Boekel de Nerée (4 ptrs, 8 asscs) The profile of the firm is largely restricted to the activities of **Hans Sachse** and his role as chief legal advisor to the STE, the Dutch securities regulator. Commended as an experienced regulatory and securities expert, he also acts for a number of other banks, brokers and financial institutions. Other partners handle asset and structured finance. In addition to STE work, the practice has assisted Citibank in setting up its Dutch warrant program, and has established an internet mortgage lending business for the Bank of Scotland. **Clients:** STE; Citibank; Bank of Scotland.

Communications

THE NETHERLANDS
Leading firms (Communications)

Band	Firm
1	Allen & Overy
	Clifford Chance
	Houthoff Buruma
	Stibbe
2	De Brauw Blackstone Westbroek
	Freshfields Bruckhaus Deringer
	Kennedy Van der Laan
	NautaDutilh

Firms are listed alphabetically in each band.

Leading individuals (Communications)

Band	Individual
1	**DOMMERING Egbert** *Stibbe*
	EIJSVOOGEL Peter *Allen & Overy*
	FLEURY Joachim *Clifford Chance*
	GEUS Marjolein *Houthoff Buruma*
	OTTOW Annetje *Houthoff Buruma*
2	**DRION Coen** *Kennedy Van der Laan*
	SIPPENS GROENEWEGEN Piet *NautaDutilh*
	VAN DER KLIS Geert *Clifford Chance*
3	**HOBBELEN Hein** *Freshfields Bruckhaus Deringer*
	SANDERS Maarten *Stibbe*
	SNOEP Martijn *De Brauw Blackstone Westbroek*

Individuals are listed alphabetically in each band.

Allen & Overy (5 ptrs, 20 asscs; 6-7 lawyers handle IT matters) There is general agreement over the firm's placing in the upper echelon. Possessing expert regulatory lawyers, the team advises on both mobile and fixed telephony, on matters ranging from interconnection to price regulation, frequency allocation and dispute resolution. It has represented state telecoms giant KPN in more than 20 disputes before the Dutch telecoms regulator, OPTA. The transactional practice has been equally active. A number of prominent corporate partners have been noted for their input on KPN deals.

Much of the credit for the firm's leading position is considered to lie with regulatory supremo **Peter Eijsvoogel***, chief legal advisor to KPN. A former litigator, he is *"hugely skilled and an outstanding expert,"* although occasionally seen to be somewhat conservative. The firm advised KPN on its global €10 billion equity offering to finance its newly acquired UMTS licences, and represented KPN Mobile in the formation of a strategic partnership with the Japanese mobile operator, NTT DoCoMo. **Clients:** KPN; Viatel.

Clifford Chance (2 ptrs, 10 asscs) Widely found by *Chambers'* researchers to be commended for its breadth, the group is respected equally for its transactional and regulatory prowess. Corporate partner **Joachim Fleury*** (*"highly impressive"*) is pre-eminent among transactional telecoms practitioners. He is a *"supremely well-organised managerial figure"* and has advised on a number of major deals, including representing NTT DoCoMo on its acquisition of a 15% stake in KPN Mobile for €4 billion, and a 20% stake in Hutchison 3G Holdings for €2 billion. The firm also advised UPC on a $2.8 billion stock and cash acquisition of the outstanding shares of SBS Broadcasting, a Luxembourg-based television and radio group.

Regulatory weight is provided by the *"skilful technical abilities"* of **Geert van der Klis***. A *"pleasant operator,"* he brings a mix of competition and regulatory knowledge to work such as advising mobile operator Libertel on its UMTS bid, and representing UPC in litigation against Canal+ over access to digital cable networks. **Clients:** NTT DoCoMo; UPC; Libertel; ENECO; Multikabel; Paribas Deelnemingen; Advent International.

Houthoff Buruma (Telecoms 3 ptrs, IT 3 ptrs, 15 asscs) The communications sector is one of the firm's strongest suits. Despite the absence of an international network to match its leading competitors, the firm's client roster comprises an enviable array of domestic and foreign operators, including many new entrants, in both the fixed and mobile telephone markets. The team is acknowledged for its expertise on interconnection tariffs, local loop unbundling and wireless matters.

"Impressive operator" **Marjolein Geus*** is noted for her breadth of practice, encompassing telecoms, IT and media. She is ably supported by **Annetje Ottow***, a leading player in competition-related and regulatory telecoms matters. *"Incredibly determined,"* she has a *"great understanding of the technical side of the business."*

The firm advised Deutsche Telekom on a joint venture with Belgacom and Tele Danmark, and on its bid for a UMTS licence. Also acted for Mediakabel, a joint venture of Dutch cable TV operators in connection with the introduction of interactive digital TV via cable TV networks. The IT/e-commerce team has advised on the establishment of internet 'shopping plazas' and portals, outsourcing projects for Origin and Hewlett Packard, and the bellen.com start-up, the brainchild of Dutch teenage internet entrepreneur Ben Woldring. **Clients:** BT; Deutsche Telekom; Mediakabel; United Telekabel; Libertel; Global Crossing; MCI WorldCom; ATOS Origin; Hewlett Packard; SIDN; bellen.com.

Stibbe (5 ptrs, 20 asscs) Although the firm has endured a difficult year, the telecoms team continues to enjoy an undiminished status. A powerful transactional capability is reinforced by regulatory advice on UMTS auctions, interconnection and unbundling of the local loop. At the helm is one of the Dutch legal profession's leading lights, *"original thinker"* and guru **Egbert Dommering***. A professor with an extensive résumé in academia, *"the market couldn't do without him."* Frequently acting for new entrants, he is an *"insightful and principled lawyer,"* and has been in the vanguard of the push for new regulatory developments in the telecoms industry.

The corporate side of the practice is in the care of the experienced **Maarten Sanders***, who looks after the interests of a number of major clients. The firm acted for VersaTel Telecom on a court appeal challenging the design of the UMTS auction. Other contentious work saw the group advising TV company CLT-UFA on a High Court challenge to the Dutch regulator, and representing Canal+ on several disputes over cable access. In conjunction with the firm's other offices, the transactional team acted for Competel, a $500 million telecoms start-up, which was floated on the Paris Bourse. **Clients:** VersaTel Telecom; CLT-UFA; Canal+; SBS; Competel.

De Brauw Blackstone Westbroek (2 ptrs, 4 asscs) The firm's blue-chip old economy client base has contributed to its comparatively low profile in communications. Expertise continues to stem largely from the firm's esteemed competition department, which has made inroads into the increasingly liberalised telecoms market.

Promising competition partner **Martijn Snoep*** is seen as the team's leading practitioner. About one third of his practice deals with telecoms clients, including advice on interconnection, number portability, number allocation, registrations and licences. His principal client is BT subsidiary Telfort, which he advised on the Dutch UMTS auction and subsequent litigation against the Government over a WLL licence. The firm represented Vizzavi (a joint venture owned by Vodafone and VivendiNet) on the acquisition from Libertel of its mobile internet portal business in the Netherlands. **Clients:** Telfort; Vizzavi.

Freshfields Bruckhaus Deringer (4 ptrs, 3 asscs) *"Clearly an up and coming force,"* the firm has embarked on a sustained recruitment drive to propel itself into the top eight communications operations. Not a specialist team, it draws on the abilities of highly rated lawyers from the competition, corporate and tax departments.

Senior associate **Hein Hobbelen*** is seen as the nearest thing to a specialist. Having learnt his trade at Stibbe, he has brought experience of regulatory and competition issues to his new firm. Best known for its work on behalf of Versatel, the team represented the company on litigation against the Dutch government over the UMTS auctioning process. Other activity has included acting for Hutchison Whampoa on its application for a TMT-2000 mobile licence, advising Deutsche Telekom on its proposed acquisition of an interest in BEN, and representing Dutchtone, a France Telecom subsidiary, in litigation against the Dutch government concerning the auction of DCS 1800 frequencies. **Clients:** France Telecom; Dutchtone; Hutchison Whampoa; Deutsche Telekom; VersaTel Telecom; QS Communications Benelux; Holland Media Group; first e-group; NeSBIC Groep; NCM Holding.

Kennedy Van der Laan (26 lawyers handle IT, telecoms and media) Newly rated this year, this progressive firm has *"organised its departments in a market-driven way"* and is considered *"ideal for a small Dutch regulatory matter."* Although not yet seen as an international force, the team is said to be *"youthful, effective and knowledgeable,"* and has *"successfully exploited commercial opportunities in the new economy."*

In spite of an increase in telecoms regulatory work, the firm's niche strength is felt to remain in IT, where a *"simply great"* team advises leading suppliers and users, government agencies and start-up companies. **Coen Drion*** is the *"main man"* for IT expertise, and is acclaimed for his technical ability and knowledge. **Clients:** A range of IT and telecoms companies, both domestic and international.

NautaDutilh (5 ptrs, 9 asscs) The firm maintains a moderate profile in the telecoms market and represents a high-powered clientele on a variety of corporate, competition, regulatory and litigation matters, notably in mobile telephony. **Piet Sippens Groenewegen*** continues to be highly respected by his peers. Substantial recent activity has centred around Dutchtone, which has been advised on extensive litigation in respect of facility sharing for sites and antenna masts. **Clients:** AT&T; Dutchtone; France Telecom; Talkline.

Competition/Anti-trust

Allen & Overy (2 ptrs, 10 asscs) A fine corporate client base in concert with a pair of outstanding partners pushes the firm into the elite of the Dutch anti-trust market. Acting for a mixture of incumbents and challengers, the firm is a constant presence in energy, communications and retail.

"Intelligent and strong-willed," **Paul Glazener*** spends at least 50% of his practice time on energy and utilities regulatory matters, particularly the implications of recent gas and electricity legislation. Accomplished at handling contentious matters, he is a *"thorough litigator with a great eye for detail."* **Tom Ottervanger*** *("shrewd, capable and pragmatic")* is equally acclaimed. Dividing his time between Brussels and Amsterdam, he has expertise in a vast range of anti-trust matters. *"You can't go wrong with him – he's even-handed and level-headed."* Long known for his state aids and energy regulatory work, he has recently turned his hand to telecoms, representing indus-

*See leaders' profiles on pages 501-506

THE NETHERLANDS Leading firms (Competition/Anti-trust)
1 Allen & Overy
De Brauw Blackstone Westbroek
2 Freshfields Bruckhaus Deringer
3 NautaDutilh
Stibbe
4 Clifford Chance
Houthoff Buruma
Nolst Trenité

Firms are listed alphabetically in each band.

Leading individuals (Competition/Anti-trust)
1 **BIESHEUVEL Mark** *De Brauw Blackstone*
BROUWER Onno *Freshfields Bruckhaus*
GLAZENER Paul *Allen & Overy*
KNIBBELER Winfred *Freshfields Bruckhaus*
OTTERVANGER Tom *Allen & Overy*
PIJNACKER HORDIJK Erik *De Brauw Blackstone*
2 **FEENSTRA Jaap** *NautaDutilh*
SLOTBOOM Marco *Nolst Trenité*
SNOEP Martijn *De Brauw Blackstone*
SWAAK Christof *Stibbe*
VAN DER WOUDE Marc *NautaDutilh*
VAN EMPEL Martijn *Stibbe*
VAN SASSE VAN YSSELT Charles *Clifford Chance*
VERLOREN VAN THEMAAT Weyer *Houthoff*
3 **OTTOW Annetje** *Houthoff*
VAN DER KLIS Geert *Clifford Chance*
VAN DER WAL Gerard *Barents & Krans*

Individuals are listed alphabetically in each band.

try heavyweight KPN, as well as clients in markets as diverse as brewing and supermarket retailing.

The team acted on the acquisition of Cruzcampo by Heineken. This created the largest Spanish brewery group and was the first case ever referred to Spain by the EU Commission. Recent second phase NMA approvals include Schuitema/A&P and Laurus/Groenwoudt. **Clients:** UPS; KPN; NUON; EPON; Aegon; Sara Lee; Buhrmann; Vendex KBB; Dutch Premier League.

De Brauw Blackstone Westbroek (4 ptrs, 14 asscs) Pace-setters for twenty years, the team is still regarded by many as the one to beat. The firm frequently defends incumbent monopolists in liberalised industries and is considered to have *"the numerical capacity and the right approach to the job."*

Mark Biesheuvel* is one of a clutch of highly recommended lawyers. *"Witty and fast-thinking,"* his clients include big guns Shell and Unilever. He attracted attention for representing KLM on its now aborted merger talks with British Airways. He also assisted the airline on its proposed merger with Alitalia, which was cleared by the EC, and on its alliance with NorthWest Airlines. **Erik Pijnacker Hordijk*** *("packs a punch")* is one of the best-known names in the Netherlands. A *"formidable talent,"* his competition practice is highlighted by a specialist knowledge of public procurement, on which he wrote the standard Dutch text. Although he *"can be blunt,"* he is widely described as *"legally brilliant"* and *"perfect for desperate cases when you need a fighter not a peacemaker."* Widely tipped as a future star, **Martijn Snoep*** *("their real young quality")* enters the lists this year. A partner since late 99, he is closely linked to the telecoms sector, notably for core client Telfort (a BT subsidiary) which he represented in the Dutch UMTS auction and subsequent litigation.

The firm successfully nullified a fine levied on client ENCI by the Commission in Brussels for alleged cartel infringements. Other principal cases include an appeal on behalf of SEP against a fine inflicted by the NMA, and a merger notification role on the takeover of NBM by BAM. **Clients:** KLM; Shell; Unilever; Telfort; ENCI; Sky Radio; Radio Noordzee FM; Gasunie; DSM; Philips; Rotterdam Port Authorities.

Freshfields Bruckhaus Deringer (2 ptrs, 8-10 asscs) The firm is considered to have *"arrived with a loud bang,"* making an instant impact through two high-profile lateral hires. Geared towards merger control work, the team can call on unparalleled pan-European corporate and anti-trust strength, and is expected to progress still further.

Onno Brouwer* is hailed by some as the best competition lawyer in the Netherlands, and his arrival from Stibbe was a massive coup. *"Bright and unaggressive,"* he has a *"unique multi-layered understanding of European law unmatched by others."* He focuses on behavioural matters, notably cartel cases, and appears frequently before the courts in Brussels, The Hague and Luxembourg. The media and telecoms industries are notably prolific areas of his caseload. **Winfred Knibbeler***, *"a brilliant young lawyer – ambitious and skilful," "has really come of age"* since his arrival from NautaDutilh, and completes a formidably hard-working spearhead. An expert on energy matters, he has represented Essent, the largest energy company in the Netherlands, on issues such as electricity tariff regulation.

The firm advised publisher Wegener in successful litigation against the Dutch Competition Authority, following the acquisition of VNU newspapers. Other highlights include representing the Dutch Bar Association in a case against PWC, the Holland Media Group, in the high profile Telegraaf / TV data case, and Martinair on its merger with KLM. **Clients:** Essent; Wegener; ABN AMRO; Holland Media Group; Dutch Bar Association; Martinair.

NautaDutilh (4 ptrs, 10 asscs) With the loss of key partner Winfred Knibbeler to Freshfields and the firm's perceived lack of international strategy, the anti-trust practice has suffered a roller-coaster year. However, the group is acknowledged to retain extensive resources, and benefits from the proximity of a respected Brussels office. Particularly prolific domestically, the firm has advised on a number of merger control cases and a raft of cartel, litigation and article 81/82 matters.

Jaap Feenstra* is now the focal point of the Dutch practice. He is a *"thorough proceduralist and legally precise,"* as well as a *"bright, pleasant advocate who communicates well."* He has raised his profile by advising on key broadcasting and publishing matters, including representing Wegener and NOS Television in a case involving De Telegraaf concerning access to data on television programmes. In Brussels, **Marc van der Woude*** *("one of the best around")* is well thought of by the legal community. *"He's my top choice for client referrals,"* said a leading Dutch practitioner. A former European Commission official, he has built up a practice that acts for a mixture of Dutch and European clients before the NMA and the EC. His energy focus has seen him defend a major oil company in a cartel case concerning alleged fixing of petrol prices in the Netherlands. **Clients:** Wegener; NOS; UNA; EZH; Ajax FC; Seagram; Esso; ABN AMRO; VNU; EDF.

Stibbe (2 ptrs, 7 asscs) The practice has endured a tough time since losing its star performer, Onno Brouwer, a lawyer regarded by some as the best in the business. Although its profile has undoubtedly diminished, a reliable corporate clientele and a department with *"definite specialist experience"* keeps it in the reckoning. The emerging younger partner is **Christof Swaak***, a lawyer with a track record in academia who specialises in article 81 and 82 issues and state aids cases, and is *"starting to assume more responsibility."* In addition to his Dutch practice, he spends a proportion of his time before the courts in Brussels and Luxembourg. Older and more established support is provided by the *"Nestor of the department,"* **Martijn van Empel*** *("bags of experience")* who had been teaching at Rome University. Since the loss of Onno Brouwer, he has returned to full time fee-earning duties in Amsterdam.

The firm acted on the Aventis merger notification, was instructed on the oral hearing before the European Court of Justice in the Marca Mode/Adidas case, and represented the Dutch Association of Jewellers against the See Buy Fly campaign at Schiphol Airport. **Clients:** Akzo Nobel; Yamanouchi; Aventis; Dutch Association of Jewellers.

Clifford Chance (2 ptrs, 5 asscs) The firm has always been regarded as something of an underperformer on the European competition stage. In spite of the advantages of a pan-European integrated structure, the firm's Amsterdam office is still felt to lack the heavyweight personnel of its leading rivals. However, the team has a varied caseload, ranging from big-ticket merger control advice to state aids (notably on banking and electricity matters) and cartel matters.

The department's best-rated performer is **Charles van Sasse van Ysselt***. A Dutch lawyer with twenty years' experience at the firm, he is based primarily in Brussels but divides his time between the two nations, acting for Dutch clients and appearing before the NMA and the EC. *"Massively underrated,"* he is *"accurate, precise and easy to work with."* **Geert van der Klis*** originally developed his competition practice as an associate at Loeff Claeys Verbeke. Now a partner, his emphasis has shifted to focus on regulatory advice for clients in the telecoms, media and e-commerce sectors.

The firm handled the merger control aspects of CVC's acquisition of Accordis, the largest transaction ever handled by the Amsterdam office. It also advised on UPC's acquisition of the Greater Rotterdam Area Cable Network. **Clients:** CVC; GE Capital; UPC; Sony Music; NBM-Amstelland.

Houthoff Buruma (3 ptrs, 7 asscs) The competition practice reflects the firm's acknowledged expertise in the new economy. A *"polder-like"* Dutch client base comprises a series of telecoms, media and IT companies.

Like many Dutch firms, the practice has a strong presence in Brussels, home to its best known practitioner **Weyer Verloren van Themaat*** *("pleasant, visible and more than competent")* who is rarely out of the limelight for both Dutch and EC matters. He advises on merger control, Article 81/82 cases and cartel work, and advised on the high-profile acquisition by Telegraaf Holdings of the regional newspaper publisher Uitgeversmaatschappij De Limburger. In Brussels, the firm operates exclusively under the banner of Liedekerke Siméon Wessing Houthoff, a pan-European joint venture which includes a number of other esteemed Brussels competition lawyers. Telecoms heavyweight **Annetje Ottow*** continues to be noted for her competition expertise which supports her prolific regulatory involvement in the sector. The team acted for internet search engine ILSE, the target of a shareholding purchase by VNU, and advised the Nederlandse Spoorwegen on the competition aspects of its participation in the high-speed link from Brussels to Amsterdam. **Clients:** Telegraaf Holdings; ILSE; Nederlandse Spoorwegen; Produktschap Vee en Vlees; BT; Global Crossing.

Nolst Trenité (3 ptrs, 7 asscs) To increase its international merger potential, the firm split into two separate organisations in early 2001. The existence of its well-regarded Brussels office is currently being deliberated, throwing into doubt the pan-European integration of this frequently recommended unit. The team handles the usual mixture of merger notification, public procurement and litigation for clients in areas such as energy, trade, agriculture, health and pharmaceuticals.

Marco Slotboom* has become increasingly prominent. Like other competition partners at Dutch firms, he is qualified under Dutch and Belgian law, based in Brussels, but handling both EC and NMA matters for an international clientele. He has a *"young, dynamic and open character"* and is *"technically highly proficient."* The firm was instructed on a challenge to the NMA's approval of the KBB/Vendex tie-up, and handled a major IP litigation case for watch manufacturer Ecoswiss against Benetton before the European Court of Justice. **Clients:** Pfizer; Ecoswiss; Aruba government.

Other Notable Practitioner Gerard van der Wal heads the small Brussels division of Dutch firm Barents & Krans, and has *"a deep knowledge and understanding of EC machinery."* He is also a regular fixture on the Dutch circuit, acting for clients such as BMW, L'Oreal and the Dutch flower industry before the NMA and courts in other EC member states.

N

Corporate/M&A

Allen & Overy (18 ptrs, 75 asscs) The results of our research show the practice to be *"one of the leaders no doubt – the name of the game now."* Since absorbing leading Benelux corporate firm Loeff Claeys Verbeke, Allen & Overy has established itself as a major competitor at the high end of the Dutch market. Mixing an acquired continental corporate clientele with renowned international financial clout, the firm has instantly proved its worth. Described as a *"progressive"* operation, the corporate team acts for a number of heavyweight clients in sectors such as energy, telecoms and retail. *"Always there – omnipresent,"* the department includes well known and connected **Steven Schuit***, a *"hard-working prince of M&A"* who *"really knows how to organise a deal"* and is adept at *"forming a good team around him."* His major clients include incumbent state telecoms operator KPN in addition to large energy companies. **Sietze Hepkema*** is another seasoned M&A figure. *"He's a top negotiator and always knows the tone to take in deals."* Regarded as a dynamic rising star, popular younger partner **Jan Louis Burggraaf*** has been prolific on a number of cross-border mergers and joint ventures. An *"excellent operator,"* he is *"legally skilled"* and *"works incredibly hard."* **Maarten Muller*** is a *"practical, gentlemanly lawyer,"* a *"pleasure to work opposite,"* and *"really knows the processes and how to work them through from A to B."* Big deals of recent times include acting for Statoil, the Norwegian state oil company in an oil refinery cross participation venture with Shell. The team also represented a consortium including UBS Capital and Scandinavian Industri Kapital in the $1.6 billion sale by Tetra Laval of the Alfa Laval Group. In the retail sector, the team acted for Schuitma on its acquisition of Sperwer. **Clients:** AEGON; Statoil; EPON Electrabel; KPN; UBS Capital; Industri Kapital; Schuitma; NeSBIC; Bührmann-Ubbens.

Clifford Chance (10 ptrs, 44 asscs) Dutch in character, the Amsterdam office of this UK giant is felt to have kept pace with the threat posed by increasingly tough Anglo-Saxon competition. The firm boasts a corporate team at least the equal of its highly acclaimed and profitable finance practice – *"this is a real quality outfit which is a benchmark for the market."* Many of the firm's M&A lawyers combine their practices with

*See leaders' profiles on pages 501-506

N

THE NETHERLANDS
Leading firms
(Corporate/Mergers & Acquisitions)

Band	Firm
1	Allen & Overy
	Clifford Chance
	De Brauw Blackstone Westbroek
2	Freshfields Bruckhaus Deringer
	NautaDutilh
	Stibbe
3	Houthoff Buruma
	Nolst Trenité/Van Doorne
4	Caron & Stevens/Baker & McKenzie
	Loyens & Loeff

Firms are listed alphabetically in each band.

Leading individuals
(Corporate/Mergers & Acquisitions)

Band	Individual
1	**FLEURY Joachim** *Clifford Chance*
	HOOGHOUDT Hein *NautaDutilh*
	LEIJTEN Alfons *Stibbe*
	SCHUIT Steven *Allen & Overy*
	WAKKIE Peter *De Brauw Blackstone Westbroek*
2	**BARBAS Constant** *Clifford Chance*
	DE BEAUFORT Hector *Clifford Chance*
	EISMA Sjoerd *De Brauw Blackstone Westbroek*
	THIJSSEN Jeroen *Freshfields*
3	**BURGGRAAF Jan Louis** *Allen & Overy*
	DE WAARD Tom *Clifford Chance*
	HEPKEMA Sietze *Allen & Overy*
	JAAKKE John *Nolst Trenité/Van Doorne*
	JITTA Marius Josephus *Stibbe*
	MULLER Maarten *Allen & Overy*
	VAN DER STAAY Jan Willem *Freshfields*
	VAN LEEUWE Jean-Pierre *Nolst Trenité/Van Doorne*
	VAN MARWIJK KOOY Johan *NautaDutilh*
	VAN VERSCHUER Philip *Loyens & Loeff*
	VLETTER Bas *Loyens & Loeff*

Individuals are listed alphabetically in each band.

equity capital markets and private equity work.

Heavy hitter **Joachim Fleury*** is noted for the transactional acumen he lends to the telecoms practice. He is *"always popping up on deals in this hot sector,"* such as those for NTT DoCoMo Inc and UPC. With his *"helicopter vision,"* father figure **Constant Barbas*** has the *"ability to look to the end point and see deals all the way through."* The team was strengthened by two high-profile partner acquisitions from Stibbe in 2000. **Hector de Beaufort*** runs a split M&A/capital markets practice and advises a number of major companies and investment banks. The experienced **Tom de Waard*** brings a number of substantial energy clients with him. He and Hector de Beaufort worked together on the sale of the construction division of NBM-Amstelland to BAM , the largest ever creation in the Dutch construction market, with a combined annual turnover of NLG5.6 billion. They also advised on the delisting of Gelderse Papiergroep, acquired by the Italian Favini. Other highlight deals of the past year have included advising European Aeronautic Defence & Space Company (EADS) on the Dutch law aspects of its IPO, the first simultaneous offering on three European exchanges (Paris, Frankfurt and Madrid), valued at €15.3 billion. **Clients:** Cap Gemini; GIMV; Vredestein; Koninklijke Ten Cate; NBM-Amstelland; Gelderse Papiergroep; European Aeronautic Defence & Space Company (EADS); NTT DoCoMo; United Pan-Europe Communications (UPC); Norit; Gilde Investment Fund; GVB; Kempen; Samenwerkende Elektriciteits Produktiebedrijven; ASM Litography Holding.

De Brauw Blackstone Westbroek (30 ptrs, 70 asscs) With history, tradition and a supreme reputation for quality, the corporate team is regarded by many as the most formidable in the Netherlands. Omnipresent on the big-ticket deals (*"they have a hand in everything"*), the group has a glittering client base of established Dutch blue-chips which is the envy of its competitors. This *"refined"* clientele has *"only improved with the coming of Linklaters."* The firm is noted for its depth of resources, and is perceived to have an academic culture and scientific approach to client relations, although its influence is not as strong among younger 'new technology' companies.

Influential Rotterdam-based **Peter Wakkie*** holds the managerial reigns and remains one of the foremost names in the market. He is said to be *"pragmatic," "legally on the ball,"* and has *"presence and drive."* Adept at tying up the big transactions, he is *"flamboyant, shrewd and great at handling clients."* An acknowledged litigator, in addition to his M&A pedigree, he is handling the largest corporate litigation matter in the Netherlands, the battle between Gucci and LVMH. Well-connected in Dutch boardrooms, **Sjoerd Eisma*** is more understated, but has *"tremendous in-depth knowledge"* and *"gets the deals done without yelling and shouting."* One fellow lawyer labelled him the *"perfect person to refer to on a complicated matter."*

The firm acted for KLM on its abortive merger talks with British Airways and for Sphinx Gustavsberg on its recommended cash offer merger with Sanitec Corporation of Finland. The team also advised on the public offer by Groothoofdspoort for all outstanding shares of Dordtsche Petroleum-Industrie Maatschappij, and Landal GreenParks Holding when acquiring the entire share capital in Exploitatiemaatschappij Port Greve and all assets in Horeca Park Port Greve. **Clients:** Shell; Unilever; Philips; KLM; Reckitt Benckiser; Sphinx Gustavsberg; SEP; Gazunie; Campina Melkunie/Menken Holding; Prada; Internatio-Müller; Tessag; Rémy Cointreau; BAM Groep; HBG; Wegener; Ahold; Krasnapolsky Hotels & Restaurants; Landal GreenParks Holding; Vopak; VNU.

Freshfields Bruckhaus Deringer (14 ptrs and 38 asscs, of whom 3 ptrs are full-time M&A) Since opening in May 1999, the increasing impact of the Amsterdam office of this corporate behemoth has been acutely felt. They *"chose the high road"* and *"having entered the market with a bang, have made an instant impact."* Although its size has still to grow to its maximum, the practice is *"definitely on the scene,"* albeit not yet felt to be at the very top of the tree. However, competitors expect the practice to present a major threat in the future as it seeks to exploit the firm's expertise in big-ticket cross-border M&A.

Following its aggressive entrance into the Dutch market, the firm had been considered to need a *"more friendly and accessible face."* The lateral hire of a number of respected local practitioners has succeeded in reinforcing a genuinely Dutch flavour to the office. Among them is the well-connected **Jan Willem Van Der Staay***, formerly of Loeff Claeys Verbeke, regarded as *"a shrewd and superb lawyer."* The poaching of senior partner **Jeroen Thijssen*** in early 2001 from NautaDutilh was another major coup for the office. A well-known and recommended figure, he runs a practice with an emphasis on structured finance as well as straightforward corporate advice. The practice has a broad raft of clients for whom it acts on public and private M&A matters, frequently in tandem with its acclaimed tax practice. Examples include acting for Ford on the Dutch aspects of its multi-jurisdictional acquisitions of Daewoo's motor business, and General Motors on its joint venture with Fiat. The team also advised UBS Warburg on its acquisition of a stake in Calvé Delft, Alpinvest on a management buy-out and Kamps on its acquisition of Quality Bakers Europe. **Clients:** Deutsche Bank; NH Hoteles; UBS Warburg; Pinault Printemps-Redoute; Daimler Chrysler; AstraZeneca; General Motors; Alpinvest; Buhrmann; Essent; Kamps; Stichting Van Leer Group Foundation; Otra; NeSBIC Groep; Halder Holdings; Tyco; Morgan Stanley; Hutchison Whampoa; Orion Capital Managers; Ford Motor Company; Swiss Re; Bass; Avis Europe.

NautaDutilh (50 ptrs, 150 asscs) Something of a *"stable giant,"* the practice has shown little sign of dynamic expansion, but remains a leading contender in the corporate league tables. This is by virtue of a solid roster of Dutch blue-chip clients, substantial resources, a top quality domestic finance practice and some fine individual talents. The corporate practice is felt by some to lack the identifiable international strategy of its principal competitors and recently suffered the loss of senior corporate finance partner Jeroen Thijssen to Freshfields. There is, however, little doubt over **Hein Hooghoudt**'s* standing as one of the country's leading M&A performers. A premier technician, he is felt to be at the pinnacle for accuracy and precision, and is a *"sophisticated senior operator with excellent negotiation and drafting skills."* Appreciated by colleagues in the profession, other lawyers like the fact that *"you can always refer conflicts to him without any fear that he will steal your client!"* Rotterdam-based partner **Johan Van Marwijk Kooy*** is considered to be a promising up and coming name.

While the firm is appreciably stronger in the finance sector, it has expertise in public and private M&A in sectors such as energy, telecoms and private equity. Handled the cash public offer by Huhtamäki Oyj for the share capital of Royal Packaging Industries Van Leer listed on the Amsterdam Stock Exchange, a transaction valued at NLG2.1 billion. In another public bid, the team represented Alpinvest as its shares were bought by GIMV and subsequently for a higher amount by the National Investment Bank (NIB Capital). The value of both bids totalled NLG3.5 billion. The firm also acted on the abortive IPO and listing on the AEX of DSB Groep N.V, advising the underwriters Rabo Securities and Merrill Lynch, and represented the Dutch government during merger talks between KLM and British Airways. **Clients:** Huhtamäki Oyj; Alpinvest Holding; Rabo Securities; Merril Lynch; NIB; ABP; Stork.

Stibbe (15 ptrs, 40 asscs) The loss of key partners to market rivals has underlined the department's difficulties during the past year. Top M&A man Hector de Beaufort left for Clifford Chance along with Tom de Waard, a senior lawyer with key energy clients. The department's most renowned name and its perennial rainmaker, Paul van den Hoek, has scaled down his active fee-earning caseload to concentrate on board memberships and other commitments. However, *"quality firms don't disappear overnight,"* and the organisation still carries weight in the M&A sector, thanks to a chunky client base and some outstanding individuals.

Considered by many to be the best lawyer at the firm, top all-rounder **Alfons Leijten*** is *"technically superb,"* has a *"100% attractive public M&A practice,"* and crops up on a huge number of corporate and finance deals. **Marius Josephus Jitta*** is another recommended name who fuses his corporate practice with some litigation (notably on behalf of LVMH in the high profile Gucci case). In conjunction with Slaughter and May, the firm advised British Airways on its failed merger talks with KLM, and also acted for Cap Gemini on its merger with Ernst & Young and for Baan on its take-over by Invensys. On behalf of the German Tengelmann Group, the firm negotiated the sale of the A&P supermarkets and hypermarkets in the Netherlands. Also represented Tele Atlas (database operator) as it was listed in May 2000 on the Frankfurt Neuer Markt. **Clients:** British Airways; Cap Gemini; Baan; Endemol; Tengelmann Group; LVMH; Tele Atlas; VIB.

Houthoff Buruma (30 ptrs, 85 asscs) It is generally felt that the firm has performed creditably this year, despite the recent Anglo-Saxon onslaught in Holland. Felt to be *"pushing quite hard,"* the firm has the resources to act on bigger deals, but its impact is still limited to traditional areas of strength, such as communications, energy/utilities and venture capital. Typically, the team acts for companies of small to medium size, both from the Netherlands and abroad. Although not possessing international clout, the firm is considered a progressive and modern unit with an emphasis on new economy clients, and is expected to prosper.

On behalf of Shanks, a waste company, the team oversaw the acquisition of Waste Management, one of the largest waste companies in the Netherlands, a deal worth around NLG700 million. Acted for Kerr McGee Corporation, a large US oil and gas exploration company, on the NLG600 million acquisition of two chemical plants from Kemira, a Finnish chemical company. The team has an active involvement in the venture capital market and represented ABN AMRO Participations and NPM Capital fund on the MBO of Hyva, a world-wide operating manufacturer and distributor in the automotive industry. **Clients:** BT; Deutsche Telecom; ntl; Cable & Wireless; Origin; Hewlett Packard; Computer Associates; NPM Capital; Gilde Investments; NIB Capital; ABN AMRO Participations; RWE; Atag (household appliances); Shanks; Kerr McGee; Start; Ad Value; Future Friday; Unwired Concepts.

Nolst Trenité/Van Doorne (40 ptrs, 80 asscs) The future of the firm was thrown into doubt in 2001 by its decision to split the Rotterdam and Amsterdam offices into separate operations, and dispense with the office in The Hague. Despite an array of well-known European clients and a large pool of legal resources, the corporate team does not have the profile of others in the market. The firm's strength lies in its breadth of activity, acting for medium to large sized corporate clients in sectors as diverse as transport, leisure, manufacturing and communications.

Executive chairman **John Jaakke*** (Amsterdam/Van Doorne) remains an established senior figure at the firm, and in tandem with the *"old-school and gentlemanly"* **Jean Pierre van Leeuwe*** at Nolst Trenité in Rotterdam, continues to be singled out by the market. Work highlights for the department include advising internet business accelerator GorillaPark on its European roll-out and its $60 million first and second finance round. Also acted as Dutch counsel to AssetTRADE.com in the acquisition of the public auctioneering company of Troostwijk Titania Holding, and advised Société de Technologie Michelin in its joint venture with WOCO Franz Josef Wolf Holding and The Goodyear Tyre and Rubber Company. **Clients:** AT&T; Netherlands Investment Bank; GorillaPark; AssetTRADE.com; Energis Communications; AVR; CSM; Koopmans Koninklijke Meelfabrieken.

Caron & Stevens/Baker & McKenzie (5 ptrs, 35 asscs) *"Definitely a corporate competitor,"* albeit not at the highest level, the firm exploits a productive network of world-wide offices to act for a series of medium sized clients, both Dutch and foreign, on cross-border deals. As much as 50% of the firm's business arrives via these channels. The department is complemented by the office's first-rate tax practice, and handles M&A, banking, capital markets, IPOs and venture capital. Handled two large equity flotations for Numico, a large Dutch listed company, in deals totalling around $3 billion. In the communications industry, the firm acted for Bell South in a $40 billion deal, where KPN acquired the German E-Plus division, now its mobile subsidiary. **Clients:** Numico; Bell South; NIB Capital.

Loyens & Loeff (17 ptrs, 80 asscs) Formerly tax firm Loyens & Volkmaars, on January 1st, 2000 it acquired the services of a substantial number of lawyers from the now defunct corporate giant Loeff Claeys Verbeke. At a stroke, this independent firm entered the corporate marketplace, thus giving support to its matchless traditional tax practice. Tax remains the bedrock of the firm, but its M&A strength is perceived to have increased markedly in the last 12 months – *"some high quality individuals and a solid clientele have remained intact from the Loeff days."*

N

*See leaders' profiles on pages 501-506

Also a litigator, **Bas Vletter*** is a *"steady M&A lawyer"* and a *"thorough deal processor."* **Philip van Verschuer*** was also identified as another key individual, running a public and private M&A practice with an emphasis on energy and telecoms. Acted for Station 12 on the $300 million satellite business joint venture between KPN and Telstra Corporation. Also represented Excite Chello in a JV between UPC and Excite. **Clients:** KPN; Station 12; Excite Chello; Banque International Luxembourgh; Newconomy; Boskalis; BCP; Linde; Kemira; Detron; Vivendi.

Energy & Natural Resources

THE NETHERLANDS Leading firms (Energy & Natural Resources)	
1	Allen & Overy
	De Brauw Blackstone Westbroek
	NautaDutilh
	Stibbe
2	Freshfields Bruckhaus Deringer
	Houthoff Buruma
3	Clifford Chance
	Nolst Trenité

Firms are listed alphabetically in each band.

Leading individuals (Energy & Natural Resources)	
1	**DE KEIJZER Jaap** *De Brauw Blackstone*
	FONTEIJN Chris *NautaDutilh*
	IN DE BRAEKT Martin *Stibbe*
2	**DE WAARD Tom** *Clifford Chance*
	GLAZENER Paul *Allen & Overy*
	KOSTER Weero *Houthoff Buruma*
	LEIJTEN Alfons *Stibbe*
	OTTERVANGER Tom *Allen & Overy*
	PERRICK Steven *Freshfields Bruckhaus Deringer*
	SCHUIT Steven *Allen & Overy*
3	**BOS Jos** *Nolst Trenité*

Individuals are listed alphabetically in each band.

Allen & Overy (7 ptrs, 15 asscs) Although lacking dedicated high-profile energy practitioners, the firm's corporate and competition departments generate sufficient work and market commendation to ensure its position among the leaders. Particularly effective in gas, electricity and waste, the group has acknowledged regulatory and transactional expertise.

The two competition partners with energy expertise, **Paul Glazener*** and **Tom Ottervanger*** are *"rock solid and well respected."* Glazener is *"brilliant at handling big electricity regulation,"* while prolific author Tom Ottervanger has *"moved into the sector with ease."* He applies his *"superb regulatory skills"* to the electricity and gas markets, although energy is only one strand of his varied practice. Ubiquitous senior corporate figure **Steven Schuit*** has *"lots of drive"* and an extensive transactional track record in the electricity industry. Core distribution client NUON has been a stimulus to the practice. The firm advised NUON and Essent, shareholders in the prominent Dutch generator EPON, on the NLG6 billion sale of EPON to Electrabel, the Belgian energy giant. **Clients:** NUON; EPON; EnergieNed; AEP; Enron.

De Brauw Blackstone Westbroek (5 ptrs, 10 asscs) As in many areas of practice, the firm's client roster includes several of the industry's traditional heavyweight clients. Such notable names as Shell, SEP and Gazunie give the firm a strong hand. Belying its conservative image, the group has added a number of new entrants, such as Centrica and Gaz De France, to its traditional base of incumbents. The workload has also broadened, from an original focus on oil, to embrace the liberalisation of the electricity and gas markets. In addition, the team has increasing experience of the nuclear industry.

Corporate partner **Jaap de Keijzer*** is *"a leading technical specialist"* with a solid energy background, and *"always gets the deals done."* The firm advised on the NLG900 million acquisition of the Eindhoven utility NRE for Endesa, and the acquisition of TransCanada's continental shelf oil and gas assets for Gaz de France, a NLG1 billion deal. It has also acted on behalf of SEP on the prospective sale of the national grid operator Tennet and the decommissioning and sale of the nuclear power plant at Dodewaard. Joint ventures have included advising Centrica on its energy trading joint venture with Essent, and Shell on a similar venture with Eneco. **Clients:** Shell; SEP; Gazunie; Centrica; NAM; Tennet; Gaz de France; Southern Energy; Endesa; EnergieNed.

NautaDutilh (6 ptrs, 6 asscs) (6 ptrs, 6 asscs) A *"prominent name,"* rated by many competitors as *"among the most visible in the sector."* The dedicated energy team draws on expertise from the firm's competition, litigation and tax departments, and has advised on regulatory matters in the cross-border leasing of gas and electricity networks. The client base comprises a selection of national and foreign clients although it is felt to lack the international breadth of some of the firm's leading rivals.

Our researchers found the major name to be **Chris Fonteijn***, an *"organised managerial lawyer who runs projects with ease."* Experienced in oil and gas exploration, his practice also includes regulatory and transactional advice in the electricity and chemicals industries. The firm represented Eneco and REMU on litigation against other energy companies concerning import restrictions, and handled a similar matter for key power client EZH against NUON. It also advised the selling municipalities in the areas of Haarlemmermeer and Zeist on the divestiture of their utility businesses, and acted for the Dutch Government on the acquisition of the share capital of Tennet, the national grid systems operator. **Clients:** EZH; Eneco; REMU; Mobil; Corus.

Stibbe (3 ptrs, 4 asscs full-time, 6 asscs part-time) The team has weathered a recent storm of uncertainty and is still a recognised force in the market. Despite the loss of Tom de Waard to Clifford Chance and accompanying work for Reliant/UNA, the group still offers a powerful combination of regulatory and transactional expertise, notably in electricity.

Martin In de Braekt* is widely regarded as one of Holland's leading energy lawyers. His versatile practice includes transactional and regulatory work, both in gas and electricity, for large industrial customers, producers and distribution companies. One of the country's leading M&A heavy hitters, **Alfons Leijten***, has an outstanding track record in energy-related M&A, and also comes warmly recommended. The firm has advised headline client EPZ, one of the Netherlands' four electricity producers, both on the issue of 'stranded costs' and its recent de-merger. Other work has involved advising Reliant on the acquisition of the remaining part of UNA, and Electrabel on the acquisition of EPON. The latter was the largest single acquisition in the Dutch energy sector. The group also represented Norsk Hydro on a complaint against SEP in front of the Dutch Competition Authority, resulting in the first fine ever imposed by the Authority. **Clients:** EPZ; Reliant; Electrabel; Norsk Hydro.

Freshfields Bruckhaus Deringer (2 ptrs, 2 asscs) Although yet to acquire the resources of the market leaders, this *"high quality unit"* is considered to have *"the potential to seize much of the market."* The team's position in the Dutch market owes much to its work on behalf of Essent. One of the largest energy concerns in the country, it corners as much as 40% of the distribution market share. In common with many of its rivals, the group adopts a cross-departmental approach, and can call on the services of partners from the tax, litigation and, most notably, competition departments.

Steven Perrick* has extensive experience in the electricity industry, and originally established his reputation at the now defunct Loeff Claeys Verbeke. Around half of his practice is dedicated to advising Essent. The firm advised Essent on the creation of its joint venture with UK based Centrica, through the formation of Access Energy. It also represented them on the proposed de-merger with EPZ and on litigation with Dutch generator EPON. Elsewhere, the team advised Enron on the Dutch aspects of its interests in energy projects in Poland and Turkey. **Clients:** Essent; Pechiney Nederland; Preussen Elektra; EZH; NUON; Delta; Enron Corporation.

Houthoff Buruma (5 ptrs, 16 asscs) Respected team with a sound name for advising domestic distributors, typically in the electricity industry, where its expertise on stranded costs is widely acknowledged. Although not normally associated with the international market, the firm has advised foreign bidders on the acquisition of Dutch gas distribution and exploration companies, and has an established M&A record in the oil and water markets.

Weero Koster* *("he's certainly on the scene and knows the regulations")* is a prominent and popular practitioner. He heads a group with particularly close ties to Delta, the Dutch distributor covering the southern region of the country. The firm advised on the restructuring of the Dutch electricity industry and formation of the central Dutch electricity utility (GPB), and was involved in the joint venture between Norsk Hydro and EDON, involving a co-generation plant at Sluiskil. **Clients:** Delta; EPZ; Dutch Railways; GPB; Stork.

Clifford Chance (3 ptrs, 15 asscs) The arrival of the high-profile **Tom de Waard*** *("sparky and punchy")* from Stibbe has had a dramatic effect on the firm's energy profile. *"A well-connected figurehead and deal-maker,"* he has brought with him close relationships with key clients Reliant and UNA, instantly boosting the firm's credibility. While clearly lacking the depth of the market leaders, the firm continues to advise generation companies on stranded costs and the liberalisation of the electricity industry. In concert with Allen & Overy, the firm advised the combined electricity production sector in the Netherlands (UNA/Reliant, EPON/Electrabel, EZH/EON, EPZ/Essent) on the settlement of NLG8 billion worth of stranded costs. **Clients:** Reliant/UNA; Enron.

Nolst Trenité (2 ptrs, 18 asscs) In spite of the recent upheaval at the firm, resulting in the split of the Amsterdam and Rotterdam offices, the energy team retains its position in the market, albeit some distance from the top practices. Medium and big-ticket M&A transactions, often for an international client, comprise a substantial part of the workload. **Jos Bos*** has a reputation as a sound practitioner.

Highlights include the merger of seven regional energy distribution companies into Eneco, the third largest national energy distribution company, a deal worth approximately NLG7 billion. The group acted for all seven companies involved. It also advised TransCanada on the $800 million sale of its Dutch exploration and production activities to Gaz de France International. In conjunction with its Brussels office, the firm assisted PreussenElektra on its NLG2.3 billion take-over of the Dutch power producer EZH. **Clients:** TransCanada; Eneco; Preussen Elektra.

Tax

THE NETHERLANDS Leading firms (Tax)
1 Loyens & Loeff
2 Freshfields Bruckhaus Deringer
3 Caron & Stevens/Baker & McKenzie
Clifford Chance
Stibbe
4 Allen & Overy
De Brauw Blackstone Westbroek
NautaDutilh

Firms are listed alphabetically in each band.

Loyens & Loeff (55 tax partners, 325 other tax fee-earners) A *"solid rock of tax advice,"* the group is considered *"top of the list due to sheer size, history and reputation."* Tax firm Loyens & Volkmaars was joined last year by the rump of the former Loeff Claeys Verbeke, thereby adding corporate strength to an already formidable operation. Excelling in its core area of tax planning, the firm also offers tax advisory and compliance services, and is increasingly involved in premium cross-border transactions.

A deep pool of resources includes the *"technically brilliant"* **Paul Simonis***, rated for his tax advice on financial products, who acts for institutional investors, funds and private equity houses. **Jan van Kempen*** *("outstanding")* is a well-established national figure and has *"always been one of the best."* New blood is represented by **Maarten van der Weijden***, the subject of numerous market plaudits. The team advised on the merger of Group 4 Securitas with Falck AS, a transaction valued at DKK30 billion, the FF9 billion restructuring of Sita/BFI and the multi-billion guilder acquisition by Tractabel of Epon. **Clients:** Merrill Lynch; UBS; Deutsche Bank; Bank Of America; United Technologies; Ford Motors; Rodamco; ING; ENI; Sara Lee; Robeco.

Freshfields Bruckhaus Deringer (5 ptrs, 17 asscs) Widely considered through our research to have the leading transactional tax practice, the firm has demonstrated its commitment to the sector in its new Amsterdam office by relocating a London partner to head the team. Although it lacks the enormous critical mass of its principal rivals, the team's global base of premium corporate clients makes it the leading candidate to challenge the supremacy of Loyens and the accountancy firms. Specific areas of expertise include stock option plans, e-commerce and telecoms.

A number of lateral hires emphasise the firm's ambitions. Joining from Loyens in late 1999, **Hans Galavazi*** and **Dick Hofland*** drew universal praise from the market for their technical ability. *"Coming man"* **Machiel Lambooij*** is *"sharp, ambitious and uses his creativity to dream up inventive tax planning ideas."* A high-calibre team is completed by **Charles Langereis***, for-

*See leaders' profiles on pages 501-506

Leading individuals (Tax)
1
DE VOS Frank *Clifford Chance*
GALAVAZI Hans *Freshfields Bruckhaus*
HOFLAND Dick *Freshfields Bruckhaus*
LAMBOOIJ Machiel *Freshfields Bruckhaus*
LANGEREIS Charles *Freshfields Bruckhaus*
SIMONIS Paul *Loyens & Loeff*
VAN KEMPEN Jan *Loyens & Loeff*
VAN WEEGHEL Stef *Stibbe*
2
DE HOSSON Fred *Caron & Stevens*
MARSEILLE Hans *De Brauw Blackstone*
VAN DER LANDE Maarten *Caron & Stevens*
VAN DER WEIJDEN Maarten *Loyens & Loeff*
Individuals are listed alphabetically in each band.

merly of Stibbe, who has a fine reputation as a tax litigation specialist. The team acted for DaimlerChrysler on the Dutch tax aspects of the establishment of the European Aeronautic and Defence Company (EADS). International tax planning work includes advising AstraZeneca on the de-merger of its agrochemicals business and the merger with Novartis of Switzerland, and representing UBS Warburg on its acquisition of a stake in Calvé Delft. **Clients:** ABN AMRO; Fortis; NCM; Reed Elsevier; Gucci; Intel; Adidas; Citibank; ING; Balfour Beatty; Immarsat; Fort James; General Motors; Deutsche Telekom; Hutchison Whampoa; Rothschilds Tyco; Hoek Loos; GATX.

Caron & Stevens/Baker & McKenzie (14 ptrs, 50-60 asscs) Considered as a *"law firm with a tax face,"* it has one of the largest integrated tax advisory and transactional teams in Holland, the result of a commitment to tax law dating back almost 50 years. Said to combine well with the corporate transactional practice, the group is split into three units, handling either domestic or international matters.

Fred de Hosson* is a *"great technician"* and has advised on a series of big-ticket deals, while younger colleague **Maarten van der Lande*** has also caught the market's eye. The group advised on a tax-effective project financing of offshore oil field exploration by Petrobras of Brazil, and acted for SHV, a large, privately owned business, on the world-wide structuring of its tax operations. Also advised the government pension fund ABP on tax matters relating to its property portfolio. **Clients:** Hewlett Packard; Lucent Technologies (Avaya); ABP; SHV; Petrobras.

Clifford Chance (3 ptrs, 10 asscs) *"The practice there is small but the quality levels are good."* A consistent volume of transactional work helps the tax team to maintain a sound reputation, notably in its forte of financial products.

Well-known leader **Frank de Vos*** heads the firm's global tax practice. Despite his management commitments, he has a first-class reputation for his advice on structured finance, international capital markets and securitisation transactions. His team advised Morgan Stanley on two complex tax-structured property securitisations for Sainsburys backed by a number of its supermarkets, only the second securitisation of retail property in Europe. The firm also acted for Dresdner Kleinwort Benson and Merrill Lynch on an innovative tender offer for Eurotunnel, and for ABN AMRO on Holland's first securitisation of consumer loans. Work for corporates includes representing NTT Docomo on a €4 billion capital injection in KPN Mobile, advising Siemens on a €2 billion exchangeable notes issue, and acting for EADS on its merger structure and subsequent international IPO, worth €15 billion. **Clients:** ABP; Robeco; ABN AMRO; Morgan Stanley; Goldman Sachs; NTT DoComo; Banco Santander Central Hispano; ASML; Rabobank; TPG pension fund; KPN pension fund; Schroder Salomon Smith Barney; UBS Warburg; EADS; Siemens.

Stibbe (4 ptrs, 10 asscs) In spite of the firm's recent troubles, it has obvious strength in the tax sector, building on its leading corporate reputation. It differs from other firms employing tax advisors, by insisting that they are all members of the local bar. Corporate and financial transactions and tax litigation are the cornerstones of the caseload, and the team has been involved in areas such as banking and finance, energy and transport. An international client base includes key investment banks such as Goldman Sachs and Merrill Lynch.

Stef van Weeghel* is the driving force of the unit and is considered one of the smartest practitioners in the market. He has an *"international mind-set"* and *"always delivers quality opinions."* The firm has offered tax advice to Euronext, the merger of the Dutch, Belgian and French Stock Exchanges, and advised British Airways on the Dutch tax aspects of its abortive merger with KLM. Also acted on the Reliant Energy/UNA utility deal and represented the investment bank involved in both Philips/Seagram (sale of Polygram) and the Unilever superdividend. **Clients:** Goldman Sachs; Merrill Lynch; British Airways; ABN AMRO; AIG Financial Products; Citibank; West LB; Euronext; Merck & Co; Caterpillar; Randstad Holding.

Allen & Overy (3 ptrs, 9 asscs) The tax practice is relatively small and is considered a novice by comparison with its more established rivals. However, it has attracted a growing number of respected practitioners, and the team's profile is felt to be moving in the right direction. Focusing largely on corporate tax, the group advises a number of blue-chip clients in a range of industry sectors.

The firm acted for Italian internet service provider Tiscali on the tax aspects of the acquisition of World Online, through a public offer of the WOL shares and the rollover of the employee stock option plans. Other matters include advising Hartford, the US insurance company, on the auction of its Dutch subsidiary Zwolsche Algemene and its pre-sale restructuring, and sports manufacturer Head on its listing on the New York and Vienna Stock Exchanges. **Clients:** Tiscali; Hartford; Head; Dresdner Kleinwort Benson; UPC; KPN.

De Brauw Blackstone Westbroek (8 ptrs, 20 asscs) The collapse of the firm's relationship with the former Loyens & Volkmaars has resulted in the development of an embryonic tax practice here, which is felt to have genuine potential. Typically, the team provides corporate tax advice for its powerful stable of premium Dutch and international clients. An established name with vast experience, **Hans Marseille*** is the group's leading practitioner. The firm advised on the acquisition by Reckitt & Coleman of Benckiser, and on the restructuring of the European operations of Coca-Cola Enterprises. **Clients:** Coca-Cola; Interbrew; Andersen Consulting.

NautaDutilh (5 ptrs, 30 asscs) Large practice, renowned for its international tax planning advice, which also offers support on M&A, capital markets and structured finance deals. The firm's New York office is considered to play a significant role in assisting on key transactions. The team has acted on venture capital transactions for 3i in the Netherlands and abroad, and the reorganisation of Eureko. Also assisted the French government on Daimler/Aerospatiale, represented EZH on its acquisition by Preussen Elektra, and advised on securitisations for Fortis and Morgan Stanley. **Clients:** Fortis; Morgan Stanley; NIB; Buhrmann; Lycos; Versatel; Sonae; Gambrö; 3i; Eureko; EZH.

Leaders' profiles – Netherlands

BARBAS, Constant
Clifford Chance, Amsterdam +31 20 711 9000
constant.barbas@cliffordchance.com
Recommended in Corporate/M&A
Specialisation: Specialises in general company and commercial work, corporate finance, and mergers and acquisitions.
Prof. Memberships: Secretary of the CCBE Special Committee on Company Law (since 1984); Raadsheer Plaatsvervanger (Deputy Judge) at the Amsterdam Court of Appeal.
Career: Joined *Clifford Chance* in 1972, partner 1974.
Personal: Attended Université de Toulouse (Baccalauréat Philosophie, 1962), Leiden University (Law, 1968) and Columbia University Law School (LLM, 1970).

BIESHEUVEL, Mark
De Brauw Blackstone Westbroek N.V. (member firm of Linklaters & Alliance), The Hague
+31 70 328 5471
markbiesheuvel@dbbw.nl
Recommended in Competition/Anti-trust
Specialisation: Partner in Anti-trust/EU Department. Main area of work is EU & Competition Law.
Publications: Report for the Dutch Association of European Law on Article 6 of the European Human Rights Convention and European Community Law (1988). Report for the Dutch Association of Competition Law on the New Dutch Competition Act (1997). Various articles in Dutch Law Review.
Career: Qualified in 1987. Joined *De Brauw Blackstone Westbroek* in 1987, partner in 1990. (1982-1986 Legal Secretary EC Court of Justice (Luxembourg), 1977-1982 Assistant Professor at the University of Leyden).
Personal: Born 4 January 1953. Attended University of Leyden (1972-1977). Visiting scholar Law School Columbia University, NY (1979-1980).

BLOM, Marc
NautaDutilh, Amsterdam +31 20 541 4646
Recommended in Banking & Finance

BOELE, Bas
Houthoff Buruma, Amsterdam +31 20 577 2000
Recommended in Banking & Finance

BOS, Jos A.M.
Nolst Trenité, Rotterdam +31 10 404 2164
jambos@trenite.com
Recommended in Energy & Natural Resources
Specialisation: Managing partner in Company & Commercial Law Section and Head of the Energy Group. Main area of work is energy law and policy, corporate law and competition law, mergers and acquisitions. Acted on take-over of a Dutch power producer, the merger of seven distribution companies, the take-over of an exploration and production company, a unitisation dispute, a merger between two upstream companies, price regulation disputes, corporate restructurings, set up of new energy companies; energy sales and transportation agreements, set up of network companies.
Prof. Memberships: Member of the International Bar Association amd member of the Council of the Section on Energy and Resources Law. Chairman of the Gas Committee of the Section on Energy and Resources Law of the International Bar Association. Honorary tutor of the Centre for Energy, Petroleum & Mineral Law & Policy (CEPMLP), Dundee, Scotland. Member of the Board of Euroforum B.V. Member of the Netherlands Centre of Managing and Supervisory Directors('NCD').
Publications: Author of articles in the Journal of Energy and Natural Resources Law, Petroleum Economist and 'Het Financieele Dagblad'. Author of a commentary on the Dutch Electricity Act 1988 (in preparation). Co-founder and co-editor of a new series of energy books called 'Energie en Recht' (Energy and Law). Co-author of 'Bestuur en Toezicht' (Management and Management Supervision in companies under Dutch law). Former columnist in a Dutch management magazine covering legal and other developments affecting boards of supervisory directors of Dutch companies. Former co-editor of 'Praktijkboek Commissarissen' (Practical Guide for Supervisory Directors).
Career: 1972-1977 Law Faculty of State University of Utrecht, The Netherlands. 1977-1980: Junior Lawyer ('advocaat-stagiaire') admitted to Dordrecht Bar in The Netherlands. 1980-1988: Business lawyer with Shell.
Personal: Born 18 July 1951. Married, three children. Hobbies: Classical music; golf; skiing.

BROUWER, Onno
Freshfields Bruckhaus Deringer, Amsterdam
+31 20 488 0900
onno.brouwer@freshfields.com
Recommended in Competition/Anti-trust
Specialisation: Specialises in competition and trade, including EU and Dutch competition law. Has particular expertise in regulatory controls affecting the telecoms and energy sectors.

BURGGRAAF, Jan Louis
Allen & Overy, Amsterdam +31 20 674 1000
Recommended in Corporate/M&A

CITROEN, René
Clifford Chance, Amsterdam +31 20 711 9000
rene.citroen@cliffordchance.com
Recommended in Banking & Finance
Specialisation: Specialises in structured finance, acquisition finance and securitisation. Most recent activites have been in the area of securitisation, acquisition finance and structured finance, particularly in relation to (i)US Lilo and service contract transactions, thereby acting for Dutch energy companies with assets consisting of a.o. electricity networks and electricity plants; and (ii)sythetic lease transactions.
Career: Joined *Clifford Chance* Amsterdam as a partner in 1992.
Personal: Attended University of Amsterdam; graduated in 1971.

DE BEAUFORT, Hector
Clifford Chance, Amsterdam +31 20 711 9000
hector.debeaufort@cliffordchance.com
Recommended in Corporate/M&A
Specialisation: Mergers and acquisitions, capital market transactions and private equity.
Career: *Hughs Hubbard & Reed, Stibbe Simont Monahan Duhot*, Amsterdam and New York, 1983-2000. Partner *Clifford Chance* since 2000.
Personal: Studied law at University of Utrecht (1981) and University of Pennsylvania (1982). Admitted to the Dutch bar and the New York bar.

DE BOUTER, Eduard C.
De Brauw Blackstone Westbroek N.V. (member firm of Linklaters & Alliance), Amsterdam
+31 20 577 1771
ecdebouter@dbbw.nl
Recommended in Banking & Finance
Specialisation: Partner in Financial Services Department. Main areas of work are banking & securities, and corporate finance.
Career: Joined *De Brauw Blackstone Westbroek* in 1977, becoming a partner in 1985. Has several publications in Spanish Law journals on Dutch corporate and securities law.
Personal: Born 8 December 1949. Attended University of Utrecht (1967-1972). Harvard Law School, LLM (1973), Harvard Law School, SJD (1978). Languages: Dutch, English, Spanish.

DE HOSSON, Fred
Caron & Stevens/Baker & McKenzie, Amsterdam
+31 20 551 75 55
Recommended in Tax
Specialisation: Main area of work is international and corporate tax law with a special focus on treaty and European law issues. Has handled major cases before Supreme and European Courts. Advises banks on structured finance products. Acts for clients like Volvo, SHV, Wolters Kluwer, Texas Instruments, Lehman Brothers. Has written extensively on international and European issues. Chief-editor of 'Intertax'. Member editorial board of 'EC Tax Review'.
Prof. Memberships: IFA, NOB
Publications: 'The EC Direct Tax Measures', author; co-author 'The US-Netherlands Tax Convention.'
Career: Qualified in 1974; lecturer/professor Leyden University and University of Florida; became *B&M* partner in 1989; member of Board Dutch Commercial Law Society.
Personal: Born in 1948, attended Leyden University 1970-1974.

DE KEIJZER, Jaap
De Brauw Blackstone Westbroek N.V. (member firm of Linklaters & Alliance), Amsterdam
+31 20 577 1771
jthadekeijzer@dbbw.nl
Recommended in Energy & Natural Resources
Specialisation: Partner in Corporate Law Department. Main areas of work are energy, mergers & acquisitions, company law, privatisation and project finance.

Publications: 'Non-voting shares', NIBE-Bankjuridische reeks deel 21, 1994; 'Public Pocurement in the Energy Sector in the Netherlands', in 'Oil and Gas Law and Taxation Review', January 1996; 'Electricity Liberalisation in the European Union, The Netherlands', in 'Oil & Gas Law and Taxation Review', October 1998.
Career: Qualified in 1990. Joined *De Brauw Blackstone Westbroek* in 1989, becoming a partner in 1998.
Personal: Born 26 October 1962. Attended University of Utrecht (MSc Geology), University of Utrecht (LLM), University of Rotterdam (MBA).

N

DE SERIÈRE, Victor
Allen & Overy, Amsterdam +31 20 674 1000
Recommended in Banking & Finance

DE VOS, Frank
Clifford Chance, Amsterdam +31 20 711 9000
frank.de_vos@cliffordchance.com
Recommended in Tax
Specialisation: Head of Global Tax at *Clifford Chance* specialises in international tax, with emphasis on securitisation, repackaging, asset backed finance, structured finance, cross-border leasing, fund structures and international corporate (re)structurings.
Career: *Loyens & Volkmaars*, Amsterdam and Hong Kong, 1983-1990. Partner *Clifford Chance* since 1991.
Personal: Studied law at University of Leiden; graduated 1982.

DE WAARD, Tom
Clifford Chance, Amsterdam +31 20 711 9000
tom.dewaard@cliffordchance.com
Recommended in Corporate/M&A, Energy & Natural Resources
Specialisation: Specialises in mergers and acquisitions, transborder and capital market transactions, arbitration and mediation. Also has experience in the field of privatisation projects, in particular in the energy sector.
Career: Qualified in 1971. *Stibbe Simont Monahan Duhot*, Amsterdam and New York, 1971-2000. Partner *Clifford Chance* since 2000. President, Dutch Bar Association, 1993-1995. Board member of ST Microelectronics, Reliant UNA and BESI.
Personal: Studied law at Leiden University; graduated 1971.

DOMMERING, Egbert
Stibbe, Amsterdam +31 20 546 0454
egbert.dommering@stibbe.nl
Recommended in Communications
Specialisation: Areas of practice include media; telecommunications; intellectual property; product liability. Specialises in telecommunications law, media law and entertainment law. Represents Dutch and European clients, including public and private broadcasting companies, telecommunications operators, Internet providers and newspapers.
Prof. Memberships: Bar of The Hague, 1968. Bar of Amsterdam, 1995. International Bar Association. Editorial Board, Computer Recht (Computer Law) and Informatierecht AMI (Law on Information and Copyright). Member of Advisory Committee of the Dutch Government on Copyright.
Career: Prior to joining *Stibbe*, was a member of the Hoge Raad der Nederlanden (Netherlands Supreme Court) at The Hague, where was involved in several landmark cases. Professor of information law at the University of Amsterdam and serves as the Director of its Institute for Information Law. Regular commentator on the judgements of the European Court of Human Rights for the Nederlandse Jurisprudentie (Netherlands Case Law).
Personal: Amsterdam University, 1968. Speaks Dutch and English.

DRION, Coen
Kennedy Van Der Laan, Amsterdam +31 20 550 6666
Recommended in Communications

EIJSVOOGEL, Peter
Allen & Overy, Amsterdam +31 20 574 1292
Recommended in Communications

EISMA, Sjoerd
De Brauw Blackstone Westbroek N.V. (member firm of Linklaters & Alliance), The Hague +31 70 328 5328
Sjoerd.Eisma@dbbw.nl
Recommended in Corporate/M&A
Specialisation: Corporate, banking and securities (litigation).
Prof. Memberships: Orde van advocaten: Vereniging voor de Vergelijkende Studie van het recht van Nederland en Belgie.
Career: Partner of *De Brauw* since 1978, Professor in Banking and Securities Law at Leiden University, non-executive director of Rabobank Nederland, Hal Holding N.V., SDU Publishers, ANT Trust and the Kroller-Moller Museum.

FEENSTRA, Jaap
NautaDutilh, Rotterdam +31 10 224 0000
feenst@nautadutilh.nl
Recommended in Competition/Anti-trust
Specialisation: EC and Competition Law Partner of the firm. Has advised clients in the various fields of EC and competition law, amongst others on issues relating to the rules on the free movement of goods and services within the EC, a public procurement (and privatisation) and on cases relating to anti-trust procedures (investigations of cartels and abuse of dominant positions and notifications of concentrations). In recent years, special focus has been on media (role of public broadcasting, newspaper mergers) and energy cases. Assisted in the field of production and distribution of energy as well as major customers on issues relating to public law regulations and free competition, like the allocation of electricity importation capacity, electricity tariffs, long term exclusive supply agreements, access to networks as well as co-operation and mergers between energy companies. Represented clients in disputes and procedures before the EC Commission, Netherlands Courts, the Netherlands competition law authority NMa and other Netherlands supervising bodies.
Career: Joined *Nauta Dutilh* in 1987.
Personal: Born 1956. Based in the Rotterdam Office.

FLEURY, Joachim
Clifford Chance, Amsterdam +31 20 711 9000
joachim.fleury@cliffordchance.com
Recommended in Communications, Corporate/M&A
Specialisation: Head of *Clifford Chance's* International Communications and Technology Group. Specialises in telecommunications law, M&A, take-overs and joint ventures. Co-founder of the Dutch Association for Information Technology and Law (NVIR).
Career: Qualified in 1985. Joined *Clifford Chance* in 1984, becoming a Partner in 1992.
Personal: Attended the University of Amsterdam (LLM, cum laude); graduated 1984.

FONTEIJN, Chris
NautaDutilh, Rotterdam +31 10 224 0371
Recommended in Energy & Natural Resources

GALAVAZI, Hans
Freshfields Bruckhaus Deringer, Amsterdam +31 20 488 0900
hans.galavazi@freshfields.com
Recommended in Tax
Specialisation: Partner in the tax department, advising particularly on cross-border mergers and acquisitions, joint ventures, corporate re-organisations and property investments. Practised in Germany for many years.

GEUS, Marjolein
Houthoff Buruma, Amsterdam +31 20 577 2000
Recommended in Communications

GLAZENER, Paul
Allen & Overy, Amsterdam +31 20 574 1337
Recommended in Competition/Anti-trust, Energy & Natural Resources

GRAAF, Frank
Clifford Chance, Amsterdam +31 20 711 9000
frank.graaf@cliffordchance.com
Recommended in Banking & Finance
Specialisation: Partner specialising in banking, securities and financial services related work, including, in particular, banking and securities regulation, domestic and international capital market offerings, OTC derivatives, repo's and securities lending, securitisation and repackaging transactions.
Career: *Clifford Chance* Amsterdam 1983 to date; made partner 1990. Co-founder and board member of The Netherlands Association for Securities Law.
Personal: Studied law at University of Leiden; graduated 1983.

HEPKEMA, Sietze
Allen & Overy, Amsterdam +31 20 574 1143
Recommended in Corporate/M&A

HOBBELEN, Hein
Freshfields Bruckhaus Deringer, Amsterdam +31 20 488 0900
hein.hobbelen@freshfields.com
Recommended in Communications
Specialisation: Member of the Competition and Trade group.

HOFLAND, Dick
Freshfields Bruckhaus Deringer, Amsterdam +31 20 488 0900
dick.hofland@freshfields.com
Recommended in Tax
Specialisation: Partner in the tax group with substantial experience of international tax work includ-

ing M&A, corporate structuring and financial products. Practised in the US for a number of years.

HOOGHOUDT, Hein
NautaDutilh, Amsterdam +31 20 541 46 46
Recommended in Corporate/M&A

IN DE BRAEKT, Martin
Stibbe, Amsterdam +31 20 546 0242
martin.indebraekt@stibbe.nl
Recommended in Energy & Natural Resources
Specialisation: Main areas of practice include Taxation, Mergers & Acquisitions, Joint-Ventures, Corporate Reorganisations, Tax Litigation and Energy Law. Advises Dutch and foreign corporations on matters relating to business and financial transactions in the above mentioned areas, with a particular emphasis on tax aspects of reorganisations, mergers and acquisitions and joint-ventures and on projects and transactions in the energy sector.
Prof. Memberships: Bar of Amsterdam, 1988. Bar of Paris, 1992. Paris Bar Association. Amsterdam Bar Association. European-American Tax Institute in Europe. International Fiscal Association. Association Internationale des Jeunes Avocats (International Association of Young Lawyers). International Bar Association.
Career: Practised in the Paris office of *Stibbe Simont Monahan Duhot* from 1990 to 1994.
Personal: Speaks Dutch, English, French and German.

JAAKKE, John C.
Van Doorne, Amsterdam +31 20 6789 123
Recommended in Corporate/M&A
Specialisation: Partner in Mergers and Acquisitions Department. Main area of work: corporate law, principally mergers, acquisitions and general advice on Dutch corporate law. Has handled acquisitions of Dutch companies. Acts for a number of (listed) top 50 companies in the Netherlands and abroad.
Prof. Memberships: Member of the Dutch Bar, member of the IBA section on business law.
Career: Qualified in 1981. Former assistant to managing director of the energy division of Steenkolen Handels Vereniging, the largest family owned Dutch company (1982-1984); joined *Trenite Van Doorne* in 1984, becoming a partner in 1990. Vice Chairman of the Board of Directors of NPS (a Dutch broadcasting company); member of the Board of Supervisory Directors of Elephant Dental BV (a subsidiary of Degussa Huls AG); member of the Board of Stiching Prioriteit en Continuiteit Versatel Telecom International; former member of the International Committee of the Amsterdam Chamber of Commerce; former Chairman of the Board of Management of *Trenite Van Doorne* (1997-2000).
Personal: Born 3 July 1954. Attended Vrije Universiteit in Amsterdam (1976-1981).

JOSEPHUS JITTA, Marius W.
Stibbe, Amsterdam +31 20 546 0130
marius.josephusjitta@stibbe.nl
Recommended in Corporate/M&A
Specialisation: Areas of practice are Mergers and Acquisitions, Financing Venture Capital, Bankruptcy.
Prof. Memberships: Bar of Amsterdam, 1973.
Personal: Speaks Dutch, English and French. Leiden University, 1970. Bowdoin College Maine, United States, 1965. Paris University, 1971.

KELLERMAN, Joanne
NautaDutilh, Amsterdam +31 20 541 46 46
Recommended in Banking & Finance

KNIBBELER, Winfred
Freshfields Bruckhaus Deringer, Amsterdam +31 20 488 0900
winfred.knibbeler@freshfields.com
Recommended in Competition/Anti-trust
Specialisation: Partner in the Competition and Trade group, with particular experience in the electricity and telecoms sectors. Also an expert on Dutch Public Procurement.

KOSTER, Weero
Houthoff Buruma, Amsterdam +31 20 577 2000
Recommended in Energy & Natural Resources

KOTHE, Tineke
Clifford Chance, Amsterdam +31 20 7119 000
tineke.kothe@cliffordchance.com
Recommended in Banking & Finance
Specialisation: Specialises in banking and securities law, securitisation and repackaging, capital market offerings, investment funds and financial services.
Prof. Memberships: Dutch Bar Association, Netherlands Association for Securities Law.
Career: *Baker & McKenzie* 1990-1991. Joined *Clifford Chance* in 1991, becoming partner in 1999.
Personal: Studied law at the University of Leiden.

LAMBOOIJ, Machiel
Freshfields Bruckhaus Deringer, Amsterdam +31 20 488 0900
machiel.lambooij@freshfields.com
Recommended in Tax
Specialisation: Partner in the finance group with specialist expertise in the areas of group finance structures and of telecoms and e-commerce. Has particular experience of cross-border projects in Spain and Switzerland.

LANGEREIS, Charles
Freshfields Bruckhaus Deringer, Amsterdam +31 20 488 0900
charles.langereis@freshfields.com
Recommended in Tax
Specialisation: Partner in the tax group. Specialises in Dutch corporate, partnership and individual taxation (both domestic and international) and with an emphasis on mergers and acquisitions, reorganisations, joint ventures, structured financing, financial products and cross border leasing transactions. Expertise includes tax litigation.

LEIJTEN, Alfons
Stibbe, Amsterdam +31 20 546 0409
fons.leijten@stibbe.nl
Recommended in Corporate/M&A, Energy & Natural Resources
Specialisation: Areas of practice include Mergers and Acquisitions, Energy and Natural Resources, Corporate Finance, Corporate Law, Corporate Litigation, and Financial and Securities Law. Advises and counsels Dutch and foreign corporations, and has particular experience in the areas of merger and acquisition process management, strategic planning and conflict resolution.
Prof. Memberships: Bar of Amsterdam, 1984. International Bar Association.
Career: Teaches three courses about corporate conflict resolution, buyout proceedings and warranties in M&A transactions as part of the post-doctoral program at the University of Nijmegen and the University of Rotterdam.
Personal: Amsterdam University, 1983. California University (LLM), 1984. Speaks Dutch and English.

MARSEILLE, Hans
De Brauw Blackstone Westbroek N.V. (member firm of Linklaters & Alliance), Amsterdam +31 20 5771 771
Recommended in Tax

MEERBURG, Dirk C.
De Brauw Blackstone Westbroek N.V. (member firm of Linklaters & Alliance), Amsterdam +31 20 577 1771
dcmeerburg@dbbw.nl
Recommended in Banking & Finance
Specialisation: Partner in Banking & Securities Law Department. Main areas of work are corporate finance, banking & securities transactions.
Career: Qualified in 1973. Joined *De Brauw Blackstone Westbroek* in 1977, becoming a partner in 1982.
Personal: Born 23 August 1949. Attended University of Utrecht (law degree 1973), Harvard Law School (LLM, 1975) and visiting scholar Harvard Law School (September 1997-March 1998).

MEESTERS, Bart J.M.A.
Allen & Overy, Amsterdam +31 20 574 1332
Recommended in Banking & Finance

MULLER, Maarten
Allen & Overy, Amsterdam +31 20 674 1000
Recommended in Corporate/M&A

OTTERVANGER, Tom R.
Allen & Overy, Amsterdam +31 20 674 1000
Recommended in Competition/Anti-trust, Energy & Natural Resources

OTTOW, Annetje
Houthoff Buruma, Amsterdam +31 20 577 2000
Recommended in Communications, Competition/Anti-trust

PERRICK, Steven
Freshfields Bruckhaus Deringer, Amsterdam +31 20 488 0900
steven.perrick@freshfields.com
Recommended in Energy & Natural Resources
Specialisation: Partner in the corporate law practice group, with wide experience in corporate and securities law and advises many listed companies and financial institutions.

PIJNACKER HORDIJK, Erik
De Brauw Blackstone Westbroek N.V. (member firm of Linklaters & Alliance), The Hague +31 70 328 5381
ehpijnackerhordijk@dbbw.nl
Recommended in Competition/Anti-trust
Specialisation: Specialises in competition law, public procurement law, utilities regulation and EU law

generally. Has a particularly strong track record in high profile litigation before the European Courts, national courts and arbitrators in all four areas of practice. Handles a significant amount of notification work before the Commission and the Dutch Competition Authority. Represents clients in sectors such as gas, electronics, electricity, railways, water, chemicals, construction and related sectors, foodstuffs and agriculture, health care.
Prof. Memberships: President of the EC Law Commission of the Union Internationale des Advocats; Secretary/treasurer of the Dutch Association for Competition Law; Member of the Board of Editors of Markt & Mededinging.
Publications: Author of the leading Dutch textbook on European and Dutch public procurement law and of numerous articles in areas of specialisation.
Career: Admitted at The Hague Bar (1983). Joined *De Brauw Blackstone Westbroek* in 1983, to become partner in 1991.
Personal: Resident in Brussels from 1987 until 1999. Languages: Dutch, English, French and German.

RANK, Pim
NautaDutilh, Amsterdam +31 20 541 46 46
Recommended in Banking & Finance

RUYS, Willem
NautaDutilh, Amsterdam +31 20 541 46 46
Recommended in Banking & Finance

SACHSE, Hans
Boekel de Nerée, Amsterdam +31 20 431 3131
Recommended in Banking & Finance

SANDERS, Maarten
Stibbe, Amsterdam +31 20 546 0162
maarten.sanders@stibbe.nl
Recommended in Communications
Specialisation: Areas of practice include Corporations, mergers and acquisitions, telecommunications, corporate finance, bankruptcy and litigation. Advises telecommunications operators on corporate and regulatory matters. Clients include financial stakeholders in telecommunications and IT related ventures.
Prof. Memberships: Bar of Amsterdam, 1987. International Bar Association (Communication Law Committee).
Personal: Amsterdam University, 1987. Speaks Dutch, English, French and German.

SCHLINGMANN, Francine
De Brauw Blackstone Westbroek N.V. (member firm of Linklaters & Alliance), Amsterdam +31 20 577 1771
fmschlingmann@dbbw.nl
Recommended in Banking & Finance
Specialisation: Capital Markets (emphasis on equity transactions, IPO's). Acted as Dutch legal adviser to Royal Ahold in its offering of shares and convertibles in May 2000 and to VNU N.V. in its accelerated global tender of shares in September 2000. Involved in regulatory practice, giving regulatory advice in complex financial structures and in structured finance.
Prof. Memberships: IBA.
Publications: Section 'Netherlands' in loose leaf CCH reporter. 'Securities Markets in Europe'; various publications in Dutch legal periodicals.
Career: 1987 - 1988: Traineeship at *Stephenson Harwood*, London. 1988 - date: *De Brauw Blackstone Westbrook* since 1 January 1997 as a partner.
Personal: Born 6 January 1966; 1987 - Law degree from Utrecht University.

SCHROEDER, Piet
Caron & Stevens/Baker & McKenzie, Amsterdam +31 20 551 7555
piet.l.a.m.schroeder@bakernet.com
Recommended in Banking & Finance
Specialisation: International partner and head of the Banking & Finance section of the Amsterdam office. Extensive experience in all types of debt financing, secured and unsecured and including project and acquisition financing; issues of structured and unstructured debt instruments on the domestic and international capital markets; investment banking, structured financing and securitisation; banking and securities regulations, securities lending, custody and settlement; repo's and derivatives.
Publications: Inter alia, on security interests in international transactions, cross-border leasing, securities lending and repo's.
Personal: Born: 1947; LLM, State University in Groningen (1970), Masters in Business Law, City of London Polytechnic (1971). In-house counsel Algemene Bank Nederland N.V. (now: ABN AMRO Bank N.V.) (1972-1976); joined *Caron & Stevens/Baker & McKenzie* in 1976.

SCHUIT, Steven
Allen & Overy, Amsterdam +31 20 674 1000
Recommended in Corporate/M&A, Energy & Natural Resources

SIMONIS, Paul
Loyens & Loeff, Rotterdam +31 10 224 6224
paul.simonis@loyensloeff.com
Recommended in Tax
Specialisation: Joined *Loyens and Loeff* (formerly *Loyens & Volkmaars*) in 1982, and is working in the corporate tax practice with specialisation in M&A, Corporate Restructurings, and (De)Mergers. Clients are MNO's. Over the last 10 years has built up expertise in the telecom and energy industry.

SIPPENS GROENEWEGEN, Piet
NautaDutilh, Amsterdam +31 20 541 46 46
Recommended in Communications

SLOTBOOM, Marco Marinus
Nolst Trenité, Rotterdam +31 10 404 2111
sloboom@trenite.com
Recommended in Competition/Anti-trust
Specialisation: Partner in EC and Competition Department. Advises Dutch and foreign clients in issues involving EC and Dutch competition law and EC regulatory enforcement generally. Represents industry and governments before the national and European Commission and the Dutch Competition Authority.
Prof. Memberships: Admitted to the Bar of Rotterdam.
Publications: 'The Hormones case: an increased risk of illegality of sanitary and phytosanitary measures', Common Market Law Review 471-491 (1999); 'Dutch competition law: not tied to EC competition law, 47', Sociaal-Economische Wetgeving 151-159 (1999) (in Dutch); 'The Technology Transfer Regulation – a practitioner's perspective', The International Lawyer 1-25 (1998, Volume 32, no.1) (co-authored with P.V.F. Bos); 'Dock-dues in the French overseas departments: the application of EC law to intrastate trade', Cahiers De Droit Europeen 9-30 (1996, nos.1-2) (in French); 'State aid in EC law: a broad or narrow definition?', 20 European Law Review 289-301.
Career: Qualified in 1992. Joined *Trenite Van Doorne* in 1990, becoming a partner in 2000.
Personal: Born 29 May 1965. Attended College of Europe (Bruges), University of Leiden – School of Law 1985-1989, University of Leiden – Faculty of Arts (French language and literature) 1983-1988.

SNOEP, Martijn
De Brauw Blackstone Westbroek N.V. (member firm of Linklaters & Alliance), Amsterdam +31 20 5771 771
Recommended in Communications, Competition/Anti-trust

SWAAK, Christof
Stibbe, Amsterdam +31 20 546 0606
Recommended in Competition/Anti-trust
Specialisation: Partner at *Stibbe*, dealing in particular with European and competition law. Advises clients and appears in proceedings before the European Court of Justice in Luxembourg, the European Commission in Brussels, the Dutch Competition Authority and Dutch courts. Within the firm, is part of an International Practice Group that deals with European law, competition law and WTO-law, with bases in Paris, Brussels and Amsterdam. Has been directly involved in a wide range of significant cases of EU law and Dutch competition law. These include the process that led to the imposition by the European Commission of certain conditions on the parties that merged into Aventis; the oral hearing before the European Court of Justice in Luxemburg in the case Marca Mode C.V./Adidas A.G.; the legal proceedings of the Dutch Association of Jewellers against the See Buy Fly-campaign at Schiphol; and the concentration proceedings before the Dutch competition authority regarding the acquisition by Schuitema of the Hermans' chain of A&P-supermarkets. Was also involved in the UMTS auction in the Netherlands and the problems created by the liberalisation of the Dutch electricity sector. Clients are multi-national companies in various sectors such as Akzo Nobel, Yamanouchi and a number of major financial institutions.
Publications: Wrote and defended PhD thesis on 'European Community Law and the Automobile Industry' (published by Kluwer in 1999). Has written and (co-)edited a number of books on competition law. Published a large number of articles and annotations in legal journals on various topics including European law, Dutch competition law and intellectual property law. Co-editor of the 'Nederlands Tijdschrift voor Europees recht' (Dutch journal of European law) and correspondent for 'Markt en Mededinging' (Dutch competition law journal) and 'European Public law'.
Career: Graduated in Dutch Civil law in 1987

(University of Leiden), studied European law at the College of Europe in Brugge, Belgium. Became an attorney at the bar of Amsterdam in 1988. Spent a year as a foreign associate at a law firm in the US. Lecturer at the University in Leiden and has been external examiner for European law at the University of Edinburgh, Scotland. Acts as ad hoc judge at the District Court in The Hague.

THIJSSEN, Jeroen
Freshfields, Amsterdam +31 20 488 0900
Recommended in Corporate/M&A

VAN DE VIJVER, Niels
Allen & Overy, Amsterdam +31 20 674 1000
Recommended in Banking & Finance

VAN DER KLIS, Geert
Clifford Chance, Amsterdam +31 20 7119 000
geert.vanderklis@cliffordchance.com
Recommended in Communications, Competition/Anti-trust
Specialisation: Specialises in general commercial, corporate and regulatory law, concentrating on telecommunications and competition law. In-depth knowledge of the markets for mobile, broadcasting and internet service provision. Guest lecturer at University of Amsterdam.
Career: Qualified in 1990. *Loeff Claeys Verbeke* Brussels and Amsterdam, 1990-1996. Joined *Clifford Chance* in 1997, becoming partner in 2000.
Personal: Degrees in Dutch and International Law, University of Amsterdam.

VAN DER LANDE, Maarten
Caron & Stevens/Baker & McKenzie, Amsterdam +31 20 551 7555
maarten.l.b.van.der.lande@bakernet.com
Recommended in Tax
Specialisation: Partner in tax group. Main areas of work are corporate tax law and international tax law. Has handled the tax aspect of complex reorganisations, mergers, and split-offs. Advises mainly on international tax planning. Has coordinated a study, commissioned by the Dutch government, on the effective tax burden in the European Union member states. Specialises also in transfer pricing. Member of the Baker & McKenzie European Tax Steering Committee. Is General Secretary of the Dutch Tax Academy (Vereniging voor Belastingwetenschap). Has spoken at various conferences on transfer pricing.
Prof. Memberships: Nederlandse Orde van Advocaten (Dutch Bar Association), Nederlandse Orde van Belastingadviseurs (Dutch Tax Advisors Association).
Publications: Has published articles on a wide range of different topics.
Career: Started career in 1975 as a tax advisor. Joined *Baker & McKenzie* in 1987 and became international partner in 1988.
Personal: Born 1950. Holds a JD from Leijden University (1974) and an MCL from the University of Miami School of Law (1980).

VAN DER STAAY, Jan Willem
Freshfields Bruckhaus Deringer, Amsterdam +31 20 488 0900
janwillem.vanderstaay@freshfields.com
Recommended in Corporate/M&A
Specialisation: Partner in the Corporate Group, specialising in mergers and acquisitions, joint ventures, IPO's, listings and equity issues, management buy-outs and corporate litigation.

VAN DER WAL, Gerard
Barents & Krans, The Hague +32 2 661 3250
barentskrans@skynet.be
Recommended in Competition/Anti-trust
Specialisation: Specialises in general EU law, as well as in EU and Dutch competition law. Advises national and multinational companies, governments and trade associations in matters concerning European law and competition law in all its aspects. Has also represented individuals on staff cases. Expertise ranges from matters of competition law to European intellectual property law, free movement of goods, freedom to provide services, state aid, the common agricultural policy, public procurement and pharmaceuticals. Wide experience in litigation before the Commission, the European Courts and the national judiciary of several European countries. Has been involved in cases on intellectual property (RTE/Magill, Loendersloot/Ballentine, Generics/Smith Kline, BMW/Deenik), freedom to provide services (Alpine Investments), agricultural policy and external relations (Emesa) and public access to documents (Van der Wal/Commission).
Prof. Memberships: Member of the advisory committee on legislation on competition and regulatory matters of the Dutch Bar Association. Recently appointed as deputy judge with the Court of Appeal in The Hague (the Netherlands).
Career: Practising law since 1977. Became managing partner of the Brussels branch of *Barents & Krans* in January 1987.

VAN DER WEIJDEN, Maarten
Loyens & Loeff, Amsterdam +31 20 578 5785
maarten.van.der.weijden@loyensloeff.com
Recommended in Tax
Specialisation: Corporate tax, international taxation, emphasis on US – Netherlands related matters.
Prof. Memberships: IFA.
Career: *Loyens & Loeff* (formerly *Loyens and Volkmaars*) since 1986. From 1987-1989 and 1996-1999 in New York, from 1990-1995 and from 2000 in Amsterdam.
Personal: Rijksuniversiteit Leiden, Master of Law (Taxation) 1986. New York University LLM, Taxation, 1988.

VAN DER WOUDE, Marc
NautaDutilh, Amsterdam +31 20 541 4646
Recommended in Competition/Anti-trust

VAN EMPEL, Martijn
Stibbe, Amsterdam +31 20 546 0188
martijn.vanempel@stibbe.nl
Recommended in Competition/Anti-trust
Specialisation: Areas of practice include European Community Law and Antitrust. Practice is focused on EC law and competition law at European level and under Netherlands law. Regularly represents clients before the national courts and authorities and the European courts and commissions.
Prof. Memberships: Bar of Amsterdam, 1983. International Bar Association. Union Internationale des Avocats (International Lawyers Association). Ligue Internationale de Droit de la Concurrence (International League of Competition Law). Nederlandse Vereniging voor Europees Recht (Netherlands Association for European Law).
Career: Professor of Law, University of LUISS Luigi Carli, Rome, Italy.
Personal: Leiden University, 1965. Paris University, 1966. Speaks Dutch, English, French, German and Italian.

VAN EVERDINGEN, Huib
NautaDutilh, Amsterdam +31 20 541 46 46
Recommended in Banking & Finance

VAN KEMPEN, Jan
Loyens & Loeff, Amsterdam +31 20 578 5785
jan.van.kempen@loyensloeff.com
Recommended in Tax
Specialisation: Tax partner in the Amsterdam office of *Loyens & Loeff.* Has a typical corporate tax practice, providing tax guidance in a broad range of areas for large multinational companies. Has been involved in various take-overs, reorganisations and de-mergers.
Career: Joined *Loyens & Volkmaars* (formerly *Loyens & Loeff*) in 1974.
Personal: Born 1942, graduated in tax law from Leyden University (1970).

VAN LEEUWE, Jean-Pierre
Nolst Trenité, Rotterdam +31 10 404 2111
leeuwe@trenite.com
Recommended in Corporate/M&A
Specialisation: Partner in the Corporate Law Department. Specialised in corporate law with an emphasis on mergers and acquisitions, joint ventures and corporate restructurings. Has handled acquisitions and joint ventures of companies in various divisions of industry and trade, both domestic and international. Has conducted several corporate restructurings of internationally operative groups. Client group consists of inter alia international pharmaceutical and chemical industries, international and domestic building material manufacturers and merchants, real estate investment companies, venture capitalists and other foreign and domestic institutional and private investors. Is a member of the firm's legal opinion committee and speaks at domestic and international mergers and acquisitions seminars.
Prof. Memberships: Dutch Bar Association; Rotterdam Bar Association; Netherlands Securities Law Association.
Career: Graduate of Leiden University – the Netherlands Civil Law (1980) and Notarial Law (1982). Was a university lecturer in Civil Law at Leiden University during 1981-1982. Joined *Trenité Van Doorne* in 1982 and became a partner in 1989.
Personal: Born 13 August 1957. Attended Leiden University 1975-1980 and 1980-1982. Leisure interests include outdoor activities such as sailing. Lives in Schiedam, The Netherlands.

VAN LEEUWEN, Gijs CL
Houthoff Buruma, Amsterdam +31 20 577 2342
Recommended in Banking & Finance

N

N

VAN MARWIJK KOOY, Johan
NautaDutilh, Amsterdam +31 20 541 46 46
Recommended in Corporate/M&A

VAN SASSE VAN YSSELT, Charles
Clifford Chance, Amsterdam +31 20 711 9000
charles.vansassevanysselt@cliffordchance.com
Recommended in Competition/Anti-trust
Specialisation: Specialises in Dutch and EU competition law and concentration control, state aid and public procurement. Sectors include banking, broadband, energy and media. In addition, practises EU trade law. Head of the Dutch competition law group. Practises from Amsterdam and Brussels. Admitted to the Dutch bar.

VAN VERSCHUER, Philip
Loyens & Loeff, Amsterdam +31 20 578 5785
philip.van.verschuer@loyensloeff.com
Recommended in Corporate/M&A
Specialisation: Partner in the Amsterdam Office of *Loyens & Loeff.* Practice consists of providing transactional advice and services to all types of business organisations, including energy production and distribution companies, companies operating in the ICT sector and venture capitalists. The practice focuses on both public and private M&A, joint ventures and strategic alliances, management buy-outs and leverage buy-out transactions. Within the energy sector acted as lead counsel for the sale of UNA NV to Reliant Inc. UNA being the first and largest privatisation of an energy company in the Netherlands. Also assisted various foreign energy companies in the auction procedures for the other energy producing companies, including Electrabel's winning bid for EPON N.V. In respect of the energy distribution sector, acted as lead counsel for the sellers of the largest remaining independent energy distribution company. Involved in a number of M&A and joint venture transactions in the ICT Sector involving telecom operating companies, satellite companies, internet providers and other ICT companies. Has been lead counsel on behalf of the largest telecom operator in the Netherlands in an infrastructure and internet provider joint venture with one of the leading operators in the US. In the satellite sector, represented one of the Inmarsat market leaders in a world-wide joint venture with one of its competitors. Represents a number of national and international players in the area of venture capital.

VAN WEEGHEL, Stef
Stibbe, Amsterdam +31 20 546 03 82
stef.vanweeghel@stibbe.nl
Recommended in Tax
Specialisation: Areas of practice include international taxation; taxation of banks; structured finance; financial products; mergers and acquisitions; financial and business joint ventures; corporate reorganisations; tax litigation; taxation and electronic commerce. Advises clients on a broad range of domestic and international tax issues in connection with mergers and acquisitions, initial public offerings, innovative financial transactions and financial instruments. Has been involved in a number of major cross-border transactions on behalf of investment banks and corporate clients. Part-time professor of international tax law at the University of Amsterdam and author and co-author of several books and numerous articles on international taxation.
Prof. Memberships: Member of the Amsterdam Executive Committee of Stibbe and a member of the international Board of the firm. Bar of Amsterdam, 1987. American Bar Association (Tax Section). International Fiscal Association. American Tax Institute in Europe (Member Advisory Board). Association for Tax Research (Vereniging voor Belastingwetenschap) (Member Executive Board).
Publications: Correspondent/Contributor: BNB (Beslissingen in belastingzaken Nederlandse Belastingrechtspraak), FED Fiscaal Weekblad, European Taxation.
Personal: Leiden University (Dutch Law, 1983); (Tax Law, 1987). New York University (LLM in Taxation, 1990). University of Amsterdam (Doctor of Law, 1997). Languages: Dutch, English, French, German, Russian.

VERLOREN VAN THEMAAT, Weyer
Houthoff Buruma, Amsterdam +31 20 577 2000
w.verloren_van_themaat@lswh.be
Recommended in Competition/Anti-trust
Specialisation: Handles full range of Dutch and EU competition law as well as EU law in general. Particular experience in merger filings and cartel investigations. Work during 2000 has included cartel investigations in the automotive sector and various merger filings, inter alia in the fields of daily newspapers, shipyards, and e-commerce.
Prof. Memberships: Dutch Association for Competition Law; Dutch Association for European Law.
Publications: Report for the Dutch Association of Competition Law on 'To what extent do, or should competition laws regulate oligopolistic markets?' (1996); 'The Dutch competition Act of May 22, 1997', ECLR (1997); 'Mededingingswet in Kort Bestek' (with Annetje T. Ottow), VUGA (1998); Cremers Mededingingsrecht (1996); various other articles on competition in Dutch and English law journals.
Career: Qualified 1990; partner 1998; first resident partner of *Houthoff Buruma* in the joint EC law office *Liedekerke Siméon Wessing Houthoff* (for more information see: www.lswh.com) as of 1997.
Personal: Married, with two children. Interests include modern art.

VLETTER, Bas
Loyens & Loeff, Rotterdam +31 10 224 6224
bas.vletter@loyensloeff.com
Recommended in Corporate/M&A
Specialisation: Member of the practice group in corporate law and the *Loyens & Loeff* TMT Team (Technology Media Telecom), the Venture Capital Team and the Banking and Securities Team. Specialises in company law, mergers and acquisitions, controlled auctions, public offers, public take-overs, IPOs, venture capital and (inter)national ventures. Acted as counsel to Dresdner Kleinwort Benson in the public take-over of the Koninklijke Dordtsche Petroleum NV and for Stonehaven Holding B.V. and its shareholders HAL and Egeria in the public bid on Koninklijke Ahrend N.V. Furthermore acted as counsel for Keppel Fels in the take-over of Verolme Botlek and as counsel to the German Metro Group in the sale of Gastronoom to Ahold, Office Centers B.V and Vobis B.V.
Career: Admitted as attorney 1984, joined the firm 1984 and became a partner in 1990.
Prof. Memberships: International Bar Association and Commercial Law Association.
Personal: Born 1960, graduated Leyden University (1984). Lectures on a wide range of company law topics such as shareholder liability and MBOs and LBOs.

WAKKIE, Peter
De Brauw Blackstone Westbroek N.V. (member firm of Linklaters & Alliance), Rotterdam
+31 10 240 6636
pnwakkie@dbbw.nl
Recommended in Corporate/M&A
Specialisation: Company law and corporate finance, including mergers and acquisitions, takeovers and issues. Also specialises in corporate litigation. Acted for Gucci in court against LVMH's takeover attempt.
Career: Qualified in 1972. Became a partner in 1979. Head of New York office 1978-1982. Presently chairman of the managing board of *De Brauw Blackstone Westbroek.*

WILLEUMIER, Jaap
Stibbe, Amsterdam +31 20 546 0405
jaap.willeumier@stibbe.nl
Recommended in Banking & Finance
Specialisation: Areas of practice include banking, securities, corporate and structured finance, cross-border leasing, and M&A. Advises corporate clients, banks and other financial institutions on international financial transactions, including debt and equity capital market transactions, syndicated secured lending transactions, securitisations, project finance, cross border leasing, corporate restructurings and mergers and acquisitions. In addition to transactional work, counsels clients on bank and securities regulatory matters. Was recently involved in the merger of the Amsterdam, Brussels and Paris securities exchanges forming Euronext.
Prof. Memberships: International Bar Association (Business Law Section). American Bar Association (Business Law Section). Vereniging voor Effectenrecht (Dutch Association of Securities Lawyers). Member of the editorial board, Vennootschap & Onderneming (monthly legal reporter on company and financial law). Member of the Supervisory Boards of several Dutch companies. Member of the Board, Koninklijke Nederlandse Reddingmaatschappij (KNRM; Royal Netherlands Sea-rescue Society).
Career: From 1989 through 1994 was a resident partner in the New York office of *Stibbe Simont Monahan Duhot.* In 1994, established *Stibbe*'s London office and was a resident partner there until returning to Amsterdam in 1996. Currently a non-executive member of the Board of the firm.
Personal: Amsterdam University 1979. Speaks Dutch and English.

NEW ZEALAND

Index

OVERVIEW: While the size of the legal spend overall has shrunk during the last year there has been a flurry of activity on the corporate side largely due to the low value of the NZ dollar. Inward investment has increased, attracted by a number of major sell offs including that of NZ giant Fletcher Challenge. Although a change of government has led to a drying up of the privatisation programme, it is offset by an increase in M&A activity and the implementation of new takeovers codes due in 2001. The banking market also remains relatively vibrant with the major trend being towards the rationalisation of New Zealand offices to their Australian parents.

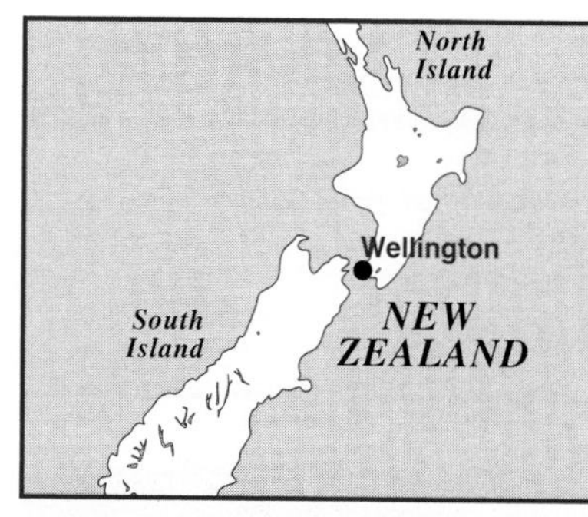

N

Banking & Finance

NEW ZEALAND Leading firms (Banking & Finance)
1 Chapman Tripp Sheffield Young
Russell McVeagh
2 Bell Gully
3 Buddle Findlay
Simpson Grierson

Firms are listed alphabetically in each band.

Leading individuals (Banking & Finance)
1 A'COURT Alan *Russell McVeagh*
JONAS Michael *Chapman Tripp Sheffield Young*
ROSS Dermot *Chapman Tripp Sheffield Young*
WETHERELL Dave *Russell McVeagh*
2 FLYNN Steve *Simpson Grierson*
LUSK John *Russell McVeagh*
REESE Mark *Chapman Tripp Sheffield Young*
3 FLACKS Prue *Russell McVeagh*
HUNT Hilary *Buddle Findlay*

Individuals are listed alphabetically in each band.

Chapman Tripp Sheffield Young (8 ptrs, 20 asscs) Excellent reputation in general banking, with a slant towards corporate borrowing and issuing and structured finance. The lending side, however, remains vibrant, with an impressive client base featuring all the major NZ banks.

The firm's bedrock is considered to be its collection of *"outstanding, top-rank practitioners."* **Michael Jonas***, *"an exceptionally good technician,"* and **Dermot Ross***, an *"excellent and thorough"* recent recruit from rivals Buddle Findlay, are viewed as *"two of the major stars of NZ banking."* Complementing them is **Mark Reese***, *"a good commercial practitioner, universally liked by his fellow lawyers."* A highlight of the year was representing United Network on its re-financing. **Clients:** Bank of New Zealand; Westpac Trust; Citibank; HSBC.

Russell McVeagh (5 ptrs, 23 asscs) A purposeful, *"cutting-edge attitude"* characterises the work of this renowned name in the market. The practice is primarily built around structured financing, project financing and securitisation. Largely eschewing pure banking work, the team also has an acknowledged specialisation in syndicated loans.

Spearheading a respected team are the *"extremely able"* **Alan A'Court***, and **Dave Wetherell***, whose *"tough, hard-nosed approach is appreciated by his clients."* **John Lusk*** continues *"a long-standing and distinguished career,"* working alongside the younger but *"highly rated"* **Prue Flacks***. The firm acted for the banks on the NZ$1.6 billion re-financing of Power NZ, and the recent re-financing of United Network. **Clients:** Westpac Trust; Deutsche Bank; National Bank of New Zealand.

Bell Gully (8 ptrs, 8 asscs) Although seen to be *"moving away from specialist banking,"* the firm retains a strong practice in this area. Still noted for the *"strength and depth"* of its client base, it acts for the majority of leading banks in New Zealand. Particularly active in the field of high value mortgage processing and structured finance, the group is uniformly strong in Auckland and Wellington. Although lacking a pre-eminent practitioner, the team is said to be of a *"consistently good standard."* Advised Banque National de Paris on the establishment of its banking operations in New Zealand and represented the Reserve Bank of New Zealand on proposed netting legislation. **Clients:** ANZ Banking Group; Bank of New Zealand; Citibank.

Buddle Findlay (5 ptrs, 11 asscs)Historically, banking has formed this firm's bedrock. Long-term principal legal advisors to Bank of New Zealand and BNZ Finance, it acts for other major NZ banks as well. While reservations have been voiced at the departure of former leading lawyer Dermot Ross to Chapman Tripp, a diverse practice remains *"sound and effectively administered."* **Hilary Hunt*** has attracted growing market commendation. The firm acted as NZ counsel to Deutsche Bank on the US$800 million financing of Southern Cross Cable, and advised HSBC on the Sealord re-financing. **Clients:** Bank of New Zealand; BNZ Finance; ABN AMRO.

Simpson Grierson (7 ptrs, 20 asscs) The hallmarks of this *"dependable second tier firm"* are its relations with the Westpac Banking Corporation, and its ties to local government. The Westpac connection affords exposure to numerous cases involving complex lending issues, while a sound borrowing practice has seen the group advise more than 30 local authorities in respect of their debt arrangements. *"On the rise"* **Steve Flynn*** *"is good both technically and at getting deals done."* Among those deals was the first retail bond issued by Auckland City Council (value NZ$300 million) as part of its restructuring of local authority funding. **Clients:** Westpac; Deutsche Bank; Brierley Investments.

*See leaders' profiles on pages 509-510

Corporate/M&A

NEW ZEALAND Leading firms (Banking & Finance)
1 Bell Gully Chapman Tripp Sheffield Young Russell McVeagh
2 Buddle Findlay Rudd Watts & Stone Simpson Grierson

Firms are listed alphabetically in each band.

Leading individuals (Corporate/Mergers & Acquisitions)
1 **FAMILTON Keith** *Bell Gully* **HARMOS Andrew** *Russell McVeagh* **KING John** *Russell McVeagh* **OLDFIELD Paul** *Russell McVeagh* **THURSTON William** *Bell Gully*
2 **BROWN Barry** *Chapman Tripp Sheffield Young* **CASTLE Peter** *Bell Gully* **FREEMAN Mark** *Bell Gully* **ROWE Peter** *Rudd Watts & Stone* **STROWGER John** *Chapman Tripp Sheffield Young*
Individuals are listed alphabetically in each band.

Bell Gully (36 ptrs, 78 asscs) The largest firm in the country provides an across the board service, catering to an established, international client base, as well as a substantial proportion of New Zealand's top companies. Many of the firm's clients are of long standing, and lend weight to its reputation for tradition and for being *"the embodiment of the institution of law."*

Leading from the front is Chairman of Partners, **Keith Familton***, *"a strategist and thinker with a good team behind him."* **Bill Thurston*** *"blends experience with great judgement"* and has enjoyed a particularly high profile following his work on the sell-off of major client Fletcher Challenge Ltd. He was assisted on this transaction by rising star **Mark Freeman***. **Peter Castle***, specialist in corporate privatisation, is *"commercial, practical and popular with clients."*

Highlights of the year include the sale of FCL Paper to Norske Skogg (a deal worth NZ$5.6 billion), and the sale of TransAlta Corporation's entire New Zealand investment portfolio (NZ$834 million.) The firm also advised on the merger of PowerCo and Central Power to form the country's fourth largest energy network company, a deal worth NZ$600 million. **Clients:** Fletcher Challenge; AltaVista; Air New Zealand; New Zealand Dairy.

Chapman Tripp Sheffield Young (26 ptrs, 75 asscs) Highly regarded corporate team specialising in big-ticket M&A deals and anti-trust legislation. Boasting strong links with the establishment and government, especially in Wellington, it is seen as *"the place to go to get chapter and verse on the law."* Energy and telecoms are two areas of notable strength. Considered to possess a *"wealth of home-grown talent,"* the group includes **John Strowger*** who is an *"excellent operator,"* and **Barry Brown*** who *"commands respect"* and *"keeps the transactional momentum going."* Mark O'Regan has become a High Court judge.

The firm advised the Natural Gas Corporation on its NZ$1.2 billion takeover of TransAlta NZ, and represented Shell Oil and Apache on their acquisition of Fletcher Challenge Energy. **Clients:** Natural Gas Corporation; Telecom NZ; Shell.

Russell McVeagh (13 ptrs, 60 asscs) Acting for an enormous slice of the NZ listed companies sector, the corporate team is one of the country's major players. Driven by a strong work ethic, it is a *"sharp, aggressive outfit,"* targeting top-end transactional work. Its strong client base is serviced by *"a core of accomplished corporate lawyers,"* led by the *"senior and well-respected"* **John King***. **Paul Oldfield***, *"one of the best commercial lawyers in NZ,"* possesses *"a concise style which shines through on major deals."* *"Slick lawyer"* **Andrew Harmos*** is said to have returned from New York *"with a new lease of life."* The firm advised the Australian Stock Exchange on its proposed merger with its NZ counterpart, and acted for the Westfield Trust on its NZ$800 million merger with the St. Luke's Group. **Clients:** Carter Holt Harvey Ltd; Ports of Auckland; Auckland International Airport.

Buddle Findlay (28 lawyers) Traditionally a banking firm, it is considered to have successfully diversified into corporate and commercial work, and is said to be *"on an upswing."* Although still lacking heavyweight individual practitioners, the team is increasingly involved in headline IPOs. The firm advised on Norske Skogg's acquisition of Fletcher Challenge Paper, and on the float of Contact Energy, New Zealand's largest privately owned generator. **Clients:** Norske Skogg; Singapore Airlines; Brierley Investments.

Rudd Watts & Stone (19 ptrs, 45 asscs) A member of the Australian-led Minter Ellison Group since 1989, this *"solid full-service firm"* handles clients from small businesses to multi-national corporations with *"an efficiency which ensures you are not going to waste your time."* Seen as a relatively young partnership with a *"modern image,"* the firm has acquired a reputation for its work in the telecoms industry. **Peter Rowe*** is regarded as *"a lawyer of integrity, who is a delight to deal with."*

The firm advised on the first migration of a listed company (Nufarm Ltd) from NZ to Australia. Also acted for three of the potential acquirers in the Fletcher Challenge break-up and represented BT plc on the Inmarsat project. **Clients:** BT, NZ Dairy Board; Vodafone; Bank of NZ.

Simpson Grierson (18 ptrs, 60 asscs) Acting for city councils and more than 96% of all local authorities, a strong local government practice continues to form this venerable firm's backbone. Its corporate practice is further enhanced by strong involvement in the energy and competition law sectors, while niche expertise in telecoms was emphasised by the group's involvement in the multi-billion dollar outsourcing of all IT services by Telecom NZ to EDS.

Although the firm suffered a blow with the departure of star name Mark Verbiest to an in-house position at Telecom NZ, it is still considered to offer a *"thoroughly reliable"* service. It advised the consortium which purchased Ansett NZ on its agreement with Qantas to operate under the franchise of Qantas New Zealand. **Clients:** BP Oil; Telstra Satellites; Fisher and Paykel.

*See leaders' profiles on pages 509-510

Leaders' profiles – New Zealand

A'COURT, Alan S.J.
Russell McVeagh, Wellington +64 4 499 9555
Recommended in Banking & Finance

BROWN, Barry J.
Chapman Tripp Sheffield Young, Wellington
+64 4 498 4916
barry.brown@chapmantripp.co.nz
Recommended in Corporate/M&A
Specialisation: Advises New Zealand and multinational clients on mergers and take-overs, business acquisition, disposition and development strategies and general corporate and business structuring. Particular experience includes advising the National Bank of New Zealand (wholly-owned by Lloyds TSB plc) on its acquisition of Countrywide Bank and the Rural Bank of New Zealand; advising HJ Heinz Company on its New Zealand investments; representing New Zealand Government on the restructuring of the Bank of New Zealand and the subsequent sale of the Government's interest to National Australia Bank and on the sale of Telecom Corporation of New Zealand; advising the Fijian Government on the restructuring of the state-owned National Bank of Fiji; advising RJR Nabisco on the sale of its New Zealand and Asian processed foods businesses; advising Ford Motor Company on its Mazda joint venture; serving as New Zealand counsel for international banks in relation to their funding of New Zealand businesses and representing Air New Zealand and other major New Zealand corporations in connection with the raising of funds in the international captial markets.
Prof. Memberships: New Zealand Law Society.
Career: Joined *Chapman Tripp* in 1972. Apart from 3 years overseas, has been with the firm since that time. Partner since 1980, and former managing partner of the Wellington office. Chairman of the firm's National Board.
Personal: Born 1950. Attended Victoria University of Wellington (LLB (Hons)). Leisure activities include skiing, golf, tennis, and family.

CASTLE, Peter R.
Bell Gully, Wellington +64 4 473 7777
Recommended in Corporate/M&A

FAMILTON, Keith R.
Bell Gully, Auckland +64 9 916 8800
Recommended in Corporate/M&A

FLACKS, Prue
Russell McVeagh, Auckland 1 +64 9 367 8000
Recommended in Banking & Finance

FLYNN, Steve
Simpson Grierson, Wellington +64 4 499 4599
sbf@sglaw.co.nz
Recommended in Banking & Finance
Specialisation: Advises banks, financial institutions, governmental agencies, State-owned enterprises, corporates, trustee companies and local authorities on a full range of financing issues. Has practised in this area for 18 years. Has considerable experience in capital markets financing – covering Eurobond and Euronote issues, commercial paper programmes, transferable loan certificate facilities, domestic bond and note issues, convertible and capital note issues, structured financing, syndicated, transactional and bilateral banking and derivatives transactions. Also advises on corporate securities law and insolvency, receiverships and statutory management. Acts for several prominent chartered accountancy firms when they are appointed as receivers or liquidators. Clients include major New Zealand and international entities such as Westpac Banking Corporation, Brierley Investments, AXA, AMP, Guinness Peat Group, TelstraSaturn, Rabobank, the New Zealand Treasury, KPMG, Overseas Union Bank, Government Superannuation Fund, UBS Warburg and ABN-Amro.

FREEMAN, Mark W.
Bell Gully, Wellington +64 4 473 7777
Recommended in Corporate/M&A

HARMOS, Andrew W.
Russell McVeagh, Auckland 1 +64 9 367 8000
Recommended in Corporate/M&A

HUNT, Hilary
Buddle Findlay, Wellington +64 4 499 4242
Recommended in Banking & Finance

JONAS, Michael D.
Chapman Tripp Sheffield Young, Auckland 1
+64 9 357 9016
michael.jonas@chapmantripp.co.nz
Recommended in Banking & Finance
Specialisation: Corporate partner in banking and finance department. Specialises in corporate finance, acting for both lenders and borrowers. Particular expertise in structured financing, securitization, tax effective funding structures (domestic and cross-border) as well as major debt restructuring. Has recently worked extensively on cross border transactions for major financial institutions raising funding in foreign jurisdictions or investing in foreign debt and equity structures.
Prof. Memberships: New Zealand Law Society.
Career: Qualified in New Zealand in 1981. Joined *Chapman Tripp* as a partner in 1997.
Personal: Born 1957. Attended University of Auckland 1977-81 (LLB). Leisure activities include flying, diving, alpine climbing, and skiing.

KING, John C.
Russell McVeagh, Auckland 1 +64 9 367 8000
Recommended in Corporate/M&A

LUSK, John O.
Russell McVeagh, Auckland 1 +64 9 367 8000
Recommended in Banking & Finance

OLDFIELD, John Paul H.
Russell McVeagh, Auckland 1 +64 9 367 8000
Recommended in Corporate/M&A

REESE, P. Mark
Chapman Tripp Sheffield Young, Wellington
+64 4 498 4933
mark.reese@chapmantripp.co.nz
Recommended in Banking & Finance
Specialisation: Partner in Banking and Finance Department. Active in full range of banking and finance transactions. Has particular interest in international capital markets and cross-border asset based and structured finance transactions. Has acted on Swedish, Japanese, US and German cross-border leases of electricity and telecommunications equipment and rolling stock. Has acted for a number of New Zealand issuers, including Westpac Banking Corporation, Telecom New Zealand, Transpower New Zealand and Housing New Zealand, on Euro and US MTN programmes and other international capital raisings. Acted on a number of mortgage-backed securitisation programmes. Two years asset financing experience in a London firm.
Prof. Memberships: New Zealand Law Society, The Law Society.
Career: Qualified in New Zealand (1983) and admitted as a solicitor of the Supreme Court of England and Wales in 1990. Joined *Chapman Tripp* in 1982. Two years at *Freshfields*, London from 1987 to 1990. Became a partner at *Chapman Tripp* in 1991. Past member of the firm's management, incomes and staff committees.
Personal: Born 1960. Canterbury University, Christchurch 1979-1982 (LLB (Hons)). Leisure interests include sport and other outdoor activities.

ROSS, Dermot
Chapman Tripp Sheffield Young, Auckland 1
+64 9 357 9068
dermot.ross@chapmantripp.co.nz
Recommended in Banking & Finance
Specialisation: Partner in Banking and Finance Department. Principal practice areas are in syndications, capital market programmes, workouts and other complex transactions. Has acted in many substantial acquisition projects by foreign companies in New Zealand. Frequently speaks on finance and company law matters at industry seminars and conferences.
Prof. Memberships: New Zealand Law Society; The Banking Law Association Limited (Australia).
Career: Qualified in New Zealand (1980). Worked in the banking and finance division of *Coward Chance* in London from 1980 to 1984. Admitted as a solicitor of The Supreme Court of England and Wales in 1984. Joined *Buddle Findlay* in Wellington in 1984, and was a partner in that firm until 2000. Currently a director and committee member of The Banking Law Association Limited (Australia), and is a New Zealand editor of the Journal of Banking & Finance Law and Practice.
Personal: Born 1956. Attended Victoria University of Wellington 1974 to 1979 (LLM). Leisure activities include reading, golf, family and travel.

ROWE, Peter J.
Rudd Watts & Stone, Auckland +64 9 353 9700
Recommended in Corporate/M&A

STROWGER, W. John
Chapman Tripp Sheffield Young, Auckland 1
+64 9 357 9081
john.strowger@chapmantripp.co.nz
Recommended in Corporate/M&A
Specialisation: Partner in commercial department, specialising in corporate law, contract law, securities law, and M&A. Has had significant involvement in various corporatisation/privatisation exercises undertaken in New Zealand, and also in M&A, corporate restructurings and takeovers in the New Zealand market. Has a particular professional interest and involvement in management/leveraged buy-outs and buy-ins, and private equity transactions for institutional investors. Acted for Fletcher Challenge in relation to its takeover of minority interests in Southern Petroleum No Liability, for Goldman Sachs led syndicate and a leverage buy-out of Skellerup Group Limited, for Blue Star Group Limited in its takeover/acquisitions of U-Bix Business Machines, Wang New Zealand Limited, Whitcoulls Group and McCollam Printers Limited, and for Cullen Investments Limited on its takeover offer in respect of Pacific Retail Group Limited. Has had a long involvement in the establishment and subsequent business of Direct Capital Private Equity, New Zealand's first listed direct investment/venture capital vehicle, and execution of various investment and divestment transactions on its behalf. Principal corporate adviser to a number of New Zealand's listed entities, providing advice on listing rule and securities legislation related issues on a day to day basis.
Prof. Memberships: New Zealand Law Society.
Career: Admitted to the Bar in 1987. Joined *Chapmann Tripp Sheffield Young* in 1986, becoming a partner in 1993.
Personal: Born 3 October 1962. Attended Canterbury University, New Zealand 1980-84 (Bachelor of Law with Honours). Leisure interests include music and marathon running (when time permits), business and economic issues.

THURSTON, William G.
Bell Gully, Auckland +64 9 916 8800
Recommended in Corporate/M&A

WETHERELL, Dave
Russell McVeagh, Auckland 1 +64 9 367 8000
Recommended in Banking & Finance

NICARAGUA

Corporate/Commercial

NICARAGUA Leading firms (Corporate/Commercial)
1 Taboada & Asociados
2 Alvarado y Asociados
Munguia Vidaurre Chavez

Firms are listed alphabetically in each band.

Leading individuals (Corporate/Commercial)
1 CHAVEZ ESCOTTO Luis *Munguia Vidaurre Chavez*
DE ALVARADO Gloria Maria *Alvarado*
TABOADA Jose Evenor *Taboada & Asociados*
2 MUNGUIA ALVAREZ Juan Alvaro *Munguia Vidaurre Chavez*

Individuals are listed alphabetically in each band.

Taboada & Asociados (3 ptrs, 14 asscs) *Chambers'* researchers were impressed with the weight of market recommendation for a firm viewed as *"the leading corporate practice in the country."* Providing commercial and corporate advice to its foreign clients, the firm is representing private foreign clients in the current privatisation of the telecommunications sector. It also acted on loans from multilateral institutions to the Nicaraguan government. **Jose Evenor Taboada*** has an excellent reputation as *"an experienced and well-connected corporate lawyer."* **Clients:** IFC; CDC; Philip Morris; Sonu; Volvo; Hamilton Bank; Crédit Agricole.

Alvarado y Asociados (2 ptrs, 4 asscs) A *"high profile"* firm, strong in corporate, banking and trademark law. Its broad coverage includes mining, privatisation, tourism, telecommunications and the administration of ports. The *"networked"* firm advised a client in its bid to build a hotel in Nicaragua. **Gloria Maria de Alvarado*** is described by rivals as *"the firm's driving force."* **Clients:** Banks; mining companies; foreign corporates.

Munguia Vidaurre Chavez (3 ptrs, 5 asscs) A *"strong firm with exceptional lawyers,"* its corporate work includes foreign investment and trademarks advice. It is heavily involved in the privatisation of the Nicaraguan telecommunications sector. **Luis Chavez Escotto*** is *"devoted to the practice"* while **Juan Alvaro Munguia Alvarez*** is *"an entrepreneur and a fine lawyer."* **Clients:** Texaco; banks; American companies; finance houses.

Leaders' profiles – Nicaragua

CHAVEZ ESCOTTO, Luis
Munguia Vidaurre Chavez, Managua +505 266 7102

DE ALVARADO, Gloria Maria
Alvarado y Asociados, Managua +505 277 4028

MUNGUIA ALVAREZ, Juan Alvaro
Munguia Vidaurre Chavez, Managua +505 266 7102

TABOADA, Jose Evenor
Taboada & Asociados, Managua +505 268 3839 taboada@taboada.com.ni
Specialisation: Business and banking law, contracts, energy, telecommunications and privatisation.
Prof. Memberships: ABA and IBA.
Career: Admitted 1969, Nicaragua. President of the Central Bank of Nicaragua, 1992-1997; President of the Financiera Nicaraguense de Inversiones (a second tier bank), 1992-1997; Member of the Board of Directors of the Superintendency of Banks and Financial Institutions, 1992-1997; Professor of Law.
Personal: Born 7 February 1947. Education: Universidad de Chile (1969), Georgetown Law Center (1973), Parker School of Foreign and Comparative Law (1974), Cornell University (JSD Doctor of Science of Law, 1976). Program of Instructions for Lawyers PIL Harvard Law School 1999 and 2000.

N

NIGER

Corporate/Commercial

NIGER Leading firms (Corporate/Commercial)
1 Cabinet Kouaovi

Firms are listed alphabetically in each band.

Leading individuals (Corporate/Commercial)
1 KOUAOVI Bernard-Olivier *Cabinet Kouaovi*

Individuals are listed alphabetically in each band.

Cabinet Kouaovi (2 lawyers) Created two years after independence in 1962, this is the oldest law firm in Niger with a long history of experience in M&A, privatisation and restructuring. After interviews with clients & foreign experts our researchers found that, having succeeded his father in 1996, **Bernard-Olivier Kouaovi** is for some *"the only lawyer to use in Niger."* The firm acts for a number of high-profile French clients.
Clients: Groupe Castel (Braniger); Exxon; Société Financière Internationale; ICRISAT; France Telecom.

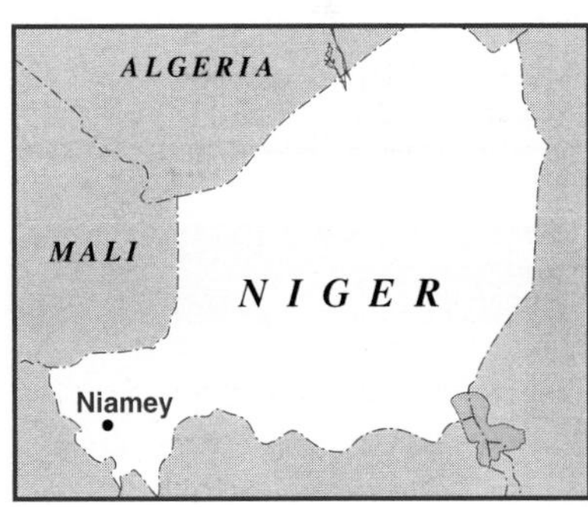

Leaders' profiles – Niger

KOUAOVI, Bernard-Olivier
Cabinet Kouaovi, Niamey +227 73 43 49

NIGERIA

Index

OVERVIEW: Over the past two years, Nigeria's first civilian government since 1983 has done much to help the continent's most populous nation emerge as a credible business environment. Law firms tend to be large by African standards, with those regularly engaged in international corporate and commercial work invariably found in Lagos. Many lawyers are western educated and more than capable of handling the scope and intensity of work Nigeria should witness over the next few years. The government's privatisation programme ranging from telecoms, electricity and petroleum refineries to banks, tourism and cement plants is creating a substantial deal flow. Energy is a particularly important sector; crude petroleum (at over two million barrels per day) accounts for more than 90% of total exports.

Corporate/Commercial

NIGERIA Leading firms (Corporate/Commercial)
1 Ajumogobia & Okeke
Aluko & Oyebode
2 Adepetun Caxton-Martins & Agbor
Banwo & Ighodalo
FO Akinrele & Co
Olaniwun Ajayi & Co
Udo Udoma & Belo-Osagie
3 Chief Rotimi Williams' Chambers
Strachan Partners

Firms are listed alphabetically in each band.

Leading individuals (Corporate/Commercial)
1 **AJAYI Koyinsola** *Olaniwun Ajayi & Co*
OKEKE Chris *Ajumogobia & Okeke*
2 **CAXTON-MARTINS Afolabi** *Adepetun Caxton*
IGHODALO Asue *Banwo & Ighodalo*
OYEBODE Gbenga *Aluko & Oyebode*
WILLIAMS Rotimi *Chief Rotimi Williams*
3 **AGBOR Dan** *Udo Udoma & Belo-Osagie*
AJUMOGOBIA Odein *Ajumogobia & Okeke*
AKINRELE Ade Dolapo *FO Akinrele & Co*
BELO-OSAGIE Myma *Udo Udoma & Belo-Osagie*
CANDIDE-JOHNSON Yemi *Strachan Partners*

Individuals are listed alphabetically in each band.

Ajumogobia & Okeke (6 ptrs, 17 asscs) A full service corporate/commercial law firm which acts exclusively for multi-national clients. The team has specific strength in project finance, foreign investment, privatisation, international trade and banking and finance. Also expanding into environmental law, the firm represented Mobil Oil following an oil spill.

"*Rainmaker and business-getter*" **Chris Okeke*** is a "*supremely versatile practitioner,*" renowned for advising the British government. His colleague **Odein Ajumogobia*** is "*a brilliant corporate lawyer with a lucid manner.*" The firm acted for South African Airways on its acquisition of the Lagos to New York route. **Clients:** Colgate-Palmolive; Philip Morris; Credit Suisse; SAA; foreign law firms.

Aluko & Oyebode (5 ptrs, 16 asscs) "*One of the best firms in the country,*" highly regarded at home and abroad, has built a broad-based corporate practice since its split from Ajumogobia & Okeke. Known for energy, banking and corporate finance, the firm's growth areas include telecommunications and the electricity industry.

A "*bright and effective team*" is headed by "*tough negotiator*" **Gbenga Oyebode***, admired for "*vigorously defending and promoting his clients' interests.*" Clients informed our researchers that he adopts a "*practical approach to most problems*" and is working with the IFC on the privatisation of the Lagos State Water Corporation. The firm also represented Mobile Telephone Networks South Africa on their Nigerian GSM bid. **Clients:** Citibank; Chase Manhattan; Morgan Stanley; SmithKline Beecham; Enron Inc.

Adepetun Caxton-Martins & Agbor (6 ptrs, 12 asscs) Relatively young commercial law firm which, although it has not enjoyed "*the head start of the older firms,*" will "*undoubtedly be one of the leading firms if they continue as they are.*" A notably eclectic workload includes energy, project finance, securitisation, banking, privatisation and M&A. "*Rugged and determined*" **Afolabi Caxton-Martins*** is noted for paying "*close attention to detail.*" The firm has recently advised major multinational corporations, banks and other financial institutions with respect to corporate restructurings, acquisitions and project finance transactions. **Clients:** IFC; Sodexho SA; Ajinomoto Inc Japan; Eiffel SA; Maersk Nigeria Ltd.

Banwo & Ighodalo (3 ptrs, 9 asscs) A "*forthright, honest*" firm with a substantial oil and gas practice, which also advises on capital markets, project finance, foreign investment, privatisation, telecommunications regulation, IPP work, and IP. Recently completed a $70 million capital markets transaction on behalf of Nigerian Breweries plc. "*Meticulous*" **Asue Ighodalo*** "*brings commercial realism to the table*" and has "*serious political connections.*" The firm advised Heineken on the acquisition of a stake in a Nigerian Brewery worth over $11 million. **Clients:** Heineken BV; NL Power; Cadbury Nigeria; Lever Brothers Nigeria; Unatrac International; National Council on Privatisation.

FO Akinrele & Co (4 ptrs, 11 asscs) Our researchers were told by competitors that this firm has a "*A young, dynamic and gung-ho team which has modernised its image.*" Especially renowned for energy and shipping advice, the firm has a reputation for "*meeting deadlines.*" **Ade**

Dolapo Akinrele* heads the commercial side of the firm, and is *"on his way to becoming one of the top lawyers in the country."* The firm represented Ocean & Oil Services Ltd on its $15 million acquisition by Unipetrol plc. **Clients:** International oil companies; Heidelberg Druckmaschinen AG.

Olaniwun Ajayi & Co (4 ptrs, 13 asscs) *"A force to be reckoned with,"* which handles cross-border M&A, securities, privatisations, banking, capital markets and project finance work. The *"focal point of the firm"* is capital markets specialist **Dr Koyinsola Ajayi***. He is described as *"highly intelligent, hard-working, thorough and impressive."* The firm acted with Arthur Andersen and Norton Rose on the privatisation of Nigerian Airways on a mandate from the IFC. **Clients:** Blue Circle Industries plc; British American Tobacco; Citibank; IFC; Nigeria LNG Ltd; Scancem International.

Udo Udoma & Belo-Osagie (6 ptrs, 10 asscs) The firm continues to thrive, with influential government connections said to *"give them access to a lot of big work."* A full-service corporate and commercial practice focuses on energy, privatisation, corporate restructuring and banking, serving a blue-chip clientele. **Dan Agbor*** *"anchors the firm,"* while **Myma Belo-Osagie*** is *"one of the leading lawyers in Nigeria,"* who can be *"trusted with complicated transactions."* The firm advised the Akwa Ibom Investment and Industrial Promotion Council over the privatisation of Champion Breweries and is working on the proposed merger of two major oil companies. **Clients:** Foreign and domestic merchant and investment banks; oil exploration companies; engineering companies; manufacturers and traders.

Chief Rotimi Williams' Chambers (5 ptrs, 24 asscs) Traditionally *"the foremost firm in Nigeria,"* the group is not considered to retain the profile of its salad days. It is best known for its litigation, but is also active in banking, foreign investment, arbitration and IP. At the heart of the firm is **Chief Rotimi Williams***. Although now 80 years of age, he is such an institution in Nigeria that he is known as *"Rotimi the law."* **Clients:** Shell; Médicins Sans Frontières; SmithKline Beecham; UPS; United Bank of Africa; G. Pappa.

Strachan Partners (3 ptrs, 7 asscs) The firm is clearly *"moving on to bigger and better things,"* and has made its name primarily in shipping and maritime work and also handles insurance, banking, aviation, telecommunications and government corporate work. When the vice-president of Nigeria appointed a telecoms sector reform implementation committee in February 2000, **Yemi Candide-Johnson*** was the only legal expert named on the committee. He is also a *"strong shipping lawyer."* The firm advised KLM on its aborted alliance with Alitalia. **Clients:** KLM; SDV; Torm Lines; Far Eastern Shipping Company of Russia; Texaco Panama Incorporation; United Bank for Africa plc; Ecobank International.

N

Energy & Natural Resources

NIGERIA Leading firms (Energy & Natural Resources)
1 Adepetun Caxton-Martins & Agbor
Aluko & Oyebode
Banwo & Ighodalo
2 Ajumogobia & Okeke
FO Akinrele & Co
Udo Udoma & Belo-Osagie

Firms are listed alphabetically in each band.

Leading individuals (Energy & Natural Resources)
1 ADEPETUN Sola *Adepetun Caxton-Martins*
IGHODALO Asue *Banwo & Ighodalo*
OYEBODE Gbenga *Aluko & Oyebode*
2 AJAYI Koyinsola *Olaniwun Ajayi & Co*
AKINRELE Ade Dolapo *FO Akinrele & Co*

Individuals are listed alphabetically in each band.

Adepetun Caxton-Martins & Agbor (2 ptrs, 2 asscs) A firm with *"vast experience"* in all matters relating to petroleum law. Energy expert **Sola Adepetun*** is on the executive board of the African Institute of Petroleum and lectures on oil and gas across the continent. The group advised two independent power producers on their establishment in Nigeria. **Clients:** Sasol Ltd; Texaco Overseas (Nigeria) Petroleum Co Ltd; PGS Exploration; Marathon Oil; Ocean Energy; JGC Group.

Aluko & Oyebode (2 ptrs, 2 asscs) A prominent firm in the oil and gas sector, which carries out both transactional and regulatory work. The *"experienced"* **Gbenga Oyebode*** is a *"strong practitioner."* The firm represented Brass Exploration Ltd (a subsidiary of Baker Hughes) in obtaining regulatory approvals and raising $120 million in financing for the development of the block. Also advised Shell Capital on a $14 million loan to aid the development of Nigerian oil fields. **Clients:** Baker Hughes; Schlumberger; Diamond Offshore Drilling; Sedco Forex Drilling; Petrobrás; Agip; Mobil Producing; Niger Delta Petroleum.

Banwo & Ighodalo (1 ptr, 3 asscs) The firm specialises in drafting joint venture agreements and offers corporate and tax advice to existing international companies. **Asue Ighodalo*** is *"prominent in the energy sector"* and has been involved on an arbitration on behalf of a major oil company in connection with a gas utilisation project. **Clients:** Agip; Shell; Elf.

Ajumogobia & Okeke (2 ptrs, 4 asscs) Notably active on energy financing, the team advised Credit Suisse First Boston on the international financing of Bonny Gas Transport Company. Also represented a consortium of European bankers in financing the development of new Nigerian oil fields, and advised the IFC on the LNG project. **Clients:** Mobil; international finance companies.

FO Akinrele & Co (2 ptrs, 3 asscs) **Ade Dolapo Akinrele*** is *"getting quite involved in the development of the privatisation of electricity,"* as well as being an established figure in the oil and gas industry. The firm works with ENP companies from the outset, establishing them in Nigeria, offering corporate legal advice and assisting them in liaising with the Nigerian Ministry of Petroleum Resources and the Nigerian tax authorities, Federal Inland Revenue. The firm advised Canadian Petroleum on the negotiations and arrangements leading up to the acquisition of a 40% interest (the legal maximum for foreign equity participation) in a Nigerian OPL. **Clients:** Exxon; Mobil; Canadian Petroleum; Conoco; BP Amoco.

Udo Udoma & Belo-Osagie (2 ptrs, 3 asscs) An active firm in the energy sector which regularly advises on contracts and the structure of long-term finance for oil companies. Also advised the

*See leaders' profiles on pages 514-515

National Electric Power Authority in relation to the establishment of the first industrial power project in Nigeria. **Clients:** National Electric Power Authority; international oil companies.

Other Notable Practitioner Dr Koyinsola Ajayi* of Olaniwun Ajayi & Co has an established reputation for advising local and foreign oil companies such as Shell, Elf, Agip and Niger Offshore. He is a veteran of the Nigerian LNG project, advised on the first IPP in Nigeria and worked on the West African Gas Line Project.

Leaders' profiles – Nigeria

N

ADEPETUN, Sola
Adepetun Caxton-Martins & Agbor, Lagos
+234 263 2164
sadepetun@nova.net.ng
Recommended in Energy & Natural Resources
Specialisation: Specialises in oil concession contracts, licensing and acquisitions, oil industry accreditation procedures, joint ventures, project structuring and financing, power purchase agreements and independent power projects.
Prof. Memberships: Nigerian Bar Association, International Bar Association, Executive Board, African Institute of Petroleum, International Faculty of the African petroleum Management Institute and the Oil and Gas Sector Reform Implementation Committee of the National Council on Privatisation in Nigeria.
Publications: Author 'Production Sharing Contracts – the Nigerian Experience', 'Nigeria: The Liquefied Natural Gas Project' and 'Inside Nigerian Oil'.
Career: Qualified in 1981; joined *O.O Koleoso & Co.*, Lagos in 1985; Partner, Energy Law Unit, *Adepetun, Caxton-Martins & Agbor*, 1991 to date.
Personal: Born 16 July, 1960. Attended University of Lagos,1977-81; London School of Economics, 1984 (LLM). Enjoys walking and playing scrabble.

AGBOR, Dan
Udo Udoma & Belo-Osagie, Lagos
+234 1 263 4831
uubo@infoweb.abs.net
Recommended in Corporate/M&A
Specialisation: Banking, finance, capital markets, power projects, taxation, joint ventures, and privatisation. Created first Nigerian global depository receipts programme. Currently, advising National Electric Power Authority on implementing various independent power projects, merger of two major oil companies, reviewing telecommunications laws for Nigerian government.
Prof. Memberships: Nigerian Bar Association, International Bar Association.
Publications: Several, on banking, capital markets, joint ventures.
Career: Lecturer, Rivers State College of Education: 1980-1981. Called to Nigerian Bar: 1986. Associate, *Ajumogobia, Okeke and Oyebode*: 1986-1987. Legal Officer (1987-1988); Product Manager (1988): Nigerian International Bank Limited (Citibank Nigeria). Associate (1990-1996), Partner (1996 to date), *Udo Udoma & Belo-Osagie*.
Personal: Born 7 January, 1960. Attended University of Calabar (BSc, political science: 1980); University of Benin (LLB 1985). Married with children. Enjoys reading, music and golf.

AJAYI, Koyinsola
Olaniwun Ajayi & Co, Lagos +234 1 264 2551
Recommended in Corporate/M&A, Energy & Natural Resources

AJUMOGOBIA, Odein
Ajumogobia & Okeke, Lagos +234 (01) 263 1138
odein@ajumogobiaokeke.com
Recommended in Corporate/M&A
Specialisation: Partner in the commercial litigation and arbitration department. Main areas of work include handling a range of corporate and commercial disputes before the Federal and State High Courts, the Court of Appeal and the Supreme Court of Nigeria. Very active in the area of international commercial arbitration. Lead advisor/counsel representing a major oil producing company in an oil spill matter, and co-ordinator of the resulting multi-party litigation involving over 700 cases.
Prof. Memberships: ICC International Court of Arbitration (Paris); Fellow of the Chartered Institute of Arbitrators FCI Arb. (London); Nigerian Bar Association; Nigerian Society of International Law; International Bar Association; American Society of International Law; American Bar Association (Associate Member).
Career: Admitted to Nigerian Bar July 1979; Assistant Lecturer, Department of Commercial & Industrial Law; University of Lagos 1979-1980; joined *Fred Egbe & Co* 1980-1983; Nigerian LNG Consultants 1983; Partner *Ajumogobia & Okeke* since 1984.
Personal: Born Lagos, Nigeria June 29 1956. Attended University of Lagos (LLB Honours, June 1978); Harvard Law School, Cambridge Massachusetts (LLM 1998). Leisure interests include squash and music.

AKINRELE, Ade Dolapo
F.O. Akinrele & Co, Lagos +234 1 269 3998 9
dolapo.akinrele@foakinrele.com
Recommended in Corporate/M&A, Energy & Natural Resources
Specialisation: Head of Corporate and Oil & Gas Department. Handled several corporate acquisitions, privatisations and mergers between 1990 and 2000. In 2000, acting for Ocean & Oil UK Limited on the acquisition of the 30% (US$14 million) shares of the Nigerian Government in Unipetrol Plc. 1998-1999, for CHIYODA Corporation (Japan) – corporate restructuring of Nigerian subsideries. 2000 – Adivising EXXON Corporation on Nigerian aspects of ExxonMobil merger. 1998 - 2000, advising Heidelberg Druckmanschinen AG on acquisition of graphics division worldwide of E.A.S. Limited, Denmark.
Prof. Memberships: Nigerian Association of Petroleum Explorationists; Nigerian Maritime Law Association; Nigerian Bar Association; International Bar Association.
Publications: Co-author, 2nd Edition – Nigerian Petroleum Law by Etikerentse. The Legal Implications of the Nigerian Energy Crises for Business Organisation.
Career: Called to the bar 1987, joined *F.O. Akinrele & Co* 1990, became Managing Partner 1999. Member – Editorial Board, Nigerian Maritime Law Journal. Nigerian delegate to the Comite Maritime International 1990. Life member, Bentham Law Society, University College, London. External legal counsel to: Exxon Nigeria and affiliates (now ExxonMobil); BP AMOCO Nigeria and affiliates; Canadian Petroleum (Nigeria) Limited (former subsidiary of Canadian Occidental Inc.) and affiliates between 19993 to date. Advised on acquisition of new ventures, oil prospecting licenses/mining leases in the Nigerian Petroleum Sector. Negotiated on their behalf, Production Sharing Contracts, tax and fiscal incentives with the Nigerian Government. Legal correspondent in Nigeria: The North of England (Protection & Indemnity Association), The American Club (Steamship Owners Mutual Protection & Indemnity Association Inc.). Advising Tanker owning members as regards Oil & Gas related Maritime Issues and Pollution matters. Presentation of papers at conferences and seminars in particular 'Legal aspects of Investment in the Nigerian Oil & Gas Industry', Houston (1992) and Calgary Oil & Gas show, Canada (1993) and West Africa Committee Seminar in London (1992).
Personal: Born 23 November 1964. Attended Clifton College, Bristol 1979-82, University of East Anglia and University College, London 1982-1986 (LLB, LLM). Interests include polo. Lives in Lagos, Nigeria.

BELO-OSAGIE, Myma
Udo Udoma & Belo-Osagie, Lagos
+234 1 263 4831
uubo@infoweb.abs.net; mybel@infoweb.abs.net
Recommended in Corporate/M&A
Specialisation: Energy, natural resources, telecommunications, foreign investment, privatisation. Current assignments: merger of major oil companies, reviewing telecommunications laws for Nigerian government.

Prof. Memberships: New York State Bar Association, Nigerian Bar Association, American Bar Association, Ghana Bar Association, International Bar Association, Telecommunications Lawyers' Association, ICC Group.
Publications: 'Foreign Investment in Nigeria', articles on petroleum and environmental law.
Career: Called to Ghanaian Bar (1977); New York Bar (1983); Nigerian Bar (1984). Associate, *Udo Udoma & Co.* (1983), Partner (1984). Member, Study Group on Monetisation of Fringe Benefits (1992); Nigerian Economic Summit Group.
Personal: Born 22 February 1954. Attended University of Ghana (LLB, 1975), Harvard Law School (LLM 1978), (SJD 1985). Trustee, various non-profit organisations. Enjoys travel, scrabble, reading. Married with four children.

CANDIDE-JOHNSON, Yemi
Strachan Partners, Lagos +234 1 263 4919
Recommended in Corporate/M&A

CAXTON-MARTINS, Afolabi
Adepetun Caxton-Martins & Agbor, Lagos +234 1 263 1960
aca@linkserve.com.ng
Recommended in Corporate/M&A
Specialisation: Partner in Coporate/Commercial Department. Specialising in general corporate affairs, mergers & acquisitions, foreign investment law and commercial matters. Diverse experience in establishment of local subsidiaries of foreign multinationals, foreign equity importation/repatriation, agency/shareholders agreements, technology transfer agreements and intellectual property protection. Consultant to commercial sections of various foreign embassies in Nigeria assisting in trade and investment promotion and protection.
Prof. Memberships: Nigerian Bar Association; International Bar Association; Pharmaceuticals Trade Marks Group, Vice President, AIPPI National Group in Nigeria.
Publications: Co-author of 'IP and the pharmaceutical industry in Nigeria'. A Euromoney 'Managing Intellectual Property' publication.
Career: Partner of *Adepetun, Caxton-Martins & Agbor* 1991 to present.
Personal: Born 18 June, 1961. Qualified University of London 1983. Leisure interests include golf. Lives in Ikoyi, Lagos.

IGHODALO, Asue
Banwo & Ighodalo, Lagos +234 1 2694724
Recommended in Corporate/M&A, Energy & Natural Resources

OKEKE, Chris
Ajumogobia & Okeke, Lagos +234 (01) 263 0586
chris@ajurmogobiaokeke.com
Recommended in Corporate/M&A
Specialisation: Partner in the corporate department. Main areas of work include rendering legal services to numerous corporate clients, by assisting them in setting up and organising their business in Nigeria; general corporate finance work, including acquisitions, divestitures and restructuring of private companies and businesses, shareholder and joint venture arrangements, banking and financial services work, including equity offerings; serves on various company boards and charitable organisations.
Prof. Memberships: Memberships: Nigerian Bar Association; International Bar Association; American Society of International Law.
Career: Admitted to Nigerian Bar July 1980; Joined *U.U. Uche & Associates* 1980-1982; *Tomisin, Thomas & Co.* 1982-1983; Partner, *Ajumogobia & Okeke* since 1984. Honorary Legal Advisor to Her Majesty's Government in Nigeria since 1989.
Personal: Born Sapele, Delta State, January 15 1952. Attended Xavier University of Louisiana (BSc 1975); Southern University of Louisiana (Juris Doctor 1978); Georgetown University Law Centre, Washington DC (LLM 1979). Leisure interests include sailing, music and art.

OYEBODE, Gbenga
Aluko & Oyebode, Lagos +234 1 260 0080
goyebode@aluko-oyebode.com
Recommended in Corporate/M&A, Energy & Natural Resources
Specialisation: Heads Corporate and Commercial, Natural Resources, and Telecommunications practices; experienced negotiator. Highlights: advising Enron International, currently implementing the first private independent power production initiative in Nigeria; representing Shell Capital Services Limited extending a facility to an indigenous petroleum company for the financing and development of oil mining blocks; advising Mobile Telephone Networks International Limited currently bidding for a telecommunications licence; advised Electronic Media Network Limited, South Africa and SuperSport International Holdings, South Africa in the first dual listing of a foreign company on The Nigerian Stock Exhange; has presented papers at various international conferences.
Prof. Memberships: Nigerian Bar Association; American Bar Association; American Society of International Law; International Bar Association (Section on Energy and National Resources Law).
Career: Managing Partner in *Aluko & Oyebode* (Barristers, Solicitors and Trademark Agents), 1993 to date; partner in *Ajumogobia, Okeke, Oyebode & Aluko* (Barristers, Solicitors & Notaries), 1985-1992; Associated with *White & Case*, 14 Wall Street, New York, 1982-1983, Gulf Oil Company, Lagos and Houston, 1983-1985.
Personal: Born 30 March 1959. University of Ife, Ile-Ife (LLB Hons) 1979; University of Pennsylvania, Philadelphia (LLM) 1982.

WILLIAMS, FRA Rotimi
Chief Rotimi Williams' Chambers, Lagos +234 1 496 1916
Recommended in Corporate/M&A

NORTH KOREA

Corporate/Commercial: Foreign Firms

NORTH KOREA: Foreign Firms Leading firms (Corporate/Commercial)
1 Coudert Brothers
Kim & Chang
Lee & Ko

Firms are listed alphabetically in each band.

Leading individuals (Corporate/Commercial)
1 CHU HYUN Hong *Kim & Chang*
JONES Jeffrey *Kim & Chang*
LEE Tae Hee *Lee & Ko*
O'BRIEN Timothy *Coudert Brothers*

Individuals are listed alphabetically in each band.

Coudert Brothers (Hong Kong) (1 ptr) Tim **O'Brien** is regarded as a specialist representing Korean businesses in the US. The firm advised Aurora Partners Ltd (APL) in connection with its joint venture with the Korea Magnesia Clinker Industry Group, a North Korean government agency. This is the first joint venture in North Korea of an American-owned company. **Clients:** Mainly US clients.

Kim & Chang (Seoul) (2 ptrs, 5 asscs) A large South Korean firm, it advises potential investors in North Korea on infrastructure, commercial, financial and transportation issues. Head of the US Chamber of Commerce, **Jeffrey Jones** has a *"fine reputation born of many years of dedicated service"*, while colleague **Hong Chu Hyun** is *"highly respected and busy"* in this area. **Clients:** ING; Shell.

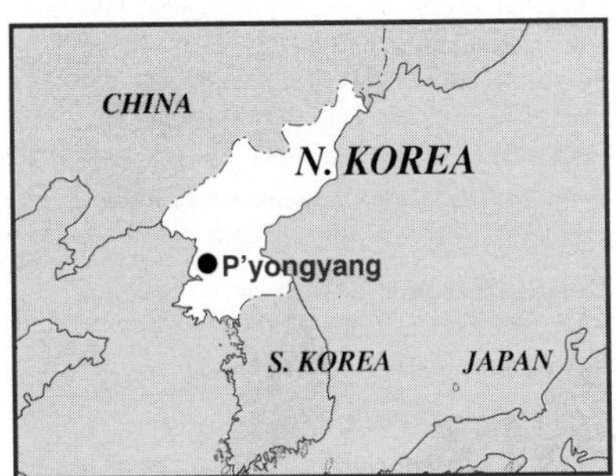

Lee & Ko (Seoul) Key to the firm's success is the solid reputation of **Tae Hee Lee**, regarded as an active player in the foreign investment market. A full service firm, it focuses on corporate M&A, restructuring, telecoms and IP. **Clients:** Kpco and other leading companies in South Korea.

Leaders' profiles – North Korea

CHU HYUN, Hong
Kim & Chang, Seoul +82 2 3703 1114

JONES, Jeffrey
Kim & Chang, Seoul +82 2 3703 1114

LEE, Tae Hee
Lee & Ko, Seoul +82 2 772 4000
cen@lawleeko.co.kr
Specialisation: Founding and senior partner of *Lee & Ko*. Main areas of work are in international investment, licensing, arbitration, insurance and aviation matters. Has acted as chief legal counsel in handling an extensive range of legal work for Korean Air, including the coordination of relevant litigation and dealings with insurers in all cases relating to Korean Air accidents; has acted as legal counsel in connection with *Lee & Ko*'s representation of the LG Group in the LG Group's sale of its controlling interest in its semiconductor subsidiary to Hyundai; has acted as legal counsel in connection with *Lee & Ko*'s representation of Hanil Bank in connection with the formation of Hanvit Bank (Korea's largest banking institution) out of the merger of Hanil Bank and Commercial Bank of Korea; has established at *Lee & Ko* a highly-regarded intellectual property department of 14+ patent attorneys and a client list that includes Silicon Graphics and Sybase; has lectured on various aspects of international business law at numerous law conferences, symposiums and other gatherings of professional, business and governmental associations both in Korea and overseas; has written articles on numerous and diverse legal topics.
Prof. Memberships: Korean Bar Association; California Bar Association; American Bar Association; International Bar Association; Inter-Pacific Bar Association; International Association of Defense Counsel; Korea-Japan Lawyers Association; Licensing Executives Society; Korean Patent Attorneys Association; International Association for the Protection of Industrial Property; International Trademark Association.
Career: Admitted to Bar: 1963 (Korea), 1976 (California). Career History: Judge Advocate Officer, Korean Army, 1963-66. Judge: Seoul District Civil Court, 1966-68; Seoul District Criminal Court, 1969-71; Foreign Associate, *Graham & James*, Los Angeles, 1974-77; Arbitrator, Korean Commercial Arbitration Board, 1978 - present; Conciliator, International Centre for Settlement of Investment Disputes, 1980 - Present; Lecturer, Judicial Research and Training Institute, Supreme Court of Korea, 1982 - Present; Legal Counsel, Korean Foreign Trade Association, 1985 - Present; Arbitrator, American Arbitration Association, 1986 - Present; Arbitrator, China International Economic & Trade Arbitration Commission, 1993 - Present; Arbitrator, Singapore International Arbitration Centre, 1998 - Present; Arbitrator, British Columbia International Commercial Arbitration Centre, 1998 - Present.
Personal: Born May 9, 1940 in Korea. Education: College of Law, Seoul National University (LL.B., 1962); Graduate School of Law, Seoul National University, 1962-63; Harvard Law School (LL.M., 1971; J.D., 1974). Has a wife and 3 children. Lives in Seoul, Korea.

O'BRIEN, Timothy
Coudert Brothers, Hong Kong +852 2218 9100

NORWAY

Index

OVERVIEW: Norway's energy sector has been expanding with new oil projects coming on line and liberalisation in the hydro-electric sector. The government is considering structures to actively manage its participation, including the disposal of up to a third of Statoil, and reorganisation in the Gas industry. These are good conditions for newly merged Arntzen de Besche. Arntzen Underland's energy practice, edging ahead this year under Christian Michelet, gains greater critical mass and financial expertise from de Besche & Co. In the long term, IT and anti-trust work should become more important in the corporate sphere, while medium sized firms are set to struggle in an increasingly, competitive international market.

N

Banking & Finance

NORWAY Leading firms (Banking & Finance)
1 Bugge, Arentz-Hansen & Rasmussen
Wiersholm, Mellbye & Bech
Wikborg, Rein & Co
2 Advokatfirmaet Schjødt AS
Thommessen Krefting Greve Lund
3 Arntzen de Besche
Kluge Advokatfirma ANS
Simonsen Musæus

Firms are listed alphabetically in each band.

Leading individuals (Banking & Finance)
1 **BJØRNSTAD Finn** *Wikborg, Rein & Co*
HAUKALI Bernhard *Wikborg, Rein & Co*
MYHRE Finn *Bugge, Arentz-Hansen*
RAMM Erik *Wiersholm, Mellbye & Bech*
2 **DAMM Wilhelm** *Advokatfirmaet Schjødt AS*
DOBROWEN Kim *Thommessen Krefting Greve*
IRGENS Einar *Advokatfirmaet Schjødt AS*
LIND Erling *Wiersholm, Mellbye & Bech*
RINGDAL Rolf Johan *Bugge, Arentz-Hansen*
3 **BRECHAN Peter** *Haavind Vislie*
BRUN-LIE Nicolas *Wiersholm, Mellbye & Bech*
HOLM Sverre *Kluge Advokatfirma ANS*
LANGE Viggo *Kluge Advokatfirma ANS*
STEEN Sven Iver *Arntzen de Besche*

Individuals are listed alphabetically in each band.

Bugge, Arentz-Hansen & Rasmussen (5 ptrs, 5 asscs) *"Business-like"* department with a tough, commercial attitude, which is considered by clients and competitors to occupy *"one of the strongest positions in the Norwegian market."* Transactionally oriented and with a presence in London, the firm has particular strength working for international and Scandinavian investment banks. Capital markets work forms the core of the practice, although the team is also involved in such matters as loan agreements, commercial paper programmes, acquisition financing and syndicated lending. *"Real gentleman"* **Finn Myhre*** is *"an experienced and skilled finance lawyer,"* while *"respected business lawyer"* **Rolf Johan Ringdal*** is *"a serious and reliable practitioner."* The team assisted the banks providing the syndicated loan for the acquisition by Nordic Capital of Nyco Pharma. **Clients:** Postenbank; Fokus Bank; KLP; Storebrand; Industri Kapital.

Wiersholm, Mellbye & Bech (6 ptrs, 7 asscs) Traditionally renowned for its banking expertise, the firm still has one of the largest practices in this sector. A comprehensive caseload includes advice on all types of asset financing, acquisition financing and syndicated loans, as well as capital markets work. Regularly representing a number of Norwegian and international banks, the group also undertakes an increasing number of securitisations.

The *"outstanding"* **Erik Ramm*** is considered by rivals to be *"thorough, experienced and civil in negotiations, even though he's as tough as stone."* He is assisted by a strong department including the experienced **Erling Lind***, *"a good, practical finance lawyer,"* and the *"technically adept"* **Nicolas Brun-Lie***. The team advised Union Bank of Norway and Den Norske Bank on a NOK4.8 billion loan to TRG Europe BV for the acquisition of shares in Aker RGI. **Clients:** Danske Bank; Christiania Bank; Den Norske Bank; Union Bank of Norway; Fokus Bank ASA; SEB; Finansbanken ASA.

Wikborg, Rein & Co (15 ptrs, 25 asscs) *"Among the largest and most ambitious in this sector,"* the firm is regularly seen advising both established Norwegian banks and leading international financial institutions. Particularly strong in the equity market, the firm was involved in many of last year's leading IPOs, as well as increasing its profile in debt financing and project financing. An expanding department also maintains an involvement in acquisition finance, as well as assisting banks in regulatory work.

"Easy to work with and very professional," **Bernhard Haukali*** was recommended to our researchers for his *"excellent"* drafting skills, while **Finn Bjørnstad**'s* commercial acumen continues to be well received. The firm represented Christiania Bank over the acquisition financing of Swebus, a complex mezzanine financing involving US bonds and the total refinancing of the Swebus group. **Clients:** Nordic Capital; ABN AMRO; Deutsche Bank; CBK; Den Norske Bank; Union Bank of Norway; CSFB; Goldman Sachs; Alfred Berg; Crédit Agricole; First Securities.

Advokatfirmaet Schjødt AS (3 ptrs, 3 asscs) *"Definitely on the way up,"* the firm is considered by the market to be expanding and *"improving its activity in this area."* Often seen on ship financings, the group has good relations with a number of domestic banks, as well as assisting international

*See leaders' profiles on pages 521-525

financial institutions entering Norway, especially on the regulatory side. *"First class"* **Wilhelm Damm*** is *"technically superb,"* while the *"versatile"* **Einar Irgens*** is *"business focused."* The firm acted for Christiania and a syndicate of banks on the financing and most recent refinancing of Prosafe. The team was also involved in the financing by which Leif acquired 50% of Høegh, involving the takeover by the latter of seven vessels from Ugland. **Clients:** Föreningspar Banken; Unibank; Christiania Bank; Sparbanken Mit Norge.

N

Thommessen Krefting Greve Lund (3 ptrs, 6 asscs) Famed for its corporate prowess, the firm's banking and finance profile has not been as noticeable this year. The team's leading player, the *"outstanding"* **Kim Dobrowen***, is *"a fine negotiator with a breadth of experience which demands your attention,"* but his corporate/M&A practice also claims much of his time. Nevertheless, this is a *"high-quality firm,"* whose varied workload includes big-ticket international financings, drafting loan documentation and capital markets transactions for a mix of foreign and domestic clients. The firm advised Thorne on the securitisation of its Nordic rental businesses. **Clients:** MeritaNordbanken; Thorne.

Arntzen de Besche (6 ptrs, 8 asscs) Held in high regard among clients and competitors for its work on framework agreements, the firm is seen more on regulatory matters, where **Sven Iver Steen*** has an estimable name. However, this newly merged operation also advises on a broader portfolio of finance and securities transactions, and has substantially increased its profile in capital markets and aircraft financing, where it represents two Norwegian commercial airlines. Additionally, the team has advised a number of domestic commercial and savings banks, recently assisting a number of them on the acquisition of Dyno. **Clients:** BN Bank; MCB; Den Norske Bank; Gjensidige Nor.

Kluge Advokatfirma ANS (3 ptrs, 2 asscs) Generally to be seen advising lenders, the firm has assisted a number of banks on transaction structures, loan documents and securities. Also involved in syndicated loans, aircraft and ship financing, asset leasing and acquisition financing, the group acts for a range of foreign and domestic financial institutions. *"A clever ship finance lawyer,"* **Sverre Holm*** is *"a sound lawyer,"* while **Viggo Lange*** is *"easy-going and good to work with."* The team advised Chase Manhattan on a short-term credit facility for a private client. **Clients:** Chase Manhattan International Ltd; CBK; Nordlandsbanken.

Simonsen Musæus (3 ptrs, 2 asscs) Historically strong in ship, aircraft and project finance, the firm *"certainly has the people and the skills"* in these areas, but also performs secured lending work, mainly for German and Dutch banks. Increasingly active in public regulatory work, the team has been involved in the establishment of credit finance institutions and the granting of concessions by Norwegian authorities. The team represented the arranging banks on a syndicated loan to Russian-controlled shipping groups, and advised on the debt restructuring of a Norwegian shipping company. **Clients:** Christiania Bank; Nordlandsbanken; Landesbank Schleswig-Holstein; Hamburgische Landesbank.

Other Notable Practitioner Peter Brechan* of recently merged firm Haavind Vislie is seen working for clients such as Handelsbanken, CBK and SEB Finance, and is considered *"a pleasant and able"* practitioner by his peers.

Corporate/M&A

Bugge, Arentz-Hansen & Rasmussen (11 ptrs, 26 asscs) In the opinion of the market this firm is *"beyond the rest."* Although competition is stiff, BAHR's fantastic client base, M&A focus and *"machine-like"* efficiency keep it slightly ahead of the pack. Active on the range of transactional work, the firm has particular strength in financial services, energy and the emerging sectors of IT, telecoms and pharmaceuticals and is an important advisor to the government on privatisations such as the Telenor IPO. The *"dominant presence"* here is renowned client-getter **Knut Brundtland***, *"a fine negotiator and team leader." "Charismatic"* **Bjørn Reed*** is *"good at getting business,"* while *"academically strong"* **Gudmand Knudsen*** has a high standing for his advisory work and makes his debut in the rankings this year. **Trond Sanfelt*** *"has a good brain"* and is visible on the tax aspects of transactional work. The firm represented Star Cruises on its NOK8.9 billion acquisition of NCL Holding, and also advised on the acquisition by Aker Maritime of a 26.5% stake in Aerner. **Clients:** Aker RGI ASA; Volvo; General Electric; Storebrand; GlaxoWellcome; Netcom; Morgan Stanley; Goldman Sachs; Deutsche Bank; the Norwegian Government.

Thommessen Krefting Greve Lund (6 ptrs, 12 asscs) *"You never go wrong if you use Thommessen."* Although the firm has an established tradition of acting for 'old money' clients, it is considered by competitors to have modernised skilfully, gaining a reputation for advice in hi-tech matters and a client base ranging from traditional industry to the new economy. *"Soft-spoken"* **Kim Dobrowen*** is *"strong academically"* and *"exudes quality,"* while **Carl-Erik Krefting*** is *"commercial, smart and good at making things happen."* The firm acts for a variety of Norwegian clients and an increasing proportion of international corporates and investment banks on big-ticket M&A and international IPOs. Represented Dyno on its acquisition by Industricapital for around NOK5.5 billion and Elkjop on its £444 million sale to Dixons. **Clients:** MeritaNordbanken; Dyno; Telenor; Norsk Hydro.

Wiersholm, Mellbye & Bech (8 ptrs, 17 asscs) *"Certainly on the rise,"* the firm is widely known for a first class banking and finance practice, but its *"energy and ambition"* have also cemented the corporate team's place among the market leaders. Active in cross-border M&A, restructurings and joint ventures, the team's client base comprises major global and national companies, with notable strength in the financial sector. *"Technically good"* **Erik Thyness*** *"gets it right and enjoys a good rapport with clients"* and the firm's increasing profile can largely be attributed to his efforts. *"Solid"* and *"user-friendly"* **Per Raustøl*** also wins market plaudits, while newly ranked **Andreas Mellbye*** is *"a deal-doer"* with *"important clients."* Acted for NCL Holding on its acquisition by Star Cruises for NOK8.9 billion, and Norsk Hydro on its NOK3.8 billion sale of Hydro Seafoods. The team also represented the joint global co-ordinators on the privatisation of Telenor. **Clients:** Norsk Hydro; Umoe; Morgan Stanley; Scandinavia Online; NCL Holding ASA.

Wikborg, Rein & Co (14 ptrs, 20 asscs) Traditional strength in shipping at the firm is considered to have been *"efficiently re-focused on capital markets and M&A."* Increasingly focused on emerging markets, the firm has strength in IT, telecoms, banking and finance, while last year's acquisition of three partners from Gundersen &

NORWAY Leading firms (Corporate/Mergers & Acquisitions)
1 Bugge, Arentz-Hansen & Rasmussen
2 Thommessen Krefting Greve Lund
Wiersholm, Mellbye & Bech
Wikborg, Rein & Co
3 Advokatfirmaet Schjødt AS
4 Arntzen de Besche
Advokatfirmaet Selmer DA
5 Kluge Advokatfirma ANS
Advokatfirmaet Steenstrup Stordrange DA

Firms are listed alphabetically in each band.

Leading individuals (Corporate/Mergers & Acquisitions)
1 **BRUNDTLAND Knut** *Bugge, Arentz-Hansen*
DOBROWEN Kim *Thommessen Krefting*
KJØRNÆS Arne Didrik *Wikborg, Rein & Co*
THYNESS Erik *Wiersholm, Mellbye & Bech*
2 **CHRISTIANSEN Erling** *Advokatfirmaet Schjødt AS*
GISVOLD Marius *Wikborg, Rein & Co*
KREFTING Carl-Erik *Thommessen Krefting*
REED Bjørn *Bugge, Arentz-Hansen*
3 **ENDRESEN Clement** *Kluge Advokatfirma ANS*
GREVE Einar *Wikborg, Rein & Co*
JANSEN Jan *Arntzen de Besche*
KNUDSEN Gudmand *Bugge, Arentz-Hansen*
MELLBYE Andreas *Wiersholm, Mellbye & Bech*
RAUSTØL Per *Wiersholm, Mellbye & Bech*
SANFELT Trond *Bugge, Arentz-Hansen*
STEENSTRUP Morten *Steenstrup Stordrange DA*
TYSLAND Sverre *Advokatfirmaet Selmer DA*

Individuals are listed alphabetically in each band.

Co has improved the department's influence within traditional industry. The addition of a Singapore office to existing UK and Japanese offices testifies to the global ambitions of an organisation which is active in big-ticket M&A for a range of Norwegian and international clients. Pre-eminent in a strong team is *"hard-working"* **Arne Didrik Kjørnæs***, praised by clients and rivals for his *"breadth of understanding of the issues."* **Marius Gisvold*** is *"clever, able and enthusiastic,"* while *"terrier"* **Einar Greve*** is respected for his commercial acumen. The firm acted for Dixons on its £444 million acquisition of retail group Elkjop and advised Telia mobile on its acquisition of a 51% stake in Netcom for $2.58 billion. **Clients:** General Electric Canada Inc; Christiania Bank; Merkantildata ASA; Telia; Software Innovation ASA.

Advokatfirmaet Schjødt AS (7 ptrs, 13 asscs) Large and ambitious, the firm has grown rapidly and now has offices in most of areas of Norway. Traditionally associated with Norwegian brokerage firms, the department also works closely with US companies, representing large foreign industrial investors as well as an impressive range of domestic clients. Especially active in the energy and financial service sectors, the firm's strength in venture capital gives it a high profile in the IT and telecoms sectors. *"Knowledgeable, experienced and clever"* **Erling Christiansen*** is felt in the market to be *"the core of the practice."* The firm represented ABB on its acquisition of the offshore assets of Umoe, and acted for Stepstone on the Norwegian aspects of its £500 million IPO. **Clients:** ABB; Stepstone; Enitel ASA; Nera ASA; Panfish ASA; Exxon.

Arntzen De Besche (6 ptrs, 6 asscs) A high quality practice whose niche strength in energy and *"real blue-chip clients"* drives its corporate work. Formerly Arntzen, Underland & Co, the firm has *"a larger proportion of leading lawyers than their size suggests."* The firm's merger with former Denton International firm De Besche & Co has been well-received in the market. Alongside energy, the firm works regularly with international companies entering Norway and financial institutions, and has diversified into the new economy. A talented team includes *"gifted young lawyer"* **Jan Jansen***. The team acted for Shell on its acquisition of Mongstad and its acquisition of Fina's portfolio of petrol stations. **Clients:** Shell; Microsoft; BN Bank; Total Fina; Carneval Corporation.

Advokatfirmaet Selmer DA (10 ptrs, 20 asscs) *"Pretty active,"* the practice has grown fast into one of the country's largest firms. Strongly transactionally focused, the corporate team regularly advises on cross-border deals, typically involving Norwegian target companies. M&A, restructurings, divestitures and general corporate advice constitute the core of the caseload, and the firm is involved on a small but growing number of IPOs. **Sverre Tysland*** is one of the firm's highest-profile partners and is considered by rivals to be *"a fine ambassador."* The team represented Sparebank 1 Gruppen AS on its NOK3.3 billion acquisition of VÅR Gruppen. **Clients:** Rolls Royce; Xerox; Proctor & Gamble; Kraft Foods; Norsk Hydro; SEB.

Kluge Advokatfirma ANS (6 ptrs, 6 asscs) *"Known for the consistently good quality of its work,"* the firm is home to a number of *"excellent lawyers,"* although it is considerably smaller than the market leaders. Advising a predominantly domestic clientele, the corporate team has been involved on some big-ticket cross-border transactions. *"Tough"* and *"academic"* **Clement Endresen*** is a *"good all-round lawyer"* who *"knows the financial sector."* The firm represented Lyse Energi in the sale of ElTele Rogaland to Tele1 Europe, and the NOK200 Million sale of Alliance Informasjonssystemer AS. **Clients:** Rasmussen Group; Kverneland Group; IPC Group; Frontline Management.

Advokatfirmaet Steenstrup Stordrange DA (7 ptrs, 12 asscs) *"By far the most ambitious law firm in Norway,"* it has most recently opened an office in Trondheim. Heavily indebted to *"able, ambitious and aggressive"* **Morten Steenstrup***, the firm represents a range of international and domestic concerns and is especially active in the new economy, including the media and healthcare sectors. Assisted Tele1 Europe on its NOK 717 million acquisition of ElTele Rogaland and advised Getronics on its NOK1.8 billion take over by Merkantil Data. **Clients:** UPC; Tele1 Europe; Cello; KPM Quest; Razorfish; Danske Bank.

N

*See leaders' profiles on pages 521-525

Energy & Natural Resources

NORWAY Leading firms (Energy & Natural Resources)
1 Arntzen de Besche
2 Advokatfirmaet Schjødt AS
3 Bugge, Arentz-Hansen & Rasmussen
Kvale & Co
Thommessen Krefting Greve Lund
4 Wikborg, Rein & Co
5 Hjort
Advokatfirmaet Selmer DA
Wiersholm, Mellbye & Bech
6 Haavind Vislie

Firms are listed alphabetically in each band.

Leading individuals (Energy & Natural Resources)
1 **KVALE Anders** *Kvale & Co*
MICHELET Christian *Arntzen de Besche*
2 **BRUUSGAARD Christian** *Thommessen Krefting*
SAMUELSEN Erik *Thommessen Krefting*
SVOREN Rune *Bugge, Arentz-Hansen*
3 **SOLLUND Stig** *Bugge, Arentz-Hansen*
4 **HØEG RASMUSSEN Annikken** *Schjødt AS*
JANSEN Jan *Arntzen de Besche*
REIN John *Wikborg, Rein & Co*
STINESSEN Stein Erik *Hjort*
Individuals are listed alphabetically in each band.

Arntzen de Besche (4 ptrs, 6 asscs) *"Serious competitors to everyone,"* the firm is renowned primarily for its oil and gas expertise and the strength of its clientele. Acting on all offshore and some on-shore legal work for Shell and TotalFina, it advises on all energy-related regulatory and transactional matters. Our researchers were impressed by the weight of recommendation for *"energetic and capable,"* **Christian Michelet*** who is *"a key player in the Norwegian market,"* while **Jan Jansen*** *"cleverly combines energy law with taxation expertise."* Indeed, the firm is considered to have one of the country's top three energy taxation practices. Not so well known in electricity, the firm still provides assistance to producers and network companies on issues including electricity sales contracts and gas purchase contracts.

The firm represented the Statfjord Group on a NOK 500 million royalty claim against the Norwegian state, and advised the Ministry of Oil and Energy on the possible privatisation of Statoil and the reorganisation of the Norwegian gas industry. **Clients:** TotalFina; Shell; Ministry of Oil and Energy; Naturkraft.

Advokatfirmaet Schjødt AS (8 ptrs, 2 asscs) *"Among the leaders in oil and gas litigation,"* the firm is acknowledged by rivals to have established a superb client base of major international and domestic clients. Although Arnold Rørholt is now concentrating largely on his board appointments, the department retains a number of highly experienced practitioners, including **Annikken Høeg Rasmussen***, who *"has been doing oil and gas since the industry arrived in Norway,"* and is currently leading a team on the Balder dispute, the largest Norwegian litigation in history. With long experience of working on complex cases, the firm is active in areas such as contract law and devising joint operating agreements, and is increasingly visible in the electricity sector acting for producers and distributors. Advised a Nordic power exchange in establishing a new power exchange abroad. **Clients:** BP Amoco; Exxon Mobil; Fortum Petroleum; Idemitsu.

Bugge, Arentz-Hansen & Rasmussen (5 ptrs, 9 asscs) Historically one of the leading oil and gas firms in Norway, it has the strength in depth to enable it to represent a diverse client base of international and Norwegian firms on complex issues involving, for example, the relationship between licensees and the ministry. However, market opinion has identified the move of Ola Mestad (*"their leading player in oil and gas"*) into a consultancy role as a potential source of weakness.

In electricity, the firm has particular experience in transactional work and a strong department which includes **Rune Svoren***, *"a project leader and a strong individual."* The respected **Stig Sollund*** fronts one of the best energy taxation practices in Norway. The team acted on the NOK 10 billion purchase by Statkraft of minority controlling ownership of three publicly-owned companies. **Clients:** Statkraft; Oslo Energi Holdings ASA; Navion; Aker Maritime.

Kvale & Co (2 ptrs, 3 asscs) *"Always on the other side,"* despite its smaller size, the firm continues to take high ranking. *"In quality terms, they belong among the best."* Traditionally more visible in oil and gas, the team's profile owes much to its work for state-owned giant Statoil, notably in litigation. Although conflicts still limit the amount of work the firm can do for other oil companies, it is now increasingly active in transactional work and general commercial advice within the electricity sector. Name partner **Anders Kvale*** is respected in the market as a *"skilled professional"* with years of relevant experience. The firm represented Statoil and Norsk Hydro on a major dispute relating to the ownership rights of the Troll field. **Clients:** Statoil; Norsk Hydro.

Thommessen Krefting Greve Lund (3 ptrs, 2 asscs) Generally seen as the leading electricity firm, it *"certainly has more work on traditional electricity matters than anyone else."* Pre-eminent in this field is **Erik Samuelsen***, who is an *"intelligent and forthright"* electricity litigation expert. Although less well known for its oil and gas practice, the firm does represent oil producers on restructuring and litigation, and has an excellent energy taxation department, headed by the *"top-rank"* **Christian Bruusgaard***. The firm has advised the Ministry of Oil and Energy on the privatisation of Statoil and the reorganisation of the state's direct financial interest in the North Sea. **Clients:** Eurokraft; CPP-Transgas; Agip.

Wikborg, Rein & Co (4 ptrs, 6 asscs) Considered to have a well-balanced oil and gas and electricity profile, *"the firm retains a fairly strong position"* overall. Tilted towards international clients, especially in the electricity sector, the team advises on issues including electricity purchase and sale agreements, gas contracts, licensing issues, fabrication contracts and the reorganisation of the gas sector. Although also active in other areas, *"good generalist"* **John Rein*** still has a commended energy practice and was recommended by competitors for his *"understanding of the industry."* The firm acted on the sale and acquisition of Norwegian electricity assets, and advised foreign companies seeking licences to operate on the Norwegian continental shelf. **Clients:** Vattenfall; Eastern Group; Enron Europe.

Hjort (5 ptrs, 5 asscs) The firm's position as advisors to the union of municipalities gives it *"a special role within the electricity sector."* This involves advising the association and its 154 members on issues such as mergers and acquisitions, restructuring, tax and the sale of shares. Its work in lobbying the government on behalf of the municipalities, and advising on licence and tax legislation in the aftermath of the liberalisation of the energy sector, has given it a reputation for *"a fine understanding of how the regulatory framework works."* *"Impressive character"* **Stein Erik Stinessen*** is the team's stand-out practitioner. The firm recently headed the lobbying for the municipalities in connection with Parliament's pro-

*See leaders' profiles on pages 521-525

posed energy taxes. **Clients:** Association of Hydro Power Municipalities (LVK).

Advokatfirmaet Selmer DA (4 ptrs, 4 asscs) *"A force on the distribution side,"* this ambitious, expanding firm is seen *"doing a lot in the electricity trading sector"* and has a good reputation for the quality of its restructuring work. The team has expertise on M&A within the energy sector, reorganisation and conversions of local authority interests and negotiating concessions, as well as advising on the legislative framework. Much less visible in oil and gas, the firm nonetheless advises on small-ticket transactions and contractual work. Represented Vestfold Kraft on its merger with SKK and its NOK 4.8 billion private placement. **Clients:** Vestfold Kraft AS; Oslo Energi Produksjo AS; Viken Energinett AS.

Wiersholm, Mellbye & Bech (3 ptrs, 3 asscs) More involved in the electricity sector than oil and gas, the firm has been less visible in the market this year. Nevertheless, its large client base and depth of expertise, particularly in financing, tax structuring and corporate acquisitions, involves it in substantial transactional work. The team has advised on a number of transactions and restructurings involving production facilities owned by municipalities. Assisted a loan syndicate in granting a $90 million secured revolving credit facility to Fred Olsen Drilling. **Clients:** Statnet; Statkraft; Hafslund.

Haavind Vislie (6 ptrs, 6 asscs) Once the leading authority for advice on the establishment of power plants, this newly merged firm has *"a sound position in the electricity sector."* Typically representing power companies, the firm advises shareholders on issues such as incorporation. In the oil and gas field, the team generally acts on behalf of suppliers. The group has advised on a number of mergers between local power companies and incorporations. **Clients:** TBL; Around 50% of the Norwegian Municipalities.

N

Leaders' profiles – Norway

BJØRNSTAD, Finn
Wikborg, Rein & Co, Oslo +47 22 82 75 00
finn.bjornstad@wrco.no
Recommended in Banking & Finance
Specialisation: Majority of clients among Norwegian and foreign banks and shipping companies; Den norske Bank ASA, Christiania Bank og Kreditkasse ASA, Union Bank of Norway, Chase Manhattan Bank N.V., ABN AMRO Bank N.V., Den Danske Bank, Deutsche Bank AG, Fortis Bank (Nederland) N.V. and Crèdit Agricole Indosuez. Has in recent years worked particularly with Norwegian and cross border acquisition project financing and various types of other structured financing. Also assisting clients working in the private equity market, including the Pareto Group and the Fearnley Group.
Prof. Memberships: Norwegian Bar Association.
Career: University of Bergen (Candidate of Jurisprudence, 1985), associate with *Wikborg, Rein & Co.* from 1986, qualified 1987, a partner of the firm since 1990, resident lawyer at the London office of *Wikborg, Rein & Co.* 1990-1993.
Personal: Born in Arendal 1958. Married to Taran. Three boys, born in 1991, 1995 and 1999. Hobbies include bicycling, skiing, jogging and other physical activities.

BRECHAN, Peter
Advokatfirmaet Haavind Vislie DA, Oslo
+47 22 40 21 00
Recommended in Banking & Finance

BRUN-LIE, Nicolas
Wiersholm, Mellbye & Bech, Oslo +47 210 210 00
Recommended in Banking & Finance
Specialisation: International Banking & Finance, Maritime, Mergers & Acquisitions/Corporate. Has been involved in different restructurings, including one for a major Norwegian airline. Has represented Norwegian and foreign clients in connection with acquisitions, mergers, financing and general corporate matters.
Prof. Memberships: Norwegian Bar Association.
Career: Graduated from the University of Oslo, Faculty of Law 1983. Joined the Torvald Klaveness Group immediately thereafter as in-house counsel. Held various positions within the group and left for *Wiersholm, Mellbye & Bech* in 1987, becoming a partner in 1990.
Personal: Born 24 June 1955, married, two children, leisure interests include outdoor activities.

BRUNDTLAND, Knut
Bugge, Arentz-Hansen & Rasmussen, Oslo
+47 22 83 02 70
kb@ba-hr.no
Recommended in Corporate/M&A
Specialisation: Partner in *BA-HR* from 1993.
Personal: Born 1961. Graduated in law: 1988.

BRUUSGAARD, Christian
Thommessen Krefting Greve Lund, Oslo
+47 23 11 11 11
christian.bruusgaard@tkgl.no
Recommended in Energy & Natural Resources
Specialisation: Principal area of practice is tax, primarily taxation of operations on the continental shelf; finance and business law. Also a board member of a number of companies.
Prof. Memberships: Norwegian Bar Association (Member of Board of Governors and Chairman Tax Committee); International Fiscal Association.
Career: Education: University of Oslo (Candidate in Jurisprudence 1974); admitted 1978; Supreme Court of Norway (1983). Career history: Directorate of Tax 1975-76; Associate *Thommessen Krefting Greve Lund* 1977; Partner 1982.
Personal: Born 1947, married, two children.

CHRISTIANSEN, Erling
Advokatfirmaet Schjødt AS, Oslo +47 22 01 88 00
erling.christiansen@schjodt.no
Recommended in Corporate/M&A
Specialisation: Specialises in corporate finance related work, including M&A transactions and banking. Acts for investment banks as well as investors, venture capital companies and target companies, both domestic and foreign.
Prof. Memberships: Member of various committees on securities law, including the committee of the Norwegian Bar Association.
Publications: Publishes law books relating to securities law and stock exchange regulations in Norway.
Career: Received a law degree from the University of Oslo in 1976, and an LLM from New York University in 1981. Joined *Schjødt* in 1981, becoming a partner in 1985. Admitted to the Supreme Court in 1997. Has spoken at various conferences. Heads the firm's corporate finance group.
Personal: Born 21 November 1951. Leisure interests include outdoor activities.

DAMM, Wilhelm
Advokatfirmaet Schjødt AS, Oslo +47 22 01 88 00
wilhelm.damm@schjodt.no
Recommended in Banking & Finance
Specialisation: Main areas of practice are international finance, shipping, and international contracts. Mainly assists banks and financial institutions, both Norwegian and foreign, with financing of ships, projects and companies, including cross-border transactions.
Prof. Memberships: Norwegian Bar Association.
Career: Law Degree, University of Oslo, 1978. Deputy Judge. Trainee, London. Partner with *Schjødt* since 1991.
Personal: Born 17 June 1954. Married with one child. Leisure interests include both summer and winter outdoor activities.

DOBROWEN, Kim
Thommessen Krefting Greve Lund, Oslo
+47 23 11 11 11
kim.dobrowen@tkgl.no.
Recommended in Banking & Finance, Corporate/M&A
Specialisation: Main areas of practice are capital market transactions and corporate law including IPO's, share and debt offerings, public offers, mergers

and acquisitions, as well as banking and corporate finance.
Prof. Memberships: Norwegian Bar Association; International Bar Association.
Career: Education: University of Oslo (Candidate in Jurisprudence 1982). Career history: Scientific Assistant, Scandinavian Institute of Maritime Law 1980-81; Legal Consultant, Ministry of Justice, Department of Legislation 1983-1985; Associate *Thommessen Krefting Greve Lund* (London office) 1985-87; Partner from 1988; Managing Partner from 1998.

ENDRESEN, Clement
Kluge Advokatfirma ANS, Stavanger
+47 5157 1477
clement.endresen@kluge.no
Recommended in Corporate/M&A
Specialisation: Partner in Corporate Department. Main areas of work are corporate law, stock exchange regulations, mergers and acquisitions, privatisations and restructuring of businesses in general, and energy law. Acts for a number of listed and other large corporations. Permanent legal advisor to the Government Bank Investment Fund concerning inter alia the on-going reprivatisation of the major Norwegian banks. Is or has been a member of the board of directors of businesses in the following areas:- banking, financing, industry, petroleum, shipping and trade.
Prof. Memberships: Law Society, Law Society's stock exchange and securities committee, Stavanger Law Society.
Publications: Contributor to the Norwegian Journal of Business Law.
Career: Law degree 1974. Assistant Professor at the University of Oslo 1975-77. Deputy Judge 1977-79. Attorney at the office of the Solicitor General 1979. Supreme court Barrister 1989.
Personal: Born 1949. Attended the University of Oslo.

GISVOLD, Marius Moursund
Wikborg, Rein & Co, Oslo +47 22 82 75 00
marius.gisvold@wrco.no
Recommended in Corporate/M&A
Specialisation: Main areas of work are in corporate, securities and restructuring, principally in mergers, acquisitions, restructuring and work associated with derivatives, but also in joint venture agreements. Has handled a substantial number of mergers and acquisitions for both national and international clients, mainly in the IT, banking and energy sectors, but also in manufacturing industry. Acted as lead for Merkantildata ASA, the largest Norwegian IT company, in about ten such transactions last year, as lead for General Electric in its acquisition of major hydro and thermal-power manufacturer Kvaerner Energy AS and as co-lead for Christiania Bank in its planned merger with two other national banks in the same period; has acted for several large entities including, for example, leading hardware producer Norsk Data and leading department store Steen & Strøm in taking them through financial restructuring both within and outside formal insolvency proceedings, focusing on the preservation of business; has acted as lead in connection with several joint ventures, new listings, IPOs and other securities transactions.
Prof. Memberships: Norwegian Bar Association, International Association of Insolvency Practitioners.
Career: Candidate of jurisprudence, University of Oslo 1983, research assistant and temporary assistant professor, Scandinavian Institute of Maritime Law 1980-83, HM King Olav's Gold Medal for 'Contracts in the Petroleum Industry', 1983, qualified 1985, associate and partner (1990) with *Wikborg, Rein & Co.* since 1983, 1986-87 as head of Scandinavian Law Office in Rotterdam. In 1987-1990 Head of *Wikborg, Rein & Co.'s* London office, partner at Oslo office since 1990, managing partner from 1995 to 1997. Served as temporary appeal court judge (Haalogaland) in 1990, appointed again for three months in 1999 (Oslo).
Personal: Born in Trondheim 1957, married with three children. Advisor to Norwegian Football Association on players contracts, licensed FIFA-agent. Member of Norwegian Non-fiction Writers Association. Leisure interests include football coaching, hunting and hiking.

GREVE, Einar J.
Wikborg, Rein & Co, Oslo +47 22 82 75 00
ejg@wrco.no
Recommended in Corporate/M&A
Specialisation: Long-term experience in a wide range of mergers and acquisitions, securitisation of assets, distribution of securities in domestic and international financings, public offerings and listings on various stock exchanges, international mergers and acquistions and public offerings/listings. Lead partner in several major mergers and acquistions in Norway and internationally. Practice involves the counselling and representation of corporate issuers, investment banks, merchant banks and commercial banks.
Prof. Memberships: The Norwegian Bar Association.
Career: University of Oslo (candidate of Jurisprudence, 1987). Associate with *Wiersholm, Mellbye, & Bech* (1987), qualified 1989, attorney at the Oslo Stock Exchange (1990-92), partner of *Wikborg, Rein & Co* since 1 January 1993.
Personal: Born in Bergen in 1960. Hobbies include art, golf, tennis, skiing and hunting.

HAUKALI, Bernhard
Wikborg, Rein & Co, Oslo +47 22 82 75 00
bernhard.haukali@wrco.no
Recommended in Banking & Finance
Specialisation: Regularly instructed by Norwegian and foreign banks in documenting corporate and secured loans, in particular to companies in the shipping industry. Clients include the Norwegian banks, Den Norske Bank ASA and Christiania Bank of Kreditkasse ASA, and international banks such as Deutsche Bank AG and Fortis Bank (Nederland) N.V. Has acted for all of the aforesaid banks in 2000 documenting several ship financing transactions totalling loans of approximately US$300 mill. Regularly instructed by Norwegian ship owners and drilling rig owners in documenting cross-border sale and leaseback, and joint venture transactions.
Prof. Memberships: The Norwegian Bar Association.
Career: University of Bergen, Faculty of Political Science, Institute of Comparative Politics (1980), University of Bergen (Candidate of Jurisprudence, 1986), associate with *Wikborg, Rein & Co.* 1986, qualified 1988, resident lawyer at the London office of *Wikborg, Rein & Co.* 1989-1993, a partner of the firm since 1992.
Personal: Born in Stavanger 1958. Married to Line. Two children, born in 1986 and 1988 respectively. Hobbies include golf, skiing and motorsport.

HOLM, Sverre André
Kluge Advokatfirma ANS, Oslo + 47 2313 9200
sverre.holm@kluge.no
Recommended in Banking & Finance
Specialisation: Senior partner in Shipping/Project Finance/Corporate Department in Oslo office. Company law; Law of Commercial Contracts; International Joint Ventures & Project Financing; Shipping/Offshore Contracts; Financial Law (Syndicated Loans, Workouts). Has handled ship/rig building contracts, financing and corporate structure for a number of clients; advisor on Norwegian banking & financial law to Manufacturers Hanover, then Chemical, now Chase Manhattan and Christiania Bank, Nordlandsbanken and certain international financing syndicates.
Prof. Memberships: Norwegian Bar Association; International Bar Association.
Career: Admitted to the Bar 1973, joined *Haneborg Holm og Lange DA* 1973 becoming partner 1981; joined *Kluge* in 1997 as senior partner.
Personal: Born 11 February 1941, 1970 – Oslo University (candidate in jurisprudence), 1970-71 – Legal Counsel to Norwegian Maritime Directorate, 1971-73 – Assistant Judge. Speaks Scandinavian languages and English.

HØEG RASMUSSEN, Annikken
Advokatfirmaet Schjødt AS, Oslo +47 22 01 88 00
achr@schjodt.no
Recommended in Energy & Natural Resources
Specialisation: Corporate law. Board member of several companies. Has worked in the following fields: Petroleum law for a number of years; contracts and disputes on both supplier and contractor side; has represented oil companies (head counsel for oil company in major dispute with contractor about delivery of floating production unit).
Prof. Memberships: Norwegian Bar Association; International Bar Association.
Career: Law degree from University of Oslo (1960). Admitted to the Supreme Court in 1971. Joined the firm in 1966, becoming a partner in 1973.
Personal: Born 2 June 1936. Married with two children and two grandchildren. Leisure interests include music, theatre and outdoor activities such as hiking, golf and cross country skiing.

IRGENS, Einar
Advokatfirmaet Schjødt AS, Oslo +47 22 01 88 00
einar.irgens@schjodt.no
Recommended in Banking & Finance
Specialisation: Main areas of practice are: International and domestic banking and financing. Acts for domestic and international banks and other financial institutions as well as investors and borrow-

ers. Also advises clients in fishing and aquaculture.
Prof. Memberships: Norwegian Bar Association and its committee for banking and financing.
Career: Law degree, University of Oslo. Admitted to the Supreme Court in 1977. Deputy Judge 1965. Legal Counsel, the Central Union of Marine Underwriters 1965-1968. Partner *Vogt & Co.* 1968-1982. General Counsel Christiana Bank og Kreditkasse 1982-1994. Partner *Schjødt* 1994 to date.
Personal: Born 26 September 1937. Leisure interests include summer and winter outdoor activities.

JANSEN, Jan
Arntzen de Besche (from Jan 2001), Oslo
+47 23 89 40 00
jansen@auco.no
Recommended in Corporate/M&A, Energy & Natural Resources
Specialisation: Main areas of work are oil and energy, corporate, mergers and acquisitions, tax and insurance. Has acted in a number of transactions and reorganisations within the oil and energy sector and mergers and acquisitions within other sectors. Tax advisor to several of the major oil companies in Norway, and represents the companies in tax litigations in the civil courts. Advisor and counsel in litigation for major insurance companies.
Prof. Memberships: Norwegian Bar Association, IFA, AIPN.
Publications: 'International Tax Problems of Partnerships' (IFA 1995). Co-author 'Forsikringsrett' (Insurance Law) (Oslo 1993).
Career: Ministry of Finance 1984-1986, Arntzen, Underland from 1986. Lecturer Tax Law University of Oslo 1986-1988.
Personal: Law degree University of Oslo 1984.

KJØRNÆS, Arne Didrik
Wikborg, Rein & Co, Oslo +47 22 82 75 00
Recommended in Corporate/M&A
Specialisation: Chairman of *Witborg, Rein & Co,* Head of *Wikborg, Rein & Co's* Merger & Acquisition Group and Corporate Law Group. Long-term experience in a wide range of mergers and acquisitions, securitisation of assets, distribution of securities in domestic and international financing, public offerings and listings on various stock exchanges. Lead partner in several major mergers and acquisitions both in Norway and internationally. Practice involves the counselling and representation of corporate issuers, investment banks, merchant banks and commercial banks.
Prof. Memberships: Chairman of the Norwegian Bar Associations (NBA) Law Committee for Securities Law; Law Committee for Accounting Law; Advisory Committee to the Oslo Stock Exchange on Securities Law; Norwegian Bar Association.
Career: University of Oslo (Candidate of Jurisprudence, 1980); University of Oslo, Associate Professor (1980-81); Deputy District Judge (1981-82); qualified 1982; associate with *Wikborg, Rein & Co.*, 1982, in charge of office in Japan from 1984-87 and partner since 1988.
Personal: Born in Oslo 1956. Married to Inger Elisabeth. Two children born 1986 and 1988. Leisure interests include outdoor activities, reading and sports.

KNUDSEN, Gudmund
Bugge, Arentz-Hansen & Rasmussen, Oslo
+47 22 83 02 70
gkn@ba-hr.no
Recommended in Corporate/M&A
Specialisation: Partner in *Bugge, Arentz-Hansen & Rasmussen* since 1992.
Publications: Author of 'Commentary on the Foundations Act'. Co-author of 'Commentary on the Limited Companies Act' and the 'Public Limited Companies Act'.
Career: Ministry of Justice, Law department 1974-1990.
Personal: Born 1946. Graduated in law 1973.

KREFTING, Carl-Erik
Thommessen Krefting Greve Lund, Oslo
+47 23 11 11 11
carl.erik.krefting@tkgl.no
Recommended in Corporate/M&A
Specialisation: Principal areas of practice are business law and finance, mergers and acquisitions, corporate law and tax law. Board member in a number of Norwegian companies.
Prof. Memberships: Norwegian Bar Association; International Fiscal Association.
Career: Education: University of Oslo (Candidate in Jurisprudence 1978), admitted 1980; Supreme Court of Norway 1996. Career history: Directorate of Taxes 1978-80; Associate *Bugge, Arentz-Hansen & Rasmussen* 1980-89; trainee *Phillips Petro Group*, Oklahoma and *Arthur Andersen & Co.*, New York, USA 1982; Member of the Royal Commission on the Accountant's Rights and Duties Towards the State, Secretary for the Royal Commission for Taxation for Group of Companies; associate *Thommessen Krefting Greve Lund* 1983; Partner 1986.
Personal: Born 1953. Married. Three children.

KVALE, Anders
Kvale & Co, Oslo +47 22 47 97 00
Recommended in Energy & Natural Resources

LANGE, Viggo
Kluge Advokatfirma ANS, Oslo + 47 2313 9200
Recommended in Banking & Finance
Specialisation: Company law; Law of Commercial Contracts; International Joint Ventures & Project Financing; Shipping/Offshore Contracts; Financial Law (Syndicated Loans, Workouts). Has handled ship/rig building contracts, financing and corporate structure for RCCL, Dyvi Offshore and others; advisor on Norwegian banking & financial law to Manufacturers Hanover, then Chemical now Chase Manhattan. Also acted for French banks Crédit Lyonnais and Société Générale, advised the Skaugen group, inter alia in connection with the Seaboard workout and in the sale of their participation in RCCL, the Rasmusssen group inter alia in their acquisition of a minority stake in Navion, and various other shipping and offshore companies.
Prof. Memberships: Norwegian Bar Association, International Bar Association.
Career: Admitted to the Bar 1977, joined Norwegian Foreign Service 1970 (1st Secretary Madrid, Moscow), joined law firm of *Haneborg Holm og Lange DA* 1976 becoming partner 1981; joined *KLUGE* law firm in 1997 as senior partner.
Personal: Born 5 October 1940, attended Lycée Corneille, Rouen, France (Baccalauréat), Oslo University (candidate in jurisprudence), 1961; Russian interpreter's course (Army)1962-63; Assistant G-2, UNOC Katanga Headquarters (Congo);1963-69 Member of group of Editors of Treaties of Norway (part time). 1968-69 Secretary, Border Commission Norway-USSR (part time) 1971-72 Assistant Judge. Languages: The Scandinavian languages, English, French, and Spanish fluently, German (conversational), Russian (conversational).

LIND, Erling
Wiersholm, Mellbye & Bech, Oslo +47 210 210 00
erling.lind@wiersholm.no
Recommended in Banking & Finance
Specialisation: Partner in the Corporate Finance and M&A departments. Main areas of work are general corporate law, corporate finance, M&A. Main clients include Norwegian and international shipping and oil service industry clients, Norwegian financial institutions, Nowegian venture funds and overseas clients investing in Norway.
Prof. Memberships: Norwegian Bar Association, International Bar Association.
Career: Graduated from the University of Oslo in 1982. Associate in *Wiersholm, Bachke & Helliesen* in 1983. Qualified in 1985. Partner in *Wiersholm, Bachke & Helliesen* from 1987, in *Wiersholm, Mellbye & Bech* from 1990. Managing Partner 1991-1995. Holds various non-executive directorships. Acted on the combination of the non-life insurance business of Storebrand, Skandia and Pohjola in 1999, the acquisition by Frontline Ltd of ICB Shipping AB in 1999, the public offerings of ordinary shares in Kvaerner ASA in 1999 and 2000, the acquisition of Stento ASA by SAIT Radio Holland in 2000 and the sale by Societé Europeénne de Communication of its ownership interests in Netcom ASA in 2000.
Personal: Born 13 June 1955.

MELLBYE, Andreas
Wiersholm, Mellbye & Bech, Oslo +47 210 210 00
andreas.mellbye@wiersholm.no
Recommended in Corporate/M&A
Specialisation: Mergers and acquisitions, corporate, transactions, litigation and IPO's. Transactions last year including the IPO of Telenor ASA: NCL Holding ASA in Connection with the bids from Carnival and later Star, for Goldman Sachs in connection with Schøyengruppen's acquisition of Swebus, for Statoil in connection with the joint bid with Hydro for all of the shares in Saga Petroleum.
Prof. Memberships: The Norwegian Bar Association.
Publications: An introduction to Norwegian Securities and Company Law, Stock Markets and Foreign Ownership of Shares. Inside trading – Assembled statement for rules in Insider Trading, including rules for duty to clearance and revert burden of proof.
Career: Norwegian Royal Navy officer. Legal Department Norsk Hydro. Partner in *Wiersholm, Mellbye & Bech* since 1989. Accepted as attorney to the Norwegian Supreme Court in 1995. Chairman of

N

the Board of Martina Hansens Hospital (Baerum), director to the Deputy Board of the Fred. Olsen-related companies Ganger Rolf ASA and Bonheur ASA.
Personal: Married with one child.

MICHELET, Christian Fredrik
Arntzen de Besche (from Jan 2001), Oslo
+47 23 89 40 00
michelet@auco.no
Recommended in Energy & Natural Resources
Specialisation: Partner. Main area of work is oil, gas and energy law, utilities, construction, corporate, mergers and acquisitions. Advisor for 20 years to oil companies and oil and gas authorities. Has acted in a number of main oil and gas disputes in Norway. Advisor to the Ministry of Petroleum and Energy on a re-organisation of the Norwegian petroleum activities.
Prof. Memberships: Norwegian Bar Association.
Publications: 'Skattefrie Sammenslutninger' (Non-Taxable Organisations), Oslo 1981, Co-author EØS-Haandboken (The EEA Handbook, 2nd edition), Oslo 1998, Co-author 'Norsk Gassavsetning' (Norwegian Gas Sales), Oslo 1998, various articles in oil, gas and tax law.
Career: Joined *Arntzen, Underland & Co.* in 1981, partner in 1985. Vice President TOTAL Norge AS, 1989-92, Partner *Arntzen, Underland & Co.* 1992-present. Chairman, Legal Committee, Norwegian Oil Industry Association, 1989-91, member, The Norwegian Petroleum Legislation Committee, 1987-92.
Personal: Born 31 December, 1953. Law Degree, University of Oslo, 1980, Masters of Business Administration, INSEAD, France 1981.

MYHRE, Finn
Bugge, Arentz-Hansen & Rasmussen, Oslo
+47 22 83 02 70
fmy@ba-hr.no
Recommended in Banking & Finance
Specialisation: Partner in *BA-HR* from 1989.
Career: Lawyer in Saga Petroleum 1973-1979. Lawyer and General Counsel in Den norske Creditbank 1979-1989. Graduated in law: 1971.
Personal: Born: 1943.

RAMM, Erik
Wiersholm, Mellbye & Bech, Oslo +47 210 210 00
erik.ramm@wiersholm.no
Recommended in Banking & Finance
Specialisation: Principal areas of work include all aspects of financing, including syndicated loan facilities, asset financing, note and bond issues, secured transactions, corporate restructuring, banking. Also acts in respect of mergers and acquisitions, as well as general corporate and commercial matters.
Career: In-house counsel with Christiania Bank og Kreditkasse ASA. Joined *Wiersholm, Mellbye & Bech* as a partner in 1990.

RAUSTØL, Per
Wiersholm, Mellbye & Bech, Oslo +47 210 210 00
per.raustol@wiersholm.no
Recommended in Corporate/M&A
Specialisation: Mergers & acquisitions; corporate law; petroleum law contracts.
Prof. Memberships: Norwegian Lawyers Association; International Bar Association.
Career: 1981-84 Lawyer *Bugge, Arentz-Hansen & Rasmussen*; 1984-87 in-house lawyer Saga Petroleum ASA; 1987 to present partner *Wiersholm, Mellbye & Bech.*
Personal: Married with one child.

REED, Bjørn Gabriel
Bugge, Arentz-Hansen & Rasmussen, Oslo
+47 22 83 02 70
bgr@ba-hr.no
Recommended in Corporate/M&A
Specialisation: Partner in *BA-HR* from 1994. Established own law firm in 1987 under the name *Lowsow & Reed.*
Publications: 'Straffbar innsidehandel' (Criminal inside Trading) 1996; 'Aksjonæravtaler' (Shareholder Agreements) 1993.
Career: Graduated in law: 1984.
Personal: Born: 1958.

REIN, John
Wikborg, Rein & Co, Oslo +47 22 82 75 00
Recommended in Energy & Natural Resources

RINGDAL, Rolf Johan
Bugge, Arentz-Hansen & Rasmussen, Oslo
+47 22 83 02 70
rjr@ba-hr.no
Recommended in Banking & Finance
Specialisation: Partner in *BA-HR* from 1987. Areas of practice: Loan documentation (in particular ship finance), M&A, securities.
Career: Assistant District Judge (Trondenes) 1983-1984. Graduated law: 1982.
Personal: Born: 1955.

SAMUELSEN, Erik
Thommessen Krefting Greve Lund, Oslo
+47 23 11 11 11
erik.samuelsen@tkgl.no
Recommended in Energy & Natural Resources
Specialisation: Principal areas of practice are energy, business and contract law; heads Litigation Department; member of the Energy Group.
Prof. Memberships: Norwegian Bar Association; AIPPI; Norwegian EDP Law Association; Association for Copyright Law.
Career: Education: University of Oslo (Candidate in Jurisprudence 1968), admitted 1972; Supreme Court of Norway 1976. Career history: Lecturer of law, University of Oslo 1969-71; member of Royal Commission on Water Resources Act 1991-94; associate *Thommessen Krefting Greve Lund* 1972, Partner 1976.
Personal: Born 1944. Married. Two children.

SANFELT, Trond
Bugge, Arentz-Hansen & Rasmussen, Oslo
+47 22 83 02 70
trond.sanfelt@ba-hr.no
Recommended in Corporate/M&A
Specialisation: Partner in *Bugge, Arentz-Hansen & Rasmussen* since 1990. Practice areas are Norwegian Tax Law, International Tax Law, Corporate Law, Mergers & Acquisitions, Monopoly, Antitrust Law and Agency Law.
Publications: Author of 1986 annual revision of Fagernaes: 'Reference book in Tax Law', 'Norwegian Tax Conventions' 1987; 'Collection of Norwegian Tax Treaties', 1987; 'Maritime Joint Ventures', 1991.
Career: Graduated law 1983. Executive Officer, 1980-1981, Senior Executive Officer, 1981-1982, Assistant Judge, 1983-83, Head of Division, 1984-85 and Assistant General Manager, 1986, Ministry of Finance.
Personal: Born: 1956.

SOLLUND, Stig
Bugge, Arentz-Hansen & Rasmussen, Oslo
+47 22 83 02 70
ss@ba-hr.no
Recommended in Energy & Natural Resources
Specialisation: Partner in *BA-HR* from 1997.
Publications: Various articles on international tax matters and petroleum tax matters in Norwegian and international tax publications.
Career: Ministry of Finance – Director General, Petroleum Department and Tax Law Department. Graduated in law 1975.
Personal: Born: 1952.

STEEN, Sven Iver
Arntzen de Besche (from Jan 2001), Oslo
+47 23 89 40 00
steen@auco.no
Recommended in Banking & Finance
Specialisation: Main area of work is bank and finance law, stock exchange law, insurance, corporate law (M&A including listed companies), contracts, competition and litigation. Has acted for banks and insurance companies in acquisition and corporate organisation matters. Broad M&A experience. Acts as counsel for the Central Bank of Norway.
Prof. Memberships: Norwegian Bar Association; previous chairman of the Committee of the law of banking, finance and currency.
Publications: Author/co-author: 'Commentaries to the Act relating to financial activities and finance institutions', 'Collection of Norwegian laws relating to finance', 'Insurance law II', 'Business laws in the Nordic Countries', contributions to Karnov.
Career: Admitted to the Supreme Court of Norway. Qualified 1986. Joined *Arntzen, Underland & Co.* 1984, becoming a partner 1989. Assistant judge 1987. Secretary of the Norwegian Government-appointed Investigation Committee on Kongsberg Vaapenfabrikk, Norwegian Public Report 1989:2. Principal secretary of the Norwegian Government-appointed Banking Law Commission: Norwegian Public Reports 1994:19 (financial agreements), 1995:25 (guarantee arrangements and public administration), 1996:24 (payment systems), 1998:14 (finance institutions).
Personal: Born 28 March 1959. Law degree, University of Oslo 1984.

STEENSTRUP, Morten
Advokatfirmaet Steenstrup Stordrange DA, Oslo
+47 2281 4500
morten@steenstrup.no
Recommended in Corporate/M&A
Specialisation: Corporate/mergers and acquisitions, arbitration, litigation, trademarks, intellectual

property, taxation, banking, securities, finance, consultations with government authorities.
Prof. Memberships: Member of the supervisory council of the Norwegian Central Bank (Norges Bank) and board member of several national and international companies. Norwegian Bar Association.
Career: 1975-1983 Member of City Council, Tonsberg; 1981-1989 Member of parliament; 1981-1983 Member of Standing Committee of Justice, MP; 1983-1989 Member of Standing Committee of Finance, MP; 1985-1986 Parliamentary Secretary to the Ministry of Finance; 1986 Parliamentary Secretary to the Prime Minister; 1986-1989 Lawyer at *Gram Hambro Garman*; 1989 Founder of *Advokatfirmaet Steenstrup Stordrange* DA; 1993 Admitted to the Supreme Court.
Personal: Education: 1972 Milton Academy, Mass., USA; 1973 Tonsberg Gymnas; 1976 Bachelor of Arts in Political Science and Sociology; 1980 Cand. jur. (law) University of Oslo.

STINESSEN, Stein Erik
Hjort, Oslo +47 22 47 18 00
Recommended in Energy & Natural Resources

SVOREN, Rune
Bugge, Arentz-Hansen & Rasmussen, Oslo
+47 22 83 02 70
rs@ba-hr.no
Recommended in Energy & Natural Resources
Specialisation: Partner in *BA-HR* from: 1989.
Career: Graduated in law 1984.
Personal: Born: 1958.

THYNESS, Erik
Wiersholm, Mellbye & Bech, Oslo +47 210 210 00
erik.thyness@wiersholm.no
Recommended in Corporate/M&A
Specialisation: Mergers and acquisitions and securities transactions. Transactions last year include advising Den Norske Bank ASA on its merger with Postbanken BA, advising Norsk Hydro ASA on the sale of its 38.1% stake in Dyno ASA to a company advised by Industri Kapital and its sale of Hydro Seafood to Nutreco, and advising Norske Skogindustrier ASA on its sale of Forestia to Moelven and its sale of the Tofte and Folla wood pulp mills to Södra Cell.
Prof. Memberships: The Norwegian Bar Association; International Fiscal Association.
Career: Law degree University of Oslo 1987. In-house counsel Norsk Hydro ASA 1988-89 and 1991-1993. Associate Judge Sør-Gudbrandsdal district court 1989-90. General Counsel Hafslund Nycomed ASA/Nycomed ASA 1993-1996. Partner in *Wiersholm, Mellbye & Bech* from 1996.
Personal: Married with three children.

TYSLAND, Sverre
Advokatfirmaet Selmer DA, Oslo + 47 23 11 65 00
Recommended in Corporate/M&A

O

OMAN

Banking & Finance

OMAN Leading firms (Banking & Finance)
1 Said Al-Shahry Law Office (in association with Richards Butler)
2 Trowers & Hamlins
3 Al Alawi, Mansoor Jamal & Co

Firms are listed alphabetically in each band.

Leading individuals (Banking & Finance)
1 NEALE Alastair *Said Al-Shahry Law Office*
2 ANGLE Sean *Towers & Hamlins*
MALIK Mansoor *Al Alawi, Mansoor Jamal & Co*

Individuals are listed alphabetically in each band.

Said Al-Shahry Law Office (in association with Richards Butler) (1 ptr, 6 asscs) The firm continues as the premier firm for banking work in the region, particularly through its connections with the Omani government. It advises on a wide range of banking and finance matters, including syndicated lending, capital markets, initial public offerings, cross-border financing, asset financing and investment and securities transactions.

Formerly in-house counsel at Arab Banking Corporation, **Alastair Neale*** is said to be *"a damn fine lawyer,"* although researchers were informed that he operates as a *"lone wolf."* Major transactions from the past twelve months include negotiating the project and financing documents for the Oman Gas Company, and advising on a number of banking mergers. **Clients:** Bank Dhofar Al Omani Al Fransi; HSBC Bank Middle East; KBC Bank (Dublin); National Bank of Oman; Nomura; Westdeutsche Landesbank.

Trowers & Hamlins (1 ptr, 3 asscs) This firm has consolidated its strength in banking over the past twelve months. *"Long established"* in the region, the team is considered by competitors to owe much to new managing partner **Sean Angle***, described as a *"powerhouse."* He heads a team which recently advised ONIC Holding on its $140 million disposal of shares in Commercial Bank of Oman. Also advised Bank Dhofar Al Omani Al Fransi on its proposed acquisition of 16 branches of Commercial Bank of Oman. **Clients:** Bank Dhofar Al Omani Al Fransi; Central Bank of Oman; Gulf Air.

Al Alawi, Mansoor Jamal & Co (2 ptrs, 8 asscs) Newly merged firm, which advises local and international banks on bond issues and syndicated loans, and is respected by clients for its *"effective service on both banking and corporate work."*

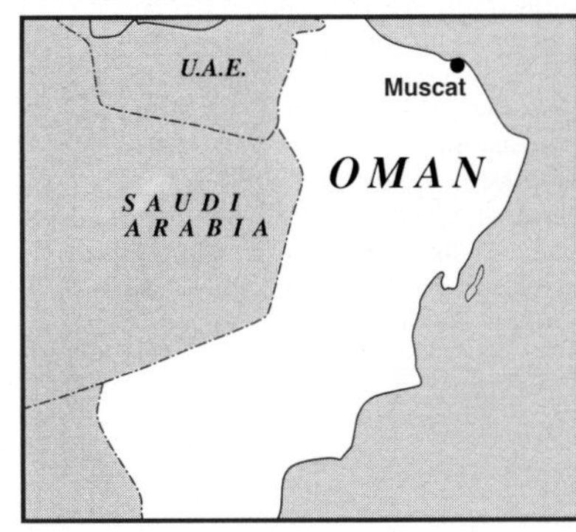

Mansoor Jamal Malik* is seen to be *"a good operator"* in banking transactions as well as corporate matters, with competitors noting that he has *"been in Oman a long time"* and *"knows the local market inside out."* Major transactions include advising on a RO4 million bond issue in Oman to be undertaken by a local finance leasing company, and representing Bank Muscat SAOG on a $150 million overseas borrowing from a syndicate of international banks. **Clients:** Alliance Housing Bank; Bank Muscat; Citibank; Habib Bank; Industrial Bank of Oman; Majan International Bank; National Bank of Oman.

Corporate/M&A

OMAN Leading firms (Corporate/Mergers & Acquisitions)
1 Trowers & Hamlins
2 Denton Wilde Sapte
3 Al Alawi, Mansoor Jamal & Co
Said Al-Shahry Law Office (in association with Richards Butler)

Firms are listed alphabetically in each band.

Trowers & Hamlins (2 ptrs, 3 asscs) The Muscat office of this firm is the largest practice in the Sultanate, acting for multi-nationals, joint venture companies, investors and funders and public bodies. It handles a range of corporate and commercial work, including general restructuring of companies, and advises franchises and foreign entities looking to invest in the country.

Nick Edmondes has recently returned to join the firm's corporate group in London after five and a half years in Oman, and has been replaced by **Sean Angle***, who is seen to have *"taken the office from strength to strength"* in both the corporate and the financial spheres. M&A work has included acting for ONIC (Oman National Investment Company) Holdings, which was the vendor on the sale of a 33% stake in Combank. **Clients:** BP; ONIC.

Denton Wilde Sapte (1 ptr, 9 asscs) The firm's office in Oman, recently acquired from Fox & Gibbons, maintains a solid relationship with the Omani government. It now provides a full range of international and domestic commercial advice, including local capital markets law, foreign investment and privatisation.

Our researchers found that the firm's competitors predicted an increasingly bright future, as the team continues to expand. Much credit is apportioned to **Alasdair Jeffrey***, who has *"accumulated a lot of knowledge at the coal face"* and is a *"great client man."*

The team has advised the Omani Government on the privatisation of the electricity and water

OMAN Leading individuals (Corporate/Mergers & Acquisitions)
1 **ANGLE Sean** *Towers & Hamlins*
JEFFREY Alasdair *Denton Wilde Sapte*
2 **AL-SHAHRY Said** *Said Al-Shahry Law Office*
MALIK Mansoor *Al Alawi, Mansoor Jamal & Co*
Individuals are listed alphabetically in each band.

desalination industries. Also acted for Bank Muscat on its merger with Commercial Bank of Oman. **Clients:** Ministry of National Economy; Shell Oman Marketing SAOG; Occidental Incorporation; Oman International Bank SAOG; National Bank of Oman SAOG; Bank Muscat SAOG; MB Petroleum Services LLC; Merrill Lynch.

Al Alawi, Mansoor Jamal & Co (2 ptrs, 8 asscs) The firm's recent merger has been commended by peers as *"a union that makes sense,"* and it has increased its profile on a variety of corporate cases for local and regional corporates. The team has specific expertise on IPOs. **Mansoor Malik*** is recommended to researchers as a *"good and competent lawyer"* and a *"real workaholic."* The firm advised the government of the Sultanate of Oman on the privatisation of the Sohar Oil Refinery Project and the establishment of a polypropylene plant, as well as the privatisation of Seeb and Salalah Airports. **Clients:** Oman Cement Co SAOG; Oman Fibre Optics Co SAOG; Oman National Electric Company SAOG; Renaissance Holding SAOG; Renaissance Hospitality Services SAOG.

Said Al-Shahry Law Office (in association with Richards Butler) (1 ptr, 6 asscs) The firm advises a variety of commercial and corporate clients, particularly in the banking and energy sectors, including those participating in the Sultanate's project financing and privatisation programmes. At the head of affairs **Said Al-Shahry*** is *"one of the best known of all the Omani lawyers."* The firm negotiated the project documentation and formation of Dhofar Power Company SAOG, and represented Oman Aviation Services on the sale of aircraft and the renewal of a concession agreement. **Clients:** Dhofar Fisheries Industries Co SAOG; DynCorp; Oman Aviation Services Co SAOG; Oman LNG LLC; Salalah Port Services Co SAOG; Sigma Paints; Total Elf Aquitaine; Yokogawa Corporation.

O

Project Finance

OMAN Leading firms (Project Finance)
1 **Towers & Hamlins**
2 **Said Al-Shahry Law Office (in association with Richards Butler)**
3 **Curtis, Mallet-Prevost, Colt & Mosle LLP**

Firms are listed alphabetically in each band.

Leading individuals (Project Finance)
1 **AL-SHAHRY Said** *Said Al-Shahry Law Office*
ANGLE Sean *Towers & Hamlins*
2 **MULLINS Bruce** *Curtis, Mallet-Prevost*
Individuals are listed alphabetically in each band.

Towers & Hamlins (1 ptrs, 3 asscs) This firm has a particular reputation for dealing with major industrial and infrastructure projects, and is the acknowledged leader for project finance work in the region. The *"multi-talented"* **Sean Angle*** is recommended by clients for his work in this area.

The firm advised Salalah Port Services Group on the latest port concession which was signed this year, and represented AES in connection with the 440MW Barka Power and Desalination Plant. Over the past twelve months, the team has also continued its involvement in the Manah Power Project, the first BOOT infrastructure project to have been completed in the Gulf. **Clients:** AES; Enron; United Power Company.

Said Al-Shahry Law Office (in association with Richards Butler) (1 ptr, 6 asscs) Over the past twelve months the firm's major focus has been on power projects, notably the ongoing gas pipeline project for the Oman Gas Company. Practice head **Said Al-Shahry*** is seen to have maintained his *"healthy profile"* in the market. The firm acted for Oman LNG in negotiating the project and lease agreements for Qalhat Housing Complex, and also negotiated the project documents for Muscat Wastewater Consortium. **Clients:** Ministry of Electricity & Water; Oman Oil Company, Oman India Fertiliser Company; Oman Air; Société Générale.

Curtis, Mallet-Prevost, Colt & Mosle LLP (1 assc) Known for its work on behalf of government institutions, the firm advises on water, electricity, telecommunications and transportation projects. However, the team's licence to practise does not extend to non-governmental clients, thus significantly limiting its scope.

Head of the office **Bruce Mullins*** is respected by his peers. Recent transactions include advising the Ministry of Communications on the effects of the sale of Sea-Land Inc to Maersk Lines on the Container Terminal Concession. Also advised the Ministry of Water Resources on the construction contract for a scheme comprising 215 kilometres of pipelines, water reservoirs and tanker points at a cost of $69 million. **Clients:** Fichtner GmbH; Government of Oman; PwC.

*See leaders' profiles on page 528

Leaders' profiles – Oman

O

AL-SHAHRY, Said Bin Saad
Said Al-Shahry Law Office (in association with Richards Butler), Muscat +968 790 577
Recommended in Corporate/M&A, Project Finance

ANGLE, Sean
Trowers & Hamlins, Muscat +968 771 5500
trowers@omantel.net.om
Recommended in Banking & Finance, Corporate/M&A, Project Finance
Specialisation: Has particular expertise in advising developers in connection with construction / EPC contracts. Has developed relationships with the various regulatory authorities and has detailed knowledge of the regulatory issues and potential problem areas (and solutions) that arise in major infrastructure projects. Also advising on international arbitrations as an expert on Omani law.
Career: Qualified in Australia in 1986, admitted in England and Wales in 1990. Joined *Trowers & Hamlins* in 1990, Partner since 1999.
Personal: Born 1961. Educated at University of Tasmania. Currently residing in Oman.

JEFFREY, John Alasdair
Denton Wilde Sapte, Muscat +968 56 43 46
dws@dwsmuscat.com
Recommended in Corporate/M&A
Specialisation: Company, Commercial, International.
Prof. Memberships: Faculty of Advocates, Glasgow, Scotland. Law Society of Scotland. Supreme Court, Oman.
Career: MA LLB Glasgow University. Partner, *Biggart, Baillie & Gifford*, Glasgow 1963-79. Partner, *Dorman, Jeffrey & Co.*, Glasgow 1979-88. Partner, *Fox & Gibbons*, Muscat, Oman 1988-99.
Personal: Married with three daughters. Leisure interests include football (Rangers fan), music (jazz pianist) and golf.

MALIK, Mansoor
Al Alawi, Mansoor Jamal & Co, Ruwi
+968 707 168
mj-co@omantel.net.om
Recommended in Banking & Finance, Corporate/M&A
Specialisation: Managing Partner in *Al Alawi, Mansoor Jamal & Co.* Main area of work is international transactions involving a diverse range of clients and projects and in arbitration, banking, commercial, construction, international corporate and project finance, mergers and acquisitions, privatisations in the power and infrastructure sector, telecommunications and civil aviation sector, insurance, listing of companies and securities and Islamic law matters.
Prof. Memberships: Chambers of Elizabeth Appleby QC and Duncan Ouseley QC; Member of Lincolns Inn.
Career: Qualified in 1982 from the University of Hull, UK and admitted to practice as barrister at law, Inns of Court (Lincoln's Inn) before moving to the Sultanate of Oman in 1986. Joined *Walker Martineu Saleem*, Oman branch, as Resident Manager, becoming a Managing Partner in *Mansoor Jamal & Co.* in 1994. Presently Managing Partner in *Al Alawi, Mansoor Jamal & Co.*, which came into existence with effect from January 1, 2000 as a result of a merger between *Mansoor Jamal & Co.*, Barristers and Legal Consultants, and *Al Safa* Legal Consultants.
Personal: Born on July 22, 1959. Primary and secondary education at schools in London, UK, from 1963-1982. Leisure interests include reading, music, sports and outdoor activities.

MULLINS, Bruce
Curtis, Mallet-Prevost, Colt & Mosle LLP, Muscat +968 607 725
Recommended in Project Finance

NEALE, Alastair
Said Al-Shahry Law Office (in association with Richards Butler), Muscat +968 790 577
Recommended in Banking & Finance

PAKISTAN

OVERVIEW: Labouring under an already weakened economy, the country faces difficulties in securing fresh loans following several defaults. A supreme court ruling against Hubco in its arbitration with WAPDA has contributed to deepening mistrust of the government by investors and the ongoing review of that judgement has assumed a crucial role in the future of the country's corporate law firms.

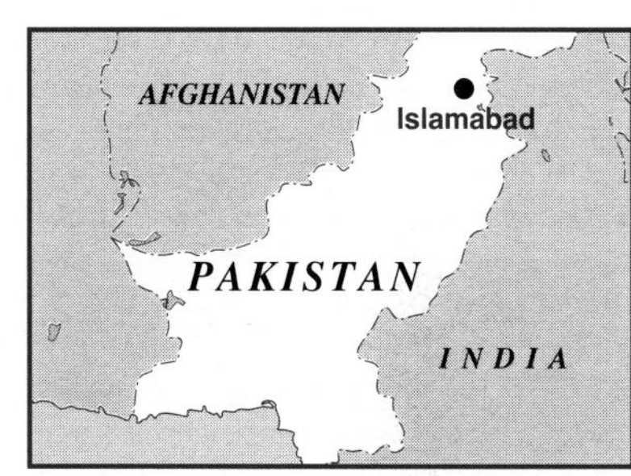

P

Corporate/Commercial

PAKISTAN Leading firms (Corporate/Commercial)

Band	Firm
1	Kabraji & Talibuddin
	Orr, Dignam & Co
	Vellani & Vellani
2	Chima & Ibrahim
	Rizvi, Isa & Co
3	Cornelius, Lane & Mufti
	Haidermota & Co
	Hassan & Hassan
	Surridge & Beecheno
4	Afridi & Angell
	Mohsin Tayebaly & Co
5	Mandviwalla & Zafar

Firms are listed alphabetically in each band.

Leading individuals (Corporate/Commercial)

Band	Individual
1	**KABRAJI Kairas** *Kabraji & Talibuddin*
	RIZVI Ahsan *Rizvi, Isa & Co*
	VELLANI Badaruddin *Vellani & Vellani*
2	**AHMAD Raufiud** *Orr, Dignam & Co*
	CHIMA Salman *Chima & Ibrahim*
	IBRAHIM Khalid *Chima & Ibrahim*
	VELLANI Fatehali *Vellani & Vellani*
3	**ANWER Khalid** *Khalid Anwer & Co*
	HAIDERMOTA Khozem *Haidermota & Co*
	HASSAN Parvez *Hassan & Hassan*
	JAFFAR Mohammed *Orr, Dignam & Co*
	KHAN Maudood *Orr, Dignam & Co*
	RIAZ Zahir *Orr, Dignam & Co*
	TALIBUDDIN Salman *Kabraji & Talibuddin*
4	**BUTT Salman** *Cornelius, Lane & Mufti*
	KHAN Aftab Ahmad *Surridge & Beecheno*
	TAYEBALY Irfan *Mohsin Tayebaly & Co*
	YUSUF Aliya *Orr, Dignam & Co*

Individuals are listed alphabetically in each band.

Kabraji & Talibuddin (2 ptrs, 7 asscs) The meteoric rise of this *"still young"* firm is almost completely due to its first-class reputation for corporate work. The team specialises in privatisations, joint ventures, inward foreign investment and cross-border M&A, and advises a blue-chip international corporate clientele. **Kairas Kabraji***, is *"knowledgeable, thorough and experienced"* and is considered by peers to be *"an authority on corporate law."* The *"gentlemanly"* **Salman Talibuddin*** is respected both as a litigator and a transactional practitioner. The firm acted for Cathay Pacific on the lease of five Boeing 747s to Pakistan International Airlines, performed due diligence for Citibank on its (abortive) acquisition of Bank of America's Pakistani interests, and advised Cable & Wireless on its investment in a locally incorporated mobile telecommunications company. **Clients:** Cable & Wireless; Cathay Pacific; Sui Southern; Citibank; Gap Inc; BHP.

Orr, Dignam & Co (6 ptrs, 18 asscs) Venerable firm, which is said by competitors to have *"a tried and tested infrastructure and an enormous clientele,"* and to be *"giving the newer firms a run for their money."* Although our researchers detected some market criticism of the firm's *"excessive caution,"* the corporate team's large contingent of foreign qualified lawyers earn high praise for expertise in cross-border M&A, project finance and Islamic finance. Financial services, pharmaceuticals and telecoms are areas of specific expertise. The highly respected **Mohammed Jaffar***, the Aga Khan's representative in Pakistan, is an established senior name, as is rainmaker **Raufiud Ahmad***. Also recommended by clients were the *"excellent"* **Maudood Khan***, who is said to have *"real commercial flair,"* the *"thorough"* **Zahir Riaz*** and *"down to earth"* **Aliya Yusuf***, who is renowned for her drafting skills and can *"fight her corner with the best of them."* The firm acted for Bank of America on its merger with Union Bank in Pakistan, advised Standard Chartered Bank on its acquisition of Grindlays Bank and represented Park Arab Refinery Company on the White Oil pipeline project. **Clients:** Bank of America; Standard Chartered Bank; Pakistan State Oil Company; American Home Products; Citibank; AT&T; SmithKline Beecham; Microsoft.

Vellani & Vellani (2 ptrs, 6 asscs) The firm specialises in IP matters but is also well regarded for its first class commercial services, including litigation. Rivals are agreed that *"trademarks are the bread and butter of this firm."* The firm's corporate clientele includes a number of overseas blue-chips, and is drawn from industries such as banking and finance, pharmaceuticals, petroleum, and telecoms. The firm's *"powerhouse"* is now held to be the *"effective"* **Badaruddin Vellani***, who follows in the footsteps of his father, **Fatehali Vellani***. The latter, although not as transactionally active as formerly, was still recommended to researchers as *"a constructive problem-solver."* The firm has acted for pharmaceuticals multi-nationals on the Pakistani aspects of two international mergers, and advised a foreign manufacturing company on its restructuring. **Clients:** Unilever; ICI; Singer Pakistan; Roche; Smithkline Beecham; Glaxo Wellcome; Warner Lambert; BAT; Shell; Rousch Power.

Chima & Ibrahim (2 ptrs, 7 asscs) Said by peers to be *"a vibrant new force,"* this *"young and energetic"* firm has been widely acknowledged for its *"excellent client base and great attention to detail."* The firm's efforts are mostly dedicated to the service of blue-chip corporate clients such as PepsiCo and Nestlé, whom the corporate team advises on inward investment and M&A transactions. The team also has niche expertise in the banking sector, advising on structured finance, acquisition finance and corporate restructurings. **Salman Chima*** and **Khalid Ibrahim*** were both applauded as *"extremely civilised and forensically precise lawyers."* **Clients:** ABN AMRO; American Express; Citibank; Crescent Petroleum International; Deutsche Bank; Motorola.

*See leaders' profiles on pages 531-532

P

Rizvi, Isa & Co (3 ptrs, 9 asscs) Present on a number of big-ticket deals, the firm covers the spectrum of corporate advice, and is particularly known for its work in financial services, energy and telecoms. Market opinion is that *"government work is the firm's speciality,"* and it has a long-held reputation for advice on privatisations. The firm's star lawyer is the *"dynamic and abrasive,"* **Ahsan Rizvi***, commended to researchers as *"one of the smartest lawyers in Pakistan."* He heads a team that advises a mixed clientele of domestic and foreign corporates and financial institutions. The firm recently advised on two high-profile mergers in the pharmaceuticals industry, and was involved in the drafting of the Pakistani government's IT regulatory framework. **Clients:** ABN AMRO; Alcatel; ALSTOM; Ciba-Geigy (Pakistan); Citibank; CDC; Crédit Lyonnais; Glaxo Wellcome Pakistan; Hoechst; ICI Pakistan; Jardine Fleming Pakistan; PepsiCo; Pfizer.

Cornelius, Lane & Mufti (4 ptrs, 14 asscs) Considered to be the leading firm in Lahore, it has grown over the last year, and is known for its *"organisation along Western lines."* Although it has recently lost a partner to duties at the High Court, the firm remains active and respected on cross-border M&A, advising agencies and international and domestic clients. The group has an especially strong banking clientele. **Salman Butt*** has *"a sound understanding of the commercial imperatives of corporate and financial transactions,"* and was strongly recommended to researchers by his competitors. **Clients:** Citibank; ABB; ABN AMRO; AES; American Express; ANZ Grindlays; Asian Development Bank; ICI; IFC; Habib Bank; Imperial Group of Companies; Mitsubishi; Siemens; Water and Power Development Authority (WAPDA).

Haidermota & Co (3 ptrs, 8 asscs) Regarded by the market as a *"small but talented"* firm, it has a particular niche in complex financial structurings and is regarded by clients as *"the firm to go to in Karachi for financial advice."* The corporate team is renowned for its privatisation expertise, having advised Merrill Lynch on its bid to become the government's financial advisor on the Oil and Gas Development Company privatisation, and represented Jardine Fleming on a similar bid in connection with the privatisation of nine oil and gas fields. The leading performer here is the *"hard-working"* **Khozem Haidermota***, a US-qualified attorney with *"sound corporate experience."* A pioneer of securitisations in Pakistan, the firm also advised Allianz on its joint venture in Pakistan with EFU Services, and represented Orix Investment Bank (Pakistan) on its bid for First Women Bank. **Clients:** State Bank of Pakistan; Government of Pakistan; ABN AMRO; Citibank; Allianz; Becton, Dickinson & Company; Jardine Fleming; Khadim Ali Shah Bukhari Co; Merrill Lynch.

Hassan & Hassan (4 ptrs, 9 asscs) This firm is regarded as a *"productive and professional"* commercial player at a medium-ticket level, generally advising overseas clients on their investments in Pakistan. The firm has particular experience of the banking and energy sectors. **Parvez Hassan*** is admiringly acknowledged by competitors to be one of the *"pioneers of corporate law in Pakistan,"* and is said by some to *"tower over his colleagues."* **Clients:** ABN AMRO; Bank of America; Cargill; Coca-Cola; Commonwealth Development Corporation; Continental AG; Deutsche Bank; HSBC; Morgan Stanley; Occidental Petroleum; Union Texas Petroleum; Volvo Pakistan.

Surridge & Beecheno Old style firm, which, in spite of recent defections, maintains a respected corporate presence, notably through its Karachi office. **Aftab Ahmad Khan*** still commands the approval of his peers, but researchers were surprised to find an absence of recommended younger lawyers here. The team still advises its loyal clientele of domestic and international companies on investments and acquisitions in Pakistan. **Clients:** Overseas and local corporates.

Afridi & Angell (2 ptrs, 7 asscs) The Islamabad office of this international firm, based in Dubai, is best known for its project finance work, especially in the energy industry. However, the corporate team is also known for its involvement in a select number of high-premium M&A transactions, generally on behalf of international entities or government agencies. The group advised on a major government initiative to introduce a national ID card scheme. **Clients:** A range of multinationals, financial institutions and governments.

Mohsin Tayebaly & Co (3 ptrs, 4 asscs) Although primarily renowned for banking and finance expertise, this smaller firm's corporate team is also regarded by competitors as *"an excellent choice for referrals."* The team advises both international financial institutions and domestic corporates on privatisations, and has niche ability in structuring documents for Islamic finance transactions. **Irfan Tayebaly*** was singled out for researchers as a *"trustworthy and thorough corporate lawyer."* The firm advised on the privatisation of United Bank, acting for the Privatisation Commission of Pakistan on the privatisation of the First Women Bank, and advised the Aries Group on the restructuring of the Investment Corporation of Pakistan. **Clients:** Standard Chartered Bank; Banque Indosuez; ABN AMRO; Allied Bank of Pakistan; Smith & Nephew Pakistan; Automobile Corporation of Pakistan; Atlas Honda.

Mandviwalla & Zafar (2 ptrs, 1 assc) This firm is known by rivals for its *"huge corporate client base and high volume of transactions,"* although its size makes it difficult to compete with the market leaders in Pakistan. Often acting for high-profile domestic companies, the firm also has a growing reputation for its commercial litigation expertise. **Clients:** Domestic corporates.

Other Notable Practitioner **Khalid Anwer** is the principal figure of the eponymous firm, which handles big-ticket commercial transactions for an array of multi-national clients. Fellow practitioners regard him as *"a great intellect, and the top corporate litigator in Pakistan by a mile."*

*See leaders' profiles on pages 531-532

Leaders' profiles – Pakistan

AHMAD, Raufiud
Orr, Dignam & Co, Karachi +92 21 241 6003/3422

ANWER, Khalid
Khalid Anwer & Co, Karachi +92 21 455 0094

BUTT, Salman Aslam
Cornelius, Lane & Mufti, Lahore +92 42 636 0868
info@clm.com.pk
Specialisation: Partner in *Cornelius, Lane & Mufti*, main area of work is corporate and banking laws, both contentious and non-contentious. Acted as counsel in respect of sale of shareholding along with transfer of management of a commercial bank, and as counsel to various power generation companies in Pakistan. Presently handling two major acquisitions of companies for purchasers. Acted as Pakistan counsel: in connection with the restructuring of AES Group Companies (in the power generation sector) in Pakistan; Mitsubishi Heavy Industries in respect of various projects being handled by it in Pakistan in the power generation sector; in connection with the securitisation of the receivables of Pakistan International Airlines Corporation in the UAE, and Saudi Arabia, for Citibank, N.A., and ABN AMRO Bank N.V. Structured and handled: the transference of shareholding between the shareholders (with management) of Dhan Fibres Limited and Dewan Salman Fibres Limited. This is the largest single transaction of this nature in Pakistan's corporate history; the first public term finance certificate issue in Pakistan, having a floating rate of profit with American Express Bank Limited; transactions for various multinational banks in respect of finance to Daewoo Corporation Motorway Project; loan restructuring of a major group (after default) in the private sector with National Development Finance Corporation and majority of Commercial Banks and Financial Institutions operating in Pakistan; swap transactions under the regulations of the State Bank of Pakistan for lending to Public/Private Sector entities; transactions under the Islamic mode of finance for local and multinational banks and financial instutions, including the DMI Group.
Prof. Memberships: Supreme Court of Pakistan Bar Association.
Personal: Born 16 July 1958. Attended Government College Lahore 1974-1978. Punjab University Law College, Lahore 1979-1981 (LLB), University of London 1984-85 (LLM).

CHIMA, Salman
Chima & Ibrahim, Lahore
+92 42 575 5233 / 575 7373

HAIDERMOTA, Khozem
Haidermota & Co, Karachi +92 21 215879097

HASSAN, Parvez
Hassan & Hassan, Lahore +92 42 636 0800

IBRAHIM, Khalid
Chima & Ibrahim, Lahore
+92 42 575 5233 / 575 7373

JAFFAR, Mohammed
Orr, Dignam & Co, Karachi +92 21 241 6003/3422

KABRAJI, Kairas N
Kabraji & Talibuddin, Karachi +92 21 583 8874
knk@digicom.net.pk
Specialisation: Partner specialising in commercial transactions of all kinds, domestic and trans-border, including project finance, privatisation, joint ventures, inward foreign investment, mergers and acquisitions, domestic and global, capital markets transactions; foreign and domestic debt and equity financings, aviation and aircraft finance.
Prof. Memberships: Advocate, High Court; Member: Sindh High Court Bar Association; Karachi Bar Association; International Bar Association.
Publications: Contributing editor, 'Capital Asia', Hong Kong; 'Custodial Services in Asia'; 'Mutual Funds in Asia'; author of chapter on Pakistan in 'Enforcement of Foreign Judgements Worldwide' (ed Plato) 1989.
Career: Associate, *Surridge & Beecheno* 1975-81; partner *Surridge & Beecheno* 1981-95; partner, *Rizvi Isa Kabraji* 1995-96.
Personal: Born 1951; education: Trinity College, Cambridge (1973 BA, (Law Tripos Parts I and II); 1975 LLM; 1976 MA).

KHAN, Aftab Ahmad
Surridge & Beecheno, Karachi 74000
+92 21 242 7292

KHAN, Maudood
Orr, Dignam & Co, Karachi +92 21 241 6003/3422

RIAZ, Zahir
Orr, Dignam & Co, Karachi +92 21 241 6003/3422

RIZVI, Ahsan
Rizvi, Isa & Co, Karachi +92 21 587 2879
ric@cyber.net.pk
Specialisation: Corporate finance, oil & gas, power sector, privatisations, mergers & acquisitions. Legal counsel for the Privatisation of Pakistan Telecommunication Company Limited, Sui Southern Gas Corporation Limited, Sui Northern Gas Pipelines Limited and Muslim Commercial Bank Limited. Legal counsel for the lenders (including World Bank, IFC, CDC, EFIC, US EXIM, ABN AMRO, Citibank and others) and project companies in the following projects: Hub Power Project, Uch Power Project, CEPA Power Project, Coastal Habibullah Power Project, Saba Power Project, Tapal Power Project and Tractebel Khaleej Power Project. Legal Counsel for Premier and Shell Pakistan B.V. dealing with all matters relating to exploration and development of oil & gas fields and Union Texas Pakistan. Legal counsel for the acquisition of Union Bank Limited and Phillips Projects business in Pakistan by Tyco Fire & Security.
Prof. Memberships: Sindh High Court Bar Association. Karachi Bar Association.
Publications: Author of various articles on legal and Islamic law matters.
Career: LLB (Hons) from London University; LLM from London University; Bar-at-Law from Lincoln's Inn; Practising corporate law in Pakistan since 1981; Taught LLM students.
Personal: Married with two daughters. Plays golf, bridge and squash. Interested in trekking and off-road bicycling.

TALIBUDDIN, Salman
Kabraji & Talibuddin, Karachi +92 21 583 8874
knk@digicom.net.pk
Specialisation: Partner specialising in a wide range of commercial and corporate matters both contentious and non-contentious, including project finance, foreign investment and joint ventures, securities and exchange, privatisation, banking, construction contracts and appearances in court and before arbitrators in civil litigation and international arbitration matters;
Prof. Memberships: Advocate High Court; Member: Karachi Bar Association; honorary member, Association of Fellows and Legal Scholars of the Center for International Legal Studies, Salzburg, Austria.
Publications: Co-author of the chapter on Pakistan in Kluwer Law International's 'Remedies for International Sellers of Goods'; co-author of the Pakistan survey for Linklaters' Internet-based Blue Flag Asia-Pacific survey.
Career: Intern, *Akin, Gump, Strauss, Hauer and Feld*, Washington DC 1981; associate, *Abraham & Sarwana, Karachi*, 1986-89; associate partner, *Saeed Salman A Al Sharif & Partners*, Dubai UAE (1989-90); associate *Surridge & Beecheno*, Karachi (1991-95); Partner, *Surridge & Beecheno*, Karachi (1995-97);
Personal: Born 1958. Education: University of Karachi (1979 BA), University of Oklahoma (1982 BA Political Science); University of Oklahoma (1986 JD); University of Warwick (1991 LLM).

TAYEBALY, Irfan
Mohsin Tayebaly & Co, Karachi +92 21 587 26 90

VELLANI, Badaruddin
Vellani & Vellani, Karachi +92 21 580 1000
bfv@vellani.com
Specialisation: Partner of the firm and practising as an advocate at Karachi since returning in 1982, became a partner in January 1984. Legal practice has concentrated on commercial matters, including corporate work, mergers, demergers, reconstructions, acquisitions, disinvestments, anti-trust matters and monopolies, corporate finance, project finance, infrastructure projects, building and construction contracts, and taxation, and has included litigation in the courts up to the High Court. In addition to general legal practice, advises on industrial property or intellectual matters including registration assignment and licensing of patent, trade marks, copyrights, unfair competition licesing and franchising, and litigation in each of these specialised areas of work. Experience gained through legal practice has led to being invited to join the boards of directors of various companies representing the interests of foreign investors. Has also been the chairman of a working group for the

P

setting up of a legal information foundation and in a project funded by the Asia Foundation for making the country's laws and regulations and the decisions of the Courts in Pakistan available through the electronic media including via the internet. Acted as a consultant on an Asian Development Bank sponsored project and carried out by the Asia Foundation for the Government of Pakistan on Pakistan Legal and Judicial Reforms. Recently participated in a Symposium organised and held in Manila in September 1999 by the Asian Development Bank on secured Transactions Law Reforms.
Prof. Memberships: Memberships: Karachi Bar Association; High Court Bar Association (Karachi); General Council of the Bar (England); the Institution of Chemical Engineers (England); Founder Member SARCLAW; General Council of the Bar, Pakistan Industrial and Intellectual Property Association, the Asia Patent and Attorneys Association the Pakistan National Committee of the International Chamber of Commerce and a member of the Task Force on Tax Administration.
Personal: Languages: Urdu and English.

VELLANI, Fatehali
Vellani & Vellani, Karachi +92 21 580 1000
khi@vellani.com
Specialisation: Senior partner of the firm. Since returning to Pakistan in 1956, has been practising as an advocate. Legal practice has concentrated on commercial matters, including corporate work, mergers, demergers, reconstructions, acquisitions, disinvestments, anti-trust matters and monopolies, corporate finance, project finance, infrastructure projects, building and construction contracts, turnkey contracts, and taxation. Experience has included litigation in the courts up to the Supreme Court of Pakistan, besides appearances before specialised tribunals and before arbitrators. In addition to general legal practice, has for over 40 years advised on industrial or intellectual property matters including registration assignment and licensing of patents, trade marks and copyrights, domain names licensing and franchising, and litigation in each of these specialised areas of work. The experience gained through legal practice has led to being invited to join the boards of directors of various companies representing the interests of foreign investors.
Prof. Memberships: Karachi Bar Association; High Court Bar Association (Karachi); Supreme Court Bar Association; American Society of International Law; General Council of the Bar (England); Chartered Institute of Patent Agents; Institute of Trade Marks Agents; Pakistan Industrial and Intellectual Property Association; Asian Patent and Attorneys Association.
Personal: Education: University College of Wales, Aberystwyth (BA, Economics, 1953). Languages: Urdu and English.

YUSUF, Aliya
Orr, Dignam & Co, Karachi +92 21 241 6003/3422

PALESTINIAN TERRITORIES

Corporate/Commercial

PALESTINIAN TERRITORIES Leading firms (Corporate/Commercial)
1 AF&R Shehadeh Law Office
AMRO & Associates Law Offices
Sharhabeel Al Zaeem & Associates

Firms are listed alphabetically in each band.

Leading individuals (Corporate/Commercial)
1 AL ZAEEM Sharhabeel
Sharhabeel Al Zaeem & Associates

Individuals are listed alphabetically in each band.

AF&R Shehadeh Law Office (4 ptrs, 4 asscs) A *"strong, established practice"* focusing on corporate and commercial work, including drafting of contracts and representing foreign businesses. Based in Ramallah, its strength lies in banking and it has a special department for IP. The firm also represents the principal two Palestinian universities. **Clients:** IFC; World Bank; HSBC; Enron.

Amro & Associates Law Offices (2 ptrs, 3 asscs) A Ramallah firm offering legal advice to international investors and handling general corporate and commercial work on behalf of banks and government organisations. The firm is associated with the prestigious practice of Ali Sharif Zu'bi & Sharif Ali Zu'bi Law Office in Jordan. **Clients:** Nomura International; Cable & Wireless; MCI WorldCom.

Sharhabeel Al Zaeem & Associates (1 ptrs, 9 asscs) The firm has extensive experience in all commercial areas in Gaza, primarily company and contract law, IP, land and taxation. It has been active in establishing the Power generating company, to create the first power station (total investment capital of $140 million) in the Gaza Strip. The firm further assisted the company in obtaining a $90 million international finance package through the Arab Bank. Recommended to Chambers' researchers **Sharhabeel Al Zaeem** is *"a master draftsman"* in both Arabic and English. **Clients:** UNRWA; Enron; Reuters; Japanese Tobacco International.

Leaders' profiles – Palestinian Territories

AL ZAEEM, Sharhabeel
Sharhabeel Al Zaeem & Associates, Gaza
+972 7 282 0445

PANAMA

Corporate/Commercial

PANAMA Leading firms (Corporate/Commercial)	
1	Alemán, Cordero, Galindo & Lee
	Arias, Fábrega & Fábrega
	Icaza, Gonzalez-Ruiz & Alemán
	Morgan & Morgan
2	Arosemena Noriega & Contreras
	Galindo, Arias & Lopez
	Patton, Moreno & Asvat
3	Mossack Fonseca & Co

Firms are listed alphabetically in each band.

Leading individuals (Corporate/Commercial)	
1	**ALEMÁN Jaime** *Alemán, Cordero, Galindo & Lee*
	ALEMÁN Roberto *Icaza, Gonzalez-Ruiz & Alemán*
	AROSEMENA Carlos *Arosemena Noriega*
	CARDOZE Fernando *Arias, Fábrega*
	MORGAN Juan David *Morgan & Morgan*
	MORGAN Eduardo *Morgan & Morgan*
2	**ALEMÁN Alvaro** *Icaza, Gonzalez-Ruiz & Alemán*
	ARANGO Ricardo Manuel *Arias, Fábrega*
	CORDERO Carlos *Alemán, Cordero, Galindo & Lee*
	DE LA GUARDIA Juan *Raul Patton, Moreno & Asvat*
	FERRER Eduardo *Morgan & Morgan*
	GALINDO Anibal *Alemán, Cordero, Galindo & Lee*
	GALINDO Mario *Galindo, Arias & Lopez*

Individuals are listed alphabetically in each band.

Alemán, Cordero, Galindo & Lee (6 ptrs, 3 asscs) Recommended to our researchers for its *"excellent lawyers, providing a high quality service to international clients."* A leading light for banking, it is actively involved in privatisation agreements and negotiations and acted for a French cement company in its bid to purchase a controlling interest in Cemento Panama. The firm continues to work on port and railroad projects. *"Literate and legalistic"* **Jaime Alemán** *"knows the commercial side of international transactions"* and **Carlos Cordero** is a *"traditional corporate/M&A lawyer."* **Anibal Galindo** is regarded by competitors as an *"intelligent and eloquent"* lawyer. **Clients:** Cable & Wireless; Citibank; Dresdner Bank; Scotiabank; Evergreen Group; Kansas City Southern Industries; Constellation Power; Siemens; Kraft; Shell.

Arias, Fábrega & Fábrega (14 ptrs, 15 asscs) An established firm with a strong *"combination of tradition and professionalism."* Acknowledged to have *"top quality lawyers"* it advises on joint ventures, company formation and offshore work. **Fernando Cardoze** is the *"senior partner who carries weight"* and **Ricardo Manuel Arango** is a *"highly intelligent young partner"* who, rivals agree, is *"building up an incredible reputation."* The firm acted on the $130 million sale of Corporación Incem to Holderbank and Cementos del Caribe and also advised Banco General on with its hostile tender offer for all the shares of Primer Grupo Nacional. **Clients:** American Airlines; Texaco; Esso; Nissan; Marriott; Kodak; Chase Manhattan; Citibank; Credit Suisse First Boston; Lehman Brothers; American Express.

Icaza, Gonzalez-Ruiz & Alemán (19 ptrs, 7 asscs) Long-established, the firm undertakes banking, insurance, M&A, privatisation, and construction work to a level that peers acknowledged *"its success is our envy."* It acted on the merger between two local insurance companies and represented a German construction company on the building of a container port. **Roberto Alemán Jr** is *"thorough, dedicated and uses sound judgement"* while his brother **Alvaro Alemán** *"works well, away from the spotlight."* The firm acted for a company bidding to build a new bridge over the Panama Canal and advised on the privatisation of the Tocumen Airport. **Clients:** Coca-Cola; Shell; Nestlé; Merrill Lynch; AT&T; Unilever; Delta Airlines.

Morgan & Morgan (7 ptrs, 4 asscs) A large, full-service firm with a well-established shipping practice, it has gained *"local corporate strength"* increasing its activity in M&A transactions. The team advised on the merger between two local banks. Active in trusts and corporate planning, it advises on economic matters to international institutions. **Eduardo Morgan Sr** has *"good international connections"* and is viewed by competitors as *"the brains behind the organisation."* The *"multi-talented"* **Juan David Morgan** is *"managing the growth of the firm"* and **Eduardo Ferrer** has *"a good grasp of corporate and offshore matters."* **Clients:** South American and European companies; banks; trusts and private companies.

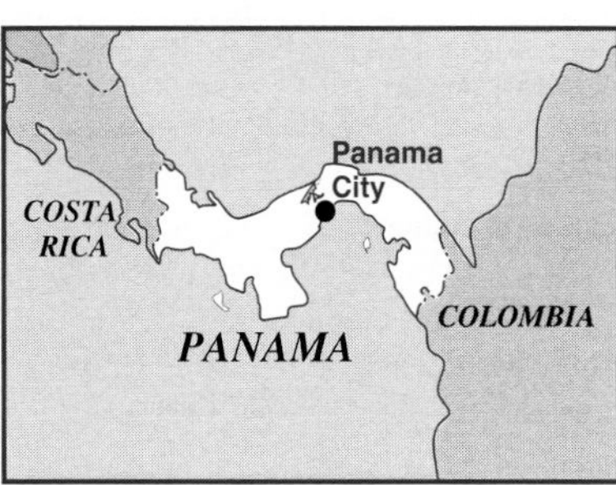

Arosemena Noriega & Contreras (6 ptrs, 6 asscs) An older firm that maintains an *"excellent local reputation,"* though seen less on the international scene. It undertakes corporate, tax, IP and admiralty work. *"Knowledgeable"* **Carlos Arosemena** is *"a senior figure in Panamanian law."* **Clients:** Banks; multinationals; manufacturers; pharmaceutical companies; oil and offshore companies.

Galindo, Arias & Lopez (10 ptrs, 10 asscs) Considered an *"improving local firm"* with a *"host of fine lawyers,"* it has a broad corporate and commercial coverage including M&A and foreign investment work. Privatisation and telecommunications are growth areas and the firm acted on the affiliation between COPA and Continental Airlines, and advised Union Fenosa in the privatisation of electrical distribution. **Mario Galindo** is a highly respected *"intellectual and scholarly"* lawyer. **Clients:** Scotiabank; Boston Bank; Schlumberger; insurance and cement companies.

Patton, Moreno & Asvat (5 ptrs, 5 asscs) Historically one of the country's leading shipping firms, it has expanded its general corporate and commercial work. The team represented an international corporate in the bidding for a local cement company and represented foreign investors in the acquisition of a business with operations throughout Central America. It is also active in hotel construction projects. **Juan Raul de la Guardia** is *"knowledgeable and well-liked."* **Clients:** Shipping companies; airlines; banks.

*See leaders' profiles on page 534

Mossack Fonseca & Co (2 ptrs, 7 asscs) The firm has an excellent reputation for its focus on *"company formation and offshore work."* It assisted on the merger between Bank of Tokyo and Mitsubishi Bank in Panama and advised on the design and organisation of the offshore corporate structure of a major South American business venture which now manages 33 airports in Argentina. **Clients:** International law firms; accountants; banks; trust companies.

Leaders' profiles – Panama

P

ALEMÁN, Alvaro
Icaza, Gonzalez-Ruiz & Alemán, Panama City
+507 263 5555

ALEMÁN, Jaime
Alemán, Cordero, Galindo & Lee, Panama City
+507 269 2620

ALEMÁN, Roberto
Icaza, Gonzalez-Ruiz & Alemán, Panama City
+507 263 5555

ARANGO, Ricardo Manuel
Arias, Fábrega & Fábrega, Panama City
+507 263 9200
rarango@arifa.co.
Specialisation: Partner since 1995, practising in the areas of securities regulations, bank and finance and mergers and acquisitions. Head of the firm's Securities Regulations Practice Group. Has acted as counsel to underwriters in connection with all issues of the Republic of Panama in recent years, including the 1996 issue of $3.2 million Brady Bonds to restructure Panama's external commercial debt; the 1997 issue of $500 million of 7 7/8% Notes; the 1997 offer to exchange Brady Bonds for $700 million of Global Bonds; the 1998 issue of $300 million of 8.25% Notes; the 1998 issue of $500 million of 9.375% Global Bonds; and the 2000 issue of $350 million of 10.75% Global Bonds. Advised Banco Latinoamericano de Exportaciones, S.A. (BLADEX) and Panamerican Beverages Co. (PANAMCO), two Panama corporations registered with the SEC, in the initial public offering of their shares in the NYSE. Also acts as counsel for Carnival Corporation, another NYSE listed company incorporated in Panama. Regularly advises clients in connection with Euro-Dollar Floating Rate Notes, Euro-Medium Term Note Programs, Euro-Commercial Paper Programs, Syndicated Loan Agreements, Revolving Credit Agreements and Securitization of Credit Card Receivables. In 2000, acted as counsel to underwriters in connection with a $125 million Commercial Paper Program for Banco Continental de Panamá, S.A. In the Panamanian market, has acted as the partner in charge of more than forty equity and debt issues of local companies, including, various bond issues of Banco General, SA; structuring the first securitisation of mortgage loans in Panama for The Chase Manhattan Bank; advising Banco del Istmo, S.A, in its initial public offering; and acting as counsel for Multi Holding Corporation, the local partner for BellSouth International Corp, in the issue of convertible securities. Also represents several local and international mutual funds. In the areas of mergers and acquisitions has participated in some of the largest mergers in Panama, including the 1996 merger between the two principal TV and radio networks to form Medcom Holdings Inc. In 1999 acted as the partner in charge of the merger between Banco General, S.A. and Banco Comercial de Panamá, S.A., at the time the largest bank merger in Panama's history, and in 2000 acted as the partner in charge of the sale of Corporación Incem, S.A., a Panama cement company, to Holderbank. From 1997 to 1999 headed the drafting efforts of the Presidential Commission appointed to prepare the country's new securities legislation enacted in July of 1999. Retained by LatinClear, S.A., Panama's custody and clearing agency, to draft its rules of operation modeled after the rules of The Depository Trust Company of New York.
Prof. Memberships: Member of the Association of the Bar of the City of New York, the American Society of Corporate Secretary, the Panama Bar Association and the National Law Center for Inter-American Free Trade.
Career: Deputy Director of The Panama Stock Exchange Inc. since 1995. With *White & Case*, New York from 1985 to 1987. Admitted to practise in New York and Panama.
Personal: Bachelor of Laws from the University of Panama in 1983, Masters of Laws from Harvard Law School in 1984 (concentration corporate law) and Masters of Law from Yale Law School in 1985 (concentration securities regulations and finance law). Fulbright Scholar, 1984-85.

AROSEMENA, Carlos
Arosemena Noriega & Contreras, Panama City
+507 265 3411

CARDOZE, Fernando
Arias, Fábrega & Fábrega, Panama City
+507 263 9200

CORDERO, Carlos
Alemán, Cordero, Galindo & Lee, Panama City
+507 269 2620

DE LA GUARDIA, Juan Raul
Patton Moreno & Asvat, Panama City
+507 264 8044

FERRER, Eduardo
Morgan & Morgan, Panama City +507 265 7777

GALINDO, Anibal
Alemán, Cordero, Galindo & Lee, Panama City
+507 269 2620

GALINDO, Mario
Galindo, Arias & Lopez, Panama City
+507 263 5633

MORGAN, Juan David
Morgan & Morgan, Panama City +507 265 7777

MORGAN SR, Eduardo
Morgan & Morgan, Panama City +507 265 7777

PAPUA NEW GUINEA

Corporate/Commercial

PAPUA NEW GUINEA Leading firms (Corporate/Commercial)
1 Allens Arthur Robinson Group
Blake Dawson Waldron
2 Gadens
3 Fiocco Posman & Kua
Warner Shand

Firms are listed alphabetically in each band.

Leading individuals (Corporate/Commercial)
1 **ALEXANDER Guy** *Allens Arthur Robinson Group*
2 **ALEXANDER Graeme** *Gadens*
FIOCCO Rio *Fiocco Posman & Kua*
SHEPHERD Geoff *Blake Dawson Waldron*
WILSON Michael *Warner Shand*

Individuals are listed alphabetically in each band.

Allens Arthur Robinson Group (1 ptr, 2 asscs) *"The leading commercial firm"* with *"good contacts,"* this definitely has *"its sights set on the future."* It was involved in the acquisition of BHP BNG oil and gas efforts worth $135 million, and acted for Niugini Mining in their merger with Liher Gold. Represented Taiheiyo Cement (the largest cement company in the world.) The firm has also been appointed by the government to act in the sale of Air New Guinea. *"Carrying the flag"* is **Guy Alexander**, *"the jurisdiction's leading commercial lawyer."* **Clients:** ANZ; Bank of South Pacific; Privatisation committee; Niugini Mining; Taiheiyo Cement.

Blake Dawson Waldron (1 ptr, 3 asscs) *"Currently in transition"* having merged with Shepherd's, this is still a *"reasonably strong"* outfit despite losing its two leading partners Richard Flynn and Philip Payne. Assisted in putting together a package for the corporatisation of Finance Pacific Ltd alongside KPMG, and has advised Lihir Gold Mine on mining, land and compensation matters. According to competitors, new partner **Geoff Shepherd** is more than capable of filling his predecessors' shoes. **Clients:** Finance Pacific Ltd; Lihir Gold Mine.

Gadens (2ptrs, 1 assc) A *"reasonably solid"* firm, *"reduced in size"* but which still benefits from its foreign connections. The firm acts for Chevron, and is advising them on the PNG side of the $3.5 billion pipeline to Queensland and also for InterOil, developer of a $180 million domestic oil refinery. The firm also acts for South Sea Tuna Corp in their joint venture with a leading American and Australian food processing company. The market rates **Graeme Alexander**. **Clients:** Chevron; InterOil; South Sea Tuna Corp.

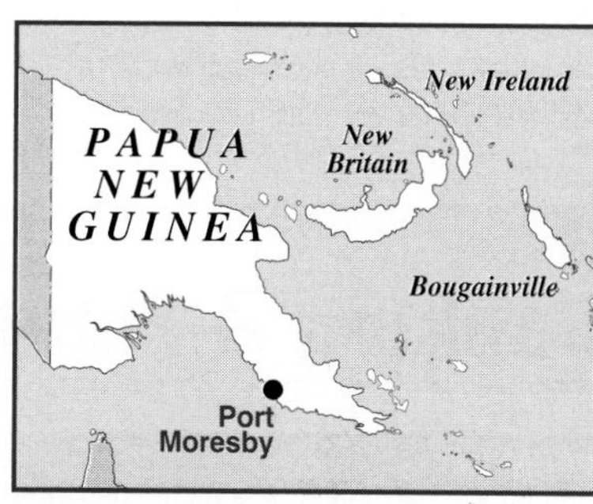

Fiocco Posman & Kua This is a *"good local firm,"* which has links to Australian firm Mallesons Stephen Jaques and is said to be *"expanding quickly."* Ex-pat **Rio Fiocco** is *"young, well qualified, competent and astute."* **Clients:** British Petroleum; UK Provident Resources; a major US oil company; Hasting & Deering.

Warner Shand (2 ptrs, 8 asscs) A firm which has recently *"recruited a lot of good, competent lawyers."* Advised the Coffee Industry Corp in the issuance of licenses and regulations relating to crops. Recommended to Chambers' researchers for its work in project development such as mining and oil exploration agreements. As owner, **Michael Wilson**'s *"reputation gets the firm a lot of business."* **Clients:** Wahgi Mek Plantations; Carpenter Group.

Leaders' profiles – Papua New Guinea

ALEXANDER, Graeme
Gadens, Port Moresby +675 321 1033

ALEXANDER, Guy David
Allens Arthur Robinson Group, Port Moresby +675 320 2000

FIOCCO, Rio George
Fiocco Posman & Kua, Port Moresby
+675 320 0127
fpklawyers@dg.com.pg
Specialisation: Partner in corporate department of *Fiocco Posman & Kua*. Associated firm – *Mallesons Stephen Jacques.* Main area of work is corporate law, principally mergers and acquisitions, liquidations, corporate restructuring and commercial law. Acted for Sime Darby Behard on the acquisition of PNG Caterpillar franchise and Pacific Helicopters Ltd on the acquisition of Airlink Ltd; acted for Abn Amro on the refinancing of Lihir Gold Ltd and BHP on the restructure of BHP Titan Ltd. Assisted PNG government on the corporatisation of Telikom PNG Ltd. Acts as general counsel to a wide range of international and local companies particularly on the establishment of their business in Papua New Guinea.
Prof. Memberships: Queensland Law Society. Papua New Guinea Law Society.
Career: Qualified in 1986 as a solicitor of the Supreme Court of Queensland, Australia and in 1987 as a lawyer of the National Court of Justice, Papua New Guinea. Partner at *Fiocco Posman & Kua* since 1993. Minister's appointee to PNG Board of Architects; Honorary Lawyer to PNG Red Cross Society Inc.
Personal: Born 13 February 1962. Attended Queensland University, 1979-1984, B.Comm. LLB (Hons). Leisure interests include marathon running, tennis and Rotary.

SHEPHERD, Geoff
Blake Dawson Waldron, Port Moresby
+675 309 2000

WILSON, Michael
Warner Shand, Boroko +675 325 4422

PARAGUAY

OVERVIEW: The first wave of privatisation in telecoms, water and rail-road rights has hit Paraguay, years after other Latin American countries. An increase in activity is expected due to the recent approval of a 'maquila' law, whereby foreign companies are able to import raw materials to factories in the country and re-export the finished product. This is hoped to provide a partial solution to the ban on foreign investors financing projects independently of the state government. It should also act as a boost to the static banking law sector that has been plagued by disputes with regulators over tax issues. Few Paraguayan firms have modernised from the traditional family outfit, though Ferrere-Lamaison's unconventionally aggressive approach has been making waves in both corporate/M&A and financial law circles.

Banking & Finance

PARAGUAY Leading firms (Banking & Finance)
1 Fiorio, Cardozo & Alvarado
Estudio Jurídico Gross Brown
Vouga & Olmedo

Firms are listed alphabetically in each band.

Leading individuals (Banking & Finance)
1 FIORIO Juan *Fiorio, Cardozo & Alvarado*
GROSS BROWN Jorge *Gross Brown*
OLMEDO Gustavo *Vouga & Olmedo*

Individuals are listed alphabetically in each band.

Fiorio, Cardozo & Alvarado (3 ptrs, 14 asscs) Led by **Juan Fiorio***, *"an excellent and versatile commercial lawyer,"* the firm is known for its work on behalf of ABN AMRO. It has specific expertise in advising on restructuring of local debt, while its insolvency prowess was highlighted by its work on the voluntary liquidation of its client Banco Corporación. The firm is also acknowledged by rivals as a leading project finance player, often acting on behalf of Exim Bank. Acted on the loan by a Norwegian governmental agency to a part Norwegian-owned Paraguayan company for the development of a coffee plantation. **Clients:** ABN AMRO; Exim Bank; Banco Corporación; Cessna Finance Corporation.

Estudio Jurídico Gross Brown (3 ptrs, 9 asscs) Known as *"the best for finance"* the firm earns recognition in this sphere for its work as counsel to Citibank, Lloyds TSB and ING. The team advises on banking M&A, syndicated loans and acquisition finance, and is led by name partner **Jorge Gross Brown***, who is *"a genuine banking expert."* **Clients:** Citibank; Lloyds TSB; ING; Private Banking Association of Paraguay.

Vouga & Olmedo (6 ptrs, 24 asscs) Advising a mixture of overseas and domestic financial institutions, the firm's banking group is regarded as an *"innovative force."* **Gustavo Olmedo*** is the resident financial expert.

The firm recently participated in the first local bond issue for China Trust and advised on the first restructuring of debt in the country involving a trust structure, representing the trustee, Multibanco, on the $50 million reorganisation of Grupo Las Palmas. Other work has included representing Dresdner Bank on its loans to Grupo Espíritu Santo and Cargill. **Clients:** CSFB; China Trust; Dresdner Bank; Merrill Lynch; domestic financial institutions.

Corporate/M&A

Berkemeyer (17 lawyers) A general commercial firm that has grown from an IP boutique to be a leading player in cross-border M&A, notably in telecoms, financial services and utilities. **Hugo Berkemeyer Jnr*** is *"a well-known all-rounder,"* and leads a team that advises a predominantly overseas clientele. The firm advised on the acquisition of a Brazilian bank by a domestic concern, and acted on the purchase of domestic soft-drinks bottler PARESA by Coca-Cola. **Clients:** Schering-Plough.

Fiorio, Cardozo & Alvarado (3 ptrs, 14 asscs) A strong commercial firm, applauded by rivals for its *"technically excellent lawyers,"* who advise an international clientele from industries such as pharmaceuticals, shipping and financial services. **Marcelo Alvarado*** and **Juan Fiorio*** are said by clients to *"inspire confidence."* **Clients:** SmithKline Beecham; Glaxo Wellcome; Kimberly Clark; ACBL.

Estudio Jurídico Gross Brown (3 ptrs, 9 asscs) An *"excellent"* firm, seen by its peers as *"one of the best corporate teams in the country,"* and which services multi-national and domestic clients from all industries. As sole representative of Shell in Paraguay, the firm is active in its retail and forestry operations, and advised on a huge investment in a port terminal in Asunción. **Jorge Gross Brown*** is the firm's outstanding practitioner.

Recent transactional activity includes assisting an international airline catering company in its acquisition of a Paraguayan corporate, and advising on a number of banking M&A matters. **Clients:** Shell; Johnson & Johnson.

Estudio Mersan (4 ptrs, 5 asscs) Said to be *"of a uniformly high standard,"* the firm's corporate team advises a blue-chip international client base on investments in Paraguay, notably in hi-tech industry. **Carlos Mersan*** was recommended to

*See leaders' profiles on pages 537

PARAGUAY
Leading firms
(Corporate/Mergers & Acquisitions)

Band	Firm
1	Berkemeyer
	Fiorio, Cardozo & Alvarado
	Estudio Jurídico Gross Brown
	Estudio Mersan
	Moreno Ruffinelli
	Peroni, Sosa, Tellechea, Burt & Narvaja
	Vouga & Olmedo

Firms are listed alphabetically in each band.

Leading individuals
(Corporate/Mergers & Acquisitions)

Band	Individual
1	**ALVARADO Marcelo** *Fiorio, Cardozo & Alvarado*
	BERKEMEYER Hugo *Berkemeyer*
	FIORIO Juan *Fiorio, Cardozo & Alvarado*
	MERSAN Carlos *Estudio Mersan*
2	**BURT Esteban** *Peroni, Sosa, Tellechea*
	GROSS BROWN Jorge *Gross Brown*
	OLMEDO Gustavo *Vouga & Olmedo*
	RUOTI Nora *Peroni, Sosa, Tellechea*
	VOUGA Rodolfo *Vouga & Olmedo*
	ZAVALA Diego *Estudio Mersan*

Individuals are listed alphabetically in each band.

researchers as *"the star of the show,"* and is supported by Yale-educated **Diego Zavala***, who also has a fine reputation for arbitration. **Clients:** Citibank; Texaco; IFC; Haliburton; Mitsubishi; Microsoft; IBM; Coca-Cola; BAT; Nike; Guess; Benetton; Mazda; Polo Lauren; Unisys; Daewoo.

Moreno Ruffinelli (7 ptrs, 11 asscs) Formerly known as a domestically inclined operation, the firm is now seen to be *"one of the leading all-round commercial players,"* acting for a mix of high-profile international and domestic clients. The team was prominent in the first wave of privatisations in Paraguay, advising both prospective investors and governmental bodies on the process. Examples include the state water company, and the securitisation of the first private road concession, where the firm acted for the successful domestic joint venture.

Other work includes acting for foreign clients on establishing branches in Paraguay, such as Newmont Gold and Telefónica de España. **Clients:** Telefónica; Alcatel; IBD; McDonald's; Toyota; PwC; Kodak; Coors; Newmont Gold; Rhone Poulenc; Paraguayan Chamber of Commerce.

Peroni, Sosa, Tellechea, Burt & Narvaja (17 ptrs) A respected corporate practice with *"an international outlook,"* which advises on cross-border M&A for a clientele of which 80% are foreign investors. Harvard-educated partner **Esteban Burt*** enjoys a healthy reputation as a rainmaker, while **Nora Lucia Ruoti*** was recommended to researchers for her *"commercial instincts,"* and has a mixed corporate and tax practice.

Typically acting on behalf of the buyer, the firm has advised on acquisitions in areas such as energy, financial services and manufacturing. **Clients:** International banks and corporates.

Vouga & Olmedo (6 ptrs, 24 asscs) The largest firm in Paraguay, it is seen by competitors as one of the leaders for work with an international flavour. The majority of the client base is composed of foreign investors, hailing from a variety of industries. **Rodolfo Vouga*** and **Gustavo Olmedo*** are highly respected by competitors.

The firm advised Hutchinson on the acquisition of a small mobile telecoms company, and acted on the Paraguayan aspects of the merger between BASF and Cyanamide. Also represented Grupo Velox, the powerful Argentinean/Uruguayan holding company, on the purchase of the local retail division of Banco Santander Central Hispano. **Clients:** Hutchinson Telecom; BASF; Delta Airlines; P&G; Colgate Palmolive; Accor; Conti Group; Allied Domecq; Schering-Plough.

P

Leaders' profiles – Paraguay

ALVARADO, Marcelo
Fiorio, Cardozo & Alvarado, Asuncion
+595 2161 0229
Recommended in Corporate/M&A

BERKEMEYER JR, Hugo
Berkemeyer, Asuncion +595 21 446 706
Recommended in Corporate/M&A

BURT, Esteban
Peroni, Sosa, Tellechea, Burt & Narvaja, Asuncion
+595 21 663 536
Recommended in Corporate/M&A

FIORIO, Juan
Fiorio, Cardozo & Alvarado, Asuncion
+595 2161 0229
Recommended in Banking & Finance, Corporate/M&A

GROSS BROWN, Jorge
Estudio Jurídico Gross Brown, Asuncion
+595 2149 4644
Recommended in Banking & Finance, Corporate/M&A

MERSAN, Carlos
Estudio Mersan, Asuncion +595 2144 7739
Recommended in Corporate/M&A

OLMEDO, Gustavo
Vouga & Olmedo, Asuncion +595 21 213 598
Recommended in Banking & Finance, Corporate/M&A

RUOTI, Nora
Peroni, Sosa, Tellechea, Burt & Narvaja, Asuncion
+595 21 663 536
Recommended in Corporate/M&A

VOUGA, Rodolfo
Vouga & Olmedo, Asuncion +595 21 213 598
Recommended in Corporate/M&A

ZAVALA, Diego
Estudio Mersan, Asuncion +595 2144 7739
Recommended in Corporate/M&A

PERU

Index

P

OVERVIEW: A meritocratic system encouraging younger lawyers to excel has started to take hold in the country. Many firms continue to be defined by associations with national politics, but this year Uría Abogados has distanced itself from a link with the incumbent Fujimori government, losing former name partner, Fernando Trazegnies, a cabinet member. It is the only firm with an international association (Uría & Menéndez of Spain) and, though the international accountancy firms are attempting to establish themselves research indicates that, so far, they have not been successful. A wave of privatisations has generated a substantial deal flow, the highlight being Lima airport, and oil, gas and mining continue to be sources of project financings.

Banking & Finance

PERU Leading firms (Banking & Finance)	
1	Estudio Luis Echecopar Garcia
	Estudio Muñiz, Forsyth, Ramírez, Pérez-Taiman & Luna-Victoria Abogados
	Rodrigo Elias y Medrano
2	Uría Abogados
3	Estudio Aurelio Garcia Sayan
	Estudio Grau
	Miranda y Amado
	Rubio Leguia Normand & Asociados

Firms are listed alphabetically in each band.

Leading individuals (Banking & Finance)	
1	**BATIEVSKY Jack** *Rodrigo Elias y Medrano*
	NOYA DE LA PIEDRA Ismael *Estudio Luis Echecopar Garcia*
	PAYET José Antonio *Uría Abogados*
2	**CASTRO Javier** *Estudio Luis Echecopar Garcia*
	FORSYTH Albert *Estudio Muñiz, Forsyth, Ramírez, Pérez-Taiman & Luna-Victoria Abogados*
	FUENTES Sandro *Rodrigo Elias y Medrano*
	GARCIA SAYAN Francisco Moreyra *Estudio Aurelio Garcia Sayan*
	NORMAND Enrique *Rubio Leguia Normand*
	REBAZA Alberto *Rodrigo Elias y Medrano*

Individuals are listed alphabetically in each band.

Estudio Luis Echecopar Garcia (3 ptrs, 5 asscs) Highly rated banking practice, which acts for a number of international financial institutions and specialises in project finance and banking M&A. Competitors regard the firm's head of finance, **Ismael Noya de la Piedra***, as *"the top man in Peru for banking transactions,"* while the *"very smart"* **Javier Castro***, recently hired from a local bank, is renowned for his bank regulatory work.

The firm advised on the financing of the Antamina mining project, acting for a syndicate of European, North American and Japanese banks. It also represented a European bank on a $90 million loan to zinc mining company Volcan, and has negotiated international loans for Banco de Crédito, Peru's largest bank. **Clients:** Chase Manhattan; Citibank; Merrill Lynch; Banco Santander Central Hispano; IFC; Dresdner Bank; BNP-Paribas; Banco de Crédito.

Estudio Muñiz, Forsyth, Ramírez, Pérez-Taiman & Luna-Victoria Abogados (3 ptrs, 9 asscs) Particularly involved in financing transactions in the telecoms and energy sectors, the firm has also advised on a number of international securities placements. **Albert Forsyth*** is the head of department, and was recommended to researchers for his *"transactional flair,"* especially in capital markets.

The firm advised Chase Manhattan on a $320 million loan facility to a Chilean corporate for the acquisition of Chilean and Peruvian companies. Also advised Citibank on a loan to Backus for the Cervesur take-over, and represented the same client as part of an international syndicate on a $114 million loan to Pluspetrol. **Clients:** BBV; Bancomex; American Express Bank; BNP-Paribas; BankBoston; Bank of America; Citibank; CSFB.

Rodrigo Elias y Medrano *"Excellent attorneys"* who have a healthy reputation for both transactional and regulatory work in the sector. The firm has been particularly active for corporate clients on issuing bonds in the local market, and acted for the largest Peruvian fishing company on the issue of $64 million worth of bonds. It has also acted for domestic electric companies Luz del Sur and Edegel and mining and telecoms entities in bond placements.

Jack Batievsky is known as the firm's international finance contact, and is respected for his transactional abilities. **Sandro Fuentes*** is a *"sound all-round finance lawyer,"* while *"rising star"* **Alberto Rebaza*** is developing a fine reputation as a practitioner who *"gets through a lot of work."* The team has advised a number of local banks on syndicated loans. **Clients:** BBV; Banco del Progreso; IDB; Banco Wiese-Sudameris; Bank One; JP Morgan; Interbank.

Uría Abogados (2 ptrs, 9 asscs) Strong capital markets team, which acts mainly for local subsidiaries of multinationals issuing bonds on the Peruvian market. According to competitors, the firm is *"in the process of passing from the second to the first tier."* This is seen to owe much to its connections with leading Spanish firm Uría & Menéndez. Managing partner **José Antonio Payet*** was recommended to researchers for his advice on pension funds and bank regulatory issues.

As part of the Telefónica share swap, the firm worked with Banco Continental and Bank Boston in raising securities. The team also handled the bond issue by Enersur, Tractabel's Peruvian subsidiary, to raise finance for an energy project. **Clients:** Banco Santander Central Hispano; Banco de Crédito; Banco Continental; Commonwealth Development Corporation.

Estudio Aurelio Garcia Sayan The firm has acknowledged lending and project finance prowess, and counts among its clients the IFC and the German finance division DEG. The banking team has advised both these clients on loans to Peruvian corporates, and is also commended for its expertise on mining projects. **Francisco Moreyra Garcia Sayan*** wins widespread acclaim for his bank regulatory work. **Clients:** IFC; Midland Bank; Wells Fargo Bank; Royal Bank of Canada; IDB; HSBC.

Estudio Grau (3 ptrs, 3 asscs) Especially active in advising on the financing of mining projects, the firm's reputation for innovation was exemplified by its handling of Peru's first combined loan and bond issue. Project finance work includes acting for Rio Algom as part of a syndicate investing $2.3 billion in the Minera Antamina. **Clients:** BankBoston; Citibank; Bank of London & South America; Lloyds Bank.

Miranda y Amado (5 ptrs, 2 asscs) A young firm with a *"promising"* banking practice, which is active in a full range of financial activities, from lending to capital markets and asset and project finance. Recommended to researchers for its transactional skill, the firm has experience of syndicated and unilateral loans, acting for borrowers and lenders. The firm advised Goldman Sachs on a recent infrastructure project. **Clients:** Banco de Crédito; BankBoston; BBVA Banco Continental; Citibank; CSFB; IFC; Merrill Lynch.

Rubio Leguia Normand & Asociados (5 lawyers) A *"well respected"* banking and finance practice that is active on bond issues in the domestic market, as well as a variety of project finance transactions. Esteemed **Enrique Normand*** is said by clients to be a *"lawyer for all seasons."*

The firm advised a local subsidiary of Newmont Mining on a $100 million loan from the IFC for the financing of the La Quinua mine project. It also assisted West LB on a $13 million revolving credit facility to Minera Rayrock, and The Bank of Nova Scotia on the restructuring of a $5 million revolving credit facility to Alicorp. **Clients:** West LB; Bank of Nova Scotia; JP Morgan; Citibank.

P

Corporate/M&A

PERU Leading firms (Corporate/Mergers & Acquisitions)	
1	Rodrigo Elias y Medrano
2	Estudio Luis Echecopar Garcia
	Rubio Leguia Normand & Asociados
3	Estudio Aurelio Garcia Sayan
	Estudio Muñiz, Forsyth, Ramírez, Pérez-Taiman & Luna-Victoria Abogados
4	Miranda y Amado
	Uría Abogados
5	Estudio Grau
	Estudio Llona & Bustamante
	Estudio Olaechea
	Osterling Arias-Schreiber Vega Orbegoso & Asociados

Firms are listed alphabetically in each band.

Rodrigo Elias y Medrano (22 ptrs, 30 asscs) *"A fine homogenous firm"* widely regarded as *"top"* for tax and privatisation, its strength lies in consistency; *"all the lawyers are good." "First class"* managing partner **Enrique Elias*** is a *" smart"* corporate expert, supported by well-known corporate stars **Jack Batievsky*** and **Julio Salas***. *"Prestigious"* tax practitioner **Humberto Medrano*** is reputed for his technical abilities.

Famed as counsel to Corporación Cervecera del Sur in its sale to Backus & Johnston breweries, the largest Peruvian M&A deal this year, the firm also advised Phelps Dodge on the acquisition of Cyprus-Amax's Peruvian interests (including the important copper mine Cerro Verde) and represented Kimberly-Clark on a merger between its local subsidiary and a domestic paper producer. The firm has a focus on niche areas including mining, where most clients are foreign investors, and the financial sector, for major local banks. **Clients:** American Airlines; Amoco; BBVA; IDB; Boeing; JP Morgan; Kimberly-Clark; McDonald's; Microsoft; Nextel; Texaco; National Grid; Viacom; Volvo; Xerox; Banco de Crédito.

Estudio Luis Echecopar Garcia (11 ptrs, 25 asscs) A *"traditional, family style"* firm recommended by peers in Lima as *"serious and reliable,"* with *"a good group of lawyers"* despite losing the founding members of Miranda & Amado. **Renato Vázquez*** is a *"prominent"* corporate player, of the *"old-style,"* who handles tax and labour matters.

The bulk of its work load is commercial contracts and M&A transactions for domestic and international corporates. The team advised Perkins Engines on the restructuring of a long-term investment and acted in the merger of two Peruvian companies that formed a leading manufacturer of machines and fish factories. **Clients:** Perkins Engines Group; international and domestic corporates in banking and industry.

Rubio Leguia Normand & Asociados (7 ptrs, 23 asscs) A *"complete"* full service firm that has a proficient corporate practice and a specialisation in mining. Among its *"serious team,"* is **Enrique Normand***, *"a stupendous lawyer and a wonderful person"* who chaired the group that re-drafted the national corporate law and advised Backus & Johnston, Peru's largest brewery, in its $150 million take-over of Cevecera del Sur, and the associated anti-trust application.

Active on privatisations in the mining, ports and airports sphere, the team has environmental expertise. The majority of the firm's clients are international corporates in the telecoms, natural resources, pharmaceutical and manufacturing sectors. **Clients:** Backus & Johnston; IFC; Mobil; YPF; American Airlines; Geotec; Cyprus-Amax; Newmont Mining; Bechtel; Telefónica; P&G; BAT.

Estudio Aurelio Garcia Sayan (6 ptrs, 13 asscs) Perceived by peers as a *"conservative"* firm (organised as a series of sole practitioners who share facilities,) it is extremely popular in its traditional *"non-aggressive"* approach. It has a fine base of clients and focuses on manufacturing and the natural resources sphere. The *"distinguished"* group of *"good people,"* is headed up by **Francisco Moreyra Garcia Sayan*** a *"first class"* commercial lawyer. Involved in foreign investment, the firm is experienced in the restructuring of domestic clients, and acted as counsel to one of the bidders for the Lima airport privatisation. **Clients:** Ford; Mobil; Swissair; Swissotel; Elf Gas;

*See leaders' profiles on page 541

PERU
Leading individuals
(Corporate/Mergers & Acquisitions)

1
ELIAS Enrique *Rodrigo Elias y Medrano*
GARCIA SAYAN Francisco Moreyra *Estudio Aurelio Garcia Sayan*
NORMAND Enrique *Rubio Leguia Normand*
PAYET José Antonio *Uría Abogados*

2
AMADO José Daniel *Miranda y Amado*
BATIEVSKY Jack *Rodrigo Elias y Medrano*
FORSYTH Albert *Estudio Muñiz, Forsyth, Ramírez, Pérez-Taiman & Luna-Victoria Abogados*
LLONA Alvaro *Estudio Llona & Bustamante*
VÁZQUEZ Renato *Estudio Luis Echecopar Garcia*

3
MEDRANO Humberto *Rodrigo Elias y Medrano*
MUÑIZ Jorge *Estudio Muñiz, Forsyth, Ramírez, Pérez-Taiman & Luna-Victoria Abogados*
OSTERLING Felipe *Osterling Arias-Schreiber Vega Orbegoso & Asociados*
SALAS Julio *Rodrigo Elias y Medrano*

Individuals are listed alphabetically in each band.

China National Petrol Corporation; Groupe GTM; Whirlpool; IDB; Newmont Gold.

Estudio Muñiz, Forsyth, Ramírez, Pérez-Taiman & Luna-Victoria Abogados (16 ptrs, 68 asscs) Perceived as an *"aggressive"* corporate practice, it is undergoing rapid growth with specialisms in mining and oil. *"An excellent group of lawyers"* includes **Albert Forsyth*** who is considered *"the one who does the bulk of work,"* and founding partner **Jorge Muñiz*** *"the wizard who built the firm."*

The firm acts for Pluspetrol and Promigas in the ongoing $2 billion Camisea gas field project, the second largest on the continent and acted for Dominion Energy in the $400 million sale of its subsidiary to Duke Energy. It also advised NBK Bank in structuring the split up of Banco Solventa and its subsequent merger into Norbank. **Clients:** Adecco; AES; Alberta Energy; Alfa Wassermann; Aventis; BellSouth; Braun; Bristol Myers Squibb; BAT; Colgate Palmolive; Cervesur; CAF; Daewoo.

Miranda y Amado (10 ptrs, 7 asscs) Formed as a spin-off of Echecopar, this young firm is a *"powerful boutique"* concentrating on transactional work for foreign investors in telecoms, utilities and consumer products. It also counsels influential Peruvian conglomerates, such as Entel, Grupo Gloria and Volcan. Founding partner **José Daniel Amado*** is an *"extremely aggressive and intelligent"* market player.

Active for prospective concessionaires in the privatisation of state ports, radio stations and electrical works, it assisted Diveo's subsidiary in the acquisition of two local radio companies. As counsel to Duke Energy, the firm acted in its purchase of Dominion's Latin American assets, and in the acquisition of a domestic electricity generator. **Clients:** Brahma; Citibank; Compaq; Diveo; Duke Energy; General Electric; Intel; Hicks Muse Tate & Furst; IFC; Nextel; Tractabel; Winstar.

Uría Abogados (3 Peruvian ptrs, 1 Spanish ptr, 26 asscs) Emerging from the controversial departure of one of its former name partners, this strong corporate player is *"aggressive and modern,"* and has an envied base of Spanish clients, due to a close relationship with Uría & Menéndez. It acted on the Telefónica share swap between the Spanish and Peruvian telecoms firms. A *"well-rounded attorney,"* **José Antonio Payet*** is recommended for his corporate expertise and strong leadership. According to one source *"the firm works from his desk."*

With a client base of mainly multi-nationals and their local subsidiaries, the firm advised on the sale of the largest Peruvian copper mine to a Mexican conglomerate. It has a focus on the energy and telecoms sector and is developing an internet practice. The firm recently recruited the former head of Arthur Andersen's Peruvian legal activities. **Clients:** Wiese Aetna; Endesa; Ferrovial; Philip Morris; Telefónica; Terra Lycos; Tractabel; PSCG.

Estudio Grau (9 ptrs, 18 asscs) A *"serious"* full service firm acclaimed for its telecoms and banking M&A and with a keen focus on mining and energy work. The team advised a consortium that included Hydro Quebec on an electrical transport line between the North and the South of the country and acted for Shell on the Camisea gas field in the early stages of its exploitation. The team also represented Unilever in the purchase of a domestic corporate and assisted EMBONOR in the acquisition of Peru's largest Coca-Cola bottling company. **Clients:** Dominion; Unisys; Rio Algom; UK-Peru Chamber of Commerce; EMI; Rio Tinto; Royal Dutch Shell; Unilever; Air France; KLM; Sony; Repsol.

Estudio Llona & Bustamante (4 ptrs, 9 asscs) A small *"prestigious"* firm said to have *"a couple of large clients,"* including concessionaires, pension and investment funds. Researchers were impressed by corporate *"leader"* **Alvaro Llona***, a *"first class lawyer."* The team advised on the merger of Progreso Bank and Norbank, to create NBK Bank and acted in the sale of the Peruvian assets of a multinational. Privatisation has proved to be a growth area – the firm acted for the successful bidders in the Jequetepeque Zaña desert development project and was involved in the sell-off of Lima's airport and the Camisea gas project. **Clients:** Domestic corporates; Banco Santander Central Hispano; Nissan; Entergy; Global One Communications.

Estudio Olaechea (9 ptrs, 14 asscs) A long-established family firm with *" nobility and seriousness"* recommended for its fine lawyers despite recent losses. It advises foreign investors and undertakes international arbitration for clients in power, mining, telecoms and banking. The firm acted for Vattenfall in its acquisition of a 60% holding in hydro-electric generator Cahua, and represented Minera Sunshine del Peru in its successful bid for the privatisation of the Mishki mining deposit. **Clients:** Adidas; AmEx; Banque Indosuez; Banque Paribas; Euromoney; Fisher Price; Fox Latin America; General Electric; Lucent; Mitsubishi; Pennzoil; SocGen; SmithKline Beecham.

Osterling Arias-Schreiber Vega Orbegoso & Asociados (14 lawyers) *"A bright practice"* with a largely domestic clientele, the firm is thought by peers to be *"keeping a steady pace,"* with its *"old style"* practice. Senior partner **Felipe Osterling*** is famed locally for his involvement in politics, and is trusted by clients as *"a very valuable person to have on your side."* **Clients:** Banco Santander Central Hispano; local insurance companies; mining companies; trade associations; Ernst & Young; L'Oreal; Nestlé; Reuters; Sanofi; SmithKline Beecham; YSL.

*See leaders' profiles on page 541

Leaders' profiles – Peru

AMADO, Jose Daniel
Miranda y Amado, Lima 27 +511 222 4747
jdamado@mafirma.com.pe
Specialisation: Main areas of work are corporate law and regulated industries. In the last twelve months has handled major industry acquisitions and merger proposals for clients such as Citibank, Duke Energy, Nextel Communications, Compaq Computer, Bank Boston, Ontario Hydro, Telmex, Televisa, Salomon Smith Barney, etc.
Prof. Memberships: Lima Bar Association, Inter-American Bar Association, International Bar Association.
Publications: In the last few months has published on state contracts, concessions, stabilisation clauses, telecommunications, electricity.
Career: Associate with *Wilmer, Cutler & Pickering,* Washington DC from 1988-1991. Partner at *Estudio Luis Echecopar Garcia* 1994-1999. Senior Partner, *Miranda & Amado Abogados.*
Personal: Graduate Program at Harvard University (Master of Laws), awarded Laylin Prize 1988 of International Law. Professor of International Economic Law, Catholic University of Peru (1991-1993).

BATIEVSKY, Jack
Rodrigo Elias y Medrano, Lima 11 +51 1 219 1900

CASTRO, Javier
Estudio Luis Echecopar Garcia, Lima
+511 372 7373

ELIAS, Enrique
Rodrigo Elias y Medrano, Lima 11 +51 1 219 1900

FORSYTH, Albert
Estudio Muniz Forsyth Ramirez Perez-Taiman & Luna Victoria Abogados, Lima 27 +51 1 422 11 22
albertf@munizlaw.com.pe
Specialisation: Specialises in banking & finance, capital markets and mergers & acquisitions.
Prof. Memberships: Lima Stock Exchange Arbitration, Controversy and Disciplinary Chambers.
Publications: Author of research work, including 'Offering of Peruvian Company Shares through American Depository Receipts'; 'Issuance of Bonds in Peru', 'Securitization of Assets'.
Career: Before joining the firm, worked for *Estudio Echecopar* specialising in civil and civil procedural law. Then served as Property Rights Program Manager for Instituto Libertad y Democracia (ILD), and ILD Manager of International Projects in El Salvador, Nicaragua, Honduras and Guatemala. Has served as Legal Manager of Tele 2000, currently BellSouth Peru.
Personal: Born 21 December 1958. Earned a Bachelor's degree in law and a law degree summa cum laude from the Catholic University of Peru School of Law, graduated in 1982. Pursued post-graduate studies in civil, commercial and international law at the Harvard University Law School, where earned a Master's Degree in Law.

FUENTES, Sandro
Rodrigo Elias y Medrano, Lima 11 +51 1 219 1900

GARCIA SAYAN, Francisco Moreyra
Estudio Aurelio Garcia Sayan, Lima 27
+51 1 440 7341

LLONA, Alvaro
Estudio Llona & Bustamante, Lima 27
+511 221 2634

MEDRANO, Humberto
Rodrigo Elias y Medrano, Lima 11 +51 1 219 1900

MUÑIZ, Jorge
Estudio Muniz Forsyth Ramirez Perez-Taiman & Luna Victoria Abogados, Lima 27 +51 1 422 11 22
jmuniz@munizlaw.com.pe
Specialisation: Specialises in Corporate Law, Commercial Law, Mergers & Acquisitions, Contracts, Foreign Investment and E-Commerce.
Prof. Memberships: E-Commerce Peruvian Institute.
Publications: Author of several works about contracts and e-commerce in dailies, magazines and academic reviews.
Career: Has filled important public positions, serving as President of the National Commision of Foreign Investment and Technology; President of the National Institute for the Defense of Competition and Intellectual Property and member of the Board of Directors of the entity in charge of supervising private investment in telecommunications. Also actively contributed to the formulation of legislation promoting and regulating e-commerce.
Personal: Born 11 August 1952. Founding partner of the Firm and graduated summa cum laude from the Catholic University of Peru School of Law. Has taken advanced courses in International Contracts at Fordhan University, New York. Has also participated in the "Visiting Professional Program" organized by New York University.

NORMAND, Enrique
Rubio Leguia Normand & Asociados, Lima 27
+51 1 442 4900

NOYA DE LA PIEDRA, Ismael
Estudio Luis Echecopar Garcia, Lima
+511 372 7373

OSTERLING, Felipe
Osterling Arias-Schreiber Vega Orbegoso & Asociados, Lima +511 442 0770

PAYET, Jose Antonio
Uría Abogados, Lima 27 +511 222 3202

REBAZA, Alberto
Rodrigo Elias y Medrano, Lima 11 +51 1 219 1900

SALAS, Julio
Rodrigo Elias y Medrano, Lima 11 +51 1 219 1900

VÁZQUEZ, Renato
Estudio Luis Echecopar Garcia, Lima
+51 1 219 1900

P

PHILIPPINES

OVERVIEW: Recent political instability has affected business confidence, with the result that foreign investments have been in decline, and the number of serious commercial law firms has shown a similar drop.

The new securities regulation code became effective in August 2000. The new law contains a mandatory tender offer, which is automatically triggered in the case of an acquisition of 15% or more of a publicly held company. This measure, together with a reported massive increase in due diligence, should keep the elite band of leading firms busy over the short and medium term.

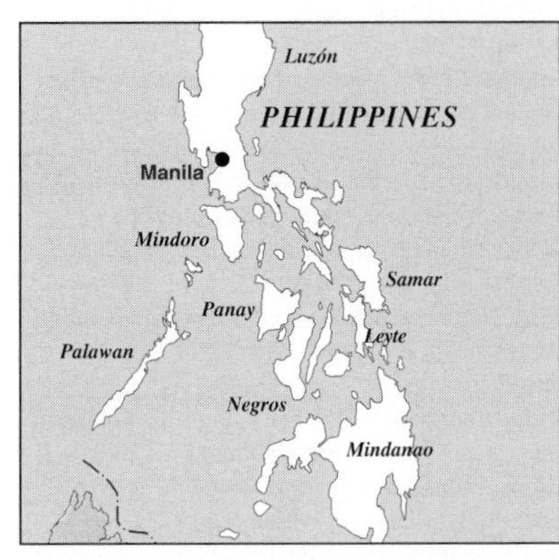

P

Corporate/Commercial

PHILIPPINES Leading firms (Corporate/Commercial)
1
Abello Concepcion Regala & Cruz
Picazo Buyco Tan Fider & Santos
Romulo Mabanta Buenaventura Sayoc & De Los Angeles
Sycip Salazar Hernandez & Gatmaitan
2
Castillo Laman Tan Pantaleon & San Jose
Quisumbing Torres
3
Platon Martinez Flores San Pedro & Leaño
Ponce Enrile Reyes & Manalastas
Siguion Reyna Montecillo & Ongsiako

Firms are listed alphabetically in each band.

Leading individuals (Corporate/Commercial)
1
REGALA Theodoro *Abello Concepcion Regala*
2
DE LOS ANGELES Eduardo *Romulo Mabanta*
PICAZO Antonio *Picazo Buyco Tan Fider & Santos*
ROMULO Ricardo *Romulo Mabanta*
STA MARIA Andres *Sycip Salazar Hernandez*
3
GATMAITAN Andres *Sycip Salazar Hernandez*
IMPERIO Angelito *Sycip Salazar Hernandez*
LAMAN Noel *Castillo Laman Tan Pantaleon*
4
BALOIS Edgardo *Siguion Reyna Montecillo*
DOMINGUEZ Leo *Quisumbing Torres*
MACARAIG Mel *Castillo Laman Tan Pantaleon*
MANALASTAS Jesus *Ponce Enrile Reyes*
PANTALEON Polo *Castillo Laman Tan Pantaleon*
SAN JOSE Roberto *Castillo Laman Tan Pantaleon*
SANTOS Gemma *Picazo Buyco Tan Fider & Santos*

Individuals are listed alphabetically in each band.

Abello Concepcion Regala & Cruz (12 ptrs, 24 asscs) Established in 1972, the firm has built a *"first-class reputation"* as a corporate leader. Specialising in M&A, foreign investments and project finance, the firm advises a range of domestic and international corporates and financial institutions. **Theodoro Regala*** is considered by peers and clients to be the most able commercial lawyer in the country and gives the firm *"world-wide exposure."*

In the largest privatisation transaction of the year, the firm represented Delphi Holdings on its acquisition of a 45% stake in the Philippine Phosphate Fertilizer Corp, a deal valued at just over PhP5 billion. Other work includes advising HJ Heinz on the acquisition of certain assets of SAFI-UFC, and acting for the International Finance Corporation on its role as principal advisor to the Metropolitan Waterworks and Sewerage System for the MWSS Privatisation Project. This scheme is reputedly the world's largest water privatisation project to date, involving $7 billion in investments. **Clients:** World Bank; IFC; Proctor & Gamble Philippines; NEC; Toyota; Itochu; Citibank; Bank of Tokyo Mitsubishi; Caltex Philippines; Deutsche Bank; San Miguel.

Picazo Buyco Tan Fider & Santos (15 ptrs, 32 asscs) *"Aggressive in pursuing business,"* the firm is invariably involved in M&A, acting both for international purchasers and local targets. A notable player in financial M&A, the team includes **Antonio Picazo***, who *"likes to get the deal done"* and was respected by our interviewees as a *"strong corporate counsel."* He receives valuable support from **Gemma Santos***, who represented BNP Paribas on the purchase of a controlling stake in Jardine Fleming Exchange Capital Group.

The firm advised Paribas Asia Equity on the merger of the Philippine subsidiaries of Banque Nacionale de Paris (BNP) and Paribas, and was involved in the merger which formed the Consolidated Orix Leasing and Finance Corporation. **Clients:** Metro Pacific; PLDT; Equitable Bank; ICTSI International Holdings; The Salim Group; BNP Paribas; Peregrine Capital.

Romulo Mabanta Buenaventura Sayoc & De Los Angeles (15 ptrs, 30 asscs) Established firm, which is primarily noted for its superb international client base and accompanying expertise in cross-border M&A in a variety of industries. The firm is also an *"obvious choice"* for securities transactions.

Eduardo de los Angeles*, a former chairman of the PSE, is a respected local figure, while **Ricardo Romulo*** has long experience of advising leading US companies and was recommended as *"a great rainmaker."* The firm has acted for Shell on its development of natural gas from the Camago-Malampaya region, and on the construction of an offshore/onshore natural gas pipeline to supply all Luzon, a deal worth $5 billion. Also represented the lead lender ABN AMRO on a $500 million syndicated loan to the Central Bank of the Philippines, and acted for the underwriters of the $1.6 billion global bond issue by the Republic of The Philippines. **Clients:** IBM; Coca-Cola; Philip Morris; Pfizer; Citibank; Royal Dutch Shell; Ford Motors; British Gas; Avon; Johnson & Johnson; Nestlé; Lufthansa; Goldman Sachs; Deutsche Bank.

Sycip Salazar Hernandez & Gatmaitan (12 ptrs, 28 asscs) Large and powerful firm, which is acknowledged by competitors to be *"among the market leaders"* and advises on big-ticket M&A

*See leaders' profiles on page 543-544

work in areas such as financial services, energy and telecoms. A blue-chip client base includes American and European investment banks. E-commerce has been a notable growth area, and the firm has advised extensively on IT start-ups.

Our researchers noted widespread commendation for a number of individuals. **Andres Sta Maria*** is respected for his expertise in financial matters, while *"strong corporate lawyer"* **Andres Gatmaitan** also maintains an excellent reputation. **Angelito Imperio*** is *"a tough but fair negotiator."*

The firm advised on several high-profile management buyouts by multinationals, including the acquisition of Smart Telecoms by PLDT. Acted as counsel to Kepco in their development of a 1200 MW natural gas fired power project in Batangas City, Philippines. **Clients:** First Pacific; Philippine Long Distance Telephone Co; Philip Morris; Tomen; ADB; JEXIM; Deutsche Bank; Citibank; Bank of Tokyo; Mitsubishi; JP Morgan; San Miguel.

Castillo Laman Tan Pantaleon & San Jose (12 ptrs, 19 asscs) Strong in mergers and acquisitions, and considered by rivals to possess excellent corporate tax capability, the firm is another to have a high-quality international clientele in which financial institutions feature prominently. Researchers had their attention drawn by the market to the firm's strength in depth. **Noel Laman*** is *"a highly regarded leader,"* **Mel Macaraig*** has a fine reputation for advising on infrastructure work, **Polo Pantaleon*** has a *"comprehensive grasp of legal problems"* and **Roberto San Jose*** also maintains his share of market approval.

The firm advised a syndicate of lenders, led by ABN AMRO (Singapore), on the San Lorenzo Gas Power project, a limited recourse financing deal worth $300 million. Also advised on the mergers of Philippine subsidiaries of pharmaceutical giants Glaxo Wellcome and SmithKline Beecham. **Clients:** Asian Development Bank; CSFB; DMCI Holdings; Merrill Lynch Direct Investment Group; General Electric; Kodak Philippines; Glaxo Wellcome; JBIC; Citibank; Inter-Continental Hotels; PepsiCo; Sony; Warner-Lambert Philippines.

Quisumbing Torres (4 ptrs, 14 asscs) The Philippine associate firm of **Baker & McKenzie** since 1963 is said to be *"thriving,"* largely as a result of the US firm's strong international network. Main areas of practice are infrastructure, banking and project finance, and the firm is said to be *"making waves in M&A."* The respected **Leo Dominguez*** is *"a deal-maker, not a deal-breaker."*

The firm acted for a German company on its acquisition of equity in the airport project, a deal worth $500 million. Also represented an Asian bank on its acquisition of a $1.2 billion stake in the entity that became the largest commercial bank in the Philippines. **Clients:** Ford Motors; Microsoft; Nike; Sony; Development Bank of Singapore; Sara Lee; Frankfurt Airport Authority; Cisco.

Platon Martinez Flores San Pedro & Leaño (8 ptrs, 16 asscs) Relatively young firm, which is *"flourishing"* because *"they know their craft."* Although lacking a heavyweight individual practitioner, the firm has niche expertise in IP, the aviation industry and e-commerce, and has handled a number of high-profile M&A transactions.

The firm advised Cable and Wireless HKT on the negotiation and implementation of its multi-million dollar joint venture with United Laboratories. Also advised Philippine Sinter Corporation on the sale of its mining operation assets to Philippine Mining Service Corporation for PhP363 million and acted for Caltex Philippines on its disposal of assets. **Clients:** ABM AMRO; Caltex; Philip Morris; Hong Kong Shanghai Bank; Coca-Cola; Air France; KLM; Cathay Pacific.

Ponce Enrile Reyes & Manalastas (7 ptrs, 8 asscs) Established in 1983 by partners from Abello Concepcion, the firm was recommended in our research as a *"prolific and respectable medium-sized firm."* Notable for its joint venture and capital markets expertise, the firm advised on the public offering and listing of Macondray Plastics on the PSE, and the reorganisation and demutualisation of the Philippine Stock Exchange.

Jesus Manalastas* is the firm's respected leading light, and acted for Sampoerna Asia on its acquisition of a cigarette manufacturing company. Other work includes advising Sun Microsystems on its equity buy-in to Philippine Systems Products, and assisting on the listing of Del Monte on the Singapore Stock Exchange. **Clients:** Citibank; Bank of America; Chase Manhattan; ING Life; Manulife; United Overseas Bank; Del Monte Philippines; Westin Philippine Plaza; Amtrust Holdings; Universal Motors; Scandinavian Motors.

Siguion Reyna Montecillo & Ongsiako (5 ptrs, 10 asscs) Although not felt to be the force of old, this venerable institution is said to be *"still surviving,"* and is active on cross-border M&A. **Edgardo Balois*** is *"a solid commercial lawyer."* The firm advised Asea Brown Boveri on its PhP72 million sale to Alstom, worked with Coudert Brothers' New York office on the sale of shares in a telecommunications holding company, and acted on the spin-off of the paper manufacturing division of Picop Resources, a deal valued at PhP1 billion. **Clients:** HSBC; Far East Bank and Trust; Shell; Caltex; Siemens; Goodyear; Gillette; Sharp; ACER; San Miguel; Bank of The Philippine Islands; Alstom.

P

Leaders' profiles – Philippines

BALOIS, Edgardo

Siguion Reyna Montecillo & Ongsiako, Makati City +63 2 810 0281
srmo@i-next.net

Specialisation: Head of Corporate Department. Specialises in mergers and acquisitions, divestments, spin-offs and hive-downs, joint venture formation, corporate restructuring and quasi-reorganisations, foreign investments, corporate finance and securities. Has handled the acquisition of mining, pulp and paper, smelting and real estate companies. Organised in the Philippines joint venture companies for Coastal Corporation and Petroleum Authority of Thailand. Recent work: Acted for Siemens on the Philippine merger of Siemens Nixdorf with Siemens Inc. Was counsel of Asea Brown Boveri in the Philippine sale of its power division to Alstom, and its subsidiary, ABB Koppel Inc to Fedders International. Represented Goodyear Akron in the sale of its Philippine rubber plantation. Acted as Philippine counsel for Rhodia Consumer Specialties Limited in the sale of the surfactant business of its Philippine affiliate to Stepan Philippines Inc. Delivered reaction papers in various conferences.

Prof. Memberships: Philippine Constitution Association, Integrated Bar of the Philippines and Inter-Pacific Bar Association.

Career: Admitted to the bar in 1976, special assistant to the Commissioner of Internal Revenue (1975-1976), joined *Siguion Reyna, Montecillo & Ongsiako* in 1976 and is now a Senior Partner, former president- IBP Makati City Chapter and currently president of the IBP Makati Foundation Inc.

Personal: Born 10 August 1949. Attended Divine Word University of Tacloban (magna cum laude), University of the Philippines (CLASP scholar and member of the Order of the Purple Feather, Phi Kappa Phi and Pi Gamma Mu honor societies).

DE LOS ANGELES, Eduardo
Romulo Mabanta Buenaventura Sayoc & De Los Angeles, Makati City +63 2 848 0114

DOMINGUEZ, Leo
Quisumbing Torres, Makati City +632 817 3016

GATMAITAN, Andres
Sycip Salazar Hernandez & Gatmaitan, Makati City 1226 +63 2 817 9811/2001

P

IMPERIO, Angelito
Sycip Salazar Hernandez & Gatmaitan, Makati City 1226 +63 2 817 9811/2001

LAMAN, Noel
Castillo Laman Tan Pantaleon & San Jose, Makati City 1227 +63 2 817 6791

MACARAIG, Mel A
Castillo Laman Tan Pantaleon & San Jose, Makati City 1227 +63 2 817 6791

MANALASTAS, Jesus M.
Ponce Enrile Reyes & Manalastas, Makati City 1227 +63-2-815-9571 to 80
pecabar@pecabar.com
Specialisation: Corporate restructuring/reorganizations, joint ventures, mergers & acquisitions, project finance and securities registration. Has handled and/or supervised various investments, mergers and acquisitions, restructuring and loan transactions for Philippine and overseas clients, including Sun Microsystems, Manulife Financial Corp, Del Monte Pacific Ltd, Air Liquide, Caltex (Asia) and Asian Hospital Inc.
Prof. Memberships: International Bar Association, Inter-Pacific Bar Association, Wharton Club.
Publications: Contributed the following articles to Mondaq Business Briefing: 'Infrastructure and Development Projects in the Philippines' and 'Business Organizations that Foreign Investors may Establish in the Philippines'.
Career: Obtained Bachelor of Laws, Cum Laude (Class Valedictorian), at the University of the Philippines in 1972 and Master of Laws from the University of Pennsylvania in 1977. Placed second in the 1972 Bar Examinations.

PANTALEON, Polo S
Castillo Laman Tan Pantaleon & San Jose, Makati City 1227 +63 2 817 6791

PICAZO, Antonio
Picazo Buyco Tan Fider & Santos, Makati City +632 810 4766

REGALA, Teodoro
Abello Concepcion Regala & Cruz (ACCRALAW), Makati City +63 2 817 09 66
accra@accralaw.com
Specialisation: Corporation law, mergers and acquisitions, international lending, joint ventures, foreign investment, and corporate reorganisation. Acted for acquiring company in November 2000 privatisation of Philphos, reportedly Asia's largest phosphatic plant. Counsel for the Yuchengco Group in recent acquisitions of a savings bank, a leading educational institution, and a credit card company. Speaker at seminars on due diligence, joint ventures and minority stockholder rights.
Prof. Memberships: Memberships: Integrated Bar of the Philippines, Inter-Pacific Bar Association (Past President).
Career: Associate, *Sullivan & Cromwell* (1960-62). Former partner, *Sycip Salazar.* Founding Partner and Senior Partner, *Abello Concepcion Regala & Cruz* (1972-date). Examiner on Mercantile Law, Philippine Bar examinations (1984).
Personal: Born 27 December 1933. University of Sydney (Bachelor of Arts - 1953), University of the Philippines, College of Law (BSJ, cum laude; LLB, cum laude - 1959), Harvard Law School (LLM - 1960). Attempts to play golf.

ROMULO, Ricardo
Romulo Mabanta Buenaventura Sayoc & De Los Angeles, Makati City +63 2 848 0114

SAN JOSE, Roberto
Castillo Laman Tan Pantaleon & San Jose, Makati City 1227 +63 2 817 6791

SANTOS, Gemma
Picazo Buyco Tan Fider & Santos, Makati City +632 810 4766

STA. MARIA, Andres B.
Sycip Salazar Hernandez & Gatmaitan, Makati City 1226 +63 2 817 9811/2001

POLAND

Index

OVERVIEW: Poland is enjoying an influx of inward investment. The privatisation process continues, particularly in the energy sector, and private equity is buoyant with close to $1 billion under management. The promised telecoms revolution has yet to materialise but January 2001 will herald major liberalisation making licensing easier and reducing investment restrictions. All this has increased demand for lawyers with transactional experience and provoked a wave of new entrants with Norton Rose, Lovells and Linklaters appearing in the market. Despite Lovells' much reported acquisition of six partners from Cameron McKenna, only Linklaters, recruiting high-profile individuals like Marek Wierzbowski, has yet to make much impression. Professor Soltysinski's new commercial code (to be introduced in 2000) has received mixed reviews with complaints that it leaves too many gaps and will increase the costs of establishing business entities.

Banking & Finance

POLAND
Leading firms (Banking & Finance)

Band	Firm
1	Allen & Overy
	Clifford Chance Pünder
2	Baker & McKenzie
	Hunton & Williams, Law Office Kacymirow, Michalski, Mrowiec LLP
	Weil, Gotshal & Manges
	White & Case W Danilowicz, W Jurecewicz & Partners
3	Soltysiñski Kawecki & Szlêzak Legal Advisors
4	CMS Cameron McKenna
	Dewey Ballantine J Grzesiak, L Redziniak, M Gmaj LLP
	Wardynski & Partners

Firms are listed alphabetically in each band.

Leading individuals (Banking & Finance)

Band	Individual
1	NAMIOTKIEWICZ Grzegorz *Clifford Chance*
2	PÊDZICH Arkadiusz *Allen & Overy*
	STAWECKI Tomasz *Baker & McKenzie*
	SWIECICKI Piotr *Baker & McKenzie*
	WADOLOWSKI Wojciech *Allen & Overy*
	WIERZBOWSKI Marek *Linklaters*
3	CZABANSKI Jacek *White & Case*
	JONAK Jacek *Allen & Overy*
	MLODZIANOWSKA Justyna *Weil, Gotshal*
	MROWIEC Zbigniew *Hunton & Williams*
	SLEDZINSKI Janusz *Wardynski & Partners*
	ZAWISLAK Piotr *Hunton & Williams*

Individuals are listed alphabetically in each band.

Allen & Overy (3 ptrs, 13 asscs) Considered by some competitors to be *"in a league of its own,"* the firm takes advantage of its superb international banking network to advise on innovative transactions, traditional lending and capital markets work. Regularly acting for major international banks, the firm's derivatives work is expanding and it is also a powerful force in structured finance, tax driven work and project finance in the power sector.

Wojciech Wadolowski is recognised by competitors as one of the top banking lawyers in Poland, while capital markets expert **Jacek Jonak** was praised by one client for his *"understanding of the complex stuff."* Among younger practitioners, *"bright, quick and well schooled"* **Arkadiusz Pêdzich** is *"one of the best of his generation."* The firm advised WestLB and ABN AMRO on a €75 million dual currency term loan for PGNiG. Also represented Crédit Lyonnais and Commerzbank as lead arrangers of the $235 million financing of the A2 Toll Motorway, the first project financing of a toll motorway in Poland. **Clients:** WestLB; ABN AMRO; Crédit Lyonnais; Commerzbank; Citibank; Chase Manhattan; CSFB.

Clifford Chance Pünder (2 ptrs, 12 asscs) Researchers were impressed by a firm which *"has all the expertise in the world,"* and which, despite the recent loss of two banking lawyers to Hunton & Williams, is said to be *"one of the few firms in Warsaw with the necessary banking resources."* The firm advises lenders and borrowers on syndicated and straight lending, commercial paper programmes and refinancing, and is increasingly active in aircraft financing, structured finance, leasing and securitisation.

The *"fantastically knowledgeable"* **Grzegorz Namiotkiewicz** is *"one of the few real specialists on the market,"* and receives the acclaim of competitors for *"maintaining a strong and focused team."* The team advised PTK Centertel on a €255 million syndicated loan and Rheinhyp-BRE Bank Hipoteczny on Poland's first post-war mortgage bond issue. **Clients:** Rheinhyp-BRE Bank Hipoteczny; PTK Centertel; PTC; Depfa Bank.

Baker & McKenzie (2 ptrs, 9 asscs) Viewed by the market as *"a good, hard-working team,"* it represents Polish banks as lead arrangers on syndicated facilities, and is most famous for capital markets expertise, which has seen the firm advise on most of the largest securities transactions of 2000. **Piotr Swiecicki** is *"the type of experienced lawyer who brings comfort to his clients,"* while rising star **Tomasz Stawecki** was recommended to researchers for his *"strong intellect."* The firm represented AWSA on the financing of the A2 Toll Motorway, comprising a €235 million secured loan arranged by Commerzbank and Crédit Lyonnais, a €275 million guaranteed loan from EIB and €235 debt and equity provided by its shareholders. Also represented DLJ and Chase Manhattan on the €200 million high-yield bond offering in Netia. **Clients:** AWSA; Chase Manhattan; Donaldson Lufkin Jeanrette; CA IB.

*See leaders' profiles on pages 552-556

Hunton & Williams, Law Office Kacymirow, Michalski, Mrowiec LLP (2 ptrs, 10 asscs) Among the country's leading capital markets firms, one client rated it *"the most versatile firm, where we find the greatest expertise"* in bonds and debt instruments. Not previously known for its pure banking strength, the team is said to be *"growing fast,"* and has recruited two new banking lawyers from Clifford Chance. *"An excellent technical lawyer with good contacts,"* **Piotr Zawislak** is especially acknowledged to have been an important hire. He joins **Zbigniew Mrowiec**, *"one of Poland's best securities lawyers."*

Domestic securitisations and lending are key elements of the department's caseload, and it advised TPSA on arranging a €400 million finance agreement with the EIB, at the time the largest Euro syndicated facility in Eastern Europe since the Russian default crisis. **Clients:** Citibank; AIB; Pekao; West Deutsche Landesbank; TPSA.

Weil, Gotshal & Manges (1 ptr, 9 asscs) Although the loss of *"well known power broker"* Marek Wierzbowski to Linklaters was clearly a setback to the firm, our researchers still noted the weight of market recommendation for *"one of the strongest young banking teams in Poland."* The firm has experience of large international syndicated loans, bonds, foreign exchange and regulatory work, and is especially strong in telecoms financing, most recently acting for Deutsche Bank and Bank Handlowy on the Polkomtel syndication.

Justyna Mlodzianowska is considered *"a top lawyer on bond issues and commercial paper programmes."* The firm represented ABN AMRO on the $200 million financing of PKN. **Clients:** Deutsche Bank; Pekao; Bank Handlowy; Bank of America; BGZ.

White & Case W Danilowicz, W Jurecewicz & Partners (2 ptrs, 3 asscs) *"Still strong in banking and finance,"* the firm received praise from clients and competitors for its securities expertise and extensive client base. The team has advised on a range of complex transactions – including derivatives and structured finance – for its clientele of large domestic and international banks. Experienced senior figure **Jacek Czabanski** is considered to be the department's leading light. The firm represented MeritaNordbanken on its acquisition of majority holdings in Bank Komunalny and BWP-Unibank in Gdansk. **Clients:** MeritaNordbanken; ING Bank; Bank Handlowy; Westdeutsche Landesbank Polska; Raiffeisen Bank; Credit Anstalt.

Soltysiñski Kawecki & Szlêzak Legal Advisors (3 ptrs, 18 asscs) *"A good, old-school firm,"* said by competitors to *"give good service on standard capital markets transactions."* Active on behalf of Polish and international borrowers, the firm is considered to be the leading wholly Polish firm in this sector. Major areas of work include restructuring bad loan portfolios for local banks and local debt and project financing for international lenders as well as regulatory work and banking M&A. It regularly represents EBRD on Polish transactions and are currently acting as local counsel on the regulatory aspects of the merger between Bank Austria and HypoVereinsbank. **Clients:** EBRD; ABN AMRO; HypoVereinsbank; Pekao; Unicredito Italiano; Bank Handlowy.

CMS Cameron McKenna (1 ptr, 5 asscs) Small but respected department, which is considered by rivals to be largely unaffected by the firm's loss of personnel to Lovells. Active on behalf of domestic and international clients on standard commercial loans and project finance, the team's greatest renown lies in its real estate finance expertise. Advised Pekao on its consolidation with three major state-owned banks. **Clients:** EBRD; Pekao.

Dewey Ballantine J Grzesiak, L Redziniak, M Gmaj LLP (2 ptrs, 5 asscs) Researchers' attention was drawn to a team that is *"making a splash"* in finance transactions. The firm's work on behalf of Merrill Lynch as underwriter on the second offering of Pekao has emphasised its credentials as a *"competent team, becoming visible on some interesting deals."* Especially focused on capital markets where its international strength comes into play, the firm also advises extensively on syndicated lending. The team acted for EBRD on bond issues and securing a loan facility. **Clients:** Merrill Lynch; HSBC; Citibank (Poland); BRE Bank; HypoVereinsbank; EBRD.

Wardynski & Partners (Up to 81 lawyers) Generally to be found advising domestic borrowers on syndicated loans, capital markets work, project finance and restructuring, the firm retains a respected – albeit low-profile – reputation for banking and finance. The *"experienced"* **Janusz Sledzinski** has a sound name among his peers. The firm represented the Polish Government on the A2 Toll Motorway, Poland's first toll motorway project financing. **Clients:** Polish Government.

Other Notable Practitioner Linklaters' recruitment campaign in Poland got off to a good start with the hiring of *"serious rainmaker"* **Marek Wierzbowski** from Weil, Gotshal & Manges. Competitors believe that his presence will help the firm to become *"a banking force in the long run."*

Communications

Allen & Overy (2 ptrs, 4 asscs) *"Promoting itself aggressively, especially on the e-commerce side,"* researchers had their attention drawn by competitors to the firm's *"top-notch telecoms practice."* Clients include government and regulatory bodies, telecommunications and cable operators, technology suppliers and investors, who are advised on a range of hi-tech matters, including M&A and financing.

Tadeusz Piatek *"has emerged as a considerable IT expert."* The firm represented National Grid International on the formation of a joint venture, and subsequently assisted the joint venture company, NGKT, on its successful negotiations with the Polish State Railways for a long-term fibre optic concession. **Clients:** National Grid International; Cable & Wireless Communications; NGKT.

Hunton & Williams, Law Office Kacymirow, Michalski, Mrowiec LLP (5 asscs) *"The key legal counsel for TPSA,"* the firm has *"solid lawyers and a reputation for quality work."* A prominent player in the telecoms market for more than three years, the team is commended by rivals for its transactional expertise. The firm represented TPSA on its $4.3 billion privatisation and its landmark €400 million corporate bond offering, the first Polish bond to be denominated in Euros. **Clients:** TPSA; Centertel; Crowley.

Weil, Gotshal & Manges (2 ptrs) *"Telecoms is a speciality"* for this respected communications team, which was especially recommended to researchers for a superb privatisation practice. The firm also advises on M&A and joint ventures

POLAND Leading firms (Communications)
1 Allen & Overy
Hunton & Williams, Law Office Kacymirow, Michalski, Mrowiec LLP
Weil, Gotshal & Manges
2 Baker & McKenzie
Clifford Chance Pünder
White & Case W Danilowicz, W Jurecewicz & Partners
3 Beata Gessel & Partners
Soltysiñski Kawecki & Szlêzak Legal Advisors
Wierzbowski & Szubielska

Firms are listed alphabetically in each band.

Leading individuals (Communications)
1 **PIATEK Stanislaw** *Sole Practitioner*
2 **BIALIK Wojciech** *Baker & McKenzie*
PIATEK Tadeusz *Allen & Overy*
WIERZBOWSKI Krzysztof *Wierzbowski & Szubielska*
Individuals are listed alphabetically in each band.

in telecoms, e-commerce, cable and terrestrial broadcasting. Acted for Netia Telekom on obtaining credit facilities from a syndicate formed by Chase Manhattan, and on its joint listing on the Warsaw Stock Exchange and Nasdaq. **Clients:** Netia Telekom; ComputerLand; Prokom; Agora.

Baker & McKenzie (1 ptr, 4 asscs) *"Part of a huge network with a lot of clients,"* the firm has been an established telecoms force in Warsaw for some time, and is singled out by clients for its *"sound knowledge of regulatory regimes."* Clients include media companies and international telecoms operators investing in Poland, and the team has experience of arranging agreements between telecoms service providers and operators and UMTS bids.

Wojciech Bialik receives market recommendation as *"an expert on the Polish law aspects"* of telecoms regulatory work. The firm represented France Telecom as part of a consortium taking a $4.3 billion stake in TPSA. **Clients:** France Telecom.

Clifford Chance Pünder (2 ptrs, 2 asscs) Superb banking and corporate teams support a telecommunications department with experience on some huge transactions. Strong in the financing and corporate sides of hi-tech work, the firm has enjoyed a marked increase in private equity investment work, and is acknowledged by competitors to have *"improved its regulatory profile."*

The firm advised the Ministry of the State Treasury on the $4.3 billion privatisation of a 35% stake in TPSA, and represented PTC, one of the three Polish GSM operators, on its UMTS bid and financing work. **Clients:** Ministry of the State Treasury; Telecom Austria; PTC; Intel; Centertel.

White & Case W Danilowicz, W Jurecewicz & Partners (1 ptr, 4 asscs) Not hitherto renowned for its telecoms work, the firm's position advising the government on the UMTS tender process has dramatically boosted its market profile. Active in e-commerce, often on behalf of venture capitalists, the firm frequently acts for companies bringing new telecoms technology and services to Poland. The group represented a consortium on its application for a UMTS licence. **Clients:** Ministry of Communications.

Beata Gessel & Partners (1 ptr, 5 asscs) A visible presence in IT and telecoms work, considered by clients and competitors to be *"a team on the rise."* A powerful client base of venture capital companies ensures the firm notable experience in the internet start-up sector, while its close ties to Elektrim have involved it in some big-ticket telecoms deals. The team represented Elektrim on its $679.4 million acquisition of 15.8% of the shares in PTC ('Era GSM,') and its $1.223 billion sale of a 49% stake in Elektrim Telekomunikacja Sp to Vivendi. **Clients:** Elektrim; ComputerLand; MCI; Ministry of Communications.

Soltysiñski Kawecki & Szlêzak Legal Advisors (1 ptr, 7 asscs) Broad-based department, with acknowledged strength in IP, wireless data transmission and drafting agreements on areas such as channel carriage, frequencies and direct satellite transmission. The firm recently advised on a 3G telephone licence bid for a consortium, assists local ISPs on investment in internet portals, and represented a major equipment provider on certification and contractual issues. Advised Canal Plus on negotiating an agreement with Polish public television to develop co-operation on certain joint projects, in return for network access. **Clients:** Canal Plus; Eurozet.

Wierzbowski & Szubielska (1 ptr, 9 asscs) Led by **Krzysztof Wierzbowski**, who was mentioned to researchers as *"an intelligent and knowledgeable co-ordinator,"* the firm is respected for its telecoms and IT advice. A leader in the field of personal data protection, it has been at the forefront of telecoms regulatory work, recently triumphing in a series of major regulatory disputes for TPSA, which changed the policy of the country's monopoly court.

The firm advised a foreign IT company on the provision of VSAT services, and represented investors and operators such as GTS, Teleglobe and COM-NET on issues involving domain addresses, ownership, acquisitions and the regulatory regime. **Clients:** TPSA; France Telecom; IBM; Pilicka Telefonia.

Other Notable Practitioner Although not a transactional lawyer, renowned sole practitioner Professor **Stanislaw Piatek** attracted enormous market recommendation as *"the most famous Polish name for regulatory telecoms work."* Clients describe him as *"the first port of call when you want a legal opinion."*

Corporate/M&A

Allen & Overy (4 ptrs, 24 asscs) *"The closest to what you see on Wall Street and in the City,"* the firm *"has the high standards you would expect from them."* Transaction oriented, the firm services major multi-nationals and large Polish companies on complex cross-border M&A and privatisations, and is especially strong in telecoms and energy deals.

The corporate team is complemented by an outstanding finance department, and includes *"leading figure"* **Andrzej Siemiatkowski**, a *"quiet, restrained guy"* with a cerebral approach. Better known for his energy work, **Michael Davies** is *"constructive and charming,"* and is recommended by clients and competitors for his corporate and managerial abilities. The firm advised Norwich Union on its sale of PTE Norwich Union to Sampo Insurance Company, and Mobil on its demerger with BP. **Clients:** Mobil; Norwich Union; Royal & Sun Alliance; Elektrim; Fosroc International; News Corporation.

Hunton & Williams, Law Office Kacymirow, Michalski, Mrowiec LLP (3 ptrs, 25 asscs) Possessing *"high standards and superb local law knowledge,"* our researchers received consistent recommendation for this firm. Much of the cred-

*See leaders' profiles on pages 552-556

POLAND
Leading firms
(Corporate/Mergers & Acquisitions)

Band	Firm
1	Allen & Overy
	Hunton & Williams, Law Office Kacymirow, Michalski, Mrowiec LLP
	Weil, Gotshal & Manges
	White & Case W Danilowicz, W Jurecewicz & Partners
2	Clifford Chance Pünder
	Soltysiñski Kawecki & Szlêzak Legal Advisors
3	Altheimer & Gray
	Baker & McKenzie
	Beata Gessel & Partners
	CMS Cameron McKenna
	Dewey Ballantine J Grzesiak, L Redziniak, M Gmaj LLP
	Domanski Zakrzewski Palinka
	Wardynski & Partners
4	Hogan & Hartson LLP
	Oles & Rodzynkiewicz

Firms are listed alphabetically in each band.

Leading individuals
(Corporate/Mergers & Acquisitions)

Band	Individual
1	**FOGELMAN Lejb** *Hunton & Williams*
	RYMARZ Pawel *Weil, Gotshal & Manges*
	SOLTYSIÑSKI Stanislaw *Soltysinski Kaweki*
	WUJEK Gabriel *Altheimer & Gray*
2	**DANILOWICZ Witold** *White & Case*
	JURECEWICZ Witold *White & Case*
	KAWECKI Andrzej *Soltysinski Kawecki*
	SIEMIATKOWSKI Andrzej *Allen & Overy*
	STUDNICKI Tomasz *Studnicki Pleszka*
3	**CHAJEC Andrzej** *Beata Gessel & Partners*
	DAVIES Michael *Allen & Overy*
	GESSEL Beata *Beata Gessel & Partners*
	GRZESIAK Jaroslaw *Dewey Ballantine*
	MICHALSKI Jacek *Hunton & Williams*
	WARDYNSKI Tomasz *Wardynski & Partners*
	WIERCINSKI Andrzej *Wardynski & Partners*
	ZAKRZEWSKI Krzysztof *Domanski Zakrzewski*
4	**FLETCHER Nicholas** *Clifford Chance Pünder*
	OLES Wieslaw *Oles & Rodzynkiewicz*
	SZLÊZAK Andrzej *Soltysinski Kaweki*

Up-and-coming individuals

Individual
GMAJ Marcin *Dewey Ballantine*

Individuals are listed alphabetically in each band.

it for its reputation is ascribed to *"gifted businessman"* and *"dynamic managing partner"* **Lejb Fogelman** who, although rarely seen on deals, is *"probably the best rainmaker and relationship person in town."* He heads *"a first-class team of lawyers who get it right,"* including **Jacek Michalski**, who is *"young, authoritative and has a good commercial brain."*

The group is noted for its contacts with large domestic clients, which it assists on privatisations, while it also acts for a blue-chip international client base in fields such as telecoms, steel, insurance, banking and aviation. The firm acted for Citibank on its merger with Bank Handlowy, and advised Allied Irish Bank on the merger of its subsidiaries WBK and Bank Zachodni to create the country's fifth largest bank. **Clients:** TPSA; AIB; Citibank; Pekao; Polish Power Grid; AXA.

Weil, Gotshal & Manges (4 ptrs, 35 asscs) Known in the market for its *"aggressive approach,"* the firm is involved in substantial big-ticket transactional work. Its bare-knuckled approach has been enhanced by its work on a number of hostile bids, notably representing Deutsche Bank in blocking the merger between Bank Handlowy and BRE Bank.

Strong on classical M&A and private equity, the firm has recently assisted in devising several multi-million dollar exit strategies, and has strong links with a range of large Polish corporates. *"Bright and intelligent"* **Pawel Rymarz** is the outstanding practitioner here, praised by one client for *"understanding all aspects of a deal."* The firm advised on last year's $1.1 billion sale of Pekao, the $700 million sale of PZU, and the $1 billion sale of PKN, the second tranche of which closed earlier in 2000. **Clients:** Deutsche Bank; PZU; PKN; ABN AMRO; CSFB; GTC; Hortex; Powerplant Belshatow.

White & Case W Danilowicz, W Jurecewicz & Partners (4 ptrs, 26 asscs) *"If there is a big transaction, you can expect White & Case to appear on the other side,"* say rivals. With a network of established clients, *"useful political connections"* and big-ticket experience, the firm is acknowledged by competitors as *"a team that you underestimate at your peril."*

An experienced department is led by managing partner **Witold Danilowicz**, *"a dedicated lawyer, who represents his clients' interests well."* He is supported by *"responsible and reliable"* **Witold Jurecewicz**, who is admired for his *"impressive analytical intelligence."* The firm advises on privatisations for its international client base, and is increasingly active in take-over defence and cross-border acquisitions for major Polish corporates. Recently advised Skanska on its $143 million acquisition of a majority stake in Poland's largest construction company, Exbud. Also acted for MeritaNordbanken on the acquisition of a stake in Bank Komunalny. **Clients:** MeritaNordbanken; Skanska; Credit Anstalt; Raiffeisen Bank; BIG Bank Gdanski; Allianz; UniCredito.

Clifford Chance Pünder (4 ptrs, 21 asscs) Known for the quality of its finance practice, the firm is less visible in straight M&A transactions, but still has the capacity for the biggest deals, as when it advised the Ministry of the State Treasury on the $4.3 billion privatisation of 35% of TPSA. Energy privatisation and private equity are expanding areas of the workload, and the firm has particular strength in the financial services sector. **Nick Fletcher** was commended to researchers as a *"commercially reasonable, relaxed and competent lawyer."* The firm represented SAir group on its $180 million acquisition of 38% of LOT Polish Airlines. **Clients:** Ministry of the State Treasury; SAir Group; Vattenfall.

Soltysiñski Kawecki & Szlêzak Legal Advisors (6 ptrs, 20 asscs) Universally acknowledged to be *"the top Polish corporate firm,"* its purely domestic character prevents it from playing a leading role in the largest cross-border transactions. However, competitors agree that *"in terms of quality, they easily compare with the top four."*

The author of the country's new commercial code, *"highly respected corporate expert"* **Stanislaw Soltysiñski** enjoys a *"unique status in Polish law." "A kind of guru,"* he is rarely seen on transactions, but his advice is valued by clients and colleagues alike. Other high-profile partners include *"professional, western-style technical lawyer"* **Andrzej Kawecki**, and prolific transactional man **Andrzej Szlêzak**. Privatisations remain the cornerstone of the practice, but private sector acquisitions and joint ventures are a large and growing area. The firm recently acted in the mergers of Petrochemica and CPN (Orlen). **Clients:** Microsoft; St Gobain; Cereol; Hachette, Bartimpex; Caterpillar; Maersk; Nutreco; Hutchinson; EBRD.

Altheimer & Gray (4 ptrs, 16 asscs) Led by **Gabriel Wujek**, *"a fantastic individual, both technically and in negotiations,"* the firm is visible in a lot of high-profile transactions, but is considered by some competitors to be over-dependent on *"one high-calibre partner."* Experienced in all areas of M&A, the firm also has a strong privatisation practice and represents both domestic and international clients.

The team assisted ITI Holdings on the $200 million sale of a 33% stake in TVN, Poland's second largest private television broadcaster, to SBS. Also acted for the Polish Ministry of Industry and Trade on a number of large transactions, including the privatisation of FSO through a joint venture with General Motors and the privatisation of FSR through a joint venture with Volkswagen. **Clients:** Ministry of Industry and Trade of Poland; Gillette; Levi-Strauss & Co; Amoco Poland; Amerbank.

Baker & McKenzie (3 ptrs, 12 asscs) *"A busy office with many sound lawyers,"* its market visibility has been hit by recent departures. The jewel in the corporate team's crown is its superb privatisation practice, which bolsters advice on share and asset acquisitions, corporate restructuring and due diligence. The firm acted for France Telecom on the privatisation of a 35% stake in TPSA, and advised Vattenfall on its acquisition of a $500 million stake in the largest Polish energy distribution company. **Clients:** France Telecom; Vattenfall; Pilkington; Readymix; Fresenius.

Beata Gessel & Partners (2 ptrs, 25 asscs) Our researchers discovered that the firm has the fastest growing corporate profile of all purely Polish firms. The corporate department is acclaimed by its clients for a *"flexible"* approach and *"transactional skill."* **Beata Gessel** is said to be *"a great negotiator,"* while **Andrzej Chajec** is the team's rising star.

Renowned for its work in private equity and telecoms, the firm is beginning to develop an energy practice, and advises an increasing number of major Polish corporates. The team advised Elektrim on the sale of several electrical machinery production companies worth $52 million, and on its $440 million Euro-linked convertible bond issue. **Clients:** Elektrim; Enterprise Investors; Bank Handlowy; WEH; KowiCapital.

CMS Cameron McKenna (2 ptrs, 13 asscs) The loss of six partners to Lovells made headlines in the legal press, but reaction in the market was muted. Competitors acknowledged that *"it wasn't exactly a tragedy for the firm,"* suggesting that it could even emerge leaner and fitter. Best known for its work in energy and insurance, the firm has extensive privatisation experience and a strong private equity practice. The firm advised the Polish State Treasury on the sale of a strategic stake in LOT Polish Airlines, and acted for Corus in connection with the privatisation of Huta Katowice. **Clients:** Corus; Rugby; Caradon; EBRD; Prokom; Orfe.

Dewey Ballantine J Grzesiak, L Redziniak, M Gmaj LLP (2 ptrs, 12 asscs) *"A growing firm, well-liked by clients,"* it has an expanding role in the region. A concerted recruitment drive has resulted in the formation of a *"dynamic young team,"* often mentioned to researchers for its work on mergers, demergers, and corporate restructuring.

Although his focus is moving towards energy and finance, peers consider **Jaroslaw Grzesiak** to have *"a good approach to clients"* and *"a sound grasp of corporate matters."* The recruitment of *"rising star"* **Marcin Gmaj** *("a smart old head on young shoulders")* from Baker & McKenzie has been applauded as a considerable coup. Increasingly visible in the financial services sector, the firm is also a force in energy and pharmaceuticals. It advised NRG Energy on the acquisition of a major power plant, and Enterprise Investors on the disposal of shares in FMCG. **Clients:** NRG Energy; South African Breweries; Howell; GE Power Controls; Enterprise Investors; Texaco.

Domanski Zakrzewski Palinka (3 ptrs, 27 asscs) Part of the Andersen Legal network, the firm has impressed competitors by *"managing to establish itself in the market as a law firm in its own right,"* and has advised on *"some good deals for Polish clients."* Particularly noted for its strong relationships with banking clients, the firm also focuses on private equity, and has specific expertise in corporate restructuring and international telecommunications deals. The Andersen link gives the firm exposure to the international market, and provides highly rated corporate tax support.

Praised by clients for his common sense, managing partner **Krzysztof Zakrzewski** is a familiar figure in the local legal community. His team represented BRE Bank and Commerzbank on an attempted merger with Bank Handlowy. **Clients:** BRE Bank; Commerzbank; Polish State Treasury; Saint Gobain Group.

Wardynski & Partners (Up to 81 lawyers) The oldest major Polish practice maintains its reputation for *"high standards"* and a solid commercial approach. Often compared to a barristers' chambers, it is seen by competitors as *"a confederation of lawyers,"* with an ethos that rejects narrow specialisation. However, the firm is acknowledged for its strength in real estate, litigation and project finance.

Tomasz Wardynski remains an influential figure at the firm, while **Andrzej Wiercinski** is an *"excellent transactional lawyer."* The firm represented one of the parties in the privatisation of TPSA. **Clients:** Leading domestic companies.

Hogan & Hartson LLP (4 ptrs, 8 asscs) Considering the size and importance of some of the firm's corporate transactions, our researchers were surprised that the team's profile was not higher. Traditionally seen acting for international companies investing in Poland, the firm has now acquired a respectable Polish clientele, and advises it on privatisations and classical M&A.

Highlight deals include advising Huta Katowice on its privatisation, the Ministry of the Treasury on its dispute with Eyreico, and PZU on the take-over battle involving BIG Bank Gdanski and Deutsche Bank. **Clients:** Smithfield; Ministry of the Treasury; PZU; Huta Katowice.

Oles & Rodzynkiewicz (2 ptrs, 10 asscs) *"Small Polish firm with expertise in derivatives and M&A,"* which, even from its Krakow base, has gained a national reputation. *"Moving spirit"* **Wieslaw Oles** is *"a clever guy with a businesslike approach."* The firm advised on the capital restructuring of BWR, in preparation for the planned investment by Deutsche Bank. **Clients:** BWR; ComArch; TECHMEX; Pekpol; Swiatowid.

Other Notable Practitioner Though the alliance between Dewey Ballantine and Studnicki Pleszka Cwiakalski Gørski has become more informal, *"charming"* **Tomasz Studnicki** spends much of his time as counsel in Krakow to the American firm. Competitors note his *"good judgement and constructive attitude to clients and opponents."*

*See leaders' profiles on pages 552-556

P

Energy & Natural Resources

POLAND Leading firms (Energy & Natural Resources)
1 CMS Cameron McKenna
2 Allen & Overy
Hunton & Williams, Law Office Kacymirow, Michalski, Mrowiec LLP
White & Case W Danilowicz, W Jurecewicz & Partners
3 Baker & McKenzie
4 Clifford Chance Pünder
Soltysiñski Kawecki & Szlêzak Legal Advisors

Firms are listed alphabetically in each band.

Leading individuals (Energy & Natural Resources)
1 DAVIES Michael *Allen & Overy*
KRASNODÊBSKI Arek *Hunton & Williams*
MIODUSKI Dariusz *CMS Cameron McKenna*
MUSZYNSKI Igor *White & Case LLP*
2 JURECEWICZ Witold *White & Case LLP*

Individuals are listed alphabetically in each band.

CMS Cameron McKenna (4 ptrs, 12 asscs) Considered by rivals to have *"probably the deepest energy expertise in Poland,"* the firm is said to be *"hard to touch for regulatory and project finance work."* Strong domestic contacts have also ensured the energy team a large slice of privatisation work.

Our researchers were struck by the degree of market recommendation for **Dariusz Mioduski**, *"a real leader with a Polish background and a western attitude."* The firm recently closed an independent power project for an American utility, involving the construction of a new coal fired power station. Also represented the Polish Power Exchange on establishing the legal framework for a clearing system for the Polish national grid. **Clients:** AES; Polish Power Exchange; Enron International.

Allen & Overy (3 ptrs, 4 asscs) Superb financial expertise and a powerful client base enable the firm to figure prominently on energy financing transactions in Poland. The team represents buyers on major energy M&A and privatisations, and advises banks on project finance. Contractual and licensing work for international traders is a notable growth area.

"Very active this year," **Michael Davies** *"is an energy lawyer from way back."* The firm represented Dresdner Kleinwort Benson on Poland's largest power project financing, the $333 million construction of a combined heat and power plant in Chorzów. Also assisted Ruhrgas on its joint venture with Conoco and Polish Oil and Gas for the exploration of on-shore gas. **Clients:** Dresdner Kleinwort Benson; Ruhrgas; Elektrim; EnBW.

Hunton & Williams, Law Office Kacymirow, Michalski, Mrowiec LLP (1 ptr, 4 asscs) An energy practice that is *"built around the Polish energy grid"* receives high praise from clients and peers alike. Historically involved in electricity and gas, the firm acts on the purchase side of the majority of long-term power agreements in Poland, and has an active project finance practice.

With Steven Horvath now relocated to London, the firm's leading energy practitioner is the *"experienced"* **Arek Krasnodêbski**, highlighted to researchers as a lawyer who *"has a good feel for the regulatory environment."* The firm represented Tractabel on its first Polish acquisition, a $84.2 million, 25% stake in the Polaniec power station, one of the largest coal-fired power plants in the country. **Clients:** Polish Power Grid; Tractabel; TXU; E.ON; Sydkraft.

White & Case W Danilowicz, W Jurecewicz & Partners (1 ptr, 6 asscs) The team has an impressive track record in project finance and also undertakes energy privatisation work, primarily representing buyers. Other work includes advice on licensing, tariffs and energy agreements.

Igor Muszynski was praised by competitors for his *"practical knowledge of the regulatory framework."* He is supported by top corporate lawyer **Witold Jurecewicz**, whose practice includes a substantial energy component.

The firm represented the state treasury on the privatisation of the Belchatow power plant, the biggest fossil fuel plant in Europe, with an attached Lagnite mine, a transaction estimated at around $3 billion. Also advised Electricité de France on the purchase of a combined heat and power plant in Gdansk. **Clients:** PESG Global; Elektrim; Gaz de France; Electricité de France.

Baker & McKenzie (2 ptrs, 6 asscs) *"A solid team without stars,"* its powerful corporate and privatisation practices keep the energy department firmly in the public eye. The practice focuses on energy M&A and project finance, advising inter alia on the A2 toll motorway. Also represented Vattenfall on the privatisation of the GZE distribution company. **Clients:** Vattenfall; International Power; Npower; AES Corporation.

Clifford Chance Pünder (3 ptrs, 2 asscs) *"Routinely involved in major transactions,"* the firm is particularly visible on M&A and financing advice in the energy industry. It also has experience of establishing joint ventures and advising on project finance. The team acted for the Polish Government on its plans to restructure the Polish oil industry, and advised Vattenfall on its acquisition of 55% of the Warsaw Thermal-Electric Power Plant for over $100 million. **Clients:** Vattenfall; BP Oil; the Polish Government.

Soltysiñski Kawecki & Szlêzak Legal Advisors (2 ptr, 5 asscs) *"Involved in a lot of major deals where there are local implications,"* the firm was consistently recommended to researchers for advice on M&A and finance transactions. With its strong privatisation practice, the firm is set to pick up a lot of work in this sector during its reorganisation in the next two years. It has been representing SGT EuRoPol GAZ in connection with the construction of the $1 billion, 600km Polish section of the Jamal peninsular gas transit pipelines. **Clients:** Cinergy; Southern Electric; Customs Coal; ABB; Siemens; Enron; E.On Polska; Ahlstrom; Foster Wheeler.

Tax

POLAND Leading firms (Tax)
1 Hunton & Williams, Law Office Kacymirow, Michalski, Mrowiec LLP
2 Soltysiñski Kawecki & Szlêzak Legal Advisors
White & Case W Danilowicz, W Jurecewicz & Partners
3 Baker & McKenzie
Linklaters
Wardynski & Partners
Wierzbowski & Szubielska

Firms are listed alphabetically in each band.

Leading individuals (Tax)
1 FISZER Janusz *White & Case*
KACYMIROW Tomasz *Hunton & Williams*
SZUBIELSKA Dorota *Wierzbowski & Szubielska*
2 KRASNODEBSKI Robert *Weil, Gotshal & Manges*
MODZELEWSKI Witold *Sole Practitioner*
3 ALEKSANDROWICZ Mariusz *Linklaters*
BIERONSKI Jaroslaw *Soltysinski Kaweki*
BORUC Slawomir *Baker & McKenzie*
JEDRZEJEWSKI Slawomir *Linklaters*

Individuals are listed alphabetically in each band.

Hunton & Williams, Law Office Kacymirow, Michalski, Mrowiec LLP (1 ptr, 5 asscs) With its *"great contacts to business and the government,"* this firm received enormous market recommendation for what one competitor described as *"the most efficient and visible tax practice on the market."* The team's main areas of expertise include structuring, litigation and complex transactional work, where its ability to engineer tax-efficient structures is at a premium.

Much of the group's success is attributed to the *"really bright"* **Tomasz Kacymirow**, who was recommended to researchers for his work on the tax aspects of M&A transactions. The firm represented Citibank on a high-profile Supreme Court judgement, concerning tax investment relief on its Warsaw office, and advised a corporate client on the tax implications of a de-merger. **Clients:** TPSA; Citibank; AIB.

Soltysiñski Kawecki & Szlêzak Legal Advisors (1 ptr, 4 asscs) One of the leading tax practices in Poland, it represents both large domestic concerns and international players on the tax aspects of multi-jurisdictional transactions. Stand out practitioner **Jaroslaw Bieronski** *"knows Polish regulations and has long experience of international tax and litigation."* The firm is active on customs and foreign exchange issues and is especially strong on the tax structuring of cross-border deals. Recently produced a tax-efficient structure for the Polish aspects of the merger between BAT and Rothmans, as well as assisting BAT on the capital restructuring of its local businesses. **Clients:** Large local and international entities including BAT and Phillips.

White & Case W Danilowicz, W Jurecewicz & Partners (1 ptr, 3 asscs) Transactionally oriented firm, concentrating largely on the tax aspects of corporate deals and tax litigation. Led by *"well-known expert"* **Janusz Fiszer**, who has *"a strong suit in international tax law,"* the department continues to be rated among Poland's leaders by competitors. The firm advised the Foundation for Polish Science on a complex dispute over corporate income tax involved in the re-investment of profits by a non-profit making organisation. With a disputed amount of $19 million at stake, this is one of the largest such disputes in Poland. The team has also acted for Volkswagen Elektrosystemy SP on personal income tax planning for expatriates. **Clients:** Foundation for Polish Science; Volkswagen Elektrosystemy SP; LOT; El Paso Energy; Pratt & Whitney Kalisz.

Baker & McKenzie (1 ptr, 4 asscs) Although not one of the highest profile tax practices, it advises on the tax aspects of M&A, and is especially experienced in the tax treatment of software imports for its many hi-tech clients. Competitors acknowledge that *"quiet and thorough lawyer"* **Slawomir Boruc** *"competes effectively with the market leaders."* The firm assisted on the complex demerger of Hewlett-Packard and Agilent, and provided tax advice for the recent A2 motorway project. **Clients:** Hewlett-Packard; Peugeot; Compaq; Informix.

Linklaters (2 ptrs, 2 asscs) The respect of clients and rivals for this *"intellectually strong team"* ensures the firm's place among Poland's leading tax practices. The firm has a twin focus on advice designed to minimise tax liability, primarily in M&A and capital markets transactions, and tax litigation involving the authorities.

The team includes respected practitioners **Mariusz Aleksandrowicz** and **Slawomir Jedrzejewski**, and recently advised on the tax elements of the acquisition of a large Polish brewery by an Austrian investor. Also advise Fiat Poland on all tax issues, especially litigation and tax planning. **Clients:** Fiat Poland.

Wardynski & Partners (11 asscs) The loss of rising star Dariusz Wasylkowski to Deloitte & Touche is considered to have severely affected the firm's profile in this area. However, our researchers discovered that *"Polish companies often choose it as tax advisor,"* taking advantage of the firm's strength in tax litigation, VAT, stamp duty, corporate income tax and international tax matters. **Clients:** Large international and domestic corporates.

Wierzbowski & Szubielska (1 ptr, 4 asscs) The move of **Dorota Szubielska** *("experienced, knowledgeable and has good relations with clients")* to this PwC-linked firm has put it on the map for tax. A high profile tax and legal advisor, she has participated in legislative work for the Ministry of Finance, and has a particularly sound reputation among clients and competitors for tax litigation and procedure.

The firm acts for foreign and domestic entities on the tax elements of investments, M&A, banking and stock exchange law, and advised on the Polish tax aspects of the de-merger of Du Pont and Conoco Poland. **Clients:** Coca-Cola; Philip Morris; GTECH; BRE Bank; Rabobank; Du Pont.

Other Notable Practitioners *"One of the best on the market,"* **Robert Krasnodebski** has moved from Clifford Chance to Weil, Gotshal & Manges, where his *"excellent knowledge of tax law, and good contacts with clients"* are employed in a corporate support role. Sole-practitioner and ex-deputy finance minister **Witold Modzelewski** is a VAT expert and is said by competitors to be *"an excellent front man on complex tax issues." "A flamboyant character,"* he is dual qualified as a lawyer and tax advisor, and also runs a tax training agency.

*See leaders' profiles on pages 552-556

Leaders' profiles – Poland

ALEKSANDROWICZ, Mariusz
Linklaters Komosa, Warsaw +48 22 828 6401
mariusz.aleksandrowicz@linklaters.com
Recommended in Tax
Specialisation: Partner in Tax Department. Main area of work is taxation of business transactions including mergers, acquisitions, capital market, insurance and leasing. Provides tax advice, serving numerous domestic and foreign clients. Has represented clients in claims with tax authorities and procedures before the Supreme Administrative Court, the Supreme Court and the Constitutional Tribunal and prepared drafts for various normative acts for the requirements of the Ministry of Finance or the National Bank of Poland.
Prof. Memberships: Member of the Warsaw Chamber of Legal Advisors, member of the Chamber of Tax Advisors. Appointed as a member of the first State Examination Commission for Tax Advisers. Chartered member and member of Supervisory Board of the Polish branch of the International Fiscal Association.
Publications: Has published numerous articles and commentaries on tax law.

BIALIK, Wojciech
Baker & McKenzie, Warsaw +48 22 635 4111
wojciech.bialik@bakernet.com
Recommended in Communications
Specialisation: Partner in the Warsaw *Baker & McKenzie.* Leads the Telecommunication and Media Practice Group in the Warsaw Office. Main areas of specialisation: telecommunications and media law, corporate and commercial law. Advised in a number of telecommunications projects including advice to major foreign telecommunications operators in connection with acquisition of significant stakes in Polish telecoms operators (recently, for example, in Telekomunikacja Polska S.A.), as well as in connection with satellite data transmission projects, establishment of fibre optic networks. Also advised operators of satellite digital TV platforms and the operator of the biggest cable TV network in Poland.
Prof. Memberships: Warsaw Bar of Legal Advisers.
Publications: Co-author of 'Telecommunications Laws in Europe', Fourth Edition, Butterworth, 1998. Contributions to *Baker & McKenzie* publications.
Career: Graduate of law from the University of Warsaw. Also holds a master's degree in Comparative Jurisprudence (MCJ) from the New York University School of Law. Prior to joining *Baker & McKenzie,* spent several years in New York acting as legal counsel in the Commercial Counsellors' Office of the Polish Embassy. Prior to that, acted as Vice Director of the Legal Service Center of the Polish Chamber of Commerce and as a legal advisor to Polish and foreign companies. Represented Poland at UNCITRAL conferences devoted to issues of international trade law and the preparation of model laws. Since August 2000, has been the Managing Partner of the Warsaw Office.
Personal: Interested in travels, different cultures, good literature.

BIERONSKI, Jaroslaw
Soltysiński Kawecki & Szlęzak Legal Advisors, Warsaw +48 22 608 7000
skslegal@warman.com.pl
Recommended in Tax
Specialisation: Partner in Tax, Customs and Foreign Exchange Department. In 2000, the department provided strategic tax advice in the merger between the local subsidiaries of Rothmans and British-American Tobacco, and tax planning in the merger of local subsidiaries of Philips. Provides advice in local and international tax matters, and represents clients in tax cases before tax authorities and the highest administrative court of Poland. Among the department's regular clients are: Canal+, Toyota, The Hachette Group, DaimlerChrysler, Vontobel Bank, Master Foods, Jeronimo Martins, Loyens & Loeff and Rothmans/BAT.
Prof. Memberships: International Fiscal Association, local branch in Poland; Warsaw Legal Counselors' Association.
Career: Admitted 1998, Poland. Legal and Tax Advisor, *Ernst & Young,* Warsaw, 1993.
Personal: Born Swiebodzin, Poland, October 3 1964. Education: University of Poznan law School (JD 1990).

BORUC, Slawomir
Baker & McKenzie, Warsaw +48 22 635 4111
slawomir.boruc@bakernet.com
Recommended in Tax
Specialisation: Partner in the Tax Department. Main areas of specialisation are: taxation of foreign entities in Poland, tax aspects of mergers and acquisitions, tax issues connected with cross border transactions, taxation of foreign individuals in Poland. Acted as advisor to many projects relating to real estate, construction, license and know how agreements. Experienced in representing clients before the tax authorities and the Supreme Administrative Court.
Prof. Memberships: IFA (International Fiscal Association), Warsaw Legal Advisors Bar Association.
Career: Joined *Baker & McKenzie* in 1992, became Partner in 1999.
Personal: Born on 28 March 1965. Attended Warsaw University 1987-92 (Faculty of Law and Administration). Leisure interests include fishing and sailing. Lives in Warsaw.

CHAJEC, Andrzej
Beata Gessel & Partners, Warsaw +48 22 690 6911
a.chajec@gessel.com.pl
Recommended in Corporate/M&A
Specialisation: Partner, Attorney at Law. Experience is mainly in commercial law, mergers & acquisitions, telecommunications law, preparing and managing international issue of bonds, venture capital transactions. Recently involved in acquisitions of significant stakes of shares of a cellular telecommunications operator, internet companies and cable TV operators.
Prof. Memberships: IBA member.
Career: Admitted to practise as a legal advisor in 1995. With *Beata Gessel & Partners* since 1993, previously lawyer and associate at *Vinson & Elkins* and *KPMG.*
Personal: Born in 1966. Graduated from the University of Warsaw, Faculty of Law and Administration. Speaks English. Leisure pursuits include sport, travelling, history and painting.

CZABANSKI, Jacek
White & Case, W Danilowicz, W Jurcewicz & Partners, Warsaw +48 22 625 3333
jczabanski@whitecase.com
Recommended in Banking & Finance
Specialisation: Partner based in *White & Case* Warsaw office with over 20 years of experience as a legal adviser in both public and private sectors in Poland. Full range of bank finance and securities law expertise.
Career: Worked previously for Polish Ministry of Finance and spent 12 years at Polish banks focusing on debt restructuring. Qualified Polish Lawyer.
Personal: Speaks Polish, French and English.

DANILOWICZ, Witold
White & Case, W Danilowicz, W Jurcewicz & Partners, Warsaw +48 22 625 3333
wdanilowicz@warsaw.whitecase.com
Recommended in Corporate/M&A
Specialisation: Head of *White & Case* Warsaw office. Wide range of corporate and finance law expertise. Acts for domestic and international investors in Poland, Polish companies abroad, the Polish government and a range of financial institutions.
Prof. Memberships: Member of Louisiana State Bar; Texas State Bar.
Career: Qualified as Polish legal adviser.
Personal: Polish and US Citizen, speaks Polish, English and Russian.

DAVIES, Michael
Allen & Overy, Warsaw +48 22 820 6100
Recommended in Corporate/M&A, Energy & Natural Resources

FISZER, Janusz
White & Case, W Danilowicz, W Jurcewicz & Partners, Warsaw +48 22 625 3333
jfiszeja@warsawwhitecase.com
Recommended in Tax
Specialisation: Partner based in *White & Case* Warsaw office. Strong reputation for both domestic and international corporate taxation. Has advised high profile corporations and financial institutions on numerous securities and mergers and acquisitions transactions.
Career: Writes and lectures broadly on chosen area of expertise. Was the co-founder of the Polish Branch of the International Fiscal Association and joined *White & Case* in 1994. Is Assistant Professor of Financial and Tax Law at the Warsaw University School of Management.
Personal: Speaks fluent Polish, English and German.

FLETCHER, Nicholas
Clifford Chance Pünder, Warsaw +48 22 627 1177
Recommended in Corporate/M&A

FOGELMAN, Lejb
Hunton & Williams, Law Office Kacymirow, Michalski, Mrowiec LLP, Warsaw +48 22 690 6100
Recommended in Corporate/M&A

GESSEL, Beata
Beata Gessel & Partners, Warsaw +48 22 690 6910 beata@gessel.com.pl
Recommended in Corporate/M&A
Specialisation: Managing Partner, Attorney at Law, arbitrator at the Arbitration Court at the Polish Chamber of Commerce, IBA member. Experience is mainly in mergers & acquisitions, venture capital, privatisation and capital markets. Developed an expertise in acquisition of public and private entities, advising venture capital funds, as well as other strategic and financial investors. Recently involved in a number of take-over transactions of telecom operators and internet companies.
Publications: 'Poland', in 'Aircraft Finance; Registration, Security and Enforcement' (Longman, London 1991). 'Poland', in 'Environmental Liabilities and Regulation in Europe' (International Business Publishing Limited, Hague 1993). 'Admissibility of arbitration clauses', in 'Rzeczpospolita' (February 6, 1998, No. 31-4891). 'Law and Stock Options Schemes', in 'Businessman Magazine' (March 1998, No. 3). 'Troubles with Venture Capital', in 'Home & Market' (February 1999, No. 2).
Career: Admitted to practice as a legal advisor in 1992; January 1993 set up a private legal office *Beata Gessel – Attorney at Law*, legal predecessor of *BGP* and since then has developed it into the existing *Beata Gessel & Partners*. Previously associate at *Weil, Gotshal & Manges, Nabarro Nathanson* (1991-1992), and also head of legal department and associate at *Arthur Anderson* in Warsaw (1990-1991); secretary of the Parliamentary Committee for Economic Co-operation with Abroad and Sea Economy (1989-1990).
Personal: Graduated from the University of Warsaw, Faculty of Law and Administration. Speaks English. Born in 1964. Leisure interests include modern art collection, climbing and hiking.

GMAJ, Marcin
Dewey Ballantine, J Grzesiak, L Redziniak, M Gmaj LLP, Warsaw +48 22 526 9950
Recommended in Corporate/M&A
Specialisation: Local partner in the Corporate Department. Main area of practice is corporate law, M&A and privatisation. Participated in a number of major privatisation transactions and other foreign investments requiring services within the scope of commercial, civil and financial law. Has been involved in the acquisition and restructuring of Polish state and private enterprises. Gained substantial experience in share transactions occurring on and out of the public market and assets transfers with a special expertise on the business as an ongoing concern. Has acquired extensive knowledge in the real property and telecommunications fields thanks to involvement in a number of deals in specific industrial sectors.
Prof. Memberships: Warsaw Bar of Advocates.
Publications: 'Enterprise as a subject of sale' (1993), 'Public Procurement Act' (1994), 'Poland's Law on Public Orders' (1994), 'New Foreign Exchange Regulations' (1995).
Career: Qualified in 1996. Joined *Dewey Ballantine* in 2000 from *Baker & McKenzie* (1991-2000).
Personal: Born 26 January 1965. Attended University of Warsaw, School of Law. Leisure interests include outdoor activities.

GRZESIAK, Jaroslaw
Dewey Ballantine, J Grzesiak, L Redziniak, M Gmaj LLP, Warsaw +48 22 526 9999 jaroslaw_grzesiak@deweyballantine.com
Recommended in Corporate/M&A
Specialisation: Partner in Corporate Department. Main area of work is corporate law, principally mergers and acquisitions (including privatisations) and capital markets transactions. Has handled acquisitions of companies and undertakings of various sorts by international clients. Has advised on transactions including the representation of PepsiCo in connection with its acquisition from the Ministry of Privatisation of shares in E. Wedel S.A., the leading Polish confectioner, PepsiCo's tender offer for all the publicly-owned shares in E. Wedel S.A. and the first delisting from the Warsaw Stock Exchange; representation of the consortium, consisting of NRG Energy and Marubeni, in connection with its proposed acquisition of shares in the state owned power company Elektrownia Rybnik S.A.; and representation of Lucent Technologies Poland in connection with its vendor loan facility to Crowley Data Poland. Recently represented the lead manager of Merill Lynch International in connection with offerings of GDRs of Bank PeKaO S.A., a leading Polish Bank and listing on the London Stock Exchange.
Prof. Memberships: Polish Advocacy Bar.
Career: Qualified as Polish advocate in 1995. Joined *Dewey Ballantine* in 1992 as its first Polish lawyer and became local partner in 2000 and international partner on January 1 2001.
Personal: Born April 27, 1966. Attended the Jagiellonian University in Cracow (1984-1990). Leisure interests include skiing and sailing.

JEDRZEJEWSKI, Slawomir
Linklaters Komosa, Warsaw +48 22 828 6401 slawomir.jedrzejewski@linklaters.com
Recommended in Tax
Specialisation: Partner in Tax Department. Main area of work is taxation of business transactions including mergers, acquisitions, privatisations and leasing. Provides tax advice, serving numerous domestic and foreign clients including Procter & Gamble, L'Oréal, Fiat, Hewlett-Packard, BA-Creditanstalt Leasing. Has represented clients in claims with tax authorities and procedures before the Supreme Administrative Court, the Supreme Court and the Constitutional Tribunal and prepared drafts for various normative acts for the requirements of the Ministry of Finance or the National Bank of Poland. Has published numerous articles and commentaries on tax law. Speaker at various seminars and conferences organised for foreign investors in Poland.
Prof. Memberships: Warsaw Chamber of Legal Advisors, International Fiscal Association.
Career: 1990-1992 expert employed in the Ministry of Finance. Member of Government delegations for negotiations on double taxation treaties, representative of the Ministry of Finance at OECD working committees dealing with currency regulations, taxation and foreign investment. Appointed as a member of the first State Examination Commission for Tax Advisers (1997-98). Chartered member and member of the managing body of the Polish branch of the International Fiscal Association.

JONAK, Jacek
Allen & Overy, Warsaw +48 22 820 6100
Recommended in Banking & Finance

JURECEWICZ, Witold
White & Case, W Danilowicz, W Jurcewicz & Partners, Warsaw +48 22 625 3333 jurcewi@warsaw.whitecase.com
Recommended in Corporate/M&A, Energy & Natural Resources
Specialisation: Partner of firm's Warsaw office. Leading reputation for work on various industrial privatisation transactions in Poland. Regular adviser to domestic and foreign investors on mergers and acquisitions and joint ventures in Poland and abroad. Has worked extensively on number of restructurings in Poland.
Career: Joined *White & Case* from *Vinson & Elkins* in 1993.
Personal: Speaks fluent Polish, English and French.

KACYMIROW, Tomasz
Hunton & Williams, Law Office Kacymirow, Michalski, Mrowiec LLP, Warsaw +48 22 690 6100
Recommended in Tax

KAWECKI, W. Andrzej
Soltysiński Kawêcki & Szlezak Legal Advisors, Warsaw +48 22 608 7000 skslegal@warman.com.pl
Recommended in Corporate/M&A
Specialisation: Areas of practice: Corporate & securities, investment company law, commercial law, mergers & acquisitions, banking & finance. Partner in Securities and Capital Markets Department. In addition to securities financing transactions, the department has for many years provided local counsel advice on capital and securities markets to several renowned international investment banks, including Morgan Stanley, Salomon Brothers, Lehman Brothers, Goldman Sachs, Merrill Lynch, Robert Fleming, IB Austria and Wasserstein Perella.
Prof. Memberships: American Bar Association.
Career: Admitted 1987, New York. Associate, *Drinker Biddle & Reath*, Philadelphia (1986-1991). Legal Advisor for Polish government, Polish Securities and Exchange Commission and Polish parliament on capital and securities markets. Founding partner of *SK&S* (1991).
Personal: Born Szczecinek, Poland, February 26 1952. Education: University of Poznan Law School (JD 1975). Institute of State and Law, Polish Academy of Sciences (SJD 1981). University of Pennsylvania Law School (LLM 1985). Senior

Fulbright Scholar, University of Pennsylvania Law School (1982-1985).

KRASNODEBSKI, Robert
Weil, Gotshal & Manges, Warsaw +48 22 520 4000
robert.krasnodebski@weil.com
Recommended in Tax
Specialisation: Tax specialist. Provides tax and legal expertise in various projects, including privatisations and the restructuring of companies, and frequently represents clients before tax governing bodies and courts.
Career: Formerly Head of Tax at *Clifford Chance* (Warsaw office). Joined the Warsaw office of *Weil, Gotshal & Manges* in January 2000.
Personal: Graduated from the University of Warsaw Law Faculty in 1991 and became a lecturer at that University's Fiscal Institute.

P

KRASNODÊBSKI, Arek
Hunton & Williams, Law Office Kacymirow, Michalski, Mrowiec LLP, Warsaw +48 22 690 6100
Recommended in Energy & Natural Resources

MICHALSKI, Jacek
Hunton & Williams, Law Office Kacymirow, Michalski, Mrowiec LLP, Warsaw +48 22 690 6100
Recommended in Corporate/M&A

MIODUSKI, Dariusz
CMS Cameron McKenna, Warsaw +48 22 520 5555
Recommended in Energy & Natural Resources

MLODZIANOWSKA, Justyna
Weil, Gotshal & Manges, Warsaw +48 22 520 4000
justyna.mlodzianowska@weil.com
Recommended in Banking & Finance
Specialisation: Field of expertise includes civil law, banking regulation, foreign exchange law, domestic and international debt issues, securitisation, derivatives (ISDA documentation). Has advised on several bond offerings by Polish issuers on international markets.
Prof. Memberships: Legal Advisors Bar.
Publications: 'Legal aspects of Municipal Bonds Issues' 1995.
Career: District Court judge (1985-1988); since 1991 senior lawyer in international law offices, at present with *Weil, Gotshal & Manges* (Warsaw).
Personal: University of Warsaw, University of London (Master in Law). Scuba diving, mountaineering.

MODZELEWSKI, Witold
Professor Witold Modzelewski – Sole Practitioner, Warsaw +48 22 810 8780
Recommended in Tax

MROWIEC, Zbigniew
Hunton & Williams, Law Office Kacymirow, Michalski, Mrowiec LLP, Warsaw +48 22 690 6100
Recommended in Banking & Finance

MUSZYNSKI, Igor
White & Case, W Danilowicz, W Jurcewicz & Partners, Warsaw +48 22 625 3333
imuszynski@whitecase.com
Recommended in Energy & Natural Resources
Specialisation: Leading lawyer based in firm's Warsaw office with formidable experience of Polish energy sector.
Career: Joined *White & Case* in 1998. Since 1993 worked for Ministry of Industry and Trade advising on restructuring and liberalisation of Polish energy sector, creation of Energy Law, Energy Charter Treaty and harmonisation of Polish and EU legal systems for energy sector. Acted in several energy sector privatisation and project finance transactions. Qualified in Poland.
Personal: Fluent Polish and English.

NAMIOTKIEWICZ, Grzegorz
Clifford Chance Pünder, Warsaw +48 22 627 1177
Recommended in Banking & Finance

OLES, Wieslaw
Oles & Rodzynkiewicz, Cracow +48 12 428 0630
kancelaria@oles.com.pl
Recommended in Corporate/M&A
Specialisation: Partner in firm. Main area of work is corporate law, principally mergers, acquisitions, corporate group reorganisations, privatisations, venture capital and private equity transactions. Acted on the first mergers of: publicly-traded companies, banks and investment fund societies in Poland and on the first market issue of the communal bonds in Poland. Has handled several acquisitions of banks, food sector companies, breweries, e-market companies, telecommunication companies, energy sector companies. Prepared restructuring programmes for polish coal mining sector and establishing South Energy Holding (the greatest producer of energy in Poland). Specialises in securitisation issues and projects regarding capital investments, represents issuers, purchasers and underwriters of securities in private capital markets, particularly venture capital investments. Advising Parliament and administration on securities law matters.
Prof. Memberships: Chamber of Legal Counsellors.
Publications: Co-author of 'Mergers & Acquisitions' and 'Transformation of companies under Polish law' (with PhD Mateusz Rodzynkiewicz).
Career: Attended Jagiellonian University in Cracow 1985-1989, university teacher at the Jagiellonian University 1989-1993, 1993 to present Legal Counsel, 1996 established his own legal firm.
Personal: Born in 1965. Collects paintings. Lives in Cracow.

PÊDZICH, Arkadiusz
Allen & Overy, Warsaw +48 22 820 6100
Recommended in Banking & Finance

PIATEK, Stanislaw
Stanislaw Piatek - Professor at Warsaw University, Niporet +48 22 676 9836
Recommended in Communications

PIATEK, Tadeusz
Allen & Overy, Warsaw +48 22 820 6100
Recommended in Communications

RYMARZ, Pawel
Weil, Gotshal & Manges, Warsaw +48 22 520 4000
pawel.rymarz@weil.com
Recommended in Corporate/M&A
Specialisation: Managing Partner of the firm's Warsaw office. Recognised as one of the leading corporate lawyers in the Central European region. Has extensive experience of acting for local and international corporations and institutional investors on mergers and acquisitions and securitites law matters both in Poland and abroad. Has worked on several international offerings by Polish issuers and assisted Polish-based entities in acquisitions in other countries. Has particular expertise in representing clients in the communications and finance sectors.

SIEMIATKOWSKI, Andrzej
Allen & Overy, Warsaw +48 22 820 6100
Recommended in Corporate/M&A

SLEDZINSKI, Janusz
Wardynski & Partners, Warsaw +48 22 622 0400
Recommended in Banking & Finance

SOLTYSINSKI, Stanislaw
Soltysiński Kawecki & Szlêzak Legal Advisors, Warsaw +48 22 608 7000
skslegal@warman.com.pl
Recommended in Corporate/M&A
Specialisation: Areas of practice: Commercial law, corporate & securities, banking & finance, mergers & acquisitions, intellectual property, antitrust law. Partner in Intellectual Property and Unfair Competition Department. Intellectual property practice offers unmatched expertise in trademark and unfair competition litigation in Poland and legal protection of software. Microsoft, Silicon Graphics, Autodesk, Skala, Johnson & Johnson, Tchibo, Rolex and Bacardi are among the corporate clients regularly using the firm's advice on various intellectual property matters.
Prof. Memberships: Poland's Legislative Council. Polish Academy of Art and Sciences. Practicing Law Institute and Commercial Practice. International Chamber of Commerce, Paris. International Association for Protection of Industrial Property, Zurich.
Publications: Author of more than a dozen books and 200 publications on commercial law, intellectual property, competition law and civil law.
Career: Admitted 1964, Poland. Visiting Professor, University of Pennsylvania Law School. Professor, University of Poznan Law School and College of Europe, Brugge. Advisor to various governmental agencies. Civil law Codification Commission and Chairman of Sub-Committee on Reform of Company Law. International Arbitrator (listed on the official rosters of arbitrators of the International Arbitration Court at the Polish Chamber of Trade, The International Arbitration Court at the Austrian Chamber of Commerce and the American Arbitration Association.
Personal: Born Poznan, Poland, May 2 1939. Education: University of Poznan Law School (JD 1961). London School of Economics (1966-67). Columbia University Law School (LLM 1973).

STAWECKI, Tomasz
Baker & McKenzie, Warsaw +48 22 635 4111
tomasz.stawecki@bakernet.com
Recommended in Banking & Finance
Specialisation: Attorney in the Banking and

Finance Department. Main areas of work include: bank lending, principally syndicated lending and other extensions of credit; major projects; project finance; public and private corporate financings; security interests structuring, in particular registered pledges under various jurisdictions. Has represented various banks and financial institutions on project financing matters. Participated in legislative working groups of the Civil Law Reform Committee, organised by the Minister of Justice, 1992-97. Recently involved in the process of establishing of the new system of registration for businesses and other legal entities.
Publications: Author of various articles relating to banking law, published in UCC Law Review, Bank, Banking gazette etc. Co-author of the commentary, The Law on Registered Pledges and the Pledge Registry (Twigger, Warsaw, 1997); the handbook, Introduction to Jurisprudence (C.H.Beck, Warsaw, 1995-96).
Career: Joined the Warsaw office of *Baker & McKenzie* in 1996. Previously practised with *Dickinson, Wright, Moon, Van Dusen, & Freeman.* Lecturer in the Department of Law and Administration at University of Warsaw.
Personal: Born 19 July 1957. Doctorate of law degree, 1991; Master's degree – Department of Law and Administration, 1980. Married with two children.

STUDNICKI, Tomasz
Studnicki Pleszka Cwiakalski Gørski, Krakow +48 12 427 2424
Recommended in Corporate/M&A

SWIECICKI, Piotr
Baker & McKenzie, Warsaw +48 22 635 4111
piotr.swiecicki@bakernet.com
Recommended in Banking & Finance
Specialisation: Banking, finance, and capital markets. Partner heading Warsaw banking and finance practice. Major transactions include international bond financing and initial public offering of major Polish telecommunications companies. Major financing projects include the A2 toll motorway and Polish segment of Yamal-Europa gas pipeline.
Prof. Memberships: American Bar Association; International Bar Association; State of Michigan Bar Association; Czech Bar Association (for foreign law advice).
Career: Joined *Baker and McKenzie* as a partner in 1996. From 1988-96, partner in *Dickinson, Wright, Moon, Van Dusen & Freeman,* including managing partner of Warsaw office, 1991-94. Advisor to the Polish Minster of Finance and Minister of Foreign Economic Relations 1990-91. Qualified in 1982.
Personal: Born 1954. Attended the University of Michigan Law School (JD 1982), Columbia University (MA 1977), Georgetown University School of Foreign Service (BSFS 1976).

SZLEZAK, S. Andrzej
Soltysiński Kawecki & Szlêzak Legal Advisors, Warsaw +48 22 608 7000
skslegal@warman.com.pl
Recommended in Corporate/M&A
Specialisation: Areas of practice: Commercial law, corporate law, mergers & acquisitions, banking & finance. During practice at *SK&S* has been involved in many pioneering privatisation transactions, such as the privatisation of Swarzedzkie Fabriyki Mebli and the Polish cement industry, the Fiat transaction and the restructuring of the Polish banking sector. Partner in Merger & Acquisition and Banking & Finance Departments.
Prof. Memberships: Poznan Legal Counselors' Association; arbitrator at Arbitration Court, Domestic Chamber of Commerce, Warsaw.
Publications: Has authored numerous publications in the areas of commercial and civil laws, dealing with several ground-breaking legal issues with which has experience as a practitioner.
Career: Admitted 1981, Poland. Professor, University of Poznan Law School (1979-1995). Visiting Scholar, University of Michigan Law School, Ann Arbor, Michigan (1985-1986). Research Scholar, University of Oxford – Pembroke and Wolfson Colleges (1989-1990).
Personal: Born Poznan, Poland, July 7 1954. Education: University of Poznan Law School (MA 1978; JD 1979; SJD 1985; Doctor Habilitatus 1992).

SZUBIELSKA, Dorota
Wierzbowski & Szubielska (Member of Landwell, correspondent law firms of PricewaterhouseCoopers), Warsaw
+48 22 523 4111
dorota.szubielska@pl.landwellglobal.com
Recommended in Tax
Specialisation: Partner in *Wierzbowski & Szubielska.* Specialises mainly in tax, banking, foreign exchange and administrative law. Provided tax advice on a number of mergers and acquisitions, and corporate restructurings. Represented clients in numerous proceedings before the Supreme Court, the Supreme Administrative Court and the Constitutional Tribunal. Was also a lecturer on numerous professional training programs and conferences for attorneys at law in financial, banking and tax law. As a tax and legal advisor has also been participating in legislative work on tax, foreign exchange and banking law as the Ministry of Finance's and Parliament's expert.
Prof. Memberships: District Chamber of Legal Advisors, Warsaw; National Board of Legal Advisors (advisor to the legislative commission of the Parliament). Since 1997 member of the State Examination Committee for Tax Consultants.
Publications: Author of numerous publications, articles and books in the area of tax and foreign exchange law and tax and administrative procedure. Most recent publications include 'Tax Implications of Mergers of Companies – Selected Aspects' (Przeglad Podatkowy Tax review) 2/2000; 'Making of in-kind contribution to company and the income tax' (Monitor Podatkowy) 7/2000; co-author of the book 'In-kind contribution to company' (published by Beck) 2000.
Career: October 1999 - present, partner in *Wierzbowski & Szubielska.* 1993 - October 1999, partner in *Domanski, Szubielska i Wspolnicy.* 1991 - 1993 vice president of ITI Poland S.A. and of-counsel in BLC law office. 1973 - 1991, Ministry of Finance, vice director of the Legal Department.
Personal: Born 31 January 1951. Attended Warsaw University, Department of Law and Administration 1969-1973 (Master of Laws). Legal advisor since 1978 and tax advisor.

WADOLOWSKI, Wojciech
Allen & Overy, Warsaw +48 22 820 6100
Recommended in Banking & Finance

WARDYNSKI, Tomasz
Wardynski & Partners, Warsaw +48 22 622 0400
Recommended in Corporate/M&A

WIERCINSKI, Andrzej
Wardynski & Partners, Warsaw +48 22 622 0400
Recommended in Corporate/M&A

WIERZBOWSKI, Krzysztof
Wierzbowski & Szubielska (Member of Landwell, correspondent law firms of PricewaterhouseCoopers), Warsaw
+48 22 523 4111
krzysztof.wierzbowski@pl.landwellglobal.com
Recommended in Communications
Specialisation: Developed practice through numerous privatisation, greenfield and joint venture projects, including the formation of Du Pont Conoco Poland, Polish-American Enterprise Fund and PTK Centertel, the first nationwide mobile operator, the sale of Polish telecommunication equipment factories to AT&T, Siemens and Alcatel, and representation of paging, mobile, local telephone and cable television operators, a local transmission provider, telecommunications equipment and network suppliers, and in numerous regulatory and litigation matters in Poland. Represented a strategic foreign investor which transferred its interest in the mobile telephone company and settled its investment dispute with the Government of Poland. Also researched the Polish legislative environment for the development of satellite telephony systems. Developed practice in the area of e-business by building a multidisciplinary team of lawyers specialising in a variety of legal aspects of e-business like data protection, intellectual property, telecoms, promotion, e-banking. The team has been involved in e-business projects for local and multinational clients as well as advised start-ups in the area of e-business and IT. Has been a speaker/chairman at conferences on foreign invesment in Poland, especially in the telecommunications sector.
Prof. Memberships: Warsaw Bar, IBA.
Publications: Published several articles on telecommunications and energy in Polish Market, International Financial Law Review, American Investor and Getting the Deal Through.
Career: Qualified in 1986. Established one of the first private law firms in Poland in 1988. Partner in *Dickinson, Wright, Moon, Van Dusen & Freeman,* a Michigan law firm; managing partner of *Dickinson, Wright, Moon, Van Dusen & Freeman* – the Warsaw office of the firm 1991-1996. Partner in *Baker & McKenzie* (after its merger with *Dickinson, Wright* 1996-1997. Since 1997 Partner in charge of the correspondent legal practice of *Price Waterhouse* and *Pricewaterhouse Coopers* (*Wierzbowski & Szubielska*).
Personal: Born 8 March 1956. Attended Warsaw

P

University 1975-79 (MA Jurisprudence); Postgraduate doctoral exam 1983. Qualified as a judge 1982. Qualified as an attorney at law (adwokat) 1986.

WIERZBOWSKI, Marek
Linklaters Komosa, Warsaw +48 22 828 6401
marek.wierzbowski@weil.com
Recommended in Banking & Finance
Specialisation: Specialist in securities, mergers and acquisitions and banking law; an internationally recognised expert on Polish securities law. Partner and Co-head of *Linklaters & Alliance* Warsaw office.

WUJEK, Gabriel
Altheimer & Gray, Warsaw +48 22 520 5000
wujekg@altheimer.co.uk
Recommended in Corporate/M&A
Specialisation: Partner and Director of Warsaw Office. Previously Director of the Legal Department of the Ministry of Foreign Economic Relations in Poland. Represented Poland in numerous negotiations relating to international commercial agreements. Served as senior negotiator for U.S. – Poland trade treaty. Legal Advisor in New York City at the Commercial Counsellor's Office of the Polish Embassy (1980-1985).
Prof. Memberships: Faculty of Central School of Economics.
Career: Warsaw University (Masters of Law, with distinction, and Doctor of Law).
Personal: Speaks French and Russian.

ZAKRZEWSKI, Krzysztof A.
Domanski Zakrzewski Palinka, Warsaw
+48 22 520 7600
Recommended in Corporate/M&A
Specialisation: Managing Partner of the firm. Specialises mainly in mergers and acquisitions, privatisations, capital markets, as well as in commercial and corporate law. Took part in legislative work carried out by the Ministry of Privatisation on the Privatisation Act, the Act on Companies with Foreign Participation and numerous introducing provisions. Participated in the privatisation of the 'first five.' Co-author and negotiator of the first takeover of a public company in Poland. Advisor to a number of Polish and international companies active in the telecommunications market in Poland in respect of regulatory and corporate issues. Advisor in many projects related to National Investment Funds. Advisor to numerous companies on all legal aspects of mergers. Speaker at numerous international conferences.
Prof. Memberships: Warsaw Chamber of Legal Advisors, International Bar Association.
Career: Qualified as legal advisor in 1994. Joined the Bureau of the Government Plenipotentiary for Ownership Transformation at the Ministry of Finance 1989-90; Deputy Head of Legal Department of the Ministry of Privatisation 1990-92; Co-founder, partner, and Vice President of the Management Board of BLC Law Office 1992-93. Since 1993 co-founder and partner of *Domanski Zakrzewski Palinka* (previously acting under the names *Szubielska, Gromek & Partners, Szubielska; Gromek, Zakrzewski, & Janiak; Domanski, Szubielska & Wsolnicy*).
Personal: Born 25 June 1964. Attended Warsaw University (Faculty of Law and Administration). Lives in Warsaw. Leisure interests include reading, skiing, sailing, bridge, and many more as time permits.

ZAWISLAK, Piotr
Hunton & Williams, Law Office Kacymirow, Michalski, Mrowiec LLP, Warsaw +48 22 690 6100
pzawislak.us@hunton.com
Recommended in Banking & Finance
Specialisation: Banking and finance: syndicated lending; property finance; derivatives. Advised Rheinhyp – BRE in the first post-war mortgage-backed bonds issue in Poland.
Prof. Memberships: Warsaw Bar Association.
Career: Present: *Hunton & Williams*; 1998-2000 *Clifford Chance*; 1993-1998 Polish Development Bank.
Personal: 1989 - Master of Law, University of Warsaw. 1992 - Legal counsel.

PORTUGAL

Index

OVERVIEW: Anglo-American firms continue to direct their gaze elsewhere and, of the English firms, only Simmons & Simmons has a presence. The auditing firms on the other hand have been creeping into the market, with the new Arthur Andersen office provoking much speculation. Associations between Portuguese, South American and Spanish firms are on the increase and, of these, the merger between Gonçalves Pereira, Castelo Branco & Associados and Cuatrecasas has been particularly fruitful.

Domestic mergers have not been so successful, with the PMBGR association widely perceived to be separating out into its constituent elements. In the market itself, M&A work is still abundant, E-banking is rising, and tax litigation is expected to increase, given that the trend to combat tax evasion is high on the political agenda.

P

Banking & Finance

PORTUGAL
Leading firms
(Banking & Finance)

Band	Firm
1	Vieira de Almeida & Associados
2	Abreu & Marques
	AM Pereira, S Leal, O Martins, Júdice & Associados (PLMJ)
	Miguel Galvão Teles João Soares da Silva & Associados
	Morais Leitão, J Galvão Teles e Associados
	Vasconcelos F Sá Carneiro, Fontes & Associados
3	Abreu Cardigos & Associados
	Gonçalves Pereira, Castelo Branco e Associados
	Grupo Legal Português
4	Albuquerque & Associados
	Antonio Frutuoso de Melo & Associados

Firms are listed alphabetically in each band.

Vieira de Almeida & Associados (4 ptrs, 12 asscs) *"Historically strong in banking,"* and *"always recognised as a market leader"* by competitors, the firm has been *"built up into an excellent practice with a great quality of service."* Active in all areas of banking, project finance and capital markets, the finance group is led by *"brilliant"* **Vasco Vieira de Almeida***. An ex-banker himself and a board member of BPA (now part of BCP,) he is said to have *"a lot of contacts, huge practical knowledge"* and to *"know how banks work."* **Pedro Cassiano Santos***, a capital markets specialist, project finance specialist **Manuel Protasio***, the *"user friendly"* **João Vieira de Almeida*** and **Margarida Couto***, *"a great bridge between banking and the new economy,"* complete a formidable team.

The firm was recently involved in the financing of two big shopping centres/retail parks in Lisbon and Oporto. Project finance work has seen the team advise on the new Lisbon bridge project and various other road and motorway concessions, as well as on energy and other large infrastructure projects. In capital markets, the firm has participated in a number of debt issues, assisting on the setting up and implementation of the majority of the existing Portuguese EMTN Programmes. It was also involved in the first AAA rated Portuguese originated debt issue. **Clients:** Large investment & retail banks; Portuguese and international corporates.

Abreu & Marques (3 ptrs, 2 asscs) An older firm, *"particularly good on traditional financing,"* which was recommended to researchers as *"the home of some first-rate lawyers."* **Luis Branco***, *"an affable young guy"* who *"carried out the first big project financing in Portugal,"* is seen as one of Portugal's leading finance lawyers. Major project finance work undertaken this year includes advising on the financing of the bridge over the River Tagus and the financing of several highways. The firm also assisted on the IPOs of companies in the paper and hi-tech industries. **Clients:** Major banks and corporates.

AM Pereira, S Leal, O Martins, Júdice & Associados (PLMJ) (3 ptrs, 2 asscs) *"Active in everything,"* the firm has been especially noted by rivals for its involvement in a number of banking/M&A and project finance transactions. A respected team includes the *"skilled, imaginative"* **Fernando Campos Ferreira***, **Jorge Brito Pereira***, mentioned to researchers as *"one of the top three capital markets lawyers in Portugal,"* and the ubiquitous **Luís Sáragga Leal***. The firm worked on the IPO of a Portuguese technology company. **Clients:** Major banks and corporates.

Miguel Galvão Teles, João Soares da Silva & Associados (3 ptrs, 3 asscs) *"Small, low-profile"* outfit which is considered by clients to have *"as much quality as the larger firms."* The firm advises major domestic banks on more complex transactions, and is considered to have particular expertise in securitisations. *"Experienced and competent"* **Miguel Galvão Teles*** and **João Soares da Silva*** are the stars of the department. The firm maintains a healthy involvement in project finance, acting on the new Portuguese airport, the Tagus Bridge financing and the financing of a number of highways. It was also involved in the organisation and structuring of a strategic alliance between a leading Portuguese group and a Spanish banking and financial services group. **Clients:** Banco Comercial Português.

Morais Leitão, J Galvão Teles e Associados (2 ptrs, 7 asscs) Noted for its involvement in capital markets on the equity side, the team, led by **António Soares*** (*"one of the best securities*

PORTUGAL Leading individuals (Banking & Finance)
1 BRANCO Luis *Abreu & Marques*
2 CAMPOS FERREIRA Fernando *PLMJ*
GALVÃO TELES Miguel *Miguel Galvão Teles*
SÁ CARNEIRO Francisco *Vasconcelos*
SOARES DA SILVA João *Miguel Galvão Teles*
VIEIRA DE ALMEIDA Vasco *Vieira de Almeida*
3 BRITO PEREIRA Jorge *PLMJ*
CASSIANO SANTOS Pedro *Vieira de Almeida*
FRUTUOSO DE MELO Antonio *A F de Melo*
PROTASIO Manuel *Vieira de Almeida*
SÁRAGGA LEAL Luís *PLMJ*
SOARES António *Morais Leitão, J Galvão Teles*
VIEIRA DE ALMEIDA João *Vieira de Almeida*
4 CARDIGOS DOS REIS Pedro *Abreu Cardigos*
COUTO Margarida *Vieira de Almeida*
OSÓRIO DE CASTRO Carlos *Carlos Osório de Castro*
REBELO DE SOUSA Pedro *Grupo Legal Português*
RICOU Maria João *Gonçalves Pereira*
VIEIRA Pedro Siza *Morais Leitão, J Galvão Teles*
Individuals are listed alphabetically in each band.

lawyers in Portugal,") has been involved in a number of privatisations this year, on behalf of both banks and corporates. Also active in project finance, where **Pedro Siza Vieira*** was especially recommended to researchers, the firm has acted on port concessions, transport (light railways,) and the Portuguese government's motorway programme. **Clients:** Banco Santander Central Hispano; Salomon Brothers; IMPRESA; Espirito Santo Group.

Vasconcelos F Sá Carneiro, Fontes & Associados (11 lawyers) *"A new law firm with young people and fresh ideas"* which is renowned for its project finance expertise, and advises BPI, one of Portugal's most important private banks. **Francisco Sá Carneiro*** is the firm's leading light. An *"experienced practitioner,"* he is said by competitors to have *"built a great reputation for himself."* The firm advised the second largest TV cable operator in Portugal on the negotiation and completion of a senior loan facility and related security to the value of €85 million, linked with a high yield bond issue in the US. Since 1999, it has also been legal advisor to the Lisbon and Oporto Stock Exchange on regulatory matters. **Clients:** BPI.

Abreu Cardigos & Associados (3 ptrs, 3 asscs) A small but active practice, recognised by the market for its capital markets expertise. Securitisations and derivatives are key elements of the workload. Former Baker & McKenzie partner **Pedro Cardigos dos Reis*** heads the practice and is highly regarded locally for his *"deep understanding of clients' needs."* The firm assisted three international banks on the securitisation of mortgage-backed assets under the new Portuguese Securitisation Law. It has also been selected to advise the Republic of Portugal on operations connected with international financial instruments, including derivatives. **Clients:** Portuguese Government.

Gonçalves Pereira, Castelo Branco e Associados (2 ptrs, 5 asscs) *"Finance expert"* **Maria João Ricou*** heads up an *"active"* practice with a reputation for representing leading domestic borrowers. The firm is recognised to possess a niche specialisation in asset finance deals, particularly cross-border leasing. Important transactions include advising a large UK investment bank on the IPO of a Portuguese company, and advising a state-owned railway company on a Eurobond issue. The firm was also strongly involved on behalf of a Portuguese construction company in the structuring and implementation of a strategic partnership with a Spanish construction company, a complex transaction involving, inter alia, stock option plans. **Clients:** State-owned railway companies; major domestic and European banks.

Grupo Legal Português Veterans of the first securitisations in Portugal, the firm's reputation for all-round capital markets expertise continues. *"High profile"* **Pedro Rebelo de Sousa*** oversees the practice. Described to researchers as *"something of a character,"* he has acquired extensive international capital markets experience from his time at Citibank/Citicorp. The firm acted for Banco Finantia on a €100 million securitisation of long term rental contracts, leasing and consumer loans. It also acted for the banks (ABN AMRO/Merrill Lynch) on an IPO for Altitude software, and for Natexis Banque Populaire on the financing of the acquisition of a holiday village. **Clients:** CSFB; Deutsche Bank; JP Morgan; NatWest Capital Markets.

Albuquerque & Associados (6 lawyers) Traditional firm with a good name and strong academic links that maintains its share of market support, particularly in shipping finance. Major activities of the year include restructuring all the finances in Portugal of a luxury hotel owner. The firm also advised a Dutch bank on its structuring of cross-border mortgage loans. **Clients:** US and European banks.

Antonio Frutuoso de Melo & Associados (18 lawyers) Since his split from Carlos de Sousa e Brito, **Antonio Frutuoso de Melo*** *("a proactive structurer of transactions")* has built up an *"effective"* practice, commended to researchers for its involvement in cross-border leasing and structured finance. The firm has also acted extensively for banks on major infrastructure projects. Local work tends to be carried out for foreign clients, often large investment banks such as Merrill Lynch and Goldman Sachs. **Clients:** Citibank; Merrill Lynch; Goldman Sachs.

Other Notable Practitioner **Carlos Osório de Castro*** of Oporto-based Carlos Osório de Castro, Eduardo Verde Pinho, JJ Vieira Peres has acquired a reputation as *"one of the best securities lawyers in Portugal."*

Competition/Anti-trust

AM Pereira, S Leal, O Martins, Júdice & Associados (PLMJ) (2 ptrs, 4 asscs) Acknowledged by competitors as clear market leaders, the firm advises on all areas of competition law, and is singled out for its expertise on merger control work. **José Luís da Cruz Vilaça*** (ex-President of the European Court of First Instance) was recommended to researchers as *"especially knowledgeable on EC law,"* while peers *"wouldn't hesitate to recommend"* **Luis Pais Antunes***, who is known for the frequency of his appearances before the competition authorities. The firm advised the Portuguese breweries in their appeal against record fines imposed by the Portuguese Council for Competition, and was in charge of all the competition issues involved in the selling of one of those breweries. It also represented several banks in competition litigation before the European Commission, and was involved in litigation against the Portuguese State concerning the imposition of illegal registration fees under EC

PORTUGAL Leading firms (Competition/Anti-trust)
1 AM Pereira, S Leal, O Martins, Júdice & Associados (PLMJ)
Pena, Machete, Botelho Moniz, Nobre Guedes, Ruiz & Associados (PMBGR)
2 Jalles Advogados
Marques Mendes & Associados
Morais Leitão, J Galvão Teles e Associados
3 Gonçalves Pereira, Castelo Branco e Asosciados
Vieira de Almeida & Associados

Firms are listed alphabetically in each band.

Leading individuals (Competition/Anti-trust)
1 RUIZ Nuno *PMBGR*
2 BOTELHO MONIZ Carlos *PMBGR*
DA CRUZ VILAÇA José Luís *PLMJ*
PAIS ANTUNES Luis *PLMJ*
3 JALLES Isabel *Jalles Advogados*
MARQUES MENDES Mario *Marques Mendes*
PINTO CORREIA Carlos *M Leitão, J G Teles*
4 ARANTES PEDROSO Filipa *M Leitão, J G Teles*
MAGALHÃES CARDOSO Antonio *Vieira de Almeida*
PEREIRA COUTINHO Frederico *Gonçalves Pereira*

Individuals are listed alphabetically in each band.

directives. It is currently advising on the privatisation of TAP, which is being acquired by Swissair. **Clients:** Domestic corporates and banks.

Pena, Machete, Botelho Moniz, Nobre Guedes, Ruiz & Associados (PMBGR) (3 ptrs, 3 asscs) The competition team is considered to remain strong, largely through the influence of *"talented"* **Nuno Ruiz*** and *"EC law and public procurements specialist"* **Carlos Botelho Moniz***. Admired by peers for its involvement in cartel, distribution and M&A work, the firm applies European and Portuguese anti-trust law to banking, telecommunications and media activities. It has advised on the investigation, launched by the European Commission, into the fees charged by Portuguese banks for the changing of Euro-block currencies. **Clients:** Domestic corporates and banks.

Jalles Advogados (3 lawyers) *"Small is beautiful"* according to competitors of this niche EC and competition law practice. **Isabel Jalles*** was recommended to researchers as *"an astute tactician."* Often involved in contentious matters, including Article 81 and 82 cases, the firm is said to have *"a good foothold in Lisbon."* Areas of expertise include internet law, data protection, and IP. **Clients:** Domestic companies.

Marques Mendes & Associados (2 ptrs, 4 asscs) Niche firm, headed by **Mario Marques Mendes***, *"one of the first lawyers to practice competition law in Portugal."* His team advises domestic and international clients on merger control, anti-cartel and state aid cases. **Clients:** American computer company; Portuguese telecoms company; Portuguese Government.

Morais Leitão, J Galvão Teles e Associados (1 ptr, 2 asscs) A *"leading competition practice"* according to rivals, the team has a strong client base, and advises on Article 81 and 82 matters, merger control work and anti-cartel cases. Both **Filipa Arantes Pedroso*** and her associate, **Carlos Pinto Correia***, are recognised faces at national and European level. The firm advised on Impresa/Soincom's acquisition of a dominant position in the largest Portuguese television channel (SIC), the acquisition of two Portuguese banks, Totta & Açores and CPP, by Banco Santander Central Hispano (BSCH), and the acquisition by Swissair of the biggest private Portuguese airline, Portugália. Other work includes defending BSCH on the investigation launched by the European Commission into fees charged by Portuguese banks for the changing of Euro-block currencies. **Clients:** Domestic and international banks and corporates.

Gonçalves Pereira, Castelo Branco e Associados (1 ptr, 2 asscs) **Frederico Pereira Coutinho***, said to be a *"promising young lawyer,"* fronts a *"small, dynamic"* practice with a reputation for advising on big-ticket merger control cases. Areas of expertise include the aviation and oil sectors. The team is felt to benefit from its link with Spanish firm Cuatrecasas, which provides access to the latter's respected Brussels office. **Clients:** Domestic and international corporates.

Vieira de Almeida & Associados (6 lawyers) Seen to provide *"invaluable support"* to the firm's highly rated corporate department, the anti-trust team advises on public procurements, commercial agreements, merger control work, telecoms and EC law. It was especially recommended to researchers for its expertise in the telecoms industry. *"Excellent all-rounder"* **Antonio Magalhães Cardoso*** heads the practice. **Clients:** Domestic and international corporates.

P

Corporate/M&A

AM Pereira, S Leal, O Martins, Júdice & Associados (PLMJ) (11 ptrs, 30 asscs) The largest firm in Portugal is said to *"offer M&A on a broader scale"* than its competitors. Now considered to function as *"a fully integrated unit,"* the firm specialises in cross-border M&A and privatisation, and has specific experience of the telecoms industry. The M&A department is considered to have *"some of the best lawyers in Portugal."* **Luís Sáragga Leal*** *("an intelligent man with a lot of experience")* was commended to researchers for his drafting skills. Peers regard **José Miguel Júdice*** as *"one of the top ten lawyers in the country."* Other notable members of the team are **Victor Réfega Fernandes*** and **Gabriela Rodrigues Martins***, *"an active and dynamic lawyer."* The firm advised on the sale of Centralcer, a large brewery, for around $500 million, and acted on the privatisation of Cimpor, the subject of a hostile takeover bid by Holderbank. **Clients:** Cimpor.

Morais Leitão, J Galvão Teles e Associados (4 ptrs, 12 asscs) Fast-growing, *"heavyweight"* firm with *"a tremendous reputation for privatisation work."* The *"outstanding"* **João Morais Leitão*** heads the corporate team, ably assisted by *"highly regarded"* **Jorge Maria Bleck*** and the *"promising young"* **Nuno Galvão Teles***.

The firm has advised on the Portuguese legal aspects of a number of high-profile transactions, including the Compaq/Digital merger and BP's joint venture with Mobil. It also advised Banco Santander Central Hispano on the acquisition of the Champalimaud Group, and IMPRESA on the acquisition of control of SIC, the owner of the largest Portuguese television network. Also assisted Vista Alegre, a porcelain and ceramic group, in its merger with Cerespor Group. **Clients:** Banco Santander Central Hispano; Salomon Brothers; IMPRESA; Espirito Santo Group.

*See leaders' profiles on pages 562-566

Gonçalves Pereira, Castelo Branco e Associados (5 ptrs, 21 asscs) Old, traditional firm, now part of the Cuatrecasas partnership, which was recommended to researchers as *"one of the big five in Portugal,"* and is a prominent player on pan-Iberian transactions. The firm includes a number of respected lawyers, including **André Gonçalves Pereira***, who has *"a name which carries weight,"* while **Manuel Castelo Branco*** is *"one of the top lawyers in the country."* Noted for its privatisation work, the firm represented Iberdrola in the privatisation of EDP and GALP, and Swissair in the privatisation of TAP. **Clients:** 3i; Credit Suisse; Fidelity; UBS.

PORTUGAL Leading firms (Corporate/Mergers & Acquisitions)
1 AM Pereira, S Leal, O Martins, Júdice & Associados (PLMJ)
Morais Leitão, J Galvão Teles e Associados
2 Gonçalves Pereira, Castelo Branco e Associados
Vieira de Almeida & Associados
3 Abreu Cardigos & Associados
Grupo Legal Português
Vasconcelos, F Sá Carneiro, Fontes & Associados
4 Abreu & Marques
Antonio Frutuoso de Melo & Associados
Barrocas & Alves Pereira
Carlos Aguiar, P Pinto & Associados
Miguel Galvão Teles, João Soares da Silva & Associados
5 Albuquerque & Associados
Carlos Osório de Castro, Eduardo Verde Pinho JJ Vieira Peres
Jardim, Sampaio, Caldas e Associados, Veiga Gomes, Marques da Cruz, Colmonero
Pena, Machete, Botelho Moniz, Nobre Guedes, Ruiz & Associates (PMBGR)

Firms are listed alphabetically in each band.

Band	Leading individuals (Corporate/Mergers & Acquisitions)	
1	**LEITÃO João Morais** *Morais Leitão, J G Teles*	**SÁRAGGA LEAL Luís** *PLMJ*
2	**BLECK Jorge Maria** *Morais Leitão, J G Teles*	**CASTELO BRANCO Manuel** *Gonçalves Pereira*
3	**DE ABREU Jorge** *Abreu & Marques*	**FRUTUOSO DE MELO Antonio** *A F de Melo*
	GALVÃO TELES Miguel *Miguel Galvão Teles*	**GONÇALVES PEREIRA André** *Gonçalves Pereira*
	JÚDICE José Miguel *PLMJ*	**OSÓRIO DE CASTRO Carlos** *Carlos Osório de Castro*
	SÁ CARNEIRO Francisco *Vasconcelos*	**SOARES DA SILVA João** *Miguel Galvão Teles*
	VIEIRA DE ALMEIDA Vasco *Vieira de Almeida*	
4	**ABREU Miguel Teixeira de** *Abreu Cardigos*	**AGUIAR Carlos** *Carlos Aguiar, P Pinto*
	ALBUQUERQUE Rui *Albuquerque & Associados*	**ALVES PEREIRA José** *Barrocas & Alves Pereira*
	BARROCAS Manuel *Barrocas & Alves Pereira*	**GALVÃO TELES Nuno** *Morais Leitão, J G Teles*
	GARRIN Duarte *Abreu & Marques*	**MARQUES Paulo** *Abreu & Marques*
	PENA Rui *PMBGR*	**RAIMUNDO Antonio** *Albuquerque & Associados*
	REBELO DE SOUSA Pedro *Grupo Legal Português*	**RÉFEGA FERNANDES Victor** *PLMJ*
	RODRIGUES MARTINS Gabriela *PLMJ*	**VIEIRA DE ALMEIDA João** *Vieira de Almeida*

Individuals are listed alphabetically in each band.

Vieira de Almeida & Associados (6 ptrs, 20 asscs) Originally a banking and finance specialist, the firm *"has broadened its scope into other areas,"* and now boasts *"a solid name"* in M&A too. *"Well connected at government level,"* it is divided into industry-related groups, each of which has an M&A capability. The firm is particularly renowned for its telecoms expertise. **Vasco Vieira de Almeida*** is commended by peers as an *"increasingly active figure in M&A,"* who *"always gives sound advice."* His son, *"proactive"* **João Vieira de Almeida***, also wins his share of market approval. The firm has provided advice on a number of domestic mergers in the telecoms, power and transport industries. **Clients:** Stagecoach; Portugal Telecom.

Abreu Cardigos & Associados Initially a niche practice specialising in M&A related tax and finance, it has developed a corporate practice with *"tremendous drive"* and *"a great future ahead of it."* **Miguel Teixeira de Abreu***, one of the brains behind the firm, is *"heavily involved in structuring acquisitions in Portugal."* Corporate restructuring and leveraged management buy-outs are areas of niche strength, and the firm advised on the MBO of one of the largest Portuguese retailers in a deal worth around $300 million. **Clients:** International and local banks and corporates.

Grupo Legal Português The association between Simmons & Simmons and F Castelo Branco, P Rebelo de Sousa & Associados has enabled the firm to *"reach a much wider audience."* Strong in telecoms, it has acted for such industry giants as BT and Telecom Italia. The firm's key player is **Pedro Rebelo de Sousa***. A former employee of Citibank/Citicorp in Brazil and New York, he is *"an active and successful practitioner."* Important transactions of the year include acting for a leading European dry cleaning company in relation to an acquisition in Portugal, and advising Scottish and Newcastle on the acquisition of 49% of Centralcer (the largest Portuguese brewery). **Clients:** Scottish & Newcastle; Toys R Us; Hewlett-Packard; Burger King.

Vasconcelos, F Sá Carneiro, Fontes & Associados A breakaway group from João Morais Leitão & Associados that has prospered since the split and is now seen by competitors as *"very much an up and coming firm."* **Francisco Sá Carneiro*** was recommended to researchers as the outstanding practitioner here. *"A nice fellow"* and a *"fine lawyer,"* he acted for a European bank on one of the largest MBOs ever carried out in Portugal. The firm has also been involved in the negotiations between a leading Portuguese retail company and the leading Dutch retailer on their joint venture. **Clients:** International and local financials and corporates.

Abreu & Marques (6 lawyers) Although particularly noted for its banking activities, this *"politically well connected firm"* also has a respected name for M&A, and has advised on a number of important cross-border transactions this year. **Jorge de Abreu***, **Paulo Marques*** and **Duarte Garrin*** are all respected by the firm's competitors. The team has advised a consortium led by Eiffagge on its tenders for several motorway concessions, and assisted Lendlease on the acquisition of one of the largest shopping centres in Portugal. **Clients:** Eiffagge; Lendlease; Sun Microsystems.

Antonio Frutuoso de Melo & Associados (18 lawyers) A *"stable, medium-sized, high-quality"* firm, comprising a core of ex-Carlos de Sousa e Brito lawyers who specialise in financial sector M&A work. The team advised the banks on the hostile take-over of the largest Portuguese cement company, Cimpor, and has been involved in a number of smaller acquisitions at a local level. **Antonio Frutuoso de Melo*** is the big-hitter here. An *"able"* lawyer with *"a strong business sense"* he is widely perceived to benefit from *"very good contacts."* **Clients:** Major US and European investment banks.

Barrocas & Alves Pereira (3 ptrs, 7 asscs) A *"fine"* firm. The result of a widely approved recent merger, it is said by peers to be able to count on *"excellent international clients and contacts."* Though primarily a corporate practice, it enjoys a good reputation in the IT sector and has also expanded its tax law department. *"Personable"* **José Alves Pereira*** and **Manuel Barrocas***, mentioned to researchers as *"an excellent client getter,"* are the firm's leading lights. **Clients:** Nortel; McDonald's; Microsoft; Bank of Tokyo-Mitsubishi; Texas Instruments; Novartis.

Carlos Aguiar, P Pinto & Associados (3 ptrs, 3 asscs) A *"small but growing"* practice with a reputation for representing financial institutions on their acquisitions. *"Vastly experienced"* **Carlos Aguiar*** (formerly of João Morais Leitão & Associados) oversees a department with a predominantly foreign client base and a particularly close association with French and Spanish banks. The firm advised on the privatisation of Cimpor, where it represented a multi-national company, and acted on a major acquisition in the mining sector. **Clients:** International and domestic banks and corporates.

Miguel Galvão Teles, João Soares da Silva & Associados (2 ptrs, 6 asscs) Specialising in big-ticket, complex transactions, and well known for its close association with Banco Comercial Português, the firm is widely acclaimed for banking-related M&A advice. **João Soares da Silva*** *("a very fine lawyer")* and *"brilliant"* **Miguel Galvão Teles***, are highly respected by their contemporaries. Major transactions include a cross-border merger that created one of Europe's largest insurance groups, a cross-border hostile take-over battle, and the merger of two banking and insurance groups to create the largest private financial group in Portugal. **Clients:** Major domestic and international financial institutions.

Albuquerque & Associados (12 lawyers) Perceived by the market to *"revolve around two brothers,"* the firm possesses *"strong academic credentials."* **Rui Albuquerque*** is the team's *"chief rainmaker,"* while **Antonio Raimundo*** brings *"a more practical perspective to legal problems."* The firm is noted for its specialisation in shipping, and acts regularly for leading companies in the ports industry. It advised on the merger that formed the largest container and transport shipping company in Portugal. Also respected for its telecoms work, the firm acted for an American communications group on its investments in Portugal. Other major activities include advising on the Portuguese aspects of the Total Fina merger, and its merger with Elf, and participation in Fisipe's acquisition of a chemical factory in Barcelona from Acordis. **Clients:** Fisipe.

Carlos Osório de Castro, Eduardo Verde Pinho, JJ Vieira Peres (4 ptrs, 6 asscs) Involved in a number of important M&A transactions in the oil, construction, media and telecommunications industries, the firm was consistently acknowledged by competitors to be the leader in Oporto. The respected and experienced **Carlos Osório de Castro***heads the team. The firm was involved in the sale of a mass media group, and advised a major Portuguese financial group on the sale of its stake in a local bank, and on its tender offer to acquire a local insurance company. **Clients:** Major financial institutions.

Jardim, Sampaio, Caldas e Associados, Veiga Gomes, Marques da Cruz, Colmonero (2 ptrs, 5 asscs) The expanded firm, which will merge fully in 2001, is considered to have *"superb political connections,"* which extend to President Sampaio himself. Full of *"experienced transactional lawyers,"* it advised on the BBV/Argentaria merger, as well as acting on two important transactions in the pharmaceuticals industry. **Clients:** International and domestic industrial and financial groups.

Pena, Machete, Botelho Moniz, Nobre Guedes, Ruiz & Associados (PMBGR) (7 ptrs, 9 asscs) An association of five different firms which merged and negotiated with Andersens to become their office in Lisbon. In spite of the failure of these negotiations, the firm still *"has some very good lawyers,"* and is seen by clients to offer *"sound advice on large M&A deals."* **Rui Pena*** in particular was singled out for market commendation. The firm has recently been involved in cases involving Grupo AON, Grupo Benckiser Portugal and Banque Rothschild Luxembourg. **Clients:** Kellogg; Honeywell; Grupo AON; Cadburys; Banque Rothschild Luxembourg.

Tax

Abreu Cardigos & Associados Noted for its participation in tax litigation and tax planning, this is an *"energetic"* tax team, led by *"knowledgeable"* **Miguel Teixeira de Abreu***. It is involved in the setting up of tax structures for financial operations, acquisitions of companies, corporate restructuring and international transactions. Members of the firm lecture on tax issues at the state university, and one partner has been invited to participate in a recently created government commission to study and propose amendments to the Portuguese tax laws governing international matters. **Clients:** Portuguese banks and corporates.

AM Pereira, S Leal, O Martins, Júdice & Associados (PLMJ) (2 ptrs, 2 asscs) Having finalised the incorporation of one of the leading tax boutique firms, that of the respected **Diogo Leite Campos***, into its tax department, the firm is considered by its competitors to have turned itself into *"one hell of a tax operation."* In addition, **João Maricoto Monteiro*** is said to add *"gravitas"* to the firm. The workload involves consultancy and tax litigation, with additional support for the firm's substantial M&A practice. Clients include banks, industrial companies, real estate companies and telecoms concerns. **Clients:** Portuguese and international banks and corporates.

Carlos Osório de Castro, Eduardo Verde Pinho, JJ Vieira Peres (1 ptr, 3 asscs) *"Financial products specialist"* **Antonio Lobo-Xavier*** is *"a well known tax expert in Portugal,"* and was cited by clients and competitors as the main factor in the tax team's eminence. He advised Caixa Geral de Depósitos on the sale of the A Champalimaud group to Banco Santander. The firm has also advised on a number of tax litigation cases, representing Barclays Bank and the national government. **Clients:** Sonae; BPI; Barclays Bank.

Gonçalves Pereira, Castelo Branco e Associados (2 ptrs, 4 asscs) With a partner from Spanish firm Cuatrecasas now installed in the Lisbon office, the team's tax profile has *"really taken off."* **Diogo Ortigão Ramos*** heads the Portuguese side of the practice, and has been involved in a variety of projects. These include the creation of funds, real estate investments for the Somague Group, cross-border leasings, stock option plans

*See leaders' profiles on pages 562-566

PORTUGAL Leading firms (Tax)
1 Abreu Cardigos & Associados
AM Pereira, S Leal, O Martins, Júdice, & Associados (PLMJ)
2 Carlos Osório de Castro, Eduardo Verde Pinho, JJ Vieira Peres
Gonçalves Pereira, Castelo Branco e Associados
Rui Barreira, Magalhaes Correia, Teresa Carregueiro e Gorjao Henriques
3 Morais Leitão, J Galvão Teles e Associados
Sérvulo Correia & Associados
Vasconcelos, F Sá Carneiro, Fontes & Associados
Xavier Bernardes e Bragança

Firms are listed alphabetically in each band.

Leading individuals (Tax)
1 **LOBO-XAVIER Antonio** *Carlos Osório de Castro*
2 **ABREU Miguel Teixeira de** *Abreu Cardigos*
BARREIRA Rui *Rui Barreira, Magalhaes Correia*
CAMPOS Diogo Leite *PLMJ*
DE SOUSA DA CÂMARA Francisco *Morais Leitão, J G Teles*
FERNANDES FERREIRA Rogerio Manuel *Sérvulo Correia & Associados*
3 **MARICOTO MONTEIRO João** *PLMJ*
MARQUES PINTO João *Vasconcelos, F Sá Carneiro*
ORTIGÃO RAMOS Diogo *Gonçalves Pereira*

Individuals are listed alphabetically in each band.

and advising banks and investment funds, such as 3i, on privatisations and buy-outs. The firm also enjoys the benefit of a strong tax litigation practice, which works mainly for corporations such as SIC, the Portuguese television station. Internationally, the firm has been involved in the structuring of investments in Madeira International Business Centre and Mozambique. **Clients:** Somague Group; Goldman Sachs; Grupo Lar; Metropolitano de Lisboa; 3i; SIC.

Rui Barreira, Magalhaes Correia, Teresa Carregueiro e Gorjao Henriques Respected niche tax firm with a particular reputation for tax litigation work. **Rui Barreira*** was recommended to researchers as an *"outstanding tax practitioner."* **Clients:** Domestic banks and corporates.

Morais Leitão, J Galvão Teles e Associados (1 ptr, 3 asscs) Regarded by peers as one of the best tax litigation groups in Lisbon, the team also provides support to corporate transactions, acting on the acquisition of the A Champalimaud financial group by BSCH and assisting a variety of multinational companies on their acquisitions. *"International tax specialist"* **Francisco de Sousa da Câmara*** is the team's leading light. His team has advised on several innovative stock options and securitisation transactions, in addition to tax issues raised by project finance operations. In tax litigation, the firm has appeared on cases relating to transfer pricing issues and tax treatment of exchange gains and losses (GE Capital Information Technology Solutions – ex-Control Data). **Clients:** Borealis; Andersen Consulting; Compaq; McKinsey; Cap Gemini.

Sérvulo Correia & Associados (1 ptr, 2 asscs) Well known tax administration firm that, in acquiring the *"highly specialised"* **Rogerio Manuel Fernandes Ferreira***, is felt to have increased its profile substantially. **Clients:** Banks; insurance companies.

Vasconcelos, F Sá Carneiro, Fontes & Associados (1 ptr) Former KPMG lawyer and esteemed practitioner **João Marques Pinto***, heads a small department specialising in tax structuring and international tax work. The firm has advised on the creation of tax structures for construction and public works companies and banking and leasing companies. **Clients:** Portuguese companies.

Xavier Bernardes e Bragança (3 ptrs, 2 asscs) Niche firm, specialising in taxation, which flourishes under the wing of Brazil-based Alberto Xavier, and uses its Brazilian connection to advise on tax planning for major Brazilian clients investing in Europe. The firm also possesses a number of Italian clients, and was involved in the Italian telecoms privatisation. **Clients:** Brazilian and Italian companies.

Leaders' profiles – Portugal

ABREU, Miguel Teixeira de
Abreu Cardigos & Associados, Lisbon
+351 21 723 1800
miguel.t.abreu@abreucardigos.com.
Recommended in Corporate/M&A, Tax
Specialisation: International and Local Tax Law; Mergers and Acquisitions; MBOs and MBIs; Financing Contracts and Capital Markets.
Prof. Memberships: Portuguese Bar Association, International Bar Association and International Fiscal Association.
Career: Assistant Professor at Faculdade de Direito da Universidade Clássica de Lisboa (Tax Law and Public Finances) 1988-1998. Associate attorney and tax counsel at *A.M.Pereira, L.Saragga Leal, Oliveira Martins, Júdice e Associados* (Lisbon) 1989-1991; Associate attorney at *Grupo Legal Portugu's (Simmon & Simmons, J. y A.Garrigues e Pinheiro Neto)* (Lisbon) 1992. Founding partner *Abreu Cardigos & Associados*, 1993-present. Conducted several professional training courses and seminars in the Tax Law and related areas; Several works published in the International Tax Planning area; Member of the Government Commission for the Reform of the International Tax Laws of the Portuguese Republic.
Personal: Born 30 July 1959. Universidade Clássica de Lisboa, Faculdade de Direito (Bachelor in Laws); London School of Economics and Political Science (LLM – Masters in International Business Law). Interests include go-karting, travelling and tennis. Resides by the coast in Oeiras.

AGUIAR, Carlos
Carlos Aguiar, P. Pinto & Associados, Lisbon
+351 21 355 2755
cappa@mail.telepac
Recommended in Corporate/M&A
Specialisation: Main area of work is corporate law. Has handled acquisitions of companies by Portuguese and foreign clients. Acts as a counsel for major industrial companies and financial institutions.
Prof. Memberships: Portuguese Bar Association; International Bar Association.
Career: Qualified in 1978; Assistant Professor, Commercial Law and Contracts, Lisbon University, Faculty of Law, 1976-80; Partner *João Morais Leitão & Associados*, 1978-93; member EC Committee Leaseurope, 1986-90; member District Council of Lisbon of the Portuguese Bar Association, 1996-98; Secretary General of the Portuguese French Chamber of Commerce and Industry.
Personal: Born 25 July 1953. Attended the Faculty of Law of the Lisbon University (Law Degree).

ALBUQUERQUE, Rui
Albuquerque & Associados, Lisbon
+351 21 343 1570
Recommended in Corporate/M&A

ALVES PEREIRA, José
Barrocas & Alves Pereira, Lisbon
+351 21 384 33 00
jalpereira@mail.telepac.pt
Recommended in Corporate/M&A

Specialisation: Senior Partner. Main areas of work are corporate, mergers & acquisitions, aviation and aerospace, banks and banking insurance, litigation, contracts and real estate. Has handled acquisition contracts representing McDonald's, Nortel, C&N Touristic and others and advised clients such as Bae Systems, Cargill, Rentokil, Cigna and others on investment, litigation and corporate matters. Speaker and moderator in several international conferences and seminars on legal matters. Arbitrator in national and international disputes.
Prof. Memberships: Portuguese Bar Association; Mozambique Bar Association; Inter-Pacific Bar Association; International Bar Association; Union Internationale des Advocats; Union of European Lawyers.
Publications: Author of 'Basic Aspects of Distribution Agreements under Portuguese Law', 'Brief Summary of the Law and Doctrine on Pre-Contractual Liability', 'Information on Legal Developments in European Countries concerning the Hague Convention on Taking Evidence Abroad in Civil and Commercial Matters – Note on Portugal', 'Note on Portuguese Employment and Labor Law', 'Agency and Distribution Agreements in Portugal', 'Insurance Intermediaries – A Survey of the Rules under which Insurance Intermediaries Operate in the European Community', 'A Practitioner's Guide to European-Corporate Insolvency Law', 'Data Protection and Privacy on Telecommunications'.
Career: Qualified in 1968 Portugal. Vice President, Executive Committee, Portuguese Bar Association, 1992-1998. Associate and Area Co-ordinator for Portugal of the American Bar Association, National President of the World Jurist Association. Admitted to the Bar of Mozambique upon its formation in 1997. Previously partner of *André Goncalves Pereira* and *Vasco Vieira de Almeida*, set up own law firm *José Alves Pereira e Associados* in 1990 and in the beginning of 2000 this firm merged with *Barrocas & Sarmento* giving place to *Barrocas & Alves Pereira*.
Personal: Born Agueda (Portugal) 1945. Attended University of Lisbon, Faculty of Law. Languages: English, French and Spanish. Leisure interests include golf and sailing. Lives in Lisbon, Portugal.

ARANTES PEDROSO, Filipa

Morais Leitão, J Galvão Teles e Associados, Lisbon +351 21 381 7400
fapedroso@mlgt.pt
Recommended in Competition/Anti-trust
Specialisation: Telecommunications and Media Law. In the Communications area, has assisted clients operating in the areas of telecommunications, cable T.V., television operators and cinema distributors. Has assisted the first private mobile telecommunications operator in the public tender for the concession of the telecommunications licence. Acted in the privatisation related to the telecommunications and media industry, and in other important mergers and acquisitions in this sector. At the same time, has been responsible for studies and legal opinions regarding several issues in the area of telecommunications operators, and assisted the third private mobile telecommunications operator in the tender which was launched in 1997. Has advised all the Portuguese television operators and one of the parties operating in Pay T.V. and Pay Per View introduced in Portugal last year. Has participated in various studies for the European Commission in the telecommunications area. Competition /Anti-trust: Assisted both at a national and European level most of the major Portugese and foreign companies acting in Portugal.
Prof. Memberships: Portuguese Law Society Association; Portuguese European Law Association.
Publications: Author of 'Merger Control' in the Portugese Society Law Review and 'Competition Law in Portugal' in 'Competition Law in Western Europe and the USA' (ed. Kluwer, updated release).
Career: Qualified in 1982. Joined *Morais Leitao, J.Galvao Telees & Associados* in 1980, becoming a partner in 1987. Member of the Portuguese Law Society, Lisbon since 1982.
Personal: Born Lisbon, Portugal, November 22, 1954; admitted to bar, 1982, Portugal. University of Lisbon Law School (1973-1978); University of Louvain, Belgium (Degrees in Law and EC Law) (1979-1980); Internship at the Commission of the EC – Competition Law (1983). Assistant Professor of Political Economics, University of Lisbon Law School (1977-1979). Languages, English, French and Spanish.

BARREIRA, Rui

Rui Barreira, Magalhaes Correia, Teresa Carregueiro e Gorjao Henriques, Lisbon +351 21 387 5167
Recommended in Tax

BARROCAS, Manuel P.

Barrocas & Alves Pereira, Lisbon +351 21 384 33 00
barrocas@mail.telepac.pt
Recommended in Corporate/M&A
Specialisation: Senior Partner. Main areas of work are corporate law, corporate finance law, mergers and acquisitions, general contracts and arbitration. Has handled acquisitions of companies and undertakings of varying sorts in Portugal and overseas such as: EDP (Portuguese Electric Company) representing RWE, AG in the acquisition of two power plants, Lisnave (Portuguese shipyard) representing the German company Thyssen Krupp, Cabelauto (Portuguese electric cable manufacturer) representing Sumitomo Corporation, Makro Group representing Metro AG, Howmedica Division of Pfizer (Portugal) representing the US company Stryker Corporation, and advised clients in a number of transactions such as: Banque Crédit Agricole, Mannesmann Eurokon, Siemens AG, Péchiney Industries, Sacilor/Usinor, WR Grace & Co., Betz Corporation, Cable & Wireless, Bank of Tokyo – Mitsubishi, British Aerospace, and many others. Speaker and moderator in several international conferences and seminars on legal matters.
Prof. Memberships: Portuguese Bar Association; Portuguese Arbitration Association (Vice President); International Bar Association; American Bar Association; The Law Society of England and Wales; European Lawyers Association; Southwestern Legal Foundation.
Publications: Author of the Portuguese chapters of a number of law books published by international publishers such as: 'Business Law in Europe', 'Acquisition of Shares in a Foreign Country', 'International Business Acquisitions', 'Structuring International Contracts', 'Pre-Trial and Court Procedures Worldwide', 'Trial and Court Procedures Worldwide', 'Civil Appeal Procedures Worldwide', 'Injunction Proceedings in Europe', 'International Tax Planning', 'Security on Movable Property and Receivables in Europe', 'Recognition and Enforcement of Foreign Judgments', 'International Conflicts of Law', 'Liability of Lawyers and Indemnity Insurance'. Editor of the comparative law book Kluwer 'Limitation of Freedom of Contracts by Mandatory Provisions of Law' (under preparation).
Career: Qualified in 1968. Professor of Commercial Law, Lisbon Business School, 1970-1978, Consultant to the Ministry of Tourism, 1968-1974, representative speaker of Portuguese Bar Association at annual meeting of CCBE (Council of the Bars and Law Societies of the European Community), appointed arbitrator by Portuguese Government for settling disputes, chairman International Relations Committee of the Portuguese Bar Association, 1981-1987. Member of the Council of the IBA/SBL 1994-1998. Current member of the Advisory Board of the US Southwestern Legal Foundation. In 1982, founded the law firm *Manuel P. Barrocas & Associados*, changed to *Barrocas & Sarmento* later on which merged in March of 2000 with *José Alves Pereira e Associados* giving place to *Barrocas & Alves Pereira*, a leading law firm in Portugal.
Personal: Born Fundão (Portugal) May 1943. Attended University of Lisbon, Law School. Languages: English, French and Spanish.

BLECK, Jorge Maria

Morais Leitão, J Galvão Teles e Associados, Lisbon +351 21 381 7439
jmbleck@mlgt.pt
Recommended in Corporate/M&A
Specialisation: Partner in and Head of Corporate & Banking Department. Main area of work is corporate law, principally mergers, acquisitions, privatisations, securities and international contracts. Has handled acquisitions of companies and undertakings of varying sorts by Portuguese and foreign clients. Acted on the privatisation of Portocel (pulp paste producer) and Brisa (highway concession); on the international IPO of Telecel (GSM concession) and Soporcel (paper producer). Has also acted on the merger of Borealis companies in Portugal; acted for Fromageries Bel on the acquisition of Lacto group; for Sunterra Inc. in the acquisition of a major resort in Portugal; for TIAA – CREF on the purchase of an important stake in one of the biggest shopping centres in Portugal. Acted for Banco Santander Central Hispano (BSCH) in the acquisition of A. Champalimaud's financial group in Portugal; for Secil on the hostile take-over of Cimpor (Portegese cement producer); and for several banks on the BOT's of motorways and shadow toll infrastructures.
Prof. Memberships: Portuguese Bar; International Bar Association – Section on Business Law and General Practice (Law Practice Management); American Bar Association – Section on Law Practice Management; Portuguese Delegation of

P

P

International Chamber of Commerce (ICC).
Career: Qualified in 1981. Was a founder of the law firm *J.M. Galvão Teles, Bleck, Pinto Leite & Associados*, later merged with *João Morais Leitão & Associados* to form the firm *Morais Leitão, J. Galvão Teles & Associados* at which is a Partner.
Personal: Born 27 December 1954, Lisbon, Portugal. Attended the University of Lisbon, Law School, 1975-1980.

BOTELHO MONIZ, Carlos
Pena, Machete, Botelho Moniz, Nobre Guedes, Ruiz & Associados, Lisbon +351 21 384 6300
Recommended in Competition/Anti-trust

BRANCO, Luis
Abreu & Marques, Lisbon +351 2 1 330 7100
Recommended in Banking & Finance

BRITO PEREIRA, Jorge
A.M. Pereira, S. Leal, O. Martins, Júdice & Associados, Lisbon +351 21 319 7300
Recommended in Banking & Finance

CAMPOS, Diogo Leite
A.M. Pereira, S. Leal, O. Martins, Júdice & Associados, Lisbon +351 21 319 7300
Recommended in Tax

CAMPOS FERREIRA, Fernando
A.M. Pereira, S. Leal, O. Martins, Júdice & Associados, Lisbon +351 21 319 7300
Recommended in Banking & Finance

CARDIGOS DOS REIS, Pedro
Abreu Cardigos & Associados, Lisbon +351 21 723 1800
pedro.c.reis@abreucardigos.com
Recommended in Banking & Finance
Specialisation: Banking and Financial Services Law; Derivatives; International Contracts; Foreign Investments and Sports Law.
Prof. Memberships: Portuguese and Brazilian Bar Associations, International Bar Association, International Section of the American Bar Association.
Career: Associate attorney at the law firm *Stroeter, Trench, Veirano e Advogados – (Baker & McKenzie,* São Paulo office) in Brazil, 1987-1989; Associate attorney at the law firm *Baker & McKenzie* (Chicago office) 1989-1990; Associate attorney at the law firm *F. Castelo Branco, Nobre Guedes & Associados*, in Lisbon, 1990-1991; Senior Associate attorney at the law firm *Veiga Gomes, Bessa Monteiro, Marques Bom e Associados*, 1992. Founding partner of *Abreu, Cardigos & Associados*, 1993-present.
Personal: Born 6 June 1964. Universidade Cat'lica Portuguesa (Bachelor in Laws); Universidade de São Paulo, Brasil (Post-Graduate in International Law); ITT, Chicago Kent School of Law (LLM, American Legal Studies); Universidade Lus'ada (Post-Graduate in Sports Law). Interest in peace education volunteer work (Children's International Summer Villages), tennis and football. Proud father of two girls.

CASSIANO SANTOS, Pedro
Vieira de Almeida Associados, Lisbon +351 21 311 3400
Recommended in Banking & Finance

CASTELO BRANCO, Manuel
Gonçalves Pereira, Castelo Branco e Associados, Lisbon +351 21 355 3800
mcastelobranco@gpcb.pt
Recommended in Corporate/M&A
Specialisation: Mergers, acquisitions and finance law. Major cases included during the years of 1998, 1999 and 2000: acquisitions in the industry and banking sector, privatisation and purchase of airline companies, project finance of motorways and cross border lending of rolling stock.
Prof. Memberships: Lisbon Law Society; American Bar Association. International Bar Association (IBA).
Career: Law degree from the Faculty of Law of the Lisbon Law School (qualified in 1976). Joined *Gonçalves Pereira, Castelo Branco e Associados* in 1980; acts as Managing Partner.
Personal: Born on 9 March 1953. Lives in Cascais, Lisbon. Leisure interests include football, golf and music.

COUTO, Margarida
Vieira de Almeida Associados, Lisbon +351 21 311 3400
Recommended in Banking & Finance

DA CRUZ VILAÇA, José Luís
A.M. Pereira, S. Leal, O. Martins, Júdice & Associados, Lisbon +351 21 319 7321
Recommended in Competition/Anti-trust

DE ABREU, Jorge
Abreu & Marques, Lisbon +351 2 1 330 7100
Recommended in Corporate/M&A

DE SOUSA DA CÂMARA, Francisco
Morais Leitão, J Galvão Teles e Associados, Lisbon +351 21 381 74 00
mlgt.lawfirm@mail.telepac.pt
Recommended in Tax
Specialisation: Partner in charge of the tax department. Main area of work is international taxation connected with transfer pricing, double taxation issues, mergers and acquisitions, project finance, capital markets and tax litigation. Acts for the leading corporations and banks present in the Portuguese market and has been successfully involved in substantial tax litigation for the last ten years. Member of several Committees of experts in charge of drafting the tax legislation in Portugal. Correspondent for the International Bureau of Fiscal Documentation, Tax Analysts, the EC Tax Journal and other journals.
Prof. Memberships: Portuguese Bar Association; Director of the Portuguese Association of Tax Consultants; Portuguese Tax Association as well as International Fiscal Association; International Tax Planning Association and Portuguese member at the Confédération Fiscale Europeénne.
Career: Also joined *João Morais Leitão & Associados* in 1986; set up tax group in 1988 and became partner in 1990. Currently is the head of the tax and public law department of *Morais Leitão, J. Galvão Teles & Associados* where manages an excellent team and is the visiting professor of international tax law of the prestigious law faculty of Lisbon's Universidade Nova (from the academic year 2000/2001 on).
Personal: Born 31 July 1961. Attended the law Faculty of the Catholic University where completed an EC post graduation (1986-1987) and an LLM in 1992.

FERNANDES FERREIRA, Rogerio Manuel
Sérvulo Correia & Associados, Lisbon +351 21 383 69 00
Recommended in Tax

FRUTUOSO DE MELO, Antonio
Antonio Frutuoso de Melo & Associados, Lisbon +351 2 1 321 8600
afmelo@afma.pt
Recommended in Banking & Finance, Corporate/M&A
Specialisation: Founder and Senior Partner of *Antonio Frutuoso de Melo e Associados.* Main area of work is banking and finance (including extensive work on structured products, securitisation, cross border and synthetic leasing), corporate, tax, mergers and acquisitions and privatisations. Acted as counsel to international investment banks in the first issues of consolidated Tier I capital for Portuguese Banks in the early 90's, for the Global Coordinators and international underwriters in the privatisation of Portuguese State owned companies, in the acquisition of several large Portuguese companies by foreign investors, and for institutional investors in various private placements. Currently acts for major international companies and financial institutions in large projects in Portugal, as well as for foreign banks established in Portugal.
Prof. Memberships: Portuguese Law Society.
Publications: Author of several articles in international magazines and collective works, dedicated to corporate finance, capital markets and M&A.
Career: Qualified in 1979. Worked for the Ministry of Labour and Social Affairs between 1971 and 1979. Teacher of Administrative Law in the Lisbon Law School 1978/1980. 1980 counsel to the Ministry for Internal Affairs. 1981 Chief of Staff to the Deputy Minister for the Council of Ministers. 1982 Chief of Staff for the Minister of Labour. 1983 Counsel to the Ministry of Public Works, Transportation and Communications. 1983/1984 National Defence Institute Studies. 1984 Joined the Law Firm *Carlos de Sousa e Brito & Associados* in Lisbon, where practised until May 1997. 1985/1987 Professor of Administrative Law Litigation by special invitation in the Lisbon Free University. In May 1997 left the previous law firm to found own law firm specially focused on banking, finance, corporate, tax and M&A.
Personal: Born 16 November 1948. Attended Coimbra and Lisbon Universities. Lives in Lisbon.

GALVÃO TELES, Miguel
Miguel Galvão Teles, João Soares da Silva & Associados, Lisbon +351 2 1382 6600
Recommended in Banking & Finance, Corporate/M&A

GALVÃO TELES, Nuño
Morais Leitão, J Galvão Teles e Associados, Lisbon +351 21 381 74 00
Recommended in Corporate/M&A
Specialisation: Partner in Corporate and Banking

Department. Main area of work is corporate and banking law, principally mergers, acquisitions, privatisations and project finance. Has handled acquisitions of companies of varying sorts by foreign clients. Also acts and leads the firm's team in the major privatisations processes in Portugal. Has been very active in the most important project finance transactions in Portugal in the past five years, including a new bridge over Tagus River and tolls and shadow tolls motorway projects. Country correspondent of the 'Journal of International Banking Law'. Author of several articles.
Prof. Memberships: Portuguese Bar Association, International Bar Association.
Career: Qualified in 1987. Joined *J.M. Galvão Teles, Bleck, Pinto Leite & Associados* in 1987, becoming a partner in 1992. Partner of *Morais Leitão, J. Galvão Teles & Associados* since 1995.
Personal: Born 4 October, 1964. Lisbon University 1982-1987. LLM in International Business Law (University of London). Resides in Lisbon, Portugal.

GARRIN, Duarte
Abreu & Marques, Lisbon +351 21 330 7100
Recommended in Corporate/M&A

GONÇALVES PEREIRA, André
Gonçalves Pereira, Castelo Branco e Associados, Lisbon +351 21 355 3800
agoncalvespereira@gpcb.pt
Recommended in Corporate/M&A
Career: Law degree, University of Lisbon Law School 1958. Admitted to Bar 1959, Lisbon. Professor of International Law, University of Lisbon since 1962. Minister of Foreign Affairs of the Republic of Portugal (1981-1982). Holder of several Decorations and Academic Degrees (Grand Cross Order of Merit, Republic of Italy, 1981. Grand Officer Légion d'Honneur, France, 1982; Grand Cross Cruzeiro do Sul, Brasil, 1982). Former representative of Portugal in the United Nations, International Monetary Fund, OECP, UNESCO, etc. Former lecturer or visiting Professor at Columbia University, Universities of Paris, Madrid, Rio de Janeiro, etc.
Personal: Born 1936.

JALLES, Isabel
Jalles Advogados, Lisbon +351 21 388 4095
Recommended in Competition/Anti-trust

JÚDICE, José Miguel
A.M. Pereira, S. Leal, O. Martins, Júdice & Associados, Lisbon +351 21 319 7300
Recommended in Corporate/M&A

LEITÃO, João Morais
Morais Leitão, J Galvão Teles e Associados, Lisbon +351 21 381 74 00
mlgtlisboa@mlgt.pt
Recommended in Corporate/M&A
Specialisation: Senior Partner of *Morais Leitão, J. Galvão Teles & Associados*, law firm which has incorporated several individual and law firms practising in Portugal since 1960. Specialises in mergers and acquisitions, project finance, insurance and international commercial arbitration. Has intervened in the main privatisation operations made in Portugal since 1985, namely the privatisation of the petrochemical sector, the public tender offers for privatisation of Banco Totta & Açores and of Secil (a cement company), the international floating of Portucl, Cimpor and EDP and the privatisation of several other state owned companies. Took the most important role in the legal advice for the project finance related with the new crossing over River Tagus, in Lisbon, acting on behalf of the winner of the concession award for the construction, financing and operation of that bridge. Such a project had an actual value of US$2 billion.
Prof. Memberships: Member of the Body of Arbitrators of the Delegation of the International Chamber of Commerce in Portugal having intervened as Arbitrator and Chairman of the Arbitral Tribunals in several important arbitration cases submitted to ICC Rules of Arbitration or to the Portugese Law of Arbitration. Former member of the Government of Portugal – Minister of Social Affairs (1980); Minister of Finance (1981); Member of the Parliament (1979-85); Vice-Chairman of the Board of the Portugese Bar Association and later on Vice-Chairman of the Supreme Body of that association until 1998.
Publications: Author of several monographs on 'Privatizations in Portugal', 'Foreign Investment in Portugal', the 'Portugese Capital Markets', 'Using State Bonds for Privatisation Bids', the 'Portugese Insurance Market, 'The New Road Crossing over the Tagus – A Case Study'.

LOBO-XAVIER, Antonio
Carlos Osório de Castro, Eduardo Verde Pinho, JJ Vieira Peres, Porto +351 22 616 6950
Recommended in Tax

MAGALHÃES CARDOSO, Antonio
Vieira de Almeida Associados, Lisbon +351 21 311 3400
Recommended in Competition/Anti-trust

MARICOTO MONTEIRO, João Filipe
A.M. Pereira, S. Leal, O. Martins, Júdice & Associados, Lisbon +351 21 319 7300
Recommended in Tax

MARQUES, Paulo
Abreu & Marques, Lisbon +351 21 330 7100
Recommended in Corporate/M&A

MARQUES MENDES, Mario
Marques Mendes & Associados, Lisbon +351 21 382 63 00
mmm@marquesmendes.pt
Recommended in Competition/Anti-trust
Specialisation: Partner at *Marques Mendes & Associados*, concentrating on EU and Portuguese competition laws, as well as general EU and international trade law matters. Extensive experience in representing clients with respect to merger control, anti-competitive practices, State aid and public procurement, in cases conducted before Portuguese and EC authorities, having handled important litigation before national and EC courts. Has advised and represented the Portuguese Government and other public sector entities as well as major national and international corporations in various sectors which include telecommunications, cement, information technology, banking and finance, energy and media, transport and transport infrastructure. Frequent speaker at conferences and seminars and has written extensively on various subjects of EU law, notably competition/antitrust, and of international trade law.
Prof. Memberships: Portuguese Bar Association (Vice-President of the Lisbon Council/1996-1998), Portuguese Association of European Law, European Association of Lawyers, Portuguese Association for the Study and Promotion of Competition and International League of Competition Law.
Publications: Relevant publications include, among others, 'Antitrust in a World of Interrelated Economies: The Interplay Between Antitrust and Trade Policies in the U.S. and the EEC' (1991); 'EC Competition Rules in National Courts: Portugal' (co-author)(1999).
Career: University of Lisbon School of Law (Lic. Dir. 1976). Admitted to the Portuguese Bar in 1976. After graduating from both the College of Europe (EU Law, 1981) and the University of Michigan Law School (LLM 1984), became Assistant-Professor of Law at the University of Lisbon School of Law and Lecturer in International Trade Law at the Center for European Studies of the Portuguese Catholic University, in Lisbon, while resuming private practice. Currently managing partner at *Marques Mendes & Associados.*
Personal: Born 11 September 1954. Recipient of Fulbright Scholarship (1983-1984), William W. Cook Fellowship/University of Michigan Law School (1983-1984); EC Commission Grant (1981-1982); Portuguese Ministry of Foreign Affairs Scholarship (1980-1981).

MARQUES PINTO, João
Vasconcelos, F Sá Carneiro, Fontes & Associados, Lisbon +351 210 308 600
vscf@mail.telepac.pt
Recommended in Tax
Specialisation: Responsible for the firm's tax department. Specialises in income tax law, both on a corporate and individual level, and in international tax planning operations. Practice also involves the reorganisation and restructuring of corporate groups. Has also been involved in cases of tax litigation. In 1999, representing the firm, was engaged by the European Union as a tax expert to coordinate a support programme to the Brazilian tax reform.
Career: Worked as a Legal Advisor to the Director of Lisbon's City Hall Tax Department between 1987 and 1989. Between 1989 and 1991 was a senior tax consultant at KPMG Peat Marwick. In 1991 joined the law firm *Barros, Sobral, Xavier, G. Gomas & Associados* as an associate. Partner at *Vasconcelos, F. Sá Carneiro & Associados* since 1996.
Personal: Graduated from Lisbon's University Law School in 1986.

ORTIGÃO RAMOS, Diogo
Gonçalves Pereira, Castelo Branco e Associados, Lisbon +351 21 355 3800
dortigaoramos@gpcb.pt.
Recommended in Tax
Specialisation: Responsible for the tax department. Divides practice between domestic and international taxation, namely mergers and acquisitions, corporate restructuring, financial operations and real estate transactions. Experience also includes advice relating to the Madeira free trade zone and tax litigation.

P

During 1999 and 2000, dealt with real estate corporate restructurings, mergers and cross border leasing of rolling stock.
Prof. Memberships: American Bar Association (ABA). Portuguese Tax Association. International Bar Association (IBA).
Career: Law degree from Lusiada University (1989). Postgraduate in tax from Intituto Superior de Gestão (1994). Joined *Gonçalves Pereira, Castelo Branco e Associados* in 1996. National reporter of the Foreign Lawyers Forum of ABA.
Personal: Born 27 January 1965. Lives in Lisbon. Leisure interests include rugby, football and music.

P

OSÓRIO DE CASTRO, Carlos
Carlos Osório de Castro, Eduardo Verde Pinho, JJ Vieira Peres, Porto +351 22 616 6950
Recommended in Banking & Finance, Corporate/M&A

PAIS ANTUNES, Luis
A.M. Pereira, S. Leal, O. Martins, Júdice & Associados, Lisbon +351 21 319 7300
Recommended in Competition/Anti-trust

PENA, Rui
Pena, Machete, Botelho Moniz, Nobre Guedes, Ruiz & Associados, Lisbon +351 21 384 6300
Recommended in Corporate/M&A

PEREIRA COUTINHO, Frederico
Gonçalves Pereira, Castelo Branco e Associados, Lisbon +351 21 355 3800
fpereiracoutinho@gpcb.pt
Recommended in Competition/Anti-trust
Specialisation: Competition and merger control, mergers and acquisitions and associated financing, corporate restructuring and real estate. During 1998, 1999 and 2000 participated in major foreign investment ventures in Portugal.
Prof. Memberships: Lisbon Law Society. Membership: International Bar Association (IBA).
Career: Law degree from the faculty of law of Lisbon University. Partner of *Gonçalves Pereira, Castelo Branco e Associados.* Former lecturer of international private law in the faculty of law of Lisbon University (1988-89) and legal advisor of the Portuguese Tourism Fund (1987-1989).
Personal: Music, art, outdoor activities, photography. Former AFS student.

PINTO CORREIA, Carlos
Morais Leitão, J Galvão Teles e Associados, Lisbon +351 21 381 74 00
Recommended in Competition/Anti-trust

PROTASIO, Manuel
Vieira de Almeida Associados, Lisbon +351 21 311 3400
Recommended in Banking & Finance

RAIMUNDO, Antonio
Albuquerque & Associados, Lisbon +351 21 343 15 70
Recommended in Corporate/M&A

REBELO DE SOUSA, Pedro
Grupo Legal Português, Lisbon +351 2 1 313 1500
Recommended in Banking & Finance, Corporate/M&A

RÉFEGA FERNANDES, Victor
A.M. Pereira, S. Leal, O. Martins, Júdice & Associados, Lisbon +351 21 319 7300
Recommended in Corporate/M&A

RICOU, Maria João
Gonçalves Pereira, Castelo Branco e Associados, Lisbon +351 21 355 3800
mjoaoricou@gpcb.pt
Recommended in Banking & Finance
Specialisation: Mergers and acquisitions, banking, corporate finance, structured finance and capital markets. Major cases during 1999 and 2000 include group restructurings in the finance sector, securitisation, cross border leasings, non-recourse finance leasings, acquisitions and sales in the industry sector; public offers.
Prof. Memberships: Member of the Lisbon Law Society. International Bar Association (IBA).
Career: Law degree from the faculty of law of The Lisbon Catholic University; joined *Gonçalves Pereira Castelo Banco e Associadosin* 1984; became partner in 1990.
Personal: Born in Lisbon in 1959; married with four children; lives in Cascais, near Lisbon.

RODRIGUES MARTINS, Gabriela
A.M. Pereira, S. Leal, O. Martins, Júdice & Associados, Lisbon +351 21 319 7300
Recommended in Corporate/M&A

RUIZ, Nuno
Pena, Machete, Botelho Moniz, Nobre Guedes, Ruiz & Associados, Lisbon +351 21 384 6300
Recommended in Competition/Anti-trust

SÁ CARNEIRO, Francisco
Vasconcelos, F Sá Carneiro, Fontes & Associados, Lisbon +351 210 308 600
vscf@mail.telepac.pt
Recommended in Banking & Finance, Corporate/M&A
Specialisation: Specialises in banking, including structured finance and acquisition finance, project finance and general corporate, especially mergers and acquisitions. Leads the firm's banking and capital markets group and co-leads the corporate group. Recently has been active in advising leading financial institutions and companies in cross-border deals, and in the road projects in Portugal, as counsel for the banks.
Career: Partner at *Vasconcelos, F. Sá Carneiro, Fontes & Associados* since 1993. Prior to 1993 was partner at *João Morais Leitão e Associados.*

SÁRAGGA LEAL, Luís
A.M. Pereira, S. Leal, O. Martins, Júdice & Associados, Lisbon +351 21 319 7300
Recommended in Banking & Finance, Corporate/M&A

SOARES, António
Morais Leitão, J Galvão Teles e Associados, Lisbon +351 21 381 74 59
afsoares@mlgt.pt
Recommended in Banking & Finance
Specialisation: Main area of work is securities law, companies law, banking law, mergers and acquisitions and privatisations. Has handled acquisitions of companies and privatisations of varying sorts by Portuguese and foreign clients.
Prof. Memberships: Portuguese Bar; International Bar Association.
Career: Degree in law. Admitted to the bar, 1988, Portugal. Assistant professor at the University of Lisbon Law School 1988-1991 and Universidade Automa 1995-96; consultant to the Lisbon Stock Exchange 1989-1991. Member of the Board of Directors of the Portuguese Securities Exchange Commission 1991-1995. Member of the Commission created by the Ministry of Finance to review the Portuguese Securities Market Code, Member of the Board of Directors of the Securities Institute. Author: 'The New Regime of Amortisation of Shares'; 'The Financial Institutions Regime and the Securities Market'; 'The Portuguese Stock Exchange Cash Market of Securities – The Lisbon Stock Exchange'; 'Privatisation – A Legal Perspective'; 'Negotiation, Settlement and Delivery of Securities Market Transactions'; ' Securities Rights'. University of Lisbon Law School; Program on Securities Enforcements and Market Oversight in the International Training Institute of the USSEC.
Personal: Born Alcobaça. Portugal, July 7, 1961.

SOARES DA SILVA, João
Miguel Galvão Teles, João Soares da Silva & Associados, Lisbon +351 2 1382 6600
Recommended in Banking & Finance, Corporate/M&A

VIEIRA, Pedro Siza
Morais Leitão, J Galvão Teles e Associados, Lisbon +351 21 381 74 00
psvieira@mlgt.pt
Recommended in Banking & Finance
Specialisation: Has been involved in most major infrastructure and transport projects carried out in the last decade in Portugal (acting for sponsors, financiers, and public bodies). Also focuses on administrative and public law.
Prof. Memberships: Ordem dos Advogados. Associação para o Desenvolvimento do Direito do Urbanismo (Vice-President). Member of the High Council of Administrative and Tax Courts.
Career: Lisbon University, Coimbra University, qualified 1988. Legal adviser to the Governor of Macau. Legal adviser to the Mayor of Lisbon. *Morais Leitão, J Galvão Teles and Associados,* 1992. Became a partner in 1997.
Personal: Born 1964, married with two children.

VIEIRA DE ALMEIDA, João
Vieira de Almeida Associados, Lisbon +351 21 311 3400
Recommended in Banking & Finance, Corporate/M&A

VIEIRA DE ALMEIDA, Vasco
Vieira de Almeida Associados, Lisbon +351 21 311 3400
Recommended in Banking & Finance, Corporate/M&A

PUERTO RICO

Corporate/Commercial

PUERTO RICO Leading firms (Corporate/Commercial)
1 Fiddler González & Rodríguez, LLP
McConnell Valdés
2 O'Neill & Borges

Firms are listed alphabetically in each band.

Leading individuals (Corporate/Commercial)
1 **ALVAREZ José Julián** *Fiddler González & Rodríguez, LLP*
CHOW Walter *O'Neill & Borges*
ESCUDERO Antonio *McConnell Valdés*

Individuals are listed alphabetically in each band.

Fiddler González & Rodríguez, LLP (12 ptrs, 15 asscs) Viewed by competitors as a *"top notch firm"* that has *"been around forever."* The corporate department handles banking and finance, insurance, tax, IP and increasing amounts of M&A work, while the firm's environmental practice has a growing reputation. Our research indicates **José Julián Alvarez** is the firm's corporate driving force. The team recently represented Masso Expo in the sale of the Plaza Masso stores to Home Depot and also represented Irizarry Acquisition in the purchase of CASCO Sales. **Clients:** American Airlines; Microsoft; Banco Bilbao Vizcaya; Bacardi; Banco Santander; Pfizer; UPS; Kodak; Chase Manhattan; Merrill Lynch; General Motors; Baxter Healthcare; BASF Pharmaceuticals; Deutsche Bank.

McConnell Valdés (18 ptrs, 15 asscs) An established *"old line"* firm and the largest on the island, it is *"the first firm one would name,"* we were told. A *"tried and true firm,"* actively involved in a wide variety of general corporate matters, corporate and public finance, M&A and secured lending work. The firm represented borrowers on two recent hotel/real estate financings and Mova Pharmaceuticals and Bristol-Myers Squibb on two tax-exempt bond deals. Managing partner **Antonio Escudero** is the firm's standout practitioner. **Clients:** American Home Products; Banco Popular de Puerto Rico; Boots; Bristol-Myers Squibb; Chrysler; Citibank; Coca-Cola; Colgate-Palmolive; Kraft; Heinz; Hewlett-Packard; IBM; Intel; Morgan Stanley; SmithKline Beecham; Unilever.

O'Neill & Borges (13 ptrs, 14 asscs) Another established law firm whose *"wonderful crop of lawyers"* are *"a pleasure to deal with."* The practice

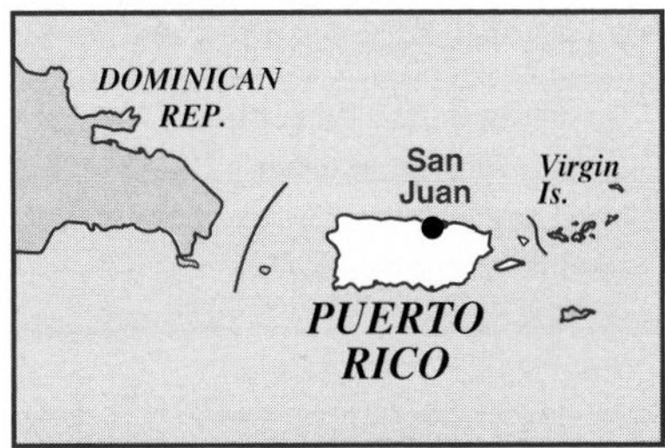

has a strong corporate department, which covers a broad spectrum of work from M&A and tax to real estate, trade regulation and environmental law. Witnessing an increase in public financing work, the firm acts as bond counsel to the Government Development Bank for Puerto Rico. Recently the firm worked as local counsel for GTE in the acquisition of the Puerto Rico Telephone Company and has been involved in the drafting of major legislative efforts in the last few years. **Walter Chow** is an *"experienced corporate attorney"* with an international reputation. **Clients:** Esso; Ford; Kmart; Polaroid; Lucent Technologies; Marriott Hotels; Sanofi-Winthrop Pharmaceutical; Santander Securities; Sara Lee; US Air; Banco Popular; Lehman Brothers.

Leaders' profiles – Puerto Rico

ALVAREZ, José Julián
Fiddler González & Rodríguez LLP, San Juan +787 753 3113

CHOW, Walter
O'Neill & Borges, San Juan +787 764 8181

ESCUDERO, Antonio
McConnell Valdés, San Juan +787 759 9292

QATAR

Corporate/Commercial

QATAR Leading firms (Corporate/Commercial)
1 Law Offices of Gebran Majdalany
2 Hassan Al-Khater Law Offices
3 Arab Law Bureau
Law Offices of Dr Najeeb Al-Nauimi (in association with Richards Butler)

Firms are listed alphabetically in each band.

Leading individuals (Corporate/Commercial)
1 **HORSFALL TURNER Richard** *Law Offices of Gebran Majdalany*
2 **MAJDALANY Gebran** *Law Offices of Gebran Majdalany*
SILVER David *Hassan Al-Khater Law Offices*
THOMPSON Hugh *Dr Najeeb Al-Nauimi*
3 **AL-KHATER Hassan** *Hassan Al-Khater*
AL-NAUIMI Najeeb *Dr Najeeb Al-Nauimi*

Individuals are listed alphabetically in each band.

Law Offices of Gebran Majdalany (10 lawyers) "*Pre-eminent*," researchers received unanimous acknowledgement for this firm, boasting experienced leaders and an established base in Doha. A large "*well staffed*" team of local, US and UK qualified lawyers undertake work relating to major projects and joint ventures, oil and gas financings and banking for a broad client base including major investment and state lending banks.

"*Doyen of the legal community*," founder partner **Gebran Majdalany*** has excellent local contacts and is "*the first port of call for legal advice.*" Running the firm's English department, former head of Allen & Overy's Dubai office **Richard Horsfall Turner*** is "*highly knowledgeable and imposing.*" "*Commercially minded and very responsive*," he "*does everything with a confident approach.*" The firm acts as key advisors in various refinancing deals relating to state owned QGPC such as the NGL4 financings and QChem's financing of QGPC's joint venture with Philips Petroleum. A recent highlight was advising four of the six bidders in relation to Qatar's first IPP. **Clients:** Leading financial institutions and corporates.

Hassan Al-Khater Law Offices (1 ptr, 2 of counsel) A small but quality practice. Clearly a major player in the region, it is heavily involved in major project financing transactions. Responsible for international corporate transactions and honorary legal advisor to the British Embassy, "*precise*" **David Silver*** is "*technically minded and knows the law well.*" The firm is also known for its excellent litigation department, headed by "*aggressive, effective*" **Hassan Al-Khater*** who practised at Trowers & Hamlins in Muscat, and Clyde & Co in Dubai. The firm acted as local counsel to the Government of the State of Qatar in two borrowings including a $1 billion bond issue. It also advised Qatar Telecommunications and Credit Suisse First Boston (Europe) on the privatisation of Qatar Telecommunications Corp, the first IPO in the State. In project finance the firm acted as local counsel to a potential bidder for the Ras Laffan Independent Power Project, the first of its kind in the State of Qatar. **Clients:** Exxon; Mobil; Occidental Petroleum of Qatar; Arco Qatar; Elf; Marubeni; Chevron; BP-Amoco; HSBC; Standard Chartered Bank; Dresdner Kleinwort Benson; CSFB; Gulf Agency; Alcatel; ABB; Interbeton; Schlumberger; the Embassies of USA, Britain and Germany.

Arab Law Bureau (5 lawyers, 1 of counsel) Researchers received clear commendation for this recently established outfit, staffed by European and US-educated Arab lawyers. Seen to be making in-roads into the legal market, it is strong in secular and Islamic banking work with clients including HSBC, Standard Charter and the Qatar Islamic Bank. Highlights include advice to Qatar Islamic Bank in establishing the Al'Namaa Global Equity Fund and in relation to an Islamic real estate deal, the first and largest of its kind. The firm represented the borrowers in the development and financing of the Four Seasons hotel complex in Doha. **Clients:** HSBC; Standard Charter; Doha Bank; Halliburton.

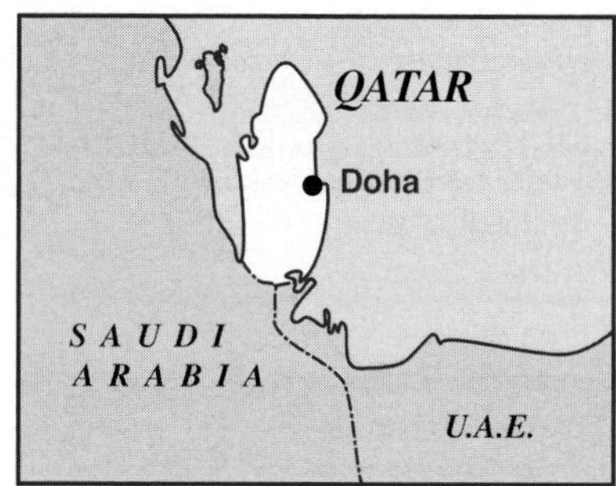

Law Offices of Dr Najeeb Al-Nauimi (in association with Richards Butler) (2 ptrs, 4 asscs) The affiliation with Richards Butler is considered to be a substantial asset to this firm, thought to be "*taking a greater share of the market.*" Its profile in banking and project financing matters is largely owed to "*competent major player*" **Hugh Thompson***, while former Minister of Justice **Najeeb Al-Nauimi*** is noted for his wide circle of excellent contacts. The firm acted as local counsel on two airbus financings to Qatar Airways and to Qatar Shipping Company and to the lending banks in relation to several ship financings. Advised a syndicate of banks on $60 million project financing of Al Ahli Hospital Project and advising lenders on $168 million financing of West Bay Complex. **Clients:** Qatar Shipping Company; Qatar National Bank; Commercial Bank of Qatar; Qatar Industrial Development Bank; Qatar Vinyl Co; Coca-Cola; Gulf International Bank.

*See leaders' profiles on page 569

Leaders' profiles – Qatar

AL-KHATER, Hassan
Hassan Al-Khater Law Offices, Doha
+974 443 7770

AL-NAUIMI, Najeeb
Richards Butler, Doha +974 4311 124
najeeb@nn-law.com
Specialisation: Commercial and civil litigation, banking and insurance, petroleum laws including oil and gas contracts, joint venture, onshore and off-shore oil exploration and exploitation pipeline and downstream industry, and commercial arbitration (local and international – major arbitration case currently being handled KHD Humboldt WEDAG AG, Germany v. Arabian Civil; Work EST., Saudi Arabia). Also patent, trade mark, copyright and intellectual property claims (represents Business Software Alliance in the Middle East), maritime claims (including arrest and release of vessel).
Prof. Memberships: International Bar Association, International Law Association, British Institute of International and Comparative Law, American Society of International Law, and World Jurist Association.
Career: Educated at Alexandria University, Egypt (LLB, 1981), received a Diploma in Petroleum Law (1983), and completed a PhD in International Law at Dundee University, UK (1987). Acted as a Legal Adviser to Qatar General Petroleum Corporation, Legal Expert at *Diwan Emiri*, later promoted to Minister Legal Adviser. Became Minister of Justice for the State of Qatar in July 1995. In June 1997 resigned from this position to start own law firm under the name *Law Offices of Dr Najeeb Bin Mohammed Al Nauimi.*
Personal: Born 21 March 1959. Leisure interests include reading and writing on social issues and environmental issues. Has a wife and five children.

HORSFALL TURNER, Richard
Law Offices of Gebran Majdalany, Doha
+974 442 8899

MAJDALANY, Gebran
Law Offices of Gebran Majdalany, Doha
+974 442 8899

SILVER, David
Hassan Al-Khater Law Offices, Doha
+974 443 7770

THOMPSON, Hugh E.
Richards Butler, Doha +974 4311 124
nnrblaw@qatar.net.qa
Specialisation: Specialist in all aspects of international banking including syndicated lending, project finance, trade finance and asset finance. Also has a wide-ranging corporate finance practice in the Middle East.
Prof. Memberships: Law Society; Union Internationale des Avocats.
Career: Qualified as a solicitor in England 1971. In-house lawyer at National Westminster Bank, and in-house legal adviser and deputy head of project finance for Standard Chartered Merchant Bank. Partner *Coudert Brothers*, London 1990. Banking Partner in *Richards Butler* since 1996; seconded to Doha 1988.
Personal: Born 1944, married with three daughters. Education, Bradfield College and Christ Church, Oxford.

Q

ROMANIA

Index

OVERVIEW: An initiative sponsored by The World Bank in association with the Romanian government has accelerated economic reform law with state companies marked for privatisiation and liquidation. Investors at present are favouring greenfield projects over formerly state-owned orgnanisations. In the banking market, Taylor Joynson Garrett has made a conscious effort to focus while the two big local firms Musat & Asociatii and Nestor Nestor Kingston Petersen maintain their dominant positions. Andy Kingston and Patricia Petersen of the latter return to the US but remain in 'of counsel' roles in Romania. Linklaters' take-over of Canadian firm Burns Schwarz signifies the first major player from London's magic circle or New York's Wall Street firms to enter Romania.

Banking & Finance

ROMANIA Leading firms (Banking & Finance)
1 Nestor Nestor & Kingston Petersen
2 Linklaters
Musat & Asociatii
Taylor Joynson Garrett
3 Altheimer & Gray

Firms are listed alphabetically in each band.

Leading individuals (Banking & Finance)
1 **DAYES Simon** *Taylor Joynson Garrett*
NESTOR Ion *Nestor Nestor & Kingston Petersen*

Individuals are listed alphabetically in each band.

Nestor Nestor & Kingston Petersen (2 ptrs, 33 asscs) Despite the return of *"financial experts"* Andrew Kingston and Patricia Petersen to America, the team is considered an outstanding financial practice which has acted on sovereign debt work for the Romanian government.

The firm acted as Romanian counsel to Mediocredito Centrale of Italy on the €99 million financing facility granted to Romtehnica RA and as Romanian counsel to Svenska Handelsbanken of Sweden in connection with its €53 million financing of the Bucharest subway system. The market agrees that **Ion Nestor*** has *"more than adequately filled the shoes"* of the absentee partners. **Clients:** Mediocredito Centrale SpA; Svenska Handelsbanken; Petrom SA; Nomura International; Demirbank TAS; Raiffeisen Zentralbank Osterreich.

Linklaters (1 ptr, 9 asscs) In banking, derivatives and secured transactions the firm has an *"experienced"* Bucharest-based team acquired from Burns Schwartz. It advises a domestic and international client base on sovereign and secured borrowings and is involved in the securitisation of currency, interest rate and commodity derivative instruments. **Clients:** State Ownership Fund; AIG; Government of Romania.

Musat & Asociatii (3 ptrs, 12 asscs) A large, highly visible Romanian team generally acknowledged as a leading banking light. The firm acted in association with Lazard and Raiffeisen Bank, conducting advisory work in the privatisation of Bank Agricola. It also advised GE Capital in its 35% acquisition of Banc Post and continues to counsel Bank Paribas, in relation to secured transactions and commercial loans. **Clients:** AIG USA; ABN AMRO; ABC USA; SocGen; Banque Paribas; Tomen Telecom.

Taylor Joynson Garrett (1 ptr, 3 asscs) Banking and finance accounts for 30% of the firm's workload, more than any other area of practice. Involved in two restructurings for Credit Suisse First Boston and acted for GE both in its sale of Pater Bank to Piraeus Bank and its exit from Banc Post. **Simon Dayes*** is *"a first rate lawyer with a fine reputation in banking."* **Clients:** Credit Suisse First Boston; Itochu Corporation; Romanian Post Privatisation Fund.

Altheimer & Gray (1 ptr, 4 asscs) Interviewees described this firm as *"a banking specialist"* although it has a relatively low profile in the market. The team acted for Raiffeisen Zentralbank in its $20 million financing of an American international school in Bucharest. **Clients:** GTE; Raiffeisen Zentralbank Osterreich.

Corporate/M&A

ROMANIA Leading firms (Corporate/Mergers & Acquisitions)	
1	Nestor Nestor & Kingston Petersen
2	Sinclair Roche & Temperley
	Taylor Joynson Garrett
3	Linklaters
	Musat & Asociatii
4	Altheimer & Gray
	Herzfeld & Rubin

Firms are listed alphabetically in each band.

Leading individuals (Corporate/Mergers & Acquisitions)	
1	NESTOR Ion *Nestor Nestor & Kingston Petersen*
2	BUZESCU Petru *Buzescu & Co*
	DAYES Simon *Taylor Joynson Garrett*
	MUSAT Gheorghe *Musat & Asociatii*
	STOICA Cristiana *Stoica & Associates*
	ZAMFIRESCU Calin *Zamfirescu & Partners*

Individuals are listed alphabetically in each band.

Nestor Nestor & Kingston Petersen (2 ptrs, 33 asscs) Supported by a large international team, this *"good group of Romanians"* is judged to be *"at or near the top"* by peers. It specialises in corporate finance, M&A, privatisations and commercial transactions. Despite returning to the US, the husband and wife team of Kingston and Petersen will remain involved in specific projects.

The firm acted in a $80 million deal for a thermo-electricity facility, an €85 million Romanian subway system project and a $25 million deal for the construction of an office complex for an Austrian Bank. The *"savvy"* **Ion Nestor*** remains at the helm. **Clients:** Lafarge; Government of Romania; IBM; GE Capital; General Motors; Philip Morris; Microsoft; AB Electrolux.

Sinclair Roche & Temperley (2 ptrs, 4 asscs) A well-established foreign firm with an office in Bucharest since 1992. Active on inward investment in Romania for multi-national companies, the firm advised an Austrian client on the structuring of its trade finance arrangements in Romania. It also advised on the sale of ships by Romanian shipyards and on a US-Romanian joint venture for the servicing and maintenance of passenger airliners. **Clients:** Romanian and international corporate clients.

Taylor Joynson Garrett (1 ptr, 1 asscs) After a recent reorganisation, the firm is cementing its *"good name"* with a number of international clients including a *"steady UK clientele."* It advised ALRO, the largest aluminium producer in central Europe, in a $40 million structured trade finance facility from London banks and acted on Interbrew's acquisition of a controlling interest in the Romanian Efes brewery.

The team also advised the Romanian Post Privatisation Fund (in which the EBRD and the EU were significant participants) on the injection of capital into six projects during the course of this year, covering telecoms, internet service provision and gas distribution companies. *"Personable"* **Simon Dayes*** is the *"back-bone of the outfit."* **Clients:** CSFB; Itochu Corporation; Romanian Post Privatisation Fund; Interbrew; Colgate Palmolive.

Linklaters (1 ptr, 9 asscs) Formerly the Canadian Burns Schwartz, this fine team is thought to be doing well by combining its contacts and reputations, old and new. It has captured a number of important mandates and occupies a niche at the top end of the overseas firms. The team advised the AIG-led consortium investment funds in connection with their $90 million acquisition of an equity stake in MobilRom, the largest single private institutional investment in Central & Eastern Europe to date.

The firm is representing the State Ownership Fund on the proposed privatisation of Sidex, Romania's largest company, and advised the Government of Romania on the proposed privatisation of Romania's national radio and telecommunications company, Radiocomunicatii. **Clients:** State Ownership Fund; AIG; Government of Romania.

Musat & Asociatii (7 ptrs, 36 asscs) A rapidly expanding Romanian practice providing corporate, commercial, taxation and property litigation and counselling. Retained by GE Capital as local counsel in the privatisation of Banc Post, the team advised the Romanian state ownership fund on the privatisation of ALRO SA, a major aluminum producer. As local counsel for SmithKline Beecham UK it advised on the acquisition of the largest private pharmaceutical group of companies in Romania.

Interviewees rated **Gheorghe Musat*** who heads a young team which recently absorbed respectable local firm Popovici & Asociatii, thus gaining its lead partner, the long-standing advisor to the Ministry of Privatisation. **Clients:** GE; Shell Romania Exploration BV; France Telecom; AT&T USA; AIG USA; ABN AMRO Bank; ABC USA; Renault; SocGen; L'Oréal; Smithkline Beecham UK; Banque Paribas; Tomen Telecom.

Altheimer & Gray (2 ptrs, 14 asscs) Researchers were told that the practice is *"emerging from its infancy"* in Romania and is *"here to stay."* The backbone of the firm is foreign investment and M&A in the telecommunications, banking and emerging energy sectors. The team is involved in the government initiative to encourage the privatisation of state companies by foreign investors and has advised on due diligence and the preparation of packages for sale. **Clients:** GTE; leading financial institutions.

Herzfeld & Rubin (11 lawyers) Established in the mid-nineties, the firm has developed fine relationships with Mediterranean clients, particularly Greek, Turkish and Israeli. It was involved in the largest US related privatisation in the country, the Resita steel works deal. It also represented Hellenic Cables in its purchase of ICME ECAB, a Romanian cable company, and acted as sole counsel to OTE, the Greek telecoms company, in the Rom Telecom privatisation. **Clients:** OTE; Mytilineos SA; Hellenic cables; Akmaya.

Other Notable Practitioners **Cristiana Stoica*** of Stoica & Asociatii and **Calin Zamfirescu*** of Zamfirescu and Partners are two local lawyers *"right at the top"* of their profession. **Petru Buzescu*** of Petru Buzescu & Asociatii is said to have *"demanding clients whom he keeps very happy."*

*See leaders' profiles on page 572

Leaders' profiles – Romania

BUZESCU, Petru
Buzescu & Co, Bucharest +40 1 335 1366
Recommended in Corporate/M&A

DAYES, Simon
Taylor Joynson Garrett, Bucharest +40 1 222 1313
sdayes@tjg.ro
Recommended in Banking & Finance, Corporate/M&A
Specialisation: UK Finance and Projects partner resident in Bucharest, leading the local office's banking and energy groups. Specialises in project finance and energy/natural resources and has twelve years' professional experience in the UK, including secondments at Bank of America and Bank Austria. Cross-border experience within Romania focuses on project and structured trade finance (syndicated and bilateral), international and domestic banking (secured and unsecured), projects in the power and minerals sectors (including IPP) and venture capital.

MUSAT, Gheorghe
Musat & Asociatii, Bucharest +40 1 223 3717
Recommended in Corporate/M&A

NESTOR, Ion I.
Nestor Nestor & Kingston Petersen, Bucharest +40 1 224 0890
ion.nestor@nnkp.ro
Recommended in Banking & Finance, Corporate/M&A
Specialisation: Partner and Head of privatisation department. Practice emphasises extensive knowledge of Romanian law (civil, commercial and corporate law), and privatisation, acquisition and restructuring matters in Romania. Acted as consultant to the Romanian Government in connection with successful privatisation of Rom Telecom upon advice of an international consortium lead by Goldman Sachs ($675m). Acted as sole legal counsel to Lafarge in the successful acquisition of a majority shareholding in Romcim, the leading Romanian cement manufacturer ($200m). Co-leader of the team of Romanian legal experts that drafted the 1999 Romanian privatisation legislation, advising the World Bank, the State Ownership Fund, the Romanian Development Agency, and other Romanian Ministries in this respect.
Prof. Memberships: Bucharest Bar Association.
Career: Counsel and Chief Legal Advisor of the Romanian Consulting Institute ROMCONSULT, 1976. Legal expert at the Institute for Legal Research of the Romanian Academy, 1983. Joined the Bucharest Bar Association, 1984. Founded *Nestor Nestor & Kingston Petersen*, 1995.
Personal: Born 24 February 1953, Bucharest, Romania. Magna cum laudae University of Bucharest Law School, 1976. Married to Manuela M. Nestor. Lives in Bucharest.

STOICA, Cristiana
Stoica & Associates, Bucharest +40 1 336 7010
Recommended in Corporate/M&A

ZAMFIRESCU, Calin
Zamfirescu & Partners, Bucharest +40 9 455 2551
Recommended in Corporate/M&A

RUSSIA

Index

R

OVERVIEW: Since the calamitous crash of 1998, investor confidence has failed to pick up and capital markets work is reduced to a trickle. Firms have been forced to downsize drastically, relocating expatriates, and in some cases closing completely. Many UK firms overly reliant on the western investment banks, and US teams tied to the energy sector were hard hit.

2001 has been greeted with cautious optimism. The leading firms have demonstrated a long-term commitment with a multi-national, multi-lingual cast of lawyers and a broad risk averse spread of clients. Clifford Chance remains the leading corporate firm on account of size, specialism and transactional flair. Many of the US stalwarts such as Akin, Gump, Strauss, Hauer & Feld, Coudert Brothers and Leboeuf, Lamb, Greene & MacRae fare well, in part due to their leading expatriate Russian specialists and energy expertise.

Corporate/M&A

Clifford Chance Pünder (8 ptrs, 40 asscs) *"Any discussion of the leading corporate firms has to start with them."* The group has high local visibility, a great client base, and by far the largest foreign presence in Russia. Although not immune to the downturn that has affected the entire Russian commercial market, its core strength in banking, finance and capital markets ensures that it remains an obvious choice in Russia for London investment banks. The firm's merger with Pünder has also given it access to work on behalf of blue-chip German investors.

John Hamilton* is rated as one of the corporate practice's major assets, and advises on financing, securities and restructuring matters. **John Balsdon*** has a similar practice, and is commended for his *"understanding of the Russian market and his high quality service."* He advised on the $22 billion London Club restructuring of the external debt of the Soviet Union. **Bruce Bean*** is a well-connected *"mover and shaker,"* a leading figure at the US Chamber of Commerce, and an *"important client developer."* He represented AT&T on its $5 billion acquisition of IBM Russia's global network assets. Although primarily known as a litigator, **Ivan Marisin*** is also recognised for his corporate practice.

The firm advised General Motors on a $500 million joint venture with Russian car manufacturer AvtoVaz, and represented Orion Capital on its $20 million acquisition of the Russian internet search system Rambler. Other deals include acting for Norwegian food producer Rieber & Son ASA on its acquisition of Russian producer Chaka, and advising BASF on the Russian aspects of the acquisition of American Home Products' Cynamid division. **Clients:** BASF; General Motors; Volvo Truck Corporation; LV Investment; Merrill Lynch; Hansa; AT&T; Deutsche Bank; BMW; Orion Capital; Rieber & Son ASA.

Akin, Gump, Strauss, Hauer & Feld, LLP (2 ptrs, 8 asscs) Consistently regarded as one of the leading US firms in Russia, it has an established clientele of major domestic corporates. Familiar figures in M&A, financing and securities, the firm is most associated with the oil and gas and telecoms industries. However, the relocation of the esteemed Robert Langer to New York in the summer of 2000 was a setback to the office, followed by the similar departure of Melissa Schwartz in early 2001.

The department represented leading mobile phone operator VimpelCom on a US SEC-registered equity offering of ADRs and convertible bonds, raising over $225 million. It also acted for Andersen Group, on the acquisition of a 50% interest in ComCor-TV, a Russian communications company, and advised the Russian Federal Commission on a two-year World Bank-funded project with the Centre for Capital Markets Development. **Clients:** Andersen Group; Caspian Pipeline Consortium; Energomash; Gazprom; Loral Space Systems; Lukoil; Media Most; Nestlé; Renaissance Hotels; Seagram; Teleglobe; Tyumen Oil Company; VimpelCom.

Allen & Overy (3 ptrs, 14 asscs) Although the firm has greatly reduced its presence in Moscow, its strengths in banking, project finance and energy maintain its position among the leaders in Russia. The corporate team has continued to advise a string of small and medium-ticket joint ventures and acquisitions for its powerful client base.

"Highly impressive" Russian partner **Irina Mashlenko*** has extensive experience in equity and debt financings, project finance and privatisations, notably in the energy industry. The firm advised the informal steering committee of foreign creditors on the restructuring of Uneximbank, and acted for the Russian Government on the proposed restructuring of Svyazinvest. **Clients:** Cargill Group; Downside Up Fund; Great Northern Telegraph; Sputnik Group; Western Union; Lukoil; WestLB; Rosneft; Russian government; ABN AMRO; BNP Paribas; DG Bank; Permtex; Standard Bank; BHP; EBRD; Gazprom; Mobil; MOL; Occidental; Shell; Uneximbank; Rossiisky Kredit; Promstroybank; Chase Manhattan.

*See leaders' profiles on pages 577-578

RUSSIA Leading firms (Corporate/Mergers & Acquisitions)	
1	Clifford Chance Pünder
2	Akin, Gump, Strauss, Hauer & Feld, LLP
	Allen & Overy
	Baker & McKenzie
	Coudert Brothers
	Freshfields Bruckhaus Deringer
	LeBoeuf, Lamb, Greene & MacRae, LLP
	Linklaters
	Salans Hertzfeld & Heilbronn
	White & Case LLC
3	Norton Rose
	Skadden, Arps, Slate, Meagher & Flom LLP

Firms are listed alphabetically in each band.

Leading individuals (Corporate/Mergers & Acquisitions)	
1	**BAUDON Jacky** *Freshfields Bruckhaus Deringer*
	ZIMBLER Brian *LeBoeuf, Lamb, Greene & MacRae*
2	**HAMILTON John** *Clifford Chance Pünder*
	JETTER Yorck *Freshfields Bruckhaus Deringer*
	MELLING Paul *Baker & McKenzie*
	TARASSOVA Jane *Salans Hertzfeld & Heilbronn*
3	**BALSDON John** *Clifford Chance Pünder*
	BEAN Bruce *Clifford Chance Pünder*
	DE CORT André *Skadden, Arps, Slate, Meagher*
	GLUHOVSKAYA Valentina *Norton Rose*
	GUTBROD Max *Baker & McKenzie*
	HEYES Philip *Linklaters*
	KEEFE Charles *Coudert Brothers*
	MARISIN Ivan *Clifford Chance Pünder*
	MASHLENKO Irina *Allen & Overy*
	VERRIER Hugh *White & Case LLP*

Individuals are listed alphabetically in each band.

Baker & McKenzie (2 ptrs, 14 asscs) Regarded by interviewees as *"one of the most important players in the domestic market,"* this full-service firm's corporate department is supported by tax, property and IP expertise, and acts for local and foreign clients on transactions in a range of industries. Our research has revealed that the group has specific experience of pharmaceuticals transactions, and is one of the few to offer specialist communications expertise, having advised on a number of Russian IPOs. A small office in St Petersburg continues to advise heavyweight clients such as Ford, Wrigleys and Tetra Laval. In Moscow, **Paul Melling***, a veteran of twelve years in Russia, and German **Max Gutbrod*** attract consistent market recommendation.

The firm acted for Italian manufacturing conglomerate Merloni on the purchase of the Stinol refrigeration plant for $120 million. It also advised IT InfoArtStars on the sale of its assets to affiliates of Golden Telecom, represented DirectNet on acquisition of shares in a Russian telecoms company, and acted for Kraft Jacobs Suchard on the establishment of a coffee packaging plant near St.Petersburg. **Clients:** Cisco; Intel; Glaxo Wellcome; Astra Zeneca; Aventis; Merloni; Hilton Hotels; Bank Austria; Evrofinance; Alrosa; Standard Bank London; HSBC; Japan Bank; Telf; Exim Bank; SNAM; DirectNet; Besser; Sud Chemie; Kraft Jacobs Suchard; Wrigley; International Paper; Ford; British Telecom; EBRD.

Coudert Brothers (4 ptrs, 14 asscs in office. 3 foreign partners) Maintaining a healthy showing in the Russian market, the firm is not generally associated with big-ticket transactions, but continues to represent Russian and foreign corporates in industries such as energy and telecoms. The corporate team is considered to have *"a sensible, pragmatic approach to Russia and a strong domestic focus."*

Charles Keefe* is a *"committed"* lawyer, respected by peers for his broad corporate and finance practice, and heads a team that advised Telenor East Invest AS in connection with its acquisition of $51 million of American Depository Shares in VimpelCom. The firm also represented the Vector Group (formerly known as the Brooke Group) on the sale of its Russian tobacco manufacture and distribution business Liggett-Ducat to Gallaher Overseas Holdings for $390 million. **Clients:** TNK; Conoco; Chevron; Exxon; Lukoil; Shell; Telenor; GTS; Crédit Lyonnais; SocGen; Sakhalin Energy Investment; Lockheed Martin Corporation; Vector Group.

Freshfields Bruckhaus Deringer (5 ptrs, 30 asscs) The addition of lawyers from the former Bruckhaus firm has created a combined unit of great depth. Both arms of the new firm have long-established reputations in Russia and close connections with domestic corporates, particularly in the energy sector. M&A, project finance and banking are major element's of the team's workload.

Ten years resident in Moscow, **Jacky Baudon*** is a name synonymous with the Russian market. He has a *"deep understanding of Russian legislation,"* and has *"brought his personal enthusiasms into the firm and guided its development."* **Yorck Jetter***, formerly of Bruckhaus, *"leaves an extremely good impression"* on opposing lawyers. The firm advised a series of international banks, including Dresdner and Chase Manhattan, on the restructuring of $750 million of Tatneft's foreign currency debt. It also advised Marconi Communications on the $60 million disposal of its 50% share in the Russian telecommunication company Comstar to Metromedia International Telecommunications. Other notable work includes serving as Russian counsel to Brooke (Overseas) on the $390 million disposal of its 99% share in the Russian tobacco company Liggett-Ducat to Gallaher Overseas Holdings. **Clients:** CSFB; Chase Manhattan; Dresdner Bank; BHF-Bank; Bankgesellschaft Berlin; Crédit Agricole Indosuez; West Merchant; Marconi Communications; Brooke Group.

LeBoeuf, Lamb, Greene & MacRae LLP (5 ptrs, 20 asscs) The firm is praised for its commitment to Russia, and its full-service office handles all aspects of corporate, finance and direct investment. Its strongest suit, however, is in the energy sector where it is regarded as one of the market front-runners. A group of expatriate partners has great experience in Moscow, and all speak fluent Russian.

The firm's greatest asset is **Brian Zimbler***, a *"true Russian specialist,"* who commands universal respect. He has *"a great understanding of Russian structures,"* and *"brings real value to meetings."* Although he will move to London in 2001, he is expected to continue to spend a large proportion of his time in Russia. The firm represented the EBRD on its $30 million investment in VimpelCom, and advised the financiers and consortium involved in the billion dollar Sea Launch project, an attempt to build a space satellite launch platform in the Pacific. **Clients:** EBRD; US-Russia Investment Fund; Caspian Pipeline Consortium.

Linklaters (3 ptrs, 15 asscs) Although the firm has closed its St Petersburg office and greatly reduced its team in Moscow, it is still considered to warrant respect for its M&A expertise on behalf of an array of international corporate clients. The firm has received increased instructions from US investment banks and also acts for the Russian Alpha Bank, one of the few to invest outside Russia. **Philip Heyes*** is *"understated, but really sharp,"* and is recommended for his mixed corporate and energy practice.

In the expanding telecoms sector, the firm advised Lucent Technologies on the creation of a manufacturing joint venture with a Russian telecoms group, resulting in a contract to supply switches to two of Russia's leading telecoms operators. Also advised Alcatel on financing matters relating to the sale of GSM equipment to VimpelCom, and acted for Morgan Stanley Dean Witter, financial advisor to Surgutneftegas, on aspects of the reorganisation of the holding company structure. **Clients:** UBS Warburg; Morgan Stanley; Lucent Technologies; Alcatel; Alpha

Bank; Lukoil; BP; Exxon; Shell; Morgan Stanley Dean Witter; Pioneer Real Estate Advisors; Reuters; ING Barings; KBC Bank; City of Moscow.

Salans Hertzfeld & Heilbronn (4 ptrs, 22 asscs) This hybrid international firm maintains impressive coverage and standing across the region, and possesses well-staffed offices in Moscow and St Petersburg. The group is considered to have *"breadth, size, commitment and US connections,"* and acts for a stock of blue-chip multi-nationals such as McDonalds and Coca-Cola. Rated for its direct investment expertise, the firm advises on transactions from a range of industries, including natural resources, telecoms, consumer goods, financial services and pharmaceuticals. **Jane Tarassova*** is *"undoubtedly one of the market leaders."*

The firm has advised the Ford Group (including Volvo Cars and Mazda) on a number of corporate and commercial matters, including litigation, while in telecoms, it advised on the creation of a project to create an overland fibre-optic link between Northern Europe and the Far East. Additionally, the group acted for Continental in acquiring a blocking minority in one of Russia's major tyre distributors, and represented a European bank on the structuring of finance for Aeroflot. **Clients:** Coca-Cola; McDonalds; Ford; Shell; Russian Central Bank; Gerald Metals; GML International; International Hotel Investments; Bouygues; City of Moscow; Volvo; Neste, Caspian Pipeline Consortium Russia; Continental; Louis Vuitton; RBA; Unilever; Isover; Colgate; Sidanco; Baltschug; UDV.

White & Case LLC (2 ptrs, 22 asscs) *"One of the strongest firms around,"* is now considered to have one of the premier US offices in Moscow, with particular expertise in incoming financing. This revolves primarily around its two core clients, the EBRD and IFC, whom the firm advises on loans to Russian corporates. Other areas of strength are M&A transactions involving oil, gas and telecoms clients, and a banking practice that usually represents lenders.

Canadian managing partner **Hugh Verrier*** has become a well-known name in the Russian market. He has *"led the practice back onto the map after some difficult times,"* and *"carved out an impressive reputation for himself."* The practice advised the EBRD on a $150 million working-capital loan to Lukoil, the EBRD's largest loan to a Russian company since 1993, and for the same client, a $35 million pre-export secured financing to Severstal, a Russian steel producer. In the telecoms sector, the practice acts as head counsel to Sonera in its acquisition of a GSM operator's licence for the city of Moscow and Moscow region. **Clients:** EBRD; IFC; Sonera; TNK; US Russia Investment Fund; Tyumen Oil Company; AIG Russia; Delta Capital; ING Bank; West LB; Société Générale.

Norton Rose (3 ptrs, 7 asscs) Although clearly not among the market leaders, the firm is respected for its general commercial expertise, advising on corporate and project finance, banking, insolvency and restructuring. It advises clients from industries such as aviation, pharmaceuticals, manufacturing and real estate. Special attention is paid to energy and natural resources, including hard minerals and precious stones, where the team acts for a number of western investors. Resident Russian partner **Valentina Gluhovskaya*** is considered to be *"a sharp operator."*

The firm advised a leading western investor on the disposal of its shareholding in the Russian open joint stock company Severalmaz, the licence holder for the exploration and development of the Lomonosov diamond deposit. It has also advised fund managers of EBRD Regional Venture Funds on projects connected with investments in small companies in the Far East, Smolensk, Moscow and Black Earth regions of Russia. **Clients:** Mineral, oil, real estate and manufacturing companies.

Skadden, Arps, Slate, Meagher & Flom LLP (1 of counsel, 5 asscs) *"Small but steady and active,"* the Moscow office of the New York corporate giant is praised for its consistent flow of M&A transactions. The firm advises on complex transactions for Russian and US clients in sectors such as telecoms and IT. Other recent activity has revolved around private equity investments, transactions in the media industry and one significant deal in the metal industry.

André de Cort* has *"accumulated extensive experience in Russia and is a quality professional."* His team represented UBS Warburg, Donaldson, Lufkin & Jenrette and Morgan Stanley Dean Witter as underwriters to the combined offerings of $75 million convertible bonds and ADSs by VimpelCom. **Clients:** Rostelecom; UBS Warburg; Morgan Stanley; Donaldson, Lufkin & Jenrette Securities Corporation; International Paper; MC-BBL Eastern Europe.

Energy & Natural Resources

Akin, Gump, Strauss, Hauer & Feld, LLP (2 ptrs, 8 asscs) Still a market leader through its status as principal external counsel to Lukoil, the firm has had to cope with the departure of Robert Langer to New York, but continues to be acknowledged for its industry-specific expertise. The team has advised Lukoil on the Caspian Pipeline Consortium Project and the refinancing of existing debt, and represented the company on its $75 million acquisition of Getty Petroleum Marketing, one of the first acquisitions of a public US company by a Russian entity. The company will take a 15-year lease on retailer Getty Realty, thereby acquiring over 1300 petrol stations, and is gearing up for an IPO, scheduled for 2001. **Clients:** Caspian Pipeline Consortium; Energomash; Gazprom; Lukoil; Tyumen Oil Company.

Coudert Brothers (4 ptrs, 14 asscs) Highly regarded for its expertise in the Russian energy market, not only in Moscow, but also in its London and New York offices, the firm has an extensive track record in major pipeline projects and financings. The esteemed John Sheedy still heads the Russian oil and gas unit from New York.

The firm was involved in the first production sharing agreement for oil and gas exploration and development in Russia, and continues to represent the Sakhalin II consortium. Continuing to advise a series of US blue-chips and Russian oil companies, the group represented Conoco in a third and final tranche of a $275 million subordinated debt financing for its Russian subsidiary, Polar Lights Company. The transaction involved a $125 million loan placed privately by Chase Securities with a syndicate of pension funds and insurance companies. Also advised Tyumen Oil Company (TNK) on its $500 million twin secured financings, backed by the Export-Import Bank of the United States, to provide funding for the rehabilitation of the Samotlor oilfield and the modernisation of TNK's Ryazan refinery. Elsewhere, the team acted for British Gas on the $28 million sale of its 50% stake in KomiArcticOil to co-shareholder Komineft, a subsidiary of Lukoil.

*See leaders' profiles on pages 577-578

R

RUSSIA Leading firms (Energy & Natural Resources)
1 Akin, Gump, Strauss, Hauer & Feld, LLP
Coudert Brothers
Freshfields Bruckhaus Deringer
LeBoeuf, Lamb, Greene & MacRae, LLP
Macleod Dixon LLP
2 Allen & Overy
Clifford Chance Pünder
Linklaters
Salans Hertzfeld & Heilbronn
3 Debevoise & Plimpton LLC
Denton Wilde Sapte

Firms are listed alphabetically in each band.

Leading individuals (Energy & Natural Resources)
1 **BAUDON Jacky** *Freshfields Bruckhaus Deringer*
BEAN Bruce *Clifford Chance Pünder*
HINES Jonathan *LeBoeuf, Lamb, Greene*
KOCHARYAN Levon *Macleod Dixon LLP*
SEFEROVICH Pat *Denton Wilde Sapte*
TARASSOVA Jane *Salans Hertzfeld & Heilbronn*

Individuals are listed alphabetically in each band.

Clients: TNK; Conoco; Chevron; Exxon; Lukoil; Shell; Sakhalin Energy Investment; British Gas.

Freshfields Bruckhaus Deringer (5 ptrs, 30 asscs) Chambers' researchers have found that this newly enlarged firm has consistently maintained a decent profile in the energy sector, with oil and gas transactions a major feature of the corporate practice. **Jacky Baudon***, considered to be one of the best expatriate corporate lawyers, has always included a substantial project finance and energy dimension to his practice.

The firm advised numerous banks, including Dresdner, Chase Manhattan and Crédit Agricole Indosuez on the restructuring of $750 million of Tatneft's foreign currency debt. It has also advised a leading Russian institution on the $100m financing of the construction of pipelines in Romania and Bulgaria, and a European company in the negotiation of production sharing agreements in Russia and the rest of the former Soviet Union. **Clients:** CSFB; Chase Manhattan; Dresdner Bank; BHF-Bank; Bankgesellschaft Berlin; Crédit Agricole Indosuez; West Merchant.

LeBoeuf, Lamb, Greene & MacRae LLP (5 ptrs, 20 asscs) *"Quality energy outfit"* which has extensive coverage across the country, and is seen as one of the undoubted leaders in Russia. Virtually all members of the multi-lingual team have had exposure to energy matters, not least the vastly experienced **John Hines***. A high-profile recruit form Debevoise & Plimpton and an *"excellent Russian oil and gas specialist,"* his hire was a *"real bonus"* to the unit. He has unique upstream experience, having worked on the Kharyaga and all three Sakhalin projects. In the latter, the firm advised the consortium of three governments and eight major oil producers in establishing the legal infrastructure for development of a $2 billion pipeline. It has also represented an American investor on one of the first active production sharing contracts in Russia. **Clients:** EBRD; US-Russia Investment Fund; Caspian Pipeline Consortium.

Macleod Dixon LLP (3 ptrs, 12 asscs) Respected Canadian energy firm, which has maintained a remarkable degree of stability in Moscow. *"They've tracked the industry well and apply a consistent level of focus."* The team retains a share of the oil and gas market, but is felt to excel in mining and minerals, having acted on a number of projects concerning gold, silver and diamond mines. The workload involves advising on mineral licences, quarrying projects and trade, generally on behalf of North American companies. **Levon Kocharyan*** is again warmly recommended as a leading energy specialist.

The firm advised Bema Gold Corporation on the restructuring of its Russian operations in respect of the Julietta Project, and assisted Kuranakh Geological and Mining Company, a Russian joint venture with 50% foreign participation, on various corporate and licensing issues. **Clients:** Halliburton; Bema; Kuranakh Geological and Mining Company.

Allen & Overy (3 ptrs, 14 asscs) Best known for its advice on energy projects and financing in the industry, the firm acts for both Western financiers and Russian oil and gas companies. A varied caseload includes acting for BHP Oil on the proposed development of the Prirazlomnoye Field, advising Gazprom on the Yamal-Europe pipeline, representing Mobil on the Russian aspects of its Europe-wide merger of downstream interests with BP, and assisting Rosneft on the proposed sale of part of its stake in the Sakhalin I PSA project. In financing, the firm acted for Lukoil on its $150 million loan facility from EBRD, the first major corporate financing by EBRD since the 1998 financial crisis. **Clients:** Lukoil; Shell; BHP Oil; Gazprom; Mobil; MOL; WestLB; Rosneft; ABN AMRO; BNP Paribas; DG Bank; Permtex; Standard Bank; Chase Manhattan; EBRD; US Eximbank; Occidental; Tomskneft.

Clifford Chance Pünder (8 ptrs, 40 asscs) Through a top-tier international energy financing practice and close links to Western investment banks, the Moscow office remains a respected force in the energy market. *"Perennial rainmaker"* **Bruce Bean*** is noted for his transactional acumen.

In addition to oil and gas work, the firm has acknowledged minerals and mining expertise, advising Deutsche Bank on the restructuring of Norilsk Nickel, the world's leading producer of nickel, copper, platinum and platinoids. The team acted for the lenders on the $1.5 billion Blue Stream financing to Gazprom, a deal designed to finance a gas pipeline from Russia under the Black Sea to Turkey. Also advised on $250 million worth of secured loans to TNK, arranged by CSFB, Deutsche Bank and ING, to enable TNK to finance its bid for the Russian oil company Onako. **Clients:** Deutsche Bank; ING; CSFB; Norilsk Nickel.

Linklaters (3 ptrs, 15 asscs) The firm has maintained a modest profile in the energy sector, acting for multi-national companies on a range of projects in Russia. The firm assisted BP on the long-running Sidanco insolvency proceedings and debt restructuring, which were successfully completed in January 2000. It advised the same client on aspects of its equity participation in, and debt and equity financing of, RUSIA Petroleum, a company with a licence to explore the giant Kovyktinskoye gas field in Eastern Siberia. Other matters include advising Morgan Stanley Dean Witter, financial adviser to Surgutneftegas, on the reorganisation of its holding company structure, and on a $15 million revolving post-production pre-payment facility for Siberian Aluminium Group. **Clients:** BP; Exxon; Lukoil; Shell; KBC Bank; Morgan Stanley Dean Witter.

Salans Hertzfeld & Heilbronn (Moscow: 3 ptrs, 15 asscs) Active in natural resources as well as energy, the firm's expertise stretches from corporate and projects advice on behalf of Russian and western energy companies, to high-end energy financing. **Jane Tarassova***, one of the first Russian energy lawyers to be made a partner in a foreign firm, is recommended for her expertise in mining, oil and gas transactions. She *"knows the details,"* and is *"much more than an average Russian lawyer."*

The practice acted for Shell AZS in the creation of a network of petrol stations in St Petersburg, and for a US holding company owning several Russian oil companies in its sale of a strategic interest to a major investment bank. It also advised a major Russian petroleum company on a public offering of shares, the restructuring of operations and an ongoing investment programme. **Clients:** Shell; Gerald Metals; Neste;

*See leaders' profiles on pages 577-578

Caspian Pipeline Consortium Russia; Sidanco; BP Amoco.

Debevoise & Plimpton LLC (1 ptr, 5 asscs) Although the firm's Moscow office lacks the transactional profile of its competitors, it still picks up substantial oil and gas work, both in exploration and development. It advises US, European and some Russian clients on production sharing agreements and a number of major pipeline projects. The loss of esteemed energy specialist John Hines to Leboeuf, Lamb, Greene & MacRae has been partially offset by an experienced lateral hire from Milbank, Tweed, Hadley & McCloy. Exxon Mobil is the team's dominant client, and has advised on various projects, including Sakhalin III, IV and V and the Caspian Pipeline Project. The firm has also represented Mitsui, a leading financial sponsor of Sakhalin II. **Clients:** Mitsui; Norsk Hydro; Exxon Mobil.

Denton Wilde Sapte (1 ptr, 10 asscs) The firm's reputation in Russia rests almost entirely on its energy practice, which is "*right up there*" for big-ticket oil and gas work, and was recently appointed to the Gazprom panel. Although the office is not considered to possess the resources of the market leaders, a "*realistic and consistent*" team keeps transactions "*ticking over nicely.*" **Pat Seferovich*** is the firm's stand-out practitioner here. In addition to the framework agreement it has signed with Gazprom, the practice represented Electricite de France on a major Russian project, UK company Teleport on a satellite telecom project in Russia, and Gastelecom on several telecom projects. It has also acted for West LB in a number of trade finance transactions involving Russian energy companies, and is principal legal advisor for the Blue Stream gas pipeline project (Snam and Gazprom/Gazexport). **Clients:** Gazprom (including Gazexport and Gaztelecom); NERA; Electricite de France; Teleport; West LB.

R

Leaders' profiles – Russia

BALSDON, John
Clifford Chance Pünder, Moscow +7 501 258 5050
Recommended in Corporate/M&A

BAUDON, Jacky
Freshfields Bruckhaus Deringer, Moscow
+7 095 363 0300
jacky.baudon@freshfields.com
Recommended in Corporate/M&A, Energy & Natural Resources
Specialisation: Specialises in corporate and commercial law, project finance and property projects. Has particular knowledge of sectors including oil, gas and hard minerals, and the food industry.

BEAN, Bruce W.
Clifford Chance Pünder, Moscow +7 501 258 5050
Recommended in Corporate/M&A, Energy & Natural Resources

DE CORT, André
Skadden, Arps, Slate, Meagher & Flom LLP, Moscow +7 501 797 4600
Recommended in Corporate/M&A

GLUHOVSKAYA, Valentina
Norton Rose, Moscow +7 095 244 3639
gluhovshayavx@nortonrose.com
Recommended in Corporate/M&A
Specialisation: Managing Partner of *Norton Rose* Moscow. Has over 9 years' experience of advising on corporate finance and mergers and acquisitions work. Widely recognised as being one of Moscow's foremost lawyers in the corporate and real estate sectors. Corporate finance experience includes acting for institutions, strategic investors and a wide range of commercial companies in a number of sectors including minerals, oil and gas, brewing, manufacturing, retail and commercial real estate. Acted for a major international manufacturing group on its acquisition of a controlling stake in a leading Russian industrial company, both by means of participation in privatisation and by secondary market acquisition; acted for an international manufacturer and distributor of consumer products on the reorganisation of its CIS business interests; advised a leading Russian restaurant group and a leading Russian brewing group on several significant private placings of shares and derivatives; advised a US company in relation to the acquisition of over 75% of shares of a well-known Russian newspaper; advised a major international institution on various disposals of shareholdings in commercial property companies.
Prof. Memberships: A member of the Moscow City Bar since 1990.
Career: Joined *Norton Rose* in 1992 and was elected to *Norton Rose's* worldwide partnership in May 1997.
Personal: Born 15 August 1965 in Moscow, Russia. Graduated from the Moscow State University (law faculty) in 1987. Languages spoken: Russian and English. Leisure interests include horse riding and cross-country skiing.

GUTBROD, Max
Baker & McKenzie, Moscow +7 095 230 6036
Recommended in Corporate/M&A
Specialisation: CIS Managing Partner in the Moscow Office of *Baker & McKenzie.* Heads the Commercial and E-Commerce Practice Groups of the Moscow Office. Regularly advises on corporate and commercial matters, joint ventures, privatisations, large mergers and acquisitions, secondary market share purchases, banking, securities and finance matters, and government regulations. Head of Financial Services Committee of the German Chamber of Commerce in Russia; member of the European Business Club and the Russian Franchising Association.
Career: Prior to joining *Baker & McKenzie* in 1993, worked with *Gleiss Lutz Hootz Hirsch,* Stuttgart/Berlin. Practising in Moscow since January 1996.
Personal: University of Munich, Germany 1985; Munich, Germany/Sao Paulo Brazil (PhD) 1990. Born in Stuttgart, 15 June 1960. Married with two daughters. Presently residing in Moscow. Fluent in German, English, Russian and Portuguese.

HAMILTON, John
Clifford Chance Pünder, Moscow +7 501 258 5050
Recommended in Corporate/M&A

HEYES, Philip
Linklaters (a member firm of Linklaters & Alliance), Moscow +7 501 797 9731
philip.heyes@linklaters.com
Recommended in Corporate/M&A
Specialisation: Advised the UK Department of Transport for more than 5 years on all aspects of the privatisation of British Rail and subsequently led teams advising on rail privatisations in Pakistan and Kenya. Also advised the Russian government on reform of transport laws. Has wide ranging corporate finance and commercial law practice, with recent transactions including the sale of GAN's UK life insurance interests and the $1 billion acquisition by Coca Cola Beverages of The Coca Cola Corporation's bottling interests in Northern Italy. Transferred to Moscow in June 1998 and became managing partner in April 1999. Practice in Moscow has included advice to leading multinational oil corporations on their investments in Russia and to global investment banks on a wide variety of corporate finance and investment products.

HINES, Jonathan H.
LeBoeuf, Lamb, Greene & MacRae, LLP, Moscow +7 095 737 5000
jhhines@llgm.com
Recommended in Energy & Natural Resources
Specialisation: Commercial, regulatory and finance work focusing on projects in the oil and gas development, pipeline, and minerals sectors, private international law generally, and international commercial arbitration. Numerous articles published in legal and energy publications, and frequent speaker at conferences and seminars.
Prof. Memberships: International Bar Association

(SERL); Association of International Petroleum Negotiators; Panel of Arbitrators of the International Commercial Arbitration Court, Russian Federation Chamber of Commerce and Industry; American Chamber of Commerce in Russia, Board of Directors.
Career: Member of New York Bar since 1981; Law Clerk for US District Court Judge Robert W. Sweet, New York, 1980-81; was with *Debevoise & Plimpton* 1981-1999 and headed its Russia/CIS Practice Group; joined *LeBoeuf, Lamb, Greene & MacCrae* as a partner in February 2000, and is resident partner in the firm's Moscow office.
Personal: Born 1952. BA Princeton University 1974. JD University of Virginia 1978. Exchange scholar at Moscow State University School of Law 1979-80. Lives in Moscow; married to Olga A. Dyuzheva; two sons.

JETTER, Yorck
Freshfields Bruckhaus Deringer, Moscow +7 095 363 0300
yorck.jetter@freshfields.com
Recommended in Corporate/M&A
Specialisation: Specialises in finance and banking.

KEEFE, Charles
Coudert Brothers, Moscow +7 095 258 5454
Recommended in Corporate/M&A

KOCHARYAN, Levon
Macleod Dixon LLP, Moscow +7 502 222 2305
levon@macleoddixon.com
Recommended in Energy & Natural Resources
Specialisation: Russian Law (State Corporate Commercial, Subsoil Securities, Anti-Monopoly, Labour, Trade, Hard Currency, Registrations, Licensing of different types of activities), International Public Law and International Private Law. Recently, has been actively involved in drafting and obtaining various acts of the President and government of the Russian Federation, regional state authorities and other state institutions regarding precious metal activities.
Prof. Memberships: International Bar Association; International Lawyers Group, Moscow; American Chamber of Trade and Commerce, Energy Committee; Russian Canadian Intergovernmental Economic Council, Mining Committee; Chairman of the Board of Directors, Russian Precious Metals Council (Russian Mining Forum).
Career: Graduated with honours from Moscow State Institute of International Relations. Completed a three year course in international economics and a five year course in international law. Partner of the Moscow office.
Personal: Born in Russia, spent most of his childhood in the United States.

MARISIN, Ivan
Clifford Chance Pünder, Moscow +7 501 258 5050
Recommended in Corporate/M&A

MASHLENKO, Irina
Allen & Overy, Moscow +7 501 725 7900
Recommended in Corporate/M&A

MELLING, Paul
Baker & McKenzie, Moscow +7 095 230 6036
Recommended in Corporate/M&A
Specialisation: Founding partner of the Moscow and Almaty offices of *Baker & McKenzie.* Resident in Moscow since 1989.
Career: Qualified in 1982. Joined *Baker & McKenzie* in 1980, becoming a partner in 1989. Faculty Member, University College London Centre for the Study of Socialist Legal Systems 1982-89; visiting scholar, Institute of State and Law Moscow 1983 and 1985. Since 1980, has advised Western investors on their business activities in the USSR/CIS. Honorary Legal Adviser to British Ambassador since 1990. Member of numerous UK government, Law Society and ICC committees devoted to trade and investment in the USSR/CIS. A frequent speaker at conferences on trade and investment in the CIS countries, and has written extensively on legal aspects of trade and investment in the region.
Personal: Born 19 March 1957. Graduated from Oxford University in 1978 (MA Jurisprudence). Fluent in English and Russian.

SEFEROVICH, Pat
Denton Wilde Sapte, Moscow +7 095 255 7900
info@dentonwildesapte.ru
Recommended in Energy & Natural Resources
Specialisation: Managing Head of *Denton Wilde Sapte's* CIS/Russia practice. Main practice areas are energy (oil & gas) and acquisitions and dispositions. Clients include mainly large US, UK, European and Russian clients.
Prof. Memberships: American Bar Association, Virginia and Colorado Bar Associations, Natural Gas Association, Rocky Mountain Mineral Law Foundation and Association of International Petroleum Negotiators.
Career: Licensed in 1981 in the US (1981 in Colorado and 1983 in Virginia). Member of Federal Bar. Joined *Denton Hall* in 1998. Prior to joining *Denton Hall*, was Senior Counsel at Occidental Petroleum Corporation (US).
Personal: Born 14 September 1946. Attended U. of Denver College of Law (1981). TC Williams School of Law, Richmond, Virginia (1978-1980) and U. of Virginia (1973), graduate School of Arts and Sciences. Married to Maria Mott Seferovich, three children: Patrick II, Amanda Wu, and Alexandra.

TARASSOVA, Jane
Salans Hertzfeld & Heilbronn, Moscow +7 501 258 3444
Recommended in Corporate/M&A, Energy & Natural Resources

VERRIER, Hugh
White & Case LLC, Moscow +7 095 787 3000
hverrier@whitecase.com
Recommended in Corporate/M&A
Specialisation: Head of *White & Case* Moscow office. Advises domestic and international corporates and financial institutions on broad range of corporate and finance law transactions within Russia and other republics of the CIS. Work includes bank finance, trade finance, investment and arbitration.
Prof. Memberships: Member of United States Supreme Court, New York State Bar and Massachusetts State Bar.
Career: Previously ran firm's Ankara office in Turkey. Broad range of privatisation experience.
Personal: Native English and French, some Russian.

ZIMBLER, Brian L.
LeBoeuf, Lamb, Greene & MacRae, LLP, Moscow +7 095 737 5000
bzimbler@llgm.com
Recommended in Corporate/M&A
Specialisation: Managing partner in the Moscow office. Concentrates on financial and investment transactions in Russia and the other former Soviet countries, generally on behalf of major foreign investors and multinational companies. Since 1986, has handled hundreds of projects in the former Soviet Union, involving a wide range of industries including energy, telecommunications and manufacturing. Has travelled extensively throughout Russia and handled legal projects in such diverse locations as Moscow, St Petersburg, the Komi Republic, Western Siberia, Tatarstan, Stavropol, and the Russian Far East.
Prof. Memberships: International Bar Association, American Bar Association.
Career: Admitted to the bar in 1986 (California) 1995 (District of Columbia). Partner at *Graham & James*, San Francisco prior to joining *LeBoeuf* in 1994. Served as President of the Moscow Lawyers Group, 1996-1998.
Personal: Born 1 March 1958. Graduate of Harvard Law School, the Fletcher School of Law and Diplomacy, and Harvard College. Served as Editor-in-Chief of the 'Harvard International Law Journal' during 1983-84.

RWANDA

Corporate/Commercial

RWANDA Leading firms (Corporate/Commercial)
1 Cabinet Batware et Nkurunziza
Cabinet Kazungu
Etude Mhayimana Isaïe

Firms are listed alphabetically in each band.

Leading individuals (Corporate/Commercial)
1 **BATWARE Jean-Claude** *Batware et Nkurunziza*
KAZUNGU Jean-Bosco *Cabinet Kazungu*
MHAYIMANA Isaïe *Etude Mhayimana Isaïe*

Individuals are listed alphabetically in each band.

Cabinet Batware et Nkurunziza (2 ptrs, 2 asscs) *"An excellent firm for banking and insurance matters,"* the firm advises most of the few foreign companies active in Rwanda. **Jean-Claude Batware** is a *"good commercial lawyer."* **Clients:** Banks; insurance companies.

Cabinet Kazungu (1 ptr, 2 asscs) The firm is respected for its work in the spheres of commercial contracts, banking, finance, insurance and transport law. Chairman of the National Bar Association **Jean-Bosco Kazungu** takes high ranking among local lawyers. **Clients:** Banks; insurance companies; public sector; local oil companies.

Etude Mhayimana Isaïe (1 ptr, 3 asscs) A strong firm which *"gets a lot of local work,"* and has niche expertise in the drafting of commercial contracts, notably in the transport sector. *"One of the most important lawyers in Rwanda"* is **Isaïe Mhayimana**. **Clients:** Transport agencies; industrial enterprises.

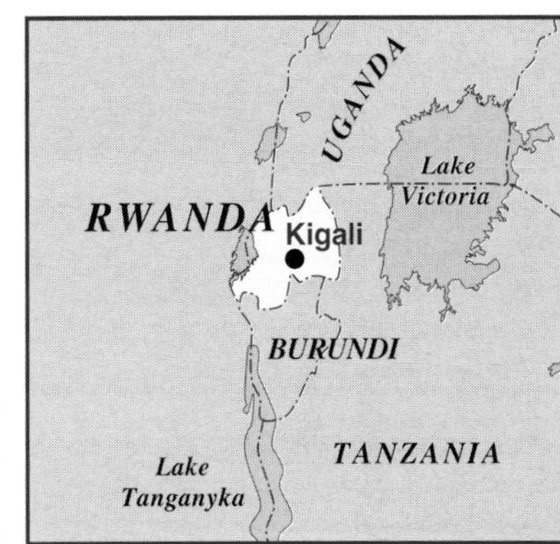

Leaders' profiles – Rwanda

BATWARE, Jean-Claude
Cabinet Batware et Nkurunziza, Kigali
+250 73432

KAZUNGU, Jean-Bosco
Cabinet Kazungu, Kigali
+250 0830 0827

MHAYIMANA, Isaïe
Etude Mhayimana Isaïe, Kigali
+250 72564/+250 0830 0698

S

SAUDI ARABIA

Banking & Finance

SAUDI ARABIA Leading firms (Banking & Finance)
1 Legal Advisors (Baker & McKenzie in association with Torki A Al Shubaiki)
2 Law Office of Hassan Mahassni (In association with White & Case LLP)
3 The International Law Firm The Law Firm of Salah Al-Hejailan

Firms are listed alphabetically in each band.

SAUDI ARABIA Leading individuals (Banking & Finance)
★ **XEFOS John** *Legal Advisors (Baker & McKenzie in association with Torki A Al Shubaiki)*
1 **HANDLEY Vernon** *The Law Firm of Salah Al Hejailan* **SIDDELL Ian** *Legal Advisors (Baker & McKenzie in association with Torki A Al Shubaiki)*
2 **CASSIN Vernon** *The International Law Firm*
Individuals are listed alphabetically in each band.

Legal Advisors (Baker & McKenzie in association with Torki A Al Shubaiki) (4 ptrs, 7 asscs) Holding a seemingly unassailable position in the banking and finance sector, this firm's enviable links with HSBC affiliate, Saudi American Bank are famed among its peers and clients. A regular presence in the projects arena, usually representing the lenders, investment banking forms 80% of the firm's portfolio. Long-standing connections render **John Xefos*** *"an integral part of the firm."* A valued lawyer, he "*projects an air of calm and self control – what you see is what you get*," while his unique view of *"the bigger picture"* is valued. *"Thorough with his advice,"* senior English lawyer **Ian Siddell*** produces "*super work*" including deals with SABIC entities involving UK law.

Advisors to the lenders on the restructuring of the US$850m term loan to Arabian Industrial Fibres Company (Ibn Rushd), the team also acted on the provision of a further $200 million revolving subordinated debt facility. It also advised the lenders on the $500 million term loan for Saudi Consolidated Electric Company in the Eastern Province (SCECO-East) for the construction of a 2400MW power plant at Ghazlan and its subsequent restructuring. **Clients:** HSBC; Saudi Arabian Monetary Agency; CSFB; Riyad Bank; Shell Oil Company; Saudi British Bank; Saudi American Bank; National Commercial Bank.

Law Office of Hassan Mahassni (in association with White & Case LLP) (Riyadh 1 ptr, 4 assc; Jeddah 1 ptr, 9 assc) Consolidating its profile won during the Saudi Chevron deal, the Jeddah office handles Islamic finance and new products development, while the majority of project finance and general banking work in Riyadh. The team advised one of the largest banks in Saudi Arabia in connection with all aspects of its online services

Active in the big ticket deals, the team represented US Exim in the $2.5 billion financing of 46 aircraft for Saudi Arabian Airlines and acted for Jadwel on the securitisation of rentals due from the Ministry of Defence. In projects, the firm acted for national oil company, Saudi Aramco, on a recent gas initiative and advised one of five bidding consortia in relation to the Captive Power Project contract. **Clients:** Saudi American Bank; The National Commercial Bank; Bank Al-Jazira; Riyad Bank; Saudi British Bank; Al Bank Al Saudi Al Fransi; Dallah Al Baraka.

The International Law Firm Researchers received warm recommendation for this firm's banking and projects related work, although it is clear that since representing the AES on the early stages of the Saudi Chevron petrochemical projects deal, the firm has had a low profile. A frequent traveller, *"pleasant, relaxed"* **Vernon Cassin*** is a *"careful lawyer who knows everything you need to know to do business in Saudi Arabia and will come out with the right answer."* Acted for Saks Fifth Avenue on its franchise arrangements with Kingdom Holding. **Clients:** Saudi American Bank; Chase Manhattan Bank; The National Commercial Bank; AES.

The Law Firm of Salah Al-Hejailan (Riyadh 20 lawyers; Jeddah 5 lawyers; Eastern Province 1 lawyer) Researchers were impressed by the market response on this *"recognised player"* in the local market. A large client portfolio within the SABIC enterprises network complements its role as the honorary legal counsel of the British Embassy in Saudi Arabia. Former associations with Clifford Chance and Graham and James promoted the firm, which undertakes a high volume of financings for both borrowers and lenders. Sought out for advice on UK aspects, the *"accurate and thorough"* **Vernon Handley*** possesses the qualities that *"paranoid bankers like to find in a lawyer."* He *"picks things up and turns work around quickly."*

The firm acted for Ibn Rushd (Arabian Industrial Fibres Company) and SABIC in the $1 billion restructuring of existing indebtedness, one of the most significant transactions of its kind. It acted for the borrowers in the $105 million revolving loan facility for Al-Jubail Fertilizer Company and a $600 million term loan facility for Arabian Petrochemical Company. **Clients:** Saudi Basic Industries Corporation (SABIC) and its affiliates; Saudi American Bank; Arab National Bank; Saudi British Bank; Riyad Bank; Kingdom Holding (the in-Kingdom investment vehicle of the Saudi billionaire Prince Alwaleed Bin Talal Bin Abdulaziz Al Saud); SmithKline Beecham; ExxonMobil; British Aerospace; Hyundai; Sumitomo.

*See leaders' profiles on pages 581-582

Corporate/M&A

SAUDI ARABIA
Leading firms
(Corporate/Mergers & Acquisitions)

Band	Firm
1	Legal Advisors (Baker & McKenzie in association with Torki A Al Shubaiki)
2	Law Office of Hassan Mahassni (in association with White & Case LLP)
3	The International Law Firm
	Law Office of Dr Mujahid M Al-Sawwaf

Firms are listed alphabetically in each band.

Leading individuals
(Corporate/Mergers & Acquisitions)

Band	Individual
1	**CASSIN Vernon** *The International Law Firm*
	SAYEN George *Legal Advisors (Baker & McKenzie in association with Torki A Al Shubaiki)*

Individuals are listed alphabetically in each band.

Legal Advisors (Baker & McKenzie in association with Torki A Al Shubaiki) (4 ptrs, 7 asscs) *"Ahead of the others"* in its ability to *"marry Western requirements with Shari'a possibilities,"* researchers received commendation for the practice's local and international advisory work. *"Creative but always realistic in his assumption,"* **George Sayen*** is the lawyer that many clients *"count on."*

The team advised a leading regional telecoms company on the establishment of the first internet service provider in the Kingdom with foreign equity participation, and advised a major Saudi group on a joint venture with power transmission and generation companies. **Clients:** The Olayan Group; National Grid; Al Zamil Group; National Industrialisation Company; CISCO; Ministry of PTT; The Al-Shoaibi Group, CMS Energy; General Dynamics.

Law Office of Hassan Mahassni (in association with White & Case LLP) (Riyadh: 1 ptr, 4 asscs; Jeddah: 1 ptr, 9 asscs) Researchers were left in no doubt that the firm *"does a credible job,"* benefiting from a strong relationship with the Ministry of Commerce. It advises on all aspects of foreign direct investment into Saudi Arabia. Coverage includes joint ventures, establishment of agency, distributorship and franchise arrangements and disputes. The team acted for a prospective strategic investor on the corporatisation and securitisation of the Saudi Telecommunications Company. **Clients:** Saudi Aramco; Saudi American Bank; The National Commercial Bank.

The International Law Firm (1 ptr, 8 asscs) Peers considered this practice to be a regular presence on commercial deals, although within the market, it has a low profile. Despite extended spells of absence, it is generally acknowledged that long-standing senior partner **Vernon Cassin*** *"provides continuity"* with his *"good commercial sense and contacts."* **Clients:** Microsoft; Autodesk; Business Software Alliance; Northrop Grumman; Otis Elevators; Gateway 2000.

Law Office of Dr Mujahid M Al-Sawwaf (2 ptrs, 3 asscs) Eschewing foreign affiliations, the firm has been a continuous presence in the Kingdom for over 20 years advising on local law, regulations and business customs. It has strong links with Allen & Overy and Millbank Tweed and benefits from referrals from international players such as Freshfields and Cleary Gottlieb. It acted as Saudi counsel to the borrowers on a $300 million guarantee by Exxon Bank, advised Lucent in the sale of $7 million of receivables and continues to represent key client General Electric in ongoing M&A deals. **Clients:** General Electric; Boeing; General Motors; British Aerospace; Mobil; Bristol Myers Squibb; SmithKline Beecham; Pfizer; Caterpillar; Caltex.

S

Leaders' profiles – Saudi Arabia

CASSIN, JR., Vernon
International Law Firm, Riyadh +966 1 462 8866
Recommended in Banking & Finance, Corporate/M&A

HANDLEY, Vernon
The Law Firm of Salah Al-Hejailan, Riyadh +966 1 479 2200
Recommended in Banking & Finance

SAYEN, George
Law Advisors (Baker & McKenzie in association with The Law Firm Torki A Al Shubaiki), Riyadh +966 1 462 9886
george.sayen@bakernet.com
Recommended in Corporate/M&A
Specialisation: Practice includes joint ventures, corporate, commercial agency, negotiable instruments, government contract, labour, litigation support, and banking matters. Has written several articles, including articles on arbitration in Saudi Arabia and the Commercial Agency Regulations.
Prof. Memberships: New York and American Bar Associations.
Career: Educated at Dartmouth College (AB 1980) and the University of Pennsylvania (JD 1986). Whilst studying for JD degree at the University of Pennsylvania completed a joint program in Middle East Studies and Islamic Law, as well as intensive Arabic language courses at Middlebury College (summer 1983) and the American University in Cairo (1984-85). Involved in handling Saudi legal matters since 1987 and has resided full time in Riyadh since joining *Baker and McKenzie* in 1988.
Personal: Born 30 July 1958. Interests include history and hiking. Has three daughters.

SIDDELL, Ian
Law Advisors (Baker & McKenzie in association with The Law Firm Torki A Al Shubaiki), Riyadh +966 1 462 9886
ian.siddell@bakernet.com
Recommended in Banking & Finance
Specialisation: Partner specialising in banking and finance matters, particularly project finance, aviation finance and structured commodity finance. Has acted for the syndicate banks on the recent internationally syndicated financings to Saudi Iron and Steel Company (Hadeed), Arabian Industrial Fibers Company (Ibn Rushd), Saudi Electricity Company, Saudi European Petrochemical Company (Ibn Zahr) and Saudi Petrochemical Company (SADAF) and on domestic financings to Saudi Telecom Company and Lucent Technologies International, Inc. Also acted for the Kingdom of Saudi Arabia in its recent $2.5 billion US Eximbank supported financing of sixty-one new aircraft operated by Saudi Arabian Airlines.
Personal: 1960 – Educated at the University of Kent, where graduated in law with first class honours and subsequently at Lincoln College, University of Oxford, (BCL). Qualified to practise in England. Resident in Riyadh since 1996.

XEFOS, John
Law Advisors (Baker & McKenzie in association with The Law Firm Torki A Al Shubaiki), Riyadh +966 1 462 9886
john.xefos@bakernet.com
Recommended in Banking & Finance
Specialisation: Acts for a number of the local banks and international banks focused on Saudi Arabia. Was involved in the first few SABIC financings that

introduced English law and security mechanisms to Saudi financings. Represented the developers in negotiating the first private sector petrochemical financing structured along classic project finance lines. On the team that developed the structure for the first privatisation and first international securitisation in Saudi Arabia, and presently involved in the telecoms privatisation and the development of a stock exchange.
Prof. Memberships: Illinois and American Bar Association.
Career: Following graduation from Cornell University, participated as one of the first students in a joint program in Middle East Studies and Islamic Law which provided a useful academic background for a legal career in Saudi Arabia. That academic background has since been tempered by the realities of a day-to-day legal practice involving Saudi matters at *Baker & McKenzie*'s Middle East Group since 1980. First came to Riyadh, where resides on a full time basis, in 1993. A member of *Baker & McKenzie*'s international Banking and Finance Practice Group and chairs the firm's Policy Committee, and also serves on the European Regional Council.
Personal: Chairs the Board of Trustees at the American International School, Riyadh. Interests include fishing and Italian food. Three daughters have been born and raised in Riyadh.

SENEGAL

Corporate/Commercial

SENEGAL Leading firms (Corporate/Commercial)
1 François Sarr & Associates
2 Etude Guedel Ndiaye & Associés
Mame Adama Gueye & Associés

Firms are listed alphabetically in each band.

Leading individuals (Corporate/Commercial)
1 **SARR François** *François Sarr & Associates*
2 **GUEYE Mame Adama** *Mame Adama Gueye*
NDIAYE Guedel *Etude Guedel Ndiaye*

Individuals are listed alphabetically in each band.

François Sarr & Associates (5 ptrs, 5 asscs) *"The largest and most important firm in the country"* is *"everyone's major competitor."* The focus is on commercial law and the firm is active in project finance, privatisation and contracts advice. It is clear from our research that *"first-class"* **François Sarr** is universally regarded as an *"excellent lawyer."* The firm represented Industries Chimiques du Sénégal in a major finance project funded by the European Investment Bank, West African Bank, AFD and BOAD. **Clients:** TOTAL Sénégal; Coca-Cola; Unilever; Lufthansa; USAID.

Etude Guedel Ndiaye & Associés (4 ptrs, 4 asscs) A *"strong corporate practice"* dealing with general corporate and commercial matters, including the establishment of foreign companies in Senegal and the drafting of commercial contracts. The market concludes that **Guedel Ndiaye** is the stand-out practitioner here. **Clients:** Mobil Oil; Crédit Lyonnais Sénégal; Shell Sénégal.

Mame Adama Gueye & Associés (4 ptrs, 1 assc) Active in banking, business, commercial, competition, contract, IP and tax law, this firm was identified in our research as a *"leading operation"*. It

has particular expertise in aviation law and acts for a number of major airlines, as well as other blue-chip international concerns. The experienced **Mame Adama Gueye** has a leading reputation. **Clients:** Air Afrique; Air Algérie; Tunis Air; AXA Insurance; Sentel GSM; NCM Credit Management Worldwide.

Leaders' profiles – Senegal

GUEYE, Mame Adama
Mame Adama Gueye & Associés, Dakar
+221 849 28 00
bg@sentoo.sn
Specialisation: Main area of work is business law (commercial, competition, banking, bankruptcy contract, intellectual property, labour law). Study on the legal environment for business in Senegal. Legal assistance for the creation of 'Technopole de Dakar'. Legal opinion at the request of Citibank International for Pre-Export Trade Financing facility for SONACOS. Legal organisational and financial study in relation to the 'Canal du Cayor' project in partnership with American consultancy firm Booz Allen & Hamilton. Legal opinion at the request of a Norwegian bank for a financing agreement with the port authority of Dakar. Legal opinion at the request of the Deutshe Investitions und Entwick Lungsgesellchaft – NBH for a financing agreement with ICS (Senegalese Chimical Industries). Legal opinion on an aircraft lease contract between BOMBARDIER Inc. and Air Senegal. Mission of modernisation of the clerk's office of the Regional Court of Dakar. National consultant for the UNDP within the framework of the study on public service ethics in Africa. Mission of setting national texts in conformity with the uniform act on arbitration law.
Prof. Memberships: Vice president of the National Association of Consultants of Senegal. Vice president of the Senegalese Business Law Association. Former member of the Bar Council (1988-1994). Referee of the centre of mediation, conciliation and arbitration of the agriculture and industry Chamber of Commerce of Dakar. Member of the international network of law firms of businesses 'LEXAFRICA'.
Career: Registered in the Senegalese Bar since 1982. Associated Manager of the law firm *Mame Adama Gueye & Associes.*
Personal: Born 20 May 1953, Dakar. Master of Business Law (University of Rennes 1979). DESS of Judiciary Law (University of Rennes 1980). DESS of business law and tax law (University of Rennes 1980). Diploma of specialised legal expert for companies. Leisure interests include sport, culture and music.

NDIAYE, Guedel
Etude Guedel Ndiaye & Associés, Dakar
+2218215858/+221 822 1075

SARR, François
François Sarr & Associates, Dakar
+221 822 2722/+221 821 4528

SEYCHELLES

Corporate/Commercial

SEYCHELLES Leading firms (Corporate/Commercial)
1 Kieran B Shah
Pardiwalla Twomey Lablache

Firms are listed alphabetically in each band.

SEYCHELLES Leading individuals (Corporate/Commercial)
1 **BOULLÉ Philippe** *Sole Practitioner*
PARDIWALLA Pesi *Pardiwalla Twomey Lablache*
SHAH Kieran *Kieran B Shah*

Individuals are listed alphabetically in each band.

Kieran B Shah (3 ptrs) *"A strong practice"* providing *"high quality work for foreign corporate clients."* It has a good name for banking and is heavily involved in insurance and aviation work. **Kieran B Shah** is *"from the old school but keeps up with modern times"* and the market agrees that he has an excellent reputation. **Clients:** Seychelles International Corp; State Assurance Corp; Seychelles Breweries; Barclays Bank.

Pardiwalla Twomey Lablache (3 ptrs, 1 assc) *"A general practice very much involved in commercial matters."* Acts as local legal counsel to overseas corporations drafting commercial contracts and working on aircraft lease transactions, with a particularly good name for insurance. This *"serious firm of lawyers on the way up"* is headed by former Attorney General **Pesi Pardiwalla** who is described as being *"professional, balanced and stable."* **Clients:** Cable & Wireless; Heinz; Citibank Hong Kong.

Other Notable Practitioner *"One of the leading senior lawyers in the Seychelles"* **Philippe Boullé** is known for his offshore work handling incorporations, foreign investment and the management of offshore companies. *"Always well researched and good in court,"* he acts on corporate and commercial matters, and admiralty related cases.

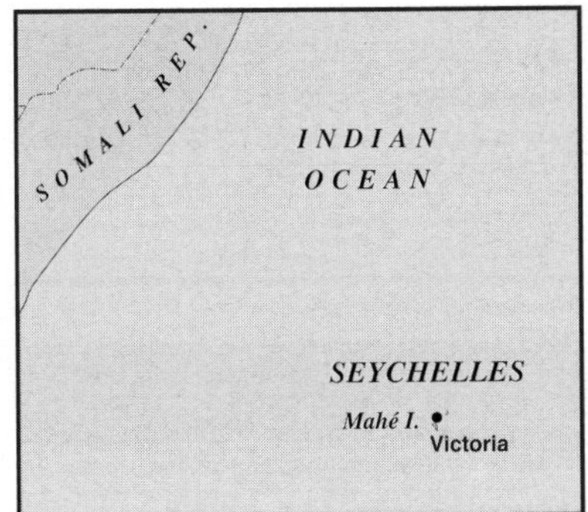

Leaders' profiles – Seychelles

BOULLÉ, Philippe
Philippe Boullé – Sole Practitioner, Victoria +248 225 633

PARDIWALLA, Pesi
Pardiwalla Twomey Lablache, Victoria +248 321 071

SHAH, Kieran
Kieran B. Shah, Victoria +248 322 608

SIERRA LEONE

Corporate/Commercial

SIERRA LEONE Leading firms (Corporate/Commercial)
1 Basma & Macaulay
Renner-Thomas & Co
Wright & Co

Firms are listed alphabetically in each band.

Leading individuals (Corporate/Commercial)
1 **MACAULAY Berthan** *Basma & Macaulay*
RENNER-THOMAS Ade *Renner-Thomas & Co*
WRIGHT Roland *Wright & Co*

Individuals are listed alphabetically in each band.

Basma & Macaulay (1 ptr, 2 asscs) *"Worthy competitors"* with an enviable client base, notably in the oil and gas sector. The firm handles corporate and commercial work on behalf of banks, insurance and shipping companies. **Berthan Macaulay** is a *"renowned practitioner of the highest standard."* **Clients:** Mobil Oil; UNDP; NGOs.

Renner-Thomas & Co (2 ptrs, 2 asscs) *"One of the leading firms in Sierra Leone"* is particularly adept at commercial and admiralty law. **Dr. Ade Renner-Thomas** is, our researchers were informed, *"an interesting person to work with or against."* **Clients:** Sierra Leone Commercial Bank; Barclays; National Development Bank; Standard Chartered Bank.

Wright & Co (2 ptrs, 6 asscs) One of the largest local firms, it is retained as counsel by the British High Commission, and carries out some international trademark work. **Roland Wright** is a highly recommended local figure. **Clients:** Foreign companies with interests in Sierra Leone.

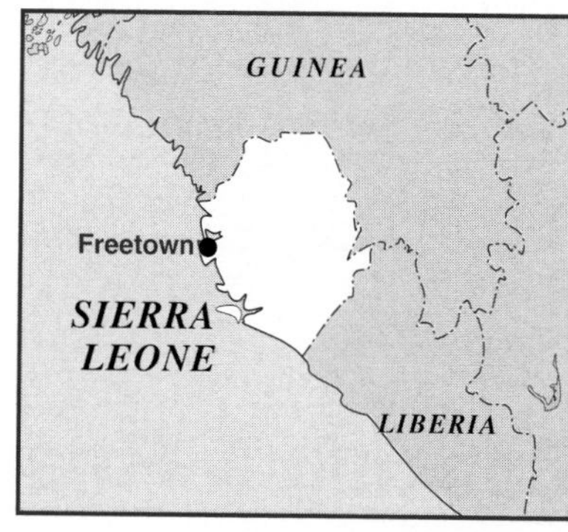

Leaders' profiles – Sierra Leone

MACAULAY, Berthan
Basma & Macaulay, Freetown +232 22 222798

RENNER-THOMAS, Ade
Renner-Thomas & Co, Freetown +232 22 225143

WRIGHT, Roland S V
Wright & Co, Freetown +232 22 227376

SINGAPORE

Index

S

OVERVIEW: In a landmark decision, licences have been granted to a select band of UK and US firms permitting the formation of joint ventures with local practices. This liberalisation of the market is widely expected to create a top tier of firms in the country, able to dominate the international banking, corporate finance and litigation sectors. Firms outside this circle face an uncertain future. The market is experiencing increased corporate activity and a boom in the technology market as Singapore consolidates its position as a major financial centre.

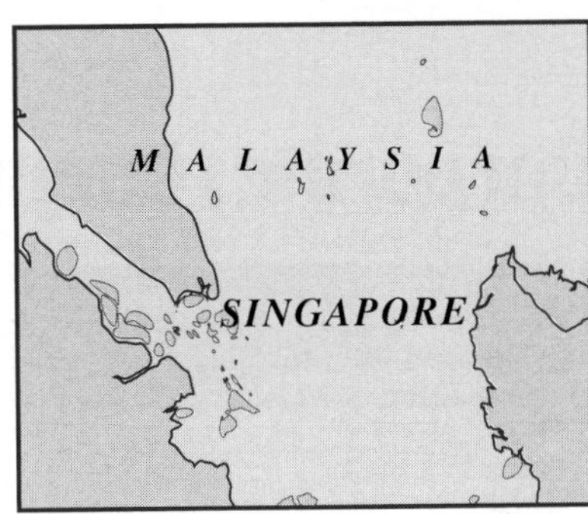

Banking & Finance: Local Firms

SINGAPORE
Leading firms (Banking & Finance)

Band	Firm
1	Allen & Gledhill
2	Lee & Lee
	Wong Partnership
3	Drew & Napier
	Shook Lin & Bok
4	Arfat Selvam & Gunasingham
	Colin Ng & Partners
	Helen Yeo & Partners
	Khattar Wong & Partners
5	Rajah & Tann

Firms are listed alphabetically in each band.

Leading individuals (Banking & Finance)

Band	Individual
1	**ANG Andrew** *Lee & Lee*
	WONG Lucien *Allen & Gledhill*
2	**LEE Suet Fern** *Stamford LLC*
	OOI Eugene *Allen & Gledhill*
	SELVAM Arfat *Arfat Selvam & Gunasingham*
	WONG Sunny *Wong Tan & Molly Lim*
	YOUNG Chee Foong *Colin Ng & Partners*
3	**ANG David** *Drew & Napier*
	CHIA Cerintha *Khattar Wong & Partners*
	HUDSPETH Mark *Allen & Gledhill*
	ONG Christina *Allen & Gledhill*
	TEO Kiang Kok *Shook Lin & Bok*

Individuals are listed alphabetically in each band.

Allen & Gledhill (6 ptrs, 7 asscs) *"A strong team which enjoys an excellent reputation"* claim clients and competitors alike. This knowledgeable team is transactionally proficient and considered to be one of the strongest local capital markets practices in Singapore. The formidable **Lucien Wong*** is *"a strong all-rounder"* seen to specialise in new banking products such as securitisation whilst **Eugene Ooi*** has a good reputation for off-shore banking work. **Christina Ong*** is recommended and **Mark Hudspeth*** focuses on syndicated loans and restructuring work.

The team advised a large shipping group based in Thailand and Singapore and its adviser, Citibank, in relation to the restructuring of the group's $284 million debts. Advised The Royal Bank of Scotland in connection with the restructuring of debts of various Indonesian property and hotel companies totalling $200 million and advised ABN Amro on a S$825 million facility for the design, procurement, installation, commissioning and operation by a Singapore telecoms company of a fixed line and cellular mobile telecommunications network in Singapore. **Clients:** DBS; OCBC; UOB; ABN Amro; Bank of America; Chase Manhattan Bank; Citibank; HSBC; Credit Lyonnais; Rabobank; Société Générale.

Lee & Lee (10 ptrs, 18 asscs) Interviewees described this quality practice as *"top-tier but conservative."* The well established **Andrew Ang*** is recommended by both clients and fellow lawyers as *"a senior practitioner,"* leading the capital finance area. The firm has advised on loans valued at up to HK$908 million, a transferable revolving credit facility valued at HK$250 million, a multi-currency RCF worth S$110 million and a multi-currency term loan facility valued at S$150 million. **Clients:** DBS; HSBC; Singapore NOL.

Wong Partnership (4 ptrs, 19 asscs) Building on a base of high profile corporate work and good political connections, the firm has developed a banking practice packed with bright lawyers. The loss of the high-profile Suet Fern Lee has been judged a blow, yet the firm maintains its major client base. Advised Jardine Fleming Securities on the placement of up to 64.5 million ordinary shares in Keppel Marine Industries.

The practice has a strong reputation for flotation work and advised in the IPO of 148 million ordinary shares in SPH AsiaOne and in the IPO of 110 million ordinary shares in SIA Engineering Company and Singapore Airport Terminal Services. **Clients:** DBS; UOB; OCBC; ING Barings; Merrill Lynch; Morgan Stanley.

Drew & Napier (7 ptrs, 16 asscs) A long established firm in the banking field yet felt by interviewees to lack a rainmaking figure. **David Ang*** has a high profile among fellow lawyers for the *"solid work"* he undertakes for local banks. The team has been involved in ten IPOs in the past year including the WizOffice.com float. Banking work has included acting for CIBC in connection with a $91.8 million replacement credit facility; acting for The Great Eastern Life Assurance Co on an S$80 million five year term loan, and for a substantial listed company in a $20 million secured inventory financing facility. **Clients:** Citibank; Canadian Imperial Bank of Commerce; StanChart; OCBC; DBS; Telecom Authority of Singapore; Ernst & Young.

Shook Lin & Bok (3 ptrs, 7 asscs) Seen by fellow lawyers as having strength in capital markets, it derives banking and restructuring work from its successful litigation practice, where the emphasis lies with quality rather than range. **Kiang Kok Teo*** has a good profile for corporate finance and capital markets work. The firm acted as Singaporean counsel to the agent and the lenders in the $205 million secured facilities for an international computer accessory manufacturer. Also acted for the lenders in syndicated loan facilities of $200 million to two Singaporean petrochemical companies and advised the lenders in the conversion of a $185 million construction loan facility to a revolving credit loan facility. **Clients:** Major banks including OCBC and DBS.

Arfat Selvam & Gunasingham (4 ptrs, 6 asscs) A niche practice with **Arfat Selvam*** admired for her expertise in corporate finance and capital markets. Acted in the restructuring of Keppel TatLee Bank, and represented DBS in the proposed share capital reorganisation of the Insurance Corporation of Singapore to create a wholly owned subsidiary. A formal alliance with Herbert Smith became effective from January 2001. In the leveraged finance field the firm acted for South East Asia Venture Investment in a S$112 million LBO of a multi-jurisdictional group based in Singapore. It represented Nera Telecommunications in its IPO of 44.4 million shares by way of public offer and placement and listing on the main board of the Singapore Exchange. **Clients:** Domestic financial institutions; Keppel TatLee Bank.

Colin Ng & Partners (6 ptrs, 10 asscs) Seen by the market as on the up with bright new recruits and a joint venture in place with strong capital markets firm White & Case. The firm has a good balance between representing the banks and major corporates. **Chee Foong Young*** who has moved over from Engelin Teh & Partners is thought to have a good off-shore practice. Both local and regional areas are covered with a range of financing matters.

The team acts for banking and finance institutions on regulatory compliance matters, enforcement and recovery matters. It has acted for parties to multi-currency loan transactions, syndicated loans and bio-credit facilities. The firm scores highly with its involvement in the restructuring of Thai and Indonesian borrowers in the production, manufacturing and commodities industries. Advised on the IPOs of Jurong Technologies Industrial Corporation, Thai Village Holdings, and Giant Wireless Technology. **Clients:** International banks and corporates.

Helen Yeo & Partners (6 ptrs, 6 asscs) Interviewees told our researchers that the firm has aggressively built a solid banking practice. It is considered to have benefited from the joint venture with Orrick Herrington & Sutcliffe cemented in October 2000. The team acted as Singaporean counsel for a US multi-national in a $100 million synthetic lease of a manufacturing facility. Also acted for a listed company in a reverse take-over involving an injection of assets aggregating over S$200 million and acted for a Singaporean issuer in a $500 million MTN programme. **Clients:** DuPont; CapitaLand; United Overseas Bank Group; Credit Suisse; PWD Corporation.

Khattar Wong & Partners (11 ptrs, 27 asscs) A highly reputed practice with an emphasis on the property market and real estate financing. Described by our interviewees as *"clever and experienced,"* **Cerintha Chia*** is active in property-based banking. The team acted for UOB, CKB in their merger and acted for banks as arrangers in transactions, including a S$550 million financing for a condominium development project in Singapore and a S$100 million syndicated loan facility to the Singapore subsidiary of a British multinational. **Clients:** DBS; UOB; OCBC; OUB; HSBS; RHB Bank; Keppel-TatLee Bank; Citibank; ABN Amro Bank; Stanchart; NTUC Income; major property developers.

Rajah & Tann (2 ptrs, 4 asscs) A practice thought to be working hard to establish itself after a late arrival on the scene. An alliance with Arthur Andersen has brought it international recognition. The team also benefits from a strategic alliance with respected US firm Weil Gotshal & Manges. Involved in the hi-tech market, the firm acted for MediaRing.com on its listing in Singapore and a global offering of 150 million new shares and acted for the SilkRoute Group of Companies in its arrangement as a domestic e-business. Also acted for a major power generating company in its S$525 million facility and medium term note programme. **Clients:** Standard Chartered; American Express; Bank of China; BNP; ABN AMRO.

Other Notable Practitioners Suet Fern Lee* of Stamford LLC is recommended as a major player in the market since her departure from the Wong Partnership. **Sunny Wong*** of Wong Tan & Molly Lim has *"good exposure"* to the markets and is *"a highly respected operator."*

Banking & Finance: Foreign Firms

Allen & Overy, Shook Lin & Bok (3 ptrs, 7 asscs) Outstanding in its reputation for quality, the production of excellent documentation and involvement in the biggest deals. Its bright partners are thought to be a pleasure to deal with and the team is a major competitor in the capital markets sphere. **Fiona Fitzgerald*** and **Chris Rushton*** both received recommendations with the latter described as *"a very able projects lawyer."* The firm acted for ABN Amro and Citicorp International as joint arrangers of the Y22 billion credit facility for the National Power Corporation in the Philippines, and acted for Hypovereinsbank on the $46.3 million credit facility for Golden Agri International (Mauritius) and on a $55 million term loan facility for the Cayman Islands subsidiary of a Singapore listed company. The team also advised the lenders to Mulia Industrindo and its subsidiaries regarding the restructuring of $500 million of bank and bond debt. **Clients:** CSFB; ABN Amro; Citibank; Bank of America; Nomura International; Chase Manhattan Bank.

Clifford Chance (3 ptrs, 7 asscs) An impressive practice admired for its structured finance work. Has increased its involvement in SEC regulated work after its link up with US firm Rogers & Wells. *"Star player"* **Sam Bonifant*** is a seasoned practitioner, *"well-liked"* and *"well-respected"* by lawyers and clients alike. Acted for Deutsche Bank, Singapore Branch in relation to the revamping of its $3 billion certificates of deposit issuance programme. The team acted for Citicorp Investment Bank (Singapore) on the issuance of the Skandinaviska Enskilda Banken S$100 million fixed and floating rate notes (due 2010) and advised The Development Bank of Singapore on the Lehman Brothers Holdings S$1000 million fixed rate notes (due 2006). **Clients:** Dresdner Bank; Deutsche Bank; IFC; ADB; EIB; The DKB; Gulf Resources.

*See leaders' profiles on pages 597-606

S

SINGAPORE: Foreign Firms Leading firms (Banking & Finance)
1 Allen & Overy, Shook Lin & Bok
Clifford Chance
2 Freshfields Drew & Napier
White & Case, Colin Ng & Partners
3 Linklaters Allen & Gledhill
Milbank, Tweed, Hadley & McCloy
Norton Rose
Slaughter and May
4 Herbert Smith
Latham & Watkins
Orrick Helen Yeo
Shearman & Sterling
5 Baker & McKenzie. Wong & Leow Pte Ltd
Denton Wilde Sapte
Sidley & Austin

Firms are listed alphabetically in each band.

Leading individuals (Banking & Finance)
1 **BONIFANT Sam** *Clifford Chance*
2 **COOPER Bruce** *Freshfields Drew & Napier*
GILES Paul *Norton Rose*
HARVEY-SAMUEL Ian *Freshfields Drew & Napier*
MEHIGAN Bertie *White & Case, Colin Ng & Partners*
ROBERTS Swain *Linklaters Allen & Gledhill*
RUSHTON Chris *Allen & Overy, Shook Lin & Bok*
3 **BRISCOE Simon** *Norton Rose*
DUFFIELD Alistair *White & Case, Colin Ng & Partners*
FITZGERALD Fiona *Allen & Overy, Shook Lin & Bok*
GALBRAITH Steven *Slaughter and May*
GALLEDARI Arman *Norton Rose*
4 **DYER Roger** *Freshfields Drew & Napier*
JOHNSTON Graeme *Baker & McKenzie. Wong & Leow*
ROBERTS Andrew *Linklaters Allen & Gledhill*

Individuals are listed alphabetically in each band.

Freshfields Drew & Napier (2 ptrs, 5 asscs) A solid broad-based practice with a high level of credibility and technically strong lawyers. **Bruce Cooper*** has a very good reputation and is liked by his peers for being *"a solid lawyer as well as a nice guy."* **Roger Dyer*** receives market recognition and **Ian Harvey-Samuel*** is *"smart on capital markets work,"* with a particular presence in Malaysia.

The team advised the international lenders arranged by Dresdner on a $350 million financing for Petronas and acted for Bank Boston as arranger on a $50 million loan to the SK Group of Korea. In the restructuring market the firm advised the Astra Group on the reorganisation of substantial foreign denominated debts. Admired for its capital markets work, the team advised Temask Holdings on an international equity offering for SMRT Corporation listed on the SXC, and advised Merrill Lynch and Warburg Dillon Read on a proposed international equity offering for an Indian Technology related group. The firm has formed a joint venture with local firm Drew & Napier. **Clients:** Asia Pulp and Paper; Renong Group; Astra; IFC; Dresdner; Bank of Tokyo-Mitsubishi.

White & Case, Colin Ng & Partners (6 ptrs, 15 asscs) Debt restructuring and a strong capital markets profile form the emphasis for this quality practice. Researchers were told that the arrival of *"smooth operator"* **Bertie Mehigan*** strengthens the team. He is thought to be *"extremely good with clients."* **Alistair Duffield*** is rated for his projects and debt work.

The practice is commended for its work in Indonesia including advising the lenders on the $1.6 billion restructuring claims against Kiani Kertas and related members of the Kalimanis Group. In Thailand the team advised on the $1.2 billion restructuring of Thai Oil and the $400 million restructuring of Jasmine International. Involved in the venture capital financing of dot.com companies and active in asset-based financings including aircraft and drilling rigs. In January 2001 the firm entered a joint venture with Colin Ng & Partners. **Clients:** Sumitomo Bank; Chase Manhattan Bank; Royal Bank of Scotland; Sanwa Bank; Citibank; Sakura Bank; Deutsche Bank; Credit Industriel et Commercial Bank of Tokyo Mitsubishi; CSFB; HSBC.

Linklaters Allen & Gledhill (1 ptr, 4 asscs) A leader in the capital markets arena, the firm is highly rated for its financings in India and Pakistan. Senior partner **Andrew Roberts*** is perceived by fellow lawyers to be an *"accomplished corporate finance lawyer,"* while **Swain Roberts*** was highly regarded for his international securities work in Indonesia.

The team scored well in its relationships with major financial institutions. Acted for JP Morgan on the S$1.5 billion establishment of the debt issuance programme by Singapore Power and advised the lead managers on the subsequent international US dollar securities issue by the latter. It also acted for Morgan Stanley & Co International and JP Morgan Securities Asia in the establishment of a debt issuance programme worth $2 billion. The formation of Linklaters Allen & Gledhill is expected to prove successful in the capital markets arena. **Clients:** Major American, European and Japanese banks.

Milbank, Tweed, Hadley & McCloy (1 ptr, 4 asscs) The practice is involved in high quality finance deals around the region. Recommended for its aggressive approach and the ability to drive a deal, the firm is particularly active on the restructuring side. It is heavily involved in capital market work for hi-tech companies. The team advised Pacific Internet, the first Singaporean company to go public, on two public offerings, and has completed eight IPOs over the last year including two dual Nasdaq, SXC listings for software, internet and pharmaceutical companies. **Clients:** Deutsche Bank; Bank of Tokyo-Mitsubishi; Fuji Bank; Canadian Imperial Commercial Bank; Bank of America; Chase Manhattan Bank, Morgan Stanley; Merrill Lynch; Pacific Internet; ING Barings.

Norton Rose (5 ptrs, 9 asscs) Traditionally strong team with a depth of experience, noted for its work in structured products and asset finance and for its recent activity in Indonesia. Although the well-respected Carol Roberts has returned to London, peers agree that she has left a robust team behind. Managing Partner of Asia **Paul Giles*** has a *"great name"* for structured leasing and asset finance while in banking **Arman Galledari*** is well regarded. **Simon Briscoe*** is thought to *"know his trade"* excelling in the area of aircraft finance.

The firm acted for the financiers to Singapore Aircraft Leasing Enterprise on seven different facilities and on an umbrella ECA supported financing for six Airbus A320 Aircraft. Also advised IBRA on the Rupiah 34 trillion recapitalisation programme for nine private sector banks. Active in Indonesia, the firm represented the equipment suppliers on the restructuring of a KSO Telecoms project. **Clients:** Chase Manhattan Bank; US Exim; HSBC Investment Bank Asia; ANZ Investment Bank; ING Bank; Singapore Aircraft Leasing Enterprise; MAS; Cathay Pacific; Credit Lyonnais; BNP Paribas.

Slaughter and May (2 ptrs, 3 asscs) Although lower in profile, this is a high quality unit that focuses on the top end of the market. **Steven Galbraith***, described to our researchers as *"an affable character and an able lawyer,"* is the team's star player. He acted for the arrangers on the Star Cruises $600 million acquisition facility. The team represented ANZ on a joint venture with OCBC for the establishment of a pan-Asian retail bank and advised the Bahrain Government and Bahrain Refinery Company on the $800 million financing for its strategic investment programme. **Clients:** ABN Amro; Standard Chartered; Bank of Nova Scotia; Morgan Stanley; DBS; Malaysian YTL; ANZ Bank.

Herbert Smith (3 ptrs, 10 asscs) A well regarded practice thought to focus on the restructuring and energy sectors. A high quality team acted for the lead arrangers for the financings of both the Ramagundam and Samayanallur power projects in India. It also advised the Bank of Scotland on the Singaporean regulatory aspects of its hostile bid for National Westminster Bank and acted for the Bank of East Asia on the acquisition of a stake in Bank Daiwa Perdania in Indonesia. Entered into a formal alliance with respected law firm Arfat Selvam & Gunasingham in January 2001. **Clients:** ING; ABN Amro; BNP; IBRA.

Latham & Watkins (3 ptrs, 8 asscs) A major player in the restructuring industry, it was described by interviewees as aggressively developing its team. Its broad coverage includes capital markets, public offerings and investment fund transactions. In restructuring, the team acted for the debtors in Gajah Tunggal and Mulia (Indonesia) and the strategic investor in Cibinong (Indonesial). Its client base includes major international financial institutions and multi-national corporates. The firm represented Chartered Semiconductor Manufacturing in its $450 million IPO listed in Singapore and New York. **Clients:** ABN Amro; Bear Stearns; Chase Manhattan Bank; Citibank; McDermott; Merck & Co; Morgan Guaranty Trust Company of New York; Salomon Smith Barney.

Orrick Helen Yeo (6 ptrs, 20 asscs) Noted for its ability to undertake complex finance work, the practice is involved in capital markets and securities work with a focus on Indonesian transactions. Its long-standing relationship with respected local firm Helen Yeo & Partners has been cemented through a formal joint venture.

The team represented the Indonesian Bank Restructuring Agency in the settlement transactions of 200 companies with an aggregate value of $13 billion and served as counsel to the Bank of Thailand in its plan to restructure the ownership of four large Thai commercial banks placed under regulatory supervision. Capital markets work includes advice to the underwriters, Lehman Brothers and Morgan Stanley, in connection with the first global IPO of Bank Central Asia. **Clients:** American Express Bank; Bank of Tokyo-Mitsubishi; Chase Manhattan Bank; DBS; Deutsche Bank; Fuji Bank; HSBC; ING Bank; Lehman Brothers; PT Danareska; Sanwa Bank; SCB; UBS Warburg Dillon Reed.

Shearman & Sterling (1 ptr, 7 asscs) Active in big-ticket restructuring and capital markets work where it focuses on the equity side for US lead arrangers. The team recently advised on the restructuring and privatisation of Radanasin Bank and Nakornthon Bank. Acted for TelecomAsia in its $1.5 billion restructuring and for the creditors on the $2.2 billion restructuring of Thai Oil.

In capital markets work the team represented the underwriters on the $275 million ADR offering and NYSE listing by ICICI. It also advised ST Assembly Test Services in its SGX and Nasdaq listing and acted for the underwriters in the proposed 144A, Reg S recapitalisation offering by Thai Military Bank. **Clients:** Citibank; Chase; Deutsche Bank; Bank of Tokyo-Mitsubishi; Kreditanstalt fur Wiederaufbau; Merrill Lynch; TD Bank; ADB; BNP Paribas.

Baker & McKenzie. Wong & Leow Pte Ltd (5 ptrs, 7 asscs) Although the practice has suffered losses on the securities side (two partners departing to Sidley & Austin), it remains active on the local front and visible in restructuring work, particularly in Indonesia. Lawyers who had worked with him recently described **Graeme Johnston*** as a *"nice guy who knows the issues."* The team acted for the issuer in a $98.8 million property securitisation and acted for the lenders in a HK$800 million facility for the acquisition of shares in a publicly listed investment company. It advised the steering committee on the $410 million debt restructuring of Japfa Comfeed Indonesia and the $280 million debt restructuring of Buna Finance Indonesia. **Clients:** International financial institutions and multi-national corporates.

Denton Wilde Sapte (3 ptrs, 2 asscs) Highly rated for its work in structured, chartered finance. The team advised Chase Manhattan Bank on a sponsored leveraged buy-out of ASAT comprising $150 million of high-yield bonds and warrants and a $65 million syndicated secured loan facility. Active in the hi-tech market, the firm advised Pacific Century Cyberworks on a $200 million bond issue and Pacific Century Internet Ventures on its subscription for shares in MediaRing.com Technologies and its subsequent IPO. It also advised Toronto Dominion on a vendor financing facility of $65 million for the purchase of equipment by an Asian telecommunications operator. **Clients:** CIBC; Media One; WestLB; Premier Oil; Nat West; IBJ.

Sidley & Austin (5 ptrs, 5 asscs) Our researchers were told that the practice is flourishing after recruiting a securities team from Baker & McKenzie, enjoying a strong presence in Indonesia and being active in US securities work. Highly rated for its flotation advice on disclosure obligations under federal and state securities law. The securities group advised the Government of Indonesia on its public offering of shares in Bank Central Asia. The team also advises strategic investors in connection with debt restructurings and asset sales.

The firm acted on the two largest asset sales by the Government of Indonesia in the past year, the $503 million sale of a controlling stake in Astra and the $368 million sale of the former Salim Group Palm Plantations companies. In the structured finance market, the team acted in a $125 million securitisation of trade receivables of Asia Pulp & Paper and advised a Singapore-based technology company in connection with a $75 million securitisation program. **Clients:** Financial intermediaries; governments and related agencies; corporates.

S

*See leaders' profiles on pages 597-606

Corporate/M&A: Local Firms

SINGAPORE Leading firms (Corporate/Mergers & Acquisitions)
1 Allen & Gledhill
2 Wong Partnership
3 Arfat Selvam & Gunasingham
Drew & Napier
4 Chang See Hiang & Partners
Lee & Lee
Shook Lin & Bok
5 Rajah & Tann
Thio Su Mien & Partners

Firms are listed alphabetically in each band.

Leading individuals (Corporate/Commercial)
★ WONG Lucien *Allen & Gledhill*
1 CHANG See Hiang *Chang See Hiang & Partners*
LEE Suet Fern *Stamford LLC*
PILLAI Philip *Shook Lin & Bok*
SELVAM Arfat *Arfat Selvam & Gunasingham*
2 ANG Andrew *Lee & Lee*
PINSLER Leena *Drew & Napier*
THIO Su Mien *Thio Su Mien & Partners*
3 NG Wai King *Wong Partnership*
PRYKE Gary *Drew & Napier*
YEO Wee Kiong *Rajah & Tann*

Individuals are listed alphabetically in each band.

Allen & Gledhill (5 ptrs, 20 asscs) Long established with an outstanding and extensive reputation. Managing partner **Lucien Wong*** is head and shoulders above the rest due to his sheer experience and exposure. Foreign and local lawyers describe him as *"very hard working"* and admire his *"tremendous market presence."* Ably supported by a large team, the firm stands at the forefront of the market. Recent acquisition work includes acting for DBS Group Holdings in its acquisition and privatisation of the Insurance Corporation of Singapore.

The firm continues to work for major local and international banks. It advised the United Overseas Bank in its acquisition and privatisation of United Overseas Finance and acted for the Bank of America in the sale of its retail banking operations in Singapore. The market anticipates an even greater profile with the formation of a joint venture with leading foreign firm Linklaters. The team also acted for Flextronics in its acquisition of JIT Holdings and for Pidemco Land on its merger with DBS Land. **Clients:** DBS; OCBC; UOB; Chase; KPMG; PriceWaterhouse Coopers; AXA Group; Alliance Group.

Wong Partnership (7 ptrs, 25 asscs) Described to researchers as aggressive in the market-place, the firm is rising on the corporate landscape. It is considered to have a good reputation with major banking houses. The firm is thought to have suffered with the departure of Suet Fern Lee. **Wai King Ng*** continues to receive market recommendation. Major corporate clients include Singapore Airlines, for whom the firm acted in connection with its S$1 billion scheme for the buyback of its shares and concerning the merger of its local and foreign share tranches. It also advised the Port of Singapore Authority in its multi-billion dollar redevelopment of the World Trade Centre building in Singapore.

In the financial services market the firm represented The Overseas Assurance Corporation in its $4.3 billion merger with Great Eastern Holdings pursuant to a scheme of arrangement. Also advised Claremont Heights, a special purpose company established by Crown Cork and Seal Company on its $240 million offer for the entirety of its issued ordinary shares. **Clients:** Group Danon; DBS; OUB; Schroders; Morgan Stanley; Exxon; Singapore Airlines; Singapore Technologies; Hong Leong Group; BNP Prime Peregrinne; Shell.

Arfat Selvam & Gunasingham (4 ptrs, 6 asscs) A smaller practice offering specialist corporate services. Top Singapore lawyers had nothing but praise for *"outstanding"* **Arfat Selvam*,** considered to have a great deal of experience with listed companies. Supported by a knowledgeable team, peers view the firm as *"terribly good"* and holding its own against the larger firms. It acted for Keppel Telecommunications & Transportation on its acquisition of the US corporation CGS for $80 million through an exchange of shares. Advised Business Trends in its multi-jurisdictional acquisition through shares and assets by Kelly Services. In the energy market the firm advised Keppel Fels Energy and Infrastructure in its offer to acquire all the issued ordinary shares in the capital of Singapore Petroleum Company. Entered into a formal alliance with Herbert Smith in January 2001. **Clients:** Mainly local financial institutions and corporates.

Drew & Napier (9 ptrs, 35 asscs) A practice recommended to our researchers for its traditional work ethic, consistency and quality. Acting from a strong litigation base, it is perceived to be actively expanding its corporate practice. **Leena Pinsler*** is described as *"competent"* and peers appreciate **Gary Pryke*** for being *"a sensible guy who doesn't waste time trying to be clever."*

In addition to advising on local M&A transactions, the firm is involved in a number of international public company takeovers. Advised Cable & Wireless (with Allen & Overy) in connection with its proposed sale of shares in Hong Kong Telecom Exchange for accommodation of cash and shares in Singapore Telecoms. The market expects regular participation in the largest deals following the joint venture with Freshfields Bruckhaus Deringer. **Clients:** Temasek Holdings Private; Port of Singapore Authority; Thomson csf; ING Baring; Canadian Imperial Bank of Commerce; OCBC; DBS; Telecom Authority of Singapore; Ernst & Young.

Chang See Hiang & Partners (5 ptrs, 5 asscs) A boutique practice specialising in commercial and corporate finance. Peers regard the quality as excellent although it is not felt to handle a similar quantity or range of deals as the larger practices. Led by the top-ranking **See Hiang Chang,*** *"a bright and able chap"* considered a *"completely competent lawyer."* Acted for two clients in the disposal of major stakes in companies listed on the Singapore Exchange valued at S$100 million and S$400 million respectively.

The firm acts for a range of companies and financial institutions in the IPO market. Clients include i-One.net International, CSE Systems & Engineering, and Parkway Laboratory Services. **Clients:** SXC listed companies; Allgreen Properties Limited; NH Ceramics; Medi-Rad Associates; financial institutions.

Lee & Lee (10 ptrs, 18 asscs) Described to researchers as a well established firm with a conservative image. Although it has a fairly low profile in the market, its reputation is based on quality, and the ability to take on the big-ticket deals. Interviewees told us that **Andrew Ang*** is a *"smart hands-on guy"* who *"has the confidence of his clients."* A cted for ANA Hotels Singapore during an offer by Roveron to acquire all its issued shares for S$118.9 million. The firm advised Hind Hotels International on a takeover offer by DBS Realty to acquire all its ordinary shares for S$165.2 million and acted for TLB Land during a takeover offer by Ambeca to purchase all ordinary stock units for S$151.5 million. The firm has recently undertaken a joint venture with Lovells. **Clients:** Major local and international financial institutions such as OCBC; property corporations.

Shook Lin & Bok (7 ptrs, 18 asscs) With former partners joining the judiciary and occupying other headline positions, the firm enjoys a high profile despite its smaller size. Although not considered a major player on the largest deals, it is recommended for its outstanding corporate finance work. The team benefits from strong relationships with the banking houses.

Research revealed that **Philip Pillai*** has good experience in dealing with the stock exchange. With an *"excellent reputation"* he is thought to be *"right up there."* Acted for TT International in an invitation in respect of 76 million shares. The firm acted for Hong Kong Telecoms in its aborted merger with Singapore Telecom. A joint venture with Allen & Overy is expected to secure greater involvement in the largest cross border deals. **Clients:** Major banks including OCBC and DBS.

Rajah & Tann (9 ptrs, 26 asscs) One of the larger local corporate practices growing in size despite entering the market later than others. Part of the Andersen Legal network, the firm has recently formed a strategic alliance with Weil, Gotshal & Manges, a major US practice. Its numbers have further been increased by the arrival of the firm Yeo Wee Kiong & Partners. **Wee Kiong Yeo*** is *"well-liked by clients,"* owing to his banker's ability to *"see the commercial side of things."* Acted for Virgin on its $1 billion mobile telephone joint venture with SingTel. The firm is involved in M&A transactions, takeovers and reverse takeovers of listed companies including Pacific Century Regional Developments and Inchcape Marketing Services. Appointed by Goldman Sachs to act in the proposed merger between SingTel and HKTel. The firm also advised Philips in the merger of its three operating subsidiaries in Singapore into a single entity. **Clients:** Government-linked companies; SIMEX; SCIOM; GES International; Pacific Century Regional Developments; Omni Industries; Datacraft Asia.

Thio Su Mien & Partners Regarded as a decent corporate finance and capital markets practice. Much of the firm's profile is tied to leader and ex-Drew & Napier managing partner **Dr Su Mien Thio***. Highly rated by fellow lawyers, she has the *"reputation, specialisation and expertise,"* to build the practice. Thought to keep a low profile, her experience and expertise allows her to do a range of corporate and corporate finance matters. **Clients:** Major local corporations.

Other Notable Practitioner Suet Fern Lee has left Wong Partnership, establishing Stamford LLC, the first corporatised law firm under the new rules. Rivals describe her as, *"an excellent lawyer"* with *"a good legal mind."*

S

Corporate/M&A: Foreign Firms

Clifford Chance (2 ptrs, 5 asscs) A professional firm considered to be well-organised and a pleasure to work with. Simon Clinton's move to the London office is viewed as a loss. However leading lawyers anticipate that a heavy work flow will promote the well-respected partners. The team acted for Heidelberger Zement in its proposed acquisition of a joint controlling interest (with the Salim group) in Indocement Tunggal. Advised the majority shareholders of Medco Energi Corporation in its $900 million joint venture with CSFB.

A major player with a global network, the firm advised Norske Skogindustrier ASA of Norway in relation to it $2.5 billion acquisition of the paper division of Fletcher Challenge Limited of New Zealand where assets of the target company were located in Malaysia, Indonesia, Australia, New Zealand and South America. **Clients:** Heidelberger Zement; Norske Skogindustrier ASA; UOB; Asia Infrastructure Development Corporation; Fijitsu; Indonesian Medico; NRG Asia Pacific; GVK.

Freshfields Drew & Napier (3 ptrs, 5 asscs) A major international player with a strong team and an admired client base in both Singapore and Malaysia. It has suffered through the loss of Andrew Bonser, but **Elaine Williams*** (made partner in May 2000) has already stamped her mark as *"a fine intelligent lawyer."* The team acted for ABN Amro on its acquisition of a controlling interest in Great Pacific Savings Bank in the Philippines.

Seen to benefit from a major client base the team advised on Asian aspects of the world-wide acquisition by GE Plastics of the plastics business of MA Hanna, and advised Dana Corporation on the Asian aspects of the world-wide disposal of Warner Electric. The firm has entered into a joint venture with highly rated local firm Drew & Napier. **Clients:** Asian Infrastructure Development; Enso Oyj (Finland); Osprey Maritime; Exxon; Charterhouse; ABN.

Linklaters Allen & Gledhill (2 ptrs, 4 asscs) An active and occasionally aggressive team, recommended for its likeable partners and its involvement in the largest transactions. **Swain Roberts**,* who has been in Singapore for nine years, *"knows what he is doing"* and is admired for being *"easy to communicate with, direct and businesslike."* The joint venture with outstanding local firm Allen & Gledhill is perceived to be a very positive move.

The team represented SingTel in its $350 million acquisition of up to 20% of the Thai mobile telecoms company, AIS, and represented PwC in the merger of accountancy practices in six Asian transactions. A global player, the team represented Exide Corporation (US) in the Singaporean and Indian aspects of its global acquisition of Pacific Dunlop's battery division. The practice is also representing BG in its world-wide corporate restructuring in advance of the Transco/BG International demerger. **Clients:** British Gas; Singapore Telecom; National Power; Merrill Lynch, Pricewaterhouse Coopers; HSBC Private Equity; Enron.

Allen & Overy, Shook Lin & Bok (1 ptr, 2 asscs) Although not as visible as our leaders, this is a strong firm with a steady deal flow which is aggressively building its practice.

Heading the team is the *"extremely competent"* **Keith McGuire*** who is *"well into all the issues."* Lawyers who have seen him in action told our researchers he was *"robust in protecting his clients' interests."*

Heavily involved in the power market, the team advised British Gas on a preference share investment in Korea Gas Corporation. It also acted for British Gas and Daesung consortium as final bidders for Korea Electric Corporation and Korea District Heating Corporation's power plant and district heating assets at Anyang and Buchon Korea. The firm advised Vivendi on the acquisition of water treatment assets within the Hyundai Daesan Petrochemical Complex in Korea. In the communications sphere, the firm acted for Cable & Wireless on its negotiations with SingTel on the sale of its HKT stake and advised TPG on its proposed international mail joint venture with Royal Mail and Singapore Post. **Clients:** British Gas;

*See leaders' profiles on pages 597-606

SINGAPORE: Foreign Firms
Leading firms (Corporate/Mergers & Acquisitions)

Band	Firm
1	Clifford Chance
	Freshfields Drew & Napier
	Linklaters Allen & Gledhill
2	Allen & Overy, Shook Lin & Bok
	Norton Rose
	Shearman & Sterling
	White & Case, Colin Ng & Partners
3	Herbert Smith
	Latham & Watkins
	Milbank, Tweed, Hadley & McCloy
	Simpson Thacher & Bartlett
	Slaughter and May
4	Ashurst Morris Crisp
	Baker & McKenzie. Wong & Leow Pte Ltd
	Orrick Helen Yeo

Firms are listed alphabetically in each band.

Leading individuals (Corporate/Mergers & Acquisitions)

Band	Individual
1	**JAMIESON William** *Norton Rose*
	ROBERTS Swain *Linklaters Allen & Gledhill*
2	**McGUIRE Keith** *Allen & Overy, Shook Lin & Bok*
	MOORE Chris *Norton Rose*
3	**GALBRAITH Steven** *Slaughter and May*
	WILLIAMS Elaine *Freshfields Drew & Napier*
4	**NEWBERY Mark** *Herbert Smith*

Individuals are listed alphabetically in each band.

Vivendi Water; Government of Singapore Investment Corporation; Cable & Wireless; American Electric Power.

Norton Rose (2 ptrs, 4 asscs) One to watch said our interviewees. Particularly strong in Indonesia and well regarded for its aggressive and commercial approach. Packed with leading practitioners including the *"solid"* **Bill Jamieson*** who is *"an excellent practitioner,"* and **Chris Moore***, an ex-Clifford Chance man who is admired for his *"commerciality."* The team advised on HSBC's acquisition of Bangkok Metropolitan Bank and represented GSS Array on the Baht 3.55 billion takeover by ACT Manufacturing of the US. It also advised KRP, a listed Thai company on a private equity investment by Prudential Asset Management Asia. **Clients:** Hong Leong; HSBC; AXA; Ericsson.

Shearman & Sterling (1 ptr, 9 asscs) Active in the M&A arena this year and building a fine reputation for work in Thailand. The emphasis here lies with quality rather than quantity. The team represented Hydro-Quebec on the acquisition of power assets in China and advised PowerGen in relation to the acquisition of a stake in the Bugok IPP developed by LG Energy. Also acted for the acquirer in the purchase of a steel production facility in Thailand and advised on the acquisitions aspect of the restructuring of a major Indonesian cement company. **Clients:** British Gas; PowerGen; InterGen; Hydro-Quebec; National Power; ABX Group.

White & Case, Colin Ng & Partners (3 ptrs, 8 asscs) A strong player, regarded by peers for the quality and size of its deals. The team was recommended to researchers for its telecommunications work in India. It advised Edison Mission Energy of California on its proposed acquisition of an equity interest in Tri Energy Company and advised Cable and Wireless in its acquisition of 25% of the shares of Daya Mitra Malindo, a KSO telecommunication company.

With a broad ranging client base the team advised a Belgian company in the execution of a co-operation agreement concerning a Southeast Asian supermarket chain, and represented the Widjaya family in connection with the $349 million sale of its interests in the captive power assets of its pulp and paper mills, as well as the formation of a joint venture with Singapore Power to operate its assets and provide power to the paper mills. The firm has formed a joint venture with Colin Ng & Partners. **Clients:** Widjaya family; Newbridge Capital; Indonesian steel manufacturer.

Herbert Smith (3 ptrs, 10 asscs) Reputed to be involved in some of the most interesting deals, it is a highly regarded participant in the market. The firm acted on Li & Fung's acquisition of Inchcape's marketing services business in the region. Advised an international water developer on investment in a number of South-East Asian water projects. Managing partner of the office, **Mark Newbery*** was recommended to our researchers for his energy work. The team advised PSEG on its acquisition of a controlling interest in the North Madras Power Project in Tamil Nadu, India. Also advised the Bank of East Asia on the acquisition of a substantial minority stake in Bank Daiwa Perdania and represented the Bank of Scotland on issues arising from the Singapore regulatory aspects of its £26 billion hostile bid for National Westminster Bank. Established a formal alliance with Arfat Selvam & Gunasingham in January 2001. **Clients:** Major corporates and financial institutions.

Latham & Watkins (3 ptrs, 10 asscs) The Singapore office of this major US firm opened in January 2000 and is judged to have hit the ground running. With ample resources and an aggressive approach, the firm is already a force possessing a base of blue chip clients. Acted as counsel to Cable & Wireless and Hongkong Telecom in the establishment of MobileOne, a joint venture formed to operate the second GSM mobile business in Singapore. The firm subsequently advised Cable & Wireless on the establishment of an internet service provider in Singapore. It also acted for Asia Pulp and Paper on the formation and negotiation of Asia based joint ventures and advised Singapore Technologies on investments in US based companies. **Clients:** ABN AMRO; Bear Stearns; Chase Manhattan Bank; Citibank; McDermott; Merck & Co; Morgan Guaranty Trust Company of New York; Salomon Smith Barney.

Milbank, Tweed, Hadley & McCloy (2 ptrs, 10 asscs) One of the most prominent US practices in Singapore and has survived the recession well. Recommended to our researchers for its involvement in the high tech field and for a prominence in Indonesia. It advised NatSteel in its $2.4 billion sale of NatSteel Electronics to Solectron. Known for its strong base of financial clients the firm represented the Indonesian Bank Restructuring Agency on the $500 million sale of Astra International to a consortium led by Cycle & Carriage. The firm continues its involvement in major M&A deals including Tractebel's purchase of Hanjin City Gas in Korea (value $100 million) and the Indonesian government's $120 million sale of Semen Gresik to Cemex. **Clients:** Pacific Internet, SembCorp Industries, IBRA, Tractebel, NTT, NatSteel, DishnetDSL, Chase, Capital Partners.

Simpson Thacher & Bartlett (1 ptr, 5 asscs) A solid team of strong all-round players considered by rivals to be building on the back of its hugely active clients. This broad practice has a tremendous US banking client base spanning global matters. A major player in the corporate finance market, it advised on a Nasdaq listed IPO for Pacific Internet, and a $650 million yankee bond offer for Petronas Oil. Also advised on the SXC listings for two subsidiaries of Singapore Airlines and represented Singapore Power in a number of acquisitions in China, Taiwan and Korea. **Clients:** Merrill Lynch; JP Morgan; Singapore Power; Asia Global Crossing; Salomon Smith Barney.

Slaughter and May (2 ptrs, 3 asscs) Although the team has a lower profile due in part to its size, it has developed a following for high-quality deals often representing its US client base in Malaysia. **Steven Galbraith*** enjoys a reputation amongst his peers for being *"a pretty effective operator."* Acted for a major European corporate on the $500 million acquisition of three publicly listed companies in Asia. The firm also acted for the shortlisted bidders on both the Kapar Power and the Pasir Gudang Power Stations and acted on a $100 million share placement for YTL Power International. **Clients:** ABN AMRO; BNP; Bank of Nova Scotia; DBS Bank; Standard Chartered Bank; Blue Circle Industries; ANZ Bank.

Ashurst Morris Crisp (2 ptrs, 4 asscs) Recommended as particularly active in the telecoms field, the firm has expertise in European-style structuring of management buy-outs. Research has found that, although the loss of high-profile Richard Gubbins was noted in the market, the firm has recruited well to fill the gap. The market predicts successful growth for the practice. **Clients:** Major corporates and financial institutions.

Baker & McKenzie. Wong & Leow Pte ltd (2 ptrs, 11 asscs) Historically major player with a solid flow of M&A deals and a strong presence in Indonesia. Benefiting from a blue chip client base, the team acted for UBS Capital in the acquisition of a 77% shareholding in MK Electron, and advised it on the formation of a joint venture with Chase Asia Investment Partners and Asia Opportunity Fund to acquire the auto parts division of Mando Machinery Corporation. Advised the purchaser in the acquisition of a light rail project in the Philippines and acted for financial investors on the acquisition of strategic interests in various toll road projects in China, Malaysia and Thailand. **Clients:** Major corporates and financial institutions.

Orrick Helen Yeo (5 ptrs, 25 asscs) A solid corporate practice thought to have been built on the back of restructuring work the firm has undertaken in Indonesia. The firm acted for the Indonesian Bank Restructuring Agency closing acquisitions for over 200 companies in many sectors of the Indonesian economy. Also represented IBRA in the sale of its interests in the Indonesian Bank Central Asia and Bank Niaga. **Clients:** Bear Stearns Asia; DBS Bank; Dresdner Kleinwort Benson; Global Crossing; Lehman Brothers; Singapore Technologies; Telenor Asia; Tomen Corporation.

S

Project Finance

Clifford Chance (3 ptrs, 5 asscs) An impressive practice particularly strong on the finance side of projects, often seen acting for lenders. **Sam Bonifant*** has a *"huge reputation."* Our researchers were told that he is *"known and liked by everyone."* **Geraint Hughes*** is *"good on project development,"* while **Kayal Sachi*** is up and coming on the financing side. The team advised Star Petroleum Refinery on the $3.8 million operating merger with the Rayong Refinery in Thailand.

It advised Gulf Indonesia Resources on all the commercial contract agreements relating to the sale of natural gas from the West Natuna Sea to Jurong Island, Singapore valued at $8 billion. Its major international client base includes Dresdner Bank, advising it as the co-ordinating arranger in a $100 billion syndicated multi-currency revolving European asset secured working capital loan facility provided to APP International Trading. **Clients:** CLP; ABB; NRG; SPI; EdF; Gulf; Santa Fe; America Hess; Exxon Mobil; Shell; Caltex; Agip Petroli; IBJ; Chase; Citibank; ABN Amro; CAI; Menta; ECAS; IFC; JBIC.

Freshfields Drew & Napier (3 ptrs, 6 asscs) Making a real mark in project development with consistently strong deals under its belt. The team is recognised for its thorough professionalism and is packed with quality practitioners. Although hit by the loss of Andrew Bonser, the *"aggressive"* **Bruce Cooper*** is pushing the profile of the practice.

It acted for the sponsors and the project company in the financing of the 815MW SembCorp Cogen cogeneration project in Singapore. The team also advised Malaysian Newsprint Industries on the $194.6 million project financing of a newsprint mill in Pahang, Malaysia and represented Dresdner Bank and Credit Agricole Indosuez on the ECA-backed (Hermes/COFACE) financing of a low density polyethylene plant in Malaysia. **Clients:** Tractebel; Malaysian Newsprint Industries; Unocal Asia-Pacific Ventures; Dresdner Bank; US EXIM; ING.

Milbank, Tweed, Hadley & McCloy (1 ptr, 5 asscs) Researchers were impressed with this professional, busy practice, thought to be particularly involved in the Singapore market. Its reputation is built around the *"perennial"* **Gary Wigmore***, who is *"everywhere for projects"* and has *"a tremendous personality."* The team acted in a $160 million financing involving a consortium of banks (BNP Paribas, Citibank, Fortis Bank, Credit Agricole Indosuez and Tokai Bank) where TotalFinalElf joined the MDX-Marubeni-lead Eastern Power deal to provide credit support and equity. Acted in the Edison Mission financing involving 100% private political risk cover in which lead arrangers SocGen, BNP Paribas, DKB and IBJ successfully syndicated the deal to a group of 15 banks. **Clients:** Citibank; Chase; Bank of America; Credit Suisse; HK China Light and Power; US Mission Energy; US InterGen; Thai EGAT; Yuliger (Malaysia); Power-Gen; Tractebel; Enron.

Allen & Overy, Shook Lin & Bok (5 ptrs, 5 asscs) Strong performer renowned for the quality of its loan documentation. **Chris Rushton*** *"really stands out"* and **Fiona Fitzgerald*** is seen by peers to have *"a real sense of confidence"* together with a broad experience of project financing. The team advised Bank of America on the $334 million financing of a 250MW lignite-fired power plant in Tamil Nadu, India and acted for the project company in the development of an LNG receiving terminal in Gujarat. The firm advised the project company in a substantial petrochemicals project in China and represented Citibank and other arrangers on the $322 million financing of the 713MW Bowin Power Project in Chonburi (Thailand.) **Clients:** ICICI; ADB; Citibank; ABN Amro; Shell; British Gas.

Linklaters Allen & Gledhill (1 ptr, 7 asscs) Although the loss of Scott Brodsky is a blow, the team continues to fly the flag on significant projects in India, Pakistan and Bangladesh where the highly regarded **Martin David*** is thought to operate. The firm acted for AES on the Haripur and Meghnaghat greenfield power projects in Bangladesh and for Kelanitissa in Sri Lanka. Also acted on the limited recourse financing of a cement plant in Bangladesh. Supported by the London office, the team acted on Enron's Metgas (LNG) project and advised CEPA on the Hirma Power Project. It advises potential investors hoping to acquire stakes in infrastructure projects in Thailand and India. **Clients:** US and European power companies; international banks.

White & Case, Colin Ng & Partners (4 ptrs, 10 asscs) Displaying great energy, this strong team has a particular focus on India. *"Impressive"* **Brian Miller*** is a long established player and **Raj**

*See leaders' profiles on pages 597-606

S

SINGAPORE
Leading firms (Project Finance)

Band	Firm
1	Clifford Chance
	Freshfields Drew & Napier
	Milbank, Tweed, Hadley & McCloy
2	Allen & Overy, Shook Lin & Bok
	Linklaters Allen & Gledhill
	White & Case, Colin Ng & Partners
3	Denton Wilde Sapte
	Norton Rose
	Orrick Helen Yeo
	Shearman & Sterling
	Slaughter and May
4	Baker & McKenzie. Wong & Leow Pte Ltd
	Herbert Smith
	Simpson Thacher & Bartlett
	Vinson & Elkins LLP

Firms are listed alphabetically in each band.

Leading individuals (Project Finance)

Band	Individual
1	**BONIFANT Sam** *Clifford Chance*
	RUSHTON Chris *Allen & Overy, Shook Lin & Bok*
	WIGMORE Gary *Milbank, Tweed, Hadley & McCloy*
2	**COOPER Bruce** *Freshfields Drew & Napier*
	GALBRAITH Steven *Slaughter and May*
	MILLER Brian *White & Case, Colin Ng & Partners*
	MILLER Calvert *Shearman & Sterling*
3	**BLAKEMORE Haywood** *White & Case Colin Ng & Partners*
	DAVID Martin *Linklaters Allen & Gledhill*
	DUFFIELD Alistair *White & Case, Colin Ng & Partners*
	FITZGERALD Fiona *Allen & Overy, Shook Lin & Bok*
	PANDE Raj *White & Case, Colin Ng & Partners*
4	**BRENNER Alan** *Simpson Thacher & Bartlett*
	HASLAM Peter *Norton Rose*
	HUGHES Geraint *Clifford Chance*
	McNEILL Michael *Baker & McKenzie. Wong & Leow Pte Ltd*
	MURRAY Stephen *Herbert Smith*
	NEWBERY Mark *Herbert Smith*
	ROBB Philip *Lovells*
	WRIGHT Oliver *Denton Wilde Sapte*

Up-and-coming individuals

Individual
SACHI Kayal *Clifford Chance*

Individuals are listed alphabetically in each band.

Pande* has a *"pretty good reputation"* for his work in India. Managing partner **Haywood Blakemore*** is *"a well known figure in the market,"* while **Alistair Duffield*** is highly rated.

The team advised the Asian Development Bank on the financing of the Thu Duc BOT water treatment plant in Vietnam and advised the project company in the Iskenderun Power Project, a 1210MW coal-fired power station in Turkey. In India the firm advised the project company on a $1 billion LNG regasification terminal and in the Philippines it acted for CBK Power Company on the 728MW hydroelectric power plant. **Clients:** Asian Development Bank; JBIC; Deutsche Bank; ABN Amro; Edison Mission Energy; Fortis Bank and other commercial banks.

Denton Wilde Sapte (2 ptrs, 2 asscs) Highly rated for its work on the project development side, where **Oliver Wright*** is judged to be a quality practitioner. The team advised two Japanese entities as co-lenders on the restructuring of the $100 million project financing of an Indonesian coal mine. It advised a Japanese trading house on the restructuring of a $90 million project financing of an Indonesian car factory and has formed part of a consortium advising the Singapore Public Utilities Board on the restructuring of the gas industry. **Clients:** National Power Corp; Gulf Resources; Conoco; Mobil; Media One; government and mulilateral organisations.

Norton Rose (4 ptrs, 4 asscs) With the departure of Carol Roberts, the strength of the team lies in project development where **Peter Haslam*** is highly rated. The team acted for Singapore Power on the $1.5 billion gas purchase arrangements and pipeline project between Indonesia and Singapore. It also advised the project company on the $1.5 billion Bang Bo IPP 350MW gas-fired power project and represented PowerGas on the construction and operation of a sub-sea pipeline from Sumatra to Singapore (a joint venture between Singapore Power and Pertamina.) **Clients:** GMS Power Public Company; Daewoo; HSBC Investment Bank Asia; Standard Chartered; ANZ Investment Bank; Tomen; Singapore Power; Rolls Royce Power Ventures; Siemens; Lucent Technologies; Ericsson.

Orrick Helen Yeo (6 ptrs, 20 asscs) Considered to have a broad coverage with particular expertise in Indonesia and on the sponsor side. The team represented the government in the $1.8 billion restructuring of the Chandra Asri petrochemical facility in Java. Active in the natural resources sector, the team advised a major oil company on its proposal for an India-Bangladesh gas pipeline and represented the sponsors on the financing of a major petrochemical facility in the Philippines. It acted on the financing of a $1 billion water fabrication facility due to be constructed in Malaysia. **Clients:** BP Amoco; Cereberus Partners; Credit Suisse First Boston; IBRA; Marubeni Corporation; Petronas; Sumitomo Corporation; Telenor Asia; Tomen Corporation.

Shearman & Sterling (1 ptr, 9 asscs) Punching above its weight in terms of quality, the firm has an excellent reputation with major financial institutions and focuses on high value transactions. **Calvert Miller*** was frequently recommended to researchers and leads a team of strong associates. The firm advised the lenders (led by ABN Amro and Citibank) in the San Lorenzo 500MW power project in the Philippines and advised the sponsors on the development of a GSM mobile network in the Asian region. **Clients:** British Gas; National Power; PowerGen; ABN AMRO; BNP; Bank Paribas; ADB; IFC.

Slaughter and May (2 ptrs, 3 asscs) The practice has an enviable list of blue-ribbon clients scoring well on complex transactions in Malaysia, Pakistan, Sri Lanka and Bangladesh. **Steven Galbraith*** is highly rated for his work in oil and gas. The team acted for the sponsor on the Express Rail Link Project in Malaysia and advised the sponsors of the Meghnaghat Power Project in Bangladesh and the Kelanitissa Power Project in Sri Lanka. **Clients:** ABN AMRO; BNP; Bank of Nova Scotia; Malaysian YTL; UK Premier Oil; Thai Rayong Refinery.

Baker & McKenzie. Wong & Leow Pte Ltd (5 ptrs, 9 asscs) Winning deals throughout the region, main player **Mike McNeill*** is described as *"pretty impressive."* The team represented CMS Energy/Keppel FELS as bidder for the proposed privatisation of the 2,400 MW Tuas power plant. In Tamil Nadu, India it acted as project counsel for the development and financing of the Jayamkondam 3 x 500MW IPP. The team advised the consortium for the Al-Khamil 250MW gas fired IPP Project in Oman and acted on the transfer of the national grid and supply of power by an existing IPP project (in conjunction with NPC) to a large industrial user in the Philippines. **Clients:** International financial institutions and project sponsors.

Herbert Smith (2 ptrs, 10 asscs) Although established later than others, peers agree that the practice is establishing a foothold in the market with a strong profile for work in India. **Stephen Murray*** has a *"big brain"* and **Mark Newbery,*** who arrived from India in 1998, has a *"strong reputation."* The team advised the lead arranger on the financing of the Ramagundam power project in India and was involved in the development and financing of two Sujana Power projects in India. It also advised ICICI Consulting on the mega power project in Orissa State India.

The practice acted for an international water developer on investment in a number of South-East Asian water projects and advised Japanese trading houses in their capacity as potential EPC contractors for an independent power project in Korea. **Clients:** European banks; investment houses; major power companies.

Simpson Thacher & Bartlett (1 ptr, 5 asscs) A practice with a good reputation, particularly on the finance side. Considered by rivals to be *"a nice guy"* **Alan Brenner*** has a strong reputation for his work with financial institutions. **Clients:** Major international financial institutions and sponsor companies.

Vinson & Elkins LLP (1 ptr, 5 asscs) A smaller *"go-getting"* practice with a focus on the energy sector (particularly in oil and gas), and considered stronger on the project development side. The team advised the Singapore consortium on the multi-billion West Natuna Gas Project and was counsel to Royal Dutch Shell on the $5 billion Malampaya Gas to Power Project in the Philippines. It also represented UniCal on the Western Region Integration Project. **Clients:** Bank of Nova Scotia; Bechtel; Chase; Dell Ventures; Enron; Gulf Canada; Lone Star Opportunity Fund; Occidental; Premier Oil; Reliance Industries; Royal Dutch/Shell; Unocal.

Other Notable Practitioner **Philip Robb*** of Lovells received market recommendation.

Shipping: Local Firms

SINGAPORE Leading firms (Shipping)
1 Rajah & Tann
2 Ang & Partners
3 Joseph Tan Jude Benny Anne Choo
4 Allen & Gledhill
Gurbani & Co
5 Colin Ng & Partners
Haridass Ho & Partners

Firms are listed alphabetically in each band.

Leading individuals (Shipping)
1 **ANG-FONG Belinda** *Ang & Partners*
CHONG Steven *Rajah & Tann*
2 **ANG Vivian** *Allen & Gledhill*
BENNY Jude *Joseph Tan Jude Benny Anne Choo*
KUEK Richard *Gurbani & Co*
3 **AJAIB Haridass** *Haridass Ho & Partners*
GURBANI Prem *Gurbani & Co*
KOH Ian *Drew & Napier*
4 **CHUA Danny** *Joseph Tan Jude Benny Anne Choo*
KWEK Winston *Colin Ng & Partners*
LEE-WAN Gina *Allen & Gledhill*
LOO Dip Seng *Ang & Partners*
MOHAN S *Gurbani & Co*
ONG Andrew *Rajah & Tann*
SEAH Collin *Rajah & Tann*

Individuals are listed alphabetically in each band.

Rajah & Tann (9 ptrs, 11 asscs) Still the market favourite, the strength of the practice stemming from its close-knit team of bright lawyers. *"Tough fighter"* **Steven Chong*** is praised by clients for his attitude and management skills. Fellow lawyers see him as a *"worthy opponent,"* with his *"English style."* His valued team includes **Collin Seah*** and **Andrew Ong*** who both received market recommendations.

The team advised the Maritime and Port Authority of Singapore in connection with the second collision case ('Evoikos' and 'Orapin Global') and acted for the owners and insurers of vessels involved in collisions in the Bangkok river. It also advised the owners of a substantial fleet of tankers in cargo claims arising from the collapse of a major oil trading company in Fujairah. **Clients:** Owners; insurers; clubs.

Ang & Partners (6 ptrs, 10 asscs) A well established practice rated for its depth of experience. Favoured more for dry matters, **Belinda Ang-Fong*** is respected at the bar and the bench. Described as *"tough but fair,"* her style is pragmatic and effective. Clients admire her ability to *"get to grips with a problem."* Of the three partners who specialise in wet work, **Loo Dip Seng*** received particular market recommendation. Peers describe him as *"notable"* in the market and possessing *"sufficient experience."*

The firm represented a Korean listed company in a dispute arising from the purchase of a floating dock for $10.8 million involving Russian sellers and an international ship broker. It represented a seafarer in a personal injury claim which concerned the scope of the Admiralty jurisdiction of the High Court of Singapore and acted for a local oil trader in litigation following the collapse of Metro Trading International. **Clients:** P&I Clubs; ship insurers; owners; brokers.

Joseph Tan Jude Benny Anne Choo (10 ptrs, 10 asscs) An ambitious practice, the first Asian firm to open an office in the shipping hub of Piraeus, it now receives instructions directly from Greek shipowners and operators. It is involved in high-profile matters such as the 'Nordic Explorer case,' the second major collision case in Singapore. **Jude Benny*** is a well-respected litigator, praised by his peers as *"articulate and street smart."* Clients appreciate the large team that has *"a good success rate in court."* **Danny Chua*** is recommended for his experience although his *"shoot from the hip"* style divides the market. Thought to have increased its shipping finance, the firm undertakes dot.com corporate work for shipping clients. **Clients:** Skuld P&I Club; Brittania P&I Club; Port of Singapore Authority Corporation; HSBC Insurance; Neptune Orient Lines; Wan Hai Lines; Malaysian National Insurance; Vestar Insurance; Andre & Cie; Lloyds Recovery; Government of Malaysia; Semco Salvage.

Allen & Gledhill (6 ptrs, 9 asscs) **Vivian Ang*** is the *"big name"* that promotes this practice. Admired by fellow lawyers for her preparation, attention to detail and ability to argue, she is *"knowledgeable and thorough."* In shipping finance, few compete with **Gina Lee-Wan*** in terms of *"market coverage and expertise."* The team acted for the shipowner in a $5.19 million claim against Metalock (Singapore). Also represented cargo interests in a claim against shipowners concerning the loss or short delivery of fuel oil worth over $21.9 million. In finance transactions it acted as Singapore counsel in a UK tax lease financing of four container ships. **Clients:** Vessel owners; banks; P&I clubs; cargo owners.

Gurbani & Co (5 ptrs, 4 asscs) A smaller practice recommended for its *"serious involvement"* in marine insurance and casualty work together with dry work such as charterparty and commodities disputes. Also active in substantial phantom, hijacking and piracy cases. **Richard Kuek*** is a *"good and aggressive"* advocate while the *"articulate and eloquent"* **Prem Gurbani*** is admired for his cross-examination. Junior partner **S Mohan*** is active in both wet and dry work and is recommended by peers as a *"good young lawyer."* **Clients:** P&I Clubs; cargo operators; marine insurers; ship-owners; traders; brokers.

*See leaders' profiles on pages 597-606

Colin Ng & Partners (3 ptrs, 5 asscs) A young and enthusiastic team known for its shipping mortgage work although less seen on intensive litigation matters. **Winston Kwek*** is popular with English law firms although rivals question the depth of team experience. Active in both wet and dry work, the team undertakes direct sales and shipping mortgage work dealing with transactions approaching the S$58 million mark. It acts for freight forwarders and for major shipyards in construction and design disputes. **Clients:** P&I clubs; marine underwriters; government-linked shipyards; shipowners.

Haridass Ho & Partners (8 ptrs, 8 asscs) Still a strong name in the market although thought to be less active since the loss of lawyers to Joseph Tan Jude Benny Anne Choo. Described as *"commercial"* and a *"superb advocate,"* **Haridass Ajaib*** has had a low profile in comparison to past years. Recent work includes acting for shipbuilders, shipowners and banks in new construction, ship finance and sale and purchase of used tonnages. In addition the firm has acted as arbitrators and mediators for shipyards, insurance companies and international organisations. **Clients:** Operators; insurers; financiers.

Other Notable Practitioner Described by clients as *"a strong advocate"* **Ian Koh*** of Drew & Napier defended a claim by cargo owners (gas and oil) relating to cargo confiscated at a Chinese port. Involved in large international shipping arbitration he acts for the PSA and American P&I Clubs.

Shipping: Foreign Firms

SINGAPORE: Foreign Firms Leading firms (Shipping)
1 Holman Fenwick & Willan
Ince & Co
2 Clyde & Co
3 Watson, Farley & Williams
4 Norton Rose
Stephenson Harwood
5 Thomas Cooper & Stibbard

Firms are listed alphabetically in each band.

Leading individuals (Shipping)
1 **LOVELL Richard** *Ince & Co*
2 **GRAY Julian** *Clyde & Co*
HAZELWOOD Steven *Ince & Co*
SACHS Mark *Thomas Cooper & Stibbard*
3 **BURKILL Steven** *Watson, Farley & Williams*
GREEN Martin *Stephenson Harwood*
McALPINE Stuart *Watson, Farley & Williams*
THOMAS Nigel *Watson, Farley & Williams*
YOUNG Iain *Stephenson Harwood*
4 **OGG Terry** *Clyde & Co*
RAY Jon *Watson, Farley & Williams*
SPOONER Guy *Norton Rose*

Individuals are listed alphabetically in each band.

Holman Fenwick & Willan (4 ptrs, 8 asscs) Recommended for wet and dry litigation and collision work, the practice is considered top tier for shipbuilding disputes. It acts on behalf of local, English, Japanese and Greek shipowners. The team represented owners and insurers in total loss cases including a loss in Malaysia involving oil pollution. Although Paul Aston has returned to London the practice is still well-respected by its peers, particularly on the wet side.

The practice has undertaken ship repair work for brokers, and advised on the Nordic Freedom case involving $6 million dollars of claims against Liverpool & London P&I Club. It is active in structural marine disputes arising from the laying of clamps on sub-sea pipelines. **Clients:** P&I Clubs; insurers; owners; brokers; shipyards; salvors.

Ince & Co (3 ptrs, 4 asscs) *"A formidable competitor"* renowned for its casualty work, the practice represented Chevron after the grounding and capsize in Indonesia of heavylift vessel 'Mighty Servant 2.' It also advised the underwriters on the sinking of the cruise ship 'Sun Vista' in the Malacca Strait. Although the team has lost John Dillon it retains star player **Richard Lovell*** who specialises in collisions, salvage and other disaster work and has good connections in Indonesia.

On the dry side the team handles commodity, shipbuilding and charterparty/MOA disputes for large shipowners, traders/charterers, shipyards and the leading clubs. A *"good theorist"* **Steven Hazelwood*** is *"highly regarded in litigation."* Clients told researchers that the firm has depth on the admiralty side. **Clients:** P&I Clubs; ship-owners; underwriters; shipyards; traders.

Clyde & Co (2 ptrs, 4 asscs) Specialising in salvage and casualty work, the team is renowned for its litigation expertise in damage to cargo cases. It advised the owners and insurers in the 'Las Sierras' case involving damage and loss of life after a collision with 'Hal Syghus' and the 'Jascon II' salvage of the tug and tow in the South China Seas. Active in dry work the firm appeared in an Islamic financing transaction for an FPSO and negotiated and drafted construction contracts for tugs. Managing Partner **Julian Gray*** is a *"well-known figure"* while **Terry Ogg*** is *"a good man for wet work."* **Clients:** CGU; Glencore Singapore; BG; Tokyo Fire and Marine; AXA; McDermott South East Asia; Inchcape Shipping Services.

Watson, Farley & Willams (4 ptrs, 12 asscs) With a broad coverage, the practice is highly regarded for its ship finance work and acted for Nedship Merchant Bank (Asia) on structured, credit enhanced and asset finance transactions for Japanese and Indian shipping companies. Involved in both wet and dry litigation, **Steven Burkill*** is the star player, while **Stuart McAlpine***, who combines technical skills with a *"commercial approach,"* and the *"well known"* **Nigel Thomas**,* lead the finance practice. Senior marine manager **Jon Ray*** is a *"competent lawyer."*

The firm advised Mees Pierson on two vessel newbuilding financings involving the provision of debt finance to a joint venture vehicle owned equally by a major Asian shipowner and a US leasing and structured finance organisation. Also advised the Bank of Nova Scotia in the purchase of a $50 million shipping loan portfolio. **Clients:** ABN AMRO Bank; Bank of Nova Scotia; Bank Sesellschaft Berlin; Citibank.

Norton Rose (6 ptrs, 8 asscs) Recommended for its broad coverage, the practice provides on-going advice to large Singaporean shipowners and managers on charter parties, newbuildings and claims. It advised on a contentious restructuring and litigation involving a $250 million Far Eastern fleet.

High profile **Guy Spooner*** is admired by peers as *"a leader in litigation"* advising shipyards on contractual issues and disputes. The firm

*See leaders' profiles on pages 597-606

advised on a LNG shipping finance into India and acted for a number of foreign banks including a large Chinese bank on its creative financing solutions for off-shore transactions. Advised a leading Japanese arranger in a $90 million financing for LPG newbuildings. **Clients:** Jurong Shipyard; Andhika; Columbia Shipmangement; HSBC; ANZ Investment Bank; insurers; owners; charterers.

Stephenson Harwood (2 ptrs, 3 asscs) A major player in ship financing, it acted for the arrangers and banks on the structuring of a substantial lease deal financing newbuildings for one of Asia's largest shipowners. The team acted for secured lenders on the debt restructuring of the Precious Shipping Group of Thailand. A budding litigation team advises Korean and Russian clients and has acted on an arbitration in Singapore for a worldwide steel producer. **Martin Green*** has 18 years experience in Asian ship financing and with **Iain Young*** forms a *"highly competent team."* **Clients:** Den Norske Bank; Fortis Bank; Nedship Bank; ING Shipping; NIB Capital; International Finance Corporation; Crédit Agricole Indosuez; Fleet National Bank; DaimlerChrysler Capital Services; CSFB; DBS Bank; Keppel Tat Lee Bank; Pohang Iron & Steel Works; Posco Asia Co; Far East Shipping Co; G. Premjee; Delta Exports; Universal Navigation.

Thomas Cooper & Stibbard (2 ptrs, 2 asscs) With strong connections in China and Japan, the practice focuses on predominantly wet matters, specialising in casualty work including collisions, cargo loss and piracy cases. It undertakes general trade disputes in relation to commodities and acted in the Global Mars case. Fluent in Mandarin, **Mark Sachs*** is considered by peers and clients to be *"a force."* **Clients:** P&I market in London & Japan; ship owners; large Japanese hull underwriters; Scandinavian owners.

S

Leaders' profiles – Singapore

AJAIB, Haridass
Haridass Ho & Partners, Singapore +65 533 2323
mail@hhp.com.sg
Recommended in Shipping
Specialisation: Managing partner and partner in the Admiralty, Shipping & Commercial Litigation department. Main area of work is litigation, principally in shipping and banking related cases. Has handled considerable litigation and arbitration work in Singapore and the region. Acts for major shipyards and rig builders in Singapore and the region. Represents shipyards in construction and repair disputes, shipowners and P&I Clubs in shipping and charterparty disputes, international, local banks and financial institutions in structured trade transactions, commodity and trade disputes, letter of credit disputes and enforcement actions. Represents oil and commodities traders in trade transactions, including structured transactions and dealing with related disputes. Represents insurance and reinsurance companies on marine and general claims.
Prof. Memberships: Appointed as Justice of the Peace. Vice Chairman of Maritime Law Association of Singapore. Accredited Member of the Singapore Mediation Centre. Singapore Academy of Law. Member of Professional Development Committee – IBA. Chairman of Hindu Advisory Board. Chairman of The Ashram Halfway House.
Publications: Contributed the chapter on 'Singapore Laws' in 'Limitation of Liability for Maritime Claims' (3rd Ed., Patrick Griggs & Richard Williams) published by LLP Limited.
Career: Called to the Bar at Middle Temple, London in 1975. Called to the Singapore Bar 1976. In practice since 1976 at the Singapore Bar. Partner in *Haridass Ho & Partner* since 1985.
Personal: Born 26 September 1949. Leisure interests include boating and golfing.

ANG, Andrew
Lee & Lee, Singapore +65 220 0666
Recommended in Banking & Finance, Corporate/M&A

ANG, David
Drew & Napier, Singapore +65 535 0733
david.ang@drewnapier.com
Recommended in Banking & Finance
Specialisation: Partner in Corporate and Finance Business Group. Main areas of practice include banking and finance, mergers and acquisitions, securitisations and corporate restructurings. Extensively involved in cross-border work dealing with English, Indonesian, Malaysian and Thai laws. Banking clients are usually financial institutions comprising both local and foreign banks and work involves loans, structured finance and issues relating to compliance. Has extensive experience in the field of mergers and acquisitions and is frequently instructed by local clients and foreign law firms and corporations. In corporate restructuring and rescue, has combined corporate and banking expertise with past litigation experience to provide clients with advice covering areas such as standstill, debt restructure, security, financial assistance, stock exchange disclosure requirements, capital reduction, scheme of arrangement, judicial management, receivership and winding-up.
Prof. Memberships: Law Society of Singapore, Singapore Academy of Law, Inter-Pacific Bar Association.
Career: Qualified in 1984. Joined *Drew & Napier* in 1984, becoming a Partner in 1989.
Personal: Born 16 March 1958. Attended National University of Singapore (LLB Hons). Enjoys swimming and tennis.

ANG, Vivian
Allen & Gledhill, Singapore +65 225 1611
vnang@gledhill.com.sg
Recommended in Shipping
Specialisation: Areas of practice include litigious and non-litigious work, marine and air cargo claims, bills of lading and charterparty disputes, freight forwarding disputes, mortgage enforcement, crew claims, ship construction and repair, oil pollution, collision, salvage, general average, towage, insurance, international trade disputes, ship sale and purchase, registration of ships, ship finance, drafting agreements relating to carriage and transportation, warehousing, international trade and shipbuilding and ship repair. Represents clients in a number of major matters, including the owners of the ORAPIN GLOBAL which collided with the EVOIKOS, resulting in the biggest oil spill in Singapore, cargo interests in a claim for loss of oil cargo valued in excess of US$22 million, and the owner of NATUNA SEA in relation to a recent oil spill. Has spoken at various conferences on the arrest of ships, arbitration and maritime law developments in Asia.
Prof. Memberships: Law Society of Singapore, the Singapore Institute of Arbitrators and the Maritime Law Association of Australia and New Zealand.
Career: Partner of *Allen & Gledhill*, Singapore's largest law firm since 1989. Head of the Shipping Department since 1995.
Personal: Born 28 March 1958. Graduated with a Bachelor's Degree in Law (2nd Upper Division) in 1980 from the University of Singapore. Awarded External Examiner's Cash Prize 1979-1980 in the Final Year for achieving the highest marks in the examinations. Obtained a Master's Degree from the University of Wales Institute of Science and Technology in Admiralty and Shipping Law in 1985. Leisure interests include music, reading, dancing and scuba diving.

ANG-FONG, Belinda
Ang & Partners, Singapore +65 224 25 30
baf@angpartners.com
Recommended in Shipping
Specialisation: Partner in Shipping Department. Main area of work is in maritime, shipping, commercial litigation and insurance. Acts on behalf of P&I Clubs, shipowners, charterers, cargo and insurance interests, shipyards, surveyors, and insurance brokers. Has spoken at various conferences.
Career: Qualified in 1974. Joined *Godwin & Co* in 1980 and was a partner from 1983-85. Co-founding partner of *Ang & Partners*, 1985. Member of the

Singapore Academy of Law Continuing Legal Education and Studies Committee, 1989-93. Member of the Singapore Academy of Law Endowment Committee, 1998. Member of the Singapore Arbitration Centre Sub-Committee on Review of Arbitration Laws, 1993. Accredited Mediator of Singapore Mediation Centre. Appointed Senior Counsel 1998. Barrister at Law, Middle Temple; Advocate and Solicitor, Supreme Court of Singapore.
Personal: Born 23 April 1954. Attended University College of Wales, Aberystwyth, LLB (Hon) 1976. Attended University College, London LLM (pass with distinction) 1979.

S

BENNY, Jude
Joseph Tan Jude Benny Anne Choo, Singapore +65 220 9388
JudeBenny@jtjb.com.sg
Recommended in Shipping
Specialisation: Founding Partner of the firm, which was established in January 1988. Developed the firm's shipping and admiralty practice, which is now arguably the largest specialist firm in Singapore. A well respected litigant, has conducted the very first international arbitration at the Singapore International Arbitration Centre, for United Engineers Berhad of Malaysia against a Norwegian company. Appeared on behalf of the Malaysian Government in a series of suits involving railway land ownership in Singapore; and the Jacques Cousteau Foundation with respect to the sinking of the famous vessel the 'Calypso'. Additionally, conducted the first major ship collision trial to go to Court in Singapore involving the vessels 'Ming Galaxy' and 'Hercei Novi'.
Prof. Memberships: Singapore Academy of Law, Law Society of Singapore.
Career: Admitted as an Advocate and Solicitor in Singapore in 1983. Commenced practice with *M/s Drew and Napier*, before founding *Joseph Tan Jude Benny* in 1988. Sits regularly as an Arbitrator in shipping and commercial disputes, and is an accredited Arbitrator of the Singapore Trade Development Board. Was conferred the title of 'Dato' by the Sultan of Pahang, Malaysia.
Personal: Born in October 1957. Graduated in 1981 from the University of London (Queen Mary College) with an LLB (Hons). Won the George Hinde Mooting Competition at Queen Mary College two years in a row (1980-81). Admitted as a Barrister to the Middle Temple in 1982, and as an Advocate and Solicitor in Singapore in 1983. Leisure interests include Go-Karting (has organised several international Kart Prix events as Chairman of the Singapore Karting Club).

BLAKEMORE, Haywood
White & Case, Colin Ng & Partners, Singapore +65 225 6000
hblakemore@whitecase.com
Recommended in Project Finance
Specialisation: Represents foreign investors throughout South East Asia and the Indian subcontinent and acts for Asian companies in their international activities. Practice spans infrastructure projects, joint ventures, mergers and acquisitions, capital markets, banking and international arbitrations.
Prof. Memberships: Admitted to the Virginia State Bar in 1979 and the District of Columbia and New York State Bars in 1980. Admitted as Gaikokuho Jimu Bengoshi to the Japanese Bar in 1990.
Career: Has practised law for 21 years including long term assignments in New York, Japan and Singapore.
Personal: Randolph Macon College (BA, 1971); College of William and Mary (MA, 1975); University of Virginia Law School (JD, 1979). US citizen.

BONIFANT, Sam
Clifford Chance, Singapore +65 535 1855
sam.bonifant@cliffordchance.com
Recommended in Banking & Finance: Singapore Foreign, Project Finance
Specialisation: Partner and head of Singapore's Finance Group with over 20 years experience of cross-border financing and project finance. Representing leading international and merchant banks as well as financial institutions on debt restructuring, project financing and project development, asset based financing and other structured and tax based finance, export credit financing and corporate lending.
Career: Admitted New Zealand (1974), England and Wales (1981). Worked at Clifford Chance, London (1976-1981), in Bahrain (1982-1985) and Singapore since 1985. Became partner (1989).

BRENNER, Alan Gordon
Simpson Thacher & Bartlett, Singapore +65 430 5100
a_brenner@stblaw.com
Recommended in Project Finance
Specialisation: A partner at *Simpson Thacher & Bartlett* and a member of the Firm's Corporate Department. Has extensive experience in international project and corporate finance transactions and regularly advises commercial banks, investment banks and other financial institutions and corporations in a broad range of financial transactions in the United States and throughout Asia. Has been a partner since 1996 and currently heads the firm's Singapore office.
Prof. Memberships: Association of the Bar of the City of New York, the American Bar Association and the International Bar Association.
Personal: Received an AB (with distinction and honors in Literature) from the University of Michigan in 1979 and a JD (cum laude) from the Ohio State University College of Law in 1983. Articles editor of the Ohio State Law Journal and elected a member of Phi Kappa Phi and the Order of the Coif.

BRISCOE, Simon N.
Norton Rose, Singapore +65 223 7311
briscoesn@nortonrose.com
Recommended in Banking & Finance: Singapore Foreign
Specialisation: Partner involved in project, aircraft and shipping finance. Based in Singapore office of *Norton Rose*. Acts for various banks, lessors, carriers, shipping companies and equipment suppliers in connection with financing, leasing and sale and purchase transactions in the Asian region. Has particular experience with limited recourse, ECA supported and Islamic financing structures. Regular speaker at conferences in Asia.
Prof. Memberships: Member, Law Society and Hong Kong Law Society.
Career: Trained New Zealand; qualified New Zealand 1984; UK 1990; Hong Kong 1993; *Chapman Tripp Sheffield Young*, New Zealand 1983-1986; *Norton Rose*, London 1987-1990; *Denton Hall Burgin & Warrens*, London, Singapore, Hong Kong 1990-1993; *Norton Rose*, Bahrain 1993-1995. *Norton Rose*, Singapore 1995 to date; partner 1997.
Personal: Born 14 November, 1961; Education: Rotorua Boys High School, New Zealand; Victoria University of Wellington, New Zealand (LLB Hons). Leisure interests include sailing, snow and water skiing, fine wine and food.

BURKILL, Steven
Watson, Farley & Williams, Singapore +65 532 5335
sburkill@wfw.com
Recommended in Shipping: Foreign Firms
Specialisation: Partner specialising in international litigation with an emphasis on charterparty, bills of lading, commodities and ship sale and purchase disputes. Also experienced in ICC, London and Asia based arbitrations involving power and large scale project disputes.
Career: Prior to joining *Watson, Farley & Williams* in 1998, spent five years in the Singapore office of *Sinclair, Roche & Temperley*.
Personal: Educated at Cambridge University (Robinson College) (MA).

CHANG, See Hiang
Chang See Hiang & Partners, Singapore +65 339 9949
Recommended in Corporate/M&A

CHIA, Cerintha
Khattar Wong & Partners, Singapore +65 535 6844
cerintha@khattarwong.com
Recommended in Banking & Finance
Specialisation: Partner in Banking, Finance and Property Department. Main area of work is banking, finance, and property law, principally loans to corporations within and outside Singapore, including syndicated loans, project finance and other types of financing products, mortgages, charges and other types of security over all kinds of real and personal property in Singapore and elsewhere. Acts for major banks and other financial institutions and major corporations. Heads the firm's international finance practice.
Prof. Memberships: Law Society of Singapore; Singapore Academy of Law.
Career: Qualified in 1980. Joined *Khattar Wong & Partners* in 1980, becoming a partner in 1986.
Personal: Born 11 October 1956. Attended University of Singapore from 1975-79. Member of the Management Committee of Paya Lebar Methodist Girl's Primary and Secondary Schools. Leisure interests include sports and music. Lives in Singapore.

CHONG, Steven
Rajah & Tann (A member of Andersen Legal), Singapore +65 535 3600
steven.s.chong@sg.rajatann.com
Recommended in Shipping
Specialisation: Has been an active litigation lawyer for the past 17 years. Senior Partner and head of the Admiralty and Shipping Department of *Rajah & Tann*. Has been involved in almost all the major shipping casualties in Singapore and in the region over the past 10 years or more. Area of practice includes ship arrest, collision, salvage, charterparty disputes, bills of lading, towage disputes, shipbuilding and ship purchases disputes, general average, oil pollution and bunker supply disputes. A significant number of shipping cases have been reported in various legal journals. Appointed Senior Counsel in 1998.
Prof. Memberships: Singapore International Arbitration Centre. Vice-Chairman of the Maritime Law section of the Inter-Pacific Bar Association (since 1997). Advisory Committee on Maritime Services to the Singapore Trade Development Board. Lecturer in charge of the Admiralty Practice course at the Postgraduate Practice Law Course since 1994. A commissioned Officer of the Singapore Navy.
Career: Graduated from the National University of Singapore in 1982. With *Drew & Napier* from 1982 to 1997 and was Joint Managing Partner at the time of departure from the firm. Joined *Rajah & Tann* in 1998 and is presently a member of the Executive Committee. Has been ranked among the leading lawyers in Asia in various publications, including the Asia Pacific Legal 500 (1998-1999: 'the country's top shipping lawyer') and Asia Law & Practice. Has also been featured in Euromoney publications, The Best of the Best, as one of the 20 top shipping and maritime lawyers in the world, as well as in the Euromoney Guide to the world's Leading Insurance & Reinsurance Lawyers, The Euromoney Guide to the World's Leading Commercial Arbitration Lawyers.

CHUA, Danny
Joseph Tan Jude Benny Anne Choo, Singapore +65 220 9388
Recommended in Shipping

COOPER, Bruce
Freshfields Drew & Napier, Singapore +65 535 6211
bruce.cooper@freshfields.com
Recommended in Banking & Finance: Singapore Foreign, Project Finance
Specialisation: Specialises in finance transactions throughout South-East Asia, particularly structured and infrastructure finance. While still active in infrastructure projects (particularly water and processing projects) and debt financing (particularly structured trade financings), has also recently been involved in a number of debt restructurings

DAVID, Martin
Linklaters Allen & Gledhill (a member firm of Linklaters & Alliance), Singapore +65 438 3800
martin.david@linklaters.com
Recommended in Project Finance
Specialisation: Specialist in project finance and construction law, worked as a civil engineer on a number of large UK infrastructure projects. Main areas of practice include project and project finance work. Transactions include advising BP on an ethylene cracker in Indonesia; the lenders on the first IPP in Tanzania; the sponsors (including PowerGen) on their 1400MW IPP in Thailand; leading the due diligence team on the US$3.4 billion acquisition of a majority shareholding in Consolidated Electric Power Asia; and advising on the potential acquisition of stakes in a number of Indian Power Projects.

DUFFIELD, Alistair
White & Case, Colin Ng & Partners, Singapore +65 225 6000
aduffield@whitecase.com
Recommended in Banking & Finance: Singapore Foreign, Project Finance
Specialisation: Partner, *White & Case*, Singapore Office. Main areas are project finance, banking and debt restructuring. Has represented finance parties, developers and project participants on major Asian project finance transactions, including: the US$750 million facilities for Rayong Electricity Generating Co. Ltd's CCGT plant in Thailand; the lenders on the US$2 billion Reliance Refinery, India; a 304MW CCGT plant in The Philippines; the 172MW coal-fired project at Him Krut, Thailand; the Basin Bridge 200MW LSWR project in India. Has developed particular expertise on fuel supply and transportation contracts for major projects; and the Thu Duc Water Project, in Vietnam. Is currently representing the developers on the coal supply and transportation for the 1200 MW Iskenderun project in Turkey. Member of the teaching faculty for CoalTrans International. Numerous speaking engagements.
Prof. Memberships: Law Society of England and Wales; Singapore Academy of Law.
Career: Admitted in England and Wales in 1980; admitted in New South Wales in 1988. Partner in *White & Case* since 1996.
Personal: Born 27 May 1955. Attended Campbell College, Belfast and Leeds University (LLB Hons). Has lived in Singapore for ten years.

DYER, Roger
Freshfields Drew & Napier, Singapore +65 535 6211
roger.dyer@freshfields.com
Recommended in Banking & Finance: Singapore Foreign
Specialisation: Partner specialising in banking and finance, restructurings, workouts and capital markets.

FITZGERALD, Fiona
Allen & Overy, Shook Lin & Bok, Singapore +65 535 1944
Recommended in Banking & Finance: Singapore Foreign, Project Finance

GALBRAITH, Steven
Slaughter and May, Singapore +65 532 1200
steven.galbraith@slaughterandmay.com
Recommended in Banking & Finance: Singapore Foreign, Corporate/Mergers & Acquisitions: Singapore Foreign, Project Finance
Specialisation: Partner specialising in general banking, energy and project finance.
Career: Educated at St Andrew's College; University of Canterbury, New Zealand (LLB Hons). Qualified in New Zealand; admitted in the UK in 1991; partner *Slaughter and May* 1996; Singapore Office 1998 to date.

GALLEDARI, Arman
Norton Rose, Singapore +65 223 1215
galledaria@nortonrose.com
Recommended in Banking & Finance: Singapore Foreign
Specialisation: Partner, based in Singapore specialising in international debt and project finance. Has advised on a significant number of transactions for lenders, borrowers, lead managers and trustees in connection with debt restructurings, structured and limited recourse financings. Specialises in energy industry and has acted for developers on a number of high profile projects, including in relation to electricity offtake, fuel supply, construction and joint venture financing. Acted for the steering committee of the creditor of Celcom Malaysia in restructuring RM2 billion of its debts, for Singapore Power on its US$8 billion gas purchase agreements from Indonesia and for the Singapore Power Group on the deregulation and restructuring of the gas and electricity industry in Singapore. Also has considerable experience in telecommunication financing having acted for Lucent, Ericsson, Siemens and Nortel.
Prof. Memberships: Law Society.
Career: Trained *Norton Rose*; qualified 1992; Singapore office 1994; Partner 1999.
Personal: Born 1963. Attended University of Essex (1989 LLB); College of Law, Chancery Law 1990.

GILES, Paul A.
Norton Rose, Singapore +65 223 7311
gilespa@nortonrose.com
Recommended in Banking & Finance: Singapore Foreign
Specialisation: International Managing Partner, *Norton Rose*, Asia Region. Experience working over 18 years in Asia. Specialises in aviation, transportation and asset finance. Work includes cross border tax transactions (including US, German, Japanese, French and UK tax leases), finance and operating leasing and export credit agency financing (utilising various structures and in combination with tax leases. Also experience of airline acquisitions, and strategic alliances; and corporate and debt restructurings. Major clients include Malaysian Airline System, and Cathay Pacific.
Prof. Memberships: Law Society.
Career: Qualified in 1973. Partner at *Johnson, Stokes & Master*, 1978-88 (in Hong Kong and Tokyo). Joined *Norton Rose* as a Partner in 1988.
Personal: Born 9 April 1948. Educated at London University.

GRAY, Julian
Clyde & Co, Singapore +65 538 7696
julian.gray@clyde.com.sg
Recommended in Shipping: Foreign Firms
Specialisation: Managing Partner of *Clyde & Co* Singapore office. Diverse and broad experience in

S

many different aspects of marine and insurance law ranging through cargo and hull insurance policy advice, recovery work, charterparty disputes, defence, general average, salvage, pollution, energy related work and multi-modal transport advice (including the past role of honorary adviser to United Arab Emirates National Committee of Freightforwarders). Has wide-ranging practice including a substantial number of regional and international insurance clients. Cases include the 'EVOIKOS', 'HUAL TRINITA', 'TENYU', and 'NATUNA SEA'.
Prof. Memberships: Law Society of England & Wales, International Bar Association and Inter-Pacific Bar Association.
Career: Qualifed in 1979 and joined *Clyde & Co* the same year, becoming a partner in 1983. Worked from 1979 to 1981 in London and from 1981 to 1985 in Hong Kong. (Admitted in Hong Kong as a solicitor in 1981). Again in London from 1986 to 1990 and Litigation Partner in Dubai from 1990 to 1996. Managing Partner in Singapore from 1996 to date.
Personal: Born 4 July 1954. Educated at Rendcomb College and Trinty College Oxford (1972-75) BA (Hons) English. Major interests are family, sports and recreational fitness and classic cars.

S

GREEN, Martin
Stephenson Harwood, Singapore +65 226 1600
martin.green@shsing.com.sg
Recommended in Shipping: Foreign Firms
Specialisation: Opened *Stephenson Harwood*, Singapore. Twelve years in Asia specialising in Asian transportation, particularly shipping and offshore finance and leasing, shipbuilding, asset sale and purchase, transportation and logistics-related IT, port and terminal development covering all of Asia and including banks, owners, contractors, shipyards, lessors and arrangers. Acted for secured lenders in restructure of Precious Shipping Group of Thailand.
Prof. Memberships: Law Society (England); Academy of Law (Singapore).
Career: Oratory School, London School of Economics and Lincolns Inn. Solicitor, England (1988) and Hong Kong (1988). Practised London 1985-87; Hong Kong 1987-1991. Singapore, 1991-present.
Personal: Hockey (Singapore Cricket Club).

GURBANI, Prem
Gurbani & Co, Singapore +65 336 7727
Recommended in Shipping

HARVEY-SAMUEL, Ian
Freshfields Drew & Napier, Singapore +65 535 6211
ian.harvey-samuel@freshfields.com
Recommended in Banking & Finance: Singapore Foreign
Specialisation: Has worked on a wide range of international capital markets transactions, including international equity and equity-related issues in Hong Kong, Indonesia, Malaysia, India, Pakistan and Thailand; international debt issues in Hong Kong, China, Malaysia, the Philippines, Sri Lanka, Thailand, Singapore and Indonesia; issues of asset-backed securities in Hong Kong, Indonesia, Korea and Singapore; OTC and exchange traded derivative products; structured financings.

HASLAM, Peter
Norton Rose, Singapore +65 223 7311
haslamp@nortonrose.com
Recommended in Project Finance
Specialisation: Partner, resident in the Singapore office. Since joining *Norton Rose* in London on qualification in 1981, has advised on most types of banking work in the UK and in Asia. Specialises in project and acquisition finance and restructuring and has been involved in a number of recent significant infrastructural projects in Thailand, Hong Kong (such as Black Point, Western Harbour, Route 3, the air cargo handling franchise for Hong Kong's new international airport, the freight forwarding centre at the airport and the River Trade Terminal) and elsewhere. Also involved in restructurings in Thailand and Indonesia (Aria West, Telecom Asia, KR Precision) and in acquisitions in the Thai market (HSBC/Bangkok Metropolitan Bank and KR Precision).

HAZELWOOD, Steven
Ince & Co, Singapore +65 538 6660
steven.hazelwood@ince.com.sg
Recommended in Shipping: Foreign Firms
Specialisation: Senior Resident Partner, *Ince & Co* Singapore, specialising in all aspects of shipping litigation with particular expertise in the field of marine insurance disputes. Has also been involved in major casualties within South East Asia including, most recently, the Sun Vista fire and sinking.
Prof. Memberships: Associate of the Chartered Institute of Arbitrators; Solicitor of the Supreme Court of England & Wales; Solicitor of the Supreme Court of Hong Kong.
Publications: Author of books and articles covering, amongst other subjects, collisions, marine insurance and P&I insurance, and speaker at international conferences and seminars on a variety of shipping and insurance related topics.
Career: University Lecturer (England and Spain):1979 to 1987. Consultant to United Nations (Geneva): 1982 to 1990. Qualified Solicitor of Supreme Court of England of Wales: 1989. Qualified Solicitor of Supreme Court of Hong Kong: 1992. Partner of *Ince & Co*, served in London from 1991, Hong Kong from 1992 to 1996, currently Senior Resident Partner of Singapore office.
Personal: Born June 1952. Graduate of University of London and University of Wales. Degrees, LLB, LLM, PhD.

HUDSPETH, Mark
Allen & Gledhill, Singapore +65 225 1611
hudspeth@gledhill.com.sg
Recommended in Banking & Finance
Specialisation: Partner in Financial Services Department. Principal area of practice is banking law, with an emphasis on acting for financial institutions and corporate borrowers in relation to Singapore, and regional transactions involving loans, structured loans and the restructuring of loans.
Prof. Memberships: Law Society of Singapore, Singapore Academy of Law.
Career: Qualified in 1989. Joined *Allen & Gledhill*, the largest law firm in Singapore, in 1993, becoming a Partner in 1996.
Personal: Born 27 January, 1962. Attended Tonbridge School, England and the National University of Singapore. Married to Celina and father of two boys, Sean and Matthew. Leisure interests include tennis and motorcycling.

HUGHES, Geraint
Clifford Chance, Singapore +65 535 1855
geraint.hughes@cliffordchance.com
Recommended in Project Finance
Specialisation: Partner in the Finance Group in Singapore and based in Asia since 1993. An infrastructure specialist with over 10 years' experience focusing on advising project companies, strategic investors and lenders on commercial contracts, project financing and corporate transactions for power, oil and gas, water and transportation deals.
Prof. Memberships: Law Society of England and Wales, Law Society of Hong Kong.
Career: Admitted in England and Wales 1991, Admitted in Hong Kong 1993.
Personal: Born: Treorchy, Wales 1967. Leisure: running, cycling, music and Anglo-Welsh literature.

JAMIESON, William
Norton Rose, Singapore +65 228 1225
jamiesonwj@nortonrose.com
Recommended in Corporate/Mergers & Acquisitions: Singapore Foreign
Specialisation: Partner in Corporate Finance Department based in Singapore. Work mostly involves corporate transactions such as mergers, acquisitions, privatisations and capital market issues in Asia, as well as securitisation. Has been advising HSBC on the acquisition of Bangkok Metropolitan Bank in Thailand. Advised the Indonesian Bank Restructuring Agency on the recapitalisation programme for nine private-sector banks. Other recent transactions include advising AXA on the reorganisation of the insurance businesses of the Guardian Royal Exchange in Hong Kong, Indonesia, Singapore and Thailand. Advised the international co-ordinator on the privatisation of Singapore Telecommunications. Produced a report for the Asia Pacific Economic Co-operation Energy Working Group on best practice in procurement of private sector investment in power infrastructure the recommendations of which were adopted by APEC energy ministers.
Prof. Memberships: Law Society.
Career: Qualified in 1982, joined *Norton Rose* in London in 1988, moved to Singapore in 1993 and became a partner in 1996.
Personal: Born 29 June 1957. Attended Oxford University: 1976-1979 (BA Hons, Jurisprudence).

JOHNSTON, Graeme
Baker & McKenzie. Wong & Leow pte Ltd. Singapore +65 338 1888
graeme.johnston@bakernet.com
Recommended in Banking & Finance: Singapore Foreign
Specialisation: Partner and head of the banking, finance and major projects department. Areas of

expertise include corporate restructuring, project finance, acquisition financing, securitisations, and capital market issues. Currently acting for the creditors in the debt restructuring of PT Bakrie Brothers Tbk, PT Bunas Finance Indonesia, PT Anwat Sierad, PT Japfa Comfeed Indonesia and PT Barito Pacific Timber.
Prof. Memberships: Law Society of Scotland; Law Society of Hong Kong; British Chambers of Commerce, Singapore.
Career: Qualified in 1986. Joined *Baker & McKenzie* in 1990, becoming a Partner in 1996. Member of *Baker & McKenzie's* Project Group, Banking and Finance Group and Asia-Pacific Corporate Restructuring Group.
Personal: Born 23 March 1964. Attended University of Aberdeen. Leisure interests include golf, rugby, and football.

KOH, Ian
Drew & Napier, Singapore +65 535 0733
ian.koh@drewnapier.com
Recommended in Shipping
Specialisation: Partner and Head of Shipping and International Trade Business Group. Active practice as a litigator in all aspects of admirality, shipping and international trade law. Shipping cases include collisions, groundings, general average, pollution, salvage, cargo and hull and machinery insurance, charterparty disputes, cargo claims, mortgagee actions, etc. Ship arrests, injunctive and enforcement work are also important areas of practice. Involved in the recent arrest of a supertanker, as well as major maritime casualties such as the 'EVOIKOS' (the largest oil spill in Singapore) and the 'SUN VISTA' (sinking of a large ferry). Frequently involved in international trade, sale of goods and trade finance issues on behalf of oil majors, trading houses and banks. Handled the Mareva Injunction for substantial sums over fleet of vessels, stocks of oil and other receivables involving complex oil trading and trade finance issues. Also active in both international and domestic arbitrations.
Prof. Memberships: Law Society of Singapore; Singapore Academy of Law; Singapore Shipping Association.
Career: Joined *Drew & Napier* in 1989.
Personal: Born in 1963. Attended Cambridge University, England (1987), BA (Hons); Barrister-at-Law of England & Wales (Middle Temple, 1988).

KUEK, Richard
Gurbani & Co, Singapore +65 336 7727
Recommended in Shipping

KWEK, Winston
Colin Ng & Partners, Singapore +65 323 8383
wk@cnplaw.com
Recommended in Shipping
Specialisation: Admiralty and shipping. Handles claims arising out of ship collisions, cargo loss or damage, charterparty disputes, oil pollution, bunkering contracts, ship sale, purchase, financing and mortgage agreements, crew employment contracts, shipboard personal injuries and accidents, construction and repair contracts, freight forwarding arrangements, maritime fraud and international trade and commodity disputes.
Prof. Memberships: Member of Law Society of Singapore, Singapore Academy of Law and Maritime Law Association of Singapore. Legal Adviser to the Southeast Asia Petroleum Exploration Society and Fut Sing Association.
Career: Admitted as an Advocate & Solicitor of the Supreme Court of Singapore in 1991.
Personal: Born Singapore, 1965. Education: National University of Singapore (LLB (Hons), 1990). Leisure interests include golf, football and music.

LEE, Suet Fern
Stamford Law Corporation, Singapore
+65 532 0409
Recommended in Banking & Finance, Corporate/M&A

LEE-WAN, Gina
Allen & Gledhill, Singapore +65 420 7582
gwlee@gledhill.com.sg
Recommended in Shipping
Specialisation: Partner in Shipping Department. Has numerous years of experience in commercial and shipping/admiralty litigation work, although in recent years has focused more on all aspects of non-contentious shipping work including ship financing, ship registration, ship sale-and-purchase and ship construction/conversion. Has been a Deputy Commissioner of Maritime Affairs for Vanuatu in Singapore since 1996.
Prof. Memberships: Law Society of Singapore; WISTA – Singapore (Women's International Shipping and Trading Association).
Publications: Has contributed to 'The Business Times', Singapore. Spoke at the IBA Conference in India in 1997.
Career: Called to the English Bar at Gray's Inn in 1980 and admitted to the Singapore Bar in 1981. Joined *Allen and Gledhill*, the largest law firm in Singapore, as a Partner in 1997. Prior to that was a Partner in *Haridass Ho & Partners* having co-established the firm in 1985.
Personal: Born 4 October 1956. Married with 2 children. Attended University of Kent 1976-79 (LLB 2nd Upper Division). Leisure interests include outdoor activities. Resides in Singapore.

LOO, Dip Seng
Ang & Partners, Singapore +65 224 2530
dsloo@angpartners.com
Recommended in Shipping
Specialisation: Partner in shipping department. Main area of work is in shipping litigation, acting for shipyards, charterers, shipowners, P&I Clubs, hull underwriters, cargo owners/insurers, bunker suppliers, mortgagees, freight forwarders and other transporters of goods. Apart from shipping related work, also handles other commercial litigation e.g. sale of goods, breach of employment contract and financial guarantees.
Career: Qualified in 1980. Joined *Godwin & Co* in 1980, becoming a partner in 1983. Co-founded *Ang & Partners* in 1885.
Personal: Born 1953. Leisure interests include scuba diving and outdoor activities.

LOVELL, Richard
Ince & Co, Singapore +65 538 6660
richard.lovell@ince.com.sg
Recommended in Shipping: Foreign Firms
Specialisation: Principal areas of specialisation are admiralty, marine insurance and cargo claims.
Prof. Memberships: Admitted as solicitor in Supreme Court of Hong Kong.
Career: After qualification practised as a marine litigator in London for 3 years, before being seconded to Hong Kong in 1986. In 1988 became the first foreign shipping litigator to relocate to Singapore in order to establish a South-East Asian litigation practice. Became a partner thereof in 1991, and joined *Ince & Co.* as a partner in 1996.

McALPINE, Stuart
Watson, Farley & Williams, Singapore
+65 532 5335
smcalpine@wfw.com
Recommended in Shipping: Foreign Firms
Specialisation: Partner in the International Finance Group of *Watson, Farley & Williams.* Co-manages the finance practice of the firm in Singapore. Specialises in international cross border asset/structured finance transactions. Client base mainly European and North American banks active in the Asia-Pacific region. Also has significant experience and expertise in advising on transactions in the Indian sub-continent and South East Asia. A regular course director for Euromoney Legal Training and the Singapore based Institute of Banking & Finance. Conducts courses on loan documentation, syndications and the financial aspects of cross-border merger and acquisition transactions.
Prof. Memberships: The Law Society of England & Wales.
Career: Qualified in England in 1986 and spent two years working as a corporate lawyer before moving to Singapore in 1988. Joined *Watson, Farley & Williams*, Singapore, as a partner on 1 September 1998.
Personal: Born 17 May 1962. Attended University College of Wales. Leisure interests include performance theatre.

McGUIRE, Keith
Allen & Overy, Shook Lin & Bok, Singapore
+65 535 1944
Recommended in Corporate/Mergers & Acquisitions: Singapore Foreign

McNEILL, Michael
Baker & McKenzie. Wong & Leow, Pte Ltd.
Singapore +65 338 1888
Michael.M.McNeill@BAKERNET.com
Recommended in Project Finance
Specialisation: Specialises in major projects and privatisations. Since joining the Singapore office has had substantial involvement with major infrastructure projects and privatisations (particularly in the energy, water, and transport sectors) throughout the region, including Malaysia, Indonesia, Taiwan, Bangladesh,Thailand, the Philippines, India, and China.
Prof. Memberships: Law Society of Scotland; Law Society of England and Wales.
Career: Partner of *Baker & McKenzie* and based in

the firm's Singapore office. Admitted to practice in Scotland (1989) and England and Wales (1992).
Personal: A keen interest in outdoor sports including rugby and sailing.

MEHIGAN, Bertie M.
White & Case, Colin Ng & Partners, Singapore +65 225 6000
BMehigan@whitecase.com
Recommended in Banking & Finance: Singapore Foreign
Specialisation: Solicitor with 15 years of experience in banking and financial transactions. Concentrates on cross-border financing transactions governed by English law, principally for international banks. Has represented Singapore and Hong Kong based banks in financial transactions in Singapore, Indonesia, Thailand, Malaysia, Korea, India, China, Pakistan, Cambodia and Vietnam. Recent work has focused on debt restructuring in Indonesia and Thailand as a result of the Asian financial crisis. Also has extensive experience representing financial institutions in connection with syndicated loans, listed and unlisted FRNS, convertible bonds, exchangeable bonds, cross-border leasing of aircraft, sovereign financings, sale and leaseback transactions and project financings. Has represented the Government of Singapore Investment Corporation in derivatives and other financial transactions and the project sponsors in the financing of a synthetic rubber plant in Thailand.
Prof. Memberships: Law Society of England and Wales; incorporated Law Society of Ireland.
Career: Admitted as Irish Solicitor in 1989 (graduated first in class), and then as Solicitor of the Supreme Court of England and Wales in 1991. Managing partner of the Singapore office of a major law firm. Practised in Singapore, London and Bahrain. Currently a member of *White & Case.*
Personal: BCL, National University of Ireland, 1983 (graduated first in class); LLB, National University of Ireland, 1984 (graduated first in class). Irish citizen.

MILLER, Brian M.
White & Case, Colin Ng & Partners, Singapore +65 225 6000
bmiller@whitecase.com
Recommended in Project Finance
Specialisation: Concentrates on international transactions especially project financings. Has advised project sponsors, lenders, product offtakers and contractors on projects in the power, shipbuilding, steel production, pulp and paper, telecommunications and various other industries. Has experience of infrastructure and industrial projects in China, India, Indonesia, the Philippines, Singapore, Thailand and Vietnam. Recent significant matters include representation of borrowers and sponsors in hydro-electric and therma power projects in the Philippines and Thailand, representation of lenders in a water treatment project in Vietnam, and representation of a major Indonesian industrial company in a debt restruction.
Career: Admitted to Massachusetts Bar in 1980. Joined *White & Case* in November 1990. Worked in the firm's Jakarta and Bangkok offices before moving to Singapore. Earlier served as the senior legal advisor for the US Agency for International Development in Manila (1984 to 1989) and in Cairo (1990) and practiced with *Rapes & Gray* in Boston (1980 to 1984).
Personal: New York University (BA, summa cum laude, 1974); University of Massachusetts (MA, 1977); Harvard Law School (JD, magna cum laude, 1980); University of Massachusetts (PhD, 1982). US citizen.

MILLER, Calvert
Shearman & Sterling, Singapore +65 230 3800
cmiller@shearman.com
Recommended in Project Finance
Specialisation: Advising clients in negotiating and structuring commercial and finance agreements for major infrastructure projects including those in the following fields: transport, mining, power and telecommunications in the U.K., Europe and Asia. Advising lenders and steering committees of creditors in relation to project finance and other major corporate restructurings in Asia. Transactions include: advising the lenders in connection with the privatisation of the coal industry in the U.K., the restructuring of the $1.3bn debt of TelecomAsia, the $2.2bn debt of Thai Oil, the $200m debt of Ital-Thai Developments, the $500m debt of AT&T Birla, the acquisition by PowerGen of LG Energy, the acquisition of an interest by Hydro-Quebec International and the $1.4bn debt of PT Semen Cibinong in a major Chinese independent power producer, advising one of the sponsors in relation to the 1000MW First Gas Santa Rita project, advising the lenders in the 500MW San Lorenzo project, advising the project company in the development and financing of a mobile telecoms network in Thailand; advising the lenders in relation to the Lihir gold project and advising the international lenders in relation to the Bangkok elevated rail MRT project. Clients include international banks and project developers.
Prof. Memberships: Law Society.
Career: Qualified in Canada in 1982 and in England in 1991. Partner, *Milbank Tweed Hadley & McCloy* 1996. Joined *Shearman & Sterling* as a partner, 1996. Managing Partner, Singapore office, 1999.

MOHAN, S.
Gurbani & Co, Singapore +65 336 7727
Recommended in Shipping

MOORE, Chris
Norton Rose, Singapore +65 228 1243
moorech@nortonrose.com
Recommended in Corporate/Mergers & Acquisitions: Singapore Foreign
Specialisation: Specialises in cross-border corporate, mergers and acquisitions, joint ventures and foreign direct investment in Europe and Asia. Industry focus on financial institutions, insurance, FMCG, energy, transport, infrastructure, telecoms, internet and technology. Advised on bank acquisitions in Indonesia for a foreign buyer, advised Axa on various acquisitions and disposals across Asia, advised Bank Daiwa on the disposal of a stake in Bank Daiwa Perdania to Bank of East Asia, advised Inchape Plc on the disposal of its Asia-Pacific marketing division, advised Osprey Maritime on its US$750 million acquisition of Gotaas Larsen, advised AIDEC on an equity investment in Lanka Bell and advised on several telecoms projects and internet acquisitions.
Prof. Memberships: Law Society.
Career: Qualified in 1992. Practised in London, Amsterdam, Warsaw, Singapore and Frankfurt before joining *Norton Rose* Singapore as a partner in January 2000.

MURRAY, Stephen
Herbert Smith, Singapore +65 536 7990
Recommended in Project Finance
Specialisation: Energy and utilities specialist including privatisations, acquisitions and the development and financing of infrastructure projects.
Prof. Memberships: The Law Society.
Career: Qualifed in England and Wales, New Zealand and New York. One year with *Russell McVeagh McKenzie Bartleet & Co*, Auckland, New Zealand. Four years with *Fried Frank Harris Shriver & Jacobson* in New York. Joined *Herbert Smith* in London in 1990.
Personal: Born 24 January 1959. Attended Mount Hermon School, Darjeeling. LLB (Hons), Victoria University, New Zealand. LLM, Harvard University, USA. Leisure interests include travel, music and theatre.

NEWBERY, Mark
Herbert Smith, Singapore +65 536 7990
mark.newbery@herbertsmith.com
Recommended in Corporate/Mergers & Acquisitions: Singapore Foreign, Project Finance, Project Finance: India Foreign
Specialisation: Managing partner of the firm's Singapore office, with experience of a wide range of corporate matters including major M&A, energy and project finance transactions. Heads the firm's electricity practice. Has acted on over 50 energy related assignments and independent power generation projects in over 20 jurisdictions. Many of these have been India related and elsewhere in Asia. Works closely with the Indonesia firm, *Hiswara Bunjamin & Tandjung*, which is associated with *Herbert Smith.*
Prof. Memberships: Law Society, City of London Law Society, International Bar Association (SERL Electricity Committee Member).
Career: Qualified 1982. Joined *Herbert Smith* in 1980, becoming a partner in 1989.
Personal: Born 28 March 1957. Attended Nottingham University 1976-1979.

NG, Wai King
Wong Partnership, Singapore +65 532 7488
nwk@wongpartnership.com.sg
Recommended in Corporate/M&A
Specialisation: Corporate transaction and advisory work with emphasis on telecommunication, corporate finance (including IPOs and other forms of fundraising through the stock exchange), mergers and acquisitions (including takeovers and private equity deals), corporate restructuring and financial services/regulatory work.
Prof. Memberships: Law Society of Singapore; Singapore Academy of Law.
Career: National University of Singapore LLB (Hons); Columbia University School of Law LLM

(Harlan Fiske Stone Scholar); seconded to General Electric Company in Hong Kong under GE's Visiting Lawyer's Program (1994); Partner, *Wong Partnership* (November 1994); part-time teacher at the Faculty of Law, National University of Singapore on certain aspects of corporate finance law.

OGG, Terry

Clyde & Co, Singapore +65 538 7696
terry.ogg@clyde.com.sg
Recommended in Shipping: Foreign Firms

Specialisation: Senior Marine Investigator & Consultant. Ex-shipmaster. Specialist in marine casualty work. Acts for ship and cargo interests, port operators, charterers, ship repairers and bunker suppliers. Both commercial shipping and offshore sector. Has particular interest in safety management.
Prof. Memberships: Member of the Nautical Institute.
Publications: In addition to giving presentations at seminars in London, Newcastle, Piraeus, Singapore, Manila, Jakarta and Kuala Lumpur, has contributed to The International Journal of Shipping Law, Seaways, Lloyd's List and the UK Club's Encyclopaedia.
Career: 1974-1978 *T & J Harrison* of Liverpool. 1978-1990 The Indo-China Steam Navigation Co, Hong Kong. Has held a British Class 1 (Master Mariner) Certificate of Competency since 1988. Eight years' experience as Master and Chief Officer in handymax bulkcarriers. Joined *Clyde & Co* in 1990. Joined *Clyde & Co's* Singapore office in 1997. Member of the Singapore Shipowners' Association Services Committee.
Personal: Born 1957.

ONG, Andrew

Rajah & Tann (A member of Andersen Legal), Singapore +65 535 3600
andrew.s.ong@sg.rajahtann.com
Recommended in Shipping

Specialisation: Partner in the Admiralty and Shipping Department. Also partner having charge of the Stockbroking litigation work of the firm. Admiralty and shipping: areas of practice include charterparty disputes, bills of lading disputes, cargo claims, crew claims, P&I matters, oil pollution, bunker disputes, oil trading disputes, personal injury claims, arrest of vessels and recovery work for ship charterers and suppliers. Stockbroking transactions and stock broking related litigation: areas of practice include the conduct of litigation for stockbroking houses in the recovery of contra losses, advising on stockbroking practices and issues, advising on stock exchange disciplinary proceedings, drafting of documentation for stockbroking houses and other forms relating to the stockbroking industry.
Prof. Memberships: Panel member Disciplinary Committee, Law Society of Singapore 1996-1999; member Continuing Legal Education Committee, Law Society of Singapore 1997; vice-chairman Continuing Legal Education Committee, Law Society of Singapore 1998-1999; member Continuing Legal Education Committee, Singapore Academy of Law 1999; chairman Finance Sub-Committee, Millennium Law Conference Steering Committee 1998-1999.
Career: Admitted as an advocate and solicitor of the Supreme Court of Singapore 1991; admitted as a solicitor England and Wales 1996; deputy registrar of the Subordinate Courts and Small Claims Tribunal Referee 1989-1990; assistant registrar of the Supreme Court 1990-1992; Gazetted as a Magistrate 1990; legal assistant *Drew & Napier* 1992-1993; senior legal assistant *Drew & Napier* 1993-1994; partner *Drew & Napier* 1995-1997; partner *Rajah & Tann* 1998 to date.

ONG, Christina

Allen & Gledhill, Singapore +65 225 1611
christina.ong@gledhill.com.sg
Recommended in Banking & Finance

Specialisation: More than 20 years' experience as a corporate and financial services lawyer. Areas of practice include banking, securities offerings, securities regulations, mergers and acquisitions, investment funds, capital markets and corporate finance. Has spoken and presented papers at various conferences including those hosted by the International Bar Association.
Prof. Memberships: Law Society of Singapore. Also active member of the International Bar Association.
Career: Graduated with a 2nd Class Upper (Hons) degree from the University of Singapore. Awarded the Aw Boon Haw and Aw Boon Par Memorial Prize for being first in Postgraduate Law Course. Admitted to Singapore Bar in 1975. Partner in *Allen & Gledhill*, the largest law firm in Singapore, as well as co-head of firm's Financial Services Department.

OOI, Eugene

Allen & Gledhill, Singapore +65 225 1611
eeooi@gledhill.com.sg
Recommended in Banking & Finance

Specialisation: Partner in the Banking Practice Group of the Financial Services Department. Advising and acting for banks and other financial institutions on general banking matters and documentation, and on trade finance structuring and documentation; advising and acting for arrangers, lenders and borrowers in domestic and cross-border lending transactions, both secured and unsecured, and in debt restructurings.
Prof. Memberships: Law Society of Singapore; Singapore Academy of Law.
Career: Called to the Middle Temple – 1977. Bank of America – 1977 to 1981. Called to the Singapore Bar 1981. Partner, *Cooma Lau & Loh* – (1982 to 1984), *Chu, Chan, Gan & Ooi* – 1984 to 1989, *Allen & Gledhill*, the largest law firm in Singapore, from 1989.
Personal: Born 14 October 1952. Schools – Victoria Institution, Kuala Lumpur, Malaysia; Anglo-Chinese School, Singapore. Read law at the London School of Economics & Political Science – 1974 to 1977.

PANDE, Raj

White & Case, Colin Ng & Partners, Singapore +65 225 6000
rpande@whitecase.com
Recommended in Corporate/Mergers & Acquisitions: India Foreign, Project Finance, Project Finance: India Foreign

Specialisation: Partner of *White & Case* in Singapore. Practice involves mergers and acquisitions, project finance and development, banking and corporate financing, capital markets and investments. Experience includes representation of principals in both US and international mergers and acquisitions and of banks, multilateral agencies and corporate borrowers in US and cross-border corporate financings. Has represented large multinational companies and investment vehicles in connection with their joint venture and direct investment activities in India. Has substantial experience in project development and finance, representing both international lenders and developers in connection with infrastructure (power, telecommunications and road) projects and greenfield industrial and refinery projects. Has particularly strong experience in power projects and has advised lenders and developers in power generation projects in India aggregating over 3,000 MW. Has substantial experience representing the firm's clients on telecommunications financing projects in India. Also counsels Indian corporations in connection with their activities outside India.
Prof. Memberships: Admitted to New York State Bar in 1988.
Career: Prior to moving to *White & Case LLP's* Singapore office, was based in the firm's New York office and worked in the firm's Tokyo office for two years.
Personal: BEng, McGill University, 1979; MBA, McGill University, 1987; LLB and BCL, McGill University, 1987. Canadian citizen. Speaks English and French.

PILLAI, Philip

Shook Lin & Bok, Singapore +65 535 1944
philip_pillai@shooklin.com.sg
Recommended in Corporate/M&A

Specialisation: Main area of work is corporate finance, securities, international finance and funds. Practice includes advising clients on Singapore and international debt, equity issues and funds, both in the public markets and private placements. Has extensive experience in advising Singapore listed companies and multinationals on major Singapore and cross-border M&A work including public takeover bids. Has also advised major clients in deregulated industries including banking, finance, media and telecommunications. Acted for the Stock Exchange of Singapore and the Singapore International Monetary Exchange in their recent merger and for the Singapore Exchange in the resolution of the CLOB International issue with the Kuala Lumpur Stock Exchange. Also a director of the Monetary Authority of Singapore and the Singapore International Foundation.
Prof. Memberships: Memberships: Law Society of Singapore; Singapore Academy of Law.
Publications: 'Company Law and Securities Regulation' (1987) Butterworths; 'Sourcebook of Singapore & Malaysia Company Law' 2nd Edition (1986) Butterworths; 'Companies & Securities Handbook' – Singapore & Malaysia (1984) Butterworths; 'State Enterprise in Singapore: Legal Importation and Development' (1983) Singapore University Press.

S

Career: Qualified in 1971 and later obtained an LLM and an SJD from Harvard University. Admitted to the Singapore bar in 1972; Joined *Shook Lin & Bok* as a partner in 1986; Managing Partner from 1992 - 1997; Senior Partner since 1998.
Personal: Born 1947; resides Singapore. Leisure interests include: Literature, opera and golf.

PINSLER, Leena
Drew & Napier, Singapore +65 531 2240
leena.pinsler@drewnapier.com
Recommended in Corporate/M&A
Specialisation: Principally involved in the area of mergers and acquisitions in the banking, finance and securities industries. Advises on regulatory issues affecting those industries as well as on the establishment of private and retail funds. Acted recently for AIB in its investment in bonds and warrants of Keppel TatLee Bank and sale of AIB's private banking and treasury businesses in Singapore, and for Temasek in its acquisitions and disposals. Heads firm's India Desk. Editor of forthcoming volume on securities of Halsbury Laws in Singapore.
Career: Qualified in 1982. Joined *Drew & Napier* in 1983. Corporate Law Committee (2000-2001). Director of the Singapore Indian Chamber of Commerce and Industry (1999).
Personal: Attended Cambridge University (1985-86), LLM; National University of Singapore (1978-82) LLB Honours; Raffles Girl's Secondary School.

PRYKE, Gary
Drew & Napier, Singapore +65 535 0733
gary.pryke@drewnapier.com
Recommended in Corporate/M&A
Specialisation: Partner in Corporate and Finance Business Groups. Main area of work is corporate finance, including securities and stock exchange related work, equity and market related finance, servicing financial institutions, local and international clients. Advises on mergers, acquisitions and corporate restructuring. Has handled the listing of companies and their initial public offerings; takeover offers for public listed companies; mergers and acquisitions of listed and unlisted businesses in Singapore and the region; group and loan restructurings.
Prof. Memberships: Law Society of Singapore, Law Society of England and Wales, International Bar Association.
Publications: Contributor to the forthcoming volume on Securities of 'Halsbury's Laws of Singapore'. Editor of Singapore Chapter in 'International Handbook on Contracts of Employment' published by Kluwer Law International and Co-author of 'International Insider Dealing' published by FT Law and Tax. Has spoken at various seminars and conferences.
Career: Qualified in 1985. Joined *Drew & Napier* in 1986, becoming a Partner in 1991. Member of the Solicitors' Accounts Rules Sub-Committee of the Law Society of Singapore.
Personal: Born 2 December 1956, originally hails from Johannesburg, South Africa. Attended University of Witwatersrand (BA); University of South Africa (LLB); University of Reading (LLB Hons). Enjoys sailing and other outdoor pursuits.

RAY, Jon
Watson, Farley & Williams, Singapore
+65 532 5335
jray@wfw.com
Recommended in Shipping: Foreign Firms
Specialisation: Senior Maritime Manager at Singapore office specialising in collision, grounding, salvage and piracy incidents, total loss, unseaworthyness, and casualty matters worldwide. Also handles issues relating to security, jurisdiction, limitation, cargo damage, marine insurance and oil pollution.
Career: Holborn College of Law, London; Fellow of the Institute of Legal Executives 1970; *Sinclair Roche & Temperley* 1975-1998; *Watson Farley & Williams* 1998 to present.

ROBB, Philip
Lovells, Singapore +65 538 0900
philip.robb@lovells.com
Recommended in Project Finance
Specialisation: Finance, including project finance, structured finance, acquisition finance, syndicated lending and restructuring; acting primarily for banks, but also for borrowers. Recently advised on the project financing of a sugar processing plant, the structured financing of sugar importations into the Philippines, the acquisition of a substantial regional loan portfolio (including loan assets in China, Taiwan, and Hong Kong), the restructuring of a listed Singapore company and its regional operations and the financing of a scheme for the acquisition of loans and shares in Indonesia. Currently advising a number of international banks in respect of proposed securitisations of loans and other receivables.
Prof. Memberships: Law Society.
Career: Qualified as a barrister in 1998 and as a solicitor in 1991. Joined *Lovells* in 1989, becoming a partner in 1998.
Personal: Born 1964. Educated at Christ's Hospital, Cambridge University, Middle Temple. Lives in Singapore.

ROBERTS, Andrew
Linklaters Allen & Gledhill (a member firm of Linklaters & Alliance), Singapore +65 438 3800
andrew.roberts@linklaters.com
Recommended in Banking & Finance: Singapore Foreign
Specialisation: Managing Partner of Asia. Specialist in international capital markets finance and company law, advising investment banks as well as corporate clients. Main areas of practice include debt and equity issues, structured finance transactions, securitisations and derivative transactions, takeover financing and general securities advice. Experienced in transactions involving European, Middle Eastern, Asian and South American issues.

ROBERTS, Swain
Linklaters Allen & Gledhill (a member firm of Linklaters & Alliance), Singapore +65 438 3800
swain.roberts@linklaters.com
Recommended in Banking & Finance: Singapore Foreign, Corporate/Mergers & Acquisitions: Singapore Foreign
Specialisation: Specialist in capital markets transactions in Asia for over nine years. In particular, specialises in equity, equity linked and debt transactions by Asian corporates, having worked on such transactions since the Singapore office opened in January 1992. More recently, has been actively involved in advising on a number of privatisations and equity issues for e-commerce and technology companies based in Singapore as well as the Indonesian Government on a number of the privatisations in its privatisation process. Practised in Australia, Indonesia and currently in Singapore.

RUSHTON, Chris
Allen & Overy, Shook Lin & Bok, Singapore
+65 535 1944
Recommended in Banking & Finance: Singapore Foreign, Project Finance, Project Finance: India Foreign

SACHI, Kayal
Clifford Chance, Singapore +65 535 1855
kayal.sachi@cliffordchance.com
Recommended in Project Finance
Specialisation: Partner in Singapore's Finance Group with over 13 years experience in banking and finance transactions representing leading banks and corporate clients in project financings, structured financings, corporate restructurings and workouts. Has advised on project finance, debt restructuring, structured and asset backed finance and trade finance, capital markets and all forms of corporate lending.
Career: Admitted in Singapore, (1984); Western Australia and Federal Court of Australia, (1986); England and Wales (1996).

SACHS, Mark
Thomas Cooper & Stibbard, Singapore
+65 438 4497
mark.sachs@tcssol.com
Recommended in Shipping: Foreign Firms
Specialisation: Shipping law with an emphasis on claims arising in China and S.E. Asia including collisions, salvage, damage to port installations, arbitration, charterparties and other commercial disputes with Chinese aspects. Recent cases include Southeast Asian vessel hijacking cases, fibre optic submarine telecoms cable damage claims and commodity futures disputes involving Chinese interests. Has been a partner of *Thomas Cooper & Stibbard*, London solicitors since May 1996 and resident partner with their Singapore office with regular attendance in China and around the region on shipping matters. Practised in the Maritime Group of *Bull Housser & Tupper* of Vancouver for 9 years, first as an associate and then as a partner, acting principally for shipowners and P&I Clubs; chief representative of *Bull & Housser*'s Shanghai office from 1988 to 1991.
Prof. Memberships: Admitted as a Solicitor and called to the Bar of British Columbia 1987. Admitted in England & Wales 1998.
Publications: Contributor to 'Kluwer's Maritime Law Handbook Part III on Judicial Sale of Vessels in China'.
Personal: Beijing University (Chinese History/Language) 1979. University of British Columbia (BA Chinese Literature) 1st Class 1982. University of British Columbia (LLB 1986).

SEAH, Collin
Rajah & Tann (A member of Andersen Legal), Singapore +65 535 3600
collin.g.seah@sg.rajahtann.com
Recommended in Shipping
Specialisation: Has handled numerous maritime casualties including the sinking of the cruise ships Royal Pacific and Sun Vista; collisions between Nanta Bhum/Kapitan Shvetsov, Herceg Novi/Ming Galaxy and Orapin Global/Evoikos; the grounding of ships by the cyclone at Kandla in June 1998. Handled the dispute over the conversion of Solitaire, and more recently the sale of a cruise ship business together with the cruise ships Sun Viva and Sun Viva II. Advises the Singapore port authority regularly on legislative and marine pollution matters.
Career: Called to the Singapore Bar 1993, became a partner in 1998. Teaches shipping law at the Singapore University.

SELVAM, Arfat
Arfat Selvam & Gunasingham, Singapore +65 538 5138
Recommended in Banking & Finance, Corporate/M&A

SPOONER, Guy
Norton Rose, Singapore +65 223 7311
spoonergda@nortonrose.com
Recommended in Shipping: Foreign Firms
Specialisation: Regional Litigation Partner based in Singapore. Main area of work is dispute resolution, arbitration and litigation in the transportation, energy and infrastructure sectors. Acts for a number of major owners, operators, builders, insurers and financiers of ships, aircraft and offshore/onshore installations in matters ranging from catastrophic loss to contractual disputes.
Prof. Memberships: Law Society of England and Wales, Hong Kong Law Society, Baltic Exchange.
Career: Qualified in England and Hong Kong (1990); 1990-1997 *Ince and Co*, joined *Norton Rose* 1997.
Personal: Born 1962. Charterhouse School and University of Southampton (LLB 1984). Married with two children. Leisure interests include tennis, golf, and hockey.

TEO, Kiang Kok
Shook Lin & Bok, Singapore +65 535 1944
kk_teo@shooklin.com.sg
Recommended in Banking & Finance
Specialisation: Partner and Head of Corporate Finance and China practices. Main areas of work are corporate finance, mergers and acquisitions. Has handled acquisitions and disposals by Singapore and foreign companies. Has advised on many public offerings of securities by Singapore and foreign companies including those from the People's Republic of China. Acted for China-Singapore Suzhou Industrial Park Development Co Ltd on the development and sale of the China-Singapore Suzhou Industrial Park.
Prof. Memberships: Called to the Bar of England and Wales (Lincoln's Inn) in 1982; admitted as an Advocate & Solicitor of the Supreme Court of Singapore in 1983.
Publications: Author of the following articles and conference papers: 'Commentary on the Companies (Amendment) Act 1984' published in Asian-Pacific Tax and Investment Bulletin (1984); 'The Giving of Investment Advice under the Securities Industry Act' published in Malayan Law Journal 1988; 'Sale of Shares in Foreign Companies in Singapore' published in Malayan Law Journal 1988; 'Market Manipulation' Conference on 'Fraud in the Securities Market' organised by the Crown Agents and Commonwealth Secretariat in January 1988; 'Going Public and Take-over/Merger Offers: Responsibilities and Liabilities of Directors at the Conference on Directors-Rights, Duties & Liabilities in June 1988; Co-author of the 'Special Report on Regulation of the Singapore Stockbroking Industry', Regulations Governing Broking Supplement to the International Financial Law Review (December 1991) (published by Euromoney). Contributing editor (since 1999) for 'International Law Office Legal Newsletter' – Corporate Finance/M&A (Singapore) & Overview. October 1999, The Asia Business Forum Conference on 'How to Successfully Position and List Your IPO'.
Career: Was an investment banker prior to legal practice. Joined *Shook Lin & Bok* in 1987; admitted as a partner in 1988; Member of the Law Reform Committee of the Singapore Academy of Law.
Personal: Born 1956; resides Singapore. Attended University of Hull. Leisure interests include reading and golf.

THIO, Su Mien
Thio Su Mien & Partners, Singapore +65 534 4877
Recommended in Corporate/M&A

THOMAS, Nigel
Watson, Farley & Williams, Singapore +65 532 5335
nthomas@wfw.com
Recommended in Shipping: Foreign Firms
Specialisation: Partner, Head of Singapore office, specialising in international finance, including structured and project finance, ship finance and international leasing structures, and acting for financial institutions, international corporations and shipping and cruise companies.
Career: Articled *Norton Rose*; qualified 1981; assistant solicitor 1981-82; manager merchant bankers Lazard Brothers & Co. 1982-87; partner *Watson, Farley & Williams* 1988; resident partner Oslo office 1988-93; head of operations Singapore office 1998.
Personal: Born 1956; resides in Singapore. Educated at Dulwich College; St Catharine's College, Cambridge (MA); London Business School.

WIGMORE, Gary S.
Milbank, Tweed, Hadley & McCloy, Singapore +65 428 2550
gwigmore@milbank.com
Recommended in Project Finance
Specialisation: Partner in charge of Asian Global Project Finance Practice. Prior to 1992, worked in *Milbank's* New York office. Practice concentrates in project finance and development, involving private power, telecoms, oil and gas, refining, mining, industrial and infrastructure projects. Representations include lenders, developers, export credit agencies, utilities and equity investors in project financings. Handled project financings, restructurings, privatisations, securitisations and mergers and acquisitions in Asia. Currently represented (i) a syndicate of bank lenders on the restructuring and refinancing of a geothermal project in Indonesia, (ii) an international developer in the acquisition of an interest in a power project in India, (iii) a group of bank lenders in a Philippine hydro project, (iv) the sponsor of a telecoms project in a financing in Indonesia, (v) the developer of an energy project in Vietnam, (vi) an international oil company in an acquisition in Thailand, (vii) the placement agent in a structured securitisation in Australia and (viii) an international developer of infrastructure in Japan. Broad finance practice in Asia has involved many pioneering transactions. Has represented a consortium consisting of InterGen and the Lippo Group in the development and financing of the 724 MW Meizhou Wan Power Project in Fujian Province, China, which was voted Deal of the Year in 1998. Currently handling a US$1 billion private power project for international developers in India In addition, has represented the senior lenders in the US$1.6 billion Bangkok Transit System elevated railway project in Thailand. A frequent speaker at conferences and seminars on the subjects of energy and project finance.
Publications: Author of 'Credit Documentation for Project Finance Transactions', published in the 1992 'Practising Law Institute Project Financing Handbook'. Recently presented a paper in Singapore entitled 'Financing Development in the Asian Water Market A Global and Regional Perspective'.
Career: Prior to joining *Milbank*, has had significant energy financing and advisory experience at JP Morgan Bank in New York and Ridgewood Energy.
Personal: Received a BA degree from the State University of New York at Oneonta, an MS degree in Management from Carnegie-Mellon University and a JD degree from Fordham Law School.

WILLIAMS, Elaine
Freshfields Drew & Napier, Singapore +65 535 6211
elaine.williams@freshfields.com
Recommended in Corporate/Mergers & Acquisitions: Singapore Foreign
Specialisation: Partner in the Corporate Group, with particular expertise in cross-border mergers and acquisitions in Asia. Handled a wide range of corporate finance and general corporate transactions in Asia and elsewhere including joint ventures and international equity and equity-related issues.

WONG, Lucien
Allen & Gledhill, Singapore +65 225 1611
lucienw@gledhill.com.sg
Recommended in Banking & Finance, Corporate/M&A
Specialisation: More than 20 years' experience as a corporate, banking and financial services lawyer. Areas of practice include banking, securities offerings, mergers and acquisitions, structured finance, project finance, derivatives instruments, capital markets instruments and securities regulations.
Prof. Memberships: Law Society of Singapore. Also active member of the International Bar Association, being a co-chairman of Committee Q

S

(Securities Committee) of the International Bar Association as well as a committee member of the Asia Pacific Forum of the International Bar Association. Member of a number of law review committees in Singapore which reviewed amendments to Singapore company and securities laws.
Career: Admitted to Singapore Bar in 1979. Managing Partner of *Allen & Gledhill*, the largest law firm in Singapore, as well as the co-head of the firm's Financial Services Department.
Personal: Graduated from the University of Singapore in 1978. Awarded Adrian Clark Gold Medal and Leow Chia Heng Prize for being first in law school class.

S

WONG, Sunny
Wong Tan & Molly Lim, Singapore 068898
+65 222 8008
swong@wtl.com.sg
Recommended in Banking & Finance
Specialisation: Head of the Corporate, Banking and Finance Department at *Wong Tan & Molly Lim.* Acts for banks and financial institutions on a wide spectrum of banking and finance work, including syndicated and project lending, structured finance and debt restructuring, in Asia (including Indonesia, Thailand, Malaysia, Philippines and China). Has advised American, European and Japanese banks on a routine basis on their standard banking documentation.
Prof. Memberships: Memberships: Law Society of Singapore, Singapore Academy of Law, Law Society of England and Wales, International Bar Association.
Career: Qualified in 1981. Joined *Freshfields* in 1981. Seconded to *Freshfields*, London in 1984. Head of Corporate, Banking and Finance Dept of *Wong Tan & Molly Lim* since 1987. Appointed Commissioner for Oaths in 1989. Appointed Notary Public in 1996.
Personal: Born 19 April 1956. Graduated with 2nd Class Upper (Hons) degree from the National University of Singapore in 1981.

WRIGHT, Oliver
Denton Wilde Sapte, Singapore +65 435 2964
olw@dentonwildesapte.com.sg
Recommended in Project Finance
Specialisation: Partner, Head of Singapore office. Practice focuses on telecommunications, energy, hotels and resorts and other projects in South-East Asia. Handles all aspects including financing, concessions, joint ventures, acquisitions and disposals, construction and disputes. In 1999-2000, acted for MediaOne (now part of AT&T) on disposals of their interests in various Asian telecommunication and cable television projects for a realised value close to US$500m. Also acted in that period on Indonesian restructuring work for Sumitomo Corporation and Marubeni Corporation, and on acquisitions from the Indonesian Bank Restructuring Agency. Has recently begun work for AES on an IPP financing in Bangladesh.
Prof. Memberships: Law Society.
Career: After a varied early career (including refugee resettlement work in South East Asia), qualified as a barrister in 1986, converting to solicitor in 1989, then returned to Asia.
Personal: Born 19 January 1955. Graduated from Cambridge 1977. Diploma in Law, City University, 1985. Languages include fluent Indonesian, Malay and German. Married with two sons.

YEO, Wee Kiong
Rajah & Tann (A member of Andersen Legal), Singapore +65 535 3600
wee.kiong.yeo@sg.rajahtann.com
Recommended in Corporate/M&A
Specialisation: Senior partner and head of corporate and capital markets practice. Main areas of work are corporate finance, initial public offerings, mergers and acquisitions, direct equity investments, cross-border investments, capital market instruments, corporate restructuring, start-up investments, etc. Has advised on many public offerings of securities by Singapore and foreign companies and of internet companies and a biotechnology corporation.
Prof. Memberships: Law Society of Singapore. Previous appointments included service on the corporate law review committee and the investment committee of the Law Society, a sub-committee of the stock exchange of Singapore, committee member of the Singapore Venture Capital Association, adviser to the Association of Small & Medium Enterprises. Current appointments include adviser to the Singapore Confederation of Industries, board member of the National Science and Technology Board and member of the advisory panel to the Registry of Companies and Businesses.
Publications: 'Singaporean M&A legislation' in the Euromoney December 1991 publication of Mergers, Acquisitions & Divestments; 'Procedures for Going Public' in the Company Secretary's Manual, published by Thomson Information (S.E. Asia) in 1997; 'Hi-tech start-ups in Singapore' June 2000 Asiamoney magazine. Has spoken and presented papers at various seminars and conferences in Singapore and the region.
Career: Served as senior investment officer from 1980 - 1984 with the Singapore government's economic development board specialising in attracting technology investments into Singapore. Was an investment banker with NM Rothschilds in Singapore from 1984 - 1988 before practising law. Joined *Drew & Napier*, one of Singapore's leading law firm in 1989 and became the equity partner heading its corporate practice in 1993. Founded *Yeo Wee Kiong & Partners*, a boutique corporate finance law practice in 1996 and merging with *Rajah & Tann* in 1999. Currently senior partner and head of corporate and capital markets practice group.
Personal: Graduated with first class honours in mechanical engineering from the University of Singapore in 1980. Awarded professional engineers board gold medal. MBA from the National University of Singapore, 1988. Interests include skiing, golfing, and investing in start-up companies.

YOUNG, Chee Foong
Colin Ng & Partners, Singapore +65 323 8383
ycf@cnplaw.com
Recommended in Banking & Finance
Specialisation: Banking and finance, covering financing, regulatory and advisory services. Domestic and international financing documentation for loans, buyer credit, debt instruments and commercial papers, ship, property, trade and project financing and debt restructuring and workouts. Regulatory and advisory work for banks and financial institutions, licensing, mergers, re-structuring, compliance and enforcement of rights and security. Bank and financial institution clients, including Singapore and major foreign banks.
Prof. Memberships: Chairman, Law Society of Singapore Committee on Professional Practice Management.
Career: Admitted as an Advocate & Solicitor of the Supreme Court of Singapore in 1987.
Personal: Born 1962; education: National University of Singapore (LLB (Hons), 1986); leisure interests include golf and reading.

YOUNG, Iain
Stephenson Harwood, Singapore +65 226 1600
iain.young@shsing.com.sg
Recommended in Shipping: Foreign Firms
Specialisation: All aspects of asset finance, particularly in relation to ships and generally in non-contentious matters related to the transportation industry including shipping, helicopter and aircraft experience. The majority of work dealt with is cross-border in nature. Acted for major Dutch bank in financing the acquisition, conversion and mobilisation of an FPSO. Currently working offshore Vietnam under contract to major Malaysian oil company.
Prof. Memberships: Law Society.
Career: Sherborne School 1976-81; St John's College, Cambridge 1982-85; The College of Law, Guildford, 1985-86; articled at *Sinclair Roche & Temperly*; joined *Stephenson Harwood* as a Singapore partner in 1996, London partner in 1999.
Personal: Married to Marcelle with three children; enjoys all sports, particularly rugby; member of Hawks & Achilles Clubs.

SLOVAKIA

Corporate/Commercial

SLOVAKIA Leading firms (Corporate/Commercial)	
1	Allen & Overy
	Linklaters
	Squire, Sanders & Dempsey
	White & Case, Feddersen
2	Cechová Rakovsky
	Cernejová & Hrbek
	Csekes, Világi, Drgonec & Partners
3	Altheimer & Gray
	Freshfields Bruckhaus Deringer

Firms are listed alphabetically in each band.

Leading individuals (Corporate/Commercial)	
1	**CERNEJOVÁ Alena** *Cernejová & Hrbek*
	MOGG Jason *Linklaters*
	PÁLKA Igor *Allen & Overy*
2	**CSEKES Erika** *Csekes, Világi, Drgonec & Partners*

Individuals are listed alphabetically in each band.

Allen & Overy (9 fee-earners) A comparative newcomer to Bratislava, the firm has fed off its superb Prague operation to make an immediate impact here. Particularly strong on banking and finance advice, the team also has an imposing cross-border practice. In **Igor Pálka***, the firm has a top-class Slovak lawyer, considered by peers to be a *"hard-working"* banking expert. The team advised AES Electric Ltd on its bid for PPC, a Slovak energy operator, and acted on the acquisition of TVS, a Slovak water company, by Suez Lyonnaise des Eaux. **Clients:** Telenor; Suez Lyonnaise des Eaux; Rhodia Industrial Yarns; Nysalter Textile Yarns; Kraft Foods International; KPN.

Linklaters (1 ptr, 13 asscs) Having acquired the bulk of the former Burns Schwartz team, this UK giant is said to have created *"a highly successful practice,"* specialising in capital markets, direct foreign investment, finance, banking and privatisation. The firm has an alliance with local practice Bolf, Nemeth and Szabova which enables it to cover domestic advice. Canadian **Jason Mogg*** has long-term experience in the region. Advising an international client base, the team represented Globtel on its investments in the Slovakian mobile telecoms market, and has acted for the City of Bratislava on its bond issues. **Clients:** Globtel; SPP State Gas Co; BASF; Bouygues SA; BP; Invensys.

Squire, Sanders and Dempsey (2 ptrs, 8 asscs) The longest established foreign firm in Bratislava, our researchers were impressed by its *"strong reputation in local corporate matters,"* and blue-chip international client base. Kevin Connor, formerly managing partner of the Bratislava office, now divides his time between here and Budapest, and will leave Slovakia during 2001. However, the firm is expected to weather his departure. Represented Tesco plc on its purchase of K-Mart Stores in Slovakia. **Clients:** Slovak Electric; Transpetrol; Slovak Telecom; Tesco plc.

White & Case, Feddersen (2 asscs) Although the firm runs much of its Bratislava practice from Prague, it remains an active player on the continuing privatisations in Slovakia. The team's M&A and venture capital practices continue to thrive, and it advised the government on the privatisation of Slovak Telecom, a deal worth €1 billion. Also advised PPC on a project financing for a cogeneration plant. **Clients:** Slovakian Government; Slovak Telecom; PPC.

Cechová Rakovsky (4 ptrs, 6 asscs) Local firm with a flourishing commercial practice and the respect of its international rivals. The group advised a committee of international and local banks on the financial restructuring of the largest steel producer in Slovakia, and represented an Austrian bank on the acquisition of a majority stake in a Slovakian bank. **Clients:** Domestic and international financial institutions.

Cernejová & Hrbek (3 ptrs, 1 assc) Although clearly unable to compete with the international big guns, the firm retains a sound reputation for its domestic corporate advice, notably in the telecoms sector. Our researchers were told that **Alena Cernejová*** *"always does a good job"* and is one of Slovakia's leading lawyers. The firm represented the foreign investor in one of the country's major privatisation transactions. **Clients:** Slovak Telecom.

Csekes, Világi, Drgonec & Partners (3 ptrs, 3 asscs) As our researchers discovered, this is a firm with a reputation as *"good local lawyers."* The firm's strengths lie in privatisation, foreign investment, corporate finance and IP. The client base includes European and US conglomerates. **Erika Csekes*** has a respected regional reputation. Represented Hungarian Mol in their acquisition of Slovnaft as well as US Steel in their acquisition of VSZ, the largest steel mill in Eastern Europe. **Clients:** US Steel; Hungarian Mol.

Altheimer & Gray (2 fee-earners) Another US operation whose Slovakian advice is primarily discharged by a powerful Prague office. The firm advises European and US clients aiming to gain a foothold in Slovakia, largely on privatisations, cross-border M&A and greenfield operations. Represented the Slovak Government on the privatisation of a Slovak bank, and advised Australian insurance company QBE on the acquisition of a Slovak rival. **Clients:** Motorola; BP; QBE.

Freshfields Bruckhaus Deringer (10 fee earners) The merger is expected to pool a formidable pair of client bases, adding Bruckhaus' German blue-chips to Freshfields' international roster. Cross-border M&A should continue to constitute the majority of the team's caseload. The team represented a major German sugar manufacturer on its joint venture with Slovak companies, a leading US software company on all licensing activities in Slovakia, and a US media company in acquiring a majority stake in a Slovak media company. **Clients:** International corporates and financial institutions.

*See leaders' profiles on page 608

Leaders' profiles – Slovakia

CERNEJOVÁ, Alena
Cernejová and Hrbek, Bratislava +421 7 5244 4019

CSEKES, Erika
Csekes, Világi, Drgonec & Partners, Bratislava +421 7 5273 1419

MOGG, Jason
Linklaters (a member firm of Linklaters & Alliance), Bratislava
jason.mogg@linklaters.com
Specialisation: Specialises in advising clients on various types of international finance and investment transactions including privatisation, emerging market equities, Euro-market debt and project finance. Has led teams of foreign and local lawyers providing advice to clients in respect of a wide variety of investment projects in Slovakia as well as elsewhere in the Central and Eastern European region.

PÁLKA, Igor
Allen & Overy, Bratislava +421 7 5441 0202

S

SLOVENIA

Corporate/Commercial

SLOVENIA Leading firms (Corporate/Commercial)
1 Jadek & Pensa
Odvetniska, Druzba, Colja, Rojs & Partners
Selih, Remec & Janezic

Firms are listed alphabetically in each band.

Leading individuals (Corporate/Commercial)
1 COLJA Marjan *Odvetniska, Druzba, Colja, Rojs*
JADEK Srecko *Jadek & Pensa*
SELIH Rudi *Selih, Remec & Janezic*

Individuals are listed alphabetically in each band.

Jadek & Pensa (2 ptrs, 2 asscs) Corporate/commercial and finance law make up the bulk of this *"active"* firm's caseload. Specific matters handled include cross-border M&A, due diligence and agreements drafting. **Srecko Jadek** is a practitioner who our researchers were told has *"a wide knowledge of the law."* The firm advised on Ford's DM100 million acquisition of an insolvent local firm, Metalflex. **Clients:** Société Générale; KPMG; Scania; Electricité de France.

Odvetniska, Druzba, Colja, Rojs & Partners (4 ptrs, 4 asscs) Respected firm which deals with cross-border M&A and has a fine reputation for litigation. The majority of the client base is comprised of international blue-chips. **Marjan Colja** was recommended to our researchers as a *"good and experienced lawyer."* Representing Goodyear in its acquisition of a Slovenian company. Also involved in the establishment of US company Bestfoods in Slovenia. Conducts debt collection work for Hypo Alpe Adria Bank AG. **Clients:** EBRD; Goodyear; Hypo Alpe Adria Bank AG.

Selih, Remec & Janezic (4 ptrs, 2 asscs) **Rudi Selih** is the *"vastly experienced"* head of an otherwise youthful team which advises international clients on IP, M&A and banking. Recent transactions include involvement in the financing of one of Slovenia's GSM operators and the performance of due diligence for the second largest bank in Slovenia. **Clients:** IBM; Philip Morris; McDonald's.

Leaders' profiles – Slovenia

COLJA, Marjan
Odvetniska, Druzba, Colja, Rojs & Partners, Ljubljana +386 1 431 5207

JADEK, Srecko
Jadek & Pensa, Ljubljana +386 1 234 2520

SELIH, Rudi
Selih, Remec & Janezic, Ljubljana +386 1 300 7650

SOUTH AFRICA

Index

The clients' choice

BUSINESS LAWYER OF THE YEAR
TONY BEHRMANN

BUSINESS LAW FIRM OF THE YEAR
WERKSMANS

Tony Behrmann and his firm, Werksmans, swept up both awards. Michael Katz, now with Nedcor Investment Bank, would have won if he had not become ineligible by leaving private practice last year.

For details see page 36.

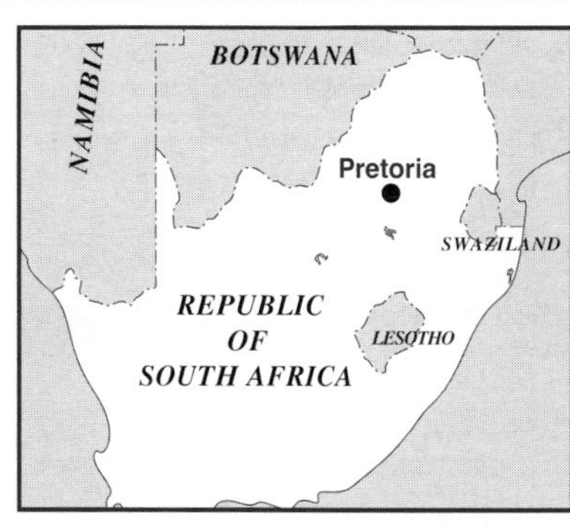

OVERVIEW: The onset of majority rule has meant an expansive renegotiation of the frontiers that delineate South African life – and it is the lawyers who effect the pragmatics of this new Rainbow Nation. Black empowerment initiatives, privatisation, labour relations, and de-regulation of markets, notably in the telecommunications sector, form the backbone of the legal market. Invariably Johannesburg based, the country's financial and banking institutions are world players. The perceived boom in banking stems, inter alia, from the rise of securitisation and loans and we profile the firms leading this market.
With many South African companies choosing to list on the LSE, domestic firms are losing out to London lawyers who take the lion's share. Tony Behrmann of Werksmans remains South Africa's doyen, his widely commended intellect and dynamism ensure his practise is recognised both at home and internationally. Although Edward Nathan's illustrious takeover by Nedcor Investment Bank, provoked much speculation, it is not expected to set a precedent despite the presence of Michael Katz, who remains something of a sui generis practitioner.

Banking & Finance

SOUTH AFRICA Leading firms (Banking & Finance)	
1	Deneys Reitz Inc
	Jowell Glyn & Marais Inc
	Jurgens Bezuidenhout Attorneys
	Webber Wentzel Bowens
	Werksmans
2	Bowman Gilfillan Inc
	Brink Cohen Le Roux & Roodt Inc
3	Bell Dewar & Hall
	Hofmeyr Herbstein Gihwala Inc

Firms are listed alphabetically in each band.

Deneys Reitz Inc (8 ptrs, 7 asscs) Traditionally known as banking experts, the firm is said by competitors to be *"getting the deals,"* and has *"powerful depth"* on export credit transactions, private structured finance deals, refinancing and restructuring, asset finance and project finance. The *"meticulous"* **Kevin Cron*** is respected for his expertise in structured finance. The firm acted for Rand Merchant Bank, Africa Merchant Bank and BOE on the financing of the Louis Trichardt Private Prison project, valued at £150 million. Also represented JP Morgan on the R1.2 billion Standard Bank bond issue, and the Kiwane Bond issue, worth R450 million. **Clients:** Rand Merchant Bank; BOE Bank; Coronation; Standard Bank; Investec Bank; JP Morgan; ING Baring; Morgan Stanley; Deutsche Bank; Société Générale; Citibank.

Jowell Glyn & Marais Inc (2 ptrs, 2 asscs) *"Strong firm"* with particular expertise in bank regulatory work, project finance and tax-based lending, and considered to be the market leader for structured finance. Growth areas include syndicated loans and export credit facility loans, typically advising the lenders. The experienced **Richard Glyn*** is seen as *"a genuine market leader."*

The team advised the consortium of lenders, headed by Rand Merchant Bank, on the N4 Toll road project, and has also handled project finance work for the Cobalt Smelting Plant. **Clients:** Absa Bank; Standard Bank; Ned Bank; Rand Merchant Bank; Rand Investment Bank; Imperial Bank; Investec Bank; Bank of America.

Jurgens Bezuidenhout Attorneys (2 ptrs, 1 assc) Seen to have *"a great following among the banks,"* our researchers discovered the firm has a reputation for producing the firm has a reputation for producing *"great technicians."* The *"intelligent"* **Jurgens Bezuidenhout*** is the stand-out figure of a team which has acknowledged capital markets expertise.

The firm advised the managers, JP Morgan and SCMB, on the listing of bonds by the Development Bank of South Africa, a transaction worth R1 billion, and also acted for the issuer, Infrastructure Finance Corporation, on its Domestic Medium Term Note Programme, worth R5 billion. **Clients:** JP Morgan; Deutsche Bank; Standard Corp. Merchant Bank; BOE; BNP Paribas; South African Futures Exchange; CORPCAPITAL Bank; Development Bank of South Africa.

Webber Wentzel Bowens (7 ptrs, 7 asscs) *"Ubiquitous"* group with an outstanding reputation for syndicated loans, securitisations, bond issues and project finance. A formidable international client base has led to an ability to act on the big-ticket cross-border deal, as when the firm advised on the financing of a R15 billion deal for Hawk and Gripen Aircraft. *"Confident draftsman"* **Stephen Meltzer*** is a respected and experienced practi-

*See leaders' profiles on pages 612-613

Leading individuals (Banking & Finance)
1 **BEZUIDENHOUT Jurgens** *Jurgens Bezuidenhout*
CRON Kevin *Deneys Reitz Inc*
GLYN Richard *Jowell Glyn & Marais Inc*
2 **BRINK Johan** *Brink Cohen Le Roux & Roodt Inc*
MELTZER Stephen *Webber Wentzel Bowens*
SCHLOSBERG Jonathan *Bowman Gilfillan Inc*
STEIN Carl *Werksmans*
Up-and-coming individuals
BAILLIE Brigitte *Webber Wentzel Bowens*
Individuals are listed alphabetically in each band.

tioner, while the emerging **Brigitte Baillie*** was seen by our interviewees as a *"rising star."*

Its strong links with international investment banks has enabled the firm to advise on a range of MTN programmes. Project finance is another forte, and the team acted on the Bakwena Platinum Corridor, a deal valued at R2.7 billion. Also represented First Rand Bank in establishing the e-commerce venture 'e-Bucks.' **Clients:** Merrill Lynch, Citibank; First Rand; Investec Bank; BOE Bank; Barclays Bank.

Werksmans (6 ptrs, 12 asscs) Although more renowned for its corporate strength, the firm's financial client base also keeps it clearly among the front-runners for banking advice. Securitisation, project finance and acquisition finance are key elements of the caseload, and the versatile **Carl Stein*** is the firm's best-known name in this area. He led the team advising on the securitisation of Telkom's properties, at R2.5 billion, the largest in South African history. The firm was also involved in one of the biggest project finance deals ever – the R2.1 billion toll highway deal between the South African Road Agency (SANRA) and the N3 Toll concession. **Clients:** Investec Bank; Standard Bank; Merrill Lynch; Liberty Life; Fedsure Group Ltd; Sage Group; Telkom; AMBAC International; SANRA; CGU International.

Bowman Gilfillan Inc (4 ptrs, 3 asscs) *"Consistent performers,"* the firm is well regarded for its work both at home and abroad. The finance group is especially acclaimed for its work on syndicated loans and derivatives. Considered to be a *"versatile strategist,"* **Jonathan Schlosberg*** is a respected practitioner.

The firm advised Standard Bank and African Merchant Bank on the project financing of the Louis Trichardt Prison Project, and advised Standard Bank on the issue of bonds on the Johannesburg Stock Exchange. **Clients:** Chase Manhattan; Credit Suisse; Donaldson Lufkin Jerette; Dresdner Bank; Barclays Capital; Standard Bank Group.

Brink Cohen Le Roux & Roodt Inc (3 ptrs, 8 asscs) *"Expert on banking products,"* the firm specialises in structured finance, loan syndication, commercial paper issues, securitisation, and repurchase agreements. Among a respected team, **Johan Brink*** is *"outstanding."* He represented TCTA (Trans Caledon Tunnel Authority) and KOBWA (Komati Basin Water Authority) on the Lesotho Highlands Water Project and Komati project respectively. The firm also advised SASOL on its MTN programme. **Clients:** SASOL; Telkom; TCTA; KOBWA; Metlife; Investec Bank; Genbel Securities; Nomura; Goldman Sachs; Merrill Lynch; Securities Lending Forum.

Bell Dewar & Hall (5 ptrs, 10 asscs) The firm created a specialist banking division in 1993 to concentrate on security documentation, negotiable instruments, letters of credit, commercial paper agreements and recovery work. Respected, although not considered to possess the depth of the market leaders, the team advises a clientele which includes a number of South African blue-chip financial institutions.

The firm acted for the arrangers of the R2.7 billion Bakwena Platinum Highway, and represented the sponsors of the Maputo Corridor Toll Road between South Africa and Mozambique – a deal worth R2 billion. **Clients:** Standard Bank; Nedcor Bank; Nedcor Investment Bank; Investec Bank; ABSA Bank; Basil Read; Stocks & Stocks; Bouygues; Saur International.

Hofmeyr Herbstein Gihwala Inc Established firm, which, although not considered by competitors to have the profile of previous years, still has a name for structured finance, credit derivatives and syndicated loans. Our researchers discovered the team is renowned for representing the principal Afrikaans finance houses. Acted on a R500 million bond securitisation scheme for Kiwane Capital holdings. Recently advised the conversion of 23% of Transnet's stake in MTN into M-Cell shares and sale of 75 million shares in M-Cell to Johnnic Communications for R2475 billion. **Clients:** Standard Bank.

Corporate/M&A

Bowman Gilfillan Inc (50 ptrs, 20 asscs) Renowned for international work, this *"competent and efficient"* firm has *"always been among the leaders."* Now moving away from public offerings to focus on capital markets and privatisation advice, the team is still felt to possess one of the strongest clienteles in the country, notably among financial institutions and mining companies. *"Sound academic"* **Charles Valkin*** is rated as one of South Africa's premier practitioners, and receives valuable support from the *"highly skilled"* **Jonathan Schlosberg***.

In the *"transaction of the year,"* the firm successfully defended STANBIC from the largest hostile take-over bid in South African history. Other highlight transactions of the past year have included the successful acquisition of PG Glass SA by the Belgian company D'ieteren, and the privatisations of Spoornet (rail division of Transnet) and special risk insurance company Sasria Ltd. **Clients:** Morgan Stanley; Merrill Lynch; Credit Suisse First Boston; Barclays Capital; Chase Manhattan.

Werksmans (40 ptrs, 45 asscs) This *"great name in commercial law"* is a specialist in international M&A and securitisation. *"A loyal clientele"* of local blue-chips and multi-nationals ensure that the firm is *"seen all the time."*

"Big league" senior partner **Tony Behrmann*** is a corporate legend in South Africa and is *"tough, fair and gets the deals done."* He was involved in the listing of South African Breweries on the London Stock Exchange, a deal worth R6 billion. **Vaughn Harrison***, respected for his *"professional approach,"* and *"solid deal maker"* **Carl Stein*** have also won widespread market acclaim. The latter assisted Mvelaphanda Platinum on their acquisition of a stake in Northam Platinum from Anglo American Platinum worth R410 million, one of the biggest 'black empowerment' deals of the year. The firm advised Swissair on its successful bid to acquire 20% of South African Airways and represented Lonmin Ltd, on its $2.5 billion disposal of shareholdings in JSE listed companies Duiker and Tweefontein. **Clients:** South African Breweries, Fedsure Holdings, BIDVEST Group, Liberty Life Holdings, Saffi, TELCOM.

SOUTH AFRICA
Leading firms
(Corporate/Mergers & Acquisitions)

Band	Firm
1	Bowman Gilfillan Inc
	Werksmans
2	Deneys Reitz Inc
	Webber Wentzel Bowens
3	Brink Cohen Le Roux & Roodt Inc
	Cliffe Dekker Fuller Moore Inc
	Jowell Glyn & Marais Inc
	Sonnenberg Hoffmann & Galombik
4	Bell Dewar & Hall
	Hofmeyr Herbstein Gihwala Inc
5	Fluxman Rabinowitz – Raphaely Weiner
	Maponya Inc

Firms are listed alphabetically in each band.

Leading individuals
(Corporate/Mergers & Acquisitions)

Band	Individual
1	**BEHRMANN Tony** *Werksmans*
	CRON Kevin *Deneys Reitz Inc*
	VALKIN Charles *Bowman Gilfillan Inc*
2	**BRINK Johan** *Brink Cohen Le Roux & Roodt Inc*
	EWING Chris *Cliffe Dekker Fuller Moore Inc*
	HARRISON Vaughn *Werksmans*
	ROODT Johan *Brink Cohen Le Roux & Roodt Inc*
	SCHLOSBERG Jonathan *Bowman Gilfillan Inc*
	SOUTHEY Ed *Webber Wentzel Bowens*
	STEIN Carl *Werksmans*

Individuals are listed alphabetically in each band.

Deneys Reitz Inc (63 ptrs, 70 asscs) With offices in Johannesburg, Durban and Cape Town, this *"long-established firm"* is *"a major force in corporate finance."* While retaining its clients in the mining and natural resources industries, the firm is now regarded as one of the country's leaders in the insurance market. *"Prominent individual"* **Kevin Cron*** is considered to be the *"major contributor"* to the firm's success, although there is some suggestion that beneath him *"the quality is not uniform."*

A highlight of the year was representing Ethos Private Equity on the acquisition by a consortium of Waco International – the largest private equity leveraged buyout in South African corporate history. The team also acted for JP Morgan on the Standard Bank bond issue, and Anglo American Platinum on the sale of interests in Northam platinum to Mvelaphanda Platinum. **Clients:** First Rand Bank; BOE Bank; De Beers; Anglovaal Mining; Anglovaal Industries; Anglo American Platinum; Western Areas; Mozal; JP Morgan; Deutsche Bank; Ethos Private Equity.

Webber Wentzel Bowens (30 ptrs, 30 asscs) One of the largest firms in South Africa, it is noted for the diversity of its client base, although its clients in the pharmaceuticals and mining industries are particularly eye-catching. The team is said to possess astute commercial lawyers, chief among them the *"reliable"* **Ed Southey***, who is also pre-eminent in the nascent competition sector.

The firm represented LPA on its acquisition by Avenge, a deal worth R1.5 billion, and was counsel to Genbel Securities on its R5 billion take-over by Sanlam. Other major recent deals include advising on the £5.5 billion listing of Dimension Data on the London Stock Exchange, and representing Anglo American Corporation and Billiton on the establishment and sale of Newcoal Company to Eyesizwe Coal. **Clients:** Anglo American; De Beers; Johnick; M-net; GlaxoWellcome; Smithkline Beecham; Pfizer.

Brink Cohen Le Roux & Roodt Inc (8ptrs, 3asscs) Respected firm founded eight years ago by partners from Bowman Gilfillan. The team's principal focus is cross-border M&A and corporate finance, with niche strength in mining and resources. Senior partner **Johan Brink*** *"knows how to manage a transaction"* while **Johan Roodt*** is seen by competition as a *"confident, forceful corporate lawyer."* The stand-out deal of the past year was the firm's involvement on the $24 billion merger of Franco Nevada and Goldfields. **Clients:** Franco Nevada; Comparex.

Cliffe Dekker Fuller Moore Inc (24 ptrs, 8 asscs) Based in Johannesburg and Cape Town, this firm has branched out from its traditional transactional base in the mining industry to increase its private equity and LBO work. **Chris Ewing***, *"a sound M&A practitioner,"* is one of the leading names in Cape Town, and advised Malback on the disposal of its subsidiary companies. The firm acts for a mixture of domestic and international concerns, advising Harmony Gold Mining Co on the successful acquisition of Kandfontein Estates, and the Coca-Cola Company and its subsidiaries on the acquisition of Cadbury Schweppes (South Africa), a transaction valued at R1.5 billion. Also advised Benco on its R430 million acquisition by Transhex. **Clients:** Malback; Coca Cola; Rand Merchant Bank; Standard Corporate; NedBank; ABN AMRO; Deutsche Bank; Harmony Goldming Co; G-Tech.

Jowell Glyn & Marais Inc (8 ptrs, 7 asscs) Part of a tripartite agreement with leading black firm Canca Inc and prolific international player CMS Cameron McKenna, the organisation is seen as a niche firm with the ability to do the big-ticket deals. Although lacking the resources of some of the market leaders, the strength of the firm's domestic financial institution client base is beyond dispute. Involved in the high-profile proposed merger between Metropolitan and client Sanlam, the firm also acted on Sanlam's buy-back of its asset management company Grenbel Securities. Represented Anglovaal Mining on the sale of its interests in Venetia, South Africa's biggest diamond mine, to De Beers. **Clients:** Sanlam; PQ Africa (Comparex); Investec Bank; South African Bank; Nedcor Bank; Anglovaal Goldmining; Engen.

Sonnenberg Hoffmann & Galombik (24 ptrs, 29 asscs) Based in the Cape, and seen as one of the region's premier organisations, the firm was dealt a blow by the departure of David Nurek to an in-house position at Investec Bank. However, peers and clients regard this as *"only a short-term reverse; the show will go on."*

The firm remains a force on big-ticket transactions as exemplified by its advice on the R4 billion merger between Distillers Corp and SFW. Also advised on the listing of Allan Gray Property Investments on the JSE, and the buy-out of Siphumelele Investment. **Clients:** Pick n Pay; Distillers Corporation/SFW; Woolworths; BP (Southern Africa); Clicks; Foschini; BOE; Trencor; Seardel; Golden Arrow Bus Services.

Bell Dewar & Hall (24 ptrs, 36 asscs) Although historically a leader in the media sector, the firm is now also a player in financial services. The firm recently joined forces with PricewaterhouseCoopers and *"it seems to be working for them."* A *"useful firm, full of integrity,"* it advised SAFCOL on a recent acquisition worth R500 million. **Clients:** Caltex; Lonrho Mining; S.A. Breweries; Southern Life Assurance; Investec Bank; Standard Bank; ABSA Bank; NEDCOR; Hollard Insurance; Volvo; McDonalds; Smithkline Beecham; Glaxo Wellcome; Johnson & Johnson; Renault.

Hofmeyr Herbstein & Gihwala Inc (8 ptrs, 7 asscs) The firm has undergone a troubled year, with merger being swiftly followed by de-merger, and a market impression that this is an organisation which *"currently lacks strategy."* However, some see the firm as the only genuinely successful multi-cultural operation, insisting that *"given time, they'll sort it out."* Possessing niche strengths in transport and sport, the firm represented Avis SA on the company's R300 million acquisition of Avis Sweden and Avis Norway. Also advised on the restructuring of the Rembrandt group. **Clients:** Placer Dome South Africa (propriety); Airports Company of South Africa; United Cricket Board of South Africa; South African Football Assoc; AVIS SA; Rembrandt; TransNet; SASOL; Vodacom.

*See leaders' profiles on pages 612-613

Fluxman Rabinowitz – Raphaely Weiner Inc (16 ptrs, 15 asscs) Although *"not yet in the big league,"* the firm is considered to have *"real commercial acumen,"* acting for a variety of clients on medium-ticket transactions. The group is best known for corporate work on behalf of publicly listed companies and international private trusts. Represented METCASH in a constitutional case against the South African government's Receiver of Revenues. **Clients:** PSG Bank; Caxton Publishers; Tiger Wheels; Accord Technologies; Tiger Oats.

Maponya Inc (9 ptrs, 8 asscs) Respected leading black firm, based in Pretoria, which is said to *"do a lot of government work."* The firm has associations with Linklaters in London and Webber Wentzel Bowen in South Africa. Known for privatisations and M&A advice, the team has *"important government contacts"* and was involved in the privatisation of Gateway Airport and TransNet's selling of Protekon. Represented the Coega Development Corporation (CDC) on the proposed development of an industrial zone at Port Elizabeth harbour, and advised Philani Health Care Group on acquisitions worth R120 million. **Clients:** South African government; Parastatals; TransNet; Protekon; Philani Health Care.

S

Leaders' profiles – South Africa

BAILLIE, Brigitte
Webber Wentzel Bowens, Johannesburg
+27 11 240 5000
brigette@wwb.co.za
Recommended in Banking & Finance
Specialisation: Partner in Corporate Department. Main areas of work are financing transactions (limited recourse/project financing, public-private partnerships/infrastructure financing, structured finance and corporate financing, including black empowerment financing) and public-private partnerships. Acted for the following: the lenders (ABSA Bank and Investec Bank) on the Mangaung Maximum Security Prison, South Africa's first privately designed, constructed, operated, maintained and financed prison; the lenders (ABSA Bank Limited, BOE Bank Limited and Genbel Securities Limited) on the financing of the GrandWest Casino; the Bakwena Platinum Corridor Consortium and Concessionaire on the N1 and N4 Platinum Highway toll road; Sun International (South Africa) and Emfuleni on the financing of the Boardwalk casino. Has also acted in a number of mergers and acquisitions in various sectors and performed due diligence investigations.
Prof. Memberships: Law Society of the Transvaal; Law Society of the Cape of Good Hope.
Publications: Euromoney Project & Infrastructure Directory 2001; PFI Focus May 2000.
Career: 1992/3 articles of clerkship – *Adams & Adams*, Intellectual Property Department; 1994 – *Adams & Adams*, Intellectual Property Department; 1995 – *Webber Wentzel Bowens*, Intellectual Property Department; 1996 – *Webber Wentzel Bowens*, Corporate Department; March 1997 – associate, *Webber Wentzel Bowens*, Corporate Department; March 1999 – partner, *Webber Wentzel Bowens*, Corporate Department.
Personal: BA LLB (UCT); LLM (Commercial and Corporate) (London); LLM (Tax) (Wits). Interests: reading, entertaining, travel and collecting African art. Unmarried.

BEHRMANN, Tony
Werksmans, Johannesburg +27 11 488 0104
abehrmann@werksmans.co.az
Recommended in Corporate/M&A
Specialisation: Senior partner at *Werksmans*, leads the firm's mergers and aquisitions team consisting of 10 partners and 8 associates. Has played a major role in many substantial mergers and aquisition transactions (particularly corporate finance aspects) both nationally and internationally and has represented many major groups.
Prof. Memberships: Director of a number of public companies listed on the Johannesburg Stock Exchange and is principally engaged in the negotiation and structuring of transactions.
Career: Has been a practising attorney for 35 years and became a senior partner of the firm in 1992.

BEZUIDENHOUT, Jurgens
Jurgens Bezuidenhout Attorneys, Parktown
+27 11 645 6040
Recommended in Banking & Finance

BRINK, Johan
Brink Cohen Le Roux & Roodt Inc, Johannesburg
+27 11 242 8000
jlbrink@bclr.com
Recommended in Banking & Finance, Corporate/M&A
Specialisation: Represents major listed companies in takeovers, mergers, acquisitions and group reorganisations and acts for multinationals in structuring their South African operations and represents them on local boards of directors. Recently advised the British Land Company plc on the acquisition of Liberty Life plc for £515 million.
Prof. Memberships: Interlaw (board member), IBA, Transvaal Law Society.
Publications: Co-author of the title 'Companies' in Butterworths' 'The Law of South Africa' (LAWSA).
Career: BCom (Pretoria) LLB (South Africa) LLM (LSE, London), H Dip Tax Law (Witwatersrand). Admitted as an attorney in 1979. Became partner at *Bowman Gilfillan* in Johannesburg in 1983. Co-founded *Brink Cohen le Roux & Roodt* Inc. in 1993.
Personal: Born 16 March 1953. Leisure interests include art, literature, wildlife and sport. Lives in Sandton, Johannesburg.

CRON, Kevin
Deneys Reitz Inc, Sandton +27 11 685 8500
Recommended in Banking & Finance, Corporate/M&A

EWING, Chris
Cliffe Dekker Fuller Moore Inc, Benmore
+27 11 290 7000
ewing@cdfm.co.za
Recommended in Corporate/M&A
Specialisation: Partner in the Corporate Department. Key specialisation areas are mergers and acquisitions and the formation and initial structuring of new business entities with particular emphasis on joint ventures. Has advised many of South Africa's major corporations and has handled various sorts of undertakings for overseas clients. Advised The Coca-Cola Corporation on its original disinvestment from South Africa and instituted the structures necessary for the re-investment in South Africa. Responsible for the listing on the Johannesburg Stock Exchange for the first company listed on the 'Venture Capital' market. Member of the legal team responsible for the listing on The Johannesburg Stock Exchange of the first company listed in the Mining Exploration sector of the Exchange. Partner in charge of the legal team responsible for the disposal by various major South African companies of their interest in Argus Newspapers Limited, and the acquisition of such interests by the Independent Newspaper Group of Ireland. Acted as legal advisor to the management teams in a number of major leveraged buyout transactions financed by local banks as a result of the recommendations made by the banks to the management team in regard to the appointment of legal advisors.

GLYN, Richard
Jowell Glyn & Marais Inc, Benmore
+27 11 784 4200
Recommended in Banking & Finance

HARRISON, Vaughn
Werksmans, Johannesburg +27 11 488 0131
vharrison@werksmans.co.za
Recommended in Corporate/M&A
Specialisation: Has extensive experience in corporate and commercial matters and as regards mergers and acquisitions and privatisation. Acts primarily for multi-nationals and overseas clients, and law firms requiring legal assistance in South and Southern Africa.
Prof. Memberships: Member of the International Bar Association and Transvaal Law Society and cur-

rently sits on the Disciplinary Committee of the Transvaal Law Society. Appointed by the Minister of Finance for a period of 5 years to the panel of Chairmen of the Special Board for the hearing of Income Tax Appeals, and appointed by the Law Society of the Transvaal to its Competition Law Committee.

Publications: Has written articles for publication including those in the International Law Review and articles recently published in respect of exchange control, telecommunications, privatisation, mining and aviation law.

Career: BA, LLB from the University of Stellenbosch and the Higher Diploma in Tax Law from the University of Witwatersrand. Joined *Werksmans* in 1978 and has been a partner since 1983. Has attended numerous, local and international conferences and presented papers on a wide-range of issues, including corporate/commercial matters, competition law, changes to company law, mergers and acquisitions, exchange control, mining and environmental matters. The aforegoing includes participating in a Euromoney conference, making a presentation on mergers and acquisitions to clients of a London firm of solicitors, co-presenting a seminar on Competition Law with *Clifford Chance*, and speaking at a conference on international joint ventures held in Paris and jointly organised by the IBA and UIA.

MELTZER, Stephen
Webber Wentzel Bowens, Johannesburg
+27 11 240 5000
Recommended in Banking & Finance

ROODT, Johan
Brink Cohen Le Roux & Roodt Inc, Johannesburg
+27 11 242 8000
jaroodt@bclr.com
Recommended in Corporate/M&A

Specialisation: Corporate law, including mergers, takeovers and acquisitions and leveraged buy-outs. Emphasis on cross-border transactions. Also involved in banking and finance, including specialised share and debt issues, financial instruments and asset securitisation. Recognised as an expert on energy and resources law.

Prof. Memberships: Council member, Section on Energy and Resources Law, International Bar Association.

Career: Admitted to practice in 1980. Director of *Bowman Gilfillan Hayman Godfrey* 1983 – 1993. Founding member of *Brink Cohen, Le Roux & Roodt* established in 1993.

Personal: Born 8 May 1953. Attended Pretoria University and University of South Africa. Leisure interests: equestrian.

SCHLOSBERG, Jonathan
Bowman Gilfillan Inc, Johannesburg
+27 11 881 9807
j.schlosberg@bowman.co.za
Recommended in Banking & Finance, Corporate/M&A

Specialisation: Principal areas of practice are corporate finance, mergers and acquisitions, and capital markets. Particular expertise lies in the structuring of complex corporate transactions for listed and unlisted companies, advising on mergers and acquisitions take-over bids and bid defences, capital market transactions (equity and debt, including local and international share and bond issues), unbundling transactions, group and corporate re-organisations and employee share incentive schemes. Representative experience includes being the lead partner or team member in most of the largest corporate transactions over the last five years in which the firm acted as advisors, including the successful hostile take-over of a listed mining company, the merger resulting in the largest coal producer in the world; the unbundling of the then largest industrial conglomerate in South Africa; the establishment of the third largest gold mining company in the country; and advising on a number of take-overs and mergers involving companies and groups in the IT, industrial and engineering sectors. Is the lead partner in a major water-related project finance transaction. Also led the firm's team which advised one of the bidders in the privatisation for the government owned forestry corporation.

Prof. Memberships: A member of the Board of Trustees of AIESEC. A former council member of the Johannesburg Attorneys Association and the Liason sub-committee between Attorneys and the Registrar of Companies. Member of the Law Society of the Transvaal.

Career: B. Comm, LLB, H Dip Tax Law (University of the Witwatersrand). Born 1953. Graduated 1976. Articles 1977/8. Admitted attorney 1979; Partner 1979. Manager of Corporate, Commercial and Financial Services Department 1993 - 1995 and again since November 2000. Serves on the firm's Executive Committee.

SOUTHEY, Ed
Webber Wentzel Bowens, Johannesburg
+27 11 240 5000
patk@wwb.co.za
Recommended in Corporate/M&A

Specialisation: Practises in the field of corporate law, mergers and acquisitions and competition law and has had a close association with the organised accountancy profession for 35 years.

Career: Joined *WWB* as an articled clerk in 1965 and has been with the firm since. Member of the Council of the Law Society of the Transvaal from 1980 to 1995; acted as president from 1985-1986. Elected as president in 1991 of the Association of law Societies of the Republic of South Africa. In 1993 recipient of the award for meritorious service to the legal profession by the Association of Law Societies.

STEIN, Carl
Werksmans, Johannesburg +27 11 488 0166
cstein@werksmans.co.za
Recommended in Banking & Finance, Corporate/M&A

Specialisation: Specialises in South African taxation, international taxation, off-shore commercial structuring, corporate law, stock exchange transactions, corporate structuring, personal financial structuring and negotiating, and structuring commerical transactions. Has given seminars and conducted workshops on topics including business in South Africa, business entities, acquisitions of businesses, companies and close corporation, and share incentive schemes.

Publications: Author of numerous articles for *Werksmans*' International Werks, Tax Werks, Law Werks, and other local and international publications such as Finance Week and Business Day.

Career: Holds the degrees B.Com, LLB, H.Dip Tax Law (Wits). Has been a partner in the corporate/commercial department of *Werksmans* since 1984.

VALKIN, Charles
Bowman Gilfillan Inc, Johannesburg
+27 11 883 4505
c.valkin@bowman.co.za
Recommended in Corporate/M&A

Specialisation: The most senior corporate lawyer in *Bowman Gilfillan Inc.* and one of the leading practitioners in his field in South Africa. Principal areas of practice are corporate finance, banking finance, commercial law and tax. Specialises in M&A transactions including JSE listed corporations and cross-border transactions. Particular expertise lies in advising on complex legal structures and the drafting of appropriate documentation. Representative experience includes leading the firm's team in the privatisation of the state-owned telecommunications company, the formation of one of the largest gold companies in the world, a bid by a leading international airport operator on the privatisation of the Airport Company and advising a leading electronics corporation in its recent successful High Court challenge of a ruling by the Securities Regulation Panel.

Prof. Memberships: Served as a past Chairman of the continuing Legal Education Programme of the Association of the Law Society of South Africa and a past member the Law Society of the Transvaal.

Career: Serves on *Bowman Gilfillan Inc's* executive committee.

S

SOUTH KOREA

Index

OVERVIEW: The present government is widely viewed as progressive, continuing to bring about reform and restructuring, while the recent North Korean detente could well trigger greater activity in the Asia Pacific as a whole. Persistent economic anxiety has seen an upturn in M&A, restructuring and insolvency work. Increasing interest from foreign firms lobbying to liberalise the legal market is a clear indication of Korea's long term lure. In the interim, local firms are experiencing bumper times exploiting a market high on transactions and low on lawyers.

S

Corporate/Commercial: Local Firms

SOUTH KOREA Leading firms (Corporate/Commercial)
1 Bae, Kim & Lee
Kim & Chang
Shin & Kim
2 Lee & Ko
3 Hwang Mok Park & Jin
Kim, Shin & Yu
Woo, Yun, Kang, Jeong & Han
4 Yoon & Partners

Firms are listed alphabetically in each band.

Leading individuals (Corporate/Commercial)
1 **JUNG Kyung Taek** *Kim & Chang*
LEE Moon Sung *Lee & Ko*
SHIN Hi Taek *Kim & Chang*
2 **KIM Soo Chang** *Lee & Ko*
KIM Doo Sik *Shin & Kim*
LEE Keun Byung *Bae, Kim & Lee*
PARK Joon *Kim & Chang*
PARK Sang Il *Hwang Mok Park & Jin*
3 **CHOI Dong Shik** *Kim & Chang*
CHOI Dyoung Seon *Shin & Kim*
KANG Hee Chul *Woo, Yun, Kang, Jeong & Han*
OH Yong Suk *Bae, Kim & Lee*

Individuals are listed alphabetically in each band.

Bae, Kim & Lee (17 ptrs, 21 asscs) Formerly recognised as litigation specialists, the firm's pronounced expansion in the corporate sector has led to greater visibility in major transactions and an improved foreign client base. A comprehensive transactional service is provided, with particular specialisation in telecoms and e-commerce, as a result of the firm's location within Seoul's 'Silicon Valley.' Growing in size, the team was recommended to researchers for its *"modern, Western way of doing business."*

Credited with having driven the practice forward is the *"excellent"* **Keun Byung Lee***, who receives sound support from the *"wholly dependable"* **Yong Suk Oh***. The team represented Citycorp Venture Capital Group on the sale of Daewoo Telecom, and advised Samsung Motors on its proposed sale to Renault. **Clients:** KEPCO; Tesco; Samsung; Korean Government.

Kim & Chang (15 ptrs, 50 asscs) The largest firm in South Korea is still expanding, and represents *"everybody's primary competitor."* With an international emphasis, the firm is considered by clients to be *"the only one-stop commercial shop for the foreign investor,"* and also acts as advisor to the government.

"Internally well organised," a strong team contains many of the country's leading lawyers, including **Hi Taek Shin***, who possesses *"a rare combination of technical expertise and client handling skills,"* **Kyung Taek Jung***, *"a ruthlessly effective transactional lawyer,"* and **Dong Shik Choi***, respected by peers for his technical skills. On the banking and securities side, **Joon Park*** is *"highly respected and utterly reliable."* The firm represented Renault on its acquisition of Samsung, and Otis on its $800 million purchase of LEIS elevators. **Clients:** GM; Motorola; Cisco; Yahoo!; Renault; BT.

Shin & Kim (13 ptrs, 50 asscs) Focusing increasingly on M&A and private equity investment in Korea the firm has been noted by the market for its visibility on a high proportion of the country's leading corporate transactions. Clients rate the team above all for its individual talent, with some claiming that the firm has *"many of the best lawyers in the country."* These include the *"impressive and industrious"* **Dyoung Seon Choi***, and the *"eminently trustworthy and reliable"* **Doo Sik Kim***. Highlights this year have included advising on AIG's $1 billion investment into Hyundai Securities and Investment Trust, and representing Fiat on the projected purchase of Daewoo Motors. **Clients:** LG Group; Citibank; Hyundai; Fiat.

Lee & Ko (7 ptrs, 23 asscs) A full service firm, which has its strongest reputation for M&A and corporate restructuring, notably in the e-commerce sector. Best known for its traditional relationship with Korean giant the Hanjin Group, the team also advises a varied international clientele.

The experienced **Moon Sung Lee*** is *"an ultimate professional, who finds no task beneath him,"* while **Soo Chang Kim*** was commended to our researchers as *"a star of the firm in M&A and financing."* The firm acted for Ford on its proposed acquisition of Daewoo; and advised the Korean Ministry of Defence on its dispute with Lockheed. **Clients:** Ford; Microsoft; Hanil Bank; Siemens; British Oxygen.

Hwang Mok Park & Jin (5 ptrs, 19 asscs) Next in size to the country's 'big four', the firm's enhanced reputation has been reflected by a recent increase in numbers and a movement to more spacious premises. Praised to researchers for its expansionist policy, the firm's Pusan office was the first branch of a law firm to be opened outside Seoul. Size has not compromised quality, as the market admiringly confirms that the team *"continues to hit the mark in satisfying clients."*

The firm specialises in cross-border M&A, international joint ventures and structured finance for its international client roster. Heading the team is **Sang Il Park***, *"an experienced practitioner with a commercial eye."* The firm advised FK Enron on the $1.5 billion acquisition of Choongnam City Gas, and Korean Airspace Industries on its $2 billion foreign equity investment. **Clients:** Daewoo; Samsung; Dow Chemical; Exxon Mobil; Citibank, Salomon Smith Barney.

Kim Shin & Yu (7 ptrs, 20 asscs) One of the oldest firms in Korea is said to have a *"long history in the international market."* Particularly active in M&A, it possesses a strong international client base and acted on behalf of foreign investors in the $500 million acquisition of Hyundai Electronics. Its corporate head Jin Ouk Kim is now less active, having moved to a more managerial role, but is recognised as having been a pioneer in his field. **Clients:** Goldman Sachs; Bank of America; Siemens; Glaxo Wellcome.

Woo, Yun, Kang, Jeong & Han (8 ptrs, 17 asscs) A smaller firm, which is acknowledged by competitors to be *"growing rapidly."* Prominent for its advice on the restructuring of KEPCO, including the first privatisation of power plants in Korea, the firm has subsequently acquired a higher profile in M&A and corporate restructuring.

"Increasingly active in the market," corporate specialist **Hee Chul Kang*** is highly respected by his contemporaries. The firm represented Hyundai Electronics on its $2.3 billion acquisition of LG Semiconductor. **Clients:** Hyundai SK; Samsung; SK Telecom; DaimlerChrysler; Mastercard.

Yoon & Partners Noticeably gaining in stature, this small firm has substantially increased its foreign client portfolio over the last year. Benefiting from a non-exclusive association with Baker & McKenzie, the firm was especially recommended to researchers for M&A and derivatives expertise. The firm also has niche ability on anti-trust matters, advising on the drafting of the country's competition legislation. **Clients:** BAT; IBM.

S

Corporate/Commercial: Foreign Firms

SOUTH KOREA: Foreign Firms Leading firms (Corporate/Commercial)	
1	Cleary, Gottlieb, Steen & Hamilton
	Clifford Chance
	Milbank, Tweed, Hadley & McCloy
	Shearman & Sterling
	White & Case LLP
2	Allen & Overy
	Simpson Thacher & Bartlett
3	Freehills
	Freshfields Bruckhaus Deringer

Firms are listed alphabetically in each band.

Leading individuals (Corporate/Commercial)	
1	HAN Jinduk *Cleary, Gottlieb, Steen & Hamilton*
	KIM Young Joon *Milbank, Tweed*
	YOON Eric *White & Case LLP*
2	KANG Hyo Young *Allen & Overy*
	O'BRIEN Timothy *Coudert Brothers*
	TURNER Edward *Shearman & Sterling*
	WALKER James *Clifford Chance*
Up-and-coming individuals	
	PARK Jin-Hyuk *Simpson Thacher & Bartlett*

Individuals are listed alphabetically in each band.

Cleary, Gottlieb, Steen & Hamilton (Hong Kong) (5 ptrs, 10 asscs) This *"first-rate firm with high quality lawyers"* is particularly active in corporate restructuring and securities. Researchers were told that the team is *"known for its integrity,"* a remark which applies equally to the *"focused, hard-working and eminent"* **Jinduk Han***. Noted for its work representing Korean creditors in the sell-off of Daewoo, it has also acted for the Carlyle Group and JP Morgan over their $400 million investment in KorAm Bank. **Clients:** Korea Telecom; Republic of Korea; Samsung; Pohang Iron & Steel; Goldman Sachs; LG Group; Hyundai; The Korea Development Bank.

Clifford Chance (Hong Kong) (1 ptr, 4 asscs) Largely active on behalf of US and European corporates and investment banks, the firm is noted for its banking practice and strong M&A team, buttressed by the presence of four Korean lawyers. *"Instrumental in driving the Korean practice forward"* is the *"financially astute"* **James Walker*** who is currently lobbying hard for the liberalisation of the Korean legal market. Major deals include acting for Prudential regarding its investment in CJ Investment Trusts and Securities. Also acted as underwriter's counsel for Korea Thrunet, the first Korean company to directly list its shares in the US. **Clients:** Korea Development Bank; Volvo; Hanil Bank; FIMAT; Citicorp International; Goldman Sachs.

Milbank, Tweed, Hadley & McCloy (Tokyo) (3 ptrs, 4 asscs) A *"top-notch, highly industrious firm,"* covering M&A, securitisation, and asset finance. At the centre of operations, **Young Joon Kim*** is a noted banking and leasing expert, with *"a superb pedigree,"* who is recommended by peers for his *"impressive negotiating skills."*

The firm has advised on strategic investments in more than a dozen Korean companies in the last year, and acted for LG Power on its acquisition of two power plants from KEPCO. Our researchers further detected a recognised specialisation in the aeronautics industry, borne out by the firm's work on behalf of Korea Air in financing the purchase of three aircraft. **Clients:** Samsung Electronics; Hyundai Electronics; Korean Air; Asiana Airlines; LG Power; Korea Development Bank.

Shearman & Sterling (Hong Kong) (3 ptrs, 3 asscs) This firm's broad-based commercial practice is reinforced by *"a strong relationship with US investment banks looking to invest in Korea."* Heading the team is **Edward Turner***, a *"senior player who has been round the block many times."* The firm is prominent in the M&A and capital markets sectors, and has been involved on a number of high profile deals.

Examples include acting for Bell Canada International and others on the $2.6 billion sale of their interest in Hansol to Korea Telecom. Also represented the Foreign Bank Committee on the $2 billion restructuring of Daewoo. **Clients:** KEPCO; LG Group; SK; Samsung.

White & Case LLP (Hong Kong) (3 ptrs, 5 asscs) Providers of international legal services to major Korean banks, companies and groups, the firm is perceived to have a *"valuable asset"* in **Eric Yoon***. A renowned banking expert, his knowledge and status as a Korean national afford him *"a secure foothold in the region"* where he assists multinational and international businesses in their outbound and inbound Korean investments. The firm advised the Korean government on the $500

*See leaders' profiles on pages 616-617

million sale of its controlling stake in Korea First Bank to a consortium led by Newbridge Capital. Also acted on the sale of the mobile phone company Hansol to Korea Telecom. **Clients:** Korean government; SK Global; AIG; Salomon Smith Barney; GE Capital.

Allen & Overy (Hong Kong) (5 ptrs, 13 asscs) Known for its strong reputation in M&A, the firm is heavily active in domestic takeovers, joint ventures and management buy-outs. In **Hyo Young Kang*** it possesses the only Korean partner in a UK firm, a standing that affords him a *"high recognition factor among native practitioners."* It acted for Kumho Corporation on its $75 million disposal of a tyre plant in China to Bridgestone, and advised British Gas on a potential equity investment in KOGAS. A heavy involvement in capital markets is illustrated by its role as advisor to KEPCO on the restructuring of its outstanding bond issues. **Clients:** KEPCO; Hyundai Securities; H&CB; Citicorp International.

Simpson Thacher & Bartlett (Hong Kong) (2 ptrs, 8 asscs) Popular amongst the leading investment banks, the firm is noted for its flourishing regional finance practice. Especially strong in capital markets, it is also known for its advice on privatisation and structured finance. Described as *"a major force in the market,"* its reputation is enhanced by the presence of a *"significant number of Korean-speaking lawyers"* on the team. **Jin-Hyuk Park*** was singled out for individual recommendation. Recent progress in the region has led some interviewees to perceive it as *"one of the very best US firms operating in South Korea."* **Clients:** Morgan Stanley; Chemical Securities; Goldman Sachs; Daewoo Securities; LG Securities; Kepco.

Freehills (Sydney) (8 ptrs, 8 asscs) A presence for the last twenty years, this is the premier Australian firm in the region. Originally acting for Koreans looking to invest in Australia, the practice has expanded to embrace all aspects of advice on inward and outbound investment. It is now associated with the restructuring of the electrical industry having, in the face of stiff competition, been retained by the Korean government to advise on KEPCO's reform programme. It is also active in the banking area, having acted for Lend Lease on the successful bid for $250 million worth of non-performing loans from the Korea Exchange Bank. **Clients:** KEPCO; LG Group; Korea First Bank; Korean Airlines; Kumho Group; Korea Foreign Trade Association.

Freshfields Bruckhaus Deringer (Hong Kong) (3 ptrs, 3 asscs) This firm's practice is *"heavily weighted towards M&A,"* acting for both international corporates and domestic companies on inward investment projects. It has acted for Jinro Whisky over its sale to Allied Domecq and advised Ford on its proposed acquisition of Daewoo. A commitment to an increased profile has been signalled by the recent recruitment of a Korean national lawyer with a view to exploiting the country's burgeoning e-commerce sector. **Clients:** Kookmin Bank; Teletech; Jinro; ICI; KEDO; KEXIM.

Other Notable Practitioner **Timothy O'Brien*** of Coudert Brothers is *"a well connected operator, fluent in Korean"* who *"has been a recognised presence in the market for a number of years."* He has recently represented foreign investors looking to obtain a stake in Korean Cable.

Leaders' profiles – South Korea

CHOI, Dong Shik
Kim & Chang, Seoul +82 2 3703 1114

CHOI, Dyoung Seon
Shin & Kim, Seoul +82 2 316 4114

HAN, Jinduk
Cleary, Gottlieb, Steen & Hamilton, Hong Kong +852 2521 4122

JUNG, Kyung Taek
Kim & Chang, Seoul +82 2 3703 1114

KANG, Hee Chul
Woo, Yun, Kang, Jeong & Han, Seoul +82 2 528 5200
Specialisation: Partner in the Corporate Department. Main area of work is corporate law (general, mergers & acquisitions, and labour & employment). Has represented many multinational corporations doing business in Korea such as GE and Daimler Chrysler in various cross-border transactions and also represented well-known Korean companies such as Hyundia Motor Company and SK Telecom in corporate governance and M&A cases. Served as editor of the Korean Bar Association Journal in 1993-2000.
Prof. Memberships: Korean Bar Association, New York Bar Association.
Career: Qualified in Korea in 1979, and in New York in 1991. Judge Advocate, Republic of Korea, Army (1981-84); Associate, *Kim & Chang*, Seoul (1984-89); counsel, General Electric Asia Pacific, Hong Kong (1990-91); Partner, *Kim & Chang*, Seoul (1990-96); Partner, *Yulchon Law Offices* (1996-97).
Personal: Born in 1958. Seoul National University, LLB (1979); Seoul National University, Graduate School of Law (1981); Judicial Training and Research Institute, the Supreme Court of Korea (1981); Harvard Law School, LLM (1990).

KANG, Hyo Young
Allen & Overy, Hong Kong +852 2974 7000

KIM, Doo Sik
Shin & Kim, Seoul +82 2 316 4114

KIM, Soo Chang
Lee & Ko, Seoul +82 2 772 4000
cen@lawleeko.co.kr
Specialisation: Partner in Banking Department. Main area of work is in international banking and financial transactions, including mergers, acquisitions, securities, and project finance. Has acted as legal counsel in handling numerous large-scale international business deals. Acted as legal counsel for several Korean bank lenders in 1999 project finance deal (US$125 million) involving acquisition of large-scale electrical power co-generation facility in Kyonggi Province (first 100% Korean Won-financed project finance deal in Korea and one of the earlier work-out transactions carried out by a chaebol (the Hyundai Group)). Also acted as legal counsel for several Korean bank lenders in 1999 project finance deal (US$109 million) involving acquisition of large-scale electrical power co-generation facility in Chungnam Province (second 100% Korean Won-financed project finance deal in Korea, another of the earlier work-out transactions carried out by a chaebol (the Hyundai Group)). Acted as legal counsel for Korean Asset Management Company (KAMCO) in 1999 large-scale sale (US$470 million) of Non-Performing Loans of Korean financial institutions, carried out by KAMCO under recently enacted Korean Asset-Backed Securitization Law. Acted as Korean counsel for purchaser in recent transaction for the sale (US$190 million) of common stock of Motorola Korea Ltd. by Motorola Asia Limited.
Prof. Memberships: Member of Korean Bar Association; International Bar Association; and Inter-Pacific Bar Association.
Career: Admitted to Bar: 1981, Korea. Career History: Judge Advocate Officer, Korean Army, 1981-84; Foreign Associate, *Milbank, Tweed, Hadley & McCloy*, New York, 1986; Arbitrator, Korean Commercial Arbitration Board, 1992 – present; Commissioner on the OECD, Subcommittee of International Finance, Committee of Financial and Industrial Development, Ministry of Finance and Economy, 1994 – present; Member of Government Advisory Group on International Economic Affairs, 1994 – present; Joined *Lee & Ko* in 1984, partner since 1990.

Personal: Born March 15, 1955 in Korea. Education: College of Law, Korea University (LLB, 1977); Graduate School of Law, Korea University, 1977-79; The Judicial Research and Training Institute, Korea Supreme Court, 1979-81. Has a wife and 2 children. Lives in Seoul, Korea.

KIM, Young Joon
Milbank, Tweed, Hadley & McCloy, Tokyo +813 3504 1050

LEE, Keun Byung
Bae, Kim & Lee, Seoul +822 3404 0001
kbl@lawyers.co.kr
Specialisation: Partner in Securities, Banking and Finance Department. Main area of work is corporate law, principally mergers and acquisitions as well as securities and financing laws involving banking regulatory framework. Has handled acquisitions of companies and undertakings of various entities by Korean and overseas clients. Acted on the joint venture project of SK-Enron for SK Group; acted for Korea Housing & Commercial Bank for strategic alliance with ING Baring; acted for Hyundai Group on IPIC-HDO joint venture; acted for UBS consortium on acquisition of Mando Climate Control Co., Ltd.; acted for Citicorp Venture Capital Consortium on acquisition of the Information and Communications Business Division of Daewoo Telecom, Ltd.; and acted for E.M. Warburg Pincus on acquisition of Jin Woong Co., Ltd. Has played a leading role on numerous matters ranging from enactment, amendment and interpretation of Korean securities and financing-related laws to a variety of overseas sales projects. Heads the firm's Securities, Banking and Finance Group.
Prof. Memberships: Korean, Seoul, New York State Bar Associations.
Publications: Co-Author of 'Overseas Bonds with Warrants issued by Korean Corporations'. Author of 'Subordinated Debt'.
Career: Admitted to the bar, Korea in 1984 and New York in 1991. Joined *Kim, Shin & Yu* in 1985; joined *Bae, Kim & Lee* in 1987; visiting attorney in *Kelley Drye & Warren* (New York) in 1991; visiting attorney in *Arendt & Medernach* (Luxembourg) in 1992; Dispute Mediator, Securities Supervisory Board in 1996; Mediator on Civil Matters, Seoul District Court in 1998; Arbitrator, Korean Commercial Arbitration Board in 1999.
Personal: Born in 1960. Graduated from Seoul National University Law School (LLB 1983). Judicial Research and Training Institute, Supreme Court of the Republic of Korea (1983-84). New York University School of Law (LLM in Corporate Law 1991). International Institute for Securities Market Development, U.S. Securities and Exchange Commission, Washington DC (1992).

LEE, Moon Sung
Lee & Ko, Seoul +82 2 772 4000
cen@lawleeko.co.kr.
Specialisation: Partner in Corporate Department. Main areas of work are foreign investment, M&A, and arbitration. Represented the Korean government in the sale of its controlling stake in Korea First Bank to Newbridge Capital; represented the LG Group in the sale of an equity interest in its credit card business to Warburg Pincus; represented the Illinois Tools Works Group in its acquisition of a speciality film business from SKC; and represented Hanwha Group in the sale of its controlling interest in power generation business to El Paso.
Prof. Memberships: Korean Bar Association; New York Bar Association; Inter-Pacific Bar Association.
Career: Admitted to Bar: 1978, Korea; 1988, New York. Career History: Judge Advocate Officer, Korean Army 1978-81; Judge, Soo-won District Court 1981-82; Foreign Associate, *Skadden, Arps, Slate, Meagher & Flom*, New York, 1987-88; Arbitrator, Korean Commercial Arbitration Board, 1992-present. Joined *Lee & Ko* in 1982, became a partner in 1990.
Personal: Born 15 April 1954 in Korea. Education: College of Law, Seoul National University (LLB 1975); The Judicial Research and Training Institute, Korea Supreme Court, 1976-78; George Washington University Law School(MCL 1987). Has a wife and 3 children. Lives in Seoul, Korea.

O'BRIEN, Timothy
Coudert Brothers, Hong Kong +852 2218 9100

OH, Yong Suk (Y.S.)
Bae, Kim & Lee, Seoul +82 2 3404 0121
yso@lawyers.co.kr
Specialisation: Head of Corporate and International Practice. Main area of work is corporate law and arbitration. Handled corporate workout of Kohap Group. Acted on business reorganisation and corporate restructuring of the Korean Electric Power Corporation. Acted for Hyundai Engineering and Constructions Co., Ltd. in an arbitration against Asian Development Bank (ADB) regarding construction of ADB headquarters in Manila, Philippines.
Career: Admitted to the Bar, Korea in 1980, New York in 1986. Joined *Bae, Kim & Lee* in 1987, serving as its managing partner since 1999. Arbitrator of Korean Commercial Arbitration Board 1996-present.
Personal: Born 25 October 1951. Attended Korea University Law School 1972-76 (LLB); Harvard Law School 1985 (LLM). Enjoys golf and running. Lives in Kuri-si, Korea.

PARK, Jin Hyuk
Simpson Thacher & Bartlett, Hong Kong +852 2514 7600
j_park@stblaw.com
Specialisation: A newly elected partner at *Simpson Thacher & Bartlett* and a member of the Firm's Corporate Department. Has a broad range of experience in M&A and capital markets transactions and has been involved in substantially all of the Korean transactions. Joined the Hong Kong office after having spent several years in the Tokyo office building up the Korea practice, including transactions involving the sale by Kookmin Bank of its equity interest to Goldman Sachs funds, KEPCO and POSCO in a number of successful offerings of American Depositary Receipts, most of the major commercial banks in Korea and other Korean issuers including Samsung Electronics, Hyundai Motor Company and state-owned enterprises.
Personal: Korean citizen and a native Korean speaker. Born in South Korea and educated largely in the United States since 10th grade. Graduated from Harvard University in 1987 and is also a 1990 graduate of University of Chicago Law School.

PARK, Joon
Kim & Chang, Seoul +82 2 3703 1114

PARK, Sang Il
Hwang Mok Park & Jin, Seoul +82 2 772 2700

SHIN, Hi Taek
Kim & Chang, Seoul +82 2 3703 1114

TURNER, Edward L.
Shearman & Sterling, Hong Kong +852 2978 8000
eturner@shearman.com
Specialisation: Firm's Managing Partner in Asia with responsibility for the Firm's practice in East Asia through offices in Beijing, Hong Kong, Singapore and Tokyo. Relocated to Hong Kong in early 1994 in connection with the opening of the Firm's office there. Previously, practised in the Firm's New York and San Francisco Offices. Current practice focuses on mergers and acquisitions, joint ventures and related financing transactions. Conducts seminars regularly for Euromoney and others on M&A topics. Is also an author of a Chapter on 'Contracts' in the treatise Start-Up Companies, New York Law Journal Seminars-Press (1999) and a speaker on various corporate law topics, including most recently Negotiating and Structuring International Joint Ventures, Partnerships and Strategic Alliances.
Prof. Memberships: Bar Admissions: California, New York and Hong Kong.
Career: Educated at Vanderbilt Law School, J.D., 1970; Corning Glass Travelling Fellowship (International Business), 1967; Harvard University, Interim Study Program; Vanderbilt University, B.A., 1966.

WALKER, James
Clifford Chance, Hong Kong +852 2825 8888

YOON, Eric S.
White & Case LLP, Hong Kong +852 2822 8700
eyoon@whitecase.com
Specialisation: Head of *White & Case's* Korean practice. Advises the firm's Korean and other clients on mergers and acquisitions, general corporate and other transactional matters. Represents clients who enter into cross-border acquisitions, divestitures and joint ventures and also is involved in credit transactions, capital markets transactions and the establishment of investment funds. Recent representations include: a private equity consortium, led by Gilbert Global Equity Partners, AIG and GIC, in a $410 million investment in Amkor Technology; Emerging Markets Partnership and AIG in a structured investment in Dreamcity Cable TV System; Hanchang Corporation in its sale of Nowcom, an Internet Service Provider, to TriGem Computer and Thrunet; Korea Deposit Insurance Corporation and Financial Supervisory Commission of Korea, in various banking sector restructuring-related matters; and establishment of M-Werks, a wireless Internet and 3G investment fund.
Career: Admitted to the New York State Bar in 1989.
Personal: Brown University (A.B., magna cum laude, 1983); Columbia University Law School (J.D., 1987). Citizen of the Republic of Korea. Speaks Korean and English.

S

SPAIN

Index

The clients' choice

BUSINESS LAWYER OF THE YEAR
SALVADOR SÁNCHEZ-TERÁN

BUSINESS LAW FIRM OF THE YEAR
URÍA & MENÉNDEZ

Uría & Menéndez *storm the poll as best firm and provides the top three nominees for best lawyer.* ***Salvador Sánchez-Terán*** *just edged ahead of his colleagues.*

For details see page 36.

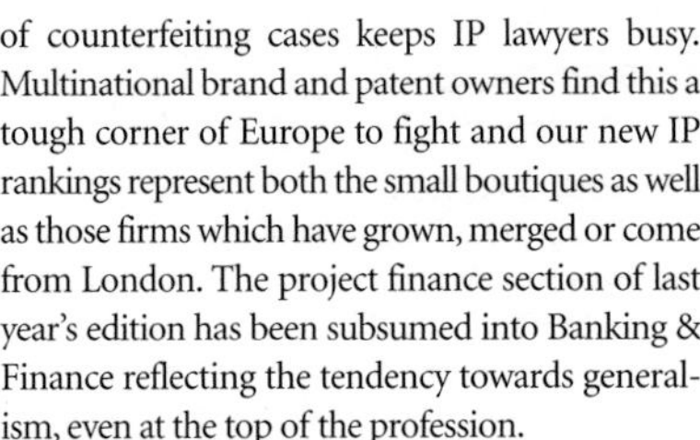

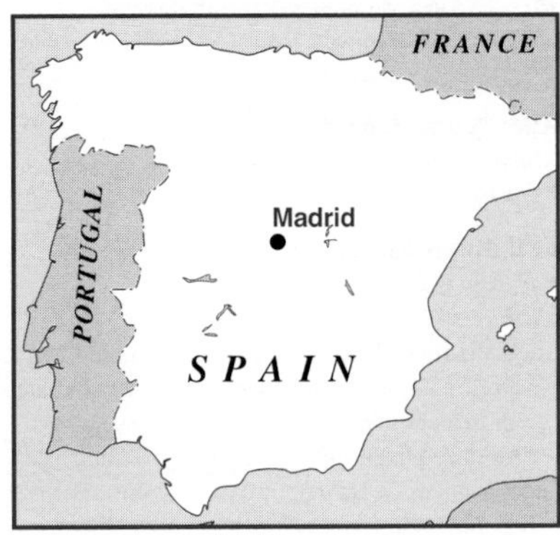

OVERVIEW: Domestic business is now no longer the preserve of the traditional Spanish law firm. The legal offices of worldwide accountancy firms and international law firms are active competitors. Whilst Garrigues & Andersen, Ernst & Young and Landwell are the strongest examples of the former, Clifford Chance and Freshfields Bruckhaus Deringer are the best of the latter.

What has led to the emergence of legal giants in a country where the family firm has held sway for so long? Spanish business is booming in its international flavour, both pan-European and as a base into the increasingly lucrative Latin American markets. The lack of Wall Street firms is striking, indeed Spanish firms have made an effort to establish a presence in New York as the portal for money headed that way.

Growth in telecoms, e-business and energy is supported by a flourishing private equity market. Merger controls have become tighter and a spate of counterfeiting cases keeps IP lawyers busy. Multinational brand and patent owners find this a tough corner of Europe to fight and our new IP rankings represent both the small boutiques as well as those firms which have grown, merged or come from London. The project finance section of last year's edition has been subsumed into Banking & Finance reflecting the tendency towards generalism, even at the top of the profession.

International firms are becoming increasingly Spanish through lateral hires of individuals or whole boutiques such as Baker & McKenzie's merger with Briones Alonso Martin (December 2000.) Clifford Chance has penetrated the domestic market in Madrid and Barcelona. Individuals like Jaime de San Roman (Clifford Chance) and Fernando Bautista (Freshfields) have taken the Anglo Saxon appeal attractive to international financial institutions and blended it with an understanding of the local market. Linklaters' office in Madrid, its 'Plan B' following the separation from former ally Uría & Menéndez, looks set to succeed with the presence of top lawyers including Álvaro Sáinz, taken from Garrigues.

Garrigues & Andersen is one of the most successful MDPs in the world and Spain's biggest billing professional firm. Senior figures Carlos Loring and Daniel García-Pita ensure the high profile of the firm despite the loss of some of its younger talent. The 'best friends' relationship between Uría & Menéndez and London's Slaughter and May appears culturally to be a successful match. What really defines Uría, however, is an almost endless list of star lawyers: Juan Miguel Goenechea, Salvador Sánchez-Terán, Luis de Carlos and many others are perceived to be quality epitomised. Cuatrecasas' corporate and finance team continues to play a vital role in the market, a major transformation from its roots as a tax-led, domestic service provider from Barcelona.

Banking & Finance

Clifford Chance (6 ptrs, 30 asscs) Benefiting from deep immersion into the Spanish finance market over the last 20 years, the firm is acknowledged by admiring rivals to be *"focused on finance,"* and to have the edge over other foreign firms, as it *"ironed out all the teething problems years ago."* Powerful both domestically and internationally, the firm advises on traditional banking matters, and has expertise in structured finance, IPOs (both for investment banks and for issuers such as Telefónica Móviles, Ya.Com and Gamesa) and securitisation.

Jaime de San Roman* *("without any doubt a star lawyer")* is *"the founder of Clifford Chance as we know it today in Spain."* Research shows that he is particularly popular with his clients. **Iñigo Gómez-Jordana*** is another partner to come in for substantial market praise, while high-profile associate **Manuel Sanchez de Movellan*** has been particularly recommended by clients. *"He really knows his stuff on capital markets. He's practical and consistent."*

In the high yield debt market, the firm advised on Jazztel's second issue and acted on Cableuropa's €200 million bond issue. **Clients:** Goldman Sachs; JP Morgan; BBVA; Nomura; Lehman Bros.

Uría & Menéndez (5 ptrs, 21 asscs) Riding high at the top of the rankings following *"a great year,"* the firm is generally found on one side or another of the majority of big-ticket transactions. Its project finance department is one of the few in Spain with genuine international expertise, while the group also advises on syndicated loans, acquisition finance and capital markets transactions. A strong relationship with investment banks gives the firm global leverage.

Luis de Carlos Bertrán* is a *"complete lawyer,"* who is considered by peers to be *"the number one capital markets lawyer in Spain."* **Emilio Díaz*** is known to be *"a financial expert, especially in futures and derivatives,"* **Rafael Sebastián*** has a particularly good reputation in traditional banking law. Project finance expert **Carlos de Cárdenas*** has also worked on a number of corporate refundings. Although better known as a corporate lawyer, **Salvador Sánchez-Terán*** has worked on large rights

SPAIN Leading firms (Banking & Finance)
1 Clifford Chance
Uría & Menéndez
2 Garrigues & Andersen
3 Freshfields Bruckhaus Deringer
4 Cuatrecasas
5 Castro Sueiro & Varela
Gomez-Acebo & Pombo
Squire, Sanders & Dempsey Abogados
6 Linklaters
Melchor, Albiñana & Suárez de Lezo
Ramón & Cajal Abogados

Firms are listed alphabetically in each band.

Leading individuals (Banking & Finance)
1 **BAUTISTA Fernando** *Freshfields Bruckhaus*
DE CARLOS BERTRÁN Luis *Uría & Menéndez*
DE SAN ROMAN Jaime *Clifford Chance*
LORING Carlos *Garrigues & Andersen*
2 **ALBELLA Sebastian** *Ramón & Cajal Abogados*
DÍAZ Emilio *Uría & Menéndez*
GÓMEZ-ACEBO Javier *Freshfields Bruckhaus*
GOMEZ-JORDANA Iñigo *Clifford Chance*
SEBASTIÁN Rafael *Uría & Menéndez*
TORRENTE Fernando *Cuatrecasas*
3 **ALBIÑANA CILVETI César** *Melchor, Albiñana*
DE CÁRDENAS Carlos *Uría & Menéndez*
DE LAS CUEVAS Fernando *Gomez-Acebo*
IGARTUA Fernando *Gomez-Acebo*
MÍNGUEZ PRIETO Rafael *Cuatrecasas*
SANCHEZ DE MOVELLAN Manuel *Clifford Chance*
SÁNCHEZ-TERÁN Salvador *Uría & Menéndez*
SANTOS Javier *Squire, Sanders & Dempsey*
SUÁREZ DE LEZO Rafael *Melchor, Albiñana*
SUEIRO Miguel *Castro Sueiro & Varela*
VARELA VARAS Angel *Gomez-Acebo*
VIVES Fernando *Garrigues & Andersen*
YBAÑEZ Javier *Garrigues & Andersen*

Individuals are listed alphabetically in each band.

offerings for banks like BSCH (€3.5 billion) and BBVA (€3 billion).

The firm advised on a €225 million syndicated credit, given to Ono Group by eight Spanish savings banks, by way of preferred shares and subordinated bonds. Also represented the Kingdom of Spain on a 'shelf programme' for the emission of US$500 million worth of bonds. High-premium IPOs include Terra Networks, Amadeus (for SBC Warburg and Merrill Lynch) and Jazztel. **Clients:** La Caixa; Fortis Bank; ING Bank; Bankers Trust Company.

Garrigues & Andersen (6 ptrs, 34 asscs) A leading force in capital markets, the firm has *"an incredible number of lawyers and economists"* and the sort of domestic geographical coverage to which most other firms cannot aspire.

Carlos Loring* is dubbed *"the king of privatisation"* and is rated as one of the firm's most influential movers and shakers, deserving his top ranking. **Fernando Vives*** (who is also known in the insurance sector) favours securities work, while **Javier Ybañez*** is known for his securities work and IPOs. *"He has clear ideas and he is straightforward in his dealings."*

The firm acted for the issuer on the IPO of Prisa, and advised the underwriting banks on the rights issues by BBVA and BSCH, the second Spanish issue of Deutsche Telekom and the rights issue by engineering group Abengoa. **Clients:** Merrill Lynch; Morgan Stanley; GE Capital; Schroeders; Argentaria.

Freshfields Bruckhaus Deringer (3 ptrs, 16 asscs) Still felt to be *"more involved in securities,"* the firm is felt to be an increasing factor in traditional bank lending. Research has shown a firm on the way up. A rapid growth in size for the finance team has been complemented by a remarkable volume of IPOs this year.

Fernando Bautista* is *"clearly their top name"* and is seen as one of the leading finance lawyers of his generation. **Javier Gómez-Acebo*** has been involved in IPOs, asset finance (an area in which the firm's Spanish offices are particularly active) and some securitisation.

In 2000, IPOs included those of Recoletas, Logista and Amadeus, on which it acted for Warburg Dillon Read and Merrill Lynch. Warburg Dillon Read also instructed the firm on the block trade of shares in Amadeus Global Travel Distribution, where the company's main shareholders sold 14 million class A shares to a small number of institutional investors. Also acted for La Caixa on its first mortgage securitisation and for the bank on the €213 million structured financing of Universal's theme park Port Aventura. **Clients:** Europa de Titulización; BNP Paribas; BBVA; JP Morgan; Angel Trains.

Cuatrecasas (4 ptrs, 17 asscs) Having grown enormously in the last five years, the firm has built on its tax base and now concentrates its efforts in the corporate and finance areas. Well-known for its secured lending and capital markets prowess, the firm's heartland is in Barcelona, although its two leading finance players both operate from Madrid.

"Mr IPO" **Fernando Torrente*** is especially well regarded, and has been joined by **Rafael Mínguez Prieto*** *("an important acquisition,")* hired from the General Directorate of the Treasury, where he has been since 1995 as Deputy Director General for Legislation.

The firm advised Morgan Stanley Dean Witter and other global co-ordinators on IPOs such as Prisa (€790 million) and Grupo Ferrovial (€1 billion). Also represented Merrill Lynch and BSCH as global co-ordinators of the €1.8 billion Iberia LAE IPO. **Clients:** European Investment Bank; Caixa Catalunya; CSFB; BNP Paribas.

Castro Sueiro & Varela (3 ptrs, 10 asscs) Renowned for M&A in the banking sector and banking litigation, the firm is considered to work *"to the highest standards,"* and is a popular choice for referrals. Research confirms that *"on infrastructure transactions, they are top quality."* **Miguel Sueiro*** is considered to be the firm's outstanding practitioner. The firm has enjoyed plenty of ship and aircraft finance work, acting for banks and leasing companies. This has included the first three financial tax lease transactions for vessels made in Spain (Ptas. 2.5 billion) completed under new regulations. In project finance it has been instructed by banks on matters including motorways and windfarms and the M45 Madrid railway. It is now working for the European agency that finances European transport infrastructure. **Clients:** Debis Financial Services Ltd; BSCH Group; Banca Commerciale Italiana, SpA; European Investment Fund.

Gomez-Acebo & Pombo *"A good firm"* with involvement in a wide range of finance and banking, capital markets and projects matters. In the latter, **Fernando Igartua*** and **Angel Varela Varas*** are recommended. In 2000, project finance matters included advice to sponsor, Edisson Mission Energy, in the structuring of the 400Mw power plant project in Aragón and to the sponsor Intergen in the 400Mw power plant in Valencia. Corporate star **Fernando de las Cuevas*** has a good reputation for finance work too. Last year the firm acted on a multitude of syndicated loans and was instructed by BBVA in the first CLO securitisation transaction in Spain, valued at ptas 200 billion. **Clients:** Société Générale; EDF; Paribas; UPSE; Spanish Institute of Official Credit; Caixa Leasing.

Squire, Sanders & Dempsey Abogados (2 ptrs, 6 asscs) Seen to have a *"strong project finance practice,"* the firm was recommended to our researchers as *"a group that is popular with the banks."* **Javier Santos*** is a *"very capable lawyer."* Advised Instituto de Crédito Oficial (as Agent) and the lenders with regard to the project financing of three different windfarm plants totalling 48MW and also for Unión Fenosa Internacional with regard to a B.O.O.M. project for a combined-cycle plant in Hermosillo, Mexico. Negotiated a $150 million project

*See leaders' profiles on pages 629-636

finance structure with a consortium of banks, acting for the Inter-American Development Bank (as Agent). The firm was instructed by BSCH (as Agent) and the lenders with regard to a $35 million multi-currency and multi-borrower credit facility in favour of Picking Pack. **Clients:** Caja Madrid; Banco Español de Crédito; Commerzbank.

Linklaters (3 ptrs, 10 asscs) Although it is comparatively new in Spain, the firm *"has the will to be there, and is putting in the effort."* Rapid expansion over the past six months has principally borne fruit in securities and IPO work. Our researchers found that the market had noted the firm's active hiring of quality lawyers from rival operations.

It has acted as both international and Spanish counsel to the underwriters on major IPOs, such as Prisa and Zeltia. In project finance, the firm has been involved with the Arcos de la Frontera power plant, and the refinancing of Seville's theme park, Isla de Magica. Also acted for CVC Partners Ltd on the LBO financing for the Spanish MBO of the Revlon Haircare business. **Clients:** HSBC; Morgan Stanley; Merrill Lynch; BSCH; Jazztel; BNP Paribas.

Melchor, Albiñana & Suárez de Lezo (3 ptrs, 9 asscs) Better known for corporate finance than pure banking, the firm is nevertheless highly regarded for its work in capital markets. The team has acted for several major Spanish companies on equity offerings on the international markets, mainly the NYSE, as well as for foreign companies on the Madrid Stock Exchange.

The names highlighted at the firm for finance work are **César Albiñana Cilveti***, who divides his practice between financial matters and corporate deals, and well-known transactional figure **Rafael Suárez de Lezo***. The firm has advised on IPOs such as Recoletos and Befesa, and reviewed the European Medium Term Note programme of BBVA. It also acted on the development in Spain of the Cash Pooling Project and Cash Concentration Systems of Credit Lyonnais. **Clients:** Caja Madrid; Banco Espirito Santo; the Lazard Group; Ericsson Credit AB.

Ramón & Cajal, Abogados (4 ptrs, 9 asscs) A respected finance practice, which is particularly rated for its securities expertise. **Sebastian Albella***, a former Secretary to the board of the Securities Commission, is felt by some to be *"at the top in capital markets."* Expanding rapidly, the firm has niche expertise in e-banking, and is considered *"a good choice for conflict referrals"* by its peers. Last year the firm acted on several capital markets transactions, including various takeover bids and global offerings of shares. It also advises on the regulations of the Comisión Nacional del Mercado de Valores. In project finance, the team has worked on alternative and renewable energy, transportation and telecommunications. **Clients:** An international bank; Spanish savings banks; investment funds; mutual fund managers.

Communications

SPAIN
Leading firms (Communications)

Band	Firm
1	Clifford Chance
	Gomez-Acebo & Pombo
	Uría & Menéndez
2	Garrigues & Andersen
	Squire, Sanders & Dempsey Abogados
3	Cuatrecasas
	Freshfields Bruckhaus Deringer
4	Baker & McKenzie/Baker & McKenzie - Briones Alonso Martin
	Cremades Abogados
	Ernst & Young Abogados
	Landwell
	SJ Berwin, Pazos, Gallardo & Asociados

Firms are listed alphabetically in each band.

Leading individuals (Communications)

Band		
1	**ARPÓN DE MENDÍVIL Almudena** *Gomez-Acebo*	**LAVILLA Juan José** *Clifford Chance*
	PÉREZ SANTOS José *Uría & Menéndez*	**PICÓN Juan** *Squire, Sanders & Dempsey*
2	**CREMADES Javier** *Cremades Abogados*	**MAYOR Pablo** *Clifford Chance*
	PÉREZ ARDÁ Javier *Garrigues & Andersen*	**PÉREZ DE LA SOTA Fernando** *Uría & Menéndez*
	REMÓN PEÑALVER Jesús *Uría & Menéndez*	
3	**CANTOS Francisco** *Freshfields Bruckhaus*	**DIEZ Maite** *Baker & McKenzie*
	GONZÁLEZ-DELEITO Nicolás *Cuatrecasas*	**HITCHINGS Paul** *Squire, Sanders & Dempsey*
	MARZO Javier *Garrigues & Andersen*	**PAZOS Carlos** *SJ Berwin, Pazos, Gallardo*
	SÁNCHEZ-PEDREÑO Antonio *Linklaters*	**SANZ Enrique** *Landwell*

Individuals are listed alphabetically in each band.

Clifford Chance (2 ptrs, 9 asscs) Advising on both transactional and regulatory proceedings, the firm is unanimously regarded as the *"best foreign firm"* in Spain, although some have argued that it could equally well be described as a pedigree Spanish operation. A heavyweight clientele receives the benefit of the firm's vast global offering of communications expertise, and the group advises Telefónica on corporate and financing issues, and BT and Auna on regulatory matters. It has also acted as general advisor to Abrared and Firstmark Communications on WLL.

"First-class" regulatory and corporate advisor **Juan José Lavilla*** has been joined by acclaimed recruit **Pablo Mayor***, who arrived in September 1999, having been Technical Secretary General in the Ministry of Development. In UMTS, the firm has worked with incubators and on licence tenders, while on Airtel it acted for BSCH, Commerzbank and Citibank, advising in connection with a €240 million performance bond facility. **Clients:** Uni2; Cableuropa; Movi2.

Gomez-Acebo & Pombo (2 ptrs, 9 asscs) Around 60% of the team's workload is telecoms related, with the rest divided between audio-visual and IT matters. Although regulatory advice is known to be a particular strength, the firm also handles commercial, start-up and corporate instructions.

Traditional telecoms leader here is the almost legendary **Almudena Arpón de Mendívil***, *"the queen of telecoms,"* who still has *"a tremendous reputation"* and *"particular expertise in regulatory issues."* She heads a team that is said to have *"great discipline."* The firm advised Nokia on the supply of equipment to UMTS licence holder Xfera, and represented long-standing client BT on its shareholding in Airtel. It has also seen a number of instructions from TV companies in relation to the creation of new channels, such as Fox, and the allocation of channels to various distributors, such as Bloomberg TV. **Clients:** Sonera; AT&T; Excite; 360 Networks.

Uría & Menéndez (3 ptrs, 6 asscs) Most of the team operates from Madrid, with a satellite office in Barcelona. For its top-grade telecoms and media clients, the firm has long taken a significant role in corporate and finance matters. Now, Uría has a team that is *"well aware of regulatory issues,"* and has redefined its role as an advisor in the telecoms sector over the last couple of years. The team advises on networks, WLL, broadband, cable services, UMTS and audio-visual matters.

José (Pepe) Pérez Santos* has a strong profile and is labelled as *"a great lawyer and a great person."* **Fernando Pérez de la Sota*** has also received substantial endorsement, along with telecoms litigator **Jesus Remón Peñalver***. The firm's broadened presence in the telecoms sector is evidenced by instructions from a number of consortia, such as Broadnet and Xfera. The firm continues to work for heavyweight operators such as Telefónica and BT, and advised Global Crossing on the establishment and operation of their networks throughout Spain. **Clients:** Airtel; UPC; Telefónica; NTL; Amena.

Garrigues & Andersen (1 ptr, 7 asscs) Part of the larger Telecoms, Entertainment and Media Group, the telecoms team has a well-established reputation, enhanced by the firm's December 2000 absorption of IT/telecoms boutique Anguiano & Asociados. Regulatory advice, licensing, public tender, strategic alliances, start-ups, joint ventures, and network agreements are all covered by the team, which has a notably good reputation for regulatory advice.

The team is led by the respected **Javier Pérez Ardá***, and also includes **Javier Marzo***. They have both contributed to a text on issues affecting new operators of telecommunications networks in Spain. The firm advised Telefónica on various auctions and 'beauty parades' for UMTS and 3G licences in the UK, Italy, France, Germany and Switzerland. **Clients:** Madritel; Telefónica Móviles; Prisa; Canal+France; Junta de Galicia.

Squire, Sanders & Dempsey Abogados (1 ptr, 7 asscs) *"Making a lot of noise"* at the moment and generally thought to deserve the attention it receives, the firm handles corporate and M&A work for several companies in the telecoms/internet arena and also gives pure regulatory advice. Former Clifford Chance transactional expert **Juan Picón*** is regarded as *"a real player,"* while **Paul Hitchings***, acknowledged for his regulatory expertise, is widely recognised in spite of his relative youth.

The firm assisted Deutsche Telekom on the tender process for a UMTS licence, advised Warner Bros on its acquisition of a stake in a satellite digital platform, and acted on Deutsche Telekom's €600 million acquisition of internet portal Ya.com from Jazztel. **Clients:** Teleglobe; MCI WorldCom; KPM Quest; Covad.

Cuatrecasas (2 ptrs, 7 asscs) The team is considered to have *"good people"* working on telecoms matters, a reputation which was underscored by the founding, in September 2000, of a separate department devoted to regulatory telecoms advice. A number of the firm's corporate lawyers have experience in transactional work for communications clients in media and communications, including fixed, wireless and mobile network provision, internet, digital audio and visual broadcasting, and satellite and submarine cable. Other matters handled include granting of and litigation over authorisations and licences, public bids and access issues.

On the regulatory side, **Nicolás González-Deleito*** is an esteemed lawyer, with a background in the firm's administrative and constitutional law department, who was previously legal secretary to the president of the Spanish constitutional committee. Covers litigation with the Administration and the regulatory bodies on a regular basis. Last year it advised Amena in the financing by the IEB of a cellular telephony infrastructure project. **Clients:** Top names in international and domestic telecoms and the audio-visual industry.

Freshfields Bruckhaus Deringer (2 ptrs, 6 asscs) Involved in a number of high profile corporate and financing transactions in the sector, the firm has far less visibility in regulatory work, although **Francisco (Paco) Cantos*** still receives market recognition. The firm acted for BT on certain aspects of the Airtel shareholding dispute and for Pearson in the joint venture between Telefónica and Recoletos. In South America, the group acted on a bond issue for Telefónica Chile, and advised UK company Broadnet on various matters in Spain, including its WLL licence application. **Clients:** Teletech; Telematrix; EMI; Broadnet.

Baker & McKenzie/Baker & McKenzie – Briones Alonso Martin (2 ptrs, 4 asscs) The telecoms lawyers are a part of the IT/Communications Group and cover both regulatory and corporate work, including a number of licence applications through public tender. **Maite Diez*** is the stand-out name here. Primary advisers to both Cisco and Nortel, the firm has represented them on commercial contracts involving equipment supply, finance and contracts with operators. **Clients:** Cable & Wireless; Formus Communications; RSL Com; Orange.

Cremades Abogados (3 ptrs, 21 asscs) Formerly Cremades & Sanchez Pintado until a major split last year, the firm is led by **Javier Cremades***, who has an established name in the industry. The firm is renowned for its *"good contacts"* and is considered to have a deep understanding of the regulatory authorities and licensing applications. In October 2000 the telecommunications law department acquired an experienced state abogado as its new director. It has also developed an incubator for internet start-ups in Spain and Latin America. The firm has a wealth of experience in licence bids – LMDS, UMTS, television and digital terrestrial radio. It was involved in the grant of the first CUG licence and advised the Spanish Government on the full privatisation of Retevision, SA. **Clients:** UPC; Colt Telecom; Ericsson; Nortel; Astra; AOC (Spanish Cable Operators association); RSL Comm; Isla Link; Atento; ICS; Madrïtel.

S

Ernst & Young Despacho Abogados (9 asscs) Operating out of Madrid and Barcelona, the team is expanding, but still lacks a partner at the helm. It is recognised most often for its IT and internet/e-commerce work, but also covers regulatory and transactional matters for telecoms clients. The firm recently advised a client on its national and pan-European restructuring. **Clients:** Domestic and international carriers; IT start-ups.

Landwell (1 ptr, 8 asscs) PwC is known to have a strong name in consultancy to the telecoms market, and its legal arm, formerly known as Estudio Legal Abogados y Asesores Fiscales (PwC), is a recognised force in the sector. It has assisted a number of operators on corporate matters, such as consortia agreements and with the preparation of bids for and judicial challenges over the awarding of licences. **Enrique Sanz*** has a corporate background and a long relationship with France Telecom, and the firm advised Tecnocom on the creation of a network to provide mobile services underground in Madrid. **Clients:** Global One; Sky Point.

S J Berwin, Pazos, Gallardo & Asociados (2 ptrs, 6 asscs) Working on behalf of niche operators, a number of them American, *"excellent"* all-round corporate lawyer **Carlos Pazos*** and his colleagues have several years of experience in the industry. The firm was instructed by AOL Europe to deal with the Spanish authorities in relation to the flat tariff negotiations. Also advised the consortium Movi2, which applied for one of the three Spanish UMTS licences that were granted by the Spanish Government. **Clients:** Cignal Global Communications Spain; LDI Telecommunications Spain; ECI Telecom Iberica.

Other Notable Practitioner **Antonio Sánchez-Pedreño*** of Linklaters has vast corporate experience in telecoms, and again comes highly recommended.

*See leaders' profiles on pages 629-636

S

Competition/Anti-trust

SPAIN Leading firms (Competition/Anti-trust)
1 Martinez Lage & Asociados Uría & Menéndez
2 Garrigues & Andersen
3 Cuatrecasas Freshfields Bruckhaus Deringer Gomez-Acebo & Pombo
4 Araoz y Rueda
5 Clifford Chance Jones, Day, Reavis & Pogue
6 Melchor, Albiñana & Suárez de Lezo M Vega Penichet SJ Berwin, Pazos, Gallardo & Asociados

Firms are listed alphabetically in each band.

Leading individuals (Competition/Anti-trust)
1 **ARAUJO Marcos** *Garrigues & Andersen* **FOLGUERA CRESPO Jaime** *Uría & Menéndez* **MARTINEZ LAGE Santiago** *Martinez Lage*
2 **ALLENDESALAZAR CORCHO Rafael** *Martinez Lage* **ARPÓN DE MENDÍVIL Almudena** *Gomez-Acebo* **CANTOS Francisco** *Freshfields Bruckhaus* **CREUS Antonio** *Cuatrecasas* **FERNÁNDEZ DE ARAOZ Alejandro** *Araoz y Rueda* **PÉREZ SANTOS José** *Uría & Menéndez*
3 **BENEYTO José María** *Gomez-Acebo* **JIMENÉZ LAIGLESIA Juan** *Jones, Day* **JIMENÉZ LAIGLESIA José María** *Jones, Day* **ODRIOZOLA Miguel** *Clifford Chance* **VEGA PENICHET Luis** *M Vega Penichet*
4 **FERNÁNDEZ Cani** *Cuatrecasas* **IGARTUA Íñigo** *Gomez-Acebo & Pombo* **ORTIZ BLANCO Luis** *Garrigues & Andersen*
Individuals are listed alphabetically in each band.

Martinez Lage & Asociados (6 ptrs, 6 asscs) *"A huge name"* in competition, this specialist boutique has the standing in the Spanish legal market to attract instructions from the largest multi-national clients, generally on contentious matters.

Santiago Martinez Lage* is *"star"* material, and a renowned rainmaker. Our research indicates that his peers regard him as the name for competition advice, primarily in litigation, where he has a wealth of experience. He is supported by a strong team, which features **Rafael Allendesalazar Corcho***, who has a sound reputation in his own right.

The firm is defending The Coca-Cola Company against claims of abuse of a dominant position brought by Pepsico. It has also acted for Canal-Satélite Digital in that company's €100 million damages claim against the Spanish Government, arising from the enforcement of national legislation relating to decoders that proved contrary to EU law. **Clients:** Airtel; El Corte Inglés; Glaxo Wellcome.

Uría & Menéndez (4 ptrs, 6 asscs) The sheer size of the firm's international M&A practice has spawned a top-class competition group, where merger control work is the chief preoccupation. The Spanish team is supported by a six-lawyer Brussels office.

A highly regarded team of associates is *"obsessed with competition law,"* and the firm is considered to be *"professional and amicable."* In control is **Jaime Folguera Crespo***, who is highly visible, *"top-class"* and is felt to have an academic mind that makes him the smart choice for complex matters. **José Pérez Santos***, while more of an all-round commercial lawyer, is also a popular choice.

The range of work here is comprehensive. The BSCH/BBV merger saw the firm acting for both banks before the Spanish authorities, while the firm also represented BSCH on its notification to the EC Commission, following its insurance tie-up with Champalimaud. High-profile work for Telefónica has included the filing of the merger with Endemol and advising on proceedings before the Spanish authorities in connection with the company's Strategic Alliance Agreement with BBVA. The Terra/Lycos merger underlined the firm's ability to deal with multi-jurisdictional filings. **Clients:** Thomson; Bertelsmann; Telefónica.

Garrigues & Andersen (1 ptr, 12 asscs) Felt to be barely a step behind the leaders, the firm has a superb reputation in merger control, abuse of dominant position, restrictive agreements and state aid cases. Since the change in regulations affecting notifications, this area of the practice has seen a notable surge.

Marcos Araujo* earns respect for his leadership of this large team, aided by **Luis Ortiz Blanco***. Together, they are considered to offer *"excellence, experience and great knowledge."* They have been joined by a former MTF economist, who brings further practical experience to the group.

The firm advised on the merger of its client Carrefour with Promodès to create Europe's largest distribution group, and represented the Basque industry association Confebask on a state aid case, defending its use of incentive schemes. **Clients:** Tabacalera; Amadeus; IBM; Argentaria.

Cuatrecasas (2 ptrs, 8 asscs) In both Madrid and Barcelona, the firm's competition lawyers are solidly endorsed for their work on state aid matters for regional governments, telecoms industry complaints, broadcasting rights in football, dominance issues concerning internet access and some energy sector work. **Antonio Creus*** has a reputation for being hard-working and popular. **Cani Fernández*** *"is sharp and holds strong views,"* and spends much of her time at the Brussels office, where she has caught the eye of a number of experienced judges. The firm has advised on numerous recent merger control cases. **Clients:** Domestic and overseas companies.

Freshfields Bruckhaus Deringer (1 ptr, 6 asscs) A magnificent pan-European competition network has helped the firm's Spanish office to mine a rich seam of high-premium cross-border M&A. The firm's pre-eminent Brussels office is home to six more Spanish associates. **Francisco (Paco) Cantos*** leads from the front, and his profile is such that some feel he is competition in the Madrid office.

The firm acted for Altidas subsidiary Logista on a Phase 2 merger investigation by the Spanish authorities, arising from the company's union with Midesa. It has also worked on the second stage investigation of Arjo Wiggins' acquisition of Chartam. EU notifications include ABN AMRO's acquisition of Barclays' leasing business in Europe. **Clients:** PepsiCo; Initec; Sotheby's.

Gomez-Acebo & Pombo (4 ptrs, 7 asscs) An accomplished competition group which deals with a substantial volume of merger control cases, such as acting for Royal Ahold NV on its acquisition of Superdiplo, as well as restrictive agreements and abuse of dominant position matters.

The team's real star is felt to be **Almudena Arpón de Mendívil***. Her practice in the telecoms sector is superb and at the interface between competition and regulatory telecoms issues, she is felt to be so good that our researchers were obliged to place her in a higher category than a number of pure competition specialists. **José María Beneyto***, although seen as more of a generalist than his colleagues, also earns his stripes. His outlook is perceived to be particularly pan-European and he has niche expertise in the German market. Based in Barcelona, **Íñigo Igartua*** *"will always put in a good appearance before the authorities."* He intervened on behalf of the Basque Government before the ECJ in relation to a state aid matter. The firm advised Dana Corporation and GKN plc on its strategic alliance, and achieved a rapid clearance from the Spanish authorities of the acquisition by Dana of GKN's propeller shaft business. It has also dealt with competition issues arising from the merger of savings entities Cajas de Ahorro de Vigo, Ourense and Pontevedra. **Clients:** Panasonic; American Nike; General Counsel of Bars of Attorneys at Law.

Araoz y Rueda (1 ptr, 2 asscs) *"Highly prestigious M&A firm"* which has also established itself as an option for both merger control work and contentious cases. Quality comes in concentrated form, with a small team under the direction of **Alejandro Fernández de Araoz***, commended to researchers as *"a worthy opponent."* The firm acted for Diageo on the clearance of its sale of Cruzcampo to Heineken, and advised Burger King on block exemption arrangements in relation to its franchising and supply agreements. Also acted for AIE and AISGE when they were fined by competition authorities for abuse of a dominant position, a case now under appeal. **Clients:** Parmalat; Imperial Tobacco Ltd; Electrabel/Tractebel.

Clifford Chance (2 ptrs, 5 asscs) Our research discovered that the Spanish market has finally accepted the firm's competition group as a serious threat. The arrival of the *"brilliant"* **Miguel Odriozola*** from Cleary Gottlieb's unsurpassed Brussels office has heralded the perception that the firm is now *"taking care of competition work."* The group has been especially busy on finance and energy transactions, notably handling the filing of Iberdrola's merger with Endesa. Also advised on the referral of TXU's attempted acquisition of Hydrocantábrico to the EU Commission. **Clients:** General Electric; JC Decaux; UPC; Forta.

Jones, Day, Reavis & Pogue (2 ptrs, 3 asscs) G&A Abogados partners, the brothers **José María Jiménez-Laiglesia*** and **Juan Jiménez-Laiglesia*** have, with their small team, signed up with strong competition practice Jones Day. They have developed a reputation as the *"hired guns"* of competition law in Spain, and are noted for a *"youthful and user friendly"* style. The US firm's strong hand in the telecoms sector now teams up with a group that has advised on high-profile gas and electricity transactions, and a variety of state aid matters. **Clients:** Domestic and international corporates.

Melchor, Albiñana & Suárez de Lezo (2 ptrs, 2 asscs) The firm owes its high profile in competition to its strong corporate team, which has provided a steady flow of merger control work. Acting for international blue-chips, the team is considered to be well-connected. During the past twelve months, it has advised on substantial matters in the drinks industry. **Clients:** The Coca-Cola Company; Heineken.

M Vega Penichet (1 ptr, 2 asscs) A traditional name in competition, it is headed by the renowned **Luis Vega Penichet***, who *"knows his stuff."* In spite of the firm's size and domestic orientation, it has a reputation in all aspects of Spanish and EU competition law. **Clients:** Multi-national Companies

SJ Berwin, Pazos, Gallardo & Asociados (2 ptrs, 2 asscs) Strong in Spanish telecoms work, the firm's Spanish office leans heavily on referrals from respected groups in the UK and Brussels. One of the Brussels office's six Spanish competition lawyers has acquired a particular reputation in competition matters affecting the fishing industry. The firm advised on the clearance of the merger between Pescafina and Pescanova. **Clients:** Swatch Group; Diageo.

S

Corporate/M&A

Uría & Menéndez (19 ptrs, 42 asscs) Research shows the firm to represent the elite of the Spanish corporate world. Still fiercely independent, following its rebuff of Linklaters, it maintains a 'best friends' relationship with UK giant Slaughter and May. Renowned for its *"quality all the way,"* the firm's expertise in cross-border M&A is beyond dispute. Investment banks, premier Spanish companies and multi-national leaders rub shoulders in an outstanding client base.

Juan Miguel Goenechea* *("one of Spain's leading lawyers")* has had a busy year, and receives high marks from clients and opponents for his consistency of performance. *"It may be difficult to negotiate with him, but it's a pleasure to have him on a deal."* **Salvador Sánchez-Terán*** is a classic *"of the Uria School; he's proactive and committed to quality."* Well-connected managing partner **Rodrigo Uría Meruéndano*** earns *"a triple gold medal"* for his business skills, while **Juan Luis Iglesias Prada*** is the most recognised of the firm's 'scholar practitioners.'

The firm has acted extensively in the banking sector, and represented both Banco Bilbao Vizcaya and Argentaria on their merger in January 2000, as well as on the subsequent €3 billion rights offering. It also acted for Terra Networks on its €15 billion acquisition of Lycos Inc in May 2000, and two months later was involved in Terra's €3.2 billion IPO. Strong connections with Latin America were exemplified by the firm's work for Telefónica in connection with Project Veronica – the acquisition of all outstanding share capital of subsidiaries in Brazil, Argentina and Peru. **Clients:** BSCH; Groupe Danone; Merrill Lynch; MeesPierson.

Garrigues & Andersen (22 ptrs, 80 asscs) The one place in Europe where MDPs not only exist, but also flourish, plays host to the best of them all. Garrigues' renowned international client base is considered by the market to have dovetailed perfectly with the Andersen strengths, producing a powerful corporate unit.

Ramon Bustillo* is a familiar figure, and those who have encountered him had *"nothing but good experiences"* to report to our researchers. Generally, he advises privately owned clients. Former managing partner **Daniel García-Pita*** has returned to full-time fee-earning, and is seen as a *"key guy"* with *"all the right contacts." "Innovative and creative,"* he has earned the name *"Mr Fix-it." "Absolutely first-class"* **Carlos Loring*** has consolidated his status as a leader in both corporate/M&A and finance work. One recent setback was the departure of Alvaro Sainz to Linklaters.

A fruitful year in domestic and cross-border M&A has included numerous highlights, among them the merger of Spanish and French tobacco companies Tabacalera and Seita into Altadis and the merger of Campofrio with Navidul in July 2000. The firm also advised on Airtours' acquisition of a leading Spanish hotel chain, and assisted NH Group on its Latin American expansion. **Clients:** BMW; Delphi; Grupo Prensa Española; Allianz Zurich.

*See leaders' profiles on pages 629-636

S

SPAIN Leading firms (Corporate/Mergers & Acquisitions)
1 Uría & Menéndez
2 Garrigues & Andersen
3 Clifford Chance
Cuatrecasas
Gomez-Acebo & Pombo
4 Araoz y Rueda
Freshfields Bruckhaus Deringer
Melchor, Albiñana & Suárez de Lezo
5 Landwell
Linklaters
Ramón & Cajal Abogados
6 Allen & Overy
Baker & McKenzie/Baker & McKenzie - Briones Alonso Martin
Garcia Añoveros & Pérez-Llorca
Jones, Day, Reavis & Pogue
SJ Berwin, Pazos, Gallardo & Asociados

Firms are listed alphabetically in each band.

Leading individuals (Corporate/Mergers & Acquisitions)
1 **BUSTILLO Ramon** *Garrigues & Andersen*
GARCÍA-PITA Daniel *Garrigues & Andersen*
GOENECHEA Juan Miguel *Uría & Menéndez*
SÁNCHEZ-TERÁN Salvador *Uría & Menéndez*
2 **ALBIÑANA CILVETI César** *Melchor, Albiñana*
BLANCO José-Luis *Cuatrecasas*
CUATRECASAS Emilio *Cuatrecasas*
GÓMEZ-ACEBO Juan *Freshfields Bruckhaus*
HERVADA Joaquín *Freshfields Bruckhaus*
LORING Carlos *Garrigues & Andersen*
PEÑA Francisco *Gomez-Acebo & Pombo*
POMBO Fernando *Gomez-Acebo & Pombo*
RUEDA Pedro *Araoz y Rueda*
SÁINZ Álvaro *Linklaters*
URÍA MERUÉNDANO Rodrigo *Uría & Menéndez*
3 **DE LAS CUEVAS Fernando** *Gomez-Acebo*
GOMEZ-JORDANA Iñigo *Clifford Chance*
IGLESIAS PRADA Juan Luis *Uría & Menéndez*
RAMÓN Y CAJAL Pedro *Ramón & Cajal*
TENA Juan *Jones, Day, Reavis & Pogue*
TORRENTE Fernando *Cuatrecasas*
4 **DE SAN ROMAN Jaime** *Clifford Chance*
FERNÁNDEZ DE ARAOZ Alejandro *Araoz y Rueda*
OJANGUREN Ignacio *Clifford Chance*
SUÁREZ DE LEZO Rafael *Melchor, Albiñana*
VALVERDE Antoni *Freshfields Bruckhaus*

Individuals are listed alphabetically in each band.

Clifford Chance (6 ptrs, 41 asscs) Now performing a volume of domestic corporate work unmatched by other Anglo-Saxon firms in Spain, the office benefits from having been established for nearly two decades. Although not as active in financial M&A last year, the firm did advise e-banking client First-e on its merger with Uno Bank S.A. However, energy and telecoms have seen a noticeable increase in instructions, and there has also been growth in private equity work, in no small part due to clients such as Dinamia and Capital Priva.

Our researchers were impressed by the market acclamation for the firm's individuals, who as a team, were described as *"the right lawyers at the right time."* *"Strong technician"* **Iñigo Gomez-Jordana*** has *"a transactionally-oriented way of operating and he knows how investment banks want things done."* **Jaime de San Roman*** is admired for his flexibility. *"He knows the law and comes up with ingenious solutions."* Also recommended is **Ignacio Ojanguren***.

In the energy sector, the team acted for TXU Europe's acquisition of a 20% stake in Hydrocantábrico for €500 million. Elsewhere, it advised Telefónica on its US$1.6 billion acquisition of mediaWays GmbH from Bertelsmann. **Clients:** Iberdrola; CVC Capital Partners; Kimberly-Clark; Philip Morris.

Cuatrecasas (14 ptrs, 75 asscs) Often seen as a Barcelona firm, it is now acknowledged to have a substantial and established Madrid practice. Historically seen on mid-sized deals, the group has been increasingly visible on bigger-ticket transactions, and is often recommended by rivals for conflict referrals. A top-notch tax practice is considered to be a vital element of the corporate team's success. Strong affiliations with firms in Brazil and Argentina have been bolstered by the opening of a six-lawyer New York office in October 2000. **José-Luis Blanco*** received rave reviews from some of our interviewees, while **Emilio Cuatrecasas*** remains one of the best known of Spain's corporate lawyers, and has been dubbed *"the best managing partner in Spain"* by some commentators. He is on the board of several Spanish companies, and acts as primary corporate advisor to a number of them. **Fernando Torrente*** is a versatile and respected commercial practitioner.

The firm has handled a number of major transactions, such as the acquisition by Vodafone of a stake in Airtel, and the merger of Terra with Lycos. It has also advised Chase Manhattan (advisor to Iberdrola) in connection with Endesa's bid to take over Iberdrola. **Clients:** Prodigios; Sol Meliá; Uno-eBank; Patagon; Suiza Foods Corp.

Gomez-Acebo & Pombo A respected independent firm with a good mixture of international and domestic clients. Although by no means the largest in Spain, the corporate group features consistently in high-end transactions in energy, the food industry and the high-tech sector.

Francisco Peña* is valued by clients for his experience on the top deals. **Fernando Pombo*** is the firm's executive chairman, as well as being treasurer of the IBA. He works on large transactions in an advisory capacity, and is also involved in arbitration work, often sitting as an arbitrator. **Fernando de las Cuevas*** receives much of the credit for the development of the firm's Latin American work. A number of the firm's lawyers are also qualified in the US, UK, Germany and France.

The team has acted for the Dutch food group Royal Ahold NV on various acquisitions in Spain, including the Kampio group and the tender offer for listed company Superdiplo (over US$1 billion). It also advised Iberdrola on its reorganisation into production, distribution and sales divisions. **Clients:** Excite; Iveco Renault; Hughes Microelectronics; BP Oil.

Araoz y Rueda (5 ptrs, 7 asscs) Small but *"young and aggressive"* firm, acting for top clients on a number of significant international transactions. The firm continues to advise Perrier-Vittel on its expansion in Latin America, and has been picking up work for General Electric. Fund and private equity work is also a key element of the workload.

"Professional" **Pedro Rueda*** is respected for his tough approach, while **Alejandro Fernández de Araoz*** is acknowledged for his transactional abilities, although our research has shown that he is even better known for competition advice. The firm advised on the sale of Cruzcampo by Diageo plc, and advises on much of the Spanish investment by UK fund 3i. The group has also established a reputation for its work in new generation telecoms, largely through its advice to Sonera, Finnish technical partner in Xfera, the successful consortium in the 3G licence auction. **Clients:** Tractebel; Yahoo!; Burger King España.

Freshfields Bruckhaus Deringer Felt to have been making *"a very big effort"* lately, the firm's ten year-old Spanish office is now an established part of the legal landscape. An omnipotent global corporate network has assisted the team in Madrid to advise heavyweight multi-nationals on important cross-border transactions across a range of industries.

Joaquín Hervada's* competitors concede that *"he always does a good job,"* while **Juan Gómez-Acebo*** takes versatility to a new level, advising on corporate matters, aircraft financing and real estate transactions. The key name in the smaller Barcelona office is **Antoni Valverde***.

The firm acted for Hewlett Packard on its Spanish de-merger and subsequent creation of Agilent Technologies, and advised Merrill Lynch and the vendors on the disposal of Burberry Spain to GUS for US$240 million. Also represented Grupo Torras on the auction sale of Torraspapel and Teletech on the all-share acquisition of CTC for US$100 million. **Clients:** Pearson; Warner; RJ Reynolds; Nabisco.

Melchor, Albiñana & Suárez de Lezo (6 ptrs, 20 asscs) Traditional firm, which is respected for its strength in administrative law and enjoys long-standing relationships with top clients, including the government. Our researchers found a corporate team that is regarded as a rising force.

César Albiñana Cilveti* is *"rated for his flexibility,"* while **Rafael Suárez de Lezo*** continues to win his share of market support. The firm advised on the Spanish aspects of Heineken's purchase of Grupo Cruzcampo from Diageo, the €165 million rights issue in Heineken's subsidiary, El Aguila, and the final merger of that subsidiary with Cruzcampo to become Heineken España S.A. Also advised Grupo Boluda on the acquisition of the operators of both Valencia's and Barcelona's shipyards. Portuguese client Group Espirito Santo instructed the firm in connection with the purchase of the Benito y Monjardin group and of Gescapital/Hiscapital. **Clients:** Repsol; Endesa; Banco Santander; Segur Iberica SA.

Landwell (8 ptrs, 72 asscs) Containing a number of ex-Garrigues and ex-Mullerat & Roca lawyers, the corporate team, which is based in Madrid and Barcelona, maintains its reputation among its peers as the best of those at the accountancy firms after Garrigues. Working with its esteemed tax department, the firm acts primarily for international clients on inward investment into Spain. In the past year its biggest instructions have come from hotels and leisure, telecoms, the automobile industry and pharmaceuticals. **Clients:** Multinationals and domestic companies.

Linklaters (7 ptrs, 20 asscs) The firm has undertaken a vigorous recruitment programme in Madrid, and Chambers' research indicates that the corporate team has benefited accordingly. **Álvaro Sáinz**'s* recent arrival from Garrigues is considered to be a major coup for the rapidly growing office. He is respected for maintaining a strong position on deals but at the same time knowing how to let them proceed. *"He's not a deal killer but a deal maker. He's that rare thing, a reasonable lawyer!"*

Advising a predominantly international clientele, the firm has been involved in a number of cross-border transactions, including the merger of Krasnapolsky and NH Hoteles, with the merged company to be listed in both Madrid and Amsterdam. The firm also represented Morgan Stanley and Warburg Dillon Read on the bid made by TXU for Hidroélectrica del Cantábrico. **Clients:** Jazz Telecom SA; National Power; HSBC.

Ramón & Cajal Abogados (3 ptrs, 4 asscs) Active and growing its profile in M&A, although the finance work of the firm is still considered to be its strong suit. **Pedro Ramón y Cajal*** has the *"qualities of a traditional Spanish lawyer,"* and is technically proficient. As a former state abogado, he is *"equipped with the right contacts."* Primarily known for its work on behalf of leading Spanish companies, the team has a consistent profile for blue-chip clients. It has been instructed by more than half of the IBEX-35, having acted for four of the top five companies. Last year it worked on the merger of national food and dairy groups and several IPOs, including Logista and Repsol. **Clients:** Major Spanish companies.

Allen & Overy (3 ptrs, 8 asscs) Although still labouring in the shadow of the more developed Anglo-Saxon firms in Spain, the firm is considered to have made a clear advance this year. Our research has shown that the catalyst was the arrival of the legal team of Satrustegui & Asociados in November 1999.

Now breaking into IPOs and advising on larger deals and spin-off transactions, the office feeds off referrals from others in the firm's European network, advising Dutch brewer Heineken on its entry into the Spanish drinks market via Cruzcampo. The firm also advised Goldman Sachs on Endesa's bid for Iberdrola. **Clients:** Campofrio; Morgan Grenfell Private Equity; KPN; Aon.

Baker & McKenzie/Baker & McKenzie – Briones Alonso Martin (7 ptrs, 33 asscs) A long-established presence in Madrid and Barcelona, the firm is best known for its *"commercial work for big international clients"* and sector-led success, notably in energy, telecoms and IP. However, it is not felt to be surging forward in the same way as corporate departments of other international law firms, although it has pioneered the introduction of virtual deal rooms. The firm acted for a client in a joint venture with a major Spanish bank in B2B exchanges in Latin America and Spain, and acted for shareholders of En Effecto on the €43 million acquisition of the group by Das Werk. **Clients:** RSL Comm; AT Kearney; Clear Channel.

Garcia Añoveros & Pérez Llorca (5 ptrs 24 asscs) M&A is a major focus for this small but rapidly expanding firm, which was started in the early 80s by two former state lawyers. In spite of the death last year of one of the firm's founders, Jaime García Añoveros, the firm continues to be recommended by our interviewees for its transactional work on behalf of French, British and American clients. Private equity work for both internet and traditional ventures is an area of niche strength.

The firm acted for US investor Capital Z Partners on its US$25 million investment in internet company Infotel, and completed a complicated disposal by Williams plc of the paints and coatings group Robbialac to Dinamia and Natwest Private Equity Partners for €124 million. **Clients:** Altadis; MCH Private Equity; BDB Midham; MyAlert.

Jones, Day, Reavis & Pogue (12 lawyers) **Juan Tena*** *("a wonderfully solid and dependable lawyer")* and his lawyers have transferred to Jones Day. The prospect of combining Tena's already respected corporate practice with the US firm's powerful international clientele, notably in the telecoms sector, is an interesting one to several of our interviewees. The firm has represented Endesa in connection with its $300 million acquisition of the Chilean mobile telephone company Smart-Com. It also represented BSCH, Royal Bank of Scotland and Charterhouse, majority shareholders of Superdiplo, in the $1.2 billion bid launched by Ahold, the Dutch supermarket chain. **Clients:** Lafarge; ABN AMRO; Acciona; Ferrovial.

SJ Berwin, Pazos, Gallardo & Asociados Reflecting the strong profile of the firm's other European offices in private equity work, the Madrid office also has *"a niche in private equity,"* especially *"in the internet start-up area."* The team includes some multi-talented lawyers. It worked on the recent merger of Pescanova and Pescafina, and also represented the shareholders in the sale of 100% of Benito y Monjardin to Banco y Espirito Santo. Also represented Buongiorno in its acquisition of Spanish Company Click Precision. **Clients:** Dresdner Kleinwort Benson; European Investment Fund; Mercapital; BSCH.

S

*See leaders' profiles on pages 629-636

Intellectual Property

SPAIN Leading firms (Intellectual Property)
1 Gomez-Acebo & Pombo
2 Clifford Chance
Bufete Mullerat
Pintó Ruiz & Del Valle
Bufete Socoró & Grau
Uría & Menéndez
3 Baker & McKenzie/Baker & McKenzie - Briones Alonso Martin
Garrigues & Andersen

Firms are listed alphabetically in each band.

Leading individuals (Intellectual Property)
1 **DE ULLOA Gonzalo** *Gomez-Acebo*
GRAU Jorge *Bufete Socoró & Grau*
MASSAGUER Jose *Uría & Menéndez*
MUÑOZ-DELGADO Jesus *Gomez-Acebo*
VALLS Carlos *Clifford Chance*
2 **ANGULO Alejandro** *Bufete Mullerat*
BERCOVITZ RODRIGUEZ-CANO Rodrigo *Bercovitz-Carvajal*
CASTAN Antonio *Elzaburu*
DEL VALLE Javier *Pintó Ruiz & Del Valle*
FERNANDEZ-NOVOA Luis *Gomez-Acebo*
GUIX Victor *Victor Guix Estudio Jurídico*
LEMA DEVESA Carlos *Estudio Jurídico Lema*
MONTAÑÁ MORA Miquel *Clifford Chance*
OTERO LASTRES José Manuel *Otero Lastres*

Individuals are listed alphabetically in each band.

Gomez-Acebo & Pombo (4 ptrs, 13 asscs) *"Number one by any definition,"* the firm has its roots in this area of law. It fields a large team and offers some of the best known names in IP. In non-contentious matters, the team handles corporate support, advisory reports on portfolio protection, structure and strategy. Its work leans more towards litigation, and within this the split between patents and trademarks is even. In the former, important clients are to be found in pharmaceuticals, chemicals and biotechnology, while the firm has acted on trademark cases in textiles, drinks and luxury goods. The firm has had substantial recent experience of domain name disputes.

Gonzalo de Ulloa* leads the team, which also includes the strongly recommended **Jesús Muñoz-Delgado***. Eminence grise **Luis Fernandez-Novoa***, who specialises in copyright advice, has a consultancy with the firm, and has been referred to as *"the father of IP in Spain."* The firm advised Bacardi on the company's claim against the Cuban Government for the recovery of the Havana Club brand. Also advised General Electric on a patent infringement action with Asahi concerning plastics produced in Cartagena. **Clients:** Nike; Chevron; Merck; Novartis; Motorola; UDV.

Clifford Chance (2 ptrs, 10 asscs) A Barcelona based IP group that will *"do it all,"* but was especially commended in our research for its *"excellent co-ordination of litigation."* Two names stand out. **Carlos Valls*** and **Miquel Montañá Mora*** are both well-known for their litigation skills, especially in patents, an area in which the firm has a good track record and acts for seven leading international pharmaceuticals laboratories. Trademark work is an increasing element of the caseload.

The firm advised Cordoniu in its high profile dispute with Freixenet, and successfully obtained a ban for Philip Morris on the parallel importation of cigarettes from outside the EU, using the 'silhouette' principle. Last year, the team handled the IP aspects of the sale of Revlon's worldwide professional haircare business. **Clients:** San Carlo; Calloway Golf; Esteve.

Bufete Mullerat (2 ptrs, 10 asscs) With most of its IP specialists in Barcelona, the firm splits the remainder between offices in Madrid and Lisbon and now Seville and San Sebastian following its merger with Echarri & Brindle in early 2001. Respected by competitors for both litigation and non-contentious work, the firm's caseload ranges from corporate support work to licensing agreements and assignment of rights to TM and patent infringement cases.

Alejandro Angulo* has built up a particularly good reputation here. He heads a team that has advised extensively on anti-counterfeiting cases across the Iberian peninsula, primarily in the clothing business. Its brand name client base is impressive, and includes companies in pharmaceuticals, textiles, food, sport and leisure. **Clients:** Domestic and European companies.

Pintó Ruiz & Del Valle (4 ptrs, 8 asscs) *"Active and successful trademark lawyers,"* the specialist IP firm of Del Valle merged with commercial practice Pintó Ruiz in 1999. Other lawyers attest that *"you always see them on cases."* Especially recommended for its work on anti-counterfeiting cases, the team includes the esteemed **Javier del Valle***, the firm's joint managing partner. Of late the firm has been a presence in anti-counterfeiting work for clients in luxury goods, especially watches, toys, sports, spirits and pharmaceuticals. In patents it has developed its plant varieties protection work. **Clients:** Multinational brand and patent owners.

Bufete Socoró & Grau (3 ptrs, 3 asscs) Described as *"a reliable and honest team of fighters,"* this Barcelona boutique has impressed everyone. Seen as *"a classic of its type,"* in a country where IP boutiques are the norm, it generally acts for the owners of patents and trademarks. The firm's client base embraces both domestic and international concerns.

Jorge Grau* *("one of the best in the business")* is the leading light of a firm that opponents admit, *"we meet a lot."* Aside from its well-known litigation work, the firm is also instructed on non-contentious matters, including copyright and unfair competition (passing off). **Clients:** Domestic and international companies.

Uría & Menéndez (2 ptrs, 7 asscs) A force in both Barcelona and Madrid, the firm acts for heavyweight names in entertainment, food, beverages and pharmaceuticals. In addition to high-profile corporate support work, the team deals with contested TM registrations and disputes among owners of marks, patents and domain names. **José Massaguer*** is a popular and respected IP advisor.

Copyright defence features heavily in the caseload, and the firm advised Zeppelin Televisión in relation to the assignment of rights for the TV show Big Brother. Its client Sol Melia, SA challenged the Spanish Audio-Visual Producers Collecting Entity (EGEDA) regarding dues payable by hotels. **Clients:** Sol Melia; Zeppelin Television.

Baker & McKenzie/Baker & McKenzie – Briones Alonso Martin (2 ptrs, 8 asscs) In offices around the world, Baker & McKenzie's IP lawyers share big name clients. In Spain, the group operates from both the Barcelona and Madrid offices, concentrating on trademarks rather than patents.

Some of the firm's associates are also qualified as TM and Industrial Property Agents. Infringement and cyber-squatting are policed for clients, including many in the fashion industry, and the team also gives copyright advice to clients in IT, book publishing and TV production. **Clients:** Domestic and international companies.

Garrigues & Andersen (1 ptr, 5 asscs) The team is part of a wider group that provides a full range of legal services relating to patents and trademarks.

The firm also has a filing and prosecution agency – G&A, Patents y Marcas. An impressive list of brand name clients in consumer goods keeps the team busy in several areas, and it also acts for a number of Spain's advertising agencies. Recently advised Spanish company Cidesport on its TM dispute with Nike. **Clients:** Rolex; Chanel; PepsiCo; Real Madrid; Gillette; Colgate Palmolive.

Other Notable Practitioners **Rodrigo Bercovitz Rodriguez-Cano*** of Estudio Jurídico Bercovitz-Carvajal Sociedad Civil is a highly reputed copyright specialist with a client base that includes significant names in music publishing such as Sony, Universal, Warner and EMI. **Antonio Castan*** is the lead lawyer within the legal unit of Spain's biggest TM and patent agency Elzaburu. Although the unit has a short history, he is firmly endorsed by his peers. **Carlos Lema Devesa*** is a well-known professor who runs a small Madrid IP boutique, Estudio Jurídico Lema. He acts for a mix of Spanish and international clients in food and drink and consumer goods, advising on patents and TMs, with some copyright work. **Victor Guix*** of Victor Guix Estudio Jurídico is respected for his advice on TMs and patents for national and multi-national clients such as Benckiser and Agrolinen. **José Manuel Otero Lastres*** is a partner at Bufete Otero Lastres. Working primarily on contentious matters, he has acted for clients such as Procter & Gamble and Danone. Last year, he acted for REGI on its dispute over motor parts with Ford.

S

Tax

Cuatrecasas (26 ptrs, 150 asscs) A powerful presence in Spanish tax law, the firm has moved well beyond its one-time reputation as a domestically oriented firm, and is now acknowledged for its international client base. The firm has grown with the economy and recently opened a New York office. On home turf, *"Cuatrecasas is king in this field."*

Javier Laorden* earns his ranking as a *"solid"* favourite, working particularly on inward investment and with domestic clients. Former tax inspector and dual-qualified lawyer/economist **Eduardo Ramírez*** is *"really brilliant, even though he's had a short career in private practice,"* and has a niche in financial products. **Alex Escoda***, who runs the international tax and corporate planning unit, and respected all-rounder **Rafael Fontana*** were also recommended to Chambers' researchers. **Clients:** Domestic and international corporates and financial institutions.

Garrigues & Andersen (45 ptrs, 227 asscs) Comprehensive coverage of all areas of tax work is provided by the firm's unmatched Spanish network of 22 offices. A primary focus on tax as an accountancy-linked law firm has been accentuated by the size and quality of the group's work, notably tax planning and transactional advice in the energy and telecoms industries.

Ex-Secretary of State for Taxes, **Santiago Ilundain*** has responsibility for the international team. Praised for being *"effective in the tax litigation field, he has a lot of ideas and he doesn't lose his nerve."* **Abelardo Delgado*** is famed for his domestic tax advice, corporate tax expert **Ricardo Gómez*** is a respected choice for referrals from other top firms; he is said to be *"someone you can rely on."* **Luis Guerreiro*** *("good on financial work")* has a high profile in the insurance industry, **Ernesto Jiménez*** advises many of Spain's leading companies, **Eduardo Gardeta*** specialises in VAT and **José Palacios*** is renowned for his international tax advice. Cesar Ortega has moved in-house at BSCH, while Dionisio Martinez has left the law. **Clients:** Domestic and international corporates and financial institutions.

Baker & McKenzie/Baker & McKenzie – Briones Alonso Martin (5 ptrs, 20 asscs) On 1st January 2001 top-class niche tax practice Briones Alonso Martin & Associados merged with Baker & McKenzie. The merger provides a powerful shot in the arm to Baker & McKenzie's tax practice. International and domestic tax expertise abounded at Briones, with particular strength existing in VAT matters and tax litigation. This *"classic, successfully grown"* niche firm had parted company with French ally Bureau Francis Lefèbvre in November 2000, as if in readiness for the merger.

Luis Briones Fernandez* is *"a leader in every sense"* and is regarded as a pioneer in his international approach to tax law. **Felipe Alonso*** is a *"good strategist,"* particularly in domestic work, with a practice that encompasses both litigation and VAT. **Enrique Leon Sanchez***, now a partner, concentrates on international work. Last year the firm successfully challenged the legitimacy of certain items of Spanish VAT law in the ECJ. **Clients:** EADS group.

Ernst & Young Abogados (30 ptrs, 266 asscs) *"Excellent tax lawyers with a good view of the market."* **Jaime Lopez Chicheri*** leads the legal side of the auditing firm. Individuals of his standing are said to instil *"a huge amount of confidence in clients."* **Eduardo Sanfrutos*** is thought by some to be the *"heir apparent."* His strength is considered to lie in his technical proficiency. **José María Cervelló*** has a broad perspective, and is praised for his commercial approach.

Found to be acting for multi-nationals around half of the time but now focusing on building up relationships with Spanish blue-chips. The firm is said to produce so many of Spain's leading tax lawyers that *"it acts as a greenhouse for the rest of the country."* It advises on tax planning and structuring, dealing with the complexities of Spanish holdings legislation and consequent group re-organisations. It has particularly strong and beneficial relationships with other E&Y offices in Europe and has recently developed a Latin American business centre in Madrid. Sector strengths appear in insurance, oil and power companies, health and pharmaceuticals and communications. E-business is on the rise. **Clients:** Multi-nationals; large Spanish companies and banks.

Landwell The firm acts for all sectors of Spanish business, as well as a number of multi-nationals. Divided into specialist groups; the tax department deals with financial, M&A, international and direct and indirect taxation work.

Former director-general of the fiscal administration, **Miguel Cruz Amoros*** is described as a *"gold medal winner"* and a real intellectual resource. **Isidro del Saz Cordero*** is the firm's leading face on transactional work, while **Juan Ramon Ramos*** is also highly recommended. Over the past year, the firm has advised extensively on the tax aspects of cross-border M&A and restructuring cases. **Clients:** Domestic and international corporates and financial institutions.

Uría & Menéndez (2 ptrs, 20 asscs) Support on corporate transactions accounts for around 50% of the tax team's work, with the remainder ranging from tax planning to litigation on behalf of its widely blue-chip clientele. The head of the tax team in Madrid is ex-fiscal inspector **Jesús López Tello***, described as *"a brilliant and well-prepared*

*See leaders' profiles on pages 629-636

SPAIN Leading firms (Tax)
1 Cuatrecasas
Garrigues & Andersen
2 Baker & McKenzie/Baker & McKenzie - Briones Alonso Martin
Ernst & Young Abogados
3 Landwell
Uría & Menéndez
4 Clifford Chance
Freshfields Bruckhaus Deringer
5 Bufete Barrilero & Asociados
Gomez-Acebo & Pombo
Estudio Jurídico Almagro
KPMG Abogados

Firms are listed alphabetically in each band.

Leading individuals (Tax)
1 **BRIONES FERNANDEZ Luis** *Baker & McKenzie*
CRUZ AMOROS Miguel *Landwell*
ILUNDAIN Santiago *Garrigues & Andersen*
LAORDEN Javier *Cuatrecasas*
2 **ALONSO Felipe** *Baker & McKenzie*
BARRILERO Eduardo *Barrilero & Asociados*
DEL SAZ CORDERO Isidro *Landwell*
DELGADO Abelardo *Garrigues & Andersen*
GUERREIRO Luis *Garrigues & Andersen*
JIMÉNEZ BLANCO José Ignacio *Clifford Chance*
LOPEZ CHICHERI Jaime *Ernst & Young*
LÓPEZ TELLO Jesús *Uría & Menéndez*
RAMÍREZ Eduardo *Cuatrecasas*
3 **CASANOVA Carlos** *Estudio Jurídico Almagro*
ESCODA Alex *Cuatrecasas*
FONTANA Rafael *Cuatrecasas*
FUSTER Rafael *Uría & Menéndez*
GARCIA LLANEZA Rafael *Uría & Menéndez*
GÓMEZ Ricardo *Garrigues & Andersen*
JIMÉNEZ Ernesto *Garrigues & Andersen*
KLINGENBERG Miguel *Freshfields Bruckhaus*
LEON SANCHEZ Enrique *Baker & McKenzie*
PALACIOS José *Garrigues & Andersen*
SANFRUTOS Eduardo *Ernst & Young*
4 **BENITEZ Carlos** *Gomez-Acebo & Pombo*
CERVELLÓ José María *Ernst & Young*
DE FRANCISCO José Antonio *Almagro*
DE ROJAS Mercedes *KPMG Abogados*
GARDETA Eduardo *Garrigues & Andersen*
RAMON RAMOS Juan *Landwell*

Individuals are listed alphabetically in each band.

lawyer." Our researchers were impressed by the warmth of recommendation for **Rafael Fuster***, who has noteworthy banking client roster. "*He may be young but he's already one of the best.*" **Rafael García Llaneza*** is recognised for his adaptability in a number of different areas of tax. Two more tax associates work from the New York office.

Last year saw advice on the tax aspects of a number of mergers between banking clients, such as Banco Santander, Hispania and Agentaria. The firm also restructured the Latin American interests of BBVA. Other important work has included the creation of a pan-European company for client Metropolitan Life to create a new structure for the sale of life assurance products. **Clients:** Telefónica; Endesa; Xfera; JP Morgan; Morgan Stanley.

Clifford Chance (1 ptr, 4 asscs) The team has almost doubled in the last 12 months, reflecting the growth in the tax business of the firm. More than half of the work is now domestic, but powerful international banks still feature prominently in the client roster.

José Ignacio Jiménez Blanco* is the real force in the tax team. He provides *"80% of the impact,"* even though he represents 20% of the manpower. In the last year, the firm has advised BSCH on the implementation of a tax lease structure for Transmediterranea's new fleet, and also advised the bank on the tax-structured financing for RENFE. Corporate support and property-related tax advice complement the finance work. Advised the managers of Ya.com on the tax aspects of its buyout by T-Online. **Clients:** HSBC; Citibank; Santander Investment; Société Générale.

Freshfields Bruckhaus Deringer (1 ptr, 7 asscs) Although it benefits from a strong relationship with financial clients and is seen to be working hard to develop that side of the tax practice, the firm's greatest impact is considered to come from its advice on the tax aspects of corporate and real estate transactions. Domestic and international tax issues are handled by the team, in which **Miguel Klingenberg*** stands out.

The firm advised Nabisco on the Spanish tax aspects of its takeover of United Biscuits. Also acted for Pearson on the transfer of its indirect shareholdings in two TV companies to RTL Group, and Goldman Sachs on a number of structured financing products. Another matter of importance was the structuring of Mahou's acquisition of the brewer San Miguel from Danone. **Clients:** JP Morgan; Morgan Stanley; Scottish Widows; Tyco International.

Bufete Barrilero & Asociados (6 ptrs, 20 asscs) Known for its *"confident"* tax structuring and strategic tax advice, the firm is based in Bilbao, and has offices in Barcelona, Madrid and Seville. **Eduardo Barrilero*** (formerly of Cuatrecasas and Garrigues) is the recommended name and is especially popular with family-owned companies and entrepreneurial clients in Spain.

Gomez-Acebo & Pombo (2 ptrs, 10 asscs) Three years after the arrival of well-regarded tax specialist **Carlos Benitez*** from Baker & McKenzie, the firm has recruited again, this time from UBS. The new arrival's specialism lies in tax advice on financial products, which is expected to dovetail effectively with the firm's existing corporate tax expertise. This embraces advice on the tax aspects of IPOs, corporate restructuring and cross-border acquisitions. **Clients:** 3i Europe plc; UBS; AXA Group; Columbia; Time Warner.

Estudio Jurídico Almagro (6 ptrs) *"Creative"* firm, which is known to advise both domestic and international clients on a range of tax matters. The senior figures here, **Carlos Casanova*** and **José Antonio de Francisco*** are both former Ernst & Young partners, and were warmly recommended to our researchers by competitors. Last year the firm was involved in the launch in the Madrid stock exchange of shares of the Prisa Group. **Clients:** Large multi-nationals and domestic corporates.

KPMG Abogados Although not possessing the profile of the other ranked accountancy firms, the group can call on the services of the managing partner of the Madrid office, **Mercedes de Rojas***, who is respected for a range of tax advice. It has experience of a number of transactions that require advice on tax planning opportunities and tax optimised structures. Recent work included acting for a Spanish client acquired by a large US-based autoparts company, including advising on due diligence and the structuring of the deal. **Clients:** medium to large Spanish companies with cross-border business.

*See leaders' profiles on pages 629-636

Leaders' profiles – Spain

ALBELLA, Sebastian
Ramón & Cajal Abogados, Madrid
+34 91 576 1900
Recommended in Banking & Finance

ALBIÑANA CILVETI, César
Melchor, Albiñana & Suárez de Lezo, Madrid
+34 91 451 9300
Recommended in Banking & Finance, Corporate/M&A
Specialisation: Senior Partner of the Firm. Main area of work is Corporate Law, mainly mergers and acquisitions, securities markets, finance, contracts and investment, Administrative Law, Arbitration, Taxation Law. Is a member of the Board of Directors of Jotsa-Holzmann, Naviera Pinillos, Aguas de Valencia, Lazard, S&C Willis Corroon. Has handled acquisitions of companies and undertakings of varying sorts of national and foreign clients. Has been active in mergers and acquisitions, securities and capital markets (e.g. on the sale of Petromed to British Petroleum; Uni'n y Fénix to AGF; of Tudor to Exide Corporation; the placement of a percentage of the capital stock of Antena 3 de Televisi'n; for Arbed on the purchase of Aceralia; for Telefonica Media on the purchase of Uniprex and Cadena Voz; for Grupo Boluda on the acquisition of Naviera Pinillos). International Public Offering of Recoletos (Person's subsidiary). Author of different articles on legal matters and speaker at various conferences.
Prof. Memberships: Madrid Bar Association since 1984.
Career: BA and Master's degree in Law, Deusto University, Bilbao and BA and Master's Degree in Business, (ICADE). Law Officer of the Estate (1982), on leave. Professor of Administrative Law at the University of Comillas, ICADE from 1984 to 1991. Member of 'Consejo de Defensa de la Competencia' (Ministry of Commerce) from 1984 to 1985. Member of the 'Comision de Fusion de Empresas' (Ministry of Economy and Finance) from 1984 to 1988. Attorney of Law for the Constitutional Court from 1985 to 1987. Joined *Melchor de las Heras, Albiñana & Suárez de Lezo* in 1995 as Partner.
Personal: Born in Madrid on October 10, 1955. Lives in Madrid.

ALLENDESALAZAR CORCHO, Rafael
Martinez Lage & Asociados, Madrid
+34 91 426 4470
Recommended in Competition/Anti-trust

ALONSO, Felipe
Baker & McKenzie-Briones Alonso Martin, Madrid
+34 91 436 4300
felipe.alonso@bakernet.com
Recommended in Tax
Specialisation: VAT, tax litigation and tax planning.
Prof. Memberships: Member of the Madrid Bar Association; Member of the Spanish Association of Lawyers specialising in Tax Law and of the Board of the Foundation for the Promotion of Studies on Financial Law.
Publications: REVISTA CARTA TRIBUTARIA - 'Deductions in VAT'; ESCUELA HACIENDA PUBLICA, 'Multiproperty and VAT', 'Systematic analysis of the limited exemptions in the Spanish Tax System'; NOTICIAS C.E.E. – 'The simplified regime in VAT'.
Career: University of Madrid (Autónoma) – Law Degree. Inspector of Finances at the Ministry of Finance, on leave; General Subdirector of Regulation and Legal Assistance in the General Directorate of Tax and Financial Inspection of the Ministry of Economy and Finances.
Personal: Chair of Financial and Tax Law in the Law Schools of Valencia and Universidad Autonoma de Madrid; School of Financial and Tax Inspection (Escuela de Hacienda Publica) and Panel member in several seminars, lectures and other teaching activities in tax related matters.

ANGULO, Alejandro
Bufete Mullerat, Barcelona +34 93 405 9300
Recommended in Intellectual Property

ARAUJO, Marcos
Garrigues & Andersen, Madrid +34 91 514 5200
marcos.araujo@garriguesandersen.com
Recommended in Competition/Anti-trust
Specialisation: Partner in charge of EC and Competition Law at *Garrigues & Andersen.* Areas of work include defence and complaints of anticompetitive behaviours, filings for individual exemptions, notification of mergers before the EC MTF and the Spanish Authorities, state aids and telecoms.
Prof. Memberships: Madrid Bar Association (1991).
Career: Law Faculty at the University of Alicante with two additional years Doctorate studies in EC Law. Joined *Garrigues & Andersen* in 1990, and became Partner in 1996. Teaches community and competition law at the Insituto de Empresa's MBA (Madrid) and Telecommunications law at ICADE. Often lectures on competition and community law matters, and has published many articles in these areas.

ARPÓN DE MENDÍVIL, Almudena
Gomez-Acebo & Pombo, Madrid +34 91 582 9100
aam@gomezacebo-pombo.com
Recommended in Communications, Competition/Anti-trust
Specialisation: Head of the Communications and Competition Group of the firm. Extensive experience in the legal advice of corporations with business in the communications area, which includes telecommunications, media and IT; has advised clients for the creation of alliances, in particular, for the submission of offers for the second and third Spanish global operators and others; intervened in the negotiations of interconnection agreements, advised alternative infrastructure companies – such as Metro de Madrid – for the provision of their networks to third parties, drafted terms and conditions for the rendering of voice and data services; handled the negotiation of contracts on Airtel's (second mobile operator) shareholding, advises foreign investors in satellite activities. On anti-trust, the Group acts before the anti-trust courts at national and European level, providing legal advice in cases of mergers, alliances and joint ventures agreements in sectors such as basic industries, telecommunications, energy, construction, pharmaceuticals, standardisation organisations, professional organisations, etc. Has initiated procedures for the removal of legal provisions and administrative actions contrary to competition in several fields – film distribution, telecommunications (several), packaging and waste.
Prof. Memberships: Spanish Bar Association (Madrid), Vice chair of the International Bar Association (IBA) Committee on Communications Law. Chair of the Regulatory Commission of the Spanish Telecommunications Users Association; Telecommunications and Information Technologies Commission of the ICC; European Space Law Centre; Management Body of the Spanish Association of Telecommunications and Information technologies Law.
Career: Qualified in 1985. Master in EC Law at the College of Bruges (1986-87); PIL at Harvard Law School (1990); Academy of American and International law at the South Western Legal Foundation (Dallas, Texas 1993). Joined *Gomez-Acebo & Pombo* in Brussels (1987-89), and from then in Madrid. Partner (1994), and member of the Management Committee (1998).

BARRILERO, Eduardo
Bufete Barrilero & Asociados, Bilbao
+34 94 479 3400
Recommended in Tax

BAUTISTA, Fernando
Freshfields Bruckhaus Deringer, Madrid
+34 91 319 1024
fernando.bautista@freshfields.com
Recommended in Banking & Finance
Specialisation: Has an estalished reputation in banking, finance and capital markets work and significant experience of Spanish privatisations, private sector IPO's and securities generally.

BENEYTO, José María
Gomez-Acebo & Pombo, Madrid +34 91 582 9100
jmbeneyto@gomezacebo-pombo.com
Recommended in Competition/Anti-trust
Specialisation: Partner in Corporate Department. Main area of work is corporate law, principally mergers, acquisitions and privatisations, as well as EC and Spanish Competition and antitrust law. Has handled acquisitions and privatisations of companies and undertakings in many different sectors (defence, utilities, industrial, telecommunications, construction, etc.) by international and Spanish clients. Acted on the privatisations of Empresa Nacional Santa Bárbara, Retevisión, and Babock Wilcox, among others; acted for Vivendi and Havas in their international joint venture with Media Planning; for the Bertelsmann Group of Companies on different acquisitions and international joint ventures; for RWE on the restructuring of its participations in

S

Spanish companies; for Daimler Chrysler, Dresdner Kleinwort Benson and Sun Microsystems on a number of different acquisition activities. Heads the firm's German Practice Group.
Prof. Memberships: International Bar Association; American Society of International Law; Madrid and New York Bar.
Career: Qualified in 1979. Civil Servant with the European Communities and Professor of Law at various German and US Universities (1982-1990), joined *Gómez-Acebo & Pombo* in 1990. Professor of European Law at the University of Madrid (USP) and Director of its Institute for European Studies. Author of various books and articles on Competition/Anti-trust law and privatisations, European Companies' Law and EC Law. Contributor to the Journal for European Economic Law, European Legal Business and European Counsel. Joint Editor of 'Gaceta Juródica de la UE y de la Competencia'.
Personal: Born 24 October 1956. Attended the University of Navarra (JD), Harvard Law School (LLM), and the Universities of Münster and Bonn, Germany (PhD in Law; PhD in History). Leisure interests include classical music, literature, languages, outdoor activities. Languages spoken: Spanish, English, German, French, Russian, Italian and Portuguese.

BENITEZ, Carlos
Gomez-Acebo & Pombo, Madrid +34 91 582 9100
cbenitez@gomezacebo-pombo.com
Recommended in Tax
Specialisation: Corporation tax law, mainly as regards mergers and acquisitions and cross-border tax issues. Tax aspects concerning transfer of technology and intellectual property as well as e-commerce.
Prof. Memberships: Madrid Law Bar (1969). Association of Spanish Tax Advisers (1973). International Fiscal Association.
Publications: 'Taxation of Technical Assistance Agreements'.
Career: Tax partner in *Ernst & Murrey (E & Y)*, *Baker & McKenzie* and *Benitez and Colmenar.*
Personal: Born 9 June 1942. Law degree at Universidad Complutense (Madrid). Master in Business Administration (Madrid School of Commerce). Married, 2 children.

BERCOVITZ RODRIGUEZ-CANO, Rodrigo
Estudio Jurídico Bercovitz-Carvajal Sociedad Civil, Madrid +34 91 445 2161
Recommended in Intellectual Property

BLANCO, José-Luis
Cuatrecasas, Barcelona +34 93 290 5500
Recommended in Corporate/M&A

BRIONES FERNANDEZ, Luis
Baker & McKenzie-Briones Alonso Martin, Madrid +34 91 436 4300
Recommended in Tax

BUSTILLO, Ramon
Garrigues & Andersen, Madrid +34 91 514 5200
ramon.bustillo@garriguesandersen.com
Recommended in Corporate/M&A
Specialisation: Partner in Corporate Department. Main area of work is corporate law, principally mergers, acquisitions and privatisations. Experience includes advice in major acquisitions of unlisted undertakings in Spain and clientele consists of US and European multinationals.
Prof. Memberships: Madrid Bar Association (1975).
Career: Bachelor at Law, Law Faculty of Seville.
Personal: Born in Seville on November 26, 1946. Speaks Spanish, English and French.

CANTOS, Francisco
Freshfields Bruckhaus Deringer, Madrid
+34 91 319 1024
francisco.cantos@freshfields.com
Recommended in Communications, Competition/Anti-trust
Specialisation: Specialises in mergers and acquisitions and joint venture work.

CASANOVA, Carlos
Estudio Jurídico Almagro, Madrid +34 91 383 0192
Recommended in Tax

CASTAN, Antonio
Elzaburu, Madrid +34 91 700 9400
Recommended in Intellectual Property

CERVELLÓ, José María
Ernst & Young Abogados, Madrid +34 91 572 7200
Recommended in Tax

CREMADES, Javier
Cremades Abogados, Madrid +34 91 426 4050
Recommended in Communications

CREUS, Antonio
Cuatrecasas, Madrid +34 1 524 71 00
Recommended in Competition/Anti-trust

CRUZ AMOROS, Miguel
Landwell Abogados y Asesores Fiscales (PricewaterhouseCoopers), Madrid
+34 91 568 4000
Recommended in Tax

CUATRECASAS, Emilio
Cuatrecasas, Barcelona +34 93 290 5500
Recommended in Corporate/M&A

DE CÁRDENAS, Carlos
Uría & Menéndez, Madrid +34 91 586 0400
ccs@uria.com
Recommended in Banking & Finance
Specialisation: Partner of the Madrid office. Main area of work is corporate law, principally mergers and acquisitions, joint-ventures and project finance.
Career: Joined the Madrid office in 1989. International associate at *Simpson Thacher & Bartlett* (New York) in 1995-1996. Resident Partner in the New York office of *Uría & Menéndez* 1997-2000.
Personal: Born 19 October 1966. Graduated, Universidad Autónoma de Madrid (Class of 1989). Several books on tender offers, corporate law and securities law and articles for Spanish and foreign law reviews. Commercial Law Professor at Universidad Pontificia de Comillas and at Centro de Estudios Universitarios, Madrid.

DE CARLOS BERTRÁN, Luis
Uría & Menéndez, Madrid +34 91 586 0400
Recommended in Banking & Finance
Specialisation: Partner in the Finance Department. Main area of work is corporate finance, mergers and acquisitions, issues and offerings of securities, takeovers, securitisation, banking and project finance. Has handled many important transactions in Spain. Author of various books and publications on banking and securities matters.
Prof. Memberships: Madrid Bar Association, International Bar Association.
Career: Doctor in Law and Licentiate in Business Administration. Joined *Uría & Menéndez* in 1983 and became a partner in 1991. Professor of Securities Law (Universidad Pontificia de Comillas).
Personal: Born 25 September 1960. Married. Languages: English and French.

DE FRANCISCO, José Antonio
Estudio Jurídico Almagro, Madrid +34 91 383 0192
Recommended in Tax

DE LAS CUEVAS, Fernando
Gomez-Acebo & Pombo, Madrid +34 91 582 9100
fcuevas@gomezacebo-pombo.com
Recommended in Banking & Finance, Corporate/M&A
Specialisation: Advises investment banks, investment fund managers and listed companies on a broad range of financial and securities matters. Has taught at the Universities of Deusto, Navarra and Madrid (Universidad Autónoma) on advanced seminars and is a frequent speaker at various national and international fora. Is an active member of international organisations such as IBA and UIA and is the Spanish correspondent of several international specialised publications in banking and securities.
Career: Graduate of the University of Deusto in 1981; obtained a joint degree in law and business administration. Holds Masters in EEC law (University of Deusto) and Economics (College of Europe, Bruges). Joined *Gómez-Acebo & Pombo* in 1982 and became partner in 1990. Since 1995 has been the partner in charge of the Financial Services Department of the firm with a broad activity in banking, securities and insurance. Managing Partner of *Gómez-Acebo & Pombo* (1998-2000). Contributor to the Journal of International Banking Law and to the World Securities Law Report.
Personal: Languages spoken: Spanish, fluent English and French, basic German.

DE ROJAS, Mercedes
KPMG Abogados, Madrid +34 91 456 3481
Recommended in Tax

DE SAN ROMAN, Jaime
Clifford Chance, Madrid +34 91 590 7500
Recommended in Banking & Finance, Corporate/M&A

DE ULLOA, Gonzalo
Gomez-Acebo & Pombo, Madrid +34 91 582 9100
gulloa@gomezacebo.com
Recommended in Intellectual Property
Specialisation: Advice and litigation in intellectual property, patents, trademarks, new technologies,

franchising. Very active in patent litigation. Partner, Head of Intellectual Property and Technology Department of *Gomez-Acebo & Pombo.*
Prof. Memberships: Admitted to the Madrid Bar in 1975. Member of Vice President of LES España-Portugal; AIPPI, Marques LIDC, IBA.
Publications: Has published articles in specialised IP magazines, and lectures regularly on this topic.
Personal: Studied at the Universities of Madrid and Strasbourg where specialised in IP and technology.

DEL SAZ CORDERO, Isidro
Landwell Abogados y Asesores Fiscales (PricewaterhouseCoopers), Madrid +34 91 568 4000
Recommended in Tax

DEL VALLE, Javier
Pintó Ruiz & Del Valle, Madrid +34 91 563 8678
Recommended in Intellectual Property

DELGADO, Abelardo
Garrigues & Andersen, Madrid +34 91 514 5200
Recommended in Tax
Specialisation: Partner of the Tax Department. Main field of work is company taxation in general with particular experience in corporate income tax, international taxation, tax proceedings and litigation. Has worked in major mergers and acquisitions including the due diligence procedures for performance of these transactions. Has also acted for different multinational groups in Spain on matters including planning their structure in Spain to payments to non-resident companies and transfer prices. Wide experience as the author of different publications in the public media and specialised journals and as professor of tax law at postgraduate training centres.
Prof. Memberships: Madrid Bar Association and of the Association of Tax Lawyers.
Career: 19 years of professional experience. Worked with the Tax Administration from 1980 to 1994. In 1995, joined *Baker & Mackenzie,* as the partner responsible for the Tax Department of the Madrid Office. In 1999, joined *Garrigues & Andersen* as a partner.
Personal: Born May 17, 1956. A Bachelor of Law from the Universidad Complutense, Madrid. State Tax Inspector on extended leave of absence.

DÍAZ, Emilio
Uría & Menéndez, Madrid +34 91 586 0400 edr@uria.com
Recommended in Banking & Finance
Specialisation: Partner in the Commercial Law Department. Main area of work is Corporate and Banking, especially derivatives. Professor (part-time) of Commercial Law at the Complutense University of Madrid. Author of several legal books and contributor to several Spanish legal Magazines and frequent speaker at Conferences on Commercial Law matters.
Prof. Memberships: Madrid Bar Association.
Career: Licenciate (1979) and Doctor (1992) in Law. Admitted to the Bar in 1980, joined *U&M* in 1981, where he became a partner in 1989.
Personal: Born August 2, 1957.

DIEZ, Maite
Baker & McKenzie-Briones Alonso Martin, Madrid +34 91 391 5950 maite.diez@bakernet.com
Recommended in Communications
Specialisation: Heads the IT/Communications Department. Main area of work is telecommunications law, including regulatory and corporate and contract law work. Has extensive experience in telecommunications gained not only in the advice on Spanish law, but also because of participation in major telecommunications privatisations in Latin America (Peru, Bolivia and El Salvador) as advisor for the Government. Acts as advisor for a number of telecommunications operators and equipment suppliers in Spain.
Prof. Memberships: Madrid Bar Association.
Publications: Publications include the chapter on Spain in the book 'Baker & McKenzie: Telecommunications Laws in Europe', Butterworths Publ., 4th Edition, London 1998 (co-author Xavier Junquera). Has spoken on telecommunications matters in various conferences.
Career: Qualified in 1986. Joined *Baker & McKenzie* in 1988 and worked for the firm's New York office in 1993/94, becoming a Partner in 1996.
Personal: Born 13 January 1963. Has a law degree and a diploma in economics from the Deusto University, Bilbao, Spain, and an LLM in International Business Legal Studies from the University of Exeter, UK. Has lived in, Bilbao, Exeter and New York, and lives now in Madrid. Married with two children.

ESCODA, Alex
Cuatrecasas, Barcelona +34 93 290 5500
Recommended in Tax

FERNÁNDEZ, Cani
Cuatrecasas, Brussels +34 932 90 55 00
Recommended in Competition/Anti-trust

FERNÁNDEZ DE ARAOZ, Alejandro
Araoz y Rueda, Madrid +34 91 319 0233
Recommended in Competition/Anti-trust, Corporate/M&A

FERNANDEZ-NOVOA, Luis
Gomez-Acebo & Pombo, Madrid +34 91 582 9100
Recommended in Intellectual Property
Prof. Memberships: Admitted, 1987 La Coruña, 1989, Madrid.
Publications: Director of the periodical Actas de Derecho Industrial. Published in Spanish, English and German: 'The International Protection of Geographics Names of Products'; 'Fundamentals of Trademark Law'; 'Studies in Advertising Law'; 'Trademark Law'. Co-author: 'Towards a New Patent System'; 'The Modernisation of Spanish Patent Law'.
Personal: Born La Estrada, 1933. Education: Universities of Santiago de Compostela, Madrid and Munich (LLD Max Planck). Professor of Commercial Law, Santiago de Compostela University since 1964. Languages: Spanish, English, French.

FOLGUERA CRESPO, Jaime
Uría & Menéndez, Madrid +34 91 586 0426 jfc@uria.com
Recommended in Competition/Anti-trust
Specialisation: Partner in the Competition Department. Main areas of work encompass merger control as well as authorisation and infringement proceedings regarding cartels and other agreements, abuses of dominant undertakings and State Aid, carried by both Spanish and European Authorities.
Career: Qualified in 1978. Diploma in European Community Law in 1982 and 1984. Master's degree in Legal advice for Businesses, 1983. Former Senior Legal adviser to the Foreign Affairs Ministry.
Personal: Born April 1954. Law degree in 1977 (University of Madrid).

FONTANA, Rafael
Cuatrecasas, Barcelona +34 93 290 5500
Recommended in Tax

FUSTER, Rafael
Uría & Menéndez, Madrid +34 91 586 0400 rft@uria.com
Recommended in Tax
Specialisation: Mainly devoted to corporate tax matters. Particular fields of experience include non resident taxation, structured finance deals and securities. Works on a permanent basis for most leading international investment banks. Also active in M&A practice and investment fund related issues. Has been professor of Tax Law at the Antonio de Nebrija University and at Instituto de Empresa.
Prof. Memberships: Madrid Bar. International Fiscal Association.
Career: Qualified in Law in 1990. Also qualified in Business Administration in 1991. Joined *Uría & Menéndez* tax department in 1991.

GARCÍA LLANEZA, Rafael
Uría & Menéndez, Madrid +34 91 586 0400 rgl@uria.com
Recommended in Tax
Specialisation: Mainly devoted to non-resident and corporate tax. Particular fields of experience include international tax planning, structured finance, design of tax driven transactions and financial products. Started the tax practice of *Uría & Menéndez* New York Office, where spent four years. Professor in the program for European Union Attorneys at San Pablo-CEU University.
Prof. Memberships: Madrid Bar.
Career: Law Degree, Madrid, 1987. Business Administration, Madrid, 1988. Accountant at Price Waterhouse from 1988-90. Joined *Uría & Menéndez* in May 1990.

GARCÍA-PITA, Daniel
Garrigues & Andersen, Madrid +34 91 514 5200 daniel.garcia-pita@garriguesandersen.com
Recommended in Corporate/M&A
Specialisation: Mergers and acquisitions, company law and commercial law in general.
Prof. Memberships: Colegio de Abogados de Madrid.
Publications: 'La Auditoria de cuentas en Derecho espanol'.
Career: Managing partner *Garrigues & Andersen.* Member of the Board of Partners of Andersen Worldwide SC.
Personal: Universidad de Madrid and Universitat zu Koln.

S

GARDETA, Eduardo
Garrigues & Andersen, Madrid +34 91 514 5200
eduardo.gardeta@garriguesandersen.com
Recommended in Tax
Specialisation: Partner with *Garrigues & Andersen*, Head of the Spanish indirect taxation practice and represents Spain in Andersen Worldwide's VAT Co-ordinators Group which brings together various specialists in the area, particularly those of the European Union. Works regularly in e-business and telecomms.
Prof. Memberships: Spanish Telecommunications Law Association; Madrid Bar Association (1986).
Career: Bachelor at Law, Madrid University (Complutense) 1986; Masters in Tax Counselling at the School of Economics and graduated in the Harvard University's Program of Instruction for Lawyers.

GOENECHEA, Juan Miguel
Uría & Menéndez, Madrid +34 91 586 0418
jgd@uria.com
Recommended in Corporate/M&A
Specialisation: Partner at *Uría & Menéndez*, specialised in Internet, M&A, banking and capital markets.
Prof. Memberships: IBA Member.
Career: Universidad Pontificia de Comillas-ICADE: Licenciate in Law and Licenciate in Business Administration. Admitted to the Bar in 1982. Associate at *Uría & Menéndez* since 1982, and Partner since 1990. Professor of Commercial Law at University Pontificia Comillas (ICADE) since 1984.
Personal: Born 2 March 1959, Cádiz (Spain). Languages: English and French.

GÓMEZ, Ricardo
Garrigues & Andersen, Madrid +34 91 514 5200
ricardo.gomez@garriguesandersen.com
Recommended in Tax
Specialisation: Partner in Tax Department at *Garrigues & Andersen's* Madrid office. Main areas of work are counselling on the finance industry, multinational groups and on mergers & acquisitions. Expertise includes group reorganisations and international deal structuring. Has worked in MBO and LBO transactions, project finance, acquisitions and product design for the banking industry. Is a frequent speaker in seminars and conferences on these matters in Spain and abroad. Is also a member of the editorial board of two of the Recoletos Group Companies (Expansiôn e Actualidad Econômica).
Career: Graduated in 1981 in Economics, Business Administration, and Law from Universidad Commercial of Deusto. Joined *Arthur Andersen* in 1982 and in 1993 was named partner of the Tax Advisory Division.
Personal: Born in Santander on July 17, 1959. Resides in Madrid.

GÓMEZ-ACEBO, Javier
Freshfields Bruckhaus Deringer, Madrid
+34 91 319 1024
javier.gomez-acebo@freshfields.com
Recommended in Banking & Finance
Specialisation: Specialises in banking, insurance and regulatory work, securitisations structured and asset finance.

GÓMEZ-ACEBO, Juan
Freshfields Bruckhaus Deringer, Madrid
+34 91 319 1024
juan.gomez-acebo@freshfields.com
Recommended in Corporate/M&A
Specialisation: Specialises in corporate restructuring, mergers and acquisitions, joint venture, commercial property and asset finance. Has particular experience in the real estate, leisure and aircraft sectors.

GOMEZ-JORDANA, Iñigo
Clifford Chance, Madrid +34 91 590 75 00
Recommended in Banking & Finance, Corporate/M&A

GONZÁLEZ-DELEITO, Nicolás
Cuatrecasas, Madrid +34 1 524 71 00
Recommended in Communications

GRAU, Jorge
Bufete Socoró & Grau, Barcelona +34 93 209 0765
Recommended in Intellectual Property

GUERREIRO, Luis
Garrigues & Andersen, Madrid +34 91 514 5200
luis.guerreiro@garriguesandersen.com
Recommended in Tax
Specialisation: Tax Partner. Financial Service Industry Group. Areas of work: private placement, M&A, investment and commercial banks, insurance companies, leasing transactions. European R&D group member. Tax advisor to the Spanish insurance and leasing associations.
Publications: Co-author of 'Life insurance in Spain'.
Career: Masters in Tax Law. Joined *Andersen Tax & Legal* in 1982. Partner in 1994. Head of FSI service line and private placement group.
Personal: Born February 4, 1961. Married, two children.

GUIX, Victor
Victor Guix Estudio Jurídico, Barcelona
+34 93 216 0560
Recommended in Intellectual Property

HERVADA, Joaquín
Freshfields Bruckhaus Deringer, Madrid
+34 91 319 1024
joaquin.hervada@freshfields.com
Recommended in Corporate/M&A
Specialisation: Specialises in corporate and commercial law, mergers and acquisitions and joint ventures.

HITCHINGS, Paul
Squire, Sanders & Dempsey LLP, Madrid
+34 91 590 2420
Recommended in Communications

IGARTUA, Fernando
Gomez-Acebo & Pombo, Madrid +34 91 582 9100
figartua@gomezacebo-pombo.com
Recommended in Banking & Finance
Specialisation: Head of the Financial Services Department. This department advises in matters regarding banking and financial services regulations and licences, acquisition and merger of such institutions, capital adequacy, securities laws, public offerings and listing of companies in the stock exchange, take-over bids, privatisation processes, term loans, credit facilities, structured finance, project finance, asset finance, securitisation, derivatives, mutual funds, pension funds, insurance law, electronic commerce. Frequently appears at conferences and seminars (both in Spain and abroad) and is a professor of several Masters courses in Spain. Author of several books and publications.
Prof. Memberships: Bar of Madrid since 1984.
Career: Studied Law and Economics at the University of Deusto, Bilbao from 1976 to 1991. Taught Civil Law from 1981 to 1983 at the University of the Basque Country in San Sebastian. Moved to Madrid in 1984 joining the University Autónoma of Madrid; read doctoral thesis in 1986 and was acting Professor of Civil Law until 1990 and became tenured professor on the same matter. Spent part of academic career at the University of Paris (1982), and at the University of California Berkeley (1987-88 was a visiting scholar). During 1991-92 worked within the English firm *Linklaters & Paines* and was a research associate at the Institute of Advanced Legal Studies at the University of London. Has been practising private law since 1984. In 1989, joined the firm *Gomez-Acebo & Pombo*, and was made a partner in 1994. Has been a member of its Management Committee (1995-97) and has headed the Financial Services Department since 1998.
Personal: Born in Eibar (Guipuzcoa) on 22 January 1959. Married, with two daughters and a son.

IGARTUA, Íñigo
Gomez-Acebo & Pombo, Madrid +34 91 582 9100
iigartua@gomezacebo-pombo.com
Recommended in Competition/Anti-trust
Specialisation: Partner in the Telecommunications and Competition Law Department. Main area of work is competition law proceedings, principally merger filings, investigation proceedings by competition authorities, authorisation requests, general advice on competition authorities, authorisation requests, general advice on competition law regarding contract drafting, acquisition of companies and other transactions. Has handled Competition Law proceedings before the European Commission, European Court of Justice, the Spanish 'Servicio de Defensa de las Competencia' and Spanish 'Tribunal de Defensa de la Competencia,' in different sorts of cases for Spanish and foreign clients. In the field of telecommunications, focused on electronic commerce related issues and the development of internet based products and services.
Prof. Memberships: Member of the Barcelona Bar.
Career: Qualified in 1988. Studied at the University of the Basque Country and then did a Masters in European Law between 1988-90 at the Free University of Brussels, Institut d'Etudes Européennes. A partner with *Gomez-Acebo & Pombo* since 1998.
Personal: Born 10 May 1965. Leisure interests include poetry, history, music, and internet. Won several literary prizes. Lives in Santa Caught, outside Barcelona.

IGLESIAS PRADA, Juan Luis
Uría & Menéndez, Madrid +34 91 586 0400
Recommended in Corporate/M&A

Specialisation: Corporate Law; Bankruptcy; Arbitration; Commercial Law.
Prof. Memberships: International Maritime Committee, since 1990. Spanish Association for the Study of European Law. Spanish Maritime Law Association. Spanish Section of the AIDA. Latin American Maritime Law Institute.
Career: PhD in Law, 1969. Admitted to the Bar, 1982 (Madrid). Joined *Uría & Menéndez* in 1981, partner in 1982. Permanent Member of the General Codification Commission, since 1988. General Technical Secretary of the Ministry of Education and Science, 1976-77. Full Member of the Academia Asturiana de Jurisprudencia, 1995. Secretary of the Board of the Universidad 'Antonio de Nebrija', 1996-present. Professor at the Universidad Autónoma de Madrid, 1970-76; Vice-Dean, Universidad Autónoma de Madrid (Law School), 1975-76; Chaired Professor of Commercial Law, Universidad Autónoma de Madrid, 1977-present.
Personal: Born November 1941. Languages: French and Italian.

ILUNDAIN, Santiago
Garrigues & Andersen, Madrid +34 91 514 5200
santiago.ilundain@garriguesandersen.com
Recommended in Tax
Specialisation: Specialises in commercial law, corporate taxation, mergers and restructuring and in international taxation. Advisor to major companies in the following sectors: banking, telecommunications, software and services. Has advised on mergers, spin-offs and group restructuring in the banking, insurance, services, construction and communication sectors.
Prof. Memberships: Madrid Bar Association, International Bar Association, European Lawyers Association and Spanish Telecommunication Law Association.
Publications: Has published numerous articles on tax and commercial law and is the co-author of 'La Reforma de la legislacion mercantil', first book on the corporate legislation reform adapting Spanish legislation to EU Directives.
Career: Madrid University (Complutense) 1967; Business Administration, University of ICADE, Masters in Taxation, Madrid Tax Studies Centre.

JIMÉNEZ, Ernesto
Garrigues & Andersen, Madrid +34 91 514 5200
ernesto.jimenez@garriguesandersen.com
Recommended in Tax
Specialisation: Partner in *Garrigues & Andersen's* Tax Department. Heads the General Taxation Group at the Madrid office. Main area of work is corporate tax, principally mergers and acquisitions. Main clients are in the utilities and telecommunications industries.
Prof. Memberships: Madrid Bar Association.
Career: Bachelor at Law, Madrid University (Complutense); Masters in Corporate Tax Counselling; qualified in 1979; joined *Garrigues & Andersen* in 1980, becoming a partner in 1990. Author of 'La Nuevas Leyes del Impuesto sobre la Renta y el Patrimonio' (1992) and 'El Impuesto sobre la Renta, comentarios a la Ley 40/1998 y a su Reglamento' (1999).
Personal: Born in Madrid in 1956. Married with three children.

JIMÉNEZ BLANCO, José Ignacio
Clifford Chance, Barcelona +34 93 344 2200
Recommended in Tax

JIMÉNEZ-LAIGLESIA, José M.
Jones, Day, Reavis & Pogue, Madrid
+34 91 561 0601
jmjimenez@jonesday.com
Recommended in Competition/Anti-trust
Specialisation: Principal areas of specialisation are Spanish and EC antitrust law, government regulation (energy and telecommunications) and general EU law.
Prof. Memberships: Madrid Bar Association.
Career: Admitted to Bar 1991. Founding partner of *G&J Abogados* in 1993, a Madrid firm specialising in antitrust law, government regulation, EC law and corporate issues. Joined *Jones Day* in October 2000 as Of Counsel. Associate Lecturer of Competition Law at the Carlos III University of Madrid, 1996-present.
Personal: Born in Madrid on 8 September 1966. 1989, Law Degree from the Complutense University of Madrid; 1990, LLM University College, London. Is fluent in English and Spanish.

JIMÉNEZ-LAIGLESIA, Juan
Jones, Day, Reavis & Pogue, Madrid
+34 91 561 0601
jjimenez@jonesday.com
Recommended in Competition/Anti-trust
Specialisation: Principal areas of specialisation are Spanish and EC antitrust law, government regulation and competition law.
Prof. Memberships: Madrid Bar Association.
Publications: Member Editorial Board 'Gaceta Jurídica de la Unión Europea y de la Competencia'.
Career: Admitted to Bar 1998. Founding partner of *G&J Abogados* in 1993, a Madrid firm specialising in antitrust law, government regulation, EC law and corporate issues. Joined *Jones Day* in October 2000 as Of Counsel. Associate Professor of Competition Law and Economics at Carlos III University of Madrid, 1998-present.
Personal: Born in Madrid on 28 August 1965. 1988, Law Degree from the Complutense University of Madrid; 1989, European Law Degree from IEE Brussels; 1991, Political Science Degree from UNED Madrid; 1991, M.B.A. from IESE Barcelona; 1999, Ph.D. from ICADE Madrid. Is fluent in English, French and Spanish.

KLINGENBERG, Miguel
Freshfields Bruckhaus Deringer, Madrid
+34 91 319 1024
miguel.klingenberg@freshfields.com
Recommended in Tax
Specialisation: Focuses on international and Spanish tax, asset management and structuring.

LAORDEN, Javier
Cuatrecasas, 28001 Madrid +34 1 524 71 00
Recommended in Tax

LAVILLA, Juan José
Clifford Chance, Barcelona +34 93 344 2200
Recommended in Communications

LEMA DEVESA, Carlos
Estudio Jurídico Lema, Madrid +34 91 316 4828
Recommended in Intellectual Property

LEON SANCHEZ, Enrique
Baker & McKenzie-Briones Alonso Martin, Madrid +34 91 436 4300
Recommended in Tax

LOPEZ CHICHERI, Jaime
Ernst & Young Abogados, Madrid +34 91 572 7200
Recommended in Tax

LÓPEZ TELLO, Jesús
Uría & Menéndez, Madrid +34 91 586 0400
jlt@uria.com
Recommended in Tax
Specialisation: Head of the firm's Tax Department since 1995. Tax law and assurance related issues. Acted for major investment banks on general financial issues; Spanish corporate leader in telecommunications on international ESOP and corporate and financial issues; foreign investors on international tax planning using Spanish Holdings; leading Spanish Bank and Electric Companies on restructuring their investments in Latin America; major ceramic manufacturer on setting up its export business.
Prof. Memberships: Madrid Bar. International Fiscal Association.
Career: Qualified in 1986 as Tax and Assurance Undertakings Inspector.

LORING, Carlos
Garrigues & Andersen, Madrid +34 91 514 5200
carlos.loring@garriguesandersen.com
Recommended in Banking & Finance, Corporate/M&A
Specialisation: Managing Partner in the Banking Finance and Stock Market Department. Main areas of work are corporate law, banking and stock market regulations, privatisations, IPOs, issues, etc. in the Spanish Market. Has handled privatisation through Public Offering of Shares in the Spanish Stock Exchange, flotation of new companies in the Madrid Stock Exchange, mergers and acquisitions of Spanish based banks, financial entities and insurance companies, and advising insurance and financial entities in group restructurisations.
Prof. Memberships: Madrid and Malaga Law Societies.
Career: Qualified in 1970. Joined *J & A Garrigues* in 1971 becoming a partner in 1977. Member of the Council of the Madrid Law Society from 1984 to 1992. Professor co-operating with Centro de Estudios Universitarios in Master Law Degrees on Private and Commercial Law.
Personal: Born in 1947. Bachelor of Law in the Madrid University 1964-1969. Lives in Madrid.

MARTINEZ LAGE, Santiago
Martinez Lage & Asociados, Madrid
+34 91 426 4470
Recommended in Competition/Anti-trust

MARZO, Javier
Garrigues & Andersen, Madrid +34 91 514 5200
javier.marzo@garriguesanderson.com
Recommended in Communications
Specialisation: Associate in corporate department.

S

Main area of work is telecom and corporate law for clients in the telecommunications and media sector, principally in M&A, IPOs, and start-ups, as well as licensing issues (programming) and regulatory advice (UMTS, cable, network construction and courses, IE, ICADE). Author of various articles on telecommunications law.
Prof. Memberships: Madrid Bar Association.
Career: Joined *Pedro Brosa & Asociados* in Barcelona in 1992. Joined *Garrigues & Andersen* in Madrid in 1995.
Personal: Law degree, Madrid Autonomous University (Spain), 1987-92. MA in International Political Economy, University of Southern California (USA), 1993-1995.

S

MASSAGUER, José
Uría & Menéndez, Barcelona +34 91 586 4590
jmf@uria.com
Recommended in Intellectual Property
Specialisation: Intellectual property, unfair competition, information technology and contract law.
Prof. Memberships: Barcelona Bar and Madrid Bar. Jury of the Asociación de Autocontrol de la Publicidad (Chairman of Section 2), Spanish Group of AIPPI (Member of Board).
Publications: 'Comentario a la Ley de Competencia Desleal' (Madrid, 1999); member of the publishing board of 'Revista General de Derecho', 'Aranzadi Civil', 'Actas de Derecho Industrial', and 'Revista de Propiedad Intelectual'.
Personal: Born October 12 1960. Fluent in Spanish, English and German. Law degree and PhD, Universidad de Valencia (1983 & 1987). Chaired Professor of Commercial Law, University Pompeu Fabra, Barcelona, since 1992.

MAYOR, Pablo
Clifford Chance, Madrid +34 91 590 7500
Recommended in Communications

MÍNGUEZ PRIETO, Rafael
Cuatrecasas, 28001 Madrid +34 1 524 7100
Recommended in Banking & Finance

MONTAÑÁ MORA, Miquel
Clifford Chance, Barcelona +34 93 344 2200
Recommended in Intellectual Property

MUÑOZ-DELGADO, Jesús
Gomez-Acebo & Pombo, Madrid +34 91 582 9100
jmunoz@acebogomez-pombo.com
Recommended in Intellectual Property
Prof. Memberships: Admitted 1986, Madrid. Member: LICD.
Personal: Born Madrid, 1959. Education: Complutense University of Madrid, 1981. IE. (Master in Business Law), 1987. Harvard Law School (PIL), 1989. Languages: Spanish, English.

ODRIOZOLA, Miguel
Clifford Chance, Madrid +34 91 590 7500
Recommended in Competition/Anti-trust

OJANGUREN, Ignacio
Clifford Chance, Barcelona +34 93 344 2200
Recommended in Corporate/M&A

ORTIZ BLANCO, Luis
Garrigues & Andersen, Madrid +34 91 514 5200
luis.ortiz.blanco@garriguesandersen.com
Recommended in Competition/Anti-trust
Specialisation: Senior Associate at the EC and Competition Law department. Former official of DGIV of the European Commission, between 1986 and 1996. Visiting Researcher at Harvard Law School in 1994-95. Worked for the Spanish Tribunal for the Defence of Competition in 1995. Focused on competition law and specialised in procedural competition matters, as well as in competition in the transport markets. Associate Professor of Competition law at the Universidad Rey Juan Carlos in Madrid.
Prof. Memberships: Segovia (1980) and Madrid Bars (1981).
Publications: Has published several books and articles, like 'EC Competition Procedure', Clarendon Press, Oxford, 1996, and 'EC Competition Law in the Transport Sector', Clarendon Press, Oxford, 1996.
Career: Joined the firm in 1998.
Personal: Attended the Complutense University in Madrid.

OTERO LASTRES, José Manuel
Bufete Otero Lastres, Madrid +34 91 458 2356
Recommended in Intellectual Property

PALACIOS, José
Garrigues & Andersen, Madrid +34 91 514 5200
jose.palacios@garriguesandersen.com
Recommended in Tax
Specialisation: Tax partner in *Garrigues & Andersen*'s Madrid office specialising in international tax planning. Coordinates the international tax practice in Spain. Specialises in Transfer Pricing, coordinates *Garrigues & Andersen*'s Transfer Pricing Group.
Prof. Memberships: Madrid Bar Association.
Publications: Co-author of the book 'Espana como plataforma de actividad empresarial internacional' awarded with the 1998 premio Circulo de Empresarios and coordinator of *G&A*'s annual publication 'A Guide to Business in Spain' published by the Spanish Institute for Foreign Trade (ICEX) of the Ministry of Economy and Finance.
Career: Attended Universidad Complutense de Madrid 1971-1976 (Law degree). After working for a firm of tax lawyers, joined *G&A* in January 1983.

PAZOS, Carlos
S J Berwin, Pazos, Gallardo y Asociados, Madrid +34 91 426 0050
Recommended in Communications

PEÑA, Francisco
Gomez-Acebo & Pombo, Madrid +34 91 582 9100
fpena@gomezacebo-pombo.com
Recommended in Corporate/M&A
Specialisation: Partner and Head of the Corporate Department of *Gomez-Acebo & Pombo* since 1989. Main area of work: M&A, Privatisations, Corporate Law, extensive work experience in Commercial Law and Tax Law in relation to acquisitions, as well as all forms of insolvency proceeding suspension of payments (receivership) and bankruptcy. Secretary of the Board of Directors of the Spanish subsidiaries of Royal Sun Alliance and member of the Board of Directors of BTTel, SA. Collaborates actively in various publications and speaks in conferences relating to business law.
Prof. Memberships: International Bar Association, Management Centre Europe.
Career: Law Degree at University Complutense of Madrid (1975). State Attorney examinations. Masters in Tax Law by 'Instituti de Empresa,' Madrid. Foreign Lawyer with *Herbert Smith & Co.* London.
Personal: Born 8 June 1952. Attended Universidad Complutense of Madrid 1970-75. Continued various postgraduate studies in business law, such as the preparation for the examination of State Attorney. Has 24 years of professional experience as a lawyer.

PÉREZ ARDÁ, Javier
Garrigues & Andersen, Madrid +34 91 514 5200
javier.perez-arda@garriguesandersen.com
Recommended in Communications
Specialisation: Specialises in administrative, mercantile and corporate law focusing on regulated sectors (banking, telecommunications & media and utilities) advising both in particular cases (as special projects or acquisition) as well as in general matters (strategic alliances, mergers.) Also deals with project finance.
Prof. Memberships: Madrid and La Coruña Bar; Spanish Commercial Court of Arbitration; Panel of Arbitration of Olympics Committee.
Career: Corps of State Attorneys (1980). Head of the Directorate General for the Treasury and Financial Policy. Professor of Administrative Law at the Universidad Nacional, Madrid. Joined *J&A Garrigues* in 1986, made partner in 1993. Speaker and author of numerous conferences, articles and chapters on project finance and other mercantile and administrative matters.

PÉREZ DE LA SOTA, Fernando
Uría & Menéndez, Madrid +34 91 586 0680
fps@uria.com
Recommended in Communications
Specialisation: Telecommunications and Commercial Law.
Prof. Memberships: IBA, 1999; Madrid, 1986; New York, 1996 (Legal Consultant not admitted to the Bar).
Career: Partner at *Uría & Menéndez* since 1995. Professor at ICADE, 1997-1999. Associate Professor at Alcalá de Henares University, 1997-1998. Legal Consultant of Appellate Division, Supreme Court, New York State, 1996. Professor at Universidad Internacional Menéndez Pelayo, summer 1996. Professor at APD, 1994-1996. Foreign Lawyer, *Sullivan & Cromwell*, 1990. Speaker at numerous conferences/seminars.
Personal: Licenciate of Law, Salamanca University, 1984. Languages: English.

PÉREZ SANTOS, José
Uría & Menéndez, Madrid +34 91 586 0446
jps@uria.com
Recommended in Communications, Competition/Anti-trust
Specialisation: Partner responsible for Communications (including telecommunications, media and e-business), entertainment (including sports and tourism), and competition. Regularly rep-

resents and advises major clients in the aforementioned economic sectors, both with respect to corporate matters and regulatory matters (such as licensing, deployment of networks, interconnection, TV, films, hiring of sport players and licensing of sports rights). Handled major competition cases, whether alleged cartels, joint ventures or concentrations (particularly in the communications and media sectors) and State aids.
Prof. Memberships: Madrid Bar and IBA.
Career: Joined *Uría & Menéndez* in 1974. Partner since 1982.
Personal: Born 5 May 1950. Law degree, Madrid Universidad Complutense. Languages: English and French.

PICÓN, Juan
Squire, Sanders & Dempsey LLP, Madrid +34 91 590 2420
Recommended in Communications

POMBO, Fernando
Gomez-Acebo & Pombo, Madrid +34 91 582 9100
fpombo@gomezacebo-pombo.com
Recommended in Corporate/M&A
Specialisation: Energy and natural resources, intellectual property, mergers and acquisitions.
Prof. Memberships: Past President of LES International; ICC Arbitrators; Spanish Arbitration Court and The Chartered Institute of Arbitrators; IBA (Chairman SLP); and others.
Career: Professor of Law, Centre for University Studies (CEU-1973-76). Visiting Professor, Institute on International Legal Studies, Salzburg (from 1985), teaching International Business Law.
Personal: Born Santander, Spain. University of Madrid, Philosophy and Law Degree, 1965. PhD studies, University of Geneva 1969-70 (with Professor Martin Archard), and Munich, Max Plank Institut (1970-71). Europa Insititute, Amsterdam (EEC law) 1979.

RAMÍREZ, Eduardo
Cuatrecasas, Madrid +34 1 524 71 00
Recommended in Tax

RAMON RAMOS, Juan
Landwell Abogados y Asesores Fiscales (PricewaterhouseCoopers), Barcelona
Recommended in Tax

RAMÓN Y CAJAL, Pedro
Ramón & Cajal Abogados, Madrid +34 91 576 1900
Recommended in Corporate/M&A

REMÓN PEÑALVER, Jesús
Uría & Menéndez, Madrid +34 91 586 0400
jrp@uria.com
Recommended in Communications
Specialisation: Practice areas: Litigation and Public Law.
Prof. Memberships: ICAM, LCIA, CIMA.
Career: Degree in law, University of Madrid. Special Law Degree Award 1981. Law Officer of the State (1985) in the General Department of the State Litigation Service, at the Madrid Government Delegation and before the Supreme Constitutional Court. Member of the Board of Directors of various State companies. Since 1992 Associate Professor of Constitutional Law at the Carlos III Madrid University. Since 1996 Partner of the *Uría & Menéndez* law firm, Madrid.

RUEDA, Pedro A.
Araoz y Rueda, Madrid +34 91 319 0233
Recommended in Corporate/M&A

SÁINZ, Álvaro
Linklaters (a member firm of Linklaters & Alliance), Madrid +34 91 781 8720
alvaro.sainz@linklaters.com
Recommended in Corporate/M&A
Specialisation: Partner in the Mergers and Acquisitions Department. Main area of work is corporate law, principally mergers, acquisitions, joint ventures, distribution contracts and project financing.

SANCHEZ DE MOVELLAN, Manuel
Clifford Chance, Madrid +34 91 590 7500
Recommended in Banking & Finance

SÁNCHEZ-PEDREÑO, Antonio
Linklaters (a member firm of Linklaters & Alliance), Madrid +34 91 781 8720
antonio.sanchez-pedreno@linklaters.com
Recommended in Communications
Specialisation: Extensive experience in corporate operations, with emphasis on M&As and corporate operations, foreign investments, guaranteed financing, debt instruments, commercial and banking operations.
Prof. Memberships: Member of the Madrid Bar Association. Member of the New York Association.

SÁNCHEZ-TERÁN, Salvador
Uría & Menéndez, Madrid +34 91 586 0400
sst@uria.com
Recommended in Banking & Finance, Corporate/M&A
Specialisation: Corporate, Financial, Securities and Banking Law. Development of new financial instruments, such as matador bonds, subordinated debt, preference shares for banks and savings banks, structures of convertible/exchangeable bonds, etc. Advisor in the 1999 BSCH merger, the largest ever in Spain at that time.
Career: Joined *Uría & Menéndez* in 1988. Partner since 1996. Professor of Commercial Law, ICADE University, Madrid, 1989-2000.
Personal: ICADE University, Madrid: Law Degree, 1987; Degree of Economics and Business Administration, 1988.

SANFRUTOS, Eduardo
Ernst & Young Abogados, Madrid +34 91 572 7200
Recommended in Tax

SANTOS, Javier
Squire, Sanders & Dempsey LLP, Madrid +34 91 590 2420
Recommended in Banking & Finance

SANZ, Enrique
Landwell Abogados y Asesores Fiscales (PricewaterhouseCoopers), Madrid +34 91 568 4000
Recommended in Communications

SEBASTIÁN, Rafael
Uría & Menéndez, Madrid +34 91 586 0430
rsq@uria.com
Recommended in Banking & Finance
Specialisation: M&A, Banking and Bankruptcy Law.
Prof. Memberships: Madrid Bar, 1980; Legal Consultant, New York Bar, 1991.
Career: Secretary of the Board, general counsel and head of legal department, Citibank España, 1982-90. Member of the Board of Directors of Citibank España, 1988-90. Professor of Commercial Law I & II (1985-1991; 1996-2000), and of the Master's program ('Bankruptcy and Insolvency', since 1997), Universidad ICADE, Madrid.
Personal: Licenciate of Law, Universidad de Deusto, Bilbao, 1976. Licenciate of Economics and Business Administration, Universidad ICADE, Madrid, 1977. Languages: English, French.

SUÁREZ DE LEZO, Rafael
Melchor, Albiñana & Suárez de Lezo, Madrid +34 91 451 93 00
rsuarez@melchorheras.com
Recommended in Banking & Finance, Corporate/M&A
Specialisation: Senior Partner of the firm. Main area of work is Corporate Law, specialising in securities markets, insolvency, mergers and acquisitions, finance, contracts and investments, antitrust law and litigation. Among others, during the last year has acted as legal counsel to Heineken on the purchase of CruzCampo, both in the contractual and antitrust aspects; has filed in Court on the suspension of payments of Mecánica de la Peña; has advised on the purchase of Segur Ibérica; has advised The Coca-Cola Company on the transaction aiming to acquire certain asset and trade marks owned by Cadbury Schweppes plc, including to represent TCC before the Antitrust Spanish Authorities and has acted as legal counsel to Hisalba on its delisting take over bid. Is a member of the Board of Directors, among others, of listed companies in the Spanish Stock Exchange.
Prof. Memberships: Madrid Bar Association since 1978.
Career: Law Degree (1977) and Economist Science Degree (1980) by Deusto University. Doctor of Law with special award, Pontifica de Comillas University (ICADE), with the thesis 'La tutela judicial en el Mercado de Valores' (Court protection in the Securities market) (1998), Professor of Commercial Law at Pontificia de Comillas University, since 1990. Joined *Melchor de las Heras* in 1978, becoming partner in 1985.
Personal: Born in Córdoba, on 14 April 1954. Lives in Madrid.

SUEIRO, Miguel
Castro Sueiro & Varela, Madrid +34 91 577 5020
msueiro@csvabogados.com
Recommended in Banking & Finance
Specialisation: Partner of the firm in Insurance and Banking Department. Other areas of work are general corporate advice and mergers and acquisitions. Has been involved as bank lawyer in several large loan transactions (mainly including project

S

S

finance and structured finance), normally syndicated ones, acting as important Spanish and foreign banks' lawyer. During 2000 advised with regards to (among others) project finance for the construction of a railroad in Madrid (M-45), project finance for the construction of two wind farms in the north of Spain (45 MW), structured finance of a 'TDW crude oil tanker' for a major Spanish oil company, and structured finance for the acquisition of three vessels (euros 150,253,026). Contributor to 'International Insurance Law and Regulation' and 'Using International Low Tax Jurisdiction'.
Prof. Memberships: Madrid Bar Association.
Career: Qualified in 1982. Joined *Uría & Menéndez* in 1982. Founding Partner of *Castro, Sueiro & Varela* in 1987. Member of the international law groups 'Insurolaw' and 'Globalaw' as contact partner. Member of the Board of Advisors of the 'Centre for International Legal Studies'.
Personal: Born 5 February 1958. Attended Complutense University of Madrid 1977-1982. Leisure interests include travelling and outdoor activities. Lives in Pozuelo de Alarcón, Madrid. Married. One son.

TENA, Juan
Jones, Day, Reavis & Pogue, Madrid
+34 91 319 28 25
jtena@jonesday.com
Recommended in Corporate/M&A
Specialisation: Principal area of specialisation is company law (mergers and acquisitions, joint ventures, capital development).
Prof. Memberships: Madrid and Barcelona Bar Associations; International Bar Association (Section on Business Law).
Career: 1973, Law Degree and Political Science Degree from the Complutense University of Madrid. Admitted to Bar 1977. Adviser to the Minister's Cabinet of the Ministry of Education and Science, 1973-74. Head of President's Cabinet of the Spanish Federation of Business Organisations-CEOE, 1978-79. Joined the law firm of *J. y B. Cremades y Asociados* as an associate in 1979 and became a partner in 1983. Founding partner of *Tena, Muñoz y Asociados* in 1993. Became partner at *Jones Day* in January 2000 on the occasion of the merger with *Tena, Muñoz y Asociados.* Has taken part in domestic and foreign arbitrations as arbitrator and counsel. Invited speaker at conferences.
Personal: Born in Madrid on 4 January 1952. Is fluent in English, French and Spanish.

TORRENTE, Fernando
Cuatrecasas, Madrid +34 1 524 7100
Recommended in Banking & Finance, Corporate/M&A

URÍA MERUÉNDANO, Rodrigo
Uría & Menéndez, Madrid +34 91 586 0400
Recommended in Corporate/M&A
Specialisation: Founder and Managing Partner of *Uría & Menéndez.*
Prof. Memberships: Chevalier de la Légion d'Honneur.
Personal: Born in Madrid on 12 January, 1941. Vice-President of the Royal Board of Trustees of the Prado Museum, member of the Board of Trustees of the Foundation Collection Thyssen-Bornemisza. Member of the Board of Directors of Barclays Bank, SA and of Altadis, SA. Chairman of St Gobain Cristalería, SA. Member of the 'Advisory Board' of 'Actualidad Económica' and 'Expansión'. Languages: English, French and Italian.

VALLS, Carlos
Clifford Chance, Barcelona +34 93 344 2200
Recommended in Intellectual Property

VALVERDE, Antoni
Freshfields Bruckhaus Deringer, Barcelona
+34 93 363 7400
antoni.valverde@freshfields.com
Recommended in Corporate/M&A
Specialisation: Specialisations include M&A, both public and private, private equity and intellectual property. Sector experience includes asset manangement, leisure, media and construction finance.

VARELA VARAS, Angel
Gomez-Acebo & Pombo, Madrid +34 91 582 9100
avarela@gomezacebo-pombo.com
Recommended in Banking & Finance
Specialisation: Responsible for *Gomez-Acebo & Pombo*'s Vigo and Santiago (Galicia) offices and partner in the financial department. Advises companies and financial institutions on: mergers and acquisitions of credit entities and other financial institutions, the Secretary of the Board of credit entities and listed companies, take-over bids, companies going public on the stock exchange, privatisation, securities loans, credit facilities, structured projects and asset finance, corporate lending, derivatives, securitisation and public offerings. Published various articles on the Securities Market and new financial products. Frequently lectures at conferences and seminars.
Prof. Memberships: Association Internationale des Jeunes Avocats; Chair, Former Students' Association of the Institute of Stock Exchange Studies; Madrid Bar Association.
Career: Salamanca University, Law Degree (1986) & Legal Training Degree, Escuela de Practica Juridica (1987); Instituto de Estudios Bursatiles, First Class Honours Masters of Stock Exchange (1989); admitted to Madrid Bar Association (1992); director of Mergers and Acquisitions at Intermediaciones y Finanzas (1990-92); Corporate Finance Department at Beta Capital SV y B SA (1989-90); lectured at Complutens University, College for European Studies, Institute for Stock Brokers' Studies, and was visiting professor at CECA Business School, at the Institute for European Legal Studies at Nebrissenssis University, among others. Joined *Gomez-Acebo & Pombo* in 1992.

VEGA PENICHET, Luis
M Vega Penichet, Madrid +34 91 431 5500
Recommended in Competition/Anti-trust

VIVES, Fernando
Garrigues & Andersen, Madrid +34 91 514 5200
fernando.vives@garriguesandersen.com
Recommended in Banking & Finance
Specialisation: Extensive experience as legal adviser to the restructuring of groups of corporations that operate within the financial sector. Mainly advises M&A, joint ventures, co-operation agreements etc. Also advises on the formation, authorisation regulation, sale and purchase of banks, securities companies, insurance companies, and other financial institutions such as investment funds and capital management companies. Wide experience in the legal practice of the securities market (ie public offerings, clearance and settlement, tender offers) and of the insurance sector (bank assurance agreements, assignment of portfolios, etc). Customary speaker at conferences and seminars on the financial law sector.
Prof. Memberships: Madrid Bar Association (Spain).
Career: Graduate in Law and in Economics and Business Administration from the Universidad Pontificia de Comillas (Madrid) in 1987. Joined *Garrigues & Andersen* the same year, becoming a partner in 1997. Professor on leave of the Universidad Pontificia de Comillas (Madrid). Assistant professor of the Centro de Estudios y Formaci'n Empresarial (Madrid).
Personal: Born 8 October 1962. Lives in Madrid.

YBAÑEZ, Javier
Garrigues & Andersen, Madrid +34 91 514 5200
javier.ybanez@garriguesandersen.com
Recommended in Banking & Finance
Specialisation: Partner in Banking, Securities and Insurance Department. Main area of work: Securities markets and banking. Advises on Public Offering of Securities (including privatisations). Syndicated and bilateral credits and project finance agreements. Securitisation (including the Spanish nuclear moratorium securitisation).
Prof. Memberships: Qualified in 1987. Joined *Garrigues & Andersen* in 1987, becoming a partner in 1998.
Personal: Born December 10, 1963. Attended Universidad Complutense of Madrid (1982-87), lives in Madrid.

SRI LANKA

Corporate/Commercial

SRI LANKA Leading firms (Corporate/Commercial)
1 FJ & G de Saram
Julius & Creasy
2 Murugesu & Neelakandan
3 John Wilson Partners
Paul Ratnayeke Associates
Tiruchelvam Associates

Firms are listed alphabetically in each band.

Leading individuals (Corporate/Commercial)
1 KADURUGAMUWA Udaya *FJ & G de Saram*
RAJAH Senathi *Julius & Creasy*
2 NEELAKANDAN Kandhia *Murugesu & Neelakandan*
3 WILSON John *John Wilson Partners*

Individuals are listed alphabetically in each band.

FJ & G de Saram (5 ptrs, 27 asscs) According to the findings of our researchers, this is the country's *"leading corporate firm which handles sophisticated matters for its important clients."* The practice is involved in project finance, insurance, telecommunications, aviation, shipping and contracts. It acted for Emirates airline of the UAE in the acquisition of a stake in Sri Lankan Airlines, and represented AIG Insurance in their establishment in Sri Lanka. *"One of the country's leading corporate practitioners,"* **Udaya Kadurugamuwa** is *"intelligent and responsive to clients' needs."* The team represented Graphitewerke in its acquisition of a graphite mine during the government's privatisation. **Clients:** IBM; Monsanto; AT&T; American Home Products; Walt Disney; Exxon Mobil; 3M; Toyota; BMW; ICI; Nokia; IMF; IFC.

Julius & Creasy (11 ptrs, 30 asscs) The *"most reputed firm in the country"* is *"well-connected,"* particularly with international law firms. With a corporate practice perceived to be *"getting stronger,"* it undertakes a broad range of work and is active in infrastructure projects. The team advised SmithKline Beecham and Glaxo Wellcome on their merger in Sri Lanka and the Asian Development Bank and ANZ on the financing of a power project. It also advised British American Tobacco on restructuring following the acquisition of Rothmans. **Senathi Rajah** is viewed by competitors as a *"senior corporate lawyer with tremendous experience."* **Clients:** Ford; Motorola; Deutsche Bank; American Express; HSBC; Colombo Stock Exchange; Shell; BAT.

Murugesu & Neelakandan (5 ptrs, 12 asscs) *"The third firm in line,"* it is *"well-known with a strong domestic client base."* Active in the incorporation of companies, contracts, project finance, admiralty and providing legal advice to banks and lenders. The team is gaining a reputation for high quality service on power projects. **Kandhia Neelakandan** is *"the corporate strength"* in the team which advised the underwriters in the AES Kelantissa power projects. **Clients:** Rolls Royce; Singer; IFC; CDC; Citibank; Standard Chartered Bank.

John Wilson Partners (2 ptrs, 4 asscs) An established firm with an excellent name for patent and trademark work, it handles general commercial work including foreign investment and hotel construction. The firm advised on a distribution agreement for a British company producing printers & peripherals and worked on a

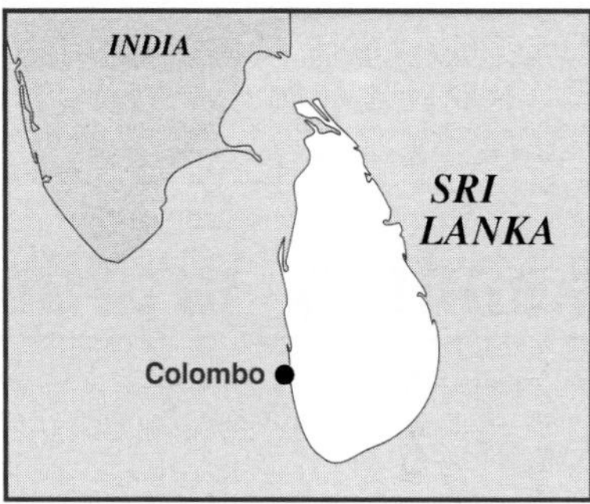

$12 million investment in a hotel resort. *"Pleasant"* **John Wilson Jr** is a *"good active young lawyer."* **Clients:** Tyco International; Morgan Stanley.

Paul Ratnayeke Associates (2 ptrs, 15 asscs) *"Climbing up the ladder,"* this *"smaller, energetic"* firm is gaining a fine reputation for its litigation, and is growing in the corporate arena. Experienced in M&A, shipping, insurance, aviation, contracts and foreign investment work, the firm recently completed the financing, sale and purchase agreement on a hotel project. **Clients:** ANZ Grindlays Bank; Ceylease Financial Services; Sri Lankan Airlines; Cathay Pacific; British Airways.

Tiruchelvam Associates (2 ptrs, 4 asscs) Perceived to be less prominent than in previous years, it is a *"good name to consider"* for its *"connections and strong client base."* The firm acts as general counsel for international corporations and works on telecoms and investment regulation work. **Clients:** NTT; Cisco; Galadari Hotels; United Brewers Lanka.

Leaders' profiles – Sri Lanka

KADURUGAMUWA, Udaya
FJ & G De Saram, Colombo +94 1 347 729

NEELAKANDAN, Kandhia
Murugesu & Neelakandan, Colombo 1 +94 1 334 949

RAJAH, R. Senathi
Julius & Creasy, Colombo 1 +94 1 422 601

WILSON JR, John
John Wilson Partners, Colombo +94 1 324 579

SUDAN

Corporate/Commercial

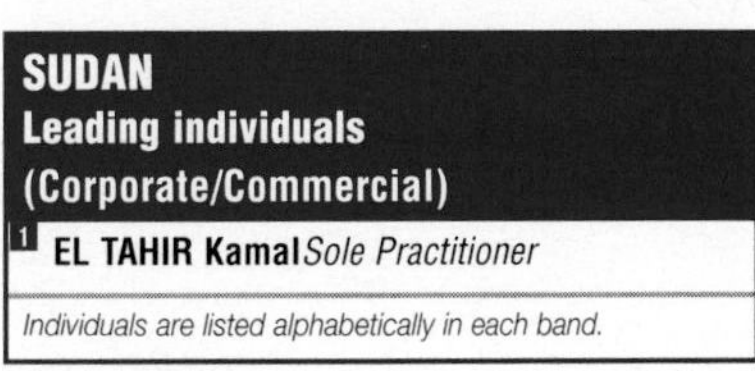

SUDAN Leading individuals (Corporate/Commercial)
1 EL TAHIR Kamal *Sole Practitioner*
Individuals are listed alphabetically in each band.

Kamal el Tahir An able local lawyer who has a sound working relationship with a number of international companies with interests in Sudan. Our researchers were impressed by the strength of commendation for the quality of his contract work and documentation. **Clients:** Domestic and foreign corporates.

Leaders' profiles – Sudan

EL TAHIR, Kamal
Kamal el Tahir – Sole Practitioner, Khartoum
+249 11 640 585

SURINAM

Corporate/Commercial

SURINAM Leading firms (Corporate/Commercial)
1 Lim A Po
2 Coster Advocaten

Firms are listed alphabetically in each band.

SURINAM Leading individuals (Corporate/Commercial)
1 HOOPLOT Edward *Law Firm Hooplot*
KRUISLAND Freddy *Lim A Po*
STRUIKEN Henk *Law Firm Struiken*
Up-and-coming individuals
SOHANSINGH Rani *Essed & Sohansingh*
Individuals are listed alphabetically in each band.

Lim A Po (4 ptrs, 3 asscs) *"Always the client's first choice,"* the firm dominates the local scene with its large size supporting a broad corporate capability. Representing the majority of established foreign investors, the firm boasts a huge portfolio of clients in mining, banking, insurance, property and telecommunications. Former public prosecutor at the Procurer General's office and current president of law society Advocaten Cereniging, **Freddy Kruisland** is the star player in a group of experienced lawyers. The team acted for ABN AMRO on the sale of a business in Surinam to Regional Bank of Trinidad & Tobago (BTT) and on a loan transaction with State Oil Company. It continues to act as counsel to Standard Bank of London and Citibank in relation to loans to the government of Surinam. **Clients:** Shell; Texaco; Billiton; State Oil Company; Golden Star Resources (Canadian Gold); BAT.

Coster Advocaten (4 ptrs) Established in 1995, this growing firm of *"enthusiastic and dedicated"* young lawyers has strength in litigation and general commercial work covering corporate, labour law and public administration. The appointment of a partner to the post of Director of Community Association (the national telecoms board) affords the firm a degree of specialisation in telecommunications work. It acted for Caribbean bank on its take-over of assets from ABN AMRO and was appointed by the Government of Surinam to act as mediators between two political parties in a local court action. **Clients:** Clico; Exmet; Burlington; Olsen; Alico.

Other Notable Practitioners: One of Surinam's oldest and most experienced lawyers with *"a good sense of commercial relationships,"* sole practitioner **Edward Hooplot** maintains a solid reputation for his work on corporate disputes, banking and commerce matters, where he acts for Energiebedrijven Suriname. **Henk Struiken** of Law Firm Struiken has *"a good track record"* in industrial property matters, his clients include Visa, Domino Pizza, Iridium and Fila. He prepared a due diligence project on the assignment of Billiton to Gencor. **Rani Sohansingh** of Essed & Sohansingh Advocaten is set to *"become one of the names talked about in years to come."* Known in political circles, she is respected for her corporate and litigation work and acted for Surinam Airways in an employment case concerning provision of work and salary disputes.

Leaders' profiles – Surinam

HOOPLOT, Edward
Law Firm Hooplot, Paramaribo +597 476 406

KRUISLAND, Freddy
Lim A Po, Paramaribo +597 473 514

SOHANSINGH, Rani
Essed & Sohansingh Advocaten, Paramaribo +597 424 231

STRUIKEN, Henk
Law Firm Struiken, Paramaribo +597 474 024

S

SWAZILAND

Corporate/Commercial

SWAZILAND Leading firms (Corporate/Commercial)
1 Robinson Bertram
2 Millin & Currie incorporating RD Friedlander & Co

Firms are listed alphabetically in each band.

Leading individuals (Corporate/Commercial)
1 CLOETE Robert *Robinson Bertram*
Individuals are listed alphabetically in each band.

Robinson Bertram (11 partners) The "*preferred firm*" for commercial work in Swaziland due to its size and expertise. Acting for a range of overseas banks, much of the focus lies in the Swaziland sugar and pulp industries. Supported by a large litigation department, it undertakes corporate, financial and M&A work. **Robert Cloete** is "*the strength behind the firm,*" and acted for Barclays and Standard Chartered on the disposal of their Swaziland interests. He also advised the Commonwealth Development Corporation on the restructuring and privatisation of three parastatals. The firm is a founder member of the Lex Africa association of law firms. **Clients:** Morgan Stanley Dean Witter; Bank of New York; Barclays; Standard Chartered; Swaziland financial institutions.

Millin & Currie incorporating RD Friedlander & Co (4 ptrs, 4 asscs) A full service firm rated by interviewees as a "*close second*" in the market. Known for its insolvency and liquidation work, it acts for major banks, corporates and the Swaziland Government in M&A work. It advised on a

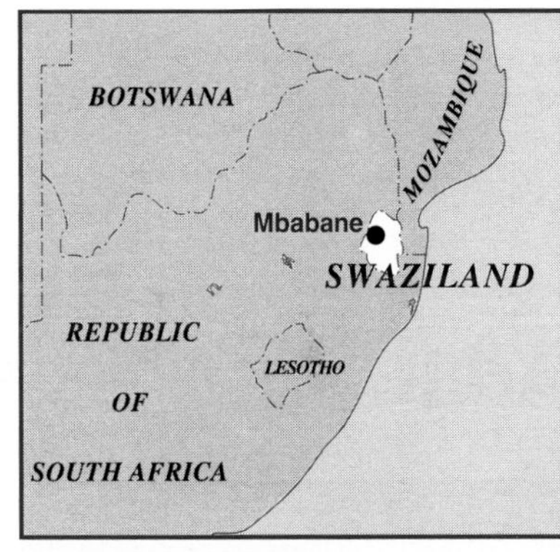

R1.6 billion transaction for Lonrho Sugar and has seen a growth in its counsel on industrial relations. **Clients:** Lonrho Sugar; Standard Bank; financial institutions and manufacturers.

Leaders' profiles – Swaziland

CLOETE, Robert
Robinson Bertram, Mbabane +268 4042826

SWEDEN

Index

The clients' choice

BUSINESS LAWYER OF THE YEAR

CLAES ZETTERMARCK, *White & Case*

BUSINESS LAW FIRM OF THE YEAR

MANNHEIMER SWARTLING ADVOKATBYRÅ

Claes Zettermarck *wins convincingly as best lawyer with established local firm* ***Mannheimer Swartling Advokatbyrå*** *picking up the award for best law firm.*

For details see page 36.

OVERVIEW: Sweden is one of the most exciting technology markets in Europe. As venture capital money has flooded in for the many startups, the fields of IT and telecoms are rapidly converging while lawyers are becoming increasingly specialised. This trend towards increased size and specialism across the country represents a preemptive strike against the threat posed by foreign competition. Though few foreign firms have entered the market, the accountancy-linked outfits are recruiting actively and many predict that they will take business from medium sized domestic firms. Smaller practices, in particular, are linking themselves to international networks or merging, with this year seeing the first genuine cross-border tie-up between Scandinavian firms. Lagerlöf & Leman, despite its international network, had another poor year. To recent personnel losses were added the defection en masse of its Gothenburg office. With its decline, Vinge cements its position as the leading banking practice, while Mannheimer Swartling has emerged as a pre-eminent corporate firm. Hans Wibom (of Vinge) continues his dominance of the corporate market while Mannheimer Swartling's recruitment of a legal team from Enskilda Securities has strengthened its corporate finance and capital markets capacity.

Arbitration (International)

SWEDEN
Leading individuals
(Arbitration (International))

Band	Name	Firm
1	**RAMBERG Jan**	*Sole Practitioner*
	ROMLOV Robert	*Advokatfirman Vinge KB*
	SÖDERMARK Bertil	*Advokatfirman Södermark*
	WERSÉN Dag	*Sole Practitioner*
	ZETTERMARCK Claes	*White & Case*
2	**BOMAN Lars**	*Advokatfirman Morssing*
	LEIJONHIELM Thorsten	*Mannheimer Swartling*
	LINDSKOG Stefan	*Wistrand Advokatbyrå*
	LUNDBLAD Claes	*Mannheimer Swartling*
	NILSSON Bo	*Rydin & Carlsten Advokatbyrå AB*
	RAMBERG Göran	*Advokatfirman Lindahl*
	SOLERUD Hans-Gunnar	*Gernandt & Danielsson*

Individuals are listed alphabetically in each band.

Sweden has a long history of arbitration and the Arbitration Institute of the Swedish Chamber of Commerce has retained its cold war reputation as a neutral ground between East and West. Particularly attractive in disputes involving parties from the US and former Soviet Union, recent arbitrations have involved China and other far Eastern countries. Chairmen are frequently justices of the Swedish court though well respected private practitioners may also be chosen. One such is former professor **Jan Ramberg***. An *"extremely talented lawyer"* he is *"one of the most notable and experienced arbitrators"* either as chair or counsel. Another lawyer equally good in the chair or on his feet is **Dag Wersén***. Until recently with Lagerlöf & Leman, he is considered by his peers to be *"an excellent arbitrator"* who is usually seen on corporate disputes. **Bertil Södermark***, by contrast, is usually appointed as counsel. *"The dean of all litigators in Sweden"* he is *"brilliant"* and our researchers were left in no doubt that he *"has all the qualities that make a good arbitrator."* Vinge's *"absolutely excellent"* **Robert Romlov***, though experienced in general commercial arbitrations, is *"particularly good in shipping"* matters, while *"high-powered"* **Claes Zettermarck*** is recognised for his arbitration expertise in construction cases.

Lars Boman* is *"a skilled lawyer"* and *"an experienced performer,"* well known for his work in shipping and insurance matters. At Mannheimer Swartling, **Thorsten Leijonhielm*** has an eclectic practice, although he stands out for his handling of corporate disputes. At the firm's Gothenburg office, **Claes Lundblad*** has established his name for shipping and general commercial disputes. *"Extremely talented and intelligent"* **Stefan Lindskog*** is felt by the market to be *"the most intellectual of all the arbitrators in Sweden,"* while **Bo Nilsson*** is perceived to take high rank among the leading arbitration lawyers of the 'next generation.' **Göran Ramberg*** at Lindahl is a *"senior, highly respected"* arbitrator with *"wide experience"* in contractual and corporate disputes, while ex-Supreme Court Justice **Hans-Gunnar Solerud*** has *"great technical ability."*

Banking & Finance

SWEDEN
Leading firms (Banking & Finance)

Band	Firm
1	Advokatfirman Vinge KB
2	Mannheimer Swartling Advokatbyrå
3	Gernandt & Danielsson Advokatbyrå
	Advokatfirman Hammarskiöld & Co
4	Advokatfirman Cederquist KB
	Lagerlöf & Leman Advokatbyrå
	Nils Setterwalls Advokatbyrå AB
5	White & Case

Firms are listed alphabetically in each band.

Leading individuals (Banking & Finance)

Band	Individual	Firm
★	WIBOM Hans	*Advokatfirman Vinge KB*
1	ANDERSSON André	*Mannheimer Swartling*
	DE HEVESY Stefan	*Advokatfirman Vinge KB*
	HÅRD Tom	*Mannheimer Swartling*
	KÄRDE Bengt	*Advokatfirman Hammarskiöld*
	LUNDQVIST Dick	*Gernandt & Danielsson*
2	DANIELSSON Karl-Erik	*Gernandt & Danielsson*
	DE GEER Carl Gustaf	*Mannheimer Swartling*
	DE GEER Stefan	*Gernandt & Danielsson*
	HÖGSTRÖM Peter	*Lagerlöf & Leman*
	HULTQVIST Svante	*Advokatfirman Cederquist*
3	EKBOM Per Gustaf	*Advokatfirman Hammarskiöld*
	ROMANDER Claes	*White & Case*
	SEDEROWSKY Peter	*Nils Setterwalls Advokatbyrå*

Individuals are listed alphabetically in each band.

Advokatfirman Vinge KB (5 ptrs, 11 asscs) Still considered *"more commercially successful"* and *"more recognised outside Sweden"* than its rivals, the firm continues to dominate the banking landscape. Active in all areas including syndicated loans, export and project finance, and capital markets work, the firm has seen rapid expansion in acquisition finance and a flood of work for buyout funds. This pre-eminence once again owes much to star performer **Hans Wibom***, who remains *"the outstanding person in this area,"* praised by competitors for his knowledge and experience, his *"low-key"* approach and for *"working around the clock." "Practical"* **Stefan De Hevesy***, meanwhile, is *"good on a technical level and good at getting a deal done."* The firm represented Nordic Capital on financing the acquisition of the Nybon and Bauwerk groups and acted for the newly established Alfa Laval group on a £1.3 billion senior credit facility and high yield bond. **Clients:** ABN AMRO; SEK; SPINTAB; SBAB; Investor AB.

Mannheimer Swartling Advokatbyrå (7 ptrs, 16 asscs) Though still a little behind Vinge in this field, there is some suggestion that, with a strong brand name and top-drawer client base, the firm has narrowed the gap. A key factor is the consistent excellence of the group's lawyers. As one rival commented to our researchers: *"When you have a lawyer from Mannheimer Swartling, you know you are going to get good work."* Active in share issues, derivatives and related tax matters, the firm has increased its profile for acquisition financing, typically acting on behalf of the banks. *"Skilful lawyer"* **André Andersson*** is *"the leading guy on banking and finance,"* while *"commercially minded"* **Carl Gustaf De Geer*** is a strong private equity player. **Tom Hård*** maintains a first-class reputation for capital markets advice and stock exchange regulation. The team advised Goldman Sachs on the issue of a high yield bond on behalf of CB Bus, the consortium acquiring Swebus from Stagecoach, a deal worth around €100 million. **Clients:** Goldman Sachs.

Gernandt & Danielsson Advokatbyrå (5 ptrs, 10 asscs) *"Generally a good quality firm"* with a broad and varied banking practice, frequently representing large Swedish and international commercial banks. Alongside traditional financings, the firm has been involved in restructurings, M&A within the banking sector and capital markets work. The team acts for companies starting up various securities, especially hedge funds, and has also picked up a lot of smaller asset management work. Considered a strong capital markets player, **Dick Lundqvist*** *"knows what he wants, gets the deal done and is technically very good as well." "Talented young lawyer"* **Stefan De Geer*** *"has solid legal knowledge but can also see the commercial implications"* and is particularly rated by the market for acquisition finance, while **Karl-Erik Danielsson**'s* name is almost inseparable from that of MeritaNordbanken. The firm advised MeritaNordbanken on its merger with Unidanmark and its proposed acquisition of shares in Christiania Bank. **Clients:** MeritaNordbanken; Lazard; Bank of America.

Advokatfirman Hammarskiöld & Co (3 ptrs, 7 asscs) A *"highly successful"* firm with *"people well qualified in banking and financing,"* including **Bengt Kärde***, *"a good lawyer on more traditional debt,"* and **Per Gustaf Ekbom*** who is often seen on structured finance deals. The team advises a wide range of Swedish and overseas clients, principally on the lenders' side, and is well known for corporate and project finance, domestic and cross-border leasing and tax-based finance. Acted recently for the lending banks on the SEK2.8 billion acquisition financing and refinancing of Swebus AB, and for Linde AG on its successful SEK4.3 billion tender for the shares in AGA and the subsequent capital increase of SEK1.5 billion. **Clients:** Deutsche Bank; Central Bank of Sweden; Goldman Sachs.

Advokatfirman Cederquist KB (3 ptrs, 5 asscs) Experienced in capital markets work, structured and project finance and syndicated loans, the firm is particularly acknowledged by clients and competitors for its expertise in leveraged transactions. *"Cederquist has a good team,"* but the presiding force is **Svante Hultqvist***, whose recruitment from Lindahl is credited with putting them on the map. *"One of the top lawyers in Sweden in this field,"* he has close links with major Swedish banks, and is visible in acquisition finance as well as traditional debt. Represented the international lender on one of the first high yield issues with a Swedish borrower, and also played a role in the financing of the Øresund Bridge. **Clients:** Large Swedish and international commercial and investment banks.

Lagerlöf & Leman Advokatbyrå (3 ptrs, 12 asscs) Though relatively weak on traditional banking work, the firm has particular strength in acquisition finance and regulatory work, and has been seen in *"several interesting capital markets transactions."* In this latter field, **Peter Högström*** was particularly recommended to our researchers. An enviable client list, especially on the international side, includes blue chip companies and a number of foreign investment banks. Currently involved in establishing an SPV joint venture for the purpose of train financing. **Clients:** Carnegie; Morgan Stanley; CSSB; Deutsche Bank; Dresdner Bank; Warburg.

Nils Setterwalls Advokatbyrå (4 ptrs, 6 asscs) Sweden's oldest firm has traditional strength in maritime finance and represents several foreign banks, especially on asset financing. The banking team also provides strategic advice on bank liabilities and opinions for foreign clients, and is active in due diligence and equity work for large investors entering the Swedish market. The firm has been involved with the Swedish government's overseas economic development arm in devising guarantee instruments and organising soft loans for Baltic governments, often in collaboration with the World Bank. *"Colourful"* **Peter Sederowsky*** has *"an impressive client portfolio,"*

S

although his profile has dipped somewhat over the last twelve months. **Clients:** Metallica SA; Scandrenting; The Swedish Government.

White & Case (2 ptrs, 2 asscs) Less involved in traditional banking finance than M&A within the banking sector, the firm undertakes banking litigation and regulatory work for larger commercial banks and the smaller Swedish brokers which act as investment banks. Acts for a number of Scandinavian companies on cross-border transactions within Scandinavia and the Baltic States, although the team also conducts a number of one-off deals for foreign investment banks, often linked to the burgeoning equity markets. Recently represented two Swedish banks, one in acquiring a Polish bank and the other in increasing its share interest in a Baltic bank. **Claes Romander*** is considered *"experienced and good to work with."* **Clients:** MeritaNordbanken; Handelsbanken; SBI.

S

Communications

SWEDEN
Leading firms (Communications)

Band	Firm
1	Mannheimer Swartling Advokatbyrå
	Advokatfirman Vinge KB
2	Gernandt & Danielsson Advokatbyrå
	Lagerlöf & Leman Advokatbyrå
	Advokatfirman Lindahl
3	Advokatfirman Cederquist KB
	Advokatfirman Delphi & Co AB
	Advokatfirman Hammarskiöld & Co
	Lindh Stabell Horten
	White & Case

Firms are listed alphabetically in each band.

Leading individuals (Communications: Telecoms)

Band	Individual
1	**BERGENSTRÅHLE Erik** *Advokatfirman Lindahl*
	DE GEER Stefan *Gernandt & Danielsson*
	RIESE Biörn *Mannheimer Swartling*
2	**AF PETERSENS Carl Johan** *Vinge KB*
	OLOFSSON Rolf *White & Case*
	WINNERBLAD Johan *Mannheimer Swartling*

Individuals are listed alphabetically in each band.

Leading individuals (Communications: IT)

Band	Individual
1	**BERNHARD Stefan** *Lagerlöf & Leman*
	CHRISTNER Anders *Advokatfirman Lindahl*
	CLEMENS Mikael *Clemens Wallén Östlund*
	LINDBERG Agne *Advokatfirman Delphi & Co AB*
2	**GUSTAVSSON Björn** *Advokatfirman Vinge KB*
	PERHARD Lars *Advokatfirman Cederquist KB*
	WINNERBLAD Johan *Mannheimer Swartling*

Individuals are listed alphabetically in each band.

Mannheimer Swartling Advokatbyrå (9 ptrs, 21 asscs in IT/media group) • **Tel:** For many people *"the first and foremost telecommunications firm,"* it has perhaps *"the broadest range of clients and work"* in Sweden and an enviable depth of practitioners. The team handles all legal matters relating to telecommunications and broadcasting, both transactional and regulatory, and also monitors and advises on legislative measures relating to the field. A superb client base includes large, listed Swedish and foreign companies, commercial and investment banks, government agencies and public utilities. Recently represented Telia on its IPO. *"A head higher than the rest,"* **Biörn Riese*** is *"a hard-working lawyer"* whose *"personality supports the transaction,"* while younger partner **Johan Winnerblad*** is considered by rivals *"a sound technical practitioner."* • **IT:** *"Young, bright and fast,"* **Johan Winnerblad**'s* broad competence sees him recommended in IT as well. Although traditionally less visible in this sector than Vinge, our researchers learned that the firm is considered to be catching up fast. Active in contractual issues such as outsourcing arrangements and systems delivery contracts, along with matters surrounding data protection, electronic markets and payment solutions. However, the firm's true expertise lies in venture capital advice, recently representing foreign banks in start-up venture capital investments ranging from £1 million to £20 million. **Clients:** Telia AB; Telefonaktiebolaget LM Ericsson.

Advokatfirman Vinge KB (5 ptrs, 15 asscs) • **Tel:** *"A huge player"* and *"the ones with the longest experience"* in this field, the firm has been involved in national and international projects relating to fixed, cellular, satellite and cable networks and has an enviable client list including Nordic, US and UK operators. *"Business minded"* **Carl Johan af Petersens*** has an *"excellent knowledge of the industry"* and *"understands the needs of his clients."* Experienced in all areas of telecoms, the firm is especially respected for broadband work, and recently represented B2 on its sale of a 25% stake to NTL Incorporated. • **IT:** *"Vinge has the best reputation."* Arguably *"the most advanced"* of the Swedish IT practices, the firm started early in this field and retains its advantage, despite losing staff to Mannheimer Swartling. *"Experienced"* **Björn Gustavsson*** is *"strong on IT law"* and *"works with flair."* Currently enjoying a dramatic increase in internet-related work, the firm advises on such areas as e-commerce and licensing strategy, portal contracts, digital signatures and data protection. On the traditional IT side the firm is active in outsourcing, licensing and system procurement, and increasingly represents disappointed purchasers in connection with large computer system contracts. **Clients:** B2; iD2.

Gernandt & Danielsson Advokatbyrå (2 ptrs, 3 asscs) • **Tel:** *"Often mentioned in connection with telecommunications,"* this strong, professional firm is well known in the market for transactional and regulatory work for international clients. *"Deal maker"* **Stefan De Geer*** *"has a good reputation"* in this sector, with his technical skills and *"great sense of humour"* smoothing the path of numerous transactions. As well as one of the three big mobile phone networks, they represent satellite and broadband operators on a range of M&A, regulatory and quasi-regulatory work, as well as such areas as programme distribution and satellite agreements. Recently acted for foreign concerns on the acquisition of a 20% stake in a Swedish broadband operator. **Clients:** Europolitan; MCI Worldcom.

Lagerlöf & Leman Advokatbyrå (5 ptrs, 15 asscs) • **Tel:** Representing Scandinavian and international telecoms clients in the Swedish market, the firm has expertise in all aspects of transactional and regulatory work. Increasingly active in the mobile phone sector, it advised several consortia on their applications for 3G licences. • **IT:** *"One of the few lawyers in Sweden who has outstanding expertise in the global sense,"* **Stefan Bernhard**'s* experience and gravity make him *"like a Supreme Court Judge in this area of law,"* and he is well known for his work within the ICC on business rules and e-commerce legislation. Active in such areas as supply and purchase agreements, outsourcing, e-commerce, on-line contracts, information security and privacy, distribution agreements and licensing, the firm assists a range of clients from established software companies to start-ups, and also advises venture capital incubators. **Clients:** TeliaAB; ACN; Swedish Microsoft; Icon Medialab.

Advokatfirman Lindahl (3 ptrs, 4 asscs) • **Tel:** Experienced in advising new entrants to the Swedish telecoms market, the firm also represents several established operators on all aspects of work from general corporate to technical regulatory issues. The client base includes major national and international companies, many of them fixed line, but also a number of cable operators. Despite a perceived weakness in the mobile field, the firm recently put together a UMTS (3G licence) application for a foreign company. *"Clients like"* **Erik Bergenstråhle***: *"He's a nice person and a reliable practitioner."* • **IT:** *"Good technical draftsman"* **Anders Christner*** has years of experience developing the Swedish industry's standard contracts, something Lindahl has been involved with since the 1980s. Works for hardware and software companies, and internet service providers on contractual issues, software licensing, e-commerce and system development and has recently advised on some major outsourcing transactions. **Clients:** IT Företagen.

Advokatfirman Cederquist (7 ptrs, 7 asscs) • **IT:** Traditionally a leading IP firm, the firm has diversified within the technology sector and is now considered *"excellent when it comes to IT."* Active in systems supply, software licensing and contractual issues, the team is increasingly visible in the e-commerce sector where it has advised on contractual issues and new service and product distribution forms. *"Experienced"* **Lars Perhard*** is praised by the market for his skills as a lecturer as well as his *"good, solid knowledge of the issues."* His work on the Millennium bug was also noted. Recently working for internet service providers on issues surrounding the development of vortals – vertical portals. **Clients:** Tele2; NetCom; Bonnier Group; Microsoft.

Advokatfirman Delphi & Co (6 ptrs, 9 asscs) • **IT:** A strong firm which has *"definitely made a name for itself"* in this sector. Experienced in all areas of IT law, it has particular expertise in IT contracts, e-business and data-security. The department's most recognised name is anti-piracy expert **Agne Lindberg***, a *"well known IT lawyer"* with a *"good combination of technical and commercial skills."* Often connected with American software and hardware companies, the firm has increasingly advised start-up internet service providers and public sector procurers of IT services. Represented a consortium of Norwegian and Swedish insurance companies in outsourcing their IT infrastructure to IBM for around SEK10 billion. **Clients:** Microsoft; Xerox.

Advokatfirman Hammarskiöld & Co (2 ptrs, 5 asscs) • **Tel:** Though *"more transactionally-oriented,"* the firm *"has an excellent reputation generally"* and is especially visible on IPO work for telecoms companies. Have been advising Tele1 Europe on a number of aspects of business including the SEK2.2 billion issue of high yield bonds and, more recently, its listing on Nasdaq and the Stockholm Stock Exchange. • **IT:** Again more prominent transactionally, the firm is also active in areas such as IT systems licensing, IT contracts and e-commerce. Worked with Scandinavia's largest computing company, TietoEnator on its merger and the subsequent public offer to shareholders in Entra Data AB, Sweden's biggest banking sector IT company. **Clients:** Tele1 Europe; Setec Oy; Siemens Elema; Sony; Telia Business Innovations.

Lindh Stabell Horten (4 ptrs, 8 asscs) • **Tel:** *"Strong in telecoms and media,"* the group represents Swedish-based telecoms operators, new entrants and international carriers, but receives greatest acclaim from the market for its advice on behalf of cable TV companies. Acts on a range of telecoms issues, including capacity leases, equipment leases, infrastructure agreements, content provision, technology licences and regulatory work. Over the past year, the team has undertaken regulatory work on a variety of telecoms mergers. **Clients:** Telecoms operators; Cable TV companies.

White & Case (1 ptr, 3 asscs) • **Tel:** *"Sweden's Mr Satellite,"* **Rolf Olofsson*** is *"cautious and business-oriented"* and *"knows satellite communications better than anyone in Sweden."* As head of White & Case's global telecoms law practice group, he has experience on such projects as the Viking, Freja, Marco Polo and Sirius 1-3 satellites. Representing satellite communications companies on the procurement of satellites and launches, joint venture agreements, corporate transactions, financing and insurance, the firm also works for financial institutions and other telecoms clients on regulatory work and frequency co-ordination. Recently involved in the acquisition by SES and the Swedish Space Corporation of shares in the Nordic Satellite Company. **Clients:** Nordic Satellite Company.

Other Notable Practitioner The *"clever and experienced"* **Mikael Clemens*** of Clemens Wallén Östlund was recommended to our researchers for his *"good insight into the business."* Widely connected in the market with Cap Gemini Ernst & Young, he also works for smaller service providers and the occasional buyer on issues such as development contracts, service contracts and IT-linked arbitration.

S

Competition/Anti-trust

Mannheimer Swartling Advokatbyrå (5 ptrs, 8 asscs) Still clearly one of the big two, the firm is known in the market for its strong position within state-owned and blue-chip industrial companies, as well as its superb record in high-profile competition litigation. Much of the firm's success rests upon the reputation and *"sound reasoning"* of the *"astute"* **Johan Coyet***, one of the first Swedish lawyers to master EC competition law. **Tommy Pettersson***, his heir apparent, has developed *"expertise in merger control,"* principally on contentious issues. The firm successfully represented a small train operator in Sweden's first predatory pricing case, and advised SAS on a price discrimination case against the Swedish Aviation Authority. **Clients:** SAS; BK Tåg; AGA; Dyno Nobel.

Advokatfirman Vinge KB (3 ptrs, 12 asscs) *"A big success with new companies,"* this high quality practice is considered to be *"stronger on merger filings"* than its competitors, although it has had a quieter time on the litigation side since the Swedish Post case. Transactionally focused, the team acts for a number of fund companies and merchant banks, along with major players in the deregulated industries and new economy. *"Meticulous"* **Carl Wetter*** has a *"fine legal mind"* and is well supported by a department *"full of talented lawyers."* Chief amongst these is **Johan Karlsson*** whose *"sharp brain"* enables him to stand out among the firm's associates. Currently increasing its profile for public procurement, the team's

*See leaders' profiles on pages 646-652

SWEDEN Leading firms (Competition/Anti-trust)
1 Mannheimer Swartling Advokatbyrå
Advokatfirman Vinge KB
2 Lagerlöf & Leman Advokatbyrå
Advokatfirman Lindahl
3 Advokatfirman Delphi & Co AB
Gernandt & Danielsson Advokatbyrå
4 Advokatfirman Cederquist KB

Firms are listed alphabetically in each band.

Leading individuals (Competition/Anti-trust)
1 **COYET Johan** *Mannheimer Swartling*
WETTER Carl *Advokatfirman Vinge KB*
2 **ERICSSON Eric** *Advokatfirman Lindahl*
PETTERSSON Tommy *Mannheimer Swartling*
3 **CARLSSON Kenny** *Gernandt & Danielsson*
HOLM Christer *Advokatfirman Delphi & Co AB*
KARLSSON Johan *Advokatfirman Vinge KB*
Up-and-coming individuals
SÖDERLIND Erik *Lagerlöf & Leman*

Individuals are listed alphabetically in each band.

caseload still overwhelmingly comprises merger control work. **Clients:** Household names within finance, industry and IT/Telecoms.

Lagerlöf & Leman (3 ptrs, 13 asscs) Although the departure of Jonas Bergh has clearly damaged its profile, the size of the competition department and its connections with Brussels have ensured that the firm remains an anti-trust force. Work is equally divided between merger filings, including multi-jurisdictional filings, and litigation, and the team represented the claimant as an interested party in the Swedish competition authority's action against SAS over its Eurobonus frequent flier scheme. *"Promising"* associate **Erik Söderlind*** was recommended to our researchers for his *"in-depth technical knowledge."* **Clients:** The Swedish Government.

Advokatfirman Lindahl (8 ptrs, 4 asscs) *"Excellent"* **Eric Ericsson** puts this practice firmly on the map. *"Low-key and competent,"* he was formerly with Vinge and is praised by competitors as *"a genuine, experienced competition lawyer."* With a focus on merger notification work and experience in litigation and public procurement, this is regarded as one of the most dynamic practices in Sweden, although yet to attain the sheer volume of cases of the market leaders. Defended Preem Petroleum against allegations of taking part in a cartel to fix the price of oil. **Clients:** Preem Petroleum; Wavin.

Advokatfirman Delphi & Co KB (2 ptrs, 5 asscs) Anti-trust specialist **Christer Holm*** heads a department which handles all aspects of competition law, but which is especially known for its strong public procurement practice. Advises a number of companies in the consumer goods and car industries including American and German multi-nationals. Currently involved in the oil industry cartel investigation before the Swedish market court on behalf of OKQ8. The team was instrumental in gaining clearance from the European Commission for the merger of the property insurance arms of three large insurance companies. **Clients:** Kraft Foods; BMW; AIG; Microsoft.

Gernandt & Danielsson Advokatbyrå (1 ptr, 3 asscs) The recruitment of competition law expert **Kenny Carlsson*** was widely felt to signal the firm's determination to develop its competition practice. The former head of the legal secretariat at the competition authority is praised for his *"legal knowledge"* and *"open-minded"* approach. The firm advises a number of clients, notably in banking and telecommunications, and is currently representing one of the parties to an oil cartel case. **Clients:** MeritaNordbanken; SEB; Förenings Sparbanken; HandelsBanken.

Advokatfirman Cederquist KB (2 ptrs, 2 asscs) Although a small department, competitors report that referrals are always *"very well dealt with."* Known for strength in IP and media, much of the competition work stems from this, though the firm also has a reputation for international public procurement and is active in competition-related litigation. Currently involved in an increasing number of cross-jurisdictional merger cases involving extensive notifications. **Clients:** Netcom; Microsoft.

Corporate/M&A

Mannheimer Swartling Advokatbyrå (12 ptrs, 21 asscs) *"Mannheimer Swartling stands for prestige."* The market suggests that, this year, the firm has taken a narrow lead over its corporate rivals. A superb client list includes a number of well-established Swedish listed companies and international household names, and competitors note rapid growth in the field of new technology. Amongst the individual lawyers, *"excellence and high quality"* is combined with *"a serious and professional attitude"* at all levels. *"Talented, experienced and efficient"* **Axel Calissendorff*** is arguably Sweden's leading technical lawyer in this sector while *"practical, pragmatic"* and *"constructive"* **Carl Gustaf De Geer*** is *"more the deal maker."* **Tom Hård***, though best known as *"the number one name in capital markets,"* is also involved in big ticket M&A. The firm advised Securitas on its acquisition of Burns International Services, the US security company, for $650 million. **Clients:** Securitas AB; Volvo; TeliaAB; Birka Energi.

Advokatfirman Vinge KB (20 ptrs, 40 asscs) Considered by clients and rivals *"a little more modern and entrepreneurial,"* Sweden's biggest law firm continues to be *"extremely successful."* Traditionally connected with the new economy, the firm is currently working for a number of investment funds and institutions acquiring dot.com start-ups. Although the loss of Bertil Villard to an in-house position is perceived to have lowered the team's corporate profile, it can still call upon *"a huge bunch of effective lawyers."* Chief amongst these is **Hans Wibom***, in the words of one competitor *"by far the most important partner they have."* Although principally known as a banking and finance lawyer, he now appears regularly on major corporate deals. *"Well regarded"* **Michael Wigge*** is considered one of the best of the younger partners. The firm also represents large listed companies on major acquisitions, divestitures, restructurings and IPOs. The firm represented Renault on th sale of its truck and bus division to Volvo and Emerson on the purchase of the Ericsson energy business. **Clients:** Emerson; Renault; Industri Kapital; Observer Ab; Statens Järnväger SJ.

Gernandt & Danielsson Advokatbyrå (5 ptrs, 15 asscs) Considered an excellent transactional unit, the corporate team advises major clients across all industry sectors, but has been especially active this year in media and new economy. *"Talented, capable and inventive,"* **Stefan De Geer*** is partic-

SWEDEN
Leading firms
(Corporate/Mergers & Acquisitions)

Band	Firm
1	Mannheimer Swartling Advokatbyrå
2	Advokatfirman Vinge KB
3	Gernandt & Danielsson Advokatbyrå
	Advokatfirman Hammarskiöld & Co
	Lagerlöf & Leman Advokatbyrå
4	Advokatfirman Cederquist KB
	Nils Setterwalls Advokatbyrå AB
	White & Case
5	Advokatfirman Delphi & Co AB
	Rydin & Carlsten Advokatbyrå AB
	Wistrand Advokatbyrå
6	Johnsson & Johnson
	Advokatfirman Lindahl

Firms are listed alphabetically in each band.

Leading individuals
(Corporate/Mergers & Acquisitions)

Band	Individual
1	**CALISSENDORFF Axel** *Mannheimer Swartling*
	DE GEER Carl Gustaf *Mannheimer Swartling*
	HAMMARSKIÖLD Peder *Advokatfirman Hammarskiöld*
	WIBOM Hans *Advokatfirman Vinge KB*
	ZETTERMARCK Claes *White & Case*
2	**BÖRRESSEN Martin** *Lagerlöf & Leman*
	DE GEER Stefan *Gernandt & Danielsson*
	HÅRD Tom *Mannheimer Swartling*
	KANTER Lennart *Advokatfirman Cederquist KB*
	LUNDIN Anders *Gernandt & Danielsson*
	LÜNING Wilhelm *Advokatfirman Cederquist KB*
	RYDBECK Otto *Nils Setterwalls Advokatbyrå AB*
3	**BERGLÖF Per** *Advokatfirman Delphi & Co AB*
	JOHNSON Claes *Johnsson & Johnson*
	WIGGE Michael *Advokatfirman Vinge KB*

Individuals are listed alphabetically in each band.

ularly linked with these sectors, while *"important player"* **Anders Lundin*** is considered more of a general M&A lawyer. The firm recently assisted MeritaNordbanken in its merger with Unidanmark, and DeutschePost in its acquisition of Swedish logistics company ASG. **Clients:** MeritaNordbanken; Caterpillar; Toyota.

Advokatfirman Hammarskiöld & Co (3 ptrs, 14 asscs) A *"strong practice"* which owes much to the energy of its name partner in building *"a good reputation for himself and the firm."* Still flourishing after its split from Lagerlöf & Leman, the firm is involved in an impressive range of large transactions, frequently involving international clients. Best known as *"a 'deal-doer',"* **Peder Hammarskiöld*** has *"particular strength in acquiring clients,"* but has also successfully retained a reputation for technical excellence. Represented German company Linde AG on its successful £2.8 billion bid for AGA, the largest ever cross-border public offer in Sweden, and Scania in negotiations with Volvo and VW. **Clients:** Scania; TeliaAB; Tele1; Central Bank of Sweden.

Lagerlöf & Leman Advokatbyrå (13 ptrs, 35 asscs) Although the problems continue for the Swedish arm of the Alliance, most recently with the defection en masse of much of its Gothenburg office, the firm still has a *"strong brand name"* and a number of top-class international clients. Although not so well represented among large domestic companies, the team advises many blue-chip multi-nationals, including large US/UK concerns and foreign investment banks. **Martin Börressen*** is praised by his peers for his *"skill and commercial understanding."* Acted recently for Altitun in its sale to ADC for SEK9 billion and for Metsä Serla in its acquisition of Modo Paper from SCA and Holman for SEK18 billion. **Clients:** ICA; Ford; CSFB; Deutsche Bank; Dresdner Bank.

Advokatfirman Cederquist KB (15 ptrs, 6 asscs) Although Rolf Andersson has moved into a consultancy role, this *"good quality"* firm still has *"a number of strong and successful lawyers." "Competent, serious and reliable"* **Wilhelm Lüning*** is rated by competitors for his M&A expertise, while **Lennart Kanter*** is considered by some *"one of the best in Sweden."* Benefiting from the nationwide increase in M&A, the firm covers all aspects of corporate and commercial work and represented AB Sequlah in its sale of an investment to a French concern. **Clients:** Daimler Chrysler; Bonnier; Industriförvaltnings Kinnevik.

Nils Setterwalls Advokatbyrå (7 ptrs, 10 asscs) A highly respected, long-established firm, particularly known for its strong niche in all aspects of maritime law. In the corporate arena, the team has a reputation for its advice on behalf of communications companies. *"Dedicated lawyer"* **Otto Rydbeck*** is the firm's stand-out transactional practitioner. The recruitment of Lindahl's Malmo office, officially due in 2001, has been augmented by the recent arrival of a number of lawyers from Lagerlöf & Leman's Gothenburg office. Highlight transactions include the acquisition of the saws and tools division of Sandvik by US company Snapon, and the sale by Telia of its 8,000 vehicle fleet to GE Capital. **Clients:** Snapon; Telia; Bidlet.

White & Case (4 ptrs, 11 asscs) *"Has a strong brand name, and it's good at what it does."* Represents banks, Swedish companies and multinational American clients, and the firm has developed a 'one stop shop' with the establishment of an international private equity practice. Benefiting from its network of international offices, the firm also has the services of newly-appointed international management board member **Claes Zettermarck***. A *"pleasant personality,"* he *"deserves a huge degree of respect"* for his *"sound judgement"* as a transactional lawyer on big ticket M&A, notably within the construction sector. Represented Nordic Capital in its majority stake acquisitions of Ahlsell, Bröderna Edstrand, Starckjohan and Reynolds from Trelleborg AB for $781 million, the region's largest private equity transaction. **Clients:** Nordic Capital; BT Industries AB.

Advokatfirman Delphi & Co AB (8 ptrs, 20 asscs) Although better known for its highly regarded IP and IT practices, the firm is also seen by competitors as *"an important corporate player"* with the ability to attract key international clients. With its *"strength in depth"* the team has taken advantage of the spate of M&A in the IT sector, and participated in a number of listings of technology companies last year, including that of Framfab, one of the largest Swedish IT concerns. *"Commercial, accessible and prompt,"* **Per Berglöf*** is highly praised by clients. **Clients:** Microsoft; Texas Instruments; Xerox; Reuters; Dupont.

Rydin & Carlsten Advokatbyrå AB (8 ptrs, 7 asscs) *"A particularly prestigious small firm,"* its *"first-rate"* IP and litigation practices complement a *"highly successful"* corporate arm. The firm has an international client base which belies its size, advising companies from traditional industry, finance and new technology. Now undertaking increasing amounts of corporate transactional work, the team represented ADC Telecommunications in its acquisition of all the shares in Altitun AB for SEK7-8 billion. **Clients:** Ford Motor Co.

Wistrand Advokatbyrå (15 ptrs, 15 asscs) The Denton International member in Sweden, although possessing a particularly strong litigation profile, has gained a marked increase of peer approval for its corporate and commercial work. Particularly influential in Gothenburg, the firm's Stockholm office has now been bolstered to 25 lawyers. The team acts for a number of smaller publicly quoted companies and typically advises on mergers and IPOs within the IT sector. **Clients:** Stena Group.

Johnsson & Johnson Advokatbyrå (2 ptrs, 4 asscs) *"A well-rounded firm"* with a reputation in the market for quality and efficiency. Its client list

*See leaders' profiles on pages 646-652

includes Swedish and international companies from traditional manufacturing industry to energy, financial services and IT. Typically acting for medium-sized concerns, the firm represented the purchasers this year in the acquisition of a listed company and a specific part of a large company's business. **Claes Johnson*** is recommended for his combination of skills and experience. **Clients:** Ericsson; SCA.

Advokatfirman Lindahl (7 ptrs, 13 asscs) Although set back by the loss of the Malmo office and other defections, the firm is *"still a player."* Traditionally strong in IT and new media, the firm has acted on a number of M&A transactions in these areas. Also involved in privatisations, the firm advises a number of venture capital companies and acted recently on the sale of an energy company for around SEK4 billion. **Clients:** Major Swedish and international companies.

S

Leaders' profiles – Sweden

AF PETERSENS, Carl Johan
Advokatfirman Vinge KB, Stockholm
+46 8 614 3000
carl_johan.af_petersens@vinge.se
Recommended in Communications: Telecoms
Specialisation: Partner and head of *Vinges's* Communications Group. Represents a broad range of domestic and international companies within the entertainment, communications and information technology industries. Engaged in a number of projects, primarily in Scandinavia, in areas such as telecoms licensing; broadband networks and services; cable and satellite television; UMTS/3G projects; data communications; mobile communications; satellite systems. Works with the firm's corporate department in major communications M&A transactions. Has spoken at several conferences.
Prof. Memberships: Swedish Bar Association.
Publications: Several articles on communications law in Swedish and international journals and books.
Career: Qualified in 1988. Joined *Vinge* in 1988, becoming a partner in 1997.
Personal: Born 6 July. Married, three children.

ANDERSSON, André
Mannheimer Swartling Advokatbyrå, Stockholm
+46 8 613 55 00
aa@msa.se
Recommended in Banking & Finance
Specialisation: Specialises in regulations in the financial sector, lending and structured financing. Work includes advice on regulatory aspects of clearing and settlement rules, and supervisory issues relating to banks and finance companies. Regularly represents banks and corporate borrowers in connection with debt financing. Recent work includes, in particular, securitisations and acquisition financing.
Career: Joined *Mannheimer Swartling* in 1987 and was made a partner of the firm in 1994. Presently the chairman of the firm's Banking and Finance Group.
Personal: Born 10 August 1959. Attended University of Lund 1979-86 (LLM and MBA), Oxford University, Christ Church, 1986-87 (Diploma in Legal Studies) and Universita per Stranieri di Siena 1998.

BERGENSTRÅHLE, Erik
Advokatfirman Lindahl, Stockholm
+46 8 670 58 00
erik.bergenstrahle@lindahl.se
Recommended in Communications: Telecoms
Specialisation: Telecommunications; transactional, regulatory as well as general corporate and commercial matters.
Prof. Memberships: Swedish Bar Association, International Bar Association, the Swedish Society for Computers and Law.
Publications: Opportunities for new entrants, European Counsel Industry Report on Telecommunications.
Career: District Court of Sodra Roslags, Scandinavian Airlines System (SAS), *Mannheimer Swartling Advokatbyrå, Dahlman Magnusson Advokatbyrå.*
Personal: Born: August 18, 1960. Education: University of Stockholm, LLM

BERGLÖF, Per
Advokatfirman Delphi & Co AB, Stockholm
+46 8 677 54 00
per.berglof@delphilaw.com
Recommended in Corporate/M&A
Specialisation: Head of *Delphi & Co.*'s Corporate Finance Department including Mergers & Acquisitions and Capital Markets. The Corporate Finance Department has more than 30 lawyers including 10 partners. Main area of practice is M&A and Capital Markets. Highlights from 1999/2000: Counsel for British Nuclear Fuel Limited and its US subsidiary, Westinghouse Inc., in its acquisition of ABB Atom AB, Counsel for Allgon AB (publ) in its acquisition of Wireless Solution, Counsel for OK petrol company in its joint venture with Kuwait Petroleum, Counsel for British Foods/Twinings in its acquisition activities in Sweden, Counsel for Skandia Insurance and Storebrand Insurance corporations in the sale of their IT businesses to IBM, Listing of Know IT AB, Listing of Biogaia AB.
Prof. Memberships: Swedish Bar Association, Delegate to the Council of the Swedish Bar Association, International Bar Association.
Career: LLM Uppsala University 1977. Court work 1978-1980. *Erik Berglunds Advokatbyrå* 1980-1983. *Advokatfirman Delphi & Co.* 1984.
Personal: Born 1952, Interests: Music, golf, skiing and ice hockey as director of the board of IK Göta Ishockey Club. Family: Wife and four children.

BERNHARD, Stefan
Lagerlöf & Leman Advokatbyrå (A member firm of Linklaters & Alliance), Stockholm +46 8 665 66 00
stefan.bernhard@lol.se
Recommended in Communications: IT
Specialisation: Partner, *Lagerlöf & Leman*, (IT/IP). Work areas cover all aspects of information technology, computer law and (tele)communications. Specially qualified in copyright, computer- and internet security (cryptography), e-commerce and convergence. Chairman of the ICC working group 'Global Information Technology Issues'. Assists the ICC, the Federation of Swedish Industry and is in governmental expert groups.
Prof. Memberships: Swedish Bar Association.
Career: Qualified in 1969 at the University of Stockholm, service with the Swedish courts, junior judge at the court of appeals, joined *Lagerlöf & Leman* in 1972.
Personal: Born 29 August 1944.

BOMAN, Lars
Advokatfirman Morssing & Nycander, Stockholm
+46 8 587 05100
Recommended in Arbitration (International)

BÖRRESEN, Martin
Lagerlöf & Leman Advokatbyrå (A member firm of Linklaters & Alliance), Stockholm +46 8 665 66 00
martin.borresen@lol.se
Recommended in Corporate/M&A
Specialisation: Partner in *Lagerlöf & Leman.* Main areas of work are all aspects of law relating to energy and other utilities such as railways, mergers & acquisitions, general corporate law and contract law. Acting for Swedish and international companies and many Swedish public and state-owned companies.
Prof. Memberships: Swedish Bar Association.
Publications: Swedish contributing editor of 'International Energy Law' and 'Taxation Review'. Co-author of 'Energy Law & Regulation in the European Union' (Sweet & Maxwell, London 1999).
Career: Qualified in 1974 at the University of Stockholm. Studies at McGill University, Montreal in 1979/1980 (Diploma in Air & Space Law). Service with the Stockholm City and at the Court of Appeal before joining *Lagerlöf & Leman* in 1980.
Personal: Born 27 April 1950.

CALISSENDORFF, Axel
Mannheimer Swartling Advokatbyrå, Stockholm
+46 8 613 5481
aca@msa.se
Recommended in Corporate/M&A
Specialisation: Head of *Mannheimer Swartling Advokatbyrå*'s M&A practice group (40 lawyers), with almost 20 years of representing international and domestic clients in transactional matters. Also a

member of the firm's Intellectual Property practice group and has wide experience as litigator and arbitrator.
Prof. Memberships: Swedish Bar Association (Deputy Chairman of the Stockholm division). The Swedish Association for Copyright.
Publications: Rättsvetenskapliga studier tillminnet av Tore Almén(1999): 'Utvecklingen av avtalen om förvärv av aktiebolag under senare delen av 1900-talet' Festskrift till Ulf. K. Nordenson (1999): Några anteckningar om personligt skadeståndsansvar for upphovsrättsintrång i en juridsk persons verksamhet' Discussion paper presented at the IBA annual meeting in September 2000: 'Can a non Anglo-Saxon purchase agreement afford adequate and satisfactory protection and if so what would the outline of such a stock purchase agreement be; and due diligence'. Rättsfall att minas (1997): Gunilla Rudlings affischer NJA 1974 94 NY juridik 1996:1: 'Interimistiska Förbud inom immaterialrätten' JT 1992 - 1993 s. 547 ff: 'Skiljedom angående svek och återgång av avtal om överlåtelse av rörelse'.
Career: Born in 1953. LLM, University of Stockholm, 1978. Law clerk at the Nacka District Court 1978-1980. Junior Judge, the Administrative Court of Appeals in Stockholm 1980-1981. *Mannheimer Zetterlöf*, 1981-1990 (member from 1986). *Mannheimer Swartling 1990* (member, executive partner 1993-1994).

CARLSSON, Kenny
Gernandt & Danielsson Advokatbyrå, Stockholm
+46 8 670 6600
Recommended in Competition/Anti-trust

CHRISTNER, Anders
Advokatfirman Lindahl, Stockholm
+46 8 670 58 00
anders.christner@lindahl.se
Recommended in Communications: IT
Specialisation: Partner in IT Department. Main area of work is IT law, principally all kinds of IT-related agreements such as outsourcing, project, system development, joint venture agreements as well as mergers and acquisitions related to IT/Internet companies. Has been legal advisor for the Swedish IT companies organisation consisting of more than 600 IT companies including all subsideries to any major foreign IT company, since 1984. Has also been the main author of all standard terms and conditions issued by the IT organisation. Has spoken at various conferences regarding IT agreements.
Prof. Memberships: Swedish Bar Association and International Bar Association.
Publications: Author of comments to IT standard agreements in Sweden and to 'Agreement 90', the leading Swedish standard document.
Career: Bachelor's degree 1975, law clerk at the District Court of Stockholm 1976-1978, joined *Advokatfirman Lindahl* 1978, became partner in 1983. Member of the Swedish Bar Association 1981. Member of the Swedish Data Protection Committee 1996-1997.
Personal: Born 11 July, 1950.

CLEMENS, Mikael
Clemens Wallén Östlund, Stockholm
+46 8 678 4000
Recommended in Communications: IT

COYET, Johan
Mannheimer Swartling Advokatbyrå, Stockholm
+46 8 613 55 00
jc@msa.se
Recommended in Competition/Anti-trust
Specialisation: Partner of *Mannheimer Swartling*, resident in Stockholm office. Chair of the firm's EC and competition practice group with over 25 years experience representing a broad range of international and domestic clients. Has worked extensively both on EC competition matters and on Swedish competition law matters representing clients before the European Commission, the Swedish Competition Authority and Swedish courts.
Publications: Author of 'Internationella Företagsconcentrationer inom EEC' (International Concentrations within the EEC, Sveriges Industriförbund. 1973), co-author of 'EG's Konkurrensrätt inom EU och EES' (Competition Law within the EU an EEA, Norstedts, 1994. Has written numerous articles on various aspects of EC- and Swedish competition law.
Career: Born in 1947. LLM, University of Stockholm 1973. Member of the Swedish Bar Association in 1978. Junior legal adviser to the Swedish Board of Commerce in 1973-74. Partner of *Mannheimer Swartling* in 1982.

DANIELSSON, Karl-Erik
Gernandt & Danielsson Advokatbyrå, Stockholm
+46 8 670 6600
Recommended in Banking & Finance

DE GEER, Carl Gustaf
Mannheimer Swartling Advokatbyrå, Stockholm
+46 8 613 55 00
cdg@msa.se
Recommended in Banking & Finance, Corporate/M&A
Specialisation: Partner of *Mannheimer Swartling*, resident Stockholm office. Practice areas: International mergers & acquisitions, stock market law, finance and securities law. Has been advising in many significant international transactions involving Swedish or Scandinavian companies.
Prof. Memberships: Member of the Swedish Bar Association; Member of the New York Bar Association.
Publications: Various articles in banking journals.
Career: Associate at *Donovan Leisure Newton Irwine*, 1981-1982. Associate at *Carl Swartling Advokatbyrå*, 1982-1989. Partner of *Carl Swartling Advokatbyrå*, 1989-1990. Partner of *Mannheimer Swartling Advokatbyrå*, 1990-.
Personal: Born in 1955. University of Stockholm (LLM, 1979); University of Pennsylvania (Master of Law, 1981).

DE GEER, Stefan
Gernandt & Danielsson Advokatbyrå, Stockholm
+46 8 670 6600
Recommended in Banking & Finance, Communications: Telecoms, Corporate/M&A

DE HEVESY, Stefan
Advokatfirman Vinge KB, Stockholm
+46 8 614 3000
www.vinge.se
Recommended in Banking & Finance
Specialisation: Partner in Bank and Finance department. Main area of work is capital markets including structured finance, securitisation, property financing and leasing. Is also active in acquisitions and mergers, specifically in relation to properties.
Prof. Memberships: Member of the Swedish Bar Association since 1986.
Career: Served at the District Court in Gothenburg 1980-1983. Joined *G. Sandströms Advokatbyrå* in 1989. Partner in *Advokatfirman Vinge* since 1991.
Personal: Born 8 June 1955. Attended Stockholm's University 1976-1980 (juris kandidat, LLM, 1980). Leisure interests include tennis, skiing and other outdoor activities.

EKBOM, Per Gustaf
Advokatfirman Hammarskiöld & Co, Stockholm
+46 8 578 450 00
Recommended in Banking & Finance
Specialisation: Specialising in Banking and Financial law. The work focuses on structured finance, i.a. asset finance, acquisition finance and project finance, with a particular strength in aviation finance.
Prof. Memberships: Professional Membership: Swedish Bar Association.
Publications: Swedish Banking Legislation, published in 'International Banking' supplement to International Financial Law Review, 1992; Swedish Legal Aspects of Aircraft Financing, published in 'Aircraft Finance, Recent Developments and Prospects', Kluwer Law International, 1995; Swedish Leasing Market (together with Christer Bois and Anders Köhlmark), published in supplement to 'Asset Finance International', 1996.
Career: LLB 1985, Stockholm University. Junior Judge 1985-1987. Attorney *Lagerlöf & Leman Advokatbyrå* 1997; since 1998 partner in *Hammarskiöld & Co.* Lecturer in financing law at Stockholm University.
Personal: Born October 25, 1960.

ERICSSON, Eric
Advokatfirman Lindahl, Stockholm
+46 8 670 58 00
eric.ericsson@lindahl.se
Recommended in Competition/Anti-trust
Specialisation: Competition Law, Public Procurement Law, and general EU law.
Prof. Memberships: Swedish Bar Association; International Bar Association.
Career: University of Lund (LLM, 1989); Diploma in EC Law, King's College (1990).

GUSTAVSSON, Björn
Advokatfirman Vinge KB, Stockholm
+46 8 614 3000
bjorn.gustavsson@vinge.se
Recommended in Communications: IT
Specialisation: Partner and head of the information technology department within *Vinge's* practice group for IT, telecommunications and media. Represents a

S

wide range of domestic and international clients on information technology matters, including traditional licensing and procurement arrangements as well as matters relating to the internet and electronic commerce. Clients include both suppliers and purchasers. Has spoken at several conferences.
Prof. Memberships: Memberships: Swedish Bar Association, International Bar Association.
Career: Joined *Vinge* in 1983, was qualified 1986 and became a partner 1988.
Personal: Born 27 December 1951. Married with two children. Degrees in Business Administration (University of Lund, Sweden and University of Colorado, USA) and Master of European Law (College of Europe, Belgium).

S

HAMMARSKIÖLD, Peder

Advokatfirman Hammarskiöld & Co, Stockholm
+46 8 578 450 00
peder.hammarskiold@hammarskiold.se
Recommended in Corporate/M&A
Specialisation: Main areas of work are mergers and acquisitions, banking, finance and corporate law. Has participated in several of the most significant M&A transactions in Sweden in the last few years. Acts regularly both for Swedish and foreign clients. Acted for Deutsche Bank and Industrivärden AB in the acquisition of Sandvik AB from Skanska AB. Has acted for Scania AB in the Volvo/Scania bid, which so far is the largest public acquisition in Sweden. Also acted for Linde A.G. in the acquisition of AGA AB which is the largest cross-border public acquisition in Sweden, and acted in the merger of the Swedish insurance companies Wasa and Länsförsäkringar. Acts for a large number of major companies, banks and insurance companies on matters ranging from corporate finance issues to general corporate law matters.
Prof. Memberships: Swedish Bar Association and the banking committee of ICC.
Publications: Author of Swedish section, 'Banks Abroad – Establishment Operation, Supervision' (Kluwer 1986); 'A World Guide to Exchange Regulations' (1992); 'The GT Guide to World Equity Markets' (Euromoney 1987-1999); 'Mergers & Acquisitions Yearbook' (1997); 'The Consequences of Class Actions in Sweden – Some Critical Comments' (JT 1995/96 No.7); 'DOCDEX – A New Dispute Resolution System for Documentary Credits' (JT 1996/97 No.4). Numerous other articles in legal journals and magazines.
Career: LLB 1974 Uppsala University, legal studies at Hamburg University, Germany, Junior Judge 1979-1982; Member of the Swedish Bar Association 1984; Attorney and Partner, *Lagerlöf & Leman Advokatbyrå* (1984-1997); Lecturer Stockholm Univ. (1982-1994); Managing partner in *Hammarskiöld & Co.* Appointed as special banking and arbitration expert to the ICC Committee on Rules for Documentary Credit Dispute Resolution, DOCDEX.
Personal: Born 24 July 1955.

HÅRD, Tom

Mannheimer Swartling Advokatbyrå, Stockholm
+46 8 613 55 00
th@msa.se
Recommended in Banking & Finance, Corporate/M&A
Specialisation: Partner of *Mannheimer Swartling*, Stockholm. Head of Corporate Finance. Specialises in securities law as well as corporate law. Has served as counsel to the Federation of Swedish Industries for many years and has also served as the Secretary General to the Swedish National Committee of the ICC and as Managing Director of the Securities Council.
Prof. Memberships: Swedish Bar Association (1992).
Career: LLM, University of Stockholm, 1974; served in Swedish Courts before entering private practice; joined *Mannheimer Swartling* in 1990 and became a partner in 1993.
Personal: Born in 1945.

HÖGSTRÖM, Peter

Lagerlöf & Leman Advokatbyrå (A member firm of Linklaters & Alliance), Stockholm +46 8 665 66 00
peter.hogstrom@lol.se
Recommended in Banking & Finance
Specialisation: Partner in charge of *Lagerlöf & Leman's* M&A and corporate department. Main area of work is mergers and acquisitions, corporate finance and structured financing. Including equity and debt issues, mergers and acquisitions, reorganisations as well as securitisations. Recently acting for QXL on their bid for Bidlet, REMEC Inc on the public bid for Allgon AB and the floatation of ENIRO AB.
Prof. Memberships: Swedish Bar Association.
Publications: Is a frequent lecturer in mergers and acquisitions and related topics and is the author of the Swedish section in the Kluwer publication "Corporate Acquisitions and Mergers".
Career: Qualified in 1987 at the University of Lund and joined *Lagerlöf & Leman* in 1989.
Personal: Born 17 February 1961.

HOLM, Christer A.

Advokatfirman Delphi & Co AB, Stockholm
+46 8 677 54 00
christer.holm@delphilaw.com
Recommended in Competition/Anti-trust
Specialisation: Head of *Delphi & Co's* EU and competition law department. Main areas of work are competition law (EU and domestic), distribution, insurance and re-insurance, as well as directors' and officers' liability. Has acted on behalf of a number of international clients, including BMW, Tupperware, Kraft Foods Int, AIG, and Kuwait Petroleum in cases before both the Swedish Competition Authority and the European Commission in Brussels regarding both mergers and cases regarding articles 81 and 82.
Prof. Memberships: Swedish Bar Association; American Bar Association; International Bar Association; Asia-Pacific Bar Association.
Career: Office of Public Prosecutor of Stockholm 1978-79; District Court Clerk, Stockholm 1980-81; Mannheimer Zetterlöf 1981-85; *Advokatfirman Delphi Co* 1985.
Personal: Born 8 May 1954 in Stockholm. Attended Stockholm University LLM, in Law 1979. Leisure interests include physical training, jogging, boating, literature, US politics, and history.

HULTQVIST, Svante

Advokatfirman Cederquist KB, Stockholm
+46 8 463 65 00
svante.hultqvist@cederquist.se
Recommended in Banking & Finance
Specialisation: Partner in Corporate Finance Department. Main area of work is banking and corporate finance work, principally acquisition finance, project finance, assets backed finance, capital markets, syndicated loans and acquisitions and disposals. Has handled financial transactions of varying sorts by Swedish and overseas clients. Acts for a number of national and international banks and financial institutions as well as borrowers in connection with a wide range of banking and financial issues. Has spoken at various conferences and publishes regularly in Swedish and international magazines.
Prof. Memberships: The Swedish Bar Association and the International Bar Association.
Career: Junior Judge between 1987 and 1989. Joined *Lindahsl* in 1989 and became a partner in 1995. Joining *Cederquist* as a partner in 2000.
Personal: Born 11 April 1959. Attended University of Stockholm 1983-1987. Leisure interests include outdoor activities, literature and music. Lives in Stockholm.

JOHNSON, Claes

Johnsson & Johnson, Stockholm +46 8 665 9070
info@jjlaw.se
Recommended in Corporate/M&A
Specialisation: Corporate & Commercial and Financing. Main area of work includes acquisitions, joint-ventures, general commercial, including partnership agreements, distributorship agreements and purchasing and agency agreements, leasing, and aircraft financing. Has acted for Swedish and foreign clients in acquisitions of companies and business entities, is representing Swedish companies with domestic and international activities in general corporate matters and has participated in a number of cross-boarder leases and aircraft financing transactions.
Prof. Memberships: Swedish Bar Association; Inter Pacific Bar Association.
Career: Uppsala University (juris kandidat, LLM, 1976), Swedish Courts 1977-1979, joined *Hedberg & Runeland* in 1979, South Western Legal Foundation, Dallas 1982, member of the Swedish Bar Association 1982, partner of *Johnsson & Johnson* since 1988.
Personal: Born in Linköping, Sweden on 21 May, 1951.

KANTER, Lennart

Advokatfirman Cederquist KB, Stockholm
+46 8 463 65 00
lennart.kanter@cederquist.se
Recommended in Corporate/M&A
Specialisation: Partner. Main areas of practice are mergers and acquisitions, intellectual property, media and advertising law. Also advises on other aspects of business law, especially company/corporate law. Represents a wide range of international and Swedish clients in various businesses.
Prof. Memberships: Swedish Bar Association, International Bar Association.
Career: University of Uppsala 1975-1980. Service in

Swedish Courts 1980-1982, Junior Judgeship. Associated with *Advokatfirman Cederquist* 1982, worked 1984-1989 in *Advokatfirman Cederquist's* London office, partner 1990.
Personal: Born 1956.

KÄRDE, Bengt

Advokatfirman Hammarskiöld & Co, Stockholm
+46 8 578 450 00
bengt.karde@hammarskiold.se
Recommended in Banking & Finance
Specialisation: Partner and head of the firm's Finance and Banking law specialist group. Main area of work is banking and finance, including regulatory, corporate lending, capital markets and structured finance. Acted on behalf of clients in a considerable number of both domestic and international financing transactions. Recently acted for Deutsche Bank in its capacity as arranger in connection with a credit guarantee issue by the Swedish Export Credits Guarantee Board in connection with US$550 million facility agreement concerning the financing of mobile telephone equipment exports and Tele 1 Europe BV's US$150 millions / ECU 100 million high yield bond issue.
Prof. Memberships: Swedish and International Bar Associations. Active in Union Internationale des Avocats (Financial Services Commission).
Career: LLB 1973 and BA 1974 Stockholm University; Junior Judge 1975-1976; Attorney, *Wetter & Wetter Advokatbyrå* 1976-1978; General Counsel, the Swedish National Debt Office 1978-1984; Attorney and partner, *Lagerlöf & Leman Advokatbyrå* 1984-1997; Lecturer in international finance and insolvency law at the Stockholm University 1997-present; Partner, *Advokatfirman Hammarskiöld & Co.* Publications: Co-author of 'Sovereign Borrowers' published by Commonwealth Secretariat, the Kluwer International book on 'Securitisation', Butterworths book on 'Cross-Border Security' and a number of articles in 'International Financial Law Review' and other publications.
Personal: Born 10 March 1948.

KARLSSON, Johan

Advokatfirman Vinge KB, Stockholm
+46 8 614 3000
Recommended in Competition/Anti-trust
Specialisation: Member of *Vinge's* EU and Competition Law Department. Main area of work is EU and competition law, including merger control and antitrust litigation. Has acted for major Scandinavian and European companies in a number of in-depth merger control investigations and other proceedings before the European Commission and the Swedish Competition Authority, and has coordinated numerous multiple filings. Has wide experience in antitrust audits and investigations and has considerable knowledge of liberalisation, especially in telecom and postal services. Has also wide experience of application of competition law within the 'new-economy', including e-commerce and B&B exchanges.
Prof. Memberships: Swedish Bar Association.
Publications: Author of 'Konkurrenslagen i praxis' (1995, incl. supplements 1996 and 1997) and 'Konkurrenslagen – en handbok' (1999, around seven hundred pages), which is a comprehensive competition law handbook. Has published a number of articles and is a regular speaker at various conferences. Lectured EU and competition law at the University of Uppsala.
Career: Joined *Vinge* in 1993. Assigned to *Vinge's* Brussels office 1996-1998.
Personal: Born August 16, 1967. University of Uppsala (Sweden) 1988. K.U. Leuven (Belgium) 1992-1993. LLM in 1993. Leisure interests include haute route skiing, mountainbiking and golf. Speaks Swedish and English.

LEIJONHIELM, Thorsten

Mannheimer Swartling Advokatbyrå, Stockholm
+46 8 613 55 00
tl@msa.se
Recommended in Arbitration (International)
Specialisation: Partner in *Mannheimer Swartling Advokatbyrå*. Highly specialised in litigation and arbitration, as counsel and as arbitrator. Practice in these fields is general but with emphasis on disputes relating to board members liability, mergers and acquisitions, and liability in tort. Has chaired a number of arbitral tribunals in proceedings under the rules of the Arbitration Institute of the Stockholm Chamber of Commerce.
Prof. Memberships: Member of the Swedish Bar Association, IBA and the LCIA.
Career: Graduated with a law degree from the University of Stockholm in 1973. Served with the Swedish courts until 1978. Joined *Carl Swartling Advokatbyrå* and became a partner in 1985. After the merger of *Carl Swartling Advokatbyrå* and *Mannheimer Zetterlof Advokatbyrå* in 1990, became head of the merged firm's Stockholm practice group for Arbitration and Litigation.
Personal: Born in 1947.

LINDBERG, Agne

Advokatfirman Delphi & Co AB, Stockholm
+46 8 677 54 00
agne.lindberg@delphilaw.com
Recommended in Communications: IT
Specialisation: Head of *Delphi & Co.'s* IT department. IT law, in particular IT contracts, outsourcing, e-commerce, jurisdiction on Internet, data protection, domain name disputes, intellectual property, software piracy and telecommunications law. Highlights of the last year: Counsel for a group of Scandinavian insurance companies' outsourcing of their IT-infrastructure to IBM, a contract with a value of US$1 billion; counsel to insurance company regarding establishment of internet sales of mutual funds; counsel to major bank regarding Internet banking.
Prof. Memberships: Swedish Bar Association; American Bar Association; co-chair of sub-committee on International Transactions in Cyberspace; Member of the legal council of the Swedish trade organisation for IT companies; member of the legal observatory of the Swedish Government's IT commission; member of the Swedish Computer Law Association; member of the Copyright Association of Sweden; member of the International Bar Association.
Publications: Author of approximately 100 articles on IT law in Swedish and International Media; author of 'IT Law in Practice', a major publication on Swedish IT Law; co-author of 'Standard Contracts for IT Business in Sweden'; co-author of 'EDI – legal aspects'; author of 'Electronic documents and Electronic Signatures'.
Career: LLM, Uppsala, 1987; Court work, 1987-89; *Adokatfirman Delphi & Co.*, 1989-90; *Advokatfirman Smitt*, 1990-92; *Advokatfirman Delphi & Co.*, 1992-present.
Personal: Leisure interests; skiing, cooking, ice-skating. Family; wife and three children, 9, 6, and 1 year.

LINDSKOG, Stefan

Wistrand Advokatbyrå, Stockholm
+46 8 50 72 00 00
Recommended in Arbitration (International)

LUNDBLAD, Claes

Mannheimer Swartling Advokatbyrå, Stockholm
+46 615 5500
clu@msa.se
Recommended in Arbitration (International)
Specialisation: International and domestic arbitration and litigation.
Prof. Memberships: Swedish Bar Association; American Bar Association; International Bar Association.
Publications: Various articles on arbitration.
Career: Partner of *Mannheimer Swartling*, chairman of the firm and the firm's Arbitration & Litigation Practice Group, member of the board of governors of the Swedish Bar Association.
Personal: Born 1946, LLM Lund University 1969. Resident in Stockholm and Gothenburg.

LUNDIN, Anders

Gernandt & Danielsson Advokatbyrå, Stockholm
+46 8 670 6600
Recommended in Corporate/M&A

LUNDQVIST, Dick

Gernandt & Danielsson Advokatbyrå, Stockholm
+46 8 670 6600
dick.lundqvist@gda.se
Recommended in Banking & Finance
Specialisation: Partner since 1998. Main area of work is corporate and company law, principally capital markets, banking and finance in Sweden and private equity related matters. Has acted as counsel to the Swedish Government in connection with privatisations and other matters. Acts for a number of Swedish and non-Swedish investment banks, financial institutions and private equity funds on matters ranging from private placements, IPO's, take-overs, new issues and debt financing in various forms to general matters, including M&A work for private equity funds. Also acts for asset managers on issues in connection with the establishing of various securities funds, i.e., hedge funds in Sweden.
Prof. Memberships: Swedish Bar Association.
Publications: Authhor of articles for Law Business Research Ltd, International Financial Law Review and FT Tax & Law.
Career: Worked as in-house counsel in one of the leading Swedish commercial banks within corporate finance and project finance departments before joining *Gernandt & Danielsson* in 1994.

S

Personal: Born 7 September, 1962. University of Lund 1983-1987 (LLM 1987). Married with one child. Leisure interests include cooking and spending time with friends and family. Resides in Stockholm.

LÜNING, Wilhelm
Advokatfirman Cederquist KB, Stockholm
+46 8678 0170
wilhelm.luning@cederquist.se
Recommended in Corporate/M&A
Specialisation: Head of the Corporate Finance Department of *Cederquist*. The Corporate Finance Department is divided into four sub-groups: banking and finance; securities and securities markets; mergers & acquisitions; company law. Advises in mergers & acquisitions, securities and securities market regulations. Has handled acquisitions of Swedish listed and non-listed companies on behalf of Swedish and foreign clients. Furthermore, has handled a number of IPOs on behalf companies and underwriters. Acts for a number of securities market institutes, governmental and non-governmental bodies and listed companies.
Prof. Memberships: Member of the Swedish Bar Association since 1993; International Bar Association.
Publications: Editor of various publications of securities market regulations.
Career: LLM 1987. Associated with *FöretagsJuridik Nord & Co* AB 1985 - 1990. *Advokatfirman Vinge* KB 1990 - 1993. Partner of *Advokatfirman Cederquist* KB since 1993.
Personal: Born 1959, married, two children. Atty-languages: Swedish and english.

NILSSON, Bo
Rydin & Carlsten Advokatbyrå AB, Stockholm
+46 8 679 51 70
bo.nilsson@rydinlaw.se
Recommended in Arbitration (International)
Specialisation: Head of *Rydin & Carlsten Advokatbyrå AB's* arbitration and litigation practice. Regularly appointed by the Stokholm Chamber of Commerce in international arbitrations.
Prof. Memberships: IBA; ILA; LCIA; European Council; Swedish Bar Association (Board Member); list of arbitrators by Russian Chamber of Commerce and Industry.
Publications: Various articles on arbitration and litigation including chapters on 'Sweden in International Execution Against Judgement Debtors' 1993 Sweet & Maxwell; 'International Civil Procedures' 1995 Lloyds of London Press Ltd.; 'Handbook of International Dispute Resolution Rules 1999 Carswell.
Career: Swedish courts 1975-1979; Associate *Wetter & Wetter* 1979-1982; Partner *Rydin & Carlsten* 1983.

OLOFSSON, Rolf
White & Case LLP, Stockholm +46 8 506 32 300
rolofsson@whitecase.com
Recommended in Communications: Telecoms
Specialisation: Partner and well-respected corporate law adviser based in the Stockholm office of *White & Case*. Has a broad-ranging corporate law practice from M&A to project finance, with a particular focus on transactions involving space and satellites. Counsels on space-related ventures including treaty negotiations, satellite acquisitions, launches, transponder leases, R&D, insurance contracts and satellite financings.
Prof. Memberships: Member of both the Swedish and New York bars.
Career: Joined the firm from *Mannheimer Swartling* in 1994.
Personal: Speaks fluent Swedish and English.

PERHARD, Lars
Advokatfirman Cederquist KB, Stockholm
+46 8 463 65 00
lars.perhard@cederquist.se
Recommended in Communications: IT
Specialisation: Chairman of information technology, internet and e-commerce group of *Cederquist* and provides advice to users and suppliers of IT on all aspects of computer, internet and web-related law. In addition to giving advice to companies, also assists the Swedish Agency for administration development and from time to time Swedish authorities.
Prof. Memberships: Swedish Bar Association (member of the board of the Stockholm division 1985-1990); International Bar Association; UIA/International Association of Lawyers (UIA International Vice President for Sweden, 1999-onwards, vice president of the UIA Standing Committee on Information Technology and Telecom 1999- onwards); and Computer Law Association.
Publications: Publishes Regularly in Swedish and international magazines.
Career: Stockholm University (juris kandidat, LLM, 1973), junior judge District Court of Stockholm 1974-1975, member of the Swedish Bar 1979, partner in 1980. Left *Lagerlöf & Leman* 1998 in order to join *Advokatfirman Cederquist* as partner. Continuously conducts a number of seminars in the field for among others the Faculty of Law of the University of Stockholm, the Stockholm Chamber of Commerce and the Swedish Bar Association. Active in other practice areas: Arbitration and litigation; contract law; general commercial law; and corporate law. Atty-languages: Swedish, English and French (reads German).
Personal: Born 1950, married, two children.

PETTERSSON, Tommy
Mannheimer Swartling Advokatbyrå, Stockholm
+46 8 613 55 00
tpe@msa.se
Recommended in Competition/Anti-trust
Specialisation: Partner of *Mannheimer Swartling*, resident in the Stockholm office. Member of the firm's EC and Competition practice group and specialises in EC law, competition law and trade law. Worked extensively both on EC competition matters and on Swedish competition law matters representing international and domestic clients before the European Court of Justice, the European Commission, the Swedish Competition Authority and Swedish courts. Written numerous articles and has been a speaker at several seminars in the field of EC and Competition Law.
Career: Born in 1958. LLM, University of Uppsala 1985. Member of the Swedish Bar Association in 1990. Joined *Mannheimer Swartling* in 1987, was seconded to *Clifford Chance* in Brussels 1990-1991 and became a partner of *Mannheimer Swartling* in 1993. Between 1993-1998 was the resident partner in the firm's Brussels office.

RAMBERG, Göran
Advokatfirman Lindahl, Helsingborg
+46 42 17 53 00
goran.ramberg@lindahl.se
Recommended in Arbitration (International)
Specialisation: Has practised general business law since 1958 and gradually, over many years come to occupy himself to a large extent, now mainly, with commercial arbitration, to some extent as counsel for parties but mostly as arbitrator. Arbitrational experience includes all fields of commercial law, national and international, as partly appointed arbitrator and as chairman, elected by fellow arbitrators or institute appointed. Is one of the most experienced arbitrators in Sweeden in the field of compulsory purchase of minority shares. Served between 1992 and 1995 as an expert on the government committee on commercial arbitration which drafted the new Swedish Act on Arbitration.
Prof. Memberships: The Swedish Bar, IBA, LES and the Association of Arbitration Law of Southern Sweden.
Publications: Author of various articles in legal journals.
Career: Member of the Swedish Bar from 1961. Partner in a law firm later merged into *Advokatfirman Lindahl*, and in *Advokatfirman Lindahl*, from 1965. Chairman of *Advokatfirman Lindahl* 1990-1994. Has held a number of positions within the Swedish Bar, among them as a member of its Board, chairman of one of its two standing committees and chairman of its Southern district.
Personal: Loves to read history and plays bad golf.

RAMBERG, Jan
Jan Ramberg – Sole Practitioner, Täby
+46 8 756 6225
Recommended in Arbitration (International)

RIESE, Biörn
Mannheimer Swartling Advokatbyrå, Stockholm
+46 8 613 55 00
br@msa.se
Recommended in Communications: Telecoms
Specialisation: Partner of *Mannheimer Swartling* resident in Stockholm office. Chair of the firm's Computer, Communications and Media practice group. Wide experience of commercial and legal issues within the Swedish and international telecoms, computer and software industry. Member of the Swedish National Committee on Telecommunications and Information Technologies of the International Chamber of Commerce among other bodies. Has been involved in many international consortia and joint ventures applying for telecoms licenses in and outside Europe, advising on commercial, corporate and regulatory matters and is regularly advising on traditional information technology matters such as matters related to provision of services, licensing and technology transfer, systems integration and outsourcing.
Career: Born in 1953. Studied at the University of

Stockholm (LLM, 1978; MBA, 1980). After service in Swedish courts and work as a law firm associate (1982-1983), joined *Carl Swartling Advokatbyrå* as associate (1984-1988) and partner (1989-1990). Partner of *Mannheimer Swartling* in 1990.

ROMANDER, Claes
White & Case LLP, Stockholm +46 8 506 32 300
cromander@whitecase.com
Recommended in Banking & Finance
Specialisation: Partner in the firm's Stockholm office. Represents local and international lenders and borrowers on the full range of banking and securities transactions. Consulted by Swedish Financial Supervisory Authority as an expert in financial instruments, advised several securities broker-dealer corporations about creation of new financial instruments and formed legal framework for first computerised broker system for anonymous trade in money market instruments in Sweden.
Career: Worked previously for *Advokatfirman Verum*, Stockholm.
Personal: A Native Swedish speaker, also fluent in German and English.

ROMLOV, Robert
Advokatfirman Vinge KB, Göteborg
+46 31 722 35 00
robert.romlov@vinge.se
Recommended in Arbitration (International)
Specialisation: International commercial arbitration, particularly in shipping, shipbuilding, natural resources and distribution. About 160 arbitrations as sole arbitrator, chairman, co-arbitrator and counsel in ICC, Stockholm Chamber of Commerce, UNCITRAL and Swedish ad hoc arbitrations.
Prof. Memberships: Memberships: Swedish Bar, IBA, Fellow of the Chartered Institute of Arbitrators, Member of the Panel of Arbitrators of ICSID, Member of the LCIA, Titulary Member of Comite Maritime International, Chairman of the Board of the Foundation for Commercial Law in Gothenburg.
Publications: Contributor for Sweden to Kluwer Maritime Handbook: Arrest, Enforced Sale, Registration, Mortgages on Vessels.
Career: Senior Partner with *Advokatfirman Vinge.*
Personal: LLB, research student in procedural law, Diplome Superieur de Droit Compare.

RYDBECK, Otto
Nils Setterwalls Advokatbyrå AB, Stockholm
+46 8 598 890 00
otto.rydbeck@setterwalls.se
Recommended in Corporate/M&A
Specialisation: Banking and finance, commercial and corporate law. Partner and member of the executive board, partner in charge of the banking and finance, corporate, and M&A departments.
Career: Educated at the University of Lund. During 1993-94 appointed by the Swedish Government and the Swedish Bank Support Authority to investigate the credit losses in the state owned banks Nordbanken and Gota Bank. Has conducted a number of investigations in various other companies regarding the liability of management and directors. Has been appointed by the Governmental Committee for the Revision of the Banking Legislation as an expert on bank secrecy and liability for negligent credit approvals.
Personal: Speaks English and Swedish.

SEDEROWSKY, Peter
Nils Setterwalls Advokatbyrå AB, Stockholm
+46 8 598 890 00
peter.sederowsky@setterwalls.com
Recommended in Banking & Finance
Specialisation: Partner of the firm and a member of the banking and finance department. Works predominantly with structured transactions in the field of corporate finance, derivatives, capital markets and project finance. Recent transactions include: the project financing and the refinancing of the high speed railway between Stockholm and Arlanda Airport; various debt programmes for Swedish issuers; index linked bonds as well as the ongoing structuring of housing loans in Sweden for securitisation purposes. Also responsible (as adviser to the arranger and purchasers) for the creation of the first Swedish Convertible Preferred Shares to be issued by a Swedish listed company. This transaction is now followed by numerous others, involving both debt and equity instruments achieving the same goal.
Career: Holds law degrees from the University of Lund, as well as the University of California-Berkeley, and is a Fulbright Fellow.

SÖDERLIND, Erik
Lagerlöf & Leman Advokatbyrå (A member firm of Linklaters & Alliance), Stockholm +46 8 665 66 00
erik.soderlind@lol.se
Recommended in Competition/Anti-trust
Specialisation: Member of the *Lagerlöf & Leman* department for Competition law, EU Law and public procurement. Main areas of work are all aspects of Swedish national and EU competition law. Has been involved in a majority of the court proceedings concerning allegations of abuse of dominance that have taken place in Sweden under the current national competition act, i.e. since 1993.
Prof. Memberships: Swedish Bar Association.
Publications: Co-author of the leading work on the Swedish Competition Act. Has spoken at various conferences.
Career: Qualified in 1988 at the University of Stockholm. Has thereafter worked in the office of the Swedish Näringsfrihetsombudsman and the legal secretariat of the Swedish Competition Authority before joining *Lagerlöf & Leman* in 1995.
Personal: Born 15 April 1959.

SÖDERMARK, Bertil
Advokatfirman Södermark, Stockholm
+46 8 670 57 50
Recommended in Arbitration (International)

SOLERUD, Hans-Gunnar
Gernandt & Danielsson Advokatbyrå, Stockholm
+46 8 670 6600
hans-gunnar.solerud@gda.se
Recommended in Arbitration (International)
Specialisation: Arbitrator and Chairman of Arbitral Tribunals in a great number of domestic and international commercial disputes.
Prof. Memberships: Member of the Swedish Bar Association and the International Bar Association.
Publications: A few articles in legal magazines on arbitration and other legal subjects.
Career: 1963 - 1966 Assistant judge in a district court; 1966 - 1968 Secretariat of the Stockholm Chamber of Commerce; 1968 - 1973 *Associate Wetter & Swartling Advokatbyrå*, Stockholm; 1973-1974. In-house counsel AB SKF (publ), Gothenburg; 1974-1985 Partner *Carl Swartling Advokatbyrå*, Stockholm; 1986-1997 Justice of the Supreme Court; 1991-1993 Member of the Law Council; Since 1997 partner *Gernandt & Danielsson Advokatbyrå AB*, Stockholm; 1985 and since 1998 Deputy member of the Board of the Swedish Bar Association; 1986-1993 Chairman of the Arbitration Institute of the Stockholm Chamber of Commerce; 1987-1993 Deputy Chairman of the Securities Council; 1990-1991 Chairman of Government Committee on legal requirements for the use of radio transmitters and the assignment of radio frequencies (the Swedish Government Official Reports No. 1991:107); 1991-1994 Chairman of Government Committee revising the Act on Accounting implementing EEC directives (the Swedish Government Official Reports No. 1994:17); 1992-1994 Expert to a Government Committee revising the Swedish Act on Arbitration; 1992-1999 Chairman of the Information Practices Committee of the Association of the Swedish Pharmaceutical Industry and the Association of Representatives of Foreign Pharmaceutical Industries; 1993 – Deputy Chairman of the Disciplinary Committee of the Stockholm Stock Exchange; 1996 – Chairman of the Board of Bonus Presskopia (collecting society handling remuneration to copyright holders).
Personal: University of Uppsala, LLM 1963.

WERSÉN, Dag
Dag Wersén – Sole Practitioner, Stockholm
+46 8 663 77 22
dag@wersenadv.se
Recommended in Arbitration (International)
Specialisation: Arbitration, litigation, general corporate, finance.
Prof. Memberships: President of the Council of the Bars and Law Societies of the European union, CCBE; Member of the Swedish Bar Association; Member of LCIA.
Career: LLB Stockholm University 1961; Admitted to the Swedish Bar 1966; *Lagerlöf & Leman Advokatbyrå* 1962-1990, partner 1970-2000; Practice in *Advokatfirman Wersen* since 2000.

WETTER, Carl
Advokatfirman Vinge KB, Stockholm
+46 8 614 3000
carl.wetter@vinge.se
Recommended in Competition/Anti-trust
Specialisation: Senior Partner and Head of *Vinge's* EU and Competition Law Department. Main area of work is EU and competition law, including merger control and antitrust litigation, especially in deregulated markets. Has acted for major Scandinavian and European companies in a number of in-depth merger control investigations and other antitrust proceedings before the Court of Justice, the European Commission, the Swedish Market Court, the Stockholm District Court (Antitrust section) and the Swedish Competition Authority. Has wide experi-

S

ence in antitrust audits and investigations and has considerable knowledge of liberalisation, especially in telecom and postal services. Member of the permanent legislative reference group for competition law of the Swedish Ministry for Trade and Industry.
Prof. Memberships: Swedish Bar Association, International Bar Association, ICC Sweden's Reference group for competition.
Publications: Author of 'Konkurrenslagen i praxis' (1995, incl. supplements 1996 and 1997); also author of 'Konkurrenslagen – en handbook' (1999) which is a comprehensive competition law handbook. Has published a number of articles on EU and Swedish competition law. Is a regular speaker at various conferences on these subjects.
Career: Swedish Ministry for Foreign Affairs 1976-77. Joined *Vinge* in 1977 and became a Partner in 1983. Head of *Vinge*'s Brussels office between 1989 and 1998.
Personal: Born January 29, 1949. University of Uppsala (Sweden) 1969. BA, in 1974 (Russian, Economics and Business Administration). LLM, in 1977. Leisure interests include sailing and tennis. Speaks Swedish, English, French and German.

WIBOM, Hans
Advokatfirman Vinge KB, Stockholm
+46 8 614 3000
Recommended in Banking & Finance, Corporate/M&A

WIGGE, Michael
Advokatfirman Vinge KB, Stockholm
+46 8 614 3000
michael.wigge@vinge.se
Recommended in Corporate/M&A
Specialisation: Managing partner in Stockholm. Main area of work is corporate law, principally mergers & acquisitions, both public and negotiated transactions representing corporate clients, financial institutions and investment banks.
Prof. Memberships: Swedish Bar; AIYA.
Career: Graduated from the University of Stockholm (jurs kandidat, LLB) in 1984 and served with the Swedish courts between 1984 and 1986. Joined *Vinge* in 1986 and became partner January 1994. During 1989 up to 1991, was located at *Vinge*'s office in London. Partner in Corporate Departement in Stockholm.
Personal: Born in Gothenburg, 4 February 1957.

WINNERBLAD, Johan
Mannheimer Swartling Advokatbyrå, Stockholm
+46 8 613 55 00
jwi@msa.se
Recommended in Communications: IT, Communications: Telecoms
Specialisation: Specialises in the TIME sector (telecoms, IT, media and entertainment) and represents both clients who are conducting business in this sector as well as clients who invest in such companies. Significant part of the matters concern the representation of domestic and foreign venture capitalists in their day-to day investment activities and the representation of clients in traditional M&A transactions. Chairman of the firm's Sports and Entertainment practice group and a member of Computers, Communications and Media group.
Prof. Memberships: Swedish Bar Association; Swedish Society for Computers and Law; Society for Computers and Law; Computer Law Association and Association Internationale des Jeunes Avocats.
Career: Staff Attorney IBM Svenska AB (1990-1991), associate (1992-1997) and partner (1998 to date) *Mannheimer Swartling Advokatbyrå.*
Personal: Born in 1967. LLM (Jur kand.) University of Stockholm 1990. Leisure activities include sports and restoration of home.

ZETTERMARCK, Claes
White & Case LLP, Stockholm +46 8 506 32 300
czettermarck@whitecase.com
Recommended in Arbitration (International), Corporate/M&A
Specialisation: Leading arbitration lawyer, both representing clients directly and acting as an arbitrator. Regularly advises on major international arbitrations. Also highly regarded for work in the M&A arena acting for sellers, investors, management and financial institutions on high profile corporate transactions. [PRP] Member of the Swedish Bar Association.
Career: Joined *White & Case* from Swedish firm, *Palm-Jensen & Roos* in 1983. Also served as a junior judge at Swedish Court of Appeals and a law clerk at District Court of Södertörn.
Personal: Speaks fluent Swedish and English.

SWITZERLAND

Index

The clients' choice

BUSINESS LAWYER OF THE YEAR
PETER ISLER, *Niederer Kraft & Frey*
PETER KURER, *Homburger Rechtsanwälte*

BUSINESS LAW FIRM OF THE YEAR
HOMBURGER RECHTSANWÄLTE

***Peter Kurer** and **Peter Isler** tie as best lawyer finishing well ahead of the field. **Homburger Rechtsanwälte** tops the best firm table, well above the opposition.*

For details see page 36.

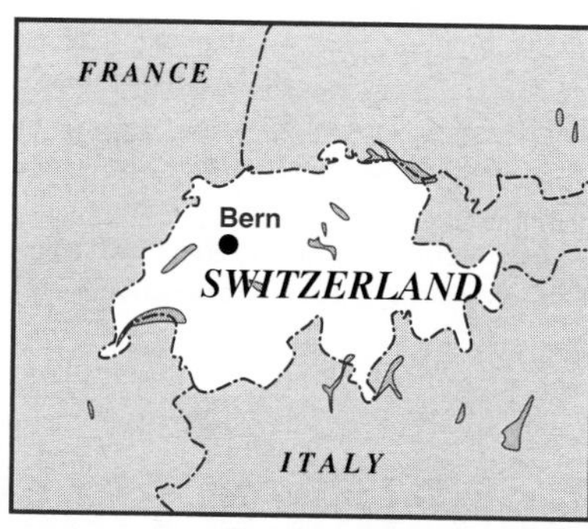

OVERVIEW: Despite Switzerland's importance as a financial centre, there are few foreign firms entering the market. The independently minded Swiss firms are well equipped to service multinational clients and Swiss clients have yet to be convinced of the one stop shop concept; they expect their lawyers to be generalists.
One of the few foreign firms to establish market presence is Baker McKenzie and although von Erlach Klainguti Stettler Wille joined the CMS Group in July 2000 there has been little cross border movement. With complementary offices in Zurich (Anglo-German clients) and Geneva (French speaking clients), Schellenberg Haissly and Brunschwig Wittmer merged (creating Schellenberg Wittmer.) Elsewhere, Walder Wyss boosted its banking team by acquiring a group of banking lawyers from Altenburger & Partners. The M&A and the new economy industries are flourishing although the capital markets front has yet to reach the heights of its neighbouring countries. Known globally for its neutrality and stability, Switzerland is one of the natural choices for international arbitration.

Arbitration (International)

SWITZERLAND Leading individuals (Arbitration (International))	
1	**BLESSING Mark** *Bär & Karrer*
	BRINER Robert *Lenz & Staehelin*
	KARRER Pierre *Pestalozzi Gmuer & Patry*
	LALIVE Pierre *Lalive & Partners*
	PETER Wolfgang *Python Schifferli Peter & Ptnr*
	POUDRET Jean-François *Jean-François Poudret*
	REYMOND Claude *Reymond, Bonnard, Maire*
2	**KAUFMANN-KOHLER Gabrielle** *Schellenberg*
	SCHNEIDER Michael *Lalive & Partners*
3	**DE COULON Philippe** *Lenz & Staehelin*
	GIOVANNINI Teresa *Lalive & Partners*
	KNOEPFLER François *Knoepfler Gabus Gehrig*
	PATOCCHI Paolo Michele *Lenz & Staehelin*
	RONCA Marc *Schellenberg*
	TERCIER Pierre *Pierre Tercier*
	TSCHANZ Pierre-Yves *Tavernier Tschanz*
4	**LÉVY Laurent** *Schellenberg*
	WEHRLI Daniel *Gloor & Sieger*
	WIRTH Markus *Homburger Rechtsanwälte*

Individuals are listed alphabetically in each band.

One of the biggest European international arbitration centres, Switzerland is home to a number of outstanding practitioners in both Geneva and Zurich.

The *"omnipresent"* **Mark Blessing*** at Bär & Karrer is said to be *"full of ideas,"* and handles a number of M&A, anti-trust and infrastructure project arbitrations. Researchers were told that he is *"a walking encyclopedia,"* who sits as an arbitrator on international disputes.

President of the International Court of Arbitration of the International Chamber of Commerce in Paris, the *"pragmatic and effective"* **Robert Briner*** remains a respected practitioner, while at Lenz & Staehelin, **Philippe de Coulon*** is *"a reliable craftsman"* of similar vintage. Also at Lenz & Staehelin, **Paolo Michele Patocchi*** is regarded by his rivals as *"a quick thinker with a big future ahead of him."* Young for an arbitrator, he has advised on joint venture agreements, licensing agreements and construction projects.

The president of the Swiss Arbitration Association, **Pierre Karrer*** of Pestalozzi Gmuer & Patry, is considered to be *"a number one choice,"* for his great experience. Fluent in several languages, he advises on a broad range of cases, including joint ventures, product liability and commercial contracts.

The venerable **Pierre Lalive*** has been *"an outstanding arbitrator for decades,"* and remains influential, although seen less often than in his heyday. His colleague at Lalive & Partners is **Michael Schneider***. Interviewees were fulsome in their praise for his *"far-sighted, skilled and elegant"* style, notably on construction arbitrations. At the same firm, **Teresa Giovannini*** is a *"tough and enthusiastic fighter,"* who acts as counsel on a number of Italian cases.

Gabrielle Kaufmann-Kohler* at Schellenberg Wittmer *"has a quick and analytical mind,"* according to her contemporaries. She is the president of the arbitration commission for the Olympic Games, and has built an acknowledged reputation both as counsel and as an arbitrator. Her colleague **Marc Ronca*** is also establishing a higher profile for his advice on arbitrations in third world countries. Relatively new to the field, **Laurent Lévy*** has also caught the eye of a number of good judges.

At Python Schifferli Peter & Partner, **Wolfgang Peter*** is said to be *"a superb negotiator,"* and is valued by clients for his *"business acumen."*

Claude Reymond* at Reymond, Bonnard,

*See leaders' profiles on pages 658-664

Maire, Freymond, Tschumy is another outstanding member of *"Switzerland's arbitration old guard,"* and is seen to be a lawyer in the mould of Pierre Lalive. Another with a similar reputation is **Jean-François Poudret***, *"a sharp and forthright lawyer,"* who now spends the majority of his time lecturing at the University of Lausanne.

"Thorough and meticulous," **Pierre Tercier*** is another outstanding sole practitioner/academic, this time at the University of Fribourg. As the former president of the Swiss Anti-trust commission, he is often sought as an arbitrator for competition cases.

François Knoepfler* of Knoepfler Gabus Gehrig, is a professor at the University of Neuchatel, and has a leading reputation as an arbitrator on cases involving distribution contracts, IP and construction law.

Pierre-Yves Tschanz* at Tavernier Tschanz is respected for his specialism in arbitrations relating to the hi-tech industry.

In Zurich, the *"deceptively understated"* **Daniel Wehrli*** at Gloor & Sieger sits as an arbitrator in many ad hoc cases in Switzerland, but is also known for his work at international tribunals, such as in Kuala Lumpur and Yugoslavia. **Markus Wirth*** *("calm, serious and conscientious")* at Homburger Rechtsanwälte, is a familiar figure on commercial, corporate and M&A-related cases.

S

Banking & Finance

SWITZERLAND Leading firms (Banking & Finance)
1 Homburger Rechtsanwälte
Lenz & Staehelin
Niederer Kraft & Frey
2 Bär & Karrer
Walder Wyss & Partners
3 Pestalozzi Gmuer & Patry
Schellenberg Wittmer
4 Wenger Vieli Belser

Firms are listed alphabetically in each band.

Leading individuals (Banking & Finance)
1 AESCHIMANN Jean-Paul *Lenz & Staehelin*
FURTER Robert *Pestalozzi Gmuer & Patry*
ISLER Peter *Niederer Kraft & Frey*
NIEDERER Hans *Niederer Kraft & Frey*
WATTER Rolf *Bär & Karrer*
WIDMER Peter *Homburger Rechtsanwälte*
2 BÖSCH René *Homburger Rechtsanwälte*
KROLL Markus *Walder Wyss & Partners*
STEINMANN Christian *Bär & Karrer*
3 BIANCHI François M. *Niederer Kraft & Frey*
DAENIKER Daniel *Homburger Rechtsanwälte*
LANZ Martin *Schellenberg Wittmer*
STEINER Hans Rudolf *Walder Wyss & Partners*
VON PLANTA Andreas *Lenz & Staehelin*
4 DU PASQUIER Shelby *Lenz & Staehelin*
PFENNINGER Markus *Walder Wyss & Partners*
Up-and-coming individuals
HUENERWADEL Patrick *Lenz & Staehelin*

Individuals are listed alphabetically in each band.

Homburger Rechtsanwälte (4 ptrs, 6 asscs) The firm has steadily grown in this sector, and has a strong reputation for advising on structured finance, IPOs and bond issues. Senior partner **Peter Widmer*** is a *"charismatic lawyer for the big transactions"* and advised on the high-profile Holocaust bank accounts case. The *"studious"* **René Bösch*** has an established reputation for advising on bond issues and structured debt financing, while **Daniel Daeniker*** *("a real problem solver")* is said by rivals to have *"profound knowledge of securities regulations."*

The firm acted for Leica Geosystems Holdings on its IPO, and advised JP Morgan on Swiss Re's $1 billion debt issue. Also advised Credit Suisse Group on the structuring, launch and completion of three tier 1 issues. **Clients:** Swisscom; Siemens; VEBA; Credit Suisse Group; JP Morgan; Leica Geosystems Holdings; Goldman Sachs.

Lenz & Staehelin (8 ptrs, 19 asscs) The firm has offices in Zurich and Geneva, but its banking and finance centre is to be found in Geneva, where a team of younger partners is said to be *"on the move."* Leading the team is **Jean-Paul Aeschimann***, who has established an *"outstanding banking reputation over many years."* His young team includes **Andreas von Planta*** *"who has an effective, easy-going style"* and collective investment schemes expert **Shelby du Pasquier***. **Patrick Huenerwadel*** is an up and coming practitioner who is said to *"focus on the important issues."* The firm recently advised Serono, a Swiss listed company, on the issue of bearer shares and their listing on the Swiss Exchange as well as on the New York Stock Exchange. It has also advised Crédit Suisse and UBS on project finance and structured finance projects, as well as acquisition financing and MBOs. **Clients:** Credit Suisse; UBS; Affichage Holding; Serono.

Niederer Kraft & Frey (8 ptrs, 12 asscs) Superb finance-oriented firm, which focuses on the structuring of new capital market products, investment funds matters, bank regulatory, acquisition finance and asset finance. **Hans Niederer*** is seen as *"the doyen of the local bond market,"* and can draw on a wealth of experience. **François Bianchi*** is viewed by competitors as Niederer's protégé, and was recommended to researchers as *"a pragmatic lawyer with unlimited potential."* **Peter Isler*** supplements his renowned corporate practice with in-depth experience of complex capital markets transactions.

The firm represented CSFB/UBS Warburg on the creation of Syngenta, a transaction worth around CHF10 billion. Also advised Chase Manhattan International on the financing of the acquisition of the Cablecom Group by NTL. **Clients:** Credit Suisse First Boston/UBS Warburg; Chase Manhattan International; Unique Airport Zurich.

Bär & Karrer (3 ptrs, 6 asscs) Although best known for corporate expertise, the firm's expanding banking and finance department is acknowledged to cover *"all aspects of banking law"* on behalf of an international banking clientele. M&A guru **Rolf Watter*** *"has an eye for the important points,"* and has a first-class reputation for his IPO work. His colleague, the *"well-organised"* **Christian Steinmann*** has a broad practice, ranging over straight banking, corporate financing and capital markets. The firm recently acted as local counsel to the underwriter of the IPO of the Israeli med-tech company, SHL Telemedicine. **Clients:** Morgan Stanley; Goldman Sachs; UBS; Commerzbank; Bank Austria.

Walder Wyss & Partners (5 ptrs, 10 asscs) The firm is considered to have grown stronger in the sector, with several new banking and finance lawyers having joined the team. Of these, the most visible is **Markus Kroll***, said to be *"the father of Swiss asset-backed finance."* **Hans Rudolf Steiner*** is another respected capital markets specialist, recommended to researchers for having *"all the right contacts."* **Markus Pfenninger*** is considered to be a rising star, and is described by clients as *"serious, meticulous and reliable."*

The firm acted for Glencore on the securitisation of commodity trade receivables through the issue of CP and MTN, and advised UBS on the structuring of a synthetic securitisation transaction worth CHF2.5 billion. **Clients:** Glencore; UBS Warburg; UBS; CSFB; Citibank; Morgan Stanley.

Pestalozzi Gmuer & Patry (5 ptrs, 5 asscs) Long established firm in the sector with its offices in Zurich and Geneva, which has kept its position as a respected mid-tier firm. The firm's leading practitioner is **Robert Furter***, who has extensive experience of cross-border deals, in particular handling debt financing.

He acted on the secondary offering by Card Guard on the SWX New Market, a complex listing that achieved a capital increase of CHF180 million. Senior partners of the firm sit on the board of numerous major international companies and top American banks in Switzerland, thus boosting connections in the industry. **Clients:** Credit Suisse; Clariden Bank; Swissnet Bank; Merrill Lynch; Deutsche Bank; UBS Warburg; Card Guard; Crédit Agricole Indosuez.

Schellenberg Wittmer (2 ptrs, 4 asscs) The recent merger between Schellenberg & Haissly and Brunschwig Wittmer unites two firms with decent reputations in this sector. The combined firm's main capital markets specialist is the *"flexible"* **Martin Lanz*** in Zurich, who has a national reputation for advising on bond issues on behalf of an international client base. The Geneva office is best known for bank regulatory issues.

The firm advised a foreign bank on the structuring of perpetual subordinated syndicated loans to a Swiss bank, and also has a niche in e-banking. **Clients:** National and international financial institutions.

Wenger Vieli Belser (7 ptrs, 8 asscs) Recently formed through the merger between Belser Altorfer & Partner and Wenger & Vieli, the firm is respected for regulatory banking and litigation matters, and has a substantial reputation for private banking advice. Although it advises both domestic and international financial institutions, the firm is best known for its substantial network of Swiss banking clients. **Clients:** UBS; Zurich Financial Service Group; Deutsche Bank; Credit Suisse.

S

Communications

CMS von Erlach Klainguti Stettler Wille (3 ptrs, 2 asscs) Part of the worldwide CMS group since May 2000, the firm is best known for its telecoms practice, and represents Orange Communications SA on regulatory and transactional matters, including advising on a successful bid for its GSM licence. **Hans Wille*** and his younger colleague **Oliver Blum*** are said to be *"versatile"* lawyers, both handling telecoms and IT transactions.

SWITZERLAND Leading firms (Communications)	
1	CMS von Erlach Klainguti Stettler Wille
	Homburger Rechtsanwälte
	Niederer Kraft & Frey
2	Bär & Karrer
	Walder Wyss & Partners
	Wiederkehr Forster Rechtsanwälte
3	Pestalozzi Gmuer & Patry
	Zürcher Blickenstorfer & Widmer
4	Python Schifferli Peter & Partner
	Thomann Fischer

Firms are listed alphabetically in each band.

On the IT side, the team acts on M&A transactions, as well as debt and equity financing, licensing and procurement. It advised one of the prospective buyers of the national CATV monopoly Cablecom. **Clients:** Orange Communications SA; several WWL companies.

Homburger Rechtsanwälte (3 ptrs, 6 asscs) Acting on both telecoms and IT, the firm is known for its *"deep business sense."* The firm covers contractual work for systems integration projects, and also advises on copyright issues and e-commerce projects for an international client base.

The *"highly professional"* **Franz Hoffet*** comes from a transactional background, but also handles the necessary regulatory matters for the firm's largest telecoms client, Swisscom. Originally an IP lawyer, **Georg Rauber*** is said to have *"a thorough understanding of IT."*

The firm represented Swisscom on the unbundling of the local loop, as well as on the UMTS process. **Clients:** Swisscom; Apple Schweiz; Unisys; Kirch Group.

Leading individuals (Communications)		
1	**NEUENSCHWANDER Peter** *Zürcher Blickenstorfer*	**RAUBER Georg** *Homburger Rechtsanwälte*
	WEBER Rolf *Wiederkehr Forster Rechtsanwälte*	
2	**AUF DER MAUR Rolf** *Vischer*	**BLUM Oliver** *CMS von Erlach Klainguti*
	JETZER Rolf *Niederer Kraft & Frey*	**THOMANN Felix** *Thomann Fischer*
	WILLE Johann *CMS von Erlach Klainguti*	
3	**BERNASCONI Michele** *Bär & Karrer*	**BRINER Robert** *Pestalozzi Gmuer & Patry*
	GUROVITS András *Niederer Kraft & Frey*	**SANGIORGIO Didier** *Walder Wyss & Partners*
4	**GUNTER Pierre-Yves** *Python Schifferli Peter*	**HOFFET Franz** *Homburger Rechtsanwälte*

Individuals are listed alphabetically in each band.

Niederer Kraft & Frey (2 ptrs, 4 asscs) One of the largest firms in Switzerland, it handles a broad range of transactional and regulatory matters. The communications team is perceived to have a focus on telecoms, due to its exclusive relationship with diAx (the second largest mobile and fixed net provider in Switzerland) on all contractual, corporate and competition issues.

Rolf Jetzer* was recommended to researchers as *"a draftsman and negotiator of the highest quality,"* and has advised diAx on its interconnection agreements with Swisscom, and on its UMTS licence bid. **András Gurovits*** is seen as *"a knowledgeable specialist,"* who handles IT cases from the contractual and litigation angle. These cases range from integrated systems solutions and developing e-commerce projects to outsourcing and data protection matters. **Clients:** diAx; multi-national IT operators; software and hardware manufacturers.

Bär & Karrer (2 ptrs, 5 asscs) Leading corporate firm, with a strong focus on IT and telecoms. In

IT matters, the team advises on networking, outsourcing, establishing of internet portals and e-commerce banking projects. In telecoms, the firm advises new entrants, on both operational and regulatory matters, acting for a number of bidders for GSM and UMTS licences.

The telecoms specialist here is **Michele Bernasconi***, commended by clients for his *"dynamic and hands-on approach."* He handles both regulatory and transactional telecoms cases, and was a prominent figure on the UMTS bidding process. The team represented Tiscali-World Online on its merger. **Clients:** Tiscali-World Online; Sunrise; UEFA.

Walder Wyss & Partners (3 ptrs, 3 asscs) Perceived to be focused on the IT sector, the firm advises its international clientele on software protection, licensing issues, systems integration contracts, data processing contracts, data protection and e-commerce. At the forefront of the team's efforts is **Didier SanGiorgio***, commended by clients for *"speaking our language."* The team advised a client on the establishment of a joint venture in relation to the provision of internet services, including cross licences.

In telecoms, the firm handles transactional work as well as regulatory matters, and advised on the UMTS licence auction. **Clients:** Microsoft; Business Software Alliance; UUNET; Interroute; i-21 Switzerland; Telenor.

Wiederkehr Forster Rechtsanwälte (2 ptrs, 2 asscs) The firm's profile in this sector is primarily ascribed to **Rolf Weber***, described by his admirers as *"the doyen of Swiss telecoms."* He handles both regulatory and transactional work, and has also branched out into IT, advising on project contract work. Apart from the firm's work for Sunrise, one of the big name telecoms players in Switzerland, the firm also acted for two different Swiss companies on the Cablecom take-over. **Clients:** Sunrise Communications

Pestalozzi Gmuer & Patry (2 ptrs, 2 asscs) Predominantly active in the IT sector, the firm also handles some telecoms work, notably on the transactional front. All IT issues, including classical software contract work, licensing, data protection and distribution outsourcing and e-commerce are handled here.

Robert Briner*, seen by competitors as *"a man for all seasons,"* is an IP/IT lawyer with a strong arbitration practice. The firm represents one of the largest US telecom providers in Switzerland on negotiations for commercial telecoms contracts and interconnection agreements. It also acted for COCOM, a WLL operator in Switzerland, on its dealings with the Federal Office for Communications and in establishing its business in Switzerland. **Clients:** Swissnet Bank; COCOM.

Zürcher Blickenstorfer & Widmer (2 ptrs, 2 asscs) Another IT specialist which owes its strong showing to one man, in this case the *"straight-talking"* **Peter Neuenschwander***. His *"first hand technical experience,"* acquired from his days as in-house counsel at Digital was mentioned to researchers as his greatest strength, and he has a strong niche in project contracts work. The firm also advises on distribution contracts, licence contracts and outsourcing.

Highlight matters include acting on one of the largest local IT roll-out deals, and advising a government client on one of the largest ERP (Enterprise Resource Planning) implementations in Switzerland. **Clients:** Compaq.

Python Schifferli Peter & Partner (2 ptrs, 4 asscs) Geneva-based firm that is renowned for its telecoms capability, and represents both Francophone Swiss and international clients. **Pierre-Yves Gunter*** was recommended to researchers as a telecoms specialist with *"an Anglo-Saxon touch,"* who handles substantial litigation and arbitration work in the sector. Often acting for new entrants in Switzerland, the firm handles both regulatory and transactional work. Its IT practice, although comparatively low-profile, advises on e-commerce projects, domain name disputes and digital signature issues.

The firm represents about ten fixed mobile WLL operators in Switzerland and advised France Telecom on the sale of Cablecom by Swisscom. **Clients:** France Telecom; Global One; Broadnet (WLL operator).

Thomann Fischer (2 ptrs, 1 assc) Basle-based specialist IT firm, which has a strong profile for contractual and licensing work on behalf of software clients, and also advises start-ups on IPOs and in e-commerce issues. The spearhead here is the *"impressive"* **Felix Thomann***, whose IP background earns him respect for domain name disputes.

The firm has advised on content management work for a leading Swiss technology company, and has been involved in several mergers and acquisitions in the IT field. **Clients:** Swiss and foreign technology companies.

Other Notable Practitioner **Rolf auf der Maur***, an *"active and intelligent technician,"* is the leading light at Vischer, and has been widely recommended for his mixed IT/IP practice.

Corporate/M&A

Bär & Karrer (8 ptrs, 11 asscs) Acknowledged as one of the top firms in Zurich, the firm places heavy emphasis on big-ticket cross-border M&A, representing both targets and acquirers. The outstanding practitioner here is **Rolf Watter***, consistently praised to researchers as *"a high-calibre lawyer, with a lightning quick grasp of complex issues."* **Felix Ehrat***, regarded by clients as *"a direct and straightforward negotiator,"* and the *"versatile"* **Nedim Peter Vogt*** were also strongly recommended.

The firm's client base is largely drawn from the financial services sector, but also includes a number of the world's leading pharmaceuticals concerns. The team acted for Algroup in its merger with Alcan Aluminium and for Novartis on its merger with AstraZeneca's agrochemical businesses to form Syngenta. **Clients:** Novartis; UBS; Algroup.

Homburger Rechtsanwälte (5 ptrs, 10 asscs) Active for an array of domestic and international clients, the firm advises on high value M&A work, and is respected by rivals and clients alike. Loved by his clients, **Peter Kurer*** *"knows how to make the deal happen,"* and has niche expertise on cases involving US law. His colleague **Heinz Schärer*** is regarded as a *"solid all-round commercial lawyer."*

The firm represented SAirGroup, the holding company of Swissair in its acquisition of Sabena, the Belgian flag carrier. Another deal highlight of the last year was representing Compagnie Financière Richemont on its CHF3 billion acquisition of the Mannesmann Watch Group. The firm was also counsel to Zurich Financial Services on the merger of two holding companies, Swiss listed Zurich Allied AG and UK listed Allied Zurich plc. **Clients:** SAirGroup; Compagnie Financière

SWITZERLAND
Leading firms
(Corporate/Mergers & Acquisitions)

Band	Firm
1	Bär & Karrer
	Homburger Rechtsanwälte
	Lenz & Staehelin
2	Baker & McKenzie
	Niederer Kraft & Frey
3	Pestalozzi Gmuer & Patry
	Schellenberg Wittmer
4	Prager Dreifuss
	Walder Wyss & Partners

Firms are listed alphabetically in each band.

Leading individuals
(Corporate/Mergers & Acquisitions)

Band	Individual
1	**ISLER Peter** *Niederer Kraft & Frey*
	KURER Peter *Homburger Rechtsanwälte*
	SCHENKER Urs *Baker & McKenzie*
	TSCHÄNI Rudolf *Lenz & Staehelin*
	WATTER Rolf *Bär & Karrer*
2	**FREY Martin** *Baker & McKenzie*
	HÖHN Jakob *Pestalozzi Gmuer & Patry*
	OERTLE Matthias *Lenz & Staehelin*
	PULVER Urs *Niederer Kraft & Frey*
	REINHARDT Christoph *Lenz & Staehelin*
	SCHÄRER Heinz *Homburger Rechtsanwälte*
3	**BOLLMANN Hans** *Pestalozzi Gmuer & Patry*
	EHRAT Felix *Bär & Karrer*
	LANZ Martin *Schellenberg Wittmer*
	VISCHER Markus *Walder Wyss & Partners*
4	**DOMENIG Gaudenz** *Prager Dreifuss*
	VISCHER Bernard *Schellenberg Wittmer*
	VOGT Nedim Peter *Bär & Karrer*

Individuals are listed alphabetically in each band.

Richemont; AstraZeneca; Unaxis; Siemens; Swisscom.

Lenz & Staehelin (9 ptrs, 26 asscs) Considered to possess *"a high quality, well balanced corporate team,"* the firm is renowned for its powerful Swiss client base, and is an influential corporate force in both Zurich and Geneva. Clearly the leading man here is **Rudolf Tschäni***, praised to researchers as *"a superb organiser and a pragmatic negotiator."* His younger colleague **Matthias Oertle*** is a *"brilliant and client-friendly technician,"* who is especially commended for his drafting skills. The *"industrious"* **Christoph Reinhardt*** also maintains his share of market support. The firm represented the Mannesmann Group on the sale of its Watch Group for CHF3 billion. **Clients:** Mannesmann Watch Group; Alcan Aluminium; Compania Roca Radiadores.

Baker & McKenzie (6 ptrs, 9 asscs) The only foreign firm to carry any weight in Switzerland continues to be recommended to researchers for its transactional expertise. The corporate team is led by **Urs Schenker***, an *"aggressive and tough negotiator"* with long experience of cross-border deals. The *"constructive"* **Martin Frey*** has established a name both for M&A and venture capital work.

The team advised on the takeover of Dobbs Inc. by Gate Gourmet (a subsidiary of the SAirGroup), and on the acquisition of BTP by Clariant. **Clients:** SAirGroup; Clariant.

Niederer Kraft & Frey (6 ptrs, 10 asscs) Better known for its work in the financial sector, the firm nevertheless advises its vast financial institution clientele on substantial M&A transactions. Renowned both in banking and corporate circles, **Peter Isler*** is a *"meticulous and effective"* transactional lawyer. He is backed by the *"persistent"* **Urs Pulver***, who is an M&A specialist. If it is a corporate legal opinion that is needed, this firm has the top man in Peter Forstmoser (*"an academic star in corporate matters"*).

The firm acted for the Credit Suisse Group on its CHF20 billion acquisition of Donaldson, Lufkin & Jenrette, and represented LVMH Möet Hennessy Louis Vuitton on its acquisition of TAG Heuer International. Also advised Sumitomo Bank on the sale of its majority shareholding in Banca del Gottardo to Swiss Life. **Clients:** Morgan Grenfell Private Equity; Sumitomo Bank; Bloomberg; Merrill Lynch; Siemens; Swiss Re; ABN AMRO; Crédit Lyonnais.

Pestalozzi Gmuer & Patry (4 ptrs, 8 asscs) Although not perceived to have the profile of the market leaders, the firm advises a host of mainly American Fortune 500 clients on their investments in Switzerland. **Hans Bollmann*** is regarded as *"a notable rainmaker,"* while **Jakob Höhn*** is an *"uncomplicated transactional lawyer."*

The firm recently handled the acquisition of several banks and has broad experience in international joint ventures for SWX New Market companies. It recently advised Crown Castle International, a NASDAQ listed company, on its bid for the acquisition of the Broadcasting Service Unit of Swisscom, and represented Triton Advisors UK on its bid for Slumberland, part of Valora. **Clients:** Johnson & Johnson; The Leading Hotels of the World Ltd; Chase Manhattan; Merrill Lynch; MCI WorldCom; Deutsche Post.

Schellenberg Wittmer (5 ptrs , 10 asscs) Having increased its size and profile in Zurich and Geneva by the merger of Schellenberg & Haissly and Brunschwig Wittmer in May 2000, the firm now caters for a French and German-speaking clientele. In Zurich, **Martin Lanz*** is seen by his peers as a *"capable and persevering"* lawyer, who divides his practice between capital markets and corporate advice. **Bernard Vischer*** is also highly recommended. **Clients:** Gretag Imaging Group.

Prager Dreifuss (3 ptrs, 4 asscs) Small firm with a flourishing corporate/M&A profile and experience of a number of domestic M&A deals. **Gaudenz Domenig*** is respected as an *"excellent client man."* The team advised NTL on its acquisition of Cablecom. **Clients:** NTL; watch industry; listed companies.

Walder Wyss & Partners (5 ptrs, 12 asscs) Perceived to be active in the banking and finance sector, the firm also handles a fair amount of M&A/corporate cases, and advises clients from industries such as banking, insurance, pharmaceuticals and IT.

Markus Vischer* is a respected transactional name. He acted for UBS on the acquisition of the Eurogate project, one of the largest building projects ever in Switzerland. The firm also advised on the demutualisation and restructuring of Swiss Life, the country's largest insurance Company. **Clients:** UBS; Swiss Life.

*See leaders' profiles on pages 658-664

Leaders' profiles – Switzerland

S

AESCHIMANN, Jean-Paul
Lenz & Staehelin, Geneva +41 22 318 70 00
jean-paul.aeschimann@lenzstaehelin.com
Recommended in Banking & Finance
Specialisation: Partner in Banking and Finance Department. Main areas of work: General Banking, Corporate Finance and Capital Markets. Member of the Board of Directors of a number of banks and finance institutions.
Career: Universities of Neuchatel and Harvard. Admitted to the Bar since 1961. Partner of *Lenz & Staehelin* since 1967.

AUF DER MAUR, Rolf
Vischer, Zurich +41 1 254 3400
ram@vischer.com
Recommended in Communications
Specialisation: Partner and head of IP/IT practice. Main area of work is intellectual property, information technology, media and entertainment law. Acts on behalf of major ISPs, ASPs, entertainment and publishing companies.
Prof. Memberships: Vice President of sima swiss interactive media association, member of the executive board of the International Association of Entertainment Laywers, Zurich, Swiss and International Bar Association, LES, AIPPI.
Career: Studied in Zurich and Los Angeles, qualified 1991, practised with major firms in Zurich and London, became a partner of a mid-sized firm in Zurich in 1996, joined *Vischer* as a partner in 2000, lecturer for online law, various publications in the area of intellectual property and online law.

BERNASCONI, Michele
Bär & Karrer, Zurich +41 1 261 5150
Recommended in Communications

BIANCHI, François M.
Niederer Kraft & Frey, Zurich +41 1 217 10 00
francois.m.bianchi@nkf.ch
Recommended in Banking & Finance
Specialisation: Principal areas of work are Swiss capital market and stock exchange law, investment fund law, banking and corporate law, particularly derivative transactions, domestic and international debt and equity financings, structured products, collective investment schemes, initial public offerings and private banking matters. Serves as a member of the board of directors of various banking institutions in Switzerland.
Prof. Memberships: Zurich Bar Association. Swiss Bar Association. International Bar Association.
Career: Admitted to the Zurich Bar in 1984. Joined *Niederer Kraft & Frey* in 1987, became a partner in 1996.
Personal: Born in 1955. Married, with two children. Doctor of Law from University of Zurich in 1981. Master of Laws from the University of Miami, School of Law in 1986.

BLESSING, Mark
Bär & Karrer, Zurich +41 1 261 5150
Recommended in Arbitration (International)

BLUM, Oliver
CMS von Erlach Klainguti Stettler Wille, Zurich +41 1 285 1111
o.blum@vonerlach.ch
Recommended in Communications
Specialisation: Telecommunications, mergers and acquisitions, corporate finance, IT. Telecommunications clients include Orange Communications SA, Callahan Broadband Wireless Switzerland GmbH, FirstMark Communications Switzerland AG, as well as a number of other international telecommunications companies with a Swiss market presence. Acted on numerous cross-border acquisitions, offering a full range of services, including negotiations, due dilligence, drafting of agreements, regulatory affairs, closing and post-closing measures. Acted on international corporate finance transactions, acting for borrowers and lenders.
Prof. Memberships: Zurich and Swiss Bar Association.
Publications: Author of 'The Regulatory Environment for Telecom Operators in Switzerland', 'The Client-Attorney Privilege in the Age of E-Mail – A Replication from the Point of View of the Practitioner' (contribution to Schweizerische Juristenzeitung), 'The lawyer adn E-Mail: Security Aspects'; co-author of 'The Swiss Tax System from the Viewpoint of the Foreign Investor', 'International Business Acquisitions in Switzerland, Major Legal Issues' (contribution to 'International Business Acquisitions – Major Legal Issues and Due Dilligence', Kluwer Law International).
Career: Admitted to the bar 1997. Joined *CMS von Erlach Klainguti Stettler Wille* 1995.
Personal: Born October 15, 1967. Attended University of Zurich 1987-1993 (licenciatus iuris), University of Basle 1993-1994 (Master of Advanced European Studies), Northwestern University School of Law, Chicago 1997-1998 (Master of Law).

BOLLMANN, Hans
Pestalozzi Gmuer & Patry, Zurich +41 1 217 91 11
Recommended in Corporate/M&A
Specialisation: Main area of work is business law (including M&A and private banking law), litigation/arbitration and international legal assistance matters (where again private banking aspects are of importance). Advises and represents in particular Swiss subsidiaries of foreign (mostly US and European) corporations in the above areas.
Prof. Memberships: Zurich Bar Association (former member Ethics Committee), American and New York Bar Associations, International Bar Association, IFA, Swiss-American Chamber of Commerce (past Chairman of the Legal Committee), Swiss Arbitration Association, and others.
Career: Graduated from University of Zurich in 1970 (Dr. iur.), admitted to the bar in 1972. 1972/73 associate in a major New York law firm. Joined *Pestalozzi Gmuer & Patry* in 1974 and became Partner in 1976. Member of several boards of directors of Swiss companies, but also of three welfare foundations.
Personal: Born 15 October 1943. Married, two children. Leisure interests cover travel, history (author of various articles on military history) and outdoor activities such as riding and hiking. Languages: German, English, French, some Italian.

BÖSCH, René
Homburger Rechtsanwälte, Zurich +41 1 265 35 35
rene.boesch@homburger.ch
Recommended in Banking & Finance
Specialisation: Partner and head of the Banking and Finance Practice Team. Main area of work is banking law, financial service regulation and securities law, principally domestic and international bond and equity-linked offerings, hybrid financial instruments and structured financings. Other areas of interest include corporate finance and corporate law.
Prof. Memberships: Zurich and Swiss Bar Associations, International Bar Association. Member of the Legal Committee of the Swiss-American Chamber of Commerce.
Career: Qualified in 1990. Joined *Homburger Rechtsanwälte* in 1989, becoming partner in 1998.
Personal: Born 1959. Graduated as Dr. iur. from the Zurich University in 1987 and received a master's degree (LLM) from the University of Chicago in 1991.

BRINER, Robert
Lenz & Staehelin, Geneva +41 22 318 70 00
robert.briner@lenzstaehelin.com
Recommended in Arbitration (International)
Specialisation: International arbitration.
Publications: Various publications, especially on arbitration, including 'Switzerland: National Report', 3 Yearbook Commercial Arbitration 181 (1978), 7 Y.B. Com. Arb. 70 (1982) and 14 Y.B. Com. Arb. 1 (1989) and International Handbook on Commercial Arbitration (P. Sanders, ed.).
Career: Counsel in the law firm *Lenz & Staehelin*, Geneva. Chairman of the International Court of Arbitration of the International Chamber of Commerce, Paris. Chairman, Panel 4 of Commissioners of the United Nations Compensation Commission, Geneva. Member of the Claims Resolution Tribunal for Dormant Accounts in Switzerland, Zurich. Former President of the Iran-United States Claims Tribunal, The Hague.
Personal: Doctor of Law, University of Zurich.

BRINER, Robert
Pestalozzi Gmuer & Patry, Zurich +41 1 217 91 11
Recommended in Communications
Specialisation: Joined *Pestalozzi Gmuer & Patry* in 1999.
Publications: Author of articles on the subject such as software inventions, copyrights on works for hire and the legal position of internet service providers.
Career: Has professional experience as a law clerk in the District Court of Meilen and in a Zurich law firm, and was admitted to the bar in 1981. Professional work has at all times been focused on industrial property and in particular on computer law; contributed to the revision of the Swiss copy-

right law (software protection) in 1987. Lectures in postgraduate courses, and is a member of many associations in the field of intellectual property and of information technology.
Personal: Born 1949. Graduated from the University of Zurich in 1979 (Dr. jur.) with a thesis on civil procedural law. During studies, worked for a Zurich patent attorney firm and was involved in trademark and patent matters. Professional languages are German, English and French.

DAENIKER, Daniel
Homburger Rechtsanwälte, Zurich +41 1 265 35 35
daniel.daeniker@homburger.ch
Recommended in Banking & Finance
Specialisation: Practice focuses on capital markets law, particularly domestic and international equity offerings and IPOs. Other areas of work include financial services regulation, private equity and venture capital transactions, and mergers & acquisitions.
Prof. Memberships: Zurich and Swiss Bar Associations.
Publications: Author of 'Swiss Securities Regulation', a primer on the regulation of the Swiss financial market.
Career: Qualified in 1990. Joined *Homburger Rechtsanwälte* in 1991, becoming partner in 2000.
Personal: Born 1963. Graduated as Dr.iur. from the University of Zurich in 1992. Also studied at the University of Chicago (LLM, 1996).

DE COULON, Philippe
Lenz & Staehelin, Geneva +41 22 318 70 00
philippe.decoulon@lenzstaehelin.com
Recommended in Arbitration (International)
Specialisation: Partner in the International Arbitration Group.
Career: University of Geneva. Admitted to the Bar in 1954. Partner of *Lenz & Staehelin* since 1960, Counsel since 2001. Former Chairman of the Geneva Bar Association (1979-1980).

DOMENIG, Gaudenz
Prager Dreifuss, Zurich +41 1 254 5555
Recommended in Corporate/M&A

DU PASQUIER, Shelby
Lenz & Staehelin, Geneva +41 22 318 70 00
shelby.dupasquier@lenzstaehelin.com
Recommended in Banking & Finance
Specialisation: Partner in Banking and Finance Department. Main areas of work: Banking Law, Financial Services, Mutual Funds, Corporate Law, Capital Markets and Mergers and Acquisitions. Acts for a number of Swiss and non-Swiss banking and financial groups.
Publications: Author of co-author of various publications and articles on company law and mutual funds; contributor to the Oceana publication 'International Securities Report Switzerland'.
Career: Born in 1960. Geneva University Business School and School of Law. Columbia University School of Law. Admitted to the Bar in 1984. Partner since 1994.

EHRAT, Felix
Bär & Karrer, Zurich +41 1 261 5150
Recommended in Corporate/M&A

FREY, Martin
Baker & McKenzie, Zurich +41 1 384 1414
Martin.Frey@bakernet.com
Recommended in Corporate/M&A
Specialisation: Partner in Corporate Department. Main area of work is corporate law, principally mergers, acquisitions, venture capital and private equity investments in Switzerland. Advised various trade buyers and financial investors on the acquisition of companies as well as MBOs, joint ventures and similar transactions.
Prof. Memberships: Swiss and Zurich Bar Associations.
Career: Qualified in 1984. Member of the Legal Department of Coopers & Lybrand, Zurich, from 1984-89. Foreign associate with *Arnold & Porter*, Washington DC 1987-88. Joined *Baker & McKenzie* in 1991, becoming a partner in 1996.
Personal: Born 18 December 1956. Attended the University of Berne Law School as well as Georgetown University Law Centre (LLM Common Law Studies). Fluent in German, English and French.

FURTER, Robert
Pestalozzi Gmuer & Patry, Zurich +41 1 217 91 11
Recommended in Banking & Finance

GIOVANNINI, Teresa
Lalive & Partners, Geneva +41 22 319 8700
tgiovannini@lalive.ch
Recommended in Arbitration (International)
Specialisation: Partner, International Litigation, Arbitration and Art Law.
Prof. Memberships: Swiss Arbitration Association; International Chamber of Commerce; Swiss National Committee (Panel of Arbitrators); Chamber of National and International Arbitration of Milan (Member, Arbitral Council); Institute of International Business Law and Practice (Corresponding Member); International Law Association (Swiss Alternate Member); International Bar Association (Member: Dispute Settlement Committee; Arbitration Committee).
Publications: Author of various publications in the areas of Civil procedure, Corporate governance and Arbitration.
Career: Internship with Law Firm *Turrettini and L'Huillier*, Geneva, 1981-1983; Foreign Counsel with *Chiomenti & Partners*, Rome, 1983-1985; Associate and Partner, *Lalive Budin and Partners*, Geneva, 1985-1994. Partner, *Lalive & Partners*, 1994-. Speaker: International Development Institute, Rome; ICC Institute of International Business Law and Practice, Paris; China International Economy, Science-Technology, Law and Expertise Society, Beijing; Centro de Estudios Constitucionales y Politicos de Ministerio de Justicia de la Nacion, La Plata, Argentina; Libera Universita Internazionale degli Studi Sociali (LUISS), Rome; Chartered Institute of Arbitrators, London; International and Comparative Law Center, Dallas.
Personal: University of Fribourg Law School (Lic.jur.). Hague Academy of International Law. Admitted Geneva Bar, 1983.

GUNTER, Pierre-Yves
Python Schifferli Peter & Partner, Geneva
+41 22 347 46 45
Recommended in Communications

GUROVITS, András
Niederer Kraft & Frey, Zurich +41 1 217 10 00
andras.a.gurovits@nkf.ch
Recommended in Communications
Specialisation: Principal areas of work are telecommunications, information technology and e-commerce law as well as infrastructure, sports and competition law.
Prof. Memberships: Zurich Bar Association. Swiss Bar Association. Deutsche Gesellschaft für Recht und Informatik. Swiss Forum of Communications Law.
Publications: Author and co-author of several publications, for example regarding IT-consulting contracts, the Swiss Telecommunications Law and the Swiss Railway Law.
Career: Software developer and marketing specialist with a major IT provider in Switzerland from 1979 to 1994. Admitted to the Bar in 1991. Joined *Niederer Kraft & Frey* in 1994, becoming a partner in 2001. Lecturer at Zurich University in IT Law since 1994.
Personal: Born in 1960, married, two children. Law degree from University of Zurich in 1987, Doctor of Law in 1993.

HOFFET, Franz
Homburger Rechtsanwälte, Zurich +41 1 265 35 35
franz.hoffet@homburger.ch
Recommended in Communications
Specialisation: Partner in IP/IT and Antitrust Practice Group. Heads the firm's domestic and EU antitrust and competition practice. Main area of work is merger control and investigations of agreements restraining competition and abuses of dominance. Other areas include corporate, mergers & acquisitions and communications law.
Prof. Memberships: Zurich and Swiss Bar Associations, International Bar Association, Studienvereinigung Kartellrecht e.V.
Publications: Co-editor and co-author of a leading treatise on Swiss Competition Law, several publications on Swiss Competition Law.
Career: Qualified in 1986. Joined *Homburger* in 1988, becoming Partner in 1994. Chairman of the Zurich Bar's Competition Law Committee, Vice-Chairman of the Swiss Bar's Antitrust Law Committee.
Personal: Born 1956, Graduated as Dr.iur. from Zurich University in 1991 and received master's degree (LLM) from the University of Chicago in 1988.

HÖHN, Jakob
Pestalozzi Gmuer & Patry, Zurich +41 1 217 91 11
jakob.hoehn@pgp.ch
Recommended in Corporate/M&A
Specialisation: Practices mainly in the areas of corporate law, including shareholders litigation, mergers and acquisitions, securities law and contract law.
Career: University of Zurich (Dr. iur. 1990); Georgetown University (LLM, 1991). Admitted to the bar in 1988. Law clerk at the District Court of Meilen; Associate in an international law firm in

S

Zurich; assistant at the University of Zurich Corporate Law Departments; Foreign Associate in a firm in New York. Joined *Pestalozzi Gmuer & Patry* in 1991. Partner since 1996.
Personal: Born 1960. Practices in English and German.

HUENERWADEL, Patrick
Lenz & Staehelin, Zurich +41 1 204 1212
patrick.hunerwadel@lenzstaehelin.com
Recommended in Banking & Finance
Specialisation: Partner in Banking and Finance Department. Main areas of work: Banking and Capital Market Law, Lease Finance, Trade, Corporate and Contract Law.
Publications: Publications in the area of Corporate Law.
Career: Admitted to the Bar in 1987. Partner since 1994. Lecturer on Corporate and Contract Law at University of St. Gallen.
Personal: Born in 1959. University of St Gallen; Boston University. Morin Center for Banking Law. Languages: German, English, French.

S

ISLER, Peter R
Niederer Kraft & Frey, Zurich +41 1 217 10 00
Peter.R.Isler@nkf.ch
Recommended in Banking & Finance, Corporate/M&A
Specialisation: Principal areas of work are Swiss banking and corporate law, particularly domestic and international debt, equity financings, acquisitions, public take-overs, initial public offerings and private banking matters. Serves as member of the board of directors of various listed and non-listed companies.
Prof. Memberships: Zurich Bar Association, Swiss Bar Association and International Bar Association.
Career: Admitted to the Zurich Bar in 1977; joined *Niederer Kraft & Frey* in 1977; became a Partner in 1981. Teaching-Fellow at the University of Zurich, School of Law, since 1978; Member of the Zurich Bar Examination Committee since 1984.
Personal: Born in 1946. Married with three children. Doctor of Law from University of Zurich in 1973. Master of Law from Harvard Law School in 1974.

JETZER, Rolf
Niederer Kraft & Frey, Zurich +41 1 217 10 00
Recommended in Communications

KARRER, Pierre A.
Pestalozzi Gmuer & Patry, Zurich +41 1 217 91 11
pierre.karrer@pgp.ch
Recommended in Arbitration (International)
Specialisation: One of the leading arbitration lawyers in Switzerland. Served in over 150 international commercial arbitrations in Switzerland and elsewhere, mostly as chairman, but also as sole and party-appointed arbitrator.
Prof. Memberships: President of ASA, the Swiss Arbitration Association, Vice-Chairman of Committee D (arbitration and ADR) of the International Bar Association, Fellow of the Chartered Institute of Arbitrators (FCIArb), a member of the Board and Co-chairman of the Arbitration Court of the Zurich Chamber of Commerce, a court member of the London Court of International Arbitration and a listed arbitrator of the Vienna, Singapore, Hong Kong, Prague and other centres.
Publications: Has published numerous articles in the field of international arbitration.
Career: Göttingen, Padova, The Hague, Zurich (Dr. iur., summa cum laude, 1967) and Yale (LLM, 1970). Admitted to the bar in 1969. Partner with *Pestalozzi Gmuer & Patry* since 1976. Assistant Professor of Law at Tulane University, in New Orleans, and is currently teaching international arbitration at the University of Zurich graduate program.
Personal: Born 1941. Speaks fluent English, French, German, Italian and Dutch, some Spanish.

KAUFMANN-KOHLER, Gabrielle
Schellenberg Wittmer, Geneva 3 +41 22 707 8000
gabrielle.kaufmann@swlegal.ch
Recommended in Arbitration (International)
Specialisation: Focuses primarily on international commercial arbitration. Acted as counsel, presiding/sole arbitrator or arbitrator in about 80 complex commercial disputes involving international business transactions, joint venture contracts, acquisitions and shareholders' agreements, and construction contracts. In addition, was involved in approx. 30 sports law disputes. Specialises in Swiss private international law, in particular international civil litigation, international commercial arbitration and international contracts, as professor at the Law School of Geneva University. President of the ad hoc Division for the Olympic Games and of the Ordinary Division of the Court of arbitration for sports. Author of numerous publications in the area of international arbitration, international contracts, international civil procedure, sports law, art law, e-commerce and Internet law.
Prof. Memberships: International Council for Commercial Arbitration (ICCA); Executive Board of the Swiss Arbitration Association; International Council for Sports Related Arbitration; Executive Committee of the Swiss International Law Society; Geneva Bar and New York State Bar Associations; Swiss Group of International Law Association.
Career: Professor (Private International Law), Geneva University Law School (from 1997); practising attorney, partner with *Schellenberg Wittmer*, formerly *Brunschwig Wittmer* (from 1996); adjunct professor (Private International Law), Geneva University Law School (1993-97); Partner (1985-95) and associate (1981-85) with *Etienne Blum Stehle Manfrini & Partners, Baker & McKenzie*; associate with *Baker and McKenzie* New York (1981); admitted to New York Bar (1981); legal adviser, Union Bank of Switzerland, New York Branch (1980); admitted to Geneva Bar (1976).
Personal: Born 3 November 1952; Law degree, University of Geneva, 1974; Doctorate (summa cum laude), University of Basle, 1979.

KNOEPFLER, François
Knoepfler Gabus Gehrig, Neuchatel
+41 32 724 3522
avokgg@bluewin.ch
Recommended in Arbitration (International)
Specialisation: Professor, law faculty, Neuchâtel University, Switzerland. Private International Law, Comparative Law, International arbitration and the Brussels/Lugano Conventions on enforcement of civil decisions. Main research interest: contracts and international commercial arbitration. Practising lawyer and arbitrator (president, sole arbitrator or party-appointed arbitrator) or counsel in over 70 arbitration proceedings involving all types of international contracts, especially in the field of construction (in several industry sectors), transfer of technology, intellectual property, energy, communication, insurance and joint venture.
Prof. Memberships: Vice-chairman of the Swiss Arbitration Association (ASA), member of the World Intellectual Property Arbitration and Mediation Centre, chairman of the Law Committee of the Swiss Federation of Watch Industry. Co-drafter of the future Court of Arbitration for Football.
Publications: Publication of a large number of contributions regarding contracts and international commercial arbitration. Responsible, with Philippe Schweizer, for the yearly review of the jurisprudence on arbitration in the Swiss Review of International and European Law.
Career: Qualified 1965. Doctor's Degree 1967. Expert for the codification of the Swiss Private International Law 1973-1978. Dean of the Law faculty 1986-1987. Visiting fellow at Wolfson College, Cambridge, UK.
Personal: Basic legal eduation in Neuchâtel, Switzerland. Specialisation in the field of international law at the Max Planck-Institute in Hamburg, Germany and The Hague, the Netherlands.

KROLL, Markus J.
Walder Wyss & Partners, 8022 Zurich
+41 1 265 75 11
mkroll@wwp.ch
Recommended in Banking & Finance
Specialisation: Banking; domestic and international financings (including project finance, asset finance and restructurings) as well as financial services. Serves a client roster of blue-chip Swiss and international financial institutions. Speaks German, English, Italian and French.
Prof. Memberships: International Bar Association (IBA); Alternative Investment Management Association (AIMA); European Derivative Investments and Funds Association (EMFA); The Futures and Options Association (FOA); Association for the Application and Promotion of Electronic Technologies (APTE).
Career: University of Zurich (lic. oec., 1987, Dr. oec., 1991, lic. iur., 1992); UBS AG, Investment Fund and Investment Research Department and Section for the Administration and Trading of Rescheduled Syndicated Loans (1987-1988); associate, law firm *Zurich-Zollikon* (1990-1992); London School of Economics and Political Science (LLM, 1992); partner, law firm *Zurich-Zollikon* (1992-1999).
Personal: Born 26 July 1960.

KURER, Peter
Homburger Rechtsanwälte, Zurich +41 1 265 35 35
peter.kurer@homburger.ch
Recommended in Corporate/M&A
Specialisation: Mergers and acquisitions, corporate and commercial law, banking, securities, capital market and corporate finance. Has acted as counsel in

numerous domestic and cross-border transactions during the last 20 years.
Prof. Memberships: International Bar Association, Swiss Bar Association, Zürich Bar Association, Swiss Lawyers' Association, Swiss Arbitration Association, Swiss Association for International Law, British-Swiss Chamber of Commerce (Legal and Tax Chapter).
Career: Admitted to Zürich Bar in 1980. Joined *Homburger Rechtsanwälte* as Associate in 1980 and became Partner in 1985. Member of the Board of various companies including Danzas Holding AG, Holderbank Financière Glarus AG, Rothschilds Continuation Holdings AG, Unisys (Schweiz) AG.
Personal: Born 28 June 1949. Lic.Jur., University of Zürich, 1974; Dr.Jur., University of Zürich, 1978; LLM, University of Chicago, 1976. Married, three children. Lives in Herrliberg (near Zürich). Leisure interests include sports, literature, music and movies.

LALIVE, Pierre
Lalive & Partners, Geneva +41 22 319 8700
Recommended in Arbitration (International)
Specialisation: Senior Partner in the Geneva based international law firm *Lalive & Partners*. Counsel or arbitrator in over 200 international arbitration proceedings under various rules (ICC, UNCITRAL, ICSID, PCA, WTO etc.). Cases concern mainly public and private international law, international commercial transactions, concessions, State contracts and joint ventures. Counsel for several Governments before the International Court of Justice. Member of various governmental commissions on legal matters and Delegate of the Swiss Government to several international conferences. One of the seven experts appointed by the Swiss Government to draft the new Code of Private International Law.
Prof. Memberships: Elected Member of the Institut de Droit International (Chairman: 1989-1991) and of the International Academy of Comparative Law. Honorary President of the Swiss Arbitration Association. Member of the International Council for Commercial Arbitration, IBA, ICCA, AAA (Panel of Arbitrators), Geneva Law Society, Swiss Society of Jurists, Swiss Society of International Law, ILA (Swiss Branch), British Institute of International and Comparative Law.
Publications: Author of more than 150 publications, mainly in the fields of private and public international law, international business law and arbitration.
Career: Professor of Law (mainly Private international law) at the Geneva Faculty of Law (1955-1983) and Professor of International Trade Law at the Geneva Graduate Institute of International Studies (1961-1986). Was awarded the Balzan Prize for International Law and four doctorate honoris causa (Paris, Lyon, Brussels, Rome). Former Head of the Department of Private International Law, Geneva Law School. Former Dean of Geneva Law School and President of the Geneva University Council
Personal: Lic. Lit., Law Degree, University of Geneva; Ph D, Cambridge University.

LANZ, Martin
Schellenberg Wittmer, Zurich +41 1 215 52 52
martin.lanz@swlegal.ch
Recommended in Banking & Finance, Corporate/M&A
Specialisation: Main area of work is corporate law, principally mergers and acquisitions, as well as banking and capital market and other finance transactions. Has handled major restructurings of businesses, spin-offs and joint ventures and is often instructed in private equity and IPO matters. Assisted several listed and non-listed companies in the structuring of ESOPs and advised domestic and foreign clients in legal and regulatory aspects affecting stock exchange and investment fund activities in Switzerland.
Prof. Memberships: Zurich Bar Association, International Bar Association
Publications: Co-author of a commentary on the Swiss Stock Exchange Act, recent publications in the area of ESOPs, business reorganisations and investment fund law.
Career: Partner with *Schellenberg Wittmer* (formerly *Schellenberg & Haissly*) in Zurich since 1995, associate with the same firm since 1991, vice-president in the legal department of the capital markets division of Swiss Bank Corporation from 1984 - 1990.
Personal: Born 25 July 1958 in Lucerne, attended law schools of the universities of Basel and Neuchâtel, bar exam in 1983.

LÉVY, Laurent
Schellenberg Wittmer, Geneva 3 +41 22 707 8000
laurent.levy@swlegal.ch
Recommended in Arbitration (International)
Specialisation: Focuses primarily on international arbitration. Acted as counsel, chairman or arbitrator in over 100 disputes. Such disputes related notably to joint venture and consortium agreements, stockholders contracts, banking, licence agreements, oil production, refining, bunkering and transportation (esp. by pipelines), construction contracts, transfers of technology. Author of publications about arbitration, international company law and civil procedure.
Prof. Memberships: Geneva Bar; International Bar Association (IBA); Fédération Suisse des Avocats (FSA); London Court of International Arbitration (LCIA); The International Arbitration Club London; Association suisse de l'arbitrage (ASA); Société Genevoise de Droit et de Législation (SGDL) (former chairman); Comité Français de l'Arbitrage; Groupe suisse de l'Association Henri Capitant; Institut pour l'Arbitrage International (IAI) (correspondent for French Switzerland); Institute of World Business Law of the ICC (member of Council); former member of the Arbitration Committee of the Geneva Chamber of Commerce and Industry (CCIG).
Career: Partner with *Schellenberg Wittmer* (from 2000); partner with *Brunschwig Wittmer* (1990-2000); partner with *Brunschwig, Biaggi, Levy* (1981-1989); admitted to the Geneva Bar (1974); assistant at the Universities of Paris, Wurzburg and Geneva (1969-1977).
Personal: Born 1 March 1948; Law degrees, University of Paris (1969) and University of Geneva (1972); Doctorate, University of Paris (1983).

NEUENSCHWANDER, Peter
Zürcher Blickenstorfer & Widmer, Zürich +41 1 224 66 00
Recommended in Communications

NIEDERER, Hans
Niederer Kraft & Frey, Zurich +41 1 217 10 00
Hans.Niederer@nkf.ch
Recommended in Banking & Finance
Specialisation: Principal areas of work are Swiss banking and corporate law, particularly domestic and international debt and equity financings, acquisitions, public take-overs, initial public offerings and private banking matters. Serves as member of the board of directors of various companies, in particular banking institutions in Switzerland.
Prof. Memberships: Zurich Bar Association, Swiss Bar Association and International Bar Association.
Career: Admitted to the Zurich Bar in 1971; joined *Niederer Kraft & Frey* in 1970; became a Partner in 1973.
Personal: Born in 1941; married, two children. Doctor of Law from University of Zurich in 1968; Master of Law from the University of California, Berkeley in 1970.

S

OERTLE, Matthias
Lenz & Staehelin, Zurich +41 1 204 1212
matthias.oertle@lenzstaehelin.com
Recommended in Corporate/M&A
Specialisation: Partner in the Corporate Department. Main areas of work include general corporate, mergers and acquisitions and corporate finance.
Career: University of Zurich. Admitted to the Bar in 1988. Partner of *Lenz & Staehelin* since 1996. Publications in the areas of company law and corporate finance.

PATOCCHI, Paolo Michele
Lenz & Staehelin, Geneva +41 22 318 70 00
paolo.michele@lenzstaehelin.com
Recommended in Arbitration (International)
Specialisation: Partner in the International Arbitration Group.
Career: University of Geneva; Hague Academy of International Law; King's College, University of London. Admitted to the Bar of Geneva in 1985. Partner of *Lenz & Staehelin* since 1997. Lecturer at the University of Geneva, Faculty of Laws, since 1989. Various publications in international commercial arbitration and international litigation.

PETER, Wolfgang
Python Schifferli Peter & Partner, Geneva +41 22 347 46 45
Recommended in Arbitration (International)

PFENNINGER, Markus D.
Walder Wyss & Partners, 8022 Zurich +41 1 265 75 11
mpfenninger@wwp.ch
Recommended in Banking & Finance
Specialisation: Banking; finance; securities; corporate; M&A and restructuring of banks, financial institutions and insurance companies. Regularly advises banks and financial institutions on all aspects of banking, capital markets and securities laws. Advised insurance company on its demutualisation and another insurance co-operative on its restructuring. Speaks regularly on conferences and has published extensively. Speaks German, English and French.

Prof. Memberships: Zurich and Swiss Bar Associations; International Bar Association (IBA).
Career: University of Zurich (lic. iur., 1989, Dr. iur., 1995); Morin Center of Banking Law Studies, Boston University (LLM, 1994); foreign associate, Boston financial management company and law firm (1994-1995).
Personal: Born 3 July, 1963; admitted 1991.

POUDRET, Jean-François
Jean-François Poudret – Sole Practitioner, Pulli +41 21 728 1077
Recommended in Arbitration (International)

PULVER, Urs
Niederer Kraft & Frey, Zurich +41 1 217 10 00
urs.pulver@nkf.ch
Recommended in Corporate/M&A
Specialisation: Principal areas of work are Swiss banking, securities and capital market law, corporate law, M&A including public take-overs, merger control law, litigations particularly relating to banking matters.
Prof. Memberships: Zurich Bar Association; Swiss Bar Association; International Bar Association.
Career: Admitted to the Zurich Bar in 1989; joined *Niederer Kraft & Frey* in 1989; became a Partner in 1997.
Personal: Born in 1957. Doctor of Law from University of Zurich in 1986; secondments with two London City law firms in 1992/1993.

RAUBER, Georg
Homburger Rechtsanwälte, Zurich +41 1 265 35 35
Recommended in Communications

REINHARDT, Christoph
Lenz & Staehelin, Zurich +41 1 204 1212
christoph.reinhardt@lenzstaehelin.com
Recommended in Corporate/M&A
Specialisation: Partner in Banking and Finance and Corporate Department. Main areas of work include international finance leases, capital markets and mergers and acquisitions.
Career: University of Zurich, College of Europe. Admitted to the Bar in 1979. Partner of *Lenz & Staehelin* since 1981.

REYMOND, Claude
Reymond, Bonnard, Maire, Freymond, Tschumy, Lausanne +41 21 320 68 51
Recommended in Arbitration (International)

RONCA, Marc
Schellenberg Wittmer, Zurich +41 1 215 52 52
marc.ronca@swlegal.ch
Recommended in Arbitration (International)
Specialisation: Main area of work is international arbitration. Involvement in more than 40 cases, as counsel, sole arbitrator, co-arbitrator and president of arbitral tribunals. Arbitrations ad hoc as well as under ICC, LCIA and UNCITRAL Rules in Zurich, Geneva, Paris, London and under CIETAC Rules in Beijing. Accredited Mediator with CEDR (Centre for Dispute Resolution, London).
Prof. Memberships: Zurich Bar Association; Association Suisse de l'Arbitrage; Union Internationale des Avocats, International Arbitration Commission.
Career: Admitted to the bar 1967; Master of Comparative Law, University of Michigan 1969; Foreign Associate with *Debevoise Plimpton* 1969/70; Doctor of Law, University of Geneva, 1971. General Legal Counsel with Landis & Gyr (measuring instruments etc) 1973-83. Since 1984, Partner with *Schellenberg Wittmer.*
Personal: Born 1941. Languages: German, English, French, Italian, (Spanish).

SANGIORGIO, Didier
Walder Wyss & Partners, 8022 Zurich
+41 1 265 75 11
dsangiorgio@wwp.ch
Recommended in Communications
Specialisation: Information technology, telecommunication, corporate, restructuring, mergers and acquisitions, intellectual property, arbitration. Has extensively advised telecom companies in the area of corporate, contracts, intellectual property, application and auction bids for and transfer of licenses, registrations, sharing/co-using of infrastructure, third-party access and data protection. Regularly advises on the IT side software publishers, hardware manufacturer, system integrators, internet service providers, information providers and customers of IT services. Has spoken at various conferences and published several articles. Speaks German, English and French.
Prof. Memberships: Zurich Bar Association (member, supervisory commission on attorney's fees); Swiss Bar Association; IBA(Vice Chairman committee L, Intellectual Property); AIPPI; Swiss Institute for Industrial Property Law (INGRES); Computer Law Association; Swiss Arbitration Association (ASA); lecturer, postgraduate program intellectual property, Swiss Federal Institute for Technology (ETH) Zurich. Chairman of Softnet Competence Center for IT Law, sponsored by the Federal Government.
Career: University of Zurich (lic. iur., 1984, Dr. iur., 1996); clerk, District Court (1985); Georgetown University Law School, Washington D.C. (LLM, 1992); foreign associate, Pittsburgh USA law firm (1992).
Personal: Born 8 May, 1959; admitted 1989.

SCHÄRER, Heinz
Homburger Rechtsanwälte, Zurich +41 1 265 35 35
heinz.schaerer@homburger.ch
Recommended in Corporate/M&A
Specialisation: Partner in the corporate and M&A practice team of *Homburger Rechtsanwälte*. Main areas of work include M&A, corporate, corporate finance and capital market.
Prof. Memberships: Swiss and Zurich Bar, International Bar Association.
Career: Qualified in 1982. Joined *Homburger Rechtsanwälte* in 1982, became partner in 1988. Board Member of various Swiss companies including Axantis Holding AG.
Personal: Born 1953. Graduated as lic. iur, University of Fribourg in 1977; Dr. iur. from the University of Fribourg in 1981 and received master's degree (MCL) from Southern Methodist University School of Law, Dallas, in 1981. Married with two children.

SCHENKER, Urs
Baker & McKenzie, Geneva +41 22 346 70 70
Recommended in Corporate/M&A
Specialisation: Main area of work is corporate law, principally mergers, acquisitions, new issues, and tender offers in Switzerland. Has handled acquisitions of companies and undertakings by Swiss and overseas clients and acted on various IPOs and tender offers. Has published articles on corporate law and tax issues of such transactions, and spoken at various conferences on the subject.
Prof. Memberships: Bar Association of Zurich.
Career: Educated at the University of Zurich (lic.jur., summa cum laude, 1981; Dr.jur., summa cum laude 1984) and Harvard Law School (LLM, 1985). Joined *Baker & McKenzie* in 1986, becoming a partner in 1991.
Personal: Born 27 September 1957.

SCHNEIDER, Michael
Lalive & Partners, Geneva +41 22 319 8700
meschneider@lalive.ch
Recommended in Arbitration (International)
Specialisation: Partner, International contracts, Government contracts, Construction, International Arbitration, private and public international law.
Prof. Memberships: Executive Board of the Swiss Arbitration Association; Leader of the Forum on Arbitration and New Fields of the ICC Commission on International Arbitration; member of several of the ICC Commission Working Parties, including the one on the Revision of the ICC Arbitration Rules (1995-1997); Chairman of Committee T7 (Construction Disputes) of the International Bar Association / SBL (1996-2000). Member of UNCITRAL Expert Groups; Member of: WIPO Arbitration and Consultative Commission; Scientific Council, Swiss and International Construction Law institute (Fribourg); American Bar Association.
Publications: Author of numerous publications in the areas of arbitration and other forms of dispute settlement, international contracts, public international law.
Career: Admitted to the Bar in Munich, Germany, and authorised to practise as a foreign lawyer in Geneva. Associate and Counsel with *Lalive Budin and Partners*, 1970-1994; in-house Counsel to UNEFICO, Swiss Bank Corporation Consultants Group, 1978-1987; various academic assignments at the Geneva Law School and the Geneva Graduate Institute of International Studies; Director of Studies and Research in International Law and International Relations at the Hague Academy of International Law Academy, (1987 Transnational Arbitration and State Contracts).
Personal: Universities of Munich, Bonn and Geneva; AIESEC trainee, Shell Company, Sierra Leone (1962); Comprehensive doctoral exam, Graduate Institute of International Studies, Geneva (1965-1968).

STEINER, Hans Rudolf E.
Walder Wyss & Partners, 8022 Zurich
+41 1 265 75 11
hrsteiner@wwp.ch
Recommended in Banking & Finance
Specialisation: Banking; finance; securities; corpo-

rate; commercial; arbitration. Regularly advises banks and financial institutions on all aspects of banking, capital markets, and securities. Has regularly contributed to national and international publications in these areas. Has served and serves as member of the board of directors of several banks. Speaks German, French, English, Italian and Spanish.
Prof. Memberships: Zurich Bar Association (board member 1979-1984, chairman 1983-1984); Swiss Bar Association (board member 1986-1992); International Bar Association (IBA; chairman, Committee Q: Issues and Trading of Securities (1993-1996); council member, Section on Business Law (1998); member, committee on globalisation of law (1999)); Swiss Arbitration Association (ASA).
Career: University of Zurich (Dr. iur., 1968); Harvard Law School (LLM, 1971); foreign associate, Boston and New York law firms (1971-1972).
Personal: Born 3 November, 1942; admitted 1970.

STEINMANN, Christian
Bär & Karrer, Zurich +41 1 261 5150
Recommended in Banking & Finance

TERCIER, Pierre
Pierre Tercier – Sole Practitioner, Fribourg +41 26 425 4848
Recommended in Arbitration (International)

THOMANN, Felix
Thomann Fischer, Basel +41 61 226 2424
Recommended in Communications

TSCHÄNI, Rudolf
Lenz & Staehelin, Zurich +41 1 204 1212
rudolf.tschaeni@lenzstaehelin.com
Recommended in Corporate/M&A
Specialisation: Partner in Corporate Department. Main areas of work include general corporate, mergers and acquisitions and public tender offers.
Career: University of Zurich, College of Europe, Harvard Law School. Admitted to the Zurich Bar in 1979 and New York Bar in 1981. Partner of *Lenz & Staehelin* since 1987. Publications in the areas of company law, tax law and European law.

TSCHANZ, Pierre-Yves
Tavernier Tschanz, Geneva +41 22 704 3700
tschanz@ttv.ch
Recommended in Arbitration (International)
Specialisation: International arbitration as counsel and arbitrator. Experienced in approximately 90 cases, including ICC, AAA, ICSID, CCIG, ZCC, ad hoc under UNCITRAL rules and others. Current or recently completed cases include pharmaceutical and technology licensing, construction, joint venture, petroleum.
Prof. Memberships: Swiss Arbitration Association (member of Executive Committee); American Society of International Law; International Bar Association; Geneva Bar Association.
Publications: Co-author with Prof. A. Bucher of treatise 'International Arbitration in Switzerland'. (1989).
Career: Admitted to the Bar of Geneva and the New York Bar. Practised in New York for five years in litigation department of two major law firms; training program of National Institute for Trial Advocacy (NITA). Practised in Paris for three years with a major law firm.
Personal: Born 1952. Married with two children.

VISCHER, Bernard
Schellenberg Wittmer, Geneva 3 +41 22 707 8000
bernard.vischer@swlegal.ch
Recommended in Corporate/M&A
Specialisation: Main areas of work are in corporate law, banking and finance, mergers and acquisitions. Has had conduct of the relocation of company headquarters, and establishment of subsidiaries in Switzerland, especially Geneva, for several multinational companies. Through a network of contacts in the shipping world (particularly in London), is often instructed in banking and finance aspects of shipping and trade matters. Having led an aircraft securitisation and airline acquisition has developed significant experience in aviation law. A regular contributor to the Swiss trade journal 'Banque & Finance'.
Prof. Memberships: Bar Association, Geneva.
Career: From 1990, Partner with *Schellenberg Wittner*. 1983-1989 Associated with *Helg, Picot & Wittmer*, Geneva. 1981-1984, Teaching assistant at the University of Geneva Law School for corporations and banking regulations. 1983 University of Pennsylvania, Law School, LLM 1978-1980 Associated with *Lalive & Budin* in Geneva.
Personal: Born 26 March 1956, attended University of Geneva, Law School.

VISCHER, Markus
Walder Wyss & Partners, 8022 Zurich +41 1 265 75 11
mvischer@wwp.ch
Recommended in Corporate/M&A
Specialisation: Partner. Main area of work is corporate law, principally mergers, acquisitions, business reorganisations and privatisations. Has handled acquisitions of companies and undertakings of varying sorts in Switzerland and abroad by UK, continental, non-continental and Swiss clients. Acted on the acquisition of Corange Holding and its subsidiary Boehringer Mannheim by Roche; advised a French bank in its bid for a majority shareholding in a to-be-privatised Romanian bank. Acted on over thirty M&A transactions in the past two years. Has spoken at various conferences and published several articles.
Prof. Memberships: Zurich and Swiss Bar Associations; International Bar Association (IBA); International Association of Young Lawyers (AIJA); Swiss Arbitration Association (ASA); London Court of International Arbitration (LCIA); Judge (part-time), Zurich Appellate Tax Court (1992-98).
Career: Admitted 1988. Joined *Walder Wyss & Partners*, becoming Partner in 1995. Attended University of Zurich (lic.jur. 1984, Dr. jur. 1986); Research Assistant, University of Zurich (1984-85); Clerk, District Court (1986-87); Trainee, Zurich tax law firm (1988-89); Queen Mary College, London University (LLM 1991).
Personal: Born 26 August 1960.

VOGT, Nedim Peter
Bär & Karrer, Zurich +41 1 261 5150
Recommended in Corporate/M&A

VON PLANTA, Andreas
Lenz & Staehelin, Geneva +41 22 318 70 00
andreas.vonplanta@lenzstaehelin.com
Recommended in Banking & Finance
Specialisation: Partner in Banking and Finance Department. Main areas of work: Mergers and Acquisitions, Banking and Capital Market Law, Capital Market Transactions, Share Issues and Listing, Trade, Corporate and Contract Law, Product Liability.
Publications: Author or co-author of various publications in the field of corporate law, private international law, commercial law.
Career: Born in 1955; Doctor of Law, University of Basle; Columbia University School of Law; Partner since 1988. Languages: German, English, French.

WATTER, Rolf
Bär & Karrer, Zurich +41 1 261 5150
Recommended in Banking & Finance, Corporate/M&A

WEBER, Rolf
Wiederkehr Forster Rechtsanwälte, Zürich +41 1 215 12 12
Recommended in Communications

WEHRLI, Daniel
Gloor & Sieger, Zürich +41 1 254 6161
dwehrli@gloor-sieger.ch
Recommended in Arbitration (International)
Specialisation: International and domestic arbitration, acting as arbitrator (chairman, sole arbitrator and co-arbitrator) in about sixty arbitrations and as counsel in about twenty arbitrations concerning construction law (including infrastructure projects), stock purchase agreements, joint ventures, brokerage and other mandate agreements, purchase and long-term delivery agreements, license and franchise agreements, tooling contracts, loan agreements and investment agreements subject to Swiss, German and Austrian Law and in one case subject to US Law (several cases including the UN-Sale Convention). Advisor in contract law, in particular in the above mentioned areas.
Prof. Memberships: Zurich and Swiss Bar Association, Member of the Executive Committee of ASA (The Swiss Arbitration Association), Member of Committee D (Arbitration and ADR) and T (International Construction Projects) of the International Bar Association, Co-Chairman of the Arbitration Court of the Zurich Chamber of Commerce, Member of DIS (German Institution of Arbitration) and listed Arbitrator of the Swiss – Italian Chamber of Commerce and other institutions.
Career: Internships with banks in Zurich and London during semester holidays (1969-1973). Lic. iur. University of Zurich (1974) and Dr. iur. (1976). Admitted to the bar in 1978. Associate with law firms in Zurich, New York and Rome (1977-1981). Partner with *Mueller, Wehrli & Partners* (1982-1992). Partner with *Gloor & Sieger* (since 1993), Honorary Consul General of the Kingdom of Norway (since 1988).
Personal: Born 1950. Fluent in German, English, Italian and French.

S

WIDMER, Peter
Homburger Rechtsanwälte, Zurich +41 1 265 35 35
peter.widmer@homburger.ch
Recommended in Banking & Finance

Specialisation: Practice concentrates on all aspects of financial markets law. Areas of interest include bank regulatory law, broker-dealer regulation, securities laws and corporate finance and banking litigation. Large litigation cases involve areas outside financial markets, in particular officers', directors', and auditors' liability. Has significant experience in large US-litigation involving European banks.
Prof. Memberships: Zurich and Swiss Bar Associations.
Career: Received bar admission in 1967. Joined *Homburger Rechtsanwälte* as an associate in 1968 and has been a Partner since 1974. At present, the Senior Partner of *Homburger Rechtsanwälte.* Also an alternate judge at the Zurich Court of Cassation, the highest appellate court in the Canton of Zurich in procedural matters.
Personal: Born 1940. Graduated from Zurich University in 1965. Master's degree from the University of Chicago in 1968.

WILLE, Johann
CMS von Erlach Klainguti Stettler Wille, Zurich +41 1 285 1111
h.wille@vonerlach.ch
Recommended in Communications

Specialisation: Mergers and acquisitions, corporate finance, banking law, telecommunications, international tax planning, competition law. Telecommunications clients include Orange Communications SA, Callahan Broadband Wireless Switzerland GmbH, FirstMark Communications Switzerland AG, as well as a number of other international telecommunications companies with a Swiss market presence. Acted on numerous cross-border acquisitions, offering a full range of services, including negotiations, due dilligence, drafting of agreements, regulatory affairs, closing and post-closing measures. Acted on numerous national and international corporate finance transactions, acting for borrowers and lenders.
Prof. Memberships: Zurich and Swiss Bar Association.
Publications: Swiss contribution to 'Handbuch des Vertriebsrechts' (Distribution Law Manual).
Career: Admitted to the bar 1973. Joined *CMS von Erlach Klainguti Stettler Wille* 1976, becoming a partner in 1981.
Personal: Born July 5, 1947. Law degrees from the Law Faculty of the University of Berne (1973) and the University of Michigan Law School, Ann Arbor (1975).

WIRTH, Markus
Homburger Rechtsanwälte, Zurich +41 1 265 35 35
markus.wirth@homburger.ch
Recommended in Arbitration (International)

Specialisation: Partner in the Litigation and Arbitration Practice Team. Main area of work is international arbitration involving cross-border sale and long-term supply contracts, joint ventures and industrial cooperation, mergers and acquisitions, construction and operation of industrial facilities etc. Acted as party counsel in over 40 international arbitrations representing Swiss and foreign companies, foreign governments and state organisations. Acted as chairman, co-arbitrator and sole arbitrator in over 50 international arbitrations.
Prof. Memberships: Memberships: Zurich and Swiss Bar Association, IBA, Swiss Arbitration Association, Chartered Institute of Arbitrators (Fellow).
Publications: Publications Include 'International Arbitration in Switzerland', Kluwer Law International, 2000, Commentary on Art. 188 and 189 Swiss Private International Law Act; 'Interim or Preventive Measures in Support of International Arbitration in Switzerland', ASA Bulletin 2000/1.
Career: Qualified in 1977. Partner of *Homburger Rechtsanwälte* since 1981. Executive Committee Swiss Arbitration Association, Panel of Chairmen Arbitration Court Zurich Chamber of Commerce, Supervisory Board on Attorneys Zurich Court of Appeals.
Personal: Born 1945, graduated lic. iur., and Dr. iur., from University of Zurich (1969/1976), LLM, from University of Toronto (1972). Married, two children. Lives in Zurich and likes outdoor activities.

SYRIA

Corporate/Commercial

SYRIA Leading firms (Corporate/Commercial)
1 Hakim Law Firm
Law Offices of Dr Moustafa Al-Sayed
2 Nahlawi Law Office
Syrian Arab Consultants Law Office

Firms are listed alphabetically in each band.

Leading individuals (Corporate/Commercial)
1 **AL-SAYED Moustafa** *Law Offices of Dr Moustafa Al-Sayed*
EL-HAKIM Jacques *Hakim Law Firm*

Individuals are listed alphabetically in each band.

Hakim Law Firm (2 ptrs, 6 asscs) The firm handles all commercial issues including international contracts, arbitration, foreign investment, IP and the incorporation of foreign companies. Head of the commercial law department at Damascus University, **Jacques el-Hakim** is *"a good international commercial lawyer."* **Clients:** Airlines; industrial companies.

Law Offices of Dr Moustafa Al-Sayed (2 ptrs, 3 asscs) With a former foreign minister as name partner, the firm advises on general commercial matters including incorporation and banking. It provides assistance to joint ventures on their investments in Syria and is known for its *"oil corporation clients."* **Moustafa Al-Sayed** is *"an experienced commercial lawyer"* with *"good contacts."* **Clients:** Telecommunications companies; foreign multinationals.

Nahlawi Law Office (5 ptrs, 5 asscs) A *"good firm with a first rate reputation"* which is felt to focus on civil law, but undertakes corporate and commercial work for its local client base. **Clients:** Damascus Chamber of Commerce.

Syrian Arab Consultants Law Office: (3 ptrs, 3 asscs) A *"good law firm rated for its commercial law practice,"* it executes studies for foreign companies looking to establish a presence in Syria. It has strength in joint ventures, international contracts, stock divisibility, labour, tax, patent and trademark matters. **Clients:** Overseas corporates.

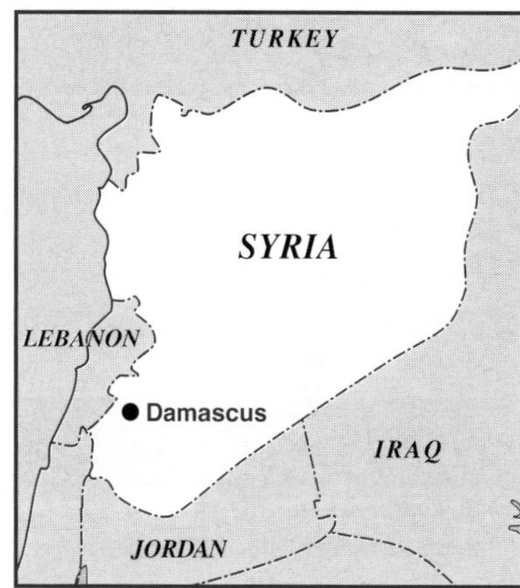

Leaders' profiles – Syria

AL-SAYED, Moustafa
Law Offices of Dr Moustafa Al-Sayed, Damascus +963 11 231 9177

EL-HAKIM, Jacques
Hakim Law Firm, Damascus +963 11 223 3577

TAIWAN

Corporate/Commercial

TAIWAN Leading firms (Corporate/Commercial)
1 Lee and Li
2 Baker & McKenzie
Tsar & Tsai
3 Jones, Day, Reavis & Pogue
4 Formosa Transnational
Perkins & Coie LLP

Firms are listed alphabetically in each band.

Leading individuals (Corporate/Commercial)
1 **HSU Paul** *Lee and Li*
HUANG Remington *Baker & McKenzie*
LIU Lawrence *Lee and Li*
2 **BRYSON William** *Jones, Day, Reavis & Pogue*
HALLOCK Michael *Tsar & Tsai*
HUANG Jack *Jones, Day, Reavis & Pogue*
TSAI Paul *Tsar & Tsai*
3 **CASSINGHAM Paul** *Perkins & Coie LLP*
CHEN John *Formosa Transnational*

Individuals are listed alphabetically in each band.

Lee and Li (7 ptrs, 38 asscs) The country's largest firm, *"the big star on the block,"* provides a *"specialised service"* to its *"wide range of clients."* It undertakes incorporation, joint ventures, foreign investment applications, M&A, securities offerings and infrastructure projects.

"*Bright and engaging speaker*" **Paul Hsu*** is a *"senior statesman"* recommended by competitors as *"careful, smart and able"* while **Lawrence Liu*** displays the firm's *"real corporate strength."* The team acted on behalf of Taiwan Semiconductor Manufacturing in its merger with Worldwide Semiconductor Manufacturing, represented Core Pacific Securities in its merger with Yuanta Securities and acted for Suntory in its acquisition of Country House. **Clients:** Ford; DuPont; IBM; Hewlett-Packard; McDonald's; Sony; Mitsubishi; Siemens; Pfizer; Toshiba; Exxon Mobil; General Instruments.

Baker & McKenzie (6 ptrs, 13 asscs) The firm's presence in Taipei is *"as strong as ever"* and the corporate practice is growing. It represented Illinois Tool Works in a $15 million acquisition of the shares in Tien Tai Electric Co and represented UK Prudential in the $100 million acquisition of Charlton Life Insurance .

"*Careful and conservative*" **Remington Huang*** is responsible for the firm's projects practice and is *"involved in many transactions."* He acted for Evergreen in the $375 million Hsin Tao IPP. **Clients:** Airlines; banks; An Feng Steel; Arsys Technology; EMC; Everfortune Everpower IPP; KLA; Michelin; SmartDisk; 3Com; Lucky Cement.

Tsar & Tsai (12 ptrs, 36 asscs) Highly rated firm, recommended to our researchers for the *"quality of its lawyers and clients."* A large general corporate department handles M&A, infrastructure, construction and power projects. The team advised American and Asian telecom companies on inbound investment. **Michael Hallock*** is a *"good general inbound foreign investment practitioner"* and **Paul Tsai*** is an *"experienced senior lawyer."* **Clients:** Multinationals; banks; financial institutions; local companies; manufacturers.

Jones, Day, Reavis & Pogue (2 ptrs, 13 asscs) Although a smaller Taipei based team, it has an excellent reputation for *"representing Taiwanese companies in outbound investment."* The firm is actively involved in hi-tech M&A transactions, securities work and restructuring. The *"excellent and smart"* **Jack Huang*** has *"good connections with large local concerns"* and **William Bryson*** is an internationally recognised lawyer. The firm

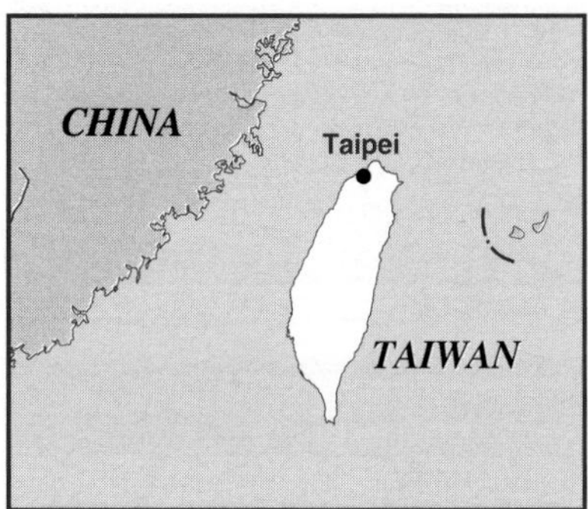

represented kimo.com in its acquisition by Yahoo! and acted for Infoserve in its acquisition by Singapore Telecom. The firm also advises on the establishment of venture capital funds. **Clients:** Yulon Group; Systex; Uni-President Enterprises; Texas Instruments; Citibank.

Formosa Transnational (3 ptrs, 4 asscs) A *"strong local law firm"* with an excellent reputation for litigation. The corporate practice, active in M&A, joint ventures, foreign investment and commercial contracts, handled a major share acquisition for a large Taipei hotel. **John Chen*** is the leading light at this firm. **Clients:** IBM; Dai-Ichi Kangyo Bank; Taiwan Power Company; Central Trust of China; Hitachi; Toyota.

Perkins & Coie LLP (3 ptrs, 3 asscs) *"A growing reputation"* in Taiwan, the firm handles inbound foreign investment, joint venture agreements and infrastructure projects. The *"excellent"* **Paul Cassingham*** is the key player in a team which represented ABN AMRO in the acquisition of the consumer banking service of Bank of America and Kwang Hua Securities Investment and Trust co. It has also been active in telecoms transactions. **Clients:** Yahoo!; ABN AMRO; AT&T.

*See leaders' profiles on pages 667

Leaders' profiles – Taiwan

BRYSON, William E.
Jones, Day, Reavis & Pogue, Taipei
+886 2 2704 6808
webryson@jonesday.com
Specialisation: Extensive experience in international investment, M&A, financing, technology licensing, construction, and other corporate transactions. Has consulted, in conjunction with locally licensed colleagues, on a variety of construction, contracting and other dispute resolution cases in Taiwan. A member of the American Bar Association's Business Law and Litigation Section and is a proctor member of the Maritime Law Association of the United States, where also serves on the Marine Finance Committee.
Prof. Memberships: American Chamber of Commerce in Taipei, currently serving as first vice president and on the chamber's board of governors. Also managing chair of the chamber's Capital Markets Committee and chair of the Publications Policy Committee. Active in the chamber's lobbying efforts with both the ROC and US governments and is an advisor to the chamber's annual Taiwan White Paper.
Career: Taipei partner. Admitted 1984 in Illinois, and 1988 in New York. Joined the firm in 1999. Educated at Duke University (BA cum laude, 1980) and Tulane University (JD magna cum laude, 1984). Law Clerk to Judge Thomas R. McMillen, United States District Court, Northern District of Illinois (1984-85). Prior to joining *Jones Day* was a senior consultant in another law firm in Taipei for several years, and before that, was an associate lawyer at a New York maritime law firm from 1985-88, specialising in maritime finance matters.

CASSINGHAM, Paul
Perkins & Coie LLP, Taipei +886 2 2778 1177

CHEN, John
Formosa Transnational, Taipei +886 2 2755 7366

HALLOCK, Michael
Tsar & Tsai, Taipei +886 2 2781 4111

HSU, Paul
Lee and Li, Taipei 105 +886 2 2715 3300

HUANG, Jack J.T.
Jones, Day, Reavis & Pogue, Taipei
+886 2 2704 6808
jhuang@jonesday.com
Specialisation: Partner-in-charge of Taipei Office and Chairman of the Firm's Greater China Practice. Main area of work is corporate law, principally mergers, acquisitions, corporate finance and securities offerings, infrastructure projects and technology transactions. Has represented numerous major U.S, European and Asian industrial and high-tech companies, investment banks and venture capital firms in such transactions in the US and Asia.
Prof. Memberships: Taipei Bar Association, American Bar Association, and the Association of the Bar of the City of New York.
Career: Qualified in Taipei in 1976 and in New York in 1983. Joined *Lee and Li* in Taipei in 1977-78, *Coudert Brothers* in Hong Kong in 1979-1980 and then in New York in 1983 - 1986. Joined *Jones, Day, Reavis and Pogue* in New York in 1986, becoming a partner in January 1990 and opening the Taipei office in July 1990.
Personal: Born October 11 1952. Attended National Taiwan University (LLB with distinction, 1975), Northwestern University (LLM, 1979), and Harvard University Law School (SJD 1983); served in various capacities in many civic and charitable organisations. Leisure interests include reading, music, travel, tennis and golf.

HUANG, Remington
Baker & McKenzie, Taipei +886 2 2715 7232
remington.huang@bakernet.com
Specialisation: Major construction projects and litigation, principally transportation infrastructure projects, independent power plants, incinerators, as well as construction related disputes. Acted on Taiwan High Speed Railway, CKS International Airport-Taipei Mass Rapid Transport Project, Ho-Ping and Ever Power IPP Projects, and various incinerator projects. Handled various significant litigation and arbitration for multinational companies.
Prof. Memberships: Tapei Bar Association; National Bar Association of the Republic of China; and Taiwan Law Society.
Career: Holds both a Bachelor of Laws and Master of Laws from the National Taiwan University. Qualified in 1978. Joined *Baker & McKenzie* in 1982. Spent two years on the *Baker & McKenzie* Associate Training Program in Frankfurt, Germany. Elected as a partner of *Baker & McKenzie* in 1992. Elected as President of Taipei Bar Association in 2000. Law school lecturer on 'Legal Ethics'. Has spoken at various conferences.
Personal: Married with 3 children. Leisure activities include mountain climbing and reading.

LIU, Lawrence
Lee and Li, Taipei 105 +886 2 2715 3300

TSAI, Paul
Tsar & Tsai, Taipei +886 2 2781 4111

T

TANZANIA

Corporate/Commercial

TANZANIA Leading firms (Corporate/Commercial)
1 Mkono & Co
2 Ishengoma, Masha, Mujulizi & Magai Advocates
Maajar, Rwechungura, Kameja & Nguluma
3 Sinare, Shiyo & Mwandambo Advocates

Firms are listed alphabetically in each band.

Leading individuals (Corporate/Commercial)
1 **KAPINGA Wilbert** *Mkono & Co*
2 **ISHENGOMA Protase** *Ishengoma, Masha*
MAAJAR Mwanaidi *Maajar, Rwechungura*
MKONO Nimrod *Mkono & Co*
3 **SINARE Hawa** *Sinare, Shiyo & Mwandambo*

Individuals are listed alphabetically in each band.

Mkono & Co (6 ptrs, 8 asscs) *"Far and away the best firm in Tanzania,"* the firm's lead has been consolidated this year by a newly-formed association with UK firm Denton Wilde Sapte, bringing them an increased number of international clients and access to the latest technology. Advising clients from a broad range of industries, the firm is active in all areas of commercial law, and is considered to have particular expertise in privatisation and company formation. The well-connected **Nimrod Mkono*** is considered to be *"one of the most influential rainmakers in town,"* and the firm also boasts the services of **Wilbert Kapinga*** who has become the *"point of reference for M&A transactions."* **Clients:** Domestic and international corporates.

Ishengoma, Masha, Mujulizi & Magai Advocates (5 ptrs, 4 asscs) Clients consider this growing firm to be *"a responsive and sophisticated operation."* **Protase Ishengoma*** is a leading name at the firm, particularly respected for his work on corporate restructurings. The firm's clientele is drawn from domestic and international companies, particularly in banking and mining, and the department has also had experience of advising industry and government institutions, most recently winning the tender for the privatisation of utilities from the government. **Clients:** Financial institutions; mining companies.

Maajar, Rwechungura, Kameja, Nguluma (3 ptrs, 3 asscs) A long established operation that is part of the Lex Africa network. The firm is noted for expertise in mining finance work and privatisations, acting on behalf of a predominantly international client base. **Mwanaidi Maajar*** is regarded as *"one of the country's leading lawyers."* **Clients:** International mining companies; domestic and foreign banks.

Sinare, Shiyo & Mwandambo Advocates (3 ptrs) A small practice dealing exclusively with corporate and commercial work. In the past year, the client base has increased, with the banking portfolio now including 60% of the banks in Tanzania. The firm is active in all areas of commercial law, with domestic and international clients drawn mainly from the financial and mining sectors. **Hawa Sinare*** is the stand-out practitioner here. Represented HSBC Equator (USA) as advisors to the Tanzanian Government in the proposed privatisation of six major hotels. **Clients:** HSBC Equator (USA) Inc; HSBC; Citibank Tanzania Ltd; Commonwealth Development Corporation.

*See leaders' profiles on pages 669

Leaders' profiles – Tanzania

ISHENGOMA, Protase Rwenzahura
Ishengoma, Masha, Mujulizi & Magai Advocates, Dar Es Salaam +22 212 0469

KAPINGA, Wilbert
Mkono & Co, Dar Es Salaam +255 22 211 8790 Wilbert.Kapinga@mkono.com
Specialisation: Corporate restructuring and parastatal reorganisation; mergers and acquisitions; telecommunications law particularly telecom licenses and interconnection agreements; employment and labour law; commercial litigation and arbitration; environmental law; energy and minerals; regulatory and anti-trust law.
Prof. Memberships: Tanganyika Law Society; East Africa Law Society. Law Association of Tanzania; International Third World Legal Studies Association. African Society of International and Comparative Law.
Career: Partner, *Mkono & Co*, Advocates since 1997. Formerly Dean of the Faculty of Law and Senior Lecturer in Law, University of Dar es Salaam. Associate, *Mkono & Co*, Advocates since 1989; Advocate, High Court of Tanzania since 1986; Teaching/Research Staff, Faculty of Law, University of Dar es Salaam 1982-97. Apprenticed as State Attorney, Attorney General's chambers, 1981. 1981, University of Dar es Salaam, LLB (Hons.); 1985, University of Dar es Salaam, LLM; 1991, Columbia University, Law School, New York, LLM; 1995, North Eastern University, Boston, PhD.
Personal: Born 1954 Mbinga, Tanzania.

MAAJAR, Mwanaidi
Maajar, Rwechungura, Kameja Nguluma, Dar Es Salaam +255 22 211 4291/899/213 7191

MKONO, Nimrod Elireheemah
Mkono & Co, Dar Es Salaam +255 22 211 8790/211 4664 Nimrod.Mkono@mkono.com
Specialisation: Main areas of practice are international commercial arbitration, banking, corporate restructuring and finance, commercial litigation, insolvencies, mergers & acquisitions, privatisation/divestitures, debt-conversions & rescheduling and corporate taxation. Has handled numerous consortium arrangements, leading a variety of consortia in bids for various acquisitions including the National Bank of Commerce and the Tanzania Telecommunications Company Limited.
Prof. Memberships: F.C.I.S., (UK) Tanganyika Law Society; East Africa Law Society; Zanzibar Law Society; TerraLex.
Career: Managing Partner, *Mkono & Co*, Advocates. Company Secretary and Legal Advisor to Tanzania Development Finance Company Limited (TDFL), Resident Magistrate, Civil and Criminal Jurisdiction. LLB, University of East Africa, University College of Dar es Salaam, 1970. Chartered Secretaryship Final Examination (C.I.S.) South West London College, 1975. MA (Bus.Law), Council for National Academic Awards, City of London Polytechnic, 1976. Honours Honorary Legal Counsel to the British High Commissioner and The Royal Swedish Ambassador.
Personal: Born Musoma, Tanzania, 1943.

SINARE, Hawa
Sinare, Shiyo & Mwandambo Advocates, Dar es Salaam +255 22 211 32 03

T

THAILAND

Banking & Finance

THAILAND Leading firms (Banking & Finance)
1 Baker & McKenzie
Freshfields Bruckhaus Deringer
Johnson Stokes & Master
Linklaters
2 Allen & Overy
Chandler & Thong-ek Law Offices
Clifford Chance Wirot
White & Case LLP
3 International Legal Counsellors Thailand
Siam Premier International Law Office Ltd

Firms are listed alphabetically in each band.

Leading individuals (Banking & Finance)
1 CHANDLER Albert *Chandler & Thong-ek*
LAWDEN James *Freshfields Bruckhaus Deringer*
MILLER Stephen *Johnson Stokes & Master*
VAJASIT Surasak *Freshfields Bruckhaus Deringer*
2 CHINSANGARAM Chinnavat *White & Case LLP*
DUNN Charles *Linklaters*
JEFFARES Tim *Clifford Chance Wirot*
OKANURAK Wilailuk *Linklaters*
SETHSATHIRA Pises *Allen & Overy*
SETHSATHIRA Sawanee *Baker & McKenzie*
3 BUKHAMANA Thinawat *Baker & McKenzie*

Individuals are listed alphabetically in each band.

Baker & McKenzie (19 ptrs, 27 asscs) By far the largest firm in Bangkok, this is a fundamentally Thai practice with 90% local lawyers, although our researchers were told that the department enjoys a *"solid relationship with both local and international clients."* **Sawanee Sethsathira*** currently heads the banking and finance group of the Bangkok office, and has had vast experience in working for a number of financial institutions and multinational companies on project financing of power, petrochemical, steel infrastructure and transportation projects. **Thinawat Bukhamana*** is also recommended by peers.

The firm has worked for TelecomAsia in restructuring debt against major Japanese and German telecommunication suppliers and contractors, and provided legal advice in the establishment of an asset management company to manage the non-performing loans for Sukhumvit AMC Company. **Clients:** NPC Power; TelecomAsia Corporation; Siam City Cement; Sukhumvit AMC; Effective Planner.

Freshfields Bruckhaus Deringer (4 ptrs, 10 asscs) Renowned for its banking and finance department in Thailand, the firm was particularly commended to researchers for its prowess in syndicated loans and project finance. **James Lawden*** is said by peers to *"lead from the front,"* while **Surasak Vajasit*** is respected for his bankruptcy and project finance expertise.

The firm acted for Lehman Brothers on the purchase of a distressed loan portfolio from DBS Thai Danu Bank, worth $150 million. This was the first sale of assets by a Thai bank for the purpose of clearing non-performing loans. The team also advised ABN AMRO as arrangers of Bht20 billion of syndicated facilities for Total Access Communication. **Clients:** DBS; ABN AMRO.

Johnson Stokes & Master(6ptrs, 5 asscs) Known for its regional banking expertise, the firm has been involved in several purchases of local banks by Hong Kong financial institutions. **Steve Miller*** has been devoted to the TPI restructuring case for over two years, and was recommended to researchers for his *"consistently sound advice."* **Clients:** Regional corporates and financial institutions.

Linklaters (3 ptrs) Advising on the corporate restructuring work and project financing that has been available in Thailand, the firm is noted for its powerful international banking client base. Led by *"strong finance lawyer"* **Charles Dunn***, the team has advised Chase Manhattan and Sakura Bank on their purchases of distressed debt, and acted for Goldman Sachs and GE Capital on their loan portfolios. *"Self-confident, positive and forthright"* **Wilailuk Okanurak*** also receives a high degree of market recommendation. **Clients:** Chase Manhattan; Goldman Sachs; GE Capital.

Allen & Overy (3 ptrs, 18 asscs) The team profits from the firm's powerful regional network, and advises an international clientele on e-banking, syndicated loans and project finance. Securities specialist **Pises Sethsathira*** is highly respected

by his peers. The firm represented Phillip Securities (Thailand) plc on drafting the first on-line Thai securities trading account agreement in Thailand. **Clients:** Phillip Securities (Thailand); Navis Capital.

Chandler & Thong-ek Law Offices (3 ptrs, 4 asscs) Best known for its banking and finance department, the firm has a strong reputation for syndicated loans, project financing and restructuring loans. The team has represented lenders on restructuring loans to 13 corporate debtors, including Telecom Holding. With 30 years of experience under his belt, **Al Chandler*** was recommended to researchers as one of the country's leading banking lawyers. The firm has advised Standard Chartered Bank on drafting routine bank loan agreements, and acted as lenders' counsel on the Ratchaburi generating project. **Clients:** Standard Chartered Bank; Thai financial institutions; Thai government.

Clifford Chance Wirot (3 ptrs, 8 asscs) Clients perceive the firm to be a market leader in the area of corporate restructuring, while the team also has extensive experience of asset finance and syndicated loans. **Tim Jeffares***, joint managing partner of the office, is well known locally for his banking expertise. The firm advised the creditors' committee on the $1.3 billion restructuring of TPI Polene, and represented US Exim and ECGD on the $550 million lease financing for five Boeing 747 and 777 aircraft. **Clients:** Wireless Communication Services; United Overseas Bank of Singapore; Biman Corporation; BPB plc; Siam City Cement; Lombard Investment; IFC.

White & Case LLP (3 ptrs, 10 asscs) Respected for its debt restructuring advice, this growing team represents a varied clientele of international corporates and financial institutions. The firm represented Ciments Français on its recent acquisition and restructuring of Jalaprathan Cement Public Company Ltd. This was the first deal to be successfully completed under the Thai government's new corporate debt restructuring programme. Competitors regard **Chinnavat Chinsangaram*** as a *"sensible and effective finance lawyer."* The office represented the creditors of a Thai subsidiary of a Scandinavian car manufacturer on its proposed debt restructuring. Also advised the Thai manufacturing and distribution agent for a German automobile company on the restructuring of its debt. **Clients:** Thai Mui Group; Sahaviriya Steel Industries; Securities One; Quality House; Property Perfect; US Exim Bank.

International Legal Counsellors Thailand Despite the rise of international firms in Thailand, this team retains *"a substantial market presence."* It advises banks, finance companies and insurance companies on banking regulatory matters, and has acted on several international loans.

The firm represented syndicates of Japanese banks in connection with loans to the Royal Thai government, has assisted on the drafting of multicurrency loans, and has advised on a variety of innovative financing instruments. Highlight transactions include advising on Thai legal aspects of the global mergers of the Bank of Tokyo with Mitsubishi Bank and Chemical Bank with Chase Manhattan. **Clients:** Rayong Power Plants; Thai government.

Siam Premier International Law Office Ltd (4 ptrs, 10 asscs) Independent firm, recommended to researchers as an *"up and coming"* force in banking and finance. The firm acted as Thai counsel for the Boeing Company on the termination of interim financing arrangements for five aircraft. Acted for banks on the successful debt and corporate restructuring of City Realty, and advised Ch Karnchang on issues of debentures secured against shares and bank accounts by way of private placement. Clients: Bank of Thailand; Sansiri; Bangkok Bank; SG Asia Credit; DBS; United Overseas Bank; Meiji Life; Goldman Sachs; Boeing Company; City Realty; Ch Karnchang.

T

Corporate/M&A

THAILAND
Leading firms
(Corporate/Mergers & Acquisitions)

Band	Firm
1	Baker & McKenzie
2	Freshfields Bruckhaus Deringer
	Linklaters
	White & Case LLP
3	Allen & Overy
	Chandler & Thong-ek Law Offices
	Clifford Chance Wirot
	International Legal Counsellors Thailand
4	Johnson Stokes & Master
	Siam Premier International Law Office Ltd

Firms are listed alphabetically in each band.

Baker & McKenzie (13 ptrs, 13 asscs) Known as *"one of the best offices in the B&M franchise,"* the Bangkok team enjoys *"a solid reputation with local and international clients."* Particularly strong in the financial services sector, the firm was widely applauded to researchers for its work on cross-border M&A and corporate restructuring.

The *"easy-going"* **Kitipong Urapeepatanapong*** enjoys *"good relationships with the Thai business community,"* and is described by competitors as *"a lawyer who takes good care of his clients."* **John Hancock***, while less involved in transactional matters, is well known as *"a rainmaker who brings a lot of corporate work."* The firm advised on the acquisition of shares in a Thai agro-industrial company for a US food industrial group, and acted on the acquisition of an ice cream manufacturer by a Singapore food company. **Clients:** Thai Farmers Bank; Merrill Lynch; DBS; BG Thailand Ltd; Teledisc.

Freshfields Bruckhaus Deringer (3 ptrs, 10 asscs) Despite being a firm that has *"more of a reputation for finance in Thailand,"* its corporate team remains an active presence, advising a high-powered international client base on a wide range of big-ticket M&A and privatisation matters. **James Lawden***, respected by clients for his *"detailed and commercial mind,"* has four years experience in Thailand.

The firm advised Ciments Français on its acquisition of a controlling interest in Asia Cement, worth $300 million and acted for Colas SA on its acquisition of a strategic stake in TIPCO Asphalt. Also represented the underwriters on the offering of shares in Ratchaburi Electricity Generating Holding, and acted for UK Orange on a strategic investment in a wireless communication service worth $350 million. **Clients:** Ciments Français; Colas SA; Telstra; Hewlett-Packard; ICI; Usha Martin.

Linklaters (2 ptrs, 7 asscs) Acknowledged by some commentators as *"top for big deals,"* the firm has enjoyed a successful year, advising a predominantly international clientele on its investments in Thailand. The group was especially commended to researchers for its prowess in the telecoms industry.

Chris King*, who heads the office, is *"knowledgeable and easy to deal with."* Considered by competitors to be *"a safe pair of hands,"* he has vast experience of the Thai legal market. The firm advised Singapore Telecommunications on its acquisition of a 20% interest in the sole operator of GSM mobile phones in Thailand and of 30% of the new shares in PointAsia.com. Also advised Groupe Casino on its acquisition of a substantial shareholding in Big C Supercenter. **Clients:** Groupe Casino; Singapore Telecommunications.

White & Case LLP (3 ptrs, 10 asscs) One of the most rapidly expanding firms in Bangkok, it has been *"hiring aggressively"* and is regarded by its rivals as *"serious competition."* The firm's recent merger with Thai firm Nopadoll & Khaisri has added further critical mass and local expertise to the office. Noted for advising on international M&A and corporate restructuring, the firm has a notably strong clientele of telecoms companies and financial institutions. *"Clever and shrewd"* **Weerawong Chittmittrapap***, formerly of Baker & McKenzie, is considered by some clients to be *"far and away the best Thai corporate lawyer."*

The firm advised Credit Suisse First Boston on the purchase of convertible preference shares and warrants in Malee Sampran Factory. Another major transaction was advising UCOM and its subsidiary TAC on Telenor's investments in the com-

*See leaders' profiles on pages 673-674

THAILAND Leading individuals (Corporate/Mergers & Acquisitions)
1
BUNNAG Jayavadh *International Legal*
CHITTMITTRAPAP Weerawong *White & Case LLP*
KING Christopher *Linklaters*
LAWDEN James *Freshfields Bruckhaus Deringer*
URAPEEPATANAPONG Kitipong *Baker & McKenzie*
2
HANCOCK John *Baker & McKenzie*
LEERABANDHU Rashane *Clifford Chance Wirot*
MAKINSON Simon *Allen & Overy*
MILLER Thomas *Siam Premier International*
POONSUWAN Wirot *Clifford Chance Wirot*
3
POONSOMBUDLERT Ratana *Chandler & Thong-ek*
PRICE Harvey *Deacons*
SAHACHAIYUNTA Pradit *International Legal*
SUBPAISARN Dumnern *Allen & Overy*
WESKOSITH Nipaporn *Johnson Stokes & Master*
Individuals are listed alphabetically in each band.

panies. This deal constituted the largest foreign private investment in Thailand to date. **Clients:** UCOM; Credit Suisse First Boston; Digital Phone Corp; Sahaviriya Steel Industries; Quality House.

Allen & Overy (3 ptrs, 18 asscs) Following its merger with MPS & Associates in 1998, the firm enjoys *"a strong local base on top of the quality one expects from them."* Recommended for strength in financial services, the firm is a familiar player on cross-border M&A deals.

Simon Makinson* is respected by peers as an *"impressive commercial lawyer"* while, newly arrived from ILCT, **Dumnern Subpaisarn*** maintains his share of market approval. The firm represented Navis Capital on the acquisition of a listed company in Thailand, and advised M-Web on the acquisition of KSC. **Clients:** Navis Capital; M Webb.

Chandler & Thong-ek Law Offices (5 ptrs, 16 asscs) Although the arrival of major foreign firms has altered the firm's once impregnable position in Thailand, the corporate team retains a respected position, handling company registration, M&A, reorganisations and liquidations. The firm's client base includes more than 200 Thai limited companies. **Ratana Poonsombudlert***, although a relatively young commercial lawyer, is considered to have *"unlimited potential."* The firm advised on the acquisition of 26% of Thaioil Power by PTTEP and the acquisition of BPE by NPC. **Clients:** Petroleum Authority of Thailand; Thai financial institutions; Thai government.

Clifford Chance Wirot (3 ptrs 11 asscs) The firm's merger with Wirot International appears to have *"bedded down satisfactorily,"* in the words of one rival. The corporate team is involved in corporate restructuring and substantial cross-border M&A work, advising regional and international clients. Finance and telecoms are notable areas of strength.

Wirot Poonsuwan* is said to be *"a clever and tenacious M&A specialist,"* although researchers noted that his *"aggressive style"* did not meet with unanimous market approval. Although adopting a lower profile, **Rashane Leerabandhu*** *"really stands out,"* according to clients. The firm advised on the corporate restructuring and subsequent sale of Wireless Communication Services. Other work includes the purchase of Radanasin Bank for United Overseas Bank of Singapore, and the privatisation of Bangladesh Airlines for Biman Corporation. **Clients:** Wireless Communication Services; United Overseas Bank of Singapore; Biman Corporation; BPB; Siam City Cement; Lombard Investment; IFC.

International Legal Counsellors Thailand *"The firm 30 years ago,"* it continues to be recommended to our researchers for its privatisation and domestic M&A expertise. However, the departure of talented lawyers to overseas firms continues; the team recently lost the services of Dumnern Subpaisarn to Allen & Overy.

Pradit Sahachaiyunta* is a *"capable and client-friendly commercial lawyer,"* while competitors regard **Jayavadh Bunnag*** as a *"vintage front line"* corporate player. The firm handled the privatisation of the Rayong Power Plants and represented the Rayong Power Plants in the Hopewell Project. **Clients:** Rayong Power Plants; Thai Telephone and Telecommunications.

Johnson Stokes & Master (3 ptrs, 10 asscs) Hong-Kong-based firm which has acknowledged corporate restructuring expertise, although it remains a low-profile M&A presence in Thailand. **Nipaporn Weskosith*** was recommended to researchers as a *"corporate expert,"* and heads a team which advised on the debt restructuring of TPI. **Clients:** Local and regional corporates.

Siam Premier International Law Office Ltd (4 ptrs, 9 asscs) *"Modest sized local firm"* with a fine reputation for litigation, and a corporate team that rivals see as a *"quality operation."* **Thomas Miller*** is a *"workmanlike lawyer"* with a *"good, honest reputation."* The firm acted for the Bank of Thailand on the sale of Radanatun Finance, and for Sansiri, a subsidiary of the Starwood Corporation, on the acquisition of a 25% stake in the Starwood Thailand Mutual Fund. **Clients:** Bank of Thailand; Sansiri; Bangkok Bank; SG Asia Credit; DBS; United Overseas Bank; Meiji Life; Goldman Sachs.

Other Notable Practitioner **Harvey Price*** of Deacons is a well-known corporate figure in Thailand and is commended by competitors for his *"technical competence."*

*See leaders' profiles on pages 673-674

Leaders' profiles – Thailand

BUKHAMANA, Thinawat
Baker & McKenzie, Bangkok +66 2 636 2000
thinawat.bukhamana@bakernet.com
Recommended in Banking & Finance
Specialisation: International Partner of *Baker & McKenzie* in Bangkok and the head of its Banking and Finance Practice Group. Main practice areas include loans, secured financing, project financing, financial products and derivatives, debt restructuring and banking regulations. Representation of owners and lenders in various project financings, including telecommunication (2.6 million Bangkok telephone lines project), petrochemical plants, and hotel projects. Also representing commercial banks and debtors in debt restructuring transactions involving telecommunication, pipelines, real estate and agricultural projects. Acting for foreign banks in mergers and in acquiring branches in Thailand. Acting for International Swaps & Derivatives Association Inc (ISDA) in relation to ISDA Master Agreement and British Bankers' Association in connection with IFEMA, ICOM, and FEOMA in Thailand.
Prof. Memberships: Thai Bar Association and the Law Society of Thailand.
Publications: Author of Pacific Basin Legal Developments Bulletin articles (January 1991).
Career: Joined *Baker & McKenzie* in 1989 and became an international partner in 1999. Lecturer at various universities on financial and business law and a frequent speaker at local and regional seminars.
Personal: Born 1963, Bangkok, Thailand. Chulalongkorn University (LLB, 1985); Southern Methodist University (LLM in International and Comparative Laws, 1989).

BUNNAG, Jayavadh
International Legal Counsellors Thailand, Bangkok +662 679 6005
Recommended in Corporate/M&A

CHANDLER, Albert
Chandler & Thong-ek Law Offices, Bangkok +66 2 266 6485
Recommended in Banking & Finance

CHINSANGARAM, Chinnavat
White & Case (Thailand) Limited, Bangkok +662 656 1721 to 32
cchinsangaram@whitecase.com
Recommended in Banking & Finance
Specialisation: Partner of *White & Case* (Thailand), specialising in corporate restructurings, banking, mergers and acquisitions, joint ventures, foreign investment, aviation and maritime practices.
Prof. Memberships: Member of the Thai Bar Council; (admitted 1983) The Law Society of Thailand and Asia Pacific Lawyers Association.
Career: LLB, Chulalongkorn University 1981; Barrister-at-law The Institute of Legal Education, Thai Bar Association 1983; MCL University of Miami 1985; LLM, in Admiralty, Tulane University 1986. Joined *White & Case* in 1996 and became partner in 1999.

CHITTMITTRAPAP, Weerawong
White & Case (Thailand) Limited, Bangkok +662 656 1721 to 32
Recommended in Corporate/M&A

DUNN, Charles
Linklaters (a member firm of Linklaters & Alliance), Bangkok +662 305 8000
charles.dunn@linklaters.com
Recommended in Banking & Finance
Specialisation: Projects and Asset Finance, particularly project financing, commercial contracts and asset finance. Involved in a number of power station projects in the UK and India. Financing and refinancing experience. Expertise also encompasses aircraft leases, the Orange PCN network, acquisition of North Sea Oil Fields, acting for banks on the building of exhibition and sports facilities, UK tax-based financing of Italian hotels, flotation of oil tanker companies, and acting for sponsors on a variety of projects for example the design, build, financing and operation of information system infrastructures and the take over, operation and maintenance of the power delivery system of London Underground Ltd. Currently very active on a number of workout and debt restructuring transactions in Thailand.
Publications: Published 'Current legal issues on the structuring of acquisition as divestiture transaction in Thailand', delivered at a Bangkok conference on Energy Asset Divestitures and Acquisitions.

HANCOCK, John
Baker & McKenzie, Bangkok +66 2 636 2000
john.w.hancock@bakernet.com
Recommended in Corporate/M&A
Specialisation: With over 25 years of practice in Thailand, has been involved in the planning, negotiation, completion (and related financing and tax planning aspects) of a significant number of major acquisitions and major projects in Thailand, in a wide range of industries. Heads the major projects group, and is also focused on and manages a broad range of clients in servicing the general corporate legal and local aspects of their investments in Thailand. Various publications and speeches.
Prof. Memberships: Law Society of South Australia; Law Society of Victoria.
Career: Attended University of Adelaide, St Marks College (LLB, 1969). Admitted in South Australia in 1970 and Victoria in 1982; permitted as a Legal Advisor in Thailand. Joined *Baker & McKenzie* in 1975 and became an international partner in 1978. Established the Bangkok office of *Baker & McKenzie* in 1977 and is currently the Chairman. Has also worked in the New York, Hong Kong and Singapore offices of *Baker & McKenzie*. Member of the International Management Committee of *Baker & McKenzie* (1993-1995); Chairman of *Baker & McKenzie Asia/Pacific* (1994-1995); and Chairman of the International Firm Policy Committee of *Baker & McKenzie* (1995-1997); and currently Chairman of the Nominating Committee. International Chamber of Commerce (Member of Thailand National Committe and Chairman of the Commission on Competition Law); American, Australian (former President), British and German Chambers of Commerce in Thailand.
Personal: Born 15 June 1946, Adelaide, South Australia. Governor Thai Country Club. Leisure interests include trekking, sailing and golf. Lives in Bangkok, Thailand.

JEFFARES, Tim
Clifford Chance Wirot, Bangkok +66 2 263 2250
Recommended in Banking & Finance

KING, Christopher
Linklaters (a member firm of Linklaters & Alliance), Bangkok +662 305 8000
christopher.king@linklaters.com
Recommended in Corporate/M&A
Specialisation: Main practice areas include debt restructuring, securities, mergers and acquisitions, banking, privatisations, project finance and general corporate matters, representing many major Thai and international finance institutions, industrial companies and project developers. These have included Kumagai Gumi in connection with the US$2 billion Phase 1 Second Stage Expressway Project in Bangkok, Merrill Lynch on the US$68 million acquisition of controlling interest in Phatra Securities Co Ltd, Thai Petrochemical Industry plc and affiliates on the development and financing of US$5 billion petrochemical and cement complexes, and Goldman Sachs and GE Capital Corporation on their joint bids for automobile contracts and commercial loans auctioned by Thailand's Financial Sector Restructuring Authority.
Career: Managing Partner of Bangkok office.

LAWDEN, James
Freshfields Bruckhaus Deringer, Bangkok +66 2 344 9200
james.lawden@freshfields.com
Recommended in Banking & Finance, Corporate/M&A
Specialisation: Main areas of practice include restructurings, mergers and acquisitions, banking and project finance, business law, derivatives, investments, capital markets and securitisation.

LEERABANDHU, Rashane
Clifford Chance Wirot, Bangkok +66 2 263 2250
Recommended in Corporate/M&A

MAKINSON, Simon
Allen & Overy, Bangkok +662 263 7600
Recommended in Corporate/M&A

MILLER, Stephen
Johnson Stokes & Master, Bangkok +66 2 638 0880
Recommended in Banking & Finance

MILLER, Thomas
Siam Premier International Law Office Ltd, Bangkok +66 2 679 1333
Recommended in Corporate/M&A

OKANURAK, Wilailuk
Linklaters (a member firm of Linklaters & Alliance), Bangkok +662 305 8000
wilailuk.okanurak@linklaters.com
Recommended in Banking & Finance
Specialisation: Project finance, restructuring and commercial contracts with extensive works on power, transport and telecommunications projects under government concessions or agreements with state enterprises. Involved, in 1999, in a number of debt restructuring and project finance transactions.

POONSOMBUDLERT, Ratana
Chandler & Thong-ek Law Offices, Bangkok +66 2 266 6485
Recommended in Corporate/M&A

POONSUWAN, Wirot
Clifford Chance Wirot, Bangkok +66 2 263 2250
Recommended in Corporate/M&A

PRICE, Harvey
Deacons, Bangkok 10120 +66 2 679 1844
Recommended in Corporate/M&A

SAHACHAIYUNTA, Pradit
International Legal Counsellors Thailand, Bangkok +662 679 6005
pradits@mail.ilct.co.th
Recommended in Corporate/M&A
Specialisation: Securities, banking, corporate/project finance, corporate recovery, mergers & acquisitions.
Prof. Memberships: Thai Bar Association, Thai Lawyers Association, Honorable Society of Gray's Inn.
Personal: Ramkhamhaeng University (LLB 1974). Institute of Legal Education, Thailand (Barrister-at-Law, 1975). University of London (LLB Hons. 1984). Institute of Legal Education, London (Barrister-at-Law Hons., Gray's Inn 1985).

SETHSATHIRA, Pises
Allen & Overy, Bangkok +662 263 7600
Recommended in Banking & Finance

SETHSATHIRA, Sawanee
Baker & McKenzie, Bangkok +66 2 636 2000
sawanee.sethsathira@bakernet.com
Recommended in Banking & Finance
Specialisation: Responsible for the banking and finance, debt restructuring and power practice groups. During 15 years of practice, has had vast experience working for a variety of financial institutions as well as borrowers, particularly on project financing (for example power, petrochemical, steel, infrastructure and transportation projects) and debt restructuring. Has also participated in a leadership role in a number of debt restructuring cases.
Prof. Memberships: International Bar Association; Thai Bar Association; and The Law Society of Thailand.
Career: Joined *Baker & McKenzie* in 1983 and became an international partner in 1992. Has also worked in the Sydney and Melbourne offices.
Personal: Born 1959, Bangkok, Thailand. Chulalongkorn University (LLB, Honours, 1981); and Cornell Law School (LLM, 1983).

SUBPAISARN, Dumnern
Allen & Overy, Bangkok +662 263 7600
Recommended in Corporate/M&A

URAPEEPATANAPONG, Kitipong
Baker & McKenzie, Bangkok +66 2 636 2000
kitipong.urapeepatanapong@bakernet.com
Recommended in Corporate/M&A
Specialisation: Head of the capital markets and securitisation, corporate and debt restructuring, and tax practice groups. Has extensive experience with tax planning and providing legal advice in respect of mergers and acquisitions, capital markets and securitisation, and corporate and debt restructuring. Deals include the workout and debt restructuring of Thai Petrochemical Public Company Limited, one of the biggest debt restructuring transactions in Thailand, and the restructuring of various other listed companies. Has also acted for Thai commercial banks in recapitalisations and has extensive experience with mergers and acquisitions involving both financial institutions and manufacturing and trading companies.
Prof. Memberships: Thai Bar Association; The Law Society of Thailand; and The International Bar Association.
Career: Joined *Baker & McKenzie* in 1978 and became International Partner in 1990. Has also worked in the firm's Singapore and Toronto offices. Author of numerous books and articles on Thai law, and lecturer at various universities on tax and business law.
Personal: Born 1955, Yala, Thailand. Chulalongkorn University (LLB, Honours, 1976; LLM, 1983); University of British Columbia (LLM, 1987); Institute of Legal Education (Thai Barrister-at-Law, 1976).

VAJASIT, Surasak
Freshfields Bruckhaus Deringer, Bangkok +662 344 9200
surasak.vajasit@freshfields.com
Recommended in Banking & Finance
Specialisation: Extensive experience in corporate and financing transactions, including a number of high profile project financings and public issues of debt and equity securities; also been involved in privatisation transactions, restructuring and bankruptcy related matters.

WESKOSITH, Nipaporn
Johnson Stokes & Master, Bangkok +66 2 638 0880
Recommended in Corporate/M&A

TOGO

Corporate/Commercial

TOGO Leading firms (Corporate/Commercial)
1 Etude Agboyibo
Aquereburu & Partners

Firms are listed alphabetically in each band.

Leading individuals (Corporate/Commercial)
1 AGBOYIBO Yawovi *Etude Agboyibo*
AQUEREBURU Coffi Alexis *Aquereburu & Ptnrs*

Individuals are listed alphabetically in each band.

Etude Agboyibo (1 ptr, 4 asscs) A firm with a *"strong corporate and commercial practice."* Advises banks, insurance companies, petrol distribution companies and financial institutions. The *"experienced"* **Yawovi Agboyibo** is recommended. **Clients:** Mobil Oil Togo; Texaco Togo; SFI; banks; insurance companies.

Aquereburu & Partners (3 ptrs, 1 assc) *"The foremost firm in the country"* has a strong commercial practice which handles foreign investment in Togo. **Coffi Alexis Aquereburu** is highly recommended. The team advised on an international tender for the privatisation of a national electric energy supply company in West Africa. **Clients:** World Bank; African Development Bank; West African Cement; Togo Shell; Crustafric; GARI.

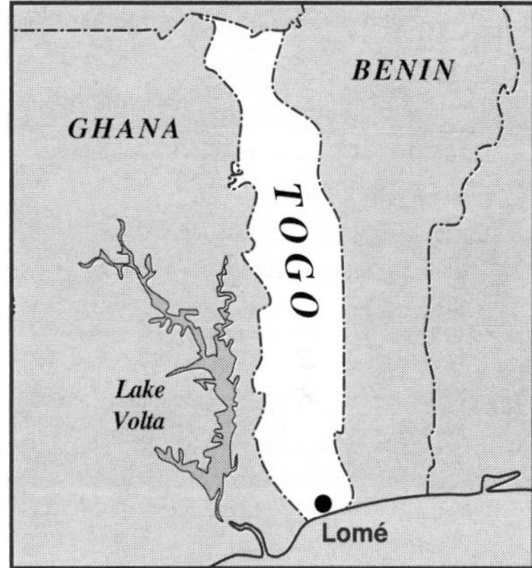

Leaders' profiles – Togo

AGBOYIBO, Yawovi
Étude Agboyibo, Lomé +228 21 27 64
yagboyibo@bibway.com
Specialisation: Commercial law, banking law, civil law, insurance law, maritime law, arbitration, international finance, debt recovery, industrial law and tax law. Links with *Me Teisserenc* and *Jeantet & Associés* in Paris, France.
Prof. Memberships: Head of Bar Association 'L'Ordre des Avocats du Togo' (1987-1990). President of 'L'Union des Barreaux de l'Afrique de l'Ouest' (1995-1997).
Publications: Co-author of 'L'Encyclopédie Juridique pour l'Afrique' (1989). Author of 'Combat pour un Togo Démocratique – une méthode politique' (Editions Karthala, 1999).
Career: Admitted in 1969. Previously worked with Maître Anani Santos (1969-1971) and Maître Raymond Viale (1971-1978). In charge of law courses at L'Ecole Nationale d'Administration de Lomé-Togo (1981-1985). President of the National Commission for Human Rights of Togo (1987-1990). Member of the Sub-Committee for Human Rights of the United Nations in Geneva (1988-1989). Member of the Committee for Human Rights of the Interparliamentary Union in Geneva (1988-1993). Member of the Pope's Council for "Justice and Peace" at the Vatican (1989-1994). President of the political party 'Comité d'Action pour le Renouveau' (April 1991 to date). President of the 'Union des Partis Africains pour le Développement at la Démocratique' – UPADD.
Personal: Born 1 January 1943. Masters in Law (Orléans, France); Diplomé d'Etudes Approfondies en Droit Privé (Abidjan, Cote d'Ivoire). Married with children.

AQUEREBURU, Coffi Alexis
Aquereburu & Partners, Lomé +228 21 05 05
eaquereb@cybercom.Tg
Specialisation: Specialises in the financial system, taxation, business law, intellectual property, penal matters and human rights. Has participated, through co-operation with the World Bank, in the making of several legal texts relating to the disengagement of the State from the Public Enterprises. Assisted the State with several privatisation and divestment procedures and is on the African Development Bank roster as a consultant.
Prof. Memberships: Arbitration Society of Togo.

TRINIDAD & TOBAGO

Corporate/Commercial

T

TRINIDAD & TOBAGO Leading firms (Corporate/Commercial)
1 Fitzwilliam, Stone, Furness-Smith & Morgan
2 M Hamel-Smith & Co
Pollonais, Blanc, De La Bastide & Jacelon
3 De Nobriga, Inniss & Co
JD Sellier & Co

Firms are listed alphabetically in each band.

Leading individuals (Corporate/Commercial)
1 **CAMACHO Cecil** *De Nobriga, Inniss & Co*
COLLIER Edward *Pollonais, Blanc*
FITZWILLIAM Daniel *Fitzwilliam, Stone*
HAMEL-SMITH Timothy *M Hamel-Smith & Co*

Individuals are listed alphabetically in each band.

Fitzwilliam, Stone, Furness-Smith & Morgan (11 ptrs, 5 asscs) *"Set apart"* from competitors with its leading corporate and commercial team where the *"thorough"* senior partner **Danny Fitzwilliam*** is renowned for the *"lengths he goes to."* Boasting an impressive portfolio of clients, the firm advised the BP Amoco Corporation on a joint venture for the development of a LNG plant in Trinidad and in negotiations with the government on project and environmental agreements. In capital markets work, it represented the Trinidad and Tobago Stock Exchange on the establishment of a centralised securities depository system and advised Citibank and CSFB on sovereign bond issues. **Clients:** Morgan Stanley; Citibank; Pepsico; BP Amoco, Nestlé; OPEC.

M Hamel-Smith & Co Interviewees regarded this firm as a leading light, renowned for its *"aggressive"* approach to the market. High profile senior partner **Timothy Hamel-Smith*** has won acclaim for the *"thoroughness of his work."* He is considered, both by clients and rivals, to be *"a first rate corporate lawyer; hardworking and diligent."* **Clients:** Leading financial institutions and corporates.

Pollonais, Blanc, De La Bastide & Jacelon (11 ptrs, 5 asscs) Growing in strength, the firm has a sound corporate practice focused on energy and communications. It has advised on the establishment of processing and manufacturing plants for US corporations, is active in the expanding telecoms sector and acted on the refurbishment of petro-chemical plants. The well-respected **Edward Collier*** is recommended for his *"all round reliability."* **Clients:** Republic Bank; Atlantic LNG; BWIA.

De Nobriga, Inniss &Co (6 ptrs, 13 asscs) The firm merged recently with a firm in Barbados entering the Ernst & Young Lex network. With an already impressive clientele including Coca-Cola, British Gas, Deutsche Bank and major financial institutions in Trinidad and Tobago, the firm is judged by the market to be growing in strength. **Cecil Camacho*** is famed for his *"analysis"* and *"practical business advice."* The team has a broad corporate coverage including expertise in oil and natural gas, and advised Atlantic on a LNG project. **Clients:** Coca-Cola; Citibank; British Gas; Deutsche Bank; Development Finance; First Citizen Bank; Titan Methanol Company; Atlantic LNG.

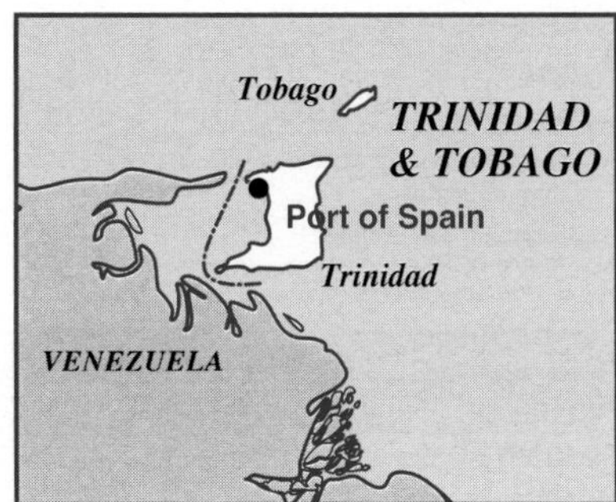

JD Sellier & Co (9 ptrs, 10 asscs) A full service law firm with a strong corporate offering, its clients are found in the banking, petroleum, industrial, agricultural and investment sectors. With a focus on oil companies and downstream industries, the practice often acts for foreign corporations establishing joint ventures in the steel, methanol, chemical and oil industries. **Clients:** Texaco ISPAT; T&T Methanol; Phoenix; BP Amoco.

*See leaders' profiles on pages 677

Leaders' profiles – Trinidad & Tobago

CAMACHO, Cecil
De Nobriga, Inniss & Co, Port of Spain
+1 868 628 9255

COLLIER, Edward
Pollonais, Blanc, De La Bastide and Jacelon, Port of Spain +1 868 623 5461

FITZWILLIAM, Daniel John
Fitzwilliam, Stone, Furness-Smith & Morgan, Port of Spain +1 868 623 1618
dfitz.fsfsm@wow.net
Specialisation: Partner with specialisation in Corporate, Commercial, Finance, Oil and Gas. Main area of work is foreign investment in major industrial projects requiring joint venture agreements, incorporation or registration of project companies and Government agreements on taxation and other incentives. Projects include major Government privatisation in iron and steel industry, joint ventures in ammonia and methanol industries, investment in iron carbide facility in a free zone and a power generation project with associated power purchase agreement and Government guarantee. Has also acted, from inception, in the formation and expansion of a major liquefied natural gas project as well as Government and environmental agreements and financing for same. Has also acted in take-over bids on the Stock Exchange and initial public offerings. Has a wide practice acting for several upstream Oil and Gas companies with attendant advice in relation to the Petroleum legislation and revision of petroleum licences and production sharing contracts.
Prof. Memberships: Law Association of Trinidad and Tobago, Association of International Petroleum Negotiators.
Publications: 'The Unanimous Shareholder Agreement – A Bane or Boon for Shareholders?' delivered at Faculty of Law's 1st Caribbean Commercial Law Workshop in Barbados August, 1999 and published in the Caribbean Law Review, 2000.
Career: Qualified in 1979. Joined *Fitzwilliam, Stone, Furness-Smith & Morgan* in 1979 and became a Partner in 1982. Associate Tutor, Hugh Wooding Law School, Trinidad, 1981 to 1986; Member, Rules Committee of the Supreme Court of Judicature, Trinidad, 1988 to 1994; Member, Committee of the Law Association of Trinidad and Tobago on proposed amendments to the Companies legislation, 2000.
Personal: Born 18 February, 1954; Attended University of Western Ontario, Ontario, Canada, BA Hons. Business Administration; University of the West Indies, LLB Honours 1977; Hugh Wooding Law School – Legal Education Certificate of Merit, 1979.

HAMEL-SMITH, Timothy Tristram
M Hamel-Smith & Co, Port of Spain, Trinidad
+1 868 623 4237
timothy@trinidadlaw.com
Specialisation: Senior Partner in Corporate/Commercial Department. Main area of expertise is commercial law, principally banking and finance. Has been engaged in several complex transactions such as project financing of the: (1) Atlantic LNG plant arranged by ABN Amro, Citibank N.A. and Barclays; (2) methanol and ammonia plants arranged by KFW; and (3) Ispat's iron and steel plant arranged by IFC, as well as both corporate and project financings throughout the Caribbean. Has been a presenter on Project Finance at various conferences in the Caribbean.
Prof. Memberships: The Law Association, the U. K. Law Society, Lex Mundi and Amcham.
Publications: Author of: (1) 'Securities Market Regulations: Trinidad & Tobago' – Euromoney Publications 1994; (2) 'Investor's Guide to Trinidad and Tobago' – www.trinidadlaw.com; and (3) 'FAQ – Companies Act 1995' – Express 1998.
Career: Qualified in 1973. Joined *M. Hamel-Smith & Co.* in 1968, becoming a Partner in 1978. Appointed head of the Corporate/Commercial Department in 1988. Member of the Parliamentary Sub-Committee to review the Companies Act.

T

TUNISIA

Corporate/Commercial

TUNISIA Leading firms (Corporate/Commercial)
1 Adly Bellagha & Associés
Ferchiou & Associés
Salaheddine Caid Essebsi & Associés
2 Abdelly & Associés

Firms are listed alphabetically in each band.

Leading individuals (Corporate/Commercial)
1 BELLAGHA Adly *Adly Bellagha & Associés*
CAID ESSEBSI Salaheddine *Salaheddine Caid*
FERCHIOU Noureddine *Ferchiou & Associés*
2 ABDELLY Samir *Abdelly & Associés*

Individuals are listed alphabetically in each band.

Adly Bellagha & Associés (2 ptrs, 5 asscs) A growing firm, internationally recognised for expertise in the oil and gas industry. The team undertakes a variety of commercial work, specialising in M&A and privatisation. **Adly Bellagha** is *"a serious, hard-working lawyer."* The firm advised Cimentos de Portugal on the privatisation of cement plants worth $245 million. **Clients:** Caterpillar; energy and telecommunications companies.

Ferchiou & Associés (4 ptrs, 6 asscs) One *"can't have a bad thing to say"* about this firm, which carries out a broad range of corporate and commercial work on behalf of an international clientele. Clients informed our researchers that the *"knowledgeable and dynamic"* **Noureddine Ferchiou** is *"the expert on foreign investment in Tunisia."* The firm advised on the merger of the three premier banks in Tunisia, and advised Merrill Lynch on the issue of a global summary bond on the Japanese market on behalf of Tunisian Central Bank worth ¥50 billion. **Clients:** Banks; Coca-Cola; IBM, Telefónica; energy companies.

Salaheddine Caid Essebsi & Associés (2 ptrs, 4 asscs) This *"commercially focused and reliable"* firm specialises in the financing and leasing of aircraft and also advises on banking, finance, energy, mining and M&A. *"Old hand"* **Salaheddine Caid Essebsi** is *"a cut above most other lawyers."* **Clients:** Hilton; Barclays, IFC; Exim Bank.

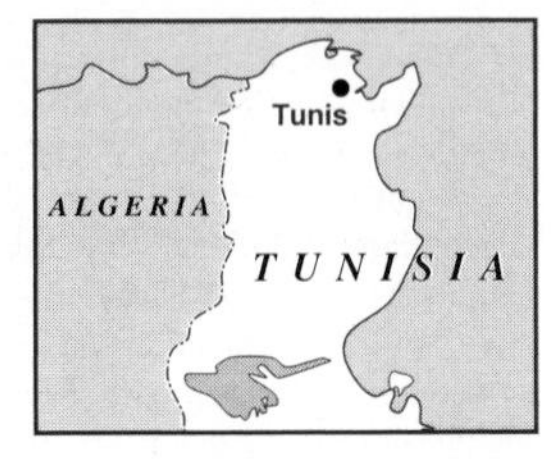

Abdelly & Associés (1 ptr, 3 asscs) The firm has offices across the Maghreb, and handles M&A, mutual funds and banking and finance. However, its true strength lies in the energy industry, particularly hydrocarbon and mining law. *"Internationally well-connected"* **Samir Abdelly** recently acted on the privatisation of the national cement factories in Tunisia, a $340 million package. **Clients:** Mobil Oil; Brickwater Resources; Fina; Baker Hughes; CGG; Atlantis; international law firms.

Leaders' profiles – Tunisia

ABDELLY, Samir
Abdelly & Associés, Tunis +216 1 849 410

BELLAGHA, Adly
Adly Bellagha & Associés, Tunis +216 1 327 122
a.bellagha@gnet.tn
Specialisation: Oil and gas, mining, commercial mergers and acquisitions and general practice.
Prof. Memberships: International Bar Association. Association of International Petroleum Negotiators. Tunis Bar Association.
Career: Graduated from Paris Law School, qualified in 1977. Senior negotiator and advisor of public and private investors.
Personal: Born 29 March 1954. Leisure interests include tennis and sailing.

CAID ESSEBSI, Salaheddine
Salaheddine Caid Essebsi & Associés, Tunis +216 1 785 611
scaidessebsi@planet.tn
Specialisation: Banking, finance, business law, capital market law, commercial law, communications & media, competition law, construction, consumer law, enviromental law, arbitration, financial leasing law, foreign exchange, foreign investment law, insolvency & bankruptcy law, information technology, intellectual property (trademark, patent, know-how), labour law litigation, mergers and acquisitions privatisation law, real estate law, securities law, tax law and telecommunications.
Prof. Memberships: Member of Bar Association of Tunisia, and the American Society of International Law.
Career: Admitted to bar on April 27 1961.
Personal: Born on May 28 1933. Qualifications: Law & Economics degree, University of Paris, Business High Studies Diploma.

FERCHIOU, Noureddine
Ferchiou & Associés, Tunis +216 1 345 373
noureddine.ferchiou@planet.tn
Specialisation: Main areas of work include corporate law, finance, banking, privatisation, mergers and investments. Well known in the business community for strong negotiating skills and problem solving abilities. Has acted as local counsel for the Consortium formed by Sithe Power International, Marubeni Power Holding B.V and PSEG International Limited, for the first privatisation of a power plant (B.O.O.) in Tunisia. Is currently working with Paribas and KPMG on the merger of Tunisia's 3 most important banks. Has also acted as counsel in several privatisation matters at times for the investor or the Tunisian government. Is well versed in matters of finance, project financing, feasibility of banking transactions, national and international public bond issues, securities transactions.
Publications: Author of various articles on investment in Tunisia in specialised magazines and publications (Gazette du Palais, Cahiers Juridiques et Fiscaux de L'Exportation). Contributor to the Salomon Smith Barney Guide to World Equity Markets.
Career: Qualified in 1981 at Tunis, founded *Ferchiou & Associés* in 1984, which employs at present 29 attorneys and staff. Succesfully leads the firm into becoming the first law firm in Tunisia, North Africa and in the Arab countries to obtain the ISO certification. Speaker at various conferences.
Personal: Born October 30, 1954. Attended University of Tunis (MA Private Law) 1978; Paris University (DEA in Business law and DEA in Private Law). Accomplished yachtsman.

TURKEY

Index

OVERVIEW: Little prospect for change in Turkey's over-regulated legal market – the Turkish bar has recently clamped down on Turkey-based international firms acting in association with domestic firms, while retaining the laws that make it almost impossible for domestic firms to grow. That said, international firms continue to loom large on the scene, with White & Case notably active on the ground, while from abroad, Linklaters, Shearman and Sterling and Clifford Chance dominate project finance deals.

Firms have witnessed an increasing volume of M&A work and a storm of changes, with new laws introducing a banking supervisory board, and allowing the privatisation of three state-owned banks.

This year, in response to the Turkish Bar's increasingly stringent behaviour towards Turkey-based international firms acting in association with domestic firms, we do not allude directly to those well-known associations that exist between international and domestic firms.

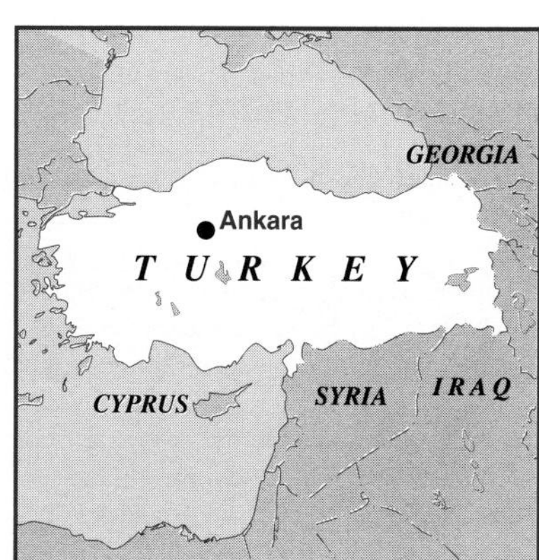

T

Banking & Finance: Local Firms

TURKEY Leading firms (Banking & Finance)
1 Derman Ortak Avukat Bürosu
Hergüner, Bilgen & Özeke
Pekin & Pekin
2 Birsel Law Offices
M Fethi Pekin & Sefika Pekin Law Firm
Somay Hukuk Bürosu
3 Dogru Law Office
Okur & Okur
Paksoy & Co

Firms are listed alphabetically in each band.

Leading individuals (Banking & Finance)
1 BIRSEL Mahmut *Birsel Law Offices*
PEKIN Ahmed *Pekin & Pekin*
2 DERMAN Emre *Derman Ortak Avukat Bürosu*
PAKSOY Serdar *Paksoy & Co*
REISOGLU Seza *Reisoglu Ensari Budak Law Firm*
SOMAY Metin *Somay Hukuk Bürosu*
3 DOGRU Halil *Dogru Law Office*

Individuals are listed alphabetically in each band.

Derman Ortak Avukat Bürosu (1 ptr, 6 asscs) Capital markets specialist **Emre Derman*** and his team were recommended to researchers for work on IPOs, privatisations and project finance. On the capital markets side, the firm closed six deals in 2000 and has been instructed on nine mandates set to close in 2001. It acted on the issue of shares for Batisöke Söke Çimento (cement manufacturing,) Sezginler Gida (fast moving consumer goods,) TÜPRAS (petroleum/refinery) and Türkiye Garanti Bankasi (banking.) The firm is frequently instructed by White & Case. **Clients:** Batisöke Söke Çimento; Sezginler Gida; TÜPRAS; Türkiye Garanti Bankasi; TEB; Yazicilar Otomotiv.

Hergüner, Bilgen & Özeke (3 ptrs, 14 asscs) *"The number one choice for international firms seeking Turkish counsel,"* this *"top-class"* act is considered an energetic player with a particular focus on the telecoms sector and privatisation issues. Noted for its government connections, it assisted the Republic of Turkey on the privatisation of Is bank. Also advised a major multi-lateral development bank on equity stakes and projects in Turkey including a benchmark multi-million dollar securitisation of lease receivables. **Clients:** Bilateral lending agencies; leading financial institutions.

Pekin & Pekin (4 ptrs, 8 asscs) A well-established firm with an outstanding international clientele. *"Striking"* **Ahmed Pekin*** heads a stellar team that includes a former vice president of the Central Bank of the Republic of Turkey. Peers rate the team's note issue work for both Turkish banks and the Republic of Turkey. It assisted the latter on more than 75% of its note issues. The firm also advised on the securitisation of floating rate certificates by Turkiye Is Bankasi and Pamukbank, and acted on the Birlesik Turk Korfez Bankasi $100 million term loan facility, and on the Turk Ekonomi Bankasi $80 million multi-currency loan. **Clients:** Turkish Government; Turkiye Is Bankasi.

Birsel Law Offices (1 ptr, 6 asscs) A key element in the firm's success lies with the strong banking relationships of the *"charming"* and *"able"* **Mahmut Birsel***. The team acts as local counsel to OPIC, the US Exim Bank and DEG-Deutsche Investitions und Entwicklungsgesellschaft in their investments in Turkey. It advised major international banks on access to the Turkish banking sector and in secured or unsecured loan financing made available to the Turkish Government and public institutions. A seasoned player in the debt restructuring market, the team is also active in the note issues of Osmanli Bankasi and Yapi ve Kredi Bankasi. **Clients:** Osmanli Bankasi; Yapi ve Kredi Bankasi.

M Fethi Pekin & Sefika Pekin Law Firm (6 lawyers) Competitors speak of a productive team which is frequently instructed by international law firms and possess strong ties to banks such as Goldman Sachs and Morgan Stanley Dean Witter. Considered *"strong on capital markets,"* its

*See leaders' profiles on page 683

expertise spreads to loan transactions and Turkish banking regulations. Advised Morgan Stanley Dean Witter on the IPO of the NYSE quoted Turkcell. **Clients:** American Express Bank; Finans Bank; JP Morgan Guaranty Trust Co; CSFB; Morgan Stanley Dean Witter; Goldman Sachs.

Somay Hukuk Bürosu (16 lawyers) Recommended as *"good at general financing and involved in major private equity deals,"* **Metin Somay*** exploits his accountancy and tax background to good advantage. His large full service firm is noted for its ties with AIG investment bank. Financial leasing is a strength, with the team advising on cross-border leasing deals for aviation companies. The firm has a long working relationship with the US law firm Arnold & Porter. **Clients:** AIG; investment banks.

Dogru Law Office (1 ptr, 7 asscs) A small capital markets boutique led by former Istanbul Stock Exchange inspector **Halil Dogru***, that focuses on public offerings, IPOs and local due diligence. It advised Enron on derivative transactions, Demir Bank on note issues and acted in the secondary offering of the electronics company, Yestel. **Clients:** Yestel; Enron.

Okur & Okur An older law firm with a respected French clientele that has a low-key reputation in the market. The team is active in debt restructuring and traditional banking arrangements for European investment banks. **Clients:** European banks and financial institutions.

Paksoy & Co (2 ptrs, 8 asscs) A spin-off from Hergüner, Bilgen & Özeke, this team has a powerful presence in the capital markets and telecoms sphere. *"Sharp, reasonable"* **Serdar Paksoy*** heads up this full-service offering, which is notably active in interesting project financings. It represented HSBC International as underwriters to the equity offering of AK Energy, and advised on the IPO of Turkcell, the largest to date, raising a $1.9 billion NYSE and Istanbul Stock Exchange listing. It also advised the Turkish Privatisation Administration on the strategic sale of shares in Turkish Airlines. **Clients:** HSBC International; Turkish Privatisation Administration.

Other Notable Practitioner **Seza Reisoglu*** of Reisoglu Ensari Budak (based in Ankara) is a prominent scholar, and regularly advises the Is Bank.

Banking & Finance: Foreign Firms

TURKEY: Foreign Firms Leading firms (Banking & Finance)
1 White & Case LLP
2 Altheimer & Gray

Firms are listed alphabetically in each band.

Leading individuals (Banking & Finance)
1 BASGOZ Asli *White & Case LLP*

Individuals are listed alphabetically in each band.

White & Case LLP (2 ptrs) *"Notably active on securitisations,"* the firm enjoys a powerful reputation and *"regularly services Turkish banks."* Its pre-eminence is attributed by peers to **Asli Basgoz***, whose broad expertise includes debt offerings and project finance. The team advised Turkiye Is Bankasi on its debut future flow securitisation backed by US-dollar denominated remittances, and acted on the equity offerings made by Batisöke Söke Çimento, Sezginler Gida, TÜPRAS and Türkiye Garanti Bankasi. **Clients:** Batisöke Söke Çimento; Sezginler Gida; TÜPRAS; Türkiye Garanti Bankasi; TEB; Yazicilar Otomotiv; Turkiye Is Bankasi.

Altheimer & Gray (2 ptrs, 5 asscs) A US firm with a local presence that has been established in Turkey for quite some time. The team represented Turkcell Iletisim Hizmetleri in a $300 million high yield global note offering, and assisted Azercell Telecom, an Azerbaijani GSM company, on its $100 million senior bank credit facility. **Clients:** Turkcell Iletisim Hizmetleri; Azercell Telecom.

Corporate/M&A: Local Firms

Hergüner, Bilgen & Özeke (3 ptrs, 14 asscs) An energetic firm with *"excellent government contacts"* and a *"high standard of professionalism."* Recognised to be *"reaching international standards"* in its telecoms and privatisation work. In the hi-tech sector, the team represented foreign firms in proposed acquisitions of internet companies in Turkey, and assisted a consortium of Turkish IT companies on joint venture negotiations with a major multi-national firm. Key to the firm's success is the *"creative, intelligent"* **Ümit Hergüner***. Onlookers are *"impressed by his ability to work through a deal from a local law perspective."* Other work includes acting as local counsel to a leading international radiator manufacturer on the sale of its European plumbing division, and advising a leading global transport holding company on its acquisition of a Turkish freight forwarder. **Clients:** Local hi-tech companies; international corporates.

Derman Ortak Avukat Bürosu (1 ptr, 6 asscs) A *"well-established, quality"* firm, frequently instructed by White & Case, and headed by *"joint ventures specialist"* **Emre Derman***. Possessing an international clientele which includes internet and e-commerce companies, the firm has acted for household names such as Coca-Cola, Enron, Toyota Motors, and Pirelli. In 2000, the team closed four major M&A transactions. **Clients:** Enron; Mobil; Toyota; Lexel; Coca-Cola; ITE; Pirelli; Huhtamaki Oy.

Duygen Yarsuvat & Ömür Yarsuvat (2 ptrs, 3 asscs) Father and son general practice firm, specialising in M&A and project finance with a notable reputation in the energy field. An international practice favoured by inbound business, the firm has advised companies in the health, advertising and power industries. **Clients:** Foreign and domestic industrial companies.

Law Offices of M Fadullah Cerrahoglu (3 ptrs, 6 asscs) *"Extremely able"* **M Fadullah Cerrahoglu*** oversees a small yet active practice with a strong

TURKEY Leading firms (Corporate/Mergers & Acquisitions)
1 Hergüner, Bilgen & Özeke
2 Derman Ortak Avukat Bürosu
3 Duygen Yarsuvat & Ömür Yarsuvat
Law Offices of M Fadullah Cerrahoglu
Özel & Özel
Pekin & Pekin
4 Birsel Law Offices
Ece Güner Ünlü Law Office
Mehmet Gün & Co

Firms are listed alphabetically in each band.

Leading individuals (Corporate/Mergers & Acquisitions)
1 **CERRAHOGLU M Fadullah** *Law Offices of M Fadullah Cerrahoglu*
HERGÜNER Ümit *Hergüner, Bilgen & Özeke*
ÖZEL Haluk *Özel & Özel*
2 **BIRSEL Mahmut** *Birsel Law Offices*
DERMAN Emre *Derman Ortak Avukat Bürosu*
GÜN Mehmet *Mehmet Gün & Co*
GÜNER-ÜNLÜ Ece *Ece Güner Ünlü*

Individuals are listed alphabetically in each band.

track record of corporate work for international companies. Frequently instructed by White & Case, the firm's broad industry coverage includes the automotive, paper, pharmaceutical, oil and computer sectors. **Clients:** Large industrial and hi-tech companies.

Özel & Özel (2 ptrs, 5 asscs) **Haluk Özel*** heads an active practice that is *"well thought of"* by the market, and known for its work with Altheimer & Gray. The firm is heavily involved in communications. It advised long-standing client, Turkcell Iletisim Hizmetleri, on the acquisition of a 60% stake in a German telephony company, and represented Cukurova Group Companies on restructuring the group's media, telecoms and IT companies under a Dutch entity. The team also acted for BPB Gypsum in the acquisition of 100% of the shares in a Turkish gypsum company, and assisted Hedef Holding in their sale of stock to Alliance Unichem. **Clients:** Turkcell Iletisim Hizmetleri; Cukurova Group companies; BPB Gypsum; Hedef Holding.

Pekin & Pekin Researchers were impressed by the depth of market approval for the firm's banking related M&A work. The team advised a German bank on its share acquisition in a Turkish brokerage house, and acted for a locally incorporated bank (belonging to a major Japanese group) on its acquisition by a major local group. Also active in the communications sector, it advised on a joint venture between a Turkish media holding company and a Fortune 500 Turkish conglomerate to provide B2C internet access and portal services. **Clients:** Domestic and foreign banks.

Birsel Law Offices (1 ptr, 2 asscs) With offices in Istanbul, Izmir and Ankara, this large local firm has a strong reputation in infrastructure projects and the private power industry. Leading arbitration lawyer **Mahmut Birsel*** is recommended for his M&A work, in particular advising on joint ventures between foreign investors and local business partners. The firm advised Kingfisher in its joint venture with Koc Holding, and assisted Taylor Nelson Sofres in setting up a partnership in Turkey. **Clients:** Koc Holding; Taylor Nelson Sofres.

Ece Güner Ünlü Law Office (14 lawyers in total, includes 3 Denton Wilde Sapte asscs) Young firm developing an international client base in association with Denton Wilde Sapte. Increasing its M&A flow in general, the team advised regular client Haci Omer Sabanci Holding on its Du Pont joint venture. It also advised Balfour Beatty on the acquisition of a major stake in a construction company, and Ontex on the acquisition of a diaper company.

"Capable, well-educated" **Ece Güner-Ünlü*** has been on maternity leave this year, but her return to active practice, together with the arrival of an M&A partner from Denton Wilde Sapte is anticipated to boost the practice. **Clients:** De Ceuninck; Sabanci Holding; Balfour Beatty; Ontex.

Mehmet Gün & Co (3 ptrs) A commercial and corporate firm with a predominantly foreign client base. The team recently advised on a joint venture in the fish farming sector. It was also active on acquisitions in the oil and gas, advertising and logistics sectors. Peers note that e-commerce is a growth area, with the firm exploiting its strong IP background. *"Reputable"* **Mehmet Gün*** heads up the practice. **Clients:** Foreign investors.

T

Corporate/M&A: Foreign Firms

TURKEY: Foreign Firms Leading firms (Corporate/Mergers & Acquisitions)
1 White & Case LLP
2 Altheimer & Gray
3 Gide Loyrette Nouel

Firms are listed alphabetically in each band.

White & Case LLP (2 ptrs) The oldest international firm in Turkey hit problems this year over its association with domestic law firms. It nevertheless retains its reputation as the best international practice in the country. *"Particularly good on joint ventures,"* the firm has *"close contacts with big corporate clients"* and *"a fine reputation"* for its work on cross-border transactions. It represents non-Turkish investors in all phases of their investments in Turkey, including acquisitions, liaison offices, wholly-owned subsidiaries and joint ventures with Turkish partners. **Clients:** Foreign investors; financial institutions.

Altheimer & Gray (2 ptrs, 5 asscs) In Turkey for quite some time and, according to market perception, *"focused on construction projects,"* but the firm also retains an involvement in M&A work. Represented Turkcell Iletisim Hizmetleri in its joint venture with a Ukrainian GSM company and advised Aygaz on its acquisition of fifty percent of the shares in a Ukrainian gas company. **Clients:** Aygaz; Turkcell Iletisim Hizmetleri.

Gide Loyrette Nouel (1 ptr, 4 asscs) Set up as a Turkish advice bureau under the name of GLN Müsavirlik, the firm represents leading French corporates in the mid tier market. The only French firm currently providing services in Turkey, it has been increasingly active in M&A, supported by a knowledgeable tax partner and its well-connected Brussels office. Active in the energy and banking sectors, the team advised a large Spanish owned electricity producer on its acquisition of a Turkish electricity producer, and acted for a large European bank on the acquisition of a Turkish bank. **Clients:** TotalFina Elf.

*See leaders' profiles on page 683

Project Finance: Local Firms

TURKEY Leading firms (Project Finance)
1 Çakmak Ortak Avukat Bürosu
Hergüner, Bilgen & Özeke
2 Birsel Law Offices
Duygen Yarsuvat & Ömür Yarsuvat

Firms are listed alphabetically in each band.

Leading individuals (Project Finance)
1 **ÇAKMAK Mesut** *Çakmak Ortak Avukat Bürosu*
HERGÜNER Ümit *Hergüner, Bilgen & Özeke*
ÖZEKE Ender *Hergüner, Bilgen & Özeke*

Individuals are listed alphabetically in each band.

Çakmak Ortak Avukat Bürosu (1 ptr, 9 asscs) A *"well-known,"* Ankara-based firm headed by *"highly regarded"* **Mesut Çakmak***, who is lauded by competitors and clients alike as a power projects specialist. Involved in the development of the BOT model in Turkey, the team also acted as lead counsel in Turkey's largest project finance deal to date, the Siemens/STEAG financing of a $1.45 billion power plant in Iskenderun.

Its broad-based practice covers oil and gas, mining, water/sewage, and transportation projects, including the CGEA-led development of a waste treatment plant in Izmir, and the construction of a new international airport complex in Istanbul. **Clients:** Enron; Hamilton Companies; El Paso; Etibank; CGEA; Government of Turkey; Ansaldo; BM Holding.

Hergüner, Bilgen & Özeke (3 ptrs, 12 asscs) *"Probably the best of the local firms,"* this *"expert,"* energy-focused outfit is involved in a variety of major pipelines, private power financings and other infrastructure projects, often seen acting on behalf of the sponsor. *"Polished, well-connected"* **Ümit Hergüner*** and the *"commercial"* **Ender Özeke*** *("I'd recommend him unhesitatingly")* are key reasons for the firm's success.

The team acted on the Baku-Tbilisi-Ceyhan main export pipeline, the Russia to Turkey trans-Balkan pipeline and the Marmara Ereolisi gas-fired power plant project. Elsewhere, it advised on the Izmit Bay crossing bridge and motorway project, and the Antalya water and sewage infrastructure. **Clients:** Foreign corporations; multinational companies and institutions.

Birsel Law Offices (2 ptrs, 2 asscs) *"Perfectly solid and helpful"* firm, seen to concentrate on investment projects in the areas of power, infrastructure and tourism for a client base that includes export credit agencies, commercial banks, and international financial institutions. It advised US Eximbank, OPIC, IFC, KfW, OeKB and Dresdner Bank in the four ongoing power projects in Gebze, Adapazari, Izmir and Iskenderun.

Participated in seven of the nine projects in Turkey involving the construction, installation and operation of gas-fired, wind energy, hydro-electric power plants. Advised Alstom Enterprise as contractor in the Istanbul Metro. **Clients:** US Eximbank; OPIC; IFC; KfW; OeKB; Dresdner Bank; ALSTOM Enterprise.

Duygen Yarsuvat & Ömür Yarsuvat (1 ptr, 2 asscs) Small father and son practice with *"a strong reputation for its project finance work,"* and a focus on the energy sector. Clients comprise foreign companies investing in Turkey and the firm recently advised on a significant power project. **Clients:** Foreign companies.

Project Finance: Foreign Firms

TURKEY: Foreign Firms Leading firms (Project Finance)
1 White & Case LLP

Firms are listed alphabetically in each band.

Leading individuals (Project Finance)
1 **BASGOZ Asli** *White & Case LLP*

Individuals are listed alphabetically in each band.

White & Case LLP (2 ptrs) A *"strikingly good"* team led by *"experienced,"* New York qualified **Asli Basgoz***. Involved in the largest project finance deal in Turkey, the team represented the sponsors STEAG (90%) and Siemens Power Ventures (10%) on the $1.45 billion, 1210MW imported coal Independent Power Project in Iskenderun, Southern Turkey. The project was the culmination of over two and a half years' work. **Clients:** Enron; STEAG; Siemens Power Ventures.

*See leaders' profiles on pages 683

Leaders' profiles – Turkey

BASGOZ, Asli
White & Case LLP, Istanbul +90 212 275 7533
abasgoz@whitecase.com
Recommended in Banking & Finance: Turkey Foreign, Project Finance: Turkey Foreign
Specialisation: Head of firm's Istanbul office. Acts for domestic and international clients in Turkey on a wide range of bank finance, M&A, projects and structured finance transactions.
Personal: Turkish citizen, speaks fluent Turkish and English.

BIRSEL, Mahmut
Birsel Law Offices, Alsancak-Izmir
+90 232 489 0519
Recommended in Banking & Finance, Corporate/M&A

ÇAKMAK, Mesut
Cakmak Ortak Avukat Bürosu, Ankara
+90 312 442 4680
Recommended in Project Finance

CERRAHOGLU, M Fadullah
Law Offices of M Fadullah Cerrahoglu, Istanbul
+90 212 270 7014
Recommended in Corporate/M&A

DERMAN, Emre
Derman Ortak Avukat Burosu, Istanbul
+90 212 275 7155
ederman@doab.com
Recommended in Banking & Finance, Corporate/M&A
Specialisation: Well-respected partner of firm based in Turkey. Range of international corporate, bank finance and securities law transactional experience. Acts for domestic and international investors in Turkey and abroad.
Career: Worked previously at *EBRD*. Qualified to practise in Turkey, speaks fluent Turkish and English.

DOGRU, Halil
Dogru Law Office, Istanbul +90 212 212 8882
Recommended in Banking & Finance

GÜN, Mehmet
Mehmet Gün & Co, Istanbul
+90 212 275 90 03
Recommended in Corporate/M&A

GÜNER-ÜNLÜ, Ece
Ece Güner Ünlü Law Firm, Istanbul
+90 212 282 4385
dentonguner@superonline.com
Recommended in Corporate/M&A
Specialisation: Has specialised in project finance, particularly in the energy and infrastucture works sector and in all types of commercial contracts, company/corporate transactions, mergers and acquisitions as well as privatisation, telecommunications and media work. Seen as a specialist in power and more generally BOT issues. Has been invited to speak at many prestigious conferences. Has acted for numerous international companies in their acquisition projects in Turkey including CNN, Turner Broadcasting (CNN), BP, Ontex NV, Balfour Beatty plc, Statoil. Advised on development of several major Independent Power Plant projects in partnership with Turkish conglomerates for Enron Europe Limited, Sumitomo Corporation, EnbW International GmbH and Enelpower. Advised Hutchison Whampoa and Nokia on telecoms projects.
Career: January 1996 to date *DGF&G*, Managing Partner. February 1995-January 1996: independent practice as an international lawyer. Worked in 12 different countries for several large investment groups. June 1991-February 1995: Salaried Partner at *Okur & Okur* Law Firm, one of the prominent local firms advising international clientele.
Personal: Qualified from University of Law of Paris II (Pantheon-Assas, attached to the Sorbonne); Masters Degree with a major in Commercial and Tax Law and a minor in International Private Law with the Highest Honour Degree, 'Menton Tres Bien'. One year Certificate from Faculty of State of Florida, USA, course taken in Business Law. Undergraduate 1986/1987. Married, one child and lives in Istanbul.

HERGÜNER, Ümit
Hergüner, Bilgen & Özeke, Istanbul
+90 212 236 57 07
Recommended in Corporate/M&A, Project Finance

ÖZEKE, Ender
Hergüner, Bilgen & Özeke, Istanbul
+90 212 236 57 07
Recommended in Project Finance

ÖZEL, Haluk Can
Özel & Özel, Istanbul +90 212 324 2040
hcozel@altheimer.co.uk
Recommended in Corporate/M&A
Specialisation: Partner. A business lawyer representing multinational companies investing and doing business in Turkey. Has extensive experience representing international companies. Activities include mergers and acquisitions, leveraged buyouts, joint ventures, government contracts, project financing, trademark, copyrights and general corporate matters.
Prof. Memberships: Istanbul, International and American Bar Associations.
Career: Istanbul University Law Faculty (LLB). Served legal apprenticeship at Istanbul courts. Served as Legal Advisor in Deva Holdings. Authored the chapters on Turkey in 'International Execution Against Judgement Debtors'. Speaks Turkish and English.

PAKSOY, Serdar
Paksoy & Co, Istanbul +90 212 290 2350
Recommended in Banking & Finance

PEKIN, Ahmed
Pekin & Pekin, Istanbul +90 212 253 3710
Recommended in Banking & Finance

REISOGLU, Seza
Reisoglu Ensari Budak Law Firm, Ankara
+90 312 467 9103
Recommended in Banking & Finance

SOMAY, Metin
Somay Hukuk Bürosu, Istanbul +90 212 216 7562
Recommended in Banking & Finance

T

UGANDA

Corporate/Commercial

UGANDA Leading firms (Corporate/Commercial)
1 Mugerwa & Masembe Advocates
Shonubi, Musoke & Co
2 Katende Ssempebwa & Co
Sebalu & Lule Advocates and Legal Consultants
3 Hunter & Greig

Firms are listed alphabetically in each band.

Leading individuals (Corporate/Commercial)
1 BYAMUGISHA Joseph *Byamugisha & Rwaheru*
2 KATENDE John *Katende Ssempebwa & Co*
MASEMBE KANYEREZI Timothy *Mugerwa & Masembe Advocates*
SHONUBI Alan *Shonubi, Musoke & Co*
3 KARUGABA Phillip *Mugerwa & Masembe Advocates*
LULE Godfrey *Sebalu & Lule*
NKAMBO-MUGERWA PJ *Mugerwa & Masembe Advocates*
SSEMPEBWA Edward Frederick *Katende Ssempebwa & Co*

Individuals are listed alphabetically in each band.

Mugerwa & Masembe Advocates (2 ptrs, 3 asscs) Researchers received concerted approval for this *"top notch"* commercial practice, noted for its aggressive litigation style. Ugandan and foreign financial institutions dominate the firm's client base, including oil and insurance sectors and government peristatals. It represented the Central Bank on the licensing of commercial banks and recovery of monies owed by collapsed debtor banks. *"Articulate and intelligent"* **Timothy Masembe Kanyerezi*** *"drives the show,"* while peers believe that the recent addition of *"brilliant"* academic **Phillip Karugaba*** has further elevated the firm's status. *"Persuasive and diligent,"* his former roles at the Ministry of Finance's Privatisation Unit and Central Bank are a continuing source of instruction. Former Attorney General and First Solicitor Advocate **P J Nkambo-Mugerwa*** is highly respected although now less of a transactional force. **Clients:** Bank of Uganda; Barclays Bank of Uganda; Uganda Commercial Bank; Citibank Uganda; Uganda Breweries; Diamond Trust Bank of Uganda; Petro Uganda; Coffee Marketing Board.

Shonubi, Musoke & Co (3 ptrs, 7 asscs) This *"dynamic"* fast growing young firm specialises in corporate finance and banking transactional work and handles contentious matters. It counts major local and international banks and foreign investors as clients. The firm advised Westmont Asia BHD against the government in a banking dispute involving tribunal arbitration hearing at the ICC. Credited with having *"singlehandedly"* secured the firm's successful profile, **Alan Shonubi*** *"knows how to deliver a result for the client"* and is the one who *"foreign investors seek to get an objective view."* The firm represented CDC and CDC (Euro) in the debt buyout of one of Uganda's largest textile companies, Nytil Picfare, and advised on the privatisation of Uganda Telecom and the recapitalisation of CellTel. It also advised MTN (Uganda) on a note issuance programme to be floated on the Uganda Stock Exchange. **Clients:** Grindleys International; IFC; CDC; CDC Europe; Diageo Group; Golf Course Holdings; Bank of Uganda; Bank of Baroda; Orient Bank; Guinness Group; Clifford Chance; International Distillers (Uganda); Maersk Uganda; Insurance Company of East Africa.

Katende Ssempebwa & Co (2 ptrs, 15 asscs) *"Still one of the leading firms"* with strength in commercial litigation, and clients ranging from middle tier local companies to blue chip multinationals. Reputed to be somewhat abrasive, the market admired the firm's large team of *"high quality, young lawyers."* Key figure **John Katende*** is a *"vision player"* who *"knows how to get business,"* while *"seasoned lawyer"* **Edward Frederick Ssempebwa*** is *"cool and always in control."* The firm recently concluded a $45 million class action settlement for the East Africa Community former workers and represented Capricorn Canopy Consortium (US international tax planning) in a new $25 million East African pilot project. **Clients:** Shell (Uganda); Tanzania Cigarette Corp; Kinyara Sugar Works; Kenya Airways; Government of Uganda; National Water & Sewage Corp; Central Bank; Uganda Development Bank.

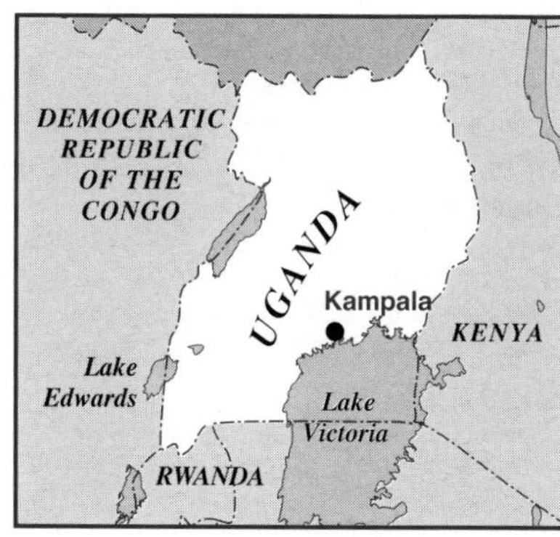

Sebalu & Lule Advocates and Legal Consultants (4 ptrs, 4 asscs) *"One of the old guard,"* considered a *"consistent market presence."* Some interviewees, however, commented on the advancing seniority of its leaders. Clients include domestic and international banks and local companies. Active on behalf of former workers in the East African repossession cases, former Attorney General **Godfrey Lule*** continues to be highly regarded for his litigation skills. **Clients:** Standard Chartered Bank; Uganda Commercial Bank; Nile Bank; Bank of Uganda; Roko Construction; Bata.

Hunter & Greig (2 ptrs, 1 assc) Researchers received universal recommendation for this strong team that has *"stood the test of time"* despite the loss of key players over the years. A popular outfit established by British expatriates in 1903, it specialises in commercial banking transactions including advice to local and foreign banks on project financing and loan agreement documentation. **Clients:** Stanbic Bank; Bank of Baroda; Crane Bank; Trans Africa Bank; Uganda Electricity Board; Uganda Coffee Development Authority; Svenska Handlesbanken (Swedish bank); Eksportfinance (Norweigan bank); National Insurance Corporation; Unilever; American Insurance Group; Xerotech Uganda; Save The Children Fund; Uganda Red Cross; St John Ambulance.

Other Notable Practitioner **Joseph Byamugisha*** of Byamugisha & Rwaheru Advocates is *"scholarly and thorough,"* and has *"the highest standing"*

*See leaders' profiles on pages 685

among his peers. Known for his representation of larger government peristatals on large scale litigation and transactional work, he is key advisor to the Central Bank and acted on the public flotations of British American Tobacco and Uganda Credit on the Kampala Stock Exchange. **Clients:** Bank of Uganda; Uganda Commercial Bank; National Insurance Corp.

Leaders' profiles – Uganda

BYAMUGISHA, Joseph
Byamugisha & Rwaheru Advocates, Kampala
+256 41 341898

KARUGABA, Phillip
Mugerwa & Masembe Advocates, Kampala
+256 41 343 859

KATENDE, John W.
Katende Ssempebwa & Co, Kampala
+256 41 233 770
Specialisation: Founding firm partner. Has over thirty years experience in the practice of Law in Uganda. Has been involved in a lot of ground breaking and law creating litigation and has contributed significantly to the development of the law and its practice in Uganda. Outside the courtrooms, is a leading practitioner in areas relating to business, corporate and commercial law. Has been involved in the structuring and planning of many of the largest commercial ventures in Uganda and continues to routinely advise leading commercial concerns in Uganda on a daily basis. Developed expertise in the areas of Corporate Law, Finance, International Commercial Transactions, Mergers and Acquisitions and litigation generally.
Prof. Memberships: Uganda Law Society, East African Law Society.
Career: Graduate of the University of East Africa at Dar-es-Salaam and Harvard Law School in the United States of America. Has lectured in law at Uganda's Makerere University and served as an external examiner for the Universities of Dar-es-Salaam, Zambia, Malawi and Nairobi for several years. Authored many learned treatises including 'The Law of Business Associations in East and Central Africa'.

LULE, Godfrey S
Sebalu & Lule Advocates and Legal Consultants, Kampala +256 41 232 604
Specialisation: Insolvency practice, company law, commercial law (banking), property litigation and family law. Corporate legal services, labour law, land law, tax law, defamation, constitutional law, intellectual property law, arbitration, mergers and acquisitions, aviation law, joint ventures and privatisation transactions. Registration of business associations, trademarks, patents and notaries public.
Prof. Memberships: Uganda Law Society; Non Performing Assets Recovery Trust Tribunal (1966 to date); East African Law Society; Indian Bar.
Career: 1962: India Chambers of the Attorney General of Mysore State – Legal Assistant. 1963-65: Uganda Government – State Attorney. 1965-1966: Uganda Government – Administrator General; Registrar General; Registrar of Trade Marks & Patents (1965-71). 1971-1973: Uganda Government – Solicitor General. 1973-1977: Uganda Government – Attorney General, Minister of Justice. 1978-1980: Private Practice in UK under *Hosking & Company*, at Bournemouth and London. 1980-date: Private practice in Uganda – Senior Partner *Sebalu & Lule Advocates*. Additional professional activities: 1966-1968: Uganda's delegate to the negotiation and establishment of the World Industrial Property organisation (WIPO) in Geneva, Switzerland, which resulted into the establishment of regional offices such as the one in Zambia for East and Central African countries. 1969-1970: Uganda's delegate to the International conference negotiating the Patent Cooperation Treaty (PCT) which was ultimately adopted in Washington D.C. in 1970. It granted concession to developing countries on transfer of technology.
Personal: University of Bombay, India – LLB.

MASEMBE KANYEREZI, Timothy
Mugerwa & Masembe Advocates, Kampala
+256 41 343 859

NKAMBO-MUGERWA, P J
Mugerwa & Masembe Advocates, Kampala
+256 41 343 859

SHONUBI, Alan
Shonubi, Musoke & Co, Kampala +256 41 230 384
alans.shonubi@starcom.co.ug
Specialisation: Senior partner and head of the Corporate and Commercial department. Widely experienced in a broad range of corporate and commercial matters. Has advised and/or acted for numerous local and international clients regarding diverse issues (contentious and non-contentious) including banking, corporate finance, investment law, mining, privatisation and telecommunications law. Acted for Mobile Systems International Cellular Holdings B.V. in its acquisition of the largest ISP in Uganda, advised Uganda Travel Bureau and Speedbird Travel Bureau when they merged to form the largest tour and travel agency in Uganda, acted for CDC Group plc during the receivership of a major textile mill in Uganda, acted for IFC and East African Development Bank during the financing of a major telecoms company and advised Westmont Land Asia BHD in a major arbitration before an ICC Tribunal based in London. Acts for various financial institutions, international agencies, international law firms and multinational corporations in a range of matters including structuring of transactions and transactional negotiations.
Prof. Memberships: Uganda Law Society.
Publications: 'Managing a Legal Practice', published 2000.
Career: Enrolled 1986. 1985-1987 Claims Manager, Sun International Insurance. 1988-1990 Senior Legal Officer, The Co-operative Bank.
Personal: Born 1958. Attended Makerere University Law School 1978-1981. Member Rotary Club of Kampala East (Past President) and holds two Paul Harris Fellow honours.

SSEMPEBWA, Edward Frederick
Katende Ssempebwa & Co, Kampala
+256 41 233 770
Specialisation: Founding firm partner. An authority on matters relating to revenue law and taxation and Constitutional Law. Has practised law both within and outside the courtrooms with distinction for over thirty years now and is a leading consultant in several areas of practice in Uganda. Has meritoriously earned the title of 'Senior Counsel' in the Courts of Uganda. Areas of particular interest and specialisation include: Revenue Law and Taxation, Constitutional Law, Contracts, Conveyancing and General Litigation.
Prof. Memberships: Uganda Law Society, East African Law Society.
Career: Graduate of the University of East Africa at Dar-es-Salaam and Queen's University Belfast, Ireland. A celebrated Professor of Law at Makerere University in Uganda and the Universities of Dar-es-Salaam and Zambia. Author of many learned articles and is widely published in many of the world's leading journals. Several times been the President of the Uganda Law Society and has also been a Minister in the Government of Uganda. Was a member of the Uganda Constitutional Commission, which drafted the current Constitution of the Republic of Uganda.

UKRAINE

Corporate/Commercial

U

UKRAINE Leading firms (Corporate/Commercial)
1 Altheimer & Gray
Baker & McKenzie
2 Vasil Kisil & Partners
3 Salans Hertzfeld & Heilbronn
Squire, Sanders & Dempsey LLP
4 BC Toms & Co
Proxen
Sergiy Koziakov & Partners
5 Frishberg & Partners
Grischenko & Partners
Konnov & Sozanovsky

Firms are listed alphabetically in each band.

Leading individuals (Corporate/Commercial)
1 KISIL Vasil *Vasil Kisil & Partners*
2 JOHNSON Jaroslawa *Altheimer & Gray*
3 BAIBARZA Volodymyr *Altheimer & Gray*
KOZIAKOV Sergiy *Sergiy Koziakov & Partners*
KRYSHTALOWYCH Helen *Squire, Sanders*
MYCYK Adam *Altheimer & Gray*
SCOTT David *Baker & McKenzie*
ZADOROZHNIY Alexander *Proxen*
4 BATIUC Olegh *Salans Hertzfeld & Heilbronn*

Individuals are listed alphabetically in each band.

Altheimer & Gray (3 ptrs, 13 asscs) *"One of the top two firms"* in the Ukraine, this outfit is heavily involved in privatisation on both the buy and sell side. Key elements of the workload include direct foreign investment, general corporate and debt restructuring. The team serves as financial advisor to the government and prepares packages for privatisation, as well as acting for a number of western companies, including a major investment bank, a cigarette company and a western European electricity company.

US-educated *"powerhouse"* **Jaroslawa Johnson*** leads the practice and is spending her third term on the Western NIS Enterprise Fund, while **Volodymyr Baibarza*** is seen by competitors as a *"strong and professional Ukrainian lawyer"* working on IP and finance matters. Newly ranked **Adam Mycyk*** has made a good impression on the market. **Clients:** Philip Morris; Crédit Suisse First Boston; Kraft Foods.

Baker & McKenzie (3 ptrs, 9 asscs) The office advises on banking and finance, capital markets, corporate finance, tax, M&A and privatisation, and has particular niches in real estate, telecoms and energy. Managing partner **David Scott*** was recommended to researchers as a *"competent and energetic commercial lawyer."* The firm advised a US investment fund on the equity financing of an agricultural services company, and acted for an international bank on underwriting an IPO for a Russian/Ukrainian telecoms company. **Clients:** EBRD; IFC; Cisco Systems; ING Barings; AT&T; Chase Manhattan; Ford; Deutsche Bank; Kimberly Clark; Samsung; Unilever.

Vasil Kisil & Partners (7 ptrs, 15 asscs) *"Professional and successful"* local firm, which enjoys a reputation unparalleled by any of its Ukrainian counterparts. It is said by clients to have a *"niche in commercial litigation and arbitration"* and **Vasil Kisil*** was recommended to researchers as *"one of the leading academics in civil law."* The firm represented a client on the purchasing of shares in a Ukrainian energy station, a transaction worth $480 million. Also successfully represented McDonald's in the Ukraine on a number of product liability cases. **Clients:** Cargill; Du Pont de Nemours; Pioneer; André & Cie SA; ING Barings; CME Media Enterprises; McDonald's; Ukrainian Mobile Telecommunications.

Salans Hertzfeld & Heilbronn (1 ptr, 10 asscs) The Kiev office of this strong regional firm advises a predominantly local client base on joint ventures, M&A and privatisations. Close relationships with governmental institutions are highlighted by work for the State Property Fund (the chief privatisation body of the Ukraine), Anti-Monopoly Committee, National Bank and State Securities and Stock Market Commission. **Olegh Batiuc*** is *"an experienced lawyer with common sense,"* for whom peers predict *"a bright future."* **Clients:** State Property Fund of Ukraine; Black Sea Shipping Company.

Squire Sanders & Dempsey LLP (1 ptr, 7 asscs) Full-service commercial firm, covering areas such

as securities, banking and finance, capital markets, privatisations and joint ventures. Telecoms and energy are key areas of expertise. **Helen Kryshtalowych*** runs the office, and is acknowledged as *"the firm's main business-getter."*

The firm has assisted a number of foreign companies on attaining majority stakes in local organisations. **Clients:** Foreign investors.

BC Toms & Co (2 ptrs, 12 asscs) Particularly active in the energy sector, the firm is said to *"work for a number of good domestic clients."* The firm's focus is entirely on Ukrainian law, and it was involved in the founding of the British/Ukrainian chamber of commerce. The team recently advised on a large energy project, sponsored by the EBRD. **Clients:** Domestic companies.

Proxen Mentioned to researchers as *"a cosmopolitan Ukrainian law firm,"* it works mainly with Ukrainian businesses on joint ventures and the establishment of offshore companies. The *"well-connected"* **Alexander Zadorozhniy*** is the head of the firm and is a *"renowned businessman and politician."* **Clients:** Domestic companies.

Sergiy Koziakov & Partners (6 ptrs, 3 asscs) Noted for its work on behalf of international companies investing in the Ukraine, the team is led by respected local figure **Sergiy Koziakov***. The group represented US company Tectonic Capital on the purchase of 50.2% of shares in Rivne Linen factory, and represented several offshore companies buying shares in an oil refinery plant. **Clients:** Avon; Bosch; Diffusion Finance; Kap; McDonald's; Tectonic Capital.

*See leaders' profiles on pages 687

Frishberg & Partners (2 ptrs, 5 asscs) The firm has a reputation for joint ventures and privatisation, and generally advises western European companies on their Ukrainian acquisitions. The firm has worked in conjunction with Commerzbank, Crédit Commercial de France and Electricité de France on privatisations in the soda production, cement production and electricity industries. **Clients:** Baltic Beverages Holding; CA IB; Bank Austria; Creditanstalt Leasing; Skanska East Europe; EBRD.

Grischenko & Partners (5 ptrs, 13 asscs) One of the oldest local law firms, it was recommended to researchers for its *"high profile among Ukrainian clients,"* and specialises in project finance, IP, inward investment, tax and labour law. The team also represents agencies and overseas corporates, representing the EBRD and Ericsson on a multi-million dollar transaction with Kievstar, and advising Carlsberg on the acquisition of a Ukrainian brewery. **Clients:** Carlsberg; Ukrtelecom; EBRD; Ericsson.

Konnov & Sozanovsky (2 ptrs, 5 asscs) Well known in the domestic field, the firm advises a substantial local client base on corporate reorganisations, acquisitions and liquidations. Also advises on regulatory issues, drafting contracts for various categories of commercial transactions and providing legal support to a range of business projects. **Clients:** AGCO; LG International Corp; LG Information and Communications; Xerox; Ukrainian Independent TV Corporation (Inter network); Carat Ukraine; Style S.

Leaders' profiles – Ukraine

BAIBARZA, Volodymyr
Altheimer & Gray, Kyiv +380 44 230 2534
vib@altheimer.kiev.ua
Specialisation: Partner with two decades of Ukrainian law experience; was engaged in the establishment of joint ventures with foreign investments in Ukraine, and advising on privatisation-legislation. Has acted as outside counsel to a variety of European and North American law firms.
Career: Began with *Injurcolleguia* Law Firm as a Legal Adviser (1977) and later as a Senior Legal Adviser. For ten years occupied leading legal and managerial positions at the Copyright Agency of Ukraine. Joined the Kyiv Regional Collegium of Advocates (1991). Kyiv State University, Faculty of International Relations and International Law (JD, MA, both with honours). Speaks Ukrainian, English and Russian.

BATIUC, Olegh
Salans Hertzfeld & Heilbronn, Kiev
+380 44 246 52 46

JOHNSON, Jaroslawa Zelinsky
Altheimer & Gray, Kyiv +380 44 230 2534
johnsonj@altheimer.com
Specialisation: Partner and director of Kyiv office. Practises in international transactions, mergers and acquisitions, secured transactions and government relations. Graduate of Goucher College; University of Wisconsin Law School (JD). Editor-in-Chief, 'Wisconsin Law Review'. Law clerk to Chief Judge Thomas E Fairchild, U.S. Court of Appeals for the Seventh Circuit. Founding member and Chairman, America Ukraine Business Council. Currently editor-in-chief of Martindale-Hubbel's 'Ukraine Law Digest'. Appointed by U.S. President Bill Clinton to Board of Directors of $150 million Western NIS Enterprise Fund (1994), established by Congress to promote private sector development in Ukraine, Moldova and Belarus.

KISIL, Vasil
Vasil Kisil & Partners, Kiev +380 44 220 5900

KOZIAKOV, Sergiy Y.
Sergiy Koziakov & Partners, Kyiv +380 44 251 1011

KRYSHTALOWYCH, Helen Z
Squire, Sanders & Dempsey LLP, Kiev
+380 44 228 8900

MYCYK, Adam M
Altheimer & Gray, Kyiv +380 44 230 2534
amm@altheimer.kiev.ua
Specialisation: Partner. Specialises in joint ventures, foreign investment, corporate matters, and complex financing transactions (extensively involving the National Bank of Ukraine and the Ministry of Finance).
Career: Admitted, Maryland and District of Columbia bars. Licensed to practise by the Ministry of Justice in Ukraine. Previously a senior associate with a Kyiv firm and an associate at a Washington, DC firm (represented clients in transportation industry). Was Law Clerk to the U.S. Equal Employment Opportunity Commission, Office of Commissioner Joy Cherian.
Personal: George Washington University (BA); Columbus School of Law, Catholic University of America (JD), Law Review member. Speaks English, Ukrainian, Russian.

SCOTT, David
Baker & McKenzie, Kyiv +380 44 490 7070
Specialisation: Managing Partner of the Kyiv office of *Baker & McKenzie.* Has practised as an English solicitor since 1987. Has been residing in Kyiv since 1997. Specialises in banking and finance, capital markets, and acquisitions/reorganizations. Member of *Baker & McKenzie's* Global Banking & Finance Practice Group. Has acted on numerous finance and acquisition transactions, including the rescheduling of sovereign debt, structured financings, privatisations (and related investments by strategic investors), acquisitions and corporate restructurings of major enterprises.
Career: Admitted to practice Law in England and Wales. Prior to joining *Baker & McKenzie* in 1994, worked in London, Tokyo and Moscow with a leading London City firm.
Personal: Born 15 September 1961. Graduate of King's College, London and Universite de Paris I (Pantheon-Sorbonne) (English and French Law). Fluent in English, French and Russian.

ZADOROZHNIY, Alexander
Proxen, 2533125 Kiev +380 44 512 7000

UNITED ARAB EMIRATES

Banking & Finance

UNITED ARAB EMIRATES Leading firms (Banking & Finance)
1
Allen & Overy
Clifford Chance
2
Simmons & Simmons
3
Afridi & Angell
Al Tamimi & Co
Bryan Cave LLP
Clyde & Co
Denton Wilde Sapte
Key & Dixon
Trowers & Hamlins

Firms are listed alphabetically in each band.

Leading individuals (Banking & Finance)
1
O'HARE Caroline *Clifford Chance*
RODERICK Simon *Allen & Overy*
2
CAMERON Ewan *Clifford Chance*
DE BELDER Richard *Bryan Cave LLP*
3
AFRIDI Ali *Afridi & Angell*
DIXON Christopher *Key & Dixon*
MUBAYDEEN Ibrahim *Simmons & Simmons*
SILVER Jonathan *Clyde & Co*

Individuals are listed alphabetically in each band.

Allen & Overy (2 ptrs, 10 asscs) Research confirms the firm's reputation as undisputed leaders in the banking and finance sector. They are often mentioned with Clifford Chance as the *"biggest hitters"* in the market. Clients agreed that the team's track record, breadth of resources and consistent quality across the range of finance disciplines placed it in a *"band of its own."*

The Dubai team is led by the experienced **Simon Roderick***, recommended as an *"ever better banking lawyer".* The firm acted for ANZ Investment Bank as arranger of a $60 million facility to finance the acquisition by the Cupola Group of the marketing business of Inchcape. It also advised regular clients Barclays Bank and Commercial Bank of Dubai on the $500 million loan and $100 million Islamic tranche to Thuraya Satellite Telecommunications. **Clients:** ANZ Investment Bank; Union National Bank; Barclays; Emirates Bank International; Gulf International Bank.

Clifford Chance (1 ptr, 3 asscs) *"World-class branding"* and a strength of purpose ensures that the firm has capitalised on expansion in the Dubai banking market. The team provides a specialist and highly professional service, with three new banking lawyers appointed this year. *"Fine negotiator"* **Caroline O'Hare*** is felt to have a *"positive influence"* on the team and **Ewan Cameron*** has a *"full understanding of Middle East culture and law."*

The firm acts for both conventional and Islamic financial institutions, governments, and corporates in domestic Gulf and international banking transactions. Structured and asset finance lies at the core of the deal flow, including ship and aircraft financing, equipment leasing and property construction. **Clients:** National Bank of Abu Dhabi; National Bank of Dubai; National Bank of Qatar; Chase Manhattan Bank; Bank of America.

Simmons & Simmons (3 ptrs, 7 asscs) A leading light in the Abu Dhabi banking market, it is heavily linked to the projects market. Our researchers found that the *"impressive"* **Ibrahim Mubaydeen*** made a substantial contribution to the team's activities, securing prestigious clients.

It advised on the establishment of the ADIB Al Hilal Fund managed by Abu Dhabi Islamic Bank, one of the first to offer a number of portfolios which invest in accordance with the principles of Islamic Shari'a. The firm also acted on the drafting of the security package and financing documents for Taweelah A1 project and advising BNP Paribas on a $77.5 million syndicated facility agreement. **Clients:** National Bank of Abu Dhabi; Prudential Securities; Barclays; SocGen; AIG International; Deutsche Bank.

Afridi & Angell (3 ptrs, 3 asscs) Dubai-based, the part-American origin makes this firm popular with US clients operating out of Saudi Arabia and India, seeking advice in the UK-dominated UAE legal market. The *"brilliant"* **Ali Afridi*** is key to the team's success.

Active across the board for both western and Islamic clients, advising on credit facilities, syndications and work-outs, the team also has exper-

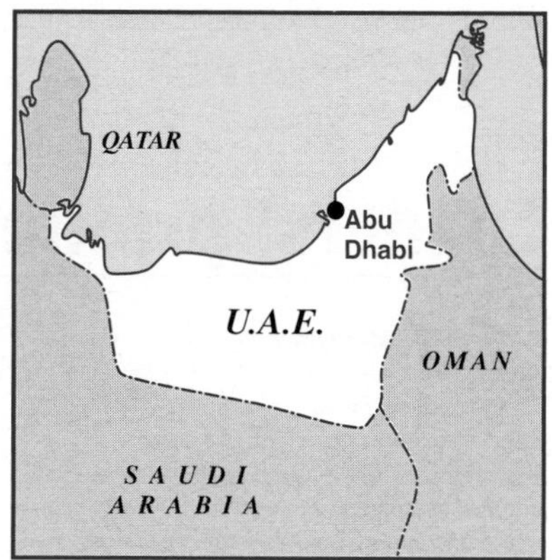

tise in regulatory matters. The heart of the banking practice is the firm's project financings on behalf of UAE based banks and the development of banking projects including Treasury, cash management and bond related products. **Clients:** ANZ Grindlays Bank; Dubai Islamic Bank; Emirates Bank International; Government of Sharjah (Finance Department); Lloyds TSB.

Al Tamimi & Co (5 ptrs and 25 asscs in total) A highly respected, professional local firm with a *"brilliant mix of qualities,"* regarded by clients as providing the *"whole package."* All the banking lawyers are bilingual. The firm advised on the entrance of financial institutions in the UAE, such as Coutts & Co, Bank of Bahrain & Kuwait and Dow Jones. Longstanding, prestigious clients include HSBC Middle East Bank, United Arab Bank and Arab Bank. The firm acted for Arab Bank in relation to a term loan of AED24 million to Abu Dhabi National Industrial Project for the construction of a pharmaceutical plant. **Clients:** Lloyds TSB; Emirates Bank International; HSBC Middle East Bank; United Arab Bank and Arab Bank.

Bryan Cave LLP (3 ptrs, 3 asscs) The only major US firm with offices in Abu Dhabi and Dubai, it practices in association with Al-Mehairi Legal Consultants, serving a broad international client base. The firm acted as counsel to GCC banks on the launch of investment funds et al with a market value of nearly $1 billion.

Researchers were told that *"first class banking lawyer"* **Richard de Belder*** deserves the credit for the firm's prestigious status. He advised on TABREED, a syndicated facility and continues act for regular clients Abu Dhabi Investment Company and Union National Bank. **Clients:** Dubai Islamic Bank; Union National Bank; Abu Dhabi Investment Company.

Clyde & Co (5 ptrs, 7 asscs) Renowned for its strengths in shipping and the insurance sectors, the firm is active across the board. It focuses on the syndication of loan arrangements, facility letters, performance bonds and regulatory matters. Leading light, **Jonathan Silver*** is recommended for his experience and well established profile in the region. The Dubai office advised on $150-200 million corporate debt restructurings in which three major European financial institutions and a UAE bank were involved. Also advised on a working capital facility for a new project start-up in the UAE worth $60 million. **Clients:** Multinational European and American financial institutions; local banks.

Denton Wilde Sapte (2 ptrs, 6 asscs) Regarded as a reputable and *"steady"* banking practice, the market anticipates it will prove to be a *"considerable force"* in the region. Predictably, the Dubai office conducts the most prestigious banking work although it is supported by a strong Abu Dhabi office. The firm has acted for mainstay client, Merrill Lynch, on the establishment of is Dubai branch office including employment matters and securities law.

The team advised HSBC on a syndicated loan facility to New Dubai Retail City including provision for separate ECA and Islamic tranches. The Abu Dhabi office advised ABN Amro as lead bank in an AED37 million syndicated loan. The team advised on various jurisdictional matters in relation to a virtual bank and advised Abbey National on licensing and regulatory issues in the UAE. **Clients:** Merrill Lynch; Abu Dhabi Commercial Bank; ANZ Grindlays; Emirates Bank International; Barclays Bank; HSBC Bank Middle East.

Key & Dixon (2 ptrs, 5 asscs) Associate firm of Nabarro Nathanson in Dubai, it operates an able if low profile banking practice. Peers acknowledge that it scores well with governments and governmental agencies as key clients. **Christopher Dixon*** remains a familiar sight to most in the region. The firm is instructed by institutional lenders and syndicates in various multibank financings in the Gulf (principally UAE and Saudi Arabia) and regularly advises on the raising of capital, credit transactions, secured financing and derivative transactions. **Clients:** DUBA; DUGAS; ENOC; DUCAB.

Trowers & Hamlins (3 ptrs, 3 asscs) Although less a leader in terms of volume, the team's excellent credentials and long-standing UAE presence continue to capture important deals, often in the projects field. Active in asset finance, including aircraft finance and equipment leasing, it has provided local advice on every Gulf Air financing of aircraft since the mid 1980s. The team has advised financial institutions on setting up and management of project funds. **Clients:** Abu Dhabi Islamic Bank; Emirates Bank International; Abu Dhabi Islamic Bank.

U

Corporate/M&A

Allen & Overy (2 ptrs, 8 asscs) Regarded as one of the top players in Dubai, operating a *"quality corporate practice"* although the market continues to refer to the firm's banking activities. *"Bright and able"* main hitter, **Simon Roderick*** has 13 years of experience in the region and is judged one of the team's most valuable assets, while project finance lawyer **Duncan Macnab*** was recommended by rivals and clients as having a *"very good corporate background"*.

The Dubai office undertakes transactions in the UAE, Egypt, Jordan, Lebanon, Oman and Qatar. It advised Emirates on its acquisition of Maritime and Mercantile International LLC from Gray MacKenzie & Partners. Capitalising on the internet boom, the firm acted on the establishment of Tejari.com, the first B2B exchange in the UAE. **Clients:** Emirates; ABN AMRO; DIC; Abela & Co; Marks & Spencer.

Al Tamimi & Co (5 ptrs, 25 asscs) Highlighted as *"the best local firm going,"* this rapidly expanding corporate team is the largest non-affiliated law firm in the country with offices in Dubai, Abu Dhabi and Sharjah. A licensed local counsel with international lawyers, it is instructed by a variety of major US and UK legal practices. With a client base ranging from small-scale entrepreneurs to multi-national companies, peers agreed that the firm has a real *"edge."* **Essam Al Tamimi*** has a *"high profile,"* displaying expertise in business structuring, agency and distribution work. The team has advised the commercial arms of the Dubai Government in relation to high profile projects. **Clients:** Microsoft; IBM; Roche Pharmaceuticals; Jebel Ali Free Zone; Emirates Airlines.

Clifford Chance (2 ptrs, 25 asscs) Interviewees believed it to be *"at least twice the size of any other corporate finance practice there,"* and an undoubted leader across the Gulf in cross border corporate finance, privatisation and Islamic products transactions. It has witnessed an increase in telecoms and e-commerce activity. The team has established an in-house advocacy capability while the association with Hadef Al-Dhahiri resulted in a valuable presence in Abu Dhabi.

Both peers and clients alike agreed that the *"charming"* **Ewan Cameron*** has *"extensive knowledge of the region."* The Dubai office led advice to both the Government and Saudi Telecoms Company on its privatisation by way of strategic sale and international IPO. It also acted on the privatisation of Saudi Arabian airlines and the establishment of a B2B exchange for the oil industry. **Clients:** GE, Kvaerner; Heinz; National Power; Shell; Coca-Cola; Philip Morris.

Simmons & Simmons (3 ptrs, 7 asscs) An efficient, international firm described as a *"one stop shop."* Competitors felt that the bulk of local work was secured by the *"talented"* **Ibrahim Mubaydeen*** with his *"remarkable combination of qualities"* and the highly rated **Andrew Ward***.

Dominating the market for offset agreements, the team advised Offsets Group on data protection and IT law issues surrounding the establishment of an extranet system and is retained as offsets' adviser on the $8-10 billion project Project Dolphin for the extraction and treatment of gas in Qatar. It advised the Abu Dhabi Securities Market on the establishment of a stock exchange and in the telecoms sphere continues to provide a wide range of intellectual property issues. **Clients:** Abu Dhabi Investment Authority; Visa International; British School of Motoring; UAE Offsets Group; Regus; Hong Kong Air.

Afridi & Angell (17 lawyers) *"Consistently doing well,"* the firm is well regarded for deals involving

*See leaders' profiles on pages 692-694

UNITED ARAB EMIRATES
Leading firms (Corporate/Mergers & Acquisitions)

Band	Firm
1	Allen & Overy
	Al Tamimi & Co
	Clifford Chance
	Simmons & Simmons
2	Afridi & Angell
	Al-Sayegh Richards Butler
	Clyde & Co
3	Denton Wilde Sapte
	Trowers & Hamlins
4	Berrymans Lace Mawer
	James Berry & Associates

Firms are listed alphabetically in each band.

Leading individuals (Corporate/Mergers & Acquisitions)

Band	Individual
1	**MUBAYDEEN Ibrahim** *Simmons & Simmons*
	RODERICK Simon *Allen & Overy*
2	**AL TAMIMI Essam** *Al Tamimi & Co*
	CAMERON Ewan *Clifford Chance*
	TREW Anthony *Al-Sayegh Richards Butler*
3	**ADAMS Simon** *Clyde & Co*
	BIBBINGS Jennifer *Towers & Hamlins*
	LEWIS Rhys *Al-Sayegh Richards Butler*
	MACNAB Duncan *Allen & Overy*
	MICHELMORE Peter *Al-Sayegh Richards Butler*
	O'TOOLE Niall *Denton Wilde Sapte*
	SILVER Jonathan *Clyde & Co*
	WARD Andrew *Simmons & Simmons*

Individuals are listed alphabetically in each band.

multiple jurisdictions with support from its US and Pakistani offices. The partners have developed extensive professional contacts across the region. The corporate group encompasses securities work, asset based and lease financings and has seen a growth in venture capital and private equity transactions. Lawyers in the UAE are proficient in Arabic, Urdu, Hindi, Pushtu, Tamil and French. **Clients:** American President Lines; Kelloggs; Microsoft; Mitsubishi; Texaco.

Al-Sayegh Richards Butler (3 ptrs, 2 asscs) Despite the departure of the group's managing partner in London, it retains *"a real Middle Eastern presence."* Leading light **Anthony Trew***, concentrates on broad strategic commercial advice and remains the chairman of the British Business Group in Abu Dhabi. **Rhys Lewis*** is rated by peers as an *"experienced commercial lawyer"* and **Peter Michelmore*** has his *"finger on the commercial pulse."*

An expanding regional practice, it has mainstay clients from construction and airline industries. It acted for Gulf Aircraft Maintenance Company (GAMCO) in establishing its joint venture with GE, and advised Mohammed Bin Masaood & Sons in the replacement by Sequa Corporation of Kvaerner as the technology partner in Masaood John Brown, the industrial gas turbine and manufacturing business. **Clients:** Hughes; Dyncorp; Microsoft; Norwich Union; Umbro.

Clyde & Co (3 ptrs, 7 asscs) The Dubai office operates throughout the Gulf and is a *"sound commercial practice"* which offers a high degree of expertise. The experienced **Jonathan Silver*** is said to *"know his way around the market"* and **Simon Adams*** is familiar player. Multi-national corporates form the backbone of its client base which also services locally owned business covering the retail, IT, manufacturing, construction and shipping industries. The team acted in a $90 million disposal involving seven regional jurisdictions, and also advised on the restructuring of distribution arrangements across the Middle East for a global manufacturer. **Clients:** Property developers, IT, retail and telecoms companies.

Denton Wilde Sapte (1 ptr, 1 assc) Interviewees perceived the firm as *"fresh thinking and a corporate specialist,"* developing its volume in energy related fields. *"Superb lawyer"* **Niall O'Toole*** was singled out for his ability to maintain the firm's broad swathe of clients. The team advised mainstay client BP on gas and oil deals and corporate joint venturing and has lately seconded an assistant solicitor to BP's offices in Abu Dhabi. It acted on major property and infrastructure developments in Abu Dhabi and advised the Gulf Business Centre on e-commerce matters. **Clients:** BP; Amcoific Century; Gulf Business Centre.

Trowers & Hamlins (3 ptrs, 6 asscs) With vast experience and a strong regional emphasis, clients are impressed with the firm's personal service and *"quality partner involvement."* **Jennifer Bibbings*** in Dubai is *"a breath of fresh air and common sense."* The team is active in the structuring of companies, joint ventures and general corporate work. The corporate practice has also acquired a strong blue chip profile, acting for clients both in the Gulf and neighbouring states. **Clients:** Marks & Spencer; McDonalds; Walt Disney; Dubai Investments.

Berrymans Lace Mawer (2 asscs) Regarded as a *"top notch insurance firm,"* and despite the loss of senior lawyers such as Jason Blich it is *"business as usual."* An association agreement with James Berry & Associates has meant that the firm is able to concentrate on cementing existing relationships (it survived the panel cuts in the UK) and winning valuable new clients. The firm advised on the Group Pension Scheme on behalf of Alliance Insurance, aimed at expatriates living and working in the UAE. **Clients:** Royal Sun Alliance; Alliance Insurance; Commercial Union; General Accident.

James Berry & Associates (1 ptr, 3 asscs) Known for its consulting work, the firm has expertise a wide spectrum of corporate and commercial transactions including joint ventures, manufacturing and licensing agreements, and international trade and patents. Managing partner, James Boyd Berry (UK qualified barrister) is described as *"approachable and efficient."* The team also has a private client capability and has developed a division focusing on information technology, IP, e-commerce and e-banking. **Clients:** International petroleum and construction companies.

Project Finance

UNITED ARAB EMIRATES Leading firms (Project Finance)
1 Allen & Overy
Clifford Chance
Shearman & Sterling
2 Afridi & Angell
Simmons & Simmons
Trowers & Hamlins
3 Al-Sayegh Richards Butler
Denton Wilde Sapte
Hadef Al Dhahiri & Associates
Key & Dixon

Firms are listed alphabetically in each band.

Leading individuals (Project Finance)
1 **CREED Adrian** *Trowers & Hamlins*
DUNDAS Philip *Shearman & Sterling*
McNAIR Alastair *Hadef Al Dhahiri & Associates*
WILLIAMS Nicholas *Simmons & Simmons*
2 **CAMERON Ewan** *Clifford Chance*
KEY Jeremy *Key & Dixon*
MACNAB Duncan *Allen & Overy*
MICHELMORE Peter *Al-Sayegh Richards Butler*

Individuals are listed alphabetically in each band.

Allen & Overy (2 ptrs, 10 asscs) Although the firm remains best known in the banking sphere, it is also among the leaders for project finance work. Strong on telecoms and energy projects, the firm's banking pre-eminence has ensured its position as counsel to the lenders for all but one of the major projects in the UAE. The Dubai office is led by one of the *"top players in the region,"* **Duncan Macnab***.

The firm advised the arrangers of the Thuraya Satellite Telecommunications project, and acted for the lenders on the financing of the Iso-Octane project. Other matters include advising Dubai Investments on the BOT sewage project for its Dubai Investments Park. Regionally, the office has been especially active in Yemen, acting for the Ministry of Electricity and Water. **Clients:** Cable & Wireless; Oman Gas Company; Thuraya Satellite Telecommunications.

Clifford Chance (2 ptrs, 25 asscs) A rapid increase in the number of lawyers based in the Dubai office has meant that the team no longer needs to rely on the London or New York branches for support. Our research found a group that *"does a huge amount of regional work,"* and conducts *"proper projects work"* on behalf of both sponsors and lenders. Regionally active in Oman, Saudi Arabia, Jordan, Bahrain and Qatar, the firm is considered to have enhanced its quality of work and its client base through its mergers with Rogers & Wells in the US and Pünder in Germany.

The team's biggest hitter, **Ewan Cameron***, is described as a *"safe pair of hands."* The firm advised on the Shweihat Independent Water and Power Project, valued at $1.5 billion, and acted for the sponsors, SPIC, in connection with the new Urea/Amonia green field project. Also represented the government on the Seeb and Salalah Airports privatisation. **Clients:** AES; SPIC; Oman Gas Company.

Shearman & Sterling (1 ptr, 2 asscs) Recognised as one of the leading firms in project finance, this *"client-oriented group"* was primarily recommended to researchers for its oil and gas expertise. The Abu Dhabi office has represented the national oil company, ADNOC, in numerous matters including the development of its full contractual regime for the sale of crude oil, refined products and gas in all aspects of the ADGAS LNG project and the GASCO LPG project. The office's managing partner **Philip Dundas*** is held in high esteem in the region and is *"a familiar figure in the market."* The firm advised on IPIC's acquisition of 50% of the Hyundai Oil Refinery Company, and continues to represent ADNOC on the Borealis Polyethylene project. **Clients:** ADNOC; UAE Offsets Group; ADGAS; Abu Dhabi Investment Company.

Afridi & Angell (16 lawyers) One of the largest foreign firms in the UAE, it has offices in Dubai, Abu Dhabi and Sharjah. Its history in the region dates back more than 25 years and the practitioners are said to be *"familiar and experienced"* local players. The firm advised Enron, bidders on the Taweelah A2 project, and represented Marubeni on the second privatisation project in the Abu Dhabi water and power sector, Taweelah A1. **Clients:** Emirates National Oil Co; Enron; Marubeni; Teledesic.

Simmons & Simmons (3 ptrs, 7 asscs) The Abu Dhabi office continues to be heavily involved in projects, and is considered to have a *"winning team of lawyers."* A close relationship with the Offsets Group and sound government contacts ensure that the firm inevitably is involved in a number of leading energy, telecoms and infrastructure projects in the region.

Project finance team leader **Nicholas Williams*** was recommended to our researchers as *"competent and highly experienced."* He leads a group that continues to advise on Project Dolphin, a project for the extraction and treatment of gas in Qatar and its transportation by pipe to Abu Dhabi, Dubai, Oman and Pakistan. Recent substantial work includes advising Abu Dhabi Water and Electricity Authority (ADWEA) on the $1.2 billion Taweelah A1 Power and Water project as well as the $1.3 billion Shuweihat Power and Water Project, both of which will be developed on a BOO basis. Other work includes advising the General Authority for the Support and Development of Health Care in Abu Dhabi on the suite of contracts for the supply of an integrated computer system linking all hospitals and clinics in the UAE. The firm continues to advise Hughes Space and International Inc in relation to the Thuraya satellite project. **Clients:** UOG; ADWEA; Alstom Power; Abu Dhabi Securities Market.

Trowers & Hamlins (3 ptrs, 6 asscs) Since the award of the Taweelah A1 project's award in favour of Tractebel rather than the firm's own client CMS Energy, its profile is considered to have lost some of its lustre. Nevertheless, the firm remains one of the most respected and well-known in Abu Dhabi, and specialises in energy and petrochemicals projects. **Adrian Creed*** is a long-term resident of the UAE, and is recommended by peers and clients as *"reliable, competent and knowledgeable."* The firm acted as lead counsel, both international and local, for Borealis A/S in all aspects of the development and financing of a world-wide petrochemicals joint venture with ADNOC, valued in excess of $1 billion. **Clients:** Borealis A/S; Borouge; CMS Energy.

Al-Sayegh Richards Butler (3 ptrs, 2 asscs) The Abu Dhabi office has an excellent reputation for its *"steady workload"* in project finance. The majority of the practice is devoted to deregulation and privatisation of various industrial sectors, mostly in the water and electricity industries. These projects, initiated by regional governments, have seen the firm acting for clients in both pre- and post-bid phases.

Peter Michelmore* was recommended by competitors as *"a sound technician"* with a *"good head on his shoulders."* His team has advised clients involved in major waste management, power transmission and distribution and security projects in Egypt, Oman, Kuwait, Saudi Arabia

*See leaders' profiles on pages 692-694

and the UAE. The firm has represented consortia on three power plant projects, acted for ESB International on power projects all over the Middle East, and for Babcock Borsing Power in relation to power projects in Kuwait and the UAE. **Clients:** Babcock Borsing Power; ESB International; Bechtel.

Denton Wilde Sapte (2 ptrs, 6 asscs) A strong force in regional energy projects, the firm acts both for lender and sponsors. On power work, the firm is acting for Babcock Borsing Power in relation to power projects in Kuwait and UAE, as well as advising ESB International on power projects in Oman, Saudi Arabia and the UAE. The Dubai office has been heavily involved in the proposed financing of a large retail development on behalf of key client HSBC. **Clients:** Babcock Borsing Power; HSBC; BAT; Flag Telecom.

Hadef Al Dhahiri & Associates (3 ptrs, 4 asscs) *Chambers'* researchers were impressed by the consistent market recommendation for this *"unique"* firm, which *"get things done in Abu Dhabi."* The group has grown substantially in the last few years, and its association with Clifford Chance has also raised its profile. Strong local connections have enabled the *"sensible and commercially-minded"* **Alastair McNair*** to boost the group's presence in regional projects, usually advising borrowers.

The firm acted for Tractebel on the Taweelah A2 project, as well as providing advice on the Thuraya satellite financing. **Clients:** Tractebel; Abu Dhabi Container Lines; ISO Octane; International Petroleum Investment Company; Total-Fina Elf.

Key & Dixon (2 ptrs, 4 asscs) Highly recommended for its work on oil and gas projects, the firm represents both government and corporate organisations on a broad range of deals, including up and downstream advice, and documentation for the construction of new refineries. **Jeremy Key*** is said to be an *"influential"* regional figure. Acting on a Caspian project development and financing and additional phases of a container terminal development. **Clients:** ENOC; DUGAS; VOPAK.

U

Leaders' profiles – United Arab Emirates

ADAMS, Simon
Clyde & Co, Dubai +971 4 331 1102
simon.adams@clyde.co.ae
Recommended in Corporate/M&A
Specialisation: Partner in the Corporate Commercial Department. Main area of work is corporate law, mergers and acquisitions, commercial agreements, principally agency, distribution and franchising and ship finance. Has acted on the acquisition by local interests of a UK Plc's operations in the Arabian Gulf; the disposal of a UK Plc's non-core business in the Arabian Gulf; the disposal by a UK construction company of its soil testing and analysis business in the UAE; the restructuring for a major oilfield supplies company of its UAE operations; the acquisition by local businesses of franchises for Planet Hollywood, Manchester United Plc and Brannigans Restaurants. Acted for National Oil Company in the purchase and financing of two product tankers. Written articles on agency law in the Arabian Gulf and insolvency and restructuring in the UAE.
Career: Educated at Sedbergh School. Qualified in 1975. Joined *Clifford Turner* in 1976. Manager of Dubai office of *Clifford Turner* 1982-84. Joined *Clyde & Co* 1990, Partner 1992.
Personal: Married, leisure interests include collecting maritime watercolours, bad golf and good wine.

AFRIDI, Ali
Afridi & Angell, Dubai +971 4 330 3900
aafridi@afridi-angell.com
Recommended in Banking & Finance
Specialisation: Specialises in international transactions involving a diverse range of clients and projects and in arbitration, banking, commercial, construction and Islamic Law matters.
Prof. Memberships: The ICC International Court of Arbitration (Pakistan representative); International Bar Association.
Publications: Correspondent: International Construction Law Review, published quarterly by Lloyd's of London Press Ltd.
Career: Partner, *Orr Dignam & Co.*, Pakistan, 1964-74 and UAE 1974-79. Resident partner *Chadbourne Parke & Afridi*, 1980-91. Partner, *Afridi & Angell*, UAE, 1991-present.
Personal: Born Karachi, Pakistan, February 2, 1936. Admitted to Bar 1958, Pakistan. Education: Peshawar University (LLB 1958).

AL TAMIMI, Essam
Al Tamimi & Co, Dubai +971 4 331 7090
essam@tamimi.com
Recommended in Corporate/M&A
Specialisation: The firm's founder and Managing Partner. Main areas of work include commercial, banking and finance, maritime law, project finance, corporate law including advising clients on re-structuring their businesses by mergers and acquisitions, assisting clients in setting up in the UAE and in the GCC countries, intellectual property, energy, litigation and international arbitration.
Prof. Memberships: International Bar Association (Co-chairman, Arab Regional Forum); American Bar Association; Dubai Chamber of Commerce & Industry.
Publications: Author of 'Arbitration Law in the United Arab Emirates' (1997), 'United Arab Emirate Court of Cassation Judgements 1989-1997' (1998), 'Setting up in Dubai' (2000).
Career: Admitted, 1985, United Arab Emirates. Trained at *Clifford Chance*, London. Started own firm in 1989, Sharjah, E.A.E.
Personal: LLB, Al Ain, 1983. LLM degree, Harvard Law School, USA.

BIBBINGS, Jennifer
Trowers & Hamlins, Dubai +971 4 351 9201
dubai@trowers-hamlins.com
Recommended in Corporate/M&A
Specialisation: Specialises in commercial law as well as joint ventures, and construction projects (including BOT), distribution and franchising, employment law and all aspects of foreign investment.
Prof. Memberships: Deputy Chairman and Hon. Secretary of the British Business Group, Dubai and Northern Emirates.
Publications: Has spoken at a variety of seminars and conferences in Dubai and London.
Career: Joined *Trowers & Hamlins* 1987, qualified 1989. Partner at *Trowers & Hamlins* since 1997.
Personal: Educated University of Surrey. Married, two children. Lived in Dubai since 1993. Keen sailor and skier.

CAMERON, Ewan
Clifford Chance, Dubai +971 4 331 4333
Recommended in Banking & Finance, Corporate/M&A, Project Finance

CREED, Adrian
Trowers & Hamlins, Abu Dhabi +971 2 626 7274
abudhabi@trower-hamlins.com
Recommended in Project Finance
Specialisation: Advising on major international infrastructure projects with a particular emphasis on Build Own Operate Schemes. Recently led the team advising CMS Energy on the Taweelah A2 Independent Water and Power Project in Abu Dhabi.
Prof. Memberships: Law Society of England and Wales.
Career: Qualified in 1990, joined *Trowers & Hamlins* 1988. Partner with *Trowers & Hamlins* since 1997.

Personal: Born 1964. Married. Two children. Educated at Wolverhampton Grammar School and Birmingham University. Currently residing in Abu Dhabi.

DE BELDER, Richard T.
Bryan Cave LLP, Abu Dhabi +971 2 340 522
rtdebelder@bryancave.com
Recommended in Banking & Finance
Specialisation: Partner specialising in banking, project finance, Islamic finance, corporate finance, capital markets and investment funds acting for both banks and borrowers in the UAE and throughout the region.
Prof. Memberships: Law Society (1978); Member of California Bar (1985).
Career: Business Studies Degree 1974; qualified as English Solicitor in 1978 and admitted to California Bar in 1985. Has practised in Abu Dhabi, Dubai, Oman, London and Chicago. Has spent 13 years in the Middle East.
Personal: Born – August 9, 1953.

DIXON, Christopher Drew
Key & Dixon, Dubai +97 1 4359 0096
Recommended in Banking & Finance

DUNDAS, Philip
Shearman & Sterling, Abu Dhabi +971 2 274477
pdundas@shearman.com
Recommended in Project Finance
Specialisation: Practice involves mainly energy and project matters. Partner in the firm's worldwide Project Development and Finance Group. Has worked on energy matters since 1977 advising on major LNG, LPG, petrochemical and infrastructure projects; construction and project management contracts; feedstock arrangements; crude oil, refined product and gas sales arrangements; transportation arrangements; project financing (international bank syndicated and export credit); and major international arbitrations. In addition, devotes significant time to shipping matters, including contracts for newbuilds, sale and leaseback transactions and charters. Also has represented numerous US and foreign bank clients of the firm in financing transactions. Acted on the acquisition of 50% of Hyundai Oil Refinery Co. Ltd. by International Petroleum Investment Company, on the Borouge Petrochemical joint venture for the Abu Dhabi National Oil Company and on an investment in Teledesic by certain institutional investors.
Prof. Memberships: Admiralty and Maritime Committee of the New York State Bar Association. Section of Energy and Natural Resources Law of the International Bar Association. Listed in Euromoney's 1999 Guide to the World's Leading Energy and Natural Resource Lawyers.
Career: Joined *Shearman & Sterling* in 1973 becoming a Partner in 1981 and is at present resident managing partner of the firm's Abu Dhabi office. Attended Washington and Lee University School of Law, JD, 1973 and Wesleyan University, BA, 1970.
Personal: Born April 29, 1948.

KEY, Jeremy
Key & Dixon, Dubai +97 1 4359 0096
Recommended in Project Finance

LEWIS, Rhys
Al Sayegh Richards Butler, Abu Dhabi
+9712 6313 010
rl@richardsbutler.com
Recommended in Corporate/M&A
Specialisation: Corporate, commercial and project finance primarily in relation to deregulation/privatisation in the Middle East Region. In addition advising international clients on cross border joint ventures, acquisitions and investment strategy.
Prof. Memberships: Law Society.
Career: *Nabarro Nathanson* (1988-1992), *Fox & Gibbons* (1992-1995). Joined *Richards Butler* in 1995 as a partner.
Personal: Born 1957; married. Educated Nottingham University (LLB Hons). Interests include literature, history and sport.

MACNAB, Duncan
Allen & Overy, Dubai +971 43323 190
Recommended in Corporate/M&A, Project Finance

McNAIR, Alastair J.
Hadef Al Dhahiri & Associates, Abu Dhabi
+9712 6276 622
alastair_mcnair@hadalaw.co.ae
Recommended in Project Finance
Specialisation: Project finance. Main area of work is project finance, corporate finance, banking and investment (internal and external) with commercial and construction experience. Has handled major privatisation projects for Total Fina Elf/Tractebel (Taweelah A1 Power and Desalination Plant) and other major investment projects. Acted for International Petroleum Investment Company in its acquisition of a major interest in Borealis A/S of Denmark, together with supervision of the underlying transactions and for ISO Octane in relation to its project finance. Acts for a number of major institutional and corporate clients – both from outside and within the U.A.E.
Prof. Memberships: Writer to H.M. Signet. Qualified Scotland (1979) and England and Wales (1991).
Career: Qualified 1979. First worked in the Middle East in 1982 seconded by *Clifford Turner* to their associated Riyadh Office. Worked in industry 1986 to 1990. Rejoined *Clifford Chance* in 1990 in the Banking Department and subsequently seconded to Crescent Petroleum in Sharjah, U.A.E. as General Manager, Contracts. Since 1995 has worked with *Hadef Al Dhahiri & Associates*, living in Abu Dhabi, U.A.E.
Personal: Born 12 January 1954. George Watsons College, Edinburgh. Aberdeen University (LLB). Centre of Petroleum and Mineral Law Studies (Diploma in Petroleum and Mineral Law).

MICHELMORE, Peter
Al Sayegh Richards Butler, Abu Dhabi
+9712 6313 010
pgm@richardsbutler.com
Recommended in Corporate/M&A, Project Finance
Specialisation: Specialising in corporate, commercial, energy and project finance and Regional Operations Director for Middle East and South West Asia, based in the firm's Abu Dhabi Office. Partner and former member of Partnership Board acting in UK, Middle East and South West Asia for public and private companies, in their mergers, acquisitions, disposals, joint ventures and financing; acting for energy clients engaged in administration of agreements concerning oil pollution liability.
Prof. Memberships: Law Society, International Bar Association, Middle East Association.
Publications: 'United Arab Emirates IBA' (1981); 'Establishing a Commercial Presence in the Emirate of Abu Dhabi' (IFLR 1980).
Career: Joined *Richards Butler* 1974; assistant solicitor in company department 1976-82. Abu Dhabi 1978-80, partner *Richards Butler* 1983, moved to Abu Dhabi office 1998.
Personal: Born 1951; married. Education: Sherborne School, Bristol University (1973 LLB Hons). Interests include riding and running.

MUBAYDEEN, Ibrahim
Simmons & Simmons, Abu Dhabi +971 2 6275 568
ibrahim.mubaydeen@simmons-simmons.com
Recommended in Banking & Finance, Corporate/M&A
Specialisation: Practises corporate, banking and commercial law, and specialises in water and power projects (having advised the Abu Dhabi Government on the first Independent Water & Power Producer's Project undertaken in the United Arab Emirates on a BOO basis), construction projects, privatisation and banking. Extensive experience in regulation (having drafted the Arabic version of the law on regulation of the water and electricity sector in Abu Dhabi); oil and gas supply agreements, project finance, international and local funds and Islamic banking. Board member of the Regulation and Supervision Bureau for the Water and Electricity Sector in the Emirate of Abu Dhabi.
Prof. Memberships: The Law Society of England & Wales and the Jordanian Bar Association.
Career: Joined *Simmons & Simmons* as a partner in 1999. Graduated from the University of Jordan in 1985, from the University of Bristol with a Diploma in English Legal Studies in 1986 and from the University of London with a Masters degree in Corporate and Commercial Law in 1987. Qualified in Jordan in 1988; Advocate at *Yousef Al Mubaideen* Law Firm 1988-90; completed Law Society finals in 1991; *Osborne Clarke* 1991-1993; in-house counsel (subsequently senior legal adviser) for a UK subsidiary of Al Rajhi Banking and Investment Corporation (1994-1996). Prior to joining *Simmons & Simmons* was a partner at *Al Tamimi & Company* and head of its Abu Dhabi Office (1996-99).

O'HARE, Caroline
Clifford Chance, Dubai +971 4 331 4333
Recommended in Banking & Finance

O'TOOLE, Niall
Denton Wilde Sapte, Abu Dhabi +971 2622 3858
dentonad@emirates.net.ae
Recommended in Corporate/M&A
Specialisation: Managing Partner, Abu Dhabi. Main areas of work are company commercial matters, M&A and banking. Acts for a variety of local and foreign companies doing business in the UAE.

U

Clients include Coca-Cola, Eskom South Africa, BP, United Eastern Group, ADNOC, ADGAS, Pacific Century and a variety of banks including ABN AMRO, Barclays, BNP, Bank of New York, HSBC, Abu Dhabi Commercial Bank, Merrill Lynch, Commercial Bank of Oman.
Prof. Memberships: Incorporated Law Society of Ireland, Law Society of England and Wales, Gibraltar Bar Council, Institute of Taxation in Ireland, Society of Trust and Estate Practitioners, International Bar Association. Qualifications include BCL, LLB, AITI and TEP.
Personal: Married with two children. Leisure interests include golf and running.

U

RODERICK, Simon
Allen & Overy, Dubai +971 43323 190
Recommended in Banking & Finance, Corporate/M&A

SILVER, Jonathan
Clyde & Co, Dubai +971 43 311102
Recommended in Banking & Finance, Corporate/M&A

TREW OBE, Anthony
Al Sayegh Richards Butler, Abu Dhabi +9712 6313 010
algt@richardsbutler.com
Recommended in Corporate/M&A
Specialisation: Corporate and commercial law as practised in the UAE. More than 20 years' experience as a legal consultant living and working in Abu Dhabi. Regularly advises a broad range of leading international companies and UAE commercial interest in relation to their corporate and business affairs in the UAE and the Gulf.
Prof. Memberships: Law Society, International Bar Association.
Career: Articled *Hextall, Erskine;* qualified 1968; joined *Richards Butler* 1970; partner 1974. Resident partner Abu Dhabi having established the firm's first overseas office there 1978 to present. Co-contributor with other *Richards Butler* colleagues, to the UAE section of Jordan's International Corporate Procedures.
Personal: Born 20 March, 1942. Educated Haileybury (four children); Chairman since 1995 of British Business Group, Abu Dhabi; Governor nominated by H.E. British Ambassador, Al Khubairat Community School – The British School Abu Dhabi since 1987; interests include swimming, bicycling and occasionally sailing a Drascombe Lugger. Freeman of the City of London. Club: Reform.

WARD, Andrew
Simmons & Simmons, Abu Dhabi +971 2 6275 568
andrew.ward@simmons-simmons.com
Recommended in Corporate/M&A
Specialisation: Managing Partner, *Simmons & Simmons*, Abu Dhabi specialising in corporate finance and company law matters, including joint ventures, public share offerings, take-overs, mergers and acquisitions, commercial transactions and telecommunications projects. Also specialises in utility and telecommunications regulation and has advised a number of governments on legislation in these sectors.
Career: Joined *Simmons & Simmons* in 1984; made a partner in the London Corporate Department in 1992; moved to Abu Dhabi in 1996.

WILLIAMS, Nicholas
Simmons & Simmons, Abu Dhabi +971 2 6275 568
nicholas.williams@simmons-simmons.com
Recommended in Project Finance
Specialisation: Mining, energy, rail and other infrastructure projects in the UK, Africa, Asia and the Gulf including projects such as a worldscale mine and refinery project in Africa, 'Project Dolphin', presently the single largest integrated gas project in the world, Railtrack Plc's re-organisation of its freight haulage operations and West Coast mainline project and fuel supply agreements to IPPs in India.
Career: Qualified at *Simmons & Simmons* in London in 1985. Transferred to *Simmons & Simmons'* Paris office from 1990 to 1995. Admitted to the Paris Bar. Partner since 1992. Transferred to *Simmons & Simmons* Abu Dhabi office in 1998.

UNITED KINGDOM

Index

The clients' choice

BUSINESS LAWYER OF THE YEAR
NIGEL BOARDMAN, *Slaughter and May*

BUSINESS LAW FIRM OF THE YEAR
SLAUGHTER AND MAY

Nigel Boardman *is the clear client's favourite lawyer, whilst his firm,* ***Slaughter and May*** *received twice as many nominations as their nearest rivals for best firm.*

For details see page 36.

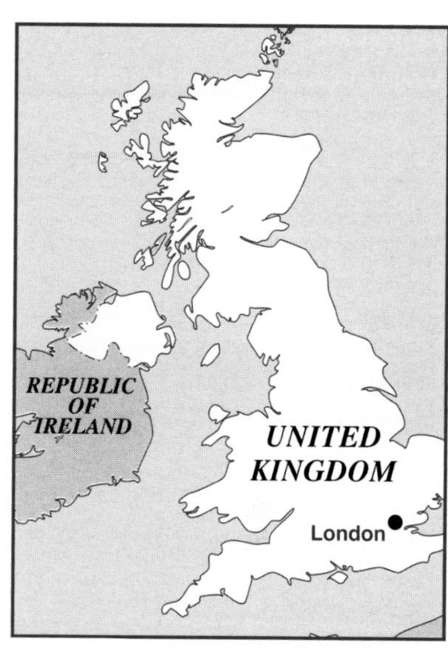

OVERVIEW: There has been no shortage of work for lawyers in the City of London. Recruitment levels were stepped up, the level of market competitiveness underlined by decisions to massively increase starting salaries for newly qualified solicitors. Many US firms continued to blaze a trail in London, paying huge bonuses to associates in an effort to retain staff and compete with the homegrown's finest. A cautionary note was sounded in early 2001 with news that many firms were bulking up their insolvency practices in anticipation of a possible economic downturn.

Clifford Chance remains *Chambers'* best-scoring UK firm. Despite having its sights fixed firmly on the globe, the banking and finance powerhouse is defiantly strong in London. Similarly, finance supremos Allen & Overy, and Linklaters, with its flourishing European alliance, have moved closer to achieving international goals without sacrificing domestic success. Both have turned in impressive UK performances across the range of practice areas as Linklaters practitioners dominate the leading capital markets, while A&O enjoys the presence of pre-eminent banking star David Morley. As a measure of its transactional credentials, Linklaters advised SmithKline Beecham on the £114 billion merger with Glaxo Wellcome while star corporate partner David Cheyne advised Vodafone in the £25 billion disposal of Orange to France Telecom.

Freshfields has been busy on an extended overseas offensive, but despite a raft of European consolidation, it remains market front-runner in its UK domains – M&A, tax and competition. Like other City firms with European M&A aspirations, it has had a productive year muscling in on a series of big-ticket corporate and financial transactions. Of the top City firms, only Slaughter and May is open to the accusation of insularity, with its European 'best friends' policy yet to show any visible signs of merger progress. However, the stalwart London office, a superb source of premium M&A, tax and competition advice, continues to prop up the firm's reputation. Head of corporate Nigel Boardman and tax doyen Steve Edge are clear individual stars.

Beyond the Magic Circle, Lovells has pushed hard with added German firepower and Ashurst Morris Crisp chases the City leaders. The latter scores impressively in banking, capital markets and jointly shares top spot in private equity. Here, practice head Charles Geffen is distinguished as the most highly sought after lawyer in the sector. The efforts of Herbert Smith's corporate practice in challenging the market leaders haven't gone unnoticed, while Denton Wilde Sapte maintains its impressive status as a leading energy firm. Our tables this year also reflect the strength of sector focused firms, such as Bird & Bird, top for e-commerce and IT, rising star Olswang and IP front runner Bristows.

*See leaders' profiles on pages 741-782

U

Arbitration (International)

UNITED KINGDOM
Leading firms (Arbitration (International))

Band	Firm
1	Clifford Chance
2	Freshfields Bruckhaus Deringer
	Herbert Smith
3	Allen & Overy
4	Linklaters
	Lovells
	Masons
	Norton Rose
	Wilmer, Cutler & Pickering
5	Baker & McKenzie
	Clyde & Co
	CMS Cameron McKenna
	Debevoise & Plimpton
	Holman Fenwick & Willan
	Ince & Co
	Richards Butler
	Shearman & Sterling
	Simmons & Simmons

Firms are listed alphabetically in each band.

Leading individuals (Arbitration (International))

Band	Individual
1	**BEECHEY John** *Clifford Chance*
	LEW Julian *Herbert Smith*
	MARRIOTT Arthur *Debevoise & Plimpton*
2	**BORN Gary** *Wilmer, Cutler & Pickering*
	CAPPER Phillip *Lovells*
	GILL Judith *Allen & Overy*
	RAWDING Nigel *Freshfields Bruckhaus Deringer*
	SUTTON David *Allen & Overy*
3	**BLACKABY Nigel** *Freshfields Bruckhaus Deringer*
	BRYNMOR THOMAS David *Herbert Smith*
	COLBRIDGE Christopher *Shearman & Sterling*
	CROALL Philip *Freshfields Bruckhaus Deringer*
	KNUTSON Robert *Masons*
	LAMBERT Robert *Clifford Chance*
	MITCHARD Paul *Wilmer, Cutler & Pickering*
	NAIRN Karyl *Simmons & Simmons*
	SHEPPARD Audley *Clifford Chance*
	STYLE Christopher *Linklaters*
Up-and-coming individuals	
	FRASER David *Baker & McKenzie*
	MORGAN Simon *Simmons & Simmons*
	O'CONOR John *Allen & Overy*
	SHACKLETON Stewart *Simmons & Simmons*
	SHORE Larry *Herbert Smith*
	WINTER Jeremy *Baker & McKenzie*

Individuals are listed alphabetically in each band.

Clifford Chance (4 ptrs, 12 asscs) The clear leaders in London, seen to be handling *"top level"* work. The excellent team fields *"trustworthy and pragmatic opponents"* from its *"army"* of people. Headed by the *"savvy"* **John Beechey***, a *"truly dedicated"* international practitioner. Other members of the team, said not to *"miss a trick,"* include *"shrewd"* and *"thorough"* **Audley Sheppard*** and **Robert Lambert***. **Highlights/work:** This year has seen a dispute between a multinational, multi-party entity and a major energy firm over a power station in Europe. The case will be heard in Geneva under UNCITRAL rules. Also instructed to act for a joint Japanese-British venture in a claim brought by a subcontractor in relation to the construction of an LNG plant in the Middle East. Again under UNCITRAL rules, this time in Paris. Representing a government in respect of a claim made by an offshore entity in the national telecoms industry.

Freshfields Bruckhaus Deringer (4 ptrs, 11 asscs) A close second place. The firm's first class international arbitration practice is led from its strong Paris office, strengthened by the sheer quality of Freshfields offices world-wide. London still has a way to go to match the 'superstar' reputation of Paris. The team is led by the *"excellent"* **Nigel Rawding*** who is said to be doing a *"good job."* He is assisted by **Philip Croall*** and **Nigel Blackaby***, a *"smart guy."* **Highlights/work:** Dominated by oil but this is certainly not all the firm does. In the past year the firm has been acting for a consortium of more than ten international oil companies in respect of disputes arising under a production sharing agreement with a Caspian Sea state-owned oil company. Also acted on a case involving an American oil company in disputes with three other international oil companies over exploration projects in South America. Lead counsel for France Telecom in a much publicised dispute with Deutsche Telekom, which they believe to be the largest ICCL arbitration ever.

Herbert Smith (4 ptrs, 8 asscs) Out of a firm traditionally viewed as the UK's litigation giant, a significant international arbitration force is emerging. Of over 70 new instructions in the last year over half come from outside the UK. The *"lightning rod"* for the practice is the *"learned"* **Dr Julian Lew***. However, **David Brynmor Thomas*** is now considered by some to be of equal stature. Others give similar recognition to **Larry Shore***, a new entry to the table, said to be *"as good as the best."* **Highlights/work:** Representing a US petroleum services company in an ICC arbitration in Singapore concerning indemnities in a service contract. Also advising claimants against the ruler of a Middle-Eastern state in an ICC arbitration over the expropriation of businesses worth many millions of dollars. Representing a major pharmaceutical company in respect of the dispute arising from the licensing and distribution of pharmaceutical products in the Far East, valued at $10 million. Advising one of the parties involved in a dispute arising from a large turnkey project in the Far East, worth in excess of $25 million.

Allen & Overy (5 ptrs, 13 asscs) Snapping at the heels of Herbert Smith, this firm is seen more by the International Court of Commerce than any other in our tables. The consensus is that the London team is increasing its profile in arbitration. *"Elder statesman"* **David Sutton*** still commutes from Paris to head up the practice. The *"wonderful"* **Judith Gill*** may not be a keen self-promoter but is nonetheless universally well spoken of. **John O'Conor*** remains in the up and coming list – well-respected but *"not quite in the thick of things yet."* **Highlights/work:** Acting in claims totalling $3.6 billion against a central Asian state and entities arising out of oil and gas ventures. Arbitrations under ICC rules in the USA and Europe. Instructed by a major pharmaceutical company in their $190 million claim against insurers. The dispute turns on the proper interpretation of the policy governed by New York law.

Acting for an English company in relation to a claim against an Eastern Europe state entity, worth $295 million, and on two related $135 million claims in a dispute between shareholders for a mobile phone company in eastern Europe.

Linklaters (5 ptrs, 10 asscs) Those in the know see the firm acting in many arbitrations at the *"highest level"* such as the longest running ICC arbitration over the cancellation of a major weapons system. *"Smart operator"* **Christopher Style*** heads the team which is both *"active"* and *"effective."* The derivatives arbitration practice is increasingly busy and the Alliance partners add a global capability not easily matched. **Highlights/work:** Acting in a widely reported dispute for an independent power producer against the Pakistan Water and Power Development Authority over terms of the tariff for electricity generated by it. The ICC arbitration clause is subject to injunction proceedings in the Supreme Court of Pakistan and has drawn criticism by the IMF and the World Bank. Also conducted two arbitrations for Bankers Trust against defaulting companies in swap transactions in Indonesia under LCIA rules and related litigation.

Lovells (15 ptrs, 19 asscs) Seen to suffer slightly from a lack of big names, although *"tough"* ex-Masons man **Phillip Capper**'s* contacts with the international arbitration bodies and his construction arbitration credentials should help in this regard. The firm is said to be doing some *"big ones"* and *"getting respect."* **Highlights/work:** Acting for a major international oil company in an arbitration under UNCITRAL rules in London. Dispute is with a West African joint venture co-licensee and subject to the law of a West African state. Also acting as principal counsel in a dispute over the design and manufacture of complex electrical and mechanical engineering equipment. One aspect is before arbitration in Spain, while related issues are referable to two other distinct European jurisdictions.

Masons (15 ptrs, 15 asscs) The construction firm and *"fantastic"* at it. Lesser known for international commercial arbitration but now *"making strides."* Doing battle all over the world with many of our interviewees on a surprising range of issues this firm seems equally at home with silicon as with bricks. *"Formidably clever"* **Robert Knutson*** (sole arbitrator in multi-million dollar power station dispute) takes over from Phillip Capper as top man here. **Highlights/work:** Represented an Asian state utility in three UNCITRAL arbitrations involving complex claims worth over $3 billion, arising from the construction and operation of a thermal power plant. The firm regularly acts for governments and major international companies on engineering, energy, technology and other issues.

Norton Rose (5 ptrs, 16 asscs) Having advised clients in arbitrations conducted under virtually every set of rules available this firm has an *"impressive"* reputation. Known for particular expertise in commodities, shipping, insurance and construction the firm is reportedly involved in a *"huge"* number of arbitrations. **Highlights/work:** Acted for an Indian publishing company in an LCIA arbitration against a European corporation and for an American company in an ICC arbitration against a major European corporation concerning supply of equipment and technology.

Wilmer, Cutler & Pickering (3 ptrs, 11 asscs) Currently the highest ranking of the US firms, impressive considering the size of the team compared to the company it keeps. This is in no small measure due to the *"innovative"* **Gary Born*** who is so *"energetic"* he caused at least one interviewee to ask *"does he ever sleep?"* Add the *"immensely impressive"* **Paul Mitchard*** who is said to be *"overwhelmed with work"* and the firm's ranking is assured. **Highlights/work:** Represented a European telecommunications provider in a multi-billion dollar arbitration under ICC rules. Acted in a large LCIA arbitration in London arising from disputes in the financial services sector worth nearly $1 billion.

Baker & McKenzie (3 ptrs, 6 asscs) Two new names in our lists are getting recognition for the *"substantial"* cases handled by the firm. *"Awfully good"* **Jeremy Winter*** is working closely with Dr Urs Zenhäusern of B&M's Zurich office in an arbitration between a German equipment supplier (their client) and an American engineering company. The arbitration concerns the construction of three power plants in Latin America, and the value of the claim is $38 million. He is joined in the tables by **David Fraser*** who is doing a *"huge number"* of important arbitrations. The practice's international credentials are augmented by its offices in over 35 jurisdictions. It has acted in arbitrations arising out of manufacturing, construction, engineering projects and telecommunications disputes among others. **Highlights/work:** Acting for six industrial enterprises in Kazakhstan in four LCIA and two UNCITRAL arbitrations arising out of management disputes worth over $200 million. Acting for an Italian equipment manufacturer in defending an arbitration claim by an Asian purchaser over alleged deficiencies in equipment supplied.

Clyde & Co (4 ptrs, 10 asscs) Does an *"enormous"* amount of international arbitrations. Primarily known as one of the leading shipping firms, the practice however has a much broader client base. It has been involved in some 300 arbitrations over the past year, many non-shipping related. Has acted for oil companies, insurers, trading houses and government departments. **Highlights/work:** Acted in a $200 million claim under a non-marine reinsurance treaty in an LCIA arbitration. Also involved in substantial claims arising out of losses incurred on Russian pipelines against former states of the USSR.

CMS Cameron McKenna (6 ptrs, 14 asscs) The International Arbitration Group is focusing on central and eastern Europe and is said to be doing some *"good stuff."* The transnational legal services organisation, CMS, adds a European dimension to the firm's dispute resolution services. **Highlights/work:** Acting for US reinsurers in a series of London arbitrations with claims exceeding £280 million. The firm is also acting for a European party in two ICC arbitrations in relation to the construction of manufacturing plants in the middle-east with claims exceeding $200 million.

Debevoise & Plimpton (1 ptr, 3 asscs) An *"excellent operation"* under the *"terrific"* and *"ingenious"* **Arthur Marriott QC*** who is an *"eminence grise"* on the international arbitration scene. Initial excitement over his acquisition has slightly abated, however, as he is not felt to benefit from the support he deserves. Nevertheless, the practice continues to pull in work and receives many referrals from the New York office. **Highlights/work:** Acted on an ICC arbitration for a Japanese client arising out of a joint venture in a developing country. Also acted for a leading Asian vehicle manufacturer in an ad hoc arbitration against a European vehicle manufacturer.

Holman Fenwick & Willan (40 ptrs, 50 asscs) Another leading shipping and commodities practice with a lesser-known yet substantial international commercial arbitration practice. **Highlights/work:** Acted in an ICC arbitration involving a US commodities house in dispute with a PRC oil company over an LNG development. Acted in dispute between a major international consulting and systems integration services company and a transport logistics plc concerning design and development of a Y2K compliant software system.

Ince & Co (43 ptrs, 50 asscs) This *"first-rate"* shipping firm has substantial practices in insurance/reinsurance, commodities and energy. Unlike many others in our list, this firm takes the view that specialists in those areas need be proficient themselves in arbitration, rather than maintain a specialist arbitration section. **Highlights/work:** Represented the owners of the 'Aegean Sea' in an arbitration arising out of the loss of the vessel and cargo of crude oil and related environmental claims. Acted for a contractor in connection with a dispute arising from the construction of two FPSOs for the oil and gas industry, in multi-million dollar arbitrations in London.

Richards Butler (27 ptrs, 29 asscs) The firm is a market leader in physical commodities work and shipping. It is seen mainly on arbitrations in these sectors. Known to have a long portfolio of cases, and currently active in some 200 arbitrations, Richards Butler is generally held to be a decent player. **Highlights/work:** A substantial supply contract dispute worth at least $100 million and two linked counter trade disputes valued at around $140 million. Also acting in a $300 million LCIA arbitration arising out of a shipbuilding contract dispute.

U

*See leaders' profiles on pages 741-782

Shearman & Sterling (7 asscs) The only practice in our tables with no partners in the team – yet . This *"classy"* firm seems to be building up its London practice nicely under the *"charming"* **Christopher Colbridge*** who is *"very good indeed."* Aided by a strong Paris team. **Highlights/work:** Acting in a $500 million arbitration in Singapore for an Asian Television company. The practice is also advising an EU institution on designing, implementing and running its dispute resolution systems. Represented a multi-national mining corporation in a $1.6 billion dispute arising out of a joint venture. Represented a US construction contractor against an African owner in a $100 million power dispute subject to ICC arbitration in the Hague.

Simmons & Simmons (7 ptrs, 12 asscs) **Karyl Nairn*** heads this team which is felt to be *"pushing hard."* The *"academic"* **Stewart Shackleton*** is considered to be an asset to the practice, as is former Hong Kong Attorney General **Simon Morgan*** who adds to the Asian expertise of the practice. **Highlights/work:** Acted for Esso against the UK subsidiaries of three international petroleum companies in a multi-party dispute over a participation agreement for the construction and operation of an oil pipeline. The firm brought one of the first successful challenges to an award in the English courts under the Arbitration Act of 1996.

U

Banking & Finance

Allen & Overy Perceived to have retained the *"quality edge"* over Clifford Chance on the domestic scene, this *"first class"* firm's banking output is described as *"top products produced by focused and tough negotiating players"* who *"never make mistakes."* Although non-transactional, *"senior guru"* **Philip Wood***, currently involved on internal knowledge-management programmes, continues to generate enormous influence amongst peers as the *"wise old man of banking."* The banking department's managing partner is the *"young yet vastly experienced"* **David Morley***. Regarded as *"urbane, easy to deal with and well organised,"* Morley is *"the one to turn to if you need to raise money in a hurry."* Lawyers admire him for being *"comfortable with billions"* and most observers see in him *"the quintessential banking lawyer."* He accordingly moves to a top band in our lists. Other highly rated practitioners include the *"solid and practical project manager"* **Michael Duncan*** and **Peter Schulz*** (representing Citibank & UniCredito Italiano in their revolving credit facility for Gucci in Italy, the Netherlands, Luxembourg, France and the USA – value €1 billion). The *"influential"* veteran **Jonathan Horsfall Turner*** and the *"tenacious"* **Tony Humphrey*** are active in both banking and projects.

The bulk of the firm's work is for lenders, with around 20% of the client base consisting of large borrowers such as GEC and British Aerospace. One of the stand-out features of the banking practice is the *"great lengths the firm goes to to teach the juniors what is in the documents."*

Split into five groups, the *"balanced and constructive"* London banking team has around 150 lawyers whose total billings increased by over 20% in 1999, advising 800-plus banking and borrower clients. London is still the centre of gravity for financial transactions in Europe, although its continental offices (particularly Amsterdam, Paris and Frankfurt) continue to gain in strength and prestige. Already, over 40% of the firm's banking partners are based outside the UK, a number that is set to increase. This translated into acting on more than 40 cross-border deals worth over $100 billion in the past year. These deals include advising an 11-bank syndicate financing a €30 billion loan for Vodafone's hostile bid for Mannesmann (at the time thought to be the largest ever syndicated loan), and advising KPN on its $13 billion loan to purchase E-Plus Mobilfunk GmbH. Other large deals include Repsol's acquisition of YPF ($16 billion) and Air Liquide's joint bid for the BOC Group ($8 billion).

In pure acquisition finance, leading lights include the *"dogged and tough"* **Tony Keal***, who is *"irascible, but one of the best; not a lot goes by him."* Lawyers acting opposite the *"pleasant"* **Stephen Gillespie*** regard him as *"so client-wise that you're scared he'll steal yours."*

Rising practitioners, the *"progressive and solid"* **Trevor Borthwick*** and *"Tony Keal protégé"* **Euan Gorrie*** continue to receive recommendations. In other banking areas the firm worked with Clifford Chance and the LMA on efforts to standardise primary documentation for syndicated loans. It has additionally launched 'newchange', an internet-based deal-room allowing the firm to manage complex transactions on the web, considerably reducing delay in documenting, amending and concluding transactions.

Represented Citibank in a loan facility for Lehman Bros Ltd worth $1 billion. Represented the lenders to MobilCom on a €8.4 billion senior debt financing for a German 3G mobile licence. Advised JP Morgan Securities Ltd and The Royal Bank of Scotland plc as arrangers and underwriters of a €100 million financing for Virgin Mobile. Advised Barclays Capital as arranger and underwriter of senior and mezzanine facilities totalling £680 million, provided in connection with the leveraged acquisition of Rank's holiday division by a consortium comprised of Bourne Leisure Group, Candover and Legal & General. **Clients:** Goldman Sachs; Barclays; Citibank; Bank of America; Crédit Agricole.

Clifford Chance *"They are still the firm with the broadest spread of office and as a result have the geographical edge on A&O."* A practice which has grown dramatically and continues to do so enables the firm to have a base of specialists, a depth of practice and a range which keeps them at the top of the pile. This has been further developed with the addition of strong US and German banking capabilities. The firm's recent mergers have added expertise in other financial areas – Rogers & Wells includes a leading finance litigation practice whilst Pünder has an active securities practice. Finance as a whole (including asset finance and capital markets) now takes up 35% of the firm's workload (of which banking is half.) Additionally, there has been a 30% increase in the turnover of the banking team in 1999.

The market perceives the upper echelons of CC's banking practice to be peopled with *"charmers."* These include **Michael Bray***, who although not fee-earning is vastly influential, the *"sensible, constructive and fantastic"* **Stuart Popham*** and the *"classic CC men"* – **Mark Campbell*** (*"relaxed, sensible and good on the commercial argument"*) and **Malcolm Sweeting*** (*"easy going, commercial, quick and effective"*). In acquisition finance, where **Mark Stewart*** has a name, the firm has been joined by **James Johnson*** formerly of Wilde Sapte, widely regarded as an important capture. Some market reservations have been expressed over the consistency of quality at junior level. Nevertheless, it was widely accepted that *"when they dedicate themselves to a task and resource it properly"* they *"get it right and don't mess around."*

UNITED KINGDOM Leading firms (Banking & Finance)
1 Allen & Overy
Clifford Chance
2 Freshfields Bruckhaus Deringer
Linklaters
3 Lovells
Norton Rose
Slaughter and May
4 Ashurst Morris Crisp
Denton Wilde Sapte
Herbert Smith
Shearman & Sterling

Firms are listed alphabetically in each band.

Leading individuals (Banking & Finance)
★ **MORLEY David** *Allen & Overy*
1 **BRAY Michael** *Clifford Chance*
EREIRA David *Freshfields Bruckhaus Deringer*
POPHAM Stuart *Clifford Chance*
PULESTON JONES Haydn *Linklaters*
WOOD Philip *Allen & Overy*
2 **ALLEN Maurice** *White & Case LLP*
BALFOUR Andrew *Slaughter and May*
HUMPHREY Anthony *Allen & Overy*
JOHNSON James *Clifford Chance*
KEAL Anthony *Allen & Overy*
SLATER Richard *Slaughter and May*
STEWART Mark *Clifford Chance*
SWEETING Malcom *Clifford Chance*
3 **CAMPBELL Mark** *Clifford Chance*
DUNCAN Michael *Allen & Overy*
EVANS Edward *Freshfields Bruckhaus Deringer*
GILLESPIE Stephen *Allen & Overy*
HORSFALL TURNER Jonathan *Allen & Overy*
PIERCE Sean *Freshfields Bruckhaus Deringer*
4 **COTTIS Matthew** *Lovells*
CULLINANE Lee *Clifford Chance*
ELLIOTT Robert *Linklaters*
FOX Ruth *Slaughter and May*
INGLIS Alan *Clifford Chance*
POLGLASE Timothy *Norton Rose*
SCHULZ Peter *Allen & Overy*
SPENDLOVE Justin *Ashurst Morris Crisp*
TUCKER John *Linklaters*
VICKERS Mark *Ashurst Morris Crisp*
Up-and-coming individuals
BORTHWICK Trevor *Allen & Overy*
GORRIE Euan *Allen & Overy*

Individuals are listed alphabetically in each band.

The majority of deals are of a cross-border nature, and include financing France Telecom's takeover of Orange. Other major transactions include the bond issue in Olivetti, handled by the *"bright"* **Alan Inglis***, and acting for Deutsche Bank in financing Mannesmann purchases from Olivetti. The main relationship partner for Chase Manhattan, **Lee Cullinane***, is another warmly recommended practitioner.

The majority of the firm's clients are financials, with Chase Manhattan, Citibank, Merrill Lynch and Morgan Stanley among the firm's largest sources of fees. The firm advised on the financing on such deals as the British Steel/Hoogevens link-up, RMC's acquisition of Rugby Group, Cable & Wireless' investment in the One2One network and the attempted Air Products/BOC link-up. Buy-out activity saw the firm active on Akzo Nobel, the Money Store, Findus European frozen fish and Thomson Directories buy-outs. The firm is becoming more active in new areas such as telebanking, e-commerce and intra-day trading, and has introduced an on-line deal room.

Represented Merill Lynch International in an equity offering of 345 million shares in Banco Santander Central Hispano in Euros and SEC, registered through ADRs listed on the New York Stock Exchange. Represented Goldman Sachs, Merill Lynch and Warburg Dillon Reed in a bonus issue of additional value shares & resale by shareholders through a bank facility. **Clients:** Chase Manhattan; Citigroup; JP Morgan; Halifax; Morgan Stanley; Fuji Bank; Goldman Sachs; UBS; Nomura; CSFB; KKR; CVC; WestLB; NatWest; Barclays; Deutsche; ABN AMRO; HSBC; Candover Partners; Apax Partners; Electra Fleming; PPM Ventures; Schroder Venture Advisers.

Freshfields Bruckhaus Deringer Known for its borrower client base, the firm is widely respected for its work on large cross-border lending work, including Repsol's acquisition of YPF, Air Liquide's joint bid for BOC, Thomson-CSF's for Racal and Generali's bid for INA. **David Ereira*** is a *"class act"* whose *"vast experience," "keen mind"* and *"commercial ability"* see him move into a top band this year. Other notable individuals include the *"affable"* **Edward Evans*** and **Sean Pierce***. The latter also moves up a band this year, with observers praising his *"original thinking"* and *"pragmatic approach."*

Two factors contribute to the Freshfields reputation as a banking team concentrated on borrowers – the immense reputation of the corporate teams and the firm's historic relationship with the Bank of England. This was a relationship which once seemed to preclude the firm from developing close relationships with private lenders. However, although heavily involved in acquisitions generated from the corporate side, the banking practice now also advises lending clients such as Citibank and Chase Manhattan, and borrower clients such as One2One, who have no relationship with the corporate team. Not regarded as a *"volume outfit,"* the firm is considered to do an *"excellent job"* on complex transactions, including tax-driven work.

Represented SSSB, Goldman Sachs RBS in the second sterling based asset-backed securitisation to refinance Punch's purchase of allied Domecq pubs, valued at £1.484 billion. **Clients:** Citibank; Chase Manhattan; Cinven; HSBC; WetsLB; Morgan Stanley; Zurich Financial Services; Rolls Royce.

Linklaters Making inroads into lender work, this *"supremely competent"* banking team is seen to have *"come on apace"* to such an extent that many see them *"slightly ahead of the rest,"* although still below the two London banking giants. The group has hired extensively during the year and is perceived to be *"a good crowd to deal with."* Moving into the top tier of individuals is *"number one man"* **Haydn Puleston Jones***. *"Relentless in his pursuit of perfection,"* he is a *"grinding, wonderful technician"* who some regard as the *"best draftsman in the City."* Other rated individuals include the *"serious"* **Robert Elliott***, who is also an insolvency player, and **John Tucker*** *("has a great intellect")*, the global head of banking.

As a whole, work for the lenders takes up around 60% of the practice's workload, yet owing to the firm's famed corporate capacity, borrowers tend to dominate in M&A-related financings (the firm advised Vodafone on corporate and financing issues for its Airtouch and Mannesmann bids). In 1999, the team acted on 54 M&A related financings totalling $93.8 billion. The firm utilises the reach of its Alliance network to advise on cross-border financings, advising US and continental-based banks and venture capital houses.

Deals this year for the lenders include advising HSBC on facilities provided to John Mansfield Group and Barclays Capital for the £1.05 billion take-over financing of Trinity prior to its merger with Mirror Group. On the borrower side, as well as the Vodafone financings, the team advised Jazz Telecom, a Spanish start-up telecoms provider, on a €300 million secured syndicated loan facility.

Represented AMBAC (Monoline) Insurance UK in the second sterling based asset backed securitisation to refinance Punch's purchase of Allied Domecq pubs, worth £1.484 billion. Acting for Chase Manhattan Bank and Hong Kong and Shanghai Banking Corporation Limited on the $7 billion Credit Facility to TIW UMTS UK. **Clients:** Barclays Capital; Chase Manhattan;

U

NatWest; ABN AMRO; HSBC; Halifax; Dresdner Bank; Morgan Stanley; Crédit Lyonnais; Lehman Brothers; Commerzbank; Anglo-American; Billiton; BP Amoco; British Telecom; Coca-Cola; Vodafone AirTouch.

Lovells The firm has been dealt a blow with the untimely death of the popular head of UK-based banking, John Penson. *"Considered and pensive"* **Matthew Cottis*** moves up a tier this year, his *"easy going, intelligent and understated approach"* being widely appreciated.

The practice is seen to be *"excellent"* on MBOs and general acquisition finance and has an active retail banking and bank regulatory practice. High-profile deals this year include advising Merrill Lynch as bridge finance provider and Schroders and Merrill Lynch as financial advisers on the £1.16 billion bid by Hicks Muse for United Biscuits. The team also represented Deutsche Bank on the £230 million financing of Pipetronix by Pipeline Integrity International. Other work includes advising new client, CIBC World Markets, on the £220 million buyout of Thomson Directories by Apax Partners, acting for the Bank of Scotland on the £215 million buyout of PHS by Charterhouse and advising Dresdner Kleinwort Benson on the £114 million take-private of Sanderson Group by Alchemy Partners. **Clients:** Dresdner Kleinwort Benson; Bank of Scotland; Barclays; KBC Bankl; EBRD; Prudential Bank; CSFB; Standard Bank; Barclays Capital Group.

Norton Rose The firm takes a 'precision bombing approach' to banking, concentrating resources on specific financial areas. Although the banking team is perceived to be a large one, it does not have the resources for 'commodity' (i.e. high volume) lending work. New to our rankings is the *"clever and able"* **Tim Polglase***, highly regarded for his *"technical and careful approach."* Concentrating on acquisition finance, he has the highest profile of a team which is a *"pleasure to work with."*

Main areas of work include acquisition finance, bid financing and telecoms financing, with additional competence in trade finance, export credit work, sovereign and regulatory work. Perceived to be *"pulling the international side together,"* the finance team has a total of 40 banking partners around the world. Correspondingly, the proportion of international work is increasing. Complementary finance areas, such as asset finance and capital markets, are flourishing, thereby boosting the banking practice.

Transactions this year include advising banks on a £1.5 billion financing of TeleWest Communications Networks to finance ongoing expenses, a £585 million financing for Iliad 6 in relation to the acquisition of Zeneca and financing the acquisition of Hillsdown Holdings. The team additionally advised AXA on its recommended offer for GRE and acted on the £1.6 billion refinancing of Mercury Personal Communications. **Clients:** Chase Manhattan; HSBC; CIBC Wood Gundy; ANZ; Société Générale; ABN AMRO; UBS; Deutsche; Lloyds TSB; Royal Bank of Scotland.

Slaughter and May The firm's specialist financiers **Richard Slater*** and **Andrew Balfour*** both continue to attract regular market plaudits. Balfour is regarded as a *"clever, knowledgeable and commercial lawyer,"* whilst Slater is simply *"excellent."* Whilst the corporate firm tag sticks to Slaughters, the firm is also doing *"high quality"* and *"effective"* banking work. It is a testament to this ability that, although not perceived by peers to have the volume of the more banking-centric City firms, the team has nevertheless acted on some of the largest financings of the year, including acting for Telecom Italia's banks on the defence of Olivetti's takeover. Acting at the top end of acquisition finance work, the practice has also been involved on legal developments in the bank lending area, as part of the LMA's working group on loan agreements.

The strength of the firm's domestic and international client base means that it has experience dealing at the highest end of acquisition finance deals. Large deals where the firm advised the banks include a €13 billion facility for KPN (for the E-Plus acquisition) and a €2.6 billion facility for companies within the Royal Numico Group. Major lending clients include JP Morgan, CSFB and ABN AMRO. On the borrower side, the firm worked on raising £1 billion for Punch Taverns' bid for Allied Domecq's retailing business, and the firm has advised borrowers including British Steel, Huntsman and Mannesmann on financing activities. The firm also acts for the corporate treasury function of major corporates, including Diageo and Bunzl. Particularly strong on cross-discipline transactions, the team is regularly seen on tax-driven transactions. The firm is also noted for banking regulatory work, where the *"able and versatile"* **Ruth Fox*** is well-known to the market.

Represented Punch Taverns Group in the second sterling based asset backed securitisation to refinance Punch's purchase of allied Domecq pubs (£1.484 billion). **Clients:** Dresdner Kleinwort Benson; Abbey National; Norwich Union; Tomkins.

Ashurst Morris Crisp The *"high-quality"* finance team is perceived to have *"clawed back some ground,"* and is now consolidating after recent departures. **Justin Spendlove*** *"knows what he's doing,"* and was recommended as a *"broad-shouldered"* banking man. *"Top notch intellectual"* **Mark Vickers*** impresses clients through his *"rolled-up sleeves approach"* and organisational skills.

Although the team's quality is beyond dispute (particularly in European high-yield transactions,) it is not felt to have the broad international punch of some of its rivals. Felt to have a comparatively narrow banking focus, the firm is seen most frequently on the corporate side, acting for the predators on MBO transactions where the practice is deemed to be *"ultra-active."* Transactions include advising on National Express Group acquisitions and related financings of £750 million and acting for Imetal on its £750 million public bid for English China Clays. The team also advised Lehman Brothers as underwriter of the £745 million facilities in respect of the Candover-backed bid for Hillsdown Holdings. **Clients:** Merrill Lynch; Lehman Brothers; Paribas; Deutsche Bank; Alfred McAlpine; Bank of Scotland; RBS; SG; WestLB.

Denton Wilde Sapte The *"sensible"* and *"complementary"* merger between Denton Hall and Wilde Sapte has created one of the largest banking practices in the country. Although market perception is that the departure of big names (such as James Johnson) from the former Wilde Sapte is a setback, it is acknowledged that the merger provides a welcome boost in areas such as bank regulatory work and trade finance. Overall, observers predict that with a *"challenging year ahead of them,"* this *"strong team will respond."*

The former Denton Hall's powerful international network (especially in Eastern Europe) now gives the new firm one of the largest international networks of any operation. Although still felt to rely heavily on major client NatWest, the team has expanded its lender client base, and has offered advice on financing in areas such as telecoms, energy and the media.

Transactions this year include acting for NatWest Acquisition Finance in relation to a refinancing facility for Bioglan Pharma, incorporating two loans totalling £40 million. The team also acted for the Bank of Scotland in relation to a £60 million loan facility for acquiring shares in Really Useful Holdings. On the borrower side, the department advised Ardagh on financing the acquisition of the glassware business of Rockware. **Clients:** CSFB; Citibank; Lloyds TSB; RBS; ABN AMRO; J Sainsbury; National Westminster Bank; Morgan Stanley; SocGen; HSBC.

Herbert Smith On the strength of the deals it completed in 1999, this *"cruising"* banking practice is *"one to watch,"* as it gains a *"volume of work* *comparable to the traditional banking firms."* Internationally, the practice's profile is increasing, following its advice on financing aspects of the Olivetti/Telecom Italia and BoS/NatWest takeover bids and the British Steel/Koninklijke Hoogovens and Time Warner/EMI link-ups. The banking practice has increased its turnover fourfold in as many years, and although more recognised for its borrower profile, has developed its lending client base. With all round debt financiers in the banking practice, the team has advised groups such as Chase Manhattan and Barclays on a range of banking, property and projects financial work. Private equity groups also make up some of the practice's client base and the firm has worked on a number of public-to-privates in the last year. On the borrower side, the firm has advised BSkyB on a number of financing matters. Only the absence of a recognised big-hitter mars an otherwise rosy picture. **Clients:** Bank of Tokyo Mitsubishi; Bank of Scotland; Chase Manhattan; Barclays.

Shearman & Sterling With a UK:US lawyer ratio of 2:1, the firm has a leading reputation as an arranger of mixed US/UK law financings. The firm's leading US high yield capital markets expertise can also be found in London, which it has combined with UK bank debt proficiency to create what is arguably London's leading leveraged financing practice. The strength of this *"big buy out"* capability sees the team move up a band this year.

Stephen Mostyn-Williams has now gone in-house. The team is felt to have *"the potential to make the big time,"* having *"built one of the best launch pads."* However, the team's relatively narrow focus means that it is less active on standard transactions, where it has not yet threatened the dominance of the traditional City firms. The practice has acted on a number of multi-jurisdictional financings, straight private equity group acquisitions and public-to-private deals. The London office worked on a number of the largest European LBOs of 1999.

Represented Turkcell Iletism Hizmetleri on a simultaneous IPO of Turkcell on the Istanbul Stock Exchange and New York Stock Exchange. **Clients:** DLJ; Goldman Sachs; Morgan Stanley; Merrill Lynch; WDR.

Other Notable Practitioner *"Super, classic banking man"* **Maurice Allen***, formerly with Weil Gotshal & Manges, has moved with some of his banking team to international firm White & Case. He has a particular reputation for acquisition finance expertise.

U

Capital Markets: International Debt & Equity

Allen & Overy (37 ptrs, 143 asscs) Clients' perceptions of the practice are summarised by the comment of one investment banker: *"We use them particularly on anything nasty; they offer a consistently high standard and the associates are well trained."* An expanding international practice, with expertise recognised in key continental and far eastern jurisdictions. Also has a *"serious and quality"* US capability in capital markets and complementary areas including tax.

Although perceived as a loss to the team, the retirement of Richard Sykes has not significantly dented the firm's abilities in the area. While lacking the numbers of high profile individuals available to Linklaters, the team is still felt to have the *"quality and the experience"* to remain at the top. The team's principal focus is on debt work, but most lawyers in the group have expertise outside straight debt work. Often referred to as *"the MTN firm,"* the team has a *"successful"* and prolific volume debt practice, and a strong profile in high-yield work.

Practice manager **Boyan Wells*** is a *"first rate lawyer"* who has been *"immersed in it for years."* Most lawyers find him a *"good guy to have on the other side,"* and clients appreciate his *"technical excellence and sense of humour"* and use him for strategic matters. New to the rankings is client favourite **Stephen Miller***, a capital markets all-rounder known for his debt and structured work. He is regarded as someone who *"gets the deal done without confrontation, doesn't mess around and is clever and personable."*

With the convergence of many aspects of domestic and international floats, a separate equity capital markets group was launched in 2000. Members of the team advised on around 30 equity offerings in 1999, often acting for the underwriters. Although it is not perceived to have as high a profile as its immediate competitors in equity transactions, the practice is still viewed as *"active and quality,"* both domestically and internationally.

Other practitioners to enter the rankings this year are **Roger Wedderburn-Day*** *("reliable and technically excellent")* and **Daniel Shurman***, who is especially respected for his emerging markets work.

Matters handled this year include advising the banks on Halifax's issue of £245 million and €415 million of preferred securities, and Bank Austria Creditanstalt on a $100 million multi-currency commercial paper issue for Pliva (the Croatian pharmaceutical company). MTN work includes advising the dealers on the establishment of a new EMTN Programme for EDP and advising Alpha Credit Bank on the establishment of its EMTN Programme (Greece's first non-sovereign programme). Last year saw the firm advise on 19 convertible and exchangeable bond issues, including advising Deutsche Bank as lead manager of €1.2 billion exchangeables into shares of Total Fina. On the equity side, work includes advising KPNQwest in relation to its $1.05 billion flotation and advising the sponsor and financial adviser to The eXchange Holdings on the company's £200 million flotation. **Clients:** ABN AMRO; BSCH; Bear Stearns; CIBC; CSFB; Goldman Sachs; ING Barings; Lehman Brothers; HSBC; JP Morgan; Merrill Lynch; Morgan Stanley DW; Paribas; WDR; West Merchant Bank; Deutsche Bank; Salomon Smith Barney; Nomura International; Citibank; Barclays Capital; British Aerospace; Government of Singapore.

Linklaters (21 ptrs, 111 asscs) *"They have a superb capital markets practice and have had for a long time."* Particular strengths are in free-standing bond issues and emerging market debt and equity. The team advised lead managers on 193 stand alone bond issues in 1999. With its traditionally strong M&A side, the firm has strength in equity issues (including internet issues) and is recognised as the most balanced of the volume capital markets players. The team's international network is expanding and it has a recognised US capacity, with a leading position on Rule 144A transactions. Most clients appreciate the partner involvement on deals, the strength at associate level and note the *"effort the firm puts into us."*

The team's lawyers all do a mix of debt and equity work, with domestic equity issues usually dealt with by the corporate finance team. The popular **Lachlan Burn*** is considered *"the senior honcho on the technical points"* – a *"judgement call man."* He is a combination of *"law and lore,"* and clients appreciate his *"knowledge of the history and of what's going on now."* Market consensus is that he is *"second to none on regulatory matters."* **Nick**

*See leaders' profiles on pages 741-782

UNITED KINGDOM Leading firms (Capital Markets: Debt & Equity)	
1	Allen & Overy
	Linklaters
2	Clifford Chance
3	Freshfields Bruckhaus Deringer
4	Slaughter and May
5	Ashurst Morris Crisp
	Baker & McKenzie
	Herbert Smith
	Lovells
	Norton Rose
	Simmons & Simmons
	Weil, Gotshal & Manges

Firms are listed alphabetically in each band.

Leading individuals (Capital Markets: Debt & Equity)	
1	**BURN Lachlan** *Linklaters*
	CANBY Michael *Linklaters*
	EASTWELL Nicholas *Linklaters*
	WELLS Boyan *Allen & Overy*
2	**DUNNIGAN David** *Clifford Chance*
	EDLMANN Stephen *Linklaters*
	FRANK David *Slaughter and May*
3	**BROWN Jane** *Linklaters*
	MILLER Stephen *Allen & Overy*
	PITKIN Jeremy *Freshfields Bruckhaus Deringer*
	THOMSON Keith *Linklaters*
4	**BICKERTON David** *Clifford Chance*
	CLARK Charles *Linklaters*
	DUNLOP Stuart *Clifford Chance*
	SHURMAN Daniel *Allen & Overy*
	THIEFFRY Gilles *Garretts*
	WEDDERBURN-DAY Roger *Allen & Overy*

Individuals are listed alphabetically in each band.

Eastwell* *("a good person to have on your side")* is primarily known for his equity work in emerging markets, but can turn his hand to many things. Clients find in him *"an investment banker, regulator and accountant as well as a lawyer,"* while others praise his *"business acumen, technical ability and charm."* Also *"excellent with a client"* is the *"outstanding"* **Michael Canby***. He is *"astute and able to see the point quickly"* and is appreciated for his *"commitment and sleeves rolled up approach."* Practice leader **Stephen Edlmann*** *("you can tell he's got bags of experience")* divides his time between management and transactional work. **Charles Clark*** remains respected for his technical ability and for his *"basic courtesy – he sticks by his word."* Joining the rankings this year are the *"technical and thorough"* **Jane Brown***, who *"doesn't miss a point"* and the *"excellent"* all-rounder **Keith Thomson*** *("reliable and not over-ambitious.")* Both are respected for their debt work.

Equity issues this year include advising the banks on the listing of South African Breweries, of Freeserve, of Thus and of ebookers.com, the last being a London-driven global offering including a listing on Nasdaq and the Neuer Markt. The team advised on Adecco's convertible notes and share offering to raise approximately $700 million. It also advised on the first ever issue by a UK bank of tax-deductible Tier 1 capital, advising Halifax on a £500 million issue of guaranteed, non-voting, non-cumulative preferred securities. Work on the debt side includes a $235 million high yield bond issue by Jazztel.

Acted as US counsel to Kreditanstalt fur Wiederaufbau (agency of the German Government) in Deutsche Telekom's offering of 200 million shares in the form of shares and American Depositary Shares. Deal value – €13.3 billion. **Clients:** CSFB; JP Morgan; Robert Fleming & Co; Barclays Capital; Goldman Sachs; Lehman Brothers; Merrill Lynch; Nomura; Paribas; Salomons/Citibank; UBS Warburg.

Clifford Chance (20 ptrs, 115 asscs) A mainstream capital markets practice with strengths on free-standing bond work, MTN programmes and non-UK equity, particularly emerging markets work. Members of the team are *"helpful and responsive,"* with *"a high degree of commerciality."* Concerns were raised about the perceived high turnover of the group and the consistency of quality in some of the firm's continental offices (although offices in Southern Europe and Germany are considered *"excellent."*) Post-mergers, the distinguishing feature of the firm continues to be its international orientation. *"Hands-on client man"* **David Dunnigan*** is *"a great networker who, if he doesn't know, knows someone who does."* New to our lists are the *"accommodating"* **David Bickerton*** and the *"personable"* **Stuart Dunlop***. Bickerton is *"diligent and technically extremely good,"* and is known for his expertise on warrants and project bonds. Client favourite Dunlop is *"in the David Dunnigan mould"* – he *"gets the deal done."*

Traditionally thought of as a debt capital markets practice, the merger with Pünder, which has a significant IPO practice, helps balance the team on a European level. Deals this year include the Olivetti take-over financing and British Aerospace's £596 million exchangeable to shares of Orange. High-yield bond deals include those of TDL Infomedia Group and ONO/Cableuropa. The team also worked on the largest ever non-gilt sterling offering with a guarantee by the UK Government, the London & Continental Railways Eurobond offer. **Clients:** LIFFE; British Bankers Association; The Bond Market Association; The Futures and Options Association.

Freshfields Bruckhaus Deringer (30 ptrs, 30 asscs) The head of the capital markets practice, **Jeremy Pitkin***, is *"a joy to have on a deal."* The practice is *"not at the top for the range of debt work,"* principally because it is not perceived to have gone for the debt commodity business as most of its immediate competitors have. In debt however, the firm has advised on a number of MTN programmes this year, for arrangers and for issuers such as AXA, Kingfisher and the Republic of Lebanon. *"Good on free standing bonds,"* stand-alone issues include offerings by Repsol, Compass, China Telecom and Pearson, for a mix of issuers and arrangers.

The general feeling is that the practice is *"much stronger on equity,"* where it is rated *"at the top,"* both for UK and non-UK company work. Internationally, particular developments this year have been a strengthening of teams in European offices, particularly France and Germany, and continued recognition for strength in Southern Europe. Also has recognised US capacity. Cross-border work includes the first ever listing of a UK plc on the Neuer Markt and the Easdaq, the IPO by Dialog Semiconductor and advising on an Alpha Credit Bank issuance, listed in Athens, with GDRs in London and a US Rule 144A component. The firm has been active this year, advising on the IPOs of service providers, companies providing technologies for access to the web over wireless networks and other internet businesses. Issues include those of Thus, lastminute.com and The eXchange Holdings. Other work includes a €336 million listing for MG and equity and bond issuances for groups such as Fortis and Stagecoach. **Clients:** CIBC; Deutsche Bank/Bankers Trust; DKB; Financial Security Assurance; Goldman Sachs; JP Morgan; RBS; Salomon Smith Barney; Nomura; WDR; Paribas; AIG Financial Products; AMP.

Slaughter and May (12 ptrs, 15 asscs) The firm is not considered to have the emphasis on capital markets of its immediate rivals – *"they are client-led, not product-led, so they only go in when their clients tap the market."* It is testament to the firm's ability that competitors can regard the firm as having de-emphasised capital markets, yet still concede that the firm is a leader for UK and non-UK equity work (notably Scandinavian equity). Regarded as *"superb company people"* with *"some of the best lawyers,"* the firm tends to appear principally on the side of the underwriters. While most of the principal M&A and banking partners were mentioned as leaders for equity issuance, the capital markets standout name is the structured debt-oriented **David Frank***. *"Long-standing and well-known,"* his work includes banking, and he is considered *"hard-working and diligent."*

Work this year includes advising the Enron Corporation on its debut Eurobond issue of €400 million, Abbey National on a new $15 billion MTN programme and debt issues for domestics such as Diageo, Unilever, Cadbury Schweppes and Bradford & Bingley. The group has also represented foreign companies such as United Utilities and Oesterreichische Kontrollbank.

Equity work has involved a €775 million global offering for Fortis, a £700 million placing for Colt Telecom, the ebookers flotation, the Old Mutual demutualisation and global offer, and advising the banks on a British Aerospace issue to GEC shareholders. Other work includes the £438 million Millennium & Copthorne and £162.5 million Eurotunnel rights issues. International work has encompassed advice on convertible bonds for Société Foncière Lyonnaise, advising on issues such as Finmatica for the underwriters and Parques Reunidos for the global co-ordinators. **Clients:** Fortis; Abbey National Treasury Services; Enron Corporation; Unilever; Deutsche Bank; Moody's; RBS; UBS Warburg.

Ashurst Morris Crisp (3 ptrs, 7 asscs) A well respected group which is not seen as a *"bread and butter outfit."* However, it is particularly noted for its equity and European high-yield debt work. High-yield work this year includes advising on Clubhaus £50 million issue and a subsequent £10 million tranche, and on an issue for Atlantic Telecom Group. Other debt work involved advising on Imperial Tobacco's €2 billion debt issuance programme and its €650 million first drawing, and advising on $530 million's worth of exchangeable notes for Swiss Re. Project bonds are also an area of expertise. Equity tends to be dealt with by the corporate department, and here the firm advised the issuers on a £100 million placing for Kingston Communications and a $665 million rights issue for Henlys Group, following its acquisition of Blue Bird Corporation. **Clients:** Abbey National Financial Products/Treasury Services; Swiss Re; ING Barings; Daiwa SBCM Europe; Sumitomo; Invesco; WestLB.

Baker & McKenzie (7 ptrs, 14 asscs) Focused on international transactions, the team is particularly known for its work on equity offerings for emerging European companies. This year has seen a string of deals out of Central and Eastern Europe and Egypt. These include advising Al Ezz Steel Rebars SAE on an offering and listing of shares in Cairo, Alexandria and London and advising the lead underwriter CSFB, in a MATAV share offering. Strength in telecoms work has seen the practice advise on telecoms offerings in Eygpt, Lithuania, Hungary, Poland and Croatia. The firm also advised on the $175 million US/German dual listing of PrimaCom and on a high yield issue for Pannon GSM Tavkozlesi Rt. On the structured side, the firm was international and Italian counsel to WestLB as arranger of the €118 million securitisation of Italian lease receivables by Landes Srl. **Clients:** CSFB; Schroders; CAIB; DLJ; Chase Securities; PrimaCom; Pannon GSM Tavkozlesi Rt; Al Ezz Steel Rebars SAE.

Herbert Smith (16 ptrs, 45 asscs) Although involved on some of the most important internet IPOs of the year, the undoubted ability of the capital markets practice has not translated into a high market profile in this area. Two significant internet IPOs were the Freeserve and QXL.com IPOs, with London and New York listings. Other equity work saw the team advise Stagecoach on the first open offer using book-building techniques. On the debt side, the practice advised on a £1.2 billion bond issue by Edison First Power and advised LCR on the issue of £2.65 billion worth of government guaranteed bonds to finance the construction of section 1 of the Channel Tunnel Rail Link. Other work includes advising Olivetti in connection with their refinancing of borrowings following the hostile takeover of Telecom Italia. The firm has also been active on a range of securitisation and derivatives work. **Clients:** BSkyB; Credit Lyonnais; Lazards; CSFB; Merrill Lynch; Eurotunnel; Colonial Financial Services.

Lovells (6 ptrs, 16 asscs) A balanced practice working for an even mix of issuers and lead managers, domestically and internationally. Active this year on high-yield issues, in emerging markets and in the hi-tech sector. Has an expanding US capability. Debt work this year has seen the firm active on Kappa Beheer €370 million high yield bond issue and Barclays Bank's £4 billion debt issuance programme. Equity work includes advising on the South African Breweries IPO for £3.5 billion, the Finmatica €67.5 million combined Italian public offer and international institutional offer, and the £305 million IPO of Morse Holdings. **Clients:** Bank of Scotland; Barclays Bank; CA Indosuez; DLJ; Dresdner Kleinwort Benson; Henderson Investors; ING Barings; Société Générale; Alstom; Slough Estates; Xerox Corporation; Granada; BNP Paribas; JP Morgan; Rothschild.

Norton Rose (5 ptrs, 12 asscs) A comparatively small team with recognised strengths in debt and securitisation. The year has seen a vast increase in the firm's derivatives capacity and the first full year for the US securities team. A balanced team whose steady growth and increased profile has seen it break into the market for US investment bank work this year. This is London's up and coming capital markets practice.

Debt practice leader **Gilles Thieffry*** is a debt all-rounder, working on straight debt and convertible issues, and has expertise in the insurance world. The team advised the EBRD on 24 bond issues of various denominations (totalling approximately €4 billion) under its EMTN programme. The practice advised Lehman Brothers on a €110 million upper tier II issue by Cofinoga and a $100 million issue for French reinsurance company SCOR. Work for BNP Paribas included four issues of embedded option bonds of $50 million each and four issues of $55 million each and floating rate notes.

Equity work is handled out of the corporate finance department and the firm has a strong emerging markets capacity. The team acted on a $3 billion share offering by HSBC and advised the lead managers on the $100 million share and global depository receipt issue by Al Ezz Steel Rebars of Egypt. **Clients:** BNP Paribas; Lehman Brothers International; Bank of Ireland; HSBC; EBRD; BMW; Kingdoms of Sweden and Belgium; AXA; Ashanti; Lukoil; Fox Kids.

Simmons & Simmons (13 ptrs, 28 asscs) Works on debt and equity for a variety of lead managers and issuers, and is praised for its perceived strength in the high-yield arena. Debt work this year saw the group act for the banks on Jazztel's high yield debt issue and on £400 million of exchangeables for Railtrack. On the equity side, the firm advised on the HK$4.8 billion international offering of New World China Land. Other work includes a secondary listing on the LSE for Esprit and for AlliedSignal after its merger with Honeywell. The team also advised the Indian Government on the GDR issue of the Gas Authority of India. The non-exclusive link-up with Fried Frank of the US gives the firm a strong US securities capacity as well as strength on structured matters. Corporate Treasury and Corporate Trustee work are also active areas. **Clients:** Deutsche Bank; NatWest; BAT; Railtrack; Dresdner Kleinwort Benson; Fuji International; Barclays Capital.

Weil, Gotshal & Manges (6 ptrs, 18 asscs) A mix of US and English partners in a firm particularly known for its securitisation and structured work. The practice nevertheless provides a broad range of debt and equity advice. *"Clearly trying to compete with the Magic Circle,"* the departure

U

*See leaders' profiles on pages 741-782

of high-profile names on the banking side has *"hurt their firepower,"* but clients still believe that the firm has *"retained strong people just below partner level."* The firm advised the MediaOne Group on its $1.129 billion offering of mandatory exchangeable notes into ADRs of Vodafone Airtouch and acted for Hicks Muse in a $299 million offering and £75 million high yield notes in connection with the buyout of Hillsdown Holdings. Also acted on Matsushita's €1.5 billion SEC-registered IPO of EPCOS, a former Siemens/Matsushita joint venture. The firm's Warsaw and London offices combined on the largest international offering in Eastern Europe in 1999, representing Nafta Polska on the sale of 30% of the Polish Oil Corp (PKN), with a subsequent listing in London and Warsaw. **Clients:** JP Morgan Securities; Morgan Stanley; Deutsche Bank; Telewest Communications; Hicks Muse; CSFB; Chase; Merrill Lynch; NatWest; Nikko Europe.

U

Capital Markets: Securitisation

Clifford Chance (8 ptrs, 40 asscs) The depth of the team, international reach, volume of deals and breadth of practice make the firm's securitisation practice stand out. Lateral hires, internal promotions, partners returning from overseas offices and departmental moves have doubled the size of the practice's partnership in the last year.

UNITED KINGDOM Leading firms (Capital Markets: Securitisation)	
1	Clifford Chance
2	Allen & Overy
	Freshfields Bruckhaus Deringer
3	Linklaters
4	Sidley & Austin
5	Ashurst Morris Crisp
	Lovells
	Norton Rose
	Simmons & Simmons
	Slaughter and May
	Weil, Gotshal & Manges

Firms are listed alphabetically in each band.

Head of the London practice is the *"charming and well-connected"* **Chris Oakley***, who is appreciated for his *"painstaking and meticulous"* approach. The popular **Kevin Ingram*** is considered *"an awesome mind who is not a cheap point scorer. The only problem is getting hold of him."* He is regarded by some as the *"best concepts guy"* – *"you get him to think and his partners to draft and you have a dream combination."* The *"user-friendly"* **John Woodhall*** enters our rankings this year, following his return from Hong Kong. **Andrew Forryan*** also enters our lists this year. *"Urbane, sensible, polite and professional,"* he is regarded as a *"bright guy,"* particularly on property-related work. Further boosting the team's capability was the arrival of the highly regarded **Peter Voisey*** from Lovells.

Main areas of work are UK and European public bond issues, private placement conduit work and property securitisations. A *"strong franchise"* spread through Europe, Asia and the Americas, significant deals this year have involved multi-office co-ordinations, including the Formula One, Amstel and INPS transactions, as well as the $1 billion Gracechurch Card Funding (No. 1). The practice advised BNP on the first synthetic CLO transaction to be realised by a bank incorporated in the European Union using credit default swap technology. Also advised the banks on the Iberbond 1999 securitisation of lease receivables and, closer to home, acted on the St James's Park Finance securitisation. Represented Cygnus in securitising a portfolio of loans (valued at €4.3 billion).

Leading individuals (Capital Markets: Securitisation)		
1	**FALCONER Ian** *Freshfields Bruckhaus Deringer*	**KRISCHER David** *Allen & Overy*
2	**BEDFORD Paul** *Allen & Overy*	**FULLER Geoff** *Allen & Overy*
	INGRAM Kevin *Clifford Chance*	**KELLY Jacky** *Weil, Gotshal & Manges*
	RAINES Marke *Shearman & Sterling*	**TROTT David** *Freshfields Bruckhaus Deringer*
3	**FORRYAN Andrew** *Clifford Chance*	**HUGHES Richard** *Linklaters*
	MACKENZIE Marcus *Freshfields Bruckhaus Deringer*	**OAKLEY Chris** *Clifford Chance*
	PENN Graham *Sidley & Austin*	**RUSSELL John** *Brown & Wood LLP*
	SMITH Michael *Ashurst Morris Crisp*	**VOISEY Peter** *Clifford Chance*
	VOISIN Michael *Linklaters*	**WALSH Jonathan** *Norton Rose*
	WOODHALL John *Clifford Chance*	
4	**BEAUMONT Rupert** *Slaughter and May*	**BRESSLAW James** *Simmons & Simmons*
	HANDLING Erica *Weil, Gotshal & Manges*	**HUDD David** *Lovells*
	RICE Jim *Linklaters*	**SMITH Christopher** *Slaughter and May*
	SMITH Sarah *Sidley & Austin*	**TUCKER Julian** *Allen & Overy*

Individuals are listed alphabetically in each band.

Allen & Overy (37 ptrs, 143 asscs-whole capital markets team) Considered to have a smaller practice than Clifford Chance, the team is still perceived to be a balanced unit which has had *"a really good year considering the size of their team."*

While not denting the team's capacity, the departure of Marke Raines (to Shearman & Sterling) and a high profile associate is seen to have affected the forward momentum of the practice. A top name in securitisation is *"motivator"* **David Krischer***, regarded as *"light years ahead in terms of technical excellence."* He is a dual qualified US/UK lawyer. He is *"going from strength to strength"* and is *"the main guy for a client to go to."* With his *"non-confrontational"* approach, the *"charming and delightful"* **Paul Bedford*** is *"the one to front a deal."* A *"details man,"* highly regarded for his brainpower, he comes from a corporate trustee background. **Julian Tucker*** enters our rankings this year following strong market recommendation for his *"commercial approach,"* with clients appreciating his *"flamboyant nature, refreshing in an area where the hours are enough to drive you potty."* An all-rounder, he has experience in property-related work.

Large deals this year include advising on the landmark £1.54 billion securitisation of the Broadgate Estate in the City of London, and the Madame Tussaud's securitisation, the first backed by leisure assets. The team was also involved on the Unique Pubs Group securitisation and the £610 million securitisation of rental income within the Trafford Centre in Manchester. In addition, the group was involved on the world's first ever securitisation of airport revenues without an external guarantee (London City Airport.)

In the more discreet world of repackaging, **Geoff Fuller*** is one of London's top names. In 1999, the practice advised on approximately 160 repackaging issues, dealing with a wide range of financial instruments. Advised Deutsche Bank on the establishment of a secured repackaging programme for Repackaged Offshore Collateralised Kredit (ROCK), the first repackaging programme with an issuer incorporated in Gibraltar. The practice also represented Nomura International in connection with the ¥32.4 billion repackaging of a variety of Japanese corporate credits.

Freshfields Bruckhaus Deringer (30 ptrs, 30 asscs) A *"high-quality"* team *"involved on the more interesting deals."* While the practice is considered to have international breadth, notably in Germany following the historic merger with Bruckhaus, it is not yet considered to have the critical mass of its immediate competitors.

Ian Falconer's* reputation precedes him. He has *"all the attributes one would look for,"* and is a *"great draftsman who gets deals done without aggro."* Such is his reputation, that some comment that he is *"hopelessly overworked."* Competitors have *"excellent dealings"* with **David Trott*** and **Marcus Mackenzie***. Trott is *"technically extremely good, and he knows it."* Mackenzie, new to the rankings, is well regarded and has *"a nice way about him."*

The team works on complex matters across Europe and has been involved this year on securitisation transactions involving mortgages, pub businesses, rolling stock, ferry businesses, autoloans, student loans and care homes businesses. Advised JP Morgan as lead manager of Abbey National's benchmark £1 billion residential mortgage securitisation through Holmes Funding No 1. Also represented on the first transaction in the Eurobond markets involving the issue of enhanced secured aircraft notes.

Linklaters (10 ptrs, 28 asscs) *"Aggressive on price,"* the securitisation team is *"chasing hard."* The firm has made a push in the area with the recruitment of the well-regarded **Richard Hughes*** *("he will make a good practice out of it.")* He is new to our rankings, as is securitisation all-rounder **Jim Rice***. The firm's dominant figure for repackaging work, Andrew Carmichael, resides in the Hong Kong office. **Michael Voisin*** is an all-rounder, well regarded for his structured work in repackaging and credit-linked notes. Clients described him as *"technical"* and a *"thinker."*

Strengths are found in the non-conforming ('sub-prime') mortgage sector and in the credit card market. Acted for the banks on the £600 million residential mortgage securitisation for Northern Rock, and on the $1 billion Gracechurch Card Funding (No.1), at the time the largest UK credit card securitisation.

Acting for Barclays Capital on the first securitisation by Barclays Bank of its credit card portfolio (Barclaycard), the largest UK credit card securitisation to date, which had an issue amount of $1 billion and was sold directly into the United States, the first time this has been achieved with a European credit card portfolio.

Sidley & Austin (13 ptrs, 21 asscs) Well-known in the securitisation field, with a large team and a perceived focus on asset-backed conduit work. With complementary practices in areas such as tax and regulatory work, the firm is considered to have *"brought in the armoury,"* and many view the firm as *"the leader of the US practices."* Practice leader is the *"technically excellent"* **Graham Penn***, while newly-ranked **Sarah Smith*** is a *"sensible and clever lawyer."*

Known for its work for rating agencies such as Duff & Phelps (recently merged with Fitch IBCA), the firm has a broad range of clients including originators, issuers of securities and liquidity providers. Work this year includes the £360 million European Loan Conduit No.2 acting for Morgan Stanley. This was the first European commercial mortgage securitisation in which the notes were offered for sale in the US under Rule 144A. The practice also acted for a Dutch bank sponsor in the creation of a US/Euro $10 billion commercial paper, and for Morgan Stanley in the securitisation of a portfolio of pubs by Alehouse Finance.

In the murky waters between securitisation and derivatives, the firm advised credit derivatives leader BCI in its capacity as originator of a synthetic CLO transaction involving the use of a credit default swap (€280 million).

Ashurst Morris Crisp (3 ptrs, 5 asscs) The *"busy"* **Michael Smith***, who *"does a bit of everything,"* is particularly well regarded for his structured work. In this area the firm is considered to be *"one of the more experienced London outfits"* for CDO work. Work this year includes acting for Immediate Capital Group on the Eurocredit CDO 1, issue of €416,000,500 asset backed notes, the first euro-denominated high yield CDO transaction closed in the Euro Markets. The team also advises on a broad range of derivatives issues.

Lovells This is an area of strength for the firm but the recent departure of Peter Voisey to Clifford Chance is perceived by the market to have affected the team's capacity. However, *"figurehead"* **David Hudd*** remains well regarded for his structured work. The firm is regarded as having a *"niche in repackaging"* where it has acted this year on repackagings of financial instruments for clients such as BNP Paribas, DLJ and CA Indosuez. A highlight of the year was acting on the First Active Financial securitisation of flexible mortgages, a first for the UK. The team advised on credit card receivables securitisations such as the Citibank Credit Card Master Trust 1's €1 billion credit card participation certificates. The team has also acted on the securitisation of car and personal loan receivables.

Norton Rose (4 ptrs, 8 asscs) *"Nice guy"* **Jonathan Walsh*** has a *"great reputation"* in securitisation. He heads a team which acted on a $5 billion conduit (Loch Ness) for Royal Bank of Scotland, a £116 million securitisation of a Boeing 747-400 by KLM and a £120 million commercial property securitisation for Workspace Group. The team also acted for SG in relation to a credit card receivable securitisation for a company providing credit card services to major UK retailers.

Simmons & Simmons (13 ptrs, 28 asscs) The firm is known for its focus on structured finance and structured securities (repackaging) work, an area where securitisation expert **James Bresslaw*** continues to be respected. The departure of John Russell and a fellow partner to Brown & Wood is perceived to have weakened the team, although it is still regarded as *"good for the lead managers on securitisation."*

The firm advised on the securitisation of revenues generated by London City Airport and advised British Land in the £1.54 billion Broadgate Development securitisation. The team acted on approximately 350 repackaging trades last year. Major clients continue to be UBS Warburg, Merrill Lynch, CSFB and Deutsche, the last of which was advised on more than 280 structured securities offerings during the year. The structured practice is closely connected to the derivatives side, where as well as credit derivatives, the practice has strengths in metals and energy-related transactions.

Slaughter and May (12 ptrs, 15 asscs) **Rupert Beaumont*** is *"a legendary figure,"* who *"built up the market in the early days."* He is still active in the area, mainly on energy deals. **Christopher Smith*** is also a respected name. Owing to the nature of the firm, which tends to spawn generalists, securitisation is not an area where the firm is felt to have genuine specialists. Thus, although the quality and complexity of the work is unquestioned, the individuals do not have the profile of the market leaders.

The practice advises underwriters and lead managers, rating agencies and bank originators.

*See leaders' profiles on pages 741-782

Advised on the issue of asset-backed notes by West Coast Train Finance, and Eastern Electricity (part of TXU Group) on a £550 million electricity receivables programme. Along with German 'best friend' Hengeler Mueller, the firm advised on a €4 billion asset-backed global commercial paper programme for BILLS Securitisation.

Weil, Gotshal & Manges (3 ptrs, 12 asscs) Both **Jacky Kelly*** and **Erica Handling*** received praise from the market for building up a strong and busy practice. Client favourite Handling is new to the rankings, and is an all-rounder particularly rated for collateralised debt/loan/bond obligation work.

The practice is mainly known for its work on the synthetic securitisation side as opposed to traditional securitisation, and is *"particularly strong on the CBO, CLO and structured side."* Worked on the First Flexible transaction, which JP Morgan arranged for First Active, the first securitisation in the UK of flexible mortgages. Other work includes an asset-backed conduit for Greenwich, while the team was involved in almost 50% of the residential mortgage-backed deals completed in the UK and Ireland in 1999. The practice also advised Morgan Stanley as the arranger on the first ever CDO with a wholly Euro-denominated European asset portfolio.

Other Notable Practitioners A major move this year was the arrival at Shearman & Sterling of **Marke Raines*** *("a real thinker")* from Allen & Overy. With the firm making a push in providing a comprehensive range of UK finance advice, his arrival will *"change its profile"* in securitisation. The capital markets all-rounder **John Russell*** at Brown & Wood has a high profile in the repackaging world. Recently arrived with another colleague from Simmons & Simmons, his reputation fortifies the UK practice of the *"pre-eminent asset-backed practice in the US."*

U

Capital Markets: Derivatives

UNITED KINGDOM Leading firms (Capital Markets: Derivatives)
1 Allen & Overy
Clifford Chance
2 Freshfields Bruckhaus Deringer
Linklaters
3 Norton Rose
4 Baker & McKenzie
Slaughter and May

Firms are listed alphabetically in each band.

Leading individuals (Capital Markets: Derivatives)
1 **GOLDEN Jeffrey** *Allen & Overy*
HENDERSON Schuyler *Norton Rose*
MOTANI Habib *Clifford Chance*
2 **BENTON David** *Allen & Overy*
BROWN Claude *Clifford Chance*
FIRTH Simon *Linklaters*
3 **HADDOCK Simon** *Allen & Overy*
LEVINE Iona *Baker & McKenzie*
RUDIN Simeon *Freshfields Bruckhaus Deringer*
WARNA-KULA-SURIYA Sanjev *Slaughter and May*

Individuals are listed alphabetically in each band.

Allen & Overy (37 ptrs, 143 asscs-whole capital markets team) Popular US lawyer **Jeffrey Golden*** maintains a high profile as the *"big picture man"* of the practice, and is primarily recognised for his ISDA work. Among an *"active and able"* team, **David Benton*** and *"moderniser"* **Simon Haddock*** stand out. The team is regarded as especially proficient in OTC derivative advice, although it is recognised for its general breadth and depth – *"they can bring a range of guns to bear against you."* Although involved in structured work, the practice's high profile stems more from its involvement on plain vanilla transactions and for acting as European and South East Asian counsel to ISDA. The team's strong relationship with ISDA continues, helping it to advise both central banks and Governments. This year, the practice advised the Hungarian Forex Association on the development of standard form documentation for the Hungarian domestic market. Transactional work has seen the firm involved in the credit derivatives market and, increasingly, in energy and commodity derivatives.

Clifford Chance (9 ptrs, 32 asscs) The *"pleasant"* and *"drop-dead smart"* **Habib Motani*** leads the derivatives group. **Claude Brown*** enters the rankings this year following market recommendation. Respected for his credit derivatives expertise, he *"knows the business side of things and presents the facts well."* This is seen as a global practice which is increasing its volume of business. Considered to have *"depth on exchange traded"* derivatives in addition to its recognised OTC capabilities. In conjunction with other departments, the group advised BNP on the first synthetic CLO transaction to be realised by a bank incorporated in the European Union using credit default swap technology. The practice also acted for the Bond Market Association on a Cross Product Master Netting Agreement, and has represented ISDA on European regulatory matters.

Freshfields Bruckhaus Deringer (30 ptrs, 30 asscs) Part of the structured finance practice, the derivatives practice is primarily known for its advice on structured work rather than on straight derivatives matters. On structured matters, **Simeon Rudin*** is considered *"the main man,"* with a particularly strong grasp of tax issues. The practice does cover the breadth of derivatives work, from standard schedules to ISDA Master Agreements and synthetic securitisations, the latter being a niche strength. The team advises trade organisations, financial institutions and end-users, and has recently been active in insurance derivatives.

Linklaters (10 ptrs, 21 asscs) The popular **Simon Firth*** *("terrific as a pure derivatives lawyer and good on structured deals")* leads the derivatives practice. Less high profile than CC's or A&O's, the team has a broad practice and is known for its regulatory work. As well as straight derivatives work, the practice has been heavily involved in credit derivatives and has handled a number of synthetic CLOs. The team has also been advising on structures which enable insurance companies to tap the derivatives market.

Norton Rose (2 ptrs, 7 asscs) The arrival of **Schuyler Henderson*** from Baker & McKenzie has propelled the firm to the ranks of serious players in derivatives. The *"eminent senior guy in the field,"* some call him simply the *"grandfather of derivatives."* A broad practice with a name in ISDA-related work, it is seen to have *"made a particular effort in credit derivatives."* Work includes advising on hedging transactions in relation to the EBRD's EMTN programme.

Baker & McKenzie (1 ptr, 2 asscs) The departure of Schuyler Henderson and another partner was initially seen to have crippled the derivatives practice. However, the recruitment of the former head of HSBC's Global Treasury & Capital Markets legal team, **Iona Levine***, from Hammond Suddards, has breathed new life into the derivatives team. She is considered to have a *"focus on derivatives, notably on OTC work where she has considerable experience."*

Slaughter and May (12 ptrs, 15 asscs) **Sanjev Warna-Kula-Suriya*** is a structured finance all-rounder, working on capital markets, securitisation and derivatives. Clients say that he *"can sometimes be professorial,"* but emphasise that this is compensated by his commercial experience gained from his time working in the derivatives field for Credit Suisse Financial Products. He is considered to be *"overworked, but if you can isolate him, we would go for him any day."*

The firm itself is held to be a *"class act"* which works on a range of derivatives matters. The group is advising on an online website for Enron, making contracts available on a bilateral basis, and acted on Yosemite 2, the securitisation of energy-linked financial contracts for an international energy company. Additionally, the firm has advised on product creation for Morgan Stanley, Fortis, Zurich Capital Markets and the Emerging Markets Clearing Corporation.

U

Communications: Telecoms

UNITED KINGDOM Leading firms (Communications: Telecoms)	
1	Bird & Bird
	Clifford Chance
2	Allen & Overy
3	Baker & McKenzie
	Denton Wilde Sapte
	Freshfields Bruckhaus Deringer
	Linklaters
	Olswang
	Simmons & Simmons

Firms are listed alphabetically in each band.

Leading individuals (Communications: Telecoms)	
1	**HIESTER Elizabeth** *Clifford Chance*
	KERR David *Bird & Bird*
	LONG Colin *Olswang*
2	**LISTON Stephanie** *McDermott, Will & Emery*
	MERCER Edward *Taylor Joynson Garrett*
	SCHWARZ Tim *Clifford Chance*
	STRIVENS Peter *Baker & McKenzie*
	WATSON Chris *Allen & Overy*
	WHEADON Tom *Simmons & Simmons*
	WRIGHT Claire *Allen & Overy*

Individuals are listed alphabetically in each band.

Bird & Bird (25 ptrs, 35 asscs) *"The firm is very clever in its strategy."* Highly rated for domestic work, the team is acknowledged as the top infrastructure player: *"They are very much the tops – an IBM choice."* **David Kerr***, leader of the group, firm chairman and *"tough negotiator,"* is one of the giants of the field. His profile somewhat overshadows the excellent support he receives from the team, enhanced in 1999 by the addition of an OFTEL lawyer. The scope of industry involvement of the practice is impressive, although the market perceives that the team does not always get the corporate support it needs.

Known for being *"BT's lawyers,"* the team has acted for BT on its international ventures (such as the AT&T/BT concert joint venture). The practice also advised Telefónica in its 3G mobile spectrum licence auction efforts and acted for Racal Telecommunications in its reorganisation to facilitate its £1 billion sale to Global Crossing. In fibre swaps, the group acted for Worldwide Fibre Networks on its deal with Telia. On commercial matters, the team advised Viatel on UK matters of the establishment of their European network, and acted for Eurotunnel on a series of dark fibre leases through the Channel Tunnel. Litigation and arbitration round out a *"well-balanced"* portfolio. The firm represented British Telecommunications plc in their increased holding in VIAG Interkom to 90%, valued at €7.4 billion. **Clients:** British Telecommunications; Video Networks; Viatel.

Clifford Chance (11 ptrs) *"Superb in most respects,"* the team is led by the *"intimidatingly sharp"* **Liz Hiester***, who receives admirable support from **Tim Schwarz***, *"technically first-rate and doesn't take cheap points."* Benefiting from the world-wide brand name, and *"always a feature"* on the big cross-border corporate transactions, the firm's London office is a full-service affair, with expertise in regulatory, competition, infrastructure and privatisations. The team acts for a range of international governments, operators and private companies, advising on proposed investments in global satellites, and representing overseas states on the creation of a new legal and regulatory framework for their telecoms sectors. As well as acting on numerous overseas privatisations, notably in Africa and the Middle East, the firm has advised a leading international player on a range of commercial agreements relating to submarine and terrestrial cable networks. **Clients:** Financial institutions; operators; multinationals.

Allen & Overy (8 ptrs, 30 asscs) *"A very professional outfit – they give the impression of being committed to the area."* A&O's telecoms team is making waves for two reasons. The first is its respected work for the government on the 3G mobile spectrum licence auction. *"Easy to work with,"* **Claire Wright*** earned praise for her 3G work and moves up the rankings this year. Secondly, the recruitment of **Chris Watson*** from Simmons & Simmons has gained unanimous approval *("a really valuable acquisition for them")*. Respected for his regulatory and technical skills, Watson's arrival is evidence of further commitment to the sector. Regulatory work includes advising the Government of Pakistan on the creation of a telecoms regulatory framework.

However, the firm's major track record has been in its corporate and financing deals. The team acted for KPN Telecom on its €20 billion joint venture with BellSouth to acquire the German cellular operator, E-Plus, for KPN Mobile on the €5 billion sale of a 15% slice of its share capital to NTT DoCoMo, and for Cable & Wireless on the $38.1 billion takeover bid by PacificCentury CyberWorks for Cable & Wireless HKT, Hong Kong's major telecoms operator. In financing the group advised the eleven-bank syndicate footing the facility for Vodafone AirTouch's offer for Mannesmann, said to be the largest ever. Equipment financing and high yield issues are also part of the firm's repertoire. The practice recently advised Marconi on the formation of a new joint venture with Railtrack, 'EuroMast.' **Clients:** Cable & Wireless; Radio Communications Agency; KPN Telecom.

Baker & McKenzie (9 ptrs, 9 asscs) Well respected worldwide, the team combines its telecoms

*See leaders' profiles on pages 741-782

nous with IT expertise. The market still mentions Stephanie Liston's departure from the telecoms team and the consequent loss of profile, and the practice may well suffer from industry consolidation. However, **Peter Strivens*** leads the group in a *"laid back, pragmatic"* style and elicited praise from peers as *"someone you can work towards a common objective with".* Known as a regulatory and commercial practice, the team represented AOL Europe in its 'Stop the Clock' campaign to end BT's current practice of charging by the minute for internet access. Another highlight was marshalling its network to act for Pangea on the negotiation, construction and related financing of a $436 million fibre optic network to connect eight European countries.

Represented SFX Entertainment Inc in its $3.3 billion merger with Clear Channel Communications Inc. **Clients:** AOL Europe; Cisco Systems; Pangea.

Denton Wilde Sapte (8 ptrs, 12 asscs) The telecommunications practice has clearly gained from the 2000's combination of Wilde Sapte's telecoms financing expertise with Denton Hall's *"far-flung"* regulatory and privatisation practice. For new client Energis, the team handled four acquisitions (including the $600 million acquisition of EnerTel). The team has been involved in numerous international matters, including representing Fibernet on its European roll-out, advising the Telecoms Regulatory Authority on creating a new legal and regulatory framework for Egypt, and advising on the sale of MediaOne's interest in TITUS and Singapore CableVision.

Although the team can handle telecoms dispute work, it is better known for its financing of industry initiatives. Acted for ABN AMRO on financing for Tele 2 Europe incorporating guaranteed long-form notes issued by Tele 2, and for Nokia in relation to vendor financing £215 million worth of equipment to the Dolphin Group. Represented Liberty Media in a $5.3 billion transaction with UnitedGlobalCom. **Clients:** Nokia; SG; MediaOne.

Freshfields Bruckhaus Deringer (18 ptrs, 57 asscs) A firm famed for its corporate finance and competition work for telecoms players and the media/dotcom world is said to have *"a good grasp of convergence."* Advised AirTouch and Mannesmann in response to Vodafone's advances, and acted for Telewest Communications on its £10.5 billion merger with Flextech. They were also seen acting for the global co-ordinators of Telefónica's Yellow Pages subsidiary, and raised their profile by acting on the IPO of Thus. *"You know you're in good hands"* say clients. The team acted for CSFB and Chase as Esat's financial advisers in respect of bids by Telenor and BT, as well as being instructed by London Transport in the PFI outsourcing of the LUL's transmission network and radio system.

On a more regulatory basis, the group advised a bidder in the 3G mobile telephony licence auction. The practice represented numerous clients on interconnection proceedings before the Regulatory Authority for Telecommunications and Post, and advised, amongst others, GEC and ICO on telecoms equipment financings. Brussels capability is integral to the practice and well-respected, but the team lacks a high-profile individual in London. **Clients:** Modern Times Group; Telewest Communications; MCI Worldcom.

Linklaters (8 ptrs, 36 asscs) *"A successful regulatory practice"* but one that falls in the shadow of the firm's high profile corporate and financing work for the telecoms industry. The firm has a strong relationship with Vodafone, acting in a high profile flurry of telecoms mergers, including with AirTouch Communications and more recently with Mannesmann. It also acted for Vodafone in the 3G mobile telephony licence auction. Kingston Communications was advised on numerous regulatory issues, while Linklaters acted for Robert Fleming and Deutsche Bank on Kingston's well-received 1999 IPO. In addition to supply contract and outsourcing work, the firm has also undertaken a variety of telecoms privatisations, including those of Turk Telecom and Kenya Telecom. Acted for the global co-ordinators of the Telecom Eireann IPO, while continuing to advise the newly listed company on regulatory issues. A mighty presence in telecoms financing matters, the firm helped Vodafone AirTouch with a syndicated facility for its Mannesmann bid. Advised on the re-structuring of Cable & Wireless Communications, involving the sale of minority interests in CWC DataCo and CWC ConsumerCo. **Clients:** Vodafone AirTouch; Freeserve; Bell Canada.

Olswang (10 ptrs, 17 asscs) Said to be building into a force on the regulatory and commercial side, this telecoms practice is known for its good domestic work and for convergent matters. In **Colin Long***, *"the guru of private telecoms law,"* the practice has a heavyweight practitioner who is *"without doubt the most experienced telecoms lawyer in the market."* On the regulatory side, the team acted for MCI Worldcom on its 3G mobile telephony licence auction efforts, and is working with One2One and Telewest on regulatory initiatives and developments, such as internet access pricing and unbundling of the local loop. Strong on the e-commerce side, the telecoms team is known for the role it plays advising ISPs such as Demon Internet and Freeserve. Acted for Thus in its £2.2 billion LSE/Nasdaq float and was involved in the reorganisation of Virata and in advising Esat Telecom in its defence of the Telenor bid. **Clients:** UUNet; Esat Telecom; Thus.

Simmons & Simmons (9 ptrs, 11 asscs) *"Focused on getting and keeping clients and giving them what they want."* Although *"unlikely to benefit from Chris Watson's departure,"* the team has recruited four new senior members to bolster the team. Highlights of the year included advising Telespazio (a subsidiary of Telecom Italia) on its investment and involvement in one of the largest satellite deals of late, the global broadband wireless business of Astrolink. Also advised Telewest on its purchase of an intelligent network platform from Alcatel Telecom, and Global TeleSystems in its acquisition of Esprit Telecom. The London office worked with Hong Kong in representing Century Pacific CyberWorks on its $38 billion acquisition of C&W HKT. On financing matters, the team acted for First Telecom and Geneva Technology in their venture capital raisings.

One2One was represented on its bid in the 3G mobile telephony licence auction and in judicial review applications. Respected for his *"outstanding"* commerciality **Tom Wheadon*** is *"a real deal-maker."* Advising on numerous regulatory issues in convergent communications, the team acted for AIG on the establishment of a central world marketplace to trade telecoms band widths on the internet. **Clients:** FLAG Atlantic UK; LDInet; First Telecom.

Other Notable Practitioners Stephanie Liston of McDermott, Will & Emery retains an excellent reputation for regulatory telecoms expertise. Although most in the market believe that it is too early to rate the firm, it is acknowledged that this should ultimately be a foregone conclusion. **Ted Mercer**'s* efforts to build up Taylor Joynson Garrett's practice have garnered praise.

Communications: Information Technology

UNITED KINGDOM Leading firms (Communications: IT)
1 Baker & McKenzie
Bird & Bird
Clifford Chance
2 Lovells
Olswang
3 Allen & Overy
Masons
Osborne Clarke OWA
Taylor Joynson Garrett
4 Denton Wilde Sapte
Field Fisher Waterhouse
Kemp & Co
5 Freshfields Bruckhaus Deringer
Herbert Smith
Linklaters
Rowe & Maw
Slaughter and May
Tarlo Lyons

Firms are listed alphabetically in each band.

Leading individuals (Communications: IT)
1 **KEMP Richard** *Kemp & Co*
MILLARD Christopher *Clifford Chance*
SANDISON Hamish *Bird & Bird*
2 **McCALLOUGH Robert** *Masons*
REES Christopher *Herbert Smith*
RENDELL Simon *Osborne Clarke OWA*
SMALL Harry *Baker & McKenzie*
3 **ARCHER Quentin** *Lovells*
BICKERSTAFF Roger *Bird & Bird*
CHISSICK Michael *Field Fisher Waterhouse*
GARDNER Nick *Herbert Smith*
GRAHAM Rory *Osborne Clarke OWA*
GRIFFITHS David *Clifford Chance*
JACOBS Lawrence *Allen & Overy*
MAHONY Michael *Hammond Suddards Edge*
MAUGHAN Alistair *Shaw Pittman*
NICHOLSON Kim *Olswang*
PEARSON Hilary *Bird & Bird*
ROWE Heather *Lovells*
SINGLETON Susan *Singletons*
SMITH Graham *Bird & Bird*
SWYCHER Nigel *Slaughter and May*
WARD Conor *Lovells*
WEBSTER Michael *Nicholson Graham & Jones*

Individuals are listed alphabetically in each band.

Baker & McKenzie (5 ptrs, 15 asscs) *"Well-known, established practice"* that is one of London's finest and is seen to benefit from a *"good European geographic spread"* (especially in Germany.) Also said to treat IT as *"less of a corporate service arm than many other large firms."* Active across the entire span of IT work, the practice's centres of excellence are in outsourcing agreements, IT litigation, digital media and IT/telecommunications convergence matters. **Harry Small*** is best known for his litigating skills and is a frequent speaker at conferences and seminars. Large soft/hardware suppliers, many of them American, form a substantial part of the practice's extensive client portfolio. Advised Compaq over the provision of software systems, over the Internet, to Cable & Wireless' new Triangle venture. **Clients:** Sony (all corporate); 3com; Apple; Cisco Systems; Oracle; Compaq; Orange; Symbian; Nortel Networks; Viasoft.

Bird & Bird (7 ptrs, 33 asscs) *"Focused"* team with a massive reputation in the field and *"strong US connections."* Despite its superlative name however, quality is sometimes seen to be *"patchy,"* in part due to the perception that recent junior recruits do not match the ability of the firm's leading lights. The stand-out name here is *"public sector guru"* **Hamish Sandison***, who *"went in with all guns blazing and turned the practice around."* Other recommended practitioners include **Roger Bickerstaff***, whose forte is in public sector procurement, litigator **Hilary Pearson*** *("dry but nice,")* and the *"bloody good"* **Graham Smith***. The team acted for HM Prison Service on a project installing a new IT infrastructure (including voice telephony) in all prisons in England and Wales, and for the Foreign & Commonwealth Office on a worldwide new voice and data network (including internet service provision) to all of the FCO's embassies. It also completed a contract to outsource The Woolwich's *"open plan"* service, the first WAP-enabled home banking service. **Clients:** SEMA Group; CCTA; BA/POCL; Inland Revenue; Census Office.

Clifford Chance (8 ptrs, 38 asscs)With *"great all-round expertise"* across the 'convergence' spectrum (IT, e-commerce, telecoms, media and corporate), the City leviathan certainly has *"the power to make it"* in the field, where it has long been a distinguished combatant. While some see the IT practice as intimately linked to the firm's corporate activities (though less so than at other 'magic circle' firms), *"you can never, never discount them – they have a lot of top clients."* The mainstay of the practice remains **Christopher Millard***, *"an absolute leader and one of the best IT lawyers in London."* Another key player is **David Griffiths***, while Vanessa Marsland, a highly respected IT litigator, moves to our IP section, where the bulk of her practice now rests. **Clients:** Large financial institutions and banks; equipment suppliers; internet start-ups.

Lovells (6 ptrs, 12 asscs)Although possessing a comparatively low-key profile, (the team is considered *"safe if not that dynamic"*) the firm's quality is beyond dispute. *"They're a real blue-chip organisation with quality people."* A broad-based department specialises on advising clients in the insurance and financial services industries on IT-related matters. The team is headed by **Quentin Archer***, who has extensive industry experience from his time in-house at Acorn. Other key players include **Heather Rowe*** *("Ms Data protection")* and **Conor Ward*** *("knowledgeable, personable and always impressive")*. The group recently advised on the IT aspects of three significant acquisitions in the insurance sector: Britannia Life by Britannic, Scottish Equitable by Aegon and National Provident Institution by AMP. **Clients:** Nintendo; Barclays; Pearson Group; Prudential Corp; Union America; Aegon; Scottish Equitable.

Olswang (5 ptrs, 11 asscs) *"Extremely go-ahead, trendy"* firm with an impressive breadth of experience in 'convergence' practice areas. Commonly perceived to be the *"media darling,"* the firm has successfully expanded beyond those roots into 'pure' IT, internet/e-commerce, digital mixed media and telecoms work. Active across the IT spectrum, the firm's clients include both suppliers and users from home and abroad. Work conducted ranges from procurement contracts and software distribution agreements to outsourcing and IT litigation. **Kim Nicholson***, who hails from a telecoms background, is seen to be *"raising her profile"* in the IT field. Currently advising Warner Music International in respect of the outsourcing of its billing systems throughout Europe to Cap Gemini. The team advised Tao Group in respect of a Sony Investment in that group and the licensing of Tao Technology to Sony. **Clients:** Thus (formerly Scottish Telecom); Motorola; RSPCA; BBC Worldwide; Bloomberg LP; Warner Music (International and UK); MCI WorldCom; Viacom.

Allen & Overy (3 ptrs, 15 asscs) *"Quality outfit"* with a *"down to earth"* and professional approach

*See leaders' profiles on pages 741-782

who *"don't haggle too much – they want to get the deal done."* Renowned for its *"innovative approach,"* the firm is *"becoming a serious player"* in the IT field, especially on corporate-related matters, and rises in the rankings this year. **Lawrence Jacobs*** *"picks up on points straight away"* and is considered *"quite a guru."* Outsourcings are a major source of revenue for the practice, which was involved in over 15 transactions with an individual value of over £100 million each. This includes advising EDS on a wide range of technology projects, acting for Unisys, Lloyds TSB and Barclays on a major outsourcing joint venture and for Accenture on a major outsourcing project with Sainsburys. **Clients:** NatWest; Chase Manhattan; Unisys; Nestle; Mobil; EDS; Fage Business Pages; Lloyds TSB; Barclays; Accenture.

Masons (7 ptrs, 15 asscs) Renowned for IT litigation, the firm is held to lack similar punch on the non-contentious front. Non-contentious activities include IT system procurements, data protection, computer games, outsourcings, software supply/services contracts, distribution and licensing. Group head **Rob McCallough*** is a *"great communicator at all levels."* Advising Standard Chartered Bank on an agreement to relocate all IT systems in one location, and ICL Group and ICL Pathway in relation to the £1 billion Pathway/Horizon project with Post Office Counters Ltd. **Clients:** ICL Group; ICI; Bank of Ireland; Standard Chartered Bank; CGU; The Law Society; Kingston Technology.

Osborne Clarke OWA (7 ptrs, 22 asscs) Respected team that is *"edging ever upwards"* in this area. With offices in Reading and Bristol, in addition to London, the firm is held to be in a *"geographically ideal"* situation and reputedly enjoys *"great non-City work."* Acts for a broad range of clients from major suppliers to company users, with fortes in the e-commerce and computer games arenas. **Simon Rendell*** *("on the ball and on top of developments")* is the best known name at the firm, though **Rory Graham*** *("tough to be up against")* is also a respected practitioner. The firm advised accounting giant KPMG on its accounting and payroll management contracts with several clients and on its back-to-back agreement with Compaq for data centre services. **Clients:** Communications & Control Electronic; Prudential Corp; Infobank; Carlton Screen Advertising; KPMG.

Taylor Joynson Garrett (15 ptrs, 17 asscs) *"Cracking"* team with *"good people and a great client-base."* Although lacking a 'star' practitioner, the team is said to *"exceed the sum of its parts."* The department is particularly strong on outsourcing, IT supply/procurement, computer games and US in-bound investments. Clients range from IT suppliers and overseas software suppliers to computer games companies. Advising Britannia Airways on the outsourcing of procurement, support and maintenance of desk-top computing operations. In contentious matters, the firm is acting for Sony Computer Entertainment on its anti-piracy programme, a process tackling the re-chipping of PlayStations to allow the playing of counterfeit discs. **Clients:** Alliance & Leicester; Eidos; Genesys; Britannia Airways; Hiscox; Rank Group; Citrix Systems; NCR; Sony Computer Entertainment Europe.

Denton Wilde Sapte (10 ptrs, 22 asscs) The firm has been less visible than in previous years, although it acts across the IT spectrum, including contentious, retail and public sector work and projects. The past year has also seen an increase in the number of IT suppliers for which the firm acts. The team acted for a leading IT supplier on a range of projects, including strategic acquisitions for wireless data operating systems, and has advised on numerous IT disputes, including database infringement cases. **Clients:** IT suppliers; retail groups; public sector organisations.

Field Fisher Waterhouse (6 ptrs, 14 asscs) The firm is seen as one of the *"success stories"* of recent years in the field, and has specific expertise in IT procurement and outsourcing agreements. **Michael Chissick***, a frequent speaker on the conference circuit, is *"developing a great following"* and continues to be perceived as the firm's leading name. Currently advising Thomas Cook Longhaul on a systems integration system for holiday reservations. **Clients:** London Transport; London Underground; Sun Microsystems; Granada Media; Pizza Hut.

Kemp & Co (3 ptrs, 2 asscs) Niche firm that concentrates on IT, internet/e-commerce and telecoms. *"Clearly a player,"* the practice is said to offer *"competitive services and prices."* Ex-Garretts man and *"visionary,"* **Richard Kemp*** is *"truly innovative"* and is seen to have *"done a really good job"* with an *"extremely loyal"* client base. Clients include major IT buyers, software developers, service suppliers/software houses and equipment suppliers. Work highlights include advising Deloitte Consulting on a large scale public sector development contract and on-going advice to the AFR Consortium (of 34 UK Police Authorities) on various projects. These include the AFIS (automatic fingerprint identification system) services contract with SAGRM SA. **Clients:** Microsoft Europe; AFR Consortium; Deloitte Consulting.

Freshfields Bruckhaus Deringer (5 ptrs, 23 asscs) Although best-known for its role in providing support to the firm's vast existing corporate client base, the department has also advised on outsourcing work and restructuring for a high-profile IT clientele. The team advised on the IT and data protection aspects of the demerger of Hewlett-Packard, and acted for Deutsche Bank on outsourcing its payroll systems to KPMG. **Clients:** GEC; Logica; Quadriga.

Herbert Smith (4 ptrs, 15 asscs) With what is *"probably the largest IT litigation group in the country,"* the firm is also making a *"big splash"* in e-commerce and internet start-ups. Large IT PFI/PPP projects are another forte. **Nick Gardner*** is considered a *"highly effective litigator,"* while recent addition **Christopher Rees***, formerly at Bird & Bird, is described as a *"super all-rounder."* The team is currently advising the Civil Aviation Authority on the implementation of major new air traffic control facilities, reportedly one of the largest IT projects in the UK. **Clients:** IBM; Capita Group; Amstrad; BSkyB; Network Solutions; Vodafone; Jardine Matheson; Cable & Wireless.

Linklaters (3 ptrs, 15 asscs) *"Corporate driven"* with *"loads of quality clients,"* the firm *"does not appear terribly serious about stand-alone IT,"* and lacks an outstanding individual player. However, *"one always has to take them into account,"* and the team acts on outsourcing, dispute resolution, and IT-related railway/transport systems work. Advised Microsoft UK on all its Y2K problems. **Clients:** ICL; Microsoft; BP Amoco; BBC; BA; Dixons; Freeserve; Ernst & Young.

Rowe & Maw (6 ptrs, 16 asscs) Respected unit with an especially good name for big-ticket outsourcing projects. However, the high-profile departure of Michael Webster to Nicholson, Graham & Jones is considered to be a setback to the team's profile. The team has an established reputation for advice on outsourcing, internet start-ups and data protection. Advised on the restructuring of Cable & Wireless Communications' IT outsource arrangements with IBM and acted for Zeneca Agrochemicals on the strategic outsourcing of elements of their systems to Cap Gemini, Compaq and BT. **Clients:** Cable & Wireless; M&G; Vignette.

Slaughter and May (2 ptrs, 13 asscs) *"The blue-chip solicitors"* are *"moving in"* on the IT sector. While some argue that they *"only care about the big ticket M&A work,"* most acknowledge that these *"quality generalists"* can *"turn their hand to anything." "Extremely bright, outgoing and forth-*

right," **Nigel Swycher*** is a *"class act"* credited with *"putting Slaughters on the IT map."* The team is acting for the DETR on the proposed PPP of National Air Traffic Services and advising the New Scottish Centre on systems procurement. **Clients:** Symbian; Psion; Cambridge Positioning Systems; HSS; Abbey National; Enron; Colgate Palmolive; Inchcape; Reuters; JP Morgan.

Tarlo Lyons (7 ptrs, 10 asscs) *"Have made a big effort in the IT sector."* Some have characterised this ambitious group as excessively *"pushy,"* but many others comment on the team's depth, one source even describing it as a *"smaller Bird & Bird."* Active across the 'convergence' areas, the practice's forte lies in high-level software patent disputes. Other work covered includes outsourcing and procurement issues. **Clients:** Internet suppliers; financial institutions.

Other Notable Practitioners: Singleton's *"phenomenal"* **Susan Singleton*** is *"eminently sensible and knows her stuff."* She has advised on two large outsourcing agreements, in addition to writing several highly respected publications. **Alistair Maughan*** of Shaw Pittman is held to be *"an impressive guy who knows his stuff."* **Michael Webster***, of Nicholson Graham & Jones, is considered to be a *"smooth, commercial lawyer"* and is *"seen a lot"* in IT legal circles. The respected **Michael Mahony*** is Hammond Suddard Edge's leading light and a regular on the conference circuit.

U

Communications: E-commerce

Bird & Bird *"Tremendous commercial lawyers who get the deal done,"* though some felt the quality of their work was, on occasion, of a *"variable"* standard. One of the first firms to venture in to the internet/e-commerce arenas, they are currently active in the fields of digital distribution and media, internet joint ventures and dot.com start-ups. The team is especially noted for its advice to venture capitalists. *"Original thinker"* **Graham Smith*** is one of the pre-eminent e-commerce practitioners, although the loss of the Mark Haftke to KLegal will deal the group's client base an obvious blow. Offering a well established corporate finance service, and seen as *"hard negotiators, expanding dramatically,"* the firm is broadening its client base to include acting for internet investors such as GE Capital and Global Retail Partners on equity financing. Advised Orchestream on four rounds of VC funding leading to its £200 million IPO. **Clients:** Amazon.co.uk; Demon Internet/Thus; Carlton Online; Emap; Loot.com; The Electronic Telegraph; Lastminute.com.

UNITED KINGDOM Leading firms (Communications: E-commerce)	
1	Bird & Bird
	Olswang
2	Clifford Chance
3	Baker & McKenzie
	Denton Wilde Sapte
	Field Fisher Waterhouse
4	H2O (Henry Hepworth Organisation)
	Harbottle & Lewis
	Herbert Smith
	Kemp & Co
	Paisner & Co
	Taylor Joynson Garrett

Firms are listed alphabetically in each band.

Olswang *"Head and shoulders above the rest,"* in the view of several interviewees, the firm certainly has what one of London's premier internet e-commerce practices. A genuine full internet service 'convergence' practice with a focus on internet content (a real forte), digital TV and WAP related issues. Key hitters in the team include **John Enser*** *("he really stands out from the crowd")* and the well known **Kim Nicholson***, who hails from a corporate background. **Matthew Cowan*** was also recommended. The firm has recently recruited two private equity specialists from Berwin Leighton to bolster its capacity to assist funding start-up and pre-flotation clients. Advising Freeserve on the launch of its women's portal, iCircle, and on content deals including People Bank and Lastminute.com. Also acting for Demon Internet in a leading defamation case concerning on-line libel. In what is seen as an innovative service to attract internet based start-ups, the firm has launched Long Acre Partners, a corporate finance house, in conjunction with JP Morgan. The corporate team has a well established reputation for AIM listings and advised Gameplay.com and VitualInternet on their floats. Also acts for internet incubator funds such as Bain Lab and AntFactory.

Represented RAMAR Technology in its acquisition by Advanced Technology for £13 million and represented Granada Media Group in its establishment of a new dot.com company owned by Liverpool FC and GMG, a deal worth £40 million. **Clients:** peoplesound.com; sportal.net; Freeserve; Demon Internet; BBC Worldwide; BSkyB; Granada Media; Dixons; worldpop.com; First Tuesday.

Leading individuals (Communications: E-commerce)		
1	ENSER John *Olswang*	HAFTKE Mark *KLegal*
	McNEIVE Liam *McNeive Solicitors*	MILLARD Christopher *Clifford Chance*
	SMITH Graham *Bird & Bird*	
2	CHISSICK Michael *Field Fisher Waterhouse*	KEMP Richard *Kemp & Co*
	SMALL Harry *Baker & McKenzie*	SUMMERFIELD Spencer *Travers Smith Braithwaite*
3	CALOW Duncan *Denton Wilde Sapte*	COWAN Matthew *Olswang*
	EDWARDS Gareth *Pinsent Curtis*	HENRY Michael *Buchanan Ingersoll*
	KAYE Laurence *Garretts*	NICHOLSON Kim *Olswang*
	PHILLIPS Mark *Harbottle & Lewis*	ROSEFIELD Stephen *Paisner & Co*
	TURNER Mark *Herbert Smith*	WILLIAMS Alan *Denton Wilde Sapte*

Individuals are listed alphabetically in each band.

Clifford Chance None of the 'Magic Circle' City firms, are felt to have established themselves in the internet/e-commerce sphere as successfully as Clifford Chance. *"Thoroughly intelligent,"* **Chris Millard*** *("amongst the best")* is not only *"one of the UK's leading data protection lawyers,"* he is also known as an academic in the sphere. Particularly noted for its work on IPOs, and often chosen for its global capacity, the team advised Orchestream on the bulk of its £214 million flotation on the London Stock Exchange. **Clients:** Orchestream; dot.com start-ups.

*See leaders' profiles on pages 741-782

Baker & McKenzie "*Its international contacts are key to the firm's success,*" and the team also benefits from the firm's strengths in the 'hard' IT and telecommunications sectors. Seen to have upped their profile over the past year, online data protection and IP/IT related matters are this full-service team's key specialities in the internet/e-commerce field. "*Intelligent and personable,*" **Harry Small*** is still "*the best at Baker Mac*" though generally perceived to be more of a 'pure' IT man. Advising Hewlett Packard on the supply of servers to Stelios Hadji-Ioannou's online venture EasyEverything Stores. **Clients:** Hewlett-Packard; Oracle; Orange; Sony; Cisco Systems; Compaq.

U

Denton Wilde Sapte While rated by some as "*incredibly impressive on e-commerce,*" especially for internet start-ups, others felt that the firm's profile simply wasn't what it used to be. "*Bright bloke*" **Duncan Calow*** is tipped as "*definitely one to watch,*" while **Alan Williams*** continues to be recognised for his niche forte in publishing related e-issues. Building on the Wilde Sapte banking reputation and Denton Hall's entertainment business, the firm has "*ridden the dot.com wave*" with an increase in IPOs, acting for institutional investors. **Clients:** Tadpole Technology, Apax Partners.

Field Fisher Waterhouse Seen to have "*made a splash*" in the internet/e-commerce arena, thanks partly to the superlative marketing skills of **Michael Chissick***, a "*very good ambassador for his firm in the e-commerce space.*" Venture capital funding, website development and online data protection matters are the department's primary areas of activity. Has successfully capitalised on its traditional profile in this market (which includes taking equity stakes in clients), "*aggressive growth*" includes advising Level 3 Communications. **Clients:** Boo.com, Thomas Cook, BAT, Doubleclick.com.

H2O (Henry Hepworth Organisation) Perhaps best known for its strength in the content and copyright ('soft IP') arenas, the firm was one of the very first to venture into the e-commerce space. One of the original pioneers of this move, Michael Henry, has now left to join the London office of US firm Buchanan Ingersoll; something of a blow. The practice advised Hay & Robertson on a number of e-commerce deals, including online merchandising agreements for Manchester United and the English Cricket Board. **Clients:** UFI (University for Industry); Arena Leisure; Hay & Robertson.

Harbottle & Lewis "*Astute*" firm, best known for its superb computer games practice. Has expanded its client base beyond its traditional media and charities focus to embrace clients from all walks of the internet/online industry, from major ISPs and key web and content providers, to incubator funds, network clubs and 'e-channels.' Particularly active in the fields of interactive television, domain names and WAP related matters. Also currently acting for around 100 internet start-ups (dot.coms and dot.co.uks.) **Mark Phillips*** is the best known name in the team. The firm has advised Chrysalis on its JV with rivals.com to form the world's largest network of sports speciality web sites, and advised Dawney, Day & Lander, the UK's first privately financed internet incubator fund, on its alliance with FBR a US technology focused investment bank (total funds £30 million.) **Clients:** Chrysalis; Virgin.com; Amazon Online; Virgin.net.

Herbert Smith A respectable internet/e-commerce practice, though some felt the firm's "*confrontational approach*" might not go down too well in 'e-arena.' Offer an across the board service to clients in the sector, with internet financings considered a real forte. Also currently active on behalf of US dot.coms setting up in the UK. **Mark Turner*** is the team's best known name. Acting for Time Warner on the UK/European aspects of its merger with AOL and advising WH Smith on an agreement with Microsoft to develop a fully fledged free access internet portal containing a range of educational and entertainment material. Established a strong reputation in the IPO field by acting for the global co-ordinators for the £3.3 billion listing of Freeserve (Credit Suisse First Boston and Cazenove & Co) and the £263 million placing of QXL.com (Credit Suisse First Boston.) **Clients:** Time Warner; CSFB; BSkyB; WH Smith; Network Solutions.

Kemp & Co Definitely on an upward curve, this specialist convergence 'boutique' has increased its standing in the e-arena over the past year. Concentrating solely on IT, telecoms and internet matters, the firm is led by "*driven*" name partner **Richard Kemp*** ("*very bright*") who will do "*absolutely anything for his clients.*" Continue to advise Microsoft on a range of issues relating to its MSN portal and have been instructed by US based internet infomediary AllAdvantage (known for their 'viral marketing') on the launch of their UK and European operations. More recently, the practice has advised Artism on the contractual and regulatory aspects of their new online talent service, Dolphin Telecom on their IT procurement arrangements, DG Bank on a range of e-banking contractual issues and Viatel on the roll out of their dedicated and dial up internet access contracts for ISPs and SMEs. **Clients:** Microsoft; Expedia; AllAdvantage; FTSE International; Primark; Cognotec.

Paisner & Co "*Noteworthy*" practitioners in the field, who entered the e-arena with a background in electronic publishing. On-line financial services, data protection advice and delivery of entertainment and information are considered the team's fortes. So too is lobbying, the firm having industry involvement with the new e-commerce related EU Directives. In September 2000 the firm lost Laurence Kaye to Garretts. "*Excellent*" corporate partner **Stephen Rosefield*** is seen to provide an impetus to the firm's entrepreneurial client base which sits well with its strong private equity practice. The firm acted for Apax Partners on its investment in QXL.com. The practice is currently providing contractual, regulatory and other advice to the FT on the establishment of its new personal finance site – FTYourmoney.com – and the launch of the revised FT.com site. Also acting for Beenz.com in various strategic alliances, including those with Excite UK and leading Italian portal Kataweb. **Clients:** Point Four Consulting; FTYourmoney.com; FT.com; Espresso Productions; Virtual Jukebox.com; UpMyStreet.com; Fish4; This is Britain.

Taylor Joynson Garrett "*Pulling ahead with a strong private equity offering*" and some "*serious US clients*" in the internet/e-commerce sphere, the firm enters our tables this year as "*something of a rising star.*" Its client portfolio is not held to be as impressive, however, when it comes to European clients. Advised Digital Ventures II and ePartners on their investments in London based e-commerce start-up Eyestorm.com, and 365 Corporation on its $1.65 million agreement and merger plan to acquire US based sports content company e-Merchants.

Advised Ask Jeeves in a $125 million joint venture with Carlton Communications and Granada Media Group.

Other Notable Practitioners. **Mark Haftke** ("*knows all the relevant people*") has joined KLegal from Bird & Bird. Regarded as one of the leading players in the sector, he takes with him a slew of impressive clients, including Amazon.com. Well-known "*veteran*" **Laurence Kaye*** ("*good on newspaper-related internet issues*") has moved from Paisner & Co to Garretts. The "*superb*" **Liam McNeive***, of McNeive Solicitors, "*certainly knows his onions*" and is a well-known name in his field. Seen by some to "*semi-house*" for long-standing client AOL, he advised QXL on all the legal strategic aspects of its European expansion. In a corporate finance capacity, **Spencer Summerfield*** of Travers Smith Braithwaite is said to *"know his stuff."* He acted for NTL on its acquisition of the cable business of Cable & Wireless Communications (value £9.8 billion.) **Gareth Edwards*** of Pinsent Curtis is said to be *"trustworthy and supportive"* and has a growing reputation acting for the corporate needs of start-ups and established players alike. He acted for Just2Clicks on its £130 million AIM floatation and for Blakes Clothing on its transference to AIM to form e-xentric. In a coup for the London office of US firm Buchanan Ingersoll, **Michael Henry***, formerly of H2O, has now joined the team. He is best known as one of the original legal e-commerce pioneers, and remains a prolific name in the sector.

Competition/Anti-trust

UNITED KINGDOM Leading firms (Competition/Anti-trust)
1 Freshfields Bruckhaus Deringer
Herbert Smith
Linklaters
Slaughter and May
2 Lovells
3 Allen & Overy
Ashurst Morris Crisp
Clifford Chance LLP
Denton Wilde Sapte
SJ Berwin & Co
4 Norton Rose
Simmons & Simmons

Firms are listed alphabetically in each band

Freshfields Bruckhaus Deringer (6 ptrs, 65 asscs) Clearly an anti-trust powerhouse with *"corporate professionalism an overriding feature of the firm." "Imaginative and tough,"* **Nick Spearing*** and **Deirdre Trapp*** are *"major players"* who *"cut to the quick."* Spearing is *"good on the deal side,"* working on a broad range of competition matters, whilst Trapp *("proactive, responsive, first rate")* is perceived to be more oriented to behavioural work. The firm's Brussels-based partners all still command immense market respect. Economists find the London team *"particularly easy to deal with; they get you involved early and don't tell you your job."* While some perceive the work to be *"skewed towards M&A,"* the team is nevertheless considered to have many other strengths.

Merger expertise has been highlighted by such work as the AstraZeneca/Novartis, RBS/NatWest and Telewest/Flextech link-ups. Non-merger work includes Competition Commission inquiries into grocery retailing and milk, and work in the financial services, brewing, media, telecoms and railway sectors. Litigation is another expanding area. Truly pan-European, particularly in the wake of the stunning merger with German powerhouse Bruckhaus Westrick Heller Löber, the practice is officially known as the European Competition and Trade Group, with clients and economists confirming the cross-office capability and mode of functioning. The practice has also worked on most major European cartel cases in sectors such as banking, cement, gas, graphite electrodes, media, newsprint, steel beams and pipes. Other international work includes the Formula One EU Investigation, PepsiCo's complaints to EU and national authorities on alleged abuse of dominance by Coca-Cola, and advising the Mexican government in their negotiation of an FTA with the EU. **Clients:** Telewest; Tesco; Milk Marque; GEC/BAe; Kingfisher; Scottish Telecom; RBS; BNFL; Sotheby's; PepsiCo; Mars.

Herbert Smith (7 ptrs, 15 asscs) After knocking on the door for two years, this *"extremely strong"* practice moves into the top tier this year. A broad and balanced team, the partners all do a range of work. Working on media and telecoms matters of late, **Dorothy Livingston*** *"has been enormously impressive in steering through BSkyB."* She *"reduces things to a sensible level"* and *"intellectually has most people licked."* On the utilities side, **Elizabeth McKnight*** is regarded as *"fantastic to work with"* by economists, who appreciate her persuasiveness with regulatory bodies. Clients find her *"hugely impressive"* as she is *"switched on and gets to grips quickly with issues."* The *"pretty bullish"* **Jonathan Scott*** *"sticks his neck out for you and he gets it right."* A competition all-rounder, he is known for his litigation skills, and is regarded as *"user-friendly, personable, practical and effective."* He advised General Mills on EC competition aspects of its acquisition of the Pillsbury Company from Diageo.

Now involved in the firm's management, **Richard Fleck*** also adds weight to the team, and remains the relationship partner for clients such as Time Warner and Stagecoach. The firm additionally has partners respected for newspaper regulation and transport work. The year has also seen the hiring of Lord Brittan, the ex-EC trade commissioner, as a consultant.

A wide range of competition and regulatory work is dealt with, including mergers and takeover battles such as those of First Choice with Kuoni and Airtours and NatWest with Bank of Scotland and RBS. In the newspaper industry, the firm advised Trinity on the competition aspects of its proposed acquisition of the Mirror Group. In utilities, the firm advised water and electricity companies on their price control reviews and gas shippers on issues arising from new gas trading arrangements. Other work includes defending BSkyB's exclusive contract to televise live Premier League football, advising the FIA on the Formula One investigation and advising the Indian and Armenian governments on trade issues. Advised Chevron on the competition aspects of its planned $100 billion merger with Texaco, and Time Warner on the European issues of its $183 billion merger with AOL. **Clients:** London Electricity; Viridian Group; North West Water; First Choice; Pilkington; BSkyB; Federation Internationale de L'Automobile; BAT; Stagecoach; Chiquita.

Linklaters (6 ptrs, 17 asscs) Whilst many in the market observed that David Hall's retirement, added to Chris Bright's departure last year, left *"two pretty big holes,"* clients still commented on the *"strength in depth"* of the team. Partners and young associates alike are *"all impressive,"* and while *"there are few superstars, that is part of their attraction."* Linklaters & Alliance operates an integrated European practice group, and the market also noted the strength of some of the firm's Brussels players. *"Quiet and full of common sense,"* the *"superlative"* **Bill Allan*** *"doesn't make a drama out of a crisis."* Among the younger partners, **Gavin Robert*** is *"tremendous,"* and clients like *"bright"* **Michael Cutting***.

Well known for its merger work, the practice advised on the link-ups of BAT/Rothmans, Vodafone/Airtouch, Vodafone/Mannesmann, Lafarge/Blue Circle, Scottish & Newcastle/Kronenburg, BP Amoco/Castrol, BAe/GEC Marconi, NatWest/RBS and other multi-jurisdictional mergers. With its Alliance partners, the firm has acted on more than 10% of EU merger notifications in the past year. Other work includes regu-

U

UNITED KINGDOM Leading individuals (Competition/Anti-trust)		
★	**AITMAN David** *Denton Wilde Sapte*	**BRIGHT Christopher** *Clifford Chance*
	KON Stephen *SJ Berwin & Co*	**NICHOLSON Malcolm** *Slaughter and May*
	WHISH Richard *Sole Practitioner*	
1	**ALLAN Bill** *Linklaters*	**CARSTENSEN Laura** *Slaughter and May*
	LIVINGSTON Dorothy *Herbert Smith*	**McKNIGHT Elizabeth** *Herbert Smith*
	POLITO Simon *Lovells*	**SPEARING Nicholas** *Freshfields Bruckhaus*
	TRAPP Deirdre *Freshfields Bruckhaus Deringer*	
2	**FREEMAN Peter** *Simmons & Simmons*	**FRIEND Mark** *Allen & Overy*
	PARR Nigel *Ashurst Morris Crisp*	**PHEASANT John** *Lovells*
	SCOTT Jonathan *Herbert Smith*	
3	**CHAPPATTE Philippe** *Slaughter and May*	**FINBOW Roger** *Ashurst Morris Crisp*
	LEIGH Guy *Theodore Goddard*	**MARTIN ALEGI Lynda** *Baker & McKenzie*
	SMITH Martin *Simmons & Simmons*	
4	**AINSWORTH Lesley** *Lovells*	**COHEN Ralph** *SJ Berwin & Co*
	COOK John *Norton Rose*	**FLECK Richard** *Herbert Smith*
	OSBORNE John *Clifford Chance*	**ROBERT Gavin** *Linklaters*
	ROWE Michael *Slaughter and May*	**WHEATON James** *Clifford Chance*
	WOTTON John *Allen & Overy*	
Up-and-coming individuals		
	CUTTING Michael *Linklaters*	**FARQUHARSON Melanie** *Simmons & Simmons*
	HOLMES Simon *SJ Berwin & Co*	**LOUVEAUX Bertrand** *Slaughter and May*
	WEITZMAN Polly *Denton Wilde Sapte*	

Individuals are listed alphabetically in each band.

latory (particularly utilities) and advisory work. The team advised British Airways in connection with travel agents' commissions and the launch of Go, and has also been involved in the milk and car Competition Commission investigations. Cartel work and trade law work are also an important feature of the practice, with a recent arrival boosting the WTO practice. **Clients:** Vodafone; British Airways; Allied Domecq; BG; Centrica.

Slaughter and May (5 ptrs, 23 asscs) This year, the firm provoked a wide range of sharply differing opinion. The practice is *"not everyone's cup of tea."* Some mentioned their *"confrontational"* approach. However, all agree that the practice is *"extremely good at representing a client",* that it *"instils trust"* and is *"tough and often right." "The lawyer to go to in London if there's a problem,"* **Malcolm Nicholson*** *"goes down very well with clients"* for his *"imaginative, aggressive and tough"* approach. Equally appreciated is all-rounder **Laura Carstensen***, who *"gets it right from the company's perspective," "understands the authorities"* and whose *"intelligence and eye for detail"* make her drafts *"so good."* **Philippe Chappatte*** *("doesn't give an inch")* is best known for his telecoms and media work. Of the younger generation, **Michael Rowe*** continues to win plaudits and the *"excellent"* **Bertrand Louveaux*** enters the ratings this year. The latter *"is down to earth and relates well to the client."*

Like all firms with top M&A practices, the competition team is sometimes seen to be a merger shop. However, the practice is also considered to be *"top on behavioural work,"* advising on Article 81 and 82 cases and restructurings in the broadcasting, electricity and building products industries. Merger work this year encompassed the uncompleted Telia/Telenor merger (the first attempted merger of two incumbent telcos) and on the attempted Airtours/FirstChoice merger. Rothmans/BAT, Kingfisher/Asda, British Steel/Hoogovens and Reckitt & Colman/Benckiser were also headline transactions in which the firm featured strongly. The group also offered advice at inquiries into the ice cream, supermarkets, public medical insurance and hospital services industries. **Clients:** Telenor; Airtours; Unilever; ASDA; BUPA; NATS; First Hydro; Home Office.

Lovells (10 ptrs, 23 asscs) With **John Pheasant*** *("a class act")* now the firm's international partner, he splits his time between management issues and competition issues, where he has been involved on shipping and cartel matters. **Simon Polito*** is now considered the *"main name"* and a *"top operator"* who is *"suited to slightly political and difficult cases."* Whilst some in the market commented that Polito *"has to do a lot on his own,"* clients also observed that he *"works well as part of a team."* His colleague **Lesley Ainsworth*** is *"sensible, practical and down to earth."* London operates as one group with the Brussels office, where the practice remains a key player. Lauded for its *"highly commercial"* character, the team maintains a leading reputation for its non-merger control competition expertise. Trade law and a *"pre-eminent marine competition practice"* are of particular note. However, the practice is perceived to be less involved than its foremost competitors on the higher profile merger and utilities work.

Advised on the attempted Telia/Telenor merger, and on a joint venture between Alsthom and ABB. Other work includes advising on the clearance for the pooling and rating agreements of the International Group of P&I Clubs, who insure the third party risks of 90% of the world's ocean-going tonnage. Inquiry work includes advising Mars in the ice cream 'wars,' and working on appeals subsequent to the 'steel tubes' and 'steel beams' investigations. **Clients:** Aegon; Albright and Wilson; AMP; British Energy; Granada; Johnson & Johnson; Schroders; Vickers; Port of Singapore.

Allen & Overy (4 ptrs, 21 asscs) A *"solid"* team, whose stand-out practitioner in London is **Mark Friend***. He is particularly rated for his work on matters which straddle the line between competition and regulation. **John Wotton*** *(" thoroughly likeable")* is respected for his experience in broadcasting and media matters. Although felt to lack nothing in quality, the team is felt to need *"more weight at the top."*

The high-tech area is one where the team is a recognised leader, drawing on a large Silicon Valley client base. Anti-cartel advice is another specific area of expertise. Acted for Cable & Wireless on the sale of One2One, on the clearance of the Global One alliance, and for the General Electric Company in connection with its acquisition of the heavy-duty gas turbine business of Alsthom. The practice advised Singapore Airlines on the competition and regulatory aspects of its proposed acquisition of a 49% interest in Virgin Atlantic and represented Thomas Cook in Phase II of the attempted Airtours/First Choice merger. Contentious cases have included acting for Coca-Cola before the Court of First Instance on the appeal against the Commission's decision on the Coke/Cadburys link-up. **Clients:** Bass; Cable & Wireless; Coca-Cola & Schweppes Beverages;

General Electric Company; Global One; Nissan; Northern Electric; Sprint; Time Warner; 20th Century Fox.

Ashurst Morris Crisp (6 ptrs, 15 asscs) A *"responsive"* team whose main name is **Nigel Parr***, someone who *"moves transactions forward"* with a *"balanced and practical"* approach. He is regarded as one of the *"top names for stand-alone competition work."* The *"sound"* **Roger Finbow*** works primarily on competition issues in broadcasting and sport. The team includes in-house economists and its legal-economic expertise is felt to be *"second to none."* As a consequence, *"you don't see the economic howlers in their documents that you do in others."*

On commercial transaction work, the team acted on the link-ups of United News and Media/Carlton Communications, Imetal/English China Clays, Lufthansa/British Midland and Express Dairies/Avonmore Waterford. Stand-alone competition work has involved working on the cars and milk inquiries and on major litigation, while WTO trade law advice is also a feature of the department. **Clients:** Allied Domecq; BT; Centrica; Cinven; Coca-Cola; IBM; Motorola; Royal & Sun Alliance; Ford Motor Company.

Clifford Chance (6 ptrs, 20 asscs) **Chris Bright*** is certainly perceived to have given the practice *"more credibility"* since he arrived from Linklaters, as well as some new clients. Clients like him for his *"exceedingly good grasp of commercial realities."* He is considered a *"great team leader,"* a heavyweight who *"knows the right people and knows how to handle them."* A competition generalist, he advises principally on anti-trust and regulation (utilities). Perceptions of the practice as a *"one man band"* have been allayed by the presence of **Jim Wheaton*** and **John Osborne***, both praised as *"easy to get on with."*

The US and German mergers have given an added dimension to the team, now capable of serving both the Washington and Brussels anti-trust hubs on contentious and non-contentious, merger and non-merger work. Represented clients on a quarter of Phase II investigations last year. The year has seen the firm heavily involved in merger work, working on the BP Amoco/ARCO, Aérospatiale/DASA, Carrefour/Promodès, Edison Mission/Powergen, Wessex Water/Enron, and Futjitsu/Siemens link-ups. Other work has seen the practice advise NTL on the Competition Commission's inquiry into its acquisition of Cable & Wireless' UK businesses. The team has additionally been acting for two clients in each of the cars and supermarkets inquiries. State aids cases have been a growth area in the past year. The firm's litigation capacity has been consolidated through the formation of a litigation division dubbed EUCLID. **Clients:** Coca-Cola; British Energy; CVC Capital Partners; General Electric Company (USA); Kimberly-Clark; Pfizer; Philip Morris; Suez-Lyonnaise; Schroder Ventures; Air Products; Edison Mission; Reuters.

Denton Wilde Sapte (5 ptrs, 9 asscs) *"Smooth operator"* **David Aitman*** *("thoughtful and skilled")* is the firm's outstanding practitioner. He has a *"particular niche in broadcasting and media"* yet is considered to be *"excellent in every respect"* – a *"bloody good anti-trust and regulatory man with a bit of flair."* He heads a *"well rounded practice"* with *"good sensible people,"* where **Polly Weitzman*** has made a name for herself, leading on a conclusive victory against the OFT in the Premier League case (successfully defending the collective selling of football rights to television). As well as advising on sports-related matters, she has also been active in gas regulatory and merger issues.

The newly-merged firm has added strength in finance and aviation, and the team acted for easyJet in its claim in the High Court against British Airways for abuse of a dominant position. Media-related work continues, with the team successfully defending the joint venture between Paramount, Universal and MGM before the EU Commission, and acting for the FA in opposing the BSkyB bid for Man Utd. The firm also advised on the clearing of EDF's acquisition of London Electricity and (indirectly) of SWEB. **Clients:** Premier League; UIP; J Sainsbury; EDF; Energis; RFU; Mastercard/Europay; Bertelsmann; Rentokil.

SJ Berwin & Co (7 ptrs, 11 asscs) *"Mighty oak"* **Stephen Kon*** continues to cast a long shadow here. Clients and lawyers comment that he is *"getting even better,"* and admire him for *"spotting and exploiting a case."* He is *"incredibly dynamic and intellectually sound"* and impresses with his ability to guide a client. However, the perception that this is a one-man band is fading as other members of the team make their mark. *"Healthy billers"* **Ralph Cohen*** and **Simon Holmes*** also received recommendations this year. The former has *"good instincts"* and *"gives sensible trade law advice."* Holmes, a *"steady"* all-rounder, is *"as bright as a button"* and *"highly commercial."*

Around half of the practice's work last year was merger-related, including opposing the Rhone Poulenc/Hoechst healthcare deal. Work this year includes advising on Diageo's disposal of Cruzcampo to Heineken, British Land's acquisition of Meadowhall, the purchase of Shell's polystyrene business and a number of private equity and venture capital transactions. Inquiry work saw the team advising on the Formula One investigation and in the supermarkets case. The team also acted for Rado/Tissot and Omega (Swatch Group) on a contested distribution agreement and is highly rated for its advice on contentious matters. **Clients:** Ladbroke Group; Universal Music Group; Qantas; Merck Generics; Coca-Cola Enterprises; Diageo; Aerolineas Argentinas; NM Rothschild & Sons.

Norton Rose (4 ptrs, 17 asscs) A substantial merger control practice with a significant contentious element. Utilities, transport, IT/IP and mergers form the backbone of the department's caseload. Perceived to have kept a lower profile this year, the team was at least able to celebrate the return of prodigal son **John Cook*** from MacFarlanes. He acted for Thomson in opposing the proposed Airtours take-over of First Choice. Telecoms has been a strong area this year, with clients such as France Telecom, Siemens and Mannesmann. Financial and insurance work saw the firm advise on the AXA/GRE link-up, and advise Switch Card and Halifax on competition matters. In energy and utilities, the team advised the AES Corporation on the acquisition of the Drax power station and on regulatory issues. The firm also advised car manufacturers during the Competition Commission's inquiry. **Clients:** Cinven; Carlsberg-Tetley; William Grant & Sons; United Airlines; TXU Europe (Eastern Electricity); Kelda (ex-Yorkshire Water); Hydrogas UK.

Simmons & Simmons (6 ptrs, 11 asscs) A strong core practice in mergers and cartel work, with a highly respected regulatory practice in utilities, transport and media. The *"able and experienced"* **Peter Freeman*** is a *"clever lawyer,"* who is *"good with the authorities."* The head of the group, he is an all-rounder, working on mergers and active on railway and broadcasting work. The *"absolutely straightforward"* **Martin Smith*** *("he knows what he's doing and is easy to collaborate with")* has recent experience in the brewing, utilities and telecoms sectors, doing substantial merger control work. **Melanie Farquharson*** is a younger name said to be *"coming through."*

Merger control work includes acting on the Bass/Punch Taverns and Vivendi/BSkyB deals. Investigation work has seen the firm active in seamless steel tubes, newsprint, vitamins, cement and airlines. The firm continues to provide regulatory advice in transport (Railtrack), telecoms, utilities and broadcasting (ITC). **Clients:** Interbrew; EFPIA (pharmaceuticals); Elkem ASA; UK MoD; Cadbury Schweppes; GKN; Aventis Pharma; Gallaher Group; BA; One2One.

*See leaders' profiles on pages 741-782

Other Notable Practitioners The *"guru we all respect,"* **Richard Whish***, is still in demand, despite his reduced level of 'coal-face' activity. He is *"a rare example of an individual who can carry a substantial practice,"* and has a reputation as *"an academic with practical experience."* Some believe that *"in terms of legal knowledge he has no equal in the country."* Clients, lawyers and economists particularly appreciate his ability to give fresh views. *"You go to him for strategy and deep thought,"* and he is felt to be *"an ideas and knowledge man rather than a proceduralist."* Theodore Goddard's leading light is the *"down to earth and coherent"* **Guy Leigh***, the Chairman of the UK Competition Law Association. Head of Baker & McKenzie's practice is the *"outstanding"* **Lynda Martin Alegi***. She is *"pragmatic and down to earth"* and is regarded as being *"so client-friendly that she gets the respect of the most obnoxious and difficult clients."* Global work includes multi-jurisdictional filings, cartel and trade work.

U

Corporate/M&A

UNITED KINGDOM Leading firms (Corporate/Mergers & Acquisitions)	
1	Freshfields Bruckhaus Deringer
	Linklaters
	Slaughter and May
2	Allen & Overy
	Clifford Chance
	Herbert Smith
3	Norton Rose
4	Ashurst Morris Crisp
	Lovells
5	Simmons & Simmons
6	CMS Cameron McKenna
	Denton Wilde Sapte

Firms are listed alphabetically in each band.

Freshfields Bruckhaus Deringer (50 ptrs, 170 asscs) European M&A opportunities are said to be behind the merger with Bruckhaus Westrick Heller Löber and this has strengthened the firm's expansionist policy, setting out its stall to be the pre-eminent European firm. This fits well with market perception of it *"leading the global domination charge."* A *"centrally-led, tight management structure"* has led to *"rigorous quality"* at partner level and a collegiate atmosphere which encourages its younger partners to gain invaluable experience on big ticket deals.

Head of Corporate Finance and Investment Banking, **Barry O'Brien*** (represented Pearson in merger of Pearson Television with CLT UFA, worth £12 billion) prospers under his reputation as *"the institutions' favourite"* with clients such as Merrill Lynch (on its agreed £3.1 billion cash bid for Mercury Asset Management) and BZW (on proposed sale of its equity and corporate advisory business to CSFB). He is a *"top-drawer operator"* who *"infuses deals with his common sense"* and receives praise for his successful rapport with clients, managing the team and running day to day transactions with enthusiasm. **Anthony Salz*** now faces increased managerial responsibilities with his role as senior partner of the merged firm and is perceived by the market to be the firm's trouble-shooter. Used as a *"check on the most complex matters, particularly when a wall is hit,"* he has *"the most astute brain in the City"* and *"sees the most important parts of the deal,"* although he is now regarded as less of a transactional force.

Will Lawes* (representing PowerGen in the acquisition of LG&E Energy Corporation, valued at $3.2 billion) is admired by the banks as *"the brightest lawyer in the City," "approachable, sharp and innovative"* and often seen on the most complex hostile work. His media work received particular praise and includes acting for Scottish Media Group on its merger with Grampian and for Pearson on the UK aspects of its acquisition of Simon & Schuster. *"Delightful"* **Mark Rawlinson*** is recommended for big ticket M&A work. He is *"the first port of call for complex hostile deals,"* and has *"excellent legal knowledge and a fantastic bedside manner."* Seen to strike a good balance between acting for corporates and financials, recent transactions include advising EMI on the merger between its music businesses and Time Warner, and advising P&O on its proposed demerger. He also continues his role as the Morgan Stanley relationship partner. Insurance specialist **Philip Richards*** *"never utters a dud word,"* and received universal praise for his work which includes advising AMP on its world wide demutualisation and listing. *"Charming"* **Charles ap Simon*** has been indisposed for part of the year but retains his reputation, particularly for his work with GEC.

Tim Emmerson* (*"incredibly bright and intelligent"*) is perceived to be an aggressive force for his clients with a substantial reputation for his IPO work, and has also acted for Bass on the sale of its brewing business (worth £2.3 billion). A familiar face due to her committee profile (as Chairman of the City of London Law Society: Company Law), **Vanessa Knapp*** is recommended as *"an intellectual lawyer."* **James Davis*** is a *"charming client man"* whose work for Cinven is *"excellent."* Respected for his private equity work, **Edward Braham*** has a wide client base which includes Kingfisher (he acted on its bid for Asda). Recognised as the rising star of the firm, **Julian Long*** is *"hard-working, sensible, calm and not adversarial,"* and is a familiar name on big-ticket deals including advising AstraZeneca on the demerger of its agricultural chemicals business, subsequently merged with Novatis. He is representing TI Group in their agreement to merge on a share for share basis with Smiths Industries, valued at £1.9 billion. *"Hardworking"* **Tom Joyce***, head of the international securities group at Freshfields Bruckhaus Deringer was acknowledged to be *"ultra aware of corporate issues."* US peers proudly regard him as a *"fantastic example to London lawyers."* Joyce acted on the US law aspects of Kingfisher's 1999 bid for the Asda group.

The team is representing Salomon Smith Barney in the drafting of a memo for the £7 billion merger between Ernst & Young and Cap Gemini, and advising Young & Rubicam in its merger with WPP, worth $4.7 billion. **Clients: Corporates:** Alcan; Avis; AstraZeneca; BNFL; BT; Bass; Caradon; Compass; EMI; Enron; Ford; Hays plc; Hewlett Packard; ICI; Kingfisher; Marconi; Pearson Group; P&O; Powergen; Prudential; Tesco. **Financials:** CSFB; Deutsche Bank; Goldman Sachs; Société Générale; Warburg Dillon Read; Morgan Stanley; Dresdner Kleinwort Benson; Schroders; Salomon Smith Barney; Lazard Brothers; Merrill Lynch; NM Rothschilds & Sons; Lehman Brothers; Allied Zurich; Warburg Pincus.

Linklaters (47 ptrs, 160 asscs) Currently facing a massive management challenge as it spreads its *"philosophy of control and seduction"* throughout the Alliance partners, yet perceived by the market to have already *"achieved amazing inroads, acting on a global scale."* The firm has a culture of commerciality with *"lawyers bred to think about the client first."* However, it is occasionally felt to have too heavily pursued a cult of the personality which overshadows its junior partners.

"Charming" **David Cheyne*** is *"an impressive presence," "thoroughly nice but very tough,"* and *"likes hostile transactions or anything he can get his*

UNITED KINGDOM
Leading individuals (Corporate/Mergers & Acquisitions)

Band		
★	**BOARDMAN Nigel** *Slaughter and May*	**CHEYNE David** *Linklaters*
1	**CANN Anthony** *Linklaters*	**GODDEN Richard** *Linklaters*
	LAWES William *Freshfields Bruckhaus Deringer*	**MACAULAY Anthony** *Herbert Smith*
	O'BRIEN Barry *Freshfields Bruckhaus Deringer*	**PAUL Alan** *Allen & Overy*
	PESCOD Michael *Slaughter and May*	**RAWLINSON Mark** *Freshfields Bruckhaus Deringer*
	SALZ Anthony *Freshfields Bruckhaus Deringer*	**UNDERHILL William** *Slaughter and May*
2	**ASHWORTH Chris** *Ashurst Morris Crisp*	**BOND Richard** *Herbert Smith*
	BROWNLOW Jeremy *Clifford Chance*	**COOKE Stephen** *Slaughter and May*
	EMMERSON Tim *Freshfields Bruckhaus Deringer*	**FRANCIES Mike** *Weil, Gotshal & Manges*
	HATTRELL Martin *Slaughter and May*	**LEWIS David** *Norton Rose*
	MIDDLEDITCH Matthew *Linklaters*	**PALMER James** *Herbert Smith*
	RICHARDS Philip *Freshfields Bruckhaus Deringer*	**SIGNY Adam** *Clifford Chance*
3	**ALLEN-JONES Charles** *Linklaters*	**ANDERSON Neil** *Sullivan & Cromwell*
	AP SIMON Charles *Freshfields Bruckhaus Deringer*	**BRAHAM Edward** *Freshfields Bruckhaus Deringer*
	CHILDS David *Clifford Chance*	**CLARK Tim** *Slaughter and May*
	CLARK Adrian *Ashurst Morris Crisp*	**CLARKE Tim** *Linklaters*
	CRANFIELD Richard *Allen & Overy*	**EVANS Stuart** *Simmons & Simmons*
	HATCHARD Michael *Skadden, Arps, Slate*	**HENDERSON Giles** *Slaughter and May*
	JAMES Glen *Slaughter and May*	**KNIGHT William** *Simmons & Simmons*
	KNIGHT Adrian *Shearman & Sterling*	**LONG Julian** *Freshfields Bruckhaus Deringer*
	McCARTHY Jack *Davis Polk & Wardwell*	**PARSONS Chris** *Herbert Smith*
	PEARSON Chris *Norton Rose*	**PECK Andrew** *Linklaters*
	RANDELL Charles *Slaughter and May*	**SACKMAN Simon** *Norton Rose*
	WIPPELL Mark *Allen & Overy*	**WOOTTON David** *Allen & Overy*
4	**BARNARD Stephen** *Herbert Smith*	**BERINGER Guy** *Allen & Overy*
	BIRD Alistair *Simmons & Simmons*	**CHARNLEY William** *McDermott, Will & Emery*
	DAVIDSON John *Lovells*	**DAVIS James** *Freshfields Bruckhaus Deringer*
	ELLARD John *Linklaters*	**GODFREY Keith** *Allen & Overy*
	GOODALL Caroline *Herbert Smith*	**HOLLAND Peter** *Allen & Overy*
	HYMAN Neil *Slaughter and May*	**JONES Arfon** *CMS Cameron McKenna*
	JOYCE Tom *Freshfields Bruckhaus Deringer*	**KING Peter** *Linklaters*
	KNAPP Vanessa *Freshfields Bruckhaus Deringer*	**MACFARLANE David** *Ashurst Morris Crisp*
	MURPHY Frances *Slaughter and May*	**NEWHOUSE Anthony** *Slaughter and May*
	PEARSON David *Clifford Chance*	**PELL Marian** *Herbert Smith*
	READ Nigel *Lovells*	**SIMPSON Scott** *Skadden, Arps, Slate*
	STEPHENSON Barbara *Norton Rose*	**STERN Robert** *Slaughter and May*
	SULLIVAN Michael *Linklaters*	**WATSON Sean** *CMS Cameron McKenna*
Up-and-coming individuals		
	BELLIS Tim *Herbert Smith*	**COPPIN Jonathan** *Norton Rose*
	NORMAN Guy *Clifford Chance*	**RYDE Andy** *Slaughter and May*
	TWENTYMAN Jeff *Slaughter and May*	**VON BISMARCK Nilufer** *Slaughter and May*

Individuals are listed alphabetically in each band.

teeth into." He is praised for inspiring loyalty in his clients and securing the biggest deals, which include acting for Vodafone on its hostile bid for Mannesmann, as well as its merger with Airtouch, and the defence of NatWest from a hostile bids from RBS (£21 billion) and the Bank of Scotland (£25 billion). Representing Vodafone AirTouch in the disposal of Orange to France Telecom, worth £25 billion. **Anthony Cann*** has *"a brilliant mind"* and is said to be a pleasure to work with. He has *"nothing to prove and no need to score points."* As Global Head of Corporate he does have other responsibilities, but appears to have no intention of taking a back seat. This year he has advised Scottish & Newcastle on its acquisition of the pubs and restaurant business from Greenalls.

Richard Godden*, perceived as *"the brainbox,"* is praised by his clients as *"a creative thinker"* but is said to have *"an intense, parsonical manner."* Seen to handle large cross-border transactions including advising Dixon Group on its bid for Elkjop Group, he is said to have the *"delicate touch"* needed to run a smooth deal.

"Outstanding" **Matthew Middleditch*** has produced *"calm authoritative work"* this year, and is praised by clients for *"achieving complex commercial objectives."* Seen to inspire loyalty in the investment banks, he has a growing portfolio of corporate clients. Acted for Unigate on its merger with Dairy Crest and for AXA Sun Life on its acquisition of Provincial. Representing Sun Life and Provincial Holdings in AXA's acquisition of 44.7% shares it does not already own (£2.4 billion). Slightly removed from transactional work as senior partner, **Charles Allen-Jones*** is seen as a key client man. He continues his role as relationship partner for Goldman Sachs.

"Valuable asset" **Andrew Peck*** is said to be *"a complete terrier"* with *"a fantastic control over huge deals,"* particularly in hostile takeover situations, although he has also received praise for his building society demutualisation work. Acted for M&G on its sale to Prudential for £1.9 billion. **Tim Clarke*** is respected for his large-scale privatisation work, and is responsible for the firm's international privatisation practice. He was heavily involved with the South African government in the role of lead counsel on the privatisation of South African Airways (SAA). Recognised for his strong tax background and his work in the telecoms field, **John Ellard*** has also advised Coca-Cola Beverages on its £4 billion merger with Hellenic Bottling Company. **Michael Sullivan*** has had a lower profile this year but is recommended for his international M&A energy deals which include the National Power demerger into two listed companies, and the sell-off of power stations. *"Phenomenally bright"* **Peter King*** is universally respected for his privatisations and high level securities work where he is said to be *"impressive, clear headed and easy to work with."* Representing RWE in their agreement to acquire Thames Water.

The team also has partners focusing on specialist industry groups such as healthcare, telecoms and IT, utilities and transport.

The team is representing MEPC in the takeover by Leconport Estates, valued at £1.9 billion. Advising SmithKline Beecham on its merger with Glaxo Wellcome (£114 billion) to create the world leader in the pharmaceuticals industry.

Clients: Corporates: BP Amoco; BT; Scottish & Newcastle; SmithKline Beecham; Vodafone Air-

*See leaders' profiles on pages 741-782

touch; Unigate; Cable & Wireless Communications; Benckiser; AstraZeneca; ICI; Dixons; Gucci Group IV; National Westminster Bank. **Financials:** Morgan Stanley; CSFB; Goldman Sachs; ABN Amro; Paribas; Dresdner Kleinwort Benson; Warburg Dillon Read.

Slaughter and May (60 ptrs) *"Traditionally the best franchise of the three"* with an enviable dominance of the global plc market. The question most posed by the market is the credibility of its *"best friends"* policy. This international strategy has divided opinion with the firm seen as *"conservative," "uniquely British, holding a dominant position"* and *"certainly no fool"* in its relationships with highly regarded firms such as Hengeler Mueller Weitzel Wirtz (Germany) and Uria y Menendez (Spain). However, the huge consolidation in the European corporate market has led concerned competitors to opine that a strong marriage will be more effective than friendships in the long run.

Regarded as having *"excellence through and through,"* the team is praised for encouraging a *"rich tier of senior assistants." "Charming, with a striking intellect,"* **Nigel Boardman*** maintains his reputation as *"the kingpin of the practice," "a fantastic force for the City."* He is *"highly commercial, a great tactician"* who, like Cheyne, is seen to relish the most complex transactions and always puts up *"a spirited battle."* Like all good operators in the hostile market he can be *"belligerent,"* but there is no dispute that he has succeeded in satisfying an enviable client base of major global corporates and powerful financial institutions. Acted for Orange on its sale to France Telecom (includes the assumption of £1.8 billion of debt), for Hyder on bids from St David's Capital and the unilateral cash offer from WPD. **Michael Pescod*** (representing Unilever in a merger agreement with Bestfoods, valued at $20.3 billion) is *"an excellent old school M&A man"* who clients say *"combines a wealth of experience with an astute business mind." "Charming with his own inimitable, playful style"* he is praised for developing client relationships for the practice as well as transactional work which includes acting for Unilever on its proposed acquisition of Bestfoods and for Glaxo Wellcome on its merger with SmithKline Beecham (combined market capitalisation of £114 billion).

"The well known aggressor of the firm" **William Underhill*** is *"bright and rumbustious"* and underpins his work with *"the strength of a superb generalist."* He is praised as *"an original thinker"* but is perceived as *"more inflexible than most."* Recent big-ticket deals include acting for Blue Circle Industries in its successful defence of a takeover bid by Lafarge and Prudential Corporation on its flotation of Egg, its internet banking subsidiary. *"A leading light for major public companies,"* **Stephen Cooke*** is said to be *"pragmatic"* and *"technically minded."* Representing BA in its proposed merger with KLM (£5 billion), also representing Diageo/Pillsbury in the proposed merger of the worldwide Pillsbury operation with General Mills ($10.5 billion). Acted for Scottish Media Group on its acquisition of Ginger Media Group. *"Impressive"* **Martin Hattrell*** is *"technically excellent"* and a *"super bloke to deal with who only ever delivers the best."* He is well regarded for his work acting for Whitbread on the sale of its brewing business to Interbrew of Belgium and the disposal of the pubs and restaurants acquired as part of the Swallow Group acquisition.

Senior partner **Giles Henderson*** is more removed from day to day transactions, but continues to be regarded as a *"powerful force"* in terms of client development. **Tim Clark*** is seen to undertake huge transactions with *"the minimum of fuss,"* and is *"thoroughly capable, not overly aggressive and certainly not vain."* He is well regarded for his work and advised BOC on its £7.15 billion break up and Carlton Communications on its £7.8 billion merger with United News & Media. Also advised Abbey National in the £1.8 billion business transfer of Scottish Provident. **Glen James*** has *"an outstanding legal brain"* and is an *"inventive"* practitioner with particular expertise in insurance work. He acted for Norwich Union on its merger with CGU (to form CGNU, a merger effected through a scheme of arrangement), and advised (with Hattrell) Schroders on the disposal of its investment banking business to Salomon Smith Barney. With the benefit of his *"excellent international experience"* (he ran the Frankfurt office) **Charles Randell*** is said to be *"demanding and uncompromising"* in his desire for excellence and *"has the makings of a future senior partner."* Advised Bertelsmann on the merger of CLT-UFA and Pearson's Televison business to form Audiofina, and in conjunction with Hengeler acted for QXL.com on its merger with ricardo.de (uniting two of Europe's largest online auction companies).

Frances Murphy* has the reputation as the firm's technician. She is *"tenacious and commercial"* but can be *"a bit of a stickler."* Has acted for Marconi on its disposal of the Avery Berkel Group and tends to be a favourite with similar industrial clients. **Anthony Newhouse*** is said to be the man to turn to with *"crisis work."* He advised troubled United Assurance Group on the agreed £1.6 billion bid by Royal London (largest takeover of a listed company by a mutual in the UK). The *"accomplished"* **Robert Stern*** is a *"helpful and personable"* practitioner and received praise for his recent big-ticket deals, including acting for C&N Touristic, the German travel group, on its £1.3 billion bid for Thomson. **Neil Hyman*** is admired by his peers for being *"succinct and easy to deal with."* His recent big ticket transactions include acting for Panmure West LB on the Unigate disposal and for Punch Taverns on its battle with Whitbread for the Allied Domecq chain of pubs where *"his achievements were remarkable."* Such deals have led to a perception that he is *"racier than the usual Slaughters mould."*

Andy Ryde* (representing Texas Instruments in their acquisition of Burr-Brown Corp, worth $7.6 billion) joins our up and coming ranking for his increased prominence on major deals, including acting for Regus on its delayed £250 million IPO. He has the *"right attitude"* to produce a smooth deal, and is a *"skilled negotiator."* **Nilufer von Bismarck*** is *"one of the unsung heroes,"* and received recognition for her *"commerciality and pragmatic business solutions."* She has acted for Sun Life & Provincial on its sale of Guardian Royal Exchanges to Aegon UK (£759 million). Developing an enviable client base, **Jeff Twentyman*** has *"excellent legal knowledge"* and has achieved particular prominence with his work for Blue Circle and in the telecoms sector.

The team is representing Thames Water in their acquisition by RWE, valued at £6.4 billion, and representing Electronic Data Systems in the integration of their existing relation with Rolls Royce into a 12.5 year global and IT outsourcing agreement ($2.1 billion). **Clients: Corporates:** Old Mutual; E-Bookers; Mannesmann; British Steel (merger with Hoogovens); Reckitt & Colman (merger with Benckiser); Inchcape; Lex Holdings; Sun Life & Provincial; BAT (merger with Rothmans); Shire Pharmaceuticals; Carlton Communications; Ladbrokes; Asda; Kwik-Fit; Blue Circle Industries; FirstGroup; Hanson; Whitbread. **Financials:** Norwich Union; GRE; Standard Chartered; Schroders; JP Morgan; Robert Fleming; Cazenove; Dresdner Kleinwort Benson; GE Capital; 3i Group.

Allen & Overy (32 ptrs, 25 asscs) A firm which had *"made a fortune with its remarkable banking and securities practice"* is perceived to be moving out of that shadow with heavy investment in the corporate team. That said, the team is still perceived to *"lack clout with the corporates"* and is more often seen acting as counsel for the financials in the largest M&A transactions, such as the finance arrangers for Vodafone's bid for Mannesmann. The international network, particularly strong in Germany, France, Italy and Spain, has led to extensive *"impressive, deal-generating capabilities"* both in cross border transactions and those requiring multi-jurisdictional advice.

In his new role as Head of Corporate, **Richard**

Cranfield* has received less exposure to the transactional market, although he did advise Cable & Wireless on the sale of One2One to Deutsche Telekom (value £8.4 billion). He is thought to be well-suited to his role as *"a great cheerleader"* for the corporate team, and it is seen as a *"major boost for the firm to have such a high profile political animal in its corner."* **Alan Paul*** is seen to be the *"driving force"* transactionally. He is *"thorough, straight as an arrow"* and *"impressive to watch."* He inspires loyalty in his clients, who agree *"he puts commerciality first"* and *"can turn his hand to anything."* This has also led to suggestions that he is in danger of spreading himself too thinly. Paul is also the focus for the firm's strong reputation in private equity financing. Acted for Heineken on the acquisition of Cruzcampo (Spain's largest brewer, value $1 billion) and for CSFB and Morgan Stanley on Bank of Scotland's £22 billion bid for NatWest. Senior partner **Guy Beringer*** is well regarded as the firm's *"rainmaker,"* and although not thought to be a key transactional figure, *"is there when it matters most to the client."*

"General corporate heavyweight" **David Wootton*** is a senior M&A figure, advised Whitbread on its £578 million recommended cash offer for Swallow Group and acted for Singapore Airlines on its £600 million investment in Virgin Atlantic. Representing Smiths Industries, UK in a merger with TI Group, valued at £1.9 billion. *"Charming"* **Keith Godfrey*** is seen as an *"old guard"* corporate presence and is respected for his cross-border experience. **Peter Holland*** *"plays a sensible hand"* and is thought of as *"reliable not pushy, an excellent corporate lawyer"* who *"knows the building society market like the back of his hand."* **Mark Wippell*** (representing UPC in their acquisition of a $5.3 billion, 25% stake in Telewest) has *"great takeover code experience"* and *"a highly commercial approach."* Acted for global consumer packaging group Rexam on its recommended cash offer for American National Can Group (£1.3 billion).

Sector strengths include telecoms and energy, where the international network and repeat business from financials is seen to generate a high profile. A recent example of this work was advising Thomas Cook on its joint venture with Carlson and Preussag which covered 40 jurisdictions.

Representing Finnmeccanica in a joint venture between Westland Helicopters and Augusta Helicopters worth £2.1 billion. Represented Citibank/UniCredito Italiano in a revolving credit facility for Gucci Group worth €1 billion. **Clients: Corporates:** Cable & Wireless; ICI; BAe; Singapore Airlines; United News & Media; United Biscuits; Welcome Break; Thomson Travel Group; Smiths Industries; WPP Group; Ericsson; Siemens; SWEB; Yorkshire Electricity. **Financials:** Morgan Grenfell; ABN Amro; Barclays Bank; Commerzbank; GE Capital; HSBC Investment Bank; Merrill Lynch; Warburg Dillon Read; Goldman Sachs; DLJ Phoenix; Deutsche Bank; Schroders.

Clifford Chance (35 ptrs, 125 asscs) *"Proud of what they have done for the London profession"* is a universally reflected view of the firm's international strategy. Its multi-jurisdictional capabilities and, in particular, the merger with Rogers & Wells and Pünder, Volhard, Weber & Axster has strengthened the M&A resource in North America, Asia and across Europe, also providing an essential securitisation facility. The firm is now able to boast 200 partners world-wide. A prime example of this transatlantic approach appeared in the integrated US and UK advice given to Lend Lease Corporation on the acquisition of Bovis from P&O. However, overall perception is of increased volume rather than value, and the team is said to need a boost in the number of big ticket practitioners as *"it lacks the level of 30-40 year old deal makers necessary to generate the flow."*

Adam Signy* is thought to be the main face for transactional work. He is *"insightful, pragmatic and effective"* and has advised both CGU on its merger with Norwich Union and Morgan Stanley on the formation of Allied Zurich into a single holding company valued at £24 billion. **Jeremy Brownlow*** is a senior M&A figure highly praised for his work on hostile public company takeovers. He has particular client responsibilities which lessen his transactional profile (such as for Volvo) and is said to be *"similar to Salz in his big ticket work."*

Global Head of Corporate **David Childs*** is seen to benefit from a strong banking background in forging strong client relationships with financial institutions, and is *"an impressive dealmaker."* He acted for Energis on its unsuccessful bid for Racal's telecoms arm and advised Chase Manhattan on its successful bid for Flemings. **David Pearson*** also has a strong following with institutional investment banks. He is said to be *"a rising star," "with a good feel for his clients' needs."* He advised Nomura's Principal Finance Group and Unique Pubs on its securitisation, and Tudor Street Acquisitions on its purchase of Inn Partnership from Greenalls. **Guy Norman***, who joins our up and coming ranks, is praised for *"his fantastic energy"* and is said to have *"a real taste for the complex hostile side"* and *"gravitas beyond his years."* He is establishing a *"fine client base"* since a two year secondment on the Takeover Panel.

The firm overall is said to lack *"that necessary base of anchor clients"* to dominate pan-European transactional work. Nevertheless, its global performance is increasing in profile with deals such as advising Carrefour on its merger with Promodes. The firm also continues to hold firm with the major financials: acted for Merrill Lynch and Goldman Sachs on RBS's hostile bid for NatWest, advised Goldman Sachs and Warburg Dillon Read on Vodafone's bid for Mannesmann and acted for Morgan Stanley on NTL's acquisition of C&W's cable television division.

Advising NTT DoCoMo on a joint venture worth £6 billion, and Woolwich in a £5.5 billion proposed takeover by Barclays. Involved in United Biscuits buy-out (£1.3 billion) and the Electra/Candover backed Newmond acquisition of Baxi Heating (£750 million).

Overseas deals include Cinven's acquisition of Frans Bonhomme (£243m), Dutch private equity firm Gilde Investments' acquisition of Armstrong Installation Products (£230m) and the US Berkshire Partners-backed Salterweigh-Tronix acquisition of Avery Berkel (£200m). **Clients: Corporates:** CGU; Coca-Cola; HJ Heinz; Kimberley-Clark; Intel; Siemens; Volvo; British Energy; Air Products; Reuters; Philip Morris; Lend Lease; Carrefour; Lagardere. **Financials:** CSFB; GE Capital; Goldman Sachs; Merrill Lynch (includes the €37.7 billion merger of Banco Bilbao Vizcaya and Argentaria); Morgan Stanley; Schroders; UBS Warburg; KKR.

Herbert Smith (40 ptrs, 110 asscs) *"Refocused well and made great strides."* The firm is praised across the board for promoting *"hard working, fine individuals"* into the driving seat of its major deals, thereby producing a *"bright, intelligent"* team who are *"fired up."* This is reflected in the number of high profile partners recommended to our lists. Big-ticket deals have been abundant this year, particularly *"out of the ordinary cross border transactions"* in the IT sector, and the team is felt to be a clear beneficiary from others' conflicts. However, the lack of a clearly-defined international strategy is considered by many to be a drawback for the firm's future prospects, and it is felt that *"it will be difficult for them to sustain growth in a primarily international field."*

"Bloody good" **Anthony Macaulay*** is a senior figure with *"a keen mind and bags of experience"* and is recommended for his work with investment banks. He has advised Publicis on its £4 billion acquisition of Saatchi & Saatchi. His *"demanding style"* has meant he is not to everyone's taste, and he is considered at his best in hostile, complex transactions. **James Palmer*** is *"a good communicator"* and can be *"a tough negotiator."* Clients respond to his *"commercial acumen"* which helps him *"take advantage of the law."* He is rapidly becoming one of the firm's most high-

*See leaders' profiles on pages 741-782

profile transactional lawyers as a result of acting for Time Warner on the European and EU aspects of its merger with AOL and on its acquisition of EMI's music business. Senior partner **Richard Bond*** has a strong reputation, is *"admired by clients and lawyers alike"* and is seen to be a strong force for developing client relationships. Transactional work includes advising Amerada Hess on its strategic alliance with Petronas.

"Quick-witted" **Chris Parsons*** has increased his profile hugely with his work on Olivetti's successful hostile bid for Telecom Italia (€26 billion). He also advised Dorling Kindersley on the recommended offer from Pearson. **Stephen Barnard*** has a low profile but is well regarded for corporate restructurings and reorganisation, has advised the London Stock Exchange on its demutualisation and continues to provide advice to PricewaterhouseCoopers on the reorganisation of its global network. As the recently appointed head of corporate finance, **Caroline Goodall*** is anticipated to be less visible on transactions, but is recommended for her work for Hoogovens on its proposed merger with Bristish Steel, where Herbert Smith advised on English and US securities law. Her *"energetic and robust"* personality must fill the void left by Edward Walker-Arnott, who has retired but will retain a role as consultant. Insurance specialist **Marian Pell*** is *"pragmatic"* and respected for work which includes acting for AXA on the restructuring of the inherited estate of AXA Equity and Law and advising Standard Chartered Bank on the Bancassurance joint venture with CGU in the Far East. Younger partner **Tim Bellis*** is gaining stature as a *"proactive"* practitioner and has acted for Loot on its sale to Scoot. He was also involved in the British American Tobacco/Rothmans merger (with Palmer), and on the subsequent restructuring of BAT following the BAT/Zurich deal.

The firm's outstanding reputation for attracting technology clients has seen a growth in e-commerce IPOs, building on *"a superb track record"* in acting for major global arrangers. Advised CSFB on the QXL.com's listing and IPO.

Acted for the joint venture partners (Ashanti Goldfields Company and AngloGold) and for the borrower (Ashanti Goldfields Tanzania) on the $135 million project financing of the Geita Gold Mine in Tanzania. Acted for British Telecommunications on the acquisition of 45% of VIAG Interkom from E.ON for £3.6 billion, BSkyB in its acquisition of Open, the TV shopping and interactive services company, and Publicis on its £4 billion merger with Saatchi and Saatchi. **Clients: Corporates:** Time Warner; Olivetti; Automobile Association; Securicor; Pearson; Stagecoach Holdings; First Choice Holidays; BAA; Hillsdown Holdings; BAT BSkyB; Sears (on demerger of Selfridges); De La Rue; Hillsdown Holdings; Tottenham Hotspur. **Financials:** CSFB; Cazenove & Co; Goldman Sachs; Lazard Capital Markets; Warburg Dillon Read; Deutsche Bank; ABN Amro; Hoare Govett; Kleinwort Benson Securities; Henderson Investors; Invesco Enterprise Trust.

Norton Rose (33 ptrs, 75 asscs) *"In the ascendancy,"* owing to its presence on major headline deals, this firm is currently *"punching above its weight."* With strong connections overseas, particularly in Asia, the firm is said to be *"undertaking complex transactions that the Big 5 would envy."* Senior partner **David Lewis*** is an established presence in the M&A market and *"a good chap to have in your corner"* with his *"professional attitude and bright intellect."* He has acted for the AA committee members on the £1.1 billion sale to GB Gas Holdings. **Simon Sackman*** has also benefited from *"big-ticket experience"* but his drive for technical accuracy has left some to consider him *"sticky."* He is one of NR's high-profile deal-doers and has acted for Finalrealm (and its backers, Paribas, Cinven and Deutsche Bank) on its £1.25 billion bid for United Biscuits and advised Prudential on the sale of its UK equity business to Deutsche Asset Management for £12 billion.

Managing partner of the Corporate Finance team, **Barbara Stephenson*** is strongly recommended for her relationship with investment banks, which has *"pushed NR into a healthy run of placings."* Her style is said to be *"feisty,"* which may have overshadowed her *"undoubted ability,"* particularly with public company takeovers and placings. She advised Citigroup and Salomon Smith Barney (jointly with Skaddens) on the acquisition of Schroders Investment Banking Division. Advising QBE Insurance Group in recommended cash offer to acquire shares in Limit , worth £375 million. *"Bright"* **Jonathan Coppin*** *"has the right attitude"* and is recommended to our up and coming lists primarily for his work advising P&O on the disposal of Bovis (£315 million) and for advising utilities group Kelda on its plans to turn Yorkshire Water into a mutual company.

"A real star," **Chris Pearson*** runs a *"first rate deal"* and *"always pulls in the best clients."* He has a strong reputation for his telecoms experience, which includes acting for Mannesmann on its £19.5 billion bid for Orange and its defence of the £86.6 billion hostile bid from Vodafone Airtouch. This specialist experience may be forced to the forefront now that the firm has lost its corporate head of Media & Telecoms to Clifford Chance. The firm advised France Telecom on its initial investment in NTL and its joint bid for the third generation mobile phone licences. Concentrating on the domestic and European corporate markets has raised the firm's profile over the last year, yet the perception is that the firm needs to *"avoid being marginalised on the international scene."*

Acted for BNP Paribas and Citibank as lead arrangers on the $1.015 billion debt financing of the Taweelah A1 Power Generation and Sea Water Desalination Project in Abu Dhabi. This is the largest power project financing to have reached financial close in the Middle East to date. **Clients: Corporates:** Mannesmann; Norsk Hydro; Kelda (formerly Yorkshire Water) P&O; Taylor Woodrow; Trinity Mirror; Automobile Association; Robert Bosch; Siemens; Harvey Nichols Group; Mansfield Brewery; Blacks Leisure Group. **Financials:** HSBC; Credit Lyonnais; Deutsche Bank; Schroders; Cinven; Dresdner Kleinwort Benson; Baxi; Warburg Dillon Read; Hawkpoint Partners; Investec Henderson Crosthwaite; Merrill Lynch; Mercury Asset Management.

Ashurst Morris Crisp (43 ptrs, 140 asscs) The failed mergers talks with Latham & Watkins (and previously Clifford Chance) have raised market concerns that *"this is not a happy ship."* While universal perception is of an *"overall unsettling effect"* the corporate team is perceived to have *"an excellent client base and a sound business."*

David Macfarlane is a *"strong plus"* for the team with his *"excellent deal knowledge"* and strong client relationships, particularly with the banks. He *"keeps his eye on the ball"* during transactions such as advising ING Barings on the disposal of Cambridge Water to Spanish utility Union Fenosa ACEX. **Chris Ashworth*** is *"more punchy"* but retains that *"laid-back Ashursts style."* He is the name seen on big-ticket deals such as advising BTP on its takeover of Clariant AG and its listing on the Swiss and Frankfurt Stock Exchanges, and acted for Henlys Group on its £420 million takeover of Blue Bird Corp. **Adrian Clark*** is said to be a *"favourite of the UK investment banks"* and advised Goldman Sachs International on Preussag's recommended cash offer (£1.8 billion) for Thomson Travel Group.

The firm is still a force on big-ticket deals and acted for Nabisco Holdings Corp on its joint bid (with Hicks Muse) for United Biscuits. The M&A practice is somewhat overshadowed by the strength and popularity of its buyouts team, which forms the basis of a well respected dominance of the private equity market.

"A strong cultural identity" with telecoms and energy specialisms has led to interesting deals such as acting for Virgin on its joint venture with One2One to create Virgin Mobile Communications Ltd, acting for Kingston Communications

on its £800 million flotation and for NRG Energy on its acquisition of the Killingholme Power Station for £410 million. Clients admire the firm's *"pragmatic, commercial approach,"* and it is seen to be building a reputation for *"solid"* work with investment banks.

Acting on Carphone Warehouse Group IPO of 25% of the company to be listed on the London Stock Exchange (up to £1.8 billion). **Clients: Corporates:** Deutsche Telekom; Nabisco Holdings Corp; Celcius; Virgin Group; Kingston Communications; PowerGen; National Power; Henlys Group United News & Media; Skansa; The Carlyle Group; Express Dairies Plc; Dunlop Slazenger; McBride; Bovis. **Financials:** Barclays Capital; Deutsche Bank; Bank of Scotland; Chase Manhattan; Chase Capital Partners; Salomon Smith Barney; West LB Panmure.

Lovells (22 ptrs, 50 asscs) The firm has recently been noted operating on mid-sized transactions and is felt to lack global clout with corporates of the market leaders. Considered to have pursued a *"sensible strategy"* internationally, the firm's merger with German firm Boesebeck Droste has been generally approved by the market. However, investment bank relationships remain an area in which the firm is said to be *"playing catch up."*

The team itself is said to *"lack a face"* now that highly regarded Dan Mace has retired (he retains a consultancy role for client relationships). **Nigel Read*** has a well-established reputation with the investment banks as a former Lazards man. He is *"pleasant to work with"* but is said to lack a continuous *"high impact"* deal profile. He is leading the charge in bolstering the team's investment bank work, acting for JP Morgan on the £4 billion TRW bid for Lucas Varity, and is advising Preussag on its recommended £1.8 billion bid for Thomson Travel. Represented Granada Media in its acquisition of United News and Media's ITV franchise, worth £1.75 billion. *"Pragmatic"* **John Davidson*** is said to be a *"sensible"* practitioner who runs a *"smooth"* deal. He ran a major international equity offering this year, acting for South African Breweries on its IPO and listing on the London Stock Exchange (£3.5 billion) and Aegon on its offer for Guardian Royal Exchange.

The team *"has a fine spread"* of clients and focuses on the particular growth areas of telecoms, e-commerce, retail and manufacturing. It acted on Racal Electronic's sale of its telecoms business to Global Crossing (£1 billion) and acted for Baltimore Technologies on its Nasdaq float. Like Ashursts, the firm is seen as strong on the private equity front and has demonstrated its international securities capabilities. Cross-border activity benefits from a strong Paris office which proved important on the IPO of Laurent Perrier where the firm acted as French counsel to the joint global co-ordinators JP Morgan Securities and Banque Nationale de Paris.

Represented Doughty Henson in the sale of Tomkins European food manufacturing business (RHM) (£1.139 billion). **Clients: Corporates:** Racal; South African Breweries; Microsoft; Mirror Group; Ford; Vickers; Interpublic; Granada. **Financials:** JP Morgan; Schroders; Lazards; Merrill Lynch; Lehman Brothers.

Simmons & Simmons (26 ptrs, 54 asscs) A firm with a *"spirited attitude"* that has inspired loyalty in its core clients. However, a rather turbulent year has seen the loss of the firm's capital markets association with Fried Frank Shriver & Jacobson which had bolstered the team's reputation with US investment banks, an area it must now fight to retain.

"Terrific" **Stuart Evans*** may be *"an eccentric character"* but there can be no doubting his big-ticket appeal. He has successfully traded on the respect garnered by acting for Wal-Mart on its £6.8 billion bid for Asda. He is said to be *"fun to work with"* and has impressed peers and clients alike. Evans advised Interbrew (of Belgium) on its £400 million acquisition of the Whitbread beer company business. The firm is said to have the ability to mobilise large teams at short notice and run deals concurrently.

"Superb lawyer" **William Knight*** is less transactional as senior partner, but retains his reputation as an intelligent practitioner *"with a great deal-doer's mind." "Adored"* by clients, he is now the firm's leading developer of new relationships. **Alistair Bird*** is recommended for his *"easy manner"* and his *"attention to detail."* He is felt to benefit from his international experience (previously managing partner in the New York office) and is developing a strong telecoms reputation.

Represented Booker in their £960 million merger with Iceland Group. **Clients: Corporates:** Bass Brewers; Cadburys Schweppes; Invensys; Internet Technology Group; Booker; Railtrack; Shell International; Sea-Land Service; Wal-Mart Stores. **Financials:** Deutsche Bank; Charterhouse Bank; Hawkpoint; Lloyds TSB Group; ABN Amro; CDC Group; DLJ Phoenix Private Equity.

CMS Cameron McKenna (28 ptrs, 35 asscs) Well known in the market as an international operator, with particular strength in Central and Eastern Europe through the firm's CMS network. The firm has a low profile for its domestic M&A work, although prominent for Eastern European mid-tier deals. It is packed with *"personable lawyers"* producing *"quality work"* the main complaint appears to be a lack of *"consistent deal flow."*

Sean Watson* maintains his high profile, particularly as a *"sound and able presence"* in the energy market. He advised the National Grid both on its £2 billion acquisition of the New England Electric System (US) and on the sale of its 25% stake in Energis. *"Excellent"* **Arfon Jones*** *("bright and clever")* is seen as a mainstay of the firm, part of the older generation, and has a profile due in part to his membership of the CLSC committee.

The firm advised Erste Bank on the proposed acquisition of Česká Spořitelna (The Czech Savings Bank). Cross-border activity is an important part of the corporate fabric with 32 offices in 19 jurisdictions undertaking transactional work resulting in a number of new clients. The team advised Swets & Zeitlinger on the acquisition of BH Blackwell and US subsidiaries to form an $11 billion subscription agency in London and Utrecht. The practice has a traditionally *"impressive"* profile in the pharmaceutical and biotech market acting for Warner Lambert and the Wellcome Trust. It has also made inroads into the internet technology market and has a strong reputation for flotation work. Nevertheless, the firm is still felt to lack a significant presence with major financial institutions. **Clients: Corporates:** Fortnum Oil & Gas; Energis; National Grid Group; NSB Retail Systems; Post Office; Roland Berger; Swets & Zeitlinger; Warner Brothers; Blockbuster Entertainment; Camelot; Warner Lambert; George Wimpey; Black & Decker; Vivendi. **Financials:** NatWest Equity Partners; Lloyds TSB; HSBC; Banque Nationale de Paris; Hawkpoint Partners.

Denton Wilde Sapte (30 ptrs, 50 asscs) The merger between Denton Hall and Wilde Sapte has created *"a fascinating firm"* but one not considered by the market as a *"mainstream corporate finance"* player. Despite the loss of key players in the WS banking team, the firm has capitalised on the strength of its debt financing team. The firm acted for a bidder of the Swedish Telia Cable TV Network (value £1 billion) with assistance from the Denton International Swedish office and has the capacity to advise on a mix of debt and equity financing.

The firm is active in a number of industry sectors, including energy, media, insurance and aviation. However, it lacks a big-hitter for corporate work and is felt to *"face an uphill struggle"* to climb the domestic pecking order. The firm's excellent energy regulatory practice is a prime generator of big-ticket deals. Acted for Energis on its £352 million acquisition of EnerTel and for

U

*See leaders' profiles on pages 741-782

Petronas on its subscription with Amerada Hess for £136 million worth of new shares in Premier Oil. Media and entertainment is another productive source. The team acts for Bertelsmann and also competes with Freshfields and Herbert Smith for Pearson's corporate work. E-commerce IPOs have also increased, with the firm acting for Tadpole Technologies, an internet incubator.

Said to have *"lots of bodies"* to throw at major deals, the firm is starting to build a profile with the financials, and has acted for Greenwich NatWest on its sale of two leasing subsidiaries, NatWest Asset Leasing and Corporate Leasing Facilities (aggregate value £500 million).

Represented Premier League in an implementing strategy for the sale of audio-visual rights in UK & Ireland (£1.6 billion). **Clients: Corporates:** Shell; J Sainsbury; Allied Leisure; London Electricity; Brambles; Energis; Tibbett & Britten Group; Dixons; Tadpole Technology; Bertelsmann; Pearson; Rentokil International; Microsoft. **Financials:** Greenwich Lloyds Underwriters; Greenwich NatWest; GE Capital.

Corporate/M&A: US Firms acting from London

UNITED KINGDOM Leading firms (Corporate Finance: US firms acting from London)
1 Shearman & Sterling
Weil, Gotshal & Manges
2 Skadden, Arps, Slate, Meagher & Flom LLP
3 Cleary, Gottlieb, Steen & Hamilton

Firms are listed alphabetically in each band.

Shearman & Sterling (3 ptrs, 16 asscs) Regarded as one of the few established US firms in the market making a determined effort to build a London presence. *"Impressive cross-border"* activity is the key for a team in which the *"intelligent"* **Adrian Knight*** *"makes his mark"* on the deal process. The team's transactional work is 80% pure M&A, aiming to provide a one-stop shop for its major US and European corporate client base. Provided advice on both US and UK law to BT on its white knight bid for East Telecom Group. The team has an enviable showing amongst private equity houses. The London office advised Soros Private Equity Partners on two UK (includes acquisition of Storm Telecommunications), and two US focused transactions. Although unable to rely on organic growth, the firm has undertaken a European recruitment strategy mirroring that of the magic circle, and has benefited from the break-up of Schilling Zutt & Anschutz in Germany. Acted for British Steel on the international aspects of its merger with Hoogovens to form Corus Group (market capitalisation £3 billion). **Clients: Corporates:** British Steel; BG; BT; Concentric Network Corp; Danone. **Financials:** Soros Private Equity Partners; Morgan Stanley; Deutsche Bank.

Weil, Gotshal & Manges (6 ptrs, 18 asscs) Seen to have risen above the mid-tier market with big ticket transactions, the firm's stability in London has been rocked by recent departures. However, *"class act"* **Mike Francies*** is *"a real fighter"* whom clients are said to follow loyally. Thought to have leveraged the firm's traditional relationships with international investment banks, it has also developed strengths in the hi-tech arena, including telecoms, media and biotech. Although the firm continues to bolster its full-service offering, it was able to provide support structures when advising MediaOne on the £8.4 billion sale of its 50% sale of stake in One2One to Deutsche Telekom. The team additionally acted for US private equity fund Hicks Muse on its successful bid for UK public company Hillsdown Holdings (includes the use of high yield bonds to fund the acquisition). Currently advising Flextech on its proposed merger with Telewest (aggregate value £12 billion). **Clients: Corporates:** MediaOne; Flextech; Pirelli (on its $2.15 billion sale to Cisco Systems); SUN Brewing; Simply Internet; Burford Group; Sara Lee (on hostile bid for Courtaulds Textile). **Financials:** GE Capital; Hicks, Muse, Tate & Furst; Nomura International.

Skadden, Arps, Slate, Meagher & Flom **Michael Hatchard*** maintains his outstanding reputation. *"Incredibly bright,"* he is said to *"have the presence of a leader."* **Scott Simpson*** has a loyal following of clients who consider him *"excellent for dealing with the US aspects of cross-border deals."* Simpson coordinated Skadden's representation of Gucci in its defence against a hostile takeover by LVMH. UK-based clients find the team offers *"impressive advice,"* noting the firm's experience in dual US and European listings as a major attraction. The success of the corporate team has split views; it is said to be *"an after thought,"* servicing the Wall Street giant's international strategy, or *"most active of the bunch,"* capturing instructions concerning dual-listed companies with increasing regularity. Also recommended for its growing portfolio of Nasdaq listings. Highlights of the year include advising Cendant Corporation on the disposal of Green Flag Holdings to Direct Line (value £220 million). **Clients:** Cendant Corporation.

Cleary, Gottlieb, Steen & Hamilton (9 ptrs, 34 asscs) Seen to be well established in the European market, the firm has notable strength in Brussels and Eastern Europe. The corporate team lacks a figurehead, and is seen to rely on rotating a number of US partners as transactions dictate. US capacity is intrinsic to the nature of practice, such as acting as US adviser to Goldman Sachs over Prudential's offering of shares in Egg. Highlights of the year include advising Robert Fleming & Co on its £4.8 billion takeover by Chase Manhatten and acting for HSBC Holdings on its acquisition of Credit Commercial de France (value £6.6 billion). **Clients: Corporates:** Abbey National; Cable & Wireless; Deutsche Telekom. Financials: Goldman Sachs; Dresdner Kleinwort Benson; Morgan Stanley; HSBC

Other Notable Practitioners **William Charnley** of McDermott, Will & Emery (*"work sticks to him"*) is well regarded for his market presence and is said to bring a *"larger than life personality"* to the deal process. Hi-tech venture capital investment is a prominent area for him.

There were also a handful of recommended practitioners based in London who are better known for their international work.

These include *"innovative"* **Neil Anderson*** of Sullivan & Cromwell who was described as a *"hugely influential figure on the global market."*

Jack McCarthy* at Davis Polk & Wardwell, known for his *"sharp commercial mind,"* advises Royal Bank of Scotland and acted for Esat Holdings in its defence of a hostile bid by Telenor. Also represented Nabisco Holdings in its bid (backed by Hicks, Muse) for United Biscuits.

Energy & Natural Resources

UNITED KINGDOM Leading firms (Energy & Natural Resources)
1 Denton Wilde Sapte
Herbert Smith
2 CMS Cameron McKenna
3 Allen & Overy
Clifford Chance
Linklaters
Norton Rose
4 Freshfields Bruckhaus Deringer
Slaughter and May
5 Ashurst Morris Crisp
Coudert Brothers
Lawrence Graham
Lovells
Nabarro Nathanson
Simmons & Simmons
Vinson & Elkins LLP

Firms are listed alphabetically in each band.

Leading individuals (Energy: Oil & Gas)
1 **BOND Richard** *Herbert Smith*
CAVE-BROWNE-CAVE Myles *Denton Wilde Sapte*
DALLAS James *Denton Wilde Sapte*
GRIFFIN Paul *Herbert Smith*
SALT Stuart *Linklaters*
WOOD Charles *Denton Wilde Sapte*
2 **BEHARRELL Steven** *Coudert Brothers*
DAVIES Roger *Allen & Overy*
PICTON-TURBERVILL Geoffrey *Ashurst Morris*
ROBERTS Martin *Slaughter and May*
STANGER Michael *Lovells*
3 **CARVER Jeremy** *Clifford Chance*
DAVEY Henry *Herbert Smith*
HIGGINSON Tony *Baker Botts LLP*
JONES Gareth *Nabarro Nathanson*
KHAN Rafique *CMS Cameron McKenna*
REES Jonathan *Freshfields Bruckhaus Deringer*
SAUNDERS Mark *Dewey Ballantine LLP*
TYNE Sally *CMS Cameron McKenna*
VERRILL John *Lawrence Graham*
4 **BRETTON Linda** *Lawrence Graham*
DOEH Doran *Denton Wilde Sapte*
PEGG Garry *LeBoeuf, Lamb, Greene & MacRae*

Individuals are listed alphabetically in each band.

Denton Wilde Sapte (19 ptrs, 64 asscs) Many say *"it's the best energy firm in London."* With energy forming almost 20% of the firm's workload, this is a key focus. Respected for its *"breadth and depth,"* this large team is encountered at every turn, on technical and industrial as well as corporate matters. Financing aspects are felt to have benefited from the 2000 merger with Wilde Sapte. In short, it is a *"very, very solid practice, difficult to knock."*

Strength in the power sector centres on regulatory and restructuring matters. Although involved at management level, the *"commercial"* **David Moroney*** maintains an excellent reputation as *"a good deal doer."* The team's recent work in the sector includes advising OFGEM on the new electricity trading arrangements, notably drafting the new balancing and settlement code. Also advised London Electricity on its proposed joint venture with Eastern Electricity in connection with the distribution businesses of two public electricity suppliers. Extensive regulatory and restructuring work has also been done for the governments of Ireland and Lesotho and the Sultanate of Oman, while corporate work includes advising London Electricity on its £160 million acquisition of SWEB and involvement in EDF's acquisition of London Electricity.

A broad upstream oil practice, which is also strong on gas issues, comprises a host of established names. *"Tremendously reliable"* **Myles Cave-Browne-Cave*** is renowned as *"tenacious and understanding of clients' needs"* as well as for his relationships with Total Fina and big players in the UK gas industry. He remains *"one you want on your team."* The *"grade A quality"* **Charles Wood*** has a strong reputation for his gas regulatory work: *"he eats, sleeps and drinks it."* Senior figure **James Dallas*** *"knows when to take a commercial point"* and is a *"vital element"* of the team. During the year the firm set up a new independent UKCS gas company, Consort Resources, where ex-group head Malcolm Groom has gone to play a management role. His *"huge experience"* is expected to be a loss to the team. However, the *"well-connected"* **Doran Doeh*** is considered to have settled in well in the year following his move from Allen & Overy's Moscow office.

The team advised Petronas on its investment in Premier Oil (with Amerada Hess) and acted for Premier Oil on the West Natuna gas production and pipeline project. Downstream, the firm has advised on the introduction of the New Gas Trading Arrangements (effective from 1 October 1999) and continued to advise British Gas on the Network Code. Abroad, there has been a notable role in advising the sub-Caucasus states and Central Asian republics on the legal requirements of the Energy Charter Treaty. **Clients:** Gazprom; Commission for Electricity Regulation; Northumbrian Water Group; Petronas; Premier Oil.

Herbert Smith (18 ptrs, 38 asscs) *"Undoubtedly right up at the top,"* this is one of the best all-round energy firms. Of special note are its power expertise, a healthy oil and gas practice, a leading profile in water and a litigation track record which stands alone. The energy team is felt to combine *"know-how with bloody hard work."*

The client base includes many electricity companies. *"At the heart of the new trading arrangements,"* the team is currently acting for the 14 PESs on the introduction of supply competition in the UK, and for 10 RECs concerning the new wholesale trading arrangements to replace the Electricity Pool. Here the *"reasonable"* **Adrian Clough*** is *"heavily involved,"* although some in the market have commented that the London office has not yet recovered from the departure of *"serious player"* Mark Newbery to Singapore.

Other recent work includes advice to Northern Ireland Electricity/Viridian on the restructuring of the electricity industry in the Republic of Ireland. The team is also acting for the MRA Executive Committee on the administration of the retail electricity market in the UK, as well as the Karnataka Electricity Board (India) on its restructuring.

Clearly, the department has an outstanding litigation profile, and has capitalised on the recent upturn in oil and gas litigation to act in some high-profile cases. Among them was one for BP Amoco concerning litigation arising from a drilling contract for the world's largest jack-up rig.

On the oil and gas transactional side, experienced *"first class operator"* **Richard Bond*** is widely respected. Also known for his gas expertise, as well as retaining a name in the power industry, is **Henry Davey***, who is helping to *"drive the practice forward."* He is acting on the sale of Meterpoint Limited (a UK energy metering firm) by Seeboard to Invensys. The recent acquisition of **Paul Griffin*** from Cadwalader Wickersham & Taft emphasises the strength in depth of the team. Traditionally strong in North Sea oil financing, the team recently advised Chase Manhattan on a number of deals, including a $220 million refinancing facility for Intrepid Energy North Sea, and a limited recourse financing for an oil and gas field in Burma. M&A work

*See leaders' profiles on pages 741-782

remains a focus: Davey advised Petroplus on its Cressier oil refinery acquisition and Bond represented Amerada Hess in its strategic alliance with Petronas for a £136m equity stake in Premier Oil. Acting for BP Amoco on litigation resulting from a drilling contract for use of Gorilla V, the world's largest jack-up rig. **Clients:** St Clements Services; Enterprise Oil; Yorkshire Water; Petroplus.

CMS Cameron McKenna (28 ptrs, 47 asscs) *"One has to hand it to them; they have a great profile."* The energy team won widespread accolades and is now ranked alone just behind the two market leaders. Known for technical expertise, the department is considered to have *"made a virtue out of energy – especially power."*

Rated as the *"first port of call"* for power privatisations, the group is headed by **Fiona Woolf***, who has *"a name that goes before her"* in regulatory matters. She is felt to have *"done wonders"* in exporting the UK grid model to the rest of the world, and is commended for *"going in and getting the work."* Both she and the *"sensible"* **Robert Lane*** are strong on industry market structures, and act for a number of transmission companies. The power work for the past year has been seasoned with international highlights. In Canada, the team represented the municipal and distribution utilities in preparation for the new Ontario electricity markets, while it advised the Mexican regulator on the development of that country's new electricity trading system. The group has also acted for developers in power projects in Africa.

Now held to possess *"a sound mainstream North Sea practice,"* the firm has been aided by an office in Aberdeen. In London, the *"extremely competent"* **Sally Tyne*** is rated for her North Sea upstream work by peers and clients alike. The *"pragmatic"* **Rafique Khan*** also has a good name for his work in the developing oil and gas markets. The team worked on the Catchment Area Project to finalise the Neptune Field Agreements. Other work has included advice in connection with the acquisition of Soco UK Onshore for Star Energy. In contentious matters, the firm has acted in North Sea litigation concerning the Banff field.

During the year 2000, the Electricity Markets Team completed its work on Phase 1 of the Thailand Electricity Supply Industry Reform Project, on behalf of the Thailand National Energy Policy Office (NEPO).

It was also retained by the South African Department of Minerals and Energy to advise on the restructuring of the electricity distribution industry in South Africa. **Clients:** Mobil North Sea Ltd; Transgas; World Bank; Star Energy.

Allen & Overy (20 ptrs, 40 asscs) *"Commercial and rational, this is a group that knows its business."* Particularly feared when energy transactions involve the use of *"their terrifically skilled finance lawyers,"* the firm recently established an 85-lawyer European Energy Group. This is led by the high profile **Ian Elder*** *("a good intellect with a real grasp of his subject")* who is best known for his project finance ability. The group as a whole covers all aspects of the energy sector: corporate, regulatory, trading and finance.

In power deals, the group advised South Western Electricity on the sale of its electricity supply business to London Electricity, TXU-Europe Group on its joint venture with EdF London Investments, and acted on several international power projects for National Grid Company.

"A name from way back," the head of the oil and gas team is *"internationally experienced lawyer"* **Roger Davies***. Upstream work has seen the group acting for Hungarian giant MOL Rt on its proposed merger with the Croatian INA, as well as advising Eastern Power & Energy Trading on the acquisition of interests in the North Sea Oil Fields. Davies was also the lead partner advising Mobil on the European aspects of its merger with Exxon. Abroad, the team has handled gas and petrochemicals privatisations in Oman and Poland.

Acted for the arrangers of the bank finance for AES's acquisition of the Drax power station from National Power, the largest power station in the UK and the second largest in Europe. Advised Barclays Capital on a £550 million loan for Eggborough Power, a subsidiary of British Energy. The facility will be used to refinance British Energy's purchase of the 2000MW coal fired Eggborough plant from National Power. **Clients:** Vivendi; TXU Europe Group; South Western Electricity.

Clifford Chance (17 ptrs, 68 asscs) *"Ubiquitous in the domestic power market,"* the team is best known for its energy projects both domestically and abroad (particularly India.) Here **Peter Blake*** has a huge IPP reputation and is recognised for his advice to the British Energy Group. **Paul Simpson*** also retains his position among the leading lights in power. Generally seen more on the financing side, the perception is that *"they're making an effort to ensure they understand the energy business."* Clients have particularly commented on the group's levels of experience in projects. Apart from their role for InterGen, lead sponsor of Egypt's $480 million Sidi Krir Project, they acted for the sponsors in Hungary's BorsodChem Industrial Power Plant Project and for the arrangers in the Budapest $110 million Ujpest CHP Power Project. In addition, the London team acted for the arrangers of a $11 billion securitisation of stranded costs in the Spanish electricity sector.

In oil and gas, where the firm's profile is not as high, it has still been involved in its share of big-ticket work. The group is acting for Petrobras in the financing of gas separation facilities and oil fields in the Campos Basin, and represented Royal Dutch Shell, as part of a successful $992 million bid for a controlling stake in Comgas.

Contentious matters are also a feature of the department. Here, the respected **Jeremy Carver*** has been involved in a number of matters, including sanctions, decommissioning and oil trading. The team is currently advising Ireland's Bord Gais on a number of issues, including the establishment of that country's energy trading operations and Network Code.

Newly-ranked **Michael Cuthbert*** is well-regarded in the mining and minerals sector. His team's work for the Zambian government in its privatisation of Zambia Consolidated Copper Mines earned particular market approbation. The firm is also advising Chase Manhattan on its $800 million restructuring of Ashanti Goldfields.

Represented the Government of the Republic of Zambia in connection with the privatisation of Zambia Consolidated Copper Mines involving nine major mining and smelting asset disposals. Advising America Mineral Fields, on its joint venture with Anglo American on the Kolwezi Tailings joint venture in the Democratic Republic of the Congo and the Kipushi Project with Iscor, also in the DRC. **Clients:** Mount Isa Mines; InterGen; IVO; Royal Dutch Shell.

Linklaters (15 ptrs, 30 asscs) The market knows this energy team primarily for an *"across the board"* service, its work on behalf of BP Amoco and for key partner, the *"first-class"* **Stuart Salt***. He is felt to combine an understanding of the financial and technical aspects of both oil and gas and electricity in a manner which *"few others emulate."* His team of assistants has also been mentioned for its *"obvious potential."*

"Strong corporate relationships" are the key to the group's success, with a large volume of overseas deals. *"Adversarial"* in style, the team is seen as *"a potent force on the other side of the table,"* particularly in power project development. The team has acted for National Power in numerous disposals, the most high profile of which was the $3 billion disposal of the Drax Power Station.

Oil and gas work has been dominated by M&A and projects/PFI deals. The team acted on the $26 billion BP Amoco-Arco merger and BP Amoco's $4.7 billion acquisition of Burmah Castro. In addition, the group advised the sponsors of the $400 million exploration and development of oil and gas reserves in the Caspian Sea. Numer-

UNITED KINGDOM Leading individuals (Energy: Electricity)
★ WOOLF Fiona *CMS Cameron McKenna*
1 LANE Robert *CMS Cameron McKenna*
SALT Stuart *Linklaters*
2 BLAKE Peter *Clifford Chance*
CLOUGH Adrian *Herbert Smith*
ELDER Ian *Allen & Overy*
MORONEY David *Denton Wilde Sapte*
PICTON-TURBERVILL Geoffrey *Ashurst Morris*
STACEY Paul *Slaughter and May*
3 DAVEY Henry *Herbert Smith*
ROWEY Kent *Freshfields Bruckhaus Deringer*
SIMPSON Paul *Clifford Chance*
TUDWAY Robert *Nabarro Nathanson*
WALLACE Patrick *Freshfields Bruckhaus Deringer*
Individuals are listed alphabetically in each band.

Leading individuals (Energy: Mining)
1 HURST Philip *Ashurst Morris*
2 CUTHBERT Michael *Clifford Chance*
Up-and-coming individuals
KELLY Christopher *Linklaters*
Individuals are listed alphabetically in each band.

ous downstream gas projects occupy the team from India to Brazil. Involved in many water PFI deals, recent projects included work for Asurix in its bids for water distribution and wastewater concessions in Egypt and Morocco.

In mining the team has a fine name, maintaining a host of blue-chip corporate relationships. M&A work in the sector has included advice on the merger of AngloAmerican with Minorco. Significant project work is also being done, where newly-ranked, up and coming assistant **Chris Kelly*** has developed an enviable reputation.

Acting for the lenders to the Changsa Power Project, a 2x360MW coal fired power station in Hunan Province, China, in a deal worth $750 million. Acting for the lenders on the $1.2 billion refinancing for the 512MW ISAB Energy integrated gasification combined cycle power station in Sicily, Italy. Acting for the lenders in relation to the closure of Chernobyl and the construction of two new replacement nuclear power stations (Value: $1.5 billion). **Clients:** Enron; National Power; Edison Mission Energy; Marubeni; BP; BG; Exxon; Shell; Azurix; International Water; Hyder; Anglo American Group; De Beers, Billiton; Rio Tinto; Glencore.

Norton Rose (11 ptrs, 47 asscs) A rising energy department has earned high marks for its projects work, in addition to being *"sound on the financing angles"* and having a recognised M&A capacity. Michael Taylor has now moved to Italy.

In electricity the group is known for its early and consistent involvement in IPP projects, which plays to the firm's strengths in project finance. The client base is evenly split between lenders and developers. New projects in the sector include the first coal-fired IPP in the country, Fifoots Point and waste to energy PFI projects are particular niches. Overseas, independent power project advice has been given to the National Electricity Company of Bulgaria.

Transactionally, the team acted for AES on the £1.875 billion acquisition of Drax UK from National Power.

"A fine upstream oil and gas practice" includes FPSO financing. Downstream, the team advised Nigeria LNG on the $2 billion expansion of its gas project and LUKOIL Petrol on the $101 million acquisition of the Neftochim oil refinery in Bulgaria. In contentious matters, the firm acted for Teeside Gas Transportation (an Enron subsidiary) in its Court of Appeal action over send or pay payments relating to the CATS sub-sea pipeline.

In mining, the firm's niche is in African transactions, advising Ashanti Goldfields in a number of cases, and De Beers as majority shareholder in AngloAmerican. **Clients:** Mobil Services Company; Scottish Power; Archangel Diamond Company.

Freshfields Bruckhaus Deringer (24 ptrs, 37 asscs) Although many consider that the firm *"hasn't yet fully turned its mind to the sector,"* the department has *"some good people"* and takes advantage of an expanding network of international offices. London partners include group leader **Jon Rees***, who has *"all the technical and commercial skills – he's taken the trouble to get to know the industry"* and **Patrick Wallace*** *("he can see the wider picture")* who is known for his power station work.

There is a large projects and corporate finance component in the group's case-load, as well as notable power privatisation experience. **Kent Rowey*** has *"great projects expertise,"* and recently acted for Enron on Croatia's first IPP. The highly-rated energy litigation team is acting for National Grid in an arbitration against National Power over charges for connection to the transmission grid.

In oil and gas the team is well-known for litigation and arbitration, acting for the owners of the North Sea Hewett field in a £70 million dispute with British Gas Trading. For Arco the team acted in a dispute against Chevron over Venezuelan oil operations. Elsewhere, it acted for co-venturers Gazprom and Wintershall in the development and financing of the Prirazlomnoye oil project off the coast of Northern Russia. Downstream work has included the development and financing of a trans-Caspian gas pipeline. The team can call on the services of a specialist tax partner who devotes all his time to oil and gas tax issues. **Clients:** Enron; PSG International; Goldman Sachs.

Slaughter and May *"Never underestimate them,"* warn competitors, while clients *"don't like them acting against us."* Although not as specialised as other teams *("but if a deal changes, they can handle it")* the year has seen significant work in electricity, oil and gas and mining. In electricity, much of the firm's advice has been on acquisitions and disposals. The team acted for SWALEC on the disposal of its electricity and gas supply business to British Energy and for Entergy in the sale of London Electricity. Advice was also given to the Electricity Pool and other clients on the introduction of the new electricity trading arrangements in England and Wales. Here, the *"efficient"* **Paul Stacey*** is *"synonymous with quality."* The group advised the Estonian Eesti Energia on the privatisation of the Eesti and Balti oil shale-fired power stations.

In oil and gas, the experienced **Martin Roberts*** is respected on the financing side. Upstream, the team handled privatisation work in Poland, Nigerian development financing and advised Premier Oil on its joint venture with Shell Exploration in Pakistan. The firm also acted for Lasmo in its £600 million bid for Monument Oil & Gas. In mining, the group has a heavyweight roster of mining and minerals houses clients, which it has represented on a number of M&A transactions. Acted for Shell in the sale by auction of its worldwide coal business and for Alcan Aluminium in the sale of its Aughinish alumina refinery in Ireland to Glencore. **Clients:** Shell; AngloAmerican; Midlands Electricity.

Ashurst Morris Crisp (9 ptrs, 22 asscs) Hard-hit by a number of high profile departures recently, the firm is not yet considered to have recovered its former lustre. While the team's energy litigation is highly praised and the corporate transactions continue to pay their way, the market view is that *"there's no real industry partner at the moment." "Solid, dependable, all round good guy"* **Geoffrey Picton-Turbervill*** is currently the major name at a department with a traditionally strong gas practice. Increasingly active abroad, the firm has been noted *"developing the international dimensions of the practice."*

*See leaders' profiles on pages 741-782

U

In upstream oil and gas last year the group acted for Hunt Oil in selling its interest in the Beatrice Field and associated decommissioning arrangements. In addition, it advised Lundin Oil to finance oil fields in Libya. Downstream, the team continues to act as UK counsel to the Azerbaijan IOC in developing export pipelines from Baku to Western markets.

Less recognised in the electricity sphere, the firm nevertheless advised NRG Energy on its $410 million acquisition of the Killingholme power station from National Power.

With the well-known **Philip Hurst*** at the helm of the mining practice, the group has one of the most recognised exploration and development operations. It is especially well-known in *"highly politicised"* climates. The team has acted for AngloAmerican on matters including the Zarshuran Project, a greenfield precious and base metals mining project in Iran – the first foreign investment in Iran since the revolution and the result of four years' work. The practice has also advised CDC Group on its acquisition of stakes in Indian power stations and Zambian copper mines. **Clients:** SOCO International; Unocal Corp; Anglo American.

Coudert Brothers (3 ptrs, 4 asscs) Possessing *"genuine energy and project capability"* and the *"personable"* **Steven Beharrell***, the team surprises some in the market by its comparatively low profile in London. The geographical spread of the firm's network of offices gives this team extensive experience of advising on issues relating to Russia and the CIS. Project and trade finance are the primary areas of focus, especially in oil and gas, where they generally act for sponsors. The team is also held to be knowledgeable on production sharing agreements. Recent work includes advising the Williams Companies on its acquisition of a controlling stake in a Lithuanian oil refinery and advising the sponsors on project financing a power plant in Mombasa. In the ongoing Sakhalin LNG project in Russia, the team is now advising on the next phase. Currently, the group is advising the Irish State Electricity Board on gas supply issues, as well as Electricité de France (which supplies England with 5 percent of its power) on sales and contractual matters. **Clients:** EDF; Mitsui & Co Ltd; Conoco.

Lawrence Graham (3 ptrs, 3 asscs) A low profile oil and gas practice which is seen principally in Middle East work, UKCS matters and on a variety of deals for key client Lasmo. However *"they do pop up"* and have also acted for Burlington Resources, as well as handling overflow work from in-house teams. Head of the practice, **John Verrill***, *"understands the problems and has a no-nonsense approach to negotiation."* **Linda Bretton***, *"loved at Lasmo for day to day work"* is also recommended as *"good, solid and dependable,"* and moves up the rankings. Recent work has included acting for Lasmo on the £90 million sale of gas assets to Gaz de France, as well as upstream oil and gas financing for CIBC, pipeline agreements, assignment of oil and gas interests and decommissioning work.

In the water sector, the firm acts for the trade association and advises the Water Grid on a number of issues. **Clients:** Lasmo; Water Grid.

Lovells (7 ptrs, 16 asscs) Although still felt to be a *"solid corporate-focused energy team,"* market perception is that the loss of Tony Higginson to Baker Botts leaves a gap that will be difficult to fill.

Known for acting as principal counsel in the UK to Exxon, the group advised on the secondary London listing of Exxon Mobil shares following that merger. Respected for its expertise in finance aspects of the industry, the firm represented JP Morgan on its financial advice to BP during the BP-Amoco merger. In contentious matters, the team has been occupied with extensive litigation and arbitration on FPSOs, dealing with, inter alia, construction and decommissioning. Other contentious work involved advising on a production sharing and joint operating agreement in South America, and contractual disputes over quantity obligations.

On the transactional and regulatory side, as well as continuing to handle claims validation arrangements, for which the team has a long-standing reputation, advice has been given to energy companies on the liberalisation of the European gas market, Interconnector and Network Code issues. Well known to the UK gas community, the *"excellent"* **Michael Stanger*** is held in high regard. At home, the group acted for an international oil and gas company on an Irish power station joint venture and the construction of a power station in England. **Clients:** Exxon Corporation; JP Morgan.

Nabarro Nathanson (6 ptrs, 8 asscs) Domestically-focused energy group, which has been perceived to suffer from the consolidation of the industry and consequent stiffer competition. More positively, the team has carved out a niche (around 15-20% of the market) in CHP power projects, advising on both industrial heating and district heating schemes. Clients like Pilkington Glass, Hays Chemicals and London Electricity have kept the practice as one of the most focused in this area. **Robert Tudway*** continues to be recognised for his abilities as a projects-oriented lawyer. In regulatory issues, the group has advised Slough Heat & Power and others on the licensing and regulation of distribution systems. Importantly, the firm is one of four on the panel of regulator OFGEM. **Gareth Jones*** has solid regulatory expertise and is *"a clever guy."*

The oil and gas team has a new group head, and recently advised Dragon Oil on its EBRD financing for an oil and gas development in Turkmenistan. It also advised BP Amoco on compliance with international trade sanctions imposed by the UN, EU and UK. **Clients:** English Partnerships; Elf; OFGEM.

Simmons & Simmons (15 ptrs, 25 asscs) Broadly based energy practice with a strong regulatory and corporate base and an international presence. In spite of the lateral hire of three new partners, the group does not have as high a profile as might be expected. When the market did comment, however, it was generally positively. *"They advise OFGAS and have done a really good job."* Leading light Charles Bankes is currently on a two-year secondment to OFGEM, and the practice is now one of four on the OFGEM panel.

In non-contentious matters, the highlight was advising government venture capital house UAE Offsets Group on the Project Dolphin joint venture, developing a cross-border gas pipeline project to connect Qatar, the UAE and Oman. The team is regularly involved in litigation on behalf of Esso and Shell and received a boost to its profile by representing ten major oil and gas companies involved in hydrocarbon exploration in the North Atlantic in judicial review proceedings brought by Greenpeace. In the water sector, the firm acted for Spanish company Union Fenosa in its recent acquisition of Cambridge Water and has acted for many years for General Utility (now part of Vivendi). **Clients:** OFGEM; UAE Offsets Group; Shell International.

Vinson & Elkins LLP (7 ptrs, 9 asscs) A global energy presence which joins the rankings for the first time after 25 years in London. Described as *"the only sensible US energy practice in London,"* this is *"a first-class outfit"* which has gained in visibility recently. An expansion drive has netted six additions to the team, mainly from City firms. Renowned for its strong link with Enron, the firm's breadth of work has ushered it into the spotlight. It acts for numerous developer clients on energy-related projects, M&A transactions and capital markets work.

Expertise in pipeline projects has been highlighted by advice on cross-border pipelines in the Baltics, Russia and Central Asia. Downstream the team handles refinery and petrochemicals work, representing a Finnish company to divest its chemicals business to a European private equity fund.

The power industry has seen the team on projects in West Africa, Andalucia and India, primarily on behalf of developers. It has also advised on credit and commodity derivative contract securitisations and private equity fund energy investment into Europe. **Clients:** Enron Corp; Fortum; EBRD.

Other Notable Practitioners Much interest has been occasioned by the departure of **Tony Higginson*** *("has a good bedside manner")* from Lovells to Baker Botts. His challenge is to build a recognised practice at the firm, which hitherto has not shone in London. The high-profile **Mark Saunders*** of Dewey Ballantine also continues to have his champions in the market. At LeBoeuf, Lamb, Greene & MacRae, **Garry Pegg*** is especially known for his work for Claims Validation Services.

U

Intellectual Property

UNITED KINGDOM
Leading firms
(Intellectual Property: Patent)

Band	Firm
1	Bird & Bird
	Bristows
2	Simmons & Simmons
	Taylor Joynson Garrett
3	Herbert Smith
	Linklaters
	Lovells
	Wragge & Co
4	Clifford Chance
5	Baker & McKenzie
	Eversheds
6	Allen & Overy
	Hammond Suddards Edge
	Roiter Zucker
	Stringer Saul

Firms are listed alphabetically in each band.

Bird & Bird (Patent 7 ptrs, 16 asscs; General 17 ptrs, 22 asscs) *"No rubbish or time-wasting"* from this powerhouse of IP. Perceived to be edging more to a technology base by some whilst also acknowledged to have a growing commercial side to the firm. Litigation, however, is what the team is best known for and it sits without question at the top of both the Patent and General league tables. Why? One expert explained it quite simply in terms of *"quality of solicitors and quality & quantity of work. It is a whole firm dedicated to this area of law."* Bird & Bird was in on IP ahead of almost everyone else in the game and the same can be said of the emerging technology sectors. Any talk in the market about a diminished profile is largely explained by the fact that some of their really big patent cases in the last couple of years have now settled. *"Smooth operator"* **Trevor Cook*** *"has a realistic approach to litigation"* whilst senior partner **David Harriss*** is described as *"a fantastic lawyer and an elder statesman in the business."* **Morag MacDonald*** and **Miles Gaythwaite*** each have a fearsome reputation, she as a *"tough opponent"* and he as a *"fierce litigator."* The well-known focus areas of biotech, hi-tech and pharmaceuticals belie a thoroughly impressive client list across the board. Conducted trademark and passing off litigation for Associated Newspapers in relation to the METRO trade mark against the Guardian Group and Modern Times Group. **Clients:** Pfizer; Nestlé; One2One.

Bristows (Patent 11 ptrs, 20 asscs; General 19 ptrs, 33 asscs) If Bird & Bird are still perceived as a niche firm, Bristows are doubly so. Finally free of the *"old family firm image,"* Bristows has emerged once more as an all round leader and a truly *"class act."* It occupies the position of overall joint leader despite the fact that it does not have a giant-sized commercial practice behind it and as a result has an overwhelming bias towards litigation. A common sentiment of the department's work is that it is *"first rate and you know it will always be incredibly thorough."* The fact that so many of them are so well known speaks volumes. *"Clients are guaranteed to like"* **Sally Field***: *"she's very amenable"* and *"gets on with things."* **Ian Judge*** is a man *"looked up to"* by the profession. **David Brown*** *"is a very experienced and competent patent lawyer"* who does *"wonderful work."* Effective **Edward Nodder***, who is seen to be *"involved in so much,"* is promoted in this year's rankings. On the brands side, **Paul Walsh*** *"speaks a lot of sense and he's got – and he keeps – good clients."* In addition to the team size shown, the firm fields two senior IP consultants. Plenty of grey goods actions and a thriving brands prosecution practice has helped see the non-patent work increase at an even faster pace in the last year than the patent work. The numbers of overseas clients instructing on litigation continues to grow. Advising United Distillers & Vintners on brand protection, transactions and co-ordination of foreign litigation. **Clients:** Monsanto/Searle (Pharmacia); Sara Lee UK; Sony Computer Entertainment Europe.

Simmons & Simmons (General 6 ptrs, 15 asscs) Whatever has been happening in the rest of the firm, the IP team has remained immune and it is as strong as ever. Traditionally very good on soft IP, on the patents side, it is now recognised as an equally potent force and is involved in plenty of big cases. **Kevin Mooney*** has put together a *"superb department"* and has a *"strong reputation"* which attracts work to the firm. Other patent litigators commended **Rowan Freeland*** for being *"easy to deal with"* and perhaps *"the backbone of the operation"* at Simmons. He is one of only three lawyers that rose in our leaders' table and now joins the enthusiastically endorsed **Helen Newman***. *"She's quick and efficient and you can't pull a fast one on her!"* **Gerry Kamstra*** heads the firm's pharmaceuticals and biotechnology practice. The pharmaceuticals sector is clearly behind much of Simmons' success but chemicals and electronics are also significant. The practice now manages big-ticket European litigation rather than concentrating purely on domestic bound disputes. The firm has a TM filing practice. Acted for Procter & Gamble on the CA interlocutory hearing concerning disclosure in the patent amendment action with Kimberley-Clark. **Clients:** SmithKline Beecham; 3M; Time Warner Entertainment Co LP.

Taylor Joynson Garrett (Patent 4 ptrs, 7 asscs; General 8 ptrs, 19 asscs) Seen to be really *"holding their own"* and working on *"great cases."* A large department which has come from a smaller start than the other three leaders, the style is seen as distinctively aggressive, and for this reason a few practitioners commented that they were not always the easiest opponents. Others went no further than acknowledging a *"firm but fair"* approach. Litigation is the engine room to the IP practice and there is a self-proclaimed preoccupation with winning. Leading name, *"top notch"* **Mark Hodgson*** *"shows common sense"* and falls squarely within the *"firm but fair"* category. **Gary Moss*** *"is a good operator and he'll fight hard"* and **Richard Price*** is both *"great for PR"* and a tough litigator. **James Marshall***, who specialises in patents, holds a Higher Courts Advocacy Certifi-

*See leaders' profiles on pages 741-782

UNITED KINGDOM Leading firms (Intellectual Property: General)
1 Bird & Bird
Bristows
2 Clifford Chance
Linklaters
Simmons & Simmons
Taylor Joynson Garrett
3 Baker & McKenzie
Eversheds
Herbert Smith
Lovells
Rouse & Co International in association with Willoughby & Partners
4 Allen & Overy
Arnander Irvine & Zietman
Denton Wilde Sapte
Olswang
Slaughter and May
Wragge & Co
5 Ashurst Morris Crisp
CMS Cameron McKenna
DLA
Field Fisher Waterhouse
Freshfields Bruckhaus Deringer
Roiter Zucker
Rowe & Maw

Firms are listed alphabetically in each band.

cate. All the assistants on the patent side have science or technology qualifications. Clients vary enormously from tobacco, food and pharmaceuticals manufacturers through to charities, oil and computer games. The emphasis is on contentious work, but the broader nature of the firm also ensures a modest helping of corporate support work. **Clients:** Eli Lilly; Amgen; Hoechst; Hasbro; Reckitt & Benckiser.

Herbert Smith (Patent 13 asscs; General 3 ptrs, 17 asscs) On a roll at the moment, and clearly more visible than a few years ago. Head of the combined IP/IT department **Bill Moodie*** shows *"intelligence and common sense"* but some question whether his time is spent more on IT matters these days. Nick Gardner, who has performed well in our tables and whose IP record is greatly admired, appears in our IT table, indicating that this now comprises the larger part of his work. *"Effective"* **Mark Shillito*** and **Andrew Rich*** are both involved in massive biotech and pharmaceuticals actions. Rich is running the Erythropoietin patent litigation for Roche Diagnostics and Genetics Institute. Shillito is, in addition to the patent work, keeping his profile on softer matters. There is also strength in counterfeit work and transactional and advisory matters, including handling all the TM work on the BSkyB bid for Manchester United.

The team represented Aventis CropScience in the widely reported hearing on whether Chardon LL (a variety of genetically modified forage maize) should become the first genetically modified agricultural crop to enter the UK National List. **Clients:** Harrods; Vodafone; Formula One Administration.

Linklaters (Patent 4 ptrs, 13 asscs; General 7 ptrs, 25 asscs) The strength of Linklaters' recent reputation in IP is unsurprising. An acknowledged *"steady flow of work"* has involved the very highest profile cases. It is seen to be *"getting the kind of clients every firm would want"* and has *"endless reams of top quality lawyers"* to look after them. In particular, at partner level, **Jeremy Brown*** is unshiftable in the upper reaches of our rankings. He shares this elevated status with **Robin Whaite***, a *"very capable academic lawyer who knows his stuff"* and rises accordingly. At the bar, Whaite is known to *"be thorough in preparation and always have all points of evidence covered – there are never any surprises."* Some regard **Ian Karet*** as *"the most talented young IP lawyer in the City today."* His focus is a very commercial one and he *"gets things done."* An *"established character,"* **Robert Swift*** displays great sense and *"a close understanding of all the issues"* on a case. **Nigel Jones*** concentrates on pharmaceuticals and biotechnology and chairs the firm's Healthcare Group. Further down the line, the practice is felt to have a stack of *"good youngsters."* 23 of the assistants have science or engineering degrees. The integrated TM filing practice is admired by others who operate in that particular field. Acted for the successful patentee in American Home Products v Novartis and on the Davidoff v A&G Imports grey goods case. Retained by Hewlett Packard to co-ordinate multi-jurisdictional litigation against a number of suppliers of components, and continues to represent Microsoft in its anti-counterfeiting work. **Clients:** Lancaster Group/Davidoff; British Airways; Centrica; Forte/Granada; Gucci; Hermes; Lloyds TSB; Matsushita/Panasonic; SmithKline Beecham.

Lovells (Patent 5 ptrs, 18 asscs; General 2 ptrs, 8 asscs) Some high profile patent work has kept Lovells in the limelight and there is a distinct feeling that it has consolidated its position in the biotech/pharmaceuticals and chemicals sectors. Of those specialising in patent work, nine have scientific degrees. Two names stand out: head of department **Robert Anderson***, who is seen to be a tough litigator and can be a *"devil in the detail"* and **Nicholas MacFarlane***, who leads on many of the firm's high profile patent cases. Certain of the more junior members of the department have been noted for their contribution to mediation work. Lovells' merger with German firm Boesebeck Droste is expected to pay dividends in the IP field. The new millennium brought it success on one of the biggest biotech patent trials to date, Monsanto v Merck. Instructed on piracy and other matters by the PRS/MCPS. **Clients:** Exxon; BBC; Reuters.

Wragge & Co (Patent 3 ptrs, 4 asscs) Until its recent merger with Birmingham powerhouse Wragge & Co, Needham & James was an established boutique firm. It was felt to be *"excellent at handling small to medium sized litigation,"* particularly patents, with a really *"sensible"* approach. That market perception didn't quite factor in the size of many of the clients. In terms of size they may have been *"a minnow"* but they were swimming with the big fish daily. Big City players were often surprised that Wragge & Co didn't have a London presence. Their activity in Birmingham rippled through anyway and the marriage with Needham & Grant looks set to provide each of the two firms with what they were looking for. *"Wonderful man"* **Gregor Grant*** *"is getting superb results with a minimalist style." "Effective"* **Adam Cooke*** is seen to have an *"aggressive"* style, whilst **David Gibbins*** is an excellent draftsman and *"fair to deal with."* Acting for Unilever in the action against Nestlé & Ors. **Clients:** Thames Water; Kone; Yamanouchi Pharmaceuticals.

Clifford Chance (General 5 ptrs, 21 asscs) Strong in IP work for the IT sector, including domain names and database rights issues, the team is also recognised for financial services branding, software and confidential information issues. A Goliath in brand management and TM filing, it manages some 30,000 marks. It has embraced the EC trademark office, becoming one of the largest filers in that venue. The firm's foreign offices in Europe have placed CC in a good position to handle multi-jurisdictional disputes. Thought to have been spending a fair amount of time in the US, **David Perkins*** is a *"good ambassador for the firm."* He's *"very commercial and clients love him." "Thorough and meticulous"* **Vanessa Marsland*** is often perceived as an IT lawyer, but her time is more devoted to IP work and not exclusively for IT clients. **Peter Taylor*** is highly regarded for his TM work. Acted for HSBC in its defence of passing off proceedings by HFC which went to the CA in January 2000. On the patents side, the team battled in the so-called 'Kettle Wars' and visited the CA four times in January on the litigation that has arisen from the Bourns v Raychem dispute. **Clients:** Allergan; Volvo; Nike.

UNITED KINGDOM
Leading individuals (Intellectual Property)

Band		
★	**COOK Trevor** *Bird & Bird*	**FIELD Sally** *Bristows*
	GRANT Gregor *Wragge & Co*	**HODGSON Mark** *Taylor Joynson Garrett*
	JUDGE Ian *Bristows*	**MOONEY Kevin** *Simmons & Simmons*
	WILLOUGHBY Anthony *Rouse & Co International in association with Willoughby & Partners*	
1	**ANDERSON Robert** *Lovells*	**BROWN David** *Bristows*
	BROWN Jeremy *Linklaters*	**DAVIES Isabel** *Eversheds*
	FREELAND Rowan *Simmons & Simmons*	**HARRISS David** *Bird & Bird*
	MACDONALD Morag *Bird & Bird*	**MACFARLANE Nicholas** *Lovells*
	MARSLAND Vanessa *Clifford Chance*	**MOSS Gary** *Taylor Joynson Garrett*
	NEWMAN Helen *Simmons & Simmons*	**NODDER Edward** *Bristows*
	PERKINS David *Clifford Chance*	**STARR Ian** *Ashurst Morris Crisp*
	WALSH Paul *Bristows*	**WHAITE Robin** *Linklaters*
2	**COHEN Laurence** *McDermott, Will & Emery*	**COOKE Adam** *Wragge & Co*
	HICKSON Chris *Slaughter and May*	**INGLIS Andrew** *Olswang*
	JONES Stephen *Baker & McKenzie*	**KARET Ian** *Linklaters*
	LLEWELYN David *White & Case LLP*	**PRICE Richard** *Taylor Joynson Garrett*
	SMITH Catriona *Allen & Overy*	**SWIFT Robert** *Linklaters*
	SWYCHER Nigel *Slaughter and May*	
3	**GAYTHWAITE Miles** *Bird & Bird*	**GIBBINS David** *Wragge & Co*
	HARRIS Paul *Eversheds*	**HART Michael** *Baker & McKenzie*
	IRVINE James *Arnander Irvine & Zietman*	**JONES Nigel** *Linklaters*
	KAMSTRA Gerry *Simmons & Simmons*	**MACDONALD-BROWN Charters** *Gouldens*
	MARSHALL James *Taylor Joynson Garrett*	**MARTINDALE Avril** *Freshfields Bruckhaus Deringer*
	MOODIE Bill *Herbert Smith*	**RICH Andrew** *Herbert Smith*
	SHILLITO Mark *Herbert Smith*	**TAYLOR Peter** *Clifford Chance*
4	**BARRY Robert** *Allen & Overy*	**RAWLINSON Paul** *Baker & McKenzie*
	THORNE Clive *Denton Wilde Sapte*	**WOOD Ian** *Rowe & Maw*

Individuals are listed alphabetically in each band.

Baker & McKenzie (Patent 2 ptrs, 5 asscs; General 5 ptrs, 10 asscs) This is a practice which is remarkably strong in the telecoms/IT sector, and as such its reputation in IP can be somewhat overshadowed. However, the department deals with a lot of counterfeiting work and numerous fashion, perfumes and pharmaceuticals clients. Big brand names rest side by side on a long and impressive client roster. *"As long as their people are there they will be doing good work,"* we were told. *"Charming man"* and ex-patent agent **Stephen Jones*** has given it *"a big plus"* on the patent side. Harry Small is ranked in our IT and e-commerce tables as it is in these areas that he spends most of his time. **Michael Hart*** and **Paul Rawlinson*** each have a good name in brand work, particularly in fashion. The department includes a TM filing practice. Acted for co-claimant Pfizer in the patent infringement action against Merck brought by Monsanto and Searle. **Clients:** Sony Corp/Sony UK; Calvin Klein; L'Oréal.

Eversheds (Patent 3 ptrs, 7 asscs; General 6 ptrs, 11 asscs) Strong in media-related copyright and TM work, and exerting a presence in patent litigation on matters such as the Boston Scientific dispute with various Johnson & Johnson subsidiaries and the defence of Hewlett Packard on infringement proceedings. It is for TMs that the team is better known though, and *"high performer"* **Isabel Davies*** is a *"tough cookie"* who commands recognition in this area. Both Davies and **Paul Harris*** (who is also commended for being an exceptionally good speaker on IP matters) conduct patent work in addition to a heavy workload of brand issues, passing off and confidential information cases. It is sometimes said that the London office gets the pick of the best cases attracted to the firm nation-wide, and certainly clients of different regional departments are served by the capital's lawyers on many occasions. Advised Unilever companies on its OXO TM litigation with General Housewares. **Clients:** Nabisco; Porsche; Mothercare.

Allen & Overy (General 4 ptrs, 18 asscs) Generally felt to be still in need of a heavyweight patent litigator but superb for transactional work. It is said of the team that *"they understand deals and have good people who understand IP and the value of it to a deal."* **Catriona Smith*** is *"someone you can do business with."* Praised for sense, calm and versatility, she *"turns her hand to many things."* The team has very recently been expanded at partner level as a result of **Robert Barry**'s* defection from one of Eversheds' northern offices. Acted for Nestlé on the disposal of the Findus brand and for Beckman Coulter and Affymetrix in their litigation with Oxford Gene Technology concerning DNA array chips. It has recently acted for William Hill in their litigation with the British Horse Racing Board on the first ever case in the UK on database rights. **Clients:** Nestlé; Beckman Coulter; William Hill.

Hammond Suddards Edge (Patent 2 ptrs, 6 asscs; General 4 ptrs, 11 asscs) From the Hammonds side of this recently merged firm, there has been an unquestionably strong patent litigation practice, although some find the style a little aggressive and unforgiving. The Edge input is an unquantifiable factor at present. Most work is patents based for the electronics, biotech and pharmaceuticals/agrochemicals markets. The *"serious and established"* Laurence Cohen, however, has left for US firm McDermott, Will & Emery, a move which must be considered a drastic blow. As a whole, the IP team is noted as *"prepared to put itself out"* for clients. Most advocacy is conducted in-house and the firm is looking more to pan-European issues. Acted for the defendant in the OXO TM litigation, Unilever v General Housewares. **Clients:** Aventsis; Thomson Licensing; Imprint Systems.

Roiter Zucker This niche firm which acts for a number of pharmaceutical clients, including generic drugs companies, has built up a splendid reputation through a number of well known patent actions. It features in our Patent table as well as our General IP table this year. It has a focused team which, given its size, associates freely with far bigger outfits. Regarded as a paradigm of a high-achieving niche practice. **Clients:** Pharmaceutical companies.

Stringer Saul (Patent 4 ptrs, 4 asscs) *"A nice little niche outfit"* which is *"highly focused"* in pharmaceuticals and biotech work. New to our Patent table following appointments to major biotech and pharmaceuticals names for patent litigation and licensing work. Involved in multi-jurisdiction litigation for large clients. **Clients:** Celltech Medeva; British Biotech; Antisoma.

*See leaders' profiles on pages 741-782

U

Rouse & Co International in association with Willoughby & Partners (General 6 ptrs, 12 asscs) *"A lovely practice"* with a *"pretty impressive range of clients."* This firm has *"an element of sexiness to it,"* with its Docklands location and collection of ex-City lawyers now working together purely on IP for big brand names. The main man **Anthony Willoughby*** attracts the comment *"Tony is who he is!"* and he is one of IP's most recognisable names. Others describe him as *"best of breed,"* a true TM specialist who has made the firm the equivalent in TM work to Needham & Grant in patent work. Willoughby leads a band of youngsters deemed to be *"competent and enthusiastic."* Acted in the parallel imports litigation between SmithKline Beecham and GlaxoWellcome and in the well-publicised Mont Blanc pens litigation. The team additionally includes two full time senior consultants and a barrister. **Clients:** The Ford Motor Company; Cadbury Schweppes; Coca-Cola.

Arnander Irvine & Zietman (General 7 ptrs, 7 asscs) In the aftermath of the departure of big names from the firm last year, notably David Llewelyn and followers to White & Case, the remaining team has maintained a good profile and a substantial portion of its client base. **James Irvine*** has impressed on some significant litigation. **Clients:** GlaxoWellcome; Ryanair.

Denton Wilde Sapte (General 3 ptrs, 8 asscs) In the short term, the Denton Hall/Wilde Sapte merger is not felt to have altered DH's previous IP capability. However, with fresh talent now bubbling under, it is thought unlikely that **Clive Thorne*** will remain the firm's sole entrant in our Leading Individuals table indefinitely. He heads the combined department. A burgeoning media practice sits alongside the IP/IT contentious team and non-contentious technology team. From each of these three focal points, IP work is drawn. Strong in the financial services industry, media and brand clients, DWS covers all aspects of IP work. Acted for Sony Corporation in its registered design action against Manwa over the 'Sports' personal stereo. **Clients:** Abbey National; Mattel; Honda Motors (Europe) and (Japan).

Olswang (General 2 ptrs, 7 asscs) Although still having to deal with a *"more media"* image, in reality media clients provide just a portion of the IP work. **Andrew Inglis*** packs a *"fair old punch"* in litigation. The caseload can be split into four almost equal servings: TM litigation, patent litigation, licensing and TM filing. Clients come from manufacturing, retail (including internet) media and financial services. Acting for the Czech brewer in the CA litigation over the Budweiser TM. **Clients:** De Beers; The Guardian; RSPCA.

Slaughter and May (General 2 ptrs, 13 asscs) *"Very commercial"* deal man **Nigel Swycher*** splits his time between IP and IT related matters. He is ranked in both tables but in a lower band to reflect the fact that he is not exclusively devoted to either. Litigator **Chris Hickson*** has been described as *"laid back"* with a *"good attitude."* On the transactional side, S&M is deeply respected, but it is felt that it needs to bring on the litigation in order to compete at a higher level all round. Its clients are essentially all large plcs in a broad range of sectors. It advised Cadbury Schweppes on the disposal of its beverage business in several countries to Coca-Cola and concluded and settled patent proceedings for APV (Siebe Group) against Tetrapak. **Clients:** Stena Lines; EMAP; Richemont.

Ashurst Morris Crisp (General 3 ptrs, 20 asscs) A busy practice perceived to be occupied with a large volume of transactional work and parallel imports cases, but in reality covering a fairly extensive range of brand related litigation. **Ian Starr*** is the team's big name. Acting for Johnson & Johnson in the 'no more tears' TM litigation. **Clients:** Nike; Motorola; Galen Holdings.

CMS Cameron McKenna (General 2 ptrs, 12 asscs) Heavily involved with pharmaceuticals, biotech and medical devices clients. Also dealing with a volume of IP related matters pertaining to the internet. The team divides its time equally between corporate support and contentious instructions; most matters are on the softer side although four of the lawyers deal with patent litigation. Acting for Eli Lilly in a High Court case on the repackaging of Prozac, which is now being referred to the ECJ. **Clients:** Asari Medical; Amazon.com; The Post Office.

DLA (General 4 ptrs, 7 asscs) Part of the Communications & Technology group, this is a somewhat lesser known London IP practice. Clients from the media and publishing worlds make up a healthy proportion of the client base on the trade-marks side. This side of the practice is counterbalanced by the activity of the patent specialists within the team. The firm offers a TMs One Stop Shop and the number of marks under management has again leapt up this year. Acting for Unilever in relation to the protection of TMs for Persil and Dove. **Clients:** B Elliott; NTL Group; Yorkshire Television.

Field Fisher Waterhouse (General 11 ptrs, 67 asscs) Best known for its serious TM filing and prosecution practice, it is the recent victim of a break up between the two heads of this element of the practice. The firm's original head has gone to Nabarro Nathanson. This is a department that carries out almost no corporate support work; and its various focus groups are kept busy on stand-alone work. Split into non-contentious (licensing, merchandising and sponsorship) and contentious (mostly TM, design and domain name disputes) in addition to the TM filing practice, the firm also separates out its very successful IT and online unit. Instructed by Ordnance Survey in proceedings against the AA in relation to Crown Copyright in maps. **Clients:** Laura Ashley; Logica; Coca-Cola.

Freshfields Bruckhaus Deringer (General 3 ptrs, 21 asscs) *"Serious people"* who have *"strengthened their corporate support role."* The team is one part of a larger IP network of teams worldwide. The name in London is **Avril Martindale***. Advised Hewlett-Packard in the IP aspects of the demerger, including issues in 40 jurisdictions. **Clients:** AstraZeneca; Wella; Microsoft.

Rowe & Maw (General 6 ptrs, 13 asscs) A very decent practice which has historically come from a corporate support base. Patent and TM litigation now features more prominently. Patent clients tend to be more on the mechanical than pharmaceutical side but the team has done some chemicals work for ICI and some biotech matters for Monsanto. **Ian Wood*** may appear *"relaxed and laid back"* but *"he knows his onions."* Has acted for BP Amoco in the protection of its 'green' TM registrations. **Clients:** AstraZeneca; C&A; Corning Communications.

Other Notable Practitioners **David Llewelyn,** now with White & Case, holds onto his reputation following his move from Llewelyn Zietman. The strong figure at Hammond Suddards Edge, **Laurence Cohen***, *("one of the most industrious lawyers you'll ever meet")* has now moved to McDermott, Will & Emery. At Gouldens, **Charters MacDonald-Brown*** *"leads a young team"* of *"competent"* lawyers.

Private Equity: Buyouts

UNITED KINGDOM Leading firms (Private Equity: Buyouts)
1 Ashurst Morris Crisp
Clifford Chance
2 Allen & Overy
3 Dickson Minto WS
Lovells
4 Macfarlanes
Travers Smith Braithwaite
5 CMS Cameron McKenna
DLA
SJ Berwin & Co

Firms are listed alphabetically in each band.

Leading individuals (Private Equity: Buyouts)
★ GEFFEN Charles *Ashurst Morris Crisp*
1 BAIRD James *Clifford Chance*
DICKSON Alastair *Dickson Minto WS*
LAYTON Matthew *Clifford Chance*
2 BARTER Charles *Travers Smith Braithwaite*
CLARKE Julia *Clifford Chance*
COMPAGNONI Marco *Lovells*
GREEN Geoffrey *Ashurst Morris Crisp*
HALE Chris *Travers Smith Braithwaite*
HANTON Bruce *Ashurst Morris Crisp*
PAUL Alan *Allen & Overy*
TUFFNELL Kevin *Macfarlanes*
3 BEDDOW Simon *Ashurst Morris Crisp*
BOWN Christopher *Freshfields Bruckhaus Deringer*
DAVIS Steven *SJ Berwin & Co*
MARTIN Charles *Macfarlanes*
SHEACH Andrew *CMS Cameron McKenna*
SHELDON Jeremy *Ashurst Morris Crisp*
WAYTE Peter *DLA*
WHITE Graham *SJ Berwin & Co*

Individuals are listed alphabetically in each band.

Ashurst Morris Crisp (7 ptrs) *"The private equity firm of choice,"* benefiting from the momentum of *"a host of excellent players."* Head of Private Equity **Charles Geffen*** has won a huge following with his *"commercial, constructive advice"* and *"sparkling personality." "Never flustered,"* he is *"the man most wanted"* for the largest private equity deals. Although widely perceived to have a managerial, client relationship role, there can be no doubting **Geoffrey Green**'s* position as the firm's *"rainmaker,"* offering a *"huge boost"* to the team's visibility and gravitas. Clients appreciate **Bruce Hanton*** for his *"intelligence and organisational skills,"* and **Simon Beddow*** is widely respected as a *"get on and do it man."* **Jeremy Sheldon*** joins our lists, recommended as a *"capable, trustworthy"* lawyer. Although European offices, in particular Paris and Frankfurt, are adding a credible capability to the London offering, critics fear the team will find it difficult to sell *"the complete package"* without further international refocusing. Advised Nabisco on its joint £1.3 billion bid with Hicks Muse for United Biscuits and the Electra/Candover backed Newmond acquisition of Baxi Heating. The practice also acted for Coller Capital in its £670 million acquisition of NatWest Private Equity Interests. **Clients:** Advent International; Apax; Candover; Cinven; Legal & General Ventures; PPM Ventures; Berkshire Partners; Deutsche Morgan Grenfell.

Clifford Chance (6 ptrs) *"An excellent client base"* and an *"integrated product offering"* contribute to the success of this *"great"* team. Cross-border activity and a steady deal flow from Europe have been well served by the firm's recent mergers. Rogers & Wells is perceived to offer closer links with US-based private equity houses (and the high yield market,) with the team increasing the number of transactions for KKR. The *"terrific"* **James Baird*** is *"unflappable"* and is praised for developing relations with influential equity houses. **Matthew Layton*** is *"energetic and bright"* and **Julia Clarke*** is said to have *"the right attitude."* Collectively, clients appreciate the firm as *"excellent deal-doers."* The practice advised Schroder Ventures in the $2.3 billion purchase of VEBA Electronics Group, from Germany based E.ON. It also acted for CVC Capital Partners in the $400 million cross-border acquisition of the sealing systems business of Invensys, and on the MBO of the stockbroking firm Collins Stewart from the Singer and Friedlander Group. **Clients:** CVC Capital Partners; Schroder Ventures; NatWest Private Equity; PPM Vantures; Industri Kapital; Candover; KKR; Apax; Citigroup; Chase Manhattan; Bankers Trust/Deutsche Bank; Barclays Capital; Merrill Lynch; CSFB.

Allen & Overy (3 ptrs) Eclipsed somewhat (and occasionally conflicted) by a strong hold in debt financing, the equity team is pushing forward on the back of a strong international presence. **Alan Paul*** is *"excellent"* but is in danger of being *"spread too thinly."* The team has a reputation for complex, cross-border deals, but lacks the depth of the market leaders. The practice acted for KKR on its £627 million buy-out of conglomerate Wassell, the team's first transaction for the US-based private equity house. **Clients:** Morgan Grefell Private Equity; KKR; CVC; Lafarge Platres International; Barclays; Deutsche Bank; Fuji Bank; Goldman Sachs International; Salomon Smith Barney; JP Morgan; Lehman Brothers Chase Manhattan.

Dickson Minto WS (4 ptrs) A small team seen to offer *"high quality solutions."* Though lacking the fire-power of an international network or a strong banking practice, this team is praised for its *"clear focus."* **Alastair Dickson*** is envied by peers for inspiring client loyalty and is said to be *"an excellent deal-maker."* **Clients:** Mercury Private Equity; Cinven; Apax Partners; Charterhouse Development Capital; Royal Bank of Scotland; Commerzbank; West LB Leveraged Finance.

Lovells (5 ptrs) The merger with Boesebeck Droste has been met with approval by the market for the stability and concerted effort this presence will bring to its private equity clients based in Germany. The group has been dealt a blow by the departure of Allan Murray-Jones although it is still too early to tell to what extent this loss will affect the practice. The main focus for the equity team remains the *"energetic"* **Marco Compagnoni***, *"sharp, intelligent and quick-witted."* He acted for Doughty Hanson on the cross border MBO of Umbro International (£98 million) and for January Investments on the MBI of Sears plc (£519 million). **Clients:** Doughty Hanson & Co; Mercury Asset Management; 3i Group; PPM Ventures; Mercury Private Equity; CSFB; Bank of Scotland; Barclays Bank; Crédit Agricole Indosuez.

Macfarlanes (6 ptrs) Capitalising on strengths in the domestic market but said to be hampered by the lack of a strong debt finance team. This *"quality"* team is starting to build on its international contacts in overseas law firms. **Kevin Tuffnell*** brings a *"great presence"* to deals which are *"always extremely well managed."* **Charles Martin*** is a *"major asset"* to the private equity team and is widely respected for advising Alchemy Partners on its failed bid for Rover.

Recent deals in the private equity/buy-out arena include acting for Alchemy on the public to privates of Brooks Service Group and William Baird for £26.1 million and £107.5 million respectively. **Clients:** Cinven ; Candover; Legal & General Ventures; Alchemy Partners; William Baird.

Travers Smith Braithwaite (6 ptrs) A leading firm for private equity, it is seen as an *"active"*

*See leaders' profiles on pages 741-782

buy-out team with a sound base of institutional clients such as Candover and NatWest. **Chris Hale*** is *"technically sound and practical"* and is seen as the mainstay of the team. **Charles Barter*** runs deals with a *"pleasant manner"* and *"inspires confidence."* Although perceived as having a primarily domestic focus, the firm is establishing relationships in key European markets (most successfully in Paris) to undertake cross-border transactions. Highlights include advising the management team on the £220 million MBO of Thomson Directories and acting for Denitz Media on its £92 million public to private MBI of Adscene group. **Clients:** NatWest Equity Partners; Candover; 3i; DLJ Phoenix.

CMS Cameron McKenna (6 ptrs) A *"sizeable"* and well regarded team with an *"international reach which lacks the penetration of the leaders."* The firm's CMS network is thought not to have provided the transactional depth required. **Andrew Sheach*** is *"going from strength to strength"* as he builds up a solid following with the equity houses. He *"controls deals well,"* but is thought to lack support. Highlights for the team include acting for ABN AMRO Capital on the MBO of the toiletries business of UK medical group Smith & Nephew, a deal valued at £170 million.

Advised Legal & General Ventures (LGV) in the sale of Golden Wonder Holdings, a secondary MBO worth £156.5 million. Also acted for NatWest Equity Partners (now Bridgepoint Capital,) in relation to the disposal of the entire issued share capital of RIVA Clubs, valued at £90 million. **Clients:** NatWest Equity Partners; Advent International; Mercury Asset Management; Legal & General Ventures; Lloyds TSB Development Capital.

DLA (7 ptrs) *"A fine but limited practice"* which is seen to build on its national base with *"big ticket regional buy-outs as its bread and butter."* **Peter Wayte*** maintains his reputation as a leading player in the equity market. The team has acted on substantial deals including for HSBC Private Equity/Newco on the institutional buy-out of Col-Art International Holdings (value £100 million). **Clients:** CVC Capital Partners; HSBC Private Equity; Barclays Ventures; Gresham Trust; Bank of Scotland; Royal Bank of Scotland.

S J Berwin & Co (4 ptrs) Acting from the base of a strong investment funds practice, this team is admired for its strong following with major private equity houses. This is a young team, *"improving with each transactional experience."* *"Impressive and proactive"* **Steven Davis*** is said to be *"valuable for his strategic knowledge."* **Graham White*** is *"an asset"* and a *"user-friendly point man"* for the team. He advised Candover on the £210 million MBO of First Leisure's bar and nightclub operation. **Clients:** Apax Partners; Phildrew Ventures; Atlas Venture; Candover; Barclays Private Equity.

Other Notable Practitioner **Christopher Bown*** of Freshfields Bruckhaus Deringer has a *"bright, positive attitude"* and has focused the team towards larger, international deals.

Project Finance

UNITED KINGDOM
Leading firms (Project Finance)

Band	Firm
1	Allen & Overy
2	Clifford Chance
	Linklaters
3	Freshfields Bruckhaus Deringer
	Norton Rose
4	CMS Cameron McKenna
	Denton Wilde Sapte
	Herbert Smith
5	Ashurst Morris Crisp
	Lovells
	Milbank, Tweed, Hadley & McCloy
	Shearman & Sterling
	Slaughter and May
	White & Case LLP

Firms are listed alphabetically in each band.

Allen & Overy (27 ptrs, 50 asscs) **Projects:** A *"stunningly brilliant"* projects team packed with *"big personalities,"* it is seen to be pulling away from the chasing pack with a successful combination of banking expertise and recent moves into the sponsor market. The firm advises on all industry sectors with particular strengths in power, energy and transport and has a truly international penetration. **Graham Vinter*** is universally recognised as *"a star"* and the mainstay of the projects team alongside the seasoned **Jonathan Horsfall Turner*** *("a get it done lawyer")* and **David Sedgley*** *("technically strong,")* who is also seen as active in the PFI sphere. Experienced players **Anthony Humphrey*** *("a good head for complex documentation")* and **Brian Harrison***, who is *"sensitive without being soft,"* are joined by a new name to our list, **Stephen Gillespie***, receiving praise for his *"excellent finance mind."* Advised Japan Bank for International Co-operation on its involvement in the $1.6 billion limited recourse financing of oil and gas reserves in Brazil.

PFI: A star player in the PFI market, **Anne Baldock*** is *"extremely bright, personable and practical,"* leading the PFI/PPP side of this practice which has a good mix of clients, notably the firm's traditional bias towards lenders, but also sponsors and concession granting authorities. Growth areas are health, defence, accommodation and transport. Acted for lenders on resurrected treasury building projects including refurbishment and subsequent facilities management, and acted for a joint sponsor of St George's Hospital project who contributed both equity and debt to the project. Recent PFI/PPP instructions have come from Germany, South Africa and Portugal.

Other highlights include advice to Bank Hapolim in its capacity as senior lender to the Cross Israel Highway and in relation to the inter-creditor issues between itself and Newcourt Capital, arrangers of bond financing and the providers of other debt financing to the project.

The practice also advised the banks financing the £2.4 billion WIND Telecommunications fixed line and mobile phone network project in Italy, and advised the Export-Import Bank of Japan in relation to the $700 million Cabiunas Pipeline Project in Brazil. **Clients:** The Japan Bank for International Co-operation; Barclays Bank; Premier Prison Services.

Clifford Chance (20 ptrs, 55 asscs) **Projects:** *"Impressive"* practice praised for its *"flexibility and cohesion,"* which has an enviable reputation acting mainly for sponsors and banks. London Projects Group head, **Peter Blake***, is recognised for his expertise in the energy field, and his enthusiasm has played a leading role in successful projects such as Sidi Krir Power Project in Egypt (for sponsors) and Ujpest CHP Power Project in Hungary (for lenders). He is ably supported by a balanced team including **Tim Soutar***, who has long overseas experience. **David Bickerton***, *"commercially astute and pragmatic,"* is praised for his construction work, and the *"excellent"* **Margaret Gossling*** is a strong force in the banking aspects of project finance. **Chris Wyman*** has

UNITED KINGDOM
Leading individuals (Projects)

Band	Name	Firm
1	**BARRATT Jeffery**	*Norton Rose*
	BLACK Alan	*Linklaters*
	SALT Stuart	*Linklaters*
	VINTER Graham	*Allen & Overy*
2	**BLAKE Peter**	*Clifford Chance*
	HORSFALL TURNER Jonathan	*Allen & Overy*
	MACRITCHIE Kenneth	*Shearman & Sterling*
	SEDGLEY David	*Allen & Overy*
3	**BELLHOUSE John**	*White & Case LLP*
	BUCKWORTH Nicolas	*Shearman & Sterling*
	ELSEY Mark	*Ashurst Morris Crisp*
	FINLAY Peter	*White & Case LLP*
	FLETCHER Philip	*Milbank, Tweed*
	FOX Jason	*Herbert Smith*
	GILLESPIE Stephen	*Allen & Overy*
	GOSSLING Margaret	*Clifford Chance*
	HARRISON Brian	*Allen & Overy*
	HUMPHREY Anthony	*Allen & Overy*
	RANSOME Clive	*Linklaters*
	ROWEY Kent	*Freshfields Bruckhaus Deringer*
	WEBER David	*Linklaters*
	WYMAN Chris	*Clifford Chance*
4	**BICKERTON David**	*Clifford Chance*
	CRANE David	*Norton Rose*
	HALL Peter	*Norton Rose*
	LEVINE Marshall	*Linklaters*
	McCORMICK Roger	*Freshfields Bruckhaus*
	McQUATER Gavin	*Lovells*
	PHILLIPS Robert	*CMS Cameron McKenna*
	PREECE Andrew	*Herbert Smith*
	SOUTAR Tim	*Clifford Chance*
	TEMPLETON-KNIGHT Jane	*Hunton & Williams*

Individuals are listed alphabetically in each band.

Leading individuals (PFI)

Band	Name	Firm
★	**BALDOCK Anne**	*Allen & Overy*
	BLISS Nick	*Freshfields Bruckhaus Deringer*
	WHITE Bruce	*Linklaters*
1	**MATHEOU Michael**	*Lovells*
	NOBLE Perry	*Freshfields Bruckhaus Deringer*
	STEADMAN Tim	*Clifford Chance*
	TOTT Nick	*Herbert Smith*
2	**COULTER David**	*Norton Rose*
	DUFFICY Frank	*CMS Cameron McKenna*
	ELSEY Mark	*Ashurst Morris Crisp*
	FOX Jason	*Herbert Smith*
	JOHNSTON Bruce	*Weil, Gotshal & Manges*

Individuals are listed alphabetically in each band.

spent the bulk of the year increasing the practice's presence in India, resulting in advice on 27 IPPs but a diminished profile in the domestic market. Acted as local counsel for lenders in the $575 million Flag Atlantic telecoms deal in the US, and as foreign sponsor counsel for Phillips Petroleum on the $1 billion Q-Chem petrochemical project in Qatar. More recent highlights include advice to the lead arrangers in relation to the financing of a pipeline between South West Chad and the Cameroon Coast.

Advised IFC, DEG and CDC Group in relation to the construction of a 74MW diesel-engine, heavy fuel-oil fired electricity-generating plant located near Mombassa in Kenya. This was the first IPP in eastern Africa and one of only a very small number of power deals ever to be completed in Sub-Saharan Africa.

PFI: Perceived by the market as a balanced practice in terms of UK domestic PFI and international projects, the practice has been involved in high profile deals such as advising the consortium (Rotch Property Group and J Henry Schroder & Co) on the Chichester NHS Trust project which involved a £1 billion bond monoline wrapped programme for public sector related projects. Prominence across the board including defence (MoD Tornado Simulator Project,) accommodation (advice to bidding consortium on transfer of Inland Revenue and Customs & Excise property portfolio STEPS) and transport (A13 Thames Gateway). The integrated team includes *"first class"* **Tim Steadman***, a strong-minded player who is recognised for his construction work. He is also seen as the force pushing international PFI deals which include the Beira Interior road project in Portugal (advising project company) and Nedco N4 Platinum Toll Highway in South Africa (advising lenders.)

Recently acted for Modus Services and its sponsors throughout the negotiations which led to the successful award of a contract worth £1.6 billion over its 30 year duration with MoD to design and redevelop the MoD's headquarters in Whitehall. **Clients:** Abbey National Treasury Services; Banque Paribas; Babcock & Brown; Hyder Investments.

Linklaters (36 ptrs, 90 asscs) **Projects:** Recommended for *"consistent"* quality of work and a smooth operating process, this practice is headed by **Alan Black*** *("sharp mind, impressive style")* who has a strong reputation in the energy markets. The *"marvellous"* **Stuart Salt*** is seen as a commercially minded and pragmatic deal-doer who occupies the top spot in our rankings. *"Old hand"* **David Weber*** is highly rated for his work on the Chad-Cameroon pipeline. **Clive Ransome*** maintains his reputation for international work. As a new name **Marshall Levine***, prominent for for his construction work, is *"always on the ball."* With a well balanced client base, this practice has strengths in power generation and distribution, transport, water, telecoms and infrastructure work. The practice advised the Greek Government on a $2.5 billion project financing of a ring-road around Athens. Also acted for the sponsor consortium (affiliates of ExxonMobil, Petronas and Chevron) on the $4 billion Chad-Cameroon Oilfield Development and Petroleum Export System project, and for the lenders to the Changsha Power Project in China, a 2x360MW coal fired power station in Hunan Province ($750m).

PFI: The integrated team benefits from the presence of **Bruce White***, universally recommended as *"a star"* for his leadership skills, huge personality and following in the banking sector. Growth areas for the practice this year include defence (MoD Skynet 5 projects) and education (Glasgow Schools.) Acted for the sponsors of the £340 million London CityLink radio transmission project, for the lenders in the refinancing of Fazakerley prison and for the sponsors on the £60 million IT PFI project for HM Customs & Excise.

Advising Financial Security Assurance (UK) as monoline insurer, and Deutsche Bank as lead manager and underwriter, on the £406 million monoline wrapped senior bond issue to finance the project for the provision of serviced accommodation to GCHQ in Cheltenham, under the UK Private Finance Initiative. This is the largest PFI bond issue and the largest single government accommodation project under the PFI. **Clients:** National Power; ABN AMRO; Deutsche Bank; Carillion; Enron; Edison Mission Energy; Marubeni; BP; BG; Shell; Bank of America; EBRD.

Freshfields Bruckhaus Deringer (25 ptrs, 50 asscs) **Projects:** A significant practice in project finance, with an outstanding focus on PFI. The team is said to be *"slicker than most,"* with a strong international presence acting on both the sponsor and lender side. The market was fulsome in its praise of the team's *"financial acumen."* Head of the global project finance practice **Kent Rowey*** is *"a highly skilled, personable chap,"* and is joined in the rankings by the *"diligent"* **Roger McCormick***. Strengths include transport (advised Derech Eretz Highways on the $1.35 billion financing of the Cross-Israel Toll Road project, the largest in Israel) and energy. The department advised OPIC on the financing of the $600 million Cuiaba Integrated Power project, one of first combined pipeline and power station projects to be financed on a limited recourse basis.

*See leaders' profiles on pages 741-782

PFI: With major clients in all sectors of the market and a firm grip on the domestic scene, this side of the practice is seen as particularly impressive. **Nick Bliss*** remains the leading light and is recommended as *"commercial, aggressively bright and a value for money lawyer."* The team is further strengthened by **Perry Noble***, who is admired for his London Transport work and is praised as *"experienced, trustworthy and intelligent."* Advised Warburg Dillon Read on the financing of Section 2 of the Channel Tunnel Rail Link and over the last three years has advised London Underground on the Connect (digital communication) project. The firm was also recognised for its work with Financial Security Assurance in advising on the Eurobond issuance programme of up to £1 billion for the financing of PPP and public sector-related projects. **Clients:** Warburg Dillon Read; Financial Security Assurance; London Transport; Conoco.

Norton Rose (12 ptrs, 52 asscs) **Projects:** *"Delightful"* projects team praised across the board for its international presence and pre-eminence in the energy and infrastructure market, with a balanced client base acting for financiers, multi-laterals and developers. The seasoned team is led by **Jeffery Barratt***, who is *"traditional"* and *" excellent in attitude and skill."* Michael Taylor has moved to Italy, where he features in our tables. The team is joined by other newly ranked names. **Peter Hall*** is recommended for his skilled construction work and **David Crane*** is felt to bring specialist contractual strengths to power deals *("he handles complex issues with ease, distilling points clearly and accurately.")* However, the firm is perceived to suffer from a lack of US capacity and a weakness in capital markets which sets it apart from the three market leaders. Acted for AES Corporation and achieved financial close of the acquisition of Drax power station from National Power (£1.875 billion.) Also advised Paribas in connection with the TotalFina/Tractabel consortium bid for Taweelah A1 independent power and water project. Also advised the project company in the Athens Ring Road project ($3 billion.)

PFI: Perceived by the market as a minor focus for the projects finance team, PFI activity has nevertheless included a number of high profile clients. *"Charismatic"* **David Coulter*** is praised for his focus on this area and his reputation within the financial sector. Acted for Bank of America, RBS, Toronto-Dominion Bank and Bayerische Landesbank in the funding of the London Underground Project Connect. Advised the consortium of Taylor Woodrow and London & Regional Properties on the £130 million Sheffield, Heart of the City regeneration project. **Clients:** Paribas; RBS; Charterhouse Bank; Norsk Hydro (UK).

CMS Cameron McKenna (22 ptrs, 50 asscs) **Projects:** Recommended as a *"professional"* team with a niche strength in electricity, the practice is finding it hard to shake off the public sector tag which has historically generated the most work. The *"excellent"* **Robert Phillips*** is perceived to be making the push into international project finance and is praised for his strong leadership style. The firm has a niche strength in electricity, both in the domestic and international market, and has advised Budapest Eromu (a joint venture between Fortum of Finland and Tomen Corporation of Japan) on Hungary's second independent power project. **PFI:** With a background in construction, **Frank Dufficy*** is praised as *"a commercial, capable lawyer, a deal maker."* Advised the British Government on the restructuring of Channel Tunnel Rail Link (including raising £2.65 billion of new financing) and advised private sector sponsors on concession agreements, finance agreements and other project documents for the first local authority DBFO (A130) road project (£80 million). **Clients:** Department of Transport; Cinergy Global Power.

Denton Wilde Sapte (27 ptrs, 12 asscs) **Projects:** Market perception of the February 2000 merger is *"a natural fit with obvious synergies,"* with the team benefiting from the traditional Wilde Sapte banking strengths and the Denton Hall energy market domination. However, the jury is still out on the strategy needed to lift the team out of the chasing pack, with the firm's smaller international offices not considered sufficient to compete evenly with the market leaders. The projects team has a focus on the areas of energy/power, telecoms and infrastructure. Active overseas, it has recently advised ECGD on prospective financing to the $1.4 billion Visakhapatnam Power project in India and advised Oman LNG and Abu Dhabi Gas Liquefaction Co on supply arrangements for Enron's Dabhol power project Phase II.

PFI: Continued as advisors on MoD's nationwide water and waste water project and acted for a Carillion-led consortium on healthcare projects, including a major acute hospital project for Swindon and Marlborough NHS Trust. **Clients:** MoD; Laing Hyder; Total Oil UK; Virgin Rail; Standard Chartered Bank.

Herbert Smith (30 ptrs, 50 asscs) **Projects:** Perceived to be a leading figure in the domestic market, but lacking the banking strengths and overseas presence necessary to threaten the leaders. The team is felt to have a more balanced client base than most, acting for its traditional base of public sector outfits as well as a growing number of funders and sponsors. Leading figures ranked in the tables for both Projects and PFI are **Jason Fox***, recommended as *"a delight to work with,"* and *"old hand"* **Andrew Preece***, who advised London and Continental Railways on its reorganisation and the joint venture with Railtrack on the £5 billion bond and loan financing of the Channel Tunnel Rail Link construction. The practice also acted as international counsel for ICICI, the lead arranger in relation to the Samayanallur power project in Tamil Nadu, India, and advised Chase Manhattan on the limited recourse financing arrangement for an oil and gas field in Burma.

PFI: Renowned for its big ticket work for the public sector, the firm has advised bidding consortia (Bechtel, GKN/McDonnell Douglas) and banks (Bank of Tokyo Mitsubishi, Bank of America, Deutsche Bank, Barclays.) **Nick Tott*** is praised as *"a professional, clever person with good ideas"* and *"handles complex documentation with a clear head."* The team as a whole receives mixed reviews, with commendations for a *"pleasant"* office, *"working to a common purpose,"* countered by fears over a lack of quality support at assistant level. Advised Bank of Tokyo Mitsubishi on its debt financing of the IT infrastructure transaction for HM Customs & Excise and advised Bombardier Group on the £150 million PFI project providing aircraft and services to the RAF's Light Aircraft Flying Task. **Clients:** Bank of Tokyo Mitsubishi; GCHQ; Highways Agency; Bechtel.

Ashurst Morris Crisp (8 ptrs, 17 asscs) **Projects:** Recognised as a sponsor-led practice active in energy, transport and the niche sector of mining, it also benefits from international exposure with Europe, Africa and India being particularly strong areas for work. Department head **Mark Elsey*** is recommended both in project finance and PFI work but is perceived to receive *"variable"* support.

Acted for the winning bidder, N3TC, for the N3 toll road project in South Africa and acted for Marubeni (sponsors) and EPC (contractor) on the $300 million PPN power project in Tamil Nadu, India. Also advising the Hong Kong Government on the HK$16 billion Cyberport project in Hong Kong.

PFI: A number of big-name construction clients have driven this area of the practice which is also active in exporting PFI principles to Portugal (acting for Aenor consortium on North Toll Road project) and Japan (representing Vivendi/Marubeni consortium on water and waste treatment projects.) The team acted on the £150 million Treasury Building project (GOGGS) for Exchequer Partnership consortium (Bovis, Stanhope and Chesterton,) and for Integrated Accommodation Services on the £450 million GCHQ New Accommodation project. This is the largest PFI bond financed project to achieve financial close to date. **Clients:** National Power; Marubeni; Barclays Bank; Amey; Sir Robert McAlpine Ltd.

Lovells (12 ptrs, 15 asscs) **Projects:** Perceived by the market to be most active in PFI, the team has yet to achieve similar recognition for its international project finance work. It has nevertheless benefited from the merger with Boesebeck Droste and a greater access to European-based clients. Group head **Gavin McQuater*** is well respected *("good finance brain")* but is thought to spread himself over a wide spectrum of work. On the international front, acted for Nissho Iwai Corporation (sponsor and senior lender) on the $344 million combined-cycle power plant in Playas de Rosicrito, Mexico. Domestically, acted for Sport England (Lottery funder and original promoter) on the £480 million Wembley National Stadium project.

PFI: Good reputation for both its public sector and private client capacity. **Michael Matheou***, *"strong in corporate documentation and commercially pragmatic,"* has recently advised the government on the standardisation of PFI documentation. Acted for the Inland Revenue and Customs & Excise on the STEPS project, and acted for National Air Traffic Services on its high profile planned PPP.

Recently advised King's Healthcare Trust as contracting authority on their PFI scheme to design, build, finance and operate a new hospital and refurbish a portion of their existing hospital premises. Also represented one of the sponsors in connection with the provision of services and accommodation to the Ministry of Defence at HMS Drake, Devonport, as part of the Armada project. **Clients:** Inland Revenue; Nissho Iwai Corporation; Sport England.

Milbank, Tweed, Hadley & McCloy (6 ptrs, 4 asscs) A force to be reckoned with on the global market and perceived to be the one US firm active in the domestic energy market, advising NatWest in relation to the £200 million Shoreham power project. A strong base within the banking sector and pre-eminence in the energy market has given the team the depth to develop niche sectors such as the financing of wind farms and satellite projects. Led by **Philip Fletcher*** *("a strong personality,")* the team is thought easily able to weather the defection of Jane Templeton-Knight to Hunton & Williams. Advised CSFB on the $160 million financing for construction and delivery of Nigeria LNG's expansion project to transport gas to Europe. The practice continues to be strong in India ($1 billion North Chennai power project, for the lenders) and the Middle East (Taweelah A1 power and desalination facility in Abu Dhabi for the consortium of Total and Tractqbel), and continues to dominate the Italian power market. **Clients:** CSFB; NatWest.

Shearman & Sterling Renowned for banking strength and global presence, the *"well-established"* London team is highly regarded in the oil, gas and telecoms fields and is perceived to be a team of *"international stars"* rather than competitors on the domestic scene. Highly regarded department head **Kenneth MacRitchie*** is *"a great lawyer with a top level intellect"* and is supported by the increasingly high-profile **Nicolas Buckworth***, praised for his *"sensible"* work in Eastern Europe. They advised Barclays Capital on the Taweelah A2 Power and Desalination project and the arranging banks (including ABN AMRO, Citibank, Crédit Lyonnais and West LB) on the $450 million San Lorenzo gas-fired power project. Also acted for InterGenENKA on their 3 BO projects in Turkey, creating 2,800MW of new gas fired generation in Turkey at a total cost of over $2 billion, and for AES in the Banka IWPP in Oman. **Clients:** ABN AMRO; Barclays Capital; BG; P&O Ports.

Slaughter and May (28 ptrs) **Projects:** Considered by the market to lack interest in this area, the *"blue-blooded"* team draws on the talents of partners and associates from across the whole firm. A lack of international leverage has also been cited as a hindrance to the firm in this area of practice. Despite this, the firm is seen acting on big-ticket projects and PFIs, thanks to a *"stunning"* client base. The practice is particularly recommended for its strength in tax and complex financial documentation. Advised RBS on the Virgin Trains project, providing new rolling stock for West Coast Main Line. Internationally prominent deals include acting for Eastern Power & Electricity Trading on funding for a hydro-electric power project in Svartisen, Norway. **PFI:** High-profile work in this arena has included advising the Department of the Environment, Transport and the Regions on the PPP for National Air Traffic Services, and acting for the arranging banks for the preferred bidders on the MoD redevelopment of offices in Whitehall. **Clients:** NATS; RBS; Eastern Power & Electricity Trading.

White & Case LLP (4 ptrs, 18 asscs) *"Serious projects people,"* praised for their *"versatility, the quality of work and balanced client base."* Market perception remains that while they are a powerful force on the global scene, domestic project/PFI work is a lesser focus. Department head **Peter Finlay*** has the *"exposure to major international clients"* and is recognised for establishing the London office. He is supported by the *"seasoned"* **John Bellhouse***, recommended for his construction expertise. Margaret Cole has moved to Singapore. Domestically, the team has advised the National Grid Company on the first project financing for the 40MW electrical interconnector, linking the Isle of Man to the electricity pool of England. International deals include representing the state-owned Cross-Israel Highway Authority on the $1.3 billion road toll project (Israel's first BOT project) and representing senior lenders (IFC, Asian Development Bank and CDC) on the $240 million financing of a container terminal in Colombo, Sri Lanka. **Clients:** IFC; Asian Development Bank; National Grid.

Other Notable Practitioners At Weil, Gotshal & Manges, *"impressive"* **Bruce Johnston*** is *"a diligent, highly-rated operator."* **Jane Templeton-Knight*** of Hunton & Williams has a reputation for *"understanding complex transactions."*

*See leaders' profiles on pages 741-782

Shipping

UNITED KINGDOM
Leading firms (Shipping: Dry)
1 Holman Fenwick & Willan
Ince & Co
2 Clyde & Co
3 Hill Taylor Dickinson
Richards Butler
4 Norton Rose
Sinclair Roche & Temperley
Stephenson Harwood
5 Clifford Chance

Firms are listed alphabetically in each band.

Leading firms (Shipping: Wet)
1 Holman Fenwick & Willan
Ince & Co
2 Clyde & Co
3 Hill Taylor Dickinson

Firms are listed alphabetically in each band.

Leading firms (Shipping: Finance)
1 Norton Rose
2 Watson, Farley & Williams
3 Allen & Overy
Stephenson Harwood
4 Clifford Chance
Sinclair Roche & Temperley

Firms are listed alphabetically in each band.

Holman Fenwick & Willan (Dry 27 ptrs, 33 asscs; Wet 9 ptrs, 11 asscs) Seen as a *"supremely confident"* outfit, the firm's individual litigators are perceived to *"get to the merits of a dispute quickly."* While the firm's worldwide reputation for salvage work is felt to be *"beyond compare,"* the team move up in our dry table, largely due to their involvement in heavyweight foreign litigation. The firm's continuing global expansion (particularly the recent opening of the Shanghai office) has noticeably lifted its profile in this area. For wet work, salvage expert **Archie Bishop***, while less involved in day to day work, is still thought to be the figurehead. He is the principal architect of the well-publicised SCOPIC clause. Fellow wet lawyer **James Gosling*** *("an absolute gent")* receives high praise from the London market. His ability to *"turn his hand to anything"* is much admired. The firm is known to be well connected within the German, Far East and Greek owner markets. For dry work, **Hugh Livingstone*** *("the rainmaker,")* **Robert Wilson*** *("committed to his clients,")* **Richard Crump*** *("outstanding – a good fighter,")* **Marcus Bowman*** and **Michael Donithorn*** were singled out for mention. The team has strong ties with the Scandinavian club market. **Clients:** Owners; clubs; charterers.

Ince & Co (Dry 39 ptrs, 46 asscs; Wet 10 ptrs, 10 asscs) Ubiquitous shipping practice *("they seem to be everywhere at the moment")* who have a *"big reputation and some loyal clients."* The market views the firm's ability to secure both *"volume and quality"* from a diverse client-base as the main driving force behind its success. The practice is seen by many to be *"more rounded"* than the immediate competition. Particularly respected for marine casualty work, the team has acted on a host of pollution incidents. Despite the retirement of respected practitioner Richard Williams, the team retains its strength in the field. **Richard Sayer*** has a reputation as *"one of the eminences grises,"* **Bob Deering*** *("goes the extra mile")* is felt to have had a particularly good year and **Paul Herring*** *("straightforward and excellent to deal with")* is highly recommended for charterparty work. **James Wilson*** and **Colin de la Rue*** are seen as *"true heavyweights"* for their admiralty work, while **Jonathan Lux*** and **Malcolm Strong*** also maintain their reputations. An acknowledged ability in dry work is highlighted by the firm's huge caseload on behalf of container operators. The team has advised clients, *inter alia*, on the termination of charters by reason of the operation of war clauses. **Clients:** Container operators; P&I clubs; insurers; underwriters.

Clyde & Co (Dry & Wet total 47 ptrs, 69 asscs) An extremely diverse practice *("the firm is clearly not embedded in any one house")* which, although historically aligned with cargo interests, has a substantial owner and banking client base. However, while the firm is clearly a major shipping force *("you ignore them at your peril,")* its sustained push into corporate work has led to market opinion that it lacks the punch of the leading pair for pure shipping instructions.

The quality of the individual partners, particularly towards the top end of the notepaper, is beyond doubt. Of those recommended, **Clive Thorp*** *("enthusiastic,")* cargo claims expert **Derek Hodgson*** *("a true problem-solver,")* **Benjamin Browne***, **Tony Thomas*** and **Simon Fletcher*** *("the archetypal cargo man")* all receive strong market feedback. The team has seen increased work on behalf of owners, P&I clubs, charterers and salvors, and advised on collisions such as 'Bukhta Uliss/Olympic Frost' and casualty instructions from such clients as the owners of the 'Giovanna.' A successful litigation practice and a number of leading salvage cases (the firm is counsel to Lloyd's and IUA on all salvage and general average matters) round out a high-profile portfolio. **Clients:** Lloyd's; IUA; salvors; P&I clubs; charterers; oil companies; banks.

Hill Taylor Dickinson (Dry 8 ptrs, 14 asscs; Wet 6 ptrs, 3 asscs) This *"ambitious"* firm is accorded respect from the London market, not least because of the *"absolute quality"* of its individual litigators. **Andrew Johnson*** *("the thinking man's lawyer")* is an *"impressive"* character who, despite his seafaring background, focuses predominantly on dry work – marine insurance and coverage disputes are particular areas of expertise. Fears that the team's strong Lloyd's connections may be detracting from its pure shipping profile have been allayed, although there is no doubt that the departure of Kevin Sach will hurt the practice in the short term. A traditional focus on salvage and hull market work has been bolstered by a strong owner presence in both wet and dry instructions – the team is known to be well-connected in continental Europe, Japan and Scandinavia. The firm's wet practice is particularly well respected, although its ability to compete for the headline casualty work is thought to be hampered by a paucity of foreign offices. Nonetheless, **Tim Taylor***, **Robert Wallis*** and **John Evans*** *("very bright – rarely gets it wrong")* are much admired by their competitors. The group has acted on a number of charterparty disputes, including unsafe port claims, and has been instructed in several recent salvage and insurance claims cases. **Clients:** P&I clubs; owners; insurers.

Richards Butler (Dry 14 ptrs, 21 asscs) Felt to be *"in the ascendancy,"* the shipping group has recovered its strong reputation within the London market. Although known historically as a dry practice, the team are making a play for a greater share of wet work, with ex-seafarer **Richard Harvey*** *("gets straight down to business")* newly recommended by his peers. The team has been involved in major collision and salvage work, including the 'Sea-Land Mariner' and 'Maersk Tokyo' cases. On the dry side, the team are respected for *"making a point properly and not being unduly aggressive."* **Lindsay East*** *("great clients, liked by the clubs,")* **Andrew Taylor*** *("sensible, knows what he's talking about")* and **Graham Harris*** *("facilitates the deal – doesn't posture unnecessarily")* all come highly recommended. Strong owner and club connections are especially notable in Italy, and the team gets a lot of spin-

UNITED KINGDOM Leading individuals (Shipping: Dry & Wet)	
★ **BISHOP Archie** *Holman Fenwick & Willan*	**SAYER Richard** *Ince & Co*
VLASTO Tony *Clifford Chance*	
1 **CRUMP Richard** *Holman Fenwick & Willan*	**DEERING Bob** *Ince & Co*
GOSLING James *Holman Fenwick & Willan*	**HERRING Paul** *Ince & Co*
HODGSON Derek *Clyde & Co*	**ROOTH Tony** *Watson, Farley & Williams*
TAYLOR Timothy *Hill Taylor Dickinson*	**TAYLOR Andrew** *Richards Butler*
WALLIS Robert *Hill Taylor Dickinson*	**WILSON James** *Ince & Co*
WILSON Robert *Holman Fenwick & Willan*	
2 **EAST Lindsay** *Richards Butler*	**EVANS John** *Hill Taylor Dickinson*
FLETCHER Simon *Clyde & Co*	**GHIRARDANI Paolo** *Stephenson Harwood*
HARVEY Richard *Richards Butler*	**HOBBS Christopher** *Norton Rose*
JOHNSON Andrew *Hill Taylor Dickinson*	**LIVINGSTONE Hugh** *Holman Fenwick & Willan*
LUX Jonathan *Ince & Co*	**STRONG Malcolm** *Ince & Co*
THOMAS Anthony *Clyde & Co*	**THORP Clive** *Clyde & Co*
3 **ATKINSON Joe** *Sinclair Roche & Temperley*	**BLANCH Juliet** *Norton Rose*
BOWMAN Marcus *Holman Fenwick & Willan*	**BROWNE Benjamin** *Clyde & Co*
DE LA RUE Colin *Ince & Co*	**DONITHORN Michael** *Holman Fenwick & Willan*
HARRIS Graham *Richards Butler*	**LOWE Steven** *Stephenson Harwood*

Individuals are listed alphabetically in each band.

Leading individuals (Shipping: Finance)	
1 **SHELTON John** *Norton Rose*	**WATSON Martin** *Watson, Farley & Williams*
2 **FARLEY Alastair** *Watson, Farley & Williams*	**SMITH David** *Allen & Overy*
3 **GIBB Jeremy** *Norton Rose*	**RUSSELL Mark** *Stephenson Harwood*
WARDER David *Watson, Farley & Williams*	
4 **TURNER Paul** *Clifford Chance*	
Up-and-coming individuals	
HARTLEY Simon *Norton Rose*	

Individuals are listed alphabetically in each band.

off litigation work from the firm's established ship financing arm. Acting for the liquidators, the team has handled all the disposals, selling and arresting relating to the liquidation of the Romanian state shipping fleet Navron. **Clients:** Louis Dreyfus; Steamship Mutual.

Norton Rose (Dry 12 ptrs, 34 asscs; Finance 8 ptrs, 20 asscs) Although historically considered a bolt-on to the firm's superior asset financing arm, the firm's litigation team is now being taken seriously in its own right. Known for the strength of its dry and commodities practices, the firm is acknowledged to be building up wet side strength, making a number of lateral hires. Overseas offices in Piraeus and Singapore have also been key elements in raising the firm's all-round profile. **Chris Hobbs*** *("smooth and good with clients")* is the club man (particularly within the Italian market,) although he is also known for his oil and gas commodities work. **Juliet Blanch***, meanwhile, straddles both wet and dry, and is particularly prominent in the US and Mediterranean cruise and passenger ship markets. On the ship financing side, the firm's profile is on the up, with both **John Shelton*** (debt re-structuring) and **Jeremy Gibb*** (leasing) considered practitioners of unusual merit. **Simon Hartley*** *("well organised and calm")* is ranked for the first time this year. The team acts for a range of owners, managers, clubs and underwriters, and acted for ANZ Investment Bank in documenting a large syndicated loan facility in connection with the construction of the first LNG carrier for transportation from the Middle East to the Dabhol power plant in India. The firm has also acted on the 'Ya Mawlaya' collision action. **Clients:** Columbia Ship Management; North of England P&I; A Bilbrough & Co; Stena Group; P&O Group.

Sinclair Roche & Temperley (Dry 14 ptrs, 16 asscs; Finance 6 ptrs, 7 asscs) After some much-publicised personnel departures in recent years, the firm continues to surprise the market with the speed with which it has turned things around. Although still viewed as lacking 'big hitters', the firm moves up in wet and receives good market feedback for its impressive financing arm. Indeed, it is for ship financing work that the firm is best known, due mainly to its impressive international banking clients. Bolstered by the recent addition of two specialists from Constant & Constant, the team is particularly strong in the German and Scandinavian markets where it has long-standing connections. The team notably represented Kreditanstalt für Wiederaufbau in a complex structured UK tax lease transaction for a £250 million containerships contract. Also active in the cruise ship and ferry markets. On the wet side, **Joe Atkinson*** is ranked for the first time and is viewed to be *"quietly yet competently"* increasing the firm's market presence. The practice is widely perceived to get a high volume of litigation (wet and dry) referrals from its banking clients. Well connected within the German, South East Asian and Korean owner markets, the team also acts for a range of owners and charterers. **Clients:** Kreditanstalt fur Wiederaufbau; Commerzbank; Daewoo; Den Norske Bank; owners/charterers/tankers.

Stephenson Harwood (Dry 5 ptrs, 3 asscs; Finance 3 ptrs) The firm attracts mixed views from the market this year, possessing undoubted *"pockets of excellence"* although appearing to lack identity as a group. The firm's reputation in this area continues to lie with its ship financiers whose competitive fee structures and volume output afford the team excellent market coverage. Lead partner **Mark Russell*** *("an intelligent practitioner")* is known to act predominantly for international shipyards and owners – the firm is particularly well-connected in Piraeus and Singapore where it has established offices. The finance department provides the dry litigators with a substantial amount of court-approved sales and mortgage enforcement work. The litigation team is known for its involvement in complex foreign litigation, with **Paolo Ghirardani*** *("forever on your back but does an unbelievable job for his clients")* considered a star performer for his asset tracing work. **Steven Lowe*** is also mentioned for his shipping and re-insurance practice.

The team acted for a P&I club to assist in negotiations leading to the release of a crew held hostage on the 'Dubai Valour' for two years in an inland Nigerian port. **Clients:** Greek owners; banks; owners; clubs; insurers.

U

*See leaders' profiles on pages 741-782

Clifford Chance (Dry 3 ptrs, 11 asscs; Finance 4 ptrs, 12 asscs) Perceived as a *"mega-case"* firm which, whilst lacking market profile for day to day shipping work, is known to be largely synonymous with the bigger-ticket deals. On the litigation side, the team's reputation rests on the shoulders of charismatic partner **Tony Vlasto*** *("a superstar in the City")* who receives overwhelming praise from the London market. Known historically for the quality of his wet practice, his caseload now straddles most aspects of contentious shipping including some mortgage enforcement work. The team continues to advise NYK on a significant dispute with the shipyard CIBC, involving three new buildings. On the ship financing side the team is active in the highly remunerative cruise and ferry markets. Notable examples of work include cruise industry projects for Star Cruises, Norwegian Cruise Line and ResidenSea. **Paul Turner*** enters our tables for the first time and is known to be well connected within the Korean owners' market. **Clients:** Owners; clubs; insurers; charterers.

Watson, Farley & Williams (Finance 27 ptrs, 54 asscs) Considered an *"immense force"* in international financings although, for the more complex structured deals, it is thought to lack the substantial capital markets expertise of its nearest competitor. Nonetheless, the firm's strength in New York and Paris cannot be underestimated and gives the London team its edge. Led by **Martin Watson*** *("a phenomenon")* and ex-senior partner **Alastair Farley*** *("now back at the coal-face")*, the team acts for both banks and owners and has particularly strong connections within the French and Scandinavian markets. **David Warder*** *("intellect, tenacity and ability")* enters our tables for the first time this year. On the dry litigation side, **Tony Rooth*** *("brilliant")* appears to have steadied the ship and is building an impressive practice. Known to have strong, long-standing Turkish owner connections, the team is kept busy by the firm's overall blue chip client base, and a smaller amount of P&I Club work. **Clients:** Owners; clubs.

Allen & Overy (Finance 18 ptrs, 25 asscs) A relative newcomer to the ship financing world, the firm is being carefully watched by the more established market players *("you never underestimate A&O.")* Although its current penetration is thought to be relatively small, the team is establishing a reputation for undertaking some extremely *"sexy"* (i.e. complex and highly remunerative) transactional work. The firm's superior capital markets and banking expertise is an obvious advantage. The focal point of the team is (ex-Wilde Sapte partner) **David Smith*** *("aggressive when required")* who is considered an expert on structured leasing deals. The team acts predominantly for banks, although two ship owners have been added to the client base this year. Advised on the headline $262 million financing for the construction of 'ultra-luxury' apartments at sea. **Clients:** Banks; owners.

Tax

Freshfields Bruckhaus Deringer (13 ptrs, 31 asscs) Most solicitors clearly regard the practice as London's number one, due to the *"sheer number of quality people." "It has the full range, talent is widespread and there are no weak links in the chain."* Most acknowledged that this was the first team to spring to mind for cross-border work, a position reinforced by the Bruckhaus link-up.

The growing London practice, headed by all-rounder **Richard Ballard*** (a *"bright, knowledgeable and common sense"* practitioner) is involved on the majority of high-profile UK and cross-border M&A and specialist financing transactions. It also has strong reputations in insurance and energy as well as in general corporate advisory, traditional litigation and investigation work. The internationalisation of the practice continues apace, with cross-referrals from Continental offices on the increase. Around half the practice's work is self-generated, consisting mainly of pure corporate consultancy work and advisory work for investment banks on financial products.

The asset finance and securitisation practices of the firm are market leaders and as these are tax-heavy areas, it is no surprise that the firm is considered to have a leading finance tax team. Head of the tax finance practice is the *"super"* **David Taylor***, a leasing and structured finance expert who *"can turn his hand to anything"* and who is appreciated for his drafting skills and *"commercial and non-combative approach."* **Sue Porter*** is a *"technical and sensible"* capital markets and securitisation expert who *"takes a focused approach."* The *"easy to get on with"* **Ben Staveley*** is considered *"real quality."* His work is primarily in banking and derivatives, though he was praised for securitisation and other structured finance work.

Head of the corporate finance practice is **Timothy Ling***, a highly rated lawyer who is perceived to have *"eschewed the limelight."* The popular **Francis Sandison*** is well regarded on VAT matters, but is principally known for his M&A corporate tax work. He is appreciated for his *"clear-thinking and sense of humour."* All in the market find **Sarah Falk*** *"impressive,"* and she is *"bright, pleasant and on top of things."* Maintaining his reputation in a more specialist area is **Michael Thompson***, an energy specialist. High profile merger work this year includes the RBS bid for NatWest (£26.5 billion,) the AirTouch merger with Vodafone (£37.5 billion,) the EMI music business merger with Time Warner (£12 billion) and reorganisations of AstraZeneca and ICI. **Clients:** Goldman Sachs; Deutsche; ING; Chase Manhattan; HSBC; Warburg Pincus; General Motors; Ford; L'Oréal; ICI; Monsanto; Nestlé; RJR Nabisco; IBM; Olivetti; Matra Marconi; MCI WorldCom; Nokia; Reuters; Siemens; Lloyd's of London; Marsh & McLennan; AMP; SwissRe; RJB Mining; Enron; Gazprom; Airbus; Virgin Atlantic; Associated Newspapers; Bank of England; EMI Group; Sotheby's; Tesco.

Slaughter and May (8 ptrs, 25 asscs) While rivals like to suggest that the firm is *"missing out on the big finance deals"* and *"not keeping up internationally,"* all concede that the practice has exceptional strength for major City work. As well as M&A-related tax, where *"they are top,"* the practice is highly regarded for structured finance work, particularly asset finance and financial product development work. What really keeps the practice at the top and differentiates it from the competition is its *"confident and robust"* attitude towards tax advice, summed up by one US investment banker: *"If they think it'll work they'll say so and they'll believe what they say."*

The doyen of tax lawyers remains **Steve Edge*** who *"stands alone."* He is a *"seriously able practitioner"* who some say is *"a victim of his own success as it is hard to pin him down."* He works on a mix of M&A and structured finance, with more of a bias towards financial work and consultancy for US clients. While his *"creativity and experience"* alone entitle him to respect, it is his *"appreciation of commercial imperatives and how markets*

UNITED KINGDOM Leading firms (Tax)
1 Freshfields Bruckhaus Deringer
Slaughter and May
2 Clifford Chance
Linklaters
3 Allen & Overy
4 Ashurst Morris Crisp
Herbert Smith
Lovells
Macfarlanes
Norton Rose
SJ Berwin & Co

Firms are listed alphabetically in each band.

Leading individuals (Tax)
★ **EDGE Steve** *Slaughter and May*
1 **BALLARD Richard** *Freshfields Bruckhaus*
FRENCH Douglas *Clifford Chance*
LEWIS David *Allen & Overy*
MARTIN David *Herbert Smith*
MEARS Patrick *Allen & Overy*
NORFOLK Christopher *Norton Rose*
NOWLAN Howard *Slaughter and May*
STAVELEY Ben *Freshfields Bruckhaus*
TAYLOR David *Freshfields Bruckhaus*
2 **AIRS Graham** *Slaughter and May*
ELMAN Jonathan *Clifford Chance*
FALK Sarah *Freshfields Bruckhaus*
FRASER Ross *Herbert Smith*
NOBLE Nicholas *Field Fisher Waterhouse*
PORTER Susan *Freshfields Bruckhaus*
RUPAL Yash *Linklaters*
SANDISON Francis *Freshfields Bruckhaus*
THOMPSON Michael *Freshfields Bruckhaus*
WALTON Miles *Allen & Overy*
WATSON John *Ashurst Morris Crisp*
3 **BALDWIN Mark** *Macfarlanes*
BEARE Tony *Slaughter and May*
BRANNAN Guy *Linklaters*
CRAWFORD Sue *Ashurst Morris Crisp*
DORAN Nigel *Macfarlanes*
ELLIOTT Peter *Clifford Chance*
GREENBANK Ashley *Macfarlanes*
HARDWICK Michael *Linklaters*
JOHNSON Ian *Ashurst Morris Crisp*
LING Timothy *Freshfields Bruckhaus*
MEHTA Nikhil *Linklaters*
ROSS Howard *Clifford Chance*
SCOTT Thomas *Linklaters*

Individuals are listed alphabetically in each band.

work," as well as his *"helpfulness,"* which are really appreciated by clients and peers alike. He has *"seen and done everything" – "a client would say fine to the most creative and innovative idea, but would want to get Steve's blessing."*

One of the *"understated tax heroes of the City"* is **Howard Nowlan***, traditionally an M&A tax expert. He is *"one of a dying breed,"* an all-round adviser who *"balances common sense, charm, a sense of humour and technical expertise."* He is said to have *"a clear understanding of the objectives he's working to, he is not distracted by irrelevant detail and he gets things done."* **Tony Beare*** is an all-rounder, especially appreciated by financial clients, while **Graham Airs*** is regarded as a *"creative international tax man."*

This is a broad practice which, as well as providing advice for the firm's well-known UK clients, also advises US and other international corporates and financials. A high proportion of the team's work is pure tax consultancy, and the department includes an ex-Inland Revenue investigation team for investigatory and litigation work. High profile M&A transactions this year include the Reckitt & Colman/Benckiser, Astra/Zeneca, BAT/Rothmans and Carlton/United News & Media link-ups. Other corporate transactions include the disposals involving Allied/Punch, Guardian Royal Exchange/Aegon and Huntsman/ICI and the demutualisations of Old Mutual and Canada Life. The team also advised on asset finance transactions for groups such as RBS (Virgin Rail West Coast Financing) and British Airways. **Clients:** Royal Bank of Scotland; British Airways; Punch; Reckitt & Colman; Carlton; Guardian Royal Exchange; Old Mutual.

Clifford Chance (17 ptrs, 36 asscs) The team offers a *"technically proficient and never less than reasonable service."* While some view the practice as *"a bit of a sleeping giant,"* clients and solicitors alike comment on the *"range of expertise at partner level."* This is especially seen on the finance side, where the team is seen as *"the first choice."* In particular, the practice is felt to have *"a huge share of the securitisation market."* Advice here is generally regarded as *"sound and cautious rather than aggressive."*

Head of the practice is the popular and *"commercial"* **Douglas French***, known primarily for his M&A work. He *"makes sure you have an answer. He always knows who knows and quite often he knows himself."* **Jonathan Elman*** is a leader for structured finance work. He is *"extremely perceptive"* and *"highly creative; nothing is to difficult for him."* Although *"he can be abrasive,"* no-one doubts his commitment. He is admired for *"going the extra mile, he really cares."* Although retired as an equity partner, **Howard Ross*** continues to run the tax litigation practice, and is admired for his *"experience and wide knowledge."* All-rounder **Peter Elliott*** maintains his reputation.

Financial highlights this year were the Barclays Credit Card and Formula One securitisations. M&A work includes the attempted Air Products/Air Liquide joint bid for BOC and mergers in areas such as telecoms and insurance. The tripartite international merger has encouraged an increasing number of instructions across the network, such as advising on the Merrill Lynch and HSBC joint venture in internet private banking. **Clients:** ABN AMRO; Barclays; Candover; Chase Manhattan; Coca-Cola; Deutsche; Dresdner; GE Capital; Goldman Sachs; KKR; Merrill Lynch; Nomura Securities; Morgan Stanley Dean Witter; VW/Audi; Whitbread; Société Générale; Paribas; CVC Capital Partners; Carlton.

Linklaters (11 ptrs, 24 asscs) Whilst involved on the major corporate deals of the year, the practice is generally viewed by the market to have *"lost a bit of punch"* as a result of Tony Angel's move to managing partner. Of the younger generation, **Yash Rupal*** *("a clever financial products person")* is seen as one of the team's torchbearers, and his secondment to Merrill Lynch's M&A department is perceived to have deprived the practice of a leading light on the finance side, though the long-term benefits may be greater. The firm is perceived to have a practice skewed heavily towards M&A as opposed to structured finance, especially when compared to leading rivals.

However, the tax team is still considered to be *"strong and steady,"* and *"still appears on the top deals."* Internationally, clients praise the *"ideas and ability to implement them"* at the firm, as well as the consistent quality of the drafting. Corporate tax all-rounder **Guy Brannan*** is *"good to deal with."* Other rated M&A-connected practitioners include **Michael Hardwick*** and the *"tough"* **Thomas Scott***, who also works on financial issues. He advised BG on its £13 billion restructuring, preparatory to its proposed demerger. **Nikhil Mehta*** is respected for international work, works on financial issues and is also head of the practice's contentious group.

Corporate work includes the Vodafone/Airtouch/Mannesmann and Reckitt & Colman/Benckiser link-ups, NatWest's bid defence, BP Amoco's acquisitions and Lloyds TSB's acquisition of Scottish Widows. Major reorganisations were those of Allied Domecq, Cable & Wireless, BAe and Tarmac. The practice advised Halifax on the first issue by a UK bank of tax-deductible Tier 1 Capital, and National Power's £8.4 billion demerger into Innogy and International Power. **Clients:** Allied Domecq;

*See leaders' profiles on pages 741-782

Bass; British Airways; BG; BP; BT; Elf; Enron; Rio Tinto; Unigate; AstraZeneca; Sedgwick; Scottish & Newcastle; National Power; Jardines; Halifax; CitiGroup; CSFB; DLJ; Goldman Sachs; Merrill Lynch.

Allen & Overy (7 ptrs, 30 asscs) Seen to have *"gone for it in a big way,"* the tax practice has *"beefed up and considerably raised its profile."* It is especially well regarded for finance work (although corporate work makes up nearly half the practice's workload,) but is not yet considered to possess the profile of its most direct competitor in tax finance work, Clifford Chance. The team has a reputation for *"professional, technically good and conservative advice."* All-rounder **Patrick Mears*** *("a careful lateral thinker")* is recognised as the driving force behind the growth of the practice, which includes talent at all levels. **Miles Walton*** has an excellent reputation in the financial world. On corporate matters, the *"meticulous and streetwise"* **David Lewis*** is *"a joy to work with."*

The team advised on the Punch Taverns saga and on disposals for Cable & Wireless. Work includes advising on the Drax power station acquisition and the Vodafone/Airtouch/Mannesman deal, advising on the Broadgate and London City airport securitisations and on British Aerospace exchangeables into Orange. Tax investigation and litigation advice are other fortes. **Clients:** Hill Samuel Asset Management; ING Barings; Misys; NatWest; Citibank; Chase Manhattan; Deutsche Bank; IBJ; Bass; Cable & Wireless; Morgan Stanley; WDR; Lehman Brothers; Goldman Sachs; Barclays; Bank of America; British Aerospace; Flemings; TI Group; Rexam; News International.

Ashurst Morris Crisp (5 ptrs, 20 asscs) A growing corporate and financial practice held in high regard for its venture capital expertise. Commentators have immense respect for the *"unique"* **John Watson*** who heads the department. The *"impressive"* **Sue Crawford*** has *"real energy, she puts a lot into it."* **Ian Johnson*** is *"nobody's fool"* on the financial side, and clients find him *"great for brainstorming."*

Outside traditional tax work (corporate, property and financial advisory,) the practice advises on a range of issues, including litigation and VAT matters. Work this year includes advising venture capital houses Cinven and CVC on their joint £825 million acquisition of William Hill, acting for Nabisco Holdings on its £1.5 billion recommended offer for United Biscuits in conjunction with Hicks Muse and advising NRG Energy in its $640 million power station acquisition. Expanding areas include e-commerce, property (enterprise zones) and private company work. **Clients:** Deutsche Telekom; ABM AMRO; Electra Fleming; Imperial Tobacco; Virgin; Yahoo!; IBM; Royal & Sun Alliance; iMeta; Finmeccanica; Invesco; AMVESCAP; Candover; Cinven; Barclays Private Equity.

Herbert Smith (4 ptrs, 16 asscs) The team is especially recommended for property, energy, insurance, projects, VAT and M&A. The team also gained recognition for its work on collective investments. Regarded to have the *"slight edge in M&A"* over its immediate competitors, clients praised the team for its *"technical ability"* and for *"understanding our corporate culture."*

Ross Fraser* is an all-rounder, especially well regarded for insurance work, while **David Martin**'s* primary reputation is in the corporate arena.

The practice continues to be strong for contentious work and is increasing its e-commerce and internet workload. Work includes advising Merrill Lynch in connection with its role as lead manager of £1.2 billion of bonds issued by Edison First Power to finance power station acquisitions, advising Securicor on tax aspects of the £3.15 billion disposal of its share in Cellnet to BT, and advising CSFB and Cazenove on the Freeserve IPO. **Clients:** Pearson; Highland Distillers; Hammerson; Automobile Association; Lazards; Goldman Sachs; Bombardier Group; Moorfield Estates; BAT; Merrill Lynch.

Lovells (9 ptrs, 10 asscs) A *"creative and pragmatic"* team, rated for its *"technical expertise."* A broad practice, particularly well regarded for property and VAT work. A range of talented individuals is making its mark in a practice with *"genuine depth."* Work includes advising Racal on the £1 billion disposal of Racal Telecoms to Global Crossings, Granada on a joint venture with Nomura, Wyndham International on the disposal of a hotel chain and Texaco on the sale and leaseback of its UK corporate headquarters at Canary Wharf. **Clients:** Racal; Wyndham International; Texaco; Granada Group.

Macfarlanes (3 ptrs, 4 asscs) A small, concentrated team, generally regarded to be doing cutting-edge work on public and private corporate matters. *"They have done well, especially in M&A, and the individual partners are bloody good."* The *"superb"* **Mark Baldwin*** *"does everything,"* and is known for investment funds and property work. He is also considered a *"bright guy and good bloke"* on VAT matters. **Nigel Doran*** and **Ashley Greenbank*** maintain their reputations in corporate, funds and private (entrepreneurial) client work. Private equity and property fund work are growth areas. Advised on Vivendi's acquisition of Medi-Media, Virgin's sale of a stake in Virgin Atlantic to Singapore Airlines and Hawkpoint on the buy-out of the company from NatWest. **Clients:** Cordiant Communications; Abbey Life; Deutsche Morgan Grenfell; Legal & General; Alchemy; 3i; Scottish Life; Vivendi.

Norton Rose (6 ptrs, 11 asscs) An *"intelligent"* team, *"capable of acting on major work"* and rated as one of the best for asset finance-related work. Also received praise from solicitors and clients for other structured finance work. The senior player of the team is the *"clever, experienced and sensible"* **Chris Norfolk***. *"The complexity of the deal is why we went to him,"* commented one client after a recent major acquisition in the financial sector. He has an *"unbelievable work capacity"* and is *"great for uncovering technical problems."* Corporate work accounts for around half the practice's workload. Growing areas include collective investment scheme advice. **Clients:** AES; Mannesmann; Finalrealm; AIG; Anheuser-Buch Group; Carlsberg International; Deutsche Morgan Grenfell; HSBC; KLM; Lloyds Leasing; Mitsubishi Trust & Banking Co; Siemens; P&O; Stena Group.

SJ Berwin & Co (6 ptrs, 10 asscs) This *"transactional"* practice is regarded as being *"at the forefront of venture capital and collective investment scheme work."* Commentators mentioned the difficulty of picking out individuals from a team regarded as *"top from the technical point of view."*

The team works on private equity, public M&A, restructuring, property, film financing, share schemes and partnership disposals/mergers. Advised on Candover's acquisition of the nightclub and bars operations of First Leisure and on Future Publishing's admission to the LSE and its acquisition of Imagine Media. On the property side, the team acted for Chelsfield on its acquisition of the City Gate complex and British Land on its acquisition of Sheffield's Meadowhall shopping centre. **Clients:** The British Land Company; Abbey National; Candover; Apax partners; Electra Fleming; Delancey Group; Deutsche Bank; Schroder Ventures; Paribas Principal Investments; Dresdner Kleinwort Benson; J Sainsbury.

Other Notable Practitioner **Nicholas Noble*** of Field Fisher Waterhouse has an established reputation as a leading tax player.

*See leaders' profiles on pages 741-782

Leaders' profiles – United Kingdom

AINSWORTH, Lesley
Lovells, London +44 20 7296 2000
lesley.ainsworth@lovells.com
Recommended in Competition/Anti-trust
Specialisation: Head of EU and Competition Law group in London. Advises on EC and UK competition law. Represents clients under investigation by the European Commission and the UK office of Fair Trading and Competition Commission including monopoly investigations. Involved in handling dawn raids and the development of competition compliance programmes. Advises on merger clearance applications and other competition aspects of M&A and joint venture transactions. Advises on the regulatory regimes for utilities. Frequent lecturer on competition law. Recent jobs include OM Gruppen bid for London Stock Exchange, Competition Commission investigation into the supply of motor cars, Doughty Hanson & Co/Ranks Hovis McDougall, CSF Thomson/Racal, advising leading record company on AOL/Time Warner/EMO mergers.
Prof. Memberships: Law Society, City of London Solicitors Company.
Career: Qualified in 1981 at *Lovells.* Practised in the firm's Brussels office in the mid – 1980's and subsequently spent time on secondment to the anti-trust department of New York law firm before returning to London. Became a partner in 1988.

AIRS, Graham
Slaughter and May, London +44 20 7600 1200
graham.airs@slaughterandmay.com
Recommended in Tax
Specialisation: Principal area of practice is corporate tax. Particular experience of privatisations, securitisations, mergers and acquisitions. Author of chapter on 'EC Direct Tax Measures' in Tolley's Tax Planning.
Prof. Memberships: The Law Society's Revenue Law Committee, The Law Society, European American Taxation Institute.
Career: Qualified in 1978 after articles at *Slaughter and May* and stayed at firm until 1980. Partner in *Airs Dickinson* 1980-1984. Returned to *Slaughter and May* 1984 and became a Partner in 1987.
Personal: Born 8 August 1953. Married Stephanie 1981. Educated Newport (Essex) Grammar, Emmanuel College, Cambridge.

AITMAN, David
Denton Wilde Sapte, London +44 20 7242 1212
dca@dentonwildesapte.com
Recommended in Competition/Anti-trust
Specialisation: Partner, Head of Competition and EC department, advising on all areas of EC and domestic competition law, particularly in the energy, transport, manufacturing, retail, communications and media sectors. Also on regulation, in connection with privatised utilities. Practice covers notifications and complaints to the European Commission, the Office of Fair Trading, the Monopolies and Mergers Commission, Oftel, the Restrictive Practices Court and the DTI.
Prof. Memberships: Competition Law Association, International Bar Association.
Publications: Editor of section on intellectual property licensing in Butterworths' 'Encyclopedia of Competition Law', of the sections on competition law in 'Practical Intellectual Property', in the 'Yearbook of Media Law' and author of telecoms chapter in 'Bellamy & Child'.
Career: Qualified in 1982 after articles at *Denton Hall.* Became a partner of the firm in 1988.
Personal: Born 1956. Educated at Clifton College, Bristol, then Sheffield University 1975-78 (English Literature) and the Royal Academy of Music (1978). Leisure interests include music, theatre, reading, wind-surfing and skiing.

ALLAN, Bill
Linklaters (a member firm of Linklaters & Alliance), London +44 20 7456 2000
bill.allan@linklaters.com
Recommended in Competition/Anti-trust
Specialisation: Specialist in EC and UK anti-trust law, mergers and acquisitions, and other competition and trade-related areas of the law. Has extensive experience in the UK and EC context, representing clients from diverse industries including utilities, food, transport, brewing, leisure, chemicals, construction materials and computers. Publications include 'Competition Laws of the United Kingdom and Republic of Ireland'.
Career: Head of the EU and Competition Law Group since 1999.

ALLEN, Maurice
White & Case LLP, London +44 20 7397 3690
mallen@whitecase.com
Recommended in Banking & Finance
Specialisation: One of the City's leading lawyers. Has extensive experience in advising on all aspects of banking law with particular expertise in acquisition finance. Leads the banking practice of *White & Case* in London. Joined the firm from *Weil, Gotshal & Manges* and was previously a partner at *Clifford Chance.*

ALLEN-JONES, Charles
Linklaters (a member firm of Linklaters & Alliance), London +44 20 7456 2000
charles.allen-jones@linklaters.com
Recommended in Corporate/Commercial
Specialisation: Senior Partner and Co-chairman *Linklaters & Alliance.* Head of *Linklaters* HK 1976-81. Specialist in corporate matters, particularly equity issues, public and private acquisitions, reorganisations and projects. Responsible for managing the firm's relationships with several key clients.

ANDERSON, Neil T.
Sullivan & Cromwell, London +44 20 7710 6500
andersonn@sullcrom.com
Recommended in Corporate Finance: Mergers & Acquisitions
Specialisation: Actively involved in corporate matters for almost 30 years, focusing primarily on mergers and acquisition transactions in the U.S. and Europe, hostile takeovers and hostile takeover defense, dispositions, joint ventures and proxy contests. Involved in numerous significant M&A transactions for domestic and foreign clients of the firm and has acted for companies and investment bankers in many larger contested takeover battles. Recent M&A transactions include representation of Union Carbide in its pending merger with Dow; Royal Philips Electronics in the sale of its PolyGram subsidiary to Seagram, its friendly acquisition of ATL Ultrasound and its successful unsolicited tender offer acquisition of VLSI Technology; Grand Metropolitan in its merger with Guinness creating Diageo; Upjohn in its merger with Pharmacia; Pharmacia & Upjohn in its merger with Monsanto; and Western Resources in its unsolicited tender offer for Kansas City Power.
Prof. Memberships: American Bar Association.
Publications: Frequent speaker and faculty member on professional seminars and programs dealing with M&A and related matters.
Career: Entire professional career at *Sullivan & Cromwell,* starting in 1971. Became partner in 1979. Senior member of Mergers and Acquisitions Group.
Personal: Born in Jamestown, New York. U.S. Army, 1969-1974. Graduate of Columbia College and Columbia Law School.

ANDERSON, Robert
Lovells, London +44 20 7296 2000
robert.anderson@lovells.com
Recommended in Intellectual Property
Specialisation: Intellectual property and technology. Patent litigation – has particular experience of cases with a chemical, pharmaceutical and biotechnological content. Designs, copyright, trade secrets and trade marks. R&D agreements and acquisitions and joint ventures involving technology based businesses. Also other matters involving computers, pharmaceuticals, biotechnology or otherwise having a high technology content. Lectures on patent litigation for the Bristol University IP Diploma and at Edinburgh University for the LLM course.
Prof. Memberships: AIPPI, Associate Member Chartered Institute of Patent Agents, Solicitors European Group, City of London Law Society Intellectual Property Sub-Committee, IPLA.
Career: BSc Edinburgh (Natural Sciences), 1968. Articled *Bristows Cooke and Carpmael,* admitted 1972; joined *Lovells* 1974; partner 1978.

AP SIMON, Charles
Freshfields Bruckhaus Deringer, London +44 20 7936 4000
charles.apsimon@freshfields.com
Recommended in Corporate/Commercial
Specialisation: Partner in Corporate Department, specialising in mergers and acquisitions, securities offerings, public takeovers, private company acquisitions and disposals, right issues and share placements. Sector experience includes defence, electronics and leisure.

U

ARCHER, Quentin
Lovells, London +44 20 7296 2000
Recommended in Communications: IT
Specialisation: Partner specialising in all aspects of IT law, both contentious and non-contentious, particularly computer contracts, electronic commerce and the introduction of new technology. One of the first lawyers to move (in 1985) from the IT industry back into private practice. Most clients outside the IT sector are in the financial services, defence, and media fields.
Prof. Memberships: Law Society; US Computer Law Association.
Career: Qualified 1981. In-house solicitor at Acorn Computer Group PLC, 1984-85. Rejoined *Lovells* in 1985, partner 1987.

ASHWORTH, Chris
Ashurst Morris Crisp, London +44 20 7638 1111
chris.ashworth@ashursts.com
Recommended in Corporate/Commercial
Specialisation: Head of mergers and acquisitions and telecommunications group. Extensive experience of mergers, acquisitions, corporate finance, private equity and insolvency generally and in the telecommunications sector. Has advised on various UK telecommunications and media mergers, including United News and MAI, Deutsche Telekom and One2One and the acquisitions of HMV and Waterstones, Henlys and Bluebird, Garban and Intercapital. Participated in ARABSAT restructuring, advised on flotations, joint ventures and alliances of various telecom companies. Clients include Deutsche Telekom, BT, Virgin and Kingston.

ATKINSON, Joe
Sinclair Roche & Temperley, London
+44 20 7452 4000
joe.atkinson@srtlaw.com
Recommended in Shipping
Specialisation: Litigation, arbitration and public enquiry work arising from the full spectrum of marine casualties – collisions with fixed and floating objects, salvage, groundings, wreck removal, actual and constructive total loss, fire and explosion, oil pollution and emergency response.
Prof. Memberships: Association of Average Adjusters.
Publications: Written a number of articles for the Trade Press on a variety of 'wet' topics . A regular speaker at seminars, both in the UK and overseas.
Career: Joined *Sinclair Roche & Temperley* 13 years ago and from the outset was involved in high-profile casualties such as the Khark v. Kowloon Bridge and 'Herald of Free Enterprise'. Became a partner in 1995 and head of the admiralty department in 1996. Has been involved in a number of major casualties over the past decade including 'Nassia', 'Mighty Servant II'/North Nember Project, 'DG Harmony', 'ABT Summer', 'Patraikos II'.
Personal: Born 30 November 1962. Graduated from Aberystwyth University with an honours degree in law and economics.

BAIRD, James
Clifford Chance, London +44 20 7600 1000
Recommended in Private Equity: Buyouts

BALDOCK, Anne
Allen & Overy, London +44 20 7330 3000
Recommended in PFI

BALDWIN, Mark
Macfarlanes, London +44 20 7831 9222
mark.baldwin@macfarlanes.com
Recommended in Tax
Specialisation: Partner in corporate tax group. Handles a broad spectrum of work, including private equity transactions and cross-border investment. Has particular expertise in indirect tax (particularly VAT), property investment, development and finance and the structuring of collective investment vehicles (particularly domestic and pan-European private equity and real estate funds) and associated carried interest and co-investment structures.
Prof. Memberships: Member of the Law Society's VAT and Duties Sub-Committee, VAT Practitioners Group, IBA.
Publications: Regular conference speaker and writer, and a contributor to 'De Voil's Indirect Tax Intelligence'. Reporter on UK taxes for the 1999 & 2000 IBA Conferences.
Career: Qualified in 1987. Assistant Solicitor at *Freshfields* between 1987 and 1995; subsequently returned to *Macfarlanes*, becoming a partner in May 1997.
Personal: Born 24 January 1963. German speaker.

BALFOUR, Andrew
Slaughter and May, London +44 20 7600 1200
andrew.balfour@slaughterandmay.com
Recommended in Banking & Finance
Specialisation: Works mainly on banking and capital markets transactions. Particular experience in syndicated loans, structured finance, project finance, acquisition finance, international equity issues, bonds, commercial paper and medium term notes. Also advises banks and corporate clients on general banking and treasury matters.
Prof. Memberships: The Law Society.
Career: Qualified 1981 and became a Partner of *Slaughter and May* in 1988. Resident partner in New York office 1991-1993.
Personal: Educated at Nailsea School (1968-75) and Manchester University (1975-78).

BALLARD, Richard
Freshfields Bruckhaus Deringer, London
+44 20 7936 4000
richard.ballard@freshfields.com
Recommended in Tax
Specialisation: Specialises in corporate finance (including mergers, demergers, reconstructions and cross border transactions); tax-based and structured financing; capital markets work, including structured bond issues as well as securitisation and derivatives transactions of all types.

BARNARD, Stephen
Herbert Smith, London +44 20 7374 8000
stephen.barnard@herbertsmith.com
Recommended in Corporate/Commercial
Specialisation: Partner in Corporate Division. Heads one of the firm's corporate groups and deals with a broad range of company and commercial work including corporate finance, mergers and acquisitions, venture capital and leveraged transactions, privatisations and major projects. Work involves acting for listed clients as well as financial intermediaries, institutions and government. Has been involved in the largest and most complex transactions. Recent transactions include the global organisation of PricewaterhouseCoopers and the demutualisation of, and often for, the London Stock Exchange.
Career: Qualified in 1974. Partner at *Herbert Smith* since 1983.
Personal: Educated at Southampton University.

BARRATT, Jeffery
Norton Rose, London +44 20 7283 6000
barrattjvc@nortonrose.com
Recommended in Projects
Specialisation: Partner, Head of Global Projects Group. All areas of banking, financing and capital markets debt instruments, in particular, project related financings. Involved in many complex infrastructure and other project financings in the UK and worldwide, acting for banks, sponsors, project companies, export credit agencies and multilateral agencies. On the Editorial Board of Butterworths' Financial Law and Practice.
Career: Qualified 1973, joined *Norton Rose* 1976, Partner 1979. Established and ran Bahrain office 1979-82. Training Partner 1987-91. Headed South East Asian Project Finance Group, based in Hong Kong 1993-95. Chairman, Partnership Committee 1997.

BARRY, Robert
Allen & Overy, London +44 20 7330 3000
Recommended in Intellectual Property

BARTER, Charles
Travers Smith Braithwaite, London
+44 20 7295 3000
Charles.Barter@TraversSmith.com
Recommended in Private Equity: Buyouts
Specialisation: Corporate finance, in particular private equity, buyouts, buyins, disposals and reconstructions. Highlights of the last year include Stoll Moss Theatres – joint venture; Golden Wonder – secondary buyout; Thomson Directories – sale.
Prof. Memberships: Member of the Law Society and City of London Solicitors Company.
Career: Articled Clerk 1985; Partner *Travers Smith Braithwaite* 1995.
Personal: Motorcycling, gardening, natural history and Church.

BEARE, Tony
Slaughter and May, London +44 20 7600 1200
tony.beare@slaughterandmay.com
Recommended in Tax
Specialisation: Corporate Tax. Qualified 1987. Partner 1994. Main area of practice is corporate tax and, in particular, structured finance, corporate finance and capital markets.
Prof. Memberships: The Law Society.
Personal: Born 30 November 1959. Educated at Durban High School, Haberdashers' Aske's, Elstree, St. Catharine's College, Cambridge and St Edmund Hall, Oxford.

BEAUMONT, Rupert
Slaughter and May, London +44 20 7600 1200
rupert.beaumont@slaughterandmay.com
Recommended in Capital Markets: Securitisation
Specialisation: Structured finance and securitisation; project finance.
Prof. Memberships: Association of Corporate Treasurers (Honorary Fellow).

BEDDOW, Simon
Ashurst Morris Crisp, London +44 20 7638 1111
simon.beddow@ashursts.com
Recommended in Private Equity: Buyouts
Specialisation: M&A Corporate Finance and Corporate, particular specialisation in private equity transactions acting for both private equity funders and management.
Prof. Memberships: Law Society, City of London Solicitors Company.
Career: University of Bristol (LLB 1986); qualifed 1989; partner *Ashurst Morris Crisp* 1998.
Personal: Married with three children. Lives in London.

BEDFORD, Paul
Allen & Overy, London +44 20 7330 3000
Recommended in Capital Markets: Securitisation

BEECHEY, John
Clifford Chance, London +44 20 7600 1000
john.beechey@cliffordchance.com
Recommended in Arbitration (International)
Specialisation: Partner and global head of international commercial arbitration practice, dealing with all arbitration, ADR, contentious construction and commercial litigation.
Prof. Memberships: Fellow of the Chartered Institute of Arbitrators; *Clifford Chance* representative on the Corporate Counsel Committee of the American Arbitration Association since 1987; appointed to the AAA Arbitrators' Panel in 1991; Member of the Board of the AAA (2000); Member of the ICC UK Arbitration Panel since March 1992 and a British representative on the ICC Commission. Member of the Council of the ICC Institute of World Business Law; appointed to the Arbitrator panel of the Regional Centre for International Arbitration in Cairo and of the Korea Commercial Arbitration Board in 1995; Member of the Board of the London Court of International Arbitration. Member of the Advisory Board to the Modern Languages Faculty of the University of Oxford.
Career: MA, (Oxon) French and German. Partner *Clifford Chance* 1983.

BEHARRELL, Steven
Coudert Brothers, London +44 20 7248 3000
beharrells@london.coudert.com
Recommended in Energy: Oil and Gas
Specialisation: Senior Partner, *Coudert Brothers*, London. Specialises in corporate finance, energy and natural resources, infrastructure investment and privatisation. Has 30 years experience advising on oil and gas law and has been involved in electricity and other privatisations since the late 1980s. Regularly addresses conferences and seminars on the subject of M&A, energy and privatisation law.
Prof. Memberships: International Bar Association.
Career: Assistant solicitor, *Denton Hall* 1966-72; partner 1972-90. Partner, *Coudert Brothers* since 1990.

BELLHOUSE, John
White & Case LLP, London +44 20 7397 3605
jbellhouse@whitecase.com
Recommended in Projects
Specialisation: Executive partner of the London office of *White & Case*. Accomplished project finance law adviser and litigator. Advises on project documentation for disputes relating to major international infrastructure projects, with a particular emphasis on construction contracts.
Career: Qualified to practice in the UK and in Hong Kong. Was a partner with *Cameron McKenna* until 1994.

BELLIS, Tim
Herbert Smith, London +44 20 7374 8000
tim.bellis@herbertsmith.com
Recommended in Corporate/Commercial
Specialisation: Partner in Corporate Division. Has concentrated particularly in the areas of mergers and acquisitions, corporate finance, securities offerings and capital markets transactions on international stock exchanges (London, Hong Kong and Luxembourg) and investment and joint venture work.
Career: Qualified in 1981 and became Partner in 1987.

BENTON, David
Allen & Overy, London +44 20 7330 3000
Recommended in Capital Markets: Derivatives

BERGER, Julian
Linklaters (a member firm of Linklaters & Alliance), London +39 06 478 751
julian.berger@linklaters.com
Recommended in Corporate/Commercial
Specialisation: Partner in the Corporate Department seconded to the Milan office of *Gianni Origoni & Partners*. Spearheads the firm's cross-border M&A practice. Represents, in particular, foreign corporations doing business in Italy as well as Italian companies involved in international transactions. Practice areas include M&A, international joint ventures, acquisition finance, venture capital, financial services and international securities offerings. Recent deals include acting for GKN Westland on its joint venture with the Agusta division of Finmeccanica, BTR plc (now Invensys) on its Italian acquisitions and disposals, Bass plc and Lloyds TSB.

BERINGER, Guy
Allen & Overy, London +44 20 7330 3000
Recommended in Corporate/Commercial

BICKERSTAFF, Roger
Bird & Bird, London +44 20 7415 6000
Recommended in Communications: IT
Specialisation: Partner in Company Department. Principle area of practice is information technology. Particular work focus is large-scale IT-infrastructure projects, including outsourcing, partnering and PFI projects. Other specialities include dispute resolution, protection of rights, e-commerce, the impact of EC legislation and impact of new technology. Also advises on all aspects of EC/GATT procurement law. Clients include many government departments and major private sector IT purchasers.
Prof. Memberships: Society for Computers and Law. Works on a part-time secondment basis as head of CCTA's legal services.
Career: Qualified in 1990. At *Linklaters & Paines* 1990-92. Joined *Bird & Bird* in 1992 and became a Partner in 1995.
Personal: Born 1961. Attended King's College, Cambridge 1980-84. Lives in London.

BICKERTON, David
Clifford Chance, London +44 20 7600 1000
Recommended in Capital Markets: Debt & Equity, Projects
Specialisation: Structured finance including: debt and equity capital markets, project bonds, acquisition finance and PFI/PPP. Recent highlights include: Tier 1 capital raisings for UK financial institutions, PFI/PPP Bond and Bank financings and refinancings including: MoD Main Building Refurbishment, Kings Hospital Bonds, A13 Road Bond and University Funding Bonds.
Career: *Clifford Chance* 1987 to date. Seconded to Citibank (1992) and Bankers Trust (1993). Partner 1997.
Personal: Education: Downing College, Cambridge – MA. Family Details: three daughters.

BIRD, Alistair
Simmons & Simmons, London +44 20 7628 2020
Recommended in Corporate/Commercial
Specialisation: Partner specialising in corporate matters, particularly public and private acquisitions and venture capital.
Prof. Memberships: Law Society.
Career: Qualified 1980; articled at *Slaughter and May*; Partner at *Simmons & Simmons* since 1986 and Managing Partner of the New York office 1994-98.
Personal: Born 1955; married with two young boys living in London; interests include photography, fly fishing and cycling.

BISHOP, Archie
Holman Fenwick & Willan, London
+44 20 7488 2300
Archie.Bishop@hfw.co.uk
Recommended in Shipping
Specialisation: Main area of practice is Admiralty law, with an emphasis on collision, salvage, oil pollution and marine insurance. Legal advisor to International Salvage Union.
Prof. Memberships: Law Society; British Maritime Law Association; City of London Solicitors Company; Royal Institute of Navigation; Average Adjusters Association; Secretary, Admiralty Solicitors Group.
Career: Deck officer with P&O Line 1954-60. Joined *Holman Fenwick & Willan* 1960, became a Partner in 1971 and Senior Partner in 1989. Retired as Senior Partner and became a consultant in November 2000. Appointed Examiner in Admiralty 1996. Contributes a variety of articles to specialised marine publications. Regular speaker at conferences and seminars. Visiting Lecturer to International Maritime Law Institute of Malta.

Personal: Born 21 July 1937. Thames Nautical Training College HMS Worcester 1952-54. British First Mates Foreign Going Certificate 1959, Solicitor 1971. Leisure pursuits: horse riding, golf, art and music. Lives in Farnham.

BLACK, Alan
Linklaters (a member firm of Linklaters & Alliance), London +44 20 7456 2000
alan.black@linklaters.com
Recommended in Projects
Specialisation: Head of Projects and Project Finance. Main area of practice has been international projects. Extensive experience of acting for governments, sponsors and lenders on major projects for transport, airports and aviation, oil, gas, and derivative products, and projects involving concessions granted by governments to private developers in both civil law and common law countries.

U

BLACKABY, Nigel
Freshfields Bruckhaus Deringer, London
+44 20 7936 4000
nigel.blackaby@freshfields.com
Recommended in Arbitration (International)
Specialisation: Specialises in international commercial arbitration, including acting as counsel in ad hoc arbitrations and arbitrations under the rules of the AAA, LCIA, ICC and UNCITRAL with a particular focus on Latin American disputes. Also advises on the drafting of arbitration clauses in international contracts.

BLAKE, Peter M.W.
Clifford Chance, London +44 20 7600 1000
Recommended in Energy: Electricity, Projects

BLANCH, Juliet
Norton Rose, London +44 20 7283 6000
blanchjs@nortonrose.com
Recommended in Shipping
Specialisation: Partner in the shipping energy and international trade group of the commercial litigation department and head of both the marine insurance and the international arbitration groups. Specialises in passenger/cruise ships, disaster litigation, marine insurance, all types of charterparty and bill of lading disputes. Has major casualty experience in connection with lost passenger vessels, together with all related insurance aspects. Also experienced in oil and commodity disputes, ship building and ship repair disputes, and banking and international trade disputes. Regular speaker at international conferences on shipping law and editor of the *Norton Rose* Disputes Resolution Newsletter. Recent cases include: representing owners and their P&I Clubs in relation to the losses of the 'Pegasus', 'Oceanos' and 'Katerina SG' and representing hull and machinery underwriters of the 'Achille Lauro'; representing cruise indemnity underwriters in relation to the 'Saga Rose', 'Starship Oceanic' and 'Odysseus'; representing steel traders Transworld on multi-jurisdictional dispute; representing diamond producers Archangel Diamond Corporation in exploration and production dispute. Clients include all the major P&I Clubs; CoeClerici; Fortum Oil and Gas Oy; Royal Olympic Cruises; Varnima and the Transworld Group.
Prof. Memberships: London Maritime Arbitrators Association; London Court of International Arbitration; The Baltic Exchange; City of London Solicitors Company; Treasurer of the London Branch of the European Court of Arbitration.
Career: Articled *Norton Rose* 1986-88. Qualified 1988; Partner 1997.
Personal: Married with 3 children.

BLISS, Nick
Freshfields Bruckhaus Deringer, London
+44 20 7936 4000
nicholas.bliss@freshfields.com
Recommended in PFI
Specialisation: Specialises in project finance and PFI.

BOARDMAN, Nigel
Slaughter and May, London +44 20 7600 1200
nigel.boardman@slaughterandmay.com
Recommended in Corporate/Commercial
Specialisation: M&A, corporate finance, corporate and commercial. Has been voted Business Lawyer of the Year in each of the past three years in Chambers surveys.
Career: Qualified in 1975 while with *Slaughter and May*. Joined the Corporate Finance Department of *Kleinwort Benson Limited* before returning to *Slaughter and May*, becoming Partner in 1982 and Head of Corporate in 1996.

BOND, Richard
Herbert Smith, London +44 20 7374 8000
richard.bond@herbertsmith.com
Recommended in Corporate/Commercial, Energy: Oil and Gas
Specialisation: Senior partner. Wide ranging experience of corporate transactions, particularly in the fields of energy and natural resources, utilities and privatisations.
Prof. Memberships: Council Member of the Energy and Natural Resources Section of the International Bar Association.
Career: Qualified in 1969. Partner with *Herbert Smith* since 1977.

BORN, Gary
Wilmer, Cutler & Pickering, London
+44 20 7872 1000
gborn@wilmer.com
Recommended in Arbitration (International)
Specialisation: Partner of *Wilmer, Cutler & Pickering*. Leading authority in the fields of international arbitration and litigation. Recent significant matters include representation of a major European telecommunications company in a series of related ICC arbitrations sited in Brussels and Geneva with amounts in dispute exceeding 30 billion Euro; representation of a German company in a multibillion Euro ICC arbitration sited in Zurich; representation of an international media company in an LCIA arbitration sited in London against a Greek Company; representation of a major oil company in an ICSID arbitration against an Asian state; representation of a Scandinavian manufacturer against a German conglomerate in two related ICC arbitrations in Stockholm; representation of US governmental agency in an AAA arbitration; representation of a major US manufacturer of capital goods in multiple ICC construction and other arbitrations; representation of a North American contractor in an ICC arbitration sited in the Hague; representation of a Latin American financial institution in an LCIA arbitration; representation of state of Eritrea in an ad hoc arbitration against Republic of Yemen; representation of a major US media company in an ICC arbitration sited in Singapore; representation of an English company in an AAA arbitration sited in London; representation of an Asian state in an ICC arbitration concerning infrastructure project; representation of a Latin American purchaser of capital equipment in an UNCITRAL arbitration in Mexico City; representation of a US supplier of capital equipment in an ICC arbitration in London; representation of a Dutch exporter in an UNCITRAL arbitration in London; representation of a Middle Eastern company in an ICC arbitration in Paris; representation of a Swiss company in an ICC arbitration in Switzerland; representation of a Belgian company in an ICC arbitration in Belgium; representation of a Dutch company in an ICC arbitration in London. Also sits as arbitrator in both institutional and ad hoc arbitration. Has extensive experience in international litigation, particularly in US courts. Recent significant matters include representation of various European entities in the Holocaust Assets and Forced Labor litigations; representation of a major creditor in BCCI proceedings; and involvement in the Wells Fargo, Laker Airways, Aerospatiale, and Mitsubishi Motors case. Served as an expert witness on aspects of US private international law in foreign and US proceedings.
Prof. Memberships: Member of the American Law Institute.
Career: Graduate of Haverford College (BA, 1978, summa cum laude, Phi Beta Kappa) and the University of Pennsylvania (JD, 1981, summa cum laude). Following graduation from law school, clerked for Judge Henry J. Friendly at the US Court of Appeals for the Second Circuit for a year, then clerked a year for Justice William H. Rehnquist at the US Supreme Court. Joined *WCP* in 1984 and became a partner in 1988. Taught law at Pepperdine University, University College London, Georgetown Law School, and the University of Arizona College of Law. Served on the Executive Council of the American Society of International Law, and as co-chair of the ABA International Section, Committee on International Aspects of Litigation. Proficient in German.

BORTHWICK, Trevor
Allen & Overy, London +44 20 7330 3000
Recommended in Banking & Finance

BOWMAN, Marcus
Holman Fenwick & Willan, London
+44 20 7488 2300
Marcus.Bowman@hfw.co.uk
Recommended in Shipping
Specialisation: Partner in shipping litigation department. Specialising in maritime litigation with emphasis on marine insurance, charterparty and bill of lading disputes; P&I claims handler for seven years.

Career: Oceanus P&I club, 1980-83; Britannia P&I club, 1983-87; articled *Holman Fenwick & Willan*; qualified 1990; partner 1993; solicitor of the Supreme Court of England and Wales.
Personal: Born 1954. University of Cape Town (BA); University of London (LLM). Resides London.

BOWN, Christopher
Freshfields Bruckhaus Deringer, London +44 20 7936 4000
christopher.bown@freshfields.com
Recommended in Private Equity: Buyouts
Specialisation: Partner in the Corporate Group specialising in mergers and acquisitions, buyouts and securities on an international scale.

BRAHAM, Edward
Freshfields Bruckhaus Deringer, London +44 20 7936 4000
edward.braham@freshfields.com
Recommended in Corporate/Commercial
Specialisation: Partner in Corporate Department specialising in major domestic cross-border public and private mergers and acquisitions and corporate finance matters.

BRANNAN, Guy C.H.
Linklaters (a member firm of Linklaters & Alliance), London +44 20 7456 2000
guy.brannan@linklaters.com
Recommended in Tax
Specialisation: Partner and Head of Tax Department. Specialises in corporate tax matters. Main areas of practice include mergers and acquisitions, reorganisations, reconstructions, cross-border transactions, capital markets and finance transactions, EC tax law and tax litigation. Co-editor of 'Taxation of Companies and Company Reconstructions' (2nd and 3rd editions).
Prof. Memberships: Member of the permanent Tax Commission on the Union Internationale des Avocats. Member of the American Bar Association (Taxation Section).
Career: New York office 1989-93.

BRAY, Michael
Clifford Chance, London +44 20 7600 1000
michael.bray@cliffordchance.com
Recommended in Banking & Finance
Specialisation: Banking, project finance and debt restructuring.
Career: Liverpool University. Partner *Clifford Chance* 1976.

BRESSLAW, James
Simmons & Simmons, London +44 20 7628 2020
Recommended in Capital Markets: Securitisation

BRETTON, Linda
Lawrence Graham, London +44 20 7379 0000
Recommended in Energy: Oil and Gas

BRIGHT, Christopher
Clifford Chance, London +44 20 7600 1000
chris.bright@cliffordchance.com
Recommended in Competition/Anti-trust
Specialisation: Head of European Competition and Regulation Practice comprising 80 lawyers across major European jurisdictions. Main areas of work include merger clearances, anti-trust litigation, cartel and abuse of market power investigations in the UK and EC together with strategic international anti-trust advice and risk management. In addition, a specialist in EC and UK utility issues particularly in the rail, water and energy sectors and on state aid and public procurement. Recent merger cases include GE/Honeywell, Pfizer/Warner Lambert, Microsoft/Telewest, ntl/CWC, BUPA/CHG, Air Liquide/Air, Products/BOC, Kvaerner/Ahlstrom, Apollo/Shell resin business, Schroder Ventures/EON, TXU/Cantabrica, Nedcor/Stanbic. Major regulatory work includes OFGEM abuse of market power investigation into Edison; Competition Commission inquiry into Wholesale Electricity Market; Severn Trent High Court action under the procurement rules; advising generators on UK energy market reforms; advising UK government on restructuring regulation of UK railways; advising a number of water and electricity companies on price regulation in UK. Competition clients include Anderson Consulting, Sun Microsystems and KKR.
Prof. Memberships: Law Society.
Career: Qualified in 1985 at *Linklaters*, elected to Partnership 1992, joined *Clifford Chance* as Head of European Competition 1999. Seconded to Competition Policy Division of Department of Trade in Industry for 2 years.
Personal: BSC, (Econ) University of Wales 1980; LLM, Dalhousie School of Law 1981; BCL, Jesus College Oxford 1982.

BROWN, Claude
Clifford Chance, London +44 20 7600 1000
Recommended in Capital Markets: Derivatives

BROWN, David
Bristows, London +44 20 7400 8000
Recommended in Intellectual Property

BROWN, Jane
Linklaters (a member firm of Linklaters & Alliance), London +44 20 7456 2000
jane.brown@linklaters.com
Recommended in Capital Markets: Debt & Equity
Specialisation: Partner, Capital Markets practice. Experience covers a wide range of international securities work, including advising underwriters and issuers in connection with issues of debt, equity and equity-related securities, as well as derivative and structured products.
Career: At *Linklaters* NY office 1987-88.

BROWN, Jeremy
Linklaters (a member firm of Linklaters & Alliance), London +44 20 7456 2000
jeremy.brown@linklaters.com
Recommended in Intellectual Property
Specialisation: Head of Intellectual Property and Technology Department. Co-head of the IP Practice Group of *Linklaters & Alliance*. Degrees in chemical engineering and law. English solicitor and South African patent attorney. Many years' experience in IP practice, particularly issues affecting the pharmaceuticals, chemical, electronics and luxury goods industries. Experience includes UK and multi-jurisdictional patent and trade mark litigation, combating unlawful parallel imports, advising on exhaustion of IP rights in Europe and internationally, and advising on EC competition law implications of patent and technology licences and other IP-related collaborations. Past President of LES International (1996) and of LES Britain and Ireland (1991-92). Long-standing member of Council of AIPPI UK.

BROWNE, Benjamin
Clyde & Co, Guildford +44 1483 555 555
ben.browne@clyde.co.uk
Recommended in Shipping
Specialisation: Partner in Marine Casualty Department. Specialises in all aspects of marine casualties, in particular salvage, collision, oil pollution, general average, transhipments, marine insurance and disputes arising from contracts of carriage of goods by sea. Advises marine cargo, hull and P&I insurers, shipowners, charterers and oil companies on shipping problems. Advised the Ocean Marine Members Action Group (a P&I insurance dispute) and drafted the international Union of Marine Insurers' proposals for the Reform of General Average. Advisor to the International Underwriting Association of London and Lloyd's Underwriters' Association on salvage matters. Member of Lloyd's Open Forum (Salvage) Working Party, Salvage Liaison Group, three man SCOPIC Drafting Committee and British Maritime Law Association General Average Sub-committee. Has contributed many articles, chapters and papers on salvage, collision, general average and oil pollution. Has a special interest in the Middle East where he helped establish the firm's Middle East regional office in Dubai.
Prof. Memberships: Fellow of the Institute of Advanced Legal Studies, Member of Comite Maritime International, subscriber to Average Adjusters' Association, Middle East Association, Indian Maritime Association.
Career: Qualified in 1978 while at *Lovell White & King*. *Morrell Peel & Gamlen*, Oxford 1979-81. Joined *Clyde & Co* in 1981 and became a Partner in 1985.
Personal: Born 18 May 1953. Educated Eton College and Trinity College, Cambridge.

BROWNLOW, Jeremy
Clifford Chance, London +44 20 7600 1000
jeremy.brownlow@cliffordchance.com
Recommended in Corporate/Commercial
Specialisation: Main area of work is corporate finance and mergers and acquisitions. Principally advising public companies and investment banks on recommended and hostile public takeovers and domestic and international corporate transactions.
Career: St Catharine's College, Cambridge. Qualified 1970; partner 1973.

BRYNMOR THOMAS, David
Herbert Smith, London +44 20 7374 8000
david.brynmor.thomas@herbertsmith.com
Recommended in Arbitration (International)
Specialisation: Partner specialising in international commercial arbitration and litigation, particularly in disputes arising from major infrastructure and engineering projects.
Prof. Memberships: Law Society, London Court of International Arbitration, Chartered Institute of

U

Arbitrators (MC/Arb), GCC Commercial Arbitration Centre.
Career: University of Edinburgh, and College of Law, Guildford. Qualified in 1993, Partner *Herbert Smith* since 2000.

BUCKWORTH, Nicolas
Shearman & Sterling, London +44 20 7655 5000
nbuckworth@shearman.com
Recommended in Projects
Specialisation: Partner in Project Finance Department. Advising project developers and financial institutions on all aspects of the structuring, negotiation, development and financing of major infrastructure projects particularly in the power and transportation sectors. Currently involved in advising on projects in Turkey, the Middle East and North Africa, as well as in Hungary, Italy and the United Kingdom. Regular participant in industry conferences and in client focused presentations and working groups.
Career: Qualified in 1986. With *Clifford Chance* 1984-94. Partner *Milbank, Tweed, Hadley & McCloy* 1994- November 1996. Partner, *Shearman & Sterling* November 1996.
Personal: Born 2 February 1961. Educated at Dundee University (LLB, Hons, 1983). Leisure activities include skiing, squash, golf, music and cinema.

BURN, Lachlan
Linklaters (a member firm of Linklaters & Alliance), London +44 20 7456 2000
lachlan.burn@linklaters.com
Recommended in Capital Markets: Debt & Equity
Specialisation: Partner, International Finance Department. Specialises in banking and capital markets issues, with over 24 years' experience in the field. Typical matters handled include GDRs, convertible bonds and derivatives of all types. Advisor to the International Primary Market Association. Seconded to the Paris office from 1982-86.

CALOW, Duncan
Denton Wilde Sapte, London +44 20 7242 1212
dcc@dentonwildesapte.com
Recommended in Communications: E-commerce
Specialisation: Senior solicitor specialising in publishing and digital media work. Advises content owner, producer and distributor clients on a wide range of projects including Internet, on-line and e-commerce services; print, CD-Rom, DVD and video games publishing; broadband, interactive television and mobile services.
Publications: Has written and spoken widely on the legal issues of digital media including contributions to specialist and legal press, national newspapers, radio and television. Contributor (with Alan Williams) to 'Halsburys Laws on Internet Publishing', Butterworths (1999) and author (with Alan Williams and Nicholas Higham) of 'Digital Media: Contracts, Rights and Licensing', Sweet & Maxwell Second Edition (1998).
Career: University of Nottingham; joined *Denton Hall* 1992; qualified 1994.
Personal: Born 1970; leisure interests include art, sport, comedy and politics.

CAMPBELL, Mark
Clifford Chance, London +44 20 7600 1000
Recommended in Banking & Finance

CANBY, Michael
Linklaters (a member firm of Linklaters & Alliance), London +44 20 7456 2000
michael.canby@linklaters.com
Recommended in Capital Markets: Debt & Equity
Specialisation: Partner, Capital Markets practice. Specialist in capital markets transactions including debt and equity financings, derivative products and documentation (involved in the drafting of the various stages of industry standard documentation) and structured financings.
Career: Seconded to New York 1982-84; Paris 1989-95 (and Managing Partner of the Paris office 1992-95). Head of London Global Securities Group 1995 to present.

CANN, Anthony
Linklaters (a member firm of Linklaters & Alliance), London +44 20 7456 2000
anthony.cann@linklaters.com
Recommended in Corporate/Commercial
Specialisation: Specialises in company law, corporate finance, M&A, takeovers and issues, with responsibility for relationships with several major public companies. Transactions include advising BG plc's demergers of Centrica and Lattice; Scottish Newcastle's acquisition of Courage Brewing, Chef & Brewer; Greenall Whitley pub business and Kronenbourg; National Westminster Bank's bid for Legal & General and its defence to Bank of Scotland's bid; British Airways on several transactions; Allied Domecq's acquisition of Pedro Domecq and the sale of its UK retail business; Racal Electronics' defence to Williams Holdings' bid; Elf Aquitaine's joint venture with Enterprise Oil; Zeneca Group's demerger from ICI; Bell Cablemedia plc's listing and then merger into Cable & Wireless Communications, Cable & Wireless Communications on its separation of businesses and sale to Cable & Wireless and NTL; Chubb Security's takeover by Williams Holdings and Willis Corroon Group's takeover by KKR.

CAPPER, Phillip
Lovells, London +44 20 7296 2000
phillip.capper@lovells.com
Recommended in Arbitration (International)
Specialisation: Partner specialising in International Arbitration, Engineering and Construction. Recognised authority on engineering and construction risks and contracts. Substantial experience of international arbitration, as advisor, advocate and arbitrator. Worked on projects for highways, rail, power, defence, and process plant, building and construction in many countries worldwide. Lead counsel for TML, the Channel Tunnel contract consortium, under English and French law – keynote speaker on this at US AAA DART conference. Advised foreign state electricity generator/distributors, national gas distributors, high-speed rail authorities and suppliers, metro and light rail projects, and privately financed infrastructure projects. Has sat as Arbitrator in ICC and LCIA arbitrations. Drafted the disputes clauses in standard forms NEC 2nd ed and ICE 7th. Engaged as expert by French Association of International Contractors (SEFI) to evaluate FIDIC's EPC Silver Book.
Prof. Memberships: UK member of ICC Commission on International Arbitration in Paris, and of European Advisory Committee of the CPR Institute for Dispute Resolution, New York. Directs the International Diploma of the Chartered Institute of Arbitrators.
Publications: For CIRIA's 'Client's Guide to Risk in Construction' wrote legal risk management. Founding editor of 'Construction Industry Law Letter' from 1983 to 1990. Recent publications include 'Construction Industry Arbitrations' in Sweet & Maxwell's 'Handbook of Arbitration Practice' 3rd edition, and former General Editor of 'Emden's Construction Law'.
Career: Formerly partner in construction and engineering and Head of International Arbitration at *Masons*. Visiting Professor in Construction Law and Arbitration at King's College London, and before moving to London in 1988 was Chairman of the Faculty of Law at the University of Oxford. Fellow of Keble College Oxford for 23 years.

CARSTENSEN, Laura
Slaughter and May, London +44 20 7600 1200
laura.carstensen@slaughterandmay.com
Recommended in Competition/Anti-trust
Specialisation: Partner, Competition Department. Practice in UK and EU Competition law, predominantly in relation to strategic corporate events (M&A; key changes in business policy and practice) and contentious situations (cartel/abuse of dominance inquiries). Extensive experience before the European Commission, Office of Fair Trading and Competition Commission.
Prof. Memberships: The Law Society.
Career: Qualified 1987 with *Slaughter and May* and became a Partner in 1994.
Personal: Born 11 November 1960. Educated Withington Girls School, Manchester then St.Hilda's College, Oxford (English Lang. & Lit.). Lives in Hampstead, London.

CARVER CBE, Jeremy
Clifford Chance, London +44 20 7600 1000
Recommended in Energy: Oil and Gas

CAVE-BROWNE-CAVE, Myles
Denton Wilde Sapte, London +44 20 7242 1212
mcbc@dentonwildesapte.com
Recommended in Energy: Oil and Gas
Specialisation: Partner; extensive experience in both industry and private practice in all aspects of the exploration for, production, transportation, processing, marketing and sale of oil and gas in the UK and continental Europe. Also experience in the Middle East and Japan.
Career: Qualified 1974. Joined *Denton Hall* 1975. Partner, *Denton Hall* 1980.
Personal: Born 1949.

CHAPPATTE, Philippe
Slaughter and May, London +44 20 7600 1200
philippe.chappatte@slaughterandmay.com
Recommended in Competition/Anti-trust
Specialisation: Competition law specialist. Provides a wide range of UK and EU competition

law advice in connection with transactions, litigation and regulatory investigations. Recent excamples of EU cases include acting for Telenor in the Telia/Telenor merger; for Shell in the Shell/BASF joint ventures; for Monsanto and Pharmacia & Upjohn in their merger; for British Airways in the proposed KLM merger; and for Anglo-American in its acquisition of Tarmac. Recent UK cases include acting for Punch in its contested acquisition of the Allied pub estate and Carlton in relation to its proposed merger with United News and Media.
Prof. Memberships: Co-founder of European Competition Lawyers Forum. Contributor to Bellamy & Child 'Common Market Law of Competition'.
Career: Bryanston School, Oxford University (BA Law, First Class). Université Libre de Bruxelles (Lic.Sp.Dr.Eur., Highest Distinction). Qualified *Slaughter and May* 1982. Partner 1989. Responsible for running and development of Brussels office between April 1991 and August 1996.
Personal: Three children.

CHARNLEY, William
McDermott, Will & Emery, London
+44 20 7577 6900
wcharnley@europe.mwe.com
Recommended in Corporate/Commercial
Specialisation: Head of Corporate/Senior Partner. Principal area of practice is corporate finance covering flotations, mergers and acquisitions and capital raising for companies acting for underwriters and issuers of securities, private equity transactions and general corporate advice.
Prof. Memberships: Member of the Law Society, Institute of Chartered Secretaries and Administrators and The Drapers Company.
Career: Articled at *Slater Heelis* in Manchester 1985-87, then joined *Booth & Co* and became a Partner in 1990; joined *Simmons & Simmons* as a Partner in 1994; joined *McDermott, Will & Emery* in November 1998.
Personal: Born 21 August 1960. Attended Rivington and Blackrod Grammar School 1971-78, Bolton Institute 1978-80, Sheffield Hallam University (formerly Sheffield City Polytechnic) 1980-81, Lancaster University 1981-83 and Manchester Metropolitan University (formerly Manchester Polytechnic) 1984-85. Trustee of Children's Heart Surgery Fund, Killingbeck Hospital. Non-executive director Sanderson Bramall Motor Group plc 2000-. Leisure pursuits include country sports, art, opera and wine. Lives in London.

CHEYNE, David
Linklaters (a member firm of Linklaters & Alliance), London +44 20 7456 2000
david.cheyne@linklaters.com
Recommended in Corporate/Commercial
Specialisation: Head of Corporate Department. Involved in a wide range of corporate transactions including M&A work, flotations, general corporate finance work and Stock Exchange-related matters.
Career: Hong Kong office, 1981-1986.

CHILDS, David
Clifford Chance, London +44 20 7600 1000
david.childs@cliffordchance.com
Recommended in Corporate/Commercial
Specialisation: Head of the Global Corporate Practice. Specialises in corporate finance particularly M&A.
Career: Sheffield University; University College, London (LLB, LLM). Articled *Clifford Chance*; qualified 1976; partner *Clifford Chance* since 1981.
Personal: Born 1951; resides Sevenoaks.

CHISSICK, Michael
Field Fisher Waterhouse, London +44 20 7861 4000
Recommended in Communications: E-commerce, Communications: IT
Specialisation: Head of IT and E-commerce Law Group which comprises a team of 7 partners and 15 specialist lawyers. Main areas of practice include: outsourcing projects, data protection, digital mixed media, electronic commerce and m-commerce contracts, linking agreements, software contracts and internet law. In the past year has advised on several major outsourcing projects, including advising London Underground on an outsourcing to ITNET and Thomas Cook on its e-commerce project.
Prof. Memberships: Law Society; Computer Law Association.
Publications: Author of 'Internet Law' published in October 1997 by FT Publications and co-author of 'Electronic Commerce Law and Practice' published in 1999 and 2000 by Sweet & Maxwell.
Career: 1st Class Degree in Law (LLB); Law Society Finals 1st Class; Masters Degree in IT and Telecommunications.

CLARK, Adrian
Ashurst Morris Crisp, London +44 20 7638 1111
adrian.clark@ashursts.com
Recommended in Corporate/Commercial
Specialisation: Company Department.
Career: Educated – Peterhouse, Cambridge (MA). Qualified 1983. *Slaughter and May* 1981-86; *Ashurst Morris Crisp* 1986 onwards. Partner 1990. Seconded to Take-over Panel 1988-90.

CLARK, Charles
Linklaters (a member firm of Linklaters & Alliance), London +44 20 7456 2000
charles.clark@linklaters.com
Recommended in Capital Markets: Debt & Equity
Specialisation: Partner, International Finance Department and Head of Derivatives – global securities group. Extensive experience of international securities issues and derivatives transactions.

CLARK, Tim
Slaughter and May, London +44 20 7600 1200
tim.clark@slaughterand may.com
Recommended in Corporate/Commercial
Specialisation: Principal area of practice is UK and international corporate work, corporate finance and mergers and acquisitions (including public takeovers, flotations, international equity offerings), advising corporate and investment bank clients. Practice also involves demutualisations (building societies and insurance companies). Joint Head of Electronic Commerce Group.

Prof. Memberships: The Law Society.
Career: Qualified 1976 with *Slaughter and May*. Became Partner in 1983.
Personal: Born 9 January 1951. Educated at Sherborne School and Pembroke College, Cambridge. Interests include theatre, sport, Italy and flying. Lives in London.

CLARKE, Julia
Clifford Chance, London +44 20 7600 1000
julia.clarke@cliffordchance.com
Recommended in Private Equity: Buyouts
Specialisation: Partner specialising in private equity and management buy-outs and buy-ins including cross-border European deals and with broad experience of general corporate and corporate finance transactions.
Career: Guildford County School; St Hugh's College, Oxford (MA, Oxon 1984). Articled *Clifford Chance*; qualified 1989; partner 1994.
Personal: Born 1962; Interests: Tennis, sailing, skiing, travel, theatre.

CLARKE, Tim
Linklaters (a member firm of Linklaters & Alliance), London +44 20 7456 2000
tim.clarke@linklaters.com
Recommended in Corporate/Commercial
Specialisation: General corporate finance practice including public and private M&A, takeovers and joint ventures. Particular experience of UK and international privatisations having advised on more than 20 internationally. These include British Aerospace, Rolls-Royce, CEGB/National Power, British Telecom, Cable & Wireless and Railtrack. Recent international privatisation experience includes advising the South African Government on the privatisation of SAA and the Kenyan Government on the privatisation of Telkom Kenya. Speaks at privatisation conferences in numerous countries. Other recent transactions include advising Wickes plc on its successful defence against hostile bid from FDIA, leading the team advising National Power in its demerger into International Power and Innogy and advising a bidder in the proposed air traffic privatisation in the UK.

CLOUGH, Adrian
Herbert Smith, London +44 20 7374 8000
adrian.clough@herbertsmith.com
Recommended in Energy: Electricity
Specialisation: Partner in *Herbert Smith*'s Projects Group, specialising in privatisation, major restructurings and infrastructure projects, particularly in the electricity and transport sectors. Involvement with the electricity sector began when part of the team which advised the Area Boards of England and Wales on the 1990 restructuring and their subsequent privatisation. Has continued to advise various members of the industry on contractual and regulatory issues. Had day to day responsibility for the *Herbert Smith* team advising the 14 Public Electricity Suppliers in Great Britain on the major revisions to the industry's contractual and regulatory structure which were necessary to enable full supply competition to be introduced in 1998. Has also advised British Gas in relation to the Northern Ireland elec-

U

tricity privatisation and the Magnox division of Nuclear Electric on the restructuring that preceded the privatisation of British Energy. Currently advising various RECs and industry bodies (including the Electricity Association) on the implementation of the New Electricity Trading Arrangements in England and Wales and the implementation of the Utilities Act 2000 (in particular the supply/distribution split). Has recently advised two RECs on the disposal of their metering businesses.
Career: Educated at Christ Church, Oxford (MA); qualified as a solicitor 1988; partner at *Herbert Smith* since 1995. Seconded for two years as an Assistant Director of the Office of Passenger Rail Franchising, leading the development of the new contractual and regulatory structure of the railway industry as it developed.

U

COHEN, Laurence J.
McDermott, Will & Emery, London +44 20 7577 6900
Recommended in Intellectual Property
Specialisation: Partner – Intellectual Property Unit. Contentious and non-contentious intellectual property matters including patents, trademarks, copyright, design right and trade secrets. Also deals with regulatory law, particularly in the area of agrochemicals and medicines and genetically modified organisms. Acted in Chiron v. Murex (client), Harrods Limited (client) v. Harrods (Buenos Aires) Limited, GEC v. FKI (client), Coin Controls (client) v. Suzo and Philips Electronics v. Ingman (client); R v DETR ex p Watson (Adventa Seeds intervening-client). Author of 'World Litigation Law and Practice: Unit B1 England and Wales' (1986) and CIPA/ ITMA Trademarks Handbook section on Civil Litigation (1992). Contributor of numerous articles to a variety of specialist publications on intellectual property topics and regular conference speaker.
Prof. Memberships: CIPA, ITMA, INTA, IBA, Law Society.
Career: Qualified 1976. Assistant solicitor with *Bristows Cooke & Carpmael* from 1976, and became a partner in 1981. Joined *Hammond Suddards* in 1992. Joined *McDermott, Will & Emery* in 2000 and is currently Head of Contentious Intellectual Property.
Personal: Born 12 September 1951. Attended Emmanuel College, Cambridge 1970-73. Leisure pursuits include tennis, cycling and skiing. Lives in Radlett, Hertfordshire.

COHEN, Ralph
S J Berwin & Co, London +44 20 7533 2222
Recommended in Competition/Anti-trust
Specialisation: Partner specialising in EC and UK Competition Law and EC Trade and Customs Law. Has extensive experience representing clients before the OFT, MMC and European Commission across a wide range of industries. Practice areas include EC and UK merger clearances and coordinating multi jurisdictional filings, advising on compatibility of commercial agreements with competition law compliance, anti-dumping investigations, WTO and general customs related issues.
Prof. Memberships: Solicitors European Group.
Career: Qualified 1983. Partner at *S J Berwin & Co* 1991.
Personal: Born 10 May 1959. Attended Clifton College, and University of Southampton. Married with three sons.

COLBRIDGE, Christopher
Shearman & Sterling, London +44 20 7655 5000
ccolbridge@shearman.com
Recommended in Arbitration (International)
Specialisation: Represents *Shearman & Sterling's* International Commercial Arbitration Group in London. Has acted as Counsel in international arbitrations, both institutional (ICC, LCIA, ICSID and other rules) and ad hoc around the world. Has represented multi-national corporations and governments in disputes involving international contracts, particularly investments, infrastructure and energy projects. Also specialises in law and practice of international litigation, conflict of laws and jurisdiction.
Prof. Memberships: London Court of International Arbitration. International Arbitration Institute. IBA.
Career: Qualified England & Wales, 1992. Admitted to Paris bar, 1999. *Clifford Chance* 1990-99.
Personal: Born 1967. Educated at Kings College, University of London (LLB, Hons), 1987. University of Paris I Panthéon-Sorbonne (Licence and Maitrise in French private law), 1989.

COMPAGNONI, Marco
Lovells, London +44 20 7296 2000
marco.compagnoni@lovells.com
Recommended in Private Equity: Buyouts
Specialisation: Specialises in a range of mergers and acquisitions work and corporate law. A particular specialisation is private equity transactions (MBOs and MBIs) acting primarily for institutional investors. Has acted regularly for the Equity institutions of Mercury Asset Management and Doughty Hanson. Also has extensive experience of joint ventures, purchase and sales companies and businesses (both domestic and cross border). Significant transactions include acting for ING in its purchase of Barings.
Prof. Memberships: The British Venture Capital Association, the British Italian Law Association and the City of London Solicitors Company.
Career: Articled at *Lovells*; qualified in 1987 and became a partner in 1993.

COOK, John
Norton Rose, London +44 20 7283 6000
cookcj@nortonrose.com
Recommended in Competition/Anti-trust
Specialisation: Partner, competition and EC department. Competition law, EC law, (including international trade, public procurement and state aids), transport and utilities regulation and public law/judicial review. A regular conference speaker and writer; author, with C.S. Kerse, of 'EC Merger Control', the leading text book on EC merger control – published by Sweet & Maxwell – third ed. December 1999.
Career: Called to the Bar of Grays Inn in 1975. Lectureship, Magdalen College, Oxford 1976-81. UK government legal service 1976-88. Joined *Norton Rose* in 1988 and headed Competition and EC Department from then until 1997.

COOK, Trevor
Bird & Bird, London +44 20 7415 6000
Recommended in Intellectual Property
Specialisation: Partner in Intellectual Property Department. Main areas of practice are litigation, advisory and transactional work in relation to patents, copyright, trademarks and other intellectual property rights and regulatory law issues, particularly in the information technology and pharmaceutical/biosciences sectors.
Prof. Memberships: Treasurer of the International Association for the Protection of Industrial Property (AIPPI) (UK Group), member of Licensing Executives Society, associate member of Chartered Institute of Patent Agents, Secretary of British Copyright Council Working Group on Copyright & Technology.
Publications: Contributor to 'Information Technology and the Law', 'CIPA Guide to Patents Act' and 'European Patents Handbook and Database Law'; co-author of 'Pharmaceuticals Biotechnology and the Law' and 'Practical Intellectual Property Precedents'; author of 'The Protection of Regulatory Data'. Frequent writer and speaker on various intellectual property and regulatory topics.
Career: Qualified in 1977. Joined *Bird & Bird* in 1974, became a Partner in 1981.
Personal: Born 1951. Attended Southampton University (BSc Chemistry, 1973).

COOKE, Adam
Wragge & Co, Birmingham +44 870 903 1000
adam_cooke@wragge.com
Recommended in Intellectual Property
Specialisation: Partner specialising in all aspects of intellectual property law across the full range of patents, trade marks, copyright, designs and trade secrets, both litigation and non contentious work. Leading cases include Wellcome v Genentech, Unilever v Gillette, Glaverbel v British Coal and Gerber v Lectra.
Prof. Memberships: CIPA, ITMA, AIPLA, AIPPI, LES (member of EEC Laws Committee).
Career: Qualified in 1986 at *Bristows Cooke & Carpmael.* Seconded to *Arnold White & Durkee* Houston, Texas, US patent attorneys 1989-90. Assistant with *Stephenson Harwood* 1991-93. Joined *Needham & Grant* in 1993, partner from 1994, partner at *Wragge & Co*, 2000.
Personal: Born 1960. Attended Durham University (BSc 1981). Married with 3 children. Interests include travel, gardening and architecture. Lives in London.

COOKE, Stephen
Slaughter and May, London +44 20 7600 1200
stephen.cooke@slaughterandmay.com
Recommended in Corporate/Commercial
Specialisation: Principal area of practice is company and commercial work with particular emphasis on M&A.
Prof. Memberships: The Law Society.
Publications: Publications include 'Takeovers' (Legal & Commercial Publishing, 1997).
Career: Qualified in 1984 with *Slaughter and May.* Worked in the New York office 1989-90, and became a Partner in 1991.

Personal: Born 7 March 1959. Educated Lincoln College, Oxford (1978-81). Lives in London.

COPPIN, Jonathan
Norton Rose, London +44 20 7283 6000
coppinjds@nortonrose.com
Recommended in Corporate/Commercial
Specialisation: Main area of practice is corporate finance in particular mergers and acquisitions, flotations and international securities offerings. Recent transactions include Texas Utilities/The Energy Group, AXA/GRE, AXA/Sun Life and Provincial Holdings, and P&O's disposal of Bovis to Lend Lease.
Prof. Memberships: Member of the Law Society's Company Law Committee.
Career: Articled at *Norton Rose* 1987-1989, Partner Corporate Finance Department *Norton Rose* 1996.
Publications: Author of numerous articles in professional publications.
Personal: Married (Lucy). Hobbies include sailing and running.

COTTIS, Matthew
Lovells, London +44 20 7296 2000
matthew.cottis@lovells.com
Recommended in Banking & Finance
Specialisation: Expertise in management buy-outs/buy-ins, bids and takeovers and other types of acquisition finance, property development finance and general syndicated loans.
Career: Articled *Lovells 1985-87,* Partner *1993.*

COULTER, David
Norton Rose, London +44 20 7283 6000
coulterdx@nortonrose.com
Recommended in PFI
Specialisation: PFI, Project Finance, Asset Finance, Public Sector Finance and Banking – PFI Projects in last year have included Scottish Water Project at Dalmuir; Hereford and Worcester Magistrates Courts; Oldham Schools; Islington and Newham HRA Housing PFI; Eden Project; National Physical Laboratory.
Prof. Memberships: Law Society, Law Society of Scotland, City of London Solicitors Company.
Career: Mainholm Academy, Ayr to 1979; Edinburgh University LLB (1984), DIPLP (1985); Admitted Scotland (1986), Notary Public (Scotland) (1986); Admitted England & Wales (1989).
Personal: Sailing, hillwalking and travel. Married (Catriona Rose) – one daughter, Fiona, one son, Alasdair.

COWAN, Matthew
Olswang, London +44 20 7208 8888
mac@olswang.com
Recommended in Communications: E-commerce
Specialisation: Commercial and corporate work in the Internet and telecommunications fields. Acted on the establishment of Worldpop.com and flotation of Netstore plc. Practice includes venture capital funding and acquisitions in the Internet and telecommunications fields.
Career: Joined *Olswang* in 1993 upon qualification and became a partner in 1999. Attended Bristol Grammar School 1979-86, then Exeter University 1986-90.
Personal: Born 31.3.67. Lives in Surrey.

CRANE, David
Norton Rose, London +44 20 7283 6000
Recommended in Projects
Specialisation: Partner in the projects group, specialising in project finance and asset finance. Also handles general commercial work. Has advised on numerous major plant leasing transactions, on sales of leasing companies as well as other company acquisitions and joint ventures. Also has considerable experience of public sector financing, particularly relating to local authorities.
Prof. Memberships: Law Society.
Career: Articled at *Norton Rose.* Qualified 1975. Partner since 1985.

CRANFIELD, Richard
Allen & Overy, London +44 20 7330 3000
Recommended in Corporate/Commercial

CRAWFORD, Sue
Ashurst Morris Crisp, London +44 20 7638 1111
sue.crawford@ashursts.com
Recommended in Tax
Specialisation: Partner in Tax Department. Principal area of practice is corporate tax with particular emphasis on corporate reorganisations, mergers, de-mergers, and acquisitions including cross-border transactions. Also specialises in oil and gas tax; all aspects of property taxation and taxation of financial institutions/transactions (including tax based structured financing), extending to securitisation and enterprise zones.
Career: Articled *Coward Chance (Clifford Chance)*; qualified 1984. Partner *Ashurst Morris Crisp* since 1994.
Personal: Educated at Wycombe Abbey School; Girton College Cambridge University.

CROALL, Philip
Freshfields Bruckhaus Deringer, London +44 20 7936 4000
philip.croall@freshfields.com
Recommended in Arbitration (International)
Specialisation: Partner specialising in arbitration, ADR and commercial litigation. Handles all aspects of international commercial arbitration work. Has appeared on Counsel in arbitrations under rules of the major arbitration institutions including the ICC, the LCIA as well as in ad hoc arbitration under the UNCITRAL Rules.

CRUMP, Richard
Holman Fenwick & Willan, London +44 20 7488 2300
Richard.Crump@hfw.co.uk
Recommended in Shipping
Specialisation: Partner in Commercial Litigation Department. Practice encompasses all areas of shipping litigation, including charterparty disputes, cargo claims, ship sale disputes, joint venture and pool agreement disputes and related commercial litigation. Has spoken at seminars in Athens and Bombay. Accredited CEDR Mediator.
Prof. Memberships: Law Society.
Career: Qualified in 1981 having joined *Holman Fenwick & Willan* in 1979. Became a Partner in 1987.
Personal: Born 6 September 1957. Educated at St. Paul's School, London 1970-74, Oriel College, Oxford 1975-78 and College of Law, Guildford 1979. Lives in London.

CULLINANE, Lee
Clifford Chance, London +44 20 7600 1000
Recommended in Banking & Finance

CUTHBERT, Michael
Clifford Chance, London +44 20 7600 1000
Recommended in Energy: Mining

CUTTING, Michael
Linklaters (a member firm of Linklaters & Alliance), London +44 20 7456 2000
michael.cutting@linklaters.com
Recommended in Competition/Anti-trust
Specialisation: Partner, competition and regulatory law group, specialist in EU and UK competition, utility law and practice, and competition law. Experience includes advising British Gas plc and subsequently BG Group plc and Lattice plc since 1992. Considerable experience of competition law in telecoms, leisure and transport sectors. Recent merger control experience includes BP Amoco's acquisition of Burmah Castrol and Bass on its sale of Coral betting shops to Ladbroke plc.

DALLAS, James
Denton Wilde Sapte, London +44 20 7242 1212
jad@dentonwildesapte.com
Recommended in Energy: Oil and Gas
Specialisation: Chairman of *DWS.* Partner in Energy and Infrastructure group. Experienced in oil and gas and electricity work, including project finance, gas, electricity and rail privatisation and regulation in the UK and internationally. Regular speaker at conferences on privatisation and regulation issues. Editor of the 'Utilities Law Review'.
Prof. Memberships: Centre for the Study of Regulated Industries (committee member).
Career: Articled City firm. Qualified 1979. Joined *Denton Hall* in 1985, became a partner in 1986 and Chairman 1996. Non-Executive Director AMEC plc.
Personal: Born 1955. Attended Eton College and St Edmund Hall, Oxford 1973-76 (MA Jurisprudence).

DAVEY, Henry
Herbert Smith, London +44 20 7374 8000
henry.davey@herbertsmith.com
Recommended in Energy: Electricity, Energy: Oil and Gas
Specialisation: Energy: involved in the privatisation and restructuring of electricity industries and international power and transmission projects. Advises on innovative electricity and gas trading contracts. Advises on oil and gas projects, including field developments, asset acquisitions and disposals, and on all aspects of oil and gas contracts, including joint ventures and joint operating agreements; advises on gas sales and transportation agreements, licensing and concession agreements and development contracts in various jurisdictions.
Prof. Memberships: IBA; United Kingdom Energy Lawyers Group.
Career: Partner at *Herbert Smith* since 1996. Joined the firm as a trainee in September 1986; qualified in 1988. MA Cantab (Queens' College), Law; Nottingham High School.

U

DAVIDSON, John
Lovells, London +44 20 7296 2000
john.davidson@lovells.com
Recommended in Corporate/Commercial
Specialisation: Is a member of Lovells' corporate finance group, specialising in public and private UK and cross-border mergers and acquisitions and joint ventures, international equity offerings and private equity investments, and is a member of the firm's market-leading corporate insurance and Lloyd's practice. Recent major transactions have included advising South African Breweries plc on its £4 billion listing on the London Stock Exchange and its admission to the FTSE 100 Index in March 1999, AEGON UK plc on its £759 million acquisition of Guardian Life in September 1999, and Goldman Sachs International as sponsor of the £1.4 billion IPO of Egg plc in June 2000.
Career: Articled *Lovells*, qualified 1985; partner 1991; resident partner New York office 1991-95.

DAVIES, Isabel
Eversheds, London +44 20 7919 4500
Recommended in Intellectual Property
Specialisation: Partner and head of intellectual property at *Eversheds*, London. Head of *Eversheds* national Intellectual Property Group. Work includes patents, trademarks, copyright, designs, competition and EC law. Cases have included Jif, Boston Scientific v Palmaz 1998, Prince Internet Litigation 1998, Tommy Hilfiger v Tesco 1998 and Elvis TM appeal (CA) 1999, Denny v Instance 2000, Unilever v American Housewares Inc (Oxo). Editor of Sweet and Maxwell's 'European Trade Mark Litigation Handbook'. Co-editor of *Eversheds* 'IPEye'. Legal Editor of 'Journal of Brand Management', Editorial Board of Trademark World and Country Correspondent for EIPR. Has spoken widely at conferences on IP issues, often taking the Chair.
Prof. Memberships: ITMS, CIPA, INTA, ACG. Member of Intellectual Property Sub-committee of the Law Society.
Career: Qualified in 1976. Partner at *Wragge & Co*, 1979-85. Joined *Woodham Smith* (*Taylor Joynson Garratt*) as Partner in 1986, then *Jaques & Lewis* (now *Eversheds*) in 1994.
Personal: Born 30 May 1952. Attended St Albans Girls' Grammar School, Leicester University and Guildford College of Law. Leisure interests include travel, theatre, squash, skiing, food and wine. Lives in Chelsea.

DAVIES, Roger
Allen & Overy, London +44 20 7330 3000
Recommended in Energy: Oil and Gas

DAVIS, James
Freshfields Bruckhaus Deringer, London
+44 20 7936 4000
james.davis@freshfields.com
Recommended in Corporate/Commercial
Specialisation: Specialises in general corporate advice, public and private mergers and acquisitions, private equity work and equity issues.

DAVIS, Steven
S J Berwin & Co, London +44 20 7533 2222
steven.davis@sjberwin.com
Recommended in Private Equity: Buyouts
Specialisation: Member of *S J Berwin & Co.*'s corporate finance department, specialising in public and private UK and cross-border mergers and acquisitions and joint ventures. A member of the firm's market leading private equity practice with a particular focus on leveraged buy-outs, venture and development capital investments, and exits whether by way of trade sale or flotation. Equity institutions for whom acts regularly include Apax Partners and Phildrew Ventures. Recent transactions include the flotation of The Future Network plc, the public to privates of Appollo Metals plc, The Denby Group plc, UPF Group plc and The Limelight group plc and advising NM Rothschild on the take private of United Biscuits.
Prof. Memberships: Member of the New York Bar.
Career: Qualified in 1987 with *S J Berwin & Co.* Seconded to *Debevoise & Plimpton*, New York office 1992-1993 and became a partner in 1994.
Personal: Born 1965. Educated Clifton College, Bristol and Manchester University. Married with one child. Leisure pursuits include golf, squash and cooking. Lives in London.

DE LA RUE, Colin
Ince & Co, London +44 20 7623 2011
colin.delarue@ince.co.uk
Recommended in Shipping
Specialisation: Has acted in most major oil pollution incidents worldwide in the last 15 years and on a day-to-day basis advises shipowners, oil companies, P&I Clubs, marine underwriters and others. Extensive experience of claims under compensation conventions and on the commercial ramifications of the subject. Has spoken on marine pollution and disaster response at seminars and conferences in many countries around the world.
Prof. Memberships: British Maritime Law Association Pollution Sub-Committee; elected titulary member of the Comité Maritime International in 1994.
Publications: General Editor of 'Liability for Damage to the Marine Environment' and co-author of 'Shipping and the Environment' (LLP, 1998), the main textbook on the subject; Visiting Lecturer in Shipping Law at the City University Business School in London 1986-96.
Career: Bar Finals 1977; admitted as solicitor 1980; partner *Ince & Co* 1986; head of firm's pollution group.
Personal: Born 11 October 1953. Education: Elizabeth College, Guernsey and Pembroke College, Cambridge (modern languages and law). Married with three children. Lives in Woodbridge, Suffolk. Spare time activities include golf and natural history.

DEERING, Bob
Ince & Co, London +44 20 7623 2011
bob.deering@ince.co.uk
Recommended in Shipping
Specialisation: Involved in all aspects of the firm's shipping practice, and represents a number of substantial ship owners and P&I Clubs, both in their own capacity and on behalf of their shipowner members. Currently acts for underwriters in the investigation of hull claims. Leader of the firm's Dry Shipping business group.
Prof. Memberships: Law Society.
Career: Joined *Ince & Co* 1976, qualified 1978, partner 1985.
Personal: Pembroke College, Cambridge. Married with three children. Enjoys both watching and playing sport.

DICKSON, Alastair R.
Dickson Minto WS, London +44 20 7628 4455
alastair.dickson@dmws.com
Recommended in Private Equity: Buyouts
Specialisation: Mergers and acquisitions; leveraged buy-outs; acting for major financial institutions and banks. Deals in 1999/2000 include: The Tussauds Group (£350 million); Ross Breeders (£100 million); Mappin & Webb (not disclosed); Cantrell & Cochrane (Euro 750 million); Zeneca Speciality Chemicals (£1.3 billion); PHS (£215 million); Greycoat plc (£535 million); General Healthcare Group Limited (£1.275billion); Merger of Trade media Group (£950million).
Prof. Memberships: Law Society of Scotland. Writer to Her Majesty's Signet.
Career: Educated Edinburgh University 1971. *Dundas & Wilson* 1971-1973. *Maclay Murray & Spen* 1973-1976. *Dundas & Wilson* 1976-1985 (partner from 1978). Founding partner of *Dickson Minto* 1985.
Personal: Golf, squash, hill walking.

DOEH, Doran
Denton Wilde Sapte, London +44 20 7242 1212
dxd@dentonwildesapte.com
Recommended in Energy: Oil and Gas
Specialisation: Widely experienced in all aspects of petroleum and minerals transactions domestically and internationally, including licensing, production sharing agreements, upstream and downstream joint ventures, pipelines, gas sales, oil trading, privatisation, acquisitions and disposals, financing and securities. Has dealt with Russia and Central Asia since 1991.
Prof. Memberships: Fellow, Society for Advanced Legal Studies; Honorary Associate, Centre for Energy, Petroleum and Mineral Law and Policy, University of Dundee.
Career: Barrister 1973; solicitor 1987. 1975-86 Legal Adviser, Burmah Oil North Sea Limited/The British National Oil Corporation/Britoil Plc. Joined *Allen & Overy* 1986, partner *Allen & Overy* based in Moscow 1995, London 1998, partner *Denton Hall* 1999; *Denton Wilde Sapte* 2000.
Personal: Born 1948 in New York. Educated Dartmouth College (USA), Oxford University (England), London University (England).

DONITHORN, Michael
Holman Fenwick & Willan, London
+44 20 7488 2300
michael.donithorn@hfw.co.uk
Recommended in Shipping
Specialisation: Partner in Commercial Litigation Department. Principal area of practice is marine liti-

gation. Specialises in commercial disputes arising from casualties. Particular experience of bulk and liner trades, P&I insurance and liability insurance generally. Other areas of practice are marine insurance and international sale of goods. Clients include major P&I clubs, liner operators, time charter operators, bulk vessel owners, gas carrier owners and market underwriters. CEDR Accredited Mediator.
Prof. Memberships: Law Society, BMLA, LMAA (supporting member), Member of Baltic Exchange.
Career: Called to the Bar 1974. Practised at the Bar 1974-76. Lawyer for West of England P&I Club 1976-78. Joined *Coward Chance* 1978. Admitted Solicitor 1980. Partner at *Coward Chance* (subsequently *Clifford Chance*) 1984-94. Joined *Holman Fenwick & Willan* as a Partner in 1994.
Personal: Born 27 January 1951. Educated at Cannock Grammar School 1962-69, Balliol College, Oxford 1969-72 (BA Hons, Modern History 1972, MA 1979) and the College of Law, Chancery Lane 1972-74. Leisure pursuits include farming. Lives in Surrey.

DORAN, Nigel J.L.
Macfarlanes, London +44 20 7831 9222
njld@macfarlanes.com
Recommended in Tax
Specialisation: Partner in the corporate tax group at *Macfarlanes*, where advises generally on corporate tax matters but with a particular emphasis on the taxation of investment funds and employment tax. Associate of the Chartered Institute of Taxation and a member of its Corporate Tax Sub-Committee. Also a member of the Revenue Law Sub-Committee of the City of London Law Society. Member of the AUTIF tax committee.
Prof. Memberships: City of London Law Society (Revenue Law Subcommittee), Chartered Institute of Taxation, Association of Certified Accountants, Chartered Institute of Bankers.
Publications: 'Taxation of Corporate Joint Ventures', published by Butterworths, and the tax section of 'Collective Investment Schemes: the Law and Practice', published by Sweet & Maxwell. Member of the editorial board of 'The Corporate Taxation Review', published by Kay Haven.
Career: Qualified in 1984 having joined *Macfarlanes* in 1982. Became a Partner in 1988.
Personal: Born 11 March 1950. Educated at Trinity College, Glenalmond 1963-69 and St. Edmund Hall, Oxford 1969-73. Leisure interests include golf and modern languages. Lives in Twickenham.

DUFFICY, Frank
CMS Cameron McKenna, London
+44 20 7367 3000
Recommended in PFI

DUNCAN, Michael G.
Allen & Overy, London +44 20 7330 3000
Recommended in Banking & Finance

DUNLOP, Stuart
Clifford Chance, London +44 20 7600 1000
Recommended in Capital Markets: Debt & Equity

DUNNIGAN, David
Clifford Chance, London +44 20 7600 1000
David.Dunnigan@cliffordchance.com
Recommended in Capital Markets: Debt & Equity
Specialisation: Partner in international capital markets group specialising in Eurobonds, Euro medium term notes, structured private placements, Euro commercial paper, certificates of deposit and warrants.
Career: Nottingham University (LLB 2.1) 1980-1983. Articled *Turner Kenneth Brown*; qualified 1986; *Coward Chance/Clifford Chance*; partner *Clifford Chance* since 1992.
Personal: Born 1961; resides Highgate.

EAST, Lindsay
Richards Butler, London +44 20 7247 6555
lte@richardsbutler.com
Recommended in Shipping
Specialisation: Partner. Previously Head of shipping group for six years. Main area of practice is shipping and insurance. Acts for owners and charterers direct or through their insurers (P&I and defence clubs) in all contractual disputes, charterparty, bill of lading, MOA, and building contracts. Particular expertise in drafting and advising on club rules and shipbuilding disputes. Also handles general marine and non-marine insurance, acting for cargo insurers and reinsurers and war-risk underwriters. Cases have included 'Antaios', 'Antares', 'Antonis P. Lemos', 'Standard Steamship v. Gann', 'Aditya Vaibhav', 'Aegean Maritime v. Flender Werft' and 'Sagheera'. Recently sucessfully defended a P&I Club in a close action claim by 2,500 American seaman involving alleged asbestos related diseases. Speaker at and chairman of various seminars.
Prof. Memberships: Baltic Exchange.
Career: Qualified in 1973, having joined *Richards Butler* in 1971. Became a Partner in 1977.
Personal: Born 24 March 1949. Attended Skinners School to 1966, then Worcester College, Oxford 1967-70. Leisure interests include cricket, opera and travel. Lives in Rickmansworth, Herts.

EASTWELL, Nicholas W.
Linklaters (a member firm of Linklaters & Alliance), London +44 20 7456 2000
nick.eastwell@linklaters.com
Recommended in Capital Markets: Debt & Equity
Specialisation: Partner, Capital Markets Department. Specialises in capital markets transactions, including issues of debt, equity-related debt, equity and depository receipts in international markets, particular emphasis on emerging markets in Central and Eastern Europe, the Middle East and Africa. Areas of practice include repackagings of bonds, funds and other financial assets, debt issuance programmes and derivatives.

EDGE, Steve
Slaughter and May, London +44 20 7600 1200
steve.edge@slaughterandmay.com
Recommended in Tax
Specialisation: Partner and principal area of practice in corporate taxation with a particular emphasis on corporate finance and structured asset finance. Expertise in investment funds, financial instruments, cross border financial transactions, securitisations and other capital markets work. Advises many UK and non-UK multinationals and banks on a wide range of tax matters. Contributes to a number of publications on corporate tax.
Career: Qualified in 1975 while with *Slaughter and May* and became a Partner in 1982.
Personal: Born 29 November 1950. Attended Canon Slade Grammar School, Bolton 1962-69, then Exeter University 1969-72. Lives in London.

EDLMANN, Stephen R.R.
Linklaters (a member firm of Linklaters & Alliance), London +44 20 7456 2000
stephen.edlmann@linklaters.com
Recommended in Capital Markets: Debt & Equity
Specialisation: Partner in the firm's Capital Markets practice. Over 20 years' experience in debt and equity capital markets and related matters. Main areas of practice include debt, equity and equity-related issues and associated listings.
Prof. Memberships: International Bar Association.
Publications: Contributed to legal text books on capital markets products, including 'The Law & Practice of International Banking', Sweet & Maxwell, 1987.

EDWARDS, Gareth
Pinsent Curtis, London +44 20 7418 7000
Recommended in Communications: E-commerce
Specialisation: Head of Corporate Department, London. Corporate finance and company law including M&A, Stock Exchange and AIM primary & secondary issues and City Code take-overs. Major transactions: Flotations of Intrinsic Value plc; Just2Clicks plc; Fulcrum Pharma plc; secondary issues for e-xentric; Transacsys plc.
Prof. Memberships: Solicitors European Group
Career: Articles: *Daultry & Keen* 1983-1985. Assistant solicitor: *Reynolds Porter Chamberlain* 1985-87: *Lewis Silkin* (partner 1988): *Pinsent Curtis* 1998 to date.

ELDER, Ian
Allen & Overy, London +44 20 7330 3000
Recommended in Energy: Electricity

ELLARD, John
Linklaters (a member firm of Linklaters & Alliance), London +44 20 7456 2000
john.ellard@linklaters.com
Recommended in Corporate/Commercial
Specialisation: Partner in the Corporate Department with extensive experience of tax and corporate finance. Particular experience in the field of privatisations, most notably in the telecommunications and transport industries; international equity offers; mergers and acquisitions, especially in the Coca-Cola System.

ELLIOTT, Peter
Clifford Chance, London +44 20 7600 1000
peter.elliott@cliffordchance.com
Recommended in Tax
Specialisation: Partner specialising in corporate and financial taxation matters including international cross-border structures and transactions. Frequent speaker at taxation related seminars.

U

Prof. Memberships: Active member of the International Bar Association, the International Fiscal Association and the Institute of Fiscal Studies.
Publications: Author of numerous articles in professional publications.
Career: Partner *Clifford Chance* 1980.

ELLIOTT, Robert
Linklaters (a member firm of Linklaters & Alliance), London +44 20 7456 2000
robert.elliott@linklaters.com
Recommended in Banking & Finance
Specialisation: Partner in the Banking Department since 1990. Global Head, Restructuring and Insolvency. Transactions include advising Innogy on the acquisition of the supply business of Independent Energy (in administrative investership); acting for the Hedge Conterparties to Ashanti Goldfields; advising the European banks in relation to Harnischfeger Industries; advising Merrill Lynch as underwriter of Senior and Mezzanine Debt on Zanussi vending/Wittenborg LBO; advising Citigroup/Schroder, Salomon Smith Barney, Royal Bank of Scotland and Bank of Ireland on financing of Greencove's takeover of Hazlewood Foods.

ELMAN, Jonathan
Clifford Chance, London +44 20 7600 1000
jonathan.elman@cliffordchance.com
Recommended in Tax
Specialisation: Partner specialising in the taxation of corporate and financing transactions with particular emphasis on international matters.
Career: Partner 1994.

ELSEY, Mark
Ashurst Morris Crisp, London +44 20 7638 1111
Mark.Elsey@ashurst.com
Recommended in PFI, Projects
Specialisation: Acts for governments, sponsors, contractors and lenders in relation to UK and international infrastructure and energy projects. Head of the firm's Projects Group (including PFI/PPP projects).

EMMERSON, Tim
Freshfields Bruckhaus Deringer, London
+44 20 7936 4000
tim.emmerson@freshfields.com
Recommended in Corporate/Commercial
Specialisation: Partner in the Corporate Department specialising in mergers and acquisitions, takeovers, flotations, corporate reconstructions, equity capital markets, financial services, securities and derivatives law.

ENSER, John
Olswang, London +44 20 7208 8888
jxe@olswang.com
Recommended in Communications: E-commerce
Specialisation: Principal area of practice: commercial, regulatory and competition law advice for Internet, interactive TV, television and music industries. Specialises in all aspects of e-commerce solutions in business to business and consumer markets. Clients include free and pay ISPs, leading websites, digital TV platform operators, internet technology providers, major film and record companies, retailers and insurers.
Prof. Memberships: ICC.
Career: Qualified: 1989. *Frere Cholmeley* 1987-94 (Brussels 1993-94). *Olswang* 1994 to date. Partner since 1996. School: Queen Elizabeth's Hospital, Bristol 1975-82. Pembroke College, Oxford 1982-85.
Personal: Born 21 October 1964. Married (one son). Lives in London.

EREIRA, David
Freshfields Bruckhaus Deringer, London
+44 20 7936 4000
david.ereira@freshfields.com
Recommended in Banking & Finance
Specialisation: Partner in finance group. Specialises in bankings, acting for banks, international institutions and borrowers in all aspects of banking and finance related work as well as property finance.

EVANS, Edward
Freshfields Bruckhaus Deringer, London
+44 20 7936 4000
edward.evans@freshfields.com
Recommended in Banking & Finance
Specialisation: Partner in finance department. Main areas of practice are banking and project and asset finance. Also handles energy law work.

EVANS, John
Hill Taylor Dickinson, London +44 20 7283 9033
John.Evans@htd-london.com
Recommended in Shipping
Specialisation: Shipping and insurance litigation. A partner for 20 years, who has practised shipping and marine insurance litigation/arbitration throughout career. Wide experience of resolution of disputes and pursuit of claims arising from major maritime casualties including actual and constructive total losses of vessels. Group leader of one of the firm's maritime and insurance litigation groups, leading a team of professional staff, including two solicitors who were formerly Master Mariners. Reported cases of interest include Ventouris v. Mountain (Italia Express); Choko Star; Royal Volker Stevin v. Mountain (Dutch Dredgers); Star Sea; Apostolis and Tjaskemolen. Partner in London responsible for the firm's Piraeus office.
Prof. Memberships: A supporting Member of LMAA, and inter alia, British Italian Lawyers' Association; BMLA; IBA and Liveryman of Worshipful Company of Shipwrights.
Personal: Llandovery College; University College of Wales, Aberystwyth (1972 LLB). Resides Stebbing.

EVANS, Stuart
Simmons & Simmons, London +44 20 7628 2020
Recommended in Corporate/Commercial
Specialisation: Head of Corporate Finance at *Simmons & Simmons*. Led teams advising: Interbrew on its £2.7 billion acquisition of the beer businesses of Whitbread and Bass; Pacific Century CyberWorks on its US$27 billion acquisition of Cable and Wireless HKT; Wal-Mart on its £6.8 billion acquisition of Asda.
Publications: Transactions in 'A Practitioner's Guide to the FSA Listing Rules'. Formerly Chairman of the Patrons of New Art Tate Gallery; director of Hackney Business Venture, and Islington International Festival st.art 2000.
Career: Qualified in 1972. With *Slaughter and May* 1972-79. Joined *Simmons & Simmons* in 1979, Partner since 1981.
Personal: Born 31 December 1947. Educated Royal Grammar School, Newcastle-upon-Tyne 1956-66, Leeds University 1966-69. Reader, C of E and contemporary art.

FALCONER, Ian
Freshfields Bruckhaus Deringer, London
+44 20 7936 4000
ian.falconer@freshfields.com
Recommended in Capital Markets: Securitisation
Specialisation: Partner in finance department. Main area of practice is complex structured capital markets transactions, in particular securitisations and repackagings.

FALK, Sarah
Freshfields Bruckhaus Deringer, London
+44 20 7936 4000
sarah.falk@freshfields.com
Recommended in Tax
Specialisation: Partner in Tax Department. Main area of practice is corporate tax. Work covers corporate tax planning and corporate finance.

FARLEY, Alastair
Watson, Farley & Williams, London
+44 20 7814 8000
afarley@wfw.com
Recommended in Shipping: Finance
Specialisation: Partner in International Finance Group. Main area of work is international finance, commercial shipping, ship finance and general corporate work.
Career: Qualified 1971; founding partner *Watson, Farley & Williams* 1982; senior partner 1982-99; non-executive director, Close Brothers Group plc and Stirling Shipping Company Ltd; Warden, Worshipful Company of Shipwrights; member, City of London Solicitors Company.
Personal: Born 1946; MA Jesus College, Cambridge.

FARQUHARSON, Melanie
Simmons & Simmons, London +44 20 7628 2020
Recommended in Competition/Anti-trust
Specialisation: EC and competition law and regulation, with particular focus on utilities, transport (air and rail) pharmaceuticals and food and drink.
Prof. Memberships: International Bar Association. Solicitors' European Group. Competition Law Association.
Career: Qualified 1988. Partner 1994.
Publications: 'Parallel Trade in Europe' (Sweet & Maxwell, 1998), Editor of the Rail Transport Section of Butterworth's 'Competition Law' (5-volume looseleaf Practitioner's textbook).
Personal: Graduate from St. Catharine's College, Cambridge.

FIELD, Sally
Bristows, London +44 20 7400 8000
Recommended in Intellectual Property

FINBOW, Roger
Ashurst Morris Crisp, London +44 20 7638 1111
roger.finbow@ashursts.com.
Recommended in Competition/Anti-trust
Specialisation: Carries out a wide range of corpo-

rate and commercial work. Specialising in competition law, in particular, merger regulation including, in 2000, Air Canada/Canadian Airlines; United News/Carlton; and Locker/Sylvan. Also head of the firm's Sports Group. A regular adviser on Competition Commission and ECMR enquiries. Clients include Allied Domecq, Smith & Nephew, National Express and Imperial Tobacco Group. Responsible for recruitment and solicitor personnel matters.
Personal: Governor of Seckford Foundation. Director of Ipswich Town Football Club.

FINLAY, Peter
White & Case LLP, London +44 20 7397 3603
pfinlay@whitecase.com.
Recommended in Projects
Specialisation: Head of *White & Case*'s project finance practice in EMEA from 1991/2000. Recent projects include leading *White & Case* team advising sponsors of the Isken Power project financing in Turkey; the Enron led Nowa Sarzyna project financing in Poland; the Ghazlan II Power financing in Saudi Arabia; and advised the Lenders on the Oman/India Fertiliser Project in Oman.
Career: Qualified to practice under US, UK, French and Irish law.

FIRTH, Simon
Linklaters (a member firm of Linklaters & Alliance), London +44 20 7456 2000
simon.firth@linklaters.com
Recommended in Capital Markets: Derivatives
Specialisation: Partner in the firm's Financial Markets Group, Corporate Department and head of its derivatives practice, specialising in the structuring and documentation of derivative products, the structuring of financial services, and head of its derivative practice businesses and the regulatory capital treatment of financial products. Part of development team for Blue Flag Confirms (the system which enables ISDA-based derivatives confirmations to be generated electronically), and Blue Flag Derivatives on online database; legal advice about the ability of counterpartis in Europe to enter into derivative transactions.

FLECK, Richard
Herbert Smith, London +44 20 7374 8000
richard.fleck@herbertsmith.com
Recommended in Competition/Anti-trust
Specialisation: Practice development partner. Has extensive experience of references of merger and monopoly situations to the Monopolies and Mergers Commission and of other competitive and regulatory matters such as investigations under the Competition Act, as well as experience with the European Commission, Department of Trade and Industry and the Bank of England. Other areas of expertise include advising accounting firms and the Institute of Chartered Accountants on technical and auditing matters, and on partnership matters.
Prof. Memberships: Law Society.
Career: Studied law at the University of Southampton. Qualified in 1973; partner *Herbert Smith* 1979; only lawyer on the Auditing Practices Board (appointed 1986).

FLETCHER, Philip
Milbank, Tweed, Hadley & McCloy, London +44 20 7448 3000
PFletcher@milbank.com
Recommended in Projects
Specialisation: Partner (Project Finance Group). Specialising in the development and financing of major infrastructure projects, including power plants, pipelines, roads and satellites. Has represented parties in relation to projects in Europe, the US and Asia, including: the Orion Satellite Project, and recent Arianespace Satellite Projects; Taweelah A1 Power Project, Abu Dhabi; the Yanpet Petrochemicals Project, Saudi Arabia; the Birecik and Marmara Ereglisi Power Projects, Turkey; the Tapada Power Project and the Sines LNG Project, Portugal; the Drax, Shoreham and Medway Power Projects, UK; the Teverola, Ferrara, Serene, Lomellina and Rosen Power Projects, Italy; the Jawa Power Project, Indonesia; the Bonny Gas LNG ship financing, Nigeria; the LG Energy Power Project, Korea and over fifteeen U.S. and Canadian power projects. Lecturer at conferences on negotiation of project documentation and has particular experience in structuring non-recourse capital markets issuances in Europe and the U.S.
Career: Has been with *Milbank, Tweed* since 1983 and was resident in the firm's Hong Kong office in 1987 and 1988.
Personal: Born 16 September 1957. Educated at Georgetown University School of Foreign Service (BS 1979), Fletcher School of Law & Diplomacy (MA, 1983) and the University of California, Berkeley (JD, 1983).

FLETCHER, Simon
Clyde & Co, Guildford +44 1483 555 555
Recommended in Shipping
Specialisation: Partner in Marine Casualty Department handling: Salvage, collision, transhipment, general average and related insurance policy disputes for insurer, cargo, ship, salvor and banking clients with special interest in Japan, Norway, USA, Turkey and Egypt. Recent cases: 'Ever Decent' / 'Norwegian Dream', 'Mighty Servant 2', also handling substantial commercial energy litigation for insurers, oil companies and contractors in commercial disputes including construction and operating problems e.g. 'Piper Alpha' and 'Sleipner A', secondment to an oil company for 18 months on an FPSO construction dispute. Now involved in disputes involving flexible riser failures, process skid and FPSO mooring construction disputes.
Prof. Memberships: Chairman of BMLA Sub-Committee for Offshore Structures. Regular conference speaker.
Publications: Contributor to GARD P&I Handbook on collision, salvage and towage and to The International Journal of Shipping Law.
Career: LLB (Hons) Manchester 1968. Joined *Clyde & Co.* 1971. Became a partner 1975.

FORRYAN, Andrew
Clifford Chance, London +44 20 7600 1000
Recommended in Capital Markets: Securitisation

FOX, Jason
Herbert Smith, London +44 20 7374 8000
jason.fox@herbertsmith.com
Recommended in PFI, Projects
Specialisation: Partner, Projects Group. Advising the public sector, corporates and banks on all aspects of the structuring, development and financing of projects in a variety of sectors including oil and gas, power, water, property and public infrastructure. Main area of practice is advising on public/private partnership projects.
Career: Qualified in 1987 with *Herbert Smith* and became a partner in 1994. Seconded to the Private Finance Panel Executive, February to September 1994. Author (jointly with Nicholas Tott) of 'The Private Finance Initiative Handbook' (Jordans, December 1998).

FOX, Ruth
Slaughter and May, London +44 20 7600 1200
ruth.fox@slaughterandmay.com
Recommended in Banking & Finance
Specialisation: Practice covers a wide range of commercial work, with an emphasis on banking and capital markets, now focusing on financial regulation. Has acted extensively for banks and also for building societies, including acting in relation to conversions, and for corporate trustees.
Prof. Memberships: The Law Society.
Career: Qualified in 1979 with *Slaughter and May.* Became a Partner in 1986.
Personal: Born 3 October 1954. Educated at St Helena School, Chesterfield and University College, London. Married with three sons. Lives in London and Hertfordshire.

FRANCIES, Mike
Weil, Gotshal & Manges, London +44 20 7903 1000
Recommended in Corporate/Commercial
Specialisation: Head of the London office and a member of the firm's thirteen-member management committee. Practice is in both the UK/US axis and across Europe. Specialises in public and private mergers and acquisitions, equity issues (IPOs and secondary), private equity/venture capital/MBOs and joint ventures. Clients span the telecommunications and new technology sectors, and include major corporates as well as financial advisers and private equity funds.

FRANK, David
Slaughter and May, London +44 20 7600 1200
david.frank@slaughterandmay.com
Recommended in Capital Markets: Debt & Equity
Specialisation: Extensive eurobond and international equity experience. Also handles corporate and banking work with a number of listed plc clients and is active in the venture capital and project financing areas.
Prof. Memberships: The Law Society. International Bar Association.
Career: Qualified 1979. Assistant Solicitor, *Slaughter and May*, 1979-86. Partner *Slaughter and May*, 1986. Head of Capital Markets, 1993.
Personal: Born 29 April 1954. Educated Shrewsbury School 1967-1972. University of Bristol 1973-76. Interests include cars and lawn tennis. Lives in Surrey.

U

U

FRASER, David
Baker & McKenzie, London +44 20 7919 1000
david.fraser@bakernet.com
Recommended in Arbitration (International)
Specialisation: Business disputes with experience in the areas of insurance and reinsurance, trade finance, sovereign immunity, professional liability, carriage by sea, telecommunications and corporate joint ventures. Has acted as counsel in and managed several major commercial arbitrations in England and elsewhere and has brought a number of cases to trial in the Commercial Court and the Court of Appeal in London. Has recently represented the owners of the Kazakhstan metals industry in complex arbitration proceedings against former joint venture partners. Led the team acting for Geest in the banana wars with Fyffes. Acts for a number of professional consultancy firms including Tillinghast and LEK. Led the team acting for Camelot in proceedings for judicial review of a decision by the National Lottery Commission on granting a new licence. Adviser on crisis management and senior management responsibilities. Member of City Disputes Panel Users Committee and LCIA.
Prof. Memberships: The Law Society and New York Bar.
Publications: 'Arbitration of International Commercial Disputes Under English Law' – The American Review of International Arbitration 1997/vol.8. no.1.
Career: Qualified in 1973. Joined *Baker & McKenzie* in 1975, becoming a partner in 1982.
Personal: Born 1948. University of Birmingham. Lives in London.

FRASER, Ross
Herbert Smith, London +44 20 7374 8000
ross.fraser@herbertsmith.com
Recommended in Tax
Specialisation: Main practice areas include insurance company mergers and acquisitions (highlights of the last year include acting on the acquisition of United Assurance Group by Royal London) and various structured finance transactions. On the non-insurance side, recent transactions include the acquisition by Iceland Group of Booker.
Career: London School of Economics (LLM 1970); qualified 1973; partner *Herbert Smith* 1982.

FREELAND, Rowan
Simmons & Simmons, London +44 20 7628 2020
rowan.freeland@simmons-simmons.com
Recommended in Intellectual Property
Specialisation: Intellectual Property litigation particularly patents and designs. Major cases include Texas Instruments v. Hyundai Electronics, Allied Colloids v American Cynamid, General Instrument v Intel, Southco v Dzus and Hallen v Brabantia. Also IT law.
Prof. Memberships: AIPPI, AIPLA, TIPLO.
Personal: Born 1956. Education Wellington, St Catherines College Oxford (BA 1978). Joined *Simmons & Simmons* 1980, qualified 1982, partner 1988. Married with three daughters. Interests reading, gardening, opera.

FREEMAN, Peter
Simmons & Simmons, London +44 20 7628 2020
peter.freeman@simmons-simmons.com
Recommended in Competition/Anti-trust
Specialisation: Main areas of practice are the EC and UK competition and regulatory law, including mergers. Industrial sector specialisations include television regulation, railways and gas. Joint General Editor (with Richard Whish) of 'Butterworths Competition Law'. Author (with Richard Whish) of 'A Guide to the Competition Act 1998', (Butterworths 1999). Chairman of the Regulatory Policy Institute, Oxford.
Prof. Memberships: IBA, UIA, Law Society, Competition Law Association.
Career: Qualifed in 1977. Joined *Simmons & Simmons* in 1973 and became a Partner in 1978.
Personal: Born 2 October 1948. Attended Goethe Institut, Berlin, 1967, Trinity College, Cambridge 1967-71, and Université Libre de Bruxelles 1972-73. Leisure interests include naval history and music.

FRENCH, Douglas
Clifford Chance, London +44 20 7600 1000
douglas.french@cliffordchance.com
Recommended in Tax
Specialisation: Managing Partner of the Tax, Pensions and Employment Practice in *Clifford Chance* London. Advises on tax issues relating to M&A, floatations, group reorganisations and reconstructions, buy-outs and joint ventures.
Prof. Memberships: Member of the Corporate Tax Sub-committee of Chartered Institute of Taxation and the Tax Committee of the British Venture Capital Association.
Career: Oxford (MA, Law) ATII. Partner *Clifford Chance* since 1988.
Personal: Married, two sons, one daughter.

FRIEND, Mark
Allen & Overy, London +44 20 7330 3000
Recommended in Competition/Anti-trust

FULLER, Geoff
Allen & Overy, London +44 20 7330 3000
Recommended in Capital Markets: Securitisation

GARDNER, Nick
Herbert Smith, London +44 20 7374 8000
nick.gardner@herbertsmith.com
Recommended in Communications: IT
Specialisation: Partner in intellectual property and information technology department. Deals with intellectual property and technology, specialising in matters involving technical issues in the computing and electronics field. Contentious and non-contentious work. Admitted as a Solicitor Advocate with rights of audience in all civil proceedings. Appointed expert for internet domain name determinations by the World Intellectual Property Organisation.
Career: A number of years experience in the electronic and computing industries before becoming a solicitor. Qualified in 1988 and became a partner at *Herbert Smith* in 1994. Handled the first Internet domain name case in front of the English courts, acting for Harrods. Acted for Amstrad in its record breaking £50 million plus judgment against Seagate Technology. Handles a wide range of internet and e-commerce work as well as traditional hardware and software contracts. Also deals with data protection matters and has advised a number of utilities in relation to Data Protection Tribunal Proceedings.
Personal: Educated at the University of Nottingham.

GAYTHWAITE, Miles
Bird & Bird, London +44 20 7415 6000
Recommended in Intellectual Property
Specialisation: Consultant to Intellectual Property Group. Principal area of practice is patents, patent and know-how licensing, trade marks and copyright. Also pharmaceuticals and software. Important cases handled include L.B. Plastics v Swish; Holtite v Jost; Unilever v Gillette; Societe Francaise Hoechst v Allied Colloids Ltd; Kakkar v Ferring; BICC plc v Burndy Corporation; Amersham v Corning; Hässle v SmithKline Beecham, Cynamid and Knoll; Connaught Laboratories v SmithKline Beecham and Napro Biotherapeutics v Bristol Myers Squibb.
Prof. Memberships: Chartered Institute of Patent Agents, Licensing Executives Society, APRAM.
Career: With *Elkington & Fife*, Chartered Patent Agents 1967-74. Qualified as a Chartered Patent Agent in 1972. Joined *Bird & Bird* in 1974 and became a Partner in 1978.
Personal: Born 1943. Educated at Glasgow University 1960-64 (BSc, Chemistry) and Cambridge University 1964-67 (PhD, Organic Chemistry). Lives in London.

GEFFEN, Charles
Ashurst Morris Crisp, London +44 20 7638 1111
charlie.geffen@ashursts.com
Recommended in Private Equity: Buyouts
Specialisation: Head of Private Equity at *Ashurst Morris Crisp*. Advises many of the leading buy-out houses in the UK and US as well as domestic and overseas corporate clients, seven of which are publicly quoted companies. Has wide experience of corporate and commercial activities, with particular emphasis on leveraged buy-outs, cross-border transactions, fund-raisings, mergers and acquisitions and other corporate finance matters.
Career: Joined *Ashurst Morris Crisp* as a trainee in 1982. Qualified as a solicitor in 1984. Partner in 1991.

GHIRARDANI, Paolo
Stephenson Harwood, London +44 20 7329 4422
paolo.ghirardani@stephensonharwood.com
Recommended in Shipping
Specialisation: Partner, Head of the Dry Litigation Group. Handles all areas of dry shipping litigation. Has gained a reputation as a tough, determined and well-respected lawyer. Developed a highly successful niche practice area in shipping fraud, with a particular emphasis on Africa. To quote one of Chambers sources for the 2000-2001 edition of Chambers Guide to the Legal Profession 'Forever on your back but does an unbelievable job for his clients'. With own team of lawyers regularly represents the interests of leading shipowners, P&I Clubs and underwriters. They investigate fraudulent cargo shortage claims – in bulk and containerised cargoes. Has made over 30 investigative trips to West Africa, including sailing on client vessels to conduct 'undercover' investigations.

Most of the cases involve complex evidence, the threat of prolonged arrests of clients' vessels in foreign jurisdictions and innovative legal tactics, especially on jurisdictional issues. Has lectured at various seminars in the UK and abroad on fraud investigation and prevention in containerised and bulk cargoes. Reported cases include: A/S D/S Svendborg & Another v Mohamed Wansa (t/a 'Melbourne Enterprises') [1996] 2 Lloyd's Law Rep. 559- Clarke J; A/S D/S Svendborg & Another v Mohamed Wansa (t/a 'Melbourne Enterprises') [1997] 2 Lloyd's Law Rep. 193- Court of Appeal.
Career: Qualified in November 1985 at *Holman Fenwick & Willan.* Joined *Stephenson Harwood* in 1989 and became partner in 1992.
Personal: Born 11 October 1959. Educated at St George's College, Weybridge, Surrey; University College Cardiff BA, (Hons) Law and Spanish 1978-82. Married. Interests include wine making (from real grapes). Languages: fluent Spanish, a little French and Italian.

GIBB, Jeremy S.P.
Norton Rose, London +44 20 7283 6000
gibbjsp@nortonrose.com
Recommended in Shipping: Finance
Specialisation: Principal area of practice is asset finance, especially for ships and aircraft. In particular has considerable expertise in domestic and cross-border leasing structures. In the shipping field has over 15 years experience in the City of London, acting for financiers and owners of all types of vessels, including cruise ships and offshore vessels, and has been involved in numerous FPSO financings. Also deals with acquisition finance, especially acquisition and disposal of leasing companies.
Prof. Memberships: Law Society, Connecticut Maritime Association.

GIBBINS, David
Wragge & Co, Birmingham +44 870 903 1000
david_gibbons@wragge.com
Recommended in Intellectual Property
Specialisation: Intellectual property litigator. Main technical areas are electronics, computers, mechanical and electrical engineering; also significant experience in passing off and trademarks.
Career: Practised at patent bar 1969-79 (chambers of J Whitford QC); director of anti-piracy operations at IFPI for 3 years; re-qualified as solicitor, partner in *Needham & Grant* since 1984; consultant for *Wragge & Co*, 2000.
Personal: MA (Cantab), lives in Kent. Married, 3 children. Interests include astronomy, playing golf and fast cars.

GILL, Judith
Allen & Overy, London +44 20 7330 3000
Recommended in Arbitration (International)

GILLESPIE, Stephen
Allen & Overy, London +44 20 7330 3000
Recommended in Banking & Finance, Projects

GODDEN, Richard
Linklaters (a member firm of Linklaters & Alliance), London +44 20 7456 2000
richard.godden@linklaters.com
Recommended in Corporate/Commercial
Specialisation: Partner, Corporate Department. Wide experience both in general corporate advisory work and corporate transactions. Advises corporate clients, investment banks and professional partnerships on public mergers and takeovers, joint ventures, private merger and acquisition transactions, public share offerings and other corporate equity fund raising. Advises corporations of various sizes in relation to their on-going affairs. Secretary to Takeover Panel, 1988-90.

GODFREY, Keith
Allen & Overy, London +44 20 7330 3000
Recommended in Corporate/Commercial

GOLDEN, Jeffrey
Allen & Overy, London +44 20 7330 3000
Recommended in Capital Markets: Derivatives

GOODALL, Caroline
Herbert Smith, London +44 20 7374 8000
caroline.goodall@herbertsmith.com
Recommended in Corporate/Commercial
Specialisation: Specialises in corporate work, in particular corporate finance and mergers and acquisitions. Has been involved as adviser to both companies and to investment banks, in numerous takeovers, international mergers and acquisitions, international share issues, IPOs, rights issues and placings. Has also advised on a number of cross border transactions and complicated international joint ventures. Leading deals include acting for Koninklijke Hoogovens N.V. in relation to its merger with British Steel; acting for Lazard Brothers, financial advisers to Electra Investment Trust plc, on the hostile £1.2bn bid by 3i Group plc and the alternative proposals by Electra for a share buy back and related restructuring; for BSkyB in relation to its IPO and £623m offer for Manchester United plc; for Friends Provident in relation to its £744m offer for the London and Manchester Group; and for Allied Colloids on hostile contested bids from Hercules Inc. (£1.2 billion) and Ciba Specialty (£1.4 billion).
Prof. Memberships: City of London Solicitors' Company.
Career: Admitted in 1980 and became a partner in 1987. Head of the Corporate Division.

GORRIE, Euan
Allen & Overy, London +44 20 7330 3000
Recommended in Banking & Finance

GOSLING, James
Holman Fenwick & Willan, London
+44 20 7488 2300
James.Gosling@hfw.co.uk
Recommended in Shipping
Specialisation: Partner in Admiralty Department. Principal areas of practice are salvage, collision, total loss, wreck removal and pollution, acting mainly for salvors, shipowners, hull underwriters and P&I Clubs. Also handles marine insurance, general shipping and commercial law MOA disputes, charterparty disputes and cargo claims. Important cases have included Scandinavian Star, Mineral Dampier collision with Hanjin Madras, Happy Fellow collision with Darfur, Europa collision with Inchon Glory, Belgrave and Smit Tak B.V. v Selco Salvage. Clients include several leading salvage companies, ship owners, P&I Clubs, hull underwriters, ship managers, insurance brokers and one southern hemisphere tycoon. Is on the editorial board of the International Maritime Law. Has lectured on Admiralty Law in Mexico and Venezuela in Spanish, and in London and Piraeus.
Prof. Memberships: Instituto Ibero-Americano De Derecho Maritimo.
Career: Qualified in 1980. Became a Partner in 1988.
Personal: Born 28 June 1955. Educated at Ampleforth College, York and at St.Catharine's College Cambridge. Leisure interests include rugby, skiing, tennis, sailing, rowing, motor cycling, antiques and crosswords. Speaks French and Spanish. Lives near Saffron Walden.

GOSSLING, Margaret
Clifford Chance, London +44 20 7600 1000
margaret.gossling@cliffordchance.com
Recommended in Projects
Specialisation: Partner specialising in international project finance (especially power, oil, gas and natural resources) and general banking and bank mergers.
Career: St Anne's College, Oxford (MA, Hons) 1980-1983. Articled *Coward Chance*; qualified 1986; partner 1993.
Personal: Married; resides London.

GRAHAM, Rory
Osborne Clarke OWA, London +44 20 7809 1116
rory.graham@osborneclarke.com
Recommended in Communications: IT
Specialisation: Partner in Technology, Media & Telecoms. Work includes advising on over 50 outsourcing transactions. Clients include financial institutions, major corporate users and local and central government. Advised on major software development agreements and hardware and system procurement. EDI and e-commerce experience includes advising a major UK telecommunications company on the launch of its internet service, advising a major internet advertising agency on 'push' technology and commercial contracts and setting up and advising an e-commerce community in the insurance industry. Wide international experience, with emphasis on the US and European jurisdictions.
Prof. Memberships: The Network Outsourcing Association (Director, Legal Affairs), British Computer Society Committee on IP law.
Publications: Articled at *Stephenson Harwood* (London) and *Stephenson Harwood & Lo* (Hong Kong). Assistant at *Bird & Bird* from May 1990; partner from January 1994. Joined *Osborne Clarke OWA* 1998. Co-author of 'Internet Law & Regulation' (1997).

GRANT, Gregor
Wragge & Co, Birmingham +44 970 903 1000
gregor_grant@wragge.com
Recommended in Intellectual Property
Specialisation: Partner and Head of Intellectual Property. Patent litigator, main technical areas being mechanical, chemical and biotechnology. Long hands-on experience in numerous patent actions in

U

these fields, with many cases reported in RPC and FSR. Also deals with trademark and design litigation.
Prof. Memberships: CIPA, AIPPI, IPLA, ITMA.
Career: Articled with *Hempsons*, assistant solicitor with *Bird & Bird*, co-founder of *Needham & Grant* in 1971, which merged with *Wragge & Co* in April 2000.
Personal: Born in Glasgow, lives in North London. Married, 4 children. Interests include jazz, piano, sketching, cooking, riding bikes.

GREEN, Geoffrey
Ashurst Morris Crisp, London +44 20 7638 1111
Recommended in Private Equity: Buyouts
Specialisation: Head of the firm's Company Department from 1994 until appointment as the firm's Senior Partner in 1998. Has extensive experience of major corporate transactions in the UK and overseas, particularly public and private mergers and acquisition work, including privatisations. One of the UK's leading practitioners in larger private equity transactions, is highly experienced at leading a co-ordinated team, including overseas legal advisors. Has advised many buy-out companies through to flotation and thereafter on equity issues, acquisitions and bids.

U

GREENBANK, Ashley
Macfarlanes, London +44 20 7831 9222
ashley.greenbank@macfarlanes.com
Recommended in Tax
Specialisation: Partner in the Corporate Tax Group specialising in UK and cross-border tax aspects of corporate finance transactions, mergers and acquisitions and venture capital work.
Prof. Memberships: Law Society (Corporation Tax Sub-Committee of the Revenue Law Committee); BVCA (Tax Committee).
Career: Qualified 1988. Articled at *Freshfields* (1986-1988). Assistant solicitor *Freshfields* Tax Department (1989-1994). Assistant solicitor *Macfarlanes* Company Commercial and Banking Department (1994-1997). Partner 1997.
Personal: King Edwards School Birmingham, Selwyn College Cambridge MA (1985), Lincoln College Oxford BCL (1989).

GRIFFIN, Paul
Herbert Smith, London +44 20 7374 8000
paul.griffin@herbertsmith.com
Recommended in Energy: Oil and Gas
Specialisation: Partner in energy and project finance. Wide experience in energy and project finance, in particular in the oil, gas (including LNG) and power sectors, both in the UK and overseas. Deals with a variety of projects and transactions in the energy field, together with privatisations. Involved in the re-negotiation of long-term contracts in liberalised gas and electricity markets and has also been much involved in energy related disputes in court and before experts and arbitrators. Experience in the related areas of competition and regulation. Writes and lectures widely.

GRIFFITHS, David
Clifford Chance, London +44 20 7600 1000
Recommended in Communications: IT

HADDOCK, Simon A.
Allen & Overy, London +44 20 7330 3000
Recommended in Capital Markets: Derivatives

HAFTKE, Mark
KLegal, London +44 20 7694 2500
Recommended in Communications: E-commerce
Specialisation: Partner, head of eBusiness and Digital Media practice. Internet specialist since 1995. Negotiates and drafts contracts for the complete e-enabled supply chain, advises on all related issues: e-payment, privacy and data protection, technology licensing, consumer protection legislation, copyright and trade mark/domain name infringement, digital distribution of content (including rights clearances and collection societies), defamation, regulatory compliance and the EU initiatives covering the regulation of E-commerce, distance selling and electronic signatures. Clients mainly blue chip, analogue and Internet including retailers and fulfillers, newspapers and publishers, ISPs, banks and media conglomerates. Also works with dotcom startups and on major technology JVs. Recent work includes many agreements for interactive digital television platforms and WAP deals.
Publications: Author of Internet chapter in 'Copyright & Designs Law' by Merkin & Black (Sweet & Maxwell) and chapters on Contract and Copyright in CFI's 'Practitioner's Guide to the Internet'.
Career: Joined *KLegal* as Partner June 2000; *Bird & Bird* (1995-2000 made partner 1997); *Russells* (1988-1995 made partner 1992); qualified as barrister 1986; re-qualified as solicitor 1992; BA Jurisprudence St Edmund Hall (1982-1985) MA (Oxon).

HALE, Chris
Travers Smith Braithwaite, London
+44 20 7295 3000
Chris.Hale@TraversSmith.com
Recommended in Private Equity: Buyouts
Specialisation: Head of *Travers Smith* Private Equity Group. Advises leading buy-out houses in the UK. Also advises on new issues and a number of listed companies, financial advisers and larger private companies on equity raising and mergers and acquisitions. Known particularly for working on more complex, larger buyouts and cross-border transactions
Prof. Memberships: Hon. Treasurer and Executive Committee member of Society of Advanced Legal Studies.
Career: Qualified as a solicitor in 1981 with *Kingsley Napley*, joined *Travers Smith Braithwaite* in 1983 and became partner in 1987.
Personal: Educated at King's College School, Wimbledon, Emmanuel College, Cambridge (MA) and Wolfson College, Cambridge (LLM). Leisure interests include football, reading, gardening, walking and legal history.

HALL, Peter
Norton Rose, London +44 20 7283 6000
Recommended in Projects
Specialisation: A Partner in the Construction and Engineering Group with considerable experience of the construction and engineering aspects of infrastructure projects around the world, including project finance and PFI deals. Recently acted for the commercial lenders on the Connect project, for the developers on a number of recent independent power projects and on a series of road and rail projects. Contentious work encompasses High Court and international arbitration claims.
Career: Member of the Technology and Construction Court Solicitors Association, an accredited adjudicator and an associate of the Chartered Institute of Arbitrators.

HANDLING, Erica
Weil, Gotshal & Manges, London +44 20 7903 1000
erica.handling@weil.com
Recommended in Capital Markets: Securitisation
Specialisation: International finance partner and co-head of the capital markets group. Has experience of a wide range of international financing transactions with particular expertise in structured capital markets transactions. Most recently has advised in connection with a large number of CDO's, including the first ever wholly Euro-denominated CDO, for which in 1999 the team won Legal Business's Capital Markets Team of the Year Award. Also advises on more traditional debt capital markets transactions and other structured finance products such as credit derivatives and repackagings.
Career: Prior to joining the firm, worked at *Allen & Overy* in both London and New York.
Personal: Graduated from Exeter University.

HANTON, Bruce
Ashurst Morris Crisp, London +44 20 7638 1111
bruce.hanton@ashursts.com
Recommended in Private Equity: Buyouts
Specialisation: Specialises in corporate finance and private equity. Recent transactions include IPDS of The Carphone Warehouse Group plc and Inflexion plc, the investment by Texas Pacific Group and Colony Capital in Punch Group Limited, acquisition of William Hill by Cinven and CVC, and acquisition by Nikko Europe Plc of Roadchef plc and Roadchef's subsequent acquisition of Blue Boar and Take-a-Break. Also acts for several corporate clients, including Alexon Group plc., Fitness First plc., United News and Media plc.

HARDWICK, Michael J.
Linklaters (a member firm of Linklaters & Alliance), London +44 20 7456 2000
michael.hardwick@linklaters.com
Recommended in Tax
Specialisation: Partner in Tax Department. Specialist in corporate taxation, with particular experience advising on tax issues in relation to corporate reorganisations, disposals, acquisitions, takeovers, mergers, joint ventures, and flotations and private finance initiative projects.
Prof. Memberships: Member, Revenue Law Committee of City of London Law Society; Chairman, Law Society's Corporation Tax Sub-Committee; Member, Law Society's Revenue Law Committee and International Tax Sub-Committee; International Fiscal Association.
Publications: Joint author of 'Taxation of Companies and Company Reconstructions' (7th edition).

HARRIS, Graham D.
Richards Butler, London +44 20 7247 6555
gdh@richardsbutler.com
Recommended in Shipping
Specialisation: Wide experience of dispute resolution and commercial negotiation in the shipping and transportation industries including shipbuilding, sale and purchase, charterparties, bills of lading, through transport documentation and insurance.
Career: Qualified October 1981, *Norton Rose*, then *Richards Butler*. Partner at *Richards Butler* 1988.
Personal: Born 28 September 1956. Educated at King's School, Canterbury and Oriel College Oxford (MA Jurisprudence, First Class Hons). Lives in London.

HARRIS, Paul
Eversheds, London +44 20 7919 4500
Recommended in Intellectual Property
Specialisation: Partner *Eversheds* London Intellectual Property Group. Patents, trademarks, copyright, designs. Notable cases include Coloplast [1993]; Wagamama v City Centre Restaurants [1995]; Electrolux v Black & Decker [1996]. Author of various IP articles; regular lecturer including Bristol University: IP Diploma course.
Prof. Memberships: ITMA; CIPA; INTA (Chair of the European Legislation Analysis Sub-committee); AIPPI; UNION; Royal Society of Chemistry; Chariman of the Whittington Committee of the City of London Law Society.
Career: Qualified in 1987. *Bristows Cooke & Carpmael*; *McKenna & Co* (1988-92); *Taylor Joynson Garrett* (1992-94); *Eversheds* formerly *Jaques & Lewis[* (1994), became Partner in 1995.
Personal: Born 17 May 1961; Keele University; Leisure interests include fitness; running; theatre; Italian wine. Lives in Westminster.

HARRISON, Brian
Allen & Overy, London +44 20 7330 3000
Recommended in Projects

HARRISS, David
Bird & Bird, London +44 20 7415 6000
david.harriss@twobirds.com
Recommended in Intellectual Property
Specialisation: Partner in Intellectual Property Department. Main area of practice is intellectual property litigation. Includes UK and international patent infringement litigation, trademark infringement, passing off, copyright infringement, design infringement and breach of confidence. Acted in Akzo/ Du Pont, PLG/Ardon, BP/Hoechst Celanese, BP/Union Carbide and Exxon/ Lubrizol. Member of Editorial Board of Patent World. Chairman of Law Society I.P. Working Party.
Prof. Memberships: Law Society, Chartered Institute of Patent Agents (Fellow).
Publications: Co-editor of 'International IP Litigation' (Sweet & Maxwell).
Career: Qualified as Patent Agent 1969. Worked for AA Thornton & Co. 1965-70, then Langner Parry from 1970-73 (Chartered Patent Agents). Joined *Bird & Bird* in 1973. Qualified as a Solicitor 1977. Partner 1977.
Personal: Born 1943. Attended Epsom College 1956-61, then Christ's College, Cambridge 1961-64. Lives in Chobham, Surrey.

HART, Michael
Baker & McKenzie, London +44 20 7919 1000
michael.hart@bakernet.com
Recommended in Intellectual Property
Specialisation: Partner in Intellectual Property and Information Technology Law Department. Principal area of practice is contentious and non-contentious IP and IT Law. Work includes copyright, trade marks and passing off, patents and trade secrets and IT disputes. Also deals with government regulations and trade libel. Has represented various trade bodies in IP/IT lobbying activities relating to UK and EU legislative proposals, including the copyright in the Information Society Directive. Has acted in numerous IP and IT court actions representing companies such as Fila, McLaren, Seiko, Versace, Apple Computer and Sony.
Prof. Memberships: Anti-counterfeiting Group, AIPPI, Intellectual Property Lawyers Association.
Career: Qualified in 1983. With *Linklaters & Paines* 1983-87. Joined *Baker & McKenzie* in 1987 and became a Partner in 1990.
Personal: Born 12 August 1959. Educated at City of London School 1970-77 and Exeter College, Oxford 1977-80. Leisure activities include theatre, cinema, horse racing and tennis. Lives in London.

HARTLEY, Simon
Norton Rose, London +44 20 7283 6000
hartleysr@nortonrose.com
Recommended in Shipping: Finance
Specialisation: Specialising in shipping finance representing shipping companies, banks, lessors, export credit agencies and other financial institutions in connection with all types of ship lending and leasing, capital raising, sale and purchase of second-hand ships, ship registration, shipbuilding contracts, bareboat chartering, management agreements and related financial arrangements. The shipping finance group is one of the leading shipping finance practices in London, working closely with other *Norton Rose* lawyers experienced in advising shipping industry clients on competition and regulatory matters, taxation, litigation, insurance, mergers and acquisitions and corporate finance for the shipping industry.
Prof. Memberships: Member of the Law Society and Baltic Exchange.
Career: Trained *Norton Rose*; qualified 1988; partner 1997.
Publications: Has been a regular contributor to the 'Euromoney Shipping Finance Annual' over the last three years.
Personal: Married with one child. Leisure interests are sport and hill walking.

HARVEY, Richard
Richards Butler, London +44 20 7247 6555
rhjph@richardsbutler.com
Recommended in Shipping
Specialisation: Heads the firm's casualty response team of mainly legally qualified ex-seafarers, which handles all types of casualty including fires and explosions, groundings, salvage, collisions, wreck removal, reef damage and pollution, and their associated insurance and general average issues. Acts for Clubs, Hull underwriters, shipowners and major salvors. Has handled for owners such cases as the Europa/Inchon Glory, MSC Samia /Carina, Lula 1/Graceous, Polydefkis P/Anna Spiritou collisions and the Sea-Land Mariner fire and explosion. Acted for salvors in the European Gateway and for owners in the salvage of the MSC Rosa M as well as in the Maersk Tokyo, Erika and World Discoverer; more recently has been closely involved in the 'Ievoli Sun' sinking and the Hatfield rail crash.
Prof. Memberships: Law Society; British Maritime Law Association; BMLA Arrest Convention subcommittee, City of London Admiralty Solicitors Group.
Career: Served as an officer in the British Merchant Navy before qualifying as a solicitor in 1980. Became a partner in *Richards Butler* in 1983.
Personal: Educated at Christ Church, Oxford (MA); Southampton College of Technology. Interests include sailing, gardening, music, photography and engineering.

HATCHARD, Michael
Skadden, Arps, Slate, Meagher & Flom LLP, London +44 20 7519 7000
mhatchard@skadden.com
Recommended in Corporate/Commercial
Specialisation: Partner specialising in corporate finance and M&A. Principally mergers, acquisitions and joint ventures and the full range of securities distribution transactions, particularly where significant UK/US implications arise.
Career: Qualified 1980 with *Theodore Goddard*, partner 1985. Joined *Skadden, Arps* as a partner in 1994 with responsibility for the English legal and regulatory aspects of global securities offerings and cross-border transactions.
Personal: Born 21 November 1955.

HATTRELL, Martin
Slaughter and May, London +44 20 7600 1200
martin.hattrell@slaughterandmay.com
Recommended in Corporate/Commercial
Specialisation: Corporate Department. Principal area of practice is corporate and commercial law, in particular mergers and acquisitions.
Prof. Memberships: The Law Society.
Career: Qualified in 1987 with *Slaughter and May* and became a Partner in 1994.
Personal: Born 9 August 1961. Educated at Ampleforth College, Yorkshire and The Queen's College, Oxford.

HENDERSON, Schuyler
Norton Rose, London +44 20 7283 6000
Recommended in Capital Markets: Derivatives
Specialisation: Practice covers the full range of lending, credit enhancement and securities transactions. Since moving to London in 1977, has worked closely with many international financial institutions in creating, developing and documenting swaps and related derivatives and structured finance products and advising with respect to enforcement, regulatory, tax and capacity issues.
Personal: Obtained his undergraduate degree (BA) from Princeton University in 1967 and his law degree (JD) and business degree (MBA) from the University of Chicago in 1971 and is a member of the New York and Illinois bars.

U

HENDERSON CBE, Giles
Slaughter and May, London +44 20 7600 1200
giles.henderson@slaughterandmay.com
Recommended in Corporate/Commercial
Specialisation: Senior Partner and Partner in Corporate Department. Corporate, corporate finance and commercial law, with particular experience in privatisations.
Prof. Memberships: The Law Society; Financial Reporting Council; Chairman, Law Group, UK/China Forum; Hampel Committee on Corporate Governance.
Career: Qualified 1970. Partner since 1975. Senior Partner since 1993.
Personal: Born 1942. Educated at Michaelhouse School, South Africa and at Witwatersrand University, South Africa (BA) and Magdalen College, Oxford (MA, BCL).

HENRY, Michael
Buchanan Ingersoll, London +44 20 7920 3700
Recommended in Communications: E-commerce

HERRING, Paul
Ince & Co, London +44 20 7623 2011
Recommended in Shipping
Specialisation: Specialises in carriage of goods by sea, charterparty, bills of lading, sale and purchase, new building disputes and shipbrokers/shipmanagers' negligence. Regular lecturer on sale and purchase and charterparty issues.
Career: Articled at *Ince & Co.* in 1979 and became a partner in 1987.
Personal: First Class Honours Degree in Law from Leicester University. Leisure interests include golf.

HICKSON, Chris
Slaughter and May, London +44 20 7600 1200
chris.hickson@slaughterandmay.com
Recommended in Intellectual Property
Specialisation: Head of group specialising in contentious and non-contentious intellectual property and information technology matters. Practice comprises principally litigation and advice on patents, trade marks, passing off, copyright and designs, the protection of trade secrets, and advertising. Has a wide experience of IP in the context of corporate transactions, licensing and general litigation.
Prof. Memberships: ITMA, ACG, INTA, AIPPI.
Career: Admitted 1977. With *Slaughter and May* since 1975. Became a Partner in 1984.
Personal: Born 10 December 1951. Educated at St. Joseph's College, Beulah Hill and Birmingham University (LLB). Interests include stamps, books and mountaineering. Lives in Surrey.

HIESTER, Elizabeth
Clifford Chance, London +44 20 7600 1000
elizabeth.hiester@cliffordchance.com
Recommended in Communications: Telecoms
Specialisation: Partner in corporate practice area with primary responsibility for telecommunications, computer, IT and media industry practice group, focusing on international and domestic projects, commercial contracts, joint ventures, regulatory advice and anti-trust and intellectual property law issues pertinent to those sectors.
Prof. Memberships: Law Society of England and Wales; International Bar Association Communication Sub-Committee; America Bar Association; International Telecommunications Committee; Telecommunications Industry Association; Royal Television Society; INTUG; International Institute of Communications.
Publications: Author of 'Telecommunications' in 'UK and EC Competition Law Encyclopaedia' (Butterworth).
Career: Manchester (LLB, 1st class Hons 1973); Amsterdam (Diploma in European Integration 1974). Articled *Clifford Chance* 1980-1982; qualified 1982; lecturer in law University of Kent 1974-1980; solicitor *Clifford Chance* 1982-1988; partner since 1988.
Personal: Music. Born 1952; resides Canterbury.

HIGGINSON, Tony J.
Baker Botts LLP, London +44 20 7778 1400
Recommended in Energy: Oil and Gas
Specialisation: Energy & Natural Resources: advising both in the UK and internationally on energy projects, including: concession and production sharing contracts; corporate and asset transactions; gas supply and marketing contracts; LNG; transportation and tariffing; downstream refining and product sales and power generation.
Prof. Memberships: International Bar Association; Institute of Petroleum; Association of International Petroleum Negotiators. In 1997 and 1999, named as one of world's leading energy and natural resources lawyers by Euromoney Publications in London.
Career: Articled *Herbert Smith*; legal adviser Vickers Plc, 1974-76; attorney Phillips Petroleum Company Europe – Africa and Phillips Petroleum Company, Oklahoma 1976-84; General Counsel Sun Oil International; Managing Director Sun Oil Britain Limited, Far East Regional Manager, Sun Oil, 1984-92; Partner *Lovell White Durrant* 1996-99. Partner *Baker Botts* from 1 January 2000.
Personal: MA, Emmanuel College, Cambridge (1971); Graduate PMD Harvard Business School 1987.

HOBBS, Christopher
Norton Rose, London +44 20 7283 6000
hobbsc@nortonrose.com
Recommended in Shipping
Specialisation: Partner in the Shipping Litigation Group at *Norton Rose* who handles a broad range of shipping and shipping-related international commercial disputes ranging from major casualties, together with insurance aspects arising, through to oil and other commodity trading, and all aspects of carriage of goods by sea and charterparty disputes. Has particular expertise in relation to tankers. Has acted for the owners in total losses including 'Pel Hunter' off Sicily, 'Oceanos' off South Africa and the 'Melete' in the Indian Ocean. Has also acted in the grounding of the 'Sea Empress' in Milford Haven and in the 'Daylam' which was a leading case on a 'follow lead underwriters' provision in insurance contracts. Also represented the owner of the 'Seaflower' in a leading (reported) dispute involving the effect of loss of oil major approvals for a tanker. Has represented shipyards in Korea and Europe in a number of major cases and presently represents a number of oil and gas majors in a variety of disputes. Has wide experience in court and arbitration both in England and internationally. Speaks regularly at shipping conferences and contributes regularly to 'Lloyd's List' and 'Fairplay'. Has qualified for Fellowship of the Institute of Risk Management.
Career: Articled *Norton Rose*; qualified 1986; assistant solicitor *Herbert Smith* 1990-91; assistant solicitor *Norton Rose* 1991; partner 1995; Commission in 3rd Royal Tank Regiment as tank troop commander 1980-83.

HODGSON, Derek
Clyde & Co, London +44 20 7623 1244
derek.hodgson@clyde.co.uk
Recommended in Shipping
Specialisation: Partner in Marine Department since 1981. Shipping/marine/insurance. Experienced in representing shipowners/P&I Clubs/hull underwriters, charterers and trading companies in High Court actions and arbitrations. Has represented shipowners on numerous high profile casualties, including container explosions at sea. Particular speciality in Thailand, Greece, South America and Africa.
Personal: Educated at Tonbridge School and University College London (1970-72).

HODGSON, Mark
Taylor Joynson Garrett, London +44 20 7300 7000
mhodgson@tjg.co.uk
Recommended in Intellectual Property
Specialisation: Specialises in advising pharmaceutical, medical device and biotechnology companies on intellectual property, regulatory, product liability and parallel importation matters. Represented clients successfully before the UK courts, The European Patent Office and the ECJ. Acted this year for Lilly ICOS in the high-profile patent revocation action against Pfizer concerning the patent for Viagra. Lectures extensively.

HOLLAND, Peter Rodney James
Allen & Overy, London +44 20 7330 3000
Recommended in Corporate/Commercial

HOLMES, Simon
S J Berwin & Co, London +44 20 7533 2222
simon.holmes@sjberwin.com
Recommended in Competition/Anti-trust
Specialisation: A wide range of work including: extensive range of merger work acting for the parties, complainants or third parties; advising on dominance issues (pricing/discounts/parallel imports etc); and a wide range of commercial arrangements both on and off-line. Coordinator of *S J Berwin*'s e-commerce group.
Prof. Memberships: Recent Chairman, Law Society's European Group.
Career: 1st Class Honours, Law and Economics from Cambridge. Grande Distinction, Licence Speciale en Droit Européen, Brussels University.
Personal: Married, 2 daughters. Walking, cycling, tennis, film.

HORSFALL TURNER, Jonathan
Allen & Overy, London +44 20 7330 3000
Recommended in Banking & Finance, Projects

U

HUDD, David G.T.
Lovells, London +44 20 7296 2000
david.hudd@lovells.com
Recommended in Capital Markets: Securitisation
Specialisation: Partner specialising in capital markets and securitisation. Extensive experience of securitisations and repackagings, debt issues, international equity and equity-linked offerings and derivatives.
Prof. Memberships: City of London Solicitors' Company; Law Society.
Career: Christ Church, Oxford University 1977-80 (MA Jurisprudence). Qualified 1983. *Linklaters* 1981-85; Paribas 1985-90; Sanwa International 1990-93; Indosuez 1993-94; joined *Lovells* as a partner in 1994.

HUGHES, Richard
Linklaters (a member firm of Linklaters & Alliance), London +44 20 7456 2000
richard.hughes@linklaters.com
Recommended in Capital Markets: Securitisation
Specialisation: Partner, securitisation, asset finance, syndicated loans and property finance. Has led the teams on the BarclayCard and Arran (RBS) securitisations, the first euro-denominated non-conforming mortgage securitisation, the financing of the world's largest dredger and the project financings of the new stands at Chelsea and West Ham football clubs.
Publications: United Nations: 'The Privatisation of African Airlines'.

HUMPHREY, Anthony R.
Allen & Overy, London +44 20 7330 3000
Recommended in Banking & Finance, Projects

HURST, Philip
Ashurst Morris Crisp, London +44 20 7638 1111
philip.hurst@ashursts.com
Recommended in Energy: Mining
Specialisation: Partner, Energy & Natural Resources Group. Leading practitioner in natural resources law, especially in Africa, Middle East and South Asia. Extensive experience in advising sponsors of independent power projects and greenfield mining projects. Currently advising on greenfield mining project in Iran, and on power/mining projects in Zambia and Tanzania. Visiting lecturer in natural resources law, Imperial College, London.
Career: BA, LLB(ANU), MA, LLM (Virginia) FRGS. 1981-85 associate *White & Case*, New York; 1985-87, World Bank, Washington DC.

HYMAN, Neil
Slaughter and May, London +44 20 7600 1200
neil.hyman@slaughterandmay.com
Recommended in Corporate/Commercial
Specialisation: Partner specialising in mergers, acquisitions and disposals; joint ventures and general company commercial; particular emphasis in the drinks, pubs and leisure industry and in the telecommunications and media fields.
Career: Articled *Slaughter and May*; qualified 1988; Hong Kong office 1990-92; partner 1995.
Personal: Born 1962; educated at Arnold School and Birmingham University (LLB Hons 1st class); resides in London; member Dyrham Park Golf & Country Club.

INGLIS, Alan
Clifford Chance, London +44 20 7600 1000
alan.inglis@cliffordchance.com
Recommended in Banking & Finance
Specialisation: Partner specialising in banking, corporate finance, insolvency and corporate reconstruction.
Career: Exeter School; Birmingham University (LLB). Articled *Clifford Turner/Clifford Chance*; qualified 1985; partner *Clifford Chance* since 1992.

INGLIS, Andrew
Olswang, London +44 20 7208 8888
api@olswang.com
Recommended in Intellectual Property
Specialisation: Partner specialising in intellectual property, particularly patents and trade marks. Also deals with copyright issues for media clients of the firm. Heads *Olswang*'s Intellectual Property Group which comprises 20 lawyers. The practice spans substantial patent and trade mark practices (including patent and trade mark filing practices), as well as meeting the needs of the more traditional clients of the firm in the areas of media, IT and e-commerce. Time is split between litigation and commercial matters. Considerable expertise in advertising and marketing. Important reported cases include British Coal Corporation v Glaverbel SA, R Bance & R Bance & Co Ltd's Licence of Right (copyright) Application, Mecklermedia v DC Congress and the most recent "Budweiser" trade mark appeal on behalf of the Czech Brewery. Acted for Dyson in their recent patent win against Hoover.
Career: Originally qualified in Australia in 1981 and practised there before moving to England. After qualifying in England in 1990 became a partner at *Nabarro Nathanson* from 1991-97, and has been a partner at *Olswang* since 1997. Active in contributing articles to publications such as the European Intellectual Property Review and public speaking on intellectual property issues.

INGRAM, Kevin
Clifford Chance, London +44 20 7600 1000
kevin.ingram@cliffordchance.com
Recommended in Capital Markets: Securitisation
Specialisation: Partner in the Finance Area specialising in debt securitisation, principal finance, asset backed commercial paper conduits, structured products, secured lending and all types of structured finance transactions.
Prof. Memberships: Member of the Executive Committee of the European Securitisation Forum.
Career: St Cyres Comprehensive School, Penarth; University College, Oxford University (1987 BA, Jurisprudence 1st class honours, 1989 Bachelor of Civil Law 1st class honours). Trainee and Assistant at *Clifford Chance* 1989-98; partner at *Clifford Chance* since May 1998.
Personal: Born in Cardiff in August 1966; resides in Surrey.

IRVINE, James
Arnander Irvine & Zietman (Formerly Llewelyn Zietman), London +44 20 7842 5400
Recommended in Intellectual Property

JACOBS, Lawrence
Allen & Overy, London +44 20 7330 3000
Recommended in Communications: IT

JAMES, Glen William
Slaughter and May, London +44 20 7600 1200
glen.james@slaughterandmay.com
Recommended in Corporate/Commercial
Specialisation: Practice covers all work in the fields of company/corporate finance, including mergers and acquisitions, issues and flotations and corporate restructurings. Additional interest in non-contentious insurance and reinsurance work.
Prof. Memberships: The Law Society; Securities Institute.
Career: Qualified 1976. Articled at *Slaughter and May* 1974-76. Assistant Solicitor 1976-83. Partner since 1983.
Personal: Born 22 August 1952. Educated at King's College School, Wimbledon and New College, Oxford.

JOHNSON, Andrew
Hill Taylor Dickinson, London +44 20 7283 9033
Recommended in Shipping

JOHNSON, Ian
Ashurst Morris Crisp, London +44 20 7638 1111
ian.johnson@ashursts.com
Recommended in Tax
Specialisation: Partner in Tax Department. Involved in advising on the taxation implications of a wide range of corporate transactions advising both overseas and UK clients.
Prof. Memberships: Associate of the Chartered Institute of Taxation.
Publications: Co-author of Butterworth's 'Taxation of Loan Relationships, Financial Instruments and Foreign Exchange'.
Career: Graduated in law from Edinburgh University. Qualified as solicitor in 1992 and partner in 1996.

JOHNSON, James
Clifford Chance, London +44 20 7600 1000
Recommended in Banking & Finance

JOHNSTON, Bruce
Weil, Gotshal & Manges, London +44 20 7903 1295
bruce.johnston@weil.com
Recommended in PFI
Specialisation: Head of the project finance practice in London. Project finance experience covers a range of sectors including infrastructure, electricity, oil and gas, telecoms, transportation and waste and water. Recent projects include: Athens Ringroad in Greece, Stirling Water in Scotland, Poznan Water in Poland, Belchatow II in Poland, Telewest in the UK, Kangal Power in Turkey and VSZ in Slovakia. Frequent speaker at conferences and author of articles.

JONES, Arfon
CMS Cameron McKenna, London
+44 20 7367 3000
Recommended in Corporate/Commercial

JONES, Gareth
Nabarro Nathanson, London +44 20 7524 6000
Recommended in Energy: Oil and Gas

JONES, Nigel
Linklaters (a member firm of Linklaters & Alliance), London +44 20 7456 2000
nigel.jones@linklaters.com
Recommended in Intellectual Property
Specialisation: Specialist in intellectual property and technology-related matters, particularly in the pharmaceuticals field. Chairman of the firm's Healthcare Group. Main areas of practice include IP aspects of corporate transactions and IPOs; drafting and negotiating technology agreements; IP litigation, including patent litigation (particularly in the biotech and general healthcare fields), breach of confidence actions and trade mark and copyright disputes.
Prof. Memberships: Fellow of the Chartered Institute of Arbitrators; Licensing Executives Society, International: Immediate Past Chair, European Committee. Licensing Executives Society, Britain & Ireland: Member of Council and Chairman of EC Laws Committee. Associate Member of the Chartered Institute of Patent Agents and American Intellectual Property Lawyers Association. Member of Editorial Board of BioScience Law Review.

JONES, Stephen
Baker & McKenzie, London +44 20 7919 1000
stephen.jones@bakernet.com
Recommended in Intellectual Property
Specialisation: Intellectual property litigation and advice work including patents, trade marks, designs and copyright; passing off; technology related litigation and dispute resolution; IP aspects of corporate transactions; commercial agreements, in particular in the pharmaceuticals and healthcare industries; partner in charge of Trade Marks Unit, responsible for applications for trade marks and registered designs.
Prof. Memberships: CIPA (Fellow); EPI; ITMA; INTA; ECTA; LES; AIPPI (British Group); PTMG; Royal Society of Chemistry (Associate).
Career: BSc (Chemistry) Imperial College; ARCS; LLB (London); Chartered Patent Agent; European Patent Attorney; Registered Trade Mark Agent; European Trade Mark Attorney; solicitor; partner *Baker & McKenzie*, London.
Personal: Born 22 January 1956; married with three children.

JOYCE, Tom
Freshfields Bruckhaus Deringer, London +44 20 7936 4000
tom.joyce@freshfields.com
Recommended in Corporate Finance: Mergers & Acquisitions
Specialisation: Member of the Corporate Department specialising in securities. Primarily advises on US legal aspects of equity and debt offerings.
Prof. Memberships: Association of the Bar of the City of New York and President of the Society of English and American Lawyers.

JUDGE, Ian
Bristows, London +44 20 7400 8000
Recommended in Intellectual Property

KAMSTRA, Gerry
Simmons & Simmons, London +44 20 7628 2020
Recommended in Intellectual Property
Specialisation: Partner in Intellectual Property Department. Principal area of practice is intellectual property law, including financings, commercial transactions and litigation within the pharmaceutical and biotechnology industries. Clients include Astra Zeneca, 3M, Bayer, Bristol-Myers Squibb, Guidant Corporation, Alizyme plc and Inhale Therapeutic Systems. Has written numerous articles and lectures widely.
Prof. Memberships: Member Intellectual Property Advisory Committee of BioIndustry Association and Associate Member of Chartered Institute of Patent Agents.
Career: Qualified in 1986. Joined *Simmons & Simmons* 1986 where became a Partner in 1992.
Personal: Born 13 May 1954. Educated at Hymers College, Hull, Keble College, Oxford (Psychology & Physiology), Leicester University (PhD in Neuroendocrinology) and Trent Polytechnic.

KARET, Ian
Linklaters (a member firm of Linklaters & Alliance), London +44 20 7456 2000
ian.karet@linklaters.com
Recommended in Intellectual Property
Specialisation: Specialist in IP and technology matters. Main areas of practice include IP and IT aspects of acquisitions and disposals, corporate fund raising and licensing. IP litigation and arbitration, including patent litigation (biotech, pharmaceutical and chemicals). Software exploitation and IT dispute resolution.
Prof. Memberships: Assistant Reporter General of AIPPI. Associate Member of the Chartered Institute of Patent Agents. Member of the Royal Society of Chemistry. Fellow of the Chartered Institute of Arbitrators. Editorial Board of EIPR.

KAYE, Laurence
Garretts, member firm of Andersen Legal, London +44 20 7344 0344
laurence.kaye@glegal.com
Recommended in Communications: E-commerce
Specialisation: Partner and Head of Technology and e-Business Practice. Advises a wide range of clients on e-business and in the publishing and digital media industries. Clients range from internet start-ups to multinationals. Recent work has included e-commerce, joint ventures and partnership agreements in the information, financial services, and e-tailing sectors, site licences for the use of electronic journals, media joint ventures, co-publishing agreements, agreements for interactive television services. Was a member of the evaluation team which formally evaluated the ground-breaking UK Pilot Site Licence Initiative under which several publishers granted site licences allowing web-based access to their materials to the higher education sector. In addition to transaction-based work, also advises a number of media industry bodies on digital media and e-commerce legal issues. Advised the Cross-Industry Working Group which made representations to the UK government on behalf of the publishers on the implementation of the Database Directive into UK law. Also legal adviser to the European Publishers Council – a member of the Brussels-based Rightsholders Alliance which is actively involved in representing media owners' interests on proposed new copyright and regulatory laws, particularly the forthcoming EU Copyright Directive.
Prof. Memberships: Law Society, Society for Computers & the Law.
Career: Qualified in 1975, having joined *Brecher & Co.* in 1973. Left in 1980 to co-found company and commercial department at *Saunders Sobell.* Joined *The Simkins Partnership* in 1994. *Paisner* 1998 – 2000.

KEAL, Anthony C.
Allen & Overy, London +44 20 7330 3000
Recommended in Banking & Finance

KELLY, Christopher
Linklaters (a member firm of Linklaters & Alliance), London +44 20 7456 2000
christopher.kelly@linklaters.com
Recommended in Energy: Mining
Specialisation: Partner, Co-head of the e-Commerce Business Group. Specialist in corporate law, including M&A, takeovers, privatisations, joint ventures, securitisations and corporate reorganisations. Key focus on the technology sector. Also specialist in mining-related corporate and projects work.
Prof. Memberships: Solicitor of Supreme Court of England and Wales. Solicitor of Supreme Court of Queensland, Australia.

KELLY, Jacky
Weil, Gotshal & Manges, London +44 20 7903 1000
jacky.kelly@weil.com
Recommended in Capital Markets: Securitisation
Specialisation: Head of the firm's securitisation practice in London working closely with counterparts in New York and in the firm's other offices worldwide. Has been closely involved in the UK securitisation market since its inception, with securitisation experience in a number of jurisdictions extending across a number of asset types and structures, including real estate assets, trade receivables, consumer assets, corporate loans, intellectual property rights, future flow transactions and operating company deals. Also has in-depth experience of a range of other structured finance products, including asset backed conducts, structured investment vehicles and structured derivatives.

KEMP, Richard
Kemp & Co, London +44 20 7600 8080
Recommended in Communications: E-commerce, Communications: IT
Specialisation: Practice covers intellectual property, competition/EU regulatory and general business law for the full range of IT, e-commerce and telecoms sectors.
Prof. Memberships: Computer Law and Security Reports – Editorial Board Member. Guide to the World's Leading IT Lawyers (1999); Telecoms Lawyers (2000); one of top 20 global IT lawyers ('Best of the Best') (2000).
Career: *Clifford-Turner* (1978-1984); *Hopkins & Wood* 1984-1991 (Partner 1985); *Hammond*

Suddards (1991-1995 (head of IT Group; Founder Partner London Office)); *Garrett & Co.* (Partner 1995, IP/IT London Office Group Head 1996; IP/IT European Service Line Head, 1997). Set up *Kemp & Co* in November 1997 to specialise in commercial, corporate and employment work in the IT, e-commerce and telecoms sectors – firm now has 17 lawyers and 25 staff.
Personal: Born 8 July 1956. Educated Oakham School, St. Catharine's College Cambridge, Université Libre de Bruxelles.

KERR, David
Bird & Bird, London +44 20 7415 6000
Recommended in Communications: Telecoms
Specialisation: Partner in Company Department. Main area of practice is corporate and commercial work involving deals in the telecommunications, digital media and information technology sectors. Has extensive experience of major transactions in these areas, including acquisitions, joint ventures, project finance, privatisation and outsourcing agreements. Frequent speaker at conferences on telecommunications and information technology.
Prof. Memberships: Communications Lawyers Association, IBA, Law Society.
Career: Qualified in 1985. Joined *Bird & Bird* in 1985, becoming a Partner in 1987.
Personal: Born 1960. Attended Jesus College, Cambridge (MA Hons, 1982). Lives in London.

KHAN, Rafique
CMS Cameron McKenna, London
+44 20 7367 3000
rzk@cmck.com
Recommended in Energy: Oil and Gas
Specialisation: Specialises in oil and gas particularly in the areas of natural gas production, transportation and supply with an additional emphasis on project-financed CCGT Power Projects. Has extensive experience of the European natural gas industries both in the commercial and regulatory field. Speaker on legislative, regulatory and commercial issues facing the gas industries in the UK, elsewhere in the European Union and Central and Eastern Europe.
Prof. Memberships: Law Society of England and Wales; The Institute of Petroleum.
Career: Graduated in 1982 from the University of Leeds; articled clerk and senior legal adviser at British Gas 1984-1992. In 1992, joined *McKenna & Co* as Assistant Solicitor and since 1994 has been a Partner in the Energy, Projects and Construction Group.
Personal: Cinema, Opera, Eating, Walking and Climbing.

KING, Peter
Linklaters (a member firm of Linklaters & Alliance), London +44 20 7456 2000
peter.king@linklaters.com
Recommended in Corporate/Commercial
Specialisation: Partner. Corporate Department. Co-Head of International Equities Practice. Experienced in all aspects of corporate finance, including, in particular, international equity offers, privatisations, mergers and acquisitions and advice to financial institutions on regulatory matters.

KNAPP, Vanessa
Freshfields Bruckhaus Deringer, London
+44 20 7936 4000
vanessa.knapp@freshfields.com
Recommended in Corporate/Commercial
Specialisation: Partner in Corporate Department specialising in mergers and acquisitions, securities offerings, corporate finance law and financial services regulation.

KNIGHT, Adrian
Shearman & Sterling, London +44 20 7655 5000
aknight@shearman.com
Recommended in Corporate/Commercial
Specialisation: Partner in M&A and Corporate Finance. Specialises in mergers and acquisitions, corporate finance and private equity transactions.
Career: Qualified in March 1984 with *Allen & Overy*. Became a Partner at *Ashurst Morris Crisp* in 1992. Resigned from *Ashurst Morris Crisp* becoming a partner at *Shearman & Sterling* in June 1999.
Personal: Graduated from Cambridge University in 1980.

KNIGHT, William
Simmons & Simmons, London +44 20 7628 2020
Recommended in Corporate/Commercial

KNUTSON, Robert
Masons, London +44 20 7490 4000
Recommended in Arbitration (International)
Specialisation: International commercial arbitration and sale of goods; international construction contracts and disputes; comparative law and conflicts of law; practising arbitrator.
Prof. Memberships: Canadian member, ICC Court of Arbitration and ICC Commission on International Arbitration; member, Canadian ICC Arbitration Committee (member qualifications sub-committee); member ICC working parties on ADR, electronic commerce, prevention of extortion, bribery, and model contract forms; Fellow, Chartered Institute of Arbitrators (England); CIA registered Construction Industry Adjudicator; member, IBA Committees on International Sale of Goods and sub-committee Chairman International Construction Projects (Newsletter Editor for committee and Publications sub-committee chairman); ABA Associate member; member of Swiss Arbitration Association; member, Society of Construction Law; co-founder, and Treasurer, International Arbitration Club; member European Panel of Distinguished Neutrals of the (US) CPR Institute, supporting member, London Maritime Arbitrators Association; member of British Institute of International and Comparative Law; LCIA Panelist and Fellow of the Indian Council of Arbitration.
Career: LLB University of British Columbia, 1982; Barrister and Solicitor, Canada, 1983; LLM, LSE, 1984; Solicitor, England and Wales, 1988; MSc Construction Law and Arbitration, 1991; partner, *Masons* 1996; MPhil University of London 1997; practised in Canadian, American and English law firms, numerous publications; regular speaker on international construction and arbitration. Recently nominated as an arbitrator in International Sale of Goods, construction, telecommunications and shareholders disputes.
Personal: Born 22/10/56; lives in Dulwich, married, two children.

KON, Stephen
S J Berwin & Co, London +44 20 7533 2222
stephen.kon@sjberwin.com
Recommended in Competition/Anti-trust
Specialisation: Head of the EU and Competition Department at *S J Berwin & Co.* Extensive experience in representing clients in contentious and non-contentious EU and domestic competition work, as well as general EU law. Regularly represents clients in proceedings before the Office of Fair Trading, the Monopolies and Mergers Commission, the European Commission and the Court of First Instance and the European Court of Justice in Luxembourg. Represented the European Commission in a number of competition cases before the CFI and the ECJ and has acted in a number of significant merger clearance enquiries; for example, for Guinness in the EU clearance of its merger with Grand Metropolitan, for which the team won the Legal Business Competition Team of the Year award, for Mediaset in its pan-European joint venture with Kirch and for Universal in its successful opposition to the Time Warner/EMI concentration. Has written and lectured extensively on various subjects relating to EU and competition law and numerous articles in most of the leading European law reviews, and most recently *SJ Berwin*'s major loose leaf publication 'The Competition Law of the UK'.
Prof. Memberships: 1986 Chairman of the Law Society's Solicitors' European Group. International Bar Association. Law Society's Solicitors European Group.
Career: With *S J Berwin & Co.* since formation in 1982, previously with a major City law firm and subsequent to that taught European Community and Competition Law at the Universities of Sussex and Reading. Most recently visiting lecturer at University of Oxford.
Personal: Sussex University; College of Europe, Bruges. Born 26 September 1949. Lives in London.

KRISCHER, David S.
Allen & Overy, London +44 20 7330 3000
Recommended in Capital Markets: Securitisation

LAMBERT, Robert
Clifford Chance, London +44 20 7600 1000
robert.lambert@cliffordchance.com
Recommended in Arbitration (International)
Specialisation: Partner specialising in the law and practice of international arbitration, conflict of laws and jurisdiction. Particular experience in disputes involving international engineering, construction and infrastructure projects. Represents clients as counsel (advocate) before domestic and international arbitral tribunals. Regularly advises on the drafting of dispute resolution provisions for projects and other commercial contracts.
Career: Oxford University (St Edmund Hall), BA, (Hons) Law (1st class). Trained *Clifford Chance*; qualified 1989.

LANE, Robert
CMS Cameron McKenna, London
+44 20 7367 3000
Robert.Lane@cmck.com
Recommended in Energy: Electricity
Specialisation: Partner specialising in utilities law

U

U

and regulation. Extensive experience of electricity projects and restructurings in the UK and overseas. Adviser to The National Grid Company plc. From 1988 to 1990 advised on the restructuring of the England and Wales electricity industry, including drafting the Grid Code for the England and Wales system, with extensive involvement in the design of the regulatory regime and pooling arrangements and in drafting and advising on many of the documents (e.g. those dealing with connection to and use of the system). Continues to advise on these topics and on the development and reform of the market structure, including extensive involvement in the introduction of the New Electricity Trading Arrangements (NETA) and the Connection and Use of System Code (CUSC). Also adviser to Northern Ireland Electricity plc on its re-structuring and privatisation and on the further recent restructuring in the Northern Ireland markets to introduce the requirements of the European IME Directive, which introduces bi-lateral trading and balancing mechanisms. Advised the ESI Reform Unit of the State Government of Victoria on the restructuring of the electricity market there, which involved consideration of and scoping of the regulatory, contractual and code structures and critiquing the licences, codes and contracts. Has also advised on power purchase agreements relating to Electricidade de Portugal and the Public Power Corporation of Greece and advised on all aspects of the restructuring of the electricity supply industry in Orissa, India. Advised Electricity Supply Board in Eire and Ontario Hydro in Canada. Advising in a number of jurisdictions on the implementation of the European IME Directive, including drafting, implementation and structure of electricity legislation and transitional regimes, which has also involved advising a major Western European integrated utility on its compliance with the Directive including advising on Grid Code, connection and use/access agreements, legislation, licensing and ancillary services and writing electricity legislation for Greece. Regular speaker at conferences throughout the world.
Prof. Memberships: International Bar Association (Member of Section on Energy and Natural Resources Law and co-chairman of Utilities Law Committee).
Career: Qualified in 1982. Joined *McKenna & Co.*, now *CMS Cameron McKenna*, in 1988.
Personal: Educated at University College, London.

LAWES, William
Freshfields Bruckhaus Deringer, London +44 20 7936 4000
will.lawes@freshfields.com
Recommended in Corporate/Commercial
Specialisation: Specialises in public bids, mergers and demergers, private acquisitions and disposals, venture capital and equity issues of all types. Sector experience includes publishing, radio and television, services sector and electricity.

LAYTON, Matthew
Clifford Chance, London +44 20 7600 1000
Recommended in Private Equity: Buyouts

LEIGH, Guy
Theodore Goddard, London +44 20 7606 8855
Recommended in Competition/Anti-trust
Specialisation: Head of the firm's competition and regulation group, based in both London and Brussels. Practice focuses on EC and UK competition and regulatory work. Extensive experience of merger joint venture, technology transfer, state aids and other competition, regulatory and compliance issues, and has advised in relation to such issues particularly in the IT, media and communications, sports, pharmaceutical and healthcare, telecommunications, and transport sectors. Experience includes representing the Intellectual Property Owners Inc. of the US before the European Court of Justice in the Magill TV Listings case, and advising a leading software manufacturer with regard to a wide range of EC competition law issues. Also dealt with the merger control aspects of the acquisition by MAID plc, now The Dialog Corporation plc, of Knight-Ridder Information Inc. and Knight-Ridder AG. Past experience includes involvement with the TSB vesting and flotation, the acquisition by British Airways of British Caledonian, a major Monopolies and Mergers Commission reference concerning the bus industry and a number of newspaper merger references.
Prof. Memberships: Chairman of the English Competition Law Association, first Vice President and a past Reporter General and International Reporter of the International League for Competition Law. Also a member of the Brussels-based European Competition Lawyers Forum and of the Law Society Bar Joint Working Party on Competition.
Publications: Co-author of 'The EEC and Intellectual Property', the author of various articles on EC law and a frequent speaker at the competition law conferences.

LEVINE, Iona
Baker & McKenzie, London +44 20 7919 1000
iona.levine@bakernet.com
Recommended in Capital Markets: Derivatives
Specialisation: Head of the Derivatives Practice. Undertakes a wide range of derivatives and treasury related work. Advises on new products and structured transactions, exchange traded and OTC matters. Advises on the newer areas of global energy trading and e.trading. Advises on the standard key issues which are of concern to the derivatives markets, e.g. Netting, Collateral and Legal Risk Management e.trading. Acts for banks, securities houses, brokers, fund managers, energy companies, corporates and e-commerce entrepreneurs. Recent experience includes: undertaking a high level consultancy assignment with a major international bank in which acted as the senior in-house derivatives counsel providing derivatives expertise and management experience and helped the bank to restructure its derivatives legal and documentation teams. Providing legal advice and support to enable a US Securities house to establish its global equities broking business. Enabling various institutions to develop and revise their netting policies. Involved in the purchase of, and undertook the English due diligence in relation to, the purchase of a prime brokerage business. Providing advice on a variety of structured transactions and notes. Undertaking derivatives litigation. Other experience includes: responsibility for setting global policy and for providing treasury and capital markets legal advice throughout the Hong Kong Banking Group. Helping to establish the world's first clearing house for the multilateral netting of foreign exchange transactions ('Echo'). Chairing the London part of the British Bankers Association/New York Foreign Exchange Legal Committee which was responsible for drafting and developing the first version of International Foreign Exchange Master Agreement (IFEMA).
Career: Pre-1984, Qualified as a Barrister. 1984-86 Citibank Legal Counsel advising on a wide range of international commercial banking matters. 1986-95, Hong Kong and Shanghai Banking Corporation/Midland specialised in Treasury, Capital Markets, Banking, Emerging Markets and Payment Systems – ultimately head of the Global Treasury and Capital Markets Legal Department. 1996 to 2000, Head of the Derivatives Practice at *Hammond Suddards*. 2000- to Date, Head of Derivatives Practice, *Baker & McKenzie.*
Personal: Educated at London School of Economics and The Inns of Court School of Law. Member of Lincoln Inn called February 1982. General Editor of 'Derivatives and Related Markets: Law and Documentation' published by Sweet & Maxwell Autumn 2000.

LEVINE, Marshall
Linklaters (a member firm of Linklaters & Alliance), London +44 20 7456 2000
marshall.levine@linklaters.com
Recommended in Projects
Specialisation: Partner and Head of the Construction and Engineering Group. Involved in a wide range of construction and engineering matters, including advice in relation to many construction and engineering projects and major real estate joint ventures, property developments and construction financing. Highly experienced in drafting construction contracts, and advising on dispute resolution over a wide variety of projects including process plants, civil engineering, substantial headquarter office developments, relocations and refurbishments as well as PFI transactions in the health, property, transportation and waste water sectors. Since being involved in the BR privatisaton, has developed 'railways' expertise.
Publications: 'Construction Insurance' (Lloyds); 'Commercial Development Property Precedents' (Longman); Construction and Engineering Precedents (Sweet & Maxwell) and Consultant Editor on Butterworth's PFI Manual.

LEW, Julian
Herbert Smith, London +44 20 7374 8000
julian.lew@herbertsmith.com
Recommended in Arbitration (International)
Specialisation: Head of International Commercial Arbitration Practice Group. Partner in Litigation and Arbitration Division. Main area of practice is international commercial arbitration, acting as an adviser and representing clients in different forms of arbitrations: concerning all kinds of international contracts,

particularly engineering and infrastructure projects, investments, distribution, intellectual property licences and joint ventures. Has also been appointed as an arbitrator in ICC, LCIA, AAA, Ad hoc and other arbitrations. Head of the School of International Arbitration, Centre for Commercial Law Studies, Queen Mary, University of London.
Prof. Memberships: British Institute of International and Comparative Law, London Court of International Arbitration, Chartered Institute of Arbitrators, American Society of International Law, American Bar Association, Swiss Arbitration Association, French Arbitration Committee, Hong Kong International Arbitration Centre, International Bar Association, Arbitral Centre of the Federal Economic Chamber, Vienna.
Publications: Author of numerous publications including: 'Applicable Law in International Commercial Arbitration' (1978). Editor, 'Contemporary Problems in International Commercial Arbitration' (1985), 'The Immunity of Arbitrators' (1990) and 'Enforcement of Foreign Judgements' (1994).
Career: 1970 (Bar); 1981 (Solicitor); 1985 (Attorney-at-Law, New York).
Personal: Born 3 February 1948. LLB (Hons) London, 1969; Academy of International Law 1970-71; and Doctorat Special en Droit International, Université Catholique de Louvain, Belgium, 1977.

LEWIS, David
Norton Rose, London +44 20 7283 6000
lewisdtr@nortonrose.com
Recommended in Corporate/Commercial
Specialisation: Partner in Corporate Finance Department; Senior Partner. Main area of practice is corporate finance, including take-overs (public and private) flotations, stock exchange work of all types, MBOs, schemes of arrangement, international global offerings, all types of commercial agreements, and debt restructurings. Has handled over 100 listings and numerous take-overs including HSBC Holdings/ Midland, GEC Siemens/ Plessey, Imperial Group/ Hanson/ UB, BA/ B-Cal, BMW/ Rover, Redland/ Steetley, Ladbroke/ Hilton, Dixons/ Currys, Guiness/ Grandmet, Ciba/ Allied Colloids, BMW/ Rolls Royce. Author of articles in Gazette and PLC; also the *Norton Rose* Guide to Take-overs. Has chaired and spoken at numerous conferences. Member of the Law Society of London Company Law Committee 1982-97. Hon Fellow Jesus College, Oxford.

LEWIS, David
Allen & Overy, London +44 20 7330 3000
Recommended in Tax

LING, Timothy
Freshfields Bruckhaus Deringer, London
+44 20 7936 4000
timothy.ling@freshfields.com
Recommended in Tax
Specialisation: Partner in Tax Department. All aspects of corporate tax, and particularly UK and cross-border mergers and acquisitions, reconstructions, joint ventures, demergers, private company acquisitions and disposals, new issues.

LISTON, Stephanie
McDermott, Will & Emery, London
+44 20 7577 6900
sliston@europe.mwe.com.
Recommended in Communications: Telecoms
Specialisation: Partner in Corporate Department leading European Communications and Technology practice. Communications work includes advising upon, drafting and negotiating communications related contracts and commercial transactions and providing strategic and regulatory advice in connection with UK and European telecommunications and broadcasting activities.
Career: Admitted to the Texas Bar in 1985, District of Columbia, 1988 and qualified in England and Wales in 1994. Associate with *Fulbright & Jaworski* in London; Houston, Texas; and Washington DC. 1984-89. Senior Attorney with MCI 1990-92. *Freshfields* 1992-95. *Baker & McKenzie* London 1995-99. Joined *McDermott, Will & Emery* in July 1999.
Personal: Born 15 March 1958. Attended The Colorado College (BA in History/Political Science 1980), University of San Diego Law School 1980-82 and University of Notre Dame London Law Centre 1982-83 (Juris Doctor 1983). Attended Trinity Hall, Cambridge University (LLM in English Law – 1st Class – 1994).

LIVINGSTON, Dorothy
Herbert Smith, London +44 20 7374 8000
dorothy.livingston@herbertsmith.com
Recommended in Competition/Anti-trust
Specialisation: Areas of expertise cover the full range of EU and UK competition law including restrictive agreements, monopolies, anti-competitive practices, abuse of dominant position, mergers, public procurement. State aids and utility regulation; in financial and banking matters, areas of procurement expertise include European Monetary Union, guarantees by States and financing of international joint ventures. Deputy head of the firm's European and Competition Law Group and head of the firm's Procurement Law Unit. Highlights of the year include acting for BSkyB in relation to 'Open....' (acquisition of controlling interest) regulatory review of Vivendi stake in BSkyB, Kirch (acquisition of joint control) and Sports Internet Group (acquisition).
Prof. Memberships: Chairman Banking Law sub-committee of the City of London Law Society. Competition Law sub-committee of the City of London Law Society, Financial Law Panel Working Party on State Aids and Advisory Board, Centre for European Law at King's College, University of London.
Career: Qualified in 1972; partner, *Herbert Smith*, 1980; author of several books and articles including 'Competition Law Practice' (Sweet & Maxwell, 1995); 'The Competition Act' (Sweet & Maxwell, for publication January 2001).
Personal: Educated Central Newcastle High School, GDST; St Hugh's College, Oxford, BA Jurisprudence. Leisure interests include photography.

LIVINGSTONE, Hugh
Holman Fenwick & Willan, London
+44 20 7488 2300
Hugh.Livingstone@hfw.co.uk
Recommended in Shipping
Specialisation: Partner in commercial litigation department, specialising in all types of marine litigation on behalf of shipowners, charterers and insurers (P & I and market), as well as sellers and buyers of ships.
Career: Admitted 1976 (South Africa), 1985 (England and Wales) and 1986 (Hong Kong). Partner in *Holman Fenwick & Willan* 1986. Resident Partner in Hong Kong office 1986-88 and subsequently at London office.
Personal: Educated University of Cape Town (BA LLB) and University College London (LLM).

LLEWELYN, David
White & Case LLP, London +44 20 7397 3607
dllewelyn@whitecase.com
Recommended in Intellectual Property
Specialisation: Heads the 10-strong London-based intellectual property practice of *White & Case*, working closely with IP specialists across the firm worldwide. Practice encompasses both contentious and non-contentious matters. In addition, works as an adviser to the information technology, e-commerce and pharmaceutical sectors.
Career: Joined *White & Case* in September 1999 from *Llewelyn Zeitman* having worked previously at *CMS Cameron McKenna* and *Linklaters & Paines.*

LONG, Colin
Olswang, London +44 20 7208 8888
cdl@olswang.com
Recommended in Communications: Telecoms
Specialisation: Joint head of the firm's telecommunications group. Has guided many of the world's leading telecommunications companies over the years in a variety of deals related to fixed, mobile and satellite-based services. Work encompasses regulation and competition law, commercial legal issues, corporate transactions, M&A, joint ventures and start-ups, as well as development funding in the communications, IT and general high-tech sectors. Was involved in advising bidders in both the 3G mobile and broadband wireless auctions.
Prof. Memberships: Former chairman of the Communications Law Committee of the International Bar Association and founder of the UK Communications Lawyers Association.
Publications: Author of the leading textbook 'Global Telecommunications Law and Practice', a guest speaker at numerous conferences and a frequent writer of articles on competition and regulatory issues.
Career: Trained at *Clifford Turner* before becoming a partner at *Bird and Bird* and later *Coudert Brothers*, before moving to *Olswang* in 1998.
Personal: Graduate of Bristol University.

LONG, Julian
Freshfields Bruckhaus Deringer, London
+44 20 7936 4000
julian.long@freshfields.com
Recommended in Corporate/Commercial
Specialisation: Partner in the Corporate Group specialising in European M&A. Sector experience includes pharmaceuticals, food, publishing and water.

U

LOUVEAUX, Bertrand
Slaughter and May, London +44 20 7600 1200
bertrand.louveaux@slaughterandmay.com
Recommended in Competition/Anti-trust
Specialisation: Provides a broad range of UK and EC Competition Law. Has wide experience before the European Commission, the Office of Fair Trading and the Competition Commission (including both merger and monopoly enquiries). Recent merger cases have included Shell/Exxon (EC), British Steel/Hoogovens (EC), BAT/Rothmans (EC), Kodak/Imation (EC), Victoria Wine/Threshers (UK), Lincoln/Charter(UK) and Carlton/United/Granada (UK). On the contentious front, recently acted for Nomura/GPC in obtaining the landmark Article 81 'pubco' decision. Regularly advises clients on Article 81 and 82 EC Treaty and 1998 Competition Act.
Career: Qualified 1994 with *Slaughter and May.*
Personal: Born 28 April 1967. Educated London School of Economics (MSc Economics). Married with two children.

LOWE, Steven
Stephenson Harwood, London +44 20 7329 4422
steven.lowe@stephensonharwood.com
Recommended in Shipping
Specialisation: Partner, Insurance and Reinsurance Group. Commercial shipping and insurance litigation and arbitration, both domestic and international (US, several European countries, ICC arbitration etc), including new building/sale and purchase disputes (frequently involving complex issues of naval architecture or marine engineering), charterparty, ship management, banking and oil trading disputes, insurance coverage issues (especially P&I, marine hull and reinsurance), advising on policy wordings and drafting policy/Club Rule changes.
Prof. Memberships: BMLA.
Career: Qualified 1972 *Holman Fenwick & Willan* and became partner in 1976. Joined *Stephenson Harwood* as partner in 1989.
Personal: Born 1946. Educated at Cambridge University, BA (Classics and Law) 1966-69. Married with one son. Interests include music, wine, (intermittently) books and golf.

LUX, Jonathan
Ince & Co, London +44 20 7623 2011
Jonathan@ince.co.uk
Recommended in Shipping
Specialisation: Partner since 1983 specialising in shipping, international trade and insurance advice and litigation.
Prof. Memberships: Law Society, London Maritime Arbitrators Association, Chartered Institute of Arbitrators, CEDR, ADR Net, British Academy of Experts, International Bunker Industry Association, International Bar Association.
Publications: Co-author of 'The Law of Tug, Tow and Pilotage' and 'The Law and Practice of Marine Insurance and Average' and 'Bunkers'. Editor of 'Classification Societies'. Author of various other publications in the fields of maritime law and international trade. Regular speaker at conferences and seminars on shipping, international trade and insurance subjects.
Career: Qualified and joined *Ince & Co* in 1975.
Personal: Born 30 October 1951. Holds LLB (Hons) (Exhib), 1973, and DES from the University of Aix-Marseilles, 1974. Freeman of the City of London, Liveryman of the Worshipful Company of Solicitors, Chairman of the Committee 2 (Trial Observations and Interventions) of the International Bar Association's Human Rights Institute. Leisure interests include opera, theatre, golf, sailing and single-seater motor racing (holder of a national licence). In the cause of raising funds for human rights participated in the Argentinean Mille Migle (2000) and the Peking to Paris Car Rally (1997) finishing First in Class and awarded gold medal. Lives in London.

MACAULAY, Anthony
Herbert Smith, London +44 20 7374 8000
anthony.macaulay@herbertsmith.com
Recommended in Corporate/Commercial
Specialisation: Experienced in company and commercial matters, especially corporate finance work, including takeovers and flotations. Has particular expertise in relation to the Takeover Code and insider dealing.
Career: Educated at Keble College, Oxford; qualifed in 1974; became Partner at *Herbert Smith* in 1983; secretary to the Takeover Panel 1983-85; Editorial Board, Partner's Corporate Law.

MACDONALD, Morag
Bird & Bird, London +44 20 7415 6000
Recommended in Intellectual Property
Specialisation: Partner in Intellectual Property Department. Work includes litigation, transactional and advisory work in relation to patents, trade marks, copyright and other intellectual property rights. Also handles electronics and computer law. Acted in Mentor/Hollister, Compaq/Dell, Richardson Vicks/Reckitt & Colman, Chocosuisse/Cadbury, Unilever/Johnson Wax, Research Corporations SPC, Swiss Miss, Baxter/Pharmacia Upjohn and Genetics Institute, Cartonneries de Thulin/White Knight, Stolt Comex Seaway/Coflexip, Novo Nordick/DSM.
Prof. Memberships: CIPA, ITMA, INTA, ECTA, British Computer Society.
Career: Called to the Bar in 1984. Qualified as a Solicitor in 1988, having joined *Bird & Bird* in 1985. Became a Partner in 1989. Contributor on IP issues to 'Internet Law and Regulation' (Sweet & Maxwell, 2nd edition, December 1997), UK section of 'The New Role of Intellectual Property in Commercial Transactions' (Wiley 1994) and the Legal Aspects chapter of 'Essential IT' (Gee Publishing 1996). Co-author of 'Designs & Copyright Protection of Products: World Law & Practice' (Sweet & Maxwell).
Personal: MA in Mathematics, Physics and Law from Cambridge.

MACDONALD-BROWN, Charters
Gouldens, London +44 20 7583 7777
Recommended in Intellectual Property
Specialisation: Head of Intellectual Property Group. Advised in numerous patent, copyright, design, trade mark and other IP cases. Executive Council of AIPPI (UK). Honorary adviser to the Legal and Parliamentary Committee of the Royal Society of Chemistry. Regular conference speaker. Lectures on IP courses at Bristol University and QMW (part of London University).
Prof. Memberships: Law Society, IBA, CIPA, ITMA, AIPPI, ABA, AIPLA, INTA, ECTA, LES, Pharmaceutical Trademark Group.
Career: Qualified 1974. Partner from 1977.

MACFARLANE, David
Ashurst Morris Crisp, London +44 20 7638 1111
Recommended in Corporate/Commercial

MACFARLANE, Nicholas
Lovells, London +44 20 7296 2000
nicholas.macfarlane@lovells.com
Recommended in Intellectual Property
Specialisation: Patents; trade marks; passing-off; copyright; misuse of confidential information; trade libel and other allied areas of competition law; largely involved in litigation. Involved in many leading intellectual property cases concerning inter alia pharmaceutical, chemical and mechanical patents; patentability of software; the movement of patented pharmaceuticals within the EU; extent of relief in Anton Piller Orders; comparative advertising and counterfeiting.
Prof. Memberships: Founder Member of and former Secretary of Intellectual Property Lawyers Association; Council Member British Group of AIPPI; associate member Chartered Institute of Patent Agents and Institute of Trade Mark Agents; member European Trade Mark Association (Anti-Counterfeiting Committee).
Career: Lancaster University 1974 BA (Hons). Articled *Richards Butler*, qualified 1977. *Faithfull Owen & Fraser* partner 1980. 1985 *Lovells.*

MACKENZIE, Marcus
Freshfields Bruckhaus Deringer, London
+44 20 7936 4000
marcus.mackenzie@freshfields.com
Recommended in Capital Markets: Securitisation
Specialisation: Partner in finance department specialising in a wide variety of capital markets, derivatives and securitisations transactions, acting for lead managers, originators and issues.

MACRITCHIE, Kenneth
Shearman & Sterling, London +44 20 7655 5000
kmacritchie@shearman.com
Recommended in Projects
Specialisation: Joint Global Head of Project Finance Group. Advising clients on financing of major infrastructure projects, including transport; mining; power; water; oil and gas and telecommunications. Clients include international banks and project developers.
Prof. Memberships: Law Society, Law Society of Scotland.
Career: Qualified in 1976. Partner, *Clifford Chance* 1991-94. *Milbank, Tweed, Hadley & McCloy* in 1994 - 1996. Joined *Shearman & Sterling* as a partner, 1996.

MAHONY, Michael
Hammond Suddards Edge, London
+44 20 7655 1000
micheal.mahony@hammondsuddardsedge.com
Recommended in Communications: IT
Specialisation: All aspects of legal work for users and suppliers of information technology products

and services including e-commerce, licensing and distribution, development, systems integration, outsourcing, telecommunications and dispute resolution.
Career: Articled Clerk at *Ashurst Morris Crisp* 1986 and Assistant Solicitor in 1988. Counsel *IBM United Kingdom Limited* 1990 to 1993. Assistant Solicitor 1993 and then Partner 1996 at *Hammond Suddards*.
Personal: Born 1964. Resides in London.

MARRIOTT QC, Arthur
Debevoise & Plimpton, London +44 20 7786 9000
Recommended in Arbitration (International)

MARSHALL, James
Taylor Joynson Garrett, London +44 20 7300 7000
jmarshall@tjg.co.uk
Recommended in Intellectual Property
Specialisation: All areas of intellectual property, contentious and non-contentious: patent and trade mark litigation, licensing.
Prof. Memberships: Solicitor's Association of Higher Courts Advocates; Associate of Chartered Institute of Patent Agents; AIPPI; IP Advisory Committee of BioIndustry Association.
Career: BSc (Mathematics and Physics), University of Bristol. Called to the Bar in 1986 with pupillage in Chambers of (then) Stephen Gratwick QC, subsequently requalifying as a solicitor. 1995 obtained Solicitor-Advocate (Higher Courts Civil) qualification. 1997 joined partnership of *Taylor Joynson Garrett.*

MARSLAND, Vanessa
Clifford Chance, London +44 20 7600 1000
Recommended in Intellectual Property
Specialisation: Partner specialising in intellectual property including copyright, patents, trademarks, and designs. Particular emphasis on digital products and e-commerce IP issues.
Career: St Leonard's, Mayfield; King's College Cambridge. Admitted 1981; intellectual property partner in *Clifford Chance* since 1987; former director of the Computer Law Association Inc. and director of the Federation Against Software Theft (FAST), the UK's software anti-piracy body; specialist editor of 'Copinger & Skone James on Copyright' (14th Edition).
Personal: Born 1957; resides London.

MARTIN, Charles
Macfarlanes, London +44 20 7831 9222
charles.martin@macfarlanes.com
Recommended in Private Equity: Buyouts
Specialisation: Mergers and acquisitions, private equity, IPOs, and securities work. Work in 2000 includes Alchemy's proposed purchase of Rover, the sale of General Trailers France to Apax and the sale of Eutectic & Castolin to Messer/Carlyle.
Personal: Merchant Taylor's School, Northwood, Bristol University (Law, 1982). Married with three children. Lives in London.

MARTIN, David
Herbert Smith, London +44 20 7374 8000
david.martin@herbertsmith.com
Recommended in Tax
Specialisation: Partner heading the firm's tax section, advising on all kinds of business-related tax matters. Has played a significant role in many high-profile transactions including company reorganisations, demergers, disposals and acquisitions of companies and businesses; has also been involved in many finance leasing transactions and other financing methods as well as advising on several substantial tax litigation matters.
Career: Qualified 1979; partner, *Herbert Smith*, 1986.
Personal: Educated at St John's College, Cambridge.

MARTIN ALEGI, Lynda
Baker & McKenzie, London +44 20 7919 1000
lynda.martin.alegi@bakernet.com
Recommended in Competition/Anti-trust
Specialisation: Partner in EC, Competition and Trade Department. Main area of practice is competition law. Also distribution, franchising, computers and IT.
Prof. Memberships: Law Society, Competition Law Society. International Bar Association.
Publications: Author of competition chapter in Sweet & Maxwell's 'Encyclopaedia of Information Technology Law'.
Career: Qualified in 1977, having joined *Baker & McKenzie* in 1975. Became a Partner in 1981. Member of the CBI Competition Panel. Member of the International Chamber of Commerce UK Competition Law Committee.
Personal: Born 7 March 1952. Educated at Cambridge University (MA in Law, 1973) and the Institute of European Studies, Brussels (1975). Lives in London.

MARTINDALE, Avril
Freshfields Bruckhaus Deringer, London +44 20 7936 4000
avril.martindale@freshfields.com
Recommended in Intellectual Property
Specialisation: Partner specialising in intellectual property, IT and e-commerce work. Main area of practice covers non-contentious intellectual property and information technology. Deals with commercial, advisory and transactional aspects of intellectual property and information technology.

MATHEOU, Michael
Lovells, London +44 20 7296 2000
mike.matheou@lovells.com
Recommended in PFI
Specialisation: Working in the firm's Project Finance Unit advising on privatisation, financiers and public sector on PPP/Private Finance Initiative projects (all sectors) and international limited recourse financial projects. Heavily involved in PFI/PPP work across a range of sectors including transport (London Underground PPP/DBFO Roads and light rail), Healthcare (New Royal Infirmary of Edinburgh; South Buckinghamshire NHS Trust), Government Accommodation (DSS PRIME; STEPS project). Also worked on a range of infrastructure projects internationally including BOT Waste Water Project in Oman, Bauxite mine and harbour development in Guyana and Oil refinery and petro-chemicals project in India.
Prof. Memberships: Law Society.
Career: *Lovells*, London and Hong Kong since 1980, Partner 1989. LLB (Hons) Nottingham University.

MAUGHAN, Alistair
Shaw Pittman, London +44 20 7847 9500
Recommended in Communications: IT

McCALLOUGH, Robert
Masons, London +44 20 7490 4000
Recommended in Communications: IT
Specialisation: Partner and Head of Information & Technology Group. Has international experience in handling large commercial and technology-related disputes involving arbitration, litigation and alternative dispute resolution relating to hardware and software procurement, project management, product liability, licensing, outsourcing and PFI contracts. Specialises in legal risk management and dispute resolution for the computer, telecommunications and other technology-related industries. Also lectures widely upon commercial and legal issues relevant to the IT industries.
Prof. Memberships: Hong Kong Law Society; English Law Society; the N.C.C.; European workshop for resolution of telecommunications disputes and the Worshipful Company of Information Technologists.
Career: Qualified in 1975. At *Hill & Perks*, Norwich 1975-78. Member of Attorney General's Chambers in Hong Kong 1978-83. Joined *Masons* (Hong Kong) in 1983. Became a Partner in 1984.

McCARTHY, Jack
Davis Polk & Wardwell, London +44 20 7418 1300
Recommended in Corporate Finance: Mergers & Acquisitions

McCORMICK, Roger
Freshfields Bruckhaus Deringer, London +44 20 7936 4000
roger.mccormick@freshfields.com
Recommended in Projects
Specialisation: Specialises in project finance in virtually all sectors and in all countries.

McKNIGHT, Elizabeth
Herbert Smith, London +44 20 7374 8000
elizabeth.mcknight@herbertsmith.com
Recommended in Competition/Anti-trust
Specialisation: Partner specialising in all aspects of European Community Law with particular expertise relating to competition law, intellectual property law and the regulation of financial services and insurance business; also experienced in the application of competition and regulatory law to privatised utilities.
Prof. Memberships: International Bar Association; Law Society.
Career: Qualified in 1988; partner, *Herbert Smith*, 1994. Jesus College, Oxford (BA, First Class Hons Literae Humaniores); London School of Economics and Political Science (LLM EC Law).

McNEIVE, Liam
McNeive Solicitors, London +44 20 7253 0535
Recommended in Communications: E-commerce

McQUATER, Gavin J.
Lovells, London +44 20 7296 2000
Recommended in Projects

MEARS, Patrick M.
Allen & Overy, London +44 20 7330 3000
Recommended in Tax

U

MEHTA, Nikhil
Linklaters (a member firm of Linklaters & Alliance), London +44 20 7456 2000
nikhil.mehta@linklaters.com
Recommended in Corporate/Mergers & Acquisitions: India Foreign, Tax
Specialisation: Corporate taxation with particular emphasis on international and structured finance, derivatives, cross-border structures, joint ventures, M&A structures, warrants and hedging instruments, preference share issues, US/UK and other cross-border offerings (public and private), bank finance.
Career: Practised as tax advocate in Bombay, 1977-80. Head of the India Business Group. Head of Contentious Tax Group since 2000. Qualified Indian Advocate and Solicitor of the Supreme Court of England and Wales.

U

MERCER, Edward
Taylor Joynson Garrett, London +44 20 7300 7000
tmercer@tjg.co.uk
Recommended in Communications: Telecoms
Specialisation: Head of IT/Telecommunications Group. Specialises in the regulatory, competition and commercial aspects of running telecoms systems worldwide. Particular expertise in the regulatory field, interconnect, procurement agreements and the cable industry. Through extensive contracts is able to provide advice on telecoms projects throughout Europe and in Asia. Frequent lecturer at seminars on cable and telecoms issues in the UK and Europe.

MIDDLEDITCH, Matthew
Linklaters (a member firm of Linklaters & Alliance), London +44 20 7456 2000
matthew.middleditch@linklaters.com
Recommended in Corporate/Commercial
Specialisation: Partner. Corporate Department. Specialises in UK corporate finance and company law. Main areas of practice include advising companies and investment banks on mergers and acquisitions, including public takeovers and private acquisitions of shares and businesses; flotations; secondary issues, including acting on rights issues, vendor placings and open offers; reorganisations; joint ventures and general corporate work.

MILLARD, Christopher
Clifford Chance, London +44 20 7600 1000
Recommended in Communications: E-commerce, Communications: IT
Specialisation: Partner in the Media, Computer and Communications Group, specialises in e-commerce, e-business and data protection compliance projects. Responsible for NextLaw®, a *Clifford Chance* online service providing guidance on managing legal and regulatory risks in multi-jurisdictional e-business projects.
Prof. Memberships: Visiting Professional Fellow University of London teaching on LLM course in IT Law, Internet Law and Telecommunications Law; past chairman Society for Computers and Law, past president International Federation of Computer Law Associations; general editor OUP 'International Journal of Law and Information Technology'; joint editor of 'Data Protection Laws of the World' (Sweet & Maxwell) and on the editorial boards of many IT, Internet and communications journals.
Career: Manchester Grammar School; University of Sheffield (LLB Hons 1980); University of Toronto (MA 1982, LLM 1983). Articled *Clifford Turner*, qualified 1986; partner *Clifford Chance* since 1992.
Personal: Music. Born 1959; married with two children; resides London.

MILLER, Stephen
Allen & Overy, London +44 20 7330 3000
Recommended in Capital Markets: Debt & Equity

MITCHARD, Paul
Wilmer, Cutler & Pickering, London +44 20 7872 1000
Recommended in Arbitration (International)

MOODIE, Bill
Herbert Smith, London +44 20 7374 8000
bill.moodie@herbertsmith.com
Recommended in Intellectual Property
Specialisation: Head of the intellectual property and technology department. Specialises in intellectual property law, particularly patents, copyright and trade marks involving the electronics, communications and the IT and digital media industries. Extensive litigation experience but also substantial non-contentious practice. Clients include Quantel, Cable & Wireless, Guinness, Formula One, BSkyB, Bridgestone/Firestone, PricewaterhouseCoopers, Warner, Vodafone, Bourns, WH Smith, BAT.
Career: South African patent agent and attorney – 1975; Solicitor in England and Wales – 1979; Partner at *Herbert Smith* – 1984; Head of Intellectual Property and Technology Department 1996.
Personal: Education – University of Cape Town (BSc Elec. Eng.) First Class Honours – 1969; University of South Africa (LLB) – 1975.

MOONEY, Kevin
Simmons & Simmons, London +44 20 7628 2020
kevin.mooney@simmons-simmons.com
Recommended in Intellectual Property
Specialisation: Senior Partner in Intellectual Property Department. Principal area of practice is patent litigation. Clients include Ericsson, Smith Kline Beecham, Eli Lilly, Bristol Myers Squibb, Pharmacia & Upjohn, 3M, Union Carbide, Procter & Gamble, Intel Inc and Norsk Hydro. Member of Nuffield Bioethics Council Working Party on Human Tissue (April 1995). Experienced speaker at conferences.
Prof. Memberships: ABA, AIPLA, AIPPI, City of London Solicitors Company (Member of Intellectual Property Sub-Committee).
Career: Qualified in 1971. Partner at *Simmons & Simmons* since 1973.
Personal: Born 14 November 1945. Educated at Bristol University (LLB, 1968). Leisure activities include gardening and supporting Q.P.R. Lives in Ealing, West London.

MORGAN, Simon
Simmons & Simmons, London +44 20 7628 2020
Recommended in Arbitration (International)
Specialisation: International Commercial Arbitration.
Prof. Memberships: International Bar Association; Chartered Institute of Arbitrators; London Court of International Arbitration; Institute for Transnational Arbitration, Inter Pacific Bar Association; International Chamber of Commerce (Commission Member); CEDR; CPR, European Advisory Committee; The Law Society.
Career: Joined *Simmons & Simmons* in 1981, from 1986 to 1988 and 1996 to 2000, Partner in the firm's Litigation Department in London, from 2000, Litigation Department Managing Partner, from 1988 to 1995 Head of Commercial Litigation and Arbitration in the firm's Hong Kong office. Admitted as a solicitor in England and Wales (1980) and Hong Kong (1985).
Personal: Married with three children.

MORLEY, David
Allen & Overy, London +44 20 7330 3000
Recommended in Banking & Finance

MORONEY, David
Denton Wilde Sapte, London +44 20 7242 1212
dfm@dentonwildesapte.com
Recommended in Energy: Electricity
Specialisation: Partner specialising in energy and natural resources law, especially large-scale projects, foreign investment and regulation. Recent matters include independent power projects in the UK and Asia, electricity privatisation and regulatory design in Europe and Asia, mining investment and financing in Africa and Asia and upstream and downstream oil and gas projects in the US, Eastern Europe, Asia and Africa. Has been involved in projects and investments in over 50 countries.
Career: International Managing Partner, *Denton Hall*. Formerly Head of Projects, Asia. Admitted 1969 (Australia). Became a partner at *Denton Hall* in 1989 after a career in industry with Burmah Oil, BNOC, Deminex, Western Mining Corporation and International Energy Development Corporation. Chairman of the IBA Section on Energy & Natural Resources Law. Read Law at Sydney University, Australia.
Personal: Married with two grown-up daughters.

MOSS, Gary
Taylor Joynson Garrett, London +44 20 7300 7000
gmoss@tjg.co.uk
Recommended in Intellectual Property
Specialisation: Practice covers all areas of intellectual property and has particular expertise in patents, biotechnology, IT, technology tranfers and partnering.
Career: Regularly writes and lectures on IP topics and is a member of the Editorial Boards of the Journal of Brand Management and of the Biotechnology Law Review.

MOTANI, Habib
Clifford Chance, London +44 20 7600 1000
Recommended in Capital Markets: Derivatives

MURPHY, Frances
Slaughter and May, London +44 20 7600 1200
frances.murphy@slaughterandmay.com
Recommended in Corporate/Commercial
Specialisation: General practice consists principally of acting for corporate clients and investment banks

on corporate finance and M&A transactions, both in England and overseas, and generally on corporate matters. Wide experience of acquisitions and disposals (both public and private), joint ventures and of equity and debt financing structures. Also has a significant practice in relation to demutualisation of building societies.
Prof. Memberships: The Law Society.
Career: Qualified in 1983 after articles with *Slaughter and May*. Became a Partner in 1990, after a year in the Hong Kong office.
Personal: Born 24 September 1957.

NAIRN, Karyl
Simmons & Simmons, London +44 20 7628 2020
karyl.nairn@simmons-simmons.com
Recommended in Arbitration (International)
Specialisation: Major cases in 2000-2001 include institutional and ad hoc arbitrations for various international financial organisations, a worldwide banking consortium, a British transport company, a worldwide media company, US/European fashion companies, and European telecommunications company. Counsel to a dispute resolution working group advising the European Telecommunications Platform.
Prof. Memberships: Member LCIA. Fellow, Chartered Institute of Arbitrators. Member for Australian (alternate), International Court of Arbitration of the ICC.
Career: Qualified as barrister and solicitor, Supreme Court of Western Australia, 1988; admitted as a solicitor in England and Wales in 1991. Joined *Simmons & Simmons* 1991; Partner in 1996; Head of International Arbitration Group.
Personal: University of Western Australia (BJuris(Hons), LLB(Hons) and LSE, University of London (LLM).

NEWHOUSE, Anthony J.R.
Slaughter and May, London +44 20 7600 1200
anthony.newhouse@slaughterandmay.com
Recommended in Corporate/Commercial
Specialisation: General corporate and commercial law, predominantly mergers and acquisitions and insurance work.
Prof. Memberships: A.F.S.A.L.S.

NEWMAN, Helen
Simmons & Simmons, London +44 20 7628 2020
helen.newman@simmons-simmons.com
Recommended in Intellectual Property
Specialisation: Partner and Managing Partner of Intellectual Property Department. Principle areas of practice include advising on contentious and non-contentious intellectual property matters including the acquisition, disposal, restructuring and exploitation of intellectual property rights portfolios; conducting trademark, patent, copyright, know-how and designs litigation in the UK and co-ordinating corresponding litigation overseas.
Prof. Memberships: International TradeMark Association, Institute of Trade Marks, MARQUES Anti Counterfeiting Group, Pharmaceuticals TradeMarks Group.
Career: Articles with *Simmons & Simmons* Qualified – 1980. Became partner – 1985.

NICHOLSON, Kim
Olswang, London +44 20 7208 8888
kan@olswang.com
Recommended in Communications: E-commerce, Communications: IT
Specialisation: Partner and Head of IT and Telecommunications Unit. Practice covers on the corporate side: corporate finance, venture capital, syndicated equity funding, mergers and acquisitions, IPOs, takeovers, all within the online, communications and technology industries; on the commercial side: contracts for exploitation of products, licensing, content deals, distribution exploitation and carriage deals in or related to the online and communications industry for clients ranging from multi-national plcs through to internet start ups, for example Thus plc, NetStore plc, Sportal International, Peoplesound.com, UUNet Technologies Inc and Motorola Inc.
Career: Qualified 1985. Joined *Olswang* as a Partner in 1993.
Personal: Born 30.11.60. Educated at Birmingham University and College of Law, London. Interests include opera, music, hill walking, art and antiques.

NICHOLSON, Malcolm
Slaughter and May, London +44 20 7600 1200
malcolm.nicholson@slaughterandmay.com
Recommended in Competition/Anti-trust
Specialisation: EU, competition and regulatory law. Head of *Slaughter and May's* Competition Group. Practice covers the full range of UK and EU antitrust work for a number of blue chip clients (including RECs and other utilities), governments and regulatory authorities. On the UK competition front, has extensive experience before the Competition Commission, including both merger and monopoly enquiries, and deals regularly with the OFT. On the European front, has been engaged in a number of competition cases before the Commission and Court of Justice and in obtaining regulatory clearances from the Merger Task Force. Was heavily involved in the regulatory and competition aspects of the major UK privatisations and currently advises a number of electricity and water utilities with regard to price controls and other regulatory matters.
Career: Qualified in 1974 with *Slaughter and May*, and became a Partner in 1982.
Personal: Born March 1949. Educated Haileybury, Cambridge University, Brussels University. Married with six children.

NOBLE, Nicholas
Field Fisher Waterhouse, London +44 20 7861 4000
Recommended in Tax
Specialisation: Partner and Head of Tax Department. Practice covers the taxation of UK and international transactions, and in particular companies and company reorganisations, securities and transactions in securities. Co-author of 'Butterworths Company Reorganisations: Tax and Tax Planning' and 'Butterworths International Taxation of Financial Instruments and Transactions' and joint editor of and contributor to 'Butterworths Tax Planning Service'.
Prof. Memberships: ATII.
Career: Qualified in 1979 having joined *Field Fisher Waterhouse* in 1977. Became a partner in 1984.
Personal: Born 1 October 1953. Educated at Winchester College and Durham University. Recreations include fencing, walking and reading.

NOBLE, Perry
Freshfields Bruckhaus Deringer, London
+44 20 7936 4000
perry.noble@freshfields.com
Recommended in PFI
Specialisation: Partner in the finance group specialising in project financing transactions and general and investment banking. Sector experience includes transport (particularly light and heavy railways) and telecoms.

NODDER, Edward
Bristows, London +44 20 7400 8000
Recommended in Intellectual Property

NORFOLK, Edward Christopher Dominic
Norton Rose, London +44 20 7283 6000
norfolkecd@nortonrose.com
Recommended in Tax
Specialisation: Partner in Commercial Tax Department. Principal area of work involves advising on tax aspects of mergers and acquisitions, corporate structuring (domestic and international), banking, oil and gas. Author of 'Taxation Treatment of Interest and Loan Relationships' (Butterworths, 3rd Ed. 1997). Member of Editorial Committee 'Practical Law for Companies'. Frequent speaker at conferences and seminars.
Prof. Memberships: Law Society (Revenue Law Committee; Chairman, International Tax Sub-Committee); Chartered Institute of Taxation (FTII), International Bar Association, International Fiscal Association, American Bar Association (Chairman, Foreign Lawyers Forum of the Section of Taxation).
Career: Articled at *Longmores* in Hertford, then joined *Gabb & Co.* in Abergavenny. Joined *Norton Rose* in 1975 and became a Partner in 1979.
Personal: Born 8 August 1948. Attended St. John's School, Leatherhead 1962-66, then Southampton University (LLB) 1966-69. Leisure pursuits include skiing and fishing. Lives in Wimbledon and Somerset.

NORMAN, Guy
Clifford Chance, London +44 20 7600 1000
Recommended in Corporate/Commercial

NOWLAN, Howard
Slaughter and May, London +44 20 7600 1200
howard.nowlan@slaughterandmay.com
Recommended in Tax
Specialisation: Corporate tax – general, restructurings, demutualisations, transfer pricing.

O'BRIEN, Barry
Freshfields Bruckhaus Deringer, London
+44 20 7936 4000
barry.obrien@freshfields.com
Recommended in Corporate/Commercial
Specialisation: Partner in corporate department. Specialises in corporate law, privatisations, hostile takeovers, mergers and acquisitions and securities offerings.

U

U

O'CONOR, John
Allen & Overy, London +44 20 7330 3000
Recommended in Arbitration (International)

OAKLEY, Chris
Clifford Chance, London +44 20 7600 1000
Recommended in Capital Markets: Securitisation

OSBORNE, John
Clifford Chance, London +44 20 7600 1000
Recommended in Competition/Anti-trust
Specialisation: Partner in European Competition and Regulation Group. Full range of EC and UK competition law from merger control, strategic alliances, joint ventures and commercial agreements to monopoly and cartel investigations. Extensive experience in conducting cases and investigations before the EC Commission, the OFT, the MMC and the CFI/ECJ for parties and complainants, and co-ordinating clearances in cross-border transactions. Acts for clients across a wide-range of business sectors including banking, financial services and broadcasting. Also advises on the EC law generally and utility regulation. Original contributing editor and author of 'Butterworths Competition Law' division on permitted horizontal agreements.
Prof. Memberships: IBA, Solicitors European Group, Competition Law Association.
Career: Qualified 1973. Partner 1980.
Personal: Born 23 October 1947. LLB Bristol (1968); LLM London School of Economics (1969). Leisure interests include military history, cricket and horseracing. Lives in Richmond.

PALMER, James
Herbert Smith, London +44 20 7374 8000
james.palmer@herbertsmith.com
Recommended in Corporate/Commercial
Specialisation: Principal areas of work are UK and cross-border mergers and acquisitions, corporate finance and general corporate, including takeovers, equity capital markets, demergers, schemes of arrangement and joint ventures. Significant involvement in internet/technology/media IPOs/M&A and in the financial services sector.
Prof. Memberships: City of London Solicitors Company, Company Law Sub-Committee.
Career: Joined 1986, qualified 1988, Partner 1994.
Personal: Born 10.9.1963. Educated at Winchester College and Queens' College Cambridge 1982-85.

PARR, Nigel
Ashurst Morris Crisp, London +44 20 7638 1111
nigel.parr@ashursts.com
Recommended in Competition/Anti-trust
Specialisation: Specialises in all aspects of UK and EC competition law and utilities regulation, particularly merger control. Has acted in relation to 25 UK Competition Commission inquiries including monopoly investigations, merger and anti-competitive practices and in relation to a number of bids to the utility sector. Regularly acts for clients in relation to notifications and investigations by the EC Commission.
Career: LLB, LLM, PhD, qualified 1989, partner 1994.

PARSONS, Chris
Herbert Smith, London +44 20 7374 8000
chris.parsons@herbertsmith.com
Recommended in Corporate/Commercial
Specialisation: Extensive corporate finance experience acting for leading investment banks and major corporate clients. One of the key relationship partners for CSFB. Practice includes cross-border M&A and international equities work. Also head of *Herbert Smith*'s Italian Practice Group. Has advised Olivetti on its successful bid for Telecom Italia.

PAUL, Alan D.
Allen & Overy, London +44 20 7330 3000
Recommended in Corporate/Commercial, Private Equity: Buyouts

PEARSON, Chris
Norton Rose, London +44 20 7283 6000
pearsoncc@nortonrose.com
Recommended in Corporate/Commercial
Specialisation: Main area of practice is public company and stock exchange transactions, including public company takeovers, other mergers and acquisitions, flotations, securities offerings, and company reconstructions and institutional investments. Also international transactions, including cross-border mergers and acquisitions and joint ventures. Important public company transactions include Guiness/Grand Metropolitan (£22 billion); Mannesmann/Orange (£20 billion); Texas Utilities/The Energy Group (£4.45 billion); Ciba Speciality Chemicals/Allied Colloids (£1.42 billion); Trinity/Mirror Group (£1.1 billion) and Airtours/Carnival, a subscription and partial offer involving Carnival acquiring 29.5% of Airtours for some £200 million. Securities transactions include the 'trombone' rights issue by Trinity International Holdings to raise £182 million in connection with the acquisition of regional newspaper interests of The Thomson Corporation and the HSBC Holdings Enhanced Scrip Dividend Scheme. Other mergers and acquisitions include the linked disposal by Siemens of its shareholding in GPT Holdings to GEC and acquisition of GEC's shareholding in Siemens GEC Communication Systems (£700 million). International transactions include the formation of a cross border joint venture between Redland and Koramic in respect of brick products in Belgium and Holland (to create the largest facing brick manufacturer in continental Europe) and the establishment of a joint venture, Sun International Investments (owned by Royale Resorts, Caledonia Investments and World Leisure Group) to invest over US$100 million in the billion dollar Paradise Island resort project in the Bahamas.
Prof. Memberships: Law Society; City of London Solicitors Company; Royal Automobile Club; City of London Law Society Company Law Sub-Committee.
Personal: Married. Leisure interests include squash, tennis, rugby, theatre and cinema.

PEARSON, David
Clifford Chance, London +44 20 7600 1000
Recommended in Corporate/Commercial
Specialisation: Partner specialising in corporate finance, takeovers, flotations, mergers and acquisitions and secondary issues, also venture capital, management buy-outs and buy-ins.
Career: Ashville College, Harrogate; Downing College, Cambridge (MA Law). Articled *Clifford Chance*; qualified 1989; made partner 1996.
Personal: Golf, skiing, running. Born 1964; resides London.

PEARSON, Hilary
Bird & Bird, London +44 20 7415 6000
Recommended in Communications: IT
Specialisation: Partner in Information Technology and Intellectual Property Groups. Main areas of practice are intellectual property and computer law. Barrister in patent chambers then worked in Silicon Valley 1980-83, becoming involved in the start of the personal computer industry. Since then has represented a wide range of hardware, software and component suppliers. Work includes intellectual property and computer contract litigation and non-contentious issues.
Prof. Memberships: American Bar Association, Computer Law Association (Board Member), Licensing Executives Society, American I.P. Law Association.
Publications: Author of 'Computer Contracts' (1983) and 'Commercial Exploitation of Intellectual Property' (1990). Contributor to 'Internet Law and Regulation' (1996, 1997).
Career: Qualified 1976. New Court, Temple 1977-80; *Rosenblum, Parrish & Bacigalupi*, San Francisco 1980-83; *Arnold White & Durkee*, Houston 1983-90. *Simmons & Simmons*, London 1990-95. Joined *Bird & Bird* in 1995. Member of the Californian Bar 1981 and Texas Bar 1985; US Patent Attorney.
Personal: Born 1943. Holds BA, MA, (Oxon) Hons Physics 1965-69, and LLB, (London) 1975.

PECK, Andrew
Linklaters (a member firm of Linklaters & Alliance), London +44 20 7456 2000
andrew.peck@linklaters.com
Recommended in Corporate/Commercial
Specialisation: Partner in the Corporate Department of since 1983 and group leader with the Corporate Practice. Deals with wide range of company law matters, including new issues, takeovers and mergers, sales and purchases of private companies and company reorganisations, extensive experience in the financial services sector, including insurance companies and building societies.
Career: Corporate Finance Department, N.M. Rothschild & Sons Limited 1976-81.

PEGG, Garry
LeBoeuf, Lamb, Greene & MacRae, LLP, London +44 20 7459 5000
gjpegg@llgm.com
Recommended in Energy: Oil and Gas
Specialisation: Main areas of specialisation are corporate and commercial work focusing on projects, particularly in the Energy and Natural Resources Sector, and Private International Law generally. Numerous articles published in legal and energy publications and has been a frequent speaker at conferences and seminars.
Prof. Memberships: Law Society, International Bar

Association (SERL), Association of International Petroleum Negotiators and the UK Energy Lawyers Sub Group.
Career: Qualified as a Barrister in 1981 and requalified as a solicitor in 1994. Began career with the West of England P&I Club, was staff legal adviser at Chevron UK Limited between March 1986-1990, and Senior International Counsel at BHP Petroleum Limited between 1990 – 1992. Was with *Clifford Chance* between 1992-1995 and joined *LeBoeuf, Lamb, Greene & MacRae* as a partner in June 1996, and has been the joint managing partner of its London office since April 1999. Currently acts as a Director of a number of energy companies including Claims Validation Services Limited.
Personal: Born 1958. BA (Hons) Law Class 2.1 University of Kent 1981. Lives in London.

PELL, Marian
Herbert Smith, London +44 20 7374 8000
marian.pell@herbertsmith.com
Recommended in Corporate/Commercial
Specialisation: Partner and head of insurance section of corporate division. Specialises in corporate insurance and reinsurance transactions, and financing involving mutual and proprietary life and general insurance companies, including mergers and acquisitions, demutualisations and the restructuring of insurance businesses.
Career: Qualified in 1976 and became a partner at *Herbert Smith* in 1984.
Personal: Educated at Southampton University.

PENN, Graham
Sidley & Austin, London +44 20 7360 3600
gpenn@sidley.com
Recommended in Capital Markets: Securitisation
Specialisation: Securitisation, structured finance, banking and bank regulation.
Career: Partner *Cameron Markley Hewitt* 1988-1994. Partner *Sidley & Austin* since 1994.

PERKINS, David
Clifford Chance, London +44 20 7600 1000
Recommended in Intellectual Property
Specialisation: Partner and head of intellectual property department specialising in patents, trademarks, designs and pharmaceuticals.
Prof. Memberships: The Law Society; City of London Solicitors Company; The Intellectual Property Lawyers Association [IPLA]; International Bar Association; Chartered Institute of Patent Agents (Associate Member); Institute of Trade Mark Agents (Associate Member); European Communities Trade Mark Practioners' Association; Union of European Practioners in Industrial Property (Council Member of the British Group); AIPPI (Associate Internationale pour la Protection de la Propriete Industrielle); International Trade Mark Association (Foreign Member); American Bar Association (Foreign Member); American Intellectual Property Law Association (Foreign Member): International Sub-Committee Chair of Anti-trust Law Committee and Co-Chair of International Developments Sub-Committee of the ADR Committee; Common Law Institute of Intellectual Property (Council Member); World Intellectual Property Organisation: listed as WIPO Mediator/Arbitrator; The Intellectual Property Lawyers Organisation [TIPLO]: (Council Member).
Career: Newcastle Preparatory School; Uppingham School; Newcastle University. Partner *Clifford Chance* 1975.
Personal: Golf; tennis. Born 1943; divorced; three sons, one daughter; resides London.

PESCOD, Michael
Slaughter and May, London +44 20 7600 1200
michael.pescod@slaughterandmay.com
Recommended in Corporate/Commercial
Specialisation: Partner 1977. Corporate Department. Main areas of practice are general commercial and corporate law, with emphasis on mergers and acquisitions.

PHEASANT, John
Lovells, London +44 20 7296 2000
john.pheasant@lovells.com
Recommended in Competition/Anti-trust
Specialisation: EC competition law in all its aspects, including merger control, contentious proceedings and competition policy/regulation. Significant experience as an advocate before the Commission in administrative proceedings, and before the Court of First Instance and European Court of Justice on appeals (including interim measures). Co-author 'Competition Law' (Butterworths) and Editor of division on prohibited horizontal agreements.
Prof. Memberships: Advisory Board of the Regulatory Policy Institute, Oxford.
Career: Articled *Lovells*. Qualified 1979; Partner since 1985 *Lovells* Brussels office; 1980-1983 and 1986 to present.

PHILLIPS, Mark
Harbottle & Lewis, London +44 20 7667 5000
Recommended in Communications: E-commerce

PHILLIPS, Robert
CMS Cameron McKenna, London +44 20 7367 3000
Recommended in Projects
Specialisation: Public/private partnerships for infrastructures. Main practice areas are major infrastructures and utility projects, development of regimes for private sector participation; development of procurement regimes for private sector participation; advising governments and the private sector on public/private partnerships internationally. Transactions include high speed rail linking the Dutch/Belgian border with Schipol and one of the key TENS projects. Also, advising the Department of Environment, Transport, and the Regions on the Channel Tunnel Rail Link and Birmingham Northern Relief Road; advising one of the bidders for LUL Infrastructure PPP on strategic issues advising on power-related projects in Sub-Sahara Africa, and advising on port and airport projects including two in India and Africa.
Prof. Memberships: Major Projects Association.
Career: Joined *McKenna & Co* in 1975, becoming a partner in 1979. Partner at *CMS Cameron McKenna* in 1997.

PICTON-TURBERVILLE, Geoffrey
Ashurst Morris Crisp, London +44 20 7638 1111
geoffrey.picton-turber@ashursts.com
Recommended in Energy: Electricity, Energy: Oil and Gas
Specialisation: Specialises in UK and international energy and project work, in particular mergers and acquisitions, joint ventures and corporate and commercial law. Partner, *Ashurst*'s Energy and Natural Resources Group. Regular clients include Unocal Corporation, Kuwait Petroleum Corporation, PowerGen, Oranje-Nassau, Repsol, Mitsui, Lundin Oil. Opened *Ashurst*'s office in New Delhi in 1994-95, now heads *Ashurst*'s India and Japan Groups. Has published numerous articles on energy related matters and speaks frequently at conferences.

PIERCE, Sean
Freshfields Bruckhaus Deringer, London +44 20 7936 4000
sean.pierce@freshfields.com
Recommended in Banking & Finance
Specialisation: Practice encompasses all aspects of banking work with particular emphasis on acquisition and leveraged financing.

PITKIN, Jeremy
Freshfields Bruckhaus Deringer, London +44 20 7936 4000
jeremy.pitkin@freshfields.com
Recommended in Capital Markets: Debt & Equity
Specialisation: Partner specialising in debt and equity capital markets, offerings and privatisations.

POLGLASE, Timothy
Norton Rose, London +44 20 7283 6000
polglaset@nortonrose.com
Recommended in Banking & Finance
Specialisation: Principal area of practice is structured finance, including the financing of leverages buy-outs and public bids, telecoms finance and project finance.
Career: Articled *Norton Rose*; qualified 1986; seconded to *Milbank, Tweed, Hadley & McCloy* (New York) 1988-1989; seconded to Banking Supervision Division, Bank of England 1990-1991; partner *Norton Rose* 1994.
Personal: Born 1962. Educated at St. John's College, Oxford.

POLITO, Simon
Lovells, London +44 20 7296 2000
simon.polito@lovells.com
Recommended in Competition/Anti-trust
Specialisation: Partner and Head of the EU and UK Competition Law group in London. Since the late 1970s has represented clients in proceedings under the EC's competition rules (including the EC Merger Regulation) and equivalent UK laws involving the Office of Fair Trading and Monopolies and Mergers Commission (now the Competition Commission). Clients represented cover a wide range of manufacturing, service and media companies. EC cases include Eemland (Wilkinson Sword; Gillette; Elopak/TetraPak I & II; Elopak/Odin; BBI/Boosey & Hawkes; Akzo/Nobel; Swedish Match/Kav; UK Tractor Registrations Exchange; Ford New Holland; Alstom/ABB; International Group of P&I Clubs.

OFT/MMC cases include: Granada/Forte; Granada/United News & Media/Carlton; car body panels; perfumes; newspaper distribution; ice cream; mobile phones.
Prof. Memberships: Law Society; Joint Working Party on Competition Laws of the UK and Irish Bars and Law Societies; ICC UK Committee on Competition Law; European Competition Lawyers Forum.
Career: Barrister (Middle Temple) in 1972; became a solicitor with *Lovells* in 1976 and a Partner in 1982. In the firm's Brussels office from 1977 to 1981, including a stage with the European Commission. Returned to Brussels as one of the Resident Partners in 1988. Now based primarily in London.

POPHAM, Stuart
Clifford Chance, London +44 20 7600 1000
stuart.popham@cliffordchance.com
Recommended in Banking & Finance
Specialisation: Partner. Global Head of Banking and Finance. Principal area of work relates to finance for corporates including acquisition financing, work-outs, syndicated and capital market financing, structured and tax driven financing, acting for lenders and borrowers.
Career: Southampton University (LLB 1975). Qualified 1978; made partner 1984.

PORTER, Susan
Freshfields Bruckhaus Deringer, London
+44 20 7936 4000
susan.porter@freshfields.com
Recommended in Tax
Specialisation: Specialises in corporate tax and corporate tax planning, the tax aspects of capital markets, banking and securitisation transactions, and structured products. Sector experience includes banking, building societes, consumer finance and media.

PREECE, Andrew
Herbert Smith, London +44 20 7374 8000
andrew.preece@herbertsmith.com
Recommended in Projects
Specialisation: Partner and Head of International Projects Group. Has considerable experience in major projects work including project finance, lease finance and general commercial work, with particular expertise in oil and gas and infrastructure matters, and including numerous PFI and PPP transactions, both domestic and international. Also in complex projects and lease and property financings. In 1999, led the *Herbert Smith* team advising London and Continental Railways on its successful tender to acquire Eurostar UK and build the Channel Tunnel Rail Link, and on its subsequent reorganisation. Also advising one of the consortium holding for the Dutch High Speed Links South.
Prof. Memberships: Law Society, International Bar Association, Major Projects Association, UK Energy Lawyers Group, Finance & Leasing Association.
Career: Qualified in 1970. Became a Partner at *Herbert Smith* in 1977.
Personal: Educated at Selwyn College, Cambridge.

PRICE, Richard
Taylor Joynson Garrett, London +44 20 7300 7000
rprice@tjg.co.uk
Recommended in Intellectual Property
Specialisation: Specialises in patent, trade mark and trade libel litigation and in IP-intensive acquisitions, disposals and licensing. Cases include cancer-inhibiting genetic engineering, artificial vascular grafts and complementary medicines including the leading UK case on genetic trade marks. Recognised as one of the leading patent and trade mark litigators in the UK.

PULESTON JONES, Haydn
Linklaters (a member firm of Linklaters & Alliance), London +44 20 7456 2000
haydn.puleston_jones@linklaters.com
Recommended in Banking & Finance
Specialisation: Head of Banking Management team, *Linklaters & Alliance.* Principal area of practice is banking. Areas of specialisation include M&A financing, other syndicated, secured and structured financings and corporate rescues and recoveries. Extensive experience of advising banks, syndicates, steering committees and distressed companies on UK and international defaults and reschedulings.
Prof. Memberships: Member of The Law Society and (from 1994 to 1998) Chairman of Banking Law Sub-Committee of the City of London Law Society. Member of the Loan Market Association's Working Party on Primary Documentation for the syndicated loan market.

RAINES, Marke
Shearman & Sterling, London +44 20 7655 5000
mraines@shearman.com
Recommended in Capital Markets: Securitisation
Specialisation: Partner, Head of English Law Securitisation Group. Securitisation and structured finance. Acts for investment banks and corporates in developing a wide range of UK and international securitisation structures and top rated structured investment vehicles.
Prof. Memberships: ABA; IBA; City of London Solicitors' Company; Fellow of the Society for Advanced Legal Studies.
Career: Called to the Bar in Ontario (1982) and New York (1990). Admitted as a solicitor in England and Wales (1990). Practised with *Stikeman, Elliott* (1982-89) and *Clifford Chance* (1991-94). Joined *Allen & Overy* in 1994 (Partner from 1996). Joined *Shearman & Sterling* as partner in 2000. Senior Visiting Fellow at Queen Mary and Westfield College, University of London (2000).
Personal: Born 17 June, 1953. Educated at Simon Fraser University (BA), University of British Columbia (LLB), and Trinity Hall, University of Cambridge (LLM). Interests include flying, skiing and motorcycling.

RANDELL, Charles
Slaughter and May, London +44 20 7600 1200
charles.randell@slaughterandmay.com
Recommended in Corporate/Commercial
Specialisation: Company/Commercial.
Career: Articled *Slaughter and May*; qualified 1982; partner 1989.
Personal: Educated at Trinity College, Oxford.

RANSOME, Clive
Linklaters (a member firm of Linklaters & Alliance), London +44 20 7456 2000
clive.ransome@linklaters.com
Recommended in Projects
Specialisation: Partner in the Project and Asset Finance Group, London. Hong Kong-based 1993-98. Has worked on a number of major projects, project financing and structured financings in the UK, Europe and Asia. These include the Channel Tunnel (acting for the arranging banks), London Electricity's purchase of Cottam Power Station, Citylink's £400 million financing and telecommunications installations on London Underground, the US$1.3 billion restructuring of the Star refinery project in the gulf of Thailand (representing IFC and the offshore banks), Southern's US$2.7 billion acquisition of CEPA (acting for Southern) and power, telecommunications and oil and gas projects in the PRC, Thailand and Indonesia.

RAWDING, Nigel
Freshfields Bruckhaus Deringer, London
+44 20 7936 4000
nigel.rawding@freshfields.com
Recommended in Arbitration (International)
Specialisation: Partner in dispute resolution group. International dispute resolution specialist representing clients in major commercial disputes involving litigation, international arbitration and ADR procedures. Litigation experience comprises a wide variety of High Court commercial cases.

RAWLINSON, Mark
Freshfields Bruckhaus Deringer, London
+44 20 7936 4000
mark.rawlinson@freshfields.com
Recommended in Corporate/Commercial
Specialisation: Partner in the Corporate Department specialising in mergers and acquisitions, both domestic and cross border. Also covers general corporate finance (including IPOs, rights issues and other issues) and joint ventures and securities issues. Sector experience includes pharmaceuticals, oil and gas and telecoms.

RAWLINSON, Paul
Baker & McKenzie, London +44 20 7919 1000
paul.rawlinson@bakernet.com
Recommended in Intellectual Property
Specialisation: 'Soft' intellectual property litigation including trade marks, copyright, unfair competition: particular emphasis on 'brand' industries where anti-counterfeiting/infringement work is undertaken for clients such as inter alia, Calvin Klein, Polo/Ralph Lauren, Tommy Hilfiger, L'Oreal, Lancome and Stussy.
Prof. Memberships: Steering Committee of the Anti-Counterfeiting Group. International Anti-Counterfeiting Coalition. French Chamber of Commerce.
Publications: Written articles for 'European Intellectual Property Review'; contributor 'Encyclopedia of Information Technology Law' (Sweet & Maxwell); editor *Baker & McKenzie* 'Guide to Intellectual Property Laws in Central & Eastern Europe'; co-editor of 'Guide to Famous Marks'; edi-

tor 'Trade Marks in Europe' and 'Global Brand Protection' publications.
Career: Trainee with *Baker & McKenzie*; qualified 1988; partner 1995; also admitted Hong Kong; lecturer for ITMA.
Personal: Born 1962, resides London. Education: St Peter's Grammar School; University of Kent (1983 BA Law); University of Paris XI (1984 Licence en Droit). Enjoys football, golf, wining and dining and waterskiing. Speaks fluent French and some Spanish and Italian.

READ, Nigel
Lovells, London +44 20 7296 2000
nigel.read@lovells.com
Recommended in Corporate/Commercial
Specialisation: Mergers & acquisitions, corporate finance, securities and general corporate law. Particular expertise in public takeovers, both recommended and hostile, and Stock Exchange flotations and secondary issues. Advises corporate clients across a wide range of industry sectors, particularly media, leisure and property. Also acts for a number of investment banks in their capacity as sponsors, financial advisers and underwriters.
Prof. Memberships: Law Society, City of London Solicitors Company.
Career: Qualified at *Freshfields* in 1984. Investment banker at Lazard Brothers & Co., Limited 1990-93. Joined *Lovells* in 1993 and became a partner in 1996.
Personal: Educated at Marlborough College and St Catharines College, Cambridge. Leisure interests include golf, tennis, skiing and watersports.

REES, Christopher
Herbert Smith, London +44 20 7374 8000
Recommended in Communications: IT

REES, Jonathan
Freshfields Bruckhaus Deringer, London
+44 20 7936 4000
jonathan.rees@freshfields.com
Recommended in Energy: Oil and Gas
Specialisation: Partner in the Corporate Group and specialises in international energy and natural resources related ventures providing mergers and acquisitions, commercial and regulatory advice to clients in the energy sector.

RENDELL, Simon
Osborne Clarke OWA, London +44 20 7809 1000
simon.rendell@osborneclarke.com
Recommended in Communications: IT
Specialisation: Head of Technology, Media & Telecoms. Advises on the Internet, multimedia software development, intellectual property, contractual negotiations, outsourcing and systems integration. Advises carriers, service providers and re-sellers and users of telecom services on legal and regulatory issues and developments. Consultant editor for IT Law Today and International Computer Law Adviser.
Prof. Memberships: FAST Legal Advisory Group, Public Network Operators Interest Group, Competition Law Association.
Career: Appointed Partner and Head of Department in 1991. Previously qualified as a Barrister in 1986. Joined *Osborne Clarke* as Head of Department in 1996.

RICE, Jim
Linklaters (a member firm of Linklaters & Alliance), London +44 20 7456 2000
jim.rice@linklaters.com
Recommended in Capital Markets: Securitisation
Specialisation: Over 15 years' experience in international capital markets, typically including such matters as eurobonds, equity and equity-related issues, medium term notes, repackagings/structured financings, securitisations. Now a member of the Structured Finance Group specialising in securitisation and other types of structured financings.
Career: Solicitor of High Court of the Hong Kong Special Administrative Region, as well as of the Supreme Court of England and Wales.

RICH, Andrew
Herbert Smith, London +44 20 7374 8000
andrew.rich@herbertsmith.com
Recommended in Intellectual Property
Specialisation: All areas of intellectual property law, contentious and non-contentious. Has been involved in a number of the leading cases in this area including the Roche/GI and Amgen patent litigation (recombinant erythropoietin), the SKB v Connaught appeal, the Sandvik v Iscar and Sandvik v Emporia patent actions, an action for Roche concerning the PCR patents, actions brought by the owners of the UK Quiksilver trade marks to prevent parallel imports, the patent action between Carter-Wallace and Unilever relating to pregnancy test kits, a contested application by BASF for a supplementary protection certificate and a number of oppositions in the European Patent Office.
Prof. Memberships: Member of the Intellectual Property Advisory Committee of the UK BioIndustry Association. Member of the Council of the British Group of AIPPI, member of IPLA and associate member of CIPA and ITMA.
Career: Degree in Biology from Liverpool University (First Class Honours), 1984. Articled at *Lovell White Durrant*, 1987-89. Joined *Hammond Suddards* in Yorkshire in 1992. Joined *Herbert Smith* in 1994. Partner 1996.

RICHARDS, Philip
Freshfields Bruckhaus Deringer, London
+44 20 7936 4000
philip.richards@freshfields.com
Recommended in Corporate/Commercial
Specialisation: Partner in Corporate Department specialising in mergers and acquisitions, equity capital markets and other transactional work, particularly for insurance, banking and fund management clients. Also active in private equity transactions.

ROBERT, Gavin
Linklaters (a member firm of Linklaters & Alliance), London +44 20 7456 2000
gavin.robert@linklaters.com
Recommended in Competition/Anti-trust
Specialisation: Partner in EU competition and regulatory department, with expertise in EU and UK competition law, public procurement, state aid, other aspects of EU law and WTO. Particular focus on multimedia, healthcare, food and drink and energy. Recent major cases include proceedings for Alpharma before the European Court of First Instance regarding the EU ban on antibiotics in animal feed, and obtaining EU merger clearance for SmithKline Beecham's merger with Glaxo Wellcome and Lafarge's hostile bid for Blue Circle. Brussels office 1994-99.

ROBERTS, Martin
Slaughter and May, London +44 20 7600 1200
martin.roberts@slaughterandmay.com
Recommended in Energy: Oil and Gas
Specialisation: Has been involved in more than fifty oil & gas and energy-related projects (acting for purchasers, sellers, sponsors and financiers) since the mid 1970s and more recently Power Station and other infrastructure projects (including road and rail) in the UK and overseas. Has acted for both sponsors and banks on major PFI projects.
Prof. Memberships: The Law Society, City of London Solicitors Company, International Bar Association.
Career: *Slaughter and May* 1967, qualified in 1969 and became Partner 1975.
Personal: Born 20 March 1944, attended Shrewsbury School and Trinity Hall, Cambridge.

ROOTH, Tony
Watson, Farley & Williams, London
+44 20 7814 8000
trooth@wfw.com
Recommended in Shipping
Specialisation: Partner in International Litigation Group. Shipping litigation including charterparty, bill of lading disputes, cargo claims, maritime casualties and marine insurance (co-editor Gard P&I Handbook). Acts principally for shipowners, charterers, P&I and defence insurers. Has represented most of the leading P&I and defence clubs.
Career: Partner *Clyde & Co* 1979-1998 (opened their Hong Kong office 1981). Partner *Watson, Farley & Williams* 1998.
Personal: BA Queens' College, Cambridge.

ROSEFIELD, Stephen
Paisner & Co, London +44 20 7353 0299
Recommended in Communications: E-commerce

ROSS, Howard
Clifford Chance, London +44 20 7600 1000
Recommended in Tax
Specialisation: Consultant, having retired as a partner in 2000. Specialises in corporate and commercial tax, international corporate tax planning, transfer pricing, oil and gas taxation and tax disputes; continues to head up both the Firm's Transfer Pricing group and its Tax Disputes. Frequent speaker and has published many articles.
Career: LLB (first class) LSE. Partner 1981.
Personal: Married with three children.

ROWE, Heather
Lovells, London +44 20 7296 2000
heather.rowe@lovells.com
Recommended in Communications: IT
Specialisation: Non-contentious information technology, telecommunications and multimedia work, including matters relating to electronic commerce, electronic banking, electronic data interchange and

U

agreements and regulation of the IBA; Chairman UK editorial board 'Droit de l'Informatique et des Telecoms'; consultant editor, 'IT Law Today' and 'Computer Law and Security Report'; correspondent 'Computer and Telecommunications Law Review'; editorial panel 'World Telecoms Report', and 'World Internet Law Report', 'Communications Law' and 'Banking Technology'; editorial Board Butterworths Journal of International Banking and Financial Law.
Prof. Memberships: Chairman ICC International Working Party on Data Protection and Privacy; Chairman ICC UK Computing, Telecommunications and Information Policies Commission; member International Telecommunication Users Group and Telecommunications Users Association.
Career: Articled *Wilde Sapte*, London: Qualified 1981 with *Wilde Sapte*; Assistant Solicitor, *S J Berwin & Co*: Assistant Solicitor, *Lovells*; Partner 1988.

U

ROWE, Michael
Slaughter and May, London +44 20 7600 1200
michael.rowe@slaughterandmay.com
Recommended in Competition/Anti-trust
Specialisation: All aspects of EU and UK competition law with particular expertise in M&A-related competition issues. Recent matters include proceedings before the European Courts in relation to impulse ice-cream freezer cabinet exclusivity and acting for Unilever in relation to its acquisition of Bestfoods. Gained experience of US M&A anti-trust practices and procedures whilst on secondment to *Cravath Swaine & Moore* in New York in 1999.
Prof. Memberships: The Law Society, Solicitors' European Group.
Career: Qualified with *Slaughter and May* in 1994. Has practised in the firm's Competition group since that date.
Personal: Born 1968. Educated at Wesley College, Dublin, Trinity College, Dublin (LLB) and Christ Church, Oxford (BCL).

ROWEY, Kent
Freshfields Bruckhaus Deringer, London
+1 202 777 4500
kent.rowey@freshfields.com
Recommended in Energy: Electricity, Projects
Specialisation: Specialises in project finance representing lenders, sponsors, contractors and other participants in project finance transactions. Sector experience includes power projects, natural resources projects and transportation and other infrastructure projects. Works out of London and Washington DC.
Prof. Memberships: State Bar of California, American Bar Association, International Bar Association.

RUDIN, Simeon
Freshfields Bruckhaus Deringer, London
+44 20 7936 4000
simeon.rudin@freshfields.com
Recommended in Capital Markets: Derivatives
Specialisation: Partner in the finance department advising on all aspects of capital markets work, including private and public debt and equity and commodity linked debt issues, tax structured financings, securitisations, repackagings and all aspects of derivatives transactions. Advises extensively on product development.

RUPAL, Yash
Linklaters (a member firm of Linklaters & Alliance), London +44 20 7456 2000
yash.rupal@linklaters.com
Recommended in Tax
Specialisation: Partner, Tax Department. Specialises in general corporate tax with particular emphasis on structured finance/product development, derivatives and other financial instruments. Recent deals have included: acting for Liberty Life on its global offering of convertible bonds – the first ever global convertible issue by a South African issuer; acting for several leading investment banks in developing tax efficient financing structures; acting for Orange plc on its recent restructuring, syndicated loan facility and global offering.

RUSSELL, John
Brown & Wood LLP, London +44 20 7778 1800
Recommended in Capital Markets: Securitisation

RUSSELL, Mark A.
Stephenson Harwood, London +44 20 7329 4422
mark.russell@stephensonharwood.com
Recommended in Shipping: Finance
Specialisation: Partner, Head of Ship Finance Group. All aspects of non-contentious shipping law, acting for lenders and shipowners. Specialises in project finance and in the energy, oil and gas and natural resources fields. Has strong experience in acting for banks and other lending institutions in a wide variety of cross-border ship finance transactions. Lectures on syndicated loans, loan transfers, loan participations and work-outs. Speaks at the Annual Ship Finance Seminar hosted by *Stephenson Harwood* in conjunction with Euromoney.
Career: Qualified October 1983. *Simmons & Simmons* as Assistant Solicitor 1983-84. *Sinclair Roche & Temperley* in 1984 and became partner in 1989. Joined *Stephenson Harwood* in 1995 as partner. Head of Ship Finance Group in 1996.
Personal: Born 7 October 1958. Educated at Bradfield College; Bristol University, LLB 2:1 1980. Married with two children. Interests include theatre. Resides Harpenden.

RYDE, Andy
Slaughter and May, London +44 20 7600 1200
andy.ryde@slaughterandmay.com
Recommended in Corporate/Commercial
Specialisation: Partner specialising in general corporate and corporate finance; acts for a number of listed companies and investment banks in connection with mergers and acquisitions and corporate finance transactions.
Publications: Author of 'Share Dealings – Restrictions and Disclosure Requirements', a chapter in the 'Practitioner's Guide to the City Code on Takeovers and Mergers'.
Career: Articled *Slaughter and May*: qualified 1989: partner 1996.
Personal: Born 1964. Educated at the Minster School, Southwell, Nottinghamshire, and Wadham College, Oxford (1986 MA Hons Jurisprudence). Resides Northwood. Interests: sports.

SACKMAN, Simon
Norton Rose, London +44 20 7283 6000
sackmansl@nortonrose.com
Recommended in Corporate/Commercial
Specialisation: Partner and Head of Corporate Finance. Main practice area is mergers and acquisitions (public and private), flotations and other equity issues, demergers and other restructurings and investment trusts. Also experienced in regulatory investigations and the hotel sector. Important transactions include the sale of Hambros Bank to Société Générale and the subsequent restructuring of Hambros plc, the restructuring of GPA Group, the flotation of Harvey Nichols, the enquiry into Lanica's bid for CWS and numerous hotel acquisitions, including the Caledonian in Edinburgh and the Landmark of London. Clients include merchant banks (Samuel Montagu, Hambros, Morgan Grenfell and Charterhouse), hotel groups and investment trusts.
Prof. Memberships: Law Society, City of London Solicitors Company, International Bar Association.

SALT, Stuart
Linklaters (a member firm of Linklaters & Alliance), London +44 20 7456 2000
stuart.salt@linklaters.com
Recommended in Energy: Electricity, Energy: Oil and Gas, Projects
Specialisation: Partner in the Project and Asset Finance Group. Main area of practice has been international projects. Extensive experience of acting for governments, sponsors and lenders on major projects in the power, energy and transport sectors. Recent transactions include advising; the project sponsors on the development and financing of the 670MW Phase 1 naptha fired Dabhol power project; the purchase of 4,000MW of generating capacity in the UK from Powergen and the arranging banks on the multi-sourced financing of the 700MW Changsha power plant in Hunan Province.

SALZ, Anthony
Freshfields Bruckhaus Deringer, London
+44 20 7936 4000
anthony.salz@freshfields.com
Recommended in Corporate/Commercial
Specialisation: Senior Partner and Partner in Corporate Department. Main area of practice is cross-border mergers and acquisitions, joint ventures and securities offerings, acting for investment and merchant banks and corporate clients worldwide.

SANDISON, Francis
Freshfields Bruckhaus Deringer, London
+44 20 7936 4000
francis.sandison@freshfields.com
Recommended in Tax
Specialisation: Partner in tax department. Experience extends to all fields of Tax Law with current focus embracing international taxation and corporate transactions as well as VAT and Property Taxation.

SANDISON, Hamish
Bird & Bird, London +44 20 7415 6000
Recommended in Communications: IT
Specialisation: Partner in Company Department and Co-Chair of Information Technology Group.

Main area of practice is IT law. Acts for both public bodies and private sector companies on IT procurement, including major IT PFI projects. Heads team representing CCTA (the Government's Central Computer and Telecommunications Agency). Member of DSS and BBC legal advisers panels. Intellectual property, e-commerce and multimedia work is also covered, especially advising on copyright law. Clients include Motion Picture Export Association of America and numerous scientific and technical publishers.
Prof. Memberships: Council of Intellectual Property Institute, FAST Legal Advisory Group, Intellectual Property Committee of the British Computer Society.
Publications: Co-author of 'Computer Software Protection Law', 1989. Contributing Editor 'International Copyright and Neighbouring Rights', 1990. Lectures frequently in both UK and US. Often interviewed on TV and Radio.
Career: Admitted to Washington DC Bar 1980. Qualified in UK 1989. Joined *Bird & Bird* 1992 as a Partner.
Personal: Born 1952. Attended University College School, London 1960-70, Jesus College, Cambridge 1971-74, then University of California, Berkeley 1974-75. Lives in Usk, Monmouthshire.

SAUNDERS, Mark
Dewey Ballantine LLP, London +44 20 7456 6121
Mark_Saunders@deweyballantine.com
Recommended in Energy: Oil and Gas
Specialisation: Partner specialising in all aspects of energy law and corporate law. A London-based partner in the firm's energy and projects group specialising in all aspects of energy law, particularly oil and gas. Seconded to a major oil and gas company in the mid 1980s. Outside counsel to a number of the integrated majors as well as service companies within the sector. Also solicitor to oil industry environmental response collective. Frequent speaker at energy conferences worldwide, contributed to Sweet & Maxwell's 'Upstream Oil and Gas Agreements' and to 'Energy Law & Regulation in the European Union'. Listed in Chambers Survey of Leading UK Commercial Lawyers as one of the eight leading commercial lawyers in the United Kingdom 1997-1998. Cited last year and throughout the preceding ten years as one of the outstanding private practice energy law specialists in Chambers and the Legal 500. Voted one of the World's Top 20 Lawyers in Euromoney's 'Best of the Best' 2000-2001.

SAYER, Richard
Ince & Co, London +44 20 7623 2011
richard.sayer@ince.co.uk
Recommended in Shipping
Specialisation: Partner covering maritime law. Main areas of practice are admiralty (collision, salvage and other casualties), charter party disputes, sale and purchase litigation and maritime fraud. Acted for owners of numerous headline casualties, including 'The Braer' following the Shetland disaster in 1993. Also a member of the four-man FERIT (Far East Regional Investigation Team) established by all the major Far East insurance associations to investigate the incidence of maritime fraud in the South China Sea in the 1970s.
Prof. Memberships: Chairman (since 1991) of the City of London Admiralty Solicitors Group (Secretary 1972-91), Chairman of the BMLA Salvage Sub-Committee, member of the Baltic Exchange, supporting member of the Association of Average Adjusters and of the London Maritime Arbitrators Association, member of the Admiralty Court Committee since 1986, and member of the Lloyd's Form Working Party. Member of Maritime London Steering Committee. Assistant to the Court of the Worshipful Company of Shipwrights. Appointed Examiner in Admiralty by Lord Taylor C.J. 1996.
Career: Qualified in 1966, having joined *Ince & Co.* in 1962. Became a Partner in 1970. Was admitted in Hong Kong in 1979 and spent five months there opening the firm's Hong Kong office. Became Senior Partner in 1995, stepping down in 2000.
Personal: Born 7 May 1943. Attended Framlingham College 1956-61. Leisure interests include golf, cricket and jazz. Lives in London.

SCHULZ, Peter F.
Allen & Overy, London +44 20 7330 3000
Recommended in Banking & Finance

SCHWARZ, Tim
Clifford Chance, London +44 20 7600 1000
tim.schwarz@cliffordchance.com
Recommended in Communications: Telecoms
Specialisation: Partner focusing on international telecoms, internet, posts and IT.
Career: Oxford University (BA Jurisprudence); Oxford University (BCL); Université de Bruxelles (Première et deuxième licences en droit européen); trainee lawyer *Clifford Chance* 1987-89; seconded to OFTEL's Legal Department 1989-90; associate *Clifford Chance* 1989-95; main telecoms lawyer World Bank Legal Department 1995-97; Partner *Clifford Chance* 1997.

SCOTT, Jonathan
Herbert Smith, London +44 20 7374 8000
jonathan.scott@herbertsmith.com
Recommended in Competition/Anti-trust
Specialisation: Principal area of expertise is anti-trust (competition) law, involving references to the regulatory authorities both in the EU and UK and anti-trust and competition litigation, much of which has a European element. Has appeared before the regulators of the recently privatised utilities in the UK, and has been involved with enquiries by the EU and UK competition authorities into several industries including television, glass, wines and spirits, oil and gas, water, electricity, travel, distribution, retail and fast moving consumer goods industries.
Prof. Memberships: International Bar Association.
Career: St Catharine's College, Cambridge. Qualified 1981; partner 1988; first resident partner Brussels office 1989-1994, returned to London 1994.

SCOTT, Thomas A.
Linklaters (a member firm of Linklaters & Alliance), London +44 20 7456 2000
tom.scott@linklaters.com
Recommended in Tax
Specialisation: Partner in Tax Department. Specialist in the corporate taxation aspects of domestic and cross-border mergers, acquisitions and capital restructurings, and capital marketing, with 20 years' experience in this area.
Publications: Publications include 'Tolley's Tax Company Acquisitions Handbook'.

SEDGLEY, David
Allen & Overy, London +44 20 7330 3000
Recommended in Projects

SHACKLETON, Stewart
Simmons & Simmons, London +44 20 7628 2020
Recommended in Arbitration (International)
Specialisation: Has acted in over 80 international commercial and construction arbitrations, institutional (including ICC, LCIA, SCC, ICSID) and ad hoc (UNICTRAL). Counsel and arbitrator in public international law disputes, including arbitration involving States, State entities and public international organisations. Advises on jurisdiction and conflicts of law disputes. Practice also includes advising on challenges to arbitral awards in France and England; acting in multi-jurisdictional banking and commercial litigation; advocacy before courts in France and before international arbitral tribunals in French and English; acting in CEDR administered international mediation proceedings. Sitting as party-appointed arbitrator, chairman and sole arbitrator in ICC proceedings.
Prof. Memberships: Member for Canada, ICC Commission on International Commercial Arbitration; London Court of International Arbitration; Fellow, Chartered Institute of Arbitrators; Swiss Arbitration Association; French Arbitration Association; French Arbitration Committee; Indian Council of Arbitration; British Institute of International and Comparative Law; British Columbia International Commercial Arbitration Centre; Vice-President of the European Lawyer's Association; Member for Canada of the International Arbitration Committee, International Law Association.
Career: Has practised in Canada, Hong Kong, Paris and London. Avocat au Barreau de Paris (1994) (conseil juridique stagiaire 1991-94); Solicitor of the Supreme Court of England and Wales (1994); Solicitor of the Supreme Court of Hong Kong (1995); Barrister, Ontario (1993).
Personal: MSc in Construction Law and Arbitration (University of London); DEA in Public International Law (University of Paris I); DSU in Private International Law (University of Paris II); Maîtrise en Droit Civil – mention droit des affaires (University of Paris II); DEA in African Law (University of Paris I); Diplôme in Comparative Law (University of Paris II); LLB (University of Western Ontario). Working languages: French, English and Scandinavian languages, knowledge of German and Spanish.

SHEACH, Andrew
CMS Cameron McKenna, London
+44 20 7367 3000
ajs@cmck.com
Recommended in Private Equity: Buyouts
Specialisation: Partner in corporate department. Advises both private equity houses and management

U

teams on all types of private equity transactions. In the last twelve months has acted on a number of MBOs and take privates with a value ranging from £5-£220 million including transactions involving Continental Europe and the United States.
Career: 1985 joined *Cameron Markby*; 1987 qualified; 1993 partner. Regular speaker at conferences on private equity topics.
Personal: Born 1963, educated Ilford County High School and Pembroke College Cambridge, 1984, BA (Hons).

U

SHELDON, Jeremy N.
Ashurst Morris Crisp, London +44 20 7638 1111
jeremy.n.sheldon@ashursts.com
Recommended in Private Equity: Buyouts
Specialisation: Extensive experience of domestic and international corporate transactions. Specialises in private equity transactions and the formation of private investment funds, including private equity, mezzanine, corporate recovery, biotechnology and emerging markets funds. Also advises clients in the telecommunication and cable industries on a variety of transactions including mergers and acquisitions, strategic alliances, equity placings and high yield issues.
Prof. Memberships: Vice President of the M&A Commission for Union Internationale des Avocats. Member of the Speachem Investment Funds Subcommittee of the International Bar Association.

SHELTON, John H.
Norton Rose, London +44 20 7283 6000
sheltonjh@nortonrose.com
Recommended in Shipping: Finance
Specialisation: Shipping finance, acting for owners, lenders, builders, and others.
Prof. Memberships: The Law Society, The Baltic Exchange.
Career: Articled at *Pinsent & Co*, Birmingham, joined *Norton Rose* on qualifying in 1981. Became partner 1987.
Personal: Married, four children. Principal interests: fatherhood.

SHEPPARD, Audley
Clifford Chance, London +44 20 7600 1000
audley.sheppard@cliffordchance.com
Recommended in Arbitration (International)
Specialisation: Partner in the firm's International Commercial Arbitration Group specialising in the resolution of investment and engineering/construction disputes arising out of infrastructure projects in Europe, Middle East, Asia, and the Americas. NZ representative on the ICC Commission. Co-Rapporteur of the International Law Association Committee on International Commercial Arbitration. Co-editor, International Bar Association Committee D Newsletter. Editorial Board International Arbitration Law Review.
Prof. Memberships: Law Society, International Bar Association, International Law Association, Chartered Institute of Arbitrators (Fellow), London Court of International Arbitration.
Career: Articled *Bell Gully Buddle Weir*, NZ; qualified Barrister and Solicitor NZ 1985, Solicitor England 1990. Joined *Clifford Chance* in 1986, worked in firm's Dubai office 1994, partner 1995.
Personal: Born 1960, New Zealand. Educated Victoria University of Wellington, NZ (LLB Hons 1983; Bcommerce 1984) and Cambridge University, UK (LLM 1986).

SHILLITO, Mark
Herbert Smith, London +44 20 7374 8000
mark.shillito@herbertsmith.com
Recommended in Intellectual Property
Specialisation: All aspects of intellectual property work, contentious and non-contentious; extensive trial experience; has acted in a number of the leading cases in the fields of patents including biotech (Chiron v Organon Teknika; Strix v Otter; Fort Dodge v Akzo); trade marks (Vodafone v Orange); plant variety rights (Germinal v Fell & Rowsell); copyright (BSkyB v PRS; Newspaper Licensing Agency Ltd v Marks & Spencer plc); and breach of confidence (Berkeley Administration v McClelland). Specific expertise in law relating to genetically modified organisms.
Prof. Memberships: AIPPI; AIPLA; CIPA; ITMA; INTA; IPLA; TIPLO.
Career: Articled at *Herbert Smith*; qualified 1989; partner 1996. University College London (LLB Hons). Queen Mary & Westfield College, London (Dip.IP).

SHORE, Larry
Herbert Smith, London +44 20 7374 8000
laurence.shore@herbertsmith.com
Recommended in Arbitration (International)
Specialisation: Counsel, acting in international commercial arbitrations.
Prof. Memberships: London Court of International Arbitration; Research Advisory Committee of the Global Center for Dispute Resolution Research.
Publications: 'The Advantages of Arbitration for Banking Institutions', 'Journal of International Banking Law' (Nov. 1999); 'Making Applicants Take Evidence Properly: Challenges to Letters of Request,' 'International Commercial Litigation' (July/August 1998); 'Southern Capitalists' (U. of N. Carolina Press 1986).
Career: Joined *Herbert Smith* in 1995. Became a partner in 1999. 1989-1995: associate, *Williams & Connolly* (Washington DC). 1995: Attorney Adviser International, Office of the Legal Adviser, US State Department.
Personal: Born 3 December 1954. JD with distinction, Emory Univ. School of Law; PhD (History) The Johns Hopkins University; MA (History) The Johns Hopkins University; BA with highest honours, The University of North Carolina at Chapel Hill.

SHURMAN, Daniel
Allen & Overy, London +44 20 7330 3000
Recommended in Capital Markets: Debt & Equity

SIGNY, Adam
Clifford Chance, London +44 20 7600 1000
adam.signy@cliffordchance.com
Recommended in Corporate/Commercial
Specialisation: Partner specialising in corporate finance and Mergers and Acquisitions.
Career: City of London School; Sussex University (Economics). Articled *Clifford Chance*; qualified in 1982; partner *Clifford Chance* since 1987.
Personal: Born 1955; married with three children; resides Suffolk and London.

SIMPSON, Paul
Clifford Chance, London +44 20 7600 1000
paul.simpson@cliffordchance.com
Recommended in Energy: Electricity
Specialisation: Partner specialising in infrastructure projects and project financings, particularly oil and gas, electricity, transport and Public Private Partnership projects.
Career: Edinburgh University (2(1) LLB Hons 1974). Articled *Norton Rose*; qualified Scotland 1976, England and Wales 1980; assistant solicitor *Fox & Gibbons* 1980-1982; assistant solicitor *Clifford-Turner* (now *Clifford Chance*) 1982-1988; partner 1989.
Personal: Born 1952; resides London.

SIMPSON SR., Scott V.
Skadden, Arps, Slate, Meagher & Flom LLP, London +44 20 7519 7000
Recommended in Corporate Finance: Mergers & Acquisitions

SINGLETON, Susan
Singletons, Pinner +44 20 8866 1934
Recommended in Communications: IT

SLATER, Richard
Slaughter and May, London +44 20 7600 1200
richard.slater@slaughterandmay.com
Recommended in Banking & Finance
Specialisation: Partner in Financial/Commercial Department. Head of Banking Stream. Principal area of practice is debt financing of all types, including syndicated loan facilities, structured financings, project financings and bond and note issues. Has also acted on international equity offerings, flotations, privatisations and corporate and commercial work of a general nature.
Prof. Memberships: The Law Society.
Career: With *Slaughter and May* throughout. Articles 1970, qualified 1972, Partner 1979. Hong Kong office 1981-86.
Personal: Born 18 August 1948. Educated at University College School, Hampstead (1956-65), Lycée Michelet, Paris (1965-66) and Pembroke College, Cambridge 1966-69. Lives in London.

SMALL, Harry
Baker & McKenzie, London +44 20 7919 1000
harry.small@bakernet.com
Recommended in Communications: E-commerce, Communications: IT
Specialisation: Partner in Intellectual Property and Information Technology Law Department. Principal area of practice is IT Law including computer litigation, software protection and IT contracts (especially e-commerce and outsourcing). Other main area of work is IP law covering enforcement of IP rights, copyright and designs law and multimedia contracts. Acted in many significant computer systems and high technology disputes including, amongst others, Exel -v- Dun & Bradstreet Software and Vodafone -v- Orange. Regularly addresses conferences and is lecturer on designs on Bristol University Intellectual

Property Diploma course. Expert to EU Economic and Social Committee on various IT and IP related draft legislation. Chair, Society for Computers & Law.
Prof. Memberships: Law Society, Computer Law Group, Patent Solicitors Association.
Publications: Contributor to Sweet & Maxwell 'IT Encyclopaedia' and Sweet & Maxwell 'Outsourcing Practice Manual.' Author of numerous articles on IP and IT law for various legal periodicals.
Career: Articled with *Linklaters & Paines* 1979-81 and then Assistant Solicitor 1981-86. Joined *Baker & McKenzie* in 1986 and became a Partner in 1989.
Personal: Born 20 April 1957. Attended St. Alban's Grammar School 1968-75, then Oriel College, Oxford 1975-78. Leisure pursuits include travel, railways, computers, books and sleeping. Lives in London.

SMITH, Catriona
Allen & Overy, London +44 20 7330 3000
Recommended in Intellectual Property

SMITH, Christopher
Slaughter and May, London +44 20 7600 1200
christopher.smith@slaughterandmay.com
Recommended in Capital Markets: Securitisation
Specialisation: Main areas of practice include securitisations, structured financings and the full range of capital markets and banking transactions.
Career: Qualified 1980, partner 1987.

SMITH, David
Allen & Overy, London +44 20 7330 3000
Recommended in Shipping: Finance

SMITH, Graham
Bird & Bird, London +44 20 7415 6000
Recommended in Communications: E-commerce, Communications: IT
Specialisation: Partner. Computer project disputes, commercial litigation in computer and telecommunications industries. Evidence, document imaging and computer records. Internet law including domain name disputes, website advice, Internet/e-mail use policies and regulatory issues. Intellectual property disputes. Gave evidence to the House of Lords Science and Technology Select Committee on Digital Images as Evidence. Advised Guernsey on its e-commerce legislation. Contributes a section on Non-Contractual Liability to the loose-leaf 'Encyclopedia of Information Technology Law' (Sweet & Maxwell). Editor and a co-author of the book 'Internet Law and Regulation' (Sweet & Maxwell, 2nd edition December 1997). Speaks and writes regularly in the UK and abroad mainly on IT and Internet legal issues.
Prof. Memberships: American Intellectual Property Law Association. Council Member, Society for Computers and Law. Computer Law Association. E centre UK Legal Advisory Group. Fellow of the Society for Advanced Legal Studies.
Career: Qualified 1978. Joined *Bird & Bird* 1983. Partner 1985.
Personal: Born 1953. Educated Uppingham School, Rutland; Bristol University (LLB 1975). Lives London.

SMITH, Martin
Simmons & Simmons, London +44 20 7628 2020
martin.smith@simmons-simmons.com
Recommended in Competition/Anti-trust
Specialisation: Main area of practice is European Community Law with particular emphasis on competition and regulatory work (both EC and UK). Has experience of dealing with all EC and UK competition law authorities. Advises on EC and UK merger control and regularly co-ordinates multiple merger filings. Experience extends to a number of regulated industries, notably water, broadcasting and radio. Also undertakes more general commercial work, usually with a significant competition law or regulatory element. Author of two major divisions of the five-volume 'Butterworths Competition Law'. Has also written a number of articles. Frequently speaks at conferences and seminars.
Prof. Memberships: Law Society, City of London Solicitors' Company Competition Law Sub-Committee, CBI Competition Panel, Solicitors European Group.
Career: Qualified in 1981. Joined *Simmons & Simmons* in 1977 becoming Partner in 1986, having worked at *Dechert Price and Rhoads* (Philadelphia) 1978 and *Linklaters & Paines* 1983-85.
Personal: Born 27 August 1955. Attended St Catharine's College, Cambridge 1974-77 (MA) and University of Pennsylvania (LLM) 1978-79. Governor of Brooklands Primary School. Leisure interests include sport, music and walking. Lives in London.

SMITH, Michael
Ashurst Morris Crisp, London +44 20 7638 1111
Recommended in Capital Markets: Securitisation
Specialisation: Securitisation, structured finance, repackagings and derivatives.
Prof. Memberships: Law Society.
Career: Partner *Ashurst Morris Crisp* 1997.

SMITH, Sarah
Sidley & Austin, London +44 20 7360 3600
sarah.smith@sidley.com
Recommended in Capital Markets: Securitisation
Specialisation: Securitisation; structured finance; banking and financial services regulation.
Career: Qualified 1990; Partner 1995.

SOUTAR, Tim
Clifford Chance, London +44 20 7600 1000
tim.soutar@cliffordchance.com
Recommended in Projects
Specialisation: Partner in London office specialising in project finance, banking and energy, oil, gas, and natural resources. Project finance experience includes power, refinery, petrochemical and transport infrastructure projects: Shajiao B, Shajiao C, Pagbilao and Sual Power Projects – Hopewell/CEPA Group, Zhuhai Power Project – HSBC/CDFC, Star Refinery Project, Thailand – Caltex and PTT, Yanpet Petrochemical Project – Arranging Banks, NODCO Refinery Expansion – NODCO/QGPC, Luton Airport Expansion – AGI Consortium, Chad – Cameroon Oil Transportation Project.
Prof. Memberships: Power Sector Working Group.
Career: Bradford Grammar School; St Catherine's College, Oxford (BA Jurisprudence 1977); University of East Asia, Macau (Diploma in Chinese Law 1987). Articled *Coward Chance*; qualified 1980, Hong Kong 1983; assistant solicitor banking practice *Coward Chance* 1980-82; *Clifford Chance* Hong Kong 1982-88; partner Hong Kong 1988.
Personal: Distance running, golf. Born 1955, resides Kent.

SPEARING, Nicholas
Freshfields Bruckhaus Deringer, London +44 20 7936 4000
nicholas.spearing@freshfields.com
Recommended in Competition/Anti-trust
Specialisation: Partner in the Competition and Trade practice group. Specialises in competition law, commercial law, agency and distribution and joint ventures.

SPENDLOVE, Justin
Ashurst Morris Crisp, London +44 20 7638 1111
justin.spendlove@ashursts.com
Recommended in Banking & Finance
Specialisation: Head of *Ashurst*'s banking and capital markets department until appointment (October 2000) as the firm's Managing Partner. Specialises in international structured finance transactions for mergers and acquisitions and corporate funding, generally acting for financial institutions and international corporations.

STACEY, Paul
Slaughter and May, London +44 20 7600 1200
paul.stacey@slaughterandmay.com
Recommended in Energy: Electricity, Project Finance: India Foreign
Specialisation: Partner in the Commercial Department. Principal areas of practice include energy-related work, banking and project finance.
Prof. Memberships: The Law Society.
Career: With *Slaughter and May* throughout. Articles 1981, qualified 1983, Partner 1990. Hong Kong Office 1986-88.
Personal: Born 9 May 1959. Educated at Dulwich College and Trinity College, Cambridge.

STANGER, Michael A.
Lovells, London +44 20 7296 2000
michael.stanger@lovells.com
Recommended in Energy: Oil and Gas
Specialisation: Practice covers a wide range of energy and projects work; energy work related primarily to the gas industry; heavily involved in the structural changes in the UK, acting on behalf of gas shippers in relation to the drafting of the Network Code and the 'Claims Validation' agreements; and acting for the Bacton Agent's Group in relation to gas flows through the Interconnector to Continental Europe. Practice also covers gas trading agreements, gas supply agreements, gas storage and work related to the development of independent gas pipeline systems.
Prof. Memberships: Law Society, City of London Solicitors Company, Institute of Petroleum, UK Energy Lawyers Group.
Career: Field Engineer in the oil industry for SPE Schlumberger, mainly in Africa, 1975 to 1978; articled *Lovells*; qualified 1981; Partner 1986.

U

U

STARR, Ian
Ashurst Morris Crisp, London +44 20 7638 1111
ian.starr@ashursts.com
Recommended in Intellectual Property
Specialisation: Patent, trade mark, confidential information and copyright, particularly litigation in the UK and across Europe. Clients range from a number of multi-national telecommunications, computer and healthcare companies to both large and small UK and foreign companies in the general engineering and fmcg industries.
Prof. Memberships: Active member of, and speaker at, a wide range of specialist intellectual property and competition law organisations. Chairman of City of London Solicitors' Company, IP sub-committee.

STAVELEY, Ben
Freshfields Bruckhaus Deringer, London +44 20 7936 4000
ben.staveley@freshfields.com
Recommended in Tax
Specialisation: Specialisations include the tax treatment of capital markets, derivatives and securities transactions and the tax position of banks and other financial institutions.

STEADMAN, Tim
Clifford Chance, London +44 20 7600 1000
Recommended in PFI
Specialisation: Partner and head of Construction Group. Member of PFI/PPP Group, specialising in concession and construction aspects of Public Private Partnerships, BDT concessions and project finance transactions in the UK and internationally.
Prof. Memberships: European Construction Institute; IBA committee "T"; CBI Procurement Committee.
Career: Hertford College, Oxford University. Trainee and assistant *Lovell White & King* 1976-1982; associate *Baker & McKenzie* 1982-1985; partner *Baker & McKenzie* 1985-1997; partner *Clifford Chance* since March 1997.
Personal: Born 1955; resides London.

STEPHENSON, Barbara
Norton Rose, London +44 20 7283 6000
Recommended in Corporate/Commercial
Specialisation: Main area of practice is public company and Stock Exchange transactions, including public company takeovers, other mergers and acquisitions, initial public offerings, securities offerings and company reconstructions and institutional investments. Also international transactions, including cross-border, mergers and acquisitions and joint ventures. Important transactions handled include the £2.5 billion takeover of Eastern Group by Hanson, the £1.4 billion acquisition of the investment banking business of Schroders by Citigroup by way of scheme of arrangement and non Code offer and the flotation of Fox Kids Europe on the Amsterdam Stock Exchange. Corporate clients include Taylor Woodrow, Pillar Property, Fox Kids Europe, Old Mutual, QBE, Blacks Leisure Group, Matsushita Electric Europe and TBI. Investment banks include Schroders Salomon Smith Barney, Credit Agricole Indosuez, HSBC, SG Hambros, Credit Lyonnais, West LB and ABN Amro.
Prof. Memberships: Member of the Law Society.
Personal: Married with three daughters.

STERN, Robert
Slaughter and May, London +44 20 7600 1200
robert.stern@slaughterandmay.com
Recommended in Corporate/Commercial
Specialisation: General practice consists principally of acting for corporate and investment bank clients on corporate finance and M&A transactions, both in England and overseas and generally on corporate matters. Wide experience of acquisitions and disposals (both public and private), joint ventures and of equity and debt financing structures.
Career: BA in French and German at The Queen's College, Oxford. Qualified as a solicitor in 1986. Became a Partner in 1993.

STEWART, Mark
Clifford Chance, London +44 20 7600 1000
mark.stewart@cliffordchance.com
Recommended in Banking & Finance
Specialisation: Partner dealing with general corporate banking with an emphasis on acquisition financings.
Career: University College School, London; Bristol University. Articled *Richards Butler*, qualified 1983; trainee and assistant solicitor 1983-86; *Clifford Chance* 1986-90; partner since 1990.
Personal: Born 1958; resides London.

STRIVENS, Peter
Baker & McKenzie, London +44 20 7919 1000
peter.strivens@bakernet.com
Recommended in Communications: Telecoms
Specialisation: Partner and the Head of the Telecommunications Practice Group. Work includes advice on licensing and regulatory issues in the UK and other jurisdictions, investments and joint ventures in the telecommunications industry and advising on a wide range of industry issues, including contractual negotiations and disputes. Has extensive experience of cross-border transactions and telecoms privatisations and is currently working on telecommunications privatisation and regulatory assignments in Eastern Europe and the Middle East. Gives frequent conference presentations on telecommunications issues and has written the UK and International Chapters of '*Baker & McKenzie* – Telecommunications Laws in Europe', Butterworths 1998. Qualified in 1984 with *Baker & McKenzie* and became a Partner in 1990.
Career: Educated at St Johns College, Johannesburg, University of Witwatersrand (1971-75) and Balliol College, Oxford (1979-81).
Personal: Born 15 December 1954. Leisure activities include painting, tennis and looking after a growing family. Lives in London.

STRONG, Malcolm
Ince & Co, London +44 20 7623 2011
Malcolm.Strong@ince.co.uk
Recommended in Shipping
Specialisation: Sale and purchase and finance of ships including related corporate, insurance, charterparty and other aspects. Was partner in the Niobe (House of Lords case on sale of ships in 1995).
Prof. Memberships: Law Society. Supporting member London Maritime Arbitrators' Association.
Career: Partner in *Ince & Co.* since 1970.
Personal: Cambridge University (Sidney Sussex College) MA, LLM Married with one daughter. Interests: music, cinema, theatre, rugby and cricket.

STYLE, Christopher
Linklaters (a member firm of Linklaters & Alliance), London +44 20 7456 2000
christopher.style@linklaters.com.
Recommended in Arbitration (International)
Specialisation: Commercial arbitration and litigation. Conducts numerous arbitrations, both ad hoc and institutional (ICC, LMAA, LCIA), both as arbitrator and as counsel. Has practised in proceedings before courts in England and other countries both as arbitrator and as counsel. Extensive experience of all forms of urgent injunctive relief, specialist in jurisdictional issues and questions of conflict of laws.
Prof. Memberships: London Solicitors Litigation Association; International Bar Association and the City of London Solicitors' Company. Fellow of Chartered Institute of Arbitrators; Solicitor Advocate (Higher Courts Civil) and Accredited Mediator.

SULLIVAN, Michael
Linklaters (a member firm of Linklaters & Alliance), London +44 20 7456 2000
michael.sullivan@linklaters.com
Recommended in Corporate/Commercial
Specialisation: Partner, Corporate Department. Specialist in corporate law including mergers and acquisitions, initial and secondary public offerings, corporate reorganisations and demergers and privatisations. Significant transactions include National Power plc's demerger, CMG plc's acquisition of Admiral plc, British Telecommunications' acquisition of the minority interests in BT Cellnet; the UK Government's sale of shares in Railtrack and British Telecommunications plc, the formation of Anglo American plc.

SUMMERFIELD, Spencer
Travers Smith Braithwaite, London +44 20 7295 3000
Spencer.Summerfield@TraversSmith.com
Recommended in Communications: E-commerce
Specialisation: Corporate finance; company; highlights of the year: £8 billion acquisition of Consumer Co operations of Cable & Wireless Communications plc.
Prof. Memberships: Law Society.
Career: Chigwell School; Cambridge University, Gonville & Caius College; College of Law, London; joined *Travers Smith Braithwaite* as a trainee solicitor in 1987; made a partner in 1997.
Personal: Interests include cinema/theatre, aerobics, rugby. Married to Karen.

SUTTON, David
Allen & Overy, London +44 20 7330 3000
Recommended in Arbitration (International)

SWEETING, Malcom
Clifford Chance, London +44 20 7600 1000
Recommended in Banking & Finance

SWIFT, Robert
Linklaters (a member firm of Linklaters & Alliance), London +44 20 7456 2000
robert.swift@linklaters.com
Recommended in Intellectual Property
Specialisation: Partner, Intellectual Property and

Information Technology Department. Specialist with over 30 years' experience in intellectual property. Typical matters include: resolving disputes about trade marks, copyright, designs and unfair trading through negotiations and litigation where necessary, interim injunctions and damages assessments against 'pirates' and 'counterfeiters'; protection of computer software; drafting and negotiating licence agreements of various IP rights; EC and UK competition law issues arising out of complex licensing structures; IP aspects of major corporate transactions.

SWYCHER, Nigel
Slaughter and May, London +44 20 7600 1200
nigel.swycher@slaughterandmay.com
Recommended in Communications: IT, Intellectual Property
Specialisation: Intellectual property and information technology law, including IP and IT aspects of acquisitions, disposals, flotations and privatisations. Involved in technology, licensing and transfer, franchising and sponsorship and IT procurement and development. Joint Head of the firm's Electronic Commerce Group.
Prof. Memberships: ITMA.
Career: Admitted 1987 with *Slaughter and May.* Partner 1994.
Personal: Born 6 June 1962. Educated at Denstone College, Staffordshire and Durham University. Magician.

TAYLOR, Andrew
Richards Butler, London +44 20 7247 6555
Recommended in Shipping
Specialisation: Partner in Shipping Unit. Specialises in charter disputes, cargo liabilities; casualty response; P&I Clubs, Rules and covers issues, sale and purchase.
Publications: Co-author of 'Voyage Charters' – Lloyds of London Press.
Career: Qualified in 1980. Partner at *Richards Butler* since 1983.
Personal: Born 1952. Educated at Magdalen College School and Lincoln College, Oxford (MA).

TAYLOR, David
Freshfields Bruckhaus Deringer, London
+44 20 7936 4000
david.taylor@freshfields.com
Recommended in Tax
Specialisation: Partner in Tax Department. Main area of work is corporate tax including banking, asset and structured finance, and corporate finance.

TAYLOR, Peter
Clifford Chance, London +44 20 7600 1000
Recommended in Intellectual Property

TAYLOR, Timothy
Hill Taylor Dickinson, London +44 20 7283 9033
Recommended in Shipping

TEMPLETON – KNIGHT, Jane
Hunton & Williams, London +44 20 7427 7850
Recommended in Projects

THIEFFRY, Gilles
Garretts, member firm of Andersen Legal, London
+44 20 7344 0344
gilles.thieffry@glegal.com
Recommended in Capital Markets: Debt & Equity
Specialisation: Partner and Head of Capital Markets Practice (from April 2001). International securities transactions. Leading expert on the implications of EMU on financial markets and on cross border capital raising. Leading expert on settlement and clearing issues.
Prof. Memberships: Member of the Paris Bar (Avocat). Member of the New York Bar. Solicitor of the Supreme Court of England and Wales.
Publications: Author of several articles on securities law, on the implications of EMU on capital markets and on the impact of the internet on securities trading. Speaker at seminars and conferences on securites law.
Career: Head of the International Securities Group and partner at *Norton Rose* (1995 – 2001). Head of Legal Department at BNP Capital Markets Ltd. (1992-95). Director of Legal Services UBS *Phillips & Drew* (1988-92).

THOMAS, Anthony
Clyde & Co, London +44 20 7623 1244
Recommended in Shipping
Specialisation: Partner in Shipping and Litigation Department. Main area of practice is shipping litigation. Has considerable experience in litigation in the Commercial Court in London, London Arbitration and proceedings overseas. Handles cargo claims and marine insurance disputes. Author of numerous articles. Has spoken at a number of lectures around the world.
Prof. Memberships: Law Society.
Career: Qualified in 1976, joining *Clyde & Co* the same year. Partner 1981.
Personal: Born 27 May 1952. Attended Leamington College 1963-70, then Manchester University 1970-73. Leisure interests include sport, art and architecture. Lives in Grayshott, Surrey.

THOMPSON, Michael
Freshfields Bruckhaus Deringer, London
+44 20 7936 4000
michael.thompson@freshfields.com
Recommended in Tax
Specialisation: Partner in tax practice group. Advises all tax aspects of corporate transactions including public and private acquisitions and disposals, mergers, demergers, reorganisations, financing and on group tax planning. Has extensive experience of advising clients in the oil and gas sectors. Specialises in structuring the financing of all types of receivable through securitisation techniques. Acts for a number of oil and gas companies and banks.

THOMSON, Keith
Linklaters (a member firm of Linklaters & Alliance), London +44 20 7456 2000
keith.thomson@linklaters.com
Recommended in Capital Markets: Debt & Equity
Specialisation: Specialist in capital market transactions; advising both lead managers and issuers in respect of issues of debt, equity-related debt, equity and depositary receipts in the international capital market. Also advises clients in relation to medium-term note programmes, commercial paper programmes, and dreivative transactions. Has acted in relation to securities transactions in such jurisdictions as Australia, Scandinavia, Switzerland, Holland, Spain, South Africa and the UK and in such emerging markets as Turkey, Greece, Russia, Zimbabwe, Indonesia, India, Pakistan, Thailand and Kazakhstan.

THORNE, Clive
Denton Wilde Sapte, London +44 20 7242 1212
cdt@dentonwildesapte.com
Recommended in Intellectual Property
Specialisation: Partner and Head of Intellectual Property Litigation group. Specialises in contentious intellectual property work, including copyright law, patents, trade marks, passing off, marketing law, computer law and trade secrets. Also commercial litigation, arbitration and employment law. Fellow of the Chartered Institute of Arbitrators. Leading cases have included: Alan Clark v. Associated Newspapers; Halifax B.S. v. Urquhart Dykes; Interlego A.G. v. Tyco Industries; Sony Corporation v. Saray Electronics; Robin Ray v. Classic FM; Dormeuil v. Nicolian; Dormeuil v. Ferlaglow; Karoon v. Bank of Tokyo.
Prof. Memberships: A founding member of The Intellectual Property Lawyers Organisation. Member of Patent Solicitors Association, International Trade Mark Association, Institute of Trade Mark Agents (Associate Member), Anti-counterfeiting Group, Computer Law Group, Chartered Institute of Patent Agents (Associate Member), panel of arbitrators WIPO and Patents County Court.
Publications: Co-author of 'Intellectual Property – the New Law', joint author of 'Sony Guide to Home Taping' and 'User's Guide to Copyright'. Lectures on and has written numerous articles about intellectual property.
Career: Qualified in 1977. Articled *Clifford Turner.* Admitted in Hong Kong in 1984 and Victoria, Australia in 1985. Joined *Denton Hall* as a partner in 1987.
Personal: Born 1952. Educated at Trinity Hall, Cambridge 1971-74 (BA Hons in Law). Interests outside the law include politics, flute playing, opera and English music.

THORP, Clive
Clyde & Co, London +44 20 7623 1244
clive.thorp@clyde.co.uk
Recommended in Shipping
Specialisation: Partner in Marine Department. Main areas of practice are charterparties, commodities, oil, freezing and search orders, payment of judgment debts, sovereign immunity and demurrage arbitrations. Also handles enforcement of judgments. Acted in 'Sonangol v. Lundquist', privilege against self-incrimination; and 'Griparion' on indemnity costs. Lectures on freezing and search orders, demurrage and shipbroker commissions.
Prof. Memberships: Baltic Exchange. Law Society Committee on Arbitration. City of London Committee Member London Court of International Arbitration.
Career: Qualified 1976. Worked at *Holman Fenwick and Willan* 1976-79, joining *Clyde & Co.* in 1979. Became Partner in 1982.
Personal: Born 28 August 1950. Attended Malvern College 1963-68, Hull University 1969-72 and College of Law. Common Councillor. Chairman, Association for Research into Stammering in Childhood.

U

TOTT, Nick
Herbert Smith, London +44 20 7374 8000
nicholas.tott@herbertsmith.com
Recommended in PFI
Specialisation: Principal areas of work include all forms of financing, particularly asset finance, leasing, project financing and Private Finance Initiative Projects. Seconded to the Private Finance Panel Executive (1994, 1995) with responsibility for PFI Projects in Scotland, Northern Ireland and the Ministry of Defence. Publications include 'Public Finance in the UK' in Leasing Finance (Euromoney 1997, 3rd Edition.) Co-author of 'The PFI Handbook' (Jordans, March 1999).
Career: Qualified Scotland (1985), England and Wales (1991). Partner 1992.

TRAPP, Dierdre
Freshfields Bruckhaus Deringer, London
+44 20 7936 4000
dierdre.trapp@freshfields.com
Recommended in Competition/Anti-trust
Specialisation: Specialises in EU and UK competition law, including merger control, joint ventures, monopolies, restrictive practices, privatisations and utility regulation.

TROTT, David
Freshfields Bruckhaus Deringer, London
+44 20 7936 4000
david.trott@freshfields.com
Recommended in Capital Markets: Securitisation
Specialisation: Has worked extensively in the banking and capital markets field acting for lenders, borrowers and arrangers on secured and unsecured transactions. Specialises in asset-backed and structured transactions.

TUCKER, John C.
Linklaters (a member firm of Linklaters & Alliance), London +44 20 7456 2000
john.tucker@linklaters.com
Recommended in Banking & Finance
Specialisation: Head of Banking. Areas of specialisation include syndicated lending, secured and structured financings, acquisition and project finance and reorganisation work. Represents banks, bank syndicates and other creditors as well as borrowers in both UK and international financing transactions.
Career: Admitted as a Barrister and Solicitor in South Australia in 1980 and as a solicitor in England and Wales and Hong Kong.

TUCKER, Julian
Allen & Overy, London +44 20 7330 3000
Recommended in Capital Markets: Securitisation

TUDWAY, Robert
Nabarro Nathanson, London +44 20 7524 6000
Recommended in Energy: Electricity

TUFFNELL, Kevin
Macfarlanes, London +44 20 7831 9222
kevin.tuffnell@macfarlanes.com
Recommended in Private Equity: Buyouts
Specialisation: Partner in the Company Commercial and Banking Department specialising in corporate finance work, including flotations, acquisitions and disposals. Broad experience of management buy-outs and other private equity transactions, acting both for investing institutions and management teams.
Prof. Memberships: Law Society, City of London Law Society.
Career: Graduated in law at Sidney Sussex College, Cambridge in 1981; joined *Macfarlanes* in 1982; qualified in 1984; became a partner in 1989.
Personal: Born 1959; lives in London; leisure interests include sailing and walking.

TURNER, Mark
Herbert Smith, London +44 20 7374 8000
mark.turner@herbertsmith.com
Recommended in Communications: E-commerce
Specialisation: Partner specialising in transactional and advisory work in the IT and e-commerce industries. Works regularly for government departments and agencies, multinationals and leading edge internet and new media businesses, usually with a strong international element. Is at the forefront of developments in e-commerce, advising on on-line exchanges, contracts and payment on the internet, regulation of business on-line and e-commerce issues generally. Work includes acting for BSkyB on new technologies; Freeserve on the acquisition of Smartgroups.com and the joint venture with Barclays Bank, clearlybusiness.com; Credit Suisse First Boston, Goldman Sachs, Bear Stearns and Schroders on IT and e-commerce issues arising from IPOs, listings and other transactions by their clients.
Personal: Born 1956. Educated Latymer Upper School and University College, Oxford (Exhibitioner).

TURNER, Paul
Clifford Chance, London +44 20 7600 1000
Recommended in Shipping: Finance
Specialisation: Main area of practice is commercial shipping covering the negotiation of ship sale contracts, shipbuilding contracts, joint venture and management agreements, finance agreements, and maritime securities.
Publications: Part author and general editor of 'Ship Sale and Purchase'.
Career: Educated at Peterhouse, Cambridge (MA). Joined *Clifford Chance* in 1982. Worked in Hong Kong between 1985 and 1988. Now working in London.

TWENTYMAN, Jeff
Slaughter and May, London +44 20 7600 1200
jeffrey.twentyman@slaughterandmay.com
Recommended in Corporate/Commercial
Specialisation: Mergers and acquisitions, corporate finance, public and private equity finance, joint ventures and commercial contracts, acting for listed and unlisted companies and investment banks; also acts extensively for companies and investors in the telecommunications and technology sectors, significantly in the last twelve months advising Bell Atlantic on the demerger of Cable & Wireless Communications, the SpectrumCo consortium in the UK 3G licence auction and Reuters on its telecommunications networking joint venture with Equant to create Radianz.
Career: Articled *Slaughter and May*, qualified 1991; *Morgan Grenfell & Co. Limited* (1993-94); *Slaughter and May* 1994; partner 1998.
Personal: Born 1965. Educated at Sackville School, East Grinstead and the University of Newcastle-upon-Tyne (1987 LLB). Resides London; one daughter.

TYNE, Sally M.
CMS Cameron McKenna, London
+44 20 7367 3000
smt@cmck.com
Recommended in Energy: Oil and Gas
Specialisation: Specialises in oil and gas, with particular emphasis on acquisitions and disposals of UKCS and international petroleum interests via share or asset deals. Extensive experience of oil industry contracts and joint venture issues. Speaker on licensing, unitisation, JOAs and oil & gas acquisition agreements.
Prof. Memberships: United Kingdom Energy Lawyers Group (IBA); Law Society.
Publications: Co-author of second edition of 'Taylor & Winsor on Joint Operating Agreements' (standard industry textbook).
Career: Educated Trinity College, Oxford. Joined *Cameron Markby Hewitt* (prior to merger with *McKenna & Co*) as an oil & gas partner in London, reinforcing the firm's strong existing energy practices in London and Aberdeen. Previously specialised in oil & gas for ten years at *Norton Rose*.
Personal: Married with three children.

UNDERHILL, William
Slaughter and May, London +44 20 7600 1200
william.underhill@slaughterandmay.com
Recommended in Corporate/Commercial
Specialisation: Specialises in corporate finance, including acting for underwriters and issuers of securities, M&A, London Stock Exchange rules and regulations and FSA compliance. Also experienced in mortgage and other asset securitisation, and other mortgage-backed financing. Editor of Weinberg and Blank on 'Takeovers and Mergers'.
Career: Qualified 1983 with *Slaughter and May*. Partner 1990.

VERRILL, John
Lawrence Graham, London +44 20 7379 0000
Recommended in Energy: Oil and Gas

VICKERS, Mark
Ashurst Morris Crisp, London +44 20 7638 1111
mark.vickers@ashursts.com
Recommended in Banking & Finance
Specialisation: Corporate banking and international finance: specialising in UK and cross-border acquisition finance and leveraged acquisitions, particularly management buy-outs/buy-ins and institutional purchases; structured finance; global syndicated lending.
Publications: Author: 'Public to Private Takeovers: The New Paradigms' and 'The Senior Debt Market for Management Buyouts'.
Career: Head of Banking at *Alsop Wilkinson* from 1990; National Head of Banking at *Dibb Lupton Alsop* following the firm's merger in 1996. Joined *Ashurst Morris Crisp* December 1999.
Personal: Helicopter pilot.

VINTER, Graham
Allen & Overy, London +44 20 7330 3000
Recommended in Project Finance: India Foreign, Projects

VLASTO, Tony
Clifford Chance, London +44 20 7600 1000
tony.vlasto@cliffordchance.com
Recommended in Shipping
Specialisation: Partner in International Maritime, Trade and Insurance Group. Head of Admiralty Practice Group, specialising in particular in all aspects of casualty work, covering also a wide range of general maritime work including charterparty and bill of lading disputes, marine insurance litigation/arbitration, sale and purchase disputes and offshore oil work.
Prof. Memberships: Baltic Exchange; BMLA, City of London Admiralty Solicitors Group; supporting member of the London Maritime Arbitrators Association and the Association of Average Adjusters; Steering Committee member of the London Shipping Law Centre.
Career: LLB 1972. Qualified 1975; partner 1981.

VOISEY, Peter G.
Clifford Chance, London +44 20 7600 1000
peter.voisey@cliffordchance.com
Recommended in Capital Markets: Securitisation
Specialisation: Partner specialising in international asset securitisation and structured finance transactions.
Prof. Memberships: City of London Solicitors' Company. Law Society.
Career: Articled at *Lovells*; qualified 1987, partner 1994-2000.
Personal: Brentwood School, Brentwood. Trinity Hall College, Cambridge University 1978-1982 (MA (Hons) Modern Languages).

VOISIN, Michael
Linklaters (a member firm of Linklaters & Alliance), London +44 20 7456 2000
michael.voisin@linklaters.com
Recommended in Capital Markets: Securitisation
Specialisation: Partner, general capital markets specialist with particular emphasis on sophisticated financial products, note programmes and regulatory capital raising for financial institutions. Responsible for development of medium-term note programme practice and one of the core partners in derivatives practice. Practice mainly comprises repackagings, CBOs/CLOs and other forms of securitised structured products, medium term note and commercial paper programmes, eurobonds, regulatory capital raising for financial institutions, securitised derivatives, such as warrants and credit-linked notes, and swaps, OTC derivatives and other treasury products.

VON BISMARCK, Nilufer
Slaughter and May, London +44 20 7600 1200
nilufer.vonbismarck@slaughterandmay.com
Recommended in Corporate/Commercial
Specialisation: Partner specialising in corporate finance, general company and commercial work and some banking.
Career: Articled *Norton Rose* 1986-90; qualified 1988; *Slaughter and May* 1990 to date; partner 1994.
Personal: Born 1961. Educated at James Allen's Girls' School and Trinity College, Cambridge (1983 BA Law 2 (1)). Resides London.

WALLACE, Patrick
Freshfields Bruckhaus Deringer, London
+44 20 7936 4000
patrick.wallace@freshfields.com
Recommended in Energy: Electricity
Specialisation: Specialises in international energy and natural resource projects, project financing, privatisations and related commercial contracts and regulatory issues. Sector experience includes electricity, transport and infrastructrue, agriculture and commercial contracts.

WALLIS, Robert
Hill Taylor Dickinson, London +44 20 7283 9033
Recommended in Shipping

WALSH, Jonathan
Norton Rose, London +44 20 7283 6000
walshjgf@nortonrose.com
Recommended in Capital Markets: Securitisation
Specialisation: Securitisation/repackaging. Acts for investment banks, corporates, arrangers and sponsors on a variety of UK and international securitisation and repackaging transactions, both in respect of term issuance and commercial paper conduit structures.
Prof. Memberships: Law Society.
Career: Kings College, London, LLB, called to the bar in 1984, requalified as a solicitor 1988. Partner 1997. Head of International Securities Group.
Personal: Member of The Oriental Club. Obscure rock music (pop trivia bore), cooking and mixing cocktails, swimming, skiing and surfing (very badly).

WALSH, Paul
Bristows, London +44 20 7400 8000
Recommended in Intellectual Property

WALTON, Miles
Allen & Overy, London +44 20 7330 3000
Recommended in Tax

WARD, Conor
Lovells, London +44 20 7296 2000
conor.ward@lovells.com
Recommended in Communications: IT
Specialisation: Partner in the firm's computer, communications and media unit. Work includes advising on the contentious and non-contentious aspects of systems acquisition and development; facilities management and outsourcing (including telecommunications services); electronic commerce, electronic signatures and encryption technologies, anti-piracy and computer crime. Practises exclusively in the information technology field, often where the technological issues are most complex. Recent work includes advising in relation to the setting up of the e-commerce protection scheme in the UK; advising several banks in relation to the launch of their Identrus Trust Services in the UK; a major strategic alliance between a major teleco and a handset manufacturer relating to WAP technology; Baltimore Technologies in its acquisition of Content Technologies.
Prof. Memberships: The British Computer Society Legal Affairs Committee, The Computer Law Association, member of the editorial board of the Computer and Telecommunications Law Review published by Sweet and Maxwell. Director of the Federation Against Software Theft (FAST) and Chairman of the legal advisory group of FAST.
Career: 1980-1984 The Queen's University, Belfast (Law LLB Hons). 1984-1988 IBM United Kingdom Laboratories Limited – development programmer. 1987 called to the Bar of England and Wales. 1988-1990 *Heald Nickinson* – assistant. 1990 to date *Lovells* – assistant solicitor. 1998 partner.

WARDER, David
Watson, Farley & Williams, London
+44 20 7814 8000
dwarder@wfw.com
Recommended in Shipping: Finance
Specialisation: Managing partner and partner of the firm's International Finance Group. Acts for financial institutions engaged in shipping finance, specialising in asset-backed finance and structured or project-based transactions; particular experience in UK and cross-border tax-based leasing.
Career: *Norton Rose* 1973-1982; partner *Watson, Farley & Williams* 1982.
Personal: Trinity College, Cambridge (1973 BA).

WARNA-KULA-SURIYA, Sanjev
Slaughter and May, London +44 20 7600 1200
sanjevwks@slaughterandmay.com
Recommended in Capital Markets: Derivatives
Specialisation: Partner specialising in capital markets, derivatives, securitisation and structured finance.
Career: Articled *Slaughter and May*; qualified 1990; partner 1997.
Personal: Born 1964. Educated at King's College, London University (1986 LLB First Class Hons). Resides London. Leisure: Cricket, theatre.

WATSON, Chris
Allen & Overy, London +44 20 7330 3000
Recommended in Communications: Telecoms

WATSON, John G.
Ashurst Morris Crisp, London +44 20 7638 1111
Recommended in Tax
Specialisation: Head of the Tax Department. Extensive experience of general commercial tax. Advises on unquoted equity funds and leads the IFMA's negotiations with the UK authorities in relation to pension fund pooling vehicles. Specialises in setting up investment funds, joint ventures, capital allowances and enterprise zones.
Prof. Memberships: Honorary legal counsel to the enterprise zone Property Trust Association.
Career: Mathematics graduate, Cambridge. Joined *Ashurst*'s in 1983 after five years in the Tax and Tax Consultancy departments of Neville Russell, Chartered Accountants.

WATSON, Martin A.
Watson, Farley & Williams, London
+44 20 7814 8000
mwatson@wfw.com
Recommended in Shipping: Finance
Specialisation: Partner in International Finance

U

Group. Main area of practice is STET finance, covering STET, commercial leasing, banking, asset finance and corporate restructuring; acts for ship-owners, operators, shipbuilders, and financial institutions providing finance of various types to the sector.
Career: Founding Partner of *Watson, Farley & Williams* 1982.
Personal: Educated at St Catharine's College, Cambridge (BA).

WATSON, Sean
CMS Cameron McKenna, London
+44 20 7367 3000
smw@cmck.com
Recommended in Corporate/Commercial
Specialisation: Partner in Corporate Department. Advises corporate, investment bank and venture capital clients on all areas of corporate and corporate finance including M&A, reconstructions, take-overs, flotations, securities offerings and venture capital transactions.
Prof. Memberships: Law Society, City of London Solicitors Company.
Career: Qualified in 1972. Joined *McKenna & Co* in 1979, becoming a Partner in the same year.
Personal: Born 5 April 1948. Attended The Leys School, Cambridge, 1961-66 and Manchester University 1966-69. Leisure interests include tennis, golf, skiing, gardening and family. Lives in Weybridge, Surrey.

WAYTE, Peter B.
DLA, London +44 (0) 8700 111 111
Recommended in Private Equity: Buyouts

WEBER, David
Linklaters (a member firm of Linklaters & Alliance), London +44 20 7456 2000
david.weber@linklaters.com
Recommended in Projects
Specialisation: Partner, Project and Project Finance Department. Co-founder of Project Department. Experience in structuring, negotiating and documenting complex projects and bringing them to financial closing. Experience includes advising and representing sponsors, project companies and lenders, including Multilateral Lending Agencies (MLAs). Particular expertise in multi-sourced financings, involving ECAs, MLAs, capital markets and commercial banks. Projects worked on span UK, North Sea, Continental Europe, Asia and Africa and include a number of large and complex multi-jurisdictional projects. Specific fields of work include oil and gas, power generation, infrastructure, transportation and telecommunication. Recent major projects include: Channel Tunnel (UK/France), Hub Power Project (Pakistan), Doba Oilfields and Transportation System (Chad-Cameroon).

WEBSTER, Michael
Nicholson Graham & Jones, London
+44 20 7648 9000
Recommended in Communications: IT
Specialisation: Computer & Telecoms, software & service supply contracts, ranging from software development & distribution contracts, VAR & financing, turnkey supply and systems integration agreements, Internet, EDI, e-commerce and web site issues, multi-media rights, joint ventures, technology transfer, outsourcing & long term supply of services agreements.
Prof. Memberships: Society for Computers & the Law, British Computer Society, Computer Law Group, Software Business Network, Worshipful Company of Information Technologists.
Publications: Long term involvement with specialisations has led to many invitations to speak and write articles on a number of topics such as outsourcing, joint ventures and liability arising from computer contracts.
Career: Articled *Herbert Smith*, qualified in 1967, partner *Rowe & Maw* 1973.
Personal: Born 1942. Educated at Berkhamsted School and Bristol University (LLB hons). Interests include tennis, golf, long distance walking and tree felling. Member of The Honourable Artillery Company and Liveryman of the Worshipful Company of Upholders.

WEDDERBURN-DAY, Roger
Allen & Overy, London +44 20 7330 3000
Recommended in Capital Markets: Debt & Equity

WEITZMAN, Polly
Denton Wilde Sapte, London +44 20 7242 1212
fmaw@dentonwildesapte.com
Recommended in Competition/Anti-trust
Specialisation: EU and UK competition law specialist advising on non-contentious (mergers, joint ventures, restrictive agreements) and contentious (cartel, restrictive practices, abuse of market power) issues with particular experience in the media and energy sectors. Extensive experience before the European Commission, Office of Fair Trading, Competition Commission and Restrictive Practices Court. Most recent major case is the successful defence of the collective and exclusive selling arrangements for the television rights to the Premier League Championship before the Restrictive Practices Court. Editor of section on gas in Butterworths 'Encyclopaedia of Competition Law'.
Prof. Memberships: Competition Law Society; The Law Society.
Career: Qualified in 1988 with *Denton Hall*. Became a partner in 1995.
Personal: Born 1961. Educated Godolphin & Latymer School, London; then Edinburgh University (Modern History).

WELLS, Boyan S.
Allen & Overy, London +44 20 7330 3000
Recommended in Capital Markets: Debt & Equity

WHAITE, Robin
Linklaters (a member firm of Linklaters & Alliance), London +44 20 7456 2000
robin.whaite@linklaters.com
Recommended in Intellectual Property
Specialisation: Partner, Intellectual Property and Technology Department, since 1989. Considerable experience in commercial and litigious matters involving IP rights and technology. Particular knowledge of issues in the healthcare and computer industries. Main areas of practice include patent, copyright, trade marks and trade secrets litigation; technology joint ventures and IP aspects of corporate finance and restructurings; technology transfer generally, including European anti-trust and competition law considerations; pharmaceutical law, including regulatory affairs. Represents the British Chambers of Commerce on the Government's Standing Advisory Committee on Intellectual Property; editorial board, 'Managing Intellectual Property'; committee of the IP Lawyers Association.

WHEADON, Tom
Simmons & Simmons, London +44 20 7628 2020
tom.wheadon@simmons-simmons.com.
Recommended in Communications: Telecoms
Specialisation: Specialisation is in the law, regulation and policy of telecommunications, the Internet and e-commerce. Is regarded as one of the 25 Best Business Lawyers in the UK, as well as being a 'Leading Individual' in Legal Directories. Is recommended as one of the 'Digital Dozen' in 'The Insider's Guide to Legal Services'. Advises a wide range of clients including the UK Government, industry, established corporates in Internet start-ups. Recently actively involved wet and dry telecoms infrastructure projects and in the conception of MatchCo, a new online service providing entrepreneurs in the technology sector with access to financial resource and expertise. Is a regular conference speaker and contributor to specialist journals.
Prof. Memberships: Law Society and International Bar Association.
Publications: Joint author of 'Telecommunications – The EU Law'.
Career: Southampton University, Guildford Law School, admitted as a Solicitor in England and Wales in 1989. 1987-89: Trainee Solicitor, *Ashurst Morris Crisp*. 1989-95: Assistant Solicitor, *Ashurst Morris Crisp*. 1995-96: Corporate and Regulatory Affairs Solicitor, Videotron Corporation Ltd. 1996 to date: Partner, Communications Practice at *Simmons & Simmons*.
Personal: Married to Kate with three sons, Fred, Henry and George.

WHEATON, James
Clifford Chance, London +44 20 7600 1000
Recommended in Competition/Anti-trust
Specialisation: Partner specialising in EU and competition law.
Career: Birmingham (LLB). Qualified 1973; partner *Clifford Chance* 1978.

WHISH, Richard P.
Richard Whish – Sole Practitioner, London
+44 20 7848 2237
Recommended in Competition/Anti-trust

WHITE, Bruce
Linklaters (a member firm of Linklaters & Alliance), London +44 20 7456 2000
bruce.white@linklaters.com
Recommended in PFI
Specialisation: Partner, Project Finance Group. Focuses on UK PFI projects. Recent projects include acting for lenders for the Durham, Edinburgh, Worcester and Swindon hospital projects, advising the sponsors on the London Underground Power and Radio projects, and advising lenders and/or bidders on other PFI projects in the transport, water, defence, education and other sectors.

WHITE, Graham
S J Berwin & Co, London +44 20 7533 2222
graham.white@sjberwin.com
Recommended in Private Equity: Buyouts
Specialisation: Partner in the corporate department specialising in Private Equity transactions.
Prof. Memberships: Law Society of Scotland.
Career: 1984-86, *Iain Smith & Co* Aberdeen, 1987 *Simmons & Simmons* London, 1988-1998 *Dickson Minto WS* London. 1999 *SJ Berwin & Co.*

WILLIAMS, Alan
Denton Wilde Sapte, London +44 20 7242 1212
apw@dentonwildesapte.com
Recommended in Communications: E-commerce
Specialisation: Head of Digital Media practice. Work includes digital media, the internet and e-commerce, electronic publishing, traditional publishing, copyright, libel, commercial contract and theatre. Lectures for Hawksmere, PIRA and others.
Prof. Memberships: Law Society, Publishing Law Group of the Publishers Association.
Publications: Co-author with Michael Flint and Clive Thorne of 'Intellectual Property: the New Law'; contributes to 'Publishing Agreements' edited by Charles Clark. Author with Duncan Calow and Nicholas Higham of 'Digital Media: Contracts, Rights and Licensing', Sweet & Maxwell, Second Edition (1998).
Career: Qualified in 1969, having joined *Denton Hall & Burgin* in 1967. Became a partner in 1972.
Personal: Born 1944. Attended Merchant Taylors' School 1957-63, then Exeter University 1963-66. Clubs include MCC, Groucho, Whitefriars, Omar Khayyam, Magic Circle, Richard III Society, City Law Club, Liveryman of the Worshipful Company of Pewterers, Fellow of the Royal Society of Arts, Friend of Shakespeare's Globe. Leisure interests include theatre, music, cricket and walking. Married, one daughter. Lives in London.

WILLOUGHBY, Anthony
Rouse & Co International in association with Willoughby & Partners, London +44 20 7345 8888
Recommended in Intellectual Property

WILSON, James
Ince & Co, London +44 20 7623 2011
Recommended in Shipping
Specialisation: Initially worked mainly on the charterparty and cargo claims side of the firm's business. More recently has concentrated on the wet side of the practice, with increasing involvement in marine casualties, for example those of the Braer and Sea Empress. Client base is drawn from across the maritime industry and includes owners, clubs and marine underwriters.
Career: Joined *Ince & Co.* in 1983 and on completion of his Articles joined *Ince & Co's* Hong Kong office for 3 years. Became a partner in 1991. Co-leader of Admiralty Business Group.
Personal: Graduated from Cambridge with an Honours Degree in Law. Leisure interests include golf, squash and shooting.

WILSON, Robert
Holman Fenwick & Willan, London
+44 20 7488 2300
Robert.Wilson@hfw.co.uk
Recommended in Shipping
Specialisation: Senior Partner of the firm and Partner in Commercial Litigation Department. Principal area of practice is shipping and maritime law. Work covers commercial legal advice, handling and resolving disputes, negotiations, conducting litigation and arbitration: including newbuildings, conversion and repair (ship/offshore), MOA, pools, charters, bills of lading, P&I and Defence Club work, marine insurance (including total losses), international trade, especially tankers and the oil trade. Also deals with insurance, commercial and banking law where related to shipping and trading interests. House of Lords and Court of Appeal cases include Delfini (title to sue), Kyzikos (laytime), Evpo Agnic (arrest), Arta (shipbrokers negligence), Apj Priti (safe berth) and Padre Island (P&I club/third party claims), Factortame (European law) and Haji-Ioannou v Frangos (European Convention and ship arrests).
Prof. Memberships: Law Society, London Maritime Arbitrators Association (supporting member).
Career: Qualified in 1977, having joined *Holman Fenwick & Willan* in 1975. Became a Partner in 1982. Senior Partner in November 2000.
Personal: Born 8 February 1952. Educated at Watford Grammar School 1962-69 and Corpus Christi College, Cambridge 1970-74 (MA Maths, History; Law). Interests include family, golf and travel. Lives in Hadley Wood, Herts.

WINTER, Jeremy
Baker & McKenzie, London +44 20 7919 1000
jeremy.winter@bakernet.com
Recommended in Arbitration (International)
Specialisation: Partner and Head of Construction & Projects Department, Solicitor Advocate. Resolution of construction and projects disputes by arbitration, litigation and ADR. Particular expertise in civil engineering matters. 18 years' experience in a total of 30 countries around the world (particularly Europe, Africa and the Middle East). Conducts own advocacy in arbitration and in High Court. Frequent speaker and writer on construction and arbitration topics. Chairman of Society of Construction Law Working Group on delay analysis.
Prof. Memberships: Hon Fellow of Institution of Civil Engineering Surveyors, Society of Construction Law, Technology and Construction Solicitors Association (Member of IT Sub-committee). Member of Association for Project Management, Fellow of the Geological Society. Member of LCIA.
Career: Qualified 1979. Joined *Baker & McKenzie* London 1980. Worked in *Baker & McKenzie* Sydney Office 1982-84. Partner 1987.
Personal: Born 26 December 1953. Warwick University (LLB Hons 1975). Lives in Toys Hill, Kent.

WIPPELL, Mark
Allen & Overy, London +44 20 7330 3000
Recommended in Corporate/Commercial

WOOD, Charles
Denton Wilde Sapte, London +44 20 7242 1212
cwcw@dentonwildesapte.com
Recommended in Energy: Oil and Gas
Specialisation: Partner; experience includes commercial contracts and regulation in gas and electricity sectors and LNG projects. Adviser to BG Transco on UK network code and to Ofgem/the NETA Programme on the new electricity trading arrangements (NETA).
Career: Articled at *Denton Hall.* Qualified 1980. Partner 1984.
Personal: Born 1955.

WOOD, Ian
Rowe & Maw, London +44 20 7248 4282
Recommended in Intellectual Property
Partner intellectual property department.
Specialisation: All aspects of intellectual property law, including patents, trade marks and copyright and allied rights, although primarily involved in the area of dispute resolution. Acts for a broad range of clients from large multinational corporations to smaller more locally based businesses, covering a broad spectrum of industries and services extending from those involved in newly emergent technologies to those in more established areas of business. Responsible for the conduct of several notable actions in the High Court, including the following leading reported patent infringement actions: Molnlycke v. Procter & Gamble; Nidek v. VISX; Unilever v. Akzo and Chefaro; Honeywell v. ACL. Other leading cases include Burton v. Burton Snowboards and BP Amoco v. Kelly. Also (with *Rowe & Maw's* WTO team) advising the European Commission in connection with WTO disputes regarding international obligations on patents. Author of several articles and regularly invited to speak at conferences and seminars (including those attended by fellow professionals).
Prof. Memberships: CIPA; ITMA; INTA; AIPPI; IPLA.
Personal: Born 1950. Attended Durham University (BSc Physics and MSc Nuclear Physics). Qualified as a solicitor in 1977.

WOOD, Philip
Allen & Overy, London +44 20 7330 3000
Recommended in Banking & Finance

WOODHALL, John
Clifford Chance, London +44 20 7600 1000
Recommended in Capital Markets: Securitisation

WOOLF, Fiona
CMS Cameron McKenna, London
+44 20 7367 3000
fiona.woolf@cmck.com
Recommended in Energy: Electricity
Specialisation: Energy Projects and Construction Group. Main areas of practice are electricity restructurings and privatisations, regulation and the introduction of wholesale and retail competitive markets in the power sector, projects and financings. Worked exclusively on banking and project finance transactions in Bahrain, 1982-85. Acted in the Channel Tunnel project as one of the lead negotiators on the Concession Agreement and the Treaty with British

U

and French Governments. Led a team of 40 people acting for The National Grid Company plc on the privatisation of the Electricity Supply Industry in England and Wales and advised on the Northern Ireland Electricity restructuring and privatisation. Advised Electricidade de Portugal on the Tapada do Outeiro and Pego power projects and the project to bring natural gas to Portugal. Worked on independent transmission projects in Pakistan and Malaysia and the privatisation of the transmission system of Argentina. Has worked on power sector restructurings, utility regulation and privatisations in Australia, Canada, India, California, the Republic of Ireland, Central America and South Africa.

Prof. Memberships: Council Member of the Law Society.

Publications: Contributor to 'Utilities Law Review' and the Electricity Journal; regular speaker at conferences.

Career: Qualified in 1973. Worked at *Coward Chance* 1973-78 before joining *McKenna & Co.* in 1978. Became a Partner in 1981.

Personal: Born 11 May 1948. Attended Keele University 1966-70. Leisure interests include wine and opera. Lives in Esher, Surrey.

WOOTTON, David

Allen & Overy, London +44 20 7330 3000

Recommended in Corporate/Commercial

WOTTON, John

Allen & Overy, London +44 20 7330 3000

Recommended in Competition/Anti-trust

WRIGHT, Claire

Allen & Overy, London +44 20 7330 3000

Recommended in Communications: Telecoms

WYMAN, Chris

Clifford Chance, London +44 20 7600 1000

chris.wyman@cliffordchance.com

Recommended in Project Finance: India Foreign, Projects

Specialisation: Partner specialising in project finance, banking and energy, oil, gas, natural resources.

Career: Epsom College; Cambridge University. Articled *Coward Chance/Clifford Chance*; qualified 1981; partner *Clifford Chance* since 1986.

U

USA

Index

OVERVIEW: In the world's biggest market for legal services it has yet again been a boom year. Waves of consolidation have taken over the global corporate markets and the US, with its much sought after liquidity, has captured the lion's share. Skadden Arps scored a first by breaking the $1 billion barrier for annual gross revenue, and the New York M&A giants continue to benefit from high value activity in financial services, energy, and the communications markets. The current bull market can sustain all comers but interesting options face these expanding practices. A global rush continues as the might of firms such as Cleary Gottlieb, Shearman & Sterling, White & Case and Skadden Arps stretches across the globe. That said, Wachtell with its "boutique like" focus competes from a US base. Or consider Davis Polk with its five overseas offices advising solely on US law; it is currently reliant on powerful alliances to Slaughter and May (UK) and Hengeler Mueller (Germany.) In this wave of competition one thing has not changed: the long vaunted threat of the accountancy firms has yet again failed to appear with the ABA firmly voting against the concept of profit sharing in MDPs.

This year we cast an eye on the biggest players on the East Coast. Although few big-ticket transactions take place in the urban centres outside New York, a corporate old guard is active in each major city from Boston to Miami. The most successful corporate practices have well established offices with a large and diverse client base. Northern Virginia in particular has become a hub of hi-tech activity, with the result that many West Coast firms are making a pilgrimage over for the rich pickings to be had in the region.

Washington DC continues to be the regulatory centre of the US. The federal anti-trust agencies (FTC and DOJ) are busier than ever in a constant review of merger activity, while lawyers anticipate a further hardening of the ways, particularly on cross border activity. In the communications market, open access issues and foreign ownership of US telcos are key areas for precedent setting rulings. While the financial centres of New York and Chicago continue to dominate the market for corporate tax advice, DC specialist firms are accruing an international reputation for tax controversy and strategic planning cases.

Chicago, the heartland of the Mid West corporate market, sustains a stable legal environment with most high level transactions covered by a handful of old line Chicago firms, of which Mayer Brown & Platt and Sidley & Austin are the most established. The trend, however, is a transcendence of traditional regional boundaries. East and West Coast firms such as Skadden Arps and Latham & Watkins have made successful inroads into the midwestern market, while many institutional Chicago firms have expanded their scope, with developed practices across the US. Chicago firm

The clients' choice

BUSINESS LAWYER OF THE YEAR

MARTIN LIPTON,
Wachtell, Lipton, Rosen & Katz
RODGIN COHEN, *Sullivan & Cromwell*

BUSINESS LAW FIRM OF THE YEAR

SKADDEN, ARPS, SLATE, MEAGHER & FLOM

*Our nation-wide survey showed that NY based law firms are the most popular with clients throughout the USA. **Martin Lipton** and **Rodgin Cohen** win as best business lawyer with **Skadden Arps** as best firm.*

For details see page 36.

*See leaders' profiles on pages 848-903

Kirkland & Ellis is known nationally as a market leader in private equity transactions. In this edition of Chambers Global we also profile the leading midwestern corporate firms outside of Chicago.

In the South research indicated two main areas of corporate law: Houston for energy, and Dallas and Austin leading the telecoms and dot.com market. Houston is one of the greatest 'oil 'n gas' cities in the world and in energy M&A, regulation and grand pipeline projects these firms are the equal of any. Subject to a rapid growth, the hi-tech focus is a cause for concern in some quarters with many firms fearing an invasion of West Coast giants.

Los Angeles is a centre for corporate work on the West Coast but Silicon Valley is the heart of the region's legal market. An increasing number of New York firms are arriving in Palo Alto and Menlo Park due to the vast amount of hi-tech work, although as Shearman & Sterling found, it has not always been an easy ride. There has been a substantial increase in intellectual property work across the States as a whole. Many full service commercial firms are devoting time and resources to developing strong IP practices to challenge the position of the established boutiques. Like their cousins on the East Coast, these corporate players are benefiting from a boom in private equity financings although the formation of funds remains a primarily New York/Boston game.

Skadden Arps continues its reign as the premier energy practice on the East Coast in both electricity and oil and gas, with its blue-chip corporate client base and complementary regulatory muscle in DC. Lebouef Lamb's electricity practice is still acknowledged as one of the finest in the country, but its oil and gas practice is just a step behind Skaddens at present. The Texan-based firms as a rule have proved to be less dominant off their home turf, and stronger in the oil and gas field than for electricity work, with Vinson & Elkins the pick of the bunch for its projects and regulatory presence in both DC and New York.

In international arbitration, Debevoise & Plimpton and White & Case continue to rule the roost in New York and Washington DC respectively, with both able to draw on support from their European offices and both maintaining strong profiles for their Latin American work. White & Case's arbitration legend Charlie Brower recently retired from private practice, but the firm still retains a fine crop of talent.

The New York shipping market is very clearly divided into those firms who practice predominantly shipping-related finance work and those whose practice consists mainly of litigation, whether this be charter party, cargo or casualty work. That said, firms at the top of the tree, Haight Gardner Holland & Knight and, to a lesser extent, Healy & Baillie, are both instructed in a variety of wet and dry work.

With the downturn in the high yield debt markets, creativity is the order of the day in banking and finance. While project financiers continue to use capital markets to raise funds, often companies are developing multiple projects or acquiring major utility assets to stay ahead of the game. The creation and design of new financial products continues apace including the rise of internet platforms for the trading of securities. With recent tie ups in the banking market such as JPMorganChase and CSFB/DLJ, one must consider the effect on the law firms currently instructed. Market speculation suggests that it is Davis Polk & Wardwell who stand to lose out if the merged entities decide to streamline their counsel although *Chambers Global* has found little evidence to expect such a drastic change.

A concentration of large and long established midwestern banks has endowed Chicago with an importance on the national banking and finance scene, second only to New York. Again, the oldest firms Mayer Brown & Platt and Sidley & Austin fare best, with secured and structured finance capabilities on a par with their New York competitors. A number of other Chicago practices, Goldberg Kohn and Sonnenschein Nath & Rosenthal among them, have made their names through handling a volume of middle market and asset based lending for midwestern financial institutions. The implementation of the Gramm-Leach-Bliley Act essentially opened the domestic financial services market place allowing commercial banks to engage in merchant banking (such as mutual funds, equity derivatives) and encouraging even greater competition (and mergers) in an already brutally competitive market.

Arbitration (International): East Coast

Debevoise & Plimpton (New York 7 ptrs, 20 asscs) The firm's New York office handles a range of commercial disputes, encompassing failed joint ventures, concession agreements and sales disputes throughout the world. Working closely with similarly respected offices in London and Paris, the team is particularly acknowledged for its expertise in Latin America.

Research unearthed unanimous acclamation for the group. Described as *"one of the highest profile arbitration practices in the US,"* its *"solid international offering"* has often been put to work on behalf of US multi-nationals doing business abroad. An excellent litigation practice is seen to provide a solid springboard for the arbitration group's pre-eminence.

USA: EAST COAST Leading Firms (Arbitration (International))	
1	Debevoise & Plimpton
	White & Case LLP
2	Hughes Hubbard & Reed
	Simpson Thacher & Bartlett
	Sullivan & Cromwell
3	Shearman & Sterling
	Skadden, Arps, Slate, Meagher & Flom LLP
4	Baker & McKenzie
	Wilmer, Cutler & Pickering
5	Covington & Burling
	Freshfields Bruckhaus Deringer

Firms are listed alphabetically in each band.

David Rivkin* and **Don Donovan*** are both considered to be *"right up at the top,"* and are commended as *"erudite practitioners."* The firm has around half a dozen cases involving foreign sovereigns, including an ICSID arbitration against the government of Venezuela, several other cases against European governments, and a case involving a Pacific Island nation.

White & Case LLP (New York 4 ptrs, 6 asscs; Washington DC 3 ptrs) The team has an established reputation for advising clients on ICC, ICSID and international AAA arbitrations. Able to draw on support from powerful Paris, London and New York offices, the firm is a market leader on arbitrations involving state entities. It has a notably strong reputation in Latin America. The firm's greatest reputation has always rested in Washington, and it is too early to judge to what extent the recent retirement of arbitration legend Charles Brower will affect this.

Carolyn Lamm* is widely seen as *"heir apparent to Brower,"* and was recommended to researchers as *"an effective advocate"* with *"good academic experience."* **Paul Friedland*** is chair of the AAA's Arbitration Practice Committee, and is *"articulate, experienced and credible,"* and a *"first-rate trial lawyer."* **Abby Cohen Smutny*** is another of *"Charlie Brower's protégés,"* and is seen as *"an astute tactician."* The firm's New York office acted in concert with Paris on the Saudi Cable/AT&T arbitration.

Hughes Hubbard & Reed (New York 18 ptrs, 10 asscs; Washington DC 2 ptrs) Broadly-based group with a specialisation in technology-based arbitrations relating to licences, know-how and trade secrets, as well as major projects and service contracts. Its reputation for excellence is undiminished, but our researchers were left in no doubt that its profile *"just can't be compared with White & Case or Debevoise."* **John Townsend*** is said to be *"super at general commercial arbitrations,"* and is still seen to be the *"star"* of the practice. The firm represented Arco Chemical Company on an ICC arbitration in Paris involving the enforcement of an arbitration clause in a secret manufacturing process licence.

Simpson Thacher & Bartlett (New York 4 ptrs) *"An excellent litigation practice"* has assisted the firm's reputation as a leading force in domestic arbitration, notably in the insurance sector. However, the firm is still considered to lack the Europe-wide coverage of the market leaders, although its high-profile and successful ICC arbitration concerning Andersen Consulting has drawn gasps of admiration from competitors.

John Kerr* is *"even-tempered, smart and knows the international scene,"* having done a number of the *"sovereign debt cases"* as well as the *"heavy lifting in the Andersen case – if you needed deep digging, you'd go to Kerr."* **Robert Smit*** is said to be *"thoroughly knowledgeable"* and *"a very bright guy,"* and was *"the lead counsel on the Andersen Consulting case – an earthquake in international arbitration."* Former President of the New York Bar Association **Conrad Harper*** is *"newer to the field"* than Robert Smit or Jack Kerr, but is said to have *"great gravitas"* and a *"very high profile name"* due to having also been a *"State Department legal adviser."*

Sullivan & Cromwell (New York 5 ptrs, 10 asscs) The firm's superb blue-chip clientele is the basis of its reputation in international arbitration. It continues to be involved in investment disputes and failed joint ventures in the oil and gas, minerals, software and pharmaceutical industries, as well as disputes in the banking and general finance sectors. **James Carter*** *"undoubtedly belongs in the top rung"* agreed rivals. He is the man credited with building the practice in New York. **Joseph Neuhaus*** is also *"terrific"* and is noted for his Latin American arbitrations. However, his versatility has also seen him undertake an increasing amount of litigation. The firm has recently been acting for private investors in a dispute in Venezuela and also acted in a dispute con-

Leading Individuals (Arbitration (International))		
★	AKSEN Gerald *Thelen Reid & Priest LLP*	
1	CARTER James *Sullivan & Cromwell*	DONOVAN Donald Francis *Debevoise & Plimpton*
	RIVKIN David *Debevoise & Plimpton*	
2	KERR John *Simpson Thacher & Bartlett*	NEUHAUS Joseph *Sullivan & Cromwell*
	NEWMAN Lawrence *Baker & McKenzie*	PARK William *Sole Practitioner*
	SMIT Robert *Simpson Thacher & Bartlett*	TOWNSEND John *Hughes Hubbard & Reed*
3	FRIEDLAND Paul *White & Case LLP*	GARFINKEL Barry *Skadden, Arps*
	HARPER Conrad *Simpson Thacher & Bartlett*	LAMM Carolyn *White & Case LLP*
	REED Lucy *Freshfields Bruckhaus Deringer*	ROVINE Arthur *Baker & McKenzie*
	VOLLMER Andrew *Wilmer, Cutler & Pickering*	WEISBURG Henry *Shearman & Sterling*
4	ASTIGARRAGA José *Astigarraga Davis*	CLAGETT Brice *Covington & Burling*
	FREYER Dana *Skadden, Arps*	GOLDSTEIN Marc *Proskauer Rose*
	HORNICK Robert *Morgan, Lewis & Bockius LLP*	SCHILLER Jonathan *Boies, Schiller & Flexner*
	SCHNABL Marco *Skadden, Arps*	
Up-and-coming individuals		
	SMUTNY Abby Cohen *White & Case LLP*	LINDSEY David *Clifford Chance Rogers & Wells*

Individuals are listed alphabetically in each band.

*See leaders' profiles on pages 848-903

cerning a bank and the sellers of another bank in Columbia.

Shearman & Sterling (New York 4 ptrs, 5 asscs; Washington DC 1 ptr) The firm's international arbitration practice falls into four broad areas, namely ICSID, AAA, ICC and ad hoc arbitrations. While the New York office still comes in for substantial market support, the heart of the firm's international arbitration practice remains in Paris, where *"Emmanuel Gaillard is their real superstar."* Although not possessing Gaillard's reputation, **Henry Weisburg*** continues to win market respect in New York.

In the past twelve months, the firm has advised on a number of AAA and ICC arbitrations of South American origin. IP arbitrations are an area of niche excellence. The firm represented TV Azteca, a Mexican television company, on an ICC arbitration against NBC, and advised the Slovakian government on a dispute with a large Czech bank.

Skadden, Arps, Slate, Meagher & Flom LLP (New York 4 ptrs, 7 asscs) Continuing to undertake a wide range of arbitration work for both US and non-US clients in a number of industries, the firm has been active in construction, manufacturing, metals and mining, and energy cases. Clients and peers agree that this is an *"aggressive"* and active team, which gains substantial work through its huge existing corporate client base.

Barry Garfinkel* is *"a salty, effective litigator,"* who has wide experience of, and is a prolific writer about arbitration. **Dana Freyer*** is a respected veteran of numerous project finance arbitrations, while **Marco Schnabl*** is *"an erudite, scholarly lawyer"* with *"good international contacts."*

The firm advised a Polish conglomerate on a breach of contract action against a US venture capital firm and a Polish telecommunications company, and appeared before the Netherlands Institute of Arbitration on a $600 million claim involving a breach of contract with respect to the sale of a biotech company.

Baker & McKenzie (New York 4 ptrs, 10 asscs; Washington DC 1 ptr, 3 asscs) The firm's International Commercial Arbitration Group handles a cross-section of global corporate and commercial disputes. The firm acts as legal counsel in arbitrations administered by institutions including the AAA, CIETAC, ICC, LCIA, HKIAC, ICSID, the Chambers of Commerce of Austria, Singapore and Stockholm, and regional arbitration centres, as well as advising on a wide range of ad hoc references.

In New York, **Lawrence Newman*** is said to be *"a player of real substance in international disputes,"* having gained much of his experience from handling a number of the Iran-US Claims Tribunal hostage cases in the 1980s. **Arthur Rovine*** is said to have a *"long-standing reputation in the area,"* although his profile is felt to have declined recently.

The New York office acted for Methanex on its $1 billion claim against the US Government under UNCITRAL rules. This related to the banning by the State of California of Methanex's product MTBE on the grounds of alleged toxicity. Another recent matter was an ICC arbitration between German and US construction contractors, concerning power plants in Latin America.

Wilmer, Cutler & Pickering (Washington DC 4 ptrs, 10 asscs) The firm has extensive experience in international dispute resolution matters, with noted experience of cases involving foreign states. A *"superb"* Washington office is led by **Andrew Vollmer***, who, although sometimes seen as *"more of an international litigator,"* is a *"learned individual with good insights into both arbitration and litigation."* A regular on the conference circuit, he is especially associated with his work at the ITA (Institute of Transnational Arbitration.) The firm recently advised on an AAA arbitration on behalf of a US government agency.

Covington & Burling (Washington DC 15 ptrs; New York 5 ptrs) DC-based firm, whose arbitration practice has handled proceedings in a wide range of industries, often on behalf of major US companies, including Exxon, Eli Lilly and Owens Corning. Our researchers were particularly impressed by market approval of the firm's expertise in insurance-related arbitration.

Brice Clagett* is said to *"put the firm on the map"* as an arbitration force, having served as lead counsel to Amoco and other clients before the Iran-US Claims Tribunal. His department successfully defended Bacardi in an arbitration in London, defeating an attempt to unwind a billion-dollar corporate transaction. For Exxon, the firm acted as lead counsel in proceedings against Lloyd's of London over coverage for the Exxon Valdez, which led to a settlement recovery of $780 million. The workload within the past year has also included ICC, LCIA and ad hoc arbitrations in Washington, London, Paris, and Singapore, for such clients as Qualcomm (telecommunications), New Skies (satellites), and Eli Lilly (product liability insurance.) The firm represented the State of Qatar in successfully resisting enforcement of an ICC award.

Freshfields Bruckhaus Deringer (New York 1 ptr, 3 asscs) A worldwide team of lawyers practises international arbitration, conducting ICC and other arbitrations in established venues in Europe and Asia. *"The first of the English firms to establish a serious arbitration practice in New York,"* it is acknowledged as the world leader in Europe. However, our research found no evidence that the New York office is yet regarded in a similar category. Although *"it should do very well,"* market opinion was that *"they need to acquire critical mass before they are regarded in anything like the league of their London and Paris arbitration teams."*

Lucy Reed* has *"a good and growing reputation"* in New York, but is felt to lack substantial support. She heads an office that acted on an arbitration in London between two US oil companies over a Venezuelan joint venture. The team also advised on the Claims Resolution Tribunal for Dormant Accounts in Switzerland, the arbitration court set up to return World War II bank accounts to Holocaust survivors.

Other Notable Practitioners **Gerry Aksen*** from Thelen Reid & Priest in New York is widely regarded to be *"top of the class – both as a practitioner and an arbitrator."* He is a *"masterful chair of arbitration panels,"* having been *"counsel of the AAA when it first started to look internationally,"* and does *"most, if not all"* of his firm's international commercial arbitrations. In Boston, sole practitioner **William 'Rusty' Park*** is said to be *"always in touch with the latest developments,"* and maintains his *"good reputation in Geneva."* **Robert Hornick*** from Morgan Lewis & Bockius in Washington DC is a *"splendid international arbitration lawyer,"* who has particular experience in Indonesian law. **Jonathan Schiller*** from Boies & Schiller in Washington DC undertakes complex commercial arbitrations on behalf of US and European multi-nationals against foreign sovereign states. His practice is a mix of arbitration and litigation. **David Lindsey*** from Clifford Chance Rogers & Wells in New York is a *"thoughtful"* and respected construction arbitration specialist, while in **Marc Goldstein*** of Proskauer Rose in Washington DC, our researchers uncovered a *"good, able player"* with a growing reputation. **José Astigarraga*** has recently left the Miami office of Steel Hector & Davis to form his own firm Astigarraga Davis in Miami, from where he is especially active in the insurance arbitration sector.

Banking & Finance: Chicago

Mayer, Brown & Platt (20 ptrs, 45 asscs) The firm's historical relationship with Continental Bank (now Bank of America), combined with its leading international project finance capabilities, gives the group a reputation as a *"top-tier international banking practice."* Interviewees describe the firm as a banking *"powerhouse"* for its sheer manpower and global coverage. Much of the group's syndicated loan work is co-ordinated with the firm's New York and London offices. The team also has extensive experience in ESOP, debtor-in-possession mezzanine financings, and Rule 144A offerings of indebtedness. In addition to substantial traditional acquisition finance and corporate lending work, the firm has a heavy focus on securitisation, under the direction of *"pre-eminent securitisation lawyer"* **Jason Kravitt***. Kravitt works heavily with federal bank regulators such as the Federal Reserve Board and SEC and also with international regulatory agencies in designing new products.

Admired by rivals for its *"fluid"* internal structure, in which *"everyone floats between different clients,"* the team was praised for its *"overall depth"* and *"good even quality."*

"Solution-oriented" **Rob Baptista*** is the *"name you come across most often"* in connection with acquisition financings. He represents both borrowers and issuers in a variety of capacities, including representation of senior and subordinated lenders, equity participants, and management in leveraged buy-outs, recapitalisations, and restructurings. Baptista recently led the representation of Bank of America as administrative agent in a revolving credit agreement and three term loan agreement for United Rentals with total credit exposure of over $2 billion to finance acquisitions and working capital.

Baptista is assisted by *"confident"* **Bill Tompsett***, a former in-house Continental Bank lawyer, who is highly regarded for his lending work on behalf of insurance companies. Tompsett led the representation of Bank of America as agent in the restructuring of debt for insurance holding company Conseco Inc.

Doug Doetsch* is heavily involved in cross-border finance, and has lately been active in a number of large transactions in Latin America. He represented Acesita SA as originator and servicer in the issuance of $150 million of medium term notes of Acesita, backed by contingent support agreements by Usinor SA

The firm also has a leading reputation in project finance work, representing developers and financial institutions in project and lease financings in the electricity, oil and gas, and gaming industries as well as major exposition and sports projects both in the US and abroad. *"Knowledgeable"* **Paul Forrester*** was recommended to our researchers for his technical ability, while **John Lawlor**'s* potential has also been noted. Lawlor was recently involved in the representation of ABN AMRO in connection with the workout and subsequent bankruptcy of Tokheim Corporation. **Clients:** Bank of America; Bank One; LaSalle Bank; Northern Trust; First Union; Bank of Nova Scotia; Industrial Bank of Japan.

USA: CHICAGO Leading Firms (Banking & Finance)	
1	Mayer, Brown & Platt
	Sidley & Austin
2	Latham & Watkins
	Winston & Strawn
3	Chapman and Cutler
	Goldberg, Kohn, Bell, Black, Rosenbloom & Moritz Ltd
4	Katten Muchin Zavis
	McDermott, Will & Emery
	Skadden, Arps, Slate, Meagher & Flom LLP
5	Kirkland & Ellis
	Sonnenschein
	Vedder, Price, Kaufman & Kammholz

Firms are listed alphabetically in each band.

Leading Individuals (Banking & Finance)		
★	**BERNSTEIN Bruce H.** *Sidley & Austin*	
1	**BAPTISTA Rob** *Mayer, Brown & Platt*	**CLARK James** *Sidley & Austin*
	CRUMBAUGH David *Latham & Watkins*	**KOHN Richard** *Goldberg, Kohn, Bell, Black*
	MURRAY Gregory *Winston & Strawn*	
2	**ALBRECHT Thomas** *Sidley & Austin*	**BARTLETT Sara** *Sidley & Austin*
	FORRESTER Paul *Mayer, Brown & Platt*	**KRAVITT Jason** *Mayer, Brown & Platt*
	McMENAMIN Robert *McDermott, Will & Emery*	**PICKENS Scott** *Schiff Hardin & Waite*
	ROKOSZ Ronald *Chapman and Cutler*	**SCHWARTZ Donald** *Latham & Watkins*
	WILLIAMS Douglas *Sidley & Austin*	
3	**BOEHRER Charles** *Winston & Strawn*	**DOETSCH Douglas** *Mayer, Brown & Platt*
	JACOBSON Ronald *Winston & Strawn*	**LATIMER Kenneth** *Duane, Morris & Heckscher LLP*
	STERN Gary *Sidley & Austin*	**TOMPSETT Bill** *Mayer, Brown & Platt*
4	**BARROW Peter** *Neal Gerber & Eisenberg*	**DRANOFF David** *Goldberg, Kohn, Bell, Black*
	FRANSON Marc *Chapman and Cutler*	**GILBERT Victoria** *Sonnenschein*
	GOLD Michael *Sidley & Austin*	**KURTZ David** *Skadden, Arps, Slate, Meagher & Flom*
	LEVIN Charles *McDermott, Will & Emery*	**LOOMAN James** *Sidley & Austin*
	SCHULRUFF Stuart *Katten Muchin Zavis*	
Up-and-coming individuals		
	LAWLOR John *Mayer, Brown & Platt*	**MASON David** *Goldberg, Kohn, Bell, Black*

Individuals are listed alphabetically in each band.

Sidley & Austin (15 ptrs, 20 asscs) The group's twenty year tenure as primary counsel to Bank One (formerly First National Bank of Chicago) has given the team an *"unrivalled depth of experience"* in high value loans and secured lending. The group recently advised Bank One in connection with a $120 million revolving credit facility to SK Global America.

Team members typically handle large syndicated, multi-bank loans, many with cross-border elements, and multi-currency provisions. A highly respected international tax practice and close ties to the firm's London branch both contribute to Sidley's reputation for complex structured finance. The group also has strength in workouts and restructurings arising from bankruptcy, handling a volume of debtor-in-possession and exit financings.

Sometimes accused of *"inflexibility,"* the firm nevertheless boasts a number of practitioners who are rated by their contemporaries in a variety of financial sectors.

Many attribute the firm's pre-eminence in the sector to the *"high visibility"* of *"gentleman and scholar"* **Bruce Bernstein***. As General Counsel to the Commercial Finance Association, Bernstein receives recognition from peers for his *"enormous contributions to the banking communi-*

U

ty" through his involvement in legislative initiatives and his work drafting amicus briefs for the CFA in a number of important cases. Considered the department's *"chairman emeritus,"* he has a lower profile for day-to-day transactional matters. Nevertheless, this *"financial guru"* retains his *"top notch"* reputation for his *"vast experience of secured lending and insolvency related finance."*

Bernstein is said to have passed on much of his asset based lending expertise to *"protégé"* **Jim Clark***. The *"unflappable"* Clark works predominantly on behalf of Bank One but is also frequently seen representing GE Capital, Chase Manhattan and Citibank. This *"gracious and hardworking fellow"* undertakes a substantial share of international multi-currency acquisition transactions and has a growing reputation for syndicated loan work. The group acted for Bank of America in relation to both a $200 million bilateral credit facility to Caterpillar, and Caterpillar Finance Services Corporation and the bank's $36 million secured debtor-in-possession financing for Einstein/Noah Bagel Corporation.

The firm places considerable emphasis on securitisation and is considered to benefit from the presence of the esteemed **Thomas Albrecht*** and **Gary "Skip" Stern***. It has further boosted its capacities in this area by poaching four partners from Katten Muchin & Zavis to create an insurance and financial services practice. Recent transactions in this area include acting as counsel in a life settlement securitisation structured by DG Bank and funded through commercial paper conduit Autobahn Funding Company LLC.

"Reliable" **Douglas Williams*** was recommended to our researchers for his straight commercial finance work for Chase Manhattan. In addition to assisting Clark in representing Bank One, **Sara Bartlett*** is active in borrower representation of corporate clients and was rated for her *"persistent but personable manner."* The *"thoughtful"* **James Looman*** focuses on leveraged lease financing, equipment leasing and securitisation and is said to combine the *"proper proportions of cynicism and intelligence."*

Another junior partner **Mike Gold*** acts principally for lenders, but also devotes a substantial proportion of his practice to troubled credit restructurings. In addition, he advises small business investment companies and their affiliates on transactional, compliance and organisational matters. Sidley & Austin recently represented the underwriter and structurer in connection with a $1 billion dollar investment grade collateralised debt transaction. **Clients:** Citibank; BankOne; Chase Manhattan; Bank of America; Wells Fargo; Fleet Group; GE Capital Group; The CIT Group; ING Barings; MBIA; DG Bank; Morgan Stanley; Canadian Imperial Bank of Commerce; Rabobank.

Latham & Watkins (14 ptrs, 14 asscs) Considered to have a *"broader national practice"* than many of its direct Chicago competitors, the group also benefits from work coming in through the firm's NY and LA offices. While the firm is best known on a national level for its unsurpassed project finance capabilities, the Chicago office has distinguished itself in banking through its volume of asset based lending transactions. The group represents many of the Midwest's key middle market lenders such as Heller Financial, Antares, and Foothill Capital.

A recognised strength in bankruptcy has seen many practitioners specialise in the finance aspects of insolvency and workouts. The group advised Bank of America Business Credit on a $650 million debtor-in-possession financing for Fruit of the Loom, and has handled a variety of restructurings in the steel, air transport, and manufacturing industries.

"Exceptional" **Don Schwartz*** heads the firm's banking group. A *"banking generalist,"* he maintains a diversified practice covering secured finance, borrower representation and insolvency issues. As the Associate General Counsel to the CFA, Schwartz is well known in the asset-based lending field.

"Making a strong name for themselves in a tight market," the firm's work on behalf of lenders has increased significantly since its 1997 acquisition of *"major rainmaker"* **David Crumbaugh***. A *"direct and tough negotiator with a wonderful sense of humour,"* he brought a substantial amount of GE Capital work with him from Winston & Strawn, representing them on a $300 million cash flow secured loan for Icon Health and Fitness. **Clients:** Bank of America Business Credit (subsidiary of Bank of America); Antares Capital Corp; Liberty Hampshire; Heller Financial; Fleet Capital; Royal Bank of Canada; ABN-AMRO/LaSalle National Bank; Crédit Lyonnais; BankOne; Wells Fargo; Foothill Capital.

Winston & Strawn (14 ptrs, 20 asscs) The firm's recent merger with NY's Whitman Breed Abbott & Morgan is considered to add further ballast to an already *"vibrant"* banking practice. The team has been especially recommended to researchers for secured finance. An *"aggressive"* presence on large syndicated financings, the firm numbers BankersTrust and Bank of America among its regular clients.

Renowned for advising US banks on financing UK tender offers, the firm represented Bankers Trust and Deutsche Bank in a structured syndicated leverage transaction for the UK sale of ICI Chemicals to Hunstman.

The firm is also highly regarded for its niche in aircraft leasing. The leveraged leasing team represents a variety of major international airlines in private and publicly funded transactions and has also been active on the leasing of rolling stock.

"Mover and shaker" **Greg Murray*** maintains a diversified practice and is acclaimed by clients for *"knowing the ins and outs of the business."* In addition to substantial lending work for Bank One, he frequently represents borrowers on acquisition transactions.

Chuck Boehrer* is said to have an *"expanding lending practice,"* representing Deutsche Bank and Bank of America in leveraged syndicated financings. He is acting as agent's counsel for the financing of BF Goodrich's announced sale of its chemicals unit for $1.4 billion and is also visible representing corporate borrowers Lear Corporation, Keebler and FMC Corporation.

"Bright and hard-working" **Ron Jacobson*** has made a name for himself in the commercial finance area and is known to have a tremendous client following among asset-based lenders such as GE Capital and Lasalle Bank. **Clients:** Deutsche Bank; Subsidiary Bankers Trust Comp; Heller Financial; Bank of America; Fleet Bank; BankOne; General Electric Capital; Salomon Smith Barney; Chase Manhattan.

Chapman and Cutler (20 ptrs, 13 asscs) Synonymous with its mainstay client Harris Bank, the group still acts as the bank's principal counsel on real estate lending and large syndicated credits. Also respected for its synthetic and leveraged leases on behalf of Bank of America and ABN AMRO, the firm is considered by some to be one of the more *"conservative"* in Chicago.

Rivals envy the firm's *"tremendous municipal bond practice,"* seen by many as a point of entry to more complex securitisation work, and the group has also carved a niche in representing insurance companies on mezzanine loans.

Ronald Rokosz* devotes much of his practice to representing ABN AMRO on syndicated loan transactions. Recent transactions include a $90 million telecom financing, with Fleet as a co-lender, a substantial gold consignment financing, and the confirmation of letters of credit issued by banks in Pakistan.

The firm has also built up a *"robust consumer financial services practice,"* headed by *"details man"* **Marc Franson***. *"An expert in consumer credit,"* he has substantial experience in credit card banking and home equity lending. He recently acted on the sale of a joint venture worth $1 billion in receivables between Bank of Boston, Bank of Montreal and credit card consultants First Anapolis Consulting. **Clients:** Harris Bank; Bank of Montreal; Bayerische Landesbank; Westdeutsche Landesbank; Landesbank Hessen Thyringen; HypoVereinsbank; Tokai; Fuji Bank;

ABN AMRO; Bank of America; American General Finance.

Goldberg, Kohn, Bell, Black, Rosenbloom & Moritz Ltd (10 ptrs, 12 asscs) Boutique firm, specialising in *"pure finance,"* which has long been respected in Chicago for its *"high quality practice,"* representing a range of banks and commercial finance companies. Despite the firm's relatively small size, it is generally acknowledged that there is *"no one better in the city for middle-market secured lending."* Most transactions involve acquisition finance or loans to provide working capital to companies, secured by accounts receivable, collateral, equipment or IP rights. The banking group works closely with the firm's strong bankruptcy department, advising lenders on workout issues, representing inter alia Citibank, Bank One, Heller Financial, and Bank of America.

"First class" **Richard Kohn*** is the leading name in the team, whose position as associate General Counsel to the CFA gives him high visibility in asset-based lending. Said by clients to be *"a lawyer who listens with all his senses,"* he is a frequent beneficiary of other firms' conflict. Additionally recommended to our researchers for a strong cross-border practice, he often represents US lenders on their loans to domestic companies wishing to acquire foreign affiliates. His team recently represented Bank of America, NA as agent for a syndicate of lenders in connection with the workout of a $100 million credit facility to a US company with operations in the UK, Belgium, Germany, Australia and Mexico.

An *"excellent transactional attorney,"* **David Dranoff*** also maintains a *"huge practice among the middle market finance crowd."* Known for his *"quick turnaround of documents,"* he is particularly skilled in US credit agreements. His *"flexible approach"* is considered to give him the *"knack of pushing deals along."*

David Mason* reportedly produces *"well presented documents written with economy,"* and enters our tables as an up and coming practitioner. He concentrates chiefly on cash flow loans, and was commended to our researchers for his ability to *"look at issues in a businesslike way."* The firm was chosen to represent UK lender Burdale Financial Limited in documenting the Swiss and German aspects of a loan facility to a UK borrower and its affiliates. **Clients:** Bank of America; Heller Financial; Foothill Capital; Antares Capital Corporation; LaSalle National Bank; Bank One; Harris Bank; GE Capital; General Motors Acceptance Corporation; Congress Financial Group; CIT Business Credit.

Katten Muchin Zavis (13 ptrs, 12 asscs) Strengths in leveraged finance product areas and structured loans provide this respected local firm with its highest profile. Transactions range from asset-based and cash flow loans to multi-currency and cross-border transactions. A highlight was the firm's advice to an affiliate of Bankers Trust Company on a $1 billion syndicated senior credit facility to a national retail chain.

Although best known for representing Heller Financial on commercial finance transactions, the firm has a widespread reputation in real estate finance, which brings it into a number of capital markets transactions, frequently acting on the borrower side. The team represented iStar Financial, a large publicly traded REIT, on its securitisation of a pool of mezzanine loans, and has negotiated mortgage loans destined for securitisation on behalf of Greenwich Capital, Heller Financial, Inc, General Motors Acceptance Corporation and LaSalle Bank National Association.

Although the firm's securitisation practice has been dealt a blow by the defection of four insurance finance practitioners to Sidley & Austin, the group retains some highly regarded securitisation specialists involved in municipal bond derivatives, commercial paper conduits and receivables financings. Recent work includes a settlement involving the securitisation of insurance policies on holders with mortal illnesses.

Stuart Shulruff* is said to *"have a lot of backbone,"* and has built up a *"strong following among private equity companies."* As co-chair of the traditional finance department, he serves as primary contact for clients Heller Financial Inc, Lasalle Bank, Fleet Capital Corporation and Antares Capital Corporation. His *"good communication skills"* make him a popular choice with clients. He led the group representing Antares Capital Corporation on a $160 million syndicated senior secured credit facility to an international manufacturer and distributor of sports optics products. **Clients:** Bankers Trust Company; Heller Financial, Inc; Fleet Capital Corporation; Antares Capital Corporation; LaSalle Bank National Association; Harris Trust and Savings Bank; First Source Financial, Inc; Household International, Inc; Greenwich Capital; Transamerica Commercial Finance; General Motors Acceptance Corporation; ABN AMRO.

McDermott, Will & Emery (10 ptrs, 12 asscs) An integrated practice combines bank representation and private placement with other financial transactions involving securitisation, workouts and commercial-backed or mortgaged security. The firm has less of a profile for traditional lending work than some of its competitors, and has its principal reputation in private banking and trust service areas. A key client is National Bank of Canada, on whose behalf the firm has acted on a handful of financings within the $50-200 million range.

A notable clientele of pension and mutual funds has instructed the group on a variety of private placements, while the team also acts for institutional investors on private equity and mezzanine finance transactions, leveraged loans, secured and unsecured synthetic finance.

"Senior player" **Bob McMenamin*** was commended to our researchers by all sections of the market. *"A bright and thoughtful attorney,"* he is most visible representing banks on their loans to hi-tech ventures, although he also has extensive experience of securitisation and structured finance transactions. Many credit him for the firm's ability to *"hold on to a piece of the old Continental Bank work."*

Charles Levin*, recently of Jenner & Block, is one of the firm's newest acquisitions. He represents lenders in venture capital and public transactions, and has acted for Lehman as underwriter in the financing of the Chicago Public School Board. **Clients:** Bell & Howell; Rabobank; National Bank of Canada; Lehman Brothers; CSFB; Industrial Bank of Japan; Northern Trust; New York Life Insurance Company; Northwestern Mutual Life Insurance Company; Transamerica Business Credit; Bank of America; Bank One; Harris Bank; Northern Trust; ABN Amro; IBJ; Astaris; Motorola Credit; CIGNA Corporation; Allstate Life; Burns International; Prudential Insurance Company of America; Budget Rent A Car; Guardian Life Insurance Company of America.

Skadden, Arps, Slate, Meagher & Flom LLP (3 ptrs, 11 asscs) This team of *"solution-oriented transactional lawyers"* is primarily recommended for its work on behalf of borrowers. Its national reputation for huge M&A work translates into a substantial volume of acquisition finance and IPOs. The team acted for Brera Western LLC in connection with a $120 million acquisition financing. Additionally, the practice was increasingly recommended to researchers for its advice on structured products and securitisation.

Much of the group's success is attributed to the *"immensely talented"* **David Kurtz***, *"one of the leading bankruptcy attorneys in the country."* Most of the firm's major insolvency work is handled out of the Chicago office, and Kurtz's enormous profile has helped bring in some substantial deals for the banking group. The group also handles debt and equity securities for both issuers and financial institutions. Corporate clients appreciate the *"good commercial instincts"* that practitioners bring to transactions. The team advised Deutsche Bank, on a $100 million debtor in possession facility to Kitney Jungle Stores of America.

Aircraft financing continues to be an area of niche expertise, with a focused team of 20 lawyers

*See leaders' profiles on pages 848-903

U

representing both lessees and lessors of equipment and facilities. Recent transactions in this field include the group's advice to Bank One NA on a synthetic lease of corporate aircraft. **Clients:** CSFB; Goldman Sachs Credit Partners; Chase Manhattan; Deutsche Bank; Eastman Chemical Company; Barclays Bank plc; BNP Paribas.

Kirkland & Ellis (5 ptrs, 7 asscs) While not known for traditional banking work, the firm ranks as the group seen most often on *"the other side of the table"* on behalf of borrowers in financial transactions. In acting for the firm's large base of international corporates and private companies, team members have acquired substantial experience of structuring and negotiating credit arrangements.

The group also has a small lender representation practice in secured senior and subordinated debt. Lending clients tend to be institutional banks and private financing groups putting together loan funds. The group is known to be particularly active in mezzanine lending in conjunction with equity investments and regularly advises Bankers Trust, Bank One and Deutsche Bank in mezzanine and bridge loan facilities.

Thanks to the firm's huge reputation in private equity, the group is called upon to undertake substantial finance work in venture capital transactions. Most notably, the group represents the venture capital arms of banks such as CSFB, Citicorp Venture Capital and other Citicorp affiliates.

Ties with foreign offices bring in solid cross-border financing transactions. Recently the group has been called upon to provide guarantees and a US securities package for transactions originating in London. **Clients:** Deutsche Bank; First Union; Bank One; Bank of Scotland; HSBC; Toronto Dominion; Société Générale; GMAC.

Sonnenschein (7 ptrs, 6 asscs) Acting primarily on middle tier transactions, the team undertakes traditional lending work for a few key clients such as Bank of America and Citigroup. Newly acquired asset-based lending clients include The Bank of Nova Scotia, Toronto Dominion and State Street Bank. The firm has its highest profile in real estate lending, in which it acts for large national and international banks on major syndicated transactions. The group represents both banks and borrowers in connection with unsecured syndicated credit facilities. In 2000, the practice completed the recapitalisation of Kansas City Southern Industries, Inc (KCSI), in order to facilitate the spin-off of its financial services businesses. It also completed a $600 million financing for Stilwell Financial Inc and Janus Capital Corp.

Key practitioner **Victoria Gilbert*** has caught the eye of competitors as *"an experienced hand on unusual financings,"* including a number of sports franchise financings. The practice's other niche is in transport financings involving rolling stock and aircraft structured finance for clients LaSalle Bank, GE Capital, and CIT Group. The group tailors loan documents to wealthy private clients in 'private banking' transactions, and recently represented Comark in a private label vendor financing. **Clients:** GE Capital; The Bank of Nova Scotia; Toronto Dominion; State Street Bank; Citigroup; Bank of America; Comark Inc; Sun Microsystems; LaSalle Bank NA; CIT Group.

Vedder, Price, Kaufman & Kammholz *"Banking is a strong suit"* at this small Chicago firm, covering a range of transactions within the fields of commercial finance, banking M&A and bank regulatory work. The team was commended for its *"bright, efficient"* partners with a *"great grasp of business issues."* The firm's finance group represents banking and savings institutions ranging in size from $50 million to more than $300 billion in assets. The workload includes loan and lease documentation, conversion to stock form of mutual savings institutions, public equity and debt offerings and the representation of underwriters in senior and mezzanine debt financing.

However, the group is most frequently seen in the field of asset-based lending, and is best known for its work in equipment and project finance. Its relationship with United Airlines has given the group a name in leveraged leasing and aircraft finance. The team also advises on SEC investment company registrations and acts for corporate clients on ERISA and employee benefit plans. **Clients:** Fleet Business Credit Corporation; LaSalle Banks; American National Bank; Finova GMAC.

Other Notable Practitioners *"Bright and knowledgeable"* **Scott Pickens** of Schiff Hardin & Waite is well known for commercial finance and is admired by peers for *"developing a practice in a firm not known for banking work."* **Ken Latimer*** at Duane, Morris & Heckscher is considered a *"solid player,"* active in a range of loan workouts and real estate lending, and maintains an active asset-based lending practice for Foothill Capital, Corus Bank, and Coast Capital Corp. Former in-house Continental Bank lawyer **Peter Barrow*** at Neal Gerber & Eisenberg *"runs a one-man band,"* representing lenders and borrowers on secured financings and syndicated facilities

Banking & Finance: New York

Cravath, Swaine & Moore (6 ptrs) Regarded by rivals as *"strong, quality players"* with a *"tight-knit"* focus. Its banking practice is dominated by a successful relationship with acquisition financing giant Chase Manhattan, whose grip on the lending market gives the firm a *"hugely effective"* LBO capacity. Under a *"fluid team structure,"* associates are acknowledged to have *"the perspective of experience"* from an early age. The firm produces *"constructive deal doers"* with excellent technical skills who are commended by clients for their *"focus on the issues not the minutiae."*

The *"power player"* for leveraged acquisition finance is **Allen Parker***. *"Personally charming,"* he is *"consistently practical and constructive."* **Jamie Vardell*** is *"low-key but effective."* *"A pleasure to work with,"* he is recommended by clients for his commerciality. He advises, inter alia, Chase, JP Morgan and Lucent Technologies. *"Bright spark"* **Mike Goldman*** is known for his complex LBO financings. Much of his high-profile work is for CSFB. **Rob Kiessling*** is *"incredibly smart,"* although opponents have suggested that *"he can be brash."* Respected for his ability to *"bridge the gap"* between pure bank lending and regulatory counsel, he represented Citibank on its $1 billion restructuring finance and new money facility for Rite Aid, the pharmaceutical retailers. **Jim Cooper*** is *"understated"* but *"effective,"* and clients *"can rely on him to get the job done."* A regular advisor to Chase, Cooper is accepted as a primary player in the investment grade market.

With substantial focus on telecoms and high-tech work, the firm has arranged financings for 360 Networks, Exodus Communications and VoiceStream Wireless. In sport, the team advised Chase on the structuring and syndication of a $190 million financing of San Francisco Giants' Pacific Bell Park and a $400 million credit facility for acquisitions of the Texas Rangers and Minesota Vikings franchises. **Clients:** Chase Manhattan; CSFB; Morgan Stanley; Goldman Sachs; Citibank.

Davis Polk & Wardwell (10 ptrs) Market speculation surrounds the outcome of the continued consolidation of the US banking market, with Chase acquiring JP Morgan and CSFB merging with DLJ. This is of particular interest to Davis Polk, as DLJ is one of the firm's mainstay clients. Rivals believe that the firm's *"old and deep"* roots in the banking community will provide it with continued prosperity.

A *"uniformly excellent"* team maintains its outstanding profile. Head of the Credit Transactions group, **Brad Smith*** is a veteran, regarded by peers and clients as a *"calm, co-operative, incredibly smart"* lawyer. Seen on much of JP Morgan's work, he was involved in the restructuring of Rite Aid which involved $2.6 billion of exposure. *"Intelligent"* **Peter Levin*** *"knows how to run a deal."* He represented Bank of New York on a $1.1 billion acquisition arrangement for SFX Entertainment, and is also heavily involved in the derivatives market. **Larry Wieman*** is a *"bright star,"* recommended for syndicated bank financings for acquisitions, with DLJ a particularly active client. A strong cross-border element extends to the Latin American market, where **Jim Florack*** is *"a familiar sight,"* and the group is reckoned to benefit from a strong presence in London and Hong Kong.

The firm advised JP Morgan and Merrill Lynch on the $13 billion financing of Norfolk Southern's bid for Conrail, and advises on senior secured lending and bridge financing for client such as DLJ Bridge Fund, Morgan Stanley and Swiss Bank. **Clients:** JP Morgan; DLJ; Morgan Stanley; CSFB; Bank of America; Lehman Bros.

USA: NEW YORK Leading Firms (Banking & Finance)	
1	Cravath, Swaine & Moore
	Davis Polk & Wardwell
	Simpson Thacher & Bartlett
2	Shearman & Sterling
3	Milbank, Tweed, Hadley & McCloy
	White & Case LLP
4	Skadden, Arps, Slate, Meagher & Flom LLP
	Sullivan & Cromwell
5	Mayer, Brown & Platt
	Weil, Gotshal & Manges

Firms are listed alphabetically in each band.

Simpson, Thacher & Bartlett (10 ptrs) *"Strong across the spectrum,"* the firm produces *"extremely capable"* attorneys with *"fine technical skills."* At the forefront of the syndicated lending market, it benefits from an excellent client base, which includes a substantial share of the Chase Manhattan deal flow. The team acted for Chase on a $7 billion syndicated multi-currency credit facility for Air Products and Chemicals Inc, thereby financing the acquisition of certain BOC Group assets. Deal flow including bridge financing, high yield debt and mezzanine financing is also generated from a strong base in private equity. The team has represented the lenders on Silverlake's $2 billion acquisition of Seagate and KKR's acquisition of Laporte.

"Intelligent and a great deal doer" **Frank Huck*** wins widespread praise from clients. His *"constructive, commonsense approach"* coupled with a *"personable, easy-going nature"* has marked him out as a *"star."* He represented the syndicate (including Chase, Citibank and Morgan Stanley) on the $4.5 billion bridge credit facility for the finance company arm of Warner EMI Music, and advised the banks on the $3.5 billion Conseco restructuring. **Greg Weiss*** brings a *"deal awareness"* and *"stacks of enthusiasm"* to the table. Known for his acquisition financing advice, he also advised Chase on a $2 billion corporate credit agreement and a $1 billion bridge loan for Global Crossing. **James Knight*** is recommended for his work on behalf of Blackstone Group, and is *"a good name for complex deals."* **Hartwell Hylton*** is a *"capable deal-doer,"* although some have remarked on his *"occasionally abrasive"* manner. He has a solid track record of advice to Lehman Brothers and Chase.

The firm has a prominent cross-border presence, featuring a steady flow of Latin American restructurings over the last year. Acted for the London office of Chase Manhattan on its $2.1 billion LBO of the Zeneca Specialty Chemicals from AstraZeneca, and advised Lehman Brothers on a syndicated credit facility for Premiere Parks Inc, refinancing existing debt and funding acquisitions across Europe. **Clients:** Chase; Lehman Bros; CIBC; SocGen; Bankers Trust; JP Morgan.

Shearman & Sterling (16 ptrs, 35 asscs) The firm has a strong reputation for cross-border transactions, successfully building on its presence in London, Paris, Dusseldorf and Frankfurt. A strong client base includes, but is no longer dominated by, Citibank. Active for Morgan Stanley on senior debt financings, the firm is also heavily involved in the acquisition finance market. Commended for its *"many superb lawyers,"* the department is said by competitors to be *"full of deal makers."*

Bill Hirschberg* brings a *"calming influence"* to the negotiating table. It is *"his skill and knowledge that brings their clients on board."* He represented Bank of Nova Scotia and Citibank as lead debt co-ordinators of the $2.6 billion debt refinancing by Warnaco Inc. Possessed of *"first-rate intellect,"* **Vladimir Rossman*** is admired by clients for his ability to *"solve any problem in minutes." "Colourful and idiosyncratic,"* he is a *"doggedly persistent lawyer"* who *"attacks everything with zeal."* Much of his practice has an international slant, and he advised Global TeleSystems Group on its bank financings and OPIC-sponsored public financings of its Russian and Ukrainian joint ventures.

The firm itself has a strong reputation for its communications work and has recently represented Bank of America (lead lender) on the $1.34 billion acquisition financing for Valor Telecommunications. **John Millard*** has a historically strong reputation for international financings in Latin America, particularly Argentina, while

Leading Individuals (Banking & Finance)		
1	**HIRSCHBERG William** *Shearman & Sterling*	**HUCK Francis** *Simpson Thacher & Bartlett*
	KIESSLING Rob *Cravath, Swaine & Moore*	**PARKER Allen** *Cravath, Swaine & Moore*
	SMITH Brad *Davis Polk & Wardwell*	
2	**BERG Eric** *White & Case LLP*	**COOPER Jim** *Cravath, Swaine & Moore*
	GEARY Sean *White & Case LLP*	**HALLIDAY Joseph** *Skadden, Arps*
	LINDAUER Erik *Sullivan & Cromwell*	**PULEO Frank** *Milbank, Tweed, Hadley*
	ROSSMAN Vladimir *Shearman & Sterling*	**WOJCIECHOWSKI Mark** *Mayer, Brown & Platt*
3	**DOKOS Daniel** *Weil, Gotshal & Manges*	**DOUGLAS James** *Skadden, Arps*
	FLORACK James *Davis Polk & Wardwell*	**HYLTON Hartwell** *Simpson Thacher & Bartlett*
	LEVIN Peter *Davis Polk & Wardwell*	**MILLARD John** *Shearman & Sterling*
	MORTIMER Peter *Milbank, Tweed, Hadley*	**VARDELL James** *Cravath, Swaine & Moore*
	WEIR Michael *Sullivan & Cromwell*	**WEISS Gregory** *Simpson Thacher & Bartlett*
	WIEMAN Lawrence *Davis Polk & Wardwell*	
4	**BERLIN Emily** *Shearman & Sterling*	**GOLDMAN Mike** *Cravath, Swaine & Moore*
	HANRAHAN Marc *Skadden, Arps*	**KNIGHT James** *Simpson Thacher & Bartlett*
	NECKLES Peter *Skadden, Arps*	**SIMMS Marsha** *Weil, Gotshal & Manges*
	URDA KASSIS Cynthia *Shearman & Sterling*	**WISEMAN Michael** *Sullivan & Cromwell*

Individuals are listed alphabetically in each band.

*See leaders' profiles on pages 848-903

Emily Berlin* is a *"capable"* practitioner, known for her work with Citibank. Although **Cynthia Urda Kassis*** also devotes her time to project finance, she is recommended by clients for pure bank lending work, and is an *"eloquent and constructive lawyer."*

The firm has seen a recent increase in highly leveraged financings, and represented Merrill Lynch as lead lender in connection with the $825 million acquisition of Advance Paradigm from Rite Aid. In one of the largest syndicated loans ever arranged, the team advised Goldman Sachs (lead) on the $30 billion syndicated credit agreement in connection with AT&T's acquisition of MediaOne. It also advised Société Générale and Citibank in connection with the $900 million financing of Amkor Technologies' purchase of three plants in Korea. **Clients:** Citibank; Bank of America; Merrill Lynch; Morgan Stanley.

Milbank, Tweed, Hadley & McCloy (5 ptrs) A *"talented team"* which benefits from a first-rate reputation as an international project finance powerhouse. Renowned in the US for its worldwide reach, the group is recommended for its work in Latin America, and has recently advised a group led by Salomon Smith Barney and Citibank on a $120 million financing for Usiminas of Brazil, and represented Chase Securities Inc on its $800 million financing for Telefonica Argentine SA. The team acts for both Chase and Citibank in the syndicated loan market and on acquisition finance, and represented an international group of financial institutions (led by Salomon and Chase) for the $140 million financing of Telecomunicaciones de Guatemala.

"Formidable character" **Frank Puleo*** is described by peers as *"a great regulatory advisor."* Like other practitioners at the firm, he has a strong background in the securities markets and is known for his relationship with Chase. Co-head of the Global Corporate Finance department **Peter Mortimer*** is a *"smart lawyer"* who maintains a *"reasonable"* approach to deals. Active in the telecoms market, the firm advised on the $5 billion syndicated credit facility for Nextel Communications Inc, arranged by Chase Securities and Banc of America Securities. **Clients:** Citibank; Chase; Bank of Nova Scotia.

White & Case LLP (8 ptrs in acquisition finance + separate banking group) A high profile in acquisition finance is derived from a strong traditional relationship with Bankers Trust, whom the firm advised on its merger with Deutsche Bank. The team advised on the arrangement of a $2 billion financing for Buhrman (known as Corporate Express in the US) and represented Deutsche bank on the $3.2 billion financing of Capstar. Clients have judged the team's overseas network to be *"particularly attractive."* Active across Europe and Asia, the firm has developed a strong six-partner office in London.

Head of the Bank Finance practice, **Eric Berg*** is seen as *"the driver"* and *"chief business-getter." "Phenomenally efficient,"* he is also known for his *"aggressive negotiating style,"* and is the relationship partner for Deutsche Bank. **Sean Geary*** is a senior figure at the firm, and *"knows how to hold a deal together,"* although his level of day-to-day involvement has slightly decreased. He was lead counsel for the lenders on the RJR Nabisco LBO and the Time-Warner merger. Joint counsel for Morgan Stanley, the firm acted on the financing of NTL's acquisition of assets from Cable & Wireless. **Clients:** Bank of America; Bankers Trust; Deutsche Bank; JP Morgan; Morgan Stanley; BNP Paribas.

Skadden, Arps, Slate, Meagher & Flom LLP (70 lawyers in Banking & Institutional Investing group) Although thought to lack a huge institutional client base, the team is *"a credible force,"* and has deep resources. The firm is most visible for its work on behalf of borrowers.

The development of the practice is credited to **Joe Halliday*** who has *"successfully leveraged"* its corporate client base. Head of the group, he is a *"smooth negotiator,"* according to opponents. On the borrower side, he represented Sunbeam Corporation on its $1.7 billion financing arrangements. *"Focused and personable"* **James Douglas*** consistently offers *"practical advice."* He is the most visible for acquisition finance and *"always does a good job."* **Marc Hanrahan*** is *"a rising star." "Easy to work with,"* he is known for his work with Goldman Sachs and CSFB. *"Sound and sensible"* **Peter Neckles*** has a good reputation for restructuring and refinancing. He recently advised Aladdin Hotel and Casino in Las Vegas on the financing of the hotel redevelopment. The firm represented CSFB and Goldman Sachs as managing underwriters of the Metlife Inc IPO, raising $5.2 billion in financing, and acted for Goldman Sachs on the $850 million Rule 144A offering by KPNQwest. Strong in aircraft financing, the firm represented US Airways on a $500 million revolving credit facility. **Clients:** Goldman Sachs; Bankers Trust; Chase Manhattan; Bank of America; CSFB.

Sullivan & Cromwell (5 ptrs, 10 asscs) Although it possesses *"a consistently high level of quality lawyers,"* the firm is not felt to have the banking focus of its leading rivals. The group benefits from a pre-eminent reputation in banking M&A, and is recommended for its regulatory expertise. Bank of New York continues to provide an active flow of acquisition finance and the firm is also picking up syndicated loan work from UBS.

Erik Lindauer* *"is great at everything he does."* He is active for both the borrower and sponsors on projects and continues to be the most visible for acquisition finance. Advised Bank of New York on a $1 billion syndicated finance facility for Winstar Communications. The firm is heavily involved in the refinancing and restructuring market for borrowers. Senior figure in the banking group, **Michael Wiseman*** has a formidable reputation for acquisition finance and regulatory matters with an emphasis on the insurance markets. **Michael Weir*** has also been recommended for his transactional acumen. In the telecoms sector the firm advised a Global Crossing regional affiliate on a bank bridging loan, and is preparing a multi-billion facility for a joint venture between SBC Corporation and Singular Wireless. **Clients:** Bank of New York; Bankers Trust; Citibank.

Mayer, Brown & Platt (11 ptrs) Acting from a pre-eminent Chicago base, this *"well established"* New York office is *"technically excellent." "Working hard at it,"* the firm is developing a broad client base, although it is said not to be a regular fixture on the biggest deals. Also benefits from a growing London office and a profile for international project finance. The group undertakes all levels of debt, new financial products and regulatory advice for mainstay client Bank of America. *"Highly rated"* by the New York market, **Mark Wojciechowski*** leads the Bank of America relationship. **Clients:** Bank of America; CIBC; Scotiabank; DLJ.

Weil, Gotshal & Manges (6 ptrs) Thought to be *"breaking into the mix,"* with a growth in representations from leading investment banks such as Salomon Smith Barney, Citibank and Lehman Brothers. However it does not possess the long-term relationships which drive our banking leaders. The team is said to benefit from opportunities created by a leading corporate recovery practice.

Ron Daitz's move to the London office has been viewed as an indication of the importance of the international network. London is assisting in the cultivation of Citibank as a substantial client, and a strong profile in the private equity market has helped the firm to act on highly leveraged acquisition finance. The firm continues to be most visible in its work for the borrower. *"A good recruit for the firm,"* **Dan Dokos*** (ex-Sidley & Austin) has cemented his high profile in asset-based lending. *"Personable and intelligent"* **Marsha Simms*** is recommended for her skill in negotiating acquisition financing and restructuring documentations. The firm advised on the $1.1 billion financing for Hydro Quebec's acquisition of TRANSELEC in Chile. **Clients:** Lehman Bros; Bankers Trust; Citigroup; Dresdner Bank.

Capital Markets: Debt & Equity: New York

Cravath, Swaine & Moore (20 ptrs, 100 asscs form Capital Markets Group) An *"always impressive"* and hugely prominent team owes much to *"outstanding relationships"* with leading underwriters such as CSFB, Chase Securities and Salomon Smith Barney. The real driving force over the past year has been an active, if turbulent, technology market, where the firm represented the underwriters and Juno Online, Razorfish and Mail.com. On the issuer side, the team acted for Infinity Broadcasting on its $3.2 billion IPO, while the group advised the underwriters (Goldman Sachs and Schroder Salomon Smith Barney) on the AOL Latin America IPO and on the financing of Americanas.com.

Our research unearthed an array of rated practitioners. **John White*** *"combines tremendous practicality with an excellent technical knowledge of securities law."* His *"calm demeanour"* ensures the smoothness of any deal. He acted for the underwriter on the Monsanto IPO. *"Likeable"* **Kris Heinzelman*** has an *"excellent grasp"* of the high yield debt market. Active for both the issuer and underwriter, **Bud Rogers*** is prominent for his *"fantastic securities law knowledge."* His move (planned for summer 2001) to head up the firm's London office, has been deemed by clients and rivals to strengthen the international securities offering. Possessing a *"great equities practice,"* **Marc Rosenberg*** is known for his work with blue-chip issuers.

Mainstay corporate clients continue to use the equity markets as a source of financing, with Lucent Technologies, IBM and Dreamworks all showing notable recent activity. The firm also scores well in the debt markets, advising Sprint on its $5 billion bond offering to finance the expansion of its wireless network, and represented AXA in its $1.9 billion multi-tranche global subordinated bond offering. In the Eurobond market the firm advised Atlantic Telecoms Group plc on its high-yield offering, raising €332 million. **Clients:** Salomon Smith Barney; CSFB; Chase Securities.

USA: NEW YORK Leading Firms (Capital Markets: International Debt & Equity)
1 Cravath, Swaine & Moore
Davis Polk & Wardwell
Sullivan & Cromwell
2 Shearman & Sterling
Simpson Thacher & Bartlett
Skadden, Arps, Slate, Meagher & Flom LLP
3 Cleary, Gottlieb, Steen & Hamilton
4 Cahill Gordon & Reindel
Latham & Watkins
5 Weil, Gotshal & Manges

Firms are listed alphabetically in each band.

Leading Individuals (Capital Markets: International Debt & Equity)	
1 **MALLOW Matthew** *Skadden, Arps*	**QUINN Linda** *Shearman & Sterling*
WHITE John *Cravath, Swaine & Moore*	**WILLIAMS William** *Sullivan & Cromwell*
2 **BELLER Alan** *Cleary, Gottlieb, Steen & Hamilton*	**DAVENPORT Kirk** *Latham & Watkins*
HARTNETT Bill *Cahill Gordon & Reindel*	**MORISON Frank** *Davis Polk & Wardwell*
SANDLER Richard *Davis Polk & Wardwell*	**THALACKER Arbie** *Shearman & Sterling*
3 **FORD Paul** *Simpson Thacher & Bartlett*	**HARMS David** *Sullivan & Cromwell*
HEINZELMAN Kris *Cravath, Swaine & Moore*	**KROUSE George** *Simpson Thacher & Bartlett*
MESTRES Ricardo *Sullivan & Cromwell*	**PISANO Vince** *Skadden, Arps*
SMALL Jeff *Davis Polk & Wardwell*	**SOUSSLOFF Andrew** *Sullivan & Cromwell*
4 **CLARK Jim** *Cahill Gordon & Reindel*	**CONRAD Winthrop (Wit)** *Davis Polk & Wardwell*
COOPER Stephen *Weil, Gotshal & Manges*	**EVANS Robert** *Shearman & Sterling*
GOLDSCHMIDT David *Skadden, Arps*	**KESSEL Mark** *Shearman & Sterling*
KORFF Phyllis *Skadden, Arps*	**ROGERS William (Bud)** *Cravath, Swaine & Moore*
ROSENBERG Marc *Cravath, Swaine & Moore*	**TEHAN John** *Simpson Thacher & Bartlett*

Individuals are listed alphabetically in each band.

Davis Polk & Wardwell (14 ptrs) *"A top notch operation"* with a *"global reach,"* best exemplified by its work with the firm's Tokyo and Hong Kong offices in advising the Japanese Ministry of Finance on the $15.9 billion equity offering from NTT. Only the *"impossible to predict"* fall-out of mergers between CSFB/DLJ and Chase/JP Morgan, casts the slightest shadow on the firm's superb client base. Researchers were impressed by market approval for the firm's strong mix of *"old timers"* and *"bright young stars gaining valuable, independent experience."*

Considered a senior player in the market, **Frank Morison*** is *"sensible and practical."* His *"exceptional market knowledge"* is seen as a valuable resource for the firm. He has a close relationship with Morgan Stanley, and regularly acts as underwriters' counsel to General Motors and GMAC. *"One of the bright stars,"* **Richard Sandler*** is a *"major talent"* in the high-yield debt markets. His practice also focuses on both the domestic and international IPO market. **Jeff Small*** is head of the Capital Markets group. Clients praise *"his rare ability in a crisis to step back and work though the problems."* He advised the underwriters on the $5.5 billion IPO of UPS and on the $150 million IPO of Martha Stewart Living Omnimedia. **Wit Conrad*** generates *"a huge amount of respect"* from the market for his advice to both issuers and underwriters in securities offerings.

Leaders in the high yield debt market, the firm advised Salomon Smith Barney, Lehman Brothers, and Merrill Lynch as lead managers of a Rule 144A issuance of high-yield notes by Williams Communications Group. The firm's recently opened Menlo Park office has helped to capitalise on the technology IPO market. In conjunction with Menlo Park, the New York team advised Goldman Sachs, Merrill Lynch and Salomon Smith Barney as global co-ordinator for the $10.6 billion offering of tracking stock of AT&T Wireless Group. **Clients:** Morgan Stanley; JP Morgan; DLJ.

Sullivan & Cromwell (33 ptrs, 57 asscs in Corporate & Finance Group) A creative practice with an outstanding international reputation. Partners are *"flexible"* and their breadth of experience is supported by the team's *"sheer volume of deals."*

Possessing a *"great depth of market knowledge,"* **Bill Williams*** is considered to be *"a first class expert."* Although prominent in the transactional field, he is also *"a wonderful academic resource"* for the firm. **Andrew Soussloff*** is always *"reasonable."* Managing partner of the firm's corporate and finance group, he has an extensive international practice, advising Santa Fe International on a $1.2 billion equity offering and representing the managers of a $2.4 billion Republic of Argentina Brady bond exchange offer. Elsewhere in Latin America, the firm has represented the managers on a $5.1 billion global bond issue in Brazil. **David Harms*** is recommended for international high-yield offerings. Known to be active for Latin American issuers, he has also recently focused on Asia, notably on offerings from Global Crossing and NTT. Less visible on the transac-

*See leaders' profiles on pages 848-903

tional front, **Ricardo Mestres*** is renowned as a *"rainmaker."* Formerly chairman of the firm, he is credited with cementing a strong relationship with Goldman Sachs, the firm's principal client. The group acted as issuers' counsel on the $5 billion SEC registered offering of China Unicom, and represented ENEL (Italian electricity company) on its $19 billion IPO. **Clients:** Goldman Sachs; Deutsche Bank; Siemens.

Shearman & Sterling (33 ptrs, 119 asscs) Successfully following an expansionist model, the firm has *"made a big investment in Europe,"* consequently snaring a number of substantial deals. The team acted in conjunction with the Paris office on the $1.7 billion Wanadoo (multi-media) IPO. *Chambers'* researchers were consistently reminded of the firm's *"great scope"* and its major investment banking clientele, including such names as Morgan Stanley and Merrill Lynch. The group acted for Merrill Lynch and Mediobanca as underwriters to the $19 billion IPO of ENEL.

Linda Quinn* is respected for her expertise in the regulatory aspects of securities law. A former Director of the Division of Corporate Finance of the SEC, she is viewed as *"the oracle"* in this market. *"Incredibly experienced and knowledgeable,"* **Arbie Thalacker*** is said to be *"always fair and professional."* Continuing his association with Ford, he advised Ford Credit on the $8.6 billion debt offering of Global Landmark Securities. **Robert Evans*** works extensively with Merrill Lynch, and is recommended for his strong knowledge of SEC securities law. **Mark Kessel*** is *"highly skilled,"* and considered a leading practitioner in the biotech, pharmaceutical and hi-tech market. The firm acted for Toyota Motor Corp on its global share offering, worth $1.5 billion. **Clients:** Morgan Stanley; Merrill Lynch; CSFB; Goldman Sachs.

Simpson Thacher & Bartlett (23 ptrs in Capital Markets group) Having *"capitalised successfully"* on the LBO boom of the 80s, the firm can now rely on *"strong institutional relationships."* Highly rated on both the issuer and underwriter side, the team is especially prominent in advising foreign issuers gaining access to the US capital markets. Chairman of the international practice **Paul Ford*** was instrumental in establishing offices in Tokyo, Hong Kong and Singapore, and is credited by peers with *"stealing a march on the Asian markets."* He advised the underwriters on the IPO of Hanaro Telecom, the South Korean internet and telecom service provider. Head of the corporate department, **George Krouse*** is hugely active in the arrangement of financings for key client Seagram, including its extensive acquisition programme. He also counselled Wachovia Corp on a $2 billion financing program. **John Tehan*** is a *"leading light"* for his overseas work. He is also closely associated with KKR and its portfolio companies, advising on high-yield debt and IPOs.

In the hi-tech market the firm benefits both from a growing Palo Alto office, and its close association with Lehman Brothers, whom the firm advised as underwriters to the IPOs of China.com, ITXC Corp and Pacific Internet Ltd. Well-regarded for its focus on debt structures, the firm acted for the underwriters (includes Lehman, Chase and CSFB) on the $600 million senior notes issue by Globix Corp, and advised Alcatel Alsthom and the arranger on a $1.5 billion Global note program (Rule 144A transaction.) The team also represented the underwriters on the financing of Verizon. **Clients:** Lehman Brothers; Chase Securities; Seagram; Global Crossing.

Skadden, Arps, Slate, Meagher & Flom LLP (150 lawyers in Corporate Finance) *Chambers'* researchers discovered an *"incredibly talented group of lawyers,"* considered by the market to be *"productive and effective"* in both high yield debt and domestic and international equities. Possessing a first-rate client base, it advised Cable & Wireless Optus on its $2.15 billion IPO.

"Statesman" **Matt Mallow*** *"is one of the great stars and has been for an age."* Head of the finance practice, he maintains a first rate international reputation. *"Consistently winning good work,"* **Vince Pisano*** has a high profile for equities work in Latin America. He has worked with Merrill Lynch to develop trust-preferred securities, and advised them as lead underwriter to the IPO of Infinity Broadcasting. **Phyllis Korff*** is a *"delight to work with."* Highly regarded for her international work, she has a strong focus on Israeli companies raising funds in the US. She advised Bank Hapoalim on its Rule 144A equity offering and acted for the underwriters on the demutualisation and $5.2 billion IPO of insurance firm MetLife Inc. **David Goldschmidt*** has a strong reputation for his work in the hi-tech field, advising Compaq and its subsidiary Alta Vista on its financings, and deltathree.com Inc on its IPO.

The firm acted for Goldman Sachs on a $850 million Rule 144A offering by KPNQwest, and subsequently advised Morgan Stanley as lead underwriter to the company's $1 billion IPO. The firm is a renowned player in the debt markets, and advised the underwriters in connection with the most recent $1 billion global bond offering by the People's Republic of China. Following the £4.2 billion IPO for Conoco, the firm represented EI du Pont de Nemours in one of the largest split-off exchange offers to date, valued at around $11.7 billion. **Clients:** Goldman Sachs; Morgan Stanley; Bank Hapoalim.

Cleary, Gottlieb, Steen & Hamilton (12 ptrs in Securities group) Picking up *"the higher profile, better quality deals,"* the firm is recognised as a leader in equity offerings. It advises a powerful stable of US issuers such as UTC, McDonalds, Interpublic and Northern Telecom. Long-standing relationships with investment banks such as Salomon Smith Barney and Goldman Sachs ensure that the firm also scores highly for underwriters. However, the firm's *"extremely strong international practice"* is said by many to *"overshadow domestic work."*

Headline transactions include acting as counsel to the Republic of Argentina on a public global bond offering worth $250 million, and since mid-1999, the group has advised on the issue of over $4 billion of debt securities. It also continues as counsel to governments in the emerging markets on debt restructuring issues, and has developed expertise in high-yield financing for industries including technology, media and manufacturing.

"The rocket scientist of securities law," **Alan Beller*** *"can do it all."* Clients recommend him as *"a great deal maker"* in both the debt and equity markets, and he acts as a consultant for other offices across the firm's substantial international network. On the equity front, the firm advised Tycom Ltd (undersea fibre-optics) on its $2 billion IPO, and represented the underwriters on Goldman Sachs' $3.49 billion secondary equity offering. **Clients:** Goldman Sachs; Salomon Smith Barney; Morgan Stanley; CSFB.

Cahill Gordon & Reindel (16 ptrs, 40 asscs) *"Specialists in high yield debt,"* the firm was described to our researchers as a *"flexible organisational structure"* with *"expertly trained"* attorneys. The firm continues to advise a number of major investment banks, and is thought to have overcome the national slump in the high-yield market. Although lacking a substantial international network, the firm has a growing office in London, and advised the underwriters on the first US IPO for a Greek TV company and for the underwriters in the Golden Telecom (Russia) IPO.

"One of the biggest names," **Bill Hartnett*** was the automatic choice of competitors and clients as *"the number one high-yield player in New York."* **Jim Clark*** *"provides level-headed advice"* and has a good reputation for all levels of securities work. With a strong international following, he is often seen working in conjunction with the London office, and elicited the comment that *"everyone loves Jim."*

Doughty competitors on the equity market, the firm advised the Canadian-based 360 Networks on its IPO and initial high-yield financings. Also represented Merrill Lynch, Warburg Dillon

Reed and Citicorp Securities in connection with an offering of senior subordinated notes and preferred stock by HMV Media Group plc. **Clients:** Goldman Sachs; JP Morgan; Merrill Lynch; Salomon Smith Barney; CSFB.

Latham & Watkins (100 lawyers group wide) Of the out-of-town firms that have settled in New York, this is *"the one with the best credentials."* A hugely prominent high-yield practice has great experience in the use of underwritten Rule 144A hybrid financings. Recent activity includes a series of high-yield bond financings for Global Crossing. *"Personable"* **Kirk Davenport*** is a *"bright, get the deal done lawyer."* Our research showed a firm with an *"aggressively expansionist"* policy, assisted by a respected London office. Benefiting from the firm's obvious connections on the West Coast, the New York team has scored well in the IPO start-up market, although equity offerings remain overshadowed by the high-yield practice. Heavily involved in the REIT, gaming and hospitality industry, the firm also acted for Goldman Sachs and Lehman Brothers as underwriters to the IPO of Orion Power. **Clients:** Goldman Sachs; DLJ; Lehman Brothers; Bear Stearns.

Weil Gotshal & Manges (16 ptrs) *"Capable, qualified and hard-working,"* the firm is still said by the market to lack a primary focus in the area. A fully integrated Capital Markets group is able to draw on its base of major corporate clients and is supported on its debt financing by a first rate bankruptcy and restructuring practice. *"Likeable"* **Stephen Cooper*** was the name suggested to our researchers as a credible player in New York.

The firm advised the arrangers, led by Bear Stearns, on the offering of $250 million of senior notes for Planet Hollywood, and acted for AK Steel on a Rule 144A deal, offering $450 million of senior notes. The firm has a good reputation for technology-based IPO, and is seen to work well in tandem with its London office. A sound base of investment bank clients includes Bear Stearns, CSFB and DLJ, and the firm also benefits from strong links to private equity houses such as Hicks Muse. **Clients:** CSFB; Citibank; Bear Stearns.

U

Capital Markets: Securitisation

USA: NEW YORK
Leading Firms
(Capital Markets: Securitisation)

Band	Firm
1	Brown & Wood LLP
	Orrick, Herrington & Sutcliffe
	Skadden, Arps, Slate, Meagher & Flom LLP
2	Cadwalader, Wickersham & Taft
	Mayer, Brown & Platt
3	Cleary, Gottlieb, Steen & Hamilton
4	Cravath, Swaine & Moore
	Simpson Thacher & Bartlett
5	Sidley & Austin
	Stroock & Stroock & Lavan LLP
6	Dewey Ballantine LLP
	Fried, Frank, Harris, Shriver & Jacobson
	Thacher Proffitt & Wood
	Weil, Gotshal & Manges

Firms are listed alphabetically in each band.

Leading Individuals (Capital Markets: Securitisation)

Band		
1	**DE SEAR Edward** *Orrick, Herrington & Sutcliffe*	**KUNZ Thomas** *Skadden, Arps*
	MARTIN Renwick *Brown & Wood LLP*	**SHAW Gregory** *Cravath, Swaine & Moore*
2	**AUERBACH Reed** *Stroock & Stroock & Lavan*	**COWAN Cameron** *Orrick, Herrington & Sutcliffe*
	CURTIS Susan *Skadden, Arps*	**KAPLAN Cathy** *Brown & Wood LLP*
	PALMA Laura *Simpson Thacher & Bartlett*	**SCHETMAN Richard** *Cadwalader, Wickersham*
	WIPPERMAN Robert *Stroock & Stroock & Lavan*	
3	**CITRON Diane** *Mayer, Brown & Platt*	**DIANGELO Christopher** *Dewey Ballantine LLP*
	EISENBERG David *Simpson Thacher & Bartlett*	**GLASS Adam** *Sidley & Austin*
	ISAACSON Laurence *Fried, Frank, Harris*	**KADLICK Richard** *Skadden, Arps*
4	**GLICK Anna** *Cadwalader, Wickersham & Taft*	**KUDENHOLDT Stephen** *Thacher Proffitt & Wood*
	NOCCO Frank *Weil, Gotshal & Manges*	**PODOLSKY Andrea** *Cleary, Gottlieb, Steen*
	RUDDER Richard *Willkie Farr & Gallagher*	

Individuals are listed alphabetically in each band.

Brown & Wood LLP (24 ptrs 75 asscs) With the firm's immense concentration on the securitisation market, it came as no surprise to our researchers that it should be universally rated as one of the three market leaders here. *"An immense volume"* of work is performed by a *"skilled team."* Although primarily known for its dominance of the commercial mortgage market (and a long-standing relationship with Fannie Mae), the firm is also at the forefront of cutting-edge asset class work. In the first transaction of its type, the firm advised New York City on the securitisation of its share ($709 million) of the $206 billion nationwide tobacco settlement, and has also been retained by other states exploring similar structures.

"Superb" **Ren Martin*** has an *"easy going, calming"* influence. His *"wealth of experience"* and *"effective intelligence"* makes him *"perfect for complicated transactions."* Substantial international experience has helped establish **Cathy Kaplan*** as *"clearly a leading player."* She is recommended for her structuring of new products, including CLOs and CBOs, such as SBC Glacier Finance Deutsche Bank's Blue Stripe.

The firm maintains a strong cross-border involvement, and advised Mexican banks on the securitisation of US$ denominated credit card receivables. An established London office has assisted the New York team on offshore CBO structures, often based on portfolios of mortgage and other asset-backed securities. The team has advised heavyweight financial institutions such as BankBoston, Sanwa Bank and SocGen on the structuring and drafting of CLOs, while in the commodity market, the firm maintains a high level of involvement in credit card receivables, auto loans and healthcare receivables. **Clients:** Countrywide; Fannie Mae; Merrill Lynch; Real Estate Investment Trust.

Orrick, Herrington & Sutcliffe (75 lawyers) Recommended for its *"complex and innovative work,"* the firm was commended to researchers for its *"perspective on what is important."* The group's reputation owes much to its substantial volume of residential and commercial mortgage-backed deals. A sound repackaging capacity has enabled the firm to advise extensively in the credit card and tobacco markets. The group represented 13 law firms in the securitisation of legal fees from the claimant in tobacco litigations, and has also been involved in the securitisation of mutual fund distribution fees.

"An intelligent and creative problem solver," **Ed de Sear*** can be relied upon to *"get a deal done efficiently."* Head of the Structured Finance group, he is commended for his work in the buoyant

*See leaders' profiles on pages 848-903

credit card market. **Cameron Cowan*** is a *"great deal lawyer."* Based in Washington, he has a strong financial institutions practice, and is involved in the structuring, issuance and purchase of both asset-backed and mortgage-backed securities. The firm advises JP Morgan on its CP conduits, and continues to be active in stranded costs and catastrophe securitisations. **Clients:** JP Morgan; Residential Funding Corp; MBNA America Bank.

Skadden, Arps, Slate, Meagher & Flom LLP (12 ptrs, 38 asscs) Boasting *"skilled lawyers"* and a *"deep pool of resources,"* the firm's chief strength lies in the traditional and commodity-backed markets, where clients agree that it achieves *"quality and diversity."*

Tom Kunz* (head of Structured Finance) has *"his finger on the pulse."* A *"great figurehead"* for the firm, he is said to *"display fantastic skill"* in new product development. Involved in the securitisation of the first credit card master trust, he is also a player in more esoteric structures, such as timber securitisation for the Pacific Lumber Corporation. **Susan Curtis*** has *"a most interesting practice,"* with a particular focus on Ford Motor Credit securitisations. Indeed, she and the firm act for Ford on all its auto receivables and auto-leasing securitisations. *"Focused and attentive"* **Richard Kadlick*** is known for his relationships with Chase Bank One and JC Penny. He also advised Merrill Lynch on the financing of the World Financial Centre for World Financial Properties.

The firm handles the CBO and CP conduit work for Chase, acting for arrangers, collateral managers and originators in their CLO work. A huge M&A engine has provided valuable spin-off work such as the securitisation of the telephone leasing business acquired by UBS from Lucent Technologies (acquired for $97 million and raising $215 million on its securitisation.) Other work includes representing the arrangers on the establishment of global guaranteed, investment contract-backed note programmes for John Hancock, Allstate and Principal Life. **Clients:** CSFB; Chase Manhattan; UBS; Goldman Sachs; Excel.

Cadwalader, Wickersham & Taft (55 lawyers) Research has established that the firm's greatest visibility lies in commercial and residential mortgage-backed securities. Major financial institutions such as Morgan Stanley, UBS, and Lehman Brothers have been advised on single asset securitisations of investment grade, high profile properties. Other work has included advising CSFB, WestLB and The Prudential on mortgage-backed securities, acting on repackagings for Lehman Brothers and counselling on CP-financed CLOs for Deutsche Bank.

"A great lawyer with a varied practice," **Richard Schetman*** offers *"intelligent and considered advice."* He represents underwriters and issuers on credit card receivables, auto loans and trade receivables, and is also renowned for his repackaging work and structuring of commercial paper vehicles. **Anna Glick*** is known for her focus on commercial mortgage-backed securitisations. Her major clients include Morgan Stanley and CSFB.

The firm has advised on the repackaging of tax-exempt debt and on combining derivative products, such as interest rate and currency swaps, to create synthetic securities. An international focus has seen the London office build up an expertise in asset-backed CP, and the firm has advised Goldman Sachs on catastrophe bonds. **Clients:** Lehman Brothers; Morgan Stanley; AIGFP.

Mayer, Brown & Platt (60 lawyers) A number of high profile defections, most notably those of Frank Nocco and Laura DeFelice, have rocked the group recently. However, the firm's established New York office continues to run a *"busy"* securitisation practice.

Diane Citron* is *"prominent"* in the residential and commercial mortgage markets, while Goldman Sachs and Solomon Brothers continue to be prime clients for CMBS work, and the team undertakes CDO work for Morgan Stanley Deutsche Bank and Merrill Lynch. Competitors were particularly impressed by the firm's expertise in commercial paper-developing structures to make CP vehicles less capital intensive for commercial banks.

The firm advised Bank of America on the structuring of an SPV to purchase receivables funded through the issue of $4 billion of commercial paper. **Clients:** Bank of America; GECC; UBS.

Cleary, Gottlieb, Steen & Hamilton (12 ptrs, 35 asscs) An important firm, undertaking *"large scale, complex securitisations."* Although *"heavily involved"* in the New York market, it is the firm's *"excellent"* cross-border practice which researchers found to score most highly with the market. The team has developed structures for asset-backed securitisation (including telephone, oil and power receivables and EXIMBank-guaranteed obligations) in Europe, Latin America and Asia, and recently advised on two residential global offerings by Abbey National in the UK.

A leader in the development of commercial mortgage securitisation, the firm's Washington office acted as underwriters' counsel on both Fannie Mae and Freddie Mac offerings. The team advised Goldman Sachs, Nomura Securities and DLJ as underwriters of the $688 million Commercial Mortgage Asset Trust.

Andrea Podolsky* is a *"bright, thoughtful lawyer,"* prominent for her work in the CLO and CBO field for clients such as Morgan Stanley, Merrill Lynch and Deutsche Bank. The team has worked in conjunction with London and Frankfurt on the offering of Euro-denominated CDOs, and has long experience of IP rights, cat bonds, credit cards, autos and other consumer receivables. **Clients:** Pemex; PDVFA.

Cravath, Swaine & Moore (3 ptrs, 5 asscs) Competitors asserted to our researchers that *"no-one can ever question the quality of this offering."* Although its ambitions are limited by its size, the firm offers a remarkably broad securitisation practice, which is especially commended for its work on innovative new products. Said to approach the market hand in hand with Citibank, the firm also benefits from a blue-chip issuer client base. Involved in credit card securitisation for Citigroup and Providian and advised Financial Security Assurance in connection with CLOs, CBOs, and CDOs. Also advised major Californian utilities, Allegheny Energy and Philadelphia Electric Company on stranded utility cost securitisation.

Greg Shaw* *"has a real sense of what will work and what won't,"* and has now developed a profile for advising on developments in the securitisation of credit card receivables. Restructured the $50 billion Citibank credit card securitisation programme so that investors purchase debt securities rather than participation certificates (other greater flexibility in classes a maturities.) **Clients:** Citibank; AT&T; Capital One; Chrysler Wholesale.

Simpson Thacher & Bartlett (4 ptrs) Although a *"small, selective"* department, the firm is recognised by rivals and clients alike for its presence on the most complex transactions. Much of the firm's status derives from its work on public transactions for Chase Securities, such as a $4 billion asset-backed financing of the commercial fleet leasing assets of a subsidiary of Avis Rent a Car. The team has a historical focus on financial institutions, performing substantial work for clients such as Chase Manhattan, Chase Securities, CSFB, GE Capital and Swiss Bank. It represented Chase Manhattan on the restructuring of its offerings of credit card-backed securities.

Laura Palma* is highly respected for *"absolutely quality"* work. Recommended for the most complex of transactions, she is heavily involved in the rental car financing market, including auto loans and leases. **David Eisenberg*** has a broader practice, which includes a strong corporate finance element, yet has a *"huge* *following of fans*" for his asset-backed securitisation work. He has a tremendous reputation for his expertise in securitisation in the Korean markets. The firm's standing in the emerging markets has been enhanced by its work in assisting asset utilisation in Latin America, Asia and Europe. A more esoteric deal saw the firm advising American Reinsurance Corp on the issue of an index-based catastrophe bond. **Clients:** Swiss Bank; Chase; Manufacturers Hanover Trust Company.

Sidley & Austin (12 ptrs, 27 asscs) Although the firm is dominated by its *"stellar"* Chicago office, researchers found that the New York team *"still gets plenty of exposure."* Its *"greatest success"* has been in the CP market, representing insurance companies and investment banks on synthetic CLOs. The firm also represents entities investing in US government-guaranteed loans under customised programs such as US EXIMBank and OPIC. A wide range of asset classes are covered including IP rights, credit card receivables, consumer loans and commercial loans.

Adam Glass* is a *"capable, level-headed"* player. Most prominent of the New York partners, his practice focuses on financial assets (franchise loans/leases) and synthetic securities, including CLOs. He also represented underwriters in SEC-registered resecuritisation of corporate debt, and advised on corporate bond repackaging for Texaco, involving credit enhancers. The firm has also served as principal counsel on catastrophe bonds, securitising the insurance on work such as the NeHi (New England and Hawaii) $41 million floating rate notes issue for Vestar Insurance.

Emerging markets are a strong focus of activity, notably in areas such as consumer finance and the future flow of crude oil receivables. The firm represented Ambac MBIA and Excel Insurance on cross-border credit enhanced transactions, and advised on Yen-denominated consumer finance receivables, involving the issuance of $3 billion of CP notes in the US. **Clients:** CSFB, MBIA Insurance.

Stroock & Stroock & Lavan LLP (4 ptrs) Considered to have a *"genuine focus"* on structured finance, the firm advises a broad base of issuers and underwriters, and obtains substantial repeat business from blue-chip names such as CSFB, Goldman Sachs and Merrill Lynch. 20 years of experience of real estate transactions and consumer loans have enabled the firm to develop a healthy niche in asset-backed securities and the CP markets. The firm has advised The Bond Market Association in its application to the US Department of Labour, requesting the expansion of underwriters' exemptions, allowing pre-funding of certain asset-backed transactions.

His competitors admit to Chambers' researchers that it is *"great to see"* **Robert Wipperman*** on a deal, admiring his *"strong market knowledge."* His primary strength lies in the residential mortgage market, including prime/subprime mortgages and HELOC. **Reed Auerbach*** has a high profile for his work with CSFB. *"Incredibly intelligent,"* he is said to undertake *"cutting-edge"* work in both auto receivables (interest only certificates) and the real estate market. The firm has also been involved in more innovative asset-backed securities, including entertainment royalties, IP rights and catastrophe insurance risks. **Clients:** CSFB; Lehman Brothers; Residential Funding Corporation; Toyota.

Dewey Ballantine LLP (5 ptrs, 20 asscs) It is traditional mortgage and auto and credit card-backed deals that give this team its high profile in the market. The firm also has a fine record in more abstruse areas, such as royalty payments and lottery receivables. In single asset deals, the firm has securitised the income streams of a stadium and a cruise ship.

Maintaining its reputation for a diversified practice, the group acts on future flow transactions, CP conduits and public and private offerings with an international flavour. One New York partner handles a substantial volume of cross-border work in Mexico and Turkey. Other areas of focus in the emerging market include Latin America and Asia, where work includes the use of securitisation in project finance, and the repackaging of debt obligations in off-shore offering vehicles.

Chris DiAngelo* is an experienced practitioner who remains *"up to date with the market."* The firm's client base includes major financial institutions and substantial issuers such as Household International (for consumer loans and credit cards), American Honda and credit rating agency Fitch. Growth in CLO activity has allowed the team to advise on structured note trusts, asset swaps and other derivative-based asset classes. **Clients:** Morgan Stanley; Merrill Lynch; Fitch; CGA Investment Management.

Fried, Frank, Harris, Shriver & Jacobson (2 ptrs, 15 asscs) Focusing on *"high end work,"* the firm is considered by rivals to owe much of its prominence in this area to the head of the structured finance group, **Larry Isaacson***. *"A big factor in the CBO market,"* he has *"made the practice what it is."* He is involved in the issuance of CBOs, CLOs and other credit linked offerings for Bear Stearns, Goldman Sachs and the Morgan houses. In a headline-grabbing deal, he arranged the first ever CBO of CBOs in the ZAIS Investment-Grade Limited transaction.

Although the market noted the firm's comparatively low profile in the mortgage field, it has acted for the Federal Agricultural Mortgage Corporation in connection with guaranteed agricultural mortgage-backed securities. Other asset classes include work for JP Morgan on the sale of future oil receivables by YPF. Large BISTRO transactions continue, with the firm representing JP Morgan in big-ticket OTC credit default swaps during the past year. The firm also represented World Financial Properties on its $1.3 billion single asset securitisation of the World Financial Centre and related leases. **Clients:** JP Morgan; Goldman Sachs; Morgan Stanley; Paine Webber; Bear Stearns.

Thacher Proffitt & Wood (14 ptrs 35 asscs) A pioneer in residential and commercial mortgage-backed securitisation, the firm has expanded its horizons to include the future flow CP and asset-backed markets. The latter includes auto loans, equipment leases, healthcare receivables, music royalties, credit card and student loans. The firm has also been involved in off-balance sheet warehouse facilities and the use of swaps and derivatives in asset-backed transactions. A healthy underwriter client base includes institutions such as CSFB and Salomon Smith Barney.

Chairman of the Structured Finance practice, **Stephen Kudenholdt*** is a respected player, known for his work in the residential mortgage field. He has recently been heavily active in off-shore resecuritisation transactions. The firm has an affiliate office in Mexico, and has worked on a programme to securitise export receivables in this area. In a landmark public transaction, it advised on CNL Funding 2000-A, securitising a pool of franchised restaurants. CLO and CBO continues to be a growth area and the firm has securitised business loans held by mid-sized banks. **Clients:** Salomon Smith Barney; CSFB; Bear Stearns; Residential Funding Corporation.

Weil, Gotshal & Manges (10 ptrs, 25 asscs) Said to have *"recruited well,"* this *"substantial, credible practice"* is felt to have achieved the desired critical mass. Our researchers received sufficiently strong recommendation from clients and competitors to rank the firm in this area for the first time. A broad practice has moved from a mortgage base to focus on the asset-backed market. Credit card receivables, insurance premium finance loans, and student loans are notable areas of expertise, and the firm has advised on the securitisation of hotels, VAT reclaim receivables and tobacco receivables. A high-profile relationship with BMW led to the firm advising on its $1.5 billion retail instalment lease securitisation. It also represented ANC Rental on a $5 billion rental car fleet financing.

*See leaders' profiles on pages 848-903

Frank Nocco* has *"a good eye for detail"* and is a respected player in the structured finance market. Formerly with Mayer Brown & Platt, he is credited with the development of an important relationship with Lehman Brothers. He advised them on the formation of a $1.5 billion secured liquidity note and term note conduit, sponsored by Alliance Capital, and on the formation of a $2 billion offshore secured note facility, sponsored by Zion's Bank. With the support of a strong London office, the firm is also building a reputation in the cross-border CLO and CBO market. **Clients:** Lehman Brothers; Deutsche Bank; BMW.

Other Notable Practitioner Dick Rudder* of Willkie Farr & Gallagher has a fine reputation for the more esoteric asset backed securitisations. With clients such as Merrill Lynch, CSFB and SocGen he has been involved in the securitisation of tobacco settlement receivables and government contracts.

U

Capital Markets: Derivatives

USA: NEW YORK
Leading Firms
(Capital Markets: Derivatives)

Band	Firm
1	Cleary, Gottlieb, Steen & Hamilton
	Cravath, Swaine & Moore
	Sullivan & Cromwell
2	Cadwalader, Wickersham & Taft
3	Davis Polk & Wardwell
	Shearman & Sterling
4	Skadden, Arps, Slate, Meagher & Flom LLP
	Stroock & Stroock & Lavan LLP
5	Mayer, Brown & Platt

Firms are listed alphabetically in each band.

Leading Individuals
(Capital Markets: Derivatives)

Band	Individual
1	**CUNNINGHAM Dan** *Cravath, Swaine & Moore*
	RAISLER Ken *Sullivan & Cromwell*
	ROSEN Edward *Cleary, Gottlieb, Steen*
	WEST Holland *Shearman & Sterling*
2	**BELLER Alan** *Cleary, Gottlieb, Steen*
	BRANDOW John *Davis Polk & Wardwell*
	GROSSHANDLER Seth *Cleary, Gottlieb, Steen*
	HEFTLER Thomas *Stroock & Stroock & Lavan*
	MITCHELL David *Cadwalader, Wickersham*
	OSBORN John *Skadden, Arps*
3	**COLLINS Joseph** *Mayer, Brown & Platt*
	GILBERG David *Sullivan & Cromwell*
4	**GOLDSTEIN Marvin** *Stroock & Stroock & Lavan*
	KLEIN Linda *Dewey Ballantine LLP*
	REEDER Robert *Sullivan & Cromwell*
	STROMFELD Lary *Cadwalader, Wickersham*

Individuals are listed alphabetically in each band.

Cleary, Gottlieb, Steen & Hamilton (4 ptrs, 10 asscs) *"Competing on a global scale,"* this is a practice that *"brings the entire package to the table."* The firm is renowned for its premier OTC and structured practice on both the transactional and regulatory front. It brings *"innovation"* to the complex equity derivatives market, advising on a range of interest rate, currency swaps and commodity-linked products.

Ed Rosen* has *"a creative mind,"* and is prominent in his role as primary derivatives counsel for Morgan Stanley. Heavily involved in the development of new products, he is said to be an *"expert in commodities,"* and respected for his knowledge of US commodities law regulation. At the forefront of the firm's capital markets practice, **Alan Beller*** was recommended to researchers for his *"extraordinary knowledge"* of derivatives regulatory issues. *"Advisor to the Street"* **Seth Grosshandler*** is known for his insolvency expertise, and his work with regulated financial institutions. He has a fine name for the structuring of AAA derivative vehicles. The team also benefits from a strong financial products tax practice.

A strong broker dealer practice has seen the firm advise FX Alliance, (derivatives exchange) EBS (forex trading systems) and BrokerTec Global. The firm also acts as derivatives counsel to the Government Securities Clearance Corporation, and overseas, is advising governments in Latin America. **Clients:** Sovereign issuers; foreign banks; end-users; credit rating agencies.

Cravath, Swaine & Moore (3 ptrs, 10 asscs) As counsel to *"marquee client"* International Swaps and Derivatives Association (ISDA), the firm is *"at the forefront of everyone's consciousness."* Although said to be *"narrower in scope"* than its principal rivals, this large team continues to produce important work on the drafting of master agreements and opinions with a focus on the OTC market.

Research has pinpointed **Dan Cunningham*** as *"a superb derivatives lawyer who shaped the industry."* Although seen less on transactions, he is *"the leading expert on opinions on rights of issuers"* and is seen as *"the arbiter of the industry."* Much of the firm's reputation rests with him, and his presence ensures that it is involved in new product development and compliance issues. Elsewhere, the firm is a powerful lobbyist across the globe for derivatives legislation changes. Advised Blackbird, the first operational e-trading platform for interim rate derivatives. **Clients:** ISDA; Salomon Smith Barney; Nomura Capital Services; Chase Manhattan; JP Morgan.

Sullivan & Cromwell (6 ptrs) *"One of the broadest derivative practices,"* is said to have an enviable balance between transactional capacity and regulatory skills. Although occasionally considered *"unduly conservative,"* our researchers were left in no doubt that the firm's deal flow from major investment banks entitles it to a position among the leaders.

Having built on an initial focus in the commodities market, the team now advises on trade, credit and insurance derivatives. In the buoyant e-trading facilities market, the firm advised Enron on compliance issues and the launch of EnronOnline, an internet-based transaction system for wholesale energy and other commodities.

"Putting the practice on the map," head of the Commodities, Futures and Derivatives Group **Ken Raisler*** is *"one of the brightest lawyers around."* A former Chairman of the CFTC, much of his reputation lies in the depth of his regulatory knowledge. He has advised on AAA derivative products for Nomura, and is principal counsel to global fixed income securities firm Cantor Fitzgerald. **David Gilberg*** is said to be a major transactional figure. He recently advised on proprietary e-trading sites, developed and sponsored by major institutions, and represented Goldman Sachs and Morgan Stanley on the development of an intercontinental exchange trading facility focused on physical commodity derivatives. *"A major player in the securities market,"* **Bob Reeder*** is recommended for his work on the launch of AAA derivative products for investment banks, as well as Section 16 disclosure issues.

The team advised Morgan Stanley, Merrill Lynch and Salomon Smith Barney on the organisation of TheMuniCenter, the largest web based B2B marketplace for the trading of municipal derivatives. **Clients:** Bank of America; CSFB; Goldman Sachs; AIG; Cantor Fitzgerald.

Cadwalader, Wickersham & Taft (35 lawyers) *"An old hand"* in the derivatives market, this *"strong team"* is felt to strike a good balance between regulatory expertise and transactional capability. Well integrated with its strong securitisation team, the derivatives group has developed a following for its combining of derivative products (interest rate, currency, swaps and credit derivatives) with asset-backed structures.

David Mitchell* is highly regarded for his expertise in futures and securities regulatory matters, and is seen to provide intellectual ballast for the team. Clients admire his *"sharp mind,"* and he also focuses on servicing a base of financial services clients on OTC derivatives and other transactional areas. **Lary Stromfeld*** has *"great market presence"* and a focus on OTC fixed income products and municipal finance. He structures credit derivatives, total return swaps, currency swaps, and fixed income swaps for clients such as Nomura, Morgan Stanley and Merrill Lynch. Active in the structuring of e-trading, the firm has advised Creditex, an internet-based platform for credit derivatives. **Clients:** Lehman Brothers; Nomura; Morgan Stanley.

Davis Polk & Wardwell (25 structured finance lawyers) Described to Chambers' researchers as *"the specialists in equity derivatives,"* the team is considered to have *"adopted a highly focused approach that certainly works."* Prominent for producing *"quality"* work on behalf of Morgan Stanley, the firm advises on all its global equity derivative activities. It is also heavily involved in product development for JP Morgan, CSFB and DLJ for retail distribution or institutional investors.

John Brandow* inspires *"a great deal of confidence,"* with his *"sound and reasonable advice."* He focuses on the design of new products, OTC hedging strategies, tax structures and regulatory issues. He represented DLJ on hedging its stake in Liberty Media, and advised Bell Canada on the hedging of its stake in Nortel. His team advised Morgan Stanley on the creation of Reg S programmes, designed to produce favourable results for equity-linked products. **Clients:** Morgan Stanley; Bank of America; DLJ; AIG.

Shearman & Sterling (60 lawyers in Global Structured finance group) *"Excellent resources and a substantial client base"* characterise this highly respected firm. Covering 15 jurisdictions, this is a team with a global perspective, focusing on exchange traded and OTC derivatives (equity, credit and commodity driven). Both on the regulatory and transactional compliance side of e-trading, the firm has advised on over 20 internet based e-trading systems. A sub group of six partners looks after the broker dealer regulatory group.

"A supreme business getter," **Holland West*** has *"succeeded in boosting the firm"* with *"the force of his personality."* Head of the Structured Products & Derivatives group he is *"a first rate lawyer,"* who is known for his work in OTC structured products. The firm continues to be active in the field of embedded derivatives, hedging and credit enhancers. **Clients:** Merrill Lynch; CSFB; Citigroup; Deutsche Bank; Salomon Smith Barney.

Skadden, Arps, Slate, Meagher & Flom LLP (6 ptrs) Unquestionably *"skilled players,"* the firm's lack of a *"cohesive focus"* on derivatives was consistently mentioned to our researchers. Generally associated with new product development, the firm has designed exchange traded and OTC derivative structures for Bank of America and First Union. Unlike many of its competitors, the firm's clientele is corporate-oriented, and is advised on credit derivatives that concentrate on beneficial tax and accounting treatments.

John Osborn* *"has created a team capable of matching its M&A excellence."* Head of the Derivative Financial Products, he is known for his creative product development with a particular focus on institutional end-users. Although of counsel (and so not ranked in our list), Philip Johnson continues to provide outstanding regulatory advice from the DC office. Acknowledged leaders in the energy field, the team has been active in producing derivative products based on energy swaps and the sale of greenhouse gas trading allowances, thereby supporting a flourishing projects practice. The firm is also active in reinsurance-related financings. **Clients:** Merrill Lynch; Citibank.

Stroock & Stroock & Lavan LLP (5 ptrs, 6 asscs) The firm's *"exceptional focus on capital markets"* is underlined by its expertise in the commodities market, which has seen a huge growth in the energy markets in North America and Europe. The team has been involved in the design of web trading platforms for partnerships or investment banks such as Goldman Sachs.

Managing partner **Tom Heftler*** has a *"terrific knowledge of the e-trading environment."* His practice focuses on commodities and derivatives transactions and includes extensive experience in energy, metals, currencies and index notes. **Marvin Goldstein**'s* *"strong market knowledge"* has a particular focus on physical commodities, swaps and options. With a strong knowledge of SEC regulations and compliance issues, the team handles complex equity derivative transactions (using features to achieve liquidity or asset protection) and debt instruments with embedded derivatives. **Clients:** AIG Trading; Banc of America Securities; Goldman Sachs; UBS; Hess Energy Trading; Orion Power; Sempra Trading; Tosco.

Mayer Brown & Platt (6 ptrs, 10 asscs) In addition to its relationships with *"enormous players"* such as UBS, it is the firm's willingness to *"undertake bulk documentation"* that was mentioned to our researchers as the factor that puts it on the derivatives map. It is also recommended for its in-depth knowledge of the Chicago exchanges and its expertise in the design of new, complex products. The workload includes advising on exchange traded instruments (swaps, foreign currency), credit and equity derivatives. The team includes a number of former advisors to the CFTC and SEC and accordingly has a balanced regulatory and transactional practice. Considered to offer *"expert commodities advice,"* **Joe Collins*** has a good knowledge of the futures market, and counsels on new product development, regulation and compliance. Structuring of e-trading platforms has been a growth area for the firm. Possessing an international client base both on the dealer and advisor side, the firm has served clients seeking to include embedded derivatives in other capital markets transactions. **Clients:** Bank of America; SocGen; UBS; First Union; Refco.

Other Notable Practitioner *"Eloquent"* **Linda Klein*** of Dewey Ballantine LLP is a *"high quality lawyer,"* whose varied practice includes fixed income, interest rate and currency derivatives.

Communications: Transactional: East Coast

USA: EAST COAST Leading Firms (Communications: Transactional)
1 Cravath, Swaine & Moore
Shearman & Sterling
Skadden, Arps, Slate, Meagher & Flom LLP
Willkie Farr & Gallagher
2 Milbank, Tweed, Hadley & McCloy
3 Cleary, Gottlieb, Steen & Hamilton
Simpson Thacher & Bartlett
Wachtell, Lipton, Rosen & Katz
Weil, Gotshal & Manges
4 Covington & Burling
Hale and Dorr
Mayer, Brown & Platt

Firms are listed alphabetically in each band.

Cravath, Swaine & Moore Described by competitors as *"one of the most prestigious M&A firms."* At its heart lies a *"spectacular communications client base"* with a track record in public company M&A *"to end all others."* This is the firm that represented Time Warner on its $165 billion merger of equals with AOL. Also assisted the former in the negotiations of open access agreements for other internet service providers to use their cable lines.

"One of the greats," **Allen Finkelson*** has a *"fantastic M&A telecoms practice."* Chambers' researchers were told that **John Gaffney*** is a major player on the *"biggest public telecoms deals."* His active clients include DLJ and Goldman Sachs. Not considered to be an outsourcing powerhouse, Cravath has more than its fair share of mature internet clients.

On the corporate front it advised Lycos on its $12 billion merger with Terra SA and represented Ford on its joint venture dealer network to create the Ford Direct internet site. Although the proposed acquisition of Sprint was ultimately unsuccessful, the firm also advised MCI WorldCom on its $6 billion acquisition of Intermedia, including a controlling interest in Digex, a provider of application services for internet-based businesses. In mass media, the firm represented Time Inc in its acquisition of Times Mirror Magazine from Tribune Co. Always at the cutting edge of the market, the team advised AirTV on the introduction of live TV into airborne aircraft. **Clients:** CBS; IBM; Time Warner; SBC; Dreamworks; Jacor Communications; Pearson; Teligent.

Shearman & Sterling Chambers' researchers were told that this M&A practice has *"always had a keen eye for the tech market."* Although rivals commented on the *"rough ride"* the west coast office has had, here the firm is *"reloading and ready."* Its *"effective cross-border strategy"* has scored well in the light of the global consolidation in this market.

With a strong European background, **John Madden*** *("fine transactional lawyer")* has guided British Telecom through its corporate transactions. In conjunction with the London office, the team advised BT on its $2.5 billion recommended white knight offer for Esat Telecom Group plc (Irish telco.)

"Blue-blooded" **Creighton Condon*** is *"known for his big hi-tech deals."* A dominant force in the broadcast arena, he advised Viacom on its $2.8 billion acquisition of BET Holdings and its $36 billion merger with CBS. **John Marzulli*** was recommended for his public utility work. He advised GE on its merger with Honeywell (formerly AlliedSignal) in the year's largest industrial deal. Although not drawn along industry lines, the firm has *"strong ties to active investors"* such as Morgan Stanley and Citibank, making it a *"powerful competitor."* Advised France Telecom on the US aspects of its $37.6 billion purchase of Orange plc from Vodafone, including its subsequent $1.37 billion acquisition of E.ON's 42.5% Orange shares. Also advised on public offerings from Looksmart, Active Software and eBay. **Clients:** NBC; British Telecom; France Telecom; General Electric Capital; Hewlett-Packard; Apollo Computers.

Skadden, Arps, Slate, Meagher & Flom LLP (120 lawyers) *"Expansionist"* in its outlook, the team is involved in the financing and corporate work for household names and emerging start-ups. *"Extremely broad,"* the firm is said by some to *"dominate the communications M&A market."* It has a significant national and international presence, with offices in Boston and North Virginia focusing on the start-up market, as well as a prominent DC regulatory practice.

Chambers' researchers were struck by the warmth of recommendation for the *"incredibly bright and personable"* **Tom Kennedy***. Advising some of the *"biggest clients,"* he is credited with building up the technology practice. Although heavily involved in the telecoms market, much of his profile lies with his *"thriving"* IT practice. He advised NTL on its £8.2 billion acquisition of the consumer business of Cable & Wireless.

Head of the e-commerce practice, **Stuart Levi*** has *"picked up the most interesting deals."* An IP/IT transactional man, he has advised Citigroup on a joint venture with AOL to provide payment services and advised Estée Lauder on the creation of cosmetics portal gloss.com. The team advised a consortium of IBM, Chase and Bank of America on the formation of Viewpointe Archive Services. **Clients:** AOL; Alcatel; Compaq; NBC; Register.com; TheStreet.com; Digital Equipment Corporation; Priceline.com; Honeywell; CMGI; ChrisCraft; NTL; THLee. Putnam Internet Partners; Bear, Stearns & Co; Merrill Lynch.

Willkie Farr & Gallagher *"A huge presence in the market,"* due in part to *"a real desire for both telecoms and IT work."* It has a strong balance of work for corporates, such as Level 3 and McLeod on senior secured debt issues, and active underwriter clients such as UBS Warburg. Dominance in the satellite systems sector has been highlighted by extensive work on behalf of mainstay client Loral, while overseas, the firm has expanded into Rome, Milan and Frankfurt.

"Charming" **John D'Alimonte*** *"knows his way around a deal."* Considered the most visible transactional player, he is recommended for his broad international scope, undertaking broad corporate financings for Level 3.

Chambers' researchers were told by competitors that **Bruce Kraus*** is a *"familiar sight"* on the most complex telecoms M&A and restructuring transactions. He is supported by a strong regulatory practice and a broad client base, notably featuring traditional telecom clients seeking a move into web hosting.

The team advised Sprint in connection with the introduction of a major new service offering and on consolidation trends in the local telephone industry. Advised EXO Communications on its private equity financings and has been involved in bank loans work for 360Networks. A growing involvement in IP/IT transactional matters has seen the firm act for heavyweights such as Bloomberg, Winstar and Intel. **Clients:** Level 3; Bloomberg; NEXTEL; Winstar; Teligent; Loral; Orion; Teledisc; GlobalStar.

Milbank, Tweed, Hadley & McCloy (35 lawyers) Considered to cover *"a true cross section of the communications market,"* the team received warm recommendation from rivals for its telecoms and satellite projects, including work for lenders on the Iridium project. It has been involved in the financing and development of fixed-line, wireless, cable and satellite systems and the internet. Supported by a fine international network, the team is particularly active in Latin America, where it acted for the lenders on the $1.75 billion refi-

USA: EAST COAST Leading Individuals (Communications: Transactional (Telecoms))	
1	**COGUT Charles** *Simpson Thacher & Bartlett*
	CONDON Creighton *Shearman & Sterling*
	D'ALIMONTE John *Willkie Farr & Gallagher*
	FINKELSON Allen *Cravath, Swaine & Moore*
	LEWKOW Victor *Cleary, Gottlieb*
2	**CHATZINOFF Howard** *Weil, Gotshal & Manges*
	GERSTELL Glenn *Milbank, Tweed*
	GROLL William *Cleary, Gottlieb*
	KRAUS Bruce *Willkie Farr & Gallagher*
	MADDEN John *Shearman & Sterling*
3	**GAFFNEY John** *Cravath, Swaine & Moore*
	GOTTDIENER Scott *Simpson Thacher*
	GREEN Frederick *Weil, Gotshal & Manges*
	LEVINE Hank *Levine, Blaszak, Block & Boothby*
	MARZULLI John *Shearman & Sterling*
	ROSENBLUM Steve *Wachtell, Lipton*

Individuals are listed alphabetically in each band.

Leading Individuals (Communications: Transactional (IT))	
1	**KENNEDY Tom** *Skadden, Arps, Slate, Meagher*
	MUMMERY Dan *Milbank, Tweed*
2	**MASUR Dan** *Mayer, Brown & Platt*
	ZAHLER Robert *Shaw Pittman*
3	**BURGESS John** *Hale and Dorr*
	EPSTEIN Michael *Weil, Gotshal & Manges*
	LEVI Stuart *Skadden, Arps*
	LYNCH Alex *Gunderson Dettmer Stough*
	MILLSTEIN Julian *Brown Raysman*
	SMITH Brian *Mayer, Brown & Platt*
	SMITH Scott *Covington & Burling*

Individuals are listed alphabetically in each band.

nancing of bridge loans to BCP for its construction of a B-Band cellular network in São Paulo. In Asia, the group advised NTT on a $10.5 billion offering of common stock.

"*Mainstay*" of the firm's telecoms practice is **Glenn Gerstell***. With an "*in-depth understanding of the market,*" he "*always does a great job.*" Former senior partner of the Asian offices, he is a fixture on the international stage. "*Fantastic*" **Dan Mummery*** is "*an intelligent lawyer*" who "*inherited a burgeoning practice and really made it his own.*" Competitors acknowledge that he is one of the leading outsourcing specialists in the country. He represented AT&T on a series of outsourcing transactions and advised United Airlines on web-hosting agreements and portal ISP negotiations. Although the e-commerce practice has focused on larger established companies, financial services and investment banks, it has a growing reputation for the financing of emerging companies. **Clients:** Qualcom; Alestra; AT&T; Global Crossing; NTT; United Airlines; Lockheed Martin; Hughes Electronics; Pacific Internet; Metiom; Xerox; Dupont; Bell South; BT; Alcatel; ABN Amro; Soc Gen; Bank of America; JP Morgan Chase; Citibank.

Cleary, Gottlieb, Steen & Hamilton Thought to have capitalised on the flow of foreign investors into the US communications market, the firm's broad international network "*gives it the jump on other firms,*" and it has a global client base "*second to none.*" The team advised Nortel Networks on its proposed acquisition of Alteon WebSystems Inc (value $7.8 billion.) Prominent for both its M&A experience and a highly rated capital markets team.

"*An excellent M&A player,*" **Victor Lewkow**'s* name is based on his "*stunning client relationships.*" Although a broad based M&A player, his work with Telecom Italia marks him out as a "*one of the big name guys.*" M&A specialist **Bill Groll*** has a high profile for his work with Deutsche Bank. The team advised the underwriters on the $2.3 billion SEC registered offering of convertible subordinated debt by AOL. Known for cross border public company deals, advised Goldman Sachs and Warburg Dillon Read in their role as financial advisors in Vodafone AirTouch's acquisition of Mannesmann. **Clients:** Nortel; Telecom Italia; Deutsche Telekom.

Simpson Thacher & Bartlett A corporate powerhouse with "*extremely qualified*" attorneys. The bulk of the team's work centres around advising established public companies on both financing and M&A. A first-rate banking client base particularly impresses competitors. The firm advised the banks on Vodafone Airtouch's acquisition of Mannesmann ($136 billion), Olivetti's acquisition of Telecom Italia ($65 billion) and the joint venture between Bell Atlantic and Vodafone Airtouch. The mainstay client is Global Crossing, for whom the team has always undertaken M&A, financing and commercial contact negotiation. Work includes the $3.8 billion acquisition of Ixnet, a provider of IP-based network services to the financial community. Media client Seagram has also been active and the firm has advised on its tripartite merger with Canal+ and Vivendi.

"*Intelligent*" **Casey Cogut*** has a reputation for the "*biggest of the complex restructuring and corporate deals.*" Head of M&A, he is credited with the development of the Global Crossing relationship, and advised Teleport Communications Group on its sale to AT&T, and Bay Networks Inc on its purchase by Northern Telecom Limited. Chambers' researchers were told that **Scott Gottdiener*** has become the "*point man*" for Global Crossing. He advised on three separate offerings of $3.5 billion of convertible preferred stock and senior notes. Elsewhere, the firm advised Bank of America on the $500 million financing for Globalstar LP, a low earth orbit satellite-based digital communications system. **Clients:** Esprit Telecom; Symbol Technologies; Qwest Communications; Teleglobe; Jaan Telekom; Internet Inc.

Wachtell, Lipton, Rosen & Katz Although the firm has recently shelved plans to open a West Coast office, its activity in the communications sector from its New York base continues to receive unanimous market plaudits. Competitors acknowledge that key client AT&T provides "*an unbelievable deal volume,*" although it is thought by some that this relationship has its limits on the scope of the practice.

His relationship with AT&T makes **Steve Rosenblum*** "*an important figure in anyone's book.*" Recommended for the most complex cross-border transactions, he advised AT&T on its joint venture with BT, expected to deliver $11 billion of revenue. The team also advised AT&T on a massive restructuring programme creating a family of four publicly held companies covering wireless, broadband, business and consumer services. **Clients:** AT&T; Motorola; Tribune Company; National Semiconductor.

Weil, Gotshal & Manges (8 ptrs) Competitors with a major international network and the pick of "*the choicest clients,*" the firm has increased its profile in the venture capital financing of emerging companies, and benefits from a strong IP and technology practice on the West Coast.

"*Highly visible*" on telecoms deals, **Howard Chatzinoff*** works closely with the firm's well established global clients on both transactional and strategic issues. He advised SBC Communications, the biggest local US phone company, on its $3.9 billion acquisition of Sterling Commerce, boosting his client's presence in the B2B e-commerce field. "*Senior member of the team*" **Fred Green*** is known for his M&A and corporate finance counselling to major manufacturers and service providers. He has a strong profile for his Latin American work and has advised Alestra (Mexico's second largest service provider) and PanAmSat on its commercial geostationary satellite network.

Other areas of specific expertise here include mass media broadcasting, cable and the internet. The firm advised on the strategic alliance between

*See leaders' profiles on pages 848-903

DirecTV and America Online. **Michael Epstein*** is a highly rated IP transactional attorney who *"has made the cross over"* and is *"heavily involved in restructuring and financing hi-tech companies."* Rivals see him taking on the mantle of the e-commerce practice. The team represented NYNEX on its $31 billion merger with Bell Atlantic, and is currently representing Bell Atlantic on international issues arising from its proposed merger with GTE. **Clients:** Telewest; Hughes Electronics; Deutsche Telekom; MTV; US Networks; Lifetime Television; Showtime Networks; Computer Associates; General Electric Capital Corp; CBS; Applied Materials; Wit Capital Group.

Covington & Burling (25 lawyers) Although overshadowed by its first rate regulatory practice, this transactionally active team provide *"high quality"* securities advice. Chambers' researchers were impressed with the success of a particularly smooth merger with Howard, Smith & Levin, and the consequent blending of accomplished regulatory and hi-tech corporate finance teams. **Scott Smith*** is considered to be a *"key player in the broadcast market."* He acted for the principal stockholder of Gemstar on its merger with TV Guide. The team also acted on a cross border transactions involving Qualcomm and advises USA Networks on corporate matters **Clients:** Microsoft; Computer Associates; Mediconsult.com; USA Networks; Sprint PCS; The Washington Post; National Geographic; PBS; CBS; NBC; San Francisco Chronicle; Raycom (TV.)

Hale and Dorr (12 ptrs, 24 asscs) *"Increasingly visible"* in the market, the firm has experienced substantial growth in VC funding. Chambers' researchers were told that the firm is *"extending its hold on the technology market,"* as its clients mature. It advised Bookham Technology on its $300 million IPO, as well as representing CGMI and Nortel on joint ventures and capital raising. Also acting for a powerful array of investment banks, the team advised Goldman Sachs on the $6.3 billion flotation of Infineon Systems.

Considered *"the main port of call for international work,"* **John Burgess*** is credited with developing the firm's overseas profile. He represented Irish microchip designer Parthus on its $188 million IPO (both Nasdaq and LSE) and further raising of $130 million. The firm has successfully run a joint venture with Brobeck Phleger & Harrison in the UK (Brobeck Hale & Dorr) and is known globally for its securities work. A leader in hi-tech M&A, it has been particularly active on the sale of companies to Lucent Technology, including Nexabit ($1 billion) and Xedia ($285 million). **Clients:** Wang Global Corporation; Analog Devices; CMGI; CareerBuilder; Proxicom; Prodigy; E Trade; Discover On Line.

Mayer, Brown & Platt (8 ptrs, 12 asscs IT, 2 ptrs e-commerce) *"One of the leading firms for IT outsourcing,"* the firm is considered to have a superb client base of Fortune 1000 entities, and has developed a global operation based on the new economy. The team has a balanced mix of vendor and customer clients and has seen a growth in the B2B trade exchanges. It advised a major aerospace contractor on the outsourcing of its data centre processing, midrange and desktop systems, and hardware and software maintenance.

"A true specialist," **Dan Masur*** is known for his expertise in outsourcing. A former general counsel of a hi-tech firm, he is said to know *"both sides of the issues facing his clients."* **Brian Smith*** is recommended for his work in the e-commerce market, particularly on behalf of financial services clients. The firm advised MapQuest on its $1.1 billion acquisition by AOL and represented eCharge, the online payment system, and Pantheon on the outsourcing of voice, data and video networks. **Clients:** IBM; Ameritech; GEC.

Other Notable Practitioners *"An important and visible part of the market,"* **Robert Zahler*** of Shaw Pittman has a *"firm grasp on the convergence of IT and telecoms."* Former Brobeck partner, **Alex Lynch*** of Gunderson Dettmer Stough Villeneuve Franklin & Hachigian, is *"doing great things in the start-up market."* His move to the recently opened New York office of this West Coast player is considered a critical step in building east coast credibility. **Julian Millstein*** of Brown Raysman and Millstein is a *"solutions oriented"* outsourcing specialist, who *"knows his clients well."* Competitors acknowledge that **Hank Levine*** of Levine, Blaszak, Block & Boothby is *"requested by the biggest telcos."* An *"effective advocate,"* he has a strong regulatory background and his *"market knowledge is fantastic."*

Communications: Regulatory: East Coast

Covington & Burling (70 lawyers) *"A vast media practice,"* which, as Chambers' researchers were reminded, has been *"a major force for many years."* Although considered to focus *"on a core traditional broadcasting market,"* it produces lawyers who are *"skilled across the board."* A full service firm, it offers transactional counsel and IP protection to a broad client base, which includes start ups in the hi-tech field and *"long established"* relationships with Fortune 100 corporates.

"Key senior figure" **Jonathan Blake*** *"grew up with the FCC,"* and is recommended for his work in the broadcast arena. He represents a major trade association on its efforts to establish digital TV. The firm has been heavily involved in the launch of new services such as PCS, cellular and satellite services. It also advises local exchanges and regional telephone companies, and has acted for an overseas government on its efforts to stimulate competition in offshore telecoms. **Clients:** CBC; NBC Affiliates Association.

Mintz Levin Cohn Ferris Glovsky and Popeo (45 lawyers) From a traditional focus on telecoms regulatory issues, the group has developed into a broad-based hi-tech practice. A pool of *"talented individuals"* has built up a *"deep well of experience,"* and the firm is seen to have recruited heavily from the FCC, thereby establishing *"ties to those who shape the industry."* The firm's client base includes wired and wireless carriers, cable and online service companies and manufacturers.

Sought after for his *"great base of knowledge,"* **Charles Ferris**, former Chairman of the FCC, has *"keen experience of the issues that face policy makers,"* and is recommended for his role on the international scene. A *"major name"* for his work with TDS Telecom, **Howard Symons*** is an important element in the group's success. He advises telecoms companies and trade associations on regulatory and legislative matters, and is commended for his advice on regulatory issues affecting the deployment of broadband services.

The team has advised its cable clients on the issues raised by entry to the market of telephone companies, direct broadcasting satellites and other delivery facilities. **Clients:** TDS Telecom.

Swidler Berlin Shereff Friedman LLP (10 ptrs, 70 asscs) *"Competing at the highest level,"* this is a team of *"good, strong battlers,"* often seen before the FCC and state public service commissions. A

USA: EAST COAST Leading Firms (Communications: Regulatory)
1 Covington & Burling
Mintz Levin Cohn Ferris Glovsky and Popeo
Swidler Berlin Shereff Friedman LLP
Wiley Rein & Fielding
2 Hogan & Hartson LLP
Latham & Watkins
Skadden, Arps, Slate, Meagher & Flom LLP
Willkie Farr & Gallagher
Wilmer, Cutler & Pickering
3 Arnold & Porter
Harris, Wiltshire & Grannis LLP
Kelley Drye & Warren
Kellogg, Huber, Hansen, Todd & Evans
Paul Weiss Rifkind Wharton & Garrison
Sidley & Austin

Firms are listed alphabetically in each band.

Leading Individuals (Communications: Regulatory)
1 **BLAKE Jonathan** *Covington & Burling*
EPSTEIN Gary *Latham & Watkins*
FERRIS Charles *Mintz Levin Cohn Ferris*
LIPMAN Andy *Swidler Berlin Shereff Friedman*
SYMONS Howard *Mintz Levin Cohn Ferris*
VERVEER Philip *Willkie Farr & Gallagher*
WILEY Richard *Wiley Rein & Fielding*
2 **LAKE William** *Wilmer, Cutler & Pickering*
ROHRBACH Peter *Hogan & Hartson LLP*
SPECTOR Phillip *Paul Weiss Rifkind Wharton*
3 **HARRIS Scott** *Harris, Wiltshire & Grannis LLP*
KELLOGG Michael *Kellogg, Huber, Hansen*
QUALE John *Skadden, Arps*
ROSENSTEIN Mace *Hogan & Hartson LLP*
ST LEDGER-ROTY Judith *Kelley Drye & Warren*
STERN Martin *Preston Gates & Ellis LLP*
WADLOW Clark *Sidley & Austin*

Individuals are listed alphabetically in each band.

leading player in the development of the internet sector from its inception, it has a broad client base of start-ups, telephone common carriers, and wireless, cable and satellite services.

Andy Lipman* is thought to have been *"hugely successful in making the start-up market his own."* Indeed, some believe that *"the whole practice is built on him."* He testified before a US House of Representatives' sub-committee on behalf of a German competitive carrier association on issues of foreign government ownership of American telcos. In playing a key advisory role on behalf of MFS Communications – the largest local service provider – he has promoted the opening of US markets.

The firm has advised on a number of FCC license transfer proceedings, including the first competitive local service and interconnection agreements in Europe and the first competitive fibre network application in Japan. **Clients:** Vodafone; Global Crossing; Level 3; RCN; McLeod.

Wiley Rein & Fielding (70 lawyers) *"Dominating the upper echelons,"* the firm is considered by rivals to be *"hugely successful, operating on the cutting edge of federal decisions."* The firm is especially recommended by clients for its handling of large complex disputes and transactions in telecoms and broadcasting. *"Senior statesman of the industry,"* **Dick Wiley*** is *"always at the forefront of the market."* Former Chairman of the FCC, he is said to have *"created a great firm."* Advising on both domestic and international considerations, the firm has been active in market access rulings (including foreign ownership limitations), transborder satellite issues and channel allocations. Although now known as a major transactional firm, *"old time contacts"* have seen the firm advise major corporates on consolidation in the broadcasting market. The team has advised the National Association of Broadcasters and The Radio-Television News Directors Association on the FCC's 'fairness doctrine.' **Clients:** Major domestic and foreign corporates.

Hogan & Hartson LLP (9 ptrs) The communications practice has been recommended to Chambers researchers as *"one of the great regulatory practices in DC."* A strong international network – comprising seven European offices – has assisted the firm in representing telecoms carriers and users on both domestic and overseas issues. Active on international wireless and satellite communications matters, the firm's enviable client roster keeps it firmly in the public eye.

Thought to be *"occasionally feisty,"* **Peter Rohrbach*** is a *"thorough and capable lawyer."* His work includes telephone industry regulation, satellite communications and broadcast law, and his relationship with NewsCorp has set him out as a leader in this market. **Mace Rosenstein*** has a fine reputation for his work in the broadcast field. He has acted before the FCC on broadcast networks' financial interests and syndication rights, and foreign ownership of US broadcast stations. The firm has advised on the entry of Bell operating companies into the long distance marketplace. **Clients:** NewsCorp; major domestic and multi-national corporates.

Latham & Watkins *"Broad coverage"* of the sector and an international transactional profile lead to high praise for a firm that is said to contain *"strong attorneys, able to spar in all arenas."* The team was especially commended to our researchers for its FCC work. The *"talented"* **Gary Epstein*** *"has a great relationship with the agencies."* Former Chief of the Common Carrier Bureau of the FCC, his focus lies in telecoms, satellite and the broadcast market. He advised the divested Bell Operating companies on regulatory issues, including local access and the convergence of cable and telephone technologies. Has also advised DirecTV on domestic and international satellite regulation. The firm is active in providing advice to foreign corporates on ownership restrictions and authorisations for international services. **Clients:** Major domestic and foreign corporates.

Skadden, Arps, Slate, Meagher & Flom LLP (1 ptr, 11 asscs) Although the firm has suffered the loss of two key regulatory figures, interviewees told our researchers that this is merely a *"stumble,"* as the firm has *"always been greater than the sum of its parts."* The firm continues to attract major global corporates such as Fox to its stable, scores highly on transactional matters and represented SBC in front of the FCC over issues surrounding its merger with Ameritech. The team has also represented Teligent in state proceedings, and before the FCC and Congress.

Other work has included advising Allied Riser Communications on regulatory matters, licence agreements and corporate ventures arising from its offering of highspeed broadband services.

"Personable" **John Quale***, formerly of Wiley Rein, has a high profile for his broadcast work and *"extending the breadth of the practice."* As well as his advice on transactional arrangements, he is recommended for his experience in FCC ownership issues and broadcast and cable regulations. In broadcasting, the team advised the National Association of Broadcasting on legislative issues, and it has also acted for Northpoint Technology on the use of satellite frequencies to serve the terrestrial market. **Clients:** NewsCorp; Fox; Verizon; SBC.

Willkie Farr & Gallagher (7 ptrs) A *"first rate combination"* of transactional advice and regulatory expertise is considered by competitors to make the team a prominent feature in the DC market. A broad based practice, it advises long distance telecoms operators, satellite companies and equipment manufacturers. The team is heavily involved in cross-border transctions, and has a strong relationship with broadband giant Motorola.

Philip Verveer* is *"the engine of the practice."* Highly regarded by clients for his *"sound, reasoned decisions,"* he advised Sprint on is failed

*See leaders' profiles on pages 848-903

merger with WorldCom and on its opposition to the opening of the long distance communications market to local telephone companies. The firm has advised established clients – such as Bloomsbury – on issues thrown up by its expansion into the internet market, notably content licence. Also advised Winstar and Teligent on the building of access channels to service residential and office users. **Clients:** Sprint; McLeodUSA; Allegiance Telecom.

Wilmer, Cutler & Pickering (12 ptrs, 20 asccs) Principally active in the telecoms sector, the firm handles traditional common carriage issues and emerging technologies such as PCS. Chambers' researchers were told that the firm is *"a big name in broadcasting,"* with a focus on the federal regulation of commercial and public broadcast stations and cable operators. It represented MCI in Latin America on service agreements and advised a Chilean company on PCS and competitive long distance activities. *"A major talent,"* **Bill Lake*** *"has his finger on the federal pulse,"* although much of his practice has a cross-border element. He advised Deutsche Telekom on its acquisition of VoiceStream, and represented it before Congress on issues surrounding foreign government ownership of American telecoms companies. The firm acted for Valor Communications on its purchase of access (rural exchanges) from GTE. **Clients:** Deustche Telekom; Yahoo!; Valor Communications; Iridium.

Arnold & Porter (13 ptrs) Described to our researchers as *"traditional old time players"* in the regulatory market, the firm is not considered to have developed any superstar figures, although its trade and regulatory group continues to be an active force. The team covers a wide spectrum of broadcasting, cable, satellite and wireless communications. It is also renowned for its work in the public sector, advising both local governments and national associations on the franchising and regulation of cable television systems. The team has counselled more than 60 cities on changes to federal and state laws. Working closely with its peerless anti-trust team, the firm advises on FCC regulations concerning the structuring of financial transactions. Also advised on the establishment of a cellular telecoms company in the US, and the development of a mobile satellite network. **Clients:** Major US and foreign corporates; municipal and state affiliates.

Harris, Wiltshire & Grannis LLP (3 ptrs, 7 asscs) A smaller *"highly specialised"* firm that, although *"new on the scene,"* has had *"a very definite impact on the market."* Competitors believe it is *"thoroughly excellent"* and packed with *"talented individuals."* The emphasis here lies on emerging technology and international issues, and the group represented a consortium of PSC providers on issues surrounding standards for next generation wireless technologies.

Managing partner **Scott Harris*** is the former Chief of the International Bureau of the FCC, and is a *"well connected"* national figure. In the telecoms market, the team has assisted common carriers before the FCC and counselled on a range of domestic and international regulatory issues. It has also advised international satellite operators on obtaining FCC licences, and handled policy debate over wireless technical standards. **Clients:** Level 3; AOL; AT&T.

Kelley Drye & Warren (55 lawyers) Chambers' researchers were told that this practice has *"recruited aggressively"* (particularly from the FCC), and has grown into an *"important fixture on the DC scene."*

Head of the telecoms practice is the *"outstanding"* **Judith St Ledger-Roty***, who is recommended for her international experience and a particular focus on the mobile phone market. On the regulatory side, the firm has niche expertise in reciprocal compensation issues under the Communications Act, concerning termination of traffic and revenues set for new entrants to the market. The team advises domestic and foreign companies on obtaining federal common carrier service authorisation, and has also prosecuted ILEC networks before state regulatory commissions and the FCC over interconnection complaints. **Clients:** PSINet; NextLink; Lucent Technologies; Lockheed Martin.

Kellogg, Huber, Hansen, Todd & Evans (29 lawyers) Possessing lawyers with *"great credentials,"* the firm is praised by peers for its *"polished legal product."* The firm has made its name for regulatory counsel on behalf of industry leaders, and is recommended for its appellate work focused on trials and appeals in federal and state courts across the US.

"Skilled" **Michael Kellogg*** is an *"on the ball lawyer."* His competitors see him as *"a troubleshooter"* within the industry, and much of his profile is linked to activity on behalf of the Bell Operating Companies. He advised them on open network rules and modifications to the AT&T consent decree to allow entry to new businesses. **Clients:** Fortune 100 companies.

Paul Weiss Rifkind Wharton & Garrison (13 ptrs, 22 asscs) Although heavily involved in transactional work, our interviewees recommended the regulatory team as *"excellent players, working hard on the international front."* Supported by a first rate Asian practice, the team advises both foreign and domestic clients on a variety of regulatory issues.

"A strong and seasoned leader," **Phillip Spector*** is chair of the firm's Communications & Technology Practice Group, and is a *"knowledgeable and familiar sight at the FCC."* In both a regulatory and transactional capacity, he acted as counsel to SkyBridge, a $6 billion satellite project spearheaded by Alcatel, in front of the FTC and ITU. The firm has a strong focus on the wireless and satellite sectors, advising large fixed line telcos, manufacturers, fibre optic cable companies and ISPs. **Clients:** BT; NTT; Singapore Telecom; Alcatel

Sidley & Austin (3 ptrs, 3 asscs in DC) Recommended to our researchers for its broadcast regulation expertise and the opening of new markets, the team liaises with its powerful Chicago office to provide advice on corporate, litigation and regulatory work in the wireless/cellular markets. It has represented both foreign governments and communication carriers such as NTT on regulatory, privatisation and competition issues in the US market.

Head of the Communications Group **Clark Wadlow*** is a *"major player,"* whose name is often linked with AT&T, which he has represented in regulatory matters before the state courts, the FCC and the Supreme Court. His team is often seen on the biggest corporate deals, and advised the Tribune Company on its $8 billion acquisition of Times Mirror, involving an appearance before the FCC. **Clients:** NTT; AT&T; Fox Affiliates Association.

Other Notable Practitioner **Marty Stern** of Preston Gates & Ellis LLP is a prominent regulatory figure, best known for his lobbying work before the FCC.

Communications: IT/e-commerce: West Coast

Wilson Sonsini Goodrich & Rosati (120 ptrs, 675 asscs) *"The dominant firm in Silicon Valley"* is *"head and shoulders above the rest in terms of market share."* This *"excellent full-service law firm"* with *"a most impressive client roster"* is particularly active in the spheres of corporate finance, corporate securities, IPOs, technology licensing, tax and employee benefits. Communications and networking are major growth areas. Our researchers were repeatedly informed that *"nobody is as well known in Silicon Valley"* as the *"fabulously talented and creative"* **Larry Sonsini***. Described as *"a force of nature,"* he *"casts a huge shadow over the practice." "Strong on corporate securities,"* **Jeff Saper*** is *"a first rate lawyer who never tries to bluff you."* According to clients, he always *"takes the time to figure out what is going on."* **Mike Kennedy*** is the firm's M&A specialist, while **Mario Rosati*** is a *"tremendous business developer with a great practice." "Focused"* **Marti Korman*** is highly regarded and the more experienced **Mark Bertelsen*** has an established name in the Valley. **Judith O'Brien*** is seen as *"technical yet practical"* and always *"works towards a realistic solution."* The younger **Steve Camahort***, believed to be *"experienced beyond his years,"* is noted for his *"easy-going negotiating style."* The firm acted on the sale of Etec Dynamics to JDS Uniphase for $20 billion and represented Hewlett Packard in the spin-out of Agilent. **Clients:** Hewlett-Packard; Apple; Sun Technology; Goldman Sachs; Morgan Stanley; Network Associates; Boeing; Infosys; Commerce One.

USA: WEST COAST Leading Firms (Communications: IT/e-commerce)	
1	Wilson Sonsini Goodrich & Rosati
2	Cooley Godward
	Fenwick & West
3	Brobeck Phleger & Harrison
	Gray Cary Ware & Freidenrich LLP
	Gunderson Dettmer Stough Villeneuve Franklin & Hachigian
	Venture Law Group
4	Latham & Watkins
5	Gibson, Dunn & Crutcher LLP
	Pillsbury Winthrop
	Skadden, Arps, Slate, Meagher & Flom LLP
6	Heller Ehrman White & McAuliffe LLP
	Morrison & Foerster
	Orrick, Herrington & Sutcliffe LLP

Firms are listed alphabetically in each band.

Leading Individuals (Communications: IT/e-commerce)		
★	**SONSINI Larry** *Wilson, Sonsini, Goodrich & Rosati*	
1	**DAVIDSON Gordon** *Fenwick & West*	**GALLO Greg** *Gray Cary Ware & Freidenrich LLP*
	GUNDERSON Bob *Gunderson Dettmer Stough*	**JOHNSON Craig** *Venture Law Group*
	MENDELSON Alan *Latham & Watkins*	
2	**CLIMAN Richard** *Cooley Godward*	**DEL CALVO Jorge** *Pillsbury Winthrop*
	GREEN Josh *Venture Law Group*	**KAUFMAN Christopher (Kit)** *Latham & Watkins*
	KELLER Don *Venture Law Group*	**SAPER Jeff** *Wilson, Sonsini, Goodrich & Rosati*
3	**DETTMER Scott** *Gunderson Dettmer Stough*	**FRANKLE Diane** *Gray Cary Ware & Freidenrich LLP*
	KENNEDY Mike *Wilson, Sonsini*	**KING Ken** *Skadden, Arps*
	MROZEK Therese *Brobeck Phleger & Harrison*	**TANOURY Mark** *Cooley Godward*
	TONSFELD Steve *Venture Law Group*	
4	**BERTELSEN Mark** *Wilson, Sonsini*	**CALOF Lawrence** *Gibson, Dunn & Crutcher LLP*
	DILLON Christopher *Gunderson Dettmer Stough*	**KORMAN Marti** *Wilson, Sonsini*
	LESSER Henry *Gray Cary Ware & Freidenrich LLP*	**O'BRIEN Judith** *Wilson, Sonsini*
	ROSATI Mario *Wilson, Sonsini*	**SIMONS Laird** *Fenwick & West*
	SMITH Greg *Skadden, Arps*	**SPECTOR Scott** *Fenwick & West*
Up-and-coming individuals		
	CAMAHORT Steve *Wilson, Sonsini*	**FLAUM Keith** *Cooley Godward*
	KOSHLAND Jim *Gray Cary Ware & Freidenrich*	**VETTER Jeff** *Fenwick & West*

Individuals are listed alphabetically in each band.

Cooley Godward (52 ptrs, 222 asscs) *"One of the seven sisters,"* this is a full-service firm that *"just wants to get deals done."* Although the team has recently lost some of its major players, most notably the departure of Alan Mendelson to Latham & Watkins, it maintains its *"great brand name"* and the *"second largest market share."* The firm recently closed one of the biggest M&A telecommunications deals when i2 Technologies acquired Aspect Development for $9.3 billion. *"Clearly the name for M&A"* is *"national figure"* **Ric Climan*** who is, competitors told our researchers, *"strong-willed, with good business sense."* The firm's other leading name is **Mark Tanoury***, who exhibits *"good instinct, knows how to build a team"* and has *"emerged from Mendelson's shadow."* **Keith Flaum*** is a young M&A lawyer with a growing reputation. The firm represented Alteon Web Systems on its sale to Nortel Networks for $7 billion and Etec Systems when it was acquired by Applied Materials for $3 billion. **Clients:** Applied Materials; Siebel Systems; Sun Micro Systems; Conexant Systems; eBay Inc; Qualcomm; Copper Mountain Networks; Texas Pacific Group.

Fenwick & West (26 ptrs, 95 asscs) An *"excellent firm with a tremendous franchise."* Although not possessing the depth of some of its market rivals, the team is noted for *"high quality work for a variety of heavyweight IT players."* The firm offers the full range of services for Silicon Valley hi-tech companies, from start-up through to IPOs, M&A and beyond, and has a particular reputation for the level of its strategic advice. *"Smart and effective"* **Gordi Davidson*** was universally recommended to our researchers as *"one of the class acts of Silicon Valley."* He offers *"excellent senior-level advice"* and is thought of as *"a technically superb lawyer and all-round nice guy."* He represented Verisign when the company was acquired by Network Solutions for $25 billion. **Scott Spector*** *"is vastly underrated,"* while *"top IPO lawyer"* **Laird Simons*** has more experience in this field than most in the Valley. *"Highly conscientious, thoughtful"* **Jeff Vetter*** is a younger lawyer with a growing reputation. The firm represented Siara Systems on its acquisition by Redback Networks for $10 billion and completed the IPO for ONI Systems worth $2 billion. **Clients:** Intuit; VERITAS; Excite

Brobeck Phleger & Harrison (13 ptrs, 98 asscs) The firm has regained its position as a *"serious competitor"* in the Valley. Our researchers were advised that they have been *"strategic in their marketing"* and have once again *"built up a good name."* The firm's reputation in the valley is synonymous with that of its major client: *"When you*

*See leaders' profiles on pages 848-903

think of Brobeck, you think of Cisco." Possessing a large business and technology practice group, covering traditional corporate finance, M&A, start-ups, venture capital, fund formation, corporate securities, underwritings and IPOs. There is a widely held view that this is a department with *"a strong team ethos and no individual stars."* The most notable lawyer here is the *"tenacious"* **Therese Mrozek*** who has *"devoted her life to Cisco,"* representing them on their $6 billion acquisition of Arrow Communications. **Clients:** Cisco; E-trade; Broadcom; GTE; DoubleClick.

Gray Cary Ware & Freidenrich LLP (49 ptrs, 98 asscs) A full service firm active in corporate securities, transactional work, M&A and public offerings, whose client base comprises a number of venture capital organisations and start-up companies. Considered to do *"a good job on middle-market technology deals,"* the firm is *"more than holding its own"* in the Valley. *"The leader of the firm"* and major *"business-getter"* is the *"terrific"* **Greg Gallo***, one of the leading lights in the Valley, while **Jim Koshland*** is, competitors informed our researchers, considered to be *"an increasingly valuable part of their practice."* Joint heads of the M&A department are former Heller Ehrman man **Henry Lesser***, respected for his expertise on hostile takeovers, and *"experienced transactional lawyer"* **Diane Frankle***. The firm represented Datapath Systems on its acquisition by LSI Logic Corporation for $532 million in July 2000 and Dot Wireless on its acquisition by Texas Instruments for $475 million. Also advised Finisar Corporation on its secondary offering for $770 million and Telocity Inc. on its IPO worth $132 million. **Clients:** Abode Systems Inc; Agile Software Corp; Calico Commerce Inc; Dupont Corp; Extreme Networks Inc; Maxtor Corp; Telocity.

Gunderson Dettmer Stough Villeneuve Franklin & Hachigian LLP (25 ptrs, 70 asscs) Boutique firm maintaining its focus on internet start-up companies, which has been *"firing on all cylinders"* this year, largely due to its seemingly eternal ability to *"attract very good clients at early stages."* The department represents emerging technology companies and venture funds on fund formations, while the corporate securities group handles financing, organisation, IPOs and M&A transactions. *"Seen it all, done it all"* **Bob Gunderson*** is *"one of the greatest marketers of all time and a fine lawyer,"* famous for his venture capital and private equity work. *"Everybody's favourite lawyer in the Valley"* is corporate partner **Scott Dettmer***. He is, our researchers were told, *"practical, effective and smart – a good lawyer to do a deal with,"* and he can *"make points for his clients without causing undue antagonism on the other side."* He represented Promatory Communications in their $800 million sale to Nortel and acted for Onebox.com when they sold Phone.com for $850 million. **Chris Dillon** *"can manage a large volume of work"* and is regarded as *"an excellent hire"* from Shearman & Sterling. The firm advised Xros when it was acquired by Nortel for $3.5 billion, and Chromatis when it was acquired by Lucent for a similar fee. **Clients:** Redback; Scient; Ariba; Cacheflow; Equinix; WalMart.com; Benchmark; Austin Ventures; Morgan Stanley; Goldman Sachs.

Venture Law Group (20 ptrs, 80 asscs) The vast majority of this boutique firm's clients are early stage technology start-ups. It is not a full service firm, but a pure business law concern, acting for those clients from birth to IPO stage. Many are then passed on to Orrick, Herrington & Sutcliffe, who have an alliance with VLG. Seen as a *"highly profitable buzz firm,"* the team is considered to possess *"great talent under one roof."* Founding partner **Craig Johnson*** *("creative, smart and entrepreneurial")* is a *"great leader"* and *"one of the visionaries of the valley."* Hands-on practitioners at the firm to gain market commendation, are **Josh Green***, who rises in the lists after constant client recommendation, and the *"thoughtful, excellent"* **Don Keller***. The respected **Steve Tonsfeld*** leads the firm's M&A team, which represented Cerent when it was acquired by Cisco for $7 billion, and Yahoo! on its acquisitions of Broadcast.com and Geocities. **Clients:** Yahoo!; Intuit; Preview Travel; X.com; SmartPipes; Phone.com; Amber Networks.

Latham & Watkins (12 ptrs, 36 asscs) *"The potential is there"* for this firm to have a *"huge presence in the Valley."* The team is, clients were keen to inform our researchers, already *"a potent force, quality-wise"* and is *"taken seriously"* by the major players in the region. The firm offers the full range of hi-tech services, from corporations, dealing with semi-conductors, life sciences, the internet and software for an eclectic mix of corporates and financial institutions. **Alan Mendelson*** is someone who *"plays to win"* and *"picking him up (from Cooley Godward) was an inspired move." "Any firm which has him will be a player in the Valley." "Smart and creative"* **Kit Kaufman*** is *"a high quality lawyer with a phenomenal work ethic."* The firm represented VLSI in connection with a hostile takeover by Philips valued at over $1.2 billion, and advised Chartered Semiconductor Manufacturing on its $575 million IPO. **Clients:** Amgen Inc; TiVo Inc; Marconi Communications; CV Therapeutics; Morgan Stanley Dean Witter; Credit Suisse First Boston; Chase Capital Partners.

Gibson, Dunn & Crutcher LLP (10 ptrs, 20 asscs) *"A really energised firm"* that is definitely *"on its way up."* The firm offers the full range of services that one can expect from a Valley practice, with financing and M&A the major growth areas. In **Lawrence Calof***, the firm possesses a *"wonderful lawyer who does a good job for them."* He represented Nortel Networks on the company's $3.25 billion acquisition of Qtera and $3.5 billion acquisition of Xros. **Clients:** Intel; Nortel Networks.

Pillsbury Winthrop (21 ptrs, 72 asscs) Start-ups are at the core of this growing firm's caseload, with networks and communications the niche areas of expertise. The 2001 merger between Pillsbury Madison & Sutro and Winthrop, Stimson, Putnam & Roberts sees it continue to expand. The corporate group works on securities, licensing, IPOs and M&A, and represented Network Solutions on one of the largest internet secondary public offerings in history, worth $2.2 billion. *"Impressive, pragmatic and bright"* **Jorge del Calvo*** is *"enormously successful at generating business."* This *"freewheeling spirit"* as he was described to our researchers is renowned for his *"casual style"* and his transactional expertise. The firm acted on the sale of Savoir Technology Group to Avnet for $170 million. **Clients:** Guidant; S3 Inc; Tivia; Webex; Support.com; Alliance Fibre Optic; Docent; Raza Foundries.

Skadden, Arps, Slate, Meagher & Flom LLP (7 ptrs, 37 asscs) The firm is *"making a real effort"* in the Valley and has developed well since opening an office there. Considered *"first-rate at doing their thing,"* the team's forte, as in New York, lies in high-end M&A deals. However, a diverse caseload also includes start-up company financing and venture capital funding. *"Easy to deal with"* **Ken King*** *"understands the business imperatives of a transaction,"* while **Greg Smith*** is also an *"established name in the Valley."* Represented Ascend Communications on its $20 billion acquisition by Lucent Technologies, and Inktomi Corporation on the acquisition of Fast Forward Networks for $1.3 billion. Also advised phone.com on its merger with software.com with a combined market capitalisation of $14 billion. **Clients:** Phone.com; Inktomi Corp; Altavista; Tumbleweed Communications; Zindart Corp; The Dialog Corp plc; Plumtree Software.

Heller Ehrman White & McAuliffe LLP (25 ptrs, 70 asscs) The firm addresses all areas of technology advice, including finance, M&A, patent prosecution and securities, but niche strength lies in life sciences. Although the loss of Henry Lesser to Gray Cary Ware & Freidenrich has been a recent setback, the team is still considered to carry weight in the region. Represented Maxygen on its $100 million IPO and $150 million secondary offering, and advised Alza on a convertible debt offering worth several hundred million dollars. **Clients:** Microsoft; Alza; Maxygen; Atmel; Lam Research.

Morrison & Foerster (20 ptrs, 50 asscs) The firm, our researchers discovered, is less prominent in the Valley than in former years, and has *"not penetrated the market to the same extent"* since the loss of Mike Philip to an in-house position at JDS Uniphase. He had worked on the company's $41 billion acquisition of SDL Inc. Although the firm is now better known for its IP capacity, it did represent Verio Inc on its $5 billion offer acquisition by NTT Communications. **Clients:** JDS Uniphase Corp; Fujitsu Corp; DoubleClick Inc; Oracle Corp.

Orrick, Herrington & Sutcliffe LLP (5 ptrs, 20 asscs) Has *"the makings of a strong hi-tech firm"* and is best known for its alliance with Venture Law Group. Perceived by some to be *"living off the scraps of VLG,"* others believe that the firm is *"getting a real boost out of the relationship."* The team's caseload is primarily focused on IT, telecoms and infrastructure for the internet. Represented Promedix.com when it was acquired by Chemdex (now known as Ventro) for $1.2 billion and represented Snap Track in its acquisition by Qualcom for $1.1 billion. **Clients:** Nokia; Apple; Silicon Graphics; private companies.

U

*See leaders' profiles on pages 848-903

Competition/Anti-trust: New York

Clifford Chance Rogers & Wells (30 attorneys in New York and DC) Now considered a *"global operation, going from strength to strength,"* the firm's recent merger is judged to be *"much more than a marketing tool."* The group is also felt to benefit from its strong presence in continental Europe. Recommended to *Chambers'* researchers for a broadly based caseload including numerous contentious cases in the healthcare, insurance, telecommunications and financial services industries.

Credited with *"growing the practice into an immense force,"* former Director of the FTC's Bureau of Competition, **Kevin Arquit*** is one of the country's leading anti-trust names. *"Incredibly intelligent,"* he is said to *"see all angles of a problem and consistently comes up with the goods."* The firm has acted for MasterCard International on a class action suit brought by 4 million retailers, and on the defence of a DOJ anti-trust enforcement action to restructure the governance and operations of both MasterCard and Visa. In a securities litigation, the firm also represented Merrill Lynch in federal class actions arising from Sumitomo Corporation's purported $2.6 billion copper trading loss and alleged efforts to manipulate the world's copper markets. **Clients:** MasterCard; Shell.

USA: NEW YORK Leading Firms (Competition/Anti-trust)	
1	Clifford Chance Rogers & Wells
	Weil, Gotshal & Manges
2	Boies, Schiller & Flexner
	Cravath, Swaine & Moore
	Simpson Thacher & Bartlett
3	Skadden, Arps, Slate, Meagher & Flom LLP
4	Davis Polk & Wardwell
	Debevoise & Plimpton
	Shearman & Sterling
	Sullivan & Cromwell
5	Fried, Frank, Harris, Shriver & Jacobson

Firms are listed alphabetically in each band.

Weil, Gotshal & Manges (21 ptrs, 45 asscs) *"Intellectual, analytical lawyers and practical litigators,"* this substantial team is said to have *"across the board strength."* A highly regarded merger control practice is complemented by extensive experience in litigation before the FTC and DOJ, and includes niche strength in the media sector.

"Pragmatic and a good tactician," **Helene Jaffe*** is *"an incredibly intelligent problem-solver."* Although her practice covers a range of Hart-Scott-Rodino rulings, she is also well regarded for her focus on advertising infringements. *"Charming"* **Peter Standish*** is recommended for his *"top flight merger compliance work,"* while *"senior market figure"* **Paul Viktor*** has a respected international anti-cartel practice. Said to possess *"energy and enthusiasm,"* he acts for a variety of major corporates across the globe. **Jay Fastow*** is seen by competitors as a *"financial services specialist,"* consistently offering *"sensible advice"* as well as effective litigation. Representations in the consumer credit and credit card field are notable cases on his resumé. **Bruce Rich*** maintains his share of market support, while the *"skilled"* **Debra Pearlstein*** is said to offer *"great analytical advice,"* and advised Texas Instruments on its $7.6 billion acquisition of Burr-Brown. Recommended for its breadth of coverage in industry sectors for both US and foreign corporates. Successfully defended Matsushita and JVC on the 'Go Video' jury litigation alleging conspiracy and anti-trust. **Clients:** CBS; Estee Lauder; Kawasaki Steel; Nutrasweet; Cendant; Hughes Electronics; KPMG; Sotheby's.

Leading Individuals (Competition/Anti-trust)		
1	**ARQUIT Kevin** *Clifford Chance Rogers & Wells*	**BOIES David** *Boies, Schiller & Flexner*
	HAWK Barry *Skadden, Arps*	**JOFFE Bob** *Cravath, Swaine & Moore*
2	**HARTY Ronan** *Davis Polk & Wardwell*	**JAFFE Helene** *Weil, Gotshal & Manges*
	LOGAN Kenneth *Simpson Thacher & Bartlett*	**WARDEN John** *Sullivan & Cromwell*
3	**BLUMKIN Linda** *Fried, Frank, Harris*	**CHESLER Evan** *Cravath, Swaine & Moore*
	COLLINS Wayne Dale *Shearman & Sterling*	**EVANS Martin (Rick)** *Debevoise & Plimpton*
	FLEXNER Don *Boies, Schiller & Flexner*	**GOLDEN Arthur** *Davis Polk & Wardwell*
	GOLDFEIN Shepard *Skadden, Arps*	**KOOB Charles** *Simpson Thacher & Bartlett*
	ROLFE Ron *Cravath, Swaine & Moore*	**STANDISH Peter** *Weil, Gotshal & Manges*
	STOLL Neal *Skadden, Arps*	**VICTOR Paul** *Weil, Gotshal & Manges*
4	**ABUHOFF Dan** *Debevoise & Plimpton*	**BARTEL Paul** *Davis Polk & Wardwell*
	BURKE Arthur *Davis Polk & Wardwell*	**FASTOW Jay** *Weil, Gotshal & Manges*
	GOLD Stuart *Cravath, Swaine & Moore*	**JOHNSTON Elaine** *White & Case LLP*
	KEZSBOM Allen *Fried, Frank, Harris*	**KUBEK Gary** *Debevoise & Plimpton*
	MEIKLEJOHN Stuart *Sullivan & Cromwell*	**PEARLSTEIN Debra** *Weil, Gotshal & Manges*
	PRINCE Kenneth *Shearman & Sterling*	**QUEEN Eric** *Fried, Frank, Harris*
	RICH Bruce *Weil, Gotshal & Manges*	**SACKS Ira** *Fried, Frank, Harris*
	TRINGALI Joseph *Simpson Thacher & Bartlett*	**WAYLAND Joseph** *Simpson Thacher & Bartlett*

Individuals are listed alphabetically in each band.

Boies, Schiller & Flexner (11 ptrs, 24 assocs) *"Growing in leaps and bounds,"* and *"first order for any anti-trust litigation work,"* the group has a superb reputation as lead counsel in class action suits, as exemplified by its litigation against vitamin manufacturers. Although lacking the corporate power base to feed through merger notification cases, the firm has a strong independent reputation for counselling high profile international corporates.

The star appeal of this practice lies with *"showman"* **David Boies***, formerly with Cravath Swaine & Moore. Said to be *"a bit between the teeth litigator,"* and now a household name, much of his public profile is based on his successful conduct of abuse of a dominant position charges against Microsoft. *"A skilled manipulator of the court room,"* at home with the limelight, Boies is a *"truly effective force of nature,"* recommended for his powers of concentration and memory. *"Superb"* **Don Flexner*** *"brings huge gravitas,"* with his background at the FTC adding *"an extra dimension"* to the firm. He represented SBC Communications on its opposition to the proposed MCI WorldCom/Sprint merger. The firm acted as lead counsel in the class action suit against Sotheby's and Christie's concerning collusion to fix commission prices. **Clients:** Napster; CBS; SBC Communications; Federal Government.

Cravath, Swaine & Moore (5 ptrs) A firm with a *"strong team ethos"* which inspires *"big deal confidence."* Although the anti-trust team's forte is considered to lie in litigation, a wealth of M&A transactions ensures an almost equally impressive merger compliance reputation. Researchers were told that the group also has a strong profile for defence of class action suits, and is currently representing BAT against price-fixing claims in over 25 federal and state class actions.

The team's litigators are said to combine *"hard-hitting"* tactics with *"pure quality"* anti-trust advice. *"Classy"* **Bob Joffe*** is regarded as a *"world class litigator,"* so prominent that some feel he has *"been around since the year dot."* He advised Time Warner on the implications of its merger with AOL. **Ron Rolfe*** is another leading litigator well known for his merger compliance work, who acted for Guinness on its merger with Grand Metropolitan and has long experience of the tobacco market, representing Brown & Williamson in a suit (with RJ Reynolds & Lorillard) against Philip Morris. **Evan Chesler*** is reckoned to be a *"fantastic presence in court,"* always *"in command of the law."* Recommended for his merger compliance work, **Stuart Gold*** is *"in the typical Cravath mould"* of a strong all-rounder *"most at home in court."* The firm acted for glass manufacturer PPG Industries against 30 price-fixing claims, and advised Pillsbury on the anti-trust issues surrounding its acquisition by General Mills. **Clients:** Lucent Technologies; BAT; Jones Apparel; Nestlé, PepsiCo; Unilever.

Simpson Thacher & Bartlett (6 ptrs) An anti-trust group containing *"a deep well"* of *"impressive"* lawyers, which is considered to have capitalised on the firm's leading corporate practice to establish a substantial reputation for the anti-trust aspects of cross border M&A transactions. Traditional strength exists in pharmaceuticals and the entertainment industry, and the firm advised UK-based Reckitt & Coleman on its merger with Benckiser.

A distinguished group of *"highly focused litigators"* includes the *"intuitive"* **Ken Logan***, who offers a *"low key approach and great strategic finesse."* He has developed a leading name in the media and telecoms industries and advised American Home Products on the $58.3 billion merger with Warner Lambert. The firm also represented AHP as co-ordinating counsel in major class actions brought by retailers against pharmaceutical manufacturers and wholesalers. **Charles Koob*** is *"a great litigator,"* recommended for a versatile practice which includes both civil and criminal anti-trust work for a blue-chip corporate client base. He represented Appleton Papers Inc, a paper manufacturer, on a criminal price-fixing trial and has an established reputation in the public company and private equity transactional market. **Joe Tringali*** is prominent for his civil antitrust actions and merger notification work, while **Joe Wayland*** is another litigator to attract market commendation. The firm advised Associates First Capital on its $31.1 billion sale to Citigroup, and represented Seagram on its tripartite merger with Vivendi & Canal Plus. **Clients:** American Home Products; KKR; Seagram; Virgin Group; Appleton Papers Inc; Reckitt & Coleman.

Skadden, Arps, Slate, Meagher & Flom LLP (15 ptrs nationwide) The huge M&A engine that drives the firm is of huge benefit to a *"high quality"* anti-trust practice, which is a leading player on merger compliance cases. The firm has advised corporate giants Honeywell before the DOJ and the EU over its merger with AlliedSignal Inc and on the US aspects of its merger with GE. A *"successfully integrated"* global anti-trust network includes an active office in Washington DC and a top-class Brussels operation.

"Legendary" **Barry Hawk*** is said to be *"one of the true anti-trust stars," "incredibly sharp"* and renowned for his litigation prowess. *"Ahead of his time"* in recognising the importance of globalisation, Hawk is equally admired in Brussels, where he is regarded as *"a fantastic deal-maker."* **Shep Goldfein*** is a renowned litigator who *"commands respect in a court room."* He is closely associated with the sports sector and has defended the NFL against a monopoly claim. Seen on the *"biggest transactions,"* **Neal Stoll*** has made his name in big-ticket merger clearance work. He advised Champion International on its acquisition by International Paper for $7.3 billion, and is a familiar figure in front of the FTC and DOJ. The firm represented Christie's Inc in a class action suit alleging price-fixing of commission charges and fees for other auction services. **Clients:** Honeywell Inc; American Stock Exchange; MGM; NFL; Champion International.

Davis Polk & Wardwell (9 ptrs, 35 asscs) *"A substantial, merger-driven"* practice, seen to benefit from cross-border transactions and a high-profile relationship with European firms such as Hengeler Mueller Weitzel Wirtz and Slaughter and May. The firm acted with Hengeler on behalf of E.ON AG on its $2.35 billion sale of VEBA Electronics to a mixed US and UK consortium. The firm is also known for class actions suits, primarily for its defence against private or government challenges.

"An outstanding commercial lawyer," **Ronan Harty*** is said to have *"removed the excessively conservative tendencies"* from the group. Recommended by rivals for cross-border transactions, he advised Zeneca (UK) on the anti-trust aspects of its merger with Astra (Sweden), as well as on the defence of a huge private anti-trust action brought by retailers and consumers over price-fixing allegations. **Arthur Golden*** has a high profile for his merger compliance work and acted for RJR Nabisco Holdings on the $8 billion sale of its tobacco unit to Japan Tobaccco. In criminal and civil anti-trust litigation, he has represented Hoffmann-La Roche on an alleged vitamin price-fixing case. *"Seasoned"* **Arthur Burke*** has advised Central Newspapers on its $2.6 billion acquisition by Gannett, as well as working on alleged price-fixing cases in the pharmaceuticals industry and the sale and marketing of agricultural products. *"Smart"* **Paul Bartel*** is recommended for his cross-border transactional practice. He advised Medical Manager on its $5 billion sale to Healtheon and Bertelsmann on its acquisition of Random House. **Clients:** AstraZeneca; ICI; GE; Compaq; Texas Instruments; Texaco; Hoffman-La Roche; Bertelsmann.

Debevoise & Plimpton (5 ptrs, 15 other litigators) An *"old line firm,"* respected for its merger control work, but now also seeing an increase in its government enforcement work, including private class actions and price-fixing litigation. Major civil and criminal anti-trust challenges are serviced by a strong litigation department, which covers industries as diverse as telecoms, airlines, credit cards and insurance. The group is able to co-ordinate its work on cross-border mergers through respected offices in London and Paris.

"Always down to earth," **Gary Kubek*** is considered to be the most prominent transactional anti-trust figure at the firm. He advised AXA financial on the sale of DLJ to CSFB, and represented a pharmaceuticals client in actions brought by the FTC and private plaintiffs as well as a vitamin manufacturer over allegations of vitamin price-fixing. Veteran partner **Rick Evans*** *"has a great track record."* Although less visible on day-to-day matters, this renowned litigator continues to be seen as *"a figure who inspires trust."* **Dan Abuhoff*** is a prominent team member who has appeared extensively before the DOJ and FTC, and has a particular focus on merger compliance issues. He represented Eni (Italian oil and gas company) on the US aspects of its plans to buy British Borneo Oil & Gas for $1.26 billion. Elsewhere, the firm advised on Phelps Dodge's proposed acquisition of two leading copper producers and acted for France Telecom on its joint venture with Sprint. **Clients:** Phelps Dodge Corporation; Eni; AXA financial; France Telecom.

Shearman & Sterling (4 ptrs, 15 asscs) Much of the anti-trust team's work revolves around its prime multi-national client base, and is supported by a strong international network, particularly notably in London and Paris. An *"excellent"* team has a balanced caseload, mixing merger control work with a strong litigation capacity that has been highlighted by major representations in

*See leaders' profiles on pages 848-903

the recent vitamin price fixing case and the carbon electronics industry. Historically prominent in the pharmaceuticals/chemicals and broadcasting sectors, the department is acknowledged to have increased its market share in areas such as e-commerce (B2B) and finance.

The *"star"* of the team is *"intellectual heavyweight"* **Dale Collins***. Said to undertake the bulk of *"the heavy lifting,"* he operates a renowned merger control practice, and advised Georgia-Pacific (paper manufacturer) on its $11 billion acquisition of Fort James. *"Strong all-rounder"* **Ken Prince*** is also recommended for his merger compliance experience. His multi-national client base includes British Steel (whom he advised on its $4.3 billion merger with Koninklijke Hoogovens,) BASF, BOC and Cadbury/Dr Pepper. **Clients:** British Steel; Cadbury Schweppes; Georgia-Pacific.

Sullivan & Cromwell (Approx 60 attorneys nationwide) Although it has had *"a strong reputation both before and since the Microsoft trial,"* the department's recent profile has been dominated by the ongoing defence of Microsoft against challenges by the anti-trust division of the DOJ and 19 states, covering aspects of product development and distribution. Said to be *"driven by the litigation department,"* the anti-trust team also benefits from the firm's massive corporate capability, which provides abundant merger compliance work.

"Intelligent" **John Warden*** is the firm's *"pre-eminent litigator."* A *"tough operator,"* he is considered to be the person to *"go to for a battle." "Punchy"* **Stuart Meiklejohn*** has a growing reputation for anti-trust counselling, and has a resumé that includes the vitamin price-fixing case and big-ticket merger compliance work. The firm advised Glaxo Wellcome on its merger with Smithkline Beecham and BP on its acquisition of Amoco. **Clients:** Royal Philips Electronics; British Airways; Alumax; Goldman Sachs; BP.

Fried, Frank, Harris, Shriver & Jacobson (6 ptrs) A *"substantial practice,"* seen to be producing strong litigators. While Hart-Scott-Rodino filings are the department's staple diet, it has also advised on contentious cases, including Six West vs Loews and the Potash litigations.

"Level-headed" **Linda Blumkin*** is seen as a *"practical problem solver."* She represented El Paso Energy on its $6 billion merger with Sonat Inc and its pending $20 billion combination with the Coastal Corporation. **Allen Kezsbom*** displays *"great prowess as a litigator,"* and is known for his blue-chip client base, including Bell South (Yellow Pages Solutions v. Bell Atlantic et al.) and Delta Pineland (Delta & Pineland v. Monsanto.) A senior figure at the firm, he is considered to be an *"excellent intellectual resource"* for the team. **Eric Queen*** has a *"nice, balanced practice,"* while **Ira Sacks*** has a *"fine analytical mind,"* and has been active in the Potash price fixing litigations. The firm represented Bell South on its $74 billion wireless joint venture with SBS Communications and WPP Group on its $4.7 billion acquisition of Young & Rubicam. **Clients:** Sony Pictures Entertainment Inc; Minnesota Mining; El Paso Energy; Bell South.

Other Notable Practitioner **Elaine Johnston*** of White & Case LLP is recommended for her *"strong international practice,"* and her work in structuring arrangements for mergers. She advised Saatchi & Saatchi on its £1.9 billion sale to French agency Publicis.

Competition/Anti-trust: Washington DC

Arnold & Porter (33 ptrs, 23 asscs) A *"powerhouse of a practice"* with the *"deepest bench"* of talent in Washington. Attorneys in London provide support on UK and EU competition and regulatory issues, and a cross-border merger control portfolio sees the group advising on the largest transactions, including acting for General Electric on the US and Canadian anti-trust aspects of its $43 billion merger with Honeywell. Seen to have *"an institutional reputation,"* the team is able to draw on the skills of a group of *"long-established veterans."*

"A class act with a stellar reputation," **Mike Sohn*** has *"a keen sense of the important aspects of each transaction." "Above board and straight as an arrow,"* he is said to be *"a man you can trust,"* and advised Arco on its $26.8 billion acquisition by BP Amoco. The year 2000 saw the return to the firm of two high-profile agency officials, thereby cementing the firm's reputation for efficiency in front of the commission. Former Director of the FTC's Bureau of Competition, **Bill Baer*** is said to be a *"major asset."* Recommended for his intellectual capacity, he is considered to be a hugely influential lobbyist. **Donna Patterson***, previously Deputy Assistant Attorney General in the anti-trust division of the DOJ, rejoined the firm in August. Her *"superb knowledge of the law"* and of agency policy is beyond dispute.

Richard Rosen* is widely regarded as a strong litigator, who is comfortable in front of the FTC. His practice focuses on IT and telecoms, with a client list that includes SBC Communications and Xerox. **Ken Letzler*** is a *"great transactional lawyer,"* who acted for Monsanto on its acquisition by AHP, and has provided counselling to pharmaceutical giant Glaxo Wellcome. An *"assertive court-room presence"* marks **Douglas Wald*** out as one of the leaders of the next generation of Arnold & Porter stars. He has represented Philip Morris Inc and Random House on contentious anti-trust matters, and advised Merck & Co on a number of joint ventures and acquisitions. Researchers were told that **Deborah Feinstein*** displays *"fine legal skills,"* and is *"gaining stature"* in cross- border merger control cases. She advised GE on its acquisition of Greenwich Air Services. **Clients:** Arco; Bank America Corp; Occidental Petroleum; Philip Morris; Unilever; Monsanto; GE; Merck; Computer Associates; Glaxo Wellcome.

Cleary, Gottlieb, Steen & Hamilton (5 ptrs, 20 asscs) *"A substantial practice"* with an *"impressive global operation,"* which includes respected offices in Paris and Rome and a pre-eminent reputation in the hub of EU competition, Brussels. A substantial profile for M&A transactional work has been enhanced by advice to Dow Chemical on its $11.6 billion acquisition of Union Carbide Corp, creating the world's second largest chemical company. The firm recruits heavily from government agencies and accordingly, also enjoys a leading reputation for its appearances before the FTC and DOJ. It represented Delta Airlines on a class action suit brought by travel agents alleging conspiracy to cap commissions.

"Personable and level-headed" **George Cary*** *"brings weight"* to the team. His high reputation for regulatory issues partly derives from his background as a Deputy Director of the FTC's Bureau of Competition. **David Gelfand*** is one of the firm's *"brighter stars,"* and is said to take a *"sensible, reasonable approach"* to litigation. He advised Tosco on the $800 million acquisition of its Avon refinery by Ultramar Diamond Shamrock. *"Excellent"* **Mark Leddy*** is commended for the *"strong international flavour"* to his practice. **Michael Laz-**

USA: WASHINGTON DC Leading Firms (Competition/Anti-trust)
1 Arnold & Porter
2 Cleary, Gottlieb, Steen & Hamilton
Jones, Day, Reavis & Pogue
3 Covington & Burling
Wilmer, Cutler & Pickering
4 Gibson, Dunn & Crutcher LLP
Howrey Simon Arnold & White
5 Clifford Chance LLP / Pünder / Rogers & Wells
Hogan & Hartson LLP
6 Collier Shannon Scott
Crowell & Moring LLP

Firms are listed alphabetically in each band.

Leading Individuals (Competition/Anti-trust)
1 RILL James *Howrey Simon Arnold & White*
RULE Charles (Rick) *Fried, Frank, Harris*
SIMS Joseph *Jones, Day, Reavis & Pogue*
SOHN Michael *Arnold & Porter*
2 BAER William *Arnold & Porter*
CARY George *Cleary, Gottlieb*
KOLASKY William *Wilmer, Cutler & Pickering*
LOFTIS Jim *Gibson, Dunn & Crutcher LLP*
McDAVID Janet *Hogan & Hartson LLP*
ROSEN Richard *Arnold & Porter*
SUNSHINE Steve *Shearman & Sterling*
3 GELFAND David *Cleary, Gottlieb*
LEDDY Mark *Cleary, Gottlieb*
LETZLER Kenneth *Arnold & Porter*
NEWBORN Steve *Clifford Chance Rogers & Wells*
PROGER Phillip *Jones, Day, Reavis & Pogue*
4 DENGER Michael *Gibson, Dunn & Crutcher LLP*
EGAN James *Clifford Chance Rogers & Wells*
FEINSTEIN Deborah *Arnold & Porter*
KATTAN Joseph *Gibson, Dunn & Crutcher LLP*
LAZERWITZ Michael *Cleary, Gottlieb*
MACLEOD William *Collier Shannon Scott*
PATTERSON Donna *Arnold & Porter*
SMITH Randolph *Crowell & Moring LLP*
WALD Douglas *Arnold & Porter*

Individuals are listed alphabetically in each band.

erwitz* has solid experience of anti-cartel cases, in addition to a broad merger control practice. He has advised clients on the congressional and DOJ investigations into political campaign financing. **Clients:** Smithkline Beecham; Dow Chemical; AlliedSignal; Elf Aquitaine/ Sanofi; Fred Meyer.

Jones, Day, Reavis & Pogue (10 ptrs) Part of the Government Regulation Group, the anti-trust team is a versatile one, with strengths in merger control, general counselling and litigation before the agencies. Noted cross-border expertise is boosted by strong offices in Brussels, Paris, London and Frankfurt. The firm has been active in the vitamin cartel cases for clients such as Aventis, and is renowned for its activity in the healthcare sector.

Joe Sims* is a *"tough negotiator, a keen analyst and a straight talker,"* who wields *"serious firepower"* and provided anti-trust advice to AOL on its merger with Time Warner. The experienced **Philip Proger*** *"never loses sight of the object of a deal."* Recommended for his work in the global merger market, he is *"heavily involved at all stages of the process."* Prominent in the energy sector, he advised Ultramar Diamond Shamrock on its $800 million acquisition of Tosco Corporation's Avon refinery. In the communications sector, the firm advised TV Guide on its $9.2 billion acquisition by Gemstar. **Clients:** Aventis; AOL; CBS; Ultramar Diamond Shamrock.

Covington & Burling (18 ptrs) Although its highest profile lies in Washington, the firm also offers EU competition advice from offices in Brussels and London. The firm recruits heavily from government agencies, and is acclaimed for its regulatory work, advising clients from industries such as telecoms, energy, sports and healthcare.

Much of the firm's anti-trust reputation was felt to lie with Rick Rule and his recent move to Fried, Frank, Harris, Shriver & Jacobson is a major blow to an operation that now lacks his *"superstar"* profile. That said, as a traditional fixture on the DC scene, this seasoned team is anticipated to weather the storm. The firm was also involved in the government investigation of alleged price-fixing among Ivy League colleges and universities, and represented US Airways over the EU's review of the proposed alliance of American Airlines and British Airways. **Clients:** Benetton; CBS Affiliates; Exxon; MCI WorldCom; Microsoft; National Football League; Washington Post.

Wilmer, Cutler & Pickering (12 ptrs) A renowned internationally oriented team, packed with *"bright, cutting-edge lawyers,"* and closely associated with high-profile agency-backed investigations. The firm's respected Brussels office lends weight to a sound cross-border merger control offering. Especially acclaimed expertise in the telecoms market was highlighted to *Chambers'* researchers in advice to Deutsche Telekom on obtaining clearance for the acquisition of VoiceStream and Powertel.

Bill Kolasky* has a *"smart deal sense."* He advised Bestfoods on securing anti-trust compliance for its $60 billion merger with Unilever. Contentious work has included acting on the recent credit card cases and advising a broker-dealer in connection with the DOJ and SEC investigations into the manipulation of the NASDAQ securities market. The firm acted as lead counsel to credit card issuing national banks, including Citibank, First Chicago and Bank One, in defence of class action suits challenging fee practices. **Clients:** BAe Systems; Deutsche Telekom; Bestfoods.

Gibson Dunn & Crutcher (40 attorneys nationwide) Seen to have recruited successfully and attained *"critical mass,"* this west coast operation is now considered to have a *"classic"* regulatory DC practice. Growing offices in London and Paris support an increasingly cross-border workload. The team is primarily recommended by clients and competitors for its influence in the technology market, and has successfully defended both Hewlett-Packard and Intel against monopoly charges.

Having *"made a big splash"* with his move from Collier Shannon Scott, **Jim Loftis*** is *"an excellent lawyer"* who has *"given this firm a face."* *"Senior player"* **Mike Denger*** is recommended as a specialist in class action defences, while his practice also includes advice on trade regulation and false advertising law. **Joe Kattan*** offers *"excellent counsel."* With a strong background in IP, he is often cited as the key figure for high-tech domestic and foreign clients.

On the transactional front, the firm has advised Northrop-Grumman on a DOJ Section 7 lawsuit, challenging its proposed merger with Lockheed Martin. The team also acted for American Airlines on a pending monopoly case, which includes predatory pricing issues. **Clients:** AKZO Nobel; American Airlines; Hewlett-Packard; Union Carbide; Intel.

Howrey, Simon, Arnold & White (120 attoneys focus) *"Going great guns now,"* the firm's revival in fortunes owes much to its *"clear focus"* and *"substantial depth."* Thought to be *"more oriented towards litigation,"* the team benefits from a thriving IP practice, and stands out for its defence of class action suits. The firm advised both Nestlé and Heinz in defence of class action suits alleging horizontal price-fixing in the baby food market.

Last year's merger with Arnold White & Durkee is considered to have cemented the firm's reputation in the technology market. The firm represented GTE Corp before the DOJ, FTC and the European Commission in connection with the proposed merger between MCI and Worldcom. Recently recruited from Collier Shannon Scott, **Jim Rill*** is *"a dean of the anti-trust bar"*

*See leaders' profiles on pages 848-903

who *"carries his reputation to the agencies." "Always ahead of the game,"* he is a prime mover behind the firm's global plans, including an international competition practice in Brussels. The firm advised both Exxon and Mobil over FTC investigations into their proposed merger. **Clients:** Amoco; Exxon; Mobil; GTE Corp; Nestlé; Heinz.

Clifford Chance Rogers & Wells (30 attorneys nationwide) Seen to benefit from its active, high-profile New York office, the Washington team plays a greater role at the FTC, and is considered as a respected stand-alone practice. *"Capable and astute"* **Steve Newborn*** plays a *"principal part in the DC market."* Occasionally viewed as *"abrasive,"* he is a skilled litigator with *"a good grasp of the market."* **Jim Egan*** is a *"fantastic trial lawyer,"* recommended for his involvement in the brand name vitamin cases. He is primarily associated with his work in the healthcare anti-trust market. The firm has extensive experience in price-fixing, false advertising and facilitating practices. Acting on an international scale, it is recommended by rivals for EU and international anti-trust issues. **Clients:** Major domestic and foreign corporates.

Hogan & Hartson LLP (25 attorneys) Star practitioner **Jan McDavid*** receives widespread commendation for her *"analytical and tactical skills,"* which, combined with a *"great intellect"* have raised the prominence of this strong regulatory team. She acted as lead counsel to Mobil on its merger with Exxon. A recent round of recruitment from German firm Oppenhoff & Rädler has reinforced the firm's substantial European presence and cross-border merger control capability. The firm acted for an international telco in obtaining clearance for its global joint venture with a US communications company and investments in Japan. **Clients:** Mobil.

Collier Shannon Scott (7 ptrs, 16 asscs) The loss of star players Jim Rill and Jim Loftis has been seen as *"a major blow"* to this long-established practice. However, anti-trust is the *"engine"* that drives the firm, and it continues to be recommended as a *"strong counselling shop."* The firm has strengths in horizontal and vertical restraints, advertising and defence of FTC disputes, and advises, inter alia, retail, petroleum and high-tech clients.

Bill MacLeod* is a *"fine, capable lawyer,"* who acted for General Mills on its $10.5 billion acquisition of Pillsbury, and represented the State of Alaska in connection with the BP Amoco acquisition of Arco. The team also advised RJ Reynolds on challenges to its Joe Camel advertisements. **Clients:** General Mills; General Motors; RJ Reynolds Tobacco; Procter & Gamble.

Crowell & Moring LLP (12 ptrs, 15 asscs) *"An effective team"* which has nevertheless suffered from the departure of Don Flexner to Boies, Schiller & Flexner. Maintaining its *"appetite for a large volume of work,"* the firm has represented major domestic and international corporates to obtain merger clearance from the DOJ. The team has advised pharmaceutical companies on class actions suits claiming price discrimination, and has also been involved in a wide range of criminal anti-trust cases and grand jury investigations, including bid-rigging and market allocation.

The group's most prominent anti-trust specialist, **Randy Smith***, is held in *"the highest regard"* by the market. Respected for its work in the high-tech market, the firm recently defended AOL in an anti-trust action brought by News Corporation, (Kesmai v AOL) which alleged use of a monopoly to dominate the games market. **Clients:** Fortune 500 companies, including AOL.

Other Notable Practitioner *"A leading name"* in Washington, **Steve Sunshine*** of Shearman & Sterling advised SmithKline Beecham on its merger with Glaxo Wellcome, and has acted on criminal anti-trust litigations in the pharmaceuticals industry. The DC office of Fried, Frank, Harris, Shiver & Jacobson has scored a major coup in securing **Rick Rule*** (formerly Covington & Burling) to lead the practice. Regarded as *"one of the smartest lawyers around,"* he is said to be *"conservative, but a major client getter."* He advised Microsoft in connection with DOJ investigations.

Corporate/M&A: Chicago

USA: CHICAGO
Leading Firms (Corporate/M&A)

Band	Firm
1	Kirkland & Ellis
	Mayer, Brown & Platt
	Sidley & Austin
2	Skadden, Arps, Slate, Meagher & Flom LLP
3	Winston & Strawn
4	Katten Muchin Zavis
	McDermott, Will & Emery
5	Schiff Hardin & Waite
	Sonnenschein Nath & Rosenthal
6	Latham & Watkins

Firms are listed alphabetically in each band.

Leading Individuals (Corporate/M&A)

Band	Individual
★	**COLE Thomas** *Sidley & Austin*
1	**HELMAN Bob** *Mayer, Brown & Platt*
	LEVIN Jack *Kirkland & Ellis*
	LOWINGER Frederick *Sidley & Austin*
	MULANEY Charles *Skadden, Arps*
	WALL Robert *Winston & Strawn*
	WANDER Herb *Katten Muchin Zavis*
2	**DAVIS Scott** *Mayer, Brown & Platt*
	EMERSON Carter *Kirkland & Ellis*
	EVANICH Kevin *Kirkland & Ellis*
	KIRSCH Bill *Kirkland & Ellis*
	KUNKEL William *Skadden, Arps*
	LUBIN Don *Sonnenschein*
	MEADOWS Stanley *McDermott, Will & Emery*
	THOMAS Frederick (Fritz) *Mayer, Brown & Platt*
	TOTH Bruce *Winston & Strawn*
3	**GOODMAN Stuart** *Schiff Hardin & Waite*
	HAMMES Jeffrey *Kirkland & Ellis*
	OSBORNE Robert *Kirkland & Ellis*
	QASIM Imad *Sidley & Austin*
	SHEPRO Rick *Mayer, Brown & Platt*
4	**CHOI Paul** *Sidley & Austin*
	CULLEN Gary *Skadden, Arps*
	FRIEDLI Helen *McDermott, Will & Emery*
	FROY Michael *Sonnenschein*
	GERSTEIN Mark *Latham & Watkins*
	HAHN Arthur *Katten Muchin Zavis*

Up-and-coming individuals

Individual
AIZENSTEIN Neal *Sonnenschein*
LITWIN Stuart *Mayer, Brown & Platt*

Individuals are listed alphabetically in each band.

Kirkland & Ellis (51 ptrs, 106 asscs) *"Cut from a different cloth,"* the firm differs from most corporate Chicago firms in its dominant focus on private equity advice. The group has long been the top name in town for highly leveraged acquisitions and major debt financings. Although overshadowed by the private equity practice, the firm's capacity for big-ticket M&A work on behalf of publicly quoted companies is also beyond dispute.

Interviewees frequently describe the in-house style as *"combative and uncompromising."* The team has acquired the reputation of being *"ruthless on transactions,"* and it has been said that *"there's more blood on the floor when you negotiate with them."*

The firm's status is felt to owe much to the pioneering efforts of the *"father of the practice"* **Jack Levin***, reckoned to be the *"undisputed king of venture capital lawyers."* With a background in tax and corporate work, many consider him a *"renaissance man of corporate transactions."* According to some, he *"invented private equity practice,"* and has built up a core of loyal public company and private equity house clients, including Willis Stein & Partners. While the lecture circuit has increasingly removed him from day to day transactions, he is still considered to *"practise from a high altitude,"* disseminating his *"vast experience"* throughout the firm.

The group has experienced a growth in its fund formation practice, raising as many as 20 funds over the last year for investment banks and equity houses. *"Tough but fair"* **Kevin Evanich*** has been particularly active in this field, advising GTCR on the creation of a $2 billion fund. As primary counsel to Code, Hennessy & Simmons, he has advised on negotiations with sellers, banks and buyers, and is recommended for his *"intuition about what type of approach works best in the negotiating room."*

"Levin's right hand man," **Bill Kirsch*** has earned a considerable reputation both for his *"booming practice,"* representing prestigious national and international private equity funds, and his *"take no prisoners"* attitude. A *"tireless worker,"* he is the firm's relationship partner for Madison Dearborn Partners, whom he advised on the formation of its $4 billion fund and $3 billion acquisition of Packaging Corporation of America from Tenneco Packaging.

The *"incisive"* **Jeffrey Hammes*** is sometimes described as *"the other bookend to Kirsch."* Known for *"figuring out a way to create value for the client,"* he is applauded for his *"deep understanding of business principles."* He represented Bain Capital on its acquisition of ChipPac from Hyundai Electronics Industries, following its $550 million recapitalisation.

Bob Osborne*, *"a first-rate securities lawyer,"* is renowned for his work on behalf of General Motors, whom he has represented in corporate deals for more than a decade, most recently in a $9 billion global exchange offer.

Carter Emerson's* practice is a mix of private equity and public company corporate work, which includes advising on SEC compliance and working with venture capital groups on high-tech financing. Said to be *"an exception to the firm's aggressive norm,"* he is considered to be a *"measured diplomat, always willing to listen."* He advised Ohio utility company DPL on the $425 million sale of its gas business. **Clients:** General Motors; DPL; Exide Corporation; Leo Burnett Company; Madison Dearborn Partners; CIVC Partners; First Chicago Venture Corporation; ABN Amro; Willis Stein & Partners; GTCR Golder Rauner; Thoma Cressey Equity Partners; Code, Hennessy & Simmons; River Road Partners; William Blair & Company.

Mayer, Brown & Platt (25 ptrs, 50 asscs) Recognised as a Chicago *"institution,"* the firm is frequently compared to Sidley & Austin for its historical stranglehold on the Chicago market and large blue-chip client base. Although sometimes accused of being *"excessively conservative,"* the group is consistently recommended for its *"blend of world-class technical skills and user friendly attitude."*

The firm's reputation is greatest for corporate finance, but it nevertheless undertakes an impressive array of M&A transactions for publicly owned companies. Restructurings, public offerings and private placements of security round out the workload.

An *"icon"* in corporate Chicago circles, **Bob Helman*** occupies the *"senior statesman"* role within the group, dispensing knowledge gleaned from years of representing clients such as the Northern Trust Corporation. While no longer in the front line for deals, *"Helman's advice is still the best that money can buy." "Conscientious"* **Scott Davis***, praised for *"listening to his clients,"* is emerging as a leading name for big-ticket public company M&A. He represented Dow Chemical on its merger negotiations with Union Carbide, a deal with an estimated value of $11.6 billion.

Fritz Thomas* spans the divide between Mayer Brown & Platt's corporate division and its 25 lawyer IT group. In addition to his traditional joint ventures and M&A practice, he oversees

*See leaders' profiles on pages 848-903

many of the firm's new economy deals, advising clients from the telecoms, IT and e-commerce industries. He represented W.W. Grainger on its acquisition of a minority stake in Works.

Rick Shepro* specialises in M&A in the insurance and reinsurance market, advising CNA Financial Corporation on its $2.8 billion sale of its personal insurance business to Allstate. Recommended as an up and coming practitioner, **Stuart Litwin*** is seen to greatest effect on corporate restructurings. **Clients:** ACE (insurance); Abbott Laboratories; GATX; Dow Chemical; Cargill; Sears Roebuck; Brunswick Corp; Monsanto; Burlington Northern Santa Fe; Whirlpool; Case Corporation; GEC; BICC; Nicor; WW Grainger; Tenneco Automotive; Ryerson Tull Steel Products; US Can; Nestlé; Bank of America; Credit Suisse First Boston; Goldman Sachs; Salomon Smith Barney.

Sidley & Austin (15pts, 25 asscs) Perceived to have a slight edge in terms of transactional volume over its nearest competitors, the firm advises a similarly imposing selection of Fortune 500 clients. Seen to be making a play for new economy work, the group is increasing its presence in both private equity and high-tech circles, acting for clients such as First Data and incubator fund Constellation. Big-ticket cross-border transactions have included NTT Communications acquisition of Verio for $5.5 billion.

Commended for its singleness of purpose, the group occasionally falls prey to charges of *"an absence of creativity"* in negotiations. However, the team is acknowledged for its depth of quality: *"They're full of bright young people, dedicated to achieving goals."*

"*Polished*" **Tom Cole*** is said to have *"360 degree vision,"* and retains his solo position at the head of the rankings. A *"national legend,"* his prominence is recognised well beyond the confines of Chicago. In spite of his position as chairman of the firm, he is transactionally active, representing the Harris family, controlling shareholders of Pittway Corporation, in Honeywell's $2.2 billion acquisition of Pittway.

Corporate head **Fred Lowinger*** is an accomplished exponent of defences to hostile takeovers. An *"articulate and insightful attorney,"* he is considered by peers and clients to have *"an IQ in 15 digits."* He served as principal advisor to major VoiceStream shareholder TDS on the $50.7 billion merger between VoiceStream and Deutsche Telekom. His protegé is **Paul Choi***, said to represent the *"next generation of Sidley lawyers,"* who exercises *"superb judgement"* in negotiations. Choi represented KPMG on its $3.7 billion IPO.

"Personable" **Imad Qasim*** spearheads the e-commerce M&A practice, and is particularly active in the development of B2B exchanges. Commended for *"not over-lawyering,"* he *"keeps on an even keel"* throughout negotiations, and attracts praise for his ability to *"relate both to clients and other parties in transactions."* He represented Tellabs on its $300 million acquisition of SALIX Technologies. **Clients:** AT&T; Starwood Hotels & Resorts; RR Donnelly; Kimberley Clark; Mariner Post-Acute Network; Aon Corporation; Apollo Advisors; General Electric; NTT; General Mills; Pilsbury; First Data; Tellabs; JP Morgan; Wasserstein Perella; Merrill Lynch.

Skadden, Arps, Slate, Meagher & Flom LLP (6 ptrs, 22 asscs) Although a comparatively small office, the Chicago branch of the New York M&A giant is felt to benefit considerably from the firm's high-powered brand name. The firm has already captured a substantial share of the local market, representing a predominantly public company client base in high-end transactions. A notable track record on hostile bids has seen the group represent both the target and the potential acquirer. A vast international network brings in a number of cross-border deals such as representation of Wesley Jessen Vision Care in its sale to Novartis (begun as hostile tender), while the team also advises on corporate restructurings, spin-offs and M&A deals involving financially troubled companies.

The tremendous success of the Chicago office is often ascribed to the presence of the *"unflappable"* **Charles Mulaney***. He represented Sara Lee in connection with the IPO of 20% of Coach. A lawyer who can see *"the big picture,"* Mulaney* "*ably marshals the firm's resources*" and was commended for his tutelage of the firm's younger lawyers. Under his guidance, rising players such as **Gary Cullen*** have flourished. Cullen has recently been active in telecoms transactions and acted on behalf of Matanuska Telephone Association in its sale to Alaska Communications Systems.

The *"pragmatic"* **Bill Kunkel*** received endorsement from clients and peers alike. Known for working *"23 hours a day,"* he has extensive experience of negotiated and contested takeovers, stock and asset acquisitions and divestitures and venture capital transactions. His *"thoughtful manner"* and *"good commercial sense"* render him a *"consummate professional"* and place him in demand for big-ticket transactions. Kunkel recently represented US Airways in its securities offerings. **Clients:** Abbott Laboratories; US Airways; Wesley Jessen VisionCare; Cash Station; Safeguard International; Agritope; Prudential; Churchill Downs; Ivex Packaging Corporation; Koch Industries; SBC Corporation; Sears Roebuck & Co.

Winston & Strawn (20 ptrs, 40 asscs) Already recognised for a heavy-hitting litigation practice, the firm is felt to be *"building up a good practice"* towards the top end of the public company M&A market. Its chief hindrance is the persistent market perception that, despite offices in New York and Washington, the firm's influence does not extend beyond its Chicago parish. Nevertheless, the group does act for such multi-national giants as Lear Corporation and Monsanto Company.

A *"user friendly team"* has been noted for the rapid growth of its high-tech clientele, having acted as advisors for start-ups from incorporation through to public offering and beyond. The group advised on the merger of two public internet companies, SPR and Leapnet a $160 million transaction.

However, the firm is best known for its strong ties to both local and national banks. The team draws on corporate finance, banking and bankruptcy expertise to advise on work-outs and complex financial restructurings.

"*Easygoing, straight-shooting*" **Bob Wall*** is described as *"the leading lawyer for the investment banking community."* Having represented targets, bidders, stock-holders and investment banks in hostile takeovers, he currently divides his time between M&A, financings, and venture capital advice. His *"keen understanding of what lies behind a deal"* is felt to serve him well in the boardroom. He recently represented rail, truck and auto component manufacturer Amsted Industries in connection with its $790 million acquisition of Varlen Corporation.

Bruce Toth* maintains close associations with financial institutions such as Deutsche Bank and DLJ, and represented Keebler Foods on its $250 million acquisition of Austin Quality Foods. Clients appreciate his *"low-key style"* and willingness to give *"practical business advice that takes into account more than just the legal aspects of a transaction."*

Other transactional highlights for the firm include advising SFX Entertainment on a $3.4 billion acquisition by Clear Channel Communications through a merger in which Clear Channel stock was issued to SFX shareholders. **Clients:** Keebler Foods; Heller Financial; Amsted Industries; SFX Entertainment; Corporate Brand Foods America; uBid; Huntsman Packaging Corp; DLJ; Deutsche Bank; Lear Corporation; Monsanto.

Katten Muchin Zavis (13 ptrs, 25 asscs) The firm is known throughout Chicago for handling a volume of *"middle-market"* transactions for a mix of public and privately owned companies. Most deals range from $10 million to $100 million, although the firm occasionally undertakes big-ticket transactions, usually on behalf of large private companies. Many of the firm's clients are companies that began as small family ventures over 60 years ago and have since expanded and either gone public or sold to other private investors.

A *"service-oriented"* group is said to provide *"tremendous value"* to its large, *"entrepreneurial"* client base. Noted for its *"aggressive growth,"* the firm has recently strengthened its corporate/M&A department through the acquisition of two partners from Jenner & Block.

Of late, the team has been particularly active on IT matters, representing a number of internet and software companies on mergers, sales, and consolidation proceedings. The team represented Whittman-Hart on its merger with USWeb Corporation, valued in excess of $1 billion.

"Scholarly" **Herb Wander*** is highly esteemed for exercising *"wonderful judgement"* in securities and M&A transactions. His tax law expertise makes him an asset in any negotiation, as does his ability to remain *"calm in the midst of everything."* He advised Commercial Intertech on its 2000 merger with Parker-Hannifin.

Arthur Hahn's* practice is largely focused on transactions involving technology companies and financial institutions. As the representative for divine interVentures since its inception, he has acted on the company's acquisition of the e-business software company mindwrap, and its joint venture with the Chicago branch of UBS to form Parlano. **Clients:** Whittman-Hart; Commercial Intertech Corp; Duff & Phelps Credit Rating Co; Centerprise Advisors; Madison Capital Partners; Pfingsten Partners; NovaMed Eyecare; divine interVentures; National Veterinary Associates.

McDermott, Will & Emery (20 ptrs, 20 asscs) Although much better known for its highly regarded tax and real estate departments, the firm has a comprehensive corporate team, particularly renowned for its expertise in healthcare mergers. Not seen to be a presence on premium value public company work, the group acts chiefly on medium-ticket deals, with the bulk of its transactions between $10 million and $400 million. The rapid development of the firm's London office has resulted in increased cross-border success on behalf of a broad base of entrepreneurial and international clients. Active in telecommunications, insurance and the food industry, the firm also represented Consolidated Papers on its $4.8 billion sale to Stora Enso, a Finnish forest products company.

"Corporate transactional generalist" **Stanley Meadows*** handles a range of M&A, joint ventures, public and private offerings of securities and corporate restructurings. Although he has recently stepped down from his position as chairman of the firm's corporate department, he is still visible as a *"consummate deal-maker,"* and is envied for his *"excellent corporate contacts."* He represented the seller of interests in Enertel to UK company Energis for approximately $625 million.

"Bright young lawyer" **Helen Friedli*** enters our tables as a market leader. She acts for a number of buyout fund clients, and led the team acting for Westell Technologies on its $240 million acquisition by Teltrend. **Clients:** Consolidated Paper; Opti-Systems; SightPath; MacNeal Health Services Corporation; Heico Companies; MCK Communications; Motorola; JW Childs Equity Partners; ABN Amro; Donaldson Lufkin & Jenrette.

Schiff Hardin & Waite (20 ptrs, 20 asscs) Despite its history as Chicago's oldest major law firm, the corporate group is not seen as frequently on larger M&A deals as its leading rivals. Nevertheless its ties with such clients as the highly acquisitive Newell (now Newell Rubbermaid), have ensured that the group remains in the public eye. The firm acted for Newell Rubbermaid on its acquisition of the stationery business of The Gillette Company. Newell's principal outside counsel for more than 25 years has been department head **Stuart Goodman***. A *"respected general corporate and securities lawyer,"* he maintains a reputation for astuteness in combating poison pill takeover defences.

In other matters, the firm represented NiSource on its $8.5 billion acquisition of Columbia Energy Group, and advised on Northern Trust's recent acquisitions of Ulster Bank Investment Services and Carl Domino Associates. **Clients:** NiSource; Newell Rubbermaid; ABC-NACO; Anixter; Laidlaw; Antec Corporation; AAR Corp; Northwestern Corporation; Northern Trust Corporation; Marquette Savings Bank; OBS Financial Corp; Leland National Bancorp.

Sonnenschein Nath & Rosenthal (15-20 lawyers) The firm's corporate department rates highly for the *"quality and knowledge"* of its lawyers, and maintains its profile by dint of long-standing relationships with valuable institutional clients such as McDonalds and Molex. With offices in San Francisco, New York, and Los Angeles, the firm has successfully extended its influence beyond Chicago, and is now considered by some to be *"as much of a New York firm as a Chicago one."*

The group has been active on a number of business to business internet deals, and receives instructions from investment banks William Blair and Lazards on technology transactions. Particularly recommended for its corporate governance expertise, the team advised PriceWaterhouse Coopers in setting up a $1.1 billion outsourcing arrangement in which PwC assumed the financial reporting, accounts-payable and accounting responsibilities for BP Amoco's US chemical, oil exploration and production units.

"Superb senior practitioner" **Don Lubin*** is reported to be *"one of the most respected guys in town."* Having served for 35 years on the McDonalds board of directors, he has acquired a *"good bit of experience in public M&A, private equity and venture capital"* in both the US and abroad. *"No longer in the trenches as much,"* he is seen to have passed the torch to younger partners such as the *"personable"* **Mike Froy***. Principal counsel to electrical and fibre-optic manufacturers Molex, he oversaw the company's acquisition of Cardell Corporation and investment in Lumenon Lightwave Technologies. Additionally, he represented Juno Lighting's $400 million leveraged recapitalisation merger with private equity investor Freemont Partners.

Another *"Lubin protegé,"* the *"hard-working"* **Neal Aizenstein*** was recommended as one of the *"young stars"* of the group. **Clients:** McDonalds; Boeing; Prudential Insurance; All State Insurance; Monsanto; Emerson Electric; General Electric; Sara Lee Corporations; Juno Lighting; Molex; CitiCorp; Bank One; Morgan Stanley Dean Witter.

Latham & Watkins (7 ptrs, 15 asscs) Although clearly not as visible in the market as the premier Chicago-based firms, the Chicago office of this national organisation boasts a number of high-end transactions for an impressive base of Midwest and national clients. The firm continues to advise long-standing client Sears, Roebuck and Co, most recently on its $3.5 billion disposition of Homart Development Co, acquisition of Orchard Supply Hardware, and disposals of HomeLife and Prodigy businesses.

The team has a greater reputation for corporate finance, but is now seen to be a viable M&A force, particularly in the new economy area, through its work for a host of venture funds and technology companies such as Click Commerce and William Blair New World Ventures.

Mark Gerstein* is considered an *"excellent lawyer"* with specific expertise in corporate governance. Credited with *"building the Chicago office,"* he frequently represents special committees of boards of directors, bidders and financial advisors on take-private transactions. He advised on the $5.2 billion merger of equals between Health Care and Retirement Corporation and Manor Care. **Clients:** Motorola; Navistar International; Sears Roebuck and Co; IDEX Corporation; Hyatt Corporation; Rand McNally & Company; Libbey ; Deloitte & Touche.

*See leaders' profiles on pages 848-903

Corporate/M&A: East Coast (excluding New York)

USA: EAST COAST (excluding New York) Leading Firms (Corporate/M&A)	
1	Arnold & Porter
	Dechert
	Greenberg Traurig
	Hale and Dorr
	Hogan & Hartson LLP
	Hunton & Williams
	King & Spalding
	Kirkpatrick & Lockhart LLP
	Morgan, Lewis & Bockius LLP
	Piper Marbury Rudnick & Wolfe LLP
	Ropes & Gray
	Steel Hector & Davis

Firms are listed alphabetically in each band.

Arnold & Porter (95 lawyers) The firm's Washington office handles corporate and securities transactions, and advises issuers, underwriters, acquirers and targets. The firm's clients range from multi-national corporations to regional companies, and also includes start-ups and entrepreneurs.

Although Washington DC is widely seen to be *"more of a regulatory and litigation market"* than a corporate centre, this firm is widely seen to be *"one of the old guard"* in DC and has *"built up a highly respectable corporate client base over the years."* Competitors are also impressed by the firm's *"sheer size"* and the *"broad base of high quality work."*

The firm represented Quebecor World, a Canadian corporation, in connection with its acquisition of World Color Press, a Deleware corporation, for a total value of approximately $2.7 billion, which created the largest commercial printer in the world. Also advised Bull, a French computer company, in the acquisition by Diebold of the worldwide financial self-service terminals business of Bull and Getronics for approximately $166 million, and served as counsel to US Investigation Services in the ground-breaking privatisation of the US Government's Office of Personnel Management. **Clients:** Avis; DynCorp; PNC Bank Corp; Republic Engineered Steels; Software AG Systems.

Dechert (80 lawyers) Involved in transactions in a broad spectrum of industries, including manufacturing, retail, life sciences and IT, the firm represents buyers (both strategic and financial), sellers and underwriters on acquisitions, takeover defences for publicly-held companies and troubled restructurings. Market comment characterises the firm as *"always impressive"* for general corporate work, with *"some sensational lawyers"* and particular strength in the *"M&A and securities areas."* The firm's merger with London firm Titmuss Sainer Dechert is considered to give it an important European base to expand its cross-border offering.

The Philadelphia office represented Comcast Corporation on its $840 million stock tender offer for shares of Jones Intercable, a publicly traded cable company based in Colorado. Also advised Dyckerhoff, one of Europe's largest producers of cement, concrete, building materials, and finishing products, on its $1.2 billion acquisition of Lone Star Industries. **Clients:** Bruckmann; Citicorp Venture Capital; Comcast Corporation; Internet Capital Group; Morgens; Pfizer; Rosser; Sherrill & Co.

Greenberg Traurig (10 ptrs, 18 asscs) The firm undertakes a wide range of corporate work, including general corporate and securities work, mergers and acquisitions and venture capital work. It is particularly active in relation to public offerings, and currently provides securities representation to more than 70 public companies. Securities experience also extends to private placements, venture capital investments and traditional and leveraged acquisitions. Other areas of expertise include the representation of start-up and other businesses in the negotiation and structuring of joint ventures and limited partnerships.

Competitors are of the opinion that the firm is a *"significant and well-established presence in Miami."* However, its profile is increasing both nationally and abroad, and the firm was labelled by one interviewee, *"Florida's leading firm."* Represented Terra Networks, the internet business of Spain's Telefonica (telephone company) in its agreement to acquire Lycos, an internet portal, for $5.7 billion. Also represented Rexall Sundown, (a developer of vitamins and consumer health products) in relation to its $1.8 billion acquisition by Royal Numico, the world's biggest vitamin maker. In addition acted for issuers on a number of IPOs, including the $87.9 million offering of Concord Camera Group, the $112 million offering of H Power Corp (a leading fuel cell development company) and the $125 million offering of Silverline Technologies. **Clients:** Investment banking firms; public companies; start-ups.

Hale and Dorr (62 ptrs, 82 asscs) Outstanding private equity firm, which also advises on IPOs and debt and equity transactions for a clientele in which new economy clients are prominent. It currently serves as primary outside corporate counsel to more than 75 public companies, and is also frequently retained by established companies for guidance through IPOs and acquisitions.

Said to be *"top of the heap in Boston,"* the firm was recommended to researchers for its *"mixture of old economy and new economy clients,"* and its sheer volume of transaction.

The firm advised ArrowPoint Communications on its acquisition by Cisco Systems for approximately $5.7 billion. Further transactions include acting for Spyglass on its merger agreement with OpenTV Corp, a transaction valued at approximately $2.5 billion. **Clients:** Analog Devices; Millennium Pharmaceuticals; Open Market; Staples; Thermo Electron Corporation.

Hogan & Hartson (100 ptrs, 150 asscs) Advising across the spectrum of corporate matters, the firm has a particularly high profile on cross-border M&A deals. Other work includes public and private offerings of equity and debt securities, privatisations, leveraged buy-outs, private equity and venture capital work. It represents a broad range of clients, including leading US and foreign companies, private investors, financial institutions and government entities. Specific areas of expertise include hi-tech, telecommunications and media.

The firm represented Havas Advertising Company on its $2.1 billion acquisition of Snyder Communications, as well as Ciena Corporation in its $500 million acquisition of Omnia Communications. In addition, the firm has represented Telebank Financial Corporation on its $1.8 billion merger with E*Trade, an online securities trading and brokerage firm. **Clients:** Deutsche Bank Alex • Brown; Goldman Sachs; Lehmann Brothers; Marriott; Merrill Lynch; NewsCorp.

Hunton & Williams (70 lawyers) The firm's mergers and acquisitions group regularly acts on domestic and international transactions, with a particular emphasis on energy, technology, financial services and consumer products. In Virginia, the firm has played a leading role in the development of corporation law, and in the creation and use of limited liability companies. The firm is respected for its real estate practice, and is said by clients to provide *"excellent advice for Virginia-based companies."* Although a huge number of new firms have set up in Virginia, *"the Silicon Valley of the Mid-Atlantic coast,"* Hunton & Williams *"easily remains pre-eminent in the region."* A respected European network of offices assists the firm's cross-border transactional capacity.

Recent transactions include acting for Philip Morris on its successful acquisition of Nabisco for approximately $19 billion, and Carolina Power & Light on its acquisition of Florida Progress. Also advised Spain's Terra Networks on its $12.5 billion acquisition, via statutory share exchange, of a leading internet portal. **Clients:** Carolina Power & Light; Chesapeake Corporation; Citibank; Philip Morris.

King & Spalding (20 ptrs, 30 asscs) Georgia-based, the firm has offices across the nation, and has a respected big-ticket transactional capacity. The client base encompasses a number of industries, including healthcare, technology, telecommunications, energy, banking, insurance and pharmaceuticals.

"Clearly the premier firm in Atlanta," the group is renowned for the breadth of its workload. Over the past twelve months, the firm has represented Georgia-Pacific Corporation on its $4.1 billion spin-off and sale of its Timber Group to Plum Creek Timber Company. Also advised Sprint Corporation on the $4 billion sale of its interest in the Global One joint venture to France Telecom.

Further transactions include advising Lockheed Martin Corporation on the $510 million sale of its Control Systems business to BAE Systems North America. **Clients:** The Coca-Cola Company; General Electric Company; Georgia-Pacific Corporation; The Home Depot; Sprint Corporation; United Parcel Service.

Kirkpatrick & Lockhart LLP (210 lawyers) Principally known for domestic M&A, the firm also advises on corporate finance and securities for clients ranging from emerging technology enterprises to Fortune 50 manufacturers. It also acts as issuers' or underwriters' counsel in public and private offerings of equity, debt and hybrid securities. Competitors were moved to note that *"none of the other firms in Pittsburgh has a regional reputation to compare with them."* Recent transactions have included the acquisition of a controlling interest in the largest US airline, and the acquisition of one of the nation's largest metropolitan daily newspapers. **Clients:** Allegheny Technologies; Spenser Trask Securities; United Technologies Corporation; Vertex Pharmaceuticals.

Morgan, Lewis & Bockius LLP (34 ptrs, 94 asscs) The Philadelphia office of this firm is the network's oldest, and acts for a sizeable chunk of the city's established business community. These clients range in size from large publicly-held corporations to family-owned enterprises, and include manufacturing and mercantile companies, banks and hi-tech companies. A substantial presence in Philadelphia is now augmented by *"a growing reputation outside the region"* for corporate work. Recent significant transactions have included representing Verizon Communications (formerly Bell Atlantic) in negotiating its $70 billion strategic alliance agreement with Vodafone Airtouch, with the resulting new company now the largest wireless business in the country. The firm also represented Union Pacific Resources, a Texas-based oil and gas exploration and production company, in its $10 billion merger with Anadarko Petroleum Corporation. A furher matter was representing half.com, an online auctioneer of used merchandise, in its $400 million sale to eBay. **Clients:** Bell Atlantic Corporation; Citicorp Venture Capital; Consolidated Natural Gas Company; IKON Office Solutions, Union Pacific Resources Group.

Piper Marbury Rudnick & Wolfe LLP (14 ptrs, 21 asscs) Said to produce *"good work across the board,"* the firm is regarded as *"streets ahead of the rest of Baltimore."* It undertakes a variety of corporate work, including M&A and securities offerings, representing emerging companies, venture capital firms and securities firms. Also has a long-standing relationship with Deutsche Bank Alex. Brown, whom it has advised as underwriters' counsel on a number of equity and debt transactions. The firm advised T Rowe Price Associates in connection with its $780 million buyout of the interest of its partner, Robert Fleming Holdings, in an international joint venture. The firm also acted for Omnipoint in connection with its $4.6 billion acquisition by Voicestream Wireless Corporation, and Sylvan Learning Systems, in connection with the $775 million sale of its computer based testing business to Thomson Corporation. **Clients:** Credit Suisse First Boston; Deutsche Bank Alex • Brown; Marriott International; McCormick & Company; Net2000 Communications; The Ryland Group.

Ropes & Gray Renowned for private equity work, the firm also advises on a range of other corporate matters including complex national and international transactions. The firm's corporate practice includes subgroups such as investment companies and advisors, banking and finance, leveraged buyouts, venture capital and securities. Acted as counsel to numerous companies on their initial and subsequent public offerings, and as underwriter's counsel in connection with public offerings of securities. Along with Hale and Dorr, the firm is said by competitors to have *"distinguished itself above all other firms in Boston."* **Clients:** Public and privately held companies.

Steel Hector & Davis (60 lawyers) The firm's corporate, securities and finance practice advises clients in the United States, Latin America and the Caribbean on complex corporate matters that arise both in their own countries and abroad. It represents large and capital-intensive corporations in public and private securities offerings, commercial loan financings, mergers and acquisitions, corporate tax issues and a broad range of general corporate matters. The firm's clients include large public and private companies based in Florida and elsewhere and a broad range of emerging businesses, as well as banks and financial and venture capital firms who invest in developing companies. It is considered to have particular expertise in advising clients on takeovers, proxy contests and defensive measures, and has an increasingly cross-border element in its transactional work. The firm is primary outside counsel to Florida Power & Light Group and general counsel to a number of other public and privately held companies. Recent significant transactions include the investment in Yupi Internet Inc (the firm's client) by Sony and other investors, where the the total investment was to the value of $100 million. Another transaction was the representation of Challenge Air Cargo, a major air cargo carrier to South America, in the sale of its business to UPS. **Clients:** Collier Enterprises; Florida Power & Light Group; GE; Guardian International; Microsoft; Ryder System; US Can Corporation; The Vincam Group; Weitzer Homebuilders Incorporated.

U

*See leaders' profiles on pages 848-903

Corporate/M&A: Mid-West (excluding Chicago)

USA: MID-WEST (excluding Chicago) Leading Firms (Corporate/M&A)

Band	Firm
1	Bryan Cave
	Dorsey & Whitney LLP
	Foley & Lardner
	Jones, Day, Reavis & Pogue
	Squire, Sanders & Dempsey LLP
2	Faegre & Benson LLP
	Thompson Hine & Flory LLP

Firms are listed alphabetically in each band.

U

Bryan Cave (26 ptrs, 32 asscs) The firm is divided into client service groups covering transactions and corporate governance, corporate finance and securities. Most transactions stem from the firm's established base of public and private companies, although the practice can sometimes be seen representing investment banks and intermediaries in commercial transactions. Anheuser-Busch is a particularly active and long-standing client. Another major relationship is with Monsanto, who instructed the firm on the sale of its sweetener ingredient business (including NutraSweet) to JW Childs Equity Partners II, and its sale of Kelco Biopolymers to an investment group led by Lehman Bros/Hercules Chemical.

Strong in technology and IP, the firm has advised WorldCom on a number of transactions, including its $350 million acquisition of Australian company OzEmail, and the $1.8 billion acquisition of Skytel Communications.

Other major work includes representation of Sigma-Aldrich Corp in the $425 million sale of its B-Line System subsidiary to Cooper Industries and acting for Gabriel Communications in its merger with TriVergent Communications. **Clients:** Anheuser-Busch Companies; Emerson Electric Co; MCI WorldCom; Boeing; Marriott International; Monsanto; DaimlerChrysler; Bridge Information Systems.

Dorsey & Whitney LLP (29 ptrs, 40 asscs) This *"Wall Street style firm in the Twin Cities"* receives widespread recognition as a full service corporate firm. The firm has done well in handling a large volume of middle market M&A deals, and was regularly recommended to our researchers for its sheer volume of work. Frequently called on to handle hostile takeovers, the group acts predominantly for the buyer on acquisitions, and advised ADC Telecommunications on its $1.51 billion acquisition of PairGain Technologies and its acquisition of Altitun AB for $872 million.

The group also acted on Valspar's $762 million acquisition of Lilly Industries and represented EM.TV & Merchandising in their $680 million acquisition of The Jim Henson Company.

The firm also has a significant niche practice in American Indian law, and a dedicated Indian Law Group represents tribes in connection with business acquisitions, taxable and conventional financing of resorts and gambling developments, and the establishment of tribal corporations. **Clients:** ADC Telecommunications; e-Funds Corporation; HB Fuller Company; MGI Pharma; Rochester Medical Corporation; SUPERVALU; United Health Group; LetsBuyIt.com; StepStone ASA; FreeShop.com; Dain Rausher Corporation; Great Plains Software.

Foley & Lardner (18 ptrs, 22 asscs) Heavily involved in M&A work throughout the US, the firm *"stands out in terms of size and national reputation."* The team has a large market share of midwestern legal work, advising public and private companies of all sizes.

The group covers all aspects of corporate acquisitions, divestitures, LBOs and restructurings, and is particularly strong in acquisition related services. The real estate sector is one of particular strength, and the firm has been active on a number of shopping centre acquisitions. These include representing Regency Realty Corporation on its $185 million acquisition of Branch Properties and on its $250 million asset acquisition of Midland Development Group.

Also recommended for its work on behalf of software and e-commerce companies, the corporate department works closely with the firm's much-vaunted IP department. It represented Aliant Communications on its $1.6 billion stock merger with ALLTEC Corporation.

The firm was enthusiastically endorsed to researchers in connection with its banking and finance capabilities. Its strength in this area led to involvement on the $125 million merger between FCB Financial Corp and Anchor Bankcorp Wisconsin Inc. **Clients:** MGIC Corporation; Midwest Express Holdings; Firstar Corporation; Johnson Worldwide Associates; Alliant Energy; Oshkosh Truck; Johnson Controls; LaCrosse Footwear; Harley-Davidson; Regency Realty Corp; Snap-on Incorporated; Sykes Enterprises.

Jones, Day, Reavis & Pogue (48 lawyers) This global firm *"covers the waterfront,"* and with 25 offices worldwide, is recognised by competitors for its *"enormous spread"* and ability to co-ordinate work internationally. Large institutional clients such as Federated Department Stores are shared between a number of offices, while local office branches take on work from smaller regional clients on an exclusive basis.

The Cleveland and Chicago offices are particularly strong in the telecoms and e-commerce fields, and receive a substantial number of instructions from new technology companies. The group represented FunBrain.com on the sale of the company to Family Education Network. Other highlights include representing CTG Resources on its $575 million proposed stock-for-stock merger with Energy East Corporation, and acting for Unicom Corporation on the $31.8 billion proposed merger with PECO Energy Company to create Exelon Corporation. **Clients:** ABC Rail Products Corporation; CTS Corporation; FirstEnergy Corp; FleetPride; Consolidated Natural Gas Company; Trillium Digital Systems; Preferred Payment Systems; Salomon Smith Barney; Unicom Corporation.

Squire, Sanders & Dempsey LLP (16 ptrs, 15 asscs) An active Ohio-based group has noted strength in institutional and public finance work. The firm is best known for its work on the issue of government bonds, but also has a solid profile in M&A and securities, while a powerful global network of offices enables it to act on international transactions including acquisitions, divestitures, restructuring activities, joint ventures, spin-offs and securities issues.

The firm represented a consortium of investors led by Callahan Associates International on a multi-billion dollar joint venture with Deutsche Telekom for the purpose of owning and operating a broadband communications business in the Nordrhein-Westphalen region of Germany, a transaction led from the Cleveland office. Energy and pharmaceuticals are significant areas of expertise.

The group acted on behalf of long-standing client Essef Corporation on their merger with Pentair. **Clients:** Ferro Corporation; Essef Corporation; Eagle-Picher Industries; The Chart Group; BF Goodrich Company; Lubrizol Corporation; OM Group; A Schulman.

Faegre & Benson LLP (30 ptrs, 29 asscs) The Minneapolis office remains the hub of the firm's activity, with most of the firm's principal clients located in the Twin Cities area. Recognised by rivals for its securitisation capabilities and close relationship with US Bank National Association, the firm represents buyers, sellers, investment banks and lenders in connection with various acquisitions, public offerings and private placements. The firm was commended to researchers for the *"quality and cohesion"* of its corporate team, with many competitors asserting that they would refer work to the firm in instances of conflict. *"The nod goes to Faegre & Benson for integrity and vigour."*

The group acted on the $3.9 billion MBO of IBP. Other highlights include acting as co-counsel with Wachtell Lipton in ReliaStar Financial Corp's $6.1 billion sale to The ING Group, and representing Fingerhut on its $1.7 billion sale to Federated Department Stores. Other areas of expertise include medical technology, agriculture and retail. **Clients:** US Bancorp; Wilsons The Leather Experts; Digi International; ReliaStar Financial Corp; IntraNet Solutions; Northwest Mortgage Services; Sasol Chemical Industries; Honeywell; Health Decisions International; Fingerhut Companies.

Thompson Hine & Flory (12 ptrs, 13 asscs) Largely Ohio-focused firm with offices in Cleveland, Dayton, Columbus and Cincinnati, which handle a wide variety of M&A transactions, primarily for a stable base of Midwest public companies. On the private company side, the firm offers business planning, tax and succession planning services. Well-known for its IPO and private placement expertise, the firm has developed a niche in e-commerce.

A strong real estate department is visible on a number of large transactions involving shopping mall sales, while in the chemicals industry, the firm maintains ties with a number of local chemical supply companies. **Clients:** Leading local corporates

Corporate/M&A: New York

Wachtell, Lipton, Rosen & Katz (50 lawyers concentrate on pure M&A) *"Extraordinarily successful"* corporate-driven practice that has a *"laser-like focus"* on the M&A market. Through its *"boutique aura,"* the firm has created a reputation as *"the specialists"* with a renowned expertise in takeover defence. Although not quite the legendary 1:1 ratio (partners to associates), the practice is praised by clients for its senior attorney predominance. Junior associates are said to be *"groomed for excellence"* and the partnership itself contains *"the highest level of uniform quality."* Also recommended for its strong bankruptcy practice, the firm is said to *"have done a splendid job"* in encouraging institutional clients, and receives praise for avoiding the full service route.

Founded in 1965 and thought to act as a *"self-contained"* unit from New York, the firm has shown a reluctance to join the rush for overseas offices. Recent discussions surrounding a West Coast office are no longer proceeding, although the firm is perceived to have reacted swiftly to the technology boom. A New York focus has not hindered this *"Lear jet"* of a business model, and the firm is applauded for its involvement in the most complex cross-border transactions.

"Legendary" **Marty Lipton*** is universally praised as *"the guru of defence to hostile takeovers,"* and his name is synonymous with the popular 'poison pill' defensive strategy originating from the boom market of the 80s. *"Greatest when seen in a complex hostile situation"* and *"immensely creative,"* Lipton is said to *"shoot from the hip"* with the *"finesse"* that encourages *"half the general counsel in the US to think they have forged a personal relationship."* Bringing *"enormous credibility to the firm,"* he is perceived to have developed a role as *"client magnet/trouble-shooter"* and maintains a high level of transactional involvement.

Senior partner **Dick Katcher*** is said to be *"a quality operator," "light on his feet"* in complex transactions. *"Confident,"* he is seen on the biggest cross border deals and recently advised AT&T on its $56 billion acquisition of MediaOne (includes $20 billion in cash.) *"Battle-hardened"* **Ed Herlihy*** has a *"keen eye for what makes a deal"* and is thought to be *"a fantastic force"* in the financial services industry. He advised Donaldson Lufkin Jenrette (alongside Davis Polk) on its sale to Crédit Suisse First Boston (value $11.5 billion.) With his *"stellar reputation,"* he is perceived to have been instrumental in developing the firm's strong relationships with investment banks.

"Thorough and astute" **Adam Emmerich*** can *"see past the horizons of a deal."* Often thought of as *"punchy,"* his major transactions include acting for United Asset Management on its $2.2 billion sale to South Africa's Old Mutual, tripling the latter's funds under management to $275 billion. **Craig Wasserman*** is said to be a *"favourite"* with financial institutions and *"following in Herlihy's footsteps." "Sharp and intelligent,"* he is also praised for displaying *"a strong grasp of market forces"* in cross-border transactions. Advised Spain's Terra Networks (Telefonica's internet arm) on its $12.5 billion merger with internet portal Lycos and Wasserstein Perella on its sale to Dresdner Bank.

David Katz* is *"no stranger to big deals"* and is said to be the firm's *"rising star."* A *"prodigious talent"* who is praised for his lack of artifice, *"he doesn't need to posture."* Advised Pinault Printemps Redoute on its acquisition of a stake in Gucci and biotech specialist Life Technologies on its sale to Invitrogen.

As the firm is felt to be *"client-driven,"* it is no surprise to find **Pat Vlahakis*** developing a role as the firm's *"new media giant."* She acted for Young & Rubicam (alongside Lipton) on its $4.7 billion takeover by WPP group. **Andy Brownstein*** is a *"no-nonsense," "experienced"* practitioner who runs deals *"without bluster."* He advised Amoco on its agreed takeover by BP. **Andrew Nussbaum*** joins our up and coming list, praised for his *"straight as an arrow attitude"* to deal management. With Marty Lipton, he advised Philip Morris on its acquisition of Nabisco Holdings for $18.9 billion including net debt. **Clients:** AT&T; Amoco; Bankers Trust; Bank Boston; General Mills (purchase of Pillsbury); Philip Morris; Wells Fargo; Young & Rubicam; United Asset Management (UAM); Voicestream.

Skadden, Arps, Slate, Meagher & Flom LLP (30 ptrs) M&A forms the *"enormous engine"* for this firm with an enviable international network and full service offering. *"Professional, sharp and capable,"* Skadden's attorneys can also be *"aggressive"* and *"pack a punch"* on behalf of their clients. The network of 21 offices (ten in the US) is recognised to have *"superb judgement of the international markets."* This grand scale is thought to generate a high volume (and value) of cross-border activity such as advising Mannesmann on its merger with Vodafone. *"Incredible"* growth has also led to some accusations of *"variable quality,"* but the firm's brand image continues to flourish.

"Great talent" **Peter Atkins*** is a *"joy to work with"* and is regarded as one of the most significant talents in New York. Described as a *"powerhouse,"* he is involved on the largest deals, such as advising US Airways on its £11.6 billion acquisition by United Airlines (includes debt and $5.8 billion in aircraft operating leases). Head of the corporate practice areas, **Roger Aaron*** is an *"M&A giant,"* whose *"incisive, creative"* mind has led to comparisons with Joe Flom. Recommended for his deal management, (*"you can't slip anything by him, but he won't waste time,"*) he acts for major corporates including Viacom and repre-

*See leaders' profiles on pages 848-903

USA: NEW YORK Leading Firms (Corporate/M&A)
1 Wachtell, Lipton, Rosen & Katz
2 Skadden, Arps, Slate, Meagher & Flom LLP
3 Cravath, Swaine & Moore
Simpson Thacher & Bartlett
Sullivan & Cromwell
4 Davis Polk & Wardwell
Shearman & Sterling
5 Debevoise & Plimpton
Fried, Frank, Harris, Shriver & Jacobson
6 Cleary, Gottlieb, Steen & Hamilton
Weil, Gotshal & Manges
Willkie Farr & Gallagher

Firms are listed alphabetically in each band.

Leading Individuals (Corporate/M&A)	
★ **LIPTON Martin** *Wachtell, Lipton*	
1 **AARON Roger** *Skadden, Arps*	**ATKINS Peter** *Skadden, Arps*
BEATTIE Richard *Simpson Thacher & Bartlett*	**COGUT Charles** *Simpson Thacher & Bartlett*
COHEN Rodgin *Sullivan & Cromwell*	**FINKELSON Allen** *Cravath, Swaine & Moore*
FLEISCHER Arthur *Fried, Frank, Harris*	**FLOM Joseph** *Skadden, Arps*
HERLIHY Ed *Wachtell, Lipton, Rosen & Katz*	**HERSCH Dennis** *Davis Polk & Wardwell*
STAPLETON Benjamin *Sullivan & Cromwell*	**VOLK Stephen** *Shearman & Sterling*
2 **BLOCK Dennis** *Cadwalader, Wickersham & Taft*	**GELSTON Philip** *Cravath, Swaine & Moore*
HELENIAK David *Shearman & Sterling*	**KATCHER Richard** *Wachtell, Lipton*
LEWKOW Victor *Cleary, Gottlieb, Steen*	**STEPHENSON Alan** *Cravath, Swaine & Moore*
3 **AQUILA Frank** *Sullivan & Cromwell*	**BASON George (Gar)** *Davis Polk & Wardwell*
BIALKIN Kenneth *Skadden, Arps*	**BROWN Meredith** *Debevoise & Plimpton*
CONDON Creighton *Shearman & Sterling*	**EMMERICH Adam** *Wachtell, Lipton*
FOGG Blaine (Finn) *Skadden, Arps*	**JACOBS Stephen** *Weil, Gotshal & Manges*
KATZ David *Wachtell, Lipton*	**KRAMER Morris** *Skadden, Arps*
NUSBAUM Jack *Willkie Farr & Gallagher*	**SPATT Robert** *Simpson Thacher & Bartlett*
WASSERMAN Craig *Wachtell, Lipton*	
4 **BEDRICK Mel** *Cravath, Swaine & Moore*	**BROWNSTEIN Andy** *Wachtell, Lipton*
CERABINO Thomas *Willkie Farr & Gallagher*	**COOPERSTEIN Gary** *Fried, Frank, Harris*
CUNNINGHAM Dan *Cravath, Swaine & Moore*	**DOUGLAS Peter** *Davis Polk & Wardwell*
DUNN Douglas *Milbank, Tweed*	**FINLEY John** *Simpson Thacher & Bartlett*
FRAIDIN Stephen *Fried, Frank, Harris*	**GITTES Franklin** *Skadden, Arps*
GROLL William *Cleary, Gottlieb, Steen*	**HALL Richard** *Cravath, Swaine & Moore*
KADEN Lewis *Davis Polk & Wardwell*	**KENNEDY Tom** *Skadden, Arps*
KRIEGER Sanford *Fried, Frank, Harris*	**LEDERMAN Lawrence** *Milbank, Tweed*
LOWY George *Cravath, Swaine & Moore*	**MADDEN John** *Shearman & Sterling*
MILLS Philip *Davis Polk & Wardwell*	**MORPHY James** *Sullivan & Cromwell*
PIERCE Mort *Dewey Ballantine LLP*	**RINALDI Joseph** *Davis Polk & Wardwell*
RUEGGER Philip (Pete) *Simpson Thacher & Bartlett*	**SCHELL Michael** *Skadden, Arps*
SORKIN David *Simpson Thacher & Bartlett*	**VLAHAKIS Patricia** *Wachtell, Lipton*
WHITE Fred *Skadden, Arps*	
Up-and-coming individuals	
NUSSBAUM Andrew *Wachtell, Lipton*	**SAEED Faiza** *Cravath, Swaine & Moore*

Individuals are listed alphabetically in each band.

sented Lazard Brothers as advisor to Gemstar on its $14.3 billion acquisition of TV Guide.

Credited with *"creating M&A,"* **Joe Flom*** ranks alongside Marty Lipton for his innovative, strategic vision, now *"part of the fabric of Skaddens."* Less visible on the transactional front nowadays, his *"immense stature"* towers over the M&A market. Seen as a *"critical symbol"* to corporate America, Flom is known for his influence with global corporations. *"Senior statesman"* **Kenneth Bialkin**'s* *"enormously successful"* relationship with Citigroup and Travellers cements a huge profile. Perceived to be *"point man"* in terms of client development, he *"knows absolutely everyone"* and brings an *"extraordinary intelligence"* to the deal table. He advised Citigroup on its acquisition of Associates First Capital for $31.1 billion (creating a total of $791 billion of assets under management.)

"Incredibly sharp" **Morris Kramer***, strongly associated with complex hostile transactions, is said to *"love a fight."* Marked as *"one of the cream of the crop,"* his *"down to earth attitude"* consistently generates warm recommendation. He represented United News & Media on its sale of broadcasting interests to UK's Granada (value $2.7 billion.) Senior figure **Finn Fogg*** is *"a great communicator"* of legal issues with a particular reputation for negotiated mergers. He has advised Champion International on its acquisition by International Paper for $7.3 billion (outplaying an offer from Finnish UPM-Keymmene.) **Frank Gittes*** has a *"great M&A name"* and is seen to handle *"top drawer"* transactions which include the sale of timber manufacturers John Manville to an investor group led by Hicks Muse and Bear Stearns ($3 billion including debt.) **Fred White*** is said to be *"consistently in control"* of a deal, a *"first rate"* financial services attorney. He acted on behalf of BankBoston Corporation in its $16 billion merger with Fleet Financial Group.

The firm, however, is still considered by the market to lag behind Wachtell in its development of younger partners. Two do stand above the herd. *"Unassuming and bright,"* **Tom Kennedy*** is said to *"cut to the chase"* in transactions and is building a strong profile in the communications arena. *"Smart"* **Mike Schell*** is a *"big name"* in public company M&A with a fine reputation for hostile transactions. He advised biotech company Dexter Corporation on its sale to Invitrogen. **Clients:** Mannnesmann; Warner-Lambert Co; Bank Boston Corp; Honeywell ($15.5 billion merger with Allied Signal); NTL; Ascend Communications; Sterling Software ($4 billion acquisition of Computer Associates Int); Assicurazioni Generali; NBC; United News & Media; Goldman Sachs; UBS Principal Finance; Warburg Dillon Read; CSFB; Merrill Lynch; Salomon Smith Barney.

Cravath, Swaine & Moore (12 ptrs 40 asscs) *"Pre-eminent reputation"* based around an *"exceptional blue-chip client base"* that is the envy of New York. Its success is tied firmly to the *"extraordinary quality, top to bottom"* spanning both associates and partners. The *"brightest lawyers,"* perhaps, though some find them *"occasionally aggressive"* on transactions, while others believe a fine line is drawn between *"arrogance and the confidence of fantastic global experience."* The market perceives little disruption to the firm from the loss of leading light Rob Kindler, as this is a firm *"not built around the cult of the individual,"* but a place where *"quality is uniform."*

Bringing *"gravitas"* to the firm and considered

"*still as sprightly as ever,*" **Allen Finkelson*** has "*no need to show off.*" Seeing complex deals with "*360 degree vision*" he can spot "*precisely what is important.*" Partner for IBM, he also acted for United Airlines on its purchase of US Airways and for MCI Worldcom on its acquisition of Sprint. "*Excellent through and through,*" **Philip Gelston*** is said to "*fight his corner superbly.*" Seen as a confident deal manager, he "*thinks on his feet*" and is developing a strong reputation for cross-border M&A. He acted for Marconi on the purchase of MSI ($900 million cash and stocks) and for FSA Holdings on its $2.6 billion acquisition by Dexia. "*Approaching a deal from all angles,*" **Alan Stephenson*** is recommended as a major player in the complex market. He represented IPALCO Enterprises, a utility holding company, on its sale to AES Corporation ($3 billion including $890 million debt.) Younger partner **Richard Hall*** also acted on the transaction and is said to have "*a good hold on major deals.*" Clients feel he has an "*acute awareness of the financial markets,*" and he advised Salomon Smith Barney as financial advisers to the MGM Grand on its acquisition of Mirage Resorts ($4.4 billion.) "*Forceful*" **Mel Bedrick*** is said to bring "*great stature*" to the table and is regarded as a "*get it done lawyer.*" A senior figure at the firm, he advised BAe Systems on its $510 million cash purchase of Lockheed Martin's control systems.

"*Old hand*" **George Lowy*** is less visible but is considered a "*shrewd tactician*" in developing relationships with investment banks such as Morgan Stanley and Lazard Brothers. He is advising AXA Group on its purchase of the remaining stake in AXA Financial on the completion of CSFB's acquisition of DLJ. Also known for his capital markets work, **Dan Cunningham*** has "*a growing presence*" on cross-border M&A, which includes recognition of "*excellent*" work acting for Unilever (Anglo-Dutch) on its purchase of Bestfoods for $24.3 billion including debt. Rising star **Faiza Saeed*** is rated for her "*down to earth attitude*" doing "*some of the biggest limelight deals.*" She is lead partner advising Vivendi on its tripartite merger with Canal+ (French) and Seagram (Canadian) by way of a share-swap deal worth $34 billion. **Clients:** Unilever; United Airlines; MCI Worldcom; Viacom; Vivendi; Time Warner; CBS; IBM; International Network Services; BAe Systems; BAT; Lycos, Peco Energy Co; Salomon Smith Barney; CSFB.

Simpson Thacher & Bartlett (30 ptrs 60 asscs) "*Pure blue-chip operators*" with "*corporate M&A the top priority.*" This is no surprise, considering that the firm is managed by LBO doyen **Dick Beattie***. Placed in a "*powerful*" position by its long-standing relationship with leading buy-out firms KKR and Blackstone Group, the firm is seen to act for highly acquisitive funds and corporates undertaking cross-border transactions. Using these relationships, which also include a close link with Chase Manhattan, the firm has broadened its clientele.

Relationship partner for KKR, the "*exceptional*" Dick Beattie is also credited with the firm's focus on Chase. "*A remarkable figurehead*" said to carry the weight of the firm on "*business-like shoulders,*" he can "*pack a punch*" during transactions. Led the advice to AOL on its plans to merge with Time Warner ($160 billion) and is acting for Chase Manhattan in its acquisition of JP Morgan. "*Financially astute and razor sharp*" **Casey Cogut*** is a major figure in both private equity and M&A. In solving corporate problems, he is thought to include "*strategic and political calculations,*" while his "*great international profile*" is seen on both sides of the Atlantic. He advised American Home Products on its receipt of a $1.8 billion break-up fee, ending its contract with Warner-Lambert.

Well respected for his work in the media market, **John Finley*** "*has an acute eye for the details*" of a deal. Reflecting the firm's reputation for cross-border work, he has acted for Seagram (client relationship partner) in its merger with Vivendi and on the sale of US based FoodService to Royal Ahold. A name linked to both KKR and major corporates, "*bright*" **Rob Spatt*** "*offers no display of ego.*" Seen to be "*picking up interesting transactions,*" he advised Frontier Corporation on its $11.2 billion sale to Global Crossing and TV Guide on its $14.3 billion sale to Gemstar International Group.

Like a number of the firm's corporate partners, **Pete Ruegger*** has a strong profile for both M&A and buy-out work. A "*prime*" player with a strong tie to Blackstone Group, he acted for Teleglobe on its sale to Bell Canada. Thought of as "*a rising star of the firm,*" **David Sorkin*** worked with Beattie and Ruegger on the AOL/Time Warner merger and is the lead partner for Associates First Capital on its $31 billion sale to Citigroup. **Clients:** Seagram Georgia-Pacific; American Home Products; CNET; Harcourt General; Scottish Hydro Electric; Warner Lambert; Dun & Bradstreet; Fred Meyer; Owen Illinios; Stagecoach; MCI Worldcom; KKR; Blackstone Group; First Capital Corp; Lehman Brothers; CSFB; Merrill Lynch;Goldman Sachs.

Sullivan & Cromwell (12 ptrs, 36 asscs) "*Phenomenally successful*" M&A practice that is seen to have "*stamped its identity on a strong overseas network.*" Its cross-border activity is aided by a formidable base in both Asia and Europe. Occasionally thought of as "*somewhat academic,*" attorneys are said to possess "*the confidence of inbred seniority*" when approaching major deals. Alongside a blue-chip corporate client base which includes Glaxo Wellcome, BP Amoco and Olivetti, the firm is commended for its relationship with global investors Goldman Sachs. Transactionally this gives them an "*enviable visibility*" in the market.

Ben Stapleton* is "*an intellectual dancer*" who is praised for his "*light-footed creativity.*" Thought of as the firm's "*giant,*" and a "*complete gentleman,*" his "*level-headed*" deal management is consistently praised. Visible on a wealth of the largest transactions, he advised Vodafone on its merger with Mannesmann. "*Premier act*" **Rodgin Cohen*** is "*the financial services guru*" with a strong reputation for transactional and regulatory work. Now Chairman of the firm and considered a "*deal powerhouse,*" he is thought to have heavily influenced the M&A practice towards a successful control of the investor market. He acted for UBS on its acquisition of PaineWebber for $12.4 billion.

On the UBS deal, Cohen was assisted by "*extremely sharp*" **Jim Morphy***, managing partner of the M&A practice. "*Intelligent,*" Morphy is said to "*stay one step ahead of the pack*" while keeping the deal process smooth. He represented Sanford Bernstein on its $3.5 billion stock and cash sale to Alliance Capital Management and is lead counsel to Goldman Sachs on its $7.4 billion acquisition of Spear, Leeds & Kellogg. "*Straight-forward*" **Frank Aquila*** is developing a reputation for advising major global corporates. He acted for Diageo on the $10.5 billion sale of Pillsbury to General Mills. **Clients:** BP Amoco; BA Diageo; Ziff-Davis Olivetti (bid for Telecom Italia); Vodafone Airtouch (sale of Orange); Dexia; Cap Gemini; Allianz; Merrill Lynch; Goldman Sachs; New Bridge Networks (sale to Alcatel); UBS; ING; CSFB.

Davis Polk & Wardwell (25 ptrs) Perceived to have "*quality throughout the firm,*" this traditional M&A practice is seen to benefit greatly from its long established relationship with Morgan Stanley. The firm also has a strong international presence with global offices providing a platform for cross border M&A, although it confines itself to offering US counsel. A 'best friends' policy with Hengeler Mueller Weitzel & Wirtz (Germany) and Slaughter and May (UK) filled any gaps created by this strategy.

The firm is considered to mix a "*decent and honourable attitude*" with "*100% technical excellence.*" A recently opened office in Menlo Park, California reflects the firm's commitment to a global technology practice.

"*Pure M&A old school*" **Dennis Hersch*** is

U

*See leaders' profiles on pages 848-903

thought to be *"one of the greats,"* who always *"treads the reasonable path"* on deals. He acted for International Paper on its acquisition of Champion International ($7.3 billion.) An important figurehead, he is seen as *"a client magnet"* whose *"heavyweight intelligence"* has promoted the firm internationally. **Gar Bason*** is a strategist who *"keeps you on your toes."* Well established and *"business-like,"* Bason is gaining a reputation as a corporate power broker. He is advising DLJ on its sale to CSFB.

"Perfectly superb" **Lewis Kaden*** is senior figure and has a strong profile in insurance based M&A. He displays a *"great level of control"* over transactions and is most prominent for his work for insurance giant Aetna. **Peter Douglas*** is felt to be *"bright and innovative,"* with a solid reputation for his mix of corporate and financial services clients. He advised Burns International on its $650 million sale to Securitas.

"Analytical and hardworking" **Philip Mills*** is *"terrifically aware"* of all aspects in a deal. He is seen to tackle the most complex transactions with ease and receives market approval for his negotiating skills. He advised P&O on its North American strategic acquisition and divestiture program. **Joe Rinaldi*** brings a *"splash of colour"* to the table, and is recommended for his work on *"interesting"* deals. He represented Promus Hotel Corporation on its $4 billion sale to Hilton Hotels and Reed Elsevier on its $5.65 billion acquisition of Harcourt General. **Clients:** Comcast; Nabisco Holdings; Terra Networks; Network Solutions; Emerson Electric; EMI; NatWest; Esat; Alliance Capital Management (acquires Sandford Bernstein); Repsol; P&O; Morgan Stanley; Aetna; JP Morgan; BSCH; DLJ Merchant Banking Partners.

Shearman & Sterling (9 ptrs 40 asscs) Having invested heavily in an international infrastructure the firm is felt to have *"reaped the rewards"* of increased cross-border activity. This broader base aproach has also supported growth in the hi-tech area, with the firm representing the Bell Canada family of companies on convergence deals such as BCE's acquisition of Emergis, the internet supplier. Perceived to have evolved from the 80's slant towards financial institutions to a balanced client base with major global corporations. Strong connections to the investment banks remain, with the firm acting for Goldman Sachs as lead arranger on a $30 billion syndicated credit agreement in connection with AT&T's $58 billion acquisition of Media One.

"Visionary" of the firm **Steve Volk*** is *"just a great deal-closer"* and hugely respected for his *"innovative mind."* As an *"international star"* said to be *"a phenomenal business generator,"* Volk is thought to have *"aggressively promoted global M&A resources."* Head of M&A **John Madden*** has a *"strong transactional presence"* and a *"clear-headed, no-nonsense"* approach. Previously managing partner of the European offices (based in Paris and an avocat of the Paris bar), he is considered an experienced cross-border practitioner. He represented BT in its proposed merger with MCI Communications and its subsequent sale of MCI Investments to WorldCom.

"First rate" **David Heleniak** *is a *"mover and shaker"* at the firm who *"handles complex deals with ease and efficiency."* As head of the international practice, he is *"most visible"* on the biggest deals such as advising CSFB on its acquisition of DLJ and advising Thomson on its acquisition of Primark (financial information) for £1.1 billion including debt. *"Smart and practical"* **Creighton Condon*** *"never lets details slip between the cracks."* Said to have the *"flair"* to tackle complex transactions. Associated with major corporate clients, he has acted for Viacom on its acquisition by CBS and for Georgia Pacific on its acquisition of Fort James (value $11 billion including debt.) In the biggest industrial deal of the year the team advised General Electric on its $45 billion agreed merger with Honeywell. **Clients:** Viacom; Alcatel; LM Ericsson; British Telecommunications; France Telecom; Siemens; Georgia Pacific; SmithKline Beecham; Morgan Stanley; Merrill Lynch; CSFB; Goldman Sachs; Salomon Smith Barney.

Debevoise & Plimpton (25 ptrs, 56 asscs) *"A classic corporate practice"* seen to benefit from a dominance of niche strengths in the insurance field and with investment companies. A highly acquisitive buy-out practice and strong fund formation lawyers have boosted its reputation for private equity transactions. Although less visible on the international scene, a network of six offices supports a growing proportion of cross-border transactions. *"Insurance kings,"* the firm is said to have a strong relationship with active insurance giants like Metropolitan Life and AXA Financial, and is acting for the latter on the acquisition of DLJ by CSFB (AXA owns 70% of DLJ.)

"Gentleman's gentleman" **Meredith Brown*** is highly rated for his *"grasp on the investment market."* Said to be *"a strong intellectual resource"* his influence is felt to pervade the firm, and has much to do with the group's *"confident style."* A strong international profile has seen Brown advising Thames Water on the US aspects of its RWE offer and in connection with the $600 million acquisition of E'Town Corporation.

The firm is also developing a niche in media and entertainment, representing Hasbro, Oxygen Media, Rede Globo's Globo.com and Henson. Less seen on public company transactions, private M&A remains the team's core activity. **Clients:** AT&T AXA Financial; Aetna; Hasbro; Waste Management; North Castle Partners; Providence Equity Partners; Phelps Dodge Corporation; Clayton Dubilier & Rice; Kelso; Greenwich Street; Schroder Ventures; Merrill Lynch; Salomon Smith Barney; DLJ; Goldman Sachs; Deutsche Banc Alex Brown.

Fried, Frank, Harris, Shriver & Jacobson (50 ptrs, 150 asscs) A *"well established"* M&A practice seen to devote *"considerable energy"* to the field. Often seen on the largest deals, the firm represented Best Foods on its acquisition by (Anglo-Dutch) Unilever (value $24.3 billion including debt), and was said to display a strong grasp of the international markets. Relationships with investment banks such as Goldman Sachs, Merrill Lynch and Lazard Brothers continue to promote the firm's visibility as counsel to financial advisers in acquisitions and divestitures. Also prominent for its work on leveraged buyouts representing major firms such as Fortsmann Little, this practice is seen to have a broad base of blue chip clients.

"Master of the complex deal" **Arthur Fleischer*** continues to be the force behind the practice. Considered *"the third father of M&A"* and an *"eminence grise,"* his level-headed approach to deal management is widely commended. Represented WPP on its $4.7 billion acquisition of Young & Rubicam. *"Bright"* **Sandy Krieger*** is said to *"really know how to close a deal."* A strong international reputation is coupled with *"a tough-talking New York style."* He advised Invensys on the $810 million sale of its paper technology division to Apax. Offices in London and Paris often work alongside the US attorneys supporting cross-border transactions. **Stephen Fraidin*** is recommended for displaying *"intelligent consideration"* in both public M&A and private equity buyouts deals where his name carries great weight. He represented Pioneer Hi-Bred International in its $7.6 billion sale to DuPont. *"An astute deal doer"* **Gary Cooperstein*** is said to *"manage any room he walks into."* A strong reputation for transactions in the utility industry has seen him acting for General Electric. The firm acted for El Paso in its $15.68 billion acquisition of Coastal Corporation. **Clients:** Bestfoods; WPP; GPU; First Energy; Bell South; Kroger; Allied Waste; Gulfstream Aerospace; Procter & Gamble; Merck; El Paso; Merrill Lynch; ING; Goldman Sachs; DLJ.

Cleary, Gottlieb, Steen & Hamilton Although less visible on the largest deals, the firm's *"wonderful international presence"* marks it as a leader for cross border M&A. This is exemplified by advice on such transactions as Deutsche

Telekom's proposed $55.7 billion acquisition of VoiceStream Wireless. Drawing comparisons with Skaddens for the profile of the nine office international network, the firm is said to offer *"all things to all men,"* but is still thought to lack the volume of headline deals of New York's principal players. A strong institutional client base has seen the firm acting for major investment banks. In Europe, the firm has developed a strong relationship with Goldman Sachs and is said to assist the New York practice with a number of multi-jurisdictional transactions.

"Senior figure" **Viktor Lewkow*** is said to *"roll his sleeves up and get involved." "Practical, intelligent"* and above all *"incredibly client friendly,"* Lewkow is thought to be *"the key to the firm's success."* A familiar name on the largest deals, he represented HSBC on its acquisition of Republic New York and Safra Republic for a total of $10.3 billion. A traditional strength with financial institutions saw the firm acting for Deutsche Bank on its acquisition of Bankers Trust. On transactions, **Bill Groll*** is said to be *"hands-on and knowledgeable."* Clients appreciate his *"responsive and hardworking"* attitude. Recognised for his work with the investment fund Zell/Chilmark, Groll has a *"strong presence"* and a balanced corporate client base. **Clients:** Deutsche Telekom; Nortel; Cable & Wireless; Hellman & Friedman Fleet Financial Group; Zell/Chilmark; Goldman Sachs; Texas Pacific Group.

Weil, Gotshal & Manges (15 ptrs) *"Quality"* practitioners who *"always deliver"* but do not have the profile of their market rivals. A major national firm, with a 12-office European network which has facilitated a number of deals with an international flavour. A respected London office also offers UK law expertise, and from New York the firm acted as US counsel to BMW Group on its sale of Land Rover to Ford Motor Company.

Much of the firm's visibility is tied to its buyout activity for US giant Hicks Muse Tate & Furst. Its investment banking relationships are often seen to take the form of highly acquisitive merchant banking funds.

In the wake of the departure of Dennis Block to Cadwaladers, the firm is said to lack a full bench of headline stars. That said, it is acknowledged to breed *"a happy, cohesive bunch." "The cream of the firm"* remains **Steve Jacobs***, *"an excellent M&A leader."* He acted for Synder Communications on its $2.1 billion sale to global giant Havas Advertising. Respected for his role as *"a first rate client developer,"* Jacobs carries the weight of the firm's blue-chip corporate client base.

Convergence in the telecoms, media and technology markets has also proven to be a growth area for the firm. A combined team from Dallas and New York acted for Texas Instruments on its $7.6 billion acquisition of Burr-Brown, creating a leading provider of data converters in the semiconductor industry. **Clients:** General Motors; Excel Communications; Matsushita; Pfizer; The Energy; CSFB; DLJ; Lehman Brothers; Hicks, Muse, Tate & Furst.

Willkie Farr & Gallagher (21 ptrs) *"A practice that commands respect,"* although currently less prominent compared with its high-profile 1980s work for corporate raiders. Much of the firm's current reputation is tied to its strong relationship with buyout fund Warburg Pincus, the firm advised on the $435 million buyout of Atlanta-based Centennial Health. Building on a successful Paris office, the firm has opened offices in Milan, Rome and Frankfurt. The basis for this expansion is thought to be M&A and international telecoms markets, the latter being a specific focus for the firm.

"Impressive" **Jack Nusbaum*** has *"excellent, across the board corporate strengths"* and is thought to *"carry the prestige of the practice."* As Chairman of the firm, he is considered less transactional and is credited with developing the major client relationships, including Goldman Sachs and Lazard Brothers. However, he is still the 'go-to' figure for the practice's complex deals, and advised Veritas Software Corp on its $20 billion stock and cash take private of Seagate Technology. *"Energetic"* **Tom Cerabino***, said to be *"growing in stature,"* is a major name for complex transactions and fund work.

Strengths are noted in insurance and the REITs, and the team is recognised as a major presence in the media and telecoms market. Recent deals include representing Nextlink Communications on its $2.9 billion acquisition of Concentric Network Corp and CalEnergy in its $5.5 billion acquisition of MidAmerican Energy Holding. **Clients:** Amax Gold; J Crew; Cal Energy; Zurich Insurance Co; Warburg Pincus.

Other Notable Practitioners **Larry Lederman*** of Milbank, Tweed, Hadley & McCloy is praised for being *"at the forefront of the LBO revolution"* and is comfortably the firm's most recognised corporate performer. *"Renowned utilities specialist"* **Doug Dunn***, also of Milbanks, is said to be *"easy going"* yet *"sharp"* on a deal, and advised Scottish Power on its $12 billion purchase of PacifiCorp. *"A straight talker,"* **Mort Pierce*** of Dewey Ballantine has *"developed a substantial, healthy"* M&A practice best known for his relationships with investment banks, in particular CSFB. *"Fiery"* **Dennis Block*** has stamped his mark on Cadwalader Wickersham & Taft's corporate practice. *"A force of nature,"* he is said to *"epitomise the concept of a New York lawyer"* and with an *"unbelievably loyal client base"* has maintained a high profile. He advised US West on its merger with Qwest Communications (backing out of an agreement with Global Crossing.)

Corporate/M&A: South

Vinson & Elkins LLP (36 ptrs, 68 asscs) This *"top-flight"* firm sits at the pinnacle of Texas corporate law, considered by clients to have *"distanced itself from everybody else."* Said to be *"superbly managed,"* the firm is renowned for its corporate securities practice, but is *"strong across the board,"* in cross-border M&A, IPOs and private placements. The firm's matchless energy clientele provides the corporate department with access to a number of notable big-ticket deals, while the team also advises underwriters and some of New York's premier investment banks. The recent acquisition of the 27-lawyer corporate securities practice from Andrews & Kurth has further cemented the firm's position ahead of its rivals.

Mark Kelly* co-heads the practice and is universally admired for his *"commercial savvy,"* while **Joe Dilg*** and *"corporate heavyweight"* **Michael Wortley*** are *"stalwart, smart practitioners."* The latter is known for his close relationship with Hicks Muse Tate & Furst. **Michael Harrington*** has also caught the market's eye.

The firm advised Duke Energy Field Services on an issue of notes for approximately $1.7 billion, acted for the underwriters on a sale of common stock by Electronic Data Systems Corporation for approximately $784 million, and represented Enron Corp on the $2.1 billion sale of Portland General Electric to Sierra Pacific Resources. Also represented AMFM on the $23 billion merger with Clear Channel Communications. **Clients:** Enron Corp; Duke Energy Corp; Apache Corp; Dynergy; Mission Critical Soft-

USA: SOUTH
Leading Firms (Corporate/M&A)

Band	Firm
1	Vinson & Elkins LLP
2	Baker Botts LLP
3	Andrews & Kurth
	Fulbright & Jaworski LLP
	Haynes and Boone LLP
	Hughes & Luce
	Weil, Gotshal & Manges
4	Bracewell & Patterson LLP
	Gardere Wynne Sewell LLP
	Jenkens & Gilchrist
	Locke Liddell & Sapp LLP
5	Akin, Gump, Strauss, Hauer & Feld, LLP

Firms are listed alphabetically in each band.

Leading Individuals (Corporate/M&A)

Band	Individual
1	**JEWELL Robert** *Andrews & Kurth*
	KELLY Mark *Vinson & Elkins LLP*
	O'LEARY Michael *Andrews & Kurth*
2	**DILG Joe** *Vinson & Elkins LLP*
	KIRKLAND David *Baker Botts LLP*
	MASSAD Stephen *Baker Botts LLP*
	STILL Charles *Fulbright & Jaworski LLP*
	SWANSON Joel *Baker Botts LLP*
	WORTLEY Michael *Vinson & Elkins LLP*
3	**BOGDANOW Alan** *Hughes & Luce*
	BOONE Michael *Haynes and Boone LLP*
	CONLON Michael *Fulbright & Jaworski LLP*
	HARRINGTON Michael *Vinson & Elkins LLP*
	MARSTON Edgar *Bracewell & Patterson LLP*
	McCORMICK Bill *Hughes & Luce*
	OXFORD Patrick *Bracewell & Patterson LLP*
	SCHOENBRUN Larry *Gardere Wynne Sewell LLP*
	WEST Glenn *Weil, Gotshal & Manges*

Individuals are listed alphabetically in each band.

ware; Xpedior; Stone Energy Corp; The Shaw Group; Randall's Food Markets; Unocal Corp; Halliburton Company; Hicks Muse Tate & Furst.

Baker Botts LLP (25 ptrs, 40 asscs) *"Significant across the board,"* the firm profits from its superb energy department to advise on a host of cross-border oil and gas transactions. However, it is also noted for its presence in the hi-tech industry, and was recommended to researchers for its expertise on equity funds. An impressive client list and some top class lawyers ensure the continuing success of this practice, in Houston at least. Among an *"experienced and impressive team,"* **Steve Massad***, **David Kirkland***, and **Joel Swanson*** stand out. The firm acted for Reliant Energy Mid Atlantic Power Holdings on a $1 billion non-recourse leveraged lease for power plants, and advised the Azerbaijan International Operating Company on its oil and gas exploration of the Caspian Sea. Other matters include representing Transocean Sedco Forex on its acquisition of R&B Falcon Corporation, valued at $8.8 billion, and advising BP Amoco on the $3.6 billion sale of Altura Energy to Occidental Petroleum. **Clients:** Reliant Energy; Global Marine; Valero Energy Corp; Centex Corp; Cabot Oil & Gas Corp; Schlumberger; Electronic Data Systems; Equistar Chemicals; Lennox International; ARCO; Cadbury Schweppes; Merrill Lynch; Goldman Sachs.

Andrews & Kurth (15 ptrs, 20 asscs) Although damaged by the loss of the heart of its securities practice to Vinson & Elkins, the firm is still considered to be a leader in Texas, although *"they're definitely hurting."* The firm specialises in cross-border M&A, acting for both buyers and targets, and also has long experience of debt offerings and IPOs. Energy and technology are areas of niche strength.

Both clients and competitors pay tribute to the *"stars of the practice,"* **Bob Jewell*** and **Mike O'Leary***, who are both recommended for their *"commercial acumen."* Highlight transactions include acting for PG&E Energy Group on its $840 million acquisition by El Paso Energy Corp, advising Santa Fe Snyder on its $5 billion acquisition by Devon Energy Corp, and representing Lexicon Genetics on its $250 million IPO. **Clients:** US Propane; Santa Fe Snyder; PG&E Energy Group; Morgan Stanley Dean Witter; CSFB; Williams Companies; Lexicon Genetics.

Fulbright & Jaworski LLP (24 ptrs, 31 asscs) Although it has a fine reputation for litigation, the firm's corporate offering in Houston has been widely praised by rivals. Principally known for its work in the energy sector, the corporate team is said to be *"well served"* by **Charles Still*** and the *"outstanding, smart and practical"* **Michael Conlon***. The group acted for EOG Resources on its acquisition of Somerset Oil & Gas Co and advised ATOFINA Petrochemicals on the sale of various assets to Alon Israel Oil Company. **Clients:** Shell Oil; Duke Energy; EOG Resources.

Haynes and Boone LLP (40 ptrs, 80 asscs) Renowned for its transactional expertise in the hi-tech sector, the firm advises foreign clients as well as domestic concerns, and has a niche specialism in developing Mexican companies in the shipping and transport industries. The team is felt by clients to owe much to **Michael Boone***, a *"superb lawyer and leader,"* and a familiar figure on big-ticket transactions.

Highlights include acting for Bargo Energy Company on the $161 million acquisition of the oil and gas properties from Texaco Exploration & Production and advising epicRealm on a $75 million VC financing. The team also advised the Tandy Corporation on the formation of an e-commerce venture with Microsoft. **Clients:** Novistar; 1travel.com; EnerVest Energy LP; Alamosa PCS; AAON; Tandy Corporation; RadioShack.com.

Hughes & Luce (13 ptrs, 12 asscs) Researchers were told by this Dallas-based firm's competitors that *"we hear only good things about them."* Although lacking the international muscle of the market leaders, the firm has a superb reputation for its transactional work in the hi-tech sphere, and acts for a heavyweight, and predominantly domestic, client base. The *"redoubtable"* **Alan Bogdanow*** and the *"dependable"* **William McCormack*** are the team's outstanding practitioners.

The firm acted for EDS on a $1.5 billion joint venture with Continental Airlines for inter alia, the provision of ticketing systems. Other work includes acting for CNET on its $3 billion merger to create NBCi and for Wal-Mart Stores on its $10.8 billion cash tender for the acquisition of Asda Group. **Clients:** EDS; CNET; NBCi; Ericsson; Suiza Foods; Southwestern Bell Telephone; Dillard's; CAN Insurance; Affiliated Computer Services; Blockbuster.com; Wal-Mart Stores; Dell; Dupont; HSBC.

Weil, Gotshal & Manges (12 ptrs, 47 asscs) The Dallas office of this respected New York player has its principal reputation as a corporate specialist, particularly in private equity. Renowned for its relationship with Hicks, Muse, Tate & Furst, the firm also acts for a number of other blue-chip concerns on cross-border M&A, securities work and high profile litigation. A particular growth area is the hi-tech sector.

Managing partner of the Dallas office is the *"busy"* **Glenn West***, commended to our researchers as an *"aggressive and effective"* practitioner. The firm represented affiliates of Bear Stearns and Hicks Muse on a $3 billion LBO of Johns Manville Corporation, advised Texas Instruments on three acquisitions totalling over $8 billion, and acted for Viasystems on its IPO. **Clients:** Texas Instruments; JC Penney; Bell Helicopter; American Airlines; General Electric; Pacific Gas & Electric; Greyhound Lines; Viasystems Group; Thermadyne Holdings; Onex Corporation; Amstar Group; NextMedia Group; Hicks, Muse, Tate & Furst.

Bracewell & Patterson LLP (18 ptrs, 40 asscs) Young by Houston standards, the firm *"shows* *every sign of staying the distance,"* and has earned the respect of its peers for its work on medium-ticket transactions, generally at a domestic level. **Edgar Marston*** and **Patrick Oxford*** gain high marks for their *"user friendly"* attitude. The firm advised Group Maintenance America on its acquisition of Building One Services and the consequent formation of Encompass Services, acted for Southdown on its acquisition by Cemex and represented Benchmark Electronics on debt and equity securities issues totalling over $280 million. **Clients:** Babcock International Group; Enron Corp; Kinder Morgan; Encompass Services Corporation; The Sterling Group; Notre Capital Ventures; Southdown; Benchmark Electronics.

Gardere Wynne Sewell LLP (39 ptrs, 25 asscs) Regarded as a *"sound firm,"* notably in financial services, it is a familiar feature on medium-ticket domestic deals. Said by rivals to be *"well- connected in Dallas,"* it has a strong reputation for advising government and municipal institutions. **Larry Schoenbrun*** was recommended to our researchers as *"a figure who commands respect."* The firm represented PalEx in a number of linked transactions including its $400 million merger with IFCO Systems and the concurrent $228.8 million IPO of the combined company; for StreetAdvisor.com in rounds of private financings and in its sale to IDEA Global.com. **Clients:** PalEx; TransTexas Gas Corporation; StreetAdvisor.com; Cardinal Investment Company; Home Interiors & Gifts; Intuit Inc; SFX Entertainment; Texas Instruments; Tyler Technologies.

Jenkens & Gilchrist (28 ptrs, 34 asscs) Known as *"conservative but solid generalists,"* this full service firm has its major focus on traditional M&A and venture capital funding. Increasingly active in the hi-tech industries, the firm has been active on advising IT and telecoms clients on their joint ventures. **Clients:** IT and telecoms companies.

Locke Liddell & Sapp LLP The union of Houston-based Liddell, Sapp, Zivley, Hill & LaBoon and Dallas-based Locke Purnell Rain Harrell is said to be *"still bedding down."* Known for a strong banking practice, the firm counts foreign and domestic companies among its client base, and has particular strength in the energy sector.

The corporate department focuses on representing buyers and sellers of both public and private companies; representing issuers and underwriters on IPOs and private placement of debt and equity securities. The firm has acted for Austin Ventures on the purchase and sale of various investments and for the York Group on the acquisition of Colonial Guild. **Clients:** ACS Dataline; Dynergy; El Paso Energy; Goldman Sachs; Enron; Kent Electronics; Synagro; Blackstone Minerals; KBK Capital; Yellowstone Capital.

Akin, Gump, Strauss, Hauer & Feld, LLP (40 ptrs, 100 asscs) The Houston office of this firm is *"focused on energy,"* while the Dallas office has been strongly recommended for its transactional expertise in the hi-tech sphere. Said to be able to handle *"politically charged transactions,"* the firm is acknowledged to have *"strong Washington connections."* Broadcasting is another area of specific expertise. The team advised Clear Channel Communications on its $4.4 billion acquisition of SFW Entertainment, and Software.com on the $540 million acquisition of **Clients:** Delhaize America (Food Lion); Software.com; Stinnes AG; Westport Energy Corp; Donaldson Lufkin Jenrette; Wyndham International; Goldman Sachs.

U

Corporate/M&A: West Coast

USA: WEST COAST Leading Firms (Corporate/M&A)
1 Gibson, Dunn & Crutcher LLP
Latham & Watkins
2 Skadden, Arps, Slate, Meagher & Flom LLP
Wilson, Sonsini, Goodrich & Rosati
3 Brobeck Phleger & Harrison

Firms are listed alphabetically in each band.

Leading Individuals (Corporate/M&A)
1 BOGEN Andy *Gibson, Dunn & Crutcher LLP*
KAUFMAN Christopher (Kit) *Latham & Watkins*
SONSINI Larry *Wilson, Sonsini*
2 OLSON Gary *Latham & Watkins*
TOSETTI Paul *Latham & Watkins*
3 COBEN Jerry *Skadden, Arps*
SAGGESE Nicholas *Skadden, Arps*

Individuals are listed alphabetically in each band.

Gibson, Dunn & Crutcher LLP (33 ptrs, 90 asscs) A *"powerhouse firm,"* operating *"at the highest level,"* which has *"deep roots in California,"* and is viewed by its competitors as a *"practical group, full of good people."* A versatile team, the corporate group handles everything from general corporate finance to joint ventures and big-ticket M&A for its *"A-class"* client base, in which high-tech companies predominate.

Our researchers were informed that *"one of the most experienced M&A guys on the West Coast"* is **Andy Bogen***, who is *"at the centre of all the firm's deals,"* and is described as *"intellectual and easy to work with."* The firm represented Boeing on its recent $3.75 billion agreement to acquire the satellite manufacturing business of Hughes Electronics Corporation, and advised Hilton Hotels Corporation on its $4 billion acquisition of Promus Hotel Corporation in a cash-and-stock transaction. **Clients:** Intel; PeopleSoft; Computer Sciences; Nortel Networks; Baxter Healthcare; Western Digital; Salem Communications.

Latham & Watkins (132 lawyers) *"An extremely successful firm on the West Coast and beyond,"* it is an expanding force, with *"incredible bench strength and vast resources."* A consistent presence on high-end M&A transactions, the firm is noted for its work on venture technology, company representation and real estate investment.

Kit Kaufman* is an *"incredibly hard-working guy"* who *"covers a lot of ground,"* while the experienced **Paul Tosetti*** is a *"fine corporate securities lawyer"* and **Gary Olson*** is *"equally at home with M&A and corporate finance."* The firm represented PIMCO Advisors on its $4.7 billion acquisition by Allianz, Ortel on its $2.95 billion acquisition by Lucent Technologies and Adecco on its $1.5 billion acquisition of Olsten Corp. **Clients:** The Carlyle Group; Jupiter Telecommunications Co; PIMCO Advisors; Ortel; American Cellular; Chase Securities; Conexant Systems; Four Media; Safeway; Havas Interactive.

Skadden, Arps, Slate, Meagher & Flom LLP (125 lawyers) *"The one New York firm to come to Los Angeles in the 1980s and to have truly succeeded in becoming a major force on the West Coast,"* is a typical comment made to our researchers about this firm. The team is renowned for its vast M&A practice and is considered to have done an *"outstanding job of penetrating the market."* The client base is deep, and covers most areas of traditional industry and new technology.

"Talented" **Jerry Coben*** *"knows the ropes,"* while **Nick Saggese*** is *"energetic"* and *"seems to be everywhere."* The firm represented Global Crossing on its $10.5 billion acquisition of Fron-

*See leaders' profiles on pages 848-903

tier Corp, and acted for Times Mirror (Independent Directors) on its $8 billion acquisition by Tribune. Also advised Fox Entertainment Group on its $325 million acquisition of LA Dodgers and Dodgers Stadium. **Clients:** Oakley Inc; Texas Pacific Group; Walt Disney; Guess?; National Football League; Apollo Advisors; Occidental Petroleum; PetSmart.com.

Wilson, Sonsini, Goodrich & Rosati (61 ptrs, 343 asscs) This great IT firm is also a leading corporate presence on the West Coast, advising its high-tech clientele on a raft of acquisitions, disposals and IPOs. *"One of the most interesting stories in the history of American law,"* the firm is *"embedded in the culture of Silicon Valley"* and is *"clearly one of the leading operations in California."* The *"unbelievably successful"* **Larry Sonsini*** has *"built up an amazing practice. Virtually nobody has been as effective as him."* The firm represented E-Tek Dynamics on its $15 billion acquisition by JDS Uniphase, and E.piphany on its $3.18 billion acquisition of Octane Software. **Clients:** 3Com Corp; Goldman Sachs; Hewlett-Packard; Network Associates; Sun Microsystems; USWeb/CKS; VA Linux Systems.

Brobeck Phleger & Harrison (88 lawyers) A firm with *"good geographical reach"* is considered, our researchers were informed, to have done a *"a good job of building a corporate practice out of its technology practice."* Although lacking an individual heavyweight, the team's overall quality is beyond dispute. It represented i2 Technologies on a $9.3 billion merger with Aspect Development, advised Cisco Systems on its $6.9 billion dollar acquisition of Cerent Corporation and assisted GeoCities on its $4.6 billion acquisition by Yahoo! **Clients:** Cisco; Broadcom; eTrade; DoubleClick; Quest Software; i2 Technologies.

U

Energy & Natural Resources: East Coast

USA: EAST COAST Leading Firms (Energy: Oil & Gas)	
1	Skadden, Arps, Slate, Meagher & Flom LLP
2	LeBoeuf, Lamb, Greene & MacRae, LLP
	Vinson & Elkins LLP
3	Baker Botts LLP
	Crowell & Moring LLP
	Fulbright & Jaworski LLP
4	Andrews & Kurth
	Chadbourne & Parke LLP
	Hunton & Williams
	Steptoe & Johnson LLP
5	Jones, Day, Reavis & Pogue
	Latham & Watkins
	Pillsbury Winthrop
	Sidley & Austin
	Thelen Reid & Priest LLP

Firms are listed alphabetically in each band.

Leading Firms (Energy: Electricity)	
1	LeBoeuf, Lamb, Greene & MacRae, LLP
	Skadden, Arps, Slate, Meagher & Flom LLP
2	Steptoe & Johnson LLP
3	Jones, Day, Reavis & Pogue
	Thelen Reid & Priest LLP
	Vinson & Elkins LLP
4	Baker Botts LLP
	Chadbourne & Parke LLP
	Crowell & Moring LLP
	Hunton & Williams
	Winthrop, Stimson, Putnam & Roberts
5	Andrews & Kurth
	Fulbright & Jaworski LLP
	Latham & Watkins
	Sidley & Austin

Firms are listed alphabetically in each band.

Skadden, Arps, Slate, Meagher & Flom LLP (55 lawyers) The firm's energy and project finance practice is based in Washington DC and includes resident practitioners in New York and Houston. It advises on project development and finance, government regulation, privatisations, mergers and acquisitions, joint ventures, litigation and legislation in relation to electric power, natural gas, liquefied natural gas (LNG), oil, petrochemicals and other energy sources.

A powerful client base includes developers, equity investors, lenders, contractors, fuel suppliers and other parties involved in project financings and merchant plant and tolling arrangements. Particularly active in the development and financing of electric power-generating projects and natural gas transactions throughout the world, the firm has also advised on the development and financing of gas pipelines and LNG projects, and undertaken complex oil and gas litigation.

Clients and peers agree that the firm is *"still an obvious choice for the top position"* in oil and gas, and it is considered to *"do a fine job with its corporate clients."*

Our researchers were left in no doubt that **Lynn Coleman*** is one of the industry's giants, having been *"a leader in building Skaddens' energy practice."* He had previously worked for the Department of Energy during the Carter administration. **Clifford Naeve*** is a *"first-rate"* transactional lawyer, who has particular expertise in mergers involving utility companies. **Martin Klepper*** is *"a driving force in Skaddens' project finance practice,"* while **Bill Scherman*** is *"an excellent advisor"* with *"superb hearing room skills."*

The firm advised NRG Energy and Dynegy Power Corp on their acquisition of 1,218MW of power generation facilities from San Diego Gas & Electric and acted for Duquesne Light Co on its sale of seven power generating facilities to Orion Power Holdings. Project financing matters include representing Chase Manhattan Bank on a $240 million financing to construct and operate a 240MW gas-fired co-generation facility in Springfield, Massachusetts, and a $200 million financing for a 195MW co-generation facility in Lake Charles, Louisiana. **Clients:** Duquesne Light Company; Kansas City Power and Light Company; Mojave Pipeline Company; Pacific Gas and Electric Corporation; Southern Natural Gas Pipeline.

LeBoeuf, Lamb, Greene & MacRae LLP (70 lawyers) Still pre-eminent in the electricity sector, the firm has undertaken substantial M&A work for utilities over the past twelve months. It also continues to raise its profile in the natural gas sector, and has recently been retained by the Foreign Minister of the Saudi Arabian government to act for the country's national gas initiative.

Competitors note that the firm is *"unquestionably right up there in terms of the top energy firms in New York and DC,"* and our researchers noted the market perception that the workload is *"now showing more balance."* **Lawrence Acker*** is *"an old hand at natural gas work,"* while **Doug Hawes*** is seen to have *"written the book on the Public Utility Holding Company Act."* **William Lamb*** is *"extremely capable"* and has *"been around the block,"* and **Brian O'Neill***, head of the energy practice in the DC office has been described by clients as an *"able and active pipeline specialist."*

The firm has recently been appointed outside counsel for Western Resources in a transaction where Public Service Company of New Mexico will acquire the Western Resources electric utility operations in a tax-free, stock-for-stock transaction with a total purchase price of approximately

USA: EAST COAST
Leading Individuals
(Energy & Natural Resources)

Band	Name	Firm
1	**BOUKNIGHT Lon**	*Steptoe & Johnson LLP*
	COLEMAN Lynn	*Skadden, Arps*
	KLEPPER Martin	*Skadden, Arps*
	NAEVE Clifford	*Skadden, Arps*
	SCHERMAN William	*Skadden, Arps*
2	**ACKER Lawrence**	*LeBoeuf, Lamb, Greene*
	BAKER William	*Thelen Reid & Priest LLP*
	BAYLIS Stanley	*Miller Baylis & O'Neill*
	BERLIN Edward	*Swidler Berlin Shereff Friedman*
	DOWNS Clark	*Jones, Day, Reavis & Pogue*
	EASTMENT Thomas	*Baker Botts LLP*
	FREMUTH Michael	*Andrews & Kurth*
	HAWES Douglas	*LeBoeuf, Lamb, Greene*
	LAMB William	*LeBoeuf, Lamb, Greene*
	O'NEILL Brian	*LeBoeuf, Lamb, Greene*
3	**BERNER Frederick**	*Sidley & Austin*
	BOWE James	*Dewey Ballantine LLP*
	CONTRATTO Dana	*Crowell & Moring LLP*
	GENTILE Carmen	*Bruder Gentile & Marcoux*
	GREEN Douglas	*Steptoe & Johnson LLP*
	KIELY Bruce	*Baker Botts LLP*
	O'SULLIVAN John	*Chadbourne & Parke LLP*
	PFEIFFER Steven	*Fulbright & Jaworski LLP*
	SHAPIRO Robert	*Chadbourne & Parke LLP*
	WILLIAMS William	*Fulbright & Jaworski LLP*
4	**ANDRIL David**	*Vinson & Elkins LLP*
	BARR Mike	*Hunton & Williams*
	BLACKBURN Thomas	*Bruder Gentile & Marcoux*
	GOODWIN Lee	*Thelen Reid & Priest LLP*
	HARDEN Rick	*Pillsbury Winthrop*
	KAIL Michael	*Steptoe & Johnson LLP*
	LOWTHER Frederick	*Dickstein Shapiro*
	NORTON Floyd	*Morgan, Lewis & Bockius LLP*
	SACHS John	*Latham & Watkins*
	WATERS Jennifer	*Crowell & Moring LLP*

Individuals are listed alphabetically in each band.

$4.4 billion. Also advised National Grid Group plc on its acquisition of Niagara Mohawk Holdings, through the formation of a new National Grid holding company and the exchange of Niagara Mohawk shares for a combination of National Grid American Depository Shares (ADSs) and cash. **Clients:** CMS Energy; Consolidated Edison Company; Enron; National Grid Group; Western Resources.

Vinson & Elkins LLP Renowned for its oil and gas expertise, this is regarded as the leading Texan based firm in the East Coast market. Advising on both contentious and transactional work, the firm advises on domestic, federal and state regulation of the generation, sale and transportation of natural gas, petroleum and refined petrochemical products, and electricity. Project finance expertise includes a number of energy-related projects, including petrochemical plants, oil, natural gas and products pipelines, and LNG and LPG facilities.

Our researchers ascertained that the firm is still largely perceived as an oil and gas operation, and, although the legendary Betsy Moler has moved to an in-house position at Exelon, it is still rated by competitors as *"serious competition for the rest of us."* **David Andril*** is regularly mentioned as the DC office's outstanding practitioner, and has a strong reputation for his regulatory advice in the natural gas industry.

The firm advised on the AES Parana Project, acting as counsel to AES on an 826MW gas-fired merchant power plant in Argentina, valued at $442 million. M&A transactions have included representing Duke Solutions on its acquisition of a portfolio of eight separate power projects in the USA from Waste Management. Also represented British Gas on the development of the Atlantic LNG facility in Trinidad, a $2.5 billion project which is the largest energy project ever undertaken in the Caribbean. **Clients:** British Gas; Duke Solutions; Enron; NRG; PSEG Global; TransAlta.

Baker Botts LLP (20 lawyers) Texan firm with an outstanding reputation for oil and gas and a respected office in Washington DC. Handling a range of regulatory, restructuring and finance work in the energy sector, the firm has undertaken substantial contracts for big electrical utilities, as well as advising on the acquisition of generation assets and natural gas pipeline contracts. The market, while admiring the office's expertise on oil and gas-related matters, noted its *"dependence"* on its strong relationship with Reliant Energy.

Competitors regard **Tom Eastment*** as the firm's *"strongest regulatory lawyer in DC,"* and he is praised for his knowledge of transportation issues. **Bruce Kiely*** is the chair of the firm's Energy practice group in DC and also draws consistent market recommendation. In addition to its fuel transportation and gas pipeline work, the firm has acted for project developers and advised extensively on restructuring in the electricity industry. Overseas, the team advised on a pipeline project from Egypt through Israel to Turkey. **Clients:** Reliant Energy Inc; electrical utilities; project developers.

Crowell & Moring LLP (5 ptrs, 5 asscs) Best known for its traditional oil and gas advice, the firm was also recommended to our researchers for natural resources expertise in mining, timber, and public lands, and also has substantial experience of international projects. A strong regulatory practice concentrates on the 'unbundling' of energy commodity sales from delivery service and stranded costs cases, while transactionally, the firm has been involved in the acquisition and divestiture of utility assets. Electricity and gas projects are handled both in the US and abroad, and the firm has an especially strong presence in Latin America.

"Well-established at the heart of the natural gas industry," according to competitors, the team advises a powerful group of distribution companies.

Head of the energy group **Dana Contratto*** is respected for his projects work, while **Jennifer Waters*** has *"been around a long time"* and is rated for her gas regulatory expertise. Fred Moring retired as a partner of the firm on 1 November 2000, and is now Special Counsel to the firm.

The firm advised two large utilities on federal legislation for the restructuring of the electricity industry, and has acted on power generation projects in the US and Mexico, a large natural gas pipeline project in Bolivia, and resource development in Peru. **Clients:** BG&E; KeySpan; ONEOK; Yacimientos Petroliferos Fiscales Bolivianos.

Fulbright & Jaworski LLP (15 lawyers) Established Texan energy firm with its primary focus on oil and gas regulatory and projects work. The firm's DC office has continued to work on the Alliance Pipeline Project, which involved the construction of a 1,800 mile pipeline in Alberta, Canada with 14 compressor stations. Renowned for its appearances before FERC on natural gas transportation issues, the firm also acts on some regulatory matters from the DC office, but researchers were left in no doubt that oil and gas continues to see the team to its best advantage.

Steven Pfeiffer* remains a respected oil and gas practitioner, although his work as managing partner of the firm's London office as well as the Washington DC office has diminished his day-to-day profile considerably. **Bill Williams*** is highly rated for his work on natural gas pipeline transportation rate cases.

The firm has represented a number of Williams Companies' Pipelines, including Texas Gas and Williams Pipeline Central, on regulatory work and domain land acquisition issues. **Clients:** Alliance; IFC; Williams Companies Inc.

Andrews & Kurth (8 ptrs, 3 asscs) The traditional base of this firm's DC office has been contentious pipeline work in front of FERC. However, anti-trust work, pipeline projects, and gas regulatory advice now form a substantial part

*See leaders' profiles on pages 848-903

of the caseload. Although its *"centre of gravity"* is in Houston, the firm's East Coast presence is still respected by competitors. **Mike Fremuth*** has been commended to researchers as *"an outstanding natural gas lawyer."*

The firm advised the Pacific Gas & Energy (PG&E) Corporation in front of the Federal Trade Commission regarding the sale of its natural gas assets in Texas to El Paso Energy Corporation. Also acted for El Paso Energy Corporation in seeking regulatory approval for a contract governing the resale of one third of the El Paso Natural Gas Pipeline. **Clients:** PG&E Corporation; El Paso Energy Corporation.

Chadbourne & Parke LLP (18 ptrs, 35 asscs) Acting in concert with its superb project finance department, the energy department's reputation is greatest on domestic and overseas projects, notably in the power industry. The team advises an international clientele of investors, lenders and developers on power projects at home and abroad, as well as acting on state regulatory proceedings. Other matters covered include electric transmission pricing and reliability, wholesale electric rates, natural gas transportation and utility restructuring.

John O'Sullivan* has a superb reputation for structuring energy transactions, and was commended to researchers for his work on behalf of AES. **Robert Shapiro*** is a *"knowledgeable and familiar figure"* on electricity regulatory matters and has worked on numerous power projects in Asia and Latin America, with his principal focus being the Brazilian power sector. The firm represented OPIC (co-senior leader with US EXIM) in the financing of three natural gas fired projects in Turkey, where the total value of the projects was $1.97 billion. The firm also represented the Korean government-owned utilities, Korea Electric Power Corporation (KEPCO) and Korea District Heating Corporation in the divestiture of two 475MW combined-cycle cogeneration LNG-fired power plants (owned by KEPCO) and two district heating systems (owned by Korea District Heating). **Clients:** The AES Corporation; Cemex; Coastal Power Company; Credit Suisse First Boston; Duke Energy Corporation; International Finance Corporation.

Hunton & Williams Active on energy policy, regulatory, and transactional matters, the firm's energy practice covers domestic and international issues, ranging from domestic transmission access for the US electricity sector to the development of Tanzania's natural gas resources. The firm combines experience in electric and gas regulation with environmental compliance, commercial contracting, project finance and energy M&A.

Historically, the firm has been associated with Virginia Power, a relationship which has been fractured by that client's acquisition by Dominion Resources. However, its powerful global network of offices enables the team to advise an array of blue-chip international clients. **Mike Barr*** in the firm's New York office is seen to be a *"projects and access guy"* who *"does a lot of capital markets deals"* in the electricity sector.

The firm advised on the project documentation and financing for the purchase of the 824MW Khanom Power Plant from EGAT and thirty separate projects in Pakistan, aggregating over 5000MW. Also acted on the sale-leaseback of a 650MW cogeneration facility in the Netherlands and the development and financing of a 605MW coal-fired power station in Western Australia. **Clients:** Domestic and international energy companies.

Steptoe & Johnson LLP (15 ptrs, 35 asscs) A superb electricity offering is the centrepiece of the firm's energy team. Power expertise includes all aspects of US regulatory practice, including the Federal Power Act and the Public Utility Holding Company Act, cross-border transactions, asset sales, project development, and anti-trust work. The firm's lower-profile oil pipeline practice provides regulatory advice, litigation and transactional services.

Lon Bouknight* is the managing partner of the firm and many competitors are of the view that *"he really built the energy practice there."* He is said to have *"an enormous utility practice and power generation M&A practice,"* and has a particularly strong relationship with American Electric Power. **Douglas Green*** is *"Lon Bouknight's right hand man,"* and was recommended to researchers as a *"forensic litigator."* **Michael Kail*** also received positive feedback from the market.

The firm secured federal regulatory approval for the merger between American Electric Power Company and Central and South West Corporation, the largest electric utility merger to date in the US. Further matters include representing Duke Energy in developing the GridSouth regional transmission company proposal and continuing to represent Southern California Edison in connection with the restructured electricity markets in California. Elsewhere, the team advised the owners of Trans Alaska Pipeline System, and acted as regulatory counsel to Lakehead Pipe Line, Colonial Pipeline and Portland Pipeline. **Clients:** Consolidated Energy Company; Duke Energy.

Jones, Day, Reavis & Pogue (8 ptrs) Most of the firm's regulatory advice is provided by its Washington DC office, with a greater focus on transactional work in New York. In recent years, the firm has focused on major electricity utility mergers, including the merger between Unicom and Peaco. The group has also advised extensively on the FERC Order 2000, stipulating that utilities place their transmission assets under the authority of a Regional Transmission Organisation.

Considered a *"small but solid regulatory group,"* the firm is a *"DC player"* in the electricity field, and clients speak highly of *"a lot of good people."* **Clark Downs*** is *"a fine lawyer"* who is known for his work on the restructuring and mergers of electricity companies.

The firm has acted for American Electric Power on separating its generating assets from its wire assets, and is also acting for South Western Public Services Company to separate its generating assets from its distribution assets over the next eighteen months. **Clients:** American Electric Power; BP; Commonwealth Edison Company; Excel Energy; Exolon; Williams Energy Group; Reliant Energy.

Latham & Watkins (22 ptrs, 53 asscs) An outstanding project finance team is sometimes seen by the market as indivisible from the firm's energy department. While it does advise on transactional and regulatory issues, there is no doubt that the firm's principal reputation lies in domestic and overseas power projects. The group has focused primarily on the development and financing of merchant power plants in the US, and also advises clients on divestitures and acquisitions of existing electricity sector assets. Clients are unanimous about the firm's projects ability, although some in the market view energy work purely as a spin-off from this specialism.

Our researchers found **John Sachs*** to be *"a popular figure"* for his work on independent power projects and development.

The firm advised on the TEG/TEP Power Project, where the firm represented project sponsors Sithe Energies, Inc. and Alstom Power on the financing of a 460MW (net) electrical generating project in Tamuin, Mexico, which was valued at $687 million and constitutes the largest single foreign investment in the Mexican power generation sector to date. Also represented the sponsors of the Hamaca extra heavy crude oil project, a $3.5 billion 200,000 bpd oil recovery and enhancement project developed in Venezuela by affiliates of Petróleos de Venezuela, Phillips Petroleum Company and Texaco Inc. **Clients:** AES; BP Amoco; CMS Energy; DTE Energy; Edison Mission Energy; GPU International; Intergen; MidAmerican Energy; Mobil; NRG Energy; PGE National Energy Group; PPL Global; Sithe Energies; Southern Electricity International; TransAlta; United Technologies Energy; Unocal.

Pillsbury Winthrop (11 ptrs, 7 asscs) Commended to our researchers for its work on energy-related financings, the firm does substantial work for public utility companies, utility holding companies and independent power. Other important elements of the caseload include energy-related M&A transactions and regulatory matters before FERC. Formely Winthrop, Stimson, Putnam & Roberts, the firm's recent merger with west coast-based Pillisbury, Madison & Sutro is welcomed by the market.

Rick Harden* is widely regarded as the *"stand-out"* in the firm's New York office for his project finance work in the energy field, and is seen to have *"good relationships with a lot of underwriters and investment banks."* The firm acted for Sigcorp on its $1.9 billion acquisition of Indiana Energy Inc, and FirstEnergy's pending acquisition of GPU for $4.5 billion. Also advised on the $3.4 billion acquisition by Public Service Company of New Mexico and PP&L Global Incorporated, of Western Resources' electric utility operations. **Clients:** The AES Corporation; Big Rivers Electric Cooperative; Central Hudson Gas & Electric Company; CP&L Energy; Enron Power Development Corporation; Entergy Corporation; FPL Group; GPU Corporation; Intergen; Northeast Utilities Inc; Pacificorp; System Energy Resources Inc; TXU Corp; Washington Gas Light Company.

Sidley & Austin (15 lawyers) The firm continues to undertake utility restructuring and regulatory work out of its DC office, with emphasis on FERC-related matters. It has acted on the creation of regional transmission companies, acting predominantly for electricity companies. Well-known for its anti-trust and trade regulation expertise in DC, the firm retains a *"distinct, albeit low, profile"* among its competitors. **Fred Berner*** is a highly regarded pipeline lawyer, who has continued his involvement with the Millennium Pipeline. The firm has also acted on litigation for a natural gas producer in matters involving pipeline reimbursement rates. **Clients:** The United Illuminating Company; electricity companies.

Thelen Reid & Priest LLP (30 ptrs) The firm's Energy and Project Infrastructure Practice Group undertakes a range of work, including power sales contracts, tolling agreements, operation and maintenance agreements, and federal energy regulation work. The firm has had a strong focus on acquisitions in the past twelve months, particularly for Orion Power Holdings. Considered by peers to have made *"a massive effort in the field,"* the firm's relationship with TXU ensures that it remains in the public eye. **William Baker*** is *"the firm's resident expert on the Public Holding Company Act in New York,"* on which he is said to be *"as good as anyone around."* **Lee Goodwin*** *"has built up a substantial practice,"* and represents mainly independent power developers. The firm acted for Orion Power Holdings on its acquisition of 2600MW of power plants from the electricity utility company Duquesne, a $1.7 billion divestiture. **Clients:** Callpine Corporation; GPU; Orion Power Holdings

Other Notable Practitioners **Stanley Baylis*** from Miller Baylis & O'Neill is recommended for his work on behalf of municipal gas distribution companies, often opposing incumbent companies. **Ed Berlin*** from Swidler Berlin Shereff Friedman is a *"very fine lawyer,"* and a familiar figure as a result of his work on behalf of US Grid. **James Bowe*** from Dewey Ballantine is *"a knowledgeable"* gas lawyer, with a *"good client base,"* while **Carmen Gentile*** from Bruder Gentile & Marcoux is said to be *"the firm's most senior and well-known practitioner"* in the energy field, with a strong regulatory electricity practice. Gentile's colleague **Thomas Blackburn*** has *"an encyclopaedic understanding of the regulation of transmission business."* **Frederick Lowther*** from Dickstein Shapiro Morin & Oshinsky is seen to be doing *"amazingly well"* on an eclectic mixture of regulatory and transactional work." **Floyd (Mac) Norton*** from Morgan Lewis & Bockius is viewed by the market as a *"solid regulatory lawyer,"* who has *"traditionally represented electric utilities in FERC proceedings."*

U

Energy & Natural Resources: Texas

USA: TEXAS Leading Firms (Energy & Natural Resources)
1 Vinson & Elkins LLP
2 Baker Botts LLP
3 Akin, Gump, Strauss, Hauer & Feld LLP
Fulbright & Jaworski LLP
4 Andrews & Kurth
Bracewell & Patterson LLP
King & Spalding
5 Locke Liddell & Sapp LLP
Skadden, Arps, Slate, Meagher & Flom LLP

Firms are listed alphabetically in each band.

Leading Individuals (Energy & Natural Resources)		
1	ASMUS David *Baker Botts LLP*	BILGER Bruce *Vinson & Elkins LLP*
	GOOLSBY George *Baker Botts LLP*	
2	COGAN John *King & Spalding*	DILG Joe *Vinson & Elkins LLP*
	ROZZELL Scott *Baker Botts LLP*	STRAUSS Bob *Akin, Gump*
	UNGER Timothy *Andrews & Kurth*	
3	BRANNAN John *Vinson & Elkins LLP*	CULOTTA Ken *King & Spalding*
	DAVIS Platt *Vinson & Elkins LLP*	KELLEY Jay *Vinson & Elkins LLP*
	MOORE Charles *Akin, Gump*	
4	GREMILLION Tod *Akin, Gump*	MAY Henry *Vinson & Elkins LLP*
	THURBER Mark *Skadden, Arps*	

Individuals are listed alphabetically in each band.

Vinson & Elkins LLP (89 ptrs, 141 asscs) In Texas, this firm is the undisputed king of the hill; it has also the furthest national and global reach of any Texas-based firm. Known for *"great depth,"* and commended to researchers for *"being to Houston what Skaddens is to New York,"* the firm is known for *"consistent quality and professionalism"* in oil gas and electricity work, both transactional and regulatory.

A superb team includes the *"excellent"* **Henry May***, recognised by clients for his work on federal and state energy regulation and utility law, and **Platt Davis***, another *"outstanding"* regulatory lawyer, whose practice incorporates a substantial litigation element. **John Brannan*** is a *"thoroughly experienced"* oil and gas lawyer, while **Bruce Bilger*** is a transactional lawyer with *"tremendous business sense and flair."* **Joe Dilg*** is another recommended transactional heavyweight, who is *"rich in common sense,"* while **Jay Kelley***, a recent arrival from Andrews & Kurth, is an acclaimed energy generalist.

The firm is still most famous for its *"wonderful work"* on behalf of Enron, but it has also represented Duke Energy on the $5.5 billion merger of its natural gas business with that of Phillips Petroleum. Also advised Merrill Lynch on the $2.8 billion merger of Dynergy Inc and Illinova Corp. For Enron, the firm advised on its purchase and sale agreement with Sierra Pacific Resources for its wholly-owned electricity utility subsidiary. **Clients:** Duke Energy Corp; Merrill Lynch; Enron Corp; Unocal Corp; AES Parana SCA; Inter-American Development Bank; Citibank; Alliance RTO.

Baker Botts LLP (33 lawyers) A *"pure energy firm"* with *"broad expertise, especially in oil and gas,"* the firm was described by a number of admiring clients as *"the industry's choice."* A transactionally oriented department advises an important pool of domestic clients, and has placed increased recent emphasis on international work, notably in and around the Caspian Sea.

In charge of the oil and gas practice group, **David Asmus*** was recommended to researchers as a *"superb"* transactional energy specialist, while the *"great"* **George Goolsby*** is *"deserving of immense respect"* as *"one of the sharpest"* lawyers in Texas. His practice embraces oil and gas transportation, regulatory and transactional advice and litigation. Chair of the Energy practice group in Houston, **Scott Rozzell*** has extensive experience of appearing before state and federal regulatory bodies, and is *"one of the finest energy lawyers out there."*

The firm acted for Reliant Energy Power Generation Inc on the financing of a $475 million power plant, advised Florida Power & Light on gas transportation agreements, and represented BP Amoco on the $3.6 billion sale of its partnership interests in Altura Energy LP. **Clients:** BP Amoco; Reliant Energy; Occidental Petroleum Corporation; Conoco; Schlumberger Limited.

Akin, Gump, Strauss, Hauer & Feld LLP The real strength of this *"totally competent"* firm is felt to lie in *"excellent regulatory work."* Its capability in this field is said by rivals to be *"formidable,"* and it represents clients before all federal agencies and most state ones, as well as appellate courts, tribunals and legislatures. Experts in oil and gas regulatory matters, both upstream and downstream, the firm's transactional prowess in the industry is felt to be somewhat overshadowed.

Bob Strauss* *("has marvellous credentials")*, a former presidential aide and ambassador, is a legendary *"opener of doors,"* and serves as the firm's rainmaking supremo. **Charles Moore*** has a *"good head for litigation"* and is *"effective with clients,"* while the *"flamboyant"* **Tod Gremillion*** is the group's transactional figure, handling domestic and international oil and gas deals. **Clients:** Westport Energy Corp.

Fulbright & Jaworski LLP (34 lawyers) The firm has its primary reputation for a *"top quality transactional capacity,"* notably in oil and gas, and a creditable litigation team. Although lacking a high profile individual name, the team's *"uniformly high standard"* was commended to our researchers.

The firm acted for EOG Resources on its acquisition of Somerset Oil & Gas, and advised ATOFINA Petrochemicals on the sale of various assets to Alon Israel Oil Company Ltd. Overseas, the group advised TotalFinaElf on its acquisition of an interest in the Brazil-Bolivia pipeline from BHP Petroleum. **Clients:** British-Borneo Exploration; BG International Ltd; Duke Energy Corp; Enterprise Oil plc; Exxon Corporation; Shell Oil Company; Transco Energy Co.

Andrews & Kurth (16 ptrs, 12 asscs) Although the firm remains one of the most highly respected energy practices in Houston, the loss of a number of partners has been a severe blow. Recommended to our researchers for regulatory and transactional expertise in oil and gas matters, as well as advice on energy projects, the firm is known for its work at both state and federal levels.

The team's star lawyer remains **Timothy Unger***, whose *"great depth of knowledge,"* especially of co-generation and independent power projects, commands widespread respect. The firm advised Santa Fe Snyder Corporation on its $5 billion acquisition by Devon Energy, and PG&E Natural Energy Corporation in its $840 million acquisition by El Paso Energy. **Clients:** Enron; Shell Oil; Conoco; Duke Energy.

Bracewell & Patterson LLP (25 ptrs, 55 asscs) Seen to be *"an ambitious challenger"* to the traditional Texan hierarchy, the firm is commended by peers for its balanced energy practice, incorporating a *"strong regulatory practice"* and an established transactional capacity. Downstream oil and gas work is a particular forte, and the firm's clientele largely comprises important domestic names. **Clients:** Babcock International Group PLC; Enron Corp; Kinder Morgan Inc.

King & Spalding (17 ptrs, 23 asscs) *"Active"* firm, which has expanded markedly, through an intensive recruitment campaign. The energy group has a reputation for *"consistent quality,"* and an increasingly international transactional workload includes niche expertise in LNG and energy projects.

The *"absolutely superb"* **John Cogan*** has an *"excellent upstream oil and gas practice,"* and also advises on transportation and sale, governmental regulation and LNG. The *"outstanding"* **Kenneth Culotta*** *"does a damn good job,"* and concentrates on energy projects. The firm advised Enron in connection with the chartering of LNG tankers. **Clients:** TCT International.

Locke Liddell & Sapp LLP (33 ptrs, 29 asscs) Recently merged firm that now boasts critical mass in addition to a high quality energy practice, especially in project finance and development. It is particularly noted for its work in the power industry, and the firm's rivals anticipate that it could be *"a real force soon."*

The firm has represented the developers on a number of power projects in Texas and Louisiana, and advised Arena Power on a proposed joint venture to develop power generation assets. Also acted for a Houston-based energy major in planned acquisitions of generation assets. **Clients:** Dynergy; Constellation Power; Arena Power; Tractabel.

Skadden, Arps, Slate, Meagher & Flom LLP (5 ptrs, 12 asscs) The firm's Houston office is devoted to transactional work in the energy sector, and has advised on numerous financings and power projects. The firm is admired by peers for its *"excellent M&A work for energy clients,"* although the absence of a serious regulatory practice is felt to impose certain limitations on the department in Texas. **Mark Thurber*** is regarded as the firm's outstanding practitioner. **Clients:** Enron; Coastal; El Paso.

Intellectual Property: East Coast

USA: EAST COAST
Leading Firms (Intellectual Property)

Band	Firm
1	Fish & Neave
2	Finnegan Henderson Farabow Garrett & Dunner LLP
3	Clifford Chance Rogers & Wells
	Pennie & Edmonds
4	Fitzpatrick, Cella, Harper & Scinto
	Kenyon & Kenyon
	Kirkland & Ellis
5	Fish & Richardson
	Howrey Simon Arnold & White
	Jones, Day, Reavis & Pogue
6	Baker Botts LLP
	Weil, Gotshal & Manges

Firms are listed alphabetically in each band.

Leading Individuals (Intellectual Property)

Band	Individual
★	**DUNNER Donald** *Finnegan Henderson Farabow*
1	**FEY Albert** *Fish & Neave*
	SCHWARTZ Herb *Fish & Neave*
2	**MISROCK Leslie** *Pennie & Edmonds*
3	**BAECHTOLD Robert** *Fitzpatrick, Cella, Harper*
	FARABOW Ford *Finnegan Henderson Farabow*
	JENNER Jesse *Fish & Neave*
	KIDD John *Clifford Chance Rogers & Wells*
	LYNCH John *Howrey Simon Arnold & White*
4	**DAVIS Jim** *Howrey Simon Arnold & White*
	KATSH Salem *Shearman & Sterling*
	LEE Bill *Hale and Dorr*
	LIPSEY Charles *Finnegan Henderson Farabow*
	NEUNER Robert *Baker Botts LLP*

Individuals are listed alphabetically in each band.

Fish & Neave (6 ptrs, 20 asscs) Consistently rated by its rivals as the leading IP practice on the East Coast, *"you are in for a war when you come up against them."* This litigation-oriented firm's success is attributed largely to its *"extremely bright lawyers"* and *"phenomenal client base."* Areas of outstanding expertise include pharmaceuticals, biotechnology and telecoms. Our researchers found two of the best names in the business to be *"elegant"* **Al Fey***, *"the mainstay of the practice,"* and **Herb Schwartz*** who is a *"real talent,"* described as *"practical, hard-working and smart."* **Jesse Jenner*** is said to be the *"heir apparent"* to these two big names. The firm recently defended a patent for AT&T, and won a plaintiff case for Georgia Pacific v US Gypsum. **Clients:** AT&T; Lucent; Ford; Biogen; Polaroid.

Finnegan Henderson Farabow Garrett & Dunner LLP (80 ptrs, 120 asscs) One of the East Coast's *"major IP players"* has a first class reputation for its *"excellent appellate practice."* The firm draws on an international clientele to advise on patent, copyright, trademarks, trade secrets, technology import issues, unfair competition, IT and biotech work. The *"dean of appellate work"* **Don Dunner*** is *"scrupulously honest,"* and *"has huge influence."* **Ford Farabow*** is another of the *"region's leaders,"* while **Charles Lipsey*** is *"building up an excellent reputation as a trial lawyer."* Representative litigations that the firm has handled include Lockheed Martin Corp et al v United States, Loral Fairchild Corp v Sony Corp and Zeneca Ltd v Novopharm Ltd. **Clients:** Sony; Toshiba; Xerox; SmithKline Beecham; Hoechst AG; BP; Coca-Cola; Mattel Inc; American Home Products; Zeneca Ltd.

Clifford Chance Rogers & Wells (9 ptrs, 49 asscs) The firm is widely believed to be *"making a strong pitch in the IP arena."* Handling both transactional and litigation work, it is most noted by peers for its expertise in biotechnology and business methods patents. **John Kidd*** is commended to researchers as an *"experienced litigator."* The firm represented Aventis v Bristol-Myers in the Taxol anti-tumour drug patent case, Genetech v Glaxo Wellcome and Sharpe Corp in an ITC lawsuit. **Clients:** Genetech; Johnson & Johnson; Hoffman LaRoche; Sun Microsystems; Merrill Lynch; Goldman Sachs; Morgan Stanley.

Pennie & Edmonds (55 ptrs, 190 asscs) Traditionally one of the strongest IP practices in the country, the firm is still viewed by rivals as *"the most formidable of opponents."* Biotechnology and patent prosecution are considered to be the major strengths of a firm which also handles IP procurement, litigation and consulting in pharmaceuticals, chemicals and materials science, electronics and computer software, and the mechanical industry. Trademarks and trade regulation work are also areas of extensive experience. **Leslie Misrock*** *"has been the leader of the firm for years"* and seen by many as *"the best biotech attorney in the country."* The firm represented Cadus Pharmaceutical v Sibia Neurosciences and won a permanent injunction for BIC v Thai Merry. **Clients:** Hoffman LaRoche; Bristol-Myers Squibb; Hewlett-Packard; Fortune Brands; Barnes & Noble; Microsoft; Purdue Pharma LP.

Fitzpatrick, Cella, Harper & Scinto (50 ptrs, 80 asscs) Highly regarded for its ability to *"get in the trenches,"* and its *"excellent work ethics,"* the firm is active in all areas of IP, particularly pharmaceutical, biotech, chemical, e-commerce and consumer trademarks. **Bob Baechtold*** is a *"serious litigator"* whose name features prominently in the region. The firm defended Pharmacia v University of Rochester on an infringement suit, and represented Astra Zeneca in enforcing its patents on Omeprazole. Also defended Bausch & Lomb against patent infringement charges relating to LASIK laser eye surgery. **Clients:** Canon; Bristol-Myers Squibb; Bausch & Lomb; Astra Zeneca; Pharmacia; Pfizer; Novartis; M&M/Mars; SmithKline Beecham; Monsanto; Emory University.

Kenyon & Kenyon (40 ptrs, 160 asscs) Another of the traditionally strong IP practices, which *"still get its share of work."* The firm is noted for its ability to *"throw a lot of good lawyers at a problem,"* but in spite of this, it is felt to lack a stand-out practitioner. Active in IP litigation and patent prosecution, the firm is considered by rivals to be seen to its best advantage in computer and electronics-oriented patent work. Highlight cases include Harris Heidelberg v Mitsubishi, Bio-technology General v Genentech and Faulding Corp v Purdue Pharma. **Clients:** Novartis; BASF; Sony; Intel; AT&T; Enzo Biochem; Imclone Systems; Amgen; Nycomed Amersham; Bio-technology General.

Kirkland & Ellis (24 ptrs, 54 asscs) A Chicago-based firm with a *"strong East Coast presence,"* the firm has a history of raising *"good IP litigators."* The team covers all aspects of IP, particularly patent litigation, notably in the spheres of biotechnology, IT, computers and electronics work. It represented Micron Technology v Mosel Vitelic in four separate patent cases, and recently achieved a successful patent defence on behalf of Oxford Gene Technologies v Affymetrix. Other important matters include representing Netscape in connection with two large patent infringement cases involving IT-related patent infringement allegations, and it is currently handling two large cases for AOL. **Clients:** 3M; Hitachi; AOL.

Fish & Richardson (49 ptrs, 65 asscs) A firm with *"great depth"* is considered by clients to have an abundance of *"talent and energy,"* and excels in complex IP litigation, notably in hi-tech industry. The group represented SeaChange International v nCube Corp and obtained $18.75 million on

*See leaders' profiles on pages 848-903

behalf of Supracor Inc from Reebok International Ltd. Also defended Microsoft in a patent infringement case brought by TypeRight Keyboard. **Clients:** 3M; Intel; Microsoft; Adobe Systems; Gillette; Bose.

Howrey Simon Arnold & White (35 ptrs, 65 asscs) The merger of these two firms has produced a large IP practice. However, according to the findings of our researchers, the market remains unclear about the effect of the union. The IP focus is on litigation, patent prosecution, counselling and trademark work. *"Experienced and talented"* **Jim Davis*** has an established reputation, while *"bright and effective"* **John Lynch*** is an *"excellent trial lawyer."* The firm has represented Monsanto in a number of litigation cases. **Clients:** Intel; Monsanto; Caterpillar; Rockwell; Shell Oil.

Jones, Day, Reavis & Pogue (30 ptrs, 55 asscs) *"A real force nationwide,"* the firm's *"fine lawyers"* handle a variety of IP matters, including trademarks, copyright, litigation, patent prosecution, cyber squatting and business method patents. The team represented Texas Instruments in a patent infringement case against Hyundai and advised Acromed on a patent infringement case against Sofamor Danek. **Clients:** P&G; Texas Instruments; IBM; Sabic; PepsiCo; Johnson & Johnson.

Baker Botts LLP (15 ptrs, 30 asscs) This Texan firm has a *"highly capable New York practice,"* which is active in IP litigation, prosecution and transactional work. A particular growth area is the telecommunications industry, while the firm also has a strong clientele of infrastructure/networking companies. **Bob Neuner*** is the firm's leading lawyer in the region. He represented Alcatel v Samsung in a trade secrets case and Exxon v Mobil on a patent case. **Clients:** i2 Software; Alcatel; Cisco; Trinity Industries; Columbia University; Silicon Graphics; Efficient Networks; Fujitsu Network Communications.

Weil, Gotshal & Manges (12 ptrs, 40 asscs) Although it has suffered a number of recent departures, the firm's established IP practice still handles a diverse range of work, including patents, copyright, trademarks and trade secrets. E-commerce and music licensing work are areas of specific expertise. The firm represented Exxon in patent litigation against the US Government and Intel and Cisco in patent litigation. **Clients:** Exxon; Intel; Cisco; Estée Lauder; Pirelli; GE; Disney; Matsushita.

Other Notable Practitioners **Salem Katsh** *"has been around forever"* and now heads Shearman & Sterling's IP practice. He is active on premium prosecution work, e-commerce, internet related trade secrets and litigation for start-up dot.com companies. In Boston, **Bill Lee*** of Hale and Dorr is *"number one."* He defended Picturetel on a patent covering video conferencing, and represented Biogen v Berlex Laboratories on a patent infringement case.

Intellectual Property: West Coast

Irell & Manella (35 ptrs, 55 asscs) The firm has *"a superb reputation throughout California,"* and is devoted to corporate transactions, patent prosecutions, licensing, trademarks, copyright, trade secrets and IP litigation. A *"wonderful"* team of lawyers is said to *"leave no stone unturned,"* and is headed by *"one of the best IP litigators in the country,"* the *"superb"* **Morgan Chu***. One lawyer told our researchers he is *"an excellent speaker,"* who gives *"the best trial presentations that I've ever heard."*

The firm represented the plaintiff on the case Stac Electronics v Microsoft, and obtained a unanimous jury verdict and permanent injunction against Microsoft for patent infringements. Also advised Hewlett-Packard v Xerox in seven different cases involving patents and other issues, which was recently settled. **Clients:** Hewlett-Packard; Compaq; Affymetrix; AT&T.

Weil, Gotshal & Manges (10 ptrs, 37 asscs) An *"active and visible IP presence in the West,"* the firm is especially noted for IP litigation, strategic patent counselling, licensing and corporate transactions. The group is said to *"do two things really well: IP litigation and representing big companies on IP transactions,"* and is considered *"a major competitor because you see them on the major cases."*

"Tenacious, hard-driving litigator" **Matt Powers*** *"handles some of the biggest and best cases,"* and *"combines intelligence and thoughtfulness with the qualities of a pit-bull terrier."* The firm was lead counsel for Perkin Elmer's Applied Biosystem Division and Celera on three patent litigations involving DNA sequencing technology used in the human genome project. Also advised Phone.com on a patent litigation against Geoworks, involving basic wireless telephony standards. **Clients:** Intel; Cisco; Micron Technology; Applied Materials; Oracle; National Semiconductor; Phone.com; Perkin Elmer's Applied Biosystems Division.

Day Casebeer Madrid & Batchelder LLP (6 ptrs, 14 asscs) A two year-old firm with *"a group of first-rate lawyers"* who our researchers were informed *"should always be considered for patent litigations."* Although viewed as a specialist litigation practice, it also offers its clients some strategic counselling.

Known to handle *"make or break litigation for companies,"* the team boasts the services of **Rusty Day***, regarded as *"a cut above the rest,"* who appears on the majority of the firm's high-profile cases and *"is very close to the big league."* The firm represented Sun Microsystems against Microsoft in litigation over the Java technology. Defence work has included advising Qualcom on a patent infringement lawsuit brought by GTE Wireless, and defending Yahoo! on a business method patent infringement lawsuit brought by Herrington. **Clients:** Amgen; Qualcomm; Yahoo!; Sun Microsystems.

Fenwick & West (16 ptrs, 74 asscs) A *"big IP practice with a top-notch reputation,"* which maintains strong relationships with hardware and software clients. Over the last twelve months, the firm has advised both claimants and defendants on numerous high-profile cases. *"Outstanding"* **David Hayes*** is the number one name here.

The firm represented Napster Inc on various copyright lawsuits brought by recording companies and music publishers, alleging contributory infringement by the company for operating the Napster service. Other highlight cases include advising Intuit Inc and Broderbund Software Inc on defending a business method patent infringement lawsuit relating to online commerce, which was brought by Interactive Gift Express. **Clients:** Sun Microsystems; Apple Computers; Excite

Morrison & Foerster (9 ptrs, 36 asscs) *"A traditional firm with a strong environmental and life sciences practice,"* it handles IP litigation for a

USA: WEST COAST Leading Firms (Intellectual Property)
1 Irell & Manella
Weil, Gotshal & Manges
2 Day Casebeer Madrid & Batchelder LLP
Fenwick & West
Morrison & Foerster
Townsend and Townsend and Crew LLP
3 Finnegan Henderson Farabow Garrett & Dunner LLP
Fish & Neave
Orrick, Herrington & Sutcliffe

Firms are listed alphabetically in each band.

Leading Individuals (Intellectual Property)
★ CHU Morgan *Irell & Manella*
POWERS Matthew *Weil, Gotshal & Manges*
1 DAY Lloyd (Rusty) *Day Casebeer Madrid*
2 HAYES David *Fenwick & West*
3 DODSON Gerald *Morrison & Foerster*
JACOBS Micheal *Morrison & Foerster*
KRUPKA Bob *Kirkland & Ellis*
McMAHON Terry *Orrick, Herrington & Sutcliffe*

Individuals are listed alphabetically in each band.

high-powered clientele comprising biotechnology, electronics and software companies and dot.coms. **Jerry Dodson*** is *"an interesting lawyer, who gains fabulous results,"* and his colleague **Mike Jacobs*** also comes highly recommended.

The team advised the University of Rochester Medical Centre in a patent infringement lawsuit against Pharmacia Corporation, GD Searle and Pfizer, involving the best-selling new drug in history, Celebrex. **Clients:** DoubleClick; Chiron; Clorox; Healthion; SDLI.

Townsend and Townsend and Crew LLP (55 ptrs, 85 asscs) The largest of the IP boutiques on the West Coast is considered to be a *"high quality patent prosecution firm,"* servicing *"an interesting collection of clients."* The firm covers the whole IP sphere, with biotechnology and appeal work acknowledged as key strengths. Designated as lead counsel in the California Co-ordinated Proceedings against Microsoft, the firm also acted on the Hyundai Electronics Co Ltd v Rambus case. **Clients:** Affymetrix; Ask Jeeves; Hyundai Semiconductor; National Institutes of Health; Oracle; Yahoo!

Finnegan, Henderson, Farabow, Garrett & Dunner LLP (7 ptrs, 13 asscs) Although primarily known for its superb Washington office, the firm's IP offering on the West Coast is highly respected, particularly for litigation and appeal work. Possessing *"some excellent lawyers,"* the firm is considered to be *"serious about growing on the West Coast."* The team advised Nortel Networks v Samsung (Federal Circuit Appeal), Hewlett-Packard v Insight Development Corp and Sony America v Drexler Technology Corporation. **Clients:** Hewlett-Packard; Sun Microsystems; Hyundai Electronics; Xerox PARC.

Fish & Neave (6 ptrs, 21 asscs) New York-based firm, described as *"the premier IP boutique in the country,"* which is *"strong across the board on the litigation side,"* and has a *"great client base."* The firm primarily advises on IP litigation in biotechnology, computers and the medical sector, and represented Incyte Genomics on a pair of gene expression data base cases (Incyte v Gene Logic and Incyte v Affymetrix.) Also acted for FileNet Corporation on a computer imaging systems matter (Kodak v. FileNet.) **Clients:** Incyte; Becton Dickinson; FileNet Corp; Linear Technology.

Orrick Herrington & Sutcliffe (15 ptrs, 35 asscs) Held to be *"building up a sound practice,"* our researchers found that the firm has been *"coming on strong lately in IP litigation."* A broad IP caseload covers patents, trade secrets, copyright and trademarks. **Terry McMahon*** is the stand-out lawyer for a team which represented Affymetrix v OGT, Compaq and Seagate v Convolve and MIT, and Quantum v Papst in multi-district litigation. At the time of press, Mr McMahon announced his intention to join McDermott, Will & Emery. **Clients:** Applied Materials; Micron Technologies; Lam Research; Seagate Technologies; Quantum; Logitech; Lucent; Microsoft.

Other Notable Practitioner Kirkland & Ellis' West Coast practice is headed by **Bob Krupka***. A *"good lawyer who drives himself incessantly,"* he acted for Oxford Gene Technology v Affymetrix Inc on a victorious jury trial, represented Razor USA in a scooter braking mechanism patent case, and has also advised Motorola, General Motors, Honeywell and Pioneer.

U

Private Equity: Buyouts: New York

USA: NEW YORK Leading Firms (Private Equity: Buyouts)
1 Simpson Thacher & Bartlett
2 Davis Polk & Wardwell
3 Debevoise & Plimpton
Weil, Gotshal & Manges
4 Kirkland & Ellis
5 Latham & Watkins
6 Fried, Frank, Harris, Shriver & Jacobson

Firms are listed alphabetically in each band.

Leading Individuals (Private Equity: Buyouts)
1 **BEATTIE Richard** *Simpson Thacher*
BLASSBERG Franci *Debevoise & Plimpton*
2 **BASON George** *Davis Polk & Wardwell*
COGUT Charles *Simpson Thacher*
FRAIDIN Stephen *Fried, Frank, Harris*
NUSBAUM Jack *Willkie Farr & Gallagher*
3 **BOHM Rick** *Debevoise & Plimpton*
GOLDBERG Louis *Davis Polk & Wardwell*
JACOBS Stephen *Weil, Gotshal & Manges*
KIMMEL Roger *Latham & Watkins*
RADKE Kirk *Kirkland & Ellis*
ROBERTS Tom *Weil, Gotshal & Manges*
RUEGGER Philip (Pete) *Simpson Thacher*
4 **BICK John** *Davis Polk & Wardwell*
ETTINGER John *Davis Polk & Wardwell*
FINLEY John *Simpson Thacher*
HALL Richard *Cravath, Swaine & Moore*
Up-and-coming individuals
HOPKINSON Ronald *Latham & Watkins*

Individuals are listed alphabetically in each band.

Simpson Thacher & Bartlett (10 ptrs) *"Packed with leading LBO lights,"* the firm is recognised as *"pre-eminent in private equity."* Highly acquisitive funds such as KKR and Blackstone Group *"feed the practice,"* and produce corporate partners with an *"innate transactional sense." "Maestro"* **Richard Beattie*** is a *"hugely influential figure"* in the market. As Chairman, his involvement on transactions is less visible to our interviewees, yet his *"legendary grasp of complex structures"* often makes him the first port of call for clients. *"Excellent"* **Casey Cogut*** *"can spot the finer points of a deal."* Overseeing the relationship with KKR, he is the most visible of the firm's transactional practitioners. Recognised for his work with Blackstone Group, the *"intelligent and considered"* **Pete Ruegger*** is said to *"inspire confidence through and through."* In common with a number of his colleagues, he mixes buyout work with public company M&A. **John Finley*** is a *"senior figure"* who consistently displays *"sound knowledge of the markets."* His buyouts profile derives from his advice on behalf of highly acquisitive merchant banking funds.

The expansion of private equity houses into Europe has led to an increased level of cross border activity. Advised KKR on the acquisitions of Siemens Nixdorf and Blackstone Real Estate Fund on the purchase of two European Office towers. **Clients:** Kohlberg Kravis Roberts; Blackstone Group; Cypress Group; Vestar; Silverlake; Lehman Brothers Merchant Banking Partners.

Davis Polk & Wardwell (8 ptrs) *"A significant buyout practice"* with a strong reputation for the management of investment banking funds including DLJ and the Morgan houses. Venture capital funds, financing a high volume of acquisitions, are noticeable growth areas for a team which maintains its presence on big-ticket deals. The firm advised DLJ Merchant Banking Partners on its $900 million cash and securities acquisition of Advanstar.

The *"vastly experienced"* **Gar Bason*** is said to be *"straight as an arrow"* in negotiations. The most visible partner with a strong relationship to DLJ, he is known for involvement on big ticket, highly leveraged work. *"Strong"* **John Bick*** is seen to mix M&A with buyout work for Morgan Stanley Capital Partners (five major fund groups.) Considered *"always good news"* on a transaction, he is s senior figure at the firm. *"Immensely energetic"* **Louis Goldberg**'s* stature continues to grow. With Bick, he advises Morgan Stanley Dean Witter on a high volume of acquisitions and fund formations. **John Ettinger*** also remains a respected member of the team. **Clients:** Morgan Stanley Capital Partners; DLJ; CSFB; Morgan Stanley Dean Witter; Tiger Management; Farallon.

Debevoise & Plimpton (25 attorneys) Producing *"high quality work,"* much of the firm's *"great strength"* lies in its long-standing relationship with major LBO fund Clayton Dubilier & Rice. With a high profile for fund formation, the firm is seen to offer *"good continuity of service"* and attorneys who *"understand time imperatives."* The team advised Kelso on its sixth fund and recently closed the first general US buyout fund for Schroder Venture Partners.

"Wonderful" **Franci Blassberg*** *"knows the business like the back of her hand."* As the relationship partner for Clayton Dubilier & Rice, she is the most visible of this large team and is thought to bring a *"strong-willed"* approach to transactions. Seen to follow major funds into overseas growth markets, Blassberg advised CD&R on its investment in Fairchild Dornier, the German aircraft manufacturer (total value $1.2 billion with Allianz Capital Partners.) *"A good problem solver,"* **Rick Bohm*** is said to have *"made his mark"* with his advice on the Kelso funds. Commended for his media and technology focus, Bohm advised the Dolan family on the take-private of the Cleveland Indians baseball team, and represented Kelso on its acquisition of Charter Communications and subsequent sale to Paul G Allen for $4.6 billion. **Clients:** Clayton Dubilier & Rice; Greenwich Street Partners; Kelso; North Castle; Schroder Venture Partners; DLJ.

Weil, Gotshal & Manges (50 attorneys nationwide) The buyouts team is considered to have a *"prominent market presence,"* with a number of partners commanding major funds as clients. The New York office receives support from the firm's Dallas operation in advising its headline client Hicks Muse Tate & Furst. A well-established London office assists the firm with its cross-border transactions, a substantial portion of the workload. Chambers researchers were told that the Private Equity and Investment Management group is also respected for its focus on high technology investment funds, including internet incubators. Often seen in high yield financings, the team has a strong clientele of merchant banking funds.

"A strong personality," **Tom Roberts*** is considered a *"real force on a deal."* Renowned for his work with Hicks Muse and Capital Z, he is a *"seasoned practitioner."* **Steve Jacobs*** has a *"great reputation amongst private equity specialists."* Less visible than Roberts, owing to his role as Head of Corporate, he is thought to have adjusted well to his role as a rainmaker. The team advised Hicks Muse on the acquisition, via newly established Eubisco, of Burton's Biscuits from Associated Foods. **Clients:** Hicks Muse Tate & Furst; CSFB; Capital Z Partners; DLJ Merchant Banking Partners; Thomas H Lee Company.

Kirkland & Ellis (70 attorneys) The firm now boasts *"a sizeable New York presence,"* which is thought to have cast off the shadow of its hugely prominent Chicago operation. Considered to be *"a firm built on private equity,"* it is *"devoted"* to buyouts, and offers advice on 'cradle to grave' fund formation and leveraged acquisitions. The team has been commended by its rivals for extending its clientele from smaller venture capital funds to broad-based financial houses including Vestar and

Citicorp. Overseas investment, particularly in Asia and Western Europe is a growth area for the practice, while the firm's West Coast office has also profited from the recent wave of hi-tech funds.

The *"talented"* **Kirk Radke*** remains *"the most prominent"* of this large team. Held to be *"a great guy to work with,"* he is the department's transactional mainstay **Clients:** Bain Capital; Vestar; Thomas H Lee Company; Bear Sterns; Corner Stone Equity; CitiCorp Venture Capital.

Latham & Watkins (7 ptrs) A *"strong"* practice which has *"capitalised on the hi-tech boom"* and built on the experience of advising highly acquisitive venture capital funds. The New York office undertakes volume work for major funds such as The Carlyle Group, and is also acclaimed for high-yield debt financing. On the West Coast the firm acts for KKR, while an established London office gives the organisation cross-border clout.

"Intelligent" **Roger Kimmel*** brings *"gravitas"* to the firm's buyout operation. He *"knows all the practicalities"* of a deal and is commended for his work as acquisition counsel to Bear Sterns' Merchant Banking Group. At the time of press, Mr Kimmel announced his intention to move to the investment bank, Rothschild North America. Younger partner **Ron Hopkinson*** continues to build a name for his *"good deal knowledge."* The firm advised European huyout firm BC Partners on its $1 billion acquisition (and $950 million assumption of debt) of the US auto parts company Mark IV Industries. **Clients:** Carlyle Group, DLJ, Bear Sterns, Stamford Capital Partners.

Fried, Frank, Harris, Shriver & Jacobson (3 ptrs) *"A familiar name"* in the market, with a reputation based on the *"huge volume"* of buyout work from substantial funds such as Forstmann Little. Cross border acquisitions are increasing, with partners in London and Paris also advising US-based funds. **Stephen Fraidin*** is the most visible New York partner. He is *"a fine operator,"* who mixes M&A with the creation of LBO funds for Fortsmann Little and subsequent acquisitions and disposals. Our researchers have shown that the firm is also active in the mid-tier market, the firm advises niche LBO house AEA Investors. The team advised Forstmann Little in its $1.2 billion acquisition of a 10% equity interest in NextLink Communications Inc. **Clients:** Fortsmann Little & Co, AEA Investors, Trefoil Capital Investors.

Other Notable Practitioners Offering *"unquestionable quality,"* **Richard Hall** of Cravath Swaine & Moore has a *"a good level of expertise"* in acting for mid-level buyout funds such as Bessemer Partners, although the firm itself is felt to lack specific focus on this area of practice. **Jack Nusbaum*** of Willkie Farr & Gallagher is said to *"have adopted a rainmaker role"* in relation to the firm's buyout activity. He is a *"fantastic lawyer,"* known principally for his strong relationship with Warburg Pincus.

U

Private Equity: Fund Formation: East Coast

USA: EAST COAST Leading Firms (Private Equity: Fund Formation)
1 Debevoise & Plimpton Simpson Thacher & Bartlett Testa, Hurwitz & Thibeault LLP
2 Reboul, MacMurray, Hewitt, Maynard & Kristol
3 Davis Polk & Wardwell
4 Ropes & Gray Weil, Gotshal & Manges
5 Hale and Dorr Kirkland & Ellis

Firms are listed alphabetically in each band.

Leading Individuals (Private Equity: Fund Formation)		
1	**BELL Thomas** *Simpson Thacher & Bartlett*	**CAMPBELL Woody** *Debevoise & Plimpton*
	HARRELL Michael *Debevoise & Plimpton*	**HEWITT William** *Reboul, MacMurray, Hewitt*
	KAWATA Yukako *Davis Polk & Wardwell*	**WOLITZER Michael** *Simpson Thacher & Bartlett*
2	**MACMURRAY John** *Reboul, MacMurray, Hewitt*	**PAINTER Robin** *Testa, Hurwitz & Thibeault LLP*
	RADKE Kirk *Kirkland & Ellis*	**TESTA Richard** *Testa, Hurwitz & Thibeault LLP*
3	**BOWIE Scott** *Latham & Watkins*	**COLLINS Michael** *Testa, Hurwitz & Thibeault LLP*
	McCORMACK William *Reboul, MacMurray, Hewitt*	**TABAK Jeffrey** *Weil, Gotshal & Manges*
	TEGELER David *Testa, Hurwitz & Thibeault LLP*	
4	**MALT Brad** *Ropes & Gray*	**ROBINS Charles** *Hutchins, Wheeler & Dittmar*
	ROTHERMEL Sarah *Hale and Dorr*	**ROWE Larry** *Ropes & Gray*
	SCHWED Robert *Reboul, MacMurray, Hewitt*	**SMITH Philip** *Ropes & Gray*
	VINE Stephen *Akin, Gump, Strauss, Hauer*	**WOLF Barry** *Weil, Gotshal & Manges*

Individuals are listed alphabetically in each band.

Debevoise & Plimpton (3 ptrs) Perceived to have *"a real desire for this work,"* the firm has *"one of the best all-round fund-structuring organisations,"* active in real estate, VC and private equity funds. A substantial cross-border capability, assisted by offices in London and Paris, has seen advice both to US funds going offshore, and European and Asian entities investing in the US. The team is thought to benefit from the *"one-two knockout punch"* of its leading partners. *"Senior statesman"* **Woody Campbell*** is a *"strong, intelligent lawyer."* Head of the firm's Investment Management Practice Group, he shows *"a clear understanding of the objectives of a deal."* Compettitors claim that *"sensible and creative"* **Mike Harrell*** is *"one of the most prominent lawyers in town." "Practical"* and an *"impressive negotiator,"* he is felt to complement Campbell ideally. The firm acts for the premier South American fund Exxel and Zephyr (South Africa and Mexico.) **Clients:** Clayton Dubilier & Rice; DLJ Real Estate Partners; Greenwich Street Capital Partners; Citigroup.

Simpson Thacher & Bartlett (5 ptrs) *"Hugely prominent"* with a *"fantastic"* client base. This global private equity player has seen recent growth in the Asian markets, supported by offices in Hong Kong and Japan. Closely associated with active buyout funds such as Blackstone Group, the team is thought to be *"driven by a desire for the exit work."* Producing *"premier quality work,"* it is said to benefit from its *"historic strengths in merchant banking funds."*

"Major talent" **Tom Bell*** is credited with *"developing a firm-wide focus on fund formation."* His *"vast experience"* spans both the domestic and international sphere. The *"personable"* **Michael Wolitzer*** also *"plays a key role." "Incredible market knowledge"* is the key to his reputation as *"the rising star"* of the industry. The firm is recommended for its variety of fund work, covering buyout (Blackstone), real estate (Joseph E Roberts, Carlyle), fund of funds (CIBC, CSFB) venture capital (Draper Fisher Jurvetson, Lehman) and hedge funds. **Clients:** The Blackstone Group; Lehman Brothers; Vestar Capital

*See leaders' profiles on pages 848-903

Partners; CIBC Oppenheimer; The Cypress Group; Evercore Capital Partners.

Testa, Hurwitz & Thibeault LLP (15 ptrs) *"The pre-eminent Boston firm"* is considered to *"have the market sewn up."* Said by competitors to strike a *"good balance between investor and sponsor,"* it acts for a range of institutional and private equity houses. The investment practice is said to be *"packed with talented lawyers."* Co-founder and manager of the firm **Richard Testa*** is seen as a major *"rainmaker in private equity."* Clients *"take great comfort in knowing he is their lawyer,"* while the practice benefits from his role as *"a fantastic intellectual resource." "Proactive and creative"* **Robin Painter*** has a strong reputation for her international work, **Michael Collins***, is recommended for his work with emerging companies, and the *"incredibly smart"* **David Tegeler*** displays *"a lot of energy."* Thought to have a strong focus on venture capital, the firm has scored notable successes in the technology market, acting for the internet-focused Softbank Inc and Spectrum Equity Investors, which funds the communications industry. **Clients:** Advanced Technology Ventures; Cedar Fund; Charles River Ventures; Flag Venture Partners; Gemini Capital.

Reboul, MacMurray, Hewitt, Maynard & Kristol (10 ptrs) *"Tight-knit and focused on private equity,"* this is considered to be *"a terrific mid-sized firm."* Close ties to Welsh Carson have raised the profile of a *"talented bunch,"* who undertake both fund formation and the subsequent transactional work, and are renowned for a *"client-friendly approach."*

Bill Hewitt* is *"passionate about fund formation." "Practical"* and hugely experienced, he is said to be *"one of the best VC formation lawyers in the States."* Typically, he advises on US investments, with venture capital, buyout, and fund of funds as common structures. Operating *"at the highest level,"* **John MacMurray*** is *"the best place to go for a first consultation."* Co-founder of the firm, he has broad sponsor client base. Primarily recommended for his tax structuring of funds, **Bill McCormack*** is *"one of the old guard"* and integral to the firm's success. He has a high profile for international venture capital work, and is said to be *"a strong all-rounder."* **Bob Schwed*** is commended for his formation and corporate finance work for clients such as Welsh Carson and BCI Partners.

The firm's growing international capability was highlighted by its advice to Industri Kapital 2000 in raising a $1.5 billion fund focusing on Europe. **Clients:** Welsh, Carson Anderson & Stowe; StarVest Partners; Accolade Partners; Riverside Holdings; CIBC Electra Kingsway; DLJ Phoenix Private Equity.

Davis Polk & Wardwell (2 ptrs). Our researchers were told that this is a small team offering a consistently *"high quality of service"* to a varied clientele of financial institutions. Closely associated with the *"hugely active"* DLJ funds, the Investment Management Group has also acted for JP Morgan and CSFB on both US and offshore structures. Notable growth areas include advice on investment programmes structured for employees. **Yukako Kawata*** is *"the first and last port of call"* for many clients. *"Professional"* and with a *"keen eye for industry issues,"* she is said to display *"a striking deal sense."* Her practice has a broad base, covering private equity, VC, fund of funds and funds focusing on the new media convergence sector. The firm acted for Bain & Co on its technology-related funds and for CSFB on its IT and telecoms investments. **Clients:** DLJ; JP Morgan; Morgan Stanley Dean Witter; CSFB.

Ropes & Gray (8 ptrs) *"A classic Boston practice,"* said to *"follow the money trail,"* it has a substantial clientele of LBO funds for which it undertakes transactional work. This complements strength in venture capital, exemplified by advice to Bain Capital on its $3.5 billion programme, focused primarily on the high-tech and internet markets. The firm is also recognised for its educational funds expertise (including Harvard, Yale and Stamford) and has a substantial base of pension funds. *"Impressive"* **Brad Malt*** has a substantial profile for structuring advice and LBO transactional work. **Larry Rowe*** is a *"quality operator,"* praised for his work with large institutional pension funds and noted for a close association with Goldman Sachs. **Philip Smith*** is recommended as a formation and transactional corporate partner. The team advised Fenway Capital on its buyout funds, with $1.5 billion currently under management. **Clients:** Bain Capital Partners (LBO, hedge and CBO funds); BankBoston Capital; Goldman Sachs; Butler Capital.

Weil, Gotshal & Manges (4 ptrs) Rated a *"national powerhouse,"* the firm undertakes a wide range of fund structuring including private equity, venture capital and real estate opportunities. Benefiting from a *"huge volume"* of work and involvement with *"some of the biggest funds,"* the group is closely associated with the LBO firms Hicks Muse and Capital Z. Although it is acknowledged to *"develop its associates effectively,"* the team is considered to have suffered a setback with the move of Michael Nissan to a private, capital-raising role. *"Practical and sensible"* **Jeff Tabak*** is said to be *"well-schooled in the law,"* while the *"talented"* **Barry Wolf*** is now joint head of the Private Equity Group (with Tabak). A prominent tax specialist, he is recognised as a *"quality practitioner."* The firm is active on a number of funds across Europe and Asia, and has strengths in both the investor and sponsor market. **Clients:** Capital Z; Hicks, Muse, Tate & Furst.

Hale and Dorr (2 ptrs) *"Highly effective group of specialists,"* said to have a *"clear focus"* on technology venture capital funds. The firm advises a substantial base of high-tech companies and VC funds, and is recommended for guiding both investors and the companies themselves through all stages of financing. **Sarah Rothermel*** is the firm's most prominent partner, and is rated for her advice on all aspects of the formation of funds, including tax issues and investment activities. The team has a strong reputation for arranging first time funds, but also advises houses with an established track record. A joint venture with Palo Alto based Brobeck Phleger & Harrison (named Brobeck Hale & Dorr) has seen the firm open two offices in the UK with a focus on the technology markets. **Clients:** Greylock; Goldman Sachs; Matrix; Harvard University.

Kirkland & Ellis (2 ptrs) Although the *"big guns"* are based in Chicago, the New York office of this pre-eminent private equity practice is a *"well-established competitor." "Typical K&E man"* **Kirk Radke*** is said to exemplify the 'cradle to grave' approach of the firm, advising LBO firms on the structuring and documentation of fund formation and the subsequent transactional buyout work. *"A key figure,"* Radke is said to have *"a good grasp of movements in the markets,"* and has acted on formations for Citicorp Venture Capital and CVC Europe. Substantial cross-border investment has seen particular activity in continental Europe and Asia. Also recommended to *Chambers'* researchers for its venture capital fund advice, focusing on new media and technology. **Clients:** CIBC; Citicorp Venture Capital; Vestar Capital Partners; Thomas H. Lee Fund.

Other Notable Practitioners Benefiting from the firm's high-profile West Coast technology practice, **Scott Bowie*** of Latham & Watkins is a prominent market player who undertakes the bulk of the group's formation work in New York. *"The grand old man of private equity,"* **Charles Robins*** of Hutchins Wheeler & Dittmar, is recommended for his long-standing relationship with the Thomas H Lee funds. *"A rainmaker,"* he *"never fails to keep his eye on the ball."* **Stephen Vine*** of Akin, Gump, Strauss, Hauer & Feld is known for his work with the Soros funds, and is commended for developing a practice from hedge funds into mainstream private equity work.

Project Finance: East Coast

Latham & Watkins (5 ptrs, 17 asscs) Described to *Chambers'* researchers as a *"huge practice"* with *"excellence through and through,"* it has a *"base built on the energy markets,"* a broad coverage of domestic power projects and a truly international reach. Around 70% of domestic work is power-related, and the team advised LS Power on its $700 million sale of generating assets for NRG, and represented Chase Manhattan on the $1 billion bank and lease financing of PPL Montana's acquisition of generating assets from the Montana Power Company. The team continues to act for both sponsors and lenders, and is praised by competitors for producing *"focused, commercially-minded lawyers."* On the international front it has advised on two Rule 144A offerings in Qatar, valued at $2.4 billion.

Bill Voge* was commended to our researchers as a *"devastatingly effective star player,"* with an international reputation. *"Personable"* **Dave Gordon*** is *"one of the greatest project finance lawyers in the world."* Recently elected manager of the New York office, he retains a reputation for *"hands on"* transactional ability. Known for his telecoms work, he has represented Deutsche Bank Securities (among others) on fibre-optic project financing for Global Crossing, Global Photon and FiberNet. The team also represented CSFB on the $2.5 billion revolving construction facility for Calpine. Although nominally based on the West Coast, **Andy Singer*** spends the bulk of his time in New York where he is *"hugely active and well respected."* Younger partner **Michele Penzer*** is *"an excellent lawyer, really making her mark."*

Capable of handling commercial bank lending and capital markets solutions, the firm advised the sponsors of the $2.5 billion crude oil Hamaca project (PDVSA, Phillips Petroleum and Texaco) in Venezuela, and advised the lenders on the $2 billion project financing of Intergen Turkey project. **Clients:** Deutsche Bank; Chase Manhattan; ABN AMRO; Bank of America; SocGen; CSFB; ExxonMobil; Sithe Energy; LS Power; Sempra Energy; Ras Laffan LNG Company; ABB Energy Ventures.

USA: EAST COAST Leading Firms (Project Finance)	
1	Latham & Watkins
	Milbank, Tweed, Hadley & McCloy
	Skadden, Arps, Slate, Meagher & Flom LLP
2	Chadbourne & Parke LLP
	White & Case LLP
3	Dewey Ballantine LLP
	Shearman & Sterling
	Sullivan & Cromwell
4	Davis Polk & Wardwell
	Freshfields Bruckhaus Deringer
	Simpson Thacher & Bartlett
5	Orrick, Herrington & Sutcliffe

Firms are listed alphabetically in each band.

Leading Individuals (Project Finance)		
1	**GORDON David** *Latham & Watkins*	**MOORE Harold** *Skadden, Arps*
	SCAVONE Arthur *White & Case LLP*	**SHUTRAN Richard** *Dewey Ballantine LLP*
	SILVERMAN Eric *Milbank, Tweed*	**VOGE William** *Latham & Watkins*
	WACHSBERGER Chaim *Chadbourne & Parke*	
2	**BAECHER John** *Chadbourne & Parke*	**BURKE Ted** *Freshfields Bruckhaus Deringer*
	GOODWILLIE Eugene *White & Case LLP*	**KLEPPER Martin** *Skadden, Arps*
	RICH Frederic *Sullivan & Cromwell*	**WARD Erica** *Skadden, Arps*
	WARNER Waide *Davis Polk & Wardwell*	
3	**ALEXANDER Troy** *White & Case LLP*	**BRACH Richard** *Milbank, Tweed*
	DESANTIS Victor *White & Case LLP*	**GALVIS Sergio** *Sullivan & Cromwell*
	GREEN Jonathan *Milbank, Tweed*	**HADLEY Joseph** *Davis Polk & Wardwell*
	JACOBSON Martin *Simpson Thacher & Bartlett*	**OLIVIER Jeanne** *Shearman & Sterling*
4	**FITZGERALD Peter** *Chadbourne & Parke*	**GANNON Lawrence** *White & Case LLP*
	HARRIS Douglas *Milbank, Tweed*	**MACHLIN Barry** *Mayer, Brown & Platt*
	MEYERS Michael *Orrick, Herrington & Sutcliffe*	**ROD Jonathan** *Freshfields Bruckhaus Deringer*
	SATTY Andrea *Chadbourne & Parke*	**SINGER Andrew** *Latham & Watkins*
	URDA KASSIS Cynthia *Shearman & Sterling*	
Up-and-coming individuals		
	MANN Christopher *Sullivan & Cromwell*	**McGRAW-WEISS Donna** *Skadden, Arps*
	PENZER Michele *Latham & Watkins*	

Individuals are listed alphabetically in each band.

Milbank, Tweed, Hadley & McCloy (18 ptrs, 80 asscs worldwide) *"A permanent fixture"* in the projects world, this *"monolithic practice"* is said to represent by far the firm's strongest suit. Rivals see it *"on the largest deals,"* and it is also *"a significant volume player"* which has captured the lion's share of the lender market. Global in scope, the firm benefits from a strong London office, which, in conjunction with the New York team, advised DLJ and Goldman Sachs on the £250 million bridge financings leading to a high-yield bond issue to facilitate AES' acquisition of the 4000 MW Drax Power Station. Although renowned for its involvement in power projects, the team was also recommended to researchers for its diversity of interest, with substantial experience of mining, water, petrochemicals, aerospace and telecoms projects.

Eric Silverman* is said to be *"at the top of the game,"* although some feel that as managing partner of the *"huge"* global project finance group, his role is becoming more managerial. He advised Chase Manhattan, Citibank, SocGen and WestLB as lead arrangers on the $5 billion financing of EME's 9510 MW acquisition of generating facilities from Commonwealth Edison. **Richard Brach*** is highly regarded for his mining practice and is said to have *"extensive cross-border expertise,"* particularly in Latin America. *"Talented"* **Jonathan Green*** also has a strong Latin American practice, and advised on the Mamonal power project and the Eldorado Airport project. With *"a precise eye for detail,"* **Doug Harris*** is recommended as *"the lawyer's lawyer."* Much of his work focuses on utilities projects.

Strong agency relationships have seen the team advise the banks and export agencies on the $1.32 billion financings of the Antamina Copper-Zinc mining project. In Latin America, the firm represented senior lenders on the $1.62 billion financing of the modernisation of Pemex Madero oil refinery in Tamaulipas, Mexico. **Clients:** Chase Manhattan; Citibank; Bank of America; Sithe Energy; J-EXIM; KfW; EDC.

Skadden, Arps, Slate, Meagher & Flom LLP (15 ptrs, 75 asscs worldwide) A practice which *"covers all fronts "* is especially admired for its *"deep*

*See leaders' profiles on pages 848-903

pool of lawyers." Chambers' researchers were impressed by the firm's outstanding relationship with its broad base of sponsor clients, although it also maintains robust relationships with lenders such as Citibank and CSFB. Power projects dominate the domestic work, with leasings and bond financings as active tools. The firm advised NRG Northeast Generating LLC on its $750 million Rule 144A bond offering to finance the acquisition of several US power plants. It is also active in the use of capital markets and receivable transactions to fund Middle Eastern petrochemical projects. Benefiting from a high-powered international network, the firm works on an even balance of domestic and international transactions.

"A great intellectual," **Hal Moore*** is *"a fantastic lawyer"* who *"argues his corner with the best of them."* He advised Edison Mission Energy on its $5 billion leveraged lease financing of the Collins power station, and represented Barclays Bank as facility agent on the three tranche ($400 million each instalment) financing of the construction and upgrading of NGL-4 LNG plant in Mesaieed, State of Qatar. **Marty Klepper*** is a *"great lawyer"* with a *"powerful position in the energy markets."* He advised on the development of three independent power projects in Brazil, acting for developers and financial investors, and maintains a key role in the firm as the relationship partner for Enron. Also advised Bank of America on the financing of the San Antonio Spurs sports arena in Texas. While many *"aspire to the breadth of her practice,"* **Erica Ward*** is particularly prominent for her work on electric power projects. Advised Lehman Brothers and ABN AMRO on the $265 million Rule 144A financing of the acquisition of Dominion Energy, and the improvement of the Kincaid generating station. Although currently an associate, **Donna McGraw-Weiss*** is a *"sensational rising star"* with a *"fine grasp of legal intricacies"* and *"the confidence to run deals."*

A major player in the telecoms field, the team advised Goldman Sachs Credit Partners (senior debt provider) on the $565 million financing of the Hibernia projects, an undersea fibre-optic telecom cable system linking the US, Canada, Ireland and England. **Clients:** Enron; Edison Mission Energy; NRG Energy; Barclays Capital; Citibank; CSFB; Lehman Brothers; Goldman Sachs.

Chadbourne & Parke LLP (16 ptrs, 60 asscs) *"A top drawer offering"* that operates with a *"fine global reach."* The team has successfully survived the defections of recent years, and has a *"strong bench of practical associates,"* who are *"always good news on a deal."* A leader in the domestic power market, the firm's Washington DC office supports close relationships with multi-lateral agencies and export credit agencies such as US Exim, OPIC, IFC and EBRD. An energetic focus on Europe, the Middle East, India, Asia and Africa is supported by an expanding office in London. The New York team represented the consortium (includes El Paso, Enron, Shell, BG) in developing the $2 billion natural gas pipeline, connecting supplies in Bolivia with markets in Brazil. Head of the Project Finance group, **Chaim Wachsberger*** is *"excellent in every way,"* often consulted for his *"expert"* advice on a wide range of projects. A headline relationship with AES has made **John Baecher*** *"one of the main figures for international transactional advice"* and an IPP specialist. He advised AES as developer and sponsor of the Guayama Project, a $815 million 454 MW coal-fired co-generation plant. *"Talented"* **Peter Fitzgerald*** has a strong profile for his work in political risk. A former OPIC chief attorney, he advises lenders in connection with EXIM Bank-supported projects in Asia and the Middle East, as well as developers in a broad range of fields such as telecoms, petrochemicals and oil field projects. *"Highly commercial"* **Andrea Satty*** is developing a profile for both international and domestic power projects. She advised the consortium developing and financing the 235 MW $311 million GVK Industries power project in India. **Clients:** AES; EL Paso; Duke Energy; CSFB; Kredit Bank; IFC; OPIC; US Exim.

White & Case LLP (New York 10 ptrs, 30 asscs; Washington DC 4 ptrs, 8 asscs) Renowned for its *"multi-jurisdictional"* capability, the firm's profile is less pronounced in the domestic market. Its overseas muscle was exemplified by advice given to US Exim on the $4 billion financing of oil field development in Chad and an oil pipeline from Chad through Cameroon to the Atlantic.

"Fabulous" **Art Scavone*** was commended to our researchers as *"a thorough, results-oriented"* lawyer. *"Incredibly intelligent,"* and the main transactional *"star,"* he led the Chad-Cameroon deal and advised US Exim on the $500 million financing of the 470 MW power plant in Brazil. *"The grandfather of the projects bar"* **Gene Goodwillie** is seen less on day to day transactional matters, although *"his opinion is always valued."* Drawing an international following, he is considered an expert in natural resources. Co-head of the projects group, **Troy Alexander*** is a *"terrifically bright lawyer." "Prominent"* internationally, he advises US and foreign clients on major power and telecoms deals. He advised ABN AMRO on the $320 million TEG II power plant in Mexico. *"Effective projects man"* **Victor DeSantis*** *"knows how to run a deal." "Personable and reasonable,"* he leads the firm's relationships with multi-lateral and bi-lateral agencies in DC. He advised IFC on financing the Saltillo power plant in Mexico, sponsored by EDFI. *"Excellent"* **Larry Gannon*** has a fine reputation for his leasing work. *Chambers'* researchers were referred to a recent high-profile deal that saw him advising the lenders in the financing of Phase II of the Dabhol Power Project, one of the leading independent power projects in India. The firm also advised US Exim on the $1 billion Vesper wireless loop telecoms project in Brazil. **Clients:** US EXIM; IFC; Inter-American Development Bank; Credit Lyonnais; JBIC; SocGen; Deutsche Bank.

Dewey Ballantine LLP (14 ptrs) *"Capturing a big chunk of the US market for its size,"* this is said by clients and peers to be a *"high quality team,"* acting for lenders, underwriters, owners and sponsors. Much of the firm's prominence is felt to lie with the *"excellent"* **Richard Shutran***. He is considered to *"know the power market like the back of his hand,"* and, according to peers, has *"achieved success for his firm beyond anyone's expectations."* Researchers were left in no doubt by interviewees that the firm's main challenge is to provide Shutran with more high-profile support.

The firm advised lenders and underwriters on the non-recourse financing of the Alliance Pipeline. Domestically, the practice has a strong focus on energy and advised BNP Paribas and CSFB on the $1 billion financing for Sithe Energies. Latin America is an area of established expertise, and the team has advised Deutsche Bank on the private placement of debt for a Chilean power plant. The firm has also developed close ties with Chase Securities, and advised on a highly structured transaction (leveraged leasing and capital markets) with power producer Reliant which included its acquisition of assets from GPU. **Clients:** Chase Securities; ABN AMRO; Air Products & Chemicals; American Electric Power; Duke Energy Group.

Shearman & Sterling (12 ptrs, 42 asscs) Another firm recognised for its great prominence on large international projects, is supported by a fine global network. Although best known for its work on behalf of Citibank, the firm's activity for other lenders and sponsors has also been commended to our researchers. The team has substantial experience of working with export credit agencies and multi-laterals, and is said to have *"a firm grasp of political risk considerations."* Close ties with Latin American governments in capital markets work have crossed over to an active involvement in infrastructure projects. The team advised the arrangers on the $810 million bank and bond financing of the FertiNitro Petrochemical Plant in Venezuela.

Head of the Project Development and Finance Group, **Jeanne Olivier** *"has quite a resumé in Latin America."* Recommended for her telecoms work, she advised Citibank on the financing of Comunicación Cellular, a Colombian provider of cellular telephone services. *"Wonderful"* **Cynthia Urda Kassis*** is a *"level-headed deal-maker."* Known for her work on mining projects, she advised Dayton Mining Corporation on the project financing of the Andacollo Gold Mine in La Serena, Chile, and has been active in the restructuring of arrangements for blue-chip financials such as Deutsche Bank. At home, the team represented Bank of America on its non-recourse bridge financing bond offering (under Rule 144A) for the $1.1 billion acquisition of three co-generation power facilities by East Coast Power. **Clients:** Deutsche Bank; PSEG; InterGen; Citicorp; Ericsson.

Sullivan & Cromwell (8 ptrs, 24 asscs) A *"good quality offering,"* seen by rivals to be *"highly competitive,"* the firm's project finance team has a superb track record acting on behalf of sponsors, but is felt by the market to lack the volume of deal of its leading competitors. However, the firm's domestic and international offices are said to handle complex transactions *"with ease,"* notably in the mining industry. Other areas of expertise include petroleum and LNG. The firm represented the borrower on the $4.6 billion Sincor heavy oil project and $2.4 billion Petrozuata heavy oil project, and has acted extensively for the big three oil companies, Exxon, BP and TotalFinaElf. In mining, the group represented the borrower on the $2.2 billion Antamina mining project in Peru.

"A first-rate talent," **Frederic Rich*** is known for his work in the mining and natural resources field. He represents a group of major petroleum companies involved in the $10 billion Caspian Sea 'Mega-Project'. Considered to be *"the corporate finance specialist,"* **Sergio Galvis*** is recommended for his Latin American bond financing deals, and is credited with promoting the firm's involvement in this region. *"A bright star"* who *"really knows his stuff,"* **Chris Mann*** is rapidly becoming a *"focal point"* for the projects team.

The firm's telecoms projects have included Iridium ($6.5 billion global wireless system) and the Latin American Arcos-I submarine cable project (representing Siemens' affiliates.) **Clients:** Iridium; Barrick Gold; Anglo American.

Davis Polk & Wardwell (25 attorneys) The depth of the firm's client base was commended to *Chambers'* researchers as the principal factor behind its reputation as a *"major player."* It continues to advise Morgan Stanley and DLJ as underwriters, and draws on the expertise of a high-profile banking team. On the sponsor side, the firm is active in the telecoms industry, advising such clients as Tyco and Marubeni.

Possessing *"an excellent projects brain,"* **Waide Warner*** *"really knows the market." "A strong technical lawyer,"* and head of the Project Finance group, he is active in telecoms, natural resources and the power industry. His caseload has included major undersea fibre-optic cable projects including FLAG, Atlantic Crossing and Pacific Crossing. **Joe Hadley*** is heavily involved in limited recourse project financings in Latin America, India and the Philippines. Clients confirm that *"when you are looking at OPIC financings, he is the man."* A high-yield and structured finance expert, he advised FertiNitro joint venture on its successful combination of bank and bond market project funding. Advised AES on bond financings for the Drax power station. **Clients:** Morgan Stanley; Petroquimica de Venezuela; Comcast; OPIC; US Exim; JBIC.

Freshfields Bruckhaus Deringer (40 attorneys nationwide) Considered by peers to have *"made a huge effort"* to attain *"credibility and critical mass"* on the east coast, the team is not yet seen to match the market leaders domestically, but is rated as a serious force on the international scene. It advised IDB and IFC on the rehabilitation of the Anhanguera Highway and the construction of the Bandeirantes Extension toll road project in Brazil. On the domestic scene, the firm has scored well on deals such as advising Chase Project Finance Fund on the 5680 MW Liberty Power project.

Ted Burke* is said to have *"made a great play for the corporate financing of deals." "A major name in the market,"* he advised OPIC on the financing of the $600 million Cuiaba integrated power project, involving a power plant in Brazil and a natural gas pipeline in Bolivia and Brazil. Recommended for his international bond financings, **Jonathan Rod*** is *"extremely bright and user friendly."* The firm advised the lenders on the refinancing of an undersea fibre-optic cable. Elsewhere, the team is noted for its increased involvement in the leasing market, and represented the lenders on the synthetic lease financing of a power plant in Hawaii. **Clients:** Solomon Smith Barney; John Hancock; ABN AMRO; OPIC; US Exim; BNP Paribas; Deutsche Bank.

Simpson Thacher & Bartlett (8 ptrs, up to 50 asscs) *"Perennial participants"* in the projects market, the firm has been recommended in our research as an *"obvious choice"* for complex, premium value work. The departure of Charlie Carroll (to Global Crossing) is considered to be a blow to the growth of the practice, although the firm's blue-chip client base continues to provide *"interesting work."*

In the US markets, the firm is recommended by clients and competitors for its highly structured power deals, and is often seen acting for financial institutions. Advised the lenders (includes Citibank, SocGen and Deutsche Bank Securities) on the $710 million La Paloma Merchant Power Project in California, and SocGen on the $8 billion financing of PG&E Turbine and Project Development Financing, involving the purchase of 50 turbines and development costs.

Internationally, the group is a fixture on power, natural resources and transport infrastructure deals, aided by offices in Singapore and Tokyo. Represented the project company formed to create, own and operate the 440 MW Quezon generating station in the Philippines, the first such financing without a government guarantee of power purchase obligations. Well positioned in the telecoms sector, the firm has an outstanding relationship with the hugely active Global Crossing, and advised the sponsors (Pacific Capital Group as lead) on the $735 million financing of the Atlantic Crossing private submarine fibre-optic cable system.

"Talented and intelligent" **Marty Jacobson*** displays *"sound experience"* and carries the bulk of the firm's reputation. Many of the partners have a solid background in leasing work, attracting clients such as CSFB, and the team recently advised Union Bank of California on the $270 million construction and leveraged lease financing of MEP Pleasant Hill-Aries, a power station in Missouri. **Clients:** Global Crossing; Citibank; Société Générale; GE; GE Capital; Lehman Brothers; Bank of America.

Orrick, Herrington & Sutcliffe (50 attorneys nationwide) Fully utilising its strong structured finance group, the firm has been recommended to researchers for its focus on the leasing market and the development of complex funding arrangements. It is known domestically for its extensive work in the power market, acting for the acquirer on Central Maine Power's divestiture of its generation assets, and advising on the restructuring of project debt for wind projects in California. In the restructuring of the domestic electric industry, the firm has acted for AES on the acquisition and financing of generation assets divested by a local utility.

Michael Meyers* has a fine reputation for his capital markets work. As head of the international offices and managing partner of the infrastructure group he is credited with promoting the firm's international ambitions, which includes high-profile recruitment in Asia. In the communications field, the group advised an equipment

*See leaders' profiles on pages 848-903

vendor on the $8 billion financing for the Sprint Spectrum nationwide PCS telecoms network. Internationally, the group acted for KMR on the financing of the Terocandelaris project in Colombia, and represented the developer of two pipelines from Argentina to Chile. **Clients:** Lucent Technologies; PG&E.

Other Notable Practitioners Although based in Chicago, **Barry Machlin*** of Mayer Brown & Platt has a substantial international reputation, and is a visible presence in New York and Washington DC. He represents US Exim Bank and Inter-American Development Bank, and has a focus on power and telecoms.

Shipping: New York

USA: NEW YORK Leading Firms (Shipping)
1 Haight Gardner Holland & Knight LLP
Healy & Baillie LLP
2 Hill Rivkins & Hayden LLP
Seward & Kissel
3 Carter, Ledyard & Milburn
Nourse & Bowles LLP
Watson, Farley & Williams
4 Burlingham Underwood LLP
5 Burke & Parsons
Cichanowicz, Callan, Keane, Vengrow & Textor
Clark, Atcheson & Reisert
De Orchis Walker & Corsa
Freehill Hogan & Mahar LLP
Gilmartin, Poster & Shafto

Firms are listed alphabetically in each band.

Haight Gardner Holland & Knight LLP (25 ptrs, 20 asscs) The firm handles a wide range of transactions from traditional wet work (collisions, casualties, salvage, charter party work) through to corporate transactions and criminal maritime work. Acting for a number of high-powered financial institutions, the group also has an excellent ship financing reputation, particularly on troubled loans, and represents shipowners and salvors such as Don John Marine and Schmidt on salvage matters. In addition, the firm represents a number of P&I clubs on litigation and arbitration matters.

Our researchers discovered *"a shipping firm"* and *"a worthy adversary"* with a *"fine group of people,"* although it is seen to be *"stronger in litigation than finance"* and *"less involved in major marine casualty work than it used to be."* **Bill Honan*** is *"a tough guy and an excellent litigator,"* who is a leading figure for charterparty work, and wins the plaudits of his opponents. He is *"someone you can work with when you have a case against him – he really knows his law."* **Nancy Hengen*** is a *"competent finance lawyer,"* who is *"excellent in the asset-based lending field"* and has *"clients who seem to come back to her,"* while **Brian Starer*** has a long-established reputation for casualty advice, although his role since the firm's merger is perceived to have become more managerial. Former president of the US Maritime Law Association **Chet Hooper*** is *"one of the old school,"* and is still rated by clients for his casualty litigation. **Jovi Tenev*** is respected in ship financing circles, particularly for his expertise on new ship-building contracts.

The firm advised on the 'New World' case, which involved multi-jurisdictional litigation arising from the collision between the vessel the 'New World' (owned by the firm's client) and the Cypriot flag vessel 'Yamalaya' off Gibraltar on December 1994, which resulted in a $20 million recovery for the firm's client. Also defended a major shipowner in connection with criminal charges arising from an oil spill off the west coast of the US. In addition, the firm represented a syndicate of US financial institutions as lessors in the sale-leaseback of a $130 million FPSO, to be used by the lessee in South American waters. **Clients:** BIMCO; Citigroup; Eletson Corporation; Expedo & Co (London); Gaard; Nordisk; Skuld P&I; Smit International; The Swedish Club; Texaco.

Healy & Baillie LLP (21 ptrs, 13 asscs) Advising a mixture of financial institutions, shipowners, charterers and traders, the firm has handled a variety of large-scale litigation, as well as maritime casualty cases such as APL China. Rivals perceive the firm to be an *"aggressive outfit,"* strong on representing P&I clubs and ship-owners. In ship financing, the team has undertaken restructuring work, refinancing and a number of work-outs, representing DLJ in connection with high-yield bond problems.

John Kimball* is a *"world class"* litigator, unhesitatingly described to our researchers as *"one of the key representatives of P&I clubs in the country."* **Howard McCormack*** ended his two year term as president of the US Maritime Law Association in May 2000, and has resumed his practice. A *"quality litigator"* in maritime matters, he is *"someone you can fight with during the day and drink with during the night!"*

Charterparty and personal injury work are other dimensions to the department's workload. The firm represented an oil company in litigation involving a shipping contract dispute. **Clients:** Financial institutions; shipowners; charterers; traders.

Hill Rivkins & Hayden LLP (9 ptrs, 12 asscs) Specialists in shipping litigation and international trade law, the firm is the largest specialist marine operation in the US. Research has shown that the firm has *"the biggest share of casualty cases,"* a historical position which has *"strengthened over the past twelve months."* **Raymond Hayden*** *"continues to be one of the most capable litigators around"* and is *"at the high end of the table,"* generally appearing in litigation on behalf of cargo insurers.

The firm has advised on the 'APL China' case, the largest container loss in history, where over $700 million was lost overboard or crushed, and acted as lead US counsel for the cargo side in the 'Norwegian Dream' collision. Major charter party arbitration work and representing underwriters on a number of major explosions and fires have also been important elements of the firm's caseload. CGU (Continental Green & Cargo) work and cases for Lloyds and Ace have also kept the firm in the public eye. **Clients:** AIG; Continental Green & Cargil; MOAC; St Paul; Texaco; Tokio.

Seward & Kissel (8 ptrs, 24 asscs) The maritime group undertakes a wide range of work, including asset-based lending, leasing, public offerings, private placings, mergers and acquisitions, securitisations, restructurings, insolvency's and commercial litigation. Opponents rate the team as *"a serious player"* on shipping finance cases, both on behalf of banks and borrowers, although its profile for casualty matters is much lower.

Larry Rutowski* is the head of the maritime practice group, and generally handles asset-based lending, leasing and securitisation work. He has *"done a good job in attracting clients and building up the practice, and he's certainly a good competitor of ours,"* said one admiring rival. **Gary Wolfe*** is a *"bright and hard-working"* lawyer, who has advised on substantial securities exchange and public company work.

USA: NEW YORK Leading Individuals (Shipping: Finance)	
1	**OSBORNE John** *Watson, Farley & Williams*
	RUTKOWSKI Larry *Seward & Kissel*
	WHALEN Tom *Carter, Ledyard & Milburn*
	WOLFE Gary *Seward & Kissel*
2	**HENGEN Nancy** *Haight Gardner Holland & Knight*
	POSTER Bob *Gilmartin, Poster & Shafto*
	TENEV Jovi *Haight Gardner Holland & Knight*
Up-and-coming individuals	
	STEARNS Craig *Watson, Farley & Williams*

Individuals are listed alphabetically in each band.

Leading Individuals (Shipping: Litigation)	
1	**HAYDEN Raymond** *Hill Rivkins & Hayden LLP*
	HONAN William *Haight Gardner Holland & Knight*
	KIMBALL John *Healy & Baillie LLP*
	NOURSE David *Nourse & Bowles LLP*
2	**BURRELL Lizabeth** *Burlingham Underwood*
	COHEN Michael Marks *Burlingham Underwood*
	HOOPER Chester *Haight Gardner Holland & Knight*
	KENNEDY Don *Carter, Ledyard & Milburn*
	McCORMACK Howard *Healy & Baillie LLP*
	STARER Brian *Haight Gardner Holland & Knight*
3	**BURKE Ray** *Burke & Parsons*
	CLARK Peter *Clark, Atcheson & Reisert*
	DE ORCHIS Vincent *De Orchis Walker & Corsa*
	FREEHILL George *Freehill Hogan & Mahar LLP*
	KEANE Paul *Cichanowicz, Callan, Keane*
Up-and-coming individuals	
	GUTOWSKI Peter *Freehill Hogan & Mahar LLP*
	PARÉ Jay *Nourse & Bowles LLP*

Individuals are listed alphabetically in each band.

The firm advised on restructurings such as the Overseas Ship Holding Group securitisation and the ongoing 'Golden Ocean' bankruptcy reorganisation. Other matters include advising on the out of court restructuring for Pacific & Atlantic, the lease financing on behalf of Fleet Capital, and the private equity investment for Ultrapetrol. **Clients:** Fleet Capital; Overseas Ship Holding Group; Ultrapetrol.

Carter, Ledyard & Milburn (5 ptrs, 6 asscs) The firm splits its workload evenly between litigation and finance work, advising financial institutions, ship owners and operators. Litigation work is primarily for P&I clubs, and also includes charter party disputes. The head of the firm's shipping finance department is **Tom Whalen***. Chambers' researchers recorded consistent commendation for a lawyer who *"gets high marks"* for his *"exceptional securitisation work."* **Don Kennedy*** is well-known for his charterparty expertise, and is a *"sound litigator."*

The firm acted for the United States Trust Company in a shareholders dispute involving default and possible restructuring of the large gas carrier Navigator Gas. Also acted as counsel to Sea Containers in connection with the expansion of its ferry business into the US. In addition to a number of shipping junk bond work-outs, particularly for TBS Shipping, the group performs litigation and investment and lease financing transactions for Interpool, one of the largest container leasing companies in the world. **Clients:** First Toronto Group; North of England P&I club; Sea Containers; Stolt Nielsen Transportation Group; United States Trust Company of New York.

Nourse & Bowles (6 ptrs, 3 asscs) Best known for its contentious work, the firm advises on charter party disputes, casualty cases, bills of lading and contracts of affreightment, vessel brokerage, agency disputes and maritime personal injury and death claims. Competitors speak of a firm *"holding its own"* in New York, largely through its first-class lawyers, *"people you don't worry about at night if you're dealing with them or up against them."*

Renowned for his work on behalf of P&I clubs, **David Nourse*** is seen as an *"experienced, well-schooled and smart"* litigator, who is *"well versed in the law."* **Jay Paré** also undertakes charter party work, and is considered to have a rising profile. Significant matters include successfully arguing a case before the US Supreme Court on behalf of a major international oil company, where the client was ultimately found entitled to a maritime lien and a judgment in excess of $1 million for fuel oil supplied by the oil company to a vessel in Saudi Arabia through the company's local supplier, a decision which has altered the basis of admiralty jurisdiction in the United States. Another matter was successfully representing a shipowner in disputes against the shipper of a cargo of steel turnings which caught fire and severely damaged the ship's structure, where the shipper was found liable for all resulting damages, including port of refuge and salvage-type expenses, costs of repairs and loss of use of the vessel. A further matter was acting on behalf of a tank barge owner and its P&I Club following the vessel's explosion during discharge operations, which resulted in the largest oil spill in the history of New York Harbor. The firm carried out an immediate on-site investigation, assisted the owner in oil spill cleanup efforts and responded to the demands of numerous local, state and federal authorities, including participating in Coast Guard and National Transportation Safety Board hearings. **Clients:** P&I (protection and indemnity) Clubs; vessel owners; charterers; insurers; reinsurers; cruise lines; high-speed ferry operators; manufacturers; freight forwarders; customs house brokers; steamship agents and shipyards.

Watson, Farley & Williams (4 ptrs, 9 asscs) Representing financial institutions on both sides of the Atlantic, this UK firm also advises ship-owners and charterers on ship mortgage loans, securitisations, IPOs and restructuring of junk-bonds. A superb finance practice remains the group's mainstay, and the London-New York connection *"has definitely helped its profile."*

The *"excellent"* **John Osborne*** has a *"premier reputation as a transactional lawyer,"* and is *"up at the top for asset-based lending."* **Craig Stearns*** has been recently made partner, does marine finance work and is said to be *"hard-working, knowledgeable and energetic."* The firm recently acted for NIB in connection with the restructuring of the Pacific & Atlantic high-yield bonds, and represented Commerce Bank and its syndicate on a securitisation of a new ship-building contract. Also represented the lenders on the financing of container ships for Seaspan, a Canadian-based shipping organisation, and has advised extensively on lease financings and structuring for Citibank, and loans and bankruptcy advice for Chase Manhattan. In contentious matters, the firm defended the banks on a crew penalty wage claim case in New Orleans. **Clients:** Fortis; Nedship; TK Shipping.

Burlingham Underwood LLP (5 ptrs, 4 asscs) Smaller shipping firm, undertaking both wet and dry work, including litigation/arbitration and marine finance.

The firm continues to act for ship owners (such as OMI), chemical trading clients (such as Thibro), charterers and cargo interests, as well as oil companies, most notably TOSCO, one of the largest independent oil refiners in the US, for whom it has acted as admiralty counsel. Envied by rivals for its tremendous turnover, the firm has *"a good raft of clients."*

Michael Marks Cohen* now focuses mostly on dry marine work, although he also advises on drafting charter party clauses and conducting litigation. A respected rainmaker, he is said to have *"a loyal client following."* **Liz Burrell**'s* reputation is also greatest for dry work, and she is national secretary of the Maritime Law Association. An

*See leaders' profiles on pages 848-903

"intelligent litigator," she is said to *"write an excellent brief."*

The firm advised on the Big Red Boat 2 case (the collapse of the Premier Cruise Line), and represented the charterers on the Barge Texas litigation, involving a barge which broke away from an off-shore facility in Long Island, dropped its anchor and severed an electrical cable. Other work includes the Bin He case, where the firm argued that the decision of Great Circle be overturned so as to bring US and English law into line on subject details in charter party work. **Clients:** OMI; Thibro; TOSCO.

Burke & Parsons (7 lawyers) A small firm with a niche in litigation work, which is also acknowledged for its charterparty work. **Ray Burke*** is widely seen as *"the top gun at Burke & Parsons,"* and comes recommended for his litigation skills. The firm's client base includes MOC (the Maritime Overseas Company) and OSG (Overseas Shipping Group). **Clients:** Maritime Overseas Company; Overseas Shipping Group.

Cichanowicz, Callan, Keane, Vengrow & Textor (4 ptrs, 7 asscs) Generally handling cargo claims and charter party disputes, the firm is respected for its litigation ability, and has niche strength in the Far East market, advising owners. While the firm does a substantial amount of P&I work, it is also corporate counsel to many steamship lines, including Evergreen, CMA-CGM and Yangming. The firm is involved in administrative law practice within the US Federal Government including US Customs (especially in the area of remission of penalties in regard to illegal drugs), Immigration & Naturalisation Services (for stowaways) and the US Federal Maritime Commission (FMC) where it has an active practice in filing agreements between carriers as well as defending carriers when the FMC seeks to levy penalties.

Paul Keane* is an *"aggressive"* litigator, with great experience in cargo claims. The firm has been involved in remitting drug penalties assessed against carriers and has had several cases where penalties of over $100 million have been remitted to zero. The firm has also been active in several major stowaway cases in obtaining refunds from the US Government to carriers and the P&I clubs for penalties that were assessed by the US Immigration Authority against ocean carriers and their P&I clubs. **Clients:** Cho Yang; CMA-CGM; Evergreen; Hanjin; Hapag-Lloyd; Koch Petroleum Group; NYK; Yangming.

Clark Atcheson & Reisert (3 ptrs, 2 asscs) The firm's practice is concentrated in the representation of shipowners, charterers, shipyards, lenders, and underwriters in areas of litigation, arbitration, shipbuilding contract negotiations, ship finance and corporate law. Described to researchers as *"a good small shop,"* the firm's litigation capability is widely respected. However, it is not perceived to have the depth of the market leaders, and to rely heavily on the expertise of **Peter Clark***. A *"professional"* and *"can-do lawyer,"* he has *"done a great job of putting the firm together,"* and is a meticulous advisor on charterparty disputes and casualty cases. In addition to his litigation expertise, he also advises on shipbuilding contracts and ship repair disputes, bulk oil transportation, marine insurance and salvage. **Clients:** Shipowners, charterers, shipyards, lenders, and underwriters in areas of litigation, arbitration, shipbuilding contract negotiations, ship finance and corporate law.

De Orchis Walker & Corsa (7 ptrs, 5 asscs, 3 counsel) The firm specializes almost exclusively in admiralty and maritime law matters, with a reputation which has been developed in Federal Court litigation and arbitration proceedings involving cargo damage, hull claims, pier damage, personal injury involving crew members, longshoremen, and passengers, collision, fire, pollution, salvage, towage and charterparty disputes. Established as a *"feisty"* player on the New York litigation scene, the firm's reputation chiefly lies in charter disputes, arbitrations and other shipping litigation. Ship-owners provide a substantial component of the client base. **Vince De Orchis JR*** is a prominent and respected cargo defence lawyer, who is an active presence at the Maritime Law Association. The firm represents many major steamship lines, as well as their P&I Clubs or their underwriters. It also services several carriers by drafting many of their critical business documents including bills of lading, stevedoring and terminal agreements, charterparty and vessel sale contracts. **Clients:** Ship-owners; steamship lines; P&I clubs; underwriters; carriers.

Freehill Hogan & Mahar LLP (22 lawyers) A large litigation practice, historically known as the principal counsel to the West of England P&I club, the source of substantial recent work. **George Freehill*** is a senior New York figure, and, although perceived to be less hands-on now, remains *"a respected source of advice"* to clients. Researchers also had their attention drawn to **Peter Gutowski***, who has an *"excellent courtroom manner."* **Clients:** West of England P&I club.

Gilmartin, Poster & Shafto (4 ptrs, 1 assc in finance group; 1 ptr, 1 assc in litigation group; 1 ptr, 1 assc in shipping bankruptcy work) Boutique shipping finance team, which numbers among its clientele a powerful array of Japanese concerns. The firm also has a small litigation group which deals with ship mortgages and charter party arbitrations inter alia. In addition, the firm undertakes shipping bankruptcy work. **Robert Poster*** is a *"good, thoughtful lawyer"* with *"commercial instincts."* Over the past twelve months, the firm's major focuses in shipping have been bank loans (secured by vessel assets), synthetic leasing of shipping assets (barges, tugs, rigs, etc), acting as maritime counsel to committees of bondholders of publicly held high yield issues in varying stages of distress, reflagging of formerly US flag vessels and opposing the company proposed Plan of Reorganisation on behalf of a noteholder in the Global Ocean bankruptcy proceeding. **Clients:** bond holders; ship owners.

Tax: Chicago

USA: CHICAGO Leading Firms (Tax)
1 Kirkland & Ellis
Mayer, Brown & Platt
McDermott, Will & Emery
2 Sidley & Austin
3 Baker & McKenzie
Latham & Watkins
Skadden, Arps, Slate, Meagher & Flom LLP

Firms are listed alphabetically in each band.

Leading Individuals (Tax)
1 BOWEN Stephen *Latham & Watkins*
FREEMAN Louis *Skadden, Arps*
JAVARAS George *Kirkland & Ellis*
LEVIN Jack *Kirkland & Ellis*
SHERCK Tim *Mayer, Brown & Platt*
WILLIAMSON Joel *Mayer, Brown & Platt*
2 CRAVEN George (Buzz) *Mayer, Brown & Platt*
LIPTON Richard *McDermott, Will & Emery*
ROCAP Don *Kirkland & Ellis*
SHEFFIELD Jeffrey *Kirkland & Ellis*
WELKE William *Kirkland & Ellis*
3 LEDUC André *Skadden, Arps*
LEMEIN Gregg *Baker & McKenzie*
ZIMBLER Jay *Sidley & Austin*
4 BANOFF Sheldon *Katten Muchin Zavis*
BORDERS Thomas *McDermott, Will & Emery*
LUSCOMBE George *Mayer, Brown & Platt*
YODER Lowell *McDermott, Will & Emery*
Up-and-coming individuals
WAIMON David *Baker & McKenzie*

Individuals are listed alphabetically in each band.

Kirkland & Ellis (8 ptrs, 10 asscs) Despite recent defections, the Kirkland & Ellis tax team remains a key player both in Chicago and nationally for tax planning in relation to venture capital and M&A transactions. Off the back of the firm's enormous reputation in private equity, the tax group have cornered the market in advising private equity, LBO and buy-out companies on tax planning and fund formation. Tax litigation is also a forte, and the team has been involved in a number of recent trials and arbitrations, particularly in relation to consolidated returns and transfer price planning.

Although more active on securities and venture capital transactions, **Jack Levin***, *"the ace of them all,"* is widely recognised for his years of experience in the tax field. Admirers rate him as *"one of the finest tax lawyers in the US."* **Don Rocap***, *"Levin's heir apparent,"* now heads the firm's LBO tax practice, and recently represented Vestar Capital Partners, Willis Stein & Partners, and Code, Hennessy & Simmons on the formation of private equity funds valued at $2 billion, $1.5 billion, and $1 billion respectively. The *"talented"* **Bill Welke*** has advised on new funds created by Madison Dearborn, GTCR and Thoma Cressey.

In addition to its formidable private equity focus, the firm's tax group has an established reputation in corporate tax planning, advising on M&A, joint ventures, spin-offs and divestitures. Senior partner **George Javaras*** is considered to be *"in the top echelon of Chicago corporate tax lawyers."* He is widely recognised for representing multi-national corporations such as Sara Lee, Alcoa and Leo Burnett, in addition to advising the Chicago Board of Trade.

"Well respected" **Jeff Sheffield*** maintains a general corporate tax practice, and has specific experience of divestitures and spin-offs, particularly in the automobile industry, where he has a close relationship with General Motors. **Clients:** Bain Capital; GTCR Golder Rauner; Madison Dearborn Partners; General Motors; USG Corporation; Thoma Cressey Equity Partners; Bank of America; Sara Lee; Alcoa; Willis Stein & Partners; Pittway Corporation; Code, Hennessy & Simmons; Vestar Capital Partners; CAN Insurance.

Mayer, Brown & Platt (12 ptrs, 20 asscs) The tax group is divided into two separate departments, handling transactional tax work and tax controversy. While both practices are constantly active, the firm receives greatest recognition in the litigation field, where it has managed to distinguish itself as a *"heavyweight presence."*

Much of the group's reputation in this area rests on the shoulders of *"pre-eminent"* **Joel Williamson***, *"the tax litigator everyone thinks of in Chicago."* With thirteen years of experience at the IRS to his credit, his name attracts some multi-national clients such as Nestlé, Nabisco, and Intel Corporation. He recently represented both the Bankers Trust New York Corporation and Riggs National Corporation in disputes relating to Brazilian foreign tax credits, and the withholding of tax on interest payments for Brazilian restructured debt.

On the transactional side, *"thoughtful"* **Tim Sherck*** ranks highly as a *"knowledgeable lawyer,"* who *"provides outstanding client service."* He focuses on real estate investment matters, including tax issues relating to REITs, REMICs and limited liability companies. *"Persevering"* **Buzz Craven*** is well known in financial tax circles, and was involved in the reorganisation of Everest Re as a subsidiary of a Bermuda holding company. **George Luscombe*** also receives commendation as a *"behind the scenes guy,"* whom peers would consult if they had a major tax problem – *"his mind was made for tax."* **Clients:** Nestlé; Intel; RJR Nabisco; Hitachi; Sara Lee; First Union; Bank of America; Lehman Brothers; Merrill Lynch; Everest Reinsurance; ACE.

McDermott, Will & Emery (30 ptrs, 13 asscs) The firm possesses one of the largest tax groups in the city, and is said to be *"most like an accounting firm in terms of the number of bodies they bring to bear."* A diverse workload includes advice on a range of tax matters relating to co-operatives, partnerships, real estate, M&A, insurance and financial products. The team receives praise for its familiarity with local state tax law and employee benefits work, but is most often seen undertaking tax planning work for local mid-sized businesses and Fortune 100 corporations.

"Energetic" **Dick Lipton*** is consistently recommended for his expertise in partnership and real estate tax issues. A prolific writer and dedicated lawyer, his work ethic led one rival to say: *"I don't know what part of his life he cuts out; it must be sleep."* He recently represented BP Amoco on a $3.75 billion transaction involving the Altura Energy partnership. **Lowell Yoder*** reputedly *"doesn't work on anything unless it's very difficult,"* and *"always does a good job."* He is seen to best effect on international tax matters. The firm maintains an active eight-person tax litigation team of *"talented people who get good results."* Here, ex-IRS trial lawyer **Tom Borders*** was recommended as an *"articulate advocate."* **Clients:** BP Amoco.

Sidley & Austin (10 ptrs, 8 asscs) While many perceive the group to have been weakened by the retirement of senior practitioner Frank Battle, it maintains a high profile for domestic tax work arising from M&A and joint venture agreements. The group's strength in this area complements the firm's overall focus on substantial corporate transactions. The team was instructed on the tax aspects of the Tribune Company's $8 billion acquisition of the Times-Mirror Company. It also advises frequently on financial products, commodity pools and hedge funds, and has established a considerable niche in the field of

*See leaders' profiles on pages 848-903

low-income housing. Recent work includes advising on the securitisation of stranded costs involved in the deregulation of utility company Commonwealth Edison.

While the firm receives somewhat less recognition for tax litigation, the group does act on a variety of banking and insurance cases, such as Physicians Insurance Co of Wisconsin v Commission, regarding the calculation of loss reserves for casualty insurance. *"Analytical"* **Jay Zimbler*** receives praise for his *"first-rate"* work in international tax planning and controversy. **Clients:** Commonwealth Edison and Unicom (parent); First Data Corporation; Tribune; Bank One; Burlington Northern Santa Fe; Chicago Mercantile Exchange; RR Donnelly.

Baker & McKenzie (9 ptrs, 10 asscs) Involved in both tax planning and litigation, the group is largely oriented towards international operations. With outposts all over the world, the firm draws on a large client base of US companies investing abroad and foreign companies looking to create American subsidiaries. Consequently, the team is most frequently noted for its handling of the tax aspects of cross-border, multi-jusridictional transactions.

Although less visible in Chicago, *"dynamite"* **Gregg Lemein*** is well known in the international arena. Accounted a *"thorough litigator,"* he also offers *"high-calibre tax-planning advice."* Among the group's recent successes in the tax controversy field is the settlement of St Jude Medical v Commissioner, a case involving several million dollars in potential exposure. International litigator **David Waimon*** enters the up and coming rankings as a *"superb younger lawyer."* In the field of transfer pricing, the group achieved a ruling in favor of Compaq to set aside over a quarter billion dollars of transfer pricing adjustments proposed by the IRS and ultimately resulting in a transfer pricing adjustment in favor of the US parent corporation of approximately $21 million. **Clients:** Eli Lilly; Medtronic; Schneider; Nova Chemicals.

Latham & Watkins (3 ptrs, 5 asscs) LA-based firm, which sustains a small but highly regarded Chicago tax unit, heavily weighted towards transactional tax work. The group counsels a range of corporations, limited liability companies, banks and insurance companies on federal, state, local and international tax issues. Much of the workload involves advising clients on the tax aspects of mergers and acquisitions, joint venture agreements and securities offerings. Niche expertise lies in advising real estate investment trusts.

A substantial benefits and compensation practice provides investment counsel to pension plans and sponsors of investments, and advises fiduciaries on their ERISA duties. Tax controversy work is handled primarily from the firm's Washington DC office.

The *"name everyone knows in Chicago"* is **Stephen Bowen***, a highly respected practitioner, considered to be *"one of the top guys for M&A tax work."* One Highlight of the past year was the firm's representation of Coach in its spin-off from Sara Lee. **Clients:** Coach.

Skadden, Arps, Slate, Meagher & Flom LLP (6 ptrs, 17 asscs) An active tax group with a number of strong individuals, which operates largely as support to the firm's vast mergers and acquisitions practice. In addition to tax planning on spin-offs, restructurings, joint ventures and LBOs, the team advises on asset-based debt and pass-through offerings, involving securities backed by credit cards and auto loans. The team has particular expertise in advising REIT partnerships, and representing investment banks on tax matter concerning financial products.

Louis Freeman* is an experienced transactional lawyer with *"one of the most creative minds in the country."* He has extensive experience in federal tax planning and dispute work in relation to corporate acquisitions and disposals, both domestically and internationally. **André Leduc*** has an acknowledged reputation for international and US leveraged lease transactions and troubled company restructurings.

The group acted on the $61 billion acquisition of Ameritech by SBC, and NTL's $13 billion acquisition of CWC cable operations. **Clients:** Banc One Capital Corp.; Citigroup; Level 3 Communications; Fortress Investment Group; Foundation Health Systems; Merrill Lynch; Morgan Stanley Dean Witter; Oxydental Petroleum; Peter Kiewit Sons'; Quellos Financial Group; Unitrin; Van Kampen Funds; Westfield Holdings; The Williams Companies.

Other Notable Practitioner Although the firm does not yet have as competitive a profile in Chicago as the market leaders, **Sheldon Banoff*** at Katten Muchin Zavis receives tremendous commendation from the market as a *"tax guru,"* particularly in respect of partnership and real estate issues.

Tax: New York

USA: NEW YORK Leading Firms (Tax)	
1	Cravath, Swaine & Moore
	Sullivan & Cromwell
	Wachtell, Lipton, Rosen & Katz
2	Davis Polk & Wardwell
	Simpson Thacher & Bartlett
	Skadden, Arps, Slate, Meagher & Flom LLP
3	Cleary, Gottlieb, Steen & Hamilton
	Debevoise & Plimpton
	Fried, Frank, Harris, Shriver & Jacobson
4	Weil, Gotshal & Manges
5	Shearman & Sterling

Firms are listed alphabetically in each band.

Cravath, Swaine & Moore (5 ptrs) *"Top drawer players,"* although smaller in size than immediate market rivals. The firm is thought to generate partners with *"a broad base of skills."* Primarily an adjunct to the corporate practice, the firm also offers advice on securities and financial products and general counselling. *"Dedicating huge amounts of energy"* to transactions, **Michael Schler**'s* reputation as an *"academic"* is based on his *"vast intellect"* which he combines with *"a pragmatic deal sense." "Intellectually honest,"* he *"never camouflages a point." "You may not agree, but he will tell you exactly what he thinks."* Acted for Unilever on its acquisition of BestFoods and for UBS over PaineWebber. *"Terrifically talented"* **Lewis Steinberg*** is considered *"more user-friendly than Schler." "Incredibly astute"* and *"always confident,"* his recent merger work includes acting for Lycos on its $12.5 billion sale to Terra Networks. **Steve Gordon*** is a *"bright and creative"* practitioner who focuses on M&A and corporate restructurings. **Clients:** Unilever; UBS; Time Warner; WorldCom.

Sullivan & Cromwell (9 ptrs) *"A wonderful firm with enormous capacity,"* which has an array of respected partners who display *"tremendous energy."* Offering a *"hugely diverse,"* though mainly M&A driven tax practice, the firm is also considered to be unsurpassed for advice on debt instruments. The team was recommended to *Chambers*' researchers for its cross-border tax

USA: NEW YORK Leading Individuals (Tax)
1
CANELLOS Peter *Wachtell, Lipton*
ROSEN Matthew *Skadden, Arps*
SCHLER Michael *Cravath, Swaine & Moore*
STEINBERG Lewis *Cravath, Swaine & Moore*
TODRYS Steven *Simpson Thacher & Bartlett*
2
EINHORN David *Wachtell, Lipton*
HEITNER Kenneth *Weil, Gotshal & Manges*
SCHWARTZ Jodi *Wachtell, Lipton*
SOLOMON Andrew *Sullivan & Cromwell*
TRIER Dana *Davis Polk & Wardwell*
YOUNGWOOD Alfred *Paul Weiss Rifkind*
3
ANDERSEN Richard *Arnold & Porter*
BLESSING Peter *Shearman & Sterling*
CHINN Adam *Wachtell, Lipton*
COHEN Ben *Cahill Gordon & Reindel*
FERGUSON Carr *Davis Polk & Wardwell*
GORDON Steve *Cravath, Swaine & Moore*
INDOE William *Sullivan & Cromwell*
JACOBS Robert *Milbank, Tweed*
POLLACK Martin *Weil, Gotshal & Manges*
SCHARFSTEIN Joel *Fried, Frank, Harris*
SHACHAR Avishai *Davis Polk & Wardwell*
4
AMDUR Martin *Weil, Gotshal & Manges*
FRIEDMAN Gary *Debevoise & Plimpton*
HAIMS Bruce *Debevoise & Plimpton*
PHILLIPS Barnet *Skadden, Arps*
REINHOLD Richard *Willkie Farr & Gallagher*
ROSEN Burt *Debevoise & Plimpton*
SAMUELS Leslie *Cleary, Gottlieb*
STAFFARONI Robert *Debevoise & Plimpton*
Individuals are listed alphabetically in each band.

Leading Individuals (Tax: Financial Products)
1
DIMON Samuel *Davis Polk & Wardwell*
HARITON David *Sullivan & Cromwell*
KLEINBARD Edward *Cleary, Gottlieb*
PEASLEE James *Cleary, Gottlieb*
2
BROWN Dickson *Simpson Thacher & Bartlett*
MORGAN Charles *Skadden, Arps*
Individuals are listed alphabetically in each band.

planning work, which draws on a strong international network. *"Prolific"* **David Hariton*** has a strong bias towards financial products, and his advice is considered to be *"expert."* A high profile in the financial services sector has seen the tax team advising German insurance giant Allianz on its acquisition of a 70% stake in Pimco Advisers. *"Excellent"* **Andrew Solomon*** is said to *"understand the intricacies"* and is seen on many cross-border transactions, notably in the insurance and hi-tech industries. He acted for Dexia (Franco-Belgian) on its $2.6 billion acquisition of FSA. *"A seasoned veteran of the most complex deals,"* **Bill Indoe*** is considered the senior figure in the New York office (Willard Taylor has moved to Paris.) **Clients:** AIG; Royal Dutch Philips Electronics; SoftBank; Allianz; Goldman Sachs (Whitehall Funds); AT&T.

Wachtell, Lipton, Rosen & Katz (4 ptrs, 5 asscs) *"A superb tax practice"* benefiting from its *"huge corporate engine"* and *"a boutique structure that keeps them focused." "Strength in depth"* exists here, as associates are exposed to *"first-rate experience"* from an early stage. This *"efficient team"* is also commended for its bankruptcy and work out advice. *"Star"* **Peter Canellos*** is considered by the market as *"a giant of our generation." "Tremendous acquisition work"* includes acting for Philip Morris on its $18.9 billion acquisition of Nabisco Holdings. *"Intellectual"* **David Einhorn*** is considered a *"tough competitor"* on transactions. Described as the firm's *"hidden gem,"* he offers *"sound thoughtful advice,"* exemplified by his work on behalf of United Asset Management on its $2.2 billion sale to Old Mutual. **Jodi Schwartz*** is considered *"great for complex deals,"* such as advising VoiceStream on its $55.7 billion acquisition by Deutsche Telekom. Her *"quick intelligence"* has garnered a *"loyal following"* among blue-chip corporates. **Adam Chinn*** is *"bright and aware of all the issues." "Idiosyncratic"* and occasionally *"combustible,"* he is considered by some to be *"an acquired taste."* Nevertheless, his profile on big-ticket transactions is beyond dispute, acting inter alia for France's CDC Asset Management on its $2.2 billion acquisition of Nvest. **Clients:** AT&T; Phillip Morris; UAM; Goldman Sachs.

Davis Polk & Wardwell (10 ptrs) *"A wonderful practice"* thought to be *"heavily involved in industrial M&A."* Both rivals and clients commend it for cultivating its tax juniors: *"The younger group is excellent and ready to take the limelight." "Fabulous"* and *"personable"* **Avishai Shachar*** is said to be the *"go to"* lawyer. His *"intellectual prowess always achieves fine results."* He advised Qwest on its merger with US West. **Dana Trier*** has a *"fantastic depth of experience"* and is known for *"handling the intricacies"* of a deal. He advised Alliance Capital Management on its $3.5 billion acquisition of Sanford Bernstein. *"Terrifically smart,"* he is said at times to be *"slightly too forceful."* Less visible on the transactional front, **Carr Ferguson*** continues to *"generate great warmth and respect"* from his peers. Considered an *"enormous intellectual resource,"* he is commended for his ruling and controversy work. Adding *"diversity"* to the tax group, **Sam Dimon*** is said to be *"one of the strongest financial products men"* in the market. **Clients:** NatWest Bank; Qwest; Alliance Capital Management.

Simpson Thacher & Bartlett (5ptrs) *"A broad practice"* with *"substantial market share"* of major transactions in both public company and private equity. Seen to benefit from an *"excellent blue-chip client base,"* the tax team has also witnessed growth in its advice within the telecoms and media sectors." The key to the firm's successful tax offering is the *"unflappable"* **Steve Todrys***. *"An excellent M&A man,"* he is said to provide *"common sense"* advice. Seen to undertake the bulk of KKR's buyout transactions, Todrys also acted for Seagram on its merger with Vivendi and Canal Plus. *"An important cog in the firm's wheel,"* **Dickson Brown*** is said to be *"one of the great names." "A superb operator,"* he is head of the tax department and is primarily known for his work in financial instruments. **Clients:** Seagram; Lehman Brothers Merchant Banking; KKR; Frontier Corporation.

Skadden Arps Slate Meagher & Flom LLP (14 ptrs) *"A ubiquitous"* tax practice that has *"successfully handled the growth of acquisition work."* Seen to benefit from *"a far-flung"* domestic and international network, the team is thought to be a well integrated unit, leading the way on a number of big-ticket cross-border transactions. *"Leading light"* **Matt Rosen*** brings a *"first-rate professional attitude"* to the deal table. His *"innovative"* style coupled with *"exceptional tax knowledge"* makes him *"undoubtedly one of the best."* He advised United News & Media on the US aspects of its $2.6 billion sale to Granada. **Barnie Phillips*** is considered a *"fantastic lawyer"* who *"covers everything."* Known for his work on structured mergers and the REIT market, he acted for Citigroup on its acquisition of Associates First Capital for $31 billion. Recommended for his work on developing financial products, **Charlie Morgan*** also has a strong international reputation. Often associated with the major investment banks such as Merrill Lynch and Salomon Brothers, he is considered a *"fine creative lawyer."* **Clients:** NTL; American Express; Bankers Trust; CSFB; Sara Lee.

Cleary, Gottlieb, Steen & Hamilton (6 ptrs) A substantial international practice thought to be *"focused on developing a profile in financial instruments."* Seen to rely on well-established offices in Europe for cross-border advice on mergers, the firm is said to *"have enough expertise to cover a broad landscape."* **Les Samuels*** has given a *"major boost"* to the practice. He is recommend-

*See leaders' profiles on pages 848-903

ed for his blue-chip international client base which includes Deutsche Telekom (advised on the acquisition of VoiceStream.) His resumé includes a spell at the US Treasury Department. He brings *"a strong international flavour"* and *"the seniority of experience"* to the team. Competitors point to a *"terrific financial products practice."* Mainstays of this area are **Jim Peaslee*** and **Ed Kleinbard***. *"First-rate"* players, they are felt to *"have sewn up a substantial share of the market."* Peaslee has an *"excellent"* market knowledge and is rated for his securitisation work. Kleinbard is thought of as a *"senior figure"* and a specialist in federal income tax and equity derivative products. He advises Goldman Sachs, Merrill Lynch and Salomon Smith Barney on financial product taxation and their own tax planning. The firm has acted as counsel to Goldman Sachs in connection with the formation of investment funds and has developed an expertise in transfer pricing issues. **Clients:** Deutsche Telekom.

Debevoise & Plimpton (10 ptrs) A broad-based practice with an international presence, recommended by rivals and clients for its *"creative structuring arrangements."* The practice is felt to lack the big-ticket public M&A deals but has a strong following for its private equity buyout work. Head of tax department **Bruce Haims*** is *"an excellent deal-doer"* who brings *"the weight of experience"* to the firm. He is said to have developed a specialist practice dealing with private wealth focusing on media and entertainment. The practice has a strong reputation for cross-border tax advice. **Gary Friedman*** is recommended for his international work and his relationship with JP Morgan. With a *"strong international following,"* **Burt Rosen*** is known for his transactional practice and is said to be *"thorough and analytical."* Peers consider that **Robert Staffaroni*** *"does not get the recognition he deserves."* Said to be *"first rate for cross-border work"* he always brings a *"thoughtful approach"* to the deal process. The firm advised Chrysler in its groundbreaking tax-free combination with Daimler-Benz and it advises tax-exempt clients such as The Ford Foundation. **Clients:** Legal & General; Metlife.

Fried, Frank, Harris, Shriver & Jacobson (9 ptrs across NY and DC) Tax forms a *"traditional feature"* of this firm which has a history of producing *"some very senior figures."* Considered *"one of the greatest tax lawyers of all time,"* DC based Martin Ginsburg continues to raise the stature of the practice. However, now of-counsel, his transactional profile has dwindled, and he does not feature in this year's rankings. Much of the team's reputation now rests with the *"intelligent"* **Joel Scharfstein***. Said to be *"heavily involved in financing,"* his broad practice has been recommended for covering everything from project finance to partnership structurings. He acted for Proctor & Gamble on its $2.3 billion acquisition of The Iams Company. The team is a player in the REIT market, creating structures to attract foreign investment into the US. **Clients:** Fortsmann Little; Procter & Gamble; Guardian Royal Exchange.

Weil, Gotshal & Manges (12 ptrs) Possessing *"a deep pool of tax lawyers,"* the firm is thought to lack the *"powerhouse"* M&A engine of its principal competitors. However, the department's profile is raised by a strong bankruptcy practice and it is recommended for its tax controversy work. Said to be *"developing juniors well,"* the practice is packed with *"smart and capable"* lawyers. *"One of the great US tax lawyers,"* **Kenneth Heitner*** is an *"effective negotiator"* who *"never takes an unreasonable position."* Occasionally thought of as *"a tad conservative,"* he remains an influential figure at the firm, and acted for Old Mutual on its acquisition of UAM. **Martin Amdur*** is a *"smart"* lawyer rated for his restructuring work. He acted for GE Capital on its purchase of Japan's LTCB's $11 billion loan portfolio. **Martin Pollack*** is thought to have a broad practice focusing on partnerships, joint ventures and cross-border M&A. **Clients:** Hicks Muse Tate & Furst; Old Mutual; Synder Communications; MediaOne.

Shearman & Sterling (5 ptrs) Though considered to lack a cohesive focus, the tax practice benefits from a *"good steady deal flow."* A strong Asian presence and offices across Europe have generated a strong profile for cross-border M&A. The *"talented"* **Peter Blessing*** remains recommended for his international restructurings and strategic planning. A *"superb"* tax lawyer, he is considered to carry the weight of the practice since the departure of a senior partner to KPMG. The firm also has a strong profile in the REIT market with both public and private transactions. Advised Novartis in the spin-off and merger of its agribusiness with AstraZeneca to form Syngenta, and BT in its acquisitions of Esat Telecom Group, Control Data Systems and Yellow Book USA. **Clients:** Merrill Lynch; MEPC; Phelps Dodge.

Other Notable Practitioners *"Creative and bright"* **Alfred Youngwood**, managing partner of Paul, Weiss, Rifkind, Wharton & Garrison is said to *"cut through all the nonsense quickly."* His major clients include Time Warner and Viacom. *"A tax lawyer's tax lawyer,"* **Ben Cohen*** of Cahill Gordon & Reindel is said to have *"an encyclopaedic knowledge of the law."* An *"idiosyncratic"* practitioner, he is recommended for his work with JP Morgan and GE. **Rick Reinhold*** of Willkie Farr & Gallagher is a *"huge name in M&A."* He is recommended for his broad practice with includes international tax planning and new financial products. Leading the transactional tax practice at Arnold & Porter, **Richard Andersen*** (formerly Jones Day Reavis & Pogue) has a reputation as a *"strong and confident lawyer"* who focuses on cross-border tax planning. *"Distinguished"* **Bob Jacobs*** of Milbank Tweed Hadley & McCloy has a broad-based practice. *"A great name in any context,"* he is particularly commended for his work in the utilities field.

Tax: Washington DC

Caplin & Drysdale (25 tax attorneys) Known for recruiting *"the best and brightest from the IRS,"* this highly regarded practice has *"across the board depth and excellence."* A leading *"specialist"* boutique, known for its controversy work, it is said to communicate well with the agencies. Though not viewed as a transactional practice, the *"terrific"* attorneys are rated for their international planning work. *"Figurehead"* of the firm, **David Rosenbloom*** is *"steeped in international tax planning."* Considered to have a *"fantastic level of knowledge,"* he is also highly visible in the New York market. Recommended to *Chambers'* researchers for its advisory work with major financial institutions, a *"complete offering"* includes advising on partnership and joint venture issues. The firm is renowned for its second opinion advice on corporate transactions and obtaining rulings from the IRS. **Clients:** Major US and foreign corporations and financial institutions.

Ivins, Phillips & Barker (18 tax attorneys) *"A first-rate operation"* which generates attorneys

USA: WASHINGTON DC Leading Firms (Tax)
1 Caplin & Drysdale
2 Ivins, Phillips & Barker
Miller & Chevalier
3 McDermott, Will & Emery
McKee Nelson Ernst & Young
Skadden, Arps, Slate, Meagher & Flom LLP
4 Baker & McKenzie

Firms are listed alphabetically in each band.

Leading Individuals (Tax)
1 **McKEE Bill** *McKee Nelson Ernst & Young*
ROSENBLOOM David *Caplin & Drysdale*
2 **GOLDBERG Fred** *Skadden, Arps*
MOORE Robert *Miller & Chevalier*
OOSTERHUIS Paul *Skadden, Arps*
3 **LIBIN Jerome** *Sutherland Asbill & Brennan LLP*
NELSON William *McKee Nelson Ernst & Young*
SCHNEIDER Leslie *Ivins, Phillips & Barker*
SILVERMAN Mark *Steptoe & Johnson LLP*
TERR Leonard *Baker & McKenzie*
WELLEN Robert *Ivins, Phillips & Barker*
4 **BENNETT Mary** *Baker & McKenzie*
FARMER Scott *McKee Nelson Ernst & Young*
MAY Gregory *Freshfields Bruckhaus Deringer*
RIEDY James *McDermott, Will & Emery*

Individuals are listed alphabetically in each band.

who *"are excellent at everything they do."* One of the smaller, focused firms, it has a *"balanced"* offering, advising on transactional and controversy-based issues. The firm acts as counsel to major corporations including a substantial proportion of the Fortune 500. Major industry sectors for the practice include oil, chemicals and textiles. **Robert Wellen*** is considered to have the highest profile for merger-backed advice. He is *"one of the best for corporate reorganisations and consolidated returns." "Terrific"* **Leslie Schneider*** is highly rated for his inventory accounting advice. Active on the international front, the firm advises a broad base of US multi-nationals on tax planning and transfer pricing. The firm also has a strong reputation for tax advice on pensions and employee benefits. **Clients:** US multi-nationals and foreign corporates.

Miller & Chevalier (49 attorneys) Though recent losses at partner level have are said to have *"left the firm in a state of flux,"* it continues to be *"one of the strongest tax specialists in the US."* Considered *"closest in model to Ivins,"* the firm focuses on planning and controversy consulting work. It recruits heavily from the agencies and *"often tackles the service on major rulings." "Excellent"* **Bob Moore*** is principally known as a federal tax litigator. Much of his high profile rests with the representation of *"major clients taking stands against the IRS."* He is particularly recommended for his work with Exxon. The firm also offers advice on complex transactions including hostile cross-border takeovers. On the consulting side, the firm is known for its work on inter-company pricing and the arrangement of tax shelters. **Clients:** Major corporates with particular focus in energy and transport.

McDermott, Will & Emery (50 tax attorneys world-wide) Not known as a specialist outfit, but with a strong international M&A practice, the firm has *"a major role to play in the DC market."* Rivals acknowledge its *"substantial fire-power,"* with a number of Fortune 500 companies as clients, the firm is primarily known for counsel on statutory requirements from international to local level. Ties to the DOJ (tax division) and IRS though recruitment have emphasised the firm's reputation for regulatory work. Partners are also thought to be effective litigators. **James Riedy***, the most visible tax partner of this large team, is said to offer *"sound counsel"* and to operate an *"evenly distributed"* practice. Known for his work on international matters, he advises foreign multi-nationals on US tax consequences. A strong London office (4 tax partners) offers support on cross border M&A transactions. Advised Warner-Lambert on its $2.1 billion acquisition of Agouron Pharmaceuticals. **Clients:** Major public companies and US multinationals.

McKee Nelson Ernst & Young (35 attorneys) *"Off to a good start,"* this specialist practice formed in 1999 is seen to have *"attracted some first-rate lawyers."* The E&Y connection has promoted a reputation among competitors as *"the money firm."* Founding partners **Bill McKee*** and **Will Nelson***, both formerly of King & Spalding, are thought to have the necessary gravitas *"to grow this boutique."* They bring a strong reputation as tax shelter specialists. *"One of the major tax lawyers in the country,"* McKee is occasionally thought to *"take extreme positions"* on key issues. Described as *"an adventurer,"* he is particularly known for his advice on partnership taxation. *"Terrific"* Nelson is a *"major player"* with a profile for international tax counsel. Former head of International Tax at Miller & Chevalier, the *"excellent"* **Scott Farmer*** is considered to have broadened the firm's scope. He advises on international tax planning and IRS controversy work, with a particular emphasis on cross-border transactions. **Clients:** Exxon; GE; Sprint.

Skadden, Arps, Slate, Meagher & Flom LLP (6 ptrs in DC) *"An anomaly in DC,"* the Washington office of this *"ubiquitous"* corporate giant offers a *"distinctive mix"* of M&A, planning and controversy counsel. Although considered a *"fully integrated"* practice, with the weight resting in New York, the Washington office has an *"important"* stand-alone team, well-regarded for its international transactional and controversy matters. *"Superlative"* **Paul Oosterhuis*** has a *"great range of skills"* and is primarily known for his international transactional and non-transactional planning work. On the acquisition front he has advised NTL, Global Crossing and Daimler-Benz. Seen *"less in the trenches"* is **Fred Goldberg***, whose *"great intellect"* is said to be focused on *"sensitive opinion"* aspects of taxation. **Clients:** Hewlett-Packard; Johnson & Johnson; Pfizer.

Baker & MacKenzie (100 tax attorneys)A *"substantial"* DC office is thought to rely heavily on a major international network. Although packed with *"good, strong lawyers"* the firm is not thought to promote a star culture. Multi-jurisdictional tax planning is the firm's forté, and a tax presence in 35 countries is considered to be its chief advantage. *"Major figure"* **Len Terr*** has an *"excellent international profile."* Admired for his planning and controversy work, he is thought to promote the firm's global image. *"Definitely one to watch"* is **Mary Bennett*** who is said to be developing an international practice to follow in Terr's footsteps. **Clients:** Major public companies.

Other Notable Practitioners Chair of the tax group at Sutherland Asbill & Brennan **Jerry Libin*** has *"a great international standing."* With a major corporate client base, he is recommended for his planning and controversy work. **Mark Silverman***, head of Steptoe & Johnson's tax practice is considered a *"major name for M&A"* and is known to advise the IRS on corporate tax matters. **Greg May*** has a *"fantastic"* profile for his structured finance practice which focuses on securities and derivatives. Now with the backing of Freshfields Bruckhaus Deringer, this former head of tax at Milbank Tweed is said to be *"one of the international front-runners."*

U

*See leaders' profiles on pages 848-903

Leaders in USA

AARON, Roger S.
Skadden, Arps, Slate, Meagher & Flom LLP, New York +1 212 735 3000
RAaron@skadden.com
Recommended in Corporate/M&A
Specialisation: Senior partner in charge of all corporate practice areas, including mergers and acquisitions, finance, banking and institutional investing, tax, employee benefits, investment companies, and restructuring and bankruptcy organisation. Among the major U.S.-based companies represented: AOL Corporation, Compaq Computer Corporation, E.I du Pont de Nemours and Company, Ferro Corporation, Hasbro, Inc., H.J. Heinz Company, International Flavors & Fragrances, Mobil Oil Corporation, Owens Corning Corporation, Slim Fast Companies, USX Corporation, VNU USA, Inc. and Viacom. Major non-U.S. -based companies represented include: Alcatel, Allied Domecq, Aventis, Celanese, Montedison, S.p.A., SK Group, and VNU N.V. Has worked with investment banking and investment firms such as: Chase, Credit Suisse First Boston, Goldman, Sachs & Co., Lazard, Lehman Brothers, J.P. Morgan, Morgan Stanley & Co., Merrill Lynch & Co. and Wasserstein Perella & Co. As a member of senior management, serves on the firm's Policy Committee. Is a frequent lecturer at various seminars and symposiums on merger and acquisition, corporate and securities law matters.
Career: AB, Dartmouth College, 1964 (magna cum laude). MBA, Amos Tuck School of Business Administration, Dartmouth College, 1965 (with High Distinction), LLB, JD, Yale Law School, 1968.

ABUHOFF, Dan
Debevoise & Plimpton, New York +1 212 909 6000
Recommended in Competition/Anti-trust

ACKER, Lawrence G.
LeBoeuf, Lamb, Greene & MacRae, LLP, Washington DC +1 202 986 8000
lgacker@llgm.com
Recommended in Energy & Natural Resources
Specialisation: Partner in Energy/Utilities/Telecommunications, concentration in major complex litigation before administrative agencies involving merger, rate, tariff and refund matters, as well as appeals from agency decisions and advising on new competition developments in formerly regulated industries. Has represented Panhandle Eastern Pipeline Company, Trunkline Gas Company, Duke Energy Corporation affiliates, New Century Energy, MCI WorldCom, NextLink. Has conducted seminars on opportunities and costs associated with open access services within the United States and abroad, and written articles on litigation and open access issues.
Prof. Memberships: Bar of District of Columbia, Virginia, Minnesota, numerous United States Courts of Appeal.
Career: Member of the Bar since 1974; 1974-76 Legal Aid Society; 1976-78 *Acker & Mansfield*, Arlington, Virginia; 1978-81 Federal Energy Regulatory Commission; 1981-84 *Bracewell & Patterson*; 1984 to date *LeBoeuf, Lamb, Greene & MacRae LLP* (partner since 1987).
Personal: Born 1950; Syracuse University BA 1971; Georgetown University JD 1974; married Donna Acker; 2 children (Benjamin and Martin); leisure actives: travel, distance running; resides in McLean, Virginia.

AIZENSTEIN, Neal
Sonnenschein, Chicago +1 312 876 8000
na@sonnenschein.com
Recommended in Corporate/M&A
Specialisation: Partner in Corporate and Securities Group. Has extensive experience in corporate and securities matters, including public and private financings, acquisitions and dispositions, restructurings, joint ventures and partnerships, securities regulations, venture capital transactions and general corporate and securities counseling. Has represented purchasers, sellers and investors in acquisition and disposition transactions. Represented both issuers and underwriters in public and private financings, including IPOs and Rule 144A offerings of both equity and debt securities. Has extensive experience in representing both borrowers and lenders in a wide range of financing transactions such as asset-based loans and private placements.
Prof. Memberships: American Bar Association, Chicago Bar Association.
Career: Certified Public Accountant, Illinois, 1984. Joined *Sonnenschein* in 1986. Admitted to Illinois Bar 1987.
Personal: Born September 4 1963; Northwestern University School of Law, JD, Cum Laude, 1987, Dean's List, Editor – Journal of Criminal Law and Criminology; University of Illinois – Champaign – Urbana, BS, Accounting, 1984, Member, Bronze Tablet, CPA, Recipient of Lowden – Wigmore Prize.

AKSEN, Gerald
Thelen Reid & Priest LLP, New York +1 212 603 2000
Recommended in Arbitration (International)

ALBRECHT, Thomas
Sidley & Austin, Chicago +1 312 853 7000
talbrech@sidley.com
Recommended in Banking & Finance
Specialisation: Partner in Chicago office of *Sidley & Austin*. Practice includes domestic and international securitisations and structured finance. Head of firm's securitisation practice area. Member of the firm's Management and Executive Committees and Co-Chair of its International Operations Committee.
Prof. Memberships: Member, American Bar Association.
Publications: Co-author, 'Corporate Loan Securitisation: Selected Legal and Regulatory Issues' (Duke Journal of Comparative & International Law, Spring 1998).
Career: Received BA, (summa cum laude), 1975, University of Dayton. Received JD, (cum laude) 1979, University of Chicago Law School.

ALEXANDER, Troy
White & Case LLP, New York +1 212 819 8200
Talexander@whitecase.com
Recommended in Project Finance
Specialisation: Co-chair of the firm's Energy, Infrastructure and Project Finance Group. Concentrates in international project finance and banking in the telecommunications, power, oil and gas and mining industries. Active on behalf of the international lenders (including Inter-American Development Bank, Deutsche Bank and ABN Amro) in the Cemex Tamuin power project in Mexico; assisting El Paso International in connection with a series of equity investments in India and elsewhere; representing the international lenders (including Asian Development Bank, International Finance Corporation and ICICI) in connection with the project financing of the coal-fired Balagarh power plant in India; acted for Eximbank in the financing and conversion of the Samalayuca II power project in Mexico; representing Inter-American Development Bank in the financing of the Pegaso telecommunications project in Mexico; assisted Société Générale and others in the North Star BHP Steel project in Ohio. General corporate work has included construction projects, joint ventures, leasing, corporate acquisitions, public securities offerings and domestic and international loan transactions. Spent three and a half years based in Jakarta, working on various public and private sector matters.
Prof. Memberships: New York State Bar.
Career: Admitted to the bar in New York, 1988, became a partner in January 1996.
Personal: Born 10 February 1956. Haverford College, BA, 1980, Watson Fellowship; Princeton University, Woodrow Wilson School of Public and International Affairs, MPA, 1987; New York University School of Law, JD, 1987. Married with two children. Lives in Brooklyn, New York.

AMDUR, Martin
Weil, Gotshal & Manges, New York +1 212 310 8000
martin.amdur@weil.com
Recommended in Tax
Specialisation: New York-based partner in the firm's Tax Department. Broad-based practice, ranging from the formation of private venture capital partnerships and the structuring of their investments, including taxable acquisitions and dispositions, to tax-free spin-offs and other reorganisations involving both domestic and multinational corporations. Advises on domestic and international financings, including derivatives, sophisticated real estate investments, secured finance transactions involving receivables and other intangibles, and executive compensation. Regularly represents individuals and corporations in tax audits.

ANDERSEN, Richard E.
Arnold & Porter, New York +1 212 715 1000
Recommended in Tax

ANDRIL, David
Vinson & Elkins LLP, Washington, DC
+1 202 639 6500
Recommended in Energy & Natural Resources

AQUILA, Francis J.
Sullivan & Cromwell, New York +1 212 558 4000
aquilaf@sullcrom.com
Recommended in Corporate/M&A
Specialisation: Principal areas of practice are mergers & acquisitions and intellectual property matters. Advises U.S. and non-U.S. companies with respect to the structuring, negotiation and documentation of acquisitions, divestitures, mergers, tender offers and joint ventures. Has extensive experience with M&A transactions involving acquisitions and divestitures of divisions and subsidiaries, defense of public companies from hostile bids, mergers of equals and cross-border acquisitions. Represented Grand Metropolitan in its merger with Guinness, Upjohn in its merger with Pharmacia, the independent directors of Marion Merrell Dow in connection with its acquisition by Hoechst, Diageo in its sale of Dewar's Scotch Whiskey and Bombay Gin to Bacardi, the financial advisor to Daimler Benz in its merger with Chrysler, IMERYS in its sale of Copperweld to LTV, Pillsbury in its U.S. ice cream joint venture with Nestlé and Vodafone AirTouch in its proposed joint venture with Bell Atlantic. Clients include British Airways, Goldman Sachs, United Distillers & Vintners, Brinker International, English China Clays PLC, Grupo Imsa S.A. de C.V., Coulter Corporation, Parker-Hannifin, SITA s.c., Diageo, Pillsbury, Western Resources, Reuters and Royal Philips.
Prof. Memberships: American Bar Association; Association of the Bar of the City of New York and its Committee to Enhance Diversity in the Profession, its Committee on Minorities in the Profession, and its Task Force on Women in the Profession; New York State Bar Association.
Career: Joined *Sullivan & Cromwell* in 1983. Became a Partner of the firm in 1992.
Personal: Born 1957. Attended Columbia University (AB, 1979) and Brooklyn Law School (JD, 1983). Trustee and Executive Committee Member, St. Peter's University Hospital & Health System; National Advisory Board, NALP Foundation for Education & Research.

ARQUIT, Kevin J.
Clifford Chance Rogers & Wells LLP, New York
+1 212 878 8000
Recommended in Competition/Anti-trust

ASMUS, David
Baker Botts LLP, Houston +1 713 229 1234
david.asmus@bakerbotts.com
Recommended in Energy & Natural Resources
Specialisation: Partner in charge of Oil and Gas Practice Group. Practice focuses on oil and gas transactions, particularly asset acquisitions and sales, joint ventures, and energy-based financings.
Prof. Memberships: Member of International Bar Association (Section on Energy & Natural Resources Law) and Oil, Gas, and Mineral Law and International Law Sections of the Texas Bar. Board member of Association of International Petroleum Negotiators (AIPN) and Advisory Board of the Asia Society Texas. Frequent speaker or program committee member for seminars on oil and gas topics sponsored by AIPN, Rocky Mountain Mineral Law Foundation and others. In 1997 and 1999, named one of world's leading energy and natural resources lawyers by Euromoney Publications in London.
Career: Joined *Baker Botts* in 1985, becoming partner in 1993. Authored 'The 1995 Model Form International Operating Agreement', published in Journal of Energy & Natural Resources Vol. 14 (Feb. 1996). Geophysicist for Pennzoil Company, 1981-82.
Personal: Earned BS, in Geology and Geophysics from Yale University in 1981, studied oil and gas law at University of Texas and received JD from Harvard Law School in 1985.

ASTIGARRAGA, José I
Astigarraga Davis, Miami +1 305 372 8282
jia@astidavis.com
Recommended in Arbitration (International)
Specialisation: Main area of work is arbitration and litigation of international business disputes in United States and Latin America. Has served as arbitrator, chair or counsel in arbitrations before ICC, AAA, and London Court of International Arbitration. Also represents multi-national and other corporate clients in litigation in United States courts. Emphasis on disputes arising out of Latin American business deals. Directs and manages litigation for clients in Latin American courts. Has represented state-owned companies as well as private sector entities. Appointed by U.S. Government as one of 8 representatives to the tri-partite committee advising the NAFTA Commission on international arbitration and alternative means of resolving private commercial disputes. Consultant to the World Bank on Latin American insolvency issues. Appointed by U.S. Government to Panel of Experts drafting Model Secured Lending Law for Organization of American States. Panel of Arbitrators, Commercial Arbitration and Mediation Center of the Americas (CAMCA).
Prof. Memberships: Florida Bar; United States Supreme Court; Circuit Courts of Appeal for the Eleventh and Fifth Circuits.
Publications: Co-author, 'Latin American Insolvency Systems', World Bank 1999.
Career: Qualified 1978. Founded *Astigarraga Davis* litigation/arbitration firm in January 2000. Joined *Steel Hector & Davis* in 1978, headed international litigation/arbitration and creditors' rights groups when left in January 2000 to found new firm. Board of Directors, National Law Center for Interamerican Free Trade. Founding Member, Latin American Users' Council, London Court of International Arbitration. International Bar Association, International Arbitration Committee; International Insolvency Committee. Advisor, American Law Institute, Transnational Insolvency Project. Frequent lecturer at international conferences.
Personal: Fluent Spanish. Born July 20, 1953. University of Miami ('75 BBA summa cum laude; '78 JD magna cum laude).

ATKINS, Peter Allan
Skadden, Arps, Slate, Meagher & Flom LLP, New York +1 212 735 3000
Recommended in Corporate/M&A

AUERBACH, Reed
Stroock & Stroock & Lavan LLP, New York
+1 212 806 5400
rauerbach@stroock.com
Recommended in Capital Markets: Securitisation
Specialisation: Partner in the Structured Finance Practice. Extensive experience with interest rate swaps and derivative products, venture capital and other types of corporate financings. Has handled public offerings and private placements involving asset-backed notes and certificates, mortgage-backed bonds, mortgage pass-through certificates and collateralised mortgage obligations. Represented underwriters in the first public offering of subordinated certificates backed by automobile receivables of the finance subsidiary of a major American automaker. Also represented underwriters in connection with the first public offering of interest-only certificates backed by automobile receivables. Has counselled a variety of underwriters and placement agents, as well as issuers, with credit support provided through multi-class and senior-subordinate structures, letters of credit, reserve funds, pool policies and surety bonds.
Prof. Memberships: Admitted to practice in New York.
Career: Graduated magna cum laude from Franklin & Marshall College in 1980 with a Bachelor of Arts Degree, member of Phi Beta Kappa. Graduated from Columbia University in 1982 with a Master of Arts Degree in International Affairs. Received law degree from Columbia University in 1985. Editor of the Journal of Transitional Law at Columbia University Law School. Harlan Fiske Stone Scholar and recipient of a certificate with honors from the Parker School of International and Comparative Law.

BAECHER, John
Chadbourne & Parke LLP, New York
+1 212 408 5100
Recommended in Project Finance

BAECHTOLD, Robert
Fitzpatrick, Cella, Harper & Scinto, New York
+1 212 218 2100
Recommended in Intellectual Property

BAER, William
Arnold & Porter, Washington DC +1 202 942 5000
William_Baer@aporter.com
Recommended in Competition/Anti-trust
Specialisation: Head of *Arnold & Porter*'s anti-trust practice, concentrates on criminal and civil anti-trust and trade regulation matters.
Career: Served as Director of the Bureau of Competition from April 1995 until 1999, under Chairman Robert Pitofsky. In that capacity, oversaw the Commission's anti-trust enforcement efforts, including the successful court challenges to the Staples/Office Depot and drug wholesaler mergers, review of Time Warner's acquisition of Turner Broadcasting System and the Ciba-Geigy/Sandoz merger, as well as challenges to the alleged exclusionary tactics of Toys 'R' Us and Intel. While at the FTC, worked closely with competition agencies in Europe, Canada, Japan, Israel and Latin America. Previously practised law at *Arnold & Porter* from 1980 to 1995, helping to secure the 1994 acquittal of The Generla

Electric Company on criminal fixing charges. Prior to initial tenure at *Arnold & Porter*, served at the Federal Trade Commission from 1975 to 1980, and held a number of positions, including trial Attorney, Assistant to the Director of the Bureau of Consumer Protection, Attorney Adviser to the Chairman, and Assistant General Counsel and Director of Congressional Relations.
Personal: Education: Recieved JD from Stanford Law School in 1975 and BA from Lawrence University in 1972.

U

BAKER Jr, William
Thelen Reid & Priest LLP, New York
+1 212 603 2000
Recommended in Energy & Natural Resources

BANOFF, Sheldon
Katten Muchin Zavis, Chicago +1 312 902 5200
Recommended in Tax

BAPTISTA, Robert C., Jr.
Mayer, Brown & Platt, Chicago +1 312 701 7101
rbaptista@mayerbrown.com
Recommended in Banking & Finance
Specialisation: Practice Area Administrator for Banking and Finance. Negotiates and documents secured and unsecured lending agreements, debt restructurings, and other financing transactions. Advises in corporate matters such as borrowing transactions, sale agreements, and long-term production and licensing arrangements.
Prof. Memberships: Admitted to practice in Illinois, 1982.
Publications: Author of 'Bank Credit as Value in Article 4 of the Uniform Commercial Code', U. Ill. L. Rev. 395, 1981; 'Prior Party Set-Off as a Defense Under U.C.C. Section 3-306', U. Ill. L. Rev. 869, 1981; 'Peoria Savings & Loan Association v. Jefferson Trust & Savings Bank', 70 Ill. B.J. 191, 1981.
Career: Served as Judicial Clerk to The Honorable R. Lanier Anderson III, U.S. Court of Appeals for the Eleventh Circuit, 1982-1983. Joined *Mayer, Brown & Platt* in 1983 and became a partner in 1989.
Personal: Born September 14, 1948. Earned JD, summa cum laude, at the University of Illinois in 1982, where was editor-in-chief of the Law Review. Received MA, also summa cum laude, from Northern Illinois University in 1976 and BA from Wheaton College in 1970.

BARR, Mike
Hunton & Williams, Washington DC
+1 202 955 1515
mbarr@hunton.com
Recommended in Energy & Natural Resources
Specialisation: Practice focuses on energy project acquisition, development and finance. Extensive experience representing clients on all aspects of acquisition, sale, structuring, development and financing of electric generating facilities, gas pipelines and other energy assets throughout the world.
Prof. Memberships: Member, District of Columbia Bar. Member, American Bar Association.
Publications: 'Merchant Power Plant Financings In An Evolving Power Market', Project Finance Yearbook, 1999/2000. 'Project Finance in the United States', International Financial Law Review, USA Legal Guide, June 1998. 'The Brazilian Electric Sector', International Financial Law Review, Project Finance, March 1998.
Career: Head, Project Finance and Leasing Group, *Hunton & Williams* 1993 – present. Partner, *Hunton & Williams*, 1980 – present. Managing Partner, *Hunton & Williams*, Washington Office 1985-2000.
Personal: JD, George Washington University, 1973. BS, Georgetown University School of Foreign Service, 1970.

BARROW, Peter
Neal Gerber & Eisenberg, Chicago +1 312 269 8000
Recommended in Banking & Finance

BARTEL, Paul
Davis Polk & Wardwell, New York +1 212 450 4000
Recommended in Competition/Anti-trust

BARTLETT, Sara
Sidley & Austin, Chicago +1 312 853 7505
sbartlet@sidley.com
Recommended in Banking & Finance
Specialisation: Partner in the commercial, financial and banking transactions practice. Practice focuses on representing financial institutions and corporate clients in connection with acquisition financings, syndicated secured and unsecured financings, cross-border financings, leveraged financings, restructurings and workouts and other financial and commercial transactions.
Prof. Memberships: Member of the Illinois State, Chicago and American Bar Associations.
Personal: Educated at University of Michigan Law School (JD, 1982); Kalamazoo College (BA, cum laude, 1979).

BASON Jr, George
Davis Polk & Wardwell, New York +1 212 450 4000
Recommended in Corporate/M&A, Private Equity: Buyouts

BAYLIS, Stanley
Miller Baylis & O'Neill, Washington DC
+1 202 296 2960
Recommended in Energy & Natural Resources

BEATTIE, Richard
Simpson Thacher & Bartlett, New York
+1 212 455 2000
r_beattie@stblaw.com
Recommended in Corporate/M&A, Private Equity: Buyouts
Specialisation: Chairman of the Executive Committee of *Simpson Thacher & Bartlett* specialising in mergers and acquisitions, leveraged buyouts and corporate law and finance. Has participated in some of the larger and more complex transactions, including the merger of America Online with Time Warner, the acquisition of Frontier by Global Crossing and the merger of WorldCom Inc. with MCI.
Career: Has a long record of public service. During the Carter Administration, served as General Counsel of the Department of Health, Education and Welfare, and in 1980, was Director of the Transition and Counsel to the Secretary of Education. During the 1980s, served on the New York City Board of Education. Has served as a Special Advisor to the Secretary of State and during 1996-1997 was President Clinton's Emissary for Cyprus.
Personal: Chairman of the Board and founder of New Visions for Public Schools, a not-for-profit organisation that develops and implements programs to affect system-wide improvements in public education in New York City. Is a member of the Board of Directors of Harley-Davidson, Inc. and the National Women's Law Center, as well as a member of the Council on Foreign Relations and Vice Chairman of the Boards of Overseers and Managers of Memorial Sloan-Kettering Cancer Center and Chairman of the Board of Managers of Memorial Hospital for Cancer and Allied Diseases. Has served on the Board of Directors of the Institute for International Education, the Board of Trustees of WNET/Channel Thirteen and as a Trustee for the Carnegie Corporation. Joined *Simpson Thacher & Bartlett* in 1968 after graduating from the University of Pennsylvania Law School. Prior to law school, served four years in the Marine Corps as a jet pilot, after graduating from Dartmouth College in 1961.

BEDRICK, Mel
Cravath, Swaine & Moore, New York
+1 212 474 1000
Recommended in Corporate/M&A

BELL, Thomas
Simpson Thacher & Bartlett, New York
+1 212 455 2000
t_bell@stblaw.com
Recommended in Private Equity: Fund Formation
Specialisation: A partner at *Simpson Thacher & Bartlett* and a member of the firm's Corporate Department. Specialises in investment management matters and oversees the firm's practice in the area of private investments funds, where the firm has a pre-eminent international presence. Advises clients globally on a wide range of buyout funds, real estate funds and other kinds of private equity funds, as well as hedge funds, and other kinds of funds for 'alternative asset' categories. Co-Chair of the annual International Conference on Private Investment Funds. Responsible for representative private equity clients, such as: The Cypress Group, The Carlyle Group, Evercore Partners, The J.E. Robert Companies, Ripplewood, Rosewood Capital and Fremont Partners. Representative hedge fund clients include JWM Partners (and its predecessor firm, Long-Term Capital Management), Salomon Brothers Asset Management and Lipper & Company.
Career: Joined *Simpson Thacher & Bartlett* in 1983 and became a partner in 1992. Chair of the Subcommittee on Specialised Investment Vehicles of the International Bar Association and member of the sub-committee on Private Investment Entities of the American Bar Association.
Personal: Received a BA, summa cum laude from Dartmouth College in 1978, an MA, with Honours from New College, Oxford University in 1980 and a JD, from Yale Law School in 1983.

BELLER, Alan
Cleary, Gottlieb, Steen & Hamilton, New York
+1 212 225 2000
Recommended in Capital Markets: Debt & Equity, Capital Markets: Derivatives

BENNETT, Mary
Baker & McKenzie, Washington DC
+1 202 452 7000
mary.c.bennett@bakernet.com
Recommended in Tax
Specialisation: Partner in Tax Department, specialising in US tax planning and controversies for multinational corporations (e.g., withholding taxes, cross-border financings, foreign tax credits, controlled foreign corporations, and tax treaties). Deals regularly with IRS to obtain letter rulings, competent authority determinations, and regulatory relief, and represents companies on tax policy matters before US Treasury and Congress. Clients include Allianz, BAT, BP, Diageo, International Air Transport Association, and Zurich Insurance Company. Adjunct Professor of Advanced International Tax, Georgetown University.
Prof. Memberships: International Fiscal Association, ABA Tax Section.
Publications: A Commentary to the US-Netherlands Income Tax Convention, numerous articles.
Career: Qualified in 1979. Practised in London and Boston (1979-85). Served in US Treasury Office of Tax Policy (1985-90) as Deputy International Tax Counsel. Joined *Baker & McKenzie* in 1990 and became partner in 1992.
Personal: Born 26 February 1954. Attended Harvard University 1972-76 (AB cum laude), Université de Paris 1974-75, Columbia Law School 1976-79 (JD), and Boston University 1982-85 (LLM, Tax).

BERG, Eric L.
White & Case LLP, New York +1 212 819 8253
eberg@whitecase.com
Recommended in Banking & Finance
Specialisation: Head of *White & Case*'s Bank Finance Practice Group. Legal practice covers a broad range of finance matters with a particular emphasis on the representation of lead agents and underwriters in leveraged finance transactions. Representative clients include Deutsche Bank/Bankers Trust Company, Morgan Stanley and JP Morgan. Has advised on recent financings including the acquisition of ITT corporation by Starwood Hotels and Resorts Worldwide Inc, the acquisition of Corporate Express by Buhrman N.V., and the leveraged recapitalisations of Dominos Pizza and the Tenneco Packaging Business. Also represented the agent banks in providing senior financing to borrowers such as Harrah's, Graham Packaging, Host Marriott Corporation, Sky Chefs; Werner and Yuasa. Is typically involved in all aspects of the deal structure, negotiation and documentation including the negotiation of intercreditor relationships, compliance with margin regulations and, in the case of international transactions, structuring the financing to maximise tax efficiencies. Has extensive experience in hostile takeovers as well as in negotiated private and public acquisitions, recapitalisations and representing underwriters of high yield debt securities.
Career: Joined *White & Case* in 1981 after graduating from Cornell Law School.

BERLIN, Edward
Swidler Berlin Shereff Friedman LLP, Washington
+1 202 424 7500
Recommended in Energy & Natural Resources

BERLIN, Emily
Shearman & Sterling, New York +1 212 848 4000
Recommended in Banking & Finance

BERNER, Frederic G., Jr.
Sidley & Austin, Washington, D.C.
+1 202 736 8232
fberner@sidley.com
Recommended in Energy & Natural Resources
Specialisation: Partner in Washington, D.C. office. Has served as lead counsel for many partnerships and joint ventures of energy companies in the development of major energy projects such as the Millennium Pipeline Project and the Great Plains Coal Gasification Project. Has represented a broad spectrum of clients in the litigation of energy issues before federal and state commissions and courts. Has prepared and negotiated hundreds of construction, supply, and transportation agreements.
Personal: Educated at George Washington University (JD, 1973).

BERNSTEIN, Bruce H.
Sidley & Austin, Chicago +1 312 853 7635
bbernstein@sidley.com
Recommended in Banking & Finance
Specialisation: Partner: *Sidley & Austin*; Management Committee Member; Group Head Banking/Financial Transactions. Emphasis in asset-based lending, restructurings, corporate reorganisations, creditors' rights. 1995 to present: General Counsel, Commercial Finance Association, an international trade association for the asset-based lending and factoring industries.
Prof. Memberships: Chicago, Illinois and American Bar Associations. Fellow: American College of Bankruptcy, American College of Commercial Finance Lawyers. Member: National Bankruptcy Conference.
Career: Cornell University, BA, 1965; Harvard Law School, JD, 1968. Admitted to Illinois Bar 1968.

BERTELSEN, Mark
Wilson, Sonsini, Goodrich & Rosati, Palo Alto
+1 650 493 9300
Recommended in Communications: IT

BIALKIN, Kenneth J.
Skadden, Arps, Slate, Meagher & Flom LLP, New York +1 212 735 3000
Recommended in Corporate/M&A

BICK, John
Davis Polk & Wardwell, New York +1 212 450 4000
Recommended in Private Equity: Buyouts

BILGER, Bruce
Vinson & Elkins LLP, Houston +1 713 758 2131
bbilger@velaw.com
Recommended in Energy & Natural Resources
Specialisation: Co-head of the Firm's Business and International Section and Coordinating Head of the International practice, *Bilger's*. Practice consists primarily of domestic and international business transactions, including international infrastructure development projects, project finance, acquisitions, and other corporate transactions, particularly in the energy industry. Has represented domestic and international energy companies, financial institutions, investment funds, and internet and technology businesses.
Prof. Memberships: Member and Former Trustee: American College of Investment Counsel.
Career: Lecturer and author: programs and articles on partnership law, corporate law, merger and acquisitions, project finance, and international law topics. Attended Dartmouth College (BA, 1973, Phi Beta Kappa), University of Virginia (MBA, 1977); University of Virginia (JD, 1977); Admitted to practice (Texas, 1977).

BLACKBURN, Thomas
Bruder Gentile & Marcoux, Washington DC
+1 202 783 1350
Recommended in Energy & Natural Resources

BLAKE, Jonathan D.
Covington & Burling, Washington DC
+1 202 662 6000
jblake@cov.com
Recommended in Communications: Regulatory
Specialisation: Communications (television, cable, telephony, wireless cable, cellular, PC, satellites, new technologies), media, Internet, licensing, deals, international, regulatory, legislation and litigation. Highlights: represented first cellular and PC systems in US; helped launch digital television beginning 20 years ago; helped launch two-way wireless strategy. Chairman of the firm and works with the group of communication lawyers in *Covington & Burling*.
Prof. Memberships: American Bar Association – Chair, 1993-present, International Telecommunications Committee; US Council for International Business – Board of Trustees; Federal Communication Bar Association – President, 1984-85; Wireless Cable Association International.
Career: Numerous publications and memberships; named one of the top 100 most powerful lawyers in America by The National Law Journal, and was profiled in 'From the Top of the List' by the Washington Business Journal.
Personal: Yale University (LLB, 1964; BA 1960); Trinity College, Oxford, England (MA in Law; BA in Law); Rhodes Scholar; Yale Law Journal. Married to Elizabeth Shriver in 1977. Five children: Juliet Shagoury, Deborah Arasaratnam, Susanna Murphy, Jonathan Shriver-Blake and Molly Shriver-Blake. Enjoys sports, running, gardening, reading, travel and spending time with family.

BLASSBERG, Franci
Debevoise & Plimpton, New York +1 212 909 6000
Recommended in Private Equity: Buyouts

BLESSING, Peter H.
Shearman & Sterling, New York +1 212 848 4106
pblessing@shearman.com
Recommended in Tax
Specialisation: Partner in Tax Department. Practice involves complex cross-border and domestic commercial transactions, financings and tax-planning strategies, including providing domestic and

U

international tax planning advice and advising on cross-border mergers and acquisitions, reorganisations and joint ventures, public and structured financings, executive compensation, and investment funds and REITs. Major clients include Merrill Lynch, CS First Boston, Chase, Thomson Corporation, United Technologies Corporation, ABB Asea Brown Boveri, Danone, TrizecHahn Corporation, Eaton Vance Management and Cardinal Health. Frequent lecturer on international tax matters.
Prof. Memberships: A Fellow of the American College of Tax Counsel; Executive Committee of the New York State Bar Association Tax Section; Co-Chair of the Tax Section's Committee on Foreign Activities of US Taxpayers; Vice Chair of American Bar Association Tax Section's Committee on Foreign Activities of US Taxpayers; Board of International Tax Institute; Board of Tax Management Advisory Board on Foreign Income; Advisory Board of tax journal 'Mergers and Acquisition'; Tax Forum.
Publications: Author of treatise on US tax treaties published by Warren Gorham and Lamont. Also author of BNA Tax Management Portfolios on the US branch profits tax and the US source of income rules and of various articles on cross-border taxation.
Career: Princeton University (AB, 1973); Columbia Law School (JD, 1977); New York University School of Law (LLM, Taxation 1981). Became a partner in *Shearman & Sterling* in 1986.

BLOCK, Dennis
Cadwalader, Wickersham & Taft, New York +1 212 504 6000
dblock@cwt.com
Recommended in Corporate/M&A
Specialisation: Co-head of corporate department and head of litigation department. Specialises in mergers and acquisitions and other corporate transactions, corporate governance, securities law and corporate, business and securities litigation. Has handled numerous M&A transactions both hostile and friendly, on behalf of acquirers and targets, joint ventures, self-tender offers, spin-offs, and other corporate restructurings. Has participated in many highly visible transactions including, Pfizer Inc.'s acquisition of Warner-Lambert, U S West's merger with Qwest, RJR Nabisco's acquisition by KKR, the NCR/AT&T merger, MediaOne's merger with AT&T, the General Electric/Kemper Insurance takeover contest, U S West's acquisition of Continental Cablevision, and U S West's joint venture with Time-Warner and subsequent split-off of MediaOne, Westinghouse's acquisition of CBS, the Macy's/Federated takeover fight, J.C. Penney's acquisition of Eckerd Drugs, Hilton's acquisition of Bally's and its subsequent split-off of Park Place Entertainment, Toys 'R' Us acquisition of Baby Superstores, and the Dresser/Halliburton, Arbor Drugs/CVS and XL/NacRe transactions. Has also represented numerous Board Committees involved in corporate transactions, and public companies, investment and commercial banks and entrepreneurs in connection with major issues of public interest and debate, including the Business Roundtable regarding corporate governance issues, Texaco regarding discrimination matters, Cendant directors, Merrill Lynch (Orange County and Nasdaq in which Mr. Block was the industry negotiator on the US$1 billion settlement), General Electric in connection with Prudential and Kidder Peabody, General Motors regarding Ross Perot and its spin-off of EDS and Hughes. Is a frequent author and lecturer on corporate governance, the business judgment rule, mergers and acquisitions, federal securities laws, corporate litigation, the attorney-client privilege and professional responsibility.
Prof. Memberships: Memberships: Member of the Committee on Corporate Laws of the Section of Business Law of the American Bar Association from 1993-1998.
Publications: Participated in drafting the Corporate Directors Guidebook and portions of the Revised Model Business Corporation Act; co-author of 'The Business Judgment Rule: Fiduciary Duties of Corporate Directors' (5th ed. 1998); co-author of 'Securities Law Techniques' (A. Sommer ed. 1985); co-author of a monthly column in the New York Law Journal; co-editor of 'The Corporate Counsellor's Deskbook' (5th ed. 1999); member of the editorial boards of several legal publications.
Career: Graduated from Brooklyn Law School, where now serves as an Adjunct Professor teaching Advanced Corporate Law. Was Branch Chief of Enforcement at the New York Regional Office of the Securities and Exchange Commission.

BLUMKIN, Linda R.
Fried, Frank, Harris, Shriver & Jacobson, New York +1 212 859 8000
Recommended in Competition/Anti-trust
Specialisation: Litigation partner resident in *Fried Frank*'s New York office concentrating practice in antitrust litigation and counselling. Practice is closely linked to the firm's mergers and acquisitions practice. It runs the gamut of antitrust issues, with special emphasis on M&A (including the premerger notification requirements of the Hart-Scott Rodino Act) compliance and litigation matters. Has focused on resolving antitrust issues in transactions ranging from the contested takeovers of the 1980s to the strategic acquisitions of the 1990s. Regularly represents clients before the Federal Trade Commission and in dealings with the Antitrust Division of the Department of Justice and litigates in federal court. Representative clients include El Paso Energy Corporation, The Scotts Company and Hunter Douglas Inc.
Prof. Memberships: Past chair of the American Bar Association's Clayton Act Committee, Antitrust Section, and is a member of the ABA's Sections on Antitrust Law and Litigation. Other professional activities include the Association of the Bar of the City of New York (past member of the Committee on Trade Regulation, the Committee on Women in the Profession and the Committee on Science and Law).
Career: Qualified in 1968. Joined *Fried Frank* as an associate in 1967 and later rejoined the firm as a partner in 1979. Prior to rejoining *Fried Frank*, served as an Assistant Director for General Litigation, Bureau of Competition, Federal Trade Commission from 1977 to 1979. From 1973 to 1977, was an associate at *Breed, Abbott & Morgan*. From 1972 to 1973, was an assistant professor at Boston University's School of Management and in 1971, a lecturer at Boston University's School of Law. Writes and speaks on legal topics and co-edited 'Corporate Sentencing Guidelines: Compliance and Mitigation' (Law Journal Seminars-Press).
Personal: Born August 25, 1944, New York, NY. Attended Harvard Law School (LLB cum laude, 1967; LLM, 1973). Attended Barnard College (AB cum laude, 1964), where was elected to Phi Beta Kappa. Interests include travel, art and family activities.

BOEHRER, Charles
Winston & Strawn, Chicago +1 312 558 5600
cboehrer@winston.com
Recommended in Banking & Finance
Specialisation: Partner in the Corporate Department. Main area of work is syndicated leveraged finance working with major money centre banks on international and US based transactions. Acted as legal counsel for Deutsche Bank in connection with the US$2.07 billion senior debt for the Huntsman-ICI joint venture as well as other Huntsman debt. Acts for a number of corporations on matters ranging from merger and acquisitions to general corporate work.
Career: Joined the firm in 1985 as an associate. Partner in 1993. Chairman of the Finance Institutions-Committee of the Chicago Bar Association, 1990.

BOGDANOW, Alan
Hughes & Luce, Dallas +1 214 939 5500
Recommended in Corporate/M&A

BOGEN, Andy
Gibson, Dunn & Crutcher LLP, Los Angeles +1 213 229 7000
Recommended in Corporate/M&A

BOHM, Rick
Debevoise & Plimpton, New York +1 212 909 6000
Recommended in Private Equity: Buyouts

BOIES, David
Boies, Schiller & Flexner, New York +1 914 273 9800
Recommended in Competition/Anti-trust

BOONE, Michael
Haynes and Boone LLP, Houston +1 713 547 2000
Recommended in Corporate/M&A

BORDERS, Thomas
McDermott, Will & Emery, Chicago +1 312 372 2000
tborders@mwe.com
Recommended in Tax
Specialisation: Partner in Tax Department, main practice areas include federal tax controversies involving audits, administrative appeals, litigation and criminal investigations. Worked on numerous domestic and international tax cases involving corporate tax matters as well as analysis of tax incentive investments, valuation, finance and accounting issues.

Prof. Memberships: Member of Chicago Bar Association.
Career: Admitted to the Indiana Bar in 1974, Illinois, 1979. Also qualified for the US District Court for the Northern District of Illinois, the US Tax Court, the 7th Circuit of the US Court of Appeals, and the US Claims Court. Prior to joining *McDermott* in 1986, worked as a trial attorney for the Office of Chief Counsel with the Internal Revenue Service (1975-1985), and also held position as Adjunct Professor in the graduate tax program at IIT Chicago-Kent College of Law (1987-1993).
Personal: Born 22 April 1948. Received BA in 1970 from St. Louis University, JD from Georgtown University Law Centre in 1974, and MBA from Northwestern University in 1984.

BOUKNIGHT Jr, Lon
Steptoe & Johnson LLP, Washington DC
+1 202 429 3000
Recommended in Energy & Natural Resources

BOWE, James F.
Dewey Ballantine LLP, Washington DC
+1 202 862 1000
James_Bowe@deweyballantine.com
Recommended in Energy & Natural Resources
Specialisation: Energy (including energy project development, energy regulatory matters, energy company MRA). Project finance (US, North America, Latin America). Oil and gas law.
Prof. Memberships: Federal Energy Bar Association. American Bar Association. Member of the Bar of the District of Columbia and several federal courts.
Career: Admitted to practice 1982, District of Columbia. Private practice since 1982. Partner, *Dewey Ballantine* LLP, July 1994-present. Adjunct Professor, Oil and Gas Law, Georgetown University Law Center, 1990-1995.
Personal: Born May 17 1955. BA, Williams College, 1977. JD, Northwestern University School of Law, 1982.

BOWEN, Stephen S.
Latham & Watkins, Chicago +1 312 876 7652
stephen.bowen@lw.com
Recommended in Tax
Specialisation: Partner in the Tax Department. Main area of work is federal income taxation issues, particularly those related to joint ventures and mergers and acquisitions.
Prof. Memberships: Member of the American and Chicago Bar Associations, Fellow of the American College of Tax Counsel, member of the University of Chicago Tax Conference Planning Committee.
Publications: Published a number of articles on the federal income tax consequences of business transactions.
Career: Managing partner, Chicago office. Former chairman of the firm's global tax department. Member of the firm's Executive Committee 1993-1997. Regular participant in the Practising Law Institute's Annual M&A Tax Program.
Personal: University of Chicago (JD 1972), Order of the Coif. Wabash College (AB 1968), Phi Beta Kappa.

BOWIE, Scott
Latham & Watkins, New York +1 212 906 1285
scott.bowie@lw.com
Recommended in Private Equity: Fund Formation
Specialisation: Partner in the New York office. Represents a broad array of management buyout, venture capital, bridge debt and other investment fund sponsors, whose funds range from US$100 million to US$6 billion of committed capital. Representative clients include Kohlberg Kravis Roberts & Co., The Carlyle Group, Bear Stearns and Goldman Sachs.
Prof. Memberships: New York and California bar associations.
Career: Joined *Latham & Watkins* in 1988 and became partner in 1996.
Personal: JD, University of California-Los Angeles, 1988. Undergraduate studies were at The London School of Economics and at Occidental College, where received an AB, cum laude with Highest Honors, in 1984.

BRACH, Richard
Milbank, Tweed, Hadley & McCloy, New York
+1 212 530 5000
Recommended in Project Finance

BRANDOW, John
Davis Polk & Wardwell, New York +1 212 450 4000
Recommended in Capital Markets: Derivatives

BRANNAN, John
Vinson & Elkins LLP, Dallas +1 214 220 7700
jbrannan@velaw.com
Recommended in Energy & Natural Resources
Specialisation: Practice focuses on oil and gas law, with particular emphasis over the last 25 years on international oil and gas matters. Practised for nine years in the firm's London office. With more than 25 years of experience working on various oil and gas matters in Nigeria, also has experience in Africa, the Middle East, Australia, South America, Asia, Russia, India, and Europe. Also worked on oil and gas matters in the US and on certain mineral transactions. Has extensive work experience in Nigeria, including negotiation of oil and gas exploration and production agreements; pipeline right-of-way and construction agreements and transaction and operations agreements; disposing interests in Nigerian oil and gas properties, including disposal of stock in companies holding those assets; drafting engineering agreements for work in Nigeria; as well as drilling contract negotiations, joint operating agreements, lifing agreements, and documents related to exploration and production operations. Has also worked extensively on petroleum operations in the UK, Dutch, German, and Norwegian sectors of the North Sea.
Prof. Memberships: Member of the International Bar Association.
Career: University of Oklahoma School of Business, BBA (1963); University of Oklahoma School of Law, JD (1966); admitted to practice Oklahoma (1966) and Texas (1969); US Army, stationed in Heidelberg, Germany (1966-68).

BROWN, Dickson
Simpson Thacher & Bartlett, New York
+1 212 455 2000
d_brown@stblaw.com
Recommended in Tax: Financial Products
Specialisation: A senior member of the firm's Tax Department. Areas of concentration are federal income tax with an emphasis on financial instruments, domestic and foreign joint ventures, mergers & acquisitions and financial institutions. Advises on various financial products such as hybrid debt instruments, tracking stock, trust preferred securities and investment units, cross-border and domestic joint ventures, and structuring of foreign operations.
Prof. Memberships: Member of the Bar Association of the City of New York, the New York and American Bar Associations.
Career: Joined *Simpson Thacher* in 1971 and became a partner in 1978.
Personal: Received BA (1968) from the University of Michigan and was elected Phi Beta Kappa; received JD (1971) from University of Michigan School of Law and also elected Order of the Coif. Earned an LLM in 1975 from New York University.

BROWN, Meredith
Debevoise & Plimpton, New York +1 212 909 6000
Recommended in Corporate/M&A

BROWNSTEIN, Andy
Wachtell, Lipton, Rosen & Katz, New York
+1 212 403 1000
Recommended in Corporate/M&A

BURGESS, John
Hale and Dorr, Boston +1 617 526 6000
Recommended in Communications: Transactional (IT)

BURKE, Arthur
Davis Polk & Wardwell, New York +1 212 450 4000
Recommended in Competition/Anti-trust

BURKE, Ray
Burke & Parsons, New York +1 212 354 3800
Recommended in Shipping: Litigation

BURKE, Ted
Freshfields Bruckhaus Deringer, New York
+1 212 277 4000
ted.burke@freshfields.com
Recommended in Project Finance
Specialisation: Project finance and related banking work and has extensive experience of infrastructure projects in the US, Latin America and Asia. Has also been active in the creation of investment funds established to invest debt and equity in project financings.

BURRELL, Lizabeth
Burlingham Underwood LLP, New York
+1 212 422 7585
Recommended in Shipping: Litigation

CALOF, Lawrence
Gibson, Dunn & Crutcher LLP, Palo Alto
+1 650 849 5300
Recommended in Communications: IT

U

U

CAMAHORT, Steve
Wilson, Sonsini, Goodrich & Rosati, Palo Alto
+1 650 493 9300
Recommended in Communications: IT

CAMPBELL, Woody
Debevoise & Plimpton, New York +1 212 909 6000
Recommended in Private Equity: Fund Formation

CANELLOS, Peter
Wachtell, Lipton, Rosen & Katz, New York
+1 212 403 1000
Recommended in Tax

CARTER, James H.
Sullivan & Cromwell, New York +1 212 558 4000
carterj@sullcrom.com
Recommended in Arbitration (International)
Specialisation: Partner in Litigation Department and Coordinator of *Sullivan & Cromwell's* Arbitration Practice. Principal area of practice is international arbitration, as counsel and arbitrator, in ICC, LCIA, AAA, CPR, ad hoc proceedings and other fora. Typical cases are international joint venture, investment and intellectual property licensing disputes.
Prof. Memberships: AAA Executive Committee (Chair of Law Committee and International Arbitrator Training Development Group); AAA and CPR Arbitration Rules Revisions committees; LCIA Court member; Court of Arbitration for Sport; former Member, NAFTA Advisory Committee on Private Commercial Disputes; WIPO Arbitration Consultative Commission; Swiss Arbitration Association; former Chair, American Bar Association Section of International Law and Practice; former Chair, New York State Bar Association International Dispute Resolution Committee; former Chair, Association of the Bar of the City of New York Council on International Affairs; VP, American Society of International Law.
Career: Joined *Sullivan & Cromwell* in 1970. Became partner in 1977.
Personal: Born 1943. Graduate of Yale College and Yale Law School; Fulbright Scholar at Cambridge University.

CARY, George
Cleary, Gottlieb, Steen & Hamilton, Washington DC +1 202 974 1500
Recommended in Competition/Anti-trust

CERABINO, Thomas M.
Willkie Farr & Gallagher, New York
+1 212 728 8000
Recommended in Corporate/M&A

CHATZINOFF, Howard
Weil, Gotshal & Manges, New York
+1 212 310 8000
howard.chatzinoff@weil.com
Recommended in Communications: Transactional (Telecoms)
Specialisation: Has a wide-ranging corporate and securities law expertise coupled with extensive experience of acting for clients in the media, telecom, information technology and internet sectors. Has, for more than 23 years, represented clients in a variety of corporate and corporate finance matters relating to broadcast properties, programming services, satellite distribution, cable television, telecom and the internet. Co-leads firm's M&A practice, and is a member of its management committee.

CHESLER, Evan
Cravath, Swaine & Moore, New York
+1 212 474 1000
Recommended in Competition/Anti-trust

CHINN, Adam
Wachtell, Lipton, Rosen & Katz, New York
+1 212 403 1000
Recommended in Tax

CHOI, Paul L.
Sidley & Austin, Chicago +1 312 853 2145
pchoi@sidley.com
Recommended in Corporate/M&A
Specialisation: Partner in the Chicago office of *Sidley & Austin.* Practises in the Corporate Group focusing on public and private mergers, acquisitions, dispositions, spin-offs, joint ventures and take-over defense. Has focused on a broad variety of public and private equity and debt offerings, including initial public offerings.
Personal: Graduate of Harvard College (1986 magna cum laude) and Harvard Law School (1989 magna cum laude; Harvard Law Review; Sears Prize). Law Clerk to Hon. Laurence H. Silberman of the D.C. Circuit (1989-90).

CHU, Morgan
Irell & Manella, Los Angeles +1 310 277 1010
Recommended in Intellectual Property

CITRON, Diane
Mayer, Brown & Platt, New York +1 212 506 2520
dcitron@mayerbrown.com
Recommended in Capital Markets: Securitisation
Specialisation: Partner and Co-Head of the firm's Securitisation Practice. Represents investment banks and financial institutions in structuring and developing foreign and domestic residential and commercial mortgage-backed programs and conduits for the purpose of issuing or participating in the issuance of MBS and CMBS in the United States and global markets. Has also represented collateralised underwriters and issuers in connection with public and private offerings of asset-backed securities, including ABS backed by leases, trade receivables, automobile, high yield bond and credit card receivables as well as commercial paper programs and the acquisition and subsequent securitisation of financial assets. Experienced in interest rate, currency, and total return swaps as used in connection with various structured financings. Represents financial institutions, corporations, and development companies in issuance of corporate debt, limited partnerships, initial public offerings, thrift mergers and acquisitions, and acquisitions of commercial and residential real estate portfolios. Previous government experience.
Prof. Memberships: Admitted to practice in California, 1985, and District of Columbia, 1978. Adjunct Professor, John Marshall Law School, Real Estate LLM Program, 'Real Estate Securitization' 1995-present. Member of the American Bar Association, Business Section; Subcommittee on Securitization and the California Bar Association, Business Section.
Publications: Author of 'The Legal Aspects of Lease Securitization', Banking and Financial Services Reporter, Vol. 9, No. 16, September 29, 1993. Lectures widely on real estate securitisation and lease securitisation for Strategic Research Institute, Mortgage Banker's Association, and the California Savings and Loan Association and the American Bar Association.
Career: Joined *Mayer, Brown & Platt* as a partner in 1992. Prior law firms include *Skadden, Arps, Slate, Meagher & Flom* (1987-1992), *Brown & Wood* (1985-1987), *Orrick, Herrington & Sutcliffe*, San Francisco (1984-1985), and *Wasserman, Orlow, Ginsberg & Rubin* (1977-1980). Served as Staff Attorney, S.E.C., Division of Enforcement (1980-1983) and Senior Counsel, Federal Home Loan Mortgage Corporation (1983-1984).
Personal: Born October 9, 1953. Earned JD at Case Western Reserve University School of Law in 1978 and BA from Franklin and Marshall College in 1975. Fluent in Spanish.

CLAGETT, Brice
Covington & Burling, Washington DC
+1 202 662 6000
Recommended in Arbitration (International)
Specialisation: Partner in the public and private international law practice. Practice includes petroleum matters, foreign claims, international arbitration, international land and maritime boundaries, law of the sea, federal election laws, transportation, general federal litigation, bankruptcy, Indian Law, constitutional law, environmental law and Middle Eastern Law. Cases on which has acted as counsel include: Iran Aircraft Industries v Acco Corp, US Court of Appeals for 2d Circuit. 980 F.2d 141 (2d Cir. 19992); Amoco Iran Oil Company and Amoco International Finance Corp v Iran, Cases No. 55 and 56 in the Iran United States Claims Tribunal, 1980s; Buckley v Valeo, U.S. Supreme Court 420 US 515 (1975) and Cambodia v Thailand, International Court of Justice, 1961 1.C.J.17 (jurisdiction); 1962 I.C.J. 6 (merits) (1961-1962). Has worked on matters representing the government of the Republic of Guinea in the organisation of major bauxite development, an infrastructure project, and obtaining loans from World Bank and AID representing Pakistan in the Indus Waters Dispute with India, resolved by the Indus Waters Treaty in 1960; representing ITT with reference to confiscated properties in Cuba for purpose of the Helms Burton Act.
Publications: Publications include: 'Title III of the Helms Burton Act is consistent with International Law 434', '90 American Journal of International Law 434' (1996); 'Competing Claims of Vietnam and China in the Vanguard Bank and Blue Dragon Areas of South China Sea'; 'Oil & Gas Law and Taxation Review', vol. 13 no.10, (Oct 1995) (Part 1) and vol 13 no. 11 (Nov 1995) (Part II); and 'Present State of the International Law of Compensation for Expropriated Property and Repudiated State Contracts' Chapter 12 in 'Private Investors Abroad Problems and Solutions in International Business in 1989' (1989) (Carol J. Halgren ed).
Career: Received AB from Princeton University in 1954 and JD from Harvard Law School in 1958.

CLARK, James E.
Sidley & Austin, Chicago +1 312 853 7776
jclark@sidley.com
Recommended in Banking & Finance
Specialisation: Partner in the Chicago office. Practice focuses on commercial and banking law. Co-author of 'Legal Developments in Secured Financing' (1978-94).
Prof. Memberships: Member of the American Bar Association.
Career: Member of the Board of Editors of 'The Bankruptcy Strategist'. Chairman of the Acquisition Financing Subcommittee of the Commercial Financial Services Committee of the American Bar Association Business Law Section from 1990 to 1994.
Personal: Educated at University of Chicago (JD, 1976); Brown University (AB, 1970, Phi Beta Kappa).

CLARK, Jim
Cahill Gordon & Reindel, New York
+1 212 701 3900
Recommended in Capital Markets: Debt & Equity

CLARK, Peter
Clark, Atcheson & Reisert, New York
+1 212 297 0257
Recommended in Shipping: Litigation

CLIMAN, Richard
Cooley Godward, Palo Alto +1 650 843 5205
Recommended in Communications: IT

COBEN, Jerry
Skadden, Arps, Slate, Meagher & Flom LLP, Los Angeles +1 213 687 5000
Recommended in Corporate/M&A
Specialisation: Leader of West Coast Corporate Practice group. Concentrates in corporate finance, mergers and acquisitions, and representation of Special Committees of Boards of Directors. Represented Turner Broadcasting Systems, Inc. in its merger with Time Warner; Independent Directors of Times Mirror in connection with acquisition of Times Mirror by The Tribune Company. Also represents Merril Lynch, CIBC World markets and other investment banks in connection with debt and equity financing.
Prof. Memberships: Admitted to practice in California, New York and the District of Columbia, Member, American and Los Angeles County Bar Associations.
Publications: Co-author, 'Types of Securities', in Harroch, 'Start up & Emerging Companies: Planning, Financing & Operating the Successful Business' (Law Journal Press 2000).
Career: First admitted to practice in New York in 1969. Moved to Los Angeles in 1979 and joined *Skadden, Arps* to open Los Angeles office of firm in 1983. Director (Past President) of *Bet Tzedek Legal Services*, a not-for-profit legal services agency providing free legal services to the elderly.
Personal: Born August 24, 1944. Attended Brown University 1962-1966 (AB cum laude); New York University School of Law, 1966-1969 (JD; Root-Tilden Scholar). Leisure activities include golf, running. Lives in Los Angeles, CA.

COGAN, John P.
King & Spalding, Houston +1 713 751 3200
Recommended in Energy & Natural Resources

COGUT, Charles
Simpson Thacher & Bartlett, New York
+1 212 455 2000
c_cogut@stblaw.com
Recommended in Communications: Transactional (Telecoms), Corporate/M&A, Private Equity: Buyouts
Specialisation: Head of Mergers & Acquisitions Practice Group at *Simpson Thacher & Bartlett*, specialising in domestic and international mergers and acquisitions and leveraged buyouts. Currently oversees the firm's relationships with Kohlberg Kravis Roberts & Co., Silver Lake Partners, Ripplewood Holdings, American Home Products and Global Crossing Ltd. Also involved in unsolicited and contested transactions.
Prof. Memberships: Is an active member of The Association of the Bar of the City of New York and the International Bar Association.
Career: Joined the firm in 1973 and has been a partner since 1980. From 1990-1993, served as the Senior Resident Partner in the firm's London office. In this capacity participated in many cross-border transactions.
Personal: Received a JD, in 1973 from the University of Pennsylvania Law School after graduating summa cum laude from Lehigh University in 1969. Frequent speaker at seminars dealing with contests for corporate control and leveraged buyouts.

COHEN, Ben
Cahill Gordon & Reindel, New York
+1 212 701 3900
Recommended in Tax

COHEN, H. Rodgin
Sullivan & Cromwell, New York +1 212 558 4000
cohenhr@sullcrom.com
Recommended in Corporate/M&A
Specialisation: Primary focus on regulatory, acquisitions and securities laws matters for domestic and foreign banking and other financial institutions. Represents The New York Clearing House Association, the association of the major New York City banks. For cross-border transactions in the acquisitions area, was engaged in Société Générale-Paribas, Mitsubishi-Bank of Tokyo, Credit Suisse-First Boston, Sumitomo-Goldman Sachs, Royal Bank of Canada-Bank of Montreal, Mitsubishi-Bank of California, and acquisitions or divestitures by Barclays Bank, National Westminster, Midland Bank, Lloyds Bank, Bank of Ireland, Crédit Lyonnais and Istituto Bancario San Paolo di Torino. Has been involved in most of the major bank acquisitions in the U.S. and has worked on a number of major cross-industry acquisitions, including UBS-PaineWebber, Credit Suisse-DLJ, Mellon-Dreyfus and NationsBank-Montgomery, as well as acquisitions in the insurance industry. In the securities area, worked on the first public offering in the United States by a foreign bank (Barclays) and on a number of other offerings in the United States by foreign banks. Also has worked on public offerings by Citicorp, Chase, Chemical, Morgan Guaranty, Security Pacific, First Interstate, Bank of New York, BancOne, Mellon, First Union, Shawmut, Wachovia, First Bank System, Continental Illinois, First Fidelity, MBNA, Republic New York, KeyCorp and Norwest. Has worked on a wide variety of bank regulatory matters with the four banking regulatory agencies, as well as other governmental agencies, on behalf of many of the largest U.S. and non-U.S. banking institutions, and the New York Clearing House.
Prof. Memberships: American Bar Association; Association of the Bar of the City of New York; New York State Bar Association; West Virginia Bar Association; Westchester County Bar Association.
Publications: A frequent speaker on banking law matters and the author of numerous articles on issues in commercial banking.
Career: Joined *Sullivan & Cromwell* in 1970, named a Partner of the firm in 1977, Vice Chairman in 1999, and Chairman in 2000.
Personal: Born 1944. Graduate of Harvard College (AB, magna cum laude, 1965) and Harvard Law School (LLB, 1968). Honorary LLB, University of Charleston, 1998. Served in the U.S. Army 1968-1970. Director, One Valley Bancorp. Member of the Board of Advisors, Banking Law Review; member, the National Board of Contributors of the American Lawyer Newspaper Group; member, the Editorial Advisory Board of Banking Expansion Reporter.

COHEN, Michael Marks
Burlingham Underwood LLP, New York
+1 212 422 7585
Recommended in Shipping: Litigation

COLE, Thomas A.
Sidley & Austin, Chicago +1 312 853 7473
tcole@sidley.com
Recommended in Corporate/M&A
Specialisation: Partner in the Chicago office of *Sidley & Austin*; Chairman of the Firm's Executive Committee. Maintains an essentially full-time practice, concentrating in public company M&A. Corporate governance assignments have included acting as special counsel to boards and takeover defenses.
Career: From 1993 to 1998, taught the seminar on corporate governance at University of Chicago Law School.
Personal: University of Chicago (JD, 1975, with honours, Order of the Coif); Johns Hopkins University (AB, 1970, with honours, Phi Beta Kappa).

COLEMAN, Lynn R.
Skadden, Arps, Slate, Meagher & Flom LLP, Washington DC +1 202 371 7000
Recommended in Energy & Natural Resources

COLLINS, E. Michael
Testa, Hurwitz & Thibeault LLP, Boston
+1 617 248 7000
Recommended in Private Equity: Fund Formation

COLLINS, Joseph P.
Mayer, Brown & Platt, New York +1 212 506 2657
jcollins@mayerbrown.com
Recommended in Capital Markets: Derivatives
Specialisation: Practice Administrator in Futures, Securities, and Derivatives Law practice. Represents

U

U

brokerage firms, investment management clients, trading and investment advisors, hedge fund operators, investment companies, banks, and pension plans. Practice encompasses securities, futures, forwards, swaps, options, and hybrid securities. Lead attorney in Refco Group's acquisitions of Lind-Waldock, LFG, and Main Street Trading Company. Active in structured derivative transactions.
Prof. Memberships: Admitted to practice in Illinois (1975), U.S. District Court for the Northern District of Illinois (1977), and U.S. Court of Appeals for the Fifth Circuit (1978). Member of the American Bar Association, Vice President, Committee on Regulation of Futures and Derivatives Instruments, including Chair of 1994 Annual Meeting; Association of the Bar of the City of New York, Futures Regulation Committee, including former Chair of the Futures Commission Merchant Subcommittee; past Chairman of the Futures Law Committee of the Chicago Bar Association; Faculty member of the IIT-Kent College of Law's Graduate Program in Financial Services Law; and Member of the Illinois Secretary of State's Commodities Law Advisory Committee.
Publications: Participant at ABA Committee on Regulation of Futures and Derivatives Instruments Conferences, SIA and FIA Law and Compliance Conferences, Kent Financial Services Law Conferences, and various other panels and workshops regarding derivative instruments and securities.
Career: Joined *Mayer, Brown & Platt* as partner in 1994 following 19 years with *Schiff Hardin & Waite.*
Personal: Born April 9, 1950. Earned JD from New York University School of Law in 1975, where was Root-Tilden Scholar, and AB (magna cum laude) from College of the Holy Cross in 1972. Served as Circuit Secretary for the New York University School of Law Root-Tilden Scholarship Program.

COLLINS, Wayne Dale
Shearman & Sterling, New York +1 212 848 4000
wcollins@shearman.com
Recommended in Competition/Anti-trust
Specialisation: Specialises in the antitrust defence of mergers and acquisitions. Has represented clients in more than 175 merger investigations by federal and state antitrust enforcement agencies.
Prof. Memberships: Served as an officer and council member of the American Bar Association Section of Antitrust Law from 1991 to 1999. Fellow of the American Bar Foundation and is a member of the Bar Association of the City of New York, the American Law Institute, the American Economics Association and the Econometric Society.
Career: Admitted to the bar in New York and the District of Columbia. Joined *Shearman & Sterling* in 1978, leaving in 1981 to serve as a White House Fellow, Special Assistant to Vice President Bush in the Reagan Administration and as Deputy Counsel to the Presidential Task Force on Regulatory Relief. Following that, served as Deputy Assistant Attorney General in the United States Department of Justice Antitrust Division. Returned to *Shearman & Sterling* in 1983. From 1991 to 1995 also served as an adjunct faculty member at the Yale Law School, where taught antitrust law.

Personal: Attended California Institute of Technology (BS, Honors, 1973; MS 1974 ARCS scholar); University of Chicago Law School (JD, 1978), Law Review; University of Minnesota, PhD candidate, mathematical economics, 1979.

CONDON, Creighton
Shearman & Sterling, New York +1 212 848 4000
ccondon@shearman.com
Recommended in Communications: Transactional (Telecoms), Corporate/M&A
Specialisation: Partner. Represents United States and multinational corporations in acquisitions and sales of public and private companies and in joint ventures, and also regularly provides advice regarding issues of corporate governance and control. Clients include prominent U.S. and international corporations and investment banks.
Prof. Memberships: American Bar Association; New York State Bar Association; California State Bar Association.
Career: Qualified for the New York Bar in 1982 and the California Bar in 1984. Joined *Shearman & Sterling* in 1982 and became a partner in 1991. Based in *Shearman & Sterling*'s San Francisco office from 1984-87.
Personal: Born January 20, 1956. Attended the university of Pennsylvania (BA, Magna Cum Laude, 1978), St. John's College, Cambridge (1978-79) and Columbia Law School (JD, 1982, Harlan Fiske Stone Scholar and Editor-in-Chief, 'Columbia Journal of Transnational Law'). Frequent lecturer to business and legal groups on a wide array of legal topics, including Mergers & Acquisitions.

CONLON, Michael
Fulbright & Jaworski LLP, Houston
+1 713 651 5151/ 2026624585
Recommended in Corporate/M&A

CONRAD Jr, Winthrop
Davis Polk & Wardwell, New York +1 212 450 4000
Recommended in Capital Markets: Debt & Equity

CONTRATTO, Dana
Crowell & Moring LLP, Washington DC
+1 202 624 2500
Recommended in Energy & Natural Resources

COOPER, Jim
Cravath, Swaine & Moore, New York
+1 212 474 1000
Recommended in Banking & Finance

COOPER, Stephen H.
Weil, Gotshal & Manges, New York
+1 212 310 8000
stephen.cooper@weil.com
Recommended in Capital Markets: Debt & Equity
Specialisation: Partner, *Weil, Gotshal & Manges LLP*, New York. Represents both issuers and underwriters in public offerings and private placements of securities, including common and preferred stock, limited partnership interests, secured and unsecured senior and subordinated debt, medium term notes, convertible securities and equity derivatives. Has represented underwriting syndicates managed by firms such as Bear, Stearns; CS First Boston; Donaldson, Lufkin & Jenrette; Morgan Stanley and Salomon Smith Barney including IPOs of Avis Rent A Car and Planet Hollywood. Served as US Counsel to Reuters in its 1984 IPO. Also writes and lectures on capital markets matters and is a regular participant in various symposia.
Prof. Memberships: Member of American Bar Association's Committee on the Federal Regulation of Securities and has served for ten years as Co-Chair of its Subcommittee on International Securities Matters.
Career: Received both undergraduate and legal education at Columbia University and served as an officer in the US Navy.
Personal: Subject of biographical reference in 'Who's Who in America.'

COOPERSTEIN, Gary P.
Fried, Frank, Harris, Shriver & Jacobson, New York
+1 212 859 8000
Recommended in Corporate/M&A
Specialisation: Business lawyer engaged in structuring and negotiating complex transactions. Clients include Burlington Resources Inc., El Paso Energy Company, GE Capital Corporation, Merck & Co. Inc., and the Quaker Oats Company. Recent representations include Burlington Resources Inc.'s US$3 billion stock combination with Louisiana Land and Exploration Company and its US$3 billion acquisition of Poco Petroleums Ltd.; El Paso Energy Company's US$15 billion merger with Coastal Corporation, its US$5 billion merger with Sonat Inc., its US$4 billion acquisition of Tenneco Inc. in a Morris Trust transaction and its US$500 million acquisition of Deeptech International Inc.; Chevron Corporation in its pending US$40 billion acquisition of Texaco Inc., GE Capital Corporation's long-term operating lease of US$1.5 billion of railcars from ACF Industries Inc., and sale of US$2 billion in bank credit-card receivables; Merck & Co. Inc.'s US$7 billion acquisition of Medico Containment Sevices Inc. and its disposition of six businesses for more than US$6 billion and its joint venture with Thone-Poulenc with respect to their animal health business.
Career: Partner with *Fried Frank*'s corporate department. Resident in the New York office. Qualified in 1979. Associated with *Fried Frank* in 1977, becoming a partner in 1984.
Personal: Born 1952. Attended New York University 1977 (JD, Order of the Coif). Attended Massachusetts Institute of Technology 1974 (BS, economics). Leisure interests include astronomy, travel, music and sports.

COWAN, Cameron
Orrick, Herrington & Sutcliffe, Washington DC
+1 202 339 8488
ccowan@orrick.com.
Recommended in Capital Markets: Securitisation
Specialisation: Practice involves the representation of financial institutions, investment banks and companies with particular expertise in such matters as the structuring, issuance, and purchase of asset-backed, mortgage-backed, and derivative products.
Prof. Memberships: District of Colombia Bar; Bar Association of the City of New York; Bar of the State of New York (First Judicial District).
Publications: Co-author of 'Mortgage-Backed

Securities: Developments and Trends in the Secondary Mortgage Market'.
Career: Prior to joining *Orrick*, was with *Milbank, Tweed, Hadley, & McCloy* in Washington DC, as a partner from 1990-93. Managing Director of *Orrick's* finance practices.
Personal: Earned JD from the University of Virginia School of Law in 1981. Received an MBA from the Columbia University Graduate School of Business, and a BS magna cum laude from Syracuse University.

CRAVEN, George
Mayer, Brown & Platt, Chicago +1 312 701 7231
gcraven@mayerbrown.com
Recommended in Tax
Specialisation: Leading authority on tax aspects of financial transactions, cross-border tax arbitrage, offshore insurance arrangements, and deductibility of alternative risk transfer payments. Advises on acquisitions and dispositions of businesses, including structured financings as well as tax aspects of new financial products such as 'Section 483 Notes', 'Liquid Yield Option Notes'. International tax planning expertise includes Subpart F issues, transactions designed to accelerate or create foreign source income, and redomestication of U.S. insurance companies to foreign jurisdiction.
Prof. Memberships: Admitted to practice in Illinois, 1976, and U.S. Tax Court, 1976. Member of the American Bar Association, Section of Taxation; Financial Transactions Committee.
Publications: Lecturer on 'Tax Aspects of Securitization of Insurance Risks' at IBC Conference on Insurance Risk & Securitization, November 11-12, 1999, New York City. Moderator and panel member, 'Hot Products and Innovative Financial Instruments', University of Chicago Federal Tax Conference, November 1, 1994; 'Offshore and Captive Insurance Issues', delivered at Tax Executive Institute Seminar, May 1994; ' "Money" and "Property (Other than Money)": An Exploration of "Amount Realized" Under Section 1001(b)', Taxes, December, 1992, paper originally delivered at the 45th University of Chicago Federal Tax Conference, October, 1992.
Career: Joined *Mayer, Brown & Platt*, Chicago, in 1981 and became a Partner in 1983. Prior to that, had worked for *Sidley & Austin*, Chicago (1976-1980) and *Ogden, Robertson & Marshall*, Louisville, 1980-1981.
Personal: Born March 11, 1951. Earned JD, cum laude, from Harvard Law School in 1976 and BA summa cum laude, from the University of Notre Dame in 1973. Also studied at Sophia University, Tokyo (1970-1971).

CRUMBAUGH, David G.
Latham & Watkins, Chicago +1 312 876 7680
david.crumbaugh@lw.com
Recommended in Banking & Finance
Specialisation: Partner in the Finance and Real Estate Department and the Banking Group. Primarily represents banks and commercial finance companies in transactions. Specialises in commercial finance, corporate finance and insolvency. Represented lenders in connection with projects in the food products, distribution, credit card processing and heavy manufacturing sectors and has been lead counsel on financings in virtually every type of industry.
Prof. Memberships: Member of the American Bar Association.
Career: Co-chair of the Chicago office Finance and Real Estate Department. Joined *Latham & Watkins* in 1997; previously head of the commercial finance group at *Winston & Strawn*. Governing Board of the Commercial Finance Association Education Foundation,1995.
Personal: University of Illinois (JD 1976), Order of the Coif, managing editor of the University of Illinois Law Review. Illinois State University (BS 1973).

CULLEN, Gary
Skadden, Arps, Slate, Meagher & Flom LLP, Chicago +1 312 407 0700
gcullen@skadden.com
Recommended in Corporate/M&A
Specialisation: Partner, Chicago. Mergers and Acquisitions and Corporate Finance, representing Fortune 500, middle market and emerging companies in a wide range of industries, as well as investment banking and other financial institutions, in a variety of transactions. Has worked on behalf of buyers and sellers in auctions involving public companies and their business units, other stock and asset acquisitions and dispositions, negotiated and contested take-overs, and joint ventures. Represents issuers and investment banking institutions in initial and other public offerings and private placements of securities. Also represents clients in a range of other corporate matters including those relating to corporate governance and disclosure issues, shareholder rights plans, stockholders' agreements and other securities, corporate control issues and investment banking clients in their role as transaction financial advisors.
Career: JD, Columbia University School of Law, 1985; BA, University of Illinois, 1982.

CULOTTA, Ken
King & Spalding, Houston +1 713 751 3200
Recommended in Energy & Natural Resources

CUNNINGHAM, Dan
Cravath, Swaine & Moore, New York +1 212 474 1000
Recommended in Capital Markets: Derivatives, Corporate/M&A

CURTIS, Susan M.
Skadden, Arps, Slate, Meagher & Flom LLP, New York +1 212 735 3000
Recommended in Capital Markets: Securitisation

D'ALIMONTE, John S.
Willkie Farr & Gallagher, New York +1 212 728 8000
jdalimonte@willkie.com
Recommended in Communications: Transactional (Telecoms)
Specialisation: Senior Partner in the Corporate Department. Experience includes representing issuers (both United States and foreign) and underwriters in securities offerings in the United States and internationally, as well as all corporate structurings and restructurings in anticipation of such transactions. In addition, practice encompasses strategic corporate investments, US and cross border merger and acquisition activities (hostile and negotiated transactions), privatisations, venture capital investments, corporate joint ventures and commercial contracts and relationships of all types. Throughout career has been involved with issuers in various industries, including telecommunications, insurance and financial services.
Prof. Memberships: American Bar Association, the New York State Bar Association and the Association of the Bar of the City of New York.
Career: Admitted in 1968, has spent entire career with *Willkie Farr & Gallagher*, becoming a Partner in 1976. Board of Directors of the St John's University School of Law Alumni Association from 1977-85 and 1997 to date, and was Secretary of the Association from 1980-83. Adjunct Professor of Law at St John's University School of Law (1980 to present).
Personal: Graduate of St John's University School of Law (JD 1968) and did undergraduate work at the US Air Force Academy and Hunter College of the City University of New York (BA 1965). A frequent speaker at seminars conducted by organisations including The Practising Law Institute. Editor of a section of Sowards' 'The Federal Securities Act' and was a contributing editor to Peat Marwick McLintock's 'Guide to Acquisitions in the US' and to 'Securities Underwriting – A Practitioner's Guide'. Has written 'US Federal Securities Law Issues for Private Issuers' and 'The Use of American Depository Receipts,' and on related subjects.

DAVENPORT, Kirk A.
Latham & Watkins, New York +1 212 906 1284
kirk.davenport@lw.com
Recommended in Capital Markets: Debt & Equity
Specialisation: Partner in the New York office, Chairman of the firm's Corporate Finance Practice Group. Extensive experience in corporate finance, mergers and acquisitions, general securities and corporate matters. Represents underwriters, placement agents, initial purchasers and issuers in public and private high yield and equity offerings. Also represents broker-dealers in other engagements, including dealer manager and consent solicitation agent engagements. Clients include domestic and foreign investment banks, New York Stock Exchange listed companies, foreign corporations and leveraged buyout funds.
Prof. Memberships: Serves on an American Bar Association committee charged with revising the Model Simplified Indenture.
Publications: Recent publications include 'The SEC's Regulation FD – Fair Disclosure' and 'Public vs. Private Markets: A Review of High Yield Financing Techniques'.
Personal: JD, University of Michigan, 1984, magna cum laude, Order of the Coif. BA, Brown University, 1981.

DAVIDSON, Gordon
Fenwick & West, Palo Alto +1 650 494 0600
Recommended in Communications: IT

U

U

DAVIS, Jim
Howrey Simon Arnold & White, Washington DC+1 202 783 0800
Recommended in Intellectual Property

DAVIS, Platt
Vinson & Elkins LLP, Houston +1 713 758 2131 pdavis@velaw.com
Recommended in Energy & Natural Resources
Specialisation: Principal areas of practice are international arbitration, energy regulation and administrative law. Experience includes the representation of several clients in contested claims before the International Chamber of Commerce, the American Arbitration Association and the Iran U.S. Claims Tribunal and in ad hoc arbitrations conducted under the UNICITRAL Rules.
Prof. Memberships: Advisory Board: Institute for Transnational Arbitration; Member: Energy Bar Association, American Bar Association.
Career: The University of Texas (BA, 1966); The University of Texas School of Law (JD, 1970); George Washington University (LLM, 1974). Admitted to practice, Texas (1969); District of Columbia (1973); numerous federal, district and appellate courts.

DAVIS, Scott
Mayer, Brown & Platt, Chicago +1 312 701 7311 sdavis@mayerbrown.com
Recommended in Corporate/M&A
Specialisation: Co-Administrator of the Corporate and Securities Group. Extensive experience in mergers and acquisitions and the problems that arise when there is a real or perceived conflict of interest between a company's officers or directors and its shareholders. Major deals have included representation of Dow Chemical in the pending merger in which Union Carbide will become Dow's subsidiary (estimated value $11.6 billion as of the date of announcement); and Illinois Tool Works in the merger in which Premark became ITW's subsidiary (estimated value $3.6 billion as of the date of announcement). Also advises in litigation matters involving derivative, takeover, and securities fraud litigation.
Prof. Memberships: Vice President, Chicago Police Board, a body appointed by the Mayor of Chicago with disciplinary and supervisory powers over Chicago police officers and the Department.
Publications: Author or Co-Author of 'Liability Under Sections 10, 18 and 20 of the Securities Exchange Act of 1934', printed in Understanding the Securities Laws 2000, PLI Corp. Law & Practice Handbook Series, No. B-1198, 2000; 'Merger and Acquisition Agreements in Competitive Bidding Situations: Rights and Obligations Created by Corporation and Contract Law', 17 Securities Regulation Law Journal 3, 1989.
Career: Joined *Mayer, Brown & Platt* in 1977 and became a partner in 1983.
Personal: Born January 8, 1952. Earned JD, cum laude, from Harvard University in 1976 where was a member of the Board of Editors, Harvard Law Review. Holds a BA, cum laude, from Yale University, 1972.

DAY, Lloyd (Rusty)
Day Casebeer Madrid & Batchelder LLP, Cupertino +1 408 255 3255
Recommended in Intellectual Property

DE ORCHIS, Vincent M.
De Orchis Walker & Corsa, New York +1 212 344 4700
Recommended in Shipping: Litigation

DE SEAR, Edward
Orrick, Herrington & Sutcliffe, New York +1 212 506 5060
Recommended in Capital Markets: Securitisation
Specialisation: Specialises in asset-backed securities, both in the US and abroad. Particular expertise in the areas of securitisation of credit card receivables, auto loans, leases, trade receivables, mutual fund fees, export loans, tobacco company payments, and catastrophe risk coverage assets. Represents issuers, underwriters, credit enhancers, placement agents, and trustees.
Career: Partner and head of the Structured Finance Group. As a lecturer and panellist, participates in numerous conferences held in the US and Latin America on the subjects of asset-backed securities and securitisation.
Personal: Earned a JD from the University of Virginia School of Law in 1973. Received an AB in History from Columbia University.

DEL CALVO, Jorge
Pillsbury Madison & Sutro, Palo Alto +1 650 233 4500
Recommended in Communications: IT

DENGER, Michael
Gibson, Dunn & Crutcher LLP, Washington DC +1 202 955 8500
Recommended in Competition/Anti-trust

DESANTIS, Victor
White & Case LLP, Washington DC +1 202 626 3607 vdesantis@whitecase.com
Recommended in Project Finance
Specialisation: Partner in the Corporate Department. Concentrates on international, multi-lender project finance, and energy and cross-border transactions. Active on behalf of International Finance Corporation, Commonwealth Development Corporation, Société Générale and others in connection with the ABB/EDFI Azito power project in Coté d'Ivoire and on behalf of Deutsche Bank, Société Générale and International Finance Corporation in connection with the EDFI Rio Bravo power plant financing in Mexico; acted for Export-Import Bank of Japan and International Finance Corporation in the financing of the AES Merida power project in Mexico; assisted JP Morgan as advisor in connection with the asset auction by Connecticut Light & Power in connection with its restructuring; assisted Credit Lyonnais in the COMSIGUA hot-briquetted iron facility financing in Venezuela; represented Citibank, HSBC, Banque Paribas, ECGD, International Finance Corporation, Commonwealth Development Corporation and others in the financing of the Sual power project in the Philippines. Has represented sponsors, multi-lateral and commercial lenders and export credit agencies in various enterprises financed on a project basis. Has spoken in various conferences.
Prof. Memberships: New York State Bar, District of Columbia Bar.
Career: Admitted to the Bar in New York, 1986; District of Columbia, 1987; became a partner in January 1994.
Personal: Born 8 March 1960. Attended Yale University, 1978-1982; Harvard Law School, 1982-85. Leisure interests include jogging, biking. Married Mary Karen McCartan DeSantis. Two children, Michael, age 6, Thomas, age 4. Lives in Bethesda, Maryland.

DETTMER, Scott
Gunderson Dettmer Stough Villeneuve Franklin & Hachigian, Menlo Park +1 650 321 2400
Recommended in Communications: IT

DIANGELO, Christopher
Dewey Ballantine LLP, New York +1 212 259 8000 cdiangelo@deweyballantine.com
Recommended in Capital Markets: Securitisation
Specialisation: Partner of *Dewey Ballantine* LLP, resident in the New York office. Specialises in financial services/structured finance and heads the firm's asset-backed practice. Has over 15 years' experience in the financial services industry, and along with the other members of the group represents a wide variety of clients in the industry, including issuers, lenders, underwriters and bond insurers on a variety of programs and projects, including asset-backed debt, municipal debt, straight corporate debt and equity, warehouse lines, regulatory matters and acquisitions.
Career: Prior to joining *Dewey Ballantine* LLP, was employed by New York State working on a variety of municipal finance programs.
Personal: Graduate of Williams College (BA Economics, 1979), City University of New York (MBA Economics, 1981) and Columbia University School of Law (JD, 1984). Admitted to practice in New York in 1984.

DILG, Joe
Vinson & Elkins LLP, Houston +1 713 758 2062 jdilg@velam.com
Recommended in Corporate/M&A, Energy & Natural Resources
Specialisation: Practice focuses primarily on domestic and international business transactions, including acquisitions, divestitures, joint ventures and financings. Experience covers all aspects of the domestic and international energy business, including oil and gas and electric power generation.
Prof. Memberships: Member: State Bar of Texas; American Bar Association.
Career: Lecturer: various legal conferences on topics ranging from leveraged buy-outs to the Foreign Corrupt Practices Act. Attended Southern Methodist University (BA; Economics, 1973); The University of Texas (JD with high Honors, 1976); admitted to practice (Texas, 1976).

DILLON, Christopher
Gunderson Dettmer Stough Villeneuve Franklin & Hachigian, Menlo Park +1 650 321 2400
Recommended in Communications: IT

DIMON, Samuel
Davis Polk & Wardwell, New York +1 212 450 4000
Recommended in Tax: Financial Products

DODSON, Gerald
Morrison & Foerster, Palo Alto +1 650 813 5600
gdodson@mofo.com
Recommended in Intellectual Property
Specialisation: Partner specialising in patent litigation. Has served as lead trial and appellate counsel in many complex technology cases involving hundreds of millions of dollars. Recently, was lead trial and appellate counsel for The Regents of the University of California on patent litigation against Genetech over a human growth hormone biotechnology patent. Case settled for $200 million, one of the largest settlements in the history of patent law, the largest ever in the biotechnology field. Has also represented companies on pioneering patent cases covering medical devices, optical and electronic hardware and software fields.
Career: Admitted to practice in the State of California and before the U.S. Patent & Trademark Office. Prior to private practice, served as Chief Counsel for the Health and Environmental Subcommittee, U.S. House of Representatives, and with the Solicitor's Office, U.S. Department of the Interior. Headed the congressional investigation of Union Carbide's pesticide plant disaster in Bhopal, India. In 1988, joined the Bay Area firm of *Townsend and Townsend*, moving to *Howard, Rice, Nemerovski, Canady, Robertson, Falk & Rabkin* in 1992. Prior to joining *Morrison & Foerster* in 1999, was a partner in the Silicon Valley office of *Arnold, White & Durkee.*
Personal: B.S.M.E., Lafayette College, 1969; JD, University of Maryland Law School, 1972; LLM, George Washington University Law School, 1977.

DOETSCH, Douglas A.
Mayer, Brown & Platt, Chicago +1 312 701 7973
ddoetsch@mayerbrown.com
Recommended in Banking & Finance
Specialisation: Partner in International Corporate and Finance practice. Advises on secured and unsecured lending, including lending for leveraged buyouts, work-outs and project financings, particularly in cross-border transactions. Represents clients in cross-border securitisation transactions, particularly future cash flow securitisations, debt restructuring and debt exchange offers, with emphasis on restructuring of emerging market debt. Counsels on asset and stock acquisitions and contract negotiations. Works on joint ventures with emphasis on cross-border ventures in Latin America. Advises on Euro-securities offerings, particularly for issues of emerging market companies, and U.S. equity offerings of foreign issuers.
Prof. Memberships: Admitted to practice in Illinois, 1989 and New York, 1987. Member of the American Bar Association and the Illinois Bar Association; Chicago Council on Foreign Relations, Member of Executive Committee of Committee on Foreign Affairs; Chairman, Mid-America Chapter of U.S.-Mexico Chamber of Commerce.
Publications: Frequent author of articles, and speaker at conferences, on topics such as securitisations by emerging market issuers, international joint ventures, issuances of debt securities in the Euromarkets and issuances of American Depositary Receipts by foreign issuers.
Career: Joined *Mayer, Brown & Platt* in 1988 and became a partner in 1995. Prior to that, worked for *Cleary, Gottlieb, Steen & Hamilton*, New York (1986-1988) and, before that, worked as a Consultant for Data Resources, Inc. (1979-1982).
Personal: Born November 6, 1957. Earned JD from Columbia University in 1986, where served as Editor-in-Chief, Columbia Journal of Transnational Law. Rotary Graduate Fellow at Université de Dakar, Dakar, Senegal (1982-1983). Holds BA, magna cum laude, from Kalamazoo College (1979), where he was elected to Phi Beta Kappa. Fluent in French and Spanish.

DOKOS, Daniel S.
Weil, Gotshal & Manges, New York
+1 212 310 8000
daniel.dokos@weil.com
Recommended in Banking & Finance
Specialisation: Partner in the firm's New York office. An experienced banking law advisor, with particular expertise in secured lending and acquisition finance. Has represented both financial institutions and corporate borrowers in connection with leveraged acquisition and recapitalisation transactions, syndicated lending, asset-based lending and cross-border financings, as well as representing lenders in connection with loan restructurings, debtor-in-possession financings, workouts and exit financings.
Career: Joined the firm in 1998 from the New York office of *Sidley & Austin.*

DONOVAN, Donald Francis
Debevoise & Plimpton, New York +1 212 909 6000
Recommended in Arbitration (International)

DOUGLAS, James
Skadden, Arps, Slate, Meagher & Flom LLP, New York +1 212 735 3000
Recommended in Banking & Finance

DOUGLAS, Peter
Davis Polk & Wardwell, New York +1 212 450 4000
Recommended in Corporate/M&A

DOWNS, Clark Evans
Jones, Day, Reavis & Pogue, Washington DC
+1 202 879 3939
cedowns@jonesday.com
Recommended in Energy & Natural Resources
Specialisation: Partner in Government Regulation Group. Main areas are representation of electric utilities before Federal Energy Regulatory Commission, Nuclear Regulatory Commission, Securities Exchange Commission and state public service commissions in merger approval, transmission access, rate, facilities certification, securities issuance and related proceedings, related appellate litigation, and negotiation and structuring of electric utility mergers, acquisitions, joint ownerships and dispositions of electric generating units and power sale and transmission service agreements; and representation of utilities and investment banking firms in public and private offerings of corporate securities, in mergers and acquisitions and in related SEC and general corporate matters. Frequent speaker at industry conferences.
Prof. Memberships: American Bar Association Public Utility, Communications and Transportation (Vice Chair, Electricity Committee), Administrative Law and Antitrust Sections; Edison Electric Institute Legal Committee; District Columbia Bar; Federal Energy Bar Association.
Career: Admitted to the Illinois bar (1973) and the District of Columbia Bar (1981). Joined *Isham, Lincoln & Beale*, 1973, Partner in charge of Washington, DC office (1980-87). Joined *Jones Day*, 1988. Admitted to practice before the US Courts of Appeal for the District of Columbia Circuit and the Second Circuit and the US District Court for the Northern District of Illinois.
Personal: Born 30 July 1946. Attended Boston University (AB in English literature, 1968, and JD cum laude, 1973). US Army, (Vietnam 1970-71), Bronze Star medal for Meritorious Service. Editor, Boston University Law Review, 1971-73. Leisure interests include cello, piano, folk music, opera and choral singing. Lives in Chevy Chase, Maryland.

DRANOFF, David
Goldberg, Kohn, Bell, Black, Rosenbloom & Moritz, Ltd, Chicago +1 312 201 4000
Recommended in Banking & Finance

DUNN, Douglas
Milbank, Tweed, Hadley & McCloy, New York
+1 212 530 5062
mdunn@milbank.com
Recommended in Corporate/M&A
Specialisation: Partner of *Milbank, Tweed, Hadley & McCloy LLP* with emphasis on corporate and project financing. Chair of the Firm's Global Power & Energy Group. Practice includes the representation of several utility companies, including those registered under the Public Utility Company Act of 1935. Also serves as designated underwriters' counsel for many other utility companies. Special assignments have included the first cross-border acquisition in which a foreign company purchased a US utility and the first leveraged buyout of an electric utility. Has also given reorganisation advice in several recent large transactions for electric and gas utility companies, telecom companies or their creditors. Major recent representations include Scottish Power plc, Montana Power and Enron Corp.
Prof. Memberships: Memberships: Member of the Board of Governors of the American Bar Association; past chair, Section of Public Utility, Communications and Transportation Law, American Bar Association; former chair, committee K, International Bar Association; member, Federal Regulation of Securities Committee, Section of Business Law, American Bar Association; former member and chair, Committee on Nuclear Technology and Law, Association of the Bar of the City of New York; Fellow, American Bar Foundation.
Publications: Author of several articles, contributor to several books and frequent speaker on securities law. Formerly Associate Editor of the 'Law Review' at Vanderbilt University.
Career: Joined *Milbank, Tweed, Hadley & McCloy* in 1985. Prior to this: Senior Vice President and

Managing Director, Investment Banking Division of Shearson Lehman Brothers Inc. from 1984 to 1985, and associate, partner and member of the Management Committee of *Winthrop, Stimson, Putnam & Roberts* from 1970 to 1984.
Personal: Received a BSE from the University of Michigan and JD from Vanderbilt University. Admitted to the New York Bar in 1971, to the US District Court for the Southern District of New York in 1972, to the US Court of Appeals for the Second Circuit in 1973 and to the US Supreme Court in 1978.

DUNNER, Donald
Finnegan Henderson Farabow Garrett & Dunner LLP, Washington DC +1 202 408 4000
donald.dunner@finnegan.com
Recommended in Intellectual Property
Specialisation: Partner. Handles all areas of patent law including prosecution, licensing, litigation, validity and infringement studies, and counseling. Has technical expertise in the areas of chemical engineering, chemistry, biotechnology and pharmaceuticals. Has litigated numerous cases in the federal district courts, but is best known for appellate practice before the United States Court of Appeals for the Federal Circuit. Has had significant success overturning jury and other verdicts handed down by the lower district courts. Most notable case involved the complete reversal of an $80 million jury verdict for Mattel's Hot WheelsTM toys.
Publications: Co-Author: Court Review of Patent Office Decisions, 1969, 1973. co-Author: Patent Law Perspectives, 1970-1988; Co-Author: Court of Appeals for the Federal Circuit Practice and Procedure, 1985.
Career: Admitted in 1958, District of Columbia; 1958-1982, U.S. Court of Customs and Patent Appeals; 1963, U.S. Supreme Court; 1982, U.S. Court of Appeals for the Federal Circuit; registered to practice before U.S. Patent and Trademark Office. Served as an Examiner with the U.S. Patent and Trademark Office and as a Law Clerk to the Honorable Noble J. Johnson, Chief Judge of the U.S. Court of Customs and Patent Appeals (1956-1958). Joined the firm in 1978.
Personal: Born May 12, 1931. Purdue University (BSChE, 1953); Georgetown University Law Center (JD, 1958).

EASTMENT, Thomas James
Baker Botts LLP, Washington DC +1 202 639 7700
Recommended in Energy & Natural Resources
Specialisation: Partner in energy department. Main area of work is litigation before federal agencies and courts relating to the regulation of oil and gas pipelines and to royalty and other issues arising from oil and gas leases. Also acts as regulatory and project development counsel for oil and gas pipeline construction projects and financings.
Prof. Memberships: Member of the Federal Energy Bar Association; New York State Bar Association; Washington DC Bar Association; also admitted to the United States Supreme Court, the Courts of Appeal for the District of Columbia and for the Fifth Circuit, and the United States District Court for the District of Columbia.
Career: Gained BChE from Manhattan College in 1972 and JD from the University of Michigan in 1975. Associate *Morton, Bernard, Brown, Roberts and Sutherland* from 1975-1977 and associate in *Baker Botts* from 1977-1984. Made Partner at *Baker Botts* in 1985.

EGAN, James
Clifford Chance Rogers & Wells LLP, Washington DC +1 202 434 0700
Recommended in Competition/Anti-trust

EINHORN, David
Wachtell, Lipton, Rosen & Katz, New York +1 212 403 1000
Recommended in Tax

EISENBERG, David
Simpson Thacher & Bartlett, New York +1 212 455 2000
d_eisenberg@stblaw.com
Recommended in Capital Markets: Securitisation
Specialisation: A partner at *Simpson Thacher & Bartlett* and member of the firm's Corporate Department, concentrating on banking and corporate law and asset-backed securities transactions.
Prof. Memberships: Association of the Bar of the City of New York.
Personal: Received a BA, summa cum laude, in 1974 from Duke University and a JD in 1977 from Duke University School of Law.

EMERSON, Carter
Kirkland & Ellis, Chicago +1 312 861 2000
Recommended in Corporate/M&A

EMMERICH, Adam
Wachtell, Lipton, Rosen & Katz, New York +1 212 403 1000
Recommended in Corporate/M&A

EPSTEIN, Gary
Latham & Watkins, Washington DC +1 202 637 2200
gary.epstein@lw.com
Recommended in Communications: Regulatory
Specialisation: Partner in charge of the telecommunications practice. Advised several of the divested Bell Operating Companies on regulatory matters and DIRECTV on domestic and international satellite regulation. Serves as U.S. regulatory counsel for Telefonos de Mexico. Counsels foreign and foreign-owned companies on U.S. international policies, including ownership restrictions and authorisation for international services. Directly involved in privatisation or other restructuring of telecommunications sectors in many countries.
Prof. Memberships: American Bar Associations, District of Columbia Bar Association.
Career: Chief, Common Carrier Bureau of the Federal Communications Commission, 1981-83; Chairman, FCC's Industry Advisory Committee on Implementation of Reduced Orbital Spacing Between Domestic Fixed Satellites, 1984-86; Chairman, FCC's Industry Advisory Committee for the 1995 World Radiocommunication Conference.
Personal: JD, Harvard University, 1971, cum laude. BSEE, Lehigh University, 1968, highest honors, Tau Beta Pi, Eta Kappa Nu.

EPSTEIN, Michael
Weil, Gotshal & Manges, New York +1 212 310 8000
michael.epstein@weil.com
Recommended in Communications: Transactional (IT)
Specialisation: Partner in the New York office. A nationally recognised expert in intellectual property. Has extensive experience litigating and counselling corporations worldwide, and has negotiated and resolved some of the largest and most complex intellectual property disputes. Practice involves substantial transactional work, including significant e-commerce, structuring and negotiating technology and intellectual property acquisitions, technology transfer and licensing arrangements, and joint ventures and other targeted alliances. Chair of the firm's 90 lawyer Technology and Proprietary Rights Group, and co-chair of the firm's 130 lawyer Trade Practice and Regulatory Law Department. Author of the treaties 'Epstein on Intellectual Property and Modern Intellectual Property'. Co-author of 'On-Line Internet Law', 'International Intellectual Property', and co-editor of 'Drafting License Agreements', 'The Corporate Counsellor's Deskbook', 'The Departing Employee', 'Doing Business in Eastern Europe', 'Biotechnology Law', 'The Trademark Law Revision Act', 'Joint Ventures and Other Cooperative Business Arrangements' and 'Trade Secrets, Restrictive Covenants, and Other Safeguards'. Author of numerous articles on intellectual property law, computer law, unfair competition, trade law, licensing, and non-compete agreements. Founder and co-editor of 'The Journal of Proprietary Rights' and a member of the Editorial Boards of the 'Computer Lawyer', 'Intellectual Property Strategist', and 'Cyberspace Lawyer'.
Prof. Memberships: American Bar Association, section of Intellectual Property Law; Licensing Executive Society.
Career: *Weil, Gotshal, & Manges, LLP* 1979 to present. Co-Chair – Trade Practices and Regulatory Law Department, Chair – Technology and Proprietary Rights Practice Group.
Personal: Born 26 June 1954. Attended Lehigh University.

ETTINGER, John
Davis Polk & Wardwell, New York +1 212 450 4000
Recommended in Private Equity: Buyouts

EVANICH, Kevin
Kirkland & Ellis, Chicago +1 312 861 2000
Recommended in Corporate/M&A

EVANS, Martin Frederick
Debevoise & Plimpton, New York +1 212 909 6000
Recommended in Competition/Anti-trust

EVANS, Robert III
Shearman & Sterling, New York +1 212 848 4000
revans@shearman.com
Recommended in Capital Markets: Debt & Equity
Specialisation: Partner in *Shearman & Sterling*'s Capital Markets Group, specialising in securities offerings and advising corporate clients on various corporate and securities law matters.
Prof. Memberships: American and New York State

Bar Associations and the New York County Lawyer's Association.
Career: Admitted to the Bar in New York and Massachusetts. Joined *Shearman & Sterling* in 1990 and became a partner in 1996.
Personal: Attended Harvard College (AB, cum laude, 1982); Boston University School of Law (JD, cum laude, 1985).

FARABOW, Ford
Finnegan Henderson Farabow Garrett & Dunner LLP, Washington DC +1 202 408 4000
ford.farabow@finnegan.com
Recommended in Intellectual Property
Specialisation: Partner. Litigates jury and nonjury patent infringement cases for both patentees and for companies accused of infringement. Patent, trade secret, and licensing disputes practice focuses on the technical fields of chemistry, pharmaceuticals, chemical engineering, and materials science. Has litigated in federal district and state trial courts throughout the U.S., domestic and foreign arbitration trials, and effective use of mini-trials and other forms of Alternative Dispute Resolution. At the appellate level, has handled numerous cases in the Federal Circuit Court of Appeals and in other circuits.
Career: Admitted in 1963, South Carolina; 1965, District of Columbia; 1981, U.S. Supreme Court; 1982, U.S. Court of Appeals for the Federal Circuit; registered to practice before U.S. Patent and Trademark Office. Worked in the patent departments of Swift & Co. and Hercules Inc. prior to joining the firm. Joined *FHFG&D* in 1965.
Personal: Born January 6, 1938. Clemson University (BSChE, 1959); The George Washington University National Law Center (JD, with honors, 1963).

FARMER, Scott
McKee Nelson Ernst & Young, Washington DC
+1 202 775 8672
sfarmer@mneylaw.com
Recommended in Tax
Specialisation: Practice Area: Taxation, Tax Controversy, International Taxation. Advises clients on all aspects of international tax planning and controversy with the Internal Revenue Service. Clients include U.S. firms engaged in foreign business activities, as well as foreign-based firms operating within the United States.
Career: Prior to joining *McKee Nelson, Ernst & Young* in January 2000, was head of the International Tax Practice at *Miller & Chevalier, Chartered*, Washington, D.C. Is Vice Chair of the U.S. Council for International Business and a frequent lecturer at the World Trade Institute and the Tax Executives Institute.
Publications: Also has written frequently on international tax topics, including 'Branching Out – Reexamining Branch Rules in the Context of Check-the-Box,' 15 Tax Notes International 1951 (December 15, 1997). Received LLM in Taxation, with highest honors, from the George Washington University Law School in 1983, and JD from the University of North Carolina at Chapel Hill Law School in 1982.

FASTOW, Jay N.
Weil, Gotshal & Manges, New York
+1 212 310 8000
jay.fastow@weil.com
Recommended in Competition/Anti-trust
Specialisation: Antitrust litigator and advisor with a wide-ranging competition and financial services litigation practice, acting for corporations and financial institutions in trial-level and appellate courts from New York to Guam. Has acted as a Liaison Counsel for defendants in both Nasdaq Market-Makers Antitrust Litigation and Stock Exchange Options Trading Antitrust Litigation, as well as in Mastercard International Inc. Internet Gambling Litigation.
Publications: Speaks and writes frequently on antitrust and litigation topics.

FEINSTEIN, Deborah
Arnold & Porter, Washington DC +1 202 942 5000
Deborah_Feinstein@aporter.com
Recommended in Competition/Anti-trust
Specialisation: Concentrates on anti-trust and trade regulation matters. Represented General Electric in connection with the acquisition of Greenwich Air Services, a case in which the Department of Justice decided not to challenge the transaction after an intensive investigation. Represented T&N plc in connection with the acquisition by Federal Mogul of the entire business of T&N plc; that matter was successfully resolved with a consent order allowing the acquisition to proceed. Also represented Kroger in its acquisition of Fred Meyer's 800 grocery stores, which proceeded with divestitures of only eight stores.
Career: From 1989 to 1991, served as a special assistant to the Director of the Bureau of Competition of the Federal Trade Commission and attorney adviser to Commissioner Dennis Yao.
Personal: Recieved JD from Harvard Law School in 1987 and AB from the University of California at Berkeley in 1983.

FERGUSON, M. Carr
Davis Polk & Wardwell, New York +1 212 450 4000
Recommended in Tax

FERRIS, Charles D.
Mintz Levin Cohn Ferris Glovsky and Popeo PC, Washington DC +1 202 434 7300
Recommended in Communications: Regulatory

FEY, Albert E.
Fish & Neave, New York +1 212 596 9000
afey@fishneave.com
Recommended in Intellectual Property
Specialisation: Patent litigation. Lead trial counsel for blue chip companies including AT&T, Bell Labs, Western Electric, Lucent, Ford Motor, General Electric, Philip Morris, Georgia-Pacific, NV Philips, Varian Associates, Messerschmitt, Corning Glass, Baxter International, National Semiconductor, Becton-Dickinson, Schlumberger Ltd, Square D and Cyrix. Full-time in patent trial work for over 35 years, trying a great many cases throughout the US. Represented an even mix of plaintiffs and defendants trying cases both to the Court and more recently, increasingly to juries. Has argued cases before 80% of Courts of Appeals, including the Federal Circuit.
Prof. Memberships: Fellow in the American College of Trial Lawyers; member of the Bars of New York, Michigan, the District of Columbia and various Federal Courts including the Supreme Court and the Federal Circuit.
Career: Assistant to the Patent Counsel of General Electric Co. 1956-1959; joined *Fish & Neave* in 1959 and became a partner in 1970.
Personal: University of Michigan BSME (Tau Beta Pi); George Washington University JD (Law Review). Widowed with four grown children. Golfer, skier, and tennis player. Various community activities such as United Way, Boy Scouts, Little League, and AYSO.

FINKELSON, Allen
Cravath, Swaine & Moore, New York
+1 212 474 1000
Recommended in Communications: Transactional (Telecoms), Corporate/M&A

FINLEY, John
Simpson Thacher & Bartlett, New York
+1 212 455 2000
j_finley@stblaw.com
Recommended in Corporate/M&A, Private Equity: Buyouts
Specialisation: A senior member of the Mergers and Acquisitions Group of *Simpson Thacher & Bartlett*. Recent transactions include Seagram's announced business combination with Vivendi and Canal Plus (2000), the announced sale of Harcourt General to Reed Elsevier (2000), the sale of U.S. Foodservice to Royal Ahold (2000), the sale of Nielsen Media Research to VNU (1999) and Seagram's acquisition of Polygram (1998). Frequently represents financial advisors in connection with mergers and acquisition matters, including Goldman, Sachs & Co. in the merger of Mobil with Exxon (1998) and Lehman Brothers in the sale of MediaOne to AT&T Corporation (1999).
Career: A frequent author and speaker at conferences on mergers and acquisitions including conferences sponsored by the International Bar Association, the Law Journal Seminars-Press, the Practising Law Institute and the M&A Lawyer.
Personal: Received a BS in Economics (1978) from the Wharton School of the University of Pennsylvania, a BA in History (1978) from the College of Arts and Sciences of the University of Pennsylvania, and a JD (1981) from Harvard Law School.

FITZGERALD, Peter
Chadbourne & Parke LLP, Washington DC
+1 202 974 5600
Recommended in Project Finance

FLAUM, Keith
Cooley Godward, Palo Alto +1 650 843 5205
Recommended in Communications: IT

FLEISCHER Jr., Arthur
Fried, Frank, Harris, Shriver & Jacobson, New York
+1 212 859 8000
fleisar@ffhsj.com
Recommended in Corporate/M&A
Specialisation: Senior partner. Has led the firm's

M&A practice for the last 25 years. Represents corporate clients both as acquirers and targets and many of the leading investment banking firms. Practice encompasses negotiated as well as contested transactions. Also advises special committees formed to review buyout proposal and corporate restructings. Has advised the following clients: BellSouth Corporation in a US$100 billion offer for Sprint Corporation; Airtouch Communications, Inc in its US$65 billion acquisition by Vodafone Group plc; Chevron Corporation in its pending US$40 billion acquisition of Texaco Inc.; Kroger Co. in its US$12.8 billion acquisition of Fred Meyer, Inc.; Allied Signal Inc. in its US$15.3 billion acquisition of Honeywell Inc.; WPP Group in its US$4.7 billion acquisition of Young & Rubicam; Bestfoods in its US$24 billion acquisition by Unilever plc; Allied Signal inc. in its proposal for AMP Inc. for over US $10 billion; GTE Corporation in its proposal for MCI Communications Corporation for US$28 billion; Cowles Media Corporation in its US$1.4 billion merger with McClatchy Newspapers Inc.; Foundation Health in its US$2.2 billion merger with Health Systems International.
Prof. Memberships: Member of the American Bar Association, Section of Corporation, Banking and Business Law, Committee on Federal Registration of Securities; American Law Institute; Advisory Committee of the Securities Regulation Institute of the University of California; Association of the Bar of the City of New York.
Career: Qualified in 1959. Associated with *Fried Frank* in 1957, becoming a partner in 1967.
Personal: Born 27 January 1933, Hartford, Connecticut. Attended Yale University (LLB 1958 and BA 1953). Lives in New York.

FLEXNER, Don
Boies, Schiller & Flexner, New York +1 914 273 9800
Recommended in Competition/Anti-trust

FLOM, Joseph H.
Skadden, Arps, Slate, Meagher & Flom LLP, New York +1 212 735 3000
JFlom@skadden.com
Recommended in Corporate/M&A
Specialisation: Partner, New York. Corporate matters. Leading attorney in M&A area. Credited with pioneering many of the strategies used today by bidders, targets and investment bankers. Practice includes all forms of corporate transactions. Represented clients in connection with corporate organisation and reorganisation, banking and securities offering activity, their joint ventures and investments, and all other matters relating to success in business.
Prof. Memberships: Director, UrbanAmerica LLC (1998-present); Advisory Director, RRE Investors, LLC (1999-present); Member, Advisory Council of Bologna Centre of the Paul H. Nitze School of Advanced International Studies of The Johns Hopkins University (2000-present); Chairman, Advisory Committee of the Export-Import Bank of the United States (1995).
Career: LLB, Harvard Law School, 1948 (cum laude; Editor, Harvard Law Review); College of the City of NY; LHD, Honorary Doctorate in Humane Letters, Queens College, 1984; LLD, Honorary Doctorate of Laws, Fordham University, 1990; First associate of *Skadden, Arps* (1948); Director Wm.Wrigley Jr. Company (1977-94); Revlon Group Inc. (1990-96); Warnaco Group, Inc. (1997-present); Trustee, Petrie Stores Liquidating Trust (1996-present).
Personal: Several honours and awards including Legal Aid Society's Servant of Justice Award, 1986; and the Department of Defense's Distinguished Service Medal, 1992 among others.

FLORACK, James A.
Davis Polk & Wardwell, New York +1 212 450 4000
Recommended in Banking & Finance

FOGG, Blaine V.
Skadden, Arps, Slate, Meagher & Flom LLP, New York +1 212 735 3000
BFogg@skadden.com
Recommended in Corporate/M&A
Specialisation: Senior partner in Mergers and Acquisitions Department. Has represented a wide variety of clients in mergers, acquisitions, joint ventures, spin-off and other major transactions. In 2000, represented the sellers in transactions valued in excess of US$25 billion.
Prof. Memberships: American Bar Association; New York State Bar Association; Association of the Bar of the City of New York.
Publications: Co-Authur of 'Acquisitions Under the Hart-Scott-Rodino Anti-trust Improvements Act', Law Journal Seminars-Press (Revised Edition, 1998).
Career: Admitted to practice in 1996. Joined *Skadden, Arps, Slate, Meagher & Flom* LLP in 1996, becoming partner in 1972. Member of the Firm's Policy Committee; Chairman of the Firm's Financial Oversight and Audit Committee.
Personal: Born March 29, 1940. Attended Williams College (AB1962) and Harvard Law School (JD1965). Married, with three children and one grandchild. Interests include golf, art and travel.

FORD, Paul
Simpson Thacher & Bartlett, New York +1 212 455 2000
p_ford@stblaw.com
Recommended in Capital Markets: Debt & Equity
Specialisation: A senior partner at *Simpson Thacher & Bartlett.* Has extensive experience in Europe, Asia and Latin America and has advised on capital raisings, joint ventures, strategic alliances and acquisitions during a 30 year career, representing a broad range of financial institutions and multinational corporations. Was instrumental in establishing the firm's offices in Tokyo, Hong Kong and Singapore.
Prof. Memberships: Chairman from 1993 through 2000 of the United States Foreign Policy Association, the nation's oldest and largest non-partisan foreign policy organisation. A member of the Council on Foreign Relations, The Japan Society, and the National Committee on U.S.-China Relations. A member of the Association of the Bar of the City of New York, the American Bar Association, Union Internationale des Avocats and the International Bar Association, serving as Co-Chairman of the Business and Organizations Committee from 1996 to 2000.
Career: Has written and lectured extensively on international legal matters.
Personal: Received a BA from Boston College in 1965 and a JD in 1968 from Duke University School of Law and was an Editor of the 'Duke Law Journal'.

FORRESTER, Paul J.
Mayer, Brown & Platt, Chicago +1 312 782 0600
Recommended in Banking & Finance

FRAIDIN, Stephen
Fried, Frank, Harris, Shriver & Jacobson, New York +1 212 859 8000
Recommended in Corporate/M&A, Private Equity: Buyouts

FRANKLE, Diane
Gray Cary Ware & Freidenrich LLP, Palo Alto +1 650 833 2026
dfrankle@graycary.com
Recommended in Communications: IT
Specialisation: Mergers and acquisitions, public and private financings, anti-takeover counselling. Represented Mattson Technologies in its acquisition of CFM Technologies and a division of Steag Electronic Systems AG (US$600 million) and Maxtor Corporation in its acquisition of Quantum's HDD business in October 2000 (US$2.3 billion). Also represented Maxtor Corporation in July 1998, US$332.5 million public offering (largest California IPO in 1998, one of the largest technology offerings in United States) and secondary offering US$305 million in February 1999. Represented C2Net Software in its acquisition by Red Hat Software in September 2000 (US$38 million); Consilium in acquisition by Applied Materials (US$80 million); DSP Technology in acquisition by MTS Systems (US$50 million); and Dascom in acquisition by IBM (US$110 million).
Prof. Memberships: American Bar Association; Committee on Negotiated Acquisitions (1994 to present); Co-Chair, Task Force on Public Company Acquisitions (1997 to present); California State Bar; Business Law Section Corporations Committee (1992 to 1996), Co-Chair (1995 - 1996).
Career: *Gray Cary Ware & Freidenrich LLP* 1985 to present (formerly *Ware & Freidenrich*), Palo Alto, California; *Ginsburg Feldman & Bress* 1981-1984; Law Clerk, Senior U.S. District Judge, R. Dorsey Watkins, USDC, D. Maryland (1979-1981); JD, Magna Cum Laude Georgetown University Law Centre 1979; BA, College of Wooster, 1975 (Phi Beta Kappa). Frequent lecturer on topics relating to mergers and acquisitions, securities law issues, Board of Directors (fiduciary duties).
Personal: Married, two children. Lived in U.K. May-July 1997. Leisure interests include gourmet cooking and photography.

FRANSON, Marc P.
Chapman and Cutler, Chicago +1 312 845 2988
franson@chapman.com
Recommended in Banking & Finance
Specialisation: Consumer credit, bank regulation, payment processing systems. Transaction highlights: Sale of US$2 billion credit card portfilio by joint venture entity to major regional bank; assisting two Canadian financial institutions in joint venture of

credit card merchant acquiring business for US and Canadian business; assisted another Canadian business in sale of its credit card business.
Prof. Memberships: American Financial Services Association; Chicago Bar Association; National Home Equity Mortgage Association; Conference on Consumer Finance Law.
Publications: Publications/speaker: Conference on Consumer Finance Law Programs; Chicago Bar Association; Financial Institutions and Consumer Credit Committee.
Career: 1991 - present, *Chapman and Cutler*; 1983 - 1991, Household International (General Counsel-Credit Card Services).
Personal: BSBA, MBA, JD – Drake University. Married to Marilyn with one daughter, Elizabeth. Hobbies: Gardening, music, religious and charitable activities.

FREEHILL, George
Freehill Hogan & Mahar LLP, New York +1 212 425 1900
Recommended in Shipping: Litigation

FREEMAN, Louis
Skadden, Arps, Slate, Meagher & Flom LLP, Chicago +1 312 407 0700
Recommended in Tax

FREMUTH, Michael
Andrews & Kurth, Washington DC +1 202 662 2700 mfremuth@akllp.com
Recommended in Energy & Natural Resources
Specialisation: Involvement with all aspects of federal regulation of the natural gas industry and has been a speaker at several conferences on natural gas industry issues. Lead regulatory counsel for Transcontinental Gas Pipeline Corporation from 1991 through its purchase by the Williams Companies and now is lead outside counsel for regulatory matters for Tennessee Gas Pipeline Company. Has argued numerous cases before the Federal Energy Regulatory Commission and before the federal circuit courts. Advises natural gas companies on all regulated aspects of their businesses and on antitrust issues.
Prof. Memberships: Federal Energy (Chairman, Antitrust Committee, 1984-85). Bar Associations: State Bar of California, District of Columbia Bar.
Career: Partner in the Energy Section of the Washington, DC office. Has been with *Andrews & Kurth* since 1982 and has been a partner since 1988. Practised for six years as an antitrust attorney at *Morgan, Lewis & Bockius* law firm.
Personal: Received undergraduate degree summa cum laude and Phi Beta Kappa from Princeton University in 1969 and law degree with honors from Stanford University in 1976. Prior to attending law school, was a professional pitcher with the Detroit Tigers and Philadelphia Phillies organisations.

FREYER, Dana
Skadden, Arps, Slate, Meagher & Flom LLP, New York +1 212 735 3000
Recommended in Arbitration (International)

FRIEDLAND, Paul
White & Case LLP, New York +1 212 819 8200 pfriedland@whitecase.com
Recommended in Arbitration (International)
Specialisation: Concentrates in international commercial arbitration and complex civil litigation. Has served as lead counsel in numerous international commercial arbitrations, principally under the rules of the International Chamber of Commerce, the American Arbitration Association, and the International Centre for the Settlement of Investment Disputes. Regularly advises clients on drafting dispute resolution clauses. Serves as an arbitrator. Frequent speaker and author on international arbitration topics. Has represented clients in all phases of trial and appellate practice before U.S. federal and state courts.
Prof. Memberships: Member of New York State Bar and Paris Bar; United States District Courts for the Southern and Eastern Districts of New York; United States Court of Appeals for the Second Circuit; United States Supreme Court; Chair, AAA Arbitration Practice Committee; Committee on International Arbitrator Training; Panel of Arbitrators (International and Domestic). Board of Trustees and Arbitration Committee, U.S. Council for International Business; Board of Trustees, Institute for Transnational Arbitration.
Career: Partner of White & Case since 1997.
Personal: BA, Yale University, 1976; JD, Columbia Law School, 1980 (Law Review; Kent Scholar).

FRIEDLI, Helen
McDermott, Will & Emery, Chicago +1 312 372 2000 hfriedli@mwe.com
Recommended in Corporate/M&A
Specialisation: Partner in Corporate Department and a member of the firm's Management Committee and Compensation Committee. Main area of work is mergers and acquisitions, takeovers, strategic alliances, public and private offerings of securities and corporate law. Has represented US based purchasers of manufacturing and telcom business in Europe and European acquirors of business in the US.
Prof. Memberships: Member of the Illinois State Bar; American Bar Association; and Chicago Finance Exchange.
Career: Admitted to the Illinois Bar in 1980. Received Industrial Management degree in 1977. In 1980, received JD, and joined *McDermott, Will & Emery.*

FRIEDMAN, Gary
Debevoise & Plimpton, New York +1 212 909 6000
Recommended in Tax

FROY, Michael M.
Sonnenschein, Chicago +1 312 876 8222 mmf@sonnenschein.com
Recommended in Corporate/M&A
Specialisation: Partner. Has extensive experience in a broad spectrum of corporate, commercial and securities matters, including domestic and foreign acquisitions, dispositions, combinations and restructurings; private equity and stategic investments on behalf of private companies and institutional and corporate investors; public and private financings; corporate control/takeover defense measures; securities regulation; and general corporate, commercial and securities counseling. Has represented purchasers, sellers and investors in a variety of acquisitions and disposition transactions ranging in size from under US$1,000,000 to over US$1,000,000,000 in value. These transactions involve public and private companies, as well as individuals; businesses and assets located throughout the United States and in over 50 foreign countries; and relate to a variety of industries including: automotive parts, supplies and diagnostic equipment; brokerage, commercial finance, investment company and investment advisor and other financial services; clothing manufacturing; electrical and electronic components; health care; insurance; lighting products; lodging; media distribution; consumer product distribution; pharmaceutical; printing; real estate; recreational marine; restaurant; software; speciality food products; technology consulting services; telecommunications; and travel. Has represented issuers and underwriters in numerous public financings including initial public offerings and equity and debt offerings of existing public companies. Those transactions have involved issuers in various industries including banking, consumer and commercial product manufacturing, consumer products, delivery and logistics services, document management, electrical and electronic components, health care, insurance, retailing, real estate, specialised business services, and toys, in offerings of various amounts including in excess of US$1,000,000,000.
Prof. Memberships: Illinois State Bar.
Career: Admitted to practice in 1983; joined *Sonnenschein Nath & Rosenthal* in 1983; becoming a partner in 1990; being named co-head of the Chicago Office in 2000. Member of the Steering Committee for the Illinois/Midwest Venture Capital Conference; Member of the Executive Committee for Ray Garrett Jr. Corporate and Securities Law Institute for Northwestern University; Trustee and member of Executive Committee for Ravinia Festival; Member of City of Highland Park Ravinia Festival Community Relations Committee.
Personal: Born January 31, 1959; University of Michigan, AB, with honors and High Distinction 1979; University of Chicago, JD, 1983.

GAFFNEY, John
Cravath, Swaine & Moore, New York +1 212 474 1000
Recommended in Communications: Transactional (Telecoms)

GALLO, Greg
Gray Cary Ware & Freidenrich LLP, Palo Alto +1 650 833 2020 ggallo@graycary.com
Recommended in Communications: IT
Specialisation: Has a wide-ranging venture capital, corporate and securities law expertise coupled with extensive experience of acting for clients in the semiconductor, networking, telecom, enterprise software, internet, biotechnology, venture capital and investment banking sectors. Has, for more than 30 years,

represented clients in a variety of corporate and corporate finance matters relating to emerging growth through Fortune 500, Silicon Valley based technology and biotechnology companies.
Prof. Memberships: Admitted to practice in District of Columbia (1969), California (1973).
Career: *Kirkpatrick & Lockhart* (formerly *Hill Christopher & Phillips*), 1969 - 72; joined *Gray Cary Ware & Freidenrich LLP*, 1973 - present.
Personal: JD, Harvard University, 1969; BS, University of Wisconsin, cum laude, 1963.

U

GALVIS, Sergio J.
Sullivan & Cromwell, New York +1 212 558 4000
galviss@sullcrom.com
Recommended in Project Finance
Specialisation: Coordinator of *Sullivan & Cromwell's* practice in Latin America and a member of the firm's Project Finance and Corporate and Finance Groups. Current work includes the $1.6 billion EVM offshore oil project in Brazil; the $900 million OCP pipeline project in Ecuador; and the Consorcio Transmantaro S.A. power transmission project in Peru, among others. Has represented borrowers and sponsors in some of the recent landmark project financings, including: the Tesoro copper project in Chile (1999); the Sidor Steel Company, Venezuela's largest privatisation since 1991 (1998); the Loma de Niquel nickel mine, the first mining project financing in Venezuela (1997); the Petrozuata heavy oil project, the first large-scale project financing in Venezuela and the largest Latin American capital markets project financing completed to date (1997); the El Abra copper project in Chile; and the Collahausi copper project in Chile, at that time the largest mining senior debt project financing ever completed (1996). Has advised Latin American businesses and governments, as well as international investment banks and companies, in connection with some of the most significant transactions undertaken in Latin America over the last 16 years. Currently involved in securities offerings, privatisations, project financings and mergers & acquisitions in Argentina, Brazil, Chile, Colombia, Mexico, Peru and Venezuela.
Prof. Memberships: American Bar Association; Association of the Bar of the City of New York (former Member of the Committee on Inter-American Affairs and the Committee on Securities Regulation); International Bar Association.
Career: Judicial Clerk to the Honorable Lawrence W. Pierce, U.S. Court of Appeals (2nd Circuit) 1983-1984. Joined *Sullivan & Cromwell* in 1984. Became a Partner of the firm in 1991.
Personal: Born 1958 in Cali, Colombia. Graduated from the College of William and Mary (1980) and Harvard Law School (1983). General Counsel and a Director of the Council of the Americas. Member, the Council on Foreign Relations. Former Chairman of the Board of Trustees of LASPAU.

GANNON, Lawrence J.
White & Case LLP, New York +1 212 819 8475
lgannon@whitecase.com
Recommended in Project Finance
Specialisation: Head of firm's Equipment and Facility Finance Practice Group. Specialises in asset-based financing, including equipment and facility leasing and project finance. In U.S. has represented lessees, institutional equity investors, institutional lenders and underwriters in the negotiation and documentation of a wide variety of U.S. tax-oriented equipment and facility financings, including some of the largest credit facility lease transactions completed to date. Represented equity investors in project financing of alternative energy projects, petro-chemical facilities, resource recovery facilities and other large facilities in the United States utilising both lease and partnership structures; lessees, equity investors and underwriters in offering and sale of lease indebtedness and non-recourse project indebtedness in the public and Rule 144A/Regulation S marketplaces and equity investors in transactions involving securitisation of lease receivables and both purchasers and sellers in the sale and restructuring of lease portfolios, including one such transaction which utilissed a complex partnership structure; lenders and developers in project financing of independent power projects in India, the Philippines and Costa Rica.
Prof. Memberships: New York State Bar, admitted 1973.
Career: *White & Case* since 1990.
Personal: AB, cum laude, Lafayette College, 1968, Phi Beta Kappa, recipient, Economics and Business Prize; JD, cum laude, Fordham University School of Law, 1972, Articles Editor, Law Review.

GARFINKEL, Barry
Skadden, Arps, Slate, Meagher & Flom LLP, New York +1 212 735 3000
Recommended in Arbitration (International)

GEARY, Sean
White & Case LLP, New York +1 212 819 8300
sgeary@whitecase.com
Recommended in Banking & Finance
Specialisation: Partner in Corporate Department and member of the Bank Finance Practice with a focus on senior leveraged acquisition lending. Has acted as lead counsel for agent banks in many of the major 'LBO' financings such as the KKR acquisition of RJR Nabisco, the Time-Warner merger and the American Home Products acquisition of American Cynamid. Has represented various major leveraged acquisition lenders such as Bankers Trust Company and the Chase Manhattan Bank. Also represented Credit Lyonnais with its investment of MGM and ultimate sale thereof. Has represented Avis Rent-A-Car Inc. in various acquisitions and joint ventures.
Career: Graduated from New York University Law School in 1974, cum laude and Order of the Coif. Joined *White & Case* upon graduation and became partner in 1982.
Personal: Born 24 August 1944. Graduated from Manhattan College in 1966 and served 5 years as an officer in the US Air Force, including a tour of duty in Berlin during 1967-69.

GELFAND, David
Cleary, Gottlieb, Steen & Hamilton, Washington DC +1 202 974 1500
Recommended in Competition/Anti-trust

GELSTON, Philip
Cravath, Swaine & Moore, New York +1 212 474 1000
Recommended in Corporate/M&A

GENTILE, Carmen
Bruder Gentile & Marcoux, Washington DC +1 202 783 1350
Recommended in Energy & Natural Resources

GERSTEIN, Mark D.
Latham & Watkins, Chicago +1 312 876 7700
mark.gerstein@lw.com
Recommended in Corporate/M&A
Specialisation: Member of the Corporate Department. Practice focuses on mergers and acquisitions, corporate securities and technology companies. Particular proficiency in advancing and defending both friendly and unsolicited tender offers and representing insurgents and management in proxy contests for control of public companies. Frequent representation of equity sponsors in leveraged acquisitions. Frequent representation of special committees of boards of directors, bidders and financial advisors in going-private transactions. Also advises special committees of boards of directors on their fiduciary duties in change of control situations, and lenders and financial advisors in financial and strategic acquisitions. Also provides general corporate counselling to numerous technology companies.
Prof. Memberships: Member of the American and Chicago Bar Associations.
Career: Co-chair of the global Mergers & Acquisitions Group.
Personal: JD University of Chicago, 1984. BA University of Michigan, 1981.

GERSTELL, Glenn
Milbank, Tweed, Hadley & McCloy, New York +1 212 530 5000
Recommended in Communications: Transactional (Telecoms)

GILBERG, David J.
Sullivan & Cromwell, New York +1 212 558 4000
gilbergd@sullcrom.com
Recommended in Capital Markets: Derivatives
Specialisation: Practice involves a broad range of derivatives and related matters, including the structuring of indexed products, private funds, and other managed trading vehicles, and the development and implementation of structured transactions and trading facilities and systems. Also advises commercial banks, investment banks, trading companies, trading advisers and other types of clients on legal and regulatory issues related to derivatives transactions and products.
Prof. Memberships: American Bar Association; Association of the Bar of the City of New York (Member, Committee on Futures Regulation).
Publications: Author of several articles on derivatives and speaker at numerous derivatives industry conferences.
Career: Served as an Adjunct Professor of Law at Georgetown University Law Center, teaching a course on the regulation of derivative products. Joined *Sullivan & Cromwell* in 1992. Served as Special Counsel, 1994-1995. Became a Partner of the firm in 1996.
Personal: Born 1956. Graduated from the University of Pennsylvania (BA, MA, 1978) and Harvard Law School (JD, 1981). Admitted to the Bar in New York and Washington, DC

GILBERT, Victoria
Sonnenschein, Chicago +1 312 876 8203
vag@sonnenschein.com
Recommended in Banking & Finance
Specialisation: Practises in commercial law, primarily in the areas of secured lending, corporate finance and banking. Has represented banks, finance companies, venture capital investors, insurance companies and borrowers in a wide range of financing transactions and investments. Has been involved in structuring, documenting and negotiating acquisition loans, asset-based loans, equipment loans, revolving credit facilities, letter of credit facilities, credit enhancement arrangements, portfolio acquisitions, receivable purchase facilities, mezzanine financing, structured financings and leases of rolling stock, aircraft, computers and other equipment, the sale and participation of loans, asset securitisations, workouts, recapitalisations, intercreditor arrangements, joint ventures, contingent compensation arrangements, credit enhancement arrangements including letters of credit backing industrial development bonds and municipal issues as well as commercial paper. Represented lead banks such as Bank of America, N.A. in connection with large syndicated credit facilities as well as domestic and foreign banks that participate in such syndicated facilities. Represents the Private Bank of Citibank and assists in servicing the credit and investment needs of its high-net worth target market. In addition, has substantial experience with sports franchise financing in both the baseball and football areas and substantial experience in financing for the health care industry.
Prof. Memberships: American Bar Association's Business Law Section and its Uniform Commercial Code Subcommittee.
Career: Admitted to practice in 1985. Joined *Sonnenschein Nath & Rosenthal* in 1995 as a partner. Formerly a partner at *Katten Muchin & Zavis* in Chicago.
Personal: Born October 3, 1955. University of Illinois, BA, 1982, DePaul University, JD, 1985.

GITTES, Franklin M.
Skadden, Arps, Slate, Meagher & Flom LLP, New York +1 212 735 3000
FGittes@skadden.com
Recommended in Corporate/M&A
Specialisation: Corporate attorney, concentrating in mergers & acquisitions. Practice Leader, Mergers & Acquisitions Department. Recent representations include: Johns Manville in its US$3 billion acquisition by Hicks, Muse, Tate & Furst Inc. and The Bear Stearns Companies Inc.; MacMillan Bloedel Limited in its US2.45 billion acquisition by Weyerhauser Company; and HSB Group, Inc. in its US1.2 billion acquisition by American International Group, Inc.
Prof. Memberships: American Bar Association; New York State Bar Association; Association of the Bar of the City of New York.
Career: Admitted to the bar in 1973 in District of Columbia and in 1975 in New York. Law Clerk, Hon. John Briggs, Jr., US Court of Appeals for the Third Circuit (1973-1974). Joined *Skadden, Arps* in 1978; became a partner in 1981.
Personal: Born in Newark, N.J. in 1947. Education: Lehigh University (BSChE, 1969); Georgetown University (JD, 1973).

GLASS, Adam W.
Sidley & Austin, New York +1 212 906 2272
aglass@sidley.com
Recommended in Capital Markets: Securitisation
Specialisation: Partner, New York. Securitisation Legal Analyst, LegalMediaGroup.com. Areas of expertise include securitisation of franchise loans and net leases, residential mortgage loans and other financial assets; cash and synthetic CDOs; credit derivatives and derivative structured finance products; creation of synthetic securities by packaging fixed-income and equity securities with swap agreements; using total return swaps for off-balance sheet financing; and representation of underwriters in SEC-registered resecuritisations of corporate debt securities. Speaker in US and abroad on asset securitisation.
Career: Commenced practice 1982.

GLICK, Anna
Cadwalader, Wickersham & Taft, New York +1 212 504 6000
aglick@cwt.com
Recommended in Capital Markets: Securitisation
Specialisation: Capital Markets Partner in the Firm's New York office. Work area includes multi-class securitisation, structured mortgage finance, securitisation of commercial mortgage loans, federal securities laws issues particular to these types of securitisations, and advising on related securities compliance matters. Also works in securitisation of residential mortgage loans as well as other mortgage-related products, such as home equity and agricultural loans, Re-REMIC transactions, dissolutions and redemptions of existing transactions, and issues associated with sales and resales of securities particularly by broker/dealers and their affiliates. Represents issuers, underwriters and institutional investors active in the primary and secondary capital markets. Structures partnerships, trusts and joint ventures, established warehouse financing programs and master repurchase facilities. Works closely with the real estate department to advise on rating agency and securitisation issues (origination of large and conduit-size mortgage loans pending securitisation). Concentrates on federal securities law, registration of public securities, corporate acquisitions of stocks and assets, disposition of diverse assets in major bankruptcy context, merger of multinational corporations, structure of numerous joint ventures, financings, options an other business arrangements for closely-held corporations.
Career: JD in 1982 from New York University School of Law; member of the Law Review and Order of the Coif.

GOLD, Michael
Sidley & Austin, Chicago +1 312 853 7148
mgold@sidley.com
Recommended in Banking & Finance
Specialisation: Partner in the Chicago office. Area of practice is commercial finance and debt restructurings for banks and commercial finance companies. Focuses on secured and unsecured syndicated financings, including acquisition financings, 'workouts' and restructurings, and debtor-in-possession financings. Also advises investors and companies with respect to acquisition and other financings.
Prof. Memberships: Member of American and Illinois Bar Associations.
Personal: Educated at John Marshall Law School (JD, 1984, with distinction); University of Illinois (BS, Finance, 1981).

GOLD, Stuart
Cravath, Swaine & Moore, New York +1 212 474 1000
Recommended in Competition/Anti-trust

GOLDBERG, Fred
Skadden, Arps, Slate, Meagher & Flom LLP, Washington DC +1 202 371 7000
Recommended in Tax

GOLDBERG, Louis
Davis Polk & Wardwell, New York +1 212 450 4000
Recommended in Private Equity: Buyouts

GOLDEN, Arthur
Davis Polk & Wardwell, New York +1 212 450 4000
Recommended in Competition/Anti-trust

GOLDFEIN, Shepard
Skadden, Arps, Slate, Meagher & Flom LLP, New York +1 212 735 3000
SGoldfein@skadden.com
Recommended in Competition/Anti-trust
Specialisation: Partner, New York. Anti-trust and Trade Regulation and Litigation Matters. Handles a variety of cases from anti-trust litigation to white collar criminal investigations and mass disaster litigation. Served as one of the trial counsel who successfully defended the NFL and its member clubs against claims of monopolisation and other anti-trust violations. Also defended the NFL in the numerous lawsuits filed by NFL players challenging NFL player employment rules. Advises and has served as litigation counsel in several matters for the National Basketball Association and the National Hockey League. Successfully represented the landlords of the Happy Land Social Club, where 87 people died in an arson fire, with regard to a felony manslaughter investigation. Has litigated many treble damages class action price fixing cases. In addition, counsels clients on a host of anti-trust issues (general compliance programs to anti-trust patent licensing issues), and has worked on securities class action litigations and several anti-trust take-over cases. Co-author, monthly trade regulation column, 'NY Law Journal' (1983-Present).
Prof. Memberships: Admitted in NY and New Jersey; Chairman, Civil Practice and Procedure Committee, Anti-trust Section, NY State Bar Association (1982-1984); Chairman, Sports Law Committee, Association of the Bar of the City of NY (1999-Present).
Career: JD, Rutgers University, 1975 (Editor, Rutgers Law Review); MA, Political Science, University of Chicago, 1977; AB, Rutgers University, 1970 (Phi Beta Kappa).

GOLDMAN, Mike
Cravath, Swaine & Moore, New York +1 212 474 1000
Recommended in Banking & Finance

U

U

GOLDSCHMIDT, David
Skadden, Arps, Slate, Meagher & Flom LLP, New York +1 212 735 3000
Recommended in Capital Markets: Debt & Equity

GOLDSTEIN, Marc
Proskauer Rose, New York +1 212 969 3000
Recommended in Arbitration (International)

GOLDSTEIN, Marvin
Stroock & Stroock & Lavan LLP, New York +1 212 806 5400
mgoldstein@stroock.com
Recommended in Capital Markets: Derivatives
Specialisation: A partner in the Corporate Department, concentrating in Derivatives and Commodities Law and transactions. Has counselled a number of firms acting as dealers in the derivatives and commodities market, advising on all aspects of trading, structuring transactions, and legal matters pertaining to risk analysis and risk reduction. Has extensive experience in advising in relation to counterpart default and market disruption. Experience extends from derivatives on financial instruments (securities, currencies, interest rates and credit markets) to physical trading and commodity transactions in financial instruments and energy, metal and agricultural commodities. Also handles matters in banking, IP/software licensing and general corporate matters.
Prof. Memberships: The Association of the Bar of the City of New York; Committee on Commodities Regulation, 1994-1996, 1984-1987; Banking Law Committee 1990-1993; Chair, Forward Contracts Subcommittee 1984-1985; Committee on Commodities and Futures Law, New York State Bar Association, 1987-1991
Career: Admitted in March 1977. Joined *Stroock & Stroock & Lavan* in September 1976 and became partner in January 1985
Personal: Born 27 February 1952. Attended Yeshiva University (BA, 1973, suma cum laude), Harvard Law School (JD, 1976, cum laude).

GOODMAN, Stuart
Schiff Hardin & Waite, Chicago +1 312 258 5500
Recommended in Corporate/M&A

GOODWILLIE, Eugene
White & Case LLP, New York +1 212 819 8432
egoodwillie@whitecase.com
Recommended in Project Finance, Project Finance: India Foreign
Specialisation: Main area of work is international and U.S. corporate and financial transactions, with significant experience in foreign investment projects, international and domestic natural resource projects, international joint venture transactions and domestic and international securities transactions. Represented investors in a broad range of transactions, including venture capital investments in the high technology area. Preeminent project finance lawyer with particular experience in the field of representing hydrocarbon and hydrocarbon related industries in connection with the full range of legal issues relevant to such industries. Select client list includes: IFC; U.S. Eximbank; Japan Eximbank; Asian Development Bank; CalEnergy Company; the Arabian American Oil Company and its successor, the Saudi Arabian Oil Company, in the restructuring of Aramco and the formation of Saudi Aramco, among other deals.
Prof. Memberships: New York State Bar, admitted 1967.
Career: Partner of *White & Case* since 1975. Currently serves as Chairman of *White & Case's* Management Board. In charge of all *White & Case* overseas offices (1980-83); served on Management Committee (1983-91, 1998-2000). Named partner in charge of the firm's worldwide energy and project finance practice group (1991).
Personal: BA, cum laude, Williams College, 1963, Phi Beta Kappa; JD, cum laude, Columbia Law School, 1966, Stone Scholar.

GOODWIN, Lee
Thelen Reid & Priest LLP, New York +1 212 603 2000
Recommended in Energy & Natural Resources

GOOLSBY, George
Baker Botts LLP, Houston +1 713 229 1234
george.goolsby@bakerbotts.com
Recommended in Energy & Natural Resources
Specialisation: Partner in charge of worldwide Energy Practice Group. Primary experience is with the upstream oil and gas and hydrocarbon pipeline industries, including regulatory, transactional, contract, finance, and trial work for producers, gatherers, marketers, industrial end-users, pipelines and distribution companies. Also experienced in the power generation and transmission industry. Coordinates project teams for Baku-Tbilisi-Ceyhan Main Oil Export Pipeline and the Shah Deniz gas transportation projects in Azerbaijan, Georgia and Turkey. Represents Egyptian-Israeli group respecting proposed offshore pipeline to deliver Egyptian natural gas to Eastern Mediterranean markets.
Prof. Memberships: Member of Energy Bar Association, Advisory Board of Institute for Transnational Arbitration, London Court of International Arbitration, and Oil, Gas, and Mineral, and International Sections of State Bar of Texas.
Career: Joined *Baker Botts* in 1975, becoming partner in 1984. In 1997, and 1999, named as one of the world's leading energy and natural resources lawyers by Euromoney Publications in London.
Personal: Earned BA, degree from University of Texas in 1971, and JD, from University of Texas School of Law in 1974.

GORDON, David A.
Latham & Watkins, New York +1 212 906 1200
david.gordon@lw.com
Recommended in Project Finance
Specialisation: Represents primarily banks, financial institutions and sponsors in connection with all phases of the development and financing of energy, telecommunications and other infrastructure and industrial projects. Has practised extensively in the development and financing of private power projects and domestic and multi-jurisdictional telecommunications projects, including submarine cable, "last mile" and telecom hotel projects. Transactional experience includes the structuring of projects and the related financing, due diligence and coordination and negotiation of project and financing agreements.
Prof. Memberships: American Bar Association.
Career: Serves as Managing Partner of *Latham & Watkins'* New York office.
Personal: JD, Syracuse University College of Law, 1986 summa cum laude. BA, Cornell University, 1982.

GORDON, Steve
Cravath, Swaine & Moore, New York +1 212 474 1000
Recommended in Tax

GOTTDIENER, Scott
Simpson Thacher & Bartlett, New York +1 212 455 2000
s_gottdiener@stblaw.com
Recommended in Communications: Transactional (Telecoms)
Specialisation: A partner at *Simpson Thacher & Bartlett* and a member of the corporate department. Extensive experience in international and domestic finance (including project finance). Emphasis in telecommunications. Practice also includes commercial contracts, mergers and acquisitions, joint ventures and general corporate matters. Advises Global Crossing on finance, merger and acquisitions, joint ventures, commercial contracts and general corporate matters.
Prof. Memberships: American Bar Association and Association of the Bar of the City of New York.
Career: Joined *Simpson Thacher & Bartlett* in 1990 and became a partner in 2000. Received JD cum laude from Fordham University School of Law in 1990; member, Fordham Law Review; received BS from State University of New York at Binghamton in 1985.

GREEN, Douglas
Steptoe & Johnson LLP, Washington DC +1 202 429 3000
Recommended in Energy & Natural Resources

GREEN, Frederick
Weil, Gotshal & Manges, New York +1 212 310 8000
frederick.green@weil.com
Recommended in Communications: Transactional (Telecoms)
Specialisation: Partner in the New York office. An established practitioner with broad experience in corporate and securities transactions. Highly regarded as an advisor to the telecom and internet sectors. Serves as a lead partner in the Firm's domestic practice, and heads the Latin American Practice. Work includes business combinations (mergers, acquisitions, spin-offs and joint ventures), capital markets transactions, debt restructurings, and corporate counseling with respect to a broad range of commercial affairs. Representative transactions include the sale to Boeing of the Hughes Satellite Manufacturing Company, the merger of Computer Sciences Corporation and Nichols Research Corporation, the internet and media based strategic alliance between DirecTV and America Online, the spin-off by General Motors of the Hughes Aircraft defense business, the merger of Hughes Aircraft with Raytheon, the acquisitions of U.S. Satellite Broadcasting and of

Primestar, the divestiture by Duke Energy of its midwest natural gas pipelines, the tender offer by Duke Energy for Endesa Chile, the acquisition by General Dynamics of Gulfstream Aerospace Corporation, the merger of NYNEX Corporation and Bell Atlantic, the merger of Excel Communications with Teleglobe Inc. and the formation of Mexico's Alestra.
Career: The Wharton School, University of Pennsylvania (BS, magna cum laude 1976); Fordham Law School (JD 1979); admitted to the New York Bar, 1980; joined *Weil, Gotshal & Manges* in 1979 and became a partner in 1987; has been featured as a 'Dealmaker' by The American Lawyer; frequently lectures on mergers and acquisitions and co-authored the first 'Plain English' merger proxy statement, which was used in connection with the NYNEX – Bell Atlantic merger.

GREEN, Jonathan
Milbank, Tweed, Hadley & McCloy, New York +1 212 530 5000
Recommended in Project Finance

GREEN, Josh
Venture Law Group, Menlo Park +1 650 854 4488
Recommended in Communications: IT

GREMILLION, Tod
Akin, Gump, Strauss, Hauer & Feld LLP, Houston +1 713 220 5800
Recommended in Energy & Natural Resources

GROLL, William A.
Cleary, Gottlieb, Steen & Hamilton, New York +1 212 225 2000
Recommended in Communications: Transactional (Telecoms), Corporate/M&A

GROSSHANDLER, Seth
Cleary, Gottlieb, Steen & Hamilton, New York +1 212 225 2000
Recommended in Capital Markets: Derivatives

GUNDERSON, Bob
Gunderson Dettmer Stough Villeneuve Franklin & Hachigian, Menlo Park +1 650 321 2400
Recommended in Communications: IT

GUTOWSKI, Peter
Freehill Hogan & Mahar LLP, New York +1 212 425 1900
Recommended in Shipping: Litigation

HADLEY, Joseph
Davis Polk & Wardwell, New York +1 212 450 4000
Recommended in Project Finance

HAHN, Arthur
Katten Muchin Zavis, Chicago +1 312 902 5200
Recommended in Corporate/M&A

HAIMS, Bruce
Debevoise & Plimpton, New York +1 212 909 6000
Recommended in Tax

HALL, Richard
Cravath, Swaine & Moore, New York +1 212 474 1000
Recommended in Corporate/M&A, Private Equity: Buyouts

HALLIDAY, Joseph
Skadden, Arps, Slate, Meagher & Flom LLP, New York +1 212 735 3000
Recommended in Banking & Finance

HAMMES, Jeffrey
Kirkland & Ellis, Chicago +1 312 861 2000
Recommended in Corporate/M&A

HANRAHAN, Marc
Skadden, Arps, Slate, Meagher & Flom LLP, New York +1 212 735 3000
Recommended in Banking & Finance

HARDEN, Rick
Pillsbury Winthrop, New York +1 212 858 1000 hardenr@pillsburywinthrop.com
Recommended in Energy & Natural Resources
Specialisation: Partner in Corporate and Capital Markets Department. Primary focus is public and private securities offerings and restructurings, principally by regulated utilities and other power producers around the world. Areas of concentration include power project financings in the capital markets.
Personal: JD, Washington & Lee University School of Law, 1973 (magna cum laude; Editor, Washington & Lee Law Review; Member, Order of the Coif). BA, Washington & Lee University, 1967.

HARITON, David P.
Sullivan & Cromwell, New York +1 212 558 4000 haritond@sullcrom.com
Recommended in Tax: Financial Products
Specialisation: Practice focuses on U.S. federal income tax matters, including taxation of financial instruments and products; corporate mergers, acquisitions and distributions; international operations, investments and transactions; and domestic and foreign partnerships and trusts. Represents various clients before Treasury Department and Internal Revenue Service (actively assisted in drafting of new regulations) and in appeals and litigation of federal, state and local tax issues.
Prof. Memberships: American Bar Association (Co-Chairman of Tax Section's Subcommittee on Hybrid Debt Instruments); New York State Bar Association (Co-Chairman of Tax Section's Committee on Financial Instruments).
Publications: Has written extensively on federal income tax treatment of contingent debt instruments, debt-equity hybrids, foreign currency obligations, foreign currency swaps, equity-indexed swaps, recapitalizations, interest expense allocation, and outbound distributions and liquidations. Lectures for Practicing Law Institute, NYU Institute on Federal Income Taxation, University of Chicago Law School, and other groups.
Career: Joined *Sullivan & Cromwell* in 1985. Partner since 1994.
Personal: Born 1957 in New York, New York. Graduate of Stanford University (BA, 1981) and Stanford Law School (JD, 1985; member, Order of the Coif).

HARMS, David B.
Sullivan & Cromwell, New York +1 212 558 4000 harmsd@sullcrom.com
Recommended in Capital Markets: Debt & Equity
Specialisation: Focuses on a wide variety of general securities and corporate law matters, including SEC-registered offerings, private placements, international corporate finance, high-yield debt financing, internet offerings and trading practices and negotiated merger and acquisition transactions. Also serves as coordinator of *Sullivan & Cromwell's* broker-dealer regulation practice and co-coordinator of the firm's securities finance practice.
Prof. Memberships: Association of the Bar of the City of New York.
Publications: 'E-Offerings and the 1933 Act: Applying the Old Rules in a New Arena' in 'The Internet Age: What Securities Lawyers Need to Know to Survive', Practicing Law Institute (2000).
Career: Judicial Clerk to the Honorable Edward Weinfeld, U.S. District Court (S.D.N.Y.) 1984-1985. Joined *Sullivan & Cromwell* in 1985. Became a partner of the firm in 1992.
Personal: Born 1954. Attended the State University of New York at Purchase (BA, 1978) and New York University Law School (JD, 1984; Editor in Chief, NYU Law Review).

HARPER, Conrad K.
Simpson Thacher & Bartlett, New York +1 212 455 2000 c_harper@stblaw.com
Recommended in Arbitration (International)
Specialisation: A partner at *Simpson Thacher & Bartlett* and a member of the Firm's Litigation Department. Areas of concentration are litigation, international arbitration and mediation including commercial contract disputes, securities, product liability, environmental and insurance defense. Has served as counsel in ICC Administered Arbitrations, as counsel to a trustee in a bankruptcy and as counsel in securities and product liability litigation. Has been an arbitrator in an international arbitration and mediator in a dispute between a trustee in bankruptcy and federal regulatory authorities.
Prof. Memberships: Member of the London Court of International Arbitration and various bar associations including the International, American, National, New York State and Metropolitan Black Bar Associations, and the Association of the Bar of the City of New York, the Federal Bar Council, the American Society of International Law and the Union Internationale de Avocats.
Career: From 1971 to 1993 was an associate (1971-74); then a partner (1974-93, 1996 to present) at *Simpson Thacher*. Served as Legal Adviser of the U.S. Department of State from 1993 to 1996 and as a member of the Permanent Court of Arbitration at The Hague (1993-96; 1998 to present). Formerly a visiting lecturer at Yale Law School, Co-Chairman of the Lawyers' Committee for Civil Rights and Chancellor of the Episcopal Diocese of New York. Was President of the Association of the Bar of the City of New York from 1990 to 1992. Holds the following positions: Member of Harvard Corporation; Trustee, Metropolitan Museum of Art; Trustee, William Nelson Cromwell Foundation; Member of the Council and 1st Vice President, American Institute; Member of the Executive Committee, American Arbitration Association. Also a Fellow, American College of Trial Lawyers; Member, Council on Foreign Relations; and Fellow, American

U

Academy of Arts and Sciences. Received a BA from Howard University in 1962 and a LLB from Harvard Law School in 1965.

HARRELL, Michael P.
Debevoise & Plimpton, New York +1 212 909 6000
Recommended in Private Equity: Fund Formation

HARRINGTON, Michael
Vinson & Elkins LLP, Houston +1 713 758 2131
Recommended in Corporate/M&A

HARRIS, Douglas
Milbank, Tweed, Hadley & McCloy, New York +1 212 530 5000
Recommended in Project Finance

HARRIS, Scott
Harris, Wiltshire & Grannis LLP, Washington DC +1 202 730 1300
Recommended in Communications: Regulatory

HARTNETT, Bill
Cahill Gordon & Reindel, New York +1 212 701 3900
Recommended in Capital Markets: Debt & Equity

HARTY, Ronan
Davis Polk & Wardwell, New York +1 212 450 4000
Recommended in Competition/Anti-trust

HAWES, Douglas
LeBoeuf, Lamb, Greene & MacRae, LLP, New York +1 212 424 8000
dhawes@llgm.com
Recommended in Energy & Natural Resources
Specialisation: Of Counsel to the firm and active in *LeBoeuf's* Utility Mergers and Acquisitions practice. A leading expert in the area of utility mergers and acquisitions, has written extensively on utility holding companies as well as on topics in the fields of corporation securities, accounting and comparative law. Author of 'Utility Holding Companies' (Clark Boardman Company, 1984 with supplements).
Prof. Memberships: Member of the International Faculty for Corporate & Capital Markets Law.
Career: Admitted to practice in New York, 1958. Joined *LeBoeuf, Lamb, Greene & MacRae* in 1958, and became a partner in 1964. Former Director of Bay State Gas Company and United Water Resources, Inc.
Personal: BA, The Principia College, 1954. JD, Columbia University, 1957. MBA, New York University, 1961.

HAWK, Barry
Skadden, Arps, Slate, Meagher & Flom LLP, New York +1 212 735 3892
bhawk@skadden.com
Recommended in Competition/Anti-trust
Specialisation: Partner, New York & Brussels. US, European and International Anti-trust and Regulatory Matters. Advises clients primarily in the areas of European Union and national anti-trust laws and merger controls, European Union regulatory law, U.S. anti-trust law and merger control laws throughout the world. Has advised on EU and European Law in connection with M&A, joint ventures, privatisations, distribution and licensing, enforcement actions and litigation, public procurement, project financing, state aids or government subsidies, and various regulatory matters. Has conducted annual seminars on anti-trust law and policy for officials of the Commission of the European Communities; served as a consultant to the Commission's Legal Service and to the OECD.
Prof. Memberships: Vice Chair, Anti-trust Section, American Bar Association (1986-87); Chair, Anti-trust Section, NY State Bar Association (1986-1987); Council Member, Anti-trust Section, American Bar Association (1981-84; 1987-90); Chair, ABA Special Committee to Study International Antitrust (1990-91); Co-Chair, Associates Committee, Anti-trust Section, American Bar Association (1994-Present)
Publications: Authored many books and articles on European and U.S. anti-trust and trade laws; recently co-authored a book on European merger controls.
Career: LLB, University of Virginia School of Law, 1965; AB, Fordham College, 1962; Professor, Fordham Law School (1968-Present); Director, Fordham Corporate Law Institute; Business Advisory Panel on Anti-trust Export Issues to the National Commission for the Review of the Anti-trust Laws and Procedures (1978); Scholar in Residence, Directorate-General for Competition and Legal Service of the European Communities, Brussels (1980-81).

HAYDEN, Raymond P.
Hill Rivkins & Hayden LLP, New York +1 212 669 0600
HR_NYC_RPH@compuserve.com
Recommended in Shipping: Litigation
Specialisation: Concentrates practice in maritime litigation with emphasis on marine casualties and insurance coverage disputes.
Prof. Memberships: Association of Average Adjusters of the United States; New York State and American Bar Associations. Has served as Chairman on the Standing Committee of Admiralty Law of the American Bar Association.
Career: Joined *Hill Rivkins*, becoming a partner in 1972. Has served The Maritime Law Association of the United States in various capacities from committee member to committee chairman. From 1988-1991, served as a member of the MLA Executive Committee. Served as Membership Secretary 1996-1998; Second Vice-President 1998-2000 and First Vice-President May 2000 to date. Was a member and has served as Chairman of the Board of the State University of New York Maritime College.
Personal: Received a BS in Marine Transportation from the State University of New York Maritime College in 1960 and an LLB from Syracuse University in 1963. Admitted to practice New York 1963, United States District Courts 1964 and the United States Supreme Court 1967.

HAYES, David
Fenwick & West, Palo Alto +1 650 494 0600
Recommended in Intellectual Property

HEFTLER, Thomas
Stroock & Stroock & Lavan LLP, New York +1 212 806 5400
theftler@stroock.com
Recommended in Capital Markets: Derivatives
Specialisation: Practice focuses on derivatives and commodities transactions and includes extensive experience in connection with the representation of financial institutions in transactions involving energy, metals, and currencies. Advises clients on securities matters, acquisitions and dispositions, financing and commercial transactions, and other corporate legal issues.
Prof. Memberships: American Bar Association; Association of the Bar of the City of New York.
Career: Managing Partner of *Stroock & Stroock & Lavan LLP* member of the firm since 1977. Admitted to practice in 1968. Educated at New York University (JD cum laude 1968) and Princeton University (AB, 1965).
Personal: Born 14 May 1943. Resides in New York City. Leisure interests include amateur radio and cycling.

HEINZELMAN, Kris
Cravath, Swaine & Moore, New York +1 212 474 1000
Recommended in Capital Markets: Debt & Equity

HEITNER, Kenneth H.
Weil, Gotshal & Manges, New York +1 212 310 8000
kenneth.heitner@weil.com
Recommended in Tax
Specialisation: Tax partner in the New York office of *Weil, Gotshal & Manges* and co-head of the firm's tax group. Has been a partner with the firm since 1981. Skills as a corporate tax adviser are widely recognised and regularly acts on the full range of tax issues affecting corporations transacting their business in the United States and abroad as well as on numerous tax-efficient structures for cross-border transactions.

HELENIAK, David W.
Shearman & Sterling, New York +1 212 848 7049
dheleniak@shearman.com
Recommended in Corporate/M&A
Specialisation: Member of *Shearman & Sterling's* M&A Group. Headed the group from 1987-95, and a member of the Firm's Executive Group. Has represented clients from around the world in numerous mergers and acquisitions transactions, both friendly and contested, involving several different industries. In addition, represents a number of the major investment banks' mergers and acquisitions advisory groups both in the United States and Europe.
Prof. Memberships: Admitted to the New York bar in 1975. Association of the Bar of New York's Committee to Enhance Diversity in the Profession and has served on its Securities Regulation Committee.
Career: Joined *Shearman & Sterling* in 1974. Executive Assistant to the Deputy Secretary and Assistant General Counsel (Domestic Finance) of the United States Treasury Department, 1977-79. Returned to *Shearman & Sterling* in 1979 and became a partner in 1981. Headed *Shearman & Sterling's* Hong Kong office from 1981-84.
Personal: Born June 27, 1945. Attended the University of Michigan (AB, 1967), London School of Economics (MSc, (Econ.) 1969) and Columbia Law School (JD, 1974). Executive Committee and past president of The MacDowell Colony, an artists' colony in New Hampshire, and a former director of

the Network for Women's Services, an organisation that provides legal services to indigent women. Lives in New York City.

HELMAN, Robert A.
Mayer, Brown & Platt, Chicago +1 312 701 7020
rhelman@mayerbrown.com
Recommended in Corporate/M&A
Specialisation: Senior partner and former chairman of *Mayer, Brown & Platt.* Primary practice areas include corporate, business, financial, securities, public utility, and banking. Widely recognised for expertise in tender offers, mergers and acquisitions, corporate restructurings, and corporate governance issues.
Prof. Memberships: Member of the American Bar Association (Chairman, Section of Public Utility Law) 1983-1984; American Law Institute; Chicago Bar Association; and Chicago Council of Lawyers.
Publications: Co-Author of 'Commentaries on the Illinois Constitution of 1970' and various articles in legal and trade publications on corporate and public utility matters.
Career: Admitted to practice in Illinois, 1956, and Supreme Court of the United States, 1963. Joined *Mayer, Brown & Platt*, Chicago and became a partner in 1967 to date. Served as Chairman, *Mayer, Brown & Platt* management committee from 1984 to1998, and now serves as Senior Partner. Prior to *Mayer, Brown & Platt*, served with *Isham, Lincoln & Beale*, Chicago, from 1956 to1966.
Personal: Born January 27, 1934. Earned BSL (1954) and LLB (1956) at Northwestern University, where was a member of the Order of the Coif and Associate Editor of Northwestern University Law Review. Serves in a range of directorships and civic organisations, including Northern Trust Corporation and The Northern Trust Company; Brambles USA, Inc.; TC PipeLines GP, Inc.; Chicago Stock Exchange, 1993-2000; Zenith Electronics Corporation, 1995-1999; The Horsham Corporation, 1990-1996; Alberta Natural Gas Company, 1993-1996; Southern Pacific Transportation Co., 1987-1988; The Brookings Institution, Emeritus Trustee; Chicago Council on Foreign Relations, Trustee; Civic Committee of the Commercial Club of Chicago; Financial Research and Advisory Committee of the City of Chicago; Museum of Contemporary Art, Trustee; University of Chicago Law School Visiting Committee; Aspen Institute, Trustee, 1986-1992; Citizens Committee on the Juvenile Court of Cook County, Chairman, 1968-1983; Jewish Federation of Metropolitan Chicago, Director, 1991-1992; The Learned Hand Human Relations Award of the American Jewish Committee, Recipient, 1989; Legal Assistance Foundation of Chicago, President, 1973-1975; Northwestern University Law School Visiting Committee, Chairman, 1989-1992; United Charities of Chicago, Director, 1967-1972; and University of Chicago Hospitals, Trustee, 1982-1988.

HENGEN, Nancy
Haight Gardner Holland & Knight, New York
+1 212 513 3200
Recommended in Shipping: Finance

HERLIHY, Ed
Wachtell, Lipton, Rosen & Katz, New York
+1 212 403 1000
Recommended in Corporate/M&A

HERSCH, Dennis
Davis Polk & Wardwell, New York +1 212 450 4000
Recommended in Corporate/M&A

HEWITT, William J.
Reboul, MacMurray, Hewitt, Maynard & Kristol, New York +1 212 841 5709
whewitt@reboul.com
Recommended in Private Equity: Fund Formation
Specialisation: A corporate partner concentrating in private equity and mergers and acquisitions. Represents several buyout and venture capital firms, including Welsh, Carson, Anderson, & Stowe, in fund formation and transactions by funds and portfolio companies. Transactions in 2000 include the formation of Welsh, Carson, Anderson & Stowe IX, LP, StarVest Partners LP and Accolade Partners LP.
Prof. Memberships: New York State Bar Association; American Bar Association; Association of the Bar of the City of New York.
Career: Admitted to the Bar in New York in 1965. Educated at Harvard Law School (LLB, 1964) and Harvard College (AB, 1961).
Personal: Born 18 July 1939.

HIRSCHBERG, William E. (Bill)
Shearman & Sterling, New York +1 212 848 4000
whirschberg@shearman.com
Recommended in Banking & Finance
Specialisation: Co-head of the firm's banking practice, with extensive experience in all areas of bank financing, including acquisition and leveraged buyout financing, workouts, restructuring, intercreditor issues, structured financing and project financing. In these areas, has represented borrowers, senior lenders, and subordinated lenders, credit enhancers and sponsors. A significant part of practice involves cross-border transactions. Representation of the lead lenders in the following senior financings; the $2 billion financing of the unsolicited offer by United Rentals for Rental Service Corporation; the $1.8 billion financing of the acquisition of IXC Communications by Cincinnati Bell, Inc.; the $1.34 billion financing of the acquisition of five rural telephone companies by Valor Telecommunications, the $3 billion restructuring of the worldwide indebtedness of Warnaco Inc.; the $900 million financing of the leveraged acquisition of three semiconductor packaging and test facilities located in South Korea by Amkor Technology, Inc.; the $190 million financing of the leveraged acquisition of American Safety Razor Company; the $335 million financing of the leveraged acquisition of United Industries, Inc; the $900 million financing of the unsolicited offer by Amsted Industries for Varlen Incorporated; the $30 billion financing of the unsolicited offer by AT&T Corp for MediaOne; various financings for subsidiaries of MacAndrews & Forbes, Ronald Perelman's holding company.
Prof. Memberships: Member of the bars of New York, Illinois and the District of Columbia, Member of the American Bar Association Commercial Financial Services Committee; Chairman, Acquisition Financing Subcommittee (1987-91).
Career: Joined *Shearman & Sterling* in 1976 and became a partner in 1981. From 1972 through 1976, worked in the office of General Counsel of the Federal Deposit Insurance Corporation in Washington DC. Served as an expert witness in a trial in United States District Court (S.D.N.Y.) on the issue of agent bank/syndicated lending market practice.
Personal: Born December 28 1947. Loyola University of Chicago School of Law, JD, 1972; Indiana University, AB, 1969.

HONAN III, William J.
Haight Gardner Holland & Knight, New York
+1 212 513 3200
Recommended in Shipping: Litigation

HOOPER, Chester
Haight Gardner Holland & Knight, New York
+1 212 513 3200
Recommended in Shipping: Litigation

HOPKINSON, R. Ronald
Latham & Watkins, New York +1 212 906 1200
r.ronald.hopkinson@lw.com
Recommended in Private Equity: Buyouts
Specialisation: Partner in the Corporate Department. Specialises in mergers and acquisitions and corporate restructurings. Represents merchant banking organisations and leveraged buyout groups, including The Carlyle Group and Lazard Freres Real Estate Investors. Recent transactions include: representation of The Carlyle Group in its acquisition of the aerostructures business from Northrop Grumman; representation of First Washington Realty Trust in its sale to CalPERS; representation of Park Place Entertainment in its acquisition of Caesars World, Inc.; and representation of General Cigar Holdings in its going-private transaction with Swedish Match.
Prof. Memberships: Admitted to practice in New York and District of Columbia.
Personal: JD Harvard University, 1988, cum laude. BA Harvard University, 1984, magna cum laude, Phi Beta Kappa.

HORNICK, Robert
Morgan, Lewis & Bockius LLP, New York
+1 212 309 6000
Recommended in Arbitration (International)

HUCK, L. Francis
Simpson Thacher & Bartlett, New York
+1 212 455 2000
l_huck@stblaw.com
Recommended in Banking & Finance
Specialisation: A partner at *Simpson Thacher & Bartlett* and a member of the Firm's Corporate Department specialising in syndicated commercial lending. Over the past 20 years, has represented domestic and foreign banks in a variety of bank financing and restructuring transactions. In recent years has been especially active in leverage financing of acquisitions by private equity groups, financings for securities firms and investment companies and funds and financing for health care and media companies. Typical recent matters include the representation of the agent bank or borrower in financings for Conseco, Viasystems, Aurora Foods, U.S. Office Products, Oak Hill Securities Fund II, Andersen Consulting and CBS. Has also represented the bank lenders to the former Yugoslavia through four debt

U

restructurings beginning in 1993, and the division of the external bank indebtedness among the five successor republics in 1996 through 1998.
Prof. Memberships: An active member of the American Bar Association and the Bar Association of the City of New York.
Career: Joined *Simpson Thacher* in 1972 and became a partner in 1980. Received an AB in 1969 from Harvard University and a JD in 1972 from Stanford Law School.

HYLTON, Hartwell
Simpson Thacher & Bartlett, New York
+1 212 455 2000
h_hylton@stblaw.com
Recommended in Banking & Finance
Specialisation: A partner at *Simpson Thacher & Bartlett* and a member of the Firm's Corporate Department. Concentrates on banking law, corporate and international finance transactions. Usually represents financial institutions, including Lehman Brothers Inc. and The Chase Manhattan Bank. Joined the firm in 1975 and became a partner in 1982. Received an AB from the College of William and Mary in 1972 and a JD from the University of Virginia in 1975.

U

INDOE, William F.
Sullivan & Cromwell, New York +1 212 558 4000
indoew@sullcrom.com
Recommended in Tax
Specialisation: A member of *Sullivan & Cromwell's* Tax Group. Focuses on the tax structuring of complex financial transactions, with particular experience in mergers & acquisitions, divestitures and spinoffs. Has represented investment banks as well as principals in hundreds of complex transactions, including: tax-free mergers; cross-border acquisitions; conversions of "C corps" into real estate investment trusts; sales of privately owned businesses; divestitures accomplished through joint ventures; and transactions involving asset managers (Weiss, Peck & Greer, Wanger Asset Management and the acquisitions of PIMCO and Nicholas-Applegate (pending) by Allianz). Also renders tax advice in securities offerings. In addition to tax work, also assists in managing the firm's ERISA and employee benefits practice. In this capacity, has participated in the preparation and negotiation of employment and severance arrangements, stock option and other incentive compensation plans, and resolution of employee benefit issues both in the ordinary course and in change of control situations.
Prof. Memberships: American Bar Association; Association of the Bar of the City of New York; New York State Bar Association.
Career: Joined *Sullivan & Cromwell* in 1968. Elected a Partner of the firm in 1976.
Personal: Born 1942. Attended Lehigh University (BA, 1964) and the University of Virginia Law School (LLB, 1968). Director, RHO Management Company, Inc; Director, The Haven Capital Management Trust.

ISAACSON, Laurence B.
Fried, Frank, Harris, Shriver & Jacobson, New York
+1 212 859 8000
Recommended in Capital Markets: Securitisation

JACOBS, Micheal A.
Morrison & Foerster, San Francisco
+1 415 268 7000
mjacobs@mofo.com
Recommended in Intellectual Property
Specialisation: Partner concentrating on high-technology and intellectual property litigation matters. Most recently, has represented clients in biotechnology and information technology disputes. Has helped to shape laws governing the emerging information and entertainment technologies, and managed a litigation team in the On Command Video case, which established that video 'on demand' performances must be licensed under the copyright public performance right. Led the technical team representing Fujitsu Ltd. in its landmark operating system software arbitration with IBM. Served as a member of the editorial board of the Association of Business Trial lawyers, Northern California, and wrote a periodic column on intellectual property litigation.
Publications: Co-author, with Prof. Donald Chisum, of 'World Intellectual Property Guidebook', United States (1992, *Matthew Bender & Company*, New York).
Career: Admitted to the California State Bar in 1993. Became Partner in the San Francisco office of *Morrison & Foerster* in 1990. Is co-head of the firm's 130-person Intellectual Property Group, and served as the firm's Managing Partner for Operations from 1995 to 1997.
Personal: BA History, Stanford University, 1977, Phi Beta Kappa with honors; United States Foreign Service, assignments in Kingston, Jamaica, and Washington, DC; JD, Yale Law School, 1983.

JACOBS, Robert A.
Milbank, Tweed, Hadley & McCloy, New York
+1 212 530 5664
rjacobs@milbank.com
Recommended in Tax
Specialisation: Partner in Tax Department. Experience in mergers and acquisitions and the tax problems of troubled companies. Also handles controversies with Federal and State taxing authorities, both administratively and in courts, including the New York State Tax Tribunal, US Tax Court, US Court of Federal Claims, US District Courts, US Bankruptcy Courts and US Circuit Courts of Appeals. Serves as an arbitrator in the New York Civil Court and has served as a member of the MFY Legal Services Board of Directors.
Prof. Memberships: Memberships: Member of the American Law Institute, the American College of Tax Counsel and the Tax Club. Also serves as Chair of the Tax Forum. Has held many offices: The American Bar Association and New York State Bar Association Tax Sections. Will chair the New York State Bar Association Tax Section in 2001. Lectures frequently for NYU, ALI/ABA, PLI and others.
Career: Served as Assistant Branch Chief of the Corporate Tax Branch in the Office of the Chief Counsel for the Internal Revenue Service and as special counsel to Treasury Secretary Fowler. Also served on the Advisory Group to Senate Finance Committee Staff on Subchapter C Revision. Taught a seminar in Advanced Corporate Tax Problems at the New York University School of Law and was visiting senior lecturer in taxation at the University of California, Davis.
Publications: Published more than 20 significant tax articles, mostly in the corporate tax and bankruptcy tax field.
Personal: Graduate from the University of Texas. Received an LLB, and an LLM, in Taxation from New York University, also editor of the 'Law Review', a Root-Tilden Scholar and a member of the Order of the Coif.

JACOBS, Stephen
Weil, Gotshal & Manges, New York
+1 212 310 8000
stephen.jacobs@weil.com
Recommended in Corporate/M&A, Private Equity: Buyouts
Specialisation: Specialises in corporate takeovers representing bidders, target companies and investment advisers and lectures on these topics frequently. Recent transactions include Summit Bank's acquisition by Fleet Boston, International Speciality Products' attempt to acquire Dexter, NYNEX's mergers with Bell Atlantic, Hicks Muse's acquisition of Lin Television, L'Oreal's acquisition of Maybelline, Cineplex Odeon's merger with Loew's Theater and Leunedia National's sale of the Colonial Penn Insurance Companies.

JACOBSON, Martin
Simpson Thacher & Bartlett, New York
+1 212 455 2000
m_jacobson@stblaw.com.
Recommended in Project Finance
Specialisation: A partner at *Simpson Thacher & Bartlett* and a member of the Corporate Department. Advises clients in project and infrastructure financing as well as structured equipment financing. Has represented sponsors, lenders, underwriters and other credit providers. Has a broad range of experience involving the financing of infrastructure, industrial property and transportation equipment. Recently led a team on project financing for the Atlantic LNG Project in Trinidad and the Port Arthur Coker Company refinery upgrade project in Texas as well as in structured aircraft financing transactions for Airbus Industrie.
Prof. Memberships: American Bar Association and Association of the Bar of the City of New York and founding Chair of its Committee on Project Finance.
Career: Joined *Simpson Thacher & Bartlett* in 1979 and became a partner in 1984. Received BS summa cum laude from the University of Pennsylvania in 1969. MBA from New York University Stern School of Business in 1973 and a JD from the University of Chicago Law School in 1976. Has written and spoken on project finance and structured equipment financing on numerous occasions.

JACOBSON, Ronald H.
Winston & Strawn, Chicago +1 312 558 5600
rjacobso@winston.com
Recommended in Banking & Finance
Specialisation: Partner, Corporate Department,

Chicago office. Practice concentrated in leveraged finance, structured investment, and private equity matters. Extensive experience advising prominent financing sources in structuring, negotiating, and documenting significant leveraged transaction financings. Substantial experience in complex mezzanine financing, structured investment product, private equity, and leveraged purchase matters.
Prof. Memberships: Member, American Bar Association, Business Law Section.
Career: Admitted to Illinois Bar, 1988. Joined *Winston & Strawn*, 1990; elected as partner, 1997. Member, Commercial Finance Association's Education Foundation Governing Board. Member, Loan Syndications and Trading Association, Inc. Member, *Winston & Strawn* Associate Evaluation Committee. Annual Presenter, *Winston & Strawn* Corporate Associate Training Program.
Personal: Born July 23, 1963. Received BA, 1985, with honors, University of Illinois at Urbana-Champaign. Received JD, 1988, with honors, Loyola University Chicago School of Law; managing editor of Loyola Law Journal. Received MM, 1990, with honors, JL Kellogg Graduate School of Management, Northwestern University.

JAFFE, Helene D.
Weil, Gotshal & Manges, New York
+1 212 310 8000
helene.jaffe@weil.com
Recommended in Competition/Anti-trust
Specialisation: Joint head of the firm's trade practices and regulatory law group. Focuses on the transactional, counselling and litigation aspects of antitrust law (particularly regarding mergers, acquisitions and Hart-Scott-Rodino matters). Also has extensive experience of advising clients on a range of advertising and marketing issues.

JAVARAS, George
Kirkland & Ellis, Chicago +1 312 861 2000
Recommended in Tax

JENNER, Jesse
Fish & Neave, New York +1 212 596 9000
jjenner@fishneave.com
Recommended in Intellectual Property
Specialisation: Partner specialising in litigation and trial practice. Main area of work is as lead counsel in patent and other technical litigation. Has represented AlliedSignal, Cognex, Emerson Electric, Ford Motor Company, Pitney Bowes, Snell & Wilcox, Symbol Technologies, U.S. Philips, Tyco International, Varian Associates and many other large and small companies. Represents plaintiffs and defendants about equally. Has argued numerous cases before the US Court of Appeals for the Federal Circuit.
Prof. Memberships: Fellow, American College of Trial Lawyers, member of numerous Bar associations; admitted to New York, US Supreme Court and other Federal Courts, United States Patent and Trademark Office; Board of Directors, National Neurofibromatosis Foundation, 1989-; member, Panel Arbitrators, American Arbitration Association.
Career: Captain, US Air Force 1973-74; *Fish & Neave*, joined 1974, partner 1981; currently Managing Partner.

Personal: Born Brooklyn, New York 1947. Cornell University (BSEE, 1969); Harvard Law School (JD, 1972); Rotary International Fellowship; University of Warwick, Coventry, England, 1972-73. Married, two children.

JEWELL, Robert V.
Andrews & Kurth, Houston +1 713 220 4200
bjewell@akllp.com
Recommended in Corporate/M&A
Specialisation: Practises in all areas of corporate and securities law, including representation of issuers and underwriters in public and private offerings of equity and debt securities in a variety of industries, the negotiation and structuring of various corporate and partnership debt financings and mergers and acquisitions, both domestic and foreign. Has particular experience relating to real estate investment trusts, the forest products industry, royalty trusts and debt financings.
Prof. Memberships: Served as a member of the Corporation Law Committee of the Corporation, Banking and Business Law Section of the State Bar of Texas since 1986 where was primarily responsible for the rewriting of the Texas Real Estate Investment Trust Act in 1989 and 1995. Also a member of the Texas Business Law Foundation.
Career: Partner of the Business Section. Has been with *Andrews & Kurth* since 1978 and has been a partner since 1986.
Personal: Graduated from the University of Texas (BBA, Finance, 1975) and received law degree from Southern Methodist University School of Law (JD, 1978). Was Editor of the 'Southwestern Law Journal' from 1977-78.

JOFFE, Bob
Cravath, Swaine & Moore, New York
+1 212 474 1000
Recommended in Competition/Anti-trust

JOHNSON, Craig
Venture Law Group, Menlo Park +1 650 854 4488
Recommended in Communications: IT

JOHNSTON, M. Elaine
White & Case LLP, New York +1 212 819 8736
mejohnston@whitecase.com
Recommended in Competition/Anti-trust
Specialisation: Partner in Litigation Department. Main area of work is antitrust, principally advising on the antitrust aspects of mergers, acquisitions and joint ventures. Has particular experience in co-ordinating U.S., European and other antitrust clearances on complex cross border deals. Current and recent matters include: Metso's pending tender offer for Svedala; Deutsche Bank's pending acquisition of National Discount Brokerage; ABB's sale of its nuclear business to British Nuclear Fuels Ltd; Metso's sale of its Timberjack forest machinery business to John Deer; and VTech's acquisition of the telephone business of Lucent. Has also advised on the formation of a number of business-to-business (B2B) exchanges including Volbroker.com, a foreign currency options trading platform.
Prof. Memberships: New York State Bar; Institute of Chartered Accountants in Ireland (FCA).
Career: Admitted in New York in 1988. Joined *White & Case* in 1993, becoming a partner in 1997. Member of American Bar Association Antitrust Section; Associate Editor of the 'Antitrust Law Journal'; member of Committee on Antitrust and Trade Regulation of the Association of the Bar of the City of New York.
Personal: Attended Cambridge University 1977-80 (BA 1980, M.A. 1984) and University of Michigan Law School 1986-87 (LLM 1987). Leisure interests include reading, hiking and mountain biking. Lives in New York City.

KADEN, Lewis
Davis Polk & Wardwell, New York +1 212 450 4000
Recommended in Corporate/M&A

KADLICK, Richard
Skadden, Arps, Slate, Meagher & Flom LLP, New York +1 212 735 3000
Recommended in Capital Markets: Securitisation

KAIL, Michael
Steptoe & Johnson LLP, Washington DC
+1 202 429 3000
Recommended in Energy & Natural Resources

KAPLAN, Cathy
Brown & Wood LLP, New York +1 212 839 5300
Recommended in Capital Markets: Securitisation

KATCHER, Richard
Wachtell, Lipton, Rosen & Katz, New York
+1 212 403 1000
Recommended in Corporate/M&A

KATSH, Salem M.
Shearman & Sterling, New York +1 212 848 4000
skatsh@shearman.com
Recommended in Intellectual Property
Specialisation: Complex commercial trials and appeals, particularly involving patent, trademark, copyright, trade secret, and antitrust claims. Lead trial and appellate counsel for major companies, including General Electric Co., Oneida Ltd, Citigroup, Sequa, A.E. Staley, Matsushita, Reuters, NCR, BMW, and others. Unbroken record of liability verdicts in major jury trials.
Prof. Memberships: American and New York State Bar Associations. Bar of the State of New York. Admitted to practice in all New York State Courts, Southern, Northern, and Eastern Districts of New York, Second Ninth, and Federal Circuit Courts of Appeals, and Supreme Court of the US.
Career: New York University College of Arts and Science (BA, 1969); New York University School of Law (cum laude, Order of the Coif, 1972). Associate *Weil, Gotshal, & Manges* 1972-80, Partner 1980-97. Founder and Co-chair of *Weil, Gotshal, & Manges'* Intellectual Property Group, 1988-97. Partner and Chair of Intellectual Property Group, *Shearman & Sterling*, 1997-present.
Personal: Married with two children. Interests include mountain climbing (including two summits of Mount Ranier), fishing, music, and mythology.

KATTAN, Joseph
Gibson, Dunn & Crutcher LLP, Washington DC
+1 202 955 8500
Recommended in Competition/Anti-trust

U

KATZ, David
Wachtell, Lipton, Rosen & Katz, New York +1 212 403 1000
Recommended in Corporate/M&A

KAUFMAN, Christopher ("Kit")
Latham & Watkins, Menlo Park +1 650 463 2606 christopher.kaufman@lw.com
Recommended in Communications: IT, Corporate/M&A
Specialisation: Partner in the Corporate Department. Specialises in mergers and acquisitions, securities offerings, venture capital and start-up companies and general corporate work. Principal focus is on high-technology companies. Represents companies in hostile takeovers and proxy contests, as well as consensual acquisitions. Represents investment banks in high-tech offerings. Worked on over 400 private offerings for high-tech start-up companies, representing either issuer or investors. Venture capital clients include Mayfield Fund and Coral Ventures. Expertise in venture capital financings of Israeli companies. Experience in corporate governance and fiduciary duty responsibilities, particularly in conflict-of-interest situations where a publicly held corporation is controlled by another corporation
Prof. Memberships: Member of the American Bar Association.
Personal: JD Harvard University, 1970, magna cum laude, editor of Harvard Law Review. BA Amherst College, 1967, Phi Beta Kappa.

KAWATA, Yukako
Davis Polk & Wardwell, New York +1 212 450 4000
Recommended in Private Equity: Fund Formation

KEANE, Paul
Cichanowicz, Callan, Keane, Vengrow & Textor, New York +1 212 344 7042
Recommended in Shipping: Litigation

KELLER, Don
Venture Law Group, Menlo Park +1 650 854 4488
Recommended in Communications: IT

KELLEY, Jay
Vinson & Elkins LLP, Houston +1 713 758 2131 jkelley@velaw.com
Recommended in Energy & Natural Resources
Specialisation: Practice consists primarily of finance, energy and commercial matters, with an emphasis on project development and finance. Has worked on various projects involving LPG, LNG, extra heavy oil and power. International experience includes projects in Venezuela, Indonesia, Chile, Argentina and the United Kingdom.
Prof. Memberships: Member: State Bar of Texas, New York State Bar Association, International Bar Association and College of the State Bar of Texas.
Publications: Advisory Board: Currents: International Trade Law Journal.
Career: Lecturer: International Practice Conference on Infrastructure Development in Emerging Markets, South Texas College of Law; Houston Bar Association; 8th Annual Advanced International Law Institute. Licensed as a certified Public Accountant, Texas, 1983; attended The University of Texas (BBA Accounting, 1981) and the University of Houston (JD summa cum laude, 1985); admitted to practise law in Texas (1985) and New York (1995).

KELLOGG, Michael
Kellogg, Huber, Hansen, Todd & Evans PLLC, Washington DC +1 202 326 7900
Recommended in Communications: Regulatory

KELLY, Mark
Vinson & Elkins LLP, Houston +1 713 758 2131
Recommended in Corporate/M&A

KENNEDY, Donald J.
Carter, Ledyard & Milburn, New York +1 212 732 3200 kennedy@clm.com
Recommended in Shipping: Litigation
Specialisation: Commercial litigation, admiralty, bankruptcy, including maritime, bankruptcy, energy and natural resources matters, commercial litigation, arbitration and mergers and acquisitions.
Prof. Memberships: Maritime Law Association of the United States (Chairman; Arbitration and Mediation Committee), London Maritime Arbitrators Association, American Bar Association (Admiralty & Maritime Committee; Vice Chairman, 1991), the Association of the Bar of the City of New York (Member, Maritime Law Committee), United States Department of State, Private Sector Adviser on the UNCITRAL Working Group on Arbitration Thirty-Second Session, March 2000 (Vienna) and Thirty-Third Session, November 2000 (Vienna).
Career: 1972 - 1997 *Haight, Gardner, Poor & Havens.* 1966-69 Transportation Corps Officer, United States Army.
Personal: BA 1966 Fordham University. JD 1972 Fordham University School of Law.

KENNEDY, Mike
Wilson, Sonsini, Goodrich & Rosati, San Francisco +1 415 947 2000
Recommended in Communications: IT

KENNEDY, Tom
Skadden, Arps, Slate, Meagher & Flom LLP, New York +1 212 735 3000 tkennedy@skadden.com
Recommended in Communications: Transactional (IT), Corporate/M&A
Specialisation: Partner, New York. Mergers, Acquisitions, Corporate Finance, and other Transactions with an emphasis on the Telecommunications and Information Technology Industries. National co-ordinator of *Skadden, Arps, Slate, Meagher & Flom's* corporate technology practice. Involved in a number of significant transactions, including representation of Ascend Communications, America On-line, Compaq Computer, NTL Inc. and many more. Experience in many hostile transactions, leveraged buyouts and governance matters representing (among many) Hasbro Inc., Emhart Corporation, The Singer Company, N.V., Veuatov Group Inc. Has represented investment banks, including Donaldson Lufkin & Jenrette, Salomon Smith Barney and more in merger and acquisition transactions in recent years. Authored various books and articles.
Prof. Memberships: Association of the Bar of the City of New York, Committee on Securities Regulation.
Career: JD, Georgetown University Law Centre, 1981; BA, University of Virginia, 1978.
Personal: In 1995, profiled in the National Law Journal article, Rising Stars in the Law: 40 Young Attorneys Who Are Making Their Mark.

KERR, John
Simpson Thacher & Bartlett, New York +1 212 455 2000 j_kerr@stblaw.com
Recommended in Arbitration (International)
Specialisation: A partner at *Simpson Thacher & Bartlett* and a member of the Firm's Litigation Department. Advises clients in general litigation and arbitration matters. Most recently, has represented Ford Motor Company in a series of arbitrations in London to recover claims from Bermuda insurers on high level excess insurance policies, represented DHL International in an ICC arbitration in Paris involving a dispute under a shareholders agreement, represented Owens-Illinois in an AAA arbitration involving an intellectual property dispute and served as sole arbitrator in an ICC arbitration.
Prof. Memberships: Member of the American Bar Association, and sits on its Litigation Section and International Litigation Committee; Member of the International Bar Association and its Business Section, Litigation Committee and Dispute Resolution Committee, the Federal Bar Council and the Association of the Bar of the City of New York. Also Vice President of the American Foreign Law Association.
Publications: The author of 'Court Jurisdiction and Arbitration over Misrepresentation in U.S. Securities Transactions' (Sweet & Maxwell, London, 1999) and 'A Chart Comparing International Commercial Arbitration Rules', published in collaboration with the Parker School of Comparative Law, Columbia Law School (Juris Publishing, 1998). Until this year, wrote a regular column on U.S. Litigation in the International Financial Law Review.
Career: Joined *Simpson Thacher* in 1978 and became partner in 1983. Received an AB from Boston College in 1972, graduating summa cum laude. Received a JD from Columbia Law School in 1976, where was a Stone Scholar, an International Fellow, a National Scholar (7th Circuit) and Editor-in-Chief of the 'Columbia Journal of Environmental Law'. Clerked for Honourable Gus J. Solomon, U.S. District Court for the District of Oregon. A member of the Columbia Law School Board of Visitors.

KESSEL, Mark
Shearman & Sterling, New York +1 212 848 4000 mkessel@shearman.com
Recommended in Capital Markets: Debt & Equity
Specialisation: Partner in the Capital Markets Practice Group. Broad corporate and securities law experience, including public and private securities offerings and mergers and acquisitions. Acts as counsel to corporations and underwriters in creative off-balance sheet financings for the biotechnology, pharmaceutical and high technology sectors. Represents major industrial companies and financial institu-

tions. Recent practice includes representation of companies and financial institutions involved with e-commerce and the Internet. Also advises boards of directors and audit committees on governance and related matters. Represented Credit Suisse First Boston and Dresdner Kleinwort Benson as redistribution managers of the shares of Celanese AG resulting from the demerger by Hoechst AG; Agouron Pharmaceuticals in connection with its acquisition by Warner-Lambert Company; Merrill Lynch & Co. as managing underwriter of LYONstand and off-balance sheet financings for Elan Corporation plc.
Prof. Memberships: Admitted to practice in New York and California; Bar Association of the City of New York; American Bar Association; former Chairman, Business Law Section; the Bar Association of San Francisco.
Career: Served from 1966-1971 as a Captain in the Judge Advocate General's Corps. Joined *Shearman & Sterling* in 1971 and became a partner in 1977. Partner in charge of the San Francisco office from 1979-1990; chairman of the Firm's Pacific Rim Committee from 1988-1990; Managing Partner from 1990-1994. Head of the Corporate Finance Practice Group from 1994-1997.
Personal: Born June 14, 1941; BA with honours in Economics, CUNY, 1963; JD magna cum laude, Syracuse University College of Law, 1966. Director, Heller Financial, Inc.; Trustee, Museum of the City of New York; Board of Visitors, Syracuse University College of Law; Listed in Who's Who in American Law, Who's Who in Finance and Industry and Who's Who in America. Leisure interests include reading, running, biking and tennis.

KEZSBOM, Allen
Fried, Frank, Harris, Shriver & Jacobson, New York +1 212 859 8000
Recommended in Competition/Anti-trust
Specialisation: Senior Partner in litigation department. Main areas of practice include competition/antitrust, environmental, contract, corporate and intellectual property. Has handled major complex litigations such as Xerox monopolisation cases, Sears mislabelling litigation, complex environmental litigation for 3M, Forstman Little and others, toxic tort class action matters for 3M (breast implants), GAF (asbestos) and Velsicol Chemical, and other complex litigation. Has written and spoken extensively in all areas of practice. Major writing includes 'No Shortcut To Antitrust Analysis; The Ties that Bind The Twisted Journey of the Essential Facilities Doctrine', (Columbia Business Law Review); 'The Long and Winding Road of Corporate Parent and Successor Liability under CERCLA' (BNA Environmental Due Diligence Guide); 'The Boundaries of Groundwater Modeling Under the Law; Standards for Excluding Speculative Expert Testimony' (ABA Tort & Insurance Law Journal); 'Disputed Tender Offers in Regulated Industries' (Journal of Corporate Law); 'The Velsicol case: Significant Precedent for Mass Toxic Tort Litigation' (Toxic Law Reporter).
Prof. Memberships: American Bar Association Sections on Antitrust, Intellectual Property, Litigation and Natural Resorces. Supreme Court Historical Society, Federal Bar Council, New York City Bar Association.
Career: BA Brooklyn College (1962) (cum laude); LLB Harvard Law School (1965) (magna cum laude); Knox Fellowship (1965-1966); *Kaye, Scholer, Fierman, Hays & Handler*, 20 years (Partner) before joining *Fried, Frank* in July 1986.
Personal: Born 1941. Married, 2 grown children.

KIDD, John
Clifford Chance Rogers & Wells LLP, Washington DC +1 202 434 0700
Recommended in Intellectual Property

KIELY, Bruce F.
Baker Botts LLP, Washington DC +1 202 639 7711 bruce.kiely@bakerbotts.com
Recommended in Energy & Natural Resources
Specialisation: Partner in charge of the Washington office and the Energy Department. Specialises in domestic and international regulatory transactional and litigation matters, involving the oil, natural gas, LNG, and electric industries. This includes: counselling on energy infrastructure projects, drafting and negotiating domestic and international contracts for the production, purchase, sale, and transportation of energy products; resolution of domestic and international disputes through arbitration, administrative proceedings and trial and appellate litigation; structuring and restructuring business entities in response to the significant changes in business and regulatory conditions; and involvement in the development, sale, and acquisition of a variety of energy assets.
Prof. Memberships: Virginia Bar, District of Columbia Bar.
Career: Qualified in 1971. Joined *Baker Botts* in 1973.
Personal: Received JD from the University of Texas School of Law in 1970. Received BS degree from the University of Colorado.

KIESSLING, Rob
Cravath, Swaine & Moore, New York +1 212 474 1000
Recommended in Banking & Finance

KIMBALL, John
Healy & Baillie LLP, New York +1 212 943 3980 jkimball@healy.com
Recommended in Shipping: Litigation
Specialisation: Managing Partner. Main area of work is maritime law, including casualties, charterparty disputes, insurance, creditors rights, insolvency. Adjunct Professor of Law at NYU Law School (1986-present).
Prof. Memberships: Maritime Law Association of the United States; Fellow of the American Bar Association; Federal Bar Council.
Career: Joined *Healy & Baillie* in 1975. Graduate of Duke University (BA 1971); Georgetown University Law School (1975).
Personal: Co-author of 'Time Charters' (4th ed.) and 'Voyage Charters.'

KIMMEL, Roger H.
Latham & Watkins, New York +1 212 906 1336 roger.kimmel@lw.com
Recommended in Private Equity: Buyouts
Specialisation: Partner in Corporate Department. Significant merger and acquisition practice both domestically and internationally. Extensive experience representing both issuers and underwriters in public and private securities offerings. Represented Sithe Energies in the sale of its GPU holdings to Reliant Energy for $2.1 billion and American Cellular Corporation in its $2.3 billion sale to AT&T Wireless Services and Dobson Communication. Represented Comsat Corporation in its spinoff of Ascent Entertainment Corp., Waterhouse Securities in its merger with Toronto-Dominion Bank, and Sithe Energies in its going-private transaction, related tender offer and sale of securities to Marubeni Corporation.
Prof. Memberships: Member of the American Bar Association, The Association of the Bar of the City of New York and the New York State Bar Association.
Career: Admitted Southern District of New York 1972.
Personal: JD University of Virginia, 1971. BA George Washington University, 1968.

KING, Ken
Skadden, Arps, Slate, Meagher & Flom LLP, Palo Alto +1 650 470 4500 kking@skadden.com
Recommended in Communications: IT
Specialisation: Partner, Palo Alto & San Francisco. Corporate and securities law, including cross-border mergers and acquisitions, joint ventures, investment transactions and restructurings. In the US: M&A and equity financing, licensing and strategic partnering transactions in the information technology and biotechnology industries. Represented, among many: Ascend Communications Inc., McKesson Corporation, Phone.com, Inktom: Corporation, Hewlett Packard Company, Compaq and Alta Vista, United Airlines, Banc Boston Robertson Stephens, Fremont Partners. Internationally represented numerous U.S. and Japanese corporations (resident in the Tokyo office of *Skadden, Arps*, 1990-91). Served as Editor-in-Chief of the California Law Review, was elected to the Order of the Coif and won two American Jurisprudence and three Prosser awards. Author, 'Representing the Public Company in an LBO Transaction: Recent Developments', Practising Law Institute (1989); 'Exon-Florio Update: Final Regulations are Released', M&A Review (1992); 'Venture Capital in Focus – Warning: Rescue May Raise Risks', The National Law Journal (1997).
Prof. Memberships: President, California Law Review, Inc. (1996-98).
Career: JD, Boalt Hall School of Law (University of California at Berkeley), 1987 (Editor-in-Chief, California Law Review; Order of the Coif); BA, Stanford University, 1977; Law Clerk to the Hon. Kenneth W. Starr, U.S. Court of Appeals for the District of Columbia Circuit (1987-88).
Personal: Fluent in both spoken and written Japanese.

KIRKLAND, David
Baker Botts LLP, Houston +1 713 229 1234 david.kirkland@bakerbotts.com
Recommended in Corporate/M&A
Specialisation: Concentrates on mergers and acquisitions, securities offerings and corporate con-

U

trol and governance issues. Represents parties and investment bankers in mergers and acquisitions, including negotiated acquisitions and dispositions, controlled auctions, tender offers and related financing transactions. Involved in many of the largest merger transactions in the oilfield service sector. Represents issuers, underwriters and holders in numerous registered public offerings and in rule 144A transactions and private placements. Member of *Baker Botts*' Executive Committee, administrative co-chair of the Corporate Department, head of the office's mergers and acquisitions practice group, chair of the Technology Committee.
Prof. Memberships: State Bar of Texas, Section on Business Law, Corporate Law Committee.
Career: Joined *Baker Botts* in 1983, becoming partner in 1990.
Personal: Attended Yale College 1976-1980 (BA summa cum laude, Phi Beta Kappa); Yale Law School 1980-1983 (JD).

U

KIRSCH, Bill
Kirkland & Ellis, Chicago +1 312 861 2000
Recommended in Corporate/M&A

KLEIN, Linda B.
Dewey Ballantine LLP, New York +1 212 259 8000
lklein@deweyballantine.com
Recommended in Capital Markets: Derivatives
Specialisation: Partner in Corporate Department. Main areas of work are derivatives and financing (both in the capital markets and in bank credit arrangements), with an additional focus on other practice areas involving the emerging markets and, in particular, Latin America. Has spoken and written extensively about these subjects and is co-author of 'Documentation for Derivatives' (Euromoney) and the related Credit Support Supplement and Cross-Product Risk Management Support Supplement to that book, as well as articles on credit derivatives, case-law involving derivatives and other related matters, and co-author of 'Documentation for Loans, Assignments and Participations' (Euromoney). Has represented major participants on all sides of transactions in these fields (in derivatives, professional market participants and end users as well as rating agencies in securitisations involving derivatives; and in financing transactions, lenders, borrowers and guarantors and agents and issuers and underwriters or placement agents in capital markets transactions.
Prof. Memberships: Bar of the State of New York since 1980.
Career: With *Dewey Ballantine LLP* since 1996. Columbia University School of Law, JD, 1979; Columbia University, PhD, 1981.
Personal: Born 24 April 1947. Lives in Greenwich Village and Redding Ct. with husband and co-author, Anthony C. Gooch. Speaks Spanish fluently; understands Portuguese and French.

KLEINBARD, Edward
Cleary, Gottlieb, Steen & Hamilton, New York +1 212 225 2000
Recommended in Tax: Financial Products

KLEPPER, Martin
Skadden, Arps, Slate, Meagher & Flom LLP, Washington DC +1 202 371 7000
mklepper@skadden.com
Recommended in Energy & Natural Resources, Project Finance, Project Finance: India Foreign
Specialisation: Development, financing and acquisition of energy, transportation and other large infrastructure projects throughout the world. Has also handled major transactions related to privatisation and restructurings within the electric and gas industry, and has extensive experience in financing sports stadiums and arenas. Has been the lead lawyer representing: developers and owners of power plants and gas pipelines, and contractors, banks, underwriters and equity investors in connection with acquisitions, joint ventures and project financings (over 100 major transactions) totalling more than $10 billion and including some of the most complex transactions in recent years, such as the Dabhol Power Project in India. Has helped develop and finance projects in more than two dozen countries throughout Africa, Asia, Europe, the Indian subcontinent, Latin America and the Middle East. Often serves as a guest speaker, chairman of programs, and lecturer at project and international financing conferences across the country. Has written and edited numerous publications, including ten books and more than twenty articles.
Prof. Memberships: Board of Directors, National Independent Energy Producers (1993-1995); Member, Co-ordinating Group on Energy Law, American Bar Association (1985-1989); Chairman, Energy Law Committee, Real Property Probate and Trust Section, American Bar Association (1980-1986).
Career: JD, Rutgers Law School, 1973 (Articles Editor, Rutgers Law Review); BA, University of Pennsylvania, Wharton School, 1969.

KNIGHT, James T.
Simpson Thacher & Bartlett, New York +1 212 455 2000
j_knight@stblaw.com
Recommended in Banking & Finance
Specialisation: Partner in the firm's Corporate Department. Main area of work is representation of lenders and borrowers in leveraged loan transactions. Principle clients include The Chase Manhattan Bank, The Blackstone Group and their respective affiliates.
Personal: Received BA from Dartmouth College in 1976 (summa cum laude) and JD from Harvard Law School in 1979 (cum laude).

KOHN, Richard
Goldberg, Kohn, Bell, Black, Rosenbloom & Moritz, Ltd, Chicago +1 312 201 4000
Recommended in Banking & Finance

KOLASKY, William J.
Wilmer, Cutler & Pickering, Washington DC +1 202 663 6357
Recommended in Competition/Anti-trust

KOOB, Charles E.
Simpson Thacher & Bartlett, New York +1 212 455 2000
c_koob@stblaw.com
Recommended in Competition/Anti-trust
Specialisation: A partner at *Simpson Thacher & Bartlett* and co-head of the Firm's Litigation Department. Specialises in competition and antitrust law. Experience includes counselling clients on antitrust issues affecting mergers, acquisitions, joint ventures and distribution practices. Has represented clients before the Federal Trade Commission, the Antitrust Division of the Department of Justice and state and foreign competition authorities; defended corporate clients in both criminal and civil anti-trust litigation; represented individuals in grand jury investigations and corporate plaintiffs in major private antitrust litigation. Most recent experience includes: the successful defense of Appleton Papers Inc. in a criminal price fixing trial; the representation of Virgin Atlantic Airways in a private treble action against British Airways; and the representation of the special committee of the Board of Directors of Archer Daniels Midland in a federal grand jury investigation of price-fixing. Has also tried both large commercial and product liability actions to verdict.
Personal: Joined the firm in 1969 and became partner in 1977. Received a BA, from Rockhurst College in 1966 and a JD, from Stanford Law School in 1969. Is a trustee of the Natural Resources Defense Council; serves as Chairman of Stanford Law School's Board of Visitors.

KORFF, Phyllis
Skadden, Arps, Slate, Meagher & Flom LLP, New York +1 212 735 3000
Recommended in Capital Markets: Debt & Equity

KORMAN, Marti
Wilson, Sonsini, Goodrich & Rosati, Palo Alto +1 650 493 9300
Recommended in Communications: IT

KOSHLAND, Jim
Gray Cary Ware & Freidenrich LLP, Palo Alto +1 650 833 2000
Recommended in Communications: IT

KRAMER, Morris
Skadden, Arps, Slate, Meagher & Flom LLP, New York +1 212 735 3000
mkramer@skadden.com
Recommended in Corporate/M&A
Specialisation: Partner, New York. Mergers and Acquisitions and Contests for Corporate Control. Practice includes both friendly and hostile transactions and has involved many of the largest and most publicised deals of the last 20 years. Counsels bidders, targets and their financial advisors in non-negotiated acquisition situations, as well as having extensive experience in strategic and negotiation issues involving public and private company mergers, acquisitions and dispositions. Also advises shareholders, boards of directors and managements in leveraged and management buyouts, proxy fights and other corporate control transactions. Extensive international experience, having represented parties from around the globe in transactions into and from North America, as well as cross-border intra-European deals.
Career: LLB, Harvard University, 1966; AB, Dartmouth College, 1963.

KRAUS, Bruce R.
Willkie Farr & Gallagher, New York
+1 212 728 8000
bkraus@willkie.com
Recommended in Communications: Transactional (Telecoms)
Specialisation: Corporate finance, mergers and acquisitions and general corporate advice for telecommunications clients. Industry experience includes undersea cable, competitive local exchange carriers (CLECs), long distance and Internet backbone networks, fixed and mobile wireless networks (LMDS, PCS, SMR), paging, geosynchronous telecommunications satellites and low earth orbit satellite constellations. Transaction types include public equity offerings, private equity in public companies, high yield debt and preferred stock offerings, secured bank financing, mergers and tender offers, private acquisitions, privatisations, international project finance and strategic joint ventures.
Career: Partner, *Willkie Farr & Gallagher*; law clerk to Chief Judge, U.S. Court of Appeals. Selected conferences and articles: 1995: Practising Law Institute (PLI): 'Doing Deals: Acquisitions'. 1996: New York University: 'The World Wide Web and the Academic Medical Enterprise'. 25 August 1997: National Law Journal, 'Pyrrhic Victory in Spectrum Auction'. 1997: Satellite Financing and Strategic Alliances (Conference Chairman). 1998: Space Finance, 'Structuring Global Satellite Systems'. 1997, 1998 & 1999: PLI Conferences: 'Telecommunications Deals' (Co-Chairman, 2000 session). ALI-ABA 'The Communication Marketplace' (2000).
Personal: Born New York City 1954; Yale Law School, JD 1979 (Editor, Yale Law Journal); Harvard College, AB 1975 (magna cum laude, economics); Phillips Academy. Interests include kyudo, sea kayaking and skiing.

KRAVITT, Jason H.P.
Mayer, Brown & Platt, Chicago +1 312 701 7015
jkravitt@mayerbrown.com
Recommended in Banking & Finance
Specialisation: Founder of the firm's securitisation practice and senior partner in that practice, and participates in a variety of finance and regulatory related practices. Represents industry groups with regard to securitisation regulatory initiatives, including the Bank for International Settlements' Risk-Based Capital 1999 Consultative Paper, the FFIEC's recourse project and residual interest proposal, the FASB's new Standard for Securitization, FAS #140, the FASB's Proposed Standard for Consolidation, and SEC Amendments to Rule 2a-7.
Prof. Memberships: Adjunct Professor of Law at Northwestern University Law School, an Adjunct Professor of Finance at the Kellogg Graduate School of Management of Northwestern University, and a Fellow in the American College of Commercial Finance Lawyers.
Publications: Editor of, and contributing author to, 'Securitization of Financial Assets', Aspen Law & Business, 1996 (2nd Ed.) – the dominant treatise in its field. Co-author of 'Securitization of Project Finance Loans and Other Private Sector Infrastructure Loans', The Financier, February 1994; 'How Feasible Is the Securitization of Loans to Small and Medium-Sized Businesses?', Commercial Lending Review, Fall 1993.
Career: Admitted to practice in Illinois, 1974, and the U.S. Court of Appeals for the Seventh Circuit, 1974. Joined *Mayer, Brown & Platt* in 1973 and became a partner in 1979. Elected Co-Chairman of the firm in 1998.
Personal: Born January 19, 1948. Phi Beta Kappa graduate of The Johns Hopkins University (where he is a member of the Advisory Board to the Dean of School of Arts & Sciences). Earned JD, cum laude, from Harvard Law School in 1972 and received a diploma in comparative law from Cambridge University in 1973. Chairman of The Cameron Kravitt Foundation.

KRIEGER, Sanford
Fried, Frank, Harris, Shriver & Jacobson, New York
+1 212 859 8000
Kriegsa@ffhsj.com
Recommended in Corporate/M&A
Specialisation: Corporate transactions, including structuring private equity investments, public mergers and acquisitions, international combinations, entertainment.
Prof. Memberships: United States Supreme Court; American Bar Association; Bar Association of the City of New York.
Publications: 'Mergers & Acquisitions' – September 2000. Roundtable discussion of '20 Years of Mergers and Acquisitions'.
Personal: Harvard Law School, JD (1968), cum laude. Cornell University, BA (1965), Phi Beta Kappa, cum laude.

KROUSE Jr., George R.
Simpson Thacher & Bartlett, New York
+1 212 455 2000
g_krouse@stblaw.com
Recommended in Capital Markets: Debt & Equity
Specialisation: A partner at *Simpson Thacher & Bartlett*, specialising in corporate and securities law. Since 1991 has served as Head of the Firm's Corporate Department. Also a member of the Executive Committee, the Firm's management body. Has principal responsibility for some of the Firm's most important client relationships, including Lehman Brothers, which the Firm represents as issuer of its own securities, underwriter or placement agent for offerings in the domestic and international capital markets, financial advisor and principal in merchant banking transactions.
Prof. Memberships: Association of the Bar of the City of New York; the New York State and American Bar Associations.
Career: Has been a member of the Firm since 1979. Received AB degree cum laude from Brown University in 1967 and graduated with distinction in 1970 from Duke University School of Law, where was articles editor of the 'Duke Law Journal' and elected to Order of the Coif. Admitted to practise law in New York in 1971.

KRUPKA, Bob
Kirkland & Ellis, Los Angeles +1 213 680 8400
Recommended in Intellectual Property

KUBEK, Gary
Debevoise & Plimpton, New York +1 212 909 6000
Recommended in Competition/Anti-trust

KUDENHOLDT, Stephen S.
Thacher Proffitt & Wood, New York
+1 212 912 7400
Recommended in Capital Markets: Securitisation

KUNKEL, William
Skadden, Arps, Slate, Meagher & Flom LLP, Chicago +1 312 407 0700
Recommended in Corporate/M&A

KUNZ, C. Thomas
Skadden, Arps, Slate, Meagher & Flom LLP, New York +1 212 735 3000
Recommended in Capital Markets: Securitisation

KURTZ, David
Skadden, Arps, Slate, Meagher & Flom LLP, Chicago +1 312 407 0700
Recommended in Banking & Finance

LAKE, William T.
Wilmer, Cutler & Pickering, Washington DC
+1 202 663 6725
Recommended in Communications: Regulatory

LAMB, William
LeBoeuf, Lamb, Greene & MacRae, LLP, New York
+1 212 424 8000
Recommended in Energy & Natural Resources

LAMM, Carolyn
White & Case LLP, Washington DC
+1 202 626 3600
clamm@whitecase.com
Recommended in Arbitration (International)
Specialisation: Partner in Litigation Department, engaged primarily in international litigation, arbitration and international trade. Previously, Assistant Director Commercial Litigation at the U.S. Department of Justice. Established and served as the first Head of International Trade Practice at *White & Case*. Lead counsel for the Republic of Indonesia ICSID arbitration. Also, was special counsel on certain issues to Klockner AG in the annulment proceeding in Klockner AG et al v Camaroons ICSID arbitration 81-2. As special counsel on ICSID issues in Metalclad Mexico. Counsel to the government of Canada in a threatened ICSID arbitration (settled). Counsel to AO Technsnabexport in a Swedish Chamber arbitration. Represents the government of Uzbekistan and NAVOI Mining and Metalurical Combinat; the Ministry of Petroleum of the Kingdom of Saudi Arabia and Saudi Aramco; Nukem; represents the government of Indonesia (Ministry of Finance and Central Bank, Bank Indonesia). Frequent speaker on international trade and arbitration issues; author of many articles.
Prof. Memberships: The District of Columbia Bar (President, 1997-98); American Bar Association; ABA Section of Litigation; U.S. Secretary of State's Advisory Committee on Private International Law; Secretary of States working group on proposed Hague Convention on Jurisdiction and the Enforcement of Judgements; American Law Institute Council and Advisory Committee on International

Jurisdiction and Judgements; Board of Directors of American Uzbekistan Chamber of Commerce; American Indonesian Chamber of Commerce and American Turkish Council. Bars of New York, Florida and District of Columbia.
Career: Joined U.S. Department of Justice in 1973 under the Attorney General's programme for honour law graduates as a trial attorney in the Fraud Section, Civil Division U.S. Department of Justice, and later became Assistant Director, Commercial Litigation Branch Civil Division, U.S. Department of Justice. Joined *White & Case* 1980 and became a partner in 1984.
Personal: Married with two sons.

U

LATIMER, Kenneth A.
Duane, Morris & Heckscher LLP, Chicago +1 312 499 6700
kalatimer@duanemorris.com
Recommended in Banking & Finance
Specialisation: Partner in Corporate and Banking Departments with focus on secured financing transactions, real estate and lease financing, asset-based lending, loan workouts and reorganisations, bank regulation and letter of credit law. Has represented a number of financial institutions in mergers and acquisition, secured financing under Article 9, loan workouts and restructurings, and has advised a number of banks and bank holding companies regarding compliance with the Community Reinvestment Act.
Prof. Memberships: Elected Fellow in the American College of Commercial Finance Lawyers (1997 - present); Member of Commercial Financial Services Committee (1993 - present) and Banking Law Committee (1975-present) of the Business Law Section of the American Bar Association; former Chairman of the Illinois State Bar Association Committee on Commercial banking and Bankruptcy Law; Member of Association of Commercial Finance Attorneys; Founding and active member of the Governing Board of the Commercial Finance Association Education Foundation (1990-present).
Publications: 'What does a Blanket Lien Cover?' (chapter on Letter of Credit); ABA Section of Business Law (1998); 'A Primer on Letter of Credit'; Illinois Committee on Commercial Banking (1986); 'Handbook on Commercial Loan Documentation'; Executive Enterprises (1997); 'Handbook on Loan Workouts'; Executive Enterprises (1997).
Career: Admitted in 1969 in District of Columbia. Admitted in Illinois in 1970. Joined *Berger, Newmark & Fenchel* in 1970. Elected to partnership in 1974 at *Berger, Newmark & Renchel.* Joined *Holleb & Coff* in 1986. *Duane, Morris & Heckscher* LLP 1999-present.
Personal: Born in Chicago, Illinois. Leisure interests include travel and sports. Raised three children and resides with wife in Highland Park, Illinois. Juris Doctor, 1969, The National Law Center of The George Washington University, Washington DC; Bachelor of Arts, 1996, University of Wisconsin.

LAWLOR, John F.
Mayer, Brown & Platt, Chicago +1 312 701 7220
jlawlor@mayerbrown.com
Recommended in Banking & Finance
Specialisation: Corporate and finance. Extensive experience in representing lenders and borrowers in many types of complex financings, senior and subordinated, secured and unsecured, investment grade and non-investment grade. Major deals have included representation of Bank of America in connection with the senior bank financings of Del Monte Corporation and Rayovac Corporation, representation of ABN AMRO Bank in connection with the workout and subsequent bankruptcy of Tokheim Corporation and representation of Chrysler Financial in connection with a credit facility extended to United Auto Group.
Prof. Memberships: Admitted to practice in Illinois, 1988.
Publications: Co-Author, 'Security Interests in Technology Assets and Related Intellectual Property: Practical and Legal Considerations', The Computer Lawyer Vol. 16, no. 8, p.3 (1999).
Career: Joined *Mayer, Brown & Platt,* Chicago, in 1988 and became a partner in 1999.
Personal: Born May 22, 1963. Earned JD, cum laude, from University of Notre Dame in 1988 where was Lead Note Editor, Law Review. Holds AB from Georgetown University, 1985.

LAZERWITZ, Michael
Cleary, Gottlieb, Steen & Hamilton, Washington DC +1 202 974 1500
Recommended in Competition/Anti-trust

LEDDY, Mark
Cleary, Gottlieb, Steen & Hamilton, Washington DC +1 202 974 1500
Recommended in Competition/Anti-trust

LEDERMAN, Lawrence
Milbank, Tweed, Hadley & McCloy, New York +1 212 530 5732
LLetterman@milbank.com
Recommended in Corporate/M&A
Specialisation: Senior partner in the firm's New York office, Chairman of the firm's International Corporate practice, Head of the Global Corporate Department.
Prof. Memberships: Memberships: Member of the Panel of Arbitrators of the American Arbitration Association. Chairman of the Board of Phoenix House Development Foundation Inc. since 1981, a Director of The National Mentoring Partnership, Incorporated, since 1993, a Director of The New York Botanical Garden since 1996 and previously served as a Director of The American Chess Foundation. Adjunct Professor of Law teaching corporate law at New York University School of Law since 1974. Chairman of the Practicing Law Institute Program on Corporate Restructuring.
Publications: Author of 'Tombstones A Lawyer's Tales from the Takeover Decades,' published in March 1992 by Farrar, Straus and Giroux. Editor of the 'Law Review' at the New York University.
Career: Prior to joining *Milbank,* was a partner at *Wachtell, Lipton, Rosen & Katz.* One of the most active corporate, mergers and acquisitions lawyers in the country, has helped shape many of the major corporate legal developments that have occurred over the past twenty years.
Personal: Graduated from Brooklyn College of the City University of New York and received LLB, from New York University, a member of Order of the Coif and a John Norton Pomeroy Scholar. From 1966 to 1967, served as a law clerk for Chief Justice Roger J. Traynor, California Supreme Court.

LEDUC, André
Skadden, Arps, Slate, Meagher & Flom LLP, Chicago +1 312 407 0700
aleduc@skadden.com
Recommended in Tax
Prof. Memberships: American Bar Association; Illinois State Bar Association; Chicago Bar Association. American Law Institute Federal Income Tax Advisory Group, 1987-1995 Adjunct Professor of Law; Graduate Tax Program, Chicago-Kent College of Law, 1985-90; 1998-present.
Publications: The Treatment of Contingent Consideration in Tax-Free Corporate Acquisitions, 29 Case W. Res. L. Rev. 88 (1978); Current Proposals to Restructure the Taxation of Corporate Acquisitions and Dispositions: Substance and Process, 22 San Diego L. Rev. 17 (1985); The New Assult on Related Party Financing: How Far Will the Service Go?, 11 Int'l Tax J. 167 (1985); Two Visions of SAubchapter C: Understanding the 1986 Tax Reform Act and the 1987 Revenue Act and Predicting the Near Future, 46 Inst. on Fed. Tax'n 37(1988).
Career: Admitted to the Ohio and Illinois Bars; *Jones, Day, Reavis & Pogue,* Cleveland, Ohio, 1978-81; Counsel, US Senate Finance Committee, 1981-83; *Winston & Strawn,* Chicago, 1984-1993; *Skadden. Arps, Slate, Meagher & Flom,* Chicago, 1993-present.
Personal: Princeton University, AB, summa cum laude, 1975; Harvard Law School, JD, cum laude, 1978; Advisory Council of the Princeton University Department of History, 1980-present.

LEE, Bill
Hale and Dorr, Boston +1 617 526 6000
Recommended in Intellectual Property

LEMEIN, Gregg D.
Baker & McKenzie, Chicago +1 312 861 8013
gregg.d.lemein@bakernet.com
Recommended in Tax
Specialisation: Partner in Tax Practice Group. Practice focuses on the U.S. federal income taxation of corporations, with emphasis on international tax planning and controversies involving international tax issues. Extensive experience in (a)international mergers and acquisitions, international reorganisations, foreign tax credit planning, and the development and analysis of intercompany pricing policies; and (b)resolution of tax controversies at the audit and appeals levels of the International Revenue Service and in court.
Prof. Memberships: American Bar Association Section, Tax Section.
Publications: International Transfer Pricing Laws: Text and Commentary (loose leaf service published by CCH in December 1994 and updated quarterly) (Managing Editor and Contributing Author); numerous articles published in CCH Taxes Magazine and other publications.
Career: Joined *Baker & McKenzie* in 1976 and became a Partner in 1983.
Personal: Born February 2, 1950. Graduated from the Northwestern University Law School, Juris Doctor, magna cum laude, Order of the Coif, in

1976; the Kellogg Graduate School of Management, Northwestern University, Master of Management, with distinction, also in 1976; and the University of Illinois, Bachelor of Science in Computer Engineering, with high honors, in 1972.

LESSER, Henry
Gray Cary Ware & Freidenrich LLP, Palo Alto
+1 650 833 2425
HLesser@graycary.com
Recommended in Communications: IT
Specialisation: Main areas of practice are corporate mergers and acquisitions and corporate governance. Involved in all aspects of merger and acquisition work.
Prof. Memberships: Admitted to practice in California (1984), New York (1977), and England and Wales (1969). American Law Institute; Board of Directors of the Southern Californian Chapter of the National Association of Corporate Directors; American Bar Association, Business Law Section.
Career: Harkness Fellow of the Commonwealth Fund of New York. With *Wachtell, Lipton Rosen & Katz* (NYC), 1977-83; *Gibson, Dunn & Crutcher*, 1983-87; *Fried, Frank, Harris, Shriver & Jacobson* (Los Angeles), 1987-91; *Irell & Manella LLP* (Los Angeles), 1991-97; *Heller Ehrman White & McAuliffe*, 1997-2000; joined *Gray Cary Ware & Freidenrich LLP*, 2000.
Personal: Cambridge University, BA Law, 1968 and MA, 1972 (Squire Law Scholar, First Class Honours in Law with distinction for work of special merit); Harvard University School of Law, LLM, 1973.

LETZLER, Kenneth
Arnold & Porter, Washington DC +1 202 942 5000
Kenneth_Letzler@aporter.com
Recommended in Competition/Anti-trust
Specialisation: Partner at *Arnold & Porter*, has been extensively involved in anti-trust litigation and counseling, with particular emphasis on distribution, licensing, and pricing issues in the consumer products and pharmaceutical industries. Has represented numerous US and European pharmaceutical companies on licensing issues, acquisitions, litigation and counselling. Also functions as counsel to a leading US firm on its acquisitions in the agricultural biotechnology field and has counselled in connection with corporate transactions involving the polymerase chain reaction (PCR) technology.
Career: Prior to joining *Arnold & Porter* in 1969, clerked on the US Court of Appeals for the United States Court of Appeals for the District of Columbia Circuit.
Personal: Recieved JD, from Harvard Law School in 1968 and BA, from Columbia University in 1965.

LEVI, Stuart
Skadden, Arps, Slate, Meagher & Flom LLP, New York +1 212 735 3000
Recommended in Communications: Transactional (IT)

LEVIN, Charles E.
McDermott, Will & Emery, Chicago
+1 312 372 2000
celevin@mwe.com
Recommended in Banking & Finance
Specialisation: Partner in corporate department. Concentrates in representing financial institutions and others in lending, restructuring and other financing-related matters, as well as other companies in mergers and acquisitions and general corporate matters. Represents National Bank of Canada in various financings. Has represented Lehman Bros. in City of Chicago School Board financing. Represented Tenneco Inc., in refinancings in excess of US$4 billion in corporate spin-offs.
Prof. Memberships: Member of Chicago Bar Association, Commercial Transactions Committee; American Bar Association, Business Section; and Commercial Finance Association, Founders Leadership Counsel.
Publications: Author of article 'A Confidentiality Agreement Primer' with John L. Howard, General Cousel of Tenneco Automotive, 18 ACCA Docket 17, no.2 (1999): 18-34.
Career: Admitted to Illinois Bar in 1971. Associate at *D'Ancona & Pflaum*, Chicago, Illinois 1971-1976, Partner 1977-1990. Partner at *Jenner & Block*, Chicago, Illnois 1990-2000. Partner at *McDermott, Will & Emery*, Chicago, Illinois 2000-current. Speaker on financing topics at Commercial Finance Association and Chicago Bar Association Seminars, and as a guest of Hungarian and Czech Republic Banking Associations in Europe.
Personal: JD cum laude from Northwestern University School of Law in 1971. Northwestern University Law Review Board of Editors, 1970-71. Assistant instructor in Legal Writing and Research, Northwestern University, 1970-71. BA magna cum laude DePaul University, 1968.

LEVIN, Jack
Kirkland & Ellis, Chicago +1 312 861 2000
Recommended in Corporate/M&A, Tax

LEVIN, Peter
Davis Polk & Wardwell, New York +1 212 450 4000
Recommended in Banking & Finance

LEVINE, Hank
Levine, Blaszak, Block & Boothby LLP, Washington DC +1 202 857 2550
Recommended in Communications: Transactional (Telecoms)

LEWKOW, Victor
Cleary, Gottlieb, Steen & Hamilton, New York
+1 212 225 2000
Recommended in Communications: Transactional (Telecoms), Corporate/M&A

LIBIN, Jerome
Sutherland Asbill & Brennan LLP, Washington DC
+1 202 383 0100
Recommended in Tax

LINDAUER, Erik D.
Sullivan & Cromwell, New York +1 212 558 4000
lindauere@sullcrom.com
Recommended in Banking & Finance
Specialisation: A member of *Sullivan & Cromwell's* Commercial Banking, Project Finance and General Practice areas. Specialises in transactional banking, secured lending, commercial law (Uniform Commercial Code), corporate reorganisations and bankruptcy. Advises clients that include domestic and foreign borrowers under lending agreements in the United States and abroad, U.S. and non-U.S. banking organisations and the New York Clearing House Association. Financing experience includes work on a broad range of complex secured and unsecured financings, including project, cable television and media financings. Recently has represented the bank lenders in the Cantarell project in Mexico; the syndicated leaders to Winstar Communications, Inc.; Niagara Mohawk Power Corporation in connection with refinancing of bank lines and certain asset dispositions; and satellite and other project financings.
Prof. Memberships: American Bar Association; Association of the Bar of the City of New York (Member, Banking Law Committee); New York State Bar Association.
Career: Joined *Sullivan & Cromwell* in 1981. Elected a Partner of the firm in 1989.
Personal: Born 1956. Attended the State University of New York at Albany (BA, 1978) and the State University of New York Law School at Buffalo (JD, 1981). In 1992, spent an extended period working in Moscow with American and Russian bankers as the legal advisor to the Government Securities Working Group of the Russia-American Bankers Forum and in 1993 served as an instructor on legal matters at the Forum's Academy for Advanced Studies in Banking and Finance.

LINDSEY, David
Clifford Chance Rogers & Wells LLP, New York
+1 212 878 8000
Recommended in Arbitration (International)

LIPMAN, Andy
Swidler Berlin Shereff Friedman LLP, Washington DC +1 202 424 7500
Recommended in Communications: Regulatory

LIPSEY, Charles
Finnegan Henderson Farabow Garrett & Dunner LLP, Washington DC +1 202 408 4000
charles.lipsey@finnegan.com
Recommended in Intellectual Property
Specialisation: Partner. Concentrates on intellectual property litigation, particularly patent infringement litigation, in the district courts, the Federal Circuit, and the Supreme Court of the United States. Has handled cases involving mechanical, chemical, and electrical technologies, with emphasis on biotechnology and pharmaceutical chemistry. Has extensive experience in patent infringement litigation, patent arbitration proceedings, and patent interferences. Representative cases include: Hybritech v. Abbott Laboratories; Regents of the University of California v. Eli Lilly and Co.; Loral Fairchild, Inc. v. Matsushita et al.; and Gallo v. Montagnier. Was invited by the United States Supreme Court to brief and argue in support of the judgment of the Florida Supreme Court in Bonito Boats, Inc. v. Thundercraft Boats, Inc.
Publications: Co-Author of 'Patent Law Perspectives', Matthew Bender & Co. 1982-1988.
Career: Admitted in 1977, Virginia; 1979, District of Columbia; U.S. Court of Appeals for the Federal Circuit; registered to practice before U.S. Patent and

U

Trademark Office. Technical Advisor to the Honorable Giles S. Rich, Associate Judge, U.S. Court of Customs and Patent Appeals, (1976-1978). Patent examiner in the U.S. Patent and Trademark Office (1977-1981). Law clerk to Associate Judge Giles S. Rich of the U.S. Court of Customs and Patent Appeals, now the U.S. Court of Appeals for the Federal Circuit. Joined the firm in 1978.
Personal: Born November 27, 1950. Georgia Institute of Technology (BSChE, 1972); The George Washington University National Law Center (JD, with high honors, 1977); (LLM, Patent and Trademark Regulation Law with high honors, 1981).

U

LIPTON, Martin
Wachtell, Lipton, Rosen & Katz, New York
+1 212 403 1000
Recommended in Corporate/M&A

LIPTON, Richard
McDermott, Will & Emery, Chicago
+1 312 372 2000
rlipton@mwe.com
Recommended in Tax
Specialisation: Partner in Tax Department. Advises on partnerships, LLCs, other pass-through entities, and real estate transactions for clients which are comprised of multinational corporations including Fortune 100 companies.
Prof. Memberships: Member of Chicago Bar Association (Chair, 1991-1992; vice-chair, 1990-1991; secretary, 1989-1990; member, executive committee, 1983-1990) and American Bar Association (section of taxation: Chair-elect, 2000 -; vice-chair, 1993-1996; council director, 1990-1993; vice regional liaison, 1989-1990).
Publications: Treaties Passive Activity Losses; numerous articles on partnerships, real estate and pass-through entities.
Career: Admitted to the Illinois Bar and US Tax Court in 1977, District of Columbia, 1978; and US Court of Federal Claims, 1980. Contributor and editor to the Journal of Taxation; Journal of Pass-Through Entities; Journal of Partnership Taxation; Journal of Real Estate and Taxation and Mergers & Acquisitions Reporter.
Personal: Born 12 February, 1952. Received bachelor's degree cum laude from Amherst College in 1974 and JD, with honors from University of Chicago in 1977.

LITWIN, Stuart M.
Mayer, Brown & Platt, Chicago +1 312 701 7373
slitwin@mayerbrown.com
Recommended in Corporate/M&A
Specialisation: Partner in Finance and Corporate practices of Chicago office. Recognised as a leading expert in the securitisation and financing of auto leases, auto loans, equipment leases, dealer floor plan receivables, catastrophic and residual value risk and the creation of asset-backed securities for money market funds. Represents originators, investment banks, commercial banks, asset-backed commercial paper conduits and investors (including money market and other mutual funds) in public and private U.S. and international asset-backed securities transactions. Experience in the securitisation of virtually all asset types. Regularly represents parties in leasing transactions, including leveraged leases involving autos and other equipment. Also experienced in negotiated and contested acquisitions and mergers (including acquisitions of finance companies, banks and other financial institutions), tender offers, takeover defenses, leveraged acquisitions, asset acquisitions and dispositions of subsidiaries; public offerings and private placements of debt and equity securities; and joint ventures.
Prof. Memberships: Former Chairman of Securities Law Committee and Corporate Control Subcommittee, Chicago Bar Association.
Publications: Author of 'Equipment and Auto Lease Financing: Securitization, Leveraged Leasing and Titling Trusts' (Aspen Law & Business, 2000); 'Equipment and Auto Lease Securitization', Chapter 30 of Equipment Leasing — Leveraged Leasing, (Practising Law Institute, 4th Ed., 2000); 'Auto Lease Double Dips: Is There a Possibility?' Asset Finance International, September 1996; 'Unlocking the Mysteries of Auto Lease Securitization', The Financier, May 1996; 'Security Measures: Auto Lease Securitization', Asset Finance & Leasing Digest, March 1996; 'The Merger and Acquisition Process: A Primer on Getting the Deal Done', The Financier, November 1995; 'Investments in Asset-Backed Securities by Money Market Funds', The Securitization of Financial Assets, Prentice Hall Law & Business, 1994 edition.
Career: Joined *Mayer, Brown & Platt* in 1985 and became partner in 1994.
Personal: Born June 17, 1959. Earned JD, cum laude, and MBA from University of Chicago in 1985. Certified Public Accountant, Illinois, 1981 (Winner of Elijah Watt Sells Award on Uniform CPA Examination). Holds BS, summa cum laude and Bronze Tablet, from the University of Illinois in 1981. President of the Chicago Lawyers Committee for Civil Rights Under Law President, 1999-2000.

LOFTIS, Jim
Gibson, Dunn & Crutcher LLP, Washington DC
+1 202 955 8500
Recommended in Competition/Anti-trust

LOGAN, Kenneth
Simpson Thacher & Bartlett, New York
+1 212 455 2000
k_logan@stblaw.com
Recommended in Competition/Anti-trust
Specialisation: A litigator and antitrust practitioner at *Simpson Thacher & Bartlett* for 28 years, handling a broad range of complex litigations and transactions. Recently represented Seagram in the Seagram/Vivendi/Canal Plus merger in the US, EU and elsewhere. Represented American Home Products and acted as lead counsel for all pharmaceutical manufacturer defendants in the Brand Name Prescription Drugs Antitrust Litigations. Represented Viacom in its private antitrust action against Time Warner challenging HBO's monopolisation of the premium television business in the U.S.; has represented Paramount, Universal, MGM and UIP in connection with various proceedings before the European Commission and various national competition authorities; represented Seagram and Viacom and others in various matters before the FTC, the Justice Department, European Commission and various national competition authorities. Also conducted a range of complex commercial litigations and arbitrations for American Electric Power, Chemical (now Chase) Bank, General Motors Corporation, ITT Industries, Kohlberg, Kravis & Roberts and others.
Personal: Received a BA from Princeton University in 1967 and a JD from the University of Pennsylvania Law School in 1972.

LOOMAN, James
Sidley & Austin, Chicago +1 312 853 7133
jlooman@sidley.com
Recommended in Banking & Finance
Specialisation: Partner in the Chicago office. Focuses on banking and commercial transactions, equipment leasing, leveraged lease financing and securitisation. Speaker at 'Commercial Loan Documentation' Seminar for Banking Law Institute and Executive Enterprises, May 2000.
Prof. Memberships: Member of the Bar of Illinois and the American and Chicago Bar Associations.
Career: Chairman of Commercial and Financial Transactions Committee of the Chicago Bar Association, 1996-97. Fellow of American College of Commercial Finance Lawyers.
Personal: Educated at the University of Chicago (JD, 1978); Valparaiso University (BA, 1974).

LOWINGER, Frederick C.
Sidley & Austin, Chicago +1 312 853 7000
flowinge@sidley.com
Recommended in Corporate/M&A
Specialisation: Principal areas of practice: mergers and acquisitions and corporate finance. Experienced in public company transactions and advising boards of directors and financial advisors.
Prof. Memberships: American and Chicago Bar Associations; Chicago Committee of the Council on Foreign Relations; Lawyers Club of Chicago.
Career: Law clerk to US Supreme Court Justice Brennan (1981-82). Joined *Sidley & Austin* in 1982; became partner in 1988 and member of firm's Executive Committee in 1996. Certified public accountant. University of Chicago (JD 1980)

LOWTHER, Frederick
Dickstein Shapiro Morin & Oshinsky LLP, Washington DC +1 202 785 9700
Recommended in Energy & Natural Resources

LOWY, George
Cravath, Swaine & Moore, New York
+1 212 474 1000
Recommended in Corporate/M&A

LUBIN, Don
Sonnenschein, Chicago +1 312 876 8000
dgl@sonnenschein.com
Recommended in Corporate/M&A
Specialisation: Counsels boards and management of public and private companies on corporate restructurings, takeover defense, joint ventures, corporate governance and mergers and acquisitions. Lead counsel to Sears in its corporate restructuring. Regularly advises other public companies, including Grainger, Great Universal, Allstate, McDonald's and

Molex. Lead counsel in GUS take-over of Metromail, Safety-Kleen takeover, merger of 360° Communications and Alltel, the sale of Searle to Monsanto, the sale of Holiday Inn's International to Bass, the acquisition of Merrill Lynch Realty by Prudential; advised Lazard in Kraft/Philip Morris transaction. Serves on McDonald's Board, its Executive Committee, Nominating and Corporate Governance Committee (Chairman) and Audit Committee (Secretary). Serves on Molex Board and its Audit Committee (Chairman).
Prof. Memberships: Law Club, Economic Club, Commercial Club, Civic Committee.
Career: Joined *Sonnenschein* in 1957. Chairman of firm 1991-1996.
Personal: University of Pennsylvania, BS, 1954; Harvard Law School, LLB, 1957. Trustee, Rush-Presbyterian- St. Luke's Medical Center; Director, National Museum of American History; Chairman, Anchor Cross Society; former Chairman, Ravinia Festival Association, Highland Park Hospital; Life Trustee, Chicago Symphony Orchestra; former Director, Smithsonian Institution; former member Board of Overseers, University of Pennsylvania.

LUSCOMBE, George A. III
Mayer, Brown & Platt, Chicago +1 312 701 7099
gluscombe@mayerbrown.com
Recommended in Tax
Specialisation: Partner in Corporate Taxation Practice in Chicago. Structures acquisitions and divestitures, taxable and tax-free, business joint ventures, leveraged buy-outs, and leasing transactions. Structures partnership, joint venture, and limited liability company vehicles for real estate, natural resources, and new technologies. Structures investment vehicles and companies in various industries, including real estate acquisitions for pension plan trusts. Represents corporations, partnerships, and limited liability companies in matters related to general corporate, partnership, real estate and natural resources taxation.
Prof. Memberships: Admitted to practice in the District of Columbia, 1972, and Illinois, 1969. Adjunct Professor of Taxation, Illinois Institute of Technology/Chicago-Kent College of Law, 1987-1993. Member of American Bar Association, Section of Taxation; former Chairman, Committee on Capital Recovery and Leasing; former Editor, Tax Notes column, American Bar Association Journal; and Illinois State Bar Association, Chairman, Council of Federal Tax Section.
Publications: Author of presentations for Illinois Institute for Continuing Legal Education, American Bar Association, University of Chicago Tax Institute, Tulane Tax Institute, and Canadian Petroleum Tax Society and Canadian Property Forum.
Career: Served in Office of Chief Counsel, Internal Revenue Service, Legislation and Regulations Division, Washington, DC, from 1969 to 1973. Joined *Mayer, Brown & Platt* in 1973 and became partner in 1976.
Personal: Born October 22, 1944. Earned LLM George Washington University in 1972. Awarded JD and Order of the Coif University of Illinois in 1969, and BS with honors in 1966. Certified Public Accountant, Illinois, 1966.

LYNCH, Alex
Gunderson Dettmer Stough Villeneuve Franklin & Hachigian, New York +1 646 487 0900
Recommended in Communications: Transactional (IT)

LYNCH, John
Howrey Simon Arnold & White, Washington DC +1 202 783 0800
Recommended in Intellectual Property

MACHLIN, Barry N.
Mayer, Brown & Platt, Chicago +1 312 701 8574
bmachlin@mayerbrown.com
Recommended in Project Finance
Specialisation: Partner and Co-Chair of Global Project Finance practice. Represents international banks and financial institutions and multilateral and bilateral official lending agencies. Recent transactions include the $440 million Bajio power project (Mexico), the $800 million Quezon power project (Philippines), a CDMA telecom upgrade financing in Mexico, the $1.3 billion Paiton I project (Indonesia), and the Khalda and Qarun oil concession developments (Egypt). Also represents banks and financial institutions in syndicated lending and Eurodollar transactions, sovereigns, state-owned enterprises and investors in privatisation and restructuring matters, and parties in cross-border investment and financial transactions. Widely experienced in representing clients in connection with transactions throughout Europe, Asia and the Middle East.
Prof. Memberships: Admitted to practice in Massachusetts (1985); the District of Columbia (1987); Illinois (2000) and New York (2000).
Publications: Speaking engagements have included 'Building Infrastructure Projects in Developing Markets' at the Practising Law Institute, 'Project Finance' at the International Bar Association, and 'Venture Capital and Private Equity Investments in Emerging Markets' at the Harvard International Development Conference.
Career: Joined *Mayer, Brown & Platt* as a partner in 1997, serving first in Washington DC, and currently in Chicago. Partner (first associate) with *White & Case*, Washington DC, and London, from 1985 to 1997.
Personal: Born July 14, 1959. Earned JD from Harvard Law School in 1985 and BA, summa cum laude, from Brandeis University in 1982, where was elected to Phi Beta Kappa.

MACLEOD, William
Collier Shannon Scott, Washington DC +1 202 342 8400
Recommended in Competition/Anti-trust

MACMURRAY, John C.
Reboul, MacMurray, Hewitt, Maynard & Kristol, New York +1 212 841 5711
jmacmurray@reboul.com
Recommended in Private Equity: Fund Formation
Specialisation: Corporate lawyer whose practice principally includes representation of domestic and international private investment funds, US middle market banks and domestic and international industrial and commercial companies. Client responsibilities involve representing private equity sponsor groups in their fundraising projects and investment programs. Clients include Behrman Capital, Cinven, Cygnus Ventures, Dailey Capital, Domain Partners, HL Capital Inc., Kulen Capital, Landmark Partners, Long Point Capital, MD Sass & Co, Prime Capital, Quad-C Advisors, Wand Partners, West Private Equity Fund, and Wm Sword & Co. Co-founded the firm with Mr John W. Reboul in 1973.
Prof. Memberships: Association of the Bar of the City of New York. New York State Bar Association. American Bar Association.
Career: Admitted to the Bar in New York in 1965. Attended Columbia Law School (LLB, 1965) and Princeton University (AB, 1961).
Personal: Born 13 April 1939.

MADDEN, John
Shearman & Sterling, New York +1 212 848 4000
jmadden@shearman.com
Recommended in Communications: Transactional (Telecoms), Corporate/M&A
Specialisation: Head of M&A practice group. Main area of work is corporate M&A, divestitures, and joint ventures. Handles both negotiated and unsolicited transactions and advises clients on corporate governance matters. Has acted on several cross-border mergers and acquisitions, including representation of the BOC Group plc in the conditional bid by L'Air Liquide, SA and Air Products and Chemicals, Inc. and representation of Rhône-Poulenc SA in its merger with Hoechst AG to form Aventis. Has represented various other corporate clients in their acquisition transactions, including British Telecommunications plc, Continental AG, Munich Reinsurance Company, Billiton plc, ICO Global Communications Limited, Corning Incorporated, BCE Inc, Bell Canada International and BCE Emergis Inc. Represents several leading investment banking firms acting as financial advisors in mergers and acquisitions.
Prof. Memberships: Bars of New York and Paris (avocat).
Career: Admitted to the New York bar in 1975. Joined *Shearman & Sterling* in 1975, becoming a partner in 1983. Co-head of the Mergers & Acquisitions Group 1986-91. Managing Partner of the firm's European offices 1991-95, resident in Paris. Head of the Mergers & Acquisitions Group since 1995. Member of the firm's Policy Committee.
Personal: Born 27 May 1946. Attended University of Pennsylvania (BA 1968) and Fordham Law School (JD 1975) as Articles Editor of the Law Review. US army military service 1969-71.

MALLOW, Matthew
Skadden, Arps, Slate, Meagher & Flom LLP, New York +1 212 735 3000
Recommended in Capital Markets: Debt & Equity

MALT, Brad
Ropes & Gray, Boston +1 617 951 7000
Recommended in Private Equity: Fund Formation

MANN, Christopher L.
Sullivan & Cromwell, New York +1 212 558 4000
mannc@sullcrom.com
Recommended in Project Finance
Specialisation: Substantial experience in project

U

finance, mergers and acquisitions, general corporate and securities matters. Experience structuring joint venture arrangements in the project finance area. Partner in charge of advising sponsors in US$2 billion VLNG project in Venezuela. Other project finance assignments include representation of Minera Escondida Limitada in Chile in various financings and refinancings; WMC in Zarmitan gold project in Uzbekistan; TOTAL, PDVSA and Statoil in Sincor project in Venezuela; Credit Suisse First Boston and other senior lenders in Port Arthur Coker Company heavy oil upgrade project in Texas; Minorco S.A. in Collahuasi copper project in Chile, the Loma de Niquel nickel project in Venezuela and the Cerro Vanguardia gold and silver project in Argentina; and Ampol Exploration Limited in Kutubu oil development and production project in Papua New Guinea.
Prof. Memberships: Association of the Bar of the City of New York (Chair, Project Finance Committee); American Bar Association.
Career: Judicial Clerk to the Honorable Ralph K. Winter, U.S. Circuit Court of Appeals (2nd Circuit), 1989-1990. Joined *Sullivan & Cromwell* in 1990. Resident in firm's London office during 1993-96 and became a partner in 1998.
Personal: Born 1963 in Beaumont, Texas. Graduate of Harvard College (AB, 1985), Cambridge University (MPhil, 1987) and Harvard Law School (JD, 1989). Member of Board of Governors and Secretary, The Links.

MARSTON, Edgar
Bracewell & Patterson LLP, Houston +1 713 223 2900
Recommended in Corporate/M&A

MARTIN, Renwick
Brown & Wood LLP, New York +1 212 839 5300
Recommended in Capital Markets: Securitisation

MARZULLI, John A. Jr.
Shearman & Sterling, New York +1 212 848 4000
jmarzulli@shearman.com
Recommended in Communications: Transactional (Telecoms)
Specialisation: Partner in the Mergers & Acquisitions Group at *Shearman & Sterling* since 1988. Represents leading investment banks and principals in cross-border mergers and acquisitions, specialising in acquisitions of publicly quoted companies, defensive assignments and privately negotiated acquisitions and divestitures.
Prof. Memberships: American Bar Association, New York State Bar Association, New Jersey State Bar Association. Bar Association of the City of New York; Member of the Securities Regulation Committee.
Career: Qualified for the New Jersey Bar in 1978 and the New York Bar in 1979. Joined *Shearman & Sterling* in 1980 following a federal district court clerkship. Became a partner in 1988. Based in *Shearman & Sterling*'s London office from 1990-96.
Personal: Attended Middlebury College (BA, magna cum laude, Phi Beta Kappa, 1975) and New York University School of Law (JD, cum laude, Order of the Coif, 1978). Lives in New York City.

MASON, David
Goldberg, Kohn, Bell, Black, Rosenbloom & Moritz, Ltd, Chicago +1 312 201 4000
Recommended in Banking & Finance

MASSAD, Stephen A.
Baker Botts LLP, Houston +1 713 229 1475
stephen.massad@bakerbotts.com
Recommended in Corporate/M&A
Specialisation: Head of firm's Houston corporate department. Handles M&A, securities and other corporate work, principally for clients in the energy, power and chemicals sectors. Substantial experience with mergers, tender offers, proxy contests, public offerings, private offerings, joint ventures and corporate counseling for major companies and investment banks.
Prof. Memberships: Member of Texas Bar, as well as American and Houston Bar Associations.
Career: Joined *Baker Botts* 1975, became partner 1983.
Personal: AB Princeton University (summa cum laude, economics) 1972; JD Harvard Law School (cum laude) 1975.

MASUR, Daniel
Mayer, Brown & Platt, Washington DC +1 202 263 3226
dmasur@mayerbrown.com
Recommended in Communications: Transactional (IT)
Specialisation: Partner in the Corporate, Information Technology, Telecommunications and Outsourcing Practices. Formerly served as Vice President and General Counsel of I-NET, Inc., a rapidly growing provider of information technology, network and outsourcing services. Represents major national and international firms in a broad range of information technology, communications and outsourcing transactions. Representative transactions include the outsourcing of business processes and functions, application development and maintenance and e-commerce transaction processing and support. Such transactions also include outsourcing of the management, operation and/or support of local and wide area networks, voice, data and video communications, data centers and midrange systems, desktop and laptop computers, help desks, and leasing/procurement. Representative clients include established and emerging firms in aerospace, defense contracting, electronic commerce, financial services, insurance, pharmaceuticals, life sciences, forestry products and electric power.
Prof. Memberships: Admitted to practice in the District of Columbia (1977).
Career: Joined *Mayer, Brown & Platt* as a partner in 1997. Prior to that, served as a partner with *Reed, Smith, Shaw & McClay* (1994-1997) and as Vice President and General Counsel for I-NET, Inc. (1994-1997).
Personal: Earned JD from Georgetown University in 1977, (Editor of the Georgetown Law Journal), and BA from Marquette University in 1974.

MAY, Gregory
Freshfields Bruckhaus Deringer, Washington DC +1 202 777 4500
gregory.may@freshfields.com
Recommended in Tax
Specialisation: Wide international tax practice focuses on structured finance, derivatives and other financial products.

MAY, Henry
Vinson & Elkins LLP, Houston +1 713 758 2131
hmay@velaw.com
Recommended in Energy & Natural Resources
Specialisation: Extensive experience in the regulatory, policy and transactional aspects of the natural gas and electric industries. Has represented clients before federal and state agencies and courts, and assisted in the development of energy policy initiatives, and participated in the structuring and negotiation of domestic and international energy transactions.
Prof. Memberships: Adjunct Professor, University of Houston Law Center.
Publications: Natural Gas Contracts, published 1992. Chairman and Author.
Career: Attended: The University of Texas (BA with honors, 1969); The University of Texas School of Law (JD with honors 1971); admitted to practice (Texas, 1972; US Supreme Court; Court of Appeals of the District of Columbia; Fifth Circuit and Eleventh Circuit.

McCORMACK, Howard
Healy & Baillie LLP, New York +1 212 943 3980
Recommended in Shipping: Litigation

McCORMACK, William F.
Reboul, MacMurray, Hewitt, Maynard & Kristol, New York +1 212 841 0627
wmccormack@reboul.com
Recommended in Private Equity: Fund Formation
Specialisation: Has represented numerous international venture capital, buy-out and other private equity investment funds and firms (both as lead counsel as well as special United States counsel), including various UK firms such as Kleinwort Benson, Charterhouse, Electra Kingsway, Cinven, DLJ Phoenix, Phildrew Ventures, ECI Ventures, Granville Private Equity, Primary Capital, Pond Ventures, CapVis and Elderstreet Capital Partners; various European based firms such as Industri Kapital, the Scandinavian buyout firm, Mercapital SL, the Spanish buyout firm, Argos Soditic and the Swiss-based Index Securities SA, the South African buyout firm FirstCorp Capital, and the Norwegian high-tech firm Venture Partners Multimedia Group. Also acted as counsel for various US-based private equity and/or buy-out investment funds.
Prof. Memberships: American Bar Association; New York State Bar Association; Virginia Bar Association.
Career: Admitted to Bar, Virginia 1971; admitted to Bar, New York 1973; LLM, University of Virginia 1972; JD, Catholic University of America 1971; BS, Virginia Polytechnic University 1968.
Personal: Born 27 December 1946.

McCORMICK, Bill
Hughes & Luce, Dallas +1 214 939 5500
Recommended in Corporate/M&A

McDAVID, Janet L.
Hogan & Hartson LLP, Washington DC
+1 202 637 5600
Recommended in Competition/Anti-trust

McGRAW-WEISS, Donna
Skadden, Arps, Slate, Meagher & Flom LLP, New York +1 212 735 3000
Recommended in Project Finance

McKEE, Bill
McKee Nelson Ernst & Young, Washington DC
+1 202 775 8580
bmckee@mneylaw.com
Recommended in Tax
Specialisation: Practice Areas: Taxation. Practice encompasses all areas of federal taxation, with a special emphasis on partnership taxation.
Publications: Co-author of the treatise Federal Taxation of Partnerships and Partners (Warren, Gorham & Lamont, 3rd edition, 1997), and also co-authored Federal Taxation of Partnerships and Partners: Structuring and Drafting Agreements (Warren, Gorham & Lamont, 2nd edition, 1993).
Career: Prior to founding the firm in November 1999, was a tax partner in the D.C. office of *King & Spalding.* Joined *King & Spalding* in 1983. Served as Tax Legislative Counsel at the U.S. Treasury Department from 1981-1983. Is a member of the American Law Institute, the American College of Tax Counsel, and the National Institute for Tax Professionals. Was a Law Professor at the University of Virginia School of Law from 1969-1981. Also a visiting Professor in the Graduate Tax Program at the New York University School of Law from 1975-1977. Frequent speaker at seminars around the country on the subject of partnership taxation.
Personal: A 1966 cum laude graduate of Yale University, received a JD, magna cum laude, in 1969 from the Harvard Law School, and was an editor of the Harvard Law Review.

McMAHON, Terry
Orrick, Herrington & Sutcliffe, San Francisco
+1 415 392 1122
tmcmahon@orrick.com
Recommended in Intellectual Property
Specialisation: A partner in *Orrick's* litigation department and a member of the firm's bi-costal intellectual property group. Has over 20 years of litigation experience and has particular expertise in intellectual property litigation, representing high-technology clients. Especially well known for his work as Lead Counsel in the representation of Advance Micro Devices (AMD) in its extensive arbitration against Intel, and as lead counsel in AMD's victory over Intel in the Federal Court jury trial regarding the right to use Intel's copyright microcode. Represented Aureal in Creative Technology verses Aureal – named 'Defense Verdict of 1999' by National Law Journal'.
Prof. Memberships: Santa Clara County Superior Court Panel of Arbitrators and of the Intellectual Property Inns of Court; Santa Clara County Bar Association; San Francisco County Bar Association; American Bar Association and its Sections on Litigation, Tort, and Insurance Practice and Science and Technology.
Career: Prior to joining *Orrick*, was a partner at *Jackson, Tufts, Cole & Black, LLP* from 1987-95; served on the firm's Executive Committee. Prior to that, was a partner at *Reed, Elliott, Creech, Roth, & Mcmahon* from 1980-87. Frequently lectures on trial practice and computer law issues for such organisations as the Bar Association of San Francisco, the Santa Clara County Bar Association, Santa Clara University's Computer Law Conference, the Hastings Centre for Trial and Apellate Advocacy, and the Intellectual Property Inns of Court. Serves as a judge pro tem for the Santa Clara County Superior Court.
Personal: Attended Santa Clara University, earning a JD cum laude in 1976 and a BSc.

McMENAMIN, J. Robert
McDermott, Will & Emery, Chicago
+1 312 372 2000
rmemenamin@mwe.com
Recommended in Banking & Finance
Specialisation: Partner in the corporate department of *McDermott, Will & Emery's* Chicago office. Has 25 years' experience in banking, finance, commercial and corporate law. Experience includes project financing, leveraged acquisition financing, capital financing, asset-based lending, subordinated debt and mezzanine financing, EDOP lending, securitisation, credit enhancement, workouts and restructurings, both in the private and public markets.
Prof. Memberships: American Bar Association; The Legal Club; The Law Club and The Economic Club of Chicago. Past chairman of the Advisory Board of Holy Trinity High School.
Career: Received bachelor's degree from the University of Notre Dame in 1968 and graduated from Notre Dame Law School in 1971. Clerked in the US Court of Appeals for the 7th Circuit during 1971-72. Thereafter, practised law at *Mayer, Brown & Platt* until 1989, when joined *McDermott, Will & Emery.*

MEADOWS, Stanley
McDermott, Will & Emery, Chicago
+1 312 372 2000
smeadows@mwe.com
Recommended in Corporate/M&A
Specialisation: Partner in Corporate Department and a member of the firm's Corporate Finance Group. Focuses practice in public and private offering of securities, mergers and acquisitions, joint ventures and corporate restructuring. Has spent considerable time representing acquirers of financially distressed companies and lenders and debtors in negotiating debt restructuring for pharmaceutical, telcom and other technology companies in joint ventures, and insurance and energy companies in acquisitions, debt financing and public offerings. During the last year, has acted for purchasers of European telcom assets, a new pan-European web hosting business and several European manufacturing businesses, together with the associated financings.
Prof. Memberships: Member of the Illinois State Bar and the Florida State Bar.
Career: Admitted to the Illinois Bar in 1970. Received undergraduate degree from the University of Illinois in 1966 and JD from the University of Chicago Law School in 1970.

MEIKLEJOHN, D. Stuart
Sullivan & Cromwell, New York +1 212 558 4000
meiklejohns@sullcrom.com
Recommended in Competition/Anti-trust
Specialisation: Has advised many clients in dealing with the Antitrust Division of the United States Department of Justice, the Federal Trade Commission and the European Commission in respect of merger transactions that might be thought to raise antitrust issues, as well as matters involving potential criminal and civil liability. Has also represented clients in connection with the defense of such claims. Clients represented in this area have included Algroup, Alumax, AMAX, Amersham, BASF, BBA, Carnation, Compagnie Generale d'Investissements et Participations, DeLaRue, Eisai, Global Industrial Technologies, Hoechst, Imasco and certain of its subsidiaries, Internorth, Mallinckrodt, Microsoft, Solvay and certain of its subsidiaries and affiliates, TI Group and Upjohn. In addition to antitrust matters of this kind, advises clients in a full range of commercial litigation matters, in judicial proceedings, investigations by federal and state authorities, arbitration proceedings, and other forms of dispute resolution.
Prof. Memberships: American Bar Association; New York State Bar Association; Association of the Bar of the City of New York.
Career: Joined *Sullivan & Cromwell* in 1975. Partner since 1983.
Personal: Born 1950 in Chicago, Illinois. Graduate of Harvard College (AB, 1971) and Harvard Law School (JD, 1975). Director and Regional Vice Chairman, Lawyer's Committee for Civil Rights Under Law; Chairman, The Legal Aid Society; Chairman, Union Settlement Association.

MENDELSON, Alan C.
Latham & Watkins, Menlo Park +1 650 463 4693
alan.mendelson@lw.com
Recommended in Communications: IT
Specialisation: Partner in Corporate Department. Represents emerging and public growth companies, handling venture capital, private and public financings, mergers and acquisitions and strategic collaborations. Experienced in management issues. Serves as the corporate secretary for many public and private companies. Serves on the board of directors of Isis Pharmaceuticals, Axys Pharmaceuticals, Aviron, iScribe and US SEARCH.com. Served as Acting General Counsel of Cadence Design Systems and Amgen.
Publications: Spoken frequently on topics related to strategic alliances, financing strategies, and clinical and regulatory disclosure issues.
Career: Joined *Latham & Watkins* in May 2000. Previously a partner at *Cooley Godward LLP.*
Personal: JD Harvard University, 1973, cum laude. AB University of California, Berkeley, 1969, Phi Beta Kappa.

U

U

MESTRES Jr., Ricardo A.
Sullivan & Cromwell, New York +1 212 558 4000
mestresr@sullcrom.com
Recommended in Capital Markets: Debt & Equity
Specialisation: Practice consists principally of advising United States and non-U.S. issuers and their financial advisors in connection with merger and acquisition and corporate restructuring transactions and public offerings and private placements of equity and debt securities. Extensive securities experience includes offerings registered under the United States Securities Act of 1933 and offerings exempt from registration under Rule 144A and Regulation S of that Act. A member of the firm's Mergers and Acquisitions Group and in that capacity has advised companies and their financial advisors in acquisition and disposition matters and in preparation for and responses to unsolicited acquisition proposals.
Prof. Memberships: American Bar Association; American Law Institute; Association of the Bar of the City of New York (former member: Securities Regulation Committee; Corporation Law Committee; State Legislation Committee); New York State Bar Association; American Law Institute; Council on Foreign Relations.
Career: Joined *Sullivan & Cromwell* in 1961; partner since 1968. Chairman of the firm, 1995-2000.
Personal: Born 1933 in New York, New York. Graduate of Princeton University (AB, 1955) and Harvard Law School (LLB, 1961). Served in the United States Navy, 1955-58.

MEYERS, Michael
Orrick, Herrington & Sutcliffe, New York +1 212 506 5000
mmeyers@orrick.com
Recommended in Project Finance
Specialisation: Expert in infrastructure project development and finance, focusing on developers, lenders and equity investors in power, telecommunications, industrial and other infrastructure projects. Expertise includes both US domestic and international projects. Recent significant projects include representation of participants in US electric industry restructuring; representation of a multinational corporation in restructuring its power generation business worldwide; representation of the sellers of three power projects in Colombia; and representation of developers of power projects in Spain and Greece.
Prof. Memberships: New York, California and District of Columbia Bars.
Career: Florida State University, BS summa cum laude 1976. Stanford Law School, JD 1979. *Graham & James*, associate and partner 1979-1993. *Orrick Herrington & Sutcliffe*, partner 1993-present.

MILLARD, John A.
Shearman & Sterling, New York +1 212 848 7028
jmillard@shearman.com
Recommended in Banking & Finance
Specialisation: Partner in *Shearman & Sterling*'s Project Development and Finance Group. Broad-based practice, including oil and gas, public and private finance, debt and equity offerings of corporations, bank investment transactions and leveraged buyouts. Has worked extensively in Latin American as well as in the United States, including representation of issuers, borrowers and financial institutions in privatisations, project financings, bank financings, SEC-registered and Rule 144A/Regulation S debt and equity offerings and merger and acquisition transactions. Among the non-financial clients represented generally in Latin America are Perez Companc Family Group, MetroGas S.A. and Mastellone Hermanos S.A. Also represented numerous non-Latin American issuers, borrowers and commercial and investment banks, including Deere & Company, Goldman, Sachs & Co., Morgan Stanley Dean Witter, CS First Boston, Saloman Brothers, Inc., Lehman Brothers Inc., Citibank, N.A. and Bank of America, N.A.
Prof. Memberships: Admitted to the New York Bar.
Career: Joined the firm in 1967 and became a partner in 1976.
Personal: Graduated from Harvard Law School (LLB, 1967) and Harvard University (AB, 1963). Born in Buenos Aires, Argentina.

MILLS, Philip
Davis Polk & Wardwell, New York +1 212 450 4000
Recommended in Corporate/M&A

MILLSTEIN, Julian
Brown Raysman and Millstein Felder & Steiner LLP, New York +1 212 944 1515
Recommended in Communications: Transactional (IT)

MISROCK, Leslie
Pennie & Edmonds, New York +1 212 790 9090
Recommended in Intellectual Property

MITCHELL, David
Cadwalader, Wickersham & Taft, New York +1 212 504 6000
david.mitchell@cwt.com
Recommended in Capital Markets: Derivatives
Specialisation: Corporate partner in the New York office concentrating on futures and securities regulatory matters, including OTC derivatives, and related transactional work. Works with clients in the financial services industry on a wide range of regulatory and compliance issues, derivatives-related matters, and on structuring and documenting new financial products and trading systems. Assists clients in developing and implementing internal policies and procedures to control their derivatives trading activities and to conduct reviews of the adequacy of internal controls and supervision. Advises clients on structuring and documenting new product offerings to meet business and investment objectives and to comply with applicable legal and regulatory requirements. Speaks regularly before industry and professional groups on matters of current interest in the area of futures regulation, OTC derivatives, and novel financial products.
Publications: Author of numerous articles, including 'Demutualization of Futures Exchanges' (Futures & Derivatives Law Report, March 2000) with Edmund R. Schroeder; 'The New Part 4 Rules – A Step in the Right Direction, But Unanswered Questions Remain' (The Futures International Law Letter, September/October 1995) with James J. Hill; 'CFTC Exemptions For Swap Agreements and Hybrid Instruments' (The Review of Banking & Financial Services, May 5, 1993) with Mark W. Saks; 'Investment Advisers Act Issues For Commodity Trading Advisors' (The Review of Securities & Commodities Regulation, December 9, 1992) with Scott E. Willoughby; a chapter on 'Commodity Price Exposure Management' in The Handbook of Currency and Interest Rate Risk Management, with Thomas A. Russo (1990).
Career: BA, (summa cum laude, Phi Beta Kappa) City College (1976); JD, (magna cum laude) New York Law School (1979), member of the Law Review; LLM, New York University School of Law (1980). Admitted 1980, New York; Commodity Futures Trading Commission, Division of Trading and Markets, Office of the Chief Counsel (1980-1983).

MOORE, Charles
Akin, Gump, Strauss, Hauer & Feld LLP, Houston +1 713 220 5800
Recommended in Energy & Natural Resources

MOORE, Harold
Skadden, Arps, Slate, Meagher & Flom LLP, New York +1 212 735 3000
Recommended in Project Finance

MOORE, Robert
Miller & Chevalier, Washington DC +1 202 626 5800
Recommended in Tax

MORGAN, Charles
Skadden, Arps, Slate, Meagher & Flom LLP, New York +1 212 735 2470
cmorgan@skadden.com
Recommended in Tax: Financial Products
Specialisation: Partner, New York. Financial products and international tax matters.
Prof. Memberships: Admitted in New York and California; Certified Public Accountant; Executive Committee Member, NY State Bar Association Tax Section (1986-Present).
Career: LLM, NY University, 1981; JD, Pepperdine University, 1977; BS, Wharton School, University of Pennsylvania, 1972; Price Waterhouse, concentrating in international tax; Associate Chief Counsel, Internal Revenue Service(1984-1986); Special Assistant to the Commissioner of the Internal Revenue Service (1982-1984); joined *Skadden, Arps* in April 1986.

MORISON, Frank
Davis Polk & Wardwell, New York +1 212 450 4000
Recommended in Capital Markets: Debt & Equity

MORPHY, James C.
Sullivan & Cromwell, New York +1 212 558 4000
morphyj@sullcrom.com
Recommended in Corporate/M&A
Specialisation: Provides mergers and acquisitions advice for a wide variety of transactions, including friendly and hostile acquisitions, representing buyers, sellers and financial advisors. Recent transactions include: acquisition of Spear, Leeds & Kellogg by Goldman Sachs; merger of PaineWebber Group with UBS; acquisition of Sanford Bernstein by Alliance Capital; Hershey Foods Corporation in asset acquisition from Nabisco; Kana Communications/Silknet

Software merger; merger of Global Industrial Technologies with RHI AG; Union Camp merger with International Paper; United Healthcare in its efforts to acquire Humana, Inc.; agreement to acquire American Bankers Insurance Group by AIG; Hoechst AG in its acquisition of Celanese Corporation; representation of the Special Committee of Western National in merger with American General; acquisition of Tecnol Products by Kimberly Clark; Union Carbide hostile takeover defense; acquisition of Nellcor Puritan Bennett by Mallinckrodt; ITT Industries/Goulds Pumps merger; sale by Inco Limited of Inco Alloys International; Target Therapeutics acquisition by Boston Scientific; Wallace Computer defense against Moore Corporation; AIG's acquisition of International Lease Finance Corp. and Greater New York Savings Bank merger with Astoria Financial.
Prof. Memberships: American Bar Association; Association of the Bar of the City of New York.
Publications: Contributing author to three-volume treatise, 'New York and Delaware Business Entities: Choice, Formation, Operation, Financing and Acquisitions' (West Publishing).
Career: Joined *Sullivan & Cromwell* in 1979. Partner since 1986. Managing Partner, Mergers & Acquisitions Group.
Personal: Born in Pittsburgh, Pennsylvania. Graduate of Harvard College (BA, Phi Beta Kappa, 1976) and Harvard Law School (JD, 1979). Board of Trustees, Greenwich Academy; Board of Governors, Wianno Club.

MORTIMER, Peter
Milbank, Tweed, Hadley & McCloy, New York +1 212 530 5000
Recommended in Banking & Finance

MROZEK, Therese
Brobeck Phleger & Harrison, Palo Alto +1 650 424 0160
Recommended in Communications: IT

MULANEY, Charles
Skadden, Arps, Slate, Meagher & Flom LLP, Chicago +1 312 407 0700
Recommended in Corporate/M&A

MUMMERY, Dan
Milbank, Tweed, Hadley & McCloy, New York +1 212 530 5000
Recommended in Communications: Transactional (IT)

MURRAY, Gregory
Winston & Strawn, Chicago +1 312 558 5600 gmurray@winston.com
Recommended in Banking & Finance
Specialisation: Partner in the Corporate Department. Concentration in syndicated leveraged finance representing numerous prominent U.S. and foreign lending institutions in a variety of senior and subordinated credit facilities, cross-border facilities and structured finance transactions. Extensive experience in structuring multi-tiered acquisition and tender facilities. In recent years has represented agent bank in financings aggregating in excess of US$40 billion.
Career: Joined *Winston & Strawn* as an associate in 1974. Elected as partner in 1980. Member of firm executive committee.

NAEVE, Clifford
Skadden, Arps, Slate, Meagher & Flom LLP, Washington DC +1 202 371 7000
Recommended in Energy & Natural Resources

NECKLES, Peter
Skadden, Arps, Slate, Meagher & Flom LLP, New York +1 212 735 3000
Recommended in Banking & Finance

NELSON, William
McKee Nelson Ernst & Young, Washington DC +1 202 775 8582
wnelson@mneylaw.com
Recommended in Tax
Specialisation: Practice areas: Taxation, tax controversy. Co-founder of *McKee Nelson, Ernst & Young* LLP and a member of the Tax Group.
Publications: Co-author of the two-volume treatise Federal Taxation of Partnerships and Partners (Warren, Gorham & Lamont, 3rd edition, 1997), and also co-authored Federal Taxation of Partnerships and Partners: Structuring and Drafting Agreements (Warren, Gorham & Lamont, 2nd edition, 1993). Written articles on tax law for numerous journals, including The Tax Law Review, Taxes, and the Virginia Law Review.
Career: Previously been a tax partner in *King & Spalding's* Atlanta office, joining the firm in 1972. From 1986-1988, served as Chief Counsel for the Internal Revenue Service, returning to *King & Spalding* at the end of appointment. Frequent lecturer at various tax institutes, including the New York University Tax Institute, the University of Southern California Tax Institute, the University of Chicago Tax Institute, the University of Texas Tax Institute, the Southern Federal Tax Institute, the New England Tax Institute, the Tax Executives Institute, the American Law Institute/American Bar Association, and the Practicing Law Institute. Is a member of the American College of Tax Counsel. Received a JD from the University of Virginia School of Law in 1972, and was Editor-in-Chief of the Virginia Law Review and was named to the Order of the Coif. Graduated from Mississippi State University with highest honors in 1969.

NEUHAUS, Joseph
Sullivan & Cromwell, New York +1 212 558 4000 neuhausj@sullcrom.com.
Recommended in Arbitration (International)
Specialisation: Practice focuses on international commercial litigation in arbitral and court settings. Recent work includes antitrust, patent, and other intellectual property disputes.
Prof. Memberships: Program Chair, Institute for Transnational Arbitration; American Society of International Law; Association of the Bar of the City of New York.
Publications: Co-author of 'A Guide to the UNITRAL Model Law on International Commercial Arbitration: Legislative History and Commentary' (Kluwer, 1989).
Career: Judical clerkship for Justice Lewis F. Powell, Jr. of U.S. Supreme Court and for the Iran-United States Claims Tribunal. Joined *Sullivan & Cromwell* in 1987. Partner since 1992.
Personal: Born in Glen Ridge, New Jersey. Graduate of Dartmouth College (BA, 1979) and Columbia University (JD, 1982).

NEUNER, Robert
Baker Botts LLP, New York +1 212 408 2552 robert.neuner@bakerbotts.com
Recommended in Intellectual Property
Specialisation: Patent lawyer by training. Has tried cases throughout the United States, primarily to juries, and is admitted to practice and has argued appeals in the Federal Circuit and in many of the regional US courts of appeals.
Publications: For ten years wrote a regular column on patent and trademark law for The New York Law Journal.
Career: Lectured and written extensively on the trial and appeal of intellectual property cases, is currently president-elect of the New York Intellectual Property Law Association, and has been actively involved in other bar associations.
Personal: Earned BS in electrical engineering from Manhattan College in 1960, and JD from Fordham University in 1965.

NEWBORN, Steve A.
Clifford Chance Rogers & Wells LLP, Washington DC +1 202 434 0700
Recommended in Competition/Anti-trust

NEWMAN, Lawrence W.
Baker & McKenzie, New York +1 212 751 5700 lawrence.w.newman@bakernet.com
Recommended in Arbitration (International)
Specialisation: Partner in Litigation Department of New York office. Areas of work are litigation in the United States of transnational commercial disputes and international commercial arbitration, to a great extent in matters involving foreign languages (French, Spanish, Portuguese) and law. Lead attorney for BellSouth International in an arbitration (1994-1999) that resulted in an award of $19.5 million against a French telecommunications company on the basis of fraudulent concealment of information in the sale of shares in a cellular telephone company. Was also lead attorney in arbitration between U.S. and Mexican companies in which client obtained an award based on breach of contract and fraud.
Prof. Memberships: Member of various bar associations; a founder and former Chairman of the United States Iranian Claimants Committee (USICC), the national organisation of U.S. businesses with claims arising out of the Iranian revolution.
Publications: Co-author of 'Litigating International Disputes' (West Group 1996) 'The Practice of International Litigation' (Juris Publishing, 2d. Ed. 1999); general editor of a series of books on international litigation, including 'Enforcement of Foreign Judgments' and 'Attachment of Assets'. Since 1982 the author of column in the New York Law Journal 'International Litigation'.
Career: Member of the bar since 1961. Attorney, U.S. Securities & Exchange Commission's Special Study of Securities Markets, 1961-1963; Assistant

U

U.S. Attorney, Southern District of New York, 1964-1969. Associate and Partner, *Baker & McKenzie* New York office 1969 to present.
Personal: Born July 1935. Harvard College 1957; Harvard Law School 1960. Leisure interests include writing, publishing, travel and golf.

NOCCO, Frank
Weil, Gotshal & Manges, New York
+1 212 310 8000
frank.nocco@weil.com
Recommended in Capital Markets: Securitisation
Specialisation: Partner in the New York office of *Weil, Gotshal & Manges.* Co-head of the Structured Finance/Derivatives Group and works closely with counterparts in London and in other offices worldwide. Specialises in representing issuers, underwriters, credit enhancers and trustees in corporate and structured securities offerings, both in the U.S. and abroad. Has participated in the securitisation of auto loans, commercial loans, student loans, franchisee loans, mortgage loans, and equipment loans, credit card receivables (both MasterCard/Visa and private label), trade receivables, equipment and vehicle leases, high-yield and other non-conventional assets, such as royalty receivables, oil and gas production payments, synthetic securities and various other derivative products, insurance premium finance contracts and intellectual property. Experienced in structuring single-seller and multi-seller commercial paper vehicles, owner trusts, master trusts, grantor trusts, REMIC's and off-shore and domestic special purpose corporation vehicles that can issue a variety of debt and equity securities, including collateralised loan obligations and collateralised bond obligations. Also has experience with other kinds of securities work such as initial public offerings and subordinated debt offerings.

NORTON, Floyd
Morgan, Lewis & Bockius LLP, Washington DC
+1 202 467 7000
Recommended in Energy & Natural Resources

NOURSE, David A.
Nourse & Bowles LLP, New York +1 212 952 6200
Recommended in Shipping: Litigation

NUSBAUM, Jack
Willkie Farr & Gallagher, New York
+1 212 728 8000
jnusbaum@willkie.com
Recommended in Corporate/M&A, Private Equity: Buyouts
Specialisation: Chairman of the Firm and leads its Mergers and Acquisition practice group. In addition to mergers and acquisition, main focus includes Internal Investigations, Corporate Governance and fiduciary duties. Extensive experience has involved many of the most notable US and cross-border transactions of the past two decades including: the recently completed multi-billion dollar merger between Veritas Software, Seagate Technology and Silver Lake Partners; the merger of Nasdaq with the American Stock Exchange; the leveraged buyout of RJR Nabisco; the acquisition of McCaw Cellular Communications by AT&T; the acquisition of Magma Copper by Broken Hill Proprietary Limited; various going private transactions and various restructurings. Headed the team responsible for the 1998 Cendant Report, the internal investigation of Cendant Corporation on behalf of its Audit Committee.
Prof. Memberships: New York State and American Bar Association; the Association of the Bar of the City of New York.
Career: Admitted in 1965, has spent entire career with *Willkie Farr & Gallagher,* becoming a Partner in 1971, Co-Chairman of the firm in 1988 and sole Chairman in 1995. Director of publicly held corporations including WR Berkley Corporation, Pioneer Companies Inc, Prime Hospitality Corp, Strategic Distribution Inc., Neuberger Berman Inc. and the Topps Company Inc; Trustee of the Robert Steel Foundation, Prep for Prep and the Joseph Collins Foundation.
Personal: Graduate of the Wharton School of the University of Pennsylvania and of Columbia Law School.

NUSSBAUM, Andrew
Wachtell, Lipton, Rosen & Katz, New York
+1 212 403 1000
Recommended in Corporate/M&A

O'BRIEN, Judith
Wilson, Sonsini, Goodrich & Rosati, Palo Alto
+1 650 493 9300
Recommended in Communications: IT

O'LEARY, Michael
Andrews & Kurth, Houston +1 713 220 4200
moleary@akllp.com
Recommended in Corporate/M&A
Specialisation: Practice includes expertise in all aspects of corporate transactions including representation of public and private companies and investment in banking firms; formation of partnerships and joint ventures; public offerings and private placements of equity and debt; publicly traded limited partnerships; spin-offs; mergers, acquisitions and dispositions (by tender offer, exchange offer and otherwise) of corporations, divisions of corporations and other entities; redemptions and exchanges of preferred equity and debt; advising clients on changes of control and strategic alliances; structuring 'going private' transactions; defensive techniques; director fiduciary duties; advising special board committees; restructurings; liquidisations; project financings (including partnership and limited partnership financings); and international joint ventures and alliances. Has particular experience in energy and oilfield service companies, pipeline transportation, staff leasings, royalty trusts and forest products companies.
Prof. Memberships: The State Bar of Texas, 1980; Houston Bar Association.
Personal: Graduated from the University of Alabama (BS, Finance, cum laude, 1977) and received law degree from the Bates College of Law at the University of Houston (JD with honors, 1980).

O'NEILL, Brian
LeBoeuf, Lamb, Greene & MacRae, LLP, Washington DC +1 202 986 8000
boneill@llgm.com
Recommended in Energy & Natural Resources
Specialisation: Managing Partner and Head of the Energy law practice group in the Washington, D.C. office. Specialises in the representation of oil and natural gas pipeline companies, as well as electric companies, in regulatory matters before the Department of Energy, the Federal Energy Regulatory Commission and the federal courts. Also represents intrastate pipelines and other oil and gas entities as well as electric utilities and industrial clients with respect to corporate and regulatory matters. Provides advice to international clients as to energy privatisation and regulatory matters. Clients include electric utilities, several major interstate natural gas pipelines and one of the largest domestic oil pipelines. Has litigated regulatory proceedings involving complex ratemaking issues, new multi-million dollar construction projects and transportation and supply contract matters.
Prof. Memberships: American Bar Association (Council to the Section of Public Utility, Communications and Transportation Law); Federal Energy Bar Association (Chairman of Committees); the Florida Bar (Administrative Law Committee); and the District of Columbia Bar. Admitted to practice in the United States Courts of Appeals for the District of Columbia Circuit, Fifth Circuit, Tenth Circuit and Eleventh Circuit.
Career: A noted expert in energy law. Has published numerous papers and energy publications including the 'Energy Law Journal' and the 'Natural Gas Journal'. Contributing author for the Treatise 'Energy Law and Transactions', and has participated as a Faculty Member in numerous industry seminars.
Personal: Born 21 February 1946. Attended The Florida State University (BA and Juris Doctorate Degree). Serves on the Board of Visitors for The Florida State University College of Law and on the Board of Trustees (past Chairman) of the Academy of the Holy Cross. Interests include golf. Member of Congressional Country Club and lives in Bethesda, Maryland.

O'SULLIVAN, John
Chadbourne & Parke LLP, Washington DC
+1 202 974 5600
Recommended in Energy & Natural Resources

OLIVIER, Jeanne C.
Shearman & Sterling, New York +1 212 848 4000
jolivier@shearman.com
Recommended in Project Finance
Specialisation: Head of the Project Development and Finance Group. Has broad experience in both international and domestic financings, including acquisition financings, asset-based financings, lease financings, project financings, privatisations and sovereign and corporate restructurings. Advises sponsors and lenders in complex political risk insurance matters. Also has extensive experience in financings in the telecommunications industry and in restructurings in Latin America.
Prof. Memberships: Bars of the State of New York and the State of Louisiana.
Career: Joined *Shearman & Sterling* in 1980 and became a Partner in 1988. Is on the University of Pennsylvania Law School Board of Overseers, the Associates Board of Directors of Tulane University, the National Board of Boys Hope Girls Hope and the

Advisory Council of the International Executive Services Corps; also a former Executive Director (1981-83) of the Thomas J. Watson Foundation. Regular lecturer on 'Financing Telecommunications Projects' at the Practising Law Institute Seminar: 'Project Financing: Building Infrastructure Projects in Developing Markets' and co-authored Latin Finance Supplement, 'Project Finance in Latin America', 'Foreign Investment Regulations in Brazil, Colombia and Peru'.
Personal: Born 7 March 1953. Educated at Newcomb College of Tulane University, BA, 1975 and the University of Pennsylvania Law School, JD, 1979.

OLSON, Gary
Latham & Watkins, Los Angeles +1 213 891 8366
gary.olson@lw.com
Recommended in Corporate/M&A
Specialisation: Partner in Corporate Department. Extensive experience in mergers and acquisitions. Has expertise in representing issuers and underwriters in corporate finance transactions. Represented the Independent Committee for Board of Directors of WellPoint Health Networks in a US$1.5 billion recapitalisation transaction. Recent clients include Fortune 500 companies, such as AutoZone, Amgen, Hughes Electronics, Lehman Bros. and Sempra Energy. Represented underwriters in numerous securities offerings for Qualcomm, The Times Mirror Company and WellPoint Health Networks.
Prof. Memberships: Member of the American Bar Association, 1933 Act Subcommittee of the Business Law Section.
Career: Chair of the firm's global Corporate Department, 1989-96.
Personal: JD University of Kansas, 1968, Order of the Coif, editor-in-chief of the University of Kansas Law Review. BS Kansas State College, 1965.

OOSTERHUIS, Paul
Skadden, Arps, Slate, Meagher & Flom LLP, Washington DC +1 202 371 7000
poosterh@skadden.com
Recommended in Tax
Specialisation: Partner, Washington DC. International and Corporate Tax Law. Represents clients on a wide range of international and domestic tax matters with experience in international acquisitions, dispositions and joint venture transactions. Also represents US and non-US multinational companies in cross-border financing arrangements and non-transactional international tax planning, in cross-border acquisitions. Has represented: NTL, Global Crossing, Daimler-Benz, MCI (now MCI WorldCom), Rhone-Poulenc Rorer, and Hoescht, among others. Has represented clients such as Hewlett Packard, DuPont, 3M and Cooper Industries with respect to spin-offs of businesses in various countries (UK, Italy, Canada and France.) Structured joint venture transactions between corporations based in the US, Japan, Germany, France, the UK and Canada. Cross-border financing experience includes investments by US companies in Canada, the UK, France, Germany, Japan and Australia, as well as investments by French, German, UK, Japanese and Canadian companies in US businesses. Represents clients before the US Tax Court, the Treasury Department, the Internal Revenue Service and the Congress on tax policy matters and technical issues. Frequent lecturer before the Tax Executives Institute and the America Bar Association, and writes on a variety of tax-related topics for professional publications.
Career: JD, Harvard University, 1973 (cum laude); BA, Brown University, 1969 (magna cum laude); Legislation Attorney, Joint Committee on Taxation, US Congress (1973-1976); Legislation Counsel, Joint Committee on Taxation, US Congress (1977-1978); taught International Tax as an Adjunct Professor of Law, Georgetown University Law Center (1977-1983).

OSBORN, John
Skadden, Arps, Slate, Meagher & Flom LLP, New York +1 212 735 3000
Recommended in Capital Markets: Derivatives

OSBORNE, John
Watson, Farley & Williams, New York
+1 212 922 2200
josborne@wfw.com
Recommended in Shipping: Finance
Specialisation: Partner and Head of New York office. Primarily involved with representation of banks and other institutional lenders in connection with secured, unsecured and lease financing of maritime and other assets and corporations engaged in shipping and other industries; representation of borrowers in connection with the acquisition and financing of vessels and other assets. Co-author of 'Targeting the Capital Markets', 'Lloyd's Shipping Economist – Capital for Shipping' (1994).
Prof. Memberships: Maritime finance committee, Maritime Law Association of the United States.
Career: Associate *Milbank, Tweed, Hadley & McCloy* 1968-77; associate *Burlingham Underwood & Lord* 1977-78; partner 1979-90; partner *Watson, Farley & Williams* 1990 to date.
Personal: Born 1941. Resides in Salisbury, Connecticut. Educated Williams College, Williamstown, Mass (1963 BA); University of Michigan (1968 JD).

OSBORNE, Robert Stephen
Kirkland & Ellis, Chicago +1 312 861 2000
Recommended in Corporate/M&A

OXFORD, Patrick
Bracewell & Patterson LLP, Houston
+1 713 223 2900
Recommended in Corporate/M&A

PAINTER, Robin
Testa, Hurwitz & Thibeault LLP, Boston
+1 617 248 7000
Recommended in Private Equity: Fund Formation

PALMA, Laura
Simpson Thacher & Bartlett, New York
+1 212 455 2000
l_palma@stblaw.com
Recommended in Capital Markets: Securitisation
Specialisation: A partner at *Simpson Thacher & Bartlett* and a member of the Firm's Corporate Department. Concentrates on general corporate finance matters, with a particular focus on the representation of sponsors, underwriters, liquidity providers and credit enhancement providers in a variety of structured finance transactions, including rental car fleet financing, auto, truck and equipment loan and lease securitisations, CBO/CLO offerings and other receivable financings.
Prof. Memberships: Bar Association of the City of New York.
Career: A partner at the firm since 1995. Received a BA magna cum laude in 1980 from Dartmouth College, and was elected to Phi Beta Kappa. Received a JD in 1983 from Columbia University Law School.

PARÉ, Jay
Nourse & Bowles LLP, New York +1 212 952 6200
Recommended in Shipping: Litigation

PARK, William W.
William W. Park – Sole Practitioner, Boston
+1 617 353 3149
wwpark@bu.edu
Recommended in Arbitration (International)
Specialisation: Chairman, sole arbitrator and party-nominated arbitrator in ICC, AAA,LCIA, UNCITRAL and IACAC arbitrations, concerning inter alia joint ventures, acquisitions, construction, financial transactions, biotech licenses, equipment supply, letters of credit, insurance, oil & gas, precious metals, telecommunications, sales, agency and distribution contracts. Arbitrator, Claims Resolution Tribunal for Dormant Accounts in Switzerland (Volcker Tribunal).
Prof. Memberships: Vice President, London Court of International Arbitration. Chartered Arbitrator. Admitted to Bar, Massachusetts (1972) and DC (1980).
Publications: Published works include 'International Chamber of Commerce Arbitration' and 'Annotated Guide to the ICC Arbitration Rules' (both co-authored with Craig and Paulsson), 'International Commercial Arbitration' (co-authored with Reisman, Craig and Paulsson), 'International Forum Selection', and 'Arbitration in Finance and Banking'.
Career: Practice in Paris from 1972-79. Since 1979, Professor of Law at Boston University and service as Director of the University's Centre for Banking Law Studies. Counsel *Ropes & Gray*, Boston. Other academic appointments have included Cambridge University, Fletcher School of Law and Diplomacy, Université de Dijon, Geneva's Institut Universitaire de Hautes Etudes Internationales and University of Hong Kong.
Personal: Yale, BA; Columbia, JD; Cambridge, MA Fluent in written and spoken French.

PARKER, Allen
Cravath, Swaine & Moore, New York
+1 212 474 1000
Recommended in Banking & Finance

PATTERSON, Donna
Arnold & Porter, Washington DC +1 202 942 5000
Donna_Patterson@aporter.com
Recommended in Competition/Anti-trust
Specialisation: Partner in the anti-trust and litigation practice groups at *Arnold & Porter*. Has represented numerous clients in FTC and anti-trust divi-

U

U

sion investigations of proposed mergers and acquisitions, in state and federal court anti-trust and complex commercial litigation, and as an anti-trust counselor. Successfully litigated one of the rare full trials on the merits of a merger case, State of New York v. Kraft General Foods, Inc.
Career: From 1997 until August 2000 was Deputy Assistant Attorney General in the anti-trust division of the United States Department of Justice. During that time, supervised the investigations and litigation of dozens of proposed transactions including US v. Lockheed, US v. Primestar, and US v. Aetna. In addition, supervised the Division's Health Care Task Force. Education: Received JD, from Yale Law School in 1981 and BA, from Yale College in 1971.

PEARLSTEIN, Debra J.
Weil, Gotshal & Manges, New York +1 212 310 8000
debra.pearlstein@@weil.com
Recommended in Competition/Anti-trust
Specialisation: New York partner in the trade practices and regulatory law group, concentrating on antitrust and competition law. Work includes acting on major mergers and acquisitions transactions, appearing before competition authorities, and extends to litigation with private and governmental parties. Provides competition law advice to many of the firm's major corporate clients across a full range of industry sectors.

PEASLEE, James
Cleary, Gottlieb, Steen & Hamilton, New York
+1 212 225 2000
Recommended in Tax: Financial Products

PENZER, Michele
Latham & Watkins, New York +1 212 906 1245
michele.penzer@lw.com
Recommended in Project Finance
Specialisation: Partner in the New York office. Primary practice is project development and project financings, acting for project sponsors, banks, underwriters and issuers on projects in the U.S. and internationally. Represented Deutsche Bank, CIBC and Goldman Sachs in the financings of several fiber optic telecommunications systems and colocation facilities. Represented Ras Laffan Liquefied Natural Gas Company Limited in connection with the development and financing of a $3.4 billion liquefied natural gas project in Qatar. Represented various banks and project sponsors in connection with the financings of several power projects.
Prof. Memberships: State Bar of New York, the New York State Bar Association and the American Bar Association.
Personal: JD, Yale University, 1993. AB, Harvard University, 1990.

PFEIFFER, Steven
Fulbright & Jaworski LLP, Washington DC
+1 202 662 0200
Recommended in Energy & Natural Resources

PHILLIPS, Barnet
Skadden, Arps, Slate, Meagher & Flom LLP, New York +1 212 735 3000
bphillip@skadden.com
Recommended in Tax
Specialisation: Partner in Tax Department, specialising in tax aspects of corporate mergers, acquisitions, divestitures, leveraged buyouts, restructuring and recapitalisations and the structuring of business organisations and investment vehicles including Real Estate Investment Trusts, Regulated Investment Companies, investment partnerships and exchange funds. Tax Counsel to MacAndrews & Forbes Holdings Inc. (holding company for Revlon and Cal Fed). Representative transactions include counsel to Petrie Stores in connection with its acquisition by Toys 'R' Us; to Entergy in its amalgamations with Gulf States and Florida Power and Light; and to the consortium of investors in the bail-out and liquidation of Long-Term Capital. Contributor to Practicing Law Institute 'Real Estate Tax Forum' and 'Tax Stategies for Corporate Acquisitions, Dispositions, Spin-Offs, Joint Ventures, Financings, Reorganisations and Restructurings'.
Prof. Memberships: American Bar Association, Tax Section. National Association of Real Estate Investment Trusts.
Publications: Co-Author 'Structuring Corporate Acquisitions-Tax Aspects', Tax Management Inc., (1999).
Career: New York State Bar admission 1974. Joined *Skadden, Arps, Slate, Meagher & Flom* in 1977, becoming a partner in 1981.
Personal: Born July 5, 1948. Graduated Yale University 1970 (BA French), received JD from Fordham Law School in 1973 and LLM (Tax) from New York University in 1977. Chairman, Board of Consultants, Portsmouth Abbey School. Interests include skiing, opera, triathlon.

PICKENS, Scott
Schiff Hardin & Waite, Chicago +1 312 258 5500
Recommended in Banking & Finance

PIERCE, Morton A.
Dewey Ballantine LLP, New York +1 212 259 6640
mpierce@deweyballantine.com
Recommended in Corporate/M&A
Specialisation: Mergers and Acquisitions; Securities Law. Represented acquirors, targets, investment bankers and investors in numerous acquisitions, including: GrandMet/Guinness, Disney/Capital Cities, Turner Broadcasting System Inc/Time Warner Inc., Telecommunications Inc/Liberty Media Corporation, Luxottica/US Shoe, Eridania/American Maize, Columbia-HCA/Healthrust, Healthtrust Inc./EPIC Holdings, Harsco/Multi Serv NV., Aon/Frank B Hall, Icahn/TWA, Union Pacific Corporation/USPCI, Inc., Rhone-Poulenc/Rorer, Mitshubiushi, Estate/Rockerfeller Group Inc., Procodia/Pharmicia, American Express/Shearson and Merrill Lynch/Kikkoman/Del Monte. Participated in numerous debt and equity offerings both domestic and international, including recent offerings for Mitsubishi Estate Company Limited, Sony and Columbia HCA.
Prof. Memberships: American Bar Association: Chairman, Subcommittee on International Securities Matters (1985 - 1991); Advisory Committee to Federal Regulation of Securities Committee (1991-); Task Force on Review of the Federal Securities Laws (1991-). Association of the Bar of the City of New York: Member, Securities Law Committee (1988-1991) and Chairman, Subcommittee on Securities and Exchange Commission Enforcement Matters (1990 - 1991).
Career: JD University of Pennsylvania Law School, 1974; Oxford University, 1974-75 BA Yale University 1970. Partner, *Dewey Ballantine*, since 1986. Chairman, Mergers and Acquisitions Group; member of Managment Committee.

PISANO, Vince
Skadden, Arps, Slate, Meagher & Flom LLP, New York +1 212 735 3000
Recommended in Capital Markets: Debt & Equity

PODOLSKY, Andrea
Cleary, Gottlieb, Steen & Hamilton, New York
+1 212 225 2000
Recommended in Capital Markets: Securitisation

POLLACK, Martin
Weil, Gotshal & Manges, New York
+1 212 310 8000
martin.pollack@weil.com
Recommended in Tax
Specialisation: Co-Head, Tax Department. Federal income tax aspects of partnerships and joint ventures; federal income tax aspects of the restructuring of troubled companies.
Prof. Memberships: New York State Bar Association Tax Section; New York City Bar Association.
Publications: Co-Author of 'Partnership Buy/Sell Agreements' (Little Brown 1995).
Career: Former Adjunct Associate Professor of Tax Law at New York University School of Law; Member of the Advisory Board of Equipment Leasing Newsletter; Advisory Board of Tax Management.
Personal: John Hopkins University (BA, MA); University of Pennsylvania Law School (JD); New York University School of Law (LLM).

POSTER, Bob
Gilmartin, Poster & Shafto, New York
+1 212 425 3220
Recommended in Shipping: Finance

POWERS, Matthew D.
Weil, Gotshal & Manges, Silicon Valley
+1 650 926 6219
matthew.powers@weil.com
Recommended in Intellectual Property
Specialisation: Managing Partner of the firm's Silicon Valley office and serves on the Management Committee of the firm as a whole. Specialises in intellectual property litigation and counselling worldwide, and is recognised as one of the world's leading trial lawyers for intellectual property disputes. Regularly participates in the largest, most significant patent litigations in several industries, including semiconductors, software, medical devices and biotechnology. Was lead counsel for Cisco Systems in the patent litigation initiated by Lucent (involving over 20 patents), is lead counsel for Perkin Elmer's Applied Biosystems Division and Celera in several patent litigations against Molecular Dynamics and Amersham involving DNA sequencing technology, and for Micron Technology in the patent litigation initiated by Lucent (involving over 10 semiconductor and telecommunications patents), and several

parties in internet/software patent litigations. Was lead trial counsel for Applied Materials in its patent litigations against ASM International, N.V. and Novellus Systems, which resulted in payments to Applied Materials of well over $150 million. Regularly advises clients in Europe and Asia and often directs litigation outside the United States.
Career: JD, Harvard Law School (1982), SB Northwestern University (1979).

PRINCE, Kenneth S.
Shearman & Sterling, New York +1 212 848 4139
kprince@shearman.com
Recommended in Competition/Anti-trust
Specialisation: Practice Group Leader of *Shearman & Sterling's* Anti-trust Group (since 1992). Practice includes counselling in a wide range of industries on the anti-trust implications of mergers and acquisitions, joint ventures, horizontal arrangements among competitors, unilateral conduct by dominant firms, intellectual property licensing agreements, and distribution and pricing arrangements. Maintains an active criminal anti-trust defence practice representing clients in numerous U.S. grand jury investigations alleging Sherman Act violations, including the Vitamins case. Regularly appears on behalf of clients before the United States Department of Justice and the Federal Trade Commission. Representative matters and companies represented include: BASF: joint venture with Shell (polyolefins); Novartis: joint venture with Astra Zeneca to form Syngenta (agricultural chemicals); Ciba Vision: acquisition of Wesley Jessen (contact lens); BASF: acquisition of American Cyanamid (agricultural chemicals); The BOC Group: offer by Air Products and Air Liquid (industrial gases); Sandoz and Ciba-Geigy: merger into Novartis (life sciences); and Cadbury Schweppes acquisition of Dr Pepper/7-Up (consumer goods). European clients who consult on a regular basis include BASF, BOC, Cadbury/Dr Pepper, Corus Group,Lafarge, Lhoist and Novartis.
Prof. Memberships: American Bar Association; Association of the Bar of the City of New York; Bar Association of the State of Massachusetts.
Career: Admitted to Massachusetts Bar in 1975, New York Bar in 1976. Joined *Shearman & Sterling* in 1975, becoming a partner in 1984. Member of the Executive Committee, New York Law Institute 1984-1996.
Personal: Born 28 January 1950. Boston College Law School, JD, magna cum laude, 1975; Editor 'Boston College Law Review'; Order of the Coif. University of Pennsylvania, AB, 1972. Lives in Darien, Connecticut.

PROGER, Phillip A.
Jones, Day, Reavis & Pogue, Washington DC +1 202 879 4668
paproger@jonesday.com
Recommended in Competition/Anti-trust
Specialisation: Senior antitrust partner in the Washington DC Office of *Jones Day*. Focuses on the representation of clients in government antitrust investigations in the United States and internationally, as well as government and private antitrust litigation. Work involves investigations concerning mergers, acquisitions and joint ventures, particularly in the healthcare, retail, chemical, automotive, telecommunication and industrial products industries. Clients for whom representation is publicly known include Aetna, Alcan Aluminum Corporation, American Greetings, Bayer, CIGNA, Cardinal Health, Clear Channel Communications, Diebold, Federated Department Stores, Louisiana-Pacific, Rite Aid and Ultramar Diamond Shamrock.
Prof. Memberships: Fellow of the American Law Institute. Member of the Advisory Board of the Antitrust and Trade Regulation Reporter. Member of the American Bar Association and the International Bar Association.
Publications: Columnist on antitrust matters for The M&A Lawyer. Co-author of 'Antitrust Aspects of Mergers and Acquisitions'.
Career: Chaired the ABA's Section of Antitrust Law from 1998-1999 and is a past chair of that Section's Merger Committee. Chairs *Jones Day's* Government Regulation Group which includes, among other practices, the Antitrust & Trade Regulation Practice. Has testified before the United States Congress, the Federal Trade Commission, and the OECD.

PULEO, Frank
Milbank, Tweed, Hadley & McCloy, New York +1 212 530 5000
Recommended in Banking & Finance

QASIM, Imad I.
Sidley & Austin, Chicago +1 312 853 7094
iqasim@sidley.com
Recommended in Corporate/M&A
Specialisation: Principal practice areas are mergers and acquisitions, technology and e-commerce, corporate finance and international transactions. Played a major role in a number of large public company mergers, and public and private securities offerings. Involved in organisation of large industry consortiums and representing high tech start-ups. Has extensive international experience, including setting up joint ventures and cross-border acquisitions.
Prof. Memberships: Membership: American Bar Association. Bar Admissions: District of Columbia; Illinois; New York.
Personal: Education: Georgetown University (JD, 1982); Hamilton College (AB, 1979, with honors).

QUALE, John
Skadden, Arps, Slate, Meagher & Flom LLP, New York +1 212 735 3000
Recommended in Communications: Regulatory

QUEEN, Eric
Fried, Frank, Harris, Shriver & Jacobson, New York +1 212 859 8000
queener@ffhsj.com
Recommended in Competition/Anti-trust
Specialisation: Antitrust.
Prof. Memberships: ABA, New York Bar Association, Member of the Committee on Antitrust Trade Regulation.
Career: Partner at *Fried Frank, Harris, Shriver & Jacobson* from 1980 to present.
Personal: Columbia University School of Law, JD 1976.

QUINN, Linda C.
Shearman & Sterling, New York +1 212 848 4000
lquinn@shearman.com
Recommended in Capital Markets: Debt & Equity
Specialisation: Partner in *Shearman & Sterling's* Capital Markets Group, advising domestic and international investment banking and corporate clients on capital markets, derivatives and securities law matters.
Prof. Memberships: Serves as Co-Chairman of the American Bar Association's Task Force on Electronic Communication.
Career: Admitted to the bar in New York. Joined *Shearman & Sterling* as a partner in 1996. Spent prior 16 years with the Securities and Exchange Commission, the last 10 as director of the Division of Corporation Finance. Before joining the SEC practised securities law for more than six years and served as law clerk to Judge J. Joseph Smith, US Court of Appeals for the Second Circuit.
Personal: Attended Mount Holyoke College (BA 1969) Phi Beta Kappa and Georgetown University Law Centre (JD 1972).

RADKE, Kirk
Kirkland & Ellis, New York +1 212 446 4800
Recommended in Private Equity: Buyouts, Private Equity: Fund Formation

RAISLER, Kenneth M.
Sullivan & Cromwell, New York +1 212 558 4000
raislerk@sullcrom.com
Recommended in Capital Markets: Derivatives
Specialisation: Heads the Commodities, Futures and Derivatives Group of *Sullivan & Cromwell*, which is responsible for a full range of regulatory, transactional and litigation advice in the commodities, securities and banking areas to its brokerage, investment banking, banking and commercial clients.
Prof. Memberships: American Bar Association (Corporation, Banking & Business Law Section); Association of the Bar of the City of New York (Chairman, Committee on Futures Regulation, 1988-1991).
Career: Judicial Clerk to the Honorable Lee P. Gagliardi, U.S. District Court (Southern District of New York). Served as an Assistant United States Attorney for the District of Columbia, 1977-1982, in the Criminal and Civil Divisions. Joined the Commodity Futures Trading Commission as Deputy General Counsel and served as General Counsel of the Commission from 1983 to 1987. Partner since 1994.
Personal: Born 1951. Graduated from Yale University (BS, 1973) and New York University School of Law (JD, 1976). Admitted to the Bar in New York and Washington DC Member, the Working Group of The Group of Thirty Derivatives Project, 1992-1993; Member, Board of Directors, Futures Industry Association; member, Commodity Futures Trading Commission's Technology Advisory Committee; member, Government Relations Committee, MFA.

REED, Lucy
Freshfields Bruckhaus Deringer, New York +1 212 277 4000
lucy.reed@freshfields.com
Recommended in Arbitration (International)
Specialisation: Member of international dispute resolution and public international law group.

U

REEDER, Robert W.
Sullivan & Cromwell, New York +1 212 558 4000
reederr@sullcrom.com
Recommended in Capital Markets: Derivatives
Specialisation: Experienced in wide array of corporate and securities matters. Recent work has included general corporate advice (including advice as to Section 16 and Rule 144 matters) to public companies such as American International Group, Inc. and The Goldman Sachs Group, Inc. Has advised commercial and investment banks, including Goldman, Sachs & Co., Deutsche Bank Securities Inc., Morgan Stanley & Company, Inc. and J.P. Morgan, on derivative instruments and "restricted" and "control" securities, including securities act registration issues, Section 16 issues and margin and net capital issues. Has acted in many significant initial public offerings, including that of The Goldman Sachs Group, Inc., and advised on numerous unique and complex securities offerings, including the first ever SEC-registered convertible MIPs offering and the first ever registered offering to consumers (The Boston Beer Company). Has acted as designated underwriters' counsel for Corning Incorporated, Delta Airlines, Inc. and XTRA Corporation. Established three AAA-rated structured derivative products companies: Goldman Sachs Mitsui Marine Derivative Products, L.P., GS Financial Products U.S., L.P. (the only derivatives product company to register with the SEC), and GS Financial Products International, L.P.
Prof. Memberships: American Bar Association; Association of the Bar of the City of New York; New York State Bar Association.
Career: Judicial Clerk to the Honorable Anthony J. Celebrezze, U.S. Court of Appeals (6th Circuit),1984-86. Joined *Sullivan & Cromwell* in 1986. Became partner in 1993. Co-Head of firm's Corporate Group and member of firm's Commodities and Derivatives, Broker/Dealer and Executive Compensation and Employee Benefits Groups.
Personal: Born 1960 in Youngstown, Ohio. Graduate of Youngstown State University (BS 1981) and Ohio State University Law School (JD 1984). Director and Treasurer, Lawyers Alliance for New York; Director, Teak Fellowship.

REINHOLD, Richard L.
Willkie Farr & Gallagher, New York
+1 212 728 8000
rreinhold@willkie.com
Recommended in Tax
Specialisation: US taxation, domestic and international.
Prof. Memberships: New York State Bar Association, Tax Section, Executive Committee (Chair of the Executive Committee, 1996-1997).
Publications: 'What is Tax Treaty Abuse? (Is Treaty Shopping an Outdated Concept?)' 53 Tax Lawyer, 663 (2000); 'Section 353(e): How we got here and where we are', 82 Tax Notes, 1485 (1999).

RICH, Frederic C.
Sullivan & Cromwell, New York +1 212 558 4000
richf@sullcrom.com
Recommended in Project Finance
Specialisation: Heads the Global Project Finance Group at Sullivan & Cromwell. Also has extensive experience in international capital markets transactions by foreign sovereigns and companies, and international privatisation transactions. Has represented sponsors of and lenders to large international projects for more than 15 years, including some of the landmark oil and gas, mining and natural resource transactions during the past decade; special emphasis on projects in countries with significant political risk. Key oil and gas project work has included representation of the sponsors of the AIOC Caspian Sea "Mega-Project" which project financed their share of the Early Oil Project and associated Northern and Western Export Route Pipeline capital costs, and is currently representing participants in the financing for Phase I of Full Field Development; the sponsors of Jose Terminal, a BOOT project in Venezuela; and the financing sponsors of Kutubu, the first petroleum development project in Papua New Guinea. Mining and metal assignments have included acting for the sponsors of the first large-scale mining projects in Argentina (Alumbrera), Chile (Escondida), Kyrgyzstan (Kumtor) and Tanzania (Bulyanhulu) and other projects in Australia, Indonesia and Papua New Guinea.
Prof. Memberships: American Bar Association (former Chair, Committee on Privatization); American Society of International Law; International Bar Association.
Publications: 'Getting it Right in Privatization', International Financial Law Review, April 1994; 'Project Finance-Managing Your Political Risk', The Treasurer, September 1990; 'The Legal Regime for a Permanent Olympic Site', 15 N.Y.U. Journal of International Law & Politics 1 (1982).
Career: Joined *Sullivan & Cromwell* in 1981. Elected a Partner of the firm in 1989. Co-Managing Partner of the firm's General Practice (corporate and financial) Group.
Personal: Born 1956. Graduated from Princeton University (AB, 1977), King's College, Cambridge (Keasby Fellow, 1978) and the University of Virginia Law School (JD, 1981). Former term member, the Council on Foreign Relations. Director, Lila Acheson and DeWitt Wallace Fund for the Hudson Highlands, Inc., The Hudson River Foundation, Inc., and Scenic Hudson, Inc.

RICH, R. Bruce
Weil, Gotshal & Manges, New York
+1 212 310 8000
bruce.rich@weil.com.
Recommended in Competition/Anti-trust
Specialisation: Recognised expert in competition/antitrust and intellectual property law, in particular as they relate to the communications industries. Focus of work includes the First Amendment, music licensing, copyright, trademark and antitrust issues and extends to advising clients of the firm such as book, magazine and newspaper publishers, broadcasters, cable television entities as well as trade associations of these entities.

RIEDY, James
McDermott, Will & Emery, Washington DC
+1 202 756 8000
jriedy@mwe.com
Recommended in Tax
Specialisation: Partner in Tax Department. Main area of work includes US federal income tax law applicable to cross-border transactions and investments. Practice encompasses both US multinational investments outside the United States and non-US, multinational investments in the United States. Practice includes consulting on technical tax matters, advising on major corporate acquisitions, corporate internal restructuring and transfer pricing.
Prof. Memberships: Member of Tax Section of the American Bar Association and International Fiscal Association.
Publications: Frequent commentator and lecturer on US international tax issues.
Career: Admitted to the Kansas Bar in 1997; District of Columbia, 1981; and US Supreme Court, 1982. Joined the tax division, appellate section of the United States Department of Justice in 1977; *Lee, Toomey & Kent* from 1981 to 1993; *McDermott, Will & Emery* to the present.
Personal: Born 25 July 1952; juris doctor degree in 1977 from the University of Kansas; master of laws degree in taxation from Georgetown University in 1981.

RILL, James F.
Howrey Simon Arnold & White, Washington DC
+1 202 383 6562
rillj@howrey.com
Recommended in Competition/Anti-trust
Specialisation: Partner in, and co-chair of the firm's Antitrust Practice. One of America's foremost antitrust attorneys; has served as a former head of the Department of Justice's Antitrust Division, as well as a former head of the ABA's antitrust section. During tenure as Assistant Attorney General, negotiated the US-European Union Antitrust Cooperation Agreement of 1991, and issued the first joint FTC and DOJ Horizontal Merger Guidelines of 1992. Was responsible for initiating the largest number of formal announced merger challenges in over a decade, including challenges to major bank mergers and airline asset transactions. Appointed by Attorney General Janet Reno and former Assistant Attorney General Joel Klein to serve as Co-Chair on the U.S. Department of Justice's International Competition Policy Advisory Committee, with a mandate to recommend future policy initiatives to the Department of Justice. Until recently, served as a senior partner in the antitrust group at *Collier Shannon Rill & Scott*, where clients included PepsiCo, Inc., CSX Sealand, Albertson's, BellSouth, American Airlines, BarTech, and GTE Corporation. Since joining *Howrey*, has served as antitrust counsel in matters for the above named firms, as well as for such companies as Merck, CSX Transportation, ConAgra, and Hannaford Bros.
Prof. Memberships: ABA Tri-National NAFTA; Fellow, American Bar Foundation; Vice Chairman, International Business and Industry Advisory Committee, OECD Competition Law and Policy Committee; Chair, U.S. Committee; Vice-Chairman, United States Council for International Business; Editorial Board, Antitrust Bulletin; Advisory Board, Bureau of National Affairs, Antitrust and Trade Regulation Report.
Publications: 'ICPAC's Blueprint for Global Competition Law', Global Competition Review

(April/May 2000). Co-author, 'Corporate Planning in the High-Tech, Global Marketplace: What Role Will Antitrust Enforcement Play?', 12 International Quarterly 2, 333 (2000).

RINALDI, Joseph
Davis Polk & Wardwell, New York +1 212 450 4000
Recommended in Corporate/M&A

RIVKIN, David
Debevoise & Plimpton, New York +1 212 909 6000
Recommended in Arbitration (International)

ROBERTS, Thomas A.
Weil, Gotshal & Manges, New York
+1 212 310 8000
thomas.roberts@weil.com
Recommended in Private Equity: Buyouts
Specialisation: A senior partner in *Weil, Gotshal & Manges'* Corporate Department and a member of the Firm's thirteen-member Management Committee. Also heads the Firm's International Corporate Partners Group. Practice primarily involves domestic and cross border mergers, acquisitions and divestitures, public financings, restructuring and reorganisations, corporate governance, special committee and similar matters. Is one of a handful of lawyers who participated in the creation of the investment techniques commonly utilised in private equity investments. Clients include major foreign and domestic public and private companies, several of the leading private equity funds in the US, and a number of leading investment banks. Clients include AMR Corporation, Hicks, Muse, Tate & Furst, Capital Z Partners, Oakhill Partners, A.M. Best & Company, General Electric Company, Conseco Inc., PennCorp Financial Group, Inc., Swiss Re Corporation, Wasserstein Perella & Co and Lehman Brothers. Transactions include a variety of matters for Hicks, Muse, Tate & Furst, Capital Z and Oakhill Partners, the $3.5 billion merger of Connecticut Mutual with Massachusetts Mutual, the $3.6 billion merger of Transocean Offshore ASA with Sonat and its subsequent merger with Sedco Forex, which is the Schlumberger's offshore contract drilling business and KPMG's abandoned $18 billion merger with Ernst & Young and the restructuring of Penncorp FG and Conseco Inc. Frequent speaker on the topics of disclosure and securities issues, mergers, acquisitions, reorganisations and transactional financing and corporate governance matters.
Personal: BA and JD from Georgetown University where served on the Georgetown Law Journal.

ROBINS, Charles W.
Hutchins, Wheeler & Dittmar, Boston
+1 617 951 6600
cwr@hutch.com
Recommended in Private Equity: Fund Formation
Specialisation: Stockholder of *Hutchins, Wheeler & Dittmar* and a member of the Business Law Department concentrating in the areas of business law, corporate law, corporate and corporate transactions. Represents private investment firms in raising institutional funds for investment in buyouts, recapitalisations and other corporate transactions, as well as structuring, financing and implementing these investments. Began career with the office of the Chief Counsel, Internal Revenue Service in Washington, DC, where, amoung other responsibilties, analysed the tax structure of redemptive buyouts, the precursor of the modern leveraged buyout. Was an early pioneer in structuring and implementing leveraged buyouts, now having represented a wide spectrum of clients in almost every aspect of these type transactions. Developed innovative approaches for both private equity investment transactions and the economic allocations as between investors and transaction sponsors. Private equity clients include the Thomas H. Lee Company and Berkshire Partners LLC.
Personal: Received BA, from Bates College, 1961, and LLB, from Columbia University School of Law, 1964.

ROCAP, Don
Kirkland & Ellis, Chicago +1 312 861 2000
Recommended in Tax

ROD, Jonathan
Freshfields Bruckhaus Deringer, New York
+1 212 277 4000
jonathan.rod@freshfields.com
Recommended in Project Finance
Specialisation: Specialises in securities work, including innovative project financing in the US capital markets.

ROGERS, William
Cravath, Swaine & Moore, New York
+1 212 474 1000
Recommended in Capital Markets: Debt & Equity

ROHRBACH, Peter
Hogan & Hartson LLP, Washington DC
+1 202 637 5600
Recommended in Communications: Regulatory

ROKOSZ, Ronald
Chapman and Cutler, Chicago +1 312 845 3827
Recommended in Banking & Finance
Specialisation: Senior Partner – Banking Department. Syndicated lending, highly-leveraged transactions, asset securitisations, U.S. Eximbank financings and other cross-border political-risk insurance transactions, trade finance, synthetic lease, aircraft finance and gold consignment financing.
Prof. Memberships: Illinois Bar Association. Japan America Society. Member of Illinois Bar and U.S. Federal District Bar of Northern Illinois.
Career: Joined *Chapman and Cutler* in 1969, became Partner in 1977. Graduate of Northwestern University Law School, Order of Coif, Law Review 1969, Loyola University of Chicago BS 1966 Magna Cum Laude; Member – Firm Practicing Standards Committee.
Personal: Born 1944. Well-travelled – Holland and Japan. Plays jazz guitar. Married to Kathleen who works with the deaf community. Have one son, Christopher. Lives in Barrington, Illinois.

ROLFE, Ron
Cravath, Swaine & Moore, New York
+1 212 474 1000
Recommended in Competition/Anti-trust

ROSATI, Mario
Wilson, Sonsini, Goodrich & Rosati, Palo Alto
+1 650 493 9300
Recommended in Communications: IT

ROSEN, Burt
Debevoise & Plimpton, New York +1 212 909 6000
Recommended in Tax

ROSEN, Edward
Cleary, Gottlieb, Steen & Hamilton, New York
+1 212 225 2000
Recommended in Capital Markets: Derivatives

ROSEN, Matthew A.
Skadden, Arps, Slate, Meagher & Flom LLP, New York +1 212 735 3000
mrosen@skadden.com
Recommended in Tax
Specialisation: Co-head of the firm's Tax Department, represents clients in every aspect of tax work, with particular emphasis on acquisitions, divestitures and restructurings, both domestic and cross-border. Also handles matters involving partnerships of every type, joint ventures, foreign investments, real estate investment trusts, regulated investment companies and executive compensation. In addition, practice includes the development of financial instruments and financial products. Clients include many significant public and private companies, investment banks and investment funds. Frequently speaks at professional gatherings throughout the country and has made many presentations at American Bar Association and New York State Bar Association meetings. Topics often cover tax strategies for corporate acquisitions, financial restructurings, issues pertaining to companies with significant net operating losses and the tax implications of many corporate 'defense' techniques.
Prof. Memberships: Co-Chair, Subcommittee on Net Operating Losses, New York State Bar Association (1985-1987). Co-Chair, Subcommittee on Bankruptcy, New York State Bar Association (1988-1989). Executive Committee Member, Tax Section, New York State Bar Association (1985-1989).
Personal: LLM, New York University, 1979 (Memorial Award for Distinction). JD, Boston University, 1976 (cum laude). BA, Swarthmore College, 1973.

ROSEN, Richard L.
Arnold & Porter, Washington DC +1 202 942 5000
Richard_Rosen@sporter.com
Recommended in Competition/Anti-trust
Specialisation: Partner at *Arnold & Porter*, represents clients before the federal anti-trust agencies in merger and acquisition and other anti-trust matters, and in general anti-trust counselling and litigation. Practice focuses on clients in the information technology and telecommunications fields, including Computer Associates International, Network Solution, SBC Communications, and Micron Technology.
Career: Has served as chief of the communications & finance section of the anti-trust division at the US Department of Justice, supervising all AT&T consent decree and other anti-trust enforcement in the telecommunications, cable television, broadcasting, computer software, and financial services industries. Played important roles in the department's anti-trust case against Microsoft, the AT&T McCaw merger and other major anti-trust matters and served as lead

U

trial counsel in the 'United States v. United Tote, Inc'. merger case. Also served on the White House Information Infrastructure Task Force, working on telecommunications reform legislation, and provided assistance to foreign governments on privatisation and competition matters. From 1975 to 1984, served at the Federal Trade Commission, where held positions of Assistant Director of the Bureau of Competition and Attorney-Advisor to the Chairman. Education: Received JD from St. John's University School of Law in 1974 and SB from Massachusetts Institute of Technology (MIT) in 1970.

ROSENBERG, Marc S.
Cravath, Swaine & Moore, New York
+1 212 474 1000
Recommended in Capital Markets: Debt & Equity

ROSENBLOOM, David
Caplin & Drysdale, Washington DC
+1 202 862 5000
Recommended in Tax

ROSENBLUM, Steve
Wachtell, Lipton, Rosen & Katz, New York
+1 212 403 1000
Recommended in Communications: Transactional (Telecoms)

ROSENSTEIN, Mace J.
Hogan & Hartson LLP, Washington DC
+1 202 637 5600
Recommended in Communications: Regulatory

ROSSMAN, Vladimir R.
Shearman & Sterling, New York +1 212 848 8051
vrossman@shearman.com
Recommended in Banking & Finance
Specialisation: Partner in *Shearman & Sterling's* Bank Finance and Bankruptcy Group. Represents issuers, borrowers and lenders in a wide range of US and cross-border financings, including CBOs, CLOs and other securitisations, secured Rule 144A offerings, leverage buyouts and other asset-based financings, deleveragings, recapitalisations and restructurings. Spent most of 2000 in Hong Kong representing the Government of Guangdong Province, China, in a multibillion dollar restructuring of Guangdong Development Enterprises.
Prof. Memberships: Member of the New York Bar Association and the American Bar Association (Business Law and International Law sections). Listed in Euromoney's 'Guide to World's Leading banking Lawyers' and in 'Who's Who of Professionals'.
Career: Member of the New York State and US federal bars. Joined *Shearman & Sterling* in 1980 and became a corporate partner in 1987. Taught at the Columbia University Graduate School of Arts and Sciences from 1969 through 1977, achieving the rank of Assistant Professor.
Personal: Attended Columbia University Law School (JD, 1978); Parker School of Foreign Law (Certificate, 1978); Columbia University Graduate School of Arts and Sciences (MA, 1969; PhD, 1972); Columbia College (BA, 1968); and Juilliard School of Music (Diploma, 1968).

ROTHERMEL, Sarah
Hale and Dorr, Boston +1 617 526 6000
Recommended in Private Equity: Fund Formation

ROVINE, Arthur
Baker & McKenzie, New York +1 212 751 5700
arthur.w.rovine@bakernet.com
Recommended in Arbitration (International)
Specialisation: Partner in the Litigation Department. Main areas of work are international litigation and international arbitration. Has represented many major clients including a large number of cases involving public and private international law issues at the Iran-U.S. Claims Tribunal in the Hague, the UN Compensation Commission in Geneva, the International Chamber of Commerce in Paris, the American Arbitration Association in New York, and international litigations in U.S. Federal Courts. Has handled many claims for and against governments, including representation of Egypt in its case against Iraq at the UN Compensation Commission. Arbitration and litigation private sector clients have included Rockwell International, General Dynamics, AES Ltd, Fluor Corporation, Deloitte Touche, Tohmatsu International, Touche Ross International, Combustion Engineering, John Brown Engineering, Nuclear Electric Insurance and Singer.
Prof. Memberships: Currently President of the American Society of International Law.
Career: Prior to joining *Baker & McKenzie* in 1983, served in the office of the Legal Adviser in the U.S. Department of State from 1972-1983. Established the 'Digest of United States Practice in International Law' (1973-1974), and then named Assistant Legal Adviser for Treaty Affairs (1975-1981). Then appointed the first United States Agent to the Iran-U.S. Claims Tribunal in the Hague from 1981-1983. Prior to Government service, served as Counsel at the International Court of Justice. Taught public international law and international organization for several years at Cornell University and later at Georgetown University Law School. Visiting Lecturer in Law at the Yale Law School in 1998. Served for 10 years as a member of the Board of Editors of the 'American Journal of International Law.'
Personal: Born April 29 1937. Law degree from Harvard University, 1961; PhD from Columbia University, 1966.

ROWE, Larry
Ropes & Gray, Boston +1 617 951 7000
Recommended in Private Equity: Fund Formation

ROZZELL, Scott
Baker Botts LLP, Houston +1 713 229 1234
Recommended in Energy & Natural Resources
Specialisation: Chair of Energy Department in Houston. Broad energy practice involving all phases of regulation of the energy industry, including oil and gas producers, pipelines, and electric utilities, generators and marketers. Has 24 years of experience in rate, certification, and licensing proceedings at Department of Energy, Federal Energy Regulatory Commission, Nuclear Regulatory Commission, and Texas Public Utilities Commission.
Prof. Memberships: Past President of Houston Bar Association and currently Director of the State Bar of Texas. Member of Energy, Texas Utility Lawyers and American Bar Associations, State Bar of Texas, and Lawyer Pilots Bar Association. Fellow of American Bar Foundation, past Chair and Sustaining Life Fellow of Houston Bar Association and Sustaining Life Fellow of Texas Bar Foundation. In 1999, named as one of world's leading energy and natural resources lawyers by Euromoney Publications in London.
Career: Admitted to practise law in Texas in 1975. Joined *Baker Botts* in 1975 becoming partner in 1983.
Personal: Received JD from University of Texas School of Law in 1975 and BA from Southern Methodist University in 1971.

RUDDER, Richard D.
Willkie Farr & Gallagher, New York
+1 212 728 8000
Recommended in Capital Markets: Securitisation

RUEGGER, Philip ("Pete")
Simpson Thacher & Bartlett, New York
+1 212 455 2000
p_ruegger@stblaw.com
Recommended in Corporate/M&A, Private Equity: Buyouts
Specialisation: Partner at *Simpson Thacher & Bartlett* in the Firm's Corporate Department. Advises clients on mergers and acquisitions, leveraged buyouts, merchant banking transactions, corporate governance, corporate finance, and general corporate and securities law matters. Represented AOL in its merger with Time Warner and MCI in its merger with WorldCom. Regular clients include Blackstone, Andersen Consulting, America Online, WorldCom, SG Cowen, Vestar, C.R. Bard and Genesee & Wyoming.
Publications: Recent articles and presentations include 'M&A of High Technology Companies', Stanford Law School Directors' College 2000; 'Structuring International Acquisition Transactions', for the Third Annual Institute on Mergers and Acquisitions in February 1999; and 'Going Global, How to Do an International Deal', The M&A Journal, Vl.1, No.6.
Career: Joined *Simpson Thacher* in 1974 and became a partner in 1981. Has been a member of the Firm's Executive Committee since 1993. Received AB from Dartmouth College, magna cum laude in 1971 and was elected to Phi Beta Kappa. Received JD from the University of Virginia School of Law in 1974.

RULE, Charles F. (Rick)
Fried, Frank, Harris, Shriver & Jacobson, Washington DC +1 202 639 7000
Recommended in Competition/Anti-trust
Specialisation: Partner whose practice focuses on U.S. and international antitrust and economic regulation in the fields of transportation, communications and energy. Chair of the firm's Antitrust and Trade Regulation Practice Group. Has written and lectured on a variety of anti-trust topics.
Publications: Recent published writings include; 'Overview of Section 2 of the Sherman Act And Its Application to Microsoft' (April 29, 1998); 'The Case Against the Case Against Microsoft: Why the Justice

Department is barking up the wrong operating system', Slate Nov 12, 1997; 'The FTC is Strangling Business Mergers', 'The Washington Times', May 19 1997 at A17; 'Antitrust Liability' (co-author with David L Meyer). Chapter 11 in 'Healthcare Corporate Law'; 'Financial Liability Aspects of Healthcare Organisations' (Mark Hall, ed.) (Little Brown 1994).
Career: Admitted to the Bar in the District of Columbia. Served as Assistant Attorney General in charge of the Antitrust Division, U.S. Department of Justice, 1986-89, Deputy Assistant Attorney General, Antitrust Division, U.S. Department of Justice 1984-86; and Special Assistant to the Assistant Attorney General Antitrust Division, U.S. Department of Justice, 1982-84. Has served as distinguished adjunct professor of law at American University of Washington College of Law. Inaugural chair of the Corporations, Securities, and Antitrust Practice Group of the Federalist Society and from 1989-91 was chair of Economics Committee of the ABA Antitrust Section. Member of the Advisory Board of the Bureau of National Affairs Anti-Trust & Trade Regulation Report, of the Advisory Boards of the Washington Legal Foundation, of the Landmark Legal Foundation, and of the Visiting Committee of the University of Chicago Law School.
Personal: Graduate of Vanderbilt University, BA, 1978, and of the University of Chicago Law School, JD, 1981.

RUTKOWSKI, Larry
Seward & Kissel, New York +1 212 574 1200
Recommended in Shipping: Finance

SACHS, John
Latham & Watkins, Washington DC
+1 202 637 2264
john.sachs@lw.com
Recommended in Energy & Natural Resources
Specialisatin: Partner in the Washington DC office. Represents sponsors, lenders, governments and national utilities in all phases of the development and financing of domestic and foreign infrastructure projects, including oil and gas projects, water projects and transportation projects. Particular experience in the development and project financing of private power projects and the acquisition of existing assets in the power sector. Handles all aspects of competitive bidding solicitations, the structuring of projects, and the negotiation of the project agreements and loan documentation.
Prof. Memberships: American Bar Association, Federal Energy Bar Association.
Publications: Written and spoken frequently about energy sector regulation and private power projects.
Career: Judical clerk, Honorable Charles R. Richey, U.S. District Court for the District of Columbia, 1980-81.
Personal: JD, Harvard Law School, 1980. BA, Yale University, 1976, magna cum laude.

SACKS, Ira
Fried, Frank, Harris, Shriver & Jacobson, New York
+1 212 859 8000
ira.sacks@ffhsj.com
Recommended in Competition/Anti-trust
Personal: Antitrust, Intellectual Property.
Prof. Memberships: ABA, ABCNY, NYSBA
Publications: Numerous.
Career: Partner, *Fried Frank, Harris, Shriver & Jacobson* (1988-date); Partner, *Kaye Scholer* (1983-1987); Associate *Kaye Scholer* (1974-1982).
Personal: JD, Georgetown 1974; SB, MIT (1970).

SAEED, Faiza
Cravath, Swaine & Moore, New York
+1 212 474 1000
Recommended in Corporate/M&A

SAGGESE, Nicholas P.
Skadden, Arps, Slate, Meagher & Flom LLP, Los Angeles +1 213 687 5000
nsaggese@skadden.com
Recommended in Corporate/M&A
Specialisation: Has represented clients in connection with a variety of corporate transactions. Has been involved with numerous mergers and acquisitions, securities offerings, and corporate restructurings. Examples of recent transactions include: the acquisitions of Petco Animal Supplies, Inc. by an affiliate of *Leonard Green & Partners*, L.P., and Texas Pacific Group, AboveNet Communications, Inc. by Metromedia Fiber Network, Harveys Casino Resorts by an affiliate of Colony Capital, Inc, and bond offerings for HMH Properties, Inc., Horseshoe Gaming Holding Corp., Host Marriott, L.P., Metromedia Fiber Network, Inc., Park Place Entertainment Corporation, United Pan-European Communications N.V., and UnitedGlobalCom, Inc. Has frequently appeared on panels, has published several articles and is a co-editor and principal author of a treatise.
Prof. Memberships: Committees of both the American Bar Association and the California State Bar.
Career: JD, Loyola Law School of Los Angeles, 1980 (cum laude; Member, Loyola Law Review, St. Thomas More Law Honour Society); Member, Board of Visitors, Loyola Law School of Los Angeles. MBA, University of California at Los Angeles, 1973 (Beta Gamma Sigma Honour Society); BA, University of California at Los Angeles, 1969; worked in insurance and benefits; taught corporate finance in the California State University system.

SAMUELS, Leslie
Cleary, Gottlieb, Steen & Hamilton, New York
+1 212 225 2000
Recommended in Tax

SANDLER, Richard
Davis Polk & Wardwell, New York +1 212 450 4000
Recommended in Capital Markets: Debt & Equity

SAPER, Jeff
Wilson, Sonsini, Goodrich & Rosati, Palo Alto
+1 650 493 9300
Recommended in Communications: IT

SATTY, Andrea
Chadbourne & Parke LLP, New York
+1 212 408 5100
Recommended in Project Finance

SCAVONE, Arthur
White & Case LLP, New York +1 212 819 8710
ascavone@whitecase.com
Recommended in Project Finance
Specialisation: Co-chair of the firm's Energy, Infrastructure and Project Finance Group. Specialises in domestic and international project financings, particularly transactions in emerging markets involving multi-lateral and bi-lateral lending agencies. Has represented sponsors, commercial banks, export credit agencies, multi-lateral agencies and institutional lenders in projects involving power plants, pipelines, LNG facilities, waste water treatment facilities, fibre optic cable systems, coke batteries and other infrastructure and industrial projects. Transactions include the representation of the sponsors in connection with two power plant financings in the United States, the Export-Import Bank of the United States in connection with the Chad-Cameroon oil transportation project, the commercial banks in connection with a fibre optic cable system in Europe, the Export Import Bank of the United States in connection with a power plant financing in Brazil, and a steel company in connection with projects involving coke batteries and cogeneration plants at its steel facilities.
Prof. Memberships: Association of the Bar of the City of New York, Project Finance Subcommittee.
Career: Joined *White & Case* in 1984. Admitted to the New Jersey Bar in 1984. Admitted to the New York Bar in 1986. Became partner of *White & Case* in 1992. Worked in *White & Case* Tokyo office in 1987 and 1988.
Personal: Born 20 December 1959. Attended Muhlenberg College, magna cum laude, 1981. Fordham University School of Law, cum laude, 'Fordham Law Review'.

SCHARFSTEIN, Joel
Fried, Frank, Harris, Shriver & Jacobson, New York
+1 212 859 8000
Recommended in Tax

SCHELL, Michael
Skadden, Arps, Slate, Meagher & Flom LLP, New York +1 212 735 3000
Recommended in Corporate/M&A

SCHERMAN, William S.
Skadden, Arps, Slate, Meagher & Flom LLP, Washington DC +1 202 371 7000
Recommended in Energy & Natural Resources

SCHETMAN, Richard
Cadwalader, Wickersham & Taft, New York
+1 212 504 6000
richard.schetman@cwt.com
Recommended in Capital Markets: Securitisation
Specialisation: Capital Markets partner in the New York office. Practice is concentrated in the areas of structured finance, derivative products, other types of financing and the federal securities law. Represents underwriters, credit enhancers, issuers, institutional investors, sponsors and swap counterparties in a wide range of matters, including the securitisation of cash flows from such assets as credit card receivables, auto loans, trade receivables, home equity loans, wholesale auto dealer notes, leases and airplane contracts. Extensive experience in structuring commer-

U

cial paper vehicles and CDO vehicles for repackaging corporate, asset-backed and non-U.S. securities. Speaker at various conferences on CDOs, repackagings and other securitisation issues.
Prof. Memberships: The Association of the Bar of the City of New York and the American Bar Association.
Career: BA in History, Brown University (1980); JD (cum laude) The University of Pennsylvania School of Law (1983) and was a member of the Moot Court Board; admitted 1984, New York. Joined *Cadwalader* in 1985. Became a partner in 1993. Prior to *Cadwalader*, was an attorney at the Federal Reserve Bank of New York.

U

SCHILLER, Jonathan
Boies, Schiller & Flexner, New York
+1 914 273 9800
Recommended in Arbitration (International)

SCHLER, Michael
Cravath, Swaine & Moore, New York
+1 212 474 1000
Recommended in Tax

SCHNABL, Marco
Skadden, Arps, Slate, Meagher & Flom LLP, New York +1 212 735 3000
Recommended in Arbitration (International)

SCHNEIDER, Leslie
Ivins, Phillips & Barker, Washington DC
+1 202 393 7600
Recommended in Tax

SCHOENBRUN, Larry
Gardere Wynne Sewell LLP, Dallas
+1 214 999 3000
Recommended in Corporate/M&A

SCHULRUFF, Stuart
Katten Muchin Zavis, Chicago +1 312 902 5200
Recommended in Banking & Finance

SCHWARTZ, Donald
Latham & Watkins, Chicago +1 312 876 7631
donald.schwartz@lw.com
Recommended in Banking & Finance
Specialisation: Partner in the Finance and Real Estate Department and head of the Banking Group. Principally represents banks, commercial finance companies and other lenders in transactional and out-of-court insolvency matters, as well as entities borrowing or leasing from financial institutions. Broad experience in issues faced by lenders, including acquisitions of loan portfolios and business units and serving as lead counsel on financings in virtually every type of industry.
Prof. Memberships: Illinois and American Bar Associations. ABA Commercial Finance Services Committee and Commercial Finance Association, 1978-2000.
Career: Joined *Latham & Watkins* in 1988. *Sidley & Austin* 1974-88. Associate General Counsel, CFA. Member, Editorial Advisory Board, Journal of Bankruptcy Law and Practice.
Personal: JD University of Chicago, 1974, Order of the Coif, Associate Editor of University of Chicago Law Review. BA, Macalester College, 1971.

SCHWARTZ, Herb
Fish & Neave, New York +1 212 596 9000
hschwartz@fishneave.com
Recommended in Intellectual Property
Specialisation: Intellectual property litigation. Lead trial counsel in many high profile litigations. Most recently, trial counsel for TKT and Aventis in suit by Amgen concerning patent rights to EPOGEN. Also represented Polaroid against Eastman Kodak, Digital against Intel, Compaq against Packard Bell and eMachines, Motorola against Rockwell and Robotics, Zeneca against Rhone Poulenc, Forest against Abbott, Purdue Pharma against Boehringer Ingelheim and Endo. Many other major litigations for other companies, such as Coca-Cola, Hershey Foods, Bombardier, Textron and Nintendo.
Prof. Memberships: Fellow, American College of Trial Lawyers; Fellow, American Bar Foundation; member, American Law Institute; Past President, New York Intellectual Property Law Association (1999-2000); Litigator of the Year (Managing Intellectual Property, 1999).
Publications: 'Patent Law and Practice', Federal Judicial Center, 1988, 2d ed. 1995; 'Patent Law and Practice, Bureau of National Affairs, 2d ed. 1996; 'Principles of Patent Law', The Foundation Press, 1998; numerous other articles in various journals.
Career: US Army Signal Corps, 1957-59; Philco Corporation and Ford Motor Co., 1959-63 (applications engineer); *Fish & Neave*, 1964-present, became partner in 1972 and Managing Partner 1985-91.
Personal: MIT, BSE.E. 1957; University of Pennsylvania, MA 1964; University of Pennsylvania Law School, LLB 1964. Married with six grown children; interested in racing and cruising sail boats; member of Cruising Club of America, New York Yacht Club and Riverside Yacht Club.

SCHWARTZ, Jodi
Wachtell, Lipton, Rosen & Katz, New York
+1 212 403 1000
Recommended in Tax

SCHWED, Robert A.
Reboul, MacMurray, Hewitt, Maynard & Kristol, New York +1 212 841 0614
rschwed@reboul.com
Recommended in Private Equity: Fund Formation
Specialisation: Corporate Partner, primarily represents private equity firms and their portfolio companies in corporate finance transactions, including public and private mergers and acquisitions and public and private securities offerings. Acted as counsel to various start-up ventures and to the issuer or to the underwriters in initial public offerings for software, internet, biotechnology, airline, healthcare, information services, information technology training and other companies. Significant representations include: Amdocs Limited, a leading provider of billing and customer care software to the telecommunications industry, in its US$290 million initial public offering in June 1998; Welsh, Carson, Anderson & Stowe, one of the largest sources of private equity in the United States, in its US$1.4 billion acquisition of Centennial Cellular in January 1999; BCI Partners, a private equity firm, in the raising of its fifth investment fund, BCI Growth V LP, a US$358 million fund; Welsh, Carson and dba partners in the US$1.7 billion acquisition of local telephone exchange properties from GTE; and Alex Brown as managing underwriter of the initial public offerings of Cyberian Outpost and iTurf.
Career: Admitted to Bar, New York 1975; JD, Harvard Law School 1974 (magna cum laude), BA, Williams College 1971 (cum laude).
Personal: Born 2 April 1949.

SHACHAR, Avishai
Davis Polk & Wardwell, New York +1 212 450 4000
Recommended in Tax

SHAPIRO, Robert
Chadbourne & Parke LLP, Washington DC
+1 202 974 5600
Recommended in Energy & Natural Resources

SHAW, Gregory
Cravath, Swaine & Moore, New York
+1 212 474 1000
Recommended in Capital Markets: Securitisation

SHEFFIELD, Jeffrey
Kirkland & Ellis, Chicago +1 312 861 2000
Recommended in Tax

SHEPRO, Richard Warren
Mayer, Brown & Platt, Chicago +1 312 701 7007
rshepro@mayerbrown.com
Recommended in Corporate/M&A
Specialisation: Co-head of Corporate Securities practice. Represents and counsels on acquisitions, restructurings, and securities law; negotiations and planning for acquisitions and sale of publicly traded and private businesses, both friendly and hostile transactions; offshore corporations; insurance and reinsurance companies; venture capital and private equity fund work; proxy and consent solicitations; public and private offerings; broker-dealer and investment adviser regulation; special complex corporate planning problems; and joint ventures and other arrangements.
Prof. Memberships: Admitted to practice in California, 1981; Illinois, 1979; U.S. District Court for the Northern District of Illinois, 1981; U.S. Court of Appeals for the Ninth Circuit, 1981; U.S. Supreme Court, 1993. Member of the American Law Institute; Chicago Council on Foreign Relations; Chicago Council of Lawyers, Board of Governors, 1986-89; Chairman, Election Law Committee, 1987 to 1993. Fellow of the Chicago Bar Foundation. Board of Directors of LaSalle Club.
Publications: Co-author of 'Bidders & Targets: Mergers and Acquisitions in the U.S.' (Oxford, England and Cambridge, Massachusetts: Basil Blackwell, 1990). Has written many articles on mergers, corporate law issues, and securities law for U.S. and foreign publications, including Financial Times, Harvard Business Review, and Business Lawyer. Lecturer, University of Chicago Law School. Visiting Professor, Northwestern University School of Law. Lectured at the London Business School, Ecole des Hautes Etudes Commerciales, and at professional associations. Taught at Harvard University.
Career: Served as Law Clerk to The Honorable Judge James R. Browning, Chief Judge, U.S. Court of

Appeals for the Ninth Circuit, 1979-81. Joined *Mayer, Brown & Platt* in 1981 and became partner in 1986.
Personal: Born May 9, 1953. Earned JD cum laude from Harvard University in 1979, where served as Supreme Court Note Editor for the Law Review. Holds MSc (1976) from The London School of Economics and AB magna cum laude (1975) from Harvard University. Member of the Board of Governors of the Kohl Children's Museum. Special Assistant Attorney General of the State of Illinois, 1981-82. Staff Member, U.S. Senate Judiciary Committee, 1978-79. Speaks French and Russian.

SHERCK, Timothy
Mayer, Brown & Platt, Chicago +1 312 701 7148
tsherck@mayerbrown.com
Recommended in Tax
Specialisation: Practice Area Administrator for Corporate Taxation Practice. Represents and counsels on all tax aspects of acquisitions and dispositions of business, including consolidated return, carryforward, spinoff and asset basis issues; tax-free reorganisations; corporate joint ventures; tax aspects of business restructurings, workouts, and bankruptcy, including debt exchanges and modification, cancellation of indebtedness income, loss carryforwards, and related matters such as tax liens and tax-related aspects of bankruptcy law; acquisitions of financially troubled business; acquisitions, mergers, and restructuring of financial institutions; publicly offered REITs and REITs offered primarily to institutional investors; and preparation and handling of requests for private letter rulings before the IRS National Office.
Prof. Memberships: Admitted to practice in Illinois, 1975.
Publications: Author of 'Treatment of Options in Applying Stock Ownership Tests in the Corporate World', 66 Taxes 1988; 'Restructuring Today's Financially Troubled Corporation', 68 Taxes 881. 'Tax Attributes and Consolidation', ALI-ABA Course of Study on Consolidated Return Regulations, 1997; 'Dealing with Troubled Companies', ALI-ABA Course of Study on Advanced Corporate Tax Planning Techniques, January 1991; Member, Planning Committee, University of Chicago Law School Federal Tax Conference, 1988 and 1990.
Career: Served as Law Clerk to The Honorable Walter R. Mansfield, U.S. Court of Appeals for the Second Circuit, New York, 1974-1975. Joined *Mayer, Brown & Platt* in 1975 and became partner in 1981.
Personal: Born February 27, 1949. Earned JD, cum laude, from Harvard Law School in 1974, where was Comment Editor for the Law Review. Holds a BA cum laude (1971) from Northwestern University.

SHUTRAN, Richard
Dewey Ballantine LLP, New York +1 212 259 8000
Susan_DiMora@deweyballantine.com
Recommended in Project Finance
Specialisation: Partner of *Dewey Ballantine LLP*, resident in the New York office. Vice Chairman of *Dewey Ballantine LLP*'s Corporate Department and of the Project Finance Group. Practice involves the representation of developers, investors, underwriters and lenders in relation to the development, financing, construction, and operation of a wide range of capital-intensive projects in the energy, industrial, mining, and public infrastructure sectors both in the U.S. and abroad. Has counselled clients in all phases of projects, including structuring, contract negotiation, financing, and post-financing matters, including restructurings and acquisitions. Has extensive experience in the use of both 144A and registered capital markets offerings to finance domestic U.S. and international projects. Fluent in Spanish, and has participated extensively in transactions in Latin America. Recent engagements of note include: advising the lenders and underwriters in connection with the commercial bank and capital markets financing of the Alliance Pipeline, the largest non-recourse financing completed in North America; advising the underwriters and lenders with respect to the financing of the Iroquois Gas Pipeline; advising the developers of power generation assets to serve the mining complex and related infrastructure of P.T. Freeport Indonesia in Irian Jaya, Indonesia; advising the lenders in connection with the multi-tranche financing of the Termobarranquilla power project in Barranquilla, Colombia; advising the underwriters with respect to the financing of the expansion of the Bogota airport; advising developers with respect to the development and financing of merchant power plants in the United States; advising the Inter-American Development Bank with respect to the financing of the Termovalle Project in Colombia; advising the lenders and underwriters with respect to the commercial bank financing and the registered bond offering for the Quezon power project in the Philippines.
Career: Earned JD, cum laude, from New York University in 1978 and earned BA from Trinity College in 1974.

SILVERMAN, Eric
Milbank, Tweed, Hadley & McCloy, New York
+1 212 530 5000
Recommended in Project Finance

SILVERMAN, Mark
Steptoe & Johnson LLP, Washington DC
+1 202 429 3000
Recommended in Tax

SIMMS, Marsha E.
Weil, Gotshal & Manges, New York
+1 212 310 8000
marsha.simms@weil.com
Recommended in Banking & Finance
Specialisation: New York based partner in the firm's International Finance Group. Has a broad-based banking law practice with extensive experience as lender and borrowers' counsel in all areas of debt financing and restructuring. Also has experience in negotiating financing and restructuring documentation and has participated in transactions involving the full range of industry sectors including retail, communications, aircraft and real estate.

SIMONS, Laird
Fenwick & West, Palo Alto +1 650 494 0600
Recommended in Communications: IT

SIMS, Joseph
Jones, Day, Reavis & Pogue, Washington DC
+1 202 879 3863
jsims@jonesday.com
Recommended in Competition/Anti-trust
Specialisation: Primary antitrust counsel for such companies as America Online (for which he advised on the acquisition of Netscape and the combination with Time Warner, among a range of matters), CBS (which has represented for over two decades, including its predecessor firm Westinghouse Electric, and recently represented in its combination with Viacom Inc., to form one of the world's largest media companies), TeleCommunications, Inc. (the largest U.S. cable operator until its acquisition by AT&T) and its affiliated company, Liberty Media Corp., Procter & Gamble, Campbell Soup, Hillenbrand Industries, American Tower Corp, Gencorp, Inc., and Textron Inc. Represented Rhone-Poulenc SA in the various criminal and civil vitamins matters in the United States and other jurisdictions; represents PepsiCo in its antitrust litigation against Coca-Cola; and represents the R.J. Reynolds Tobacco Co. in a series of private treble damage actions alleging price fixing in cigarettes. Primary outside counsel for the organisers of the Internet Corporation for Assigned Names and Numbers (ICANN), the global non-profit private sector body that is gradually assuming the administrative and technical management of the infrastructure of the Internet from the United States Government.
Prof. Memberships: Member of the American Law Institute.
Career: Serves as the Chair of the Technology Issues Practice of *Jones Day*, which is the internal structure charged with co-ordinating the delivery of technology-related legal services by *Jones Day*. Joined the Antitrust Division of the Department of Justice as a trial attorney in 1970, became Special Assistant to the Assistant Attorney General in 1973, and was appointed Deputy Assistant Attorney General, the second highest rank in the Division, in 1975. Joined *Jones Day* in 1978 to establish a Washington antitrust capacity.
Personal: Admitted to practice in the United States Supreme Court and a majority of the United States Courts of Appeal. Received JD from the College of Law at Arizona State University in 1970, graduating magna cum laude and serving as a law review editor.

SINGER, Andrew
Latham & Watkins, San Diego +1 619 238 2869
andrew.singer@lw.com
Recommended in Project Finance
Specialisation: Partner in and practice group leader of the firm's project finance group. Has substantial experience representing lenders, utilities and owner/developers in project financings around the world in power, oil and gas, and undersea cable sectors. Experience includes the structuring, documentation and negotiation of financing arrangements, and the preparation and negotiation of project contracts. Also handles the coordination of the work and input of other project specialists, including investment bankers, insurance consultants, independent engineers, environmental consultants, technical con-

U

sultants and local governmental specialists.
Prof. Memberships: California and American Bar Associations.
Career: Was named one of the top 20 California lawyers under the age of 40 by California Law Business in 1999.
Personal: JD, Harvard University, 1987. BS, Cornell University, 1984.

SMALL, Jeff
Davis Polk & Wardwell, New York +1 212 450 4000
Recommended in Capital Markets: Debt & Equity

SMIT, Robert
Simpson Thacher & Bartlett, New York
+1 212 455 2000
r_smit@stblaw.com
Recommended in Arbitration (International)
Specialisation: A partner at *Simpson Thacher & Bartlett* and a member of the Firm's Litigation Department specialising in international arbitration and litigation. Represents clients in a wide range of commercial litigations and arbitrations, including joint venture, agency and distributorship matters, securities, banking and insurance litigations as well as fraud and business crimes matters. Spent over two years in Switzerland representing a major financial institution in a series of international fraud litigations before the Geneva civil and criminal courts; and has represented clients and served as arbitrator in numerous international arbitrations around the world. Has acted as counsel to Andersen Consulting in one of the largest ever ICC arbitrations, based in Geneva, Switzerland; DHL in various ICC arbitrations, including an ICC arbitration in Paris concerning the transfer of a significant share of interest in DHL under a shareholder's agreement and an ICC arbitration in Paris, Miami and Buenos Aires involving DHL's independent agent in Argentina; Ford Motor Company in an UNCITRAL arbitration in Paris arising out of Ford's sale of its agricultural equipment and tractor subsidiary.
Career: Has a JD from Columbia Law School; a graduate law degree in private international law and international arbitration from the Sorbonne in Paris; clerked in the S.D.N.Y. Federal courts; taught U.S. Commercial Law at the Sorbonne; interned at the ICC International Court of Arbitration.

SMITH, Brad
Davis Polk & Wardwell, New York +1 212 450 4000
Recommended in Banking & Finance

SMITH, Brian W.
Mayer, Brown & Platt, Washington DC
+1 202 263 3236
bsmith@mayerbrown.com
Recommended in Communications: Transactional (IT)
Specialisation: Founding partner of firm's e-commerce practice. Primary practice areas include financial institutions regulation, corporate, securities, electronic commerce. Represents financial services firms and technology companies in: transactional and regulatory matters, retail and institutional financial product development and distribution, electronic commerce, capital markets, asset management and fiduciary products.
Prof. Memberships: Admitted to practice in District of Columbia, 1975; New York, 1972; U.S. District Courts for the Southern, 1975, and Eastern, 1975, Districts of New York and District of Columbia, 1986; and U.S. Supreme Court, 1976.
Publications: Editor of Bank Investment Products Deskbook, New York, Warren, Gorham & Lamont, 1995. Author or co-author of numerous articles on e-commerce law, including 'Recent Developments in Electronic Authentication: The Evolving Role of the Certification Authority', The Banking Law Journal, April/May 1999; 'Avoiding Transborder Data Flows Interruptions: Implementing Contract Clauses', Banking Policy Report, Vol. 18, Nos. 15 & 16, August 1999, 'Banker or Big Brother?' Legal Times, Week of March 1, 1999. Frequent lecturer on the financial services industry and the law and regulations affecting it, most recently: 'A Clear View, a Steady Hand and a Firm Resolve: A Practitioner's Perspective on the Issues Facing eCommerce in Financial Services and How to Address Them'. Seminar on Current Issues in Monetary and Financial Laws (May 12, 2000).
Career: Joined *Mayer, Brown & Platt*, Washington, D.C., as partner in 1992. Managing Partner of *Stroock & Stroock & Lavan*'s Washington office, 1984-1992. Served as Chief Counsel & Member of Policy Group, Office of Comptroller of Currency, U.S. Department of Treasury, Washington, D.C., 1982-1984, Senior Vice President, General Counsel & Corporate Secretary, MasterCard International, Inc.,1974-1982; CIT Financial Corporation, New York, 1973-1974; and American Express Company, New York, 1970-1973.
Personal: Earned MS from Columbia University Graduate School of Business, 1981, JD from St. John's University School of Law, 1971, and BA from St. John's University, 1968. Selected as one of Washington's most influential people on Financial Services by American Banker, October 1986; listed in the American Banker's Banking on Top Bankers, 1990 and 1991; and listed in An International Who's Who of Internet and E-Commerce Lawyers, 1999 and 2000.

SMITH, Greg
Skadden, Arps, Slate, Meagher & Flom LLP, Palo Alto +1 650 470 4500
grsmith@skadden.com
Recommended in Communications: IT
Specialisation: Partner, Palo Alto & San Francisco. Corporate. Experience in the areas of corporate finance, including public offerings and private placements of debt and equity, mergers and acquisitions, licensing and related transactions, and corporate restructurings. Regularly represents emerging growth technology and life science companies in all stages of their development, including incorporation, venture capital financings, initial public offerings and mergers and acquisitions; also complex finance transactions, including high-yield and convertible debt securities offerings pursuant to Rule 144A and otherwise; underwriters, financial advisors and placement agents with technology and other transactions; as well as foreign and international companies with both domestic and foreign transactions. Transactions include representation of: Credit Suisse First Boston; Bear, Stearns & Co.; Tumbleweed Communications Corp.; Wavesplitter Technologica, Inc., among others.
Career: JD, Columbia Law School, 1988 (Harlan Fiske Stone Scholar); BA, Stanford University, 1985 (with distinction; Phi Beta Kappa).
Personal: Active interest and history in music and the performing arts. Winner of the Stanford Concerto Competition (piano) and co-winner of the Dean of Humanities and Sciences Award in music. Has appeared as a soloist with the Utah Symphony on several occasions and continues to perform in recital from time to time. Chairman of the Board, Friends of Music at Stanford University.

SMITH, Philip
Ropes & Gray, Boston +1 617 951 7000
Recommended in Private Equity: Fund Formation

SMITH, Randolph
Crowell & Moring LLP, Washington DC
+1 202 624 2500
Recommended in Competition/Anti-trust

SMITH, Scott F.
Covington & Burling, New York +1 212 841 1000
ssmith@cov.com
Recommended in Communications: Transactional (IT)
Specialisation: Leads the firm's corporate department, focusing on information technology and telecommunications transactions. Was the principal lawyer in four of the largest software deals ever, including Computer Associate's acquisitions of Sterling Software, Platinum Technology and Legent. Other transactions include the merger and subsequent IPO of Ticketmaster Online City Search, Granaria's buyout of Eagle-Picher industries, and the cross-border Internet merger of PrizePoint Entertainment with Uproar Ltd. Also for Computer Associates, negotiated an enterprise-wide licensing agreement with Electronic Data Systems, ending a billion dollar lawsuit that had been underway for several years. Represented SG Capital, GE Equity and other investors in OpenSite technologies when it was acquired by Siebel Systems. A principal corporate advisor to a number of investment banks and private equity and venture capital funds, including UBS Warburg and SG Capital Partners, and is relied upon by Internet entrepreneurs and emerging companies.
Career: Admitted to the New York Bar.
Personal: Born 31 January 1954, Hot Springs, Arkansas. Received a JD high honours from the University of Texas in 1980, was a member of the Order of the Coif. Received a AB, magna cum laude, from Harvard University in 1976.

SMUTNY, Abby Cohen
White & Case LLP, Washington DC
+1 202 626 3608
asmutny@whitecase.com
Recommended in Arbitration (International)
Specialisation: Partner in Washington, DC concentrating in international dispute resolution through arbitration or litigation. Wide range of commercial disputes with particular experience in matters involving State parties and investment disputes, disputes under investment treaties and claims of expropriation. Counsel in ICSID, ICSID Additional Facility,

ICC and ad hoc arbitration proceedings as well as in cases before U.S. courts.
Prof. Memberships: New York State Bar, 1990; District of Columbia Bar, 1992; United States District Court for the District of Columbia; American Society of International Law (Executive Council, Member, since 1999, Executive Committee, Member, since 2000); District of Columbia Bar Association (International Law Section, Chair, 1999-2000 and Steering Committee, Member, 1998-2000); American Bar Association: Section of International Law and Practice; International Bar Association; Southwestern Legal Foundation: Institute for Transnational Arbitration
Career: Joined *White & Case* in 1990; partner since 2000.
Personal: Vassar College (A.B., cum laude, 1986); London School of Economics and Political Science (Certificate 1985); Université des Langues et Lettres de Grenoble (Certificate 1986); University of Chicago School of Law (JD 1990).

SOHN, Michael N.
Arnold & Porter, Washington DC +1 202 942 5000
Michael_Sohn@aporter.com
Recommended in Competition/Anti-trust
Specialisation: Chairman of *Arnold & Porter.* In addition to management responsibilities, maintains a substantial anti-trust practice of international scope. A former General Counsel of the Federal Trade Commission, practice encompasses a broad range of antitrust and consumer protection matters, with particular focus on the anti-trust aspects of mergers and acquisitions and treble damage class-actions. Represented such clients as American Home Products Corporation, ARCO, Boston Scientific Corporation, General Electric Corporation, Hoffmann-La Roche Inc., Intel Corporation, Merck & Company, Inc., and Occidental Petroleum Corporation in merger investigations and litigations before the FTC and the Justice Department.
Publications: Contributing author to 'The Ernst & Young Management Guide to Mergers and Acquisitions', as well as co-author of an article on merger remedies – Shapiro and Sohn, 'Crown Jewel Provision in Merger Consent Decrees', Antitrust, (Fall 1997).
Career: Designated a council member of the Administrative Conference of the United States while at the FTC and a member of the Executive Committee of the Regulatory Council of the United States.
Personal: Education: Received LLB, from Harvard Law School in 1963 and AB, from Columbia University in 1960.

SOLOMON, Andrew P.
Sullivan & Cromwell, New York +1 212 558 4000
solomona@sullcrom.com
Recommended in Tax
Specialisation: Managing Partner of the Tax Group at *Sullivan & Cromwell.* Regularly advises clients concerning the federal income taxation of complex financial products and cross-border transactions. Has extensive international M&A experience, recently having advised Philips Electronics in several U.S. acquisitions and joint ventures, Dexia in its acquisition of Financial Security Assurance, Elf Aquitaine in its merger with TotalFina and Republic New York in its acquisition by HSBC Holdings. Has advised on numerous privatisations, including that of INA and the spin-off of its real estate subsidiary. Has been involved in organising and/or taking public various offshore insurers, reinsurers and securitisation vehicles, including the organisation of International Property Catastrophe Insurance (IPC), Global Capital Reinsurance (GCR), Georgetown Re, Pacific Re and Mosaic Re and the IPOs of IPC and GCR. Other significant transactions and representations have included: representation of American International Group in connection with its investment in 20th Century, its acquisitions of SunAmerica and HSB Group and IPC's unsolicited proposal to acquire Tempest Re; and representations of The St. Joe Company in its spin-off of Florida East Coast Industries, First Union in numerous acquisitions and joint ventures, and Bank of New York in connection with the establishment of American Depositary Receipt (ADR) programs.
Prof. Memberships: American Bar Association; New York State Bar Association (Executive Committee Member, Tax Section).
Publications: Writes and speaks frequently on the taxation of financial products and institutions and international taxation and is a contributing author of 'Taxation of Financial Products', a Clark Boadman treatise.
Career: Joined *Sullivan & Cromwell* in 1984. Elected a Partner of the firm in 1992.
Personal: Born 1953. Graduated from Brown University (AB, magna cum laude, 1975) and Harvard Law School (JD, magna cum laude, 1984; Editor, Harvard Law Review).

SONSINI, Larry
Wilson, Sonsini, Goodrich & Rosati, Palo Alto +1 650 493 9300
Recommended in Communications: IT, Corporate/M&A

SORKIN, David
Simpson Thacher & Bartlett, New York +1 212 455 2000
d_sorkin@stblaw.com.
Recommended in Corporate/M&A
Specialisation: A partner at *Simpson Thacher & Bartlett* practising in the Firm's Corporate Department. Advises clients in merger and acquisition transactions and securities law matters. Regularly advises the investment firm Kohlberg Kravis Roberts & Co and its portfolio companies, including Borden, Inc. Recent KKR representations include Duracell International in its merger with The Gillette Company and World Color Press in its merger with Quebecor Printing. Among other clients, provides on-going corporate advice to America Online Inc, including in connection with its US$165 billion merger with Time Warner Inc and other acquisitions and joint ventures. Also represents Associates First Capital Corporation in connection with its initial public offering, its spinoff by the Ford Motor Company and its US$31 billion merger with Citigroup Inc and Ford Motor Company in connection with numerous acquisitions, divestitures, joint ventures and securities law matters.
Career: Joined the firm in 1985 and became a partner in 1993. Received a BA, summa cum laude in 1981 from Williams College and a JD, cum laude in 1984 from Harvard University. From 1984 to 1985 clerked for Hon. Charles M Merrill of the US Court of Appeals for the Ninth Circuit in San Francisco.

SOUSSLOFF, Andrew D.
Sullivan & Cromwell, New York +1 212 558 4000
soussloffa@sullcrom.com
Recommended in Capital Markets: Debt & Equity
Specialisation: Twenty years of domestic and international corporate finance experience representing clients from the U.S., Mexico, South America, Canada and Europe in securities offerings and acquisitions. Has worked with major industrial companies, financial institutions and foreign governments in capital-raising activities in U.S. and international markets. International M&A experience includes cross-border takeovers and joint ventures. Notable financing transactions include representing Harris Corp. in the $1 billion spin-off and listing of Lanier Worldwide, Inc.; Pharmacia & Upjohn in the $1.9 billion secondary offering by the Kingdom of Sweden; Repap New Brunswick Inc. in a series of high yield debt financings aggregating more than $1.5 billion; the underwriters in the $2.1 billion privatisation offering of Teléfonos de México; the underwriters in the $1.2 billion secondary offering by the Government of Kuwait of part of its interest in Santa Fe International; and the underwriters in the $1 billion preferred stock offering by Microsoft, the largest high tech offering of 1996. Has had a major role in the return to the international capital markets by Latin American sovereign issuers. Firm team leader for SEC-registered global bond offerings by Argentina, Brazil and Panama and architect of Brady bond "reverse Dutch auction" exchange offers.
Prof. Memberships: American Bar Association; Association of the Bar of the City of New York. Co-Chairman, Securities Law Committee of the International Bar Association.
Career: Joined *Sullivan & Cromwell* in 1981. Partner since 1986. Co-Managing Partner of General Practice Group, which includes the firm's securities, corporate, M&A, financial institutions, project finance and real estate practice areas.
Personal: Born 1953 in Providence, Rhode Island. Graduate of the University of Pennsylvania (BA, MA, 1975) and University of Pennsylvania Law School (JD, 1979).

SPATT, Robert E.
Simpson Thacher & Bartlett, New York +1 212 455 2000
r_spatt@stblaw.com
Recommended in Corporate/M&A
Specialisation: Corporate partner at *Simpson Thacher & Bartlett* in New York since 1987, specialising in mergers, acquisitions and restructurings for buying and selling companies, their financial advisors, leveraged buy-out firms and special committees of boards of directors. Represented KKR in a number of its significant acquisitions. Recent principle transactions include representing Smithfield Foods in its bid for IBP, the Special Committee of AXA

U

Financial in its buyout by AXA Group, Frontier in its sale to Global Crossing, Global Crossing in the sale of its LEC to Citizens Communications, Artal International in its acquisitions of Weight Watchers and Keebler and Sunshine Biscuits, Nine West in its sale to Jones Apparel, and American Home Products in its acquisition of American Cyanamid and its terminated mergers with Monsanto and Warner-Lambert. Extensive practice representing financial advisors in M&A transactions, including financial advisors for NTT Communications in its acquisition of Verio and for Bestfoods in its acquisition by Unilever.
Prof. Memberships: Co-Chairman of the Tulane Corporate Law Institute, one of the leading M&A institutes in the country, and a Professional Fellow of the NYU Centre for Law and Business.
Personal: Graduated from Brown University (AB, 1977) and University of Michigan Law School (JD, magna cum laude 1980, Order of the Coif).

SPECTOR, Phillip
Paul, Weiss, Rifkind, Wharton & Garrison, New York +1 212 373 3000
Recommended in Communications: Regulatory

SPECTOR, Scott
Fenwick & West, Palo Alto +1 650 494 0600
Recommended in Communications: IT

ST LEDGER-ROTY, Judith
Kelley Drye & Warren, Washington DC +1 202 955 9600
Recommended in Communications: Regulatory

STAFFARONI, Robert
Debevoise & Plimpton, New York +1 212 909 6000
Recommended in Tax

STANDISH, Peter D.
Weil, Gotshal & Manges, New York +1 212 310 8000
peter.standish@weil.com
Recommended in Competition/Anti-trust
Specialisation: New York based senior partner in the firm's Trade Practices and Regulatory Law Department. Practice covers all areas of antitrust and trade regulation, including joint ventures, licensing, pricing, distribution and marketing issues, focusing heavily on mergers and acquisitions work. Enjoys a national reputation as an antitrust lawyer and has successfully obtained clearance for scores of strongly contested acquisitions at the Department of Justice and the Federal Trade Commission, as well as in state attorney general and private actions.

STAPLETON, Benjamin F.
Sullivan & Cromwell, New York +1 212 558 4000
stapletonb@sullcrom.com
Recommended in Corporate/M&A
Specialisation: Member of Mergers and Acquisition Group since 1978 and Senior Partner of group. Has participated in hundreds of transactions during that period and represented bidders, targets and financial advisors in both friendly and contested situations. Represented BP Amoco plc in its acquisition of Atlantic Richfield Company (ARCO), Glaxo-Wellcome in proposed merger with SmithKline Beecham and Vodafone AirTouch in its acquisition of Mannesmann. Other recent work includes representation of Vodafone in its acquisition of AirTouch, The British Petroleum Company plc in its acquisition of Amoco Corporation and SBC Communications Inc. in its acquisitions of Pacific Telesis Group, SNET and Ameritech.
Prof. Memberships: American Bar Association; Association of the Bar of the City of New York; New York State Bar Association.
Career: Joined *Sullivan & Cromwell* in 1969. Partner since 1977.
Personal: Born 1943 in Newport News, Virginia. Graduate of Harvard College (AB, 1965) and Yale Law School (JD, 1969). Director and Treasurer, The Asphalt Green, Inc.

STARER, Brian
Haight Gardner Holland & Knight, New York +1 212 513 3200
Recommended in Shipping: Litigation

STEARNS, Craig
Watson, Farley & Williams, New York +1 212 922 2200
CStearns@wfw.com
Recommended in Shipping: Finance
Specialisation: Partner in the New York office. Primarily focuses on structuring international joint ventures and mergers and acquisitions involving shipping companies. Has considerable experience representing financial institutions and borrowers in asset-based finance transactions, including vessel finance.
Prof. Memberships: Association of the Bar of New York (member, tax section); New York Country Lawyers Association; American Bar Association.
Publications: Co-author of 'Proposed conduit rules focus on US withholding tax'; 'Tax Noted International' (1994).
Career: Associate – *Wertime, Robinson & Ries*, Cohoes, NY (1985-1987); associate – *Coxeter & Coxeter*, Albany, NY (1987-1990); associate – *Watson, Farley & Williams* (1990-2000); partner – *Watson, Farley & Williams* (2000 to date).
Personal: Born 1959. Resides in Stamford, CT. Educated at Nichols College, Dudley, MA (BSBA, cum laude, 1981); Albany Law School of Union University (JD, cum laude, 1985); New York University (LLM in taxation).

STEINBERG, Lewis
Cravath, Swaine & Moore, New York +1 212 474 1000
Recommended in Tax

STEPHENSON, Alan
Cravath, Swaine & Moore, New York +1 212 474 1000
Recommended in Corporate/M&A

STERN, Gary
Sidley & Austin, Chicago +1 312 853 7267
gstern@sidley.com
Recommended in Banking & Finance
Specialisation: Practice Area: Partner in the Securitisation and Structured Finance Group since 1989. Represents investors, issuers, placement agents, credit enhancers and liquidity providers in securitisation transactions involving a variety of asset types, including, credit cards, auto loans, equipment leases, student loans, consumer loans, trade receivables, sports related revenue streams and entertainment royalties and distribution revenues. Transaction structures include multi-seller and single-seller commercial paper conduit deals, private placements and 144A issuances.
Career: Received JD, 1982, Northwestern University School of Law.

STERN, Martin L.
Preston Gates & Ellis LLP, Washington DC +1 202 628 1700
Recommended in Communications: Regulatory

STILL, Charles
Fulbright & Jaworski LLP, Houston +1 713 651 5151/+1 2026624585
Recommended in Corporate/M&A

STOLL, Neal R.
Skadden, Arps, Slate, Meagher & Flom LLP, New York +1 212 735 3000
Recommended in Competition/Anti-trust

STRAUSS, Bob
Akin, Gump, Strauss, Hauer & Feld LLP, Dallas +1 214 969 2800
Recommended in Energy & Natural Resources

STROMFELD, Lary
Cadwalader, Wickersham & Taft, New York +1 212 504 6000
lary.stromfeld@cwt.com
Recommended in Capital Markets: Derivatives
Specialisation: Capital Markets Partner in the firm's New York office. Experience in the capital markets, with particular expertise in OTC fixed income products and municipal finance. Represents numerous underwriters, commercial banks, bond insurers, derivative product companies, broker-dealers, state and local governments, and other financial institutions. Practice involves development, negotiation and documentation of financial products, including credit derivatives, total return swaps, currency swaps, and fixed income swaps. Assists clients in the creation of structured derivative products that combine securitisation techniques and derivative products. Extensive involvement in the development and use of financial products in the primary and secondary municipal markets, including tender option programs, swaps, repurchase agreements and other investment products, as well as various forms of liquidity facilities and credit enhancement. Responsible for an annual compilation of state laws authorising municipal swaps and has represented financial institutions in monitoring state legislative developments affecting the sale of derivatives and various investments to state and local governmental entities.
Prof. Memberships: Municipal documentation committee of the International Swaps and Derivatives Association, Inc.; National Association of Bond Lawyers.
Career: BA, (magna cum laude), Brandeis University, 1977; JD, University of Pennsylvania Law School, 1981; admitted New York.

SUNSHINE, Steven C.
Shearman & Sterling, Washington DC
+1 202 508 8022
ssunshine@shearman.com
Recommended in Competition/Anti-trust
Specialisation: Anti-trust – mergers, litigation, criminal investigations. Experience includes Smithkline Beecham in connection with the formation of Glaxo Smithkline, CS First Boston in acquisition of Donaldson Lufkin & Jenrette; Rhone Poulene in connection with formation of Aventes; Fiat & New Holland in connection with acquisition of Case Corporation.
Prof. Memberships: DC, NY Bars. American & New York Bar Associations.
Career: 1993-95 Deputy Assistant Attorney General in charge of Merger Enforcement, U.S. Department of Justice.

SWANSON, Joel
Baker Botts LLP, Houston +1 713 229 1330
joel.swanson@bakerbotts.com
Recommended in Corporate/M&A
Specialisation: Senior partner in Corporate Department and head of the international practice group. Main areas of practice include initial public offerings, acquisitions and international acquisitions for domestic and international clients. Special focus on energy transactions.
Prof. Memberships: ABA, Texas Bar.
Career: Licensed and joined *Baker Botts* LLP in 1972. Partner in 1980. Worked as a chemical engineer at Exxon in 1968-1969.
Personal: Born February 21, 1945. University of Texas (BS in chemical engineering – highest ranking engineering graduate); Harvard Business School (MBA 1972 – high distinction); Harvard Law School (JD 1972 – cum laude).

SYMONS, Howard J.
Mintz Levin Cohn Ferris Glovsky and Popeo PC, Washington DC +1 202 434 7300
Recommended in Communications: Regulatory

TABAK, Jeffrey E.
Weil, Gotshal & Manges, New York
+1 212 310 8000
jeffrey.tabak@weil.com
Recommended in Private Equity: Fund Formation
Specialisation: Corporate Partner. Has wide-ranging corporate and securities law practice with emphasis on private investment entities. Co-Head of the firm's Private Equity and Investment Management Practice Group. Also advises on the formation and representation of basic business structures, particularly partnerships and limited liability companies. Has written and spoken on many topics relating to private investment funds.
Prof. Memberships: American Bar Association; ABA Federal Securities Subcommittee on Private Investment Entities.
Career: Joined firm in 1982. Secretary, Museum of Jewish Heritage. Trustee, HIPPY U.S.A.
Personal: BA, Duke University, 1979; JD, Duke University, 1982. Member, Phi Beta Kappa.

TANOURY, Mark
Cooley Godward, Palo Alto +1 650 843 5205
Recommended in Communications: IT

TEGELER, David W.
Testa, Hurwitz & Thibeault LLP, Boston
+1 617 248 7000
Recommended in Private Equity: Fund Formation

TEHAN, John
Simpson Thacher & Bartlett, New York
+1 212 455 2000
j_tehan@stblaw.com
Recommended in Capital Markets: Debt & Equity
Specialisation: Partner at *Simpson Thacher & Bartlett* and a member of the Firm's Corporate Department. Concentrates in corporate finance advising both issuers and underwriters in capital raising transactions with emphasis on public and private high-yield financings and initial public offerings. Also designated by investment grade and other corporate issuers to act as underwriters counsel on an ongoing basis in connection with the offering by such issuers of their debt and equity securities. Regularly advises KKR and its portfolio companies in connection with their high yield debt and initial public offerings. On the underwriting side, primarily represents Lehman Brothers, SG Cowen Securities Corporation, Merrill Lynch, BT Alex Brown and Bear Stearns. Acts as underwriters counsel for corporate issuers such as MBNA Corporation, Halliburton Corporation, Georgia-Pacific Corporation, Genesis Health Ventures, The Ryland Group and Owens-Illinois.
Prof. Memberships: Member of the Association of the Bar of the City of New York.
Career: Member of the Firm since 1982. Admitted to the New York Bar in 1974.
Personal: Received AB from LeMoyne College in 1970 and JD from Catholic University School of Law in 1973 where was the Recent Developments Editor of The Catholic University Law Review from 1972 to 1973.

TENEV, Jovi
Haight Gardner Holland & Knight, New York
+1 212 513 3200
jtenev@hklaw.com
Recommended in Shipping: Finance
Specialisation: Airline services; banking; capital markets; equipment leasing; project finance; ship finance; workout and foreclosures.
Prof. Memberships: American and International Bar Associations; Maritime Law Association of the United States.
Publications: 'International Maritime Workouts', Business Workout Manual; 'High Yield and the High Seas: Capital Sources for Shipping', Shipping Finance Annual, 1999-2000.
Personal: Education: University of Pennsylvania (AB cum laude, 1975); Boston College (JD, 1978).

TERR, Leonard
Baker & McKenzie, Washington DC
+1 202 452 7000
leonard.b.terr@bakernet.com
Recommended in Tax
Specialisation: Partner in the Washington, DC office of *Baker & McKenzie.* Has over 20 years of experience representing US-based and foreign-based multinationals, foreign governments, international organisations and trade associations in all phases of international tax practice. Served as International Tax Counsel of the US Treasury Department from 1987 to 1989. Headed the US delegation in the negotiation of the current US Germany tax treaty, in addition to over a dozen other US tax treaties and protocols. Directed Treasury's work on international tax legislation and regulations, the transfer pricing White Paper and other US and OECD international tax policy initiatives. Responsibility for client matters in recent years include obtaining a ground breaking IRS ruling on a European US acquisition, securing a pioneering Advance Pricing Agreement for a leading foreign automobile company, obtaining a significant exemption in a new tax treaty on behalf of a foreign industry group, achieving favorable settlements of docketed tax cases involving a variety of issues and obtaining favorable Competent Authority agreements in tax controversies involving Canada, Germany, Italy, Japan, Switzerland, the UK and other jurisdictions. Routinely counsels companies engaged in international expansion and global effective tax rate reduction initiatives, assists in tax planning for major cross-border acquisitions, divestitures and restructurings, handles transfer pricing compliance, planning and controversy matters involving a variety of industries and countries and represents companies and groups in various legislative, regulatory and treaty projects.
Prof. Memberships: Sits on the American Bar Association Tax Section's Foreign Activities of US Taxpayers Committee and has chaired the Section 367 Subcommittee and currently chairs the Source Subcommittee. Serves on the Tax Section's Task Force on Global Tax Policy.
Career: Served as a Consultant to the American Law Institute project on Tax Treaties, and as an adviser or board member for Tax Notes International, Tax Management International Journal, The Journal of Corporate Taxation, and the Hartford Institute on Insurance Taxation. Is a member of the International Fiscal Association and was US National Reporter for the 1986 and 1990 Congresses. Has chaired the Washington International Tax Study Group since 1990. Served as Law Clerk to Chief Judge Wilson Cowen of the US Court of Appeals for the Federal Circuit. Is an Adjunct Professor of International Tax Law at the Georgetown University Law Center. Lectured and published widely on international tax matters.
Personal: AB, from LaSalle College, an AM, and PhD, from Brown University and a JD, from Cornell University.

TESTA, Richard J.
Testa, Hurwitz & Thibeault LLP, Boston
+1 617 248 7000
Recommended in Private Equity: Fund Formation

THALACKER, Arbie R.
Shearman & Sterling, New York +1 212 848 4000
athalacker@shearman.com
Recommended in Capital Markets: Debt & Equity
Specialisation: Partner of *Shearman & Sterling*'s

U

Capital Markets Group, specialising in international corporate finance. Represents both issuers and underwriters in investment grade debt offerings, medium-term note offerings, initial public offerings and other equity offerings, convertible and non-convertible preferred stock offerings, global bond offerings, Regulation S offerings, Rule 144A offerings and private placements. Also advises corporate clients on disclosure and other matters under the federal securities laws and state corporation laws.
Prof. Memberships: American Bar Association; the New York Bar Association and the Association of the Bar of the City of New York.
Personal: Born 17 April 1935. Attended Princeton University (AB, 1957); University of Michigan Law School (LLB, 1960). Serves as director of Detrex Corporation, Meredith Monk/The House Foundation for the Arts, Inc. and Shambhala International. Trustee of Naropa University and a vice president and trustee of the Greenwich Village Society for Historic Preservation. Married to Deborah B. Garrett and has three sons and a stepson. Lives in New York City.

THOMAS, Frederick B.
Mayer, Brown & Platt, Chicago +1 312 701 7035
fthomas@mayerbrown.com
Recommended in Corporate/M&A
Specialisation: Partner in general corporate practice in Chicago. Advises clients on stock acquisitions, asset acquisitions, mergers, joint ventures, financings, tender offers, shareholder disputes, and a variety of other matters involving U.S., foreign and multinational businesses. Extensive representation of clients in e-commerce, telecommunications and information technology businesses. Represents large U.S. corporations, other U.S. clients of various types and foreign corporations.
Prof. Memberships: Admitted to practice in Illinois, 1974. Member of the American Bar Association, Section of Business Law; Chicago Council of Lawyers; and the Planning Committee for Ray Garrett, Jr. Corporate and Securities Law Institute.
Career: Served as Law Clerk to The Honorable John C. Godbold, U.S. Court of Appeals for the Fifth Circuit, Montgomery, AL, from 1974 to 1975. Joined *Mayer, Brown & Platt*, Chicago, in 1975. Served in London office from 1978 to 1981 and became partner in 1981. Serves on Management Committee of *Mayer, Brown & Platt.*
Personal: Born August 13, 1949. Earned JD at the University of Chicago in 1974, (awarded the Joseph Henry Beale Prize and served as Comment Editor, University of Chicago Law Review). Holds AB, magna cum laude (1971), from Dartmouth College, (elected to Phi Beta Kappa). Serves on the Board of Directors of St. Gregory Episcopal School and on the Board of Trustees of LaRabida Children's Hospital and Research Center. Adjunct Professor of Law (teaching corporations) at the University of Notre Dame, London Law Center, 1980-1981.

THURBER, Mark
Skadden, Arps, Slate, Meagher & Flom LLP, Houston +1 713 655 5100
Recommended in Energy & Natural Resources

TODRYS, Steven C.
Simpson Thacher & Bartlett, New York
+1 212 455 2000
S_Todrys@stblaw.com
Recommended in Tax
Specialisation: A partner at *Simpson Thacher & Bartlett* and a member of the Firm's Tax Department. Specialises in federal income taxation, with a particular emphasis on corporate mergers and acquisitions, joint ventures, restructurings and real estate matters. Recent experience includes the business combinations of AOL and Time Warner, Seagram and Vivendi, Associates First Capital and Citigroup, CNET and ZD, Frontier Corporation and Global Crossing and the numerous buyout transactions of Kohlberg Kravis Roberts & Co.
Career: Graduated from the University of Rochester in 1975 and obtained a JD in 1978 with honours from the University of Chicago. Served as Chair of the Tax Section of the New York State Bar Association in 1998 and also served as a Co-Chair of the Committee on Corporations and Committee on Foreign Activities of U.S. Taxpayers. Admitted to practice in New York, the U.S. Tax Court and the U.S. Supreme Court.

TOMPSETT, William C.
Mayer, Brown & Platt, Chicago +1 312 701 7133
wtompsett@mayerbrown.com
Recommended in Banking & Finance
Specialisation: Partner in Chicago office finance practice. Represents commercial lenders in secured and unsecured financing transactions; letter of credit transactions; interest rate, currency and commodity derivative products; participations and syndications of loans; workouts; sale of trade receivables and commercial loans in securitisation transactions.
Prof. Memberships: Admitted to practice in Illinois in 1978 and Pennsylvania in 1974. Member of the American Bar Association and the Chicago Bar Association.
Publications: Author of 'Interbank Relations in Loan Participation Agreements: From Structure to Workout', 101 The Banking Law Journal, pp. 31-49, 1984.
Career: Joined *Mayer, Brown & Platt* as partner in 1991. Served in Continental Bank N.A., Law Department from 1977 to 1991, except two years (1982-1983) with *Seki, Jarvis & Lynch Morgan* and prior to that with *Lewis & Bockius*, Philadelphia from 1974 to 1977.
Personal: Born December 22, 1948. Earned JD from Cornell University in 1974 and BA from Haverford College in 1970 where is a member of the Founders Club.

TONSFELD, Steve
Venture Law Group, Menlo Park +1 650 854 4488
Recommended in Communications: IT

TOSETTI, Paul
Latham & Watkins, Los Angeles +1 213 485 1234
paul.tosetti@lw.com
Recommended in Corporate/M&A
Specialisation: Partner in the Corporate Department and Co-Chair of the firm's global Mergers and Acquisitions Group. Specialises in the acquisition and disposition of public and private companies, on both a solicited and unsolicited basis. Extensive experience with leveraged buyouts. Regular speaker at Practising Law Institute and academic events.
Prof. Memberships: American Bar Association, California State Bar Association, Los Angeles Bar Association.
Publications: Editor, 'Corporate Governance Advisor'.
Personal: JD Harvard University, 1981, cum laude, Supreme Court Editor of Harvard Law Review. MA Oxford University, 1979, with First Class Honours from Magdelen College. BA Harvard University, 1976, cum laude.

TOTH, Bruce
Winston & Strawn, Chicago +1 312 558 5600
btoth@winston.com
Recommended in Corporate/M&A
Specialisation: Head of the Corporate Department. Concentration in financing, securities, and mergers and acquisitions. Recent M&A transactions include representation of Keebler Foods in its US$4.2 billion sale to Kellogg Company and its acquisitions of Austin Quality Foods, Inc. and Presidents International Inc.; representation of Huntsman Packaging in the sale of the company to Chase Capital Partners in a US$1.1 billion recapitalisation transaction; representation of Corporate Brands Foods America in its acquisition by IBP, Inc.; and representation of Northland Holdings, Inc. in the sale of 50 percent of its outstanding stock to Adsteam Marine Limited.
Career: Joined *Winston & Strawn* as an associate in 1982. Elected as partner in 1987. Member of firm executive committee.
Personal: Born February 14, 1953. Received BS, summa cum laude, Georgia Institute of Technology. Received MBA, and JD, Stanford University.

TOWNSEND, John
Hughes Hubbard & Reed, Washington DC
+1 202 721 4600
Recommended in Arbitration (International)

TRIER, Dana
Davis Polk & Wardwell, New York +1 212 450 4640
Recommended in Tax

TRINGALI, Joseph
Simpson Thacher & Bartlett, New York
+1 212 455 2000
J_Tringali@stblaw.com
Recommended in Competition/Anti-trust
Specialisation: A partner at *Simpson Thacher & Bartlett* and a member of the firm's Litigation Department representing clients on antitrust and general commercial litigation. Has handled jury and bench trials in diverse areas, including antitrust, breach of contract, copyright infringement, employment discrimination and civil rights. Primarily, has litigated civil antitrust actions on behalf of both plaintiffs and defendants and counsels clients under the Sherman, Clayton, Robinson-Patman and Hart-Scott-Rodino Acts. Has handled merger transactions before the Department of Justice, the Federal Trade Commission and various state antitrust enforcement

agencies as well as coordinating competition law filings on a global basis. Work includes acting for American Home Products, Andersen Consulting, CNET, CheckFree Holdings, Global Crossing, Kohlberg Kravis Roberts, Blackstone, Vestar Capital Partners, Fred Meyer Inc., Kerr-McGee, Viacom and Nidek Co., Ltd.
Career: Joined the firm in 1983 and became a partner in 1989.
Personal: Received a BA from Wesleyan University in 1977 and a JD from the New York University School of Law in 1980.

UNGER, Timothy
Andrews & Kurth, Houston +1 713 220 4200
tunger@akllp.com
Recommended in Energy & Natural Resources
Specialisation: Representation of a variety of corporate and institutional clients. In recent years practice has focused primarily on cogeneration and independent power projects, as well as oil and gas industry financings.
Prof. Memberships: The State Bar of Texas, 1974.
Career: Partner with *Andrews & Kurth*, practising in the Business Section. Has been with the firm since 1974, and has represented a variety of corporate and institutional clients.
Personal: Received undergraduate degree from the University of Notre Dame (AB, magna cum laude, 1969) and law degree from the Univesity of Texas (JD, with honors, 1974). During law school was a member of the Texas Law Review and Order of the Coif.

URDA KASSIS, Cynthia
Shearman & Sterling, New York +1 212 848 4000
curdakassis@shearman.com
Recommended in Banking & Finance, Project Finance
Specialisation: Partner in the Project Development and Finance Group. Represents United States and foreign corporations and financial institutions in their general private financing activities, sponsors and lenders in project development and finance transactions worldwide, US and foreign corporations in joint ventures and US and foreign financial institutions in their letter of credit activities. Has also represented US and foreign corporations on general corporate matters.
Prof. Memberships: American Bar Association.
Career: Admitted to the bar in New York. Joined *Shearman & Sterling* in 1984 and became a partner in 1992.
Personal: Attended University of Virginia (BA, 1980); University of Notre Dame (MA, 1981); American University, Washington College of Law (JD, 1984).

VARDELL, James
Cravath, Swaine & Moore, New York
+1 212 474 1000
Recommended in Banking & Finance

VERVEER, Philip L.
Willkie Farr & Gallagher, New York
+1 212 728 8000
Recommended in Communications: Regulatory

VETTER, Jeff
Fenwick & West, Palo Alto +1 650 494 0600
Recommended in Communications: IT

VICTOR, A. Paul
Weil, Gotshal & Manges, New York
+1 212 310 8000
paul.victor@weil.com
Recommended in Competition/Anti-trust
Specialisation: A well regarded expert in antitrust and international trade law. Has spent the past thirty seven years representing foreign and domestic clients in some of the largest antitrust and antidumping cases ever brought. Prior to this, spent two and a half years with the Antitrust Division of the United States Department of Justice in Washington. Regularly represents corporate clients of the firm across a wide range of industry sectors.

VINE, Stephen
Akin, Gump, Strauss, Hauer & Feld LLP, New York
+1 212 872 1000
Recommended in Private Equity: Fund Formation

VLAHAKIS, Patricia
Wachtell, Lipton, Rosen & Katz, New York
+1 212 403 1000
Recommended in Corporate/M&A

VOGE, William
Latham & Watkins, New York +1 212 906 1352
william.voge@lw.com
Recommended in Project Finance
Specialisation: Partner in the New York office. Extensive experience in project development and project financings. Acted for project sponsors, banks, underwriters and other parties on electricity, oil and gas and communication projects in the U.S. and abroad. Activities include structuring complex project financings involving multiple groups and types of lenders.
Prof. Memberships: New York and American Bar Associations.
Publications: Written about political risks, environmental concerns, export credit agencies, disclosure issues, common financing conditions in international projects, and the use of Islamic capital and capital markets to finance international projects. Spoken about structuring the financing on private power, oil and gas projects in emerging markets and the issues with concurrent funding of bank facilities and capital market offerings.
Personal: JD, University of California, Berkeley, 1983. MBA, University of California, Berkeley, 1983. BS, California State University, Fresno, 1980, magna cum laude.

VOLK, Stephen R.
Shearman & Sterling, New York +1 212 848 7061
svolk@shearman.com
Recommended in Corporate/M&A
Specialisation: Senior Partner at *Shearman & Sterling*, an international law firm, since 1991. In the mid 70s, formed the firm's Mergers and Acquisitions Group, which grew from a few lawyers to over 150 members today. Has led *Shearman & Sterling's* M&A team in representing many clients in major transactions, including friendly and contested takeovers, mergers and acquisitions.
Prof. Memberships: Harvard Law School Dean's Advisory Board; American Bar Association's Committee on Securities Regulation and the Council on Foreign Relations.
Career: Joined *Shearman & Sterling* in 1960 and qualified for the New York bar in 1961. Was elected to partnership in 1968, became Deputy Senior Partner in 1988 and Senior Partner in 1991. Serves on boards of several professional and civic organisations. A frequent lecturer to business and legal groups.
Personal: Born April 22, 1936. Attended Dartmouth College (BA, 1957, Phi Beta Kappa) and Harvard Law School (JD, 1960). Lives in New York City with wife, Diane Kemelman Volk and their daughter, Anne. Also has three adult sons and seven grandchildren.

VOLLMER, Andrew N.
Wilmer, Cutler & Pickering, Washington
+1 202 663 6202
Recommended in Arbitration (International)

WACHSBERGER, Chaim
Chadbourne & Parke LLP, New York
+1 212 408 5100
Recommended in Project Finance

WADLOW, R. Clark
Sidley & Austin, Washington DC +1 202 736 8215
rwadlow@sidley.com
Recommended in Communications: Regulatory
Specialisation: Head of firm's Communications group. Taught communications law at Catholic University. Former member, Board of Trustees, licensee of educational WETA-TV/FM. Frequent participant in industry and continuing legal education programs. Co-chair, annual PLI program, Telecommunications Policy and Regulation.
Prof. Memberships: Alaska and District of Columbia bars; American Bar Association; Federal Communications Bar Association.
Career: Formerly chair, ABA Forum on Communications Law; Member-at-Large, ABA Board of Governors; President, Federal Communications Bar Association.
Personal: Harvard University (JD, 1971); Dartmouth College (AB, 1968).

WAIMON, David
Baker & McKenzie, Chicago +1 312 861 2850
david.a.waimon@bakernet.com
Recommended in Tax
Specialisation: Main area of practice is focused on tax planning relating to international transactions, reorganisations, intercompany pricing, financial products, and tax controversies.
Prof. Memberships: American Bar Association Section on Taxation, Illinois State Bar Association, US Tax Court and the Chicago Bar Association.
Publications: 'Almost a Merger: Achieving Cross-Border Shareholder Unity Without a Shareholder Exchange,' 78 TAXES 163 (2000); Using Partnerships In International Tax Planning, 73 Taxes 834 (1995); A Passive-Aggressive Approach to Anti-Deferral in the 1990s: Critical Analysis and Planning Techniques Under Section 956A, 72 Taxes 1084 (1994); Tax

U

Advisors Planning Series, Vol. 28; US Corporations Doing Business Abroad, Research Institute of America; US Taxation of Global Securities Trading, 1992 International Tax Review, (September 1992); Overview of the Proposed Section 482 Regulations, May 1992, American Bar Association, Section on Taxation; Pass-Through Rules for Financial Intermediaries: Different Routes to a Single Tax, 67 Taxes 1025 (1989).
Career: *Kirkland & Ellis*, Chicago, Illinois (April 1985-January 1991); *Baker & McKenzie* January 1991-Present; became partner in 1994.
Personal: Born July 22, 1958. Attended University of Illinois School of Law (JD, magna cum laude, 1984). Leisure interests include running and sailing. Lives with his wife in Wilmette, Illinois.

U

WALD, Douglas
Arnold & Porter, Washington DC +1 202 942 5000
Douglas_Wald@aporter.com
Recommended in Competition/Anti-trust
Specialisation: Partner at *Arnold & Porter*, specialises in anti-trust and litigation. Experience involves a broad range of anti-trust matters, including counselling, private litigation (including federal class actions), and representation before the Federal Trade Commission and Department of Justice. Has advised clients on matters involving marketing, pricing, distribution, price discrimination, monopolisation, and joint ventures and acquisitions. In addition, has represented clients in appellate matters, such as 3M Company v. Browner, 17 F.3d 1453 (D.C.Cir.).
Career: Prior to joining *Arnold & Porter* in 1980, served as law clerk to Judge William H. Timbers of the U.S. Court of Appeals for the Second Circuit.
Personal: Graduated in 1979 from Harvard Law School (JD), was an editor of the 'Harvard Law Review'. Received AB from Harvard College in 1975.

WALL, Robert
Winston & Strawn, Chicago +1 312 558 5600
Recommended in Corporate/M&A
Specialisation: Partner in Corporate Department. Concentration in mergers and acquisitions and corporate finance for public companies. Represented clients in these areas since 1977. Recently, represented Keebler Foods Company in sale to Kellogg Company; represented special committee of Shaw Industries Inc. in sale of company to Berkshire Hathaway; represented Citigroup and Salomon Smith Barney in their respective roles as bridge lender, equity participant and private placement agent in sale of U.S. Can Company to Berkshire (private LBO fund); represented Monsanto Company in $4.2 billion financing of equity, equity equivalents and debt. Frequent speaker at seminars and member of various securities and merger and acquisition organisations.

WANDER, Herb
Katten Muchin Zavis, Chicago +1 312 902 5200
Recommended in Corporate/M&A

WARD, Erica A.
Skadden, Arps, Slate, Meagher & Flom LLP, Washington DC +1 202 371 7050
Recommended in Project Finance

WARDEN, John L.
Sullivan & Cromwell, New York +1 212 558 4000
wardenj@sullcrom.com
Recommended in Competition/Anti-trust
Specialisation: Active litigation practice since 1965 covering the antitrust, banking, contract, corporate governance and securities areas. Has advised and represented Amax, Bank of New York, British Airways, British Petroleum, Eastman Kodak, First Boston, Goldman Sachs, Gulf Oil, Kennecott, TW Services and Union Carbide in major litigation. Major cases include Berkey Photo v. Eastman Kodak, the Union Carbide/GAF takeover litigation and the Bank of New York/Irving Trust takeover litigation. In addition to civil litigation, represented Amax in United States v. Amax, et al., a criminal antitrust case involving the potash industry, and has represented clients in various antitrust grand jury investigations. Also has had an extensive appellate experience, including constitutional cases and the successful appeal in United States v. D'Amato, and has acted for The New York Clearing House as amicus curiae in numerous cases in courts of appeals and the Supreme Court. Has represented Goldman Sachs in the antitrust litigation and investigations regarding the NASDAQ Stock Market and British Airways in the antitrust case brought by Virgin Atlantic. Presently acting for Microsoft in the government antitrust case.
Prof. Memberships: American College of Trial Lawyers; American Law Institute; Speaker, ABA National Institutes on Corporate Control and Governance.
Career: Joined *Sullivan & Cromwell* in 1965. Became a Partner of the firm in 1973.
Personal: Born 1941. Graduated from Harvard College (AB, 1962) and University of Virginia Law School (LLB, 1965; Editor-in-Chief, Virginia Law Review). President, University of Virginia Law School Foundation and Trustee, American Ballet Theatre.

WARNER JR, Waide
Davis Polk & Wardwell, New York +1 212 450 4000
Recommended in Project Finance

WASSERMAN, Craig
Wachtell, Lipton, Rosen & Katz, New York +1 212 403 1000
Recommended in Corporate/M&A

WATERS, Jennifer
Crowell & Moring LLP, Washington DC +1 202 624 2500
Recommended in Energy & Natural Resources

WAYLAND, Joseph F.
Simpson Thacher & Bartlett, New York +1 212 455 2000
J_Wayland@stblaw.com
Recommended in Competition/Anti-trust
Specialisation: A partner at *Simpson Thacher & Bartlett*. Practice areas include antitrust, counselling and litigation, complex commercial and securities litigation and corporate investigations. Most recently, has served as lead trial counsel in New York and California state court jury trials, including a successful six-week jury trial of contract and fraud claims arising from the sale of a major publishing company. Represents a major international airline as plaintiff in an action alleging monopolisation and monopoly leveraging of North America air routes. Also provides general antitrust counsel to major media clients and has represented numerous clients in the pharmaceutical, telecommunications, medical device and defense industries before US and European competition authorities in connection with mergers and acquisitions.
Career: Partner since 1994. Was in the Honours Programme of the Air Force General Counsel from 1984 to 1988, and was responsible for litigation of disputes concerning the acquisition of computer hardware and software.
Personal: Received a BA from Washington University in 1979, a JD from the University of Columbia Law School in 1983 and a LLM (International and Comparative Law) from Georgetown University in 1987.

WEIR, Michael W.
Sullivan & Cromwell, New York +1 212 558 4000
weirm@sullcrom.com
Recommended in Banking & Finance
Specialisation: Member of the firm's General practice Group, specialising in commercial banking matters.
Prof. Memberships: Association of the Bar of the City of New York.
Career: Joined *Sullivan & Cromwell* in 1966. Partner since 1974.
Personal: Born 1940 in Dubuque, Iowa. Graduate of Duke University (BA, 1963) and Columbia Law School (JD, 1966).

WEISBURG, Henry
Shearman & Sterling, New York +1 212 848 4000
hweisburg@shearman.com
Recommended in Arbitration (International)
Specialisation: Partner and Practice Group Leader in Litigation Department in New York. Concentrates in areas of international financial and insolvency disputes, including international arbitrations administered by the American Arbitration Association, the International Chamber of Commerce, the International Centre for Settlement of Investment Disputes, the London Court of International Arbitration, as well as pursuant to ad hoc agreements, as well as litigations in both federal and state courts. Frequently handles matters concerning commercial and sovereign restructurings, banking disputes (especially involving letters of credit, syndicated loans, a forfait transactions), investment disputes (especially involving joint ventures), and similar matters.
Prof. Memberships: American Bar Association; Association of the Bar of the City of New York (ABCNY).
Career: Trinity College BA (1973); NYU Law School JD (1977). Joined *Shearman & Sterling* 1977; became a partner 1986. Member of ABCNY Committees on International Commercial Dispute Resolution; formerly Director, American Arbitration Association.

WEISS, Gregory A.
Simpson Thacher & Bartlett, New York +1 212 455 2000
g_weiss@stblaw.com
Recommended in Banking & Finance
Specialisation: A partner at *Simpson Thacher &*

Bartlett and a member of the Firm's Corporate Department where for over 30 years has represented banks and other financial institutions and borrowers in syndicated lending transactions, including senior secured and subordinated bridge financings. In 2000, has represented numerous commercial banks in connection with senior secured financings including Canadian Imperial Bank of Commerce, the Chase Manhattan Bank, Barclays Bank, Union Bank, Fleet Bank and Société Generale. With extensive experience in the field of media and telecommunications, has also represented Sprint PCS, Global Crossing Ltd. and Aeric Networks Inc. in multibillion dollar senior secured vendor and bank financings for the development of their respective telecommunications systems.
Career: Joined *Simpson Thacher* in 1970 and became a partner in 1977.
Personal: Received an AB from Yale in 1966 and a LLB, cum laude in 1969 from the University of Pennsylvania, and was elected to the Order of the Coif. Clerked for the Honourable William Gray, U.S. District Court, Central District of California from 1969 to 1970.

WELKE, William R
Kirkland & Ellis, Chicago +1 312 861 2143
Recommended in Tax

WELLEN, Robert
Ivins, Phillips & Barker, Washington DC
+1 202 393 7600
Recommended in Tax

WEST, Glenn D.
Weil, Gotshal & Manges, Dallas +1 214 746 7700
glenn.west@weil.com
Recommended in Corporate/M&A
Specialisation: Managing Partner of the firm's Dallas office and a member of the firm's Management Committee. A member of *Weil, Gotshal & Manges'* International Corporate Group and has extensive securities and mergers and acquisition law expertise. Represents a large number of international and domestic corporations and financial institutions across a full range of industry types on corporate law matters. Has led public and private acquisition and corporate finance transactions for the following major clients, among others: Hicks, Muse, Tate & Furst Inc., Thomas Weisel Capital Partners, Greyhound Lines, Inc., Six Flags Inc., Firesytems Group, Inc., Financiere Moulin de Champagne and International Seed Holdings, L.P. Representative recent transactions (domestic and international) include the acquisition of Six Flags Entertainment Corporation by Premier Parks, Inc. (U.S.); the acquisition of Hillsdown Holdings PLC (U.K.) and the acquisition of Perrier Jouet and Mumm Champagne from Seagrams (France) by Hicks, Muse, Tate & Furst (U.K.); the investment in a Brussels efinance business (Belgium); and the acquisition of Forward Group PLC and Interconnection Systems Limited by Viasystems Group, Inc. (U.K.). Has also been involved recently in a number of venture capital transactions in internet, technology and telecommunication businesses by Hicks, Muse, Tate & Furst Inc. and Thomas Weisel Capital Partners. Also represents the Texas Rangers Baseball Club and the Dallas Stars Hockey Club, and has led the project finance for the new American Airlines Center in Dallas.

WEST, M. Holland
Shearman & Sterling, New York +1 212 848 4000
hwest@shearman.com
Recommended in Capital Markets: Derivatives
Specialisation: Partner and Co-Head of Global Corporate Finance and Investments Group. Specialises in derivative, structured product, securitisation, capital market, securities and commodities matters; assists clients globally in the development, structuring and execution of complex financing, derivative and securitisation techniques, products and structures, such as fixed income, equity, currency, commodity and credit linked swaps, forwards, notes, options and similar instruments, securities and other instruments with embedded derivatives, hybrid and synthetic products and special purpose financing vehicles; includes representation of investment advisory firms and domestic and offshore investment funds; and provides clients with regulatory, risk management and compliance counselling. Frequent lecturer and author in respect of financial product and investment management matters. Serves on the board of editors of industry journals and periodicals.
Prof. Memberships: Bars of the States of New York (1981), New Jersey (1981), and Florida (1981); International Swaps and Derivatives Association, Inc.; Futures Industry Association's Law and Compliance Division; American Bar Association's Committee on Regulation of Futures and Derivative Instruments; New York State Bar Association's Executive Committee-Business Law Section and Committee on Commodities and Futures Law; The Association of the Bar of the City of New York's Committee on Futures Regulation; International Bar Association's Committee on Business Law; Managed Futures Association; Private Investment Fund Forum.
Career: Fordham University School of Law, Juris Doctor (Honours) (1980); Associate Editor, 'Fordham Law Review'; University of the South at Sewanee, Bachelor of Arts – English Literature (Honours) (1975).
Personal: Born 26 November 1952. Married to Deborah A. Stites, with three children. Leisure interests include outdoor and sporting activities.

WHALEN, Thomas J.
Carter, Ledyard & Milburn, New York
+1 212 732 3200
whalen@clm.com
Recommended in Shipping: Finance
Specialisation: Corporate, vessel and equipment finance, creditors' rights, including corporate asset based financing involving ships, aircraft and rail equipment in bank lending, leverage lease financing and other complex structured financing transactions, domestic and cross-border leasing transactions representing both debt and equity interests.
Prof. Memberships: American College of Investment Counsel (Fellow); The Association of the Bar of the City of New York (Member, Maritime Law Committee, 1994-1997); Maritime Law Association of the United States (Member, Maritime Finance Committee); Equipment Leasing Association of America (Member, Counsel's Committee, 1986-89; Transportation Committee, 1994-96).
Career: 1981-1997 Partner *Haight, Gardner, Poor & Havens.*
Personal: BA 1967 Yale University. JD 1970 University of Michigan School of Law.

WHITE, John
Cravath, Swaine & Moore, New York
+1 212 474 1000
Recommended in Capital Markets: Debt & Equity

WHITE III, Fred B.
Skadden, Arps, Slate, Meagher & Flom LLP, New York +1 212 735 3000
Recommended in Corporate/M&A

WIEMAN, Lawrence E.
Davis Polk & Wardwell, New York +1 212 450 4000
Recommended in Banking & Finance

WILEY, Richard
Wiley Rein & Fielding, Washington
+1 202 719 7010
Recommended in Communications: Regulatory

WILLIAMS, Douglas H.
Sidley & Austin, Chicago +1 312 853 7667
dwilliam@sidley.com
Recommended in Banking & Finance
Specialisation: Partner in the Chicago office. Co-author of 'Legal Developments in Secured Lending (1978-94)'. Advisor to the National Conference of Commissioners on Uniform State Laws Drafting Committee to Revise UCC Article 6.
Prof. Memberships: Member of the Bar of Illinois; American and Chicago Bar Associations.
Personal: Educated at the University of Chicago (JD, 1977; MBA, 1977); University of Michigan (BA, 1970).

WILLIAMS, William
Fulbright & Jaworski LLP, Washington DC
+1 202 662 0200
Recommended in Energy & Natural Resources

WILLIAMS Jr., William J.
Sullivan & Cromwell, New York +1 212 558 4000
williamsw@sullcrom.com
Recommended in Capital Markets: Debt & Equity
Specialisation: Widely recognised as one of the preeminent securities lawyers in the United States. Has had extensive experience in international securities offerings by European, Japanese and Latin American issuers, including acting as the partner in charge of Sullivan & Cromwell's involvement in the privatisations of Repsol and Corporación Bancaria de España (Argentaria). Worked on the recently completed offerings of Banco Bilbao Vizcaya Argentaria, Bank Hapoalim, Repsol and Terra Networks. Played a major role in the development of SEC Regulation S, Rule 144A, Rule 15a-6 (governing the activities of non-U.S. broker-dealers in the United States) and Regulation M (the trading rules).
Prof. Memberships: American Bar Association; American Law Institute; American Society of International Law; Association of the Bar of the City

U

of New York; New York State Bar Association.
Career: Joined *Sullivan & Cromwell* in 1962. Elected a Partner of the firm in 1969.
Personal: Born 1937. Graduated from the College of the Holy Cross (AB, 1958) and New York University Law School (LLB, 1961; Editor-in-Chief, New York University Law Review). Trustee, New York University Law School Foundation; Member, New York Stock Exchange Legal Advisory Committee; Trustee, Sofia American Schools, Inc.; Member, Advisory Committee of Past Presidents, United States Golf Association.

WILLIAMSON, Joel V.
Mayer, Brown & Platt, Chicago +1 312 701 7229
jwilliamson@mayerbrown.com
Recommended in Tax
Specialisation: Administrator of Tax Litigation practice. Has tried approximately 50 U.S. Tax Court cases. Represented clients in five major international transfer pricing cases (Eli Lilly, G.D. Searle, Nestlé Westreco, Seagate Technology, Inc., and National Semiconductor). Has also represented clients in cases involving financial products (Saba Partnership [Brunswick]); captive insurance (Humana and Gulf Oil); Subpart F issues (The Limited, Inc.); constructive triangular dividends (Gulf Oil); R&D moratorium (Intel Corporation); entitlement to Brazilian foreign tax credits (Bankers Trust); Iranian losses and foreign tax credits (Continental Bank); tax accounting; sale and leaseback transactions (Comdisco); foreign source income on export sales (Intel Corporation); I.R.C. section 338 liquidations; trademark valuation, sale of assets for preferred stock and the proper role of IRS trial counsel in the audit examination process, and summons enforcement (Nestlé Holdings, Inc.).
Prof. Memberships: Admitted to practice in Illinois, 1986; Kentucky, 1970; U.S. District Court for the Northern District of Illinois; Trial Bar for the Northern District of Illinois; various Circuit Courts of Appeal; U.S. Court of Federal Claims; U.S. Tax Court; U.S. Supreme Court. Member of the American Bar Association.
Career: Special Trial Attorney, Chief Counsel's Office, United States Department of Treasury, Cincinnati, Ohio, 1972-1985. Joined *Mayer, Brown & Platt* as partner in 1986.
Personal: Born May 26, 1945. Earned JD from University of Kentucky in 1970, where was a member of the Order of the Coif, Law Review, Moot Court Board, and National Moot Court Team. Holds BA (1967) from Davidson College. Served as Officer, Criminal Trial Attorney, U.S. Army, at Ft. Bragg, N.C., and in the Republic of South Vietnam from 1970 to 1972.

WIPPERMAN, Robert
Stroock & Stroock & Lavan LLP, New York
+1 212 806 5400
rwipperman@strook.com
Recommended in Capital Markets: Securitisation
Specialisation: Partner in Structured Finance Department. Since 1988 concentrated exclusively in structured finance transactions. Regularly represents originators, servicers, issuers, purchasers, and underwriters in public offerings and private placements of mortgage-backed and asset-backed securities. (Underlying assets as well as tax and credit enhancement structures, covers full spectrum).
Prof. Memberships: Admitted to practice in Massachusetts and New York; American Bar Association and the New York State Bar Association.
Career: Graduated from Rutgers University in 1976 with a bachelor's degree in Communications. Graduated from Boston College Law School in 1979. Joined *Herrick & Smith* in Boston, MA in 1979, concentrating in corporate and securities transactions. In March 1986, joined *Brown & Wood LLP* in New York City becoming partner in 1988. In May 1991, joined *Stroock & Stroock & Lavan LLP* in New York City, as a partner, becoming a member of the executive committee in 1996.
Personal: Married with three children.

WISEMAN, Michael
Sullivan & Cromwell, New York +1 212 558 4000
wisemanm@sullcrom.com
Recommended in Banking & Finance
Specialisation: Practice focuses on banking and financial institutions law. Represents a number of domestic and foreign commercial banks, investment banks and insurance companies. Practice encompasses regulatory issues, capital markets, new products initiatives, derivative products, payment system issues, and corporate governance and counseling. Regularly advises financial institutions on principal investing, joint ventures matters, capital market products and enforcement matters. Has participated on behalf of The New York Clearing House Association in development of CHIPS settlement finality procedures and development of netting provisions in FDICIA and the New York State Banking Law. Acted as reporter for the Financial Market Lawyers Group's study of transactions between financial advisors and dealers. Currently represents the Group of Twenty leading international banks in developing continuous linked settlement system for clearing foreign exchange.
Prof. Memberships: American Bar Association; Association of the Bar of the City of New York (Former Chair, Banking Law Committee); New York State Bar Association (Member, Banking Law Committee); American Bar Foundation; American Law Institute.
Publications: 'Money Management Issues – OTC Markets' (Futures & Derivatives Law Report, February 1997); Procter & Gamble Company vs. Bankers Trust (Securities Industry Association, 1996, co-author); 'Commentary on Capital Market Risks' (Legal Times, March 17, 1986, co-author); 'Commentary on Derivative Products' (U.S. Banker, April 1994, co-author); 'Commentary on Foreign Banks in the United States' (American Banker, January 4, 1994); 'The Evolution of Banking in the United States: Comments on Present Trends' (Korea Institute of Finance, International Symposium on Universal Banking, 1996).
Career: Joined *Sullivan & Cromwell* in 1978. Partner since 1985. Managing Partner of the firm's Financial Institutions Group.
Personal: Born 1953 in New York, New York. Graduate of Harvard College (AB, 1975) and Harvard Law School (JD, 1978).

WOJCIECHOWSKI, Mark S.
Mayer, Brown & Platt, New York +1 212 506 2525
mwojciechowski@mayerbrown.com
Recommended in Banking & Finance
Specialisation: Primary practice areas include corporate, corporate finance, and private equity. Has extensive experience in mergers and acquisitions, joint ventures (domestic and international), private equity investment and venture capital, general corporate matters and transactions, and structured financing (including acquisition finance and project finance).
Prof. Memberships: Admitted to practice in New York in (1982). Member of International Law Advisory Committee of the Practising Law Institute, American Bar Association, Section on Corporation, Banking, and Business Law, the New York State Bar Association, Section of International Law and Practice, and the Association of the Bar of the City of New York.
Publications: Co-Author of 'How to Buy a U.S. Business: A Guide to Negotiated and Hostile Acquisitions' (1999).
Career: Joined *Mayer, Brown & Platt* in 1986 and became a partner in 1988. Member of the *Mayer, Brown & Platt* Executive Committee (the Policy and Planning Committee). Current head of the firm's International Committee.
Personal: Born May 4, 1954. Earned JD (cum laude) from Indiana University (Bloomington) in 1981 and AB from Columbia College in 1976.

WOLF, Barry M.
Weil, Gotshal & Manges, New York
+1 212 310 8000
barry.wolf@weil.com
Recommended in Private Equity: Fund Formation
Specialisation: Co-Head of the Private Equity Group of *Weil, Gotshal & Manges*. Regularly represents a number of private investment funds and their sponsors in their organisation and operation. Has extensive experience representing institutional investors in investing in private equity funds, providing both commercial advice as well as tax advice. Background as a tax partner provides him with a unique combination of skills in advising sponsors and investors in connection with fund formation.

WOLFE, Gary
Seward & Kissel, New York +1 212 574 1200
Recommended in Shipping: Finance

WOLITZER, Michael
Simpson Thacher & Bartlett, New York
+1 212 455 2000
m_wolitzer@stblaw.com
Recommended in Private Equity: Fund Formation
Specialisation: A partner at *Simpson Thacher & Bartlett* since 1998. Practice focuses on private investing and other facets of 'alternative asset management'. Represents some of the largest and well known sponsors of private equity funds, such as Blackstone, Lehman Brothers, Heartland Industrial Partners and Silver Lake Partners. Involved in many acquisitions of, and investments in, private investment firms.
Prof. Memberships: Chairman of the 'Private Investment Fund Forum', a group comprised of New

York City attorneys practising extensively in the private fund area. Served on the panels 'How to Negotiate Winning Partnership Terms and Conditions' at the 'Private Equity Analyst' Conference, 'Buying, Selling and Investing in Private Investment Fund Managers' and 'Employee Investment Arrangements' at the IBA/ABA Conference on Private Investment Funds and 'How to Effectively Manage Multiple Funds' at the IIR Conference on Private Equity Fund Formation.
Career: Received a JD from Columbia University School of Law in 1989 and was a James Kent Scholar, a Harlan Fiske Stone Scholar and the Administrative Editor for the 'Columbia Journal of Law and Social Problems'.

WORTLEY, Michael
Vinson & Elkins LLP, Houston +1 713 758 2131
Recommended in Corporate/M&A

YODER, Lowell
McDermott, Will & Emery, Chicago
+1 312 372 2000
lyoder@mwe.com
Recommended in Tax
Specialisation: Partner in Tax Department. Practice focuses on international tax planning for public and private multinational companies. Advises on cross-border acquisitions, mergers, leases, financings and restructurings. Advises on international tax aspects of transactions and structures regarding foreign tax credits, expense allocations, sourcing of income, Subpart F, foreign personal holding companies, passive foreign investment companies and foreign sales corporations.
Prof. Memberships: Member of the Illinois Bar Association and American Bar Association.
Publications: Author and co-author of three treaties on Subpart F of the Internal Revenue Code (rules that apply to foreign operations of US multinationals); author of numerous articles on international tax topics including on classification of foreign entities, effect of foreign losses on the use of foreign tax credits, treatment of foreign partnerships, and a variety of foreign tax planning subjects.
Career: Admitted to the Illinois Bar in 1982. Federal Clerkship, 1982 - 1983, for the Honorable James M. Sprouse, US Circuit Court of Appeals for the Fourth Circuit. Joined *McDermott, Will & Emery* in 1983. Co-chairs the firm's International Tax Practice. Adjunct Professor of Law at the University of Illinois College of Law and the Chicago – Kent College of Law. Board member of the Journal of International Taxation and the Tax Management International Journal. Frequent speaker for Practising Law Institute, Tax Executives Institute and International Fiscal Association. Named in the 1999 Euromoney Guide to the World's Leading Tax Advisors.
Personal: Born 10 October 1955. Attended University of Illinois College of Law 1979 to 1982 (Juris Doctor, magna cum laude).

YOUNGWOOD, Alfred
Paul, Weiss, Rifkind, Wharton & Garrison, New York +1 212 373 3000
Recommended in Tax

ZAHLER, Robert
Shaw Pittman, Washington +1 202 663 8000
Recommended in Communications: Transactional (IT)

ZIMBLER, Jay H.
Sidley & Austin, Chicago +1 312 853 7000
jzimbler@sidley.com
Recommended in Tax
Specialisation: Principal areas of practice: Federal income taxation. Experienced in the taxation of foreign related transactions, mergers and acquisitions, and contested tax matters.
Prof. Memberships: American Bar Association; American College of Tax Counsel Fellow.
Career: Harvard Law School (JD 1975). *Hopkins & Sutter* (1975-1996). Joined *Sidley & Austin* as partner in 1996. Certified Public Accountant.

U

URUGUAY

Index

U

OVERVIEW: Most Uruguayan firms are multidisciplinary practices, with accountants, notaries, and a significant number of law students counted among the personnel. No international firms are present in the market, though multi-nationals are active. A long-term strike by the judiciary has halted all litigation, and Uruguayan firms have turned their attention to Mercosur trade, M&A activity in the banking sector and more substantial corporate acquisitions by foreign investors, particularly in the telecoms sector. As most corporate clients have no in-house counsel, day to day counsel is required. A clear winner in finance is Guyer & Regules, which has dominated the Uruguayan banking scene since the 1980s.

Banking & Finance

URUGUAY
Leading firms (Banking & Finance)

Band	Firm
1	Guyer & Regules
2	Estudio Ferrere-Lamaison
	Jiménez de Aréchaga & Brause
3	Hughes & Hughes
	Olivera & Delpiazzo
	Posadas, Posadas & Vecino

Firms are listed alphabetically in each band.

Leading individuals (Banking & Finance)

Band	Individual
1	**HERRERA Nicolás** *Guyer & Regules*
2	**FERRERE Daniel** *Estudio Ferrere-Lamaison*
	JIMÉNEZ DE ARECHAGA Fernando *Jiménez*
	OLIVERA Ricardo *Olivera & Delpiazzo*

Individuals are listed alphabetically in each band.

Guyer & Regules (5 ptrs, 8 asscs) *"The leading financial firm"* in Montevideo is noted for its strong client base of international banks, a domination that extends back to the 1980s. Competitors admitted to our researchers that the firm appears on *"about 80% of the deals."* Considered to be an innovator in the field, the firm was one of the first in the country to deal with commercial paper, negotiable obligations, derivatives, and securitisation, and has an established reputation for advising on syndicated loans. It also handled all issues of Euronotes and Euromarket shares by Uruguayan corporates, most governmental issues of Euronotes, and the first issue of shares by a local bank in the Euromarket.

Nicolás Herrera* is *"the driving force"* in this area; his work on the re-negotiation of Uruguay's external debt and the banking experience he gained while at Shearman & Sterling in New York, have led to renown as a *"thoroughly capable"* banking specialist.

Capital markets activity includes acting for Chase Manhattan as lead manager on the issue by the Republic of Uruguay of $300 million of bonds. The firm represented the same client on the issue of U$90 million notes with a swap agreement. **Clients:** Citibank; BankBoston; Chase Manhattan; CSFB; JP Morgan; Salomon Smith Barney; HSBC Uruguay.

Estudio Ferrere-Lamaison (1 ptrs, 5 asscs) An *"aggressive"* firm that has attacked the banking market with gusto in recent times, and is now described by rivals as *"quite active"* in the field. The firm has advised on negotiating loans for the government, some placements in the local market, and collection work. Name partner **Daniel Ferrere*** is *"the guy you see for finance."*

The firm acted for Banco Surinvest on a loan to the local government of Montevideo, and represented the Interamerican Investment Corporation in the recently privatised Hotel Carrasco project. Also acted for BellSouth on the issue of debentures by its Uruguayan subsidiary. A key client is the IFC, for whom the team acted on a loan to the university of Montevideo. **Clients:** ABN AMRO; Lloyds; BBVA; Fidelity; Discount Bank; Banco Surinvest.

Jiménez de Aréchaga & Brause *"Distinguished"* firm that is traditionally strong in finance, prospering on the back of its work for a number of high-powered international banks. Financial *"expert"* **Fernando Jiménez de Aréchaga*** was consistently endorsed by his peers.

The firm's client base also includes insurance and credit card companies, and pension and investment funds. The workload covers the whole range of general commercial matters from bank regulatory work to small-ticket acquisition finance and banking M&A. **Clients:** ABN AMRO; ING; Banco Santander.

Hughes & Hughes (2 ptrs, 2 asscs) A firm that *"you could definitely approach"* for financial advice, although the department is overshadowed by its corporate counterpart. Active on syndicated loans and project finance, the group advises a number of offshore banks, and represented Banco de Galicia on its incorporation in Uruguay.

The firm advised a corporate client on a USCP program worth $75 million, and acted on the abortive privatisation of the Carastro airport for Bank Boston. Lending activity has included acting on a loan from the Bank of Estonia to finance the import of Lada cars to Uruguay. **Clients:** Banco Galicia Uruguay; Bank of New York; Banque Priveé Edmond de Rothschild; Bank of Tokyo-Mitsubishi.

Olivera & Delpiazzo Full-service firm with a banking department that owes much of its reputation to the esteemed **Ricardo Olivera***. He is best known as dean of the Montevideo University law school, but has acknowledged capability in traditional banking work. The client base includes a number of overseas banks and offshore funds. **Clients:** Banco Comercial; Banco Santander; BNP Paribas; Citco Bank; Velox Bank; ABN AMRO.

Posadas, Posadas & Vecino (5 lawyers) The firm is renowned for its financial advice to offshore clients, and has a respected, if small, banking practice. It is counsel to a number of large Brazilian banking names, as well as domestic subsidiaries of international banks. Our research has found the firm to be a popular choice for referrals. Respected for its work on lending and banking M&A, the firm advised Banco Comercial, owned by Chase, Dresdner and CSFB, on the acquisition of ING Bank Uruguay. The firm is experienced in establishing Uruguayan branches of international banks, it recently set up the local arm of Deutsche Bank. **Clients:** Banco da Bahia; Banco Boavista; BankBoston; Banco Comercial; Banco Surinvest; Deutsche Bank Brazil; Merrill Lynch Uruguay.

U

Corporate/M&A

URUGUAY
Leading firms
(Corporate/Mergers & Acquisitions)

Band	Firm
1	Estudio Ferrere-Lamaison
	Guyer & Regules
	Hughes & Hughes
	Posadas, Posadas & Vecino
2	Jiménez de Aréchaga & Brause
	Pérez del Castillo-Navarro-Inciarte-Gari
3	Bado Kuster Zerbino & Rachetti
	Estudio Hector A Viana
	Olivera & Delpiazzo

Firms are listed alphabetically in each band.

Leading individuals
(Corporate/Mergers & Acquisitions)

Band	Individual
1	**DE POSADAS Ignacio** *Posadas, Posadas*
	FERRERE Daniel *Estudio Ferrere-Lamaison*
	HERRERA Nicolás *Guyer & Regules*
	HUGHES Conrado *Hughes & Hughes*
2	**CERRISOLA Andres** *Estudio Ferrere-Lamaison*
	JIMÉNEZ DE ARECHAGA Fernando *Jiménez*
	OREGGIA Juan Carlos *Posadas, Posadas*

Individuals are listed alphabetically in each band.

Estudio Ferrere-Lamaison (4 ptrs, 27 asscs) The corporate team has *"good people and doesn't make mistakes,"* a combination that has led to its reputation as *"one of the best"* commercial firms in the country. Its *"aggressive"* culture attracts cautious respect from local lawyers, but a high level of activity is acknowledged by all. **Daniel Ferrere*** is *"clearly a national leader,"* while **Andres Cerrisola*** *"has a great future."*

Particularly active in cross-border M&A in telecoms and banking, the firm advises a high proportion of the US corporates active in Uruguay. It advised on the merger of the local operations of Rhone Poulenc/Hoechst into Aventis, and also acted on the Uruguayan aspects of the Lloyds/TSB merger. The firm has also played an active role in recent privatisations, assisting Glenby in its successful bid for the Plan Fénix concession, a large urban development project. **Clients:** AEG; BAT; British Gas; Exxon; Microsoft; Gillette; Aventis; IDB; BASF; BellSouth; IFC; Esso; IBM; Microsoft; Movicom; Procter & Gamble; Royal & Sun Alliance; Sempra; SmithKline Beecham.

Guyer & Regules (8 ptrs, 7 asscs) A multi-disciplinary firm that is considered by most Montevideo lawyers to provide stiff competition in M&A. The firm *"has serious international connections,"* acts for a blue-chip international client base and is said to have *"probably the greatest market share"* in the country. **Nicolás Herrera*** is a *"young, dynamic lawyer"* with extensive international experience.

The firm's M&A activity is focused on acting for purchasers, and includes representing Danone on the purchase of a majority stake in domestic bottled water producer, Salus. Cross-border work includes advising Telefónica on the incorporation and co-ordination of its Latin American arm, and the development of a sub-marine cable. Other telecoms work, one of the firm's niche areas, includes acting for Telepuerto Internacional Buenos Aires on the purchase of Dalinco, a local teleport. The firm was also counsel to BBV, through its local subsidiary, in the merger with Banco Exterior de América. **Clients:** Xerox; Telefónica; Unilever; Oracle; American Airlines; Walt Disney; YPF/Repsol; General Motors; Reuters.

Hughes & Hughes (6 ptrs, 8 asscs) A *"dedicated, traditional"* firm with some *"wonderful people,"* which advises both international clients and companies with *"domestic clout."* The firm is active in the forestry and telecoms sectors and has also advised several internet start-ups. The *"seriously good"* **Conrado Hughes*** heads the corporate department. Recent work includes acting on the redevelopment of a hotel by Marriott. **Clients:** Colgate-Palmolive; Enron; Fox Latin America; Hilton; IFC; KLM; MCI WorldCom; Shell; Chevron; McDonalds; Panasonic.

Posadas, Posadas & Vecino (10 lawyers) A firm that has an outstanding reputation for offshore work, and has attracted praise for its growing M&A practice. The *"gentlemanly"* **Ignacio de Posadas*** is respected by counterparts for his abilities as managing partner, and is the country's current Minister of the Economy. **Juan Carlos Oreggia*** was recommended to our researchers as a popular corporate player. The firm's clientele is a mixture of domestic and international corporates in various sectors, including food and drink producers and utilities companies.

The firm recently acted for American Beverage Co on the acquisition of a local beer and soft drink producer, and also represented Hicks Muse Tate & Furst on the purchase of Uruguay's two largest outdoor advertising companies. M&A activity in the banking sector includes the acquisition of ING Bank Uruguay by Banco Comercial. Advice on establishing joint ventures is an area of specific expertise, exemplified by the firm's work on one such arrangement between cheese producers Bongrain and local corporate Conaprole. **Clients:** Alcatel; AT&T; BT; Caterpillar; Duke Energy; Procter & Gamble; Quaker; Exxel; Delta Airlines.

Jiménez de Aréchaga & Brause (3 ptrs, 7 asscs) The firm maintains a strong corporate practice, acting for a number of multi-national big-hitters, and is described by competitors as *"an important local player."* **Fernando Jiménez de Aréchaga*** is one of the leading figures in Uruguay and has a sound reputation. The firm is especially active in handling daily corporate matters. **Clients:** PepsiCo; Nabisco; McDonalds; Ericsson; Milagro.

Pérez del Castillo-Navarro-Inciarte-Gari (4 ptrs, 15 asscs) A firm that has gained increasing exposure for corporate work recently. One of its newest and most high profile clients is Exxel, said

*See leaders' profiles on page 906

by the market to have been *"managed well."* The client base is predominantly international, and the corporate group receives referrals from Argentinian, Brazilian and Spanish firms. Apart from its substantial general corporate and M&A practice, the team has niche expertise in regional and Mercosur trade and competition. **Clients:** 3M; Adecco; Sol Melia Hotels; Iberia; Lacoste; Latinstocks.com; Levi Strauss; Polo Ralph Lauren; Exxel.

Bado Kuster Zerbino & Rachetti (4 ptrs, 4 asscs) Traditional firm, which is acknowledged for M&A work for a mixture of corporate clients, and is especially well known for its dominance of the French market in Uruguay. The partners are described as *"proactive,"* and enjoy particular repute for their work in gas, telecoms and consumer products.

The firm took part in the largest merger in Uruguay in 2000, the association between Supermercados Disco and French group Casino, and the subsequent acquisition by the merged venture of the second largest domestic supermarket chain from Exxel. It also advised on the acquisition by NH Hoteles of Spain of a Montevideo hotel. Other M&A work includes the purchase of a local record label by EMI International, while the firm's extensive experience for bidders in tender offers includes acting for a consortium of French, Italian and Spanish telecoms companies in a bid for a regional mobile phone system. **Clients:** Martini Rossi; Goodyear; Telefónica (Argentina & Spain); Peugeot; EMI; Citroën; Aguas de Barcelona; Lyonnaise des Eaux.

Estudio Hector A Viana (5 ptrs, 7 asscs) A popular Montevideo firm that has maintained its market position due to its well known work for local clients, though it now has a swelling international clientele. The firm handles the full range of commercial matters and has recently developed specialisms in telecoms and IP. It also dabbles in restructuring, acting for Galicia Capital Markets on the refinancing of the international boat operator Buquebus Group. Telecoms work includes assisting VeloCom in the preparation of a successful bid for the installation and operation of a broad band telecoms network. The firm represented Republica AFAP (the largest national pension fund) in setting up the first co-branded website in the country with StarMedia. **Clients:** Republica AFAP; Sudamtex; Guess; BankBoston; Adidas; Warner Bros; Nortel; La Nación; Embassy of South Africa.

Olivera & Delpiazzo (24 lawyers) Known by its peers to be *"strong in corporate,"* the firm has survived rocky times, having been through several mergers and splits in the past few years, including one with PwC. The firm's client base largely comprises domestic corporates, although the firm also represents a number of medical and scientific societies. **Clients:** Antel; Avis; BAT; Esso; Nike Argentina; Shell Uruguay; Sony Music; Coca-Cola Export; Kellogg's.

Leaders' profiles – Uruguay

CERRISOLA, Andres
Estudio Ferrere-Lamaison, Montevideo
+598 2 402 4243
acerrisola@ferrere.com.uy
Recommended in Corporate/M&A
Specialisation: Head of the firm's Infrastructure & Telecommunications Dept. Is a highly recognised expert on regulatory matters, particularly in telecommunications and energy.
Prof. Memberships: International Bar Association.
Publications: 'Derecho de la Empresa', Edit. AJF Montevideo, 1998; 'Las Telecomunicaciones en un Mundo de Competencia', Edit. EUDEBA, Buenos Aires, 2000.
Career: Joined *Ferrere-Lamaison* as Associate in 1986 (Partner, 1991). Director of the Institute of Law and Member of the Advisory Board, ORT University, School of Business and Social Sciences. Professor of International Trade Theory and International Finance, University of the Republic (1990-92), Professor of Economics, University of the Republic (1987-1990).
Personal: Born 1964. Graduated in the University of Uruguay (Doctor in Law and Social Sciences, 1990); Harvard Law School (Master in Law, 1992); University of Brussels (Law and Institutions of the European Community, 1992).

DE POSADAS, Ignacio
Posadas, Posadas & Vecino, Montevideo
+598 2 916 2202
Recommended in Corporate/M&A

FERRERE, Daniel
Estudio Ferrere-Lamaison, Montevideo
+598 2 402 4243
dferrere@ferrere.com.uy
Recommended in Banking & Finance, Corporate/M&A
Specialisation: Managing Partner of the firm since 1984, is in charge of the more complex deals on finance and M&A.
Prof. Memberships: Bar Association of Uruguay, International Bar Association, International Fiscal Association.
Publications: Author of seven books and more than 50 articles on banking and trade law, published in Uruguay, Argentina and Switzerland.
Career: Member of the diplomatic service of Uruguay until 1977. Joined *Ferrere-Lamaison* in 1977. Was Senior Professor of International Trade Law in the School of Laws of the University of Uruguay until 1994, and Professor of Financial Markets Regulation in the School of Management of the ORT University until 1996.
Personal: Born 1950. Graduated in the University of Uruguay (Dr. in Laws and Social Sciences, 1974) and in Harvard Law School (LLM 1976).

HERRERA, Nicolás
Guyer & Regules, Montevideo +598 2 902 1515
Recommended in Banking & Finance, Corporate/M&A

HUGHES, Conrado
Hughes & Hughes, Montevideo +598 2 916 0988
Recommended in Corporate/M&A

JIMÉNEZ DE ARECHAGA, Fernando
Jiménez de Aréchaga & Brause, Montevideo
+598 2 915 3188
Recommended in Banking & Finance, Corporate/M&A

OLIVERA, Ricardo
Olivera & Delpiazzo, Montevideo +598 2 916 5859
Recommended in Banking & Finance

OREGGIA, Juan Carlos
Posadas, Posadas & Vecino, Montevideo
+598 2 916 2202
Recommended in Corporate/M&A

UZBEKISTAN

Corporate/Commercial

UZBEKISTAN Leading firms (Corporate/Commercial)
1 Baker & McKenzie
Chadbourne & Parke LLP
2 Gouldens

Firms are listed alphabetically in each band.

Leading individuals (Corporate/Commercial)
1 **KHODADAD Nabil** *Chadbourne & Parke LLP*
TAYLOR Robert *Baker & McKenzie*

Individuals are listed alphabetically in each band.

Baker & McKenzie (3 lawyers) Part of the firm's CIS practice group, the office is, by its own admission, a satellite of the Almaty office. Active on a variety of corporate matters, the firm includes *"bright"* senior associate **Robert Taylor***, the only full-time foreign lawyer in Tashkent.

The firm advised on Ford's abortive acquisition of Daewoo, and has acted for a number of German clients involved in supply contracts for mining. Also represented the banks involved in underwriting the forthcoming privatisation of the state owned gas company, a matter worth $500 million. **Clients:** International banks and corporates.

Chadbourne & Parke LLP (3 asscs) **Nabil Khodadad***, formerly Mayer Brown & Platt's central Asia head, has transferred his practice wholesale to this New York firm. As a result, the firm is now established as a major force in the region. The firm advised Rabobank on its financing of the Uzbek government's purchase of agricultural machinery, and assisted Trinity Energy on a production sharing arrangement for its oil and gas interests. **Clients:** Heinrich Glaeser; Rabobank; Trinity Energy.

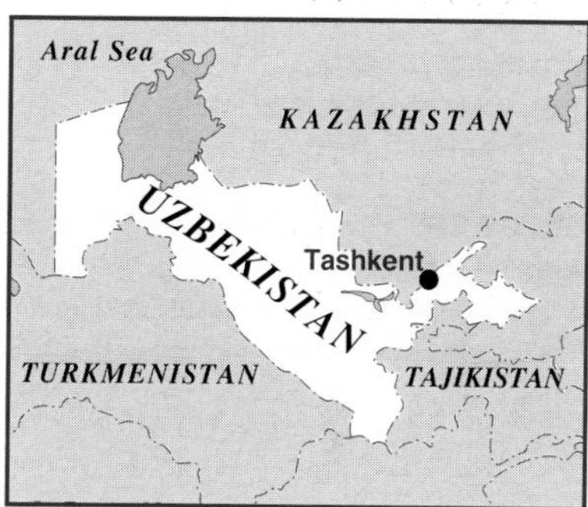

Gouldens (3 lawyers) The team consists of *"local lawyers doing small projects,"* and is recognised by peers as a *"sound operation."* It provides day to day legal advice for Elsut, an American cotton seed company, and has provided regulatory advice to two UK telecoms clients. **Clients:** Elsut; Barakat.

Leaders' profiles – Uzbekistan

KHODADAD, Nabil
Chadbourne & Parke LLP, Tashkent
+998 71 12 06 627

TAYLOR, Robert
Baker & McKenzie, Tashkent +998 13 33 643
Specialisation: Associate with the Almaty Office of *Baker & McKenzie.* Specialises in commercial and energy law. Prior to joining *Baker & McKenzie* was the Dean of International Studies for the University of the Pacific and adjunct Professor of Law at Pepperdine University and at Boston University. Member of the Alabama and Brussels Bar Associations, and practised commercial Law in Brussels. Most recently, has worked as a legal advisor to the Government of the Kyrgyz Republic through the European Union's TACIS program and continues to work closely with the international donor community there.
Publications: Published in both international trade and comparative law journals.
Career: Cumberland School of Law (JD), Samford University (BA in Roman Languages). Received an LLM in Transnational Business Practice and undertook two years of post doctoral training in French Private Law. Admitted to practice Law in Alabama (USA) and Belgium.
Personal: Fluent in English and French.

VENEZUELA

Index

V

OVERVIEW: A serious slump has hit the economy drying up new project finance work in the oil and gas sectors, formerly the major source of legal activity. All privatisations previously scheduled have been postponed, frustrating many potential foreign investors and their Venezuelan counsel. But the restucturing or extension of existing oil and gas projects provides some relief, as did the $1.6 billion acquisition by AES of Electricidad de Caracas. Firms have found their labour and corporate restructuring practices are booming, while banking experts, led by the remarkable James Rodner of Rodner Martínez, are fighting over an increasingly small pot of opportunities. Baker & McKenzie's Caracas branch continues to be its strongest in South America, while other foreign firms such as Macleod Dixon and Steel Hector & Davis are serious competitors to the local firms.

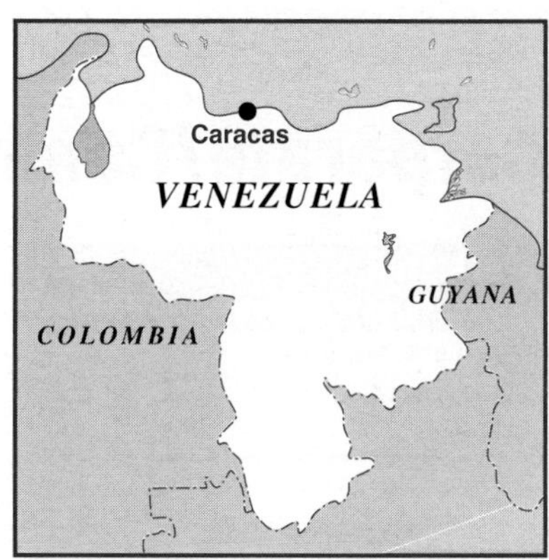

Banking & Finance

VENEZUELA
Leading firms
(Banking & Finance)

Band	Firm
1	Rodner Martínez & Asociados
2	D'Empaire Reyna Bermudez
	Hoet Pelaez Castillo & Duque
	Tinoco Travieso Planchart & Nuñez
	Torres Plaz & Araujo
	Travieso Evans Arria Rengel & Paz

Firms are listed alphabetically in each band.

Leading individuals
(Banking & Finance)

Band	Individual
1	**RODNER James** *Rodner Martínez & Asociados*
2	**CASTILLO Francisco** *Hoet Pelaez Castillo*
	REYNA Gustavo *D'Empaire Reyna Bermudez*
	TORRES Manuel *Torres Plaz & Araujo*

Individuals are listed alphabetically in each band.

Rodner Martínez & Asociados (9 ptrs, 11 asscs) *"A great name for finance"* universally admired by peers for its high degree of expertise and *"fine clients,"* the firm has a near monopoly on international banks active in the country. The team is led by the *"outstanding,"* high profile **James Rodner*** who is *"respectful of his colleagues."* Described by competitors as a *"savvy"* expert, *"he has really capitalised on the banking activity"* in Venezuela.

Project finance in oil, gas, and telecoms dominates the work load, where it has advised big-ticket US, European and Japanese clients facing the privatisation process. World Bank, OPIC and Exim Bank continue to supply strong deal flow. The team acted for Citibank and Paribas on the restructuring of a local steel mill. **Clients:** Bank of America; ABN AMRO; World Bank; OPIC; Exim Bank; Citibank; Paribas; BP.

D'Empaire Reyna Bermudez & Asociados Considered an *"important competitor,"* the firm is respected for its restructuring practice often acting for banks. It represented domestic corporate Sidererúgica del Orinoco in its $1 billion debt restructuring and $300 million capitalisation. Founding partner **Gustavo Reyna*** is known by peers as *"good for finance."*

In capital markets the team advised Electricidad de Caracas on the issuance of €200 million notes, and the CAF in its $300 million USCP Program. In banking M&A activity it acted for Colombian group Davivienda in the sale of its holding in Banco de la República. **Clients:** Corporación Andina de Fomento; Chase Manhattan; Citibank; Royal & SunAlliance; insurance companies; Barclays; Davivienda.

Hoet Pelaez Castillo & Duque Our researchers found that the firm is acknowledged to be *"an important player in Caracas"* with a focus on this sector. *"Excellent"* name partner **Francisco Castillo*** *"perceives things easily"* and is said to be *"a tough, yet nice man."* The firm has a mainly domestic banking clientele and acted in negotiations arising from a local banking dispute. **Clients:** Domestic financial institutions.

Tinoco Travieso Planchart & Nuñez The firm is regarded by leading lawyers in Caracas as having *"a good banking practice"* although it has a lesser profile than in previous years. A team of *"good people"* undertakes restructuring and credit arrangement work. **Clients:** Domestic financial institutions and corporates.

Torres Plaz & Araujo The firm is described by peers as having *"good clients"* with a mixture of international banks, domestic and international corporates. Local lawyers also admire the firm's buoyant tax practice led by banking expert and figurehead **Manuel Torres*** who has recognised strength. **Clients:** Banco Venozolano de Crédito; JP Morgan; Lehman Brothers; Merrill Lynch; Royal & SunAlliance.

Travieso Evans Arria Rengel & Paz Considered by Venezuela's top lawyers as *"first rate for banking and finance,"* the firm counts international banks among its clientele. The finance department is active in local bond issues and oil and gas project finance, where it represents big ticket clients such as Exxon Mobil, in both its upstream and downstream activities. **Clients:** Multinationals; Exxon Mobil.

Corporate/M&A

VENEZUELA Leading firms (Corporate/Mergers & Acquisitions)
1 Baker & McKenzie
D'Empaire Reyna Bermudez & Asociados
Rodríguez & Mendoza
Torres Plaz & Araujo
Travieso Evans Arria Rengel & Paz
2 Anzola Raffalli y Rodriguez
Mendoza, Palacios, Acedo, Borjas, Paez Pumar & Cia
3 Araque Reyna Sosa Viso & Pittier
Palacios Ortegay Asociados
Rodner Martínez & Asociados
Tinoco Travieso Planchart & Nuñez
4 Benson, Perez Matos, Antakly & Watts
Hoet Pelaez Castillo & Duque
Perez Luna Alvins Paoli & Asociados

Firms are listed alphabetically in each band.

Leading individuals (Corporate/Mergers & Acquisitions)
1 **ANZOLA Oswaldo** *Rodríguez & Mendoza*
CAPLAN Malcolm *Baker & McKenzie*
2 **ANZOLA J Eloy** *Anzola Raffalli y Rodriguez*
ARAUJO Federico *Torres Plaz & Araujo*
MUCI ABRAHAM José *Steel Hector & Davis*
TORRES Manuel *Torres Plaz & Araujo*
TRAVIESO Eduardo *Travieso Evans Hughes*
3 **BORJAS Arminio F** *Mendoza, Palacios, Acedo*
HERNANDEZ-BRETON Eugenio *Baker & McKenzie*
ITALIANI Fulvio *D'Empaire Reyna Bermudez*
MENDOZA Luis Ignacio *Rodríguez & Mendoza*
PALACIOS Luis Esteban *Palacios Ortega*
PLANCHART MANRIQUE Gustavo *Tinoco Travieso Planchart & Nuñez*
REYNA Gustavo *D'Empaire Reyna Bermudez*
4 **ACEDO Carlos Eduardo** *Mendoza, Palacios, Acedo*
ANTAKLY Farid *Benson, Perez Matos, Antakly*
PAZ PARRA Francisco *Travieso Evans Hughes*
PLAZ Rodolfo *Torres Plaz & Araujo*
RENGEL JR Pedro *Travieso Evans Hughes*
RODNER James *Rodner Martínez & Asociados*

Individuals are listed alphabetically in each band.

Baker & McKenzie (10 ptrs, 45 asscs) A large team with a *"strong presence,"* it is acknowledged as a leader packed with *"good people." "Key figure"* **Malcolm Caplan*** (US and Venezuelan dual qualified) is co-ordinator of the firm's activity in South America, and his expertise in tax and corporate matters in the oil and gas sectors is admired. Younger partner **Eugenio Hernandez-Breton*** is described as *"one of the most outstanding lawyers in Venezuela"* for corporate and financial work.

The firm's client base includes both domestic and multinational corporates and it is heavily involved in restructuring and labour law. It advised Telecom Italia in its purchase of Digitel's Venezuelan assets, acted for Quibarca in a $4 million merger, and represented the Conti Group in the $10 million disposal of part of its domestic operations. **Clients:** Nintendo; Reebok; Quibarca; Gruma; Conti Group; Repsol YPF; Bell Canada; 20th Century Fox; domestic corporates.

D'Empaire Reyna Bermudez & Asociados An *"excellent"* firm regarded by Caracas lawyers as *"aggressive"* and *"hardworking."* It has been in the limelight for its representation of AES in the $1.6 billion acquisition of 80% of Electricidad de Caracas – by far the largest M&A deal this year. A *"good team"* includes the *"outstanding"* young M&A and projects partner **Fulvio Italiani***, credited with being the *"mastermind"* behind the AES deal. *"Extremely strong"* managing partner **Gustavo Reyna*** is widely respected, described by rivals as *"a good negotiator"* and a businessman.

US and European clients in the electricity and telecoms sectors provide the bulk of the firm's corporate activity and it is supported by active labour law and IP practices. The team advised Telecom Italia Mobile on its acquisition of a majority shareholding in Digitel, a local telecoms provider. **Clients:** AES; Telecom Italia Mobile; BASF; Bristol Myers-Squibb; Chubb; Continental Airlines; Del Monte; McDonald's; Pérez Companc; Pfizer; Pirelli; StarMedia; Sun Microsystems; Techint.

Rodríguez & Mendoza A *"traditional and competent"* practice highly regarded for its corporate work although occasionally thought to rely on its old guard partners. A *"first rate"* team is led by the *"outstanding tax guru"* **Oswaldo Anzola***. He is vastly experienced and *"a good teacher"* to younger members. *"Prominent attorney"* **Luis Ignacio Mendoza*** is *"of the older generation,"* recognised by the market as a major player.

Recommended for its M&A, anti-trust and project finance work, clients include multinationals in telecoms, consumer products and the oil and gas industries. The team acted for Citibank in a local acquisition. **Clients:** Citibank; Microholding supermarkets; Gillette; Bunzl; Coward Corp; telecoms and TV companies.

Torres Plaz & Araujo Originally a tax boutique, the practice has established itself as full service, judged by peers to be *"an excellent corporate team."* The key to the firm's rapid growth lies with the *"high profile"* of its respected name partners. Tax expert **Federico Araujo*** is described as *"the most visible player in the firm"* and, with the *"charming"* **Manuel Torres***, *"helps to promote the firm."* **Rodolfo Plaz*** is an important element in the group's success. The firm acts for domestic and international corporates in a broad base of industry sectors. **Clients:** BAT; Cargill; Chrysler de Venezuela; IBM de Venezuela; Schering-Plough; Toyota; domestic corporates.

Travieso Evans Arria Rengel & Paz (7 ptrs, 13 asscs) Research has shown that the firm is a respected corporate player, with a blue-chip multinational client base providing valuable *"international experience." "Consolidated well,"* the team has built on experience acquired as *"one of the pioneers in foreign investment."* Name partners **Eduardo Travieso*** and **Pedro Rengel Jr*** are regarded as *"fine"* corporate and tax lawyers, while *"rainmaker"* **Francisco Paz Parra*** is seen as the *"leader"* who promotes the firm abroad.

The firm acts as Venezuelan counsel to multinationals such as Unilever and Ford, indeed 98% of its clientele are international corporates. Growth areas include telecoms where the team has been active in privatisations. **Clients:** Exxon Mobil; Unilever; Warner Lambert Group; Enron; Ford.

Anzola Raffalli y Rodriguez (3 ptrs, 3 asscs) *Chambers'* researchers were told that this small, young firm offers *"an excellent product"* and local lawyers who have *"good initiatives."* Active for foreign companies in the acquisition of Venezuelan corporates, the *"dynamic"* team is led by highly respected founder **Eloy Anzola***, known for his business acumen.

Clients are domestics and multinationals in food, oil and banking sectors while privatisation in the telecoms field continues to drive the firm. It acted for a US corporate in its acquisition of a local company and advised a local liquor client in its purchase of assets from a UK corporate. **Clients:** Domestic and multinational corporates.

Mendoza, Palacios, Acedo, Borjas, Paez Pumar & Cia (7 ptrs, 4 asscs) A *"traditional, family-focused"* practice. It has suffered with the departure of two senior partners (to form Palacios Ortega & Asociados) but despite a *"generation problem"* continues to be acknowledged as

*See leaders' profiles on pages 912-914

"effective." **Arminio Borjas*** is described by peers as a *"good corporate lawyer,"* while Paris educated **Carlos Eduardo Acedo*** is recommended in corporate and insurance work.

A strong national client base is balanced by long-term relationships with big-ticket multinationals such as Shell and IBM. It acted on the merger of a local insurance company owned by Banco Mercantil with Aetna, advised Citibank on the change in control of Banco Unión and on the merger of the latter with Caja Familia. Active in restructuring, it undertakes corporate and regulatory work. **Clients:** IBM; Sun Microsystems; Telefónica de España; CanTV; Glaxo Wellcome; Pfizer; domestic insurance companies; AT&T; CAF.

V

Araque Reyna Sosa Viso & Pittier (2 ptrs, 1 assc) A well respected general practice with a strong corporate team and expertise in labour law. It has capitalised on the current telecoms privatisation activity. The clientele contains a mix of international and national corporates, including representation of the Caracas and the US/Venezuelan chambers of commerce. **Clients:** Caracas Chamber of Commerce; US/Venezuelan Chamber of Commerce.

Palacios Ortega y Asociados (4 ptrs, 5 asscs) Regarded by competitors as a *"promising"* corporate player formed recently by two ex Mendoza Palacios lawyers and one ex in-house counsel of CANTV. Rapid growth in its first year has given the firm commercial clout. Much of its esteem is due to *"prominent"* name partner **Luis Palacios***, a prestigious player who commands respect from peers for his corporate and M&A expertise.

An impressive clientele includes multi-nationals, financial institutions and domestic corporates. The team advised on the acquisition by Banco Mercantil of Interbank to form the largest domestic bank, and advised a trust bank on the hostile takeover of a Venezuelan utilities corporate. The firm handles all of IBM's corporate law needs and has a niche in telecoms. **Clients:** Citibank; GTE; IBM; JP Morgan; Banco Mercantil; CANTV; Patagon.com; domestic corporates.

Rodner Martínez & Asociados (9 ptrs, 1 assc) A *"famous"* firm reputed for its M&A activity although somewhat overshadowed by the financial practice. *"Prestigious"* **James Rodner*** is respected for his transactional expertise. The firm's client base comprises mainly foreign investors in the telecoms, forestry, oil and gas industries, and foreign banks and governmental agencies such as OPIC. Involved in daily corporate matters, the firm is rated for its activity on corporate transactions. **Clients:** OPIC; World Bank; international corporates.

Tinoco Travieso Planchart & Nuñez A *"fine"* long-standing corporate player that has been judged by the market to be *"losing steam"* since a failed local merger. The corporate practice is led by the *"respectable"* **Gustavo Planchart Manrique***, *"a high level person"* known for his teaching at the university and as a member of several international commissions. **Clients:** Mainly domestic corporates.

Benson, Perez Matos, Antakly & Watts With its roots in the oil sector it is a practice that has *"been around for a long time."* Senior partner **Farid Antakly*** has *"an excellent reputation in international investments"* according to competitors. The team acted in the acquisition of an industrial plant in the liquor business, and advised a US paper company in its merger with two domestic corporates. It has counselled on strategic alliances between multinational clients and Venezuelan state-owned companies. The firm's client base is 70% foreign investors, largely US corporates. **Clients:** DuPont; Minnesota Mining; Federal Express; Heinz; Diageo; Lotus; Holderbank; Pillsbury; Elizabeth Arden; Kimberly-Clark.

Hoet Pelaez Castillo & Duque (11 ptrs, 25 asscs) Known as an IP specialist this firm has diversified into a *"strong"* general corporate practice which includes a former member of the Venezuelan supreme court. The majority of the firm's corporate clients are multinationals and activity in the telecoms sector is high. It assisted a US telecoms entity in setting up a Venezuelan branch of its global financial and economic news network, and continues to act for domestic telecoms operators. The team represented a Spanish hotel chain in the development of a luxury hotel in Caracas and acted for a North American explosives client in the establishment of a joint venture with a state enterprise. Members of the firm collaborated in the recent reform of the judiciary in Venezuela. **Clients:** Teléfonos de Venezuela; Movilet; international corporates.

Perez Luna Alvins Paoli & Asociados (4 ptrs, 4 asscs) An outstanding practice judged by rivals to be *"small but good"* packed tightly with *"strong partners."* The tax practice has a fine reputation locally for its daily corporate and transactional work. It acted as counsel on the negotiations surrounding the Venezuelan demerger of an accountancy firm into its two original parts. **Clients:** Chase Manhattan; international accountancy firms.

Other Notable Practitioner A senior player in the market, *"prestigious"* **José Muci-Abraham*** of Steel Hector Davis has a *"combative"* approach and is admired by rivals for his primarily US client base.

Energy & Natural Resources

Baker & McKenzie (5 ptrs, 8 asscs) Traditionally *"good for oil,"* with a branch in Maturín, the oil and gas hub of Eastern Venezuela, the team acts for blue-chip multi-national clients often referred via the international network. Founding partner of Caracas branch, **Malcolm Caplan*** is "*highly regarded*" as a key player by contemporaries. The team acted for Repsol YPF in its $55 million acquisition of the Quiriquire hydrocarbons project and on its $24 million purchase of interests in the Guarapiche oil field.

Elsewhere, it advised Seneca, a joint venture midstream electrical corporate, on a gas supply agreement with the government. It also advised clients on the ultimately aborted privatisation of the electricity sector. Active in mining, the team represented Shell Coal on the sale of its $850 million interest in the Paso Diablo-Socuy mines, a transaction that involved the disposal of coal interests in Australia and Venezuela. **Clients:** Repsol YPF; Hamaca; Shell Coal; Seneca.

Rodríguez & Mendoza Market opinion regards this firm as *"one of the leaders"* in oil and gas, with a strength in transactional matters for multinational clients. Much of the firm's activity lies in project development. It has played a part in four of the seven projects in the past three years, including a $3 billion petro-chemical financing. It has assisted in the Hamaca joint venture since its inception, representing Texaco, and in capital markets advised PDVSA on the securitisation of its oil receivers.

VENEZUELA
Leading firms
(Energy & Natural Resources)

1
- Baker & McKenzie
- Rodríguez & Mendoza

2
- Anzola Raffalli y Rodriguez
- Macleod Dixon LLP
- Torres Plaz & Araujo
- Travieso Evans Arria Rengel & Paz

3
- D'Empaire Reyna Bermudez & Asociados
- Mendoza, Palacios, Acedo, Borjas, Paez Pumar & Cia
- Steel Hector & Davis

Firms are listed alphabetically in each band.

Leading individuals
(Energy & Natural Resources)

1
- ANZOLA Oswaldo *Rodríguez & Mendoza*

2
- ANZOLA Eloy *Anzola Raffalli y Rodriguez*
- ARAUJO Federico *Torres Plaz & Araujo*
- CAPLAN Malcolm *Baker & McKenzie*
- ELJURI Elizabeth *Macleod Dixon LLP*
- HELLMUND Reinaldo *Rodríguez & Mendoza*
- TRAVIESO Eduardo *Travieso Evans Hughes*

Individuals are listed alphabetically in each band.

High profile tax practitioner **Oswaldo Anzola*** is considered in Caracas legal circles as an *"excellent"* oil and gas lawyer, and **Reinaldo Hellmund***, with *"a good reputation"* in energy, is said to *"do much of the work."* **Clients:** Hamaca; Texaco; BP; Exxon Mobil; Enron; Conoco.

Anzola Raffalli y Rodriguez (1 ptr, 1 assc) Successfully established in the energy sector over a relatively short period, the firm is renowned for its work with French oil clients such as Elf. Among its *"good people,"* **Eloy Anzola*** is a key figure as the Elf contact. On the domestic front the team represented a local company in an association with an oil multinational in the operation of an oil field. It advised a German oil client on a joint venture with a local company to operate a port, and assisted a French chemical client in the purchase of a domestic chemicals corporate. The firm also has an active mining practice involved in the acquisition of gold and coal mining companies, and has been involved in electricity privatisation plans. **Clients:** Elf; multinational and domestic corporates in oil and gas services.

Macleod Dixon LLP (6 ptrs, 14 asscs) An *"aggressive"* firm widely acknowledged to *Chambers'* researchers for its energy expertise and as counsel to the majority of Canadian oil and gas corporates active in Venezuela. That said, it has faced difficulties recently over a dispute with the local bar association. Venezuelan partner **Elizabeth Eljuri*** enjoys acclaim for her energy work, and is described by competitors as *"an exceptionally fine lawyer."* Active on several exploratory blocks, the focus lies with oil and gas work for multinationals and service companies.
The team advised on the Jose crude oil and shiploading terminal, and on the world's largest gas compression project Pigap 2. Involved in rendering advice on the forthcoming gas licence bids and the Anaco-Jose pipeline bid, the firm has close connections with PDVSA. **Clients:** BP; Burlington Resources; Chevron; Enbridge International; Halliburton; Petrobras; Shell; Nippon Oil; Perez Companc; Precision Drilling; PDVSA.

Torres Plaz & Araujo According to *Chambers'* research the firm is regarded locally as *"one of the best for energy,"* and has scored well with its involvement in a large fertiliser project. **Federico Araujo*** has tax-related energy expertise, and benefits from *"a fine group of lawyers around him."* The firm counsels international energy corporates, mainly through their Venezuelan subsidiaries and has a substantial mining practice. **Clients:** Chevron Olersas Petroleum; Delta Minerals; Newmont Mining; Petroleos de Venezuela; Petroquímica de Venezuela; Super-Octanos.

Travieso Evans Arria Rengel & Paz Rated by peers as *"a top firm"* and described as *"one of the best for energy,"* its fine reputation lies in oil and electricity. Among the firm's impressive clientele is Exxon Mobil, for whom it handles upstream and downstream work, and Pennzoil, which owns three activation blocks. Name partner **Eduardo Travieso*** *"does an awful lot of work in energy,"* and is recommended for his corporate expertise. With regional offices in the cities of Valencia and Maturín, the bulk of the firm's activity is in the negotiation of contracts in the oil sector. **Clients:** Exxon Mobil; Pennzoil; Enron.

D'Empaire Reyna Bermudez & Asociados A *"fine practice,"* although not considered *"a heavyweight"* in energy, it has attracted attention with its role in the AES deal where it represented the power multinational in its $1.6 billion take-over of the domestic Electricidad de Caracas, the largest private Venezuelan utility corporate. Much of its activity in the energy sector is transactional, though it does undertake regulatory work and project finance. It advised Electricidad de Caracas in its issuance of €200 million notes, and Sidererúgica del Orinoco, the country's largest steel manufacturer, in its $1 billion debt restructuring and $300 million capitalisation. **Clients:** AES; Energy Works; Inelectra; Minera Loma de Níquel; Sidor.

Mendoza, Palacios, Acedo, Borjas, Paez Pumar & Cia (6 ptrs, 4 asscs) A *"fine firm"* famed locally as counsel to long standing client Shell, it acts for a combination of national and international clients, mainly in the oil and gas sectors, both upstream and downstream. Growth has been seen in mining and the electricity sector where the team advises potential foreign investors. In collaboration with Freshfields, it acts as counsel on the $4.1 billion Hamaca crude oil project representing the lenders, Exim Bank inter alia. The energy team is also counsel to the IFC in the financing of a new industrial coal project, and the development of the Elkem carbonised plant project. **Clients:** Shell; PDVSA; Amoco; Enron; Petroquímica de Venezuela; Petrotrin; Sociedad de Fomento de Inversiones Petroleras.

Steel Hector & Davis (4 ptrs, 4 asscs) This *"fine"* office of a Florida based firm enjoys acclaim locally for its work with international petrochemical clients. It advised CVG Bauxilum and French corporate Pechiney on a joint venture to upgrade an alumina plant, and acted in Lasmo's project in the Dacion oil field. The team also represented AES in its greenfield electricity generation plant in the Dominican Republic and assisted Orinoco Iron's structuring of commercial operations outside Venezuela. **Clients:** PDVSA; Pequiven; Lasmo; Koch Industries; AES; Florida Power & Light; Delta Resources; Orinoco Iron; Citgo Petroleum Corp.

V

*See leaders' profiles on pages 912-914

Leaders' profiles – Venezuela

ACEDO, Carlos Eduardo
Mendoza, Palacios, Acedo, Borjas, Paez Pumar & Cia, Caracas +58 2 992 1611
ceacedo@juriscompint.com
Recommended in Corporate/M&A
Specialisation: Contracts, Torts, Insurance, Corporate Finance, Mergers and Acquisitions.
Prof. Memberships: Member of the National Society of Doctors in Law (France); the Venezuela-United States Businessmen Council; Director of several institutions, including the Venezuelan Association of Insurance Law; Arbitrator, Caracas Chamber of Commerce (affiliated to the Paris International Chamber of Commerce).
Publications: Author of two books and several articles on Contracts, Torts and Insurance.
Career: Universidad Católica Andrés Bello (Lawyer, Cum Laude, 1982); University of Paris 2 (Specialisation Diploma on Civil Law, "Bien", 1986; Diploma of Doctoral Studies, "Tres bien", 1988). Professor of Contractual Liability and Torts (1989-1992), Universidad Central de Venezuela. Joined *Mendoza Palacios* (1982), Partner (1995). Auxiliary Lawyer of the Supreme Court of Justice (1991-1994). Legal Assistant to the Minister of Finance (1994-1995).
Personal: Born August 21, 1959. Languages: Spanish, English and French.

ANTAKLY, Farid
Benson, Perez Matos, Antakly & Watts, Caracas +582 266 8292
fantakly@bpmaw.com
Recommended in Corporate/M&A
Specialisation: Senior partner in corporate department. Main areas of legal work are corporate, commercial, M&A, privatisations, foreign investments in Venezuela, transfer of technology, exchange controls and debt/equity Swaps. Has handled several acquisitions and mergers of companies, including the acquisition of local cement companies by a leading Swiss company; of local industries in the food and services sector by major US companies; and of local companies in the liquor business by a major UK company. Acted in the mergers of subsidiaries of multinational companies. Assisted clients in processes of privatisation of state-owned companies in telecommunications, aluminium, cement, and energy sectors and bidding processes for other industries.
Prof. Memberships: Bar Association of the Federal District (Caracas); International Bar Association.
Career: Admitted 1964. *Benson, Perez Matos, Antakly & Watts*, Partner 1969; Managing Partner 1979. Member of the boards of several multinational companies. Venezuelan-American Chamber of Commerce and Industry (VENAMCHAM): President 1988-90; legal advisor since 1979; Chairman of the Foreign Investment Committee 1975-87. FEDECAMARAS: Chairman of the Binational Chambers Committee and Member of the International Economic Affairs Committee 1982-87. Published works on condominium property, the treatment of foreign investments, exchange controls, and transfer of technology. Speaker at various conferences.
Personal: Awarded by the Government of Venezuela the Order of 'Francisco de Miranda', October 1985 and July 1995, and the order 'Mérito al Trabajo' (Meritorious Service), October 1990. Speaks Spanish, English, French, and Arabic.

ANZOLA, J Eloy
Anzola Raffalli y Rodriguez, Caracas +582 952 0995
Recommended in Corporate/M&A, Energy & Natural Resources

ANZOLA, Oswaldo
Rodríguez & Mendoza, Caracas +582 285 4113
ocap@telcel.net.ve
Recommended in Corporate/M&A, Energy & Natural Resources
Specialisation: Partner specialised in Tax and Energy and Natural Resources. Most important work area is Taxes, Oil and Gas as well as Corporate/Mergers and Acquisitions. Has co-operated directly with Tax Authorities in various Tax Law reforms in the Republic of Venezuela. Has counselled and continues to counsel different companies in the Oil and Gas Area, such as Petrolera Zuata, PETROZUATA, S.A., in which there are partners Conoco Inc., and Petróleos de Venezuela, S.A. Has counselled and continues to counsel different affiliates of Conoco Inc. in the Republic of Venezuela, is current counsel for companies belonging to the Pérez Companc Group, counsels Exxon Mobil Chemical in some of its projects, and has participated in the structuring of the Conoco group of companies in Venezuela at the time of the public sale by Dupont of its stock in Conoco Inc. Has participated in the negotiation of the so-called Hamaca Project, which consists of an association for the extraction of extra heavy crude oil in the Orinoco Oil Belt and where Texaco Inc., Phillips and Petróleos de Venezuela are participants. Has taken part in the international financing of the projects for the exploitation of extra heavy crude oil in the area of the Orinoco Oil Belt, specifically in the PETROZUATA project, the Hamaca project and the Sincor project. Participated in the placing of the US$ 25MM Bearer Depositary Receipts issued by Banco Union, C.A. in 1983; in the public offering by Industrias Ventane S.A. (Vengas Group) of 55 million Registered Common Shares non-convertible to Bearer Shares, in September 1992, as well as in the issuance of 909,091 Registered Class ®A® Shares of Manufacturera de Aparatos Domésticos, S.A., which took place in December, 1991. This last company was controlled at the time by Enron Corporation and The General Electric Company. Participated in the public issuance of bearer participation instruments (securitisation of receivables) of Manufacturera de Aparatos Domésticos, S.A., which took place in November, 1992. Acting as attorney at law, was leader in the European Investment Bank US$ 20 million placing.
Prof. Memberships: Active member of the Bar Association of the Federal District (Colegio de Abogados del Distrito Federal), founder and regular member of the Venezuelan Tax Law Association, and honor member of the Venezuelan Association of Financial Law. Also reporter for Venezuela to the American Bar Association, member of the International Bar Association, and member of the Tax Committee at the Venezuelan American Chamber.
Publications: Has published several articles regarding Tax and Oil in Venezuela. These have appeared in different magazines of national circulation.
Career: In 1967 graduated with honors from Andrés Bello Catholic University. Was Head of the Doctrine and Publications Department at the General Income Tax Bureau from 1967 to 1970. Joined *Rodriguez & Mendoza* in 1970, and in 1980 became a partner. Teaches Financial Law at Andrés Bello Catholic University, and teaches Tax Law, specifically on the subject of tax wrongs, at the Venezuela Central University. Was associate Judge in the First Income Tax Court.
Personal: Born September 30 1944 in Barquisimeto, Republic of Venezuela. Currently lives in Caracas, Venezuela.

ARAUJO, Federico
Torres Plaz & Araujo, Caracas +58 2 709 53 11
Recommended in Corporate/M&A, Energy & Natural Resources

BORJAS, Arminio F
Mendoza, Palacios, Acedo, Borjas, Paez Pumar & Cia, Caracas +58 2 992 1611
aborjas@juriscompint.com
Recommended in Corporate/M&A
Specialisation: Corporate finance, arbitration, securities law, mergers and acquisitions, telecommunications law and privatisation.
Prof. Memberships: Member of the Venezuelan American Chamber of Commerce (Capital Markets Committee), International Bar Association. Correspondent of the International Arbitration Law Review; Member of the Advisory Board of the World Securities Law.
Career: Educated at the Universidad Católica Andrés Bello and The American University majoring in Latin-American Politics and International Economic Development, Washington DC, USA. Professor of Social and Political Analysis of Latin-America at Universidad Simón Bolivar. 1978, Legal Practice III and Evidence at Universidad Católica Andrés Bello, and Civil Procedure at the Central University 1982-94. Designated arbitrator by the International Court of Arbitration of Paris.
Personal: Born Caracas, Venezuela, July 7 1952. Speaks both Spanish and English. Leisure interests include outdoor activities such as soft-ball, soccer, skiing and tennis.

CAPLAN, Malcolm
Baker & McKenzie, Caracas +58 2 276 5049
malcolm.caplan@bakernet.com
Recommended in Corporate/M&A, Energy & Natural Resources
Specialisation: Taxes, Corporate, Banking & Finance, Securities Regulation, Mergers and Acquisitions, Oil and Gas, Conflict of Laws, Licensing, Anti-Trust.
Prof. Memberships: New York Bar Association.
Career: Qualified in 1957. Joined *Baker & McKenzie* in 1958. Became Partner in 1960. Former Chairman of Strategic Planning Committee; Former Member of Executive Committee of *Baker & McKenzie*; Senior Partner, *Baker & McKenzie*, Caracas Office. Teaching experience: New York University Law School, Comparative Law Institute, 1958 - U.S. Constitutional, Contract and Corporate Law. Lecturer - American Management Association, British Management Institute, Venezuelan Institute of Financial Executives, Venezuelan-American Chamber of Commerce, Venezuelan National Council for Investment Promotion.
Personal: Born 14 October 1932 in Brooklyn, New York. Attended Yale University (BA 1954); Harvard Law School (LLM, 1957); New York University Law School, Comparative Law Institute, 1958 (Ford Foundation Fellow). Central University of Caracas, Venezuela Law Faculty, 1959.

CASTILLO, Francisco
Hoet Pelaez Castillo & Duque, Caracas +582 263 6644
Recommended in Banking & Finance

ELJURI, Elizabeth
Macleod Dixon LLP, Caracas +58 2 993 2777
eljurie@macleoddixon.com
Recommended in Energy & Natural Resources
Specialisation: Partner in the Energy and Corporate practice of *Macleod Dixon's* Caracas office. Represents numerous producers and energy clients in major upstream, midstream and downstream projects. Renders advice, primarily in Venezuela, in the natural resources and corporate areas.
Prof. Memberships: Caracas College of Lawyers; New York Bar; Harvard Law School Council; International Bar Association; Association of International Petroleum Negotiators.
Publications: Corporate Structuring of Oil and Gas Projects in Venezuela; Oil and Gas Profit Sharing Agreements; Legal Framework for Gas in Venezuela.
Career: Graduated with honours (valedictorian) from Universidad Católica Andrés Bello; LLM, from Harvard Law School; Professor of Contracts (UCV, 1994 - 1996); National Administrator of the Phillip C. Jessup International Law Competition; Spent nearly ten years at a major international law firm before joining *Macleod Dixon.*
Personal: Born in Caracas, spent most of childhood in Europe and lived also in the United States. Fluent in English, Spanish and spoken French.

HELLMUND, Reinaldo
Rodríguez & Mendoza, Caracas +582 285 4944
Recommended in Energy & Natural Resources
Specialisation: Capital Markets and Project Finance; Oil and Gas Law. Partner of *Rodriguez & Mendoza* specialised in oil and gas and financing transactions, including project financing and capital markets. Extensive practice in the oil and gas and the financing of oil and gas ventures. Venezuelan legal counsel to the sponsors in the financing of Petrozuata and to the underwriters in the financing of the Sincor project and the Project Financing of the Orinoco Iron Project. Participated partially in the Cerro Negro Project Financing due to the simultaneity with the Sincor Project Financing. On behalf of Texaco participated in the negotiations and drafting of the Hamaca Association Agreement from the beginning of the project, which included the negotiation of the term sheet, the definition of the corporate structure, the negotiation of the association agreement and its further modifications and the study of different financing alternatives. Also has participated intensively in the setting up of the Hamaca Project, including the negotiation and the acquisition of properties and pipelines for the operation of the association and the review of different agreements including pipeline agreements and EPCs, and has continued in all the different stages of the project. Has participated in all of the four extra heavy oil association agreements; participated in the acquisition of land and securing of servitudes for both the production areas as well as for the pipeline corridors; has dealt with, drafted or reviewed a substantial number of construction and supply agreements and permits, the agreements related to the construction of the pipelines and port facilities and the oil upgrading facilities, analysing and participating in the drafting of EPC agreements. Has also participated in all matters related to the treatment and disposition of the associated and non-associated gas in the extra heavy oil projects.
Career: Admitted 1983, Venezuela.
Personal: Born Caracas, Venezuela, October 26, 1960. Education: Catholic University Andrés Bello. London City College. Languages: English and Spanish.

HERNANDEZ-BRETON, Eugenio
Baker & McKenzie, Caracas +58 2 276 5085
eugenio.hernandez@bakernet.com
Recommended in Corporate/M&A
Specialisation: Corporate/Mergers & Acquisitions, Major Projects/Project Finance (mining, oil, gas, energy, construction, procurement), International Corporate Law.
Prof. Memberships: Caracas Bar Association.
Publications: More than 60 publications in Constitutional, Administrative, Civil, Commercial, International Private and International Civil Law.
Career: Joined Caracas Office of *Baker & McKenzie* in 1981, became a partner in 1997. Member of Firm's Banking, Finance and Major Projects Practice Group. Professor of International Private Law at Universidad Central de Venezuela, Universidad Católica Andrés Bello and Institute of High Diplomatic Studies "Pedro Gual", Caracas.
Personal: Born April 25, 1958 in Caracas, Venezuela. Attended University of Heidelberg (Dr. iur. utr., 1991); University of Tubingen (LLM, 1988); Columbia University (LLM, 1983); Universidad Católica Andrés Bello (Lawyer,1981).

ITALIANI, Fulvio
D'Empaire Reyna Bermudez & Asociados, Caracas +58 2 264 62 44
Recommended in Corporate/M&A

MENDOZA, Luis Ignacio
Rodríguez & Mendoza, Caracas +582 285 4944
lmendoza@romen.com
Recommended in Corporate/M&A
Specialisation: Partner in Corporate Department. Main area of work is corporate law, principally mergers, acquisitions and privatisations. Has handled acquisitions of companies and undertakings of varying sorts by Venezuela and overseas clients. Acted in the privatisations of hotels, a race track and others.
Publications: Author 'Nature of the Cassation Recourse and Duties of the Members of the Board of Directors of Corporations'. Author of PROLEGA, a software program to control clients, all aspects of litigation, legal opinions, etc.
Career: Qualified in 1942. Joined *Rodríguez & Mendoza* in 1942, becoming partner in 1946. Member of the Federal District of Lawyers Association. Member of the Academy of Political and Social Sciences. 1978-1980: Speaker at the University of Illinois in connection with foreign investments. 1983: Speaker at the University of Illinois in the city of Williamsburg, Virginia, to lawyers and bankers of the United States regarding restructuring of the public debt of Venezuela. Trade Union Activities: Second Vice President of the Industrial Association 'Graphic Arts' (1962). Alternate Director of 'Asociación Venezolana de Exportadores' AVEX (1962). Director of the 'Asociación de Productores de Pulpa y Papel' and President during the periods 1964-1965, 1966-1967 and 1969-1970. Awards: Libertador Comander Class; Labor Merit, First Class; Francisco de Miranda; First Class, Andrés Bello; First Class, Industrial Labor Merit, of Cámara de Industriales de Carabobo; Order of Merit of the Venezuelan Bar of Lawyers.
Personal: Born 11 December 1918. Attended Law School of Central University of Venezuela, Doctor in Political and Social Sciences. Cum Laude.

MUCI ABRAHAM, José
Steel Hector & Davis, Caracas 1060 +582 953 4006
Recommended in Corporate/M&A

PALACIOS, Luis Esteban
Palacios Ortega y Asociados, Caracas +58 2 951 3333
Recommended in Corporate/M&A

PAZ PARRA, Francisco
Travieso Evans Hughes Arria Rengel & Paz, Caracas +582 277 3333
Recommended in Corporate/M&A

V

PLANCHART MANRIQUE, Gustavo
Tinoco Travieso Planchart & Nuñez, Caracas
+582 952 9033
gplanchm@ttpn.com.ve
Recommended in Corporate/M&A
Specialisation: Senior Partner in Corporate Department. Main area of work is corporate law, principally international bank transactions, debt refinancing, bond issues. Has acted as counsel to leading Venezuelan and foreign banks as well as insurance and other major companies.
Prof. Memberships: Member of the Bar Association of the Federal District. Regular Member of the Venezuelan Academy of Political and Social Sciences, 1989.
Career: Qualified 1949. Joined *Tinoco, Travieso, Planchart & Nunez* in 1960, Tenure Professor of Constitutional Law, Central University of Venezuela, 1953-1981. Dean of the School of Law, Central University of Venezuela, 1965-1968. Chief of the Delegation, with rank of Ambasador, for the Delimitation of Marine and Submarine Areas between Venzuela and Columbia, 1979-1980, and for the Delimitation of Marine and Submarine Areas with France (Guadeloupe and Martinique), 1980. Vice President of the Advisory Commission for Foreign Relations of the Republic of Venezeula, 1979-1983. Alternate Justice of the Political-Administrative Division of the Supreme Court of Justice, 1981-1987. "Professor Emeritus", Central University of Venezuela, 1986. Member of the Superior Legal Advisory Council of the Congress of the Republic, since 1991.
Personal: Born Caracas, Venezuela, 11 September 1925. Attended the Central University of Venezuela (Law Degree and Doctor in Political Science, 1949). Leisure interests include reading and music. Lives in Caracas.

PLAZ, Rodolfo
Torres Plaz & Araujo, Caracas +58 2 709 53 11
Recommended in Corporate/M&A

RENGEL JR, Pedro
Travieso Evans Hughes Arria Rengel & Paz, Caracas +582 277 3333
Recommended in Corporate/M&A

REYNA, Gustavo
D'Empaire Reyna Bermudez & Asociados, Caracas
+58 2 264 62 44
Recommended in Banking & Finance, Corporate/M&A

RODNER, James
Rodner Martínez & Asociados, Caracas
+58 2 951 3811
Recommended in Banking & Finance, Corporate/M&A

TORRES, Manuel
Torres Plaz & Araujo, Caracas +58 2 709 53 11
Recommended in Banking & Finance, Corporate/M&A

TRAVIESO, Eduardo
Travieso Evans Hughes Arria Rengel & Paz, Caracas +582 277 3333
Recommended in Corporate/M&A, Energy & Natural Resources

VIETNAM

Corporate/Commercial: Local Firms

VIETNAM Leading firms (Corporate/Commercial)
1 Thang & Associates
2 IMAC
Vietbid Law Firm
YKVN Ltd
3 Hang Le Company Ltd
Invest Consult
Vision & Associates

Firms are listed alphabetically in each band.

Leading individuals (Corporate/Commercial)
1 BAC Pham Nghiem Xuan *Vision & Associates*
BICH Nguyen Ngoc *IMAC*
THANG Tran Quyet *Thang & Associates*
2 DANG Nguyen Thi *YKVN Ltd*
LE Hang *Hang Le Company Ltd*

Individuals are listed alphabetically in each band.

Thang & Associates (1 ptr, 3 asscs) *"One of the best firms in Vietnam,"* interviewees felt it has *"adopted Western standards, getting work done to a high quality."* **Tran Quyet Thang*** is a *"superb internationally-trained lawyer with good corporate experience"* who, having acquired the first private broking license in the country, now *"wears two hats."*

The banking practice incorporates commercial lending, structuring and project financing and was involved in a UNDP project for strengthening the capacity of the financial departments of enterprises. In M&A, the firm has advised a number of foreign investors in the acquisition of local corporations. **Clients:** HBO; Danao International Holdings.

IMAC (2 ptrs, 2 asscs) Although *"quite small"* this is a *"famous"* local law firm combining legal and business advice, mainly for local companies. Our researchers were told that *"the philosopher,"* **Nguyen Ngoc Bich***, has *"a deep understanding of the culture of the Vietnamese legal system,"* with an *"open"* approach that *"takes into account the bigger picture."* The firm advised Chiron, an American pharmaceutical company based in Italy, on corporate and commercial interests. **Clients:** Kodak; Novartis; American Standard; Housing Bank; Investment and Development Bank; Chiron.

Vietbid Law Firm (5 ptrs, 7 asscs) A broad based firm focusing on banking and finance, commercial law, property rights, and taxation. Industry-wise, it concentrates on hi-tech matters, food and packaging, and infrastructure, particularly telecoms, power, oil and gas.

With a wide international clientele, it has advised US Fortune 500 companies and small firms on the establishment of businesses in Vietnam. It has worked closely with the US Embassy and the US Foreign Commercial Services office in Hanoi, assisting on issues surrounding the entrance of US companies to the Vietnamese market. **Clients:** Leading local and international corporates.

YKVN Ltd (3 lawyers) YKVN is a Vietnamese investment consulting company with a close working relationship with White & Case and a dedicated legal team providing comprehensive Vietnamese legal advice. This *"top firm"* assisted in the London Club restructuring of Vietnam's defaulted commercial debt. The team acted with White & Case, advising foreign investors in projects, including steel mills, oil and gas, fertilizer plants, soap factories, and ceramic tile factories. Highly rated by the market, **Nguyen Thi Dang*** is the managing director of YKVN. **Clients:** International corporates and financial institutions.

Hang Le Company Ltd (2 ptrs, 1 assc) Former Freshfields lawyer, **Hang Le*** is a *"well respected"* lecturer at Hanoi Law School and a key figure in the market. The firm's work includes banking and foreign investment. It has been involved in loan agreements for Chin Son Bank, advised on commercial contracts worth $2 million for Food

Techno Corporation and acted in a dispute resolution for a cosmetics company. **Clients:** Chin Son Bank; Food Techno Corporation.

Invest Consult (50 lawyers) A law firm within a business consultancy, it is *"famous"* within the jurisdiction. The firm assists foreign investors to establish projects, acting in negotiations with local planners. Although involved with local entities, its client base is mostly foreign corporations and companies. **Clients:** Coca-Cola; IBM; Citibank; BHP; ANZ Bank; Philip Morris; Crown Cork and Seal; Asahi Glass; AT&T; Daewoo; Cargill.

Vision & Associates (10 ptrs, 15 asscs) A combined business and legal service operation which deals in foreign investment, banking, IP, labour and corporate law. It assisted in the expansion of Cargill and provides general commercial advice to Motorola. It also acts for IVK, a Danish firm producing water control systems. A recently opened office in Ho Chi Minh City supports activity there and in the southern region offering a strong IP practice. **Pham Nghiem Xuan Bac*** is *"gifted and intelligent"* with a *"hot reputation"* in IP, dispute resolution and general corporate matters. **Clients:** Daewoo; Coats Phong Phu; Mekong Project Development (an arm of IFC); Cargill; Motorola; IBM; Toyota.

*See leaders' profiles on pages 916-917

Corporate/Commercial: Foreign Firms

VIETNAM: Foreign Firms
Leading firms (Corporate/Commercial)

Band	Firm
1	Baker & McKenzie
	Freshfields Bruckhaus Deringer
	Lucy Wayne & Associates
	Phillips Fox
2	Freehills
	Russin & Vecchi Ltd
3	Deacons

Firms are listed alphabetically in each band.

Leading individuals (Corporate/Commercial)

Band	Individual
1	**FOSTER Tony** *Freshfields Bruckhaus Deringer*
	MAGENNIS Bill *Phillips Fox*
	WAYNE Lucy *Lucy Wayne & Associates*
2	**BURKE Frederick** *Baker & McKenzie*
	RUSSELL Nigel *Phillips Fox*
	SKINNER Stephen *Freehills*
	VECCHI Sesto *Russin & Vecchi Ltd*

Individuals are listed alphabetically in each band.

Baker & McKenzie (30 lawyers) Although felt to have *"down-sized,"* the group is broad in scope, advising Vietnamese companies on overseas operations and international companies in Vietnam. It has developed a focus on banking, securities, IP, real estate, taxation, construction and project work.

It acted on the equipment procurement contract for the first BOT power plant project in Vietnam, and is advising the European Union on negotiations related to trade and investment with Vietnam. *"Corporate specialist"* **Fred Burke*** has *"a broad knowledge of Vietnam."* **Clients:** Leading local and international corporates.

Freshfields Bruckhaus Deringer (1 ptr, 8 asscs) A highly successful operation with *"big contracts and a good client strategy."* The firm advised Ford on the acquisition of Daewoo Motor Corporation and advised ICI in relation to the sale of assets of a company in Vietnam to PPG Industries. The *"most reputable"* **Tony Foster*** has 15 years in the jurisdiction and has been involved in a number of BOT pipeline projects. The firm advised Hewlett-Packard on a tender for supply of computer hardware to a Vietnamese state-owned bank. **Clients:** Ford; ICI; Hewlett-Packard; Honda Motors Corporation; Citibank.

Lucy Wayne & Associates (1 ptr, 19 asscs) *"A quality service,"* 40% of its practice is concentrated on new investment, 30% on restructurings. The firm was involved in the funding of the first international standard hospital in Ho Chi Minh and advised on restructuring in the personal hygiene sector. It also advised four advertising agencies on the establishment of design companies. *"Intelligent"* **Lucy Wayne***, formerly of Coudert Brothers, is acknowledged to be *"easily as good as the other top lawyers here,"* although the firm is felt to lack the support of an international network. **Clients:** HBO; advertising agencies; pharmaceutical companies.

Phillips Fox (4 ptrs, 2 asscs) A *"good firm"* seen by interviewees as *"busy enough to be recruiting,"* and active in Vietnam's equitisation (privatisation) programme. The firm has assisted Citibank in investment in oil industry projects in Vietnam and advised Holderbank on a $390 million joint venture with a cement manufacturer, the largest operating foreign investment project. The team also assisted Nippon Telegraph and Telecommunications in a $190 million contract for upgrade and expansion of the Hanoi fixed telephone network. **Bill Magennis*** is a *"precise yet practical lawyer"* with *"many years' experience,"* and **Nigel Russell***, based in Ho Chi Minh, is a *"likeable guy"* and a seasoned practitioner. **Clients:** Citibank; Colgate Palmolive; Holderbank; Nippon Telegraph and Telecommunications.

Freehills (Hanoi 1 ptr, 2 asscs; Ho Chi Minh 1 ptr, 2 asscs) Despite the loss of senior partner John Dick, this practice is acknowledged as capable of *"fine work"* and possessing *"good, able lawyers."* Its main focus is banking, finance and securities, and it provides advice on infrastructure projects, assisting BCC in contracts and telecommunications. With a strong foreign investment practice in Ho Chi Minh, **Stephen Skinner*** is *"highly rated"* by his peers. **Clients:** BCC; international corporates.

Russin & Vecchi Ltd (2 foreign lawyers, 6 Vietnamese asscs) With 30 years in Vietnam, *"old timer"* **Sesto Vecchi*** offers *"superb practical advice."* The firm has acted in loan agreements for the Bank of America related to restructurings and represented Marriott on the opening of a hotel in Ho Chi Minh. Represented Hanna Corporation on the Vietnamese aspects of a world-wide merger. **Clients:** Bank of America; Marriott; Hanna Corporation.

Deacons (1 lawyer) Opened in 1992, Deacons' corporate practice in Ho Chi Minh and Hanoi undertakes the establishment and operation of companies in Vietnam. It also offers ongoing advice to corporate clients on taxation, import/export, labour and distribution. **Clients:** International corporates and financial institutions.

Leaders' profiles – Vietnam

BAC, Pham Nghiem Xuan
Vision & Associates, Hanoi +844 934 0629
Vision@hn.vnn.vn
Specialisation: Managing Partner of *Vision & Associates.* Main area of work is foreign investment, banking, project finance, corporate and commercial, mergers & acquisitions, privatisation, intellectual property in Vietnam, Laos and Cambodia.
Prof. Memberships: Hanoi Lawyers' Association, Nam Dinh Bar Association, LawAsia, INTA, APAA, AIPPI.
Career: Qualified in 1989. Managing Partner *Vision & Associates,* 1999 to date. Principal partner and Deputy General Director, InvestConsult Group, 1989-May 1999. Patent Examiner, National Office of Industrial Property (NOIP), 1985-1988.
Personal: Born 13 August 1961. Moscow Auto-Mechanical Institute, Russia (B.Sc., 1984). Moscow Institute for Intellectual Property laws, Russia (Postgraduate Diploma, 1985). Hanoi University, Vietnam (LLB, 1995). Henley University (UK) Program (MBA, 1999).

BICH, Nguyen Ngoc
IMAC, Ho Chi Minh City +848 829 5619

BURKE, Frederick
Baker & McKenzie, Ho Chi Minh City
+84 8 829 5585
Specialisation: Has 13 years' experience in the planning, negotiation and operation of foreign investment projects as well as in the related issues of contract law, securities, finance, construction, taxation, regulatory compliance, labour, intellectual property and technology transfer.

Prof. Memberships: Admitted in New York (1987) and Washington, D.C. (1988). Registered foreign lawyer in Vietnam (since 1996) and in Hong Kong (since 1994).
Career: Joined *Baker & McKenzie* in 1987 in its New York office, and served in its Shanghai office from 1988 through to 1991. Moved to Vietnam in 1991 and in 1993 became the firm's first chief representative in Hanoi and Ho Chi Minh City.
Personal: Stanford University (Bachelor of Arts, Honours, 1981); East China Institute of Politics & Law (Certification, 1984); Columbia University School of International Affairs (Master of International & Public Affairs, 1986); Parker School of Foreign & Comparative Law (Certification, 1987); and Columbia University School of Law (Juris Doctor, 1987).

DANG, Nguyen Thi
YKVN Ltd, Ho Chi Minh City +84 8 823 6880

FOSTER, Tony
Freshfields Bruckhaus Deringer, Hanoi
+84 4 8247 422
tony.foster@freshfields.com
Specialisation: Specialises in inward investment, infrastructure, commercial, and financing transactions in Vietnam.

LE, Hang
Hang Le Company Ltd, Hanoi +84 4 822 3986

MAGENNIS, Bill
Phillips Fox, Hanoi +84 4 822 6794

RUSSELL, Nigel
Phillips Fox, Ho Chi Minh City +84 8 822 1717

SKINNER, Stephen
Freehills, Hanoi +844 934 6239

THANG, Tran Quyet
Thang & Associates, Ho Chi Minh City
+848 825 0084

VECCHI, Sesto E.
Russin & Vecchi Ltd, Ho Chi Minh City
+84 8 824 3026/3114

WAYNE, Lucy
Lucy Wayne & Associates, Ho Chi Minh City
+84 88 244 395

V

YEMEN

Corporate/Commercial

YEMEN
Leading firms (Corporate/Commercial)

Band	Firm
1	Law Offices of Sheikh Tariq Abdullah

Firms are listed alphabetically in each band.

Leading individuals (Corporate/Commercial)

Band	Individual
1	**ABDULLAH Sheikh Khalid** *Law Offices of Sheikh Tariq Abdullah*
	MAKTARI Abdulla *Sole Practitioner*

Individuals are listed alphabetically in each band

Law Offices of Sheikh Tariq Abdullah (3 ptrs, 7 asscs) A commercial law firm with a strong shipping and energy practice, and a focus on joint venture agreements and the incorporation of foreign companies. **Sheikh Khalid Abdullah** is a key player in Yemeni commercial law and advised McDonald's on the franchise agreements concerning its entry into the country. **Clients:** Coca-Cola; Group 4 Security; Canadian Occidental; Port of Singapore Authorities; British Embassy; United States Embassy.

Other Notable Practitioner Sole practitioner, **Abdulla Maktari** advises banks and oil companies, including Exxon and BP in the negotiations and drafting of contracts. He was described to our researchers as an *"eminent, sensible, well-read and internationally oriented commercial lawyer."*

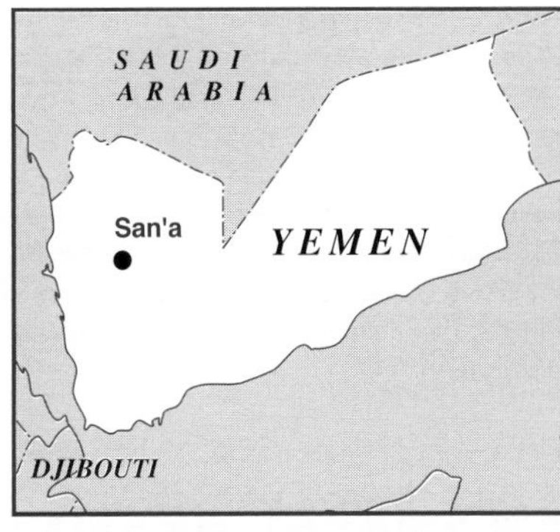

Leaders' profiles – Yemen

ABDULLAH, Sheikh Khalid T
Law Offices of Sheikh Tariq Abdullah, Aden
+967 2 255 305

MAKTARI, Abdulla
Dr Abdulla Maktari - Sole Practitioner, Yemen
+967 1 248 018

ZAMBIA

Corporate/Commercial

ZAMBIA Leading firms (Corporate/Commercial)
1 Christopher, Russell Cook & Company
Corpus Globe
Ellis & Co
2 DH Kemp & Co
Musa Dudhia & Co

Firms are listed alphabetically in each band.

Leading individuals (Corporate/Commercial)
1 **CHIMUKA Constantine** *Ellis & Co*
PATEL Kanti *Christopher, Russell Cook & Co*
2 **CHIPIMO Elias** *Corpus Globe*
MUBONDA Newton *DH Kemp & Co*
3 **CHIBESAKUNDA Mwelwa** *Corpus Globe*
DUDHIA Abdulla *Musa Dudhia & Co*

Individuals are listed alphabetically in each band.

Christopher, Russell Cook & Company (2 ptrs, 4 asscs) *"A firm of the old school, with traditional clients"* which is a by-word for stability. The firm has some *"senior lawyers who handle major work"* in company law, banking and finance, IP and conveyancing. *"Experienced"* **Kanti Patel** is reputedly *"easy to deal with, flexible and pleasant."* The firm prepared securities documentation for the IFC in connection with its loan to Zamcell. **Clients:** IFC; Stanbic Bank Zambia Ltd; mining companies.

Corpus Globe (4 ptrs, 6 asscs) *"One of the best law firms in Zambia"* which is full of *"young lawyers who have handled big transactions."* The team has a stand-out reputation for advising on securities, privatisations, energy, banking, financial services, development projects and mining. **Elias Chipimo** is regarded as one of the country's best young lawyers, and has recently returned from a stint in New York. **Mwelwa Chibesakunda** is *"an aggressive young lawyer with potential,"* who *"wants to work and makes clients feel comfortable."*

The firm has represented Anglovaal Minerals on various mining asset acquisitions, and Sun International on investment in Zambia. The team also advised the Capital Market and Securities Authority of Tanzania on the framework of the Dar es Salaam Stock Exchange, and advised Lusaka Stock Exchange on reformation of the Exchange Listing Rules. **Clients:** Metorex (Pty) Limited; Anglovaal Metals; Sun International; Anglo American; BOC Gases; Microsoft Corporation; Stanbic Bank Zambia Ltd.

Ellis & Co (5 ptrs, 5 asscs) With three offices and a traditional client base, the firm has always been one of the country's leaders, notably in banking and IP. Still viewed as *"a competent commercial and company law firm,"* the firm regularly carries out work for international clients. *"The focal point of the firm"* is **Constantine Chimuka**, *"an excellent corporate lawyer."* The firm advised UK law firm Clifford Chance on the privatisation of a mine. **Clients:** IFC and international finance houses.

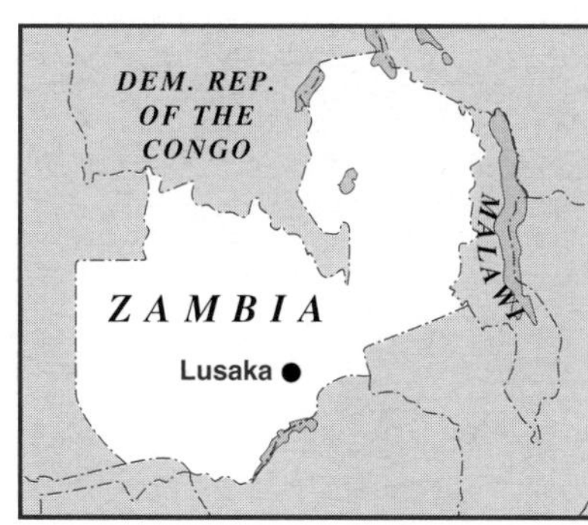

DH Kemp & Co (1 ptr, 3 asscs) The firm is considered to owe much to leading light **Newton Mubonda**, *"a thoroughly user friendly lawyer,"* our researchers were often told. He specialises in company and commercial law, and handles international work on behalf of banks and limited companies. The firm acted on behalf of a group of Zambian managers and an overseas joint venture group in the acquisition of a local company involved in the electricity industry. **Clients:** International banks and corporates.

Musa Dudhia & Co (3 ptrs, 3 asscs) *"An established family firm,"* which advises clients from a wide range of industries on all aspects of corporate finance, and banking, primarily secured lending. Principal partner **Abdulla Dudhia** is recommended for his commercial acumen. The firm was involved in the privatisation of Chilanga Cement plc. **Clients:** Banks; accountants; embassies; overseas law firms.

Leaders' profiles – Zambia

CHIBESAKUNDA, Mwelwa
Corpus Globe, Lusaka +260 1 235 479 / 235 481
corpus@zamnet.zm
Specialisation: Senior Partner. Main area of work is corporate law, dealing mainly in privatisations, corporate finance transactions, including public and private mergers and acquisitions. Acted as local counsel for Metorex Consortium in acquisition of Chibuluma Mines plc; acted for Seaboard Corporation on acquisition of National Milling Company. Significant representations include Microsoft Corporation, Southern African Enterprise Development Fund, Stanbic Bank Limited and Anglovaal Minerals.
Career: Qualified in 1991. Joined *Corpus Globe* as a partner 1996.
Personal: Attended University of Bristol 1994-1995 (LLM).

CHIMUKA, Constantine
Ellis & Co, Lusaka +260 1 252 709 / 809 / 738

CHIPIMO, Elias
Corpus Globe, Lusaka +260 1 235 479 / 235 481

DUDHIA, Abdulla
Musa Dudhia & Co, Lusaka +260 1 228 426 30

MUBONDA, Newton
DH Kemp & Co, Lusaka +260 1 252 381

PATEL, Kanti
Christopher, Russell Cook & Company, Lusaka +260 1 229 366

ZIMBABWE

Corporate/Commercial

ZIMBABWE Leading firms (Corporate/Commercial)
1 Atherstone & Cook
Coghlan Welsh & Guest
Gill, Godlonton & Gerrans
Honey & Blanckenberg
Wintertons
2 Dube Manikai & Hwacha
Kantor & Immerman
Scanlen & Holderness
Stumbles & Rowe

Firms are listed alphabetically in each band.

Leading individuals (Corporate/Commercial)
1 BACK James *Gill, Godlonton & Gerrans*
COOK Lindsay *Atherstone & Cook*
MASTERSON Alex *Coghlan Welsh & Guest*
MORGAN David *Coghlan Welsh & Guest*
PICHANICK Alan *Wintertons*
ROSETTENSTEIN Albert *Honey & Blanckenberg*
TURPIN Dick *Scanlen & Holderness*
2 CHADWICK Roger *Scanlen & Holderness*
CHIHAMBAKWE Simplicius *Chihambakwe Mutizwa & Partners*
MANIKAI Edwin *Dube Manikai & Hwacha*
STUMBLES Robert *Stumbles & Rowe*
THOMPSON Howard *Wintertons*

Individuals are listed alphabetically in each band.

Atherstone & Cook (6 ptrs, 5 asscs) A *"smaller"* and *"more general firm"* that has been active in Harare for over forty years. It has close associations with Calderwoods in Bulawayo and Edward Nathan & Friedland in Johannesburg. Clients include international law firms such as Clifford Chance, Linklaters and Freshfields. The team advised on an aborted power station project and acts for Standard Chartered Bank Zimbabwe and Stanbic Bank Zimbabwe. Senior figure **Lindsay Cook*** is *"one of the country's most senior commercial lawyers: able and aggressive,"* and continues to be a *"force to be reckoned with."* **Clients:** Clifford Chance; Linklaters; Freshfields; Standard Chartered Bank Zimbabwe; Stanbic Bank Zimbabwe.

Coghlan Welsh & Guest (6 ptrs, 5 asscs) An *"efficient"* firm with *"a lot of long-standing clients,"* the firm is rated for its general corporate practice, and the *"individual strength"* of its lawyers. **David Morgan*** is *"an aggressive and able senior partner"* while the *"tenacious and bright"* **Alex Masterson*** has a *"high media profile."* He led the Commercial Farmer's Union in a case against the government. **Clients:** Clifford Chance; Linklaters; Freshfields; Oppenheimers.

Gill, Godlonton & Gerrans (12 ptrs, 7 asscs) Packed with *"excellent people,"* the firm has a large IP department and is expanding into M&A, foreign loans, investment, mining and joint ventures. With a fine combination of local and foreign clients, **James Back*** is renowned as a *"first rate corporate lawyer."* **Clients:** Microsoft; BAT; Lonrho Africa.

Honey & Blanckenberg (10 ptrs, 9 asscs) This firm has the largest trademark and patents department in the country. An *"efficient"* team also advises on restructurings and defamations. The firm advised on a postal voting irregularities case which went to the supreme court. **Albert Rosettenstein*** is a senior lawyer recommended for his *"attention to detail."* **Clients:** Harare Municipality; Zimbabwe Newspaper Group; Main farmer's suppliers; Davis Engineering.

Wintertons (10 ptrs, 4 asscs) This *"good-sized, well-established"* firm is a key player in the corporate market. **Alan Pichanick*** is a senior lawyer with a strong following while **Howard Thompson*** is *"learning fast."* **Clients:** Leading financial institutions and corporates.

Dube Manikai & Hwacha (4 ptrs) A firm with *"big ambitions,"* which does a lot of government work. It acted as lead advisor in the recent Z$ 5 billion bond issue of a national company in Zimbabwe. The firm advised a regional media funding group, Samdef, on the restructuring of a newspaper group. **Edwin Manikai*** is a *"quality lawyer"* who advises corporate clients on the competition act in Zimbabwe. **Clients:** Domestic corporates and financial institutions.

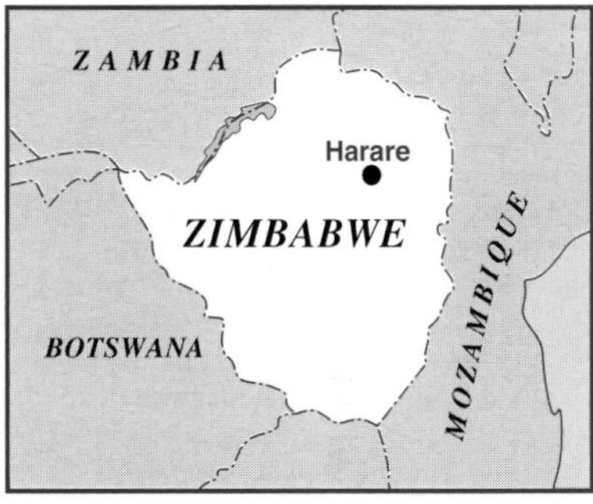

Kantor & Immerman (7 ptrs, 6 asscs) The practice is in a period of transition as Harry Kantor has shifted to a consultancy role and another partner has moved to Australia. It retains its reputation as a strong general commercial practice and continues to advise the Zimbabwe stock exchange. **Clients:** Domestic corporates and financial institutions.

Scanlen & Holderness (4 lawyers) A firm with an *"excellent reputation"* which has *"been around forever."* It acted on the demutualisation of Old Mutual and its registration in the United Kingdom as Old Mutual plc. **Dick Turpin*** is an *"aggressive senior partner,"* while the equally experienced **Roger Chadwick*** is also recommended. **Clients:** Barclays Bank; Bindura Nickel Corporation; Border Timbers; CAPS Holdings; Delta Corporation; Hippo Valley Estates; Meikles Africa; Tanganda Tea Company; Zimbabwe Alloys; Old Mutual; Central African Building Society.

Stumbles & Rowe (2ptrs, 5 asscs) This well-regarded firm has acted for international energy and mining concerns on foreign investments, restructuring, and company flotations. It has seen an increase in instructions concerning the Farmers' Union and is involved in work from other African countries and SADEC. **Robert Stumbles*** is a *"high profile"* player and personal legal advisor to the President of Malawi. **Clients:** SADEC.

Other Notable Practitioner **Simplicius Chihambakwe*** of Chihambakwe Mutizwa & Partners was warmly recommended as a *"rising star."*

*See leaders' profiles on page 920

Leaders' profiles – Zimbabwe

BACK, James
Gill, Godlonton & Gerrans, Harare +263 4 707 023

CHADWICK, Roger
Scanlen & Holderness, Harare +263 4 702 561

CHIHAMBAKWE, Simplicius
Chihambakwe Mutizwa & Partners, Harare +263 4 708 595

COOK, Lindsay
Atherstone & Cook, Harare +263 4 704 244

MANIKAI, Edwin
Dube Manikai & Hwacha, Harare +263 4 780 351
dmh@zimsurf.co.zw
Specialisation: Head Commercial and Corporate Services Department at *Dube, Manikai & Hwacha.* Main area of work is corporate law, principally mergers, acquisitions, restructurings, joint ventures, privatisations and flotations, banking and financial services. Acted for Africa Resources Limited in a US$60 million localisation of a major base mineral conglomerate from T&N plc. Acted as principal legal advisor in the recent successful flotation of the ZW$5 billion National Oil Company of Zimbabwe oil bond; acted on the merger of two merchant banks to establish one of the largest merchant banks in the country. Has conducted extensive legal due diligence reviews on target companies and more recently has advised on the Competition Act in Zimbabwe; has been involved in the privatisation of Dairibord Zimbabwe Limited, Cotton Company of Zimbabwe and was consulted in the privatisation of Rainbow Tourism Group Limited. Acts for a number of financial institutions and renders opinions in international financial agreements.
Prof. Memberships: Law Society of Zimbabwe and Commonwealth Law Association.
Career: Bachelor of Laws (Honours), University of Zimbabwe (1982-1985); qualified in 1985. Joined *Gill, Godlonton & Gerrans* in December 1985, becoming a Partner in 1992. Commonwealth Young Lawyers Alumni. President Harare Legal Practitioners Association and founding partner of *Dube, Manikai & Hwacha* in June 1998. Member of the Constitutional Commission 1999; Director of several public and private companies.
Personal: Born 13 September 1962. Keen golfer.

MASTERSON, Alex
Coghlan Welsh & Guest, Harare +263 4 758 472

MORGAN, David
Coghlan Welsh & Guest, Harare +263 4 758 472

PICHANICK, Alan
Wintertons, Harare +263 4 250 113

ROSETTENSTEIN, Albert
Honey & Blanckenberg, Harare +263 4 750 295

STUMBLES, Robert Atherstone
Stumbles & Rowe, Harare +263 4 738 903

THOMPSON, Howard
Wintertons, Harare +263 4 250 113

TURPIN, Dick
Scanlen & Holderness, Harare +263 4 702 561

GLOBAL IN-HOUSE COUNSEL

INDEX OF GLOBAL IN-HOUSE COUNSEL

For full details see the alphabetical listing of firms on pages 928-954

Cooper, Nick
Sage Group PLC

Cooperman, Daniel
Oracle Corporation

Cortone, Pier Paulo
Telecom Italia Mobile (TIM)

Costello, Thomas
Compuware

Cotone, Pier Paulo
Telecom Italia Group

Counillon, JM
TF1 - TV FRANCAISE

Courbarein, Selvie
Metropole Tv-(M6)

Creager, Steve
Tyco Electronics (formerly AMP Inc)

Cristofori, Massimo
Tiscali SPA

D'agnolo, Monique
Libertel NV

Da Rita, Luca
AEM SpA

Dacciaria, Fabio
Gruppo Editoriale L'Espresso SPA

Dacier, Paul T
EMC Corp

Dagefoerde, Casten
Aachener und Muenchener Beteiligungs AG (AMB)

Dahlberg, AW
Southern Company

Dallo, Bruno
Baloise Holding

Dawson, Grant
Centrica PLC

De Baenst, Eric
Banque Bruxelles Lambert SA

De Carvalho, Alfaia
EDP - Electricidade De Portugal SA

de Chaunac,
Hermes International

de Dorlodot, Vincent
RTL (formerly Audiofina)

de Garcia, Jean
Tractebel SA

De Haan, Pieter
DSM NV

de Lasa, Jose
Abbott Laboratories Limited

de Oliveira Cruz, Carlos Alberto
Mundial Confianca

De Ros, Rafael Mateu
Bankinter SA

Decharit, Issarachai
TPI

Deeming, Nick
SEMA Group PLC

Delaby, Luc
Groupe Danone SA

Delwiche, Francis
Agfa-Gevaert

Derendinger, Urs
Credit Suisse Group

DeRoma, Nicholas J
Nortel Networks Corporation

Derrick, James
Enron Corp

Desjardins, Daniel
Bombardier Inc

Devereux, Christopher
Gallaher Group

Devlin, Richard
Sprint Fon Group

Dewast, Phillippe
Eurotunnel SA

Dhanji, Anisa
QXL.Com PLC

Dias, Rui
Petrobras

Diethelm, Markus
Swiss Reinsurance Company

Dimitrajopoulos, George
Biohalco

Doess, Manfred
MG Technologies AG

Donghua, Ding
China Mobile (Hong Kong) Limited

Donohoo, Robert
i2 Technologies Inc

Dowdy, Robert
Weyerhaeuser Company

Dransfield, Graham
Hanson PLC

Dudognon, Marc
Legrand SA

Dull, David
Broadcom Corporation

Dungate, Albert
Arjo Wiggins Appleton PLC

Dunlap, Thomas
Intel Corp

Durand-Barthez, Pascal
Alcatel Alsthom Group

East, Anna
Britannic PLC

Edwards, Christine A.
Bank One Corp

Efimova, Olga
Unified Energy Systems

Eggers, William
Corning Incorporated

Eijsbouts, A Jan AJ
Akzo Nobel NV

Ejido, Antonio
Corporacion Financiera Alba SA

Eliopoulos, G
Hellenic Petroleum SA

Elliot, William
Gateway 2000

Ellis, JD
SBC Communications Inc

Elloriaga, Inigo
Iberdrola Energia SA

Enoch, Simon J
Baltimore Technologies PLC

Esen, Hasan
Akbank Turk Anonim Sirketi

Evans, Jeremy
United Pan-Europe Communications NV (UPC)

Everbach, George
Kimberly-Clark Corporation

Faggella, Vito
Intesa Gestione Crediti S.P.A.

Faldella, Michele
Rolo Banca 1473 SpA

Farrant, Simon
Johnson Matthey PLC

Fast, John C
BHP Limited

Fernandez, Mario
Banco Bilbao Vizcaya Argentaria SA

Fernebrand, Thomas Lopez
Amadeus Global Travel

Ferreira, Luzia Gomes
Sonae SGPS

Ferrero, Dominique
Credit Lyonnais SA

Feyza, Torlak
Yapi Ve Kredi Bankasi

Field, Bernard
Saint Gobain SA

Filos, Tasos
Hellenic Bottling

Fine, Roger
Johnson & Johnson

Fisher, Brian
Bank of Scotland

Fisk, Hayward D.
Computer Sciences Corp

Fitz, J Daniel
Cable & Wireless PLC

Flach, Roland
Wcm Beteiligungs und Grundbezits AG

Flaemig, Christian
Merck KGaA

Flodstrom, Johan
Holmen AB

Folmer, Pieter
Shell Transport & Trading Co PLC

Fontaine, Michael
MAN AG

Forsberg, Gitte Grace
Tele Danmark A/S

Foulkes Shaw, Sarah
BBA Group PLC

Fournis, Yves-Marie
Sodexho Alliance SA

Francesco, Zan
Fiat SpA

Franchini, Umberto
Italgas [Sta Italina Per it Gas pA]

Francis, Richard
CMG PLC

Frazier, Kent
Merck & Co Inc

Fredrich, William
BG Group PLC

Frezza, Francesco
Autostrade - Concessioni e Costruzioni Autostrade SpA

Frick, Hans Peter
Nestle SA

Fricklas, Michael
Viacom Inc

Friedlander, D Gilbert
EDS

Friocourt, Michel
Pinault-Printemps-Redoute

Fuchs, Reinhard
MLP Finanzdienstkeistungen AG

Fukutake, Soichiro
Benesse

Fukuzawa, Takeshi
Mitsubishi Estate Company Ltd

Galster, Wirnt
Heidelberger Druckmaschinen AG

Garber, Robert
AXA Financial

Gavin, Carol
Tellabs

Gensheimer, Joseph
Sprint PCS Group

Ghezzi, Furio Silvio
Arnoldo Mondadori Editore SpA

Ghosn, Carlos
Nissan Motor Co Ltd

Giaoui, Norbert
Lagardere

Gibber, Robert
Tate & Lyle PLC

Gierlich, Peter
BASF AG

Gladden Jnr, Joseph R
Coca-Cola Co

Glahn, William G Von
Williams Companies

Glitz, Albrecht
Heidelberger Zement AG

Gob, Natalie
Mobistar

Göhmann, Andreas
Preussag AG

Gomarasca, Alberto
Mediobanca

Gordon, Jeff
Marconi PLC

Gordon, Robert A
Safeway Inc

Gorton, Jim
Global Crossing Ltd

Gotoh, Osamu
Itochu Techno-Science

Gottschalk, Thomas
General Motors Corporation

Goulden, Ian
Exel PLC

Gradon, Michael
Peninsular & Oriental Steam Navigation Co

Grande, Carlo
ENI-Ente Nazionale Idrocarburi

Guerguerian, Gerard
ATOS Origin

Gunderson, James
Schlumberger Limited

Gust, Anne
Gap

Haeseler, Hans-Georg
Linde AG

Haesler, Pierre
Holderbank Financiere Glarus AG

Hale, James
Target Corporation

Hall, Edward R Eamonn
Eircom PLC

Hambrett, Bruce
Cable & Wireless Optus Limited

Hamburg, Marc D
Berkshire Hathaway Inc

Hanus, Jean-Claude
Peugeot SA

Hara, Yoshinari
Daiwa Securities

Harland, Philip
Great Universal Stores PLC

Harrington, Rick A
Conoco Inc

Harris, Michael S
Thomson Corporation

Harris, Neil
Shire Pharmaceuticals Group PLC

Harrysson, Lars
WM-data AB

Hartwig, Roland
Bayer AG

Hayman, Martin
Standard Chartered PLC

Heard, Robert M
BPB PLC

Heidmeier, Heiner
Degussa-Huels AG

Heineman, Ben
General Electric Company

Heinen, Nancy
Apple Computer

Heldal, Olav
Den Norske Bank

Heldman, Paul W
Kroger Co

Hellrung, Steve
Lowes Companies

Hendry, Andrew
Colgate-Palmolive Company

Heng, Lee Cheng
Development Bank of Singapore

Henniker-Smith, Ian
Halliburton Company

Herbet, Patrice
Suez Lyonnaise des Eaux

Herga, Robert
BAA PLC

Herlihy, Michael HC
Imperial Chemical Industries PLC

Hess, Beat
ABB Ltd

Hess, Donald
Pacific Century CyberWorks Limited

Hibbert, Andrew P
Alstom

Hieda, Hisashi
Fuji Television Network

Higashi, Tetsuro
Tokyo Electron

Hinman, Harvey
Chevron Corporation

Hirasawa,
Sumitomo Corporation

Hoffman, Andre
Banque Generale du Luxembourg SA

Honsel, Bernd
Allianz AG

Hosker, David
United Utilities PLC

Houdoux-Cellura, Bénédicte
Cap Gemini France SA

Hoynes Jr, Louis L
American Home Products Corporation

Huang, TK
Cathay Life Insurance Co Ltd

Hubach, Joseph
Texas Instruments Inc

Hudnut, Stewart
Illinois Tool Works

Hughes, Kathrine
Alliance & Leicester PLC

Huppe, Ulrich
E.ON AG

Hüppi, Rolf
Zurich Financial Services

Hurst, Gordon M
Capita Group PLC

Hussey, Paul N
Bunzl PLC

Husson, Christian
Renault SA

Ide, William R
Monsanto Co

Idei, Nobuyuki
Sony Corporation

Imaizumi, Isao
Bridgestone Corporation

Inoue, Masahiro
Yahoo! Japan

Irrisou, Alain-Marc
TotalFinaElf

Isaac, Anthony Eric
BOC Group PLC

Ishido, Noburo
Canon Inc

Ishikawa, Takashi
Kansai Electric Power Co Inc

Itoh, Hiroshi
Asahi Bank

Jackson, David J
PowerGen PLC

Jackson, Michael
Alltel Corporation

Jacobson, Michael
eBay Inc

Jang, Chang Ming
Trend Micro

Jarry, Francoise
Hachette Filipacchi Medias

Jenkins, John
Guidant Corp

Jenkins, Mark
Colt Telecom Group PLC

Joergensen, Niels
Unidanmark A/S

Johnson, Geoffrey
Lloyds TSB Group PLC

Johnson, Kevin
Siebel Systems

Jones, Helen
Kingfisher PLC

Jones, Jay
Veritas Software

Jones, Jonathan
Reckitt & Benckiser PLC

Jonsson, Ulla Karin
Sydkraft AB

Joseph, Ann
Reed Elsevier

Joyce, Joseph
Best Buy Co

Juelsgaard, Stephen
Genentech

Jung-Nam, Cho
SK Telecom

Junge, Michael
SAP AG

Kaden, Ellen Oran
Campbell Soup Company

Kalogeropoulos, A
OTE Telecom AE

Kalthoff, Ulrich
MobilCom AG

Kanagawa, Chihiro
Shin-Etsu Chemical Co Ltd

Kaneko, Masashi
Nikko Securities Co Ltd

Kappelle, H M
Aegon NV

Kappler, Anne
Fannie Mae

Karambelas, Agisilaos
National Bank of Greece SA

Kass, Harvey
Daily Mail & General Trust PLC

Kaufmann, Albert
Richemont AG (Cie Financiere)

Kawada, Takashi
Matsushita Communication Industrial Co

Kawashima, K
Kao Corporation

Kay, Alison B
National Grid Group PLC

Keisler, Ben
Anglo American PLC

Kelley, Russell P
Allied Domecq PLC

Kelly, Anastasia
Sears Roebuck & Co

Kelly, Janet
Kellogg

Kempf Jr, Donald G
Morgan Stanley Dean Witter & Co

Kennedy, Leonard J
NEXTEL Communications

Kenney, C
Tribune Co

Kerjouan, Jean-Pierre
Sanofi-Synthelabo

Kikuchi, Takehisa
Tokio Marine & Fire Insurance Co Ltd

Kinch, John
Safeway PLC

Kindler, Jeffrey
McDonald's Corporation

Kinoshita, Shigeyoshi
Acom Co

Kirsten, Roland
Fresenius AG

Klajnman, Gilbert
Vivendi Universal SA

Knight, Michael
Severn Trent Water Ltd

Knoll, Peter
Epcos AG

Kobayashi, Hisanori
Denso Corporation

Kobayashi, Toshiharu
Toshiba Corporation

Kohler, Klaus
Deutsche Bank AG

Kojima, Takeshi
Advantest

Komiya, Yoko
Mitsubishi Corporation

Körner, Uwe
BHW Holding AG

Koster, Tilo
GEHE AG

Kosuniak, Jacek
Telekomunikacja Polska SA (TP SA)

Kotaki, Kunio
Takefuji Corporation

Kowalska, Malgorzata
Polski Koncern Naftowy

Krasnostein, David
National Australia Bank Ltd

Kreindler, Peter
Honeywell

Krüger, Horst
Schering AG

Kuhlen, Detlef
Ergo Versicherungsgruppe AG

Kuhn, Bernard
LVMH Moët Hennessy Louis Vuitton

Kurkinen, Jyrki
Stora Enso Oyj

Kuwabara, Akira
Fujitsu Support & Services Inc (FSAS)

Kwak, Mu-Nam
Pohang Iron & Steel Co., Ltd (POSCO)

Lachaud,
Casino Guichard-Perrachon et Cie/Groupe Casino

Lacher, Jörg
Thyssen Krupp Materials & Services AG

Lamana, Cristina
Terra Networks

Lambot, Christoph
SEC

Lambright, Stephen K
Anheuser-Busch Companies Inc

Lankousky, Zenon
CVS Corporation

Laudermilk, Joey
AFLAC

Lavelle, Thomas
Xilinx Inc

Lawson, Peter
Motorola Inc

Lawton, Charles
Rio Tinto PLC

Lebedoff, Geric
Valeo SA

Leduc, Philippe
Havas

Legrez, Philippe
Michelin [Cie Generale des Etablissements]

Leitinen, Maire
Sonera

Leopoldo, Confolte
Alitalia Linee Aeree Italiane SPA

Lessig, Roland
Adidas-Salomon

Lester, Michael
BAE Systems PLC

Levy-Morelle, Jacques
Solvay SA

Lewis, Roderick
Micron Technology

Li, Godwin
Hang Seng Bank

Lilly, Charles
FI Group PLC

Lin, Larry
United Micro Electronics

Lindgern, Johan
Modern Times Group

Lochow, Stefan
Consors AG

Loechelt, Dieter
BMW Group

Loginovskaya, Ludmila
Surgutneftegaz

Lonka, Jouko
TietoEnator Corporation

Lopes, Fernando Quintaif
Banco Espirito Santo e Comercial de Lisboa

Loquet, Martine
CNP Assurances

Lorlick, John
Gemstar TV Guide International

Lubasch, Richard J
NTL Incorporated

Lundgren, Einar
Skanska AB

Lurasci, William R
AES

Lush, Paul
Billiton

Lytton, William
International Paper Company

MacCarthy, Cathal
Irish Life & Permanent PLC

MacDonald, Ian
CGNU PLC

Machida, Katsuhiko
Sharp Corporation

Mackay, David N
ARM Limited

Macleod, David
Thus PLC

Macrez, Roland
Usinor

Magnusson, Ingmar
Gambro AB

Maier, Bruno
Roche Holding Ltd

Makris, Maria
Intracom SA

Maladorno, Antonio
Unicredito

Malkin, Gwyn
Abbey National PLC

Malone, Angela
CRH PLC

Manson, Ian
Scottish & Southern Energy PLC

Marchant, Richard
Tomkins PLC

Marchat, Philippe
Ciments Francais

Marcos, Louis-Phillipe
Banco Popular Espanol

Marshall, Brian
Jefferson Smurfit Group

Mascherpa, Maria Enrica
Fininvest

Maslyaev, Ivan
Lukoil

Masterson, Kenneth
Fedex Corporation

Mater, Maud
Federal Home Loan Mortgage Corporation

Matthews, Charles
Exxon Corp

Mattout, Jean-Pierre
BNP Paribas

Maurice, Jeffrey L
Dell Computer Corporation

Mayer, Georg
Neckarwerke Stuttgart AG

Maynard, Peter
Prudential PLC

Mays, L Lowry
Clear Channel Communications

McAllister, Kenneth
Wachovia Bank

McAllister, Philippe
France Telecom SA

McCabe, Michael
Allstate Corp

McDavid, William H
JP Morgan Chase & Co

McDonnall, Glen
Cookson Group PLC

McGoldrick, John L
Bristol-Myers Squibb

McKelvie, Andrew
Energis PLC

Mehnzel, Gerhard
Axel Springer Verlag AG

Meisinger, Lou
Walt Disney Co

Melville, David
Freeserve PLC

Menendez, V
Banco Espanol de Credito SA (Banesto)

Menon, Satish
Wipro

Michael, Mark D
3Com Corporation

Mihaly, Odri
Matav Hungarian Telecommunications Co Ltd

Mijares, Juan
Grupo Televisa

Miki, Shigemitsu
Bank of Tokyo-Mitsubishi Ltd
Miller, George
Novartis Group
Miller, Paul
Pfizer Inc
Minami, Nobuya
Tokyo Electric Power Co Inc
Mintziras, Konstantinos
Lambrakis
Mitau, Lee
US Bancorp
Mitchell, Stephen
Reuters Group
Miyamura, Satoru
Nippon Telegraph & Telephone Corporation
Mizuno, Masaru
Japan Tobacco Inc
Mobley, Stacy
Du Pont (EI) De Nemours
Montagon, Javier
Telefonos de Mexico SA
Morgan, Charles R
BellSouth Corporation
Morgan, David
Royal & Sun Alliance Insurance Group PLC
Morose, Brian
Tyco International Ltd
Morris, Michael
Sun Microsystems
Moskowitz, David K
EchoStar Communications
Moss, Sara
Pitney Bowes Inc
Motte, Francois Regis
Castorama Dubois Investissements SCA
Muller, Martin
Karstadt Warenhaus AG
Müller, Georg
RWE AG
Munich, Diether
Bayerische Hypo- und Vereinsbank AG
Murase, Mitsumasa
Jafco
Murata, Tsuneo
Murata Manufacturing Co Ltd
Muromachi, Kaneo
Sanwa Bank Ltd
Murphy, Finbarr
Bank of Ireland (The Governor and Company of The)
Murphy, Lisabeth F
Elan Corporation PLC
Murray, Martin
Old Mutual PLC
Murray, Urban A
AGA AB (Linde Gas AG)
Musker, Graeme
AstraZeneca PLC
Naef, Francois
Serono SA
Naito,
Hitachi Ltd
Nakamura, Hiroshi
ORIX Corp
Nakamura, Noboru
Kyocera Corporation
Nakano, Koichi
NTT Data Corporation
Nassau, Henry
Internet Cap Group
Nauta, AW
KPN - Koninklijke PTT Nederland BV
Neate, Francis W
Schroders Investment Managment Limited
Necati,
Turkiye Is Bankasi AS
Neely, Scott
BroadVision
Neukom, William
Microsoft Corporation
Nichols, Michael C
Sysco Corporation
Nieminen, Olavi
Pohjola Group Insurance Corporation
Nigai, Noriaki
Nomura Securities Co Ltd
Nimmo, Mark
Société Générale
Nishi, Toshihisa
Japan Telecom Co Ltd
Nishikawa, Motoyoshi
Nippon Steel Corporation
Nishimura, Masao
Industrial Bank of Japan Ltd
Nithyanandan, R
Infosys Technologies
Noguera, Dominique
SAGEM SA
Noppeney, Jacques
Societe Europeene des Satellites
Nordvaller, Thomas
AB Industrivarden
Norlund, Craig
Agilent Technologies
Nyberg, Anders
Svenska Cellulosa Aktiebolaget (SCA)
O'Brien, Alan
LASMO PLC
O'Neill, Margaret
Corus Group PLC
O'Reilly, Dennis
Conexant Systems Inc
Oakley, Graham
Marks & Spencer PLC
Odre, Steven
Amgen Inc
Oettinger, Julian
Walgreen Co
Ogasawara, Hideo
Tokai Bank Ltd
Ogilvie Smals, Rufus
GKN PLC
Ohnishi, Minoru
Fuji Photo Film Co Ltd
Okada, Akishige
The Sakura Bank Ltd
Oldenburg, Dirk
Aventis SA
Oliver, Michael
Boots Company PLC
Olivier, Francis
Sidel
Ollivier, Pierre
STMicroelectronics
Ono, Teruji
Takeda Chemical Industries Ltd
Opsomer, Ann
Groupe Bruxelles Lambert
Osborne, Simon
Railtrack Group PLC
Otsuka, Mutsutake
East Japan Railway Company
Palm, Gregory K
Goldman Sachs Group Inc
Palmore, Roderick
Sara Lee Corporation
Papavasiliou, Rinia
EFG Eurobank Ergasias SA
Parent, Louise
American Express Company
Parenti, Carlo
RAS - Riunione Adriatica di Sicurta
Parlato, Ettore
Mediolanum
Parrott, Graham
Granada Compass PLC
Parson, Michael G
Smith & Nephew PLC
Patrick, Deval
Texaco Inc
Patrikis, Ernest
American International Group Inc (AIG)
Paulesu, Pasqualino
Banca Monte Dei Paschi
Pea, Barry G.
Immunex Corporation
Pederson, Bjarne Lau
RealDanmark (formerly Kapital Holding)
Perez, Arnaldo
Carnival Corporation
Persson, Eva
AB Volvo
Pesce, Simona
Holding di Partecipazioni Industriali SpA
Peters, Joachim
Mannesmann AG
Pfaffel, Leopold
Bank Austria AG
Phillips, George J
Shop At Home Inc
Phillips, Michael
JDS Uniphase
Pietzke, Rudolf
Altana AG
Pineau, Norbert
Carrefour SA
Piqueras, Rafael
Repsol YPF
Place, John
Yahoo! Inc
Ploubis, Kostantinos
Panafon
Polking, Paul
Bank of America Corporation
Porter, Alan
Imperial Tobacco Group PLC
Pottinger, Alan
Computacenter
Price, John
MEPC PLC
Prince, Charles
Citigroup Inc
Proctor, Tim
Diageo PLC
Proudfoot, Graeme
Amvescap PLC - Invesco Global
Puca, Vincenzo
Acea SpA
Pudlin, Helen
PNC Bank
Pues, Werner
DePfa Bank (Deutsche Pfandbriefbank) AG
Purtell, Lawrence
Alcoa
Pynna, Harri
Fortum Oyj
Ramos, Angel
Centros Comerciales PRYCA
Ramsay, Stephen
International Power PLC
Ramsby, Ole
Novo Nordisk A/S
Ranin, Ursula
Nokia Corporation
Rapone, Costanzo
Bulgari SpA
Rawson, Richard J
Lucent Technologies
Read, Simon
Telewest Communications PLC
Rees, David
Provident Financial PLC
Renault, Michel
CGIP (Compagnie Generale d'Industrie et de Participations)
Rentsch, Hanspeter
Swatch Group AG
Reynolds, Paul
Fifth Third Bank
Ribert, Jean-Paul
ACCOR
Ribn, Carl
Scania CV AB
Ricciardi, Lawrence
International Business Machines Corporation
Rich, Carsten
ISS System AS
Richey, Mary E
Providian Financial
Rigg, Charles
Maxim Integrated Products
Rinck, Gary
Pearson PLC
Roberti, P
Telecel Communications
Robin, Kenneth
Household International
Rodrigues, Manuel
Portugal Telecom
Roell, Hans A R
Fortis (NL) NV
Roelofs, Robert
ASM Lithography Holding NV
Rosoff, William L
Marsh & McLennan Companies Inc
Ross, Dennis E
Ford Motor Co
Rossi, Francesco
Banca Popolare di Verona - Banco S Geminiano e S Prospero
Roth, P
UBS AG
Rötheli, Jürg
Swisscom AG
Rouget, Gerard
CIC Group
Rudolph, Bernd
Thüga AG
Russ, Charles
Qwest Inc
Sabatino, Thomas
Baxter International
Saggbaken, Ivar
Christiania Bank og Kreditkasse ASA
Saito, Kenichiro
Yamanouchi Pharmaceutical Co
Saito, Shigeru
Central Japan Railway Company
Sakurai, Masamitsu
Ricoh Company Ltd
Salazar, Pedro
Schneider Electric SA
Saldin, Thomas R
Albertson's
Salehe,
NRJ
Salsbury, Michael
MCI Worldcom
Salvai, Serge
Canal+ Group
Salzbach, Christi R
Tenet Healthcare
Samuel, Mathew
Singapore Airlines Ltd
Sancho-Martinez-Pardo, Luis
Compania Espanola de Petroleos (Cepsa)
Sand, Hudeth
FöreningsSparbanken AB
Sandberg, Hans
Atlas Copco AB
Sandoval, Gabriel
Ariba
Santamaria, Vinente
Acciona SA
Sauerwein, Eleonore
Aegis Group PLC
Sawabe, Hajime
TDK
Sawch, William B
PE Corp-PE Biosystems Group

Schafer, Albrecht
Siemens AG
Schaub, LL.M, Helen
STRATEC Medical
Scheflen, John
MBNA Corp
Scheinman, Daniel
Cisco Systems Inc
Schmidt-Lorenz, Tilman
Wüstenrot & Württembergische AG
Schneiderman, AF
Linear Technology Corp
Scholten, Marianne
Randstad Holding NV
Schott, Volker
EM TV & Merchandising AG
Schwindenhammer, Alain
PUBLICIS SA
Sclavos, Stratton
VeriSign
Scott, David J
Medtronic
Scott, Derek
Stagecoach Hldgs PLC
Scott, H Lee
Wal-Mart Stores Inc
Scott, Stephen
Vodafone Group PLC
Sequeira, Isabelle
PT Multimedia
Sevaltsen, Erik
Danske Bank [Den] AS
Severin, Bo
Sandvik AB
Sharma, MK
Hindustan Lever Ltd
Sharpe, Robert
PepsiCo Inc
Shepherd, Michael
Bank of New York
Sheridan, Bryan
AIB (Allied Irish Banks) PLC
Shigeta, Yasumitsu
Hickari Tsushin
Shih, Edith
Hutchison Whampoa Limited
Shinohara, S
Fujitsu Limited
Siekman, Thomas
Compaq Computer Corporation
Simoncelli, M Pierre
L'Oreal
Siskind, Arthur Michael
News Corporation Limited
Siu, Winnie
Pacific Century Group
Sjöholm, Anders
Europolitan Holdings AB
Slider, John
Samsung Electronics (UK) Ltd
Smith, Alan
Smiths Group PLC
Smith, Lawrence
Home Depot Inc

Son, Masayoshi
Softbank Corporation
Spiegel, JW
SunTrust Banks
Spillaert, Bruno
Entreprises Et Chemins De Fer En Chine
Spyridakis, John
Commercial Bank of Greece
Stables, Jane
United News & Media PLC
Stanley, James
Scottish Power PLC
Stasinopoulous, George
Piraeus Bank
Stein, Laura
HJ Heinz Company
Stratton, Malcolm
Williams PLC
Stroup, Stanley S
Wells Fargo & Company
Sugawara,
Dai-Ichi Kangyo Bank Limited
Sugimachi, Toshitaka
Secom Co Ltd
Suzuki, Masatoshi
Chubu Electric Power Co Inc
Suzuki, Toshifumi
Ito-Yokado Co Ltd
Suzuki, Toshifumi
Seven-Eleven Japan
Svajgl, Vaclac
Cesky Telecom
Svanberg, Carl-Henric
Assa Abloy AB
Sweeney, Joseph
Applied Materials
Sweetnam, HLM
De Beers Consolidated Mines Ltd
Tachikawa, Keiji
NTT Moblie Communicatons Network Inc
Taisch, Franco
Julius Bär Holding AG
Taithe, Andre-Gilles
Lafarge SA
Takada, Kaoru
Kyushi Matsushita Electric Co Ltd
Takizaki, Takemitsu
Keyence Corporation
Taniguchi, Ichiro
Mitsubishi Electric Corporation
Tapp, Richard F
Blue Circle Industries PLC
Tarkoff, Robert
Commerce One
Taylor, Colin
Northern Rock PLC
Taylor, Leslie
Commonwealth Bank of Australia
Taylor, Peter
Thames Water PLC
Temes, Jabier
Canal Satelite Digital

Tempest, Drake
Qwest Communications Int'l
Teytaud, Cecile
CCF - Credit Commercial de France
Than, Jurgen
Dresdner Bank AG
Thibaut, Isabelle
Dexia
Thomas, Eric
EADS NV
Thomas, Eva Simon
ABN Amro Holding NV
Thompson, M.C.
Wolters Kluwer NV
Thornander, Ulf
Skandinaviska Enskilda Banken AB (publ)
Thurston, David
J Sainsbury PLC
Timms, Geoffrey
Legal & General Group PLC
Tjermell, Jan
Tele 2 AB
Tneter, Karl Otto
Orkla AS
Tomassetti, Andrea
Banca Fideuram SpA
Tonkinson, Andrew OC
South African Breweries
Trachsel, William
United Technologies Corporation
Treanor, Mark
First Union Corp
Tristano, Riccardo
Banca di Roma
Trust, Howard B
Barclays PLC
Tucker, Mark
Dow Chemical Co
Turcotte, Martine
BCE Inc
Tuttle, Alan
Gucci Group NV
Tyteca, Johan
KBC Bankverzekering
Uebel, Mats
Securitas AB
Ujiie, Seiichiro
Nippon Television Network Corporation
Ursu, John J
Minnesota Mining and Manufacturing Company
Valentine, Catherine
Intuit Inc
Van Caenegem, Jettie
UCB SA
van Der Ven, JHC
Royal Numico NV
Van Gorp, Jo
Level 3 Communications Inc
Van Graafeiland, Gary P
Eastman Kodak Company
Van Kampen,
VNU (NV)

van Maasakker, SA
Getronics NV
Van Tielraden, A.H.P.M.
Koninklijke Ahold NV
van Wassenaer, DC
ING Groep NV
Vellani, Andrew S
Scottish & Newcastle PLC
Verly, Philippe
Almanij NV - Algemene Mij voor Nijverheidskrediet
Vetter, E
AXA Colonia Konzern AG
Vieweg, Cecilia
AB Electrolux
Vogelgesang, Ralph
Munich Reinsurance Company
von Hulsen, Hans-Viggo
Volkswagen AG
von Ruckteschell, Nicolai
Deutsche Lufthansa AG
von Verschuer, Nikolaus
Alusuisse Group AG
Vyakhirev, Rem Ivanovich
OAO Gazprom
Wagner, Barry
Omnicom Group
Wagner, Thomas
ACE INA Holding
Walker, David
Logica PLC
Wall, Charles R.
Philip Morris Companies Inc
Wall, Elizabeth
Equant NV
Wallimann, Martine
Dassault Systemes
Walsh, Stephen
British Airways PLC
Wang, Elizabeth
Doubleclick
Ward-Jones, Robert
Rentokil Initial PLC
Warmsley, Derek K
EMAP PLC
Washington, Jyrl
Adecco Management & Consulting SA
Waskönig, Peter
DaimlerChrysler AG
Waterman, Bob
Columbia/HCA Healthcare Corp
Waters, Paul
Misys PLC
Webber, Michael
Woolwich PLC
Webber, Peter
Next PLC
Webbink, Mark
Red Hat
Wegner, Adam
Exodus Communications
Westerlaken, A
Philips Electronics NV
Whealy, Michael T.
First Data Corporation

Whilden Jr, Robert
BMC Software
White, John
Toronto-Dominion Bank
Whitfield, Alan
British Telecommuncations PLC
Wiedmann, Michael
Metro Cash & Carry GmbH
Willard, Richard K
Gillette Company
Williams, Stephen G
Unilever Group
Willing, Leonard Peter
Heineken NV
Wilson, Andrew
Enterprise Oil PLC
Winter, Richard
Bass PLC
Wise, William
Analog Devices
Withers, Wayne
Emerson Electric Co
Withington, Neil
British American Tobacco PLC
Woghin, Steve
Computer Associates Int'l Inc
Wohlmann, Herbert
Clariant Ltd
Woo, Seung-Sul
Korea Telecommunication
Xueref, Carol
Essilor International SA
Yagi, Nobuhito
NEC Corporation
Yakada, Yoshiyuki
SMC Corporation
Yamamoto, Masahiro
ROHM Co Ltd
Yamamoto, Yoshiro
Fuji Bank Ltd
Yamnie, Mohammed
Saudi Basic Industries Corporation (SABIC) Marketing Company Ltd
Yamuchi, Hiroshi
Nintendo Co Ltd
Yang, Lee Hsien
Singapore Telecom
Yip, Emmanuel
Cheung Kong (Holdings) Limited
Ylekartes, Same
Helsingin Puhelin Oyj (Helsinki Telephone)
Ylikortes,
Elisa Communications Oyj (formerly HPY Holding Corporation)
Youth, Tom
Internap Network Services
Yuksel, Cuneyt
H.O. Sabanci Holding A.S.
Zoeller, DC
National City
zur Nedden, Christian
Continental AG

TOP GLOBAL IN-HOUSE COUNSEL

[Based on Financial Times Global 500/Euro 500 Rankings]

3Com Corporation
Mark D Michael, General Counsel
5400 Bayfront Plaza, Santa Clara CA 95052-8145, USA
Tel: +1 408 326 5000 **Fax:** +1 408 326 5001
Website: www.3com.com

3i Group PLC
Tony Brierley, Company Secretary and Head of Legal Services
91 Waterloo Road, London SE1 8XP, United Kingdom
Tel: +44 20 7928 3131 **Fax:** +44 20 7928 0058
Website: www.3i.com

Aachener und Muenchener Beteiligungs AG (AMB)
Casten Dagefoerde, Head of Legal Department
Aachener & Muenchener Allee 9, D-52074 Aachen, Germany
Tel: +49 241 46101 **Fax:** +49 241 46 118 35
Website: www.amb.de

AB Electrolux
Cecilia Vieweg, Senior Vice President, General Counsel & Secretary
S:t Goransgatan 143, 10545 Stockholm, Sweden
Tel: +46 8 738 6000 **Fax:** +46 8 738 6335
Email: cecelia.vieweg@notes.electrolux.se
Website: www.electrolux.com

AB Industrivarden
Thomas Nordvaller, General Counsel
PO Box 5403, 11484 Stockholm, Sweden
Tel: +46 8 666 64 00 **Fax:** +46 8 661 46 28
Email: thomas.nordvaller@industrivarden.se
Website: www.industrivarden.se

AB SKF
Carina Bergfelt, General Counsel
415 50 Göteborg, Sweden
Tel: +46 31 337 10 00 **Fax:** +46 31 337 28 32
Email: carina.bergfelt@skf.com
Website: www.skf.com/group

AB Volvo
Eva Persson, Head of Legal
Volvo Bergegardsvaeg, SE-405 08 Gothenburg, Sweden
Tel: +46 31 66 0000 **Fax:** +46 31 54 5772
Website: www.volvo.com

ABB Ltd
Beat Hess, Senior Vice-President, General Counsel and Secretary
Postfach 8131, CH-8050 Zurich, Switzerland
Tel: +41 1 317 7111 **Fax:** +41 1 317 7992
Email: beat.hess@ch.abb.com
Website: www.abb.com

Abbey National PLC
Gwyn Malkin, Group Legal Services Director
Abbey House, 201 Grafton Gate East, Milton Keynes MK9 1AN, United Kingdom
Tel: +44 1908 343000 **Fax:** +44 1908 348282
Email: gwyn.malkin@abbeynational.co.uk
Website: www.abbeynational.co.uk

Abbott Laboratories Limited
Jose de Lasa, Senior Vice-President and General Counsel
100 Abbott Park Road, Abbott Park IL 60064-3500, USA
Tel: +1 847 937 6100 **Fax:** +1 847 938 6277
Email: jose.delasa@abbott.com
Website: www.abbott.com

ABN Amro Holding NV
Eva Simon Thomas, Head of Legal Affiars
Foppingadreef 22, 1102 BS Amsterdam, Netherlands
Tel: +31 20 629 5202 **Fax:** +31 20 628 4641
Email: eva.simon.thomas@nl.abnamro.com
Website: www.abnamro.nl

Acciona SA
Vinente Santamaria, Director of Legal Department
Avenida Europa 18, Parque Empresarial La Moraleja, Alcobendas, 28108 Madrid, Spain
Tel: +34 91 663 3101 **Fax:** +34 91 663 30 99
Website: www.acciona.es

ACCOR
Jean-Paul Ribert, Director of Legal Services
Tour Maine Montparnasse, 75015 Paris, France
Tel: +33 1 45 38 86 83 **Fax:** +33 1 60 77 98 90
Email: ribert_jeanpaul@accor.fr
Website: www.accor.com

ACE INA Holding
Thomas Wagner, Head of Legal
1 Liberty Place, 1601 Chestnut Street, 21st Floor, PO Box 7716, Philadelphia PA 19192-1550, USA
Tel: +1 215 640 1000 **Fax:** +1 215 761 5519
Website: www.cigna.com

Acea SpA
Vincenzo Puca, General Counsel
Piazzale Ostiense, 2, 00154 Roma, Italy
Tel: +39 06 5799 3415 **Fax:** +39 0657 9941 81
Website: www.aceaspa.it

ACESA - Autopistas Concesionaria Espanola SA
Marta Casas, Head of Legal
Plaza Gala Placidia, 1, 08006 Barcelona, Spain
Tel: +34 93 228 50 00 **Fax:** +34 93 228 50 01
Email: marta.casas@autopistas.com
Website: www.autopistas-sa.es

Acom Co
Shigeyoshi Kinoshita, President
2-15-11 Fujimi, Chiyoda-ku, Tokyo 102-0071, Japan
Tel: +81 3 3234 9120
Website: www.acom.co.jp/

Adecco Management & Consulting SA
Jyrl Washington, Senior Vice President and General Counsel
Adecco Group North America, 175 Broad Hollow Road, Melvile, New York NY 11747-8905, USA
Tel: +1 631 844 7660 **Fax:** +1 631 844 7266
Website: www.adecco.com

Adidas-Salomon
Roland Lessig, Head of Legal Department
Adi-Dassler-Strasse 1-2, D-91074 Herzogenaurach, Germany
Tel: +49 91 32 84 0 **Fax:** +49 91 32 84 874
Email: roland.lessig@adidas.de
Website: www.adidas.de

Advantest
Takeshi Kojima, General Manager
Shinjuku-NS Bldg., 2-4-1, Nishi-Shinjuku, Shinjuku-ku, Tokyo 163-0880, Japan
Tel: +81 3 3342 7500 **Fax:** +81 3 5381 7661
Website: www.advantest.co.jp

Aegis Group PLC
Eleonore Sauerwein, Group Legal Counsel
11a West Halkin Street, London SW1X 8JL, United Kingdom
Tel: +44 20 7470 5000 **Fax:** +44 20 7470 5099
Website: www.carat.com

Aegon NV
H M Kappelle, Director of Legal Affairs
Mariahoeveplein 50, Postbus 202, NL-2501 CE The Hague, Netherlands
Tel: +31 703 445 934 **Fax:** +31 703 447 346
Email: hkappelle@aegon.nl
Website: www.aegon.com

AEM SpA
Luca Da Rita, General Sectrary Legal Dept
via Della Balle dei Fontanili 29, 00168 Rome, Italy
Tel: +39 06614 2430 **Fax:** +39 066114 9936
Email: luca.darita@acotel.com
Website: www.aem.it

AES
William R Lurasci, General Counsel
1001 N. 19th Street, Arlington 22209-1722, USA
Tel: +1 703 522 1315 **Fax:** +1 703 528 4510
Website: www.aesc.com

AFLAC
Joey Laudermilk, General Counsel
1932 Wynnton Road, Columbus GA 31999-0001, USA
Tel: +1 706 323 3431 **Fax:** +1 706 324 6330
Email: jlaudermilk@aflac.com
Website: www.aflac.com

AGA AB (Linde Gas AG)
Urban A Murray, General Counsel
Linde Gas AG, Seitnerstrasse 70, D-82049 Höllriegelskreuth, Germany
Tel: +49 89 74 46 15 90 **Fax:** +49 89 74 46 10 86
Email: urbanmurray@de.linde-gas.com
Website: www.aga.se

AGF (Assurances Generale de France)
Jean Francois Bruno, General Counsel
87 Rue de Richelieu, 75113 Paris, France
Tel: +33 1 44 86 20 13 **Fax:** +33 1 44 86 20 74
Email: brunojf@agf.fr
Website: www.agf.fr

Agfa-Gevaert
Francis Delwiche, General Counsel
Septestraat 27, 2640 Mortsel, Belgium
Tel: +32 3 444 5901 **Fax:** +32 3 444 7228
Email: francis.delwiche.fd@belgium.agfa.com
Website: www.agfa.be

Agilent Technologies
Craig Norlund, General Counsel
395 Page Mill Rd, Palo Alto 94306, USA
Tel: +1 650 857 1501 **Fax:** +1 650 857 7299
Website: www.agilent-tech.com

AIB (Allied Irish Banks) PLC
Bryan Sheridan, Group Law Agent
Bank Centre, PO Box 1121, Ballsbridge, Dublin 4, Ireland
Tel: +353 1 660 0311 **Fax:** +353 1 660 4896
Email: bryan.c.sheridan@aib.ie
Website: www.aib.ie

Airtours Holidays Limited
Andy Cooper, Head of Legal
Wavell House, Holcombe Road, Helmshore, Rossendale BB4 4NB, United Kingdom
Tel: +44 1706 240033 **Fax:** +44 1706 212144
Email: lglac@airtours.com
Website: www.airtours.co.uk

Akamai Technologies
Robert Ball, Vice President and General Counsel
500 Technology Square, Cambridge 02139, USA
Tel: +1 617 250 3000 **Fax:** +1 617 250 3001
Website: www.akamai.com

Akbank Turk Anonim Sirketi
Hasan Esen, General Counsel
Sabanci Center, Fort Levent, 80745 Istanbul, Turkey
Tel: +90 212 270 0044 **Fax:** +90 212 269 9969
Website: www.akbank.com.tr

Akzo Nobel NV
A Jan AJ Eijsbouts, General Counsel
PO Box 93 00, Velperweg 76, NL-6800 SB Arnhem, Netherlands
Tel: +31 26 366 2730 **Fax:** +31 26 366 3240
Email: Jan.Eijsbouts@AkzoNobel.com
Website: www.akzonobel.com

Albertson's
Thomas R Saldin, Executive Vice-President and General Counsel
250 Parkcenter Boulevard, P O Box 20, Boise ID 83706, USA
Tel: +1 208 395 6200 **Fax:** +1 208 385 6110
Website: www.albertsons.com

Alcatel Alsthom Group
Pascal Durand-Barthez, Head of Legal
54 Rue la Boétie, Cedex 08, 75008 Paris, France
Tel: +33 1 40 76 10 10 **Fax:** +33 1 40 76 14 35
Website: www.alcatel.com

Alcoa
Lawrence Purtell, Executive Vice-President and General Counsel
390 Park Avenue, New York 10022, USA
Tel: +1 212 836 2652 **Fax:** +1 212 836 2809
Email: lawrence.purtell@alcoa.com
Website: www.alcoa.com

Alitalia Linee Aeree Italiane SPA
Confolte Leopoldo, Head of Legal
Viale Alessandro Marchetti 111, 00148 Rome, Italy
Tel: +39 06 656 21 **Fax:** +39 06656 24533
Email: confolte.leopoldo@alitalia.it
Website: www.alitalia.com

Alleanza Assicurazioni SPA
Maurizio Basso, Head of Legal
Viale Luigi Sturzo 35, 20154 Milano, Italy
Tel: +39 02 629 61 **Fax:** +39 02 629 6609
Email: maurizio.basso@mail.alleanzaassicurazioni.it
Website: www.alleanzaassicurazioni.it

Alliance & Leicester PLC
Kathrine Hughes, Head of Legal
Alliance & Leicester Unit Trust Managers Ltd, Building 3, Floor 2, Carlton Park, Narborough LE9 5XX, United Kingdom
Tel: +44 116 201 1000 **Fax:** +44 116 200 4995
Website: www.alliance-leicester.co.uk

Allianz AG
Bernd Honsel, Head of Legal Department
Königinstrasse 28, D-80802 Munich, Germany
Tel: +49 89 3800 2234 **Fax:** +49 89 3800 2152
Website: www.allianz.de

Allied Domecq PLC
Russell P Kelley, General Counsel & Company Secretary
The Pavillions, Bridgwater Road, Bedminster Down, Bristol BS13 8AR, United Kingdom
Tel: +44 117 978 5000 **Fax:** +44 117 978 5284
Website: www.allieddomecqplc.com

Allstate Corp
Michael McCabe, General Counsel and Vice President
Allstate Plaza, 2775 Sanders Road, Northbrook IL 60062-6127, USA
Tel: +1 847 402 5000 **Fax:** +1 847 402 5670
Website: www.allstate.com

Alltel Corporation
Michael Jackson, Counsel
One Allied Drive, Little Rock AR 72202, USA
Tel: +1 501 905 5459 **Fax:** +1 501 905 5489
Email: michael.t.jackson@alltel.com
Website: www.alltel.com

Almanij NV - Algemene Mij voor Nijverheidskrediet
Philippe Verly, Corporate Secretary
Schoenmarkt 33, B-2000 Antwerp, Belgium
Tel: +32 3 202 8700 **Fax:** +32 3 202 8706
Email: philippe.verly@almanij.be
Website: www.almanij.be

Alstom
Andrew P Hibbert, Executive Vice President & General Counsel
25 Avenue Kléber, 75116 Paris Cedex 16, France
Tel: +33 1 47 55 20 00 **Fax:** +33 1 47 55 28 61
Email: andrew.hibbert@chq.alstom.com
Website: www.alstom.com

Altadis
Jean-Phillipe Carrier, Head of Legal
Eloy Gonzalo 10, 28010 Madrid, Spain
Tel: +34 91 360 9000 **Fax:** +34 91 360 9018
Email: jpcarrier@altadis.com
Website: www.altadis.com

Altana AG
Rudolf Pietzke, General Counsel
Günther-Quandt-Haus, Seedammweg 55, Postfach, D-61352 Bad Homburg vor der Hohe, Germany
Tel: +49 6172 404372 **Fax:** +49 6172 404427
Email: ute.schueler@atlana.de
Website: www.altana.com

Altran Technologies SA
Christophe Brie, Responsable Juridique
251 Boulevarde Pereire, 75017 Paris, France
Tel: +33 1 44 09 64 55 **Fax:** +33 1 44 09 64 81
Email: cbrie@altran.fr
Website: www.altran.fr

Alusuisse Group AG
Nikolaus von Verschuer, Senior Vice-President
Feldeggstrasse 4, PO Box 8034, CH-8034 Zurich, Switzerland
Tel: +41 1 386 22 22 **Fax:** +41 1 386 25 85
Website: www.algroup.ch

Amadeus Global Travel
Thomas Lopez Fernebrand, Head of Legal
Amadeus Global Travel, C/Salvador de Madariaga 1, E-28027 Madrid, Spain
Tel: +34 915 820 100 **Fax:** +34 915 820 129
Email: tlopez@amadeus.net
Website: www.global.amadeus.net

Amazon. Com
Allan Carlan, General Counsel
1200 Twelfth Avenue South, Building 1200, Seattle 98144-2734, USA
Tel: +1 206 266 1000 **Fax:** +1 206 266 4206
Website: www.amazon.com

American Express Company
Louise Parent, General Counsel
American Express Tower, World Financial Center, 200 Vesey St., New York 10285, USA
Tel: +1 212 640 2000 **Fax:** +1 212 267 9061
Email: louise.parent@aexp.com
Website: www.americanexpress.com

American General Corporation
Mark Berg, General Counsel
PO Box 3247, Houston 77253, USA
Tel: +1 713 522 1111 **Fax:** +1 713 831 1322
Email: mark_berg@agc.com
Website: www.americangeneral.com

American Home Products Corporation
Louis L Hoynes Jr, General Counsel
5 Giralda Farms, Madison NJ 07940, USA
Tel: +1 973 660 5000 **Fax:** +1 973 660 7050
Email: hoynesl@ahp.com
Website: www.ahp.com

American International Group Inc (AIG)
Ernest Patrikis, General Counsel
70 Pine Street, New York 10270, USA
Tel: +1 212 770 7000 **Fax:** +1 212 425 2175
Email: ernest.patrikis@aig.com
Website: www.aig.com

Amgen Inc
Steven Odre, Senior Vice President & General Counsel
1 Amgen Centre Drive, Thousand Oaks CA 91320-1789, USA
Tel: +1 805 447 1000 **Fax:** +1 805 447 1010
Email: sodre@amgen.com
Website: www.amgen.com

Amvescap PLC - Invesco Global
Graeme Proudfoot, General Counsel
11 Devonshire Square, London EC2M 4YR, United Kingdom
Tel: +44 20 7626 3434 **Fax:** +44 20 7454 3166
Email: graeme_proudfoot@ldn.invesco.com
Website: www.invesco.co.uk

Analog Devices
William Wise, General Counsel
One Technology Way, PO Box 9106, Norwood 02062, USA
Tel: +1 781 329 4700 **Fax:** +1 781 461 3491
Email: william.wise@analogue.com
Website: www.analogue.com

Anglo American PLC
Ben Keisler, Executive Vice President, General Counsel
20 Carlton House Terrace, St James's, London SW1Y 5AN, United Kingdom
Tel: +44 20 7698 8888 **Fax:** +44 20 7698 8500
Website: www.angloamerican.co.uk

Anheuser-Busch Companies Inc
Stephen K Lambright, General Counsel
1 Busch Place, St. Louis MO 63118-1852, USA
Tel: +1 314 577 200 0 **Fax:** +1 314 865 9271
Email: stephen.lambright@anheuser-busch.com
Website: www.anheuser-busch.com

AOL Time Warner Inc
Paul Cappuccio, Executive Vice-President, General Counsel and Secretary
75 Rockerfeller Plaza, New York 10019, USA
Tel: +1 212 484 8164 **Fax:** +1 212 265 2646
Website: www.aoltimewarner.com

Apple Computer
Nancy Heinen, General Counsel
1 Infinite Loop, Cupertino 95014, USA
Tel: +1 408 996 1010 **Fax:** +1 408 974 8530
Email: heinen@apple.com
Website: www.apple.com

Applied Materials
Joseph Sweeney, Head of Legal
3050 Bowers Avenue, Santa Clara CA 95054 - 3299, USA
Tel: +1 408 727 5555 **Fax:** +1 408 748 9943
Email: joseph_sweeney@amat.com
Website: www.appliedmaterials.com

Arçelik
Ali Jen Budak, General Counsel
81719 Tuzla, Istanbul, Turkey
Tel: +90 216 395 4515 **Fax:** +90 216 395 2727
Website: www.arcelik.com

Ariba
Gabriel Sandoval, VP, General Counsel
1565 Charleston Road, Mountain View 94043, USA
Tel: +1 650 930 6200 **Fax:** +1 650 930 6300
Website: www.ariba.com

Arjo Wiggins Appleton PLC
Albert Dungate, Company Secretary and Group Solicitor
Times Place, 45 Pall Mall, London SW1Y 5JG, United Kingdom
Tel: +44 20 7941 8000 **Fax:** +44 20 7941 8008

ARM Limited
David N Mackay, Company Secretary
110 Fulbourn Road, Cambridge CB1 9JN, United Kingdom
Tel: +44 1223 400400 **Fax:** +44 1223 400410
Website: www.arm.com

Arnoldo Mondadori Editore SpA
Furio Silvio Ghezzi, Chief Executive
Via Mondadori 1, Segrate, 20090 Milan, Italy
Tel: +39 02 7542 2215 **Fax:** +39 02 7542 2537
Email: aallegri@mondadori.it
Website: www.mondadori.com

Asahi Bank
Hiroshi Itoh, Senior Managing Director
1-2 Otemachi 1-chome, Chiyoda-ku, Tokyo 100-8016, Japan
Tel: +81 3 5223 5274 **Fax:** +81 3 3213 6424
Website: www.asahibank.co.jp

ASM Lithography Holding NV
Robert Roelofs, General Counsel
De Run 1110, 5503 LA Veldhoven, Netherlands
Tel: +31 40 268 3444 **Fax:** +31 40 268 4888
Email: robert.roelofs@asml.nl
Website: www.asml.com

Assa Abloy AB
Carl-Henric Svanberg, President
Klarabergsviadukten 90, PO Box 70340, 107 23 Stockholm, Sweden
Tel: +46 8 5064 8500 **Fax:** +46 8 5064 8560
Email: carl-henric.svanberg@assaabloy.se
Website: www.assaabloy.se

Assicurazioni Generali SpA
Aldo Cappuccio, General Counsel
Piazza Duca degli Abruzzi, 2, 34132 Trieste, Italy
Tel: +39 040 6711 11 **Fax:** +39 040 6710 06
Email: aldo_cappuccio@generali.com
Website: www.generali.com

Associated British Foods PLC
Simon Bromwich, Joint Head of Legal Department
Legal Department, 3-5 Rickmansworth Road, Watford WD1 7HG, United Kingdom
Tel: +44 1923 252050 **Fax:** +44 1923 223542
Website: www.abf.co.uk

AstraZeneca PLC
Graeme Musker, Head of Legal
15 Stanhope Gate, London W1Y 6LN, United Kingdom
Tel: +44 20 7304 5000 **Fax:** +44 20 7304 5151
Email: Graeme.Musker@astrazeneca.com.
Website: www.astrazeneca.com

Asustek Computer Inc
Jessica Chen, Head of Legal
4th Floor No.150 Lide Rd, Peitou , Taiwan
Tel: +886 2 2894 3447 **Fax:** +886 2 289 43449
Email: jessica_chen@asus.com.tw
Website: www.asus.com.tw

AT&T Broadband
Rick Bailey, General Counsel
188 Inverness Drive West, Englewood CO 80112, USA
Tel: +1 303 858 3000 **Fax:** +1 303 858 5083
Website: www.attbroadband.com

AT&T Corporation
James W Ciconi, General Counsel
295 North Maple Ave, Basking Ridge 07920, USA
Tel: +1 908 221 8441 **Fax:** +1 908 630 1138
Website: www.att.com

AT&T Liberty Media Group
Rick Bailey, General Counsel
188 Inverness Drive West, Englewood 80112, USA
Tel: +1 303 858 3000 **Fax:** +1 303 858 5083
Website: www.attbis.com

Atlas Copco AB
Hans Sandberg, Senior Vice President, Legal
Sickla Industrivag 3a, SE-105 23 Stockholm, Sweden
Tel: +46 8 743 8000 **Fax:** +46 8 743 8037
Email: hans.sandberg@atlascopco.com
Website: www.atlascopco.com

ATOS Origin
Gerard Guerguerian, Group General Counsel
3 Place de la Pyramide, La Defense Cedex, 92067 Paris, France
Tel: +33 1 49 00 90 00 **Fax:** +33 1 47 73 07 63
Email: gguerguergain@atos.group.com
Website: www.atosorigin.com

Autogrill SPA
M Casu, General Counsel
Via Caldera 21, 20153 Milan, Italy
Tel: +39 02 482 61 **Fax:** +39 02 452 74 443
Website: www.autogrill.it

Automatic Data Processing
James Benson, General Counsel
1 ADP Boulevard, Roseland NJ 07068, USA
Tel: +1 973 994 5000 **Fax:** +1 973 974 3324
Website: www.adp.com

Autostrade - Concessioni e Costruzioni Autostrade SpA
Francesco Frezza, General Counsel
Via Alberto Bergamini 50, 00159 Roma, Italy
Tel: +39 06 599 3415 **Fax:** +39 06 4363 4259
Website: www.autostrade.it

Aventis SA
Dirk Oldenburg, General Counsel
Espace Europeen de l'Enterprise, Schiltigheim, 67300 Strasbourg, France
Tel: +33 3 88 99 1287 **Fax:** +33 3 88 99 1364
Website: www.aventis.com

AXA Colonia Konzern AG
E Vetter, Head of Legal
Gereonsdriesch 9-11, D-50670 Cologne, Germany
Tel: +49 221 148 32990 **Fax:** +49 221 148 32978
Website: www.axa-colonia.de

AXA Financial
Robert Garber, Executive Vice President and General Counsel
1290 Avenue of the Americas, New York 10104, USA
Tel: +1 212 554 1234 **Fax:** +1 212 707 1755
Website: www.axa-financial.com

AXA-UAP SA
Christianne Butte, General Counsel
GIE AXA, 21 Avenue Matignon, 75008 Paris, France
Tel: +33 1 40 75 56 38 **Fax:** +33 1 40 75 59 71
Email: christiane.butte@axa.com
Website: www.axa.com

Axel Springer Verlag AG
Gerhard Mehnzel, General Counsel
Axel-Springer-Platz 1, D-20350 Hamburg, Germany
Tel: +49 040 347 244 99 **Fax:** +49 040 347 255 40
Website: www.asv.de

BAA PLC
Robert Herga, Head of Legal Services
Stockley House, 2nd floor, 130 Wilton Road, London SW1V 1LQ, United Kingdom
Tel: +44 20 7834 9449 **Fax:** +44 20 7932 6811
Email: Robert_Herga@BAA.CO.UK
Website: www.baa.co.uk

BAE Systems PLC
Michael Lester, Group Legal Director
1 Brewers Green, Buckingham Gate, London SW1H 0RH, United Kingdom
Tel: +44 1252 383904 **Fax:** +44 1252 383992

Baloise Holding
Bruno Dallo, Head of Legal
Aeschengraben 21, CH-4002 Basle, Switzerland
Tel: +41 61 285 85 85 **Fax:** +41 61 285 90 48
Email: bruno.dallo@basle.ch
Website: www.baloise.com

Baltimore Technologies PLC
Simon J Enoch, Company Secretary
The Square, Basing View, Basingstoke RG21 4EG, United Kingdom
Tel: +44 1256 818800 **Fax:** +44 1256 812901
Email: senoch@baltimore.com
Website: www.baltimore.com

Banca di Roma
Riccardo Tristano, General Counsel
Vialle Tupini 180, 00144 Rome, Italy
Tel: +39 06 544 51 **Fax:** +39 06 544 52 879
Website: www.bancaroma.it

Banca Fideuram SpA
Andrea Tomassetti, Head of Legal Department
Piazzale Giulio Douhet n. 31, 00143 Rome, Italy
Tel: +39 06 59021 **Fax:** +39 06 59022634
Email: atomassetti@bancafideuram.it
Website: www.bancafideuram.it

Banca Lombarda SpA
Franco Bicci, General Counsel
Via Cefalonia 62, 25175 Brescia, Italy
Tel: +39 030 2433 1 **Fax:** +39 030 2433 242
Website: www.bancalombarda.it

Banca Monte Dei Paschi
Pasqualino Paulesu, Director, Legal Dept
Via Maravolti 15, 53100 Siena, Italy
Tel: +39 0577 294 492 **Fax:** +39 0577 46303
Email: pasqualino.paulesu@banca.mps.it
Website: www.mps.it

Banca Nazionale del Lavoro SpA
Carlo Caprodossi, General Counsel
Via Vittorio Veneto 119, 00187 Rome, Italy
Tel: +39 06 47 02 1 **Fax:** +39 06 47 02 8280
Email: carlo.caprodossi@bnlmail.com
Website: www.bnl.it

Banca Popolare dell'Emilia Romagna SCARL
C Baldoni, Chairman, Board of Directors
Via San Carlo 8-20, 4110 Modena, Italy
Tel: +39 059 20 21 111 **Fax:** +39 059 202 2033
Website: www.bper.it

Banca Popolare di Verona - Banco S Geminiano e S Prospero
Francesco Rossi, Head of Legal
Piazza Nogara, 2, 37121 Verona, Italy
Tel: +39 04 58 67 5111 **Fax:** +39 04 58 67 5131
Email: settlegale@bpv.it
Website: www.bpv.it

Banco Bilbao Vizcaya Argentaria SA
Mario Fernandez, Director of Legal Dept
Gran Via, 1, 3A Planta, 48001 Bilbao, Spain
Tel: +34 94 487 6592 **Fax:** +34 94 487 6424
Email: m.fdez@grupobbva.com
Website: www.bbva.es

Banco Comercial Português (BCP)
Manuel Campos, Head of Legal
Av. José Malhoa, lote 1686, 1°, 1070-157 Lisboa, Portugal
Tel: +351 21 720 1450 **Fax:** +351 21 720 534
Email: camarate.campos@serzibanco.pt

Banco Espanol de Credito SA (Banesto)
V Menendez, Chief Executive Officer
Paseo de la Castellana, 7, 28046 Madrid, Spain
Tel: +34 91 338 2349
Website: www.banesto.es

Banco Espirito Santo e Comercial de Lisboa
Fernando Quintaif Lopes, Director
Avenida da Liberdade 195, 1250-140 Lisbon, Portugal
Tel: +351 21 3158 331 **Fax:** +351 21 8557 698
Website: www.bes.pt

Banco Popular Espanol
Louis-Phillipe Marcos, Legal Services Manager
Velazquez 34, 28001 Madrid, Spain
Tel: +34 91 520 70 00 **Fax:** +34 91 577 0079
Email: Louis-Phillipe.Marcos@bancopopular.es
Website: www.bancopopular.es

Bank Austria AG
Leopold Pfaffel, Director & Head of the Legal Department
Vordere Zollamtsstrasse 13, A-1030 Vienna, Austria
Tel: +43 1 711 91 0 **Fax:** +43 1 711 91 56149
Email: leopold.pfaffel@bankaustria.com
Website: www.bankaustria.com

Bank of America Corporation
Paul Polking, Head of Legal
Bank of America Corporate Center, 100 N. Tryon St., Charlotte NC 28255, USA
Tel: +1 888 279 3457 **Fax:** +1 704 370 1515
Email: paul.polking@bankofamerica.com
Website: www.bankofamerica.com

Bank of Ireland
Finbarr Murphy, Head of Legal
Bank of Ireland, 2 College Green, Dublin 2, Ireland
Tel: +353 1 677 6801 **Fax:** +353 1 670 3602
Email: finbarr.murphy@boi.ie
Website: www.bankofireland.ie

Bank of New York
Michael Shepherd, General Counsel
1 Wall Street, New York 10286, USA
Tel: +1 212 495 1784 **Fax:** +1 212 635 1698
Email: mshepherd@bankofny.com
Website: www.bankofny.com

Bank of Scotland
Brian Fisher, Head of Legal
Legal Services, 1st Floor Broadstreet House, 55 Old Broad Street, London EC2P 2HL, United Kingdom
Tel: +44 20 7601 6711 **Fax:** +44 20 7601 6713
Email: brianfisher@bankofscotland.co.uk
Website: www.bankofscotland.co.uk

Bank of Tokyo-Mitsubishi Ltd
Shigemitsu Miki, Deputy President and Director of Finance
7-1 Marunouchi 2 Chome, Chiyoda-ku, Tokyo 100-8388, Japan
Tel: +81 3 3240 1111 **Fax:** +81 3 3240 4179
Website: www.btm.co.jp

Bank One Corp
Christine A. Edwards, General Counsel
1 Bank One Plaza, Mail Suite, Chicago IL 10276, USA
Tel: +1 312 732 4000 **Fax:** +1 312 732 7677
Email: chris_edwards@bankone.com
Website: www.bankone.com

Bankinter SA
Rafael Mateu De Ros, General Counsel
Paseo de la Castellana 29, 28046 Madrid, Spain
Tel: +34 91 339 75 00 **Fax:** +34 91 339 77 58
Website: www.bankinter.es

Banque Bruxelles Lambert SA
Eric De Baenst, Head of Legal
24 Avenue Marmix, B-1000 Brussels, Belgium
Tel: +32 2 547 2161 **Fax:** +32 2 412 21 94
Email: eric.de-baenst@bbl.be
Website: www.bbl.be

Banque Generale du Luxembourg SA
Andre Hoffman, Manager of the Legal Department
50 avenue John F Kennedy, L-2951 Luxembourg, Luxembourg
Tel: +352 42 42 1 **Fax:** +352 424 2359
Email: andre.hoffman@bgl.lu
Website: www.bgl.lu

Barclays PLC
Howard B Trust, Group General Counsel
54 Lombard Street, London EC3P 3AH, United Kingdom
Tel: +44 20 7699 5000 **Fax:** +44 20 7699 3414
Email: GGCO@barclays.co.uk
Website: www.barclays.co.uk

BASF AG
Peter Gierlich, Head of Central Legal Department
Carl Bosch Strasse 38, D-67056 Ludwigshafen, Germany
Tel: +49 621 604 7413 **Fax:** +49 621 604 1789
Email: peter.gierlich@basf-ag.de
Website: www.basf.de

Bass PLC
Richard Winter, Group Company Secretary
20 North Audley Street, London W1Y 1WE, United Kingdom
Tel: +44 20 7409 1919 **Fax:** +44 20 7409 8526
Website: www.bass.com

Baxter International
Thomas Sabatino, General Counsel
1 Baxter Parkway, Deerfield IL 60015-4633, USA
Tel: +1 847 948 2000 **Fax:** +1 847 948 2450
Email: sabatit@baxter.com
Website: www.baxter.com

Bayer AG
Roland Hartwig, General Counsel
Werk Leverkusen, D-51368 Leverkusen, Germany
Tel: +49 214 302 5649 **Fax:** +49 214 302 6786
Website: www.bayer.de

Bayerische Hypo- und Vereinsbank AG
Diether Munich, Chief Legal Counsel
AM Tuchapark 16, D-80538 Munich, Germany
Tel: +49 89 378 0 **Fax:** +49 89 378 29940
Email: diether.muenich@hypovereinsbank.de
Website: www.hypovereinsbank.de

BBA Group PLC
Sarah Foulkes Shaw, Group Secretary
70 Fleet Street, London EC4Y 1EV, United Kingdom
Tel: +44 20 7842 4900 **Fax:** +44 20 7353 5831
Email: czumstein@bbagroup.com
Website: www.bbagroup.com

BCE Inc
Martine Turcotte, Chief Legal Officer
1000 Rue de la Gauchetiere W., Bureau 3700, Montreal H3B 4Y7, Canada
Tel: +1 514 870 8777 **Fax:** +1 514 870 4877
Email: martine.turcotte@bell.ca
Website: www.bce.ca

Beiersdorf AG
Hans-Henning Bernhard, Head of Legal
Unnastrasse 48, D-20245 Hamburg, Germany
Tel: +49 40 49 09 0 **Fax:** +49 093 434
Email: bernhah@beiersdorf.com
Website: www.beiersdorf.com

BellSouth Corporation
Charles R Morgan, General Counsel
1155 Peachtree St. N.E., Suite 2002, Atlanta GA 30309-3610, USA
Tel: +1 404 249 2000 **Fax:** +1 404 249 5948
Website: www.bellsouthcorp.com

Benesse
Soichiro Fukutake, President
3-7-17 Minamigata, Okayama-shi, Okayama 700-8686, Japan
Tel: +81 86 225 1100
Website: www.benesse.co.jp

Benetton Group SpA
Stefano Artuso, General Counsel and Vice President Legal Affairs
Via Villa Minelli 1, Ponzano, 31050 Veneto, Italy
Tel: +39 0422 519111 **Fax:** +39 0422 519586
Website: www.benetton.it

Berkshire Hathaway Inc
Marc D Hamburg, Vice President, Chief Finance Officer and Treasurer
1440 Kiewit Plaza, Omaha NE 68131, USA
Tel: +1 402 346 1400 **Fax:** +1 402 346 3375
Website: www.berkshirehathway.com

Best Buy Co
Joseph Joyce, General Counsel
PO Box 9312, Minneapolis 55440-9312, USA
Tel: +1 952 995 4559 **Fax:** +1 952 995 4498
Website: www.bestbuy.com

BG Group PLC
William Fredrich, Deputy Chief Executive & General Counsel
100 Thames Valley Park Drive, Reading RG6 1PT, United Kingdom
Tel: +44 118 929 3367 **Fax:** +44 118 929 3327
Email: william.friedrich@bg-group.com
Website: www.bg-group.com

BHP Limited
John C Fast, Vice President and Chief Legal Counsel
BHP Tower, D Bourke Place, 600 Bourke Street, 48th Floor, Melbourne VIC 3000, Australia
Tel: +61 3 9609 3119 **Fax:** +61 3 9609 3204
Email: davies.jane.j@bhp.com.au
Website: www.bhp.com.au

BHW Holding AG
Uwe Körner, Chief Legal Officer
Lubahnstrasse 2, D-31789 Hameln, Germany
Tel: +49 5151 1842 70 **Fax:** +49 5151 1895 4270
Email: UKoerner@bhw.de
Website: www.bhw.de

Billiton PLC
Paul Lush, Group Legal Counsel
Billiton Plc, 1-3 Strand, London WC2N 5HA, United Kingdom
Tel: +44 20 7747 3800 **Fax:** +44 20 7747 3900
Website: www.billiton.com

Biohalco
George Dimitrajopoulos, Head of Legal Department
16 Himaras Street, Maroussi, Greece
Tel: +30 2 623 12025 **Fax:** +30 1 686 1258
Email: nmandi@steelmet.vionet.gr
Website: www.biznet.com

Bipop Carire
Graziano Caldiani, Head of Legal Department
Piazza Vittorio Veneto 8, 24122 Bergamo, Italy
Tel: +39 035 392 1111 **Fax:** +39 035 392 325
Email: graziano.caldiani@bpb.it
Website: www.bipop.it

Blue Circle Industries PLC
Richard F Tapp, Company Secretary/Legal Adviser
84 Eccleston Square, London SW1V 1PX, United Kingdom
Tel: +44 20 7828 3456 **Fax:** +44 20 7245 8272
Email: rftapp@bciplc.com
Website: www.bluecircle.co.uk

BMC Software
Robert Whilden Jr, General Counsel
2101 City West Blvd., Houston TX 77042, USA
Tel: +1 713 918 8800 **Fax:** +1 713 918 1110
Email: bob_whilden@bmc.com
Website: www.bmc.com

BMW Group
Dieter Loechelt, Head of Legal Department
BMW Haus, Petuelring 130, D-80788 Munich, Germany
Tel: +49 893 820 **Fax:** +89 382 26470
Email: dieter.loechelt@bmw.de
Website: www.bmwgroup.com

BNP Paribas
Jean-Pierre Mattout, General Counsel
16 Boulevard des Italiens, 75009 Paris, France
Tel: +33 1 40 14 40 09 **Fax:** +33 1 40 14 39 72
Website: www.bnpgroup.com

BOC Group PLC
Anthony Eric Isaac, Chief Executive
Chertsey Road, Windlesham GU20 6HJ, United Kingdom
Tel: +44 1276 477222 **Fax:** +44 1276 471333
Website: www.boc.com

Boeing Co
Donna Clarke, Manager of Operations, Law Department
7755 East Marginal Way South, Seattle WA 98108, USA
Tel: +1 206 655 2121 **Fax:** +1 206 655 1177
Website: www.boeing.com

Bombardier Inc
Daniel Desjardins, Vice President, Legal Services
800 Rene-Levesque Boulevard West, Montreal H3B 1Y8, Canada
Tel: +1 514 861 9481 **Fax:** +1 514 861 2740
Website: www.bombardier.com

Boots Company PLC
Michael Oliver, Company Secretary
1 Thane Road West, Beeston, Nottingham NG2 3AA, United Kingdom
Tel: +44 115 950 6111 **Fax:** +44 115 959 2727
Website: www.boots-plc.com

Bouygues
Robert Brard, Directeur Juridique
1 Avenue Eugene Freyssinet, 78065 St.Quentin-Yvelines Cedex, France
Tel: +33 1 3060 2311 **Fax:** +33 1 30 60 58 44
Email: rtb@challenger.bouygues.fr
Website: www.bouygues.fr

BP
Peter BP Bevan, Group General Counsel
Britannic House, 1 Finsbury Circus, London EC2M 7BA, United Kingdom
Tel: +44 20 7496 4013 **Fax:** +44 20 7496 4592
Email: bevanpb@bp.com
Website: www.bp.com

BPB PLC
Robert M Heard, Company Secretary
Park House, 15 Bath Road, Slough SL1 3UF, United Kingdom
Tel: +44 1753 898800 **Fax:** +44 1753 898888
Website: www.bpb.com

Bridgestone Corporation
Isao Imaizumi, General Counsel
10-1 Kyobashi 1-chome, Chuo-ku, Tokyo 104-8340, Japan
Tel: +81 3 3567 0111 **Fax:** +81 3 3535 2553
Website: www.bridgestone.co.jp

Bristol-Myers Squibb
John L McGoldrick, General Counsel
345 Park Avenue, New York 10154-0004, USA
Tel: +1 212 546 4000 **Fax:** +1 212 546 4020
Website: www.bms.com

Britannic PLC
Anna East, Company Secretary and Solicitor
1 Wythall Green Way, Wythall, Birmingham B47 6WG, United Kingdom
Tel: +44 1564 828 888 **Fax:** +44 1564 828 822
Website: www.britannic.co.uk

British Airways PLC
Stephen Walsh, Legal Director
Waterside, PO Box 365, Harmondsworth, West Drayton UB7 0GB, United Kingdom
Tel: +44 20 8738 6873 **Fax:** +44 20 8738 9962
Website: www.britishairways.com

British American Tobacco PLC
Neil Withington, Legal Director and General Counsel
Globe House, 4 Temple Place, London WC2R 2PG, United Kingdom
Tel: +44 20 7845 1000 **Fax:** +44 20 7845 2189
Website: www.bat.com

British Energy PLC
Robert M Armour, Director of Corporate Affairs and Company Secretary
10 Lochside Place, Edinburgh EH12 9DF, United Kingdom
Tel: +44 131 527 2000 **Fax:** +44 131 527 2277
Email: Robert.Armour@British-Energy.co.uk
Website: www.british-energy.com

British Land Company PLC
Anthony Braine, Company Secretary/Head of Legal
10 Cornwall Terrace, Regent's Park, London NW1 4QP, United Kingdom
Tel: +44 20 7486 4466 **Fax:** +44 20 7935 5552
Email: t.braine@britishland.co.uk
Website: www.britishland.co.uk

British Sky Broadcasting Group PLC (Sky Digital)
Deanna Bates, Head of Legal & Business Affairs
6 Centaurs Business Park, Grant Way, Isleworth TW7 5QD, United Kingdom
Tel: +44 20 7705 3000 **Fax:** +44 20 7705 3254
Email: deanna.bates@bskyb.com
Website: www.sky.co.uk

British Telecommuncations PLC
Alan Whitfield, Head of Legal
British Telecom Centre, 81 Newgate Street, London EC1A 7AJ, United Kingdom
Tel: +44 20 7356 5000 **Fax:** +44 20 7356 6638
Email: alan.z.whitfield@bt.com
Website: www.bt.com

Broadcom Corporation
David Dull, General Counsel
16215 Alton Pkwy, Irvine 92618, USA
Tel: +1 949 450 8700 **Fax:** +1 949 450 0504
Website: www.broadcom.com

BroadVision
Scott Neely, Vice President & General Counsel
585 Broadway St., Redwood City 94063-3122, USA
Tel: +1 650 261 5100 **Fax:** +1 650 261 5900
Website: www.broadvision.com

BSCH (Banco Santander Central Hispano) SA
Ignacio Benjumen, Head of Legal
Plaza Canalejas, Piso 1, 28014 Madrid, Spain
Tel: +34 91 342 4610 **Fax:** +34 91 342 4613
Email: mgc1@bancosantander.es
Website: www.bancosantander.bsch.es

Bulgari SpA
Costanzo Rapone, General Counsel
Lungotevere Marzio, 11, 00186 Rome, Italy
Tel: +39 06 68 81 01 **Fax:** +39 06 6881 0614
Website: www.bulgari.com

Bunzl PLC
Paul N Hussey, Company Secretary and Group Legal Adviser
110 Park Street, London W1Y 3RB, United Kingdom
Tel: +44 20 7495 4950 **Fax:** +44 20 7495 4953
Website: www.bunzl.com

Cable & Wireless Optus Limited
Bruce Hambrett, General Counsel
101 Miller Street, North Sydney 2060, Australia
Tel: +61 2 9234 7800
Website: www.cwo.com.au

Cable & Wireless PLC
J Daniel Fitz, General Counsel
124 Theobalds Road, London WC1X 8RX, United Kingdom
Tel: +44 20 7315 4000 **Fax:** +44 20 7315 5056
Email: daniel.fitz@cwplc.com
Website: www.cwplc.com

Cadbury Schweppes PLC
Michael Clark, Group Secretary and Chief Legal Officer
25 Berkeley Square, London W1X 6HT, United Kingdom
Tel: +44 20 7409 1313 **Fax:** +44 20 7830 5200
Email: mike.clark@csplc.com
Website: www.cadburyshweppes.com

Campbell Soup Company
Ellen Oran Kaden, Vice-President Legal & Senior Vice President
Campbell Place, Camden NJ 08103-1799, USA
Tel: +1 856 342 4800 **Fax:** +1 856 342 3936
Email: ellen_kaden@campbellsoup.com
Website: www.campbellsoup.com

Canal Satelite Digital
Jabier Temes, Head of Legal Dept
Gran Via, 32, 28013 Madrid, Spain
Tel: +34 913 965 500 **Fax:** +34 915 245 828
Email: jtemes@csatelite.es
Website: www.sogecable.es

Canal+ Group
Serge Salvai, General Counsel
85-87 Quai Andre Citroen, 75711 Paris, France
Tel: +33 1 53 78 6020 **Fax:** +33 1 44 25 1809
Email: serge.salvai@canal-plus.com
Website: www.cplus.fr

Canary Wharf Group PLC
Michael Ashley-Brown, Head of Legal
One Canada Square, Canary Wharf, London E14 5AB, United Kingdom
Tel: +44 20 7418 2000 **Fax:** +44 20 7418 2222
Website: www.canarywharf.com

Canon Inc
Noburo Ishido, General Manager, Legal Division
30-2 Shimomaruko 3-chome, Ohta-ku, Tokyo 146-8501, Japan
Tel: +81 3 3757 6666 **Fax:** +81 3 3757 9235
Website: www.canon.com

Cap Gemini France SA
Bénédicte Houdoux-Cellura, General Counsel
Immeuble Elysees, La Defence, 92056 Paris, France
Tel: +33 1 49 01 70 00 **Fax:** +33 1 49 01 70 05
Email: bhoudoux@capgemini.fr
Website: www.capgemini.com

Capita Group PLC
Gordon M Hurst, Finance Director & Company Secretary
71 Victoria Street, Westminster, London SW1H 0XA, United Kingdom
Tel: +44 20 7799 1525 **Fax:** +44 20 7799 1526
Website: www.capita.co.uk

Cardinal Health Inc
Steve Alan Bennett, General Counsel
5555 Glendon Court, Dublin OH 43016, USA
Tel: +1 614 717 5000 **Fax:** +1 614 717 6000
Website: www.cardinal-health.com

Carlton Communications PLC
David Abdoo, Company Secretary
25 Knightsbridge, London SW1X 7RZ, United Kingdom
Tel: +44 20 7663 6363 **Fax:** +44 20 7663 6300
Website: www.carlton.com

Carnival Corporation
Arnaldo Perez, General Counsel
3655 North West 87th Avenue, Miami FL 33178-2428, USA
Tel: +1 305 599 2600 **Fax:** +1 305 406 4758
Email: aperez@carnival.com
Website: www.carnival.com

Carrefour SA
Norbert Pineau, Head of Legal
123 Rue Jueles Erusdes, 92000 Le Vallois, France
Tel: +33 1 53 70 19 00 **Fax:** +33 1 53 70 19 59
Website: www.carrefour.com

Casino Guichard-Perrachon et Cie/Groupe Casino
Mr Lachaud, Director of Legal Services
24 rue de la Montat, 42008 Saint-Etienne, France
Tel: +33 477 453 131 **Fax:** +33 477 453 306

Castorama Dubois Investissements SCA
Francois Regis Motte, General Counsel
Parc d'Activites, BP 24, 59175 Templemars, France
Tel: +33 3 20 16 75 11 **Fax:** +33 3 20 16 75 75
Email: francoisregis@castorama-group.com
Website: www.castorama-group.com

Caterpillar Inc
Robert Atterbury, General Counsel
100 North East Adams Street, Peoria IL 61629-5310, USA
Tel: +1 309 675 1000 **Fax:** +1 309 675 6886
Website: www.caterpillar.com

Cathay Life Insurance Co Ltd
TK Huang, Chief Finance Officer
296 Jen Ai Road, Sec. 4, Taipei , Taiwan
Tel: +886 22 755 1399 **Fax:** +886 22 708 2167
Website: www.cathlife.com.tw

CBS Corp
Louis Briskman, Executive Vice President & General Counsel
51 West 52nd Street, New York 10019, USA
Tel: +1 212 975 4321 **Fax:** +1 212 597 4031
Email: imhaugh@cbs.com
Website: www.cbs.com

CCF - Credit Commercial de France
Cecile Teytaud, General Counsel
103, Avenue des Champs-Elysees, 75419 Paris, France
Tel: +33 1 40 70 70 40 **Fax:** +33 1 40 70 71 17
Website: www.ccf.com

Cendant
Joel Buckberg, Head of Legal
6 Sylvan Way, Parsippany NJ 07054, USA
Tel: +1 973 428 9700 **Fax:** +1 973 496 5915
Email: joel.buckberg@cendant.com
Website: www.cendant.com

Central Japan Railway Company
Shigeru Saito, Vice President
1-1-4 Meieki, Nakamura-ku, Nagoya 450-8610, Japan
Tel: +81 3 3274 9727 **Fax:** +81 3 5255 6780
Website: www.jr-central.co.jp

Centrica PLC
Grant Dawson, General Counsel & Company Secretary
Charter Court, 50 Windsor Road, Slough SL1 2HA, United Kingdom
Tel: +44 1753 758 211 **Fax:** +44 1753 758 011
Email: grant.dawson@centrica.co.uk
Website: www.centrica.co.uk

Centros Comerciales PRYCA
Angel Ramos, Head of Legal
Campezo 16, Poligono de las Mercedes, 28022 Madrid, Spain
Tel: +34 91 379 6100 **Fax:** +34 91 3331 486
Website: www.pryca.es

Cesky Telecom
Vaclac Svajgl, Director of Legal Dept
Olsanska 5, 130-34 Praha 3, Czech Republic
Tel: +420 2 7141 1111 **Fax:** +420 2 7146 9868
Email: vaclac.svajgl@ct.cz
Website: www.telecom.cz

CGIP (Compagnie Generale d'Industrie et de Participations)
Michel Renault, General Counsel
89 rue Taitbout, 75009 Paris, France
Tel: +33 1 42 85 30 00 **Fax:** +33 1 42 80 68 67
Email: m.renault@cgip.fr
Website: www.cgip.fr

CGNU PLC
Ian MacDonald,
St Helen's, 1 Undershaft, London EC3P 3DQ, United Kingdom
Tel: +44 20 7283 7500 **Fax:** +44 20 7662 8182
Website: www.cgugroup.com

Charles Schwab
Hardy Callcott, General Counsel
101 Montgomery Street, San Fransisco CA 94104, USA
Tel: +1 415 627 7000 **Fax:** +1 415 627 8840
Website: www.schwab.com

Cheung Kong (Holdings) Limited
Emmanuel Yip, Chief Legal Manager
7-12/F Cheung Kong Center, 2 Queen's Road Central, Hong Kong , Hong Kong
Tel: +852 2128 8888 **Fax:** +852 2526 9326
Website: www.ckh.com.hk

Chevron Corporation
Harvey Hinman, Head of Legal, General Counsel & Vice President
575 Market Street, 40th Floor, San Francisco CA 94105, USA
Tel: +1 415 894 7700 **Fax:** +1 415 894 7084
Website: www.chevron.com

China Mobile (Hong Kong) Limited
Ding Donghua, Chief Finance Officer
60/F The Center, 99 Queen's Road Central, Hong Kong
Tel: +852 3121 8888 **Fax:** +852 2511 9092
Website: www.cthk.com

Christian Dior
Mr Bouet, Administrative & Legal Manager
11 Bis Rue Francois Premier, F-75008 Paris, France
Tel: +33 1 40 73 54 44 **Fax:** +33 1 47 20 00 60
Website: www.dior.com

Christiania Bank og Kreditkasse ASA
Ivar Saggbaken, General Counsel
Middlethunsgt, 17, N-0107 Oslo, Norway
Tel: +47 22 48 50 00 **Fax:** +47 22 48 43 25
Website: www.kbank.no

Chubu Electric Power Co Inc
Masatoshi Suzuki, Head of Legal
1 Toshin-cho, Higashi-ku, Nagoya City 461-8680, Japan
Tel: +81 52 951 8211 **Fax:** +81 52 973 3185
Website: www.chuden.co.jp

CIC Group
Gerard Rouget, General Counsel
6 Avenue de Provence, 75009 Paris, France
Tel: +33 1 45 96 96 96 **Fax:** +33 1 45 96 96 66
Website: www.cic-banques.fr

Ciments Francais
Philippe Marchat, Head of Legal & Tax Department
Tour Ariane, 5 place de la Pyramide, La Defense Cedex, 92088 Paris, France
Tel: +33 1 42 91 76 33 **Fax:** +33 1 47 73 74 02
Email: pmarchat@cimfra.com
Website: www.cimfra.fr

Cisco Systems Inc
Daniel Scheinman, General Counsel
170 W. Tasman Drive, San Jose 95134-1700, USA
Tel: +1 408 526 4000 **Fax:** +1 408 526 7019
Email: dscheinm@cisco.com
Website: www.cisco.com

Citigroup Inc
Charles Prince, General Counsel
153 E. 53rd Street, New York 10043, USA
Tel: +1 212 793 8855 **Fax:** +1 212 793 9700
Email: princec@citigroup.com
Website: www.citigroup.com

Clariant Ltd
Herbert Wohlmann, Head of Legal
Rothausstrasse 61, 4132 Muttenz, Switzerland
Tel: +41 61 469 61 27 **Fax:** +41 61 469 65 08
Email: herbert.wohlmann@clariant.com
Website: www.clariant.com

Clear Channel Communications
L Lowry Mays, Chief Executive Officer
200 E.Basse Road, San Antonio 78209, USA
Tel: +1 210 822 2828 **Fax:** +1 210 822 2299
Website: www.clearchannel.com

CMG PLC
Richard Francis, Company Secretary/Company Solicitor
Parnell House, 25 Wilton Road, London SW1V 1EJ, United Kingdom
Tel: +44 20 7592 4000 **Fax:** +44 20 7592 4804
Website: www.cmg.com

CNP Assurances
Martine Loquet, Head of Legal
4 Place Raoul Dautry, Cedex 15, 75716 Paris, France
Tel: +33 1 42 18 88 88 **Fax:** +33 1 42 18 79 70
Website: www.cnp.fr

Cobepa
Chantel Barras, Legal Manager
Rue De La Chancellerie 2, Box 1, B-1000 Brussels, Belgium
Tel: +32 2 213 32 10 **Fax:** +32 2 513 17 02
Website: www.cobepa.be

Coca-Cola Co
Joseph R Gladden Jnr, General Counsel
One Coca-Cola Plaza, PO Box 1734, Atlanta GA 30301, USA
Tel: +1 404 6762121 **Fax:** +1 404 676 6209
Email: jgladden@na.co.com
Website: www.cocacola.com

Colgate-Palmolive Company
Andrew Hendry, General Counsel
300 Park Avenue, New York 10022, USA
Tel: +1 212 310 2000 **Fax:** +1 212 310 3302
Email: andrew_hendry@colpl.com
Website: www.colgate.com

Colt Telecom Group PLC
Mark Jenkins, Legal Services Director and Company Secretary
15 Marylebone Road, London NW1 5JD, United Kingdom
Tel: +44 20 7863 5000 **Fax:** +44 20 7390 3701
Email: colt-telecom.com
Website: www.colt-telecom.com

Columbia/HCA Healthcare Corp
Bob Waterman, General Counsel
1 Park Plaza, Nashville TN 37203, USA
Tel: +1 615 344 9551 **Fax:** +1 615 344 2266
Email: bob.waterman@columbia.net
Website: www.columbia.net

Comcast Corporation
Arthur R Block, General Counsel
1500 Market Street, Philadelphia PA 19102-2148, USA
Tel: +1 215 981 7564 **Fax:** +1 215 981 7794
Email: ablock@comcast.com
Website: www.comcast.com

Commerce One
Robert Tarkoff, General Counsel
CarrAmerica Corporate Center 4440 Rosewood Drive, Pleasanton 94588, USA
Tel: +1 925 520 6000 **Fax:** +1 925 520 6066
Email: rob.tarkoff@commerceone.com
Website: www.commerceone.com

Commercial Bank of Greece
John Spyridakis, Director of Legal Division
11 Sofokleous Street, 102 35 Athens, Greece
Tel: +30 1 32 84 000
Website: www.combank.gr

Commerzbank AG
Jochen Appell, Head of Legal Department
Neue Mainzer Strasse 32-36, D-60261 Frankfurt am Main, Germany
Tel: +49 69 136 20 **Fax:** +49 69 136 27073
Email: heidi_seitz@commerzbank.com
Website: www.commerzbank.com

Commonwealth Bank of Australia
Leslie Taylor, Chief Solicitor
Legal Dept., Bank House, 10th Floor, 309 George Street, Sydney 1155, Australia
Tel: +61 2 9378 4709 **Fax:** +61 2 9378 4792
Website: www.commbank.com.au

Compania Espanola de Petroleos (Cepsa)
Luis Sancho-Martinez-Pardo, General Legal Counsel
Avenida del Partenon 12, Campo de las Naciones, 28046 Madrid, Spain
Tel: +34 91 337 60 00 **Fax:** +34 91 721 1613
Website: www.cepsa.es

Compaq Computer Corporation
Thomas Siekman, General Counsel
20555 SH 249, Houston TX 77070, USA
Tel: +1 281 370 0670 **Fax:** +1 281 374 1740
Website: www.compaq.com

Computacenter
Alan Pottinger, Company Secretary
Link House, 19 Colonial Way, Watford WD2 4HS, United Kingdom
Tel: +44 20 7593 4505 **Fax:** +44 20 7593 4589
Website: www.computacenter.com

Computer Associates Int'l Inc
Steve Woghin, General Counsel
1 Computer Associates Plaza, Islandia NY 11749, USA
Tel: +1 516 342 5224 **Fax:** +1 613 342 4866
Email: steven.wogin@cai.com
Website: www.ca.com

Computer Sciences Corp
Hayward D. Fisk, Vice President General Counsel & Secretary
2100 East Grand Avenue, El Segundo CA 90245, USA
Tel: +1 310 615 0311 **Fax:** +1 310 322 9767
Email: hfisk@csc.com
Website: www.csc.com

Compuware
Thomas Costello, General Counsel
31440 Northwestern Highway, Farmington Hills MI 48334-2564, USA
Tel: +1 248 737 7300 **Fax:** +1 248 737 7690
Email: donna.duane@compuware.com
Website: www.compuware.com

Conexant Systems Inc
Dennis O'Reilly, Senior Vice President, General Counsel & Secretary
4311 Jamboree Road, Newport Beach CA 92660-3095, USA
Tel: +1 949 483 4600 **Fax:** +1 949 483 4078
Email: Dennis.O'Reilly@Conexant.com
Website: www.conexant.com

Conoco Inc
Rick A Harrington, General Counsel
Conoco Center, 600 North Dairy Ashford, Houston 77079, USA
Tel: +1 281 293 1000 **Fax:** +1 281 293 1054
Website: www.conoco.com

Consors AG
Stefan Lochow, Head of Legal
Johannesgasse 20, D-90402 Nurenberg, Germany
Tel: +49 911 3690 **Fax:** +49 911 369 1000
Email: stefan.lochow@consors.de
Website: www.consors.de

Continental AG
Christian zur Nedden, Head of Legal
Vahrenwalder Strasse 9, D-30165 Hanover, Germany
Tel: +49 511 938 01 **Fax:** +49 511 938 1229
Email: marga.zebulla@conti.de
Website: www.conti.de

Cookson Group PLC
Glen McDonnall, Legal Adviser and Assistant Company Secretary
The Adelphi, 1-11 John Adam Street, London WC2N 6HJ, United Kingdom
Tel: +44 20 7766 4500 **Fax:** +44 20 7747 6600
Website: www.cooksongroup.co.uk

Corning Incorporated
William Eggers, Head of Legal
One Riverfront Plaza, MP-HQ-E2-10, Corning NY 14831, USA
Tel: +1 607 9749000 **Fax:** +1607 9748656
Email: eggerswd@corning.com
Website: www.corning.com

Corporacion Financiera Alba SA
Antonio Ejido, General Counsel
Castello 77, Piso 5, 28006 Madrid, Spain
Tel: +34 91 436 37 10 **Fax:** +3491 575 6737
Email: aev@alba-cfa.com
Website: www.corporacionalba.es

Corus Group PLC
Margaret O'Neill, Director - Corporate Legal Services
15 Great Marlborough Street, London NW1 5JD, United Kingdom
Tel: +44 20 7717 4444 **Fax:** +44 20 7717 4455
Website: www.corusgroup.com

Costco Wholesale Inc
Jo Bendiel, Head of Legal
999 Lake Drive, Issaquah WA 98027, USA
Tel: +1 425 313 8100 **Fax:** +1 425 313 8114
Email: jbendiel@costco.com
Website: www.costco.com

Credit Lyonnais SA
Dominique Ferrero, Director General
19 Boulevard des Italiens, 75002 Paris, France
Tel: +33 1 42 95 70 00 **Fax:** +33 78 38 12 85
Website: www.creditlyonnais.com

Credit Suisse Group
Urs Derendinger, General Counsel
Dorfli Street 120, PO Box 400, CH-8070 Zurich, Switzerland
Tel: +41 1 333 11 11 **Fax:** +41 1 335 20 70
Website: www.credit-suisse.com

CRH PLC
Angela Malone, Company Secretary
CRH PLC, 42 Fitzwilliam Square, Dublin 2, Ireland
Tel: +353 1 634 4340 **Fax:** +353 1 676 5013
Website: www.crh.com

CVS Corporation
Zenon Lankousky, Head of Legal
One CVS Drive, Woonsocket RI 02895, USA
Tel: +1 401 765 1500 **Fax:** +1 401 766 2917
Email: zplankousky@cvs.com
Website: www.cvs.com

Dai-Ichi Kangyo Bank Limited
Mr Sugawara, Head of Legal
1-5 Uchisaiwai-cho, 1-chome, Chiyoda-ku, Tokyo 100-0011, Japan
Tel: +81 3 3596 1111 **Fax:** +81 3 3596 2179
Website: www.dkb.co.jp

Daily Mail & General Trust PLC
Harvey Kass, Legal director
Northcliffe House, 2 Derry Street, Kensington, London W8 5TT, United Kingdom
Tel: +44 20 7938 6000 **Fax:** +44 20 7937 3251
Website: www.dailymail.com

DaimlerChrysler AG
Peter Waskönig, Head Of Legal Department
Epplestrasse 225, D-70567 Stuttgart, Germany
Tel: +49 711 179 2787 **Fax:** +49 711 179 4498
Website: www.daimlerchrysler.com

Daiwa Securities
Yoshinari Hara, President and Chief Executive Officer
6-4, Otemachi 2-chome, Chiyoda-ku, Tokyo 100-8101, Japan
Tel: +81 3 3243 2100 **Fax:** +81 3 3242 0955
Website: www.daiwa.co.jp

Dampskibsselskabet Svendborg A/S
Jan Al-Erhayem, Vice President, Head of Corporate Secretariat
Esplanaden 50, K-1098 Copenhagen, Denmark
Tel: +45 33 63 33 63 **Fax:** +45 33 63 36 73
Email: cphcorp@maersk.com

Danske Bank [Den] AS
Erik Sevaltsen, Executive Vice President & General Counsel
2-12 Holmens Kanal, 1092 Copenhagen, Denmark
Tel: +45 33 44 00 00 **Fax:** +45 31 18 58 73
Email: ese@danskebank.dk
Website: www.danskebank.dk

Dassault Systemes
Martine Wallimann, Legal Officer
9 Quai Marcel Dassault, BP 310, 92156 Suresnes, France
Tel: +33 1 40 99 40 99 **Fax:** +33 1 42 04 45 81
Email: martine-wallimann@ds-fr.com
Website: www.dsweb.com

De Beers Consolidated Mines Ltd
HLM Sweetnam, Chief Legal Officer
36 Stockdale Street, PO Box 616, Kimberley 8300, South Africa
Tel: +27 53 839 4111 **Fax:** +27 53 839 4210
Website: www.edata.co.za/debeers

Degussa-Huels AG
Heiner Heidmeier, Head of Legal
Weissfrauenstrasse 9, D-60287 Frankfurt am Main, Germany
Tel: +49 69 2 18 01 **Fax:** +49 69 2 18 32 18
Email: heiner.heidmeier@degussa-huels.de
Website: www.degussa-huels.de

Dell Computer Corporation
Jeffrey L Maurice, Senior Corporate Counsel
1 Dell Way, Round Rock 78682-2244, USA
Tel: +1 512 338 4400 **Fax:** +1 512 728 7100
Email: jeff_maurice@dell.com
Website: www.dell.com

Den Norske Bank
Olav Heldal, General Counsel
Stranden 21, 0021 Oslo, Norway
Tel: +47 22 48 20 30 **Fax:** +47 22 48 28 99
Email: olav.heldal@dnb.no
Website: www.dnb.no

Denso Corporation
Hisanori Kobayashi, Senior Managing Director
1-1 Showa-cho, Kariya-shi 448-8661, Japan
Tel: +81 566 25 5511 **Fax:** +81 566 25 4520
Website: www.denso.co.jp

DePfa Bank (Deutsche Pfandbriefbank) AG
Werner Pues, Head of Legal
Paulinenstrasse 15, D-65189 Wiesbaden, Germany
Tel: +49 611 348 0 **Fax:** +49 611 348 2086
Email: werner.pues@depfa.com
Website: www.depfa.com

Deutsche Bank AG
Klaus Kohler, Head of Legal Department
Taunusanlage 12, 60325 Frankfurt am Main, Germany
Tel: +49 69 910 00 **Fax:** +49 69 910 38572
Email: klaus.kohler@db.com
Website: www.deutsche-bank.de

Deutsche Lufthansa AG
Nicolai von Ruckteschell, Senior Vice President & General Counsel
Flughafen-Bereich West, D-60546 Frankfurt am Main, Germany
Tel: +49 69 696 91304 **Fax:** +49 69 696 91305
Website: www.lufthansa.com

Deutsche Telekom AG
Manfred Balz, Head of Legal
Friedrich Ebert Allee 140, Postfach 20 00, D-53113 Bonn, Germany
Tel: +49 228 181 74000 **Fax:** +49 228 181 74008
Email: manfred.balz@telekom.de
Website: www.telekom.de

Development Bank of Singapore
Lee Cheng Heng, Head of Legal Dept
6 Shenton Way, DBS Building, Tower 1 #39 - 00, Singapore 068809, Singapore
Tel: +65 4289 317 **Fax:** +65 221 1306
Email: leecheng@dbs.com
Website: www.dbs.com.sg

Dexia
Isabelle Thibaut, Manager of Legal Dept
7-11 Quai Andre Citroen, Paris Cedex 15, 75901 Paris, France
Tel: +33 1 43 92 7777 **Fax:** +33 143 92 7000
Email: isabelle.thibaut@clf-dexia.com
Website: www.dexia.com

Diageo PLC
Tim Proctor, Group General Counsel
8 Henrietta Place, London W1M 9AG, United Kingdom
Tel: +44 20 7927 5200 **Fax:** +44 20 7927 4626
Website: www.diageo.com

Dixons Group PLC
Geoffrey Budd, Company Secretary
Maylands Avenue, Hemel Hempstead HP2 7TG, United Kingdom
Tel: +44 1442 353000 **Fax:** +44 1442 233218
Website: www.dixons-group-plc.co.uk

Doubleclick
Elizabeth Wang, General Counsel
450 West 33rd St, New York 10001, USA
Tel: +1 212 683 0001 **Fax:** +1 212 287 7845
Email: ewang@doubleclick.net
Website: www.doubleclick.net

Dow Chemical Co
Mark Tucker, Legal Executive
2030 Dow Center, Midland MI 48674, USA
Tel: +1 517 636 1000 **Fax:** +1 517 636 3228
Website: www.dow.com

Dresdner Bank AG
Jürgen Than, General Counsel
Jürgen Ponto Platz 1, D-60301 Frankfurt am Main, Germany
Tel: +49 69 263 4822 **Fax:** +49 69 263 110303
Email: jurgen.than@dresdner-bank.com
Website: www.dresdner-bank.de

DSM NV
Pieter De Haan, Director of Corporate Legal Affairs
Het Overloon 1, PO Box 6500, 6401 H Heerlen, Netherlands
Tel: +31 45 578 2870 **Fax:** +31 45 578 7087
Email: pieter-haan.de@dsm-group.com
Website: www.dsm.nl

Du Pont (EI) De Nemours
Stacy Mobley, Head of Legal
1007 Market Street, Wilmington DE 19898, USA
Tel: +1 302 774 1000 **Fax:** +1 302 892 1705
Email: stacey.mobley@usa.dupont.com
Website: www.dupont.com

Duke Energy Corporation
Richard W Blackburn, General Counsel
526 South Church Street, Charlotte NC 28202-1802, USA
Tel: +1 704 594 6200 **Fax:** +1 704 382 7705
Email: rwblackb@duke-energy.com
Website: www.duke-energy.com

E.ON AG
Ulrich Huppe, General Counsel
Benningsensplatz 1, D-40474 Dusseldorf, Germany
Tel: +49 211 45791 **Fax:** +49 211 457 9446
Email: ulrich.hueppe@eon.com
Website: www.eon.com

EADS NV
Eric Thomas, General Counsel
37 Blvd. de Montmorency, 75016 Paris, France
Tel: +33 1 42 24 24 24 **Fax:** +33 1 42 24 28 30
Email: eric.thomas@eads-nv.com
Website: www.eads-nv.com

East Japan Railway Company
Mutsutake Otsuka, Executive Vice-President and CEO
2-2-2 Yoyogi, 2-Chome, Shibuya-ku, Tokyo 151-8578, Japan
Tel: +81 3 5334 1151 **Fax:** +81 3 5334 1110
Website: www.jreast.co.jp

Eastman Kodak Company
Gary P Van Graafeiland, General Counsel
343 State Street, Rochester NY 14650-0001, USA
Tel: +1 716 724 4000 **Fax:** +1 716 724 0663
Website: www.kodak.com

eBay Inc
Michael Jacobson, General Counsel
eBay Inc, 2145 Hamilton Ave, San Jose 95125, USA
Tel: +1 408 558 7400 **Fax:** +1 408 558 7401
Email: mikej@ebay.com
Website: www.ebay.com

EchoStar Communications
David K Moskowitz, General Counsel
5701 South Santa Fe, Littleton 80120, USA
Tel: +1 303 723 1000 **Fax:** +1 303 723 1099
Email: david.moskowitz@echostar.com
Website: www.echostar.com

Edison SpA
Eugemio Bruti Liberati, General Counsel
Foro Buonaparte 31, 20121 Milan, Italy
Tel: +39 02 62 22 1 **Fax:** +39 02 6222 7250
Email: BrutiE@edison.it
Website: www.edison.it

EDP - Electricidade De Portugal SA
Alfaia De Carvalho, Head of Legal Services
Avenida José Malhoa, Lote A 13, 1070-157 Lisbon, Portugal
Tel: +351 21 726 3013 **Fax:** +351 21 720 2630
Email: alfaia.carvalho@edp.pt
Website: www.edp.pt

EDS
D Gilbert Friedlander, General Counsel
5400 Legacy Drive, Plano TX 75024-3199, USA
Tel: +1 972 604 6000 **Fax:** +1 972 605 5610
Email: Gil.Friedlander@eds.com
Website: www.eds.com

EFG Eurobank Ergasias SA
Rinia Papavasiliou, Head of Legal
Voukouiesdou Str 15, GR-10562 Athens, Greece
Tel: +30 1 333 7000 **Fax:** +30 1 337 1401
Website: www.eurobank.gr/europortal

Eircom PLC
Edward R Eamonn Hall, Chief Legal Officer
52 Harcourt Street, Dublin 2, Ireland
Tel: +353 1 671 4444 **Fax:** +353 1 679 3980
Email: ehall@eircom.ie
Website: www.eircom.com/

Elan Corporation PLC
Lisabeth F Murphy, Head of Legal
Elan Pharmaceuticals, 800 Gateway Boulevard South, San Francisco CA 94080
Tel: +001 650 877 0900 **Fax:** +001 650 794 5764
Email: LMurphy@Elancorp.com
Website: www.elancorp.com

Electrocomponents PLC
Carmelina Carfora, Group Company Secretary
International Management Centre, 5000 Oxford Business Park South, Oxford OX4 2BH, United Kingdom
Tel: +44 1865 204000 **Fax:** +44 1865 207400
Email: nicola.black@electrocomponents.com
Website: www.electrocomponents.com

Eli Lilly & Company
Jim Burns, General Counsel
Lilly Corporate Center, Indianapolis IN 46285-0001, USA
Tel: +1 317 276 2000 **Fax:** +1 317 276 6221
Email: jburns@lilly.com
Website: www.lilly.com

Elisa Communications Oyj (formerly HPY Holding Corporation)
Mr Ylikortes, Head of Legal
Korkeavuorenkatu 35-37, 00130 Helsinki, Finland
Tel: +358 102 6000 **Fax:** +358 102 6060
Website: www.elisa.com

EM TV & Merchandising AG
Volker Schott, Head of Legal Dept
Beta Str 11, D-85774 Unterfoehring, Germany
Tel: +49 89 957150 **Fax:** +49 8999 500 111
Email: volker.schott@em-ag.de
Website: www.em-ag.de

EMAP PLC
Derek K Warmsley, Company Secretary
1 Lincoln Court, Lincoln Road, Peterborough PE1 2RF, United Kingdom
Tel: +44 1733 568900 **Fax:** +44 1733 358081
Website: www.emap.com

EMC Corp
Paul T Dacier, General Counsel
35 Parkwood Drive, Hopkinton MA 01748-9103, USA
Tel: +1 508 435 1000 **Fax:** +1 508 497 6915
Email: dacier_paul@emc.com
Website: www.emc.com

Emerson Electric Co
Wayne Withers, General Counsel
8000 W. Florissant Ave., P.O. Box 4100, St. Louis MO63136-8506, USA
Tel: +1 314 553 2000 **Fax:** +1 314 553 3205
Email: wayne.withers@emerson.com
Website: www.emersonelectric.com

EMI Group PLC
Charles Ashcroft, Company Secretary and Group General Counsel
4 Tenterden Street, Hanover Square, London W1A 2AY, United Kingdom
Tel: +44 20 7667 3246 **Fax:** +44 20 7495 1308
Email: ashcroftc@emigroup.com
Website: www.emigroup.com

ENDESA
Borga Acha, Director of Legal
Principe de Vergara 187, 28002 Madrid, Spain
Tel: +34 91 566 8800 **Fax:** +34 91 213 9655
Email: bacha@endesa.es
Website: www.endesa.es

Enel SpA
Salvatore Cardillo, Legal Counsel
Viale Regina Margherita 137, 00198 Rome, Italy
Tel: +39 06 85092727 **Fax:** +39 06 85092042
Email: cardillo.salvatore@enel.it
Website: www.enel.it

Energie Baden-Wuerttemberg AG
Bernhard Beck, Director of Legal Services
Durlacher Allee 93, D-76131 Karlsruhe, Germany
Tel: +49 721 631 2190 **Fax:** +49 721 631 3175
Email: b.beck@enbw.com
Website: www.enbw.com

Energis PLC
Andrew McKelvie, Assistant Company Secretary
50 Victoria Embankment, London EC4Y 0DE, United Kingdom
Tel: +44 20 7206 5555 **Fax:** +44 20 7206 5651
Website: www.energis.net

ENI-Ente Nazionale Idrocarburi
Carlo Grande, Head of the Legal Department
Piazzale E. Mattei 1, 00144 Rome, Italy
Tel: +39 06 59821 **Fax:** +39 06 5982 2369
Website: www.eni.it

Enron Corp
James Derrick, Senior Vice-President & General Counsel
1400 Smith St, Houston TX 77002, USA
Tel: +1 713 853 6161 **Fax:** +1 713 853 3129
Website: www.enron.com

Enterprise Oil PLC
Andrew Wilson, Head Of Legal Affairs
Grand Buildings, Trafalgar Square, London WC2N 5EJ, United Kingdom
Tel: +44 20 7925 4000 **Fax:** +44 20 7925 4321
Email: andrew.wilson@london.entoil.com
Website: www.entoil.com

Entreprises Et Chemins De Fer En Chine
Bruno Spillaert, Attorney General
Rue du Bois Sauvage 17, 1000 Brussels, Belgium
Tel: +32 2 219 01 21 **Fax:** +32 22 19 23 73
Email: bruno.spillaert@surongo.skynet.be
Website: www.bois-sauvage.be

Epcos AG
Peter Knoll, Head of Legal Dept
St Martin Strasse 53, D-81541 Munich, Germany
Tel: +49 89 6362 6510 **Fax:** +49 89 6362 3050
Email: peter.knoll@epcos.com
Website: www.epcos.com

Equant NV
Elizabeth Wall, General Counsel
Gatwickstraat 21-23, Sloterdijk, NL-1043 GL Amsterdam, Netherlands
Tel: +31 20 581 8383 **Fax:** +31 20 688 0388
Email: elizabeth.wall@equant.com
Website: www.equant.com

Ergo Versicherungsgruppe AG
Detlef Kuhlen, Head of Legal
Victoria Platz 2, D-40477 Dusseldorf, Germany
Tel: +49 211 493 70 **Fax:** +49 211 477 2667
Email: detlef.kuhlen@victoria.de
Website: www.ergo.de

Eridania Beghin-Say
Catherine Chalon-Szymanek, General Counsel
14 Boulevard de General Leclerc, 92572 Neuilly-sur-Seine Cedex, France
Tel: +33 1 41 43 11 50 **Fax:** +33 1 41 43 11 55
Website: www.eridania-beghin-say.com

Essilor International SA
Carol Xueref, Director for Legal Affairs and Group Development
147 rue de Paris, 94227 Charenton-le-pont, France
Tel: +33 1 49 77 43 00 **Fax:** +33 1 49 77 43 05
Website: www.essilor.fr

Estee Lauder Inc
Paul Conney, General Counsel
767 Fifth Avenue, New York 10153, USA
Tel: +1 212 572 4200 **Fax:** +1 212 572 7941
Website: www.esteelauder.com

Europolitan Holdings AB
Anders Sjöholm, General Counsel
Biblioteksgatan 11, Box 5251, 102 46 Stockholm, Sweden
Tel: +46 8 678 09 50 **Fax:** +46 8 678 09 80
Email: anders.sjoholm@europolitan.se
Website: www.europolitan.se

Eurotunnel SA
Phillippe Dewast, Director of Legal Affairs
B.P. 69, 62 904 Coquelles Cedex, France
Tel: +33 32 1 00 61 85 **Fax:** +33 32 1 00 63 52
Email: phillippe.dewast@eurotunnel.com
Website: www.eurotunnel.com

Exel PLC
Ian Goulden, Head of legal
Ocean House, The Ring, Bracknell RG12 1AN, United Kingdom
Tel: +44 1344 744 310 **Fax:** +44 1344 301193
Website: www.oceangroup.uk.com

Exodus Communications
Adam Wegner, General Counsel
2831 Mission College Boulevard, Santa Clara CA 95054, USA
Tel: +1 408 346 2200 **Fax:** +1 408 346 2420
Email: awegner@exodus.net
Website: www.exodus.net

Exxon Corp
Charles Matthews, General Counsel
5959 Las Colinas Blvd., Irving TX 75039-2298, USA
Tel: +1 972 444 1000 **Fax:** +1 972 444 1350
Website: www.exxon.mobil.com

Fannie Mae
Anne Kappler, Senior Vice President and General Counsel
3900 Wisconsin Ave. N.W., Washington DC 20016-2892, USA
Tel: +1 202 752 4850 **Fax:** +1 202 752 4439
Email: anne_kappler@fanniemae.com
Website: www.fanniemae.com

Federal Home Loan Mortgage Corporation
Maud Mater, Executive Vice President, General Counsel & Secretary
8200 Jones Branch Drive, McLean VA 22102, USA
Tel: +1 703 903 2800 **Fax:** +1 703 903 2544
Website: www.freddiemac.com

Fedex Corporation
Kenneth Masterson, General Counsel
942 Shady Grove Road, Memphis 38120, USA
Tel: +1 901 369 3600 **Fax:** +1 901 818 7590
Website: www.fedexcorp.com

FI Group PLC
Charles Lilly, Legal Advisor
Maylands Avenue, Hemel Hempstead HP2 7TQ, United Kingdom
Tel: +44 1442 233339
Website: www.figroup.co.uk

Fiat SpA
Zan Francesco, General Counsel
Via Nizza 260, 10126 Turin, Italy
Tel: +39 011 686 2562 **Fax:** +39 011 686 2196
Website: www.fiatgroup.com

Fifth Third Bank
Paul Reynolds, General Counsel
38 Fountain Square Plaza, Cincinnati OH 45263, USA
Tel: +1 513 579 4356 **Fax:** +1 513 744 6757
Website: www.53.com

Fininvest
Maria Enrica Mascherpa, Head of Legal
Via Paleocapa 3, 20121 Milan, Italy
Tel: +39 0285 41 4283 **Fax:** +39 02 8541 4209
Email: direzione.legale@fininvest.it
Website: www.mediaset.it

Finmeccanica
Giuseppe Bono, General Manager
Piazza Monte Grappa 4, 00195 Rome, Italy
Tel: +39 06 32 47 31 **Fax:** +39 06 32 08 621
Email: vannisanti@finmeccanica.it
Website: www.finmeccanica.it

First Data Corporation
Michael T. Whealy, Executive VP, General Counsel and Chief Administrative Officer
5660 New Northside Drive, Suite 1120, Atlanta GA 30328, USA
Tel: +1 770 857 7103 **Fax:** +1 770 857 0414
Email: mike.whealy@firstdatacorp.com
Website: www.firstdatacorp.com

First Union Corp
Mark Treanor, General Counsel
1 First Union Center, 310 South College Street, Charlotte NC 28288, USA
Tel: +1 704 374 6161 **Fax:** +1 704 374 3105
Email: mark.treanor@firstunion.com
Website: www.firstunion.com

Firstar Corp
Jennie Carlson, General Counsel
777 E. Wisconsin Ave., Suite 800, Milwaukee 53202, USA
Tel: +1 414 765 4298 **Fax:** +1 414 287 3290
Email: jennie.carlson@firstar.com
Website: www.firstar.com

Flextech Television
Clive Burns, Company Secretary
160 Great Portland Street, London W1N 5TB, United Kingdom
Tel: +44 20 7299 5000 **Fax:** +44 20 7299 6000
Website: www.flextech.co.uk

Ford Motor Co
Dennis E Ross, Vice-President and General Counsel
One American Road, Dearborn 48126-2798, USA
Tel: +1 313 322 7453 **Fax:** +1 313 248 7450
Email: dross9@ford.com
Website: www.ford.com

FöreningsSparbanken AB
Hudeth Sand, Head of Legal Department
Brunkebergstorg 8, 105 34 Stockholm, Sweden
Tel: +46 8 5859 0000 **Fax:** +46 858 59 1750
Website: www.foreningssparbanken.se

Fortis (NL) NV
Hans A R Roell, Head of Legal
Archimedeslaan 6, NL-3584 BA Utrecht, Netherlands
Tel: +31 30 257 7577 **Fax:** +31 30 257 7826
Email: hans.roell@fortis.com
Website: www.nl.fortis.com

Fortum Oyj
Harri Pynna, General Counsel
Keilaniemi, PO Box 1, FIN-00048 Espoo, Finland
Tel: +358 104 511 **Fax:** +358 104 524 315
Email: harri.pynna@fortum.com
Website: www.fortum.com

France Telecom SA
Philippe McAllister, Vice President, General Counsel, International Legal Operation
6 Place d'Alleray, 75505 Paris, France
Tel: +33 1 44 44 22 22 **Fax:** +33 1 44 44 95 95
Email: philippe.mcallister@francetelecom.fr
Website: www.francetelecom.fr

Freeserve PLC
David Melville, Company Secretary and General Counsel
500 The Campus, Maylands Avenue, Hemel Hempstead HP2 7TG, United Kingdom
Tel: +44 1442 353 000 **Fax:** +44 1442 233 218
Email: david.melville@freeserve.com
Website: www.freeserve.com

Fresenius AG
Roland Kirsten, General Counsel
Else Kroener Strasse 1, D-61346 Bad Homburg v.d.H, Germany
Tel: +49 6172 608 2524 **Fax:** +49 6172 608 2251
Email: roland.kirsten@fresenius.de
Website: www.fresenius.de

Fuji Bank Ltd
Yoshiro Yamamoto, Chief Executive Officer
1-5-5 Ohtemachi, Chiyoda-Ku, Tokyo 100-0004, Japan
Tel: +81 3 32162211 **Fax:** +81 3 3216 6055
Website: www.fujibank.co.jp

Fuji Photo Film Co Ltd
Minoru Ohnishi, Chief Executive, Chairman
2-26-30 Nishiazabu, Minato-ku, Tokyo 106-8620, Japan
Tel: +81 3 3406 2111 **Fax:** +81 3 3406 2193
Website: www.fujifilm.com

Fuji Television Network
Hisashi Hieda, President and Chief Executive Officer
2-4-8, Daiba, Minato-ku, Tokyo 137-8088, Japan
Tel: +81 3 5500 8888 **Fax:** +81 3 5500 8758
Website: www.fujitv.co.jp

Fujitsu Limited
S Shinohara, Head of Legal
Fujitsu Japan, 4-1-1 Kami-Odanaka, Nakahara-ku, Kawasaki City, Kanagawa , Japan
Tel: +81 4 4754 8645 **Fax:** +81 4 4754 8503
Email: shinohara@jp.fujitsu.com
Website: www.fujitsu.co.jp

Fujitsu Support & Services Inc (FSAS)
Akira Kuwabara, President
26-1, Minami-Ohi 6-Chome, Shinagawa-Ku, Tokyo 140-8567, Japan
Tel: +81 3 5471 4700
Website: www.fsas.co.jp

Gallaher Group
Christopher Devereux, Corporate Legal Adviser
Members Hill, Brooklands Road, Weybridge KT13 0QU, United Kingdom
Tel: +44 1932 859777 **Fax:** +44 1932 832792
Email: chris.devereux@gallaherltd.com
Website: www.gallaher-group.com

Gambro AB
Ingmar Magnusson, General Counsel
Magistratsvagen 16, PO Box 10101, 220 10 Lund, Sweden
Tel: +46 46 16 90 00 **Fax:** +46 46 169 294
Email: ingmar.magnusson@gambro.com
Website: www.gambro.com

Gannett Co
Thomas L Chapple, General Counsel
1100 Wilson Blvd., Arlington VA 22234-0001, USA
Tel: +1 703 284 6000 **Fax:** +1 703 558 3897
Email: tchapple@gci1.gannett.com
Website: www.gannett.com

Gap
Anne Gust, General Counsel
1 Harrison Street, San Fransisco CA 94105, USA
Tel: +1 650 952 4400 **Fax:** +1 415 427 7007
Website: www.gap.com

Gas Natural SDG SA
Felipe Canellas, Director of the Legal Department
Avenida Portal de l'Angel 22, 08002 Barcelona, Spain
Tel: +34 93 402 5100 **Fax:** +34 93 402 5870
Website: www.gasnaturalsdg.es

Gateway 2000
William Elliot, General Counsel
4545 Town Centre Court, San Diego CA 92121, USA
Tel: +1 858 799 3401 **Fax:** +1 858 799 3442
Website: www.gateway.com

GEHE AG
Tilo Koster, Head of Legal Department
Neckartalstrasse 155, D-70376 Stuttgart, Germany
Tel: +49 711 500 1353 **Fax:** +49 711 5001 590
Email: Tilo.koester@gehe.de
Website: www.gehe.de

Gemstar TV Guide International
John Lorlick, General Counsel
135 N. Los Robles Ave., Ste. 800, Pasadena CA 91101, USA
Tel: +1 626 792 5700 **Fax:** +1 626 792 0257

Genentech
Stephen Juelsgaard, General Counsel
1 DNA Way, South San Fransisco CA 94080, USA
Tel: +1 650 225 1000 **Fax:** +1 650 952 9881
Email: stevej@gene.com
Website: www.genentech.com

General Electric Company
Ben Heineman, General Counsel
3135 Easton Turnpike, Fairfield CT 06431-0001, USA
Tel: +1 203 373 2211 **Fax:** +1 203 373 3079
Website: www.ge.com

General Motors Corporation
Thomas Gottschalk, Vice President and General Counsel
300 Renaissance Center, Detroit MI 48265, USA
Tel: +1 313 556 5000 **Fax:** +1 313 556 5108
Website: www.gm.com

Getronics NV
SA van Maasakker, Corporate Senior Vice President, Legal Services
Donauweg 10, Postbus 652, 1043 AJ Amsterdam, Netherlands
Tel: +31 20 586 1508 **Fax:** +31 20 586 1617
Website: www.getronics.com

Gillette Company
Richard K Willard, Head of Legal
Prudential Tower Building, Boston MA 02199, USA
Tel: +1 617 421 7000 **Fax:** +1 617 421 7874
Email: richard_willard@gillette.com
Website: www.gillette.com

GKN PLC
Rufus Ogilvie Smals, Head of Group Legal
PO Box 55, Ipsley House, Ipsley Church Lane, Redditch B98 0TL, United Kingdom
Tel: +44 1527 533253 **Fax:** +44 1527 533470
Email: ra.ogilvie-smals@gknghq.co.uk
Website: www.gknplc.com

GlaxoSmithKline
James R Beery, Senior Vice President, General Counsel and Corporate Secretary
1 New Horizons Court, Great West Road, Brentford TW8 9EP, United Kingdom
Tel: +44 20 8975 2000 **Fax:** +44 20 8975 6344/6177
Email: clare.a.mcclintock@sb.com
Website: www.sb.com

Global Crossing Ltd
Jim Gorton, General Counsel
Wessex House, 45 Reid Street, Hamilton HM 12, Bermuda
Tel: +310 385 5222 **Fax:** +310 281 5820
Email: jgorton@globalcrossing.bm
Website: www.globalcrossing.com

Goldman Sachs Group Inc
Gregory K Palm, Executive Vice President, General Counsel
85 Broad Street, New York NY10004, USA
Tel: +1 212 902 1000 **Fax:** +1 212 902 3000
Email: gregory.palm@gs.com
Website: www.gs.com

Granada Compass PLC
Graham Parrott, Commercial Director
Stornoway House, 13 Cleveland Row, London SW1A 1GG, United Kingdom
Tel: +44 20 7451 3000 **Fax:** +44 20 7451 3008
Website: www.granada.co.uk

Great Universal Stores PLC
Philip Harland, Head of Legal
Leconfield House, Curzon Street, London W1Y 7FL, United Kingdom
Tel: +44 20 7495 0070 **Fax:** +44 20 7495 1567
Email: harlap@gusco.com
Website: www.gusplc.co.uk

Groupe Bruxelles Lambert
Ann Opsomer, Head of the Legal and Tax Department
Avenue Marnix 24, 1000 Brussels, Belgium
Tel: +32 2 547 23 39 **Fax:** +32 2 547 22 06
Email: aopsomer@gbl.be
Website: www.gbl.be

Groupe Danone SA
Luc Delaby, General Counsel
7 rue de Teheran, cedex 08, 75381 Paris, France
Tel: +33 1 44 35 20 20 **Fax:** +33 1 42 25 67 16
Email: ldelaby@groupe.danone.com
Website: www.danone.com

Grupo Televisa
Juan Mijares, Vice President and Head of Legal Department
Avenida Chapultepec No. 28, 06724 Mexico City, Mexico
Tel: +52 5 261 2585 **Fax:** +52 5 261 2546
Email: jmijares@televisa.com.mx
Website: www.televisa.com.mx

Gruppo Editoriale L'Espresso SPA
Fabio Dacciaria, Company Secretary
Via Po 12, 00198 Rome, Italy
Tel: +39 06 847 81 **Fax:** +39 0684 78371
Website: www.repubblica.it

Gucci Group NV
Alan Tuttle, General Counsel
Rembrandt Tower, Amstelplein 1, 1096 HA Amsterdam, Netherlands
Tel: +31 20 462 1700 **Fax:** +31 20 465 3569
Email: atuttle@gucci.it
Website: www.gucci.com

Guidant Corp
John Jenkins, Vice President and General Counsel
111 Monument Circle, 29th Floor, Indianapolis IN 46204-5129, USA
Tel: +1 317 971 2000 **Fax:** +1 317 971 2041
Email: jjenkins.@guidant.com
Website: www.guidant.com

H.O. Sabanci Holding A.S.
Cuneyt Yuksel, Head of Legal Department
Sabanci Center Kule 2 K 20 4, Levent, 80745 Istanbul, Turkey
Tel: +90 212 281 6600 **Fax:** +90 212 281 0272
Email: cyuksel@sa.com.tr
Website: www.sabanci.com.tr

Hachette Filipacchi Medias
Francoise Jarry, General Counsel
149-151 rue Anatole France, 92534 Le Vallois-Perret, France
Tel: +33 1 41 34 73 07 **Fax:** +33 1 41 34 77 77
Email: fjarry@hfp.fr
Website: www.hachette-filapacchi.com

Halifax Group PLC
Harry Baines, Group Secretary
Trinity Road, Halifax HX1 2RG, United Kingdom
Tel: +44 1422 333333 **Fax:** +44 1422 333000
Email: harrybaines@halifax.co.uk
Website: www.halifax.co.uk

Halliburton Company
Ian Henniker-Smith, Senior Regonal Counsel
Hill Park Court, Springfield Drive, Leatherhead KT22 7NL, United Kingdom
Tel: +44 1372 865000 **Fax:** +44 1372 866635
Website: www.halliburton.com

Hang Seng Bank
Godwin Li, Legal Advisor
83 Des Voeux Road, Level 10, Central, Hong Kong , Hong Kong
Tel: +852 2198 1111 **Fax:** +852 2868 5923
Website: www.hangseng.com

Hanson PLC
Graham Dransfield, Legal Director
1 Grosvenor Place, London SW1X 7JH, United Kingdom
Tel: +44 20 7245 1245 **Fax:** +44 20 7235 3455
Email: logden@hanson.co.uk
Website: www.hansonplc.com

Havas
Philippe Leduc, General Counsel
19-27 Rue de Capitaine Juynemer, 92903 Paris La Defence, France
Tel: +33 1 46 96 33 87 **Fax:** +33 1 46 96 33 80
Email: PLeduc@hvae.havasvoyages.fr
Website: www.havas.fr

Hays PLC
Stephen Charnock, Company Secretary and Head Of Legal
Hays House, Millmead, Guildford GU2 5HJ, United Kingdom
Tel: +44 1483 302 203 **Fax:** +44 1483 455242
Email: stephan.charnock@hays.plc.uk
Website: www.hays-plc.co.uk

Heidelberger Druckmaschinen AG
Wirnt Galster, General Counsel
Kurfursten-Anlage 52-60, D-69115 Heidelberg, Germany
Tel: +49 6221 92 4060 **Fax:** +49 6221 92 4069
Email: wirnt.galster@heidleberg.com
Website: www.heidelberg.com

Heidelberger Zement AG
Albrecht Glitz, General Counsel
Berliner Strasse 6, D-69120 Heidelberg, Germany
Tel: +49 62 21 481 0 **Fax:** +49 62 21 481 477
Email: albrecht.glitz@hzag.de
Website: www.hzag.de

Heineken NV
Leonard Peter Willing, Director of Corporate Legal & Business Affairs
Tweede Weteringplantsoen 21, NL-1017 ZD Amsterdam, Netherlands
Tel: +31 20 523 9239 **Fax:** +31 20 626 3503
Email: l.p.willing@heineken.nl
Website: www.heinekencorp.nl

Hellenic Bottling
Tasos Filos, Head of Legal
9 Fragkoklissias St., Marousi, GR-15125 Athens, Greece
Tel: +30 1 618 3219 **Fax:** +30 1 619 5514
Website: www.3e.gr

Hellenic Petroleum SA
G Eliopoulos, Head of Legal
17th km. Athens-Corinth National Road, GR-19300 Aspropyrgos, Greece
Tel: +30 1 55 33 051 **Fax:** +30 1 55 33 050
Email: ltourlida@hellenic-petroleum.gr
Website: www.hellenic-petroleum.gr

Helsingin Puhelin Oyj (Helsinki Telephone)
Same Ylekartes, General Counsel
Korkeavuorenkatu 35-37, FIN-00131 Helsinki, Finland
Tel: +358 9 6061 **Fax:** +358 102 62 60 60
Email: same.ylekartes@elisa.fi
Website: www.elisa.fi

Henkel KGaA
Hans-Josef Acher, Head of Legal
Henkelstrasse 67, D-40589 Dusseldorf, Germany
Tel: +49 211 7970 **Fax:** +49 211 7 98 40 08
Email: hans-josef.acher@henkel.de
Website: www.henkel.de

Hennes & Mauritz [H & M] AB
Hakan Bjorkstedt, General Counsel
Norlandsg 15D9, PO Box 1421, S-111 84 Stockholm, Sweden
Tel: +46 8 796 5500 **Fax:** +46 8 228020
Email: hakan.bjorkstedt@hm.com
Website: www.hm.com

Hermes International
Ms de Chaunac, General Counsel
24 rue du Faubourg Saint-Honore, 75008 Paris, France
Tel: +33 1 4017 4949 **Fax:** +33 1 4017 4921
Email: dechaunac@hermes.com

Hewlett-Packard Company
Ann Baskin, General Counsel
3000 Hanover St., Palo Alto CA 94304, USA
Tel: +1 650 813 3332 **Fax:** +1 650 852 8452
Email: ann_baskin@hp.com
Website: www.hp.com

Hickari Tsushin
Yasumitsu Shigeta, President & Chief Executive Officer
22F Ohtemachi Nomura Bldg, 2-1-1 Ohtemachi, Chiyoda-ku, Tokyo 100-0004, Japan
Tel: +81 3 3510 2300 **Fax:** +81 3 3510 2321
Website: www.hikari.co.jp

Hilton International
J Geoffrey Chester, Solicitor, General Counsel & Secretary
Maple Court, Central Park, Reeds Crescent, Watford WD24 4SS, United Kingdom
Tel: +44 20 7850 4000 **Fax:** +44 20 7850 4001
Website: www. hilton.com

Hindustan Lever Ltd
MK Sharma, Director of Legal
PB No 409 Hindustan Lever House, 165/166 Backbay Reclamation, Mumbai 400 020, India
Tel: +91 22 287 0622 **Fax:** +91 22 2845 443
Email: mk.sharma@unilever.com
Website: www.hll-unilever.com

Hitachi Ltd
Mr Naito, Head of Legal
6 Kanda-Surugadai 4-chome, Chiyoda-ku, Tokyo 101-8010, Japan
Tel: +81 3 3258 1111 **Fax:** +81 3 3258 1334
Website: www.hitachi.co.jp

HJ Heinz Company
Laura Stein, General Counsel & Senior Vice President
600 Grant Street, Pittsburgh PA 15219-2857, USA
Tel: +1 412 456 5700 **Fax:** +1 412 456 6128
Email: laura.stein@hjheinz.com
Website: www.heinz.com

Holderbank Financiere Glarus AG
Pierre Haesler, General Counsel
Insel 14/Postfach, CH-8750 Glarus, Switzerland
Tel: +41 55 6403494 **Fax:** +41 55 222 8669
Email: pierre.haesler@hmc.ch
Website: www.holderbank.com

Holding di Partecipazioni Industriali SpA
Simona Pesce, Legal Department
Via F. Turati 16/18, 20121 Milan, Italy
Tel: +39 02 622 91 **Fax:** +39 0262 29696
Email: simona.pesce@hdp.it
Website: www.hdp.it

Holmen AB
Johan Flodstrom, Director of Legal Dept
Strandvagen 1, S-114 84 Stockholm, Sweden
Tel: +46 8 666 2100 **Fax:** +46 8 666 2174
Email: johan.flodstron@holmen.com
Website: www.holmen.com

Home Depot Inc
Lawrence Smith, Head of Legal
2455 Paces Ferry Road North West, Atlanta GA 30339, USA
Tel: +1 770 433 8211 **Fax:** +1 770 384 2337
Website: www.homedepot.com

Honda Motor Co Ltd
Richard Colliver, Executive Vice President
1-1 Minami-Aoyama 2-chome, Minato-ku, Tokyo 107-8556, Japan
Tel: +81 3 3423 1111 **Fax:** +81 3 3423 0511
Website: www.honda.com

Honeywell
Peter Kreindler, General Counsel
101 Columbia Road, PO Box 2245, Morristown 07962-2245, USA
Tel: +1 973 455 2000 **Fax:** +1 973 455 4807
Email: peter.kreindler@honeywell.com
Website: www.honeywell.com

Household International
Kenneth Robin, General Counsel
2700 Sanders Road, Prospect Heights IL 60070, USA
Tel: +1 847 564 5000 **Fax:** +1 847 205 7452
Website: www.household.com

HSBC Holdings PLC
Richard E.T. Bennett, Group General Manager, Legal and Compliance
10 Lower Thames Street, P.O. Box 506, London EC3R 6AE, United Kingdom
Tel: +44 20 7260 0500 **Fax:** +44 20 7260 3446
Email: richardbennett@hsbc.com
Website: www.hsbc.com

HSBC Trinkhaus & Burkhardt KGaA
Gunther Bottger, Head of Legal
Koenigsallee 21/23, D-40212 Dusseldorf, Germany
Tel: +49 211 9100 **Fax:** +49 2119 1616
Website: www.hsbctrinkhaus.de

Hutchison Whampoa Limited
Edith Shih, Head of Legal
Hutchison House, 22nd Floor, 10 Harcourt Road, Hong Kong , Hong Kong
Tel: +852 2 128 1188 **Fax:** +852 2128 1778
Email: ediths@hwl.com.hk
Website: www.hutchison-whampoa.com

i2 Technologies Inc
Robert Donohoo, General Counsel
i2 Technologies Inc, 117 01 Luna Road, Dallas 75234, USA
Tel: +1 469 357 1000 **Fax:** +1 469 357 6566
Email: robert_donohoo@i2.com
Website: www.i2.com

Iberdrola Energia SA
Inigo Elloriaga, Head of Legal
Gardoqui 8, 48008 Bilbao, Spain
Tel: +34 944 15 14 11 **Fax:** +34 944 057 508
Email: ielorriaga@iberdrola.es
Website: www.iberdrola.com

Illinois Tool Works
Stewart Hudnut, General Counsel, Senior Vice President, Secretary.
3600 W. Lake Ave., Glenview IL 60025, USA
Tel: +1 847 724 7500 **Fax:** +1 847 657 4329
Website: www.itw.com

Immunex Corporation
Barry G. Pea, General Counsel
51 University Street, Seattle 98101-2918, USA
Tel: +1 206 587 0430 **Fax:** +1 206 587 0606
Email: peab@immunex.com
Website: www.immunex.com

Imperial Chemical Industries PLC
Michael HC Herlihy, General Counsel
Imperial Chemical House, 9 Millbank, London SW1P 3JF, United Kingdom
Tel: +44 20 7834 4444 **Fax:** +44 20 7798 5872
Email: michael_herlihy@ici.com
Website: www.ici@ici.com

Imperial Tobacco Group PLC
Alan Porter, Legal Manager
PO Box 244, Upton Road, Southville, Bristol BS99 7UJ, United Kingdom
Tel: +44 117 963 6636 **Fax:** +44 117 988 1472
Website: www.imperial-tobacco.com

Industrial Bank of Japan Ltd
Masao Nishimura, President and Chief Executive Officer
3-3 Marunouchi 1-chome, Chiyoda-ku, Tokyo 100-8210, Japan
Tel: +81 3 3214 1111 **Fax:** +81 3 3201 7643
Website: www.ibjbank.co.jp

Infosys Technologies
R Nithyanandan, Chief Legal Counel
Electronics City, Hosur Road, Bangalore 561 229, India
Tel: +91 80 852 0261 **Fax:** +91 80 852 0362
Email: nithyar@infy.com
Website: www.infy.com

ING Groep NV
DC van Wassenaer, General Counsel
Strawinskylaan 2631, 1000 ZZ Amsterdam, Netherlands
Tel: +31 20 541 8702 **Fax:** +31 20 541 8723
Website: www.ing.com

Intel Corp
Thomas Dunlap, Senior Vice President and General Counsel
2200 Mission College Blvd., Santa Clara CA 95052, USA
Tel: +1 408 765 8080 **Fax:** +1 408 765 1859
Website: www.intel.com

Interamerican
Lavrentis Alvertis, General Counsel
117 Kifisias Ave. & St. Konstantine 59-61, 15180 Marousi, Greece
Tel: +30 1 6122222 **Fax:** +30 1 619 1246
Email: alvertisl@interamerican.gr
Website: www.interamerican.gr

Internap Network Services
Tom Youth, Head of Legal
601 Union Street, Ste 1000, Seattle 98101, USA
Tel: +1 206 441 8800 **Fax:** +1 206 264 1833
Email: tyouth@internap.com
Website: www.internap.com

International Business Machines Corporation
Lawrence Ricciardi, General Counsel
New Orchard Road, Armonk NY 10504, USA
Tel: +1 914 499 1900 **Fax:** +1 914 499 6252
Email: lrr@us.ibm.com
Website: www.ibm.com

International Paper Company
William Lytton, General Counsel
2 Manhattanville Road, Purchase NY 10577, USA
Tel: +1 914 397 1500 **Fax:** +1 914 397 1505
Website: www.internationalpaper.com

International Power PLC
Stephen Ramsay, Company Secretary & Corporate Counsel
Senator House, 85 Queen Victoria Street, London EC4V 4DP, United Kingdom
Tel: +44 20 7320 8627 **Fax:** +44 20 7320 8710
Email: stephen.ramsay@natpower.com
Website: www.internationalpowerplc.com

Internet Cap Group
Henry Nassau, General Counsel
435 Devon Park Dr, Building 600, Wayne 19087, USA
Tel: +1 610 989 0111 **Fax:** +1 610 989 0112
Email: hnassan@internetcapital.com
Website: www.icge.com

Interpublic Group of Companies Inc
Nicholas Camera, General Counsel
1271 Avenue of the Americas, New York NY 10020-1449, USA
Tel: +1 212 399 8000 **Fax:** +1 212 399 8119
Email: ncamera@interpublic.com
Website: www.interpublic.com

Intershop Communications AG
Axel Burkhardt, Head of Legal
Amsinckstrasse 57, D-20097 Hamburg, Germany
Tel: +49 40 237090 **Fax:** +49 4023 709 111
Email: a.burkhardt@intershop.de
Website: www.intershop.de

Intesa Gestione Crediti S.P.A.
Vito Faggella, Chief Executive Officer
Via Andegari 9, 20121 Milan, Italy
Tel: +39 02 8866 2945 **Fax:** +39 02 8866 3993
Email: mrusso@ambro.it
Website: www.bancaintesa.it

Intracom SA
Maria Makris, General Counsel
64 Kifissias Ave & Premetis Street 3, 151 25 Marousi, Greece
Tel: +30 1 61 05 416 8 **Fax:** +30 1 61 05 419
Website: www.intracom.gr

Intuit Inc
Catherine Valentine, General Counsel
2535 Garcia Avenue, Mountain View 94039-7850, USA
Tel: +1 650 944 6000 **Fax:** +1 650 944 3699
Email: catherine_valentine@intuit.com
Website: www.intuit.com

Invensys PLC
James C Bays, Senior Vice President, General Counsel and Chief Legal Officer
Carlisle Place, London SW1P 1BX, United Kingdom
Tel: +44 20 7821 3743/2 **Fax:** +44 20 7821 3806
Email: jim.bays@invensys.com
Website: www.invensys.com

Irish Life & Permanent PLC
Cathal MacCarthy, General Council
Irish Life Centre, Lower Abbey Street, Dublin 1, Ireland
Tel: +353 1 702 0324 **Fax:** +353 1 702 0457
Website: www.irishlifepermanent.ie

ISS System AS
Carsten Rich, General Counsel
Bredgade 30, DK-280 60 Copenhagen K, Denmark
Tel: +45 38 17 17 17 **Fax:** +45 33 93 69 83
Email: cri@group.issworld.dk
Website: www.ISS-group.com

Istituto Bancario San Paolo Di Torino
Franco Confortini, General Counsel
Piazza S. Carlo 156, 10121 Turin, Italy
Tel: +39 06 6902 3436 **Fax:** +39 06 69 022058
Website: www.sanpaolo.it

Italgas [Sta Italina Per it Gas pA]
Umberto Franchini, General Counsel
Via XX Settembre 41, 10121 Turin, Italy
Tel: +39 011 23941 **Fax:** +39 112 394850
Website: www.italgas.it

Ito-Yokado Co Ltd
Toshifumi Suzuki, President & Chief Executive
1-4, Shibakoen, 4-Chome, Minato-ku, Tokyo 105, Japan
Tel: +81 3 3459 2111 **Fax:** +81 3 3434 8378
Website: www.itoyodado.iyg.co.jp

Itochu Techno-Science
Osamu Gotoh, President
11-5 Fujimi l-Chome, Chiyoda-Ku 102-0071, Japan
Tel: +81 3 5226 1234 **Fax:** +81 3 5226 1309
Website: www.ctc-g.co.jp

J Sainsbury PLC
David Thurston, Head of Group Legal Services
Stamford House, Stamford Street, London SE1 9LL, United Kingdom
Tel: +44 20 7695 6000 **Fax:** +44 20 7695 7610
Email: david.thurston@tao.sainsburys.co.uk
Website: www.j-sainsbury.co.uk

Jafco
Mitsumasa Murase, President
Tekko Building, 1-8-2 Marunouchi, Chiyod-ku, Tokyo 100-0005, Japan
Tel: +81 3 5223 7536 **Fax:** +81 3 5223 7561
Website: webroom@jafco.co.jp

Japan Telecom Co Ltd
Toshihisa Nishi, General Manager, General Affairs Department
4-7-1, Hacchobori, Chuo-ku, Tokyo 104-8508, Japan
Tel: +81 3 5540 8000 **Fax:** +81 3 5543 1972
Website: www.japan-telecom.co.jp

Japan Tobacco Inc
Masaru Mizuno, President and Chief Executive Officer
JT Building, 2-1, Toranomon 2-chome, Minato-ku, Tokyo 105-8422, Japan
Tel: +81 3 3582 3111 **Fax:** +81 3 5572 1441
Website: www.jtnet.ad.jp

JDS Uniphase
Michael Phillips, Senior Vice-President Business Development and General Counsel
210 Baypointe Pkwy, San Jose 95134, USA
Tel: +1 408 434 1800 **Fax:** +1 408 954 0760
Website: www.jdsunph.com

Jefferson Smurfit Group
Brian Marshall, General Counsel
Beech Hill, Clonskeagh, Dublin 4, Ireland
Tel: +353 1 202 7000 **Fax:** +353 1 2600 709
Email: bmarshall@smurfitcapital.ie
Website: www.smurfit.ie

Johnson & Johnson
Roger Fine, Corporate Vice-President and General Counsel
1 J & J Plaza, New Brunswick NJ 8933-0001, USA
Tel: +1 732 524 2440 **Fax:** +1 732 524 3300
Website: www.jnj.com

Johnson Matthey PLC
Simon Farrant, Senior Legal Adviser and Company Secretary
2-4 Cockspur Street, Trafalgar Square, London SW1Y 5BQ, United Kingdom
Tel: +44 20 7269 8400 **Fax:** +44 20 7269 8476
Website: www.matthey.com

JP Morgan Chase & Co
William H McDavid, General Counsel
270 Park Ave, New York 10017, USA
Tel: +1 212 552 7813 **Fax:** +1 212 270 4288
Email: william.mcdavid@chase.com
Website: www.jpmorganchase.com

Julius Bär Holding AG
Franco Taisch, Group Legal Manager
Bahnhofstrasse 36, CH-8010 Zurich, Switzerland
Tel: +41 1 228 51 11 **Fax:** +41 1 212 11 21
Email: franco.taisch@juliusbaer.com
Website: www.juliusbaer.com

Juniper Networks
Lisa Berry, Vice-President, General Counsel and Secretary
1194 N. Mathilda, Sunnyvale 94089, USA
Tel: +1 408 745 2384 **Fax:** +1 408 745 8910
Email: lberry@juniper.net
Website: www.juniper.net

Kansai Electric Power Co Inc
Takashi Ishikawa, Executive Vice-President and CEO
3-3-22 Nakanoshima Kita-ku, Osaka 530-8270, Japan
Tel: +81 66 441 8821 **Fax:** +81 66 441 0569
Website: www.kepco.co.jp

Kao Corporation
K Kawashima, Manager, Legal Department
14-10 Nihonbashi Kayabacho, 1-chome, Chuo-ku, Tokyo 103-8210, Japan
Tel: +81 3 3660 7049 **Fax:** +81 3 3660 7942
Website: www.kao.co.jp

Karstadt Warenhaus AG
Martin Muller, Head of Legal Departmert
Theodor Althoff Str. 2, D-45133 Essen, Germany
Tel: +49 201 7270 **Fax:** +49 201 727 2055
Email: martin.mueller@karstadt.de
Website: www.karstadt.de

KBC Bankverzekering
Johan Tyteca, Manager, Legal Department
Warmoesberg 24 - 26, 1000 Brussels, Belgium
Tel: +32 2 429 5849 **Fax:** +32 2 429 5511
Email: johan.tyteca@kbc.be
Website: www.kbc.be

KDDI
Hiromu Ashina, Head of Legal
KDDI Building, 3-2 Nishishinjuku, 2-chome, Shinjuku-ku, Tokyo 163 8003, Japan
Tel: +81 3 3347 5711 **Fax:** +81 3 3347 5845
Website: www.kddi.com

Kellogg
Janet Kelly, General Counsel
1 Kellogg Square, PO Box 3599, Battle Creek MI 49016-3599, USA
Tel: +1 616 961 2000 **Fax:** +1 616 961 3276
Email: janet.kelly@kellogg.com
Website: www.kelloggs.com

Keyence Corporation
Takemitsu Takizaki, President and Representative Director
3-14 Higashi-Nakajima 1-chome, Higashi-Yodogawa-ku, Osaka 533 8555, Japan
Tel: +81 6 63791111
Website: www.keyence.co.jp

Kimberly-Clark Corporation
George Everbach, General Counsel
351 Phelps Drive, Irving TX 75038, USA
Tel: +1 972 281 1200 **Fax:** +1 972 281 1490
Website: www.kimberly-clark.com

Kingfisher PLC
Helen Jones, Company Secretary
North West House, 119 Marylebone Road, London NW1 5PX, United Kingdom
Tel: +44 20 7724 7749 **Fax:** +44 20 7724 0355
Website: www.kingfisher.co.uk

Kingston Communications (HULL) PLC
John Bailey, Company Secretary and Head of Legal Affairs
Telephone House, 37 Carr Lane, Hull HU1 3RE, United Kingdom
Tel: +44 1482 602 614 **Fax:** +44 1482 210765
Website: www.kingston-comms.co.uk

Koc Holding
Prof Allangoya, General Counsel
Azizbey Sok. No. 1, Kuzguncuk, 81207 Istanbul, Turkey
Tel: +90 216 5310000 **Fax:** +90 216 3918268
Email: selimk@koc.com.tr
Website: www.koc.com.tr

Koninklijke Ahold NV
A.H.P.M. Van Tielraden, General Counsel
Albert Heijnweg 1, NL - 1507 Zaandam, Netherlands
Tel: +31 75 659 5604 **Fax:** +31 75 659 8366
Website: www.ahold.com

Korea Electric Power Corporation
Young-Shik Chang, President
167, Samsong-dong, Kangnam-Gu, Seoul 135-791, South Korea
Tel: +82 2 3456 3633 **Fax:** +82 2 3456 3699
Website: www.kepco.co.kr

Korea Telecommunication
Seung-Sul Woo, President
Sambu Building 5-8 Floor, 676 Yoksam-Dong, Kangnam-Gu, Seoul 110-777, South Korea
Tel: +82 2 527 0707 **Fax:** +82 2 527 0700
Website: www.kt.co.kr

KPN - Koninklijke PTT Nederland BV
AW Nauta, Head of Legal
PO Box 3000, 2500 GA The Hauge, Netherlands
Tel: +31 70 332 3278 **Fax:** +31 70 332 3675
Email: a.w.nauta@kpn.com
Website: www.kpn.com

Kroger Co
Paul W Heldman, General Counsel
1014 Vine Street, Cincinnati OH 45202-1100, USA
Tel: +1 513 762 4000 **Fax:** +1 513 762 1400
Website: www.kroger.com

Kyocera Corporation
Noboru Nakamura, Executive Vice President
6 Takeda Tobadono-cho, Fushimi-ku, Kyoto 612-8501, Japan
Tel: +81 75 604 3500 **Fax:** +81 75 604 3501
Website: www.kyocera.co.jp

Kyushi Matsushita Electric Co Ltd
Kaoru Takada, Head of Legal
1048, Kadoma, Osaka 571-8501, Japan
Tel: +81 6 6908 1121 **Fax:** +81 6 6906 2836
Website: www.kme.panasonic.co.jp

L'Air Liquide SA
Laurent Blamoutier, General Counsel
75 quai d'Orsay, 75321 Paris, France
Tel: +33 1 40 62 55 55 **Fax:** +33 1 47 62 50 00
Website: www.airliquide.com

L'Oreal
M Pierre Simoncelli, Directeur Juridique
41 Rue Martre, 92117 Clichy Cedex, France
Tel: +33 1 47 56 87 41 **Fax:** +33 1 47 56 75 01
Email: psimoncelli@dgc.loreal.com
Website: www.loreal.com

Lafarge SA
Andre-Gilles Taithe, Senior Vice President Legal Affairs
61 rue des Belles Feuilles, 75116 Paris, France
Tel: +33 1 44 34 11 11 **Fax:** +33 1 44 34 11 48
Email: andre-gilles.taithe@lafarge.com
Website: www.lafarge.com

Lagardere
Norbert Giaoui, Head of Legal
4 Rue de Presbourg, 75116 Paris, France
Tel: +33 1 4069 1600 **Fax:** +33 1 4069 1718
Email: ngiaoui@lagadere.fr
Website: www.lagardere.fr

Lambrakis
Konstantinos Mintziras, General Counsel
Panepistimou 18, 10672 Athens, Greece
Tel: +30 1 3686 452 **Fax:** +30 1 3686 445
Email: kmintziras@dolnet.gr
Website: www.dol.gr

Land Securities PLC
Clive Ashcroft, Legal Manager
5 Strand, London WC2N 5AF, United Kingdom
Tel: +44 20 7413 9000 **Fax:** +44 20 7925 0202
Website: www.landsecurities.co.uk

LASMO PLC
Alan O'Brien, General Counsel, Company Secretary and Head of Legal.
101 Bishopsgate, London EC2M 3XH, United Kingdom
Tel: +44 20 7892 2705 **Fax:** +44 20 7892 9292
Email: alan.o'brien@lasmo.com
Website: www.lasmo.com

Legal & General Group PLC
Geoffrey Timms, Group Head of Legal
Legal & General House, Kingswood, Todworth KT20 6EU, United Kingdom
Tel: +44 1737 370370 **Fax:** +44 1737 376144
Email: geoffrey.timms@landg.com
Website: www.legalandgeneral.co.uk

Legrand SA
Marc Dudognon, General Counsel
128 avenue de Lattre de Tassigny, PO Box 523, Cedex, F-87045 Limoges, France
Tel: +33 5 55 06 87 87 **Fax:** +33 5 55 06 13 41
Email: marc.dudognon@legrand.fr
Website: www.finance.legrandelectric.com

Level 3 Communications Inc
Jo Van Gorp, General Counsel
66 Prescott Street, London E1 8HG, United Kingdom
Tel: +44 20 7864 0223 **Fax:** +44 20 7864 0391
Website: www.level3.com

Lexmark International
Vincent J Cole, Vice President, General Counsel and Secretary
740 West New Circle Road, Lexington 40550, USA
Tel: +1 859 232 2000 **Fax:** +1 859 232 3128
Website: www.lexmark.com

Libertel NV
Monique D'agnolo, Manager Legal Dept
Avenue Ceramique 300, NL-6221 Maastricht, Netherlands
Tel: +31 43 3555555 **Fax:** +31 43 355 7048
Email: m.d.agnolo@libertel.nl
Website: www.libertel.nl

Linde AG
Hans-Georg Haeseler, Head of Legal Department
Abraham-Lincoln-Strasse 21, D-65189 Wiesbaden, Germany
Tel: +49 6 11 770 0 **Fax:** +49 611 770 453
Email: sanda.stoiacovici@linde.de
Website: www.linde.de

Linear Technology Corp
AF Schneiderman, General Counsel
1630 McCarthy Boulevard, Milpitas 95035, USA
Tel: +1 408 432 1900 **Fax:** +1 408 434 0507
Website: www.linear-tech.com

Lloyds TSB Group PLC
Geoffrey Johnson, Group Chief Legal Adviser
71 Lombard Street, PO Box 215, London EC3P 3BS, United Kingdom
Tel: +44 20 7626 1500 **Fax:** +44 20 7929 1654
Website: www.lloydstsb.co.uk

Logica PLC
David Walker, Group Legal Adviser
Stephenson House, 75 Hampstead Rd, London NW1 2PL, United Kingdom
Tel: +44 20 7637 9111 **Fax:** +44 20 7872 8994
Email: williamsf@logica.com
Website: www.logica.com

Lowes Companies
Steve Hellrung, Head of Legal
State Hwy 268 E, North Wilkesboro 28659, USA
Tel: +1 336 658 4000 **Fax:** +1 336 658 4766
Website: www.lowes.com

Lucent Technologies
Richard J Rawson, Senior Vice President, General Counsel and General Counsel
600 Mountain Ave., Murray Hill NJ 07974-0636, USA
Tel: +1 908 582 8500 **Fax:** +1 908 508 2576
Email: execoffice@lucent.com
Website: www.lucent.com

Lukoil
Ivan Maslyaev, Director of Legal Directorate
11 Sretenski Boulevard, RU-101000 Moscow, Russia
Tel: +7 095 927 1654 **Fax:** +7 095 927 1653
Website: www.lukoil.com

Lundbeck
Mette Carlstedt, General Counsel
Ottiliavej 9, DK-2500 Copenhagen, Denmark
Tel: +45 36301311 **Fax:** +45 36 302 732
Email: meco@lundbeck.com
Website: www.lundbeck.com

LVMH Moët Hennessy Louis Vuitton
Bernard Kuhn, Director of Legal Affairs
30 Avenue Hoche, F-75008 Paris, France
Tel: +33 1 44 13 22 22 **Fax:** +33 1 44 13 21 19
Email: b.kuhn@lvmh.fr
Website: www.lvmh.fr

MAN AG
Michael Fontaine, General Counsel
Ungererstrasse 69, D-80805 Munich, Germany
Tel: +49 89 3 60 98 0 **Fax:** +49 89 36 09 82 50
Website: www.man.de

Mannesmann AG
Joachim Peters, General Counsel
Mannesmannufer 2, Postfach 103641, D-40213 Dusseldorf, Germany
Tel: +49 211 8 20 0 **Fax:** +49 211 8 20 2493
Email: joachim.peters@mm.mannesmann.de
Website: www.mannesmann.de

Marconi PLC
Jeff Gordon, Head of Legal
1 Bruton Street, London W1X 8AQ, United Kingdom
Tel: +44 20 7493 8484 **Fax:** +44 20 7409 7748
Website: www.marconi.com

Marks & Spencer PLC
Graham Oakley, Company Secretary & Group Legal Adviser
Michael House, 37-67 Baker Street, London W1A 1DN, United Kingdom
Tel: +44 20 7935 4422 **Fax:** +44 20 7487 2670
Email: graham.oakley@marks-and-spencer.com
Website: www.marks-and-spencer.co.uk

Marsh & McLennan Companies Inc
William L Rosoff, Senior Vice-President and General Counsel
1166 Avenue of the Americas, New York 10036-2774, USA
Tel: +1 212 345 5000 **Fax:** +1 212 345 4647
Email: w.rosoff@mmc.com
Website: www.marchmac.com

Matav Hungarian Telecommunications Co Ltd
Odri Mihaly, Director of Legal Dept
Krisztina Korut 55, 1013 Budapest, Hungary
Tel: +36 1 457 4000 **Fax:** +36 1 458 7295
Email: odri.mihaly@ln.matav.hu
Website: www.matav.hu

Matsushita Communication Industrial Co
Takashi Kawada, President
3-1 Tsunashima-Higashi, 4-chome, Kohoku-ku, Yokohama 223-8639, Japan
Tel: +81 45 531 1231 **Fax:** +81 45 544 3285
Website: www.mci.panasonic.co.jp

Maxim Integrated Products
Charles Rigg, General Counsel
120 San Gabriel Drive, Sunnyvale 94086-5150, USA
Tel: +1 408 737 7600 **Fax:** +1 408 737 7194
Website: www.maxim-ic.com

MBNA Corp
John Scheflen,
1100 North King Street, c/o MBNA America Bank, Wilmington DE 19884, USA
Tel: +1 302 453 9930 **Fax:** +1 302 432 0753
Website: www.mbnainternational.com

McDonald's Corporation
Jeffrey Kindler, General Counsel
McDonald's Plaza, Oak Brook IL 60523, USA
Tel: +1 630 623 3000 **Fax:** +1 630 623 7409
Email: jeffkindler@mcd.com
Website: www.mcdonalds.com

MCI Worldcom
Michael Salsbury, Head of Legal
515 East Amite Street, Jackson MS 39201-2702, USA
Tel: +1 601 360 8600 **Fax:** +1 601 974 8350
Website: www.wcom.com

Mediobanca
Alberto Gomarasca, General Counsel
Via Filodrammatici 10, 20121 Milan, Italy
Tel: +39 02 8829 1 **Fax:** +39 02 8829 367
Website: www.mbres.it

Mediolanum
Ettore Parlato, Head of Legal
Via Francesco Sforza, 20080 Basiglo, Italy
Tel: +39 02 90491 **Fax:** +39 02 904 924 06
Email: eparlato@notes.mediolanum.it
Website: www.mediolanum.it

Medtronic
David J Scott, Senior Vice President, General Counsel and Secretary
7000 Central Ave. N.E, Minneapolis MN 55432, USA
Tel: +1 763 514 4000 **Fax:** +1 763 572 5459
Email: david.j.scott@medtronic.com
Website: www.medtronic.com

Mellon Bank Corp
Michael Bleier, General Counsel
1 Mellon Center, 19th Floor, Pittsburgh PA 15258-0001, USA
Tel: +1 412 234 5000 **Fax:** +1 412 236 4814
Website: www.mellon.com

MEPC PLC
John Price, Company Secretary
103 Wigmore Street, London W1U 1AH, United Kingdom
Tel: +44 20 7911 5503 **Fax:** +44 20 7911 5361
Email: jprice@mepc.co.uk
Website: www.mepc.com

Merck & Co Inc
Kent Frazier, Senior Vice-President and General Counsel
1 Merck Drive, Whitehouse Station NJ 8889, USA
Tel: +1 908 423 1000 **Fax:** +1 908 735 3184
Website: www.merck.com

Merck KGaA
Christian Flaemig, Head of Legal
Frankfurter Strasse 250, D-64293 Darmstadt, Germany
Tel: +49 6151 72 0 **Fax:** +49 6151 72 7773
Website: www.merck.de

Merrill Lynch & Co Inc
Michael Constantine, Assistant Vice President, Compliance Third Party Processing Division
Global Headquarters, World Financial Center, North Tower, 250 Vesey Street, New York NY 10281, USA
Tel: +1 212 670 0280 **Fax:** +1 212 236 4384
Email: michael_constantine@ml.com
Website: www.ml.com

Metro Cash & Carry GmbH
Michael Wiedmann, General Counsel
Schluterstrasse 17-19, D-40235 Dusseldorf, Germany
Tel: +49 211 969 3083 **Fax:** +49 211 969 3089
Email: Michael.Wiedmann@metro-mcc.de
Website: www.metro-cc.com

Metropole Tv-(M6)
Selvie Courbarein, General Counsel
89 Avenue Charles de Gaulle, 92200 Neuilly-sur-Seine, France
Tel: +33 1 41 92 66 66 **Fax:** +33 1 41 92 61 59
Website: www.m6.fr

MG Technologies AG
Manfred Doess, Head of Legal Department
Bockenheimer Landstrasse 73-77, D-60271 Frankfurt am Main, Germany
Tel: +49 69 711 990 **Fax:** +49 711 99 122
Email: manfred.doess@mgtechnologies.com
Website: www.mgtechnologies.com

Michelin [Cie Generale des Etablissements]
Philippe Legrez, Head of Legal
Sgd Batiment A7, 23 Place de Carmes, 63040 Clermont Ferrand, France
Tel: +33 473 98 5900 **Fax:** +33 4 73 32 61 48
Website: www.michelin.fr

Micron Technology
Roderick Lewis, General Counsel
8000 South Federal Way, Boise ID 83707-0006, USA
Tel: +1 208 368 4000 **Fax:** +1 208 368 4540
Email: rodlewis@micron.com
Website: www.micron.com

Microsoft Corporation
William Neukom, General Counsel
1 Microsoft Way, Building 8 N Suite 2211, Redmond WA 98052-8300, USA
Tel: +1 425 882 8080 **Fax:** +1 425 936 7329
Website: www.microsoft.com

Minnesota Mining and Manufacturing Company
John J Ursu, General Counsel
3M Center, St. Paul MN 55144, USA
Tel: +1 651 733 1110 **Fax:** +1 651 736 7859
Email: jjursu@mmm.com
Website: www.mmm.com

Misys PLC
Paul Waters, Company Secretary
Burleigh House, Chapel Oak, Salford Priors WR11 5SH, United Kingdom
Tel: +44 1386 871 373 **Fax:** +44 1386 871045
Website: www.misysplc.com

Mitsubishi Corporation
Yoko Komiya, Head of Legal
6-3 Marunouchi, 2-chome, Chiyoda-ku, Tokyo 100-8086, Japan
Tel: +81 3 3210 2121 **Fax:** +81 3 3210 8935
Website: www.mitsubishi.co.jp

Mitsubishi Electric Corporation
Ichiro Taniguchi, President and Chief Executive Officer, Mitsubishi Electronics America
Mitsubishi Denki Bldg, 2-2-3 Marunouchi, Chiyoda-ku, Tokyo 100-8310, Japan
Tel: +81 3 3218 2111 **Fax:** +81 3 3218 3537
Website: www.Mitsubishielectric.com.

Mitsubishi Estate Company Ltd
Takeshi Fukuzawa, President
2-7-3 Marunouchi, Chiyada-ku, Tokyo 100-8330, Japan
Tel: +81 3 3287 5100 **Fax:** +81 3 3212 3757
Website: www.mec.co.jp

MLP Finanzdienstkeistungen AG
Reinhard Fuchs, General Counsel
FORUM 7, D-69126 Heidelberg, Germany
Tel: +49 6221 308 740 **Fax:** +49 6221 308 158
Website: www.mlp.de

MobilCom AG
Ulrich Kalthoff, Head of Legal
Hollerstrasse 126, D-24782 Budelsdorf, Germany
Tel: +49 43 31 69 11 75 **Fax:** +49 43 3169 2522
Website: www.mobilcom.de

Mobistar
Natalie Gob, General Counsel
149 Rue Colonel Bourg, 1140 Brussels, Belgium
Tel: +32 2 745 71 11 **Fax:** +32 2 745 8649
Email: ngob@mail.mobistar.be
Website: www.mobistar.be

Modelo Continente SGPS
Alice Castanho, General Counsel
Modelo Continente SGPS, Lugar do Espido, Via Norte, 4470 Maia, Portugal
Tel: +351 22 940 4349 **Fax:** +351 22 940 4532
Email: esmachado@sonae.pt
Website: www.modelcontinente.pt

Modern Times Group
Johan Lindgern, CFO
Skeppsbron 18, PO Box 2094, SE-10313 Stockholm, Sweden
Tel: +46 8 56200050 **Fax:** +46 8 205074
Email: marita.asp@mtg.se
Website: www.mtg.se

Monsanto Co
William R Ide, General Counsel
800 N. Lindbergh Blvd., St. Louis MO 63167-0001, USA
Tel: +1 314 694 1000 **Fax:** +1 314 694 6399
Email: bill.ide@monsanto.com
Website: www.monsanto.com

Montedison SPA
Piergiuseppe Biandrino, General Counsel
Piazzetta Maurilio Bossi 3, 20121 Milan, Italy
Tel: +39 02 62701 **Fax:** +39 02 62705290
Email: p.biandrino@montedison.it
Website: www.montedison.it

Morgan Stanley Dean Witter & Co
Donald G Kempf Jr, Executive Vice President, Chief Legal Officer and Secretary
World Headquarters, 1585 Broadway, New York NY 10036, USA
Tel: +1 212 761 4000 **Fax:** +1 212 761 0086
Website: www.msdw.com

Motorola Inc
Peter Lawson, Head of Legal
1303 E Algonquin Road, Schaumburg IL 60196-1079, USA
Tel: +1 847 576 5012 **Fax:** +1 847 576 3628
Website: www.motorola.com

Mundial Confianca
Carlos Alberto de Oliveira Cruz, Chairman
Largo Do Chiado, 8, 1249-125 Lisbon, Portugal
Tel: +351 21 341500

Munich Reinsurance Company
Ralph Vogelgesang, General Counsel
Königinstrasse 107, D-80802 Munich, Germany
Tel: +49 89 38 91 0 **Fax:** +49 89 3891 4515
Email: rvogelgesang@munichre.com
Website: www.munichre.com

Murata Manufacturing Co Ltd
Tsuneo Murata, Senior Executive Director
Nagaoka Office, 26-10,, Tenjin 2-chome, Nagaokakyo-shi, Kyoto 617-8555, Japan
Tel: +81 75 955 6502 **Fax:** +81 75 954 7720
Website: www.iijnet.or.jp/murata

National Australia Bank Ltd
David Krasnostein
500 Bourke Street, GPO Box 84A, Melbourne 3000, Australia
Tel: +61 3 8641 3500 **Fax:** +61 3 8641 4916
Website: www.national.com.au

National Bank of Greece SA
Agisilaos Karambelas, Head of Legal
86 Eolou Street, Cotzia Square, 102 32 Athens, Greece
Tel: +30 1 3341562 **Fax:** +30 1 3346550
Email: lbk@nbg.gr
Website: www.ethniki.gr

National City
DC Zoeller, General Counsel
National City Center, 1900 East 9th St., Cleveland OH 44114, USA
Tel: +1 216 575 2000 ext: 2978 **Fax:** +1 216 575 2336
Website: www.national-city.com

National Grid Group PLC
Alison B Kay, Company Secretary & General Counsel
National Grid House, Kirby Corner Road, Coventry CV4 8JY, United Kingdom
Tel: +44 24 76537 777 **Fax:** +44 24 76423 620
Email: fiona.smith@ngc.co.uk
Website: www.ngc.co.uk

NEC Corporation
Nobuhito Yagi, General Manager, Legal Division
7-1 Shiba, 5-chome, Minato-ku, Tokyo 108-8001, Japan
Tel: +81 3 3798 6534 **Fax:** +81 3 3798 1510
Website: www.nec-global.com

Neckarwerke Stuttgart AG
Georg Mayer, Head of Legal
Lautenschlagerstrasse 21, D-70167 Stuttgart, Germany
Tel: +49 711 2890 **Fax:** +49 711 2894 220
Website: www.nws-ag.de

Nestle SA
Hans Peter Frick, General Counsel
Ave Nestle 55, CH-1800 Vevey, Switzerland
Tel: +41 21 924 2111 **Fax:** +41 21 924 4568
Email: hans-peter.frick@nestle.com
Website: www.nestle.com

News Corporation Limited
Arthur Michael Siskind, Senior Executive Vice President and Group General Counsel
Fox Entertainment Group, 1211 Avenue of The Americas, New York 10036, USA
Tel: +1 212 852 7111 **Fax:** +1 212 852 7145
Email: asiskind@newscorp.com
Website: www.fox.com

Next PLC
Peter Webber, Head of Legal Department
Desford Road, Enderby, Leicester LE9 5AT, United Kingdom
Tel: +44 116 286 6411 **Fax:** +44 116 284 2642
Email: peter_webber@next.co.uk
Website: www.next.co.uk

NEXTEL Communications
Leonard J Kennedy, General Counsel
2001 Edmund Halley Drive, Reston 20191, USA
Tel: +1 703 433 4000 **Fax:** +1 703 433 4036
Email: len.kennedy@nextel.com
Website: www.nextel.com

Nike Inc
Jim Carter, General Counsel
1 Bowerman Drive, Beaverton OR 97005-6453, USA
Tel: +1 503 671 6453 **Fax:** +1 503 671 6300
Email: jim.carter@nike.com
Website: www.nike.com

Nikko Securities Co Ltd
Masashi Kaneko, President and Chief Executive Officer
3-1 Marunouchi 3-chome, Chiyoda-ku, Tokyo 100-8325, Japan
Tel: +81 3 5644 4431 **Fax:** +81 3 5644 4555
Email: nikko@nikko.co.jp
Website: www.nikko.co.jp

Nintendo Co Ltd
Hiroshi Yamuchi, President
11-1 Hokotate-cho, Kamitoba, Minami-ku, Kyoto 601-8501, Japan
Tel: +81 75 541 6112 **Fax:** +81 75 541 5127
Website: www.nintendo.cc.jp

Nippon Steel Corporation
Motoyoshi Nishikawa, Director
6-3 Otemachi 2-chome, Chiyoda-ku, Tokyo 100-8071, Japan
Tel: +81 3 3242 4111 **Fax:** +81 3 3275 5607
Website: www.nsc.co.jp

Nippon Telegraph & Telephone Corporation
Satoru Miyamura, Senior Vice President
3-19-2 Nishi-Shinjuku Shinjuku-ku, Tokyo 163-8019, Japan
Tel: +81 3 5359 5111
Website: www.ntt.co.jp

Nippon Television Network Corporation
Seiichiro Ujiie, President
14, Niban-cho, Chiyoda-ku, Tokyo 102-8004, Japan
Tel: +81 3 52751111 **Fax:** +81 3 5275 4012
Website: www.ntv.co.jp

Nissan Motor Co Ltd
Carlos Ghosn, COO
6-17-1 Ginza 6-chome, Chuo-ku, Tokyo 104-8023, Japan
Tel: +81 3 5565 2004 **Fax:** +81 3 5565 2019
Email: yafuko-s@mail.nissan.co.jp
Website: www.global.nissan.co.jp

Nokia Corporation
Ursula Ranin, Vice President, General Council
Keilalahdentie 4, FIN-02150 Espoo, PO Box 226, FIN-00045 Nokia Group, Finland
Tel: +358 9 180 71 **Fax:** +358 9 605 042
Email: ursula.ranin@nokia.com
Website: www.nokia.com

Nomura Securities Co Ltd
Noriaki Nigai, Head of Legal
1-9-1 Nihonbashi, Chuo-ku, Tokyo 103-8011, Japan
Tel: +81 3 3211 1811 **Fax:** +81 3 3278 0420
Email: noriaki.nigai@nomura.co.jp
Website: www.nomura.co.jp

Nordea
Tord Arnerup, Head of Law Department
Hamngatan 10, SE-10571 Stockholm, Sweden
Tel: +46 8 614 78 28 **Fax:** +46 8 6148770
Email: tord.arnerup@ng.se
Website: www.nb.se

Norsk Hydro AS
Odd Ivar Biller, General Counsel
Bygdoy allé 2, 0240 Oslo, Norway
Tel: +47 22 53 8100 **Fax:** +47 22 53 2725
Email: odd.ivar.biller@hydro.com
Website: www.hydro.com

Nortel Networks Corporation
Nicholas J DeRoma, Chief Legal Officer
8200 Dixie Road, S.100, Brampton L6T 5P6, Canada
Tel: +1 905 863 1301 **Fax:** +1 905 863 8423
Website: www.nortelnetworks.com

Northern Rock PLC
Colin Taylor, Director - Compliance and Legal Services
Northern Rock House, Gosforth NE3 4PL, United Kingdom
Tel: +44 191 285 7191 **Fax:** +44 191 284 8470
Email: colin.taylor@northernrock.co.uk
Website: www.northernrock.co.uk

Novartis Group
George Miller, Deputy General Counsel
Legal Services, CH-4002 Basel, Switzerland
Tel: +41 61 324 2745 **Fax:** +41 61 324 3894
Email: george.miller@group.novartis.com
Website: www.novartis.com

Novo Nordisk A/S
Ole Ramsby, Head of Legal Department
Novo Alle 1, DK-2880 Bagsvaerd, Denmark
Tel: +45 44 44 8888 **Fax:** +45 4498 0555
Email: ofr@novonordisk.com
Website: www.novonordisk.com

NRJ
Mme Salehe, General Counsel
22, RUE BOILEAU, CEDEX 16, 75203 Paris, France
Tel: +33 1 40 71 42 43 **Fax:** +33 1 44 14 92 15
Website: www.nrj.fr

NTL Incorporated
Richard J Lubasch, General Counsel
110 East 59th Street, 26th Floor, New York NY 10022, USA
Tel: +1 212 906 8470 **Fax:** +1 212 906 8497
Email: lubasch@ntli.com
Website: www.ntl.com

NTT Data Corporation
Koichi Nakano, Head of Legal
Toyosu Center, Bldg. 3-3, Toyosu 3-chome, Tokyo 135-6033, Japan
Tel: +81 3 5546 8141 **Fax:** +81 3 5546 2405
Website: www.nttdata.co.jp

NTT Moblie Communicatons Network Inc
Keiji Tachikawa, President and Chief Executive Officer
10-1 Toranomon, 2-chome, Minato-ku, Tokyo 105-8436, Japan
Tel: +81 3 5563 7015 **Fax:** +81 3 3568 8942
Website: www.nttdocomo.com

Nycomed Amersham Plc
Robert Allnutt, Group Legal Adviser and Company Secretary
Amersham Place, Little Chalfont HP7 9NA, United Kingdom
Tel: +44 1494 544 000 **Fax:** +44 1494 542 266
Email: robert.alnutt@uk.nycomed-amersham.com
Website: www.nycomed-amersham.com

OAO Gazprom
Rem Ivanovich Vyakhirev, Chairman of the Management Board
16 Nametkina St., 117884 Moscow, Russia
Tel: +7 095 719 4600 **Fax:** +7 095 719 8327
Website: www.gazprom.ru

Old Mutual PLC
Martin Murray, Company Secretary
3rd Floor, Lansdowne House, 57 Berkeley Square, London W1X 5DH, United Kingdom
Tel: +44 20 7569 0109 **Fax:** +44 20 7569 0209
Website: www.oldmutual.com

Olivetti SPA
Loris Bisone, Director of Legal Department
via Jervs 77, Ivrea, 10015 Turin, Italy
Tel: +39 0125 152 39 15 **Fax:** +39 0125 522989
Email: l.bisone@olivetti.it
Website: www.olivetti.it

Omnicom Group
Barry Wagner, General Counsel
437 Madison Avenue, New York 10022, USA
Tel: +1 212 415 3600 **Fax:** +1 212 415 3470
Email: barry_wagner@omnicomny.com
Website: www.omnicomny.com

OMV AG
Jürg Cabjolsky, General Counsel
Otto Wagner-Platz 5, Postfach 15, A-1090 Vienna, Austria
Tel: +43 1 404 40 36 **Fax:** +43 1 404 40 91
Email: Juerg.Cabjolsky@omv.com
Website: www.omv.com

Oracle Corporation
Daniel Cooperman, Senior Vice President, General Counsel, and Corporate Secretary
500 Oracle Parkway, Redwood Shores CA 94065, USA
Tel: +1 650 506 7000 **Fax:** +1 650 506 7200
Email: dcooperm@us.oracle.com
Website: www.oracle.com

ORIX Corp
Hiroshi Nakamura, Head of Legal
3-2 2-8 Shipa Minato-Ku, Tokyo 105-8683, Japan
Tel: +81 3 5419 5102 **Fax:** +81 3 5419 5901
Email: hiroshi_nakamura@orix.co.jp
Website: www.orix.co.jp

Orkla AS
Karl Otto Tneter, Company Lawyer
PO Box 423, Skoyen, 0213 Oslo, Norway
Tel: +47 22 54 40 00 **Fax:** +47 22 54 44 92
Website: www.orkla.com

OTE Telecom AE
A Kalogeropoulos, Chief Legal Officer
99 Kifissias Ave, Marousi, 151 81 Athens, Greece
Tel: +30 1 611 1250 **Fax:** +30 1 611 7235
Email: dianelia@ote.gr
Website: www.ote.gr

Overseas Chinese Banking
Than Aung, General Counsel
65 Chulia Street, OCBC Centre, Singapore 049513, Singapore
Tel: +65 530 1779 **Fax:** +65 534 3986
Website: www.ocbc.com.sg

Pacific Century CyberWorks Limited
Donald Hess, General Counsel of Legal and Regulatory Affairs, Company Secretary
39th Floor, Hongkong Telecom Tower, Taikoo Place, 979 King's Road, Quarry Bay , Hong Kong
Tel: +852 2888 2888 **Fax:** +852 2962 5725
Email: donald.j.hess@hkt.com
Website: www.pccw.com

Pacific Century Group
Winnie Siu, General Counsel, Business Development
38th Floor Citibank Tower, Citibank Plaza, 3 Garden Road, Central, Hong Kong 070, Hong Kong
Tel: +852 2514 8888 **Fax:** +852 2514 8627
Email: general@pcg-group.com
Website: www.pcg-group.com

Panafon
Kostantinos Ploubis, General Counsel
44 Kifissias Avenue, 151 25 Marousi, Greece
Tel: +30 1 61 60 000 **Fax:** +301 6160 148
Email: ploubis@panafon.gr
Website: www.panafon.gr

PE Corp-PE Biosystems Group
William B Sawch, General Counsel
761 Main Avenue, Norwalk 06859-0001, USA
Tel: +1 650 638 5800 **Fax:** +1 203 761 5000
Website: www.pebio.com

Pearson PLC
Gary Rinck, General Counsel
3 Burlington Gardens, London W1S 3EP, United Kingdom
Tel: +44 20 7411 2000 **Fax:** +44 20 7411 2390
Website: www.pearson.com

Pechiney SA
Pierre Alain, General Counsel
7 place du Chancelier Adenauer, Cedex 16, 75116 Paris, France
Tel: +33 1 56 28 25 77 **Fax:** +33 1 56 28 33 38
Website: www.pechiney.com

Peninsular & Oriental Steam Navigation Co
Michael Gradon, Group Legal Director and Company Secretary
79 Pall Mall, London SW1Y 5EJ, United Kingdom
Tel: +44 20 7321 4515 **Fax:** +44 20 7930 6042
Email: mlilisons.legal@p-and-o.com
Website: www.p-and-o.com

PepsiCo Inc
Robert Sharpe, Senior VP & General Counsel
700 Anderson Hill Road, Purchase NY 10577, USA
Tel: +1 914 253 2000 **Fax:** +1 914 249 8166
Website: www.pepsico.com

Pernod Ricard
P-M Châteauneuf, General Counsel
142 boulevard Haussmann, 75008 Paris, France
Tel: +33 1 40 76 77 78 **Fax:** +33 1 45 63 34 23
Email: pmchateauneuf@pernod-ricard.fr
Website: www.pernod-ricard.fr

Petrobras
Rui Dias, Legal Counsel
Avenida Chile 65, 20035-900 Rio de Janeiro, Brazil
Tel: +55 21 534 4477 **Fax:** +55 21 534 1200
Email: ruiderford@petrobras.br
Website: www.petrobras.com.br

Peugeot SA
Jean-Claude Hanus, General Counsel
75 Ave. de la Grande Armée, 75116 Paris, France
Tel: +33 1 40 66 55 11 **Fax:** +33 1 40 66 44 21
Email: hanus@psa.com
Website: www.psa.fr

Pfizer Inc
Paul Miller, Executive Vice Pres. and Gen. Counsel
235 E. 42nd St., New York 10017, USA
Tel: +1 212 573 2323 **Fax:** +1 212 808 8924
Email: paul.s.miller@pfizer.com
Website: www.pfizer.com

Pharmacia & Upjohn
Richard Collier, General Counsel
100 Route 206 North, Peapack NJ 07977, USA
Tel: +1 908 901 8000 **Fax:** +1 908 901 7700
Website: www.pnu.com

Philip Morris Companies Inc
Charles R. Wall, Senior Vice President and General Counsel
120 Park Avenue, New York 10017, USA
Tel: +1 917 663 5000 **Fax:** +1 917 663 2167
Website: www.philipmorris.com

Philips Electronics NV
A Westerlaken, General Counsel
PO Box 77900, 1070 MX Amsterdam, Netherlands
Tel: +31 20 597 7237 **Fax:** +31 20 597 7150
Email: a.westerlaken@philips.com
Website: www.philips.com

Pinault-Printemps-Redoute
Michel Friocourt, Head of Legal
18 Place Henri Bergson, 75008 Paris, France
Tel: +33 1 44 90 61 00 **Fax:** +33 1 44 90 62 77
Email: mfriocourt@pprgroup.com
Website: www.pprgroup.com

Piraeus Bank
George Stasinopoulous, Head of Legal Dept
20 Amalias Avenue & 5 Souri Street, 10557 Athens, Greece
Tel: +30 1 333 5699 **Fax:** +30 1 333 599
Email: athanassakiv@piraeusbank.gr
Website: www.piraeusbank.gr

Pirelli SpA
Mr Boschetti, Head of Legal
Viale Sarca 222, 20126 Milan, Italy
Tel: +39 026 4421 **Fax:** +39 264 423329
Email: oscar.boschetti@pirelli.com
Website: www.pirelli.com

Pitney Bowes Inc
Sara Moss, General Counsel
1 Elmcroft Road, Stamford 06926, USA
Tel: +1 203 356 5000 **Fax:** +1 203 351 7984
Email: sara.moss@pb.com
Website: www.pitneybowes.com

PNC Bank
Helen Pudlin, General Counsel
One PNC Plaza, Fifth Avenue and Wood Street, Pittsburgh , USA
Tel: +1 412 762 2889 **Fax:** +1 412 768 2875
Website: www.pncbank.com

Pohang Iron & Steel Co., Ltd (POSCO)
Mu-Nam Kwak, President
Pohang Iron & Steel Co., Ltd (POSCO), Kaedang-dang, Nam-ku, Pohang City, Kyangsangpuk 790-600, South Korea
Tel: +82 562 220 0114 **Fax:** +82 562 220 6000
Website: www.posco.co.kr

Pohjola Group Insurance Corporation
Olavi Nieminen, General Counsel
Lapinmaentie 1, FIN-00013 Helsinki, Finland
Tel: +358 10 559 2452 **Fax:** +358 10 559 6813
Email: olavi.nieminen@pohjola.fi
Website: www.pohjola.fi

Polski Koncern Naftowy
Malgorzata Kowalska, Head of Legal Department
Chemikow 7, 09-411 Plock, Poland
Tel: +48 24 365 3667 **Fax:** +48 24 365 5583
Email: malgorzata.kowalska@orlen.pl
Website: www.petrochemia.pl

Portugal Telecom
Manuel Rodrigues, General Counsel
Rua Andrade, Corvo 6, 3rd Floor, 1500 Lisbon, Portugal
Tel: +351 21 357 3791 **Fax:** +35 1 21 357 4711
Email: manuel.g.rodrigues@telecom.pt
Website: www.telecom.pt

PowerGen PLC
David J Jackson, Company Secretary and General Counsel
Westward Way, Westward Business Park, Coventry CV4 8AG, United Kingdom
Tel: +44 24 76424 453 **Fax:** +44 24 76642 5248
Email: david.jackson@pgen.com
Website: www.pgen.com

Preussag AG
Andreas Göhmann, Head of Legal Department
Karl-Wiechert-Allee 4, D-30625 Hanover, Germany
Tel: +49 511 56600 **Fax:** +49 511 566 1748
Email: goehmann.andreas@preussag.de
Website: www.preussag.de

Procter & Gamble
Carroll Bodie, General Counsel
One Procter & Gamble Plaza, Cincinnati OH 45202, USA
Tel: +1 513 983 1100 **Fax:** +1 513 983 9369
Email: bodie.ca@pg.com
Website: www.pg.com

Provident Financial PLC
David Rees, Group Legal Advisor
Colonnade, Sunbridge Road, Bradford BD1 2LQ, United Kingdom
Tel: +44 1274 731 111 **Fax:** +44 1274 727 300
Email: david.rees@provident.co.uk
Website: www.providentfinancial.co.uk

Providian Financial
Mary E Richey, General Counsel
201 Mission Street, 28th Floor, San Francisco 94105, USA
Tel: +1 415 543 0404 **Fax:** +1 415 278 6028
Website: www.providian.com

Prudential PLC
Peter Maynard, Group Legal Services Director
Laurence Pountney Hill, London EC4R 0EU, United Kingdom
Tel: +44 20 7548 3737 **Fax:** +44 20 7548 3191
Email: peter.maynard@prudential.co.uk
Website: www.prudential.co.uk

Psion PLC
Andrew J Bodenham, Company Secretary
1 Red Place, London W1Y 3RE, United Kingdom
Tel: +44 20 7317 4100 **Fax:** +44 20 7317 4266
Website: www.psion.com

PT Multimedia
Isabelle Sequeira, Head of Legal Dept
Rua Andrade Corvo, No. 30, 1065 Lisbon, Portugal
Tel: +351 21 500 1754 **Fax:** +351 21 500 5585
Email: isabelle.v.sequeira@telecom.pt
Website: www.ptmultimedia.pt

PUBLICIS SA
Alain Schwindenhammer, General Counsel
133 Champs-Elysees, 75008 Paris, France
Tel: +33 1 44 43 70 00 **Fax:** +33 1 44 43 75 47
Email: a.schwin@gps.publicis.fr
Website: www.publicis.fr

Publigroupe SA
Jean-Denis Briod, (Secretary to the board)
Avenue des Toises 12, CH-1002 Lausanne, Switzerland
Tel: +41 21 3177111 **Fax:** +41 21 3177555
Email: jdbriod@publigroupe.com
Website: www.publigroupe.com

Publix Super Markets Inc
John Attaway, General Counsel
PO Box 407, Lakeland FL 33802-0407, USA
Tel: +1 863 688 1188 **Fax:** +1 863 284 5532
Website: www.publix.com

Qualcomm
Steve Altman, General Counsel
5775 Morehouse Drive, San Diego 92121, USA
Tel: +1 858 587 1121 **Fax:** +1 858 658 2110
Website: www.qualcomm.com

Qwest Communications Int'l
Drake Tempest, Executive Vice President & General Counsel
1801 California Street, Suit 50200, Denver 80202, USA
Tel: +1 303 992 1400 **Fax:** +1 303 296 5947
Website: www.qwest.com

Qwest Inc
Charles Russ, General Counsel
1801 California Street, Denver 80202, USA
Tel: +1 303 391 8300 **Fax:** +1 303 296 2916
Website: www.uswest.com

QXL.Com PLC
Anisa Dhanji, Company Secretary
Floor 4 & 10, Landmark House, Hammersmith Bridge Road, London W6 9DP, United Kingdom
Tel: +44 20 8962 7100 **Fax:** +44 20 8962 7303
Email: anisa_dhanji@QXL.com
Website: www.qxl.com

Railtrack Group PLC
Simon Osborne, Company Secretary & Solicitor
Railtrack House, Euston Square, London NW1 2EE, United Kingdom
Tel: +44 20 7557 8000 **Fax:** +44 20 7557 9000
Website: www.railtrack.co.uk

Randstad Holding NV
Marianne Scholten, General Counsel
Diemermere 25, 1112 TC Diemen, Netherlands
Tel: +31 20 569 5623/91 **Fax:** +31 20 5 695 855
Email: marianne_scholten@randstad.nl
Website: www.randstadholding.com

RAS - Riunione Adriatica di Sicurta
Carlo Parenti, General Counsel
Corso Italia 23, 20122 Milan, Italy
Tel: +39 02 7216 2371 **Fax:** +39 02 7216 5025
Email: carlo.parenti@rasnet.it
Website: www.ras.it

RealDanmark (formerly Kapital Holding)
Bjarne Lau Pederson, General Counsel
Silbegede 8, DK-1113 Copenhagen, Denmark
Tel: +45 433 070 50 **Fax:** +45 4330 7068
Website: www.realdanmark.dk

Reckitt & Benckiser PLC
Jonathan Jones, Senior Vice President, Global Legal Affairs / Company Secretary
67 Alma Road, Windsor SL4 3HD, United Kingdom
Tel: +44 1753 835 835 **Fax:** +44 1753 835 830
Website: www.reckittbenckiser.com

Red Hat
Mark Webbink, General Counsel
2600 Meridian Pkwy, Durham 27713, USA
Tel: +1 919 547 0012 **Fax:** +1 919 547 0024
Email: mwebbink@redhat.com
Website: www.redhat.com

Reed Elsevier
Ann Joseph, Head of Legal
25 Victoria St., London SW1H 0EX, United Kingdom
Tel: +44 20 7222 8420 **Fax:** +44 20 7227 5799
Website: www.reed.co.uk

Renault SA
Christian Husson, Directeur Juridque
13 - 15 Quai le Gallo, Billancourt Cedex, 92109 Boulogne, France
Tel: +33 1 41 04 62 72 **Fax:** +33 1 41 04 68 18
Email: christian.husson@renault.com
Website: www.renault.com

Rentokil Initial PLC
Robert Ward-Jones, Company Secretary and Legal Director
Rentokil House, Garland Road, East Grinstead RH19 2DR, United Kingdom
Tel: +44 1342 833 022 **Fax:** +44 1342 835 672/410 637
Email: rward-jones@rentokil-initial.co.uk
Website: www.rentokil-initial.com

Repsol YPF
Rafael Piqueras, Head of Legal Department
P° de la Castellana, 278-280, 28046 Madrid, Spain
Tel: +34 91 348 8172 **Fax:** +34 91 348 9494
Email: rpiqueras@repsol-ypf.com
Website: www.repsol-ypf.com

Reuters Group
Stephen Mitchell, General Counsel
85 Fleet Street, London EC4P 4AJ, United Kingdom
Tel: +44 20 7250 1122 **Fax:** +44 20 7542 5896
Email: stephen.mitchell@reuters.com
Website: www.reuters.com

Rexel
Martine Coiquaud, General Counsel
25 rue de Clichy, 75009 Paris, France
Tel: +33 1 42 85 85 00 **Fax:** +33 1 42 85 09 98
Website: www.rexel.com

Rhodia
Chris Beasley, Director of Legal
Oak House, Reeds Crescent, Watford WD1 1QH, United Kingdom
Tel: +44 1923 485513 **Fax:** +44 1923 485928
Email: chris.beasley@eu.rhodia.com
Website: www.rhodia.com

Richemont AG (Cie Financiere)
Albert Kaufmann, Corporate Counsel
Rigistrasse 2, CH-6300 Zug, Switzerland
Tel: +41 41 710 33 22 **Fax:** +41 41 711 71 02
Email: albertkaufmann.com
Website: www.richemont.com

Ricoh Company Ltd
Masamitsu Sakurai, President
15-5 Minami-Aoyama, 1-chome, Minato-ku, Tokyo 107-8544, Japan
Tel: +81 3 3479 3111 **Fax:** +81 3 3403 1578
Website: www.ricoh.com

Rio Tinto PLC
Charles Lawton, Legal Adviser
6 St James's Square, London SW1Y 4LD, United Kingdom
Tel: +44 20 7753 2345 **Fax:** +44 20 7753 2197
Email: Charles.Lawton@riotinto.co.uk
Website: www.riotinto.com

RMC Group PLC
Michael Collins, Head of UK Legal Department
RMC House, High St, Feltham TW13 4HA, United Kingdom
Tel: +44 1932 568 833 **Fax:** +44 20 8751 6439
Email: collinsm@rmc-readymix.co.uk
Website: www.rmc-group.com

Roche Holding Ltd
Bruno Maier, Head of Corporate Law
Grenzacherstrasse 124, CH-4070 Basle, Switzerland
Tel: +41 61 688 11 11 **Fax:** +41 61 688 13 96
Email: bruno.maier@roche.com
Website: www.roche.com

ROHM Co Ltd
Masahiro Yamamoto, Manager, Legal Affairs Division
21 Saiin mizosaki cho, Ukyo-ku, Kyoto 615 8585, Japan
Tel: +81 75 311 2121 **Fax:** +81 75 315 0172
Website: www.rohm.co.jp

Rolls-Royce PLC
Brian Baker, General Counsel
65 Buckingham Gate, London SW1E 6AT, United Kingdom
Tel: +44 20 7222 9020 **Fax:** +44 20 7227 9170
Email: brian.baker@rolls-royce.com
Website: www.rolls-royce.com

Rolo Banca 1473 SpA
Michele Faldella, General Counsel
Via Zamboni 20, 40126 Bologna, Italy
Tel: +390 51 640 8111 **Fax:** +390 51 640 7082
Website: www.rolobanca.it

Royal & Sun Alliance Insurance Group PLC
David Morgan, Head of Legal (UK Operations)
Leadenhall Court, 1 Leadenhall Street, London EC3V 1PP, United Kingdom
Tel: +44 20 7337 5141/7283 9000 **Fax:** +44 20 7337 5133
Email: john.berg@rsa12.royalsun.com
Website: www.royalsunalliance.com

Royal Bank of Canada
David Allgood, Executive Vice-President and General Counsel
1 Place Ville Marie, Montreal H3B 3A9, Canada
Tel: +1 416 974 9241 **Fax:** +1 416 974 4555
Website: www.royalbank.com

Royal Bank of Scotland Group PLC
Derek Arnott, Head of Group Legal Services
PO Box 31, 42 St Andrew Square, Edinburgh EH2 2YE, United Kingdom
Tel: +44 131 5232412 **Fax:** +44 131 557 2927
Website: www.rbs.co.uk. / www.royalbankscot.co.uk

Royal Numico NV
JHC van Der Ven, General Counsel
Rokkeveenseweg 49, 2712 PJ Zoetemeer, Netherlands
Tel: +31 79 353 9000 **Fax:** +31 79 353 9671
Website: www.numico.com

RTL (formerly Audiofina)
Vincent de Dorlodot, General Counsel
45 Boulevard Pierre Frieden, L-1543 Luxembourg, Luxembourg
Tel: +352 42 142 5090 **Fax:** +352 42 142 2753
Email: vincent.de.dorlodot@rtl-group.com
Website: www.rtl-group.com

RWE AG
Georg Müller, General Counsel
Opernplatz 1, D-45128 Essen, Germany
Tel: +49 201 1200 **Fax:** +49 201 12 15 283
Email: monica.braun@rwe.de.com
Website: www.rwe-dea.de

Safeway Inc
Robert A Gordon, Senior Vice-President and General Counsel
5918 Stoneridge Mall Road, Pleasanton CA 94588-3229, USA
Tel: +1 925 467 3000 **Fax:** +1 925 467 3321
Website: www.safeway.com

Safeway PLC
John Kinch, Company Secretary
Safeway Stores PLC, 6 Millington Road, Hayes UB3 4AY, United Kingdom
Tel: +44 20 8848 8744 **Fax:** +44 20 8756 1069
Website: www.safeway.co.uk

Sage Group PLC
Nick Cooper, Head of Legal and Group Secretary
Sage House, Benton Park Road, Newcastle upon Tyne NE7 7LZ, United Kingdom
Tel: +44 191 255 3000 **Fax:** +44 191 255 0306
Website: www.sage.com

SAGEM SA
Dominique Noguera, Head of Legal
27 Rue Leblanc, 75512 Paris Cedex 15, France
Tel: +33 1 40 70 63 63 **Fax:** +33 1 47 20 39 46
Email: dominique.noguera@sagem.com
Website: www.sagem.com

Saint Gobain SA
Bernard Field, General Counsel
Les Miroirs, 18 Avenue d'Alsace, Cedex 27, La Défense Cedex, 92096 Paris, France
Tel: +33 1 47 62 30 00 **Fax:** +33 1 47 62 31 69
Email: bernard.field@saint-gobain.com
Website: www.saint-gobain.com

SAirgroup
Karin Anderegg Bigger, General Counsel and Secretary
Legal Affairs, CH-8058 Zurich, Switzerland
Tel: +41 1 812 56 03 **Fax:** +41 1 812 90 71
Email: kandereg@sairgroup.com
Website: www.sairgroup.com

Samsung Electronics (UK) Ltd
John Slider, Deputy Managing Director
Samsung Avenue, Samsung Wynyard Park, Billingham TS22 5SS, United Kingdom
Tel: +44 1740 660000
Website: www.samsungelectronics.co.uk

Sandvik AB
Bo Severin, General Counsel
Storgatan 2, SE-811 81 Sandviken, Sweden
Tel: +46 26 261081 **Fax:** +46 26 261086
Email: bo.severin@sandvik.com
Website: www.sandvik.com

Sanofi-Synthelabo
Jean-Pierre Kerjouan, General Counsel
174 Avenue de France, Cedex, 75013 Paris, France
Tel: +33 1 53 77 42 30 **Fax:** +33 1 53 77 40 85
Email: jean-pierre.kerjouan@sanofi-synthelabo.com
Website: www.sanofi-synthelabo.fr

Sanwa Bank Ltd
Kaneo Muromachi, President and Chief Executive Officer
3-5-6, Fushimi-machi, 3-chome, Chuo-ku, Osaka 541-8530, Japan
Tel: +81 6 6206 8111 **Fax:** +81 3 3215 1776
Website: www.sanwabank.co.jp

SAP AG
Michael Junge, General Counsel
Neurottstrasse 16, Postfach 1461, D-69190 Walldorf, Germany
Tel: +49 62 27 74 74 74 **Fax:** +49 62 27 75 75 75
Email: info.germany@sap.com
Website: www.sap.com

Sara Lee Corporation
Roderick Palmore, Head of Legal
3 First National Plaza, Chicago IL 60602, USA
Tel: +1 312 726 2600 **Fax:** +1 312 345 5706
Website: www.saralee.com

Saudi Basic Industries Corporation (SABIC) Marketing Company Ltd
Mohammed Yamnie, Director of Legal Dept
Dubab Street, Riyadh 11422, Saudi Arabia
Tel: +966 1 401 2033 **Fax:** +966 1 401 2045

SBC Communications Inc
JD Ellis, General Counsel
175 E. Houston, San Antonio TX 78205, USA
Tel: +1 210 821 4105 **Fax:** +1 210 351 2699
Website: www.sbc.com

Scania CV AB
Carl Ribn, Senior Vice-President and General Counsel
Jarnag 33, 15187 Sodertalje, Sweden
Tel: +46 8 55 38 10 00 **Fax:** +46 8 55 38 10 37
Email: maja.sondberg@scania.com
Website: www.scania.com

Schering AG
Horst Krüger, General Counsel
Muellerstrasse 178, D-13342 Berlin, Germany
Tel: +49 30 468 12799 **Fax:** +49 30 468 14086
Email: horst.krueger@schering.de
Website: www.schering.de

Schering-Plough Corporation
Joseph C Connors, Executive Vice-President and General Counsel
2000 Galloping Hill Road, Kenilworth 07033-0530, USA
Tel: +1 908 298 4000 **Fax:** +1 908 298 1960
Website: www.sch-plough.com

Schlumberger Limited
James Gunderson, General Counsel
277 Park Ave., New York 10172-0266, USA
Tel: +1 212 350 9400 **Fax:** +1 212 350 9440
Email: gunderson@new-york.sl.slb.com
Website: www.slb.com

Schneider Electric SA
Pedro Salazar, Directeur Juridique
Schneider Electric SA, 43/45 Boulevard Franklin Roosevelt, 92500 Rueil Mal Maison, France
Tel: +33 1 41 29 70 00 **Fax:** +33 1 41 29 71 97
Website: www.scheider-electric.com

Schroders Investment Managment Limited
Francis W Neate, Group Legal Director
Schroder Property Investment Management Ltd, 31 Gresham Street, London EC2V 7QA, United Kingdom
Tel: +44 20 7658 7447 **Fax:** +44 20 7658 3960
Website: www.schroders.com/www.schroder.co.uk

Scottish & Newcastle PLC
Andrew S Vellani, Group Legal Director
33 Ellersly Road, Edinburgh EH12 6HX, United Kingdom
Tel: +44 131 528 2000 **Fax:** +44 131 528 2311
Email: andrew.vellani@scottish-newcastle.co.uk
Website: www.scottish-newcastle.com

Scottish & Southern Energy PLC
Ian Manson, Director of Legal Services
200 Dunkeld Road, Perth PH1 3AQ, United Kingdom
Tel: +44 1738 456000 **Fax:** +44 1738 456520
Email: ian.manson@scottish-southern.co.uk
Website: www.scottish-southern.co.uk

Scottish Power PLC
James Stanley, Legal Director
1 Atlantic Quay, Glasgow G2 8SP, United Kingdom
Tel: +44 141 6364 514 **Fax:** +44 141 566 4642
Email: james.stanley@scottishpower.plc.uk
Website: www.scottishpower.com

Sears Roebuck & Co
Anastasia Kelly, Executive Vice-President, General Counsel and Secretary
3333 Beverly Road, Hoffman Estates IL 60179, USA
Tel: +1 847 286 2500 **Fax:** +1 847 286 8351
Website: www.sears.com

Seat Pagine Gialle Spa Torino
Alfredo Bonfiglio, Head of Legal
Via Aurelio Saffi 18, 101 38 Turin, Italy
Tel: +39 011 43 51 **Fax:** +39 0114 352 642
Email: alfredo.bonfiglio@seat.it
Website: www.seat.it

SEC
Christoph Lambot, Financial Analyst & Controller
75 Route de Longwy, L-8080 Bertrange, Luxembourg
Tel: +352 45 71 45 1 **Fax:** +352 27 752 331
Email: christophlambot@tele2.com
Website: www.sec.lu

Secom Co Ltd
Toshitaka Sugimachi, President and Representative Director
Shinjuku Normura Building, 26-2, Nishi-Shinjuku, 1-chome, Shinjuku-ku 163-0555, Japan
Tel: +81 3 5381 5642
Email: info@secom.co.jp
Website: www.secom.co.jp

Securitas AB
Mats Uebel, Company Lawyer
Lindhagensplan 70, PO Box 12307, S-18229 Stockholm, Sweden
Tel: +46 8 657 74 00 **Fax:** +46 8 657 70 72
Email: mats.uebel@securitas.se
Website: www.securitasgroup.com

SEMA Group PLC
Nick Deeming, Chief Legal Counsel and Company Secretary
233 High Holborn, London WC1V 7DJ, United Kingdom
Tel: +44 20 7830 4225 **Fax:** +44 20 7830 4206
Email: nick.deeming@sema.co.uk
Website: www.semagroup.com

Serono SA
Francois Naef, General Counsel
Chemin des Mines 15bis, PO Box 54, CH1211 Geneva 20, Switzerland
Tel: +41 22 739 3000 **Fax:** +41 22 739 3070
Email: francois.naef@serono.com
Website: www.serono.com

Seven-Eleven Japan
Toshifumi Suzuki, Chairman & Chief Executive Officer
1-4, Shibakoen, 4-chome, Minato-ku, Tokyo 105-0011, Japan
Tel: +81 3 3459 3711 **Fax:** +81 3 3438 3724
Website: www.sej.co.jp

Severn Trent Water Ltd
Michael Knight, Company Solicitor
2297 Coventry Road, Birmingham B26 3PU, United Kingdom
Tel: +44 121 722 4951 **Fax:** +44 121 722 4228
Email: michael.knight@severntrent.co.uk
Website: www.severn-trent.com

Sharp Corporation
Katsuhiko Machida, President & Chief Executive Officer
22-22 Nagaike-cho, Abeno-ku, Osaka 545-8522, Japan
Tel: +81 6 6621 1221 **Fax:** +81 6 6627 1759
Website: www.sharp-world.com

Shell Transport & Trading Co PLC
Pieter Folmer, Legal Director
Shell Centre, York Road, London SE1 7NA, United Kingdom
Tel: +44 20 7934 5113 **Fax:** +44 20 7934 7043
Website: www.shell.com

Shin-Etsu Chemical Co Ltd
Chihiro Kanagawa, Chief Executive Officer - President
2-6-1 Ohtemachi 2-chome, Chiyoda-ku, Tokyo 100-0004, Japan
Tel: +81 3 3246 5011 **Fax:** +81 3 3246 5350
Website: www.shinetsu.co.jp

Shire Pharmaceuticals Group PLC
Neil Harris, Head of Legal Affairs
East Anton, Andover SP10 5RG, United Kingdom
Tel: +44 1264 333 455 **Fax:** +44 1264 333460
Website: www.shiregroup.com

Shop At Home Inc
George J Phillips, Executive Vice President & General Counsel
5388 Hickory Hollow Parkway, Nashville 37230-5249, USA
Tel: +1 615 263 8090 **Fax:** +1 615 263 8911
Email: GPHILLIPS@SATH.com
Website: www.isshopathome.com

Sidel
Francis Olivier, Head of Legal
Avenue de la Patrouille de France, Octeville sur Mer - BP 204, 76 053 Le Havre Cedex, France
Tel: +33 2 32 85 86 87 **Fax:** +33 2 32 85 81 00
Email: secretariat_general@fra.sidel_com
Website: www.sidel.com

Siebel Systems
Kevin Johnson, General Counsel
2207 Bridgepionte Parkway, San Mateo 94404, USA
Tel: +1 650 295 5000 **Fax:** +1 650 295 5116
Email: kjohnson@sibel.com
Website: www.siebel.com

Siemens AG
Albrecht Schafer, Head of Legal
Wittelsbacherplatz 2, 80333 Munich, Germany
Tel: +49 89636 33537 **Fax:** +49 89 636 32477
Email: albrecht.schaefer@zf.siemens.de
Website: www.siemens.de

Singapore Airlines Ltd
Mathew Samuel, Senior Vice President, Corporate Affairs
Airline House, 25 Airline Road, Singapore 819829, Singapore
Tel: +65 541 4010 **Fax:** +65 545 4231
Website: www.singaporeair.com

Singapore Telecom
Lee Hsien Yang, President and Chief Executive Officer
31 Exeter Road, Comcentre, Singapore 239732, Singapore
Tel: +65 838 3388 **Fax:** +65 738 3769
Website: www.singtel.com

SK Telecom
Cho Jung-Nam, President
99 Seorin-dong, Jongro-Gu, Seoul 110-110, South Korea
Tel: +82 2 2121 2114 **Fax:** +82 2 2121 3964
Website: www.skelecom.com

Skandia Insurance Company Ltd
Jan-Mikael Bexhed, General Counsel and Company Secretary
Sveavagen 44, S-10350 Stockholm, Sweden
Tel: +46 8 788 2500 **Fax:** +46 8 788 1680
Website: www.skandia.se

Skandinaviska Enskilda Banken AB (publ)
Ulf Thornander, General Counsel and Company Secretary
SEB Group, Kungsträdgårdsgatan 8, S-10640 Stockholm, Sweden
Tel: +46 8 763 8000 **Fax:** +46 8 611 9425
Email: ulf.thornander@seb.se
Website: www.seb.se

Skanska AB
Einar Lundgren, General Counsel
Klarabergsviadukten 90, PO Box 1195, SE-111 91 Stockholm, Sweden
Tel: +46 8 753 88 00 **Fax:** +46 8 753 3752
Email: einar.lundgren@skanska.se
Website: www.skanska.com

SMC Corporation
Yoshiyuki Yakada, President
1-16-4, Shimbashi, Minato-ku, Tokyo 105, Japan
Tel: +81 3 3502 8271 **Fax:** +81 3 3508 2480
Website: www.smcworld.com

Smith & Nephew PLC
Michael G Parson, Group Company Secretary & Legal Adviser
Heron House, 15 Adam Street, London WC2N 6LA, United Kingdom
Tel: +44 20 7401 7646 **Fax:** +44 20 7930 3353
Email: michael.parson@smith-nephew.com
Website: www.smith-nephew.com

Smiths Group PLC
Alan Smith, Solicitor
765 Finchley Road, Childs Hill, London NW11 8DS, United Kingdom
Tel: +44 20 8458 3232 **Fax:** +44 20 8458 4380

Société Air France
Jean-Marc Bardy, Vice President, Legal Affairs
45 Rue de Paris, Roissy Cedex, 95747 Paris, France
Tel: +33 1 41 56 78 00 **Fax:** +33 1 41 56 67 19
Email: jmbardy@airfrance.fr
Website: www.airfrance.net

Société Europeene des Satellites
Jacques Noppeney, Legal Affairs Manager
Chateau de Betzdorf, Betzdorf, Luxembourg, L-6815
Tel: +352 710 7251 **Fax:** +352 710 7252 22
Email: jacques_noppeney@scs-astra.com
Website: www.scs-astra.com

Société Générale
Mark Nimmo, Executive Director, Group Legal
SG House, 41 Tower Hill, London EC3N 4SG, United Kingdom
Tel: +44 20 7676 6000 **Fax:** +44 20 7676 8888
Website: www.socgen.com

Sodexho Alliance SA
Yves-Marie Fournis, Head of Legal
3 Avenue Newton, 78180 Montigny le Bretonneux, France
Tel: +33 1 30 85 75 00 **Fax:** +33 1 30 85 50 05
Email: yvesmarie.fournis@sodexho-alliance.fr
Website: www.sodexho.com

Softbank Corporation
Masayoshi Son, President and Chief Executive Officer
24-1 Nihonbashi-Hakozakicho, Chuo-ku, Tokyo 103-8501, Japan
Tel: +81 3 5642 8005 **Fax:** +81 3 5641 3401
Website: www.softbank.co.jp

Solectron Corp
Robert Aeschliman, General Counsel
847 Gibraltar Drive, Building 5, Milpitas 95035, USA
Tel: +1 408 957 8500 **Fax:** +1 408 956 6096
Email: robertaeschliman@ca.slr.com
Website: www.solectron.com

Solvay SA
Jacques Levy-Morelle, Corporate Secretary & General Counsel
Rue de Prince Albert 33, Ixelles, B-1050 Brussels, Belgium
Tel: +32 2 509 61 11 **Fax:** +32 2 509 66 17
Email: jacques.levymorelle@solvay.com
Website: www.solvay.com

Sonae SGPS
Luzia Gomes Ferreira, Head of Legal
Lugar do Espido, Via Norte, PO Box 1011, 4471 Maia Codex, Portugal
Tel: +351 22 940 4786 **Fax:** +351 22 940 4722
Email: ls@sonnae.pt
Website: www.sonae.pt

Sonera
Maire Leitinen, Group General Counsel
Teollisuuskatu 15,, PO Box 106, 000510 Helsinki, Finland
Tel: +358 20401 **Fax:** +358 2040 58521
Email: maire.leitinen@sonera.com
Website: www.sonera.com

Sony Corporation
Nobuyuki Idei, President and Chief Executive Officer
7-35, Kitashinagawa 6-Chome, Shinagawa-ku, Tokyo 141-0001, Japan
Tel: +81 3 5448 2111 **Fax:** +81 3 5448 2244
Website: www.world.sony.com

South African Breweries
Andrew OC Tonkinson, Group Company Secretary
2 Jan Smuts Avenue, Braamfontein, PO Box 1099, Johannesburg 2000, South Africa
Tel: +27 11 407 1700 **Fax:** +27 11 339 1830
Website: www.sabplc.com

Southern Company
AW Dahlberg, Chief Executive
270 Peachtree Street NW, Atlanta GA 30303, USA
Tel: +1 404 506 5000 **Fax:** +1 404 506 0455
Website: www.southernco.com

Spirent PLC
Michael Arnaouti, Company Secretary
Spirent House, Crawley Business Quarter, Fleming Way, Crawley RH10 2QL, United Kingdom
Tel: +44 1293 528 888 **Fax:** +44 1293 541905
Website: www.bowthorpe.com

Sprint Fon Group
Richard Devlin, General Counsel
2330 Shawnee Mission Pwy., Westwood KS 66205, USA
Tel: +1 913 624 8440 **Fax:** +1 913 624 8426
Email: richard.devlin@mail.sprint.com
Website: www.sprint.com

Sprint PCS Group
Joseph Gensheimer, General Counsel PCS
4900 Main, Kansas City 64112, USA
Tel: +1 816 559 2500 **Fax:** +1 816 559 1498
Email: jgensh01@sprintspectrum.com
Website: www.sprintpcs.com

Stagecoach Hldgs PLC
Derek Scott, Company Secretary
10 Dunkeld Rd, Perth PH1 5TW, United Kingdom
Tel: +44 1738 442 111 **Fax:** +44 1738 643 648
Email: dscott@stagecoachholdings.com
Website: www.stagecoachholdings.com

Standard Chartered PLC
Martin Hayman, Head of Legal
1 Aldermanbury Square, London EC2V 7SB, United Kingdom
Tel: +44 20 7280 7021 **Fax:** +44 20 7280 7112
Email: martin.hayman@uk.standard.chartered.co.uk
Website: www.standardchartered.com

STMicroelectronics
Pierre Ollivier, Vice President Legal Corporate & IP
20 Route de Pré-bois, ICC Bldg., CH-1215 Geneva 15, Switzerland
Tel: +41 22 929 5877 **Fax:** +41 22 929 5878
Email: pierre.ollivier@st.com
Website: www.st.com

Stora Enso Oyj
Jyrki Kurkinen, Senior Vice President Legal Affairs General Counsel
Kanavaranta 1, 00101 Helsinki, Finland
Tel: +358 204 6131 **Fax:** +358 204 621 471
Website: www.storaenso.com

STRATEC Medical
Helen Schaub, LL.M, Manager of Legal Affairs
Eimattstrasse 3, CH-4436 Oberdorf, Switzerland
Tel: +41 61 956 61 11 **Fax:** +41 61 965 66 00
Website: www.stratec.com

Suez Lyonnaise des Eaux
Patrice Herbet, Head of Legal
1 Rue d'Astorg, 75008 Paris, France
Tel: +33 1 40 06 65 58 **Fax:** +33 1 40 06 66 22
Website: www.suez-lyonnaise-eaux.fr

Sumitomo Corporation
Mr Hirasawa, Head of Legal
5-33 Kitahama 4-chome, Cho-ku, Osaka 540-8666, Japan
Tel: +81 6 6220 6000 **Fax:** +81 6 6220 7714
Website: www.sumitomocorp.co.jp

Sun Microsystems
Michael Morris, General Counsel
901 San Antonio Road, Palo Alto CA 94303, USA
Tel: +1 650 960 1300 **Fax:** +1 650 336 0530
Email: michael.morris@corp.sun.com
Website: www.sun.com

Sunevision Holdings Limited
Jeremy Cheng, Legal Counsel
21 Sun Hung Kai Centre, 30 Harbour Road, Wanchai, 1017, Hong Kong
Tel: +852 2802 0022 **Fax:** +852 2627 9299
Website: www.sunevision.com

SunTrust Banks
JW Spiegel, Executive VP
303 Peachtree Street, NE, Atlanta GA 30308-3201, USA
Tel: +1 404 588 8594 **Fax:** +1 404 588 7495
Email: john.speigel@suntrust.com
Website: www.suntrust.com

Surgutneftegaz
Ludmila Loginovskaya, General Counsel
Kukuevitskogo 1, Surgut, 628-415 Tyumen, Russia
Tel: +7 095 928 9895/+7 346 2 466 424 **Fax:** +7 346 233 3235
Website: www.surgutneftegas.ru

Svenska Cellulosa Aktiebolaget (SCA)
Anders Nyberg, General Counsel
Stureplan 3, PO Box 7827, 10397 Stockholm, Sweden
Tel: +46 8788 5100 **Fax:** +46 8 678 2324
Email: anders.nyberg@hq.sca.se
Website: www.sca.se

Swatch Group AG
Hanspeter Rentsch, General Counsel, Senior Vice President
Faubourg du Lac 6, CH-2501 Biel, Switzerland
Tel: +41 32 343 68 11 **Fax:** +41 32 343 6923
Website: www.swatchgroup.com

Swiss Life Insurance & Pension Co
Hans Peter Conrad, Director of Legal Services
General Guisan-Quai 40, CH-8002 Zurich, Switzerland
Tel: +41 1 284 3311 **Fax:** +41 1 284 6566
Email: hanspeter.conrad@swisslife.ch
Website: www.swisslife.com

Swiss Reinsurance Company
Markus Diethelm, General Counsel
Mythenquai 50/60, PO Box 8022, CH-8022 Zurich, Switzerland
Tel: +41 1 285 21 21 **Fax:** +41 1 285 34 05
Email: markusu_diethelm@swissre.com
Website: www.swissre.com

Swisscom AG
Jürg Rötheli, General Counsel
Alte Tiefenau Strasse 6, 3050 Berne, Switzerland
Tel: +41 31 3421111 **Fax:** +41 31 3427608
Email: juerg.roetheli@swisscom.com
Website: www.swisscom.com

Sycamore Networks
Margaret Cohen, Senior Corporate Counsel
150 Apollo Drive, Chelmsford 01824, USA
Tel: +1 978 250 2900 **Fax:** +1 978 256 3434
Website: www.sycamorenet.com

Sydkraft AB
Ulla Karin Jonsson, Head of Legal Affairs
Carl Gustafs Vag 1, 205 09 Malmo, Sweden
Tel: +46 40 25 50 00 **Fax:** +46 40 970116
Email: ulla-karin.jonsson@sydkraft.se
Website: www.sydkraft.se

Sysco Corporation
Michael C Nichols, Head of Legal
1390 Enclave Parkway, Houston TX 77077-2099, USA
Tel: +1 281 584 1390 **Fax:** +1 281 584 2721
Email: nichols.michael@corp.sysco.com
Website: www.syscosmart.com

Taiwan Semiconductor Manufacturing Company Ltd (TSMC)
Kok-Choo Chen, General Counsel
No. 121, Park Avenue III, Science-Based Industrial Park, Hsin-Chu , Taiwan
Tel: +886 35 780 221 **Fax:** +886 3578 1545
Email: kc_chen@tsmc.com.tw
Website: www.tsmc.com.tw

Takeda Chemical Industries Ltd
Teruji Ono, General Manager, Legal Department
1-1 Doshomachi 4-chome, Chuo-Ku, Osaka 540-8645, Japan
Tel: +81 6 6204 2111 **Fax:** +81 6 6204 2880
Website: www.takeda.co.jp

Takefuji Corporation
Kunio Kotaki, Senior Managing Director
15-1, Nishi-Shinjuku, 8-chome, Shinjuku-ku, Tokyo 160-8654, Japan
Tel: +81 3 33658000
Website: www.takefuji.co.jp

Target Corporation
James Hale, General Counsel
777 Nicollet Mall, Minneapolis 55402-2055, USA
Tel: +1 612 370 6948 **Fax:** +1 612 370 5502
Email: jim.hale@target.com
Website: www.target.com

Tate & Lyle PLC
Robert Gibber, General Counsel
Sugar Quay, Lower Thames Street, London EC3R 6DQ, United Kingdom
Tel: +44 20 7626 6525 **Fax:** +44 20 7623 5213
Email: robertgibber@tateandlyle.com
Website: www.tateandlyle.com

TDK
Hajime Sawabe, President and Chief Executive Officer
1-13-1 Nihonbeshi, Chuo-ku, Tokyo 103-8272, Japan
Tel: +81 3 5201 7102 **Fax:** +81 3 5201 7114
Website: www.tdk.co.jp

Tele 2 AB
Jan Tjermell, Head Jurist
Box 62 164, 94 Kista, Sweden
Tel: +46 8 562 64000 **Fax:** +46 8 562 64200
Email: Jan.Tjermell@tele2.se
Website: www.tele2.se

Tele Danmark A/S
Gitte Grace Forsberg, Senior Vice President and General Counsel
Nørregade 21, DK-0900 Copenhagen, Denmark
Tel: +45 33 43 76 16 **Fax:** +45 33 43 76 88
Email: gf@tdk.dk
Website: www.teledanmark.dk

Telecel Communications
P Roberti, Chief Financial Officer
Rua Tomas Fonseca, Torre A-14, 1600 Lisbon, Portugal
Tel: +351 21 722 50 00 **Fax:** +351 21 721 38 78
Website: www.telecel.pt

Telecom Italia Group
Pier Paulo Cotone, General Counsel
41 Corso D'Italia, 00198 Rome, Italy
Tel: +39 06 36881 **Fax:** +39 06 3688 2333
Website: www.tim.it

Telecom Italia Mobile (TIM)
Pier Paulo Cortone, General Counsel
Telecom Italia Mobile (TIM), 41 Corso d'Italia, 00198 Roma, Italy
Tel: +39 06 36881 **Fax:** +39 06 3688233
Website: www.tim.it

Telefonaktiebolaget LM Ericsson
Carl Olof Blomquist, Senior Vice President and General Counsel
Telefonvagen 30, 126 25 Stockholm, Sweden
Tel: +46 8 719 8250 **Fax:** +46 8 719 9527
Email: carlolof.blomqvist@lme.ericsson.se
Website: www.ericsson.com

Telefonica De Espana SA
Heliodoro Alcaraz, General Counsel
Gran Via 28, 28013 Madrid, Spain
Tel: +34 91 584 0306 **Fax:** +34 91 580 5931
Website: www.telefonica.es

Telefonos de Mexico SA
Javier Montagon, Head of Legal
Parque Via 190, Colonia Cuauhtemoc, 06599 D F Mexico, Mexico
Tel: +52 5 222 2519 **Fax:** +52 5 592 8833
Website: www.telmex.com.mx

Telekom Malaysia Berhad
Khir Bin Abdul Rahman, Chief Executive
Tingkat 2, Jalan Pantai Baharu, Kuala Lumpur 50672, Malaysia
Tel: +60 3 208 9494 **Fax:** +60 3 755 4747
Website: www.telekom.com.my

Telekomunikacja Polska SA (TP SA)
Jacek Kosuniak, Head of Management Board Legal Services
3 Swietokrzyska, 00945 Warsaw, Poland
Tel: +48 22 661 7232 **Fax:** +48 22 827 8689
Website: www.tpsa.pl

Telewest Communications PLC
Simon Read, Director of Legal Services
35 Old Queen Street, London SW1A 9JA, United Kingdom
Tel: +44 1483 750900 **Fax:** +44 1483 295 183
Email: simon.read@telewest.co.uk
Website: www.telewest.co.uk

Tellabs
Carol Gavin, General Counsel
4951 Indiana Avenue, Lisle IL 60532, USA
Tel: +1 630 378 8800 **Fax:** +1 630 852 7346
Email: carol.gavin@tellabs.com
Website: www.tellabs.com

Telstra Corporation Limited
Bruce Akhurst, Group Managing Director, Legal and Regulatory
Level 41, 241/2 Exhibition Street, Melbourne VIC 3000, Australia
Tel: +61 3 9634 3128 **Fax:** +61 3 9634 2358
Email: bruce.j.akhurst@team.telstra.com
Website: www.telstra.co.au

Tenet Healthcare
Christi R Salzbach, Head of Legal
PO Box 31907, Santa Barbara CA 93130, USA
Tel: +1 805 563 7011 **Fax:** +1 805 563 6857
Email: christi.salzbach@tenethealth.com
Website: www.tenethealth.com

Terra Networks
Cristina Lamana, Head of Legal
Via de las Dos Castillas, 33 Complejo Atica, Edificio 1, Pozuelo de Alarcon, 28223 Madrid, Spain
Tel: +34 91 452 3000 **Fax:** +34 91 452 3147
Email: cristana.lamana@corp.terra.com
Website: www.terra.es

Tesco Stores PLC
John Bailey, Company Secretary
Tesco House, PO Box 18, Delamare Road, Waltham Cross, Cheshunt EN8 9SL, United Kingdom
Tel: +44 1992 632222 **Fax:** +44 1992 630794
Email: johnbailey_tesco@hotmail.com
Website: www.tesco.co.uk

Texaco Inc
Deval Patrick, Vice President and General Counsel
2000 Westchester Ave., White Plains NY10650, USA
Tel: +1 914 253 4000 **Fax:** +1 914 253 4477
Email: patricdl@texaco.com
Website: www.texaco.com

Texas Instruments Inc
Joseph Hubach, General Counsel
8505 Forest Lane P.O. Box 660199, Dallas TX 75266-0199, USA
Tel: +1 972 995 3773 **Fax:** +1 972 995 4360
Website: www.ti.com

TF1 - TV FRANCAISE
JM Counillon, Head of Legal Department
1 Quai du Point du Jour, 92656 Boulogne, France
Tel: +33 1 41 41 12 34 **Fax:** +33 1 41 41 21 35
Email: jml@tf1.fr
Website: www.tf1.fr

Thames Water PLC
Peter Taylor, Head of Legal Services
Blake House, Manor Farm Road, Reading RG2 0JN, United Kingdom
Tel: +44 118 939 9259 **Fax:** +44 118 959 3599
Website: www.thames-water.com

The Sakura Bank Ltd
Akishige Okada, Chief Executive - President
3-1 Kudan-Minami 1-chome, Chiyoda-ku, Tokyo 100-8611, Japan
Tel: +81 3 3230 3111 **Fax:** +81 3 3239 1022
Website: www.sakura.co.jp/bank/index-e.htm

Thomson Corporation
Michael S Harris, General Counsel
Metro Centre, One Station Place, Stamford CT 06902, USA
Tel: +1 203 969 8711 **Fax:** +1 203 328 8385
Website: www.thomson.com

Thomson-CSF
Pierre Chareton, General Counsel
173 Boulevard Haussmann, Cedex 08, 75008 Paris, France
Tel: +33 1 53 77 80 00
Website: www.thomson-csf.com

Thüga AG
Bernd Rudolph, Head of Legal
Mandlstrasse 3, D-80802 Munich, Germany
Tel: +49 89 3 81 97 0 **Fax:** +49 893 819 7511
Email: rudolph@thuega.de
Website: www.thuega.de

Thus PLC
David Macleod, Company Secretary
Dalmore House, 310 St Vincent Street, Glasgow G2 5BB, United Kingdom
Tel: +44 141 567 1234 **Fax:** +44 141 566 3010
Website: www.let-it-be-thus.com.

Thyssen Krupp Materials & Services AG
Jörg Lacher, Senior Legal Counsel
Thyssen Trade Centre, Hans-Gunther-Sohl-Str 1, D-40235 Düsseldorf, Germany
Tel: +49 211 967 0 **Fax:** +49 211 967 7680
Email: petersen@tkms.thyssenkrupp.de
Website: www.thyssenkrupp.com

TI Group PLC
Stephen Clarke, Director of Legal Affairs
Lambourn Court, Abingdon OX14 1UH, United Kingdom
Tel: +44 1235 705555 **Fax:** +44 1235 705570
Website: www.tigroup.com

TietoEnator Corporation
Jouko Lonka, Head of Legal Dept
Kutojantie 10, PO Box 33, 02361 Espoo, Finland
Tel: +358 9 862 6000 **Fax:** +358 9 8626 3091
Email: jouko.lonka@tietoenator.com
Website: www.tietoenator.com

Tiscali SPA
Massimo Cristofori, Legal Officer
Via Pieprasanta 14, 20141 Milan, Italy
Tel: +39 0230 9011 **Fax:** +39 0230 901 400
Email: cristofori@tiscali.it
Website: www.tiscali.it

TNT Post Group
Jeroen Brabers, General Counsel/Company Secretary
Neptunusstraat 41 - 63, 2132 JA Hoofddorp, Netherlands
Tel: +31 20 500 6371 **Fax:** +3120 500 7984
Email: jeroen.brabers@tntpost.com
Website: www.tpg.nl

Tokai Bank Ltd
Hideo Ogasawara, President Chief Executive Officer
3-21-24 Nishiki Naka-ku, Nagoya 460-8660, Japan
Tel: +81 52 211 0394 **Fax:** +81 52 219 2609
Website: www.csweb.co.jp

Tokio Marine & Fire Insurance Co Ltd
Takehisa Kikuchi, Chief Finance Officer
2-1 Marunouchi, 1-chome, Chiyoda-ku, Tokyo 100-8050, Japan
Tel: +81 3 3212 6211 **Fax:** +81 3 3214 3944
Website: www.tokiomarine.co.jp

Tokyo Electric Power Co Inc
Nobuya Minami, President
Thibiya Chunichi Bldg 1-4, Uchisaiwai-cho, Chiyoda-ku, Tokyo 100-0011, Japan
Tel: +81 3 3501 8111 **Fax:** +81 3 3596 8438
Website: www.tepco.co.jp

Tokyo Electron
Tetsuro Higashi, President and Chief Executive Officer
TSB Broadcast Center, 3-6 Akasaka 5-chome, Minato-ku, Tokyo 107-8481, Japan
Tel: +81 3 5561 7000 **Fax:** +81 3 5561 7400
Website: www.tel.co.jp

Tomkins PLC
Richard Marchant, Administration Director and Company Secretary
East Putney House, 84 Upper Richmond Road, London SW15 2ST, United Kingdom
Tel: +44 20 8871 4544 **Fax:** +44 20 8877 9700
Website: www.tomkins.co.uk

Toronto-Dominion Bank
John White,
Trinton Court, 14-18 Finsbury Square, London EC2A 1DB, United Kingdom
Tel: +44 20 748 8372 **Fax:** +44 20 7638 1042
Website: www.tdbank.ca

Toshiba Corporation
Toshiharu Kobayashi, Head of Legal
1-1-1 Shibaura Minato-ku, Tokyo 105-8001, Japan
Tel: +81 3 3457 2096 **Fax:** +81 3 5444 9202
Email: toshiharu.kobayashi@toshiba.co.jp
Website: www.toshiba.co.jp

TotalFinaElf
Alain-Marc Irrisou, Group General Counsel
2 place de la Coupole, 92400 Courbevoie, France
Tel: +33 1 47 44 45 05 **Fax:** +33 1 47 44 48 76
Website: www.totalfinaelf.com

TPI
Issarachai Decharit, Vice President of Legal Department
Tungmahamek, Sathorn, Bangkok 10120, Thailand
Tel: +66 2 6785050 **Fax:** +66 1 678 5247
Website: www.tpigroup.co.th

Tractebel SA
Jean de Garcia, Head of Legal
Place du Trone 1, B-1000 Brussels, Belgium
Tel: +32 2 510 70 93 **Fax:** +32 2 510 70 97
Email: Jean.deGarcia@tractebel.be
Website: www.tractebel.com

Trend Micro
Chang Ming Jang, President & Chief Executive Officer
Trend Micro, Odakyu Southern Tower, Tenth Floor, 2-2-1 Yoyogi, Shibuya-ku, Tokyo 151-8583, Japan
Tel: +81 3 5334 3600 **Fax:** +81 3 5334 3653

Tribune Co
C Kenney, Vice President/General Counsel and Secretary
435 N. Michigan Ave., Chicago 60611, USA
Tel: +1 312 222 9100 **Fax:** +1 312 222 4206
Email: ckenney@tribune.com
Website: www.tribune.com

Trinity Mirror PLC
Charles Collier-Wright, Group Legal Manager
1 Canada Square, Canary Wharf, London E14 5AP, United Kingdom
Tel: +44 20 7293 3000 **Fax:** +44 20 7293 3613
Website: www.trinity-mirror.co.uk

Turkiye Garanti Bankasi A/S
John Camvehdi, Head of Legal Department
65 Buyukdere Caddesi, Maslak, 80670 Istanbul, Turkey
Tel: +90 212 335 35 35 **Fax:** +90 212 2863301
Email: camv@garantibank.com.tr
Website: www.garantibank.com.tr

Turkiye Is Bankasi AS
Mr Necati, Head of Legal
Pembegal Sok, 4 Levent, 80620 Istanbul, Turkey
Tel: +90 212 316 0000 **Fax:** +90 312 413 9074
Website: www.isbank.net.tr

Tyco Electronics (formerly AMP Inc)
Steve Creager, Head of Legal
PO Box 3608, 441 Friendship Road, Harrisburg PA 17105 - 3608, USA
Tel: +1 717 564 0100 **Fax:** +1 717 592 4022
Website: www.amp.com

Tyco International Ltd
Brian Morose, General Counsel
1 Tyco Park, Exeter NH 03833, USA
Tel: +1 603 778 9700 **Fax:** +1 603 778 7330
Email: bmorose@tyco.com
Website: www.tyco.com

UBS AG
P Roth, Group General Council
Bahnhofstrasse 45, CH 8098 Zurich, Switzerland
Tel: +41 1234 2061 **Fax:** +41 1234 6363
Website: www.ubs.com

UCB SA
Jettie Van Caenegem, Group General Counsel
Allee de le Recherche 60, B-1170 Brussels, Belgium
Tel: +32 2 559 9999 **Fax:** +32 2 559 9491
Email: jettie.vancaenegem@ucb-group.com
Website: www.ucb-group.com

Unicredito
Antonio Maladorno, Head of Legal Dept
Piazza Cordusio 2, 20123 Milan, Italy
Tel: +39 02 8862 3895 **Fax:** +39 02 88 62 2342
Website: www.credit.it

Unidanmark A/S
Niels Joergensen, Director of Legal Services
Strandstraede 3, Postboks 850, 0900 Copenhagen, Denmark
Tel: +45 33 33 3333 **Fax:** +45 33 33 1004
Email: bolt@unibank.dk
Website: www.unibank.dk

Unified Energy Systems
Olga Efimova, Senior Legal Counsel
7 Kitaigorodskiy, Proyezd, 103-074 Moscow, Russia
Tel: +7 095 220 4001
Website: www.rao-ees.ru

Unilever Group
Stephen G Williams, Joint Secretary and General Counsel
Unilever House, Blackfriars, PO Box 68, London EC4P 4BQ, United Kingdom
Tel: +44 20 7822 5252 **Fax:** +44 20 7822 5817
Website: www.unilever.com

Union Electrica -Fenosa SA
Alejandro Sanchez Bustamante, General Counsel
Capitan Haya 53, 28020 Madrid, Spain
Tel: +34 91 550 7700 **Fax:** +34 91 567 7301
Email: asanchezb@uef.es
Website: www.uef.es

United Micro Electronics
Larry Lin, Director of IPR/Legal Affairs
No 3, Li-Hsin 2nd Road, Science-Based Industrial Park, Hsinchu City , Taiwan
Tel: +886 3 578 2258 **Fax:** +886 3 579 8506
Website: www.umc.com

United News & Media PLC
Jane Stables, Head of Legal and Personnel
Ludgate House, 245 Blackfriars Road, Blackfriars, London SE1 9UY, United Kingdom
Tel: +44 20 7921 5000 **Fax:** +44 20 7921 5047
Email: shamliant@unm.com
Website: www.unm.com

United Pan-Europe Communications NV (UPC)
Jeremy Evans, Senior Legal Counsel
Boeing Avenue 53, PO Box 74763, Schiphol Rijk, 1119 PE Amsterdam, Netherlands
Tel: +31 20 778 9840 ext 9959 **Fax:** +31 20 778 9841
Email: jevans@upccorp.com
Website: www.upccorp.com

United Technologies Corporation
William Trachsel, General Counsel
1 Financial Plaza, Hartford CT 6101, USA
Tel: +1 860 728 7000 **Fax:** +1 860 728 7982
Website: www.utc.com

United Utilities PLC
David Hosker, Legal Services Manager, North West Water Ltd
North West Water Ltd, Dawson House, Liverpool Road, Great Sankey, Warrington WA5 3LW, United Kingdom
Tel: +44 1925 234000 **Fax:** +44 1925 233360
Website: www.unitedutilities.com

UPM-Kymmene Corp
Reko Aalto-Setala, Head of Legal
Eteläesplanad 2, PO Box 380, 00101 Helsinki, Finland
Tel: +358 204 15 111 **Fax:** +358 204 15 0304
Email: reko.aalto-setala@upm-kymmene.com
Website: www.upm-kymmene.com

US Bancorp
Lee Mitau, General Counsel
US Bank Place, 601 Second Avenue South, Minneapolis MN 55402, USA
Tel: +1 612 973 1111 **Fax:** +1 612 973 4333
Website: www.usbank.com

Usinor
Roland Macrez, Group General Legal Counsel
11-13 Cours Valmy, 92800 Puteaux, France
Tel: +33 1 4125 8000 **Fax:** +33 1 4125 5675
Email: roland.macrez@usinor.com
Website: www.usinor.com

Valeo SA
Geric Lebedoff, General Counsel
43, rue Bayen, 75017 Paris, France
Tel: +33 1 40 55 20 22 **Fax:** +33 1 40 55 21 62
Email: geric.lebedoff@valeo.com
Website: www.valeo.com

VeriSign
Stratton Sclavos, Chief Executive Officer
1350 Charleston Road, Mountain View 94043, USA
Tel: +1 650 961 7500 **Fax:** +1 650 961 7300
Website: www.verisign.com

Veritas Software
Jay Jones, General Counsel
1600 Plymouth Street, Mountain View 94043, USA
Tel: +1 650 335 8000 **Fax:** +1 650 335 8050
Website: www.veritas.com

Verizon
Bruce Brafman, Senior Vice-President and Deputy General Counsel
1095 Avenue of the Americas, 39th Floor, New York 10036, USA
Tel: +1 212 395 1086 **Fax:** +1 212 597 2586
Website: www.verizon.com

Viacom Inc
Michael Fricklas, Executive Vice President, General Counsel and Secretary.
1515 Broadway, New York NY 10010-3630, USA
Tel: +1 212 258 6070 **Fax:** +1 212 258 6099
Email: michael.fricklas@viacom.com
Website: www.viacom.com

Vivendi Universal SA
Gilbert Klajnman, General Counsel
42 Avenue de Friedland, Paris, France
Tel: +33 1 71 71 1000 **Fax:** +33 1 71 71 1001
Website: www.vivendiuniversal.com

VNU (NV)
Mr Van Kampen, General Counsel
Ceylonpoort 5-25, 2037 AA Haarlem, Netherlands
Tel: +31 23 546 3463 **Fax:** +31 23 546 3938
Email: t.van.kampen@hq.vnu.com
Website: www.vnu.com

Vodafone Group PLC
Stephen Scott, Company Secretary/Head of Legal
Fairfax House, London Road, Newbury RG14 1JX, United Kingdom
Tel: +44 1635 682 802 **Fax:** +44 1635 580 857
Email: stephen.scott@vf.vodafone.co.uk
Website: www.vodafone.co.uk

Voicestream Wireless
Alan Bender, Senior Corporate Counsel
12920 SE 38th Street, Bellevue 98006, USA
Tel: +1 425 653 4600 **Fax:** +1 425 378 4000
Email: alan.bender@voicestream.com
Website: www.voicestream.com

Volkswagen AG
Hans-Viggo von Hulsen, General Counsel
Berliner Ring 2, D-38436 Wolfsburg, Germany
Tel: +49 53 61 90 **Fax:** +49 53 61 92 82 82
Email: anja3.frank@volkswagen.de
Website: www2.vw-online.de

Wachovia Bank
Kenneth McAllister, General Counsel
100 North Main Street, Winston-Salem NC 27150, USA
Tel: +1 336 770 5000 **Fax:** +1 336 732 2281
Email: kenneth.mccallister@wachovia.com
Website: www.wachovia.com

Wal-Mart Stores Inc
H Lee Scott, President & Chief Executive Officer
702 S.W. Eighth Street, Bentonville AR 72716, USA
Tel: +1 501 273 4000 **Fax:** +1 501 273 1917
Website: www.wal-mart.com

Walgreen Co
Julian Oettinger, Senior Vice-President General Counsel
200 Wilmot Road, Deerfield IL 60015, USA
Tel: +1 847 940 2500 **Fax:** +1 847 914 2804
Website: www.walgreens.com

Walt Disney Co
Lou Meisinger, General Counsel
500 S. Buena Vista Street, Burbank CA 91521-0001, USA
Tel: +1 818 560 1000 **Fax:** +1 818 560 1930
Website: www.disney.com

Washington Mutual
Fay Chapman, Head of Legal
1201 Third Ave., Seattle WA 98101, USA
Tel: +1 206 461 2000 **Fax:** +1 206 461 5739
Website: www.wamu.com

Wcm Beteiligungs und Grundbezits AG
Roland Flach, Member of the Management Board
Opernplatz 2, Postfach 17 05 45, 60313 Frankfurt, Germany
Tel: +49 69 900 26 0 **Fax:** +49 69 900 26 110
Website: www.wcm.de

Wells Fargo & Company
Stanley S Stroup, Executive Vice President and General Counsel
420 Montgomery St., San Francisco CA 94163, USA
Tel: +1 415 396 6019 **Fax:** +1 415 677 9031
Website: www.wellsfargo.com

Westpac Banking Corp
Ilana Atlas, Group Secretary & General Counsel
60 Martin Place, Sydney NSW 2000, Australia
Tel: +61 2 9226 3584 **Fax:** +61 2 9226 1234
Website: www.westpac.com.au

Weyerhaeuser Company
Robert Dowdy, Head of Legal
33663 Weyerhaeuser Way S., Federal Way WA 98003, USA
Tel: +1 253 924 2345 **Fax:** +1 253 924 3253
Website: www.weyerhaeuser.com

Whitbread PLC
Simon Barratt, Legal Affairs Director and Company Secretary
The Brewery, Chiswell Street, London EC1Y 4SD, United Kingdom
Tel: +44 20 7606 4455 **Fax:** +44 20 7615 1000
Email: simon.barratt@whitbread.com
Website: www.whitbread.co.uk

Williams Companies
William G Von Glahn, Senior Vice President and General Counsel
1 Williams Center, Tulsa OK 74172-0000, USA
Tel: +1 918 573 2000 **Fax:** +1 918 573 5942
Email: bill.vonglahn@williams.com
Website: www.williams.com

Williams PLC
Malcolm Stratton, Company Secretary
Pentagon House, Sir Frank Whittle Road, Derby DE21 4XA, United Kingdom
Tel: +44 1332 202 020 **Fax:** +44 1332 295339
Email: marie.rhodes@williams-plc.com
Website: www.williams-plc.com

Wipro
Satish Menon, Company Secretary
88 M.G. Rd, S.B. Towers, Bangalore 560025, India
Tel: +91 80 844 0012 **Fax:** +91 80 844 0054
Website: www.wipro.com

Wm Morrison Supermarkets PLC
Martin Ackroyd, Company Secretary
Hilmore House, Thornton Road, Bradford BD8 9AX, United Kingdom
Tel: +44 1274 494 166 **Fax:** +44 1274 494831
Website: www.morrisons.co.uk

WM-data AB
Lars Harrysson, President & Chief Executive Officer
Sandhamnsgatan 65, PO Box 27030, 102 51 Stockholm, Sweden
Tel: +46 8 670 20 00 **Fax:** +46 8 670 22 90
Email: lahar@wmdata.com
Website: www.wmdata.com

Wolseley PLC
David A Branson, Group Company Secretary
PO Box 18, Vines Lane, Droitwich WR9 8ND, United Kingdom
Tel: +44 1905 777200 **Fax:** +44 1905 777219
Email: susan.lacey@wolseley.com
Website: www.wolseley.com

Wolters Kluwer NV
M.C. Thompson, Legal Counsel
Apollolaan 153, PO Box 75248, 1070 AE Amsterdam, Netherlands
Tel: +31 20 607 0400 **Fax:** +31 20 607 0490
Email: mthompson@wolterskluwer.com
Website: www.wolters-kluwer.com

Woolwich PLC
Michael Webber, Chief Solicitor
Corporate Headquarters, Watling Street, Bexleyheath DA6 7RR, United Kingdom
Tel: +44 20 8298 5000 **Fax:** +44 20 8298 4783
Email: michael.webber@woolwich.co.uk
Website: www.woolwich.co.uk / www.thewoolwich.co.uk

WPP Group PLC
David Calow, Group Legal Adviser
27 Farm Street, London W1X 6RD, United Kingdom
Tel: +44 20 7408 2204 **Fax:** +44 20 7409 0242
Email: dcalow@wpp.com
Website: www.wpp.com

Wüstenrot & Württembergische AG
Tilman Schmidt-Lorenz, General Counsel
Gutenbergstrasse 30, D-70176 Stuttgart, Germany
Tel: +49 711 662 1439 **Fax:** +49 711 662 2016
Email: tilman.schmidt-lorenz@wuertembergische.de
Website: www.ww-ag.com

Xerox Corporation
Christina Clayton, Vice-President and General Counsel
800 Long Ridge Road, Stamford CT 06904, USA
Tel: +1 203 968 3000 **Fax:** +1 203 968 4301
Website: www.xerox.com

Xilinx Inc
Thomas Lavelle, President & Chief Executive Officer
2100 Logic Drive, San Jose 95124-3400, USA
Tel: +1 408 559 7778 **Fax:** +1 408 559 7114
Website: www.xilinx.com

Yahoo! Inc
John Place, VP & General Counsel
3420 Central Expressway, Santa Clara CA 95051, USA
Tel: +1 408 731 3300 **Fax:** +1 408 731 3301
Website: www.yahoo.com

Yahoo! Japan
Masahiro Inoue, President
24-1 Nihonbashi, Hakozakicho, Chuo-ku, Tokyo 103, Japan
Tel: +81 3 5469 5401 **Fax:** +81 3 5469 6859
Website: www.yahoo.co.jp

Yamanouchi Pharmaceutical Co
Kenichiro Saito, Head of Legal
2-3-11, Nihonbashi-Honcho, Chuo-ku, Tokyo 103-8411, Japan
Tel: +81 3 3244 3000 **Fax:** +81 3 3244 5811
Email: saitouk@yamanouchi.co.jp
Website: www.yamanouchi.com

Yamato Transport
Keiji Aritomi, President
2-16-10, Ginza, Chuo-ku, Tokyo 104-8125, Japan
Tel: +81 3 354 13411 **Fax:** +81 3 3542 1979
Website: www.kuronekoyamato.co.jp

Yapi Ve Kredi Bankasi
Torlak Feyza, Head of Legal Department
Yapi Kredi Plaza, Buyukdere Caddesi Levent, 80620 Istanbul, Turkey
Tel: +90 212 3397000 **Fax:** +90 212 3396128
Email: ftorlak@ykb.com
Website: www.ykb.com

Zurich Financial Services
Rolf Hüppi, Chairman and CEO, Zurich Financial Services and Zurich Allied; Deputy Chairman, Allied Zurich
Mythenquai 2, 8000 Zurich, Switzerland
Tel: +41 1 625 2525 **Fax:** +41 1 625 3555
Website: www.zurich.com

FIRM PROFILES

A & L GOODBODY

HEAD OFFICE

International Financial Services Centre, North Wall Quay,
Dublin 1, Republic of Ireland
Tel: +353 1 649 2000 **Fax:** +353 1 649 2649
Email: law@algoodbody.ie
Website: www.algoodbody.ie

FIRM OVERVIEW

Managing partner: Frank O'Riordan
Number of partners worldwide: 64
Number of other lawyers worldwide: 148

AREAS OF PRACTICE:

Banking and finance	*%
Commercial litigation	*%
Commercial property	*%
Company and commercial	*%
Employment	*%
EU and competition	*%
Funds	*%
M&A	*%
Media and entertainment	*%
Property	*%
Technology, IT and telecommunications	*%

*Workload % not disclosed

WORLDWIDE OFFICE CONTACTS

BELGIUM
17-19 Rue Montoyer, Boite 3, 1000 **Brussels**
Tel: + 322 512 3333 **Fax:** + 322 512 1353
Email:

REPUBLIC OF IRELAND
International Financial Services Centre, North Wall Quay, **Dublin** 1
Tel: +353 1 649 2000 **Fax:** +353 1 649 2649
Email: law@algoodbody.ie

UNITED KINGDOM
4th Floor, Augustine House, Austin Friars, **London** EC2N 2HA
Tel: +44 207 382 0800 **Fax:** +44 207 382 0810
Email: info@algoodbody.com

USA
Suite 3800, One Financial Center, 38th Floor, **Boston** MA 02111
Tel: + 1 617 348 1800 **Fax:** + 1 617 348 3018
Email: afbrowne@aol.com

Suite 816, Ten Rockefeller Plaza, **New York** NY 10020
Tel: + 1 212 582 4499 **Fax:** + 1 212 333 5126

A

FIRM PROFILE: Established over a century ago by Alfred and Lewis Goodbody, A&L Goodbody is Ireland's largest law firm, with offices in London, New York, Boston and Brussels. It offers an extensive range of commercial legal services both to Irish and non-resident clients, as well as to other professionals requiring advice on Irish legal or commercial issues.

INTERNATIONAL EXPERIENCE: The firm has advised international companies seeking to invest in Ireland, in particular from the US, UK, Europe and the Far East, and advises Irish companies on their overseas activities. The firm's public private partnership experts acted as advisers in a range of major transactions in Ireland and the UK. M&A work in 2000 included advising Banco Bilbao Vizcaya Argentaria (BBVA) and Terra Networks on the proposed joint venture with enba plc to create Unofirst Group. The firm has acted for Elan since its IPO and recent acquisitions include the Liposome Company, Inc. and its worldwide subsidiaries and Dura Pharmaceuticals, Inc. with a value of £1.8 billion. The firm's technology law group provides a 'cradle to heaven' legal service to dot.com and other technology clients. The firm acts for a number of hi-tech companies at pre-IPO stage, assisting in bringing in venture capital or investment from other sources and for venture capitalists active in the sector, and has the largest team of legal tax specialists in Ireland. The firm has been involved in a range of high profile international and commerical litigation and has represented the Office of the Director of Telecommunications Regulation in the appeal by Orange Communications Limited against the Directors' decision to award the country's third mobile telephone licence to Meteor Mobile Communications Limited.

INTERNATIONAL CLIENTS: The firm's clients include major international organisations particularly in the field of technology, financial services, biotechnology and manufacturing.

MAIN INTERNATIONAL AREAS OF PRACTICE:
Company and commercial: The firm has particular expertise in the areas of high-tech, electronic, medical devices and software development.
Banking and finance: The firm has one of the largest banking practices in Ireland. Work includes asset financing, funds management, treasury operations, structured financing and general banking.
Technology/IT/telecoms: This group advises technology companies on all aspects of their business including licensing, intellectual property, M&A, corporate finance and e-commerce.
Employment: The firm's dedicated employment unit has advised on the employment aspects of M&A deals, inward investment projects and other significant projects.
Funds: The funds group has a well established client base including international and Dublin based banks, fund administration groups, global custodians, fund managers and other financial services groups.
M&A: The firm is extremely busy in the M&A field. Irish companies have been active in the domestic market, the UK market and often further afield, while on the inward investment front changes in the capital gains tax regime have stimulated market activity. The firm advised Irish Permanent on its intended acquisition of the TSB.
EU and competition: The firm's full-time EU and competition unit in Dublin acts for the Office of Director of Telecommunications Regulations and is advising on the third mobile telephone licence.
Media and entertainment: The unit has a particular focus in relation to film and TV work. It has also doubled its activity in the music sector. The firm also acts for major Irish and international media organisations including Irish and overseas newspapers.
Commercial litigation: The firm's practice in this area continues to grow, and includes large-scale long-running cases as well as specialist expertise in key niche areas. The firm is involved in advising a range of clients in connection with three major tribunals of inquiry.
Commercial property: The firm advised the vendors of the highest-selling piece of land in Dublin, the largest office developments sale of the year and a number of major retail development sales including Airside Retail Park, Phase 1.

LANGUAGES: Cantonese, Dutch, French, German, Malay, Mandarin

ABDELLY & ASSOCIÉS

HEAD OFFICE

Carthage Center, Regus Building, Tour. A, Les Berges Du Lac, 2035,
Tunis Tunisia
Tel: +216 1 849 410 **Fax:** +216 1 845 915

Email: sabdelly.lawyercenter@gnet.tn

WORLDWIDE OFFICE CONTACTS

TUNISIA
Carthage Center, Regus Building, Tour. A, Les Berges Du Lac, 2035 **Tunis**
Tel: +216 1 849 410 **Fax:** +216 1 845 915
Email: sabdelly.lawyercenter@gnet.tn

FIRM OVERVIEW

Senior partner: Abdelly Samir

Number of partners worldwide: 4
Number of other lawyers worldwide: 10

AREAS OF PRACTICE:

Energy	40%
Corporate, M&A and privatisation	20%
Banking and finance	10%
Litigation and arbitration	10%
Telecommunications and IT	10%
Insurance and reinsurance	5%
Real estate	5%

FIRM OVERVIEW: Abdelly & Associés was established by Samir Abdelly. It has grown considerably and plans to expand further in the future. The firm offers comprehensive legal advice to clients with international business interests, focusing on natural resources, banking and finance, telecommunications, and M&A. The firm aims to be responsive to the needs of its clients, achieve effective results, and act with integrity.
A&A does not participate in any formal alliances or networks. It prefers to maintain close links with various firms worldwide, including a number of Algerian and Libyan firms. The decision of which firm to work with is based on the merits of individual transactions.

INTERNATIONAL EXPERIENCE: During 2000 A&A acted in over 30 major transactions and acquisitions and advised on the establishment and registration of foreign companies in Tunisia, Libya and Algeria. It also acted as counsel for major international companies in North Africa.

INTERNATIONAL CLIENTS: The firm's clients include oil and mining companies, major international banks, telecommunication companies, and a range of companies in the franchising, tourism, construction and financial industries.

MAIN INTERNATIONAL AREAS OF PRACTICE:

Energy: A&A has a large oil, mining and natural resource practice. It advises mining companies on permits (prospecting, exploration and concessions), negotiating with governments and public and private companies, conventions, JOAs, accounting procedures, farm outs, joint ventures, and purchase and sale agreements. The firm is a member of the IAPN.
Corporate, M&A and privatisations: A&A advises a wide range of commercial clients on the structuring, negotiation and documenting of commercial transactions. The firm also advises on public offerings and private placements, public ventures, privatisations, bank mergers, mutual funds, corporate reorganisations, M&A, and take-overs. The firm handles issuer bids, proxy contests and preparation, directors' circulars, and annual meeting reports.
Telecommunications and IT: The firm advises on all aspects of telecommunication and IT law.
Banking and finance: A&A handles all aspects of banking and finance including secured and syndicated loan transactions and guarantees, structured finance, project finance, leasing and tax based finance.
Insurance and reinsurance: The firm advises on all aspects of insurance and reinsurance.
Litigation and arbitration: The firm's litigation practice advises on corporate and commercial, employment, labour relations, insurance, constitutional, maritime, energy regulation, construction, and environmental law. It represents clients before trial and appellate courts, boards, commissions and tribunals in relation to commercial and regulatory disputes, as well as individual rights. The firm recognises that litigation is no longer the only avenue for dispute resolution, and where appropriate, recommends mediation, arbitration or alternative dispute resolution as a more effective response to the needs of its clients.
Real estate: A&A advises on several major real estate, construction and investment projects in Tunisia.

LANGUAGES: Arabic, English, French, German, Italian

For other recommended firms see pages 1485-1520

ABELLO CONCEPCION REGALA & CRUZ (ACCRALAW)

HEAD OFFICE

ACCRA Building, 122 Gamboa St, Legaspi Village
Makati City 0770, Philippines
Tel: +63 2 817 09 66 **Fax:** +63 2 816 01 19

Email: accra@accralaw.com
Website: www.accralaw.com

FIRM OVERVIEW

Managing partner: Victor P. Lazatin
Co-managing partner: Marcial G. de la Fuente

Number of partners worldwide: 31
Number of other lawyers worldwide: 60

AREAS OF PRACTICE:

Litigation and arbitration	32%
Corporate	30%
Labour	16%
Intellectual property	10%
Immigration	8%
Tax	4%

FIRM OVERVIEW: Abello Concepcion Regala & Cruz Law Offices (ACCRALAW) is a cohesive multi-disciplinary team of legal professionals who possess in-depth knowledge of specialised fields of law backed by extensive experience. The firm was formed in 1972 and has grown rapidly in many respects. From six lawyers when it was first set up, it now has more than eighty lawyers. Its clientele has also expanded to include hundreds of local and multinational companies. Initially with one office in Makati City, it has branched out and opened offices in Cebu City and Davao City to better cater to the needs of its clients in these areas of the country. The firm has established close affiliations and links with overseas clients and law firms, as well as with international bar associations. Ready access to this network of valuable contacts is possible through advanced e-mail technology which enables the firm to have an expanded information resource base on a global scale. ACCRALAW is the Philippine member in Commercial Law Affiliates (CLA) and Terralex.

INTERNATIONAL EXPERIENCE: The firm and its lawyers are regularly consulted by international law firms acting on behalf of clients who require advice and representation in the Asian region. The firm is one of the strongest law firms in the fields of business organisations and foreign investments, privatisations and build-operate-transfer (BOT) projects. The firm acted as counsel in various international public offerings of equity and debt securities of leading Philippine companies, such as Philippine Long Distance and Telephone Company, San Miguel Corporation, and Philippine Airlines. The firm also acted as counsel for International Finance Corporation in the privatisation of the Metropolitan Waterworks and Sewerage Systems, reputed to be the largest water privatisation project in the worth US$ 7B.

INTERNATIONAL CLIENTS: The firm acts for clients in sectors including telecommunications, power generation and distribution, construction, manufacturing, wholesale and retail trade, aviation, transportation and communication, real estate, financing, banking and insurance.

MAIN INTERNATIONAL AREAS OF PRACTICE:

Corporate: The firm handles matters including due diligence, joint ventures, M&A, reorganisations and restructurings, privatisations, project financing, e-commerce transactions, loan syndications, incentives registration, securities transactions, the establishment of business organisations in the Philippines, proxy contests and intracorporate disputes. The firm also renders legal services to general retainer clients required in the ordinary course of business such as consultation and advice, preparation of ordinary contracts and legal documents, rendering of opinions and notarial services as well as ancillary corporate secretarial services.

Intellectual property: The firm represents clients in all aspects of intellectual property protection issues on services involving trademarks, patents, and copyrights and domain names (including registration and post-registration of intellectual property rights and prosecuting or defending any litigation matter involving intellectual property); assistance in the preparation of documentation and the recordation of assignments, licensing agreements, franchise agreements, technology transfer agreements involving intellectual properties, and related agreements such as distributorship agreements and confidentiality agreements. The firm has expanded its practice to include information technology and entertainment law.

Employment: The firm handles all matters involving labour/management relations, such as negotiation of collective bargaining agreements, administrative investigation of cases involving employees, dismissal and suspension of employees, money claims and damages arising from employer-employee relations.

Litigation: The firm represents clients before regular courts of law, administrative agencies, quasi-judicial tribunals and arbitral bodies, both international and local covering all aspects of commercial litigation and arbitration, including intracorporate disputes, rehabilitation and insolvency proceedings; actions to enforce obligations under international transactions; maritime and admiralty; insurance; violation of banking laws; public utilities; actions for damage; product liability cases; actions for foreclosure of mortgages and other disputes involving e-commerce, real estate conveyances, mortgages and leases; and criminal actions.

Tax: The firm advises on the entire field of national and local taxation, customs and anti-dumping laws, employee benefits, estate planning and international taxation.

Immigration: The firm is involved in representation before government agencies involved in defining the terms and conditions of an alien's authorized stay in the Philippines, as well as representation before the courts in connection with petitions for the acquisition of Philippine citizenship.

LANGUAGES: English, Filipino, French, Japanese, Mandarin, Spanish

WORLDWIDE OFFICE CONTACTS

PHILIPPINES
6/F Cebu Holdings Center, Cebu Business Park (Ayala), Archbp. Reyes Avenue 6000, **Cebu City**
Tel: +63 32 231 4223 **Fax:** +63 32 231 3614
Email: accralaw@pacific.net.ph

11/F Pryce Tower, Pryce Business Park, J.P. Laurel, Bajada, **Davao City** 8000
Tel: +63 82 224 0996 **Fax:** +63 82 224 0983
Email: accralaw@mazcom.com

ACCRA Building, 122 Gamboa St, Legaspi Village, **Makati City** 0770
Tel: +63 2 817 09 66 **Fax:** +63 2 816 01 19 / 812 48 97
Email: accra@accralaw.com

A

For other recommended firms see pages 1485-1520

ABREU CARDIGOS & ASSOCIADOS

HEAD OFFICE

Praça Nuno Rodrigues dos Santos, 14-B,
1600 - 171 Lisbon, Portugal
Tel: +351 21 723 1800 **Fax:** +351 21 723 1899

Email: general@abreucardigos.com
Website: www.abreucardigos.com

FIRM OVERVIEW

Managing partner: Miguel Teixeira de Abreu

Number of partners worldwide: 5
Number of other lawyers worldwide: 28

AREAS OF PRACTICE:

Banking and finance .... *%
Capital markets .... *%
Employment .... *%
EU law .... *%
M&A/corporate restructuring .... *%
Public and administrative law .... *%
Real estate and environmental law .... *%
Sports .... *%
Tax and tax planning .... *%
* Workload % not disclosed

FIRM OVERVIEW: Abreu Cardigos & Partners is a Portuguese law firm mainly acting for corporate entities. It offers specialist legal advice and a range of complementary services. The firm focuses on M&A, corporate restructuring and emerging areas of legal practice.

INTERNATIONAL EXPERIENCE: The firm's international experience was initially grounded on the founding partners' experience with major international law firms. This expertise provides the firm with a substantial network referral of international clients as well as experience of international standards of client service.

INTERNATIONAL CLIENTS: The firm's client base includes some of the largest international companies operating in Portugal, covering a wide range of sectors such as the automotive industry and automotive suppliers, financial and banking services, managed funds, telecommunications and e-commerce, public works, construction firms, engineering, pharmaceuticals, chemical, distribution and retailing.

MAIN INTERNATIONAL AREAS OF PRACTICE:

M&A/MBOs/MBIs: The firm provides legal and tax advice with regard to the purchase or disposal of Portuguese companies. It frequently undertakes due diligence work and handles acquisitions and/or disposals of Portuguese companies. It also handles restructurings, including mergers, split-offs, flotations and asset divisions. Recently, the firm advised Portugal Telecom on the outsourcing of its information systems department, a deal involving over 500 employees and worth $US1billion over ten years.
Banking and Financial Services: Through the Public Debt Management Institute, the firm acts as consultant to the Portuguese government advising on operations connected with international financial instruments, including derivatives. In 2000 the firm advised on the securitisation of receivables and mortgage backed assets of their Portuguese clients. Currently, the firm is providing legal and tax assistance to three leading international banks on their securitisation activities. The firm also advises a number of national and international banks, as well as other credit institutions and financial services providers, on issues related to financial products, including derivatives and complex tax structures.
Local and international taxation and tax planning: The firm provides specialist advice on several issues of local and international taxation to resident and non-resident corporations, as well as to other law firms in Portugal and abroad. The firm has been involved in the establishment of tax structures regarding financial operations, acquisitions of companies, corporate restructuring and international transactions for resident and non-resident corporations. The firm has also been retained in respect of the issuance of tax opinions related to securitisations transactions in Portugal.
Capital markets: The firm regularly advises resident and non-resident investors on their duties before the Portuguese Capital Markets Regulatory Authorities. The firm has also been involved in the admission and listing of several Portuguese companies on the Lisbon Stock Exchange.
Industrial and Intellectual property and IT Law: Further to the lateral hiring of Dr Cesar Bessa Monteiro along with his IP and IT teams, the firm is able to provide first-rate advice on industrial and intellectual property law issues as well as on IT law matters. Dr Monteiro is also an official industrial property agent, with more than 25 years experience in this field. He has been invited to join a government commission created to study and review the Portuguese Industrial Property Code. Currently, the firm advises more than 300 international clients on all matters relating to industrial intellectual property and IT law including but not limited to trademark protection, trademark litigation, counterfeiting, copyright protection, software protection and domain name registration and protection.
EU/anti-trust/competition law: The firm regularly advises Portuguese companies on the implications of EU law. It has represented many multinational companies before the anti-trust authorities in connection with mergers and other concentration operations. The firm has successfully represented a number of companies before the Portuguese courts.
Telecommunications: The firm advises resident and non-resident telecom companies on their entry into the recently deregulated Portuguese telecom market. The firm is also currently representing the Portuguese telecom operator on a number of restructuring deals.
Environmental law: Members of the firm founded EURONATURA, a NGO dedicated to environmental law and policy. The firm is regularly consulted on national and European environmental matters. A member of the firm has recently been invited as a surrogate member of the European Council for Environmental Law.
Employment: As part of its commercial law department, the firm has been increasingly consulted on employment matters and represents one of the major international consultancy firms in this area. The firm recently advised on all matters concerning the establishment of one of the largest international retail groups in Portugal.
Other areas: Other areas include construction and public works (the firm advised on the reconstruction of the Formula 1 track, including the preparation of the bidding process and of public contests, review of documentation presented by bidders, preparation of the adjudication sessions, drafting and negotiating construction contracts and supervising all legal work pending construction and delivery of works); real estate; sports and leisure law.

LANGUAGES: English, French, German, Portuguese, Spanish

WORLDWIDE OFFICE CONTACTS

PORTUGAL
Praça Nuno Rodrigues dos Santos, 14-B, 1600 - 171 **Lisbon**
Tel: +351 21 723 1800 **Fax:** +351 21 723 1899
Email: rita.osorio@abreucardigos.com

A

For other recommended firms see pages 1485-1520

ADEPETUN CAXTON-MARTINS & AGBOR

HEAD OFFICE

38/40 Strachan Street, P.O. Box 55285, Falomo
Lagos Nigeria
Tel: +234 1 263 1960 **Fax:** +234 1 2647374
Email: aca@linkserve.com.ng

FIRM OVERVIEW

Partners: Sola Adepetun, Afolabi Caxton-Martins Funke Agbor, Yinka Agidee, Kemi Segun

Number of partners worldwide: 5
Number of other lawyers worldwide: 11

AREAS OF PRACTICE:

Corporate and commercial	20%
Energy and natural resources	20%
Foreign investment and international trade	15%
Intellectual property	10%
Litigation and arbitration	15%
Shipping and maritime	10%
Banking and finance	5%
Tax	3%
Other	2%

FIRM OVERVIEW: Established in 1993, Adepetun, Caxton-Martins & Agbor (ACA) has developed into one of the top ten corporate law firms in Nigeria. It offers a full range of legal services to clients with both local and international business interests. The firm's areas of specialisation include corporate and commercial law, banking and finance, oil and gas, foreign investments and international trade, litigation and arbitration, shipping and maritime, intellectual property, property law, and tax.

INTERNATIONAL EXPERIENCE: ACA has advised several international organisations and has assisted a number of international corporations in the establishment of subsidiary companies in Nigeria.

INTERNATIONAL CLIENTS: The firm's international clients include major multinational E&P companies, oil service companies, manufacturing companies, banks, shipping companies, and foreign embassies.

MAIN INTERNATIONAL AREAS OF PRACTICE:

Corporate and commercial: The firm specialises in corporate and commercial work. It advises on a range of issues including sole proprietorship, joint ventures, partnerships, corporate financing, diversification efforts, reconstruction or mergers, and dissolution. The firm also provides company secretarial services to both local and foreign organisations.

Banking and finance: ACA handles the preparation of all forms of security and financial documentation for banks and other financial institutions including secured and syndicated loan agreements and guarantees, mortgages, bills of sale, project finance, equipment leasing, and debt rescheduling documentation.

Intellectual property: The firm advises on all aspects of patent and trademark law including searches, filing and prosecution, patent and trademark surveillance and opposition, transactional work, licensing, franchising and joint ventures. The firm is a member of the International Trademark Association (INTA).

Shipping and maritime: ACA provides comprehensive legal services to ship owners, their local agents and representatives, shippers, charterers and marine insurers including P&I Clubs in matters relating to bill of lading disputes, charter parties and other contracts of affreightment, agency agreement, ship sales and purchases, and the application of the Hague/Hamburg rules.

Foreign investment and international trade: The firm advises foreign companies/individuals interested in establishing business in Nigeria. It also advises clients on Nigerian law compliance issues and assists foreign companies in obtaining the relevant licenses and approvals required for operating in Nigeria.

Energy and natural resources: The firm provides specialised legal representation and advice to oil companies, oil service companies, oil traders and oil industry financiers on every aspect of the oil and gas industry. Work handled includes oil concession licensing and acquisition, oil industry accreditation, petroleum taxation issues, oil field service agreements, project finance issues, communal disputes, and compliance with environmental law standards. The firm is also keenly involved in Nigeria's developing power industry and advises on the legal framework and contractual components relating to the development of Nigeria's independent power projects.

Tax: The firm has a team of experienced tax lawyers. It provides services in respect of petroleum taxation and mergers and acquisitions.

Litigation and arbitration: ACA is continuously engaged in commercial dispute negotiation on behalf of its clients. The firm's lawyers are well versed in court procedures and provide legal representation in areas of contractual disputes arising from agency relationships, supply of goods and services, property related matters, employment issues, and infringement of intellectual property rights. ACA also represent clients in commercial arbitration within and outside Nigeria.

LANGUAGES: English

WORLDWIDE OFFICE CONTACTS

NIGERIA
38/40 Strachan Street, P.O. Box 55285, Falomo, **Lagos**
Tel: +234 1 263 1960 **Fax:** +234 1 2647374
Email: aca@linkserve.com.ng

2 Wokekoro Street, Old GRA, **Port Harcourt**
Tel: +234 084 233126 **Fax:** +234 084 233126
Email: aca@phca.linkserve.com

A

AFRIDI ANGELL & KHAN

HEAD OFFICE

Emirates Towers, 35th Level, Sheikh Zayed Road, P.O. Box 9371
Dubai United Arab Emirates
Tel: + 971 4 330 3900 **Fax:** + 971 4 330 3800

Email: dubai@afridi-angell.com

FIRM OVERVIEW

Senior partner: M.A.K. Afridi

Number of partners worldwide: 11
Number of other lawyers worldwide: 18

AREAS OF PRACTICE:

Arbitration and litigation .... *%
Banking and financial services .... *%
Capital market and privatisation .... *%
Corporate and commercial .... *%
Employment .... *%
Insurance .... *%
Intellectual property .... *%
International commerce .... *%
IT and e-commerce .... *%
Maritime and shipping .... *%
Project finance .... *%
Regional coordination .... *%
* Workload % not disclosed

FIRM OVERVIEW: Afridi & Angell is an international law firm with offices in Dubai, Abu Dhabi, Jebel Ali, Sharjah, Islamabad, Karachi, New York and Washington DC. The firm conducts a general corporate and financial legal practice and an international practice specialising in the Middle East, North Africa and South Asia.

INTERNATIONAL EXPERIENCE: The firm advises clients seeking advice on domestic transactions as well as inward and outward investment activities.

INTERNATIONAL CLIENTS: The firm's clients include multinational corporations, businesses, entrepreneurs, financial institutions, and governments.

MAIN INTERNATIONAL AREAS OF PRACTICE:
Corporate and commercial: The firm handles securities work, mergers and acquisitions, reorganisations, leveraged buyouts, asset-based and lease financings, commodities transactions, futures, and other derivatives.
Banking and financial services: The firm advises international and domestic banks (including US branches of regional banks) on lending matters. Afridi & Angell has one of the most active banking practices in the UAE and Pakistan.
Insurance: Afridi & Angell advises on corporate and regulatory issues facing insurers, brokers and agents (including problem investments), permitted insurance activities, director and officer liability, and insurance and reporting requirements.
Intellectual property: The firm advises on patents, trademarks, copyrights, know-how and other intellectual property matters.
IT: Afridi & Angell have worked on a range of projects involving IT and telecommunications companies.
International commerce: The firm advises clients on WTO issues, US, UN and other sanctions, and boycotts. It also handles issues involving the US Foreign Corrupt Practices Act and other bribery prohibitions.
Arbitration litigation: Afridi & Angell handles multi-jurisdictional dispute resolution, including the representation of US and other parties in arbitration proceedings.
Regional coordination: Afridi & Angell coordinates work involving multiple jurisdictions. The firm also recommends, briefs and supervises local counsel in relevant jurisdictions.
Maritime and shipping: Afridi & Angell advises ship owners, protection and indemnity clubs, banks and financial institutions on all aspects of maritime law (including financing and environmental pollution claims).

LANGUAGES: Arabic, English, French, Hindi, Urdu

WORLDWIDE OFFICE CONTACTS

PAKISTAN
Affridi Angell & Khan, 94 W Jinnah Avenue, Blue Area, **Islamabad** 44000
Tel: +92 51 2823 110 **Fax:** + 92 51 2823 009
Email: islamabad@afridi-angell.com

Affridi Angell & Khan, House D-3/1, Kehkashan, Clifton, Block 7, **Karachi**
Tel: +92 21 583 3503 **Fax:** + 92 21 583 3022
Email: karachi@afridi-angell.com

UNITED ARAB EMIRATES
Bin Hamoodah Building, P.O. Box 3961, **Abu Dhabi**
Tel: +971 2 627 5134 **Fax:** + 971 2 627 2905
Email: abudhabi@afridi-angell.com

Emirates Towers, 35th Level, Sheikh Zayed Road, P.O. Box 9371, **Dubai**
Tel: + 971 4 330 3900 **Fax:** + 971 4 330 3800
Email: dubai@afridi-angell.com

Jebel Ali Free Trade Zone, P.O. Box 61276, **Jebel Ali**
Tel: +971 4 881 6010 **Fax:** + 971 4 881 6774
Email: dubai@afridi-angell.com

Al-Boorj Avenue, P.O. Box 5925, **Sharjah**
Tel: +971 6 554 4062 **Fax:** + 971 6 554 7336
Email: sharjah@afridi-angell.com

USA
Afridi, Angell & Pelletreau,LLP, 599 Lexington Avenue, Suite 2806,
New York NY 10022-6030
Tel: +1 212 705 5000 **Fax:** +1 212 705 5125
Email: firm@afridi.com

Afridi, Angell & Pelletreau,LLP, 1025 Connecticut Ave, N.W.,
Washington DC 20036
Tel: +1 202 518 8900 **Fax:** +1 202 518 8903
Email: ldunn@afridi.com

A

For other recommended firms see pages 1485-1520

AIRD & BERLIS

HEAD OFFICE

BCE Place, Suite 1800, PO Box 754
Toronto, Ontario M5J 2T9, Canada
Tel: +1 416 863 1500 **Fax:** +1 416 863 1515
Website: www.airdberlis.com

WORLDWIDE OFFICE CONTACTS

CANADA
BCE Place, Suite 1800, PO Box 754, **Toronto,** Ontario M5J 2T9
Tel: +1 416 863 1500 **Fax:** +1 416 863 1515

FIRM OVERVIEW

Managing partner: Diane Harris
Number of partners worldwide: 94
Number of other lawyers worldwide: 26

AREAS OF PRACTICE:

Banking and financing .... *%
Corporate and commercial .... *%
Corporate finance .... *%
Entertainment .... *%
Insolvency and restructuring .... *%
Litigation .... *%
Real estate and planning .... *%
Tax .... *%
Technology .... *%
*Workload % not disclosed

FIRM OVERVIEW: Aird & Berlis is a major and well-respected full-service Canadian law firm with a large diversified practice, counselling the domestic and international business community in the corporate, financial, industrial and governmental sectors. The firm has been established for more than 80 years. The firm is renowned for its creative and cost-effective advice, particulaly the complex securities, mergers and acquisitions, bank finance, tax counselling, regulatory advice, emerging technology, venture capital, mining, real estate and cross border transaction areas. Several partners are ranked as leading Canadian lawyers and many more are ranked at the highest standards of their profession by authoritative sources. Aird & Berlis is affiliated with Owen Bird in Vancouver and is a member of Interlaw, an international association of independent law firms in major world centres.

INTERNATIONAL CLIENTS: Clients of Aird & Berlis include commercial banks, insurance and other financial institutions, public utilities, venture capital and private equity firms, industrial and service corporations, partnerships, pension and mutual funds, profit and non-profit organizations, government and government agencies, entrepreneurs and individuals.

MAIN INTERNATIONAL AREAS OF PRACTICE:

Corporate finance and M&A: The Corporate Finance Group assists clients in international and domestic public and private financings and rights offerings. The firm is also recognised for its development of innovative financing techniques, takeover bids and M&A transactions, going-private transactions and financial derivative products. It acts for private and public corporations, financial institutions, investment dealers, mutual funds and limited partnerships in the structuring of transactions and advising on securities legislation and stock exchange regulations in Canada. The M&A Group acts for managers in MBOs, promoters of LBOs, senior and subordinate debt lenders and equity investors in leverage and cash flow-based transactions. Aird & Berlis also acts on numerous cash flow and asset-based lending transactions both internationally and nationally and advises on the syndication of large asset-based loans and the public financing of asset-backed securities.

Taxation: The Tax Group provides international tax planning advice to international and domestic clients. They also advise on the structuring of tax-advantaged transactions, including corporate finance, real estate, e-commerce, mergers and acquisitions, and both private and public company transactions. Working closely with the firm's corporate finance group, the tax group ensures that its clients' business transactions, arrangements and strategies produce the most favourable tax consequences.

Banking and financing: The banking and financing group acts for international lending syndicates (both as lead counsel for syndicates and as Canadian counsel for foreign-led syndicates) and represents major chartered banks, trust companies, insurance companies and the full spectrum of other asset-based lending institutions. It also provides advice to major financial institutions with respect to the regulatory framework in Canada, corporate governance issues, related party transactions, conflict of interest rules, business and investment powers and ownership issues, including foreign ownership.

Natural resources: The mining group has an extensive international natural resource practice having carried out assignments in more than 45 different countries in the last decade. It acts for both Canadian and foreign exploration, development and producing companies as well as domestic and international lending and financial institutions in all facets of the mineral cycle from grass roots exploration to mineral fabrication. It has expertise in due diligence in commercial mining transactions and advises governments, stock exchanges and international funding agencies on mineral policy and mineral strategy issues.

Entrepreneurial corporate and commercial: The firm works closely with entities on short and long-term strategies in negotiating and structuring business transactions with domestic and cross-border implications, regulatory requirements, including corporate acquisitions; corporate governance issues; reorganizations; corporate restructurings; divestitures; arrangements for the commercial exploitation and use of technology; and intellectual property matters relating to patents, trade-marks and copyright.

Technology: Clients include established and emerging technology companies and their financial and strategic partners with global interests. Members of the emerging technology group integrate knowledge and experience from the core areas of licensing, technology transfers, corporate finance, tax and related business, which they use to assemble teams that are tailored to the specific needs and substantive legal issues faced by clients of the firm.

Litigation: The broad-based practice of the Litigation Group includes commercial, securities, intellectual property, construction, employment/labour, energy/regulatory, family, first nations, insurance, libel and slander, and professional negligence litigation. The firm combines its advocacy expertise with the expertise from other practice groups of the firm, which leads to effective litigation avoidance advice. It also acts extensively in arbitrations and mediations internationally and in Canada. This includes acting for non-Canadian clients seeking redress using Canadian or non-domestic law, as well as the rules of the International Chamber of Commerce.

Canadian investments: The firm specialises in counselling foreign companies conducting business in Canada (Investment Canada Act and the Competition Act).

LANGUAGES: Armenian, Chinese, Czech, English, French, German, Greek, Gujarati, Hebrew, Hindi, Italian, Portuguese, Serbian, Spanish, Ukranian

For other recommended firms see pages 1485-1520

AJUMOGOBIA & OKEKE

HEAD OFFICE

NAL Towers, 20 Marina,
Lagos Nigeria
Tel: +234 01 264 7460-3 **Fax:** +234 01 263 5585

Email: ao@ajumogobiaokeke.com
Website: www.ajumogobiaokeke.com

FIRM OVERVIEW

Managing partner: C.N. Okeke
Senior partners: H.O. Ajumogobia, C.N. Okeke

Number of partners worldwide: 5
Number of other lawyers worldwide: 20

AREAS OF PRACTICE:

Area	%
Commercial litigation and arbitration	40%
Company/commercial	30%
Energy resources and environment	15%
Banking and finance	10%
Maritime and aviation	5%

WORLDWIDE OFFICE CONTACTS

NIGERIA
NAL Towers, 20 Marina, **Lagos**
Tel: +234 1 264 7460-3 **Fax:** +234 1 263 5585
Email: ao@ajumogobiaokeke.com

CFAO Building, 8 Nnamdi Azikiwe Road, **Port Harcourt,** Rivers State
Tel: +234 84 234 267 Fax: +234 84 235 796
Email: ao@ajumogobiaokeke.com

A

FIRM OVERVIEW: Founded in January 1984, Ajumogobia & Okeke has established a reputation for its commitment to serving its client's businesses, utilising strong and long-standing contacts throughout the commercial sector. A successful merger with Ukiri & Shasore in 1999 (arguably the first in Nigeria between law firms) resulted in the creation of the largest and most dynamic full service commercial law firm in Nigeria.

INTERNATIONAL EXPERIENCE: The firm benefits from extensive correspondent relationships with international law firms in Europe, Asia, the United States and other parts of Africa. This enables the provision of an efficient and cost effective service to clients on a coordinated global basis.

INTERNATIONAL CLIENTS: The firm's clients include local and international public and private businesses, individuals, Sovereign Governments, and humanitarian agencies.

MAIN INTERNATIONAL AREAS OF PRACTICE:
Company/commercial: The firm's clients benefit from extensive experience in a wide range of transactions and corporate finance work. In addition to comprehensive legal advice on new ventures in the Nigerian market, the firm offers advice in the areas of acquisitions, divestitures and restructuring of local companies. The firm advises and provides support to inhouse counsel and is positioned to participate fully in the privatisation programme in Nigeria, to which the government is fully committed.
Commercial litigation and arbitration: The firm's litigation team handles a range of corporate and commercial disputes before the Federal and State High Courts, the Court of Appeal and the Supreme Court of Nigeria. The team draws on its intimate knowledge of clients' businesses and has an ability to respond creatively to their problems. Litigation lawyers offer expertise in contract claims of varied complexity, admiralty and shipping; insolvency and tax appeals; intellectual property; multi-party/multijurisdictional representative actions. The firm's experienced and highly qualified arbitrators provide the advice vital for effective alternative methods of resolving disputes.
Banking and finance: The firm's banking and finance division advises financial institutions on both general advisory and transactional capacities. It advises clients on syndicated and non-syndicated financing transactions, incuding secured and unsecured loans; liquidity facilities; senior and subordinated credit facilities; acquisition credit and leveraged buy-outs involving both public and private companies; debt conversion and global depository receipts.
Maritime and aviation: The firm represents and counsels companies and their underwriters exposed to a range of risks ranging from traditional 'blue water' shipping; personal injury, cargo, longshore and towage operations to 'brown water' oil and gas actvities and transporatation. The firm's lawyers also offer expertise in cargo and carriage claims; all aspects of international trade insurance; pollution and marine collisions. The firm regularly advises clients in aircraft financing; bilateral negotiations; and regulatory matters with national and international aviation authorities.

LANGUAGES: English, French, German, Hausa, Igbo, Itsekiri, Kalabari, Urhobo, Yoruba

For other recommended firms see pages 1485-1520

AKINJIDE & CO

HEAD OFFICE

4th Floor, NCR Building, 6 Broad Street,
Lagos Nigeria
Tel: +234 1 263 5315 **Fax:** +234 1 264 5525

Email: akinjideco@compuserve.com

FIRM OVERVIEW

Principal partner: Richard Akinjide
Managing partner: Jumoke Akinjide-Balogun
Partner: Omobola Ajao

Number of partners worldwide: 3
Number of other lawyers worldwide: 7

AREAS OF PRACTICE:

Corporate and commercial	20%
Litigation	20%
Oil and gas	20%
Arbitration and dispute resolution	15%
Shipping and admiralty	10%
Banking and tax	5%
Intellectual property	5%
Privatisation	5%

FIRM OVERVIEW: Established over 40 years ago, Akinjide & Co is one of Nigeria's leading law firms. With offices in Lagos and Ibadan, and an association with barrister's chambers in London, the firm is able to advise both national and international clients. It advises on a broad range of legal issues, specialising in work of a commercial and international nature.

INTERNATIONAL EXPERIENCE: The firm has handled several major international transactions including Star Deep Petroleum Limited in a US$3 billion oil and gas arbitration; Shell Development Petroleum Company (Nigeria) Limited in an international arbitration held in London; Ashland Inc in its dispute with Perenco (Nigeria) Ltd. The firm is currently representing the Federal Government of Nigeria in a dispute with the Republic of Cameroon over the Bakassi Peninsula at the International Court of Justice, The Hague, Netherlands.

INTERNATIONAL CLIENTS: The firm's international clients include a wide range of multinational oil companies, banks, shipping companies, insurance companies and private individuals.

MAIN INTERNATIONAL AREAS OF PRACTICE:

Oil and gas: Akinjide & Co advises multinational and indigenous oil companies, the Nigerian National Oil Company, and oil regulatory bodies.
Corporate: The firm advises on all areas of general corporate and securities law, corporate insolvency, joint ventures, partnerships and other forms of co-operative arrangements.
Banking and corporate finance: Work handled includes all areas of banking and security rights, domestic and international trade, and export credit financing.
Litigation: Akinjide & Co advise multinational companies, local companies and institutions, the Federal Government of Nigeria and State Governments. The firm regularly represents clients before the Federal and State High Courts, the Federal Court of Appeal, and the Supreme Court.
Shipping and admiralty: The firm handles all aspects of shipping law including ship arrests and releases, ship sale and purchase, disputes arising out of charter parties, bills of lading, collisions, insurance and other marine related matters. It advises ship owners, charterers, shippers, and marine insurers (including P&I clubs).
Arbitration and dispute resolution: The firm advises clients in the energy, intellectual property and construction industries. It has a team of experienced lawyers, many of whom are accredited by the Chartered Institute of Arbitrators (UK).
Intellectual property: Akinjide & Co advises on the protection and registration of intellectual property rights including patents, trademarks, copyrights and designs. It also handles intellectual property litigation.
Privatisations: The firm advises on the reform and privatisation of the oil, gas and aviation industries in Nigeria. A member of the firm serves on restructuring committees of the National Council of Privatisation.

LANGUAGES: English, French

WORLDWIDE OFFICE CONTACTS

NIGERIA
4th Floor, NCR Building, 6 Broad Street, **Lagos**
Tel: +234 1 263 5315 **Fax:** +234 1 264 5525
Email: akinjideco@compuserve.com

ASSOCIATED OFFICES

UNITED KINGDOM
10 King's Bench Walk, Temple, LONDON EC4Y 7EB
Tel: +44 20 7353 2501 **Fax:** +44 20 7353 0658
Email:

AKINJIDE & CO

For other recommended firms see pages 1485-1520

ESTUDIO ALEGRIA

HEAD OFFICE

Av. Santa Fe 1621, 4°, 5° y 6° piso,
C1060ABC Buenos Aires, Argentina
Tel: +54 11 4812 5500 **Fax:** +54 11 4812 6245

Email: info@est-alegria.com.ar
Website: www.est-alegria.com.ar

FIRM OVERVIEW

Managing partner: Hector Alegria
Senior Partners: Ricardo M. Richards, Pablo A. Buey Fernández, Gabriel H. Fissore and Miguel Montemerlo

Number of partners worldwide: 5
Number of other lawyers worldwide: 17

AREAS OF PRACTICE:

Corporate	20%
Insolvency	20%
Litigation and arbitration	20%
Mergers and acquisitions	15%
Banking and finance	10%
Administrative law	5%
Telecommunications and computer law	5%

A

FIRM OVERVIEW: Estudio Alegria was formed in July 1976. Since then it has become one of the most successful law firms in Argentina, specialising in commercial, financial and corporate matters, as well as administrative, constitutional and tax law. The firm is currently composed of 20 attorneys and two certified public accountants, together with 16 other employees and a national and international structure of correspondent law firms that provide a full range of services for national and international clients. Work undertaken is varied with particular emphasis on corporate consulting, contracts, insurance and trust law, foreign investments, banking, corporate and capital markets law, notes and securities, international business and financial transactions, restructuring proceedings under the Bankruptcy Act, insolvency and litigation, privatisations, debt-to-equity conversion programmes, mergers and acquisitions, e-commerce and internet law, administrative law, tax counseling and integration law (MERCOSUR - NAFTA and EU) practices.

INTERNATIONAL CLIENTS: The firm's clients include Shell C.A.P.S.A; Global Environmental Fund; Hoescht Argentina S.A.; CTI; HASBRO (U.S.A.); Fuchs Petrolub A.G. (Germany); CYDSA GROUP (México); Harteneck, López y Cía. (Coopers & Lybrand); Acindar Industria Argentina de Aceros S.A.; Roggio S.A.; Tetra Tech Argentina S.A.; Banca Comerciale Italiana; Banco Sudameris (Buenos Aires); Banco Portugués do Atlántico; Kalpakián S.A.; Banco Piano S.A.; Juan Minetti S.A. (Portland); SOCMA S.A.; Sideco Americana S.A.; Cerámica Zanón S.A.; Bonafide S.A.; Georgalos Hnos. S.A.I.C.A.; Necon S.A.; B.G.H. S.A.; Metrovías S.A.; Grupo Exxel; Infotel (España); ACH (Cámara Compensadora de Valores); Argenclear S.A. (Compensadora de Valores de Mercado Abierto); Banco Caja de Ahorro S.A.; Mercado Abierto Electrónico; Banco Indosuez; Banco Mariva; Bunge & Born; Westphere Investment Management; Colorin (Pinturas); Torneos y Competencias S.A.; I.M.P.S.A.; Droguería Americana; Mercado a Término de Buenos Aires; CILFA (Cámara Industrial de Laboratorios Farmacéuticos); Distribuidora Gas del Centro; Latinstocks.com; Axesor.com.

WORLDWIDE OFFICE CONTACTS

ARGENTINA
Av. Santa Fe 1621, 4°, 5° y 6° piso, C1060ABC **Buenos Aires**
Tel: +54 11 4812 5500 **Fax:** +54 11 4812 6245
Email: info@est-alegria.com.ar

MAIN INTERNATIONAL AREAS OF PRACTICE:

Commercial: The firm handles corporate consulting, assisting with the drafting of documents (such as forms, notes and standard documents for transactions with third parties), agreements and the multidisciplinary design of development and managerial strategies, as well as providing solutions to more specific issues. All aspects of commercial law are covered.
Banking: The firm provides a full range of services to national and international financial institutions and investors, including the organisation and chartering of commercial and investment banks, foreign investments in the banking industry, mergers and acquisitions, rescheduling and restructuring negotiations, loan agreements, representation before the Central Bank and matters related to this practice, banking guarantees and regulatory compliance. The firm was involved in the debt to equity conversion plan implemented by the Argentine economic authorities in 1987. The firm has represented international banks, holding companies and major local corporations in many of the largest transactions closed under these regulations.
Corporate/capital markets: The firm advises major domestic and foreign corporations on a wide range of transactions, including mergers, acquisitions, spin-offs, take-overs, public offerings of securities, authorisations for listing on the Stock Exchange, corporate financing, foreign investments and transfer of technology. The firm advise clients on commercial law matters, representing them before administrative agencies and associations regulating exchange and open market transactions. The firm has been acting in an advisory capacity in some of the largest transactions in the Buenos Aires Stock Market, as well as in the first stock issuance in the capital market made under the debt-to-equity conversion programme.
Litigation: The firm handles all aspects of litigation, ranging from banking regulation or eventual breaches of public offering regulations to all types of cases arising from commercial transactions and international commercial arbitration.
Administrative law: The firm advises clients on tax, customs and administrative law. It acts as consultant to federal agencies and is currently advising local and foreign clients on subjects arising from the international treaties signed by Argentina within the framework of Mercosur (Southern Cone Common Market). Estudio Alegria is actively involved in this development, having organised the first international legal seminar on the subject.
Other areas: The firm is actively involved in the privatisation of state-owned companies, mainly utilities, oil, gas, and defence related enterprises, advising international and major local clients on the bidding process. It also advises on matters such as structuring financial packages to meet tender requirements, represents clients in foreign debt swaps and establishes joint ventures and other business organisations to participate in bidding processes for privatisation purposes. The firm is developing a new department for e-commerce and internet-related issues.

LANGUAGES: English, French, Italian, Portuguese, Spanish

For other recommended firms see pages 1485-1520

ALFARO NAVARRO

HEAD OFFICE

Avenida Córdoba 1184,
CP 1055 Buenos Aires, Argentina
Tel: +54 11 4371 8181 **Fax:** +54 11 4371 9292
Email: a-n@alfaro-navarro.com.ar
Website: www.alfaro-navarro.com

FIRM OVERVIEW

Managing partners: Carlos E. Alfaro, Alberto Navarro
Number of partners worldwide: 5
Number of other lawyers worldwide: 38

AREAS OF PRACTICE:

Area	%
M&A	15%
Banking, finance, project finance and capital markets	10%
Foreign investments	10%
Cross-border transactions, joint ventures	8%
Employment and personnel expatriate	8%
Property and real estate development	8%
Oil, gas and energy	6%
E-business and intellectual property	5%
International trade and trade finance	5%
Litigation	5%
Regulatory and public utilities	5%
Securities and commodities	5%
Other	4%
Insurance	3%
Tax	3%

FIRM OVERVIEW: Alfaro-Navarro is a full corporate service international law firm with broad experience in M&A, intellectual property and e-business, project finance transactions and hedging/trading of securities and commodities. Its lawyers are highly trained and many have attended universities abroad.

INTERNATIONAL EXPERIENCE: Alfaro-Navarro has offices in Buenos Aires and New York, and representative offices in London and Madrid. It has established a strategic alliance with the Brazilian firm Tozzini, Freire, Teixeira e Silva, under the Mercosur Alliance of Law Firms. Its regional and international presence enables the firm to respond effectively to clients' needs. More than half of the firm's clients are foreign companies with investments in Latin America.

INTERNATIONAL CLIENTS: Clients include Bell Helicopter Textron, Sun Microsystems Inc., Celanese, Heinz, Wal-Mart (M&A issues), Georgia Pacific Corporation, The Williams Corp., Newsweek, Parsons & Whittmore, Sennheisser Gmbh, Ralston Purina, First International Bank, Morgan Stanley, Inter-American Development Bank, the Overseas Private Investment Corporation, Sandel, Farallon Capital, J. Aron (Goldman Sachs), Hess Trading Corporation (Amerada Hess), BSI, Intertek, UBS Warburg, Merrill Lynch, Cantor Fitzgerald, The Exxel Group, Acindar S.A., Pirelli Cables S.A., Supermercados Norte S.A., Musimundo S.A., OCA S.A., Grupo Socma, Grupo Industrial Saltillo, Yale la Font, Foodpack S.A., Itron, MTC, SEPSA, veritas.com, Halcyon and DomainNames.com.

MAIN AREAS OF INTERNATIONAL PRACTICE:

M&A: The firm handles matters ranging from structuring and negotiating transactions, implementing deal strategies, and performing due diligence, relating to environmental issues, cross-border takeovers and buy-out transactions.
E-business and intellectual property: The firm's intellectual and e-business practice group advises on all aspects of information technology, patenet, trademark protection, licensing, copyright, domain names registration, technology transfer agreements and investors relations. The firm represents both start-ups and venture capitalists.
Banking, finance, project finance and capital markets: The firm handles all areas of banking and finance, including drafting contracts, implementing local and offshore facilities, structured finance, leasing, and tax based finance. The firm also advises on project finance, including cross-border projects.
Property and real estate development: The firm has been actively involved in a number of transactions, such as the acquisition, leasing and construction of more than 130 supermarkets and 50 mega stores. It has a broad experience in investment funds and real estate developments.
Tax: The firm advises on all aspects of this area, including Mercosur's tax regulations.
Foreign investments: The firm provides advice in compliance and tax planning including Foreign Corrupt Act issues.
Employment and personnel expatriate: The firm has a specialist department in this area and is experienced in immigration, labour and cross-cultural consulting services.
Securities and commodities: The firm advises on private and public offerings, disclosure issues, compliance with securities regulations, placement memoranda and related documentation. It also assists investment firms in the structuring and licensing of their operations.
Oil, gas and energy: The firm advises on exploration and production permits, concessions and contracts. It represents clients in the negotitation, contract drafting and dispute resolution of matters related to the construction operation and financing of power projects, transmission lines and pipelines. The firm also has expertise in regulatory issues.
International trade and trade finance: Alfaro-Navarro advises on trade defence, the filing of dumping and countervaling duty cases, and on transactional and regulatory issues related to importing and exporting, and the import of turn-key projects.
Cross-border transactions, joint ventures: The firm advises on cross-border transactions and joint ventures and has experience in planning and implementing joint ventures and strategic alliances.
Mining projects and investments: The firm advises on government regulations, tax benefits, the acquisition of mining rights and the import of mining equipment.

LANGUAGES: English, French, Italian, Portuguese, Spanish

WORLDWIDE OFFICE CONTACTS

ARGENTINA
Avenida Córdoba 1184, CP 1055 **Buenos Aires**
Tel: +54 11 4371 8181 **Fax:** +54 11 4371 9292
Email: a-n@alfaro-navarro.com.ar

SPAIN
Calle Españoleto No.4, 1° Izquierda, 28010 **Madrid**
Tel: +34 91 593 1776 **Fax:** +34 91 593 1776
Email: alejandro.vanderbroele@alfaro-navarro.com

UNITED KINGDOM
16 Hanover Square, **London** W1R 9AJ
Tel: +44 20 7408 9450 **Fax:** +44 870 137 4630
Email: antf@btinternet.com

USA
630 Fifth Avenue, 25th Floor, Suite 2518, Rockefeller Center,
New York NY 10111
Tel: +1 212 698 1140 **Fax:** +1 212 698 1144
Email: antf@mercosur.alliance.com

A

ALLENDE & BREA

HEAD OFFICE

Maipú 1300, 10th Floor,
C1006ACT Buenos Aires, Argentina
Tel: +54 11 4318 9900 **Fax:** +54 11 4318 9999
Email: lex@allendebrea.com.ar
Website: www.allendebrea.com

Managing partners: Enrique Garrido, Rafael La Porta Drago
Senior and managing partner: (New York office) Osvaldo J Marzorati
Number of partners worldwide: 21
Number of other lawyers worldwide: 70

FIRM OVERVIEW

AREAS OF PRACTICE:

Corporate	21%
E-commerce	20%
Oil, gas and energy	14%
Mergers and acquisitions	12%
Banking and insurance	10%
Mining	8%
Telecommunications	8%
Tax and others	7%

A

FIRM OVERVIEW: Allende & Brea is a 45 year old law firm which offers a wide range of services. The firm is known for its work in M&A, Internet, energy and telecoms with 65% of its clientele being international. Allende & Brea is a member of PRAC (Pacific Rim Advisory Council). As such, it has strong ties and professional relationships in Malaysia, Taiwan, Singapore, India, Japan, Indonesia, Philippines, New Zealand, Australia, South Africa and all Latin American countries.

INTERNATIONAL EXPERIENCE: The firm has advised on international matters including privatisations, mining, oil, gas and electricity, mergers and acquisitions, mining and forestry, telecommunications, e-commerce, banking and capital markets, distribution law and intellectual property.

INTERNATIONAL CLIENTS: The firm's client base includes Bank of America, Banca Nazionale del Lavoro, Hicks Muse Tate and Furst, Microsoft, Chase Capital Partners, United Utilities plc, Odebrecht, Bechtel, Boeing, Met Life, Aetna, New York Life, Renault, Telecom Italia, The AES Corp, Mobil Oil, Benetton, British Petroleum, Coastal, Dresdner Kleinwort Benson, Placer Dome, SC Johnson, Fidelity Investments, PA Consulting Group, NCR, Templeton, Eagle Star, Bayerische Hypo-und Vereinsbank AG, Hydro-Quebec, Bombardier International, Texaco Inc., Donaldson, Lufkin & Jenrette, The Williams Company and Orient Energy.

MAIN INTERNATIONAL AREAS OF PRACTICE:

Corporate: The firm assists and represents clients in connection with all activities and issues relating to the formation, governance, management and general conduct of business by corporations.
E-commerce: Since the very inception of Internet in Argentina, Allende & Brea has dedicated a specialised group of professionals for advising start-ups, incubators, private equity funds and other companies interested in developing or investing in the digital economy.
Oil, gas and energy: Since its foundation the firm has been actively involved in the development of the oil and gas industry, becoming one of few Argentine law firms specialising in this area. The firm advises on preparing and negotiating exploration permits, operating concessions, assignment of existing exploration and operation agreements, and transportation and distribution contracts. The firm also advises on matters such as title and record inspections, project financing, and preparing bids for oil and gas exploration and development. Allende & Brea has participated in the privatisation of the electricity industry from the very start. This led to the creation of a specialised team which has earned an outstanding track record in advising electric utilities.
Mergers and acquisitions: The firm has expertise in acquisitions and divestitures in areas including regulated industries such as food and drugs, utilities and telecommunications. The firm handles transactions involving complex antitrust, intellectual property, labour, securities, tax and environmental issues. The firm has designed innovative corporate structures aimed at protecting minority stockholders and providing for fair exit mechanisms.
Mining: Since the deregulation of the mining industry the firm has been concerned with major mining companies worldwide and has been actively involved in the drafting of environmental legislation affecting the mining industry. The firm advises such companies on creating local subsidiaries, obtaining development permits and negotiating leasing agreements with the owners of the areas to be mined.
Banking and finance: Allende & Brea advises several major international banks and other financial institutions on day-to-day operations and on specific transactions.
Tax: The firm aim to minimise tax liabilities while strictly ensuring compliance with the law and most of the firm's tax experts trained in the national revenue service or the tax courts.
Telecommunications and media: The firm was retained by one of the two international consortia awarded the concession for the country's newly-privatised telephone system. Following privatisation, the firm has been serving as legal counsel for the local international carrier. In addition, the firm advises several television cable companies and has participated as counsel in one of the largest merger and acquisition transactions in the country.

LANGUAGES: English, French, German, Italian, Korean, Portuguese, Spanish

WORLDWIDE OFFICE CONTACTS

ARGENTINA
Maipú 1300, 10th Floor, C1006ACT **Buenos Aires**
Tel: +54 11 4318 9900 **Fax:** +54 11 4318 9999
Email: lex@allendebrea.com.ar

USA
10 Rockefeller Plaza, Suite 1001, **New York** 10020
Tel: +1 212 698 2230 **Fax:** +1 212 489 7317
Email: allendebr@aol.com

WORLDWIDE OFFICES

USA

10 Rockefeller Plaza, Suite 1001, New York 10020

Number of lawyers: 3
Office profile: The office provides advice on Argentine Law to local Allende & Brea clients visiting the United States and needing immediate and personal attention. It serves as a liaison between these clients and their U.S. attorneys in cases related to countervailing duties or dumping allegations, arbitration proceedings brought before U.S. panels, and other similar matters requiring close logistical support. To foreign clients, this office offers on-the-spot legal advice. The firm provides Argentine clients immediate access to information regarding the legal and political environment of the country.

ALLEN & GLEDHILL

HEAD OFFICE

36 Robinson Road, #18-01 City House,
Singapore 068877
Tel: +65 225 1611 **Fax:** +65 224 8210

Email: a_g@gledhill.com.sg
Website: www.gledhill.com.sg

WORLDWIDE OFFICE CONTACTS

SINGAPORE
36 Robinson Road, #18-01 City House, **Singapore** 068877
Tel: +65 225 1611 **Fax:** +65 224 8210
Email: a_g@gledhill.com.sg

FIRM OVERVIEW

Managing partner: Lucien Wong

Number of partners worldwide: 68
Number of other lawyers worldwide: 116

AREAS OF PRACTICE:

Banking .... *%
Capital markets and corporate finance .... *%
Corporate .... *%
Financial services .... *%
Intellectual property and technology .... *%
Litigation and arbitration .... *%
Real estate .... *%
Shipping .... *%
* Workload % not disclosed

FIRM OVERVIEW: The firm was founded by Rowland Allen and Joseph John Gledhill in 1902, making it one of the oldest law firms Singapore. It is a full-service firm with 68 partners and over 180 lawyers in total.

INTERNATIONAL EXPERIENCE: The firm has a broad international practice, and has acted in a number of large corporate, commercial and litigation matters of an international nature. It has established strong working relationships with law firms worldwide.

INTERNATIONAL CLIENTS: In line with the firm's international perspective, it has set up specialist sections under the leadership of its senior lawyers to assist clients in their investments in China, India, Vietnam and the ASEAN countries.

MAIN INTERNATIONAL AREAS OF PRACTICE:

Banking: Work includes syndicated loans, secured financing, project finance and structured finance. The firm has also advised on note issuance facilities and provides general advice on banking law.
Capital markets: The firm is active in capital markets work in Singapore and the region, having acted for managers, issuers, and trustees in bond, warrant, convertible and medium-term notes issues. It has also acted on swap transactions and other derivative products and the listing of Dragon Bonds.
Corporate finance: Work covers flotation, rights issues, private placements, takeover offers, privatisation, corporate restructuring, schemes of arrangement and leveraged buyouts. The firm also advises generally on securities regulations in Singapore.
Corporate: Expertise includes corporate administration, employment and environmental law, futures transactions (regulated and unregulated), immigration law, incorporation and registration, joint ventures and M&A.
Intellectual property and technology: Work divides broadly into three main areas. They are protection of IP rights (trade marks, patents, designs, copyrights and layout designs), IP enforcement (infringement proceedings, injunctions and search and seizure) and transactional IP (licensing and exploitation, IT issues and computer contracts, internet/e-commerce and technology transfer).
Litigation and arbitration: Services cover the whole spectrum of contentious work, including banking, building contracts, company law, contract and commercial law, employment law, family law, futures and commodities trading, insurance, land law, securities and trust.
Real estate: The department has been involved in international and regional property work, including advising on joint ventures between local and foreign partners and acting for foreign developers marketing their projects in Singapore.
Shipping: The firm deals with all aspects of contentious and non-contentious marine, air and other transport law including related insurance matters. It has represented both local and international clients including shipowners, managers, agents, charterers, P&I clubs and insurers.

LANGUAGES: Bahasa Indonesia, English, French, Hindi, Italian, Malay, Mandarin (and various Chinese dialects), Tamil

For other recommended firms see pages 1485-1520

ALLEN & OVERY

HEAD OFFICE

One New Change,
London EC4M 9QQ, United Kingdom
Tel: +44 20 7330 3000 **Fax:** +44 20 7330 9999

Email: information@allenovery.com
Website: www.allenovery.com

FIRM OVERVIEW

Managing partner: John Rink
Senior partner: Guy Beringer

Number of partners worldwide: 349
Number of other lawyers worldwide: 1,127

AREAS OF PRACTICE:

Banking .... *%
Business reconstruction and insolvency .... *%
Communications, media and technology .... *%
Corporate and commercial .... *%
Derivative products .... *%
EC and competition law .... *%
Employment, pensions and incentive law .... *%
Environmental .... *%
Financial services .... *%
Insurance .... *%
Intellectual property .... *%
International capital markets .... *%
Litigation .... *%
MBOs .... *%
Mergers, acquisitions and take-overs .... *%
PFI/PPP .... *%
Private clients .... *%
Projects and project finance .... *%
Property (commercial) .... *%
Securitisation .... *%
Tax (corporate) .... *%
* Workload % not disclosed

FIRM OVERVIEW: Founded in 1930, Allen & Overy has over 340 partners and some 3,600 staff. It has offices in 24 major cities and is committed to global expansion and full localisation, where regulations permit. The network of international offices includes local lawyers and English solicitors who combine local expertise with international transaction management skills. In 1999, Allen & Overy was awarded a Queen's Award for Export Achievement in recognition of its success in exporting legal services around the world.

INTERNATIONAL EXPERIENCE: Through its network of 25 offices, Allen & Overy advises businesses, financiers and governments wherever there is a need for legal advice from experienced international practitioners. The combination of local expertise and experience with international transaction management skills, ensures clients receive consistency of quality. Deals can be controlled round-the-clock where necessary, and each overseas office has a support group in London comprising lawyers with experience in that particular country, able to provide back-up when required.

LANGUAGES: Throughout its 25 offices, Allen & Overy offers clients an extensive range of language capabilities.

WORLDWIDE OFFICE CONTACTS

ALBANIA
Veve Business Centre, Suite 108, Bulevaedi Zog 1, **Tirana**
Tel: +355 42 28966 **Fax:** +355 42 28985

BELGIUM
Uitbreidingstraat 80, 2600 **Antwerp**
Tel: +32 3 287 72 22 **Fax:** +32 3 287 72 44

European Union Office, 60 avenue de Cortenburgh, B-1000 **Brussels**
Tel: +32 2 739 5000 **Fax:** +32 2 739 5099

Tervurenlaan 268A, B-1150 **Brussels**
Tel: +32 2 780 2222 **Fax:** +32 2 780 2244

CHINA
Unit 518, Tower 2, Bright China Chang An Building, No 7 Jianguomemei Dajie, Dongcheng District, **Beijing** 100005
Tel: +86 10 6510 2368 **Fax:** +86 10 6510 2378

CZECH REPUBLIC
Krakovskà 9, 4th Floor, 110 00 **Prague** 1
Tel: +42 02 22 107111 **Fax:** +42 02 22 107107

FRANCE
Edouard VII, 26 boulevard des Capucines, 75009 **Paris**
Tel: +33 1 40 06 54 00 **Fax:** +33 1 40 06 54 54

GERMANY
Taunustor 2, 14th Floor, 60311 **Frankfurt am Main**
Tel: +49 69 2648 5000 **Fax:** +49 69 2648 5800

HONG KONG
9th Floor, Three Exchange Sq, Central, **Hong Kong**
Tel: +852 2974 7000 **Fax:** +852 2974 6999

HUNGARY
Madàch Trade Center, Madàch Imre utca 13-14, H-1075 **Budapest**
Tel: +36 1 483 2200 **Fax:** +36 1 268 1515

ITALY
Via Manzoni, 43, 20121 **Milan**
Tel: + 39 02 290 491 **Fax:** + 39 02 290 49333

Corso Vittorio Emanuele II, 284, 00186 **Rome**
Tel: +39 06 684 271 **Fax:** +39 06 684 27333

Corso Vittorio Emanuele II, 68, 10121 **Turin**
Tel: + 39 011 51121 **Fax:** + 39 011 5112333

JAPAN
NTB°M Building, 5th Floor, 2-2-9 Shinbashi, Minato-ku, **Tokyo** 105-0004
Tel: +81 3 5521 8400 **Fax:** +81 3 5521 8444

LUXEMBOURG
58, rue Charles Martel, BP 5017, L-1050 **Luxembourg**
Tel: +352 444 4551 **Fax:** +352 444 4552 22

NETHERLANDS
Apollolaan 15, PO Box 75440, 1070 AK **Amsterdam**
Tel: +31 20 674 1000 **Fax:** +31 20 674 1111

POLAND
Sienna Centre Building, ul. Zelazna 28/30, 00-832 **Warsaw**
Tel: +48 22 820 6100 **Fax:** +48 22 820 6199

RUSSIA
Dmitrovsky pereulok 9, 103031 **Moscow**
Tel: +7 501 725 7900 **Fax:** +7 501 725 7949

For other recommended firms see pages 1485-1520

ALLEN & OVERY

WORLDWIDE OFFICES

ALBANIA

Veve Business Centre, Suite 108, Bulevaedi Zog 1, Tirana
Contact: Enyal Shuke

Number of lawyers: 2

Office profile: The Tirana office opened in 1998. It works closely with the Rome office and practises Albanian law. The firm's Albanian lawyers advise mainly international financial institutions and foreign investors on project finance work (including concessions and BOT transactions), secured banking transactions, privatisations and equity investments. The office has been involved in many major transactions in the country in the last two years. The nature of the practice is to work in integrated teams of Albanian, Italian and English lawyers and, where relevant, lawyers from other jurisdictions.

BELGIUM

Allen & Overy Belgium
Uitbreidingstraat 80, Antwerp 2600

Tervurenlaan 268A, B-1150 Brussels

Contact: Wim Dejohnghe

Number of lawyers: 85

Office profile: On 1st January 2001, 139 lawyers from Loeff Claeys Verbeke's offices in Antwerp and Brussels joined Allen & Overy. The firm now has a major presence in the Benelux region with some 670 partners and staff. Allen & Overy Belgium offers a full legal service including intellectual property, employment, corporate, public and environmental law, litigation, tax, banking and finance, capital markets, property, energy, telecommunications, IT and media. The offices advise multinationals, growth companies and start-ups, working in Dutch, English, French, German, Italian, Spanish and Russian. Allen & Overy Belgium combines Loeff Claeys Verbeke's in-depth knowledge of the local Belgian market with Allen & Overy's global presence and expertise.

European Union Office
60 avenue de Cortenburgh, B-1000 Brussels

Contact: Michael Reynolds

Number of lawyers: 10

Office profile: Opened in 1979, the EU office in Brussels acts for corporate clients in the UK, North America, the Far East and other parts of the world. The office specialises in advice on EU competition laws and has acted in some of the leading EU competition cases before the Commission and the ECJ. It has close contacts with Commission officials responsible for formulating and implementing EU competition policy, in particular with senior officials in the cabinet of the Competition Commissioner, the Merger Task Force and other parts of DG IV. It also advises on a wide range of other areas of EU law, including in relation to air transport; biotechnology and pharmaceutical; e-commerce and the internet; energy; intellectual property, information technology and media; public procurement; single market issues; State aids; telecommunications; and trade law. It provides effective lobbying and monitoring services in all areas, as well as advice and guidance on current EU policy and its future development.

CHINA

Unit 518, Tower 2, Bright China Chang An Building, No 7 Jianguomemei Dajie, Dongcheng District, Beijing 100005

Contact: Bill Shouyun Tong

Number of lawyers: 4

SINGAPORE
1 Robinson Road, #18-00 AIA Tower, **Singapore** 048542
Tel: +65 535 1944 **Fax:** +65 435 7474

SLOVAKIA
Obchodnà 2, 811 06 **Bratislava**
Tel: +421 7 5441 0202 **Fax:** +421 7 5441 0203

SPAIN
Antonio Maura 7-5°, 28014 **Madrid**
Tel: +34 91 521 2654 **Fax:** +34 91 523 0458

THAILAND
22nd Floor, Sindhorn Building III, 130 Wireless Road, **Bangkok** 10330
Tel: +662 263 7600 **Fax:** +662 263 7699

UNITED ARAB EMIRATES
PO Box 3251, 1603 API World Tower, Sheikh Zayed Road, **Dubai**
Tel: +971 43323 190 **Fax:** +971 43323 192

UNITED KINGDOM
One New Change, **London** EC4M 9QQ
Tel: +44 20 7330 3000 **Fax:** +44 20 7330 9999

USA
10 East 50th Street, **New York** NY 10022
Tel: +1 212 610 6300 **Fax:** +1 212 610 6399

Office profile: Allen & Overy has been providing legal advice in China for over 10 years and was one of the first UK firms to be granted a licence to practise in Beijing in 1993. The office is headed by Chief Representative Bill Shouyun Tong who has over ten years of China experience. The firm has excellent working relationships with a number of leading local law firms and regularly assists clients in foreign trade and investment matters in China such as joint ventures, technology licensing, sales of capital equipment, financial transactions, documenting complex projects, the resolution of international commercial disputes and much more. Allen & Overy's Beijing office is supported by the firm's regional headquarters in Hong Kong and includes lawyers who have substantial and broad experience in advising clients on business transactions in China.

CZECH REPUBLIC

Krakovskà 9, 4th Floor, 110 00 Prague 1

Contacts: Stephen Polland, Mikuláš Touška, Václau Valvoda

Number of lawyers: 12

Office profile: Opened in 1992, the Prague office has been involved in a large number of major Czech transactions. It practises in English, Czech, Slovak and EU law, advising both Czech international corporate, banking and financial clients. The office has an integrated Slovakian law capability and handles Slovak transactions directly from Bratsilava.

FRANCE

Edouard VII, 26 boulevard des Capucines, 75009 Paris

Contact: Edouard Didier

Number of lawyers: 62

Office profile: Established since 1989, Allen & Overy, Paris offers its international and French clients a comprehensive French and English law service in the key business areas of banking and finance, capital markets, mergers and acquisitions, corporate matters (including competition, public/administrative and employment law) and all tax-related questions. The office has undergone considerable expansion in recent years and is now one of Allen & Overy's key offices in Europe.

ALLEN & OVERY cont'd

GERMANY

Taunustor 2, 14th Floor, 60311 Frankfurt am Main

Contacts: Arndt Overlack, Mark Welling

Number of lawyers: 60

Office profile: Allen & Overy was established in Frankfurt in 1994 and the office focuses on corporate commercial, international capital markets and banking. Its lawyers work in integrated teams of German, English and, where relevent, lawyers from other jurisdictions. The office has doubled in size over the last 18 months.

HONG KONG

9th Floor, Three Exchange Sq, Central, Hong Kong

Contact: Chris Roberts

Number of lawyers: 84

Office profile: The Hong Kong office was established in 1988 and provides a comprehensive legal service covering banking, business reconstruction and insolvency, China, communications, media and technology, corporate finance, derivatives, employment, insurance, intellectual property, international capital markets, litigation and dispute resolution, M&A, project finance, property and regulatory (including investment products). The office also has a dedicated Korean practice comprising Korean-speaking lawyers who have an understanding of Korean business and social culture, and a specialist Taiwan team. The office is staffed by over 80 lawyers, trained in Hong Kong and other juridictions. The office advises on English, Hong Kong and US law. It has a large number of lawyers who speak and write several Chinese dialects, Asian and European languages including Bahasa Malay, French, German, Hindi, Italian, Japenese, Korean and Thai.

A

HUNGARY

Madàch Trade Center, Madàch Imre utca 13-14, H-1075 Budapest

Contacts: Jonathan Porteous, Eva Hegedus

Number of lawyers: 11

Office profile: Allen & Overy is one of the leading law firms in Budapest. The office combines its international experience in managing corporate and finance transactions and its expertise in new and complex areas with local advice provided by Hungarian lawyers. The office's team of Hungarian and non-Hungarian lawyers specialise in M&A, banking, securities, derivatives, project finance and communications, media and technolgy.

ITALY

Via Manzoni, 43, 20121 Milan
Corso Vittorio Emanuele II, 284, 00186 Rome
Corso Vittorio Emanuele II, 68, 10121 Turin

Contacts: Davide D'Angelo (Milan), Carlo Pavesio (Turin), G. Massimiliano Danusso (Rome)

Number of lawyers: 94

Office profile: Since January 1, 1998 Allen & Overy has had offices in Rome, Milan and Turin, following its merger with the Italian law firm Brosio, Casati e Associati. The Italian practice has over 90 lawyers, many of whom worked or studied in the US or UK. The firm forms teams of English, Italian and US lawyers to handle complex cross-border financings and other transactions and advises on major energy projects in Italy, and large banking and project finance deals. In the last 12 months the firm has advised on over 20 international equity offerings in Italy. During 1999 Allen & Overy established an Italian desk in London which provides a high-quality service to Allen & Overy's Italian and international clients in connection with all aspects of Italian finance law and practice.

Main areas of work: M&A, capital markets, project finance, corporate and commercial, banking and finance, energy, litigation and arbitration, communications, media and technology, US labour law, derivatives.

JAPAN

NTBoM Building, 5th Floor, 2-2-9 Shinbashi, Minato-ku, 105-0004 Tokyo

Contacts: Aled Davies, Salim Nathoo, David Wainer

Number of lawyers: 14

Office profile: The firm's Tokyo office opened in 1988, and has since grown to become one of the largest international law firms in Japan. In April 2000, the office entered into a joint venture with Akatsuki International Law Office, providing clients with access to Japenese law capabilities, particularly in the areas of securitisations, project finance and banking. The Tokyo office advises banks, securities houses and companies on English, EU, US and Japanese law. The practice is split into two principal areas - international capital markets and banking and project finance. Project finance work mostly concerns transactions with Japanese investment.

LUXEMBOURG

58, rue Charles Martel, BP 5017, L-1050 Luxembourg

Contact: Mark Feider

Number of lawyers: 14

Office profile: The Luxembourg office opened on 1st January 2000 following the merger with Beghin & Feider. The office advises both local and foreign companies, as well as foreign bodies, on all aspects of commercial, corporate, civil, administrative, real estate, employment, intellectual property, tax, financial services and banking law, including the incorporation of holding and financial companies, and the formation of investment funds. Its lawyers represent clients before all the Luxemburg Courts - the European Community Court of Justice, the Benelux Court of Justice and the Courts of the Member States of the European Community. The office works closely with Allen & Overy's international offices on many cross-border transactions.

NETHERLANDS

Apollolaan 15, Amsterdam, 1070 AK

Contact: Sietze Hepkema

Number of lawyers: 104

Office profile: The Amsterdam office opened on 1st January 2000. Lawyers, (deputy) civil notaries and tax lawyers work together in an integrated practice, providing legal services to corporates, financial institutions and governmental bodies requiring advice on Dutch, English and European Community law. Several of its partners are qualified to practise US law and one is qualified to practise German law. The lawyers in Amsterdam advise on general corporate, banking and finance, competition and regulatory, telecommunications, media and entertainment, intellectual property and information technology, litigation, employment and tax law, advising Dutch clients doing business abroad and clients from all around the world doing business in the Netherlands.

POLAND

Sienna Centre Building, ul. Zelazna 28/30, 00-832 Warsaw

Contacts: Michael Davies, Andrzej Siemiatkowski

Number of lawyers: 35

Office profile: Allen & Overy Warsaw opened in 1991 as one of the first international law firms in Poland. It provides a comprehensive legal ser-

For other recommended firms see pages 1485-1520

vice for major Polish and international clients seeking to do business in Poland. The office has Polish and English lawyers, operating as a combined team, providing a combination of international experience with local expertise.

RUSSIA

Dmitrovsky pereulok 9, 103031 Moscow

Contact: Peter Timchur

Number of lawyers: 15

Office profile: Allen & Overy has been advising on Russian transactions since the early 1970s and opened its Moscow office in 1993. The office has worked on a broad range of innovative transactions, particularly in the corporate and project finance and restructuring sectors. It has also peformed an increased amount of litigation work over the past year. It provides a comprehensive legal service in English, Russian and New York law to corporations and financial institutions, and works closely with the firm's other offices, particularly London, New York, Frankfurt and Tokyo.

SINGAPORE

1 Robinson Road, #18-00 AIA Tower, Singapore 048542

Contact: Philip N. Pillai

Number of lawyers: 18

Office profile: In September 2000, Allen & Overy Shook Lin & Bok Joint Law Venture (JLV) was established in Singapore. This JLV combines the expertise of two organisations highly regarded in their respective markets. The office offers Singapore, UK and US law capabilities within practice areas such as banking, capital markets, derivatives, securitisations, project finance and corporate. Allen & Overy opened ints Singapore office in 1992 and Shook Lin & Bok was established in Singapore in 1964.

SLOVAKIA

Obchodnà 2, 811 06 Bratislava

Contacts: Hugh Owen, Igor Pàlka

Number of lawyers: 2

Office profile: The Bratislava office opened in 1999, following the recruitment in July 1999 of senior Slovak lawyer, Igor Pálka, to build on the reputation that it had already established for providing a professional and comprehensive service to clients wishing to do business in the Slovak Republic. The firm provides a fully integrated service in Slovak transactions, combining international commercial, banking and financial experience with local expertise and knowledge of local conditions. Allen & Overy acts for corporate, banking and financial clients, advising international and Slovak clients alike and has been involved in advising on a large number of major Slovak transactions.

SPAIN

Antonio Maura 7-5°, 28014 Madrid

Contact: Graham Donnell

Number of lawyers: 15

Office profile: The firm opened its Madrid office in 1990. It practises Spanish, English and EU law and provides a comprehensive legal service to both local and international clients, specialising in areas including corporate, finance, M&A, projects, banking, litigation, property and capital markets.

THAILAND

22nd Floor, Sindhorn Building III, 130 Wireless Road, Bangkok 10330

Contact: Simon Makinson

Number of lawyers: 39

Office profile: The firm's Bangkok office is the second largest within the firm's Asian region network and has significantly enhanced capabilities with the recent arrival of a team of Thai banking, capital markets and litigation specialists. The office comprises six partners and some 30 lawyers whose clients include many major Thai companies and a number of the world's leading international corporates. Working closely with lawyers in the firm's other regional offices, the Bangkok office is well placed to meet the needs of clients working on cross-border deals. With other regional offices located in Hong Kong, Singapore, Beijing and Tokyo, the firm stays at the forefront of legislative and regulatory developments in Asia and provides advice on strategic and commercial issues affecting business in Thailand. The office's presence in Thailand is supported by the resources of the firm's Thailand Practice Group which comprises partners and fee-earners based in Allen & Overy offices around the world who have specialised knowledge and experience of working with Thai organisations, or advising businesses looking to invest in Thailand.

UNITED ARAB EMIRATES

PO Box 3251, 1603 API World Tower, Sheikh Zayed Road, Dubai

Contact: Simon Roderick

Number of lawyers: 10

Office profile: Allen & Overy opened in Dubai in 1978. It provides a professional legal service to large companies, banks, governments and individuals on their activities throughout the region. It also provides advice to clients based in the Middle East on business, investment and other matters outside the region. The Dubai office comprises 10 legal staff including Arabic, Farsi, French and Urdu speakers. In addition, several of these lawyers are qualified in more than one jurisdiction.

USA

10 East 50th Street, New York NY 10022

Contact: Carl Sheldon

Number of lawyers: 39

Office profile: Opened in 1985, the New York office of Allen & Overy has extensive experience of all areas of international finance, with specialist knowledge of project finance, capital markets and banking transactions, swaps and other derivative products, asset finance and leasing, US tax, securitsation and corporate and M&A work. The office serves clients around the globe, and can advise on US federal, securities and tax law, New York law, Delaware corporations law, Dutch law and Netherlands Antilles law and English law. Typical transactions include: Rule 144A placements; securitisations and asset-backed, offerings; single and syndicated bank loans, trade finance facilities; tax-driven asset finance; tender offers; SEC registered transactions; swaps and other derivative products; project financings; M&A; and US domestic and cross-border leasing. These transactions include geographic areas such as Latin America, Europe and Russia and the former Soviet Union Republics. The New York office also works closely with other offices to provide integrated and responsive legal services wherever and whenever clients' needs so require.

ALLEN & OVERY

ALSTON & BIRD LLP

HEAD OFFICE

One Atlantic Center, 1201 West Peachtree Street,
Atlanta GA 30309-3424, USA
Tel: +1 404 881 7000 **Fax:** +1 404 881 7777
Email: info@alston.com
Website: www.alston.com

FIRM OVERVIEW

Managing partner: Ben F. Johnson III
Senior partner: Philip C. Cook
Number of partners worldwide: 199
Number of other lawyers worldwide: 295

AREAS OF PRACTICE:

Intellectual property/technology	23%
Litigation/antitrust	20%
Capital markets/finance	12%
Health care	10%
Tax/employee benefits	10%
Real estate	7%
Financial services	5%
Environmental and land use	3%
Bankruptcy, reorganisation and workouts	2%
International	2%

A

FIRM OVERVIEW: Founded in 1893, Alston & Bird is based in Atlanta, Georgia, with offices in Charlotte and the Research Triangle (North Carolina) and Washington, DC. Its 199 partners and 295 other lawyers offer services in virtually every practice area, specialising in intellectual property and technology. It makes extensive use of technology such as intranets, extranets, laser discs and video conferencing in its work, and groups its lawyers into client-based skill teams rather than into large departments.

INTERNATIONAL EXPERIENCE: The firm's international practice group assists clients with joint ventures and alliances, acquisitions, licensing arrangements, tax matters and manufacturing abilities in growing customer markets in Europe, Latin America and Asia. It has extensive experience in planning, structuring and implementing business deals in all the major commercial jurisdictions worldwide. The team also helps clients plan and structure their US operations. Firm members have conducted over 100 international arbitrations, as well as US litigation involving parties from around the world.

INTERNATIONAL CLIENTS: Clients include American Airlines, Inc, ARCADIS NV, Bass Hotels and Resorts, Inc, Boral Industries, Inc, Borden, Inc, Celpage, Inc, CGW Southeast and Affiliates, Dry Branch Kaolin Company, Fortis, Inc, Genuine Parts Company, Verizon Communications, Komatsu America International Company, LHS Group, Inc, London International Group plc, Matsushita Electric Industrial Co, Ltd, National Data Corporation, Paragon Trade Brands, Inc, Premiere Technologies, Inc, Printpack, Inc, Umbro International and United Parcel Service.

MAIN INTERNATIONAL AREAS OF PRACTICE:

Intellectual property: Patent solicitation expertise includes work in emerging and cutting-edge technologies such as genetic engineering, immunology, microelectronics, computer hardware and software, and Internet and business method patents, as well as the traditional areas. Trademark work is also worldwide. The transactional practice advises clients in the entertainment, sports and IT industries. It has spent the last five years developing experience in electronic commerce, the Internet and telecommunications issues.

WORLDWIDE OFFICE CONTACTS

USA
One Atlantic Center, 1201 West Peachtree Street, **Atlanta** GA 30309-3424
Tel: +1 404 881 7000 **Fax:** +1 404 881 7777
Email: info@alston.com

1211 E. Morehead Street, P.O. Box 34009, **Charlotte** NC 28234-4009
Tel: + 1 704 331 6000 **Fax:** + 1 704 334 2014
Email: info@alston.com

Research Triangle Office, 3605 Glenwood Avenue, Suite 310, **Raleigh** NC 27612-4957
Tel: + 1 919 420 2200 **Fax:** + 1 919 420 2260
Email: info@alston.com

601 Pennsylvania Avenue NW, North Building, 11th floor, **Washington, DC** 20004-2601
Tel: + 1 202 756 3300 **Fax:** + 1 202 756 3333
Email: info@alston.com

Technology: The group represents developers and suppliers of computer software, hardware and services; personal communications service providers; cable and broadcast interests; biotechnology enterprises; venture capitalists; e-commerce companies; and companies engaged in major acquisitions or outsourcings of technology-related systems and services.
Real estate: Acts for traditional construction and permanent lenders, conduit lenders, developers, pension funds and their advisors, REITs, institutional owners and investors, landlords, tenants and corporate users.
Tax: The practice serves all the planning and dispute-related needs of US and foreign clients, including coordination of multi-country tax planning, transfer pricing and tax treaty work. It also undertakes tax advocacy where this is the best way to address clients' problems.
Litigation: The firm's litigation teams have tried hundreds of jury and non-jury cases in the last several years, and participate in mediations and arbitrations nearly every day.
Antitrust and investigations: The group represents blue chip clients in complex litigation on a national and international basis. It represents clients before European antitrust authorities and has litigated in Japan.
Bankruptcy: The group has been particularly active in the communications, technology and health care sectors.
Environmental and land use: The group has a long history of working with federal and state environmental agencies and local zoning officials. Litigators regularly handle complex environmental cases.
Capital markets and investments: The firm has completed more than 500 M&A transactions and over 160 public offerings in the past five years. The firm has closed business combination transactions at the rate of one every three days and closed securities offerings at the rate of one every 11 days.
Leveraged capital: The group advises borrowers, lenders and underwriters on virtually every type of commercial finance transactions. The firm's main concern is to protect clients' interests, whilst recognising that the aim of these transactions is to allocate not eradicate risk.
Financial services: Since 1981 the group has been involved in more than 300 transactions with an aggregate value of almost US$50 billion. The group has particular expertise in electronic commerce.
Health care - corporate finance: One of the largest corporate finance practices in the country working exclusively in health care. Clients range from health care services and managed care companies to medical IT, pharmaceutical and biotech companies, and customary financing sources.
Health care - regulatory: Work includes defending antitrust and false billing cases, forming provider networks, interpreting and applying legislation and establishing compliance programmes.

For other recommended firms see pages 1485-1520

ALTHEIMER & GRAY

HEAD OFFICE

10 South Wacker Drive,
Chicago, Illinois 60606, USA
Tel: +1 312 715 4000 **Fax:** +1 312 715 4800
Email: goldmanl@altheimer.com
Website: www.altheimer.com

FIRM OVERVIEW

Managing partner: Jeffrey N. Smith
Co-chairmen: Gery Chico, Louis B. Goldman, Phillip Gordon, S. Michael Peck
Number of partners worldwide: 128
Number of other lawyers worldwide: 208

AREAS OF PRACTICE:

Bankruptcy ....*%
Corporate, corporate finance and securities ....*%
Employment ....*%
Estate planning and administration ....*%
Government ....*%
Intellectual property and IT ....*%
Internet and high-tech ....*%
Litigation ....*%
Real estate ....*%
Tax ....*%
* Workload % not disclosed

FIRM OVERVIEW: Established in Chicago in 1915, Altheimer & Gray has more than 335 attorneys in nine offices in Chicago, Prague, Warsaw, Kyiv, Istanbul, Bratislava, Bucharest, Shanghai and London. It serves corporate and business clients, providing cross-border and domestic legal advice in Europe, the US and China.

INTERNATIONAL EXPERIENCE: The international practice group consists of lawyers with experience in finance and banking, acquisitions, securities, antitrust, real estate, tax, litigation and arbitration, patents, licensing and intellectual property and insurance. As well as advising clients on inward and outward bound business and financial transactions, the firm serves clients involved in foreign investment in the US; direct US investment abroad; the licensing of technology abroad; international joint ventures; Eurocurrency/Eurodollar financing transactions; international arbitration; international taxation; complex financings; international real estate transactions and construction projects and international acquisitions and divestitures. The firm is particularly involved in the developing markets of central, eastern and southern Europe. Unlike most international firms in the region, it decided to staff its foreign offices predominantly with prominent local lawyers, who work closely with US lawyers experienced in cross-border transactions.

INTERNATIONAL CLIENTS: The firm's international clients comprise major US and European multinationals and financial institutions and large real estate companies and leading corporations from emerging market countries. Representative projects include numerous telecommunication acquisitions, joint ventures, privatisations, and global security offerings; representation of the developers of the Warsaw Financial Centre; the representation of Aero Vodochody (the leading Czech aircraft manufacturer) in connection with a $200 million high-yield note offering; the representation of Danka plc in connection with certain strategic dispositions and a strategic investment into Danka by the Cypress Group; and the representation of major international petroleum, food and tobacco companies in connection with privatisations, acquisitions and greenfield projects.

WORLDWIDE OFFICE CONTACTS

CHINA
Shanghai Kerry Centre, 1515 Nanjing West Road, **Shanghai** 200040
Tel: +86 21 6289 0990 **Fax:** +86 21 6289 9911
Email: general@altheimer.cn

CZECH REPUBLIC
Platnérská 4, 110 00 **Prague 1**
Tel: +420 2 2481 2782 **Fax:** +420 2 2481 0125
Email: agprague@altheimer.cz

POLAND
Warsaw Financial Center, ul. Emilii Plater 53, 00-113 **Warsaw**
Tel: +48 22 520 5000 **Fax:** +48 22 520 5001
Email: ag@warsaw.altheimer.pl

ROMANIA
Pitar Mos 5, Sector 1, 70151 **Bucharest**
Tel: +40 1 212 3791 **Fax:** +40 1 212 3796
Email: bucharest.office@altheimer.ro

SLOVAKIA
Námestie SNP 15, 811 06 **Bratislava**
Tel: +421 7 5293 2144 **Fax:** +421 7 5296 1566
Email: agba@altheimer.sk

TURKEY
Buyukdere Cad. 195, Buyukdere Plaza 6, Levent, 80640 **Istanbul**
Tel: +90 212 324 2040 **Fax:** +90 212 324 2032
Email: istanbul@altheimer.com.tr

UKRAINE
11 Mykhailivska Street, 01001 **Kyiv**
Tel: +380 44 230 2534 **Fax:** +380 44 230 2535
Email: office@altheimer.kiev.ua

UNITED KINGDOM
7 Bishopsgate, **London** EC2N 3AR
Tel: +44 20 7786 5700 **Fax:** +44 20 7786 0000
Email: london@altheimer.co.uk

ASSOCIATED OFFICES

HUNGARY
Ban, S. Szabo & Partners, Szerb utca 17-19, 1056 **Budapest**
Tel: +36 1 266 35 22 **Fax:** +36 1 266 35 23
Email: office@bansszabo.hu

MAIN INTERNATIONAL AREAS OF PRACTICE:

Corporate, corporate finance and securities: The firm has handled a large number of investment, financing, privatisation, joint venture and real estate development transactions in established and emerging markets. The firm has established a substantial practice in private equity and management-led investment groups, acting as lead counsel in hundreds of successful transactions. Work also includes follow-on investments and add-on acquisitions. In recent years, the firm has handled global securities issues and complex financings representing a wide range of clients in Rule 144A and registered offerings. The firm has become increasingly involved in takeovers involving public companies and representing special committees.

Banking and finance: The firm represents major financial institutions and multilateral financial institutions in connection with secured and unsecured credit facilities, securitisations, and global securities offerings of high-yield and other debt. The firm has particular experience in developing such structures in emerging market economies.

Insurance: The firm advises on all aspects of insurance law for corporate and insurance industry clients. Matters handled range from drafting insurance contracts, reinsurance audits and a broad range of insurance litiga-

For other recommended firms see pages 1485-1520

tion and arbitration cases for foreign and domestic insurers and reinsurers, as well as major national and international insurance brokers. The firm advises on the insurance laws and markets of Western, Central and Eastern Europe and China, and has experience with ministries and insurers in these areas.

Bankruptcy, workout and insolvency: The department combines new loan documentation with workout and bankruptcy and represents institutional investors, unsecured creditors, creditors' committees and business debtors.

Intellectual property and IT: The department works in the US and in established and emerging markets. It provides comprehensive litigation, patent, trademark, copyright, technology and trade secrets services and advises on the development of worldwide intellectual property strategy.

Internet and high-tech: The firm advises on e-commerce strategies, M&A, start-ups, venture investing, government incentives and site acquisitions.

Litigation: The firm handles civil and criminal matters and international arbitrations. It is able to field cross-jurisdictional teams of lawyers to handle complex arbitrations involving the laws of multiple jurisdictions.

Real estate: The firm has experience in structuring complex commercial and financial transactions throughout the world. It advises financial investors, developers, property managers, architects, construction companies, hotel owners and developers and others in connection with a wide variety of real estate projects ranging from industrial to retail to hotels to commercial office buildings and mixed use facilities. The firm represents major multinational corporations who have outsourced all of their global real estate legal work.

Tax: The firm helps to design business structures, and advises on the international, federal, state and local tax implications of various alternatives. It also litigates in all the administrative tribunals, federal and state courts.

LANGUAGES: Belarusian, Chinese (Mandarin and Shanghainese), Czech, English, French, German, Hungarian, Italian, Norwegian, Polish, Russian, Slovak, Spanish, Swahili, Turkish, Ukrainian

WORLDWIDE OFFICES

CHINA

Shanghai Kerry Centre, 1515 Nanjing West Road, Shanghai 200040

Managing director: Edward J. Epstein
Number of lawyers: 8
Office profile: Opened in 1996, the Shanghai office specialises in M&A, joint ventures, WFOEs, corporate restructuring transactions, real estate matters, intellectual property, environmental law, tax and labour. Clients include American, Canadian, European and Chinese clients in the oil, chemical and petrochemical, automobile and auto parts industries.

CZECH REPUBLIC

Platnérská 4, 110 00 Prague 1

Number of lawyers: 27
Office profile: The firm was one of the first Western law firms to open a Prague office, in 1991 at the request of the Czech Ministry of Privatisation, the firm advised senior officials on privatisations and was the principal draughtsman of the form purchase agreements used during the first wave of privatisation. The firm advises Western clients on transactions and operations in the Czech Republic, including capital markets work, acquisitions, privatisation, joint venture, real estates and 'greenfield' projects. It serves privatised Czech companies and the Czech subsidiaries of multinational companies.

POLAND

Warsaw Financial Center, ul. Emilii Plater 53, 00-113 Warsaw

Managing partner: Gabriel Wujek
Number of lawyers: 26
Office profile: Opened in September 1990, Altheimer & Gray was the first US firm to open an office in Poland. The office has been involved in over 100 Polish privatisations. It has also been active in M&A, joint ventures and greenfield projects for multinationals, as well as significant real estate and insurance work. Clients include the Polish ministries of industry and trade, privatisation, foreign economic relations and finance, as well as major US, European and Asian multinationals.

ROMANIA

Pitar Mos 5, Sector 1, 70151 Bucharest

Managing partner: Obie L Moore
Number of lawyers: 14
Office profile: Opened in1997, clients include major European financial institutions in connection with privatisation and investment funds and a variety of investment banking activities; Western private equity funds; a major international brewery in connection with the acquisition of three Romanian breweries, a Western multi-line insurance company, and a range of clients involved in consumer products, cement, defence technology, telecommunications and other industries.

TURKEY

Buyukdere Cad. 195, Buyukdere Plaza 6, Levent, 80640 Istanbul

Managing partner: Haluk Çan Özel
Number of lawyers: 12
Office profile: Opened in 1994, the Istanbul office is staffed by top local professionals and US lawyers experienced in cross-border transactions. The practice focuses on representing multinational companies investing or doing business in Turkey, and Turkish companies doing business abroad. It advises on M&A, global securities offerings, joint ventures, government contracts, privatisations, project financing, trademark, copyrights and general corporate matters.

UKRAINE

11 Mykhailivska Street, 01001 Kyiv

Managing partner: Jaroslawa Zelinsky Johnson
Number of lawyers: 13
Office profile: The Kiev office was opened in July 1993. Clients are from agrochemical, pharmaceutical, oil exploration and refining, machinery, telecommunications, food processing, fast food, tobacco and consumer product industries. The firm advises on foreign investment, including joint ventures, subsidiaries, due diligence inquiries, document negotiation and preparation, all aspects of Ukrainian tax law, and real estate development.

UNITED KINGDOM

7 Bishopsgate, London EC2N 3AR

Managing partner: Robert C. Bata
Number of lawyers: 32
Office profile: The London office was opened in July of 1999 and is focused on five core areas: corporate finance and securities, project finance, real estate/property, M&A and telecommunications/IT. Most of its lawyers are UK admitted solicitors. The office runs a domestic United Kingdom practice, as well as acting as a hub for the firm's work across Europe.

For other recommended firms see pages 1485-1520

ALUKO & OYEBODE

HEAD OFFICE

35 Moloney Street, PO Box 2293, Marina,
Lagos, Nigeria
Tel: +234 1 260 0080 **Fax:** +234 1 263 2249

Email: ao@aluko-oyebode.com
Website: www.info.martindale.com/aluko&oyebode

FIRM OVERVIEW

Managing partner: Gbenga Oyebode
Number of partners worldwide: 5
Number of other lawyers worldwide: 15

WORLDWIDE OFFICE CONTACTS

NIGERIA
35 Moloney Street, PO Box 2293, Marina, **Lagos**
Tel: +234 1 260 0080 **Fax:** +234 1 263 2249
Email: ao@aluko-oyebode.com

UNITED KINGDOM
9 Mason's Yard, Duke Street, St James's, **London** SW1Y 6BU
Tel: +44 20 7930 8444 **Fax:** +44 20 7930 7774
Email: ao@aluko-oyebode.com

AREAS OF PRACTICE:

Area	%
Energy	30%
Litigation and arbitration	20%
Corporate and commercial	15%
Banking and finance	12%
Privatisation	8%
Intellectual property	6%
Telecommunications and computer law	5%
Other	4%

FIRM OVERVIEW: Aluko & Oyebode is one of the largest law firms in Nigeria. It provides a comprehensive range of specialist legal services to both national and international clients. Established in January 1993, the firm currently has five partners and a full complement of highly qualified professional staff.

INTERNATIONAL EXPERIENCE: Aluko & Oyebode has advised on cross-border transactions in addition to the establishment of multinational businesses and foreign companies in Nigeria. The firm has acted as Local Attorney for the first dual listing of a foreign company on the Nigerian Stock Exchange and is currently acting as Local Attorney to the first private independent power production initiative in Nigeria.

INTERNATIONAL CLIENTS: The firm has a diverse client base including top-tier international and multinational clients operating in the banking, energy, telecommunications, manufacturing, aviation/shipping and public sectors.

MAIN INTERNATIONAL AREAS OF PRACTICE:

Corporate and commercial: The firm advises on all aspects of general corporate and commercial law including the operation of businesses in Nigeria; joint ventures; advising on compliance with corporate legislation; business law; laws relating to foreign investments in Nigeria and the establishment of foreign businesses in Nigeria; liquidations; receiverships; schemes of arrangements and reconstruction and company secretarial services; employment law; commercial property transactions and conveyancing.
Banking and finance: The firm advises in all areas of banking and finance, including general banking law, loan documentation, asset-based finance, construction finance, off-balance sheet and lease transactions, local and offshore secured and syndicated loan transactions and guarantees, project finance, structured trade finance, securitisation, debt advisory and rescheduling, foreign exchange regulations and hedging mechanisms.
Litigation and arbitration: Aluko & Oyebode has an experienced team of barristers led by a Senior Advocate of Nigeria who is also a Fellow of the Chartered Institute of Arbitrators. The firm advises on all aspects of commercial, national and international litigation and arbitration, and ADR. It handles a broad range of cases before the Nigerian Courts and has advised on International Chamber of Commerce regulations.
Privatisation and commercialisation: Aluko & Oyebode advises on the regulatory framework for investment, preparing and reviewing requisite documentation and advising on governmental approvals and permits in the Nigerian power, water, telecommunications and solid minerals industries.
Intellectual property: The firm advises on all aspects of intellectual property including registering, protecting, using and enforcing trademarks, copyrights, patents, designs and trade secrets, licensing, franchising, technology transfer, packaging, labelling manufacturing and distribution agreements.
Telecommunications and computer law: Aluko & Oyebode advises on the regulations governing the Nigerian telecommunications industry and handles all information technology matters. It also handles government approvals and the filing of necessary documentation with the Nigerian Communications Commission and Ministry of Communications.
Energy: The firm has played an active role in the development of law in this area. Aluko & Oyebode's transactions include the first private independent power production initiative in Nigeria, the proposed privatisation of Nigeria's largest state-owned water corporation, financing of exploration and production agreements in the oil sector.
Capital markets: Aluko & Oyebode advises on matters relating to the Nigerian Stock Exchange; public company flotations and other types of capital funding; divestment of equity, securities, takeovers, management buy-outs; mergers and acquisitions, and reorganisations. It also assists investment companies and trust fund structures with the licensing of their operations.
Aviation and shipping: The firm advises on the leasing, registration and financing of aircraft and ships, ship arrests, shipbuilding and ship repair contracts. It also advises on regulatory issues, procuring governmental approvals and permits, hull and cargo claims, contracts of affreightment, marine insurance, P&I insurance, oil pollution, mortgages, salvage and collision.
Tax: The firm advises on tax matters in various industries including oil and gas, manufacturing, and power sectors.

LANGUAGES: English, French, Hausa, Ibo, Yoruba

AMARCHAND & MANGALDAS & SURESH A SHROFF & CO

HEAD OFFICE

Lentin Chambers, Dalal Street, Fort
Bombay 400 023, India
Tel: +91 22 265 0500 **Fax:** +91 22 432 4980

Email: amss.bombay@amarchand.com

FIRM OVERVIEW

Managing partners: Cyril S Shroff, Shardul S. Shroff

Number of partners worldwide: 13
Number of other lawyers worldwide: 65

AREAS OF PRACTICE:
Banking and finance .... *%
EU, commercial and anti-trust .... *%
M&A .... *%
Real estate and planning .... *%
Telecommunications, IT and intellectual property .... *%
*Workload % not disclosed

A

FIRM OVERVIEW: The firm, headquartered in Bombay, was established 80 years ago and since then has established a presence in several regions in India. It has a significant practice in New Delhi in addition to its branches in Bangalore, Ahmedabad and Calcutta. Amarchand & Mangaldas & Suresh A Shroff & Co is a full service law firm.

INTERNATIONAL CLIENTS: The firm serves clients in a wide range of sectors.

MAIN INTERNATIONAL AREAS OF PRACTICE:
The firm handles a full service range of work in a broad range of categories, undertaking contentious and non-contentious work.

LANGUAGES: English, Hindi and other Indian languages.

WORLDWIDE OFFICE CONTACTS

INDIA
Apartment No. 4b, Premchand House Annexe, Highcourt Way, Ashram Road, **Ahmedabad** 380 009
Tel: +91 79 658 5310 **Fax:** + 91 79 653 7354
Email: amssah@satyam.net.in

201 Midford House, Midford Garden, Off M.G. Road, **Bangalore** 560 001
Tel: +91 80 558 4870 **Fax:** + 91 80 558 4266
Email: amssblr@blr.vsnl.net.in

Anand Lok, 227 AJC Bose Road, (Lower Circular Road), **Calcutta** 700 020
Tel: +91 33 247 0508 **Fax:** + 91 33 247 2349
Email: amsscal@cal.vsnl.net.in

41/42 Lloyds Centre Point, Appa Saheb Marathe Marg, Prabhadevi, **Mumbai** 400 025
Tel: +91 22 432 4455 **Fax:** + 91 1 22 4324980
Email: cyril.shroff@amarchand.com

Lentin Chambers, Dalal Street, Fort, **Mumbai** 400 023
Tel: +91 22 265 0500 **Fax:** +91 22 432 4980
Email: amss.bombay@amarchand.com

Presidential Towers, 3 L.S Complex, Pamposh Enclave, **New Delhi** 110048
Tel: +91 11 628 7825 **Fax:** + 91 11 628 7829
Email: shardul.shroff@amarchand.com

13, Abul Fazal Road, Bengali Market, **New Delhi** 110 001
Tel: +91 11 335 5147 **Fax:** + 91 11 335 5149
Email: pallavi.shroff@amarchand.com

For other recommended firms see pages 1485-1520

AMARO, STUBER E ADVOGADOS ASSOCIADOS

HEAD OFFICE

Av. Paulista 1499, 18° e 19° andares,
São Paulo, SP CEP 01311-928, Brazil
Tel: +55 11 284 9911 **Fax:** +55 11 283 0483

Email: lawyers@amarostuber.com
Website: www.amarostuber.com

WORLDWIDE OFFICE CONTACTS

BRAZIL
Av. Paulista 1499, 18° e 19° andares, CEP 01311-928, **São Paulo**
Tel: +55 11 284 9911 **Fax:** +55 11 283 0483
Email: lawyers@amarostuber.com.br

FIRM OVERVIEW

Managing and senior partners: Walter Douglas Stuber,
Abel Simão Amaro

Number of partners worldwide: 4
Number of other lawyers worldwide: 20

AREAS OF PRACTICE:

Tax - consultation/litigation	35%
Banking and finance	30%
Corporate	20%
Mergers and contracts	10%
Litigation - labour/civil/commercial	5%

FIRM OVERVIEW: Amaro, Stuber e Advogados Associados was founded on August 1, 1992 by former partners of a prominent São Paulo law firm. It currently has a staff comprising more than 40 professionals. The firm is the Brazilian member of GLOBALAW, the International Law Group, an international network of law firms in the United States, Canada, Europe, Latin America, Asia and the Middle East. The firm is also a member of the International Bar Association (IBA), American Bar Association (ABA), Inter-Pacific Bar Association (IPBA), American Arbitration Association (AAA), and the International Fiscal Association (IFA). It has also been legal counsel for the Brazilian Commercial and Multiple Banks Association ('Associação Brasileira de Bancos Comerciais e Múltiplos - ABBC') since 1992.

INTERNATIONAL EXPERIENCE: The firm has a major international practice which provides legal advice in Brazil and abroad. It has experience in diverse jurisdictions including South Korea, the US, the UK, South Africa, Argentina, and Canada. The firm has advised multinational companies on joint venture and merger and acquisition strategies, as well as commercial litigation via arbitration.

INTERNATIONAL CLIENTS: The firm's client base is diverse and engages in banking, insurance, industry, trade, services, imports and exports, vehicle assembly, mining, telecommunications, and cosmetics. Many of its clients are established in Brazil, the US, Mexico, Canada, Europe, Latin America, and Asia.

MAIN INTERNATIONAL AREAS OF PRACTICE:
M&A: The firm's transactions in this area range from small technology companies to major financial institutions. The firm is experienced in representing sellers, buyers, investors, investment banks, commercial banks, venture capitalists and companies in a range of M&A transactions.
Tax litigation and tax planning: The tax practice includes challenging tax inspections and charges as well as assisting clients in planning domestic, cross-border and transnational operations. It advises multinationals and medium-sized companies with international operations and public-sector companies on risk prevention, tax optimisation, management and negotiation of projects, corporate tax consulting, profit repatriation planning, indirect tax, transfer pricing, strategic tax consulting, banking and financial products taxation.
Banking and finance: It advises several major multinational banks, insurance companies and financial related service companies regarding a vast array of financial issues including Central Bank regulations governing international monetary transactions, negotiation and preparation of documents for foreign loans, hedging transactions, structuring and issuance of security placements abroad, hybrid securities and real estate investment funds, Brazilian capital market transactions, negotiation of leasing transactions, foreign trade and other domestic and international financial and banking transactions.
Corporate and contracts: The firm's lawyers are constantly advising clients in Brazil and overseas on corporate and international contract matters (i.e. leasing, project finance, service rendering, joint ventures).
Employment: The firm is very active in advising on Brazilian employment law in consultative and litigation areas.
Internet and communications: The firm is experienced in advising Internet related business and communication companies in Brazil regarding domestic and international domain name registration and disputes, website development and ownership rights, drafting of online and electronic commerce contracts, and electronic publishing issues.
Financial markets securities: The firm has experience advising international and domestic financial institutions and investors on Brazilian law involving funds, securities, and derivatives.
Intellectual property: The firm is experienced in negotiation and drafting of technology transfer and technical assistance agreements, including patent and trademark licenses, and registration of agreements with the National Institute of Industrial Property and Central Bank of Brazil. It provides general consulting regarding the informatics law, software and copyright protection, negotiation and drafting of appropriate documentation.
Real estate: The firm advises on real estate titles, performs drafting and filing of contracts to convey, assign or encumber real estate for national or foreign companies. It also negotiates rental and lease agreements and drafts the respective documents. The firm has acted as consultant on real estate investment funds.
Environmental: The firm provides general consulting on the legal requirements for urban development, zoning, and environmental protection. It has advised clients on environmental aspects of commercial transactions and has provided environmental assessment of projects.
Project finance: The firm provides legal counseling in all phases of project finance to domestic and international clients interested in undertaking infrastructure projects as well as public works, including the supply of water, electricity, oil, gas, telecommunications, and transportation.

LANGUAGES: English, French, Portuguese, Spanish

For other recommended firms see pages 1485-1520

AMOSH LEGAL SERVICES & ARBITRATION

HEAD OFFICE

El-Rabiah, PO Box 950452,
Amman 11195, Jordan
Tel: +962 655 40 456 **Fax:** +962 655 40 459

Email: amoshlsa@nets.com.jo

FIRM OVERVIEW

Managing partner: Dr. Ibrahem Amosh

Number of partners worldwide: 2
Number of other lawyers worldwide: 5

AREAS OF PRACTICE:

- **Corporate, commercial and securities** 30%
- **Intellectual property** 15%
- **Litigation and arbitration** 15%
- **Telecommunications** 15%
- **M&A and joint ventures** 10%
- **Banking and finance** 5%
- **Insurance** 5%
- **Tax and employment** 5%

WORLDWIDE OFFICE CONTACTS

JORDAN
El-Rabiah, PO Box 950452, **Amman** 11195
Tel: +962 655 40 456 **Fax:** +962 655 40 459
Email: amoshlsa@nets.com.jo

ASSOCIATED OFFICES

OMAN
M. Alkiyumi & Associates, OCC Office No. 512, PO Box 1108, 112
Muscat Oman
Tel: +968 790 455 **Fax:** +968 787 261

A

FIRM OVERVIEW: Amosh Legal Services & Arbitration was established at the start of 2000. Currently comprising two partners and five other lawyers, the firm has established two specialised departments. Through its corporate law department and intellectual property department the firm provides a range of comprehensive legal services, with particular expertise in corporate, commercial and securities law, telecommunications, privatisations, intellectual property, M&A and joint ventures, litigation and arbitration. Other important areas of practice are banking, tax, employment law and insurance.

INTERNATIONAL EXPERIENCE: During 2000, the firm advised several international clients on a range of transactions including privatisations, tax, joint ventures, intellectual property (including copyright, patents, industrial designs, trademarks, trade names, integrated circuits, geographical indications, and plant varities), WTO and its impact on local laws, import and export, corporate law and commercial law in general.

INTERNATIONAL CLIENTS: The firm acts for a number of foreign corporations and industrial groups in Lebanon, Saudi Arabia, Sultanate of Oman, UAE, Syria, Tunisia, the Palestinian National Authority, the UK, the US, and the Republic of Moldova. The firm's local clients include the government of Jordan, Jordan Telecom Plc, Mobilecom LLC, Jordan Investment Trust Plc, Moldtech Co. LLC, University of Jordan, Jordan Electricity Plc, and Jordan Petroleum Refinery Plc.

MAIN INTERNATIONAL AREAS OF PRACTICE: The firm advises clients on business and investment including mergers, acquisitions and take-overs; securities law and financial markets; joint ventures; tax; intellectual property and telecommunications; employment; insurance.

LANGUAGES: Arabic, English

For other recommended firms see pages 1485-1520

ANDERSEN LEGAL

HEAD OFFICE

1 Surrey Street,
London WC2R 2PS, United Kingdom
Tel: +44 20 7489 6225 **Fax:** +44 20 7438 3431

Website: www.andersenlegal.com

FIRM OVERVIEW

Chief executive: Alberto Terol
Managing partners: Patrick Bignon, Tony Williams

Number of partners worldwide: 490
Number of other lawyers worldwide: 2,928

AREAS OF PRACTICE:

Area	%
Corporate and commercial	29%
Tax	25%
Litigation and arbitration	10%
Banking and finance	9%
Employment	9%
Intellectual property and IT	9%
Real estate	9%

FIRM OVERVIEW: Andersen Legal is an international organisation of high quality law firms operating in more than 35 countries around the world. It brings together some of the world's leading legal practices and delivers an integrated approach based on common technology, methodologies and commitment to quality client service. Andersen Legal is able to provide clients with a full range of legal expertise in areas covering corporate/commercial work including extensive experience in mergers and acquisitions. It also has a rapidly growing banking and finance practice and a large amount of experience and expertise in advising clients on e-business and other new economy related areas of law. Andersen Legal also advises clients in other areas including labour law (including pensions and share schemes work), real estate, competition and trade and litigation and arbitration. Andersen Legal can provide its clients with a multi-disciplinary approach to solving business problems. Through its association with Andersen Worldwide SC, Andersen Legal has unique access to the professional services of Arthur Andersen and therefore an unmatched ability to provide integrated legal and business solutions to clients. Andersen Legal has invested heavily in on-line delivery of information and project management. Andersen Legal is one of the world's pioneers in the use of secure extranets to manage deal information on behalf of clients. Called 'Dealsight', this service is very valuable when handling cross-border projects across multiple time zones. In 1991 Andersen Legal reported worldwide fee income of US$528 million, an increase of 30 percent on the previous financial year. During the same year Andersen Legal completed two mergers – in Germany with Luther & Partners to create Andersen Luther, and in Brazil where Brazilian law firm Thiollier e Pinheiro Advogados merged with Branco Advogados Associados to create Thiollier, Pinheiro e Branco-Advogados. The year also saw the recruitment of high profile lawyers Tony Williams from Clifford Chance, Jean Thibaud from Gide Loyrette Nouel and Gilles Thieffry from Norton Rose.

INTERNATIONAL EXPERIENCE: Europe is the leading region for the organisation but it also has thriving practices in Asia/Pacific and Latin America. Law firms within the Andersen Legal organisation are strong players in their respective domestic marketplaces, not foreign office transplants. Andersen Legal firms have a thorough understanding of their marketplace

WORLDWIDE OFFICE CONTACTS

ARGENTINA
Arthur Andersen Asesores Legales, 25 de Mayo 487, 1002 **Buenos Aires**
Tel: +54 11 4311 6644 **Fax:** +54 11 4312 8647

AUSTRALIA
Andersen Legal, 363 George Street, **Sydney** NSW 2000
Tel: +612 9993 6600 **Fax:** +612 9993 6650

BRAZIL
Thiollier, Pinheiro e Branco - Advogados, Praia de Botafogo, 300 - 7 andar, 22250-040 **Rio de Janeiro**
Tel: +55 21 559 4350 **Fax:** +55 21 551 8151

COLOMBIA
Andersen Legal, Carrera 7 No. 74-09 Piso 6, **Bogota**
Tel: +57 1 312 3232 **Fax:** +57 1 217 8088

CZECH REPUBLIC
Weinhold Andersen Legal, Husova 5, 110 00 **Prague** 1
Tel: +420 2 2440 1510 **Fax:** +420 2 2440 1389

DENMARK
Rønne & Lundgren, Midtermolen 1, DK-2100 **Copenhagen**
Tel: +45 35 25 25 35 **Fax:** +45 35 25 25 36

ECUADOR
Arthur Andersen & Co., Av. Amazonas 3837 y Corea, **Quito**
Tel: +593 2 468 6677 **Fax:** +593 2 46 94 94

FRANCE
Andersen Legal Association d'Avocats, Neuilly-sur-Seine: 41 rue Ybry, 92576 **Neuilly-sur-Seine** Cedex (see entry page 983)
Tel: +33 1 55 61 10 10 **Fax:** +33 1 55 61 15 15

GERMANY
Andersen Luther Rechtsanwaltsgesellschaft mbH, Ludwigstr. 8, 50667 **Cologne**
Tel: +49 221 92597710 **Fax:** +49 221 92597772

GUATEMALA
Arthur Andersen S.A., Diagonal 6 10-01, Zona 10, Centro Gerencial Las Margaritas, Torre II, 60 Nivel, **Guatemala City** 01010
Tel: +502 332 7939 **Fax:** +502 339 2731

HUNGARY
Burai-Kovács & Partners, Attorneys at Law, River Estates Building, Váci út 35, H-1134 **Budapest**
Tel: +36 1 451 7170 **Fax:** +36 1 451 7179

ITALY
Studio di Consulenza Legale e Tributaria
Largo Donegani, 2, 20121 **Milan**
Tel: +39 02 6240 1 **Fax:** +39 02 659 80 61

MALAYSIA
Zaid Ibrahim & Co., Level 19 Manara Milenium, Jalan Damaniela, Pusat Bandar Damansara, Damansara Heights, **Kuala Lumpur** 50490
Tel: +60 3 2579999 **Fax:** +60 3 2544888

MEXICO
Ruiz, Urquiza y Cía, SC, Bosque de Duraznos 127, Bosques de las Lomas, 11700 Mexico, D.F **Mexico City**
Tel: +52 5 326 6413 **Fax:** +52 5 326 8969

NETHERLANDS
Wouters Advocaten & Notarissen, Prof. W.H. Keesomlaan 8, 1183 DJ Amstelveen, PO Box 75381, 1070 AJ **Amsterdam**
Tel: +31 20 880 8700 **Fax:** +31 20 880 8787

and many are independently ranked in the top 5-10 law firms for that country. The firms have handled a number of high profile projects for clients around the world. These include advising Spanish bank Argentaria on its merger with Banco Bilbao Vizcaya, worth approximately US$38 billion, to create the second largest bank in the 'Eurozone'; advising Bank of Scotland on its outsourcing of IT needs to IBM, worth approximately US$1 billion over ten years and estimated to be Europe's largest ever outsourcing contract; advising Polish Bank, BRE Bank S.A., and its main shareholder, Commerzbank AG, on a contested merger with Bank Handlowy worth US$2 billion; advising Virgin on its US$1 billion mobile telephone joint venture (Virgin Mobile) which will be based in Singapore, with SingTel Mobile (a subsidiary of Singapore Telecom); advising clients on five different licence applications in different countries across Europe for the third generation of mobile telephone networks known as UMTS (Universal Mobile Telecommunications System); advising on a number of telecommunications and Internet IPOs including the public offering of Telefónica Móviles for US$2.81 billion and the flotation of UK based TTP Communications plc via an international offer that valued the company at £542 million; handling projects from a number of governments around the world to assess and draft e-business legislation and handle procurement of e-business related services. In addition, the network completed a 20 jurisdiction report for an airline/travel industry client on e-business regulations as well as producing with the European insurance trade body, Comité Européen des Assurances (CEA), a pan-European report on the impact of eBusiness legislation on the insurance industry. It also handled a multi-billion dollar M&A project in Norway and New Zealand, two billion-dollar transactions in Germany as well as advising on a US$1 billion merger in Australia.

INTERNATIONAL CLIENTS: Clients of firms within Andersen Legal include leading US and international investment and commercial banks as well as global and regional corporates drawn from all parts of the economy including financial services, manufacturing, hospitality and leisure.

MAIN INTERNATIONAL AREAS OF PRACTICE: Andersen Legal's lawyers handle a broad range of work including all aspects of corporate and commercial, tax, litigation and arbitration, employment, real estate, intellectual property and IT, banking and finance.

LANGUAGES: All major languages are spoken including Czech, Danish, Dutch, English, French, German, Hungarian, Italian, Malay, Norwegian, Polish, Portuguese, Russian, Spanish and Swedish.

Wouters Advocaten, Jupiterstraat 8, P.O. Box 721, Willemstad, **Curaçao**
Tel: +599 9 461 7782 **Fax:** +599 9 465 8443

NEW ZEALAND
Andersen Legal, Level 16, Arthur Andersen Tower, 209 Queen Street, PO Box 1523, **Auckland** 1015
Tel: +64 9 980 6100 **Fax:** +64 9 980 6111

NORWAY
Andersen Legal ANS, Drammensveien 165 Postboks 228 - Skøyen, 0213 **Oslo**
Tel: +47 22 92 84 00 **Fax:** +47 22 92 89 04

PERU
Arthur Andersen Abogados y Asesores, Tributarios S.R. Ltda, Av. Pardo y Aliaga 699, Sexto Piso, San Isidro, **Lima** 27
Tel: +51 12 2 1060 **Fax:** +51 12 2 1061

POLAND
Domański, Zakrzewski, Palinka, Warsaw Financial Center, ul. Emilii Plater 53, 00-113 **Warsaw** (see entry page 1109)
Tel: +48 22 520 76 00/01 **Fax:** +48 22 520 88 10

RUSSIA
Andersen Legal International B.V., 52/2 Kosmodamianskaya nab, 113054 **Moscow**
Tel: +7 095 755 9700 **Fax:** +7 095 755 9710

SINGAPORE
Rajah & Tann, 4 Battery Road #26-01, Bank of China Building, **Singapore** 049908 (see entry page 1348)
Tel: +65 535 3600 **Fax:** +65 538 8598

SLOVAKIA
Weinhold Andersen Legal, Panska 14, 811 01, **Bratislava**
Tel: +421 7 5441 9864 **Fax:** +421 75441 9863

SOUTH AFRICA
Arthur Andersen & Associates, Andersen Park, 5 Summit Road, **Johannesburg** Dunkeld 2196
Tel: +27 11 328 3000 **Fax:** +27 11 328 3117

SPAIN
Garrigues & Andersen, José Abascal 45, 28003 **Madrid**
Tel: +34 91 514 52 00 **Fax:** +34 91 399 24 08 (see entry page 1142)

SWEDEN
Archibald Advokatbyrå KB, Södra Hamngatan 53, 411 20 **Gothenburg**
Tel: +46 31 771 74 00 **Fax:** +46 31 80 12 02

SWITZERLAND
Andersen Legal Rechtsanwälte, Attorneys at Law, Binzmühlestrasse 14, 8050 **Zurich**
Tel: +41 1 308 17 70 **Fax:** +41 1 308 17 71

UKRAINE
Arthur Andersen (Kyiv) Co. Ltd., Ukrainian House, 2 Khreshshatyk St., 252601 **Kiev**
Tel: +380 44 462 0555 **Fax:** +380 44 228 6388

UNITED KINGDOM
Garretts, 180 Strand, **London** WC2R 2NN
Tel: +44 20 7344 0344 **Fax:** +44 20 7438 2518

Dundas & Wilson, Saltire Court, 20 Castle Terrace, **Edinburgh** EH1 2EN
Tel: +44 131 228 8000 **Fax:** +44 131 228 8888

VENEZUELA
Romero-Muci, Briceño & Asociados, Torre Credicard, Piso 17, Av. Principal de El Bosque con, Avenida Santa Lucia, El Bosque **Caracas,** 1050
Tel: +58 2 953 9097 **Fax:** +58 2 953 9617

Andersen Legal has a correspondent office in Belgium and a representative office in New York.

ANDERSEN LEGAL ASSOCIATION D'AVOCATS

A MEMBER OF ANDERSEN LEGAL

HEAD OFFICE

41, Rue Ybry,
Cedex 92576 Neuilly-sur-Seine, France
Tel: +33 1 55 61 10 10 **Fax:** +33 1 55 61 15 15
Email: avocats@fr.andersenlegal.com
Website: www.andersen-legal.avocat.fr

FIRM OVERVIEW

Managing partner: Frédéric Donnedieu de Vabres
Number of partners: 40
Number of other lawyers: 460

AREAS OF PRACTICE:

Corporate ..... *%
Competition and distribution ..... *%
E-Business ..... *%
Insolvency and bankruptcy ..... *%
Intellectual property ..... *%
Litigation and arbitration ..... *%
* Workload % not disclosed

FIRM OVERVIEW: Founded in 1883, SG Archibald formed an association with Arthur Andersen International in 1995. It is a full-service French firm, with offices in Paris, Lyon and Strasbourg, advising French and international corporations on business and investment. Many of the firm's lawyers have received multi-jurisdictional training and qualifications. The firm has ISO 9001 accreditation since January 2000.

INTERNATIONAL EXPERIENCE: Recent international work includes advising on the acquisition by a French energy group of two oil companies located in Nigeria and controlled by a US group; advising a French wholesaler in the Czech Republic; advising a US group on the cross-border acquisition of a bicycle manufacturer owned by a German group with three plants in France; negotiating building contracts and sub-contracts for the renovation of town centre buildings to host the French outlets of an English retailer; setting up an international franchise network in Switzerland, Germany, Benelux, the UK, Turkey, Lebanon and Israel; advising a Japanese financial and industrial group on the financing of an aircraft fleet.

INTERNATIONAL CLIENTS: Includes a wide range of businesses, including investment funds, banks, pharmaceuticals, telecoms, software companies, foodstuffs manufacturers, packaging companies and hotel groups, mainly from the US but also from the UK and Japan.

MAIN AREAS OF INTERNATIONAL PRACTICE:

Tax practice: The firm has roughly 250 lawyers specialising in domestic and international taxation and all tax-related areas. It advises multinationals and medium-sized companies with international operations, as well as public-sector companies, government agencies and individuals on risk prevention, tax optimisation, management and negotiations of projects, corporate tax consulting, profit repatriation planning, indirect tax, tax arbitration and mediation, personal tax planning, transfer pricing, strategic tax consulting, executive tax services, valuation services, value-added tax issues, banking and financial products taxation.

M&A: The firm advises US-based clients on transactions in France, including all the indirectly-related aspects such as competition and environmental obligations. It has acted, for example, for pharmaceutical and healthcare companies on the acquisition of French concerns, on a joint venture with a European partner (and its later liquidation) and on European group reorganisation and the subsequent mergers of several entities in five different jurisdictions. Work includes M&A, negotiating and drafting agreements, establishing distribution networks, handling litigation, obtaining market authorisation and making filings.

Banking and finance: Work includes setting up and documenting cash-pooling agreements, structuring, negotiating, documenting and implementing cross-border financial leases, defeasance structures and related transactions, as well as regulatory and other classic banking matters. Recent major projects include advising a UK bank, negotiating credit agreements and designing and documenting French security packages and advising a large French group on a proposed internal European cash-pooling system to and from France. In aircraft finance the firm regularly advises a US law firm on developing, validating and documenting double- and triple-dip aircraft leasing structures or modifying existing ones.

Employment: The firm advises international clients on employment contracts, handling redundancies and relations with trade unions, remuneration and incentive systems, pension funds and social security audits, expatriation and secondment and the application of EU regulations. Clients come from sectors as varied as the metalworking, chemical, automotive, aeronautics, information and advanced technology, transportation, advertising and hotel industries, as well as from banking, finance, the media and professional sports.

Telecommunications: The firm has advised new entrants into the French telecommunications market in negotiations with the French Postal and Telecommunications Services Department (DPT) and France Telecom, as well as in the context of a ministerial working group on interconnection. It has conducted a large study of the French telecommunications industry for a European operator and one on frequency allocation, as well as case studies for the European Commission regarding liberalisation. Other work includes negotiating contracts for call centres and, with a major French airline, for in-seat telephones.

Real estate: The firm has represented numerous buyers and sellers of French real estate or mortgage-back receivables, as well as property developers, shopping center promoters, banks, hotel and leisure groups, commercial and industrial groups and others in acquiring, disposing of, building, restructuring or financing French property. Recent matters include property tenders offer documentation, data rooms and sales agreements for sales of properties ranging from large office promises to shopping centers and industrial warehousing facilities, as well as acquisitions and financings of portfolios of investment properties or real estate loan receivables.

LANGUAGES: English, French, German, Malagasy, Spanish, Swedish

WORLDWIDE OFFICE CONTACTS

FRANCE

Tour Crédit Lyonnais, 129 rue Servient, 69326 **Lyon** Cedex 03
Tel: +33 4 78 63 1717 **Fax:** +33 4 78 631700
Email: avocats@fr.andersenlegal.com

48 Rue Jacques Dulud, 92521 **Neuilly-sur-Seine** Cedex
Tel: +33 1 55 61 10 00 **Fax:** +33 1 55 61 16 16
Email: avocats@fr.andersenlegal.com

136 Avenue Charles de Gualle, 92207 **Neuilly-sur-Seine** Cedex
Tel: +33 1 55 61 10 10 **Fax:** +33 1 55 61 14 14
Email: avocats@fr.andersenlegal.com

Tour Europe, 20, Place des Halles, 67000 **Strasbourg**
Tel: +33 3 88 22 87 70 **Fax:** +33 3 88 22 87 99
Email: avocats@fr.andersenlegal.com

A

ANDREAS NEOCLEOUS & CO

HEAD OFFICE

Neocleous House, 199 Arch Makarios III Avenue, PO Box 50613
Limassol CY-3608, Cyprus
Tel: +357 5 362818 **Fax:** +357 5 359262

Email: info@neocleous.com
Website: www.neocleous.com

FIRM OVERVIEW

Senior partner: Andreas Neocleous

Number of partners worldwide: 8
Number of other lawyers worldwide: 40

AREAS OF PRACTICE:

Corporate	35%
Litigation and arbitration	25%
Banking and finance	15%
Maritime	10%
Insurance and reinsurance	5%
Intellectual property	5%
M&A	3%
Telecommunications	2%

A

FIRM OVERVIEW: The firm is an international organisation and has a broad based practice offering a full range of legal services. It has an international clientele and is considered to be one of the leading firms in the Eastern Mediterranean region, employing approximately 110 people, of whom 60 are fee earners, 48 are qualified lawyers and five are tax consultants. The firm has established links with international law firms, especially in relation to international corporate finance and tax law. It is the Cypriot member of Globalaw, the Euro-American Lawyers Association and the International Attorneys' Club. Andreas Neocleous & Co is the only law firm in Cyprus to be awarded the ISO 9002 Standard of Quality Management System by Bureau Veritas Quality International (BVQI).

INTERNATIONAL EXPERIENCE: In 2000, Andreas Neocleous & Co advised on over 40 corporate finance transactions and ten cross-border joint venture projects. The firm acted as Cypriot project council to a consortium of international banks in the financing of a new desalination plant under a 'built-operate-transfer' scheme.

INTERNATIONAL CLIENTS: The firm's client base includes multinational companies in the hotel, tourism and leisure industry, energy companies, multinational companies in the mobile telecommunication industry, multinational media and entertainment industry, commercial and investment banks, building societies, stock broking companies, investment companies, and software houses.

MAIN INTERNATIONAL AREAS OF PRACTICE:

Corporate and corporate finance: Andreas Neocleous & Co has extensive experience in corporate and commercial law both in Cyprus and internationally. The firm has considerable experience in advising and assisting western corporations expanding into central and Eastern Europe and the CIS, and central and Eastern European corporations expanding into other parts of the world.

Banking and finance: Andreas Neocleous & Co acts on behalf of borrowers and lenders. The firm's client base includes foreign and local commercial banks, trust companies, investment banks and underwriters.

WORLDWIDE OFFICE CONTACTS

CYPRUS
Neocleous House, 199 Arch Makarios III Avenue, PO Box 50613,
Limassol CY-3608
Tel: +357 5 362818 **Fax:** +357 5 359262
Email: info@neocleous.com

Xenios Business Centre, Arch., Makarios Avenue, **Nicosia** 1076
Tel: +357 2 376 868 **Fax:** +357 2 376 7644
Email: chrisc@neocleous.com

Othon Galaxias Court, 7 Kyniras Street, 8132 **Paphos**
Tel: +357 6 953 240 **Fax:** +357 6 953 238
Email: soteroup@neocleous.com

CZECH REPUBLIC
Hradebni 3, 11000 **Prague** 1
Tel: + 420 2 248 26605 **Fax:** + 420 2 248 26614
Email: grubner-bansky@telecom.cz

HUNGARY
Balassi B. u. 25, H-1055 **Budapest**
Tel: +361 311 3135 **Fax:** +361 311 3135
Email: tuller.neolaw@mail.matav.hu

RUSSIA
14 Zhitnaya Str, Office 1107, 117049 **Moscow**
Tel: +7 095 287 7965 **Fax:** +7 095 287 6108
Email: neolaw@user.ru

UKRAINE
24/7 Institutska Str, Office 12, 01021 **Kiev**
Tel: +38 44 293 4495 **Fax:** +38 44 293 4495
Email: irina@neocleous.kiev.ua

M&A: In 1999, Andreas Neocleous & Co advised on 15 acquisitions. The Cypriot Merger Control Law (1999) have increased the volume of merger control-related work handled by the firm.

Intellectual property law: The firm advises on all aspects of patent and trademark protection, design registration, copyright and licensing of technology.

Telecommunications and corporate law: Andreas Neocleous & Co has established an e-business group. The group offers a broad spectrum of legal services relating to online business, information technology and telecommunications.

EU and competition: As a result of Cyprus' progress in its accession negotiations with the EU the firm handles an increasing volume of work in this area. Members of this department are involved in projects concerning the harmonisation of Cypriot law with the EU's 'acquis communautaire'.

Securities and financial markets: Andreas Neocleous & Co advises on Cypriot law in relation to securities and international collective investment schemes. The firm acts for several Cypriot companies seeking a listing on the Cyprus Stock Exchange.

Litigation and arbitration: Andreas Neocleous & Co has a large litigation practice, covering all areas of general and commercial law. The firm conducts both domestic and international arbitration under internationally recognised arbitration bodies.

LANGUAGES: Czech, English, French, German, Greek, Hungarian, Italian, Russian, Ukrainian

For other recommended firms see pages 1485-1520

ANDRÉ TINOCO & ASOCIADOS

HEAD OFFICE

Los Yoses Av 10, Calles 37-39, PO Box 11745-1000
San José Costa Rica
Tel: +506 283 3070 **Fax:** +506 283 3234

Email: aandre@sol.racsa.co.cr
Website: www.andretinoco.com

WORLDWIDE OFFICE CONTACTS

COSTA RICA
Los Yoses Av 10, Calles 37-39, PO Box 11745-1000, **San José**
Tel: +506 283 3070 **Fax:** +506 283 3234
Email: aandre@sol.racsa.co.cr

FIRM OVERVIEW

Managing partner: Arnoldo Andre

AREAS OF PRACTICE:

Banking and finance 15%
Corporate 15%
Labour and tax law 15%
Litigation and arbitration 15%
Intellectual property 10%
Mergers and acquisition 10%
Free Trade Zone (Zona Franca) Regulations 5%
Immigration 5%
Lobbying and negotiation 5%
Offshore Services 5%

FIRM PROFILE: Founded in 1984, the firm is well known for its integrated practice in corporate law, international business transactions, including tax law and foreign investment counseling, as well as litigation. The firm also provides independent advice on political and economic conditions in the region, estate planning and offshore structures, intellectual property and real estate development. Other services, such as administration of assets, trustee and financial services, tourism project development and accounting, are provided.

INTERNATIONAL EXPERIENCE: The firm advises mainly foreign corporations and individuals doing business in Costa Rica, as well as the German, Swiss and Norwegian Embassies. Dr. André is the General Consul of Norway in Costa Rica. M&A and international franchise Agreements and Disputes are increasing in the region. The recognition of foreign judgments in Costa Rica is also a field of interest.

INTERNATIONAL CLIENTS: The firm's client base includes large and medium size companies, banks and other financial institutions, high net worth individuals and law firms from abroad.

MAIN INTERNATIONAL AREAS OF PRACTICE:

Corporate law: The firm covers all aspects of corporate and commercial law. The firm advises on and prepares the incorporation of companies. AT&A provides a complete service regarding the company's by-laws, its shares, shareholder meetings, administration and representation, including the powers of attorney. The firm's attorneys supervise the corporation, initiate transformations, joint ventures and all necessary forms of co-operation with other legal entities.

Mergers and acquisitions: The firm supports companies and individuals involved in mergers and acquisitions, including due diligence and corporate restructuring. The firm's attorneys are regularly implicated in purchasing and selling concepts for companies, as well as the resolution of bankruptcy problems.

Labour law: The firm deals with all matters concerning foreign employees and their working permits, working hours, holidays and vacations, sick leave, maternity leave, leave for work-related injuries, wages, salaries and other compensation methods such as stock sharing plans.

Tax law: AT&T's lawyers are accustomed to working closely with the clients' accountants and auditors in order to prevent legal problems with taxation. The firm are prepared to devise solutions that meet client goals in the most tax efficient way. As Costa Rica bases its tax system upon the territorial principle, corporate clients face specific advantages and disadvantages.

Offshore services: AT&A renders a complete service regarding offshore-operations based in Costa Rica.

Free Trade Zone (Zona Franca) Regulations: The firm has been active in the development of foreign investment incentive programs and their regulations since the 1990s.

Lobbying and negotiation: AT&A has experience in presenting and introducing clients to the decision-makers, both in the private and public sector of Costa Rica. Members of the firm also belong to the diplomatic community in the country and therefore keep regular contact with foreign representatives.

Litigation: The firm has a full-service litigation practice, with particular strengths in the areas of commercial law, intellectual property, banking, financial services, securities and labor law.

Intellectual property: AT&A is very active in the area of trademark patent and copyright registration. The firm's attorneys advise clients on registration procedures, rights and protection under the new intellectual property regulations, including trade secrets and other privileged information.

Immigration: AT&A provides full immigration services to our corporate clients as well as to individual applicants. Its longstanding expertise in this field guarantees satisfactory solutions for every foreigner desirous to work or live in Costa Rica, or who simply wishes to have a 'second home'.

LANGUAGES: English, German, Spanish

ANDRÉ TINOCO ABOGADOS - ATTORNEYS IN COSTA RICA

A

ANDREWS & KURTH LLP

HEAD OFFICE

600 Travis Suite 4200,
Houston TX 77002, USA
Tel: +1 713 220 4200 **Fax:** +1 713 220 4285
Email: webmaster@akllp.com
Website: www.akllp.com

FIRM OVERVIEW

Managing partner: Howard T. Ayers
Senior partner: Robert V. Jewell
Number of partners worldwide: 96
Number of other lawyers worldwide: 299

AREAS OF PRACTICE:

Bankruptcy	*%
Business transactions	*%
Corporate and finance	*%
Employment	*%
Energy	*%
Environmental	*%
Litigation	*%
Tax	*%

* Workload not diclosed

FIRM OVERVIEW: Andrews & Kurth represents established companies and emerging businesses around the globe. The firm has a multi-disciplinary approach that enables it to handle complex legal issues by combining knowledge and experience. It aims to provide efficient, effective and valuable legal services. Andrews & Kurth has offices in major corporate and government centres on two continents. In addition to its founding office in Houston, it advises clients from offices in Dallas, London, Los Angeles, New York, The Woodlands, and Washington DC.

INTERNATIONAL EXPERIENCE: Andrews & Kurth has international experience in a number of practice areas, specialising in business transactions, energy, and project finance matters. The firm has been heavily involved in the privatisation of the Argentine oil and gas industry. It has advised a range of clients on a broad spectrum of projects including electric generating facilities, gas gathering systems, industrial plants (e.g. chemicals and fertilizer projects), alternative fuels, pipelines, paper recycling, waste-to-energy, storage facilities, and other infrastructure projects. Lawyers in the firm's project finance practice group have played a leading role in a number of recent precedent setting transactions, including acting as lead finance counsel for Mega in connection with the Mega Liquefied Natural Gas Project.

MAIN INTERNATIONAL AREASOF PRACTICE:

Bankruptcy: The firm specialises in commercial bankruptcies and reorganisations, and has significant retail, oil and gas, and restaurant industry experience. Andrews & Kurth' s diverse client base includes individual creditors, creditors' committees, bank groups, equity committees, trustees and debtors. It also represents creditors and borrowers in commercial workouts and out-of-court debt restructurings, and assists high-yield funds in buying and selling bankruptcy claims.

Business transactions: The firm advises a wide range of clients, with specific emphasis on transactional matters related to banking, public and private financing, and real estate. Work handled includes project and structured finance, syndicated lending, leasing, swaps and loan workouts, and restructuring. It also advises on the acquisition, development and financing of a variety of commercial, industrial and public projects. The firm advises a number of energy related businesses. It has handled a range of issues related to energy exploration, production, processing, refining, transportation, trading and marketing, and has significant experience in the development of energy projects in the US and internationally.

Corporate and finance: In the last two years Andrews & Kurth was involved in more than 78 securities offerings totalling approximately US$18.7 billion. The firm advises public and private corporations, partnerships, joint ventures, national and regional investment banks, merchant banks, venture capital firms, capital market groups of commercial banks, and individual clients. Andrews & Kurth has a reputation as one of the leading securities firms for the energy industry and has been particularly active in the high yield debt offering market. The firm is involved in the development of the standard covenant packages for energy companies in the markets for high yield debt and crossover investment grade debt.

Energy: The energy practice specialises in federal and state regulation of the natural gas, oil and electric industries. The energy group has significant experience concerning regulatory matters that affect natural gas pipelines, oil pipelines, gathering companies, independent power producers, natural gas and electricity end users, energy marketing companies, power project developers, co-generators, NGL processors, and other related businesses.

Environmental: Andrews & Kurth advises on all aspects of environmental law. It counsels industrial and commercial clients including oil and gas producers and transporters, environmental service companies, petrochemical companies, manufacturers, recyclers, real estate companies, lenders and investors. It also has a growing international environmental practice, with projects in Mexico and South America.

Employment: The firm represents management in all aspects of labour and employment law. Emphasis is placed on advising clients on employment obligations and rights. The firm represents employers in all aspects of traditional employment law including union avoidance, representation elections, collective bargaining, grievances, arbitrations and unfair labour practice charges before the National Labour Relations Board.

Tax: The firm advises on a broad spectrum of services for corporations, partnerships, individuals, trusts (both business and personal), estates and foundations, including asset securitisation; reorganisations, mergers, acquisitions and dispositions, and employee benefits and executive compensation.

LANGUAGES: Chinese, English, French, German, Italian, Portuguese, Russian, Spanish, Taiwanese

WORLDWIDE OFFICE CONTACTS

UNITED KINGDOM
Level 16 City Tower, 40 Basinghall Street, **London** EC2V 5DE
Tel: +44 20 7382 0550 **Fax:** +44 20 7614 0012

USA
1717 Main Street, Suite 3700, **Dallas** TX 75201
Tel: +1 214 659 4400 **Fax:** +1 214 659 4401

600 Travis Suite 4200, **Houston** TX 77002
Tel: +1 713 220 4200 **Fax:** +1 713 220 4285

601 South Figueroa, **Los Angeles** California 90017
Tel: +1 213 896 3100 **Fax:**

1701 Pennsylvania Avenue NW, Suite 300, **Washington DC** 20006
Tel: +1 202 662 2700 **Fax:** +1 202 662 2739

A

For other recommended firms see pages 1485-1520

ANG & PARTNERS

HEAD OFFICE

150 Beach Road, 32-00, The Gateway West,
Singapore 189720
Tel: +65 224 25 30 **Fax:** +65 225 36 80

Email: mail@angpartners.com
Website: www.angpartners.com

WORLDWIDE OFFICE CONTACTS

SINGAPORE
150 Beach Road 32-00, The Gateway West, **Singapore,** 189720
Tel: +65 224 25 30 **Fax:** +65 225 36 80
Email: mail@angpartners.com

FIRM OVERVIEW

Managing partner: Loo Dip Seng
Senior partners: Christopher Lau SC, Belinda Ang Fong Saw Ean SC, Goh Kok Leong

Number of partners worldwide: 11
Number of other lawyers worldwide: 14

AREAS OF PRACTICE:

Admiralty and maritime	*%
Building and construction	*%
Corporate and securities	*%
Intellectual property and information technology	*%
Litigation and arbitration	*%
Tax	*%

*Workload % not disclosed

FIRM OVERVIEW: The firm was established in February 1985 by three lawyers as a niche practice specialising in admiralty and maritime, litigation and arbitration. It has in the past year expanded its practice areas to corporate and securities, construction and information technology by recruiting partners and associates with particular expertise in these areas. There are three Senior Counsel in the firm, two of whom are partners and the other a consultant to the firm. Professor Francis M B Reynolds of the University of Oxford, acts as a consultant in English law to the firm.

INTERNATIONAL EXPERIENCE: The firm's lawyers have experience in both domestic and cross-border transactions, litigation and arbitration.

INTERNATIONAL CLIENTS: Clients include financial institutions, merchant banks, investment intermediaries, technology and telecommunication companies, listed companies, co-operatives, venture capitalists, P&I Clubs, corporations engaged in shipping, insurance and construction.

MAIN INTERNATIONAL AREAS OF PRACTICE:
Admiralty and maritime: Ang & Partners handles the full range of shipping matters, such as claims for loss of or damage to cargo, defending cargo claims, charterparty disputes, collision, salvage, oil pollution and bunker disputes. Other types of shipping work handled include the sale and purchase of vessels, ship repair claims, shipping fraud, disputes under sale and purchase of vessels, ship repair contracts, enforcement of crew and shipboard personal injury and fatal accidents. They also advise on aviation matters including air forwarder and air courier operations.
Building and construction: The firm's building and construction practice offers a comprehensive range of services in construction and engineering such as advising on legal issues that arise during construction, drafting, advising and vetting of construction contracts and associated documentation, arbitrating and litigating disputes that arise from construction projects or resolving these through mediation or other alternative dispute resolution procedure.
Corporate and securities: The firm advises on, structures, negotiates and prepares documents in relation to: corporate and commercial transactions including mergers and acquisitions, joint ventures, venture capital financing, corporate reorganisations, corporatisations, privatisations, asset securitisations and employee compensation schemes; corporate finance and capital market transactions including the issue, offering and placement of equity and debt securities by way of public offerings, rights issues and private placements, and the establishment of medium term note programmes, unit trusts and close-end funds; and derivatives transactions involving exchange-traded and over-the-counter derivatives, including swaps, futures, forwards and options.
Information technology: The firm advises on issues relating to electronic commerce and the internet such as electronic payment systems, user agreements, privacy policy, electronic data interchange, website development and hosting and the construction of internet hubs and portals. The firm also has experience in preparing and negotiating software licences, franchises, computer contracts, confidentiality agreements, agency agreements, technology transfer agreements and other corporate-related aspects of electronic commerce and technology-related transactions.

LANGUAGES: English, Malay, Mandarin

For other recommended firms see pages 1485-1520

ANTONIO FRUTUOSO DE MELO & ASSOCIADOS

HEAD OFFICE

Av.da. Liberdade, 38, 7th Floor,
1250-145 Lisbon, Portugal
Tel: +351 2 1 321 8600 **Fax:** +351 2 1 321 8686

FIRM OVERVIEW

Managing and senior partner: Antonio Frutuoso de Melo

Number of partners worldwide: 10
Number of other lawyers worldwide: 18

AREAS OF PRACTICE:
Finance, banking, securities and capital markets 50%
Corporate 30%
Securitisation 10%
Other 10%

FIRM OVERVIEW: Antonio Frutuoso de Melo e Associados was established in May 1997, specialising in legal financial and commercial areas of practice. It was incorporated by a group of lawyers with several years' experience working in various large law firms. Senior partner, António Frutuoso de Melo, has practised in the corporate, finance and tax fields for the last 15 years, mainly for international clients, including large investment banks, other financial institutions and corporations.

INTERNATIONAL EXPERIENCE: Since its foundation, the firm has represented financial companies and international banks on bad debt mortgage loans recovery and asset securitisation in Portugal. Other work includes representing American investors and international banks in US Cross Border Leasing in the transport area in Portugal; acting for several international banks in financing for the acquisition of a large bank in Portugal; representing national and international banks in the issue of bonds in the international markets, and the structure of sophisticated transactions, namely TRS; and acting for a major Portuguese TV broadcasting company, having undertaken legal liability for the negotiation of the contractual terms of several external loans and pertinent swaps. The firm has been involved in a major takeover bid of a listed Portuguese company.

INTERNATIONAL CLIENTS: The firm's main clients are large investment banks, other financial institutions and international corporations acting from various commerce and industry sectors.

WORLDWIDE OFFICE CONTACTS

PORTUGAL
Av.da. Liberdade, 38, 7th Floor, 1250-145 **Lisbon**
Tel: +351 2 1 321 8600 **Fax:** +351 2 1 321 8686

ASSOCIATED OFFICES

Quintas, Jardim Fernandes & Associados
Rua dos Ferreiros, 260, 9000 Funchal, **Madeira**
Tel: +291 224 707 **Fax:** +291 224 897

MAIN INTERNATIONAL AREAS OF PRACTICE:
Banking and finance: Work handled covers all aspects, including structured finance and issue of bonds in international markets. In the last year the firm acted for a bank in the set-up and legal structuring of the issue of €2.5 billion Floating Rate Notes.
Corporate: The firm handles the incorporation of companies with international shareholders and branches of international companies, including in the current year the incorporation of a specialised securities market manager with 12 international partners, all major European and American banks; and the legal restructure of Portuguese branches of international companies including a large European bank.
Securitisation: The firm have been involved in the structuring and securitisation transactions of two major international American banks.
Tax driven transactions: The firm was involved in the negotiation of all the US cross border lease transactions in Portugal. The senior partner developed a new 'Portuguese synthetic leasing' for railway equipment, where he has acted for financiers. The firm is currently handling the tax aspects of cross-border equipment and lease transactions.

LANGUAGES: English, French, German, Italian, Portuguese, Spanish

A

For other recommended firms see pages 1485-1520

ANZOLA RAFFALLI Y RODRIGUEZ

HEAD OFFICE

Torre Centuria, piso 8, Av. Venezuela, El Rosal,
Caracas 1060, Venezuela
Tel: +582 952 0995 **Fax:** +582 952 4415

Email: arr@arr.com.ve
Website: www.arr.com.ve

WORLDWIDE OFFICE CONTACTS

VENEZUELA
Torre Centuria, piso 8, Av. Venezuela, El Rosal, **Caracas** 1060
Tel: +582 952 0995 **Fax:** +582 952 4415
Email: arr@arr.com.ve

FIRM OVERVIEW

Managing partner: J. Eloy Anzola
Senior partner: J. Eloy Anzola

Number of partners worldwide: 7
Number of other lawyers worldwide: 9

AREAS OF PRACTICE:

Administrative and constitutional	15%
Corporate	15%
M&A	15%
Tax	15%
Employment	10%
Litigation and arbitration	10%
Anti-trust	5%
Intellectual property	5%
Mining, oil and energy	5%
Telecommunications	5%

FIRM OVERVIEW: Founded in 1990, the firm comprises 16 lawyers. Many of the firm's members have studied in the US and Europe, and one of the firm's lawyers has been admitted to practice in the State of New York. Anzola Raffalli y Rodriguez aim to provide foreign and local corporate clients with an efficient and high quality legal service.

INTERNATIONAL EXPERIENCE: The firm have advised South American, US and European clients on a broad range of legal issues including M&A, joint ventures, privatisations, corporate law, employment and tax.

INTERNATIONAL CLIENTS: Anzola Raffalli y Rodriguez advise clients operating in a range of industries including banking, insurance, capital markets, telecommunications, entertainment, food, chemicals, pharmaceutical, and energy.

MAIN INTERNATIONAL AREAS OF PRACTICE:

Corporate: The firm advise on all aspects of corporate law including incorporation of local companies and subsidiaries, and domiciling of local branches of foreign corporations in Venezuela.

M&A: The firm act as local counsel to foreign clients in mergers and acquisitions, either advising purchasers or sellers in share or asset purchase transactions.

Tax: Anzola Raffalli y Rodriguez handle a substantial amount of tax related work. They advise on the adoption of worldwide income taxation and the taxation of dividends and transfer prices. The firm also advise on tax litigation, both on an administrative and judicial level.

Administrative and constitutional: The firm advise clients on relationships with government agencies at national, state and municipal level. They also advise on public bidding, direct adjudication procedures, license applications, and authorisations and concessions from all public organisations.

Mining, oil and energy: Anzola Raffalli y Rodriguez handle all matters relating to the exploration process in the mining and oil industries, and advise on the application, granting, renewal and amendment of concession titles (vein and alluvium). The firm have been involved in the acquisition of gold and coal mining companies. They also advise European oil companies on the marginal fields program of PDVSA.

Telecommunications: The firm advise several major telecommunication companies on all telecommunication issues. They have close links with the telecommunications regulatory office (CONATEL) and advise on the newly enacted Organic Telecommunications Law.

Foreign investments and technology transfer: The firm specialises in the registration and updating of direct investments in Venezuela and the superintendence of foreign investments and other government agencies including the Ministry of Energy and Mines. They also advise on regional and local regulations governing the repatriation of capital, investment protection, and payments of dividends abroad.

Intellectual property and e-commerce: Anzola Raffalli y Rodriguez advise on all intellectual property and e-commerce matters including trademarks, patents, and copyright.

Litigation and arbitration: The firm represents clients in civil, commercial, administrative, employment, tax and intellectual property litigation in all Venezuelan courts. Two of the firm's partners are arbitrators of the Conciliation and Arbitration Centre of the Caracas Chamber of Commerce and the Venezuelan American Chamber of Commerce.

LANGUAGES: English, French, Italian, Spanish

A

ARENALES & SKINNER-KLÉE

HEAD OFFICE

13 Calle 2-60, Zona 10, Edificio Topacio Azul, Oficina 701
Guatemala City 01010, Guatemala
Tel: +502 363 1178 **Fax:** +502 363 1208

Email: arenales@arenales.com.gt

WORLDWIDE OFFICE CONTACTS

GUATEMALA
13 Calle 2-60, Zona 10, Edificio Topacio Azul, Oficina 701,
Guatemala City 01010
Tel: +502 363 1178 **Fax:** +502 363 1208
Email: arenales@arenales.com.gt

FIRM OVERVIEW

Senior partners: Alfredo Skinner-Klée, Alejandro Arenales Farner
Counsel members: Jorge Skinner-Klée, Alejandro Arenales Catalan

Number of partners worldwide: 6
Number of other lawyers worldwide: 7

AREAS OF PRACTICE:
Banking and finance .... *%
Constitutional and administrative .... *%
Corporate, commercial and intellectual property .... *%
Litigation .... *%
Real estate .... *%
Tax .... *%
* Workload % not disclosed

A

FIRM OVERVIEW: Arenales & Skinner-Klée was established recently as a result of the merger between Arenales & Associates and Skinner-Klée, Attorneys. The firm has expanded and diversified its operations and is now a full service law firm. Based in Guatemala City, the firm aims to provide its clients with comprehensive and quality legal services. The firm has a dynamic team of lawyers, juridical assistants and support personnel who are continually receiving academic and professional training. The firm has prestigious and experienced correspondents in North, Central and South America, the Caribbean and Europe.

INTERNATIONAL CLIENTS: The firm's clients include prestigious national and international companies, banking and financial institutions, government enterprises (privatised) and individuals.

MAIN INTERNATIONAL AREAS OF PRACTICE:
Constitutional and administrative: The firm advises companies on matters relating to the government of Guatemala, its bodies and agencies. It also handles privatisations, concessions, public biddings, quotations and contracts in general. The firm has handled several privatisations involving state owned Guatemalan services including telephone services, postal services, railroads, passports, and driving licenses. It also advises on the design of the corresponding regulatory frame in some privatisations. The firm regularly advises private companies in relation to infrastructure, power generation and national and foreign investment.
Banking and financial: The banking and financial practice handles a wide range of banking and finance issues including advising on the Guatemalan regulatory framework. The firm also advises on the constitution of trusts, design of credit and financial operations, financial leasing, factorage, refinancing, issuance and negotiation of securities and other stock exchange transactions, as well as in insurance and bonds. The firm has advised several banks on establishment and on authorisation to operate in Guatemala.
Corporate, commercial and intellectual property: Arenales & Skinner-Klée specialises in mergers and acquisitions, intellectual property (copyrights, trademarks, patents, domain names), agencies and distribution contracts and other contracts of business cooperation, such as franchises, transfer of technology, licenses and joint ventures. The firm handles the negotiations involved in national and international commerce, maritime law and foreign investment. It also advises on arbitration and conciliation matters.
Tax: The firm advises on legal opinions, reports, counselling and fiscal planning. It is also handles issues arising from objections, appeals for annulment and motions to set aside, fiscal administrative lawsuits, cassations and relieves.
Real estate: The firm advises investors (companies or individual persons) who develop and promote real estate projects in the Republic of Guatemala. It designs the legal and administrative aspects of such projects and prepares the documentation and required contracts.
Litigation: The firm's litigation practice handles civil, mercantile, employment and criminal litigation.
Other: Other work handled includes employment, immigration and environmental law.

LANGUAGES: English, Spanish

For other recommended firms see pages 1485-1520

ARNOLD & PORTER

HEAD OFFICE

555 Twelfth Street NW,
Washington, DC 20004-1206, USA
Tel: +1 202 942 5000 **Fax:** + 1 202 942 5999

Website: www.arnoldporter.com

FIRM OVERVIEW

Chairman Michael N Sohn
Managing partner: James J Sandman

Number of partners worldwide: 218
Number of other lawyers worldwide: 360

AREAS OF PRACTICE:

Antitrust and trade regulation	*%
Bankruptcy	*%
Benefits and employment law	*%
Corporate and securities	*%
Environmental	*%
Financial institutions	*%
Food, drug and medical devices	*%
Government contracts	*%
Health care	*%
Intellectual property and technology	*%
International	*%
Legislative	*%
Litigation	*%
Product liability	*%
Project finance	*%
Public policy	*%
Real estate	*%
Tax	*%
Telecommunications	*%

* Workload % not disclosed

FIRM OVERVIEW: Arnold & Porter, founded in 1946, is one of the largest law firms based in Washington DC. With additional offices in London, New York, Los Angeles, Century City, CA, Denver, and lawyers organised into over 25 practice areas, it maintains an international practice spanning a broad spectrum of the law. The firm's core areas of practice are litigation, transactional matters and regulatory issues. The firm conducts business with companies in many jurisdictions spanning the globe including North America, Europe, Latin America, and Asia.

INTERNATIONAL EXPERIENCE: The firm has an international practice representing clients in a full range of legal and policy processes affecting the international economy and international business. In the past 10 years, Arnold & Porter has assisted in the formation of more than 100 joint ventures involving participants based in more than 20 nations, including countries without the legal and regulatory structures to support sophisticated transactions. Recently the firm has: represented major pharmaceutical and medical device companies on product safety issues, serving as national counsel for such clients as Hoffmann-LaRoche, Inc and Pfizer Inc; served as national counsel for a blood-banking organization in cases brought by individuals who allegedly contracted the AIDS virus from blood transfusions; represented Philip Morris Inc in lawsuits seeking to hold the company liable for illnesses allegedly caused by smoking; represented the governments of Brazil, Israel, Panama, Turkey and Venezuela in offerings aggregating more than $20 billion; represented Xerox in antitrust challenges; represented a former Counsel to the President of the United States in the Whitewater matter; and represented PNC Bank Corp in its $240 million acquisition of BlackRock Financial Management. The firm successfully defended General Electric against charges that it had conspired with DeBeers to fix the price of industrial diamonds. In New York and other money centres, the firm represents issuers and underwriters in financings and M&A activity involving a wide range of industries, including financial institutions, telecommunications, real estate, pharmaceuticals, medical devices and information technology

WORLDWIDE OFFICE CONTACTS

UNITED KINGDOM
Tower 42, Old Broad Street, **London** EC2N 1HQ
Tel: + 44 20 7786 6100 **Fax:** + 44 20 7786 6299

USA

One Norwest Center, 1700 Lincoln Street, **Denver,** CO 80203-4540
Tel: + 1 303 863 1000 **Fax:** + 1 303 832 0428

777 South Figueroa Street, 44th Floor, **Los Angeles,** CA 90017-2513
Tel: + 1 213 243 4000 **Fax:** + 1 213 243 4199

Suite 1700, 1900 Avenue of the Stars, **Los Angeles**,CA 90067
Tel: + 1 310 552 2500 **Fax:** + 1 310 552 1191

399 Park Avenue, 44th
Floor, **New York**, NY 10022-4690
Tel: + 1 212 715 1000 **Fax:** + 1 212 715 1399

555 Twelfth Street NW, **Washington, DC** 20004-1206
Tel: +1 202 942 5000 **Fax:** + 1 202 942 5999

INTERNATIONAL CLIENTS: Arnold & Porter's clients range from Fortune 500 corporations to high-tech start-ups, and include entities based in North America, South America, Europe, Africa, Asia and Australia. Among the firm's clients are: Hoffmann-LaRoche Inc; Pfizer Inc; the governments of Brazil, Israel, Panama, Turkey and Venezuela; Philip Morris Inc; the City of New York; General Electric; a former Counsel to the President of the United States; PNC Bank Corp; Xerox; Braniff Airways Inc; Air Partners; The Kroger Co; Guinness plc; Armco; DynCorp; Municipality of Rio de Janeiro; the Argentine Republic; the Government of Israel's integrated chemical and mining company; Inter-American Investment Corporation; CANTV; First American National Bank.

MAIN INTERNATIONAL AREAS OF PRACTICE:

Antitrust and trade regulation: The firm has a strong tradition in antitrust policy and trade regulation policy. Lawyers work with clients from a broad range of industries, and represent them in matters under federal, state and European laws governing competition, pricing, distribution, advertising and intellectual property.

Bankruptcy: The firm has represented clients in prominent US cases in such matters as airline bankruptcies, real estate bankruptcies, holders of unsecured claims, trade creditors, insurance insolvencies, asset purchases, as well as purchase and sale of claims.

Benefits and employment law: The firm represents employers and employees, pension plans, unions, corporations, and non-profit organisations in matters ranging from tax qualification requirements to the use of employee stock ownership plans (ESOPs) in buyouts and other takeovers.

A

ARNOLD & PORTER cont'd

Corporate and securities: The firm's corporate practice has particular experience in mergers and acquisitions and corporate control matters involving banks, savings associations, and other financial institutions. The firm also represents issuers, underwriters, security holders and indenture trustees in a full range of public and private offerings of debt and equity securities.

Environmental: Arnold & Porter represents corporations, developers, utilities, and public agencies in a wide range of environmental matters. Litigation is a prominent aspect of the firm's work in this area.

Financial institutions: The firm's practice covers every aspect of the legal, business and regulatory issues encountered by financial institutions, including growth and expansion, regulatory matters, financial products and services, capital markets and corporate governance.

Food, drug and medical devices: Arnold & Porter advises and represents clients in the food, drug, medical device and other industries that are regulated by the Food and Drug Administration (FDA) on such issues as unfair competition, product liability risk control, crisis management for embattled products, and traditional regulatory questions.

Government contracts: The firm works with companies doing substantial business with government agencies. It advises on matters such as white collar crime, compliance programmes, litigation, corporate transactions, privatisation, outsourcing, policy and legislation.

Health care: The firm has acted for major health care organisations in a wide range of regulatory and litigation work. It has represented hospitals and health care providers in acquisitions and joint ventures and has represented health care and biotechnology clients in matters relating to intellectual property and technology assets.

Intellectual property and technology: This group has wide experience in the acquisition, protection, exploitation and enforcement of intellectual property rights. It is particularly knowledgeable in the areas of computer and information technology, the internet, pharmaceuticals and biotechnology.

International: The firm represents domestic and foreign corporations, governments, government agencies, international organisations, trade associations, labour unions, nongovernmental organisations, investors, banks, financial institutions and individuals in virtually all aspects of international activity.

Legislative: This practice includes advocacy on legislative and regulatory policy matters before the US Congress, the White House, cabinet departments and independent regulatory agencies. The firm also advises clients on compliance with federal and state campaign finance laws, as well as lobbying and ethics requirements.

Litigation: This is a major area of the firm's work, with almost half of its domestic lawyers involved. Anti-trust and securities have been a traditional area of strength, but the firm's work is diverse and includes civil and criminal, regulatory and commercial, national and international matters.

Product liability: The firm co-ordinates wide-ranging legislative and lobbying programmes at the state and federal levels, representing companies whose products have come under congressional investigation. It has experience with such issues as liability damage caps, tort liability protection, professional standards, protective orders, tort reform and charitable immunity.

Public policy: This group provides strategic planning to deal with public policy, analyses legislation, advocates for clients' positions, monitors developments and gathers information, organises coalitions and co-ordinates visibility campaigns.

Real estate: Arnold & Porter structure and negotiate real estate deals locally, nationally and overseas for a diverse clientele, including publicly traded hoteliers, government contractors, investment bankers, pension funds and European developers.

Tax: With approximately 30 attorneys in the firm's Washington and New York offices, the tax practice provides representation in all major areas of corporate, partnership, employment, individual, trusts and estates, and gift tax law.

Telecommunications: The firm provides regulatory, administrative, litigation, and legislative advice to corporations, government entities, institutions, and individuals. Governments and enterprises from other countries also seek the firm's advice on the domestic and international implications of existing and emerging technologies and on new regulatory and marketplace structures in the United States and at home.

LANGUAGES: Arabic, Bengali, Chinese, Ebrou, Estonian, Farsi, Filipino, French, German, Greek, Hebrew, Hindustani/Punjabi/Urdu, Hungarian, Italian, Japanese, Konkani (Indian), Latin, Marathi, Portuguese, Russian, Sesotho, Spanish, Turkish, Vietnamese.

WORLDWIDE OFFICES

UNITED KINGDOM

Tower 42, Old Broad St, London EC2N 1HQ

Number of lawyers: 21
Number of dual qualified lawyers: 3
Number of locally qualified lawyers: 18

Office profile: The firm first established a presence in London in the early 1990s. In 1996 it opened a full office in response to a growing demand for cross border financing and European transactional and regulatory work. The office has broad capabilities in the areas of business, finance and EU competition and policy matters. The office's work is developing as new lawyers join, and is backed up by the full resources of the firm in the United States. The office has established contacts with other English lawyers to provide specialist English law advice in areas that it cannot cover. It is also part of a network of firms in the EU and Central and Eastern Europe on whom it can call for multijurisdictional projects.

ARNOLD & PORTER

A

For other recommended firms see pages 1485-1520

ARNTZEN DE BESCHE AS

HEAD OFFICE

PO Box 1424 Vika, N-0115 Oslo, Norway
Tel: +47 23 89 40 00 **Fax:** +47 23 89 40 01

Email: mail@arntzendebesche.no
Website: www.arntzendebesche.no

WORLDWIDE OFFICE CONTACTS

NORWAY
PO Box 1424 Vika, N-0115 **Oslo**
Tel: +47 23 89 40 00 **Fax:** +47 23 89 40 01
Email: mail@arntzendebesche.no

FIRM OVERVIEW

Managing partner: Ingeborg Moen Borgerud
Managing director: Anja Munro

Number of partners worldwide: 21
Number of other lawyers worldwide: 39

AREAS OF PRACTICE:

Oil and gas/energy	20%
IT/telecommunications/IP	14%
Employment	14%
Litigation and arbitration	14%
Corporate and M&A	12%
Banking and finance	11%
Insurance	10%
Competition and marketing	5%

FIRM OVERVIEW: On January 1st, 2001 a merger took place between the law firms Arntzen, Underland & Co and de Besche & Co. The new firm, Arntzen de Besche has 60 lawyers and a total staff of 90. The merger was driven by the wish to create a stronger firm to benefit Norwegian and international clients. Arntzen de Besche covers all core business related areas and aims to take a leading position in disciplines such as securities/finance, oil and energy, information technology and intellectual property rights, labour legislation, commercial real estate and aviation. The firm will also further emphasise developing its already extensive litigation practice.
In order to meet its clients' requirements, extensive resources have been put in to developing business insight and understanding. Several of the firm's partners have extensive working experience in the energy and finance sectors, as well as in the public sector.
The firm's experience in international projects, such as finance, M&A, and telecom/e-business, gives it unique experience enabling it to compete in complex processes as advisors to 'new economy' clients.

INTERNATIONAL EXPERIENCE: Arntzen de Besche has acquired extensive experience in dispute settlements on an international scale. This includes international contracts and contract negotiations within a wide range of business areas, corporate law aspects of establishing companies and operations abroad, international tax legislation, acquisitions, mergers and financing, as well as general representation of foreign branches and subsidiaries in Norway. The firm's attorneys have training and professional experience from foreign organisations, companies and legal institutions. This provides valuable insight into the legal systems of many of Norway's most important trading partners and their cultural traditions and business practices. The firm can draw on a global network of legal services through its co-operation with Baker & McKenzie, Stockholm, Sweden.

INTERNATIONAL CLIENTS: Arntzen de Besche's client portfolio has traditionally comprised a substantial number of foreign companies with ownership interests in, or business associations with, Norway.

MAIN INTERNATIONAL AREAS OF PRACTICE:
Insurance: Insurance law is one of the firm's specialist fields. The department handles material damage cases, third party interests and liability insurance, personal insurance and personal injury issues, both in connection with the preparation of insurance terms and legal advice to insurance companies in case of disputes.
Employment: The firm handles collective and individual labour law matters. Employees and employers are advised on all types of industrial and commercial matters.
Oil and gas and energy: Ever since petroleum was first discovered on the Norwegian Continental Shelf in the mid-1960s, the firm's attorneys have been engaged as legal advisors to the oil companies. They have experience advising on all types of operations in the oil and gas sector although the majority of work handled is in oil company operations.
Banking and finance: The firm has long served as advisor to both Norwegian and foreign clients, and has been engaged in preparing official reports and in legislative work. The firm's clients include individuals, companies and institutions, some of which are major players in the world of finance and banking.
IT, telecommunications and IP: The firm has a number of clients which are leading players in the IT and telecommunication sectors. It also has a number of clients within the media and entertainment sectors. Arntzen de Besche has broad experience in intellectual property law.
Corporate and M&A: The firm offers advice on all aspects of corporate law. Within the area of M&A the firm's transactions range from small private acquisitions to cross-border take-overs.
Competition and marketing: The firm has been active in these areas for many years and provides guidance to both Norwegian and international companies.
Litigation and arbitration: A substantial part of the firm's activities is related to litigation and arbitration in domestic as well as international disputes.

LANGUAGES: English, French, German and the Scandinavian languages.

ARTHUR COX

HEAD OFFICE

Earlsfort Centre, Earlsfort Terrace,
Dublin 2, Ireland
Tel: +353 1 618 0000 **Fax:** +353 1 618 0618

Email: mail@arthurcox.ie
Website: www.arthurcox.ie

FIRM OVERVIEW

Managing partner: Eugene McCague
Chairman: James O'Dwyer

Number of partners worldwide: 52
Number of other lawyers worldwide: in excess of 90

AREAS OF PRACTICE:

Corporate and commercial	60%
Litigation	20%
Property	20%

FIRM OVERVIEW: The firm is one of the largest in Ireland, with over 130 lawyers. It is a full-service corporate and business firm, focusing in particular on M&A, corporate finance, inward manufacturing investment, investment through Ireland's International Financial Services Centre (IFSC), commercial property and commercial litigation.

INTERNATIONAL EXPERIENCE: A large proportion of the firm's clientele is international. Much of its international work consists of cross-border M&A, securities offerings, international commercial agreements and dispute resolution, advice on financial products and services in the IFSC, and overseas investment in Ireland.

INTERNATIONAL CLIENTS: The firm represents multinational high-tech, industrial and service companies, international banks and financial institutions with interests in Ireland. Arthur Cox's international clientele comprises predominantly European and North American companies but also includes a significant number of clients from the Pacific Rim, the Middle East, South Africa and Latin America.

MAIN INTERNATIONAL AREAS OF PRACTICE:

M&A and corporate finance: M&A is a core activity of Arthur Cox and a large proportion of it is cross-border. The firm's corporate finance practice is also a core strength. It advises on Irish flotations and public offers, MBO's and share acquisition financing and acted for Telecom Eireann plc (now eircom plc) in its IR£6.8b privatisation and flotation in July 1999.

Banking and financial services: Arthur Cox has one of Dublin's largest specialist banking and financial services practices. The firm advises a wide range of international banks and financial services companies on project and asset finance (including public private partnership), secured, unsecured, senior, mezzanine and subordinated lending (both syndicated and bilateral), funds, derivatives and insurance.

WORLDWIDE OFFICE CONTACTS

REPUBLIC OF IRELAND
Earlsfort Centre, Earlsfort Terrace, **Dublin** 2
Tel: +353 1 618 0000 **Fax:** +353 1 618 0618
Email: mail@arthurcox.ie

NORTHERN IRELAND
Stokes House, 17-25 College Square East, **Belfast** BT1 6HD
Tel: +44 28 9023 0007 **Fax:** +44 28 9023 3484
Email: bt@arthurcox.ie

UNITED STATES
570 Lexington Avenue, 28th Floor, **New York**, NY 10022
Tel: +1 212 759 0808 **Fax:** +1 212 688 3237
Email: matson@arthurcox.com

Inward investment: Arthur Cox's Inward Investment Group is dedicated to advising overseas companies investing in Ireland. The firm's US office, which was established in 1980, is designed primarily to serve North American clients investing in Ireland. The firm has particular expertise in technology, e-commerce, teleservices and manufacturing projects.

Litigation and arbitration: The litigation department offers international clients advice in both contentious and non-contentious matters. Arthur Cox's litigation practice has grown significantly in recent years, particularly in the areas of international arbitration and international commercial disputes.

LANGUAGES: English, French, German, Italian, Spanish

For other recommended firms see pages 1485-1520

ALLENS ARTHUR ROBINSON GROUP (AAR)

HEAD OFFICE

Arthur Robinson & Hedderwicks, Stock Exchange Building, 530 Collins Street
Melbourne VIC 3000, Australia
Tel: +61 3 9613 8637 **Fax:** +61 3 9614 4661
Email: Tom.Poulton@arh.com.au
Website: www.arh.com.au

FIRM OVERVIEW

Managing partners: Tom Poulton (Melbourne)
Ian McGill (Sydney)
Jeremy Schultz (Adelaide)
Number of partners worldwide: 192
Number of other lawyers worldwide: 503

AREAS OF PRACTICE:

Corporate and commercial 28%
Banking and finance 18%
IT/intellectual property 15%
Energy, resources and infrastructure 12%
Tax 12%
Competition and anti-trust 9%
Property 6%

FIRM OVERVIEW: The strategic alliance between Arthur Robinson & Hedderwicks, Allen Allen & Hemsley and Finlaysons forms the Allens Arthur Robinson (AAR) Group - one of Australasia's largest and most successful group of lawyers. The group advises leading corporations on landmark corporate and commercial matters. The group handles matters in the three key areas of banking and finance, corporate and commercial, and litigation and dispute resolution. The firm is actively involved in creating new equity and debt structures, developing new financial products and leading the way forward in newly emerging areas of law.

INTERNATIONAL EXPERIENCE: The group offers legal services across the Asia Pacific region with a network which covers Singapore, Hong Kong, Shanghai, Port Moresby, Jakarta, Bangkok, Phnom Penh and Australia.

INTERNATIONAL CLIENTS: Clients include ABN AMRO; Bank of America; Bank of Tokyo; Barclays Bank PLC; Chase Manhattan Bank; Deutsche Morgan Grenfell; General Electric Capital Corporation; HSBC; Morgan Stanley; News Corporation; PepsiCo; Sony Music; Telecom NZ.

MAIN INTERNATIONAL AREAS OF PRACTICE:

Banking and finance: The group specialises in the financing of landmark infrastructure and resource projects, intricate corporate financing and capital market issues for key market players. These include corporate and government borrowers and issuers, as well as trading, investment and merchant banks.
Capital markets: The group handles innovative, complex and sophisticated banking deals. The group is distinguished by the highly advanced deal management techniques used by its lawyers.
Communications: The group's expanding communications practice advise on all aspects including the outsourcing of communications requirements, telecommunications legislation, shared facilities access, litigation, privacy and competition laws.
Competition: The group handles sensitive competition issues, advising on M&A; joint ventures; supply, distribution and agency agreements; 'market power' issues; authorisations and notifications in respect of restrictive trade practices; and misleading and deceptive conduct allegations.
Corporate and commercial: The group advises many of Australia's leading companies and major international corporations on mergers, takeovers, sales, acquisitions, joint ventures, capital raisings and securities issues.
Energy: The group advises on all aspects including building, owning and operating energy projects; electricity and gas purchase contracts; coal and gas supply; transportation agreements; transmission agreements; hedging agreements and commodity marketing arrangements.
Information technology: The group is involved in e-commerce transactions; software licences; facilities management; outsourcing; alliance of IT services providers; IT consulting; business acquisitions and dispute resolution.
Intellectual property: The group handles matters ranging from seeking patent, trade mark and design protection to licensing those rights, and where necessary, undertaking litigation to protect clients' rights
Mergers and acquisitions The group has expertise in M&A transactions including public company takeovers; share and asset acquisitions; government privatisations; joint ventures and other alliances; and other forms of business amalgamation and partition.
Project finance/infrastructure The group has achieved international recognition for its advice to government and corporate bidders on many of Australia's most significant privatisation and infrastructure deals.
Property: The group's practice covers every aspect of property law.
Tax: The group advises corporate clients on the tax implications of all types of transactions and circumstances including M&A; offshore loans and investments; restructuring; employee share schemes and new financial products.
Other: Other complementary areas of expertise of the AAR Group include insurance; health and life sciences; superannuation and funds management; media and entertainment; construction and arbitration; environment and planning; employment and industrial relations.

LANGUAGES: Arabic, Cantonese, Chinese, English, French, German, Greek, Hindu, Indonesian, Italian, Japanese, Malay, Mandarin, Russian

WORLDWIDE OFFICE CONTACTS

AUSTRALIA
Finlaysons, 81 Flinders Street, GPO Box 1244, **Adelaide** SA 5000
Tel: +61 8 8235 7400 **Fax:** +61 8 8232 2944
Email: Jeremyschultz@finlaysons.com.au

Allen Allen & Hemsley, Level 31, The Riverside Centre, 123 Eagle Street, **Brisbane** QLD 4000
Tel: +61 7 3334 3000 **Fax:** +61 2 7 3334 3444
Email: Ken.MacDonald@allens.com.au

Arthur Robinson & Hedderwicks, Stock Exchange Building, 530 Collins Street, **Melbourne** VIC 3000
Tel: +61 3 9613 8637 **Fax:** +61 3 9614 4661
Email: Tom.Poulton@arh.com.au

Arthur Robinson & Hedderwicks, Level 8, Wesfarmers House, 40 The Esplanade, **Perth** WA 6000
Tel: +61 8 9420 4222 **Fax:** + 61 8 9481 1954
Email: Bill.Manning@arh.com.au

Allen Allen & Hemsley, Level 14, 50 Cavill Avenue, **Surfers Paradise** QLD 4217
Tel: +61 7 5585 3600 **Fax:** +61 7 5585 3666
Email: Ken.MacDonald@allens.com.au

Allen Allen & Hemsley, Level 17, The Chifley Tower, 2 Chifley Square, **Sydney** NSW 2000
Tel: +61 2 9230 4000 **Fax:** +61 2 9230 5333
Email: Ian.McGill@allens.com.au

ASHURST MORRIS CRISP

HEAD OFFICE

Broadwalk House, 5 Appold St,
London EC2A 2HA, United Kingdom
Tel: +44 20 7638 1111 **Fax:** +44 20 7638 1112

Email: enquiries@ashursts.com
Website: www.ashursts.com

FIRM OVERVIEW

Managing partner: Justin Spendlove
Senior partner: Geoffrey Green

Number of partners worldwide: 106
Number of other lawyers worldwide: 517

AREAS OF PRACTICE:

Area	%
Company and commercial	49%
Litigation	17%
Real estate	16%
Banking and Capital Markets	13%
Tax	5%

A

FIRM OVERVIEW: Ashurst Morris Crisp is an international law firm with offices in Brussels, Frankfurt, London, Milan, New York, Paris, Tokyo and Singapore as well as a liaison office in New Delhi. Founded in 1822, the firm has 106 partners and 517 other lawyers. The firm focuses on all aspects of business and financial law and also has a number of cross-departmental groups to provide specialist coverage in areas including intellectual property, commercial contracts and EU law.

INTERNATIONAL EXPERIENCE: A significant proportion of the firm's work has an international dimension. Ashursts works with its clients and intermediaries to anticipate their future requirements and adapt to changing market conditions. In particular Ashursts has responded effectively to its clients' growing involvement in larger, increasingly complex and international deals.

INTERNATIONAL CLIENTS: The firm's clients include @Entertainment Inc., Bell Atlantic Corporation, Candover, Chase Capital, Cinven, Deutsche Bank, Société Générale, Deutsche Telekom, Imetal, Imperial Tobacco, Kingston Communications, Legal & General Ventures, Lehman Brothers, Liechtenstein Global Fund Management, Marubeni Corporation, Merrill Lynch, Oakhill Capital, Paribas International, Telecom Eireann, Texas Pacific, Thuraya Satellite Communicatons and Videocon International.

MAIN INTERNATIONAL AREAS OF PRACTICE: The firm provides a comprehensive range of services in the areas of banking and capital markets; buy outs/private equity; commercial litigation; commercial real estate; construction and engineering; e-commerce; employment; employee benefits; energy and natural resources; environmental risk management; EU and competition; film; information technology; insurance and reinsurance; intellectual property; international arbitration and dispute resolution; investment banking; investment funds; life sciences; media; pensions; product liability; projects; property litigation and licensing; pubic international law; rail; reconstruction and insolvency; sports; tax; telecommunications; and trade.

WORLDWIDE OFFICE CONTACTS

BELGIUM
Avenue Louise 375, 1050 **Brussels**
Tel: +32 2 626 1900 **Fax:** +32 2 626 1901

FRANCE
22, Rue de Marignan, 75008 **Paris**
Tel: +33 1 53 53 53 53 **Fax:** +33 1 53 53 53 54

GERMANY
Oberlindau 76-78, 60323 **Frankfurt am Main**
Tel: +49 69 97 11 26 **Fax:** +49 69 97 20 52 20

INDIA
(Liason Office), 6 Aurangzeb Road, D-1, **New Delhi** 110011
Tel: +91 11 301 4054 **Fax:** +91 11 301 4089

ITALY
Via C Finocchiaro Aprile, 14, 20124 **Milan**
Tel: +39 02 620 227 225 **Fax:** +39 02 620 227 226

JAPAN
Kioicho Building, 8th Floor, 3-12 Kioicho, Chiyoda-Ku, **Tokyo** 102-0094
Tel: +81 3 5276 5900 **Fax:** +81 3 5276 5922

SINGAPORE
6, Battery Road, #15-08, **Singapore** 049909
Tel: +65 221 2214 **Fax:** +65 221 5484

UNITED KINGDOM
Broadwalk House, 5 Appold St, **London** EC2A 2HA
Tel: +44 20 7638 1111 **Fax:** +44 20 7638 1112

USA
712 Fifth Avenue, **New York** NY 10019
Tel: +1 212 245 4540 **Fax:** +1 212 245 4335

For other recommended firms see pages 1485-1520

ATANASKOVIC HARTNELL

HEAD OFFICE

Atanaskovic Hartnell House, 75-85 Elizabeth Street,
Sydney NSW 2000, Australia
Tel: +61 2 9777 7000 **Fax:** + 61 2 9777 8777

Email: info@ah.com.au
Website: www.ah.com.au

FIRM OVERVIEW

Managing partner: Mark Pistilli
Senior partners: John Atanaskovic, Tony Hartnell

Number of partners worldwide: 9
Number of other lawyers worldwide: 25

AREAS OF PRACTICE:

Corporate and commercial	45%
Commercial litigation	15%
IT&T and media law	15%
Banking and finance	10%
Tax	10%
Competition and anti-trust	5%

FIRM OVERVIEW: Atanaskovic Hartnell is a focused corporate and commercial law firm practising Australia-wide and internationally from its Sydney base. A number of its partners are recognised worldwide as experts in their fields, having practised for some years at the firm, and previously at other national and international law firms. Between them, the firm's partners have handled some of the most significant legal matters which have arisen in Australia in the last 20 years.

INTERNATIONAL EXPERIENCE: Atanaskovic Hartnell acts for many foreign clients conducting business in Australia, throughout Asia, and worldwide.

INTERNATIONAL CLIENTS: Atanaskovic Hartnell's clients include major Australian and international corporates such as AMP; Arthur Andersen; Babcock & Brown; Bankers Trust; Broken Hill Proprietary; Capital Z Asia; Cable and Wireless Optus; Can-West Global Communications; Chase Manhattan Bank; Commonwealth Bank of Australia; Competitive Foods Group; Cyprus; Glencore International; Goodman Fielder; Haliburton Company; HIH Insurance; Japan Telecoms; Leighton Holdings; Macquarie Bank; Merrill Lynch; Murdoch Family; News Corporation; Petronas; Phelps Dodge; RAG Coal International; Sydney Organising Committee for the Olympic Games; TransCanada International.

MAIN INTERNATIONAL AREAS OF PRACTICE:

Corporate and commercial law: Atanaskovic Hartnell is one of the leading mergers and acquisition firms in Australia, having acted in many of Australia's largest and most complex takeovers. The firm is also active in other areas of corporate and commercial law including capital raisings, joint ventures, competition law, IT&T and media law

Banking and finance: The firm has acted for a number of Australian companies raising funds in Australia and offshore.

Tax: The firm's tax practice specialises in advice on tax matters for worldwide corporate groups.

Energy and natural resources: The firm has been involved in most of the significant energy and resources deals in Australia over the past two years. It acts for international miners such as Phelps Dodge Corporation, Cyprus, RAG Coal International, BHP and Glencore International.

Complex Litigation: The firm has acted in matters such as the worldwide Arthur Andersen/Andersen Consulting arbitration, and has assisted many interntional corporates handle disputes in Australia.

LANGUAGES: Chinese dialects, English, French, German, Greek, Italian, Vietnamese

WORLDWIDE OFFICE CONTACTS

AUSTRALIA
Atanaskovic Hartnell House, 75-85 Elizabeth Street, **Sydney** NSW 2000
Tel: +61 2 9777 7000 **Fax:** + 61 2 9777 8777
Email: info@ah.com.au

ATANASKOVIC HARTNELL
LAWYERS - CORPORATE, FINANCE & TAXATION

A

For other recommended firms see pages 1485-1520

AWOONOR LAW CONSULTANCY

HEAD OFFICE

42 Dr. Isert Road, North Ridge,
Accra PO Box CT2629, Ghana
Tel: +233 21 227 307 **Fax:** +233 21 244 900

Email: awoonor@ighmail.com

FIRM OVERVIEW

Managing partner: Ekow Awoonor

Number of partners worldwide: 4
Number of other lawyers worldwide: 12

AREAS OF PRACTICE:

Corporate finance	60%
Banking and finance	15%
Litigation	10%
Mining and energy	10%
Capital markets	5%
Privatisation	5%

A

FIRM OVERVIEW: Founded in 1984, Awoonor Law Consultancy is an alternative to the wholesale practice of law in Ghana. The firm was established in response to the changing economies of the developing world. It aims to provide innovative and unique problem solving skills to the corporate, financial, and investment needs of its clients.

INTERNATIONAL EXPERIENCE: The firm advises foreign multinationals and global corporations on investment and corporate activities in Ghana. Awoonor Law Consultancy is the Ghanaian counsel advising the consortium of private operators working with the West African States of Nigeria, Benin, Togo, and Ghana on the proposed West African Gas Pipeline project.

INTERNATINAL CLIENTS: The firm's clients include Modern Africa Fund, Accor Hotel Group, TotalFina, and other multinationals.

MAIN INTERNATIONAL AREAS OF PRACTICE:
Corporate finance and securities: The firm handles all aspects of corporate finance and securities law, and regularly acts for local and international financial institutions and public listed companies. It has acted as adviser to the government of Ghana in respect of its holdings in Ashanti Goldfield Corporation (a company listed on the London, New York, Zimbabwe, Australian, and Ghana stock exchanges).
Banking and finance: The firm has experience in banking and finance, advising on all aspects of finance law. It advises local and multinational banks, and international financial institutions on large transactions and project financing in Ghana.
Mining and energy: The firm regularly advises mining companies, and is currently advising the consortium involved with the construction and operation of the West African Gas Pipelines project.
Litigation: The firm advocates alternative dispute resolution, and handles corporate and commercial litigation.
Capital markets: The firm advises on Ghanaian securities law with regard to IPOs, public offerings, cross-border listing, as well as collective investment schemes. It is a consultant to the Ghana Stock Exchange in training and licensing dealers and brokers.
Privatisation: The firm has been closely involved in the privatisation of state owned enterprises in Ghana, principally advising on the privatisation process through the Stock Exchange or by sale and purchase agreement. The firm has experience of handling due diligence investigations, prospectus preparation, and listings on the Ghana Stock Exchange.

LANGUAGES: English, French, Ga, Twi

WORLDWIDE OFFICE CONTACTS

GHANA
42 Dr. Isert Road, North Ridge, **Accra** PO Box CT2629
Tel: +233 21 227 307 **Fax:** +233 21 244 900
Email: awoonor@ighmail.com

ASSOCIATED OFFICES

NIGERIA
Victor & Charles, 11 Eleto Street, Victoria Island, PO Box 54331, Falomo, **Lagos**
Tel: +234 1 261 6036 **Fax:** +234 1 262 5944
Email: vcharles@infoweb.abs.net

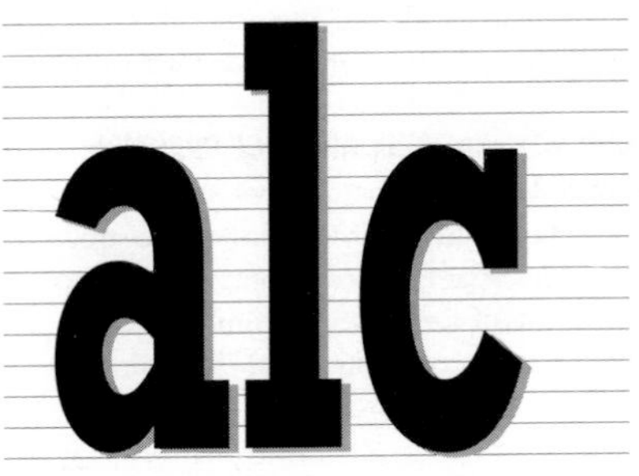

For other recommended firms see pages 1485-1520

AZEVEDO SETTE ADVOGADOS

HEAD OFFICE

Rua Paraíba 1000, 14th Floor,
MG 30130-141 Belo Horizonte, Brazil
Tel: +55 31 3261 6656 **Fax:** +55 31 3261 6797
Email: fsette@azevedosette.com.br
Website: www.azevedosette.com.br

WORLDWIDE OFFICE CONTACTS

BRAZIL

SCS - Quadra 07 - Bl. A, Executive Tower, 9º. andar - Shopping Pátio, DF - 70300-911 **Brasília**
Tel: +55 61 322 5052 **Fax:** +55 61 224 84 04
Email: jbatella@azevedosette.com.br

Rua Israel Pinheiro, 2801 Suite 310, Centro, **Governador Valadares**
Tel: +55 33 3276 8870 **Fax:** +55 33 3225 0138
Email: asagv@azevedosette.com.br

Rua Gomes de Carvalho 1306, 2nd floor, SP 04.547-005 **São Paulo**
Tel: +55 11 3845 5553 **Fax:** +55 11 3845 9660
Email: osette@azevedosette.com.br

FIRM OVERVIEW

Senior partner: Ordelio Azevedo Sette
Managing partner: Fernando Sette
Number of partners worldwide: 17
Number of other lawyers worldwide: 76

AREAS OF PRACTICE:

Anti-trust	*%
Corporate, M&A, joint ventures	*%
Intellectual property	*%
International trade	*%
Litigation and arbitration	*%
Privatisation and infrastructure	*%
Project finance	*%
Tax	*%

*Workload % not disclosed

FIRM OVERVIEW: Founded in 1967, Azevedo Sette Advogados is a full-service business law practice firm. Comprised of highly qualified and specialised attorneys, the firm upholds standards of excellence in accordance with the highest level of international practice.

INTERNATIONAL EXPERIENCE: Azevedo Sette Advogados has conducted several cross-border mergers, acquisitions and joint ventures. The firm advises foreign companies and investment funds on entering the Brazilian market and conducting day-to-day business operations. In 2000, the firm advised on over 120 international transactions. It has recently advised both governments and investors in the privatisation of the infrastructure sector in Brazil. Azevedo Sette Advogados is the Brazilian member of Legal Network International.

INTERNATIONAL CLIENTS: The firm's clients include Microsoft Corporation, General Electric, Business Software Alliance, Xerox, Santander, Citibank, General Motors, Gilat, Alcoa, Gessy Lever, Federal Express, Du Pont, Nike, Exxon, Siemens, IBM, Global Environment Fund. Azevedo Sette Advogados has worked for the World Bank and the Inter-American Development Bank in privatisations in Brazil and in Africa.

MAIN INTERNATIONAL AREAS OF PRACTICE:

M&A: The firm advises buyers and sellers in a range of M&A transactions. It specialises in conducting due diligence operations in local target companies, including an on-site evaluation and an investigation of the company's legal status before federal, state and municipal government bodies and administrative agencies.

Corporate: The firm specialises in establishing and incorporating companies and joint ventures in Brazil and representing its clients before the CVM - Comissão de Valores Mobiliários (Brazil's equivalent to the Securities and Exchange Commission). It offers a full-range of services including assisting clients in going public, underwriting, issuing of debentures, maintenance of control in public corporations, counsel to majority or minority of shareholders in takeovers or corporate disputes, drafting shareholders agreements, and implementing innovative capital structures for the purpose of acquiring or selling equity interest.

Privatisation and infrastructure: The firm advises government bodies on privatising state-owned companies, as well as advising prospective investors. It has acted in over 25 transactions including privatisations of state banks, mining and telecom companies. The firm's privatisation team has a unique experience in the privatisation of the infrastructure sector. It has been responsible for creating and structuring regulatory agencies that will regulate the water treatment, water supply and sewage services after the privatisation of state-owned companies in five Brazilian states.

Intellectual property and IT: The firm offers preventive consulting to companies wishing to comply with recently passed Brazilian software laws. The firm also specialises in intellectual property, including patent and trademark registration, copyright, transfer and licensing of technology, as well as patent and trademark litigation.

Tax: The firm provides tax consulting, planning and litigation services to clients in connection with all Brazilian taxes, including state sales tax, federal excise tax on manufactured products, municipal service tax, individual and corporate income taxes and social contributions, and social security contributions.

Anti-trust: The firm works with anti-trust agencies, such as CADE (Administrative Counsel of Economic Law), SDE (Secretary of Economic Law), and DECOM (Consumer Department), in proceedings related to the abuse of economic power, market concentration, trust, M&A, free competition, dumping, and other commercial practices.

International trade: Azevedo Sette Advogados has advised a range of industries, associations, and trade associations on subsidies, safeguards, surcharges, fiscal barriers and countervailing duties imposed on Brazilian products. With regard to the MERCOSUR entities, Azevedo Sette has defended sectorial or specific interests of Brazilian industries related to fiscal impositions or restrictions made by other member countries.

Project finance: Azevedo Sette Advogados has worked with US and UK law firms as legal counsel for banks, investments funds and other institutions, in addition to financing infrastructure projects such as water supply and sewage, telecommunications, highways and transportation.

Litigation and arbitration: The firm represents corporate, institutional and individual clients in all types of litigation before State Courts, Special Appeal Courts, and the Supreme Court. Azevedo Sette Advogados also advises on litigation in administrative cases before government agencies, including the Central Bank of Brazil, in extra-judicial liquidation of financial institutions and representation of managers or controllers. The firm's attorneys have participated in international arbitration committees. It assists clients involved in arbitration in Brazil and abroad, including arbitration under the International Chamber of Commerce and the American Arbitration Association rules.

LANGUAGES: English, French, German, Italian, Portuguese, Spanish

For other recommended firms see pages 1485-1520

BC TOMS & CO

UK OFFICE

64 London Wall,
London EC2M 5TP, United Kingdom
Tel: + 44 20 7638 7711 **Fax:** + 44 20 7382 9360

Email: bt@bctoms.com
Website: www.bctoms.com

WORLDWIDE OFFICE CONTACTS

UKRAINE
18/1 Prorizna Street, Apartments 1/2, **Kyiv** 252001
Tel: + 380 44 228 1000 / 490 6000 **Fax:** + 380 44 228 6508
Email: bt@bctoms.com

Additional office in **Odessa**

ASSOCIATED OFFICES

Baku, Azerbaijani; Minsk, Belarus; Tibilisi, Georgia; Chisinau, Moldova; and Simferopol, Ukraine.

FIRM OVERVIEW

Managing partner: B.C Toms

Number of partners worldwide: 2
Number of other lawyers worldwide: 15

AREAS OF PRACTICE:

Acquisitions and investments	30%
Corporate	30%
Real estate	20%
Banking and finance	10%
Litigation and arbitration	10%

B

FIRM OVERVIEW: BC Toms & Co is a law firm comprising Western and Ukrainian lawyers specialising in Ukrainian law. The firm was the first from the West to found a Ukrainian law practice following Ukrainian independence in 1991. It is among the largest law firms in Ukraine and is the only Western firm with an office in Odessa. In the last three years, the firm has handled transactions amounting in value to over US$1.5b of investments and loans into Ukraine. The firm was founded by BC Toms, who was previously a partner in a multi-national law firm and has substantial experience practising in the US and Western as well as Eastern Europe.

INTERNATIONAL EXPERIENCE: BC Toms & Co has handled most oil, gas and electricity legal work in Ukraine for Western firms and joint ventures with Western investment. They have also dealt with numerous Western investments in real estate development, large international loans to Ukraine, telecommunications projects, green-field factory developments and acquisitions of Ukrainian businesses, among other projects.

INTERNATIONAL CLIENTS: BC Toms represents major multinational companies and other foreign companies focusing on Ukraine. The firm also acts for international and multinational organisations (including for lending and debt restructuring) and some individual investors. In particular, the firm represents oil and gas exploration and development, electricity generation, telecommunications, pharmaceuticals, food processing, hotel and real estate development companies, banks and securities firms. It also acts for clients acquiring and renovating or constructing office buildings and factories, and companies producing industrial products. The firm has established numerous branches and subsidiaries in Ukraine for its European, North American and Asian clients.

MAIN INTERNATIONAL AREAS OF PRACTICE:

Investments and acquisitions: Since it began its Ukrainian practice following Ukrainian independence in 1991, the firm has advised on and documented acquisitions of and investments into Ukrainian businesses, including the purchase of factories, office buildings and other assets.
Project finance and construction: The firm has a major Ukrainian project finance and construction law practice. It has handled many of the largest projects in Ukraine, in particular in the energy and property development sectors.
Oil and gas and electricity: The firm has handled legal work for most of the significant oil and gas projects in Ukraine, including four public offerings by western companies to raise funding in the West for Ukrainian oil and gas development. It is currently responsible for the legal work for the largest electricity project in Ukraine to rebuild and expand a major co-generation plant in Kyiv.
Securities law: The firm acts for a number of multinational and local Ukrainian securities firms, and has handled both securities offerings and provided advice on securities regulation. It has also been involved in establishing banking activities in Ukraine for foreign banks and advising on bank regulatory issues.
Real estate: The firm has handled numerous significant real estate developments in Ukraine over the past nine years.
Privatisation: The firm is involved in the privatisation of Ukrainian state enterprises, in particular in the energy and telecoms sectors.
Tax, customs and exchange control law: The firm advises on all aspects of Ukrainian tax, customs and exchange control law, including on multinational tax structuring for inward investments (for which the firm has expertise in the laws of certain other jurisdictions particularly relevent to Ukraine). It has a successful record negotiating the resolution of tax and customs disputes with the state tax and customs authorities in Ukraine.
Labour: The firm covers all aspects of Ukrainian labour law.
Bankruptcy: The firm handles both voluntary liquidations and the involuntary liquidation of bankrupt firms as well as the purchase of assets out of bankruptcies.
Litigation: The firm has an active litigation practice and, in particular, has successfully obtained numerous large judgements in Ukrainian courts for foreign companies against local debtors. The firm has also been involved in a number of arbitrations.

LANGUAGES: English, French, Russian, Ukrainian

For other recommended firms see pages 1485-1520

BAKER BOTTS LLP

HEAD OFFICE

One Shell Plaza, 910 Louisiana,
Houston TX 77002-4995, USA
Tel: +1 713 229 1234 **Fax:** +1 713 229 1522
Email: joel.swanson@bakerbotts.com
Website: www.bakerbotts.com

FIRM OVERVIEW

Managing partner: Richard C. Johnson

Number of partners worldwide: 198
Number of other lawyers worldwide: 377

AREAS OF PRACTICE:

Antitrust .... *%
Corporate .... *%
Energy, oil, gas andreal estate .... *%
Environmental .... *%
Finance .... *%
Government contracts .... *%
Intellectual property .... *%
Labour and employment .... *%
Litigation .... *%
Tax and benefits .... *%
Trade .... *%
*Workload % not disclosed

FIRM OVERVIEW: Founded in 1840 in Houston, the firm has offices in London (opened 1998) and Baku (opened 1998) in addition to its five US offices. The firm is known principally for advising energy clients around the world, such as a consortium of major energy companies developing Caspian Sea resources and export oil pipelines. However, it is also involved in major transactions for non-energy multinationals as well as providing full services in other practice areas. James A. Baker III, United States 61st Secretary of State, is the firm's most prominent international lawyer. For more information about the international practice of Baker Botts, please contact Joel Swanson in the Houston office at +1 713-229-1234

INTERNATIONAL EXPERIENCE: Baker Botts has been active internationally for more than 100 years with global energy clients among the firm's principal clients.Through years of representing clients with global interests, the firm developed an international practice to serve clients' needs in the Middle East, Asia, Latin America, the UK and elsewhere. Longstanding representation of energy, petrochemical and electric companies, in combination with business and financing experience support the firm's increasing activity in international project development and project finance. The firm's experience with these transactions dates from the 1970's when it became involved in LNG production and shipping facilities in Indonesia. In more recent years, the firm has developed its intellectual property and international trade practices in response to increased global activity by technology clients.

Major international deals handled recently include assisting Occidental Oil and Gas Corporation in a four country, US$1 billion international asset swap with Royal Dutch/ Shell; representing Odebrecht Oil and Gas Services Ltd in securing rights to the Bijupira and Salema fields offshore Brazil, including negotiating and drafting a joint bid agreement with Enterprise Oil and a participation agreement and joint operating agreement with Enterprise Oil and Petrobras; representing Occidental Oil and Gas Corporation with the Tangguh LNG Project, the first new greenfield LNG project in Indonesia in several decades; assisting Reliant Energy in its US$2.4 billion acqisition of N.V. UNA, a Dutch electric generation company. Representing Lyondell Chemical Company in the US$2.4 billion sale of its polyols chemical business to Bayer A.G., a German conglomerate, and in their related propylene-oxide joint venture; assisting Philippine National Oil Company in a farm-in transaction in the US$4.5 billion offshore Malampaya gas-to-power project; representing Azerbaijan International Operating Company as principal outside counsel to the US$4 billion main export pipeline project through Turkey and negotiation of the US$700 million 'early oil' export project routes over Russia and Georgia.Representing Transocean Sedco Forex Inc. in the project financing of the drillship Enterprise and the upgrade of a rig through a US$238 million securitisation transaction of charters of the vessels to BP Amoco, and in its planned US$8.8 billion acquisition of R&B Falcon Corporation, the largest oilfield services industry transaction in history, creating the world's largest offshore drilling company; assisting Light-Serviços de Electricidade S.A., the electric utility company in Rio de Janeiro, Brazil, in connection with its successful bid for Eletropaulo Metropolitana Electricidade de São Paulo S.A. and the negotiation (and subsequent renegotiation and extension) of US dollar denominated debt to finance the acquisition.

INTERNATIONAL CLIENTS: Light-Serviços de Electricidade S.A.; Lyondell Chemical Company; Occidental Oil & Gas; Philippine National Oil Company; AES China Generating Co. Ltd; AGFA-Gevaert NV; Aventis S.A.; Azerbaijan International Operating Company; Cadbury Schweppes; German Federation of Industries; Honeywell; IBM; Japan Export Trade Organisation; LUKArco; Lukoil BV; Middle East Airlines; Mitsubishi Corporation; Mosbacher Power Group; Novartis Corporation; Rhodia

WORLDWIDE OFFICE CONTACTS

AZERBAIJAN
6-10 Vagif Mustafa-zadeh Street, Third Floor, Icheri Sheher, 370004 **Baku**
Tel: +99 412 976 388 **Fax:** +99 412 976 391
Email: jay.kolb@bakerbotts.com

UNITED KINGDOM
45 Ludgate Hill, **London** EC4M 7JU
Tel: +44 20 7778 1400 **Fax:** +44 20 7778 1450
Email: jay.kolb@bakerbotts.com

USA
1600 San Jacinto Center, 98 San Jacinto Blvd., **Austin** TX 78701-4039
Tel: +1 512 322 2500 **Fax:** +1 512 322 2501
Email: robb.voyles@bakerbotts.com

2001 Ross Avenue, **Dallas** TX 75201-2980
Tel: +1 214 953 6500 **Fax:** +1 214 953 6503
Email: jack.kinzie@bakerbotts.com

One Shell Plaza, 910 Louisiana, **Houston** TX 77002-4995
Tel: +1 713 229 1234 **Fax:** +1 713 229 1522
Email: joel.swanson@bakerbotts.com

599 Lexington Avenue, **New York** NY 10022-6030
Tel: + 1 212 705 5000 **Fax:** + 1 212 705 5125
Email: john.huggins@bakerbotts.com

30 Rockefeller Plaza, **New York** NY 10112-4498
Tel: + 1 212 408 2500 **Fax:** + 1 212 705 5020
Email: john.huggins@bakerbotts.com

The Warner, 1299 Pennsylvania Avenue, NW, **Washington DC** 20004-2400
Tel: + 1 202 639 7700 **Fax:** + 1 202 639 7890
Email: bruce.kiely@bakerbotts.com

B

(Brazil); Volkswagen; Dell Computers; Electronic Data Systems; MasterCard International; Nissho Iwai Bank; Occidental Petroleum Corp; Schlumberger Limited.

MAIN INTERNATIONAL AREAS OF PRACTICE:

Corporate: The firm advises on joint ventures, acquisitions and financings, particularly for energy, petrochemical and electric companies.

Tax: The firm handles the structuring of all types of international projects.

Energy, oil and gas, real estate: The firm advises on production sharing contracts, acquisitions and dispositions of petroleum interests, pipeline and LNG projects and real estate development.

Intellectual property and technology: Baker Botts LLP has over 100 lawyers involved in all phases of intellectual property.

Project finance: The firm advises on power plants, pipelines, offshore rigs, and LNG Projects.

Litigation: The firm handles arbitration and international boundary disputes.

Environmental: The firm handles a range of environmental related work, focusing on Latin America.

Trade: The firm advises on trade regulation and controls with a focus on high technology.

Other: In the United States, it is a large general practice firm with expertise in almost all commercial areas.

WORLDWIDE OFFICES

AZERBAIJAN

6-10 Vagif Mustafa-zadeh Street, Third Floor, Icheri Sheher, 370004 Baku

Contact partner: Jay Kolb

Number of lawyers: 4

Office profile: Baker Botts has been active in transactions involving Azerbaijan since 1992. In 1998, the firm opened an office in Baku which has four resident Azeri lawyers who work closely with the firm's US and London partners. The firm has worked with the Azerbaijan International Operating Company (AIOC) from its inception, and continues to represent the consortium on various matters, including the development of the main export pipeline project. Other clients include PennzEnergy (now Devon Energy Corporation) with respect to several major investments in natural resource production and processing in the country, BP Amoco with respect to natural gas export, LukArco, the LukOil/Atlantic Richfield joint venture on its investments in the Azeri energy sector, and various independent companies and service organisations operating in the region. The office also advises on a variety of other matters, including sales contracts, tax advice and transportation. The firm also assists clients with interests in Georgia and has represented AIOC and its Georgian project affiliate with respect to the early oil pipeline and the development of the main pipeline option through Georgia. The firm has also assisted Georgian businessmen on various projects such as the Tbilisi office of an international courier service. Baker Botts has a good working relationship with Georgian Law firms and several Georgian lawyers have worked as interns in the firm's Washington DC office.

UNITED KINGDOM

45 Ludgate Hill, London EC4M 7JU

Contact partner: Jay T Kolb

Number of lawyers: 12

Office profile: Although Baker Botts established its London office in 1998, the firm's attorneys have been active in London for decades in representations on commercial matters as well as commercial litigation and dispute resolution. The London resident partners have substantial experience in international projects, including mergers and acquisitions, joint ventures, industrial contracts, 'greenfield' industrial development and infrastructure projects, US corporate securities, real property and other transactional matters. Additionally, the London office assists clients in a broad range of contested matters and arbitration. Attorneys in the London office support clients doing business in various areas, particularly in transactions involving the energy, chemical and technology sectors. Currently, the firm is actively involved in some of the largest joint ventures in the international oil and gas industry, and will continue to emphasise and expand this capability as European and international markets evolve and consolidate. The London office has eight UK qualified solicitors and four US qualified attorneys, three of whom are dually qualified as UK solicitors. Baker Botts expects to continue to expand its London-based capabilities. The London office also serves as the support base for the firm's representations in various regions including Asia, the Middle East and the CIS. It works closely with the firm's Baku office and is integrally involved with the firm's alliance with Afridi and Angell, a leading law firm in the Middle East. Attorneys in the London office are experienced in emerging market transactions, and in addressing issues in connection with establishing operations in regions around the world. This office also monitors developments in international trade and business, including developments in the European Union that affect banking, financing and similar transactions.

For other recommended firms see pages 1485-1520

BAKER & McKENZIE

HEAD OFFICE

One Prudential Plaza, Suite 2500, 130 East Randolph Drive
Chicago IL 60601, USA
Tel: +1 312 861 8800 **Fax:** +1 312 861 8823

Website: www.BakerNet.com

FIRM OVERVIEW

Chairman of the executive committee: Christine Lagarde

Number of partners worldwide: 589
Number of other lawyers worldwide: 2,394

AREAS OF PRACTICE:

Anti-trust and competition .... *%
Banking and finance .... *%
Construction, property and real estate .... *%
Corporate .... *%
Energy and power .... *%
Environmental law .... *%
EU law .... *%
Health care and pharmaceuticals .... *%
Information technology/e-commerce .... *%
Insurance .... *%
Intellectual property .... *%
International dispute resolution .... *%
Labour, employment and employee benefits .... *%
Litigation .... *%
M&A .... *%
Major projects/project finance .... *%
Securities .... *%
Tax .... *%
Telecommunications .... *%
Venture capital .... *%
World trade (WTO) .... *%
*Workload % not disclosed

FIRM OVERVIEW: Baker & McKenzie services clients across the full spectrum of commercial law through 2,800 lawyers operating from the most financial centres of any law firm. Drawing on a pool of experience, know-how, and resources from 61 offices in 35 countries, the firm provides unparalleled client service on cross-border matters and applies global-best-practice standards to everything it does. Baker & McKenzie was established in Chicago in 1949, decades before the concept of 'globalisation' emerged. When operating seamlessly across markets and time zones is considered essential for success, the firm's global strategy and structure are being replicated throughout the legal industry. The firm's global revenues totaled US$935 million in 2000.

INTERNATIONAL EXPERIENCE: Baker & McKenzie was the first law firm to recognise the importance of a global perspective. While competitors focused only on domestic markets, Baker & McKenzie looked further afield with a foresight that enabled the firm to service its clients wherever their businesses dictated. Baker & McKenzie offices are staffed by internationally experienced yet locally qualified lawyers who are intimately familiar with the legal and business practices of their country and region. The firm's multinational culture, which has grown 'organically' rather than through mergers and acquisitions, is founded upon strong personal relationships among its attorneys and reflects the firm's belief that the best cross-border service comes from lawyers who know each other and practice law with each other on a daily basis.

WORLDWIDE OFFICE CONTACTS

ARGENTINA
Avenida Leandro N Alem 1110, Piso 13, 1001 **Buenos Aires**
Tel: + 54 11 4310 2200 **Fax:** + 54 11 4310 2299
Email: Pablo.Dukarevich@BakerNet.com

AUSTRALIA
Level 39, Rialto 525 Collins Street, **Melbourne** VIC 3000
Tel: + 61 3 9617 4200 **Fax:** + 61 3 9614 2103
Email: David.Nathan@BakerNet.com

Level 26, AMP Centre, 50 Bridge Street, **Sydney** NSW 1223
Tel: + 61 2 9225 0200 **Fax:** + 61 2 9223 7711
Email: David.Nathan@BakerNet.com

AZERBAIJAN
The Landmark Building, 96 Nizami Street, 6th Floor, 370010 **Baku**
Tel: +99 412 97 18 01 **Fax:** + 99 412 97 18 05
Email: Daniel.Matthews@BakerNet.com

BAHRAIN
6th floor, Al Salam Tower, PO Box 11981, **Manama**
Tel: + 973 538 800 **Fax:** + 973 533 379
Email: John.Xefos@BakerNet.com

BELGIUM
149 Avenue Louise, Eighth Floor, 1050 **Brussels**
Tel: + 32 2 639 36 11 **Fax:** + 32 2 639 36 99
Email: Francois.Gabriel@BakerNet.com

BRAZIL
Trench, Rossi e Watanabe, SCN-Q2, Bloco A-Ed. Corporate Financial Center, 3 andar, Sala 301, 70712-900 **Brasilia**
Tel: + 55 61 327 3273 **Fax:** + 55 61 327 3274
Email: Tulio.f.do.Egito.Coelho@BakerNet.com

Trench, Rossi e Watanabe, Av. Rio Branco, 1-19th floor, Sector B, 20090-003 **Rio de Janeiro**
Tel: + 55 21 206 4900 **Fax:** + 55 21 206 4949
Email: Luis.F.Pacheco@BakerNet.com

Trench, Rossi e Watanabe, Av. Dr. Chucri Zaidan, 920, 8th floor, Market Place Tower, 04583-904 **São Paulo**
Tel: +55 11 3048 6800 **Fax:** +55 11 5506 3455
Email: Juliana.Viegas@BakerNet.com

CANADA
BCE Place, 181 Bay Street, Suite 2100, PO Box 874, **Toronto** ON M5J 2T3
Tel: + 1 416 863 1221 **Fax:** + 1 416 863 6275
Email: Edward.J.Kowal@BakerNet.com

CHILE
Cruzat, Ortuzar & Mackenna, Nueva Tajamar 481, Torre Norte, Piso 21, Las Condes, **Santiago**
Tel: + 56 2 367 7000 **Fax:** + 56 2 362 9875
Email: Leon.Larrain@BakerNet.com

CHINA
Suite 2526, China World Tower, China World Trade Centre, 1 Jianguomenwai Dajie, **Beijing** 100004
Tel: +86 10 6505 0591 **Fax:** +86 10 6505 2309
Email: Danian.Zhang@BakerNet.com

COLOMBIA
Raisbeck, Lara, Rodriguez & Rueda, Calle 35 No. 7-25, 4th Floor, **Bogota**
Tel: + 57 1 285 1400 **Fax:** + 57 1 285 6908
Email: Alvaro.Correa@BakerNet.com

CZECH REPUBLIC
Praha City Center, Klimentská 46, 110 02 **Prague 1**
Tel: + 420 2 2185 5001 **Fax:** + 420 2 2185 5055
Email: John.Hewko@BakerNet.com

For other recommended firms see pages 1485-1520

INTERNATIONAL CLIENTS: Baker & McKenzie services the leading bricks-and-mortar and clicks-and-mortar businesses of our time, as well as emerging 'new economy' enterprises. The firm has an extensive list of both domestic and multinational clients in its various offices around the world - many of whom engage the firm on a multijurisdictional basis. In particular, its client list includes major corporations, financial institutions, and other business organisations in almost every industry and service sector, as well as governments and multilateral agencies. It is the policy of the firm not to disclose the names of its clients.

MAIN INTERNATIONAL AREAS OF PRACTICE: Baker & McKenzie offers forward-thinking practice expertise coupled with an individually tailored understanding of a client's specific business, no matter where in the world that business takes place. The firm's legal services are individual and singular, and yet the scope encompasses awareness and ability in every major commercial and financial centre throughout the world. In keeping with the firm's global perspective, Baker & McKenzie offers clients the benefits of global practice groups, which are augmented by practice groups at the regional and national levels. The strength of each practice group is having the right people possessing the right skills positioned precisely in the right places. As a result, Baker & McKenzie is able to offer seamless integration of global, regional, and local capabilities.

Banking and finance: Baker & McKenzie regularly represents sophisticated providers and users of debt, including banks, funds, and other financial institutions, in a wide range of capital market and other financial transactions. A significant strength of its practice is the ability to deliver co-ordinated, multijurisdictional advice in cross-border transactions. The firm brings together money centre expertise in structuring and documenting financial transactions with the ability to tailor transactions to meet legal, regulatory and tax requirements in the locations where financing is to be provided. The firm's practice is focused in the following areas – project finance, capital markets, asset securitisation, debt restructuring, leveraged leasing, credit facilities, aircraft finance, derivatives, global custody, and transfers of electronic and other uncertified securities.

Information technology/e-commerce: Baker & McKenzie's information technology/e-commerce expertise is at the forefront of the digital economy. Whether drafting legislation for states, countries, or the United Nations, doing first-of-their kind transactions and initiatives, writing ground-breaking publications, addressing key industry groups or legal associations, or litigating cutting-edge issues, Baker & McKenzie attorneys are extending the boundaries of e-commerce law throughout the world. Drawing on the firm's extensive experience with the legal issues raised by emerging technologies, the Internet, and e-commerce, as well as the firm's exceptional ability to cross legal disciplines and jurisdictions, Baker & McKenzie offers clients significant resources in navigating the continually changing legal issues of a dot.com world. The firm provides the full spectrum of legal services to information technology clients and enterprises engaging in e-commerce, including tax, corporate, securities, finance, venture capital, antitrust and competition law, telecommunications, advertising and content regulations, e-banking, e-contracting, insurance, employment, employee benefits and stock options, intellectual property, information technology and privacy.

Intellectual property: The firm boasts an unparalleled global IP practice with expertise in patents, trademarks, copyright, design and unfair competition laws. It acts for the world's leading intellectual property owners across industries, including pharmaceuticals and healthcare, fashion and apparel, information technology and telecoms companies, food and beverages, and other manufacturing industries. Services range from filing to securing registered protection, advising on the protection and exploitation of IP rights, and full enforcement capability. The firm provides international clients with cross-border assistance to secure injunctions, damages

EGYPT
Helmy & Hamza, World Trade Centre, 1191 Cornich El Nil, 18th Floor, **Cairo**
Tel: + 20 2 579 1801 **Fax:** + 20 2 579 1808
Email: Taher.S.Helmy@BakerNet.com

FRANCE
32 Avenue Kleber, 75116 **Paris**
Tel: + 33 1 44 17 53 00 **Fax:** + 33 1 44 17 45 75
Email: Eric.M.Lasry@BakerNet.com

GERMANY
Friedrichstrasse 79-80, 10117 **Berlin**
Tel: +49 30 20 38 7 600 **Fax:** +49 30 20 38 7 699
Email: Ulrich.Hennings@BakerNet.com

Neuer Zollhof 3, 40221 **Dusseldorf**
Tel: +49 211 31 11 6 0 **Fax:** +49 211 31 11 6 199
Email: Juergen.Mark@BakerNet.com

Bethmannstrasse 50-54, 60311 **Frankfurt am Main**
Tel: +49 69 29 90 80 **Fax:** +49 69 29 90 8 108
Email: Guenther.Heckelmann@BakerNet.com

Theatinerstrasse 23, 80333 **Munich**
Tel: + 49 89 55 23 8 0 **Fax:** + 49 89 55 23 8 199
Email: Walter.Henle@BakerNet.com

HONG KONG
14th Floor, Hutchison House, 10 Harcourt Road, **Hong Kong**
Tel: + 852 2846 1888 **Fax:** + 852 2845 0476
Email: Lawrence.Lee@BakerNet.com

HUNGARY
Martonyi és Kajtár/Baker & McKenzie, Andreássy-út 102, 1062 **Budapest**
Tel: + 36 1 302 3330 **Fax:** + 36 1 302 3331
Email: Geza.Kajtar@BakerNet.com

ITALY
3 Piazza Meda, 20121 **Milan**
Tel: + 39 02 76231 1 **Fax:** + 39 02 76231 620
Email: Corrado.Bartoli@BakerNet

Via degli Scipioni 288, 00192 **Rome**
Tel: + 39 06 328 38-1 **Fax:** + 39 06 320 3502
Email: Fabio.M.Brembati@BakerNet.com

JAPAN
Tokyo Aoyama Law Office (Attorneys At Law) Baker & McKenzie (Attorneys at Foreign Law Office) Qualified Joint Enterprise Office, 410 Aoyama Building, 2-3, Kita Aoyama 1 Chome, Minato-Ku, **Tokyo** 107-0061
Tel: + 81 3 3403 5281 **Fax:** + 81 3 3470 3152
Email: Hiroshi.Kondo@BakerNet.com

KAZAKHSTAN
8th Floor, 155 Abai Avenue, 480009 **Almaty**
Tel: + 7 3272 50 99 45 **Fax:** + 7 3272 50 95 79
Email: Mark.Lockwood@BakerNet.com; Curtis.B.Masters@BakerNet.com

MEXICO
Abogados, SC, PT de la Republica 3304, Piso 2, 32330 **Cd. Juárez**
Tel: +52 16 29 1300 **Fax:** +52 16 29 1399
Email: Andrés.Ochoa-B̧nsow@BakerNet.com

Edificio Country Empresarial - Piso 2, Prolongación Américas 1592, Col. Country Club, 44620 **Guadalajara**
Tel: +52 3819 0300 **Fax:** +52 3819 0399
Email: Andres.Ochoa-Bünsow@BakerNet.com

Edificio Plaza Inverlat, Blvd M Avila Camacho No 1-12o, Col. Lomas de Chapultepec, 11560 **Mexico City**
Tel: + 52 5 230 2900 **Fax:** + 52 5 557 8829
Email: Raymundo.E.Enriquez@BakerNet.com

B

For other recommended firms see pages 1485-1520

and other remedies, ranging from anti-counterfeiting work to patent, trademark and copyright infringements. Baker & McKenzie is at the forefront of advising clients on strategies to secure IP protection in the dot.com world. This includes advice and clearance of domain names, anti-cybersquatting action as well as cross-border advice on content issues. The firm also has expertise in lobbying for the introduction and improvement of IP legislation on a national and international level.

International dispute resolution: The firm's global team of dispute resolution lawyers is expert in the full range of skills needed to prevent and resolve commercial conflicts. These include litigation, arbitration, and all forms of ADR and global risk assessments. The firm's disputes lawyers act as advocates and are skilled negotiators. The global team has grown organically over a 50-year period, and its members are used to working together on some of the world's most significant and complex disputes. The fact that the firm's offices are staffed by locally qualified but internationally experienced lawyers enables it to devise the most practical strategies and tactics to deal with conflict.

Labour, employment and employee benefits: Comprised of more than 300 practitioners, the firm's practice provides comprehensive employment-related legal services to multinational employers in all major jurisdictions of the world. Members of the practice group provide employment and labour law counseling and advice to businesses on a wide variety of labour, employment, and employee benefits issues; specialise in the defense of employers and management in all types of employee-initiated litigation, as well as the prosecution of claims on behalf of companies against former employees; specialise in advising companies on immigration, tax, and other legal problems and solutions attendant the transfer of personnel to and from foreign countries; and design, implement, and administer all types of employee benefits, and executive compensation programs, and global equity services.

Major projects/project finance: Ranked the Number 1 Global Adviser for privately financed infrastructure projects in Privatisation International's 1999 and 2000 league tables, Baker & McKenzie advises clients in relation to major projects for the development of infrastructure facilities and large-scale manufacturing and processing systems throughout the world, in both established and emerging markets. Coverage includes nearly every jurisdiction where privatised or privately financed project development is now underway. The practice combines an understanding of the politics and culture of each country with experience in international construction, finance and commercial law, as well as a strong grasp of relevant technologies and industry practices. The firm advises lenders, sponsors, and operators on a broad spectrum of infrastructure projects, such as motorway and road, port, airport, water and power sector projects, as well as oil and gas and mining transactions.

M&A: Baker & McKenzie provides structuring and execution advice for all types of M&A transactions, including takeovers/tender offers, hostile, contested and agreed; private company acquisitions and disposals, both domestic and multijurisdictional; and privatisations. The firm has an unrivalled capacity to handle multijurisdictional M&A work, combining money-centre experience with local-market expertise.

Securities: With significant securities capability in all of the world's money centres and a greater presence in the world's emerging market countries than any other law firm, Baker & McKenzie is a leading adviser to investment banks and companies in equity and debt offerings. The firm has done pioneering work in emerging markets capital raisings in the People's Republic of China, South East Asia, Central and Eastern Europe, Latin America and the Middle East. The scope of the firm's work includes IPOs (domestic and international), equity linked and debt issues, including high-yield debt. The firm has significant industry experience with offerings by telecommunications and Internet-related companies.

Abogados SC, Oficinas en el Parque - Piso 10, Blvd Antonio L Rodriguez 1884 Pte, 64650 **Monterrey**
Tel: + 52 8 399 1300 **Fax:** + 52 8 399 1399
Email: Andrés.Ochoa-Bünsow@BakerNet.com

Abogados SC, Blvd. Agua Caliente 10611 - 1er Piso, Edificio Centura, 22420 **Tijuana**
Tel: + 52 6 633 4300 **Fax:** + 52 6 633 4399
Email: Andrés.Ochoa-Bünsow@BakerNet.com

NETHERLANDS
Caron & Stevens, Leidseplein 29, 1017 PS **Amsterdam**
Tel: +31 20 551 75 55 **Fax:** +31 20 626 79 49
Email: Mark.P.Bongard@BakerNet.com

PHILIPPINES
Quisumbing Torres, 11th Floor, Pacific Star Building, Makati Ave. cor. Sen. Gil J. Puyat Ave, **Makati City** 1200
Tel: + 63 2 817 3016 **Fax:** + 63 2 811 5640
Email: Juan.G.Collas@BakerNet.com

POLAND
Gruszczynski & Partners Law Offices, ul. Dluga 26, 00-238 **Warsaw**
Tel: +48 22 635 4111 **Fax:** +48 22 635 9447
Email: Wojciech.Bialik@BakerNet.com

RUSSIA
Bolshoi Strochenovsky Pereulok, 22/25, 113054 **Moscow**
Tel: +7 095 230 6036 **Fax:** +7 095 230 6047
Email: Max.Gutbrod@BakerNet.com

Bolshaya Morskaya, 57, 190000 **St Petersburg**
Tel: + 7 812 325 8308 **Fax:** + 7 812 325 6013
Email: James.Hitch@BakerNet.com

SAUDI ARABIA
Legal Advisors, King Faisal Foundation Building, King Fahad Road, PO Box 4288, **Riyadh** 11491
Tel: + 966 1 462 9886 **Fax:** + 966 1 463 2657
Email: John.Xefos@BakerNet.com

SINGAPORE
#27-01 Millenia Tower, 1 Temasek Avenue, **Singapore** 039192
Tel: + 65 338 1888 **Fax:** + 65 337 5100
Email: Kien.Keong.Wong@BakerNet.com

SPAIN
Avda.Diagonal, 652, Edif D, 8th Floor, 08034 **Barcelona**
Tel: +34 93 280 5900 **Fax:** + 34 93 205 4959
Email: Alex.Valls@BakerNet.com

Paseo de la Castellana, 33, Edificio Fénix - 6th Floor, 28046 **Madrid**
Tel: + 34 91 391 5950 **Fax:** + 34 91 391 5145
Email: Cristina.Bustillo@BakerNet.net

SWEDEN
Linnégatan 18, PO Box 5719, SE-11487 **Stockholm**
Tel: + 46 8 566 177 00 **Fax:** + 46 8 566 177 99
Email: Bo.Lindqvist@BakerNet.com

SWITZERLAND
Rue Bellot 6, 1206 **Geneva**
Tel: + 41 22 346 70 70 **Fax:** + 41 22 347 02 84
Email: Denis.Berdoz@BakerNet.com

Zollikerstrasse 225, PO Box 8034, **Zurich**
Tel: + 41 1 384 1414 **Fax:** + 41 1 384 1284
Email: Philip.Marcovici@BakerNet.com

TAIWAN
3F, No 11, Park Avenue II, Hsinchu Science-based Industrial Park, **Hsinchu**
Tel: + 886 3 564 1177 **Fax:** + 886 3 564 1561
Email: Michelle.Gon@BakerNet.com

B

BAKER & McKENZIE cont'd

Tax: Baker & McKenzie's tax practice has had an international focus since the firm was established in 1949. More than 50 years of development has produced an unparalleled level of experience and network of professional resources. Clients can call upon the expertise of more than 350 tax attorneys in 35 countries, including over 100 tax attorneys in North America. The firm provides seamless national and international tax advice and combines global tax solutions with multi-country legal implementation. The firm's tax practice offers comprehensive global tax advice on a full range of domestic and international tax consulting and tax dispute resolution/litigation services, including transfer pricing, mergers and acquisitions, e-commerce, global tax minimisation, VAT and private banking.
World trade (WTO): The WTO practice group consists of a core of international trade practitioners linked with attorneys specialising in other WTO-related areas. Through this structure, the group offers global, regional, and local guidance on traditional international trade matters, on national implementation of WTO rules, and on other WTO substantive areas. Key areas of work include services, investment, intellectual property, technical barriers, health and safety standards, subsidies, trade remedies, public procurement, customs, agriculture, competition, and dispute settlement. With an integrated group across five continents, the firm offers an unequalled resource for corporations, large and small, facing the demands of local laws, regulations and practices when accessing new markets or competing in existing ones. The firm also maintains a global pro bono programme through which it counsels Least-Developed Countries.

LANGUAGES: Afrikaans, Aguacateco, Arabic, Azerbaijani, Belarusan, Bulgarian, Catalan, Cebuano, Chinese (Cantonese, Chiochow, Fujanese, Hakka, Hokkien, Min Nan, Putonghua, Shanghainese, Taechew), Croatian, Czech, Danish, Dutch, English, Farsi, French, Galician, German, Greek, Gujarati, Hebrew, Hindi, Hungarian, Ilonggo, Indonesian, Italian, Japanese, Kazakh, Korean, Latvian, Lithuanian, Malay, Maltese, Marathi, Norwegian, Polish, Ponapean, Portuguese, Romanian, Russian, Serbian, Sindhi, Spanish, Swedish, Tagalog, Taiwanese, Tamil, Telegu, Thai, Ukrainian, Urdu, Uzbek, Vietnamese, sign language

BAKER & McKENZIE

15th Floor, Hung Tai Center, No. 168 Tun Hwa North Road, **Taipei** 105
Tel: + 886 2 2712 6151 **Fax:** + 886 2 2716 9250
Email: Michelle.Gon@BakerNet.com

THAILAND
25th Floor, Abdulrahim Place 990, Rama IV Road, **Bangkok** 10500
Tel: +66 2 636 2000 **Fax:** +66 2 636 2111
Email: Siripong.Silpakul@BakerNet.com

UKRAINE
48 Bohdana Khmelnytskoho Street, 01030 **Kyiv**
Tel: + 380 44 490 7070 **Fax:** + 380 44 490 6787
Email: David.Scott@BakerNet.com

UNITED KINGDOM
100 New Bridge Street, **London** EC4V 6JA
Tel: +44 20 7919 1000 **Fax:** +44 20 7919 1999
Email: Russell.Lewin@BakerNet.com

USA
One Prudential Plaza, Suite 2500, 130 East Randolph Drive, **Chicago** IL 60601
Tel: +1 312 861 8000 **Fax:** +1 312 861 2899
Email: David.P.Hackett@BakerNet.com

2300 Trammell Crow Center, 2001 Ross Avenue, **Dallas** TX 75201
Tel: + 1 214 978 3000 **Fax:** + 1 214 978 3099
Email: Robert.H.Albaral@BakerNet.com

Chevron Tower, 1301 McKinney, Suite 3300, **Houston** TX 77010-3019
Tel: +1 713 427 5000 **Fax:** +1 713 427 5099
Email: J.Richard.Hammett@BakerNet.com

1200 Brickell Avenue, 19th Floor, **Miami** FL 33131
Tel: + 1 305 789 8900 **Fax:** + 1 305 789 8953
Email: Donald.J.Hayden@BakerNet.com

805 Third Avenue, **New York** NY 10022
Tel: + 1 212 751 5700 **Fax:** + 1 212 759 9133
Email: Gerald.J.Hayes@BakerNet.com

660 Hansen Way, **Palo Alto** CA 94304
Tel: + 1 650 856 2400 **Fax:** + 1 650 856 9299
Email: Edward D. Burmeister@BakerNet.com

101 West Broadway, Twelfth Floor, **San Diego** CA 92101
Tel: + 1 619 236 1441 **Fax:** + 1 619 236 0429
Email: Abby.B.Silverman@BakerNet.com

Two Embarcadero Center, 24th Floor, **San Francisco** CA 94111-3909
Tel: + 1 415 576 3000 **Fax:** + 1 415 576 3099
Email: Edward.D.Burmeister@BakerNet.com

815 Connecticut Avenue, NW, **Washington DC** 20006-4078
Tel: + 1 202 452 7000 **Fax:** + 1 202 452 7074
Email: Nicholas.F.Coward@BakerNet.com

VENEZUELA
Despacho de Abogados, Torre Edicampo, PH, Avenida Francisco de Miranda cruce con Avenida Del Parque, Urbanizacion Campo Alegre, **Caracas**
Tel: + 58 2 276 5111 **Fax:** + 58 2 264 1532
Email: Francisco.Palma@BakerNet.com

Edificio Torre Venezuela, Piso No 4, Av Bolivar cruce con Calle 154 (Misael Delgado), Urbanizacion La Alegria, **Valencia**
Tel: + 58 41 2487 11 **Fax:** + 58 41 2461 66
Email: Omar.Benítez@BakerNet.com

VIETNAM
3rd Floor, 63 Ly Thai To Street, Hoan Kiem District, **Hanoi**
Tel: + 84 4 825 1428 **Fax:** + 84 4 825 1432
Email: Fred.Burke@BakerNet.com

12th Floor, Saigon Tower, 29 Le Duan Blvd., District 1, **Ho Chi Minh City**
Tel: + 84 8 829 5585 **Fax:** + 84 8 829 5618
Email: Fred.Burke@BakerNet.com

For other recommended firms see pages 1485-1520

BAKER & MCKENZIE - BRIONES ALONSO MARTIN

HEAD OFFICE

see Worldwide Office Contacts

Website: www.BakerNet.com

FIRM OVERVIEW

Contact partners: Cristina Bustillo
Luis Briones

Number of partners: 15
Number of other lawyers: 77

AREAS OF PRACTICE:

Banking ....*%
Capital markets ....*%
Construction ....*%
Corporate ....*%
Employee benefits ....*%
Employment ....*%
Environmental ....*%
Financial services ....*%
Intellectual property ....*%
IT/communications ....*%
Litigation ....*%
M&A ....*%
Project finance ....*%
Real estate ....*%
Tax ....*%
Workload % not disclosed

FIRM OVERVIEW: The merger between Baker & McKenzie and Briones Alonso y Martin in Madrid, effective January 1, 2001, has led to the creation, together with Baker & McKenzie in Barcelona, of the largest international law firm in Spain with a network of almost 140 lawyers and other fee earners. The firm is full service, but brings particular expertise to the areas of tax, mergers and acquisitions, employment, intellectual property, information technology and telecommunications, and securities law. The newly merged office in Madrid will be able to draw on the global Baker & McKenzie network, particularly it's unrivalled presence in Latin America.

INTERNATIONAL EXPERIENCE: The firm advises Spanish companies with cross-border business in Europe, Latin America and the US, as well as foreign companies operating in Spain. The firm is very active in cross-border operations in France, Portugal, Luxembourg, the Netherlands, Brazil and Venezuela.

INTERNATIONAL CLIENTS: The firm has an extensive list of both domestic and multinational clients, many of whom engage the firm on a multijurisdictional basis. In particular, its client list includes major corporations, financial institutions, and other business organisations in almost every industry and service sector. It is the policy of the firm not to disclose the names of its clients.

WORLDWIDE OFFICE CONTACTS

SPAIN

Baker & McKenzie, Avda. Diagonal, 652, Edificio D, 8th floor, 08034 **Barcelona**
Tel: +34 93 280 59 00 **Fax:** +34 93 205 49 59
Email: Alex.Valls@BakerNet.com

Baker & McKenzie - Briones Alonso Martin, Paseo de la Castellana 33, Edificio Fénix 6th floor, 28046 **Madrid**
Tel: +34 91 436 4300 **Fax:** +34 91 575 5744
Email: Luis.Briones@BakerNet.com

MAIN INTERNATIONAL AREAS OF PRACTICE: Work handled includes banking; executive transfers; capital markets; construction; corporate compliance and trade regulation; corporate and securities; employee benefits and executive compensation; employment counselling and litigation; environmental law; financial services; information technology and communications; intellectual property; international trade; litigation; mergers and acquisitions; project finance; real estate; tax controversies, tax planning and advice.

LANGUAGES: Catalan, English, French German, Italian, Spanish

Please also see the Baker & McKenzie entry on pages 1003-1006

BANWO & IGHODALO

HEAD OFFICE

98 Awolowo Road, SW Ikoyi,
Lagos, Nigeria
Tel: +234 1 2694724 **Fax:** +234 1 2694576

Email: banwigho@linkserve.com.ng

FIRM OVERVIEW

Managing partner: Asue Ighodalo
Senior partner: Femi Olubanwo

Number of partners worldwide: 3
Number of other lawyers worldwide: 8

AREAS OF PRACTICE:

Commercial	20%
Securities and capital markets	20%
Banking and corporate finance	15%
Corporate/M&A	10%
Intellectual property	10%
Oil and gas	10%
Shipping and admiralty	5%

B

FIRM OVERVIEW: Established in 1991 as a partnership, Banwo & Ighodalo focuses on advising clients on all aspects of the traditional and emerging disciplines of law. Members of the firm have wide and varied experience in both corporate and commercial law. The firm regularly monitors the progress of new legislation likely to affect client's interests, researching the impact of new developments in the law. They also seek, directly and indirectly, to influence legislation impacting the creation of an enabling investment climate in Nigeria. In October 1998, one of the firm's partners was involved in advising the Federal Government on the review and repeal of anti-competition and investment unfriendly laws. The firm was also recently invited by the House of Representatives to advise on the review of the country's telecommunications laws in general and the new telecommunications policy in particular. The firm has been actively involved in the ongoing privatisation programme, acting as legal consultant in the divestment by Government of its 16.58% equity stake in the country's largest cement manufacturing enterprise, valued at US$25 million.

INTERNATIONAL EXPERIENCE: Banwo & Ighodalo advise offshore clients involved in capital market issues and project finance transactions. In 1998/1999, they advised a foreign multinational company and carried out extensive due diligence with regard to the acquisition of a US$15 million controlling stake in a local company engaged in the assembly and distribution of heavy industrial machinery. In 1999, the firm provided local legal representation to a foreign multi-national company in the acquisition of a controlling stake in a local tobacco manufacturing company.They have provided local representation and advice on transaction structure, with extensive due diligence and legal advisory services to a foreign brewery in the acquisition of a substantial stake in a large Nigerian brewery. Since 1996, the firm has been engaged by one of the largest tobacco manufacturing concerns in the world in the establishment of its trademark portfolio in Nigeria, and has been similarly engaged on behalf of one of the global telecommunications services providers.

INTERNATIONAL CLIENTS: Banwo & Ighodalo's clients include Shell International Ltd, London; Baker & McKenzie, London; NAL Merchant Bank, Lagos; National Council on Privatisation (NCP), Abuja; John D and Catherine T McArthur Foundation, Chicago; British American Tobacco, London; Nigerian Agip Oil Company Limited, Lagos; Eli Lilly International Corporation, London; Heineken International Beer B.V., Amsterdam and Elf Petroleum Nigeria Limited, Lagos.

MAIN INTERNATIONAL AREAS OF PRACTICE:

Corporate/M&A: The firm advises local and overseas clients on all aspects of Nigerian and International business law, particularly on laws and procedures relating to investment in Nigeria. It undertakes work for public and private companies and other commercial enterprises, individuals and corporate investors, financial institutions and participants in development and venture capital transactions. It has negotiated and prepared shareholders' and other pre-incorporation contracts, advised on the formation and structuring of corporate entities, the purchase, asset sale, acquisition, restructuring or mergers of companies and in transactions involving the sale or transfer of shares and stocks held by foreign and local entities.

Foreign investments and divestments: The firm represents international clients in the manufacturing, investment, technology and service sectors, and has considerable experience with international companies and individuals wishing to establish business in Nigeria.

Oil and gas: The firm has vast experience in oil and gas law, offering advice and acting on behalf of multinational oil companies operating in Nigeria, on various aspects. The firm review and draft transactions, lease assignments and operating documentation. Partners have been involved in complex energy and project finance transactions.

Securities and capital market issues: The firm is active in the Nigerian Capital market, acting for issuing houses, appointed trustees, and security issuing companies. It assists in raising funds through public offerings either by way of offer for sale or for subscription, or by private placements or loan debenture stock. The principal areas of work are the preparation of prospectuses, underwriting and vending agreements, placement memoranda, trust deeds and debentures and issuing general advice on the offer structure.

Commercial: The firm advises on all aspects of commercial transactions. It has considerable experience in taxation, commercial contracts, sale of goods, insurance law and claims, partnership and trade disputes and receivership matters.

Banking and corporate finance: The firm acts for merchant and commercial banks and other financial institutions operating in Nigeria. Partners have represented major international financial institutions.

Intellectual property: Work handled includes protection of ideas, concepts, business operating plans and information, know-how, product or service information, works of authorship and advertising. It advises on registration of trademarks, patents, designs and inventions and the protection of trade names and copyrights, and has been engaged in the transactional aspects of intellectual property ownership, such as licensing and franchising, offering advice on joint venture relationships. Litigation arising from the infringement of clients' proprietary interests is also undertaken.

Shipping and admiralty: The firm handles the arrest and release of ships and cargo as well as ship mortgages and charterparty disputes. Its members have also been involved in admiralty procedings concerning claims as to ownership, damage to and shortloading or loss of cargo.

LANGUAGES: English, French

WORLDWIDE OFFICE CONTACTS

NIGERIA
98 Awolowo Road, SW Ikoyi, **Lagos**
Tel: +234 1 2694724 **Fax:** +234 1 2694576
Email: banwigho@linkserve.com.ng

For other recommended firms see pages 1485-1520

BARBOSA, MÜSSNICH & ARAGÃO

HEAD OFFICE

Av. Almirante Barroso 52, 32nd Floor,
20031-000 Rio de Janeiro, Brazil
Tel: +55 21 3824 5800 **Fax:** +55 21 262 5536

Email: mailbox@bmalaw.com.br

FIRM OVERVIEW

Senior partners: Paulo Cezar Aragão, Francisco Antunes Maciel Müssnich, Plinio Simões Barbosa

AREAS OF PRACTICE:

M&A	40%
Banking and finance	20%
Corporate	20%
Litigation and arbitration	10%
Telecommunications and computer law	10%

FIRM OVERVIEW: Barbosa, Müssnich & Aragão, founded in 1995, provide specialised knowledge and understanding of the legal and economic scene of Brazil. The firm deals with all matters concerning business law such as mergers and acquisitions; privatisations; private equity; capital market financings and investment; corporate restructurings; partnerships; joint ventures. The firm is active in a number of other areas including corporate, tax, administrative, antitrust, litigation, intellectual property, technology, labour and environmental law.

INTERNATIONAL EXPERIENCE: The firm has acted as legal advisor in several complex M&A transactions with parties located in different countries, and has acted as counsel in Brazilian issues of debt and equity securities abroad.

INTERNATIONAL CLIENTS: The firm's client base includes large companies, commercial and investment banks, insurance companies and Brazilian companies conducting cross-border business.

MAIN INTERNATIONAL AREAS OF PRACTICE:
Mergers and acquisitions: Transactions in this area range from small private acquisitions to cross-border acquisitions of foreign companies by Brazilian clients. The firm has acted as counsel in matters involving the acquisition and sale of Brazilian companies by foreign clients.
Banking and finance: Barbosa, Müssnich & Aragão has been actively involved in areas of banking and finance, including secured and syndicated loan transactions, structured finance and project finance.
Insurance and reinsurance: The firm acts for large insurance companies in Brazil.
Telecommunications and computer law: The firm advises on all aspects of this field of practice. They have relevant experience acting for the Brazilian Government in the US$19 billion reorganisation and privatisation of the Brazilian Telecommunication Holding Company.
Litigation and arbitration: The firm deals with civil and commercial litigation. Its lawyers are frequently involved in cases before the Brazilian Courts, including the Federal Supreme Court, and have experience in international arbitration, being represented in the Commission on International Arbitration of the International Chamber of Commerce.
Corporate: The firm advises on all aspects of general corporate law, including the drafting of Brazilian and international contracts.
Employment: The firm handles all matters relating to Brazilian employment law.
Securities and financial markets: The firm advises clients on Brazilian law pertaining to private equity and mutual securities and derivatives.
Internet law: The firm has been actively involved in the incorporation and funding of internet ventures as well as in the roll-up of Brazilian internet companies into foreign holding companies.

LANGUAGES: English, French, German, Portuguese, Spanish

WORLDWIDE OFFICE CONTACTS

BRAZIL
Av. Almirante Barroso 52, 32nd Floor, 20031-000 **Rio de Janeiro**
Tel: +55 21 3824 5800 **Fax:** +55 21 262 5536/5537
Email: mailbox@bmalaw.com.br

Av. Pres.Juscelino Kubitschek 50, 4th Floor, Itaim Bibi, 04534-000
São Paulo
Tel: +55 11 3365 4600 **Fax:** +55 11 3044 3479
Email: mailbox.sp@bmalaw.com.br

WORLDWIDE OFFICES

BRAZIL

Av. Pres.Juscelino Kubitschek 50, 4th Floor, Itaim Bibi, 04534-000 São Paulo

Resident partners: Paulo Cezar Aragão and Leandro Luiz Zancan
Number of lawyers: 19

Office profile: The office, founded at the beginning of 2000, comprises partners from the firm's head office and local lawyers. The office aims to provide better services to local existing and new clients.

BARDEHLE PAGENBERG DOST ALTENBURG GEISSLER ISENBRUCK

HEAD OFFICE

Galileiplatz 1,
Munich 81679, Germany
Tel: +49 89 92 80 50 **Fax:** +49 89 92 80 54 44

Email: info@muc.bardehle.de
Website: www.bardehle.com

FIRM OVERVIEW

Contact Partner: Reinhardt Schuster

Number of lawyers worldwide: 45

AREAS OF PRACTICE:

- **Antitrust** .... *%
- **Computer & IT law** .... *%
- **Copyright** .... *%
- **Design protection** .... *%
- **Industrial and intellectual property law** .... *%
- **Intellectual property searches** .... *%
- **Licensing** .... *%
- **Patent trade mark** .... *%
- **Software protection** .... *%
- **Trademarks** .... *%

* Workload % not disclosed

FIRM OVERVIEW: The firm was established in 1977 as a combined partnership of attorneys and patent attorneys specialised exclusively in the field of industrial and intellectual property law and litigation before all German courts, as well as licensing and prosecution before the European and the German Patent Office. In 1992, offices were founded in Paris and Düsseldorf, with further offices opening in Mannheim and Alicante in 1996 as well as a liaison office in Shanghai in 1998. The firm has 15 partners and 48 associates with a total staff of about 200. It comprises patent attorneys and lawyers, exclusively specialising in all fields of international German, French, US and European industrial and intellectual property law. The firm is active in prosecution, litigation and counseling, and is a member of the Information Technology Law Group, Europe.

LANGUAGES: Dutch, English, French, German, Hungarian, Italian, Polish, Portuguese, Romanian, Russian, Spanish

WORLDWIDE OFFICE CONTACTS

CHINA
435 Guiping Road, 200233, **Shanghai**
Tel: + 86 21 64 85 41 64 **Fax:** + 86 21 64 85 50 62
Email: info@sha.bardehle.com

FRANCE
14 bd Malesherbes, 75008, **Paris**
Tel: + 33 1 53 05 15 00 **Fax:** + 33 1 53 05 15 05
Email: info@par.bardehle.com

GERMANY
Uerdinger Str.5, 40474, **Düsseldorf**
Tel: + 49 211 47 81 30 **Fax:** + 49 211 47 81 331
Email: info@dus.bardehle.de

Theodor-Heuss-Anlage 12, 68165, **Mannheim**
Tel: + 49 621 42 27 10 **Fax:** + 49 621 42 27 131
Email: info@man.bardehle.de

Galileiplatz 1, 81679, **Munich**
Tel: +49 89 92 80 50 **Fax:** +49 89 92 80 54 44
Email: info@muc.bardehle.de

SPAIN
Explanada de Espana 3, 03002, **Alicante**
Tel: + 34 965 209 899 **Fax:** + 34 965 205 744
Email: info@ali.bardehle.com

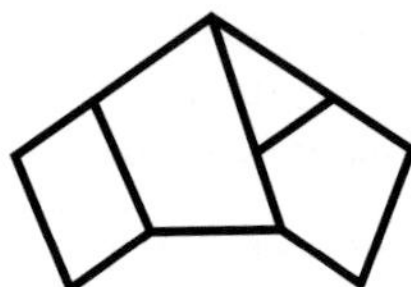

BARDEHLE • PAGENBERG • DOST
ALTENBURG • GEISSLER • ISENBRUCK

For other recommended firms see pages 1485-1520

BÄR & KARRER

HEAD OFFICE

Seefeldstrasse 19,
CH-8024 Zurich, Switzerland
Tel: +41 1 261 5150 **Fax:** +41 1 251 3025

Email: zurich@baerkarrer.ch
Website: www.baerkarrer.ch

FIRM OVERVIEW

Managing partner: Felix R. Ehrat
Senior partner: Christian Steinmann

Number of partners worldwide: 22
Number of other lawyers worldwide: 48

AREAS OF PRACTICE:

Corporate and commercial	30%
Banking and finance	20%
International arbitration	20%
EU and competition	10%
Intellectual property	10%
Taxation	10%

FIRM OVERVIEW: Bär & Karrer, founded in 1969, is organised as a partnership with 22 partners and 50 associates/lawyers providing advice both nationally and internationally. The firm works with Swiss, foreign and corporate clients in Switzerland and abroad. The firm provides a broad range of services in the area of corporate and commercial law. Its lawyers are admitted to practice in the region of Zurich and all other major regions of Switzerland. It has branch offices in Geneva, Lugano, Zug and London. Bär & Karrer also has an affiliate, BK-Services AG, which provides accounting and administrative services to the firm's clients.

INTERNATIONAL EXPERIENCE: The firm maintains an extensive network of foreign correspondents located in almost all major cities of the world. The firm has intentionally not entered into any close association or cross-border alliance.

INTERNATIONAL CLIENTS: The firm does not publicise names of clients.

MAIN INTERNATIONAL AREAS OF PRACTICE: Work undertaken includes banking and finance, corporate and commercial, EU and competition, intellectual property, international arbitration and tax.

LANGUAGES: English, French, German, Italian

WORLDWIDE OFFICE CONTACTS

SWITZERLAND

12, quai de la Poste, CH-1211 **Geneva** 11
Tel: +41 22 318 91 91 **Fax:** +41 22 318 91 92
Email: geneve@baerkarrer.ch

Riva Albertolli 1 (Palazzo Gargantini), CH-6901 **Lugano**
Tel: +41 91 913 44 10 **Fax:** +41 91 913 44 19
Email: lugano@baerkarrer.ch

Baarerstrasse 8, CH-6301 **Zug**
Tel: +41 41 711 46 10 **Fax:** +41 41 710 56 04
Email: zug@baerkarrer.ch

Seefeldstrasse 19, CH-8024 **Zurich**
Tel: +41 1 261 5150 **Fax:** +41 1 251 3025
Email: zurich@baerkarrer.ch

UNITED KINGDOM

1 Pemberton Row, Fetter Lane, **London** EC4A 3BG
Tel: +44 20 7583 1940 **Fax:** +44 20 7583 1941
Email: london@baerkarrer.co.uk

WORLDWIDE OFFICES

UNITED KINGDOM

1 Pemberton Row, Fetter Lane, London EC4A 3BG

Number of lawyers: 3

Office profile: Opened in 1999, the London office of Bär & Karrer, supported by the resources of the head-office in Zürich, offers advice and assistance on Swiss legal issues primarily in the areas of banking, financial and capital markets, M&A and a wider range of commercial and corporate transactions.

B

For other recommended firms see pages 1485-1520

BUFETE BARRILERO & ASOCIADOS

HEAD OFFICE

Alda Urquijo nº 12, entreplanta izda,
48008 Bilbao, Spain
Tel: + 34 94 479 34 00 **Fax:** + 34 94 479 34 01

Email: bbarlaw@ctv.es

FIRM OVERVIEW

Managing partner: Eduardo Barrilero

Number of partners worldwide: 6
Number of other lawyers worldwide: 68

AREAS OF PRACTICE:

Tax 25%
Commercial 15%
Company restructuring 15%
Administrative law 15%
Litigation 10%
Foreign investment 5%
Insolvency 5%
Employment 5%
Crime 5%

WORLDWIDE OFFICE CONTACTS

SPAIN
Alda Urquijo nº 12, entreplanta izda, 48008 **Bilbao**
Tel: + 34 94 479 34 00 **Fax:** + 34 94 479 34 01
Email: bbarlaw@ctv.es

Velazquez nº 12-2º, 28001 **Madrid**
Tel: + 34 91 576 34 24 **Fax:** + 34 91 575 75 17
Email: bbamadrid@ctv.es

Avda Diagonal nº 652, Edif B, 6º 2ª, 08034 **Barcelona**
Tel: + 34 93 204 85 12 **Fax:** + 34 93 204 75 52
Email: bbabcn@ctv.es

Ciudad de Ronda nº 8-3º dcha, 41004 **Seville**
Tel: + 34 95 454 09 11 **Fax:** + 34 95 454 18 29

B

FIRM OVERVIEW: Founded in 1991, Bufete Barrilero & Asociados has achieved considerable standing nation-wide, providing advice to companies as well as high net worth individuals particularly on tax and commercial matters. Whilst developing other areas of expertise, the firm covers all areas related to company law including restructuring, administrative law, foreign investments, insolvency, employment, litigation and criminal law.

INTERNATIONAL EXPERIENCE: The firm acts for some of Spain's largest commercial and industrial entities, handling all international matters. It also acts for foreign companies investing in Spain as well as domestic firms investing abroad.

INTERNATIONAL CLIENTS: The firm represents large domestic commercial and industrial corporations as well as banks, insurance and real-estate companies, among others.

MAIN INTERNATIONAL AREAS OF PRACTICE:

Tax: This is the one of the firm's core practice areas. It advises corporations as well as individuals on all aspects of national and international taxation.
Commercial: International contracts work and the negotiation of transactions in other jurisdictions have become key practice areas for the firm.
Company restructuring: The firm handles group restructuring of multinational corporates, including takeovers, mergers, joint ventures and other forms of company reorganisation.
Administrative law: Advice is offered in all situations pertaining to the administration with special reference to town planning and urban management.
Litigation: This is a core practice area. The firm acts on behalf of individuals and companies from overseas in Spanish Tribunals.
Foreign investment: This is also a key practice area within the firm. The firm advises business groups investing in Spain and abroad.
Insolvency: The firm has experience acting for foreign companies facing liquidation proceedings initiated in Spain.
Employment: The firm undertakes all types of work involving employment and social security law in Spain.
Crime: The firm also handles criminal matters, and is able to offer to foreign citizens services in this area ranging from pre-trial advice through to representation before Spanish tribunals.

LANGUAGES: Spanish, English, French, German, Basque, Catalan

BUFETE BARRILERO & ASOCIADOS

For other recommended firms see pages 1485-1520

BARROCAS & ALVES PEREIRA

HEAD OFFICE

Amoreiras Torre 2, 16th Floor,
1070-274 Lisbon, Portugal
Tel: +351 21 384 33 00 **Fax:** +351 21 387 02 65
Email: bap-lis@mail.telepac.pt

FIRM OVERVIEW

Managing and contact partners: Manuel P Barrocas, José Alves Pereira (Lisbon)

Number of partners worldwide: 9
Number of other lawyers worldwide: 23

AREAS OF PRACTICE:

Banking and finance .... *%
Construction and public procurement .... *%
Corporate and M&A .... *%
Employment and labour .... *%
Environment, planning and real estate .... *%
EU law and competition .... *%
Intellectual property .... *%
Licensing and franchising .... *%
Litigation and arbitration .... *%
Maritime, shipping and transport .... *%
Tax .... *%
Telecommunications and internet .... *%
*Workload % not disclosed

WORLDWIDE OFFICE CONTACTS

PORTUGAL
Amoreiras Torre 2, 16th Floor, 1070-274 **Lisbon**
Tel: +351 21 384 33 00 **Fax:** +351 21 387 02 65
Email: bap-lis@mail.telepac.pt

PORTUGAL
Rua Júlio Dinis, 891, 4th Floor, 4050-327 **Porto**
Tel: +351 22 600 80 02 **Fax:** +351 22 609 43 83
Email: bap-por@mail.telepac.pt

ASSOCIATE OFFICES

The firm has associated offices in Faro (Algarve), Funchal (Madeira), Maputo (Mozambique), and Luanda (Angola).

B

FIRM OVERVIEW: Founded in March 2000 as a result of the merger between Barrocas & Sarmento and José Alves Pereira & Associados, Barrocas & Alves Pereira is a leading Portuguese law firm. Comprising nine partners and 23 associate lawyers, the firm offers a full range of legal services.

INTERNATIONAL EXPERIENCE: The firm has experience in a range of international transactions. The firm has handled a number of significant international transactions in the areas of telecommunications, energy, construction, utilities, banking, project finance, chemical, automotive industry, electronics, insurance, shipping, hotel operation and distribution. The firm has an extensive network of correspondent law firms worldwide.

INTERNATIONAL CLIENTS: The firm's client base includes a number of large multinational companies.

MAIN INTERNATIONAL AREAS OF PRACTICE:

Corporate and M&A: The senior partners have over 30 years' experience in international mergers and acquisitions and advise international clients on the setting up of their businesses in Portugal in various sectors, as indicated above.

Shipping and transport: The firm is one of the few in Portugal with a consistent shipping and transport practice. The practice extends to all areas of work related to transportation, from accidents to sale and purchase, leasings and finance transactions.

Telecommunications and internet: The firm advises large net operators, software and high-tech companies, both national and international.

Construction and public procurement: The firm advises some of the largest construction companies and international joint ventures in Portugal. It is currently dealing with the largest public works project under construction and advises clients regularly on public procurement matters.

Licensing and franchising: Portugal's largest fast-food franchise is a client of the firm. It deals with all matters including selection of sites, rentals, real estate purchases, assistance to franchisers and franchisees and other related matters. It also has international clients and extensive experience in the fields of agency, distribution and licence agreements.

Environment, planning and real estate: The firm advises clients in the fields of real estate, planning, urbanisation, management and environment problems, both in tourism, where it has advised some of the major developments in the south of Portugal, and in commercial property for office occupation.

Intellectual property: Work includes copyright, trademark, patent and related litigation. The firm provides regular legal assistance to major international clients in the software, film, video and audio industries.

Litigation and arbitration: In addition to an active commercial litigation department, including product liability, unfair competition, shareholder's rights, insurance and tort liability, the firm has a specific white collar defence department, and is particularly active in arbitration and mediation proceedings.

Tax: The firm provides specialist advice to companies in the fields of tax planning and tax litigation.

Employment and labour: The firm advises institutional clients in the fields of labour law, safety, social security and regulatory compliance. It has participated in collective employment issues and due diligences related to employment matters.

EU and competition law: Provides anti-trust, competition and related advice to companies operating in the Portugese market.

Other services: The firm can handle cases in all areas of commercial law, real estate law, financial and banking transactions, insurance and other fields related to institutional investors in Portugal.

LANGUAGES: English, French, Italian, Portuguese, Spanish

BARROS & ERRÁZURIZ ABOGADOS

HEAD OFFICE

Avenida Isidora Goyenechea N°2939, 11th Floor,
Santiago Chile
Tel: +56 2 378 9777 **Fax:** +56 2 362 0387

Email: barros.errazuriz@bye.cl

WORLDWIDE OFFICE CONTACTS

CHILE
Avenida Isidora Goyenechea N°2939, 11th Floor, **Santiago**
Tel: +56 2 378 9777 **Fax:** +56 2 362 0387
Email: barros.errazuriz@bye.cl

FIRM OVERVIEW

Managing and senior partners: Fernando Barros, José Tomás Errázuriz

Number of partners worldwide: 4
Number of other lawyers worldwide: 22

AREAS OF PRACTICE:
Anti-trust: .... *%
Finance and securities: .... *%
Corporate: .... *%
Energy and public utilities: .... *%
Environmental: .... *%
Litigation and arbitration: .... *%
M&A: .... *%
Real estate: .... *%
Tax: .... *%
Telecommunications and IT: .... *%
* Workload % not disclosed

B

FIRM OVERVIEW: Founded in 1988, Barros & Errázuriz Abogados has a strong local and international practice, advising several multinational corporations, financial institutions, and formerly state-owned companies on a broad range of matters. It specialises in financing, securities, mergers and acquisitions, tax, project finance, privatisation, environmental, and litigation. The firm has close links with firms in Latin America, the US and Europe. Its members have a range of expertise and skills, many of which are gained from study and work experience overseas.

INTERNATIONAL EXPERIENCE: The firm has extensive experience in cross border transactions involving financing, corporate restructuring, mergers and acquisitions and international joint ventures. In 2000, the firm handled some of the largest cross border transactions in Chile including toll road financing, international bidding process of utilities companies, takeovers of electricity generating companies, and telecom companies. The firm has also represented major investment banks, commercial local and international banks, private equity funds, and controlling shareholders in cross border transactions.

INTERNATIONAL CLIENTS: The firm's client base includes large companies, investment banks, investment funds, insurance companies and public or international institutions conducting cross-border business.

MAIN INTERNATIONAL AREAS OF PRACTICE:
M&A: M&A is one of the firm's core practice areas. Its transactions range from small private acquisitions to cross-border takeovers of listed companies. Barros & Errazuriz has been involved in many of the largest M&A transactions in Chile.
Finance and securities: Barros & Errazuriz handles a range of banking and finance and securities issues including secured and syndicated loans, transactions and guarantees, structured finance, project finance, leasing, and tax-based finance. The firm has been involved in ADR programs, local and international bond offerings (representing both issuers and underwriters), and the listing of companies on local stock exchanges. It has expertise in securities law and has advised several publicly traded companies and many investment funds.
Telecommunications and IT: The firm advises local and international companies and handled the privatisation of the telecom industry in Chile. Barros & Errázuriz also advises several online service providers, incubators, and venture capitalists in the IT industry.
Corporate: The firm provides general corporate advice including the establishment of companies and representing clients before the Chilean authorities. The firm also handles joint ventures and partnerships between local and international clients. The firm acts as counsel to a variety of local and international clients in a range of areas including real estate and construction, stock brokerage and investment funds, pharmaceuticals, media enterprises (TV), private ports, hotel and tourism, agricultural, and forestry.
Tax: The firm handles tax planning and advises on legislative changes. It also provides tax advice to local and international clients on incorporations, recapitalisations, and liquidations.
Energy and public utilities: The firm is playing an active role in the development of law in the recently deregulated energy sector. It acts as counsel to electricity generating companies and water and sewage companies.
Anti-trust: The firm has advised on major anti-trust cases before Chilean anti-trust agencies in the telecom industry. The firm has been retained in several other anti-trust matters.
Litigation and arbitration: The firm has a permanent litigation department comprising lawyers and paralegals acting in a range of cases before civil courts. Barros & Errazuriz specialises in commercial litigation, insolvency, and corporate restructuring cases. The firm also counsels several clients in local and international arbitrations.
Real estate: The firm represents a variety of clients in all major real estate activities. The firm has been involved in several major real estate developments during the last decade in Chile.

LANGUAGES: English, French, German, Spanish

**Barros & Errázuriz
Abogados**

For other recommended firms see pages 1485-1520

BASHAM, RINGE Y CORREA, SC

HEAD OFFICE

Paseo de los Tamarindos No. 400-A, 9° Piso, Bosques de las Lomas,
05120 Mexico City, DF, Mexico
Tel: +52 5 261 0400 **Fax:** +52 5 261 0496

Email: basham@basham.com.mx
Website: www.basham.com.mx

FIRM OVERVIEW

Managing partner: Javier F. Becerra

Executive committee: Luis Ortiz-Hidalgo /
Daniel del Río
Martín Michaus

Number of partners worldwide: 19
Number of other lawyers worldwide: 70

AREAS OF PRACTICE:

Area	%
Intellectual property	24%
Corporate and real estate	16%
Tax	16%
Employment	11%
Civil and commercial litigation	8%
Criminal	8%
Telecommunications	7%
Foreign trade	6%
Environmental	3%
Immigration	1%

FIRM OVERVIEW: Founded in 1912, Basham, Ringe y Correa, is a full-service law firm. Comprising nearly 90 lawyers, the firm's aim is to provide its clients with quality, creative legal advice. One of the most senior firms in Mexico, Basham draws upon nearly a century of experience in assisting its well-known international and domestic clients conducting business in Mexico. Many of the firm's lawyers have degrees and/or completed other higher education abroad. Based in Mexico City, it has opened a Monterrey office to attend to the needs of its clients in the northern region of the country, especially in-bond manufacturing operations.

INTERNATIONAL EXPERIENCE: The firm's international work covers most of its practice areas. It has experience in corporate representation of major international corporations, and in dealing with cross-border transactions. Recent transactions have involved advising on foreign investment in local companies, establishment and operation of contract manufacturing facilities, global mergers and acquisitions, anti-trust filings and litigation, labour strategies for international operations, hiring of expatriates by local companies and granting of global benefits by multinational corporations, loan facilities by foreign banks to local companies, tax planning and regulatory compliance, commercial, tax and intellectual property litigation involving parties from different countries, trademark and patent registrations, and litigation.

INTERNATIONAL CLIENTS: International clients include Ford Motor Company, JC Penney, Federal Express, The Coca-Cola Company, VF Corporation, Mattel Inc., Colgate Palmolive Company, Union Pacific, Newell-Rubbermaid, Citibank, Hilton Hotels, Compagnie de Saint-Gobain, Accor, Cannon, Obrascon Huarte Line, and Sandvik.

WORLDWIDE OFFICE CONTACTS

MEXICO
Paseo de los Tamarindos No. 400-A, 9° Piso, Bosques de las Lomas,
05120 **Mexico City**
Tel: +52 5 261 0400 **Fax:** +52 5 261 0496
Email: basham@basham.com.mx

Batallón de San Patricio No. 109, 16° Piso, Col. Valle Oriente, San Pedro Garza García, N.L. 66269 **Monterrey**
Tel: +52 8 299 2100 **Fax:** +52 8 299 2109
Email: basham_mty@basham.com.mx

MAIN INTERNATIONAL AREAS OF PRACTICE:
Corporate and commercial: The firm handles a broad range of corporate and commercial transactions. It has advised a number of international clients operating in Mexico, and advises on the intricacies of Mexican law and practice.
Real estate: The firm advises on acquisition, transfer and sale real estate transactions, including all matters relating to foreign ownership.
Employment: Due to the special features of Mexican labour law, the firm offers different alternatives for the efficient operation of the labour force. It represents clients in union contract negotiations and litigation.
Tax: The firm is involved in all domestic and international tax-related issues from the planning stages to specialised litigation.
M&A: The firm handles all phases of the acquisition process, including due diligence review, contract drafting and negotiations, and anti-trust filings and litigation.
Intellectual property: The firm handles trademark, patent, copyright and Internet related registrations and litigation.
Foreign trade: The firm specialises in NAFTA and EU commerce, and in anti-dumping and countervailing taxes.
Legal translation: To efficiently handle international transactions and litigation, the firm has developed its own in-house (English-Spanish/Spanish-English) legal translation department.

LANGUAGES: English, French, Spanish

For other recommended firms see pages 1485-1520

BASILICO FERNANDEZ MADERO & DUGGAN

HEAD OFFICE

Macelo T. de Alvear 684, 2nd Floor,
C1058AAH Buenos Aires, Argentina
Tel: +54 11 4310 3900 **Fax:** +54 11 4311 3903

Email: bfmd@bfmd.com.ar
Website: www.bfmd.com.ar

WORLDWIDE OFFICE CONTACTS

ARGENTINA
Macelo T. de Alvear 684, 2nd Floor, C1058AAH **Buenos Aires**
Tel: +54 11 4310 3900 **Fax:** +54 11 4311 3903
Email: bfmd@bfmd.com.ar

FIRM OVERVIEW

Managing partner: Carlos A Basilico

Number of partners worldwide: 7
Number of other lawyers worldwide: 24

AREAS OF PRACTICE:

Administrative	*%
Banking	*%
Capital markets	*%
Corporate	*%
Customs law and foreign trade	*%
Employment	*%
Internet and e-commerce	*%
Litigation and arbitration	*%
Privatisations	*%
Tax	*%

* Workload % not disclosed

B

FIRM OVERVIEW: Basilico Fernandez Madero & Duggan (BFM&D) was established under its present name in 1978. BFM&D is a full service corporate law firm which provides quality, cost effective advice by maintaining close contact with its local and international clients. The firm specialises in complex structuring of mergers and acquisitions, corporate finance, capital markets, telecommunications, e-commerce, and media.

INTERNATIONAL EXPERIENCE: BFM&D has experience in international and multi-jurisdictional legal transactions. Many of the firm's lawyers have studied and practiced law abroad.

INTERNATIONAL CLIENTS: The firm counts among its clients a major US based international manufacturer of medical specialities, and the Export-Import Bank. The firm has also advised OPIC, the US government political risk insurance and project financing agency, US, UK, French, Swiss, Dutch, and Brazilian banks, a computer and office equipment company, and a number of leading European companies. Other international clients include a US oil company, an international chemical cargo company, a US investment fund active on the Latin American stock exchange, a Mexican oil and gas company, a large US communications company, and a Swedish steel and pharmaceutical manufacturer.

MAIN INTERNATIONAL AREAS OF PRACTICE:

Corporate: BFM&D handles all aspects of corporate law. It advises on the creation and restructuring of corporate vehicles, organising corporate governance, corporate conflict, and corporate finance matters. BFM&D also handles mergers and acquisitions.
Banking: The firm is general counsel for a number of banks. It also handles representation before the regulatory authorities and litigation issues.
Capital markets: In the last three years the firm has been involved in more than 40 international transactions including both public and private placements of debt and equity securities. BFM&D advises both issuers and investment banks.
Administrative: The firm has experience representing companies before the federal and provincial governments, public administration, and regulatory agencies. It also advises state-owned companies.
Litigation and arbitration: BFM&D represents clients before all courts in Buenos Aires. Through a network of correspondents, BFM&D also handles litigation in other jurisdictions within Argentina.
Tax: BFM&D is one of the few law firms in Buenos Aires that provides highly specialised tax advice and representation. Relying on sound commercial awareness and knowledge of Argentine tax law, the firm's team of experts handles a wide range of tax-related issues.
Customs law and foreign trade: BFM&D handles a wide range of customs law and foreign trade issues, both in court and extra judicially.
Employment: BFM&D advises on all aspects of employment relations including collective bargaining and litigation.
Privatisations: The firm has played a prominent role in the privatisation process that Argentina has undergone in recent years.
Internet and e-commerce: The firm has a specialised Internet and e-commerce department. The firm advises ISPs and provides legal and regulatory assistance in a range of diverse issues related to the Internet, e-commerce, and web sites.

Languages: English, French, German, Hungarian, Portuguese

BFM&D
BASILICO, FERNANDEZ MADERO & DUGGAN

For other recommended firms see pages 1485-1520

BBLP MEYER LUSTENBERGER

HEAD OFFICE

Forchstrasse 452, PO Box 832,
CH-8029 Zurich, Switzerland
Tel: +41 1 396 91 91 **Fax:** +41 1 396 91 92

Email: info@bblp.ch
Website: www.bblp.ch

FIRM OVERVIEW

Managing partners: Thomas Lustenberger, Martin Ammann, Christoph Heiz

Number of partners (Switzerland): 11
Number of other lawyers (Switzerland) 15
Number of partners worldwide: 75
Number of other lawyers worldwide: 470

AREAS OF PRACTICE:

Arbitration and litigation, forensic services	*%
Banking, capital markets	*%
Company, securities and commercial law	*%
Competition and antitrust, public procurement	*%
Intellectual property	*%
Media, IT, and telecommunications	*%
Mergers and acquisitions	*%
Tax	*%

* Workload % not disclosed

WORLDWIDE OFFICE CONTACTS

SWITZERLAND
Zugerstrasse 50, PO Box 2024, CH-6302 **Zug**
Tel: +41 41 768 11 11 **Fax:** +41 41 768 11 12
Email: zug@bblp.ch

OTHER BBLP OFFICES WORLDWIDE:
Beijing, Berlin, Budapest, Düssledorf, Frankfurt, Hanoi, Hong Kong, Leipzig, London, Lyon, Milan, Moscow, Munich, New York, Nuremberg, Padua, Paris, Postdam, Prague, Rome, Singapore, St. Petersburg, Turin, Warsaw

ASSOCIATED OFFICES

SWITZERLAND
Croisier & Gillioz, 61 Rue du Rhône, PO Box 3127, CH-1211 **Geneva**
Tel: +41 22 319 09 09 **Fax:** +41 22 319 09 11
Email: mail@cglaw.ch

B

FIRM OVERVIEW: Meyer Lustenberger has merged with Beiten Burkhardt Mittl & Wegener of Germany; Pavia e Ansaldo of Italy; and Moquet Borde & Associés of France to form a partnership under the name BBLP. With more than 480 attorneys and tax advisers, a total staff of nearly 800 and 26 offices in 14 countries worldwide, BBLP is one of the largest law partnerships on the European continent.

INTERNATIONAL EXPERIENCE: BBLP Meyer Lustenberger advises on cross border mergers and acquisitions, capital markets transactions, finance lease transactions, international joint ventures, distribution and other commercial agreements.

INTERNATIONAL CLIENTS:
The firm's client base is diverse and international, including major industrial companies, banks, travel companies and airlines, international organisations and private individuals.

MAIN INTERNATIONAL AREAS OF PRACTICE
Mergers and acquisitions: The firm advises on national and cross border M&A activities, including financing and corporate restructuring.
Banking, capital markets: The firm is involved in the formation of banks, ongoing advice on bank regulatory issues, bank documentation, initial public offerings, stock market regulations, financial products, bonds, and derivatives.
Company, securities and commercial law: The firm handles the formation of companies, corporate transactions and reorganisations, and general corporate advice.
Tax: The firm advises on fiscal and financial structuring of domestic and international transactions, property tax and VAT issues and international tax planning for corporate and private clients.
Intellectual property: The firm advises on Swiss and European patent law, trademarks and marks of origin, designs and models, and copyrights.
Competition, anti-trust, public procurement: Work undertaken by the firm includes competiton law, Swiss and EU merger control and cartel law, federal and local public procurement.
Media, IT and telecommunications: The firm advises on contractual and regulatory issues for audiovisual and print media, IT and telecommunications.
Arbitration and litigation, forensic services: The firm handles international arbitration, litigation before Swiss courts, and forensic services for public authorities and private companies.

LANGUAGES: English, French, German, Italian, Spanish, Portuguese

BBLP

MEYER LUSTENBERGER
RECHTSANWÄLTE - ATTORNEYS AT LAW

For other recommended firms see pages 1485-1520

BBLP MOQUET BORDE & ASSOCIÉS

FRENCH ADMINISTRATIVE OFFICE

30 Avenue de Messine, 75008 Paris, France
Tel: + 33 1 42 99 04 50 **Fax:** + 33 1 45 63 91 49

Email: bblp@bblp-fr.com
Website: www.bblp-fr.com

FIRM OVERVIEW

Managing partner: Dominique Borde

Number of partners worldwide: 9
Number of other lawyers worldwide: 94

BBLP OVERVIEW

President of the Executive Committee: Dr. Jürgen Burkhardt
Vice President of the Executive Committee: Agostino Migone de Amicis

Number of partners worldwide: 75
Number of other lawyers worldwide: 475

AREAS OF PRACTICE:

M&A	*%
Securities and financial markets	*%
EU and competition	*%
Intellectual property and media	*%
Tax	*%
Public law	*%

* Workload % not disclosed

FIRM OVERVIEW: BBLP Moquet Borde, established in Paris in 1976, is one of four firms to merge on January 1, 1999 to form the BBLP international partnership. Beiten Burkhardt Mittl & Wegener from Germany, Meyer Lustenberger from Switzerland and Pavia e Ansaldo from Italy are the other founding member firms. The partnership has no one head office, but is managed by an Executive Committee, with equal representation of each member firm. A Managing Partner and Vice-Managing Partner run the Executive Committee on a two year rotating basis.
With more than 450 lawyers, a total staff of almost 800, and 27 offices worldwide, BBLP is one of the largest law partnerships on the European continent. Its practice is international in focus and nearly 50% of work is transnational in nature. The partnership has a strong presence throughout Europe and Asia. Worldwide offices are: Beijing, Berlin, Budapest, Düsseldorf, Frankfurt, Hanoi, Hong Kong, Leipzig, London, Lyon, Milan, Moscow, Munich, New York, Nuremburg, Padova, Paris, Potsdam, Prague, Rome, Singapore, St Petersburg, Tokyo, Turin, Zug, Zurich. BBLP Moquet Borde's offices in Paris, Brussells Lyon, Geneva, Budapest and Tallinn are particularly experienced in providing legal advice and litigation services on French and European law to French and foreign clients and correspondent law firms.

INTERNATIONAL EXPERIENCE: During 1999 and 2000, the firm advised on numerous international mergers and acquisitions in banking, petroleum, mining and telecommunications and also advised on numerous international transactions involving airline, travel and finance companies.

INTERNATIONAL CLIENTS: The firm's client base is over 40% non-French, including major manufacturing companies. It also includes representatives from the banking and finance, energy and, minerals and telecommunications and media sectors.

WORLDWIDE OFFICE CONTACTS

FRANCE
BBLP Moquet Borde, 11 Place Bellecour, 69002 **Lyon**
Tel: + 33 4 78 38 70 00 **Fax:** + 33 4 72 41 98 62

HUNGARY
BBLP Moquet Borde, Kossuth Ter 16-17, H-1055 **Budapest**
Tel: + 36 1 353 1255 **Fax:** + 36 1 353 1229
Email: 100324.1022@compuserve.com

ESTONIA
Moquet Borde Raidla & Partners, Roosikrantsi 2, 6th Floor, 10119 **Tallinn**
Tel: + 372 6 407 170 **Fax:** + 372 6 407 171
Email: email@mba.ee

MAIN INTERNATIONAL AREAS OF PRACTICE:
M&A: A major part of the firm's work load is concentrated on national and cross-border M&A activity, including financing and corporate restructuring.
Tax: The tax department works with all other departments, and oversees specific tax issues and tax adjustments for corporations and individual executives.
Securities and financial markets: The firm has been involved in most of the major stock exchange transactions on the Paris and Brussels markets, advising on the issue and placement of shares and specialised financial products.
EU and competition: BBLP Moquet Borde is experienced in EU law, especially in the areas of competition, technology transfer and distribution.
Intellectual property and media: The firm has significant experience in different aspects of intellectual property law, particularly in the audio visual and print media.
Public law: The firm has a strong administrative law practice, stemming from its participation in privatisations, where it represents public regulatory authorities as well as the corporate sector on cases of public law.
Other: Litigation, arbitration, white collar crime, real estate and labour law.

LANGUAGES: English, Estonian, French, German, Hungarian, Italian, Spanish

BBLP

MOQUET BORDE & ASSOCIÉS
SOCIÉTÉ CIVILE PROFESSIONNELLE D'AVOCATS

For other recommended firms see pages 1485-1520

BEACHCROFT WANSBROUGHS

HEAD OFFICE

100 Fetter Lane,
London EC4A 1BN, United Kingdom
Tel: +44 20 7242 1011 **Fax:** +44 20 7831 6630
Email: lordhunt@bwlaw.co.uk
Website: www.bwlaw.co.uk

FIRM OVERVIEW

Managing partner: Robert Heslett
Senior partner: The Rt Hon the Lord Hunt of Wirral MBE
Number of partners worldwide: 132
Number of other lawyers worldwide: 349

AREAS OF PRACTICE:

Insurance 48%
Commercial 30%
Health 22%

FIRM OVERVIEW: The commercial law firm Beachcroft Wansbroughs is a dynamic and progressive national partnership providing a strong regional office network with major offices in the City of London. The firm's services are structured around client market sectors, primarily in the commercial, health and insurance arenas, supported by multi-disciplinary partner-led teams focused on serving client needs. With a particular reputation in defendant litigation, Beachcroft Wansbroughs provides a comprehensive legal service to the health and insurance sectors, supported by an in-depth capability for the commercial, financial and public and private sectors. As well as being an integral member of two European wide legal networks, Beachcroft Wansbroughs also has a fully integrated Brussels office which provides advice on competition law and all European issues.

INTERNATIONAL EXPERIENCE: The firm's European law team is supported by its partner led office in Brussels. Having a partner at the centre of European Government law ensures that the firm responds quickly to any changes that occur and has an excellent understanding of the EU law making process.

INTERNATIONAL CLIENTS: The firm's international client list includes, amongst others, banks, insurance companies, hotel chains, automotive manufacturers, advertising, the soft drinks industry, oil & gas, clothing manufacturers, electronics manufacturers and telecommunications organisations.

MAIN INTERNATIONAL AREAS OF PRACTICE: The firm is structured into three market-focused divisions – commercial, health and insurance and five functional departments comprising – corporate services, property, litigation, employment and projects and PFI.
Insurance: The firm's insurance practice has taken full account of the radical changes that the insurance industry continues to undergo. With corporate mergers and acquisitions leading to the rationalisation and increased concentration within the sector, Beachcroft Wansbroughs has responded effectively to help the sector to meet cost effectiveness and productivity challenges, through IT initiatives and the use of specialist services. The firm provides a comprehensive range of services to cover all aspects of the insurance industry's activities including claims management, contentious and non-contentious work, investment, strategy and operations. The firm works closely with insurers and brokers to develop existing and new products and is regularly instructed by the leading general insurers, re-insurers, Lloyds' syndicates, underwriting agencies, governing bodies and companies which self-insure. Beachcroft Wansbroughs handles a wide range of professional indemnity, employers' product and public liability, personal injury and motor claims, policy coverage disputes and has specialist knowledge and experience of major international product liability claims. Beachcroft Wansbroughs provides general claims advice and cross-border litigation advice across sixteen countries in Europe through a number of alliances.
Health: Beachcroft Wansbroughs' health division carries out a vast range of work for both private and public healthcare providers. In addition to a comprehensive health litigation capability, work covered includes a wide range of healthcare advice, governance, employment, property, PFI, IP/IT, procurement, construction and commercial matters.
Commercial: Beachcroft Wansbroughs looks after the needs and requirements of private and public sector clients across a wide range of disciplines. Solutions are delivered through skills based teams from across the departmental spectrum.
Corporate services: A high profile City presence and expansive nationwide coverage guarantees clients a seamless service. The department includes commercial litigation and corporate finance capabilities. It handles the full range of commercial disputes in the courts, arbitration tribunals and mediation. It advises on a comprehensive set of issues from intellectual property and product liability to insolvency. It also has a strong capability in M&A, disposals, listings, new issues, capital restructuring and joint ventures for a variety of UK and international clients. This is supplemented by additional specialist expertise in European Union law and in the advertising and media, construction, education, information technology, retail, sports and water sectors.
Employment: The firm works with a diverse range of businesses, providing up-to-date knowledge on the legal implications of human resource management. It undertakes employment work for both the public and private sector covering the full range of contentious and non-contentious matters, including High Court and tribunal actions and all forms of discrimination and industrial relations matters.
Property: With a team of more than 60 property lawyers the property department is one of the largest practices in the UK. The team provides a full range of services in property management, property investment and finance, dispute resolution and property litigation, planning and environment, construction, lease negotiation and total facilities management.
Projects and PFI: The projects team has a market leading reputation and a track record to match with clients extending across the public and private sectors. The firm's lawyers are experienced in structuring complex, large-scale, high value transactions, working with clients in construction, IT, facilities management and the provision of major services.

LANGUAGES: English, French, German, Hindi, Hungarian, Italian, Portuguese, Punjabi, Spanish, Swedish, Urdu

WORLDWIDE OFFICE CONTACTS

BELGIUM
85 rue du Prince Royal, 1050 **Brussels**
Tel: +32 2 511 9126 **Fax:** +32 2 511 9525
Email: jnazerali@bwlaw.co.uk

B

For other recommended firms see pages 1485-1520

BEAUCHAMPS

HEAD OFFICE

Dollard House, Wellington Quay,
Dublin 2 Republic of Ireland
Tel: +353 1 418 0600 **Fax:** +353 1 418 0699

Email: securemail@beauchamps.ie
Website: www.Beauchampslaw.com

WORLDWIDE OFFICE CONTACTS

REPUBLIC OF IRELAND
Dollard House, Wellington Quay, **Dublin** 2
Tel: +353 1 418 0600 **Fax:** +353 1 418 0699
Email: securemail@beauchamps.ie

FIRM OVERVIEW

Managing partner: Imelda Reynolds

Number of partners worldwide: 15
Number of other lawyers worldwide: 47

AREAS OF PRACTICE:

Area	%
Commercial litigation	20%
Commercial property	20%
Corporate/commercial	30%
Insurance litigation	10%
Private client	20%

B

FIRM OVERVIEW: Beauchamps was formed in 1974 when three well-known Dublin law firms amalgamated. The firm practised under the name Hickey Beauchamp Kirwan & O'Reilly until 1990 when it changed its name to Beauchamps.The firm's size enables it to provide a comprehensive range of services to clients, although it remains small enough to provide a personalised and client-focused service. The firm is also extremely competitive on price and aims to provide a comprehensive, pro-active and cost-effective service. Beauchamps uses state-of-the-art technology in order to provide an efficient document production service, and an efficient file and accounts recording information system.The firm operates a continuing in-house training programme designed to ensure that all legal personnel are regularly updated on legal developments. In addition, its solicitors attend and speak at a variety of external conferences both nationally and internationally.

INTERNATIONAL EXPERIENCE: Beauchamps is a member of an international network of medium to large law firms based in over 30 jurisdictions, including firms with offices in London, Brussels, Paris and Boston. This network is an informal, non-exclusive arrangement, and Beauchamps has relationships and contacts with other major international law firms. Beauchamps is also a founding member of ECOMLEX, the first European e-commerce organisation of lawyers, established with the aim of leading the way in legal advice on the new economy.

INTERNATIONAL CLIENTS: The firm's clients include leading companies, financial institutions, public bodies and private clients.

MAIN INTERNATIONAL AREAS OF PRACTICE:

Corporate and commercial services: The commercial group acts for corporate, business and banking clients, both Irish and international, in a number of areas including joint ventures, mergers and acquisitions, management buyouts, corporate re-structuring, franchising, distribution and agency agreements, asset financing and commercial lending.The commercial group also regularly advises international clients regarding inward investment in Ireland and assists these clients with all of their requirements in this process. The firm is also active in the area of Private Finance Initiatives, both from the State and business client point of view and is well regarded for its service in this area.

Intellectual property: Beauchamps employs a number of European Trademark Attorneys and has a rapidly growing intellectual property department servicing the needs of a number of leading companies. All aspects of the intellectual property requirements of clients are covered including registration, enforcement and commercial agreements.

Information technology, communications and e-commerce: Beauchamps is a prominent firm in the area of information technology, communications and e-commerce and advises a large number of business clients in this rapidly expanding area.

EU and competition law: Beauchamps has a highly respected practice in EU and competition law and advises a large number of its clients in all aspects of competition and European law. In-house personnel are particularly skilled in the area of public procurement and advise state bodies and businesses in relation to European and domestic requirements.

Commercial property: Beauchamps acts on behalf of many of the largest commercial and residential property developers in Ireland and has been involved in many of the largest commercial and residential property transactions during recent years.

Employment law and employee benefits: Beauchamps acts for a large number of business and industrial clients in relation to their employment law requirements and regularly advises and represents clients in employment and industrial relations matters. The firm's employment team advises a large range of corporate and personal clients in the area and has been involved in a number of significant cases. Beauchamps has also assisted clients in establishing share participation and share option schemes.

Media and sport: Beauchamps has rapidly gained a profile in the area of media and sport law and acts for a number of publications and media groups and a number of sports regulators both private and public.

Commercial arbitration and litigation: Beauchamps employs a number of qualified arbitrators to assist commercial clients in international and domestic arbitrations. Beauchamps has an exceptionally cost-effective corporate recovery and insolvency department using state of the art technology yielding particularly good results for corporate clients.

For other recommended firms see pages 1485-1520

ESTUDIO BECCAR VARELA

HEAD OFFICE

Cerrito 740, piso 16,
C1010AAP Buenos Aires, Argentina
Tel: +54 11 4379 6800 **Fax:** +54 11 4379 6860

Email: estudio@beccarv.com.ar

WORLDWIDE OFFICE CONTACTS

ARGENTINA
Cerrito 740, piso 16, C1010AAP **Buenos Aires**
Tel: +54 11 4379 6800 **Fax:** +54 11 4379 6860
Email: estudio@beccarv.com.ar

FIRM OVERVIEW

Senior partner: Damian F Beccar Varela
Managing partners: Alberto Lasheras Shine, Roberto A. Fortunati and Horacio E. Beccar Varela.

Number of partners worldwide: 22
Number of other lawyers worldwide: 68

AREAS OF PRACTICE:

Corporate, insurance, tax and administrative 46%
Banking and finance/capital markets 20%
M&A 18%
Litigation and arbitration 15%

FIRM OVERVIEW: Founded in 1897 by the late Dr. Horacio Beccar Varela, Estudio Beccar Varela advises on all aspects of corporate and financial law. The firm's reputation is built on its sound and reliable counselling and litigation practices. For almost 30 years Estudio Beccar Varela has been a member of the Club de Abogados, an organisation formed by law firms in Latin America and Europe and currently expanding its membership to the Far East. With no formal ties, the relationships developed through the network are essential when dealing with international clients. In July 2000 the firm entered into a Cooperation Agreement with Pinheiro Neto, Advogados (Brazil), Gómez-Acebo & Pombo (Spain) and Vieira de Almeida & Associados.

INTERNATIONAL EXPERIENCE: The firm has been involved in major Argentine banking, industrial and commercial transactions.

INTERNATIONAL CLIENTS: The firm's client base comprises international banking institutions, large multinational European and American companies, banks and insurance companies. Many clients have been served for over 50 years, the oldest being Citibank, N.A., a client since 1914.

MAIN INTERNATIONAL AREAS OF PRACTICE:
M&A: The firm's transactions range from small private acquisitions to listed companies. The practice is capable of handling various deals simultaneously.
Banking and finance: Estudio Beccar Varela covers all areas of banking and finance, including local and foreign currency secured and syndicated loan transactions and guarantees, structured finance, leasing and project finance for very large projects. During 1999 the firm was involved in some of the largest debt restructurings in Argentina.
Insurance and reinsurance: The opening of the Argentine insurance market to foreign capital has led to the expansion of the firm's insurance department.
Intellectual property: The firm specialises in trademarks, patents, and copyrights. Estudio Beccar Varela's lawyers act in the negotiation of license agreements and advise on infringement disputes and other aspects of IP law.
Energy, telecommunications, oil and gas: The firm played an active part in the privatisation of these industries and is now heavily involved in the development of each respective market.
Litigation and arbitration: Estudio Beccar Varela has a specialist litigation and arbitration practice appearing before both federal and provincial courts and international arbitration panels.
Corporate law and capital markets: The firm handles all aspects of general corporate law, including the drafting of Argentine and international contracts. Some of the firm's lawyers conduct various open market transactions.
Employment and social security law: The firm handles all matters relating to Argentine employment and social security laws, including collective bargaining agreements.
Tax and administrative law: The firm advises clients at all levels of federal, provincial and municipal governments.

LANGUAGES: English, French, German, Italian, Portuguese, Russian and Spanish

BECH-BRUUN & TROLLE

HEAD OFFICE

Nr Farimagsgade 3,
DK-1364 Copenhagen K, Denmark
Tel: + 45 33 12 12 33 **Fax:** + 45 33 15 25 55

Email: bbt@bbtlaw.dk
Website: www.bbtlaw.dk

WORLDWIDE OFFICE CONTACTS

BELGIUM
Avenue de Tervueren, 155, B-1150 **Brussels**
Tel: + 32 2 736 05 23 **Fax:** + 32 2 736 20 51
Email: brux@bbtlaw.dk

DENMARK
Nr Farimagsgade 3, DK- 1364 **Copenhagen**
Tel: + 45 33 12 12 33 **Fax:** + 45 33 15 25 55
Email: bbt@bbtlaw.dk

FIRM OVERVIEW

Managing director: Lasse Bjerggaard
Number of partners worldwide: 23
Number of other lawyers worldwide: 46

AREAS OF PRACTICE:

Aviation	*%
Banking and finance	*%
Capital markets	*%
Competition and EU	*%
Construction	*%
Environmental	*%
Insolvency	*%
Insurance	*%
Intellectual property	*%
International arbitration	*%
IT and telecommunications	*%
Employment	*%
Media	*%
Oil and mineral resources	*%
Real estate	*%
Tax	*%

* Workload % not disclosed

FIRM OVERVIEW: Bech-Bruun & Trolle was established in 1990 by a merger of the law firms Bech-Bruun and Trolle, Damsbo & Lund-Andersen. Bech-Bruun celebrated its centennial in 1988. Trolle, Damsbo & Lund-Andersen was established in 1979.

INTERNATIONAL EXPERIENCE: Bech-Bruun & Trolle has rendered legal advice in relation to exploration and extraction of oil and gas in the North Sea for 30 years, and has also advised a number of international clients in relation to mineral exploration projects in Greenland.

INTERNATIONAL CLIENTS: The firm's client base includes foreign lawyers seeking advice on Danish law and on the implementation and application of EU law in Denmark, the European Commission, and other authorities, commercial organisations, foundations, foreign businesses and private individuals conducting cross-border activities.

MAIN INTERNATIONAL AREAS OF PRACTICE:

Intellectual property: The firm provides legal advice on patents, utility models, copyrights, designs and know-how, as well as in disputes with third parties, including trademark infringements and injunction proceedings. They also assist in the formulation and implementation of protection programmes including trademark registration and watching.
Insolvency: The firm provides assistance to creditors in securing their outstanding accounts and to debtors in securing the continuation or liquidation of their business. The firm also has considerable experience in the administration of bankruptcy estates, suspension of payments, compositions and voluntary arrangements with creditors.
Competition and EU: Legal services in this field comprise drafting agreements, safeguarding business interests in relation to the competition authorities and formulating compliance programmes and instructions for unannounced inspections by the competition authorities. Advice is also offered on EU rules on public procurement.
M&A: The firm sets up project teams to deal at short notice with M&As, even large-scale and highly complex ones, providing contract terms and due diligence reports.
Banking, capital markets and finance: The firm has experience in matters of international capital markets, in connection with major financing and investment products and with the development of new financial instruments.
Tax: The practice deals with the taxation of dividends and capital gains affecting ownership and transfers of shares across a spread of countries worldwide. Tax matters and litigation advice is offered on both a personal and corporate level, whether it be a public or private limited liability company, a co-operative society or a foundation.
Construction: The firm undertakes planning and drafting agreements (traditionally governed by the law applicable in the country of establishment), when turnkey projects are established abroad.
Media and IT: The firm's advice covers all branches of trade and industry involved in the fields of media and IT, including production and license agreements, in the areas of TV and films, telecommunications, computer and internet law, multimedia in compliance with Danish and international governing.
Company: The firm provides advice on all aspects of company law and other legal and practical issues relating to establishment in Denmark and international developing markets. The practice also covers all aspects of national and transnational company law and securities regulation, as well as advice on estate planning.

LANGUAGES: Dutch, English, French, German, and the Scandinavian languages.

 For other recommended firms see pages 1485-1520

BEDELL CRISTIN

HEAD OFFICE

PO Box75, 26 New Street,
St Helier JE4 8PP, Jersey
Tel: +44 1534 814 814 **Fax:** +44 1534 814 815

Email: enquiries@bedellcristin.com
Website: www.bedellcristin.com

WORLDWIDE OFFICE CONTACTS

JERSEY
PO Box75, 26 New Street, JE4 8PP, St Helier, **Jersey**
Tel: +44 1534 814 814 **Fax:** +44 1534 814 815
Email: enquiries@bedellcristin.com

FIRM OVERVIEW

Managing partner: Michael Richardson
Senior partner: Anthony Dessain

Number of partners worldwide: 12
Number of other lawyers worldwide: 16

AREAS OF PRACTICE:

Financial services	60%
Litigation	20%
Private client	20%

FIRM OVERVIEW: Established more than 60 years ago, the firm has been at the forefront of providing legal advice to the banking and finance industry in Jersey for over 30 years. Consistently ranked one of the top three firms in Jersey and highly rated for the professionalism and technical expertise of its partners and associates, Bedell Cristin aims to provide a first class service tailored to the commercial needs of clients and intermediaries from all over the world. The firm has been responsible for the establishment of a significant proportion of the banks, mutual funds and structured finance vehicles carrying on business from Jersey. The firm was ranked amongst the top 3 by number and value of investment fund clients in Jersey in a 1999 survey of the Jersey Fund Management Industry and the leading firm of lawyers and administrators for securitisations. Bedell Cristin has established a professional association with Guernsey law firm, Babbé Le Pelley Tostevin (following the merger of Babbé Le Poidevin Allez and Le Pelley & Tostevin on 1st June, 2000), the principal purpose of which is to allow the provision of "one stop" advice in matters of Jersey and Guernsey law to clients of both firms and to emphasise the unitary nature of the Channel Islands for financial services purposes.

INTERNATIONAL EXPERIENCE: Innovative securitisation transactions handled recently include acting for Barclaycard in a US$1 billion credit card backed securitisation, acting for Commerzbank in a EUR 5 billion ECP conduit, for Bank Gesellschaft Berlin in a EUR 3 billion CP conduit and for Rabobank in a EUR 250 million synthetic securitisation.

INTERNATIONAL CLIENTS: Include ABN AMRO, Aberdeen Asset Management, ABSA Fund Managers, Bacob Bank, Bank of America, Bank Gesellschaft Berlin, Banca Commerciale Italiana, Barclays Capital, Barclays Global Investors, Barclaycard, Bank of Ireland Securities Services, Capital One Bank, Chase Bank, Citibank, Commerzbank, CSFB, Deutsche Bank International, Foreign & Colonial, HSBC, Lombard Odier & Cie, MBNA International, Merrill Lynch/Mercury, Pictet & Cie, Prudential, Rabobank, N.A. Rothschild, Royal Bank of Canada (CI), Royal Bank of Scotland, Schroders, Swissca Fund Management.

MAIN INTERNATIONAL AREAS OF PRACTICE:

Financial services: The capital markets and structured finance practice area has considerable experience in asset backed financing having acted as Jersey counsel in some of the most innovative securitisation transactions in the market, and is rated as a market leader in securitisation. The dedicated structured finance practice area is organised to provide the highest level of service. Together with Bedell Cristin Trust and Bedell SPV Management (Jersey) Limited (a joint venture SPV administration specialist jointly owned by Bedell Cristin Trust and SPV Management Limited) the practice area provides a "one stop shop" for establishing special purpose vehicles in Jersey.

Investment funds and pensions: The investment funds and pension schemes practice area focuses on the establishment and legal servicing of pooled investment structures qualifying as public collective investment funds or non-public collective investment schemes and defined contribution pension schemes. Sponsorship and listing services in connection with the Channel Islands Stock Exchange are available through Bedell Channel Islands Limited, which is a category 1 sponsorship member of the Exchange.

Banking and corporate finance: Bedell Cristin's banking and corporate finance practice area provides banking and regulatory advice to a high proportion of the 60 plus banks having a branch or subsidiary in Jersey. Advice and legal opinions on matters of Jersey law are also provided to banks and multinationals from all over the world whose customers may have assets in Jersey or who seek to structure transactions in Jersey. In such cases, advice on corporate, trust and regulatory law is often sought through other professional firms in leading finance centres around the world.

Trust and Company: The trust and company law practice area advises trust companies, banks and other professionals, locally and internationally, on all matters concerning Jersey trusts and companies including the use of Jersey trusts in employee benefit schemes.

Litigation: The litigation group comprises four partners and nine assistants. Particular emphasis is placed on contentious trust, company and probate litigation; serious fraud and other cases involving asset tracing, freezing and disclosure orders; areas of compliance and regulatory law which involve disclosure and insolvency proceedings. Anthony Robinson, Anthony Dessain, Mark Taylor and Simon Young are the partners in the group. The group has a good deal of experience in construction disputes and information technology issues and all other aspects of litigation including professional and medical negligence.

Private client & local business: The private client and local business group is headed by Guy Le Sueur and advises on a wide range of Jersey property matters as well as running a private client practice including matrimonial matters and estate planning and probate. Local business clients are also advised within this group with the additional assistance of Simon Young who advises on IT and telecoms matters for Jersey Telecoms and with other IT industry clients.

LANGUAGES: French, Portuguese, Spanish

B

For other recommended firms see pages 1485-1520

BELL GULLY

HEAD OFFICE

Royal & SunAlliance Centre, 48 Shortland Street, PO Box 4199
Auckland, New Zealand
Tel: + 64 9 916 8800 **Fax:** + 64 9 916 8801
Email: aklenquiries@bellgully.com
Website: www.bellgully.com

FIRM OVERVIEW

Chief executive: Ian Wilson
Number of partners worldwide: 63
Number of other lawyers worldwide: 230

AREAS OF PRACTICE:

Corporate commercial 42%
Commercial litigation 24%
Property 21%
Banking and corporate finance 13%

B

FIRM OVERVIEW: Bell Gully is one of New Zealand's largest commercial law firms, the result of a merger in 1984 between Bell Gully & Co of Wellington and Buddle Weir & Co of Auckland, firms which have operated in New Zealand since 1840 and 1860 respectively. Today, the firm provides legal services to New Zealand and international companies, government agencies and leading financial institutions. Bell Gully's extensive range of services is focused on four core areas of banking and finance, corporate and commercial (including tax), litigation and commercial property.

INTERNATIONAL EXPERIENCE: Bell Gully has established strong international links spanning Australia, Asia, Canada, the UK and the US. Recent international experience includes the sale of Fletcher Challenge Paper to Norske Skog for NZ$5.6 billion – the largest ever New Zealand corporate transaction by dollar value; the sale of all TransAlta Corporation's investments in New Zealand, including its 76% stake in the New Zealand listed company TransAlta New Zealand, the capital notes held in TransAlta and the debt held in the Taranaki Combined Cycle Power Station for a total purchase price of NZ$834 million; Air New Zealand's purchase of 50% of Ansett Holdings (which it did not already own); Sky City Limited's purchase of Adelaide Casino; Edison Mission Energy's acquisition of a 40% cornerstone shareholding of Contact Energy Limited; acting for GCU Plc and Norwich Union Plc on the New Zealand competition law aspects of their global merger; advising The Coca-Cola Company on the New Zealand competition law implications arising from its US$1.1 billion worldwide purchase of the beverage brands of Cadbury Schweppes Plc and acting on the initial public offering of shares in eVentures - a venture between epartners (Softbank and News Corporation) and Craig Heatley.

INTERNATIONAL CLIENTS: Fletcher Challenge Paper, TransAlta Corporation, Air New Zealand, Sky City Limited, Edison Mission Energy, CGU Plc/Norwich Union Plc, The Coca-Cola Company/Schweppes, eVentures, Microsoft, Vodafone, Hewlett Packard, Heinz Wattie's Australasia, Mitsui, Bridgestone Tyre Corporation, Warner Lambert, Generics (UK) Limited, CSR.

MAIN INTERNATIONAL AREAS OF PRACTICE:

Banking and finance: The banking and finance group has specialist knowledge attained through international experience in, and a thorough understanding of, global financial markets. Bell Gully provides services to leading banks, sharebrokers, merchant and investment banks and other financial institutions within New Zealand and overseas.

WORLDWIDE OFFICE CONTACTS

NEW ZEALAND

Royal & SunAlliance Centre, 48 Shortland Street, PO Box 4199, **Auckland**
Tel: + 64 9 916 8800 **Fax:** + 64 9 916 8801
Email: aklenquiries@bellgully.com

IBM Centre, 171 Featherston Street, PO Box 1291, **Wellington**
Tel: + 64 4 473 7777 **Fax:** + 64 4 473 3845
Email: wlgenquiries@bellgully.com

Corporate and commercial law: The corporate and commercial group is acknowledged as one of New Zealand's foremost legal practices, having the greatest depth and partner numbers of the major New Zealand firms.
M&A: In the M&A area, the firm can offer expertise and experience handling complex initial public offerings, due diligence, listings and other securities issues. Bell Gully has been involved in the majority of the listed company mergers and acquisitions in New Zealand.
E-business: Bell Gully leads New Zealand in providing legal services to users and providers of information technology, including the Internet and e-business. It has an impressive international client list in these developing areas. Work handled includes outsourcing, venture capital, international software licensing, capital raising, joint ventures and alliances.
Telecommunications: The telecommunications group is at the cutting edge of the telecommunications industry in New Zealand. Bell Gully has an unparalleled client list and is strong on both the commercial and regulatory aspects of the telecommunications industry.
Energy: One of Bell Gully's key strengths is the energy sector, particularly electricity, petroleum and gas. The electricity group has been closely involved in advising on the reform of the electricity industry in New Zealand since the outset of the reform process in 1987. Bell Gully has extensive experience with major exploration companies nationally and internationally. The firm acts for the major participants in exploration and production industries and has extensive experience in the gas contracting area.
Litigation: The firm's litigation group has developed a highly respected reputation based on appropriate and measured responses to each individual case. Commercial focus, pragmatism and experience have ensured optimal outcomes for its clients before the courts, specialist tribunals and commissions. The litigation team also includes highly experienced mediators and Alternative Dispute Resolution (ADR) practitioners.
Property: The property group is directly responsible for managing offshore investment into New Zealand (particularly for investors in Asia) as well as advising on construction contracts, property management contracts and a wide range of developmental projects.
Tax: Bell Gully has the largest and strongest law firm tax group in New Zealand. It has in-depth knowledge of every aspect of corporate taxation and advises clients on matters relating to corporate structure, tax-effective finance raising, joint ventures involving New Zealand offshore companies, development of new financial products, GST-related matters and government taxation policy.
Trade group: The trade group provides commercial solutions to trade law issues combining legal expertise with a pragmatic approach and practical experience. The trade group is unique in the New Zealand legal environment. It not only combines legal and non-legal talent but offers a truly international advisory service to a global client base.

LANGUAGES: Afrikaans, Arabic, Cantonese, Chinese, Croatian, Dutch, English, French, German, Greek, Hebrew, Hindi, Indonesian, Italian, Japanese, Korean, Malay, Mandarin, Maori, Polish, Portugese, Russian, Samoan, Spanish, Thai, Ukranian

For other recommended firms see pages 1485-1520

STUDIO LEGALE BELTRAMO

HEAD OFFICE

Via Lazio 20/C,
00187 Rome, Italy
Tel: +39 06 481 7747 **Fax:** +39 06 482 0281

Email: slblex@tin.it

OFFICE CONTACTS

ITALY
Via Lazio 20/C, 00187 **Rome**
Tel: +39 06 481 7747 **Fax:** +39 06 482 0281
Email: slblex@tin.it

ASSOCIATED OFFICE CONTACTS

ITALY
Zambelli Luzzati & Meregalli – Milan
Agostoni-Ceccon Polettini – Padua

FIRM OVERVIEW

Contact partner: Susanna Beltramo

Number of partners worldwide: 1
Number of other lawyers worldwide: 4

AREAS OF PRACTICE:

Area	%
Corporate and financial	68%
Commercial litigation	18%
Tax	5%
EU and competition	3%
Intellectual property	3%
Property	3%

FIRM OVERVIEW: Founded in 1993 by a group of partners and associates from Studio Avv. Ercole Graziadei (no longer in existence), Studio Legale Beltramo has a diverse and extensive international practice dealing with a wide range of corporate, commercial and financial work for Italian, overseas and international clients. The firm has developed close working relations with the leading independent law firms around the world so that the best local advice and service is available to its clients.

INTERNATIONAL EXPERIENCE: Work handled has included the US$1.5bn Global Medium Term Note Program for the region of Lazio and the related issues thereunder; US$300m Global Medium Term Note for the city of Florence and the related issues thereunder; €250m Medium Term Note Programme for the province of Naples, 1999 and the related issues thereunder; region of Sicily Note Issues during 1999 in various tranches for an aggregate amount of ITL 1,700bn; ENEL €1bn fixed rate notes due 2008; ENEL €2.2bn fixed and floating rate notes due 2004 and 2001; Parmalat Capital Finance Limited Guaranteed Preference Shares; US$5bn Continuously Offered Euro Depositary Receipt Programme for Banca Monte dei Paschi di Siena Spa and related issues thereunder; US$5bn Euro Medium Term Note Programme for Crediop Overseas Bank Limited and Crediop Spa and related issues thereunder; Cassa di Risparnio in Bologna €1bn debt issuance programme; Api Energia Spa Falconara project financing, Elcogas project financing in Spain; Elekta Instruments acquisition transaction from Philips; Goodyear/Sava dd joint venture agreement.

INTERNATIONAL CLIENTS: Major clients of the firm include Merrill Lynch International; UBS acting through their Warburg Dillon Read division; Deutsche Bank; Bank of Tokyo Mitsubishi; The Sumitomo Bank Ltd; Fox International Inc; Abbott Laboratories; Goodyear; ENEL S.p.a. and Elekta Instruments.

MAIN INTERNATIONAL AREAS OF PRACTICE: Studio Legale Beltramo's practice covers a broad spectrum of corporate, commercial and financial work. Clients include industrial and commercial companies from diversified business sectors, banks, financial institutions and professional firms as well as governments, public bodies and other organizations. The principal areas of practice comprise:

Banking and capital markets: Work handled includes international debt, equities issues and derivatives; international and domestic lending, structured finance and project an dasset finance including aviation.

Corporate and corporate finance: The firm advises on securities issues, flotations, mergers and acquisitions and corporate and commercial transactions generally.

EC and competition: The firm provides advice on competition law, particularly in relation to acquisitions and mergers and joint ventures.

Environment: providing specialist advice on a broad spectrum of environmental issues.

Financial regulation: The firm deals with the regulatory aspects of corporate finance, fund management, securities and derivatives as well as supervision and regulation of banks and insurance companies.

Intellectual property: The firm advises on all aspects of the creation and ownership of intellectual property rights including the acquisition, development and licensing of computer systems and programmes.

Litigation and arbitration: Studio Legale Beltramo deals with a wide range of commercial proceedings and disputes up to the Court of Cassation including domestic and international arbitrations.

Property: The firm handles all types of commercial property transactions as well as advice on construction and engineering projects.

Tax: It advises on the tax aspects of corporate transactions and activities, including development of tax-efficient structures and instruments.

BENNETT JONES

HEAD OFFICE

4500 Bankers Hall East, 855 - 2nd Street SW,
Calgary AB T2P 4K7, Canada
Tel: +1 403 298 3100
Fax: +1 403 265 7219

Email: firmwatch@bennettjones.ca
Website: www.bennettjones.ca

FIRM OVERVIEW

Chairman: Clifton D O'Brien
Managing Partner: William S. Rice

Number of partners worldwide: 103
Number of other lawyers worldwide: 115

WORLDWIDE OFFICE CONTACTS

CANADA
4500 Bankers Hall East, 855 - 2nd Street SW, **Calgary** Alberta T2P 4K7
Tel: +1 403 298 3100 **Fax:** +1 403 265 7219
Email: firmwatch@bennettjones.ca

1000 ATCO Centre, 10035, 105 Street, **Edmonton,** Alberta T5J 3T2
Tel: + 1 780 421 8133 **Fax:** + 1 780 421 7951
Email: firmwatch@bennettjones.ca

Toronto Suite 3400, 1 First Canadian Place, PO Box 130, **Toronto,** Ontario M5X 1A4
Tel: +1 416 863 1200 **Fax:** +1 416 863 1716
Email: firmwatch@bennettjones.ca/toronto

AREAS OF PRACTICE:

Banking and financial services	*%
Commercial and civil litigation	*%
Energy and natural resources, regulatory/environmental	*%
Insolvency/debt restructuring	*%
International business	*%
M&A	*%
Real estate (commercial)	*%
Securities	*%
Taxation and tax litigation	*%
Technology and intellectual property	*%

* Workload % not disclosed

B

FIRM OVERVIEW: Founded in 1922 by RB Bennett, later the prime minister of Canada, Bennett Jones is a 200+ lawyer firm with complementary corporate and litigation practices. The practice encompasses virtually all business sectors, with particular emphasis on the energy sector, including a substantial amount of M&A. In addition to providing legal servcies in traditional areas of law such as civil litigation and corporate finance, the firm increasingly advises in emerging fields such as technology law.

INTERNATIONAL EXPERIENCE: The firm has a substantial amount of international energy work experience. Recent deals in which it has acted as counsel include representing Hunt Oil Company in its $760 million friendly takeover bid for Newport Petroleum Corporation and Petrobank Energy and Resources Ltd in its $16 billion takeover bid for Langer Oil Limited, including Ranger's North Sea, African and Middle East assets. Other deals include the US$2 billion Sudan Petroleum Project; Gulf Canada's $593 million sale of UK North Sea assets; ATCO Power's Thames Power Project; Suncor's Shale Oil Project in Australia; the Sable Island Gas Development Project, which included cross-border financing and pipeline development; Gulf Canada's $150 million sale of its Australian assets; Burlington Resources' US$2.5 billion acquisition of Poco Petroleums, which included cross-border securities issues; Canadian Natural Resources and Penn West Petroleum's $1.7 billion joint acquisition of BP Amoco's Canadian oil properties; and Talisman's $1.7 billion acquisition of Rigel, which included Rigel's North Sea assets.The firm has worked extensively in the former Soviet Union. It has advised the Ukraine government on its new production sharing laws and foreign investment, and provided comprehensive legal services to a number of international energy companies.International independent power project work also forms a significant part of the firm's practice. Recent IPPs include the Barking Expansion (England), the Bord Gais Joint Venture (Ireland), Bulwer Island (Australia), Darnyka (Ukraine), Osborne Cogeneration Project (Australia), Pomalaa Power Project (Indonesia), Tanzania Gas to Power Project (Tornado), Termotasajero Power Plant (Colombia), Thames Power (London), Waste-to-Energy Facility Project (Taiwan), various projects in China (Northland Power) and various projects in the Ukraine (Northland Power).

INTERNATIONAL CLIENTS: The firm advises companies, international development finance organisations, banks and investment banks involved in resource projects, joint ventures, power generation projects, financings, securities, acquisitions and dispositions, international tax planning, regulatory and environmental issues in North America and around the world. It has worked with clients in the US, Mexico, China, Taiwan, Malaysia, Vietnam, Japan, Hong Kong, Indonesia, Venezuela, Colombia, Argentina, the UK, Australia, Hungary, Russia, Kyrgystan, Ukraine and various countries in Africa and the Middle East.

MAIN INTERNATIONAL AREAS OF PRACTICE: These include M&A, energy, independent power projects, taxation, trade, immigration and intellectual property, and encompass services relating to corporate finance, export and trade, arbitration and alternative dispute resolution, international contracts, export and import permits, foreign investment laws, Canadian legislation, regulations and policies, joint ventures and tariffs, duties and taxes.

LANGUAGES: Cantonese, Czech, English, French, German, Greek, Italian, Japanese, Punjabi, Spanish, Vietnamese

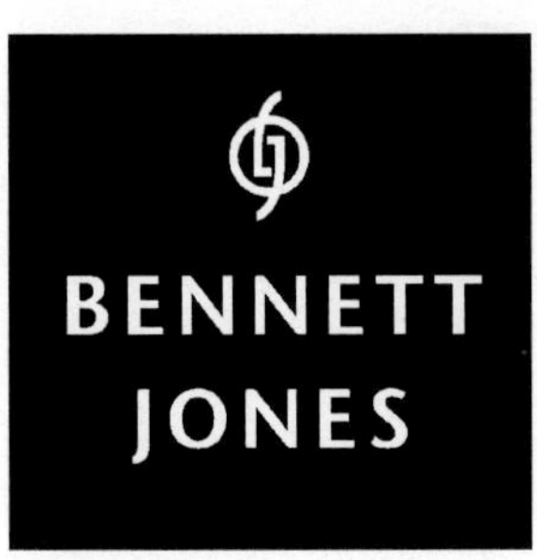

For other recommended firms see pages 1485-1520

BENTSI-ENCHILL & LETSA

HEAD OFFICE

1st Floor Teachers Hall Annex, Educational Loop (off Barnes Road),
PO Box 1632, Accra Ghana
Tel: +233 21229396 **Fax:** +233 21 226129
Email: belm@africaonline.com.gh

FIRM OVERVIEW

Partners: Kojo Bentsi Enchill, D.K.D Letsa, Ace A. Ankomah
Senior associates: Sadia Chinery-Hesse, Rosa A. Kuduadzi Kwakyewaa Cantamantu-Koomson

Number of partners worldwide: 3
Number of other lawyers worldwide: 8

AREAS OF PRACTICE:

Aviation and shipping	*%
Corporate	*%
Energy	*%
IT and technology	*%
M&A	*%
Project finance	*%

* Workload % not disclosed

WORLDWIDE OFFICE CONTACTS

GHANA
1st Floor Teachers Hall Annex, Educational Loop (off Barnes Road),
PO Box 1632, **Accra**
Tel: +233 21229396 **Fax:** +233 21 226129
Email: belm@africaonline.com.gh

ASSOCIATED OFFICES

NIGERIA
Udoma and Belo-Osagie, 9 Military Street, LAGOS
Tel: +234 1 2636880 **Fax:** +234 1 263 3541
Email: uubo@infoweb.abs.net

FIRM OVERVIEW: The firm was founded in 1988 by Kojo Bentsi-Enchill. It became Bentsi-Enchill & Letsa when DKD Letsa joined in 1990. The firm advises international and local corporations, as well as financial institutions on all legal and regulatory aspects of investment, corporate finance and business in Ghana. The firm has extensive experience in designing tax and corporate structures that achieve client objectives within the framework of local laws, regulations and practices. The firm also has experience handling project financing, and has a strong track record in energy, telecommunications, and mining projects. Bentsi-Enchill & Letsa maintains close links with Udoma and Belo-Osagie in Nigeria. The firm is currently investing in its IT and communications systems in order to enhance its capacity to give rapid, well informed advice.

INTERNATIONAL EXPERIENCE: During 2000, Bentsi-Enchill & Letsa handled a number of major transactions including Samsung Corporation's US$157 million RFCC project in relation to Tema Oil Refinery; IFC on its US$100 million loan investment in Ghana Telecom; OPIC on its US$12 million loan to PhotoRyker-Bermuda and Photo-Ryker-Ghana; World Bank on financial and business legislation in Ghana; KBC Ltd on its refinancing of US$55 million facility for Ghana Airways Ltd; IFC on its loan to Enterprise Insurance Company; State Insurance Company on corporate structuring options; Starkist sa and Ghana subsidiary, PFC; Chevron on the West African Gas Pipeline.

INTERNATIONAL CLIENTS: The firm's client base includes a range of international and local corporations, and financial institutions. These include Samsung Corporation, IFC, OPIC, Ghana Telecom, KBC Ltd, and Chevron.

MAIN INTERNATIONAL AREAS OF PRACTICE: The firm advises on project finance, loan and equity investments, privatisation, tax, mergers and acquisitions, commercial litigation, IT, real estate, energy, mining and natural resources, aviation, shipping and insurance, and trusts. Through its subsidiary, Trustee Services Ltd, the firm has the capacity to advise on due diligence and company secretarial services.

LANGUAGES: English, French, Spanish

B

BERKEMEYER

HEAD OFFICE

Benjamin Constant 835, Edificio Jacaranda, 4to. Piso, PO Box 285
Asuncion, Paraguay
Tel: +595 21 446 706 **Fax:** +595 21 449 694

Email: law@berke.com.py
Website: www.berke.com.py

WORLDWIDE OFFICE CONTACTS

PARAGUAY
Benjamin Constant 835, Edificio Jacaranda, 4to. Piso, PO Box 285,
Asuncion
Tel: +595 21 446 706 **Fax:** +595 21 449 694
Email: law@berke.com.py

FIRM OVERVIEW

Senior partner: Hugo T. Berkemeyer

Number of partners worldwide: 3
Number of other lawyers worldwide: 9

AREAS OF PRACTICE:

Anti-trust	*%
Commercial	*%
Corporate	*%
Employment	*%
Energy	*%
Immigration	*%
Intellectual property	*%
Tax	*%

* Workload % not disclosed

FIRM OVERVIEW: Founded in 1951, Berkemeyer is one of the most prestigious law firms in Paraguay. Comprising 13 lawyers, 12 paralegals and more than 40 administrative professionals, it is an established and technologically advanced firm with offices in the country's capital, Asuncion. Berkemeyer has embraced the changes that have occurred in the legal profession over the past twenty years. It provides a broad range of legal services and specialises in international transactional work such as mergers and acquisitions, joint ventures, and foreign investment. The firm has an historical strength in intellectual property and rights protections. An increasingly important part of its practice centers on the agreement to create a common market among the Mercosur Countries of South America and the economic liberalisation policies that are propelling the region into the mainstream of the world economy.

INTERNATIONAL CLIENTS: The firm's clients comprise foreign corporations and individuals seeking legal advice in Paraguay.

MAIN INTERNATIONAL AREAS OF PRACTICE:

Commercial: The firm advises on structuring and drafting supply, distribution, and representation contracts; research, development and technology transfer contracts; leases of property and equipment leases; and contracts for the acquisition and divestment of fixed assets. It also handles the development of franchising and licensing agreements and the transfer of franchising rights.

Corporate: The firm advises clients on selecting the best business structure to meet their particular interests, taking into consideration pricing, tax, regulatory and liability issues. It also advises on reorganising and restructuring individual and joint undertakings, and on the purchase and sale of businesses and the structuring of complex ventures. Berkemeyer handles sophisticated cross-border transactions; due diligence investigations; regulatory approvals; tax structuring; developing and negotiating purchase agreements; structuring of articles of incorporation and bylaws; stock issues; acquisition and divestment of corporate assets or shares; and receiverships and liquidation.

Tax: Berkemeyer handles all tax aspects of business purchase agreements and the tax structuring and restructuring of individual and joint undertakings. It advises clients on obtaining tax credits for investments of capital in Paraguay, and assists in tax audits and appeals. For clients with foreign interests, the firm also advises on foreign tax liability, tax credits and relevant double taxation treaties or provisions. Berkemeyer provide tax planning advice and legal counsel on corporate pricing issues; social security and other employee taxes

Intellectual property: Berkemeyer specialises in intellectual property. Its clientele ranges from start-up ventures to Fortune 500 corporations who are advised on all areas of intellectual property law including patent, trademark and copyright procurement; litigation and licensing; the protection and international transfer of property rights in technology, software, literary and artistic works, trademarks, designs, and trade secrets. Further areas of specialisation include anti-piracy; industrial designs; industrial property; intellectual property infringement; intellectual property licensing; intellectual property litigation; computer and software patents; electronic and mechanical patents; chemical, biochemical and pharmaceutical patents; and other varied industrial property protections.

Employment: Berkemeyer handles employment agreements; dismissals; negotiated settlement and cancellation agreements; business transfers; layoffs and plant closings; and proceedings concerning Paraguayan regulations and collective bargaining agreements. It also acts for clients in disputes before all labour courts and before administrative panels and arbitration boards.

Energy, telecommunications, water supply and sewage: The firm advises on energy, telecommunications, water supply and sewage projects. It advises clients entering the deregulated telecommunications market and the soon-to-be deregulated water supply and sewage sector. It also advises on energy projects and regulatory compliance relating to these sectors.

Immigration: Berkemeyer handles the preparation of documents needed for temporary, permanent and residency permits; work visas for foreigners; preparation and processing of applications for temporary foreign employees and their dependents; representation of non-immigrant foreigners concerning permit renewals; housing, goods, automobiles and other issues relating to residency in Paraguay.

Anti-trust: Berkemeyer specialises in anti-trust and unfair competition law, reviewing contracts and preparing advisory opinions. It advises on compliance with, and prosecution of enforcement actions for, unfair trade practices. The firm monitors and actively pursues any anti-competitive conduct by its clients' competitors, prosecutes actions for unlawful advertising, illegal promotions, trademark or product logo infringement, institute dumping and countervailing duty actions, and obtains preventive actions and injunctions in the courts to prevent continued anti-competitive activities.

LANGUAGES: English, French, German, Spanish

For other recommended firms see pages 1485-1520

S J BERWIN & CO

HEAD OFFICE

222 Gray's Inn Road,
London WC1X 8XF, United Kingdom
Tel: +44 20 7533 2222 **Fax:** +44 20 7533 2000

Email: info@sjberwin.com
Website: www.sjberwin.com

FIRM OVERVIEW

Senior partner: David Harrel

Number of partners worldwide: 93
Number of other lawyers worldwide: 207

AREAS OF PRACTICE:

Corporate	49%
Commercial property	21%
Litigation and dispute resolution	16%
EU/competition/trade	8%
Tax	6%

FIRM OVERVIEW: Established in 1982, S J Berwin & Co is a London-based corporate and commercial law firm, with additional offices in Brussels (opened 1990), Frankfurt (opened 1998), Madrid (opened 1999), Berlin (opened 2000) and Munich (opened 2000). S J Berwin is a member of Interlaw, a worldwide association of independent law firms.

WORLDWIDE OFFICE CONTACTS

BELGIUM
Square de Meeûs 19, B-1050 **Brussels**
Tel: +32 2 511 5340 **Fax:** +32 2 511 5917
Email: brussels@sjberwin.com

GERMANY
S J Berwin Knopf Tulloch Steininger, Kurfürstendamm 63, 10707 **Berlin**
Tel: +49 030 88 71 71 10 **Fax:** +49 030 88 71 71 77
Email: berlin@sjberwin.de

S J Berwin Knopf Tulloch Steininger, Poseidon Haus, Hamburger Allee 1, 60486 **Frankfurt am Main**
Tel: +49 69 5050 32 500 **Fax:** +49 69 5050 32 499
Email: info@sjberwin.de

S J Berwin Knopf Tulloch Steininger, Maria-Teresiastr. 5, 81675 **Munich**
Tel: +49 089 89 08 10 **Fax:** +49 089 89 08 1100
Email: munich@sjberwin.de

SPAIN
SJ Berwin, Pazos, Gallardo y Asociados, Serrano, 38-5°, 28001 **Madrid**
Tel: +34 91 426 0050 **Fax:** + 34 91 426 0066
Email: madrid@sjberwin.com

UNITED KINGDOM
222 Gray's Inn Road, **London** WC1X 8XF
Tel: +44 20 7533 2222 **Fax:** +44 20 7533 2000
Email: info@sjberwin.com

INTERNATIONAL EXPERIENCE: The firm acted for Intermedia Film Equities Limited, on the admission of IM Internationalmedia AG to the Frankfurt Neuer Markt. Other matters in which the firm was involved include: acting for Interactive Investor International PLC on its £246 million flotation; acting for Granville Baird with the sale of Elmeg GmbH; acting for Future Network on the Acquisition Imagine Media Inc; acting for Hellman & Friedman LLC, in its acquisition of a 37.5% interest in Formula One Holdings Ltd; acting for France Telecom Movidos in conection with a UMTS licence tender; acting for Nova Chemicals Corporation on the acquisition of Shell's Polystyrene Division; advising N M Rothschild & Sons Ltd in connection with Finalrealm's £1.25 billion acquisition of United Biscuits; and acting for Pierre Et Vacances in the acquisition of Center Parcs from Scottish & Newcastle of the value of £670 million.

INTERNATIONAL CLIENTS: The firm's clients include Apax Partners & Co., Bridgepoint Capital, Marks & Spencer, Hilton International, Generics, Fyffes Plc, Diageo Plc, Interactive Investor, Guardian iT plc, IM Internationalmedia, Akzo Nobel, Universal Music Group, Coca-Cola Schweppes Beverages, Mediaset, oneswoop.com, ABN Amro, Bellsouth Corp., Deutsche Bank, Musgrave Group, Future Network, Schroder Ventures, MWB Group, UBS Capital, Tradepoint, Barclays Private Equity, West LB, Lighthouse Holdings, Atlas Venture, Jeld-Wen Inc., Nova Corp. ENIC, Pescafina, Société Générale, Banque Internationale à Luxembourg, Société Européenne des Satellites, Sony Corp., Merck, World Wrestling Federation (WWF), Commission of the European Communities, and EASDAQ.

MAIN INTERNATIONAL AREAS OF PRACTICE:

Corporate: The firm offers a full range of corporate finance services, including mergers and acquisitions, management buy-outs and securities regulation. A special focus area is private equity and venture capital, including funds formation and transactions.

Tax: National and international taxation advice, including the structuring of international transactions and property development is provided by the firm's tax group. Estate planning and asset protection advice is given to private clients in the UK and overseas.

EU, competition and trade: The firm advises on domestic and EU mergers and acquisitions, competition, anti-trust and anti-dumping, regulatory work and judicial review proceedings.

Commercial property: All aspects of commercial property work are handled for various clients, including property companies, developers, institutions, retailers and hoteliers. In addition, specialist groups advise on property finance, public and private funding programmes for major infrastructure projects, construction and local government finance issues.

Litigation: The firm deals with a broad range of substantial international and domestic commercial litigation, as well as mediation and arbitration, which is undertaken by the specialist ADR Services Unit. The practice also includes a specialist property litigation group and an advocacy group.

Insolvency: Activities include corporate insolvency and bankruptcy, as well as reconstructions

Intellectual property: International trade mark, copyright and patent litigation, international trade mark registration and the identification, exploitation and protection of intellectual property rights are undertaken by a specialist intellectual property group.

LANGUAGES: Afrikaans, Arabic, Cantonese, Catalan, Czech, Dutch, French, German, Greek, Gujerati, Hebrew, Hindi, Italian, Kiswahili, Malay, Maltese, Polish, Punjabi, Romanian, Russian, Slovak, Spanish, Swedish, Turkish, Urdu, Welsh

For other recommended firms see pages 1485-1520

S J BERWIN & CO cont'd

WORLDWIDE OFFICES

BELGIUM

Square de Meeûs 19, B-1050 Brussels

Resident partner: Ramon Garcia Gallardo
Number of lawyers: 3
Number of dual qualified lawyers: 2
Number of locally qualified lawyers: 1

Languages: Dutch, English, French, German, Italian, Spanish
Office profile: The main emphasis of S J Berwin & Co's Brussels office is EU law, in particular competition matters, regulatory work, agriculture and food law especially fishery law, international market, trade law and litigation. Lawyers at the office regularly represent clients before National Authorities, the European Commission, the European Parliament, Court of First Instance and the European Court of Justice. A key aspect in all operations undertaken by the office is the close monitoring of European legal developments and their impacts at national level. The Brussels office works closely with the firm's head office in London, allowing joint involvement in the provision of advice and assistance to clients in the corporate and commercial law aspects. The office handles international transactions from a multi-jurisdictional stand point.

GERMANY

S J Berwin Knopf Tulloch Steininger, Kurfürstendamm 63, 10707 Berlin

S J Berwin Knopf Tulloch Steininger, Poseidon Haus, Hamburger Allee 1, 60486 Frankfurt am Main

S J Berwin Knopf Tulloch Steininger, Maria-Teresiastr. 5, 81675 Munich

Number of lawyers: 37
Number of locally qualified lawyers: 10

Languages: Danish, English, German, Greek
Office profile: Mergers and acquisitions, private equity, venture capital, corporate finance, project finance, investment law (onshore and offshore funds), tax law, audits, due diligence, business evaluations, corporate and commercial law, labour law, industrial property, trade marks.

SPAIN

SJ Berwin, Pazos, Gallardo y Asociados, Serrano, 38-5°, 28001 Madrid

Resident Partners: Carlos Pazos, Julio Veloso and Javier Morera

Number of lawyers: 20
Number of dual qualified lawyers: 2
Number of locally qualified lawyers: 18

Top clients: Banco Santander, Banco Comercial Portugues, Bank Von Tobel, Apax, 21 Invest, Suala Capital, Granville, European Investment Fund, Zeltia, Pharmamar, Musgrave, Multitel, Globalnet, Webraska, Cable & Wireless and Carrier.

Languages: Arabic, English, French, German, Italian, Portugese, Spanish.
Office profile: Established in May 1999, SJ Berwin & Co's Madrid office provides corporate legal services with a strong focus on M&A and private equity work. This includes both fund structuring and deal work for the major venture capital and private equity houses. The firm also has a major focus on telecommunications and internet and IT related work.

S J Berwin & Co

For other recommended firms see pages 1485-1520

BIRD & BIRD

HEAD OFFICE

90 Fetter Lane,
London EC4A 1JP, United Kingdom
Tel: +44 20 7415 6000 **Fax:** +44 20 7415 6111

Email: info@twobirds.com
Website: www.twobirds.com

FIRM OVERVIEW

Chief executive: David Kerr

Number of partners worldwide: 74
Number of other lawyers worldwide: 186

AREAS OF PRACTICE:

Banking .... *%
Commercial litigation .... *%
Communications .... *%
Corporate and banking .... *%
EU law .... *%
Health and pharmaceuticals .... *%
Intellectual property, brands and trademarks .... *%
Media and entertainment .... *%
Sport .... *%
* Workload % not disclosed

FIRM OVERVIEW: Working with some of the world's most innovative and technologically advanced companies, Bird & Bird has established a formidable reputation for advice at the cutting edge of law. Its approach is also strongly commercial enabling clients to capitalise on business opportunities and manage change effectively. Sectoral focus has been pivotal to the firm's success. The firm offers a fully comprehensive service across the sectors of e-commerce, communications, IT, intellectual property, sport, media and entertainment, pharmaceuticals and biotechnology. With offices in London, Brussels, Paris, Hong Kong and Sweden, the firm's lawyers are strategically placed to offer local expertise within a global context.

INTERNATIONAL EXPERIENCE: The firm has worked on projects in the UK, US, the Asia Pacific region, Belgium, France, the Netherlands, Italy, Hungary, India, Middle East, Spain and the Ukraine.

INTERNATIONAL CLIENTS: Alta Vista Company, Applied Materials Inc, BP Amoco plc, British Telecommunications plc, Carlton On-line, CCTA, Compaq Computer Corporation, Diageo, Dresdner Kleinwort Benson, Energis plc, European Bank for Reconstruction and Development, Exxon Chemicals, Foreign and Commonwealth Office, Glaxo Wellcome, Hoechst Marion Roussel, Last Minute Networks, Madge Networks, MGM Home Entertainment (Europe) Ltd, Nestlé, Orchestream Ltd, Pharmagene plc, Philips, Pfizer, Sema Group plc, Telefonica InterContinental, Unilever.

MAIN INTERNATIONAL AREAS OF PRACTICE:

Banking: Working with leading banks and financial institutions, the firm advises on a full range of banking issues including e-commerce, project finance, PFI, secured and syndicated lending, insolvency, corporate reconstruction and banking litigation.
Commercial litigation: The firm offers specialist dispute resolution advice, both in the UK and internationally, focusing on the communications, IT and sports sectors.
Commercial property: The firm advises telecoms providers, government departments and financial institutions on matters ranging from PFI structures and commercial agreements to pan-European regulatory issues.
Communications: The firm advises telecoms users and suppliers on a variety of domestic and international issues including major infrastructure projects; regulatory issues; joint ventures and strategic alliances; M&A; interconnection agreements, outsourcing arrangements and 3g licences.
Corporate: The firm offers a comprehensive range of corporate services, including tax. The firm's corporate lawyers undertake a wide variety of transactional work spanning M&A, joint ventures, strategic alliances, investments, equity financing, venture capital and public offerings.
E-commerce: Bird & Bird is one of Europe's leading practices in e-commerce and advises on all aspects including VC and incubators funds, 'dot-com' start-ups, funding and IPO's. In addition it advises established businesses on developing an internet presence and on e-banking.
Employment: Working with companies and individuals, the firm advises on both non-contentious and litigious issues, ranging from employee contracts and termination agreements to changes in employment regulation.
EU: With substantial offices in both Brussels and Paris the firm has a significant EU and competition capability, concentrating on anti-trust enforcement and legislative developments.
Intellectual property: The firm is one of the largest IP practices in Europe, offering comprehensive expertise across all areas. The firm advises on brands and trademark strategy, advertising, media and internet domain name issues. It has established a strong reputation for conducting successful patent actions and providing transactional and litigation advice.
Information technology: The firm has considerable experience gained in-house within the IT industry and specialist backgrounds. The firm advises both IT users and suppliers from the public, private and utilities sectors on a variety of major projects.
Media and entertainment: Expertise in music, film, TV, publishing and computer games with a particular focus on negotiating and drafting finance and distribution agreements, publishing deals and issues of digital convergence.
Pharmaceuticals and biotechnology: The firm advises on IP, corporate and commercial issues, to diverse UK and multi-national companies within these sectors.
Sport: Experience of advising governing bodies, rights purchasers, broadcasters, sponsors and leading sportsmen and women.

WORLDWIDE OFFICE CONTACTS

BELGIUM
15 rue de la Loi, 1040 **Brussels**
Tel: +32 2 282 6000 **Fax:** +32 2 282 6011
Email: info@twobirds.com

FRANCE
Centre D'Affaires Edouard VII, 3 Square Edouard VII, 75009 **Paris**
Tel: +33 1 42 68 60 00 **Fax:** +33 1 42 68 60 11
Email: info@twobirds.com

HONG KONG
Suite 602-4, 6/F Asia Pacific Finance Tower, Citibank Plaza, 3 Garden Road, Central, **Hong Kong**
Tel: +852 2248 6000 **Fax:** +852 2 2248 6011
Email: infohk@twobirds.com

SWEDEN
Stureplan 2, SE 102 47 **Stockholm**
Tel: +46 8 611 80 90 **Fax:** +46 8 611 35 51
Email: info@twobirds.com

B

For other recommended firms see pages 1485-1520

WORLDWIDE OFFICES

BELGIUM

15 rue de la Loi, 1040 Brussels

Managing partner: Jean-Paul Hordies

Number of lawyers: 31

Languages: Dutch, English, Flemish, French

Office profile: Established since 1991, the Brussels office provides comprehensive legal and commercial advice with a focus on EU and competition law across the firm's core capabilities of communications, e-commerce, IP, media and broadcasting, sports and IT.

FRANCE

Centre D'Affaires Edouard VII, 3 Square Edouard VII, 75009 Paris

Managing partner: Frèdèrique Dupuis-Toubol

Number of lawyers: 37

Languages: English, French

Office profile: Opened in January 2000, Bird & Bird's office in Paris offers clients a full service approach across all of the firm's core sectors. The Paris office has a particular capability in communications and IT, advising many leading companies across the European Union.

HONG KONG

Suite 602-4, 6/F Asia Pacific Finance Tower, Citibank Plaza, 3 Garden Road, Central, Hong Kong

Managing partner: Matthew Laight

Number of lawyers: 8

Languages: Chinese (Cantonese and Mandarin), English, French

Office profile: Opened in 1995, Bird & Bird's Hong Kong office offers corporate and commercial advice in the core areas of e-commerce, communications, intellectual property and IT, servicing Hong Kong, China, and the Asia Pacific Region (including Australasia). With its network of established local contacts, the firm is able to offer multi-jurisdictional advice throughout the region.

SWEDEN

Stureplan 2, SE 102 47 Stockholm

Managing partner: Michael Frie

Number of lawyers: 29

Languages: English, French, German, Italian, and the Scandinavian languages.

Office profile: Following a recent merger with one of Sweden's leading law firms, Gedda & Ekdahl, on 1 December 2000, the Stokholm-based firm assumed the name Bird & Bird. The Stockholm office services clients in Scandinavia's burgeoning high-tech economy and has a particular focus on the e-commerce, IT, communications, media and entertainment sectors.

 For other recommended firms see pages 1485-1520

BLAKE, CASSELS & GRAYDON LLP

HEAD OFFICE

Box 25, Commerce Court West, Toronto
Ontario, Canada M5L 1A9
Tel: +1 416 863 2400 **Fax:** +1 416 863 2653

Email: toronto@blakes.com
Website: www.blakes.com

FIRM OVERVIEW

Managing partner: Rob Granatstein

Number of partners worldwide: 205
Number of other lawyers worldwide: 211

AREAS OF PRACTICE:
Corporate .... *%
M&A .... *%
Intellectual property and technology .... *%
Banking and project finance .... *%
Competition .... *%
Infrastructure .... *%
*Workload % not disclosed

FIRM OVERVIEW: Blake, Cassels & Graydon LLP was founded in 1857. Originally exclusively in Toronto, the firm is now one of Canada's leading law firms, with over 400 lawyers in offices in Vancouver, Calgary, Toronto, Ottawa, London and Beijing. The firm provides advice on diverse areas of business law to both domestic and international clients. M&A is one of Blakes' main activities, and the firm has been involved in many of Canada's largest mergers and acquisitions, acting for buyers, sellers, target companies, investment dealers, banks and other lenders and financial intermediaries. The firm is a member of both Lex Mundi, an association of independent law firms with members in over 140 jurisdictions, and TechLaw, an international network of major law firms working with businesses, institutions and individuals involved in technology. Blakes' lawyers have also been at the forefront of civil litigation in Canada, representing clients in every forum, from trial and appellate courts to administrative and regulatory tribunals.

INTERNATIONAL EXPERIENCE: The firm has a broad international practice with particular emphasis on M&A, finance and trade law. Through its six offices, and its relationships with major international legal and accounting firms, Blakes provides a co-ordinated service for Canadian businesses operating or financing outside Canada, and for foreign businesses entering, operating and financing in Canada. In the field of international finance, the firm is very active in the public and private placement of debt and equity of Canadian entities abroad, as well as in the placement of foreign securities in Canada. It is also frequently involved in international syndicated loans, note facilities and ECP programs, for Canadian issuers or their foreign affiliates. Blakes is involved on a regular basis with diverse aspects of international commercial law, ranging from advice on the North American Free Trade Agreement (NAFTA) and WTO matters to antidumping and technology transfers.

INTERNATIONAL CLIENTS: The firm's clients include some of the best known firms in Canadian business, ranging from major corporations and financial institutions to start-ups in manufacturing and knowledge-based industries.

LANGUAGES: Cantonese, English, French, German, Mandarin, Spanish

WORLDWIDE OFFICE CONTACTS

CANADA
Box 25, Commerce Court West, **Toronto**, Ontario M5L 1A9
Tel: +1 416 863 2400 **Fax:** +1 416 863 2653
Email: toronto@blakes.com

CHINA
Suite A - I, 21st Floor, Hanwei Plaza, 7 Guanghua Road,
Chaoyang District, **Beijing** 100004
Tel: +86 10 6561 1515 **Fax:** +86 10 6561 0667
Email: rymkwauk@public.bta.net.cn

UNITED KINGDOM
7th Floor, 10 Lloyd's Avenue, **London** EC3N 3AX
Tel: +44 20 7680 4600 **Fax:** +44 20 7680 4646
Email: london@blakes.com

B

WORLDWIDE OFFICES

UNITED KINGDOM

7th Floor, 10 Lloyd's Avenue, London EC3N 3AX
Email: london@blakes.com

Senior partner: David Glennie

Number of lawyers: 3

Office profile: Established in 1986, Blakes' London office advises Canadian clients with interests in the UK, Europe and emerging markets. The office has considerable experience in the representation of corporations in the high technology, mining, oil and gas sectors. In addition, lawyers in the London office assist European businesses considering Canadian acquisitions, joint ventures and financings. The office also advises on all aspects of Canadian competition, tax, securities, trade and business law.

CHINA

Suite A–1, 21st Floor, Hanwei Plaza, 7 Guanghua Road, Chaoyang District, Beijing 100004

Email: rymkwauk@public.bta.net.cn

Senior partner: Robert Kwauk

Number of lawyers: 2

Number of locally qualified lawyers: 1

Office profile: The goal of Blakes' Beijing office, opened in 1998, is to assist Canadian and other international companies to conduct their business affairs in China and the Pacific Rim. The firm is one of only two Canadian national law firms granted approval by the Chinese government to operate in Beijing. This office advises clients on all aspects of doing business in China, including establishing representative offices, structuring and documenting joint ventures and wholly foreign-owned enterprises, arranging intellectual property protection and assisting in dispute resolution. Blakes lawyers also assist Chinese clients to expand into Canadian and other Western markets through a variety of means including securities offerings, stock market listings and establishing corporations in Canada.

For other recommended firms see pages 1485-1520

BLAKE DAWSON WALDRON

HEAD OFFICE

Level 41, 225 George Street,
Sydney NSW 2000, Australia
Tel: +61 2 9258 6000 **Fax:** +61 2 9258 6999
Email: legal.info@bdw.com.au
Website: www.bdw.com.au

FIRM OVERVIEW

CEO: John Colvin
Chairman of Partners: Richard Fisher
Number of partners worldwide: 182
Number of other lawyers worldwide: 681

AREAS OF PRACTICE:

Competition .... *%
Corporate .... *%
Financial services .... *%
Intellectual property .... *%
IT and communications .... *%
Litigation and dispute resolution .... *%
Tax .... *%
* Workload % not disclosed

FIRM OVERVIEW: Blake Dawson Waldron (BDW) is one of Australia's leading international law firms, with more than 180 partners and 1,400 staff. The firm's strength is underpinned by its national partnership structure, giving the firm a strong presence in each of its offices within Australia as well as the offshore offices and the associated offices in Jakarta and Hong Kong. BDW is dedicated to providing quality, value-added legal services for all aspects of commercial activity and government operations.

INTERNATIONAL EXPERIENCE: The firm undertakes a considerable level of international commercial work. The offshore offices serve as a liaison for clients with business interests in Australia and for Australian clients doing business offshore. In the past year, BDW has acted for significant multinational organisations in the areas of mergers and acquisitions, intellectual property, project financing and infrastructure projects.

WORLDWIDE OFFICE CONTACTS

AUSTRALIA
Riverside Centre, 123 Eagle Street, **Brisbane** QLD 4000
Tel: +61 7 3259 7000 **Fax:** +61 7 3259 7111

Level 11, 12 Moore Street, **Canberra** ACT 2601
Tel: +61 2 6234 4000 **Fax:** +61 2 6234 4111

Level 39, 101 Collins Street, **Melbourne** VIC 3000
Tel: +61 3 9679 3000 **Fax:** +61 3 9679 3111

Forrest Centre, 221 St George's Terrace, **Perth** WA 6000
Tel: +61 8 9366 8000 **Fax:** +61 8 9366 8111

225 George Street, **Sydney** NSW 2000
Tel: +61 2 9258 6000 **Fax:** +61 2 9258 6999

CHINA
Suite 628, Shanghai Centre, 1376 Nanjing Road West, **Shanghai** 200040 PRC
Tel: +8621 6279 8069 **Fax:** +8621 6279 8109

PAPUA NEW GUINEA
Mogoru Moto Building, Champion Parade, (PO Box 850), **Port Moresby**
Tel: +675 309 2000 **Fax:** +675 399 2099

UNITED KINGDOM
66 Gresham Street, **London** EC2V 7PL
Tel: +44 20 7600 3030 **Fax:** +44 20 7600 3392

ASSOCIATED OFFICES

HONG KONG
Kwok & Yih, 37th Floor, Gloucester Tower, The Landmark,11 Pedder Street, Central, **Hong Kong**
Tel: +852 2523 1000 **Fax:** +852 2530 4300
Email: Info@KnY.com

INDONESIA
Soebagjo, Jatim Djarot, 17th Floor, Plaza Mashill, Jalan Jenderal Sudirman Kav 25, **Jakarta** 12910
Tel: +62 21 522 9765 **Fax:** +62 21 522 9752

INTERNATIONAL CLIENTS: The firm serves a wide range of commercial, trading, financial and industrial corporations as well as governments, institutional organisations and statutory corporations. Its clients include organisations such as Telstra, BHP Limited, Goodman Fielder Limited, Qantas Airways, ANZ Bank, Macquarie Bank, Woolworths Limited, Australian Department of Defence, Australian Commonwealth Office of Asset Sales and IT Outsourcing (OASITO), Asea Brown Boveri and Unilever.

MAIN INTERNATIONAL AREAS OF PRACTICE:

Financial services: The Financial Services Group provides a full range of legal services to facilitate the activities of banks, financial institutions and corporate and government sector borrowers in domestic and international financings.

Corporate: The firm's Corporate Advisory Group provides advice for both the 'old' and 'new' economies including; mergers and acquisitions; privatisations and ongoing advice to privatised utilities; general corporate and securities law, ASX Listing Rules, corporate governance and dealings with the Australian Securities and Investments Commission; capital raisings, IPOs and floats on stock exchanges; structured products including those involving futures, warrants and tax structuring; and general commercial transactions such as franchising, distribution, agency, partnership, trade and supply.

Intellectual property: The firm acts for organisations in securing, maintaining and enforcing intellectual property rights in Australia and overseas. Its unique OZMARK® software enables it to manage significant intellectual property portfolios, and to generate reports and trade mark schedules tailored to meet individual client needs.

Litigation and dispute resolution: BDW's leading litigation and dispute resolution team provides advice on commercial disputes, contract enforcement, corporate regulation, litigation arising from mergers and acquisitions, trade practices, product liability, taxation disputes and defamation. The practice also focuses on the successful conduct of mediation, arbitration, and other methods of alternative dispute resolution.

Competition: BDW is recognised as pre-eminent in the field of trade practices and competition law. It advises corporate and government clients on matters concerning mergers, horizontal and vertical business arrangements, access to infrastructure, misleading and deceptive conduct and consumer protection and product liability.

LANGUAGES: Afrikaans, Arabic, Bengali, Cantonese, Croatian, Czech, Dutch, Fijian, Filipino, Finnish, French, German, Greek, Hebrew, Indonesian, Italian, Japanese, Korean, Latin, Maltese, Mandarin, Russian, Spanish

B

For other recommended firms see pages 1485-1520

BOEKEL DE NERÉE

HEAD OFFICE

Atrium Building, Strawinskylaan 3037 1077 ZX, PO Box 2508, 1000 CM, Amsterdam, The Netherlands
Tel: +31 20 431 3131 **Fax:** +31 20 431 3143

Email: boekel.de.neree@bdn.nl
Website: www.bdn.nl

WORLDWIDE OFFICE CONTACTS

NETHERLANDS
Atrium Building, Strawinskylaan 3037, PO Box 2508, 1077 ZX
Amsterdam
Tel: +31 20 431 3131 **Fax:** +31 20 431 3143
Email: boekel.de.neree@bdn.nl

FIRM OVERVIEW

Managing partner: Els H. Swaab

Number of partners worldwide: 34
Number of other lawyers worldwide: 106

AREAS OF PRACTICE:

Corporate, M&A, banking and securities 38%
Real estate, administrative, environmental 29%
Employment 16%
Maritime, aviation and insurance 11%
Intellectual property, media and ICT 6%

FIRM OVERVIEW: Boekel De Nerée is a full service business law firm employing 140 lawyers, civil law notaries and tax advisers. The firm specialises in cross-border legal work and advises foreign clients operating in the Netherlands. The firm has an Anglo-American Advisory group lead by the firm's English solicitor partner. Boekel De Nerée is a member of Eversheds International who have 18 offices in Europe and three associated offices in Asia. It also has excellent ties with a number of close correspondent law firms throughout the world.

INTERNATIONAL EXPERIENCE: In 2000 Boekel De Nerée advised 15 major multi-jurisdictional transactions including a major British publisher entering into a complex strategic alliance with its Dutch counterpart. The firm has advised a major Dutch company on the highly complex sale of its shares to a large French company and acted for a British plc in the acquisition of a company partly owned by the Dutch government. Boekel De Nerée has also acted for a UK listed company on its acquisition of a major Dutch listed ICT company. Boekel De Nerée represents various international clients who are looking to increase their market share in the Netherlands.

INTERNATIONAL CLIENTS: The firm acts for many international companies and financial institutions including a large number of UK and US clients conducting cross-border business.

MAIN INTERNATIONAL AREAS OF PRACTICE:

Corporate and M&A: The firm specialises in cross-border transactions, mergers and acquisitions, company reorganisations and joint ventures. The firm's Anglo-American Advisory Group advises clients from the UK, US and other English speaking countries on M&A and other commercial transactions taking place in the Netherlands.
Corporate finance, banking and securities: Boekel De Nerée advises on national and international financing transactions and advises on a wide range of securities matters including regulatory, primary and secondary markets, listings and OTC trade.
Real estate and construction law: The firm is the largest real estate practice in The Netherlands. Clients comprise investment and operating companies, property and development companies, real estate agents, financial institutions and private investors.
Administrative: The firm handles all matters involving government at both local and national levels including litigation for the administrative courts and the handling of permits.
Employment: Boekel De Nerée acts for employers and employees in labour disputes and settlement negotiations. It also offers advice on international labour contracts, industrial relations and mass lay-offs.
Intellectual property: The firm advises clients on the acquisition, exploitation and protection of intellectual property rights. It also handles franchising matters and related disputes/litigation.
Media and ICT: Boekel De Nerée advises national and international clients on film, video, radio and television including pay-TV and broadcasting by cable and satellite. It also advises on theatre productions, concerts and touring, recording, publishing, artists and management. The firm deals with all aspects of information and communication technology law (ICT) and new media. It specialises in ICT related business issues and has extensive litigation experience in complex ICT cases.
Maritime, aviation and traffic law: The firm handles all aspects of maritime, aviation and traffic law and is highly specialised in logistics matters and in the outsourcing of warehousing and logistics operations.
Insurance: Boekel De Nerée represents insurance companies, brokers and insured parties and provides a full advisory and litigation service at national and international levels.

LANGUAGES: Dutch, English, French, German, Italian, Spanish

For other recommended firms see pages 1485-1520

BONILLA MONTANO & TORIELLO

HEAD OFFICE

Avenida Reforma 15-54, Zona 9, Edificio Reforma Obelisco Niviel 3
Guatemala City C.A. 01009, Guatemala
Tel: +502 334 8155 **Fax:** +502 332 2361

Email: bmytlaw@guate.net

WORLDWIDE OFFICE CONTACTS

GUATEMALA
Avenida Reforma 15-54, Zona 9, Edificia Reforma Obelisco Niviel 3,
Guatemala City C.A. 01009
Tel: +502 334 8155 **Fax:** +502 332 2361
Email: bmytlaw@guate.net

FIRM OVERVIEW

Managing partner: Jorge Rolando Barrios

Number of partners worldwide: 5
Number of other lawyers worldwide: 9

AREAS OF PRACTICE:

Area	%
Banking and finance	20%
M&A	20%
General corporate and commercial	10%
International trade and foreign investments	15%
Litigation and arbitration	10%
Administrative and immigration	5%
Intellectual property	5%
Oil and mining	5%
Real estate, construction and insurance	5%
Central American Common Market regulations	3%
Tax	2%

B

FIRM OVERVIEW: Bonilla, Montano & Toriello was established in 1964. Regarded as one of Guatemala's leading law firms, the firm specialises in corporate, commercial and international transactions, and is committed to an international outlook. With over 14 attorneys and professionally qualified staff, the firm comprises two basic practice groups - the Corporate/Commercial Group and the Litigation Group.

INTERNATIONAL EXPERIENCE: Bonilla, Montano & Toriello has advised national and international clients on commercial and financial transactions.The firm has close links with correspondent law firms throughout the world and provides coordinated legal services in Central America.

INTERNATIONAL CLIENTS: Bonilla, Montano & Toriello's clients have included A&E Products (Tyco International); Bausch & Lomb; Becton Dickinson; Cadbury Schweppes; Cargill Incorporated; Cessna; Commonwealth Development Corporation (CDC); Communications Satellite Corporation (COMSAT); Compañía General de Combustibles (Argentina oil company); Constellation; Quality Suites; Data General Corporation; Deutsche Bank; Dial Corporation; Duke Energy; EDCS; ESPN; Export-Import Bank of the United States (EXIMBANK); Federal Express; Florsheim Shoe Company; Foreign Credit Insurance Association (FCIA); General Electric Company; GST International; Herbalife; Inter-American Investment Corporation (IIC-BID); Intrepid Minerals Corporation; Isuzu Motors; JC Penney Company, Inc.; Kellogg's Corporation; Kimberly-Clark Corporation; Lykes Pasco, Inc.; Maersk; McDonald's Corporation; MCI Communications Corporation; Merrill Lynch International Bank Limited (Merrill Lynch); Microsoft Corporation; NCNB National Bank (NCNB); Northern Telecom International Ltd.; Ochsner Clinic; Oxford University Press; Paine Webber; Panamco; Scott Paper Company; Seminis Vegetable Seeds; SMV America, Inc.; Textron Inc. (Bell Helicopter Textron); The Associated Press (AP); Thomson Consumer Electronics; Votocel; Walt Disney; Warner Lambert; Western Union Financial Services Inc.

MAIN INTERNATIONAL AREAS OF PRACTICE: The firm's main practice areas include foreign investments; international transactions; joint ventures; international trade; foreign debt transactions; general corporate and commercial work; mergers and acquisitions; international and domestic banking and finance; litigation and arbitration; taxation and exchange controls; central American Common Market regulations; telecommunications; privatisation; agency work; franchise and copyrights; licence agreements; real estate; construction and insurance; oil and mining; administrative and integration.

LANGUAGES: English, Spanish

For other recommended firms see pages 1485-1520

BORDEN LADNER GERVAIS LLP

HEAD OFFICE

see Worldwide Office Contacts

Email: info@blgcanada.com
Website: www.blgcanada.com

WORLDWIDE OFFICE CONTACTS

CANADA
Borden Ladner Gervais LLP, 1000 Canterra Tower, 400 Third Avenue S.W., **Calgary,** Alberta T2P 4H2
Tel: +1 403 232 9500 **Fax:** +1 403 266 1395

1000 de La Gauchetiere Street, Suite 900, **Montreal,** Quebec H3B 5H4
Tel: +1 514 879 1212 **Fax:** +1 514 954 1905

1000 - 60 Queen Street, **Ottawa,** Ontario K1P 5Y7
Tel: +1 613 237 5160 **Fax:** +1 613 230 8842

Scotia Plaza, 40 King Street West, **Toronto,** Ontario M5H 3Y4
Tel: +1 416 367 6000 **Fax:** +1 416 367 6749

1200 Waterfront Centre, 200 Burrard Street, P.O. Box 48600, **Vancouver**, British Columbia V7X 1T2
Tel: +1 604 687 5744 **Fax:** +1 604 687 1415

FIRM OVERVIEW

National managing partner: Sean Weir
Regional managing partners: Doug Mitchell (Calgary), Ian Taylor (Montreal), Guy Pratte (Ottawa), John Warren (Toronto), Kenneth Bagshaw (Vancouver)
Number of partners worldwide: 318
Number of other lawyers worldwide: 301

AREAS OF PRACTICE:

Capital markets	20%
Finance	20%
ADR	10%
M&A	10%
Technology and intellectual property	10%
Transportation	10%
Construction, surety and fidelity	5%
Energy and natural resources	5%
Environment	5%
International trade	5%

FIRM OVERVIEW: Borden Ladner Gervais LLP is one of the largest law firms in Canada, comprising over 600 lawyers, intellectual property agents and other professionals. Borden Ladner Gervais LLP is a full-service law firm, offering fully bilingual legal, patent and trademark services throughout Canada and around the world. Borden Ladner Gervais LLP is the result of the unique merger between Howard, Mackie (Calgary), McMaster Gervais (Montreal), Scott & Aylen (Ottawa), Borden & Elliot (Toronto), and Ladner Downs (Vancouver).

INTERNATIONAL EXPERIENCE: The firm has acted in a range of international transactions including the resolution of international trade disputes and litigation; international banking transactions (including sovereign risk lending); international insolvencies, liquidations and restructurings; international joint ventures, reorganisations and acquisitions; international communications networks and commercial contracts. The firm's international law group has acted as counsel for transactions in regions including South East Asia and the Far East, Europe, The Middle East, and Latin America and the Caribbean.

MAIN INTERNATIONAL AREAS OF PRACTICE:

ADR: Borden Ladner Gervais LLP represents clients before, and acts as members of, international arbitration and mediation panels in a broad spectrum of litigation and alternative dispute resolution issues. Work undertaken includes toxic torts, product liability and commercial, banking, environmental, international trade and investment, energy, and securities matters.

Capital markets: The capital markets group provides experienced legal representation in all types of corporate and securities transactions, both domestic and trans-border. Borden Ladner Gervais LLP has acted for underwriters, issuers, selling security holders and investors in a wide variety of domestic and cross-border financings.

Construction, surety and fidelity: Borden Ladner Gervais LLP advises clients on all aspects of international engineering, procurement, and construction projects. It handles the preparation of joint venture, bid, construction and financing documents, negotiation and implementation of technology supply, license and service agreements, project implementation, and project management agreements.

Energy and natural resources: Borden Ladner Gervais LLP's energy practice advises on oil, gas and petrochemical projects, and in particular the development, financing and building of oil and gas pipelines, offshore energy projects, and other natural resource projects. The firm also advises on mining related projects in a number of Latin American countries.

Finance: Borden Ladner Gervais LLP's financial services law group has a multidisciplinary team of lawyers with expertise in banking, lending, securities, real estate, insurance, trust, tax and litigation law, and other relevant specialties including international business, communications and environmental law. The firm provides a wide range of services to major Canadian and foreign banks, trust companies, insurance companies and investment dealers. The group also represents numerous corporate borrowers in diverse sectors of the economy.

International trade: Borden Ladner Gervais LLP advises clients on a full range of public and private international trade law issues, including routine import and export matters and questions arising under anti-competition, anti-bribery legislation, negotiations of international trade agreements, and government dispute settlement. The firm also advises on clearance issues relating to the international aspects of proposed cross-border business transactions and anti-trust investigation issues.

M&A: Borden Ladner Gervais LLP structures, negotiates, implements and manages complex business and corporate re-organisations, restructurings, insolvencies, combinations, organisations, and mergers. As part of this work, the firm obtains regulatory approvals, designs international tax strategies, and deals with multi-jurisdictional legal issues that arise in international M&A transactions.

Technology and intellectual property: Borden Ladner Gervais LLP advises both technology suppliers and users on international technology transactions. The firm also assists clients on international registration and transfer of technology involving several jurisdictions and tax issues.

Transportation: The firm has handled the preparation of bid responses for the establishment of an airport link between a major US airport and one of the busiest urban centres in North America. It has also advised a leading international transportation company in connection with the development and construction of a subway system in Europe.

LANGUAGES: Members of the firm can speak approximately 30 languages.

B

For other recommended firms see pages 1485-1520

BORENIUS & KEMPPINEN

HEAD OFFICE

Yrjönkatu 13 A,
FIN-00120 Helsinki, Finland
Tel: +358 9 615 333 **Fax:** +358 9 6153 3499

Email: info@borenius.fi
website: www.borenius.fi

FIRM OVERVIEW

Managing partner: Jyrki Tähtinen

Number of partners worldwide: 8
Number of other lawyers worldwide: 21

AREAS OF PRACTICE:

Intellectual property	25%
M&A	25%
Private equity and venture capital	25%
Litigation, arbitration and mediation	7%
Capital markets	7%
Telecommunications and IT	5%
Insolvency	3%
Competition	3%

WORLDWIDE OFFICE CONTACTS

FINLAND
Yrjönkatu 13 A, FIN-00120 **Helsinki**
Tel: +358 9 615 333 **Fax:** +358 9 6153 3499
Email: info@borenius.fi

RIGA
Lauris Liepa, Sworn Advocates Office
5A Blaumana **Riga** LV1011
Tel: +371 722 2794 **Fax:** +371 728 5511
Email: advocats@liepa.lv

B

FIRM OVERVIEW: Established in 1911, Borenius & Kemppinen is one of Finland's older law firms. It is a full-service firm which advises both domestic and international institutional and corporate clients. One of its 29 lawyers is dually qualified practising in Finland and in the state of New York, USA as Member of the New York Bar.

INTERNATIONAL EXPERIENCE: Much of the firm's international work involves Scandinavian, Eastern Europe and the Baltic states. M&A deals in which it has acted for the investors include the supply of fishing trawlers for the Barents Sea, lubrication oil production in Latvia, forest machines in United States and packaging material production in Russia. International finance work includes syndicated loans such as the Sonera MDEM1,000 revolving credit facility in Finland and the first privately-funded highway.

INTERNATIONAL CLIENTS: Clients include sovereign states, investment banks, financial institutions, foreign private equity investors and trade buyers, and Finnish unlisted and listed companies investing and operating abroad. The majority of the firm's Foreilu clients are from Europe and North America.

MAIN INTERNATIONAL AREAS OF PRACTICE:

M&A: The practice has advised investors, MBO and MBI teams, private equity and venture capital funds and industrial buyers and sellers on a broad spectrum of deals involving clients ranging from energy companies to internet service providers. It is supported by the IP, corporate, finance and employment teams.
Capital markets: Work includes acting for several growth companies such as Rocla, PK Cables, PMJ automec on their IPOs in Helsinki. The firm is a member of the EASD tax and legal committee and can advise on New York law from Helsinki.
Venture capital and private equity: Clients include private equity and venture capital fund management firms and investors in several of the latest fund documentations. The firm has acted in numerous acquisitions, MBOs and MBIs and in venture capital exits through trade sale or IPOs.
Intellectual property: The firm advises on patents, copyrights, trademarks, biotechnology, internet and multimedia.
Telecommunications and IT: Clients include leading Finnish digital media publishers, telecoms, internet content providers and mobile telephone and telecom infrastructure manufacturers. Firm members have been active in e-commerce issues such as contracting on the internet, consumer protection and the protection of personal data.
Litigation, arbitration and mediation: Commercial litigation has traditionally been one of the firm's cornerstone practice areas, and the firm was also one of the first to introduce mediation in Finland. Group members have substantial experience as arbitrators.
Insolvency: Experience includes acting as trustees in several of Finland's largest bankruptcies and corporate restructurings.

LANGUAGES: English, Finnish, French, German, Spanish, Swedish, Latvian, Russian

 For other recommended firms see pages 1485-1520

BOWMAN GILFILLAN INC

HEAD OFFICE

9th Floor Twin Towers West, PO Box 785812,
Sandton, Johannesburg Metropolitan Area, 2146, South Africa
Tel: +27 11 881 9800 **Fax:** +27 11 883 4505
Email: m.doherty@bowman.co.za
Website: www.bowman.co.za

FIRM OVERVIEW

Chairman: Mike Adcock
Chief executive: Michael Doherty
Number of partners worldwide: 67
Number of other lawyers worldwide: 88

AREAS OF PRACTICE:

Corporate, commercial and financial services	27%
Intellectual property	22%
Employment	10%
Litigation	10%
Property and conveyancing	9%
Construction and engineering	5%
Maritime	5%
Environmental, mining and energy	4%
Broadcasting and telecommunications	2%
Estates and trusts	2%
Insolvency and corporate recovery	1%
Matrimonial and family	1%
Public law	1%

FIRM OVERVIEW: Bowman Gilfillan, one of the largest law firms in South Africa, was formed through the merger of three South African law firms: Findlay & Tait (established 1889), Bowman Gilfillan Hayman Godfrey (established 1902) and John & Kernick (established 1923), with offices in Johannesburg, Midrand, Cape Town and London.

INTERNATIONAL EXPERIENCE: The firm advises corporate clients in bids for the privatisation of major state-owned enterprises, on financing acquisitions and concession projects and on the new competition legislation. It advises major South African corporations in outward investment and international offerings and placings. The London office primarily deals with cross-border transactions, international tax planning, the establishment of off-shore structures, joint ventures, acquisitions and international investment in South Africa. The firm is the sole South African member of Lex Mundi, a global association of 146 independent law firms. The firm also has long-standing relationships with leading law firms in New York and London.

INTERNATIONAL CLIENTS: Major domestic and multinational corporations, investment banks, financial institutions, governments, state authorities, international agencies and medium-sized companies in diverse fields. Amongst the firm's corporate clients are: ABB, Bank of New York, Chase Manhattan, Credit Suisse, DaimlerChrysler, Donaldson, Lufkin & Jenrette, Ford Motor Credit, GEC P.L.C., General Motors, Hewlett-Packard, IBM, Merck International, Morgan Stanley, Pfizer, SBC Communications, Toyota, UBS and Warburg.

MAIN INTERNATIONAL AREAS OF PRACTICE:

Corporate, commercial and financial services: The practice covers corporate, finance, banking finance, capital markets and derivatives, as well as commercial law and tax. The firm has extensive experience in advising on transactions in various sectors, including financial services, mining and energy, pharmaceutical, health care, manufacturing, IT, construction and engineering.

Broadcasting and telecommunications: In South Africa these fields have been extensively liberalised over the past few years. The firm has acted for the regulatory authorities for the first private free-to-air television licence and the applications for the third cellular mobile phone licence.

Construction and engineering: The practice deals with all legal aspects of the construction and engineering industries. Expertise includes intellectual property, contracts and negotiations advice, arbitrations and mediations.

Employment: The firm has been involved in the development of employment law jurisprudence and represents state-owned enterprises, local government institutions, development corporations as well as major listed and unlisted domestic and international corporations and employers organisations.

Environmental, mining and energy: This field is undergoing rapid legislative change in South Africa. The firm regularly advises the government on the development of key environmental laws. Mining and mineral law as well as off-shore oil and gas exploration are other areas of specialisation.

Intellectual property: The firm advises on IP issues including the optimisation of rights in product life cycles and marketing. It has a domestic and international client base with particular experience in African countries.

Litigation: The firm offers expertise in alternative dispute resolution. Some of the firm's partners are qualified mediators and arbitrators, with particularly strong representation in construction, employment, engineering and intellectual property law.

Insolvency and corporate recovery: The firm has been involved in major South African bankruptcies and corporate recoveries as well as in proceedings in foreign jurisdictions.

Public law: The firm advises clients on the validity and interpretation of new laws and acts and represents clients in proceedings before various boards and councils and in applications for licences.

Maritime services: Experience in the field dates back more than a century, and covers the whole range of services. The firm has an extensive South African and international client base, including several overseas P&I clubs.

Property and conveyancing: Clients include major domestic and international banking and financial institutions, listed and unlisted corporations, property developers and consultants, commercial and residential real estate agents and private individuals.

LANGUAGES: English

WORLDWIDE OFFICE CONTACTS

SOUTH AFRICA
SA Reserve Bank Building, 60 St Georges Mall, Cape Town 8001, PO Box 248, **Cape Town** 8000
Tel: +27 21 480 7800 **Fax:** +27 21 424 1688
Email: enquiries@fandt.co.za

Kernick House, Howick Close, Waterfall Park, Midrand, PO Box 3511, Halfway House, **Midrand** 1685
Tel: +27 11 315 7400 **Fax:** +27 11 315 7444
Email: info@africaip.com

9th Floor Twin Towers West, PO Box 785812, **Sandton** 2146
Tel: +27 11 881 9800 **Fax:** +27 11 883 4505
Email: m.doherty@bowman.co.za

UNITED KINGDOM
35 John Street, **London** WC1N 2AT
Tel: +44 20 7430 0888 **Fax:** +44 20 7430 2030
Email: d.anderson@bowmangilfillan.co.uk

B

BOXALLS

HEAD OFFICE

Queensgate House, PO Box 1234, George Town
Grand Cayman, Cayman Islands
Tel: +1 345 949 9876 **Fax:** +1 345 949 9877

Email: boxalls@boxalls.com.ky
Website: www.boxalls.com.ky

WORLDWIDE OFFICE CONTACTS

CAYMAN ISLANDS
Queensgate House, PO Box 1234, George Town, **Grand Cayman**
Tel: +1 345 949 9876 **Fax:** +1 345 949 9877
Email: boxalls@boxalls.com.ky

FIRM OVERVIEW

Partners Ian Boxall, James Bagnall, James Bergstrom, William Helfrecht

Number of partners worldwide: 4
Number of other lawyers worldwide: 8

AREAS OF PRACTICE:

Corporate, commercial banking and finance	45%
Litigation	40%
Real estate and private client	15%

B

FIRM OVERVIEW: Over the last ten years Boxalls has developed a reputation as a responsive and cost-effective alternative to the larger firms in the Cayman Islands and is now one of the jurisdiction's top four law firms. The firm is divided into three practice areas: commercial, litigation, and private client and property. Boxalls is also a listing agent for the Cayman Islands Stock Exchange. The firm's affiliated corporate management company, Ironshore Corporate Services Limited, provides registered office services.

INTERNATIONAL CLIENTS: Boxalls clients include international banks and financial institutions, investment advisors, insurance companies, airlines and multinational corporations.

MAIN INTERNATIONAL AREAS OF PRACTICE:
M&A: The firm's experience ranges from private acquisitions and disposals to cross border take-overs of listed companies.
Banking and finance: The firm advises on all areas of banking and finance including secured lending and guarantees, structured finance, project finance and finance leasing.
Insurance: Boxalls advises on the establishment and operation of captive insurance companies.
Mutual funds: A major part of Boxalls' practice is in advising administrators, promoters and investment managers on the structuring, establishment and operation of all forms of mutual funds, including hedge funds, private equity funds and listings on the CSX.
Litigation: Boxalls advise on a wide range of litigation such as company disputes (including all aspects of directors duties and responsibilities), corporate finance and merger disputes, enforcement of foreign judgments and awards in the Cayman Islands, minority shareholders rights and actions, mutual funds disputes (including rights and duties of administrators and managers), personal and corporate insolvency proceedings (including liquidators' duties), probate, banking and securities disputes, professional negligence actions, rights of investors, transnational asset tracing and recovery, challenges to and variations in and validity of trust deeds, beneficiaries rights and trustees' and protectors' duties.
Private client and property: The firm advises on all aspects of trusts, wills, probate and administration of estates in the Cayman Islands, real estate purchases and sales, property development and leasing, immigration and business licensing for both private and commercial clients. It also acts for a number of leading banks in advising on mortgage securities.

LANGUAGES: English, French, German, Russian, Spanish

For other recommended firms see pages 1485-1520

BREDIN PRAT

HEAD OFFICE

130 Rue de Faubourg Saint-Honoré, 75008 Paris, France
Tel: + 33 1 44 35 35 35 **Fax:** + 33 1 45 63 14 07

FIRM OVERVIEW

Senior partners: Jean-Denis Bredin, Jean-François Prat

Number of partners worldwide: 19
Number of other lawyers worldwide: 46

AREAS OF PRACTICE:

M&A .... *%
Finance and capital markets .... *%
EU & competition .... *%
Litigation and arbitration .... *%
* Workload % not disclosed

WORLDWIDE OFFICE CONTACTS

BELGIUM
Avenue Lloyd Georges 6, 1000 **Brussels**
Tel: +32 2 639 27 10 **Fax:** +32 2 646 03 11
Email: bredin.prat@bredin-prat.law.be

FRANCE
130 Rue de Faubourg Saint-Honoré, 75008 **Paris**
Tel: + 33 1 44 35 35 35 **Fax:** + 33 1 45 63 14 07
Email: bredinprat@bredinprat.com

FIRM OVERVIEW: Founded in 1965, Bredin Prat & Associés specialises in business law, in particular high-level mergers and acquisitions (including major French privatisations.) It also undertakes work in finance and capital markets, competition law and commercial and white-collar criminal litigation and arbitration. The firm is not organised into departments; its lawyers remain multi-disciplinary and form themselves into teams as required. In particular, the firm does not separate its litigation and transaction practices. Bredin Prat has decided not to significantly expand above its present size, as well as continuing to focus on "what it does best" rather than becoming a broad-based commercial practice.

INTERNATIONAL EXPERIENCE: Approximately a third of the firm's clients are international, in particular from the US, UK and from the main jurisdictions in continental Europe. The firm advises on a large number of cross-border and multi-jurisdictional corporate transactions, as well as undertaking international litigation and arbitration. Bredin Prat remains independent from law firm network organisations which would require the firm to work with designated firms or offices outside of France. The firm has instead chosen the route of developing strong working relationships with firms in all the European capitals and in the United States (and to a more limited extent in Asia) that can be called upon to form the appropriate international team for specific transborder or multi jurisdictional transactions. Three of the firm's partners are American and admitted to the New York bar and one of the firm's partners is English and admitted to the bar of England and Wales (barrister).

MAIN AREAS OF INTERNATIONAL PRACTICE:

M&A: Cross border mergers or acquisitions, particularly involving publicly traded companies.
Finance and capital markets: Co-ordination of securities issues on foreign markets (particularly in the European Union and the US), advice on venture capital investments, co-ordination of multiple listings and privatisations.
EU and competition: Frequently in connection with M&A practice.
Litigation and arbitration: Major corporate litigation with an emphasis on stock exchange-related litigation and international investment disputes.

LANGUAGES: English, German, Italian, Spanish

WORLDWIDE OFFICES

BELGIUM

Avenue Lloyd Georges 6, 1000 Brussels

Number of lawyers: 3

Office profile: The Brussels office was opened in early 1999. It practises EU law, in particular competition law, complementing the firm's competition capabilities in Paris.

B

For other recommended firms see pages 1485-1520

BRONS & SALAS

HEAD OFFICE

Marcelo T de Alvear 624, 1st Floor,
C1058AAH Buenos Aires, Argentina
Tel: +54 11 4891 2700 **Fax:** +54 11 4311 7025
Email: brons@brons.com.ar
Website: www.brons.com.ar

FIRM OVERVIEW

Managing partner: Alfredo L. Rovira
Senior partners: Hernán Celorrio, Eduardo E. Represas, Gustavo Ferrante
Number of partners worldwide: 11
Number of other lawyers worldwide: 64

AREAS OF PRACTICE:

Litigation	26%
Energy	17%
Intellectual property	14%
Tax	14%
Corporations and securities	8%
Real estate	8%
Administrative, customs and privatisations	3%
Employment	3%
Environmental	3%
Banking and finance	2%
E-commerce	2%

FIRM OVERVIEW: Brons & Salas was established in 1967 by Stanley A. Brons and Acdeel E. Salas. The firm's lawyers are all members of the Buenos Aires Bar Association and many participate in other professional and academic associations. Its lawyers are also involved in bar association committees and other bar activities.

INTERNATIONAL EXPERIENCE: The firm has advised prominent Argentine and international clients on their investments and business activities in Argentina.

MAIN INTERNATIONAL AREAS PRACTICE:

Administrative, customs, privatisations: The firm acts on behalf of numerous companies, both Argentine and foreign, in submitting bids in tenders issued by the National and different Provincial Governments. It has acted on behalf of public agencies in the transformation of the National and Provincial Governments advising on the various processes involved in the privatisation of public utilities. The firm was actively involved in the privatisation of Electric Energy, the Post Office and designed the legal system for the privatisation of Argentine Airports. The firm has played an active role in the commercial integration of Argentina with its neighbor countries, particularly in the MERCOSUR regulatory processes. Brons & Salas advises corporate clients on import and export issues, particularly antidumping cases, free trade zones, special customs zones and all matters concerned with the automotive industry compensated interchange system.
Banking and corporate finance, foreign investments: Brons & Salas advises clients including international financial entities on loans and financial transactions. The firm handles large scale legal audits of banking entities and advises on mergers and corporate acquisitions. Due to the growth of the Argentine capital market, the firm has acted on behalf of issuing parties in the public offerings of bonds, securities and stock equity. The firm has a special division to handle banking and financial law and capital market transactions and has experience in M&A, syndicated loans, equity-linked products, securitisation, IPO, and in providing support to capital market products.

WORLDWIDE OFFICE CONTACTS

ARGENTINA
Marcelo T de Alvear 624, 1st Floor, C1058AAH **Buenos Aires**
Tel: +54 11 4891 2700 **Fax:** +54 11 4311 7025
Email: brons@brons.com.ar

ASSOCIATED OFFICES

ARGENTINA
Reyna & Asociados, Bolivar 553 Piso 1°, 5000 **Córdoba**
Tel: +54 351 425 6881 **Fax:** +54 351 423 9241
Email: arovira@brons.com.ar

Racciatti & Hourquescos, Paraguay 777, piso 12°, 2000 **Rosario**
Tel: +54 0341 425 5791 **Fax:** +54 0341 426 0980
Email: estudio@estudioracciatti.com.ar

URUGUAY
Ituzaingó 1324, Piso 8°, **Montevideo** 1100
Tel: +59 82 916 2121 **Fax:** +59 82 916 3583
Email: arozyasoc@redfacil.com.uy

Corporations and securities: Brons & Salas advises domestic and foreign clients on issues involving the organisation, administration and development of the corporate structure of their businesses. The firm enjoys a close relationship with both controlling stockholders and with the directors and managers of its corporate clients. In the area of mergers and corporate acquisitions, the firm is involved in the initial negotiation and due diligence procedures.
Intellectual property: The firm's patents and trademarks department advises domestic and foreign clients on matters such as trademarks; patents; copyrights; and performers' and discographic producers' rights, including the registration and protection of software. The firm focuses on conflicts arising from the protection of persons' names and the right to their own image.
Litigation: The firm represents clients at both trial and appellate levels before Provincial and National Courts throughout Argentina. It handles all kinds of litigation such as commercial, civil and administrative and is experienced in the areas of contractual damages and torts; insurance; divorce and related proceedings; enforcement of judgments; mortgage and pledge foreclosures; and collections in general. The firm has also been actively involved in estates, bankruptcies and insolvency proceedings.
Energy: Brons & Salas advises National and Provincial public agencies with mining policy-making and advises foreign companies interested in setting up business in Argentina to engage in mining exploration and exploitation. The firm is involved in processing registrations with the Mining Investment Register; analysing titles to mining concessions and claims located in several Argentine Provinces; drafting mining contracts; and setting up mining easement. The firm has advised clients on the submission of tenders in bidding processes for the award of hydrocarbon areas and other aspects involved in their relationship with YPF, a recently privatised company. Clients include companies engaged in the exploration and exploitation of oil and companies engaged in the gas industry.
Tax: The firm specialises in the transformation, reorganisation, merger and spin-off of companies and transfer of stocks-in-trade, advising on their implementation under the tax-free system. The firm offers specific advice on all kinds of administrative and court proceedings relating to inspections; verifications and assessment of taxes; special summary proceedings for infringements; and closing of establishments and criminal tax charges.

LANGUAGES: English, French, German, Italian, Portuguese, Spanish

For other recommended firms see pages 1485-1520

BROWN & WOOD LLP

HEAD OFFICE

One World Trade Center,
New York NY 10048-0557, USA
Tel: +1 212 839 5300 **Fax:** +1 212 839 5599

Email: firstinitialsurname@brownwoodlaw.com
Website: www.brownwoodlaw.com

FIRM OVERVIEW

Managing partner: Thomas R. Smith, Jr

Number of partners worldwide: 124
Number of other lawyers worldwide: 290

AREAS OF PRACTICE:

Corporate/securities	25%
Securitisation	25%
Pooled investment entities	12%
Litigation	10%
Tax	10%
M&A	8%
Public finance	6%
Real estate	3%
Private clients	1%

FIRM OVERVIEW: Brown & Wood comprises over 400 lawyers in seven offices throughout the world. Founded in New York City in 1914, the firm is recognised as a leader in providing legal services to major participants in the world's capital markets. Brown & Wood handles a diverse range of work, with an emphasis on structuring complex financial transactions, both domestic and international, and in providing a broad variety of legal services, primarily to financial institutions, other business interests, public entities and institutional end-users of financial products.

INTERNATIONAL EXPERIENCE: Brown & Wood handles a significant number of global financial transactions and continues to strengthen its international practice. The firm practices US, English and Hong Kong law and has successfully built a globally integrated US/UK practice. The London office, which is active in corporate finance, cross-border structured finance and securitisation activity, handled financial transactions in 1999 totalling approximately US$85 billion. Brown & Wood recently expanded its presence in Hong Kong, and through its Beijing and Hong Kong offices, continues its representation of the Ministry of Finance of the People's Republic of China, the China Development Bank and The Export-Import Bank of China. The firm has maintained a Japanese practice for more than 20 years, representing large industrial corporations, trading companies, entertainment companies, securities companies, commercial banks and financial services firms in Japan. The firm has one of the most successful and established practices of any US law firm in the area of Latin America securities transactions, and has helped structure a large number of securities offerings for Latin American issuers as well as working on significant M&A transactions. Significant international transactions handled by the firm in 1999 include: representing Grupo Mexico in the all-cash hostile tender offer for ASARCO Inc. which involved US$1.8 billion of financing committed by The Chase Bank; acting as underwriter's counsel for Merrill Lynch in connection with the US$1.3 billion stock offering by Grupo Televisa, S.A.; representing the financial advisor to the Royal Bank of Scotland Group plc for its successful US$2.2 billion tender offer for all outstanding shares of the National Westminster Bank plc; acting as underwriter's counsel in connection with the US$550 million IPO of iCable Communications in Hong Kong.

WORLDWIDE OFFICE CONTACTS

CHINA
China World Tower, 1 Jian Guo Men Wai Avenue, **Beijing** 100004
Tel: +8610 6505 5359 **Fax:** +8610 6505 5360
Email: hding@brownwoodlaw.com

HONG KONG
Bank of China Tower, One Garden Road, Central, **Hong Kong**
Tel: +852 2509 7888 **Fax:** +852 2509 3110
Email: kcote@brownwoodlaw.com

UNITED KINGDOM
Princes Court, 7 Princes Street, **London** EC2R 8AQ
Tel: +44 20 7778 1800 **Fax:** +44 20 7796 1807
Email: cmead@brownwoodlaw.com

USA
10877 Wilshire Boulevard, **Los Angeles** CA 90024-4341
Tel: +1 310 443 0200 **Fax:** +1 310 208 5740
Email: cdyba@brownwoodlaw.com

One World Trade Center, **New York** NY 10048-0557
Tel: +1 212 839 5300 **Fax:** +1 212 839 5599
Email: tsmith@brownwoodlaw.com

555 California Street, **San Francisco** CA 94104-1715
Tel: +1 415 772 1200 **Fax:** +1 415 397 4621
Email: ppringle@brownwoodlaw.com

1666 K Street, NW, **Washington DC** 20006-1208
Tel: +1 202 533 1300 **Fax:** +1 202 533 1399
Email: jarnholz@brownwoodlaw.com

ASSOCIATED OFFICES

JAPAN
Kioicho Building, 3-28 Kioicho, Chiyoda-Ku, **Tokyo** 102
Tel: +813 5276 0045 **Fax:** +813 5276 0049
Email: yshimada@brownwoodlaw.com

B

INTERNATIONAL CLIENTS: The firm's clients include Allied Irish Banks plc, Anglo Irish Bank, Banco Mercantil del Norte, Banco Santander, Banque et Caisse d'Epargne de l'Etat, Banc of America, Bayerische Landesbank, Catalonia, China Development Bank, China Import Export Bank, Citigroup Inc., Core Pacific-Yamaichi Capital Ltd, Countrywide Credit Industries Inc., Credit Lyonnais, Credit Suisse First Boston, Deutsche Bank, Deutsche Morgan Grenfell, Dresdner Kleinwort Benson, GE Capital, Goldman, Sachs & Co., Grupo Mexico, Lehman Brothers, Merrill Lynch International, Morgan Stanley & Co., Nomura Securities Co., Ltd., Northern Rock, People's Republic of China - Ministry of Finance, Puerto Rico Government Development Bank, Salomon Smith Barney International, Scotia Holdings, Société Générale, Standard Life Bank, Swiss Bank Corporation, Tokai Bank, Union Bank of Norway, Westdeutsche Landesbank Girozentrale.

MAIN INTERNATIONAL AREAS OF PRACTICE:
Corporate/securities: Brown & Wood advises major securities firms, sovereign and private issuers, borrowers and other participants on a broad range of public and private securities transactions in the US, Europe, Latin America and the Asia-Pacific region. The firm has been at the forefront of structuring and developing innovative securities and banking products and in structuring multi-jurisdiction and global equity and debt transactions. The firm's experience with debt and equity products and transactions enables it to provide efficient and effective legal services in the development

of new financial products and transactions, and in the execution of financial transactions generally.

Global venture and technology: The firm advises venture, technology and new economy clients on a wide variety of matters and transactions including angel and seed investments; venture capital financings; mergers and acquisitions; intellectual property, including patent, trademark and copyright law; and employment compensation and employment law.

Securitisation: The firm has vast experience in the development of asset securitisation programs, having first pioneered mortgage-backed securities in the 1970's, subsequently developing programs for credit card receivables, automobile loans and consumer loans. The firm is actively involved in the growing market for international securitisation programs, with securitisation specialists in each of its offices worldwide.

Pooled investment entities: The firm handles a broad range of legal developments in the area of investment companies and related pooled investment entities. Work handled includes counselling of funds and their directors and advisers, private investment entities, private swap-based structured note programs, and the development of other private offshore and onshore vehicles.

Tax: Brown & Wood advises financial institutions and corporations around the world on tax aspects of their securities transactions. Working with the firm's other practice areas, the tax group provides a full range of tax support to clients, including structuring debt and equity financings and asset-backed financings, compensation arrangements, restructurings, acquisitions, divestitures and tax-oriented investments.

M&A: Brown & Wood specialises in the structuring, negotiation and financing of a broad range of merger and acquisition transactions as well as in the design and implementation of structural defenses to unsolicited takeover proposals. It handles public company acquisitions (including the representation of special committees of independent directors), tender offers, privately negotiated transactions, auctions, proxy solicitation and various forms of related financings.

Litigation: Brown & Wood manages disputes on behalf of a wide variety of corporations and individuals in the world's financial markets including broker-dealers, issuers, underwriters, accountants, investment companies, partnerships and others. The firm specialises in securities litigation and contract disputes involving financial services and transactions, arbitration and mediation, employment litigation, corporate reorganisation and bankruptcy, anti-trust, intellectual property issues, tax disputes, governmental investigations and white collar crime.

Intellectual property: Brown & Wood advises US and foreign companies on patent, trademark, copyright, trade secret and computer law issues, and prepares and prosecutes patent and trademark applications for domestic and international clients.

Real estate: Brown & Wood represents a broad spectrum of clients in all major aspects of real estate activity, including development, financing, joint venture, and sales and leasing. The firm also advises owners, lenders and underwriters on sophisticated real estate capital markets transactions.

Private clients: Brown & Wood offers estate planning for both US and non-US individuals, utilising sophisticated techniques designed to effect tax-efficient transfers. The firm coordinates all aspects of global estate planning, along with pre-residency tax planning and expatriation, for both US and multinational families.

LANGUAGES: Chinese, French, German, Hebrew, Italian, Japanese, Korean, Norwegian, Portuguese, Russian, Spanish, Swedish

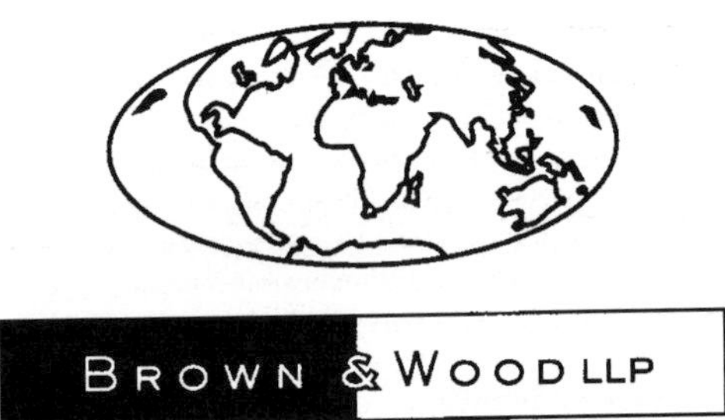

For other recommended firms see pages 1485-1520

BRUCHOU, FERNÁNDEZ MADERO, LOMBARDI & MITRANI

HEAD OFFICE

Ing. Enrique Butty 275 Piso 12°,
C1001 AFA Buenos Aires, Argentina
Tel: +54 11 5288 2300 **Fax:** +54 11 5288 2301

Email: bfmyl@bfmyl.com.ar
Website: www.bfmlym.com

Number of partners worldwide: 8
Number of other lawyers worldwide: 63

WORLDWIDE OFFICE CONTACTS

ARGENTINA
Ing. Enrique Butty 275 Piso 12°, C1001 AFA **Buenos Aires**
Tel: +54 11 5288 2300 **Fax:** +54 11 5288 2301
Email: estudio@bfmyl.com.ar

FIRM OVERVIEW

AREAS OF PRACTICE:

Antitrust	*%
Banking and finance	*%
Capital markets	*%
E-business	*%
Leasing	*%
Litigation	*%
M&A	*%
Project finance	*%
Public sector finance	*%
Restructuring	*%
Structured products and derivatives	*%
Tax	*%

* Workload % not disclosed

FIRM OVERVIEW: Founded in 1989, Bruchou, Fernández Madero, Lombardi & Mitrani is one of Argentina's leading business law firms. It frequently handles some of the largest and most complex transactions involving Argentine parties and/or local assets. During the 1990s the firm handled some of the largest privatisations carried out by the Argentine government. It also handled some of the largest international equity and debt offerings by Argentine private entities, and was involved in many of the largest mergers and acquisitions. The firm is well known for its work in M&A, project finance, secured lending transactions (including leveraged buy-out financings), securitisation, leasing and other forms of structured finance. In addition, the firm has been developing a specialist e-business service.

INTERNATIONAL CLIENTS: The firm's clients include major industrial and commercial companies from all business sectors; leading banks, financial institutions and professional firms; governments, public bodies and other organisations. These include Citibank N.A., Citigroup, Salomon Brothers, Chase Manhattan Bank, Bankers Trust/Deutsche Bank, Merrill Lynch, Goldman Sachs, Morgan Stanley, CS First Boston Group, Bear Stearns, Lehman Brothers, BankBoston, Bank of America, Banco Río de la Plata, Banco Frances, Banco de Galicia y Buenos Aires, Banco Nacional de México, Banco Bansud, HSBC Bank Argentina, Crédit Agricole, Société Générale, ING Bank, UBS, ABN Amro Bank, Rabobank, The Interamerican Development Bank, Standard & Poors, Perez Companc, Perez Companc Family Group, Techint Group, Algoma Steel Tubes, Confab Industrial, Dalmine SpA, NKKTubes, SIAT, Siderca, Sidor, Tubos de Acero de México, Tubos de Acero de Venezuela, Molinos Rio de la Plata, AT&T, Consolidar AFJP, La Nación, The Exxel Group, Lucent Technologies, Royal Ahold and Capex.

MAIN INTERNATIONAL AREAS OF PRACTICE:

Banking & finance: The firm regularly represents domestic and international financial institutions in the full scope of their lending activities, and has experience in secured and syndicated lending and acquisition finance. It recently acted for the Exxel Group to acquire Argentina's second-largest supermarket chain, with a US$220 million financing arranged by a group of banks led by Merrill Lynch and Bankers Trust. This was the first US-style LBO in the region. Since then, LBOs have become the most widely used structure in acquisition finance.
Project finance: The firm represented Citibank and CS First Boston as co-lead agents in the US$685 million financing of the Mega Project sponsored by YPF Petrobras and Dow Chemical. It also acted for Inter-American Development Bank and the Japan Exim-Bank, as financiers, and ING Barings, Bank of Tokyo-Mitsubishi and West LB, as arrangers, in the $450m AES Parana Project Financing for a new 826 MW gas-fired combined-cycle generation plant in Argentina. Both deals were the only two Latin American transactions awarded by "Project Finance" magazine as deals of the year, 1999.
Public sector finance: The firm has a substantial track record in public sector finance, particularly in structuring secured finance transactions for Argentine provinces and public sector entities. Members of the firm acted for the bank working committee in the implementation of the Republic of Argentina Brady Plan. The firm advises as underwriter counsel in almost every international bond offering made by the Republic of Argentina, and has a broad privatisation practice.
Capital markets: The firm represents both issuers and underwriters in local and international capital markets transactions, in structuring and implementing corporate bond offerings, MTN programmes, USCPs, global equity offerings, Yankee bonds, structured notes, high yield bonds, project bonds, FRNs, IPOs, tender offers and exchange offers. It also has a strong securitisations practice, acting both for arrangers and underwriters in a number of innovative local and international transactions.
Mergers & acquisitions: The firm was involved in many of the most significant transactions carried out in Argentina during the last decade, representing both sellers and buyers in the various industry sectors. In 1999, it participated in the structuring of a $13 billion tender for the entire capital stock of YPF, the first hostile takeover and the largest deal ever in Argentina.
E-business: The firm advises local and international investors and entrepeneurs in Internet-related deals, including start-ups, seed and angel financing, outsourcing, licensing agreements and strategic alliances. Many of its old-economy clients request the firm's assistance for the development of both B2C and B2B projects.
Restructuring: The firm has participated as bank counsel in many workouts involving Argentine companies and has broad experience dealing with standstill agreements, restructuring agreements, the structuring of applicable collateral packages and handling complex reorganisation and bankruptcy filings in court.
Litigation: The firm handles conflicts arising from its clients' corporate finance transactions before federal and provincial trial and appellate courts and administrative tribunals, and in arbitration and other alternative dispute resolution procedures. The head advisor was a judge and District Attorney of the Courts of Appeal for 25 years.

LANGUAGES: English, French, German, Italian, Portuguese, Spanish

BUGGE, ARENTZ-HANSEN & RASMUSSEN

HEAD OFFICE

Stranden 1A, PO Box 1524 Vika,
N-0117 Oslo, Norway
Tel: + 47 22 83 02 70 **Fax:** + 47 22 83 07 95

Email: post@ba-hr.no
Website: www.ba-hr.no

WORLDWIDE OFFICE CONTACTS

NORWAY
Stranden 1A, PO Box 1524 Vika, N-0117 **Oslo**
Tel: + 47 22 83 02 70 **Fax:** + 47 22 83 07 95
Email: post@ba-hr.no

FIRM OVERVIEW

Contact partners: Anders Eckhoff, Rolf Johan Ringdal

Number of partners worldwide: 27
Number of other lawyers worldwide: 68

AREAS OF PRACTICE:

Banking	*%
Capital Markets	*%
Competition law	*%
Debt financing	*%
IT & IP	*%
M&A	*%
Pharmaceuticals	*%

* Workload % not disclosed

B

FIRM OVERVIEW: The firm was established in 1966 as a specialised business law firm. Over the years through organic growth it has grown to 95 lawyers (27 partners, 68 associates), making it one of the largest law firms in Norway. The firm has developed a sophisticated practice as a leading Norwegian law firm in domestic and cross-border business law. The firm is a true partnership with the aim of providing high quality efficient and practical legal and strategic advice. The firm has developed international practice enjoys the benefits of close, although non-exclusive, co-operation with leading law firms in relevant jurisdictions.

INTERNATIONAL EXPERIENCE: The firm offers legal services to international clients with interests in Norway and abroad. The firm often manages major transactions and processes, involving co-operation and alignment with other professionals such as accountants, engineers and consultants. It frequently organises multi-jurisdictional legal teams, but keeps its international practice rooted in the domestic tradition.

INTERNATIONAL CLIENTS: The clients are predominantly large and medium-sized Norwegian and international companies within banking/finance, investment services, industry, trade, shipping, oil and gas, telecommunications, pharmaceuticals and IT. The firm also frequently acts for governmental bodies and agencies in relation to privatisations and conduct of business. It focuses on the business community and rarely acts for individuals or in criminal cases or non-business matters.

MAIN INTERNATIONAL AREAS OF PRACTICE: The firm provides services and assistance in the broad range of business law, with a particular focus on domestic and cross-border transaction work. A leading specialist presence within capital markets, M&A, debt financing and banking, is supplemented by a strong general practice as advisor to leading industrial companies, shipowners, insurance companies and oil and gas companies. The firm is frequently engaged in competition law matters, as well as IT, pharmaceutical law and intellectual property matters. The firm has expanded its litigation work and frequently acts before the regular courts and arbitration panels.

LANGUAGES: English, French, German, Norwegian

For other recommended firms see pages 1485-1520

BULL & CO ANS

HEAD OFFICE

Nedre Vollgt 4, PO Box 552 Sentrum,
0105 Oslo, Norway
Tel: +47 23 01 01 01 **Fax:** +47 23 01 01 11

Email: bull@bullco.no
Website: www.bullco.no

FIRM OVERVIEW

Managing partner: Bjørn Blix

Number of partners worldwide: 12
Number of other lawyers worldwide: 8

AREAS OF PRACTICE:
Company and commercial 50%
Intellectual property 35%
IT and telecoms 15%

FIRM OVERVIEW: Established in 1864, Bull & Co is a Norwegian law firm comprising 27 lawyers. The firm is particularly experienced in the fields of intellectual property , company and commercial, insolvency, competition and EU law, and is continually expanding in the field of IT and telecommunications. Bull & Co services a large number of foreign clients, and is a member firm of the Association of European Lawyers (AEL) and the Legal Network International (LNI).

INTERNATIONAL EXPERIENCE: Recent work includes acting for Reichhold Chemicals Inc (US) in its acquisition of Fotun Polymer Holdings AS.

MAIN INTERNATIONAL AREAS OF PRACTICE:
Intellectual property: The firm is one of the strongest in this field and has become actively involved in patent disputes within the pharmaceutical industry.
IT law: The firm has expanded its website with interactive legal services. Users of the internet can obtain formation of a limited liability company, formation of a partnership, the registration of Sole Proprietorship, as well as stock options and employment agreements.The firm has several new 'dot.com' clients and advises in the field of e-commerce.
Company and commercial: Recent work includes acting for German firm APCOA in the acquisition of Norwegian firm Europark, and for BMC Software in the international merger with Boole and Babbage.

LANGUAGES: Danish, English, French, German, Norwegian, Swedish

WORLDWIDE OFFICE CONTACTS

NORWAY
Nedre Vollgt 4, PO Box 552 Sentrum, 0105 **Oslo**
Tel: +47 23 01 01 01 **Fax:** +47 23 01 01 11
Email: bull@bullco.no

B

For other recommended firms see pages 1485-1520

BUSTAMANTE & BUSTAMANTE

HEAD OFFICE

Avenues Patria & Amazonas, Cofiec Building, 10th Floor, P.O. Box 17-01-02455
Quito, Ecuador
Tel: +593 2 562 680 **Fax:** +593 2 564 069

Email: bustamanteybustamante@bustamante.com.ec
Website: www.bustamanteybustamante.com

FIRM OVERVIEW

Managing partners: Juan Carlos Bustamante
José Rafael Bustamante

Number of partners worldwide: 13
Number of other lawyers worldwide: 12

AREAS OF PRACTICE:
Banking and finance ....*%
Corporate ....*%
Insurance and reinsurance ....*%
Intellectual property ....*%
Litigation and arbitration ....*%
M&A ....*%
Oil, energy and mining ....*%
Tax and labour ....*%
Telecommunications and computer law ....*%
* Workload % not disclosed

FIRM OVERVIEW: Established in 1956, Bustamante & Bustamante has been serving international corporate clients conducting business in Ecuador for more than forty years. It is a large firm with 13 senior partners, 12 associates and over 80 supporting staff members, all largely bilingual. The firm provides legal assistance on all corporate law areas including banking, insurance, mining, oil and gas, foreign investment, incorporation and administration of corporations, tax and labour advice; immigration, public procurement and various other legal services, including litigation. Bustamante & Bustamante has vast experience in the intellectual property field.

INTERNATIONAL EXPERIENCE: The firm maintains a system of co-operation with law firms throughout the Andean Pact subregion, which is particularly important for handling foreign investment and intellectual property matters. Bustamante & Bustamante is a member of MULTILAW, an association of independent law firms in private practice throughout the world, whose purpose is to aid members in serving their international clients, and of Bomchil, Castro, Goodrich, Claro, Arosemena & Associates, an association of Latin American law firms providing services to international clientele.

MAIN INTERNATIONAL AREAS OF PRACTICE: The firm handles a wide range of work covering various sectors. Some of these include banking and finance; corporate; insurance and reinsurance; intellectual property; litigation and arbitration; mergers and acquisitions; oil energy and mining; tax and employment; telecommunications and computer law.

LANGUAGES: English, French, Spanish

WORLDWIDE OFFICE CONTACTS

ECUADOR
Avenues Patria & Amazonas, Cofiec Building, 10th Floor, P.O. Box 17-01-02455, **Quito**
Tel: +593 2 562 680 **Fax:** +593 2 564 069
Email: bustamanteybustamante@bustamante.com.ec

ASSOCIATED OFFICES

SPAIN
Av. Maisonave 28 bis, 2da - oficina 8, E-03003 **Alicante**
Tel: +34 96 598 4004 **Fax:** +34 96 598 4004
Email: byl@arrakis.es

ASSOCIATED OFFICES

SPAIN
Av. Maisonave 28 bis, 2da - oficina 8, E-03003 Alicante

Managing partner: José Antonio López
Senior partners: José Rafael Bustamante, Thomas R. Schmuhl, Luis Giménez Guitard

Office profile: Bustamante & Bustamante, in association with Duane, Morris & Heckscher LLP, Lopez and the Bufete Gimenez Torres, established the firm Bustamante, Lopez, Duane, Morris & Gimenez Torres, in Alicante, Spain. Alicante is the European Unión headquarters for marks and designs, as well as the headquarters for the court responsible for the Union's trademark matters, with jurisdiction on all these issues related to the European Union.

For other recommended firms see pages 1485-1520

BUZESCU & CO

HEAD OFFICE

Splaiul Independentei 17, Bl. 101, Ap 57, Sector 5,
705011 Bucharest, Romania
Tel: +401 335 1366 **Fax:** +401 335 1735

Email: pblex@bx.logicnet.ro

WORLDWIDE OFFICE CONTACTS

ROMANIA

Splaiul Independentei 17, Bl. 101, Ap 57, Sector 5, 705011 **Bucharest**
Tel: +401 335 1366 **Fax:** +401 335 1735 WRONG
Email: pblex@bx.logicnet.ro

FIRM OVERVIEW

Managing partner: Petru Buzescu

Number of partners worldwide: 1
Number of other lawyers worldwide: 4

AREAS OF PRACTICE:

Admiralty .... *%
Anti-trust .... *%
Commercial .... *%
Foreign investment .... *%
Intellectual property .... *%
Joint ventures .... *%
M&A .... *%
Privatisation .... *%
Real estate .... *%
Tax .... *%
Telecommunications .... *%
* Workload % not disclosed

FIRM OVERVIEW: Buzescu & Co was founded by Peter Buzescu in 1992. The firm specialises in foreign investment, joint ventures, project finance, privatisation, M&A, anti-trust, tax, admiralty, intellectual property and real estate.

INTERNATIONAL EXPERIENCE: The firm has advised foreign companies investing in Romania since 1992.

INTERNATIONAL CLIENTS: The firm's clients include AB Electro-Invest; Amoco; ARCO; British American Tobacco; Becton Dickinson; Bell Helicopter Textron; Canadian Oxy Ltd; Chevron; The Coca-Cola Company; Colgate-Palmolive (US); Danisco Seed; Deloitte & Touche; Delta Air Lines; Drapantex BVBA; Efes; Elite International BV; EUnet International; Ferrero S.p.A.; Fin-Part S.p.A; Exxon; Forasol; General Electric; Glencore; The Greenbrier Companies; Heineken; Henkel Austria Gruppe; Hilton International; IKEA AG; Iguacu de Cafe Soluvel; Interamerican Hellenic Life Insurance; International Water Ltd; Jacobs Holdings Plc; Johnson Wax S.p.A; Jones Lang & Wootton; McDonald's; Medochemie Ltd; Merck Sharp & Dohme Idea Inc; Meubelfabrick De Toekomst BV; Mobil; Molino Holding S.A; Monsanto; Motorola International Network Ventures, Inc; National Foods; Ogden Services Corporation; Ozgorkey Group; Pak Holding A.S; Palsgaard Industry A/S; Price Waterhouse Ltd; Pratt & Whitney Canada Inc; Precision Castparts Corp; Roswell Navigation Corp; Schlumberger Petroleum Services CV; Sepulchre Luxembourg s.a.r.l.; Shell Aviation; Starion International; Tabacmesa S.A; Timken; Unilever Export B.V; Voest Alpine Intertrading GmbH; Whirlpool; Worldspan Services Limited; Yasar.

MAIN INTERNATIONAL AREAS OF PRACTICE: Work undertaken includes foreign investment, joint ventures, privatisations, M&A, anti-trust, tax, admiralty, intellectual property, real estate, telecommunications, and commercial.

LANGUAGES: English, French, Romanian

For other recommended firms see pages 1485-1520

BYAMUGISHA & RWAHERU ADVOCATES

HEAD OFFICE

East African Development Bank Building, 4 Nile Avenue, PO Box 9400
Kampala Uganda
Tel: +256 41 341898 **Fax:** +256 41 341898
Email: byam@africaonline.co.ug

WORLDWIDE OFFICE CONTACTS

UGANDA
East African Development Bank Building, 4 Nile Avenue,
PO Box 9400, **Kampala**
Tel: +256 41 341898 **Fax:** +256 41 341898
Email: byam@africaonline.co.ug

FIRM OVERVIEW

Partners: Joseph Byambara Byamugisha, Constantine Rwaheru

Number of partners worldwide: 2
Number of other lawyers worldwide: 2

AREAS OF PRACTICE:

Litigation and arbitration	40%
Banking and finance	30%
Corporate	10%
Intellectual property	8%
Securities and financial markets	6%
Tax	6%

FIRM OVERVIEW: Byamugisha & Rwaheru Advocates was established in 1974. Comprising two partners and two associate lawyers, the firm advises large companies, as well as individuals, on all aspects of Ugandan law. It also advises new and established foreign investors in Uganda. Byamugisha & Rwaheru Advocates specialises in banking, insurance and finance, trademarks and copyright, constitutional protection of property rights, conciliation and arbitration, debentures and IPOs for bonds and shares on the Uganda Securities Exchange, local and foreign investment, repatriation of capital, dividends, profits, and taxation. The firm is also actively involved in litigation in the High Court, Court of Appeal and the Supreme Court.

INTERNATIONAL EXPERIENCE: Byamugisha & Rwaheru Advocates has advised international development banks, international banks and other financing institutions on principal lending, as well as on lending agreements. The firm has also advised international development banks on bond issues on the local stock exchange; on IPOs for local companies where foreign investors were invited to participate; advised on foreign acquisition of local companies by foreign investors; advised the government and foreign investors on the privatisation of public corporations in Uganda. The firm has also handled trademark registration and protection proceedings for foreign companies. It has handled ICC and local arbitrations.

INTERNATIONAL CLIENTS: Byamugisha & Rwaheru Advocates clients include large companies, foreign investors, banks, and individuals.

MAIN INTERNATIONAL AREAS OF PRACTICE:
M&A: The firm has handled the merger and acquisition of interest by a foreign bank in a local bank and it also handled the general reconstruction and recapitalisations of the bank. It handled the acquisition of a subsidiary of a large foreign oil company by another foreign oil company. It has recently been advising both government and foreign investors on the privatisation of governmental parastals.
Banking and finance: The firm advises on all aspects of banking and finance including loan agreements and guarantees.
Intellectual property: The firm handles trademark registration, advising on infringement and passing off and handling protection proceedings.
Litigation and arbitration: The firm handles commercial litigation for foreign clients and conducts national and international arbitration, including ICC arbitration.
Corporate: The firm has drafted, and advised on, many international contracts for foreign clients or attorneys.

LANGUAGES: English, Luganda, Rukiga, Swahili

 For other recommended firms see pages 1485-1520

CÁRDENAS CASSAGNE & ASOCIADOS

HEAD OFFICE

Reconquista 360, Piso 6,
Buenos Aires, C 1003 ABH, Argentina
Tel: +54 11 4321 8000 **Fax:** +54 11 4325 5533

Email: ccasoc@ccas.com.ar
Website: www.ccas.com.ar

WORLDWIDE OFFICE CONTACTS

ARGENTINA
Reconquista 360, Piso 6, C 1003 ABH, **Buenos Aires**
Tel: +54 11 4321 8000 **Fax:** +54 11 4325 5533
Email: ccasoc@ccas.com.ar

SPAIN
Goya 15, 2do. Piso, 28001, **Madrid**
Tel: +34 91 577 9506 **Fax:** +34 91 781 1402
Email: ccasmadrid@trc.es

FIRM OVERVIEW

Senior partners: Emilio J. Cárdenas, Juan Carlos Cassagne

Number of partners worldwide: 20
Number of other lawyers worldwide: 46

AREAS OF PRACTICE:

Administrative and environmental .... *%
Banking, finance and capital markets .... *%
Corporate and business law .... *%
Employment and labour .... *%
Energy, natural resources and mining .... *%
Litigation .... *%
Taxation .... *%
Telecommunication law .... *%
* Workload % not disclosed

FIRM OVERVIEW: The firm is the product of the 1991 merger of three prominent Buenos Aires law firms. The firm offers a full range of legal services to corporate and individual clients, both domestic and international. In 2000 CC&A opened a representative office in Madrid.

INTERNATIONAL EXPERIENCE: CC&A is actively involved in handling international transactions. The structural reforms implemented in Argentina during the last decade have resulted in drastic changes in the political, financial and legal arenas. These changes have led to the deregulation and privatisation of various sectors of the economy. Consequently, foreign and domestic investments were significantly fostered and the firm's lawyers have played an active role in the legal structuring of new private ventures.

INTERNATIONAL CLIENTS: The firm's international client base covers a wide range of sectors including telecommunications, energy, mining, industrial, finance, banking, waste and water, food and beverage, transport and dredging.

MAIN INTERNATIONAL AREAS OF PRACTICE:

Administrative and environmental law: The firm acts for corporations and individuals with federal, provincial and municipal administration matters. CC&A offers services in particular, to corporations in relation to the government's intervention in the economy, in such matters as governmental technical regulations, police power and public utilities regulatory frameworks.

Banking, finance and capital markets: CC&A's banking practice offers advice to investment and commercial banks on product development and regulatory matters. It advises issuers and underwriters on the conversion of cash-generating assets into marketable securities and Argentine Government Bonds, and covers a full scope of tax, litigation and other support services. CC&A has been actively involved in debt/equity financing in relation to the privatisation process that took place in Argentina. Since the mid-1980s the firm has represented domestic and foreign banks, in the rescheduling of public debt and the issuance of bonds placed by the Republic of Argentina in international markets.

Corporate and business law: The firm provides legal services to domestic and foreign companies in structuring commercial transactions. CC&A has handled some of the most notable mergers and acquisitions to take place in the last decade, acting as counsel to purchasers and sellers, both in Argentina and overseas. Work handled has covered practically all areas of industry including oil, banking, food, chemicals, transportation, communications, e-commerce, energy, utilities and services. Recently, the firm has developed specialisation in the hotel industry, a business that has recently experienced a boom in Argentina. CC&A also offers legal advice on anti-trust law.

Tax: The firm's tax department provides expert advice on all tax matters arising from conducting business in Argentina. This includes all aspects of federal, provincial, local and international tax planning for foreign and domestic business entities and individuals.

Energy, natural resources and mining: The firm has been particularly active in the deregulation process taking place in the energy industry (oil, gas and electricity). It has been involved in most of the international public bids carried out to date. The firm's client base includes leading international and local mining companies. In addition, the firm has had an active and successful participation in the privatisation process of mining deposits owned by the State.

Litigation: The firm represents clients, both as plaintiffs and defendants, in cases heard in federal and provincial courts. It has a broad network of correspondent lawyers in the provinces, enabling it to offer legal services in all provincial jurisdictions, in a prompt and efficient manner.

Emloyment and social security: The firm's employment department advises corporate clients, on all issues related to employment and social security law. It also advises on all matters arising from mergers, privatisations and shutdowns. The firm also advises on employment contracts, employment of foreign personnel and related immigration issues, retirement plans and additional benefits.

Telecommunications: The firm has been particularly active in this area advising on the introduction of the cellular phone system to the Argentine telecommunications market. It has also advised shareholders with interests in the recently privatised telephone companies. The firm's telecommunications department also offers advice on Internet related issues.

LANGUAGES: English, French, Italian, Portuguese, Spanish

For other recommended firms see pages 1485-1520

CAREY LANGLOIS

HEAD OFFICE

PO Box 98, 7 New Street,
St. Peter Port, Guernsey GY1 4BZ, Channel Islands
Tel: +44 1481 727272 **Fax:** +44 1481 711052

Email: info@careylanglois.com
Website: www.careylanglois.com

FIRM OVERVIEW

Managing partner: John Greenfield
Senior partner: John Langlois

Number of partners: 7
Number of other lawyers: 15

AREAS OF PRACTICE:

Banking and finance	*%
Captive insurance	*%
Commercial property	*%
Corporate and commercial	*%
Litigation	*%
Matrimonial and probate	*%
Private client, trust and tax planning	*%
Securitisation	*%

* Workload % not disclosed

FIRM OVERVIEW: Established in 1898, the firm is a member of both Lex Mundi and the Association of European Lawyers. It undertakes contentious and non-contentious work especially in the investment funds, banking, financial services and private client fields. It also has the only dedicated trust department and independent trust company, Carey Langlois Trust Company Limited.

INTERNATIONAL EXPERIENCE: The firm acts for a significant number of institutional clients, based both in Guernsey and internationally, who are involved in large multi-jurisdictional transactions. The firm is able to provide a round-the-clock service on international deals. Recent work includes acting for one of the largest non-life and life reassurance groups in the world, advising on and establishing a Guernsey-based structure to raise up to US$1 billion by the issue of zero coupon convertible bonds on the Luxembourg Stock Exchange. The bonds have been assigned an AAA rating by Standard & Poor.

INTERNATIONAL CLIENTS: Include large multinational companies, banks based both in Guernsey and elsewhere, insurance companies and wealthy individuals seeking expert tax planning.

MAIN INTERNATIONAL AREAS OF PRACTICE:

Banking and finance: Work covers all areas of banking and finance, including securitisation, listing on the Channel Islands Stock Exchange and other exchanges, guarantees, structured finance, leasing and other loan transactions.

Corporate and commercial: The firm advises on a wide range of corporate and commercial transactions. It also specialises in M&A, acting in smaller private acquisitions and increasingly in large cross-border acquisitions and takeovers.

Securitisation: The firm can advise on securitisation issues, and can also administer them through its trust company. It also has its own in-house listing sponsor.

Captive insurance: Carey Langlois formed the first captive insurance company in Guernsey in 1922. The firm is active in new developments in the captive insurance industry, such as the use of protected cell companies.

Litigation: The department offers a full range of litigation advice encompassing asset tracing, insurance, banking, funds litigation and trust litigation. The firm has Guernsey's only dedicated injuction team, and has been involved in a large number of high-value injunctions and disclosure applications.

Private client, trust and tax planning: Clients include a number of major institutional trust providers and law firms in many jurisdictions. Particular specialities include pension trusts and employee benefit trusts. The firm also provides tax and estate planning advice to individual international clients.

Matrimonial and probate: The firm provides matrimonial advice to any international clients with assets in Guernsey and elsewhere. It also provides probate advice and executorship services to a wide range of international clients.

Commercial property: Clients include many high-profile international property groups.

LANGUAGES: English, French, German

WORLDWIDE OFFICE CONTACTS

CHANNEL ISLANDS

PO Box 98, 7 New Street, St. Peter Port, **Guernsey** GY1 4BZ
Tel: +44 1481 727272 **Fax:** +44 1481 711052
Email: info@careylanglois.com

CAREY LANGLOIS
—— ADVOCATES AND NOTARIES PUBLIC ——

For other recommended firms see pages 1485-1520

CAREY Y CIA

HEAD OFFICE

Miraflores 222, Floor 24,
Santiago 65 00 786, Chile
Tel: +56 2 365 7200 **Fax:** +56 2 633 1980

Email: info@carey.cl
Website: www.carey.cl

WORLDWIDE OFFICE CONTACTS

CHILE
Miraflores 222, Floor 24, **Santiago** 65 00 786
Tel: +56 2 365 7200 **Fax:** +56 2 633 1980
Email: info@carey.cl

FIRM OVERVIEW

Senior partner: Jorge Carey
Managing partner: Diego Peralta

Number of partners worldwide: 13
Number of other lawyers worldwide: 70

AREAS OF PRACTICE:

Banking, finance and capital markets	25%
Corporate and commercial	25%
Energy and infrastructure	10%
Litigation and arbitration	10%
Mining	10%
Tax	10%
Telecommunications, e-commerce and internet	10%

FIRM OVERVIEW: Founded in 1905, Carey y Cia is one of Chile's largest law firms. In the last 20 years the firm has expanded significantly to meet the needs of international business clients especially in the banking, finance and capital market sectors. Careys also advises clients operating in Chile's expanding internet and e-commerce industry. The firm is a member of the Pacific Rim Advisory Council (a strategic alliance of independent law firms serving major international clients) and Terralex (a network of international firms specialising in international matters).

INTERNATIONAL EXPERIENCE: In recent years Careys has been involved in the majority of the most significant transactions in Chile. The firm has advised on major international banking and financial deals including bond and eurobond issues, initial primary offerings, securities, structured finance, lending and cross border lending, pensions and insurance, project financing (especially in relation to mining, fisheries and forestry) and asset leasing. It has also advised on acquisitions, mergers, take-overs, joint ventures, corporate reconstructions, employment, intellectual property, retail law, competition and anti-trust matters. Careys has acted on the deregulation and the acquisition of interests in the electricity and water industries, and advised on the financing of power plants and road concessions. It also advises leading telecommunication service providers and acts on behalf of internet and e-commerce start-ups and backers.

INTERNATIONAL CLIENTS: The firm's clients include ABN Ambo Bank NV, American Express Co, Banco Santander, BankBoston NA, Bank of America NA, Biwater SA, Blue Circle Plc, Boeing Corporation, Chase Manhattan Bank, Codelco, Deutsche Bank, EntelChile SA, GlaxoWellcome PLC, HSBC Bank Plc, ING Group, Motorola, National Grid Plc, The Home Depot Inc, The Pillsbury Company, and UBS AG.

MAIN INTERNATIONAL AREAS OF PRACTICE:

Banking, finance and capital markets: The firm handles all banking, finance, and capital markets related work, specialising in bond and Eurobond issues. During 2000 the firm advised Banco BNP Paribas, Dresdner Bank AG, JP Morgan Securities and Salomon Brothers International Limited on a US$1 billion Eurobond issue for Enersis electricity and a US$1 billion Eurobond issue for Endesa electricity. Also in 2000, Careys advised Chase Manhattan Bank International Limited on a bond issue by the Republic of Uruguay for sale in the USA to Chilean investors.

Corporate and commercial: The firm handles a range of corporate and commercial related work including M&A, joint ventures, corporate reconstructions, employment, intellectual property, retail law, competition and anti-trust. Careys represented the Finnish Danisco in the sale of fishing interests in Chile to the Norwegian Statkorn Holding ASA for US$90 million and to a local group for an undisclosed amount. The firm also advised on the merger between Igemar (owned by the Angelini Group and the largest fishing company in Chile) and Pacific Protein's fishing business in Chile for a combined book value of US$125 million. Careys represented Statkorn Holding ASA in an agreement to purchase Salmones Mainstream SA for an approximate US$140 million, and acted on behalf of the Canadian Silvagen Inc (now Celfor Inc) in the formation of Genfor SA, a joint venture with Fundación Chile for the development of a forest biotechnology business in the Southern Cone of South America. In the health industry, the firm handled the merger between Banmedica and the Penta group for a combined value of US$300 million.

Energy and infrastructure: Careys has advised the Chilean Government on the privatisation of ESVAL, the Chilean water utility. It also represented the Swedish investor Skanska and the Spanish investor Dragados in their successful bid to build a US$500 million toll road and its subsequent financing with international lenders.

Mining: The firm advised Aur Resources of Canada on the financing of its purchase of a controlling interest in the Chilean copper producer Quebrada Blanca (approximate value US$190 million) and on the subsequent refinancing of Quebrada Blanca's external debt.

Telecommunications, e-commerce and internet: Careys represented National Grid Plc in its investment of US$80 million in Telefonica Manquehue and in its investment, of an undisclosed amount, in Southern Cone Communications (a broadband network linking Argentina and Chile).

LANGUAGES: All lawyers are bilingual in English and Spanish. Other languages spoken include French, German and Japanese.

CARIOLA DIEZ PEREZ-COTAPOS Y CIA LTDA

HEAD OFFICE

Avenida Andres Bello 2711, 19th Floor, Las Condes
Santiago Chile
Tel: +56 2 360 4000 **Fax:** +56 2 360 4030
Email: cariola@cariola.cl
Website: www.cariola.cl

FIRM OVERVIEW

Senior partner: Sebastián Obach
Number of partners worldwide: 11
Number of other lawyers worldwide: 45

AREAS OF PRACTICE:

Banking and finance .... *%
Corporate .... *%
Employment .... *%
Energy and public utilities .... *%
Environmental .... *%
Insurance .... *%
Intellectual property .... *%
Litigation and arbitration .... *%
M&A .... *%
Media, telecommunications and e-commerce .... *%
Mining .... *%
Tax .... *%
* Workload % not disclosed

C

FIRM OVERVIEW: Cariola Diez Perez-Cotapos y Cia Ltda is one of Chile's leading law firms. The firm specialises in industry, banking, international trade, communications, international transportation, and large-scale mining issues. It comprises lawyers with postgraduate qualifications from US law schools and professional experience in major US and UK law firms.

INTERNATIONAL EXPERIENCE: The firm advises foreign companies operating in Chile or entering into joint venture operations with Chilean companies. Work handled includes corporate and tax issues, foreign investment and financial matters, foreign exchange regulations, intellectual property, and anti-trust. The firm also advises a number of foreign investors, foreign banks and financial institutions carrying out financial transactions and/or structuring project financing in Chile.

INTERNATIONAL CLIENTS: The firm's clients include large and medium size companies and corporations, banks, financial institutions, governments, and multilateral agencies.

MAIN INTERNATIONAL AREAS OF PRACTICE:

General corporate: The firm handles a range of general corporate work including preparing, drafting, and execution of contracts and agreements such as purchase agreements, leasings, incorporation of companies and corporations, loan agreements, constitution of guarantees, labour agreements, and board resolutions and general shareholders meetings.
M&A: The firm handles corporate, tax, finance, litigation, anti-trust, and employment issues. It advises on the preparation of acquisition strategies and purchase offers, tender offers, analysis of contingencies, preliminary purchase agreements, negotiation and drafting of the purchase contracts, shareholder agreements, preliminary approvals, and structuring financing and guarantees.
Mining: The firm represents the largest mining corporations and projects in Chile, and has advised foreign companies undertaking prospecting activities, acquisition of mining properties, project finance, joint venture agreements, option agreements, mining exploitation agreements, and incorporation of mining companies.
Finance: The firm advises banks and financial institutions on financial laws and regulations in Chile, and assists in the preparation and execution of term sheets, loan agreements, project financing, underwriting and other financial transactions. It has represented investment banks in equity placements in Chile and abroad, including ADR programs and debt placements, private placements, Yankee Bonds and Eurobonds.
Tax: The firm advises on a range of tax issues including corporate, personal and salaried personnel income tax, sales tax or VAT, stamp taxes, and real estate taxes. The firm handles tax strategies in company restructures, tax contingencies arising from M&A transactions, foreign capital contributions. The firm also represents clients before Chilean tax authorities in obtaining tax exemptions and rulings, tax refunds and the application of special tax regimes.
Employment: The firm undertakes the preparation of labour contracts with foreign personnel and work permits for expatriates, the filing and prosecution of Central Bank's authorisation for the payment of wages in foreign currency, and the remittance of social security payments to foreign pension funds.
Litigation: The firm advises on civil, commercial, white collar, criminal and labour cases. The firm has also engaged in a range of administrative proceedings including anti-trust, tax, municipal, environmental, and consumer protection matters. Its arbitration practice handles arbitration proceedings before international arbitrators and local arbitration of business disputes.
Energy and public utilities: The firm has advised foreign and domestic corporations within the energy and water sectors on the structuring of joint ventures in the construction stage of projects, management agreements and privatisation of state owned power plants and utilities. It advises on production, transportation and distribution of power, and regulations applicable to water companies and companies involved in gas transportation and distribution.
Media and telecommunications: The firm has acted as local counsel for foreign telecom companies investing in local companies, and in the structuring of joint ventures. It has advised several companies in acquiring or selling important interests in domestic telecoms and has also assisted the main local telecom company in negotiating foreign joint ventures and performing investments in foreign markets. The firm has also advised on the purchase of important assets and companies, including a private television project.
Insurance: The firm advises foreign insurance companies on the structuring of contracts and insurance policies necessary to comply with Chilean insurance regulations including life insurance plans, civil liability, life annuities and liability insurance to third parties. It has also participated in the structuring of life insurance and retirement plans for corporate clients in Chile. Cariola Diez Perez-Cotapos y Cia Ltda also reviews risk coverage in civil liability, including general liability against damage to property, arson, aircrafts, ships and cargo liabilities.
E-commerce: The firm supports leading Internet start up companies, in relation to the establishment and operation of B2B and B2C websites. It has advised investment banks and other investors in the financing of Internet companies and assisted them in drafting various contracts related to e-business.

LANGUAGES: English, French, German, Italian, Spanish

WORLDWIDE OFFICE CONTACTS

CHILE
Avenida Andres Bello 2711, 19th Floor, Las Condes, **Santiago**
Tel: +56 2 360 4000 **Fax:** +56 2 360 4030
Email: cariola@cariola.cl

For other recommended firms see pages 1485-1520

CARLOS AGUIAR, P. PINTO & ASSOCIADOS

HEAD OFFICE

Avenida da Liberdade, N 200-4° Esq, 1250-147 Lisbon,
Lisbon, Portugal
Tel: +351 2 1355 2755 **Fax:** +351 2 1355 2756

Email: cappa@mail.telepac.pt

WORLDWIDE OFFICE CONTACTS

PORTUGAL
Avenida da Liberdade, N 200-4° Esq, 1250-147 Lisbon, **Lisbon**
Tel: +351 2 1355 2755 **Fax:** +351 2 1355 2756
Email: cappa@mail.telepac.pt

FIRM OVERVIEW

Managing partner: Carlos Aguiar

Number of partners : 3
Number of other lawyers: 9

AREAS OF PRACTICE:

Corporate and commercial 45%
Banking and finance 30%
Employment law and industrial relations 15%
Commercial litigation and arbitration 10%

FIRM OVERVIEW: Founded at the beginning of 1995, the firm has concentrated on all major areas of corporate and business law and has strengthened its practice in banking and finance. It also maintains close contacts with firms based in Europe and the United States.

INTERNATIONAL EXPERIENCE: The firm advises multinational and Portuguese companies in their business dealings in Portugal. It is actively involved in cross-border deals, project finance for Portuguese motorways and the acquisition by foreign clients of financial stakes in partially privatised companies and other major Portuguese companies.

INTERNATIONAL CLIENTS: The firm's clients comprise large and medium sized foreign companies, from countries such as the UK, France, the US, Spain, the Netherlands, Canada, Belgium, Germany and Switzerland. Clients' activities cover a wide range of sectors including banking and financial services, telecommunications, e-commerce, engineering, construction, public works and real estate, cement, mining, textiles, media and advertising, office equipment, distribution, optics, food processing, healthcare and cosmetics.

MAIN INTERNATIONAL AREAS OF PRACTICE:
Corporate and commercial: The firm provides general corporate advice, mergers and acquisitions and the constitution of joint ventures and restructuring operations.
Banking and finance: The firm acts as local counsel to Portuguese, Spanish, French and American banks and financial institutions. It is currently advising major Spanish and French companies in the concession and project finance involved in the construction of motorways in Portugal. The practice also covers syndicated loan transactions, guarantees, leasing and securitisation.
Employment law and industrial relations: The firm has been involved in collective dismissal proceedings, as well as industrial relations matters.
Commercial litigation and arbitration: The firm represents clients in civil, commercial, labour and administrative litigation. Members of the firm have represented clients in arbitration proceedings.

LANGUAGES: English, French, Portuguese, Spanish

For other recommended firms see pages 1485-1520

SOCIEDADE DE ADVOGADOS CARLOS OLAVO E ASSOCIADOS

HEAD OFFICE

Avenida Sidónio Pais. n.º 10- 5º Dto,
1050- 214 Lisbon, Portugal
Tel: +351 21 3171390 **Fax:** +351 21 3153673

Email: olavolex@mail.telepac.pt

WORLDWIDE OFFICE CONTACTS

PORTUGAL
Avenida Sidónio Pais. n.º 10- 5º Dto, 1050- 214 **Lisbon**
Tel: +351 21 3171390 **Fax:** +351 21 3153673
Email: olavolex@mail.telepac.pt

FIRM OVERVIEW

Managing partner: Isabel Magalhães Olavo
Senior partner: Carlos Olavo

Number of partners worldwide: 2
Number of other lawyers worldwide: 2

AREAS OF PRACTICE:
Banking and finance 30%
Corpoarte and commercial 30%
Intellectual property and copyright 30%
Other 10%

C

FIRM OVERVIEW: Founded in 1985, Sociedade de Advogados Carlos Olavo e Associados comprises two partners and two associates. It is a small niche firm that provides a full range of legal services, specialising in corporate, banking, financial, and intellectual property matters.

INTERNATIONAL EXPERIENCE: The firm has advised several foreign firms setting up business in Portugal, and advised Portuguese and foreign firms in cross-border transactions. It is member of the International Chamber of Commerce, the Chambre de Commerce et d' Industrie Luso-Francaise, the American Chamber in Portugal, and the Clube de Empresários do Brasil.

INTERNATIONAL CLIENTS: The firm's international clients include companies seeking advice in corporate, banking, finance and industrial property matters.

MAIN INTERNATIONAL AREAS OF PRACTICE:
Corporate and commercial: The firm advises national and foreign companies on all investment and corporate matters. It specialises in the structuring of foreign investment enterprises.
Intellectual property: The firm advises on infringement disputes, license agreements and other aspects of intellectual property. Its senior partner, who chaired the Annual Meeting of ECTA held in Lisbon, is a Portuguese and European patent and trademark attorney and member of the Consultative Boards of the Portuguese Industrial Property National Institute (INPI) and of the Portuguese Foundation for the National Scientific Computation (FCCN).
Banking and finance: The firm covers all aspects of banking and finance including incorporating banking and finance companies and assisting with licensing their operations. It handles secured and syndicated loan transactions and guarantees, structured finance, project finance, and securities.
Litigation and arbitration: The firm handles with commercial litigation and national and international arbitration. It operates under the rules of the International Chamber of Commerce.

LANGUAGES: English, French, Portuguese, Spanish

For other recommended firms see pages 1485-1520

CARLOS OSÓRIO DE CASTRO, EDUARDO VERDE PINHO, JJ VIEIRA PERES

HEAD OFFICE

Avda da Boavista 3265, 5.2, Edificio Oceanus,
4100 137 Porto, Portugal
Tel: +351 22 616 6950 **Fax:** +351 22 616 3810

FIRM OVERVIEW

Managing partner: Eduardo Verde Pinho

Number of partners: 5
Number of other lawyers: 14

AREAS OF PRACTICE:

M&A, securities, construction and tourism	20%
Banking and finance	15%
Corporate	15%
Tax	15%
Telecommunications and computer law	15%
EU and competition	5%
Marketing law	5%

WORLDWIDE OFFICE CONTACTS

PORTUGAL
Av. Eng. Duarte Pacheco, Amoreiras, Torre 2, 17°, 1070-102 **Lisbon**
Tel: + 351 21 3825810 **Fax:** + 351 21 3825819
Email: advogadoslx@castropinhoperes.pt

Avda da Boavista 3265, 5.2, Edificio Oceanus, 4100 137 **Porto**
Tel: +351 22 616 6950 **Fax:** +351 22 616 3810
Email: advogados@castropinhoperes.pt

ASSOCIATED OFFICES

PORTUGAL
A.M. Pereira, Sáragga Leal, Oliveira Martins, Júdice & Associados, Avenida da Liberdade, 224, 1250 - 148 **Lisbon**

C

FIRM PROFILE: Established in 1989, Carlos Osório de Castro, Eduardo Verde Pinho e J.J. Vieira Peres - Sociedade de Advogados is one of the most renowned law firms in northern Portugal with five senior partners, thirteen associates and seven trainees. The firm has strong academic ties and currently nine of its members lecture in prestigious universities in Oporto, Lisbon and Coimbra. The firm's areas of practice include commerce and trade law, mergers and acquisitions, securities, capital markets, taxation, finance, EU and competition, corporations, real estate, construction and tourism, consumer, insurance, employment, energy, telecommunications, administrative law and litigation. In addition to their practice, the senior partners have taken an active role in shaping Portuguese legislation. António Lobo Xavier is considered to be one of the country's leading tax experts and Carlos Osório de Castro was a member of the drafting committee of the new Portuguese Securities Code.

INTERNATIONAL EXPERIENCE: The firm has advised in several M&A transactions and in the establishment of foreign companies in Portugal, as well as in other forms of foreign investment. It has also been involved in major international projects concerning industrial investments, energy and telecommunications. These include incorporation of companies, shareholders agreements, operation and maintenance, construction, financing (recourse and non-recourse) and tax planning.

INTERNATIONAL CLIENTS: The firm's clients include some of the largest private companies, natural gas, telecommunications and construction companies as well as banks.

MAIN AREAS OF PRACTICE:

Corporate: The firm has advised on investment and business matters to both national and foreign companies and aided in the structuring of foreign investments enterprises. These include equity and contractual joint ventures, wholly foreign-owned enterprises and holding companies.

M&A: Over the past few years, the firm has had extensive involvement in the acquisition and restructuring of Portuguese businesses and has set up both market and off-market operations. The firm's strong business connections and history has lead to the specialisation of many of the lawyers in this area.

Tax: António Lobo Xavier has established a solid reputation in the various aspects surrounding tax law and has trained his team to advise on the tax structure for financial operations, acquisitions of companies, corporate restructuring and international transactions for resident and non-resident companies.

Financial and capital markets: The firm regularly advises residents and non-residents of their duties before the Portuguese Capital Market Regulatory Authorities. Past experiences have included initial public offerings, take-overs, mergers and privatisation. Carlos Osório de Castro is a nationally renowned name in this area both at an academic and professional level. The firm also covers the main areas of banking and finance including syndicated loan transactions and guarantees, structured finance, project finance and tax.

EU and competition: The firm regularly advises some of the most important Portuguese groups on anti-trust matters, both at the national and European levels. The firm is currently involved in several cases before the European Court of Justice.

Energy and telecommunications: The firm is the legal adviser to three of Portugal's gas distributors. It handled the legal aspects of the launching of a GSM operator, a new fixed line operator and internet portal including licensing and all business development aspects.

Public and administrative law: The firm advises clients on various areas of public law including public tenders and construction and concessions contracts as well as energy and public utilities matters.

Real estate, construction and tourism: Experience covers a wide range of matters such as infrastructure projects, construction and engineering contracts, property zoning, building and commercial leases and various chain restaurant and hotel businesses seeking to establish franchises in Portugal.

Consumer law and marketing law: The firm has a solid background in all aspects of consumer law and product liability matters, including regulatory issues and consumer disputes.

Employment: The firm has aided its corporate clients in handling a wide rage of employment related issues and the practice is growing steadily.

LANGUAGES: English, French, German, Italian, Portuguese, Spanish

CARNELUTTI STUDIO LEGALE

HEAD OFFICE

Via Principe Amedeo, 3,
20121 Milan, Italy
Tel: +39 02 655 851 **Fax:** +39 02 655 855 85

Email: carnelutti@carnelutti.com
Website: www.carnelutti.com

FIRM OVERVIEW

Managing partner: Luca Arnaboldi
Senior partner: Marino Bastianini

Number of partners worldwide: 13
Number of other lawyers worldwide: 62

AREAS OF PRACTICE:

M&A	25%
Banking and corporate finance	15%
General corporate and commercial	15%
Media, broadcasting and telecommunications	15%
Litigation and arbitration	10%
Real estate	10%
Tax	10%

WORLDWIDE OFFICE CONTACTS

FRANCE
Cabinet Carnelutti, 6 Avenue George V, 75008 **Paris**
Tel: +33 1 47 23 31 81 **Fax:** +33 1 47 20 25 09

ITALY
Via Principe Amedeo, 3, 20121 **Milan**
Tel: +39 02 655 851 **Fax:** +39 02 655 855 85
Email: carnelutti@carnelutti.com

Viale Gramsci, 14, 80122 **Naples**
Tel: +39 081 761 4277 **Fax:** +39 081 680 176
Email: naples@carnelutti.com

Piazza Eremitani, 18, 35121 **Padua**
Tel: +39 049 8774890/8756225 **Fax:** +39 049 8783705/663061
Email: padua@carnelutti.com

Via Parigi 11, 00185 **Rome**
Tel: +39 06 4620241 / 473901 **Fax:** +39 06 48906285 / 4819833
Email: studio@carneluttirome.com

C

FIRM OVERVIEW: The firm, founded by Francesco Carnelutti, offers its services on a wide range of corporate, financial, commercial and dispute resolution matters, with an organisation comprising more than 150 partners and associates in Italy. Carneletti has an extensive and international practice with offices in Milan, Rome, Padua, Naples and Paris and contacts include lawyers practising in most other commercial centres throughout the world. Through its organisation of offices the firm provides an effective service to companies and institutions of all types and sizes in the new global economy. The firm offers a comprehensive and wide range of legal services in several areas of practice, including international business law and corporate and financial transactions, advising international and Italian clients operating abroad.

INTERNATIONAL EXPERIENCE: Carnelutti has expertise in advising international and transnational transactions, having advised both Italian and non-Italian clients in connection with crossborder transactions. It has experience in advising on international mergers and acquisitions, international joint ventures, cross-border transactions, media and telecommunications, project finance and tax planning. The firm's international capabilities are strengthened by its network of affiliated offices and by correspondence relationships with leading law firms in all the major countries.

INTERNATIONAL CLIENTS: The firm advises and represents major international industrial and financial players, including media, entertainment and telecommunications of a large range of nationalities particularly in Europe, North America and Asia.

MAIN INTERNATIONAL AREAS OF PRACTICE

M&A: The firm handles transactions and projects such as mergers and acquisitions through the purchase of stocks or the purchase of assets including MBO and LBO, joint ventures, Stock Exchange and Consob regulatory requirements.

General corporate and commercial: Work includes corporate reorganisations and assistance in the negotiating and drafting of contracts. The firm has considerable experience in the protection of shareholders' rights and interests in private and public companies, and in advising on proxy voting.

Banking and corporate finance: Work includes public offerings and leveraged buyouts; public offerings and public tender offers; organisation of companies licensed to provide financial services, organisation of project finance, banking, securities and finance, capital markets, domestic and international loans.

Media, broadcasting and telecommunications: The firm advises major international and domestic companies. It is a leading law firm in Italy and has expertise in the media, telecommunications, television and entertainment industry.

Real estate: The firm handles a variety of property related transactions, providing services to investors, developers, land-owners, tenants and lenders in relation to industrial, commercial and personal properties and is regularly involved in the acquisition of real estate portfolios.

Tax: The firm's tax department provides a complete service, including local and international tax planning, tax litigation and general advice on tax aspects related to national and international matters.

Litigation and arbitration: The department represents clients in all the Italian courts, as well as in national and international arbitration.

Other areas: The firm also advises on entertainment, intellectual property, advertising and marketing competition, employment, real estate, sports law, chemistry and life sciences, energy and EU law (particularly through its Paris office).

LANGUAGES: English, French, German, Italian, Spanish

For other recommended firms see pages 1485-1520

CASTRÉN & SNELLMAN

HEAD OFFICE

Erottajankatu 5 A, PO Box 233,
FIN-00130, Helsinki, Finland
Tel: + 358 9 228 581 **Fax:** + 358 9 601 961

Website: www.castren.fi

WORLDWIDE OFFICE CONTACTS

FINLAND
Erottajankatu 5 A, PO Box 233, FIN-00131 **Helsinki**
Tel: + 358 9 228 581 **Fax:** + 358 9 601 961
Email: firstname.surname@castren.fi

Ylistönmäentie 31, 40500 **Jvyäskylä**
Tel: +358 14 445 1590 **Fax:** +358 14 445 1591
Email: firstname.surname@castren.fi

RUSSIA
24 Nevsky Prospekt, 3rd Floor, 191186 **St Petersburg**
Tel: + 7 812 325 8085 **Fax:** + 7 812 325 8086
Email: firstname.surname@castren.fi

FIRM OVERVIEW

Managing partner: Pekka Jaatinen
Senior partner: Pekka Sirvio

Number of partners worldwide: 15
Number of other lawyers worldwide: 31

AREAS OF PRACTICE:

Mergers and acquisitions	25%
Banking and finance	20%
Insolvency	15%
EU and competition	15%
Litigation & arbitration	10%
Corporate	4%

FIRM OVERVIEW: Founded in 1888, Castrén & Snellman is the oldest law firm in Finland. Its growth has been particularly rapid in the past decade, with both domestic and international M&A projects playing a significant role. Since Finland joined the European Union, the firm has been involved in competition law and international arbitration, but capital markets work including international securities offerings currently form the bulk of its international work. Finance and securities assignments range from listings to various loan arrangements and project financing. The firm, which has represented international financial institutions in capital markets projects in the Baltic States and Russia, also has an office in St Petersburg. The branch office of Castrén & Snellman Attorneys at Law in Jyväskylä was opened on 1 February, 2000 to offer high quality legal services to companies located in Central Finland.

INTERNATIONAL EXPERIENCE: M&A projects and corporate finance work are at present the main elements of the firm's international practice. Major deals and transactions over the last couple of years have included advisng in the re-organisation of the group structure combined with a sale of shares and listing of HPY Holdings/Helsinki Telephone, a major telecom operator, and the privatisation and listing of Sonera, a state owned telecom company. The firm also advised, among others, on the formation of Fortum (the merger of state-owned energy companies Neste and Ivo), and in the various capital market transactions of Neptun Maritime, a shipping company.

INTERNATIONAL CLIENTS: Castrén & Snellman represents several multinational companies and financial institutions from all over the world with interests in Finland. International clients are advised on all aspects of business law.

MAIN INTERNATIONAL AREAS OF PRACTICE:

Mergers and acquisitions: The increasing interest in buying Finnish companies is reflected in the firm's growing M&A department, which handles both Finnish and international transactions. Castrén & Snellman has experience in drafting comprehensive international acquisition agreements, but the firm also cooperates with other international law firms in this regard.

Insolvency: The recession in the early 1990s led to thousands of bankruptcies and restructurings. The firm's lawyers have acted in several notable cases as receivers, administrators of the estate or representatives of the creditors.

Litigation and arbitration: Many of Castrén & Snellman's lawyers have acted as members and chairmen of Finnish and international courts of arbitration, giving the firm a broad background in dispute resolution.

Banking, finance and securities: The firm handles banking and corporate finance projects, as well as securities-related matters. It has also represented international financial institutions in capital markets projects in the Baltic States and Russia. Services include stock exchange listings and related issues, cross-border leasing and a range of investment services matters (securities brokerage, assets management etc).

Competition: Since Finland's entry into the European Union, the firm has regarded competition law as an important part of its services. The firm helps its clients take preventative measures in the preparation and drafting of agreements, recommends measures to eliminate hidden risks and represents them in proceedings before Finnish and EU authorities.

Contract Law: Castrén & Snellman prepares and reviews agreements ranging from employment contracts to extensive acquisition documents.

Corporate: The firm assists its clients with all stages of their structural and operational development, including general and limited partnerships.

Other areas: Include IT, IP, marketing law and employment.

LANGUAGES: English, Estonian, Finnish, French, German, Italian, Russian, Swedish

CASTRÉN & SNELLMAN

C

CASTRO SUEIRO & VARELA

HEAD OFFICE

Alcalá, 75-1°,
Madrid 28009, Spain
Tel: +34 91 577 5020 **Fax:** +34 91 431 5931
Email: csueiroy@idecnet.com

WORLDWIDE OFFICE CONTACTS

SPAIN
Alcalá, 75-1°, 28009, **Madrid**
Tel: +34 91 577 5020 **Fax:** +34 91 431 5931
Email: csueiroy@idecnet.com

FIRM OVERVIEW

Managing partners: Juan Carlos Castro, Miguel Sueiro , José Ramon Varela

Number of partners worldwide: 3
Number of other lawyers worldwide: 14

AREAS OF PRACTICE:

Banking, finance and capital markets	25%
General corporate	15%
Insurance	15%
M&A	15%
Litigation	10%
Telecommunications	10%
Aviation	5%
Tax	5%

C

FIRM OVERVIEW: Founded in 1987 by three lawyers with a variety of legal experience, the firm specialises in providing global legal advice to business clients, mainly foreign and multinational companies. Each case is entrusted to one of the firm's partners, who then works together with one or more assistant lawyers specialising in the subject concerned. The firm is independent, but is a member of the Statecapital international law group and the European group Insurolaw.

INTERNATIONAL EXPERIENCE: The firm has advised on a large number of international transactions, particularly in banking, insurance and M&A. It advises foreign investors on the law on exchange control and foreign investment as it affects the establishment of subsidiaries and branches, the acquisition of Spanish companies, investment on the stock exchange and the acquisition of property. It also advises Spanish clients on the possibilities and means of investing abroad.

INTERNATIONAL CLIENTS: 60% of the firm's clints are international. These come principally from other EU countries and the United States, and from the banking, insurance and computer sectors.

MAIN INTERNATIONAL AREAS OF PRACTICE:
M&A: The firm has been involved in the acquisition of one of the largest European Television producers by a spanish company; sale of the third largest printing group in Spain to a foreign company; acquisition of one of the most important food distribution comapny; merger of three distribution companies.
Banking, financing and capital markets: The firm has been involved in a large number of financing transactions during the last year. It has advised a Spanish lease company in the financial lease of three oil tanker vessels for an oil company; it has structured the first three financial tax lease transactions for vessels made in Spain under the new regulation. The firm has advised banks in the financing of vessels for an amount of US$300 million; it has advised banks in other projects such as windfarms and motorways. The firm is working for a european agency that finances European transport infrastructure.
Insurance: The firm advises foreign insurance companies (either life insurance or various general insurance businesses) operating in Spain through branches and subsidiaries or under the freedom to provide services regime. It also acts for leading private insurance brokers. Recently it has advised the largest USA insurance company covering nuclear risks.
Telecommunications: The firm has a specialised team dedicated to this field. It advises an American company that is a member of the consortium that has obtained one of the three licences for the establishment and exploitation of a public network for nationwide fixed wireless broadnet radio access by the Spanish government. It has also advised on two complex transactions related to cable TV and to the transfer of a Spanish internet business to a foreign European listed company.
Aviation: The firm has a high profile in this area and is currently advising the sponsors of the future first international private airport in Spain. The firm recently advised leasing companies in the acquisition and lease of several aircrafts.
Tax: The firm offers comprehensive advice on personal income tax, corporate tax, tax planning for non-residents, international and cross-border tax issues, the tax implications of property transactions, VAT and tax proceedings of all kinds.
Litigation: The department advises on, institutes and defends clients in proceedings including debt recovery, insolvency proceedings, contractual litigation and enforcement of foreign judgments.

LANGUAGES: Arabic, English, French, Italian, Spanish

 For other recommended firms see pages 1485-1520

CAVELIER ABOGADOS

HEAD OFFICE

Edificio Siski, Carrera 4 No 72-35, Bogota 8, Colombia
Tel: +571 347 3611 **Fax:** +571 217 9211

Email: cavelier@colomsat.net.co
Website: www.cavelier-abogados.com

WORLDWIDE OFFICE CONTACTS

COLOMBIA
Edificio Siski, Carrera 4 No 72-35, **Bogota** 8
Tel: +571 347 3611 **Fax:** +571 217 9211
Email: cavelier@colomsat.net.co

FIRM OVERVIEW

Managing partner: Emilio Ferrero
Administrative partner: Germán Cavelier

Number of partners worldwide: 7
Number of other lawyers worldwide: 27

AREAS OF PRACTICE:

Banking	*%
Business law and contracts	*%
Foreign investment	*%
Intellectual property	*%
Internet and IT	*%
Health registrations	*%
M&A	*%

* Workload % not disclosed

FIRM OVERVIEW: Founded in 1953, Cavelier Abogados combines experience and innovation and is active in several fields of law. The firm's lawyers have degrees from Colombia and abroad and the firm places particular emphasis on legal training. The application of technology in the form of its multilingual library and legal databases allows the firm to keep up to date with legal developments.

INTERNATIONAL EXPERIENCE: In Latin-America the firm is among the leaders in obtaining pre-trial interpretations from the Andean Court of Justice, and is a promoter of the development of patents and trademarks law. The firm advises companies, individuals and non-profit entities worldwide.

INTERNATIONAL CLIENTS: The firm advises a large volume of clients covering a wide range of sectors in various jurisdictions.

MAIN AREAS OF PRACTICE:
Litigation: The firm handles civil and administrative work before the local courts, appellate courts, Supreme Court of Justice, constitutional courts and Council of State.
Andean community law: The firm advises Andean group countries including Bolivia, Ecuador, Peru and Venezuela on commercial law, industrial property, intellectual property, and litigation.
Industrial and intellectual property: The firm advises on patents, utility models and designs, industrial secrets, genetic resources, plant varieties, trademarks and service marks, slogans, commercial names, trade emblems and denominations of origin. It also handles copyright, software and transfer of technology.
Information technology: The firm advises on domain name registration, e-mail contracts and electronic commerce contracts.
International public law: The firm handles litigation in international courts, acting for governments, private companies and individuals.
Business law: The firm advises on all commercial contracts including sale, leasing, rentals, representation, distribution, consignment, supply, loans and consulting.
Corporate: The firm advises local companies and branches of foreign companies on legal management and maintenance.
Health regulation: The firm handles issues in relation to human, animal and plant products.

LANGUAGES: English, French, Spanish

CAVELIER
ABOGADOS

For other recommended firms see pages 1485-1520

ČECHOVÁ RAKOVSKÝ

HEAD OFFICE

Hurbanovo nám. 5,
811 03 Bratislava, Slovakia
Tel: +421 7 5441 4441 **Fax:** +421 7 5443 4598

Email: cechrak@internet.sk
Website: www.cechrak.sk

WORLDWIDE OFFICE CONTACTS

SLOVAKIA
Hurbanovo nám. 5, 811 03 **Bratislava**
Tel: +421 7 5441 4441 **Fax:** +421 7 5443 4598
Email: cechrak@internet.sk

FIRM OVERVIEW

Managing partner: Katarína Čechová

Number of partners worldwide: 4
Number of other lawyers worldwide: 5

AREAS OF PRACTICE:
Antimonopoly .... *%
Banking and finance .... *%
Civil .... *%
Commercial and business law .... *%
Corporate .... *%
Corporate and project financing .... *%
M&A .... *%
* Workload % not disclosed

C

FIRM OVERVIEW: Čechová Rakovský was founded over ten years ago. It is a commercial law firm with considerable international experience and a large client base. Comprising four partners, the firm provides high quality legal advice. It has advised international and domestic clients on a number of commercial transactions ranging from standard deals to complicated transactional structures.

INTERNATIONAL EXPERIENCE: Čechová Rakovský has a well-established international reputation. It provides a wide range of legal services, and is able to compete on an international scale. The majority of the firm's clients are foreign companies or their local subsidiaries or branches. Recently, the firm has been involved in a number of significant foreign investments in the Slovak Republic.

INTERNATIONAL CLIENTS: The firm's client base includes banks, financial institutions, and large and medium-sized international and multinational companies involved in diverse areas of industry and services. Clients are located in Western and Central Europe, North America, Asia, and Australia.

MAIN INTERNATIONAL AREAS OF PRACTICE:
Banking and finance: Čechová Rakovský advises a number of foreign banks and financial institutions on syndicated loans to Slovak corporations (private companies, partially state owned companies or local banks). It also advises on various banking and finance structures and has handled some of the largest syndicated loans to take place in the Slovak Republic. The firm also assisted the managers on the number of Eurobond issues, some of which were the first transactions of such nature in the Slovak Republic.
Project finance: Čechová Rakovský has handled the restructuring of financial schemes in connection with a number of proposed acquisition transactions. Recently the firm has advised co-ordination committees of international and local banks in successful financial restructuring and reorganisation of the largest steel producer in Slovakia.
M&A: Čechová Rakovský has handled a number of transactions, advising its clients on acquisition of shares and other ownership participation in local companies, as well as mergers and joint ventures. The firm has also been involved in a range of privatisation transactions including the acquisition of shares in a monopoly telecommunication operator, a large Slovak bank, a major industrial electronics corporation, a mechanical product manufacturer, and a leading international lime producer.
Corporate: The firm has handled a number of standard and non-standard corporate matters and procedures including corporate financing, advising either local subsidiaries of multinationals on local legal matters or multinationals in connection with a local subsidiaries establishment, operation or acquisition.
Antimonopoly: Čechová Rakovský handles all matters related to Slovak antimonopoly law, including representing its clients in front of the Slovak Antimonopoly Office.

LANGUAGES: Czech, English, Russian, Slovak

For other recommended firms see pages 1485-1520

ADVOKATFIRMAN CEDERQUIST KB

CONTACT OFFICE

Nybrokajen 15, PO Box 1670,
111 96 Stockholm, Sweden
Tel: + 46 8 463 65 00 **Fax:** + 46 8 678 01 70

WORLDWIDE OFFICE CONTACTS

SWEDEN

Nybrokajen 15, PO Box 1670, 111 96 **Stockholm**
Tel: + 46 8 463 65 00 **Fax:** + 46 8 678 01 70
Email: advokat@cederquist.se

FIRM OVERVIEW

Managing partner: Lars Johansson

Number of partners worldwide: 16
Number of other lawyers worldwide: 19

AREAS OF PRACTICE:

Corporate/M&A	30%
Intellectual property and media	15%
Litigation and arbitration	15%
Banking and finance	10%
IT and telecommunications	10%
EU and competition	10%
Others	10%

FIRM OVERVIEW: Founded in Stockholm in 1953, Advokatfirman Cederquist represents a wide range of Swedish and international clients, for whom it provides both general corporate advice on a regular basis and specialist advice in connection with particular business transactions or litigation matters. The majority of clients are corporations, partnerships, trade organisations, government entities, banks and other financial institutions.

INTERNATIONAL EXPERIENCE: Major international deals and transactions handled by the firm include acting as legal adviser in a number of corporate acquisitions of Swedish companies on behalf of foreign corporations, investment banks and law firms, as well as acquisitions of companies outside Sweden in Scandinavia, UK, US, Western and Eastern Europe and other parts of the world on behalf of Swedish companies. The firm acts as legal adviser on behalf of foreign corporations, entities, organisations, funds, investment banks and law firms in all areas of practice in Sweden. It also handles all kinds of legal matters on behalf of Swedish companies abroad.

INTERNATIONAL CLIENTS: The firm's international clients include leading business corporations and major foreign companies within areas such as banking, media, IT, transportation, entertainment, heavy industry and pulp and paper, as well a governmental entities, supranational institutions, banks and other financial instituations.

MAIN INTERNATIONAL AREAS OF PRACTICE:
M&A: The firm represents major foreign companies in their acquisitions and divestments of Swedish companies, and Swedish clients in sales and acquisitions of foreign companies.
Company and commercial: The firm is frequently retained in major company law matters. It handles privatisation of governmental agencies or state/municipal companies and restructuring and mergers in the private sector.
Corporate finance, banking and insurance: The firm draws on its internal expertise and its broad network of external cooperation partners throughout Europe and around the world.
Intellectual property: Work includes copyright, trademarks, design rights and patent rights. The firm has a long history of representing leading companies in industries in which intellectual property law is particularly important.
Computer/IT: The firm frequently represents clients who are newly active on the IT and telecommunications markets. Its experience in intellecual property law ensures a thorough understanding of the developments affecting IT companies.
EU/competition: Competition law has become an area of increasing focus as Sweden's competition legislation has radically changed as a result of adaptation to EU rules. The firm advises on national and international legislation with regard to such things as acquisitions and distributorship agreements.
Litigation and arbitration: The firm's lawyers are retained as arbitrators and counsel in arbitration proceedings concerning both Swedish and foreign disputes.
Employment: The firm advises, assists and represents clients in all aspects of employment law, including employment contracts, business transfer agreements and complicated legislation arising from staff reductions, incorporation, mergers and so on.
Tax: The firm's tax department deals with all types of national and international corporate tax issues. In transactions between Swedish and foreign entities it also cooperates with a network of foreign lawyers with regard to, inter alia, the interpretation and application of double taxation treaties. Advice is provided to Swedish and foreign companies, municipalities, foundations and non-profit organisations and also to private individuals.
Public procurement: The firm advises on contractual aspects regarding the acquisition of various types of goods and services. It has been retained as adviser on public procurement legislation and related subjects in foreign countries - notably in Eastern Europe - by the World Bank and governments concerned.

LANGUAGES: English, French, Swedish

ADVOKATFIRMAN
CEDERQUIST

For other recommended firms see pages 1485-1520

CERHA HEMPEL & SPIEGELFELD

HEAD OFFICE

Parkring 2,
A-1010 Vienna, Austria
Tel: +43 1 514 350 **Fax:** +43 1 514 35 35

Email: chs@chs.at
Website: www.chs.at

FIRM OVERVIEW

Senior partner: Karl Hempel
Contact partner: Edith Hlawati

Number of partners worldwide: 18
Number of other lawyers worldwide: 26

AREAS OF PRACTICE:
Equity and debt offerings .... *%
Litigation and arbitration .... *%
M&A .... *%
Privatisations .... *%
Project finance .... *%
Real estate .... *%
Telecommunications and IT .... *%
* Workload % not disclosed

WORLDWIDE OFFICE CONTACTS

AUSTRIA
Parkring 2, A-1010 **Vienna**
Tel: +43 1 514 350 **Fax:** +43 1 514 35 35
Email: chs@chs.at

BELGIUM
Avenue Louise, 65, 1050 **Brussels**
Tel: +32 2 535 77 11 **Fax:** +32 2 535 77 00
Email: chs@chs.at

HUNGARY
Buday László u. 12., H-1024 **Budapest**
Tel: +36 1 438 31 11 **Fax:** +36 1 438 31 13
Email: chs@chs.at

FIRM OVERVIEW: Founded in 1921, Cerha Hempel & Spiegelfeld is one of Austria's largest law firms. Comprsing 18 partners and 26 associates, the firm has two members admitted as New York attorneys, one associated attorney professor, and one associated attorney admitted in Hungary.

INTERNATIONAL EXPERIENCE: In the last year the firm has advised on various cross-border M&A transactions for Austrian and international clients, IPOs and secondary offerings (including the IPO of Telekom Austria), several cross-border facility lease transactions, restructurings of entities held by the Republic of Austria for the preparation of privatisations, and various debt restructurings.

INTERNATIONAL CLIENTS: Cerha Hempel & Spiegelfeld represents international clients in M&A, banking and finance, capital markets, real estate, telecommunications and information technology, energy and public law. The firm's clients are national and international banks, major publicly listed or other large and medium sized entities, investment and real estate funds, telecommunication and information technology companies and the Republic of Austria.

MAIN INTERNATIONAL AREAS OF PRACTICE:
M&A and corporate: Work handled includes strategic planning of M&A transactions, due diligence, a range of corporate transactions (including optimisation and tax driven restructurings), setting up of companies, corporations and partnerships, mergers, demergers, and spin-offs.
Privatisations: The firm advises on the restructuring of entities held by the Republic of Austria by way of spin-offs or any other corporate measure, and the sale of shares by way of controlled auctions or IPOs.
Banking and finance: Work handled includes general banking matters, structured financings and securitisation issues, cross-border facility and QTE leases, settlement terms for the new stock exchange, and investment funds (distribution and compliance).
Capital markets: The firm advises on IPOs and secondary offerings (including dual listings on the NYSE/Vienna Stock Exchange and Neuer Market), and pan-European and international offerings involving Austrian capital markets law aspects.
Telecommunications and IT: Cerha Hempel & Spiegelfeld advises the Austrian telecommunications operator on interconnection agreements, interconnection pricing, unbundling procedures, frequency allocation and licenses applications. It also advises Austrian and international investment and commercial banks on cross-border rendering of electronic banking and capital markets services.
EU and competition: The firm handles all work relating to large scale M&A cross border transactions such as compliance matters, merger control, state aid and public procurement issues.
Real estate: Cerha Hempel & Spiegelfeld advises investment and development companies on the acquisition of real estate, particularly office buildings, shopping malls and hotels. It also advises on project management (including acquisition of property and financing), due diligence, tax structuring issues, review of lease and other related agreements.
Litigation and arbitration: Members of the firm act as arbitrators, conciliators and mediators under the rules of the Austrian Federal Economic Chamber, in ICC and in ad hoc arbitrations; advice to national and international clients in all kinds of large scale business disputes.

LANGUAGES: Croatian, English, French, German, Hungarian, Italian, Russian, Spanish

C

For other recommended firms see pages 1485-1520

CERNEJOVÁ AND HRBEK

HEAD OFFICE

Kycerského 7, 811 5 Bratislava
Slovakia
Tel: +421 7 5244 4019 **Fax:** +421 7 5244 2650

Email: chplaw@chplaw.sk

WORLDWIDE OFFICE CONTACTS

SLOVAKIA
Kycerského 7, 811 5 **Bratislava**
Tel: +421 7 5244 4019 **Fax:** +421 7 5244 2650
Email: chplaw@chplaw.sk

FIRM OVERVIEW

Partners: Alena Cernejová, Milan Hrbek Peter Stavrovsky

AREAS OF PRACTICE:

Corporate 35%
Banking and finance 20%
Competition law 20%
Mergers and acquisitions 20%
Litigation and arbitration 5%

FIRM OVERVIEW: Founded in 1992 as a partnership, Cernejová and Hrbek has considerable international experience and a large client base. The firm provides high standards of service advising international and domestic clients on Slovak law, varying from standard deals to complicated transactional structures and from ad hoc advice to ongoing legal assistance.

INTERNATIONAL EXPERIENCE: The firm advises foreign clients on banking transactions, commercial and corporate matters including corporate finance, mergers & acquisitions, operations on banking and financial and capital markets in the Slovak Republic.

INTERNATIONAL CLIENTS: The firm's client base includes large corporations in various industry sectors and banks.

MAIN INTERNATIONAL AREAS OF PRACTICE:
Banking and finance: The firm has experience in banking debt transactions and advises foreign banks and financial institutions on syndicated and other loans to Slovak borrowers, including securing of such loans under Slovak law, or any other forms of financing.
Corporate: The firm has extensive experience advising on standard and non-standard corporate matters and procedures.
Litigation and arbitration: Members represent the clients before the court and arbitration authorities in the Slovak Republic.
Mergers and acquisitions: The firm advises foreign clients on the acquisition of Slovak entities in various forms, including acquisitions in the privatisation process and acquisitions of assets or shares. The firm also advises on transactions involving the due diligence process as well as structuring the legal means of an acquisition.
Competition law: The firm deals with mergers within the acquisition process. Cernejová and Hrbek represent clients before the Slovak anti-monopoly authorities. In addition it represents clients in matters of negative clearances with respect to agreements restricting competition.

LANGUAGES: English, Slovak

CHANCERY CHAMBERS

HEAD OFFICE

Chancery House, High Street,
Bridgetown Barbados
Tel: +1 246 431 0070 **Fax:** +1 246 431 0076
Email: chancery@caribsurf.com

FIRM OVERVIEW

Principal: Trevor A. Carmichael, QC

Number of staff worldwide: 25

AREAS OF PRACTICE:

Arbitration .... *%
Banking and finance .... *%
Charities (international and local) .... *%
Corporate .... *%
Insurance and reinsurance .... *%
Intellectual property .... *%
M&A .... *%
Telecommunications and IT .... *%
* Workload % not disclosed

WORLDWIDE OFFICE CONTACTS

BARBADOS
Chancery House, High Street, **Bridgetown**
Tel: +1 246 431 0070 **Fax:** +1 246 431 0076
Email: chancery@caribsurf.com

USA
17th Floor, 300 Park Avenue, **New York**
Tel: +1 212 572-4832 **Fax:** +1 212 572-6499

FIRM OVERVIEW: Founded in 1977, the firm maintains contacts with various firms worldwide and offers a comprehensive legal service to clients with international business interests. It focuses on banking and finance, mergers and acquisitions, insurance and reinsurance, international development consulting and domestic as well as international charities, and environmental law.

INTERNATIONAL CLIENTS: The firm's client base includes large companies, banks, insurance companies and public or supranational institutions conducting cross-border business, as well as some national governments.

MAIN INTERNATIONAL AREAS OF PRACTICE:

M&A: The firm's transactions in this area range from small private acquisitions to cross-border takeovers of listed companies.
Banking and finance: Chancery Chambers covers all areas of banking and finance, including secured and syndicated loan transactions and guarantees structured finance, project finance, leasing and tax-based finance.
Insurance and reinsurance: The demutualising and restructuring of insurance groups as well as the setting up of captive insurance companies and related transactional work are all undertaken by the firm.
Intellectual property: The firm specialises in trademarks, patents, and copyrights. Its lawyers participate in the negotiation of license agreements and advise on infringement disputes and other aspects of IP law.
Economic development consulting: The firm advises governments, regional and international organisations as well as development banks. It provides legal consulting services to these entities and works on feasibility and pre-feasibility studies.
Telecommunications and IT: The firm advises on all aspects of this area.
Charities law: The firm represents many international charities and is actively engaged in the work of local charities and the advising of charities with international connections.
Marketing law: Clients range from large multinationals to local enterprises, and the firm has substantial experience in dealing with marketing guidelines, consumer disputes, regulatory issues and producer liability matters.
Arbitration: Chancery Chambers deals with commercial litigation, national and international arbitration, and alternative dispute resolution.
Environmental law: The firm advises domestic and international clients on a full range of environmental matters including assistance with environmental impact assessments and statements.
Employment: The firm handles all matters relating to Barbados employment law.
Securities and financial markets: Chancery Chambers advises clients on Barbados law pertaining to funds, securities and derivatives. It also assists investment firms structure and license their operations.

LANGUAGES: English, French, Hindi, Mandarin, Spanish, Swedish

For other recommended firms see pages 1485-1520

CHANDLER & THONG-EK LAW OFFICES

HEAD OFFICE

Bubhajit Building, 7th Floor, 20 North Sathorn Road,
Bangkok 10500, Thailand
Tel: +66 2 266 6485 **Fax:** +66 2 266 6483

Email: chandler@ctlo.com
Website: http://ctlo.com

FIRM OVERVIEW

Founding partner: Albert T. Chandler
Senior partner: Niwes Phancharoenworakul
Managing partner: Ratana Poonsombudlert

Number of partners worldwide: 8
Number of other lawyers worldwide: 24

AREAS OF PRACTICE:

Banking and project finance	20%
Corporate and acquisitions	15%
Major investment projects	15%
Energy, petroleum and minerals	10%
International business transactions	10%
Restructuring	10%
Dispute resolution	5%
E-commerce	5%
Government contracts and tax	5%
Securities	5%

FIRM OVERVIEW: Chandler & Thong-ek was established in 1974 by Albert T. Chandler. The firm currently has eight partners, 23 associates, one foreign consultant and over 50 non-professional staff. It handles Thai business and finance matters and represents a number of major Thai and international clients in a wide range of investment projects and financial transactions. Taking account of commercial considerations, the firm advises on tax issues, regulatory and other legal matters.

INTERNATIONAL EXPERIENCE: The firm deals with a range of legal and administrative issues arising from cross-border transactions, delivery of services and financial transactions. These include exchange control, tax, licensing, customs, and intellectual property issues. The firms advises Thai clients on foreign investment transactions, utilising a network of lawyers in foreign jurisdictions including all leading financial centres.

INTERNATIONAL CLIENTS: Clients comprise international companies from the banking, finance, petroleum, minerals and energy sectors. Major foreign corporate clients include Phelps Dodge Corporation, Heinz, Kimberly Clark, McDonald, Seagate Technology, Volvo, Allegiance Healthcare and Solvay. Major restructuring works include CMIC, Finance One, Feul Pipeline Transportation, One Holding, Ital-hai, Nikko Hotel, Siam Yamaha, TT&T, Thai Tank Terminal, Aromatics, Sri Racha Harbour, Siam Strip Mill, PTK Metal, and Central Trading.

MAIN INTERNATIONAL AREAS OF PRACTICE:

Energy, petroleum and minerals: Chandler & Thong-ek specialises in energy and natural resource matters. It advises international agencies and Asian governments on mineral policy and legislation.
The firm has experience with business transactions in Lao PDR, Myanmar, Nepal and Vietnam. It advised the lenders on the 'operating alliance' between Star Petroleum Refining Co Ltd and Rayong Refinery (1999) and currently advises the Petroleum Authority of Thailand on its joint development project with Petroliam Nasional Berhad, the national oil company of Malaysia, in connection with a US$1 billion project to construct, own and operate the Trans-Thailand-Malaysia Pipeline. The project includes the establishment of a gas separation plant in the Songkhla province of Thailand.
Banking and project finance: The firm advises on all aspects of banking and finance. It is lead counsel to lenders of Ratchaburi Electricity Generating Co Ltd, which is acquiring a 3, 645MW power plant from EGAT. The firm also advises the lenders of Eastern Power and Electric Co Ltd (third IPP to achieve financial close in Thailand). The firm was the Thai legal advisor to the Financial Sector Restructuring Authority (FRA) in connection with the sale of all core asset programmes of 56 suspended finance companies.
E-commerce: The firm recently established an e-commerce group to follow the development of law and policy in Thailand relating to e-commerce and information technology.
Tax: The firm advises on tax planning for Thai projects including shareholders, officers, and EPC contractors, and is familiar with the numerous tax treaties to which Thailand is party. The firm has close links with the leading international accounting firms in Thailand, which assist in providing responsive and comprehensive advice on Thai tax issues.
Corporate and acquisitions: The firm handles all types of company registration, M&A reorganisation and liquidation work, and peforms corporate secretarial work for over 200 Thai limited companies. It advises on the registration of branch offices of foreign corporations, representative offices, regional offices, applications for US Treaty protection, and conversions to public limited companies.
Employment: The firm advises on all aspects of employment law including the employment of aliens in Thailand, work permits, visas, and related government approvals. The firm published an English translation of the Labour Protection Act which came into force in August 1988, and the Alien Business Operation Act which came into force in March 2000.
Restructuring: The firm represents creditors, creditor committees and debtors in due diligence work and restructuring of corporate debt, and advises on reorganisation proceedings under the amended Bankcruptcy Act and under CDRAC. The firm published an English translation of the amended law 1999, and co-published *Restructuring Eurobond Debt in Thailand.*
Dispute resolution: The firm represents clients in a number of Thai courts and in arbitration proceedings. It has substantial experience in the resolution of construction industry disputes, enforcement of foreign arbitration awards, and arbitration under the rules of the Arbitration Office of the Ministry of Justice.

LANGUAGES: English, French, Japanese, Lao, Thai

WORLDWIDE OFFICE CONTACTS

THAILAND
Bubhajit Building, 7th Floor, 20 North Sathorn Road, **Bangkok** 10500
Tel: +66 2 266 6485 **Fax:** +66 2 266 6483
Email: chandler@ctlo.com

ASSOCIATED OFFICES

MYANMAR
Suite 106, International Business Center, 88 Pyay Road, 6 1/2 Miles, Hlaing Township, **Yangon**
Tel: +95 1 650 740 **Fax:** +95 1 650 466
Email: MyanmarLegal@mptmail.net.mm

C

For other recommended firms see pages 1485-1520

CHANG SEE HIANG & PARTNERS

HEAD OFFICE

9 Temasek Boulevard #15-01, Suntec Tower 2,
Singapore 038989, Singapore
Tel: +65 339 9949 **Fax:** +65 338 0500

Email: all@cshnp.com.sg

WORLDWIDE OFFICE CONTACTS

SINGAPORE
9 Temasek Boulevard #15-01, Suntec Tower 2, **Singapore** 038989
Tel: +65 339 9949 **Fax:** +65 338 0500
Email: all@cshnp.com.sg

FIRM OVERVIEW

Senior partner: Chang See Hiang

Number of partners worldwide: 5
Number of other lawyers worldwide: 5

AREAS OF PRACTICE:

Commercial ....*%
Corporate ....*%
Corporate banking ....*%
Corporate finance and planning ....*%
Foreign investments ....*%
Joint ventures ....*%
M&A ....*%
Property ....*%
Stocks and securities ....*%
Tax ....*%
* Workload % not disclosed

C

FIRM OVERVIEW: Founded in 1996 by Mr Chang See Hiang, the firm specialises in corporate finance, commercial and securities work. Comprising 10 fee-earners, the firm has remained small for strategic reasons. The firm's senior partner has been active in the corporate, commercial and securities sectors for more than 23 years.

INTERNATIONAL EXPERIENCE:
The firm has experience in international public offers and regional cross-border corporate and commercial transactions. Some of the firm's lawyers are qualified to practice and have practical experience in other jurisdictions such as Malaysia.

INTERNATIONAL CLIENTS: The majority of the firm's clients are listed on the Singapore Exchange. It advises clients from a range of industries including technology, info-communications, media and publishing, healthcare, food and beverage, shipping, plantation, property development, hotel ownership, securities brokerage, and financial services.

MAIN INTERNATIONAL AREAS OF PRACTICE:
Corporate finance and securities: The firm specialises in corporate finance. It plays a prominent role in Singapore's corporate, commercial and securities transactions, with experience in a range of transactions including takeovers, mergers and acquisitions, initial public offers, and other fund raising exercises. The firm has acted for clients in their initial public offers and placement exercises (domestic and international), as well as on a number of takeovers, mergers and acquisitions (including the takeover of a securities trading firm). The firm has acted as Singapore counsel to the offerers on international initial public offers and placement exercises.

Commercial and joint ventures: The firm handles corporate restructurings and reorganisations, tax issues, joint ventures, and investments in Singapore and regionally. It has advised on a number of major corporate restructurings and reorganisations. The firm has also handled due diligence work on a number of major corporations in Singapore.
Property: The firm advises on conveyancing and property development, and specialises in corporate conveyancing transactions. It has also acted for clients on acquisitions and disposals of commercial properties.

LANGUAGES: English, Malay, Mandarin

For other recommended firms see pages 1485-1520

CHAO AND CHUNG

HEAD OFFICE

2601-5, Asia Pacific Finance Tower, Citibank Plaza, 3 Garden Road, Central
Hong Kong
Tel: +852 2820 7555 **Fax:** +852 2537 5454

Email: office@chaoandchung.com

WORLDWIDE OFFICE CONTACTS

HONG KONG
2601-5, Asia Pacific Finance Tower, Citibank Plaza, 3 Garden Road, Central, **Hong Kong**
Tel: +852 2820 7555 **Fax:** +852 2537 5454
Email: office@chaoandchung.com

FIRM OVERVIEW

Senior partner: Tien-yo Chao

Number of partners worldwide: 2
Number of other lawyers worldwide: 8

AREAS OF PRACTICE:

Corporate .... *%
M&A .... *%
Direct investment .... *%
Regulatory compliance .... *%
*Workload % not disclosed.

FIRM OVERVIEW: Chao and Chung, established in 1994, focuses principally on corporate finance and company and commercial work. The firm offers clients a specialist approach in its selected areas of practice, and a thorough understanding of the business culture of the China region, including Hong Kong. The firm's dedicated team of commercial lawyers has established an impressive client list which includes major public companies, investment banks and other financial institutions. A major part of the firm's work comprises initial public offerings in Hong Kong, Shanghai and Shenzhen and substantial institutional direct investment arrangements in the region, complementing a strong practice in regulatory compliance work.

INTERNATIONAL EXPERIENCE: The firm's practice covers Hong Kong and the rest of the People's Republic of China, where the firm has a strong presence. Chao and Chung has experience handling international securities offerings, joint venture projects and other business transactions. The firm advises on transactions involving Hong Kong entities investing in Mainland China, Taiwan, Thailand and elsewhere and in foreign-sourced inward investments into Hong Kong and Mainland China.

INTERNATIONAL CLIENTS: The firm's clients include public companies, investment banks, direct investment funds and other financial institutions. The firm also undertakes domestic work referred by international law firms with no or limited Hong Kong representation.

MAIN INTERNATIONAL AREAS OF PRACTICE :
Corporate finance: The firm handles a range of corporate finance matters such as initial public offerings (including those by foreign issuers) with listings in Hong Kong, Shanghai and Shenshen and capital market transactions.
M&A: Chao and Chung advises on private M&A transactions and public company takeovers, including cross border transactions.
Direct investment: The firm is involved in debt/equity investments including by foreign institutions, in Hong Kong and mainland China businesses. The firm also advises on joint ventures.
Regulatory compliance: The firm advises on securities regulations and stock exchange rules, including those applicable to foreign market participants.

LANGUAGES: Chinese (Putonghua and Cantonese), English

C

For other recommended firms see pages 1485-1520

CHAPMAN TRIPP SHEFFIELD YOUNG

HEAD OFFICE

1-13 Grey Street, PO Box 993,
Wellington New Zealand
Tel: +64 4 499 5999 **Fax:** +64 4 472 7111
Email: ctsywn@chapmantripp.co.nz
Website: www.chapmantripp.co.nz

FIRM OVERVIEW

Managing partner: Rupert Wilson
Chief executive: Alastair Carruthers
Number of partners worldwide: 85
Number of other lawyers worldwide: 255

WORLDWIDE OFFICE CONTACTS

NEW ZEALAND
23-29 Albert Street, PO Box 2206, **Aukland** 1
Tel: +64 9 357 9000 **Fax:** +64 357 9099
Email: ctsyak@chapmantripp.co.nz

119 Armagh Street, PO Box 2510, **Christchurch** 8001
Tel: +64 3 353 4130 **Fax:** +64 3 365 4587
Email: ctsych@chapmantripp.co.nz

1-13 Grey Street, PO Box 993, **Wellington**
Tel: +64 4 499 5999 **Fax:** +64 4 472 7111
Email: ctsywn@chapmantripp.co.nz

AREAS OF PRACTICE:

Corporate/commercial	49%
Commercial litigation	22%
Other	16%
Banking, corporate finance and capital markets	13%

C

FIRM OVERVIEW: Established in New Zealand in 1875, Chapman Tripp practises in all areas of commercial, corporate, securities, property, environmental and public law. The firm's lawyers play key roles in mergers, acquisitions, dispositions, take-overs, financing, banking and capital restructurings in New Zealand and overseas. Taxation, privatisation, superannuation, litigation, dispute resolution and government relations are among the firm's specialities.

INTERNATIONAL EXPERIENCE: The firm's international work includes acting for Southern Cross Cables Limited on the establishment and project financing of a US$1.8b fibre optic submarine project linking New Zealand, Australia, California, Hawaii and Fiji; advising the New Zealand partners on the merger of PricewaterhouseCoopers; advising significant international investors in New Zealand including HJ Heinz Company, Independent Newspapers plc, International Paper Company, BHP, RJR Nabisco, Sumitomo Forestry Company Limited and Anglian Water International (NZ) Limited; advising on the New Zealand component of global mergers such as Guinness/GrandMet, Daimler-Chrysler, and Zeneca/Astra; advising China International Trust & Investment Corporation on its participation in the joint venture acquisition of an interest in Forestry Corporation of New Zealand Limited's business assets; advising foreign issuers on public offers of their products in New Zealand, including British Telecom plc and J Boag & Son Limited; Shell Exploration Company's proposed acquisition of Fletcher Challenge Energy; and acting for Telecom Corporation of New Zealand Limited on funding and related activities and general treasury operations including the recently completed current US cross-border lease of qualifying technological equipment.

INTERNATIONAL CLIENTS: The firm services large companies, banks, insurance companies and investors, including ABB, ABN Amro, AMP, Anglian Water, Bankers Trust, BHP, Brierley Investments Limited, Commonwealth Bank of Australia, Credit Suisse First Boston, Deutsche Bank, GE Capital Corporation, HIH Winterthur Insurance, HJ Heinz Company, The Hongkong and Shanghai Banking Corporation Limited, Independent Newspapers plc, Microsoft Corporation, News Corporation, RJR Nabisco, Stryker Corporation, Sumitomo Forestry Company Limited, Telecom Corporation of New Zealand, TransAlta, Waste Management and Westpac Banking Corporation.

MAIN INTERNATIONAL AREAS OF PRACTICE:

Banking, corporate finance and capital markets: The firm is experienced in advising banks, borrowers, arrangers and packagers on a wide range of matters, including domestic and international capital markets and corporate finance transactions; cross-border leasing; Euro and US MTN issues; European, Asian and US commercial paper programmes; project financing; securitisations, swaps and other derivatives and structured financing transactions in general.

Corporate and commercial law: The firm advises international clients on their New Zealand business and investments, including advising on energy, international trade, mergers, acquisitions and take-overs, overseas investment, securities law, taxation, telecommunications and competition law.

Mergers, acquisitions and take-overs: This is a core practice area for Chapman Tripp. The firm's corporate and commercial lawyers are extensively involved in mergers, acquisitions and take-overs for both local and offshore clients. This work includes major involvement with contested listed company take-over offers.

Taxation: Taxation specialists advise on all areas of corporate taxation with an emphasis on large and complex commercial transactions.

Securities law: The firm has been closely involved in reform and regulation of New Zealand's security markets, and has advised on many of the major public securities offerings in New Zealand.

Overseas investment in New Zealand: The firm advises on all matters governing offshore investment in New Zealand, including assisting businesses to plan activities, operations and strategies that comply with the country's Commerce Act and Overseas Investment Act; ensuring necessary consents are identified and obtained; advising on international and domestic equity and debt financing, and trade practice obligations.

International trade: The firm is very familiar with the impact of international trade treaties and regimes, as well as the domestic legislation giving effect to them. The firm is particularly experienced in anti-dumping.

Competition law: The firm advises on business acquisitions, restructurings, franchising and industry licensing situations, restrictive trade practice issues, price control and legislative proposals in New Zealand, Australia and other jurisdictions.

Energy: The firm's experience in this area ranges from matters concerning oil exploration through to the mining, distribution and marketing of oil, natural gas and coal. The firm is also experienced in all aspects of the electricity sector.

Telecommunications: The firm advises on the full range of corporate and commercial law issues faced by telecoms companies. The firm is particularly experienced in competition law and trade practices in this sector.

Commercial litigation: The firm has widespread experience of the New Zealand judicial system, including the High Court, Court of Appeal and Privy Council, as well as various courts throughout the Pacific.

 For other recommended firms see pages 1485-1520

CHIOMENTI STUDIO LEGALE

HEAD OFFICE

Via Antonio Bertoloni 44-46,
00197 Rome, Italy
Tel: + 39 06 809 701 **Fax:** + 39 06 809 706

Email: roma@chiomenti.net
Website: www.chiomenti.net

FIRM OVERVIEW

Managing partner: Luigi Bendi
Managing committee: Luigi Bendi, Carlo Croff, Francesco Tedeschini

Number of partners worldwide: 22
Number of other lawyers worldwide: 80

AREAS OF PRACTICE:

Corporate/M&A	25%
Securities and capital markets	25%
Banking and finance	20%
Antitrust and EU legislation	5%
Litigation and arbitration	5%
Other	5%
Real estate	5%
Tax	5%
Telecommunications and IT	5%

FIRM OVERVIEW: Chiomenti Studio Legale continues the practice started by Avv Pasquale Chiomenti in the mid-forties. The firm is currently composed of over 100 lawyers and tax counsellors, including 22 partners, and has offices in Rome, Milan, Turin, London and Brussels.
The firm has a well-develped network of national and international correspondents and routinely works with foreign attorneys.

INTERNATIONAL EXPERIENCE: Chiomenti Studio Legale has advised on a substantial number of Italy's major business transactions including: IPOs, privatisations, M&A, structured finance (project finance/securitisation/ acquisition finance), capital markets, real estate, antitrust and EU matters. The firm also represents clients in foreign arbitration proceedings. In recent months, the firm has focused its work on the application of new legal techniques in Italy with the structuring of the first securitisation transactions within the framework of Law 130/1999.

INTERNATIONAL CLIENTS: The firm's clients are predominantly Italian and foreign industrial corporations, banks, insurance companies, financial institutions and corporations. The firm has also acted for Italian state and local authorities, foreign states and public entities (including central banks), and international organisations (including the Commission of the European Communities).

MAIN INTERNATIONAL AREAS OF PRACTICE:

Banking and finance: The firm advises foreign banks and financial institutions in their establishment and activities in Italy. It also assists Italian and foreign commercial and merchant banks and finance companies in their current activities in Italy and abroad. The main aspects involved in this specialisation are banking, stock exchange and financial services regulations, banking and financial products, tax, personnel and foreign exchange.
Securities and capital markets (including IPOs and privatisations): The firm advises on the issue of debt and equity securities, loan participations, commercial papers and securities placements, currency and interest rate swaps, options, futures and other derivatives, export financing, secured lending and asset-backed financing.
Corporate/M&A: In particular, the firm is active in advising clients in connection with the formation and restructuring of companies or groups of companies; the issue of securities in Italy and abroad; shareholder agreements; relationships between minority and majority shareholders; public offers; and take-overs.
In M&A, the firm has particular experience in leveraged buy-out and management buy-out transactions and has been active in major Italian transactions of this kind.
Antitrust and EU legislation: The firm is experienced in all aspects of EU law, particularly anti-trust, state-aids, public procurement, telecommunications, energy, transport, circulation of services and goods, freedom of establishment and agriculture.
Tax: The firm assists its clients in tax matters relating in particular to income tax, value added tax and international tax. The firm represents clients before Italian tax authorities and tax courts.
Real estate: The firm advises on the legal aspects connected with town planning, construction permits, title and other related issues, including authorisations for the operation of the business.
Litigation and arbitration: The firm represents clients before all civil jurisdictions and administrative authorities and agencies in Italy, as well as in domestic and foreign arbitral proceedings.
Telecommunications and IT: The firm has been involved in several of the largest Italian transactions in these sectors in the last years and has experience of the liberalisation and privatisation of regulated or public sectors.
Other: Other practice areas include insurance and reinsurance business and various energy sectors. The firm also handles matters concerning employment relationships and employee stock option plans.

LANGUAGES: English, French, Italian

WORLDWIDE OFFICE CONTACTS

BELGIUM
41 Avenue Roger Vandendriessche, 1150 **Brussels**
Tel: + 32 2 775 9900 **Fax:** + 32 2 775 9927
Email: bruxelles@chiomenti.net

ITALY
Via Boito 8, 20121 **Milan**
Tel: + 39 02 721 571 **Fax:** + 39 02 721 272 24
Email: milano@chiomenti.net

Via Antonio Bertoloni 44/46, 00197 **Rome**
Tel: + 39 06 809 701 **Fax:** + 39 06 809 706
Email: roma@chiomenti.net

Via Lamarmora 39, 10128 **Turin**
Tel: + 39 011 568 1938 **Fax:** + 39 011 581 8853

UNITED KINGDOM
20 Berkeley Square, **London** W1J 6HF
Tel: +44 20 7569 1500 **Fax:** +44 20 7569 1501
Email: london@chiomenti.net

CHIOMENTI
STUDIO LEGALE

CLARO Y CIA

HEAD OFFICE

Apoquindo 3721, 13th Floor, Las Condes Santiago, Chile
Tel: +56 2 367 3000 **Fax:** +56 2 367 3003

Email: claro@claro.cl
Website: www.claro.cl

WORLDWIDE OFFICE CONTACTS

CHILE
Apoquindo 3721, 13th Floor, Las Condes, **Santiago**
Tel: +56 2 367 3000 **Fax:** +56 2 367 3003
Email: claro@claro.cl

FIRM OVERVIEW

Senior partner: José María Eyzaguirre

Number of partners worldwide: 10
Number of other lawyers worldwide: 35

AREAS OF PRACTICE:

M&A	20%
Banking and finance	18%
Litigation and arbitration	18%
Securities and financial markets	18%
Anti-trust	5%
Corporate	5%
Energy and public utilities	5%
Tax	5%
Insurance and reinsurance	2%
Intellectual property	2%
Telecommunications	2%

C

FIRM OVERVIEW: Founded in 1880, Claro y Cia is one of the oldest and most prestigious full service law firms in Chile. The firm advises banking and finance companies, investment advisors, and a range of corporate clients in industries including mining, energy, telecommunications, infrastructure, securities and litigation, IT and Internet. Claro y Cia is the Chilean member of Lex Mundi and is also a member of the Ibero-American section of the Club de Abogados. Its association with Bomchil, Castro, Goodrich, Claro, Arosemena y Asociados enables it to maintain close links with major law firms in Europe and Central and South America.

INTERNATIONAL EXPERIENCE: The firm has handled the planning and structuring of foreign investments in Chile, corporate restructuring, mergers and acquisitions, joint ventures and finance, and project finance. It has advised sellers, buyers, minority and majority shareholders, and state and privately owned companies for sale. It also handles diverse transactions involving mergers, spin-offs, associations, tender offers, reorganisations and other forms of restructuring.

INTERNATIONAL CLIENTS:
The firm's client base comprises mainly multinational companies operating in Chile.

MAIN INTERNATIONAL AREAS OF PRACTICE:
Corporate: Claro y Cia advises on all corporate matters including the drafting of domestic and international contracts for the purchase and sale of goods, distribution strategies, and imports and exports. The firm also advises clients on negotiation with third parties.
Securities and financial markets: The firm handles the design and structuring of complex financial transactions comprising multilateral financing and cross-border capital flows. It supports clients in developing and implementing all types of project financing, loans, public and private placement of securities, futures, derivatives and structured products.
Banking and finance: The firm has advised on the development of new financial products and innovative banking transactions that are now standard in Chilean securities and capital markets. Claro y Cia advises foreign banks with a large business presence in Chile including some of the largest international banks. It continues to develop products that are at the forefront of the banking and finance industries.
Litigation and arbitration: The firm handles commercial litigation, national and international arbitration, and ADR. Claro y Cia's litigation department consistently handles cases that demand an aggressive and efficient approach.
Intellectual property: The firm advises on trademarks and trade names, patents and industrial models, copyrights, license agreements, franchising, confidential information, unfair competitive practices and the transfer of technology. Claro y Cia's services extend to infringement control, software protection, and consumers rights.
Anti-trust: Claro y Cia handles work relating to the implementation of businesses and advises on all aspects on Chilean competition law.
Telecommunications: Claro y Cia advises telecommunications companies and firms providing data transmission, video, satellite, cable, and Internet services.
Energy and public utilities: Claro y Cia has advised on the structuring of oil and gas pipelines extending from Argentina. It has also handled projects for the construction of thermo-electric and combined-cycle power plants, and has been involved in other transactions in the electricity industry.
Insurance and reinsurance: Claro y Cia advises insurance and reinsurance companies on insurance transactions for all types of property. The firm has also assisted a number of foreign companies starting up in Chile.
Employment: Claro y Cia advises on individual and collective bargaining agreements. It also handles labour conflicts, union related and social security matters, and all aspects of Chilean employment law.
Tax: The firm advises on income tax, value added tax, and stamp tax in relation to determining the optimum structure of businesses.
M&A: The firm advises on all aspects of mergers and acquisitions from due dilligence to the drafting and completion of acquisition agreements. M&A work represents a substantial part of the firm's practice.

LANGUAGES: English, French, German, Spanish

CLARO Y CIA.

For other recommended firms see pages 1485-1520

CLAYTON UTZ

HEAD OFFICE

Levels 23-35, No 1 O'Connell Street,
Sydney NSW 2000, Australia
Tel: +61 2 9353 4000
Fax: +61 2 9251 7832
Email: cuinfo@claytonutz.com
Website: www.claytonutz.com

FIRM OVERVIEW

Chief Executive Partner: Geoff Brown
Number of partners worldwide: 180
Number of other lawyers worldwide: 551

AREAS OF PRACTICE:

Banking and financial services .... *%
Corporate .... *%
Litigation/dispute resolution .... *%
Property and construction .... *%
* Workload % not disclosed

FIRM OVERVIEW: Clayton Utz is one of Australia's leading top tier law firms, with offices in Sydney, Melbourne, Brisbane, Perth, Canberra and Darwin. Established in 1833, the firm has more than 180 partners, a further 540 lawyers and 750 support staff. The firm operates through four national practice departments – corporate, financial services, property and construction and litigation/dispute resolution. Clayton Utz has an established reputation as one of Australia's pre-eminent commercial legal firms and is recognised as a leading provider of legal services in the Asia Pacific region. Fundamental to the firm's success is its depth of knowledge of client businesses and its breadth of experience across industry sectors in Australia and the Asia Pacific region. The firm's client list includes a number of Australia's top 100 companies, as well as Federal and State Government departments and agencies. The firm's industry-specific knowledge is extensive, and includes banking, construction, insurance, information technology, e-commerce, energy production, mining, telecommunications, transport and health services. Clayton Utz is a member of two international networks, the Pacific Rim Advisory Council and Lex Mundi, enabling the firm to coordinate matters from Australia while utilising the resources of leading, local lawyers on a worldwide basis.

INTERNATIONAL EXPERIENCE: Major international transactions involving Clayton Utz over the past three years include acting for American-based Monsanto in the worldwide class action regarding IUDs, advising Coca-Cola Amatil in the A$5 billion acquisition of the Coca-Cola Philippines bottling operations from San Miguel, and advising on the financing of the Southern Cross Cable Project from California to Australia.

INTERNATIONAL CLIENTS: The firm's major international clients include Allianz AG, Cable and Wireless plc, The Morgan Crucible Co plc, Coca-Cola Amatil, The Lenfest Group, Enron Corporation, Monsanto, The Coca-Cola Company, Eli Lilly International, Alcan Aluminium Ltd, Invensys plc, Hydro Quebec, Rexel CDME, Deutsche Bank, United Distiller & Vinters (HP) Ltd, Roche Holding, Baxter Health Care Corporation and Mentor Corporation.

MAIN INTERNATIONAL AREAS OF PRACTICE:

Mergers and acquisitions: The firm has acted for Australian and international companies in some of Australia's largest and most complex takeovers, takeover defences, corporate acquisitions, and mergers and reconstructions. The firm is particularly experienced in share floats and underwritings, as well as helping corporations to achieve growth and maximise shareholder value.

Construction: The firm advises on contractual frameworks, property project documentation, tender reviews and provides advice on the construction phase, preparation and review of claims and dispute resolution, including ADR, arbitration and litigation.

Product liability: The firm's product liability lawyers are supported by Australia's largest litigation practice. They represent a wide range of manufacturers, importers and insurers in litigation involving products as diverse as drugs, consumer goods, therapeutic devices, motor vehicles, automotive components, boats and chemicals.

Technology and intellectual property: The firm advises, drafts contracts and negotiates with both local and foreign businesses in this area.

Corporatisation and privatisation: The firm has experience throughout Australia and Asia in the restructuring of airports, power, water, rail, roads and banking.

Energy and natural resources: The firm has handled several resource developments, farm-in, farm-out and other exploration and development arrangements in Australia and throughout the Pacific region, including Japan. The firm also markets products such as transport and shipping agreements, long term sales contracts and other downstream areas.

Power utilities: The firm advises on the regulatory framework and commercial environment of the power industry throughout Australia and the Asia Pacific region.

Banking and finance: The firm has one of Australia's largest banking and finance practices. It handles project finance, infrastructure, securitisation and capital markets in Australia and Asia.

Taxation: The firm regularly advises on a range of international tax questions relating to preferred structures for both inbound and outbound investments.

LANGUAGES: Afrikaans, Arabic, Croatian, Czech, Danish, Dutch, French, German, Greek, Hebrew, Hindi, Hokkien, Hungarian, Indonesian, Italian, Japanese, Korean, Macedonian, Malay, Mandarin, Polish, Russian, Serbian, Spanish, Swedish, Turkish, Ukranian, Vietnamese

WORLDWIDE OFFICE CONTACTS

AUSTRALIA
Levels 18-27, 215 Adelaide Street, Qld 4000, **Brisbane**
Tel: +61 7 3292 7000 **Fax:** +61 7 3292 7950
Email: gharley@claytonutz.com

Level 8, Canberra House, 40 Marcus Clarke Street, ACT 2601, **Canberra**
Tel: +61 2 6279 4000 **Fax:** +61 2 6279 4099
Email: rcutler@claytonutz.com

17-19 Lindsay Street, NT 0801, **Darwin**
Tel: +61 8 8943 2555 **Fax:** +61 8 8943 2500
Email: nmitaros@claytonutz.com

Levels 17-19, 333 Collins Street, Vic 3000, **Melbourne**
Tel: +61 3 9286 6000 **Fax:** +61 3 9629 8488
Email: bdoyle@claytonutz.com

Levels 35-39, Bankwest Tower, 108 St George's Terrace, WA 6000, **Perth**
Tel: +61 8 9426 8000 **Fax:** +61 8 9481 3095
Email: gberson@clayton.com

Levels 23-35, No 1 O'Connell Street, NSW 2000, **Sydney**
Tel: +61 2 9353 4000 **Fax:** +61 2 9251 7832
Email: cloveday@claytonutz.com

C

CLAYTON UTZ

CLEARY, GOTTLIEB, STEEN & HAMILTON

HEAD OFFICE

One Liberty Plaza,
New York NY 10006-1470, USA
Tel: +1 212 225 2000 **Fax:** +1 212 225 3999

Website: www.cleary.com

FIRM OVERVIEW

Managing partner: Peter Karasz

Number of partners worldwide: 146
Number of other lawyers worldwide: 452

AREAS OF PRACTICE:
Corporate/commercial .... *%
EU/competition .... *%
Litigation .... *%
Tax .... *%
* Workload % not disclosed

FIRM PROFILE: Cleary Gottlieb Steen & Hamilton is a leading international law firm widely recognised for its expertise in finance, M&A and for its tax, regulatory and litigation practice. The firm, founded in 1946, is organised and operates as an integrated worldwide partnership. Clients include corporations, banks and other financial institutions engaged in domestic and international business, as well as sovereign governments and international organisations, individuals, trusts and non-profit institutions. The firm has substantial experience in the investment banking, telecommunications, e-commerce and media sectors.

INTERNATIONAL EXPERIENCE: The firm provides advice in the areas of international capital markets transactions, mergers and acquisitions, privatisations, joint ventures, cross-border investment, tax, and EU and Member State regulation, particularly competition law. Clients also have access to a full range of litigation and arbitration expertise involving both common law and civil code jurisdictions.

LANGUAGES: Armenian, Bulgarian, Dutch, Farsi, Flemish, French, German, Greek, Hebrew, Hindi, Italian, Japanese, Korean, Malay, Mandarin, Polish, Portuguese, Russian, Spanish, Swedish, Urdu, Vietnamese

WORLDWIDE OFFICES

ASIA
Regional profile: Cleary Gottlieb has offices in Hong Kong and Tokyo. The Asian practice comprises 20 lawyers and has core practices in corporate finance and securities, sovereign and corporate debt restructurings and workouts, joint ventures, M&A, securities transactions, foreign direct investment, project finance and other transactional work.

EUROPE
Regional profile: The firm has had a European presence since 1949. The European practice comprises almost 200 lawyers, many of whom are dual-qualified and able to practice in leading European jurisdictions and in the US. Each office has a core practice in corporate finance, including capital markets, privatisations and tax, and all of them are particularly well-established in cross-border mergers, acquisitions and joint ventures. The Brussels and Rome offices have strong practices in competition and regulatory law and together with the Paris office, also provide advice in relation to litigation and arbitrations involving domestic and multinational clients, including in proceedings before the European Court of Justice and the European Commission.

USA
Regional profile: The firm has offices in New York City and Washington, D.C comprising over 400 lawyers. The New York office has core practices in capital markets and transactional work, financial institutions, M&A, joint ventures, project finance and infrastructure, privatisations, tax, sovereign debt management, litigation, real estate, intellectual property, employee benefits and trust and estates. The Washington office has core practices in antitrust, environmental law, financial institutions, corporate and regulatory advisory work, international trade, project finance and other transactional work including securities and structured finance.

WORLDWIDE OFFICE CONTACTS

BELGIUM
Rue de la Loi 57, B-1040 **Brussels**
Tel: +32 2 287 20 00 **Fax:** +32 2 231 16 61

FRANCE
41 Avenue de Friedland, 75008 **Paris**
Tel: +33 1 40 74 68 00 **Fax:** +33 1 45 63 66 37

GERMANY
Main Tower, Neue Mainzer Strasse 52, D60311 **Frankfurt am Main**
Tel: +49 69 97 1030 **Fax:** +49 69 97 103 199

HONG KONG
39th Floor Bank of China Tower, One Garden Road, **Hong Kong**
Tel: +852 2521 4122 **Fax:** +852 2845 9026

ITALY
Piazza Di Spagna 15, 00187 **Rome**
Tel: +39 06 69 52 22 1 **Fax:** +39 06 69 20 06 65

JAPAN
20th Floor, Shin Kasumigaseki Building, 3-2, Kasumigaseki 3-Chome, Chiyoda-Ku, **Tokyo** 100-0013
Tel: +81 3 3595 3911 **Fax:** +81 3 3595 3910

UNITED KINGDOM
City Place House, 55 Basinghall Street, **London** EC2V 5EH
Tel: +44 20 7614 2200 **Fax:** +44 20 7600 1698

USA
One Liberty Plaza, **New York** NY 10006-1470
Tel: +1 212 225 2000 **Fax:** +1 212 225 3999

2000 Pennsylvania Avenue, NW, **Washington DC** DC 20006-1801
Tel: +1 202 974 1500 **Fax:** +1 202 974 1999

For other recommended firms see pages 1485-1520

CLIFFE DEKKER FULLER MOORE INC

HEAD OFFICE

see Worldwide Office Contacts

Website: www.cdfm.co.za

FIRM OVERVIEW

Managing partner: Tim Jooste

Number of partners worldwide: 48
Number of other lawyers worldwide: 50

AREAS OF PRACTICE:

Corporate and commercial	22%
M&A	22%
Corporate commercial litigation and arbitration	20%
Corporate finance, banking and securities	12%
Electronic law, IT and e-commerce	10%
Employment	5%
Telecommunications and broadcasting	3%
Environmental law	2%
Mining	2%
Trade marks and copyright	2%

WORLDWIDE OFFICE CONTACTS

SOUTH AFRICA
Johannesburg Regional Office, (mailing address) Private Bag X7,
Benmore 2010
Tel: +27 11 290 7000 **Fax:** +27 11 290 7300
Email: jhb.network@cdfm.co.za

Western Cape Regional Office, (mailing address) PO Box 695,
Cape Town 8000
Tel: +27 21 481 6300 **Fax:** +27 21 424 5801
Email: ctn.network@cdfm.co.za

FIRM OVERVIEW: As one of the largest independent commercial law firms in Southern Africa, the firm's professionals offer expert legal advice on a comprehensive range of specialist legal services relating to commerce and industry, and encompassing all aspects of finance, corporate capital markets, corporate commercial litigation and dispute resolution. The firm's roots go back almost 150 years and the practice has grown strongly since the 1980s following the merger of Cliffe Dekker & Todd Inc. in Johannesburg with the Cape Town practices of Syfret Godlonton-Fuller Moore Inc. and Silberbauers.

INTERNATIONAL EXPERIENCE: With offices situated in South Africa's main financial centres (Johannesburg and Cape Town), the firm is ideally situated to act for both Southern African clients , who include many of the country's major corporations, listed companies and medium sized enterprises, and for international clients doing business in Southern Africa. The firm's growing international business and client portfolio extends through Europe, the US, Australasia and the Far East. In addition, the firm has been increasingly active in assisting its South African clients in making international acquisitions.

MAIN INTERNATIONAL AREAS OF PRACTICE:

Corporate and commercial: The firm assists international corporations in establishing a presence in South Africa and in developing a full range of business operations.

M&A: The firm has advised on a diverse range of local and international transactions, from small private acquisitions to takeovers and management buyouts of listed companies. Its lawyers are fully conversant with recent changes to competition law in South Africa.

Litigation and arbitration: The firm specialises in corporate and commercial litigation, including arbitration and alternative dispute resolution, in areas including banking, industrial, tax, liquidation, insolvency, construction, product liability, media and environmental law.

Banking and finance: The firm advises on all areas of banking, finance and securities law, including derivatives, domestic and international trade and export credit financing, securities, futures and commodities trading. It is engaged in drafting legislation governing the banking system in South Africa, and acts for retail, merchant, investment and niche banks.

Electronic law, IT and e-commerce: The firm has one of the largest, most experienced electronic law units in SA, with the capacity to provide a totally integrated IT/electronic law service.

Employment: The firm has in-depth expertise in this rapidly changing field of law in South Africa. Its professionals offer wide ranging advice on all aspects including retrenchments, transfers of businesses as going concerns, employment implications of mergers and acquisitions, due diligence investigations and trade union negotiations.

Telecommunications and broadcasting: The firm has specialist expertise in all regulatory requirements when interfacing with the regulator and for satellite telecommunication and broadcasting, licensing framework for VANS, PTNS, mobile operators and new entrants, network interconnection and facilities leasing, and radio communications management.

Environmental law: The firm's work in this area continues to expand as environmental issues gain greater prominence among local communities and in line with international requirements.

Mining: The firm has an historic association with the SA mining industry. Overall exposure in the mining sector has increased over time.

Trade marks and copyright: The firm advises on trade marks, copyright and passing-off law and unlawful competition litigation. The trade marks department operates from the firm's Cape Town offices, dealing directly with the Registrar of Trade Marks in Pretoria.

LANGUAGES: Afrikaans, Dutch, English

For other recommended firms see pages 1485-1520

CLIFFORD CHANCE LLP

HEAD OFFICE

200 Aldersgate Street,
London EC1A 4JJ, United Kingdom
Tel: +44 20 7600 1000 **Fax:** +44 20 7600 5555

Website: www.cliffordchance.com

FIRM OVERVIEW

Chairman: Keith Clark
Chief executive: Michael Bray
Chief operating officer: Garth Pollard

Number of partners worldwide: 640
Number of other lawyers worldwide: 2403

AREAS OF PRACTICE:

Corporate	30%
Finance	25%
Litigation and dispute resolution	20%
Capital markets	10%
Real estate	10%
Tax, pensions and employment	5%

FIRM OVERVIEW: Clifford Chance Limited Liability Partnership is the first (and largest) fully integrated global law firm. The firm was created through the January 1 2000 merger of three international law firms – New York - based Rogers & Wells, London-based Clifford Chance and Frankfurt-based Pünder, Volhard, Weber & Axster. The firm provides seamless global services to the world's leading financial institutions and multinational businesses, and offers expertise in Asia, the Americas, Continental Europe and the UK. The firm has over 3040 legal advisers comprising 640 partners and 2403 other fee earners. Its practice is organised around six global practice areas – banking and finance; capital markets; corporate (including M&A); litigation and dispute resolution; real estate; and tax, pensions and employment law.

INTERNATIONAL EXPERIENCE: The firm operates in all major business and financial centres worldwide, enabling it to handle disputes and provide expert legal advice on all areas of trade and commerce internationally. It operates under both common and civil law and advises clients on complex cross-border transactions with high quality advice delivered quickly and seamlessly. With offices in 19 countries, the firm is also pre-eminently positioned to advise on local law transactions and business matters.

INTERNATIONAL CLIENTS: From its 29 offices worldwide, the firm advises many of the world's leading financial institutions and corporations, as well as governments and multilateral agencies. Integrated services are provided to clients in many different industries, combining lawyers' specialist skills with multiple language, commercial and legal abilities.

MAIN INTERNATIONAL AREAS OF PRACTICE: The firm provides a comprehensive range of legal services in the areas of finance, capital markets, corporate, litigation and dispute resolution, real estate, taxation, pensions and employment.
Finance: The firm has the world's largest international finance practice with over 1000 partners and lawyers located in major financial and commercial centres worldwide. The practice provides advice across the full spectrum of financial products including banking, asset finance, derivative products, product finance, securitisation and structured finance. It is the

WORLDWIDE OFFICE CONTACTS

BELGIUM
Clifford Chance Pünder, Avenue Louise 65, Box 2, 1050 **Brussels**
Tel: +32 2 533 59 11 **Fax:** +32 2 533 59 59

BRAZIL
Clifford Chance Rogers & Wells, Rua Helena 260, 6th Floor, SP 04552-050 **São Paulo**
Tel: +55 11 3049 3188 **Fax:** +55 11 3049 3198

CHINA
Suite 730, Shanghai Center, 1376 Nanjing Xi Lu, **Shanghai** 200040
Tel: +86 21 6279 8461 **Fax:** +86 21 6279 8462

CZECH REPUBLIC
Clifford Chance Pünder, Charles Bridge Centre, Krizovnické nám 2, 110 00 **Prague** 1
Tel: +420 2 2409 7410 **Fax:** +420 2 2409 7411

FRANCE
112 Avenue Kléber, BP 163 Trocadéro, 75770 **Paris** Cedex 16
Tel: +33 1 44 05 52 52 **Fax:** +33 1 44 05 52 00

GERMANY
Clifford Chance Pünder, Katharina-Heinroth-Ufer 1, 10787 **Berlin**
Tel: +49 302 54 65 7800 **Fax:** +49 302 54 65 900

Clifford Chance Pünder, Cecilienallee 6, 40474 **Düsseldorf**
Tel: +49 211 43 550 **Fax:** +49 211 43 55 5600

Clifford Chance Pünder, Mainzer Landstrasse 46, 60325 **Frankfurt am Main**
Tel: +49 69 71 99 01 **Fax:** +49 69 71 99 4000

Clifford Chance Pünder, Burgplatz 7, 04109 **Leipzig**
Tel: +49 341 21 49 0 **Fax:** +49 341 21 49 600

Clifford Chance Pünder, Pacellistrasse 14, 80333 **Munich**
Tel: +49 89 216 320 **Fax:** +49 89 216 32 8600

HONG KONG
29th Floor, Jardine House, One Connaught Place, **Hong Kong**
Tel: +852 2825 8888 **Fax:** +852 2825 8800

HUNGARY
Köves Clifford Chance Pünder, Madách Trade Centre, Madách Imre út 14, 1075 **Budapest**
Tel: +36 1 429 1300 **Fax:** +36 1 429 1390

ITALY
Grimaldi e Clifford Chance LLP, Via Clerici, 7, 20121 **Milan**
Tel: +39 02 806 341 Fax: +39 02 806 34200

Grimaldi e Clifford Chance LLP, Via Felice Cavallotti 4, 35124 **Padua**
Tel: +39 049 804 2511 **Fax:** +39 049 880 5900

Grimaldi e Clifford Chance LLP, Via Saverio Mercadante, 32, 00198 **Rome**
Tel: +39 06 844 651 **Fax:** +39 06 844 652 00

JAPAN
Akasaka Tameike Tower, 6th Floor, 2-17-7 Akasaka, Minato-ku, **Tokyo** 107-0052
Tel: +81 3 5561 6600 **Fax:** +81 3 5561 6699

LUXEMBOURG
Kremmer Associes & Clifford Chance, 6 rue Heinrich Heine, BP 1147, L-1011 **Luxembourg**
Tel: +352 48 50 50 1 **Fax:** +352 48 13 85

C

For other recommended firms see pages 1485-1520

CLIFFORD CHANCE LLP

first firm to bring together lawyers in Europe, the United States and Asia to advise on national and international regulatory issues, including e-commerce and the relationship between regulatory systems. The firm acts for all the world's leading investment and commercial banks across many major jurisdictions as well as many corporates. It also advises regulatory authorities, supranational bodies, governments and government agencies.
Capital markets: The firm's capital markets practice comprises over 500 partners and lawyers. The practice is founded on a full-service US and UK securities law capability - the law of choice for the majority of international transactions - complemented by local securities law expertise in each of the key financial centres. This combination of local and international perspectives is brought to bear, for example, when helping to apply US disclosure standards to European, Asian and Latin American issuers. The firm acts on the whole range of securities offerings whether public or private where the proceeds may be used to finance mergers or acquisitions or for general capital. The firm is well known for its innovative approach to developing solutions and its clients include issuers, guarantors, arrangers, managers, investors, trustees and regulatory bodies such as banks and financial institutions, specialised lenders, corporate originators, security and share trustees, rating agencies, monoline insurers and swap counterparties.
Corporate: The corporate practice handles some of the world's largest and most complex M&A transactions, combining global transaction capability with a full service in English, US and civil law expertise in the key financial centres across Europe, the Americas and Asia. Apart from mainstream M&A, the firm also encompasses leading specialist practices in private equity; funds; financial institutions; e-commerce; insurance; media, computers and telecommunications; energy; real estate; commercial contracts and competition and antitrust. The firm focuses on providing practical, commercial legal advice and its clients include investment banks and financial institutions, multi-nationals and other public and private corporations, private equity providers and management teams, asset management clients, international partnerships and governments.
Litigation and dispute resolution: The firm has a team of more than 600 litigators internationally – the world's largest and most comprehensive practice of its kind – and has experience in virtually all segments of the business and financial markets across multiple jurisdictions. The firm's lawyers work with clients to resolve disputes efficiently and effectively – whether through arbitration, litigation or other techniques, in a manner that promotes their business objectives. They also work with clients to develop compliance programs and other techniques to minimise future litigation risks. The firm is currently representing clients in some of the largest and most significant actions underway, particularly in the areas of antitrust and competition law, white collar and regulatory, intellectual property, insurance and banking and securities.
Real estate: The international real estate practice is at the forefront of the sophisticated and fast changing real estate market. With an increasingly international focus, the European practice remains a market leader and has advised on some of the largest and most complex pan-European real estate and real estate transactions. The firm has a wide client base including banks, property companies, hoteliers, institutions, local and public authorities and REITs as well as open and closed real estate funds. The group advises them in their roles as investors, developers, landowners, occupiers, borrowers, funders or lenders.
Tax: The firm has the largest international tax group of any single law firm internationally, providing advice on international and domestic taxation, covering a wide range of financing, investment, corporate and commercial issues, together with advice on tax litigation, disputes and transfer pricing.

POLAND
Clifford Chance Pünder, Norway House, ul Lwowska 19, 00-660 **Warsaw**
Tel: +48 22 627 11 77 **Fax:** +48 22 627 14 66

RUSSIA
Ul. Sadovaya-Samotechnaya 24/27, Second Floor, 103051 **Moscow**
Tel: +7 501 258 50 50 **Fax:** +7 501 258 50 51

SINGAPORE
16 Collyer Quay #10-00, Hitachi Tower, **Singapore** 049318
Tel: +65 535 1855 **Fax:** +65 535 6855

SPAIN
Avda. Diagonal 682, 08034 **Barcelona**
Tel: +34 93 344 2200 **Fax:** +34 93 344 2222

Paseo de la Castellana 110, 28046 **Madrid**
Tel: +34 91 590 75 00 **Fax:** +34 91 590 75 75

THAILAND
Clifford Chance Wirot, Sindhorn Building Tower 3, 21st Floor, 130-132 Wireless Road, Pathumwan, **Bangkok** 10330
Tel: +66 2 263 2250 **Fax:** +66 2 263 2240

NETHERLANDS
Droogbak 1a, 1013 GE, PO Box 251, 1000 AG **Amsterdam**
Tel: +31 20 7119 000 **Fax:** +31 20 7119 999

UNITED ARAB EMIRATES
Dubai World Trade Centre, 18th Floor, PO Box 9380, **Dubai**
Tel: +971 4 331 4333 **Fax:** +971 4 331 3990

UNITED KINGDOM
200 Aldersgate Street, **London** EC1A 4JJ
Tel: +44 20 7600 1000 **Fax:** +44 20 7600 5555

USA
Clifford Chance Rogers & Wells, 200 Park Avenue,
New York NY-10166 0153
Tel: +1 212 878 8000 **Fax:** +1 212 878 8375

Clifford Chance Rogers & Wells, 607 Fourteenth Street N.W.,
Washington DC 20005 2018
Tel: +1 202 434 0700 **Fax:** +1 202 434 0800

ASSOCIATED OFFICES

CHINA
Pünder, Volhard, Weber & Axster, C712 Beijing Lufthansa Centre, 50 Liangmaqiao Road, **Beijing** 100 016
Tel: +86 10 6465 1808 **Fax:** +86 10 6467 1256

CLYDE & CO

HEAD OFFICE

51 Eastcheap,
London EC3M 1JP, United Kingdom
Tel: +44 20 7623 1244 **Fax:** +44 20 7623 5427

Email: firstname.surname@clyde.co.uk, info@clyde.co.uk
Website: www.clydeco.com

FIRM OVERVIEW

Senior partner: Michael Payton

Number of partners worldwide: 105
Number of other lawyers worldwide: 185

AREAS OF PRACTICE:

Area	%
Banking/corporate/commercial/tax	26%
Insurance/reinsurance	26%
Marine and transport	21%
Commercial litigation	10%
Energy and natural resources	7%
Property	7%
Employment	3%

C

FIRM OVERVIEW: Clyde & Co is a major international law firm founded on global commerce, established over 60 years ago in London. Key practice areas include insurance, reinsurance, shipping, aviation, rail and road carriage, trade, energy, commodities, corporate, commercial and IP/IT, international regulatory and competition law. Firm members are admitted in 17 jurisdictions and are fluent in more than 20 languages. In addition to its six foreign offices and one associate office, the firm has relationships with correspondent law firms in over 90 countries worldwide.

INTERNATIONAL EXPERIENCE: The firm has extensive experience in handling complex, multi-party international actions before and after litigation, and is involved in multi-jurisdictional issues. Recent work includes acting for for the Kazakh Government on the Kazakh-Iran oil swap across the Caspian Sea; on behalf of leading commodity traders; prominent involvement in multi-party litigation in the Commercial Court and elsewhere arising out of the collapse of a trading and bunkering company in the UAE; for the same clients, involvement in successful re-negotiations with banks, major oil companies and government representatives regarding the refinancing and operation of an associated refinery; acting for shareholders of a major Hong Kong based financial services company in relation to financial losses as a result of the company's collapse; multi-jurisdictional infringement and copyright claim concerning videos transmitted by satellite links worldwide; acting for reinsurers in relation to recovery of debts in the FSU, resulting in substantial arbitratration awards; the 'Natuna Sea' grounding just outside Singapore waters; acting for the contractor on the construction of of a gas pipeline from Indonesia to Singapore; acting for the owners of Cape Providence; Silver Seal cargo interest; cargo interests reference the 'Norgas Discoverer'; collision in the Straits of Melaka. The tax department conducts tax planning for multinationals and groups, while the corporate insurance department has been extensively involved in alternative risk transfer projects.

INTERNATIONAL CLIENTS: Include multinationals, banks, insurance and trading companies, credit insurers, shipowners and salvors, P&I clubs and oil companies.

WORLDWIDE OFFICE CONTACTS

FRANCE
Clyde & Co Europe, 29-31 rue Saint Augustin, 75002 **Paris**
Tel: +33 1 44 77 83 80 **Fax:** +33 1 42 60 04 18
Email: paris.office@clydeco.fr

GREECE
31 Akti Miaouli, 18535 **Piraeus**
Tel: +30 1 418 7007 **Fax:** +30 1 418 7010
Email: clyde@ath.forthnet.gr

HONG KONG
18th floor, CITIC Tower, 1 Tim Mei Avenue, Central, **Hong Kong**
Tel: +852 2 878 8600 **Fax:** +852 2 522 5907
Email: clyde@clyde.com.hk

SINGAPORE
South East Asia Office, 10 Collyer Quay #13-07, Ocean Building, **Singapore** 049315
Tel: +65 538 7696 **Fax:** +65 538 7661
Email: post@clyde.com.sg

UNITED ARAB EMIRATES
Middle East Regional Office, PO Box 7001, 3rd floor, City Tower 2, Sheikh Zayed Road, **Dubai**
Tel: +971 4 331 1102 **Fax:** +971 4 331 9920
Email: mero@clyde.co.ae

UNITED KINGDOM
3 Harbour Drive, Capital Waterside, **Cardiff** CF10 4WZ
Tel: +44 29 2082 4569 **Fax:** +44 29 2082 4200
Email: cardiff@clyde.co.uk

Beaufort House, Chertsey Street, **Guildford** GU1 4HA
Tel: +44 1483 555 555 **Fax:** +44 1483 567 330
Email: firstname.surname@clyde.co.uk

51 Eastcheap, **London** EC3M 1JP
Tel: +44 20 7623 1244 **Fax:** +44 20 7623 5427
Email: firstname.surname@clyde.co.uk, info@clyde.co.uk

VENEZUELA
Despacho de Abogados, Miembros de la Firma Internacional de Abogados Clyde & Co, Centro Comercial el Parque, Piso 8, Avenida Francisco de Miranda, Los Palos Grandes, **Caracas** 1062-A
Tel: +58 2 285 7118 **Fax:** +58 2 285 5098
Email: clyde.co@cantv.net

ASSOCIATED OFFICES

RUSSIA
Musin & Partners, Apt 2, 23 Roentgena Street, 197101 **St Petersburg**
Tel: +7 812 327 5871 **Fax:** +7 812 327 5873
Email: russia@clyde.co.uk

MAIN INTERNATIONAL AREAS OF PRACTICE:
Insurance and reinsurance: Areas of specialisation include aviation, general liability, insolvency and recovery, marine and energy, political and credit risks, professional indemnity, property and construction. The firm has a distinct corporate insurance group which specialises in insurance-related corporate transactions and regulatory matters of all kinds, including M&A, alternative risk transfer projects in the life and non-life sectors, the establishment of insurance and reinsurance companies, captives (including Lloyd's Captives Syndicates) and Lloyd's Underwriting vehicles.
Shipping and transport: The firm handles all areas of work in the shipping field, including disputes arising from salvage, collision, carriage of goods, charterparties, marine insurance policies, general average, pollution and

For other recommended firms see pages 1485-1520

ship repairs. It advises all sectors of the maritime industry on an international basis on all aspects of ship sale and purchase, new building contracts, the management and operation of ships and ship finance transactions. It has similar extensive experience in aviation and the carriage of goods by road and rail.

Corporate and commercial: The firm undertakes transactions including flotations, M&A, company refinancings and restructurings, demergers, venture capital arrangements, MBOs, MBIs, joint ventures and inward investment. It advises on intellectual property rights, data protection issues and on all types of commercial contracts including distribution and agency agreements, manufacturing, supply and warehousing agreements and licensing arrangements. The firm's specialists advise on the UK and European regulatory and competition implications of corporate transactions, financing arrangements and commercial contracts. The banking group advises on a broad range of international and domestic financing arrangements including asset and project finance.

Commercial dispute resolution and arbitration: The firm is involved in litigation and arbitration before courts and tribunals in the UK and worldwide through its international network of offices and correspondent lawyers.

Energy and natural resources: Clients include state oil companies, regulatory bodies, privatised utilities, banks, independent companies, some of the world's largest commodities traders, mining exploration and production companies.

Property: The firm advises international developers, contractors, consultants, funders and investors on property transactions.

Employment and immigration: Immigration work includes international labour law.

Taxation: The department deals with all aspects of corporate and personal taxation, including company reorganisations, refinancings, employee remuneration packages, estate planning and settlements.

Public law: The firm handles public international work before international tribunals for corporations and government agencies.

LANGUAGES: Work is handled in Arabic, Cantonese, English, French, Italian, Mandarin, Portuguese and Spanish among others.

WORLDWIDE OFFICES

FRANCE

Clyde & Co Europe, 29-31 rue Saint Augustin, 75002 Paris

Number of lawyers: 8

Main areas of work: Commercial litigation, insurance/reinsurance, shipping litigation, transportation and arbitration.

Languages: English, French

Office profile: Clyde & Co Europe has a total staff of 15 of which 8 are case handlers. The practice concentrates on commercial litigation with marine and non-marine insurance, shipping, transportation, arbitration, corporate and commercial, debt recovery and trading disputes being central to its work.

GREECE

31 Akti Miaouli, 18535 Piraeus

Number of lawyers: 1

Main areas of work: Predominantly marine, including wet and dry shipping work, contractual disputes, collision and insurance work.

Languages: English, French, Greek

Office profile: This office handles a range of activities including a wide variety of shipping work.

HONG KONG

18th floor, CITIC Tower, 1 Tim Mei Avenue, Central, Hong Kong

Number of lawyers: 23

Number of dual qualified lawyers: 20

Main areas of work: General commercial litigation, marine and non-marine insurance, aviation, personal injury defence work, intellectual property, corporate and commercial transactions, trading disputes, debt recovery and credit insurance.

Languages: Cantonese, English, French, Japanese, Mandarin

Office profile: Founded in 1981, this office has a total staff of 64, of whom 10 are partners and 18 are case handlers. The firm also carries out a broad range of corporate and commercial transactions including share/asset sale and purchase, joint venture work, corporate securities work and trade documentation and finance.

SINGAPORE

South East Asia Office, 10 Collyer Quay #13-07, Ocean Building, Singapore 049315

Number of lawyers: 6

Main areas of work: Commercial litigation, ADR, shipping and insurance, reinsurance, non-marine insurance, credit risk insurance, recovery work, commodity trading and energy business.

Office profile: The office is a regional office and its lawyers have expertise in marine insurance, reinsurance and energy work.

UNITED ARAB EMIRATES

Middle East Regional Office, PO Box 7001, 3rd floor, City Tower 2, Sheikh Zayed Road, Dubai

Number of lawyers: 20

Main areas of work: Corporate, commercial, banking, litigation, information technology, insurance including in particular credit and political risks, trading and transport disputes.

Languages: Arabic, English, French

Office profile: The office has expanded rapidly in the region in recent years and is one of the largest corporate and commercial practices in the UAE.

VENEZUELA

Despacho de Abogados, Miembros de la Firma Internacional de Abogados Clyde & Co, Centro Comercial el Parque, Piso 8, Avenida Francisco de Miranda, Los Palos Grandes, Caracas 1062-A

Number of lawyers: 5

Main areas of work: Maritime, insurance, corporate investments and finance, litigation and arbitration, transportation, energy and aviation.

Languages: English, Spanish

Office profile: This office serves the needs of clients involved in South America and has a staff of 13, supported by the London office.

ASSOCIATED OFFICES

RUSSIA

Musin & Partners, Apt 2, 23 Roentgena Street, 197101 St Petersburg

Number of lawyers: 5

Main areas of work: Inward investment, property projects, joint ventures, shipping (wet and dry), road and rail carriage, trading.

Languages: English, Russian

Office profile: The office handles a wide range of work for Russian and foreign clients. Igor Nikolaev of Clyde & Co is also based in this office.

C

For other recommended firms see pages 1485-1520

CMS CAMERON MCKENNA

HEAD OFFICE

Mitre House, 160 Aldersgate Street,
London EC1A 4DD, United Kingdom
Tel: +44 20 7367 3000 **Fax:** +44 20 7367 2000
Website: www.cmck.com

FIRM OVERVIEW

Managing partner: Dick Tyler
Senior partner: Bill Shelford
Chief executive: Robert Derry-Evans
Number of partners worldwide: 187
Number of other lawyers worldwide: 446

AREAS OF PRACTICE:
Banking and international finance .... *%
Commercial litigation .... *%
Corporate .... *%
Employee benefits .... *%
Energy, projects and construction .... *%
Environment .... *%
Financial services .... *%
Insurance and reinsurance .... *%
IT .... *%
Property .... *%
Tax .... *%
* Workload % not disclosed

FIRM OVERVIEW: CMS Cameron McKenna is a leading law firm in Europe. The firm is resourced and experienced to advise on a wide range of transactions and projects throughout the world. The firm has offices and associated offices in key business centres worldwide including the UK, Central Europe, Russia, Central, East and South East Asia, North America and South Africa and advices businesses, financial institutions, governments and public sector bodies. The firm has a significant reputation in a number of fields and has been recognised for several prestigious awards. CMS Cameron McKenna is a founding firm of CMS, the transnational legal services organisation.

INTERNATIONAL EXPERIENCE: CMS Cameron McKenna advises clients in the UK, EU, Central and Eastern Europe, CIS, Indian subcontinent, sub-Saharan Africa, Far East and North, Central and South America. The firm has advised foreign governments and state authorities on the privatisation of state assets throughout the world, in particular in Central and Eastern Europe in the early 1990s and more recently in Africa and India. The firm has advised on the privatisation of the water and sewerage services in Sofia, Bulgaria and Bucharest, Romania; Hong Kong's ports and airports development scheme; setting up the new California electricity market; advising on the privatisation of Kilimajaro airport, Tanzania; drafted new pensions legislation for Poland; advised on joint ventures in Russia, Central Asia and Central Europe; advised international clients on EU and UK competition law; advised on environmental regulations, especially in the EU for Japanese and US clients; negotiated and established the first real estate fund to operate exclusively in Poland.

INTERNATIONAL CLIENTS: 14 US Bioscience companies, Aeroflot, AIG, Amazon.com inc, AMC Europe S.A., APV, BP and approximately 11 other oil companies, Chinese, Romanian, Polish, Dutch and Maltese Governments, Coca-Cola, Delphi Automotive Systems Inc, IFC, EBRD, Saudi American Bank, United Bank of Kuwait Plc, Kredietbank, Erste Bank Sprakassen, Credit Suisse First Boston, National Australia Bank, Citibank, HSBC, Kilimanjaro Airport Authority, Mott MacDonald, Municipalities of Sofia and Bucharest, National Grid Company, Energis, Enron, Nestle, Nomura International Plc, Nykredit, Prudential Insurance Company of America (PRIOCA), Rhone Poulenc, Samancor, Stannifer, Vianova, Warsaw Stock Exchange.

WORLDWIDE OFFICE CONTACTS

BELGIUM
Avenue Louise 200, B-1050 **Brussels**
Tel: +32 2 627 5020 **Fax:** +32 2 627 5021/22
Email: info@cmck.com

CANADA
Power Budd LLP, One First Canadian Place, Suite 7210, PO Box 148, **Toronto** Ontario M5X 1C7
Tel: +1 416 640 4100 **Fax:** +1 416 640 2777
Email: info@powerbudd.com

CHINA
Room 1503, Landmark Tower One, 8 North Dongsanhuan Road, Chaoyang District, **Beijing** 100004
Tel: +8610 6590 0389 / 6229 **Fax:** +8610 6590 0102
Email: info@cmck.com

CZECH REPUBLIC
CMS Cameron McKenna v.o.s., Karoliny Svelte 25, 110 00 **Prague 1**
Tel: +420 2 2109 8888 **Fax:** +420 2 2109 8000
Email: info@cmck.comcmck@asiaonline.net

HONG KONG
7th Floor, Hutchison House, 10 Harcourt Road, Central **Hong Kong**
Tel: +852 2846 9100 **Fax:** +852 2845 3575
Email: cmck@asiaonline.net

HUNGARY
Ormai és Tarsai CMS Cameron McKenna, Bank Center, Citibank Tower, 4th Floor, Szabadsag ter 7, 1944 **Budapest**
Tel: +36 1 302 9302 **Fax:** +36 1 302 9300
Email: info@cmck.com

POLAND
Warsaw Financial Centra, ul. Emilii Plater 53, 18th Floor, 00-113 **Warsaw**
Tel: +48 22 520 5555 **Fax:** +48 22 520 5556
Email: info@cmck.com

ROMANIA
CMS Cameron McKenna S.R.L., Bulevardul Aviatorilor 52, Suite 5, Bucharest - Sector 1, **Bucharest**
Tel: +40 1 231 6470 76 **Fax:** +41 1 231 6477 78
Email: cbr@cmck.com

RUSSIA
Paveletskaya Square 2/3, 113054 **Moscow**
Tel: +7 501 258 5000 **Fax:** +7 501 258 5100
Email: info@cmck.com

SINGAPORE
CMS Cameron McKenna in association with Niru & Co, 3 Raffles Place, 08-01 Bharat Building, **Singapore** 048617
Tel: +65 534 1711 **Fax:** +65 534 3331
Email: info@cmck.com

USA
Cameron McKenna LLP, 2175 K Street, NW, Fifth Floor, **Washington DC** 20037
Tel: +1 202 466 0060 **Fax:** +1 202 466 0077
Email: info@cammckenna.com

For other recommended firms see pages 1485-1520

CMS HASCHE SIGLE ESCHENLOHR PELTZER SCHÄFER

HEAD OFFICE

Markgrafenstrasse 36, Carree am Gendarmenmarkt,
D-10117 Berlin, Germany
Tel: +49 30 203 600 **Fax:** +49 30 203 60290

Email: berlin@cmslegal.de

FIRM OVERVIEW

Managing partner: Cornelius Brandi
Senior partner: Rolf Schmidt-Diemitz

Number of partners: 136
Number of other lawyers: 123

AREAS OF PRACTICE:

Corporate and M&A 40%
Banking and finance 20%
Intellectual property 10%
Litigation and arbitration 10%
Employment and service contracts 5%
EU and competition 5%
Maritime law 5%
Telecommunications and computer law 5%

FIRM OVERVIEW: CMS Hasche Sigle Eschenlohr Peltzer Schäfer, one of Germany's four largest law firms, is also one of its leading international firms. The firm was created by the merger of Hasche Sigle Eschenlohr PeltzerRiesenkampff Fischötter, Sigle Loose Schmidt-Diemitz and Schäfer Wipprecht Schickert, three long-time leaders in the German market. The firm, with over 250 attorneys, offers a comprehensive range of all legal services required by national and international companies in all areas of corporate and commercial law. CMS Hasche Sigle Eschenlohr Peltzer Schäfer is particularly strong in the areas of mergers and acquisitions and international business transactions, with a long history of advising both German firms and international clients interested in investing in Germany. CMS Hasche Sigle Eschenlohr Peltzer Schäfer is a founding member of the international association CMS. This international alliance, with more than 1400 lawyers worldwide, offers clients integrated international legal services of the highest standard. The other firms belonging to CMS are CMS Cameron McKenna, Great Britain: CMS Derks Star Busmann Hanotiau, Netherlands and Belgium; CMS Strommer Reich-Rohrwig Karasek Hainz, Austria and CMS Klainguti Stettler Wille, Switzerland.

INTERNATIONAL EXPERIENCE: The firm has a large international practice involving most of the world's industrial countries. In particular, the corporate department, the finance department and the maritime department advise clients in Europe, the United Stated and Far East in transactional and commercial matters.

MAIN INTERNATIONAL AREAS OF PRACTICE:

M&A: Mergers and acquisitions, management buy-outs, leveraged buy-outs, privatisation of state-owned companies.
Corporate law: Corporate and partnership law, national and international joint ventures, investments in Germany and abroad, organisation and reorganisation of businesses and corporate groups, international public offerings.
Banking and finance: Securities law, advising on the issuance of shares, participation rights and bonds on the German and European capital markets, project finance, real property, investment funds, real property leasing, asset finance, ship and aircraft finance.
Telecommunication and IT law: Telecommunication, information technology, press and media law, including new media, and entertainment.
Intellectual property: Trademarks, patents, copyrights, license agreements.
Distribution law: National and international distribution law, in particular agency, distributorship and franchising.
EU and competition law: German and European cartel and merger control and antitrust unfair competition.
Maritime Law: Charter party disputes and cargo claims, maritime insurance and admiralty.
Employment: All matters relating to German employment law.
Litigation and arbitration: Civil and commercial litigation, national and international arbitration, recognition and enforcement of German judgements abroad and foreign judgements within Germany.

LANGUAGES: Dutch, English, French, Italian, Russian, Spanish, Swedish

WORLDWIDE OFFICE CONTACTS

BELGIUM
Avenue du Diamant 139, B-1030 **Brussels**
Tel: +32 2 735 3428 **Fax:** +32 2 735 2678
Email: general@dsh-law.be

GERMANY
Markgrafenstrasse 36, Carree am Gendarmenmarkt, D-10117 **Berlin**
Tel: +49 30 203 600 **Fax:** +49 30 203 60290
Email: berlin@cmslegal.de

Hartmannstrasse 7, D-09111 **Chemnitz**
Tel: +49 371 369 740 **Fax:** +49 371 369 7421
Email: chemitz@cmslegal.de

An der Dreikönigskirche 10, D-01097 **Dresden**
Tel: +49 351 826 4400 **Fax:** +49 351 826 4716
Email: dresden@cmslegal.de

Bankstrasse 1, D-40476 **Dusseldorf**
Tel: +49 211 4934 0 **Fax:** +49 211 4920 097
Email: cmslawyers@annonet.de

Friedrich-Ebert-Anlage 44, D-60325 **Frankfurt am Main**
Tel: +49 69 71 70 10 **Fax:** +49 69 71 70 11 10
Email: frankfurt@cmslegal.de

Stadthausbrücke 1-3, D-20355 **Hamburg**
Tel: +49 40 376 300 **Fax:** +49 40 376 30300
Email: hamburg@cmslegal.de

Karl-Tauchnitz-Strasse 10B, D-04107 **Leipzig**
Tel: +49 341 216 720 **Fax:** +49 341 216 7233
Email: leipzig@cmslegal.de

Brienner Strasse 11/V, D-80333 **Munich**
Tel: +49 89 238 070 **Fax:** +49 89 238 07110
Email: müchen@cmslegal.de

Schöttlestrasse 8, D-70597 **Stuttgart**
Tel: +49 711 97 640 **Fax:** +49 711 97 64900
Email: stuttgart@cmslegal.de

(cms)

CMS Hasche Sigle Eschenlohr Peltzer Schäfer

RECHTSANWÄLTE STEUERBERATER

C

CMS STROMMER REICH-ROHRWIG KARASEK HAINZ

HEAD OFFICE

Ebendorferstrasse 3,
A-1010 Vienna, Austria
Tel: +43 1 40 4430 **Fax:** +43 1 404 43 9000
Email: office@cmslegal.at
Website: www.cmslegal.at

FIRM OVERVIEW

Managing partner: Alfred Strommer
Senior partner: Alfred Strommer
Number of partners worldwide: 18
Number of other lawyers worldwide: 30

AREAS OF PRACTICE:

Corporate 25%
Arbitration and litigation 20%
Construction and commercial property 20%
Employment and pensions 15%
Banking and finance 10%
Intellectual property 5%
IT and telecommunications 5%

FIRM OVERVIEW: Established in 1970, CMS Strommer Reich-Rohrwig Karasek Hainz is a Viennese law firm with 18 partners and 30 other lawyers. In July 1999 it became one of the founder members, together with Cameron Mckenna (UK), Hasche Sigle Eschenlohr Peltzer Schäfer (Germany) and Derks Star Busman Hanotiau (Belgium and the Netherlands), of the CMS transnational legal services alliance. The alliance now also includes CMS von Erlach Klainguti Stettler Wille (Switzerland). The firm advises on all aspects of Austrian Law, focusing on corporate law and is one of Austria's leading M&A firms. Members of the firm have advised the Austrian legislature on the content of new Austrian legislation and have published numerous articles and books on Austrian and EU law, some of which are used as standard texts. In addition to their experience in Austria, lawyers of the firm have practised, studied or trained abroad.

INTERNATIONAL EXPERIENCE: The firm has international experience in corporate and commercial law, IT, utilities, construction and real estate. The firm is particularly active in the neighbouring countries of Central and Eastern Europe, especially in Slovakia, (where it has this year set up an office), as well as in Croatia, Bosnia, Bulgaria, Hungary, Poland and Slovenia, and is well placed to advise on cross-border transactions and multi-jurisdictional legal issues. The firm advised on the bid on a GSM licence in Croatia and arranged for the financing involved; advises a major Croatian telecom operator; and advised an Austrian telecom company on investments in Bosnia and Slovenia. The firm has acted for contractors on major building developments in the Czech Republic and Poland, and is currently advising a French investor on the acquisition of a major retail outlet in Slovakia.

INTERNATIONAL CLIENTS: The firm advises a wide range of large and medium-sized companies in the banking, telecommunications, computer, internet, oil and gas, pharmaceutical and automotive sectors. International clients include Abbey National, UBS, HSBC, Merrill Lynch, Morgan Stanley Dean Witter, Postabank (Hungary), Lloyds TSB Bank, Shell, Magna (Canada), ABB, Bayer, Gehe, Preussag, Viag, and VIP-net GSM (Croatia).

MAIN INTERNATIONAL AREAS OF PRACTICE:

Arbitration and litigation: The firm undertakes a large amount of work in the utilities sector and also handles construction, employment and shareholders' disputes.

Banking and finance: The firm handles all financial aspects of international projects. Recent work includes the handling of US leveraged lease transactions for lessees and lessors, and project finance.

Capital markets: The firm has acted on a number of public equity bonds and high-yield offerings, advising all three major Austrian investment banks, among other institutions.

Construction and commercial property: The firm advises a substantial number of Austria's leading construction companies. Projects, public procurement and corporate matters are dealt with at both the Austrian and international level.

Corporate: The firm advises on the entire range of legal issues arising out of the formation of companies and their operation. This includes restructuring and re-organisation programmes for industrial groups and privatisation of local utilities as well as public takeover bids.

Employment: The firm handles all matters relating to Austrian employment law, advising foreign companies on the same. It handles relations with trade unions, social security issues and collective bargaining agreements. The employment law aspects of M&A transactions are also dealt with.

EU and competition law: The firm has an established Austrian Cartel law practice and expanded its expertise to EU Competition law even before Austria's accession. The firm represents clients before the Commission and European Court.

Intellectual property: The practice encompasses copyright, patent law, trademarks and unfair competition advice to Austrian and International clients.

IT and telecommunications: The firm advises the largest Austrian GSM operator. It handles inter alia bidding procedures for GSM licences and dealings with foreign shareholders and has a strong list of technology clients.

Utilities: The firm advises five out of the ten Austrian electricity companies and represents a number of international clients in the sector.

Tax: The firm's tax department advises primarily on the domestic and international tax aspect of M&A and capital markets transactions.

White collar criminal defence: Work includes tax crime and criminal procedure.

LANGUAGES: Bosnian, Bulgarian, Chinese, Croatian, Czech, English, French, German, Macedonian, Romanian, Russian, Serbian, Slovak, Spanish

WORLDWIDE OFFICE CONTACTS

AUSTRIA
Ebendorferstrasse 3, A-1010 **Vienna**
Tel: +43 1 40 4430 **Fax:** +43 1 404 43 9000
Email: office@cmslegal.at

SLOVAKIA
CMS Camogursky Strommer Reich-Rohwirg, PO Box 21 Krizkova 9
Bratislava, SK81499
Tel: +421 7 524 500 60 **Fax:** +421 7 524 500 65
Email: office@cmslegal.sk

YUGOSLAVIA
CMS Strommer Reich-Rohrwig Karasek Hainz GmbH, Semina 1
YU 1100 **Belgrade**
Tel: +381 11 328 3096 **Fax:** +381 11 328 3097
Email: office@cmslegal.co.yu

 For other recommended firms see pages 1485-1520

CONYERS DILL & PEARMAN

HEAD OFFICE

Clarendon House, 2 Church Street, PO Box HM 666
Hamilton HM CX Bermuda
Tel: +1 441 295 1422 **Fax:** +1 441 292 4720
Email: info@cdp.bm
Website: www.cdp.bm

WORLDWIDE OFFICE CONTACTS

BERMUDA
Clarendon House, 2 Church Street, PO Box HM 666, **Hamilton** HM CX
Tel: +1 441 295 1422 **Fax:** +1 441 292 4720
Email: info@cdp.bm

HONG KONG
2901 One Exchange Square, 8 Connaught Place, Central, **Hong Kong**
Tel: +852 2524 7106 **Fax:** +852 2845 9268
Email: hongkong@cdp.bm

FIRM OVERVIEW

General Manager: John Buckley
Number of partners worldwide: 17
Number of other lawyers worldwide: 72

AREAS OF PRACTICE:

Civil litigation and arbitration ....*%
Company and commercial ....*%
E-commerce and telecommunications ....*%
Insolvency and restructuring ....*%
Insurance and reinsurance ....*%
Intellectual property ....*%
Mutual funds and partnerships ....*%
Real property ....*%
Shipping and aviation ....*%
Trusts and private client ....*%
*Workload % not disclosed

FIRM OVERVIEW: Founded in 1928, Conyers Dill & Pearman is one of the oldest and largest offshore law firms. It has contributed significantly to the development of Bermuda as one of the world's most successful 'offshore' jurisdictions and is recognised as one whose work is predominantly international in scope. It is a member of the international association of law firms, Lex Mundi. Its overseas offices in British Virgin Islands, Cayman Islands, Guernsey, Hong Kong and London concentrate on corporate and trust law and, in particular, transactions involving Bermuda and British Virgin Islands companies. They also advise on, and arrange for, the incorporation and administration of such companies.

INTERNATIONAL EXPERIENCE: Since the 1930's when Conyers Dill & Pearman formed the first exempt company, its business has been primarily international.

MAIN INTERNATIONAL AREAS OF PRACTICE:

Company/commercial: The practice covers several areas of law including the formation of companies, mutual funds, partnerships, commercial shipping transactions, aircraft financing, leasing and purchasing, liquidations, trademarks and patents and general commercial transactions. Advice and legal assistance is given on the incorporation of companies and the formation of partnerships and trusts; drafting and amending the constitutive documents of companies and partnerships; all forms of financing and loan transactions the acquisition or disposal of assets and businesses, corporate reconstructions, amalgamations, mergers and take-overs; all forms of corporate reorganisation of capital; public offers and prospectuses, private placement documentation and stock exchange particulars; facilitating the migration or continuation of a foreign company to an offshore jurisdiction, or of an offshore company to a foreign country.
Insurance: Bermuda is one of the world's largest insurance and reinsurance centres. The firm's Bermuda office provides most of the insurance law related advice. Bermuda based insurers range from large publicly owned companies to small single-parent captives.
Mutual funds and public offerings: The mutual fund business has grown dramatically since 1980. Conyers Dill & Pearman has been involved in the formation of numerous mutual funds, unit trusts and limited partnerships, many of which are quoted on stock exchanges around the world.
Partnership: The firm's lawyers are well versed in the drafting and reviewing of agreements for both general and limited partnerships. The firm handles applications to the relevant authorities for the registration of such partnerships to ensure that they are properly authorised to carry on business. Additionally, they have considerable experience in advising on offer documentation relating to partnership interests.
Shipping and aircraft: The firm advises on agreements for the purchase, leasing, financing or sale of ships or aircraft, whether registered offshore or elsewhere; the registration of ships and aircraft on their respective registers agreements relating to the operation of the companies owning and/or operating ships and aircraft.
Foreign sales corporations: In December 1988 Bermuda was designated by the US Treasury as a qualified jurisdiction for the incorporation of US owned Foreign Sales Corporations (FSCs). Since then a large number of FSCs have been incorporated in Bermuda and have been used in tax-based lease financing of major American manufactured capital equipment such as aircraft, satellites and locomotives.
Intellectual property, trademarks and patents: The registration of trademarks and patents is achieved through application to the Registrar General. The firm assists and advises with such applications and the maintenance of the ensuing registrations. It co-ordinates the international protection of intellectual property rights, utilising copyright and trademark rights for international business clients.
Liquidations: Voluntary liquidations are undertaken when the business purpose for the company has been fulfilled, or where beneficial tax reasons exist. In the case of insolvent companies, the procedures are different and a professional accountant, experienced in liquidating insolvent companies, is usually appointed as liquidator to ensure compliance with local law. The dissolution of a company incorporated in another jurisdiction, but doing business offshore, requires assistance from local offshore counsel.
Private client and trusts: The private client department offers the international client advice on overall asset owning structures, estate planning and the establishment of trusts, where necessary co-ordinating advice on international legal and tax issues affecting families of substantial wealth. It provides trustee services through its affiliated trust companies.
Modern Trust Laws: Trust laws are based on English common law and equity, ensuring a comfortable level of predictability should court decisions be necessary. Private purpose trusts, asset protection features, protection from forced heirship, protection from community property laws and certainty on conflict of laws issues are certain innovative features of local trust law that may be available.
Property: The practice covers all transactions involving residential and commercial property with particular emphasis on major hotel properties.
Litigation: Recent years have seen a marked increase in the number of commercial disputes which have been tried in the Bermuda Courts. The litigation department is involved in all aspects of civil and commercial arbitration and litigation particularly company insolvency, insurance and reinsurance, contracts, banking, trusts and personal injury claims.

For other recommended firms see pages 1485-1520

COTTLE CATFORD & CO

HEAD OFFICE

PO Box 63, 17 High Street,
Bridgetown Barbados
Tel: +1 246 426 3298 **Fax:** +1 246 426 3726

Email: lawcott@caribsurf.com

WORLDWIDE OFFICE CONTACTS

BARBADOS
PO Box 63, 17 High Street, **Bridgetown**
Tel: +1 246 426 3298 **Fax:** +1 246 426 3726
Email: lawcott@caribsurf.com

FIRM OVERVIEW

Senior partner: Allan St. Clair Watson
Partners: Phillip V Nicholls, Joyce J Griffith

Number of partners worldwide: 3
Number of other lawyers worldwide: 2

AREAS OF PRACTICE:

Property 25%
Estates and trusts 20%
Corporate and commercial 15%
Banking 10%
Offshore 10%
Civil litigation 5%
Family 5%
General practice 5%
Intellectual property 5%

C

FIRM OVERVIEW: Cottle is one of the oldest law firms in Barbados. The firm was established over 125 years ago, and has maintained its reputation for excellence in the traditional fields of conveyancing, corporate and commercial law, intellectual property, insurance and probate. Since 1972, the firm has developed into a general-practice firm, offering clients a full range of legal services and adding family law, civil litigation and off-shore services to its portfolio.

INTERNATIONAL CLIENTS: The firm's client base includes a number of regional and international corporations, banks and insurance companies, including Life of Barbados Ltd, Barclays, Barbados Mutual Life and Barbados Fire & General Insurance.

MAIN INTERNATIONAL AREAS OF PRACTICE:

Property: The firm covers all types of property transactions and is well known for the large volume of conveyancing and mortgage work that it conducts.

Offshore and financial: This is a major growth area for the firm and members of the firm are heavily involved in the promotion of offshore business in Barbados. The firm is represented on various government taskforces whose goals are to promote Barbados as a top class offshore and financial investment jurisdiction. Its clients include those investing into the island's economy and it was recently involved in the refinancing of Hilton International Barbados.

Intellectual property: The firm is an active participant in the promotion of the harmonisation of Intellectual Property legislation in Barbados. It has experience of trademark and patent registration and litigation.

LANGUAGES: English

For other recommended firms see pages 1485-1520

COUDERT BROTHERS

HEAD OFFICE

The Grace Building, 1114 Avenue of the Americas,
New York NY 10036-7703, USA
Tel: +1 212 626 4400 **Fax:** +1 212 626 4120
Email: inquiries@coudert.com
Website: www.coudert.com

FIRM OVERVIEW

Chairman: Anthony Williams
Number of partners worldwide: 224
Number of other lawyers worldwide: 610

AREAS OF PRACTICE:

Antitrust ....*%
Banking ....*%
Employee Benefits ....*%
Entertainment ....*%
Global project finance ....*%
Intellectual property ....*%
Litigation ....*%
* Workload % not disclosed

FIRM OVERVIEW: Founded in 1853, Coudert Brothers is a global partnership with a worldwide network of 27 offices in 15 countries. The firm provides legal advice on international business transactions and dispute resolution and has offices in the major world financial centers including offices in North America, Europe, Asia, Australia and associated offices in Budapest, Prague, Stockholm and Mexico City.

INTERNATIONAL EXPERIENCE: The firm works both nationally and internationally, providing legal services to large international and multinational companies as well as government and non governmental organisations, institutions and agencies in respect of domestic, international and cross border activities.

INTERNATIONAL CLIENTS: Clients include multinational consumer product corporations; commercial, investment and development banks, telecommunications and transport (including airlines); insurance companies; national and municipal governments and agencies; real estate companies; venture capital firms; high technology and Internet companies; investment funds; institutional investors; publishing companies.

MAIN INTERNATIONAL AREAS OF PRACTICE:

Antitrust: The firm advises on antitrust and EU competition issues for local and international M&A deals and joint ventures as well as litigation.
Bankruptcy/business reorganisation: The firm assists creditors, debtors, committees and opportunistic investors worldwide.
Customs: The firm represents US importers and agents, US and foreign exporters, customhouse brokers, individuals and others before the US Customs Service and federal courts.
Energy/natural resources: Work handled includes financing, regulatory, environmental, tax and dispute resolution advice on oil, gas, electricity and mining projects as well as contracts for supply, installations and infrastructure.
Entertainment: The firm advises on international licensing, distribution and financing of film, general entertainment matters, tax, intellectual property and litigation.
General corporate/commercial: Work handled includes M&A, joint ventures, privatisations, management buyouts, corporate finance and commercial agreements.

WORLDWIDE OFFICE CONTACTS

AUSTRALIA
Level 8 Gateway, 1 Macquarie Place, **Sydney** NSW 2000
Tel: + 61 2 9930 7500 **Fax:** + 61 2 9930 7600
Email: mail@sydney.coudert.com

FRANCE
52 Avenue des Champs Elysees, BP 639, 75367 **Paris**
Tel: + 33 1 53 83 60 00 **Fax:** + 33 1 53 83 60 07
Email: info@paris.coudert.com

GERMANY
Friedrich-Ebert-Anlage 14, D-60325 **Frankfurt am Main**
Tel: +49 69 7549 0 **Fax:** +49 69 7549 290
Email: info@coudert.schuermann.com

HONG KONG
39th Floor, Gloucester Tower, The Landmark, 11 Pedder Street, Central, **Hong Kong**
Tel: + 852 2218 9100 **Fax:** + 852 2868 1417
Email: info@hko.coudert.com

UNITED KINGDOM
60 Cannon Street, **London** EC4N 6JP
Tel: + 44 20 7248 3000 **Fax:** + 44 20 7248 3001
Email: info@london.coudert.com

USA
The Grace Building, 1114 Avenue of the Americas, **New York** NY 10036-7703
Tel: +1 212 626 4400 **Fax:** +1 212 626 4120
Email: inquiries@coudert.com

Other offices in Almaty, Antwerp, Bangkok, Beijing, Berlin, Brussels, Denver, Ghent, Jakarta, Los Angeles, Milan, Montreal, Moscow, Munich, Palo Alto, St. Petersburg, San Francisco, San Jose, Singapore, Tokyo. Associated offices in Budapest, Mexico City, Prague, Stockholm

Banking and finance: The firm advises on project financing, capital markets, investment funds and international securities.
International arbitration/dispute resolution: Work includes drafting arbitration clauses, representing claimants and respondents in institutional and ad hoc arbitral proceedings, and litigation.
International trade: The firm advises on import relief proceedings, rights under WTO and other agreements, commercial and regulatory trade matters.
Real property: The firm handles real estate acquisitions and divestitures, financing transactions, joint ventures, foreclosures, purchase/resale of mortgage and equity portfolios; complex construction projects; litigation.
Tax: Work includes acquisitions, financings and tax planning; international transactional work; international financing and leasing transactions and leasing products.
Telecommunications: The firm advises on technology, regulation, M&A, information traffic, finance, privatisations, joint ventures, infrastructure development, securities and commercial transactions.
Private client: Work handled includes estate planning, probate/trust administration, multi-jurisdictional estate planning for persons and estates with property in foreign countries subject to US tax laws.

LANGUAGES: Arabic, Cantonese, Croatian, Danish, Dutch, Estonian, English, Filipino, Flemish, French, German, Greek, Hebrew, Hindi, Hungarian, Indonesian, Italian, Japanese, Kazakh, Korean, Mandarin, Norwegian, Polish, Portuguese, Romanian, Russian, Serbian, Spanish, Swedish, Tamil, Thai, Ukranian, Vietnamese

C

For other recommended firms see pages 1485-1520

COVINGTON & BURLING

HEAD OFFICE

1201 Pennsylvania Avenue, NW,
Washington DC 20004-2401, USA
Tel: +1 202 662 6000 **Fax:** +1 202 662 6291
Email: jblake@cov.com
Website: www.cov.com

FIRM OVERVIEW

Chairman Jonathan D Blake
Vice Chairman Philip K Howard

Number of partners worldwide: 142
Number of other lawyers worldwide: 297

AREAS OF PRACTICE:

Litigation	27%
Corporate/tax	23%
Regulatory/legislative	18%
Technology/IP	18%
Antitrust/international trade	14%

WORLDWIDE OFFICE CONTACTS

BELGIUM
Kunstlaan-Avenue des Arts, 44/8, B-1040 **Brussels**
Tel: +32 2 549 5230 **Fax:** +32 2 502 1598
Email: dharfst@cov.com

UNITED KINGDOM
Leconfield House, Curzon Street, **London** W1Y 8AS
Tel: +44 20 7495 5655 **Fax:** +44 20 7495 3101
Email: rkingham@cov.com

USA
1330 Avenue of the Americas, **New York** NY 10019
Tel: +1 212 841 1056 **Fax:** +1 212 841 1010
Email: phoward@cov.com

601 California Street, 19th Floor, **San Francisco** CA 94108
Tel: +1 415 591 6000 **Fax:** +1 415 591 6091
Email: jsnipes@cov.com

1201 Pennsylvania Avenue, NW, **Washington DC** 20004-2401
Tel: +1 202 662 6000 **Fax:** +1 202 662 6291
Email: jblake@cov.com

C

FIRM OVERVIEW: Based in Washington, Covington & Burling was founded in 1919 and now has approximately 400 lawyers in Washington, New York, San Francisco, London and Brussels, as well as 60 lawyers at August & Debouzy, a correspondent office in Paris. Covington & Burling combined with New York firm Howard, Smith & Levin LLP in October 1999.

INTERNATIONAL EXPERIENCE: The firm represented longtime client Exxon Corporation on its merger with Mobil. It is counsel to Microsoft Corporation in a variety of matters including intellectual property, piracy and licensing. The firm represented Bacardi in its acquisition of the Dewars and Bombay brands, is counsel of record to the National Football League for litigation and general corporate matters, represents Monsanto in a variety of intellectual property litigation matters, and is counsel of record for Union Pacific in M&A and other regulations. The firm also handles numerous assignments for food, drug and cosmetic companies such as Merck, Warner-Lambert and Eli Lilly. Covington & Burling has achieved twelve consecutive Supreme court victories, including three cases in 2000: Mobil Oil Exploration & Producing Southeast v US, Harris Trust & Savings Bank v Salomon Brothers Inc and Food and Drug Administration v Brown and Williamson Tobacco Corp. As a result of the merger with Howard, Smith & Levin, the firm has expanded its capabilities in areas such as M&A, finance and securities law. In the software field, lawyers have handled four of the largest transactions ever, including computer Associates' US$4 billion acquisition of Sterling Software. The New York office also has wide experience in transactional and financial litigation, and an active white collar practice.

INTERNATIONAL CLIENTS: Include ExxonMobil, Microsoft, Bacardi, WorldCom, Benetton, the Business Software Alliance, Monsanto, Merck, Warner-Lambert, Eli Lilly, UBS Warburg, GE Capital and Zurich Financial Services.

MAIN INTERNATIONAL AREAS OF PRACTICE:

Technology and the Internet: The firm is a principal intellectual property, public policy and transactional counsel for leading software and Internet companies, such as Microsoft, Computer Associates and USA Networks. The firm is advising the Business Software Alliance and numerous companies on crafting and enforcing software anti-piracy laws worldwide and advises a wide variety of companies on data privacy, encryption and other technology issues.

Communications: The firm has a comprehensive communications practice in the US, with expertise in telecommunications, mass media, cable, satellite, PCS, international law, programming ventures, newsgathering and First Amendment issues. It represents new competitors in telecommunications, such as Sprint PCS, and entrepreneurial companies, such as Pathnet, on policy issues and transactions. It represents more than 100 TV stations, including groups such as The Washington Post Company and associations of network affiliates, and it represented National Geographic in the negotiation of a new cable channel.

Financial services: The firm is principal regulatory and legislative counsel to the Bank of America, BankBoston, Freddie Mac, Golden West and the leading trade assocations for banking and finance. As financing counsel, the firm represents international banks and insurance companies, including UBS Warburg, GE Capital and Zurich Financial Services.

M&A: The firm has a wide practice in negotiated and hostile mergers. Transactions include the 1998 Bacardi acquisitions of the Dewars and Bombay branks, the 1998 acquisition of Eagle-Picher industries by a Dutch company and actively advising the M&A Department of UBS Warburg.

Legislative and regulatory: The practice encompasses many of the leading industry trade groups, including The Coalition to Preserve the Integrity of American Trademarks, American Bankers Association, American Automobile Association, Pharmaceutical Research and manufacturers of America, Association of American Railroads and the Chemical Manufacturers Association.

Anti-trust: The firm advises on large combinations and divestitures, and on international trade issues. Recent assignments include representing Exxon in its US$80 billion acquisition of Mobil.

Litigation: The firm prosecutes and defends cases before judges and juries in US state and federal courts nationwide, before arbitration panels convened by US and international arbitral organisations, before all major US federal agencies, and in the courts of selected foreign jurisdictions. Our appellate practice extends to every federal Court of Appeal and includes 12 consecutive victories on behalf of clients before the US Supreme Court.

LANGUAGES: Arabic, Danish, Dutch, English, French, German, Greek, Hebrew, Hindi, Italian, Japanese, Korean, Mandarin, Portuguese, Russian, Spanish, Turkish, Ukranian

For other recommended firms see pages 1485-1520

COX HALLETT WILKINSON

HEAD OFFICE

Milner House, 18 Parliament Street, PO Box HM 1561,
Hamilton HM FX Bermuda
Tel: +441 295 4630 **Fax:** +441 292 7880

Email: cw@cw.bm
Website: www.cw.bm

WORLDWIDE OFFICE CONTACTS

BERMUDA
Milner House, 18 Parliament Street, PO Box HM 1561, **Hamilton** HM FX
Tel: +441 295 4630 **Fax:** +441 292 7880
Email: cw@cw.bm

FIRM OVERVIEW

Managing partner: David R Kessaram

Number of partners worldwide: 7
Number of other lawyers worldwide: 8

AREAS OF PRACTICE:

Corporate and M&A	40%
Litigation	40%
International and estate planning	10%
Real estate	10%

FIRM PROFILE: Cox Hallett Wilkinson is a mid-sized law firm, which was formed on the 1st January, 1998 by the merger of the two law firms - Cox & Wilkinson (formed in 1970) and Hallett Whitney & Patton (established in 1918). The merged firm provides wide legal experience with its main focus on corporate and commercial law, all forms of civil litigation and arbitration, property law, conveyancing and trusts. The merger has also brought together the respective subsidiaries of the firms - Coson Corporate Services Limited and Globe Corporate Services Limited, providing corporate administrative services to a variety of local and exempted companies carrying on business in the insurance, reinsurance, mutual fund, investment holding, international trade, shipping, and aircraft operation leasing, amongst others.

INTERNATIONAL EXPERIENCE: Cox Hallett Wilkinson is the exclusive Bermuda member of the Commercial Law Affiliates ('CLA'), the world's largest affiliation of independent medium-sized business law firms. Cox Hallett Wilkinson's partners are active members of the professional organisations relevant to the practice of law in Bermuda, including the Bermuda Bar Association, the International Bar Association and local and international special interest organisations. CHW attorneys serve on many local committees and sub-committees of these organisations to consider and recommend changes to the existing law and practice in Bermuda and facilitate the growth of international business.

MAIN INTERNATIONAL AREAS OF PRACTICE:
Corporate and M&A: The firm's services to clients include formation of companies, limited partnerships, joint ventures, 1978, collective investment schemes (mutual funds/unit trusts), securities work including public offerings and private placements, corporate finance, secured lending and other financial transactions, insolvency - receivership, liquidation and voluntary arrangements, shipping and aviation, including Bermuda registration, redomicile of companies, pension trust funds and share option schemes, general commercial advice including sales, distribution, manufacturing, franchising and management agreements and the establishment of captive and mutual insurance companies including registration under the Insurance Act
International and local estate planning: Bermuda's trust laws encourage the use of the island as a jurisdiction for estate planning and other financial planning purposes. Local laws, which limit the extent to which creditors can set aside transfers of property by settlors, also make Bermuda a viable jurisdiction for asset protection purposes. Cox Hallett Wilkinson's licensed trust company, State House Trust Company Limited offers many services, including acting as executor and trustee of wills; acting as trustee of pension and similar trusts; management of family assets and implementation of international estate planning; administration of private trust companies formed for the purpose of acting as trustee of a family trust or group of trusts; providing trustee services for charitable trusts and foundations whether local or international in scope; providing administrative and management facilities for subsidiary or affiliated companies.
Litigation: An increasing number of international commercial arbitrations are conducted in Bermuda because of its neutrality as a venue, convenient access, facilities and communications, agreeable climate and the enactment of the UNCITRAL Rules governing the conduct of arbitrations. The parties and their legal representatives enjoy complete freedom from government and local professional restrictions for the purposes of attending and participating in Bermuda arbitrations. The firm advises and represents clients in areas which include insurance and reinsurance litigation and arbitration, hostile take-overs and shareholder disputes, compulsory liquidations and insolvency, international trade, receiverships and breach of trust actions. Cox Hallett Wilkinson's litigation lawyers are experienced in arbitration. Its attorneys not only act as counsel to parties in arbitration but, in appropriate cases, also accept appointment as party-nominated or sole arbitrators. Although mostly oriented towards corporate and commercial work, its attorneys are experienced in most areas of law in which contention can arise. The firm makes use of international computer databanks for research needs, allowing attorneys cost effective desk-top access to the latest cases and authorities.
Real Estate: Land transactions of every type are handled by Cox Hallett Wilkinson's real estate attorneys. It is experienced in all facets of freehold and leasehold property acquisition and disposal (both commercial and residential). Foreign persons require a government licence before being able to buy a house or condominium, application for which must be made in the prescribed form with supporting character and financial references. Cox Hallett Wilkinson's attorneys assist foreign clients in all stages of the application process, advising what is required and compiling and submitting the application on their behalf.

LANGUAGES: Danish, English, German

COZEN AND O'CONNOR

HEAD OFFICE

1900 Market Street,
Philadelphia, PA 19103, USA
Tel: +1 215 665 2000 **Fax:** +1 215 665 2013

Email: postmaster@cozen.com
Website: www.cozen.com

FIRM OVERVIEW

Chairman: Stephen A.Cozen
Vice-Chairman: Patrick J. O'Connor

Number of partners worldwide: 91
Number of other lawyers worldwide: 349

AREAS OF PRACTICE:
Business law and business litigation 40%
Insurance litigation 35%
Insurance coverage 25%

C

FIRM OVERVIEW: Cozen and O'Connor is a full service, client-oriented law firm, founded in 1968 by Stephen A. Cozen. The firm's roots lie in commercial and insurance related litigation. Under the management of Chairman, Stephen A. Cozen and Vice Chairman, Patrick J. O'Connor, the firm has grown from its initial complement of four attorneys practising in Philadelphia to over 440 attorneys practising in 15 offices nationwide. In December, 1998, the firm opened its first international office in London. Within the last decade, the firm has extended its trial practice skills into the commercial arena.

INTERNATIONAL EXPERIENCE: Business, company commercial; insurance; mergers and acquisitions and significant transactions involving public and private organisations.

INTERNATIONAL CLIENTS: The firm advises clients from the insurance, banking and finance, health care insurance, high tech, industrial, service, real estate sectors.

MAIN INTERNATIONAL AREAS OF PRACTICE: Work handled includes insurance and reinsurance; insurance litigation; claim investigation; litigation management and support; subrogation and recovery; corporate and commercial matters; banking and financial services; EU law; e-commerce, information technology and telecommunications; international tax; estate planning.

LANGUAGES: English, French, German, Greek, Italian, Japanese, Portuguese, Norwegian, Spanish

WORLDWIDE OFFICE CONTACTS

USA
SunTrust Plaza, Suite 2200, 303 Peachtree Street, NE, **Atlanta**, GA 30308
Tel: + 1 404 572 2000 **Fax:** + 1 404 572 2199

One First Union Centre, Suite 2100, 301 South College Street, **Charlotte**, NC 28202
Tel: + 1 704 376 3400 **Fax:** + 1 704 334 3351

LibertyView Building, Suite 300, 457 Haddonfield Road, **Cherry Hill**, NJ 08002
Tel: + 1 856 910 5000 **Fax:** + 1 856 910 5075

222 South Riverside, Suite 1500, **Chicago**, IL 60606
Tel: + 1 312 382 3100 **Fax:** + 1 312 382 8910

2300 BankOne Center, 1717 Main Street, **Dallas**, TX 75201
Tel: + 1 214 462 3000 **Fax:** + 1 214 462 3299

3753 Howard Hughes Parkway, **Las Vegas**, NV 89109
Tel: + 1 702 892 3740 **Fax:** + 1 702 892 3741

777 South Figueroa St, Suite 2850, **Los Angeles**, CA 90017
Tel: + 1 213 892 7900 **Fax:** + 1 213 892 7999

45 Broadway Atrium, 16th Floor, **New York**, NY 10006
Tel: + 1 212 509 9400 **Fax:** + 1 212 509 9492

One Newark Center, Suite 1900, 1085 Raymond Blvd, **Newark**, NJ 07102
Tel: + 1 973 286 1200 **Fax:** + 1 973 242 2121

501 West Broadway, Suite 1610, **San Diego**, CA 92101
Tel: + 1 619 234 1700 **Fax:** + 1 619 234 7831

100 California Street, Suite 700 **San Francisco**, CA 94111
Tel: + 1 415 617 6100 **Fax:** + 1 415 617 6101

Washington Mutual Tower, Suite 5200, 1201 Third Avenue, **Seattle**, WA 98101
Tel: + 1 206 340 1000 **Fax:** + 1 206 621 8783

200 Four Falls Corporate Center, Suite 400, PO Box 800, **West Conshohocken**, PA 19428-0800
Tel: + 1 610 941 5400 **Fax:** + 1 610 941 0711

Chase Manhattan Centre, Suite 1400, 1201 North Market Street, **Wilmington**, Delaware 19801
Tel: + 1 302 295 2000 **Fax:** + 1 302 295 2013

UNITED KINGDOM
Tower 42, Level 43 25 Old Borad Street, **London** EC2N 1HQ
Tel: + 44 20 7864 2000 **Fax:** + 44 20 7864 2013

For other recommended firms see pages 1485-1520

CRAWFORD BAYLEY & CO

HEAD OFFICE

State Bank Buildings, 4th Floor,
NGN Vaidya Marg, (Bank Street),
Fort, Mumbai 400 023, India
Tel: + 91 22 266 3713 **Fax:** + 91 22 266 0355/0986

WORLDWIDE OFFICE CONTACTS

INDIA
State Bank Buildings, 4th Floor, NGN Vaidya Marg, (Bank Street),
Fort, **Mumbai** 400 023
Tel: + 91 22 266 3713 **Fax:** + 91 22 266 0355 / 0986

FIRM OVERVIEW

Senior partners: R A Shah
S N Talwar

Number of partners worldwide: 9
Number of other lawyers worldwide: 58

AREAS OF PRACTICE:
Aviation and space .... *%
Banking and finance .... *%
Company/commercial and foreign investment .... *%
Corporate, commercial and business law .... *%
Project finance .... *%
Property, conveyancing and real estate law .... *%
Shipping, admiralty and maritime law .... *%
Telecommunications .... *%
* Workload % not disclosed

FIRM OVERVIEW: Crawford, Bayley & Co has had its present name since 1916, but traces its origins back to 1830. The firm currently has nine partners, 58 associates, 15 paralegal personnel and a supporting staff of over 75 individuals. It is a full-service law firm which advises and represents local and multinational corporations banks and development on corporate law, corporate finance, project finance, banking, capital markets, shipping, real estate, trusts, corporate law, litigation and arbitration, intellectual property and media and communications.

INTERNATIONAL EXPERIENCE: The firm's recent international work includes acting for Schenectady Inc in its acquisition of BSF Worldwide's paint business and representing Hoescht AG in its sale of a speciality chemical business to Clariant International. It is currently handling three ADR cases for a large pharmaceutical company, for a well known software company and for a well known telecom company.
The firm handled the first successful ADR issue in India – Infosys, including the listing of Infosys scrips on Nasdaq Amex. It was also involved in the spin-off of Specialities Chemicals of Sandoz into Clariant, and in the amalgamation of Sandoz into Ciba to form Novartis.

INTERNATIONAL CLIENTS: The firm's international clients include: banks such as Bank of America, Banque Nationale de Paris, Credit Lyonnais, Bank of Tokyo, Deutsche Bank, Dresdner Bank, ABN-AMRO, UBS and HSBC, development agencies or international financial institutions such as the USA's Asian Development Bank, the EDC, the IBRD, IMF and World Bank, investment banks such as Daiwa Securities, GE Capital, Merrill Lynch, Peregrine and Jardine Fleming; Morgan Stanley; consulates such as the American, Australian, British High Commission, Canadian, German and Thai, pharmaceutical, chemical and personal care companies including Bayer AG, Ciba Geigy, Glaxo, Hoechst AG, Johnson & Johnson, Pfizer Inc, Procter & Gamble, Rhone-Poulenc, Unilever and Warner Lambert; engineering companies including Asea Brown Boveri, Courtaulds, Honeywell, Siemens AG, Sandvik AB and Ingersoll Rand; consumer electronics companies such Philips, Samsung, and Sony; aviation, shipping, transport and automotive companies such as Boeing, Fiat, Ford, General Motors, Lloyds Register of Shipping, Maersk Line, Mercedes Benz, Volvo and P&O Containers; petrochemical concerns such as Burmah-Castrol, Exxon, Chevron, Gulf Oil and Pennzoil; insurance companies including Prudential, Canada Life and Cologne Re; Sunlife Assurance Company of Canada; media companies such as the Financial Times and Pearsons; all the Big 5 auditors; airlines including Cathay Pacific, Delta; Swissair and energy company Enron.

MAIN INTERNATIONAL AREAS OF PRACTICE:
Capital markets: The firm has handled numerous international offerings offered by Indian corporations to date either as advisors to the offering company or to the lead managers to the offering.
Project financing and infrastructure project: The firm has handled several infrastructure projects including power, telecommunications, and road projects. It acts for lenders (domestic and international) to the projects as well as for the project companies.
M&A: The firm has successfully assisted domestic and multinational corporations in their acquisitions and mergers in India.
Joint ventures and foreign collaborations: The firm represents multinationals including Fortune 500 Companies for their joint ventures in India.
Shipping: The firm regularly advises international corporates on shipping and admiralty law and also undertakes both dry and wet litigation. The firm is also involved in advising international lenders in the areas of ship finance.

LANGUAGES: English and various Indian regional/vernacular languages.

CRAWFORD BAYLEY & CO.
Solicitors & Advocates

CREEL, GARCÍA-CUÉLLAR Y MÜGGENBURG, SC

HEAD OFFICE

Bosque de Ciruelos No. 304-2° Piso, Bosques de Las Lomas,
11700 Mexico City, Mexico
Tel: +52 5 246 0600 **Fax:** +52 5 596 3309
Email: mail@creel.com.mx

FIRM OVERVIEW

Contact partner: Samuel García-Cuéllar
Managing partner: Carlos Creel C.
Number of partners worldwide: 13
Number of other lawyers worldwide: 50

AREAS OF PRACTICE:

Corporate	20%
M&A	20%
Financial services	15%
Intellectual property	15%
Real estate and tourism	10%
Regulated industries and projects	10%
Tax	10%

C

FIRM OVERVIEW: For more than 60 years Creel, García-Cuéllar y Müggenburg has been one of Mexico's leading full service corporate law firms, serving a broad range of domestic and international clients. The firm was founded in 1936 by Luís J. Creel Luján (1912-1977) under the name Creel Abogados, and adopted its current name in 1990. The firm has thirteen partners and a solid group of associates and attorneys totaling 60 legal professionals. It is committed to offering a quality service to a limited number of clients, through a close personalised client-attorney relationship. Partners and associates may call upon other attorneys within the firm to provide the specialised advice, information and direction that a particular project may require.

INTERNATIONAL EXPERIENCE: The firm has focused its practice on corporate and financial transactions with an international component, providing a broad range of legal services to industrial, commercial and financial clients in Mexico and abroad. Creel, García-Cuéllar y Müggenburg maintains close working relationships with many leading law firms headquartered in the United States, Canada, the European Union and Latin America. In anticipation of expanding free trade areas and the enhanced interaction between the the world's economies, as well as the increasing trade and investment flows between Mexico and its NAFTA partners, the United Kingdom, Continental Europe and Latin America, the firm is actively promoting liaisons with first-rate law firms in North America, several Mercosur countries and the European Union.

INTERNATIONAL CLIENTS: The firm's list of clients includes a substantial number of North American, Asian, European and Latin American companies and funds investing in Mexico, commercial banks financing international trade and infrastructure projects, securities firms arranging or managing securities offerings and derivatives structures, as well as a host of multinational corporations doing business in Mexico. The diversity of its clientele has allowed it to better understand the problems faced by investors in their international activities and particularly, in establishing or enlarging their business in Mexico.

MAIN INTERNATIONAL AREAS OF PRACTICE:

General corporate: The firm offers expert legal advice, covering all aspects of business law relating to the incorporation, organisation and maintenance of all sorts of legal entities in Mexico, including subsidiary companies and branch offices. It advises corporations involved in the issuance and listing of equity and debt instruments, recapitalisations, restructurings and reorganisations, stock repurchases, employees' stock option plans and other types of specialised corporate transactions. The corporate law practice regularly advises clients on competition law matters, assisting them in securing clearance for mergers, acquisitions and joint ventures from the Mexican competition authorities. In addition, the firm advises on a full range of anti-trust issues, including licensing agreements, distribution issues, exclusivity arrangements, price discrimination, trade associations, the extraterritorial application of Mexican competition statutes, as well as in major antitrust practices investigations.

M&A: The firm's predominant practice area is mergers and acquisitions, handling acquisitions, divestitures, mergers, spin-offs, reorganisations, joint ventures and private equity investments, and representing foreign and domestic clients doing business in a variety of regulated and unregulated industries. The firm is involved in designing, negotiating and executing transactions.

Financial services: Creel, García-Cuéllar y Müggenburg represents a variety of Mexican and foreign commercial and investment banks, broker-dealers, public and private funds, insurance and surety institutions, financial leasing and factoring firms and securities markets. The firm advises on domestic and cross-border loan transactions, syndications, project financings, debt and equity offerings in the domestic and international capital markets, debt restructurings and reschedulings, off-balance sheet financings, derivative transactions, securitisations and asset-backed financings of all kinds. In addition, the firm advises on compliance issues affecting financial service firms established in Mexico.

Intellectual property: Creel, García-Cuéllar y Müggenburg represents clients in a wide range of trademark, patent, copyright and trade secret matters arising under Mexican law. Work includes the registration and enforcement of all forms of intellectual property rights and the negotiation of technology transfer, technical assistance, licensing and franchising agreements. This encompasses trademark, copyright, patent infringement and trade secret litigation, including amparo proceedings. Creel, García-Cuéllar y Müggenburg has been a pioneer in the fields of IT and e-commerce, multimedia and entertainment law in Mexico, representing, among others, major international software and media firms.

Real estate and tourism: The firm's real-estate practice group handles all aspects of complicated real-estate transactions and financings. It advises a variety of residential and commercial real-estate developers and managers, as well as major multinational hotel and resort chains, on the acquisition and disposition of real estate assets and businesses, the structuring of time-share schemes, and the operation of hotels and resorts.

Tax: Creel, García-Cuéllar y Müggenburg provides tax advisory services, including tax litigation.

Regulated industries and projects: The firm undertakes transactional and regulatory work for clients in regulated industries in Mexico, including mining, energy, telecommunications, transportation, aviation and railroads. The firm advises on government contracts and procurement, licensing requirements and procedures, public tenders and auctions to obtain licenses.

LANGUAGES: English, French, German, Spanish

WORLDWIDE OFFICE CONTACTS

MEXICO
Bosque de Ciruelos No. 304-2° Piso, Bosques de Las Lomas, 11700
Mexico City
Tel: +52 5 246 0600 **Fax:** +52 5 596 3309
Email: mail@creel.com.mx

For other recommended firms see pages 1485-1520

CREMADES ABOGADOS

HEAD OFFICE

Serrano 27,
28001 Madrid, Spain
Tel: +34 91 426 4050 **Fax:** +34 91 426 4052

Email: despacho@ecremades.com
Website: www.ecremades.com

FIRM OVERVIEW

Managing partner: Javier Cremades

Number of partners worldwide: 7
Number of other lawyers worldwide: 43

AREAS OF PRACTICE:

Corporate and commercial 35%
Telecommunications and new technologies 30%
Intellectual property 15%
Internet and e-commerce 15%
Administrative and civil 5%

FIRM OVERVIEW: Founded in 1994, Cremades Abogados is a leading Spanish firm. It offers comprehensive legal services to national and international clients in administrative, commercial, corporate and financial areas. The firm focuses on telecommunications law, internet law, e-commerce, intellectual property, and information technology. Cremades Abogados created the first Latin-American firm specialising in telecommunications law and Internet, by taking over one of Argentina's most important firms in this area. The firm has created the first legal incubator for Internet start-ups in Spain and Latin America. The firm established an Advisory Board chaired by Antonio Barrera de Irimo, former Chairman of Telefónica and the Spanish Minister of Economy and Finance, and has entered into collaboration agreements with economic and financial consultants, technology consultants, communications agencies, and investment banks.

INTERNATIONAL EXPERIENCE: Cremades Abogados has advised three foreign governments on audio-visual rights and telecommunications regulations, and on constitutional affairs and administrative practice in relation to the PHARE program of the European Union.

INTERNATIONAL CLIENTS: Clients include UPC, Colt Telecom, Dresdner Kleinwort Benson, Ericsson, Nortel, Telenor, Astra (Societé European des Satellites), Alcatel, Arinc (US company participated by the major Airlines), Eurosport TV, RSL Comm (Aló in Spain), Isla Link (submarine cable company), Atento (Telefonica's subsidiary), ICS (telephone operator in Spain), Internet Data House, Sainco, Televent, Tele 2 Europe, El Mundo (major Spanish newspaper), Conferencia Episcopal Española (Spanish Episcopal Conference) Grupo Códice (Spanish publishing company), Iberdrola (major Spanish company), Reuters, Edgix, Sonic, Global Metro Networks, Flag Telecom, Storm Communications, Madritel (Madrid cable operator), Supercable Andalucia (cable operator), Telecable (Asturia's cable operator), Retena (Navarra's cable operator), Reterioja (Rioja's cable operator), Agrupación de Operadores de Cable, Canal 4 Navarra (Pamplona's local television), Colegio Oficial de Ingenieros Técnicos de Comunicación, Acceso a la red de Internet, Cetecom, and Isdefe.

WORLDWIDE OFFICE CONTACTS

ARGENTINA
Av Cordoba 1233, 10B, C 1055 AC **Buenos Aires**
Tel: +54 11 4812 4840 **Fax:** +54 11 4812 4846
Email: buenosaires@ecremades.com

SPAIN
Serrano 27, 28001 **Madrid**
Tel: +34 91 426 4050 **Fax:** +34 91 426 4052
Email: despacho@ecremades.com

Cortina del Muelle, 5, 29015 **Malaga**
Tel: +34 952 06 04 32 **Fax:** +34 952 60 34 24
Email: malaga@ecremades.com

MAIN INTERNATIONAL AREAS OF PRACTICE:

Telecommunications: Cremades Abogados is one of the leading firms in Spain and is known for its expertise. The firm handles all aspects of telecommunications from regulation to licensing. The firm organises an LLM program at the university on telecommunications law, and organises multiple conferences and seminars.
Internet: The firm offers advice to start up companies on corporate, contractual and intellectual property matters and advises Internet companies on e-commerce.
New Technologies: The firm handles all matters relating to new and emerging technologies.
Intellectual property: The firm is actively involved in copyrights, trademarks and patents, and its lawyers participate in conferences and seminars.
Administrative: Cremades Abogados deals with a wide range of administrative matters, such as licensing, permits, regulation, and administrative litigation.
Civil: The firm advises on all aspects of general civil law.
Corporate: The firm advises on all aspects of general corporate law, including international contracts.
Commercial: The firm works with clients ranging from large multinational corporations to national entities and has substantial experience in this area.

LANGUAGES: English, French, German, Italian, Spanish

CREMADES
ABOGADOS
Madrid - Málaga - Buenos Aires

C

For other recommended firms see pages 1485-1520

CROSBY, HEAFEY, ROACH & MAY PC

HEAD OFFICE

1999 Harrison Street, Oakland, CA 94612-3572
Tel: +1 510 763 2000 **Fax:** +1 510 273 8832

Email: information@chrm.com
Website: www.crosbyheafey.com

FIRM OVERVIEW

Managing partner: Kurt C. Peterson
Senior partner: Robert S. Schulman
Number of partners worldwide: 122
Number of other lawyers worldwide: 122

WORLDWIDE OFFICE CONTACTS

USA
1901 Avenue of the Stars, Suite 850, **Los Angeles** CA 90067
Tel: 310 734 5200 **Fax:** 310 734 5299
Email: information@chrm.com

700 South Flower Street, Suite 2200, **Los Angeles**, CA 90017
Tel: +213 896 8000 **Fax:** +213 896 8080
Email: information@chrm.com

Two Embarcadero Center, 20th Floor, **San Francisco**, CA 94111-4106
Tel: 415 543 8700 **Fax:** 415 391 8269
Email: information@chrm.com

AREAS OF PRACTICE:

Commercial litigation	20%
Insurance	15%
Product liability	15%
Business finance and securities	10%
Corporate and commercial services	10%
Employment and labour	10%
Intellectual property	10%
Real estate	10%

C

FIRM OVERVIEW: Established in 1900, Crosby, Heafey, Roach & May employs almost 250 lawyers in offices in Oakland, San Francisco, Los Angeles and Century City, California. The firm advises clients from Fortune 500 companies to start-up entrepreneurs, on a local, national and international level. The firm advises in virtually every area of civil law, and is particularly experienced in business practice and in handling complex litigation.

INTERNATIONAL EXPERIENCE: The firm has an active international practice, representing foreign-based parties and their domestic entities in connection with their US interests, as well as representing US-based clients in connection with their overseas interests. The firm advises on all legal matters involved in conducting business in the US and acquiring US-based companies and assets.

INTERNATIONAL CLIENTS: The firm's clients include local, national and international businesses such as technology companies, manufacturers, distributors, retailers, service businesses, financial institutions and insurance companies. Representative clients include certain underwriters at Lloyd's, London; American Suzuki Motor Corporation and Suzuki Motor Company Ltd; Sony Corporation and Yokohama Tire Corporation.

MAIN INTERNATIONAL AREAS OF PRACTICE:

Business finance and securities: The firm offers a broad range of expertise in business entity formation and finance, transactions regulated by state and federal securities laws, international finance transactions and syndications and lending transactions.

Corporate and commercial services: The firm's corporate lawyers have experience in corporate law, including venture tax planning, representation of corporate and venture interest, M&A and reorganisations and other related services.

Taxation: The firm helps clients plan all types of business transactions, provides advice on business formations, liquidations, recapitalisation and reorganisations and counsels clients on ERISA, retirement plans, executive compensation and a variety of other tax issues.

Intellectual property: The firm's intellectual property lawyers are involved in all matters relating to patents, copyrights, trademarks, trade names, trade secrets, and unfair competition. These include preparing, filing and prosecuting patent and trademark applications in the US and securing similar protection around the world. The firm handles domestic and international business transactions in which intellectual property rights are a key component, including distributorship arrangements, licensing and other forms of technology transfer, joint ventures and 'teaming' arrangements in the computer software, semi-conductor, electronics, pharmaceutical and other industries.

Real estate: The firm's real estate lawyers are active in every aspect of acquiring, developing, financing, leasing and selling all types of real estate. These include commercial, industrial, agricultural and residential properties.

Product liability: The firm defends national and international manufacturers in the pharmaceutical, medical device, chemical and mechanical products industries in lawsuits involving personal injury and property damage.

Environmental: The firm's environmental lawyers assist in the assessment and proper management of environmental rights, advising on the federal, state and local environmental regulations affecting real estate transactions. The firm's lawyers also provide advise on environmental strategies both preventative and remedial.

Employment and labour: The firm's management-oriented labour practice covers the full range of issues facing employers and employees in California. Working with attorneys from the firm's environmental and litigation groups, the practice also advises on workplace safety and regulatory compliance.

Bankruptcy and creditors' rights: The firm represents both creditors and debtors in major bankruptcy reorganisations as well as pre-bankruptcy workouts. It advises clients prior to commencement of proceedings and also handles both litigious and transactional phases of such matters.

Insurance and reinsurance: The firm represents insurers and other entities engaged directly in the business of insurance. It handles numerous intra-insurer and reinsurance arbitrations, as well as binding arbitrations with insureds.

Personal estate planning: Activities include preserving and transferring family wealth. These services have been performed for clients in Canada, the United Kingdom, Western and Eastern Europe, Central America, South America and Asia.

Commercial litigation: Work includes product liability, securities, intellectual property, unfair competition, antitrust, taxes, publishing, professional malpractice, insurance, employment discrimination, immigration and construction.

LANGUAGES: English, French

For other recommended firms see pages 1485-1520

DALY & FIGGIS

HEAD OFFICE

Lonrho House, Standard Street, P.O. Box 40034
Nairobi Kenya
Tel: +254 2 310 304 **Fax:** +254 2 334 892

Email: DF@daly-figgis.co.ke

WORLDWIDE OFFICE CONTACTS

KENYA
Lonrho House, Standard Street, P.O. Box 40034, **Nairobi**
Tel: +254 2 310 304 **Fax:** +254 2 334 892
Email: DF@daly-figgis.co.ke

FIRM OVERVIEW

Senior partner: Neville Warren

Number of partners worldwide: 6
Number of other lawyers worldwide: 10

AREAS OF PRACTICE:

Banking and finance .... *%
Bankruptcy and insolvency .... *%
Corporate/commercial .... *%
Employment .... *%
Intellectual property .... *%
Litigation .... *%
Mergers and acquisitions .... *%
Real estate .... *%
Regulation of business enterprises .... *%
* Workload % not disclosed

FIRM OVERVIEW: Established in 1899, Daly & Figgis offers a comprehensive legal service to clients focusing on real estate, corporate/commercial, banking and finance, and mergers and acquisitions. The firm does not belong to any formal alliances or networks with other lawyers, preferring to maintain contacts with various firms worldwide, with which it works on individual international transactions.

INTERNATIONAL EXPERIENCE: The firm regularly handles international transactions, including mergers and acquisitions, public and private debt and equity financing, the establishment of new business enterprises in Kenya, and provision of Kenyan Law advice on transactions involving other jurisdictions.

INTERNATIONAL CLIENTS: Clients include multinational businesses operating in a wide range of industry sectors. These include banking and financial services, telecommunications, power, oil, energy and mineral exploration, pharmaceuticals, information and technology, foods and beverages, transport, hotels, tourism, leisure and agriculture. Clients come from Europe, Southern Africa, North America and the Far East.

MAIN INTERNATIONAL AREAS OF PRACTICE:

Mergers and acquisitions: Transactions in this area range from small private acquisitions, to advising on Kenyan Law implications of cross border take-overs of international companies.

Banking and finance: Daly & Figgis provide expertise in this area, including secured and syndicated loan transactions, guarantees, structured finance, project finance, leasing and tax based finance.
Corporate finance and securities: The firm advises on public and private equity and debt offerings, take-over bids, and capital markets transactions.
Corporate: The firm advises on all aspects of general Kenyan corporate law.
Licensing laws: The firm advises on licensing aspects of telecommunications, power, energy and mining, banking and insurance.
Security and financial markets: The firm advises clients on Kenyan laws pertaining to funds, securities and derivatives and advises investment firms on the structure and licensing of their operations.
Employment: The firm handles all matters relating to Kenyan employment law and Retirement Benefit Schemes.
Intellectual property: The firm advises in relation to registration in Kenya and ARIPO signatories of trade, service marks, patents and copyright.
Privatisation: The firm provides advice on privatisation operations.
Litigation: The firm provides litigation support services to its corporate and commercial clients, with particular reference to enforcement of debt securities.
Real estate: The firm advises on all aspects of Kenyan real estate and property laws.

LANGUAGES: English, French, and local Kenyan dialects.

D

DANKNER-LUSKY & CO

HEAD OFFICE

Rothschild House, 38 Rothschild Boulevard,
Tel Aviv 66883, Israel
Tel: +972 3 560 0644 **Fax:** +972 3 560 0743
Email: danlu@danlu.co.il

FIRM OVERVIEW

Managing partner: Moshe Lusky
Senior partner: Nochi Dankner, Moshe Lusky

Number of partners worldwide: 8
Number of other lawyers worldwide: 9

AREAS OF PRACTICE:

Aviation and Tourism	*%
Banking and finance	*%
Commercial	*%
Construction, development and real estate	*%
Corporate	*%
Energy, natural gas and chemicals	*%
Investments and finance	*%
Litigation and arbitration	*%
M&A	*%
Telecommunications and technology	*%
Tenders	*%

* Workload % not disclosed

FIRM OVERVIEW: Dankner-Lusky & Co was established in 1984. The firm provides a high level of services and expertise, offering a full range of legal services, specialising in domestic and international commercial transactions, investment and finance representation, real estate, development and construction, corporate matters, and litigation.

INTERNATIONAL EXPERIENCE: Dankner-Lusky & Co has advised international clients engaged in various industries.
The firm advises one of the four largest energy companies and one of the three largest natural gas suppliers in Israel. It advises one of Israel's largest retail chains and handles the purchase and construction of one of Israel's largest computerised storage systems. The firm has handled work on the 'Power Centers' project including financing, zoning and planning, construction, marketing and sale of commercial space, management and other related matters.
Dankner-Lusky & Co has advised one of the largest Israeli telecommunication cable companies on its successful tender offer to the Israeli Government to become a major operator. It has also carried out due diligence examinations in the preparation of bids in two major tender offers for companies privatised by the Israeli Government; and advised the Israeli Government on the Cross Israel Highway Project, the largest transportation project in Israel in recent years.

INTERNATIONAL CLIENTS: The firm's client base includes local and international public corporations, investment funds, insurance conglomerates, telecommunication providers, governmental institutions, developers and contractors, international department stores and franchises, cooperative societies, energy and chemical companies and private companies of all sizes.

WORLDWIDE OFFICE CONTACTS

ISRAEL
Rothschild House, 38 Rothschild Boulevard, **Tel Aviv** 66883
Tel: +972 3 560 0644 **Fax:** +972 3 560 0743
Email: danlu@danlu.co.il

MAIN INTERNATIONAL AREAS OF PRACICE:
Corporate and commercial: The firm handles all aspects of corporate transactions, finance and management (including the incorporation and tax structuring of companies), the acquisition and disposition of corporate stock and assets, mergers and acquisitions, tender offers, due diligence examinations, supply and distribution arrangements and equipment purchase and leasing agreements.
Dankner-Lusky & Co also advises tourism and airline companies on investment, finance and stock purchase agreements, aircraft lease agreements, international service agreements and aircraft maintenance contracts.
Technology: Dankner-Lusky & Co handles investments in hi-tech and R&D companies and advises start-up/high-tech companies and venture capitalists. Work handled includes raising capital from seed to IPO; purchase agreements; term sheets; due diligence; registering trademarks and patents; mergers; buyouts; capital investments; share transfer agreements; and disputes over ownership of intellectual property rights and titles.
Real estate: Dankner-Lusky & Co advises large development and construction companies on large-scale acquisitions and the development of commercial, mixed-use, hotel, shopping mall, and residential projects. The real estate department also advises on real estate tax planning, the initial acquisition/leasing of the land, the registration and zoning process, condemnation of property, title issues, expropriations, the application and negotiation with the planning authorities, project financing, the negotiation and drafting of construction contracts, and the sale/lease of the units to end users.
Litigation: Dankner-Lusky & Co provides litigation services in all areas of commercial law, contract enforcement, foreclosure of security interests, real estate matters, disputes over ownership of intellectual property, labour disputes, and liquidation.

LANGUAGES: English, French, Hebrew

DANKER-LUSKY & CO., ADVOCATES

For other recommended firms see pages 1485-1520

DARROIS VILLEY MAILLOT BROCHIER

HEAD OFFICE

69 Avenue Victor Hugo,
75116 Paris, France
Tel: +33 1 4502 1919 **Fax:** +33 1 4501 9168

Email: jmdarrois@darroisvilley.paris.barreau.fr

FIRM OVERVIEW

Managing partners: Jean-Michel Darrois, Philippe Villey

Number of partners worldwide: 9
Number of other lawyers worldwide: 14

AREAS OF PRACTICE:

M&A	50%
Corporate and tax	15%
Litigation and arbitration	15%
Finance and capital markets	10%
Regulatory and other matters	10%

FIRM OVERVIEW: Founded in 1982, Darrois Villey Maillot Brochier is a highly specialised firm comprising 23 lawyers. The firm's main activity concerns complex corporate and financial transactions including mergers and acquisitions, tender offers and tender offer defences, company reorganisations, stock exchange and company law issues, privatisations, and government transactions. The firm also handles French and international litigation and arbitration matters relating to corporate and financial transactions. It specialises in complex corporate and securities regulation issues. It also handles 'white collar' criminal matters. The firm has close links with leading international law firms including Wachtell, Lipton, Rosen & Katz in New York.

INTERNATIONAL EXPERIENCE: The firm has experience in multi-jurisdiction matters in its practice areas. The firm acts as counsel in cross-border mergers and acquisitions and advises on international securities issues and listings. The firm is experienced in the reorganisation of major multinational enterprises, and has handled a number of complex transactions in regulated industries. The firm has undertaken an increasing volume of multi-jurisdictional and arbitration matters and has advised multinational clients on investment strategies.

INTERNATIONAL CLIENTS: The firm's client base includes a number of major multinational enterprises for which it acts both as strategic adviser and transaction counsel, either alone or in cooperation with selected firms in other jurisdictions. The firm also maintains close and ongoing relationships with the major investment banks operating in key financial marketplaces.

WORLDWIDE OFFICE CONTACTS

FRANCE
69 Avenue Victor Hugo, 75116 **Paris**
Tel: +33 1 4502 1919 **Fax:** +33 1 4501 9168
Email: jmdarrois@darroisvilley.paris.barreau.fr

MAIN INTERNATIONAL AREAS OF PRACTICE:

M&A: Darrois Villey Maillot Brochier advises on major acquisitions, securities regulation and corporate financial transactions. The firm has handled privatisations and related transactions involving enterprises controlled by the state. It is currently advising the French government on several major transactions.

Litigation and arbitration: Darrois Villey Maillot Brochier has been involved in a number of high profile litigation and arbitration transactions. It advises on corporate and financial issues, specialising in transactions involving complex securities regulation. The firm handles international arbitration matters and has advised on a number of transactions, both as counsel to parties in arbitration and through the appointment of partners as arbitrators. The firm handles both civil and criminal litigation.

Finance and capital markets: Darrois Villey Maillot Brochier advises on the conception, documentation and implementation of securities issues in the capital markets in France as well as elsewhere in Europe and North America. The firm advises its clients directly, and acts in cooperation with other firms and investment banks, on structuring and coordinating securities issues.

Regulatory and administrative matters: In addition to its privatisation activities, the firm intervenes with and makes submissions to professional and administrative bodies such as the national competition Board of Directors and the tax administration. The firm maintains close relations with relevant government authorities.

Corporate and tax: The firm advises on French and international investment and tax structures and coordinates the creation and implementation of such structures. The firm handles work for investment funds from various countries and selected individual and family group investors. Its activities in these areas increasingly involve 'private equity' investments in traditional industrial and financial sectors as well as telecommunications, media and 'new technologies'.

LANGUAGES: Dutch, English, French, German, Italian, Spanish

D

DAVE & GIRISH & CO

HEAD OFFICE

1st Floor, Sethna Building, 55 Maharshi Karve Road, Marine Lines
Mumbai 400 002, India
Tel: +91 22 206 2192 **Fax:** +91 22 208 5620

Email: davegirish@vsnl.com
Website: www.lawindiadavegirish.com

FIRM OVERVIEW

Managing partner: Girish Dave

Total Partners Worldwide: 3
Total Other Lawyers Worldwide: 15

FIRM OVERVIEW: Dave & Girish & Co was founded in 1978 by Mohanlal Dave, and Girish Dave joined him in 1980. The firm has three partners, two senior counsels and ten associate advocates. It specialises in international and corporate law as well as civil litigation and arbitration. The firm has offices in Bangalore and Bombay and associate offices in Delhi and Ahmedabad.

MAIN INTERNATIONAL AREAS OF PRACTICE: The firm handles international and domestic litigation and arbitration; documentation of domestic and offshore loans; public and private placement of securities (international and domestic); formation, structuring and documentation of mutual funds (domestic and offshore); shipping finance; mergers acquisition and restructuring; joint ventures; techonology transfer; commercial contracts; project financing; power, infrastructure and telecommunication documentation; securitisation and cross-border insolvency.

LANGUAGES: English, Gujarati, Hindi, Kannada, Marathi,Tamil

WORLDWIDE OFFICE CONTACTS

INDIA
Flat No. GB, Ground Floor, Sangeeta Apartments No 13, 18th Cross
Malleswaram, **Bangalore** 560 055
Tel: +91 80 334 1508 **Fax:** +91 80 334 1508
Email: mayura@vsnl.com

1st Floor, Sethna Building, 55 Maharshi Karve Road, Marine Lines,
Mumbai 400 002
Tel: +91 22 206 2192 **Fax:** +91 22 208 5620
Email: davegirish@vsnl.com

DAVE & GIRISH & CO
Advocates

D

For other recommended firms see pages 1485-1520

DAVIES WARD PHILLIPS & VINEBERG LLP

HEAD OFFICES

1501 McGill College Avenue, 26th Floor, Montreal, H3A 3N9
Tel: +1 514 841 6400 **Fax:** +1 514 841 6499

1 First Canadian Place, Toronto, M5X 1B1
Tel: +1 416 863 0900 **Fax:** +1 416 863 0871
Email: info@dwpv.com
Website: www.dwpv.com

FIRM OVERVIEW

Managing partners: William M O'Reilly, Richard Cherney, Pierre-André Themens
Number of partners worldwide: 128
Number of other lawyers worldwide: 85

AREAS OF PRACTICE:

M&A	*%
Antitrust, competition and trade practices	*%
Tax	*%
Corporate and commercial	*%
Corporate finance and securities	*%
Banking and project finance	*%
Securitisation	*%
Financial restructuring and insolvency	*%
Technology, e-commerce and communications	*%
Litigation	*%
Commercial real estate	*%
Environmental	*%
Trusts, estates and fiduciary obligations	*%
International trade and business regulation	*%

* Workload % not disclosed

FIRM OVERVIEW: Davies Ward Phillips & Vineberg LLP is a full-service business law firm, with a particular focus on M&A and tax.

INTERNATIONAL EXPERIENCE: Recent international transactions include mergers and acquisitions in, among others, equipment manufacturing, mining, transportation, pharmaceuticals and telecommunications, tax, commercial lending transactions and international real estate joint venture development projects.

INTERNATIONAL CLIENTS: Clients range from small, single-location single-business enterprises to large multinationals, and also include governments, regulatory bodies and international agencies. Countries in which the firm has recently assisted its clients include Argentina, Australia, Chile, China, France, Germany, Ghana, Indonesia, Italy, Luxembourg, Panama, Singapore, the UK and the US.

MAIN INTERNATIONAL AREAS OF PRACTICE:

M&A: Clients include purchasers, sellers, boards of directors, independent committees of directors, investment dealers, merchant banks, with deals covering all types of mergers, acquisitions and restructurings of public and private corporations.
Antitrust, competition and trade practices: The firm advises US and overseas companies on the Canadian competition law aspects of international transactions or trans-border antitrust investigations.
Tax: Work includes the coordination of domestic and foreign tax laws, treaty interpretation and the tax implications of corporate reorganisations and transactions.
Corporate and commercial: The practice covers business organisation formation, corporate reorganisations, acquisitions and divestitures, foreign investments, licensing and technology transfers, outsourcing contracts and shareholder arrangements.
Corporate finance and securities: The firm advises on public offerings and private placements of equity, debt and derivative securities, asset-backed financings and securitisations and mutual fund and other investment vehicle offerings.
Banking and project finance: The practice spans domestic, cross-border and multi-jurisdictional transactions and includes commercial lending, structured and project finance and advice on commodities futures, options, forwards, swaps, securities lending and repos.
Securitisation: The firm has an extensive practice using single and multi-seller vehicles in both domestic and offshore markets. It designs securitisation transactions for asset classes, including credit card receivables, trade receivables, auto loans and leases, mutual fund commissions, government receivables, RRSP loans and commercial real estate mortgages.
Financial restructuring and insolvency: The focus is primarily on businesses in financial difficulty. The firm acts for debtors, institutional secured and unsecured lenders, non-institutional lenders, bondholders, lessors, trade creditors, debt traders, employee and management groups, boards and committees of directors, shareholders and investors.
Technology, e-commerce and communications: Clients include users and providers of computer hardware, software, internet services, e-commerce, systems integration, telecommunications, satellite and other information technology services.
Litigation: The practice covers business-related litigation, professional liability and discipline, administrative and constitutional law. Clients include individual directors, corporate boards, banks, financial institutions and trustees in bankruptcy.
Commercial real estate: The firm has advised on office buildings, shopping centres, hotels, condominiums, trade centres, casinos, residential buildings and mixed-use projects.
Environmental: Work includes environmental liabilities and risk management strategies, particularly in the context of purchase and sale agreements, leases, real estate developments, loans and other commercial arrangements.
Trusts, estates and fiduciary obligations: A broad-based practice covering estate planning and implementation, domestic and international trust planning and establishment, cross-border tax planning for individuals and estate and trust litigation.
International trade and business regulation: Work includes advising Canadian and international clients on the impact of international law on their business transactions; international arbitration and dispute settlement; multijurisdictional securities regulation; international insolvency; foreign investment review and investment treaties; trade sanctions; and import and export controls.

LANGUAGES: Arabic, Cantonese, English, French, German, Hebrew, Hindi, Italian, Mandarin, Russian, Spanish

WORLDWIDE OFFICE CONTACTS

CHINA
1612 Office Tower One, Henderson Centre, 18 Jianguomennei Avenue, Dongcheng District, **Beijing**, 100005
Tel: +86 10 6518 6201 **Fax:** +1 86 10 6518 6205

FRANCE
Reinhart Marville, 13, Ave.Hoche, 75008 **Paris**
Tel: +33 1 53 53 44 44 **Fax:** +33 1 53 96 04 20

USA
430 Park Avenue, 10th Floor, **New York**, NY 10022
Tel: +1 212 308 8866 **Fax:** +1 212 308 0132

D

For other recommended firms see pages 1485-1520

DE BANDT, VAN HECKE, LAGAE & LOESCH

A MEMBER FIRM OF LINKLATERS & ALLIANCE

HEAD OFFICE

Rue Brederode 13, B-1000 Brussels, Belgium
Tel: + 32 2 501 94 11 **Fax:** + 32 2 501 94 94

Email: rnieuwdorp@debandt.com
Website: www.linklaters-alliance.com

FIRM OVERVIEW

Managing partner: Roel Nieuwdorp
Senior partner: Jean-Marie Nelissen Grade

Number of partners worldwide: 54
Number of other lawyers worldwide: 165

Number of partners worldwide (Linklaters & Alliance): 586
Number of other lawyers worldwide (Linklaters & Alliance): 2,232

AREAS OF PRACTICE:

Banking	*%
Capital markets	*%
EU law	*%
Intellectual property	*%
Investment funds	*%
Litigation and arbitration	*%
Mergers and acquisitions	*%
Pensions and employee benefits	*%
Project finance	*%
Real estate	*%
Tax	*%
Telecommunications	*%

* Workload % not disclosed

WORLDWIDE OFFICE CONTACTS

BELGIUM
Graanmarkt 2, B-2000 **Antwerp**
Tel: + 32 3 203 62 62 **Fax:** + 32 3 203 62 34
Email: jpblumberg@debandt.com

LUXEMBOURG
4 rue Carlo Hemmer B.P. 1107, L-1011 **Luxembourg**
Tel: + 352 2608 1 **Fax:** + 352 2608 8888
Email: tloesch@debandt.com

UNITED KINGDOM
One Silk Street, **London** EC2Y 8HQ
Tel: +44 20 7456 5505 **Fax:** + 44 20 7456 5567
Email: ptulcinsky@debandt.com

USA
1345 Avenue of the Americas, **New York**, NY 10105
Tel: + 1 212 424 9130 **Fax:** + 1 212 424 9100
Email: dleclercq@debandt.com

OTHER LINKLATERS & ALLIANCE OFFICES

Alicante, Amsterdam, Bangkok, Berlin, Bratislava, Bucharest, Budapest, Cologne, Frankfurt am Main, Gothenburg, The Hague, Hong Kong, Madrid, Malmö, Milan, Moscow, Munich, Padua, Paris, Prague, Rome, Rotterdam, São Paulo, Shanghai, Singapore, Stockholm, Tokyo, Warsaw, Washington, DC.

FIRM OVERVIEW: De Bandt, van Hecke, Lagae & Loesch originated with the merger between De Bandt, van Hecke, Lagae, Belgium (founded 1969) and Loesch & Wolter, Luxembourg (founded 1896). It presently consists of 54 partners, three counsel and 165 associates, with a support staff of over 200 including legal assistants and paralegals. The firm is a member firm of Linklaters & Alliance, which brings together five of Europe's premier law firms including De Bandt, van Hecke, Lagae & Loesch (Belgium and Luxembourg), De Brauw Blackstone Westbroek (Netherlands), Gianni, Origoni & Partners (Italy), Lagerlöf & Leman (Sweden) and Linklaters (which practises in Germany as Linklaters Oppenhoff & Rädler). Linklaters & Alliance is one of the leading global legal practices with nearly 3,000 lawyers and other professionals operating in combined teams from 34 offices in major financial and business centres worldwide.

INTERNATIONAL EXPERIENCE: The main office of the firm is based in Brussels, the seat of the principal decision making institutions of the European Union. The firm has offices in Antwerp, one of the largest ports in the world and a major industrial area in Belgium, and Luxembourg, one of the most important financial centres in Europe, as well as in London and New York.

INTERNATIONAL CLIENTS: The clients are predominantly multinational and domestic companies active in the food and beverage, distribution, building, glass, transport, energy, banking, insurance, telecommunications and information technology sectors.

MAIN INTERNATIONAL AREAS OF PRACTICE: The firm's main international areas of practice include: mergers and acquisitions; banking; capital markets; investment funds; project finance; litigation and arbitration; EU law; pensions and employee benefits; tax; real estate; intellectual property; and telecommunications.

LANGUAGES: Dutch, English, French, German, Italian, Japanese

LINKLATERS
& ALLIANCE

For other recommended firms see pages 1485-1520

DE BRAUW BLACKSTONE WESTBROEK

A MEMBER FIRM OF LINKLATERS & ALLIANCE

HEAD OFFICE

Zuid-Hollandlaan 7, NL-2596 AL
The Hague, Netherlands
Tel: + 31 70 328 5 328 **Fax:** + 31 70 328 5 325

Email: maildhg@dbbw.nl
Website: www.linklaters-alliance.com

FIRM OVERVIEW

Managing partner: Peter Wakkie

Number of partners worldwide: 98
Number of other lawyers worldwide: 310

Number of partners worldwide (Linklaters & Alliance): 586
Number of other lawyers worldwide (Linklaters & Alliance): 2,232

AREAS OF PRACTICE:

Corporate M&A and capital markets	34%
Litigation and arbitration	14%
Employment	10%
Property	10%
Tax	8%
Banking and project finance	7%
Intellectual property and telecommunications	7%
Competition	4%
Other	6%

FIRM OVERVIEW: De Brauw Blackstone Westbroek is a leading Dutch law firm with a strong national and international practice. Since it was founded in the 19th century, clients from both The Netherlands and abroad have brought the firm their business. The firm is a member firm of Linklaters & Alliance, which brings together five of Europe's premier law firms including De Bandt, van Hecke, Lagae & Loesch (Belgium and Luxembourg), De Brauw Blackstone Westbroek (Netherlands), Gianni, Origoni & Partners (Italy), Lagerlöf & Leman (Sweden) and Linklaters (which practises in Germany as Linklaters Oppenhoff & Rädler). Linklaters & Alliance is one of the leading global legal practices with nearly 3,000 lawyers and other professionals operating in combined teams from 34 offices in major financial and business centres worldwide.

INTERNATIONAL EXPERIENCE: The practice of the firm includes a variety of areas of Dutch law. The firm has expertise in corporate, banking, commercial, securities, aircraft finance, administrative, environmental, litigation and (international) arbitration, EU, real estate, employment and health care law. Attorneys in the office in The Hague represent clients in proceedings before the Supreme Court of the Netherlands. The attorneys, civil law notaries and tax lawyers working in the corporate law departments are active in mergers and acqusitions, securities transactions and international financing. The tax advisers often render their expert advice in the transactions. Within the firm there is extensive experience in the area of privatisation of government-owned corporations and institutions. The firm has developed the highest professional standards during its many years of Supreme Court practice.

WORLDWIDE OFFICE CONTACTS

BELGIUM
rue Brederode 13a, B-1000 **Brussels**
Tel: + 32 2 505 02 11 **Fax:** + 32 2 502 02 00
Email: dbbwbru@dbbw.nl

NETHERLANDS
Tripolis 300, Burgerweeshuispad 301, NL 1076 HR **Amsterdam**
Tel: + 31 20 5771 771 **Fax:** + 31 20 5771 775
Email: mailamst@dbbw.nl

Blaak 34, NL 3011 TA **Rotterdam**
Tel: + 31 10 240 65 00 **Fax:** + 31 10 411 35 48
Email: mailrdm@dbbw.nl

UNITED KINGDOM
One Silk Street, **London** EC2Y 8HQ
Tel: + 44 20 7456 5400 **Fax:** + 44 20 7456 5567
Email: dbbwlnd@dbbw.nl

USA
1345 Avenue of the Americas, 19th floor, **New York**, NY 10105
Tel: + 1 212 424 9140 **Fax:** + 1 212 424 9100
Email: dbbwny@dbbw.nl

OTHER LINKLATERS & ALLIANCE OFFICES

Alicante, Antwerp, Bangkok, Berlin, Bratislava, Bucharest, Budapest, Cologne, Frankfurt am Main, Gothenburg, Hong Kong, Luxembourg, Madrid, Malmö, Milan, Moscow, Munich, Padua, Paris, Prague, Rome, Sao Paulo, Shanghai, Singapore, Stockholm, Tokyo, Warsaw, Washington, DC.

D

INTERNATIONAL CLIENTS: Corporate clients include a large number of leading multinational companies as well as Netherlands-based companies listed on the Amsterdam Stock Exchange.

LANGUAGES: Chinese, Dutch, English, French, German, Greek, Italian, Portuguese, Russian, Spanish

ADVOKATFIRMAN DELPHI & CO

HEAD OFFICE

Sergels Torg 12, PO Box 1432,
SE-111 84 Stockholm, Sweden
Tel: +46 8 677 54 00 **Fax:** +46 8 20 18 84
Email: stockholm@delphilaw.com
Website: www.delphilaw.com

FIRM OVERVIEW

Managing partner: Peter Utterström
Number of partners worldwide: 34
Number of other lawyers worldwide: 53

AREAS OF PRACTICE:

Corporate/M&A	25%
IT and telecommunications	25%
EU and competition law	15%
Intellectual property	15%
Banking and finance	10%
Litigation and arbitration	5%
Insurance and tort liability	3%
Insolvency law	2%

D

FIRM OVERVIEW: Advokatfirman Delphi & Co was established in 1998 through the merger of Advokatfirman Delphi (Stockholm), Advokatfirman Arnerius & Partners (Malmö), and Advokatfirman LJB (Linköping). In 1999, Friman & Carlander Advokatbyrå (Gothenburg), merged with Advokatfirman Delphi & Co. The firm is active in all areas of the law, focusing in particular on banking and finance; corporate, including M&A; IT and telecommunications; EU; competition law; and environmental law.

INTERNATIONAL EXPERIENCE: The firm represents foreign multinational and global corporations in their activities in Sweden, including cross-border transactions.

INTERNATIONAL CLIENTS: The firm's clients include a wide range of both publicly traded and privately held Swedish, US and European corporations, as well as banks, financial institutions and corporations conducting cross-border business. Many of Delphi & Co's clients are Fortune 500 companies.

MAIN INTERNATIONAL AREAS OF PRACTICE:
Banking and finance: The firm handles all types of financial transactions, such as drafting consortium agreements, loan documentation (including pledges, mortgages and other security arrangements) and due diligence.
Corporate/M&A: In its M&A work, the firm works cross-departmentally, drawing on competition, corporate finance, enviroment, tax and employment. Recent acquisitions handled by the firm have ranged in value from 100 million to 15 billion Swedish Crowns.
EU and competition law: The firm offers a wide range of advice in this area.
Insurance and tort liability: The firm assists its clients with litigation, legal opinions and claims investigations.
IT and telecommunications: The firm has one of the largest IT departments in Sweden. In this area, the firm's activities include IT contracts and digital intellectual property rights, as well as e-commerce, IT outsourcing and contracts and telecommunications permits.
Intellectual property: Working closely with corporations whose trademarks are well known and respected throughout the world, the firm specialises in patents, copyrights, trademarks, infringements and other issues.
Litigation and arbitration: The firm's litigators represent enterprises in court proceedings, in arbitration and in mediation, both in Sweden and abroad. Several of its lawyers also serve as arbitrators in domestic and international arbitrations.

WORLDWIDE OFFICE CONTACTS

SWEDEN
Östra Hamngatan 29, SE-411 10 **Göthenburg**
Tel: +46 31 17 88 10 **Fax:** +46 31 13 94 69
Email: goteborg@delphilaw.com

Stora Torget 4, PO Box 465, SE-581 05 **Linköping**
Tel: +46 13 35 62 00 **Fax:** 46 13 35 62 01
Email: linkoping@delphilaw.com

Stadt Hamburgsgatan 9B, SE-211 38 **Malmö**
Tel: +46 40 660 79 00 **Fax:** +46 40 660 79 09
Email: malmoe@delphilaw.com

LANGUAGES: English, French, German, Scandinavian languages, Spanish

WORLDWIDE OFFICES

SWEDEN

Östra Hamngatan 29, SE-411 10 Göthenburg

Number of lawyers: 16
Main areas of work: General commercial, corporate law, banking and finance, environmental law, litigation and M&A.
Office profile: The office focuses on all matters related to environmental law and banking and finance. Its client base comprises medium-sized firms as well as many large corporations including major Swedish banks in both the Gothenburg area and other parts of Sweden.

Stora Torget 4, PO Box 465, SE-581 05 Linköping

Number of lawyers: 13
Main areas of work: General commercial, corporate and M&A, commercial property, insolvency and IT.
Office profile: The office focuses on all matters of general commercial law, as well as corporate, commercial property and IT. The client base consists of medium-sized companies in the rapidly expanding areas around Linköping. Many of the clients are involved in cross-border activities.

Stadt Hamburgsgatan 9B, SE-211 38 Malmö

Number of lawyers: 12
Main areas of work: Corporate and M&A, general commercial, real estate, tax, litigation and employment.
Office profile: The office's clients include medium-sized firms as well as large corporations based in the expanding area of Malmö/Copenhagen. The office focuses on all matters related to corporate, tax and real estate.

Sergels Torg 12, PO Box 1432, SE-111 84 Stockholm

Number of lawyers: 46
Main areas of work: Corporate and finance (incl. M&A), competition and EU, IP, IT and telecommunications.
Office profile: The office acts for a number of foreign multinational corporations in their Swedish activities as well as Swedish corporations listed on the Stockholm Stock Exchange. The office advises on all corporate financial issues including M&A. Many of these transactions are cross-border. The office deals with numerous matters relating to IP, such as copyright, media, entertainment and trademark, especially trademark protection.

For other recommended firms see pages 1485-1520

DEMAREST e ALMEIDA

HEAD OFFICE

Alameda Campinas , 1070,
01404-001 São Paulo, Brazil
Tel: +55 11 888 1800 **Fax:** +55 11 888 1700

Email: da.sp@demarest.com.br
Website: www.demarest.com.br

FIRM OVERVIEW

Managing partner: Orlando Giacomo Filho

Number of partners worldwide: 31
Number of other lawyers worldwide: 320

AREAS OF PRACTICE:

Anti-trust and consumer protection	*%
Banking, finance and capital markets	*%
Civil and commercial	*%
Contract	*%
Corporate and securities	*%
Employment and social security	*%
Foreign trade	*%
Intellectual property	*%
Real estate	*%
Zoning and environmental	*%

* Workload % not disclosed

FIRM OVERVIEW: Founded in 1948, the firm was established by a Brazilian attorney, João Batista Pereira de Almeida, and an American attorney, Kenneth E. Demarest, who combined their experience to form one of Brazil's leading law firms. Demarest e Almeida has offices in major Brazilian cities and an office in New York. The firm is part of the Lex Mundi network and has an alliance with Marval O'Farrell and Mairal, one of Argentina's largest law firms.

WORLDWIDE OFFICE CONTACTS

BRAZIL
SCN-Quadra 04 - Bloco B - Sala 104, Edificio Centro Empresarial Varig, Distrito Federal 70710-926 **Brasilia**
Tel: +55 61 328 8845 **Fax:** +55 61 327 0493
Email: da.df@demarest.com.br

Avenida Humberto Mendes, 746 - Sala 39/40, Edificio Wall Street-Empresarial Center, Alagoas 57021-580 **Maceió**
Tel: +55 82 223 8422 **Fax:** +55 82 223 8422
Email: da.al@demarest.com.br

Avenida Loureiro da Silva, 2001-10° andar, Rio Grande do Sul, 90050-240 **Porto Alegre**
Tel: +55 51 227 3455 **Fax:** +55 51 226 5580
Email: da.rsl@demarest.com.br

Avenida Rio Branco, 1-6° andar-Sala 601, 20090-003 **Rio de Janeiro**
Tel: +55 21 277 9800 **Fax:** +55 21 277 9822
Email: da.rj@demarest.com.br

Avenida Tancredo Neves, 12383-Sala 601/604, Bahia 41820-021 **Salvador**
Tel: +55 71 341 2360 **Fax:** +55 71 341 4837
Email: da.ba@demarest.com.br

Alameda Campinas , 1070, 01404-001 **São Paulo**
Tel: +55 11 888 1800 **Fax:** +55 11 888 1700
Email: da.rj@demarest.com.br

USA
509 Madison Avenue, 5th Floor, **New York** NY 10022-5501
Tel: +1 212 371 9191 **Fax:** +1 212 371 5551

D

INTERNATIONAL EXPERIENCE: Demarest e Almeida has advised a range of domestic and international clients, in virtually every sector of business in Brazil. Work handled has included major cross-border mergers and acquisitions in Brazil; corporate restructuring and reorganisation of both multinationals subsidiaries in Brazil and Brazilian companies; and joint ventures and privatisations. The firm has handled a number of transactions involving banking, anti-trust, environmental, intellectual property, litigation, commercial and civil law.

INTERNATIONAL CLIENTS: The firm advises a number of international clients doing business in Brazil in a range of industries. Among its clients are major multinationals, banks, insurance companies and public institutions.

MAIN INTERNATIONAL AREAS OF PRACTICE:
M&A: The firm has represented major multinationals in their acquisitions of companies in Brazil.
Banking and finance: Demarest e Almeida has acted in a range of major transactions involving foreign and Brazilian banks, including the privatisation of Brazilian financial institutions.
Corporate: The firm advises on all aspects of corporate law.
Employment: The firm has one of the largest practices in Brazil, counselling both foreign and Brazilian companies in all matters relating to Brazilian employment law.
Competition: As Brazil experiences continuous growth of sophisticated transactions, this area has gained new prominence in the firm.
Civil and commercial: The firm has a long established tradition in civil, commercial and contract law including distributorship, licensing and agency arrangements.

LANGUAGES: English, French, German, Italian, Japanese, Portuguese, Spanish

For other recommended firms see pages 1485-1520

DENTON WILDE SAPTE

HEAD OFFICE

Five Chancery Lane, Clifford's Inn,
London EC4A 1BU, United Kingdom
Tel: +44 20 7242 1212 **Fax:** +44 20 7404 0087

Email: info@dentonwildesapte.com
Website: www.dentonwildesapte.com

FIRM OVERVIEW

Chairman: James Dallas
Managing partner: Virginia Glastonbury

Number of partners worldwide: 197
Number of other lawyers worldwide: 670

AREAS OF PRACTICE:

Corporate	34%
Litigation	25%
Banking and finance	23%
Property	18%

D

FIRM OVERVIEW: Denton Wilde Sapte is a leading international law firm based in the City of London. Formed by the merger of Denton Hall and Wilde Sapte on 1 February 2000, this truly international organisation offers a comprehensive range of the highest quality and affordable commercial legal advice. The combination of Denton Hall and Wilde Sapte has created a premier law firm which is recognised for its innovative and commercial approach. Denton Wilde Sapte has 18 offices across Europe, the Middle East and Asia - a network that is further strengthened by Denton International, a group of leading law firms that brings the overall total to 35 offices in 23 jurisdictions around the world.

INTERNATIONAL EXPERIENCE: The firm offers a comprehensive range of commercial legal advice and is particularly known for its sector strengths in banking and finance, energy and infrastructure, media and technology, property, retail and aviation. With a combination of locally trained lawyers and sector specialists, all of the firm's offices are able to provide a high level of expertise. The firm's international work is not restricted to the private sector. It has worked with a large number of governments and government agencies, particularly in drafting and reworking local legislation and regulations.

INTERNATIONAL CLIENTS: Clients include BG plc, Electricité de France, Shell, Premier Oil, Oman LNG, Itochu Corporation, Marubeni, Sumitomo, Nissho Iwai, Sony, Toshiba, Ericsson, Tomen, Westdeutsche Landesbank Girozentrale, Royal Bank of Canada, Standard Chartered Bank, Bank of Tokyo, Mitsubishi, Sanwa Bank, Daiwa Bank, Royal Bank of Scotland, Barclays Bank, UIP, Warner Bros Pictures, Sony Pictures, Universal Studios, MediaOne Group, Pearson Plc, BBC, FA Premier League, The Equitable Life Insurance Society, Virgin, the UK Government, the Government of Abu Dhabi, the Government of the Republic of Kenya and the Privatisation Agency of Bulgaria.

LANGUAGES: Afrikaans, Arabic, Bahsa Indonisian, Bahsa Malay, Bulgarian, Cantonese, Chinese Hokkien, Czech, Dutch, Finnish, Flemish, French, German, Greek, Gujarati, Hebrew/Modern Hebrew, Hindi, Igbo, Italian, Japanese, Korean, Malay, Mandarin, Norwegian, Portuguese, Punjabi, Russian, Spanish, Swahili, Swedish, Tamil, Urdu, Welsh

WORLDWIDE OFFICE CONTACTS

BELGIUM
Brussels **Tel:** +32 2 223 0621 **Fax:** +32 2 223 0482
Email: Brussels@dentonwildesapte.be

CHINA
Beijing **Tel:** +86 10 6505 4891 **Fax:** +86 10 6505 4893
Email: info@dentonwildesapte.com.cn

EGYPT
Cairo **Tel:** +202 736 5128 **Fax:** +202 736 7717
Email: dwsinfo@dwscairo.com

FRANCE
Paris **Tel:** +33 1 53 05 16 00 **Fax:** +33 1 53 05 97 27
Email: dentonsvt@de.ntonsvt.com

GIBRALTAR
Gibraltar **Tel:** +350 77750 **Fax:** +350 77800
Email: mail@dentonwildesapte.gi

HONG KONG
Hong Kong **Tel:** +852 2820 6272 **Fax:** +852 2810 6434
Email: info@dentonwildesapte.com.hk

JAPAN
Tokyo **Tel:** +81 3 5641 8455 **Fax:** +81 3 5641 8460
Email: tokyoinfo@dentonwildesapte.com

KAZAKHSTAN
Almaty **Tel:** +7 3272 581 950 **Fax:** +7 3272 581 905
Email: almaty@dentonwildesapt.kz

OMAN
Muscat **Tel:** +968 56 4346 **Fax:** +968 56 4395
Email: dws@dwsmuscat.com

RUSSIA
Moscow **Tel:** +7 095 255 7900 **Fax:** +7 095 255 7901
Email: info@dentonwildesapte.ru

SINGAPORE
Singapore **Tel:** +65 538 1551 **Fax:** +65 538 2276
Email: info@dentonwildesapte.com.sg

TURKEY
Istanbul **Tel:** +90 212 282 4385 **Fax:** +90 212 282 4305
Email: dentonguner@superonline.com

UNITED ARAB EMIRATES
Abu Dhabi **Tel:** +971 2622 3858 **Fax:** +971 2622 3586
Email: dentonad@emirates.net.ae

Dubai **Tel:** +971 4331 0220 **Fax:** +971 4331 0201
Email: dwsdubai@emirates.net.ae

UZBEKISTAN
Tashkent **Tel:** +998 71 120 6946 **Fax:** +998 71 120 6185
Email: tashkent@dentonwildesapte.kz

For other recommended firms see pages 1485-1520

DE ORCHIS WALKER & CORSA

HEAD OFFICE

61 Broadway, 26th Floor,
New York NY 10006, USA
Tel: +1 212 344 4700 **Fax:** +1 212 422 5299

Email: DWC@marinelex.com
Website: www.marinelex.com

WORLDWIDE OFFICE CONTACTS

USA
24 Hoyt Street, Stamford, **Connecticut** CT 06905
Tel: +1 203 348 5846 **Fax:** +1 203 324 5024

Routes 28 & 137, South Chatham, **Massachusetts** MA 02659
Tel: +1 508 432 4715 **Fax:** +1 508 432 2334

De Orchis Corsa & Hillenbrand, LLP, 2650 Biscayne Boulevard, **Miami** FL 33137
Tel: +1 305 571 9200 **Fax:** +1 305 571 9250

1495 Morris Avenue Union, **New Jersey** NJ 07083
Tel: +1 973 467 4740 **Fax:** +1 908 687 0255

61 Broadway, 26th Floor, **New York** NY 10006
Tel: +1 212 344 4700 **Fax:** +1 212 422 5299

FIRM OVERVIEW

Managing partner: Vincent M. DeOrchis
Senior partner: LeRoy S. Corsa

Number of partners worldwide: 11
Number of other lawyers worldwide: 23

AREAS OF PRACTICE:

Maritime and admiralty litigation	55%
Personal injury	15%
Arbitration	10%
Transport	10%
Corporate	5%
Insurance and reinsurance	5%

FIRM OVERVIEW: De Orchis Walker & Corsa was founded in 1997 with the merger of Walker & Corsa and DeOrchis & Partners. The firm's aim is to provide quality, cost effective legal advice. It emphasises the need to work with its clients to address their immediate legal problem, as well as positioning them to avoid problems in the future. The firm has developed an extensive network of correspondent law firms that enables it to advise clients anywhere in the world. Five of the firm's lawyers hold US Coast Guard merchant mariner licenses, two have Masters of Law degrees in maritime law, and one is an instructor at the US Merchant Marine Academy. The firm also maintains a visiting foreign lawyer program where the firm will host foreign lawyers with an interest in transportation law for a period of up to six months.

INTERNATIONAL EXPERIENCE: The firm has been involved in a range of international transactions. Most recently, the firm has been involved in discussions with the government of Pakistan concerning the release of a vessel; the investigation at Las Palmas of a vessel that broke in half at sea; investigations concerning hijacking of cargo in Central and South America; testimony at trial in Canada concerning the operation of bills of ladings; depositions in Korea concerning shipyard construction; investigation of cargo theft in South America; negotiation of project financing in Russia; the setting-up of new companies in Central Asia and negotiations in London on General Average and salvage matters. The firm's managing partner is participating in the CMI's efforts to draft a new international convention on liability for cargo damage.

INTERNATIONAL CLIENTS: The firm's clients include a number of P&I clubs in London and Scandinavia, well known ship owners, charterers, non-vessel owning common carriers, freight forwarders, underwriters and insurance brokers located in the US and abroad. The firm has also represented banking and financial institutions, equipment leasing companies and foreign governments.

MAIN INTERNATIONAL AREAS OF PRACTICE:

Maritime and admiralty litigation: The firm is licensed to practice in the federal and state courts of New York, New Jersey, Connecticut, Massachusetts, Florida, Texas, Pennsylvania, and Washington, DC. Much of the firm's maritime and admiralty litigation involves cargo damage, documentation issues, collision, hull damage, pollution and criminal matters.
Personal injury: The firm has a growing specialisation in transportation related personal injury litigation. It has represented ship owners and P&I Clubs in a variety of matters involving personal injury and death of crew members, passengers and longshore workers. The firm also represented ship owners and equipment leasing companies in personal injury claims arising from the use of maritime containers and chassis on public highways. With its growing client base of North American trucking companies, the firm has developed a specialty in defending against injury and death claims arising from trucking operations and warehousing.
Arbitration: The firm has represented both ship owners and charterers in a range of arbitrations ranging from collisions and allusions to cargo disputes and performance claims. The firm also has extensive experience before the American Arbitration Association in construction and warranty claims.
Trucking, rail and aviation: The firm has a rapidly developing practice dealing with all aspects of rail and trucking law. The firm has handled litigation dealing with cargo loss and damage, physical damage to equipment and premises and personal injury. It has also advised on government regulations and general corporate matters. In the field of aviation, the firm has represented underwriters in recovery actions for damage to air cargo and has represented air carriers in connection with liability resulting from the loss of aircraft.
Insurance and reinsurance: The firm has represented both insurers and assureds in coverage disputes. The firm has acted as outside counsel on behalf of individual members where there has been a conflict between two members of the same P&I Club. It has also advised clients on the establishment of insurance brokerage firms in the US.
Corporate: The firm handles a wide variety of general corporate matters. In particular, the firm has assisted in setting up US agencies for international carrier clients and representing clients before US regulators and in criminal investigations. The firm has also advised on matters such as US employment law, discrimination law and immigration matters. It has also advised foreign governments in negotiations for project finance and debt restructuring.

LANGUAGES: Finnish, French, German, Italian, Norwegian, Spanish, Swedish

D

For other recommended firms see pages 1485-1520

DE PARDIEU BROCAS MAFFEI & LEYGONIE

HEAD OFFICE

64-66 Avenue d'Iéna,
75116 Paris, France
Tel: +33 1 53 57 71 71 **Fax:** +33 1 53 57 71 70

WORLDWIDE OFFICE CONTACTS

FRANCE
64-66 Avenue d'Iéna, 75116 **Paris**
Tel: +33 1 53 57 71 71 **Fax:** +33 1 53 57 71 70

FIRM OVERVIEW

Senior partner: Charles-Henri de Pardieu

Number of partners worldwide: 18
Number of other lawyers worldwide: 47

AREAS OF PRACTICE:
Banking and finance .... *%
Capital markets .... *%
Corporate finance, securities law and private equity .... *%
EU and competition .... *%
Insolvency .... *%
Insurance .... *%
Labour law .... *%
Litigation and arbitration .... *%
M&A and general corporate .... *%
Privatisation .... *%
Real estate and environment .... *%
Telecommunications and IP .... *%

D

FIRM OVERVIEW: De Pardieu Brocas Maffei & Leygonie specialises in business law. The firm is known for its expertise in banking, finance, insurance, corporate finance, M&A, competition, telecommunications, real estate and litigation.

INTERNATIONAL EXPERIENCE: The firm has been involved in a significant number of cross-border and multijurisdictional transactions.

INTERNATIONAL CLIENTS: The firm acts for a number of multinational groups including banks, financial institutions, insurance companies and industrial groups. Foreign clients account for approximately 35% of the firm's work.

MAIN INTERNATIONAL AREAS OF PRACTICE:
Banking and finance: The firm has developed a leading practice in all types of financial transactions including syndicated loans, export credits, structured financing, project financing and documenting sureties. It is also widely recognised in bank mergers and acquisitions, debt rescheduling and defeasance schemes. The firm has wide experience in representing clients in connection with regulatory, litigation and enforcement matters, particulary in the emerging area of cyber-banking, electronic brokerage and electronic business.
Corporate finance and capital markets: The firm advises on a wealth of capital markets transactions including domestic and international issues of capital and debt securities, repurchase transactions and securities loans, documentation related to regulated and non-regulated market instruments, derivatives and securitisation.
M&A and general corporate: The mergers and aquisitions team has extensive experience in all aspects of acquisitions, mergers and restructuring transactions involving listed and non-listed companies. It regularly advises issuers, shareholders and investment banks, lenders and outside investors.
Private equity: The firm has an active LBO practice.
Privatisations: The firm advises on the privatisation of state owned companies and in the sale of assets by public bodies. It also advises private and state controlled companies participating in privatisation transactions with respect to their alliances (joint ventures, cross-holdings, cooperation agreements).
Insurance: The firm advises some of the largest French and foreign insurance companies on regulatory matters, corporate, M&A and securities matters. It is also active in insurance litigation.
EU and competition: The firm has a wealth of experience in advising on matters of French and EU competition laws. Longstanding clients include industrial groups, banks, insurance companies and trade associations, active in France and abroad.
Telecommunications: The firm has developed a leading practice in the telecommunications and information technologies sectors. In addition to advising major domestic telephone operators (fixed, mobile, cable) the telecommunications team also advises foreign operators interested in expanding their business into France. This includes defending clients before the Telecommunications Regulatory Authority in connection with disputes.
Real estate: The firm has a strong real estate practice and its client base includes banks, property companies, institutions, both French and foreign. It represents investors, developers, lenders and borrowers.
Litigation and arbitration: De Pardieu Brocas, Maffei & Leygonie handles all its clients' needs for effective representation in court at all stages of a dispute (including mediation and alternative dispute resolution procedures). Active in all areas of corporation life the practice also works with both individual and institutional clients in regulatory investigations and criminal prosecutions. The firm also handles disputes before the French and international arbitration tribunals as well as before the EU Court of Justice. Some partners' experience extends to participation in professional task forces and legislative think tanks.

LANGUAGES: Dutch, English, French, German, Russian, Spanish

For other recommended firms see pages 1485-1520

DÉRI & LOVRECZ

HEAD OFFICE

8th Floor, Váci út 99,
H-1139 Budapest, Hungary
Tel: +361 270 7430 **Fax:** +361 270 7432

Email: solicitors@deri.hu

WORLDWIDE OFFICE CONTACTS

HUNGARY
8th Floor, Váci út 99, H-1139 **Budapest**
Tel: +361 270 7430 **Fax:** +361 270 7432
Email: solicitors@deri.hu

FIRM OVERVIEW

Senior partner: Bela Deri

Number of partners worldwide: 3
Number of other lawyers worldwide: 15

AREAS OF PRACTICE:

M&A	40%
General corporate	20%
Banking and finance	10%
Capital markets	10%
Litigation and arbitration	10%
Real estate	10%

FIRM OVERVIEW: Deri & Lovrecz was founded in 1991. Comprising three partners and 15 Hungarian qualified lawyers, the firm offer a full range of legal services, specialising in M&A, capital market transactions, IPO, and private equity. The firm are part of the Klegal group.

INTERNATIONAL EXPERIENCE: In recent years the firm has advised on several greenfield projects. It has also acted as counsel for the public offering of several companies floated on the Budapest Stock Exchange.

INTERNATIONAL CLIENTS: The firm's client base includes major international companies, financial enterprises and other corporations conducting cross-border business. Clients include Pannonplast, Sanyo, Meinl AG, Credit Suisse Group, Siemens, and the Emmis Group.

MAIN INTERNATIONAL AREAS OF PRACTICE:
M&A: The majority of the firm's transactions involve medium size mergers and acquisitions.
Banking and finance: The firm specialises in specific complex regulatory and compliance matters in the banking and securities industry.
Corporate: The firm advises on all aspects of general corporate law.
Employment: Deri & Lovrecz advises on mass redundancy, stock options, and collective agreements with unions. It also handles labour litigation.
Telecommunications: The firm advised the foreign investors involved in the establishment of a nationwide telecommunication provider (PANTEL). It also advises foreign investors on Hungarian telecommunications law in relation to internet and e-commerce issues.
Securities and financial markets: Deri & Lovrecz advises clients on Hungarian law relating to funds, securities and derivatives. It also advises on the structuring of investment firms, and the licensing of operations.

LANGUAGES: English, German, Hungarian, Spanish

DÉRI & LOVRECZ

D

DEWEY BALLANTINE LLP

HEAD OFFICE

1301 Avenue of the Americas,
New York NY 10019-6092, USA
Tel: +1 212 259 8000 **Fax:** +1 212 259 6333

Email: name.surname@deweyballantine.com
Website: www.deweyballantine.com

FIRM OVERVIEW

Managing partner: Everett L. Jassy
Administrative partner: Richard Shutran

Number of partners worldwide: 134
Number of other lawyers worldwide: 394

AREAS OF PRACTICE:
Banking and finance .... *%
Corporate .... *%
Industry sectors .... *%
International trade .... *%
Legislative .... *%
Litigation .... *%
Trusts and estates .... *%
* Workload % not disclosed

D

FIRM OVERVIEW: Founded in 1909, Dewey Ballantine LLP is an international law firm with offices in New York, Washington, DC, Los Angeles, Menlo Park, London, Hong Kong, Budapest, Prague and Warsaw. The firm combines an active financial transactional practice with expertise in trade, legislative and international issues, and complex litigation and dispute resolution. Clients include industrial corporations, financial services companies, high-tech companies, utilities, developers, entertainment companies, investment and commercial banks, government entities, multilateral institutions, trade associations, charitable foundations, estates and individuals.

INTERNATIONAL EXPERIENCE: Recent international transactions include acting for COSMOTE in its US$2.7 billion IPO, the largest IPO in Greece in the year 2000; acting for Banque Centrale de Tunisie in its signing of the first Global Samurai Bond (issue of ¥35 billion bonds sold alongside a ¥15 billion issue); acting for Riverdeep Group plc in its US$85 million acquisition of Edmark Corporation from IBM; acting for Excite Chello in its US$6 billion merger of Excite's non-US assets with those of pan-European broadband provider Chello Broadband NV; acting for Merrill Lynch and Citicorp in the US$246,975,000 and €350,000,000 Floating Rate Notes securitisation of cruise ships receivables; acting for Lebanese Republic in its US$500,000,000 debt issuance and its US$2.5 billion Global MTN Program; and acting for Carphone Warehouse in its Global IPO of ordinary shares. The project finance team advised the underwriters in the El Dorado airport privatisation in Colombia, the commercial banks and underwriters in the US/Canada Alliance Pipeline, the underwriters and commercial lenders in the Quezon Project in the Philippines, the commercial banks in the Termobarranquilla power project in Colombia, the sponsors of the Irian Jaya power project in Indonesia, and the underwriters for the Marlim offshore oil project in Brazil.

INTERNATIONAL CLIENTS: The firm represents multinationals, financiers, banks, multilateral institutions and governments worldwide. Industries from which corporate clients come include telecommunications, energy, waste and water, food and beverages, industrial, finance, banking, media, and transport industries.

MAIN INTERNATIONAL AREAS OF PRACTICE: Work handled includes antitrust; bankruptcy and reorganisations; capital markets; debt finance; emerging markets; employee benefits and compensations; energy; environmental; healthcare; insurance; intellectual property; international trade; investment management; leasing; legislative; litigation; mergers and acquisitions; private equity; privatisations; project finance; real estate; securitisation; tax; technology; telecommunications; trusts and estates.

LANGUAGES: Afrikaans, Amharic, Arabic, Chinese (Cantonese and Mandarin), Czech, French, German, Greek, Hebrew, Hindi, Hindko, Hungarian, Italian, Japanese, Korean, Persian, Polish, Portuguese, Punjabi, Pushto, Romanian, Russian, Serbian, Shona, Slovak, Spanish, Swedish, Tagalog, Urdu

WORLDWIDE OFFICE CONTACTS

CZECH REPUBLIC
Adria Palace, Jungmannova 31, 5th Floor, Prague 1, 110 00 **Prague** 1
Tel: +420 2 2499 0000 **Fax:** +420 2 2499 0001
Email: christopher.caperton@deweyballantine.com

HONG KONG
Suite 701, Edinburgh Tower, The Landmark, 15 Queen's Road, Central, **Hong Kong**
Tel: +852 2509 7000 **Fax:** +852 2509 7088
Email: john.otoshi@deweyballantine.com

HUNGARY
Andrássy út 60, H-1062 **Budapest**
Tel: +36 1 374 2660 **Fax:** +36 1 374 2661
Email: andras.hanak@deweyballantine.com

POLAND
Level 14, Sienna 39, 00-121 **Warsaw**
Tel: +48 22 526 9999 **Fax:** +48 22 526 9988
Email: monika.rommel@deweyballantine.com

UNITED KINGDOM
1 Undershaft, **London** EC3A 8LP
Tel: +44 207 456 6000 **Fax:** +44 207 456 6001
Email: fred.gander@deweyballantine.com

USA
333 South Hope Street, **Los Angeles** California 90071-1406
Tel: +1 213 626 3399 **Fax:** +1 213 625 0562
Email: robert.smith@deweyballantine.com

525 Middlefield Road, Suite 250, **Menlo Park** CA 94025-3447
Tel: +1 650 462 7400 **Fax:** +1 650 462 7499
Email: robert.smith@deweyballantine.com

1301 Avenue of the Americas, **New York** NY 10019-6092
Tel: +1 212 259 8000 **Fax:** +1 212 259 6333
Email: name.surname@deweyballantine.com

1775 Pennsylvania Avenue, NW, **Washington DC** 20006-4605
Tel: +1 202 862 1000 **Fax:** +1 202 862 1093
Email: alan.wolff@deweyballantine.com

For other recommended firms see pages 1485-1520

DJINGOV, GOUGINSKI, KYUTCHUKOV & VELICHKOV

HEAD OFFICE

10 Tsar Osvoboditel Blvd,
1000 Sofia, Bulgaria
Tel: +359 2980 1358 **Fax:** +359 2980 3586

Email: dgkv@dgkv.com
Website: www.dgkv.com

WORLDWIDE OFFICE CONTACTS

BULGARIA
10 Tsar Osvoboditel Blvd, 1000 **Sofia**
Tel: +359 2980 1358 **Fax:** +359 2980 3586
Email: dgkv@dgkv.com

FIRM OVERVIEW

Managing partner: Assen A. Djingov

Number of partners worldwide: 7
Number of other lawyers worldwide: 18

AREAS OF PRACTICE:

Project finance and infrastructure	*%
Banking, corporate finance and securities	*%
Energy, oil & gas, environmental	*%
Privatisation and capital markets	*%
Competition and trade	*%
General corporate and commercial/M&A	*%
Telecommunications	*%
Tax	*%
Commercial real estate	*%

* Workload % not disclosed

FIRM OVERVIEW: The firm was founded in 1994 by its name partners to meet the unique needs of the new free market environment in Bulgaria. Since then, it has grown substantially in size, and with its 25 fully qualified lawyers it is now one of the largest and most prominent firms on the Bulgarian legal market with a strong emphasis on foreign investment. The firm has a sophisticated and extensive commercial practice, with a strong concentration on project finance, large scale infrastructure projects, banking, securities, equity investment, joint ventures, privatisation, energy and telecommunications.

INTERNATIONAL EXPERIENCE: A predominant part of the firm's practice is directed towards providing first-class service to foreign clients investing, establishing or expanding operations in Bulgaria. The firm represents major international investment and commercial banks, securities firms, international financial institutions and funds, as well as internationally recognised industrial, utilities and service companies.

INTERNATIONAL CLIENTS: Clients include: BNP; Citibank; Coca-Cola; Conoco UK; Creditanstalt Investment Bank; Deutsche Bank; DMG; Dresdner Kleinwort Benson; Dyno Industries; Eli Lilly; Enron; Entergy; EBRD; GE International; Hilton; IFC; ING Barings; KBC Bank; Merrill Lynch; Morgan Stanley; Nokia; Nomura International; OMV; Paribas; RJ Reinholds; Rheinbraun, Scudder, Stevens & Clark; Shell; Societe Generale; Standard Bank London; Volvo.

MAIN INTERNATIONAL AREAS OF PRACTICE

Project finance and infrastructure: The firm's position in the field of project finance is founded upon high expertise in all areas of lending, debt finance, securitisation, security/offshore agreements and guarantees. The firm is the legal adviser to EBRD and IFC on the financing of various infrastructure, construction and financial projects such as the structuring and securitisation of the financing of the Sofia water supply and sewerage system and the construction of a superstore in Sofia. Other significant projects include structuring the financing of the Sofia Hilton Hotel, the construction of the 'Maritsa' highway and the construction of a cascade of three dams and hydro-power plants.

Banking, corporate finance and securites: The firm acts as the legal adviser to major international commercial banks in relation to the establishment of their branches and operations in Bulgaria and has represented several major financial institutions for the acquisition of shares in large Bulgarian banks. The firm has been appointed to act as counsel in relation to the first Euro Bond issue for Bulgaria for the City of Sofia for the amount of DEM 100 million. In addition, the firm advises numerous U.S. and European investment banks and securities firms in connection with their interests and operations on the Bulgarian market of stocks, bonds and T-bills.

Energy, oil & gas, environmental: In the energy sector the firm has advised the foreign sponsors of the two principal electricity generating thermal power plants and of Bulgaria's largest lignite deposits. Infrastructure projects in which the firm has acted as counsel include the privatisation of the water supply and sewerage system of the Bourg as region, the development of the network for the second GSM operator, and the construction of a multimillion network of petrol stations throughout Bulgaria.

Privatisation and capital markets: The firm's role in the privatisation process has received strong international recognition upon the firm's appointment as counsel in the privatisation of the of the Bulgarian Telecommunications Company and Bulgartabac Holding, the country's tobacco monopoly. The firm's expertise has been reaffirmed by its involvement in the acquisition of the state-owned gasoline retail company, the three major domestic pharmaceutical companies, the Bulgarian national air carrier, as well as the three largest state-owned banks.

General corporate and commercial/M&A: The firm provides a full range of corporate advice, and acts for foreign companies and international corporations in relation to the establishment of operations in Bulgaria, acquisition of businesses and forming joint ventures, incorporation of companies, equity and debt investment, corporate governance, reorganisations and transformations, mergers, spin-offs and dissolutions.

Telecommunications: The firm has an extensive telecommunications practice developed by advising international clients on issues such as Bulgarian regulatory matters, licensing, and granting of concessions. The firm is a member of the international consortium advising the Bulgarian Telecommunications Company, and is actively involved in the process of the development of new telecommunication laws.

Tax: The firm has specialists in tax planning and all tax aspects of corporate and commercial transactions, foreign investments, setting up Bulgarian operations, M&A's.

LANGUAGES: Bulgarian, English, German, French, Russian

DJINGOV, GOUGINSKI, KYUTCHUKOV & VELICHKOV

D

DLA

HEAD OFFICE

3 Noble Street,
London EC2V 7EE, United Kingdom
Tel: +44 (0) 8700 111 111 **Fax:** +44 20 7796 6666

Email: info@dla.com
Website: www.dla.com

FIRM OVERVIEW

Managing partner: Nigel Knowles
Senior partner: Roger Lane-Smith
Number of partners worldwide: 258
Number of other lawyers worldwide: 855

AREAS OF PRACTICE:

Corporate 25%
Litigation 17%
Real estate 17%
Insurance 9%
Banking 7%
Human resources 7%
Business services 6%
Business support and restructuring 6%
Reinsurance, marine and aviation 5%
Law training 1%

D

FIRM OVERVIEW: With over 1,100 lawyers and a total staff of over 2,300, DLA, is one of the UK's largest law firms. In addition to its position in the City of London, the firm has a substantial presence throughout the UK, in Birmingham, Bradford, Edinburgh, Glasgow, Leeds, Liverpool, Manchester and Sheffield, and a growing international presence with offices in Brussels, Hong Kong and Singapore. In addition to the normal practice areas, the firm has developed a number of market-focused business groups.

INTERNATIONAL EXPERIENCE: The firm's work includes joint ventures and commercial agreements, M&A, corporate tax, competition and antitrust, lobbying, regulatory work, procurement, litigation, shipping, insurance, employment, IP, IT and e-commerce. DLA has set up an international alliance known as DLA & Partners (D&P). This is the result of exclusive association agreements with Price & Partners in Brussels, Ginestié, Paley-Vincent & Associés in Paris, Brugueras, Garcia-Bragado, Molinero y Asociados in Barcelona and J Koh & Co in Singapore. The focus at Price & Partners is on advising British and US clients on competition law issues and Belgian corporate, employment and tax laws. Ginestié is particularly strong in banking, finance and securities law, as well as French, EU and international law. Brugueras offers a full law service, whilst specialising in corporate, commercial, international and EU law transactions. In Hong Kong, the firm developed an association with Charltons in 1998 and merged with Lui & Carey in 1999 which enabled them to offer legal advice relating to collective investment schemes, mergers, corporate finance, general corporate and commercial transactions, capital markets, securities and derivatives as well as China investment. J Koh & Co in Singapore specialises in cross-border transactions, in particular, project financing, M&A, private equity investments, venture capital and equity securities.

INTERNATIONAL CLIENTS: Clients include multinational organisations, governments, banks and insurance companies.

LANGUAGES: Chinese, Danish, Dutch, English, French, German, Greek, Hindi, Italian, Japanese, Korean, Norwegian, Portuguese, Spanish, Swedish, Turkish

WORLDWIDE OFFICE CONTACTS

BELGIUM
2nd floor, 106 avenue Louise, 1050 **Brussels**
Tel: +32 2 629 6969 **Fax:** +32 2 629 6970
Email: david.church@dla.com

HONG KONG
59th Floor, Bank of China Tower, 1 Garden Road, **Hong Kong**
Tel: +852 2 524 2003 **Fax:** +852 2 810 1345
Email: stewart.crowther@dla.com

SINGAPORE
11th Floor Cosco Building, 8 Robinson Road, **Singapore** 048544
Tel: +65 236 0588 **Fax:** +65 236 0589
Email: mike.melwood.smith@dla.com

UNITED KINGDOM
Victoria Square House, Victoria Square, **Birmingham** B2 4DL
Tel: +44 8700 111 111 **Fax:** +44 121 262 5794
Email: chris.rawstron@dla.com

Napier House, 27 Thistle Street, **Edinburgh** EH2 1BS
Tel: +44 8700 111 111 **Fax:** +44 131 459 5600
Email: gordon.hollerin@dla.com

249 West George Street, **Glasgow** G2 4RB
Tel: +44 8700 111 111 **Fax:** +44 141 204 1902
Email: gordon.hollerin@dla.com

Princes Exchange, Princes Square, **Leeds** LS1 4BY
Tel: +44 8700 111 111 **Fax:** +44 113 369 2369
Email: neil.mclean@dla.com

India Buildings, Water Street, **Liverpool** L2 0NH
Tel: +44 8700 111 111 **Fax:** +44 151 236 9208
Email: michael.prince@dla.com

3 Noble Street, **London** EC2V 7EE
Tel: +44 8700 111 111 **Fax:** +44 20 7796 6666
Email: info@dla.com

101 Barbirolli Square, **Manchester** M2 3DL
Tel: +44 8700 111 111 **Fax:** +44 161 235 4111
Email: roy.beckett@dla.com

Fountain Precinct, Balm Green, **Sheffield** S1 1RZ
Tel: +44 8700 111 111 **Fax:** +44 114 270 0568
Email: paul.firth@dla.com

ASSOCIATED OFFICES

BELGIUM
Price & Partners, 106 Avenue Louise, B-1050 **Brussels**
Tel: +32 2 629 6911 **Fax:** +32 2 629 6922
Email: charles.price@price.be

FRANCE
Ginestié, Paley-Vincent & Associés, 10 Place des États-Unis, 75116 **Paris**
Tel: +33 1 53 23 40 00 **Fax:** +33 1 53 23 97 00
Email: ginestie@ginestie.com

SINGAPORE
J Koh & Co, 8 Robinson Road, **Singapore** 048544
Tel: +65 549 5600 **Fax:** +65 538 2221
Email: jkc@jkohco.com

SPAIN
Brugueras, Garcia-Bragado, Molinero y Asociados, Passeo de Gràcia 81, 08008 **Barcelona**
Tel: +34 93 467 1670 **Fax:** +34 93 487 1853
Email: carlos.ginebreda@brugueras.com

For other recommended firms see pages 1485-1520

DOMAŃSKI ZAKRZEWSKI PALINKA

A MEMBER OF ANDERSEN LEGAL

HEAD OFFICE

Warsaw Financial Center, ul. Emilii Plater 53,
00-113 Warsaw, Poland
Tel: + 48 22 520 76 00 **Fax:** + 48 22 520 88 10

FIRM OVERVIEW

Managing partner: Krzysztof Zakrzewski
Senior partner: Grzegorz Domański
Partners: Józef Palinka, Janina Ligner, Lech Zyzylewki

Number of partners worldwide: 5
Number of other lawyers worldwide: 39

WORLDWIDE OFFICE CONTACTS

POLAND
Warsaw Financial Center, ul. Emilii Plater 53, 00-113 **Warsaw**
Tel: + 48 22 520 76 00 **Fax:** + 48 22 520 88 10
Email: dzp@andersenlegal.com

ul. Paderewskiego 8, 61-770 **Poznań**
Tel: + 48 61 858 24 00 **Fax:** + 48 61 858 24 01

AREAS OF PRACTICE:

Banking	*%
General corporate law	*%
Insurance	*%
Labour	*%
M&A, privatisation	*%
Multimedia and telecommunications	*%
Real estate	*%
Securities	*%

* Workload % not disclosed

FIRM OVERVIEW: Established in 1993, Domański Zakrzewski Palinka is a full-service Polish law firm with four partners and 39 other lawyers, based in Warsaw and providing services throughout Poland. Since 1995 the firm has worked together with Arthur Andersen on both a national and international basis, enabling its lawyers to draw on the international and interdisciplinary resources of Arthur Andersen whilst retaining the advantages of being a local firm which is sensitive to the way business is done in Poland. At least two senior lawyers take responsibility for each assignment in the firm, and great emphasis is placed on the training of its lawyers, who attend specialist lectures and seminars and also follow courses in data processing technology.

INTERNATIONAL EXPERIENCE: Major international deals in the last three years have included providing full scope legal advice to NSK-RHP in its acquisitions in Poland, advice to Smithfield Foods Inc on capital markets transactions as the company invested in the Polish market, and Everest Capital Ltd on major transactions concerning national investment funds. The firm has advised on and negotiated numerous international joint ventures and acquisitions in Poland by foreign companies, sometimes representing the Polish privatisation ministry or private owners and sometimes the foreign acquirer or partner.

INTERNATIONAL CLIENTS: The firm's other major international clients include financial companies and institutions (Commerzbank, Deutsche Bank, Nykredit, International Finance Corporation, VHF, Polish-American Enterprise Fund), insurance (Hamburg Mannheimer, Commercial Union), manufacturing companies (NSK-RHP, Rieber & Son, Degussa, Saint Gobain Group, Carmeuse SA), retail (CONFORAMA SA), technology companies (Ricoh Europe BV, WPI Group) and agencies (WPP Group, Young & Rubicam, Ogilvy & Mather).

MAIN INTERNATIONAL AREAS OF PRACTICE:
Mergers: The firm has provided corporate and tax law advice in major Polish bank mergers – to the management board of BIG Bank on its merger with Bank Gdanski, the management board of Kredyt Bank on its merger with PBI SA, to Bank Pekao-Grupa Pekao on its merger with Pomorski Bank Kredytowy SA, Bank Depozytowo-Kredytowy SA and Powszechny Bank Gospodarczy SA and advice on tax and corporate issues to Bank Rozwoju Eksportu SA in its merger with Polski Bank Rozwoju SA. It has also advised on all the legal aspects of the mergers of furniture manufacturer Swarzedz SA's 26 subsidiaries.
Acquisitions: The firm has acquired expertise in negotiating and concluding important acquisitions in the course of transactions it has handled. It has been involved in share issues, share acquisitions and sales. Work includes the representation of Rieber & Son in the acquisition of shares in Delecta SA, the Polish-American Enterprise Fund in a public share acquisition involving ESPEBEPE SA, advising the shareholders in a new share issue in Lukas SA, the Minister of Privatisation in share sales in Energoaparatura SA, Hydrobudowa 6 SA, Cement Works Gorazdze SA and Ponar Zywiec SA., BRE Bank SA in the acquisition of shares in Best SA, UNP International Holdings Inc in the sale of shares in glassworks Huta Szkla Antoninek SA, Skane Grippen AB in the acquisition of furniture manufacturers Wolsztyńska Fabryka Mebli Sp zoo, BRE Bank SA and other selling shareholders in sale of shares in ERA GSM and BRE Bank SA in acquisition of Optimus SA.
Joint ventures: Work includes representing US WEST International in negotiations on a joint venture with Polska Telefonia Cyfrowa ERA GSM, the State Treasury in negotiations on the Thomson Polkolor joint venture, Kronospan AG on a joint venture with Furnel International and the Schieder Group in the Polspan deal.
Restructuring: Work includes drawing up privatisation plans for the Polish power sector, the restructuring of Polish Oil and Gas Mining, forming legal structures for the INCO-VERITAS Group drawing up plans for the Holding Energetyczny Poludnie (Southern Energy Holding) and drawing up a concept of formation for the Mostostal-Export SA holding.
Public companies: Work includes IPOs for several Polish companies including Bank Handlowy w Warszawie SA, Dom-Plast SA, Sanwil SA, Budokor SA, NIF Progress and NIF Piast. The firm has also represented brokerage houses in proceedings before the Securities Commission and advised on transactions on the public securities market, for example in the course of Carlsberg's investment in Okocim SA. The team has produced share option plan concepts and advised on the issuing of convertible bonds (for Elektrim SA) and represented clients in several public take-overs (Dom-Plast, Best).

LANGUAGES: English, French, German, Polish, Russian, Spanish

For other recommended firms see pages 1485-1520

DORSEY & WHITNEY LLP

HEAD OFFICE

220 South Sixth Street,
Minneapolis MN 55402-1498, USA
Tel: +1 612 340 2600 **Fax:** +1 612 340 2868

Website: www.dorseylaw.com

FIRM OVERVIEW

Managing partner: Peter S. Hendrixson
Senior partners: Walter F. Mondale, David Aaron

Number of partners worldwide: 284
Number of other lawyers worldwide: 393

AREAS OF PRACTICE:

Corporate and commercial transactions .... *%
Finance .... *%
Intellectual property .... *%
Trade .... *%
* Workload % not disclosed

FIRM OVERVIEW: Established in 1912, Dorsey & Whitney LLP is one of the 30 largest firms in the United States, with more than 675 lawyers and 800 support staff located in 19 offices in 14 domestic cities and five foreign countries. The firm have a focus in corporate law and litigation, but have established a wide range of other practice groups. Clients include public and private companies, nonprofit organisations, governmental bodies and individuals.

INTERNATIONAL EXPERIENCE: Members of the group provide a variety of legal services to US and foreign companies on cross-border and local issues. Outbound matters include a wide range of commercial, financial and trade matters, including acquisitions, joint ventures, licensing and distribution, capital markets, project finance, European Union laws and dispute resolution. Inbound matters include the broad range of United States legal services offered by the firm, such as acquisitions, employment, immigration, financings, intellectual property, litigation, real property, trade and other matters.

INTERNATIONAL CLIENTS: Dorsey & Whitney's international lawyers have worked closely over the years with a national and international client list, ranging from large American and foreign-based multinational corporations and financial institutions, to small American and foreign companies dealing in areas of international trade, finance, investment and telecommunications.

MAIN INTERNATIONAL AREAS OF PRACTICE:

Finance: The firm's clients in this area include issuers, underwriters and foreign commercial and merchant banks. Advises on public and private offerings of debt, equity and convertible securities in the European financial markets; global initial public offerings of European-based companies; structured Eurosecurity financings, with the use of special purpose corporations, trusts or agencies; and listings of securities of US companies on the major European stock exchanges, among other matters.
Corporate and commercial transactions: Dorsey & Whitney provides US and foreign clients with advice on a variety of corporate and commercial transactions that include the establishment of overseas subsidiaries and branches for US companies, the acquisition or divestiture of overseas businesses or assets by US companies, operations of foreign companies in the US, cross-border joint venture agreements, tax considerations involved in international operations and EU laws and regulations.
Intellectual property: The firm represents domestic and foreign clients in the acquisition, exploitation, protection and enforcement of international intellectual property rights. The firm's areas of particular experience include helping clients develop, formulate, budget for and implement intellectual property strategies and licensing programmes; advising clients on considerations related to the filing of intellectual property applications; obtaining patents and trademark and copyright registrations for US clients in foreign jurisdictions in cooperation with local counsel; and helping clients define business relationships and identify and build strategic alliances.
Trade: The firm advises large and small companies on the legal aspects of importing and exporting goods and services to and from the US and Europe. Examples of the firm's work include representing clients in proceedings concerning the proper classification and value of merchandise for US and EU purposes, penalty proceedings against importers brought by the US Customs Service, export licensing and National Security Clause proceedings before the US Department of Commerce and in legislative matters before US Congress and its committees.

LANGUAGES: Catalan, Cantonese, Chinese, Czechoslovakian, Dutch, Flemish, French, German, Gujanti, Hindi, Italian, Japanese, Korean, Lithuanian, Norwegian, Polish, Portuguese, Russian, Spanish, Swedish, Toumil

WORLDWIDE OFFICE CONTACTS

BELGIUM
35 Square de Meeûs, 1000 **Brussels**
Tel: +32 2 504 4611 **Fax:** +32 2 504 4646
Email: glazer.barry@dorseylaw.com

CANADA
Suite 500 Park Place, 666 Burrard Street, **Vancouver** BC V6C 3P6
Tel: +1 604 687 5151 **Fax:** +1 604 687 8504
Email: peterson.jeff@dorseylaw.com

CHINA
Suite 801, Citic Tower, No 1 Tim Mei Avenue, Central, **Hong Kong**
Tel: +852 2526 5000 **Fax:** +852 2524 3000
Email: zhang.zhao@dorseylaw.com

JAPAN
Shiroyama JT Mori Building 16F, 4-3-1 Toranomon Minato-Ku, **Tokyo**, 105 6016
Tel: +81 3 5403 4876 **Fax:** +81 3 5403 4877
Email: obrien.chris@dorseylaw.com

UNITED KINGDOM
Veritas House, 125 Finsbury Pavement, **London** EC2A 1NQ
Tel: +44 20 7588 0800 **Fax:** +44 20 7588 0555
Email: kohl.peter@dorseylaw.com

USA
220 South Sixth Street, **Minneapolis** MN 55402-1498
Tel: +1 612 340 2600 **Fax:** +1 612 340 2868
Email: trucano.mike@dorseylaw.com

Additional offices in Anchorage, Alaska; Orange County, California; Denver, Colorado; Washington, DC; Rochester, Minnesota; Billings, Great Falls and Missoula, Montana; Fargo, North Dakota; New York; Salt Lake City, Utah; Seattle, Washington

D

For other recommended firms see pages 1485-1520

DRAGSTED SCHLÜTER AROS

HEAD OFFICE

see Worldwide Office Contacts

FIRM OVERVIEW

General manager: Anne Granborg
Number of partners worldwide: 57
Number of other lawyers worldwide: 134

AREAS OF PRACTICE:

Banking and finance .... *%
Competition and EU .... *%
Construction, real property and environmental law .... *%
Corporate and M&A .... *%
Employment .... *%
Entertainment and media law .... *%
Insolvency and reconstruction .... *%
Intellectual property .... *%
IT and telecommunications .... *%
Maritime, transport and insurance .... *%
Tax .... *%
* Workload % not disclosed

FIRM OVERVIEW: Dragsted Schlüter Aros was established in 1999 as a result of a merger between Dragsted Schlüter Helmer Nielsen, the largest law firm in Copenhagen, and AROS Advokater, Aarhus, the largest law firm in Denmark outside of Copenhagen. Over 185 lawyers serve Danish and international companies, financial institutions, organisations and public authorities in all areas of business law.

INTERNATIONAL EXPERIENCE: The firm has provided legal advice in numerous substantial cross-border transactions, including M&As, on behalf of Danish and international clients, assisted in arbitration and litigation proceedings and in business set-ups including international taxation.

INTERNATIONAL CLIENTS: The firm's client base includes large companies and public or supranational institutions conducting cross-border business.

MAIN INTERNATIONAL AREAS OF PRACTICE:

Banking and finance: The firm provides specialised legal services in all fields of banking, finance and stock exchange law. The firm's lawyers have many years of experience in the establishment of banks, bank branches, stockbroking firms and leasing companies. In recent years, the firm has been an active adviser in connection with stock exchange flotations, secondary offerings, takeovers and de-listings, as well as structured financing in conjunction with M&A activities.
Competition and EU: The firm's specialists on EU law, international law and competition law advise Danish and international companies and institutions on Danish competition rules, EU competition law, EU public procurement policy, EU rules on the free movement of goods, export rules for agricultural goods, deregulation and WTO issues.
Construction, real property and environmental law: The firm provides specialist legal advice on construction and environmental law as well as real property with particular emphasis on commercial property. The firm offers advice to engineers, contractors, architects, building owners, sellers and purchasers of large properties. The firm has many years' experience with all environmental issues regarding real property and industrial production and often participates in environmental due diligence.
Corporate and M&A: The firm advises Danish and international companies, financial institutions and venture capitalists. Its team approach enables the firm to handle all types of corporate finance work, including the acquisition and restructuring of major, publicly held corporations, private and public offerings of securities, and the organisation of new entrepreneurial enterprises.
Insolvency and reconstruction: The firm's lawyers have considerable experience in matters of insolvency law, reconstruction and administration of estates. The firm offers advice to individual creditors, companies and financial institutions, and three members have been appointed public receivers at the Bankruptcy Division of the Court of Copenhagen.
Maritime, transport and insurance: The firm offers specialist legal services to Danish and international insurance companies, P&I clubs, insurance brokers, airlines, shipping companies, charterers, shipyards, freight forwarders, transport companies, transport organisations and financial institutions.
IT and telecommunications: Members assist internet service providers and providers of goods and services on the internet, software producers and purchasers of software as well as systems service providers and telecommunication operators. Dragsted Schlüter Aros has been involved in major infrastructure projects in Denmark in recent years.
Employment: The firm's employment group advises on individual and collective employment issues including employment contracts for employees and executives, confidentiality and non-competition clauses, the Acquired Rights Directive and works councils. It carries out due diligence investigations in relation to staff matters in connection with mergers and acquisitions and provides general advice on Danish employment legislation and the impact of EU directives.
Entertainment and media law: The firm has the largest entertainment and media law practice in Denmark. It represents Danish trade association record, film, video and game producers as well as a number of independent producers. Advice is also offered to book publishers, newspapers, magazines and other similar enterprises in Denmark.
Tax: The firm handles planning as well as litigation. It represent clients before administrative authorities, tax complaints boards, The National Tax Tribunal and the courts.

LANGUAGES: Danish, English, French, German, Italian, Norwegian, Russian, Spanish, Swedish

WORLDWIDE OFFICE CONTACTS

DENMARK
Frue Kirkeplads 4, 8100 **Arhus**
Tel: +45 89 31 00 00 **Fax:** + 45 89 31 01 01
Email:

Bredgade 6, DK-1260 **Copenhagen** K
Tel: +45 33 14 33 33 **Fax:** +45 33 32 43 33
Email:

Rådhuspladssen 4, DK-1550 **Copenhagen** V
Tel: +45 77 33 77 33 **Fax:** +45 77 33 77 44
Email: dsa@dragsted.com

RUSSIA
Tverskaja ul 24/2,, W 103009 **Moscow**
Tel: +7 095 956 49 61 **Fax:** +7 095 956 49 62
Email: arosrus@online.ru

Dragsted Schlüter Aros

DREW & NAPIER

HEAD OFFICE

20 Raffles Place, #17-00, Ocean Towers,
Singapore 048620, Singapore
Tel: +65 535 0733 **Fax:** +65 535 4906
Email: mail@drewnapier.com
Website: www.drewnapier.com

FIRM OVERVIEW

Managing partner: Davinder Singh, Senior Counsel
Number of partners worldwide: 41
Number of other lawyers worldwide: 98

AREAS OF PRACTICE:

Business and corporate	*%
Banking, finance and securities	*%
Building and construction	*%
Employment and immigration	*%
Info-communications and technology	*%
Family and matrimonial	*%
Insolvency and reorganisation	*%
Insurance and reinsurance	*%
Intellectual property	*%
Life sciences	*%
Litigation	*%
Real estate, property and conveyancing	*%
Shipping and international trade	*%
Tax, trusts, estate planning and probate	*%
Transnational and cross-border work	*%

* Workload % not disclosed

FIRM OVERVIEW: Established in 1889 by British solicitors Charles Napier and Alfred Drew, the firm now has over 140 lawyers organised into specialised business groups, making it one of the largest law firms in Singapore. It is a full service practice and is constantly innovating and expanding its legal services to keep in step with developments in business, info-communications and technology. Its IP and litigation departments are amongst the top practices in Singapore. Many of its lawyers are qualified in other jurisdictions. Together with its foreign lawyers and network of international associates worldwide, Drew & Napier provides multi-jurisdictional and multi-lingual legal advice to companies with international businesses. Drew & Napier and Freshfields Bruckhaus Deringer have entered into a joint law venture in Singapore. All international and regional corporate work will be carried out under Freshfields Drew & Napier. Drew & Napier's litigation, real estate and intellectual property practice and all other aspects of advice on Singapore law and local matters will continue to be carried out by Drew & Napier.

INTERNATIONAL EXPERIENCE: The firm advises on cross-border investments in Asia, Greater China and South Africa. It has teams of lawyers who specialise in work relating to countries such as China, India, Indonesia, Malaysia, Thailand and Vietnam. The infrastructure practice is familiar with the workings of the multilateral agencies and export agencies that fund much of the infrastructure development in Asia. Its intellectual property practice secures registrations directly in Singapore, Malaysia, Brunei and work alongside a network of associates worldwide to safeguard intellectual property rights. The firm's litigation department includes Senior Counsels and a former Judicial Commissioner. It is divided into specialisations including insolvency, banking, commercial fraud, family, infocomms and intellectual property. It regularly handles multi-party and multi-jurisdictional disputes. The firm's shipping and international trade business group represents P&I clubs, hull and cargo underwriters, shipyards and shipowners. Its InfoComms team works with some of the world's leading telecommunications, broadcast and IT companies. With the joint law venture with Freshfields Bruckhaus Deringer, it will provide a greater international and regional capacity to its clients, and the best of what its constituent firms have to offer in terms of quality, experience, network and value to all clients of the joint venture.

INTERNATIONAL CLIENTS: Comprise multi-national corporations, private and public companies, including Fortune 500 and blue chip companies, and governmental entities.

MAIN INTERNATIONAL AREAS OF PRACTICE:

Banking, finance/securities and business/corporate: The firm specialises in all areas of corporate and commercial law, including corporatisation, privatisation, mergers and acquisitions, stock exchange matters, investments in joint ventures, infrastructure, cross-border investments, corporate restructuring, schemes of arrangement, reconstruction, employment matters, company incorporation and registration and corporate secretarial.
Info-Communications and technology: Specialising in legal matters related to information technology, telecommunications, broadcasting and multimedia practices, the InfoComms and Technology Group acts for hardware manufacturers, telecommunication carriers, network operators, consultants, equipment suppliers, specialist contractors, software houses, broadcasters, programmers and international law firms.
Insolvency and reorganisation: The Insolvency and Reorganisation Group works closely with accountants, liquidators, receivers and judicial managers, and specialises both in insolvency-related matters like bankruptcy, liquidation and receivership including priority issues, claims for unfair preferences and fraudulent trading and in the restructuring and reorganisation of companies, including such areas as judicial management, schemes of arrangements and workouts.
Intellectual property: With a large intellectual property practice, the Intellectual Property Group advises on trademark protection, copyright and design rights, patent protection, intellectual property litigation, franchising, licensing, distributorship and technology transfer. The firm also has emerging life sciences expertise.
Litigation and dispute resolution: A premier litigation firm, Drew & Napier's clients include Fortune 500 and blue chip companies, and high profile individuals. The firm handles the full range of civil and commercial claims.
Shipping and international trade: The Shipping and International Trade Group has extensive experience in both dry and wet work. The firm provides advice and litigation support to its clients worldwide. Other areas of work covers ship arrests, injunctions, recovery work, charterparty dispute, salvage, general average and collisions.

LANGUAGES: Bahasa Melayu, Bahasa Indonesia, Cantonese, French, Japanese, Mandarin, Tamil, Vietnamese

WORLDWIDE OFFICE CONTACTS

MALAYSIA
Drewmarks Patents & Designs (Malaysia) Sdn Bhd, 9th Floor, Bangunan Getah Asli (Menara), 148 Jalan Ampang, 50450, **Kuala Lumpur**
Tel: +603 2162 2522 / 2162 2529 **Fax:** +603 2162 2804
Email: drewmark@tm.net.my

SINGAPORE
20 Raffles Place, #17-00, Ocean Towers, 048620, **Singapore**
Tel: +65 535 0733 **Fax:** +65 535 4906
Email: mail@drewnapier.com

VIETNAM
Room 605, CFM Building, 23 Lang Ha, Ba Dinh, **Hanoi**
Tel: +844 514 1995 / 1996 **Fax:** + 844 514 1972
Email: dnhn@hn.vnn.vn

D

For other recommended firms see pages 1485-1520

DUBE MANIKAI & HWACHA

HEAD OFFICE

DMH Commercial Law Chambers, 6th Floor, Goldbridge, Eastgate Complex, Second Street, PO BOX CR36, Cranborne
Harare Zimbabwe
Tel: +263 4 733 992/8 **Fax:** +263 4 780350

Email: dmh@internet.co.zw

FIRM OVERVIEW

Senior partner: Canaan F. Dube

AREAS OF PRACTICE:

Corporate /M&A 30%
Banking and finance 25%
Litigation and arbitration 16%
Insurance 10%
Telecommunications and computer law 10%
Intellectual property 9%

FIRM OVERVIEW: Dube, Manikai & Hwacha was established on the 1st June, 1998. The firm's aim is to be client-service oriented, to primarily deliver corporate legal services to both emerging and mature markets professionally and promptly and in a cost-efficient manner. The firm's core business is the provision of corporate legal services to both mature and emerging markets. The firm is structured and organised into specialist practice areas, which are the commercial and corporate services division, the banking and financial services division, the labour consultancy division and the conveyancing and real estate division.

INTERNATIONAL EXPERIENCE: Since inception, DMH has represented various international organisations interested in local target companies. The firm has also advised on regional intellectual property registration and is building relationships with regional trademark and patent attorneys. The firm was recently involved in the major restructuring exercise of a local newspaper group with the firm acting for a foreign media funding organisation.

INTERNATIONAL CLIENTS: The firm's international clients are in the technological and financial markets. These conduct regional business using DMH as legal consultant of the target countries in which they conduct business.

MAIN INTERNATIONAL AREAS OF PRACTICE:

Banking and finance: The firm has vast experience in drafting financial facility agreements, security forms and documentation, vetting of and rendering opinions in international financial agreements, registration of security documents, debt recoveries and foreclosures.

Commercial and corporate: The firm specialises in company formations and restructuring; acquisition/mergers and take-overs, privatisations and floatations; joint ventures; vetting and drafting of commercial agreements; liquidations/winding-up; back up tax law and related opinion work. The firm was the lead adviser in a ZW$5 billion bond flotation by a local fuel procurement company. The firm has advised on telecommunications and entertainment contracts.

Labour consultancy: The firm has a dominant reputation in reviewing and drafting of employee share-ownership schemes; employment contracts; codes of conduct; constitutions; retrenchments and human resources restructuring and general labour consultancy. It has represented a wide spectrum of clients at all labour hearings and has been involved in wage/trade union negotiations.

Conveyancing and real estate: DMH's corporate-focused profile has endowed it with experience in reviewing and drafting agreements relating to immovable property and financial security documents, registration of mortgage and notarial bonds, and immovable property. The firm has registered securities on behalf of foreign lending institutions.

Litigation and arbitration: This department is a back up and integral part of the commercial service the firm offers to its clients. Team DMH comprises some keen litigators and negotiators. The firm's litigation practice cuts across a full range of legal problems, common to financial, and other commercial entities including company and commercial disputes, construction disputes, insurance and personal injury claims, corporate governance issues, employment, civil and criminal disagreements. The firm is represented in the Chartered Institute of Arbitrators at Associate Level. In this field the firm has participated in corporate arbitrations and recommends alternative dispute resolution mechanisms (ADR) to ensure the prompt and expeditious resolution of commercial disputes in a cost-effective manner.

Intellectual property: The firm's members have participated in regional intellectual property conferences. The firm offers advice on local and regional patents, copyrights and trade marks registrations, prosecutions or infringement advice.

LANGUAGES: English

WORLDWIDE OFFICE CONTACTS

DMH Commercial Law Chambers, 6th Floor, Goldbridge, Esatgate Complex, Second Street, PO BOX CR36, Cranborne, **Harare**
Tel: +263 4 780351 **Fax:** +263 4 780350
Email: dmh@internet.co.zw

D

EITAN, PEARL, LATZER & COHEN-ZEDEK

HEAD OFFICE

2 Gav-Yam Center, 7 Shenkar Street,
PO Box 12688, Herzlia 46733,
Israel
Tel: +972 9 970 9000 **Fax:** +972 9 970 9001

Email: main@technolawgy.co.il
Website: www.technolawgy.com

WORLDWIDE OFFICE CONTACTS

ISRAEL
Omega Center, Advanced Technology Center, **Haifa** 31905
Tel: +972 4 855 0917 **Fax:** +972 4 855 0918
Email: haifa@technolawgy.co.il

2 Gav-Yam Center, 7 Shenkar Street, PO Box 12688, **Herzlia** 46733
Tel: +972 9 970 9000 **Fax:** +972 9 970 9001
Email: main@technolawgy.co.il

FIRM OVERVIEW

Senior partners: Named partners

Number of partners worldwide: 9
Number of other lawyers worldwide: 43

AREAS OF PRACTICE:

Intellectual property prosecution and litigation	40%
Licensing	28%
Tax and venture capital	20%
Mergers, acquisitions and securities	10%
Others	2%

E

FIRM OVERVIEW: Founded in 1992, the firm focuses principally on the technology industry, providing intellectual property, business, licensing and litigation services to both Israeli and international companies. It has 52 lawyers and patent attorneys/lawyers, several of whom are admitted to practise in Europe and the US. The firm has a diverse client base, from small start-ups to major high-tech companies.

INTERNATIONAL EXPERIENCE: The firm's 52 lawyers and patent attorneys/lawyers cover areas including internet, computers, telecoms, semiconductors, bio-tech, medical devices and imaging. Many are admitted to practise in Europe and the US, and have experience in high-tech companies. The firm represented Scitex Corporation Ltd in the sale of Scitex's Pre-Press division to Creo Technologies; represented Siemens Data Communication Ltd in its sale and merger with Seabridge Technologies; acted as counsel to the formation of Sequoia Seed Capital - a Venture Capital Fund in which Sequoia and Cisco are partners focusing on Israeli investments; currently representing around 12 venture capital funds raising aggregate capital exceeding US$1 billion including (in public domain) BRM, Magnum, Israel Seed and Delta Ventures.

INTERNATIONAL CLIENTS: The firm's clients include McDonald's, Siemens, 3COM, Applied Materials, Elron, Creo-Scitex, Tadiran, CheckPoint, HMR, Hewlett Packard, ECI, Vocaltec, Amdocs, Comverse, Medinol, Seiko, Intel Corporation, ST Microelectornics, Micro Swiss Advances Bonding Systems, Cadence Design Systems Limited, Saifun Semiconductors Ltd and Sequoia Capital Seed Funds.

MAIN INTERNATIONAL AREAS OF PRACTICE:
Intellectual property: Work includes the procurement, enforcement and licensing of patents, trademarks, copyrights, mask works, technical know-how and trade secrets.
Business law: The group has a dedicated start-up section specialising in emerging technology companies.
Licensing: The practice specialises in negotiating and structuring licensing and technology transfer agreements, with particular emphasis on the software, Internet and telecommunications industries.
Litigation: The firm represents litigants in disputes concerning technological issues, with an emphasis on intellectual property.
Tax: The tax practice encompasses all facets of domestic and international tax law. It represents companies and venture funds, structuring transactions in the high-tech industry, both domestic and international.
Venture capital: The venture capital group has been involved in the formation of a multitude of funds, and is responsive to the unique issues that may arise in Israel and abroad.

LANGUAGES: English, French, German, Hebrew

 For other recommended firms see pages 1485-1520

ESPINO NIETO UMAÑA & ASOCIADOS

HEAD OFFICE

83 Avenida Norte, No. 138 Colonia Escalón,
San Salvador El Salvador
Tel: +503 263 7522 **Fax:** +503 263 7504

Email: info@espinolaw.com
Website: www.espinolaw.com

WORLDWIDE OFFICE CONTACTS

EL SALVADOR
83 Avenida Norte, No. 138 Colonia Escalón, **San Salvador**
Tel: +503 263 7522 **Fax:** +503 263 7504
Email: info@espinolaw.com

FIRM OVERVIEW

Senior partner: Luis Miguel Espino

Number of partners worldwide: 3
Number of other lawyers worldwide: 13

AREAS OF PRACTICE:

Intellectual property	*%
Corporate	*%
Banking and finance	*%
Litigation and arbitration	*%
M&A	*%
Telecommunications and energy	*%

* Workload % not disclosed

FIRM OVERVIEW: Espino Nieto Umaña & Asociados was founded in 1960. It has adapted and expanded to meet the needs of its increasingly international client base and is now one of the leading law firms in El Salvador. The firm advises foreign corporations investing in El Salvador and specialises in privatisations.

INTERNATIONAL EXPERIENCE: Espino Nieto Umaña & Asociados advised the Chilean and US partnership Emel/PPL on the sale of stocks in electrical power distribution companies (1997). It advised on the privatisation of the Mexican telecommunications company Telmex (1998) and also advised the US energy firm Duke Energy Corporation on its privatisation (1999). In banking and finance, the firm assisted Citibank on the US$100 million first domestic syndicated credit to a national company (1999).

INTERNATIONAL CLIENTS: The firm advises foreign companies producing pharmaceuticals, cleaning products, chemicals and processed foods. It also advises companies operating in service sectors including banking, telecommunications, energy, film and television, entertainment and broadcasting, wholesale and retail services.

MAIN INTERNATIONAL AREAS OF PRACTICE:
M&A: The firm advises foreign corporations on local company takeovers. Espino Nieto Umaña & Asociados also advises on tax aspects of acquisitions.
Banking and finance: Espino Nieto, Umaña & Asociados covers all areas of banking and finance including syndicated loan transactions.
Corporate: The firm advises on all corporate issues including agreements review and execution and conducting due diligence.
Intellectual property: The firm advises multinational companies investing in El Salvador on registering trademarks, slogans and other intellectual property rights. The firm also handles regulatory work.
Telecommunications and energy: The firm advises on all aspects relating to telecommunications law.
Tax: Espino Nieto Umaña & Asociados advises on all aspects of taxation including on the importation of machinery and duty-free procedures. It has also advised on establishing the regulatory framework for taxation in El Salvador.
Employment: Espino Nieto, Umaña & Asociados has advised on the execution of collective labour agreements with several unions, including the Electrical Union of El Salvador.

LANGUAGES: English, Spanish

For other recommended firms see pages 1485-1520

ETAH-NAN & CO

HEAD OFFICE

Société d' Avocats, BP 4736,
Douala Cameroon
Tel: +237 42 56 09 **Fax:** +237 423 289

Email: etahnan@camnet.cm

FIRM OVERVIEW

Managing partner: Etah Akoh

Number of partners worldwide: 5
Number of other lawyers worldwide: 6

AREAS OF PRACTICE:
Banking, finance and insurance ....*%
Corporate and commercial ....*%
Energy and natural resources ....*%
Intellectual property ....*%
Joint venture ....*%
Litigation and arbitration ....*%
M&A ....*%
Maritime ....*%
Privatisation ....*%
Tax ....*%
* Workload % not disclosed

FIRM OVERVIEW: Etah-Nan & Co, founded in 1984, is the first bilingual law firm in Cameroon. The creation of the firm was in response to the bilingual nature of Cameroon, where French and English law is applicable. The firm's partners and associates are trained in both English and French law, and some specialise in comparative law (English and French law). This is the firm's most important asset as it enables it to practise in two legal systems.

INTERNATIONAL CLIENTS: The firm's clients base includes companies from Africa, Europe and Asia.

WORLDWIDE OFFICE CONTACTS

CAMEROON
Société d' Avocats, BP 4736, **Douala**
Tel: +237 42 56 09 **Fax:** +237 423 289
Email: etahnan@camnet.cm

MAIN INTERNATIONAL AREAS OF PRACTICE: Work undertaken includes corporate and commercial, banking, finance and insurance, joint venture, energy and natural resources, M&A, maritime, intellectual property, tax, privatisation, and litigation and arbitration.

LANGUAGES: English, French, Spanish

E

For other recommended firms see pages 1485-1520

EVERSHEDS

HEAD OFFICE

Senator House, 85 Queen Victoria Street,
London EC4V 4JL, United Kingdom
Tel: +44 20 7919 4500 **Fax:** +44 20 7919 4919
Email: london@eversheds.com
Website: www.eversheds.com

FIRM OVERVIEW

Managing partner: David Ansbro
Chairman: Keith James
Number of partners worldwide: 373
Number of other lawyers worldwide: 1,044

AREAS OF PRACTICE:

Corporate/commercial	35%
Litigation/dispute management	25%
Property	25%
Employment	9%
Other	6%

FIRM PROFILE: The firm has 1,900 legal and business advisers, based in 18 offices in Europe and three associated offices in Asia. Each office provides a wide range of services to the business and financial community and to the public sector. Its distinctive approach gives clients access to a large team of lawyers who combine local market knowledge with an international perspective.

INTERNATIONAL EXPERIENCE: The firm has a vast number of multi-disciplinary teams which focus on specific industry sectors and specialist services which operate across its offices. The firm's Anglo-German group offers a full bi-lingual specialist service to the Anglo-German business community through a team of dual qualified lawyers.

INTERNATIONAL CLIENTS: Eversheds advises 45 companies in the Fortune 500 index and acts for 46 of the Euro 100 companies. It has many clients from the US and Asia who look to Europe for trade, commerce, investment, acquisition or joint venture.

MAIN INTERNATIONAL AREAS OF PRACTICE:

Corporate finance: The firm advises businesses on multi-jurisdictional mergers and acquisitions, joint ventures operations, stock exchange listings and venture capital investments. The firm's financial services and banking practice advises many of the world's major investment institutions.

Commercial: Eversheds commercial team has particular expertise in multi-jurisdictional joint ventures and cross border supply contracts. Its telecommunications and procurement teams advise on the establishment of regulatory regimes in this area. The franchising team is highly renowned for its activities on a global scale. These skills are combined with a strong international trade practice and one of the strongest EU/competition law practices. The firm offers advice on all available options and strategic considerations to clients seeking a cross-border relationship or establishing their own green field operations.

Tax: The fim's international tax lawyers, which include a number of chartered accountants and a barrister as well as specialist tax lawyers, offer technical expertise coupled with commercial awareness and a proactive approach to tax planning.

Litigation and dispute management: The firm's litigation and international arbitration team is renowned both in countries in which it operates and in front of forums such as the International Chamber of Commerce and in the International Courts of Justice. The firm leads the field in public international law, advising governments and enterprises on boundary disputes, maritime delimitation issues and sanctions.

Real estate: Eversheds provides a full property service for clients across Europe, in individual jurisdictions and on a pan-European, multi-jurisdictional basis through a network of offices and close relationships with law firms in each jurisdiction.

Employment: The firm's employment team advises on all aspects of employment law and human resources consultancy, as well as in the issues arising from international mergers. The team has advised a major international company on the employment aspects of its merger, coordinating advice across 42 jurisdictions.

LANGUAGES: Danish, Dutch, English, French, German

WORLDWIDE OFFICE CONTACTS

BELGIUM
75 Avenue de Cortenberg, 1000 **Brussels**
Tel: +32 2 737 9340 **Fax:** + 32 2 737 9345

FRANCE
42 Avenue du Président Wilson, 75116 **Paris**
Tel: +33 1 44 34 71 00 **Fax:** + 33 1 44 34 71 11

MONACO
Est-Ouest, 24 Boulevard Princesse Charlotte, 98000 **Monte Carlo**
Tel: +377 93 10 55 10 **Fax:** +377 93 10 55 11

UNITED KINGDOM
Senator House, 85 Queen Victoria Street, **London** EC4V 4JL
Tel: +44 20 7919 4500 **Fax:** +44 20 7919 4919

ASSOCIATED OFFICES

BULGARIA
In association with Georgiev, Todorov & Co, 58-V Tzar Assen Street, PO Box 15, **Sofia** 1463
Tel: +359 2 951 5665 **Fax:** +359 2 952 0451

DENMARK
Østergade 27, DK-1100 **Copenhagen**
Tel: +45 33 75 05 05 **Fax:** +45 33 75 05 00

HONG KONG
Khattar Wong & Partners, 1910-1913 Hutchison House, No.10 Harcourt Road, Central **Hong Kong**
Tel: +852 2815 6292 **Fax:** +852 2815 6007

MALAYSIA
KM Chye & Murad, 6th floor, UBN Tower, Letterbox 163, No.10 Jalan P Ramlee, **Kuala Lumpur** 50250
Tel: +603 238 8055 **Fax:** +603 201 9300

SINGAPORE
Khattar Wong & Partners, 80 Raffles Place, #25-01 UOB Plaza 1, **Singapore** 048624
Tel: +65 535 68 44 **Fax:** +65 534 48 92

NETHERLANDS
Boekel De Nerée, Atriumbuilding, 2nd floor, Strawinskylaan 3037, 1077 ZX **Amsterdam**
Tel: +31 20 431 31 31 **Fax:** +31 20 431 31 43

BUFETE F.A. ARIAS

HEAD OFFICE

85 Ave. Nte. 825 Colonia Escalon,
San Salvador El Salvador
Tel: +503 257 0900 **Fax:** +503 257 0901

Email: ariaslaw@ariaslaw.com
Website: www.ariaslaw.com

FIRM OVERVIEW

Senior partner: Francisco Armando Arias Rivera

Number of partners worldwide: 4
Number of other lawyers worldwide: 14

AREAS OF PRACTICE:

Corporate	30%
Banking and finance	15%
Telecommunications and energy	15%
Intellectual property	10%
Oil and gas	10%
Tax	10%
Capital markets	7%
Employment	2%
Insurance and reinsurance	1%

WORLDWIDE OFFICE CONTACTS

EL SALVADOR
85 Ave. Nte. 825 Colonia Escalon, **San Salvador**
Tel: +503 257 0900 **Fax:** +503 257 0901
Email: ariaslaw@ariaslaw.com

ASSOCIATED OFFICES

COSTA RICA
F.A. Arias Muñoz, Centro Empresarial Forum, Edificio C, Of. ICI, Santa Ana, **San José**
Tel: +506 204 7575 **Fax:** +506 204 7580
Email: jamunoz@sol.rasca.co.cr

GUATEMALA
F.A. Arias & Muñoz, Ave Reforma 7-62, Zona 9, Edificio Aristos Reforma, 10th level, **Guatemala City**
Tel: +502 362 9328 **Fax:** +502 362 9331
Email: ariaslaw@gua.net

NICARAGUA
F.A. Arias & Muñoz, Centro BANIC, Edificio Pérez Cassar, Carretera a Masaya, Kilómetro 5 1/2, **Managua**
Tel: +505 270 0480 **Fax:** +505 270 2021
Email: pmunoz@arislaw.com.ni

FIRM OVERVIEW: Established in 1942, Bufete F.A. Arias is one of the oldest and largest law firms in El Salvador. The firm has 18 lawyers and offers legal and notary public services to individuals, national and international companies, corporations, associations, organisations and institutions both from the private and public sectors. It is committed to offering services of the highest calibre. In 1998 it established F.A Arias & Muñoz, which together with the renowned Costa Rican attorneys José Antonio Muñoz and Pedro M. Muñoz, became the only law firm in Central America working as a sole regional entity. It offers an innovative system addressing legal issues in the region with offices in Guatemala, El Salvador, Nicaragua and Costa Rica. The firm will soon be opening an office in Honduras.

INTERNATIONAL EXPERIENCE: As the firm has expanded, so has its range of international clients. It currently represents a number of well-known international companies from the US, Europe and Latin America. The firm has gained experience in a range of international transactions including contracts, international financing, and mergers and acquisitions.

INTERNATIONAL CLIENTS: The firm's clients include Citibank, Texaco, 3M, Airbus, Dresdner Bank, General Electric, Telefónica, Caterpillar, World Bank (IFC), McDonald's, Visa International, BMW, and Daimler-Chrysler.

MAIN INTERNATIONAL AREAS OF PRACTICE:
Banking and finance: The firm represents a range of local and international banks, advising them on the structuring of finance projects. It also advises the Salvadoran Banking Association. One of the firm's senior partners serves as president of the Salvadoran Banking Law Association.
Corporate: The firm advises a number of local and international corporations on a range of corporate issues.
Capital markets: The firm has advised a number of clients on the structuring of finance through capital markets and the issuance of bonds and stock for public offering.
Telecommunications and energy: The firm has worked with many international telecom companies. It participated in the acquisition of one of the two state owned telephone companies and advises internet companies and call centres. In the energy sector, the firm represents the second largest energy distribution company and has assisted other companies with projects in El Salvador.
Tax: The firm advised the Ministry of Finance in 1992 on major VAT and income tax law reforms. It has also advised a number of corporations on tax issues including tax structuring for mergers and acquisitions. One of the firm's members serves as president of the Salvadoran Tax Law Association.
Oil and gas: The firm represents one of the major oil companies doing business in El Salvador.
Employment: The firm advises all its corporate clients on a range of employment issues.
Intellectual property: The firm has a strong intellectual property department and has experience in trademark registration, patents, oppositions and all matters related to intellectual property protection. One of the firm's members currently serves on the board of the Intellectual Property Association.

LANGUAGES: English, Spanish

 For other recommended firms see pages 1485-1520

FANGDA PARTNERS

HEAD OFFICE

19/F, HSBC Tower, 101 Yin Cheng East Road,
Shanghai 200120, China
Tel: +86 21 6841 1166 **Fax:** +86 21 6841 2255
Email: email@fangdalaw.com

FIRM OVERVIEW

Managing partner: Kenneth X. Lu
Executive partner: William W. Huang

Number of partners worldwide: 8
Number of other lawyers worldwide: 28

AREAS OF PRACTICE:

Corporate finance	35%
Banking and finance	25%
General corporate and commercial	20%
M&A	10%
Telecommunications and IT	10%

FIRM OVERVIEW: Founded in 1994, Fangda Partners was one of China's first private firms. Based in Shanghai, the firm handles a range of legal transactions throughout China. As a recognised leading PRC firm in the commercial field, the firm serves international and domestic clients successfully in various industries.

INTERNATIONAL EXPERIENCE: The firm has advised a number of overseas listings of Chinese companies, international project financing and private equity funding. It has frequently been involved in multi-jurisdictional transactions in which it has advised either international or Chinese clients. Some of the partners and associates have been trained or educated overseas.

INTERNATIONAL CLIENTS: The firm's clients include New Bridge Capital, Bank of China, Citibank, PSEG, Texas Instruments, Eastman Kodak, CICC, Guotai Junan Securities, Merrill Lynch, Core Pacific-Yamaichi, New Margin, Morningside.

WORLDWIDE OFFICE CONTACTS

CHINA
19/F, HSBC Tower, 101 Yin Cheng East Road, **Shanghai** 200120
Tel: +86 21 6841 1166 **Fax:** +86 21 6841 2255
Email: email@fangdalaw.com

MAIN INTERNATIONAL AREAS OF PRACTICE:

Corporate finance: The firm advises on international and domestic IPOs, mergers and acquisitions of listed or unlisted companies, and private equity transactions.
Banking and finance: Fangda Partners handles a range of banking and finance transactions including syndicated lending, security arrangements, project finance, trade finance, and structured finance.
General corporate and commercial: The firm advises on foreign inward investment, company formation, liquidation, labour, tax, licensing, franchising, technology transfer and license, intellectual property, and foreign exchange.
Telecommunication and IT: The firm advises telecom operators, carriers and manufacturers, Internet companies, and technology and media companies on a range of legal issues.

LANGUAGES: Cantonese, English, German, Mandarin, Shanghainese

FARGOSI & ASOCIADOS

HEAD OFFICE

Tucuman 141, 1°,
C1049 AAC Buenos Aires, Argentina
Tel: +54 11 4311 5080 **Fax:** +54 11 4311 1775

Email: administracion@fargosi.com.ar

WORLDWIDE OFFICE CONTACTS

ARGENTINA
Tucuman 141, 1°, C1049 AAC **Buenos Aires**
Tel: +54 11 4311 5080 **Fax:** +54 11 4311 1775
Email: administracion@fargosi.com.ar

FIRM OVERVIEW

Senior partner: Horacio P. Fargosi

Number of partners worldwide: 16

AREAS OF PRACTICE:
Corporate 35%
Insurance and reinsurance 25%
Banking and finance 15%
M&A 15%
Litigation and arbitration 10%

FIRM OVERVIEW: Fargosi & Asociados was established in 1960 by Horacio P. Fargosi, author and co-author of various laws and legal texts, such as the Corporations Act 19550 and the Cheque Act 24452. The firm is reputed to be one of Argentina's leading law firms and a number of its lawyers are former judicial clerks and employees.

INTERNATIONAL EXPERIENCE: Fargosi & Asociados acts on behalf of major local and international corporations. The firm is actively involved in litigation and has handled both local and international arbitration. The firm advises foreign companies seeking to establish themselves in Argentina on matters such as corporate and commercial law, M&A, international business transactions (including agency, distribution, representation, franchising and leasing) and foreign commercial law. It has participated in complex M&A transactions including Siembra AFJP, Aerolineas Argentinas and Transportes Metropolitanos.

INTERNATIONAL CLIENTS: Clients include Generali (Italy); Sepi (Spain); Argentaria (Spain); Kverneland (Denmark and Scandanavia); Iberia (Spain); Pirelli (Italy); Grupo Pescarmona (Argentina); Sancor (Argentina). The firm is actively involved in the transportation industry, advising airlines (such as Aerolineas, Iberia and Austral) in aircraft lease, wet-lease, route and frequency approval, and regulatory matters; and railway and shipping companies (including Ivaran, Lykes and Norsul).

MAIN INTERNATIONAL AREAS OF PRACTICE:
Mergers and acquisitions: The firm handles matters ranging from small private acquisitions to larger and more complex M&A transactions, including full privatisation of state owned companies.
Banking and finance: The firm offers advice on all aspects of banking and finance, including pension funds. Members of the firm have held positions on the board of directors of many local and international banks and insurance companies. The firm has advised on financial products, loan transactions (including syndicated loans), and project finance.
Insurance and reinsurance: Fargosi & Asociados is actively involved in the insurance and reinsurance industry. The firm advises on matters ranging from the restructuring (including demutualising) of local and international insurance groups as well as regulatory matters. It specialises in insurance-related litigation.
Corporate law: The firm specialises in pure corporate law handling all aspects of corporate matters, such as disputes between shareholders; corporate reorganisation; insolvency and bankruptcy; stock; corporate finance; board of directors legal framework and litigation.
Litigation and arbitration: Fargosi & Asociados handles civil, commercial and administrative litigation before the Argentine Courts, including the Supreme Court. The firm undertakes local and international arbitration and its lawyers have participated in several cases under the ICC and international organisations' rules.
Admiralty and air law: The firm is retained by numerous local and international rail, shipping and airline companies.
Competition and consumer law: This sector has become more prominent since Argentina joined the Mercosur common market. Fargosi & Asociados' lawyers advise on a wide range of matters including anti-trust, competition, consumer disputes, product liability, and regulatory issues.

LANGUAGES: English, German, Italian, Spanish

For other recommended firms see pages 1485-1520

FASKEN MARTINEAU DUMOULIN LLP

HEAD OFFICE

Toronto Dominion Bank Tower, PO Box 20, Toronto Dominion Centre
Toronto, Ontario M5K 1N6, Canada
Tel: +1 416 366 8381 **Fax:** +1 416 364 7813

Email: info@tor.fasken.com
Website: www.fasken.com

FIRM OVERVIEW

Managing partners: Alan Schwartz QC (Toronto), Louis Bernier (Montreal), Sue Paish (Vancouver)

Number of partners worldwide: 285
Number of other lawyers worldwide: 192

AREAS OF PRACTICE:

Litigation, ADR and insolvency 35%
M&A 15%
Banking and corporate finance 10%
IT and telecommunications 10%
Employment and pensions 10%
Financial institutions 10%
Intellectual property 10%

FIRM OVERVIEW: Fasken Martineau DuMoulin was founded in the 1860s. Comprising nearly 500 lawyers practising in major Canadian cities, London and New York, the firm advises national and international clients on virtually all areas of law. The firm has particular experience in cross-border M&A and securities, mining and project finance, banking and financial services, computer and information technology law, and litigation and arbitration.

WORLDWIDE OFFICE CONTACTS

CANADA
Stock Exchange Tower, PO Box 242, 800, Place-Victoria, **Montréal**
Québec H4Z 1E9
Tel: +1 514 397 7400 **Fax:** +1 514 397 7600
Email: info@mtl.fasken.com

140, Grande Allée est, Bureau 800, **Québec City** Québec G1R 5M8
Tel: +1 418 640 2000 **Fax:** +1 418 647 2455
Email: info@qc.fasken.com

Toronto Dominion Bank Tower, PO Box 20, Toronto Dominion Centre,
Toronto, Ontario M5K 1N6
Tel: +1 416 366 8381 **Fax:** +1 416 364 7813
Email: info@tor.fasken.com

Suite 2100, 1075 West Georgia Street, **Vancouver**, British Columbia
V6E 3G2
Tel: +1 604 631 3131 **Fax:** +1 604 631 3232
Email: info@van.fasken.com

UNITED KINGDOM
10 Arthur Street, Fifth Floor, **London** EC4R 9AY
Tel: +44 20 7929 2894 **Fax:** +44 20 7929 3634
Email: info@lon.fasken.com

USA
Seagram Building, 375 Park Avenue, Suite 2608, **New York** NY 10152
Tel: +1 212 935 3203 **Fax:** +1 212 935 4822
Email: info@nyc.fasken.com

F

INTERNATIONAL EXPERIENCE: The firm has acted for private and public parties (including the EBRD and the World Bank) on M&A, privatisations, reorganisations and financings involving businesses located in North, Central and South America, Europe and Eastern Europe, Africa and Asia.

INTERNATIONAL CLIENTS: The firm's clients include AT&T Canada (telecommunications), Allied Domecq (spirits and wine), AXA (insurance), Caisse de dépôts et placement du Québec (financial services), Daimler Chrysler Canada (automotive), PricewaterhouseCoopers (professional services), DuPont Canada (biotechnology), CP Rail (transportation), Quebecor Printing Inc (commercial printing), Teleglobe Inc (telecommunications) and Rio Algom (mining).

MAIN INTERNATIONAL AREAS OF PRACTICE:

M&A: Transactions involve both private and listed corporations and include take-over bids (friendly and hostile), asset and share acquisitions and divestitures, privatisations, public/private partnerships, and other joint venture transactions.
Banking and corporate finance: The firm handles a range of capital markets transactions including the raising of both debt and equity capital, project finance, syndicated loans, initial public offerings including cross-border IPOs, structured finance, securitisations and investment funds regulation.
IT and telecommunications: The firm advises on both transactional and strategic issues involving the computer and information technology sector, including the impact of the Internet and e-commerce.
Financial institutions: The firm handles the establishment of financial institutions in Canada via both branches and subsidiaries including all regulatory compliance and demutualisation of insurance companies.
Intellectual property: The firm advises on the prosecution of all intellectual property rights (patents, trade marks, copyright and design), licensing, and related litigation and dispute settlement.
Employment and pensions: Fasken Martineau DuMoulin LLP advises management on all aspects of the employment relationship, both within and outside a collective bargaining relationship, and the administration of employee pension plans.
Litigation/ADR (including arbitration) and insolvency: The firm handles dispute settlement, including mediation and arbitration, before all manner of domestic and international tribunals. Core insolvency work includes multi-jurisdictional bankruptcies, insolvencies and restructurings, acting for all parties (trustees, receivers, debtors and creditor groups).

LANGUAGES: Cantonese, English, French, German, Japanese, Mandarin, Spanish

For other recommended firms see pages 1485-1520

FENECH & FENECH ADVOCATES

HEAD OFFICE

198 Old Bakery Street,
Valletta VLT 09, Malta
Tel: +356 241232 **Fax:** +356 221893

Email: f.f@fenlex.com
Website: www.fenechlaw.com

WORLDWIDE OFFICE CONTACTS

MALTA
198 Old Bakery Street, **Valletta** VLT 09
Tel: +356 241232 **Fax:** +356 221893
Email: f.f@fenlex.com

FIRM OVERVIEW

Managing partner: Tonio Fenech
Senior partner: Joseph M. Fenech

Number of partners worldwide: 7
Number of other lawyers worldwide: 9

AREAS OF PRACTICE:

Company	15%
Litigation, arbitration and ADR	15%
Maritime	15%
Aviation	10%
Banking and finance	10%
International tax planning	10%
M&A	10%
Trusts and estate planning	10%
Insurance	5%

F

FIRM OVERVIEW: The firm was established in 1897. It has grown to become one of the largest firms in Malta and is established as a general legal practice with a particular focus on the commercial, corporate, transportation, mergers and acquisitions and finance, and financial services. The largely international client base is served by 12 advocates and 4 legal procurators. The firm is supported by 25 paralegal and administrative staff. A corporate services company, a licensed nominee service and a trust company, are among the firm's subsidiaries, as well as a company specialising in the provision of alternative dispute resolution with a special emphasis on mediation.

INTERNATIONAL EXPERIENCE: Fenech & Fenech has advised on various M&A transactions both locally and on a cross-border basis. The firm has acted for a number of banks, particularly in the asset finance area, and has assisted in tax-driven structuring of corporations and other vehicles in Malta and abroad. The firm's varied maritime and aviation practice also remains a mainstay of the firm's international work.

INTERNATIONAL CLIENTS: The firm's client base includes large companies, banks, insurance companies and public or supranational institutions conducting cross-border business.

MAIN INTERNATIONAL AREAS OF PRACTICE:
Maritime: The firm's involvement in this area ranges from ship registration and finance, related assistance to full blown marine litigation.
Banking and finance: The firm advises various banks on a range of issues including the setting up of branches on the island.
International tax planning: The firm advises on the Maltese tax system and its impact on international business operations. The firm also handles an increasing amount of investment related work.
Trusts and estate planning: The firm advises on various aspects of trusts and estate planning ranging from family wealth management planning to the more commercial field of trading trusts.
M&A: The firm has advised on the acquisition of a US company by European interests, the acquisition of various Maltese companies, as well as the handling of three Italian company acquisitions.

LANGUAGES: English, French, Italian

For other recommended firms see pages 1485-1520

FENNICA ATTORNEYS AT LAW LTD

HEAD OFFICE

Erottajankatu 15-17 A,
00130 Helsinki, Finland
Tel: +358 9 622 6670 **Fax:** +358 9 622 6677

Email: contact@fennicalaw.fi
Website: www.fennicalaw.fi

WORLDWIDE OFFICE CONTACTS

FINLAND
Erottajankatu 15-17 A, 00130 **Helsinki**
Tel: +358 9 622 6670 **Fax:** +358 9 622 6677
Email: contact@fennicalaw.fi

FIRM OVERVIEW

Managing partner: Pekka Takki

Number of partners worldwide: 6
Number of other lawyers worldwide: 6

AREAS OF PRACTICE:

Area	%
IT & Telecommunications	25%
General corporate and commercial	20%
Litigation and arbitration	10%
M&A	10%
Banking and finance	5%
Capital markets	5%
Competition	5%
Intellectual property	5%
Real estate and construction	5%

FIRM OVERVIEW: Founded in 1999, Fennica Attorneys-at-law Ltd has a reputation as one of Finland's leading law firms. Specialising in IT, telecommunications and new media, the firm's objective is to offer efficient legal support based on a solid understanding of the respective areas of business. The firm offers a comprehensive legal service to a range of selected clients. The partners have between five and ten years experience in the legal profession and many have been partners or junior partners in leading Finnish law firms prior to joining Fennica.

INTERNATIONAL EXPERIENCE: The firm has experience in international M&A and other transactions. The firm's lawyers have also gained experience in similar transactions with various Finnish law firms. Fennica Attorneys-at-law Ltd handles international IT and telecommunications transactions on a daily basis.

INTERNATIONAL CLIENTS: The firm's client base includes major US and European multinational companies operating in Finland. It also advises several Finnish companies with operations worldwide.

MAIN INTERNATIONAL AREAS OF PRACTICE:

IT and telecommunications: The firm specialises in IT and telecommunications. It advises on licensing, distribution and product development arrangements, content provision, and mobile value added services. Clients include major Finnish, European and US companies. Recently the practice has expanded to include ASP agreements and consultation on locationing based services. The firm also handles aspects of intellectual property, contracts and competition law in relation to IT and telecommunications.

Competition: The firm regularly advises on all aspects of competition law including anti-trust and marketing issues. Experience includes representation before the EU Commission.
Intellectual property: The firm advises on traditional areas of intellectual property such as copyright and trademarks. These areas form an integral part of the firm's services in the IT sector. Fennica Attorneys-at-law Ltd also specialises in franchising.
M&A: The firm advises on all aspects of mergers and acquisitions.
Litigation and arbitration: The firm deals with commercial litigation, arbitration, and ADR. Two of the firm's partners are accredited mediators and most partners are qualified for the bench and have acted in a broad range of dispute resolution matters.

LANGUAGES: English, Finnish, Swedish

F

For other recommended firms see pages 1485-1520

FERCHIOU & ASSOCIÉS

HEAD OFFICE

34 Place du 7 Novembre 1987,
Tunis 1001, Tunisia
Tel: +216 1 345 373
Fax: +216 1 350 028

Email: noureddine.ferchiou@planet.tn

WORLDWIDE OFFICE CONTACTS

TUNISIA
34 Place du 7 Novembre 1987, **Tunis** 1001
Tel: +216 1 345 373 **Fax:** +216 1 350 028
Email: noureddine.ferchiou@planet.tn

FIRM OVERVIEW

Managing and senior partner: Noureddine Ferchiou

Number of partners worldwide: 9

AREAS OF PRACTICE:

Banking and finance	20%
Corporate	15%
Energy	15%
Investment	15%
M&A	15%
Privatisation	15%
Litigation and arbitration	5%

F

FIRM OVERVIEW: Founded in 1984, Ferchiou & Associés specialises in all aspects of business, commercial and corporate law, international trade and joint ventures involving both Tunisian and foreign investors. The firm advises on financial schemes, investments, and new financial products on the Tunisian market. It also handles subsidiary and branch office structuring and organisation. The firm achieved ISO accreditation in July 2000.

INTERNATIONAL EXPERIENCE: The firm has advised foreign clients (including domestic entities) and foreign investors in joint ventures with local partners. In recent years, the firm has advised on several major privatisations and projects in the energy sector.

INTERNATIONAL CLIENTS: Ferchiou & Associés' client base is predominantly international, consisting of foreign companies seeking to do business in Tunisia. Many of the firm's clients are foreign multinationals, industrials, manufacturers, retailers, financial institutions, and service suppliers.

MAIN INTERNATIONAL AREAS OF PRACTICE:
Banking and finance: The firm advises international financial institutions on the feasibility of transactions under Tunisian legislation. In recent years it has drafted prospectus's on bond loans totalling ¥10 billion and €1 billion. Other work includes financial leasing, securities, secured and unsecured lending and project finance.
Energy: The firm advises on all aspects of oil, prospecting and environment related legislation. Ferchiou & Associés have an expanding energy practice. They recently advised the foreign consortium working on the construction project of the first Tunisian power plant to be privatised, and are currently involved in other important power plant (windmill and gas) projects.
Privatisation: Ferchiou & Associates advises the Tunisian government and foreign investors on privatisation matters in the energy, textile, cement plants and tourism industries. The firm's experience includes review of tenders, due diligence reviews, legal audits, and negotiation of deals.
Investments: The firm advises on financial schemes relating to Tunisian investment incentives, tax breaks and state guarantees for the repatriation of capital and profits.
M&A: The firm advises on small private acquisitions, take-overs of listed companies, share acquisition and sale, employment issues resulting from business transactions, and corporate transition strategies. Work recently handled includes the merger of Tunisia's three most important banks (STB, BDET and BNDT), and the merger of two international shoe companies.
Corporate: The firm advises on the establishment, conduct, restructuring and liquidation of companies. It also represents foreign owned entities operating in Tunisia and advises on commercial undertakings, fiscal and labour matters, project finance, company restructuring, corporate transactions, distributorships and franchises, and various commercial agreements.
Litigation and arbitration: The firm handles commercial disputes.

LANGUAGES: Arabic, English, French, Italian

For other recommended firms see pages 1485-1520

ESTUDIO FERRERE-LAMAISON

HEAD OFFICE

Acevedo Díaz 996,
Montevideo 11200, Uruguay
Tel: +5982 402 4243 **Fax:** +598 2402 4241

Email: efl@ferrere.com.uy
Website: www.ferrere.com.uy

FIRM OVERVIEW

Managing partner: Daniel Ferrere

Number of partners worldwide: 5
Number of other lawyers worldwide: 32

AREAS OF PRACTICE:

Banking and finance	20%
Corporate	15%
Intellectual property	10%
M&A	10%
Tax	10%
Telecommunications	10%
Employment	5%
Energy	5%
Insurance	5%
IT	5%
Pharmaceutical and chemical	5%

FIRM OVERVIEW: Ferrere Lamaison was formed in 1957, but adopted its present structure and policies in the early eighties. Since then, it has become one of Uruguay's largest law firm's. The firms in-house resources (140 overall, including 37 lawyers and approximately 80 fee earners) enable it to handle large-scale transactions, notably privatisations and public bids. Most of its lawyers have studied abroad.

INTERNATIONAL CLIENTS: The services of Ferrere Lamaison are adapted to the policies and needs of its international clients. The firm's client base mainly comprises multinationals, including five of the 25 top Fortune 500 companies.

MAIN INTERNATIONAL AREAS OF PRACTICE:

Telecommunications: The firm has been involved in all aspects of the deregulation of the telecommunications sector in Uruguay. It regularly represents clients involved in cellular telephones, long distance, PCS and LMDS. It also negotiates with the government on the opening of new areas to private competition.
Computers, software and IT: Computer and software law was one of the first areas in which Ferrere Lamaison acquired local recognition. It currently represents a number of leading international companies.
Energy: The firm advised the government of Uruguay at the beginning of the deregulation of the energy market. It currently represents clients in gas transportation, gas distribution and fuel distribution.
Corporate: Corporate work comprises a significant part of the firm's practice. It advises on all relevant areas of business.
M&A: Ferrere Lamaison has been involved in a significant number of Uruguayan M&A transactions. The firm handles all transactions in-house.
Banking and finance: The firm represents several banks and has acted in a range of banking, investment and open-market operations. On behalf of large multinational lending organisations, Ferrere Lamaison has advised on a number of the largest long term financing transactions that have taken place in Uruguay.
Insurance: Since the opening of the insurance market in 1995, the firm has been heavily involved in its development. Ferrere Lamaison has worked for more than half of all the private insurance companies operating in Uruguay.
Intellectual property: Due to the firm's involvement with high tech business, intellectual property has always been a significant part of its practice. Ferrere Lamaison has been a registered Industrial Property Agent for almost 20 years.
Tax: Ferrere Lamaison's large tax practice advises clients on their day-to-day operations and on acquisition deals. The firm runs its tax practice as a multi-disciplinary unit, combining the skills of its lawyers with those of certified accountants in order to take care of clients needs.
Employment: The firm advises on collective bargaining, and has been responsible for a number of complex reorganisations.

LANGUAGES: English, French, Hebrew, Italian, Portuguese, Spanish

WORLDWIDE OFFICE CONTACTS

URUGUAY
Acevedo Díaz 996, **Montevideo** 11200
Tel: +5982 402 4243 **Fax:** +598 2402 4241
Email: efl@ferrere.com.uy

F

FIELD FISHER WATERHOUSE

HEAD OFFICE

35 Vine Street,
London EC3N 2AA, United Kingdom
Tel: +44 20 7861 4000 **Fax:** +44 20 7488 0084

Email: info@ffwlaw.com
Website: www.ffwlaw.com

FIRM OVERVIEW

Managing partner: John Price
Senior partner: John Wilson

Number of partners worldwide: 64
Number of other lawyers worldwide: 151

AREAS OF PRACTICE:

Company and commercial	25%
Commercial property	22%
Intellectual property and IT	15%
Litigation	13%
Banking and finance	11%
Professional regulation	9%
Employment	5%

WORLDWIDE OFFICE CONTACTS

BELGIUM
Avenue Louise No 65, Box 11, 1050 **Brussels**
Tel: +32 2 535 7846 **Fax:** +32 2 535 7700
Email: info@ffwlaw.com

UNITED KINGDOM
35 Vine Street, **London** EC3N 2AA
Tel: +44 20 7861 4000 **Fax:** +44 20 7488 0084
Email: info@ffwlaw.com

F

FIRM OVERVIEW: Established over 150 years ago, Field Fisher Waterhouse is based in the City of London and comprising 64 partners and 151 other lawyers. The firm has a substantial UK and international corporate and commercial practice.

INTERNATIONAL EXPERIENCE: The firm acts for numerous overseas clients and has particularly strong connections in China, France, Germany, Italy, Japan, Korea, Scandinavia and the US. It works closely with overseas firms in these and other countries, and also employs many lawyers qualified in other jurisdictions. The firm's finance practice has advised on international financings and projects of all types. The corporate finance practice includes advising on cross-border mergers, acquisitions and joint ventures. The information technology and e-commerce practice provides international solutions, often drafting English-language contracts for use in overseas jurisdictions. Its IP practice advises international brand names on worldwide portfolio management on roll-out programmes. The telecommunications practice has extensive experience of satellite operations and managing the international roll-out of clients' networks. In oil and gas, the firm advises the international consortium of energy companies operating the UK-Continent Gas Interconnector. The firm also undertakes a substantial amount of overseas franchising work for companies expanding into the EU, Eastern Europe, the CIS, the Middle East, Far East and Latin America.

INTERNATIONAL CLIENTS: Include Arab Bank Plc, Citibank, N.A., Compagnie Gervais Danone, Lehman Brothers, Merrill Lynch, Mitsubishi Corporation, Nichimen Europe plc, Orange, Robert Fleming, Salomon Brothers International, Société Générale and Thomas Cook Holdings Ltd. Other clients include Chinese banks and corporations, French and German companies and several national airlines.

MAIN INTERNATIONAL AREAS OF PRACTICE:
Banking and finance: The finance group regularly advises international banks and other providers and users of credit in all the main areas of financing and related activity. It advises on bilateral, syndicated, unsecured financing and financing secured loans on a wide range of assets including ships, aircraft, lease and other receivables. The group also advises on derivatives, international capital markets and investment funds and products.
Corporate finance: The lawyers in the corporate group have extensive experience of advising on all aspects of establishing, running, developing and funding cross-border corporate ventures.
Intellectual property: The intellectual property group has a broad range of legal, industry, scientific and engineering knowledge. It advises on brand protection, advertising and marketing strategies, the sponsorship of events, merchandising and brand extension, technology transfer and other forms of IP licensing. It includes one of Europe's largest in-house trade mark agencies.
Information technology and e-commerce: The firm advises major UK and international providers of IT and e-commerce services. Particular areas of expertise are outsourcing and procurement arrangements and advising on devising and implementing global e-commerce strategies. This group also operates anti-piracy programmes for software companies and handles internet-related proceedings.
Commercial property: The practice comprises five specialist groups: institutional and property finance, hotels and leisure, industrial property and infrastructure, retail and development.
Tax: The firm practice advises a number of international clients on tax related matters.

LANGUAGES: A wide range of European languages, Japanese, Korean, Mandarin.

For other recommended firms see pages 1485-1520

FLICK GOCKE SCHAUMBURG

HEAD OFFICE

Johanna-Kinkel-Strasse 2-4,
D-53175 Bonn, Germany
Tel: +49 228 95 94 0 **Fax:** +49 228 95 94 100

Email: bonn@fgs.de
Website: www.fgs.de

FIRM OVERVIEW

Senior partners: Hans Flick, Rudolf Gocke, Harald Schaumburg

Number of partners worldwide: 29
Number of other lawyers worldwide: 42

AREAS OF PRACTICE:

German and international tax law	50%
Corporate law	20%
M&A	20%
IPOs	10%

FIRM OVERVIEW: Set up as a specialist firm for international tax law in 1962 and formed as a partnership in 1971. The firm comprises 29 partners and 42 other lawyers in offices located in Bonn, Berlin and Frankfurt/Main. The firm has established itself as one of the leading tax law firms in Germany, combining the experience of lawyers and economists to develop tailor-made and tax efficient legal structures and solutions. In the last 10 years, the firm has extended its capacities in areas of practice closely connected to tax law, such as corporate law, M&A and capital markets law.

INTERNATIONAL EXPERIENCE: The firm's international work primarily involves international tax law, corporate law with M&A, cross-border conversions, international transfer pricing structures and implementing international holdings and joint ventures.

INTERNATIONAL CLIENTS: The firm's clients include multinational enterprises, affiliated corporations, family-owned businesses and high net worth individuals. The firm regularly acts, inter alia, for banks, investment funds and insurance companies, the telecommunications sector, chemicals companies, the energy industry, car manufacturers, mechanical engineering companies and airlines.

MAIN INTERNATIONAL AREAS OF PRACTICE:

International taxation: The firm's activities include international tax planning and application of double taxation treaties; negotiation of advance agreements with tax authorities; representation in tax audits and closing talks; tax, administrative and constitutional litigation; legal and financial analysis of investment funds; development and support of transfer pricing systems; legal representation before customs authorities and in foreign trade matters.

Corporate and business law: The firm deals with joint ventures and other forms of cooperation; drafting and amending of shareholders' agreements, articles of incorporation and partnership agreements; resolution of disputes among owners of a business enterprise; evaluation and negotiation of takeover bids and of compensation for dissenting shareholders.

WORLDWIDE OFFICE CONTACTS

GERMANY

Nürnberger Str. 67, D-10787 **Berlin**
Tel: +49 30 21 00 20 20 **Fax:** +49 30 218 46 86
Email: berlin@fgs.de

Bockenheimer Landstr. 23, D-60325 **Frankfurt**
Tel: +49 69 71 703 0 **Fax:** +49 69 71 703 100
Email: frankfurt@fgs.de

Inbound and outbound investment: The firm is active in tax efficient structuring of direct sales, permanent establishments and subsidiaries; establishing, maintaining and winding up operations in Germany and abroad; transfer of tangible and intangible property; cross-border M&A.

M&A: The firm handles tax efficient acquisitions or sales of companies and ownership interests, management buy-outs and leveraged buy-outs, the formation and reorganisation of corporations and partnerships; the incorporation and optimisation of business entities; the structuring of affiliated groups and intra-group transactions; tax efficient capital increases, contributions of property in exchange for ownership interests, divisions and other group reorganisations.

Estate planning: Advice is provided on the transfer of family-owned businesses, lifetime gratuitous transfers to prospective heirs, international estate planning, and the execution of wills.

Due diligence and special audits: The firm offers legal, tax and financial due diligence; statutory and voluntary audits; preparation of annual financial statements and balance sheets for specific events; national and international group financial statements; verification of transfer prices and other special examinations, appraisal of business enterprises and evaluation of controlling systems.

LANGUAGES: English, French, Italian

FLICK GOCKE SCHAUMBURG

F.O. AKINRELE & CO

HEAD OFFICE

188 Awolowo Road, S W Ikoyi,
Lagos Nigeria
Tel: +234 1 269 3998 9 **Fax:** +234 1 269 2889

Email: akinrele@infoweb.abs.net
Website: www.foakinrele.com

WORLDWIDE OFFICE CONTACTS

NIGERIA
188 Awolowo Road, S W Ikoyi, **Lagos**
Tel: +234 1 269 3998 9 **Fax:** +234 1 269 2889
Email: akinrele@infoweb.abs.net

Additional offices in Abuja and Port Harcourt

FIRM OVERVIEW

Managing partner: Adedolapo Akinrele

Number of partners worldwide: 4
Number of other lawyers worldwide: 14

AREAS OF PRACTICE:

Energy 38%
Corporate and project finance, M&A 25%
Marine and admiralty 20%
Commercial litigation and arbitration 15%
Intellectual property 2%

F

FIRM OVERVIEW: F.O. Akinrele & Co was founded in 1957. Since the 1960s the firm has expanded from a general law practice into the corporate sector and now specialises in handling maritime, oil and gas and corporate work. As a result of recent industry deregulations the firm handles a large amount of work in the telecommunication and downstream energy sectors. The firm currently manages a West African network of law firms encompassing 16 countries.

INTERNATIONAL EXPERIENCE:

Maritime: The firm has acted as legal advisors to the North of England P&I Club and the American Club.
Oil and gas: In recent years the firm has advised Exxon Exploration Inc, Conoco Inc, Canadian Occidental Petroleum and Amoco Corporation on exploration interests and the establishment of local subsidiaries.
Corporate: Work handled in recent years includes advising the Chiyoda Corporation on the corporate restructuring of its Nigerian subsidiaries (1998); advising Heidelberger Druckmaschinen AG on its acquisition of the graphics division of E.A.S LTD (1998); acting for Canadian Occidental Petroleum Limited on its acquisition of 40% equity interest in an oil prospecting license held by SOLGAS NIG LTD (1999); advising Engen S.A on its bid for the acquisition of 60% shares in National Oil & Chemical Marketing Plc (2000); advising Ocean & Oil Group Ltd.UK on its successful acquisition of 30% of Unipetrol shares (2000).

INTERNATIONAL CLIENTS: The firm's client base includes ship owners, protection and indemnity associations, underwriters, oil and gas exploration companies and multinationals with subsidiaries in Nigeria.

MAIN INTERNATIONAL AREAS OF PRACTICE:

Maritime and admiralty: Work undertaken ranges from representation of ship owners in the courts to advice on specialist marine issues including navigation, seamanship, classification chartering, ship registration and transfer.
Oil, gas and minerals: The firm advises on all aspects of acquisition management and disposal of oil and gas and mineral interests, including taxation.
Intellectual property: The firm advises on the negotiation, registration and defence of trademarks, patents and designs as well as the negotiation and drafting of licensing agreements.
Commercial litigation: The firm provides broad representation through arbitration and the courts in matters ranging from commercial disputes to banking and oil and gas disputes.
Corporate finance and M&A: The firm advises on the corporate investments of publicly quoted companies, share issues, corporate restructuring and mergers and acquisitions.
Project finance: The firm advises on the negotiation and drafting of agreements, syndicated loan transactions and guarantees and structured finance.

LANGUAGES: English, French

For other recommended firms see pages 1485-1520

FOURGOUX ET ASSOCIÉS

HEAD OFFICE

111, boulevard Péreire,
75017 Paris, France
Tel: +33 1 5565 1665 **Fax:** +33 1 4754 9190

Email: cabinet@avocats-fourgoux.com
Website: www.avocats-fourgoux.com

FIRM OVERVIEW

Managing partner: Jean Louis Fourgoux
Senior partners: Jean-Claude Fourgoux, Marie-Véronique Jeannin, Leyla Djavadi

Number of partners worldwide: 3
Number of other lawyers worldwide: 7

AREAS OF PRACTICE:

Area	%
Competition	30%
European union	30%
Franchising	10%
Intellectual property	10%
Litigation	10%
Corporate	5%
IT	5%

WORLDWIDE OFFICE CONTACTS

FRANCE
111, boulevard Péreire, 75017 **Paris**
Tel: +33 1 5565 1665 **Fax:** +33 1 4754 9190
Email: cabinet@avocats-fourgoux.com

ASSOCIATED OFFICES

BELGIUM
Square du Bastion 1,a, 1050 **Brussels**
Tel: +322 289 64 60 **Fax:** +322 503 48 58

FIRM OVERVIEW: Fourgoux et Associés was founded in 1947. As a middle-sized firm, it offers a full range of corporate advice. The firm specialises in the distribution and franchising aspects of competition law, and business and competition law in France and Europe. The firm acts for small to medium sized companies, multinationals and professional organisations, and is active in domestic competition litigation. The firm also acts at community level, regularly pleading before the Court of Justice. The firm has recently created a corporate and banking law department.

INTERNATIONAL EXPERIENCE: The firm has particular experience in European competition and business law. It has advised international groups established in France and in other countries including the Netherlands, Italy and the UK.

INTERNATIONAL CLIENTS: Clients include major international groups in the communications, distribution and oil industries.

MAIN INTERNATIONAL AREAS OF PRACTICE:
French and EU competition law: The firm advises on the impact of French and EU competition and anti-trust law (mergers) in relation to franchising, distribution contracts, general terms and conditions, selective distribution contracts, and parallel imports. The firm handles competition cases before the French Competition Council and the Competition Chamber of the Court of Appeal of Paris. At European level, it handles actions based on article 81 or 82 of the Treaty, competition cases before the Commission, the Court of First Instance and the Court of Justice of the European Communities.
Corporate and business: The firm acts for a wide range of clients, advising on general business law in a variety of areas including advertising, unfair competition law, general conditions of sale, and transactions. The firm also advises on all aspects of general corporate law, including the drafting of French and international contracts.
Intellectual property: The firm specialises in trademarks and copyrights. Its lawyers act in the negotiation of license agreements and advise on infringement disputes and other aspects of IP law.
Litigation and arbitration: Fourgoux et Associés handles all aspects of commercial litigation and arbitration. Its lawyers are frequently involved in cases before the French Courts, including the French Competition Council, and have participated in numerous arbitrations (sometimes acting as arbitrators).
IT: The firm specialises in IT issues in relation to commercial and distribution law.
Employment: One of the partners handles all matters relating to French employment law.

LANGUAGES: English, French, German

For other recommended firms see pages 1485-1520

FOX MANDAL & CO

HEAD OFFICE

Corporate Office, FM House, D-1109 New Friends Colony
New Delhi 110 065, India
Tel: +91 11693 4401 **Fax:** +91 11 693 4403

Email: newdelhi@foxmandal.com
Website: www.foxmandal.com

FIRM OVERVIEW

Contact partners: Som Mandal (New Delhi)
Pankaj Prakash (New Delhi)
Shourya Mandal (Calcutta)
Shuva Mandal (Bangalore)
Shreyas Patel (Mumbai)

Number of partners worldwide: 16
Number of other lawyers worldwide: 80

AREAS OF PRACTICE:

Arbitration	*%
Conveyancing and documentation	*%
Franchising	*%
Infrastructure and project finance	*%
Insurance and banking	*%
Intellectual property	*%
Joint venture and foreign collaborations	*%
M&A and take-overs	*%
Property	*%
Shipping and admiralty	*%
Tax	*%
Telecom, power	*%

* Workload % not disclosed

FIRM OVERVIEW: Established in 1896, the firm has offices in New Delhi, Bangalore, Chandigarh, Hyderabad, Mumbai, Chennai, Cochin, Bhubaneshwar and associated offices in Pune and Allahabad. Comprising approximately 90 lawyers, and a supporting staff of nearly 100, the firm is one of the largest in India. The New Delhi office is an Advocate on Record of Supreme Court of India. The firm aims to provide responsive and practical solutions to business problems, and ensure timely and cost sensitive representation.

INTERNATIONAL CLIENTS: The firm's clients include major private and public sector companies in India and a large number of major and medium sized US and international companies.

WORLDWIDE OFFICE CONTACTS

INDIA

FM House, 6/12, Primrose Road, Gurappa Avenue, **Bangalore** 560025
Tel: +91 80 559 5911 **Fax:** +91 80 559 5844
Email: bangalore@foxmandal.com

12, Old Post Office Street, **Calcutta** 700001
Tel: +91 33 248 4843 **Fax:** +91 33 248 0832
Email: calcutta@foxmandal.com

SCO, 415-416,, Sector 35C, 2nd Floor, **Chandigarh** 160022
Tel: +91 172 60 8899 **Fax:** +91 172 60 8899
Email: chandigarh@foxmandal.com

11- Gee Gee Apartments, 8 - Kasturi Estates, IIIrd Street,
Chennai 600 086
Tel: +91 44 498 6803 **Fax:** +91 44 498 6691
Email: chennai@foxmandal.com

FM House, 237, Banjara Hills, Road No. 2, **Hyderabad** 500 034
Tel: +91 40 354 0218 **Fax:** +91 40 354 0219
Email: hyderabad@foxmandal.com

Fox Mandal Eastley Lam, 301, Jahangir Building, 3rd Floor, 133 Mahatma Gandhi Road, Fort, **Mumbai** 400 023
Tel: +91 22 267 3988 **Fax:** +91 22 263 2674
Email: mumbai@foxmandal.com

1, Doctor's Lane, Gole Market, **New Delhi** 110 001
Tel: +91 11 334 6872 **Fax:** +91 11 373 2591
Email: fox_mandal@vsnl.com

Corporate Office, FM House, D-1109 New Friends Colony, **New Delhi** 110 065
Tel: +91 11693 4401, **Fax:** +91 11 693 4403
Email: newdelhi@foxmandal.com

The firm has representative offices in Cochin and Bhubaneshwar

MAIN INTERNATIONAL AREAS OF PRACTICE: The firm undertakes a wide range of work including joint venture and foreign collaborations; shipping and admiralty; mergers, acquisitions and take-overs; property; intellectual property; arbitration; infrastructure and project finance; telecommunications and power; franchising; conveyancing and documentation; insurance and banking; tax.

LANGUAGES: Bengali, English, French, Gujarati, Hindi, Kannada, Marathi, Oriya, Punjabi, Tamil, Telugu

F

For other recommended firms see pages 1485-1520

ADVOKATFIRMAET FØYEN & CO ANS

HEAD OFFICE

CJ Hambros Place 2C, PO Box 6641, St Olavs Place,
N-0129 Oslo, Norway
Tel: + 47 22 98 30 00 **Fax:** + 47 22 98 30 10

Email: law@foyen.no
Website: www.foyen.no

FIRM OVERVIEW

Chairman of the board/Managing partner: Jostein Ramse

Number of partners worldwide: 18
Number of other lawyers worldwide: 21

AREAS OF PRACTICE:

Commercial law, including M&A ....*%
European law, public sector ....*%
IT and telecom law ....*%
Real estate and construction law ....*%
* Workload % not disclosed

FIRM OVERVIEW: Established in 1969, Advokatfirmaet Føyen & Co Ans is a Norwegian-based law firm with offices in Oslo, London, New Jersey, Stockholm and Brussels. The firm's principal areas of practice are real estate and construction law, IT and telecommunications law and company and commercial law, including M&A. Much of the firm's work is international. Advokatfirmaet Føyen is part of an international group of lawyers that practises under the name Føyen, and the firm's cooperation with the international law firm Masons in London has given it a base in Brussels and strengthened its EEA and EU law practice. The firm also has an extensive international network of contacts that provide legal assistance in most areas of law.

INTERNATIONAL EXPERIENCE: Advokatfirmaet Føyen & Co has been involved in the Norwegian part of Nasdaq and LSE introduction of ECsoft Ltd, the merger of PC-Systemer Norge ASA of Norway and Scandinavian PC-Systems AB, the outsourcing of Saga Petroleum IT Services to Andersen Consulting and setting up TV-distribution agreements for Scandinavian DTH platform operators.

INTERNATIONAL CLIENTS: Include Canal Digital, Andersen Consulting ANS, Clifford Chance, Advanced Radio Telecommunications Inc, Braas Scandinavia, Bull, ICL Data, ECsoft Ltd, Schering Plough Inc, Logica plc, IMI Norgren, Leo Burnett and Crane Inc.

MAIN INTERNATIONAL AREAS OF PRACTICE:

IT, telecoms and broadcasting: The firm is active in both regulatory and transactional matters. Acting for new entrants in the liberalised market, it advises on licensing issues, international communications agreements and negotiations, as well as right of access issues. The firm negotiates outsourcing agreements, development agreements, major IT contracts of all kinds and software, data protection compliance and Y2K compliance programmes for multinational companies. It also handles satellite TV distribution agreements, and acts for satellite platform operators in the Nordic market.

WORLDWIDE OFFICE CONTACTS

NORWAY
CJ Hambros Place 2C, PO Box 6641, St Olavs Place, N-0129 **Oslo**
Tel: + 47 22 98 30 00 **Fax:** + 47 22 98 30 10
Email: law@foyen.no

BELGIUM
c/o Masons Solicitors, Avenue Louise 391, B-1050 **Brussels**
Tel: +32 2 646 0260 **Fax:** +32 2 646 7323
Email: info@masons.com

SWEDEN
Nybrogatan 15, Box 5294, S-10246 **Stockholm**
Tel: +46 8 663 0290 **Fax:** +46 8 662 1590
Email: mailbox@foyen.se

UNITED KINGDOM
30 Aylesbury Street, **London** EC1R OER
Tel: +44 20 7490 6336 **Fax:** +44 20 7490 6234
Email: info@masons.com

USA
108 Baker Street, Maplewood, **New Jersey** 07040
Tel: +1 201 762 5800 **Fax:** +1 201 762 5801
Email: 102447.150@compuserve.com

Real estate development and construction: The firm acts for some of the major players in the Nordic countries on construction contracts and real estate development. The firm acts both for developers and construction companies as well as for real estate companies. It has a significant litigation and arbitration portfolio for clients in this area.
M&A company commercial: The firm is increasing its base of M&A and company commercial work. Over the last few years, the firm has been involved in several flotations on the stock exchange. It acts for UK and US firms in due diligence work, acquisitions of Norwegian companies, negotiations of JV agreements and M&A deals.

LANGUAGES: Danish, English, German, Norwegian, Spanish, Swedish

F

For other recommended firms see pages 1485-1520

FRASER MILNER CASGRAIN

HEAD OFFICE

PO Box 100, 1 First Canadian Place, 100 King St West
Toronto ON M5X 1B2, Canada
Tel: +1 416 863 4511 **Fax:** +1 416 863 4592

Email: john.langs@fmc-law.com
Website: www.fmc-law.com

FIRM OVERVIEW

Chairman: David P. Smith PC QC
Chief executive officer: David Robottom

Number of partners worldwide: 269
Number of other lawyers worldwide: 235

AREAS OF PRACTICE:

Banking and financial services	*%
Corporate	*%
Energy and natural resources	*%
M&A	*%
Real estate	*%
Tax	*%

* Workload % not disclosed

FIRM OVERVIEW: Fraser Milner Casgrain was established in 1839 and is now one of Canada's leading business law firms, providing a comprehensive range of legal services to both Canadian and international clients. With more than 500 lawyers in six offices in Canada's major business centres, the firm offers a range of diverse legal skills, experience and resources. Fraser Milner Casgrain offers experienced counsel in all major areas of practice, including corporate and commercial law, financial services, taxation, securities, insurance, competition and anti-trust, international trade, real estate, resources (energy, forest products, mining, oil and natural gas), banking, employment and labour, construction, project financing, information technology, property trusts and estates, ADR and litigation.

INTERNATIONAL EXPERIENCE: The firm advises corporations, lenders, investors and governments on the assessment and execution of international initiatives in Canada and internationally. As one of Canada's largest full service business law firms, Fraser Milner Casgrain has the resources and experience to provide timely, strategic and comprehensive advice on national and international matters.

MAIN INTERNATIONAL AREAS OF PRACTICE:
Corporate: Work handled includes organisation and governance, incorporations, joint ventures, reorganisations, purchase and sale of businesses, management and leveraged buyouts, contracts, financing, capital market transactions and mergers and acquisitions.
M&A: M&A activity (both public and private) is a substantial part of the firm's practice. The firm acts on take over bids (hostile and friendly), amalgamations, capital and asset restructuring, spin-offs and arrangements advising bidders, targets or independent committees of boards of directors regarding all aspects of a transaction including tax, environmental, competition, employment, pension, Investment Canada requirements and intellectual property matters.
Banking and financial services: Fraser Milner Casgrain advises on banking, financing, credit transactions, restructuring, insolvency and realisations, equipment leasing, synthetic leases, asset-backed securitisations, financial instruments transactions, project financing and structured finance.

WORLDWIDE OFFICE CONTACTS

CANADA
30th Floor, Fifth Avenue Place, 237-4th Avenue S.W., **Calgary** AB 2TP 4X7
Tel: +1 403 268 7000 **Fax:** +1 403 268 3100
Email: gerry.scott@fmc-law.com

2900 ManuLife Place, 10180-101 Street, **Edmonton** AB T5J 3V5
Tel: +1 780 423 7100 **Fax:** +1 780 423 7276
Email: robert.roth@fmc-law.com

1 Place Ville-Marie, Suite 3900, **Montreal** QC H3B 4M7
Tel: +1 514 878 8800 **Fax:** +1 514 866 2241
Email: michel.brunet@fmc-law.com

Suite 1420, 99 Bank Street, **Ottawa** ON K1P 5A3
Tel: +1 613 783 9600 **Fax:** +1 613 783 9690
Email: tom.houston@fmc-law.com

PO Box 100, 1 First Canadian Place, 100 King St West, **Toronto** ON M5X 1B2
Tel: +1 416 863 4511 **Fax:** +1 416 863 4592
Email: john.langs@fmc-law.com

15th Floor Grosvenor Building, 1040 West Georgia Street, **Vancouver** BC V6E 4H8
Tel: +1 604 687 4460 **Fax:** +1 604 683 5214
Email: howard.kellough@fmc-law.com

Taxation: Work undertaken comprises tax planning (national and international) for corporations and individuals, tax-effective structuring of cross-border and domestic transactions, tax representation and advocacy.
Real estate: Advice and assistance on all types of real estate matters including acquisitions, dispositions, financing, leasing and development in all major markets across Canada.
Energy and natural resources: The firm advises petroleum, natural gas, electricity, mining, forestry and other resource-based industries on matters such as acquisitions, dispositions, reorganisations, development and regulatory approvals, royalty trusts, marketing, cross-border issues, land/facilities/operating agreements, distribution and transportation.
Securities: The firm handles mergers, acquisitions and corporate finance transactions for all types of issuers and securities offerings in both public and private markets (including initial public offerings, bought deals NIDs, special warrants, private placements, government privatisations, hybrid, derivative, asset-backed and tax related securities), reporting and disclosure requirements, and regulatory compliance.

LANGUAGES: Cantonese, Dutch, English, Finnish, French, German, Guyarati, Ukranian

FRASER MILNER CASGRAIN
Business. Advice. Success.

For other recommended firms see pages 1485-1520

FREEHILLS

HEAD OFFICE

MLC Centre, 19-29 Martin Place,
Sydney NSW 2000, Australia
Tel: +61 2 9225 5000 **Fax:** +61 2 9322 4000

Email: info@freehills.com.au
Website: www.freehills.com.au

FIRM OVERVIEW

Number of partners worldwide: 240
Number of Other lawyers worldwide: 654

AREAS OF PRACTICE:

Banking and finance ....*%
Corporate and commercial ....*%
Energy and resources ....*%
Funds management ....*%
Intellectual property ....*%
Litigation ....*%
Major projects ....*%
Property and environment ....*%
Revenue law ....*%
* Workload % not disclosed

FIRM OVERVIEW: Freehills is an Australian-based international law firm which has grown to be one of the largest commercial legal practices in Australia and South-East Asia. With 240 partners and more than 650 other legal practitioners across Australia and the Asia Pacific region, Freehills' reputation for providing excellent and innovative commercial legal advice has been built over more than 140 years.

INTERNATIONAL EXPERIENCE: Freehills has pursued a strategy of business expansion into Asia since the early 1980s when it began developing an Indonesian practice. The firm currently has two offices in Vietnam (Hanoi and Ho Chi Minh City), a formal law alliance in Singapore (with Alban Tay Mahtani & de Silva) and correspondent firms in Jakarta (Soemadipradja & Taher) and Kuala Lumpur (Lee Hishammuddin). Freehills acts as a source of business and transaction advice for international and Australian corporations investing and operating in Malaysia, Vietnam, Indonesia, Thailand, the Philippines, and other countries in the region. The firm also has close relationships in Vietiane, Seoul, Bangkok and other key Asian commercial centres.
Highlight deals: Advising Commonwealth Bank on its $10.1bn. acquisition of Colonial Limited; acting for the banks in the Bell litigation; acting for Lend Lease on the sale of MLC to the National Australia Bank; acting for Victorian Government on Longford Gas Explosion litigation; representing National Australia Bank in AUSMAQ litigation; advising the Korean, Malaysian and Philippines Governments on electricity market reform and restructure.

INTERNATIONAL CLIENTS: Phillips Oil Company, Anglo American, SmithKline Beecham, Visa, Lend Lease, Mayne Nickless, InterGen, 3M, AXA, Toyota, Deutsche Bank, Salomon Smith Barney, Granada Media, Pfizer, Shell, Microsoft, Reebok.

WORLDWIDE OFFICE CONTACTS

AUSTRALIA

Level 38, Central Plaza I, 345 Queen Street, **Brisbane** QLD 4001
Tel: +61 7 3258 6666 **Fax:** +61 7 3258 6444
Email: michael_back@freehills.com.au

London Court, 13 London Circuit, **Canberra** ACT 2601
Tel: +61 2 6240 6100 **Fax:** +61 2 6240 6222
Email: daniel_moulis@freehills.com.au

101 Collins Street, **Melbourne** VIC 3000
Tel: + 61 3 9288 1234 **Fax:** + 61 3 9288 1567
Email: paul_montgomery@freehills.com.au

AMP Building, 140 St Georges Terrace, **Perth** WA 6000
Tel: +61 8 9211 7777 **Fax:** +61 8 9211 7878
Email: peter_mansell@freehills.com.au

MLC Centre, 19-29 Martin Place, **Sydney** NSW 2000
Tel: +61 2 9225 5000 **Fax:** +61 2 9322 4000
Email: bruce_cutler@freehills.com.au

SINGAPORE

39 Robinson Road, #07-01 Robinson Point, **Singapore** 068911
Tel: +65 534 5266 **Fax:** +65 223 8762
Email: john_dick@freehills.com.au

VIETNAM

Unit 2, 2nd Floor, International Centre, 17 Ngo Quyen Street, Hoan Kiem District, **Hanoi**
Tel: +844 934 6239 **Fax:** +844 934 6238
Email: timothy_reinold@freehills.com.au

Unit 2, 10th Floor, Saigon Centre, 65 Le Loi Boulevard, District 1, **Ho Chi Minh City**
Tel: +848 824 2733 **Fax:** +848 824 2736
Email: stephen_skinner@freehills.com.au

MAIN INTERNATIONAL AREAS OF PRACTICE: Corporate and commercial; banking and finance; securities and capital markets; project finance; telecommunications; intellectual property; property; major projects/infrastructure development; energy and resources; competition law; privatisation; revenue law; funds management; litigation and dispute resolution.

LANGUAGES: Afrikaans, Arabic, Bahasa Indonesian, Cantonese, Croatian, Danish, Dutch, French, German, Greek, Hebrew, Hindi, Italian, Japanese, Korean, Macedonian, Malay, Maltese, Mandarin, Polish, Portuguese, Russian, Spanish, Vietnamese

Freehills

F

For other recommended firms see pages 1485-1520

FRESHFIELDS BRUCKHAUS DERINGER

CONTACT OFFICE

65 Fleet Street,
London EC4Y 1HS, United Kingdom
Tel: +44 20 7936 4000 **Fax:** +44 20 7832 7001

Email: email@freshfields.com
Website: www.freshfields.com

FIRM OVERVIEW

Senior partners: Anthony Salz and Christian Wilde
Chief executive: Alan Peck
Managing partner: Ian Terry

Number of partners worldwide: 436
Number of other lawyers worldwide: 1,469

AREAS OF PRACTICE:

Competition and trade	*%
Corporate	*%
Dispute resolution	*%
Employment, pensions and benefits	*%
Finance	*%
Intellectual property and IT	*%
Real estate	*%
Tax	*%

* Workload % not disclosed

WORLDWIDE OFFICE CONTACTS

UNITED KINGDOM
65 Fleet Street, **London** EC4Y 1HS
Tel: +44 20 7936 4000 **Fax:** +44 20 7832 7001
Email: email@freshfields.com

Freshfields Bruckhaus Deringer has additional offices in; Amsterdam, Bangkok, Barcelona, Beijing, Berlin, Bratislava, Brussels, Budapest, Cologne, Dusseldorf, Frankfurt, Hamburg, Hanoi, Ho Chi Minh City, Hong Kong, Leipzig, London, Madrid, Milan, Moscow, Munich, New York, Paris, Prague, Rome, Singapore, Tokyo, Vienna and Washington, DC.

ASSOCIATED OFFICES

Freshfields Bruckhaus Deringer has an associated office in Shanghai.

F

FIRM OVERVIEW: Freshfields Bruckhaus Deringer was created through the merger of Freshfields and Bruckhaus Westrick Heller Löber on 1st August 2000. The merger has formed a new leader among international law firms capable of offering leading business law advice throughout Europe, Asia and the US. With over 1,900 lawyers and a total of 30 offices in 19 countries, the firm provides its clients with a full range of business legal services and a wealth of experience in the world's major economies. The firm's international approach is founded on strong local capabilities and experience, offering clients multi-disciplinary teams from a number of jurisdictions. It now has a powerful platform for delivering the highest standards of service and achieving strength in depth across all areas.
Europe: The firm has combined international experience with in-depth local knowledge of all the major EU member states, central and eastern Europe, and assists clients with their cross-border and domestic transactions across Europe.
Asia: Freshfields Bruckhaus Deringer is a leading international law firm in Asia, practising international law and, where possible, local law through its eight Asian offices. A joint law venture has been entered into in Singapore with Drew & Napier, which will enable the firm to offer clients local legal advice. A considerable amount of work is also undertaken in those countries in which the firm does not have offices, such as India, Korea, Malaysia and the Philippines.
US: US law is another key part of the service provided to clients around the world, particularly in areas such as securities and finance. The firm now has over 125 US-qualified lawyers throughout its network. The US-based lawyers are particularly active on projects in Latin America, where they are able to offer advice across a broad range of areas.

INTERNATIONAL EXPERIENCE: Freshfields Bruckhaus Deringer has advised on many of the world's largest recent deals, including acting for Mannesmann on the £80 billion hostile take-over bid by Vodafone Airtouch, Telewest on its £10.5 billion merger with Flextech, DaimlerChrysler on the £10.3 billion merger between DASA and Aérospatiale Matra, Prada on the acquisition of Jill Sander and Tyco International on the acquisition of the electronics division of Siemens. The year has seen teams from Freshfields Bruckhaus Deringer active in places as far apart as Ireland, Israel, India and Indonesia. As well as working on complex cross-border transactions, the firm is also widely recognised as a world leader in fields ranging from international arbitration and environmental law to privatisations and aircraft finance.

INTERNATIONAL CLIENTS: The firm has advised on many complex transactions and cases around the world, working with a wide range of corporate, financial, and governmental clients. The firm is committed to maintaining and developing strong relationships with its clients, based on consistent quality of service around the world, alongside strong local knowledge and expertise. The firm's lawyers are organised into global practice and specialist industry groups to provide clients with the technical legal expertise and industry knowledge required for each transaction or case.

MAIN INTERNATIONAL AREAS OF PRACTICE: Practice groups include corporate, finance, dispute resolution, tax, competition and trade, IP/IT, real estate and employment, pensions and benefits. Specialist sector groups include telecoms, media and technology (TMT), energy and natural resources, private equity, financial institutions and insurance, pharmaceuticals and life sciences, automotive, transport and logistics, construction and public procurement. The firm has three geographical specialist groups, which are China, India, and Latin America.

LANGUAGES: Freshfields Bruckhaus Deringer offers its clients extensive language capabilities.

FRESHFIELDS BRUCKHAUS DERINGER

For other recommended firms see pages 1485-1520

FRIED, FRANK, HARRIS, SHRIVER & JACOBSON

HEAD OFFICE

One New York Plaza,
New York NY 10004, USA
Tel: +1 212 859 8000 **Fax:** +1 212 859 4000

Email: info@ffhsj.com
Website: www.ffhsj.com

FIRM OVERVIEW

Co-managing partners: Peter v.Z . Cobb, Michael H. Rauch

Number of partners worldwide: 137
Number of other lawyers worldwide: 391

AREAS OF PRACTICE:

Corporate 49%
Litigation 32%
Real estate 6%
Tax 5%
Bankruptcy 4%
Benefits/employment 3%
Trust and estate 1%

WORLDWIDE OFFICE CONTACTS

FRANCE
7 rue Royale, 75008 **Paris**
Tel: +33 140 17 04 04 **Fax:** +33 140 17 08 30

UNITED KINGDOM
99 City Road, **London** EC1Y AX
Tel: +44 20 7972 9600 **Fax:** +44 20 7972 9602

USA
350 South Grand Avenue, 32nd Floor, **Los Angeles** CA 90071
Tel: +1 213 473 2000 **Fax:** +1 213 473 2222

One New York Plaza, **New York** NY 10004
Tel: +1 212 859 8000 **Fax:** +1 212 859 4000
Email: info@ffhsj.com

1001 Pennsylvania Avenue, NW, **Washington, DC** 20004
Tel: +1 202 639 7000 **Fax:** +1 202 639 7003

FIRM OVERVIEW: Fried Frank is an international law firm with approximately 524 attorneys, located in New York, Washington, DC, Los Angeles, London and Paris. The US offices' general corporate practice is concentrated on mergers and acquisitions, capital markets transactions, complex financings and securitisations, securities regulation, compliance and enforcement, corporate governance, asset management, private investment funds and electronic commerce. The US offices' litigation practice includes securities, anti-trust, environmental, intellectual property, proxy contests, white-collar crime, government contracts, general commercial litigation and class actions and other shareholder lawsuits. The firm also handles major matters involving bankruptcy and restructuring, benefits and compensation, real estate, tax and trusts and estates.

INTERNATIONAL EXPERIENCE: Fried Frank has an established international practice with a focus on cross-border mergers, acquisitions and joint ventures; U.S. registered and Rule 144A securities offerings; cross-border non-U.S. debt and equity offerings; representation of corporate and individual borrowers and banks and other financial institutions in commercial financing transactions; structured and securitized financings; establishment of LBO funds; international trade and investment; tax; and trust and estate planning. The practice is conducted from each of its US offices and its offices in London and Paris. Recent international representations include Pacific Century CyberWorks Limited in its acquisition of Cable & Wireless HKT Limited; Bestfoods in its merger with European giant Unilever; UK's WPP Group in its acquisition of Young & Rubicam; Invensys plc in its acquisition of Baan NV; Royal Philips Electronics NV's acquisition of MedQuist Inc.; Grupo Televisa SA and Grupo Televicentro in a global secondary equity offering; Merrill Lynch & Co., and Deutsche Bank AG as underwriters in connection with a Eurobond high yield offering for Ineos Acrylics; Merrill Lynch and Credit Suisse First Boston as underwriters in connection with a Eurobond high yield offering for Jazztel; and Goldman Sachs and Deutsche Bank as underwriters in connection with a Eurobond offering for The Procter & Gamble Company.

INTERNATIONAL CLIENTS: International clients include AEA Investors Inc., AT&T Corp., Chase Securities, City Reach International plc, FirstMark Communications, Credit Suisse First Boston, Gallagher Group plc, Grupo Televisa SA, Invensys plc, Lloyd's of London, Merrill Lynch, Mettler-Toledo International Inc., Pacific Century CyberWorks Limited, The Procter & Gamble Company, Rio Tinto plc, Sara Lee Corporation, and WPP Group.

MAIN AREAS OF PRACTICE:

Corporate: The corporate practice handles business transactions such as mergers, acquisitions and dispositions; leveraged buyouts; securities offerings and financings; asset management; structured finance and securitisation; securities regulation, compliance and enforcement; and electronic commerce.
Litigation: The litigation practice advises on environmental liability and enforcement, antitrust and franchise matters, intellectual property law, white-collar crime, securities and shareholder litigation and all forms of challenging financial and commercial contract litigation.
Tax: The tax practice offers advice in the area of tax law in principal forms of commercial transactions including M&A, financial transactions, real estate, bankruptcy and complex joint ventures.
Bankruptcy and restructuring: The bankruptcy and restructuring practice advises financially troubled companies on insolvency, creditors' rights and commercial law issues that arise in complex corporate and real estate acquisitions, divestitures and financings.
Real estate: The real estate practice advises clients in property acquisitions, commercial leasing, construction and development projects, portfolio transactions, financings, sales and exchanges and joint ventures.
Benefits and compensation: The benefits and compensation practice is conducted by two separate departments with somewhat different focuses: employee benefits and plans, executive compensation and exempt organisations; and executive compensation and employee benefits.
Trusts and estates: Trusts and estates is a tax-oriented practice, specialising in counseling of high-net-worth individuals and families in their estate, tax and business planning.

For other recommended firms see pages 1485-1520

FRORIEP RENGGLI

HEAD OFFICE

Bellerivestrasse 201, PO Box 385,
CH-8034 Zurich, Switzerland
Tel: +41 1 386 60 00 **Fax:** +41 1 383 60 50
Email: zurich@froriep.ch
Website: www.froriep.com

FIRM OVERVIEW

Managing Partner: Peter J. Merz

Number of partners worldwide: 13
Number of other lawyers worldwide: 30

AREAS OF PRACTICE:

Corporate/commercial	20%
M&A	20%
Arbitration and litigation	15%
Intellectual property and competition	15%
Finance, banking and securities	10%
Private capital	10%
Miscellaneous	10%

F

FIRM OVERVIEW: Founded in Zurich in 1966, Froriep Renggli is one of the largest law firms in Switzerland, with offices in Zurich, Geneva, Zug and London. The firm's activities reflect the international commercial vitality of Switzerland, focusing on the general commercial, corporate, M&A, IP/competition, financial, arbitration and litigation sectors. International estate planning and international judicial assistance are two other areas of specialisation.

INTERNATIONAL EXPERIENCE: The firm's international practice handles mergers and acquisitions, takeovers, corporate law, banking, financing and capital markets, intellectual property, licensing and distribution, competition, computer law, aviation, commercial litigation and arbitration, bankruptcy, insolvency, immigration and taxes. The firm acted in the first hostile takeover in Switzerland, the acquisition of Holvis by BBA Group.

INTERNATIONAL CLIENTS: The firm's clients include multinational corporations and individuals, especially those based in the UK, Scandinavia and the US.

MAIN INTERNATIONAL AREAS OF PRACTICE

Transactional work: The firm focuses on acquisitions and cross-border transactions.
General corporate: Includes corporate work and commercial contracts, joint ventures, international trade.
Intellectual property: Includes trade marks, patent licensing, and related strategic advice as well as competition issues.
Arbitration: The firm's activities in this area are mainly international.
Litigation: The focus is on commercial litigation and arbitration; includes enforcement of foreign judgements and mutual assistance.
Private Capital: The firm advises on estate planning and corporate structures.

LANGUAGES: Croatian, Czech, Dutch, English, Farsi (Persian), Galician, French, German, Hebrew, Italian, Portuguese, Serbian, Spanish, Turkish

WORLDWIDE OFFICE CONTACTS

SWITZERLAND

Bellerivestrasse 201, PO Box 385, CH-8034 **Zurich**
Tel: +41 1 386 60 00 **Fax:** +41 1 383 60 50
Email: zurich@froriep.ch

4 Rue Charles Bonnet, CH-1211 **Geneva** 12
Tel: +41 22 839 6300 **Fax:** +41 22 347 7159
Email: geneva@froriep.ch

Baarerstrasse 37, CH-6304 **Zug**
Tel: +41 41 710 6000 **Fax:** +41 41 710 6001
Email: zug@froriep.ch

UNITED KINGDOM

1 Knightrider Court, St Pauls, **London** EC4V 5JP
Tel: +44 20 7236 6000 **Fax:** +44 20 7248 0209
Email: london@froriep.ch

WORLDWIDE OFFICES

UNITED KINGDOM

1 Knightrider Court, St Pauls, London EC4V 5JP

Managing Partner: Bruno W Boesch
Number of lawyers: 3

Main areas of work: Mergers and acquisitions, corporate banking, arbitration/litigation, private capital.
Top clients: Includes multinational companies and individuals, in particular from the UK, Scandinavia and the US.
Highlight deals: Includes advising on the first hostile takeover in Switzerland, the acquisition of Holvis by BBA Group.
Languages: English, French, German, Italian, Swedish

Office Profile: Opened in 1984, Froriep Renggli's London office is the largest overseas office of any Swiss law firm. It works closely with several of the major City law firms and banks in London, its lawyers frequently acting as expert witnesses in litigation matters. The office's main areas of practice are general corporate/commercial, M&A, banking and finance with respect to Swiss issues, as well as private capital.

FRORIEP RENGGLI

For other recommended firms see pages 1485-1520

FUGAR & COMPANY

HEAD OFFICE

Wesley House, Liberia Road, P. O. Box ARN 6274
Accra-North Ghana
Tel: +233 21 228 988 **Fax:** +233 21 669 589

Email: fugar@ghana.com
Website: www.fugarandcompany.com.gh

WORLDWIDE OFFICE CONTACTS

GHANA
Wesley House, Liberia Road, P. O. Box ARN 6274, **Accra-North**
Tel: +233 21 228 988 **Fax:** +233 21 669 589
Email: fugar@ghana.com

FIRM OVERVIEW

Managing partner: William Edem Fugar
Senior partner: Lawrence N. Otoo

Number of partners worldwide: 2
Number of other lawyers worldwide: 12

AREAS OF PRACTICE:

Corporate	20%
Investment	20%
Banking and finance	10%
Insurance and reinsurance	10%
Intellectual property	10%
Litigation and arbitration	10%
M&A	10%
Telecommunication and IT	10%

F

FIRM OVERVIEW: Established in 1977, Fugar & Company is one of the leading law firms in Ghana. Comprising 14 lawyers, five paralegal staff and five secretaries, the firm has expanded both in size and practice areas to become one of the largest law firms in Ghana. Essentially an international commercial law practice, the firm has strong legal expertise in a range of practice areas.

INTERNATIONAL EXPERIENCE: Fugar & Company have advised several international firms and corporations on issues relating to mining, investment law, energy and natural resources law, telecommunications, environmental law, tax, and immigration. In recent years the firm have advised the Overseas Private Investment Corporation and the International Finance Corporation.

INTERNATIONAL CLIENTS: The firm's client base includes international and multinational companies, banks and other financial institutions, telecommunication companies, industries, and estates.

MAIN INTERNATIONAL AREAS OF PRACTICE

Corporate finance and securities: The firm prepares comprehensive legal and corporate due diligence reports for a range of prospective investors in collaboration with leading law firms in the UK and the US. It advises a reputable US investment bank on foreign ownership of securities and local market practice governing trade and settlement of securities in Ghana.

Investment: The firm advises investors on obtaining the appropriate licenses from the Ghana Investment Promotion Centre and other governmental agencies. Fugar & Company has been instrumental in the setting up of major investment companies in Ghana.

Immigration: The firm advises on immigration related matters, acquisition, extension or renewal of work and residence permits, obtaining immigrant quotas and legal representation at inquiries conducted by the Ghana Immigration Services.

Tax: The firm advises on various tax structures and the fiscal and tax incentives incorporated in the Minerals and Mining Law, Ghana Investment Promotion Centre Act and the Income Tax Decree.

Energy and natural resources: Fugar & Company continues to play an important role in the development of the mineral and mining sector in Ghana. The firm represents clients at the Minerals Commission, and advises on Ghana's mining laws and regulations, project planning and documentation. It also advises on the procurement of reconnaissance, prospecting/exploration licenses and mining leases from the Minerals Commission.

Environmental: The firm specialises on compliance, liability and control. They also handle the preparation of Environmental Impact Assessment Statements and processing of applications for authorisation, licenses and premiums.

Telecommunications: Fugar & Company advises potential operators and investors on the regulatory framework of the communications industry in Ghana. It has advised a local cellular phone company on the acquisition of a majority shareholding by a major international telecommunications company.

Intellectual property: The firm advises local and foreign clients on the enforcement and protection of intellectual property rights, registration of trademarks, patents and designs. It also handles litigation in respect of copyright infringements, representing clients at arbitrations conducted by the Copyright Office, and generally advising on Ghanaian intellectual property laws. The firm's client base includes firms from Asia, Europe and North America.

Banking and finance: The firm has expertise in the structuring and documentation of loan facilities of all kinds as well as related security packages. It has represented banks on a number of large and complex transactions and has been instrumental in the establishment of banking operations and non-banking financial institutions. Fugar & Company also handles diverse legal issues including dispute resolution pertaining to the banking and financial communities.

LANGUAGES: English, French

FULBRIGHT & JAWORSKI LLP

HEAD OFFICE

1301 McKinney, Suite 5100
Houston, TX 77010-3095, USA
Tel: + 1 713 651 5151 **Fax:** + 1 713 651 5246

Email: info@fulbright.com
Website: www.fulbright.com

FIRM OVERVIEW

Managing partner: AT Blackshear

Number of partners worldwide: 311
Number of other lawyers worldwide: 461

AREAS OF PRACTICE:

Corporate/M&A	*%
Energy (incl project finance)	*%
Health	*%
IP	*%
Litigation	*%

* Workload % not disclosed

F

FIRM OVERVIEW: Founded in 1919, Fulbright & Jaworski is one of the largest firms in the US, with more than 750 lawyers in offices in Houston, New York, Washington DC, Los Angeles, Austin, Dallas, San Antonio, Minneapolis, Hong Kong and London. The firm also has a long-standing relationship with Canadian law firm, Fraser Milner Casgrain. It has experience in a wide range of legal matters, from local, state and federal litigation to complex national and international corporate and commercial transactions. Clients are based in major business, financial and governmental centres around the world.

INTERNATIONAL EXPERIENCE: The firm's international department includes lawyers from its Hong Kong, London and US offices. Work includes mergers and acquisitions, oil and gas and other energy industry transactions of all types, project finance, international joint ventures, all forms of direct investment into the US, international arbitration and ADR, international tax planning, US export law, customs and immigration law. The firm's energy practice has become increasingly international as US-based energy companies have invested outside the US and European and other energy companies have increased their presence in the US.

INTERNATIONAL CLIENTS: The firm has represented private sector and sovereign clients in many different industries, including energy, infrastructure development, financial services, chemicals, health care, textiles, consumer products, manufacturing, publishing and software, among others.

HEAD OFFICE

Number of lawyers: 296
Main areas of work: Admiralty, banking, bankruptcy, corporate, employee benefits, energy, environmental, family, health, intellectual property & technology, international, labour & employment, litigation, oil & gas, public finance & administrative, real estate, tax, trusts & estates, venture capital.
Office profile: The Houston office is the firm's oldest and largest. Its corporate, energy, litigation, tax and intellectual property practices are large and with considerable experience. The shipping practice is one of the oldest in Houston, the largest US port in terms of foreign tonnage handled. Health law is also a growth area.

WORLDWIDE OFFICE CONTACTS

HONG KONG
19th Floor, 3A Chater Road, Central **Hong Kong**
Tel: + 852 2523 3200 **Fax:** + 852 2523 3255

UNITED KINGDOM
2 St James's Place, **London** SW1A 1NP
Tel: + 44 20 7629 1207 **Fax:** + 44 20 7493 8259

USA
600 Congress Avenue, Suite 2400, **Austin**, Texas 78701
Tel: + 1 512 474 5201 **Fax:** + 1 512 320 4598

2200 Ross Avenue, Suite 2800, **Dallas**, Texas 75201
Tel: + 1 214 855 8000 **Fax:** + 1 214 855 8200

865 South Figueroa, 29th floor, **Los Angeles**, California 90017-2571
Tel: + 1 213 892 9200 **Fax:** + 1 213 680 4518

4580 US Bank Place, **Minneapolis,** Minesota 78205
Tel: +1 612 321 2800 **Fax:** +1 612 321 9600

666 Fifth Avenue, **New York**, NY 10103
Tel: + 1 212 318 3000 **Fax:** + 1 212 752 5958

300 Convent Street, Suite 2200, **San Antonio**, Texas 78205
Tel: + 1 210 224 5575 **Fax:** + 1 210 270 7205

801 Pennsylvania Avenue, NW, **Washington, DC** 20004-2615
Tel: + 1 202 662 0200 **Fax:** + 1 202 662 4643

WORLDWIDE OFFICES

HONG KONG

19th Floor, 3A Chater Road, Central Hong Kong

Managing partner: Jeffrey A Blount
Number of lawyers: 6
Main areas of work: International transactional practice, investment, finance, tax and investment in and out of greater China and Southeast Asia.
Top clients: North American and European entities and individuals doing business and investing in Asia, as well as Asian-based entities and individuals in their international business activities and investments, both in the United States and in other locations throughout the world.
Office profile: The firm's representation of its Asian-based clients includes handling project finance and other commercial transactions, including tax, foreign exchange, investment incentive and commercial laws and regulations throughout Southeast Asia.

UNITED KINGDOM

2 St James's Place, London SW1A 1NP

Managing partner: Steven B Pfeiffer
Number of lawyers: 3
Main areas of work: US corporate , commercial and tax aspects of international transactions, with particular focus on energy and trade with and investment into the US; international commercial arbitration.
Office Profile: Opened in 1972, Fulbright & Jaworski's London office is a US and international law practice which handles a broad range of international transactional, commercial, investment, finance, trade and regulatory matters, with particular emphasis on US corporate, energy and tax law. Clients include non-US based corporations and banks doing business and investing in the US, and US corporations doing business in the UK, the Middle East and Africa and sovereign national and multilateral entities.

FULBRIGHT & JAWORSKI L.L.P.

For other recommended firms see pages 1485-1520

GAIA, SILVA, ROLIM & ASSOCIADOS

HEAD OFFICE

Alameda Campinas nº 463, 12º andar,
São Paulo, Brazil
Tel: +55 11 288 7277 **Fax:** +55 11 283 3158
Email: gaiasp@gaiasilvarolim.com.br
Website: www.gaiasilvarolim.com.br

FIRM OVERVIEW

Senior partner: Fernando Gaia
Number of partners worldwide: 10
Number of other lawyers worldwide: 101

AREAS OF PRACTICE:

Bids, judicial and administrative .... *%
Commercial .... *%
Corporate .... *%
Environmental .... *%
Financial .... *%
International operations .... *%
Tax .... *%
* Workload % not disclosed

FIRM OVERVIEW: Gaia, Silva, Rolim & Associados - Advocacia E Consultoria Empresarial was founded in 1990. With branch offices in São Paulo, Rio de Janeiro, Brasilia, Belo Horizonte and Curitiba, and associate offices in Buenos Airies, Miami and New York, the firm specialises in tax, corporate and commercial, financial, and environmental law, as well as handling work relating to international trade and administrative matters.

MAIN INTERNATIONAL AREAS OF PRACTICE:

Tax: Gaia, Silva, Rolim & Associados advises on a range of tax issues.It handles all aspects of tax planning including income tax, withholding tax, profit-related social dues, added-value sales tax, service tax, and Brazilian social security and financial tax. It also handles the review of tax-related procedures including preventive analysis of levels of compliance with applicable regulations; tax contingencies in corporate diversification; creation of tax routines for companies; contingencies and credit raising; and designing of tax routines.
Corporate: The firm advises on the analysis, creation and modification of articles of incorporation (by-laws and certificates); prevention and correction of formal corporate procedures; corporate restructuring (acquisitions, mergers, splitting, transformation); incorporation of consortiums, joint ventures and corporations; designing and negotiation of shareholder agreements; issuing of debentures, commercial papers, founders shares, and succession processing; corporate agency, catering for shareholders' interests.
Commercial: The firm provides a wide range of consultancy services, covering all business needs from contract drafting and review to negotiations. Areas of particular specialisation include foreign capital in Brazil and the rules from BACEN, CVM, Susep and other similar bodies; registration of investments in Brazil (advisory services and follow-up of BACEN and VCM); profit reinvestment, remittance, and capital repatriation; regularisation of foreign capital registration; debt/equity swaps; due diligence.
Finance: The firm handles the structuring, merging, splitting and privatisation of financial institutions; negotiations and structuring of transactions at national and international level; advises on financial rules, operations and guarantees; national and international financial product design; the structuring of operations involving derivatives and other forms of risk reallocation; the structuring of sophisticated financial operations (LBOs, MBOs, MBIs and venture capital); banking and administrative contract design and review; restructuring of legal departments; debt collection and re-negotiations (isolate or by creditor pool); project finance; privatisations (corporate, commercial, labour, tax-related, operational and administrative); and adjustment and re-organisation of pension funds operations.
Environmental: Gaia, Silva, Rolim & Associados advises on environmental legislation relating to corporate environmental management; drafts and develops environmental studies in association with environmental consultants; advises on procedures for environmental licensing; handles the development of legal studies in environmental feasibility assessments for strategic development projects and major ventures; environmental management performance review in relation to bids involving major ventures and infrastructure projects; advice on the implementation of environmental management systems based on the technical standards of the ISO 14000 series; the implementation of municipal environmental management systems; mediation of environment related conflicts, devising strategies for alternative resolution of disputes involving the sustained use of natural resources.
International: The firm advises on commercial and financial contract design and review; negotiations, legal structuring and follow-up of projects and ventures involving parties from different jurisdictions; law of competition in bilateral, regional and multilateral treaties; international disputes; and capital raising.
Bids, judicial and administrative: The firm handles lawsuits involving tax, civil and commercial matters. It also acts in administrative proceedings (taxpayers council, BACEN, VCM, Susep) and advises on tax, civil and commercial matters. It also handles all bidding and privatisation matters.

LANGUAGES: English, Portuguese, Spanish

WORLDWIDE OFFICE CONTACTS

BRAZIL

Afonso Pena, 3.111 - 8º e 14º andares, CEP 30 130-008 **Belo Horizonte**
Tel: +55 31 3280 2800 **Fax:** +55 31 3280 2828
Email: gaiabh@gaiasilvarolim.com.br

SRTVN, Q. 701, Bloco B, Centro Empresarial Norte - Sl. 515 a 519, CEP 70 719-900 **Brasília**
Tel: +55 61 328 2107 **Fax:** +55 61 328 3834
Email: gaiadf@gaiasilvarolim.com.br

Rua Mal. Deodoro, 344 - 14º andar - Edifício Atalaia, CEP 80 010-909 **Curitiba**
Tel: +55 41 323 6215 **Fax:**
Email: gaiapr@gaiasilvarolim.com.br

Av. Rio Branco, 116 - 9º andar, CEP 20.040-001 **Rio de Janeiro**
Tel: +55 21 3852 3600 **Fax:** +55 21 242 9101
Email: gaiarj@gaiasilvarolim.com.br

ASSOCIATE OFFICES

ARGENTINA

Abal, Dans, Perez & Associados, Avda. Corrientes, 456 p. 19 of. 192, 1366 **Buenos Aires**
Tel: +54 14 394 9652 **Fax:** +54 14 393 1670
Email: abal_dans@ciudad.com.ar

USA

Robinson Silverman Pearce Aronsohn & Berman LLP
1290 Avenue of the Americas, **New York**, NY 10104-0053
Tel: +1 212 541 2000 **Fax:** +10212 541 4630

The firm is also associated with Freeman, Butterman, Haber & Rojas, LLP in Miami and New York.

G

For other recommended firms see pages 1485-1520

GALLANT Y.T. HO & CO

HEAD OFFICE

4th Floor, Jardine House, 1 Connaught Place
Hong Kong Hong Kong
Tel: +852 2526 3336 **Fax:** +852 2845 9294

Email: gytho@gallantho.com.hk

WORLDWIDE OFFICE CONTACTS

CHINA
Suite 2651, Dong Fang Hotel, Liu Hua Road, **Guangzhou**
Tel: +86 20 8666 9900 ext. 2651 **Fax:** +86 20 8666 9900 ext. 2697
Email:

HONG KONG
4th Floor, Jardine House, 1 Connaught Place, **Hong Kong**
Tel: +852 2526 3336 **Fax:** +852 2845 9294
Email: gytho@gallantho.com.hk

FIRM OVERVIEW

Managing partner: Vincent WS Lo

Number of partners worldwide: 17
Number of other lawyers worldwide: 22

AREAS OF PRACTICE:

Conveyancing 28%
Corporate and commercial (including IT) 22%
Banking, finance, insurance 20%
Litigation and arbitration 20%
Others 10%

G

FIRM OVERVIEW: Established in 1977, Gallant Y.T. Ho & Co. is one of the largest local firms in Hong Kong, with over 40 lawyers and 230 staff in total. Nearly all the partners and consultants are dual-qualified in Hong Kong and England, and other jurisdictions. Since 1979 the firm has been involved in cross-border work with China, opening an office in Guangzhou in 1992 which specialises in real estate, manufacturing, retail, service industries, telecommunications and other infrastructural work. The bulk of the firm's work, however, remains in Hong Kong. The recent economic recession has necessitated a particular focus on asset tracing, debt collection, restructuring, litigation and arbitration.

INTERNATIONAL EXPERIENCE: The firm's 20-year-old China practice ranges from child adoption applications to joint ventures and state enterprise listings. It has represented investors from Hong Kong, South East Asia, North America and Europe. The involvement in China began with the establishment of joint venture hotels, of which the firm helped set up over 20 in the 1980s including the Hilton in Shanghai. In the mid-1980s the firm acted for the Bank of China in the largest project financing at that time, the Ping Shuo coal mine. It has also been involved in the listing of Chinese State Enterprises in Hong Kong or Shenzhen. In 1998 the firm acted for one of the major shareholders in the restructuring of Beijing Oriental Plaza Company Limited, the single largest foreign joint venture in Beijing for the development of the much-publicised Oriental Plaza near Tiananmen Square.

INTERNATIONAL CLIENTS: Include the Bank of China Group, the China Merchant Shipping Group, the Kowloon-Canton Railway Corporation, MTR Corporation Ltd., the Shanghai Commercial Bank and Wharf (China) Ltd.

MAIN INTERNATIONAL AREAS OF PRACTICE:

Commercial conveyancing: The firm has one of the largest commercial conveyancing practices in Hong Kong, representing major developers and quasi-governmental organizations. Currently the firm acts for the individual owners of Yau Tong Bay in their joint development of a one million sq. ft. site which on completion will be one of the major urban renewal projects in Hong Kong. The firm is also working with Paul, Weiss, Rifkind, Wharton & Garrison in advising the Hong Kong SAR Government in its successful negotiation with The Disney Group to build and operate a theme park on Lantau Island. In mainland China the firm has handled over 150 real estate projects in 25 cities since the introduction of leasehold interest in May 1990.

Corporate finance: The firm has made significant growth in this area in the past five years, handling over 30 IPOs between 1995 and 2000. Listings of Chinese state enterprises include acting for the software research arm of Beijing University in its Hong Kong listing in 1995, and in 1996 the listing of Anhui Expressway Company Limited, the first expressway in China to be listed in Hong Kong. This was followed by the 1997 listing of Anhui Conch Cement Company, the largest cement manufacturer in China. Recent clients include Sinopec Kantons Holdings Limited, the first 'Red Chip' company to be listed on the Hong Kong Stock Exchange in 1999. With the stock market starting to rally after the economic recession, the firm has seen more mergers and acquisitions involving listed companies.

Banking and finance: The firm is on the list of some 50 banking institutions in Hong Kong and it routinely reviews and sets banking forms and documents for some of these banks' day-to-day operations as well as preparing loan documentation and taking enforcement actions under mortgages or pledges.

Litigation: The firm assists clients in instituting court actions in Beijing, Guangzhou, Nanjing, Shanghai, Shenzhen and Sian. The firm's senior partner is an arbitrator of the Arbitration Commissions of Guangzhou, Tianjian and Shenzhen. Since the start of the region's economic crisis in 1997, the department has acted for several international banking and financial institutions in their debt-recovery and restructuring exercises. In addition to commercial litigation and insolvency works, the firm also has a large insurance claims practice in which it acts for some of the largest international and local insurance companies as well as statutory bodies.

LANGUAGES: English, Chinese (Cantonese, Chiuchow, Mandarin, Shanghainese)

For other recommended firms see pages 1485-1520

GARCÍA AÑOVEROS & PÉREZ-LLORCA

HEAD OFFICE

Velazquez, 29-4, dcha
28001 Madrid, Spain
Tel: + 34 91 436 04 25 **Fax:** + 34 91 436 04 30

Email: central@garcia-pllorca.com

WORLDWIDE OFFICE CONTACTS

SPAIN
Diputación, 260 (4° - 2ª), 08007 **Barcelona**
Tel: + 34 93 481 3075 **Fax:** + 34 93 481 3076
Email: bcn@garcia-pllorca.com

Compostela, 8 (5 izq - A) **La Coruña** 15004
Tel: + 34 981 202881 **Fax:** + 34 981 202782
Email: central@garcia-pllorca.com

Velazquez, 29-4, dcha 28001 **Madrid**
Tel: + 34 91 436 04 25 **Fax:** + 34-91 436 04 30
Email: central@garcia-pllorca.com

FIRM OVERVIEW

Senior partners: Jaime García Añoveros
José Pedro Pérez-Llorca

Number of partners worldwide: 3
Number of other lawyers worldwide: 21

AREAS OF PRACTICE:

Commercial law and finance	40%
Real estate	30%
Bankruptcy and litigation	15%
Tax	15%

FIRM OVERVIEW: Established in 1983, García Añoveros & Pérez-Llorca is a middle-sized, independent Spanish law firm with 24 lawyers (including 3 partners) in its offices in Madrid, Barcelona and La Coruña. The firm provides advice in all major areas of Spanish law , with specialisations including real estate, corporate law and litigation. The firm advises international and domestic corporate clients, including major banks, national and regional government agencies and listed and unlisted companies, among them several of the recently-privatised companies. It deals frequently with Spanish public authorities such as the Bank of Spain, the Securities Market National Commission and the Competition Court.

INTERNATIONAL EXPERIENCE: More than 50 percent of the firm's client base is international. Typical work includes project development and financing, cross-border acquisitions, joint ventures, cross-border acquisition finance, liquidation of foreign investments, mergers and spin-offs.

INTERNATIONAL CLIENTS: The firm works with top companies from the UK, US, Canada and Australia, as well as Germany, France and Italy. Clients include major UK and French public limited companies, international banks and international insurance companies, and New York and City law firms.

MAIN INTERNATIONAL AREAS OF PRACTICE:
Commercial law and finance: The firm has been especially oriented towards mergers and acquisitions, construction and project development, foreign investment, joint ventures, financing and capital markets. The group covers the securities market, competition, environment, intellectual property, internet and telecommunications.

Real estate: The group has extensive experience in areas such as the sale and purchase, leases, mortgages, town planning and the financing and marketing of business resorts and office projects. It has a particular focus on the promotion of malls, leisure theme parks and office buildings. The practice operates throughout Spain, currently in Madrid, Barcelona, Alicante, Seville, Córdoba and La Coruña.

Bankruptcy and litigation: The practice group operates throughout Spain, mainly in the civil jurisdiction. It is active in all types of procedures, especially claims for amounts, and is also familiar with the use of injunctions. The group has broad experience in commercial litigation areas such as unfair competition, intellectual property, company, advertising and general conditions. It also has sound experience of all kinds of arbitration proceedings, with firm members having been appointed arbitrators in a number of internationally-relevant arbitration proceedings.

Tax: The tax group works in close contact with the commercial law and finance and the real estate groups, and specialises in non-resident and company taxation. Many of its clients are multinational companies, and here the firm aims to maximise clients' profits on transactions where more than one tax regime is involved.

LANGUAGES: English, French, German, Italian, Spanish

For other recommended firms see pages 1485-1520

GARRIGUES & ANDERSEN

A MEMBER OF ANDERSEN LEGAL

HEAD OFFICE

Jose Abascal, 45,
28003 Madrid, Spain
Tel: +34 91 514 5200 **Fax:** +34 91 399 2408

Website: www.garriguesandersen.com

FIRM OVERVIEW

Managing partners: Miguel Gordillo
José María Alonso

Number of partners worldwide: 97
Number of other lawyers worldwide: 839

AREAS OF PRACTICE:

Area	%
Commercial and banking	30%
Tax law	30%
General practice	20%
Litigation and arbitration	12%
Employment	8%

WORLDWIDE OFFICE CONTACTS

SPAIN

Cataluña Regional Office, Avinguda Diagonal, 654, 08034 **Barcelona**
Tel: +34 93 253 3700 **Fax:** +34 93 253 3750

Basque Regional Office, Rodriguez Arias, 15, 48008 **Bilbao**
Tel: +34 94 470 0699 **Fax:** +34 94 444 7998

Jose Abascal, 45, 28003 **Madrid**
Tel: +34 91 514 5200 **Fax:** +34 91 399 2408

Andalucia Regional Office, Americo Vespucio, 25 - Isla de la Cartuja, 41092 **Seville**
Tel: +34 95 448 9348 **Fax:** +34 93 448 9349

Valencia Regional Office, Pascual y Genis, 1, 46002 **Valencia**
Tel: +34 96 353 6611 **Fax:** +34 96 394 4734

Galicia Regional Office, Av. García Borbon, 106-1°, 36201 **Vigo**
Tel: +34 986 815 525 **Fax:** +34 984 815 535

G

FIRM OVERVIEW: Garrigues & Andersen, was formed by the merger between J&A Garrigues and Arthur Andersen Asesores Legales y Tributarios, and comprises 936 professionals in 22 offices. The firm provides a wide range of legal and tax services and specialises in M&A, banking, litigation, arbitration (domestic and international), environmental law, new technologies, labour law, insurance, security markets law and international tax. The firm's international activities are concentrated in South America and Europe, particularly England, France and Italy. Garrigues & Andersen is a member of Andersen Legal, a large international network of law firms.

INTERNATIONAL EXPERIENCE: Garrigues & Andersen provides counseling services to the largest transnational companies on international transactions and assists foreign companies that wish to invest in Spain. It is associated with legal and tax consulting firms worldwide, offering its clients additional experience and knowledge of other countries' legislation. The firm's membership of Andersen Legal also allows it to offer clients international advice on corporate and business matters, and assist them with transnational litigation.

INTERNATIONAL CLIENTS: The firm's client base includes large companies, banks, telecommunications, electricity companies and public or supranational institutions conducting cross-border business.

MAIN INTERNATIONAL AREAS OF PRACTICE:

Company and commercial: The firm advises on commercial law; formation of companies and other entities, corporate and group reorganisations, transformations, mergers, spin-offs and dissolutions; advice on and design of control procedures to safeguard the liability of directors and administrators and privatisations and public sector infrastructure projects.

Tax: The firm handles matters including tax planning and analysis of legislative changes, financing schemes, cash repatriation, holding structures, national and international double taxation advise, taxation of non-residents in Spain and of residents abroad, as well as definition and monitoring of tax consequences of international postings of employees.

Banking, insurance and securities market law: The firm provides legal and tax advice on a wide range of issues affecting financial institutions and insurance companies, including ongoing and specific planning advise on the legal, administrative and tax aspects of financial institutions and insurance companies and advise, design and administration of financing, leasing and underwriting agreements.

Employment: Garrigues & Andersen provides general and specialist advice on all matters of industrial relations, compensation policies and social security, including negotiation, planning and design of collective bargaining and company agreements, changes to working conditions, geographical and functional mobility.

Litigation and arbitration: The firm advises domestic and international clients on dispute resolution relating to commercial law as well as in pre-litigation and litigation issues on related civil and criminal matters. In arbitration the firm has an established practice that covers both domestic and international arbitration in application of ad hoc (UNCITRAL and EDF) and institutional (ICC, AAA and LCIA) arbitration rules.

Administrative law: The firm provides advisory services to government authorities, public sector agencies, state-owned companies and the private sector on administrative matters that include preparation, management and processing of claims and appeals before both the Administration and the administrative courts.

Zoning and city planning: The firm advises on urban planning law, planning management and enforcement in relation to national legislation and to the Autonomous Regional Communities litigation.

Real estate: The firm handles matters such a management of property portfolios, mortgage transactions, regularisation and continuous updating of the legal status and possession situation of properties and advise on rural and urban lease contracts and on property sales and purchases.

Industrial and intellectual property: The firm offers a wide range of legal services relating to the protection of industrial and intellectual property rights and in the fields of unfair trade practices and advertising.

EU general and competition law: The firm advises on commercial and customs matters, on the regulations arising from EU directives, on the problems of harmonisation of legislation and on the free circulation of goods.

International institutional projects: The firm provides legal and tax consulting services to foreign countries and international agencies, assisting in the development of legislation in Eastern Europe, North African and Latin American countries financed by the European Union and by other international institutions.

LANGUAGES: English, French, German, Italian, Japanese, Spanish

For other recommended firms see pages 1485-1520

GEORGIEV, TODOROV & CO

HEAD OFFICE

58-V Tzar Assen Street, PO Box 15,
1463 Sofia, Bulgaria
Tel: +359 2 951 5665 **Fax:** +359 2 952 04 51

Email: office@georg-tod.com
Website www.georg-tod.com

FIRM OVERVIEW

Managing partner: Ivan Todorov
Senior partner: Theodor Tchipev
Number of partners worldwide: 7
Number of other lawyers worldwide: 41

AREAS OF PRACTICE:

Foreign investments and project finance	30%
Litigation and arbitration	30%
Banking	10%
Tax	10%
Licenses and concessions	5%
Mergers and acquisitions	5%
Securities transactions	5%
Telecommunications	5%

WORLDWIDE OFFICE CONTACTS

BULGARIA
61 Christo Botev Street, Entrance G, 1st floor, **Bourgas**
Tel: +359 56 80 14 23 **Fax:** +359 56 80 14 23

6, Antim 1st Street, **Plovdiv**
Tel: +359 32 225 45 **Fax:** +359 32 225 45

53 Raijko Daskalov Street, **Plovdiv**
house "Levski",floor 2, office 20
Tel: +359 32 62 71 17 **Fax:** +359 32 62 71 17

16, Tzarkovna Nezavisimost Street, **Rousse**
Tel: +359 82 27 4081 **Fax:** +359 82 22 4043

20, Metodi Koussev Street, **Stara Zagora** 6000
Tel/Fax: +359 423 1953

13, Georgi Benkovski Street, Floor 2, **Varna**
Tel: +359 52 23 50 82 **Fax:** +359 52 234006

PO Box 36, 5000, **Veliko Turnovo**
Tel: +359 62 20135 **Fax:** +359 62 20472

G

FIRM OVERVIEW: The firm was established in 1991 and is one of the first Bulgarian law firms. It has five offices in the centre of Sofia with 33 lawyers among them, and further offices in the major Bulgarian towns as well as representatives in Milan, New York and Belarus. The firm also has an association with UK firm Eversheds and German firm Scheele & Partner. It is the only Bulgarian member of Lawyers Associated Worldwide. It provides corporate law services, with particular emphasis on venture capital, secured lending and litigation, acting for a large domestic client base and a range of foreign investors.

INTERNATIONAL EXPERIENCE: The firm advised the European Commission on loans to Bulgaria and to the EBRD on eight investment projects. It also advised on four post investment projects of ECM BPPF. It has also been involved in two of the largest Bulgarian privatisations, advising buyers of Bulgarian Telecommunications and Balkan Airlines. It has advised on the country's first Eurobonds issue, for the Sofia municipality, which it also represented in a joint venture with Sour Internationale in France.

INTERNATIONAL CLIENTS: The firm's clients include ABN AMRO, AVL Vervaltungsgesellschaft mbH Prof. Dr. h. c. Hans List, Austria, Bank Austria Credit Anstalt Leasing, Commerzbank, Frankfurt am Main, Germany, AT&T, Metal Traders, Bank of Toscana, the EBRD, the European Commission, ECM/Bulgarian Post Privatisation Fund, Microsoft, Oracle, Montgomery Watson S.A., Belgium, Fiat, Daewoo, Boston Consulting Group, Turner Broadcasting Europe, Taylor Nelson Sofres, Ernst & Young, Reuters, Balkan Mining Consultants, Du Pont de Nemours Lego Trading, Halcrow UK, Draeger Germany, Sneider Group Germany, Elliot Management, SACMI Group, Italy, Ko-Pac International, UK, Wisconsin Alumini Research Foundation, USA, Allied Van Lines Inc, USA, Harlequin Publishing Holland, Salini Italy, Fiat Italy, DAEWOO Korea, SGL Carbon GmbH, Germany, Snelling Personal Services, Petroconsultants Ltd, UPS Europe S.A., Belgium, OTE (Hellenic Telecommunication Organisation) Greece, Intracom Greece, Papastratos Greece, Yugoslavian Airlines.

MAIN INTERNATIONAL AREAS OF PRACTICE:

Foreign investments and project finance: In 1999 the firm advised on over 30 international transactions involving secured lending, equity acquisitions, real estate in Bulgaria and joint ventures.

Litigation and arbitration: Work includes commercial litigation, national and international arbitration and the enforcement of foreign rulings in Bulgaria. The firm has acted in three of the five biggest court cases in Bulgaria.

Banking: The firm covers all aspects, including bank establishment and licensing, day-to-day operation (including secured lending) and insolvency.

Tax: Firm members have successfully led major appeals against illegal actions by tax authorities in the collection of undue taxes. The practice advises major local and foreign individual and corporate clients on corporate tax, VAT, withholding tax and treaties on the avoidance of double taxation. The firm has successfully acted in the three biggest court cases in Bulgaria.

M&A: The firm has advised on ten complex M&A cases, including the first Bulgarian private bank merger.

Telecommunications: The firm advised the buyers in the privatisation of the Bulgarian Telecommunication Company. It has also advised telecommunications operators on licensing and has appealed illegal acts of the Committee on Post and Telecommunications (CPT). The firm specialises in licensing and operations of telecom operators.

Licences and concessions: As well as handling issuing, the firm acts in appeals against suspension and revocation.

Securities transactions: Work includes bonds and convertible bonds issues, securities acquisitions/disposals, charges over securities, taxation of securities transactions, permission and currency control.

LANGUAGES: Armenian, Bulgarian, English, French, German, Italian, Russian, Spanish

For other recommended firms see pages 1485-1520

GERNANDT & DANIELSSON ADVOKATBYRA AB

HEAD OFFICE

PO Box 5747, Nybrogatan 11,
SE-114 87 Stockholm, Sweden
Tel: +46 8 670 6600 **Fax:** +46 8 662 6101

Email: info@gda.se
Website: www.gda.se

FIRM OVERVIEW

Managing partner: Bjorn Tude
Senior partners Johan Gernandt and Karl-Erik Danielsson

Number of partners worldwide: 12
Number of other lawyers worldwide: 45

AREAS OF PRACTICE:

Corporate finance	20%
M&A	20%
Arbitration and litigation	15%
Banking and finance	15%
Competition	10%
Telecommunication	10%
Others	10%

FIRM OVERVIEW: Established in 1992 in Stockholm, Gernandt & Danielsson Advokatbyra AB employs approximately 45 lawyers. The firm specialises in corporate law, banking and financial law, contract law, competition law and arbitration and litigation proceedings. The firm is active in international matters, and has well-established connections with several large law firms in Europe and elsewhere in the world. When dealing with clients, Gernandt & Danielsson consults with or recommends the foreign law firm or expert who can best respond to a client's needs.

INTERNATIONAL EXPERIENCE: Examples of recent international transactions involving the firm include acting for MeritaNordbanken in connection with its merger with the Unidanmark group (Unibank and Tryg-Baltica Insurance) and in connection with its bid on the Norwegian bank Christiania Bank; acting for Deutsche Post in connection with its take-over of Swedish logistics company ASG; acting for Holmen in connection with its sale of Swedish paper company Modo Paper and for StoraEnso in connection with the sale of its power assets in Sweden and Finland to Fortum. The firm also represented Cap Gemini S.A., in its acquisition of Ernst & Young's management consulting business in Sweden, and Formica Corporation in its acquisition of Perstorp Surface Materials business, including the financing of such acquisition, and, Karolin Machine Tool's acquisition of Lidköping Machine Tools from SKF. The firm advised media group MTG in connection with the spin-off of Metro and the subsequent listing of Metro on NASDAQ; and advised Carnegie and other Swedish and non-Swedish investment banks in numerous IPOs, suhc as the Proffice IPO. Gernandt & Danielsson has also been involved in several financing matters. The firm acted as advisor to a bank consortium headed by Bank of America in connection with syndication of the project financing facilities to Arlanda Express, the operator of the train shuttle between Stockholm Central and Arlanda Airport.

INTERNATIONAL CLIENTS: A considerable number of Gernandt & Danielsson's clients are in the banking, financial and insurance sector and include MeritaNordbanken, Carnegie Latzard and Skandia. The firm also services clients in the service, trade, telecom and industrial sectors, including Toyota, MCI Worldcom, Europolitan, MTG, Caterpillar and Alfa Laval.

WORLDWIDE OFFICE CONTACTS

SWEDEN
PO Box 5747, Nybrogatan 11, SE-114 87 **Stockholm**
Tel: +46 8 670 6600 **Fax:** +46 8 662 6101
Email: info@gda.se

MAIN INTERNATIONAL AREAS OF PRACTICE:
Banking and finance: The firm assists Swedish and international banks and financial companies in several areas, and is particularly experienced in planning and conducting large financial transactions and market floatations.
Corporate and commercial: The firm regularly handles shareholder and joint venture agreements and acts as advisor in the restructuring of companies and business groups. The firm frequently advises clients on issues concerning board responsibility, changes in capital structure, incentive programmes for employees and annual general meetings of shareholders.
M&A The firm advises public and private companies on all types of mergers and acquisitions, including negotiated and non-negotiated transactions, public and private sales, public offers and management buy-outs.
Competition/anti-trust: The firm acts as adviser in applications for negative clearance and exemption, notifications and mergers and complaints with respect to restrictive practices and abuses of dominant position.
Public procurement: The firm has advised and counseled authorities and suppliers on a range of issues in this area.
Litigation and arbitration: The firm assists in both Swedish and international arbitration proceedings and litigation, especially banking disputes and in cases regarding compulsory share purchases. Several of the firm's lawyers are frequently appointed as arbitrators in Swedish and international arbitration matters.
Telecommunications: The firm's activities range from concessions and competition law matters to interconnect, supply and customer agreements.
Employment: The firm handles all matters relating to Swedish employment law.

LANGUAGES: English, French, German

For other recommended firms see pages 1485-1520

GIANNI ORIGONI & PARTNERS

A MEMBER FIRM OF LINKLATERS & ALLIANCE

HEAD OFFICE

Via delle Quattro Fontane 20, I-00184 Rome, Italy
Tel: +39 06 478 751 **Fax:** +39 06 487 1101
Email: fgianni@gop.it
Website: www.linklaters-alliance.com

FIRM OVERVIEW

Managing partner: Francesco Gianni
Number of partners worldwide: 27
Number of other lawyers worldwide: 151
Number of partners worldwide (Linklaters & Alliance): 586
Number of other lawyers worldwide (Linklaters & Alliance): 2,232

FIRM OVERVIEW: Established in 1988, the firm was founded with the goal of developing an international business practice. It now has five offices and with over 170 lawyers, it is one of the largest firms in Italy. The firm is a member firm of Linklaters & Alliance, which brings together five of Europe's premier law firms including De Bandt, van Hecke, Lagae & Loesch (Belgium and Luxembourg), De Brauw Blackstone Westbroek (Netherlands), Gianni, Origoni & Partners (Italy), Lagerlöf & Leman (Sweden) and Linklaters (which practises in Germany as Linklaters Oppenhoff & Rädler). Linklaters & Alliance is one of the leading global legal practices with nearly 3,000 lawyers and other professionals operating in combined teams from 34 offices in major financial and business centres worldwide. Since joining Linklaters & Allliance, Gianni Origoni & Partners has been able to offer significantly enhanced breadth and depth of service on a global basis, with integrated work on multi-jurisdictional transactions.

INTERNATIONAL CLIENTS: The firm's clients range from large Italian and foreign industrial multinationals and financial institutions to individuals seeking advice on business matters. A significant portion of the firm's clientele is represented by non-Italian corporates and financial institutions requiring advice on virtually any legal issue connected with their Italian operations or international transactions related to the Italian jurisdiction. The firm also advises major Italian companies both locally and in their business activities outside of Italy.

MAIN INTERNATIONAL AREAS OF PRACTICE:

M&A: The firm has always had an extensive M&A practice. It has advised on numerous mid-size acquisitions as well as several of the largest international acquisitions made in Italy in recent years involving leading businesses in a number of diverse markets. The firm has also advised major foreign investors as well as state-owned companies in some of the Italian government's largest privatisation projects.

Banking, finance and capital markets: The firm assists several domestic and foreign banks and financial institutions, as well as investment firms, with both their Italian and foreign operations. It drafts and negotiates documentation, provides opinions and devises complex legal structures for a wide variety of banking and finance transactions including domestic and international syndicated loan agreements, security packages, letters of credit, project and structured finance transactions and securitisations. The firm has also advised issuers, sellers and underwriters in several public offerings of financial instruments (including shares, bonds and warrants), tender offers for stakes in listed and unlisted companies as well as domestic and international private placements.

Litigation and arbitration: Firm members appear in major civil and administrative litigations in courts throughout Italy and before the Court of Cassation, the country's highest court. They also represent clients or act as arbitrators in major international arbitrations, including ICC proceedings.

Energy and natural resources: Several firm members have developed specific expertise in these areas. The firm advises several leading foreign and Italian independent energy companies on project development, sometimes through joint ventures. Work includes project finance, infrastructure projects, distribution, regulatory compliance, licensing, concession and bidding agreements.

Telecommunications and media: The firm advises foreign and Italian companies on European and Italian telecommunications and media law, including matters such as joint ventures and infrastructure projects, broadcasting rights licensing and similar agreements, and the setting up and acquisition of TV and radio stations.

Tax: The firm has specialists on the tax aspects of corporate and commercial transactions such as M&A, asset transfers, corporate restructuring and recapitalisations, licence and service agreements as well as inter-company agreements. It also advises on the tax aspects of setting up Italian operations and their day-to-day operation, as well as handling tax litigation.

Anti-trust: The firm was a forerunner in creating a department specialising in Italian anti-trust, partly because one of its largest offices is located in Rome, where the enforcement agency is based. The firm's attorneys thus have extensive experience of the area, and represent clients in major proceedings before the Italian Antitrust Authority.

LANGUAGES: English, French, German, Italian, Spanish

WORLDWIDE OFFICE CONTACTS

ITALY
Piazza Belgioioso 2, I-20121 **Milan**
Tel: +39 02 76 37 41 **Fax:** +39 02 76 00 96 28
Email: amaggi@gop.it

Via Altinate 146, I-35121 **Padua**
Tel: +39 04 969 94 41 **Fax:** +39 04 966 03 41
Email: lpavanello@gop.lt

UNITED KINGDOM
One Silk Street, **London** EC2Y 8HQ
Tel: +44 20 7456 4940 **Fax:** +44 20 7456 4941
Email: bbartocc@gop-London.co.uk

USA
1345 Avenue of the Americas, **New York,** NY 10105
Tel: +1 212 424 9170 **Fax:** +1 212 424 9100
Email: tcenci@gopny.com

OTHER LINKLATERS & ALLIANCE OFFICES

Alicante, Amsterdam, Antwerp, Bangkok, Berlin, Bratislava, Brussels, Bucharest, Budapest, Cologne, Frankfurt am Main, Gothenburg, The Hague, Hong Kong, Luxembourg, Madrid, Malmö, Moscow, Munich, Paris, Prague, Rotterdam, Sao Paulo, Shanghai, Singapore, Stockholm, Tokyo, Warsaw, Washington, DC.

LINKLATERS
& ALLIANCE

GIBSON, DUNN & CRUTCHER LLP

HEAD OFFICE

see Worldwide Office Contacts

Website: www.gibsondunn.com

FIRM OVERVIEW

Managing partner: Wesley G Howell, Jr

Number of partners worldwide: 254
Number of other lawyers worldwide: 554

AREAS OF PRACTICE:

Corporate/corporate finance	44%
Litigation	41%
Labour/employment	6%
Real estate	6%
Tax	3%

G

FIRM OVERVIEW: Gibson, Dunn & Crutcher is an international law firm with over 800 lawyers in 11 offices. The firm's clients range from the world's largest multinational corporations to high-tech leaders and real estate funds, and are active in the entire spectrum of the global economy. Gibson Dunn has well-respected expertise in corporate and securities transactions, and is particularly experienced in mergers and acquisitions and public equity transactions. Gibson Dunn also has a commercial litigation practice with litigators experienced in many forums and a distinguished appellate practice. Lawyers within the firm also specialise in anti-trust, high-yield debt, real estate finance, corporate tax, employment and labour and business restructurings and reorganisations. Gibson Dunn operates its offices on an integrated basis, drawing on the depth, expertise and other resources provided by the firm's multi-office structure.

INTERNATIONAL EXPERIENCE: The firm has long represented major multinational corporations in their acquisition, joint venture and investment activities throughout the world. Lawyers in the firm handle complex litigation and arbitration globally. The London and Paris offices have robust practices and they represent European, North American, Asian and Middle Eastern corporations, investment houses and financial institutions throughout the world. They handle cross-border mergers and complex capital markets deals. Based in New York, the firm's global projects and Latin American practices represent clients in corporate transactions and debt and equity offerings. Gibson Dunn's lawyers also counsel clients on large energy, telecommunications and investment projects.

INTERNATIONAL CLIENTS: Gibson Dunn's many thousands of clients are active in virtually every sector of the global economy, including transportation, telecommunications, entertainment, health care, leisure, electronics and finance. The firm's clients range from multinational corporations to start-up ventures.

WORLDWIDE OFFICE CONTACTS

FRANCE
166, rue du Faubourg Saint Honoré, 75008 **Paris**
Tel: +33 01 56 43 13 00 **Fax:** +33 01 56 43 13 33

UNITED KINGDOM
Telephone House, 2-4 Temple Avenue, **London** EC4Y 0HB
Tel: +44 20 7071 4000 **Fax:** +44 20 7071 4244

USA
2100 McKinney Avenue, Suite 1100, **Dallas** TX 75201-6911
Tel: +1 214 698 3100 **Fax:** +1 214 698 3400

1801 California Street, Suite 4100, **Denver** CO 80202-2641
Tel: +1 303 298 5700 **Fax:** +1 303 296 5310

4 Park Plaza, **Irvine** CA 92614-8557
Tel: +1 949 451 3800 **Fax:** +1 949 451 4220

2029 Century Park East, **Los Angeles** CA 90067-3026
Tel: +1 310 552 8500 **Fax:** +1 310 551 8741

333 South Grand Avenue, **Los Angeles** CA 90071-3197
Tel: +1 213 229 7000 **Fax:** +1 213 229 7520

200 Park Avenue, **New York** NY 10166-0193
Tel: +1 212 351 4000 **Fax:** +1 212 351 4035

1530 Page Mill Road, **Palo Alto** CA 94304-1125
Tel: +1 650 849 5300 **Fax:** +1 650 849 5333

One Montgomery Street, **San Francisco** CA 94104-4505
Tel: +1 415 393 8200 **Fax:** +1 415 986 5309

1050 Connecticut Avenue NW, **Washington** DC 20036-5306
Tel: +1 202 955 8500 **Fax:** +1 202 467 0539

GIBSON, DUNN & CRUTCHER

For other recommended firms see pages 1485-1520

GIDE LOYRETTE NOUEL

HEAD OFFICE

26, cours Albert 1er,
75008 Paris, France
Tel: +33 1 40 75 60 00 **Fax:** +33 1 43 59 37 79

Email: info@gide.fr
Website: www.gide.com

FIRM OVERVIEW

Managing partners: Gérard Tavernier, Jean-Jacques Raquin
Number of partners worldwide: 73
Number of other lawyers worldwide: 305

AREAS OF PRACTICE:

Mergers, acquisitions and corporate law	25%
Banking, finance and project financing	20%
Arbitration and litigation	15%
Real estate	10%
IP, media, IT and telecommunications	8%
Community law and competition	7%
Tax	6%
Employment	4%
Other	5%

FIRM OVERVIEW: Gide Loyrette Nouel is France's leading international law firm. Its areas of expertise cover all sectors of business law. The firm has offices in 12 countries comprising 370 lawyers and legal consultants (including 73 partners), which enables it to assist its clients worldwide.

INTERNATIONAL EXPERIENCE: Gide Loyrette Nouel has an extensive presence in Europe having opened offices in Brussels (1967), Warsaw (1991), Prague (1992), Moscow and Budapest (1993), Istanbul (1997) and Bucharest (1998). The firm is also very active in Asia. The Beijing office was opened in 1987 and now has some 28 lawyers and legal consultants. Gide Loyrette Nouel's involvement in Vietnam began in the late 1980s and the Hanoi office works actively for foreign investors and local government departments and agencies. The firm maintains close relationships with local firms and legal agents based in Tokyo, Hong Kong, Bangkok, Jakarta and Singapore. The firm also has offices in Saudi Arabia (Riyadh) and in the US (New York). For many years, the firm has represented North American companies, banks and financial institutions in connection with their business transactions in Europe. More and more US start up companies work with the New York office to create and develop their activities in France.

INTERNATIONAL CLIENTS: The firm's clients include major international groups, banks, financial institutions and government bodies.

MAIN INTERNATIONAL AREAS OF PRACTICE:

Arbitration: Gide Loyrette Nouel's arbitration department provides assistance to clients in defining their litigation strategy and settling disputes. The firm's international network has allowed the department to acquire practical experience in the courts of many countries. This, in conjunction with an understanding of all major legal systems, enables the department to provide clients with the best possible advice on managing their international litigation around the world. Contact partners, Pierre Raoul-Duval and Christian Camboulive.

Bankruptcy/insolvency: Gide Loyrette Nouel provides a full range of advice and assistance to companies in financial difficulty, ranging from preventative measures to insolvency proceedings. Its experience extends to international insolvency, buy-outs and the restructuring of companies in financial difficulty. Contact partners, Jean-Michel Lucheux and Olivier Puech.

EU law: The firm's experience in French and European Community law is based on well-established and wide ranging practice in various commercial sectors. In Paris, Gide Loyrette Nouel boasts one of the most highly-rated teams in this field. The department works in close collaboration with the firm's Brussels office which provides an effective means of access to the European institutions. Contact partners, Xavier de Roux and Joëlle Salzmann.

WORLDWIDE OFFICE CONTACTS

BELGIUM
View Building, Rue de l'Industrie, 26-38, B-1040 **Brussels**
Tel: +32 2 231 11 40 **Fax:** +32 2 231 11 77
Email: voillemot@gide.fr

CHINA
Suite 3301, Jing Guang Centre, Hu Jia Lou, Chaoyang District, **Beijing** 100020
Tel: +86 10 65 97 45 11 **Fax:** +86 10 65 97 45 51
Email: yan@gide.fr

CZECH REPUBLIC
Krakovská 9, 110 00 **Prague** 1
Tel: +420 2 22 87 11 11 **Fax:** +420 2 22 87 11 12
Email: veit@gide.fr

HUNGARY
EMKE Building, Rákóczi út 42, BP 409, 1072 **Budapest**
Tel: +36 1 268 12 36 **Fax:** +36 1 268 12 39
Email: servigny@gide.fr

POLAND
Stratos Office Centre-ul.Ks.I.Skorupki 5, 00-546 **Warsaw**
Tel: +48 22 583 67 01 **Fax:** +48 22 583 67 67
Email: dwernicki@gide.fr

ROMANIA
10-12 Strada Maior Sontu, Sector 1, **Bucharest**
Tel: +40 1 223 03 10 **Fax:** +40 1 233 03 42
Email: leroyb@gide.fr

RUSSIA
Stoleshnikov pereulok, 14, 103031 **Moscow**
Tel: +7 501 258 31 00 **Fax:** +7 501 258 31 01
Email: lasfargue@gide.fr

SAUDI ARABIA
PO Box 4615, **Riyadh** 11412
Tel: +966 1 476 60 39 **Fax:** +966 1 476 18 96
Email: info@gide.fr

TURKEY
Büyükdere Cad., Yapi Kredi Plaza, B Blok Kat 6, Levent, 80620 **Istanbul**
Tel: +90 212 325 35 81 **Fax:** +90 212 325 35 87
Email: rougier@gide.fr

USA
UBS Tower, 10 East 50th Street, **New York** NY 10022
Tel: +1 212 644 12 01 **Fax:** +1 212 644 12 05
Email: malamed@gide.fr

VIETNAM
Metropole Centre, Unit 504-1, 56 Ly Thai To, **Hanoi**
Tel: +84 4 825 19 58 **Fax:** +84 4 825 79 19
Email: glnhn@hn.vnn.vn

G

Employment: Gide Loyrette Nouel advises clients in all areas of employment law and employment protection, with particular emphasis on aspects such as restructuring, collective redundancy plans, labour agreements, working hours, negotiated departure of senior executives, health care and contingency schemes, pensions, employee savings and professional training. The firm also represents its clients before the relevant government agencies, employment tribunals and higher courts in any matter related to labour and social security issues. Contact partner, Joël Grangé.

Finance/project finance: Comprising over 50 lawyers, the finance department offers a full service banking and finance practice, including traditional bank financing, structured financing relating to all types of tangible, movable and real estate or intangible assets, securitisation, international securities and debt instrument issues, sales of securities in France, collective savings, OTC derivatives products and derivatives traded on regulated markets and also in devising financing instruments. The firm also advises numerous banking and financial institutions on the regulatory aspects of their business activities. Gide Loyrette Nouel has also developed a project finance team specialised in privatisation and project finance. Clients of the project finance team include IFIs, banks and governments as well as sponsors, construction companies and operators. The firm combines its leading position in French infrastructure and concession projects with wide experience in legislative drafting, international concession, BOT and limited recourse project financing around the world. The project finance team has significant experience in the fields of infrastructure (water and wastewater, energy, motorways, telecommunications, airports, ports), natural resources, construction and production facilities. Contact partners, Emmanuel Fontaine and Kamel Ben Salah.

Intellectual property: Gide Loyrette Nouel has long-standing experience in intellectual property law, including patents in a wide variety of technical fields, trademarks, designs, models and copyright. The firm assists clients in all areas of infringement litigation. It also negotiates and drafts assignments and licences of intellectual property rights. In addition, the firm has developed extensive experience in intellectual property issues relating to the internet. Contact partners, Arnaud Michel and Grégoire Triet.

Internet/e-commerce: Gide Loyrette Nouel has more than 50 specialist lawyers with experience in handling a wide range of legal issues arising for companies involved in the internet and e-commerce sectors. The firm's expertise in IT, media, intellectual property, competition and distribution law, capital raising and M&A has enabled it to respond rapidly to the expansion of the internet. Services offered cover the entire range of services required for new economy start-ups as well as for more traditional companies wishing to develop their e-commerce. Contact partners, Bertrand Nouel and Grégoire Triet.

Litigation/corporate crime: The firm assists, advises and represents companies both before and during litigation. Staffed by 20 lawyers (including six partners), the litigation department provides assistance with every phase of court proceedings in all the main areas of commercial law. The firm's wide-ranging experience allows it to provide its corporate clients with effective representation and comprehensive solutions to their legal problems. Contact partners, Gilles Duquet and Aurélien Boulanger.

Media, IT and telecommunications: Building on over 20 years experience in the traditional IT and media law fields, the firm was one of the first to adapt to the convergence of new technologies by offering advice, in France and abroad, to communication groups operating in the IT, media, radio, TV and telecommunications fields (film, television, radio, specialised channels, cable, satellite, Internet, telephony) and on negotiating and drafting agreements for technology transfer and the assignment of rights. The department also assists clients in preparing applications to regulatory authorities for operating licenses. Contact partners, Bertrand Nouel and Olivier Cousi.

Corporate/M&A: M&A has been one of the busiest departments since the firm was founded, particularly in the areas of nationalisation, privatisation and operations involving listed companies. In recent years, the M&A department has developed significant expertise in the area of stock market listings and securities issues. Contact partners, Youssef Djehane and Hugues Mathez.

Real estate and financing: The firm deals with all stages in real estate transactions, both in France and abroad, including structuring and financing, the purchase of real property assets, real estate companies, secured real estate claims and related litigation. The real estate transactions and financing department handles all aspects of such transactions, including taxation and the relevant town and country planning regulations. Over the last few years, the real estate transactions and financing department has advised numerous French and overseas clients in some of the largest property deals in France. It has been instructed in the acquisition of asset portfolios, consisting of offices and shopping centres, and in the buy-back of secured real estate claim portfolios belonging to banks and institutional investors on behalf of foreign investment funds. Contact partners, Gérard Tavernier and Renaud Baguenault.

Tax: Gide Loyrette Nouel's tax department provides advice to companies on all aspects of their tax strategy and management. The tax team is acknowledged, both in France and abroad, as being one of the leaders in the Paris market. Contact partners, Richard Beauvais and Olivier Dauchez.

Transportation, maritime and insurance law: This department practises in all areas relating to maritime, land and air transport, industrial risks connected with these activities and the applicable insurance systems. It also acts in collaboration with the finance and tax departments in connection with financing for ships and aircraft. Contact partner, Emmanuel Fontaine.

LANGUAGES: Arabic, Bulgarian, Chinese, Czech, English, German, Hungarian, Italian, Polish, Romanian, Russian, Spanish, Turkish, Vietnamese

For other recommended firms see pages 1485-1520

GILBERT & TOBIN

HEAD OFFICE

2 Park Street,
Sydney NSW 2000, Australia
Tel: +61 2 9263 4000 **Fax:** +61 2 9263 4111

Email: email@gtlaw.com.au
Website: www.gtlaw.com.au

WORLDWIDE OFFICE CONTACTS

AUSTRALIA
2 Park Street, **Sydney** NSW 2000
Tel: +61 2 9263 4000 **Fax:** +61 2 9263 4111
Email: email@gtlaw.com.au

FIRM OVERVIEW

Managing partner: Danny Gilbert

Number of partners worldwide: 32
Number of other lawyers worldwide: 150

AREAS OF PRACTICE:

Communications and technology	35%
Corporate and commercial	33%
Litigation	13%
Intellectual property	11%
Competition law and utilities regulation	8%

FIRM OVERVIEW: Gilbert & Tobin is a specialist commercial law firm, established in 1988 and widely recognised as the most successful new law firm to emerge in recent years. Its reputation is based on excellence in the industry sectors building the emerging digital economy. The firm is ranked among the top 10 advisers in Australia in mergers and acquisitions (as ranked by Thomson Financial Securities Data) and it was recently named one of the best companies to work for in Australia by Corporate Research Foundation (HarperBusiness 1999). Pro bono work is undertaken and the firm has two lawyers dedicated to the provision of pro bono assistance.

INTERNATIONAL EXPERIENCE: While the majority of the firm's work is based in Australia, a number of its practice areas involve international work. It advises CLEAR (a wholly-owned British Telecom subsidiary) in New Zealand on regulatory and interconnection matters. It advises Cable & Wireless HKT (formerly Hongkong Telecom) on an ongoing basis on a wide range of legal and regulatory issues. The firm has also provided regulatory and other advice to companies in Hong Kong, India, Malaysia, Singapore, South Africa, Sri Lanka, UK, US and Korea.

INTERNATIONAL CLIENTS: The firm's clients include the Vodaphone AirTouch Group, Cable & Wireless (London), Cable & Wireless HKT (formerly Hongkong Telecom), Jardine Fleming, One 2 One, SingTel, Sri Lanka Telecom, Samsung, South African Telecommunications Regulatory Authority (SATRA), Lucent Technologies Inc, Pico Holdings Inc (North American investment company), Safety Equipment Australia Pty Limited, John Hancock Mutual Life Insurance Company, Publishing & Broadcasting Limited, AGL, Macquarie Bank, Sons of Gwalia, Rural Press, Email, George Weston Foods, Capral Aluminium, CSR, Perpetual Trustees, Tourism Asset Holdings, Aristocrat Leisure, Australian Multimedia Enterprise, Australian Technology Group, Cable & Wireless Optus, Compaq, CNN, LibertyOne, MNET, MediaOne, NCR, Ninemsn, Nine Network Australia, Ozemail, Peoplesoft, Red Square, Siemens, Turner Broadcasting Systems, ecorp, AAP, ACCOR, Babcock & Brown, Paramount Pictures, Cisco and Road Runner.

MAIN INTERNATIONAL AREAS OF PRACTICE:

Communications: Telecommunications, Internet infrastructure and peering arrangements, pay and free-to-air television, broadcasting and content.
Competition law and utilities regulation: Strategic transactions, ACCC clearance for mergers and JV's, representation in ACCC inquiries and prosecutions, third party access to infrastructure and services and proactive compliance.
e-Business: Internet commerce (online retailing and other business-to-business/ business-to-consumer transaction), internet intermediaries (market makers in vertical industries, portal and content providers), internet infrastructure.
Information technology: IT&T outsourcing, IT procurement contracts, e-commerce, joint ventures, major projects, strategic transactions.
Intellectual property: Copyright, trade marks, brands and domain names, designs, patents, commercialising and enforcing intellectual property rights in the areas of music law, on-line content, publishing, film, broadcasting and television, marketing and advertising, retailing, manufacturing and technology.
Litigation: Commercial litigation, media and defamation, sport, trade practices, marketing and advertising, information technology, telecommunications, intellectual property, insolvency and reconstruction, Corporations law, industrial relations.
Projects and finance: Infrastructure, utilities, managed investments, tourism, corporate property, government property, banking and finance.
Energy: Integrated corporate, regulatory and dispute resolution advisory services for the gas, electricity and water industries.
Health: Regulatory, intellectual property, trade marks, property, corporate and commercial, IT contracts, outsourcing, on-line products, compliance products and litigation.
Privacy: Online privacy compliance and training programme, privacy review and audits, privacy code development.
Pro Bono: Gilbert & Tobin has a strong commitment to providing free legal services to those who cannot afford representation. Special consideration is given to people with disabilities, Aboriginal people, children and young people and organisations working in these areas.

LANGUAGES: Cantonese, Croatian, French, German, Greek, Indonesian, Italian, Japanese, Malay, Mandarin, Polish, Russian, Spanish

LAWYERS

For other recommended firms see pages 1485-1520

GLEISS LUTZ HOOTZ HIRSCH

HEAD OFFICE

Maybachstrasse 6,
D-70469 Stuttgart, Germany
Tel: +49 711 89 97 0 **Fax:** +49 711 85 50 96

Email: info@stu.gleiss-law.com
Website: www.gleiss-law.com

FIRM OVERVIEW

Contact: Gerhard Wegen

Number of partners worldwide: 73
Number of other lawyers worldwide: 101

AREAS OF PRACTICE:

Banking and finance .... *%
Competition law .... *%
Corporate/M&A .... *%
Employment .... *%
Environmental and pollution control .... *%
EU and anti-trust .... *%
Insurance .... *%
Intellectual property .... *%
Labour law .... *%
Media and IP .... *%
Real estate .... *%
Tax .... *%
Telecommunications .... *%
* Workload % not disclosed

FIRM OVERVIEW: Gleiss Lutz Hootz Hirsch was founded by Professor Dr Alfred Gleiss in 1949. It developed from an anti-trust boutique in the 1960's into a full service corporate firm. The Brussels office was founded for EU anti-trust purposes in 1987. Further offices were established in Frankfurt and Berlin (1990), Prague (1992), Shanghai (1996) and Warsaw (1998). Gleiss Lutz Hootz Hirsch has 174 lawyers and will be opening an office in Munich in 2001.

INTERNATIONAL EXPERIENCE: Gleiss Lutz Hootz Hirsch has had considerable international exposure through its anti-trust work in Germany and the EU and has advised foreign clients, particularly from the US. Gleiss Lutz Hootz Hirsch announced a formal association with the London based international law firm Herbert Smith, which has a particularly strong practice in Asia. Gleiss Lutz Hootz Hirsch has also agreed on an informal relationship with Cravath Swaine & Moore, Simpson Thacher & Bartlett, as well as Paul, Weiss, Rifkind, Wharton & Garrison of New York.

INTERNATIONAL CLIENTS: The firm advises a broad variety of international clients from Europe, the US and Canada as well as from Asia covering all sectors of industrial activity, in particular, financial services, manufacturing, telecommunications, pharmaceutical, software and e-commerce as well as wholesale and retail chains.

WORLDWIDE OFFICE CONTACTS

BELGIUM
Rue Guimard 7, B-1040 **Brussels**
Tel: +32 2 551 10 20 **Fax:** +32 2 512 15 68
Email: info@brx.gleiss-law.com

CHINA
Shanghai Bund International Tower, 17th Floor, 99 Huangpu Road, **Shanghai** 200080
Tel: +86 21 6393 9155 **Fax:** +86 21 6393 9156
Email: gleiss-shanghai@gleiss.com.cn

CZECH REPUBLIC
Jugoslavska 29, CR-120 00 **Prague** 2
Tel: +420 2 24007 500 **Fax:** +420 2 24007 555
Email: info@prg.gleiss-law.com

GERMANY
Friedrichstadt-Passagen, Friedrichstraße 71, D-10117 **Berlin**
Tel: +49 30 2094 6400 **Fax:** +49 30 2094 6444
Email: info@bln.gleiss-law.com

Gärtnerweg 2, D-60322 **Frankfurt am Main**
Tel: +49 69 955 140 **Fax:** +49 69 9551 4198
Email: info@ffm.gleiss-law.com

Prinzregentstrasse 50, **Munich,** D-80538
Email: info@muc.gleiss-law.com

Maybachstrasse 6, D-70469 **Stuttgart**
Tel: +49 711 89 97 0 **Fax:** +49 711 85 50 96
Email: info@stu.gleiss-law.com

POLAND
ul. Sienna 39, PL 00121 **Warsaw**
Tel: +48 22 526 5500 **Fax:** +48 22 526 5555
Email: info@war.gleiss-law.com

MAIN INTERNATIONAL AREAS OF PRACTICE: The firm practices in the areas of EU, competition and anti-trust; banking and finance; corporate; insurance; intellectual property; M&A; tax; telecommunications; and media and IP.

LANGUAGES: Czech, Dutch, English, French, German, Italian, Mandarin, Cantonese, Polish, Portuguese, Russian, Slovak, Spanish

For other recommended firms see pages 1485-1520

ADVOKATFIRMAN GLIMSTEDT

HEAD OFFICE

Hovslagargatan 5 PO Box 16108,
SE-103 22 Stockholm, Sweden
Tel: +46 8 566 11 900 **Fax:** +46 8 566 11 949

Email: stockholm@glimstedt.se
Website: www.glimstedt.se

FIRM OVERVIEW

Contact partner: Jan Litborn

Number of partners worldwide: 62
Number of other lawyers worldwide: 27

AREAS OF PRACTICE:

Banking and finance	*%
Commercial property	*%
Corporate	*%
Insolvency	*%
Litigation and arbitration	*%
M&A	*%

* Workload % not disclosed

FIRM OVERVIEW: Advokatfirman Glimstedt is one of Sweden's larger business law firms, with 12 offices in Sweden and one in Lithuania. It focuses on corporate, banking and finance and commercial property, acting for international and domestic companies, and acts for both international and domestic companies and small local businesses.The firm is a member of the Association of European Lawyers.

INTERNATIONAL EXPERIENCE: The firm has advised on several cross-border M&A transactions as well as on the establishment of foreign companies in Sweden and abroad.

MAIN INTERNATIONAL AREAS OF PRACTICE:
M&A: The firm frequently advises both international and national companies acquiring businesses and forming joint ventures in Sweden and in other locations in Europe and the rest of the world. In 1999 it advised on the formation of a successful joint venture in the Middle East and Asia.
Banking and finance: Work includes project finance, structured finance, leasing and secured loan transactions.
Commercial property: The focus is on sale and purchase as well as commercial leasehold transactions.
Corporate: The firm advises on all aspects of general corporate law, including drawing up contracts, company formations and issues regarding company instruments.
Insolvency: Several partners are certified administrators of bankruptcy estates, and have substantial experience in insolvency law. The firm handles all types of insolvency work, including company reconstructions.
Litigation and arbitration: The firm has broad experience in commercial litigation and of cases before the Swedish Courts, including the Supreme Court.
Other areas of practice: Franchising, competitition/antitrust, intellectual property, marketing and employment.

LANGUAGES: English, French, German, Lithuanian, Russian, Swedish.

WORLDWIDE OFFICE CONTACTS

LITHUANIA
A. Gostauto 12A, VII floor, LT-2001 **Vilnius**
Tel: +370 2 683 700 **Fax:** +370 2 225 649
Email: glimstedt@taide.lt

SWEDEN
Howslagargatan 5 PO Box 16108, SE-10322 **Stockholm**
Tel: +46 8 566 11 900 **Fax:** +46 8 566 11 949
Email: stockholm@glimstedt.se

WORLDWIDE OFFICES

LITHUANIA

A. Gostauto 12A, VII floor, LT-2001 Vilnius

Contact lawyer: Fredric Forsman

Number of lawyers: 10
Number of locally qualified lawyers: 9

Office profile: The Vilnius office was established in 1997. Approximately 35% of its work consists of M&A, including acting for a major world brewery acquiring Lithuania's largest brewer. Foreign investment work accounts for another 30% and is mostly for clients from Scandinavia, France, the UK and US. Privatisation work forms 20%, with deals including the privatisation of the Lithuanian State Agriculture Bank and the Mazeiku Nafta oil company, in which the office represented the Lithuanian Ministry of the Economy. The firm has also represented foreign and domestic acquirors in privatisations. Banking clients include the Lithuanian Ministry of the Economy and the World Bank, as well as international commercial and investment banks. Project finance work includes acting for a Swedish investor group in a joint venture hotel project with Vilnius City Council and representing a global UK-based bank financing the upgrading of a Lithuanian petrochemical facility.

ADVOKATFIRMAN
GLIMSTEDT

G

GOLDBERG, KOHN, BELL, BLACK, ROSENBLOOM & MORITZ, LTD

HEAD OFFICE

55 East Monroe Street, Suite 3700,
Chicago Illinois 60603, USA
Tel: +1 312 201 4000 **Fax:** +1 312 332 2196

Email: info@goldbergkohn.com
Website: www.goldbergkohn.com

WORLDWIDE OFFICE CONTACTS

USA
55 East Monroe Street, Suite 3700, **Chicago** Illinois 60603
Tel: +1 312 201 4000 **Fax:** +1 312 332 2196
Email: info@goldbergkohn.com

FIRM OVERVIEW

Number of partners worldwide: 32
Number of other lawyers worldwide: 38

AREAS OF PRACTICE:

Class action defense .... *%
Commercial finance .... *%
Corporate, tax and securities .... *%
Creditors rights and bankruptcy .... *%
Education .... *%
Employment .... *%
Intellectual property .... *%
IT and e-commerce .... *%
Litigation and ADR .... *%
Policyholders insurance coverage .... *%
Real estate .... *%
* Workload % not disclosed

FIRM OVERVIEW: Goldberg, Kohn was established in 1976 by three young partners from an established Chicago firm. The firm's growth has been primarily achieved through internal business development rather than from mergers with other firms or individual practices.

INTERNATIONAL EXPERIENCE: The firm represents US based banks and other lenders in connection with multi-jurisdictional loans as well as loan workouts and insolvency proceedings. It also advises US based manufacturing, distribution, retail and licensing clients on their operations outside of the US including acquisitions, distribution and licensing agreements, joint ventures and intellectual property registration and maintenance. The firm is a member of the Commercial Law Affiliates, through which it has developed effective working relationships with highly qualified independent law firms in over 60 countries outside the US.

INTERNATIONAL CLIENTS: The firm advises foreign businesses on acquisitions, dispositions, joint ventures and strategic alliances in the US. It also handles the establishment of US based subsidiaries and branch office and acts as US counsel to such businesses for the full range of their legal needs in the US. The firm has represented US and offshore entities in insolvency and restructuring proceedings in various countries.

MAIN INTERNATIONAL AREAS OF PRACTICE:

Class action defence: The firm defends banks, credit card and finance companies, debt collectors, attorneys in the collection industry, and consumer product companies in various courts against class actions brought under both state and federal law.
Commercial finance: The firm has represented clients in international lending transactions in Europe, Asia and South, and Central America, including taking foreign collateral or guarantees and financing cross-border acquisitions involving funding in multiple currencies.
IT and e-commerce: The firm advises clients on a variety of information technology, internet and e-commerce business issues, including privacy, cross-border data transfers, security, website design and operations, hosting, software development, licensing, supply and distibution-chain agreements, outsourcing and jurisdictional matters.
Corporate, tax and securities: The firm's corporate group represents large public companies, mid-sized and emerging businesses, limited and general partnerships and limited liability companies, some of which are multinational. The practice is diverse and includes mergers and acquisitions, reorganisation transactions, tax planning and structuring, joint ventures and other general corporate advice. The firm also represents corporate securities issuers in direct placements of a wide variety of debt and equity instruments.
Creditors rights and bankruptcy: The firm represents lenders and other creditors in bankruptcy proceedings, enforcement activity, and out-of-court workouts.
Education law: The firm's education industry group has invested significant resources towards understanding the dynamics of school reforms, including technological reforms. Through its involvement with key education experts it strives to predict and influence how legal and business issues will evolve in this dynamic environment.
Intellectual property: The firm regularly works with clients regarding all aspects of trademarks, copyrights, trade secrets and license/distribution agreements. It also advises on how best to protect such assets. Where disputes arise, it regularly handles litigation matters involving trademark infringement, unfair competition, dilution, misuse/misappropriation of trade secrets and copyright infringement. The IP group also evaluates new trademarks and other marketing efforts, including analysis of trademark searches and the review of proposed promotions and commercial symbols.
Employment: The firm advises employees on a wide variety of employment actions in courts and administrative agencies around the country. The firm also counsels clients regarding the many labour and employment issues that arise in connection with various acquisition, divestiture and reorganisation transactions.
Litigation and ADR: The firm's approach to litigation combines professional aggressiveness with legal creativity. Goldberg, Kohn looks for the solution that best serves its clients' goals.
Policyholders insurance coverage: The firm's services encompass all phases of the risk management process, including policy review and procurement, tender of claims, negotiation, and litigation of disputes.
Real estate: The firm handles every aspect of commercial property transactions including acquisitions, dispositions, developments, financings, sale and leasebacks, synthetic leasing, workouts, retail, office, industrial, specialty leasing, environmental, construction, and zoning.

LANGUAGES: Dutch, English, Flemish, French, German, Greek, Spanish

 For other recommended firms see pages 1485-1520

GOMEZ-ACEBO & POMBO

HEAD OFFICE

Castellana 164,
28046 Madrid, Spain
Tel: +34 91 582 9100 **Fax:** +34 91 345 3679

Email: abogados@gomez-acebo-pombo.com
Website: www.gomezacebo-pombo.com

FIRM OVERVIEW

Executive president: Fernando Pombo
President: Ignacio Gomez-Acebo
Managing partner: Fernando de las Cuevas

Number of partners worldwide: 31
Number of other lawyers worldwide: 138

AREAS OF PRACTICE:

Financial law	15%
Intellectual property	15%
Litigation and arbitration	15%
Mergers and aquisitions	15%
Real estate and environment	10%
Tax	10%
Telecommunications and media	10%
Employment	5%
Insurance and reinsurance	5%

FIRM OVERVIEW: The firm was founded in 1971 by Ignacio Gómez-Acebo and Fernando Pombo with the objective of providing high quality, specialised and personalised integrated legal advice. The firm has offices in the key commercial centres of Spain, such as Madrid, Barcelona, Bilbao, Las Palmas de Gran Canaria, Sevilla, Malaga, Valencia and Vigo. The firm also etablished an office in Brussels in 1985. The firm has been actively involved in the globalisation of the Spanish economy through the deregulation of exchange controls and inward investment in Spain. The firm has also helped with the integration of Spanish businesses into European and Latin-American markets and has formed alliances with Portuguese law firm Vieira de Almeida, Brazilian firm Pinheiro Neto and Beccar Varela in Argentina.

INTERNATIONAL EXPERIENCE: Half of the firm's turnover is derived from foreign clients or their Spanish subsidiaries.

INTERNATIONAL CLIENTS: Clients include British Telecom, ICI, GEC, Rolls Royce, Royal-Sun Alliance, National Westminster Bank, SmithKline Beecham, and Glaxo Wellcome from the UK, General Electric Corporation, Microsoft, and Boeing of the USA, Nomura and Dai-Ichi Bank of Japan; Dresdner Bank and Westdeutsche Landesbank of Germany, Société Générale and BNP of France, and Scadinaviska, and Enskilda Banken of Sweden.

MAIN INTERNATIONAL AREAS OF PRACTICE: Work handled is varied and includes mergers and acquisitions; intellectual property; real estate and development; foreign investment; litigation and arbitration; tax; employment; insurance; telecommunications and media.

LANGUAGES: Basque, Catalan, English, French, German, Italian, Japanese, Portuguese

OFFICE CONTACTS

BELGIUM
Rue de la Loi, 99/101, 1040 **Brussels**
Tel: +32 2 231 1220 **Fax:** +32 2 230 8035
Email: abogados.brx@gomezacebo-pombo.com

SPAIN
Diagonal, 442, 08037 **Barcelona**
Tel: +34 93 415 74 00 **Fax:** +34 94 415 84 00
Email: abogados.bcn@gomezacebo-pombo.com

Gran Vía, 31, 48009 **Bilbao**
Tel: +34 94 415 70 15 **Fax:** +34 94 415 21 80
Email: abogados.bil@gomezacebo-pombo.com

Viera y Clavijo, 48, 35002 **Las Palmas**, Canarias
Tel: +34 928 38 38 36 **Fax:** +34 928 38 38 56
Email: abogados.bcn@gomezacebo-pombo.com

Marqués de Larios, 3, 28015 **Malaga**
Tel: +34 952 12 00 51 **Fax:** +34 952 12 00 59
Email: abogados.mal@gomezacebo-pombo.com

Av. de la Constitucion, 40, **41001 Seville**
Tel: +34 95 421 66 59 **Fax:** +34 95 421 08 14
Email: abogados.sev@gomezacebo-pombo.com

Gran Via Marqués del Turia, 49, 46005 **Valencia**
Tel: +34 96 351 38 35 **Fax:** +34 96 351 60 74
Email: abogados.vlc@gomezacebo-pombo.es

Plaza de Compostela. 29, 36201 **Vigo**
Tel: +34 986 44 33 80 **Fax:** +34 986 44 30 17
Email: gapo.vig@gomezacebo-pombo.com

ASSOCIATED OFFICES

ARGENTINA
Estudio Beccar Valera,
Tel: +54 11 4379 68 00 **Fax:** +54 11 4379 68 60
Email: estudio@beccarv.com.ar

BRAZIL
Pinheiro Neto-Advogados,
Tel: +55 11 237 8400 **Fax:** +55 11 237 8600
Email: pna@pinheironeo.com.br

PORTUGAL
Vieira de Almeida-Advogados,
Tel: +351 21 311 34 00 **Fax:** +351 21 354 8939
Email: vieiradealmeida.p

WORLDWIDE OFFICES

BELGIUM

Rue de la Loi, 99/101, 1040 Brussels

Number of lawyers: 6

Office profile: The Brussels office opened shortly before Spain joined the EU, and now has six lawyers. It is one of the biggest foreign law offices in Brussels, and deals with all aspects of EU law, not only for Spanish clients but also for clients from other countries.

For other recommended firms see pages 1485-1520

GOMEZ PINZON & ASOCIADOS

HEAD OFFICE

Carrera 9 No 73-24, Piso 1,2,3,4,
Santafe de Bogota 057629 Bogota, Colombia
Tel: +57 1 310 5066 **Fax:** +57 1 310 6646

Email: gpa@gomezpinzon.com
Website: www.gomezpinzon.com

FIRM OVERVIEW

Managing partner: Alejandro Linares

Number of partners worldwide: 5
Number of other lawyers worldwide: 25

AREAS OF PRACTICE:

Banking and finance .... *%
Corporate .... *%
Energy, oil and gas .... *%
Insurance and reinsurance .... *%
Intellectual property .... *%
Litigation and arbitration .... *%
M&A .... *%
Tax .... *%
Telecommunications and computer law .... *%
*Workload % not disclosed

FIRM PROFILE: Founded in 1992, the firm has expanded rapidly in recent years both in terms of volume of work and number of attorneys. The firm has a talented group of young but experienced lawyers and a balanced portfolio of national and international clients, with an emphasis on cross-border structured finance. Other core areas of practice are privatisation, project finance, M&A, banking, capital markets and taxation.

INTERNATIONAL EXPERIENCE: The firm has been involved in most of the major cross-border infrastructure projects in Colombia. It advises extensively on international transactions with significant experience in cross-border and offshore project finance, corporate transactions, and securitisation.

INTERNATIONAL CLIENTS: The firm has a global client base including McCain Foods; Transcanada Energy; Positron PSS (Canada); Degrémont; Société Générale; Suez Lyonnaise des Eaux; Total (France); Neumann Gruppe; Veba Oil; BASF (Germany); Itochu Corporation; Japan Bank for International Cooperation; Nissho Iwai; Sumimoto; The Tokai Bank; Tomen Corporation (Japan); Cemex; Inverlat (Mexico); Norsk Hydro (Norway); Nimir Petroleum Company (Saudi Arabia); Banco Santander Investment Ltd.; Media Planning (Spain); ABN Amro Bank (Netherlands); BP Exploration Company; Heath Lambert Group; Standard Chartered Bank (UK); AT&T Capital Corporation; Bank of America; Bank of New York; Bankers Trust Company; Bear Stearns; Booz Allen & Hamilton; Bristol-Myers Squibb; Daimler-Chrysler; Computer Associates; Drummond Company, Inc.; Goldman Sachs & Co.; Gtech Corporation; Greka Energy; Harken Energy; International Generating Company; J.P. Morgan; Lehman Brothers; Lexmark; Merrill Lynch; Morgan Stanley Dean Witter; Owens-Illinois; Reliant Energy; Salomon Brothers Inc.; Scudder, Stevens & Clark; Sensormatic Electronics; Soros Fund Management; Starmedia Network; State Street Bank; Sun Microsystems; The Chase Manhattan Bank; Violy, Byorum & Partners; Westsphere Equity Investors; Whirlpool (US); C.A. Telecomunicaciones de Caracas; Inelectra (Venezuela).

WORLDWIDE OFFICE CONTACTS

COLOMBIA
Carrera 9 No 73-24, Piso 1,2,3,4, Santafe de Bogota 057629 **Bogota**
Tel: +57 1 310 5066 **Fax:** +57 1 310 6646
Email: gpa@gomezpinzon.com

MAIN INTERNATIONAL AREAS OF PRACTICE:

Project finance: The firm has broad experience as adviser for sponsors, underwriters, international private banks and developers in significant project finance operations, particularly in the areas of oil and gas, energy generation, water treatment, railroad concessions, toll road concessions, and telecommunications.

Capital markets: Gomez Pinzon & Asociados advises the managers, underwriters and placement agents in the majority of offerings of bonds and medium term notes issued by the Republic of Colombia and other governmental entities.

M&A: The firm advises large companies, banks, insurance companies, oil and gas companies and public or supranational institutions conducting cross-border operations.

Privatisations: The firm has advised on a large number of privatisations in Colombia, especially in the financial, energy, infrastructure and telecommunications areas. It has advised public entities and private companies, through the whole process of sale of state owned enterprises and the granting of licenses and concessions to operation of public services.

Telecommunications: The firm represents clients in almost all areas opened to investments, including private telephone networks, cellular phones, value added and direct satellite communication and subscription television. The firm has also acted as adviser for corporations and international banks interested in the area of telecommunications, including assistance with the regulatory framework, authorisations, licenses, financial structure and commercial operations in Colombia.

Energy, oil and gas: Gomez Pinzon & Asociados advises on matters relating to energy, gas, oil and mining, including assistance with contracts, authorisations and the financial structuring of their operations in Colombia.

Taxation: The firm advises on all aspects of this area.

Securitisation: Gomez Pinzon & Asociados represents both originators and financial institutions in a variety of asset-backed securitisation programs. It advises clients on the most appropriate funding for the issuer as well as tax issues.

Intellectual property: The firm's IP group advises in all areas of intellectual and industrial property, including trademarks, patent utility models, trade names, trade emblems copyright, and sanitary licenses. It advises on the registration and protection of their intellectual and industrial rights in accordance with the national and regional legislation and international treaties.

LANGUAGES: English, French, Spanish

For other recommended firms see pages 1485-1520

GONÇALVES PEREIRA, CASTELO BRANCO E ASSOC.

HEAD OFFICE

Praça Marquês de Pombal, 1-8th floor,
1250-160 Lisbon, Portugal
Tel: + 351 21 355 3800 **Fax:** + 351 21 353 23 62

Email: lisboa@gpcb.pt

FIRM OVERVIEW

Managing partner: Manuel Castelo Branco
Senior partner: André Gonçalves Pereira

Number of partners worldwide: 9
Number of lawyers worldwide: 54

AREAS OF PRACTICE:

M&A, general corporate law and labour law	40%
Banking and capital markets	15%
Litigation and arbitration	15%
Tax	15%
Media/telecommunications law	10%
Other	5%

WORLDWIDE OFFICE CONTACTS

PORTUGAL
Praça Marquês de Pombal, 1-8th floor, 1250-160 **Lisbon**
Tel: +351 21 355 3800 **Fax:** +351 21 353 2362 / 354 9784
Email: lisboa@gpcb.pt

Av. da Boavista, 3265-3°, No 3.3, 4100-137 **Porto**
Tel: +351 22 616 6920 **Fax:** +351 22 616 6949
Email: gpcb.porto@mail.telepac.pt

MOZAMBIQUE
Rua da Sé, 114-1°. No 16, **Maputo**
Tel: +258 1 30 86 48 / 49 / 50 **Fax:** +258 1 30 86 51
Email: cgpcb.maputo@teledata.mz

FIRM OVERVIEW: The firm was established in Lisbon in 1928, opening an office in Porto in 1989 and one in Maputo, Mozambique in 1998. In 1998 the firm signed an association agreement with the Spanish firm Cuatrecasas for the Iberian legal market. They then both signed an agreement with Machado, Meyer, Sendacz e Opice of Brazil and Perez Alati, Grondona, Benites, Arntsen & Martinez de Hoz of Argentina to cover the Ibero-American area. Today the firm has 54 lawyers, 9 of them partners, and 4 permanent paralegals with a total of 90 staff working on a permanent and exclusive basis.

INTERNATIONAL EXPERIENCE: The firm represents some of the major Portuguese companies, and advises American, European and Asian multinationals on their investments in Portugal. Among the transactions which the firm has recently handled are the privatisation of the airline industry, project finance for Portuguese motorways, US cross-border leasings for transport equipment; numerous mergers and acquisitions, the restructuring of Spanish and Portuguese banking activity, and the tax reorganisation of real estate developments.

INTERNATIONAL CLIENTS: The firm's client base covers a range of domestic and international companies in industry and banking.

MAIN INTERNATIONAL AREAS OF PRACTICE:
M&A, general corporate law and labour law: The firm's activities range from company incorporation, organisation and day-to-day functioning, to advice on mergers and acquitions and assisting in the preparation of employee agreement and issues involving trade unions, amonst others.
Banking and capital markets: The finance activities of the firm include, inter alia, tender offers, credit transactions, securities of assets and derivative transactions.
Litigation and arbitration: The firm provides advice on resolving and preventing disputes and prepares and develops argumentation before administrative, judicial and arbitral courts and tribunals.
Tax: The firm provides advice to corporate and private individuals and represents them in front of the authorities concerned.
Media telecommunications law: The firm advises clients on all aspects of media/telecommunications law, including regulatory and corporate issues.
Other: The firm is additionally qualified to provide advice in intellectual property, EU law, shipping, construction, real estate and environmental law, amongst others.

LANGUAGES: English, French, Spanish

WORLDWIDE OFFICES

MOZAMBIQUE

Rua da Sé, 114-1°. No 16, Maputo

Managing partner: Manuel Magalhaes

Number of lawyers: 8

Office profile: This office was opened in 1998, in response to the increasingly international focus of the firm's Portugal-based work. It handles corporate, banking, finance, administrative law, tax, contracts and litigation work.

GONÇALVES PEREIRA, CASTELO BRANCO
SOCIEDADE DE ADVOGADOS

GOODMAN AND CARR LLP

HEAD OFFICE

Suite 2300, 200 King Street West,
Toronto, Ontario, Canada M5H 3W5
Tel: +1 416 595 2300 **Fax:** +1 416 595 0567

Email: mail@goodmancarr.com
Website: www.goodmancarr.com

WORLDWIDE OFFICE CONTACTS

CANADA
Suite 2300, 200 King Street West, **Toronto**, Ontario M5H 3W5
Tel: +1 416 595 2300 **Fax:** +1 416 595 0567
Email: mail@goodmancarr.com

FIRM OVERVIEW

Managing partner: Gary H Luftspring

Number of partners worldwide: 62
Number of other lawyers worldwide: 56

AREAS OF PRACTICE:

Area	%
Corporate finance	30%
Commercial litigation	30%
Employment	10%
Real estate	10%
Entrepreneurial (technology, health)	10%
Tax	5%
Private client	5%

G

FIRM OVERVIEW: A full service firm created in 1965, Goodman and Carr LLP today has more than 140 legal professionals committed to providing outstanding client service. In addition to core practice areas, in excess of 20 specialty practice groups and industry-focused teams have emerged to better meet and anticipate the requirements of clients. These areas include merchant banking, initial public offerings, mergers, acquisitions and divestitures, professional liability, employment, human rights, commercial leasing, property development, franchising, health, retail, technology and private client wealth management.

At Goodman and Carr LLP each client is a client of the firm and a team approach is used to meet client requirements. The firm's ongoing objective is to leverage its experience and expertise in order to assist its clients.

INTERNATIONAL EXPERIENCE: The firm offers a broad range of services to a diversified and rapidly expanding roster of national and international clients. The firm serves as counsel and special counsel to a number of idividuals, small to medium-sized entrepreneurial clients as well as large international corporations, financial institutions, mutual funds, insurance companies and securities brokers throughout the USA and overseas. The firm has represented virtually every major merchant bank and has assisted them in establishing their operations. Goodman and Carr LLP has extensive experience in structuring and negotiating merchant banking transactions.

INTERNATIONAL CLIENTS: Goodman and Carr LLP's international client base includes large retail companies, several US corporations and private clients.

MAIN INTERNATIONAL AREAS OF PRACTICE:

Corporate finance and securities: Goodman and Carr LLP's transactions in this area include complex and sophisticated domestic and cross-border financings, amalgamations, purchase of shares and financings associated with acquisitions, corporate reorganisations and restructurings, establishment of effective tax plans and tax assisted syndications. The firm acts for Canadian capital market participants including public companies, mutual funds, investment dealers and investors. Services include debt and equity financings, initial public offerings, private placements and asset scrutinisations, acting for issuers, underwriters, special committees and shareholders.

Employment: Serving as counsel to management in a wide range of industries and represents multinational, national, regional and local employers at every stage of the employment relationship (hiring, HR issues, codes of conduct, employment contracts, terminations etc). Regularly assists international corporations with their obligations in establishing Canadian operations.

Retail: Acts for many big box retailers, anchors, shopping centre tenants and independent retail operations. Assists on sophisticated lease negotiations and documentation, franchising, import and export matters, commodities tax concerns and employment and immigration issues. Frequently consulted by retailers and lenders for advice concerning new retail opportunities.

Technology: The firm acts for high-technology businesses and includes all aspects of negotiating contracts, licensing of technology, strategic alliances, joint ventures and assessing and reorganising R&D initiatives.

LANGUAGES: Bengali, Cantonese, Dutch, English, French, German, Hebrew, Italian, Mandarin, Portuguese, Russian, Serbo-Croatian, Spanish, Turkish, Ukrainian, Yiddish

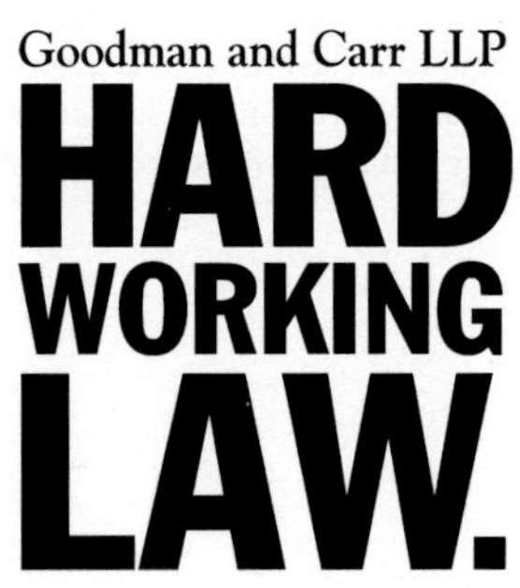

For other recommended firms see pages 1485-1520

GOODMANS LLP

HEAD OFFICE

250 Yonge Street, Suite 2400,
Toronto Ontario, Canada M5B 2M6
Tel: +1 416 979 2211 **Fax:** +1 416 979 1234

Website: www.goodmanslaw.com

FIRM OVERVIEW

Co-chairs: Dale Lastman, Allan Leibel
Managing partner: Richard Storrey

Number of partners worldwide: 80
Number of other lawyers worldwide: 92

AREAS OF PRACTICE:
Administrative law .... *%
Competition .... *%
Corporate/M&A .... *%
Finance and development .... *%
Litigation .... *%
Real estate .... *%
Sports and entertainment .... *%
Tax .... *%
* Workload % not disclosed

FIRM OVERVIEW: Goodmans, one of Canada's premier transaction law firms is well-recognised across Canada and internationally for expertise in large-scale corporate transactions as well as a broad range of key practice areas. Based in Toronto, the firm has grown to over 175 lawyers with offices in Vancouver and Hong Kong. Goodmans' primary focus remains its commitment to high quality corporate legal advice and client service and to further develop its practice areas.

INTERNATIONAL EXPERIENCE: Goodmans has represented clients from around the world, including the US, France, Asia, Australia, New Zealand and Israel. Goodmans also advises numerous Canadian clients on overseas business activities. Over the past few years, the firm has helped businesses and investment banks raise billions of dollars in equity and debt financing through public offerings and private placements. Goodmans is particularly strong globally in merger and acquisitions and takeovers; international tax structuring; negotiating and drafting joint ventures and multinational debt restructuring. Goodmans advises major domestic and international businesses, industry associations and governments on a broad spectrum of international trade matters, including WTO and NAFTA obligations and dispute settlement, investor-state dispute settlement, government procurement bid challenges, anti-dumping duties, safeguards, customs duties, export and import controls and compliance with the Corruption of Foreign Public Officials Act and money laundering legislation.

INTERNATIONAL CLIENTS: Clients range from small business enterprises to multinational corporations, financial institutions, government bodies, international agencies, regulatory bodies, as well as other organisations in fields as diverse as commercial real estate, manufacturing, retail, development financing, energy, financial services, newspapers, oil and gas, mining, high technology, forest products, telecommunications, computer software and film and television production.

WORLDWIDE OFFICE CONTACTS

CANADA
Goodmans LLP, 250 Yonge Street, Suite 2400, **Toronto** ON M5B 2M6
Tel: +1 416 979 2211 **Fax:** +1 416 979 1234

CANADA
Goodmans, 355 Burrard Street, Suite 1900, **Vancouver** BC V6C 2G8
Tel: +1 604 682 7737 **Fax:** +1 604 682 7131

HONG KONG
Goodmans, 8/F Aon China Building, 29 Queen's Road Central, **Hong Kong**
Tel: +852 2522 1061 **Fax:** +852 2835 9089

MAIN INTERNATIONAL AREAS OF PRACTICE: Goodmans is a full service business law practice with particular emphasis and expertise in, transactional matters such as corporate financings; mergers and acquisitions and restructurings, both public and private; real estate acquisition and disposition; securities; finance and development; and tax planning. Goodmans also has substantial practices in litigation, intellectual property, information technology, broadcasting, telecommunications and new media, sports and entertainment, international trade, privatisation, public/private projects and project finance, administrative law and competition.

LANGUAGES: Cantonese, English, French, German, Hebrew, Italian, Mandarin, Portuguese, Spanish

GOODMANS

G

GOULART PENTEADO, IERVOLINO E LEFOSSE ADVOGADOS

HEAD OFFICE

Rua Paes Leme 524, 6° e 7° andares,
05424-904 São Paulo SP, Brazil
Tel: +55 11 3816 7399 **Fax:** +55 11 3031-5008

Email: gpilbra@gpilbra.com.br
Website: www.gpilbra.com.br

WORLDWIDE OFFICE CONTACTS

BRAZIL

SCS, Quadra 6, bloco A, 157, sala 303, Edifício Bandeirantes, **Brasília,** DF
Tel: +55 61 322-5101 **Fax:** +55 61 322-5899
Email: gpildf@gpilbra.com.br

Rua Paes Leme 524, 6° e 7° andares, 05424-904 **São Paulo,** SP
Tel: +55 11 3816 7399 **Fax:** +55 11 3031-5008
Email: gpilbra@gpilbra.com.br

FIRM OVERVIEW

Senior Partners: João Caio Goulart Penteado, Flávio Iervolino, Geraldo Roberto Lefosse Jr.

Number of partners worldwide: 9
Number of other lawyers worldwide: 46

AREAS OF PRACTICE:

Corporate, M&A, contracts	40%
Litigation and arbitration	18%
Competition and anti-trust	10%
Tax	8%
Employment	7%
Intellectual property and IT	6%
Real estate, environmental law	6%
Capital markets, securities, project finance	5%

FIRM OVERVIEW: Founded in 1987 the firm specialises in M&A but also offers comprehensive legal advice in other areas of law. The firm has a sustainable growth policy designed to ensure high quality, creative legal advice.

INTERNATIONAL EXPERIENCE: During 1999 and 2000 the firm advised on over 50 M&A cross-border transactions.

INTERNATIONAL CLIENTS: A large number of the firm's clients are multinational companies based in North America and Europe and/or their Brazilian subsidiaries. Its clients are engaged in various fields including automotive, agricultural and industrial equipment, petrochemicals, mining, chemical and pharmaceutical products, energy, communications and telecommunications, media, information technology, agribusiness, foods and beverages, transportation and logistics, real estate, consumer goods, and services in general, including financial services.

MAIN INTERNATIONAL AREAS OF PRACTICE:

Corporate, M&A, contracts: The firm advises international clients on local and cross-border transactions, providing support in the structuring, tax planning, negotiation, compliance with governmental agencies' regulation and formalisation of corporate and all other types of contracts and agreements. It has also developed and followed up on projects involving innovative and sophisticated processes, especially in the automotive and information technology industries, creating the contractual structures for these enterprises.

Capital markets, securities, project finance: The firm assists Brazilian and international companies in privatisations and in the issuing and public offering of stock and other securities. Work includes foreign investment projects and various infrastructure projects, and the firm has acquired significant experience in structuring finance operations.

Intellectual property, information technology: Activities include advising leading information technology companies on the protection of intellectual property rights.

Competition and anti-trust: The practice is increasingly active in advising on competition law and on the structuring, application and proceedings regarding transactions that involve market concentration.

Litigation and arbitration: The firm handles litigation cases in virtually all areas of law and has substantial experience in alternative dispute resolution. Some of its partners are qualified arbitrators for local and international arbitrations.

GOULART PENTEADO,
IERVOLINO & LEFOSSE
ADVOGADOS

G

For other recommended firms see pages 1485-1520

GOWLINGS

HEAD OFFICE

Commerce Court West, Suite 4900
Toronto ON M5L 1J3, Canada
Tel: +1 416 862 7525 **Fax:** +1 416 862 7661

Email: scott.jolliffe@gowlings.com
Website: www.gowlings.com

FIRM OVERVIEW

Managing partner: R Scott Jolliffe
Chief operating officer Sharon Mitchell

Number of partners worldwide: 308
Number of other lawyers worldwide: 250

AREAS OF PRACTICE:

Litigation	35%
Corporate	30%
Intellectual property	26%
Banking	9%

FIRM OVERVIEW: Founded in 1887, Gowlings is one of the largest full-service law firms in Canada. With 570 professionals working in Canada's technological and financial centres as well as in Moscow, the firm provides a complete range of financial, corporate and commercial services, both domestically and internationally. It has a large and highly-rated IP group which provides a natural complement to the technology and e-commerce focus to much of its corporate work. The firm's credentials are enhanced by its substantial public and private sector experience on a national and international level.

INTERNATIONAL EXPERIENCE: Gowlings has a worldwide reputation as a leader in the protection of intellectual property and international trade. The firm advises clients with interests in Russia and the Commonwealth of Independent States as well as those operating in the United States, Mexico and Latin America, China and the Pacific Rim, and Western Europe.

INTERNATIONAL CLIENTS: Gowlings' international client base comprises banks and other financial institutions, multinational corporations, manufacturers, software and technology developers, and government agents.

MAIN INTERNATIONAL AREAS OF PRACTICE: During its ongoing dealings with business and government, Gowlings has established strong working relationships with government agencies, businesses and professional service firms across Canada and around the world. The firm provides legal expertise in a range of domestic and international services in areas such as corporate and commercial law; advocacy; public and administrative law; intellectual property law; banking; financial services; taxation; insolvency law; securities; real estate and environmental law.

LANGUAGES: English, French, Italian, Russian, Spanish

WORLDWIDE OFFICE CONTACTS

CANADA

Suite 1400, 700-2nd Street SW, **Calgary** AB T2P 4V2
Tel: +1 403 298 1000 **Fax:** +1 403 263 9193
Email: john.iredale@gowlings.com

Suite 560, 120 King Street West, **Hamilton** ON L8P 4V2
Tel: +1 905 540 8208 **Fax:** +1 905 528 5833
Email: robert.wilkins@gowlings.com

Suite 1020, 50 Queen Street North, **Kitchener** ON N2H 6M2
Tel: +1 519 576 6910 **Fax:** +1 519 576 6030
Email: john.doherty@gowlings.com

37th Floor 1 Place Ville-Marie, **Montreal** PQ H3B 3PY
Tel: +1 514 878 9641 **Fax:** +1 514 878 1450
Email: luc.lissoir@gowlings.com

Suite 2600, 160 Elgin Street, **Ottawa** ON K1P 1C3
Tel: +613 233 1781 **Fax:** +613 563 9869
Email: henry.brown@gowlings.com

Commerce Court West, Suite 4900, **Toronto** ON M5L 1J3
Tel: +1 416 862 7525 **Fax:** +1 416 862 7661
Email: scott.jolliffe@gowlings.com

Suite 2300, 1055 Dunsmuir Street, PO Box 49122, Bentall IV, **Vancouver** BC V7X 1J1
Tel: +1 604 683 6498 **Fax:** +1 604 683 3558
Email: shayne.strukoff@gowlings.com

RUSSIA

Prechistensky Perevlok 14, Building 1, 4th Floor, 119034 **Moscow**
Tel: +7 501 787 2070 **Fax:** +7 501 787 2071
Email: kathryn.szymczyk@gowlings.com

GRAY CARY WARE & FREIDENRICH LLP

HEAD OFFICE

400 Hamilton Avenue,
Palo Alto CA 94301-1825, USA
Tel: +1 650 833 2000 **Fax:** +1 650 833 2001

Email: info@graycary.com
Website: www.graycary.com

WORLDWIDE OFFICE CONTACTS

USA

100 Congress Avenue, Suite 1440, **Austin** TX 78701
Tel: +1 512 457 7000 **Fax:** +1 512 457 7070

400 Hamilton Avenue, **Palo Alto** CA 94301-1825
Tel: +1 650 833 2000 **Fax:** +1 650 833 2001

400 Capitol Mall, Suite 2400, **Sacramento** CA 95814
Tel: +1 916 930 3200 **Fax:** +1 916 930 3201

401 B Street, Suite 1700, **San Diego** CA 92101
Tel: +1 619 699 2700 **Fax:** +1 619 699 2701

4365 Executive Drive, Suite 1600, **San Diego** CA 699-2701
Tel: +1 858 677 1400 **Fax:** +1 858 677 1477

139 Townsend Street, Suite 400, **San Francisco** CA 94107
Tel: +1 415 836 2500 **Fax:** +1 415 836 9220

999 Third Avenue, Suite 4000, **Seattle** WA 98104
Tel: +1 206 839 4800 **Fax:** +1 206 839 4801

FIRM OVERVIEW

Chairman: J.Terence O'Malley
Managing partner (Northern region): John R. Shuman, Jr
Managing partner (Southern region): Jeffrey M. Shohet

Number of partners worldwide: 144
Number of other lawyers worldwide: 454

AREAS OF PRACTICE:

Area	%
Corporate and securities	38%
Intellectual property and technology	31%
Litigation	11%
Real estate	9%
Tax and trusts	6%
Employment	5%

G

FIRM OVERVIEW: Gray Cary Ware & Freidenrich LLP is a Silicon Valley based firm that represents emerging growth and high technology companies. Comprising more than 450 attorneys, the firm has offices in Palo Alto, San Diego, San Francisco, Sacramento, Austin and Seattle. The firm is organised into distinct practice areas based on specific industries or complementary areas of law. It provides expertise, responsiveness, and cost effective solutions in order to meet the needs of each client. Members work as business counsellors to the client's management team, providing practical, innovative solutions.

INTERNATIONAL CLIENTS: The firm's client base includes global public and private companies, ranging from start-ups to Fortune Global 500. It advises emerging growth companies in technology, telecommunications, manufacturing, software, life sciences, healthcare, real estate, media, service providers, investment banks and financial institutions, venture capitalists, entrepreneurs, and individuals.

MAIN INTERNATIONAL AREAS OF PRACTICE:
Corporate and securities: The firm advises on the negotiation of joint ventures (including due diligence on potential partners, country risk and business issues); acquiring and selling foreign companies and other business entities; US legal issues relating to foreign acquisitions of US entities (including US report requirements); structuring international channels of distribution; drafting outbound and inbound sales and service agreements, agency agreements and representation agreements.
Intellectual property: The firm specialises in protecting clients' intellectual property rights including copyrights, trademarks, and patents. They also handle the preparation of international software licensing agreements.
Other: Other international practice areas include employment, litigation, real estate, tax and trusts.

LANGUAGES: Chinese, French, German, Hindi, Hungarian, Japanese, Mandarin, Polish, Punjabi, Spanish, Urdu, Vietnamese

GRAYCARY.
TECHNOLOGY'S LEGAL EDGE®

For other recommended firms see pages 1485-1520

GRIMALDI CLIFFORD CHANCE

HEAD OFFICE

see Worldwide Office Contacts

Website: www.cliffordchance.com

FIRM OVERVIEW

Senior partner: Vittorio Grimaldi
Number of partners worldwide: 28
Number of other lawyers worldwide: 126

AREAS OF PRACTICE:

Corporate	44%
Finance	43%
Litigation	8%
Others	5%

FIRM OVERVIEW: Grimaldi Clifford Chance is the Italian branch of Clifford Chance. The firm operates as a single worldwide partnership, ensuring a consistently high level of quality across its offices and providing a solid platform for the delivery of an integrated service to clients. Grimaldi Clifford Chance has rapidly developed into a multicultural global firm, advising many of the top Italian and international leading financial institutions and corporations and playing a leading role in Italian government privatisations and stock exchange market development as well as in the Italian and international banking area. It provides a comprehensive range of legal services relating to domestic and international corporate work. The firm is organised into a number of broad service areas, most of which are divided into smaller teams and have an information legal support service. Clients of the firm frequently require multidisciplinary working groups and its structures are flexible to reflect that, especially in respect of domestic implications such as administrative, environmental, privacy, anti-trust and employment law.

INTERNATIONAL EXPERIENCE: The most relevant experience in international work is related to mergers and acquisitions, flotations (Italy, UK, US and international), structured finance, project finance, banking, regulatory, energy, oil and gas, media and telecommunications, government privatisations, domestic and EU competition, and insolvency. The firm has also a major dispute resolution practice which operates worldwide and undertakes major Italian and international commercial disputes and arbitrations.

INTERNATIONAL CLIENTS: Clients are drawn from a wide range of worldwide commercial banks, investment banks and corporations, as well as regulatory agencies, governments and government agencies. The firm acts on behalf of business companies, financial institutions and governments throughout Italy and the world, and the firm's lawyers have capabilities to advise under many different jurisdictions.

MAIN INTERNATIONAL AREAS OF PRACTICE:

Corporate M&A: The corporate M&A practice handles private equity, buyouts, mergers and acquisitions, take-overs, commercial contracts, joint ventures and corporate reorganisation. It advises both domestic and international major private equity investors and financial institutions and big and medium sized corporate organisations.

Capital markets: The firm has one of the leading international equity capital markets practices in Italy, acting for a wide range of Italian and domestic commercial banks, investment banks and corporations. The firm advises on privatisations, listings on the Italian and foreign stock exchanges, initial public offerings, domestic and international private placements including under Rule 144A, takeovers, bond issues (Italian and Luxembourg listed) and rights issues.

Banking and finance: The firm provides general advice to a number of Italian and international banks and investment companies on debt transactions (loan and capital markets), asset finance and securitisation transactions, and offerings of securities in Italy. The firm currently advises a number of investment banks in connection with the acquisition and funding of Italian real estate portfolios. It has a strong regulatory practice acting for major financial institutions and funds in connection with asset transfer transactions involving the transfer of positions on Italian securities and derivatives regulated markets.

Domestic and EU competition: The domestic and EU competition practice specialises in competition law and communications. Competition related work that the firm handles includes major abuse of dominant position cases, specially in deregulating markets, such as telecommunications, or in the IT sector, both before the Commission and the Italian Competition Authority; major cartel cases, in a wide range of industries such as cement, oil and gas, pharmaceuticals, both before the Commission and the Italian Competition Authority; merger filings, often in complex cases, such as hostile tender offers, in the banking and telecommunications industries, or filings going through second-stage procedures, in the power generation, medical, chemical and metal industry, or multi-jurisdictional filings, in the banking and fashion industry; state-aid cases before the European Commission, specially in the banking sector and concerning regional aids; non-litigation assistance; drafting and steering anti-trust compliance projects for major clients in many areas such as chemicals, pharmaceuticals, and entertainment. Communications work undertaken includes drafting and reviewing regulatory aspects concerning fibre lease agreements; assisting new entrants on regulatory aspects in Italy, including the obtainment of licenses, interconnection, carrier pre-selection, unbundling of the local loop; drafting agreements relating to strategic alliances; assisting lenders through the complete acquisition process in reviewing and following the regulatory issues stemming from the recent Telecom Italia take-over, and assisting an operator on the issues which could have derived from the merger between TI and Deutsche Telekom; and advising cable-TV operators.

LANGUAGES: English, French, German, Italian, Japanese, Portuguese, Spanish

WORLDWIDE OFFICE CONTACTS

ITALY

Via Clerici, 7, 20121 **Milan**
Tel: +39 02 806341 **Fax:** +39 02 80634200

Viale Felice Cavallotti, 4, 35124 **Padua**
Tel: +39 049 8042511 **Fax:** +39 049 8805900

Via Saverio Mercadante, 32, 00198 **Rome**
Tel: +39 06 844651 **Fax:** +39 06 84465200

UNITED KINGDOM

Clifford Chance, 200 Aldersgate Street, **London** EC1A 4JJ
Tel: +44 207 600 1000 **Fax:** +44 207 600 5555

The Clifford Chance network has 29 offices in 19 countries including Amsterdam, Bangkok, Barcelona, Beijing, Berlin, Brussels, Budapest, Dubai, Düsseldorf, Frankfurt, Hong Kong, Leipzig, London, Luxembourg, Madrid, Milan, Moscow, Munich, New York, Padua, Paris, Prague, Rome, São Paulo, Shanghai, Singapore, Tokyo, Warsaw, Washington DC.

G

GROSS, KLEINHENDLER, HODAK, HALEVY, GREENBERG & CO

HEAD OFFICE

Azrieli Center No. 1, Circular Building,
Tel Aviv 67021, Israel
Tel: +972 3 608 3333 **Fax:** +972 3 695 8397

Email: law@gkh-law.com

FIRM OVERVIEW

Chairman: Prof. Joseph Gross
Managing partner: Amir Halevy

Number of partners worldwide: 11
Number of other lawyers worldwide: 36

AREAS OF PRACTICE:
Commercial and corporate .... *%
Cross-border transactions .... *%
High-tech .... *%
Intellectual property .... *%
Investments .... *%
Litigation .... *%
M&A .... *%
Real estate .... *%
Securities and underwriting .... *%
Tax .... *%
Venture capital .... *%
* Workload % not disclosed

WORLDWIDE OFFICE CONTACTS

ISRAEL
Azrieli Center No. 1, Circular Building, **Tel Aviv** 67021
Tel: +972 3 608 3333 **Fax:** +972 3 695 8397
Email: law@gkh-law.com

FIRM OVERVIEW: Gross, Kleinhendler, Hodak, Halevy, Greenberg and Co. was established in January 2001 as a result of the merger between Greenberg & Co and Kleinhendler and Halevy. Comprising 11 partners and 36 associates, the firm offers a comprehensive range of corporate and commercial legal services, including high technology and venture finance law. Some members of the firm are licensed to practice in various states of the US and most of the firm's work is conducted in English.

INTERNATIONAL EXPERIENCE: The firm represents some of Israel's leading corporations, and multinational companies operating in Israel. It has advised high-technology companies on their financial and commercial activities; advised on investments by venture capital funds in Israeli companies; handled public and private offerings in Israel, the US and Europe; regularly handled matters relating to capital markets in Israel, the US and Europe, and foreign investments in Israel. The firm has also handled the privatisations of a number of Israeli companies. The firm's local activities bring it into frequent contact with various government ministries and agencies such as the Israel Securities Authority, The Office of the Chief Scientist, the Tel Aviv Stock Exchange, the Ministry of Communication, the Ministry of Industry and Trade, the Israel Government Companies Authority and the Bank of Israel.

INTERNATIONAL CLIENTS: The firm's client base includes large technology and telecommunication companies, investment bankers, investment companies and government agencies. The firm also advises a number of Israel's leading corporations and promising start-ups, foreign investors, government agencies, venture capital funds and international investment banks.

MAIN INTERNATIONAL AREAS OF PRACTICE:
Commercial and corporate: The firm advises on all aspects of general corporate law, including drafting of local and international contracts.
Securities and underwriting: The firm represents both issuers and underwriters in public offerings on Israeli, US and European exchanges. The firm specialises in Israeli and US securities regulations.
High-tech: The firm has a specialist department that advises on all matters ranging from the formation of start-ups, through to public and private offerings in Israel, the US and Europe.
M&A: The firm handles a variety of international mergers and acquisitions, and has experience representing both sellers and buyers. The firm handles a range of regulatory aspects, including anti-trust, securities regulations in stock purchase transactions, taxation and other government regulations relating to licensing.
Venture capital: The firm advises venture capital funds on their structure, and represents companies in their financing rounds by venture capital funds from seed round through mezzanine financing.
Intellectual property: The firm provides one-stop shop services, in particular to high-tech start-up companies, with regard to trademarks, licensing arrangements and real time consultation with international patent attorneys who work in affiliation with the firm.
Litigation: The firm's litigation department deals with commercial and employment litigation, with respect to claims filed in Israel by, or against, multinational organisations and government agencies.
Employment: The firm handles all matters relating to Israeli employment law.

LANGUAGES: Arabic, English, Flemish, French, German, Hebrew Portuguese, Spanish

For other recommended firms see pages 1485-1520

GURBANI & CO

HEAD OFFICE

Suntec City Tower 2, 9 Temasek Boulevard # 17-01,
Singapore 038989, Singapore
Tel: +65 336 7727 **Fax:** +65 336 0110
Email: gurbanis@singnet.com.sg

WORLDWIDE OFFICE CONTACTS

SINGAPORE
Suntec City Tower 2, 9 Temasek Boulevard # 17-01, **Singapore** 038989
Tel: +65 336 7727 **Fax:** +65 336 0110
Email: gurbanis@singnet.com.sg

FIRM OVERVIEW

Senior partner: Prem Gurbani

Number of partners worldwide: 5
Number of other lawyers worldwide: 4

AREAS OF PRACTICE:
Litigation and arbitration 85%
Ship and other finance 15%

FIRM OVERVIEW: The firm, founded in June 1989, works with international clients, international lawyers and on an individual basis largely in the area of litigation and arbitration. The firm does not enter into any formal alliances or other networks.

INTERNATIONAL EXPERIENCE: The firm, since its formation, has acted for P&I Clubs, Hull underwriters, cargo underwriters and owners. Around 95% of the firm's work is Shipping and Marine insurance. Both claims and investigative work are undertaken.

INTERNATIONAL CLIENTS: The firm's client base includes large insurance companies, offshore banks and P&I Clubs, including Gard of Norway, Steamship Mutual and North of England.

MAIN INTERNATIONAL AREAS OF PRACTICE:
Litigation and arbitration: The firm deals with commercial arbitration, domestic and international arbitration and ADR. The firm's lawyers are involved in cases before all levels of the courts in Singapore and have participated in numerous arbitrations under the Rules of International Chamber of Commerce and the Singapore International Arbitration Centre. Matters covered include charterparty disputes, commodity disputes, collisions and casualties, spillages, death, phantoms and piracy cases. Some non-marine insurance is also covered as is enforcement of arbitration decisions.
Ship finance: The firm has a small but active ship finance section and acts for several financial institutions in this area.

LANGUAGES: English, Hindi, Mandarin, Tamil

G

GURBANI & CO

HAARMANN, HEMMELRATH & PARTNER

HEAD OFFICE

Maximilianstrasse 35, 80539 Munich, Germany
Tel: +49 89 2 16 36 0 **Fax:** +49 89 2 16 36 133

Email: firstname_lastname@hhp.de
Website: www.hhp.de

FIRM OVERVIEW

Number of partners worldwide: 108
Number of other lawyers worldwide: 178

AREAS OF PRACTICE:

Administrative law	*%
Anti-trust	*%
Banking and finance	*%
Company and commercial	*%
Employment	*%
Energy	*%
Environmental	*%
EU and competition	*%
Initial public offerings	*%
Insolvency	*%
Intellectual property	*%
IT, media and telecommunications	*%
Litigation and arbitration	*%
M&A	*%
Real estate	*%
Tax	*%

* Workload % not disclosed

FIRM OVERVIEW: Haarmann, Hemmelrath & Partners (Haarmann Hemmelrath Hügel in Austria) is a partnership of attorneys-at-law, certified public auditors and tax consultants. It was founded in Munich in 1987 and has a staff of approximately 930. Multi-disciplinary and international teams provide solutions, integrating the experience of business consultants, Haarmann Hemmelrath Management Consultants GmbH. The firm has offered notarial services since 1999, when the co-operation between certified public auditors and notaries was permitted. Haarmann Hemmelrath is a member of several international associations such as RSM International, a leading international tax and audit network, and Salustro Robson.

INTERNATIONAL CLIENTS: The firm's clientele comprises German and foreign companies from diverse business sectors, including insurance, financial, industrial, trading and service companies. The firm also advises private individuals.

MAIN INTERNATIONAL AREAS OF PRACTICE: Work undertaken includes administrative law; anti-trust; banking, stock exchange and financing; corporate and commercial; employment; energy; environmental; EU and competition; initial public offerings; insolvency; intellectual property and patents; IT, media and telecommunications; litigation and arbitration; M&A; real estate; national and international tax.

WORLDWIDE OFFICE CONTACTS

AUSTRIA		
Vienna	**Tel:** +43 1 503 7780	**Fax:** +43 1 503 7780-40
BELGIUM		
Brussels	**Tel:** +32 2 7401 100	**Fax:** +32 2 7401 133
CHINA		
Shanghai	**Tel:** +86 21 5049 8176	**Fax:** +86 21 5047 5122
CZECH REPUBLIC		
Prague	**Tel:** +420 2 22 51 88 45	**Fax:** +420 2 22 51 88 43
FRANCE		
Paris	**Tel:** +33 1 5 35 30 280	**Fax:** +33 1 5 35 30 281
GERMANY		
Munich	**Tel:** +49 89 2 16 36 0	**Fax:** +49 89 2 16 36 133
Berlin	**Tel:** +49 30 2 64 73 0	**Fax:** +49 30 2 64 73 133
Cologne	**Tel:** +49 221 2 70 58 0	**Fax:** +49 221 2 70 58 133
Düsseldorf	**Tel:** +49 2 11 83 99 0	**Fax:** +49 2 11 83 99 133
Frankfurt am Main	**Tel:** +49 69 9 20 59 0	**Fax:** +49 69 9 20 59 133
Hamburg	**Tel:** +49 40 3 50 06 0	**Fax:** +49 40 3 50 06 133
Leipzig	**Tel:** +49 3 41 12 63 0	**Fax:** +49 3 41 12 63 133
HUNGARY		
Budapest	**Tel:** +36 1 48 40 484	**Fax:** +36 1 48 40 433
ITALY		
Milan	**Tel:** +39 02 7 71 94 111	**Fax:** +39 02 7 71 94 133
JAPAN		
Tokyo	**Tel:** +81 3 55 70 64 11	**Fax:** +81 3 55 70 64 15
POLAND		
Warsaw	**Tel:** +48 22 82 00 800	**Fax:** +48 22 82 00 888
ROMANIA		
Bucharest	**Tel:** +40 1 3 15 35 72	**Fax:** +40 1 3 15 35 77
RUSSIA		
Moscow	**Tel:** +7 501 79 79 070	**Fax:** +7 501 79 79 080
SINGAPORE		
Singapore	**Tel:** +65 8 83 1050	**Fax:** +65 8 83 1060
UNITED KINGDOM		
London	**Tel:** +44 20 738 24 800	**Fax:** +44 20 738 24 833

LANGUAGES: Bulgarian, Croatian, Czech, Dutch, English, Finnish, French, German, Hungarian, Italian, Japanese, Mandarin, Norwegian, Polish, Portuguese, Romanian, Russian, Slovak, Spanish, Swedish, Vietnamese

For other recommended firms see pages 1485-1520

HADIPUTRANTO, HADINOTO & PARTNERS

HEAD OFFICE

The Jakarta Stock Exchange Building, Tower II, 21st Floor, Sudirman Central Business District, Jl. Jenderal Sudirman Kav. 52-53
Jakarta 12190, Indonesia
Tel: +62 21 515 5090 **Fax:** +62 21 515 4850
Email: tuti.hadiputranto@bakernet.com

FIRM OVERVIEW

Managing partner: Timur Sukirno
Senior partners: Tuti Dewi Hadinoto
and Tuti (Sri Indrastuti) Hadiputranto

Number of partners worldwide: 11
Number of other lawyers worldwide: 50

AREAS OF PRACTICE:

Capital markets and securities	38%
Corporate and commercial	31%
Banking and finance	23%
Intellectual property	8%

FIRM OVERVIEW: Established in 1989, Hadiputranto, Hadinoto & Partners is the correspondent law firm of Baker & McKenzie in Indonesia, and is linked to an international network of 61 offices in 35 countries worldwide. In the wake of the economic crisis of 1997, the firm has responded to the need for debt restructuring and insolvency expertise by developing capabilities to meet growing demands in these areas.

INTERNATIONAL EXPERIENCE: The firm advises a wide range of domestic, regional and multinational clients in Indonesia and around the region. Specifically, this includes Australia, China, Hong Kong, Japan, the Philippines, Singapore, Taiwan, Thailand and Vietnam. The firm has taken a number of Indonesian companies to the American Depository Receipt market and represents many others in the offering of various debt and equity securities offshore. The firm has been successful in bidding for a number of major transactions for the Indonesian Government. It acted for Bank Danamon in the US$3.8 billion merger of nine banks, represented PT Indocement Tunggal Prakarsa in a US$1.1 billion debt restructuring and represented BCA (a bank previously under the supervision of of the Indonesian Bank Restructuring Agency) in a notable IPO.
Effective cooperation between Hadiputranto Hadinoto & Partners and Baker & McKenzie in the Asia Pacific region ensures that lawyers are able to offer a seamless service through global and regional practice group structures.

WORLDWIDE OFFICE CONTACTS

INDONESIA
The Jakarta Stock Exchange Building, Tower II, 21st Floor, Sudirman Central Business District, Jl. Jenderal Sudirman Kav. 52-53, **Jakarta** 12190
Tel: +62 21 515 5090 **Fax:** +62 21 515 4850
Email: tuti.hadiputranto@bakernet.com

INTERNATIONAL CLIENTS: The firm acts for corporations, banks and other financial institutions, government agencies and state owned companies. Clients include Goldman Sachs, CSFB, Telekom Indonesia, Indosat, Indofood, Indocement, Ford Motors and Lyonnaise des Eaux.

MAIN INTERNATIONAL AREAS OF PRACTICE: The firm is committed to providing quality legal services to clients and aims to provide international standards of legal service to support international business.
The firm's lawyers are organised into practice groups such as corporate restructuring/debt restructuring; insolvency; litigation and arbitration; foreign direct investment/corporate commercial; capital markets and securities; M&A/venture capital; projects; infrastructure and construction; tax (domestic and international); information technology; banking and finance; natural resources/environment and intellectual property.

LANGUAGES: English, French, Indonesian, Japanese

HADIPUTRANTO, HADINOTO & PARTNERS

For other recommended firms see pages 1485-1520

HAIDERMOTA & CO

HEAD OFFICE

D-79, Block 5, Clifton, K.D.A Scheme No.5, Karachi, Pakistan
Tel: +92 21 587 9097 **Fax:** +92 21 586 2329

Email: hmco@cyber.net.pk

FIRM OVERVIEW

Managing partner: A.M. Haidermota
Senior partner: A.M. Haidermota

AREAS OF PRACTICE:

Banking and finance ....*%
Corporate ....*%
Energy ....*%
Joint ventures ....*%
Legislative drafting ....*%
Litigation and arbitration ....*%
M&A ....*%
Privatisation ....*%
Real estate ....*%
Securitisation ....*%
Telecommunications ....*%
* Workload not disclosed

WORLDWIDE OFFICE CONTACTS

PAKISTAN
D-79, Block 5, Clifton, K.D.A Scheme No.5, **Karachi** 75530
Tel: +92 21 587 9097 **Fax:** +92 21 586 2329
Email: hmco@cyber.net.pk

H

FIRM OVERVIEW: Haidermota & Co was established in 1957. The firm does not participate in formal alliances or networks, preferring to maintain contacts with various firms worldwide and to choose the firms it works with on individual international transactions.

INTERNATIONAL CLIENTS: The firm's client base includes multi-national companies, banks, and insurance companies. Its international clients include Citibank N.A., Allianz AG, ABN AMRO Bank N.V., ABN AMRO Asia Limited, Merrill Lynch, Jardine Fleming, McDonald's, SNC-LAVALIN and Becton Dickinson & Co.

MAIN INTERNATIONAL AREAS OF PRACTICE:

Banking and finance: Haidermota & Co handles all aspects of banking and finance including structured finance, syndicated loan transactions, project finance and Islamic modes of financing. They also act for the State Bank of Pakistan (central bank), banks and the Pakistan Banks Association.

Privatisation: The firm is extensively involved with the privatisation process in Pakistan. They advise various financial advisers in connection with the privatisation of banks, oil and gas companies, and potential buyers in respect of various companies.

Securitisation: Haidermota & Co specialises in securitisation. Selected transactions include US$ 250 million securitisation of Pakistan Telecommunication Company Limited's international receivables, securitisation of domestic airline's ticket sales, securitisation of lease rentals, and securitisation (by way of true sale of certain receivables) of a public sector company.

Corporate: The firm advises on all aspects of general corporate law, including drafting of contracts and agreements.

Joint ventures: Haidermota & Co's transactions include various cross-border joint ventures. It has also represented various international and local clients in joint venture transactions including Allianz AG, Becton Dickinson & Company and McDonald's.

M&A: The firm's transactions include amalgamation of banks, modaraba companies, investment banks, and leasing companies. Recent transactions include advising Citibank Overseas Investment Company on the sale of their investment banking subsidiary in Pakistan; Standard Chartered Bank in respect of sale of their leasing subsidiary in Pakistan; ABN AMRO Asia Limited in respect of sale of their brokerage firm; amalgamation of three modaraba companies; State Bank of Pakistan in respect of amalgamation of Mehran Bank Limited into National Bank of Pakistan.

Litigation and arbitration: Haidermota & Co handles commercial litigation, shareholder rights litigation and international arbitration. Its lawyers are frequently involved in cases before High Courts and Supreme Court of Pakistan.

Real estate: The firm advises various local and foreign institutions in connection with purchase, sale and lease of large commercial properties in Karachi.

Securities and financial markets: Haidermota & Co advises on all aspects of funds and securities. They represent investment banks in developing various innovative financial products.

Telecommunication: The firm advises on various regulatory matters in the telecommunications industry including advising internet service providers. The firm has recently acted for a potential buyer of Pakistan Telecommunications Company Limited.

LANGUAGES: English, Gujrati, Urdu

For other recommended firms see pages 1485-1520

HAIWEN & PARTNERS

HEAD OFFICE

Room 1016, Beijing Silver Tower, No 2 Dong San Huan North Road, Chao Yang District
Beijing 100027, China
Tel: +86 10 8642 1166 **Fax:** +86 10 6410 6928

FIRM OVERVIEW

Managing partner: He Fei

Number of partners worldwide: 9
Number of other lawyers worldwide: 32

AREAS OF PRACTICE:
Corporate 60%
Litigation and arbitration 30%
M&A 10%

FIRM OVERVIEW: Haiwen & Partners is a Beijing based firm with an office in Shanghai. The firm offers a comprehensive legal service to both international and domestic clients. It specialises in securities law, direct investment, and mergers and acquisitions. Haiwen & Partners also has a strong litigation and arbitration practice.

INTERNATIONAL EXPERIENCE: Haiwen & Partners has advised major international investment banks on many PRC related capital market deals. It has also acted as legal counsel for overseas investors in their investments in the PRC.

INTERNATIONAL CLIENTS: The firm's client base includes major foreign investment banks, large overseas companies and banks.

MAIN INTERNATIONAL AREAS OF PRACTICE:
Securities: Haiwen & Partners advises on all securities related issues. The firm has recently advised PetroChina, Sinopec Corp, and Unicom's IPO on capital markets issues.
M&A: The firm advises on a range of M&A matters. It advised on the merger between Shandong Huaneng and Huaneng Power International, two overseas listed PRC power companies.
Litigation and arbitration: Haiwen & Partners handles commercial litigation and national and international arbitration. The firm's lawyers have participated in matters under the Rule of China International Economic and Trade Arbitration Commission.

LANGUAGES: Chinese, English

WORLDWIDE OFFICE CONTACTS

CHINA
Room 1016, Beijing Silver Tower, No 2 Dong San Huan North Road, Chao Yang District, **Beijing** 100027
Tel: +86 10 8642 1166 **Fax:** +86 10 6410 6928

Room2604, Shanghai Kerry Centre, 1515 Nanjing West Road, **Shanghai,** 200040
Tel: +8610 864 166 **Fax:** +86 10 6410 6928

海问律师事务所

HAIWEN & PARTNERS

H

ADVOKATFIRMAN HAMMARSKIÖLD & CO AB

HEAD OFFICE

Norra Bankogränd 2, PO Box 2278,
103 17 Stockholm, Sweden
Tel: + 46 8 578 450 00 **Fax:** + 46 8 578 450 99

Email: info@hammarskiöld.se

WORLDWIDE OFFICE CONTACTS

SWEDEN
Norra Bankogränd 2, PO Box 2278, 103 17 **Stockholm**
Tel: + 46 8 578 450 00 **Fax:** + 46 8 578 450 99
Email: info@hammarskiöld.se

FIRM OVERVIEW

Managing Partner: Peder Hammarskiöld

Number of partners worldwide: 7
Number of other lawyers worldwide: 24

AREAS OF PRACTICE:

Mergers and acquisitions: 25%
Banking and finance: 20%
Corporate and other: 15%
Insurance and reinsurance: 10%
Intellectual property: 10%
Litigation and arbitration: 10%
Telecommunications and computer law: 10%

H

FIRM OVERVIEW: Founded on January 1st 1998, this Swedish firm was established by a group of 15 lawyers who left Lagerlöf & Leman prior to its alliance with Linklaters. Hammarskiöld & Co offers a comprehensive legal service to clients with international business interests, focusing on banking and finance, mergers and acquisitions, IP and telecommunication, computer law and litigation and arbitration.

INTERNATIONAL EXPERIENCE: In 1999, Hammarskiöld & Co advised on a record number of M&A transactions, as well as on other high profile matters. The firm has participated in several of the most significant and largest cross-border M&A transactions in Sweden in recent years.

INTERNATIONAL CLIENTS: The firm's client base includes large companies, banks, insurance companies and public or supranational institutions conducting cross-border business.

MAIN INTERNATIONAL AREAS OF PRACTICE

Mergers and acquisitions: The firm's transactions in this area range from small private acquisitions to cross-border takeovers of listed companies. The firm's lawyers have acted for both sellers and buyers.
Banking and finance: Hammarskiöld & Co covers all areas of banking and finance, including secured and syndicated loan transactions and guarantees, structured finance, project finance, leasing and tax-based finance.
Insurance and reinsurance: The demutualising and restructuring of insurance groups have been major practice areas in Sweden in recent years. In such transactions, the firm has helped insurance companies to find the best legal structure. It also advises on insurance contracts, reinsurance treaties, claims-related disputes and insurance related litigation.
Intellectual property: The firm specialises in trademarks, patents, copyrights, licensing and franchising. Its lawyers participate in the negotiation of license agreements and advise on infringement disputes and other aspects of IP law.
Telecommunications and computer law: The firm advises on all aspects in this area and has been involved in some of the largest and most recent telecommunications projects. It also advises market leaders in the computer and internet industries.
Marketing law: Working with clients ranging from large multinationals to local enterprises, the firm has substantial experience in dealing with marketing guidelines, consumer disputes, regulatory issues and producer liability matters.
Litigation and arbitration: Hammarskiöld & Co deals with commercial litigation, national and international arbitration, and ADR. Its lawyers are frequently involved in cases before the Swedish Courts, including the Supreme Court, and have participated in numerous matters under the rules of the International Chamber of Commerce and the Stockholm Chamber of Commerce.
EU and competition law: This area has acquired a new prominence since the accession of Sweden to the European Union. The firm's lawyers undertake antitrust, competition and marketing-related cases involving companies in the Swedish market.
Energy and public utilities: The firm plays an active role in the development of law in the recently deregulated energy sector.
Corporate: The firm advises on all aspects of general corporate law, including the drafting of Swedish and international contracts.
Employment: The firm handles all matters relating to Swedish employment law.
Securities and financial markets: The firm advises on Swedish law pertaining to funds, securities and derivatives as well as advising investment funds on structuring and licensing.

LANGUAGES: Dutch, English, French, German, Russian

For other recommended firms see pages 1485-1520

HAMMOND SUDDARDS EDGE

HEAD OFFICE

7 Devonshire Square, Cutlers Gardens,
London EC2M 4YH, United Kingdom
Tel: +44 20 7655 1000 **Fax:** +44 20 7655 1001

Email: enquiries@hammondsuddardsedge.com
Website: www.hammondsuddardsedge.com

FIRM OVERVIEW

Managing partner: Chris Jones
Senior partner: John Heller

Number of partners worldwide: 238
Number of lawyers worldwide: 570

AREAS OF PRACTICE:

Banking	*%
Business finance and recovery	*%
Commercial dispute resolution	*%
Construction and engineering	*%
Corporate finance	*%
Employment	*%
Insurance	*%
Intellectual property	*%
Pensions	*%
Property and planning	*%

* Workload % not disclosed

WORLDWIDE OFFICE CONTACTS

BELGIUM
Avenue Louise 250, Box 65, B-1050 **Brussels**
Tel: +32 2 627 76 76 **Fax:** +32 2 627 76 86
Email: enquiries@hammondsuddardsedge.com

UNITED KINGDOM
Rutland House, 148 Edmund Street, **Birmingham** B3 2JR
Tel: +44 121 222 3000 **Fax:** +44 121 222 3001
Email: enquiries@hammondsuddardsedge.com

Pennine House, 39-45 Well Street, **Bradford** BD1 5NU
Tel: +44 1274 764400 **Fax:** +44 1274 730484
Email: enquiries@hammondsuddardsedge.com

2 Park Lane, **Leeds** LS3 1ES
Tel: +44 113 284 7000 **Fax:** +44 113 284 7001
Email: enquiries@hammondsuddardsedge.com

7 Devonshire Square, Cutlers Gardens, **London** EC2M 4YH
Tel: +44 20 7655 1000 **Fax:** +44 20 7655 1001
Email: enquiries@hammondsuddardsedge.com

Suite 688 Lloyd's, 1 Lime Street, **London** EC3M 7HA
Tel: +44 20 7327 3388 **Fax:** + 44 20 7621 1217
Email: enquiries@hammondsuddardsedge.com

Trinity Court, 16 John Dalton Street, **Manchester** M60 8HS
Tel: +44 161 830 5000 **Fax:** +44 161 830 5001
Email: enquiries@hammondsuddardsedge.com

H

FIRM OVERVIEW: The merger of Hammond Suddards and Edge Ellison on 1 August 2000 created one of the UK's largest legal practices. The firm has a formidable corporate practice in London and top-flight status in all the major financial and industrial centres in England with offices in Birmingham, Bradford, Leeds, Lloyd's of London and Manchester. The firm also has a dedicated European law unit in Brussels, Belgium. It has 185 partners, 900 lawyers and a total staff of 2000, operating as a national integrated practice delivering a seamless service to clients, irrespective of location. With an impressive range of major national and international companies and institutions on its client list, Hammond Suddards Edge advises more than 80 UK stock market-listed companies, including 18 of the FTSE 100 companies and 16 US Fortune 500 companies. The firm is recognised and respected for its enterpreneurial and innovative approach and is constantly looking for new ways to enhance client service.

INTERNATIONAL EXPERIENCE: In addition to the firm's dedicated law practice in Brussels, it acts for many domestic and overseas clients in all areas of practice. A team of 15 lawyers, headed by partner Konstantinos Adamantopoulos, advises a variety of clients on anti-dumping and anti-subsidy procedures; competition, merger control and state aids; EC funding; energy and utilities; environment issues; information technology and e-commerce; intellectual property; public procurement, and trade and customs work (including GATT and WTO).

INTERNATIONAL CLIENTS: Clients include the Government of Ukraine, International Air Transport Association, Matsushita, Tokio Marine, the P&O Group, Mita, the Japanese Chemical Industry Association, the Japanese Environmental Agency, Mirror Group plc, Murray Johnstone Ltd, Planetfootball.Com Ltd and Primary Capital.

MAIN INTERNATIONAL AREAS OF PRACTICE:

Banking: The banking unit advises financial institutions including UK and overseas banks, building societies and borrowers on a broad range of secured and unsecured transactions and restructurings.

Business finance and recovery: The business finance and recovery unit advises insolvency practitioners and banks on all aspects of their work as receivers, liquidators, trustees, administrators and supervisors. The unit also advises companies and partnerships experiencing serious financial difficulties. Much of the work has an international element.

Commercial dispute resolution: The CDR unit encompasses all aspects of commercial claims and disputes. The firm has particular expertise in ADR and arbitration, which has been recognised by the Centre for Dispute Resolution. The unit also handles regulatory work, directors' and officers' liabilities and other aspects of criminal law that presents risk for businesses. In addition, there is a growing safety, health and environmental team conducting all litigious and non-litigious work.

Construction and engineering: The construction and engineering unit is one of the largest bespoke practices in the UK. The unit acts for both employers and contractors both in the UK and overseas on all aspects of contentious and non-contentious construction law from building projects to civil, process and chemical engineering projects.

Corporate finance: The corporate finance unit advises more than 80 UK stock market-listed companies, including 18 of the FTSE 100 companies and 16 US Fortune 500 companies on all aspects of corporate finance. The unit includes teams dedicated to M&A, private equity and investment banking.

Corporate tax: The financial services and corporate tax units provide advice on tax planning at all levels, employee share options and off-shore tax advice.

For other recommended firms see pages 1485-1520

HAMMOND SUDDARDS EDGE cont'd

Employment: Hammond Suddards Edge has one of the largest employment practices in the UK with a team of dedicated lawyers in all locations. Work encompasses all aspects of contentious and non-contentious employment advice.
EU law: The firm's European law team is based in Brussels and is among the largest of those operated by UK firms in the EU capital. The unit provides specialist advice in EU, commercial and environmental law.
Financial services: The financial services unit provides advice on off-shore funds, UK investment funds, FSA regulation, regulatory compliance advice, retail financial products and FSA avoidance.
Insurance: The commercial insurance unit is the largest based at Lloyd's of London and is recognised for its expertise in professional indemnity for accountants, solicitors, surveyors, architects, engineers, computer consultants and financial institutions. The unit also advises on policy coverage disputes, product liability matters and non-contentious insurance work.
Intellectual property: The IP unit has established itself as a market leader for both contentious and non-contentious IP matters for a broad spectrum of multinationals and UK companies. The unit has teams dedicated to e-commerce, telecommunications, media and film and biotechnology and pharmaceuticals. In addition, a dedicated enterprise and technology team has expertise in advertising, brand clearance, character merchandising, computer contracts for hardware and software, domain name recovery, e-commerce, media contracts, rights agreements for sports governing bodies, companies and clubs and sales promotions.
Pensions: Pensions unit is widely recognised as one of the UK's largest and most experienced pensions advisers. The unit advises employers and trustees on all aspects of pensions arrangements from large occupational schemes to product development work for providers and unapproved top-up schemes.

Property and planning: The property and planning unit advises major national and international developers, institutions and end-users on all aspects of commercial property, particularly city centre schemes and out-of-town developments. The planning team goes from strength to strength with large-scale involvement in major national planning enquiries for UK and international companies and utilities. A dedicated retail team advises a wide range of retailers from high street names to breweries and charities.

LANGUAGES: Afrikaans, Arabic, Cantonese, Croatian, Dutch, French, German, Greek, Gujarati, Hebrew, Hindi, Italian, Japanese, Lithuanian, Malay, Marathi, Portugese, Punjabi, Russian, Spanish, Tamil, Turkish, Urdu

Hammond Suddards Edge

For other recommended firms see pages 1485-1520

HANNES SNELLMAN

HEAD OFFICE

Etelaranta 8 (6th Floor),
FIN-00130 Helsinki, Finland
Tel: +358 9 228 841 **Fax:** +358 9 177 393

Website: www.snellman-law.fi

WORLDWIDE OFFICE CONTACTS

FINLAND
Etelaranta 8 (6th Floor), FIN-00130 **Helsinki**
Tel: +358 9 228 841 **Fax:** +358 9 177 393
Email: hannes.snellman@snellman-law.fi

Lemminkaisentie 14-18B, FIN-20520 **Turku**
Tel: +358 2 2130 600 **Fax:** +358 2 2130 630
Email: hannes.snellman@snellman-law.fi

FIRM OVERVIEW

Managing partner: Juhani Makinen
Senior partner: Robert Mattson

Number of partners worldwide: 17
Number of other lawyers worldwide: 37

AREAS OF PRACTICE:

M&A	30%
General corporate and commercial	15%
Capital markets	15%
Litigation and arbitration	10%
Banking and finance	8%
Competition	8%

FIRM OVERVIEW: Founded in 1909 by Hannes Snellman, the firm is now one of the largest in Finland and continues to grow rapidly. Whilst from the beginning its focus has been on general corporate and commercial law, it practises in all substantive areas of law for a range of domestic and international clients.

INTERNATIONAL EXPERIENCE: The firm has developed a broad network of of international industrial and financial contacts. It regularly advises on international matters and maintains close ties with foreign law firms worldwide.

INTERNATIONAL CLIENTS: Hannes Snellman advises international clients on a regular basis, including leading financial institutions, major international corporations, industrial groups, leading investment banks and service companies. Geographically the clients come mostly from North America, England and continental Europe as well as Scandinavia.

MAIN INTERNATIONAL AREAS OF PRACTICE:
General corporate and commercial: The firm handles general corporate and commercial matters, ranging from formation to dissolution and including interim changes of corporate form, such as reorganisation and restructuring of companies and conglomerates. It advises on joint ventures and a variety of commercial undertakings, as well as on debt, equity and other financing arrangements.
M&A: The firm advises on domestic and international mergers and acquisitions, including MBOs, LBOs, divestitures and spin-offs of publicly listed companies and small and medium-sized business entities. There is a focus on restructuring, regulatory compliance and disclosure obligations.
Banking and finance: The firm represents domestic and international financial institutions and companies in various banking and financing transactions, such as syndicated and other loan facilities and other forms of structured finance, including lease finance, asset and project finance, securitisation and venture capital transactions. Advice includes legal and regulatory compliance.
Capital markets: Clients include Finnish and foreign financial institutions and issuers, and advice spans bond issues and equity-linked securities, specifically convertibles and other commercial paper, together with IPOs. The firm acts for investment services firms, banks and other entities on compliance with securities laws and regulations in the establishment and marketing in Finland of mutual funds, collective investment schemes and investment services.
Taxation: Tax advice is a crucial element of the firm's comprehensive legal services. Practitioners have particular experience in the fields of corporate tax and VAT.
Competition: Competition law issues emerge throughout the practice, particularly in relation to M&A, joint ventures, distribution and licensing. The firm represents clients before national and EU competition authorities and courts, and advises them on notifications in the merger control process and on developing compliance programmes.
Environmental law: Environmental regulation continues to expand in breadth and sophistication as environmental issues take precedence in Finland, Europe and around the world. The firm combines legal and technical expertise in this field and employs lawyers with additional education in natural sciences and engineering. It represents clients in matters concerning domestic and European environmental regulation, including environmental liability and due diligence in mergers, acquisitions and real estate transactions.
Intellectual property: The IP practice encompasses the traditional areas of copyright, trademark, patent and licensing law. The practice advises on issues such as trade secrets, in particular with regard to computer programs and integrated services, millennium compliance and e-commerce.
Litigation and arbitration: The group works in all areas of law, from simple contract cases to intricate corporate transactions, and represents domestic and foreign parties. Lawyers handle cases in different forums including civil and administrative courts at all levels and arbitral tribunals.

LANGUAGES: English, Finnish, French, German, Swedish

HANNES SNELLMAN

For other recommended firms see pages 1485-1520

HASSANS INTERNATIONAL LAW FIRM

HEAD OFFICE

57/63 Line Wall Road, P O Box 199, Gibraltar
Tel: + 350 79000 **Fax:** + 350 71966

Email: jahassan@gibnet.gi
Website: www.gibraltarlaw.com

WORLDWIDE OFFICE CONTACTS

GIBRALTAR
57/63 Line Wall Road, P O Box 199, **Gibraltar**
Tel: + 350 79000 **Fax:** + 350 71966
Email: jahassan@gibnet.gi

FIRM OVERVIEW

Senior partner: James Levy
Managing partner: Tony Provasoli

Number of partners worldwide: 12
Number of other lawyers worldwide: 15

AREAS OF PRACTICE:

Corporate and commercial	21%
Litigation	17%
International banking and finance	15%
Private client	13%
Trust and company administration	11%
Drafting	10%
Maritime	7%
Property	6%

H

FIRM OVERIVIEW: Hassans was founded in 1939, and is the largest law firm in Gibraltar. The firm was the first in Gibraltar to structure itself as a modern international law firm, with separate departments for different fields of specialisation. Its aim is to give a high quality, personal and effective service to its clients of whatever size or nature. Though rooted in Gibraltar, the firm has an international clientele, which it continues to develop. The firm has links with major London, Continental and US law firms.

INTERNATIONAL EXPERIENCE: Three quarters of the firm's work is related to international clients. Many of them use Gibraltar companies and trusts to structure their fiscal, fiduciary or investment requirements, and over the years strong links have been forged with major multinationals, financial institutions, banks, law and accountancy firms throughout the world. Gibraltar's status as part of the European Union is often a significant factor in attracting such institutions and businesses to it.

INTERNATIONAL CLIENTS: The firm's international clients come above all from the US, the UK, Israel and continental Europe (in particular Luxembourg, the Netherlands, Spain and Portugal). They include major multinationals, banks and building societies.

MAIN INTERNATIONAL AREAS OF PRACTICE:

Corporate and commercial: The firm provides a full range of legal services for clients ranging from small businesses to major multinationals. It advises corporate clients working in or through Gibraltar on a wide variety of cross-border transactions and financing structures. Other matters handled include international corporate restructures, joint ventures, M&A and corporate franchising, tax and e-commerce.

Litigation: The department handles most aspects of litigation, with a niche focus on international commercial and trust litigation. The firm's litigators practise as both barristers and solicitors, and provide a full range of litigation services at all levels for both local and international clients.

International finance and banking: The firm has particular experience in banking and financial markets. The firm's lawyers also advise in banking regulation and licensing work, including the establishment of offshore operations and regulatory advice, as well as the implementation of various legal and tax structures including repackaging and securitisation. It is the only firm in Gibraltar to combine specialist expertise in derivatives regulation with a substantial banking, tax and securitisation practice.

Telecommunications: The firm has advised on the privatisation of the Government of Gibraltar's telephone services and advises one of the main carriers. The firm advises on all aspects of telecommunications including broadcasting and wireless telegraphy, and was instructed by the International Telecommunications Union to report on the state of telecommunications legislation in various territories in the Caribbean region.

Private client: The firm has specialist lawyers who regularly advise on all aspects of private client matters including asset protection, trusts, domiciliation and taxation.

Drafting: The firm advised the governmnet on the transposition of EU Directives into Gibraltar law. Principally, this work has concerned legislation relating to financial services and telecommunications. Contacts have also been established with a number of other governments requiring assistance in this area.

Trust and company administration: Through an associated company (Line Management Services Ltd) the firm provides administration services for both companies and trusts. Among the users of these services are international clients who the firm advises on the use of Gibraltar trusts and offshore companies.

Maritime: The firm has strong links with major English shipping firms and has been involved in a number of significant international admiralty cases. The firm also handles ship registration and finance.

Property: The firm acts for most of the major local and international developers and builders. The firm advises in matters concerned with secured lending, mortgages and charges for most banks and building societies in Gibraltar.

LANGUAGES: English, French, Hebrew, Italian, Portuguese, Spanish

For other recommended firms see pages 1485-1520

HEIKKI HAAPANIEMI

HEAD OFFICE

Mannerheimintie 14 A, PO Box 232,
FIN-00101 Helsinki, Finland
Tel: +358 9177 613 **Fax:** +358 9 653 873

Email: haapaniemi@haapaniemi.com
Website: www.haapaniemi.com

FIRM OVERVIEW

Managing partner: Arto Kukkonen

Number of partners worldwide: 11
Number of other lawyers worldwide: 16

AREAS OF PRACTICE:

Construction, real estate and environment	*%
Corporate finance, M&A	*%
EU and competition	*%
Intellectual property	*%
IT and telecommunications	*%
Litigation and arbitration	*%
Shipping and transport	*%
Tax	*%

* Workload % not disclosed

WORLDWIDE OFFICE CONTACTS

FINLAND
Mannerheimintie 14 A, PO Box 232, FIN-00101 **Helsinki**
Tel: +358 9177 613 **Fax:** +358 9 653 873
Email: haapaniemi@haapaniemi.com

FRANCE
148 boulevard du Montparnasse, 75014 **Paris**
Tel: +33 1 43 35 23 12 **Fax:** +33 1 43 35 19 58
Email: haapaniemi@haapaniemi.com

FIRM OVERVIEW: Established in 1958, the firm provides a broad range of services, with a recent focus on corporate finance, M&A, IT, telecommunications and intellectual property. It has a network of relationships with other Scandinavian and foreign law and accountancy firms and is the Finnish correspondent firm for a number of international legal reviews. Several firm members have law degrees from abroad, including from the US, Germany and France, and they play an active part in a number of international organisations such as the International Bar Association and International Fiscal Association. In 1989 the firm opened a Paris office to facilitate its international operations and give it greater capacity in EU-related issues. It is a member of the Paris bar.

INTERNATIONAL EXPERIENCE: The firm represents major US, European and Asian corporations in M&A transactions or advises others on the establishment of subsidiaries in Finland. It provides tax advice on the restructuring of numerous companies, particularly in the IT sectors.

INTERNATIONAL CLIENTS: Include international companies and other organisations ranging from multinationals to companies operating on a national level. Sectors include banking and financial services, insurance, IT and telecommunications, construction, publishing, media, international trade and transport, pharmaceuticals and biotechnology, industry, food products, distribution, natural resources and electronics.

MAIN INTERNATIONAL AREAS OF PRACTICE:

EU and competition: The firm acts for clients ranging from large multinationals to local businesses on merger control notifications and Article 85 (3) cases with the Finnish Competition Authority and the European Commission.

Construction, real estate and environment: The firm advises many of the leading construction and real estate companies in Finland on various contract and litigation matters.

Corporate finance: Work includes IPOs and M&A.

IT and telecommunications: Firm members undertake in-house secondments advising major IT companies. Other IT and telecoms companies and associations regularly advised and represented range from listed companies and companies with substantial export activities to smaller software houses. The firm has been involved in major M&A work in the sector.

Intellectual property, marketing law: Expertise covers a range of industrial rights-related work, from handling registration applications to highly complex patent court cases, especially concerning product forgery, franchising and various industrial rights and marketing-related issues.

Litigation and arbitration: Work handled ranges from disputes connected with acquisitions, construction contracts and other contractual matters, employment law disputes including pension matters, cases with a community dimension and compensation disputes. Firm members have experience in the European Court of Justice and chair arbitration tribunals or act as arbitrators.

Shipping and transport: Heikki Haapaniemi is one of the two Finnish law firms who work for P&I clubs, mainly in the interests of various shipowners. Clients include underwriters, multinational transport operators and freight forwarders.

Tax: Clients range from individuals to multinationals, with a particular focus on the IT sector.

LANGUAGES: English, Finnish, French, German, Swedish

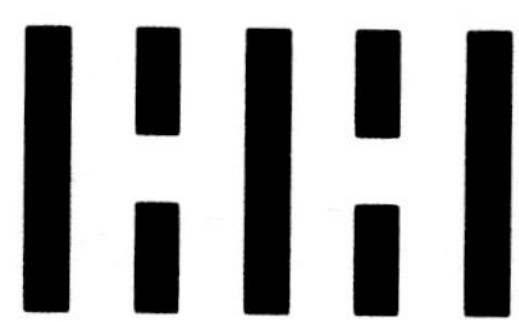

For other recommended firms see pages 1485-1520

HELLER EHRMAN WHITE & MCAULIFFE LLP

HEAD OFFICE

333 Bush Street,
San Francisco CA 94104-2878, USA
Tel: +1 415 772 6000 **Fax:** +1 415 772 6268

Email: info@hewm.com
Website: www.hewm.com

FIRM OVERVIEW

Managing shareholder: Barry S. Levin
Firmwide practice group chairs: Matthew L. Larrabee, Sarah A.O'Dowd

Number of partners worldwide: 189
Number of other lawyers worldwide: 335

AREAS OF PRACTICE:

Corporate	14%
Anti-trust	9%
Life sciences	9%
Banking and finance	8%
Intellectual property	8%
Product liability	8%
Professional liability	8%
IT	7%
Environmental	6%
Insurance	6%
Employment	5%
Real estate	5%
Tax	4%
Energy	3%

FIRM OVERVIEW: Heller Ehrman is a full-service law firm dedicated to helping clients shape the global economy. Comprising 524 lawyers, it is one of the oldest and fastest growing law firms in the US and one of the few big firms with more than a 20-year presence in Asia. Heller Ehrman lawyers work within 15 national practice groups to service its clients throughout the biotech, telecommunications, banking and computer industries. Heller Ehrman's capacity to undertake work of an international nature is enhanced by its US, Hong Kong and Singapore offices. Its offices are close to the major commercial centres of the world and its lawyers can work across different time zones in multiple languages and cultural settings.

INTERNATIONAL EXPERIENCE: Heller Ehrman lawyers practice in virtually all areas of law. A strong cadre of transactional and intellectual property lawyers, as well as international patent consultants and commercial lawyers, have a broad experience in structuring cross-border joint ventures and business alliances, strategic partnerships, mergers and acquisitions and various forms of licensing transactions. The firm has handled transactions for clients from all over the world, notably Asia and Europe.

INTERNATIONAL CLIENTS: The firm's diverse client base ranges from Fortune 500 companies to start-ups, investment banks to angel investors, and venture capital partnerships to entrepreneurs.

MAIN INTERNATIONAL AREAS OF PRACTICE: Main areas of practice include corporate; energy; financial services; information technology; life sciences; intellectual property; real estate; tax.

WORLDWIDE OFFICE CONTACTS

HONG KONG
6308-09 The Center, 99 Queen's Road, Central, **Hong Kong**
Tel: +852 2526 6381 **Fax:** +852 2810 6242
Email: info@hewm.com

SINGAPORE
50 Raffles Place, Singapore Land Tower #17-04, **Singapore** 048623
Tel: +65 538 1756 **Fax:** +65 538 1537
Email: info@hewm.com

USA
550 West 7th Avenue, Suite 1900, **Anchorage** AK 99501-3571
Tel: +1 907 277 1900 **Fax:** +1 907 277 1920
Email: info@hewm.com

601 South Figueroa Street, 40th Floor, **Los Angeles** CA 90017-5758
Tel: +1 213 689 0200 **Fax:** +1 213 614 1868
Email: info@hewm.com

2500 Sand Hill Road, Suite 100, **Menlo Park** CA 94025-7063
Tel: +1 650 234 4200 **Fax:** +1 650 234 4299
Email: info@hewm.com

711 Fifth Avenue, **New York** NY 10022-3194
Tel: +1 212 832 8300 **Fax:** +1 212 832 3353
Email: info@hewm.com

200 S.W. Market Street, Suite 1750, **Portland** OR 97201-5718
Tel: +1 503 227 7400 **Fax:** +1 503 241 0950
Email: info@hewm.com

4250 Executive Square, Seventh Floor, La Jolla, **San Diego** CA 92037
Tel: +1 858 450 8400 **Fax:** +1 858 450 8499
Email: info@hewm.com

333 Bush Street, **San Francisco** CA 94104-2878
Tel: +1 415 772 6000 **Fax:** +1 415 772 6268
Email: info@hewm.com

701 Fifth Avenue, Suite 6100, **Seattle** WA 98104-7098
Tel: +1 206 447 0900 **Fax:** +1 206 447 0849
Email: info@hewm.com

275 Middlefield Road, Menlo Park, **Silicon Valley** CA 94025-3506
Tel: +1 650 324 7000 **Fax:** +1 650 324 0638
Email: info@hewm.com

815 Connecticut Avenue NW, Suite 200, **Washington DC** 20006-4004
Tel: +1 202 263 8900 **Fax:** +1 202 785 8877
Email: info@hewm.com

ASSOCIATED OFFICES

The firm has affiliated Carnelutti offices in Milan, Rome, Paris, Padua, and Naples, as well as with Schuster & Partners in Frankfurt, Germany.

LANGUAGES: Arabic, Armenian, Dutch, Flemish, French, Gaelic, German, Hebrew, Indian, Italian, Japanese, Mandarin, Norwegian, Persian/Farsi, Polish, Portuguese, Russian, Spanish, Tagalog, Taiwanese, Thai, Turkish, Ukrainian, Vietnamese

H

For other recommended firms see pages 1485-1520

HENGELER MUELLER WEITZEL WIRTZ

HEAD OFFICE

see Worldwide Office Contacts

Website: www.hengeler.com

FIRM OVERVIEW

Managing partners: Hendrik Haag and Gerd Krieger

Number of partners worldwide: 65
Number of other lawyers worldwide: 98

AREAS OF PRACTICE:

Corporate/M&A .... *%
Private equity .... *%
Capital markets .... *%
Banking .... *%
Project finance .... *%
Competition and antitrust .... *%
Tax .... *%
Telecommunications/media/e-commerce .... *%
Environmental .... *%
Intellectual property .... *%
Employment .... *%
Insurance .... *%
Litigation and arbitration .... *%
*Workload % not disclosed

FIRM OVERVIEW: The origins of the firm date back to 1901. Since its inception, Hengeler Mueller has been widely regarded as one of the leading German firms in national and international business transactions, particularly in the areas of corporate law, M&A (including cross-border mergers, acquisitions, takeovers, and joint ventures), banking law and capital markets (including equity and debt, securitisation, and derivatives). The firm maintains its strong international presence by entertaining close relationships with Slaughter and May, London, and Davis Polk & Wardwell, New York, and other firms in New York, Paris, Madrid, Rome, Amsterdam and other financial and corporate centres around the world, believed to be clearly leading in their respective countries and areas of practice. This policy makes it possible to provide clients, through integrated teams of lawyers from the different firms, with seamless and one-stop legal services on all aspects of international business transactions and in all jurisdictions concerned.

INTERNATIONAL EXPERIENCE: Hengeler Mueller's international work is characterised by advising clients in top-league transactions in the areas listed above. The firm is often retained as lead counsel when innovative solutions are sought and new legal products must be developed. If needed to handle the transaction, Hengeler Mueller will operate through an integrated team of lawyers from leading firms in the relevant jurisdictions.

WORLDWIDE OFFICE CONTACTS

BELGIUM
Avenue de Cortenbergh 118, bte 2, B-1000 **Brussels**
Tel: +32 2 737 1530 **Fax:** +32 2 737 1531

CZECH REPUBLIC
Betlémský Palác, Husova 5, CZ-1 1000 **Prague**
Tel: +420 2 2440 1488 **Fax:** +420 2 2424 8701

GERMANY
Charlottenstrasse 35/36, D-10117 **Berlin**
Tel: +49 30 203 740 **Fax:** +49 30 203 743 33
Email: hmwwbln@hengeler.com

Trinkausstrasse 7, D-40213 **Düsseldorf**
Tel: +49 211 830 40 **Fax:** +49 211 830 4170
Email: hmwwdus@hengeler.com

Bockenheimer Landstrasse 51, D-60325 **Frankfurt am Main**
Tel: +49 69 170 950 **Fax:** +49 69 725 773
Email: hmwwffm@hengeler.com

HUNGARY
Bartók Béla, U.15/B. I./5, H-1114 **Budapest**
Tel: +36 1 372 7650 **Fax:** +36 1 372 7659

USA
712 Fifth Avenue, NY 10019, **New York**
Tel: +1 212 586 4600 **Fax:** +1 212 586 4481

INTERNATIONAL CLIENTS: Clients are typically major publicly-listed corporations and financial institutions, based in Germany and abroad and from a wide variety of industries, including American Express, Aventis, Credit Suisse First Boston, Deutsche Bank, Deutsche Telekom, General Motors, Goldman Sachs, J.P. Morgan, Lazard, Merrill Lynch, METRO, Morgan Stanley Dean Witter, RWE, Thyssen Krupp, United Technologies.

LANGUAGES: Czech, English, French, Hungarian, Italian, Spanish

HENGELER MUELLER WEITZEL WIRTZ

For other recommended firms see pages 1483-1520

HERBERT SMITH

HEAD OFFICE

Exchange House, Primrose Street,
London EC2A 2HS, United Kingdom
Tel: +44 20 7374 8000 **Fax:** +44 20 7374 0888
Email: enquiries@herbertsmith.com
Website: www.herbertsmith.com

FIRM OVERVIEW

Senior partner: Richard Bond
Practice development partner: Richard Fleck
Executive partner: Tim Parkes

Number of partners worldwide: 170
Number of other lawyers worldwide: 526

AREAS OF PRACTICE:

Competition and regulation .... *%
Energy and natural resources .... *%
Finance and banking .... *%
Insurance .... *%
Intellectual property and technology .... *%
Litigation and arbitration .... *%
Mergers and acquisitions .... *%
Projects .... *%
Property and construction .... *%
* Workload % not disclosed

FIRM OVERVIEW: Formed in 1882, Herbert Smith comprises more than 1700 staff. The firm advises major corporate organisations, governments, financial institutions and commercial organisations, globally and in all business sectors.

INTERNATIONAL EXPERIENCE: A significant proportion of the firm's work is international, involving the co-ordination and management of clients' commercial activities across many jurisdictions and in different parts of the world. The firm's international capability is resourced from offices in London, Brussels, Moscow and Paris and in Asia through offices in Bangkok, Beijing, Hong Kong, Singapore and Tokyo. It is further resourced by the offices of its associated firms, Gleiss Lutz Hootz Hirsch in Berlin, Brussels, Frankfurt, Munich, Prague, Shanghai, Stuttgart and Warsaw, and Hiswara Bunjamin & Tandjung in Jakarta. Recent corporate work has included advising Royal London on its £1.1 billion acquisition of the business of Scottish Life and the defence of the £850 million hostile offer by OM Gruppen AB and Publicis on its £4 billion merger with Saatchi and Saatchi. International projects work include advising BNP Prime Peregrine, sponsor and lead manager, in connection with the flotation on the Growth Enterprise Market of the Hong Kong Stock Exchange of techpacific.com Limited and Huaneng Power International Inc. on its listing on the Hong Kong Stock Exchange. International litigation work includes representing Marconi Communications in the successful defence of substantial litigation concerning the effect of United Nations sanctions against Iraq and advising Goldman Sachs in respect of injunction proceedings from Mannesmann seeking to prevent Goldman Sachs acting for Vodafone in any potential hostile takeover of Mannesmann. The firm's substantial international arbitration team is also conducting 130 arbitrations in 19 jurisdictions around the world.

INTERNATIONAL CLIENTS: The firm's international clients include Chevron, the European Commission, Time Warner, British American Tobacco, Sinopec, United Utilities, First Choice Holidays, BSkyB, Merrill Lynch, Nomura, Publicis, Sumitomo Bank, Sandvik, and Allied Zurich.

WORLDWIDE OFFICE CONTACTS

BELGIUM
15 Rue Guimard, B-1040 **Brussels**
Tel: +32 2 511 7450 **Fax:** +32 2 511 7772
Email: enquiries@herbertsmith.com

CHINA
1410-1415 China World Tower, 1 Jianguomenwai Avenue, **Beijing** 100004
Tel: +86 10 6505 6512 **Fax:** +86 10 6505 6516
Email: enquiries-asia@herbertsmith.com

FRANCE
20 Rue Quentin-Bauchart, 75008 **Paris**
Tel: +33 1 53 57 70 70 **Fax:** +33 1 53 57 70 80
Email: enquiries@herbertsmith.com

HONG KONG
23rd Floor Gloucester Tower, 11 Pedder Street, Central, **Hong Kong**
Tel: +852 2845 6639 **Fax:** +852 2845 9099
Email: enquiries-asia@herbertsmith.com

JAPAN
Toranomon 2-Chome Tower, 2-3-17 Toranomon, Minato-ku,
Tokyo 1-5-0001
Tel: +81 3 3508 4508 **Fax:** +81 3 3508 4509
Email: enquiries-asia@herbertsmith.com

RUSSIA
Herbert Smith CIS Legal Services, Ulitsa Nikoloyamskaya, 15, 109240
Moscow
Tel: +7 095 777 6500 **Fax:** + 7 095 777 6501
Email: enquiries@herbertsmith.com

SINGAPORE
#15-08 Ocean Building, 10 Collyer Quay, **Singapore** 049315
Tel: +65 536 7990 **Fax:** +65 536 7993
Email: enquiries-asia@herbertsmith.com

THAILAND
Herbert Smith (Thailand) Ltd, 990 Abdulrahim Building, 14th Floor, Room 1401, Rama IV Road, Kwaeng Silom, Khet Bangrak, **Bangkok** 10500
Tel: +66 2 636 0656 **Fax:** +66 2 636 0657
Email: enquiries-asia@herbertsmith.com

UNITED KINGDOM
Exchange House, Primrose Street, **London** EC2A 2HS
Tel: +44 20 7374 8000 **Fax:** +44 20 7374 0888
Email: enquiries@herbertsmith.com

HEAD OFFICE:

Number of lawyers: 534
Number of dual qualified lawyers: 26
Number of locally qualified lawyers: 534

Main areas of work: Banking, capital markets, commercial litigation, commercial real estate, construction and engineering, corporate, corporate finance, corporate recovery, defamation, EU and competition, employee incentives, employment, energy, environment, insurance, insurance litigation, intellectual property, international commercial arbitration, international fraud, international project finance, investment funds, media, mergers and acquisitions, pensions, planning and development, private equity, tax, telecoms, trusts and charities, utilities regulation.
Top clients: Include BT, Goldman Sachs, Iceland, Merrill Lynch, Nomura, and Publicis.

For other recommended firms see pages 1485-1520

Highlight deals: The firm has been involved in advising Time Warner Inc on the European issues of its US$220 billion merger with AOL; Goldman Sachs in respect of injunction proceedings from Mannesmann seeking to prevent Goldman Sachs for Vodafone in any potential hostile takeover of Mannesmann; BT on the acquisition of 45% of VIAG INTERKOM GmbH & Co from EON AG; Publicis on its £4 billion merger with Saatchi and Saatchi; Nomura on all the legal aspects of the proposed bid to acquire the Millennium Dome site and the associated land on the Greenwich Peninsula and to develop the site as Europe's first urban entertainment resort; Tata Tea (GB) Limited on the £280 million acquisition of the entire issued share capital of Tetley Group Limited from Venture Capitalists and Management; Allied Zurich plc on the £24 billion unification of Zurich Financial Services Group, including Zurich Allied AG of Switzerland under a single holding company; Iceland Group plc in relation to its proposed merger with Booker plc; Merrill Lynch in its capacity as financial adviser to Cable & Wireless on the £22.5 billion Singapore bid for Cable & Wireless HKT by Singapore Telecom and Pacific Century Cyber Works; the Birmingham Alliance in connection with two compulsory purchase orders (CPOs) for the new BullRing shopping centre in Birmingham which have been confirmed by the Secretary of State following an inquiry in February 2000.
Languages: Afrikaans, Arabic, Cantonese, Danish, Dutch, French, German, Greek, Gujarati, Hebrew, Hindi, Italian, Japanese, Malaysian, Mandarin, Norwegian, Persian, Polish, Portuguese, Punjabi, Russian, Spanish, Swedish, Turkish, Urdu
Office profile: The firm's London office, opened in 1882, provides a wide range of legal services across all areas of corporate and commercial life. The office is experienced in advising on mergers, acquisitions and takeovers and is well known for its expertise in corporate finance. The office is active in international finance and banking, most notably in the specialised field of international capital markets. The office is experienced in domestic and international litigation and arbitration, and specialises in administrative and public law, banking, civil fraud, construction, defamation, employment, energy, environment and planning, information technology, insurance and reinsurance, intellectual property, investment funds, public and private international law, professional indemnity, regulatory and compliance cases and sport. The office is also active in real estate development and investment, buying, selling and managing portfolios on behalf of several of the UK's leading property developers and investors.

WORLDWIDE OFFICES

BELGIUM
15 Rue Guimard, B-1040 Brussels

Managing partner: Stephen Kinsella
Number of lawyers: 9

Main areas of work: Anti-trust and trade regulation; communications and media, mergers and acquisitions, public procurement
Top clients: International Motorsport Federation (the FIA), Salt Union, Time Warner, Gannet, Trinity, Johnson Matthey, Allergan
Highlight deals: The office acts on many competition matters, such as the proposed merger of Time Warner with America Online (AOL) - estimated to be the largest ever in terms of total value.
Languages: Danish, Dutch, English, Finnish, French, German, Irish, Italian, Norwegian, Spanish, Swedish
Office profile: The Brussels office of Herbert Smith, which is part of the firm's European and Competition Group, advises on the application of European Union and WTO law to a wide range of commercial clients.

CHINA
1410-1415 China World Tower, 1 Jianguomenwai Avenue, Beijing 100004

Senior resident: Terence Grady
Number of lawyers: 2
Number of locally qualified lawyers: 1

Main areas of work: Finance and banking, projects and direct investment, corporate finance, dispute resolution, shipping and international trade, shipping.
Languages: Chinese (various dialects), English
Office profile: Herbert Smith opened an office in Beijing in September 1999 to deal with investment and trade activities in China.

FRANCE
20 Rue Quentin-Bauchart, 75008 Paris

Managing partner: Neil Brimson
Number of lawyers: 49
Number of dual qualified lawyers: 6
Number of locally qualified lawyers: 39

Main areas of work: The practice extends across the corporate, commercial and financial sectors, especially in mergers and acquisitions, equities and other securities, banking and capital markets, tax and commercial property.
Languages: Arabic, Dutch, English, French, German, Italian, Japenese, Spanish
Office profile: Herbert Smith has a substantial, broadly-based French and international business law practice in Paris. It is established in international projects and project financing, notably in the oil and gas, mining, transport and other infrastructure sectors. Much of this involves projects outside France especially in Africa and the Middle East. The firm provides a full French litigation service as well as its long-established international arbitration practice.

HONG KONG
23rd Floor Gloucester Tower, 11 Pedder Street, Central

Managing partner: David Willis
Number of lawyers: 63
Number of dual qualified lawyers: 32
Number of locally qualified lawyers: 55

Main areas of work: Arbitration, China investment and securities, commercial litigation, corporate finance/commercial, corporate restructuring and insolvency, insurance, intellectual property, international banking, finance and capital markets, M&A and direct investment, projects/project finance, property and conveyancing, regulatory and commercial crime, shipping and internaional trade, structured finance/asset finance.
Top clients: AXA, Bank of Scotland, Crosby, Arthur Andersen, Bechtel, Stagecoach
Highlight deals: Acting for AXA China Region on the HK$4.3 billion takeover offer made by National Mutual Holdings under the Hong Kong Takeovers and Mergers Code and the subsequent application for delisting of the company's shares on the Stock Exchange of Hong Kong; Bank of Scotland on the Hong Kong aspects of its takeover bid for National Westminster Bank; Sinopec on its initial public offering of Hong Kong Shares and American Depository Shares; and Crosby on the establishment of growasia.com.
Languages: Cantonese, Danish, English, French, German, Italian, Japenese, Mandarin (and other Chinese dialects), Portuguese, Spanish

H

For other recommended firms see pages 1485-1520

Office profile: The Hong Kong office, opened in 1982, provides a full range of legal services and, with the firm's Beijing office, acts as a base for the firm's China practices. Its lawyers are qualified to practice in Hong Kong, UK, China, USA, Singapore, Australia and New Zealand.

JAPAN

Toranomon 2-Chome Tower, 2-3-17 Toranomon, Minato-ku, Tokyo 1-5-0001

Managing partner: Steve Lewis
Number of lawyers: 9

Main areas of work: M&A, banking and finance, projects, dispute resolution and media.
Highlight deals: Acting for West Japan Railways and Central Japan Railways on the acquisition of Vodafone of a 15% stake in Japan Telecom, the country's third largest telecoms operator.
Languages: English, Japanese
Office profile: The office, opened in Tokyo in February 2000, focuses on providing legal services to international corporations in Japan and to Japanese clients with overseas investments. The Tokyo team has long-term experience of the Japanese market particularly in M&A, energy, projects, telecoms and media.

RUSSIA

Herbert Smith CIS Legal Services, Ulitsa Nikoloyamskaya, 15, 109240 Moscow

Managing partner: Alan Jowett
Number of lawyers: 6
Number of locally qualified lawyers: 4

Languages: English, French, Russian
Office profile: The Moscow practice, established in June 1999, focuses on projects, particularly energy and natural resources; banking and debt restructuring; and mergers and acquisitions.

SINGAPORE

#15-08 Ocean Building, 10 Collyer Quay, Singapore 049315

Managing partner: Mark Newbery
Number of lawyers: 15
Number of locally qualified lawyers: 1

Main areas of work: Corporate finance, energy and natural resources, insurance, international banking, finance and capital markets, arbitration/dispute resolution, M&A, privatisations, projects/project finance.
Highlight deals: Advising on a Sino-American joint venture in recovery actions in Hong Kong and civil proceedings in China, with regards to letter of credit frauds; the Bank of Scotland on Singapore regulatory aspects of its £24 billion hostile bid for Natoional Westminster Bank plc; and the Crossby Group on the creation of growasia.com.
Languages: English, French, Portuguese, Putonghua
Office profile: Herbert Smith's Singapore office, established in May 1995, focuses primarily on project development and project finance, corporate finance, privatisations, structured finance, capital markets, insurance and arbitration.

THAILAND

Herbert Smith (Thailand) Ltd, 990 Abdulrahim Building, 14th Floor, Room 1401, Rama IV Road, Kwaeng Silom, Khet Bangrak, Bangkok 10500

Director: Jonathan Pyne
Number of lawyers: 9
Number of locally qualified lawyers: 7

Main areas of work: Arbitration, banking, capital markets, commercial litigation, corporate finance, corporate restructuring and insolvency, M&A, privatisations, projects/project finance, property.
Highlight deals: Acting for a bank steering committee led by Sumitomo Bank on the restructuring of a listed machinery manufacturing company by 29 creditors with endebtedness of THB4.5 billion; European and US insurers on claim litigation conducted in Thailand and Taiwan.
Languages: English, Thai
Office profile: The Bangkok office opened in Autumn 1998 to support the firm's rapidly growing regional dispute practice, the Thai corporate restructuring practice, and Herbert Smith's banking and M&A work in Thailand and neighbouring countries.

HERBERT SMITH

For other recommended firms see pages 1485-1520

HERZOG FOX & NEEMAN

HEAD OFFICE

Asia House, 4 Weizmann Street,
Tel Aviv 64239, Israel
Tel: +972 3 692 2020 **Fax:** +972 3 696 6464

Email: hfn@hfn.co.il

WORLDWIDE OFFICE CONTACTS

ISRAEL
Asia House, 4 Weizmann Street, **Tel Aviv** 64239
Tel: +972 3 692 2020 **Fax:** +972 3 696 6464
Email: hfn@hfn.co.il

FIRM OVERVIEW

Senior partners: Michael Fox and Yaakov Neeman

Number of partners worldwide: 18
Number of other lawyers worldwide: 47

AREAS OF PRACTICE:

Area	%
Banking and finance	20%
Litigation and arbitration	20%
M&A	20%
Tax	20%
General corporate	10%
Energy	5%
Telecommunications and IT	5%

FIRM OVERVIEW: Herzog, Fox & Neeman was formed in 1972 as a firm specialising in corporate, commercial and tax matters. The firm has grown into one of the largest firms in Israel with a legal staff of over 75. The firm was founded by the late Chaim Herzog, who later became the sixth President of the State of Israel; Michael Fox, a former London solicitor who heads the corporate and foreign client department; and Dr. Yaakov Neeman, a leading tax and finance expert.

INTERNATIONAL EXPERIENCE: The majority of the firm's business comes from outside Israel and approximately half of its work is conducted in English. A high proportion of the firm's lawyers, including five of the partners, are native English speakers with foreign legal qualifications. Members of the firm are licensed to practise in various US states, the UK, and in Australia. The firm's lawyers have worked at leading international firms in the US, the UK, EEC countries, Japan, Australia, and Singapore.

INTERNATIONAL CLIENTS: The firm advises international technology companies on acquisitions and investments.

MAIN INTERNATIONAL AREAS OF PRACTICE:
Corporate: The firm has represented over half of the foreign acquiring companies in the 30 major mergers and acquisitions of Israeli technology companies in the past five years.
Banking and finance: The firm represents many large American and European banks, and has advised foreign banks on syndicated loans to Israeli corporations. The firm is involved in many infrastructure and project finance matters and has been involved in virtually all major PFI projects in Israel.
Tax: The firm has the largest tax department of all the law firms in Israel. A number of its lawyers are qulaified in both the US and UK and are CPA's. The firm is actively involved in the tax aspects of Israel's major mergers and acquisitions. The firm's tax expertise covers derivatives, real estate and employee benefits.
Litigation: The firm's litigation department deals only with commercial litigation. The practice group represents many multinational corporations, defending claims filed in Israel.
Securities: The firm's securities practice advises underwriters and issuers on a wide variety of offerings in the Israeli and international capital market.
Telecommunications: In addition to the firm's ongoing representation of a number of international telecommunications corporations, it has represented bidders in major telecommunications tenders in Israel.
Construction and property development: The practice works closely with the tax and corporate departments, and acts for foreign developers. The firm advises on all aspects from the structure to be assumed through to financing with Israeli banks and development and registration procedures. The firm has represented bidding consortia on many high profile infrastructure projects including the Cross-Israel Highway, the Carmel Tunnel, the Jerusalem Light Railway, water and desalination and several power projects.
Energy: The firm is active in the expanding area of natural gas.

LANGUAGES: English, Hebrew

HERZOG, FOX & NEEMAN

For other recommended firms see pages 1485-1520

HEUKING KÜHN LÜER WOJTEK

HEAD OFFICE

Cecilienallee 5,
40474 Düsseldorf, Germany
Tel: +49 211 600 55 00 **Fax:** +49 211 600 55 050
Email: duesseldorf@heuking.de
Website: www.heuking.com

FIRM OVERVIEW

Number of partners worldwide: 53
Number of other lawyers worldwide: 82

AREAS OF PRACTICE:

Administrative and constitutional .... *%
Arbitration .... *%
Bankruptcy and insolvency .... *%
Corporate .... *%
Employment, health and safety .... *%
Environmental, competition and state aids .... *%
Family law and law of succession .... *%
Finance and banking .... *%
International trade and customs .... *%
M&A .... *%
Product Liability Acts .... *%
Real estate and construction .... *%
Telecommunications .... *%
* Workload % not disclosed

FIRM OVERVIEW: Heuking Kühn Lüer Wojtek is one of the major German law firms, focusing particularly on business law. The firm, established in 1970, is a member of the 'Denton International Group of Law Firms'. Heuking Kühn Lüer Wojtek is internationally orientated - all lawyers are multilingual and many have foreign university degrees. The firm has an office in Brussels which maintains contacts with institutions in Brussels, particularly the European Commission.

INTERNATIONAL CLIENTS: The firm's client base comprises numerous well-known corporations from Germany and throughout Europe (especially France and the UK) and the US, as well as governments and individuals.

MAIN INTERNATIONAL AREAS OF PRACTICE:

Corporate law: The firm advises on acquisitions and mergers, incorporations and international co-operation agreements. Heuking Kühn Lüer Wojtek assists in re-organisations and due diligence reports and advises on issues of distribution and transport law. The firm structures cross-border transactions and implements such under inclusion of international tax counselling.
Finance and banking law: The firm advises on the foundation and acquisition of bank branches and all related aspects. The firm monitors investment funds and financing instruments and advises clients on initial public offerings and private placements.
Environmental, competition and state aid law: The firm offers advice on all aspects of competition law applicable in Germany and the EU, including merger control, competition restrictions and unfair competition. It also advises on industrial copyright protection (in particular, German and European trademark law), and handles aspects of technology transfer, computer rights and the protection of company information and electronic data.
Telecommunications: In addition to the traditional sector of copyright issues, Heuking Kühn Lüer Wojtek offers expert advice in the field of new media and entertainment, on aspects of German, European and international telecommunications law, including radio, television and satellite regulations.
Tax: The firm advises on individual tax assessments, enterprises and international tax structuring. The firm handles statutory and voluntary audits of company and group accounts and special audits in case of company acquisitions.
Administrative and constitutional law: The firm advises on administrative matters relating to privatisations in the new and old 'Bundesländer'. The firm advises foreign governments in structuring standards and contracts under aspects of commercial and general civil law.
Bankruptcy and insolvency: The firm focuses on bankruptcy, insolvency and insurance law.
Real estate and construction: The firm advises on public and private building law focusing primarily on questions of real estate acquisition and development and company acquisitions.
Product liability acts: The firm offers comprehensive advice on German, French and European product liability acts.
Employment: The firm handles matters such as individual and collective labour law, re-organisations, the drafting of social plans, pension benefits, and representation in labour law disputes as well as mass restructurings.
Family law and law of succession: The team at Heuking Kühn Lüer Wojtek advise on matters of family law and law of succession, including the regulation of accession. The firm handles litigation in civil and fiscal matters and represents its clients in national and international arbitration proceedings, commercial law litigation and estate planning.

LANGUAGES: English, French, German, Italian, Japanese, Russian, Spanish, Swedish

WORLDWIDE OFFICE CONTACTS

BELGIUM
Avenue Louise 140, B-1050 **Brussels**
Tel: +32 2 646 20 00 **Fax:** +32 2 646 20 40
Email: g.williamson@heuking.de

GERMANY
Tiergarten Dreieck, Klingelhöfer Strasse 5, 10785 **Berlin**
Tel: +49 30 88 45 030 **Fax:** +49 30 88 27 150
Email: berlin@heuking.de

West Strasse 49, 09112 **Chemnitz**
Tel: +49 371 3820 30 **Fax:** +49 371 3820 391
Email: chemnitz@heuking.de

Cecilienallee 5, 40474 **Düsseldorf**
Tel: +49 211 600 55 00 **Fax:** +49 211 600 55 050
Email: duesseldorf@heuking.de

Linden Strasse 37, 60325 **Frankfurt am Main**
Tel: +49 69 97 56 10 **Fax:** +49 69 97 56 12 00
Email: frankfurt@heuking.de

Bleichenbrücke 9, 20354 **Hamburg**
Tel: +49 40 35 52 800 **Fax:** +49 40 35 52 80 80
Email: hamburg@heuking.de

Magnus Strasse 11-13, 50672 **Köln**
Tel: +49 221 20 52 0 **Fax:** +49 221 20 52 1
Email: koeln@heuking.de

Hermann-Elfleinstrasse 29, 14467 **Potsdam**
Tel: +49 331 29 80 00 **Fax:** +49 331 29 80 050
Email: potsdam@heuking.de

 For other recommended firms see pages 1485-1520

HJORT

HEAD OFFICE

PO Box 471, Sentrum,
0105 Oslo, Norway
Tel: +47 22 47 18 00 **Fax:** +47 22 47 18 18
Email: advokatfirma@hjort.no
Website: www.hjort.no

FIRM OVERVIEW

Managing partner: Erik Keiserud
Senior partner: Jonas W Myhre

Number of partners worldwide: 25
Number of other lawyers worldwide: 22

AREAS OF PRACTICE:

Commercial 55%
Litigation 30%
Criminal 8%
Family 8%

FIRM OVERVIEW: The firm was originally established in Oslo in 1893. It specialises in the field of business law, with an increasingly international focus. In 1993, the firm opened an office in Brussels. An important part of the firm's business consists of advisory services and other assistance to companies operating within trade and industry, and public authorities within the field of commercial law.

INTERNATIONAL EXPERIENCE: The firm represented Statoil in litigation related to Kårstø and in litigation regarding the offshore laying of the Nor-Fra-pipeline from Norway to France. It advised Telenor and various Telenor companies on telecoms and competition matters; Norsk Hydro in various commercial matters in Russia and Italy; the Norwegian Banker's Association on state aid matters and acted on behalf of Norway's largest tobacco company with regard to two tobacco law suits recently filed with Norwegian courts.

INTERNATIONAL CLIENTS: The firm's clients include British Airways, Amerada Hess, Statoil, Telenor, Den norske Bank, Gjendsidige Bank og Forsikring, Statnett and Norsk Hydro.

MAIN INTERNATIONAL AREAS OF PRACTICE:

Litigation: The firm settles a large number of business disputes by means of arbitration, representing clients before the permanent courts of arbitration, as well as ad hoc tribunals. Several of the firm's lawyers are regularly appointed as arbitrators in the ad hoc tribunals. More than half of the partners are Supreme Court barristers.

Companies, partnerships and societies: The firm assists in the formation, conversion, merger, demerger and winding-up of companies of all kinds, including limited companies, partnerships, sole proprietorships, co-operative societies, foundations and organisations. The firm also advises on stock exchange and securities law, corporate financing and operations, including general meetings, articles of association, shareholders' agreements and shareholders' remedies. In addition, Hjort drafts all types of corporate documents and attends the registration of companies.

Contracts: The firm assists small and large enterprises in all types of industries, as well as private individuals in negotiating and drafting contracts, nationally and internationally. The firm's services include cooperation agreements, joint venture and license agreements, agreements for sole distributors and agents, franchise agreements, property development and construction contracts, energy leases and transmission agreements, as well as contracts relating to installations and operations in the offshore sector.

Real property and property development: The firm offers assistance in conjunction with the acquisition, development and operation of real estate. Concession, expropriation and tenancy law (commercial buildings and private dwellings) are areas of particular experience. The firm's activities in this field cover relations with the public authorities and cases before the courts. The firm has been involved in a number of major contracting litigations within the oil and offshore industry.

Taxes and duties: A large portion of the firm's advisory work concerns tax law-related issues, including personal and corporate taxes, wealth and property tax, income tax, value-added and investment tax, payroll tax and inheritance tax. The firm also assists in the completion of tax returns and other statements to public authorities, and deals with matters being handled by the authorities, both administratively and in cases before the courts.

Energy and public utilities: The firm acts as secretariat for the Norwegian Organisation of Hydro Electric Power Municipalities and assists the 155 members on organisational matters, changes in ownership structures, taxes and other issues related to regulation/deregulation affecting the production and distribution of hydroelectric power. The firm has a similar function for some 60 municipalities facing issues related to ownership of natural resources, wild life preservation and local vs. central government.

EEA and EU: The firm assists in drafting contracts and in the notification of contracts and joint ventures to the European Surveillance Agency and to the European Commission. It also assists in the drawing up of marketing strategies and renders assistance on competition law, including the preparation of programmes under EEA/EU law. The firm supplies information about the specific consequences that the implementation of the European Single Market could have for its clients, and offers advice on questions relating to state aid, anti-dumping and other trade policy measures, public purchasing, energy law, free capital movement and legal questions relating to banking and securities law. The firm offers advisory services in connection with free movement of goods and industrial property rights, and acts in cases relating to parallel import. Together with local lawyers, the firm assists in the establishment of businesses in the EEA/EU.

LANGUAGES: English, French, German, Italian, Russian, the Scandinavian languages.

WORLDWIDE OFFICE CONTACTS

BELGIUM
Rue de Taciturne 42, B-1040 **Brussels**
Tel: +32 2 280 0670 **Fax:** +32 2 280 7278
Email: lawoffice.hjort@skynet.be

NORWAY
PO Box 471, Sentrum, 0105 **Oslo**
Tel: +47 22 47 18 00 **Fax:** +47 22 47 18 18
Email: advokatfirma@hjort.no

WORLDWIDE OFFICES

BELGIUM

Rue de Taciturne 42, B-1040 Brussels

Number of lawyers: 2

Office profile: Hjort is the only Norwegian law firm to have an office in Brussels. Its activities include assisting with contract negotiations involving international joint venture projects, assisting with cartel investigations, drawing up compliance programmes and assisting in bringing cases before the EFTA Court. Hjort is a member of TERRALEX, a network of 139 lawfirms in 91 countries.

H

For other recommended firms see pages 1485-1520

HÖCKER RUEB & DOELEMAN

HEAD OFFICE

Van Eeghenstraat 98, 1071 GL Amsterdam,
PO Box 74654, 1070 BR Amsterdam, Netherlands
Tel: +31 20 577 7700 **Fax:** +31 20 671 9710

Email: mail@hrd.nl

WORLDWIDE OFFICE CONTACTS

NETHERLANDS
Van Eeghenstraat 98, 1071 GL,
PO Box 74654, 1070 BR **Amsterdam**
Tel: +31 20 577 7700 **Fax:** +31 20 671 9710
Email: mail@hrd.nl

FIRM OVERVIEW

Managing partner: Leo Sapir

Number of partners worldwide: 14
Number of other lawyers worldwide: 27

AREAS OF PRACTICE:

Corporate and commercial, M&A, insolvency	30%
Employment and workers' participation law	25%
Intellectual property, media and IT	20%
Other	25%

FIRM OVERVIEW: The firm was established in 1987. Höcker Rueb & Doeleman offers a commercial practice that is highly focused on corporate and insolvency law, employment law and intellectual property, media and IT law. The firm also has a general commercial practice in most areas of Dutch and international law.

INTERNATIONAL EXPERIENCE: The firm has established an extensive informal network of international contacts. The firm is a member of Lexwork International, an association of European law firms.

MAIN INTERNATIONAL AREAS OF PRACTICE:
Corporate and commercial, insolvency: The firm advises on all aspects of corporate and commercial activities, in particular on M&A, corporate finance related issues and buyouts. The main area of practice is advising on national and international joint ventures, partnerships and other strategic and operational alliances in the media and advertising business. Another important area of activity is the insolvency practice. A few of the partners frequently act as receivers in bankrupcty proceedings or as company trustees following the suspension of payments. Taking advantage of this experience, the practice also advises company management and creditors on insolvency-related matters. Contact, Antoine Endtz (corporate and commercial/M&A) +31 20 577 7711; Kees van de Meent (insolvency), +31 20 577 7760.
Employment: Höcker Rueb & Doeleman deals with all legal aspects of employer and employee relations, including employee documentation, the resolution of individual and/or collective disputes and employee benefits. The practice also covers collective employment law, worker participation law and pension schemes. The firm has extensive experience in matters where a works council's advice is needed, such as reorganisation and M&A, and frequently advises works councils and corporate groups, as well as management boards, on these matters. Contact, Otto Albers, +31 20 577 7724; Jasper van Hulst, +31 20 577 7765.

Intellectual property, media, computer and IT law: The firm has created a multi-disciplinary department to service the needs of both listed and small companies in all areas of intellectual property, media and information technology law. IT activities include resolving a wide range of disputes, drafting and negotiating agreements for the supply and maintenance of IT systems, advising on software development, licensing and distribution and the establishment and protection of technology rights, particularly in relation to the internet and e-commerce. In addition the department focuses on media and entertainment law, its clients including a large number of broadcasters and related clients as well as entertainment companies. Contact, Gijsbert Brunt (intellectual property/IT),+31 20 577 7727; Willem Roos (intellectual property and entertainment), +31 20 577 7700, Germ Kemper (media), +31 20 5777705.

LANGUAGES: Dutch, English, French, German, Italian

For other recommended firms see pages 1485-1520

ATTORNEYS AT HOFDABAKKI

HEAD OFFICE

Hofdabakki 9, 6th floor, 110
Reykjavik Iceland
Tel: +354 587 1286 **Fax:** +354 587 1247

Email: logmenn@justice.is
Website: www.justice.is

WORLDWIDE OFFICE CONTACTS

ICELAND
Hofdabakki 9, 6th floor, 110, **Reykjavik**
Tel: +354 587 1286 **Fax:** +354 587 1247
Email: logmenn@justice.is

FIRM OVERVIEW

Managing and senior partner: Hreinn Loftsson

Number of partners worldwide: 3
Number of other lawyers worldwide: 2

AREAS OF PRACTICE:

Corporate	40%
Insurance and reinsurance	20%
Litigation and arbitration	20%
M&A	10%
Banking and finance	5%
Telecommunications and IT	5%

FIRM OVERVIEW: The firm offers a full range of legal services including litigation and arbitration, general corporate and M&A work. Its principle is to offer fast and effective quality services using modern technology and specialisation in order to satisfy the increasing demand of its corporate clients. Among the firm's domestic clients are some of the largest business enterprises in Iceland. The firm acts as consultants to the government and local muncipalities. It is is a member of two international law firm networks.

INTERNATIONAL EXPERIENCE: In 1999, the firm handled the sale of a bottling company in Iceland to Coca Cola Nordic Beverages A/S in Denmark. The previous year the firm was actively involved in the merger between Sol (a soft-drinks manufacturer) and Viking (a brewery). The firm's Senior Partner, Hreinn Loftsson, has been chairman of the Icelandic Government's Executive Committee on Privatisation since 1991 and has overseen the preparation of some 20 privatisations. In 1999 the Committee completed the privatisation of a major investment bank. During the course of this year the Committee has been involved in the preparation of the potential privatisation of Iceland Telecom.

INTERNATIONAL CLIENTS: The firm's client base includes a major Icelandic power company, the largest retailer chain in Iceland, a large municipality in the Reykjavík area, as well as the local sales agency for one of the biggest insurance companies in Europe and a major local insurance brokerage.

MAIN INTERNATIONAL AREAS OF PRACTICE:
M&A: The firm has an experienced M&A practice. The firm's senior partner, Mr Hreinn Loftson, is a member of the advisory board overseeing the largest merger in Iceland involving The National Bank of Iceland and The Agricultural Bank of Iceland.
Banking and finance: Attorneys at Hofdabakki covers all areas of banking and finance, notably within the EEA area with consideration of EU laws.
Insurance and reinsurance: Attorneys at Hofdabakki advise on all aspects of insurance. The firm's lawyers are experienced in local and international insurance operations and one of the firm's members is a certified insurance broker.
Telecommunications: The firm advises on all aspects of telecommunications. It advises mainly large companies on all aspects of telecommunications law.
Litigation and arbitration: Attorneys at Hofdabakki handle commercial litigation and national and international arbitration. The firm's lawyers are frequently involved in cases before the Icelandic Courts, including the Supreme Court, and have participated in matters under the rules of the International Chamber of Commerce.
EU and competition: This area has acquired a new prominence since Iceland's inclusion in the European Economic Area. The firm's lawyers undertake competition and marketing-related cases involving companies in the Icelandic market.
Energy and public utilities: The firm plays an active role in the energy sector as lawyers to one of Iceland's major power companies.
Corporate: The firm advises on all aspects of general corporate law, including the drafting of Icelandic and international contracts.
Employment: The firm handles all matters relating to Icelandic employment law.
Securities and financial markets: Attorneys at Hofdabakki advise clients on Icelandic law pertaining to funds, securities and derivatives.

LANGUAGES: Danish, English, Icelandic

HOLLAND & KNIGHT LLP

HEAD OFFICE

195 Broadway, 24th Floor,
New York NY 10007, USA
Tel: +1 212 513 3200 **Fax:** +1 212 385 9010

Email: whonan@hklaw.com
Website: www.hklaw.com

FIRM OVERVIEW

Managing partner: Bill McBride

Number of partners worldwide: 669
Number of other lawyers worldwide: 486

AREAS OF PRACTICE:

Litigation 42%
Corporate 32%
Real estate and public land use 18%
Public law 8%

FIRM OVERVIEW: Holland & Knight LLP is one of the largest commercial law firms in the world with more than 1,100 lawyers, practising in over 100 areas of law. The firm's multi-office, one firm structure enables it to provide efficient legal advice to local and international clients.

INTERNATIONAL EXPERIENCE: Holland & Knight's international lawyers represent clients in both inbound and outbound transactions. The firm advises US and international clients on establishing manufacturing and other operating installations including feasibility, customs and taxation issues. In coordination with the tax, corporate and securities lawyers, the firm's international lawyers handle matters involving organisation of foreign operations of domestic businesses, international patents and copyrights, and customs matters. Holland & Knight has been involved in all aspects of privatisation including banking, energy, and transportation privatisations in Latin and South America, Europe, the Middle East, and Asia.The firm's global focus is enhanced by its well-established correspondent relationships with leading law firms located in the commercial centres of Europe, Latin America, Asia, the Middle East, and Africa.

INTERNATIONAL CLIENTS: The firm advises clients with business interests in banking and finance, domestic and foreign governments, aviation, maritime, high technology, telecommunications, international construction, hospitality, energy and transportation.

MAIN INTERNATIONAL AREAS OF practice:

Alternative dispute resolution: Lawyers in Holland & Knight's ADR practice group have experience in a range of international dispute resolutions.
Corporate finance: The firm represents financial institutions and other lenders in connection with the negotiation and preparation of documentation for complex secured and unsecured credit transactions.
Aviation: The firm handles international aviation work and specialises in advising on issues involving the International Civil Aviation Organisation and air ministries throughout the world. Holland & Knight's clients are based in Europe, the Middle East, and Central and South America.
Corporate: Holland & Knight advises on a range of corporate transactions including mergers and acquisitions, sales and divestitures, financings, and securities offerings. The firm also handles tax advice, negotiation, corporate planning, M&A strategic planning, and capital formation.

WORLDWIDE OFFICE CONTACTS

BRAZIL
Rue de Assembléia, nº58-10º andar, 20011-1000, **Rio de Janeiro**, RJ
Tel: +55 21 509 5050 **Fax:** +55 21 221 9035

Rue Pedrosa Alvarenga nº1-284-10º, andar-conj, 102, 04532-000
São Paulo, SP
Tel: +55 11 3079 2300 **Fax:** +55 11 3079 2004
Email: epramos@hklaw.com

JAPAN
New Otemachi Building, Suite 613, 2-2-1 Otemachi, Chiyoda-ku, **Tokyo**
Tel: +81 33 242 1289 **Fax:** +81 33 242 1290

MEXICO
Edificio Arcos Bosques Corporativo, Paseo de los Tamarindos No 400-B, Piso 2, 05120 **Mexico City**
Tel: +52 52 611 866 **Fax:** +52 52 611 867

USA
1201 West Peachtree Street NE, One Atlantic Center, Suite 2000,
Atlanta GA, 30309
Tel: +1 404 817 8500 **Fax:** +1 404 881 0470

One Beacon Street, **Boston** MA 02108
Tel: +1 617 523 2700 **Fax:** +1 617 523 6850

Huntingdon Bank Building, 1001 3rd Avenue West, Suite 600,
Bradenton FL 34205
Tel: +1 941 748 7076 **Fax:** +1 941 747 9774

55 West Monroe Street, Suite 800, **Chicago** IL 60603
Tel: +1 312 263 3600 **Fax:** +1 312 578 6666

One East Broward Boulevard, Suite 1300, **Fort Lauderdale** FL 33301
Tel: +1 954 535 1000 **Fax:** +1 954 463 2030

50 North Laura Street, Suite 3900, **Jacksonville** FL 32202
Tel: +1 904 353 2000 **Fax:** +1 904 358 1872

92 Lake Wire Drive, **Lakeland** FL 33815
Tel: +1 863 682 1161 **Fax:** +1 863 688 1186

633 West Fifth Street, 21st Floor, **Los Angeles** CA 90071
Tel: +1 213 896 2400 **Fax:** +1 213 896 2450

1499 S. Harbor City Boulevard, Suite 303, **Melbourne** FL 32901
Tel: +1 407 951 1776 **Fax:** +1 407 951 1849

701 Brickell Avenue, Suite 3000, **Miami** FL 33131
Tel: +1 305 374 8500 **Fax:** +1 305 789 7799

195 Broadway, 24th Floor, **New York** NY 10007
Tel: +1 212 513 3200 **Fax:** +1 212 385 9010

200 South Orange Avenue, Sun Trust Building, Suite 2600,
Orlando FL 32801
Tel: +1 407 425 8500 **Fax:** +1 407 244 5288

56 Exchange Terrace, East Office Building, Suite 500,
Providence RI 02903
Tel: +1 401 751 8500 **Fax:** +1 401 553 6850

Weston Center, 29th Floor, 112 East Pecan Street,
San Antonio TX 78205
Tel: +1 210 229 3000 **Fax:** +1 210 229 1194

44 Montgomery Street, **San Francisco** CA 94104
Tel: +1 415 743 6900 **Fax:** +1 415 743 6910

For other recommended firms see pages 1485-1520

HOLLAND & KNIGHT LLP cont'd

Construction: Holland & Knight's construction and design practice handles all aspects of contract drafting and negotiation, claim preparation, and dispute resolution through mediation, arbitration or litigation.
Energy: The firm provides a wide range of services to some of the largest international and US energy related companies and public authorities.
Environmental: Holland & Knight advises clients at the local, state, regional and federal levels in the US and internationally on virtually all areas of environmental law.
Government relations: The firm provides a full range of legal and consulting services to domestic and foreign clients considering, or engaged in, transactional operations. The firm advises on the political and legal systems and the cultures of various countries.
Immigration: The firm advises on a wide range of immigration, nationality, and consular laws.
Intellectual property: Holland & Knight's broad intellectual property practice handles client counseling, application/registration, prosecution, licensing, technology transfer and litigation in patents, trademarks, copyrights, trade dress, and common law rights such as unfair competition, trade secrets, and interference with business relations.
Maritime: The firm handles maritime, shipping and admiralty issues. It advises underwriters, owners, charterers, and financial institutions on issues including anti-trust, cargo claims, contracts, cruise shipping, ISM code compliance, insurance and risk management, casualties, financing, and port development.
Privatisation: Holland & Knight's international privatisation practice provides comprehensive services to governments and private sector investors, intermediaries and other participants.
Tax: The firm advises national and international clients on taxation, specialising in preventive and remedial matters.
Technology and emerging companies: Holland & Knight's technology and emerging companies team helps clients identify, troubleshoot, and resolve critical issues relating to business growth. It advises on business formation, intellectual property protection, financing, strategic partnering, initial public offerings, M&A, human capital, and tax planning/wealth transfer.
Telecommunications: The firm provides a full range of legal services in all aspects of telecommunications including litigation, complex business transactions and financing, and in regulatory and legislative areas.

LANGUAGES: The firm has the capacity to translate or interpret in all known languages.

USA
3210 First Interstate Center, 999 Third Avenue, **Seattle** WA 98104
Tel: +1 206 626 5310 **Fax:** +1 206 626 5313

200 Central Avenue, Suite 1600, **St Petersburg** FL 33701
Tel: +1 727 896 7171 **Fax:** +1 727 822 8048

315 South Calhoun Street, Suite 600, **Tallahassee** FL 32301
Tel: +1 850 224 7000 **Fax:** +1 850 224 8832

400 North Ashley Drive, Suite 2300, **Tampa** FL 33602
Tel: +1 813 227 8500 **Fax:** +1 813 229 0134

3110 Fairview Park Drive, Falls Church, **Virginia** VA 22042
Tel: +1 703 645 8600 **Fax:** +1 703 645 8610

2100 Pennsylvania Avenue NW, Suite 400, **Washington DC** 20037
Tel: +1 202 955 3000 **Fax:** +1 202 955 5564

625 North Flagler Drive, Suite 700, **West Palm Beach** FL 33401
Tel: +1 561 833 2000 **Fax:** +1 561 650 8398

ASSOCIATED OFFICES

ARGENTINA
Alvarez Prado, Cabanellas & Kelly, Estudio Petrakovsky, Reconquista le 71, Piso 1 1003, **Buenos Aires**
Tel: +54 11 4311 7392 **Fax:** +54 11 4311 7392

ISRAEL
23 Derech Petach-Tikva, 18th Floor, **Tel Aviv** 66184
Tel: +972 3 566 7666 **Fax:** +972 3 566 7667

VENEZUELA
Tinoco, Travieso, Planchart & Numez, Avenida Francisdo De Miranda, Torre Country Club, Piso 1,2 and 3, Chacaito, **Caracas** 1050
Tel: +58 2 952 9033 **Fax:** +58 2 953 1053
Email: ttpn@ttpn.com.ve

HOLLAND & KNIGHT LLP

For other recommended firms see pages 1485-1520

HOLMAN FENWICK & WILLAN

HEAD OFFICE

Marlow House, Lloyds Avenue,
London EC3N 3AL, United Kingdom
Tel: +44 20 7488 2300 **Fax:** +44 20 7481 0316
Email: holmans@hfw.co.uk
Website: www.holmanfenwick.com

FIRM OVERVIEW

Senior partner: Robert Wilson
Number of partners worldwide: 75
Number of other lawyers worldwide: 110

AREAS OF PRACTICE:

Shipping lititation 50%
Commercial litigation/international trade 20%
Corporate/marine finance and related non-contentious work ... 15%
Insurance/reinsurance 15%

H

FIRM OVERVIEW: Founded in 1883, Holman Fenwick & Willan is an international law firm specialising in shipping law, but continuing to develop its practice outside this area. It has 75 partners and 110 other lawyers in a network of offices in London, Paris, Rouen, Nantes, Piraeus, Hong Kong, Singapore and Shanghai. The firm aims to maintain a close commitment to its clients and an understanding of their business and commercial requirements.

INTERNATIONAL CLIENTS: Clients include businesses involved in all aspects of shipping, insurance underwriters and brokers, trading companies, energy majors, banks and many other forms of commercial enterprise. The firm acts for private and public companies, governments, partnerships, international agencies and trade associations.

MAIN INTERNATIONAL AREAS OF PRACTICE:

Marine: Holman Fenwick & Willan has one of the world's largest admiralty and marine litigation practices and has vast experience in this field. Areas of expertise include charter parties, bills of lading, other carriage contracts and related disputes.
Admiralty and crisis management: The firm has a pre-eminent reputation as a leader in this field and operates a 24-hour emergency service providing an immediate response to maritime casualties worldwide. It handles collisions, fire and explosions; salvage, towage, wreck removal and recovery; personal injury; damage to oil terminals, rigs and offshore structures; pollution, environment damage and clean up.
Insurance and reinsurance: The firm advises on coverage issues, policy interpretation, captive insurance/reinsurance, errors and omissions coverage, insolvency and schemes of arrangement, contract drafting and regulatory advice.
Commercial litigation and arbitration: The firm handles commercial litigation, arbitration and disputes in the areas of banking and financial disputes, engineering and construction claims, coal, oil and gas, environmental claims, professional negligence, corporate fraud, insolvency and schemes of arrangement and sovereign debt and asset recovery.
International trade and commodities: Holman Fenwick & Willan's international trade and commodity practice advises the international trading and financial community on sale, purchase and futures contracts, quality claims, damage and shortfall disputes, swaps and barter trade, trade finance, EU competition law, and transportation agreements.
Corporate and financial: The firm handles a wide range of matters including company formations, corporate finance and acquisitions, project and asset finance, joint ventures, agency and distribution agreements, EC and competition law, intellectual property and information technology, and commercial property.
Air, road and rail: The firm has extensive experience of air and land based carriage, advising operators, financiers and underwriters on transactions, litigation and regulatory issues.
Energy: The firm's energy team is well equipped to advise on exploration, development and production issues, refining, transport and sales.

WORLDWIDE OFFICE CONTACTS

CHINA
Level 24, HSBC Tower, 101 Yin Cheng East Road, Pudong, **Shanghai** 200120
Tel: +86 21 6841 3872 **Fax:** +86 21 6841 2087
Email: holmans@hfw.com.cn

FRANCE
1 rue Eugène Varlin, 44000 **Nantes**
Tel: +33 2 51 84 93 60 **Fax:** +33 2 51 84 93 69
Email: holmans@hfw.france.com

3 rue La Boétie, 75008 **Paris**
Tel: +33 1 44 94 40 50 **Fax:** +33 1 42 65 46 25
Email: holmans@hfw.france.com

47 avenue Gustave Flaubert, 76000 **Rouen**
Tel: +33 2 32 08 18 60 **Fax:** +33 2 35 89 90 54
Email: holmans@hfw.france.com

HONG KONG
15th Floor, Tower One, Lippo Centre, 89 Queensway, **Hong Kong**
Tel: +852 2522 3006 **Fax:** +852 2877 8110
Email: mail@hfw.com.hk

SINGAPORE
10 Collyer Quay, #08-02 Ocean Building, **Singapore** 049315
Tel: +65 534 0195 **Fax:** +65 534 5864
Email: hfw@hfw.com.sg

UNITED KINGDOM
Marlow House, Lloyds Avenue, **London** EC3N 3AL
Tel: +44 20 7488 2300 **Fax:** +44 20 7481 0316
Email: holmans@hfw.co.uk

ASSOCIATED OFFICES

GREECE
6th Floor, 86 Filonos Street, 185 36 **Piraeus**
Tel: +30 1 429 3978 **Fax:** +30 1 429 3118

HEAD OFFICE:

Number of lawyers: 124

Main areas of work: Admiralty and crisis management, corporate and financial, commercial arbitration and litigation, energy, EU and competition law, insolvency, insurance and reinsurance, international trade and commodities, marine litigation, personal injury, property, ship and asset finance, and transport.
Languages: 26 including English, French, German, Greek and Mandarin.
Office profile: Although Holman Fenwick & Willan has an established international presence, the firm has a main office in London. The 51 partners in this office provide advice and assistance on all matters relating to commercial litigation, arbitration and commercial contracts and transactions. The office has particular expertise in maritime law, admiralty, (re)insurance, international trade and transport.

For other recommended firms see pages 1485-1520

HOLMAN FENWICK & WILLAN cont'd

WORLDWIDE OFFICES

CHINA

Level 24, HSBC Tower, 101 Yin Cheng East Road, Pudong, Shanghai 200120

Senior partner: Chris Lockwood
Number of lawyers: 2
Number of dual qualified lawyers: 1

Main areas of work: Commercial, insurance, ship building and ship finance, shipping litigation (marine and admiralty), banking litigation and joint ventures.
Languages: English, Mandarin, Shanghainese
Office profile: Opened in June 1999, the Shanghai office is the firm's most recent addition to its international network of offices. The office has particular expertise in advising clients trading with and within China, and has experience in assisting both Chinese and non-Chinese clients with all aspects of their business ventures in the People's Republic of China. The Shanghai office allows the firm to provide on-the-spot assistance when required, to liaise with Chinese lawyers in the conduct of cases before the Chinese court, and before the many arbitration tribunals in China, and generally to advise clients conducting business there.

FRANCE

3 rue La Boétie, 75008 Paris

Senior partner: Timothy Clemens-Jones
Number of lawyers: 13
Number of dual qualified lawyers: 4
Number of locally qualified lawyers: 13

Main areas of work: All aspects of shipping including admiralty, international trade, insurance and reinsurance, litigation and arbitration, financial, company and commercial, all relevant aspects of European law, aviation
Languages: English, French
Office profile: The firm opened its Paris office in 1977. It has two further offices in France, Nantes (opened 1997) and Rouen (opened 1993), with a total of 17 lawyers. There are four French and two English partners, all experienced in shipping litigation and arbitration. About half the office's work consists of shipping and maritime litigation, with a further ten percent being admiralty work. General commercial litigation represents another 20 percent.

HONG KONG

15th Floor, Tower One, Lippo Centre, 89 Queensway, Hong Kong

Senior partner: Peter Rees Smith
Number of lawyers: 28
Number of dual qualified lawyers: 17
Number of locally qualified lawyers: 19

Main areas of practice: Shipping litigation (admiralty and marine), other admiralty, international trade and transportation, commodities, energy, insurance and reinsurance, commercial real estate, banking and insolvency/restructuring, intellectual property, corporate and other non-contentious.
Languages: Cantonese, English, Mandarin
Office profile: The firm opened its Hong Kong office in 1978. Over half its work consists of admiralty and marine litigation throughout Asia, while commercial litigation and international trade represent another 30 percent. It has particular experience in advising on problems encountered in trade and investment in and with China, including litigation and arbitration before the Chinese courts and arbitration bodies (CIETAC/CMAC) and all aspects of financial and business ventures in China. The office serves clients from all over the world, with lawyers frequently travelling to China, Vietnam, Japan, Korea, Taiwan, the Philippines, Malaysia, Singapore, Indonesia, Thailand, Myanmar and India.

SINGAPORE

10 Collyer Quay, #08-02 Ocean Building, Singapore 049315

Senior partner: Simon Davidson
Number of lawyers: 10
Number of dual qualified lawyers: 2

Main areas of practice: Shipping litigation (marine and admiralty), ship building and conversion, ship repair, oil refinery and trading, commodity trading, insurance and reinsurance, international trade, corporate shipping, ship finance, port projects, energy and natural resources
Languages: Cantonese, English, Malay, Mandarin, Tamil.
Office profile: The Singapore office was opened in 1990. In 1998, there was a major change in the development of the office, as it was strengthened by a significant increase in personnel to reflect the growth of Singapore as a major city for shipping and international trade. The office offers a complete range of services in its traditional core business areas of shipping, insurance, commodities and international trade, as well as commercial litigation, asset finance and general corporate and commercial work. The office has built up a substantial energy practice in the region. Around two thirds of the office's work consists of litigation and arbitration, while a third is non-contentious.

ASSOCIATED OFFICES

GREECE

Holman Fenwick & Willan (Consultants) OE, 6th Floor, 86 Filonos Street, 185 36 Piraeus

Senior partner: Charles Lowe

Main areas of work: Shipping litigation/admiralty, commercial litigation and marine insurance.
Languages: English, Greek.
Office profile: Holman Fenwick & Willan's Piraeus office was opened in 1993 to provide enhanced services to one of the shipping industry's most important strategic centres. The office provides consultancy services in relation to English law matters with the emphasis on shipping-related litigation (including casualties). The office has particular expertise in marine and insurance matters, including hull and cargo claims, charterparty disputes, casualty investigation and collisions, salvage, oil, pollution, sale and purchase and commodity-related and other commercial issues.

HOLMAN FENWICK & WILLAN

H

For other recommended firms see pages 1485-1520

HOMBURGER RECHTSANWÄLTE

HEAD OFFICE

Weinbergstrasse 56/58, PO Box 338,
CH-8035 Zurich, Switzerland
Tel: + 41 1 265 35 35 **Fax:** + 41 1 265 35 11

FIRM OVERVIEW

Senior Partner: Dr Peter Widmer

Number of partners worldwide: 17
Number of other lawyers worldwide: 45

AREAS OF PRACTICE:
Mergers, acquisitions and corporate restructuring: 25%
Litigation and arbitration: 20%
Banking, securities & corporate finance: 15%
Tax: 12%
Corporate and commercial: 10%
Intellectual property & copyright: 8%
Competition and anti-trust: 5%
Media, telecommunications and computer: 5%

WORLDWIDE OFFICE CONTACTS

SWITZERLAND
Weinbergstrasse 56/58, PO Box 338, CH-8035 **Zurich**
Tel: + 41 1 265 35 35 **Fax:** + 41 1 265 35 11
Email: lawyers@homburger.ch

H

FIRM OVERVIEW: Established in 1957, Homburger is now one of the largest Swiss law firms, with 62 lawyers drawn from all parts of Switzerland. The firm offers a comprehensive service in business law, though the process of European integration has seen the firm dealing increasingly with the implications of EU law for Swiss companies and for foreign and multinational enterprises with activities in Switzerland.

MAIN INTERNATIONAL AREAS OF PRACTICE:
Corporate & commercial: The firm provides advice on the establishment of companies, corporate restructuring, joint ventures, shareholders' agreements, privatisation, distribution, franchising, agency and other commercial contracts, business succession planning including estate planning and wills, product liability and employment law.
M&A: The firm handles both domestic and cross-border M&A work.
Banking, securities and corporate finance: Organisation, corporate governance and regulatory supervision of banks; capital market transactions; initial public offerings (IPOs); debt financing; securityholder protection; venture capital structures; stock exchange law and securities law; employee stock participation plans; project finance; leasing; and insurance law.
Litigation and arbitration: Representation in all commercial and civil litigation, including intellectual property, competition law and bankruptcy related matters; before cantonal courts; and before the Swiss Federal Tribunal. The firm's lawyers represent clients in arbitration proceedings and also serve as members and chairmen of arbitration panels.
Insolvency: Representation in pre-trial attachment, enforcement and insolvency proceedings.
Competition and anti-trust: Anti-trust law, including European competition and merger control law, and fair trade law.
Intellectual property & copyright: Patent law; trademark; industrial design law; licensing; copyright law, including related proprietary rights and the rights of users; and firm names and other business identity law.
Tax: The firm provides general tax advice as well as more specific advice concerning mergers and acquisitions, capital market transactions; corporate finance and restructuring, transfer pricing arrangements, estate planning, social security, pensions and telecommunications law. The firm also undertakes representation before the tax authorities and courts, especially regarding domestic and international corporate tax law.
Media, telecommunications and computer law: Includes advice on data protection, software protection and contract drafting in the areas of software and hardware, and telecommunications law.
EU: European competition law, anti-dumping, and matters relating to the free movement of goods and services.

LANGUAGES: English, French, German, Italian, Spanish

For other recommended firms see pages 1485-1520

HOPE DUGGAN & SILVA

HEAD OFFICE

Av. Leandro N. Alem 1110,
C1001AAT Buenos Aires, Argentina
Tel: +54 11 4891 1000 **Fax:** +54 11 4315 0606

Email: hds@hds.com.ar

WORLDWIDE OFFICE CONTACTS

ARGENTINA
Av. Leandro N. Alem 1110, C1001AAT **Buenos Aires**
Tel: +54 11 4891 1000 **Fax:** +54 11 4315 0606
Email: hds@hds.com.ar

FIRM OVERVIEW

Senior partners: Adrian F.J. Hope, Juan P. Duggan, Roberto E. Silva, Javier Zapiola

Number of partners worldwide: 9
Number of other lawyers worldwide: 31

AREAS OF PRACTICE:

Banking and capital markets	20%
Commercial, corporate and financial	20%
Litigation	10%
Real estate	10%
Tax	10%
E-commerce	5%
Other	25%

FIRM OVERVIEW: Hope, Duggan & Silva is a full-service law firm with a strong commercial, financial and corporate practice. The firm serves foreign and domestic clients and maintains close ties with leading law practices globally.

INTERNATIONAL CLIENTS: The firm's clients include industrial and service corporations, investment and commercial banks, public utilities, venture capital/private equity firms, investment funds and government agencies.

MAIN INTERNATIONAL AREAS OF PRACTICE:

Commercial, corporate and financial: Work includes M&A transactions; commercial contracts, competition and anti-trust; joint ventures and foreign investment matters.
Banking and capital markets: The firm handles the entire spectrum of banking and finance matters including derivatives, trade finance, bonds, security or trust instruments, banking due diligence and securities regulations.
Tax: Work undertaken includes international and domestic taxation, including tax planning, transfer pricing and use of double tax treaty mechanisms.
Real estate: The firm offers advice to investors, developers and land owners on residential and commercial real estate developments, including contractual and financial arrangements as well as zoning regulations.
E-commerce: Advice is given to clients establishing sites and/or vertical and horizontal portals; internet service providers and start-up companies.
Litigation: The firm has broad experience in commercial litigation and arbitration.
Employment: The firm advises on all matters relating to Argentine labour law.
Administrative law: The firm advises on all administrative law matters including the preparation, management and processing of all allegations and appeals before government agencies and administrative tribunals.
Competition law/anti-trust: The firm advises on applications for clearance and exemption, and on restrictive practices and abuse of dominant positions.
Telecommunications: The firm's activities range from concessions to interconnect, supply and customer agreements.
Insolvency: The firm handles all type of insolvency work, including company reconstructions.
Natural resources: The firm advises on all areas of natural resources and energy law, including acquisitions and divestitures, financing of oil and gas transactions, restructuring and disposition of oil and gas assets.
Other areas of practice: The firm is qualified to provide advice in environmental law, intellectual property, estates and wills, media and technology transfer.

LANGUAGES: English, French, German, Spanish

For other recommended firms see pages 1485-1520

HOUTHOFF BURUMA

HEAD OFFICE

Parnassusweg 126, PO Box 75505,
1070 AM Amsterdam, The Netherlands
Tel: +31 20 577 2000 **Fax:** +31 20 577 2700

Email: info@houthoff.nl
Website: www.houthoff.nl

FIRM OVERVIEW

Chairman and senior partner: Jan Mark Dingemans

Number of partners worldwide: 61
Number of other lawyers worldwide: 280

AREAS OF PRACTICE:

Corporate, financial, tax, commercial	50%
Property	25%
Insurance and reinsurance	15%
Employment	5%
Intellectual property, IT, telecom	5%

WORLDWIDE OFFICE CONTACTS

NETHERLANDS
Parnassusweg 126, PO Box 75505, 1070 AM **Amsterdam**
Tel: +31 20 577 2000 **Fax:** +31 20 577 2700
Email: info@houthoff.nl

Weena 355, PO Box 1507, 3000 BM **Rotterdam**
Tel: + 31 10 217 2000 **Fax:** + 31 10 217 2700

Scheveningseweg 66, PO Box 84046, 2508 AA **The Hague**
Tel: + 31 70 352 9500 **Fax:** + 31 70 350 3014

ASSOCIATED OFFICES

BELGIUM
Leidekerke Siméon Wessing Houthoff, Keizerslaan 3, 1000, **Brussels**
Tel: +32 2 551 1616 **Fax:** +32 2 551 1600

H

FIRM OVERVIEW: Houthoff Buruma is one of the The Netherlands' largest law firms. Comprising more than 280 lawyers, civil law notaries and tax consultants, the firm provides a full range of legal services to domestic and international clients. The firm has offices in Amsterdam, The Hague, Rotterdam and Brussels and is a member of The Conference of European Lawyers.

INTERNATIONAL CLIENTS: The firm's clients include a broad range of large and medium-sized, national and multinational companies. The firm also acts for governmental and semi-governmental bodies.

MAIN INTERNATIONAL AREAS OF PRACTICE:
Corporate and commercial: The firm advises on all general corporate and commercial matters, specialising in structuring and disputes.
Banking and finance: Houthoff Buruma handles a wide range of legal issues including derivative products, lending, structured financing, securitisations, banking regulations, the euro and financial litigation. The firm advises on the latest developments in the financial markets including the rendering of financial services via the Internet, credit derivatives, collateralisation and developments in capital adequacy regulations.
Tax: Members of the firm advise on commercial tax planning, cross-border transactions, tax litigation and VAT, particularly in relation to commercial property. Houthoff Buruma also handles a range of onshore and offshore issues, including financial instruments and investment funds.
Insurance and reinsurance: Houthoff Buruma's insurance practice is one of the largest in the Netherlands. It advises on all aspects of insurance ranging from policy drafting and coverage advice to defence work. The firm also advises on business issues arising from industry regulation, the distribution of insurance and single passport applications, professional indemnity insurance, and property insurance defence. Houthoff Buruma acts for the largest Dutch reinsurer and advises on a range of international reinsurance issues. It also handles reinsurance schemes involving captives and advises on international insurance and reinsurance disputes.
Property: Houthoff Buruma's notarial department handles complicated commercial transactions relating to immovable property. It also advises on collateral securities and complex integrated property projects including parking facilities, shops, offices, and homes.
Intellectual property: The firm advises on all trademark and copyright issues including licences, take-overs and joint ventures, conflicts regarding domain names and trademarks, protection against piracy, and the development of websites.
IT and telecommunications: The firm advises on the formation of strategic alliances and partnership agreements with large clients. It handles the review of software licences, maintenance agreements, service level agreements and project agreements.
Employment: The firm handles employment contracts, collective labour agreements, management agreements, employment conditions, employee share options, pension and pre-pension benefits and other employment law matters. The firm also advises on terminations, lay-offs, reorganisations and the setting up of redundancy arrangements and social plans.
Other: M&A, venture capital, bankruptcy, construction, administrative law and government regulation, litigations and arbitration, shipping and transport.

LANGUAGES: English, French, German, Spanish, Italian, Portuguese, Russian

HOUTHOFF BURUMA

For other recommended firms see pages 1485-1520

HOWREY SIMON ARNOLD & WHITE

HEAD OFFICE

1299 Pennsylvania Avenue, N.W.,
Washington DC 20004-2402, USA
Tel: +1 202 783 0800 **Fax:** +1 202 383 6610

Email: coucha@howrey.com
Website: www.howrey.com

FIRM OVERVIEW

Chairman: Ralph J. Savarese
Managing partner and CEO: Robert F. Ruyak

Number of partners worldwide: 191
Number of other lawyers worldwide: 253

AREAS OF PRACTICE:

Intellectual property 50%
Competition 25%
Commercial litigation 18%
International arbitration 7%

FIRM OVERVIEW: Founded in 1956 as a competition boutique, Howrey Simon Arnold & White continues to evolve to meet the changing needs of its clients. It is a leading firm in competition, intellectual property, complex commercial litigation and government and international arbitration and litigation law. With offices throughout the US and in Europe, and over 400 attorneys, Howrey Simon Arnold & White aims to be the leading legal services firm in the world for anti-trust/competition, intellectual property, complex commercial litigation, and government and international advocacy. The firm has the largest IP practice in the world. It also has the largest anti-trust practice of any law firm in the world, with over 160 competition lawyers with a wide range of experience in domestic and international mergers and acquisitions, government criminal and and civil investigations, and private anti-trust litigation. It has the most experienced group of competition lawyers outside of the federal government, and also has a large commercial trial practice with more than 200 lawyers with a wide range of trial experience and litigation expertise. The firm has litigated in over 1,500 federal and state court cases since 1995 and regularly handles international and national arbitrations of complex claims.

INTERNATIONAL EXPERIENCE: Howrey Simon Arnold & White represents an international client base that includes over 60 Global 500 companies, in industries ranging from aerospace to telecommunications. The firm houses a comprehensive in-house trial site logistics team with the ability to mobilise and deploy resources anywhere in the US and Europe in a way that maximises productivity while containing costs. Howrey Simon Arnold & White has extensive litigation experience in the US, Canada, Japan and Europe. Its attorneys play an active role in several intellectual property organisations, such as WIPO and COMPRI, competition/anti-trust organisations and international commercial arbitration and litigation entities such as the ICC. The firm has had extensive IP litigation experience, before juries and judges, in most federal district courts, the US Court of Appeals for the Federal Circuit (CAFC), the U.S. Patent and Trademark Office, the International Trade Commission, the European Patent Office as well as the Community Trademark Office (OHIM). In the last 20 years of experience, the firm has learned to combine the skills of IP professionals, commercial litigators, competition lawyers, supreme court and appellate lawyers, economists, accountants, and multimedia professionals. These teams are also supported by a group of experienced on-site trial logistics professionals. Howrey aims to develop trial teams that are tailored to meet clients' needs.

WORLDWIDE OFFICE CONTACTS

UNITED KINGDOM
1 Ropemaker Street, **London** EC2Y 9HT
Tel: +44 20 8895 4006 **Fax:** +44 20 8895 4001
Email: RASSERK@howrey.com

USA
321 N. Clark Street, #801, **Chicago** IL 60610
Tel: +1 312 595 1239 **Fax:** +1 312 595 2250
Email: coucha@howrey.com

2020 Main Street, Suite 1000, **Irvine** CA 926
Tel: +1 949 721 6900 **Fax:** +1 949 721 6910
Email: coucha@howrey.com

4225 Executive Square, #14, **La Jolla** CA 92037-9150
Tel: +1 858 622 5100 **Fax:** +1 858 622 5199
Email: coucha@howrey.com

550 South Hope Street, Suite 1400, **Los Angeles** CA 90071-2627
Tel: +1 213 892 1800 **Fax:** +1 213 892 2300
Email: coucha@howrey.com

301 Ravenswood Avenue, **Menlo Park** CA 94025
Tel: +1 650 463 8100 **Fax:** +1 415 463 8400
Email: coucha@howrey.com

1299 Pennsylvania Avenue, N.W., **Washington** DC 20004-2402
Tel: +1 202 783 0800 **Fax:** +1 202 383 6610
Email: coucha@howrey.com

MAIN INTERNATIONAL AREAS OF PRACTICE:

Intellectual property: Howrey Simon Arnold & White provides a complete range of litigation, prosecution, counselling, arbitration strategy, and mediation services in all aspects of intellectual property including patent, trademark, copyright, and trade secret matters.The intellectual property practice has combined technical knowledge of scientists and engineers with litigation expertise for the past twenty years. Today, with over 230 intellectual property attorneys and more than 30 technical advisers in Washington, DC, Houston, Los Angeles, Menlo Park, San Diego, and London, Howrey continues to be a leading IP litigation firm for clients ranging from Fortune 100 giants to emerging Silicon Valley start-ups. It offers a full array of IP services, including trademark litigation, patent prosecution and trademark prosecution before the USPTO, EPO and OHIM; patent interferences, opposition and cancellation proceedings; licensing, counselling, and related matters. Its substantial experience in alternative dispute resolution techniques and how they can effectively be used in IP disputes is invaluable to its clients. It also provides IP expertise in electronics and computer software; biotechnology and pharmaceuticals; mechanical and chemical engineering; telephony; and other disciplines.

The Trademark Practice Group at Howrey Simon Arnold & White offers the full range of trademark-related services, from portfolio planning to enforcement and litigation. The firm's strength in this practice area stems from the breadth and depth of experience provided by a large team of trademark professionals dedicated to the practice of trademark law. This group of trademark experts, located in the firm's various offices, has a wealth of experience in trademark clearance, use, registration, and enforcement. Several of its trademark attorneys have worked as Attorney-Examiners at the Trademark Trial & Appeal Board or as Trademark Examiners at the U.S. Patent and Trademark Office. Others have worked in corporations and understand the challenges faced by corporate in-house counsel and legal departments, including their relationships with corporate marketing and product groups. The firm's trademark portfolio management services are also fully developed: trademark attorneys provide a full range

For other recommended firms see pages 1485-1520

of trademark services to clients and are experienced in managing global and domestic trademark portfolios. The firm registers and maintains domestic and international trademarks for numerous corporations, from the largest Fortune 500 companies to smaller high tech start-up concerns. For some of these clients, it manages extensive domestic and international trademark portfolios. It also provides trademark prosecution, maintenance, and licensing services worldwide, including extensive work in Europe, Japan, and through the Pacific Rim countries.

Howrey Simon Arnold & White is also renowned for trial and appellate expertise in patent disputes. The firm tries cases before juries and judges nationwide on virtually every important patent-related subject. It has pioneered innovative ways to present technically complex patent cases in both bench and jury trials, and its lawyers have acquired this experience through many years of patent litigation in a broad range of technologies in courts throughout the United States. Complex technical issues combined with complex legal issues involving patent law are common elements in cases it handles. Its lawyers regularly handle procedural, evidentiary, and discovery-related legal issues that require combined legal and technical knowledge and experience. Because of its substantial number of attorneys with advanced degrees and experience in the sciences and engineering, the firm can quickly staff a first-class litigation team with the necessary depth of expertise for cases in virtually any technology. While having strength in large-scale litigation, it also handles more limited litigation with the same innovative legal strategies, and effective implementation and advocacy.

Howrey Simon Arnold & White has litigated numerous patent enforcement cases to a successful result for patent owners. It develops trial teams that are tailored to meet client needs, and can provide full array of IP services, including trademark litigation, patent prosecution and trademark prosecution before the UPSTO and the EPO; patent interferences, opposition and cancellation proceedings; licensing, counselling, and related matters.

The firm's practice is centred around its belief that IP and IP litigation must serve the business objectives of its clients, and that effective IP strategies must understand and meet these objectives.

Competition: Howrey Simon Arnold & White covers all areas of government merger and acquisitions, private litigation, and criminal anti-trust matters. Anti-trust/competition was the original practice area upon which the firm was founded and today Howrey Simon Arnold & White has one of the largest and most experienced competition practice in the world. Its practice is the global leader in anti-trust and competition law. It is the largest anti-trust practice of any law firm in the world, with approximately 160 competition lawyers with a wide range of experience in domestic and international mergers and acquisitions, government criminal and civil investigations, and private anti-trust litigation.

Howrey has the most experienced group of competition lawyers outside of the federal government. Over the last 5 years alone, its competition lawyers have worked on over 1,200 matters, including: 800 government anti-trust mergers and acquisitions; 150 government civil and criminal investigations; and 250 private anti-trust litigation matters. The practice employs lawyers that possess varied and complementary strengths. The group has substantive understanding of anti-trust principles, a strong knowledge of, and expertise in, government anti-trust policy and practises outstanding litigation and trial skills. Many of the lawyers regularly appear before, and understand the policies, procedures, and analytical constructs of, the federal anti-trust enforcement agencies. The group has successfully represented clients in the most celebrated of the federal agencies' inquiries, and litigates in private anti-trust/competition actions virtually every day and in every federal district court in the United States. The competition group has obtained two of the largest plaintiff's anti-trust jury verdicts in the United States affirmed on appeal totalling $825 million, and has won jury verdicts and summary judgements for numerous clients as defendants. It represents a substantial client group, including 35 of the Fortune 250 companies and 24 Global 500 companies, and it has access to the talents of Capital Economics, Howrey's consulting affiliate, to support anti-trust/competition matters with a staff of highly trained economists, financial analysts, and computer professionals. It also has a vast experience in solving a broad range of anti-trust/competition issues in a diverse group of industries including banking, computers, financial services, food and beverages, petroleum, pharmaceuticals, telecommunications, transportation, and utilities.

In the area of representation of merging parties, Howrey Simon Arnold and White has had substantial experience and success in obtaining federal approval of complex, large-scale mergers in concentrated industries. Its attorneys counsel corporate clients at every stage of the merger process, from an initial analysis of anti-trust feasibility and structuring of transactions through enforcement agency investigations. Although many of its clients have succeeded in avoiding lengthy government investigation of their proposed mergers, it has helped clients to efficiently resolve those transactions that do become the subject of government investigation.

In the past three years alone, Howrey has represented the following parties with mergers that were subject to federal, state, and/or foreign anti-trust agency investigation: Exxon and Mobil in their proposed merger (the firm represented both Exxon and Mobil in this proposed $80 billion merger that was investigated and approved by the Federal Trade Commission); American Stores in its merger with Albertson's (one of the largest supermarket mergers in history, it was investigated and approved by the Federal Trade Commission); ConAgra in its acquisition of International Home Foods, an important strategic transaction for ConAgra involving multiple grocery product lines; Heartland in its acquisition of Masco-Tech (the deal was cleared after a review of difficult HSR questions); Hannaford Brothers Co. in its acquisition by Food Lion (Delhaize), which was investigated by the FTC and two state attorneys general; Cargill and Continental, the largest privately held company in the United States, in a transaction that combined the first and second largest grain export businesses in the United States; CSX Lines in the sale of Sealand, its liner business, to Maersk; Entravision in its acquisition of Zradio; Ford Motor Company in its merger with Volvo; Ingram Industries in its merger with Barnes & Noble; Amoco in its $50 billion merger with BP, successfully consummated after an accelerated FTC investigation; McDonnell Douglas Corporation in its merger with The Boeing Company; Texas Pacific Group in the sale of its majority shareholding in Continental Airlines, Inc., to Northwest Airlines Corporation; Lockheed Martin Corporation in its $9.1 billion acquisition of Loral Corporation; and Texaco Inc. in its $17 billion joint venture with Shell Oil Company, combining the companies' U.S. downstream refining, transportation, and marketing operations. In December 1997, the FTC approved the transaction with a consent decree affecting a small fraction of the assets involved.

Commercial litigation: Howrey Simon Arnold & White handles complex commercial cases, including breach of contract, class action, insurance coverage, and the arbitration of complex claims.The firm can quickly staff a first-class litigation team with the necessary depth of expertise for cases in virtually any technology involving complex, multi-patent, multi-party lawsuits. For example, in Samsung Electronics Co. v. Texas Instruments, which involved 60 patents regarding DRAMs and VRAMs, the firm's successful litigation strategy led to a favourable settlement for Samsung. The firm has one of the nation's largest commercial trial and complex business litigation practices, and more than 200 lawyers with a wide range of trial experience and litigation expertise in the United States and internationally. The commercial litigation group tries complex commercial cases in federal and state courts nationwide, and handles international and national arbitrations of complex claims. It has litigated over 1,500 federal and state court cases in 49 states since 1995, and has participated in over 365 US Supreme Court

For other recommended firms see pages 1485-1520

and federal and state appeals in the last 5 years. It has demonstrated a record of success, winning a $248 million settlement on behalf of a global leader in Internet and telecommunications, and obtaining three of the largest plaintiff's anti-trust jury verdicts in US history totalling over $1 billion. It has secured more than $3 billion of insurance recoveries for mass torts, environmental liabilities, and other complex cases. Working as an integrated team, it combines seasoned trial lawyers with members of other practice areas of the firm as well as economists, scientists, and multimedia experts as required. Its expertise (plaintiff and defence) includes: competition, franchise, securities, intellectual property, white collar crime, fraud, insurance coverage, products liability, tortious interference, environmental, unfair trade and contracts.

Government and international advocacy: The firm handles a range of international arbitration and multinational litigation; environmental, chemical and export trade regulation; government contracts and environmental litigation; and trans-national policymaking. It also has extensive experience of federal anti-trust enforcement agencies, such as the US Department of Justice, Anti-trust Division and Federal Trade Commission, and works with many other federal agencies.

The firm's international arbitration and litigation practice is recognised for managing international arbitrations throughout the world, acting as advocate in arbitrations involving amounts between $25 and $270 million and obtaining arbitral awards cumulatively valued at hundreds of millions of dollars.

The firm handles arbitrated international commercial disputes between companies and between foreign governments and companies; cases involving the application of the United States Foreign Sovereign Immunities Act, obtaining of foreign discovery and related jurisdictional and procedural international litigation issues; multi-jurisdictional litigations involving same-subject-matter lawsuits in different countries. The firm advises US clients in US and foreign court litigations involving foreign representative and distributor arrangements, joint ventures, and other international commercial arrangements. It has also obtained injunctions in US federal and state courts enjoining foreign buyer demands in seller's guarantee or stand-by letters of credit, and acted as co-counsel on such actions in foreign court. Recent representative cases include $40 million ICC dispute involving three consolidated cases arising under joint-venture and related agreements between American and Scandinavian companies involving US distribution rights (sited in New York with hearings in London, New York, and Oslo); $25 million ad hoc arbitration using ICC rules (but not administered by the ICC) for claimant against NATO in a dispute under a telecommunications contract with hearings in Brussels; $30 million ad hoc arbitration under UNCITRAL rules arising under a contract between an American company and the government of Egypt (sited in Cairo with hearings in Geneva); $165 million ad hoc arbitration under UNCITRAL rules in a dispute under an air traffic controls services contract with the government of Egypt; sited in Zurich; $30 million CEPANI (Belgian arbitration forum) dispute over an asset purchase price in an information industry acquisition; $70 million International Centre for Settlement of Investment Disputes (ICSID) representing a Balkan government in an action brought by foreign investors.

Telecommunications, technology and IT: The firm's lawyers have acquired technical acumen in a wide array of diverse technologies in the large number of industries from which its clients come. Its experience includes (but is not restricted to) technologies pertaining to: wireless communications, including cellular telephones; telecommunications networks and protocols; computer hardware; software, and networks including computer architectures, network architectures, genetic algorithms, neural networks, artificial intelligence, and fuzzy logic systems; optics and its applications; solid state laser systems; automotive technologies, such as engines, brake systems, and transmissions; semiconductor architecture, manufacturing, and packaging, including processors, controllers, and memories; nuclear fusion and engineering; oil field and seismic exploration and production; telecommunications, including wireless telephony and intelligent networks; LADAR systems; missile guidance systems; electronic and industrial instrumentation and control systems; lighting systems; biomedical technologies, such as implantable biomedical instrumentation, artificial hearts and valves, dental implants, and dental components; water purification systems; portable life support systems; data storage systems; television and video processing and display; food packaging and handling; concrete production and transfer; coin and currency machines; air distribution equipment; roof assemblies; oil misters; storm drain filters; sound cancellation; pipe support springs.

In addition, many of the firm's IP professionals have advanced degrees and significant industry experience in both the R&D and the manufacturing of electronic systems, semiconductors, and computer software. These professionals keep abreast of developments in relevant technical areas, and pay specific attention to associated legal developments in litigation in numerous areas of high technology matters, including microprocessors, SDRAM, optical switching equipment, modem standards, Flash EPROMS, optical fibres, CDROM controllers, and many additional areas; the patenting and copyrighting of computer software as well as enforcement of software rights; evolution of Internet technologies, with emphasis on emerging backbone and e-commerce technologies; entertainment and software copyright litigation; and licensing and enforcement of existing patent portfolios. In addition, the firm's IP practice has seen a dramatic rise in recent years in the number of matters – litigation and prosecution-related – that it has handled in the telephony related arts. It handles a broad range of patent litigation matters for one of the RBOCs. It has handled matters relating to analog V.34 modems, 56Kbs modem technology, pair gain systems, voice recognition techniques, overvoltage protection circuitry, narrow bandwidth digital communications, satellite communications, and encrypted techniques, including STU-III telephony. A significant number of the firm's IP members have technical and legal expertise in the chemical arts. Its patent prosecution, client counselling, and litigation experience spans the broad range of chemical technologies such as: polymer chemistry, organic chemistry, physical chemistry, speciality chemistry, photochemistry, chromatographic technologies.

LANGUAGES: Arabic, Chinese, Dutch, English, French, German, Portuguese, Spanish

H

HSD ERNST & YOUNG

HEAD OFFICE

Tour Ernst & Young, Faubourg de l'Arche
11, allée de l'Arche 92037 Paris-la-Défense cedex , France
Tel: + 33 1 46 93 60 33 **Fax:** + 33 1 58 47 70 16

FIRM OVERVIEW

Chairman of the board: Pierre-Alain Molinier (Paris)
Chief executive officer: Christian Clocher (Lyon)

Number of partners: 50
Number of other lawyers: 425

FIRM OVERVIEW: HSD Ernst & Young is a French law firm member of the Hauts de Seine Bar. In 1984 it was incorporated as a Société de Conseil Juridique and subsequently transformed into a Société d'Avocats in 1991. The firm comprises 50 partners, 425 other professionals and a total staff of 670, and is active, either directly or through its subsidiaries, in 14 cities in France, one office in Monaco and countries in Western and Central French speaking Africa. The firm is a member of the Ernst & Young International network, the second largest tax and legal network in the world.

H

INTERNATIONAL EXPERIENCE: International tax and legal optimisation involving the utilisation of a DINC (Dual Incorporated Company), drafting and implementation of dual incorporated or resident companies, designing and implementation of transfer pricing policies; application for APAs (Advanced Pricing Agreements); designing of international finance structures (using inter-alia REPOs); designing an implementation of European distribution centres; international location feasibility studies; reorganisation and substantiation of industrial companies' supply chain process; conception and legal implementation of dividend access plans; optimisation of local tax burden; review of non-profit organisations' tax or legal situations; conception of remuneration and retirement policies; reorganisation/outsourcing of HR, legal, or tax functions; international acquisitions; international litigations and arbitration.

INTERNATIONAL CLIENTS: The firm provides advice to numerous medium and large business organisations in all sectors, including major global companies, governmental agencies and municipal organisations in the major business centres of France, Monaco and Africa.

MAIN INTERNATIONAL AREAS OF PRACTICE:
Corporation tax: The firm handles general corporate tax, international tax, indirect tax, custom duties and local and property taxes.
Business law: This includes company law, employment law, intellectual property law, distribution and competition law and public and environmental law, new technologies, international litigation and arbitration.
International mobility: The firm provides human resources advice and international location advice, and deals with pensions and employee benefits, personal income taxes and immigration law.
Cross disciplinary industrial expertise: Activities include banking and insurance, construction and real estate, healthcare, hi-tech and biotech industries and consumer products.
Cross disciplinary project expertise: Ernst & Young handles M&A, inbound and outbound investment, company and project financing, transfer pricing, group reorganisations and e-business and e-commerce.

LANGUAGES: Dutch, English, French, German, Italian, Russian, Spanish

WORLDWIDE OFFICE CONTACTS

FRANCE
North France regional head office, 35, avenue de la Marne,
BP 35, 59441 Wasquehal cedex, **Lille**
Tel: + 33 3 20 76 10 50 **Fax:** + 33 3 20 76 10 68
Email: marc_pourbaix@ernst-young.fr

Lyon regional office, Tour Cristal Parc, 113, Boulevard Stalingrad,
69626 Villeurbanne cedex, **Lyon**
Tel: + 33 4 72 44 19 19 **Fax:** + 33 4 72 44 18 20
Email: christian_clocher@ernst-young.fr

Mediterranean regional office, 408, avenue du Prado,
BP 116, 13267 **Marseille** Cedex 08
Tel: + 33 4 91 23 66 79 **Fax:** + 33 4 91 22 51 30
Email: evelyne_bataille@ernst-young.fr

West France regional head office, 10, rue du Président Herriot,
44000 **Nantes**
Tel: + 33 2 40 89 79 29 **Fax:** + 33 2 51 72 02 74
Email: thierry_meunier@ernst-young.fr

Tour Ernst & Young, Faubourg de l'Arche, 11, allée de l'Arche
92037 **Paris-la Défense** Cedex
Tel: + 33 1 46 93 60 33 **Fax:** + 33 1 58 47 70 16
Email: pierre-alain_molinier@ernst-young.fr

Paris Entrepreneurial office, 4, rue Auber, 75009 **Paris**
Tel: + 33 1 53 05 85 20 **Fax:** + 33 1 44 56 01 61
Email: franck_van_hassel@ernst-young.fr

SW France regional head office, Le Compans - Immeuble B,
1, place Alfonse Jourdain, 31000 **Toulouse**
Tel: + 33 5 62 21 37 31 **Fax:** + 33 5 61 21 47 96
Email: francois_beglin@ernst-young.fr

East France regional head office, Le Sebastopol,
3 quai Kiéber, 67055 **Strasbourg** Cedex
Tel: + 33 3 88 15 24 50 **Fax:** + 33 3 88 22 65 27
Email: luc_julien_saint_amand@ernst-young.fr

MONACO
SOMODECO SAM, Immeuble Les Lys,
3, rue Louis Auréglia BP 449, 98011 **Monaco** Cedex
Tel: + 377 93 25 00 52 **Fax:** + 377 93 25 58 92
Email: francis_ferrari@ernst-young.fr\

OTHER OFFICES
Offices also in Cameroon, Congo, Ivory Coast, Guinea, Gabon and Senegal, contact Africa head office.

HSD ERNST & YOUNG
SOCIETE D'AVOCATS

For other recommended firms see pages 1485-1520

HUGHES HUBBARD & REED

HEAD OFFICE

One Battery Park Plaza,
New York NY 10004-1482, USA
Tel: +1 212 837 6000 **Fax:** +1 212 422 4726
Email: info@hugheshubbard.com
Website: www.hugheshubbard.com

FIRM OVERVIEW

Chair: Candace Krugman Beinecke
Managing partner: Charles H. Scherer

AREAS OF PRACTICE:

Anti-trust and competition law ....*%
Employment ....*%
Intellectual property and technology law ....*%
International trade and customs ....*%
Liitigation and arbitration ....*%
M&A, corporate finance, banking and financial services ....*%
* Workload % not disclosed

FIRM OVERVIEW: Hughes Hubbard & Reed LLP was founded in 1937 by a group of individuals that included Charles Evans Hughes. The firm's practice includes most areas of corporate law, including M&A, banking and financial services, but has long been recognised for its work in litigation and arbitration, that combined with the firm's international experience enables it to handle multi-jurisdictional and transnational disputes including complex financial and commercial litigation, mass tort and information technology litigation and arbitration.

INTERNATIONAL EXPERIENCE: More than half of Hughes Hubbard's work involves international clients. The firm established an office in Paris more than 30 years ago that advises on all aspects of French business law and the laws and regulations of the European Community. The firm has also established bilingual attorney groups that focus on the Pacific Basin and Latin America. The firm's international arbitration and transnational litigation practice has a broad range of experience.

INTERNATIONAL CLIENTS: The firm's international clients have included foreign governments, the European Commission, foreign central banks, and large, multinational corporations including PricewaterhouseCoopers, ALSTOM, NIKON and Lazard Freres.

MAIN INTERNATIONAL AREAS OF PRACTICE:

International arbitration and litigation: During 2000, the firm advised or served as counsel or arbitrators to clients in connection with existing or potential arbitrations in the accounting; airline and surface transportation; agribusiness; automotive; banking; chemical; civil engineering; distribution; electric generation and power; franchising; hotels; information technologies; insurance; media; metals and mining; petroleum; pharmaceutical; power; online banking; and telecommunications industries. The firm's litigation practice specialises in all aspects of transnational litigation. Work undertaken has included actions on behalf of, or involving, foreign governments or their agencies, investor participants and managers in US, and foreign ventures, big five accounting firms, global manufacturing and industrial entities, and foreign banking and financial institutions.

M&A, corporate finance, banking and financial services: Hughes Hubbard has handled a number of large cross-border acquisitions and has advised on the implementation of several large multi-country joint ventures. Members of its Paris office have particular expertise in multi-jurisdiction joint ventures and acquisitions involving pharmaceuticals and medical devices. In corporate finance and financial services, Hughes Hubbard represents more than 30 foreign financial institutions including those involved in credit enhancement for commercial paper programs and trade finance facilities. The firm also represents corporate clients and investment banking entities involved with global capital markets products such as securitisations, commercial paper conduit facilities and asset backed securities, and dealers and end-users in financial products including fixed income, credit and equity derivatives. The firm advises clients on issues relating to international payment systems and international banking questions.

International trade and customs: Hughes Hubbard advises on a wide range of issues that arise in international trade and litigation. These range from customs compliance and enforcement matters, to trade litigation under the countervailing duty and antidumping laws to international trade dispute resolution under the North American Free Trade Agreement and the World Trade Organisation agreements. On the export side, the firm's lawyers counsel US and international clients on compliance and enforcement aspects of US export and re-export control laws, US antiboycott regulations, US economic sanctions programs and their extraterritorial effects, and the US Foreign Corrupt Practices Act. It also handles other international trade-related issues, including intellectual property, telecommunications, environmental law and arbitration.

Anti-trust and competition law: The firm advises on merger filings, Hart Scott Rodino 'second requests' and investigations in the US and increasingly coordinate these with foreign jurisdictions in order to have a single anti-trust strategy in countries throughout the world. Members of Hughes Hubbard's anti-trust group also actively litigate anti-trust cases in the US for both US and foreign clients. The firm's attorneys regularly handle anti-trust and competition matters for clients such as Bristol-Myers Squibb, Alstom, PricewaterhouseCoopers and Louisiana Pacific. The firm has also done extensive compliance and consulting work for these and many other clients, both US based and non-US. Members of Hughes Hubbard's anti-trust practice group have recently handled major cases, served on task forces or authored leading articles and publications on topics such as merger review, anti-trust/intellectual property issues and joint venture and competitor collaboration guidelines.

Intellectual property and technology law: The firm's work covers a variety of industries, including financial, securities, manufacturing, entertainment, publishing, semiconductor, telecommunications, multimedia, consumer electronics, video games, and Internet services and information. Hughes Hubbard's intellectual property attorneys serve a broad range of clients, including multinational corporations, in the registration, protection, enforcement and licensing of trademarks, patents and copyrights in the United States and internationally. The firm also advises US and foreign clients on a variety of e-commerce-related transactions and legal questions.

LANGUAGES: Czech, Danish, Dutch, English, French, German, Greek, Hebrew, Italian, Japanese, Korean, Portuguese, Russian, Spanish, Swedish, Thai

WORLDWIDE OFFICE CONTACTS

FRANCE
47, Avenue Georges Mandel, 75116 **Paris**
Tel: +33 1 44 05 80 00 **Fax:** +33 1 45 53 15 04

USA
350 South Grand Avenue, **Los Angeles** CA 90071
Tel: +1 213 613 2800 **Fax:** +1 213 613 2950

201 South Biscayne Boulevard, **Miami** Fl 33131
Tel: +1 305 358 1666 **Fax:** +1 305 371 8759

1775 I Street, N.W., **Washington DC** 20006-2401
Tel: +1 202 721 4600 **Fax:** +1 202 721 4646

H

HWANG MOK PARK & JIN

HEAD OFFICE

9th Floor, Daekyung Building, 120, 2-ka, Taepyung-ro, Chung-ku
Seoul 100-724, South Korea
Tel: +82 2 772 2700 **Fax:** +82 2 772 2800

Email: hmpj@hmpj.com
Website: www.hmpj.com

WORLDWIDE OFFICE CONTACTS

SOUTH KOREA
9th Floor, Daekyung Building, 120, 2-ka, Taepyung-ro, Chung-ku, **Seoul** 100-724
Tel: +82 2 772 2700 **Fax:** +82 2 772 2800
Email: infor@hmpj.com

ASSOCIATED OFFICES

USA
30 Corporate Park, Suite 103, **Irvine** CA 92606
Tel: +1 949 955 2577 **Fax:** +1 949 955 2520

FIRM OVERVIEW

Managing partner: Ju Myung Hwang

Number of partners worldwide: 11
Number of other lawyers worldwide: 28

AREAS OF PRACTICE:

Area	%
Anti-trust	*%
Corporate and M&A	*%
Employment	*%
Finance and securities	*%
Intellectual property	*%
Litigation and arbitration	*%
Maritime and insurance	*%
Real estate	*%
Tax	*%
Telecommunications	*%

* Workload % not disclosed

H

FIRM OVERVIEW: Founded in 1993, Hwang Mok Park & Jin (HMPJ) is a distinguished full service law firm. HMPJ provides cost effective services through identifying the needs, and protecting the interests, of its clients. HMPJ maintains a liaison office in Orange County, California. HMPJ does not maintain any exclusive working relationship with law firms outside Korea, preferring to maintain good working relations with a number of major international law firms.

INTERNATIONAL EXPERIENCE: The firm has handled a range of overseas financing and securities transactions, working with lawyers in foreign jurisdictions on the preparation, negotiation and implementation of contracts and/or projects. HMPJ regularly works with foreign lawyers on major international M&A transactions, joint venture projects, technology transfer transactions, litigation and arbitration. HMPJ is the Korean representative member firm of Lex Mundi.

INTERNATIONAL CLIENTS: HMPJ advises both domestic and multinational companies and financial institutions from all over the world with interests in Korea. International clients are advised on all aspects of Korean law.

MAIN INTERNATIONAL AREAS OF PRACTICE:
M&A and business restructuring: HMPJ handles all aspects of M&A transactions, from structuring deals to preparing contracts details. The firm also advises on financial restructuring, workout, sale of assets or businesses, sale of stock, combination of businesses, divestiture, and establishment of holding companies.
Fair trade: HMPJ advises on matters regulated by the fair trade law of Korea including business combination, establishment of holding company, unfair collaborative acts, unfair international contracts, as well as representing clients in litigation involving the fair trade issues.
IT and telecommunications: HMPJ advises on compliance with the legal, regulatory and technical requirements of the relevant laws governing the telecommunications industry. It also advises on disputes and proceedings before the relevant government agencies.
Food and drugs: HMPJ has represented domestic and foreign pharmaceutical companies and food companies. The firm has rendered services to its clients in connection with the reform of the Pharmaceutical Affairs Act and relevant regulations, product registrations of pharmaceutical and hygienic products with the relevant government agency, and for compliance with various unfair trade practice regulations in Korea.
Bankruptcy and reorganisation: HMPJ advises on corporate reorganisations including composition, bankruptcy, workout and corporate reorganisation proceedings.
Financial institutions consulting: HMPJ advises financial institutions in Korea including banks, securities and insurance companies, venture capitals, mutual funds, corporate restructuring companies, as well as other second-tier financial institutions, on compliance issues with the laws and regulations of the regulating agencies and for development of new products and transactions.
Corporate finance: HMPJ handles project financing, asset backed securitisation transactions, SOC projects, and other types of traditional corporate financing transactions. Major clients include domestic and the foreign banks, securities companies, investment banks, mutual funds and insurance companies.
International trade/anti-dumping: The firm advises on international trade regulations, anti-dumping regulations, countervailing duty, safeguard, and government procurement cases.
Litigation and arbitration: HMPJ's litigation team handles a wide range of litigation and arbitration cases in civil, commercial, criminal, international trade, tax, fair trade, administrative, labour, intellectual property, insurance and maritime laws.

LANGUAGES: English, French, German, Japanese, Korean

For other recommended firms see pages 1485-1520

INCE & CO

HEAD OFFICE

Knollys House, 11 Byward Street,
London EC3R 5EN, United Kingdom
Tel: +44 20 7623 2011 **Fax:** +44 20 7623 3225
Email: firstname.lastname@ince.co.uk
Website: www.ince.co.uk

FIRM OVERVIEW

Administration partner: Allan Hepworth
Senior partner: Peter Rogan
Number of partners worldwide: 57
Number of other lawyers worldwide: 130

AREAS OF PRACTICE:

Shipping, aviation 39%
Insurance, reinsurance, professional indemnity 28%
Energy, construction, pollution, environment, personal injury .. 16%
Corporate, private client, property 6%
International trade and commodities 6%
Sale and purchase 5%

FIRM OVERVIEW: Founded in 1870 in the City of London, Ince & Co is an international law firm with a global reputation in shipping, insurance, energy and international trade. Over the years the firm has expanded internationally, opening offices in Hong Kong, Singapore, Piraeus, and Shanghai. Ince & Co has a continuously manned emergency response hotline on +44 20 7283 6999.

INTERNATIONAL EXPERIENCE: In May 2000 the firm enhanced its service to clients in the Asia Pacific region when it was granted a licence to open an office in Shanghai. Its Hong Kong office has experienced steady growth since opening in 1979 and is now staffed by over 25 lawyers and consultants with a total staff of 50, covering all aspects of shipping and commodities work, insurance, reinsurance and personal injury. The firm's Singapore office has provided legal services as offshore lawyers since inception in 1991. The office also advises on a range of other areas of commerce and commercial dispute resolution. The Piraeus office opened in 1993 to provide a broad range of services on English law matters to the Greek maritime community, including all aspects of maritime law (both wet and dry), insurance, reinsurance, commercial, sale and purchase of ships, negotiating and drafting commercial contracts and general commercial litigation. In addition, the firm has significant international practices in aviation, e-commerce and finance.

Ince & Co has expanded into many other areas of commercial and corporate law covering general corporate advice, banking, e-commerce, employment, EC law and property law.

INTERNATIONAL CLIENTS: The firm's client base reflects the international and commercial breadth of its practice.

MAIN INTERNATIONAL AREAS OF PRACTICE:

Asset recovery: Work includes worldwide enforcement of ship mortgages, judgments and awards, attachment of assets, debt collection and asset tracing.
Aviation: Work includes personal injury, insurance and reinsurance, airport, carrier, collision and product liability, personal injury, subrogation recoveries, crisis management, cargo, and international litigation.
Corporate: The firm handles a diverse range of general corporate and commercial work from employment to international joint ventures.
Dispute resolution: Ince & Co advises on commercial litigation, international arbitration, ADR and mediation.

WORLDWIDE OFFICE CONTACTS

CHINA
Suite 328, Shanghai Bund No.12, 12 Zhong Shan Dong Yi Road, **Shanghai** 200002
Tel: +86 21 6329 1212 **Fax:** +86 21 6321 5468
Email: firstname.lastname@ince.com.cn

GREECE
7th Floor, 137 Filonos Street, **Piraeus** 185-36
Tel: +30 1429 2543 **Fax:** +30 1429 3318
Email: firstname.lastname@ince.com.gr

HONG KONG
38th Floor, Asia Pacific Finance Tower, Citibank Plaza, 3 Garden Road, **Hong Kong**
Tel: +852 2877 3221 **Fax:** +852 2877 2633
Email: firstname.lastname@ince.com.hk

SINGAPORE
16 Collyer Quay, #24-01 Hitachi Tower, **Singapore** 049318
Tel: +65 538 6660 **Fax:** +65 538 6122
Email: firstname.lastname@ince.com.sg

UNITED KINGDOM
Knollys House, 11 Byward Street, **London** EC3R 5EN
Tel: +44 20 7623 2011 **Fax:** +44 20 7623 3225
Email: firstname.lastname@ince.co.uk

I

E-commerce: The firm advises a range of companies, from the media industry to the shipping industry, on a range of issues including start-up financing, liability for website content, and internet regulation.
Energy and natural resources: The firm specialises in energy litigation and arbitration with specialist offshore marine and insurance expertise.
EU and competition: The firm handles all aspects of EU and UK competition law and general EU law.
Insurance and reinsurance: Building on the firm's close contacts with the London marine insurance market, the firm extends its expertise into virtually every class of insurance and reinsurance business and into all the world's major marketplaces.
International trade and commodities: The firm advises on physical commodities, the futures markets, trade finance, transport of commodities, drafting and advising on contracts, joint venture agreements, documentary aspects of trade finance and letters of credit, oil and gas, metals, and soft commodities. It also handles cargo insurance and political contingency credit and financial risk insurance.
Personal injury: The firm handles the defence of all types of claims on behalf of insurers and other corporations, large and small.
Property and private client: Ince & Co advises on a range of services to help private clients maximise their property and other assets.
Shipping: The firm represents shipowners and charterers, P&I and other insurers, shipbuilders and repairers, salvors, hull and cargo interests and other providers of maritime services.

LANGUAGES: Arabic, Armenian, Cantonese, French, German, Greek, Hakka, Hindi, Italian, Japanese, Latvian, Malay, Mandarin, Romanian, Russian, Shanghainese, Spanish, Tai-shanese, Urdu

For other recommended firms see pages 1485-1520

JALLES ADVOGADOS

HEAD OFFICE

Av. Álvares Cabral, 34, 6th floor,
1250-018 Lisbon, Portugal
Tel: + 351 21 388 4095 **Fax:** + 351 21 388 1955

Email: jalles.law@mail.telepac.pt

WORLDWIDE OFFICE CONTACTS

PORTUGAL
Av. Álvares Cabral, 34, 6th floor, 1250-018 **Lisbon**
Tel: + 351 21 388 4095 Fax: + 351 21 388 1955
Email: jalles.law@mail.telepac.pt

FIRM OVERVIEW

Managing partner: Isabel Jalles
Number of partners worldwide: 3
Number of other lawyers worldwide: 9

AREAS OF PRACTICE:
Company/corporation, commercial and competition 40%
Litigation and arbitration 20%
Banking and business 10%
Media, TV and advertising 10%
Private international law 10%
Other 10%

FIRM OVERVIEW: The firm was established in1986 with the onset of internationalisation in the Portuguese economy. The firm provides a wide range of legal services related to international and domestic business transactions and investments. It is generally involved in highly complex litigation cases, as well as in cross-border transactions.

INTERNATIONAL EXPERIENCE: The firm has gained experience providing legal services within the countries of Northern as well as Southern Europe. Its lawyers currently represent clients before all domestic courts and also within international jurisdictions, such as to the European Court of Justice and the Court of First Instance of the European Communities. The firm's core area of expertise has been developed in business law; however, it is also concerned with matters relating to the individual. This includes the effect of the application of private international laws and conventions in planning and solving intricate and complex international cases. In the last year, the firm's major transactions included cross-border mergers and acquisitions in the telecommunications, electronics and tourism industries.

INTERNATIONAL CLIENTS: The firm's client base includes large companies and corporations, as well as public or supranational institutions conducting cross-border transactions. The client base is spread over a range of countries in Europe and North America, with the majority originating from the German and English speaking market.

MAIN INTERNATIONAL AREAS OF PRACTICE:
M&A: The firm's transactions in this area range from small acquisitions to large cross-border take-overs.
Competition law: The firm specialises in EU competition law and often represents clients in this particular field at European level, namely at the European Commission in Brussels as well as the Court of Justice of the European Communities and the Court of First Instance of the European Communities in Luxembourg, apart from the national jurisdictions of all Member States.
Advertising law: The firm has established expertise in dealing with marketing guidelines, regulatory issues and product liability matters.
Litigation and arbitration: The firm currently deals with commercial litigation, both at domestic and international level.

LANGUAGES: Portuguese, English, German, French, Spanish, Italian, Dutch, Russian

JALLES ADVOGADOS

 For other recommended firms see pages 1485-1520

JAUREGUI NAVARRETE, NADER Y ROJAS S.C.

HEAD OFFICE

Torre Arcos, Paseo de los Tamarindos 400-B,
7th, 8th and 9th Floors, Colonia Bosques de las Lomas
05120 Mexico City, Mexico
Tel: +52 5 267 4500 **Fax:** +52 5 267 4598
Email: jnnr@jnnr.com.mx

WORLDWIDE OFFICE CONTACTS

MEXICO
Torre Arcos, Paseo de los Tamarindos 400-B, 7th, 8th and 9th Floors,
Colonia Bosques de las Lomas, 05120 **Mexico City**
Tel: +52 5 267 4500 **Fax:** +52 5 267 4598
Email: jnnr@jnnr.com.mx

FIRM OVERVIEW

Managing partner: Gabriel Navarrete Alcaráz
Chairman: Miguel Jáuregui Rojas

Number of partners worldwide: 16
Number of other lawyers worldwide: 50

AREAS OF PRACTICE:

Banking and finance	*%
Corporate	*%
Energy	*%
Insurance and reinsurance	*%
Intellectual property	*%
Litigation, arbitration and mediation	*%
M&A	*%
Project finance	*%
Real estate	*%
Securities	*%
Telecommunications, IT, Internet and media	*%

*Workload % not disclosed

FIRM OVERVIEW: Jauregui, Navarrete, Nader y Rojas was founded in 1974 and is one of Mexico's foremost law firms specialising in international business transactions. The firm handles M&A, banking and finance, corporate, telecommunications, IT, Internet and media, energy, project finance, securities, insurance and reinsurance, intellectual property, litigation, arbitration and mediation, real estate, and international trade.

INTERNATIONAL EXPERIENCE: The firm has advised highly regulated entities on structuring foreign equity investments. It has handled the privatisation of government owned companies, and advised on all phases of qualifications for public bid processes and negotiations of procurement, services, infrastructure and other kinds of agreements with government entities.The firm has also advised foreign governments including the US Department of Commerce on the various chapters of NAFTA, and the US Treasury Department on the US$20 billion emergency financial package for Mexico in 1995.

INTERNATIONAL CLIENTS: The firm's clients include major national and international companies.

MAIN INTERNATIONAL AREAS OF PRACTICE:

M&A and joint ventures: The firm advises on M&A, joint ventures, strategic alliances, associations, distribution and related corporate and commercial law issues. It has handled takeovers, divestitures, stock, asset and merger transactions, buyouts, reorganisations, negotiated transactions, spin-offs and regulatory matters. Work undertaken also includes the evaluation of anti-trust issues, pre-merger and pre-acquisition notification requirements with governmental regulatory entities, environmental law matters and foreign investment regulations in general. The firm has extensive experience in the structuring, preparation and negotiation of letters of intent, memorandums of agreement and understanding, joint venture agreements, shareholders agreements, subscription agreements, share control arrangements, provisions for the protection of minority shareholders, co-investments and other documents and agreements.

Banking and finance: The firm handles all aspects of banking and finance including general corporate lending, secured and syndicated loan transactions and guarantees, structured finance, securitisations, project finance, leasing, and tax-based finance.

Telecommunications, IT, Internet and media: The firm advises on all issues relating to telecom, Internet, cellular, paging, media, trunking, satellite telecommunications, broadcasting, cable television, PCS and other value added telecommunication services including other kinds of voice and data transmission services. It also handles financial, legal and tax structures related to communications projects, including the preparation, filing and processing of applications, vis-à-vis, and obtaining relevant permits.

Energy: The firm advises on natural gas transportation, distribution and storage projects, oil exploration and drilling, secondary petrochemicals, distribution of fuels and lubricants, electric power projects (including cogeneration), IPPs, BLTs, bulk sales of power, and other generation projects. It also handles transactions, joint ventures, strategic alliances, project finance, international and national public bids and general regulatory matters in the energy, oil and electricity industries.

Restructuring and workouts: The firm advises on issues ranging from debt restructurings to complicated workouts, both secured and unsecured. It handles divestitures, asset management, liquidations, debt repurchase, debt swaps and debt-to-equity swaps for which different vehicles such as commercial paper, floating rate notes and financial and leveraged leases were used. The firm also advises clients on bankruptcy and suspension of payments proceedings.

Anti-trust: The firm handles all kinds of investment and regulatory issues relating to anti-trust notifications, clearances and opinions. It advises on anti-trust implications relating to all kinds of transactions, agreements, litigation, investments, purchases, mergers and acquisitions.

Real estate: The firm advises on all aspects of real estate and infrastructure projects and handles a wide range of transactions.

Insurance and reinsurance: The firm's insurance practice handles a wide range of regulatory, organisational, operational and transactional matters.

Infrastructure: The firm has advised on a range of transactions including international toll roads and bridges, electricity generation projects, water services, natural gas distribution and transportation projects, port developments, Pemex and Federal Electricity Commission plants and infrastructure, basic telephony and other communication networks and installation, and airports.

Intellectual property: The firm advises on licensing, franchising, patent-related work, protection of IP and technology transfer.

LANGUAGES: English, French, Spanish

J

JEANTET & ASSOCIÉS

HEAD OFFICE

87 Avenue Kléber,
75016 Paris, France
Tel: +33 1 4505 8008 **Fax:** +33 1 4704 2041

Email: jeantet@jeantet.fr

FIRM OVERVIEW

Chairman, Management Committee: Georges Terrier

Number of partners worldwide: 17
Number of other lawyers worldwide: 40

AREAS OF PRACTICE:

Litigation and arbitration	20%
M&A	20%
Banking and finance	10%
Competition	10%
Tax	10%
Employment	5%
Insolvency	5%
Intellectual property, IT and telecommunications	5%

WORLDWIDE OFFICE CONTACTS

FRANCE
87 Avenue Kléber, 75016 **Paris**
Tel: +33 1 4505 8008 **Fax:** +33 1 4704 8798
Email: jeantet@jeantet.fr

USA
152 West 57th Street, Suite 26C, **New York**
Tel: +1 212 314 9499 **Fax:** +1 212 582 3806
Email: jeantet@jeantetmy.com

FIRM OVERVIEW: Founded in 1921, Jeantet is a full-service firm which has increasingly focused on high-value work such as M&A and litigation. The firm has 57 lawyers, of which 17 are partners (all members of the Paris Bar), and is structured to be able to act as a single multi-disciplinary legal and tax team. Since 1991 it has had a New York office which practises French and European law.

INTERNATIONAL EXPERIENCE: The firm has had an international focus since the 1950s, when a large proportion of its foreign clients were from the US. During the last two decades it has diversified its client base so that, while a third are still North American, a third are now large French industrial and financial groups and the remaining third are mostly European. The firm also has specialists in OHADA law, investments in Africa and related dispute resolution. Over the years it has developed close working relationships with a number of African and Middle East lawyers, many of whom are former Jeantet associates.

INTERNATIONAL CLIENTS: Although the client base still consists largely of industrial groups, the firm increasingly represents financial institutions. Non-French clients vary considerably in size, but the firm's French clients are usually large groups who retain the firm almost exclusively for complex litigation, M&A, tax or very specialised areas. The New York office mostly advises US law firms and local branches of French banks.

MAIN AREAS OF INTERNATIONAL PRACTICE:
M&A: This, together with joint ventures, has always formed a large part of the firm's practice. It handles all stages of the acquisition process, including contract negotiation, financing, due diligence, tax structuring and advice on all the related matters. Clients tend to be non-French investors, but the firm also advises a number of large French investors or sellers, as well as banks. It has considerable experience in representing both buyers and sellers in transactions concerning listed companies, where it has developed relationships with the regulatory authorities.
Litigation: The practice covers all areas of business law (general commercial, tender offers and shareholder agreements, competition, tax, white collar crime, insolvency, employment and others). The firm represents clients before French and EU courts and in arbitration (ICC and ad hoc).
Tax: The firm was one of the first French law firms to develop a tax department. The practice specialises in the tax aspects of acquisitions, corporate reorganisations, structured financing, tax litigation and also tax planning for high net worth individuals. Tax partners who specialise in corporate or structured finance are trained to handle not only the tax but other aspects of these files if the matter does not justify involving corporate or finance lawyers.
Banking and finance: Although the firm is active in various aspects of traditional banking and finance work, the finance practice is largely focused on structured and asset finance (receivables, real estate, insurance risks and so on).
Private equity: The firm has experience in venture capital, buy-out structures, investment funds, listings and tax-related issues.
Oil, gas, energy and mining: The practice covers both France and French-speaking Africa.
Competition: A two-partner department assesses the impact of French and EU competition law on major transactions and agreements, negotiates and files merger notifications, coordinates multiple national filings, helps clients develop compliance programmes and undertakes litigation.
Other specialist areas: Include intellectual and industrial property, IT, telecoms and media.

LANGUAGES: English, French, German, Italian, Spanish

JEANTET & ASSOCIÉS
Avocats

For other recommended firms see pages 1485-1520

JINGTIAN & GONGCHENG

HEAD OFFICE

11th and 15th Floors, The Union Plaza, 20 Chaoyangmenwai Dajie,
Beijing 100020, China
Tel: +86 10 6588 2200 **Fax:** +86 10 6588 2211

Website: www.jingtian.com

FIRM OVERVIEW

Managing partner: Zhang Xusheng

Number of partners worldwide: 14
Number of other lawyers worldwide: 60

AREAS OF PRACTICE:

Securities and capital markets 40%
Litigation and arbitration 20%
Banking and finance 10%
Corporate 10%
Real estate 10%
Telecom and IT 10%

WORLDWIDE OFFICE CONTACTS

CHINA
11th and 15th Floors, The Union Plaza, 20 Chaoyangmenwai Dajie,
Beijing 100020
Tel: +86 10 6588 2200 **Fax:** +86 10 6588 2211

Suite 3204-3213, Central Plaza, 381 Huaihai Road (m),
Shanghai 200020
Tel: +86 21 6391 5688 **Fax:** +86 21 6391 5166

J

FIRM OVERVIEW: Formed by the recent merger between Jingtian Associates and Gong Cheng Law Offices(established in the early 1990s), the firm has consistently maintained strong international services and client base. Comprising 14 partners and 60 other lawyers, the firm specialises in securities and capital markets work, litigation and arbitration, banking and finance, a range of corporate issues, telecommunications and IT law, and real estate.

INTERNATIONAL EXPERIENCE: During 2000, more than two thirds of the firm's securities practice involved IPOs on overseas markets. The firm also advises foreign clients in direct investment in the PRC.

MAIN INTERNATIONAL AREAS OF PRACTICE:

Securities and capital markets: The firm acted as issuer's PRC counsel for Hong Kong Gem IPO of Beijing Beida Jade Bird and Phoenix Satellite Holdings Ltd. and sponsor's PRC counsel for NYSE and HKSE IPO of PetroChina and Netease.com Inc. IPO on Nasdaq.
Litigation and arbitration: The firm's litigation department has a reputation for its strength in international arbitration, arbitration at China International Economic and Trade Arbitration Commission, as well as domestic litigations.
Banking and finance: The firm advises on secured and syndicated loans, project finance and lease arrangements.
Corporate: The firm is able to organise project specific task forces to meet the ever-changing requirements of its clients. The firm is well recognised for its overall corporate commercial practice.
Telecom and IT: The firm's telecom and IT department has expanded with the industry. It acted as the issuer's counsel in China Telecom's overseas IPO, and represented and is still representing international clients with investments in the Chinese telecommunications industry. It also advises venture capitalists investing in the IT industry.
Real estate: The firm's real estate department continues to grow with Beijing's high expectations for WTO accession.

LANGUAGES: Chinese, English, Japanese, Portuguese

競天公誠律師事務所
JINGTIAN & GONGCHENG
ATTORNEYS AT LAW

JONES, DAY, REAVIS & POGUE

CONTACT OFFICE

North Point, 901 Lakeside Avenue,
Cleveland OH 44114, USA
Tel: +1 216 586 3939 **Fax:** +1 216 579 0212
Email: counsel@jonesday.com
Website: www.jonesday.com

FIRM OVERVIEW

Managing partner: Patrick F. McCartan
Number of partners worldwide: 432
Number of other lawyers worldwide: 973

AREAS OF PRACTICE:

Litigation	47%
Business practice	39%
Government regulation	7%
Tax	7%

FIRM OVERVIEW: Founded in 1893, Jones, Day, Reavis & Pogue is one of the world's largest law firms. It has US offices in Cleveland, New York, Los Angeles, Palo Alto, Chicago, Dallas, Atlanta, Washington DC, Columbus, Irvine and Pittsburgh, six offices in Europe and seven in Asia. The firm advises approximately half the Fortune 500 companies as well as a wide variety of other entities including privately-held companies, financial institutions, investment firms, health care providers, retail chains, foundations, educational institutions and individuals.

INTERNATIONAL EXPERIENCE: The firm's international practice is significant and growing. Jones Day maintains a significant presence in the principal legal and regulatory capitals of the world. In Europe, more than 135 lawyers are based in Brussels, Frankfurt, Geneva, London, Madrid and Paris. In Asia, more than 50 lawyers are based in Hong Kong, Shanghai, Sydney, Taipei, and Tokyo. In Mumbai and New Delhi, Jones Day has an associate relationship with Pathak & Associates. The firm's international practice focuses primarily on mergers and acquisitions, joint ventures and other investment transactions; securities and finance matters; tax, labour, environmental, competition and other significant regulatory matters; and international litigation and arbitration. The firm's international practice balances US lawyers posted outside the United States and foreign lawyers experienced in representing US-based clients. The firm's lawyers are licensed in most significant jurisdictions in Europe and Asia and are fluent in virtually all principal languages relevant to international business.

INTERNATIONAL CLIENTS: In addition to representing a large number of its United States-based clients in international matters, Jones Day represents many major companies based in Europe, the Middle East, Asia, and Latin America.

WORLDWIDE OFFICES

AUSTRALIA

Governor Phillip Tower, Level 38, 1 Farrer Place, Sydney NSW 2000

Coordinator: Kevin D. Cramer
Number of lawyers: 3

Main areas of work Securities offerings.
Languages: English, German.
Office profile: Opened in 1997, the Sydney office concentrates on cross-border securities offerings, acting for Australian-based investment bankers

WORLDWIDE OFFICE CONTACTS

AUSTRALIA
Governor Phillip Tower, Level 38, 1 Farrer Place, **Sydney** NSW 2000
Tel: +61 2 9210 6921 **Fax:** +61 2 9210 6926
Email: counsel@jonesday.com

BELGIUM
Avenue Louise 480, 1050 **Brussels**
Tel: +32 2 645 14 11 **Fax:** +32 2 645 14 45
Email: counsel@jonesday.com

CHINA
Shanghai Kerry Centre, Suite 2805, 1515 Nanjing Road West, **Shanghai** 200040
Tel: +8621 5298 6568 **Fax:** +8621 5298 6569
Email: counsel@jonesday.com

FRANCE
120, Rue du Faubourg Saint-Honoré, 75008 **Paris**
Tel: +33 1 5659 3939 **Fax:** +33 1 5659 3938
Email: counsel@jonesday.com

GERMANY
Hochhaus am Park, Grüneburgweg 102, 60323 **Frankfurt am Main**
Tel: +49 69 9726 3939 **Fax:** +49 69 9726 3993
Email: counsel@jonesday.com

HONG KONG
29th Floor, Entertainment Building, 30 Queen's Road Central **Hong Kong**
Tel: +852 2526 6895 **Fax:** +852 2868 5871
Email: counsel@jonesday.com

JAPAN
Toranomon 45 Mori Building, 3rd Floor, 1-5, Toranomon 5-chome, Minato-ku, **Tokyo** 105-0001
Tel: +81 3 3433 3939 **Fax:** +81 3 5401 2725
Email: counsel@jonesday.com

SPAIN
Zurbarán, 20, 28010 **Madrid**
Tel: +34 91 319 28 25 **Fax:** +34 91 319 61 31
Email: counsel@jonesday.com

SWITZERLAND
20, rue de Candolle, 1205 **Geneva**
Tel: +41 22 320 23 39 **Fax:** +41 22 320 12 32
Email: counsel@jonesday.com

TAIWAN
8th Floor, 2 Tun Hwa South Road, Section 2, **Taipei**
Tel: +886 2 2704 6808 **Fax:** +886 2 2704 6791
Email: counsel@jonesday.com

UNITED KINGDOM
Bucklersbury House, 3 Queen Victoria Street, **London** EC4N 8NA
Tel: +44 20 7236 3939 **Fax:** +44 20 7236 1113
Email: counsel@jonesday.com

USA
3500 SunTrust Plaza, 303 Peachtree Street NE, **Atlanta** GA 30308-3242
Tel: +1 404 521 3939 **Fax:** +1 404 581 8330
Email: counsel@jonesday.com

77 West Wacker, **Chicago** IL 60601-1692
Tel: +1 312 782 3939 **Fax:** +1 312 782 8585
Email: counsel@jonesday.com

North Point, 901 Lakeside Avenue, **Cleveland** OH 44114
Tel: +1 216 586 3939 **Fax:** +1 216 579 0212
Email: counsel@jonesday.com

J

For other recommended firms see pages 1485-1520

and corporations in connection with public and private offerings into the US capital markets by foreign issuers. It also advises foreign clients on US Securities and Exchange Commission policies governing cross-border debt and equity offerings.

BELGIUM

Avenue Louise 480, 1050 Brussels

Partner-in-charge: Luc G. Houben
Number of lawyers: 16
Number of dual qualified lawyers: 4
Number of locally qualified lawyers: 12

Main areas of work: EU, corporate, tax, finance, general commercial, tax, telecommunications, environmental, US antitrust & trade law, litigation.
Languages: Dutch, English, French, German, Italian, Spanish.
Office profile: Opened in 1989. The majority of its lawyers have spent most of their legal careers in Brussels, either in private practice or with the European Commission. They have also practised in various EU jurisdictions and the US. The firm's EU practice is wide, but has a particular emphasis on competition law under articles 85 and 86 of the EC treaty, telecommunications and trade. Other areas include M&A, joint ventures, State aids, intellectual property, antidumping and the compatibility of national legislation with European law. It has considerable experience of EU notification and regulatory processes and has handled complaints before the Commission and pleadings before the ECJ. The office's corporate practice represents European, US and Japanese clients in international business transactions; the international and Belgian tax practice advises on corporate transactions and structuring; the finance practice represents financial institutions with headquarters in Brussels and other European cities on cross-border financings, acquisition financing, project and export financing, and general lending, often on a syndicated basis. The office also deals with capital markets transactions, including swaps, trading activities relating to a variety of assets, and Euromarkets fund-raising.

CHINA

Shanghai Kerry Centre, Suite 2805, 1515 Nanjing Road West, Shanghai 200040

Partner-in-charge: Mitchell D. Dudek
Number of lawyers: 5

Main areas of work: Corporate, commercial, intellectual property
Languages: Chinese (Mandarin, Shanghai), English, French.
Office profile: Opened in July 1999, the office focuses on direct investment opportunities for clients, working in conjunction with Jones Day lawyers in Hong Kong and Taipei. It advises on the structuring and maintenance of business operations, including bankruptcy-related restructuring, commercial law matters such as joint ventures, technology transfers, distributorships and other agreements, and intellectual property.

FRANCE

120, Rue du Faubourg Saint-Honoré, 75008 Paris

Partner-in-charge: Wesley R. Johnson Jr.
Number of lawyers: 53
Number of dual qualified lawyers: 12
Number of locally qualified lawyers: 24

Main areas of work: M&A, joint ventures, dispositions, general corporate, securities, banking law and stock exchange matters, employment, tax (tax-efficient acquisition and operating structures), bankruptcy, national and international dispute resolution.

1900 Huntington Center, 41 South High Street, **Columbus** OH 43215
Tel: +1 614 469 3939 **Fax:** +1 614 461 4198
Email: counsel@jonesday.com

2727 North Harwood Street, **Dallas** TX 75201-1515
Tel: +1 214 220 3939 **Fax:** +1 214 969 5100
Email: counsel@jonesday.com

5 Park Plaza, Suite 1100, **Irvine** CA 92614-8502
Tel: +1 949 851 3939 **Fax:** +1 949 553 7539
Email: counsel@jonesday.com

555 West Fifth Street, Suite 4600, **Los Angeles** CA 90013-1025
Tel: +1 213 489 3939 **Fax:** +1 213 243 2539
Email: counsel@jonesday.com

599 Lexington Avenue, **New York** NY 10022
Tel: +1 212 326 3939 **Fax:** +1 212 755 7306
Email: counsel@jonesday.com

1804 Embarcadero Road, Suite 201, **Palo Alto** CA 94303
Tel: +650 739 3939 **Fax:** +650 739 3900
Email: counsel@jonesday.com

One Mellon Bank Center, 31st Floor, 500 Grant Street, **Pittsburgh** PA 15219
Tel: +1 412 391 3939 **Fax:** +1 412 394 7959
Email: counsel@jonesday.com

51 Louisiana Avenue NW, **Washington DC** 20001-2113
Tel: +1 202 879 3939 **Fax:** +1 202 626 1700
Email: counsel@jonesday.com

ASSOCIATED OFFICES

INDIA
Pathak & Associates, 12th Floor, Express Towers, Nariman Point, **Mumbai** 400 021
Tel: +91 22 230 8989 **Fax:** +91 22 230 6564

Pathak & Associates, Dr Gopal Das Bhavan, 28 Barakhamba Road, **New Delhi** 110 001
Tel: +91 11 373 8793 **Fax:** +91 11 335 3761

Languages: English, French, German, Italian, Romanian, Spanish, Swedish, Vietnamese.
Office profile: Opened in 1970, most of the office's 53 lawyers are registered with the Paris Bar to practise French law. It advises on corporate transactions in Europe and the US, acting for European, American and Asian clients, as well as on investment and financing projects for major corporations and banks. Corporate matters include the establishment of French companies, compliance with French laws and regulations and advice on day-to-day operations. The office also has expertise in commercial lending, structured and asset-based finance and project finance. Tax work includes advice on structuring tax-efficient acquisitions both in and outside Europe, as well as a wide range of domestic French tax matters. The office has also handled major international arbitration cases before the ICC and other bodies, and coordinates multi-jurisdictional litigation.

GERMANY

Hochhaus am Park, Grüneburgweg 102, 60323 Frankfurt am Main

Partner-in-charge: Karl G. Herold
Number of lawyers: 30
Number of dual qualified lawyers: 7
Number of locally qualified lawyers: 20

Main areas of work: Mergers and acquisitions, litigation and arbitration, energy, labour, telecommunications, tax, finance and antitrust and regulatory.

Languages: Czech, Dutch, English, Farsi, French, German, Greek, Italian, Romanian.
Office profile: Opened in 1991, this office handles German corporate and international transactions. It also advises on accessing German, US and international securities markets (especially with IPOs or dual listings in Germany and the US). The office handles Central and Eastern European work. Energy work is a further area of expertise, particularly privatisations, independent power projects and project financings in Germany and Turkey. Telecommunications work includes international joint ventures and advice on EU and German regulations. The office also undertakes international dispute resolution, including multilingual arbitration, international claims proceedings and civil litigation before the German courts.

HONG KONG

29th Floor, Entertainment Building, 30 Queen's Road, Central, Hong Kong

Partner-in-charge: Kevin D. Cramer
Number of lawyers: 11
Number of dual qualified lawyers: 7
Number of locally qualified lawyers: 1

Main areas of work: Structuring and maintaining operations in Hong Kong and the PRC, real estate, joint ventures, technology transfers, distributorship agreements, stock exchange work, international lending and project finance, privatisation, M&A, restructuring, IP, litigation and arbitration.
Languages: Chinese (Cantonese, Mandarin), English, French.
Office profile: Opened in 1986. In 1996 gained permission to practise Hong Kong law. It advises on US, Hong Kong and other international legal issues. It has experience in structuring all types of investments in the PRC for US, European and Asian clients, including joint ventures, cooperative enterprises and wholly foreign-owned enterprises. The office also provides investment restructuring services for businesses whose existing China investments have underperformed. It has also acted for PRC private and state-owned enterprises in international transactions. Work for Hong Kong clients includes advice on structuring their US real estate holdings and other acquisitions, and representation in US litigation.The office also advises regionally on matters in other Pacific Rim jurisdictions, including Australia, China, Indonesia, Korea, Malaysia, New Zealand, the Philippines, Singapore, Thailand and Vietnam, in conjunction with local law firms. These include intellectual property issues such as trademark infringement and product counterfeiting, and filing registrations.

JAPAN

Toranomon 45 Mori Building, 3rd Floor, 1-5, Toranomon 5-chome, Minato-ku, Tokyo 105-0001

Partner-in-charge: John C. Roebuck
Number of lawyers: 6
Number of dual qualified lawyers: 3

Main areas of work: US corporate, securities & partnership law, structuring investments and operations in the US and the Pacific Rim, commercial, corporate finance, tax, stock exchange, project finance, asset finance, M&A, restructuring, trade disputes, litigation & arbitration.
Languages: English, French, Japanese, Chinese (Cantonese).
Office profile: Opened in 1989, the Tokyo office represents Japanese clients in connection with US and European investments, including M&A, joint ventures and commercial loans. It also advises Japanese clients on lending, project finance and asset-based lending, and on restructuring their US real estate holdings. The office is also experienced in dispute resolution for Japanese companies regarding their their investments in the US and in connection with US government antidumping investigations. Work for US-based clients includes advice on the establishment of manufacturing and other joint ventures with Japanese entities. The firm also represents US and European clients on technology transfers and related negotiations.

SPAIN

Zurbarán 20, 3rd floor, 28010 Madrid

Partner-in-charge: Juan I. Tena
Number of lawyers: 11

Main areas of work: Business practice including M&A, corporate and commercial law and real estate and construction law; finance practice including banking and structured finance, securities law and public offerings; and disputes practice including commercial litigation and international arbitration.
Languages: English, French, German, Spanish.
Office profile: Jones Day opened its Madrid office in January 2000, further expanding the firm's presence in the major European markets. It offers international clients Spanish local law capability and provides Spanish-based businesses looking to expand globally with access to the depth and experience of one of the world's largest law firms. The office is staffed by the former partners of the established Madrid law firm of Tena, Muñoz y Asociados. These lawyers have significant experience in handling a wide range of Spanish corporate and commercial matters, including M&A, securities law, banking and structured finance, commercial litigation and arbitration.

SWITZERLAND

20, rue de Candolle, 1205 Geneva

Partner-in-charge: Roy F. Ryan
Number of lawyers: 2
Number of locally qualified lawyers: 1

Main areas of work: International finance, international business transactions, international tax, international arbitration.
Languages: English, French, German.
Office profile: Opened in 1987, the Geneva office offers US and international tax advice both for businesses and private clients. It has handled numerous Geneva-based arbitrations as well as others based in Zurich, Paris and elsewhere. Although US lawyers are not admitted to practise before Swiss courts, the Geneva office supervises and coordinates the activities of local counsel in Swiss litigation. In multijurisdictional corporate transactions, the office often performs a general advisory function on general legal matters, as well as coordinating the advice from local lawyers.

TAIWAN

8th Floor, 2 Tun Hwa South Road, Section 2, Taipei

Partner-in-Charge: Jack J. T. Huang
Number of lawyers: 14
Number of dual qualified lawyers: 2
Number of locally qualified lawyers: 4

Main areas of work: Corporate transactions, general corporate, securities, real estate, construction, environmental, tax, dispute resolution.
Languages: Chinese (Cantonese, Hakka, Mandarin, Taiwanese), English.
Office profile: Opened in 1990, Jones Day's Taipei office regularly represents clients on many international corporate and financial transactions, and provides advice on a wide range of Taiwanese legal issues. The office is particularly experienced in structuring cross-border transactions for Taiwanese businesses (and also non-Taiwanese) in the People's Republic of

For other recommended firms see pages 1485-1520

China. Securities work includes international offerings such as Global Depositary Receipts, non-Taiwanese institutional investments on the Taiwan Stock Exchange, IPOs, private placements in Taiwan and the establishment of non-Taiwanese brokerage branches. Real estate and construction work includes contractual joint venture structuring and bidding assistance for Taiwanese infrastructure projects, wastewater remediation projects and large-scale cogeneration incinerator projects. The office deals with all facets of commercial and construction disputes, including discovery, depositions, motions, argument and appeal, and undertakes international arbitration.

UNITED KINGDOM

Bucklersbury House, 3 Queen Victoria Street, London EC4N 8NA

Partner-in-charge: Robert L. Thomson
Number of lawyers: 36
Number of dual qualified lawyers: 6
Number of locally qualified lawyers: 25

Main areas of work: M&A/corporate finance transactions, tax-planning and tax-based structured finance, dispute resolution, general commercial, property, employment and pensions.
Languages: English, French, German, Italian, Turkish.
Office profile: Opened in 1977, Jones Day's London office handles complex multi-jurisdictional transactions as part of the firm's international network, working closely with the other European offices and the firm's affiliated office in New Delhi. It focuses on three principal areas: M&A/corporate finance transactions, inbound to the UK from the US and Europe; corporate tax planning and tax-based structured finance; and litigation/dispute resolution (including complex multi-jurisdictional fraud ligitation). It is also able to handle the English legal issues that arise in the acquisition or divestiture of a UK company or its assets, such as employment, pensions, real estate transfers, environmental issues and competition law, as well as advising on a broad range of commercial matters including distributorship, supplier, and licensing arrangements. The office represents clients in English High Court litigation, English and other European arbitration proceedings, and ADR.

ASSOCIATED OFFICES

INDIA

Pathak & Associates, 12th Floor, Express Towers, Nariman Point, Mumbai 400 021

Languages: Bengali, English, Gujurati, Hindi, Marwari

Pathak & Associates, Dr Gopal Das Bhavan, 28 Barakhamba Road, New Delhi 110 001

Languages: English, Hindi, Punjabi

Managing partner: Anand S. Pathak
Number of lawyers: 14

Main areas of work: Corporate, commercial and financial transactions, and arbitrations.
Office profile: Opened in 1995, Jones Day's India practice services international businesses in India and Indian businesses outside India, handling all stages of transactions, including structuring, drafting, negotiating, international tax planning and the procurement of Indian governmental approvals. The firm's associate relationship with Pathak & Associates, an Indian law firm in New Delhi, allows it to provide a more comprehensive India-related legal service. Pathak & Associates 14 lawyers are all Indian nationals admitted to practice in India and in other international markets within North America, Europe and Asia.

J

ADVOCACIA JOSÉ DEL CHIARO

HEAD OFFICE

Av. Brigadeiro Faria Lima, 2012, 9º Andar - Conjunto 91,
01469-900 São Paulo, Brazil
Tel: +55 11 3816 2066 **Fax:** +55 11 3819 0537

Email: ajdc@uol.com.br

FIRM OVERVIEW

Senior partners: José Del Chiaro Ferreira da Rosa,
Selma M. Ferreira Lemes,
Maria Augusta Fidalgo

Number of partners worldwide: 3
Number of other lawyers worldwide: 9

AREAS OF PRACTICE:

ADR .... *%
Anti-trust .... *%
General corporate .... *%
M&A .... *%

*Workload % not disclosed

FIRM OVERVIEW: Advocacia José Del Chiaro comprises three partners and nine other lawyers. It specialises in business law, but has a broad and diverse practice that encompasses economic law, anti-dumping, anti-trust, regulation and consumer rights, a range of commercial and corporate issues, and tax. The firm provides consultative and preventive guidance on a range of corporate issues. It also handles administrative proceedings before the government agencies which deal with anti-trust (CADE/SDE), and anti-dumping (DECOM/SECEX). The firm also handles judicial cases before State and Federal Courts. The firm's lawyers all have strong academic backgrounds and experience, many with more than 15 years of practice in both administrative and judicial litigation and counseling. It is also assisted by experienced economic consultants.

INTERNATIONAL CLIENTS: The firm's client base includes large international companies within the food, aluminium, car, chemical, pharmaceutical, plastics, steel and tobacco industries. It also advises banks, as well as insurance, credit card, oil, media, computer and telecommunications companies.

WORLDWIDE OFFICE CONTACTS

BRAZIL

SCN, Centro Empresarial Encol, Torre A - Conj. 817, **Brasília** 70710-500
Tel: +55 61 328 1857 **Fax:** +55 61 326 5515
Email: ajdc1@attglobal.net

MAIN INTERNATIONAL AREAS OF PRACTICE:

Anti-trust: The firm advises on administrative and judicial litigation and all other matters relating to anti-trust and regulation matters and disputes.
M&A: The firm advises on the analysis and preparation of legal strategies in relation to mergers, acquisitions, incorporations, joint ventures and agreements for submission to approval by the anti-trust agency.
ADR: Work handled includes a range of alternative dispute resolution, notably mediation and arbitration.
General corporate: The firm provides legal and economic counseling in negotiations and the drafting of contracts; advises on administrative and judicial litigation and legal counseling in matters including anti-dumping, consumer relations and unfair competition; provides legal assistance in the preparation of proposals in bid procedures; provides legal and economic counseling in privatisation proceedings.

LANGUAGES: English, Portuguese, Spanish

J

For other recommended firms see pages 1485-1520

JOSE LLOREDA CAMACHO & CO

HEAD OFFICE

Calle 72 No. 5-83 5th Floor, P.O. Box 12304,
Bogota, Colombia
Tel: +57 1 3264270 **Fax:** +57 1 2126426

Email: jllcco@lloredacamacho.com
Website: www.lloredacamacho.com

WORLDWIDE OFFICE CONTACTS

COLOMBIA
Calle 72 No. 5-83 5th Floor, P.O. Box 12304, **Bogota**
Tel: +57 1 3264270 **Fax:** +57 1 2126426
Email: jllcco@lloredacamacho.com

FIRM OVERVIEW

Managing partner: Jose Antonio Lloreda

Number of partners worldwide: 7
Number of other lawyers worldwide: 18

AREAS OF PRACTICE:

Corporate and commercial	32%
Intellectual property	32%
Employment and immigration	7%
Banking and finance	5%
Litigation	5%
Tax	5%
Anti-trust and competition	4%
Energy and mining	4%
Internet and e-commerce	3%
Securities	3%

FIRM OVERVIEW: Jose Lloreda Camacho & Co was founded in 1941 by Jose Lloreda Camacho. It is a full service law firm that specialises in advising foreign and multinational clients doing business in Colombia. Emphasis is placed on the preventive aspects of law and assisting clients in business planning and projection. Jose Lloreda Camacho & Co has correspondent law firms in major cities around the world.

INTERNATIONAL EXPERIENCE: Since its foundation the firm has been involved in many international transactions.

INTERNATIONAL CLIENTS: The firm's client base includes multinational companies and local companies with international projection.

MAIN INTERNATIONAL AREAS OF PRACTICE:

Banking and finance: The firm has advised foreign banks and financial institutions on Colombian regulations governing banking, securities and corporate law. The firm handles the development of new products, securitisation of bank assets, acquisition of financial companies, and structuring of new capital instruments. It has also represented international credit institutions acting as lenders and as administrative agents of syndicated credit operations to Colombian companies.

Commercial: Jose Lloreda Camacho & Co advises national and foreign companies on the negotiation and preparation of civil and commercial agreements necessary to operate in Colombia. It advises on technical services, trademark license, distribution, agency, lease, and purchase and sale agreements.

Corporate: The firm advises Colombian and foreign companies on the legal, tax and exchange regulations involved in corporate structuring. It also has experience in business restructuring operations through mergers, acquisitions, spin-offs and privatisations. The firm advises on the legal evaluation, due diligence and liability assessment of acquisition targets, as well as on structure planning based on tax accounting and special regulatory considerations. The firm has extensive experience in liquidation and bankruptcy procedures.

Energy and mining: The firm advises oil companies, oil service companies, power generating companies, and gas and distribution mining companies. It handles the negotiation of concession agreements, oil association contracts, power purchase agreements, interconnection contracts and mining agreements.

Foreign investment and exchange regulations: Jose Lloreda Camacho & Co offers specialised legal advice to foreign companies investing in Colombia.

Intellectual property: The intellectual property department is one of the biggest in Colombia. It advises on all intellectual property matters including patents, utility models, designs, trademarks and copyrights. It specialises in prosecution, as well as in licensing and litigation. The firm's trademark department comprises six attorneys and more than fifteen paralegals. The firm handles patents in all technical areas including chemical, biochemical, pharmaceutical, mechanical and electrical. It conducts all phases of patent applications including prosecuting nullity cases against Superintendency resolutions before the Council of State. The firm also prepares and files copyright registrations, including those relating to computer software protection.

Internet and e-commerce: The firm advises software, internet and media companies on electronic commerce and internet related issues. The firm's attorneys work with intellectual property lawyers in negotiating and drafting technology agreements in relation to transaction, licenses and strategic alliances.

Employment and immigration: The firm advises on the planning of employment structures and handles a range of issues including collective bargaining, mediation, arbitration and litigation with organised labour, as well as individual employment agreements and litigation with ex-employees.

Litigation: The firm's litigation department acts as a support to all the other departments of the firm. It advises on all aspects of civil and commercial litigation including unfair competition, patent and trademark infringements, as well as all general corporate matters, employment matters and proceedings before administrative courts.

Tax: The firm advises on tax planning and determines the most efficient structures available to individual clients. It handles specific cases before the Tax Office and Administrative Courts and advises foreign companies on tax matters specifically relating to foreign investments.

LANGUAGES: English, French, Spanish

For other recommended firms see pages 1485-1520

JOSEPH TAN JUDE BENNY ANNE CHOO

HEAD OFFICE

5 Shenton Way #35-01, UIC Building,
Singapore 068808, Singapore
Tel: +65 220 9388 **Fax:** +65 225 7827
Email: jtjb@singnet.com.sg
Website: www.jtjb.com.sg

FIRM OVERVIEW

Senior partners: Joseph Tan, Jude P Benny, Anne Choo
Number of partners worldwide: 18
Number of other lawyers worldwide: 19

AREAS OF PRACTICE:

Admiralty and shipping .... *%
Civil litigation .... *%
Construction .... *%
Corporate, commercial and tax .... *%
Family and estate .... *%
Information technology/Intellectual property .... *%
Real property .... *%
* Workload % not disclosed

FIRM OVERVIEW: Reputed as the largest specialist shipping practice in Singapore, the firm merged with Koh & Choo to expand into key growth areas of the new economy such as corporate law, IT and intellectual property. The merger and consolidation of the firm's core practice areas has made it a full-facility legal practice. The firm has earned a reputation for its civil litigation practice; 12 of its 18 partners are trial lawyers. The firm's other core practice groups include: real property; construction law; family and estate; commercial and tax; and intellectual property. The overseas expansion of the firm included the establishment of a Malaysia Desk, enabling its lawyers to make direct representation in Malaysia; the opening of an office in alliance with Regency Interlaw Office in Bangkok, Thailand; and the establishment of a practice in Piraeus, Greece, called Joseph Tan Jude Benny O.E. More overseas offices are due to open in 2001 in Asia, the Middle East and Europe.

INTERNATIONAL EXPERIENCE: The firm has been involved in leading cases and transactions such as representing the Cousteau Society and their underwriters when The Calypso sank in Singapore; Bethlehem Shipyard in a highly contentious matter concerning the delivery of the John Brewer, the world's first floating hotel; the Crown Prince of U.A.E.; the Malaysian government in various suits against private individuals and corporations for misuse of Malaysian railway land in Singapore; and the Ukraine government in obtaining the release of their vessels arrested in Singapore. Other work includes the acquisition of the Nabisco food operations in Singapore; corporatisation of the Public Utilities Board, Singapore; management agreements for leading global hotel; sale and leaseback arrangements of industrial premises for MNCs; structuring of property interests for sale to purchasers; and, total chemical management contracts for Merck for the wafer-fabrication industries.

INTERNATIONAL CLIENTS: Clients include Gateway Inc, Honeywell International Asia Pacific Inc, Incepta Group Plc, NetTasking.Com, ValenceTech (part of SRS Labs Inc), 8 Layer.Com (part of North 22 Technology Services Group), General Motors, Microsoft, Starwood Hotels & Resorts Worldwide Inc, SAIT Radio Holland SA, United International Pictures and International Management Group rank among the firm's corporate/IT clientele.

WORLDWIDE OFFICE CONTACTS

GERMANY
Schaartor 1, **Hamburg,** 20459
Tel: +49 40 3690 1972 **Fax:** +49 40 3690 1978

GREECE
Joseph Tan Jude Benny O.E., K. Paleologou 5, 18535, **Piraeus**
Tel: +301 422 3820 **Fax:** +301 422 5458
Email: jtjbs@singnet.com.sg

SINGAPORE
7 Temasek Boulevard, #21-02 Suntec Tower One, **Singapore** 038987
Tel: +65 333 1611 **Fax:** +65 338 6277
Email: AnneChoo@jtjb.com.sg

Malaysian Desk, 5 Shenton Way, #35-01, UIC Building, **Singapore**
Tel: +65 220 9388 **Fax:** +65 220 7827
Email: Victor@jtjb.com.sg

ASSOCIATED OFFICES

THAILAND
JT JB-Regency Interlaw Office, 88 SSP Tower 3, 11th floor, Silom Road, Suriyawong, Bangrak, **Bangkok** 10500
Tel: +662 634 1336 7 **Fax:** +662 634 1335
Email: jtjbs@singnet.com.sg

MAIN INTERNATIONAL AREAS OF PRACTICE:

Admiralty and shipping: The firm has a 20-man shipping practice – one of the largest in Singapore. The firm advises on matters ranging from charterparty disputes and marine insurance claims to sale and purchase matters.

Construction: The firm offers legal services at every stage of the building contract process in matters relating to project management, project structuring, building contracts specifications, tenders and full litigation support.

Corporate, commercial and tax: The firm offers a full range of corporate, commercial and tax services, including formation of companies, M&A, restructuring, joint ventures, asset and share acquisitions and disposals, hotel management, total chemical management contracts, international stock options, public listings, private placements, investments, cross-border transactions, tax issues on reorganisation of group companies, stamp duty, goods and services tax, estate duty, property tax, personal income tax and corporate tax. These mainly involve multi-national corporations, new economy-based institutions and maritime-related companies.

Civil litigation: The firm handles a wide range of matters in civil and commercial litigation, domestic and international arbitration and mediation and alternative dispute resolution.

Family and estate: Practice covers all aspects of family law including probate, administration of estates, wills and trusts.

Information technology/intellectual property: Work covers agreements relating to software licensing and distribution, network management and consultancy services, disaster recovery services, software supply, development and implementation, co-branding, internet content provision and internet trading terms and conditions.

Real property: Work covers all aspects of real property law, including developmental conveyancing and lease agreement services. The firm is presently on the panel of solicitors for the Central Provident Fund (CPF) Board involving property transactions.

LANGUAGES: English, French, Greek, Hindi, Malay, Mandarin, Punjabi, Tamil

For other recommended firms see pages 1485-1520

KABRAJI & TALIBUDDIN

HEAD OFFICE

64-A/1, Gulshan-e-Faisal, Bath Island,
Karachi 75530, Pakistan
Tel: +92 21 583 8874 **Fax:** +92 21 583 8871

Email: kandt@cyber.net.pk

FIRM OVERVIEW

Senior partner: Kairas N. Kabraji

Number of partners worldwide: 2
Number of other lawyers worldwide: 7

AREAS OF PRACTICE:

Litigation and arbitration 25%
Banking and finance 20%
Corporate and commercial...................................20%
Energy and mining 15%
M&A 15%
Telecommunications and IT 5%

FIRM OVERVIEW: Founded in 1997, the firm comprises two partners and seven associates. The firm's lawyers have twenty-five years experience in commercial and corporate law in Pakistan, particularly in inward foreign investment, joint ventures, project finance, securities and privatisation. They also have experience in international commercial arbitration and litigation, as well as commercial and corporate law. The firm's associates provide support to the partners and are all encouraged to deal independently with clients within their respective areas of practice.

INTERNATIONAL CLIENTS: The firm's clients include international financial institutions (International Finance Corporation, Asian Development Bank), major international banks (Citibank and Standard Chartered Grindlays), international and domestic energy and mining companies (Exxon Mobil and BHP), telecommunications companies (Cable & Wireless, Motorola), and major domestic listed companies (Hubco), some with substantial foreign shareholding. Kabraji & Talibuddin advise international clients operating in Pakistan, including cross-border issues. The firm is also frequently instructed by major international law firms to advise their clients on all aspects of Pakistan law.

MAIN INTERNATIONAL AREAS OF PRACTICE:

M&A: The firm advises on international mergers where one or both of the merging parties have business interests in Pakistan. It also advises international and domestic clients on acquisitions and disposals (shares or assets) in Pakistan.

Banking and finance: Kabraji & Talibuddin advises foreign and domestic banks on various cross-border transactions in Pakistan, including aircraft leasing and the debt restructuring of a power project with cross-border financing.

Telecommunications and IT: Kabraji & Talibuddin advises on the satellite regulatory regime in Pakistan for a major international satellite project. It also acts as the placement agents and conduct due diligence on a proposed cross-border private placement of shares by a domestic IT company, including eventual listing outside Pakistan.

Litigation and arbitration: The firm advises major domestic power companies on litigation (including international arbitration). It also acts for a global telecommunications company in relation to litigation arising from the proposed disposal of its interests in Pakistan. Kabraji & Talibuddin advises domestic clients on general litigation and arbitration matters.

Energy and mining: Kabraji & Talibuddin acts for a number of private power companies (or their lenders), advising in relation to mineral joint ventures. It also advises domestic clients on energy related transactions involving international parties.

Corporate and commercial: The firm acts for a number of listed and private companies (mainly those with substantial foreign shareholding) in relation to their general corporate and commercial work.

LANGUAGES: English, Urdu

WORLDWIDE OFFICE CONTACTS

PAKISTAN

64-A/1, Gulshan-e-Faisal, Bath Island, **Karachi** 75530
Tel: +92 21 583 8874 **Fax:** +92 21 583 8871
Email: kandt@cyber.net.pk

K

KANGA & CO

HEAD OFFICE

Readymoney Mansion, 43 Veer Nariman Road,
Mumbai 400 001, India
Tel: +91 22 204 2288 **Fax:** +91 22 204 3726

Email: kanga@bom5.vsnl.net.in

WORLDWIDE OFFICE CONTACTS

INDIA
Readymoney Mansion, 43 Veer Nariman Road, **Mumbai** 400 001
Tel: +91 22 204 2288 **Fax:** +91 22 204 3726
Email: kanga@bom5.vsnl.net.in

FIRM OVERVIEW

Managing and senior partner: M L Bhakta
Number of partners worldwide: 16
Number of other lawyers worldwide: 10

AREAS OF PRACTICE:

M&A and project finance	25%
Banking and finance	20%
Telecommunications	20%
Corporate	15%
Litigation and arbitration	10%
Real estate	10%

K

FIRM OVERVIEW: Founded in 1890, Kanga & Co is one of the oldest and largest law firms in India. Comprising 16 partners and 10 associate lawyers the firm offers a full range of legal services, specialising in corporate law, mergers and acquisitions, and banking and finance. The firm does not have any formal alliances, but has associates in cities throughout India and works with various firms worldwide.

INTERNATIONAL EXPERIENCE: The firm has advised multi-national corporations on M&A, telecommunications, project finance, power projects and project structuring. Work recently handled by the firm includes advising on mergers and acquisitions of some of the largest industrial units and power projects in India. It has also handled company acquisitions in various industries including consumer products, chemicals, service related and support industries, and industrial equipment/machinery.

INTERNATIONAL CLIENTS: The firm's client base includes large Indian and foreign companies, banks, insurance companies including; British American Tobacco Co Ltd; UK, Pacific Century Regional Developments Ltd (Hong Kong); Smith & Nephew (UK); The Pillsbury Company (USA); Schindler Aufzuge AG (Switzerland); Thyssen Krupp AG; Carnegie Mellon University (USA) and Swiss Re (Switzerland). Some of their foreign banks include: Citibank NA; Bank of America NT & SA; The Hongkong & Shanghai Banking Corporation Ltd; Societe Generale; The Bank of Nova Scotia, Fleet National Bank; Westdeutsche Landesbank (WestLB). Some of their Indian clients and banks include; Bennett Coleman & Company Ltd; Gujarat Ambuja Cements Ltd; Hindustan Coca-Cola Bottling South West Private Ltd; International Distillers (India) Ltd; Larsen & Toubro Ltd; Reliance Industries Ltd; SKF Bearings (India) Ltd; Canara Bank; Centurion Bank Ltd; Syndicate Bank; and HDFC Bank Ltd.

MAIN INTERNATIONAL AREA OF PRACTICE:
M&A: Kanga & Co advises on structuring, spin-off and takeovers, taxation, banking and finance. It advised a major multinational company on one of the largest joint ventures and mergers of 2000-2001.
Banking and finance: The firm specialises in banking and finance (including syndicate foreign currency loans and securities), mutual funds (including off-shore mutual funds), factoring and Forfaiting.
Corporate: The firm has adapted to the liberalisation of industrial policies in India, advising some of the largest corporate houses and multinationals on all aspects of corporate law and securities regulations, including securitisation and derivatives.
Litigation and arbitration: Kanga & Co has a large litigation and arbitration practice. It handles a variety of work including writs, civil suits, taxation, and frequently represent clients before the Supreme and High Courts. The firm has advised a large US firm in a joint venture with the Government of India. It has also acted in numerous arbitration proceedings.
Real estate: The firm advises large construction companies and developers on all real estate issues.
Intellectual property: The firm advises on the registration of intellectual property including computer software, invention, drafting of agreements and contracts for transfer and assignment of intellectual property rights. It also handles litigation relating to protection from infringement of intellectual property rights and passing off.
IT: The firm advises telecommunication companies on the organisation and structuring of IT subsidiaries, drafting contracts and negotiating with government bodies and authorities.
Insurance and reinsurance: The firm advises on structuring and drafting of contracts and insurance related documents.
Environmental: The firm advises various corporate organisations on contesting several litigations.

LANGUAGES: English, Gujarathi, Hindi, Marathi

For other recommended firms see pages 1485-1520

KAPILA ANJARWALLA & KHANNA

HEAD OFFICE

7th Floor, Transnational Plaza, City Hall Way, PO Box 41144
Nairobi Kenya
Tel: +254 2 337625 **Fax:** +254 2 337620
Email: nbi@ka-legal.com

FIRM OVERVIEW

Managing partners Sheetal Kapila, Karim S. Anjarwalla
Number of partners worldwide: 7
Number of other lawyers worldwide: 10

AREAS OF PRACTICE:

Capital markets, banking and finance	25%
Corporate/commercial	25%
Civil litigation	20%
Criminal litigation	10%
Property/real estate	10%
Admiralty and maritime law	5%
Intellectual property	5%

FIRM OVERVIEW: Kapila Anjarwalla & Khanna Advocates is the product of a merger (1st January, 2000) between two well established firms in Kenya, Anjarwalla Abdulhusein & Co. and A. R. Kapila & Company. The firm is one of the largest in Kenya with a high degree of specialisation in various fields of law. The firm is unique in providing a broad range of legal services in Kenya's two main commercial centres, Nairobi and Mombasa. Kapila Anjarwalla & Khanna has a reputation for matters relating to banking, corporate and commercial law, mergers and acquisitions, admiralty and maritime law, civil and criminal litigation and private client work. The firm's client base includes industrial and commercial companies, banking and financial institutions, professional firms as well as government and public organisations both locally and internationally. Some of the banking institutions that the firm advises include Barclays Bank of Kenya Limited, ABN-AMRO Bank N.V., Citibank N.A. and Credit Agricole Indosuez. The firm also advises the British High Commission, the Swiss and Belgian Embassies and Swissair International and has advised (as part of an international consortium) the Kenyan Government on the development of independent power producer projects in Kenya. In addition, the firm acts for numerous high profile individuals and companies in Africa. The firm also has informal associations with various law firms worldwide.

INTERNATIONAL EXPERIENCE: The firm's international experience has mainly focused on corporate/commercial/M&A, infrastructure projects and civil, commercial and criminal litigation. Kapila Anjarwalla & Khanna has recently advised and acted on several major projects including acting for the developer on the project financing of a grain and fertiliser terminal in Mombasa, the then single largest private funding project in sub-Saharan Africa, financed by the IFC, CDC and other lenders; advising a UK Bank in connection with the listing of bonds on the Nairobi Stock Exchange; acquisition of an insurance group and large transport company; advising a bidder on the proposed purchase of one of the largest hotel chains in Kenya (including undertaking detailed due diligence and reviewing and advising on the terms of the share purchase agreement); and advising on the proposed merger of two large manufacturing concerns operating in East and Central Africa. The firm has also acted (together with a team of international advisors) for the World Bank in advising the Government of Kenya on the development of independent power projects.

INTERNATIONAL CLIENTS: The firm's clients include Schoeller International Engineering, Deloitte & Touche, PricewaterhouseCoopers, Safmarine Container Lines, AXA Insurance plc, PNI Clubs, Cargil, Kleinwort Benson and other international banks including Standard Bank, Coutts & Co and Habib Bank AG Zurich. The firm also advises the British High Commission, and the Swiss and Belgian Embassies and Swissport. It has acted for many international law firms including Denton Wilde Sapte, Norton Rose, Slaughter and May, CMS Cameron McKenna, Allen & Overy, Macfarlanes, Freshfields Bruckhaus Deringer, Richards Butler and Hill Taylor Dickinson.

WORLDWIDE OFFICE CONTACTS

KENYA

SKA House, Dedan Kimathi Avenue PO Box 83156, **Mombassa**
Tel: +254 11 312848 **Fax:** +254 11 312013
Email: mba@ka-legal.com

MAIN INTERNATIONAL AREAS OF PRACTICE:

Banking, finance and capital markets: The firm has considerable experience in banking regulation including advising banks on solvency ratios and capital structures. The firm also handles the drafting and negotiating of single bank and syndicated loan agreements and multiple option facilities acting for both lenders and borrowers, drafting and negotiating trade finance and project finance documentation, taking of security in connection with lending transactions including the taking of security on a multi-jurisdictional basis, mortgage and other asset securitisations and other off-balance sheet financing structures, debt restructuring documentation, listing of securities and undertaking all aspects of due diligence prior to listing.

Corporate and commercial: Kapila Anjarwalla & Khanna has considerable experience in all types of private and public company commercial work including share sales and asset sales, joint venture agreements, partnership agreements and distribution and marketing agreements. The firm acts for receivers of companies and advises on commercial conveyancing transactions (including the development of substantial residential and commercial developments); setting up of timeshare resorts; negotiating funding and development agreements for property companies; and negotiating agreements with contractors and other professionals involved in the development of commercial property.

Civil and commercial litigation: The firm's civil and commercial litigation practice has an outstanding reputation and considerable experience in the area of general property litigation, advising receivers and liquidators on receivership and winding-up of companies, enforcement of foreign judgements and arbitration awards, advising on shareholder disputes, intellectual property and passing off disputes.

Infrastructure projects: The firm has advised on the deregulation of the power and telecommunications sectors in Kenya. The firm acted (together with a team of international advisors) for the World Bank in advising the Government of Kenya on the development of independent power projects and has also advised an international company based in the US in connection with its tender for participation in the telecommunication industry in the process of privatisation.

Shipping: Kapila, Anjarwalla & Khanna advises clients on a full range of shipping and admiralty matters including the arrest of ships and towage, salvage and collision claims. The firm's experience also includes acting for crew, ship owners and shipping agents in undertaking litigation for demurrage claims, claims for hire, claims arising from collisions, claims in respect of cargo loss, cargo damage, claims arising from salvage and disputes between owners and charterers.

LANGUAGES: English, French, Kiswahili

KARTINI MULJADI & REKAN

HEAD OFFICE

Bina Mulia I Building, 5th & 6th Floor, Jalan HR Rasuna Said Kaveling 10, Jakarta 12950 Indonesia
Tel: +62 21 525 6968 **Fax:** +62 21 525 5561

FIRM OVERVIEW

Senior partner: Kartinin Muljadi

Number of partners worldwide: 5
Number of other lawyers worldwide: 28

AREAS OF PRACTICE:
Banking and finance .... *%
Capital markets .... *%
Construction .... *%
Corporate .... *%
Energy .... *%
Intellectual property .... *%
Litigation .... *%
Real estate .... *%
Telecommunications .... *%
Tourism .... *%
* Workload % not disclosed

FIRM OVERVIEW: Kartini Muljadi & Rekan was established in 1990 as the successor to the notary office of Kartini Muljadi SH. The firm has experience handling Indonesian and international legal matters.

INTERNATIONAL CLIENTS: Clients include Messer Griesheim GmbH, Aneka Gas Industri, and Makro.

MAIN INTERNATIONAL AREAS OF PRACTICE:
Corporate: The firm advises on establishing and structuring Indonesian state-owned enterprises (BUMN) as well as limited liability companies. It also handles the reorganisation and restructuring of limited liability companies including mergers, consolidations and acquisitions, bankruptcy and suspension of payment matters, private debt settlement, work-outs and advising on foreign and domestic capital investments. It also advises on domestic and international trade and commodities transactions, arranging for and obtaining licences for wholesale trading, retail trade, export and import activities. Recent clients include Messer Griesheim GmbH in the acquisition of shares held by the Indonesian government in PT and Aneka Gas Industri; Makro in the acquisition of a majority stake in PT Makro Indonesia.
Capital markets: Kartini Muljadi & Rekan advises clients on initial public offerings, rights issues, tender offers and financing issues relating to Indonesian and overseas capital market activities. Its clients include an Indonesian public company that issued debt securities registered with the US Securities and Exchange Commission through its subsidiary in the Netherlands. The firm has lawyers registered with Bapepam (Capital Market Supervisory Board) as capital specialist legal consultants.
Banking and finance: The firm advises on project financing, infrastructure and plant financing and securitisation.
Telecommunications: Kartini Muljadi & Rekan advises on all aspects of telecommunications.
Intellectual property: The firm advises on franchising documentation, the prosecution and registration of trademark, copyright and patent applications.
Real estate: The firm provides advice to real estate developers and investors.
Energy: Kartini Muljadi & Rekan advises on the preparation of agreements relating to the oil and natural gas industry and mining projects. It has also advised on the establishment of several cement factories.
Construction: The firm prepares various types of construction agreements including Build Operate and Transfer (BOT) agreements and Build Operate and Own (BOO) agreements.
Diplomatic representation: The firm represents diplomatic personnel and various foreign embassies including the British Embassy and the Dutch Embassy on specific projects.
Litigation: The firm represents inter alia IFC and several major international and domestic banks in connection with bankruptcy and related matters before the Commercial Court.

WORLDWIDE OFFICE CONTACTS

INDONESIA
Bina Mulia I Building, 5th & 6th Floor, Jalan HR Rasuna Said Kaveling 10, **Jakarta** 12950
Tel: +62 21 525 6968 **Fax:** +62 21 525 5561

For other recommended firms see pages 1485-1520

KATENDE SSEMPEBWA & CO

HEAD OFFICE

Radiant House, Plot 20, Kampala Road, PO Box 2344
Kampala, Uganda
Tel: + 256 41 233 770 **Fax:** + 256 41 257 544

Email: kats@kats.co.ug
Website: www.kats.co.ug

WORLDWIDE OFFICE CONTACTS

UGANDA
Radiant House, Plot 20, Kampala Road, PO Box 2344, **Kampala**
Tel: + 256 41 233 770 **Fax:** + 256 41 257 544
Email: kats@kats.co.ug

FIRM OVERVIEW

Senior partners: John W. Katende, Prof. Frederick Ssempebwa

Number of partners worldwide: 2
Number of other lawyers worldwide: 15

AREAS OF PRACTICE:

Aviation	*%
Banking and finance	*%
Corporate and commercial	*%
Employment	*%
Insurance and debt recovery	*%
Intellectual property	*%
Litigation and arbitration	*%
M&A and privatisations	*%
Real estate	*%
Securities and capital markets	*%
Tax	*%
Telecommunications and utility	*%

*Workload % not disclosed

FIRM OVERVIEW: Katende Ssempebwa & Co was established in 1969. It is one of Uganda's leading law firms and has maintained a significant and pioneering presence in general and specialised transactional and litigation related work. The firm has consistently advised on groundbreaking and unusually challenging assignments in Uganda.

INTERNATIONAL CLIENTS: The firm's clients includes industrial and commercial corporations, investment and commercial banks; foreign investors and their local subsidiaries, international development institutions, and multilateral agencies. Other clients include the Government of Uganda and Parastatals, non-governmental and other charitable organisations, airlines, utilities, oil and insurance companies, estates and individuals.

MAIN INTERNATIONAL AREAS OF PRACTICE:

Corporate: The firm advises on the formation, incorporation, and restructuring of companies. It also handles matters relating to equity and contractual joint ventures, wholly foreign owned enterprises and holding companies, and financial and management agreements. Katende Ssempebwa & Co has acted as in-house counsel, and as company secretaries for foreign and local clients.

M&A: The firm handles due diligence and provides legal and tax assistance with regard to the purchase or disposal of Ugandan corporations and Parastatals. It has represented both the government and international purchasers.

Banking and finance: The firm has one of the largest banking practices in Uganda and is the primary outside counsel for the country's central bank, Bank of Uganda. It also represents international finance bodies like the European Credit and Guarantee Department (ECGD) and Uganda's largest financing house, Uganda Development Bank. Its practice includes general banking, structured finance, syndicated and general lending, asset and project finance, guarantees, derivatives, debentures and charges. It has acted as counsel for numerous foreign and local investors seeking to underwrite and structure major loans and transactions within the country. The firm has represented international and local investors, foreign donor agencies and government bodies and performed due diligence and monitored the projects they have underwritten.

Litigation and arbitration: The firm has been involved in several groundbreaking, law making and landmark litigation cases that have shaped Ugandan law. The firm handles a substantial amount of arbitration, mediation and negotiation proceedings and has secured countless out of court settlements on behalf its clients

Securities and capital markets: The firm is currently advising two clients on the legal and tax aspects of their proposed listing on the Uganda Stock Exchange.

Insurance and debt recovery: The firm represents some of the largest insurance corporations in Uganda and routinely handles bankruptcy, liquidation, debt collection and receiverships for various banks, financial institutions and individuals in Uganda.

Employment: Katende Ssempebwa & Co advised the former employees of the East African Community (valued at over US$45 million) on the largest employment benefits class action settlement in East African history. It also advises international and corporate clients on employment contracts, handling redundancies and relations with trade unions, remuneration and incentive systems, pension funds and social security audits, expatriation, employee benefits and managerial compensation.

Intellectual property: The firm handles all aspects of intellectual property including trademarks, patents, designs, copyrights and layout designs. It is taking a pioneering role in the registration of internet based domain names in Uganda and is handling the first unfair competition and predatory pricing action in Uganda valued at over US $5 million.

Real estate: The firm specialises in all real estate transactions including conveyancing, mortgages, charges, debentures, purchases, sales, leases and transfers and all manner of litigation. It advises foreign and local institutional investors, developers, and surveyors and handles due diligence work regarding development projects in Uganda.

Tax: The firm advises on the tax implications of investment in Uganda, tax planning for managing directors and shareholders, mergers, reorganisations, financing, and privatisation. It specialises in local and international tax with regard to resident and non-resident corporations.

Aviation: The firm handles aircraft purchases, sales, leasing and financing, aircraft certification and registration, aviation claims, personal injuries, cargo and baggage claims. It represents numerous international and domestic airlines and Uganda's aviation authorities.

Telecommunications: The firm has represented the government of Uganda in the divestiture and liberalisation of the state-owned Parastatals in conjunction with various US law firms. The firm currently represents one of the largest private mobile telephone service providers in Uganda.

LANGUAGES: English and all local languages in Uganda

KATTEN MUCHIN ZAVIS

HEAD OFFICE

525 West Monroe Street, Suite 1600
Chicago IL 60661-3693, USA
Tel: +1 312 902 5200 **Fax:** +1 312 902 1061

Website: www.kmz.com

FIRM OVERVIEW

National managing partner Vincent A. F. Sergi

Number of partners worldwide: 200
Number of other lawyers worldwide: 260

AREAS OF PRACTICE:

Antitrust .... *%
Banking, finance and securities .... *%
Corporate .... *%
Intellectual property .... *%
Litigation .... *%
M&A .... *%
Real estate .... *%
Technology, e-business and new media .... *%
* Workload % not disclosed

FIRM OVERVIEW: Founded in 1974, Katten Muchin Zavis (KMZ) aims to provide comprehensive legal services and creative advice to top businesses and business people. Comprising more than 460 attorneys the firm has offices in Chicago, Los Angeles, New York and Washington DC. From start-ups through to multibillion-dollar transactions, KMZ attorneys distinguish themselves as legal counselors and strategic business advisors. The firm's practice areas have been carefully designed to complement, augment and protect clients' businesses. KMZ lawyers remain dedicated to helping clients anticipate change and adapt to a constantly evolving global marketplace

INTERNATIONAL EXPERIENCE: KMZ has represented clients in Eastern Europe, Japan, People's Republic of China, every major country in the European community, Mexico, Canada and Brazil. KMZ has established a worldwide network of highly qualified foreign counsel that provides global coverage and instant access.

MAIN INTERNATIONAL AREAS OF PRACTICE:

Antitrust: KMZ advises on a range of high-tech and traditional manufacturing and service industries including technology and new media start-ups, large multinational corporations, professional sports franchises, and health care providers.
Corporate: KMZ's corporate group comprises teams of corporate and securities attorneys, as well as lawyers from other disciplines such as tax and employment. Corporate services include advising on the structure, formation, funding and operation of business entities; structuring project-specific financings and IPOs; advising on merger and acquisition; conducting due diligence investigations; advising on partnerships and joint ventures; and restructuring joint ventures and other multi-party contracts.
Entertainment: KMZ advises on all aspects of the entertainment industry including television, motion pictures, licensing and merchandising, location-based entertainment, animation, publishing, labour and guilds, and music.
Intellectual property: KMZ advises on the protection and registration of patents, trademarks, copyrights, service marks and trade secrets including confidential information such as customer lists, client files and computer software.
Litigation: KMZ attorneys practice in federal and state courts, at trial and appellate level, before arbitration tribunals and administrative law judges. They also represent clients before specialty courts including the US Tax Court and the US Court of International Trade.
M&A: The firm advises on all aspects of take-overs. It has represented both targets and bidders in major hostile take-overs and has experience in defensive planning for clients through the implementation of anti-takeover devices and other defensive actions. The firm also acts for investment bankers, financial institutions and special committees of boards of directors.
Private equity and emerging growth companies: The firm regularly advises start-up companies, emerging growth companies and established firms in a wide variety of industries including conventional and high-tech businesses. KMZ undertakes the negotiation and structuring of investments for angels and private equity sources, start-up rounds, and late-stage financings through IPO and beyond. The firm handles structuring, documenting and closing investments involving common stock, straight preferred stock, convertible preferred stock, participating preferred stock, subordinated debt, warrants, capital appreciation rights and other phantom equity structures. It also handles general corporate and acquisition work.
Real estate: Comprising more than 75 lawyers, the real estate practice advises on environmental law, REITs, property tax and income taxation of real estate owners, and foreign investment and international real estate transactions.
Securities: The firm advises public and private companies on a wide range of securities matters including IPOs, private placements, proxy battles, mergers and asset securitisation transactions. It also handles issues relating to ongoing securities compliance (including insider trading policies), proxy statements and solicitations, regular reports and filings. Other ongoing securities-related matters handled range from managing relationships with analysts, market makers and the press to other general legal and business issues.
Technology, e-business and new media: The firm advises some of the US's top high-tech companies and e-businesses on antitrust, patent and trademark audit and protection, brand extension licensing, intangibles leveraging, content acquisition and exploitation, litigation, and technology licensing and distribution.

LANGUAGES: English

WORLDWIDE OFFICE CONTACTS

USA
525 West Monroe Street, Suite 1600, **Chicago** IL 0661-3693
Tel: +1 312 902 5200 **Fax:** +1 312 902 1061

1999 Avenue of the Stars, Suite 1400, **Los Angeles** CA 90067-6042
Tel: +1 310 788 4400 **Fax:** +1 310 788 4471

245 Park Avenue, 39th Floor, **New York** NY 10167
Tel: +1 212 764 6886 **Fax:** +1 212 382 3395

1025 Thomas Jefferson Street N.W, East Lobby: Suite 700,
Washington DC 20007-5201
Tel: +1 202 625 3500 **Fax:** +1 202 298 7570

K

For other recommended firms see pages 1485-1520

KELLY AFFLECK GREENE

HEAD OFFICE

One First Canadian Place, Suite 840, PO Box 489
Toronto, Ontario M5X 1E5, Canada
Tel: +1 416 360 2800 **Fax:** +1 416 360 5960

Email: info@kag.net
Website: www.kag.net

WORLDWIDE OFFICE CONTACTS

CANADA
One First Canadian Place, Suite 840, PO Box 489, **Toronto,** Ontario M5X 1E5
Tel: +1 416 360 2800 **Fax:** +1 416 360 5960
Email: info@kag.net

FIRM OVERVIEW

Partners: W.A. Kelly QC, D.S. Affleck QC, Peter R. Greene, Donald B. Houston, James C. Orr, Peter C. Wardle, Helen A. Daley, Melissa J. Kennedy

Number of partners worldwide: 8
Number of other lawyers worldwide: 7

AREAS OF PRACTICE:

Litigation 60%
Competition and anti-trust 30%
Administrative law 10%

FIRM OVERVIEW: Kelly Affleck Greene was founded in 1992 by a group of recognised litigators who had previously practiced with one of Canada's largest law firms. Comprising eight partners and seven other lawyers, the firm specialises in complex litigation cases. It aims to provide the highest quality legal representation at a reasonable cost through a combination of expertise, teamwork and practical advice.

INTERNATIONAL EXPERIENCE: During 1999 and 2000 Kelly Affleck Greene represented and advised a number of European, American and Caribbean clients in both litigation and competition law matters.

INTERNATIONAL CLIENTS: The firm's international client base includes corporations in the chemical, financial services/insurance, beverage and iron and steel industries.

MAIN INTERNATIONAL AREAS OF PRACTICE:

Commercial litigation: The firm handles a range of commercial litigation work including dispute resolution; banking and insolvency litigation (including CCAA proceeding before the Commercial Court); class actions (primarily as defence counsel in defending class actions); constitutional questions; construction contract claims (including alien claims); contractual disputes; employment litigation including wrongful dismissal actions; environmental litigation including defending prosecutions under the Environmental Protection Act and civil actions for trespass to property; fidelity bonds and all-risk crime guard policies; income tax assessment appeals and defensive criminal prosecutions; injunctions; health litigation; intellectual property claims and defences (including passing-off claims); libel, slander and defamation actions; product liability claims and defences; professional negligence (including defending claims against accountants, architects, doctors, engineers and lawyers); shareholders disputes; stock brokerage and securities litigation (primarily as defence counsel for several of Canada's leading investment houses); surety bonds; tort litigation.

Competition and anti-trust: The firm acts for clients in criminal prosecutions under the Competition Act and related statutes. It appears before the Competition Tribunal in cases involving mergers, abuse of dominance, exclusive dealing and other reviewable practices. It also represents plaintiffs and defendants in private civil actions. Kelly Affleck Greene handles a range of M&A related work including preparing pre-notification filings, obtaining advance ruling certificates and making representations to the Competition Bureau and the Competition Tribunal. It also advises clients dealing with the Competition Bureau by filing and responding to complaints, responding to search warrants, orders or requests for information, obtaining advisory opinions and making representations.
Administrative law: The firm has represented clients on a range of issues before the National Energy Board; the Ontario Municipal Board; the Ontario Securities Commission; the Toronto Stock Exchange; the Investment Dealers Association; the Liquor Control Board; the Employment Standards Tribunal; coroners inquests; Law Society Discipline Committee; Ontario College of Physicians and Surgeons; Ontario College of Pharmacists; Commercial Registration Appeals Tribunal; Human Rights Commission; Ontario Labour Relations Board.

LANGUAGES: English, French

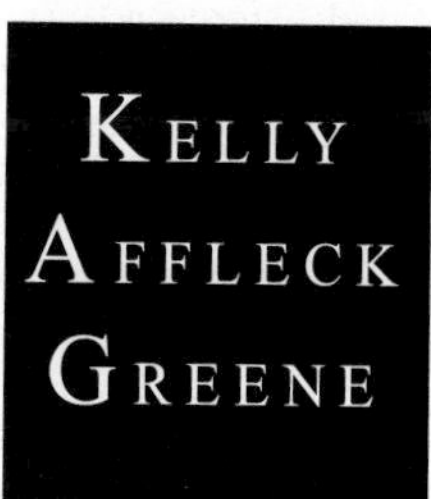

For other recommended firms see pages 1485-1520

KEMMLER RAPP BÖHLKE

HEAD OFFICE

9 Rond Point Schuman, Box 9,
B-1040 Brussels, Belgium
Tel: +32 2 230 9075 **Fax:** +32 2 230 1416

Email: krb@eurojura.be

WORLDWIDE OFFICE CONTACTS

BELGIUM
9 Rond Point Schuman, Box 9, B-1040 **Brussels**
Tel: +32 2 230 9075 **Fax:** +32 2 230 1416
Email: krb@eurojura.be

FIRM OVERVIEW

Managing partners Alexander Böhlke, Rainer Bierwagen
Number of partners worldwide: 4
Number of other lawyers worldwide: 3

AREAS OF PRACTICE:

Competition law 45%
Litigation 25%
State aid 15%
Trade 10%
Market access 5%

K

FIRM OVERVIEW: Established in the mid 1960s, Kemmler Rapp Böhlke specialises in EU law and is the longest standing Brussels-based independent EU law practice. The firm offers advocacy and advisory services. The former is essentially before the Community courts and the European Commission. Its advisory service covers all aspects of EU law and is designed to assist in forward strategic planning and dispute avoidance. The firm's partners and associates are multilingual.

INTERNATIONAL EXPERIENCE: The firm is experienced in helping to remove obstacles and opening access to markets, identifying the EU legal issues relevant to clients' businesses and providing practical advice on them. The firm advises clients on the administrative processes in Brussels and on challenges to acts which are incompatible with EU law. The firm has been involved in the EDF/Louis Dreyfus, Linde/AGA and EDF/ENBW mergers, the latter two being second phase mergers; it has been instrumental in defeating the Langnese & Baustahlgewebe appeals; active in PVC II, cement, Irish Sugar; and the appeal of regional aid and steel aid decisions. The firm has handled matters in industries such as air transport and airports, rail, telecommunications, electricity production and distribution, coal, industrial gases, tobacco, sugar, food production, pharmaceuticals and professional sport.

INTERNATIONAL CLIENTS: The firm advises large corporate clients and trade associations and acts for the European Commission in competition, Brussels Convention, tax and other matters. The firm's clients include AGA AB, EDF, Greencore and the German Government.

MAIN INTERNATIONAL AREAS OF PRACTICE:

Competition law: The firm advises on transactions falling under Articles 81 and 82 EC Treaty and the Merger Control Regulation; on the application of European competition law to agency, distribution, licensing and other commercial agreements and assisting in their negotiation and drafting; merger and commercial agreement notification; defending clients in administrative procedures before the European Commission; drawing up competition compliance programmes and training management; and drawing up procedures for handling raids by the competition authorities.

Market access: The firm handles matters such as drafting and pursuing complaints against anti-competitive practices, transactions or mergers to the European Commission and national authorities; advising on public procurement and the making and processing of tenders; and advising on trade and policy instruments for the opening of third country markets.
State Aid: The firm advises on rules relating to the giving and receipt of state aid and represents clients harmed by the anti-competitive grant of state aid to competitors.
Trade: The firm advises on dumping, subsidy and trade barriers investigations. The firm is involved in drafting complaints for European industry, defending third world exporters, and advising on international trade law issues relating to the WTO.
Litigation: The firm has wide experience of litigation before the European Court of Justice and the Court of First Instance, before which its lawyers have right of audience. The firm represents applicants, defendants and third parties in the range of areas listed above.

LANGUAGES: English, French, German, Hungarian, Spanish

For other recommended firms see pages 1485-1520

KHALID ANWER & CO

HEAD OFFICE

153-K, Block 2, P.E.C.H.S,
Karachi Pakistan
Tel: +92 21 455 0094 **Fax:** +92 21 455 7080

Email: laws@cyber.net.pk

WORLDWIDE OFFICE CONTACTS

PAKISTAN
153-K, Block 2, P.E.C.H.S, **Karachi**
Tel: +92 21 455 0094 **Fax:** +92 21 455 7080
Email: laws@cyber.net.pk

FIRM OVERVIEW

Senior partner: Khalid Anwer

Number of partners worldwide: 2
Number of other lawyers worldwide: 6

AREAS OF PRACTICE:

Area	%
Corporate and commercial litigation	40%
Banking and securities	20%
Intellectual property	15%
Power projects	10%
Admiralty and shipping	5%
Domestic and international arbitration	5%
Other	5%

FIRM OVERVIEW: Khalid Anwer & Co is a premier law firm comprising eight lawyers. Formerly known as A.K. Brohi & Co, it has offices in Karachi and associate firms in Lahore and Islamabad. It is one of the oldest and most prestigious law firms in Pakistan. The firm specialises in commercial law, but also handles constitutional matters in the Supreme Court. The firm advises clients on a wide range of issues regardless of technical complexity or geographic scope. The firm's law library is one of the finest in Pakistan and contains a complete and updated set of not only Pakistani and English law reports and treatises, but also those from other related jurisdictions.

INTERNATIONAL EXPERIENCE: The firm has acted for companies from EU countries, the US, Japan and the Far East. International work includes advising on investing or setting up business in Pakistan, international trade, finance agreements, franchising, distribution and agency agreements, litigation and arbitration. In 1993, the firm successfully persuaded the Supreme Court to take the unprecedented step of restoring a deposed Government to office. In 1996, the firm convinced the Supreme Court that the previous Government had been lawfully dismissed from office.

INTERNATIONAL CLIENTS: The firm's regular and retainer clients include various foreign and local banking companies and financial institutions, major industrial concerns, many pharmaceutical multinational companies, beverage companies, airlines and software companies.

MAIN INTERNATIONAL AREAS OF PRACTICE

Corporate and commercial: The firm provides a full range of services to many of Pakistan's leading financial, industrial and commercial enterprises including advocacy, consultancy and advisory services in civil matters encompassing the constitutional, banking, commercial and corporate areas. The firm has been successfully involved in a number of landmark commercial cases.
Banking: Clients include banks, development financial institutions and borrowers. The firm has also on several occasions advised the State Bank of Pakistan (Pakistan's central bank) and other banking institutions on major issues such as the State Bank's Prudential Regulations and other regulatory measures. The firm has advised clients on issues relating to the setting up of banks, on privatisation of banking institutions and other major issues that have recently emerged. The firm also advises the private sector banks that have emerged in Pakistan over the last few years.
Finance: The firm has handled a range of international financing of Pakistani projects. It has also advised clients on the private placement of equity in foreign markets including the first ever flotation of Euro-bonds by a Pakistani company. It has also been involved in the power sector projects that are coming up in Pakistan and has represented both lenders and project sponsors. The firm has also acted for clients in the raising of debt and equity financing in local markets. It has acted as advisors to the issue of prospectuses and the public placement of shares in Pakistan and has assisted clients in obtaining financing from banking and leasing companies. The firm anticipates a continuing involvement in this area as local capital markets develop further and more instruments and methods of raising financing become feasible.
Intellectual property: The firm is particularly active in the field of intellectual property rights. In particular, it represents a large number of multinational pharmaceutical companies operating in Pakistan. The firm is currently involved in several patent infringement suits, in all of which it successfully obtained court injunctions prohibiting the defendants from continuing the manufacture of the drug that allegedly violated the patent issued to the firm's client.
Joint venture projects: The firm has handled several joint venture projects in which a foreign partner has been involved. This included advising clients from the inception of the project (i.e. the basic joint venture agreement) all the way to the final agreements setting it up. The firm has been advising clients who are interested in participating in the government's privatisation program. The firm has on several occasions carried out due diligence on behalf of prospective buyers.

LANGUAGES: English, Urdu

For other recommended firms see pages 1485-1520

KIM & CHANG

HEAD OFFICE

Seyang Building, 223 Naeja-Dong, Chongro-ku
Seoul 110-720, South Korea
Tel: +82 2 3703 1114 **Fax:** +82 2 737 9091/3

Email: lawkim@kimchang.com
Website: www.kimchang.com

WORLDWIDE OFFICE CONTACTS

SOUTH KOREA
Seyang Building, 223 Naeja-Dong, Chongro-ku, **Seoul** 110-720
Tel: +82 2 3703 1114 **Fax:** +82 2 737 9091/3
Email: lawkim@kimchang.com

FIRM OVERVIEW

Managing partner: Young-Moo Kim

AREAS OF PRACTICE:

Area	
Banking and securities	*%
Competition and anti-trust	*%
Corporate/M&A	*%
Employment	*%
Environmental Law	*%
Insurance	*%
Intellectual property	*%
Litigation and arbitration	*%
Maritime	*%
Project finance	*%
Real estate	*%
Tax	*%
Telecommunications and IT	*%

* Workload not disclosed

K

FIRM OVERVIEW: Founded in 1972, Kim & Chang has grown to become one of the recognised leaders in the legal services market, providing high-quality services in all areas of Korean law. Many Kim & Chang attorneys are nationally renowned experts in their field.

INTERNATIONAL EXPERIENCE: For over a quarter of a century, Kim & Chang have represented international clients in successfully establishing their business ventures in Korea. In 1999, the firm advised on more than thirty large-scale M&A transactions involving Korean target companies.

INTERNATIONAL CLIENTS: The firm's international clientele includes major industrial and financial companies, most of which are on the Fortune 500 list.

MAIN INTERNATIONAL AREAS OF PRACTICE:

M&A: The practice provides a broad range of legal and tax services relating to domestic and cross-border M&A. The firm works in close association with major international investment banks, accounting firms and consulting firms covering all aspects of M&A.

Banking and securities: Made up of 50 professionals with substantial experience, this group specialises in handling international and domestic banking and securities matters.The firm advises major financial institutions, merchant banks and securities companies as well as private equity funds.

Corporate: The firm's corporate group provides legal advice and practical assistance on strategic planning, drafting contracts, obtaining business licences, and negotiating the establishment of business entities.

Environmental: Related activities include identifying potential environmental risks associated with acquisitions, conducting reviews of central, provincial or local government permit and environmental compliance status, consulting with government agencies to resolve permit, enforcement and clean-up matters.

Competiton and anti-trust: A key part of the practice, this group advises clients on anti-trust issues in the context of mergers and acquisitions. Another important aspect is the defence of clients accused of administrative/criminal violations of Korean anti-trust and fair trade law. This group includes highly experienced attorneys with whom the government regularly consults on a wide range of anti-trust issues as well as former officials with the fair-trade commission of Korea.

Insurance: This group advises and represents major insurance-related companies, including life and non-life insurance companies, reinsurance companies, surety and fidelity companies, and insurance agents and brokers.

Intellectual property: This group assists clients in acquiring, enforcing, protecting and commercialising their intellectual property rights, including patents, trademarks, designs, copyright, computer software, trade secrets, internet domain names and semiconducter layouts. Service covers most major technical fields, including electronic and electrical engineering, chemistry, pharmaceuticals, agrochemicals, biotechnology, food processing and mechanical engineering.

Employment: This group advises domestic and foreign enterprises on the legal issues inherent in employer-employee relationships and represents clients in administrative and judicial procedings arising from their status as employers.

Litigation and arbitration: This group is composed of seasoned trial attorneys, experts in all aspects of dispute resolution (including Korean civil, criminal, and appellate courts) and domestic and international commercial arbitration. The group also have extensive experience in product liability litigations.

Real estate: The group comprises attorneys as well as real estate and tax experts who together are uniquely qualified to assist clients with a wide range of real estate matters.

Tax: This group consists of tax lawyers, CPAs and former tax officials offering advice and planning in all areas of Korean taxation, including corporate, VAT, real estate, personal and customs, focusing on consulting and assistance during tax audits. The group also handle tax litigation.

Telecommunications and IT: The firm's legal advisers offer a broad range of services to clients involved or interested in the Korean communications market. The team works closely with relevant government regulatory bodies and has played a major role in drafting domestic telecommunications laws and regulations.

Trade and foreign exchange: The firm advises on trade and foreign exchange transactions and customs procedures. Expert advice in this area is vital due to the complex system of foreign exchange control regulations and foreign trade regulations in Korea.

White collar crime: The firm is experienced in white collar criminal litigation and investigation. According to the nature of a given case, the criminal group puts together a team consisting of attorneys who specialise in criminal law and attorneys who specialise in the relevant field, such as securities, finance, fair trade or tax.

LANGUAGES: Chinese, English, French, German, Japanese, Korean, Spanish

For other recommended firms see pages 1485-1520

KIM, SHIN & YU

HEAD OFFICE

12th Fl., Leema Bldg, 146-1, Susong-dong, Chongro-gu
Seoul 110-755, South Korea
Tel: +82 2 2000 5000 **Fax:** +82 2 2000 5050

Email: lawyer@ksy.co.kr
Website: www.ksy.co.kr

FIRM OVERVIEW

Senior partner: Jin Ouk Kim
Managing partner: Rok Sang Yu

Number of partners worldwide: 10
Number of other lawyers worldwide: 30

AREAS OF PRACTICE:

Corporate	25%
Litigation and arbitration	20%
M&A	20%
Banking and finance	15%
Intellectual property	10%
Insurance and reinsurance	5%
Telecommunication and IT law	5%

WORLDWIDE OFFICE CONTACTS

SOUTH KOREA
K.P.O Box 341, 5th Floor, Nong-Shim Building, #209 Seogye-dong, Yongsan-ku, **Seoul**
Tel: +82 2 3273 5822 **Fax:** +82 2 2000 5050

12th Fl., Leema Bldg, 146-1, Susong-dong, Chongro-gu, **Seoul** 110-755
Tel: +82 2 2000 5000 **Fax:** +82 2 2000 5050
Email: lawyer@ksy.co.kr

FIRM OVERVIEW: Founded in 1968, Kim, Shin & Yu is one of the pre-eminent law firms in Korea. The firm advises Korean and foreign clients on international business transactions, and its specialisation and experience in the field of international business has played a prominent role in the country's legal, commercial, and economic development. The founding partners were pioneers in providing legal services to foreign clients doing business in Korea, as well as to Korean clients interested in international business and investments. The firm has a reputation for bringing together western concepts of law and business with oriental traditions of commerce and judicature.

INTERNATIONAL EXPERIENCE: The firm has over 30 years international experience representing foreign companies investing in Korea. In the last decade, as the Korean economy expanded, Kim, Shin & Yu has advised a number of Korean companies requiring legal representation in international investment projects both in and outside of Korea.

INTERNATIONAL CLIENTS: The firm serves a broad and diversified client base ranging from small and medium-sized companies to companies listed in the Fortune 500.

MAIN INTERNATIONAL AREAS OF PRACTICE:

International trade and corporate: The firm advises on the intricacies of Korean commercial and corporate legislation, regulations and policy, taxation, foreign investment controls, and trade practices. The firm's broad domestic and international corporate practice handles partnerships/joint ventures; venture capital; M&A; incorporation/corporate formation; government relations; distributor and agency matters; shareholder and boardroom disputes; real estate matters; franchising; reorganisation and bankruptcy. One of the firm's partners was a member of the original Foreign Capital Inducement Deliberation Committee advising the Ministry of Finance.

Banking, finance and securities: Since its establishment, the firm's banking, finance and securities department has advised companies and financial institutions on various types of regulatory and financial transactions. The innovative structures of some of the transactions have served as standard practice for many transactions taking place in Korea today. These transactions include establishing foreign banks and financial institutions, dealing with regulatory governmental agencies, structuring secured and unsecured loans, underwriting public offerings, syndicating credit facilities and note issuances, and structuring lease financings and project financing.

Intellectual property: The firm specialises in transfer and licensing and the protection of intellectual property remains a key element in the full service it offers clients. Kim, Shin & Yu has been involved in several groundbreaking high-tech issues, which have served as the foundation for many industries in Korea and the firm has negotiated and drafted a large number of the licensing and technology transfer agreements that have become models for such practice in Korea. It handles all aspects of intellectual property development, registrations, licensing and protection of patents, utility models, designs, trademarks, service marks, copyright, and other intellectual property rights in Korea and abroad. Members of the firm have served as judges with the Korean Industrial Property Office. The firm also employs specialists in chemistry, biochemistry, genetic engineering, pharmaceuticals, computer software, electronics, communications, electrical engineering, mechanical engineering, and metallic engineering.

Telecommunications and IT: The firm represents a number of companies and individuals in the communications industry. As a result of deregulation, more opportunities will be available for foreign companies to participate in telecommunications in Korea. By closely monitoring proposed legislation, new laws, rules, and regulations, the firm is able to advise firms planning to submit bids for government contracts and/or seeking to comply with relevant legislation governing the industry.

Tax: The firm's tax department has expanded rapidly. It reviews each client transaction for tax ramifications in order to minimise tax liabilities. The firm also represents domestic and foreign clients in tax audits and litigations.

LANGUAGES: English, French, German, Japanese, Korean, Russian, Spanish

For other recommended firms see pages 1485-1520

KING & SPALDING

HEAD OFFICE

191 Peachtree Street,
Atlanta GA 30303-1763, USA
Tel: +1 404 572 4600 **Fax:** +1 404 572 5100

Email: kingspalding@kslaw.com
Website: www.kslaw.com

FIRM OVERVIEW

Managing partner: Walter W. Driver, Jr.
Senior partner: Griffin B. Bell

Number of partners worldwide: 192
Number of other lawyers worldwide: 438

AREAS OF PRACTICE:

Banking and finance .... *%
Corporate .... *%
Intellectual property .... *%
Litigation and arbitration .... *%
M&A .... *%
Real estate .... *%
Telecommunications and IT .... *%
* Workload % not disclosed

WORLDWIDE OFFICE CONTACTS

USA
191 Peachtree Street, **Atlanta** GA 30303-1763
Tel: +1 404 572 4600 **Fax:** +1 404 572 5100
Email: kingspalding@kslaw.com

1100 Louisiana, Suite 3300, **Houston** TX 77002-5219
Tel: +1 713 751 3200 **Fax:** +1 713 751 3290
Email: kingspalding@kslaw.com

1185 Avenue of the Americas, **New York** NY 10036-4003
Tel: +1 212 556 2100 **Fax:** +1 212 556 2222
Email: kingspalding@kslaw.com

1730 Pennsylvania Avenue NW, **Washington DC** 20006-4706
Tel: +1 202 737 0500 **Fax:** +1 202 626 3737
Email: kingspalding@kslaw.com

K

FIRM OVERVIEW: Established in 1885, the firm has offices in Atlanta, Washington DC, New York, and Houston. Since its inception, King & Spalding has provided high caliber legal counsel to clients in the United States and abroad. With over 600 attorneys, King & Spalding currently represents more than 250 public companies in over 48 practice areas.

INTERNATIONAL EXPERIENCE: The firm's international transactions group advises clients in cross-border mergers and acquisitions, trade and customs, e-commerce, energy, islamic finance and investment, intellectual property, structured finance, and international arbitration. The firm has undertaken extensive work in Latin America and in the Middle East, as well as with German companies investing in the United States.

INTERNATIONAL CLIENTS: King & Spalding's clients include Brown & Williamson Tobacco Corp, Budget Group, Inc., The Coca-Cola Company, Delta Air Lines, Inc., Enron Corp., General Electric Capital Corp., General Electric Company, General Motors Corp., Georgia-Pacific Corporation, The Home Depot, Inc., Lend Lease Real Estate Investments, Inc., Lockheed Martin Corp., Minnesota Mining and Manufacturing Company, SmithKline Beecham, Sprint Corporation, SunTrust Banks, Inc., Texaco Inc., and United Parcel Service, Inc.

MAIN INTERNATIONAL AREAS OF PRACTICE:
Banking and finance: The practice group provides legal services for domestic and non-US banks and other financial institutions. It handles all aspects of credit facilities and financial products, including traditional secured and unsecured credit facilities, asset-based financings, venture and mezzanine investments, structured financings, leveraged leases, credit enhancement arrangements, trade credits, swaps, and derivatives.
Corporate: Since 1995, the firm has served as counsel to issuers and underwriters/placement agents in over 185 public/Rule 144A offerings having an aggregate market value of over $38 billion. The firm represents issuers, underwriters, investors, and other corporate finance participants, as well as providing continuing corporate advice to public and private companies.
Intellectual property: The firm's IP lawyers concentrate on acquiring, creating, licensing, protecting, and litigating intellectual property rights, both domestically and internationally. The group advises clients on trademarks, patents, copyrights, marketing, competition and antitrust issues, joint ventures, mergers and acquisitions, and other related matters in a wide range of industries, including computer software, telecommunications, and biotechnology.
Litigation and arbitration: The firm provides litigation services in the areas of antitrust, appellate, class action, commercial litigation, product liability, shareholder and securities litigation, trade and customs, and environmental tort. The firm also has a substantial international arbitration practice.
M&A: In recent years, King & Spalding has ranked among the top 10 US law firms, measured by announced M&A transaction dollar volume, and among the top 20 US law firms, measured by the number of announced transactions. The firm's M&A experience spans a wide range of industries.
Real estate: The firm's real estate practice includes acquisition, development, financing, and leasing of commercial real estate primarily for nationally recognised developers as well as for non-US institutional and private investors and lenders. The firm has been active in asset portfolio transactions and the securitisation of real estate, including the creation of numerous real estate investment trusts.
Tax: The firm works with clients on the planning and execution of business transactions of all sizes and types arising in domestic and cross-border settings, including acquisitions, dispositions, joint ventures, and financing transactions. Advice covers the full range of federal income tax issues, with extensive experience in the corporate, partnership, and international practice areas.
Technology: The firm takes an integrated and multi-disciplined approach to technology related matters. Clients range from Fortune 50 multi-national corporations to single proprietor inventors.

LANGUAGES: Arabic, Cantonese, French, German, Gujarati, Hebrew, Italian, Japanese, Latin, Korean, Mandarin, Chinese, Portuguese, Spanish, Russian, Taiwanese, Yoruba

KING & SPALDING

For other recommended firms see pages 1485-1520

KLAVINS, SLAIDINS & LOZE

HEAD OFFICE

Blaumana iela 22, LV-1011 Riga, Latvia
Tel: +371 783 0000 **Fax:** +371 783 0001

Email: advokati@ksl.lv
Website: www.ksl.lv

WORLDWIDE OFFICE CONTACTS

LATVIA
Blaumana iela 22, LV-1011 **Riga**
Tel: +371 783 0000 **Fax:** +371 783 0001
Email: advokati@ksl.lv

FIRM OVERVIEW

Senior partners: Filip K. Klavins, Raymond L. Slaidins, Janis Loze, Anita Tamberga-Salmane, Laine Skopina

Number of partners worldwide: 5
Number of other lawyers worldwide: 7

AREAS OF PRACTICE:

Banking and finance	*%
Corporate	*%
Employment and immigration	*%
Foreign investment	*%
Intellectual property	*%
M&A	*%
Real estate	*%
Securities	*%
Tax	*%

* Workload not disclosed

FIRM OVERVIEW: Klavins, Slaidins & Loze is located in the central business district of Riga. Founded in 1992, the firm comprises twelve lawyers in all, of which there are five partners and seven associate lawyers. Four of its lawyers add valuable foreign experience to the firm, having been educated and trained in the US, England, and Germany. In addition to this legal staff, Klavins, Slaidins & Loze also has a specialist tax consultancy led by the former head of tax, legal and business advisory practice of Arthur Andersen Riga office. The firm is a member of the worldwide network Lex Mundi, and is active in the International Bar Association, American Bar Association, the Latvian Lawyers Collegium, and Latvian Lawyers Association.

INTERNATIONAL EXPERIENCE: Klavins, Slaidins & Loze has been involved in precedent setting legal work including acting as counsel to Union Bank of Switzerland as global co-ordinator of the first-ever offering of global depository receipts by a Latvian bank. It is currently acting as counsel to Metsaliitto from Finland and Sodra from Sweden in their negotiations with the Latvian government to establish a company which will investigate, finance and construct a pulp mill in Latvia - this is anticipated to be the largest foreign direct investment in Latvian history.

INTERNATIONAL CLIENTS: The firm's established clients in Latvia are Caterpillar, Coca-Cola, Kellogg's, Varner Hakon Invest, Skanska, Mid Baltic Realty, Motorola, Vereinsbank, Nordeutsche Landesbank, EBRD, Skandinaviska Enskilda Banken, TV 3, Netcom Group, Maersk, Statoil, Kodak, Air Baltic, SAS, and many more internationally prominent businesses. The firm has represented the Swedish government in establishment of both the Stockholm School of Economics in Riga and the Riga Graduate School of Law.

MAIN INTERNATIONAL AREAS OF PRACTICE:

Foreign investment: Soon after Latvia's independence the firm represented the winner of the international tender for the replacement of the Latvian telephone system, Cable & Wireless. Klavins, Slaidins & Loze has been actively working on behalf of Neste and Statoil on their ongoing major oil terminal project in the Riga Port through successive levels of administrative co-ordination, approval and planning.

M&A: The firm has played a prominent role in a number of major mergers in Latvia including Hansabanka/Zemes Banka and Hansabanka/Ventspils Apvienota Baltijas Banka in the banking industry, and the Hanzas Maiznicas group in agricultural products. The firm has extensive contacts with the Latvian Competition Council regarding issues of merger clearance and anti-trust issues. Recent major acquisition transactions include the Norddeutsche Landesbank acquisition of Riga's Pirma Banka, the acquisition by ICA AB of the food retail chain Interpegro-Latvija, and closing of the NetCom Group acquisition of one of the two Latvian mobile telephone operators Baltcom GSM.

Corporate: In addition to the handling of all aspects of company establishment and registration in Latvia, subsidiaries, branches and joint ventures, the firm assists with ongoing corporate governance issues and company relations with state and local government departments.

Real estate: The firm advises buyers and sellers of major real property in Latvia. It handles mortgage financing, construction, hotel and all other real property related work. The firm has represented numerous foreign governments with respect to their diplomatic properties in Latvia.

Banking and finance: The firm provides due diligence and legal advice to foreign banks lending in Latvia. The firm represents the EBRD with regard to many of its loans and equity investments in Latvia.

Securities: Klavins, Slaidins & Loze is very experienced in the Latvian Securities Market Commission. The firm represented Deutsche Bank in its role as arranger of the Latvijas Unibanka EMT Note Programme.

Intellectual property: The firm's lawyers include licensed trademark agents and licensed patent agents. In addition to filing and protecting intellectual property rights, the firm assists clients in licensing and royalties arrangements.

Employment and immigration: The firm provides advice regarding relations and contracts with employees. The firm has experience in reviewing various forms of international employee stock option plans under Latvian law. The firm also advises on executive work and residency permits.

Tax: The firm handles the design and implementation of tax efficient structures, corporate and shareholding structuring, structuring of business transactions such as sales, purchases, leasing and rent, financing and borrowing, transactions with intangible assets, import and export, repatriation of profits. The firm advises on compliance assurance, tax reviews and tax due diligence, and on disputes with authorities.

LANGUAGES: English, German, Latvian, Russian

KLEIN & FRANCO

HEAD OFFICE

Av Córdota 883, Piso 7,
105Y AAH Buenos Aires Argentina
Tel: +54 11 4315 4000 **Fax:** +54 11 4315 4590
Email: kyf@kleinyfranco.com
Website: www.kleinyfranco.com

WORLDWIDE OFFICE CONTACTS

ARGENTINA
Av Córdota 883, Piso 7, 105Y AAH **Buenos Aires**
Tel: +54 11 4315 4000 **Fax:** +54 11 4315 4590
Email: kyf@kleinyfranco.com

FIRM OVERVIEW

Managing partner: Guillermo Walter Klein
Senior partner: Guillermo Walter Klein
Number of partners worldwide: 6
Number of other lawyers worldwide: 26

AREAS OF PRACTICE:

Antitrust law	*%
Banking and financial transactions	*%
Corporate law and international business transactions	*%
Energy and public utilities	*%
Internet law	*%
Labour, employment and social security law	*%
Litigation and arbitration	*%
M&A	*%
Real estate	*%

*Workload % not disclosed

FIRM OVERVIEW: Founded in June, 1992, this Argentine firm is one of the successors of Klein & Mairal, a firm founded in 1970 which ended its activities in September, 1991. K&F has extensive experience in the areas of corporate and project finance, antitrust law and energy-related transactions. Some of K&F's members have had a commitment to public service, exemplified by Guillermo Walter Klein who served as the Argentine Secretary of State for Economic Planning (1976-1981), among other public positions. Also Raúl Granillo Ocampo, of counsel to the firm, served as Member and Chief Justice of the Supreme Court of Justice of the Province of La Rioja (1984-1986); Argentine Ambassador to the United States of America (1993-1997) and Argentine Minister of Justice (1997-1999).

INTERNATIONAL EXPERIENCE: K&F has advised on numerous major M&A transactions between 1997 and 2000, in acquisitions or sales in the following industries: automobile, food, supermarkets, specialised commercial stores, oil production and public services such as natural gas distribution and communications. Most of these transactions involved non-Argentine participants. K&F has also advised its clients on their business activities outside Argentina, either in other Mercosur countries (mainly in Brazil) or overseas, with the cooperation of local counsel.

INTERNATIONAL CLIENTS: The firm's client base is varied, with Argentine, U.S., European, Latin American and Asian clients, including international corporations, financial institutions, privatised companies, companies which quote on the Buenos Aires Stock Exchange, closely held companies, tax exempt organizations, start-up companies and individuals.

MAIN INTERNATIONAL AREAS OF PRACTICE:
M&A: The firm is frequently involved in Mergers & Acquisitions and in due diligence work on behalf of purchasers of Argentine companies.
Anti-trust law: The firm has wide experience in competition and anti-trust practice, providing legal assistance in the proceedings before the antitrust authorities for the obtaining of authorisation when required (under the recently enacted Antitrust Law Nbr. 25,156 for M&A transactions).
Energy and public utilities: The firm has actively participated in the privatisation process undergone by the Argentine economy, assisting investors in the purchase of state-owned companies and in the concession of public services. The firm has represented its clients through public bids and auctions in diverse areas including, inter alia, natural gas, dredging, landfill, public roads, airports, postal service, energy and operation of thermal plants and dams, etc. The firm renders legal counselling in connection with the sale, purchase, distribution and exportation of natural gas and electricity. K&F regularly handles regulatory and administrative law matters before Argentine governmental agencies and controlling bureaus.
Corporate law and international business transactions: K&F's corporate practice includes corporate planning and organisation, helping its clients to structure a wide spectrum of transactions. The firm's international contracts practice includes, inter alia, license agreements, agency and distributorship agreements, franchise agreements, construction, operation and maintenance agreements and transfer of technology agreements. Domestic and international joint ventures also constitute an important part of the firm's practice.
Banking and financial transactions: K&F is prepared to handle all aspects of federal regulation of the banking business. The practice includes issues of domestic and international financing, as well as the developing, structuring, negotiation and implementation of local and international financial operations.
Internet law: With regard to internet law, IT contracts and related matters, K&F has a specific department and is increasingly engaged in assisting in drafting or reviewing contracts and counselling on these subjects, including conflict of law and jurisdiction issues, applicable regulations and related tax aspects.
Labour, employment and social security law: K&F has an active practice in this area of law and its expertise includes litigation matters and legal counselling in areas such as collective bargaining, wrongful termination, labour arbitration, occupational safety and health, benefit determinations, personnel procedures, employee discipline, wage and hours laws and executive employment contracts.
Litigation and arbitration: The firm has represented numerous corporate clients in litigation and arbitration proceedings and appeals, both domestic and international.
Real estate: K&F advises on real estate acquisitions, development and financing, including construction, zoning, building and special issues relating to foreign ownership.

LANGUAGES: English, French, Italian, Portuguese, Spanish

For other recommended firms see pages 1485-1520

KLUGE ADVOKATFIRMA ANS

HEAD OFFICE

Gamle Forus v 17, PO Box 277,
4066 Stavanger, Norway
Tel: + 47 5157 1477 **Fax:** + 47 5157 6565

Email: stavanger@kluge.no

FIRM OVERVIEW

Senior partner: Clement Endresen
Managing partner: Snorre Hankali

Number of partners worldwide: 19
Number of other lawyers worldwide: 52

AREAS OF PRACTICE

Company, M&A and stock exchange	*%
Tax	*%
Construction	*%
Petroleum & energy	*%
Litigation	*%
Shipping, offshore, financing	*%
Competition	*%

* Workload % not disclosed

WORLDWIDE OFFICE CONTACTS

NORWAY
Gamle Forus v 17, PO Box 277, 4066 **Stavanger**
Tel: + 47 5157 1477 **Fax:** + 47 5157 6565
Email: stavanger@kluge.no

Fr Nansens pl, PO Box 1548, Vika, 0117 **Oslo**
Tel: + 47 2313 9200 **Fax:** + 47 2313 9201
Email: oslo@kluge.no

Bradbenken 1, PO Box 4139, Dreggen, **Bergen**
Tel: + 47 5555 9440 **Fax:** + 47 5532 6206
Email: bergen@kluge.no

K

FIRM OVERVIEW: Established in 1923, Kluge was joined in 1997 by the partners of Haneborg, Holm og Lange. The firm now has 52 lawyers in offices in the three major Norwegian business centres of Stavanger, Oslo and Bergen and covers all areas of commercial law as well as employment, construction and public law.

INTERNATIONAL EXPERIENCE: A substantial and growing part of the practice is international. The firm is active in international projects in Central and Western Europe and North America, advising on international contracts, mergers and acquisitions, ship finance, corporate finance, tax, oil and energy law.

INTERNATIONAL CLIENTS: Include trade, industry, shipping, aviation, oil, energy and construction sector clients, export credit agencies, banks and financial institutions as well as local and central government branches and agencies.

MAIN INTERNATIONAL AREAS OF PRACTICE:
Company, M&A and stock exchange: Clients range from small and intermediate businesses to publicly quoted companies and multinational corporations. The firm advises on the choice of company form and assists in the establishment, restructuring and liquidation of companies. Other areas of expertise are comprehensive merger transactions, buy-outs and takeovers, as well as demergers and company sales. The firm also advises on organisational questions concerning such things as administrative and decision-making policy, and advises shareholders and partners.
Tax: The firm considers this an important part of its services. It advises on tax regulations and the tax consequences of various decisions and transactions. It also advises municipal and governmental authorities on tax issues and undertakes a considerable amount of litigation.
Construction: This is a major area of work. The firm advises on all the phases of realisation of a project, from initial planning, including preparation for and liaison with municipal authorities, up to completion and final settlement. It represents major developers, construction companies, and architects as well as consulting engineers.
Petroleum and energy: The firm has over the years acquired considerable expertise in the area of petroleum and energy law, and provides assistance in dealing with questions of private law in connection with petroleum contracts and acquisition of rights to develop, concession petroleum resources and the construction of hydro electric power plants and the distribution network as well as issues of public law in this area. Kluge regularly advises a number of Norwegian and foreign service companies, and assists several foreign operating companies in this field.
Litigation: The firm has lawyers with broad experience in litigation, who represent clients in a wide range of disputes, including the Supreme Court. Several of the firm's partners also have broad experience as arbitrators.
Shipping/offshore/financing: Kluge advises Norwegian shipping companies on the choice of company form and financial structure for shipping and offshore projects, and gives advice and assistance in respect of negotiations regarding construction contracts for ships and floating platforms, time and bareboat charters, and employment contracts for drilling and service/accomodation platforms. Kluge also represents Norwegian as well as foreign companies in connection with the purchase and sale of ships and platforms, and Norwegian management companies regarding contracts for the technical management and/or crewing of vessels for shipowning companies in Norway and abroad. The firm has extensive experience in the establishment, financing, restructuring and refinancing of various projects, in particular within the shipping, offshore and aviation sectors. It advises both financial institutions, shipping companies and other investors regarding international financing, and assists in the negotiation and implementation of loan agreements.
Competition: The firm advises on Norwegian and EU competition regulations, and liaises with the competition authorities.

LANGUAGES: Danish, English, French, Italian, Norwegian, Spanish, Swedish and to some extent German and Russian

KONNOV & SOZANOVSKY

HEAD OFFICE

23 Shota Rustaveli Street, Suite 5,
01023 Kiev, Ukraine
Tel: +380 44 227 1590 **Fax:** +380 44 246 7466

Email: info@konnov.com
Website: www.konnov.com

WORLDWIDE OFFICE CONTACTS

UKRAINE
Suite 204, 13-a Komarova Street, 58017, **Chernovtsy**
Tel: + 380 3722 4 5729 **Fax:** + 380 3722 4 8700
Email:

23 Shota Rustaveli Street, Suite 5, 01023 **Kiev**
Tel: +380 44 227 1590 **Fax:** +380 44 246 7466
Email: info@konnov.com

FIRM OVERVIEW

Managing partner: Sergei Sozanovsky

Number of partners worldwide: 3
Number of other lawyers worldwide: 16

AREAS OF PRACTICE:
Corporate 25%
Litigation 25%
Intellectual property 20%
Telecommunications 15%
Tax 10%
Real estate 5%

K

FIRM OVERVIEW: Founded in 1992, Konnov & Sozanovsky has offices in Kiev and Chernovtsy. Comprising approximately 20 lawyers, the firm is considered big by Ukrainian standards. It has extensive knowledge of Ukrainian legislation and international law as well an understanding of business in Ukraine. Konnov & Sozanovsky aims to provide cost-effective legal advice to a wide range of Ukrainian and foreign clients.

INTERNATIONAL EXPERIENCE: Konnov & Sozanovsky has handled a large number of international transactions, mainly in telecommunications, foreign trade, and arbitration.

INTERNATIONAL CLIENTS: The firm advises major international companies in the production, telecom, television and music industries. It also advises banks.

MAIN INTERNATIONAL AREAS OF PRACTICE:
Anti-trust: Konnov & Sozanovsky advises on anti-trust and unfair competition issues. The firm has handled joint-stock company formation and merger proceedings before the Anti-Monopoly Committee of Ukraine (AMCU). During 1998-2000, it advised a number of clients, including leading TV networks, on several stock purchase transactions. The firm has also advised on several unfair competition investigations.
Communications: Konnov & Sozanovsky advises licensees, investors, lenders and customers on telecommunications services and equipment, cellular and other mobile services, television and radio broadcasting, cable television systems, and program production. In addition to general representation of communications clients, the firm handles a wide range of international, state and municipal issues. It has advised on acquisitions and sales of regulated companies and the formation of joint ventures to provide communications services. The firm also provides anti-trust advice to telecommunications companies and obtains state regulatory authorisation for clients transferring control of carriers and licenses and entering the telecommunications sector. The firm has also advised on communications license auctions conducted by the Ukrainian State Communication Committee.
Corporate: Konnov & Sozanovsky's practice covers a broad spectrum of corporate and business issues. The firm advises on formation, reorganisation, structuring, acquisition and liquidation of corporations, partnerships, and non-profit organisations. The firm is one of the first in the Ukraine to practise in Internet and e-commerce law. Konnov & Sozanovsky advises a range of companies, banks and non-profit organisations. Work includes advising on regulatory issues, drafting contracts for various categories of commercial transactions, and legal support to diverse business projects. Its clients are active in a variety of industries including telecommunications, mass media, entertainment, transportation, real estate, food production, and distribution.
Foreign investments: The firm specialises in legal support for foreign investors and companies operating in the Ukraine. The firm advises foreign clients on employment, immigration and visa issues, real estate transactions, rent, and privatisation.
Intellectual property: The firm advises on copyright and trademark protection, and other intellectual property issues. Konnov & Sozanovsky frequently represents plaintiffs and respondents in trademark litigation including internationally known trademarks. The firm represents major corporations, publishers, studios, producers, broadcasters, distributors and talent in matters involving intellectual property, rights ownership, and royalty accounting.
Employment: Konnov & Sozanovsky advises a range of corporate clients on employment law including the preparation of employment contracts, confidentiality agreements, non-competition agreements, personnel manuals, and employee benefit plans. It also advises employers on claims made against them by former employees in administrative proceedings and litigation (breach of contract, wrongful termination, infliction of emotional distress, defamation).
Litigation: Konnov & Sozanovsky's litigation practice specialises in complex civil and commercial disputes in state courts, arbitration panels, and appellate tribunals. The firm has been involved in case relating to anti-trust, breach of contract, enforcement of administrative agency regulations, employment, personal injury, defamation, bankruptcy, unfair competition, copyright and trademark infringements, and real estate
Real estate: Konnov & Sozanovsky advises on acquisition and sale of all types of real estate. Work undertaken includes negotiating purchase and sale agreements, organising title-holding entities, due diligence, and preparing deeds and easements. It also handles land use issues and advises landlords and tenants on the preparation and negotiation of commercial leases covering industrial and office properties.
Tax: The firm provides general tax counselling to corporations, individuals and charitable organisations. It advises on the planning, structure, negotiation, and implementation of a range of business transactions, combinations and financing for Ukrainian and foreign clients. It also handles tax-free and taxable reorganisations, spin-offs, acquisitions, restructuring, joint ventures, leasing transactions, and tax litigation.

LANGUAGES: English, German, Russian, Ukrainian

For other recommended firms see pages 1485-1520

KOO AND PARTNERS

HEAD OFFICE

22/F Bank of China Tower, 1 Garden Road, Central, Hong Kong
Tel: +852 2867 9988 **Fax:** +852 2868 1017

Email: dk@kooandpartners.com/awyc@kooandpartners.com
Website: www.kooandpartners.com

WORLDWIDE OFFICE CONTACTS

HONG KONG
22/F Bank of China Tower, 1 Garden Road, Central, **Hong Kong**
Tel: +852 2867 9988 **Fax:** +852 2868 1017
Email: dk@kooandpartners.com/awyc@kooandpartners.com

CHINA (PEOPLE'S REPUBLIC OF)
D-11B Fuhua Mansion, No 8 Chaoyangmen North Avenue, **Beijing**
Tel: +8610 6554 2740 **Fax:** +8610 6554 2726
Email: dk@kooandpartners.com

FIRM OVERVIEW

Senior partner: Donald HY Koo

Number of partners worldwide: 17
Number of other lawyers worldwide: 40

AREAS OF PRACTICE:

Corporate finance and commercial (including employment and provident funds)	20%
China project finance/asset finance	20%
Banking and finance	15%
Litigation and arbitration	15%
Insolvency and restructuring	15%
Property	15%

FIRM OVERVIEW: Koo and Partners was established in October 1993. While it maintains a focus on China and Hong Kong banking and finance transactions, it is a full service law firm servicing the domestic and international business community. The firm is one of the larger Hong Kong based law firms with a staff complement of 200, including 17 partners, 4 consultants and 50 other legal staff. Nearly all lawyers are bilingual.

INTERNATIONAL EXPERIENCE: The firm's lawyers have specific transactional experience in China, Hong Kong and other Asian countries such as Thailand, Philippines, Indonesia, Singapore, Vietnam, Cambodia and Korea. The firm maintains close working relationships with law firms throughout the PRC and the Asia-Pacific Region, Europe and the United States. The firm's China practice is in close contact with a number of Chinese governmental institutions and law firms, and advises on finance and commercial transactions relating to China. In particular, the firm is actively involved in Chinese infrastructure financings ranging from transportation (such as toll road and toll bridge) and power projects, to petrochemical, water, telecommunications and aviation related projects. Lately, the firm has been actively involved in restructuring, insolvency and litigation matters both of a local and cross-border nature.

INTERNATIONAL CLIENTS: Koo and Partners was set up initially to represent a major banking group in Hong Kong. However, it now acts for an extensive range of clients including international and domestic banks and financial institutions, venture capital outfits, developers, project sponsors, airlines, multinational corporations as well as individuals.

MAIN INTERNATIONAL AREAS OF PRACTICE:

Aviation and shipping: Services provided include transportation and services contracts and issues, aircraft/shipping, carriage of goods/passengers, finance and operating leasing, insurance, and export credits supported financings. This group also advises on domestic and cross-border equipment leasing matters.

Banking: Matters handled cover the entire spectrum of banking and finance matters including: banking forms, derivatives, leasing, trade finance, bonds, letters of credit, financial market instruments, security or trust instruments, banking procedures, credit card matters, internet and e-banking, risk management, banking due diligence and data privacy.

China and project finance: This group advises on all aspects of lending and security taking in Hong Kong, mainland China and elsewhere; including infrastructural transactional advice relating to toll road, other transportation, power plants, telecommunications and manufacturing project facilities.

Corporate finance and commercial: This group advises on business arrangements such as venture capital, joint venture, agency or distributorship arrangements, sale and purchase of businesses, listings in Hong Kong and abroad, capital market issues, construction and related matters, health and safety issues, telecommunications, intellectual property issues, employment and provident funds, data privacy and entertainment-related matters.

Litigation and arbitration: The services offered include property litigation, finance related and debt recovery litigation, commercial dispute resolution, labour dispute resolution, personal injury and insurance related litigation, construction litigation as well as arbitration and mediation services.

Property: The firm represents financiers, mortgagees, developers, vendors, purchasers and governmental bodies in conveyancing, property development, leasing and all other landed property related and secured lending matters.

Restructuring and insolvency: This group is involved in all aspects of debt and corporate restructurings, standstills and reorganisations involving creditors as well as liquidations, receiverships and bankruptcies involving Hong Kong, mainland PRC and overseas corporations and individuals. Extensive debt collection and property receivership services are provided within this group.

LANGUAGES: Chinese (Cantonese, Hokkien, Mandarin, Shanghainese), English, French, German

K

For other recommended firms see pages 1485-1520

CABINET KOUAOVI

HEAD OFFICE

Rue de la Guinée,
Niamey BP 10191, Niger
Tel: +227 73 43 49/+227 73 21 00 **Fax:** +227 73 49 23

Email: bok@intnet.ne

WORLDWIDE OFFICE CONTACTS

NIGER
Rue de la Guinée, **Niamey** BP 10191
Tel: +227 73 43 49/+227 73 21 00 **Fax:** +227 73 49 23
Email: bok@intnet.ne

FIRM OVERVIEW

Managing partner: Bernard O. Kouaovi

Number of partners worldwide: 1
Number of other lawyers worldwide: 4

AREAS OF PRACTICE:
Commercial .... *%
Company restructuring .... *%
Corporate .... *%
Litigation and arbitration .... *%
M&A .... *%
Privitisations .... *%
* Workload % not disclosed

FIRM OVERVIEW: Established in 1962, Cabinet Kouaovi is one of Niger's leading law firms. Comprising one partner, one trainee, three paralegals and seven support staff, the firm's aim is to establish personalised relationships between clients and its lawyers. It specialises in corporate, commercial (notably transfers), acquisitions, privatisations and company restructuring. The firm also assists clients in legal and administrative proceedings, as well as in domestic and international arbitrations. The firm has an extensive legal library.

INTERNATIONAL EXPERIENCE: The firm successfully represented l'U.S.A.I.D. against 104 employees following the organisation's closure. The firm is heavily involved in a number of ongoing privatisations in Niger and was chosen by French firm Gide Loyrette Nouel as the local correspondent in the creation of a multi-sector regulatory authority.

INTERNATIONAL CLIENTS: The firm's clients include Afelen, Air France, AMPN (Clinique de la Cooperation Française), Bank Of Africa Niger, Banque Commerciale Du Niger, Banque Internationale De L'Afrique, Banque Mondiale, Braniger (Castel Group), Care International, Coopération Suisse, CRS, Embassy of France, Embassy of Morocco, Embassy of US and Affiliate Members, Exxon (Esso), French Development Agency, GTZ, Hotel Gaweye Sofitel, Icrisat, Nimag Score (formerly Scoa Group), Parker Driling, Plan International, Societe Fonciere Internationale, Sonichar, Sos Kinderdorf, Total-Fina-Elf, Ugan (Group Axxa), World Vision.

MAIN INTERNATIONAL AREAS OF PRACTICE: Work undertaken includes corporate, commercial (notably transfers), acquisitions, privitisations and company restructuring. The firm also assists clients in legal and administrative proceedings, as well as in domestic and international arbitrations. It advises on employment contracts, restructuring and corporate planning, individual and collective conflicts, transfer and acquisition of businesses, M&A, transfer of commercial funds, property management and real estate negotiations.
OHADA: The firm specialises in the application of the OHADA treaty (Uniform Act in West Africa) and handles a range of commercial aspects relating either to Niger or the rest of the world.

LANGUAGES: English, French

For other recommended firms see pages 1485-1520

KUDJAWU & CO

HEAD OFFICE

D693/4 Derby Avenue, PO Box 294,
Accra Ghana
Tel: +233 21 664552 **Fax:** +233 21 668574

Email: kudjawu@africaonline.com.gh

FIRM OVERVIEW

Managing partner: N.K. Kudjawu
Senior partner: S.B Amarteifio

Number of partners worldwide: 4
Number of other lawyers worldwide: 2

AREAS OF PRACTICE:

Banking and finance	*%
Corporate	*%
Industry and employment	*%
Intellectual property	*%
Litigation and arbitration	*%
M&A	*%
Minerals and mining	*%

* Workload not disclosed

FIRM OVERVIEW: Kudjawu & Co was established as the successor to a UK based firm, Giles Hunt & Co. The firm offers comprehensive legal advice to clients with international business interests, specialising in mergers and acquisitions, corporate, commercial, mining, and intellectual property. The firm does not participate in formal alliances or networks, but maintains close working relationships with various international law firms.

INTERNATIONAL EXPERIENCE: The firm has over 35 years international experience. It has advised major international organisations on mergers and acquisitions, mining, banking and finance, and intellectual property. The firm has also provided legal services to the World Bank and International Finance Corporation. More recently, it has handled the flotation and listing of Ashanti Goldfields Company Limited on the Ghana, London and New York Stock Exchanges.

WORLDWIDE OFFICE CONTACTS

GHANA
D693/4 Derby Avenue, PO Box 294, **Accra**
Tel: +233 21 664552 **Fax:** +233 21 668574
Email: kudjawu@africaonline.com.gh

INTERNATIONAL CLIENTS: The firm's client base includes Ghanaian and foreign companies in the public and private sectors, including banks and other financial institutions, shipping and oil marketing companies, and mining companies.

MAIN INTERNATIONAL AREAS OF PRACTICE: Work undertaken includes corporate, M&A, banking and finance, intellectual property, minerals and mining, litigation and arbitration, industry and employment.

LANGUAGES: English, French

For other recommended firms see pages 1485-1520

LAGERLÖF & LEMAN ADVOKATBYRÅ

A MEMBER FIRM OF LINKLATERS & ALLIANCE

HEAD OFFICE

Strandvägen 7A, PO Box 5402,
SE-114 84 Stockholm, Sweden
Tel: +46 8 665 66 00 **Fax:** +46 8 667 68 83

Email: info.sto@lol.se
Website: www.linklaters-alliance.com

Managing partner: Rolf Johansson

Number of partners worldwide: 40
Number of other lawyers worldwide: 110

Number of partners worldwide (Linklaters & Alliance): 586
Number of other lawyers worldwide (Linklaters & Alliance): 2,232

FIRM OVERVIEW

L

AREAS OF PRACTICE:

Banking .... *%
Employment .... *%
EU and competition .... *%
Finance .... *%
Intellectual property .... *%
IT .... *%
Litigation and arbitration .... *%
M&A .... *%
Real estate .... *%
Tax .... *%
Telecommunications .... *%
* Workload % not disclosed

FIRM OVERVIEW: Lagerlöf & Leman is a top-ranked Swedish law firm, focused on modern business law. Its 150 lawyers operate from eight domestic and international offices. Clients include multinational and domestic companies active in various fields of business, as well as the Swedish Government and state-owned companies. Lagerlöf & Leman is a member firm of Linklaters & Alliance which brings together five of Europe's premier law firms: De Bandt, van Hecke, Lagae & Loesch (Belgium and Luxembourg); De Brauw Blackstone Westbroek (Netherlands); Gianni, Origoni & Partners (Italy); Lagerlöf & Leman (Sweden) and Linklaters (which practises in Germany as Linklaters Oppenhoff & Rädler). Linklaters & Alliance is one of the leading global legal practices with nearly 3,000 lawyers and other professionals operating in combined teams from 34 offices in major financial and business centres worlwide.

MAIN INTERNATIONAL AREAS OF PRACTICE: Approximately one third of Lagerlöf & Leman's business is international. The firm handles international transactions and deals within all fields. Predominantly, the firm's international areas of practice are mergers and acquisitions; EU and competition law; banking and financial markets; intellectual property; IT; telecommunications; employment and employee benefits; pensions; litigation and arbitration; real estate and tax.

LANGUAGES: English, French, German, Italian, Polish, Spanish, Swedish

WORLDWIDE OFFICE CONTACTS

BELGIUM
rue Brederode 13A, B-1000 **Brussels**
Tel: +32 2 50 50 211 **Fax:** +32 2 50 50 644
Email: info@alliancebrussels.com

FRANCE
25, Rue de Marignan, F-75008 **Paris**
Tel: +33 1 56 43 56 86 **Fax:** +33 1 43 59 50 75
Email: lagerlof.leman@wanadoo.tr

POLAND
Warsaw Towers, ul. Sienna 39, PL-00121 **Warsaw**
Tel: +48 22 526 5000 **Fax:** +48 22 526 5060
Email: cwal@consultor.com.pl

SWEDEN
Västra Hamngatan 24, PO Box 2252, SE-403 14 **Gothenburg**
Tel: +46 31 701 68 00 **Fax:** +46 31 13 56 62
Email: info.got@lol.se

Stortorget 8, SE-211 34 **Malmö**
Tel: +46 40 665 65 00 **Fax:** +46 40 97 19 17
Email: info.mlm@lol.se

UNITED KINGDOM
One Silk Street, **London** EC2Y 8HQ
Tel: +44 7456 5838 **Fax:** +44 7456 5839
Email: bertil.olgard@linklaters.com

USA
1345 Avenue of the Americas, 19th Floor, **New York** NY 10105
Tel: +1 212 424 9150 **Fax:** +1 212 424 9155
Email: lagerlof@mindspring.com

OTHER LINKLATERS & ALLIANCE OFFICES

Alicante, Amsterdam, Antwerp, Bangkok, Berlin, Bratislava, Bucharest, Budapest, Cologne, Frankfurt am Main, The Hague, Hong Kong, Luxembourg, Madrid, Milan, Moscow, Munich, Padua, Prague, Rome, Rotterdam, São Paulo, Shanghai, Singapore, Tokyo, Washington, DC

For other recommended firms see pages 1485-1520

LANDWELL

HEAD OFFICE

see Worldwide Office Contacts

Email: info@landwellglobal.com
Website: www.landwellglobal.com

FIRM OVERVIEW

Chairman: Gérard Nicolaÿ
Head of global operations – legal: Alan Morris

Number of partners worldwide: 280
Number of other lawyers worldwide: 1700

AREAS OF PRACTICE:

Corporate and commercial	40%
E-business	15%
Employment and human resources	15%
Financial services	10%
Intellectual property	8%
Real estate/environment	5%
Public law	4%
Dispute resolution	3%

FIRM OVERVIEW Landwell is the correspondent legal practice of PricewaterhouseCoopers. The Landwell network was established in October 1999, bringing together the correspondent law firms of PricewaterhouseCoopers under a common name and structure. Landwell represents a new approach to legal consulting. Landwell's lawyers are business consultants as well as experts in law. Its international network specialises in national and international solutions to complex business issues and provides in-depth advice across the spectrum of business law. The practice delivers complete solutions, adding value to the entire process from planning though to implementation and review. To provide an integrated approach, the practice draws on other specialists in tax, corporate finance, and consultancy, either in Landwell or in PricewaterhouseCoopers.

INTERNATIONAL EXPERIENCE: The Landwell network operates in over 40 different countries and, leveraging off the global skills of Pricewaterhouse-Coopers, has established a network of offices that combine in-depth local expertise with international legal consulting.

INTERNATIONAL CLIENTS: Landwell acts for a large range of multi-national and international clients and has dedicated cross-border client service teams in the areas of M&A, corporate transformation, financial services, e-business, and employment and HR. Landwell's approach is to ensure that global teams are assembled quickly and effectively, working with the client through a single point of contact.

MAIN INTERNATIONAL AREAS OF PRACTICE:

Corporate and commercial: Landwell has experience in cross-border and European M&A transactions, with over 700 specialists based in over 40 countries. It works with a full range of clients, from large national and multi-national companies to government and financial institutions. The practice works closely with consultants and other advisers in PricewaterhouseCoopers, including tax specialists. It specialises in transactions that involve complex business projects or corporate transformation.
E-business: The firm's global e-business network comprises over 150 lawyers advising clients on securing, defending and transforming their e-business enterprises. The practice advises both start-ups and established

WORLDWIDE OFFICE CONTACTS

AUSTRALIA
PricewaterhouseCoopers Legal, Tower 2, Darling Park, 201 Sussex Street, GPO Box 2650, **Sydney** NSW 1171
Tel: +61 2 8266 6666 **Fax:** +61 2 8266 6990
Email: info@pwclegal.com.au

BELGIUM
Bogaert & Vandemeulebroeke, Woluwedal 20, 1932 Sint-Stevens-Woluwe, **Brussels**
Tel: +32 2 710 78 11 **Fax:** +32 2 710 78 53
Email: info@landwellglobal.com

DENMARK
Landwell Advokataktieselskab, Strandvejen 60, DK 2900, **Hellerup**
Tel: +45 39 45 39 50 **Fax:** +45 39 45 39 60
Email: info@landwell.dk

ESTONIA
OÜ Advokaadibüroo Landwell, Narva mnt 9A, 10117, **Tallinn**
Tel: +372 6 141 990 **Fax:** +372 6 141 999
Email: tallinn@ee.landwellglobal.com

FRANCE
Landwell & Associés/Partners, 32 rue Guersant, 75017 **Paris**
Tel: +33 1 56 57 56 57 **Fax:** +33 1 56 57 56 58
Email: info@landwell.fr

GERMANY
PricewaterhouseCoopers Veltins, Im Trutz Frankfurt, 55, 60322, **Frankfurt am Main**
Tel: +49 69 15242 0 **Fax:** +49 69 15242 111
Email: info@pwc-veltins-law.com

HUNGARY
Dezsö, Réti & Antall Landwell, Wesselényi utca 16/A, 1077 **Budapest**
Tel: +36 1 461 9888 **Fax:** +36 1 461 9898
Email: info@landwellglobal.com

IRELAND
Evans & Company, Gardner House, Wilton Place, **Dublin** 2
Tel: +353 1 662 8989 **Fax:** +353 1 662 6788
Email: evansco@indigo.ie

ITALY
Pirola Pennuto Zei & Associati, Via Vittor Pisani 16, 20124 **Milan**
Tel: +39 02 669 951 **Fax:** +39 02 669 1800
Email: info@landwellglobal.com

NETHERLANDS
Landwell, Atrium Building, Strawinskylaan 3127, 1077 ZX **Amsterdam**
Tel: +31 20 568 5685 **Fax:** +31 20 568 5681
Email: info@landwellglobal.com

NORWAY
Advokatfirmaet PricewaterhouseCoopers, Karenslyst allé 12-14, 0245 **Oslo**
Tel: +47 23 16 00 00 **Fax:** +47 23 16 03 00
Email: advokatfirmaet.pwc@no.pwcglobal.com

POLAND
Wierzbowski & Szubielska, ul. Nowogrodzka 68, 02-014 **Warsaw**
Tel: +48 22 523 4111 **Fax:** +48 22 523 4755
Email: krzysztof.wierzbowski@pl.landwellglobal.com

L

LANDWELL cont'd

businesses seeking to capitalise on the e-business revolution, working with consultants and other specialists to provide a complete advisory service. This includes ensuring that clients have full ownership and effective control of products, services and brands, risk analysis and establishing the most effective business model through best use of the legal and regulatory environment.

Employment and human resources: With over 200 lawyers in the network, Landwell's lawyers provide complete advice on HR legal issues, specialising in cross-border transactions. This includes labour and employment law, social security, pensions law, and immigration law. The network provides integrated advice, often working with tax and human resources and management consultants in PricewaterhouseCoopers.

Financial services: Landwell advises on banking (including e-banking), insurance, capital markets and fund and investment management to leading international clients. This includes advice to regulators around the world. The network combines strong international legal expertise supported by lawyers based around the world to ensure effective implementation. The network frequently works with corporate financiers and other financial advisers.

Intellectual property: The network provides clients with a co-ordinated, commercial approach to global intellectual property issues. The range of services includes legal audits, implementing protection programmes, enforcement and litigation proceedings, and the intellectual property aspects of transactions.

Real estate/environment: The network advises corporate clients on flexible occupancy, freehold and leasehold occupation, outsourcing, and investment in real estate. Clients include e-business enterprises seeking premises for new operations.

Public law: Landwell provides a full range of services in government-related business law including project finance, procurement, state aid or subsidies, government contracts, privatisation, and real estate. The practice is experienced in areas such as project financing and advising regulated industries.

Dispute resolution: Landwell's support for clients includes litigation before national courts, arbitration before national and international tribunals, mediation and other alternative dispute resolution methods.

LANGUAGES: Many of Landwell's lawyers are multilingual, working in local languages and other languages, including English, as appropriate. The practice ensures that advice is provided in the language preferred by clients around the world, either to deliver solutions in individual countries or in multiple jurisdictions.

PORTUGAL
Oliveira, Martins, Moura, Esteves & Associados, Rua Dr. Eduardo Neves, 9-7o, 1050-088 **Lisbon**
Tel: +351 2 1 799 7040 **Fax:** +351 2 1 799 7041
Email: luis.m.s.oliveira@pt.landwellglobal.com

RUSSIA
PricewaterhouseCoopers CIS Law Offices, 52 Kosmodamianskaya Naberezhnaya, Building 5, 113054 **Moscow**
Tel: +7 095 967 6000 **Fax:** +7 095 967 6001
Email: info@landwellglobal.com

SOUTH AFRICA
Bell Dewar & Hall Inc, 37 West Street, Houghton, **Johannesburg**
Tel: +27 11 710 6000 **Fax:** +27 11 710 6104
Email: bdh@belldewar.co.za

SPAIN
Landwell Abagados y Asesores Fiscales, Paseo de la Castellana 53, 28046 **Madrid**
Tel: +34 91 568 4000 **Fax:** +34 91 568 4672
Email: landwellmarketing@es.pwcglobal.com

SWITZERLAND
Suter Attorneys at Law, Stampfenbachstrasse 52, CH-8035 **Zurich**
Tel: +41 1 630 48 11 **Fax:** +41 1 630 48 15
Email: info@suterlaw.ch

UNITED KINGDOM
Landwell, St Andrew's House, 20 St Andrew Street, **London** EC4A 3TL
Tel: +44 20 7212 1616 **Fax:** +44 20 7212 1570
Email: info@landwell.co.uk

The Landwell network operates through 1,700 business lawyers based in over 40 countries. Landwell firms and correspondent law firms of PricewaterhouseCoopers are listed above.

Correspondent law firms of PricewaterhouseCoopers

L

For other recommended firms see pages 1485-1520

LATHAM & WATKINS

HEAD OFFICE

633 West Fifth Street, Suite 4000,
Los Angeles CA 90071-2007, USA
Tel: +1 213 485 1234 **Fax:** +1 213 891 8763

Email: webmaster@lw.com
Website: www.lw.com

FIRM OVERVIEW

Managing partner: Robert M. Dell

Number of partners worldwide: 341
Number of other lawyers worldwide: 793

AREAS OF PRACTICE:

Corporate 32%
Litigation 32%
Finance and real estate 21%
Environmental 10%
Tax 5%

FIRM OVERVIEW: Founded in 1934 in Los Angeles, Latham & Watkins now has more than 1,100 lawyers in 11 US offices and five overseas – in London, Moscow, Hong Kong, Singapore and Tokyo. The firm is divided into five departments – corporate, environmental, finance & real estate, litigation and tax – with lawyers also working interdepartmentally in practice groups such as insolvency, project finance and transportation.

INTERNATIONAL EXPERIENCE: Latham & Watkins' global strengths are in corporate finance, capital markets, project finance and technology company matters. The firm's international practice has undertaken work involving more than 50 countries focusing on the areas of project finance, corporate finance, technology, telecommunications, privatisations, litigation and arbitration. In the project finance area, Latham & Watkins has handled the development and financing of large infrastructure projects such as electricity plants, oil pipelines, liquefied natural gas plants and telephone systems in the Middle East, Africa, Asia and Latin America. The firm's corporate finance team has been involved in equity and debt financings for companies located in Asia, Europe and Latin America. Latham & Watkins advises clients on all phases of acquisitions, including crafting anti-takeover strategies, responding to acquisition offers, advising proxy contestants, structuring acquisitions, making acquisition offers, arranging public and private financing and cross-border transactions. The firm also provides strategic legal counsel to emerging growth companies – internet, new media, e-commerce, networking, biotechnology and other technology companies – as well as incubators, accelerators, investment banks and venture capital fims that service such companies. Privatisation work has taken Latham & Watkins to countries such as Australia, Armenia, Georgia, Lebanon, Nicaragua, Poland and Russia. In the telecommunications area, the firm recently represented Jupiter Programming Co Ltd in the establishment of a new internet business for the Japanese market with @Home Corporation of the US and Sumitomo Corporation. In international arbitration, a Latham & Watkins team recently obtained awards totalling more than US$700 million on behalf of CalEnergy International from PLN, the state-owned Indonesian utility company.

LANGUAGES: Cantonese, English, French, German, Hebrew, Hindi, Italian, Japanese, Korean, Mandarin, Punjabi, Russian, Spanish

WORLDWIDE OFFICE CONTACTS

HONG KONG
20th Floor, Standard Chartered Bank Building, 4 Des Voeux Road, Central, **Hong Kong**
Tel: + 852 2522 7886 **Fax:** + 852 2522 7006
Email: joseph.bevash@lw.com

JAPAN
Kanematsu Building, 5th Floor, 2-14-1 Kyobashi, Chuo-Ku, **Tokyo** 104-0031
Tel: +81 3 5524 1900 **Fax:** +81 3 5524 1901
Email: david.shapiro@lw.com

RUSSIA
Ulitsa Gasheka 7, Ducat II, Suite 900, **Moscow** 123056
Tel: +7 095 785 1234 **Fax:** +7 095 785 1235
Email: anya.goldin@lw.com

SINGAPORE
80 Raffles Place #14-20, UOB Plaza 2, **Singapore** 048624
Tel: + 65 536 1161 **Fax:** + 65 536 1171
Email: joseph.bevash@lw.com

UNITED KINGDOM
99 Bishopsgate, 11th Floor, **London** EC2M 3XF
Tel: +44 20 7710 1000 **Fax:** +44 20 7374 4460
Email: joe.blum@lw.com

USA
Riverside Centre, 275 Grove Street, Floor 4, Newton, **Boston** MA 02466
Tel: +1 617 663 5700 **Fax:** +1 617 663 5319
Email: ian.blumenstein@lw.com

Sears Tower, 233 South Wacker Drive, Suite 5800, **Chicago** IL 60606-6401
Tel: +1 312 876 7700 **Fax:** +1 312 993 9767
Email: stephen.bowen@lw.com

650 Town Centre Drive, 20th Floor, **Costa Mesa** CA 92626-1925
Tel: +1 714 540 1235 **Fax:** +1 714 755 8290
Email: virginia.grogan@lw.com

633 West Fifth Street, Suite 4000, **Los Angeles** CA 90071-2007
Tel: +1 213 485 1234 **Fax:** +1 213 891 8763
Email: martha.jordan@lw.com

135 Commonwealth Drive, **Menlo Park** CA 94025-1105
Tel: +1 650 328 4600 **Fax:** +1 650 463 2600
Email: peter.kerman@lw.com

885 Third Avenue, Suite 1000, **New York** NY 10022-4802
Tel: +1 212 906 1200 **Fax:** +1 212 751 4864
Email: david.gordon@lw.com

One Newark Center, 16th Floor, **Newark** NJ 07101-3174
Tel: +1 973 639 1234 **Fax:** +1 973 639 7298
Email: james.tyrrell@lw.com

11400 Commerce Park Drive, Suite 200, **Reston** VA 20191-1549
Tel: +1 703 390 0900 **Fax:** +1 703 390 0901
Email: scott.herlihy@lw.com

701 B Street, Suite 2100, **San Diego** CA 92101-8197
Tel: +1 619 236 1234 **Fax:** +1 619 696 7419
Email: bruce.shepherd@lw.com

505 Montgomery Street, Suite 1900, **San Francisco** CA 94111-2562
Tel: +1 415 391 0600 **Fax:** +1 415 395 8095
Email: gregory.lindstrom@lw.com

1001 Pennsylvania Ave, NW, Suite 1300, **Washington** DC 20004-2505
Tel: +1 202 637 2200 **Fax:** +1 202 637 2201
Email: eric.bernthal@lw.com

L

For other recommended firms see pages 1485-1520

LEBOEUF, LAMB, GREENE & MACRAE, LLP

HEAD OFFICE

125 West 55th Street,
New York NY 10019-5389, USA
Tel: +1 212 424 8000 **Fax:** +1 212 424 8500
Website: www.llgm.com

FIRM OVERVIEW

Co-Chairmen Steven H Davis, Peter R O'Flinn
Number of partners worldwide: 226
Number of other lawyers worldwide: 524

AREAS OF PRACTICE:

Banking and leasing .... *%
Bankruptcy and restructuring .... *%
Corporate and finance .... *%
E-commerce/Internet business .... *%
Employee Benefits/ERISA .... *%
Energy and utilities .... *%
Environmental, health and safety .... *%
Information technology .... *%
Insolvency .... *%
Insurance and reinsurance .... *%
Intellectual property .... *%
Litigation, arbitration and mediation .... *%
Project finance .... *%
Real estate .... *%
Tax .... *%
Telecommunications .... *%
Trusts and estates .... *%
* Workload % not disclosed

FIRM OVERVIEW: LeBoeuf, Lamb, Greene & MacRae has more than 700 lawyers practising in 14 US cities and in 10 other countries. Founded in 1929, LeBoeuf has developed particular experience with the energy, utilities and insurance industries. From these historical strengths, the firm has expanded its practices in corporate finance, international, bankruptcy and litigation. With its network of offices throughout the world, LeBoeuf is positioned to assist clients in virtually every major commercial centre.

INTERNATIONAL EXPERIENCE: LeBoeuf's practice is essentially multinational, often drawing upon lawyers based in many locations to work together on local, national and international legal issues. The firm has developed expertise in cross-border insurance transactions, advising on some of the largest such deals effected to date including Aegon NV's $10.8bn acquisition of Transamerica Corporation and the $18.4bn acquisition of BAT's financial services businesses by Zurich Group. LeBoeuf also has advised on some of the largest international combinations of electric and gas utilities, highlighted by its representations of The National Grid Group plc in its US$3.2bn acquisition of New England Electric System and PacifiCorp in its US$7.9bn merger with ScottishPower plc, the first successful acquisition of US utilities by foreign purchasers.
The firm has significant experience in cross-border and offshore corporate transactions, project finance, international trade & customs practice, tax advice, environmental reviews and multijurisdictional litigation and dispute resolution. LeBoeuf also has substantial experience in international bankruptcy and insolvency practice. The firm has been selected by the European Bank for Reconstruction and Development to its legal consultancy panel.
LeBoeuf has a strong international practice in London, where the firm's office is staffed almost entirely by British professionals educated in the UK,

WORLDWIDE OFFICE CONTACTS

BELGIUM
Kunstlaan, Avenue des Arts 19H, B-1000 **Brussels**
Tel: + 32 2 227 0900 **Fax:** + 32 2 227 0909

CHINA
Room B8, 21st Floor Hanwei Plaza, No 7 Guanghau Road, Chaoyang District, **Beijing** 10004
Tel: + 8610 6561 0422 **Fax:** + 8610 6561 0425

FRANCE
130 rue du Faubourg Saint-Honoré, 75008 **Paris**
Tel: + 33 1 5393 7700 **Fax:** + 33 1 4256 0806

KAZAKHSTAN
Prospect Seyfullina 531, 480091 **Almaty**
Tel: + 7 3272 50 7575 **Fax:** + 7 3272 50 7576

KYRGYZ REPUBLIC
Ulitsa Panfilova, 205, **Bishkek**
Tel: + 996 312 22 2994 **Fax:** + 996 312 66 2233

RUSSIA
Nikitsky Pereulok 5, 103009 **Moscow**
Tel: + 7 095 737 5000 **Fax:** + 7 095 737 5050

SAUDI ARABIA
King Faisal Foundation Building, 13th Floor (North Tower), PO Box 2700, **Riyadh** 11461
Tel: + 966 1 464 8534 **Fax:** + 966 1 464 3764

UNITED KINGDOM
No 1 Minster Court, Mincing Lane, **London** EC3R 7AA
Tel: + 44 20 7459 5000 **Fax:** + 44 20 7459 5099

USA
One Commerce Plaza, Suite 2020, 99 Washington Avenue, **Albany** NY 12210-2820
Tel: + 1 518 626 9000 **Fax:** + 1 518 626 9010

260 Franklin Street, **Boston** MA 02110-3173
Tel: + 1 617 439 9500 **Fax:** + 1 617 439 0341

633 Seventeenth Street, Suite 2000, **Denver** CO 80202
Tel: + 1 303 291 2600 **Fax:** + 1 303 297 0422

200 North Third Street, Suite 300, PO Box 12105, **Harrisburg** PA 17108-2105
Tel: + 1 717 232 8199 **Fax:** + 1 717 232 8720

Goodwin Square, 225 Asylum Street, 13th Floor, **Hartford** CT 06103
Tel: + 1 860 293 3500 **Fax:** + 1 860 293 3555

1000 Louisiana, **Houston** TX 77002
Tel: + 1 713 287 2000 **Fax:** + 1 713 287 2100

50 North Laura Street, Suite 2800, **Jacksonville** FL 32202-3650
Tel: + 1 904 354 8000 **Fax:** + 1 904 353 1673

725 South Figueroa Street, Suite 3600, **Los Angeles** CA 90017-5436
Tel: + 1 213 955 7300 **Fax:** + 1 213 955 7399

125 West 55th Street, **New York** NY 10019-5389
Tel: +1 212 424 8000 **Fax:** +1 212 424 8500

One Riverfront Plaza, **Newark** NJ 07102-5490
Tel: + 1 973 643 8000 **Fax:** + 1 973 643 6111

L

For other recommended firms see pages 1485-1520

many of whom are qualified to advise in multiple jurisdictions. The same is true of the firm's presence in Moscow, Paris, Brussels, Riyadh, Johannesburg and Central Asia, where locally qualified and educated professionals predominate. Rather than sending US lawyers abroad to staff its foreign offices, LeBoeuf has instead consistently expanded by attracting local practictioners to its practice.

INTERNATIONAL CLIENTS: ACE Limited, AM Best, Aegis, Alcoa, Inc, Aegon, NV, The Allstate Corporation, Bayer Corporation, Bell Atlantic International, Canada Life Assurance Company, Caspian Pipeline Consortium, Chieftain Petroleum, China Chamber of Commerce, Daihatsu Motor Company, Enron Corporation, Entergy Corporation, European Bank of Reconstruction and Development, Finova, General Electric Capital Corporation, General Motors Corporation, the Government of Ghana, HSB Engineering, Hellenic Petroleum, HydroQuebec, Lehman Brothers, Lloyd's of London, MCI WorldCom, MOL, Morgan Stanley Dean Witter Discover, Nampower, The National Grid Group plc, National Power, National Westminster Bank, Nationwide Mutual, Nestle Corporation, Nomura Securities International, PP&L Global, Petronas, Phoenix, RAO Unified Energy Systems, Saturn Corporation, Sea Launch Company, Sun Life of Canada, Swiss Re Holding Inc, US Filter Corp, United Technologies Corporation, the Volta River Authority, Xerox Financial Services, Zambian Electricity Corporation, Zurich Group.

One Gateway Center, 420 Fort Duquesne Boulevard, Suite 1600, **Pittsburgh** PA 15222-1437
Tel: + 1 412 594 2300 **Fax:** + 1 412 594 5237

1000 Kearns Building, 136 South Main Street, **Salt Lake City** UT 84101
Tel: + 1 801 320 6700 **Fax:** + 1 801 359 8256

One Embarcadero Center, **San Francisco** CA 94111-3619
Tel: + 1 415 951 1100 **Fax:** + 1 415 951 1180

1875 Connecticut Avenue NW, Suite 1200, **Washington DC** 20009-5728
Tel: + 1 202 986 8000 **Fax:** + 1 202 986 8102

UZBEKISTAN
Ulitsa Turab Tula, 1, 700003 **Tashkent**
Tel: + 7 3712 40 6050 **Fax:** + 7 3712 40 6052

WORLDWIDE OFFICES

BELGIUM

Kunstlaan, Avenue des Arts 19H, B-1000 Brussels

Managing partner: Etienne R. Claes
Number of lawyers: 5

Main areas of practice: Anti-trust and competition, insurance, corporate, litigation, European Union advice, intellectual property.
Highlight deals: The firm's Brussels lawyers have taken leading roles in several major international transactions, including providing EU regulatory advice for US Filter Corporation's US$7.8bn merger with Vivendi SA, and advising Dutch insurer Aegon NV in its US$10.8bn acquisition of Transamerica Corporation.
Languages: Dutch, English, French, German and other major business languages.
Office profile: LeBoeuf is one of the few major law firms in Brussels that extensively practices Belgian and European law with English as its main language. The firm has had a presence in Brussels since 1985 and a fully functioning office for more than 12 years. The practice encompasses all aspects of business law that are of concern to major corporate clients. They also serve as advisors to government administrations in Europe and Central Asia.

CHINA

Room B8, 21st Floor Hanwei Plaza, No 7 Guanghau Road, Chaoyang District, Beijing 10004

Managing partner: James R Woods
Number of lawyers: 2

Main areas of practice: Insurance, corporate, international trade.
Languages: Cantonese, English, Mandarin and other major business languages.
Office profile: LeBoeuf received its licence to practice law in China in December 1998. The practice in Beijing focuses on insurance, natural resources, and facilitating new business opportunities in China.

FRANCE

130 rue du Faubourg Saint-Honoré, 75008 Paris

Managing Partners Alain de Foucaud and Rene de Monseignat
Number of lawyers: 23

Main areas of practice: Corporate and litigation.
Highlight deals: The Parisian lawyers recently led the firm's representations of Global Telesystems Inc in its US$462m acquisition of French telecommunications provider Omnicom.
Languages: English, French, German and other major business languages.
Office profile: The Paris office was opened in June 1998 with the arrival of the group formerly practicing in Paris with Donovan and Leisure. Now an integral part of Leboeuf's multinational network of offices, the Parisian lawyers represent French clients in their business dealings locally and internationally. They also assist foreign clients seeking to expand their operations in France and Western Europe.

KAZAKHSTAN

Prospect Seyfullina 531, 480091 Almaty

Managing partner: John I. Huhs
Number of lawyers: 7

Main areas of practice: Energy and utilities, corporate and litigation.
Highlight deals: The Almaty office has advised private and governmental interests in a variety of energy and utilities transactions, including privatisation and project finance matters.
Languages: English, Kazakh, Russian and other major business languages.
Office profile: LeBoeuf is a leader in Central Asian legal practice. Lawyers in the full service Almaty office, the majority locally educated and trained, counsel foreign clients on the spectrum of issues raised by Kazakh law. They have extensive experience representing clients seeking to invest in infrastructure and energy development projects.

KYRGYZ REPUBLIC

Ulitsa Panfilova, 205, Bishkek

Managing Attorneys: John Corrigan and Niyaz R Aldashev
Number of lawyers: 2

Main areas of practice: Energy and utilities, corporate and litigation.
Languages: English, Kyrgyz, Russian and other major business languages.
Office profile: LeBoeuf's office in Bishkek works in co-operation with the larger Almaty office to serve clients in Central Asia.

RUSSIA

Nikitsky Pereulok 5, 103009 Moscow

Managing partner: Brian L Zimbler
Number of lawyers: 21

Main areas of practice: Energy and utilities, corporate, litigation and tax.
Languages: English, Russian and other major business languages.
Office profile: LeBoeuf has one of the largest law offices in Moscow, with 74 lawyers and staff. The practice in Russia offers clients the full range of business services relating to Russia and the CIS. LeBoeuf's Moscow lawyers counsel domestic and foreign corporate clients in complex transactional, regulatory and dispute resolution matters.

SAUDI ARABIA

King Faisal Foundation Building, 13th Floor (North Tower), PO Box 2700, Riyadh 11461
Managing partner: Khalid A Al-Thebity
Number of lawyers: 2

Main Areas of Practice: Energy and utilities, corporate, international trade.
Languages: Arabic, English and other major business languages.
Office Profile: LeBoeuf opened its office in Riyadh, in affiliation with Saud MA Shawwaf Law Office, in January 1999, to serve clients in their business dealings in the Kingdom of Saudi Arabia. The practice in Riyadh focuses on energy and utilities, corporate finance and natural resources matters.

SOUTH AFRICA

11 Alice Lane, 2nd Floor, West Wing, Standard Bank Building, Sandton, Johannesburg, 2196
Managing partner: Jude Kearney
Number of lawyers: 2

UNITED KINGDOM

No 1 Minster Court, Mincing Lane, London EC3R 7AA

Joint Managing Partners Alan M Jones and Garry J Pegg
Number of lawyers: 59

Office profile: LeBoeuf has been based in London ever since 1978. Since then the office has expanded its practice areas and grown to be one of LeBoeuf's largest offices worldwide. The office is a multinational partnership of US lawyers and English solicitors. The London office serves clients with business interests in the UK and throughout Europe and the CIS, the Middle East and Africa as well as the United States. Located in the heart of the City of London, lawyers in the London office represent UK and international clients and advise on US, English and European law.

Main areas of practice: Corporate and finance, including cross-border mergers and acquisitions; general corporate and commercial; major projects and project finance, including shipping, aviation, oil and gas; telecommunications; insurance and reinsurance, including regulatory and litigation; insolvency; banking and leasing; commercial litigation, arbitration and mediation; energy, water and public utilities; intellectual property and information technology.
Highlight deals: The London office has been involved in some very significant international work throughout 2000. Recent deals include: representing the Kingdom of Saudi Arabia in connection with an initiative to open its natural gas industry to private investors; acting for Nationwide Mutual, the firm handled the US$1.6bn acqusition of Gartmore, an international asset fund manager; advising MCI WorldCom on the financing of the US$1.2 bn Southern Cross fibre-optic cable system linking Australia, New Zealand, Fiji and the US; concluding a joint venture and financing on behalf of Providian Financial, the fifth largest bank card issuer in the US; acting for the Government of Ghana and the state electricity generating utility in a number of transactions arising from the Takoradi power project, including negotiating with Shell/Chevron on a sales and transportation contract for a supply of gas through the West African Pipeline Project; acting for Boeing in the structuring and financing of four C17 aircraft for the Ministry of Defence; working on various projects for the European Bank for Reconstruction and Development; and acting for defendant Andrew Hughes in the Elton John case.
Languages: Arabic, English, French, German, Italian, Russian, Spanish and other major business languages.

UZBEKISTAN

Ulitsa Turab Tula, 1, 700003 Tashkent

Number of lawyers: 1

Main areas of practice: Energy and utilities, corporate and litigation.
Languages: English, Russian, Uzbek and other major business languages.
Office profile: LeBoeuf's office in Tashkent works in co-operation with their larger Almaty office to serve clients in Central Arabia.

 For other recommended firms see pages 1485-1520

LEE & KO

HEAD OFFICE

19th Floor, Marine Center Main Building, 118, 2-Ka Namdaemun-Ro,
Chung-Ku, C.P.O. BOX 8735
Seoul, South Korea
Tel: +82 2 772 4000 **Fax:** +82 2 772 4001/2

Email: cen@lawleeko.co.kr
Website: www.lawleeko.com

WORLDWIDE OFFICE CONTACTS

SOUTH KOREA
19th Floor, Marine Center Main Building, 118, 2-Ka Namdaemun-Ro,
Chung-Ku, C.P.O. BOX 8735, **Seoul**
Tel: +82 2 772 4000 **Fax:** +82 2 772 4001/2
Email: cen@lawleeko.co.kr

FIRM OVERVIEW

Managing partner and senior partner: Tae Hee Lee

Number of partners worldwide: 16
Number of other lawyers worldwide: 69

AREAS OF PRACTICE:

Corporate	28%
M&A	20%
Banking and finance	15%
Litigation and arbitration	15%
Intellectual property	10%
Telecommunications	8%
Insurance and reinsurance	4%

FIRM OVERVIEW: Founded in 1977, Lee & Ko is one of Korea's leading law firms. It provides advice on a wide range of issues to multinational and Korean clients. The firm has extensive experience in the establishment and operation of manufacturing industries and service businesses including telecommunications, information and e-commerce, franchising, wholesaling and retailing, advertising, and business consulting.

INTERNATIONAL EXPERIENCE: Lee & Ko has represented a number of international companies, mainly in M&A and foreign investment.

INTERNATIONAL CLIENTS: The firm's client base includes large companies, banks, insurance companies and public or supranational institutions conducting cross-border business.

MAIN INTERNATIONAL AREAS OF PRACTICE:

M&A: The firm's transactions range from small private acquisitions to cross-border takeovers of listed companies.
Corporate: Lee & Ko has handled a number of foreign investments, advising joint venture corporations, foreign owned subsidiaries, and branches or liaison offices of foreign corporations. It is experienced in the preparation, negotiation and counseling of corporate matters relating to foreign investment and technology transfer. Lee & Ko specialises in corporate reorganisation and bankruptcy proceedings and has advised a number of companies on composition or corporate reorganisation. The firm has also represented creditors in a range of transactions.
Banking, finance and securities: Lee & Ko advises on all aspects of banking, finance and securities including secured and syndicated loan transactions and guarantees, structured finance, project finance, leasing and tax-based finance.
Maritime: Lee & Ko's maritime department specialises in all aspects of maritime law. It has represented various ship owners, P&I clubs, underwriters, and cargo claimants based in countries around the world including the UK, US, Japan, and Hong Kong.
Intellectual property: Lee & Ko has an experienced intellectual property department comprising licensed patent attorneys, consultants and support staff. It advises on patents, trademarks, and copyright and specialises in computer software.
Telecommunications, IT and e-commerce: Lee & Ko advises on all telecommunications, IT and e-commerce related issues. The firm is committed to handling the pioneering legal issues in these rapidly developing industries.
Tax: Lee & Ko specialises in tax and tariff matters relating to foreign direct investment, technology licensing, foreign resident technicians, transfer pricing, and importation of goods and services including software.
Trade and trade regulation: Lee & Ko has experience in trade related transactions and import/export regulatory matters.
Environment: Lee & Ko has a broad range of experience in environmental law.
Aviation: The firm has experienced members in all aspects of aviation law. It has been active in some of the most significant aviation litigation cases in Korea.
Employment: Lee & Ko advises both foreign and domestic clients on every aspect of employment law. The firm advises joint venture companies, wholly owned foreign subsidiaries and branches of foreign companies.
Anti-trust and competition: Lee & Ko is one of the few law firms in Seoul that advises foreign and local clients on anti-trust and unfair trade practice issues.
Litigation, arbitration and dispute resolution: The firm's litigation department has experience in a wide range of general commercial litigation matters, both domestic and international.

LANGUAGES: Chinese, English, Japanese, Korean

For other recommended firms see pages 1485-1520

LEGA INTERCONSULT PENKOV, MARKOV & PARTNERS

HEAD OFFICE

22-A Iztok Dstr.,
Sofia 1113, Bulgaria
Tel: + 359 2 732 936 **Fax:** + 359 2 722 452

Email: office@legainterconsult.com
Website: www.legainterconsult.com

FIRM OVERVIEW

Managing partner: Vladimir Penkov

Number of partners worldwide: 4
Number of other lawyers worldwide: 14

AREAS OF PRACTICE:

Commercial and business	15%
Company	15%
Foreign investments	15%
Joint ventures	15%
Privatisation	15%
Banking and finance	5%
Competition	5%
Real estate	4%
Labour and social	3%
Tax	3%
Licensing	2%
Litigation and international arbitration	2%
Family and inheritance	1%

FIRM OVERVIEW: When Lega Interconsult was established in 1990 it was one of the first law firms in Bulgaria. At present it has 18 partners and associated members and five trainees, as well as 10 assistants and other staff, and offices in Sofia, Bourgas, Rousse, Lovetch and Dobrich. The firm has cooperation agreements (including joint offices) with Lansky & Partner in Vienna, and Punge Brenscheidt Staubach in Dortmund. It is the Bulgarian member of Lex Mundi, an associate member of Eurojuris Deutschland and Bulgarian correspondent of Torus International. On certain large projects the firm works with another Bulgarian law firm which allows it to increase the number of active qualified lawyers to 35. This ensures that 15-18 lawyers can be involved in a specific project without disturbing the general course of the firm's work.

INTERNATIONAL EXPERIENCE: One of the firm's main activities is advising foreign clients on investment opportunities and ways to establish a presence in Bulgaria. It advises on taxation, customs procedures, exports and imports, the foreign currency regime, employment and social security, all of which determine the overall investment climate in Bulgaria. The firm advises on drawing up the documents needed and acts to protect clients' interests. It has advised on a number of large investment projects involving well-known companies considering setting up a number of high-capital joint ventures.

INTERNATIONAL CLIENTS: The firm's clients include a number of large commercial and industrial companies, as well as banks and insurance companies, both national and international.

MAIN INTERNATIONAL AREAS OF PRACTICE:

Commercial and business: The firm undertakes work in most aspects of commercial and business law, including company, foreign investments, and joint ventures. It has performed extensive due diligence for a number of large Bulgarian companies involved in transactions among major investors, and in 2000 it advised on the rehabilitation program of Varna shipyard.

Privatisation: The firm has advised on numerous privatisations in the fields of banking, specialised services and the construction, brewing, glass, food, ceramics and plastics and construction industries, among others. In 2000 the firm acted as legal counsel to one of the bidders for the privatisation of Bulgartabac Holding AD, the biggest producer of tobacco products in Bulgaria. It also advised on the privatisation of State Insurance Institute, Bulgaria's biggest insurance company. In recent years the firm has also participated in other large privatisations, such as that of Post Bank (acting for the National Bank of Greece), and that of the Balkans' largest glass production plant, Druzhba Plovdiv (acting on behalf of Bareck Overseas Ltd and ending with a successful acquisition). The firm is a member of two international consortia led by Roland Berger & Partner, Germany, and RES & Co, United Kingdom, which have been assigned ten major privatisation deals under the PATA project of the PHARE SARA programme. The companies subject to privatisation under this project include DZU, Microprocessor Systems, Chavdar, ZMM-Sofia, Vidachim, Yambolen, Kapitan Dyado Nikola and Roulon-Iskar.

Project finance: The firm acted for Domaine Boyar in one of Bulgaria's largest project financings, with financing from the EBRD and ING Barings, as well as in the financing of Celhart AD by the EBRD and IFC, acting for the EBRD. It also advised the Bulgarian government on a project financing for SODI Devnya.

M&A: Work includes acting for the Greek company Titan Cement in the acquisition of one of Bulgaria's largest cement plants, Plevenski Cement AD. In 2000 the firm advised on the merger of Domaine Boyar Group and Vinprom Rousse, one of the biggest mergers in Bulgaria for that year. It also advised Telefonica Intercontinental on its privatisation bid for acquisition of shares in the Bulgarian Telecommunication Company (BTC), as well as TBI on the acquisition of BULSRAD.

Joint ventures: The firm has advised on the establishment of several dozen joint ventures with significant foreign interest, in sectors including manufacturing, agriculture, electronics, telecommunications, chemicals, soft drinks, trade and distribution.

LANGUAGES: Bulgarian, English, French, German, Russian

WORLDWIDE OFFICE CONTACTS

BULGARIA
116 Patriarch Evthimyi Str., 2nd floor, **Bourgas** 8000
Tel: + 359 56 841 173 **Fax:** +359 56 810 971
Email:

14 Nezavisimost Str., Room 508, **Dobrich** 9300
Tel: + 359 58 38443 **Fax:** +359 58 38443
Email:

41 Targovska Str., **Lovetch** 5500
Tel: + 359 68 44509 **Fax:** +359 68 44509
Email:

2 Tcherno more Str., **Rousse**
Tel: + 359 82 274 003 **Fax:** +359 82 278 460
Email:

22-A Iztok Dstr., **Sofia** 1113
Tel: + 359 2 732 936 **Fax:** + 359 2 722 452
Email: office@legainterconsult.com

For other recommended firms see pages 1485-1520

LEJINS, EDZINS, TORGANS & VONSOVICS

HEAD OFFICE

20 Kr. Valdemara,
LV-1010 Riga, Latvia
Tel: +371 782 1525 **Fax:** +371 782 1524

FIRM OVERVIEW

Managing partner: Girts Lejins
Senior partners: Kalvis Torgans, Romualds Vonsovics
Elgars Edzins, Girts Lejins

Number of partners worldwide: 5
Number of other lawyers worldwide: 5

AREAS OF PRACTICE:

Corporate	25%
Banking and finance	20%
Commercial	20%
Litigation	20%
Competition, employment, energy, intellectual property, privatisation, real estate, securities, transport	15%

FIRM OVERVIEW: The firm was established in 1994 and covers a wide range of business law. Firm members came from other law firms, government agencies, banks, audit companies, courts and academic institutions, and they continue to maintain close contacts with these communities. A number of them studied abroad for advanced degrees and undertook placements with foreign law firms, subsequently establishing informal correspondent relationships.

INTERNATIONAL EXPERIENCE: The firm has been involved in a large number of Latvia's major investment and privatisation projects, including the privatisation of the state gas company Latvijas Gaze. It has advised ministries and other state institutions on major projects, acting for the Ministry of the Economy in negotiations for oil exploration in the Baltic Sea. The firm has now been retained by the State Forestry Service to advise on a pulp mill project which is expected to become the largest foreign investment in Latvia to date. In addition, the firm has helped a number of prominent multinational companies establish local subsidiaries and representative offices, and continues to advise them on a day-to-day basis.

INTERNATIONAL CLIENTS: Multinationals include Alcatel Baltics, MasterFoods Latvia (the local subsidiary of Mars Inc), Philip Morris Eastern Europe Region, Procter & Gamble Marketing Latvia. Financial clients include EBRD, DEG, Den Norske Bank, Finnfund, Fuji Bank, Merrill Lynch, Nordic Investment Bank, OPIC, Sumitomo Bank, Swedfund and the World Bank Mission in Latvia.

WORLDWIDE OFFICE CONTACTS

LATVIA
20 Kr. Valdemara, LV-1010 **Riga**
Tel: +371 782 1525 **Fax:** +371 782 1524
Email: letv@latnet.lv

MAIN INTERNATIONAL AREAS OF PRACTICE:

Banking & finance: Over the last five years the firm has advised the foreign banks listed above and others in various financial transactions with Latvian entities, including secured loan transactions and project finance. It has also advised on obtaining banking licences and regulatory compliance. The most recent enrolment was successful counseling to Rigas Comercbanka's restructuring and rehabilitation.

Commercial: The firm drafts a wide range of commercial contracts, including sale-purchase agreements and distributorship agreements. It advises on the various local procedures and regulations governing commerce, and ensures the compliance of standard agreements with the requirements of Latvian laws.

Corporate: Work includes setting up companies, representative offices, branches and so on. The firm advises on all aspects of corporate law, including M&A.

Litigation: The litigation practice is headed by a former justice of the Supreme Court of Latvia, Romualds Vonsovics. Lawyers appear in all court instances and in all types of business dispute, on behalf of some of the biggest taxpayers in Latvia as well as foreign companies.

Real estate: The firm drafts and negotiates sale-purchase, lease and construction agreements, and conducts title clearance and registration. Clients include some of the largest real estate developers in Latvia.

LANGUAGES: English, Latvian, Polish, Russian

For other recommended firms see pages 1485-1520

LENZ & STAEHELIN

HEAD OFFICES

Bleicherweg 58,
CH-8027 Zurich, Switzerland
Tel: +41 1 204 12 12 **Fax:** +41 1 204 12 00

25, Grand' Rue,
1211 Geneva 11, Switzerland
Tel: +41 22 318 70 00 **Fax:** +41 1 318 70 01

Website: www.lenzstaehelin.com

FIRM OVERVIEW

Number of partners worldwide: 32
Number of other lawyers worldwide: 70

AREAS OF PRACTICE

Trade, corporate and contract ....*%
Tax ....*%
Litigation and arbitration ....*%
Banking and capital markets ....*%
M&A ....*%
*Workload % not disclosed

WORLDWIDE OFFICE CONTACTS

SWITZERLAND
35, rue de Romont, 1701 **Fribourg**
Tel: +41 26 347 16 30 **Fax:** +41 26 347 16 31
Email: email@lenzstaehelin.com

25, Grand'Rue, 1211 **Geneva**
Tel: +41 22 318 70 00 **Fax:** +41 22 318 70 01
Email: email@lenzstaehelin.com

2, Place St-François, 1003 **Lausanne**
Tel: +41 21 320 79 72 **Fax:** +41 21 312 97 45
Email: email@lenzstaehelin.com

Bleicherweg 58, 8027 **Zurich**
Tel: +41 1 204 12 12 **Fax:** +41 1 204 12 00
Email: email@lenzstaehelin.com

L

FIRM OVERVIEW: Lenz & Staehelin was formed in 1991 as the result of a merger between two major law firms based in Geneva and Zurich. It is now the largest law firm in Switzerland, with over 100 lawyers in its four offices. The firm offers a comprehensive legal service to clients with international business interests, with a focus on banking and finance, mergers and acquisitions and arbitration/litigation.

INTERNATIONAL EXPERIENCE: Lenz & Staehelin is one of the leading firms in advising clients in international transactions involving Switzerland. The firm is regularly retained by large corporate clients and investment banks in M&A transactions, capital markets transactions, bank financings and finance lease transactions. Traditionally, the firm has advised non-Swiss clients in the establishment of businesses in Switzerland.

INTERNATIONAL CLIENTS: Lenz & Staehelin's client base is diverse and international, and includes multinational industrial companies, banks and financial institutions, investment banks, international organisations and private individuals.

MAIN INTERNATIONAL AREAS OF PRACTICE:

Trade, corporate and contract: Incorporation and administration of companies, corporate structuring, planning for family businesses, advising of start-up companies, winding up of companies, directors' liability, drafting and advising on contracts, e-commerce, agency and distributorship agreements, rental and leasing contracts, labour law, tort law including product liability, purchase and sale of real estate.
Tax: Tax planning for companies and private individuals, including international tax law, tax consulting (ancillary to other main areas of the firm's activities), representation before the authorities and the courts.
Banking and capital markets: Establishment of banks and ongoing advice on banking law, banking documentation, investment fund law, venture capital, issues of shares, bonds and derivatives, financial products, bank supervision.
Stock exchange: Securities listings, initial public offerings, public tender offers, stock exchange reporting and disclosure rules.
Mergers and acquisitions: Corporate takeovers, mergers, joint ventures, takeover of listed companies.
Litigation: Representation before the Swiss courts, attachment, enforcement and bankruptcy proceedings, representation in matters of international legal assistance and financial crime.
Arbitration: Representation before national and international arbitration tribunals, acting as arbitrator.
International: Private international law, EU law.
Industrial property and copyright: Swiss and European patent law, trade mark law and marks of origin, design and models law, copyright law, law of business names, telecommunications and media law, licensing, representation before the courts and the authorities.
Competition: Cartel law, merger control, unfair competition, representation before Swiss and European competition authorities.
Trusts and estates: Formation and administration of trusts and foundations, wills, inheritance contracts and estate planning, executorship, administration of estates.
Administrative: Residency and work permits for foreigners, acquisition of Swiss real estate by foreign companies and private individuals, social welfare and employee welfare law, insurance law, health and food law, environmental law, construction law.

LANGUAGES: English, French, German, Italian, Spanish

For other recommended firms see pages 1485-1520

HEAD OFFICES

Sundagarðar 2, PO Box 8975, Reykjavik Iceland
Tel: +354 590 2600 **Fax:** +354 590 2606

Email: lex@lex.is
Website: www.lex.is

WORLDWIDE OFFICE CONTACTS

ICELAND
Sundagarðar 2, PO Box 8975, **Reykjavik**
Tel: +354 590 2600 **Fax:** +354 590 2606
Email: lex@lex.is

FIRM OVERVIEW

Board of directors: Jónas A. Aðalsteinsson, Helgi V. Jónsson, Helgi Jóhannesson

Senior partner: Jónas A. Aðalsteinsson

Number of partners worldwide: 9
Number of other lawyers worldwide: 6

AREAS OF PRACTICE:

Banking and finance	*%
Corporate and commercial	*%
Energy	*%
IT and e-commerce	*%
Litigation	*%
M&A	*%
Real estate	*%
Shipping and transport	*%
Tax	*%

* Workload % not disclosed

FIRM OVERVIEW: The firm was established following the recent merger with KPMG Attorneys at law. The merger created one of Iceland's largest law firms, comprising nine partners and six other lawyers. Lex Law Office is a leading Icelandic firm, specialising in corporate and commercial law, banking and finance, real estate, tax law, and M&A.

INTERNATIONAL EXPERIENCE: The firm has acted on behalf of a number of international corporations, banks and organisations. Recent deals which the firm has been involved include advising Bank Paribas as Icelandic legal advisor in a US$170 million re-finance and additional finance of an expansion of an aluminum plant in Iceland; advising an Icelandic investment bank in a US$73 million finance of a Shopping Mall in the greater Reykjavik; advising in the merger of two of the biggest commercial real estate companies in Iceland.

INTERNATIONAL CLIENTS: The firm represents a diverse group of clients on a broad range of legal issues. Its client base includes major Icelandic and international banks, financial institutions, merchants and ship owners, along with municipalities, government organisations, insurance companies and private individuals.

MAIN INTERNATIONAL AREAS OF PRACTICE:
Corporate and commercial: The firm advises on the formation, conversion, merger, demerger, and winding up of a range of companies. The firm also advises on securities law, stock exchange law and other aspect of company law.
Banking and finance: The firm advises banks, financial institutions and borrowers on all aspects of banking and finance, including loans, securitisation and project finance.
Shipping and transport: The firm acts for one of the biggest shipping and transport companies in Iceland. The firm also acts for P&I clubs and individual ship owners.
M&A. The firm advises on corporate takeovers, mergers and joint ventures.
Commercial property and real estate: work undertaken includes real estate purchase and sale, leasing and financing, planning and public law issues, environmental law and expropriation law.
IT and e-commerce: The firm advises on various aspects of IT related law and on a variety of intellectual property issues.

LANGUAGE: Danish, English, German, Icelandic

LIEDEKERKE WOLTERS WAELBROECK KIRKPATRICK & CERFONTAINE SC

HEAD OFFICE

Boulevard de l'Empereur 3, B-1000
Brussels, Belgium
Tel: +32 2 551 15 15 **Fax:** +32 2 551 14 14

Email: info@liedekerke-law.be
Website: www.liedekerke-law.be

FIRM OVERVIEW

Managing partner: Marc van der Haegen
Senior partner: Jacques de Liedekerke
Number of partners worldwide: 33
Number of other lawyers worldwide: 85

AREAS OF PRACTICE:

Corporate and M&A	33%
European law	20%
Banking and finance	15%
Litigation and arbitration	12%
Intellectual property and telecommunications	8%
Labour law	6%
Real estate	6%

L

FIRM OVERVIEW: Founded in 1965, the firm advises and represents domestic, foreign and multi-national companies in the financial, property, industrial and service sectors, public authorities and international organisations, charities and private clients. Its European Union law practice is integrated within the firm of Liederkerke Siméon Wessing Houthoff, which it has set up in conjunction with the law firms of Siméon & Associés (France), Wessing & Berenberg-Gossler (Germany) and Houthoff Buruma (the Netherlands).

INTERNATIONAL EXPERIENCE: The firm advises on a wide range of areas in business law including: the various branches of civil and commercial law, tax and accountancy law, financial law, social security and labour law, public and administrative law, white-collar criminal law. Since its foundation, the firm has enjoyed an important international client base which today represents more than 50% of its turnover. The firm has also advised in numerous major M&A and financial transactions in Belgium. Since its foundation, the firm has been actively involved in the various areas of European Union law. In 1996, it formed a dedicated EU law practice called Liederkerke Siméon Wessing Houthoff. This unit comprises more than 30 attorneys specialising in European Union law, international commercial law and the application of the free movement principles within the European Union.
In association with Siméon & Associés (France), Wessing & Berenberg-Gossler (Germany) and Houthoff Buruma (the Netherlands), the firm has set up the "Conference of European Lawyers", which combines the resources of the various firms within the areas other than European law. The "Conference" offers clients a cross-border service for transactions such as corporate reorganisations and mergers and acquisitions. It puts at its clients' disposal more than 400 attorneys, offering a whole range of multi-juridictional and multi-sectorial skills. The firm is also the Belgian member of the US-European Network, a group of non-exclusive correspondent law firms formed of North American law firms situated in major regional centres in the United States and Canada, together with ten European firms.

INTERNATIONAL CLIENTS: A major part of the practice is of a cross-border nature and the firm has long been developing relations with top-grade world corporations and foreign law firms.

WORLDWIDE OFFICE CONTACTS

BELGIUM
Meir 24, B-2000 **Antwerp**
Tel: +32 3 213 40 40 **Fax:** +32 3 213 40 45
Email: meir@liedekerke-law.be

MAIN INTERNATIONAL AREAS OF PRACTICE:

Corporate: Creation of undertakings, operation of companies, transfer of shares and assets, co-operation between undertakings.
Mergers & acquisitions: Choice of the most appropriate form of reorganisation from commercial, tax, labour and social security points of view; negotiating and drafting documents; domestic and European Union merger control units.
Banking and finance: Credit transactions; guarantees and securities; issues of bonds; securitisation; derivative financial products; stock-market transactions; national and international systems for clearing securities; domestic and cross-border asset funding; accounting and tax aspects of financial transactions. Regulation of banking activities and other financial services; regulation of investment firms; regulation of mutual funds.
EU and international economic regulation: European Union competition rules; merger control; state aids; public procurement; regulations relating to the internal market and the basic freedoms of movement; regulation of international trade.
Intellectual and industrial property rights: Product and service trade marks, patents, know-how, designs and models, copyright, media and the internet hardware and software contracts, regulation of databases.
Taxation: Advice of all tax matters and appeals before the tax authorities and the courts, including: corporate taxation and personal taxation; tax aspects of commercial and financial transactions; inheritance tax planning.
Employment relations: Negotiating and drafting of employment contracts; deferred compensation; termination of employment relations; individual dismissals, collective dismissals, early retirement, restructuring, closure; secondments; workforce elections, collective negotiations, strikes, transfers of undertakings.
Public sector: Co-operation between public authorities and private companies; privatisations; contracts with government bodies; out-sourcing of public services; administrative appeals; staff regulations.
White-collar criminal law: Advice of and defending breaches of the business, financial, employment, social security, environmental and tax laws.
Telecommunications sector: Relations with the Belgian Postal and Telecommunications Institute; service operating permits; interconnection contracts; setting up of joint ventures for obtaining and operating a licence or establishing a network.
Distribution of products and services: Distribution, agency and franchise agreements; exclusive supply contracts; parallel imports; compliance with European Union law.
Transport: Carriage contracts, regulations of transport activities; carriers' liability; purchase, leasing and financing of aircraft and other means of transport.
Real estate: Purchases and transfers of property; town and country planning rules and building permits; environment; compulsory purchases; contracts for architects and property construction and development; public procurement; financial leases of property; property-related bonds.
Regulation of economic activity: Rules of access to business sectors; operating and envirinmental permits; trade practices; price regulation; subsidies.

LANGUAGES: French, Dutch, English, German

For other recommended firms see pages 1485-1520

ADVOKATFIRMAN LINDAHL

HEAD OFFICE

Strandvagen 5A, PO Box 14240,
SE-104 40 Stockholm, Sweden
Tel: +46 8 670 58 00 **Fax:** +46 8 667 73 80

Email: reception.stockholm@lindahl.se
Website: www.lindahl.se

FIRM OVERVIEW

Managing partner: Rolf G Sjoberg

Number of partners worldwide: 45
Number of other lawyers worldwide: 51

AREAS OF PRACTICE:

International business law .... *%
Swedish business law .... *%
* Workload % not disclosed

FIRM OVERVIEW: Advokatfirman Lindahl, founded in 1918, is the result of a merger of law firms specialising in Swedish and international business law. The firm employs approximately 95 lawyers and has offices located in the main commercial centres of Sweden. The firm has close relationships with other law firms world-wide and supplies legal advice to Swedish and international clients in all areas of business law.

INTERNATIONAL EXPERIENCE: Lindahl advises on international transactions in all fields of business law. Examples of recent work include project financing, foreign acquisitions of Swedish companies, international loan agreements, competition law matters in Sweden and before the EU institutions, general legal advice on doing business in Sweden in various business areas, tax law and labour law.

INTERNATIONAL CLIENTS: Lindahl's clients include Swedish and international listed companies, small and medium-sized companies, family and other small businesses. In addition, the firm advises banks and other financial institutions, public authorities and private individuals. An increasing part of the practice consists of advising other advisers, such as foreign law firms, accounting firms, investment banks and management consultancies.

MAIN INTERNATIONAL AREAS OF PRACTICE:

Arbitration and litigation: The firm's lawyers act as arbitrators or counsel in arbitral proceedings and appear before public or administrative courts.
Banking and finance: The firm advises banks, other financial institutions and borrowers on all aspects of banking and finance, including loans, project financing and capital markets.
Corporate: The firm provides advice on all aspects of company law, such as establishment and structuring of companies, stock exchange matters, joint-ventures, compulsory purchase of minority shares and other shareholder related issues.
Contract and property: The firm provides legal advice on contract and property issues in the public and private sector, such as BOT (Build, Operate and Transfer) and DBFO (Design, Build, Finance and Operate) projects. The firm also assists in individual property transfers as well as sales of entire stocks of property, and advises on landlord and tenant issues.
Competition and EU: The firm provides advice on competition law aspects of all sorts of business transactions, and acts before relevant authorities and courts. The firm also advises on EU law matters, such as public procurement and free movement of goods, among others.

WORLDWIDE OFFICE CONTACTS

SWEDEN

Östra Hamngatan 36, PO Box 11911, SE-40439 **Gothenburg**
Tel: + 46 31 80 34 30 **Fax:** + 46 31 15 82 85
Email: reception.goteborg@lindahl.se

Stororget 2, PO Box 1214, SE-25112 **Helsingborg**
Tel: + 46 42 17 53 00 **Fax:** + 46 42 17 53 01
Email: reception.helsingborg@lindahl.se

Skomakaregatan 4, SE 211 34 **Malmo**
Tel: +46 40 664 66 50 **Fax:** +46 40 664 66 55
Email: reception.malmo@lindahl.se

Vasastrand 11-13, Box 143, SE-70142 **Örebro**
Tel: +46 19 10 48 00 **Fax:** +46 19 10 44 45
Email: reception.orebro@lindahl.se

Strandvagen 5A, PO Box 14240, SE-104 40 **Stockholm**
Tel: +46 8 670 58 00 **Fax:** +46 8 667 73 80
Email: reception.stockholm@lindahl.se

Kungsängsgatan 17-19, PO Box 1203, SE-75142 **Uppsala**
Tel: + 46 18 16 18 50 **Fax:** + 46 18 14 46 79
Email: reception.uppsala@lindahl.se

Franchising: The firm works with several of Sweden's major franchise chains.
IT and telecommunications: Within the IT field, the firm has been involved in the drafting of all the standard form agreements issued by the Swedish IT companies' trade association, and the firm assists IT suppliers in various kinds of projects and business agreements. In the field of telecommunications, the firm is experienced in providing advice on regulatory issues.
Insolvency, bankruptcy and resturcturing: The firm's lawyers act as receivers in bankruptcy or company restructurings, appointed by the courts.
Insurance: The firm advises on insurance law and all aspects of establishing and operating an insurance company.
Intellectual property: The firm provides legal assistance on patents, trade marks, copyright and design rights including registration and maintenance of such rights.
Maritime and transport: The firm acts for shipping companies, freight and charter firms, cargo owners and insurance companies.
Media: The firm's clients include commercial radio, as well as satellite, terrestrial and cable-TV companies. The firm also has experience of the media field, such as publishing and production agreements.
M&A: The firm has an extensive practice within the field of M&A, including sale, purchase and financing of companies and businesses, public offerings, take-overs, management buy-outs, venture capital projects and the specific issues related to transactions involving listed corporations.
Sports: Lindahl has a long tradition of involvement at various levels in the sporting community and the firm assists large and small sports clubs, associations and individual athletes.
Tax: The firm regularly assists corporations and their owners in all taxation matters arising in connection with commercial operations, as well as all kind of income capital taxation issues.
Environmental: The firm has a strong practice in environmental law, and is presently engaged in several larger ongoing infrastructure projects.

LANGUAGES: English, French, German Swedish

LINDAHL

For other recommended firms see pages 1485-1520

LINKLATERS

A MEMBER FIRM OF LINKLATERS & ALLIANCE

HEAD OFFICE

One Silk Street,
London EC2Y 8HQ, United Kingdom
Tel: +44 20 7456 2000 **Fax:** +44 20 7456 2222
Website: www.linklaters-alliance.com

WORLDWIDE OFFICE CONTACTS

Linklaters & Alliance has offices in Alicante, Amsterdam, Antwerp, Bangkok, Berlin, Bratislava, Brussels, Bucharest, Budapest, Cologne, Frankfurt am Main, Gothenburg, The Hague, Hong Kong, Luxembourg, Madrid, Malmö, Milan, Moscow, Munich, New York, Padua, Paris, Prague, Rome, Rotterdam, São Paolo, Shanghai, Singapore, Stockholm, Tokyo, Warsaw, Washington, DC.

FIRM OVERVIEW

Senior partner: Charles Allen-Jones
Managing partner: Tony Angel
Chief executive, Linklaters & Alliance: Terence Kyle
Number of partners worldwide (Linklaters & Alliance): 586
Number of other lawyers worldwide (Linklaters & Alliance): 2,232

FIRM OVERVIEW: Linklaters is a member firm of Linklaters & Alliance, which brings together five of Europe's premier law firms including De Bandt, van Hecke, Lagae & Loesch (Belgium and Luxembourg), De Brauw Blackstone Westbroek (Netherlands), Gianni, Origoni & Partners (Italy), Lagerlöf & Leman (Sweden) and Linklaters (which practises as Linklaters Oppenhoff & Rädler in Germany). It is one of the leading global legal practices with lawyers and other professionals operating in combined teams from 34 offices in major financial and business centres worldwide.

L

In January 2001, Linklaters and Oppenhoff & Rädler merged and now practise under the name Linklaters Oppenhoff & Rädler in Germany and Linklaters elsewhere. This represents a significant step towards achieving the aim of providing clients with a single source of premium legal advice worldwide.

INTERNATIONAL EXPERIENCE: Linklaters & Alliance was formed in response to the increasing needs of clients for access to first class, multi-jurisdictional legal advice as a result of globalisation and the growth in cross-border M&A and capital raising. Clients now benefit from access to combined technical excellence, breadth and depth of expertise and a strong tradition of providing a high quality service which is delivered consistently throughout the world.

INTERNATIONAL CLIENTS: Linklaters' clients are major corporations, banks, financial institutions and governments worldwide.

MAIN INTERNATIONAL AREAS OF PRACTICE:

Asset finance: Experience of all principal financing techniques used in the global asset finance industry, advising both on the financing of specific assets and on the acquisition, disposal and financing of asset portfolios. Contact, Ron Gibbs.
Banking: Work handled comprises bank lending, telecom acquisition, trade, project and property finance, PFI and tax structured finance. Contact, John Tucker.
Capital markets: Covers international capital markets and securities issues, debt and equity, structured and derivative products, project bonds and securitisations. Contact, Michael Canby.
Construction and engineering: Expertise covers complex domestic construction and engineering projects; major international projects; PFI/PPP work; construction finance; insolvencies; insurance contracts; and claims analysis and negotiation. Contact, Marshall Levine.
Corporate and M&A: Advice is given on finance and commercial transactions of all types, including share offerings, M&A, company restructurings and privatisations. Contact, David Cheyne.
Corporate tax: The firm's tax lawyers handle all types of corporate tax advice including large international transactions, litigation and international tax planning. Contact, Guy Brannan.
Employment, pensions and incentives: A comprehensive service is provided to corporate and individual clients, covering disputes, remuneration, benefits and pensions. Contact, Raymond Jeffers.
Environment: Identifies, quantifies, and allocates environmental risks and liabilities; prepares, litigates and defends cases on behalf of clients; advises on risk assessment and crisis management; assists clients on a variety of regulatory issues including obtaining and transfering environmental permits; and on all aspects of development and planning law, policy and practice. Contact, Ray Jackson.
EU and competition law: The department handles EU and competition/antitrust issues, including merger control, dominance and dealings with national, EU regulatory and WTO authorities. Contact, Bill Allan.
Financial regulation: The firm advises investment and commercial banks, securities houses and their affiliates providing a 'sunrise to sunset' service. Contact, Paul Nelson.
Intellectual property: The firm gives advice on the exploitation and protection of patents, trade marks and other intellectual property rights. Contact, Jeremy Brown.
Investment management: Work includes structuring and organising offshore open- and closed-ended investment companies, unit trusts, UCITS, limited partnerships, fonds communs de placement and other vehicles. Contact, Tim Shipton.
IT and communications: Commercial and regulatory advice is given to clients in e-commerce, telecoms and other forms of media. Contact, Ian Karet.
Litigation and arbitration: Handles disputes through the traditional media of litigation and arbitration, and through increasingly popular alternative dispute resolution (mediation, mini trials and adjudication). Contact, Christopher Style.
Projects: Advises on power; infrastructure; oil and gas; petrochemical; telecommunications; water; and PFI. Contact, Alan Black.
Real estate: The real estate department advises on traditional real estate matters; investment and funds; retail and leisure schemes; headquarters projects; construction and engineering matters; real estate, tax and financing; planning and environmental issues; rent review and real estate-related litigation. Contact, Simon Clark.
Restructuring and insolvency: The department handles corporate recovery and workouts, including cross-border restructuring and insolvency. Contact, Robert Elliott.
Trusts: Trusts and estate planning are handled, both domestic and offshore. Contact, Nigel Reid.

LANGUAGES: Work is handled in all commercial and local languages in the countries where Linklaters & Alliance operates.

For other recommended firms see pages 1485-1520

LINKLATERS OPPENHOFF & RÄDLER

A MEMBER FIRM OF LINKLATERS & ALLIANCE

HEAD OFFICE

Mainzer Landstrasse, 16,
D-60325 Frankfurt am Main, Germany
Tel: + 49 69 71 00 30 **Fax:** + 49 69 71 00 33 33

Website: www.linklaters-alliance.com

FIRM OVERVIEW

Senior partner: Michael Oppenhoff (from 1 May 2001 Rudolf Cölle)
Managing partner: Markus Hartung

Number of partners worldwide (Linklaters & Alliance): 586
Number of other lawyers worldwide (Linklaters & Alliance): 2,232

FIRM OVERVIEW: Linklaters practises as Linklaters Oppenhoff & Rädler in Germany and is one of the country's leading law firms. Its main activities are in the areas of commercial and tax law with a strong international focus. The firm is a member of Linklaters & Alliance, which brings together five of Europe's premier law firms including De Bandt, van Hecke, Lagae & Loesch (Belgium and Luxembourg), De Brauw Blackstone Westbroek (Netherlands), Gianni, Origoni & Partners (Italy), Lagerlöf & Leman (Sweden) and Linklaters. Linklaters & Alliance is one of the leading global legal practices with more than 2,500 lawyers and other professionals operating in combined teams from 34 offices in major financial and business centres worldwide. This enables Linklaters Oppenhoff & Rädler to provide clients with an enhanced breadth and depth of service on a global basis, with integrated work on multi-jurisdictional transactions.

INTERNATIONAL CLIENTS: Global operating corporates; financial institutions such as investment banks, banks, insurance and reinsurance companies; and medium sized companies. Some of the more significant clients include: Alcatel, Vodafone, Babcock, Pirelli, AXA, Commerzbank, Hypo Vereinsbank, Ford, Kreditanstalt fuer Wiederaufbau (KfW), e-plus, EDS, GE Capital, Metro AG.

MAIN INTERNATIONAL AREAS OF PRACTICE: Linklaters Oppenhoff & Rädler is active in practically all fields of business law with an emphasis on: asset finance; banking; capital markets; corporate and M&A; corporate tax; employment; environment; EU and competition; financial regulation; intellectual property; IT and communications; litigation and arbitration; projects; real estate and construction. Notarial services are available in Berlin and Frankfurt.

LANGUAGES: German, English, French, Japanese, Polish, Portuguese, Spanish, Swedish

WORLDWIDE OFFICE CONTACTS

Linklaters & Alliance has offices in Alicante, Amsterdam, Antwerp, Bangkok, Berlin, Bratislava, Brussels, Bucharest, Budapest, Cologne, Gothenburg, The Hague, Hong Kong, London, Luxembourg, Madrid, Malmö, Milan, Moscow, Munich, New York, Padua, Paris, Prague, Rome, Rotterdam, São Paolo, Shanghai, Singapore, Stockholm, Tokyo, Warsaw, Washington, DC.

LINKLATERS
& ALLIANCE

L

For other recommended firms see pages 1485-1520

LITTLE & CO

HEAD OFFICE

Central Bank Building, Mahatma Gandhi Road,
Mumbai 400 023, India
Tel: +91 22 265 2739 **Fax:** +91 22 265 9918

Email: littleco@bom3.vsnl.net.in

WORLDWIDE OFFICE CONTACTS

INDIA

Central Bank Building, Mahatma Gandhi Road, **Mumbai** 400 023
Tel: +91 22 265 2739 **Fax:** +91 22 265 9918
Email: littleco@bom3.vsnl.net.in

FIRM OVERVIEW

Managing partner: Ravindra Kulkarni

Number of partners worldwide: 18

AREAS OF PRACTICE:

Litigation 40%
Corporate finance 20%
Banking and finance 20%
Property 15%
Shipping 5%

FIRM OVERVIEW: Established over 140 years ago and based in Mumbai, Little & Co is a firm of advocates and solicitors with an extensive pan-India and international civil practice. The firm has advised the East India Company, many leading Indian business groups, the governments of India and successively the Bombay Presidency, Bombay State and the State of Maharashtra and is considerably involved in the privatisation of the Indian infrastructure. It has over 50 lawyers (including 18 partners), supported by a paralegal staff.

INTERNATIONAL EXPERIENCE: The firm has been involved in several trans-border transactions involving foreign investment in India both in equity as well as debt financing. Equity investment typically is by way of foreign direct investment in the joint venture projects of multi-national corporations such as Ford Motor Company, GE, Enron, Total, who have joint ventures or subsidiaries in India. The firm represents both multi-national corporations as well as Indian companies. The firm also has considerable experience syndicating financing of infrastructure projects especially in the power and telecom sector, where large international lenders lend to Indian projects on a non-recourse or limited recourse basis.
The firm has also been advising Indian corporates who have been tapping international capital markets to raise both equity and debt capital by offering securities which are listed on international stock exchanges.

INTERNATIONAL CLIENTS: The firm has a large international clientele, consisting chiefly of US, UK, European and Japanese corporations and foreign banks.

MAIN AREAS OF PRACTICE:
Banking and finance: Work includes project finance, capital markets, mutual funds. and securitization.
Corporate and commercial: The work includes joint ventures and technology transfers including intellectual property rights.
Insurance: The work includes advising large multi-national insurance companies on the opening up of the insurance sector and on their tie-up with local Indian partners for forming joint ventures in anticipation of the privatisation of the insurance sector.
Energy/Telecommunications: The firm advises several private sponsors of energy and telecommunication projects in India as well as the lenders.
Shipping: The firm is substantially involved in admiralty and maritime law related work both advisory and in litigation.
Intellectual property: The firm has an established practice in all aspects of intellectual property law including trademarks, patents, copyrights, industrial designs and e-commerce.
Property: The firm has since its constitution in the year 1854 been in the conventional practice of property law which involves documentation of property transfers including sales, mortgages, hypothecations, leases and all other forms of transfer recognised under the Transfer of Property Act 1882.
Litigation & arbitration: The firm represents clients before international and domestic tribunals.

LANGUAGES: English, French, Gujarati, Hindi, Marathi, Portuguese

LITTLE & CO
Advocates, Solicitors & Notaries

For other recommended firms see pages 1485-1520

LK SHIELDS, SOLICITORS

HEAD OFFICE

39/40 Upper Mount Street,
Dublin 2 Ireland
Tel: +353 1 661 0866 **Fax:** +353 1 661 0883
Email: email@lkshields.ie
Website: www.lkshields.ie

FIRM OVERVIEW

Managing partner: Laurence K. Shields
Number of partners worldwide: 12
Number of other lawyers worldwide: 21

AREAS OF PRACTICE:

Area	%
Corporate and commercial	21%
Commercial litigation	20%
Corporate finance	12%
Commercial property	9%
Banking and finance	8%
Intellectual property	6%
IT and e-commerce	6%
Employment	5%
EU and competition	5%
Construction	2%
Energy and natural resources	3%
Pensions	2%
Public procurement	1%

FIRM OVERVIEW: L.K.Shields was established in 1988 by three of the current partners and has grown rapidly to become one of the leading commercial practices in Ireland. It focuses on all aspects of business and financial law to include mergers and acquisitions, corporate finance, private placements and public offerings, inward investment, commercial litigation, banking and finance, intellectual property, commercial property and pensions. L.K.Shields has developed an international practice and enjoys the benefits of close co-operation with leading law firms in relevant jurisdictions.

INTERNATIONAL EXPERIENCE: The firm's M&A team frequently advises on multi-jurisdictional acquisitions and disposals. It has considerable experience of managing and co-ordinating overseas lawyers supporting such transactions and in advising on overseas investments in Ireland. The firm's banking and financial services department advises financial institutions and financial services companies on a wide variety of international financial and commercial actives and regularly handles cross-border transactions and work relating to activities carried out in Dublin's International Financial Services Centre. The firm's intellectual property team is frequently involved in the coordination of international protection and filing strategies.

INTERNATIONAL CLIENTS: The firm's client base comprises a range of domestic and international clients including significant corporate organisations, banking and financial institutions, and other businesses in almost every industry sector.

MAIN INTERNATIONAL AREAS OF PRACTICE:

Banking and finance: The firm specialises in domestic banking and international and domestic financial services. Work handled includes lending and debt transactions, syndicated credit facilities, project finance transactions, leveraged buyouts, and inter-creditor agreements. L.K.Shields also advises foreign companies and third party managers on mutual funds, hedge funds, treasury issues, asset financing and leasing, securities trading, structured finance and derivatives transactions. It acts for some of the largest international companies in the IFSC, providing advice on the establishment, authorisation and listing of securities in all types of mutual funds vehicles. The firm has been heavily involved with Internet distribution or 'fund supermarket' products and represented the first fund supermarket to be authorised by the Central Bank of Ireland.

Commercial litigation and dispute resolution: L.K.Shields regularly represent clients before the Superior Courts. The firm maintains close contacts with leading law firms in the European Union, the US and other jurisdictions that enables it to take urgent and effective action on behalf of clients in the international arena. Two of the firm's partners are fellows of the Chartered Institute of Arbitrators (Irish branch).

Commercial property: The firm has acted in a number of high value property deals in Ireland including the recent disposal of landmark buildings in Dublin. The firm handles property related work for semi-state bodies, property finance work for major financial institutions, the property portfolio for a major international discount store, and property work for large developers .

Competition: The firm advises on the competition implications of all types of commercial transactions and agreements and has handled dealings with the Competition Authority and the European Commission.

Corporate and commercial: The firm's corporate and commercial department is the largest department in the firm and advises a wide variety of Irish and international clients on all aspects of company and commercial law. It advises on the structuring and implementation of all forms of corporate transactions including agency and distribution, building society law, company law, food law, telecommunications, inward investment, life and non-life insurance regulation, and the impact of e-commerce.

M&A: The firm has acted in the acquisition and disposal of a number of high profile companies.

Corporate finance: L.K Shields advises Irish and foreign companies on public offerings and private placing of securities, on compliance issues under the Listing Rules of the Irish Stock Exchange and the rules of the Irish Take-Over Panel.

Employment: The firm advises on employer-employee relationships and on the employment law aspects of M&A and inward investments. The firm advises Irish companies on the implications of international share plans that offer shares to employees. It also advises on how to avoid tax and regulatory pitfalls. The firm also sets up local and international plans which can encompass several legal jurisdictions.

Energy and natural resources: The firm has advised a wide variety of Irish and international clients on regulatory compliance, joint venture agreements, project finance and public company compliance issues for resource companies.

IT and e-commerce: The firm handles all aspects of information technology law including electronic commerce, intellectual property and the Internet, database and software protection, digital signatures, data protection and technology contracts.

Intellectual property: The firm has an expanding intellectual property practice. It handles all aspects of intellectual property and the prosecution of trademarks and patents. The firm advises on franchise and distribution arrangements and specialises in software. The firm also handles contentious intellectual property matters and domain name disputes.

LANGUAGES: English, French, German, Italian

WORLDWIDE OFFICE CONTACTS

IRELAND
39/40 Upper Mount Street, **Dublin** 2
Tel: +353 1 661 0866 **Fax:** +353 1 661 0883
Email: email@lkshields.ie

LLINKS LAW OFFICE

HEAD OFFICE

Suites 2205 - 2206, South Tower, Shanghai Stock Exchange Building,
528 Pudong Road South, Shanghai 200120, China
Tel: +86 21 6881 8100 **Fax:** +86 21 6881 6880

Email: master@llinkslaw.com
Website: www.llinkslaw.com

WORLDWIDE OFFICE CONTACTS

CHINA
Suites 2205 - 2206, South Tower, Shanghai Stock Exchange Building,
528 Pudong Road South, **Shanghai** 200120
Tel: +86 21 6881 8100 **Fax:** +86 21 6881 6880
Email: master@llinkslaw.com

FIRM OVERVIEW

Contact partners: David Liu, Charles Qin, Christophe Han, David Yu, Alvin Cai

Number of partners worldwide: 5
Number of other lawyers worldwide: 10

AREAS OF PRACTICE:

Banking and finance	*%
Corporate and commercial	*%
Litigation and arbitration	*%
M&A	*%
Project finance	*%
Securities	*%

* Workload % not disclosed

L

FIRM OVERVIEW: Llinks Law Office is one of the fastest growing PRC law firms based in Shanghai and practising PRC law all over China. Llinks is a full-service firm. The partners, with an international education and diverse practice background, provide local and international clients with a combination of legal, linguistic and cultural skills.
Established in 1998, the firm provides legal services for international business with particular strength in banking and finance, project finance, securities, M&A, direct investment and corporate, commercial property, commercial litigation and arbitration. The firm's core areas are banking, project finance and corporate finance including mergers, acquisitions, and restructurings.
It prides itself on teamwork and its commitment to quality service and efficiency. The firm seeks solutions for clients whilst avoiding unnecessary legal exposure. Llinks keep close contacts with government agencies enabling them to keep abreast of the implementation of, or changes to, regulatory requirements. Some of Llinks' lawyers worked for government agencies before practising law and others act as legal counsel for government agencies.
Lawyers at Llinks remain actively involved in a significant number of Chinese infrastructure financings and restructurings, such as the first BOT financing project in Shanghai, the offering of the first B share in China, the first RMB syndicated loan by international banks and domestic banks, major mergers and some foreign invested enterprises.

INTERNATIONAL EXPERIENCE: The firm is often involved in cross-border transactions. It has established close relationships with top law firms in international financial centres and major cities including New York, London, Paris, Tokyo, Hong Kong and Singapore. Using this international co-operation network, the firm provides clients with extremely reliable legal services.

INTERNATIONAL CLIENTS: Llinks has many international clients. It has successfully represented a large number of international companies and financial institutions as well as many Chinese companies.

MAIN INTERNATIONAL AREAS OF PRACTICE: Work undertaken includes banking and finance, project finance, securities, M&A, corporate and commercial, and litigation and arbitration.

LANGUAGES: English, French, Mandarin, Shanghainese

 For other recommended firms see pages 1485-1520

LOPEZ RODEZNO & ASOCIADOS

HEAD OFFICE

Edificio Palmira 5°. Piso, Avenida República de Chile No.1701, Tegucigalpa MDC
Honduras
Tel: +50 4 232 8114 **Fax:** +50 4 232 4116

Email: rlopez@david.intertel.hn
Website: www.lopezrodezno.com

WORLDWIDE OFFICE CONTACTS

HONDURAS
Edificio Palmira 5°. Piso, Avenida República de Chile No.1701,
Tegucigalpa MDC
Tel: +50 4 232 8114 **Fax:** +50 4 232 4116
Email: rlopez@david.intertel.hn

FIRM OVERVIEW

Managing partner: Jorge López Loewenberg
Senior partner: René López Rodezno

Number of partners worldwide: 5
Number of other lawyers worldwide: 7

AREAS OF PRACTICE:

Corporate, M&A, joint ventures	40%
Telecommunications	14%
Banking, finance and privatisation	10%
Commercial	10%
Intellectual property	10%
Energy and public utilities	8%
Litigation	4%
Employment and immigration	2%
Real estate and tourism	2%

FIRM OVERVIEW: Founded in 1955 by Guillermo López Rodezno, the firm is one of the oldest, largest and most prestigious law firms in Honduras. The firm is a member of Club de Abogados, the International Business Law Consortium (IBLC), the Inter-American Association of Industrial Property (ASIPI) and the International Trademark Association (INTA). It maintains links with various law firms worldwide.

INTERNATIONAL CLIENTS: The firm's client base includes large companies, banks, insurance companies and international organisations conducting cross-border transactions. International clients include Banco Agrícola Comercial de El Salvador, Central American Bank of Economic Integration (CABEI), Enron, German Investment and Development Company (DEG), International Finance Corporation (IFC), Inter American Development Bank (IADB), M.D. Foods, Royal Dutch Airlines, Shrimp Culture Inc, Rover Group Ltd, SmithKline Beecham, Sun Microsystems, Telefónica Sistemas de Seguridad, Uniliver, Unibank, US Tobacco Co.

MAIN INTERNATIONAL AREAS OF PRACTICE:

Corporate, M&A and joint ventures: The firm advises on all corporate matters including the formation of commercial companies, operational and environmental permits, corporate structuring and shareholders' agreements. The firm also advises local and international clients on M&A transactions, handles due diligence matters and advises on anti-trust, environmental, industrial property, labour and tax areas.

Banking, finance and privatisations: Lopez Rodezno & Asociados has advised national and international banks and insurance companies on local lending operations. It has represented the International Finance Corporation (IFC) and the Investment and Development Company of Germany (DEG) in many lending operations in Honduras. The firm has also advised the Honduran Government and foreign clients on privatisation projects.

Commercial: The firm advises local and foreign clients on the preparation of a wide range of commercial contracts including sales, agency, representation, distribution, factoring, leasing and trust.

Intellectual property: The firm specialises in trademarks, patents, copyrights and commercial names.

Telecommunications: The firm advises on all aspects of this area.

Employment and immigration: The firm advises foreign clients in all aspects related to employment of local personnel and immigration problems of foreign executives.

Real estate and tourism: The firm handles all matters relating to property deals including transactions and disputes involving commercial and residential property. The firm has also represented international clients in the development of tourist projects, obtaining all the necessary permits and tax exemptions.

Litigation: The firm's lawyers undertake commercial and civil litigation, and are frequently involved in cases before the Honduran Courts, including the Supreme Court. They also participate in arbitration matters.

Energy and public utilities: The firm is playing an active role in the deregulated energy and public utilities sector. It represents local and international clients in the development of energy projects.

LANGUAGES: English, Italian, Spanish

L

LOVELLS

HEAD OFFICE

see Worldwide Office Contacts

Website: www.lovells.com

FIRM OVERVIEW

Managing partner: Lesley MacDonagh
Senior partner: Andrew Walker
Number of partners worldwide: 260
Number of other lawyers worldwide: 706

AREAS OF PRACTICE:

Banking .... *%
Capital markets .... *%
Commercial .... *%
Corporate .... *%
Litigation .... *%
Property .... *%
* Workload % not disclosed

FIRM OVERVIEW: Lovells is one of the leading international law firms, with more than 1,200 lawyers across 26 offices worldwide. The firm combines the expertise of two leading practices, formerly Lovell White Durrant in the UK, Continental Europe, the US and Asia; and Boesebeck Droste, with offices in the major financial and commercial centres in Germany, Spain and key Central European countries. The Milan office focuses primarily on corporate and financial work and the Rome office concentrates on administrative, regulatory and governmental matters. In Central Europe, the firm is expanding and has offices in Warsaw, Vienna, Zagreb, Prague and Moscow. Its associated offices in Budapest, Zagreb and Vienna allow the firm to advise clients who have interests in the developing economies of Central and Eastern Europe. The firm is also active in Asia. Lovells is a member of the Pacific Rim Advisory Council, an association of major law firms undertaking work in the region. The firm has three US offices which, in conjunction with the firm's other offices in Europe and Asia, provide a significant dual US/UK jurisdictional service.

INTERNATIONAL EXPERIENCE: International experience includes co-ordinating the Granada Media flotation; advising South African Breweries in its £4 billion IPO in London; advising Laurent Perrier in its €53 million IPO in Paris and New York; and acting for established clients such as Barclays, Exxon Mobil, Ford and Prudential. Other examples include the BCCI/Stigma claims case and health related litigation for BAT.

INTERNATIONAL CLIENTS: The majority of work undertaken by Lovells has an international dimension. The firm acts for some 170 of the US Fortune 500 industrials and many leading European and Asian based corporate and financial institutions.

MAIN INTERNATIONAL AREAS OF PRACTICE: Work is handled in the areas of banking; capital markets; commercial and trading law; commodities; competition; trade and European law; consumer financial services; computers; communication and media; construction; corporate; employee benefits; employment; energy; environmental law; financial services and investment funds; insolvency and business restructuring; insurance and reinsurance; intellectual property; international arbitration; litigation and dispute resolution; pensions; private equity; product liability; project finance; property and planning; and tax.

WORLDWIDE OFFICE CONTACTS

BELGIUM		
Brussels	**Tel:** +32 2 647 06 60	**Fax:** +32 2 647 11 24
CHINA		
Beijing	**Tel:** +86 10 6526 3490	**Fax:** +86 10 6526 3492
CZECH REPUBLIC		
Prague	**Tel:** +420 2 2141 1700	**Fax:** +420 2 2421 0004
FRANCE		
Paris	**Tel:** +33 1 53 67 47 47	**Fax:** +33 1 47 23 96 12
GERMANY		
Berlin	**Tel:** +49 30 8 89 19 0	**Fax:** +49 30 8 89 19 100
Dresden	**Tel:** +49 351 829 61 0	**Fax:** +49 351 829 61 99
Düsseldorf	**Tel:** +49 211 13 68 0	**Fax:** +49 211 32 44 39
Frankfurt am Main	**Tel:** +49 69 962 36 0	**Fax:** +49 69 962 36 100
Hamburg	**Tel:** +49 40 419 93 0	**Fax:** +49 40 419 932 00
Munich	**Tel:** +49 89 290 12 0	**Fax:** +49 89 290 122 22
HONG KONG		
Hong Kong	**Tel:** +852 2219 0888	**Fax:** +852 2219 0222
ITALY		
Rome	**Tel:** +39 06 675 8231	**Fax:** +39 06 675 82323
Milan	**Tel:** +39 02 720 2521	**Fax:**+39 02 720 25252
JAPAN		
Tokyo	**Tel:** +81 3 3221 8511	**Fax:** +81 3 3221 8560
POLAND		
Warsaw	**Tel:** +48 22 628 64 70	**Fax:** +48 22 629 47 02
RUSSIA		
Moscow	**Tel:** +7 095 933 3000	**Fax:** +7 095 933 3001
SINGAPORE		
Singapore	**Tel:** +65 538 0900	**Fax:** +65 538 7077
SPAIN		
Alicante	**Tel:** +34 96 514 41 05	**Fax:** +34 96 514 43 03
UNITED KINGDOM		
London	**Tel:** +44 20 7296 2000	**Fax:** +44 20 7296 2001
USA		
New York	**Tel:** +1 212 909 0600	**Fax:** +1 212 909 0666
Chicago	**Tel:** +1 312 832 4400	**Fax:** +1 312 832 4444
Washington DC	**Tel:** +1 202 783 6144	**Fax:**+1 202 783 6250
VIETNAM		
Ho Chi Minh City	**Tel:** +84 8 829 5100	**Fax:** +84 8 829 5101

ASSOCIATED OFFICES

AUSTRIA		
Vienna	**Tel:** +43 1 53 55 744	**Fax:** +43 1 53 50 649
CROATIA		
Zagreb	**Tel:** +385 1 6 15 95 95	**Fax:** +385 1 6 15 77 33
HUNGARY		
Budapest	**Tel:** +36 1 474 2080	**Fax:** +36 1 474 2081

For other recommended firms see pages 1485-1520

LYAN & ASSOCIÉS

HEAD OFFICE

145 Habib Basha El-Saad Street, Achrafieh,
Beirut 2062 4508, Lebanon
Tel: +961 1616 616 **Fax:** +961 1616 161

Email: main@lyanlaw.com
Website: www.lyanlaw.com

WORLDWIDE OFFICE CONTACTS

LEBANON
145 Habib Basha El-Saad Street, Achrafieh, **Beirut** 2062 4508
Tel: +961 1616 616 **Fax:** +961 1616 161
Email: main@lyanlaw.com

FIRM OVERVIEW

Managing partner: Najib N. Lyan
Senior partner: Nicolas N. Lyan

Number of partners worldwide: 6
Number of other lawyers worldwide: 8

AREAS OF PRACTICE:

Litigation and arbitration	25%
Telecommunications	20%
Corporate and commercial	15%
Banking and finance	10%
Intellectual property	10%
M&A	10%
Sports and entertainment	5%
Other	5%

FIRM OVERVIEW: Lyan & Associés was established in1959 by Nicolas N. Lyan, Esq. In 1990 it expanded to become one of the leading international firms in Lebanon and the Middle East. The firm has an office in Panama to serve its international corporate clients and it maintains close links with various firms worldwide. The firm offers comprehensive legal services to clients with international business interests, but focuses on banking, mergers and acquisitions, and telecommunications. In 1999, a member of the firm was elected chairman of the Beirut Bar Association. The Panama office offers services to the firm's international clients using offshore jurisdictions as a platform for their international business. Lyan & Associés has a wholly owned subsidiary, Forum Finance, a company established to provide non-legal services such as accounting, trademark and IP agency and management of companies' assets.

INTERNATIONAL EXPERIENCE: Since 1990, Lyan & Associés advised a large number of foreign companies that came to Lebanon, either to participate in the reconstruction of the country or to establish offices for its Middle East operations. The firm also acted as legal counsel on a large number of transactions, each exceeding US$200 million.

INTERNATIONAL CLIENTS: The firm's client base includes large companies, banks, telecommunications companies and public or supranational institutions conducting cross-border business. These include Gulf International Bank, Arab Banking Corporation, Universal Trust Bank of Nigeria, The Lebanese Ministry of Telecom, PSINet, The Lebanese Association of Telecom Operators, SkyBridge, TeleChoise, CH2M Hill, Hochtief, Daikin, Radian International, Tenecco, CAT, Christian Dior and Maytag.

MAIN INTERNATIONAL AREAS OF PRACTICE:

Banking and finance: The firm covers all areas of banking and finance, including secured and syndicated loan transactions and guarantees, leasing and tax-based finance. It specialises in loans between banking institutions.
Corporate and commercial: The firm advises on all aspects of general corporate and commercial law, including the drafting of Lebanese and international contracts. It is playing a leading role in the revision of the Code of Commerce.
Intellectual property: The firm specialises in trademarks, patents, and copyrights. It acts in the negotiation of license agreements and advises on infringement disputes and other aspects of IP law.
Litigation and arbitration: The firm deals with commercial litigation and national and international arbitration. It is involved in cases before the Lebanese Courts, including the Cour de Cassation, and has participated in a number of matters under the rules of the International Chamber of Commerce.
M&A: The firm's transactions in this area range from small private acquisitions to companies listed on the Beirut stock exchange market.
Sports and entertainment: Lyan & Associés represents a large number of artists, clubs and associations, including the Lebanese Soccer Federation.
Telecommunications and IT: The firm advises on all aspects of telecommunications and IT law including legal, financial and technical issues. It has drafted various RFPs and PPMs for a number of telecom companies. It also handles a large amount of work for the Lebanese telecom community and represents the Ministry of Telecom and the Association of Telecom Operators.
Employment: Working with clients ranging from multinationals to local enterprises, the firm handles all their matters relating to Lebanese employment law and social security.
Public bids: The firm has extensive experience in bidding for public contracts.

LANGUAGES: Arabic, English, French, Spanish

WORLDWIDE OFFICES

PANAMA

Plaza Centro Building, Suite #8, Ricardo J. Alfaro Avenue, El-Dorado

Managing partner: Manuel J. Berrocal
Number of lawyers: 3

Office profile: Founded in 1991, the office was established to serve the multinational clients of the firm. The Panama office offers comprehensive legal services to clients with international business interests, but focuses on banking, tax, corporate and admiralty.

L

For other recommended firms see pages 1485-1520

MACCHI DI CELLERE E GANGEMI

HEAD OFFICE

see Worldwide Office Contacts

Website: www.macchi-gangemi.com

FIRM OVERVIEW

Head of business services: Luigi Macchi di Cellere
Head of financial services: Claudio Visco
Head of taxation: Bruno Gangemi

Number of partners worldwide: 12
Number of other lawyers worldwide: 40

AREAS OF PRACTICE:

Corporate services 40%
Taxation 35%
Financial services 25%

FIRM OVERVIEW: Established in 1986, Macchi di Cellere e Gangemi is a partnership of Italian lawyers serving business clients worldwide on matters of Italian, European and international law. Its lawyers have a thorough knowledge of local laws and practices, and understand the practical demands of the European market.

INTERNATIONAL EXPERIENCE: The firm specialises in transnational operations and joint ventures, assisting foreign clients and multinational groups on matters of Italian and European law, and advising Italian clients on their investments abroad. Macchi di Cellere e Gangemi works with independent firms throughout Europe and the Mediteranean basin, North and South America, the Far East and Australia. A number of its lawyers are admitted to practise in foreign jurisdictions.

INTERNATIONAL CLIENTS: The firm's international clients come mainly from Europe and the Mediterranean basin, North and South America, the Far East and Australia. They are multinational groups and foreign companies operating in all sectors of industry, trade, services and finance, as well as international organisations and foreign agencies.

MAIN INTERNATIONAL AREAS OF PRACTICE:

CORPORATE SERVICES:

M&A/Joint Ventures: The firm handles major and mid-sized negotiated acquisitions, including LBOs and joint venture transactions, in a wide variety of sectors of industry, trade, services and finance.

Anti-trust: The firm advises on provisions of the EU Treaty and of Italian competition laws.

Arbitration and ADR: The firm has a growing practice, especially in the fields of company/commercial, engineering, construction and employment.

Business organisations/insolvency: The firm advises on the establishment, conduct, restructuring and insolvency of business entities in Italy.

Commercial transactions/international trade: The firm advises on agency, supply, distribution and franchise contracts, the licensing of trademarks, patents and know-how, engineering and construction contracts, outsourcing agreements, lease agreements, transportation by land, sea and air and insurance contracts.

Communications and IT: The firm's lawyers have broad experience in telecommunications, and specifically in matters involving fixed, mobile and satellite networks and services, acquired in assisting major multinatioanl clients and international joint ventures. The firm has also provided expert advice with respect to radio and television broadcasting, information technology and internet communications.

WORLDWIDE OFFICE CONTACTS

ITALY
Via G. Cuboni 12, 00197 **Rome**
Tel: +39 06 362 141 **Fax:** +39 06 322 21 59
Email: roma@macchi-gangemi.com

Via G. Serbelloni 4, 20122 **Milan**
Tel: +39 02 763 281 **Fax:** +39 02 7600 1618
Email: milano@macchi-gangemi.com

ASSOCIATED OFFICES

Studio Lambertini & Rubin
Contrà Porti, 13, 36100 **Vicenza**
Tel: +39 0444 547808 **Fax:** +39 0444 547840
Email: vicenza@macchi-gangemi.com

Studio Lambertini & Rubin
Corso Cavour, 44, 37121 **Verona**
Tel: +39 045 803 6115 **Fax:** +39 045 803 4080
Email: verona@macchi-gangemi.com

Energy and natural resources: The firm advises on research and exploitation of natural resources, in particular oil and gas, and represents clients in the new deregulated electricity market.

Employment and social security: The practice handles matters of social security, safety at work and the transfer of personnel between enterprises.

Litigation: The firm represents clients in corporate, commercial, banking and finance, IP, employment, real estate, environment, tax, bankruptcy and white-collar crime proceedings.

Real estate/environmental: The firm has been retained in a wide variety of real estate matters, giving advice and assistance in respect of the acquisition, disposition and lease of land, industrial and commercial buildings, hotels, resorts and residential housing. The firm is active in rendering advice and assistance in all areas of enviromental law.

FINANCIAL SERVICES:

Banking: The firm has broad experience of export credits, syndicated loans, re-financing, leasing, factoring and asset-backed/securitisation transactions.

Capital markets: The firm advises in all matters relating to the issuing and placing of shares, bonds and warrants, IPOs, MBOs and securities lending transactions, as well as in tender offers, take-over bids and various privatisation matters.

Investment funds: The firm handles all aspects of the operation of funds and investment companies.

Project financing: The firm works in the fields of energy, waste, transportation and infrastructure.

TAXATION:

Business transations: The firm has experience in all aspects of business taxation affecting the business income of corporate entities, partnerships and individuals and, in particular, in respect of cross-border corporate reorganisation, M&As, JVs, takeovers, banking, financial investment and commercial agreements, also involving real estate and intellectual property.

Tax: The firm acts for corporate entities, partnerships and individuals. It is experienced in cross-border corporate reorganisations, banking and finance, real estate and IP. It also advises on double tax treaties and indirect taxation, and acts in matters of tax litigation.

Employee benefits: The firm advises on income tax, including employee compensation issues arising as a result of mergers and transfers of businesses.

Individuals/non-profit organizations: The firm advises individuals (and in particular expatriates) on tax and tax planning.

LANGUAGES: English, French, German, Italian, Spanish

For other recommended firms see pages 1485-1520

MACFARLANES

HEAD OFFICE

10 Norwich Street,
London EC4A 1BD, United Kingdom
Tel: +44 20 7831 9222
Fax: +44 20 7831 9607

Email: cpp@macfarlanes.com
Website: www.macfarlanes.com

WORLDWIDE OFFICE CONTACTS

BELGIUM
Avenue Louise 106, B-1050, **Brussels**
Tel: + 32 2 647 0650 **Fax:** + 32 2 646 4729
Email: cpp@macfarlanes.com

UNITED KINGDOM
10 Norwich Street, EC4A 1BD, **London**
Tel: +44 20 7831 9222 **Fax:** +44 20 7831 9607
Email: cpp@macfarlanes.com

FIRM OVERVIEW

Managing partner: Paul Phippen
Senior partner: Robert Sutton

Number of partners worldwide: 52
Number of other lawyers worldwide: 175

AREAS OF PRACTICE:

Area	%
Company/commercial	49%
Property	22%
Litigation	16%
Tax and financial planning	13%

FIRM OVERVIEW: Macfarlanes is a leading City of London law firm. A significant proportion of the firm's work is cross-border or international, advising clients from outside the UK on all matters requiring English legal advice as well as working with UK clients on projects which have an international element. The firm does not have a network of international offices or alliances. Remaining independent, the firm has instead built close working relationships with leading independent law firms in other jurisdictions, aiming to provide clients with an integrated service to rival that offered by the global firms. In addition, Macfarlanes has an office in Brussels which maintains a substantial information system on European legal and policy matters to provide clients with access to up to date information on developments in the European Union.

INTERNATIONAL CLIENTS: Include substantial companies as well as private individuals, and span a diverse range of industries including advertising, media, automotive, brewing, chemical, electronic, engineering, entertainment, financial, pharmaceutical and securities.

MAIN INTERNATIONAL AREAS OF PRACTICE:

Corporate: Macfarlanes is highly regarded for its work in the areas of corporate finance and mergers and acquisitions, including private equity and take-overs. The firm's related specialist areas, such as intellectual property, corporate tax, banking and employee benefits, mean that Macfarlanes can provide its commercial clients with legal services, both in relation to corporate transactional work and at the clients' operational level. The firm has earned a reputation for advertising and marketing work as well as investment funds and financial services. Recent highlights include the firm's representation of Vivendi on its £2.5 billion acquisition of a 24% stake in BSkyB; Saint-Gobain of France in connection with its £1.04 billion bid for Meyer International; Virgin on its sale of a 49% stake in the Virgin Atlantic airline to Singapore Airlines for over £550 million; and Intercapital plc on its merger with Garban plc valued at £158 million.

Property: Work for the property sector covers all transactions involving ownership, development, investment in and financing of land. Commercial property investment and development transactions are at the core of the work of the property department whose reputation and profile continues to rise as the quality of its work and of the transactions in which it is involved are more widely recognised.

Litigation: Macfarlanes' wide range of litigation and other dispute resolution work includes: leading employment law cases; acting for insured and insurer, especially in advertising and surveying cases; IP cases and disputes over computer hardware and software; financial services regulatory issues and enquiries; Lloyd's-related work; sovereign debt, securities and other banking disputes; judicial review, breach of contract and professional negligence claims. Recent work includes working on major EU and competition disputes including acting on behalf of Thomson Holidays Ltd, where we persuaded the Court of Appeal to declare invalid the key elements of an order made by the Secretary of State for Trade and Industry in connection with the MMC report into the foreign package holiday industry; major shipping and construction arbitration; and advising on a number of jurisdictional disputes and EU jurisdiction questions. Our strong international commercial dispute resolution practice also attracts a significant volume and diversity of work

Private client: Macfarlanes is one of the leading UK firms in advising private clients and their family trusts, both domestically and internationally. Tax planning, including the creation and administration of trusts, the preparation of wills and the administration of estates are central to this work. The firm forms and advises many charitable companies and trusts. The international element is very important both for UK-based families and for overseas taxpayers seeking advice on tax and trust law. The firm is frequently instructed at the request of many of the largest US firms and private banks for this work. Partners have been appointed by courts in the UK and abroad to be trustees in place of existing trustees.

LANGUAGES: Include Dutch, English, French, German, Italian, Japanese, Romanian, Spanish

MACFARLANES

M

MACIEL, NORMAN & ASOCIADOS

HEAD OFFICE

San Martin 323, 19th floor,
1004 Buenos Aires, Argentina
Tel: +54 11 4394 4535 **Fax:** +54 11 4394 8433

Email: info@mna.com.ar
Website: www.mna.com.ar

FIRM OVERVIEW

Managing partner: Justo F. Norman
Senior partner: Rogelio N. Maciel

Number of partners worldwide: 2
Number of other lawyers worldwide: 22

AREAS OF PRACTICE:

Energy	20%
Corporate	15%
M&A	15%
Tax	15%
Banking and finance	10%
Litigation and arbitration	10%
Telecommunications	10%
Intellectual property	5%

WORLDWIDE OFFICE CONTACTS

ARGENTINA
San Martin 323, 19th floor, 1004 **Buenos Aires**
Tel: +54 11 4394 4535 **Fax:** +54 11 4394 8433
Email: info@mna.com.ar

ASSOCIATED OFFICES
Associated offices in Bolivia and Uruguay.

M

FIRM OVERVIEW: Maciel, Norman & Asociados provides a comprehensive range of legal services. Work undertaken includes general corporate and commercial work, mergers and acquisitions, taxation, financing, energy and natural resources law, labour and social security, environmental law, intellectual property and litigation.

INTERNATIONAL CLIENTS: The firm's client base includes large companies and supranational institutions conducting cross-border business such as Anadarko Petroleum Corp., Arjo Wiggins Appleton, BHP Petroleum, Bombardier Aerospace, Parker Drilling, Petrobras Internacional, Qantas Airways, Sikorsky Aircraft.

MAIN INTERNATIONAL AREAS OF PRACTICE:
Corporate and commercial law: MN&A acts on behalf of multinational corporations in connection with their investments in Argentina. Work undertaken includes advising on corporate vehicles and the structuring of joint ventures.
Taxation: MN&A advises on tax free mergers and acquisitions, transfer pricing (sales, purchases, import, export and licensing) and the tax structuring of joint ventures.
Energy: MN&A advise on acquisitions in international tenders and the negotiation of joint operating agreements for oil and gas operations in Argentina.
International trade and customs: The firm provides a comprehensive range of advisory and monitoring services both in Argentina and in the Southern Common Market (Mercosur) to clients in diverse industry sectors on import and export regimes. It is experienced in international trade law, including anti-dumping investigations, anti-subsidy measures, customs disputes and WTO issues.
Maritime law-land and multimodal transport: The firm's practice covers admiralty and shipping law, passengers and cargo claims, purchase, financing, leasing mortgage, registration and sale of ships, hull charter parties and cargo loss or damage agreements.
Aviation law: Work undertaken includes advising on aircraft sales, purchase and leasing agreements. MN&A also advises on regulatory matters including air transport licenses and operating permits, ticketing and conditions of carriage, passenger and cargo claims.
Litigation and arbitration: MN&A has broad experience in litigation involving commercial, civil, employment, administrative, environmental and tax matters before federal and local Argentine courts.
Administrative law and privatisations: MN&A has been active in every major privatisation of state owned utilities and companies during the 1990s. It has represented awardees of telecommunication services, oil production, gas transportation services and port terminal facilities.
Communications: The firm's expertise includes all areas of the communications industry from broadcasting to a full range of telecom services such as acquisition of cable television systems, obtaining of licences for the rendering of value added services and other competing telecommunication services.
Environmental law: MN&A specialises in legislation on hazardous waste, water, soil and air laws, environmental regulations on oil and gas, refineries and fuel outlets, mining and electricity..
Intellectual property: The firm represents foreign and domestic clients in all aspects of intellectual property matters and related licensing and litigation.

LANGUAGES: English, French, German, Italian, Spanish

For other recommended firms see pages 1485-1520

MACLEOD DIXON LLP

HEAD OFFICE

3700 Canterra Tower, 400 Third Avenue SW,
Calgary, Alberta, Canada T2P 4H2
Tel: +1 403 267 8222 **Fax:** +1 403 264 5973

Email: calgary@macleoddixon.com
Website: www.macleoddixon.com

FIRM OVERVIEW

Managing partner: Bill Tuer

Number of partners worldwide: 85
Number of other lawyers worldwide: 114

AREAS OF PRACTICE:

Energy and natural resources	15%
Public and trade law	15%
Project development and finance	5%
Tax	5%

FIRM OVERVIEW: Founded in Calgary in 1912, Macleod Dixon LLP focuses in particular on the energy and natural resources sectors, acting for multinational and national corporations, private businesses, governments and individuals. The firm opened a Moscow office in 1990 which is accredited with the Russian government and is licensed to practise in Mongolia. In 1995 it opened an office in Kazakhstan, the first Canadian firm to do so. The firm's Venezuela office was opened in 1997, making Macleod Dixon the first Canadian law firm to establish a fully staffed office in Latin America.

INTERNATIONAL EXPERIENCE: The firm has extensive experience in international transactions, not only in Russia, Kazakhstan, Uzbekistan, Turkmenistan, Ukraine, Kyrgystan and South and Central America, but also in Eastern Europe, the Far East, the Indian subcontinent, Africa and the Caribbean. From its CIS and Latin American offices the firm has been extensively involved in the support, negotiation and documentation of joint ventures, joint stock companies and other entities, acting mostly for Canadian, American, European, Asian and Australian companies.

INTERNATIONAL CLIENTS: These come chiefly from the renewable and non-renewable resource industries, major lending organisations and companies involved in industrial and natural resource projects. The firm also advises the Russian, Uzbek and Vietnamese governments.

MAIN INTERNATIONAL AREAS OF PRACTICE:
Energy and natural resources: The firm has worked in North America, Europe, Asia, South America and Africa, acting for exploration and production companies, mining companies, oil and gas service companies, royalty owners and governments. Work includes structuring joint ventures and other partnerships to conduct oil and gas activities, performing due diligence for oil and gas and securities transactions and providing regulatory and commercial advice on major projects such as processing plants, pipelines and cogeneration facilities. The firm has also been retained by the EBRD to advise the Uzbek government on the country's mining and mineral licensing regulations.
Project development and finance: The practice has worked extensively in the CIS and Latin America and elsewhere. Secured loan transactions in which it has acted in various capacities include the original financing of McDonalds' operations in Moscow. It has strong ties to Canadian and international banking institutions.
Public and trade: The firm has won four successive technical assistance contracts from the Russian and Canadian governments and is currently advising the Russian Ministry of Trade. It assisted the Russian government in its application to join the General Agreement on Tariffs and Trade, and subsequently the World Trade Organisation (WTO). The group has also advised the Vietnam and Barbados governments on their WTO membership applications. The firm also advises on government procurement issues involving clients in Canada, including appeals before the Canadian International Trade Tribunal.
Tax: Work includes advice on the taxation of foreign investments in Canada and outbound Canadian investments, and the taxation of public and privately-owned entities with business abroad.

LANGUAGES: Azeri, American Sign Language, Cantonese, Croatian, English, French, German, Greek, Hebrew, Italian, Kazakh, Japanese, Polish, Portuguese, Russian, Scots Gaelic, Spanish, Swedish, Turkish, Ukrainian, Vietnamese

WORLDWIDE OFFICE CONTACTS

CANADA
3700 Canterra Tower, 400 Third Avenue SW, **Calgary**, Alberta T2P 4H2
Tel: +1 403 267 8222 **Fax:** +1 403 264 5973
Email: calgary@macleoddixon.com

3900, Canada Trust Tower, BCE Place, 161 Bay Street, **Toronto**, Ontario M5J 2S1
Tel: +1 416 360 8511 **Fax:** +1 416 360 8277
Email: toronto@macleoddixon.com

KAZAKHSTAN
6th floor, 157 Prospekt Abaya, **Almaty** 480009
Tel: +73272 509380 **Fax:** +73272 509382
Email: almaty@macleoddixon.com

RUSSIA
8th Floor, Mosenka Park Towers, 17-23, ul. Taganskaya, **Moscow** 109004
Tel: +7502 222 2305 **Fax:** +7502 222 2314
Email: moscow@macleoddixon.com

VENEZUELA
Despacho de Abogados miembros de Macleod Dixon, S.C.,
Calle Orinoco, Torre Uno, Piso 5, Urb. Las Mercedes, **Caracas** 1060
Tel: +582 993 2777 **Fax:** +582 993 2611
Email: caracas@macleoddixon.com

MAISTO E ASSOCIATI

HEAD OFFICE

Piazza F. Meda, 5,
20121 Milan, Italy
Tel: +39 02 776 931 **Fax:** +39 02 776 93300

Email: info@maisto.it

FIRM OVERVIEW

Partners Avv Guglielmo Maisto, Avv Andrea Manzitti and Dott. Paolo Ludovici
Number of partners worldwide: 3
Number of other lawyers worldwide: 15

AREAS OF PRACTICE:

Domestic and multinational group taxation and tax planning	30%
Tax (capital markets, financial instruments, derivatives)	20%
Tax (M&A, corporate restructuring)	20%
Tax litigation	20%
Employee benefits	10%

M

FIRM OVERVIEW: Maisto e Associati specialises in Italian taxation law for a mainly corporate clientele. The 18 partners and associates comprise either lawyers, or accountants with a legal background and each has substantial experience in their field.

INTERNATIONAL EXPERIENCE: The firm advises large companies and groups conducting cross-border business on the fiscal aspects of various types of transactions, in particular structured finance and M&A. It also advises a variety of companies on EU concerns. Firm members have substantial experience in the international sector, having worked in the Netherlands, France and the UK. Its lawyers have held numerous international and domestic committee and advisory roles, including to the Italian Ministry for European Affairs and the Italian Association of Industry. In 1999 the firm advised on the largest take-over in Italy, which was amongst the largest in Europe, and has been involved in one of the largest Italian tax litigation cases.

INTERNATIONAL CLIENTS: The firm advises six of the top ten Fortune 500 companies. Clients include top American investment banks and other financial institutions; the leading tobacco producing firm worldwide; and the two largest Italian telecommunications companies. The firm works closely with leading companies in the venture capital market and advises major IT and consulting companies. The firm also has a strong reputation in the fashion industry.

MAIN INTERNATIONAL AREAS OF PRACTICE:
Domestic and multinational group taxation and tax planning: The firm advises on complex matters of Italian tax law for resident and non-resident companies and permanent establishments, including partnerships, limited liability companies or joint ventures. It provides tax advice on the most suitable locations for holding companies, appropriate transfer pricing arrangements, profit distribution, dividend flows, interest and royalties between related companies.
Mergers and acquisitions, corporate restructuring: The firm works within tight time constraints to structure complete domestic and cross-border mergers and acquisitions, joint ventures and leveraged buy-outs. It also advises on company reorganisation.
Capital markets, financial instruments and derivatives: The firm advises on withholding tax, corporate income tax and personal income tax. Areas of expertise include taxation of bonds and trading, the fiscal treatment of derivatives for both individuals and enterprises and stock options.
Tax litigation: The firm handles complex tax litigation, dealing with cases involving transfer pricing, issues arising from audits and international and domestic tax structuring disputes.
Employee benefits: The firm advises on contracts and the most tax effective benefit schemes for employees, including executives and expatriates. Taxation of fringe benefits is a further area of expertise.
EU tax law: The firm tackles EU taxation issues and keeps clients up to date on new developments and their implications.

LANGUAGES: English, French, Italian, Spanish

WORLDWIDE OFFICE CONTACTS

ITALY
Piazza F. Meda, 5, 20121 **Milan**
Tel: +39 02 776 931 **Fax:** +39 02 776 93300
Email: info@maisto.it

UNITED KINGDOM
Royex House, Aldermanbury Square, **London** EC2V 7HR
Tel: +44 20 7726 6560 **Fax:** +44 20 7726 6561
Email: postmaster@maisto.it

WORLDWIDE OFFICES

UNITED KINGDOM

Royex House, Aldermanbury Square, London EC2V 7HR
Senior partner: Guglielmo Maisto
Senior associate: Riccardo Michelutti
Number of lawyers: 1

Main areas of work: Italian taxation advice regarding M&A, capital markets, financial instruments, derivatives, corporate restructuring and employee compensation.
Top clients: The office works with major firms from diverse sectors and includes international banks and investment houses, consulting companies, and other international companies conducting cross-border transactions.
Languages: English, French, Italian
Office profile: The London office was opened in March 1998. As well as assisting in inbound and outbound investment, it is involved in taxation of derivatives, M&A, Italian taxation of UK residents and other financial transactions.

 For other recommended firms see pages 1485-1520

MAKES & PARTNERS

HEAD OFFICE

Menara Batavia, 7th Floor, JL KH Mas Mansyur Kav 126,
Jakarta 10220 Indonesia
Tel: +62 21 574 7181 **Fax:** +62 21 574 7180
Email: makes@indosat.net.id

WORLDWIDE OFFICE CONTACTS

INDONESIA
Menara Batavia, 7th Floor, JL KH Mas Mansyur Kav 126, **Jakarta** 10220
Tel: +62 21 574 7181 **Fax:** +62 21 574 7180
Email: makes@indosat.net.id

FIRM OVERVIEW

Managing partner: Yozua Makes

AREAS OF PRACTICE:

Banking and finance .... *%
Capital markets .... *%
Competition .... *%
Corporate/M&A .... *%
Energy .... *%
Information technology .... *%
Real estate .... *%
Telecommunications .... *%
* Workload % not disclosed

FIRM OVERVIEW: Makes & Partners is an independent Indonesian law firm providing corporate legal services to Indonesian and international clients. The firm maintains strong connections with the government, legal and business communities in Indonesia. Makes and Partners adopts a practical business approach to its dealings with clients to provide meaningful legal solutions in Indonesia. Established in the early 1990s, the firm currently has more than 20 lawyers, including foreign attorneys. The lawyers are also assisted by special counsel previously serving in senior capacities with various government ministries and the Supreme Court.

INTERNATIONAL EXPERIENCE: Makes & Partners has extensive experience in International work, having represented major multinational companies and international strategic and institutional investors in connection with their investments in Indonesia. The firm has also served as co-counsel with leading American, British, Australian and Japanese international law firms. The firm has strategic allegiances or associations with certain foreign law firms, including, Skadden, Arps, Slate, Meagher & Flom, a US international law firm prominent in corporate finance and mergers and acquisitions; Advoc, an alliance of independent business law firms in Europe and the Asia Pacific region; Sandler, Travis & Rosenberg, a US law firm that is one of the largest US organisations exclusively devoted to the representation of companies in complying with US trade (dumping) and customs laws. Notwithstanding these strategic arrangements, the firm is fully independent from the above firms.

INTERNATIONAL CLIENTS: Makes & Partners has represented major multinational companies, strategic and institutional investors, banks and investment houses in connection with their investments in Indonesia. The firm's portfolio of clients also includes Indonesian investors, issuers, underwriters and borrowers as well as the Government of Indonesia and other public entities. The firm's private clients include some of the largest Indonesian corporate groups and numerous Indonesian investment banks. International clients of Makes & Partners include major financial institutions and multinational corporations operating in a variety of industries. Makes & Partners is also representing the Government of Indonesia in its privatisation and divestment matters. The firm works closely and continuously with the Government agencies relevant to a corporate finance, capital investment and mergers and acquisitions practice.

MAIN INTERNATIONAL AREAS OF PRACTICE:
Banking and corporate finance: Makes & Partners continues to act for both domestic borrowers and international lenders in banking and finance transactions.
Capital markets: The firm has acted for domestic and international clients in capital market transactions.
Competition: The firm has advised foreign investors on Indonesia's evolving competition law regime.
Corporate/M&A: Makes & Partners' corporate/M&A clients include Indonesian and foreign investors and the Governemnt of Indonesia. The firm is actively involved in high profile and complex transactions requiring comprehensive and strategic legal services.
Information technology: The firm has acted in a number of IT matters and joint ventures.
Real estate: The firm has particular experience in regulatory issues involved with foreign investment.
Telecommunications: The firm has particular experience in regulatory issues involved with foreign investment in this sector.

LANGUAGES: English, Indonesian, Mandarin

MALLESONS STEPHEN JAQUES

HEAD OFFICE

Level 60, Governor Phillip Tower, 1 Farrer Place
Sydney NSW 2000, Australia
Tel: +61 2 9296 2000 **Fax:** +61 2 9296 3999
Email: syd@msj.com.au
Website: www.msj.com.au

FIRM OVERVIEW

Chief executive partner: Tony D'Aloisio
Number of partners worldwide: 204
Number of other lawyers worldwide: 659

AREAS OF PRACTICE:

Corporate and commercial	34%
Banking and finance	23%
Contentious business	22%
Property	14%
Tax	7%

M

FIRM OVERVIEW: Mallesons Stephen Jaques is focused on assisting major corporations and financial institutions with complex legal issues in the Asia Pacific region. The firm, established in 1832, is committed to the highest ethical and professional standards.
Mallesons Stephen Jaques has offices in Sydney, Melbourne, Perth, Brisbane and Canberra as well as Hong Kong, Beijing and London. The firm also has an associate office in Port Moresby.
The firm's client base is focused on major corporations and financial institutions, many of which have international operations.

INTERNATIONAL EXPERIENCE: The firm has a substantial international practice, with an emphasis on cross-border M&A work and international capital raisings.

INTERNATIONAL CLIENTS: Many of the firm's clients are international corporations and financial institutions. The majority are UK/European and US based and the firm acts for a number of substantial Asian corporations.

MAIN INTERNATIONAL AREAS OF PRACTICE:

Banking and finance: The firm's banking and finance lawyers advise many of Australia's blue chip lenders and borrowers and act for arrangers and underwriters of complex, benchmark transactions throughout the Asia Pacific region.
Corporate and commercial: The firm advises on all areas of corporate law including mergers, acquisitions, funds management, divestments, long term supply agreements, restructurings, directors issues, e-commerce, technology and intellectual property.
Dispute resolution: The firm has been involved in many of the major disputes in Australia. It delivers a full range of dispute resolution services in multiple jurisdictions around the world, particularly in Asia.
Energy and Resources: The firm's lawyers focus on large-scale infrastructure and resources projects, and energy and resources related mergers and acquisitions, advising sponsors, utilities, governments and financiers. The firm also advises sponsors, utilities and regulators on regulatory reform and market development in the energy sector in Australia and the Asian region.
Insolvency: The firm has a wealth of experience in Australia and off-shore. Areas of specialist practice include all forms of company appointments, informal workouts, voluntary administration, tax advice and liquidator claims.

WORLDWIDE OFFICE CONTACTS

AUSTRALIA

Level 30, Waterfront Place, 1 Eagle Street, **Brisbane** OLD 4000
Tel: +61 7 3244 8000 **Fax:** +61 7 3244 8999
Email: bris@msj.com.au

Level 10, St George Centre, 60 Marcus Clarke Street, **Canberra City,** ACT 2601
Tel: +61 2 6217 6000 **Fax:** +61 2 6217 6999
Email: can@msj.com.au

Level 28, Rialto, 525 Collins Street, **Melbourne** VIC 3000
Tel: +61 3 9643 4000 **Fax:** +61 3 9643 5999
Email: mel@msj.com.au

Level 10, Central Park, 152 St George's Terrace, **Perth** WA 6000
Tel: +61 8 9269 7000 **Fax:** +61 8 9269 7999
Email: per@msj.com.au

Level 60, Governor Phillip Tower, 1 Farrer Place, **Sydney** NSW 2000
Tel: +61 2 9296 2000 **Fax:** +61 2 9296 3999
Email: syd@msj.com.au

CHINA

Suite 701, CVIK Tower, 22 Jian Guo Men Wai Avenue, **Beijing** 100004
Tel: +86 10 6512 3565 **Fax:** +86 10 6523 2018
Email: bei@msj.com.au

HONG KONG

Suite 801, Asia Pacific Finance Tower, Citibank Plaza, 3 Garden Road, Central **Hong Kong**
Tel: +852 2848 4600 **Fax:** +852 2868 0124
Email: hk@msj.com.au

UNITED KINGDOM

2nd Floor, Aldermary House, 15 Queen Street, **London** EC4N 1TX
Tel: +44 20 7982 0982 **Fax:** +44 20 7982 9820
Email: lon@msj.com.au

Intellectual property/information technology: Clients include leading Australian and international corporations in Australia and the Asian region. The firm advises on Internet cybercasting, content and hosting agreements, e-commerce, and business to business platforms. The firm also advises on all areas of intellectual property incuding patents, copyright and trademarks and provides advice on emerging areas such as biotechnology.
Property and construction: Mallesons Stephen Jaques' property and construction lawyers specialise in large scale infrastructure projects, project alliancing and construction-related disputes. The firm has particular expertise in power, transport, water and telecommunications. Clients include local and offshore clients and advice is offered on investments, sales and development projects.
Taxation: The firm's lawyers assist clients in planning and completing complex finance and M&A transactions, combining advice on income tax, GST, stamp duty and excises. The firm also offers advice on resolving tax disputes with the revenue offices and other parties to transactions.
Telecommunications: Mallesons Stephen Jaques has a strong reputation in all regulatory and commercial aspects of the telecommunications industry, in Australia and the Asia Pacific region. The firm is actively involved in major telecommunication issues.

LANGUAGES: Arabic, Bahasa, Indonesian, Bengali, Burmese, Cantonese, English, Fijian, French, German, Greek, Hindi, Hungarian, Italian, Japanese, Korean, Macedonian, Malay, Mandarin, Polish, Portuguese, Spanish, Swedish, Vietnamese

MANNHEIMER SWARTLING

CONTACT OFFICE

Norrmalmstorg 4, Box 1711,
SE-111 87 Stockholm, Sweden
Tel: + 46 8 613 55 00 **Fax:** + 46 8 613 55 01

Email: reception@msa.se
Website: www.msa.se

FIRM OVERVIEW

Managing partner: Magnus Wallander
Chairman of the Board: Claes Lundblad

Number of partners worldwide: 66
Number of other lawyers worldwide: 157

AREAS OF PRACTICE:

Corporate/M&A 31%
Finance and securities 18%
Litigation and arbitration 17%
Corporate taxation 11%
IT/telecommunications 7%
EU, competition and marketing 6%
Environmental 5%
Intellectual property 5%

FIRM OVERVIEW: The firm, which traces its origins to 1877, is a broadly-based commercial practice, with an emphasis on M&A, banking, finance and securities and litigation and arbitration. It is not part of any formal alliance or network, but has long-standing relationships with other firms in all major jurisdictions. These, together with the firm's own foreign offices, enable it to deal with matters involving several jurisdictions.

INTERNATIONAL EXPERIENCE: The firm is involved in most major transactions on the Swedish stock market. In 1999 the firm advised 28 of the 30 most traded companies on the Stockholm Stock Exchange.

INTERNATIONAL CLIENTS: Clients include large and medium-sized Swedish and foreign companies, banks and other financial institutions, government departments and agencies, municipalities and public utilities.

WORLDWIDE OFFICE CONTACTS

BELGIUM
Avenue de Tervueren 13B, BE-1040 **Brussels**
Tel: +32 2 732 22 22 **Fax:** +32 2 736 96 52
Email: reception@msa.se

GERMANY
Mauerstrasse 83-84, DE-10117 **Berlin**
Tel: +49 30 202 20 10 **Fax:** +49 30 202 20 110
Email: reception@msa.se

Wildunger Strasse 9, DE-60487 **Frankfurt am Main**
Tel: +49 69 974 01 20 **Fax:** +49 69 741 01 43
Email: reception@msa.se

RUSSIA
Ul. Arbat 16/2 building 3, 3rd Floor 121002 **Moscow**
Tel: +7 095 234 1714 **Fax:** +7 095 234 1715
Email: reception@msa.se

Dom Shvetsii, Malaya Konyushennaya ul. 1/3a, 191186 **St Petersburg**
Tel: +7 812 329 2505 **Fax:** +7 812 329 2507
Email: reception@msa.se

SWEDEN
Lilla Torget 1, Box 2235, SE-403 14 **Gothenburg**
Tel: +46 31 10 96 00 **Fax:** +46 31 10 96 01
Email: reception@msa.se

Sodra Storgatan 7, Box 1384, SE-251 13 **Helsingborg**
Tel: +46 42 49 06 200 **Fax:** +46 42 49 06 201
Email: reception@msa.se

Stortorget 29, Box 4291, SE-203 14 **Malmo**
Tel: +46 40 25 08 00 **Fax:** +46 40 25 08 01
Email: reception@msa.se

USA
101 Park Avenue, 26th Floor, **New York,** NY 10178
Tel: +1 212 682 0580 **Fax:** +1 212 682 0982
Email: reception@msa.se

M

MAIN INTERNATIONAL AREAS OF PRACTICE:

Finance and securities: The practice covers secured and syndicated loan transactions, structured finance, project finance, leasing and tax-based finance, public offers, private placements, listings and regulatory work.
M&A: The firm's M&A group handles all types of transactions, from private acquisitions to cross-border mergers between public listed companies.
Litigation and arbitration: The firm handles disputes both in general commercial law and specialist areas such as IP, admiralty, IT and insurance. Also handles Swedish and international arbitration.
Corporate tax: The practice primarily advises on international tax issues such as the structuring of international transactions and transfer pricing.
EU, competition and marketing: The firm advises on all types of European Community law, competition law, marketing law and entertainment law.
Intellectual property: Advises on all types of intellectual property issues. It has an emphasis on issues relating to trademarks and copyright.
IT and telecoms: The firm handles legal matters relating to information technology, telecommunications, multimedia, broadcasting and new media such as the Internet, data protection and electronic markets.
Environmental law: The firm advises clients on matters such as the environmental impact assessment of proposed uses of land, environmental requirements of specific business transactions, securing operating permits and environmental due diligence.

LANGUAGES: English, Finnish, French, German, Polish, Russian, Swedish

MANNHEIMER SWARTLING

MAPLES AND CALDER

HEAD OFFICE

see worldwide office contacts

Website: www.maplesandcalder.com

FIRM OVERVIEW

Senior partner: Anthony Travers
Managing Partners: Andrew Moon, Henry Harford, Adrian Pope
Number of partners worldwide: 20
Number of other lawyers worldwide: 45

AREAS OF PRACTICE:

Banking ....*%
Capital markets/securitisation ....*%
Collective investment schemes ....*%
Commercial and private trust and commercial and trust litigation *%
Private equity ....*%
* Workload % not disclosed

WORLDWIDE OFFICE CONTACTS

CAYMAN ISLANDS
P O Box 309, Ugland House, South Church Street, **Grand Cayman,** Cayman Islands
Tel: +345 949 8066 **Fax:** +345 949 8080
Email: info@maples.candw.ky

HONG KONG
Maples and Calder Asia, 1504 One International Finance Centre, 1 Harbour View Street, **Hong Kong**
Tel: +852 2522 9333 **Fax:** +852 2537 2955
Email: info@maples.com.hk

UNITED KINGDOM
Maples and Calder Europe, 5th Floor, 7 Princes Street, **London** EC2R 8AQ,
Tel: +44 20 7466 1600 **Fax:** 020 7466 1700
Email: info@maplesandcalder.co.uk

FIRM OVERVIEW: Maples and Calder is the largest law firm in the Cayman Islands and has practised Cayman Islands law for more than 30 years. It opened affiliated offices in Hong Kong in 1995 and London in 1997 in order to develop greater proximity with the firm's client base and to provide time zone sensitive advice. There are now over 275 lawyers and staff worldwide and advice is given to leading international and domestic law firms, major financial institutions and high net worth clients although solely in relation to Cayman Islands law. The firm provides the highest quality legal advice on all aspects of Cayman Islands law, recruiting mainly English-trained lawyers who are familiar with international financial transactions. The firm emphasises a team approach. Partners of the firm sit on the Financial Secretary's Private Sector Consultative Committee and on the Financial Services Legislative Sub-Committee. This preserves close links with the Government. The intention is to ensure that, through such programmes, the Cayman Islands will continue to meet the demands of both the financial industry and international regulators thereby maintaining the reputation of the Cayman Islands as a leading financial centre.

MAIN INTERNATIONAL AREAS OF PRACTICE: Maples and Calder provides Cayman Islands legal advice in relation to banking, capital markets, securitisation, asset financing, captive insurance, international equity offerings and listings, mutual and hedge funds, venture capital and commercial and private trusts and commercial and trust litigation.
Corporate: This area forms the core of the firm's practice. Maples and Calder has extensive experience in establishing many forms of corporate vehicles available in the Cayman Islands. Expertise includes initial public offerings, cross-border mergers and reorganisations, joint venture and project finance vehicles in such areas as infrastructure development, telecommunications and inward investment of capital into emerging markets.
Capital markets: The capital markets department advises on the structuring and implementation of a broad range of financing transactions for off-balance sheet vehicles and finance subsidiaries.
Mutual funds: The firm played an important role in the development of the Cayman Islands mutual funds legislation which adopted an innovative and non-intrusive regulatory approach. Maples and Calder has an extensive practice and advises on the full range of mutual funds in corporate, trust and partnership form.
Trusts: The trusts department has assisted with the introduction of sophisticated conflicts of law and trust legislation in the Cayman Islands and handles a wide variety of commercial trusts transactions as well as private trusts and estate planning.
Banking: The Cayman Islands are one of the foremost banking centres in the world with over 575 banks and trust companies holding deposits of over US$750 billion and the firm numbers amongst its clients many of the major international financial institutions. The firm acts in relation to all types of banking matters, including establishment in the Cayman Islands, secured and subordinated lending and syndicated facilities.
Insurance: Maples and Calder was involved in the development of the captive insurance industry in the Cayman Islands, having assisted the Cayman Islands Government in the initial preparation and development of governing legislation and have been closely involved in pioneering the development of new forms of financial instruments such as catastrophe bonds through which insurers and reinsurers have been gaining access to the capital markets to transfer risk instead of using traditional reinsurance.
Aircraft and shipping: The firm acts for many major financial institutions, arrangers, airlines and shipping companies in relation to asset financing for commercial and private aircraft, ships and yachts. Maples and Calder regularly establishes and advises on both on and off-balance sheet vehicles for the world's largest airlines and shipping companies which are typically structured through the use of Cayman Islands companies, limited partnerships and trusts.
Litigation: The firm has an experienced and successful litigation department which can assemble specialist teams to provide the expertise and advocacy required by complex contentious matters in both well established fields such as trust litigation and expanding new fields such as e-commerce. The firm also provides specialist expertise in arbitrations and, if required, a qualified arbitrator for the purposes of arbitrations conducted under American Arbitration Association rules.
Local practice: The Cayman Islands offer an attractive legal, regulatory and tax environment to conduct business. In recent years there has been both an expansion in existing local businesses and an upsurge in the number of foreign businesses proposing to re-locate either the whole or part of their operations to the Cayman Islands. The firm has established a Local Business Legal Support Unit as a specialist team to offer its services on a unified basis.
Other: The firm offers a highly specialised fiduciary service to structured finance transactions through its controlling interest in QSPV Limited and QSVP (Jersey) Limited, licensed trust company administrators of Cayman Islands debt-issuing special purpose vehicles.

LANGUAGES: Cantonese, English, French, German, Italian, Japanese, Portugese, Russian, Spanish

For other recommended firms see pages 1485-1520

MARENA, BONVICINI, AGHINA E LUDERGNANI - STUDIO LEGALE

HEAD OFFICE

Via Degli Omenoni, 2,
Milan 20121, Italy
Tel: +39 02 7201 0896 **Fax:** +39 02 7202 3904

Email: milano@marlaw.it

FIRM OVERVIEW

Senior and managing partner: Francesco Marena

Number of partners worldwide: 8
Number of other lawyers worldwide: 4

AREAS OF PRACTICE:
M&A and joint ventures 60%
Corporate and commercial 20%
Other 20%

FIRM OVERVIEW: Founded in 1971, Marena, Bonvicini, Aghina e Ludergnani is a 'boutique firm' specialising in international corporate and commercial matters. The firm assists its clients in cross-border transactions, and other areas by maintaining strong relations with other independent specialised national and international law firms.

INTERNATIONAL EXPERIENCE: The firm provides advice and assistance in cross-border transactions both to Italian clients making acquisitions abroad and to non-Italian clients investing in Italy. Partners of the firm act as arbitrators in national and international proceedings (ICC and UNCITRAL).

INTERNATIONAL CLIENTS: The firm assists major consulting companies, multinational industrial companies, Italian telecommunications companies, investment banks and several players in the private equity market.

MAIN INTERNATIONAL AREAS OF PRACTICE: The firm has significant and long-standing experience in mergers and acquisitions, joint ventures, corporate law and shareholders' agreements, licensing and intellectual property, EC and national anti-trust, construction contracts, real estate transactions and commercial contracts, both Italian and cross-border. Other areas of practice include take-overs, banking and finance law, private equity funds, information technology and employee stock option plans.

LANGUAGES: English, French, Italian

WORLDWIDE OFFICE CONTACTS

ITALY
Via D'Azeglio, 21, 40123, **Bologna**
Tel: + 39 051 222 551 **Fax:** + 39 051 222 428
Email: bologna@marlaw.it

Via Degli Omenoni, 2, 20421 **Milan**
Tel: +39 02 7201 0896 **Fax:** +39 02 7202 3904
Email: milano@marlaw.it

WORLDWIDE OFFICES

ITALY
Via D'Azeglio, 21, Bologna, 40123

Number of lawyers: 5
Managing partner: Roberto Ludergnani.

Marena, Bonvicini, Aghina e Ludergnani
STUDIO LEGALE

For other recommended firms see pages 1485-1520

MARQUES MENDES & ASSOCIADOS

HEAD OFFICE

Av. Eng. Duarte Pacheco, nº 19, 12º,
1070-100 Lisbon, Portugal
Tel: +351 21 382 63 00 **Fax:** +351 21 382 63 19

Email: marquesmendes@marquesmendes.pt

WORLDWIDE OFFICE CONTACTS

PORTUGAL
Av. Eng. Duarte Pacheco, nº 19, 12º, 1070-100 **Lisbon**
Tel: +351 21 382 63 00 **Fax:** +351 21 382 63 19
Email: marquesmendes@marquesmendes.pt

FIRM OVERVIEW

Managing partner: Mário Marques Mendes

Number of partners worldwide: 3
Number of other lawyers worldwide: 9

AREAS OF PRACTICE:

Banking and finance .... *%
Corporate .... *%
Insurance and reinsurance .... *%
Intellectual property .... *%
Litigation and arbitration .... *%
M&A .... *%
Telecommunications and IT .... *%
* Workload % not disclosed

M

FIRM OVERVIEW: The firm's practice covers a wide spectrum of business and commercial law, with special emphasis on corporate, finance (including banking, insurance and securities), project financing, EU and competition/anti-trust matters, M&A, IT, intellectual property, telecommunications, energy, tax, labour and real estate matters. It also includes strong litigation and arbitration practices. The firm is proud of its long-standing approach to the legal profession and commitment to excellence.

INTERNATIONAL EXPERIENCE: The firm's practice has always been internationally oriented. Currently, the large majority of the work handled by the firm involves international clients, with or without local subsidiaries, as well as referral work from well known international law firms, with which the firm has kept strong links since its formation.

INTERNATIONAL CLIENTS: The firm represents major national and multinational companies, including some of the top ranking Fortune 500 corporations, in a variety of sectors such as information technology (including computer hardware and software), consumer electronics, automotive industry, finance (including banking, insurance and securities), project financing, telecommunications, energy, media and entertainment, plastic and cement industries, pharmaceuticals, food and beverage industry, international air transport and transport infrastructures. The firm has also been retained by EC as well as national institutions and has advised and represented major companies and national public sector entities in cross-border issues and transactions.

MAIN INTERNATIONAL AREAS OF PRACTICE:

Corporate, commercial and M&A: From its inception, the firm has acted for international clients advising on all legal aspects of their investment, establishment and activity in Portugal. It has also handled corporate restructuring operations, including take-overs and mergers, spin-offs and split-offs, having conducted, where required, due diligence procedures.
Finance: The firm covers all areas of finance, including banking, insurance, securities, structured finance, project finance, leasing and factoring.
EU, competition/anti-trust: The firm has always been active in EC law and EC law related matters, notably competition/anti-trust and regulatory issues, intellectual property, anti-dumping, state aids and public procurement. It has been retained by both EC and national institutions, advised and represented public sector entities, as well as major corporations and associations of undertakings, in proceedings before Portuguese and EC authorities, and handled important litigation before national and EC courts. The firm has also assisted clients in transnational concentration operations having filed notifications and conducted the corresponding cases before both the EC Commission and Portuguese competition authorities.
IT (including computer hardware and software): The firm has long-standing experience representing some of the key players in the IT sector, advising on all IT matters, notably on computer software licensing and related issues. The firm has also been frequently involved in the negotiation of information technology outsourcing deals.
Telecommunications: The firm provides legal assistance to multinational and local telecommunications operators, covering a wide range of areas that include regulatory licensing and operational aspects. Lawyers of the firm have also been called to assess telecommunications legal and regulatory matters and their interrelation with other areas of law, in particular EC and EC related laws, notably competition/anti-trust.
Energy: The firm has been strongly involved in several aspects of the Portuguese energy market advising clients on energy and energy-related domestic and international transactions, also assisting in cases conducted at both national and EC levels.
Employment: The firm advises clients on all aspects of employment and other labour related issues, representing clients in negotiation procedures as well as before the courts.
Entertainment and media: The firm advises on the negotiation and drafting of production and licensing agreements in the areas of TV and films. It has also represented clients in important rights infringement litigation.
Litigation and arbitration: The firm has developed specific expertise in all areas of civil, commercial and labour litigation. In the area of EC law, it is frequently involved in cases conducted before both Portuguese and EC courts. Members of the firm have served as arbitrators in arbitration proceedings, having also represented clients in some important cases.

LANGUAGES: English, French, Italian, Portuguese, Spanish

MARQUES MENDES & ASSOCIADOS
Sociedade de Advogados . Attorneys at Law

For other recommended firms see pages 1485-1520

MARVAL, O'FARRELL & MAIRAL

HEAD OFFICE

Av Leandro N Alem 928,
1001 Buenos Aires, Argentina
Tel: +54 11 4310 0100 **Fax:** +54 11 4310 0200
Email: marval@marval.com.ar
Website: www.marval.com.ar

FIRM OVERVIEW

Managing partner: Julio Fernandez Moujan
Senior partner: Ernesto O'Farrell

Number of partners worldwide: 50
Number of other lawyers worldwide: 200

AREAS OF PRACTICE:

Banking and finance ....*%
Capital markets ....*%
Commercial and competition ....*%
Corporate, foreign investments, M&A ....*%
Intellectual property ....*%
Internet and information technology ....*%
Litigation, dispute resolution and arbitration ....*%
Real estate and construction ....*%
Tax ....*%
* Workload % not disclosed

WORLDWIDE OFFICE CONTACTS

ARGENTINA
Av Leandro N Alem 928, 1001 **Buenos Aires**
Tel: +54 11 4310 0100 **Fax:** +54 11 4310 0200
Email: marval@marval.com.ar

Obispo Trejo 655, 5000 **Córdoba**
Tel: +54 351 425 7634 **Fax:** +54 351 428 2512
Email: marval@marval.com.ar

Av. España 1340, 7th Floor, 5500 **Mendoza**
Tel: +54 261 429 2143 **Fax:** +54 261 428 2512
Email: marval@marval.com.ar

SPAIN
Serrano 26, 4th Floor, 28001 **Madrid**
Tel: +34 91 586 0648 **Fax:** +34 91 586 0777
Email: marval@marval.com.ar

USA
509 Madison Avenue, Suite 506, **New York** NY 10022
Tel: +1 212 838 4641 **Fax:** +1 212 751 3854
Email: marvalny@marval.com.ar

FIRM OVERVIEW: Founded in 1923, Marval O'Farrell & Mairal is one of the largest and oldest law firms in Argentina. The firm provides high quality legal advice and offers a creative and innovative approach. Comprising over 250 members, the firm provides a wide range of legal services to financial institutions, commerce and industry, and to diverse sections of government.

INTERNATIONAL EXPERIENCE: The firm is experienced in international business issues and the complexities of multi-jurisdictional transactions. It works closely with clients in seeking solutions to the competitive challenges facing international business.

INTERNATIONAL CLIENTS: Clients include commercial and investment banks, and a range of domestic and foreign companies, including many Fortune 500 companies and international organisations such as the World Bank, the International Finance Corporation (IFC) and the Inter-American Development Bank.

MAIN INTERNATIONAL AREAS OF PRACTICE:

Banking and finance: The firm advises on secured and unsecured credit facilities, sovereign and sub-sovereign credit: trade finance, leasing transactions, vendor and leveraged-lease financings, structured finance, project finance, government guaranteed securities, buyouts, acquisition finance, bank and commercial debtor restructurings, real property financing, and bank regulatory matters.
Capital markets: The firm handles structured receivable financing, money market preferred stock issues, asset purchase and sale programmes, and commercial programmes. It also advises on debt and equity securities offerings, securitisations, derivatives; synthetic products, risk reduction techniques and hedging agreements, debt and equity transactions, financial trusts, open and closed end mutual funds, capital markets regulation, and pension funds (AFJP's).
Commercial and competition: The firm advises on international trade law, commercial agreements (including distribution and supply agreements), sale, purchase and leasing agreements, anti-trust and unfair competition issues, and product liability and consumer related matters.
Corporate, foreign investment, M&A: The firm handles inward investments by foreign investors (including private equity funds), outward investments by Argentine investors. It also advises on M&A, due diligence audits, planning and structuring of joint ventures, shareholder agreements, restructurings, and spin-offs.
Insurance and reinsurance: The firm handles the incorporation and acquisition of local insurers, drafting and adaptation of insurance plans and policies to Argentine law, and the registration of foreign reinsurers and reinsurance brokers. It also advises insurance brokers on insurance litigation and alternative dispute resolution.
Intellectual property: Marval, O'Farrell & Mairal handles intellectual property protection and management, transfer of technology and licence agreements, and international franchising agreements and licensing and registration of software. It also advises on the protection of patents, utility models and ornamental design rights, general trademark matters and worldwide trademark protection.
Internet and IT: The firm advises internet start-ups on intellectual property, tax, corporate structure and governance, employee benefits and executive and consultant compensation packages. It handles all e-commerce and internet-related issues including user agreements, disclaimers, protection of intellectual property, encryption, digital signature, consumer protection, data protection, and on-line trading issues. The firm also advises on IT contracts, hardware contracts, software licensing, development and maintenance agreements, and outsourcing contracts.
Employment: The firm advises on matters including construction, manufacturing, energy, finance, and retail distribution. It handles employee stock options and benefit plans, labour related litigation and dispute resolution.
Tax and customs: The firm advises on the creation of tax efficient structures for domestic and international transactions, strategic tax planning and innovative tax driven products. It represents clients before the Argentine tax authorities and courts on customs matters and dumping claims.
Telecommunications and broadcasting: The firm handles a range of telecommunications and broadcasting issues.

LANGUAGES: English, French, German, Italian, Portuguese, Spanish

MASON HAYES & CURRAN

HEAD OFFICE

6 Fitzwilliam Square,
Dublin 2, Republic of Ireland
Tel: +353 1 614 5000 **Fax:** +353 1 614 5001

Email: mail@mhc.ie
Website: www.mhc.ie

WORLDWIDE OFFICE CONTACTS

REPUBLIC OF IRELAND
6 Fitzwilliam Square, 2, **Dublin**
Tel: +353 1 614 5000 **Fax:** +353 1 614 5001
Email: mail@mhc.ie

FIRM OVERVIEW

Managing partner: Declan Moylan
Senior partner: Maurice Curran

Number of partners worldwide: 20
Number of other lawyers worldwide: 42

AREAS OF PRACTICE:

Corporate/commercial/IT	45%
Litigation/arbitration/dispute resolution	35%
Banking/financial services	10%
Other	10%

M

FIRM OVERVIEW: Mason Hayes & Curran was formed in Dublin in 1968. Over the past five years it has grown rapidly, trebling in both size and turnover, and is now one of Ireland's largest law firms. The firm provides the full range of legal services, with the bulk of its work being for corporate, institutional and government clients. It is dedicated to maintaining close client/lawyer relationships. The firm also has a niche recoveries, insolvency and corporate bankruptcy practice.

INTERNATIONAL EXPERIENCE: The firm has experienced particular growth in its activities for international clients. It regularly receives instructions concerning Irish law from corporate clients based in the UK, USA, Germany, Denmark and other jurisdictions. Recent work includes representing Orange in its application for Ireland's third mobile telephony licence and in subsequent judicial review and appeal litigation, representing Allied Domecq in its acquisition of 49% of Cantrell & Cochrane Group from Guinness, representing FLS Aerospace Holding in its acquisition of TEAM Dublin from TEAM Aer Lingus and representing Dole Food Company in its acquisition of the Honduras and Guatemala interests of Fyffes. Representing Air Foyle Limited in its acquisition in 1999 and disposal in 2000 of a controlling interest in CityJet Limited, Lake Communications Limited in its sale of Topology Systems Limited to Cable & Wireless, DCC plc in its sale of International Translation & Publishing Limited to SDL plc and Shandwick International Limited in its acquisition of FCC Communications Limited.

INTERNATIONAL CLIENTS: Include Allied Domecq plc, Royal Liver Assurance plc, FLS Aerospace A/S, P&O, Dole Food Company, Haribo, Chr. Hansen A/S, Orange PLC, Universal Foods Corporation, United Healthcare Inc.

MAIN AREAS OF INTERNATIONAL PRACTICE:

Corporate deals and fundraisings: The practice is expanding rapidly with the boom in the Irish economy and the increased numbers of industrial setups, mergers and acquisitions. Fundraising services include advice on syndications, tax-based lending, asset finance, structured finance, securitisations, bond issues, derivatives and acquisitions finance.

Commercial disputes: The firm's commercial litigators have handled major competition cases, cases before the European Court of Justice and a wide range of banking-related litigation. The firm also handles insolvency-related, property, contractual, joint venture and shareholders' disputes, and tort cases in fiduciary duty, use of confidential information, fraud, professional negligence and tracing. It also has international arbitration and ADR expertise.

Intellectual property: The firm provides the full range of intellectual property advice, covering patent licensing, trade mark, registered designs and copyright protection and exploitation work. The contentious IP unit acts predominantly for foreign-based multinational companies.

IT (including telecommunications): Work includes drafting and negotiating software development agreements, technology licences, hardware supply, facilities management contracts and website design agreements. In February 1999 MHC became the first Irish law firm to establish a dedicated e-commerce Unit to serve and develop its clients' growing e legal needs. In May 2000 MHC introduced eMHC the next step in client e legal service. No longer a unit but a dedicated firm within the firm, eMHC advises Irish and International clients in all areas of e law. The firm helps clients protect, exploit and enforce intellectual property rights in technology and to resolve computer contract disputes. The telecommunications unit advises several long-established companies as well as a number of newly-licensed ones. Work includes advice on regulatory and licensing issues, competition, establishing operations in Ireland and on the negotiation of commercial agreements.

Energy and other areas of deregulation: This is an increasingly important area, due to the imminent deregulation of energy supply in Ireland. The firm advises clients on the implications of liberalisation and aims to provide an effective legal framework for their future activities.

Human resources law: This includes employment, health and safety law, and is one of the firm's most significant growth areas. The practice spans both contentious and non-contentious work, represents large employers or very senior employees. It helps clients anticipate and minimise problems, and has had a significant input into the company's M&A work.

LANGUAGES: English, French, German

MASON HAYES & CURRAN

SOLICITORS

For other recommended firms see pages 1485-1520

MASONS

HEAD OFFICE

30 Aylesbury Street,
London EC1R 0ER, United Kingdom
Tel: +44 20 7490 4000 **Fax:** +44 20 7490 2545

Website: www.masons.com

FIRM OVERVIEW

Senior partner: John Bishop
UK managing partner: Peter Wood
Worldwide managing Partner: Tony Bunch

Number of partners worldwide: 92
Number of other lawyers worldwide (excluding partners and trainees): 272

AREAS OF PRACTICE:

Area	%
Construction and engineering, energy and infrastructure	53%
Information and technology	11%
Project and finance	9%
Property, planning and environment	8%
Commercial dispute resolution	6%
Corporate and commercial	6%
Property litigation	4%
Insolvency	1%
Employment and pensions	2%

FIRM OVERVIEW: Established in 1948, Masons employs over 800 people in the UK, Europe and the Asia Pacific region. The firm has a distinctive reputation for its comprehensive range of services to the Information Technology, Construction and Engineering, Energy and Infrastructure industries. In addition the firm is also highly regarded for its national and international dispute avoidance and resolution expertise. In the UK, Masons operates through a network of offices which are located in the key commercial centres of London, Bristol, Edinburgh, Glasgow, Leeds and Manchester, International matters are handled by Masons' offices in Brussels, Dublin, Hong Kong, Guangzhou (PRC) and Singapore, as well as by the firm's UK based lawyers who work regularly in continental and central Europe, Scandinavia, the Middle East, the Pacific Rim, Africa and the Indian subcontinent.

INTERNATIONAL EXPERIENCE: The firm advises on international projects worldwide including airports, tunnels, motorways, rail, ports, water systems, power stations and hospitals. Recent projects include acting for the sponsor on a major port development in Malaysia; acting for the employer on the Bangalore Mass Rapid Transit System project; advising the South African Government on a privatised prison project in South Africa, and advising in connection with the procurement of the Korean High Speed Rail Project. Recent transactions include advising the Bank of Ireland on both a major IT outsourcing joint venture with Perot Systems and on BOI Fsharp offshore internet bank; advising the state owned nuclear electricity company of the Ukraine and the EBRD in connection with the rebuilding of sarcophagus No. 4 at Chernobyl; advising the English National Stadium on the application of the EU's rules in the procurement of a new stadium for England; acting for a major offshore contractor in a high value multi-forum dispute concerning a new-build FPSO; and, advising Anglian Water International on all project documentation aspects of the consortium tender for the first BOT water treatment plant in China.

WORLDWIDE OFFICE CONTACTS

BELGIUM
Avenue Louise 391 - Bte 1, B-1050, **Brussels**
Tel: + 32 2 646 0260 **Fax:** + 32 2 646 7323

CHINA
Suites 2118-2120, Dongshan Plaza, 69 Xian Lie Road Central, **Guangzhou**, 510095
Tel: + 86 20 8778 2788 **Fax:** + 86 20 8775 7518

HONG KONG
26th Floor, Central Plaza, 18 Harbour Road, **Hong Kong**
Tel: + 852 2521 5621 **Fax:** + 852 2845 2956

REPUBLIC OF IRELAND
61 Merrion Square, 2, **Dublin**
Tel: + 353 1 638 3838 **Fax:** + 353 1 638 3888

SINGAPORE
65 Chulia Street, #40-03 OCBC Centre, 049513, **Singapore**
Tel: + 65 339 8577 **Fax:** + 65 339 5122

UNITED KINGDOM
1-4 Portland Square, BS2 8RR, **Bristol**
Tel: + 44 117 924 5678 **Fax:** + 44 117 924 6699

9/10 St Andrew Square, EH2 2AF, **Edinburgh**
Tel: +44 131 718 6006 **Fax:** +44 131 718 6100

33 Bothwell Street, G2 6NL, **Glasgow**
Tel: + 44 141 248 4858 **Fax:** + 44 141 248 6655

Springfield House, 76 Wellington Street, LS1 2AY, **Leeds**
Tel: + 44 113 233 8905 **Fax:** + 44 113 245 4285

30 Aylesbury Street, EC1R 0ER, **London**
Tel: +44 20 7490 4000 **Fax:** +44 20 7490 2545

100 Barbirolli Square, M2 3SS, **Manchester**
Tel: + 44 161 234 8234 **Fax:** + 44 161 234 8235

INTERNATIONAL CLIENTS: Include ABB Lummus Global Ltd, Adtranz, Amec, Babcock International, Balfour Beatty, Bovis Europe, Coca Cola & Schweppes Beverages, Daewoo, Ernst & Young, El Camino, Foster Wheeler, Gulf Petrochemicals Industries Co., Hollandsche Beton Groep, ICL, Kvaerner Group, McCallagh International Inc., Mowlem, Norsk Hydro, Northumbrian Lyonnais International, P & O, Rizzani de Eccher, Samwhan Construction, Savoy Hotel Group, The Sumitomo Bank Limited, Westdeutsche Landesbank Girozentrale.

MAIN INTERNATIONAL AREAS OF PRACTICE: The firm's main reputation is for its services to the information and technology, construction and engineering, energy and infrastructure sectors. It advises in the key areas of project finance, corporate, commercial, intellectual property, insolvency, tax, employment, pensions, property, planning, environment and national and international dispute avoidance and resolution. The firm's major projects expertise is divided into sectors: water, transport, energy, health, education and accommodation. Other specialities include competition law, procurement, risk management, outsourcing, data protection, e-commerce, internet based new media, insurance, bonds and guarantees, health and safety, EU law, and international asset protection.

LANGUAGES: Afrikaans, Cantonese, Chinese, Dutch, English, Foo-chow, French, Greek, German, Hebrew, Hindi, Hokkien, Irish, Italian, Japanese, Malay, Mandarin, Polish, Punjabi, Russian, Spanish, Swedish, Swiss German, Turkish, Urdu

For other recommended firms see pages 1485-1520

MATHESON ORMSBY PRENTICE

HEAD OFFICE

30 Herbert Street,
Dublin 2, Republic of Ireland
Tel: +353 1 619 9000 **Fax:** +353 1 619 9010

Email: mop@mop.ie
Website: www.mop.ie

WORLDWIDE OFFICE CONTACTS

REPUBLIC OF IRELAND
30 Herbert Street, **Dublin** 2
Tel: +353 1 619 9000 **Fax:** +353 1 619 9010
Email: mop@mop.ie

UNITED KINGDOM
Pountney Hill House, 6 Laurence Pountney Hill, **London** EC4R OBL
Tel: + 44 20 7618 2800 **Fax:** + 44 20 7618 2880

USA
375 Forest Avenue, **Palo Alto** CA 94301-2521
Tel: + 1 650 470 0810 **Fax:** + 1 650 470 0811

FIRM OVERVIEW

Managing partner: Donal Roche

Number of partners worldwide: 37
Number of other professional fee-earners worldwide: 147

AREAS OF PRACTICE:
Corporate, financial services and tax 60%
Commercial litigation 20%
Commercial property 20%

M

FIRM OVERVIEW: Established in 1825, Matheson Ormsby Prentice is one of Ireland's largest corporate law firms. The firm is based in Dublin, and also has offices in London and Silicon Valley.
The firm's corporate focus is reflected in the division of the firm into four principal departments – corporate and commercial, banking and financial services, commercial property and commercial litigation. Specialist working groups comprising representatives from each of these departments co-operate to ensure the timely delivery and implementation of integrated advice and effective business solutions to the firm's clients.

INTERNATIONAL EXPERIENCE: The firm has extensive experience in advising clients based in North and South America, Europe, Africa, Asia and Australia on inward investment and other commercial and financial services transactions throughout Ireland.

INTERNATIONAL CLIENTS: Clients include governments, government agencies, supranational organisations and many of the world's leading corporations, commercial and investment banks and other financial institutions.

MAIN INTERNATIONAL AREAS OF PRACTICE:
Banking and financial services: The group advises on all areas of banking and finance including leasing and asset finance, structured finance, asset management, investment funds and investment services as well as the establishment of banks, insurance companies and financial institutions in the International Financial Service Centre (IFSC).
Corporate tax: The firm provides a full range of tax services, both transactional and advisory, advising on cross-border transactions in conjunction with tax counsel from other jurisdictions.
Commercial property: The group advises on all areas of commercial and industrial real estate, acquisition, finance, development and disposal. International and domestic clients include many leading property developers, property investors (institutional and private), retailers, lenders and inward investors.
Corporate finance and commercial law: The group provides advice on all aspects of general commercial law and corporate finance requirements of international and domestic clients including M&A, MBOs, MBIs, venture capital funds, stock exchange listings, flotations, shareholder agreements, public take-overs, joint ventures and strategic alliances.
Commercial litigation: The litigation group provides expertise aimed at managing and resolving a broad range of commercial and other disputes in an efficient and cost-effective manner for international and domestic clients by way of negotiation, arbitration or court proceedings. The group has comprehensive experience in all aspects of international disputes.
Intellectual property: Clients include newspapers, publishers, broadcasters, software houses, film and television production companies, authors, artists and copyright collection societies, as well as industrial and service companies. The group has expertise in all areas of litigation and cross border enforcements.
Information technology: The firm was the first amongst Irish law firms to establish a dedicated group specialising in IT law. The group advises on all aspects of computer, telecommunications, e-commerce and internet law. It acts for some of the largest international and IT and telecoms companies as well as some of the largest corporate users of IT.
Project finance/PPP: The firm advises on projects under the Irish PPP programme from the initial structuring and tendering stage, including legislative and regulatory issues, to financing and final contractual negotiations.
Employment: The group is multi-disciplinary and draws on expertise from other practice areas including tax. It advises on all aspects of employer/employee relations and both Irish and European employment and pensions legislation.

LANGUAGES: Dutch, French, German, Japanese, Spanish

MATHESON
ORMSBY
PRENTICE

Dublin
London
Palo Alto

For other recommended firms see pages 1485-1520

MAW HTOON & PARTNERS

HEAD OFFICE

Dagon Tower, Suite #2, 10th Floor, No 190/192, Shwegondine Road, Bahan Township, Yangon, Myanmar
Tel: +95 1 545 537-8 **Fax:** +95 1 545 575

Email: shambhala@mptmail.net.mm

FIRM OVERVIEW

Managing partner: U Ye Htoon

Number of lawyers worldwide: 7

AREAS OF PRACTICE:
Aviation ....*%
Banking and finance ....*%
Corporate ....*%
Environmental laws ....*%
Government contacts ....*%
Insurance ....*%
Intellectual property and copyright ....*%
Investment ....*%
Labour ....*%
Litigation and arbitration ....*%
Oil and gas ....*%
Taxation ....*%
Transport ....*%
* Workload % not disclosed

FIRM OVERVIEW: The firm was founded in 1995 by Advocate U Ye Htoon, a graduate of the Bucknell University, and son of Barrister U Chan Htoon who is the former Associate Justice of the Supreme Court and the author of the first constitution of Burma. The firm is one of Myanmar's principal law firms offering legal advice to clients both domestic and foreign. It focuses on corporate, litigation, arbitration, trademarks and investment.

INTERNATIONAL EXPERIENCE: Over the years the firm has developed particular expertise in advising international clients on environmental law, infrastructure investments, oil and gas, corporate and arbitration. It has established relationships with law firms worldwide.

INTERNATIONAL CLIENTS: The firm's clients comprise foreign companies, banks and organisations including Total Oil & Gas Company of France, Daewoo Corporation of Korea, Hind International Investment of Hong Kong, Behn Meyer Chemical Company of Germany, Thai Gypsum Products Public Company of Thailand, Jim Styers' Dolphin World Company of USA.

MAIN INTERNATIONAL AREAS OF PRACTICE: The firm handles work in a wide range of areas including banking, corporate, trademarks, insurance, litigation and arbitration.

LANGUAGES: English, Japanese, Hindi, Myanmar

WORLDWIDE OFFICE CONTACTS

MYANMAR
Dagon Tower, Suite #2, 10th Floor, No 190/192, Shwegondine Road, Bahan Township, **Yangon**
Tel: +95 1 545 537-8 **Fax:** +95 1 545 575
Email: shambhala@mptmail.net.mm

M

MAYER, BROWN & PLATT

HEAD OFFICE

190 South LaSalle Street, Suite 3900,
Chicago IL 60603-3441, USA
Tel: +1 312 782 0600 **Fax:** +1 312 701 7711

Website: www.mayerbrown.com

FIRM OVERVIEW

Chairpersons: Tyrone C. Fahner, Jason H.P. Kravitt
Managing partner: Debora de Hoyas

Number of partners worldwide: 324
Number of other lawyers worldwide: 659

AREAS OF PRACTICE:

Litigation and arbitration	25%
Corporate and securities	18%
Finance, banking and insurance	15%
Oil, gas and real estate	12%
Tax	10%
Competition and trade	8%
Securitisation	8%
Other	4%

M

FIRM OVERVIEW: Founded in 1881, Mayer, Brown & Platt specialises in securitisation, banking, transfer pricing, and capital markets transactions. Other prominent practice areas include global trade, project finance, competition, international arbitration and litigation, including the foremost US appellate practice.

INTERNATIONAL EXPERIENCE:
Transatlantic fibre optic cables: The firm has represented lenders in the financing of two major undersea fibre-optic cable-laying projects. Atlantic Crossing One will link the US to the United Kingdom, Germany, and the Netherlands in a continuous loop. GlobeNet will connect the US with South America with similar technology.
Turkmenistan settlement: The firm has succesfully advised Turkmenistan's Ministry of Oil & Gas Industry and Mineral Resources on an arbitration involving claims of US$2.1 billion in alleged lost profits.
Russian gold mine: The firm represented the lenders and lead arrangers in the first mining project financing in Russia to be funded by commercial banks and not solely by multilateral lenders. It was recognised by a large financial publication as one of the most prominent deals of 2000.
Mexican power plant: The firm represented the lenders and arrangers in the financing of a US$435 million power plant in Guanajuto, Mexico. The deal included the first Ex-Im Bank construction guarantee, the first financing through commercial paper, and the first incorporating merchant capacity. It was also recognised by a large financial publication as one of the most prominent deals of 2000.
UK defence industry giant: The firm assisted General Electric Corporation (now Marconi PLC) in two major US acquisitions (a broadband switching equipment maker for US$4.5 billion and a telecom networking provider for $2.1 billion) as part of its bold transformation from the UK's leading defence industry business into a networking equipment company.
Deutsche Telekom acquisition: The firm assisted DT in the US$2 billion purchase of MediaOne assets in Poland, Hungary, and Russia, the largest acquisition ever in Eastern Europe.
China licenses: The firm has set up joint ventures with reliable partners, and secured operating licenses in China on behalf of major US companies, one of which was the third such license ever granted.

WORLDWIDE OFFICE CONTACTS

FRANCE
13 Avenue Hoche, 75008 **Paris**
Tel: +33 1 53 53 43 43 **Fax:** +33 1 53 96 03 83

GERMANY
Kaiser-Wilhelm-Ring 27-29, 50672 **Cologne**
Tel: +49 221 5771 100 **Fax:** +49 221 5771 199

UNITED KINGDOM
Bucklersbury House, 3 Queen Victoria Street, **London** EC4N 8EL
Tel: +44 20 7246 6200 **Fax:** +44 20 7329 4465

USA
Bank of America Corporate Center, 100 North Tryon Street, Suite 2400, **Charlotte** NC 28202
Tel: +1 704 377 3500 **Fax:** +1 704 377 2033

190 South LaSalle Street, Suite 3900, **Chicago** IL 60603-3441
Tel: +1 312 782 0600 **Fax:** +1 312 701 7711

700 Louisiana Street, Suite 3600, **Houston** TX 77002-2730
Tel: +1 713 221 1651 **Fax:** +1 713 224 6410

350 South Grand Avenue, 25th Floor, **Los Angeles** CA 90071-1503
Tel: +1 213 229 9500 **Fax:** +1 213 625 0248

1675 Broadway, **New York** NY 10019-5820
Tel: +1 212 506 2500 **Fax:** +1 212 262 1910

1909 K Street, N.W, **Washington DC** 20006-1101
Tel: +1 202 263 3000 **Fax:** +1 202 263 3300

ASSOCIATED OFFICES

CHINA
1504 China World Trade Center, No. 1, Jianguomenwai Avenue, **Beijing** 100004
Tel: +86 10 6505 5319 **Fax:** +86 10 6505 5323

Independent correspondent: Jáuregui, Navarrete, Nader y Rojas, S.C.Torre Arcos, Paseo de los Tamarindos No. 400-B, Col. Bosques de las Lomas, 05120, Mexico, D.F.

INTERNATIONAL CLIENTS: In addition to its traditional client base in the US, Mayer, Brown & Platt has expanded globally to represent clients in Central and Eastern Europe, Russia, Central Asia, China, Latin America, Australia, India and Africa. International clients include Credit Suisse, BASF, Deutsche Telekom, Societe Generale, ABN-AMRO, Abril, Marconi, ExIm Bank, and Daimler-Chrysler.

MAIN INTERNATIONAL AREAS OF PRACTICE Work handled includes conventional finance, structured bank finance; corporate and M&A; asset securitisation; capital markets and securities; fund management and financial services regulation; commodities and derivatives; international arbitration and global trade.

LANGUAGES: Chinese, English, French, German, Italian, Japanese, Portuguese, Russian, Spanish

For other recommended firms see pages 1485-1520

MAYORA Y MAYORA

HEAD OFFICE

15 calle 1-04, Zona 10, Edificio Céntrica Plaza, 3er. Nivel, Of. 301
Guatemala City 01010, Guatemala
Tel: +502 366 25 31 **Fax:** +502 366 25 40/41

Email: mayora&mayora@gua.gbm.net

FIRM OVERVIEW

Senior partners: Eduardo Mayora Dawe, Eduardo Mayora Alvarado

Number of partners worldwide: 2
Number of other lawyers worldwide: 6

AREAS OF PRACTICE:

Corporate	20%
Intellectual property	20%
Telecommunications	20%
Banking and finance	10%
Insurance and reinsurance	10%
Litigation and arbitration	10%
Securities and financial markets	10%

FIRM OVERVIEW: The firm was founded by Eduardo Mayora Dawe, a lawyer with over 40 years of professional experience. The firm, founded over 30 years ago, has maintained the same structure for the past 15 years and has served many clients on a continuing basis. It has also served multinational companies on a case by case basis.

INTERNATIONAL EXPERIENCE: Mayora & Mayora has been in international practice for over four decades. Many of the firm's lawyers are members of various international lawyers' associations and networks. The firm has been actively involved in a number of significant transactions covering foreign investment, franchising, privatisation and acquisitions.

INTERNATIONAL CLIENTS: The firm's client base includes large local companies such as Credomátic de Guatemala, S.A., Bolsa de Valores Nacional, S.A. GBM de Guatemala, S.A.; banks such as Citibank Sucursal Guatemala, Banco Bilbao Vizcaya, Bac Valores Guatemala; insurance companies such as Seguros Alianza; and branches or subsidiaries of foreign corporations such as Telecomunicaciones de Guatemala, Texaco Guatemala Inc. and Kellogg Company.

MAIN INTERNATIONAL AREAS OF PRACTICE:

Banking and finance: Mayora & Mayora covers all areas of banking and finance, including secured and syndicated loan transactions and guarantees, structured finances, project finance, leasing and tax-based finance.

Corporate: The firm advises on all aspects of general corporate law, including international contracts.

Insurance and reinsurance: The firm advises both local and international insurance companies.

Intellectual property: The firm specialises in trademarks, patents and other intellectual property rights. Its lawyers are involved in the negotiation of licence agreements and advise on infringement disputes and other aspects of IP law.

Litigation and arbitration: Mayora & Mayora deals with commercial litigation, national and international arbitration. Its lawyers are frequently involved in cases before the Guatemalan courts, including the Supreme Court and have been involved in various matters under the rules of the International Chamber of Commerce and the ICSID.

Securities and financial markets: Mayora & Mayora advises clients on Guatemalan law pertaining to fund, securities and derivatives. The firm also advises on the structure of investment firms and license their operations.

Telecommunications: The firm advises on all aspects telecoms and offers advice to significant parties in the telecommunications market.

LANGUAGES: English, French, Spanish

WORLDWIDE OFFICE CONTACTS

GUATEMALA
15 calle 1-04, Zona 10, Edificio Céntrica Plaza, 3er. Nivel, Of. 301,
Guatemala City 01010
Tel: +502 366 25 31 **Fax:** +502 366 25 40/41
Email: mayora&mayora@gua.gbm.net

McCANN FITZGERALD

HEAD OFFICE

2 Harbourmaster Place, International Financial Services Centre, Dublin 1, Republic of Ireland
Tel: +353 1 829 0000 **Fax:** +353 1 829 0010

Email: postmaster@mccann-fitzgerald.ie
Website: www.mccann-fitzgerald.ie

FIRM OVERVIEW

Chairman: Ronan Molony

Number of partners worldwide: 53
Number of other lawyers worldwide: over 130

AREAS OF PRACTICE:
Corporate and commercial 26%
Commercial disputes 26%
Banking and financial services 25%
Property 23%

FIRM OVERVIEW: Established in 1829, McCann FitzGerald is one of Ireland's largest law firms, with 53 partners and a total staff of over 300 based in offices in Dublin, Brussels, New York and London. It is a full service law firm with a focus on corporate and banking law, commercial property and commercial dispute resolution. The firm has experienced significant growth over the past 30 years. Its practice areas today closely mirror the sectors and activities that have seen the most significant growth in Ireland in recent years.

INTERNATIONAL EXPERIENCE: In addition to its offices in London, Brussels and New York, the firm is also represented in Belfast through the North South Legal Alliance, which it has formed with L'Estrange & Brett, one of the leading corporate and commercial law firms in Northern Ireland. They work together in matters where advice is required in both Northern Ireland and the Republic of Ireland.

INTERNATIONAL CLIENTS: Clients are predominantly corporate, comprising domestic and foreign-owned enterprises in equal proportions. They include major commercial and investment banks and financial institutions, both in Ireland and overseas, as well as Irish corporates, multinationals, regulatory bodies and state and semi-state organisations.

MAIN INTERNATIONAL AREAS OF PRACTICE:
Corporate and commercial: The firm's corporate and commercial department is the largest single department of the firm and acts for a wide variety of Irish and international clients on all areas of company and business law, including the establishment of business operations in Ireland by overseas companies in electronics, software, pharmaceuticals and healthcare.
Commercial disputes: Activities include advising clients preparing to make claims or adopt positions that may encounter opposition, as well as those seeking to avoid situations likely to give rise to claims by others against themselves. The firm also handles formal dispute resolution procedures, litigation and arbitration, along with mediation and other 'alternative' dispute resolution processes.
Banking and financial services: Activities include advising on secured and unsecured lending, aircraft finance, ship finance, film finance, project finance, commercial property finance and syndicated credits.

WORLDWIDE OFFICE CONTACTS

BELGIUM
Avenue de Cortenbergh 89, Kortenberglaan 89, 1000 **Brussels**
Tel: +32 2 740 0370 **Fax:** +32 2 740 0371
Email: postmaster@mccann-fitzgerald.ie

UNITED KINGDOM
St. Michael's House, 1 George Yard, Lombard Street, **London** EC3V 9DF
Tel: +44 20 7621 1000 **Fax:** +44 20 7621 9000
Email: postmaster@mccann-fitzgerald.ie

USA
156 West 56th Street, **New York,** NY 10019
Tel: +1 212 237 1078 **Fax:** +1 212 237 1215
Email: postmaster@mccann-fitzgerald.ie

ASSOCIATED OFFICES

NORTHERN IRELAND
North South Legal Alliance with L'Estrange & Brett, Arnott House, 12-16 Bridge Street, **Belfast** BT1 1LS
Tel: +44 28 90 230 426 **Fax:** +44 28 90 236 496
Email: law@landbrett.co.uk
Contact: Alan Hewitt

Property: The firm's activities in this area include the acquisition and disposal of property; property development, including shopping centres, office parks, industrial parks, residential developments, apartment blocks, hotels and leisure developments; financing arrangements; tax incentives/benefits; management structures; property joint ventures; planning advice and environmental advice and audits.

LANGUAGES: Afrikaans, French, German, Italian, Spanish

WORLDWIDE OFFICES

BELGIUM
Avenue de Cortenbergh 89, Kortenberglaan 89, 1000 Brussels
Contact: Damian Collins

Number of partners: 1
Number of other lawyers: 1

Office profile: With a presence in Brussels since the 1970s, it is the only Irish law firm to have a fully-staffed office there. It assists the firm's Irish and international clientele in matters of EU law.

UNITED KINGDOM
St. Michael's House, 1 George Yard, Lombard Street, London EC3V 9DF
Contact: John Cronin
Number of partners: 2
Number of other lawyers: 4

Office profile: The London office, established in 1986, is the largest London office of an Irish law firm, with two resident partners. It advises on major Irish and international corporate and financial services work. The office has close contacts with many City and UK law firms, regularly advising them and their clients on Irish law and cross-border transactions.

For other recommended firms see pages 1485-1520

McCARTHY TÉTRAULT

Suite 4700, Toronto Dominion Bank Tower,
Toronto, Ontario M5K 1E6, Canada
Tel: +1 416 362 1812
Fax: +1 416 868 0673

Email: toronto@mccarthy.ca
Website: www.mccarthy.ca

FIRM OVERVIEW

National chairman: James C. McCartney, QC

Number of partners worldwide: 362
Number of other lawyers worldwide: 395

AREAS OF PRACTICE:

Corporate finance	30%
Litigation	26%
Banking	12%
IP and high tech	8%
Property	7%
Tax	6%
Other	11%

FIRM OVERVIEW: McCarthy Tétrault is Canada's national law firm. It is a single, fully integrated national partnership consisting of more than 750 lawyers and patent and trade-mark agents who provide services in English and French from offices in Vancouver, Surrey, Calgary, London, Toronto, Ottawa, Montréal, Québec, New York and London, England. McCarthy Tétrault is the largest law firm in Canada acting in local, national and international matters in the context of a Canadian legal system which is based on common and civil law and federal and provincial legislation. The firm provides clients with legal expertise and advice in banking and insolvency; business; communications and entertainment; competition and antitrust; constitutional/administrative/regulatory law; corporate finance and securities; estates, wills and trust; intellectual property; Internet and e-commerce; labour and employment; litigation; natural resources; pensions and retirement income planning; real estate; municipal and environmental; taxation; and technology.

INTERNATIONAL EXPERIENCE: McCarthy Tétrault's international experience includes a wide variety of telecommunications, mining, oil, gas and power transactions and other work in Asia, the Middle East, Africa, North America, Central America, South America, Europe and the former Soviet Union. The firm develops innovative loan and security documentation in emerging markets where the legal structures for sophisticated secured lending transactions are not fully developed. In addition, it deals with lending, insolvency, bank financing, financial services regulation, electronic banking and innovative project finance. Examples of the firm's recent work include representation of The European Bank for Reconstruction and Development (EBRD) in different countries providing advice on telecom regulation; interconnection issues; licensing of rural telecom operators; preparation of universal service legislation; strategy for mobile licensing; bank capitalisation investments; power projects including Zimbabwe Electric Supply Authority re Gokwe North Power Station; privatisation of electricity distribution network in Philippines; mining projects including: Antamina copper project in Peru; private placement in Canada for Ivernia West; restructuring of Gencor's off-shore holdings; investment in Tunisian base metals project; reorganization of local recovery joint venture in Ukraine. The firm also undertakes international commercial arbitration.

WORLDWIDE OFFICE CONTACTS

CANADA

Suite 3300, 421-7th Avenue SW, **Calgary**, Alberta T2P 4K9
Tel: +1 403 260 3500 **Fax:** +1 403 260 3501
Email: calgary@mccarthy.ca

Suite 2000, One London Place, 255 Queens Avenue, **London,** Ontario N6A 5R8
Tel: +1 519 660 3587 **Fax:** +1 519 660 3599
Email: london@mccarthy.ca

Le Windsor, 1170 rue Peel, **Montréal**, Québec H3B 4S8
Tel: +1 514 397 4100 **Fax:** +1 514 875 6246
Email: montreal@mccarthy.ca

The Chambers, Suite 1400, 40 Elgin Street, **Ottawa**, Ontario K1P 5K6
Tel: +1 613 238 2000 **Fax:** +1 613 563 9386
Email: ottawa@mccarthy.ca

Le Complexe St-Amable, 1150 rue de Claire-Fontaine, 7e étage, **Québec**, Québec GIR 5G4
Tel: +1 418 521 3000 **Fax:** +1 418 521 3099
Email: quebec@mccarthy.ca

Suite 4700, Toronto Dominion Bank Tower, **Toronto**, Ontario M5K 1E6
Tel: +1 416 362 1812 **Fax:** +1 416 868 0673
Email: toronto@mccarthy.ca

Suite 1300, Station Tower, Gateway, 13401-108th Avenue, **Surrey**, British Columbia V3T 5T3
Tel: +1 604 583 9100 **Fax:** +1 604 583 9150
Email: ephillips@mccarthy.ca

Suite 1300, Pacific Centre, 777 Dunsmuir Street, **Vancouver**, British Columbia V7Y 1K2
Tel: +1 604 643 7100 **Fax:** +1 604 643 7900
Email: vancouver@mccarthy.ca

UNITED KINGDOM

Pountney Hill House, 6 Laurence Pountney Hill, **London,** EC4R 0BL
Tel: +44 20 7618 2888 **Fax:** +44 20 7618 2880
Email: londonuk@mccarthy.ca

USA

25th Floor, One New York Plaza, **New York,** NY 10004-1980
Tel: +1 212 785 6410 **Fax:** +1 212 785 6438

INTERNATIONAL CLIENTS: The governments of Indonesia, Jordan, Cameroon, Colombia, Costa Rica, Burkina Faso, Nepal, Morocco, Nigeria, Chad, Gabon, Sri Lanka (all telecommunications work), Kazakhstan, Ukraine, Ivernia West plc, Grupo Mexico, Impala Platinum Holdings Ltd, Lionore Mining International Ltd, Billiton (mining), Argentina, Zimbabwe, Philippines, Congo, South Africa (power work), the Secretary of Communications and Transport of Mexico, the telecommunications regulatory commissions of Sri Lanka and Jordan, the World Bank, the EBRD, the CRTC, Atomic Energy of Canada Limited, Noranda, Falconbridge, Antamina, Cornucopia, Cominco Resources, Euromin S.A. Investment, FirstMiss Gold, Hemlo Gold, Gencor/Eldorado, Korea Zinc, Northern Orion, Scorpion Minerals.

McCarthy Tétrault

M

McDERMOTT, WILL & EMERY

HEAD OFFICE

227 West Monroe Street,
Chicago IL 60606-5096, USA
Tel: +1 312 372 2000 **Fax:** +1 312 984 7700

Website: www.mwe.com

FIRM OVERVIEW

Managing partner: Larry Gerber

Number of partners worldwide: 477
Number of other lawyers worldwide: 432

AREAS OF PRACTICE:

Trial (Litigation) 21%
Corporate 20%
Regulation and government affairs 16%
Health law 13%
Taxation 13%
Intellectual property 10%
Employee benefits 5%
Estate planning 5%

FIRM OVERVIEW: McDermott, Will & Emery is an international law firm with more than 900 lawyers in three international and eight US offices. The firm represents a wide range of industrial, financial and commercial enterprises, both publicly and privately held, and is experienced in representing clients before government agencies and congressional committees on various administrative and substantive legal issues.

INTERNATIONAL EXPERIENCE: Firm lawyers have been involved in cross-border matters on every continent and in virtually every sector of business. Matters of an international nature include cross-border mergers and acquisitions; joint ventures; financings; corporate restructuring and reorganisations; the structuring of distributorship, licensing and agency arrangements; the negotiation of commercial contracts; compliance with investment laws; privatisation; cross-border tax planning; international litigation and dispute resolution; public law; enviromental; construction and real estate; banking; anti-competition; e-business and intellectual property, acquisitions, dispositions and financings.

INTERNATIONAL CLIENTS: The firm has represented clients from more than 40 countries and has advised on matters in more than 60 countries. Clients include, those in accounting, agriculture, architecture and engineering, broadcasting, commercial and investment banking, construction, consumer finance, distribution, financial services, food and beverage processing, health care, insurance, investment syndication, manufacturing, mining, oil and gas development and production, publishing, real estate, retailing, savings and loans, technology, telecommunications, utilities and venture capital.

MAIN AREAS OF PRACTICE:

Antitrust and trade regulation (competition): The practice is comprised of approximately 50 lawyers, many of whom have prior government experience with the Federal Trade Commission, the Antitrust Division of the Department of Justice or the office of a State Attorney General.
Banking and finance: The firm has an integrated finance and banking team of more than 70 lawyers, with recognised experience in all areas of US, UK and international corporate finance.
Bankruptcy: The firm represents debtors, trustees, and various creditor and equality constituencies on a regular basis, including banks, bondholders, trade creditors, credit corporations and acquirors in major restructuring.
E-business: The firm's e-business group comprises lawyers in various offices and practice groups around the world. The group is led by a core team of full time e-business lawyers with historic practices in this area. The firm's e-business group brings practical commercial experience, a familiarity with established and innovative business models, and a sophisticated level of strategic advice based upon extensive work in the field. The firm offers e-commerce 'audits' for clients ranging from the largest multinationals to new media companies and dot.com start-ups.
Environmental law: The practice includes many lawyers with substantial governmental and private experience and involves representing clients in the practical and legal aspects of environmental compliance and liability. Areas of experience include hazardous wastes, toxic substances, air and water pollution, solid waste, land reclamation, land development, wetlands regulation, storage tank regulation, OSHA hazard communication, right to know laws and environmental impact statements.
Public international law and litigation: The firm has significant experience in public international law and international litigation. The firm's lawyers also act as legal counsel to many governments, and have acted as counsel to the United Nations Organization and to OPEC. The firm's litigation lawyers are regularly involved in international arbitrations.
Labour, employment and OSHA: The practice has considerable experience in all employment-related matters, both contentious and non-contentious. Its lawyers advise on wrongful and unfair dismissal, executive severance,

WORLDWIDE OFFICE CONTACTS

LITHUANIA
Smetanos 6-16, 2600 **Vilnius**
Tel: +370 2 79 10 00 **Fax:** +370 2 22 79 55

RUSSIA
Mosenka Plaza, Sadovaya-Samotechnaya Ulitsa 24/27, 103051 **Moscow**
Tel: +7 095 792 5270 **Fax:** +7 095 792 5271

UNITED KINGDOM
7 Bishopsgate, **London** EC2N 3AQ
Tel: +44 20 7577 6900 **Fax:** +44 20 7577 6950

USA
28 State Street, **Boston** MA 02109-1775
Tel: +1 617 535 4000 **Fax:** +1 617 535 3800

227 West Monroe Street, **Chicago** IL 60606-5096
Tel: +1 312 372 2000 **Fax:** +1 312 984 7700

18191 Von Karman Avenue, Suite 1100, **Irvine,** CA 92612-0187
Tel: +1 949 851-0633 **Fax:** +1 949 851 9348

2049 Century Park East, **Los Angeles** CA 90067-3208
Tel: +1 310 277 4110 **Fax:** +1 310 277 4730

2700 Sand Hill Road, **Menlo Park** CA 94025-7020
Tel: +1 650 233-550 **Fax:** +1 650 233 5599

201 South Biscayne Boulevard, **Miami** FL 33131-4336
Tel: +1 305 358 3500 **Fax:** +1 305 347 6500

50 Rockefeller Plaza, **New York** NY 10020-1605
Tel: +1 212 547 5400 **Fax:** +1 212 547 5444

600 13th Street NW, **Washington DC** 20005-3096
Tel: +1 202 756 8000 **Fax:** +1 202 756 8087

For other recommended firms see pages 1485-1520

confidentiality and restrictive covenants, breaches of fiduciary duty, fraud by employees, sex/race/disability discrimination, early retirement programs, development of employee manuals, wage-hour compliance, workers' compensation, substance abuse programs, drug testing, equal pay, Working Time Regulations, union recognition and works councils, industrial disputes, EU employment law, corporate governance, TUPE, the employment aspects of acquisitions, disposals and outsourcing, OSHA, and general labour and employment matters.

M&A: The firm's lawyers have extensive experience and advise continuously regarding the purchase, sale and merger of businesses. The firm handles takeovers, acquisitions and disposals, MBOs and MBIs, LBOs and LBIs, and reorganisations and restructurings.

Real estate: The practice advises regarding the acquisitions, dispositions, financing, development and utilisation of commercial and industrial real estate. Several of the firm's lawyers have substantial experience in serving as landlord's or tenant's counsel in negotiating and drafting complex leases covering all forms of real property.

Securities: The firm has a significant practice relating to the public offerings of equity and debt securities. Its corporate lawyers represent issuers who are repeatedly in the public markets as well as those making a first public offering. It also represents underwriting syndicates headed by some of the largest investment banking firms in the world. This work involves all phases of the financing, from planning to closing. The practice also handles public offerings involving industrial revenue bonds and limited partnership interests.

Telecommunications: The firm's telecommunications lawyers advise on strategic, regulatory, commercial and transactional matters to telecoms operators, ISPs, investors, manufacturers and users of communications services. Experience includes working closely with businesses in the conveyancing industries of communications, IT and media.

LANGUAGES: More than 200 of the firm's lawyers are proficient in one or more foreign languages, including Afrikaans, Cantonese, Creole, Croatian, Danish, English, French, German, Greek, Haitian-Creole, Hebrew, Hindi, Italian, Japanese, Korean, Lao, Latin, Lithuanian, Mandarin, Norwegian, Polish, Portuguese, Romanian, Russian, Spanish, Swedish, Turkish, Ukrainian, Yoruba.

HEAD OFFICE:

227 West Monroe Street, Chicago, IL 60606-5096

Number of lawyers: 294

Main areas of work: Corporate, employee benefits, estate planning, health law, international law, government and regulatory affairs, intellectual property, trial law and taxation.

Office profile: McDermott, Will & Emery's head office opened in Chicago in 1934.

WORLDWIDE OFFICES

LITHUANIA

Smetanos 6-6, 2600 Vilnius

Supervising attorney: Eugenija Sutkiene
Number of lawyers: 5

Main areas of work: Lawyers in the Vilnius office advise clients on commercial law, especially in connection with establishing international joint ventures and privatisations in the Baltics. These lawyers also handle legal matters involving real estate, taxation, project and lending finance, as well as business litigation.

Top clients: Representation of companies involved in manufacturing, telecommunications, oil and gas, and construction, as well as financial institutions and health care organisations. The firm has also served as counsel to the World Bank, the European Bank for Reconstruction and Development, the Nordic Investment Bank, the Overseas Private Investment Corporation and the United States and British embassies in Lithuania.

Office profile: The Vilnius office was established in 1991. The firm's Vilnius lawyers, licensed professionals, educated in Lithuania and at institutions in the US and Europe, work closely with experienced US and UK lawyers. The office is staffed with translators who are fully conversant in English, Lithuanian and Russian terminology.

RUSSIA

Mosenka Plaza, Sadovaya-Samotechnaya Ulitsa 24/27, 103051 Moscow

Supervising attorney: Gennady M. Khareyn
Number of lawyers: 2

Main areas of work: The firm's Moscow office provides clients with advice in connection with capital markets and financial services, project finance, privatisation, joint ventures, tax compliance and planning, intellectual property, real estate, environmental regulation, litigation and corporate advice, among other areas.

Top clients: The Moscow office has advised major financial institutions. multinational corporations, start-up ventures, insurance companies, governmental agencies and numerous Western businesses and private investors. Representation also includes Russian clients regarding their US and international business activities.

UNITED KINGDOM

7 Bishopsgate, London EC2N 3AQ

Managing partner: William F. Charney
Number of lawyers: 57

Main areas of work: Banking, capital markets and financial services; corporate, corporate finance; employment; intellectual property, information technology, e-business; litigation and dispute resolution; pensions; taxation; and telecommunications.

Top clients: Bank One, BAE Systems, British Amercian Tobacco, Caterpillar, Dominos Pizza, Dredner Kleinwort Benson, Korea Asset Management Corporation, Levi Strauss, London and Regional Properties, Motorola, One.Tel, J. Sainsbury, Signet Group, State Street Bank, Storm Telecommunications, TotalFinaElf, United Airlines, and Zeus Technology.

Highlight deals: Korea Asset Management Corporation on the US$5 billion Daewoo debt restructuring; One.Tel on its bid for a UK UMTS licence; Storm Telecommunications on its buy-out from Telenor.

Office profile: The London office was established in 1998 and has grown quickly to become a full-service law practice providing comprehensive and cross-border legal services to a broad range of international and domestic corporate, institutional, governmental and private clients.

USA

28 State Street, Boston MA 02109-1775

Managing partner: Doron Ezickson
Number of lawyers: 113

Main areas of work: One of the largest firms in Boston, the lawyers in the firm's Boston office practice in areas of corporate and securities; emerging companies; employee benefits; energy services; environmental law; estate

M

McDERMOTT, WILL & EMERY

planning; health law; intellectual property; international law; labour and employment; litigation/dispute resolution; private equity; real estate; telecommunications; and tax.

USA
18191 Von Karmen Avenue, Irvine CA 92612-0187

Managing partner: Fay Morisseau
Number of lawyers: 19

2049 Century Park East, Los Angeles CA 90067-3208

Managing partner: Donald Goldman
Number of lawyers: 68

2700 Sand Hill Road, Menlo Park CA 94025-7020

Managing partner: Anthony de Alcuaz
Number of lawyers: 11

Main areas of work: The lawyers in the firm's California offices practice in the areas of corporate, emerging companies, intellectual property, labour and employment, litigation/dispute resolution, M&A, and private equity.

USA
201 South Biscayne Boulevard, Miami FL 33131-4336

Managing partner: Ira Coleman
Number of lawyers: 24

Main areas of work: The lawyers in the firm's Miami office concentrate their practice on banking, bankruptcy, construction, corporate and securities, health care, litigation/dispute resolution, maritime and real estate.

USA
50 Rockefeller Plaza, New York NY 10020-1605

Managing partner: Peter Sacripanti 1149
Number of lawyers: 110

Main areas of work: Lawyers in the firm's New York office focus their practice on anti-trust; banking; corporate; environmental law; franchising; health; international; litigation; M&A; real estate; securities; and tax.
Top clients: The New York office represents US and international clients, including some of the world's largest publicly and privately held companies; financial institutions; major health care organisations; venture capital-backed start-ups and individuals.

USA
600 13th Street NW, Washington DC 20005-3096

Managing partner: Timothy Waters
Number of lawyers: 206

Main areas of work: The firm's Washington office focuses on areas including anti-trust; corporate; e-business; employee benefits; energy services; environmental; food, agriculture and alcohol; inetellectual property; international trade; legislative; occupational health and safety; tax; and telecommunications.

McDERMOTT, WILL & EMERY

 For other recommended firms see pages 1485-1520

MCKENNA & CUNEO

HEAD OFFICE

1900 K Street N.W.,
Washington DC 20006, USA
Tel: +1 202 496 7500 **Fax:** +1 202 496 7756

Website: www.mckennacuneo.com
Email: fred_levy@mckennacuneo.com

FIRM OVERVIEW

Managing partner: James Gallagher
Number of partners worldwide: 93
Number of other lawyers worldwide: 130

AREAS OF PRACTICE:

Appellate litigation	*%
Construction	*%
Corporate (including securities and tax)	*%
Employment	*%
Energy	*%
Environmental	*%
Food and drug	*%
Government contracts	*%
Healthcare	*%
Information privacy	*%
Insurance recovery	*%
Intellectual property	*%
International trade and investment	*%
Litigation	*%
Product liability	*%
Technology business law	*%
Trusts and estate planning	*%

* Workload % not disclosed

OFFICE CONTACTS

BELGIUM
56, Rue des Colonies, B-1000 **Brussels**
Tel: +11 322 278 1211 **Fax:** +11 322 278 1200
Email: bruce_owens@mckennacuneo.com

USA
Suite 4800, 370 Seventeenth Street, **Denver**, Colorado 80202
Tel: +1 303 634 4000 **Fax:** +1 303 634 4400
Email: tom_bieging@mckennacuneo.com

28 South Waterloo Road, Suite 101, **Devon**, Pennsylvania 19333
Tel: +1 610 687 9750 **Fax:** +1 610 687 9755
Email: frank_rapoport@mckennacuneo.com

444 South Flower Street, **Los Angeles,** California 90071
Tel: +1 213 688 1000 **Fax:** +1 213 243 6330
Email: michael_kavanaugh@mckennacuneo.com

Suite 3200, Symphony Towers, 750 B Street, **San Diego,** California 92101
Tel: +1 619 595 5400 **Fax:** +1 619 595 5450
Email: robert_brewer@mckennacuneo.com

Steuart Street Tower, One Market, **San Francisco,** California 94105
Tel: +1 415 267 4000 **Fax:** +1 415 267 4198
Email: chris_volz@mckennacuneo.com

M

FIRM OVERVIEW: Since the firm's founding in 1939, McKenna & Cuneo, L.L.P. lawyers have advised on a range of complex business and regulatory issues and have handled litigation disputes in a wide variety of administrative and judicial forums. As a result of the firm's long-standing presence in Washington, it is able to marshal a range of approaches to solving problems with the government. The firm has experience in approaching decision makers at the policy-formulation level, addressing regulatory compliance issues proactively, responding to enforcement issues, and litigating when necessary. McKenna & Cuneo is distinguished by its ability to achieve results at the working level of government. The firm has proven that success in the regulatory sphere can be gained by working within a regulatory agency and by understanding the regulator's perspective and proposing cost-effective solutions.

INTERNATIONAL CLIENTS: The firm's client base is diverse, ranging from some of the world's largest corporations to small businesses in emerging, high technology industries. Its clients include major defence and aerospace contractors, telecommunications, biotechnology and information resource companies, health care providers, real estate related concerns, and trade associations. Much of the firm's work involves civil, criminal, and administrative litigation and counselling services in the fields of intellectual property, environmental, food and drug, healthcare, litigation, government contracts, international trade and business, general business, insurance recovery, labour and employment.

MAIN INTERNATIONAL AREAS OF PRACTICE: Work undertaken includes government contracts, litigation, intellectual property, corporate (including securities and tax), healthcare, insurance recovery, environmental, construction, employment, international trade and investment, product liability, trusts and estate planning, trade associations, and energy.

LANGUAGES: Arabic, Armenian, Cantonese, Chinese, Danish, Dutch, Finnish, French, German, Greek, Hebrew, Italian, Korean, Mandarin, Persian/Farsi, Polish, Portuguese, Russian, Spanish, Swedish, Vietnamese

For other recommended firms see pages 1485-1520

BUFETE MEDRANO IRIAS

HEAD OFFICE

PO Box 1233,
San Pedro Sula Honduras
Tel: +504 553 4589 **Fax:** 504 557 3151

Email: bufetemi@bmi.hn
Website: www.bmi.hn

FIRM OVERVIEW

Managing and senior partner: Leonel Medrano Irías

AREAS OF PRACTICE:

Corporate	55%
Intellectual property	20%
Maritime law	10%
Insurance and reinsurance	5%
M&A	5%
Banking and finance	3%
Telecommunications/computer software	2%

FIRM OVERVIEW: Founded at the start of 1980, this Honduran firm was established by Leonel Medarno Irias who was previously at XYZ Lawyers Office. The firm has grown to become one of Honduras' leading and largest commercial law firms. The firm has a wide base practice and corporate management experience. It maintains contacts with various firms in the US, Central and South America. Bufete Medrano Irias offers a comprehensive legal service to clients with international business interests, but focuses on all aspects of general corporate law and M&A.

INTERNATIONAL EXPERIENCE: In 2000, Bufete Medrano Irias assisted in the establishment of US and other foreign companies in Honduras.

INTERNATIONAL CLIENTS: The firm's client base includes large companies, banks, insurance companies and public or supranational institutions conducting cross-border business. These include El Volcan de Guatemala, AS Lingebygg Transmission Lines Co. Ltd. (Honduras Office), Allen & Overy (Hong Kong), Demarest & Almeida (São Paulo), Scott Paper Co., Texaco Caribbean Inc. 3M, Interpacket Networks Inc., NOL Group, API Limited (US), International Apparel Industry (Fruit of the Loom).

MAIN INTERNATIONAL AREAS OF PRACTICE:

Coporate: The firm assists in drafting international and Honduras contracts.
Intellectual property: The firm specialises in trademarks, patents and copyrights. Its lawyers participate in the negotiation of licence agreements and advise on infringement disputes as well as other aspects of IP law.
Telecommunications and computer law: The firm advises on all aspects in this area.
Securities and financial markets: Bufete Medrano Irias advise clients on Honduras law pertaining to funds, securities, and derivatives. It also assists investment firms structure and license their operations.
Other: The firm also specialises in offshore financing services; economics; feasibility studies; international marketing; the preparation of agricultural projects; economic indicators; real estate services; land tenure studies; legal surveying and mapping; commercial land valuation

LANGUAGES: English, French, Italian, Spanish

WORLDWIDE OFFICE CONTACTS

HONDURAS
PO Box 1233, **San Pedro Sula**
Tel: +504 553 4589 **Fax:** +504 557 3151
Email: bufetemi@bmi.hn

Sendero La Cumbre, Nº 1564, Altos Colonia, Miramontes,
Tegucigalpa MDC
Tel: +504 235 6524 **Fax:** +504 235 4515
Email: bufetemi@bmi.hn

M

For other recommended firms see pages 1485-1520

MEFFRE & GRALL

HEAD OFFICE

80, avenue Marceau,
75008 Paris, France
Tel: +33 1 53 57 31 70 **Fax:** +33 1 47 20 90 40

Email: meffregrall@meffre-grall.avocat.fr
Website: www.meffre-grall.avocat.fr

WORLDWIDE OFFICE CONTACTS

FRANCE
80, avenue Marceau, 75008 **Paris**
Tel: +33 1 53 57 31 70 **Fax**: +33 1 47 20 90 40
Email: jcgrall@meffre-grall.avocat.fr

FIRM OVERVIEW

Managing partner: Jean-Marie Meffre
Senior partner: Jean-Christophe Grall

Number of partners worldwide: 2
Number of other lawyers worldwide: 6

AREAS OF PRACTICE:

EU, competition and commercial	60%
Employment	15%
Litigation	15%
Intellectual property	10%

FIRM OVERVIEW: Meffre & Grall was founded in 1998, the result of the merger between the firms established by Jean-Marie Meffre (attorney at law since 1972) and Jean-Christophe Grall (attorney at law since 1992 after having exercised as legal counsel and in-house counsel). The firm belongs to the Paris Bar and works with law firms worldwide. It focuses on corporate and commercial matters and has extensive experience in anti-trust and competition law both at the domestic and EU level, consumer and marketing law. Meffre & Grall has been involved in many key decisions in diverse fields including pharmaceuticals, health and beauty, media, mobile phones, energy and food.

INTERNATIONAL EXPERIENCE: The firm has extensive experience of French and EU competition law, distribution contracts, franchising, commercial agents, licensing, mergers and acquisitions, parallel imports and the powers of the French competition Counsel and the European Commission. The firm acts for electricity companies subject to competing offers, for pharmaceutical companies regarding horizontal agreements, and in relation to consumer product supply disputes. It also handles arbitration between US and Italian companies manufacturing and distributing industrial measurement systems and applications to automobile manufacturers. The firm has recently undertaken significant work for US and UK banks and press.

INTERNATIONAL CLIENTS: The firm acts for large international companies (US and EU, especially Germany) in sectors including pharmaceuticals, health and beauty care, nutritional supplements, food and other consumer products, press/media, telecommunications, construction and electricity.

MAIN INTERNATIONAL AREAS OF PRACTICE:
French and EU competition law: The firm has extensive expertise in advising on the anti-trust-related Article 81 (ex 85) and 82 (ex 86) of the EC Treaty, vertical and horizontal agreements, distribution contracts, franchising, exclusive distribution, selective distribution, licensing, object or effect of restricting competition, the application of competition law to the public sector, M&A, the definition of the relevant market, barriers to entry, freezing out of the market, general terms and conditions, discrimination, parallel imports (v. trademark and unfair competition law), the powers of the French competition authorities and the European Commission, procedures and rights of defence, notification and other competition-related issues.
Litigation: The firm handles numerous law suits in the competition law area, unfair competition, trademark infringements and other commercial litigation.
Employment: The firm handles all matters related to French employment law.
Intellectual property: Expertise includes trademarks, patents, copyright and on-line services.
Marketing law: Work includes advice on consumer disputes, liability matters, marketing operations, consumer contests and electronic commerce.
Computer law: Expertise includes reseller agreements, customer licence terms and conditions, support and maintenance.

LANGUAGES: English, French, Italian

For other recommended firms see pages 1485-1520

MEIGHEN DEMERS

HEAD OFFICE

Suite 1100, Merrill Lynch Canada Tower, 200 King Street West,
Toronto, Canada M5H 3T4
Tel: +1 416 340 6000 **Fax:** +1 416 977 5239

Website: www.meighendemers.com

WORLDWIDE OFFICE CONTACTS

CANADA
Suite 1100, Merrill Lynch Canada Tower, 200 King Street West, **Toronto**
M5H 3T4
Tel: +1 416 340 6000 **Fax:** +1 416 977 5239
Email: jdemers@meighen.com

FIRM OVERVIEW

Contact partner: Jacques Demers
Number of partners worldwide: 19
Number of other lawyers worldwide: 25

AREAS OF PRACTICE:

Corporate finance and banking (incl project and structured finance and related tax) 40%
Commercial litigation and arbitration 18%
Corporate (and related tax) 12%
Financial restructuring and insolvency (and related tax) 14%
Mergers and acquisitions (and related tax) 12%
Intellectual property and computer law 4%

M

FIRM OVERVIEW: Established in 1976 and affiliated with a full service firm in Montreal from 1981 to 1990, the firm developed its banking and project finance practice during the mid to late 1980s. The firm terminated this affiliation in 1990 and reconstituted itself to continue to build upon its business law practice with particular focus on corporate finance (including project and structured finace, banking and securities) and tax, together with related litigation and real estate as well as sophisticated financial restructurings and insolvencies. The practice has since grown to include aircraft finance, infrastructure development, health care, aerospace, software and other high tech businesses.

INTERNATIONAL EXPERIENCE: The firm's international practice has grown steadily throughout the 1990s. Over the past several years, the firm has been active in mining project financings in Latin America and on international infrastructure development and related financings, notably the Ferihegy International Airport expansion in Budapest. In addition, the firm continues to represent and advise: (a) banks, life insurance companies and other financial institutions in respect of multi-jurisdictional corporate, project and structured financings, (b) Canadian-based and foreign manufacturers and licensors in: (i) structuring and documenting their multi-jurisdictional contracting, licensing and franchising arrangements, and (ii) dispute resolution, and (c) domestic and international financial institutions, investment houses and debtors in complex cross-border financial restructurings. Revenue generated from international practice averages between 15-25% of the firm's annual revenues.

INTERNATIONAL CLIENTS: The firm's international clients include (in addition to the international affiliates of Canadian-based clients) UK, Italian and Chinese aerospace manufacturers, UK and US software houses, UK insurance underwriters and brokers, US manufacturers of cable, wireless and satellite communication systems, European and US banks, German machine tool manufacturers and major US aircraft finance houses. Software: Apak Systems (UK), Leisure Time Technologies (US), CGI Information Systems, EMC2 (US), MIA Corporation, IVI Checkmate Corp (US), Surfen Inc (US). Aerospace: GKN-Westland, EH Industries (UK), Agusta (Italy), BIAM (China). Insurance: Lloyd's (UK). Communications: General Instrument, Home Wireless Network (US). Breweries: Shepherd Neame Ltd (UK), Noble China. Machine tools: Trumpf Inc, Krupp Industries (Germany). Aircraft finance: Textron Financial, Bombardier Capital (US). Banks and financial: ABN-AMRO, Bank of America, Barclays Bank plc, Chase, Deutsche Bank AG, Dresdner Bank AG, Euroclear System, GMAC, GE Capital, UBS, Antwerpse Diamantbank (Belgium), Textron Fiancial (US).

MAIN INTERNATIONAL AREAS OF PRACTICE:
Software/Computer law: Joint ventures, systems integration, licensing, mergers and acquisitions, taxation.
Aerospace: Government contracts, joint ventures, systems integration, finance, tax, dispute resolution.
Cross-border financial restructurings: Regularly advises domestic and international financial instituitons, investment houses, creditor committees, debtors and regulators in connection with major financial restructurings, insolvencies and receiverships, taxation.
Insurance: Regulatory compliance, broker agreements, underwriting terms, risk analysis, risk allocation.
Communications: Systems integration, research and development, product development, risk allocation, dispute resolution, taxation.
Infrastructure development: Concessions, construction, operations and maintenance, project financing (representing developer/operators, banks and underwriters), taxation.
Mining/Natural resource projects: Financings (usually representing banks or underwriters).
Manufacturers: Distribution agreements, joint ventures, import/export issues, regulatory compliance, government relations, taxation, mergers and acquisitions.
Banks: Corporate counsel, regulatory compliance, asset-based lending, project finance, structured finance, financial leasing, private banking and trust administration (both offshore and onshore), taxation.

LANGUAGES: English, French

For other recommended firms see pages 1485-1520

MELCHOR ALBIÑANA & SUÁREZ DE LEZO

HEAD OFFICE

José Abascal nº 58,
28003 Madrid, Spain
Tel: +34 91 451 93 00 **Fax:** +34 91 442 60 45

Email: melchor@arrakis.es
Website: www.melchorheras.com

FIRM OVERVIEW

Chairman José Luis López Sánchez
Managing partners Cesar Albiñana and Rafael Suárez de Lezo

Number of partners worldwide: 11
Number of other lawyers worldwide: 50

AREAS OF PRACTICE:

Corporate	25%
M&A	18%
Securities market	13%
Banking and finance	10%
Litigation and arbitration	10%
Media and intellectual property	10%
Public law	8%
Tax	7%
Employment	3%

WORLDWIDE OFFICE CONTACTS

SPAIN
Avda del Gran Capitán nº 44, piso 2º, 14001 **Cordoba**
Tel: + 34 957 496 070 **Fax:** + 34 957 486 984
Email: raranda@cordoba.melchorheras.com

José Abascal nº 58, 28003 **Madrid**
Tel: +34 91 451 93 00 **Fax:** +34 91 442 60 45
Email: melchor@arrakis.es

Avda. de la República Argentina nº 21-B, 8ºB, 41001 **Sevilla**
Tel: +34 954 28 61 02 **Fax:** +34 954 27 83 19
Email: jlorite@sevilla.melchorheras.com

FIRM OVERVIEW: The firm was founded in 1927 by Antonio Melchor de las Heras (deceased in 1986). With the liberalisation of the Spanish economy in 1958, the firm was structured as a partnership. Despacho Melchor, Albiñana & Suárez de Lezo combines the traditional concept of practising law in Spain, on a one-to-one level, providing a comprehensive service to large companies. The firm belongs to the Commercial Law Affiliates (CLA), a worldwide association of independent law firms.

INTERNATIONAL EXPERIENCE: The firm advises multinational companies from the US, the UK and continental Europe covering a wide range of industry sectors. It also acts as legal counsel on anti-trust matters before the anti-trust authorities.

INTERNATIONAL CLIENTS: The firm's client base includes large companies, banks, public or supranational institutions conducting cross-borders businesses.

MAIN INTERNATIONAL AREAS OF PRACTICE:

Corporate: The firm provides legal advice to subsidiaries of multinationals ranging from strictly corporate matters to contracts of distribution, franchise, agency, supply, and tax structures.

Securities market: The firm has advised major Spanish state and private companies on offerings in international markets such as the New York Stock Exchange. It has also advised foreign companies in the Madrid Stock Exchange. Melchor, Albiñana & Suárez de Lezo represents both issuing companies and underwriters in public or private offerings, debt financing and private equity issues.

Banking and financing: The firm's financing experience varies from intervention in very complex leveraged lease financing transactions of aeroplanes or vessels to the granting of syndicated multi-currency loans representing both borrowers and lenders.

M&A: Transactions range from small private acquisitions to cross-border take-overs of listed companies.

Litigation and arbitration: The firm's litigation department handles arbitration proceedings and a wide variety of commercial and civil litigation matters.

Tax: The firm's tax practice is mainly focused on corporate and international tax planning, particularly connected to foreign investments, mergers and acquisitions and restructurings.

Employment: The firm handles all matters relating to Spanish employment law.

EU and competition: The firm undertake anti-trust, competition and marketing-related work involving companies in the Spanish market.

Insolvency: The firm handle corporate restructuring and has been involved in a number of complex bankruptcy matters.

Public law: Melchor, Albiñana & Suárez de Lezo provide legal advice on all aspects of administrative law.

Media and intellectual property: The firm advises clients on copyright, patents, trademarks, design, technology transfers and licensing. It also handles computer, Internet, technology, telecommunications, advertising and media work.

LANGUAGES: Arabic, English, French, German, Spanish

M

For other recommended firms see pages 1485-1520

MELLO JONES & MARTIN

HEAD OFFICE

Reid House, 31 Church Street, PO Box HM 1564
Hamilton HM FX Bermuda
Tel: +1 441 292 1345 **Fax:** +1 441 292 2277

Email: mjm@mjm.bm
Website: www.mjm.bm

FIRM OVERVIEW

Managing partner: Andrew A. Martin
Senior partner: Michael J. Mello

Number of partners worldwide: 6
Number of other lawyers worldwide: 13

AREAS OF PRACTICE:
Litigation and arbitration 40%
Corporate 30%
Trusts and estates 15%
Banking and finance 10%
Insurance and reinsurance 5%

M

FIRM OVERVIEW: Mello Jones & Martin was formed in 1990 by the merger of two smaller firms. The merged partnership offers progressive, high-quality services with Bermudian barristers and attorneys supported by a team of attorneys with experience in other jurisdictions such as England, Canada, the United States and Cayman Islands. The firm's key areas of practice are commercial litigation, corporate transactions and formations, and asset protection for personal and corporate identities.

INTERNATIONAL CLIENTS: The firm's client base includes large companies, banks, insurance companies and public or supranational institutions conducting cross-border business.

WORLDWIDE OFFICE CONTACTS

BERMUDA
Reid House, 31 Church Street, PO Box HM 1564, **Hamilton** HM FX
Tel: +1 441 292 1345 **Fax:** +1 441 292 2277
Email: mjm@mjm.bm

MAIN INTERNATIONAL AREAS OF PRACTICE: Work handled includes banking and finance; corporate; insurance and reinsurance; litigation and arbitration; trusts and estates.

LANGUAGES: English

MELLO JONES & MARTIN
Barristers and Attorneys

For other recommended firms see pages 1485-1520

MENDOZA, PALACIOS, ACEDO, BORJAS, PAEZ PUMAR & CIA

HEAD OFFICE

Edificio Aba, Calle Veracruz, Las Mercedes
Caracas 1060, Venezuela
Tel: +58 2 992 1611 **Fax:** +58 2 993 1237

Email: aborjas@juriscompint.com

FIRM OVERVIEW

Number of partners worldwide: 14
Number of other lawyers worldwide: 19

AREAS OF PRACTICE:

Banking and finance 15%
Corporations and capital markets 15%
Litigation and arbitration 15%
Telecommunications and IT law 15%
Insurance and reinsurance 10%
Mergers and acquisitions 10%
Competition and anti-trust 5%
Energy 5%
Tax 5%
International arbitration 3%
Intellectual property 2%

FIRM OVERVIEW: Founded in 1896, Mendoza Palacios has offices in Caracas and Valencia, as well as correspondent offices in Puerto La Cruz, Maturín and Margarita. A number of the firm's attorneys are actively involved as researchers and professors in academic institutions. Most are proficient in English and some have expert knowledge of other European languages such as French and Italian.The firm's growth is attributed to the oil concessions of the 1920s, and has since developed to include other areas of expertise, especially in the financial, commercial and industrial sectors. The firm acts for Venezuelan clients domestically and abroad, as well as foreign individuals and corporations doing business in Venezuela. The firm's client base includes some of the largest multinational corporations and major Venezuelan industrial, commercial, financial and insurance groups. Others include individuals and charitable organisations.

INTERNATIONAL EXPERIENCE: The firm has represented international clients such as Citibank, IBM and Shell for over 60 years. It has handled privatisations, such as CANTV (local telephone company); joint ventures, such as the partnership of Aetna and Banco Mercantil; acquisitions, such as CEMEX/Venezolana de Cementos, Glaxo Wellcome/Merril Dow, Corp Banca/Banco Orinoco and Inversiones Mundial/Corporación Grupo Químico (Sherwin Williams); debt restructuring, such as CANTV US$ 1 billion, and the restructuring of Siderúrgica del Orinoco, representing the lending bank. Other work includes project finance, such as the Petrozuata project (petroleum), representing the banks, and the BHP-Sivensa project (iron). The firm has also worked on projects related to the elimination of restrictions in certain areas of the economy, such as the cellular phone business, acting for Movilnet. The firm has handled antidumping procedures, for the pre-mixed concrete and steel components industries. It has also handled anti-trust procedures, such as the Pepsi-Cola/Coca-Cola case. The firm is also active in capital markets, assisting issuers, the stock exchange and the regulatory agency.

INTERNATIONAL CLIENTS: Clients include major international companies covering a wide range of sectors. These include Citibank, IBM, Royal Dutch/Shell, Enron, PDVSA, Telefónica Internacional de España, Sun Microsystems, Norsk Hydro, Pfizer, Glaxo Wellcome, J.P. Morgan, Axsia Serck Baker, Charles Schwab & Co, International Finance Corporation, Eximbank, Inversiones Mundial S.A. (Colombia), CANTV and Mavesa.

WORLDWIDE OFFICE CONTACTS

VENEZUELA
Edificio Aba, Calle Veracruz, Las Mercedes, **Caracas** 1060
Tel: +58 2 992 1611 **Fax:** +58 2 993 1237
Email: aborjas@juriscompint.com

Centro Commercial Siglo XX1, Urb La Viña, Oficina A-1 y A-2, Piso 3°, **Valencia**
Tel: +58 41 217983 **Fax:** +58 41 257739

MAIN INTERNATIONAL AREAS OF PRACTICE:

Banking and finance: The firm represents foreign commercial banks, insurance companies, investment funds, finance companies, investments firms and other corporate lenders as well as borrowers and issuers in a wide range of international financial transactions. It has recently advised clients on several major international oil and gas projects such as Petrozuata, Fertinitro, Profalca and currently, Hamaca). Other major foreign investment projects include Orinoco Iron, Minera las Cristinas and Minera Loma de Níquel. Debt restructuring processes include CANTV, Siderúrgica del Orinoco SIDOR, Venepal and Ron Santa Teresa.

Capital markets /corporate finance: The firm has been involved in ADR and GDR issues such as the CANTV and CORIMON global offering and the EPIC initial public offering. It has also provided assistance to governmental agencies, such as the Ministry of Finance, the Ministry of Industry and Commerce and Fondo de Inversiones de Venezuela. The firm recently participated in privatisation processes of CANTV and Pequiven. It has also been involved in international joint ventures such as Banco Mercantil ñ Aetna in Seguros Mercantil.

Competition and anti-trust: The firm has handled anti-trust procedures, such as the Pepsi-Cola/Coca-Cola case.

Energy and natural resources: Prior to the nationalisation of the oil industry, Mendoza Palacios advised major oil companies on government-related and other matters. Following nationalisation, the firm continued to advise clients on their remaining —and now increasing— businesses in Venezuela. The firm also advises the national oil company. It has recently handled major investments in oil and gas projects such as Petrozuata, Fertinitro, Profalca and, currently, Hamaca.

International arbitration: The firm has participated in international arbitration processes, under ICC and AAA rules.

Litigation and arbitration: The firm's litigation department is one of the largest in Venezuela. Prior to the nationalisation of the oil industry, the firm handled most of Royal Ducht/Shell Group's litigation. Subsequently the firm handled most of PDVSA's litigation before the merger of the national oil companies. The firm also handles litigation for other international clients such as Citibank, Enron, CANTV, J.P. Morgan, and Formiconi.

Tax: Work handled includes tax planning and litigation, ranging from the negotiation of special tax regimes to the fighting of tax claims at administrative and judicial levels. Several of the firm's lawyers are permanent members of the accounting , auditing or financial committees, was internally set up by the firm's largest clients to deal with tax and related matters. In addition the firm advises on the structuring of various transactions focusing on tax implications.

Telecommunications and computer law: The firm is actively involved in the privatisation of the government-owned monopoly. Clients in this sector include CANTV and Telefónica Internacional de España. The firm is also active in e-commerce and matters regarding the leasing of equipment, licensing and software.

LANGUAGES: English, French, Italian, Spanish

MERILAMPI MARTTILA LAITASALO LAW OFFICES

HEAD OFFICE

Eteläesplanadi 22,
FIN-00130 Helsinki, Finland
Tel: +358 9 686 481 **Fax:** +358 9 6864 8484

Email: law.offices@mmllaw.fi
Website: www.mmllaw.fi

WORLDWIDE OFFICE CONTACTS

FINLAND
Eteläesplanadi 22, FIN-00130 **Helsinki**
Tel: +358 9 686 481 **Fax:** +358 9 6864 8484
Email: law.offices@mmllaw.fi

Kauppakatu 6A, FIN-33210 **Tampere**
Tel: +358 3 260 1600 **Fax:** +358 3 260 1650
Email: tampere.offices@mmllaw.fi

FIRM OVERVIEW

Managing partner: Pekka Merilampi

Number of partners worldwide: 7
Number of other lawyers worldwide: 9

AREAS OF PRACTICE:

Corporate	25%
Banking and finance	20%
Litigation and arbitration	20%
M&A	15%
Intellectual property	10%
Telecommunications and computer law	10%

M

FIRM OVERVIEW: The firm was founded in 1992 after the split of a major Finnish law firm. The new practice has been growing steadily and employs 16 lawyers. It provides a full range of national and international services, focusing mainly on capital markets transactions, corporate and general commercial law as well as litigation and arbitration. The firm is currently engaged in several major liquidations of Finnish companies and entities. The firm has a well-established clientele and good links with the Finnish business community and authorities. It has offices in Helsinki and Tampere.

INTERNATIONAL EXPERIENCE: Merilampi Marttila Laitasalo's international experience has grown substantially in the last few years and the firm regularly advise on cross-border transactions, especially in the Scandinavian market. The firm also have a strong dispute resolution practice advising international clients on disputes in Finland.

MAIN INTERNATIONAL AREAS OF PRACTICE:

Mergers and acquisitions: In recent years the firm has advised on several major transactions involving Finnish and international companies. It advised two major Finnish banks on their merger with into Merita-Bank, and Merita on their merger with Nordbanken.

Corporate and general commercial: The firm works on issues related to establishing companies, amending corporate form and structure, capital arrangements, as well as mergers, divisions, liquidation, reorganisation and winding-up of companies.

Capital markets: One of the firm's core practice areas is providing advice on public offerings, IPO's, privatisations, private placements and other aspects of finance.

Dispute resolution: The firm advises both domestic and international clients on dispute resolution. The practice covers in-court litigation and arbitration procedures. Some partners have been nominated to act as arbitrators in major disputes.

Media and intellectual property: The firm has a strong client base in the field of media. Merilampi Marttila Laitasalo also advise and assist on issues relating to different licensing and franchising arrangements. It acted as adviser when Elisa Communications, formerly Helsinki Telephone Company, was formed.

LANGUAGES: English, Finnish, German, Swedish

For other recommended firms see pages 1485-1520

MICHAEL WILSON & PARTNERS

HEAD OFFICE

36 Samal-1 5th Floor,
480099 Almaty, Kazakhstan
Tel: +7 3272 501 570 **Fax:** +7 3272 501 575

Email: mwp@nursat.kz

WORLDWIDE OFFICE CONTACTS

KAZAKHSTAN
36 Samal-1 5th Floor, 480099 **Almaty**
Tel: +7 3272 501 570 **Fax:** +7 3272 501 575
Email: mwp@nursat.kz

FIRM OVERVIEW

Managing partner: Michael E. Wilson
Executive director: Peter Reilly

Number of partners worldwide: 1
Number of other lawyers worldwide: 6

AREAS OF PRACTICE:

Foreign investments, joint ventures and partnerships	15%
Mining, natural resources, oil and gas	15%
Corporate, corporate finance and securities	10%
Intellectual property	10%
Labour and employment matters	10%
Power industry	10%
Privatisation, restructuring and reorganisation	10%
Tax and customs	10%
Banking, finance and project finance	5%
Real estate	5%

FIRM OVERVIEW: Michael Wilson & Partners (MWP) is a leading full-service law firm which also focuses on corporate finance and project development work in Kazakhstan and the rest of Central Asia. The firm is also active in Kyrgyzia, Uzbekistan, Turkmenistan, Tajikistan, Azerbaijan, Georgia and Armenia. MWP was established in July 1998. Its founding members had been practising at Baker & McKenzie for many years before forming their own practice. MWP places significant emphasis on client care, quality of service and training. It is proactive in its relationships with clients, while offering an open, creative and flexible approach to fees. MWP's lawyers have handled the legal aspects of some of the most important landmark regional projects, including privatisation and restructuring of major enterprises and businesses.

INTERNATIONAL CLIENTS: MWP's clients include some of the region's largest and most strategically important investors. The firm advises foreign and domestic business clients on all aspects of commercial and business law. Clients include multinationals involved in major industries such as energy, power generation and distribution, natural resources, mining, oil and gas industry, major banks, international financial institutions, foreign-based companies and their regional subsidiaries and affiliates.

MAIN INTERNATIONAL AREAS OF PRACTICE:

Privatisation, restructuring and reorganisation: The firm advises on regulatory and contractual issues relating to privitisation techniques in Kazakhstan. It has extensive experience and advises on business purchases, sales and mergers. It negotiates takeovers, acquisitions, joint ventures and corporate restructuring programs, and assists private borrowers and lenders in a variety of transactions, including project financings. Project work includes advice on structuring, negotiating, documenting and implementing a broad range of infrastructure and other development projects in the power generation, oil and mineral refining, telecommunications and airport infrastructure industries.

Power industry: The firm has handled the structuring, documentation, completion and implementation of almost all of the power and other utility projects undertaken to date in Kazakhstan. It has expert knowledge of and experience in relevant tax, accounting, tariff and regulatory issues with which it deals on a day-to-day basis for regulated utilities in Almaty and other regions and centres throughout Kazakhstan.

Mining, natural resources, oil and gas: The firm has substantial experience in the areas of mining, natural resources, oil and gas. It also represents clients in the practical and legal aspects of environmental compliance and liability.

Foreign investments, joint ventures and partnerships: The firm advises foreign companies on foreign investment laws and policies in Kazakhstan, devises offset programs and represents clients in numerous transactions.

Corporate finance and securities: The firm is experienced in all areas of Kazakhstani and international corporate finance. It advises underwriters, issuers and purchasers in public and private financings with all types of debt and equity instruments; structured finance; lease and project financing; public finance; commodities, futures and derivative products; investment companies, advisers and broker dealers; and private investment funds. The firm provides regulatory and transactional advice to a variety of foreign and domestic financial institutions and assists foreign companies planning to open branches, agencies or offices in Kazakhstan.

Banking and project finance: The firm advises on the full range of financial projects including banking, asset finance, product finance, securitisation and structured finance.

Tax and customs: The firm is experienced in customs matters, export licensing and other trade regulations matters as well as tax planning and optimisation, representing clients in state and local tax authorities. It advises on international and domestic taxation, covering a wide range of financing, investment, corporate and commercial issues, together with advice on tax litigation, disputes and transfer pricing.

Employment: The firm has experience in all employment-related matters. Its lawyers advise on matters such as wrongful and unfair dismissal, executive severance, confidentiality, sex/race/disability discrimination, workers' compensation, industrial disputes, the employment aspects of acquisitions, disposals and outsourcing.

Real estate: The firm advises on the acquisitions, dispositions, financing, development and utilisation of commercial and industrial real estate. Some members of the firm also have experience in serving as landlord's or tenant's counsel in negotiating and drafting complex leases covering all forms of real estate property.

Intellectual property: MWP has an international reputation for its IP work. The IP group provides a full range of services relating to the registration, protection and enforcement of IP rights, as well as litigation, transactional and advisory services as required by those concerned with the creation and protection of rights in plant varieties, technology, brands, trademarks, patents, utility models, industrial designs and copyright. The IP department encompasses the firm's e-commerce practice.

LANGUAGES: Czech, English, French, Kazakh, Russian, Spanish, Ukranian

MILBANK, TWEED, HADLEY & MCCLOY

HEAD OFFICE

1 Chase Manhattan Plaza, 47th Floor,
New York NY 10005, USA
Tel: +1 212 530 5000 **Fax:** +1 212 530 5219
Website: www.milbank.com

FIRM OVERVIEW

Managing partner and chairman: Mel M Immergut

Number of partners worldwide: 118
Number of other lawyers worldwide: 320

AREAS OF PRACTICE:

Banking, finance and capital markets	35%
Project finance	20%
Litigation and arbitration	15%
Energy	5%
General corporate	5%
Intellectual property	5%
M&A	5%
Tax	5%
Telecommunications, IT and technology	5%

WORLDWIDE OFFICE CONTACTS

HONG KONG
3007 Alexandra Hse, 16 Chater Road, Central, **Hong Kong**
Tel: +852 2971 4888 **Fax:** +852 2840 0792

JAPAN
Fukoku Seimei Building, 2-2, Uchisaiwaicho 2-chome, Chiyoda-ku, **Tokyo** 100-0011
Tel: +813 3504 1050 **Fax:** +813 3595 2790

SINGAPORE
30 Raffles Place, #14-00 Caltex House, **Singapore** 048622
Tel: +65 428 2400 **Fax:** +65 428 2500

UNITED KINGDOM
Dashwood House, 69 Old Broad Street, **London** EC2M 1QS
Tel: +44 20 7448 3000 **Fax:** +44 20 7448 3029

USA
601 South Figueroa Street, 30th Floor, **Los Angeles** CA 90017
Tel: +1 213 892 4000 **Fax:** +1 213 629 5063

1 Chase Manhattan Plaza, 47th Floor, **New York** NY 10005
Tel: +1 212 530 5000 **Fax:** +1 212 530 5219

International Square Building, 1825 Eye Street, NW, Suite 1100, **Washington DC** DC 20006
Tel: +1 202 835 7500 **Fax:** +1 202 835 7586

M

FIRM OVERVIEW: Founded in1866, Milbank, Tweed, Hadley & McCloy provides advice to the financial services industry. It advises commercial and investment banks, insurance and finance companies and self-regulatory organisations. Milbank is an international law firm specialising in project finance and related areas of corporate law, including the structuring and implementation of sophisticated financial and business transactions.

INTERNATIONAL EXPERIENCE: In recent years Milbank has closed more than 140 project financings, which have raised more than US$85 billion for infrastructure projects worldwide. The firm has also handled cross-border transactions, including joint ventures and M&A. Its global transportation finance group has devised several innovative financing structures and techniques which have become standard-bearers for the industry, and has participated in financings for companies in over 40 countries throughout North and South America, Europe, Asia, Africa and Australia.

INTERNATIONAL CLIENTS: The firm advises government agencies, investment and commercial banks, public utilities, real estate owners, developers and financiers, syndicates of investors and foreign individuals and companies.

MAIN INTERNATIONAL AREAS OF PRACTICE:
Banking and finance: The firm handles a range of corporate and other financings, representing commercial banks, institutional lenders, investment banks, investment funds, export credit and multilateral agencies, corporate and special purpose borrowers. It also assists domestic and non-US banks in corporate, capital markets and regulatory matters.
Capital markets: Milbank advises issuers, underwriters, placement agents, institutional and individual investors and selling shareholders on all aspects of public offerings and private transactions. Milbank also represents trustees and fiscal agents, as well as a number of important institutions which play a role in many capital markets transactions.
Financial restructuring: The firm advises domestic and international debtors, financial institutions, hedge funds, committees of creditors and equity security holders and debtors. In addition to general reorganisation, Milbank represents clients in large and complex financing transactions and cross-border insolvency cases.
Litigation and arbitration: Milbank advises on business disputes arising from mergers and acquisitions, proxy battles, international and domestic financings, corporate restructurings, securities offerings, class action defence, and real estate workouts.
M&A: Milbank advises on all aspects of hostile take-overs.
Project finance: The firm has handled projects in industries including petroleum (including exploration, production, refining and transportation) petrochemicals, natural gas (including pipelines), telecommunications (including satellite), electricity generation and distribution (including independent power projects), waste disposal and recycling, wastewater treatment, mining and metals, wood products, paper, transportation, toll roads, and other types of infrastructure.
Securitisation: The firm advises sponsors, underwriters, rating agencies and investors on all securitisations issues. It has been involved in several landmark transactions including the first transaction in which production risk was shared with the market, the first securitisation backed by railcar operating leases, and the first transaction to securitise rights under a floating pool of swaps and derivatives.
Technology: The firm handles all aspects of the rapidly changing technology market place. It advises on Internet, new media and e-commerce transactions, as well as more traditional information technology. The firm has played a significant role in many of the largest and most complex international and domestic outsourcing transactions completed to date.

LANGUAGES: Afrikaans, Arabic, Armenian, Bahasa, Bongall, Chinese (Cantonese, Mandarin and others), Czech, Danish, Dutch, English, Farsi, French, German, Gujarati, Hebrew, Hindi, Hungarian, Italian, Japanese, Kiswahili, Korean, Latin, Malay, Marathi, Polish, Portuguese, Rumanian, Russian, Spanish, Tagalog, Thai, Toyshanese, Turkish, Ukranian, Urdu, Vietnamese

For other recommended firms see pages 1485-1520

MINTER ELLISON

HEAD OFFICE

Aurora Place, 88 Phillip Street,
Sydney NSW 2000, Australia
Tel: +61 2 9921 8888 **Fax:** +61 2 9921 8123
Email: minters.mail@minters.com.au

FIRM OVERVIEW

Managing partner: Philip Marcus Clark

Number of partners worldwide: 277
Number of other lawyers worldwide: 854

AREAS OF PRACTICE:

Corporate	28%
Banking and finance	22%
Litigation	20%
Technology and communications	16%
Property	14%

FIRM OVERVIEW: Minter Ellison is Australia's second largest law firm, with over 1,000 lawyers working in the Asia-Pacific, Europe and the US. It is the only Australian firm with an office in New York, has the largest London office of any Australian firm, a growing presence in Asia and plans to open an office in Shanghai during 2001. The firm is recognised as a market leader in Australia and in 2000 received top rankings from a leading Asian law journal. It was also placed third in a large business magazine's annual law firm rankings for 2000, as well as being the only highly-placed Australian firm in the recent M&A legal advisory league tables.

INTERNATIONAL EXPERIENCE: The firm's international offices play a crucial role in sourcing global work requiring significant jurisdictional knowledge in the Asia-Pacific region. The London office recently secured instructions to act for Cap Gemini on the Asia-Pacific components of its acquisition of Ernst & Young's global consulting business. The only Australian firm represented in New York, the firm is frequently consulted on global transactions with an Asia-Pacific component. It acted for Castle Harlan Inc, on establishing a joint venture with Australian Mezzanine Investments - the fund is now the largest private equity fund in Australia. In Asia it provides specialist services primarily in the areas of major projects and construction. As the Hong Kong office grows it is developing a practice in e-commerce, corporate and securities.

INTERNATIONAL CLIENTS: Minter Ellison's international clients include banks, telecommunications, transport and construction companies, private individuals, charitable organisations and corporations. Specific clients include Australia's telecommunications carrier, Cable & Wireless Optus, AMP Limited, Consolidated Press Holdings, Cap Gemini Ernst & Young, Nestlé Australia, Qantas Airways, TAB and the Westfield Group.

LANGUAGES: Bahasa (Indonesia), Bahasa (Malaysia), Cantonese, English, Foochow, French, German, Hokkien, Italian, Japanese, Korean, Mandarin, Shanghainese, Thai

WORLDWIDE OFFICE CONTACTS

AUSTRALIA
1 King Williams Street, **Adelaide** SA 5000
Tel: +61 8 8233 5555 **Fax:** +61 8 8212 7518

Waterfront Place, 1 Eagle Street, **Brisbane** QLD 4000
Tel: +61 7 3226 6333 **Fax:** +61 7 3229 1066

Level 9, 15 London Circuit, **Canberra** ACT 2601
Tel: +61 2 6274 3000 **Fax:** +61 2 6274 3111

Rialto Towers, 525 Collins Street, **Melbourne** VIC 3000
Tel: +61 3 9229 2000 **Fax:** +61 3 9229 2666

Level 51, Central Park, 152-158 St George's Terrace, **Perth** WA 6000
Tel: +61 8 9429 7444 **Fax:** +61 8 9429 7666

Witheriff Nyst, 13 Nerang Street, **Southport** Goldcoast QLD 4215
Tel: +61 7 5532 5611 **Fax:** +61 7 5532 7334

Aurora Place, 88 Phillip Street, **Sydney** NSW 2000
Tel: +61 2 9921 8888 **Fax:** +61 2 9921 8123

HONG KONG
1910-13 Hutchison, 10 Harcourt Road, Central, **Hong Kong**
Tel: +852 2815 6888 **Fax:** +852 2810 0235

NEW ZEALAND
Rudd Watts & Stone, Bank of New Zealand Tower, 125 Queen Street, **Auckland**
Tel: +64 9 353 9700 **Fax:** +64 9 353 9701

Anthony Harper, 47 Cathedral Square, **Christchurch**
Tel: +64 3 379 0920 **Fax:** +64 3 366 9277

Rudd Watts & Stone, Trust Bank Centre, 125 The Terrace, **Wellington**
Tel: +64 4 498 5000 **Fax:** +64 4 498 5001

UNITED KINGDOM
20 Lincoln's Inn Fields, **London** WC2A 3ED
Tel: +44 20 7831 7871 **Fax:** +44 20 7404 6722

USA
500 Fifth Avenue, 39th floor, **New York** NY 10110
Tel: +1 212 642 2400 **Fax:** +1 212 642 2444

ASSOCIATED OFFICES

INDONESIA
Makarim & Taira S, 17th floor, Summitmas Tower 1, JL Jenderal, Sudirman no 61, **Jakarta** 12069
Tel: +62 21 252 1272 **Fax:** +62 21 252 2750

THAILAND
Matzger MacGregor, 28th floor, Lake Rajada Office Complex, 193/118 Ratchadapisek Road, Klong Toey, **Bangkok** 10110
Tel: +66 2 661 9200 **Fax:** +66 2 661 9300

For other recommended firms see pages 1485-1520

MIRANDA Y AMADO

HEAD OFFICE

Los Nardos 1018, Piso 15, San Isidro
Lima 27 Peru
Tel: +511 222 4747 **Fax:** +511 222 7400

Email: abogado@mafirma.com.pe
Website: www.mafirma.com.pe

WORLDWIDE OFFICE CONTACTS

PERU
Los Nardos 1018, Piso 15, San Isidro, **Lima** 27
Tel: +511 222 4747 **Fax:** +511 222 7400
Email: abogado@mafirma.com.pe

FIRM OVERVIEW

Managing partner: Luis Marcelo De-Bernardis
Senior partner: Jose Daniel Amado

Number of partners worldwide: 10
Number of other lawyers worldwide: 7

AREAS OF PRACTICE:
Energy and natural resources 15%
Finance and capital markets 15%
M&A 15%
Telecommunications 15%
Corporate 10%
Dispute resolution and arbitration 10%
Infrastructure 10%
Regulatory matters 10%

FIRM OVERVIEW: Miranda & Amado Abogados is one of the leading law firms in Peru. The firm has a broad-based practice covering corporate, financial and capital markets transactions and an extensive regulatory and dispute resolution practice. It handles a variety of general commercial and corporate work and advises on tax, labour, immigration and intellectual property matters. The firm specialises in the development of projects and infrastructure works, financing and regulatory matters in the energy, oil and gas, mining, banking, insurance and telecommunications sectors.

INTERNATIONAL EXPERIENCE: More than two thirds of Miranda y Amado's turnover is derived from foreign clients or their Peruvian subsidiaries.

INTERNATIONAL CLIENTS: The firm's client base includes large companies, banks, insurance companies and multilateral institutions including Amadeus; BankBoston; BBVA Banco Continental; Cía Cervejaria Brahma; Citibank; Compaq Computer Corporation; Diveo Broadband Networks; Duke Energy International; Export Development Corporation; General Electric Corporation; IDT Corporation; Intel Corp.; Hicks, Muse, Tate & Furst; Inter-American Development Bank; Inter-American Investment Corporation; International Finance Corporation; MBIA Insurance Corporation; MasterCard International; Merril Lynch; Nextel International; PanAmSat; Salomon Smith Barney; TELMEX; Televisa; Tractebel; UBS AG; Winstar International.

MAIN INTERNATIONAL AREAS OF PRACTICE:
M&A: The firm advises on cross-border mergers, take-overs and acquisitions. In recent years it has been involved in some of the largest M&A transactions in Peru.
Banking and finance: The firm advises on all aspects of banking and finance including secured and syndicated loan transactions and guarantees, structured finance, project finance, leasing and tax-based finance.
Telecommunications: The firm has a leading practice on all aspects of telecommunication law.
Litigation and arbitration: The firm advises on commercial litigation, national and international arbitration, administrative procedures and ADR.
Energy and natural resources: The firm is involved in the development of law in the recently deregulated energy sector and has substantial experience in mining and other natural resources projects.
Corporate: The firm advises on all aspects of general corporate law including the drafting of international and domestic contracts.
Securities and financial markets: The firm advises national and international clients on Peruvian law relating to funds, securities and derivatives.

LANGUAGES: English, French, Italian, Portuguese, Spanish

MIRANDA & AMADO
ABOGADOS

For other recommended firms see pages 1485-1520

MKONO & CO

HEAD OFFICE

9th Floor PPF Tower, Garden Avenue/ Ohio Street, PO Box 4369
Dar Es Salaam Tanzania
Tel: +255 22 211 8790/211 4664 **Fax:** +255 22 211 3247/211 6635

Email: info@mkono.com
Website: www.mkono.com

FIRM OVERVIEW

Managing partner: Nimrod E Mkono
Senior partner: Wilbert B. Kapinga

Number of partners worldwide: 7
Number of other lawyers worldwide: 17

AREAS OF PRACTICE:

Company, corporate finance and commercial 42%
Banking and capital markets 20%
Commercial litigation (incl construction) 18%
Employment/Intellectual property 12%
Mining and international tax planning 6%
Property (incl planning) 2%

FIRM OVERVIEW: Mkono & Co is a leading corporate practice based in the city of Dar es Salaam. On 1st May 2000 Mkono & Co set up an alliance with Denton Wilde Sapte, an international law firm. The association stops short of a merger but the expectation is that in due course the relations will come even closer. The move will build on the two law firms existing strengths in corporate and trade finance. Mkono & Co provides a range of legal services to major commercial clients from within and outside Tanzania. The firm has grown steadily over the past decade and has developed considerable experience in the corporate field, particularly in privatisation, telecommunications and banking. Its global partnership with leading law firms has enabled Mkono & Co to handle wide-ranging matters for governmental, public and private companies. Recently these have included advising the government on the privatisation of the National Bank of Commerce, Tanzania Telecommunications Company Limited, Tanzania Portland Cement Company Limited and the Southern Paper Mill Limited. The firm's corporate clients operate in many different areas including banking, capital markets, corporate finance, construction, insurance, mining, management, international trade, telecommunications, property development and construction.

INTERNATIONAL EXPERIENCE: Some of the recent work handled by the firm in 1999 includes the privatisation of the National Bank of Commerce through share sale, and the privatisation of the Tanzania Telecommunications Company Limited, on behalf of the government of Tanzania; employee share scheme, taxation and fraud litigation, acting for the Tanzania Telecommunications Company Limited; the high profile international commercial arbitration (ICSID) case involving electric power project, as well as international commercial arbitration (ICC) involving TANESCO v SIETCO and tax advice and judicial review, on behalf of the Tanzania Electric Supply Company Limited; corporate tax litigation between GAPCO Group v Tanzania Revenue Authority, acting for GAPCO Group of Companies; local arbitration, acting for GAPOIL (Tanzania) Limited; establishment and licensing of a bank, acting on behalf of Barclays Bank PLC; project finance for Barclays Bank (Bank Capital); and the privatisation of Southern Paper Mills, acting for the buyer, London Timber Co Limited as asset acquisition.

WORLDWIDE OFFICE CONTACTS

INDIA
2A, Suvas, 68-F, Nepean Sea Road, 400 006, **Bombay**
Tel: + 91 22 285 5141 **Fax:** + 91 22 363 7610
Email: kapadia@hotmail.com

TANZANIA
9th Floor PPF Tower, Garden Avenue/ Ohio Street, PO Box 4369, **Dar Es Salaam**
Tel: +255 22 211 8790/211 4664 **Fax:** +255 22 211 3247/211 6635
Email: info@mkono.com

UNITED KINGDOM
Denton Wilde Sapte, One Fleet Place, EC4M 7WS, **London**
Tel: + 44 20 7246 046 **Fax:** + 44 20 7246 7777
Email: bcm@dentonwildesapte.com

INTERNATIONAL CLIENTS: Clients of Mkono & Co include the government of Tanzania through Presidential Parastatal Sector Reform Commission; the British High Commission; Tanzania Electric Supply Ltd (TANESCO); Tanzania Telecommunications Company Ltd; PATMA, UK; GAPCO Group of Companies and Adams and Adams, South Africa.

MAIN INTERNATIONAL AREAS OF PRACTICE: Mkono & Co divides its work into the main practice areas described below. There are also a number of cross-departmental groupings which cover specialist areas such as construction, environment, insolvency, insurance, telecommunications, intellectual property, employment and employee benefits, as well as project finance pursuant to the Private Finance Initiative.

Company and commercial: The firm's company and commercial department has a strong reputation in the City and advises, amongst others, major public companies and institutions on all aspects of commercial activity including corporate finance, public company take-overs and flotations, mergers and acquisitions, joint ventures, venture capital, management buy-out, information technology, international agreements and franchise and distribution networks and agreements, as well as providing specialist support in areas such as intellectual property, pensions and employee benefits.

Banking and capital markets: The firm's banking and capital markets department advises borrowers, lenders, issuers, lead managers and trustees on corporate debt, syndicated lending, capital market issues and structured, asset and project finance. The firm advises a number of clients who are active in the secondary debt markets.

Property and planning: The firm's property and departments advise developers, institutional investors, surveyors, and other professionals on financing and planning implications.

Litigation, insurance and insolvency: The firm handles a wide variety of domestic and international commercial disputes relating to construction, defamation, employment, financial and corporate matters, insolvency, insurance and intellectual property, and has considerable experience in the field of patent and trade mark disputes. The firm's insolvency group advises insolvency practitioners and lenders on corporate recovery and insolvency.

LANGUAGES: English, Kiswahili

MOCHTAR, KARUWIN & KOMAR

HEAD OFFICE

Wisma Metropolitan II, 14th Floor, J1 Jend Sudirman Kav 31, Jakarta 12920
(PO Box 2844, Jakarta 10001) Indonesia
Tel: + 62 21 571 1130 **Fax:** + 62 21 571 1162

Email: mail@mkk.co.id

FIRM OVERVIEW

Managing partners: Dr D Sidik Suraputra and Emir Kusumaatmadja
Senior (and founding) partner: Dr Mochtar Kusumaatmadja

Number of partners worldwide: 6
Number of other lawyers worldwide: 37

AREAS OF PRACTICE:

Banking and finance 25%
Mergers and acquisitions 20%
Capital markets 15%
General corporate and commercial 15%
Oil and gas, mining and energy 15%
Infrastructure 10%

FIRM OVERVIEW: Mochtar, Karuwin & Komar was established as one of the first commercial law firms in Indonesia in 1971 and has grown considerably in size since that time. From its inception, the firm has concentrated on corporate and commercial law, with an emphasis on international finance and foreign investment in Indonesia, and oil and gas and mining law. In recent years, in addition to the firm's core practice in banking, finance and investment, the firm has represented clients participating in the privatisation of State-owned companies and infrastructure projects, including electricity generation and telecommunications. As a result of the recent economic crisis, the firm has become heavily involved in corporate and debt restructuring and has performed legal audits on a number of banks for the Indonesian Bank Restructuring Agency (IBRA).

INTERNATIONAL EXPERIENCE: Historically, approximately 90% of the firm's clients have been international investors or their local subsidiaries or international financial institutions. Major areas of international practice are mergers and acquisitions, including representation of parties to the sale by IBRA of interests in shares of P.T. Astra International Tbk., First Pacific Company Ltd., and the Salim Oleochemicals Group and sale of loans by IBRA to international investors.

INTERNATIONAL CLIENTS: The firm's clients include American Express Bank Ltd, Asian Development Bank, Bank Nationale de Paris, Bank of India, BASF, Bechtel Group, BHP, British Telecommunications, Cargill, Cemex SA, Chase Manhattan Bank, Commonwealth Development Corporation, Conoco, CS First Boston, Dai-Ichi Kangyo Bank Limited, Du Pont, Dow Chemical, Edison Mission Energy Company, Enron Power Corporation, Exxon Corporation, Fluor Daniel Corporation, GE Capital, Gillette, Hilton International, Hong Kong and Shanghai Banking Corporation, Hyatt International, IBM, Inco Limited, International Finance Corporation, Japan Exim Bank, The Kellogg Corporation, Kimberly-Clark corporation, Merrill Lynch, Mitsui & Co Ltd, Mobil Oil Corporation, Morgan Guaranty Trust, Nippon Telegraph and Telephone Corporation, Northwest Airlines, Nova Gas, Pennzoil, Pfizer, Texas Eastern corporation, Telstra, Tomen, Toyota Corporation, Union Texas Corporation, UNOCAL, Warner Lambert Corporation.

WORLDWIDE OFFICE CONTACTS

INDONESIA
Wisma Metropolitan II, 14th Floor, J1 Jend Sudirman Kav 31, Jakarta 12920, (PO Box 2844, **Jakarta** 10001)
Tel: + 62 21 571 1130 **Fax:** + 62 21 571 1162 / 570 1686
Email: mail@mkk.co.id

SINGAPORE
#22-06 Singapore Land Tower, 50 Raffles Place, **Singapore** 0104
Tel: + 65 225 3311 **Fax:** + 65 223 2191
Email: mkk.sing@pacific.net.sg

M

MAIN INTERNATIONAL AREAS OF PRACTICE:

General corporate and commercial: The firm's transactions involve representation of foreign companies in establishing (or acquiring) Indonesian companies, or in developing non-investment commercial relationships (distribution, licensing, etc).

Mergers and acquisitions: The firm represents both international investors and local companies in connection with private acquisitions or acquisitions through the stock exchange, including through tender offers.

Oil and gas, energy and mining: The firm's practice includes advice in connection with production sharing contracts (including farm-ins), contracts of work (hard mining and coal) and geothermal energy production, and representation of lenders to such companies.

Banking and finance: The firm has traditionally represented offshore and local financial institutions in extending credit to Indonesian companies either in the form of loans or other credit arrangements, including project finance. Due to the recent economic crisis in Indonesia, this work has shifted to debt restructuring in most cases.

Infrastructure privatisation: With the government's desire to privatise parts of the infrastructure (telecommunications, ports, toll roads, etc), the firm has represented many foreign investors interested in participating in these activities.

Capital markets: The firm has acted as counsel to issuers and underwriters of securities through the stock exchange, companies undertaking a tender offer for shares and general compliance issues with respect to publicly traded securities, including the creation of derivative securities based on securities listed on the stock exchange.

LANGUAGES: Dutch, English, Indonesian

Mochtar, Karuwin & Komar

For other recommended firms see pages 1485-1520

MORAIS LEITÃO, J GALVÃO TELES & ASSOCIADOS

HEAD OFFICE

Rua Castilho, 75 -1st floor,
Lisbon 1250, Portugal
Tel: +351 21 381 74 00
Fax: +351 21 381 74 96

FIRM OVERVIEW

Managing partner: João Morais Leitão

Number of partners worldwide: 13
Number of other lawyers worldwide: 38

AREAS OF PRACTICE:

M&A and others	25%
Banking and finance	20%
Privatisation and capital markets	15%
Litigation and arbitration	15%
Project Finance	15%
Taxation	10%

WORLDWIDE OFFICE CONTACTS

PORTUGAL
Rua Castilho, 75 -1st floor, 1250, **Lisbon**
Tel: +351 21 381 74 00 **Fax:** +351 21 381 74 96
Email: mlgtlisboa@mlgt.pt

SPAIN
Uría & Menéndez, Jorge Juan 6, 28001, **Madrid**
Tel: + 34 91 586 0400 **Fax:** + 34 91 586 0403
Email:

FIRM OVERVIEW: Morais Leitao, J Galvao Teles & Associados was born of the 1994 merger of two Portuguese law firms founded in the 1960s, one with a focus on international finance and corporate law, the other specialising in litigation and commercial law. By combining the respective strengths of these two firms, MLGT has developed a broad-based practice capable of providing legal services in all major areas. The firm has offices in Lisbon and Funchal, with one in Oporto that opened at the end of 1999. It also maintains close contacts with firms in Europe, the United States and Brazil, and has an association with the Spanish firm Uria & Menendez.

INTERNATIONAL EXPERIENCE: MLGT represents foreign and multinational corporations in their business dealings in Portugal, and Portuguese clients in their foreign business mainly in Brazil, Spain and the former Portuguese colonies. Recent transactions have included advising clients as sellers or purchaser in companies under privatisations and of private nature, in areas such as banking, oil and gas, electricity and multimedia.

MAIN INTERNATIONAL AREAS OF PRACTICE:

Corporate and commercial: The firm has assisted clients in areas including mergers and acquisitions, restructuring, joint ventures, management buy-outs and taxation. Its corporate law advice has covered sectors including chemical, telecommunications, food processing, oil and gas, recycling, construction and insurance.

Banking and finance: MLGT has been active in this area since the 1984 constitutional amendments which introduced private banks and other financial and credit institutions to Portugal. The firm participated in the first privatisation of a state-owned bank, and acts as local counsel to Portuguese and foreign banks.

Privatisation and capital markets: The firm has been extensively involved in the Portuguese privatisation programme, and has advised privatised companies, shareholders and global coordinators in almost every privatisation to date.

Project finance: This continues to be one of the firm's major practice areas, and further growth is forecast in light of the increasing levels of public investment in infrastructure.

EU and competition: The firm represents clients before both the Portuguese and European competition authorities. As counsel to a Portuguese company, MLGT was one of the first Portuguese law firms to appear in a European Commission proceeding, even before the country's full membership of the EU.

Taxation: Advising clients how to optimise the tax efficiency of their investments by establishing branches and subsidiaries in mainland Portugal and the International Business Centre in Madeira is one of the firm's most active areas. The firm monitors tax reform and has participated in the drafting of new tax laws.

Litigation and arbitration: The firm has extensive experience in administrative, civil, commercial, criminal and tax litigation, and has participated in many of the major criminal, commercial and transfer pricing cases in Portugal. Members of the firm serve in arbitration proceedings, both as lawyers and arbitrators.

Employment: The firm provides advice and representation in court. It has been involved in several collective dismissal proceedings.

LANGUAGES: English, French, German, Italian, Spanish

For other recommended firms see pages 1485-1520

MORALES NOGUERA VALDIVIESO & BESA

HEAD OFFICE

Avda. Apoquindo 3001, Piso 9, Las Condes
Santiago 6760342, Chile
Tel: +56 2 750 2900 **Fax:** +56 2 750 2901

Email: mnvb@mnvb.cl
Website: www.mnvb.cl

WORLDWIDE OFFICE CONTACTS

CHILE
Avda. Apoquindo 3001, Piso 9, Las Condes, **Santiago** 6760342
Tel: +56 2 750 2900 **Fax:** +56 2 750 2901
Email: mnvb@mnvb.cl

FIRM OVERVIEW

Senior partner: G. Morales
Managing partners: E. Besa, J. C. Valdivieso and D. Noguera

AREAS OF PRACTICE:

M&A	26%
Banking and finance	18%
Corporate	14%
Securities	12%
Tax	12%
Intellectual Property	10%
Litigation and arbitration	8%

M

FIRM OVERVIEW: Morales, Noguera, Valdivieso & Besa was established in 1992 by a group of leading international, finance and tax lawyers. In 1995 the firm merged with a law firm with strong domestic corporate credentials, and has continued its expansion ever since. The firm does not participate in formal alliances or networks, preferring to maintain contacts with various firms worldwide and to choose the firm it works with on individual international transactions. Morales, Noguera, Valdivieso & Besa offers a comprehensive legal service to clients with international business interests, and focuses on banking and finance, mergers and acquisitions, securities offerings, taxation and litigation.

INTERNATIONAL EXPERIENCE: The firm advises on all kinds of complex cross-border transactions, including mergers and acquisitions, debt and equity securities offerings, structured finance, project finance and tax planning. In 1999 Morales, Noguera, Valdivieso & Besa acted as special legal counsel for the Republic of Chile in its inaugural Sovereign Global Bond issuance and advised Merrill Lynch & Co. on a cross-border securitisation involving credit card sales of air tickets for a national airline carrier. The firm also represented Donaldson, Lufkin & Jenrette and Credit Suisse First Boston in the financial restructuring of a local telecommunications company trading in the New York Stock Exchange.

INTERNATIONAL CLIENTS: The majority of the firm's clients are international and include a wide variety of US and European investment banks, commercial banks, securities firms and multinational corporations engaged in such diverse areas as telecommunications, oil and gas, infrastructure and retailing.

MAIN INTERNATIONAL AREAS OF PRACTICE:

M&A: The firm has advised international and domestic buyers and sellers in acquisitions and take-over processes. Morales, Noguera, Valdivieso & Besa are a leading legal advisor in tender offers of publicly listed companies in Chile. It's privatisation practice group has represented international buyers and the government of Chile in all major transfers of Chilean state-owned assets and enterprises.

Banking and finance: The firm covers all areas of investment banking and finance, including corporate finance, leveraged buy outs, structured finance, project finance, derivatives, distressed debt and restructuring, commercial lending and syndicated loans.

Securities and financial markets: The firm is involved in advising and executing debt and equity securities offerings, securitisation of all kinds of assets, listing of companies, domestically and internationally. The firm has particular expertise in the areas of asset management and venture capital law.

Taxation: Morales, Noguera, Valdivieso & Besa is one of few local firms with a highly specialised tax practice group that provides advice on tax planning, tax driven restructurings, tax litigation and general tax advice.

Intellectual property: The firm advises on all kinds of intellectual property issues, infringement disputes and all other aspects of IP law. The practice group undertakes trademark, patent and copyright registration and litigation, although its lawyers largely perform related transactional work. The firm is actively involved in the structuring and negotiation of licensing agreements and technology agreements. The internet and its development are a principal focus.

Litigation, arbitration and ADR: The firm's group of highly skilled litigation practitioners represent the firm's clients in a variety of civil, commercial, tax, anti-trust, white collar crime and other specialised court litigation, at district, appellate and Supreme Court level. The group has experience and familiarity with domestic and international arbitration proceedings and the enforcement of foreign awards. In the area of alternative dispute resolution its attorneys are active, particularly in large infrastructure projects and engineering contracts.

Anti-trust: Chile actively enforces its antitrust statute and the firm's lawyers undertake antitrust, competition and marketing related cases involving companies in the Chilean market.

Energy, public utilities and infrastructure: Morales, Noguera, Valdivieso & Besa plays an active role in the continuing development and deregulation of the Chilean energy, utilities and infrastructure sectors. The firm has vast experience in the regulatory framework of power generation, transmission and distribution, fuel transportation and distribution, water and sewage and public works. It has advised major multinational companies that have made significant investments in power plants, gas pipelines, transmission lines and privatised toll roads.

LANGUAGES: English, French, Spanish

MORALES NOGUERA VALDIVIESO & BESA

SOCIEDAD CIVIL DE RESPONSALIBIDAD LIMITADA

For other recommended firms see pages 1485-1520

MORGAN, LEWIS & BOCKIUS LLP

HEAD OFFICE

1701 Market Street,
Philadelphia PA 19103-2921, USA
Tel: +1 215 963 5000 **Fax:** +1 215 963 5299
Email: info@morganlewis.com
Website: www.morganlewis.com

FIRM OVERVIEW

Chairman: Francis M. Milone
Number of partners worldwide: 330
Number of other lawyers worldwide: 1,100

AREAS OF PRACTICE:

Anti-trust .... *%
Business & commercial litigation .... *%
Business and finance .... *%
Corporate transactions .... *%
Employment, labour & benefits .... *%
Energy and utilities .... *%
Intellectual property .... *%
Investment management .... *%
Life sciences .... *%
Mergers and acquisitions .... *%
Personal law .... *%
Real estate .... *%
Securities .... *%
Tax .... *%
Technology .... *%
*Workload % not disclosed

FIRM OVERVIEW: Morgan Lewis is a leading law firm comprising more than 1,100 lawyers in 12 offices in the US and abroad. The firm represents many Fortune 250 companies, top biotechnology and e-commerce sector businesses, as well as leading financial services and investment banking organisations.

INTERNATIONAL EXPERIENCE: Each area of the firm's practice, from anti-trust to litigation, has a strong international component. The firm represents clients in mergers and acquisitions all over the world, resolving differing and conflicting laws in a number of jurisdictions. Its lawyers are experienced in the problems and complexities of transnational litigation and advise on US and EU regulatory matters.

INTERNATIONAL CLIENTS: The firm has a diverse client base including Fortune 250 companies, leading financial services and investment banking organisations, as well as pioneers in the e-commerce and internet sector. It also represents high net worth individuals.

MAIN INTERNATIONAL AREAS OF PRACTICE:

Anti-trust: The firm provides the full spectrum of anti-trust services, from preventative counselling and advice on the latest anti-trust issues to defence litigation.
Business and commerical litigation: The litigation practice group handles the entire range of problems associated with dispute resolution in relation to business corporations, individuals and other organisations.
Business and finance: This is one of the firm's principal strengths in M&A practices. The firm also has an active corporate finance practice.
Employment, labour and benefits: The firm handles all aspects of labour and employment issues.
Energy and utiities: The firm advises on, and negotiates, a broad range of energy-related domestic and international transactions.

WORLDWIDE OFFICE CONTACTS

BELGIUM
7 Rue Guimard, B-1040 **Brussels**
Tel: + 32 2 512 55 01 **Fax:** + 32 2 512 58 88

GERMANY
Guiollettstrasse 54, 60325 **Frankfurt am Main**
Tel: + 49 69 71 40 070 **Fax:** + 49 69 71 40 07-10

JAPAN
Yurakucho Denki Bldg, S-556, 7-1 Yurakucho 1-chome, Chiyoda-ku, **Tokyo** 100
Tel: + 81 3 3216 2500 **Fax:** + 81 3 3216 2501

UNITED KINGDOM
2 Gresham Street, **London** EC2V 7PE
Tel: + 44 20 7710 5500 Fax: + 44 20 7710 5600

USA
One Commerce Square, 417 Walnut Street, **Harrisburg** PA 17101-1904
Tel: +1 717 237 4000 **Fax:** + 1 717 237 4004

300 South Grand Avenue, Twenty-second floor, **Los Angeles** CA 90017-3132
Tel: +1 213 612 2500 **Fax:** + 1 213 612 2554

5300 First Union Financial Center, 200 South Biscayne Boulevard, **Miami** FL 33131-2339
Tel: +1 305 579 0300 **Fax:** + 1 305 579 0321

101 Park Avenue, **New York** NY 10178-0060
Tel: +1 212 309 6000 **Fax:** + 1 212 309 6273

1701 Market Street, **Philadelphia** PA 19103-2921
Tel: +1 215 963 5000 **Fax:** +1 215 963 5299

One Oxford Centre, Thirty-second floor, 301 Grant Street, **Pittsburgh** PA 15219-6401
Tel: +1 412 560 3300 **Fax:** + 1 412 560 3399

502 Carnegie Center, **Princeton** NJ 08540
Tel: +1 609 919 6600 **Fax:** + 1 609 919 6639

1800 M Street, NW, **Washington** DC 20036-5869
Tel: +1 202 467 7000 **Fax:** + 1 202 467 7176

Intellectual property: The firm advises clients on all aspects of intellectual property, including patents, trademarks and copyrights.
Life sciences: The firm advises on finance and securities law, mergers and acquisitions, licensings and collaborations, intellectual property law, FDA and other government regulations, tax, litigation, labour and employment, and immigration.
Securities: The firm has a worldwide interdisciplinary practice comprised of securities enforcement and litigation, investment management, broker-dealer and corporate finance attorneys, among others.
Tax: The firm advises clients on tax planning and litigation matters, as well as administrative and legislative matters, on behalf of domestic and foreign corporations, partnerships and individuals.
Technology: The firm represents emerging e-commerce companies and start-ups as well as established companies, Fortune 250 companies, venture capitalists and investment banks in the areas of Internet, e-commerce, telecommunications, biotech, IPOs and venture capital.

LANGUAGES: English, Flemish, French, German, Japanese, Portuguese, Spanish

MORI SOGO LAW OFFICES

HEAD OFFICE

NKK Building, 1-1-2, Marunouchi, Chiyoda-ku
Tokyo 100-0005, Japan
Tel: +81 3 5223 7700 **Fax:** +81 3 5223 7600

Website: www.morisogo.com

WORLDWIDE OFFICE CONTACTS

CHINA
Suite 813, Beijing Fortune Bldg, 5 Dong San Huan Bei Lu, Chaoyang District, **Beijing** 100004
Tel: +86 10 6590 9292 **Fax:** +86 10 6590 9290

FIRM OVERVIEW

Senior partner: Harumichi Uchida

Number of partners worldwide: 31
Number of other lawyers worldwide: 54

AREAS OF PRACTICE:

Banking and finance	*%
Bankruptcy and insolvency	*%
Corporate	*%
E-commerce	*%
Intellectual property	*%
Litigation	*%
M&A	*%
Structured finance	*%
Venture capital and private equity	*%

* Workload % not disclosed

M

FIRM OVERVIEW: One of Japan's largest law firms, Mori Sogo began as a litigation specialist. The firm has grown into a full service law firm with offices in both Tokyo and Beijing.

INTERNATIONAL EXPERIENCE: Mori Sogo has advised on a number of joint ventures and M&A transactions involving foreign companies, including representing a major Japanese securities company in its investment banking joint venture with, and sale of a substantial amount of its equity to, a major US financial group. Mori Sogo routinely represents foreign financial service firms in international banking and finance. The firm also has experience in domestic and international litigation and arbitration. Mori Sogo regularly assists in the establishment of foreign companies in Japan including start-up dot.coms in the US.

INTERNATIONAL CLIENTS: The firm's international clients include multinationals from a wide range of business sectors including banks, financial institutions, insurance, telecommunications, information technology, real estate, and manufacturing companies.

MAIN INTERNATIONAL AREAS OF PRACTICE:

Banking and finance: Mori Sogo regularly advises foreign clients on the regulatory procedures involved in the banking and finance industries in Japan. It is regular outside counsel to more than ten banks.

Bankruptcy and insolvency: Mori Sogo regularly advises clients and their financial advisers on buying companies out of insolvency proceedings and devising safe structures to undertake debtor-in-possession financings. The firm often acts as trustees or receivers for insolvent and reorganising companies.

Corporate: The firm advises on all aspects of general corporate law. It has been at the forefront of recent western style developments in Japanese corporate law, including corporate governance, tracking stock, corporate divisions, and stock option plans. It has handled major strategic alliances in the Internet and automobile industries.

E-commerce and new economy: The firm advised on the creation of, and is often counsel to, Japan's largest Internet service provider. It also advised on the establishment of Nasdaq-Japan and is counsel to several bank groups that are creating electronic payment systems.

Intellectual property: The firm's intellectual property practice handles litigation, negotiation, strategic planning, and contract drafting. Much of Mori Sogo's work has an international aspect. The firm coordinates with clients and co-counsel in infringement litigation in more than one country, particularly Asian countries and the US.

Litigation: Mori Sogo's origins as a domestic litigation firm have left it with more attorneys spending most of their time in court. It has handled several cases, which helped shape the jurisdictional and other rules applicable to international trade and investment. One such case established, through a unanimous decision of the Japanese Supreme Court, the primacy of contractual arbitration.

M&A: The firm specialises in M&A. It has handled a large number of acquisitions in the financial services industry involving takeovers of insolvent banks and insurance companies by foreign companies. Mori Sogo has also handled several take over bids for public companies, including the first hostile one between Japanese companies.

Structured finance: Mori Sogo has handled the securitisation of lease and credit card receivables, consumer loans, trade receivables, residential and commercial mortgage loans, and commercial real estate. A recent trend is to securitise office buildings and multi-use real estate projects to yield proceeds to the originator of several billion dollars.

Venture capital and private equity: With attorneys that have practiced in both Tokyo and the Silicon Valley, Mori Sogo handles substantial US-Japan venture capital work and fund organisation. It also advises US dot.com companies setting up local subsidiaries with Japanese partners.

LANGUAGES: Chinese, English, French, Japanese

 For other recommended firms see pages 1485-1520

MORRISON & FOERSTER LLP

HEAD OFFICE

425 Market Street,
San Francisco CA 94105-2482, USA
Tel: +1 415 268 7000 **Fax:** +1 415 268 7522

Email: info@mofo.com
Website: www.mofo.com

FIRM OVERVIEW

Chairman of the firm: Keith Wetmore

Number of partners worldwide: 293
Number of other lawyers worldwide: 723

WORLDWIDE OFFICE CONTACTS

BELGIUM
Avenue Molière 262, 1180 **Brussels**
Tel: +32 2 347 0400 **Fax:** +32 2 347 1824
Email: info@mofo.com

UNITED KINGDOM
21 Garlick Hill, **London** EC2V 2AU
Tel: +44 20 7815 1150 **Fax:** +44 20 7815 1159
Email: London@mofo.com

Additional offices in New York, Tokyo, Beijing, Hong Kong, Singapore, San Francisco, Los Angeles, Sacramento, Palo Alto, Orange County, Walnut Creek, Washington DC, Denver, Northern Virginia, San Diego and Buenos Aires.

AREAS OF PRACTICE:

Corporate and M&A	25%
Litigation and arbitration	25%
Technology transactions (including IP)	23%
Finance/ infrastructure	10%
Employment	5%
Tax	5%
Property	4%
Land use and environment	3%

FIRM OVERVIEW: Morrison & Foerster (MoFo) is the world's largest technology and finance law firm. Founded in 1883, the firm is headquartered in Silicon Valley/San Francisco and comprises over 1,000 lawyers in 18 offices located in key technology and financial centres in the US, Europe, Asia and Latin America. MoFo is one of a limited number of law firms with global capabilities in the technology sector, serving clients in the software, internet, e-commerce, new media, entertainment, hardware, telecoms, internet infrastructure, and life sciences areas, as well as institutions and specialist investors in these areas and 'traditional economy' clients moving into or operating in them. The firm is experienced in domestic and international corporate and corporate finance, securities and capital markets, US anti-trust and EU competition, banking and finance law. The firm's employment, tax, and litigation and arbitration practices are widely regarded as being amongst the pre-eminent practices in their respective fields.

INTERNATIONAL EXPERIENCE: The firm has extensive international experience in the areas of international capital markets, cross-border mergers and acquisitions, strategic exploitation of intellectual property rights, international tax and cross-border e-commerce issues. Recent transactions have included acting for Verio Inc. in its US$5.5 billion acquisition by NTT; acting for Vodafone AirTouch in its joint venture with Japan Telecom and BT for the development of 3G mobile phones and related services; representing Quadrem, a B2B exchange of 16 major mining companies, on EU competition law issues and contracts for auctions over the Internet; representing Fujitsu in its acquisition of ICL; acting for Hong Kong-based iAdvantage, an internet infrastructure company, in its US$100 million share swap deal with Canadian fibre-optics network builder 360 Networks; and Toshiba in its formation of a US$600 million worldwide joint venture with General Electric for the development and sale of large scale industrial drive systems.

INTERNATIONAL CLIENTS: The firm's clients include 724 Solutions Inc., @Nifty, Airports Council International, Aiwa Research & Development, AmericaOnline, Asiacontent.com, Ltd., BEA Systems Inc., Bear Stearns, BMG Entertainment, Broadband Sports, Cha! Technologies, Cheap Tickets, Inc., Checkpoint Software Technology, Chubb Insurance, Covisint, Creative Computers, CS First Boston, Curaflex Health Services, CyberSource Corporation, DirectTV, Dow Chemical, EarthWeb Inc., eBay, Fujitsu, Goldman Sachs, Home Box Office, Identrus, iAdvantage, LLC, JDS Uniphase Corporation, Net2Phone, Inc., Netscape Communications Corporation, Kiodex, Inc., Lehman Brothers, Lockheed Martin Corporation, Marconi P.L.C., McKinsey & Co., Merrill Lynch, Morgan Stanley Dean Witter, NBC Internet, Netease.com, Inc., NTT, Oppenheimer & Co., Oracle, Organic, Inc., Quadrem, Qwest, Rare Medium, Razorfish, RealNetworks, Saba Software, Sage, Inc., Salomon Smith Barney, SDL, Inc., Softbank, Tandem Computers, Inc., Toshiba, Toyota, uBid, Inc., VeriFone, Inc., Verio Inc., Vodafone AirTouch, Xoom.com, Yahoo!, Walt Disney Productions, Warburg Pincus, Whitney & Co, WinStar Communications, Working Woman Network.

MAIN INTERNATIONAL AREAS OF PRACTICE:

Corporate: The firm has extensive experience in the areas of private equity and venture capital, working on both the company and the fund side. Formed by MoFo partners, early funds such as Arthur Rock & Associates, Kleiner, Perkins, Caulfield & Byers and H & Q Ventures established the structure on which most subsequent venture funds have been based. Since 1987, MoFo has represented more than twenty venture capital funds in various aspects of their fund formation and investment activities. The firm has extensive experience advising both publically-traded and privately-held companies on domestic and cross-border mergers, acquisitions, joint ventures and strategic and financial alliances. MoFo's M&A activity has been most highly concentrated in the technology, telecommunications, multimedia and software, banking and other financial sectors. The firm represented JDS Uniphase in its $41 billion acquisition of SDL, Inc. and Verio Inc. in NTT's $5 billion tender offer for, and acquisition of, Verio, Inc. The firm is actively involved in representing a wide variety of issuers and underwriters in connection with public and private offerings of securities (including IPOs and non-IPO offerings) in a wide number of jurisdictions across Asia and the US. MoFo has acted on IPOs or secondary offerings for new or emerging companies such as Saba Software, Inc., 02Micro International Limited, Asiacontent.com Ltd., Organic, Inc., NBC Internet, Inc., and 724 Solutions, Inc. It has advised debt and equity securities issuers such as BankAmerica Corporation, The Clorox Company, Intel Corporation, McKesson Corporation and San Diego Gas & Electric. MoFo's lawyers have represented many of the major underwriting firms, including Bear Stearns, Chase, H&Q, Credit Suisse First Boston, Deutsche Bank Alex.Brown, Goldman Sachs, Lehman Bros., Merrill Lynch, Schroder, Salomon Smith Barney, Thomas Weisel Partners, WR Hambrecht & Co. and others. MoFo represents brokers, dealers and investment advisers in regulatory and disciplinary matters.

M

MORRISON & FOERSTER LLP cont'd

Technology transactions: The firm's clients include telecom operators, equipment vendors and other infrastructure-based businesses, content, software and hardware providers and purchasers, web site developers, webcasting and broadcasting companies, entertainment and 'infotainment' companies and other content developers and providers, and an extremely broad range of business-to-business and business-to-consumer players, including portal operators, search engines, retailers, auction sites and B2B exchanges. The firm's lawyers routinely advise these and other technology based businesses on corporate matters, including corporate structuring, M&A, all types of commercial matters including vendor, supplier, affiliate and sponsor agreements and joint ventures, partnerships and strategic alliances and all aspects of financing and funding as well as on the development and licensing of content (for static and dynamic media), syndicating content among online service providers, and general internet and e-commerce matters including in relation to on-line contracts and contracting, on-line liability, domain-name, copyright, trade mark, patent and other intellectual property matters, technology transfer, negotiating technology/IP licences, and privacy and data protection law. Telecoms advice involves representing telecommunications operators, service providers and providers and purchasers of telecoms equipment in contractual negotiations, regulatory issues, M&A and transactions structuring. MoFo represent numerous large government and commercial users of telecoms services in transactions and regulatory proceedings involving telecoms issues.

Biotechnology: The firm's multidisciplinary life science group draws upon the expertise of attorneys in a wide range of practice areas. The firm represents a diverse group of partitipants in biotechnology, medical technology, and health care industries, offering legal expertise for every phase of a life science company's growth cycle. Its involvement in biotechnology spans a broad range of subspecialities, including genomics, combinatorial chemistry, drug design, development biology, and drug deivery. The firm complements experience in counselling high-technology companies in many industries with internationally renowned expertise in biotechnology and a life science patent practice with skills drawn from in-house patent and scientific analysis

Intellectual property: MoFo's IP practice is drawn from an international base of lawyers advising on patents (including in relation to business methods), trade marks, passing off, copyright, confidentiality/trade secrets, data protection, unfair competition and other national and international IP matters. Over 140 lawyers provide a range of services, including representation in patent and trade mark prosecution, litigation and alternative dispute resolution, and all aspects of non-contentious IP advice including licensing transactions, applications / registrations of intellectual property rights, assignments and advising on IP issues in all corporate transactions.

Litigation: The firm has approximately 350 litigators who provide foreign and domestic clients with skilled representation in such areas as antitrust and trade regulation, IP, securities, financial institutions, land use and environmental, product liability, commercial property and communications. MoFo represented the defendant in the groundbreaking Religious Technology Center v. Netcom litigation concerning copyright infringement on bulletin boards and the liability of online service providers for the infringement of their subscribers. In conjunction with MoFo's international litigation group, the London telecoms and new media practice represents technology clients in a range of contentious issues specific to the sector. These include profit participations, copyright and trade mark matters, domain name misuse and cybersquatting, patent infringement, unfair competition, antitrust, rights and royalties, defamation, licensing and privacy issues. The office has represented Internet clients in securities fraud, antitrust and consumer class actions. The office represents providers of transmission services, computer hardware and software, video and audio programming and traditional telephone services in litigation before the courts and regulatory agencies. MoFo advised Fujitsu in its arbitration with IBM regarding its operating system software, and has since represented Fujitsu in litigation in numerous matters around the world. The firm acted for Fujitsu in the US District Courts in both California and Virginia in relation to the expiry of a cross licensing agreement with a major rival and the case was litigated before the International Trade Commission in Washington D.C. The firm also acted as co-ordinating counsel in Italy, Germany and the UK.

Finance and infrastructure: The firm's practice includes leading experts in the fields of financial services, investment management, finance and infrastructure. The 55 lawyer group encompasses expertise in both energy regulatory matters and energy and non-energy project-development and finance as well as debt, lease, securitisation, sovereign debt restructuring, debt/equity swaps and other debt, equity and derivative-based financing of all types, including Rule 144A financings of project debt. Recent work includes representing the Overseas Private Investment Corporation (OPIC) and the Export-Import Bank of the United States as lenders in the non-recourse financing of a 500MW gas-fired combined cycle power plant in Turkey (the world's largest such project to date), the representation of OPIC as lender in connection with the initial funding and current restructuring of a $2.5 billion limited recourse project financing for the construction and operation of a 1230 MW power plant in Indonesia and the representation of Azurix Corporation on privatisation projects in Latin America, including the financing of the $450 million purchase of AGOSBA, a Buenos Aires water utility.

Tax: The Tax Department advises on the planning and structuring of domestic and international transactions and all other aspects of tax related-work. The department's practice includes advising on the federal, state, and international tax implications of all aspects of business transactions. MoFo's Tax Department is one of the pre-eminent international tax practices and has broad experience in representing technology clients, corporations and investment banks in connection with cross-border transactions, acquisitions and disposals of assets and shares of public and private companies. The group has also advised corporations and investment funds in connection with strategic and venture investments, leveraged buy-outs, spin-offs, split-ups and restructurings in connection with bankruptcy and non-bankruptcy work-outs. The US Tax Department's extensive state and local practice services a diverse group of clients with advice including planning and consulting with respect to state and local tax issues, representation in the audit process and administrative controversies, and prosecution of appeals through court litigation. MoFo's tax lawyers have been involved in a number of important cases affecting state and local taxation including representing Container Corporation before the United States Supreme Court in its challenge of the California worldwide unitary method of taxation as applied to corporations operating exclusively outside the United States; and representing Colgate-Palmolive Co. in its challenge in state court and before the United States Supreme Court to California's method.

Property: MoFo's global property practice includes 55 property and land use lawyers, representing many of the largest developers and lending institutions in their activities around the world. Advice is given to clients including Bank of America, Clorox, Shea Homes, United Parcel Service, Wells Fargo and The University of California. Clients also include property investment advisers in connection with their pooled property funds and the pension fund industry with respect to their real estate investors.

LANGUAGES: Catalan, Chinese (Cantonese, Mandarin), Danish, Dutch, English, Finnish, French, German, Hebrew, Italian, Japanese, Korean, Norwegian, Portuguese, Russian, Spanish, Swedish

For other recommended firms see pages 1485-1520

MOURANT DU FEU & JEUNE

HEAD OFFICE

PO Box 87, 22 Grenville Street,
St Helier JE4 8PX, Jersey
Tel: +44 1534 609000 **Fax:** +44 1534 609333

Email: enquiry@mourant.com
Website: www.mourant.com

FIRM OVERVIEW

Managing partner: Richard Jeune
Senior partner: Conrad Coutanche

Number of partners: 21
Assistant solicitors: 24

WORLDWIDE OFFICE CONTACTS

JERSEY
PO Box 87, 22 Grenville Street, JE4 8PX, **St Helier**
Tel: +44 1534 609000 **Fax:** +44 1534 609333
Email: enquiry@mourant.com

UNITED KINGDOM
Mourant du Feu & Jeune, London, 4th Floor, 35 New Bridge Street, Blackfriars, **London** EC4V 6BW
Tel: + 44 207 332 6161 **Fax:** + 44 207 332 6199
Email: enquiry@mourant.com

AREAS OF PRACTICE:

International finance	38%
Employee benefits	25%
Private wealth management	14%
Commercial corporate	10%
Commercial litigation	8%
Property	5%

FIRM OVERVIEW: Established in Jersey in 1947, Mourant du Feu & Jeune is the largest law firm in the Channel Islands, with 21 partners heading a total staff of 400 based in Jersey and London. It specialises in offshore legal services and has been active in the development of Jersey's financial services industry. Areas of expertise include capital markets, structured finance, securitisation, funds, property holding and finance, employee benefits and commercial litigation. Recognising the importance of its City client base, the firm opened a London branch office in April 2000, the first in the Channel Islands to do so.

INTERNATIONAL EXPERIENCE: The firm acts for global financial institutions in international finance, and advises City lawyers and investment banks on the Jersey aspects of securitisation and structured finance transactions. Employee benefits clients include multinational organisations implementing global share plans. Work for collective investment funds includes advising the largest management buyout of a private equity fund in Europe and several other major European funds.

INTERNATIONAL CLIENTS: In 2000 Mourant du Feu & Jeune and Mourant & Co acted for 70% of the FTSE100 companies and 22% of the top 100 companies in Business Week Global 1000.

MAIN INTERNATIONAL AREAS OF PRACTICE:

International finance: The firm advises global financial institutions on the Jersey legal aspects of securitisation, capital markets transactions, structured and corporate finance and banking. Recent transactions include Arran One Limited, Geldilux 99-1 Limited and Geldilux 99-2 Limited, Lochness Limited, Fast 1999-1 Limited and Glencore - Energy and Metals Finance Ltd.

Commercial: The commercial team specialises in advising businesses on Jersey commercial and corporate law, in particular trust and company law, collective investments, financial services regulation, M&A and employment law.

Commercial litigation: The practice focuses on banking and trust litigation, asset tracing and fraud.

Employee share plans: The firm's associated trust company, Mourant & Co, provides administration services to employee share plans. It currently administers plans for 35% of the FTSE100 companies, together with global stock option plans for a number of blue chip multinationals based outside the UK. Assets under administration total over US$6 billion.

Private wealth management: Mourant & Co's private wealth management group manages the financial and legal affairs of high-profile individuals resident both in Jersey and outside the island.

Funds: The firm has advised on almost 50% of Jersey-domiciled collective investment funds, and specialises in particular in private equity and venture capital funds. Clients include the largest management buyout private equity fund in Europe. Its trust company, Mourant & Co, administers some of the chief European private equity funds including the largest, CVC European Equity Partners II, and has fund assets of over US$5 billion under administration.

Corporate property structures: Mourant Group advises on the establishment and administration of onshore and offshore financing and holding structures for property assets. Its services include off balance sheet financing arrangements, securitisation of property assets and joint venture structures for property co-ownership and property holding structures.

LANGUAGES: English, French, German, Italian, Portuguese, Spanish

WORLDWIDE OFFICES

UNITED KINGDOM

Mourant du Feu & Jeune, London, 4th Floor, 35 New Bridge Street, Blackfriars, London, EC4V 6BW

Number of lawyers: 2

Office profile: Mourant de Feu & Jeune opened for business in London in May 2000, the first Channel Islands law firm to do so. It provides Jersey legal advice in relation to capital markets and structured finance transactions.

M

MUGERWA & MASEMBE ADVOCATES

HEAD OFFICE

3rd Floor Diamond Trust Building, 17/19 Kampala Road,
P.O. Box 7166, Kampala Uganda
Tel: +256 41 343 859 **Fax:** +256 41 259 992

Email: info@mugmas.co.ug
Website: www.mugmas.co.ug

WORLDWIDE OFFICE CONTACTS

UGANDA
3rd Floor Diamond Trust Building, 17/19 Kampala Road, P.O. Box 7166,
Kampala
Tel: +256 41 343 859 **Fax:** +256 41 259 992
Email: info@mugmas.co.ug

FIRM OVERVIEW

Partners: P.J. Nkambo-Mugerwa, T. Masembe Kanyerezi
Associates: V. Mathias Ssekatawa, Phillip Karugaba, David Mpanga

Number of partners worldwide: 2
Number of other lawyers worldwide: 3

AREAS OF PRACTICE:

Commercial	50%
Litigation	25%
Conveyancing	20%
Probate, trust and family law	5%

M

FIRM OVERVIEW: Mugerwa & Masembe (formerly Mugerwa & Matovu) is one of the oldest established law firms in Uganda. It is associated to Hunt & Airey, Wilkinson & Hunt, Mpanga & Njuba and Mpanga & Mugerwa. The firm has two partners and three qualified lawyers, supported by a staff of approximately 14 clerks and administration staff. It has recently been admitted to Lex Africa and the Association of Commercial Lawyers (ACL). Lex Africa is a select group of law firms in Africa that co-operate to offer their clients a better service. ACL is an international association of lawyers practising commercial law. One of the firm's advocates is also a member of the International Trademark Association (INTA). Mugerwa & Masembe's law library contains most of the material available on Uganda law and relevant law reports and reference works from elsewhere in the world.

INTERNATIONAL CLIENTS: Mugerwa & Masembe's clients include Ugandan and foreign banks and financial institutions, foreign investors and their Ugandan subsidiaries and branches, oil companies, insurance companies, and international aid organisations. The firm's major clients include Bank Of Uganda, Barclays Bank Of Uganda Limited, Uganda Breweries Limited, Uganda Commercial Bank Ltd, Citibank Uganda Limited, Coffee Marketing Board Limited, Intrum Justitia International, Diamond Trust Bank Uganda Limited, Uganda National Examination Board, Snv Netherlands Development Organisation, Jubilee Investment Company Of Uganda Ltd, Sdv Transami (Uganda) Ltd, Petro Uganda Ltd, and Stanhope Finance Company Ltd.

MAIN INTERNATIONAL AREAS OF PRACTICE:
Commercial: The firm's commercial department handles a range of issues relating to commercial and corporate law, banking, securities, foreign investments, joint ventures, share issues, mergers and takeovers, receivership, liquidation, tax issues, and privatisations.
Intellectual property: The firm has a specialist intellectual property department that advises on patents, trademarks, industrial designs, and copyright issues.
Conveyancing: Mugerwa & Masembe's conveyancing department advises on land and conveyancing transactions, transfers, charges, mortgages, leases, sales and purchases, sub-divisions, changes of user, and extension of term development schemes.
Litigation: The firm offers full litigation services in the Supreme Court, Court of Appeal, the High Court, and the Magistrates' Courts and before arbitrators.
Probate, trust and family law: The firm advises on wills, estate administration, trust matters, provident and pension funds, divorce, adoption, and children's law.
Environmental litigation: Mugerwa & Masembe advises on a range of environmental concerns in Uganda.

LANGUAGES: English, Luganda, Swahili

Mugerwa & Masembe Advocates

For other recommended firms see pages 1485-1520

MULLA & MULLA & CRAIGIE BLUNT & CAROE

HEAD OFFICE

Mulla House, 51 Mahatma Gandhi Road, Fort
Mumbai 400 001, India
Tel: +91 22 285 4016 **Fax:** +91 22 285 0315
Email: mullas@vsnl.com

WORLDWIDE OFFICE CONTACTS

INDIA
209 Regency Enclave, 4 Magrath Road, **Bangalore** 560 025
Tel: + 91 80 555 0370 **Fax:** + 91 80 559 8549
Email: mullas@vsnl.net

FIRM OVERVIEW

Senior partner: J.P. Thacker
Number of partners worldwide: 20
Number of other lawyers worldwide: 110

AREAS OF PRACTICE:

Admirality and marine insurance .... *%
Infrastructure .... |*%
Insurance .... *%
IT, telecomm and broadcasting .... *%
M&A, joint ventures and privatisations .... *%
Offshore investments and securities .... *%
Oil and gas .... *%
Project finance .... *%
* Workload not disclosed

FIRM OVERVIEW: Founded in 1897 by Sir Dinshaw Mulla, the firm merged in 1952 with M/s. Craigie Blunt & Caroe, Solicitors to the East India Company. The firm has over 100 lawyers and fee earners. Partners focus on various areas of practice providing highly specialised legal, technical and commercial services to clients. Several lawyers are solicitors of the Supreme Court of England and Hong Kong. The firm has established relationships with lawyers and international law firms worldwide.

INTERNATIONAL EXPERIENCE: The firm has acted for Port of Singapore Authority in the privatisation of Pipavav, the first minor Port in India; acting for BBC in their Joint Venture with Business India Television; acting for Harvard Medical International in their Indian operations; acting for Komatsu, Japan in hiving out of L&T's engineering unit to their JV Company; acting for L.T. in acquiring Narmada Cement Co. Ltd; acting for Hindalco Industries Limited in their takeover of shares of Alcan Aluminum Limited, Canada in Indian Aluminium Company Limited; acting for the Birla Group in their Joint Venture with Sun Life Assurance Company of Canada relating to the Life Insurance Business; acting for Indian Rayon & Industries Limited in a transaction involving their purchase of Madura Coats' Garment Division; acting for Lubrizol India Limited in the Joint Venture with Lubrizol Corporation, USA and Indian Oil Corporation; acting for Tata International Limited in their Joint Venture with systems integrated Telemarketing, Netherlands BV; acting for the Birla Group in a transaction involving the merger of Birla AT & T communications Limited and Tata Cellular Limited; acting for Essar Oil Limited in a transaction involving the hiving off of their Energy Division.

INTERNATIONAL CLIENTS: ANZ, London; Air India; Amway; Bank of Nova Scotia; BBC; Birla Group of Companies; Port of Singapore Authority; ECGD; Exxon International; HPCL; HSBC; IOC; Larsen & Toubro Ltd; Saipem Italy; GE Caps; Shipping Corporation of India; Tata Group of Companies; The Great Eastern Shipping Company Limited; The Indian Hotels Company Limited (Taj Group of Hotels); Harvard Medical International; Komatsu.

MAIN INTERNATIONAL AREAS OF PRACTICE:

M&A and joint ventures: The firm has acted for numerous multinational corporations in their joint ventures in India. It represents leading Indian commercial houses, foreign companies and banks in negotiations, documentation, taxation, obtaining regulatory permissions including SEBI, FIPB, Exchange Control and advises on acquisitions/spin offs, divestments and other structuring.

Infrastructure: The firm handles work for power projects including documentation and negotiation of projects for the sale of power to SEBs and for captive consumption, as well as advice on regulatory requirements (State/Central government, electricity/environmental authorities). It advises the telecommunications sector on the submission of bids to the Department of Telecommunications and obtaining licenses to operate basic and cellular telecom services in various regions. It advises on various issues concerning financial and technical conditions of the tendered documents; and advises on the raising of foreign equity, involving Indian and international financial institutional investors, for debt financing. The firm acts for a variety of foreign and domestic corporations involved in the privatisation of the infrastructure sector such as power, telecommunications, roads, airports, and ports. The firm is also involved in transport systems projects (railways, roads, airports and ports).

Project finance and external borrowings: The firm acts for international banks and overseas lenders for major bilateral and syndicated facilities of all types including acquisition finance for aircraft, ships and industrial projects. It has been instrumental in advising and obtaining approvals from the Ministry of Finance/Reserve Bank of India. For over 30 years the firm has advised Air India and on aircraft acquisitions.

Oil and gas: The firm advises on regulatory permissions for onshore, offshore, intertidal area drilling and oil exploration, documentation relating to technical/ commercial bids on ONGC; and on regulatory requirements for oil prospecting licenses and related contracts, guarantees and other documentation.

Admiralty and marine insurance: The firm has the largest admiralty practice in India with a worldwide reputation as a specialist in every area of shipping business. It acts for numerous shipowners, charterers, hull and cargo insurers, P&I and defence clubs, salvage and tug companies, shipbuilders, and bunker suppliers.

Offshore investments and securities: The firm advises on structuring offshore investment into India through FIIs, GDRs/ADRs/FRNs and offshore schemes of domestic mutual funds.

Telecommunications, IT and broadcasting: The firm acted for a large Japanese corporation in the acquisition of shares in an Indian Telecom company. It advises Indian private Internet service providers on distribution of services in various jurisdictions, including documentation in terms distributorship agreements, end-user agreements, terms and conditions of service; leading European betting domain seeking entry into India. It also handles Indian gambling laws, tax laws and exchange control. The firm advised US-based portal – India Abroad Publications on its merger with Indianfoline.com, including regulatory compliance and due diligence. It acts for IT companies on various activities such as mergers, acquisitions, incorporation of subsidiaries, drafting and reviewing documentation, due diligence exercises, exchange control and obtaining regulatory approvals. It advises domestic and global broadcasting corporations in relation to their Indian operations; and global Satellite transponder leasing corporations.

LANGUAGES: English, Indian languages

MUNDIE E ADVOGADOS

HEAD OFFICE

Av. Juscelino Kubitschek, 50, 17th Floor,
04543-000 São Paulo-SP, Brazil
Tel: +55 11 3040 2900 **Fax:** +55 11 3040 2940

Email: central@mundie.com.br

WORLDWIDE OFFICE CONTACTS

BRAZIL
Rua do Carmo, 7, 18th Floor, 20011-020 **Rio de Janeiro** RJ
Tel: +55 21 517 5000 **Fax:** +55 21 517 5017
Email: central@mundie.com.br

FIRM OVERVIEW

Managing partner: Carlos Forbes
Senior partner: Kevin Louis Mundie

Number of partners worldwide: 6
Number of other lawyers worldwide: 27

AREAS OF PRACTICE:

Telecommunications	20%
Corporate and commercial	15%
Energy	15%
Finance	15%
M&A	10%
Privatisation, public bids and governmental contracts	10%
Anti-trust and competition	5%
Litigation	5%
Tax	5%

FIRM OVERVIEW: Established in 1996, the firm was founded with the aim of providing distinct and high quality legal services. The firm is a full service corporate law firm that specialises in telecommunications, energy, administrative, corporate, finance, commercial, contract, anti-trust and tax law. It also handles privatisations and advises on governmental contracts, and is experienced in M&A transactions. Many of the partners, and several lawyers of the firm, have professional experience in leading Brazilian, US and European law firms. Several attorneys hold postgraduate and master degrees from foreign and Brazilian universities.

INTERNATIONAL EXPERIENCE: During the last five years, Mundie E Advogados has advised clients on several major transactions. It has acted in a number of large privatisations and public bids in the telecommunications industry, and in several important projects in the energy and infrastructure sectors. Other major transactions handled include the public bids for the granting of cellular and the so called 'mirror' licenses; the public bids and licensing of microwave, satellite and spectrum surveillance, Cable TV, MMDS and other telecommunication services; the privatisation of Telebras, as well as several electric energy concessionaires; the acquisition of equity interests and the formation of joint ventures in the telecommunications, energy and other sectors; public bids for green field energy projects; and the structuring and implementation of several large cross-border and local secured facilities, syndicated loans, vendor and project finance.

INTERNATIONAL CLIENTS: The firm's clientele is diverse, covering different sectors of the Brazilian economy including telecommunications, energy, mining, computer hardware and software, e-business, institutional investors, media vehicles and content providers, entertainment companies, theme parks, credit and banking services, commodity traders, contractors, and heavy industry. The major part of the firm's clientele consists of large foreign and Brazilian corporations.

MAIN INTERNATIONAL AREAS OF PRACTICE:

Telecommunications: The firm advises on matters covering all aspects of the industry. It has been involved in almost every relevant telecommunications project in Brazil and has contributed to proposed rulemakings for the regulation of telecommunication services.

Energy: The firm handles all types of contractual and regulatory matters, including wholesale market aspects, and the granting of concessions and authorisations. The firm also has expertise in gas and the use of gas and electric energy infrastructure by telecom service providers.

Corporate, commercial, M&A, anti-trust and competition: The firm advises on every aspect of corporate activity including the drafting and negotiation of all types of agreements, structuring of foreign and local investments, incorporation of companies, mergers and acquisitions, acquisition due diligence, formation of joint ventures, shareholder agreements, acquisition and disposition of assets (including real estate), technology transfer and technical assistance arrangements, anti-trust and competition and consumer matters.

Finance: The firm specialises in finance, having participated in the structuring of several financings involving foreign lenders, the local market and Brazilian official credit agencies (including BNDES), as well as trade financing facilities. The firm has handled a number of vendor and project financings, particularly in the telecom, energy and infrastructure sectors.

Privatisation, public bids and governmental contracts: The firm has been particularly active in acting for clients in privatisations, public bids and governmental contracts. It has participated in many of the recent large Brazilian privatisations in the telecommunications and electric energy areas.

Tax: The firm advises on all aspects of Brazilian tax legislation, also in connection with the rendering of public services, as well as assisting in tax planning relating to acquisition and other transactions. The firm also offers individual tax and immigration law counseling in respect of expatriates.

Litigation: The firm has a litigation practice group qualified to represent clients in all types of civil, commercial, tax and labour litigation.

LANGUAGES: English, French, German, Portuguese

 For other recommended firms see pages 1485-1520

ESTUDIO MUÑIZ, FORSYTH, RAMIREZ, PEREZ-TAIMAN & LUNA-VICTORIA ABOGADOS

HEAD OFFICE

Las Begonias 475, 6 Piso,
Lima 27 Peru
Tel: +51 1 422 11 22 **Fax:** +51 1 421 31 04

Email: postmast@munizlaw.com.pe
Website: www.munizlaw.com.pe

WORLDWIDE OFFICE CONTACTS

PERU
Las Begonias 475, 6 Piso, **Lima** 27
Tel: +51 1 422 11 22 **Fax:** +51 1 421 31 04
Email: postmast@munizlaw.com.pe

Jirón Bolivar 200, **Trujillo**
Tel: +51 44 290779 **Fax:** +51 44 290779
Email: trujillo@munizlaw.com.pe

FIRM OVERVIEW

Senior Partners: Jorge Muñiz, Albert Forsyth, Nelson Ramirez, Jorge Pérez-Taiman, César Luna-Victoria

Number of partners worldwide: 15
Number of other lawyers worldwide: 69

AREAS OF PRACTICE:

Area	%
Commercial contracts	15%
Corporate	15%
Competition	10%
Litigation	10%
Natural resources	10%
Tax	10%
Employment	8%
Foreign trade	8%
Telecommunications, transportation and e-commerce	5%
Agriculture and fisheries	3%
Environment and native communities	3%
Tourism	3%

FIRM OVERVIEW: Muñiz, Forsyth, Ramírez, Pérez-Taiman & Luna-Victoria was founded in 1980. Comprising 84 lawyers the firm has considerable professional experience in all areas of the law and is the largest full service firm in Peru. The firm tries to develop a solid commitment and long-term relationship with its clients in order to be in a position to identify their business objectives and offer the necessary profesional support, coupled with expertise, creativity and common sense.

INTERNATIONAL EXPERIENCE: In recent years the firm has advised a number of prominent foreign companies established in Peru. The firm acts on behalf of American and European companies and advises international law firms.

INTERNATIONAL CLIENTS: The firm's client base includes large companies, banks, insurance companies and supranational institutions conducting cross-border business.

MAIN INTERNATIONAL AREAS OF PRACTICE:

Corporate: The firm advises national and foreign clients on the incorporation of companies, company organisation, and on the regulations and protection of their investments.

Banking, finance and capital markets: The firm advises on all matters related to capital markets, corporate finance, commercial and investment banking of local securities, strategic investment and privatisation processes.

Litigation: Muñiz, Forsyth, Ramírez, Pérez-Taiman & Luna-Victoria represent clients in civil, criminal, commercial and constitutional proceedings before the Judiciary and Constitutional Court, including arbitration courts.

Energy and mines: The energy and mines division includes lawyers with broad international experience in oil, gas, mining and electric power activities, including specialists in contractual, tax, labour and environmental matters.

Tax: Members of the firm's tax division work closely with members of the firm's accounting services to devise corporate tax strategies.

LANGUAGES: English, French, German, Italian, Spanish

WORLDWIDE OFFICES

PERU

Jirón Bolivar 200, Trujillo

Number of lawyers: 4

Office profile: The large economic potential shown by the department of La Libertad encouraged the firm to open an office in Trujillo on March 18, 1999. The firm was the first law office in Peru to decentralise its operations. The Trujillo office represents clients in all contentious and non-contentious proceedings brought by government authorities and other institutions in northern Peru.

MURUGESU & NEELAKANDAN

HEAD OFFICE

P.O.Box 749, Hemas Building, 3rd Floor, York Street,
Colombo 1, Sri Lanka
Tel: +94 1 334 949 **Fax:** +94 1 445 255

Email: emanden@sri.lanka.net
Website: www.muruandneel.com

WORLDWIDE OFFICE CONTACTS

SRI LANKA
P.O.Box 749, Hemas Building, 3rd Floor, York Street, **Colombo** 1
Tel: +94 1 334 949 **Fax:** +94 1 445 255
Email: emanden@sri.lanka.net

FIRM OVERVIEW

Partners: Veluppillai Murugesu, Kandiah Neelakandan, Sivananthavalli ThuraiRajah, Sashidevi Neelakandan, Nithianandan Murugesu

Number of partners worldwide: 5
Number of other lawyers worldwide: 12

AREAS OF PRACTICE:

Admiralty and shipping .... *%
Banking and finance .... *%
Corporate and commercial .... *%
Dispute resolution .... *%
Corporate and commercial .... *%
Intellectual property .... *%
Privatisation and joint ventures .... *%
* Workload % not disclosed

M

FIRM OVERVIEW: Murugesu & Neelakandan was established in 1962 by Mr Veluppillai Murugesu. Comprising five partners and nine other lawyers the firm advises on a range of legal issues, specialising in banking and finance, intellectual property, shipping and admiralty, and general corporate law.

INTERNATIONAL EXPERIENCE: The firm advises a number of multinational clients on their business in Sri Lanka.

INTERNATIONAL CLIENTS: The firm has a broad international client base including Alpha Group UK, International Finance Corporation (a member of the World Bank Group), Commonwealth Development Corporation, and Lanka Bell (Pvt). It has also acted as Sri Lankan counsel to Rolls Royce, Levis Strauss and Singers.

MAIN INTERNATIONAL AREAS OF PRACTICE:

Banking and finance: The firm advise on a range of banking, finance and investment issues. They advised the International Finance Corporation (IFC) and Commonwealth Development Corporation (CDC) on loan documentations in the Asia Power Project. Murugesu & Neelakandan advises on the Kelanitissa Project and is also local counsel for IDC, CDC and Asian Development Bank (the senior lenders to the Colombo Port development project, the largest boot project in Sri Lanka).
Intellectual property: The firm handles a large volume of IP related work, specialising in the registration of patents, designs and trademarks. They have links with law firms in the UK, US, South Africa, Hong Kong, Canada, Singapore and India.
Admiralty and shipping: The firm advises clients involved in admiralty cases.
Dispute resolution: The firm has undertaken a number of arbitrations.
Privatisation and joint ventures: The firm advised on the privatisation of duty free shops.
Litigation and arbitration: The firm has handled a number of litigation and arbitration matters.

LANGUAGES: English, Sinhala, Tamil

For other recommended firms see pages 1485-1520

MUSAT & ASOCIATII

HEAD OFFICE

Piata Charles de Gaulle, 8 Maior Gheorghe Sontu Street Sect.1, 1st District
Bucharest 71264, Romania
Tel: +40 1 223 3717 **Fax:** +40 1 223 3957

Email: general@musat.ro
Website: www.musat.ro

FIRM OVERVIEW

Managing partner: Gheorghe Musat
Senior partner: Florentin Tuca

Number of partners worldwide: 9
Number of other lawyers worldwide: 55

AREAS OF PRACTICE:

Privatisation	23%
Corporate and commercial	21%
Communication	12%
Litigation	12%
Banking and project finance	9%
Real estate	7%
Energy	5%
Intellectual property	5%
Tax	4%
Insurance	3%
Others	3%

FIRM OVERVIEW: Founded in 1993 Musat & Asociatii was one of the first law firms to be incorporated under Romanian law. In May 2000 it merged with Popovoci & Asociatii, another market leader, to form the largest practice in Romania. The firm now numbers over 55 lawyers, all admitted to practice, and 20 non-legal staff. The firm is a true multidisciplinary practice. It is a member of the Romanian Bar Association and has close contacts with law firms in the European Union and the United States. The firm has representative clients in every kind of legal transaction. Musat & Asociatii is a member of Terralex, one of the largest associations of independent law firms which includes more then over 9000 lawyers world-wide, allowing fast access to international experience in any field.

INTERNATIONAL EXPERIENCE: The firm has extensive experience of assisting foreign entities in expanding their operations in Romania. It specializes in the negotiations and documentation of international transactions.

INTERNATIONAL CLIENTS: Most of the firms' clients are drawn from Europe, North America, Japan, and the Asia Pacific region. The following is a brief description of a few major transactions on which the firm has advised: retained by Ministry of Transport in relation to the privatisation of the national airline Tarom; advised an international buyer on the privatisation of the Romanian helicopter manufacturer IAR Brasov; adviser to the Romanian state on the privatisation of two of the largest state companies, Alro and Alprom, and on the optimum sale methods for these two of the largest state processors of aluminium; retained by G.E. Capital in the privatisation of BancPost; instructed by the national oil company Petrom S.A. in connection with an equity issue in capital increase; BP Oil in connection with a fuel supply project involving a joint venture with Tarom Airlines; retained by the State Ownership Fund in connection with the privatisation of the second largest Romanian bank, Banca Agricola S.A; acted for Sidex S. A on various commercial matters regarding the restructuring of a syndicated loan which required a change in the corporate governance; acted for Banca Turco-Romana on various recourse and non-recourse financing and other banking and project finance matters; selected as Romanian legal counsel by two major syndicates consisting of international banks in connection with USD 140,000,000 loan facility for RAIF (arranged by Citibank International PLC) for the purchase of agricultural supplies; instructed by Banca Comercial Romana on various international loans and securisation issues; special adviser to Central European Media Enterprises (CME) and have acted in the PFI aspects of the sale of the shares in MOBIL ROM, as well as in all other CME's legal needs in Romania; special legal adviser to France Telecom on the project finance matters in Romania related to Mobil Rom joint venture (the largest joint venture in Romania at the moment) and on its acquisition of a GSM license.

WORLDWIDE OFFICE CONTACTS

ROMANIA
Piata Charles de Gaulle, 8 Maior Gheorghe Sontu Street Sect.1,
1st District, 71264, **Bucharest**
Tel: +40 1 223 3717 **Fax:** +40 1 223 3957
Email: general@musat.ro

MAIN INTERNATIONAL AREAS OF PRACTICE:

Privatisation: The firm advises on the privatisation of state owned companies, including the restructuring and privatisation of the oil and gas and electricity companies. It has been actively involved in privatising a major group of state owned companies in different sectors of the economy, acting for purchasers and as well as sellers.
Corporate and commercial: Specialisms include national and international, joint ventures, debt issues, loan agreements, national licensing, agency and distributorship agreements, and structuring and financing development projects and a substantial amount of competition law.
Communications: Advice has ranged in all aspects of the communication revolution from the acquisition of companies and licensees, authorisations and advice on divestiture and operation of various communication systems within the ambit of the Romanian regulatory legal system.
Real estate: Clients include landowners, tenants, financial, banks, real estate companies and developers, and work covers all types of real estate transactions.
Litigation: The firm deals with disputes concerning the entire spectrum of national as well as international transactions. It has experience in resolving conflicts before the Romanian courts and arbitration bodies for non national and national Romanian entities.
Insurance: Work handled includes employer liability, fire, flood, personal injury, product liability, reinsurance and retrocession issues, while clients may be insurers, re-insurers, brokers, or loss adjusters.
Banking and project finance: The firm has extensive experience of banking law and project finance deals, including BOT, PFI's and other specialised finance aspects of transactions. It has advised banks and other financial institutions on protecting a secured lending position when a borrower is moving towards insolvency, including an assessment of the insolvency and prompt action to enforce security rights wherever the assets are located.

LANGUAGES: English, French, German, Italian, Romanian

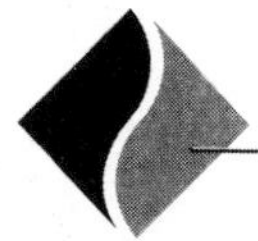

MUSAT & ASOCIATII

M

For other recommended firms see pages 1485-1520

CABINET NACIRI & ASSOCIÉS

HEAD OFFICE

52 Boulevard Zerktouni, Espace Erreda,
Casablanca Morocco
Tel: +212 22 27 46 28
Fax: +212 22 27 30 16

Email: nsm@techno.net.ma

FIRM OVERVIEW

Managing partner: Hicham Naciri
Senior partner: Mohamed Naciri

Number of partners worldwide: 2
Number of other lawyers worldwide: 5

AREAS OF PRACTICE:
Banking and finance .... *%
Corporate and project finance .... *%
Litigation and arbitration .... *%
M&A .... *%
Securities and financial markets .... *%
Telecommunications and IT .... *%
* Workload % not disclosed

FIRM OVERVIEW: Founded in the early 1930s, Cabinet Naciri & Associés handles all major areas of corporate and business law. It acts for both Moroccan and international corporate clients. Cabinet Naciri & Associés offers a comprehensive legal service to clients with international business interests, but focuses on banking and finance, mergers and acquisitions, and project finance. The firm has also developed a very strong local and international litigation and arbitration practice. The firm maintains contacts with various firms worldwide.

INTERNATIONAL EXPERIENCE: The firm has handled a large number of international transactions. Recent international transactions include acting as local counsel for ABN AMRO Bank NV on a bridge facility loan of US$350 million to the second Moroccan GSM Operator (1999); advising a syndicate of commercial (international and local) banks and IFC in a telecommunications long term financing of €1 billion (2000). The firm is currently acting for an Anglo-US consortium in a bid for a US$200 million wind farm project.

INTERNATIONAL CLIENTS: The firm acts on behalf of foreign corporations, organisations, funds, investment banks, law firms, and governmental organisations. Over half the firm's client base is international and includes large companies, textile, luxury and industrial companies, banks, insurance companies, and public or supranational institutions conducting cross-border business.

WORLDWIDE OFFICE CONTACTS

MOROCCO
52 Boulevard Zerktouni, Espace Erreda, **Casablanca**
Tel: +212 22 27 46 28 **Fax:** +212 22 27 30 16
Email: nsm@techno.net.ma

MAIN INTERNATIONAL AREAS OF PRACTICE:
M&A: Cabinet Naciri & Associés provides a full range of legal services to clients ranging from small businesses to large multinationals. It advises on the choice of company form and assists in the establishment, restructuring, and liquidation of companies. The firm has been involved in the largest Moroccan privatisation, advising a potential buyer of 35% of Maroc Telecom (the national telecommunications operator) for US$2 billion. It is currently advising a large US multinational on a major privatisation.
Corporate: The firm advises subsidiaries of multinationals on a range of corporate matters including contracts of distribution, franchise, agency, supply, and investment agreements with the Moroccan Government.
Banking and finance: Cabinet Naciri & Associés handles all aspects of banking and finance including secured and syndicated loan transactions and guarantees, structured finance, and project finance.
Telecommunications: Work handled includes regulatory as well as licence and interconnection agreements, including electronic commerce, intellectual property issues, the financing of mobile telephone networks, etc
Litigation and arbitration: The firm has an established litigation practice in civil, commercial, labour, intellectual property, criminal, maritime, and insurance law. The firm also has considerable arbitration experience.
Employment: The firm handles all matters relating to Moroccan employment law.

LANGUAGES: Arabic, English, French

 For other recommended firms see pages 1485-1520

NAJJAR IBRAHIM LAW FIRM

HEAD OFFICE

11 Madrassat El Salam Street, PO Box 116/2270,
Beirut, Lebanon
Tel: +961 1202 100 **Fax:** +961 1201 974

Email: inajjar@dm.net.lb
Website: www.najjaribrahim.com

FIRM OVERVIEW

Senior partner: Ibrahim Najjar

Number of partners worldwide: 5
Number of other lawyers worldwide: 9

AREAS OF PRACTICE:

Litigation and arbitration	45%
Family law, successions and wills	20%
Corporate	15%
Banking and finance	10%
Intellectual property	10%

FIRM OVERVIEW: Najjar Ibrahim Law Firm was founded in 1966. It advises international clients on their business activities in Lebanon and throughout the Middle East. The firm specialises in advising on litigation, domestic and international arbitration, family law, corporate activity and the establishment of offices and franchises in Lebanon. Najjar Ibrahim Law Firm has alliances with firms in Jordan, Egypt, Syria, Tunisia, France, UK, Switzerland, Canada and the US.

INTERNATIONAL EXPERIENCE: The firm has advised Lebanese, European and Arab clients on litigation.

INTERNATIONAL CLIENTS: The firm's client base comprises multinational franchises, international sports organisations, Arab holding companies, and investors wishing to initiate business interests either within Lebanon or internationally.

MAIN INTERNATIONAL AREAS OF PRACTICE:

Successions, wills and family law: The firm advises on all matters relating to family law.

Private law, litigation and arbitration: The firm advises Lebanese and international clients on all aspects of private law litigation and arbitration including the settlement of estates with multinational interests. The firm has expertise in lease agreements, shareholders agreements and the establishment of corporations under Lebanese law and in assisting clients in obtaining the necessary administrative authoritisation for the purchase of real estate in Lebanon. The firm's clients include franchisees of major international corporations, government bodies and private investors. The firm has experience in issuing legal opinions on matters of Lebanese and foreign law, as requested by parties to arbitration proceedings. The firm also advises on the enforcement of international decrees and awards in Lebanon.

Banking, finance and capital markets: The firm has played a major role in the adoption of modern Lebanese legislation in the banking, finance and capital markets sectors. The firm advises on fiduciary contracts, banking secrecy and other banking and capital markets issues.

Intellectual property: The firm has handled some of the most significant intellectual property cases in Lebanon. It has advised on the implementation of the new Lebanese Legislation on intellectual property, trade marks, and patents.

LANGUAGES: Arabic, English, French, Spanish

WORLDWIDE OFFICE CONTACTS

LEBANON
11 Madrassat El Salam Street, PO Box 116/2270, **Beirut**
Tel: +961 1202 100 **Fax:** +961 1201 974
Email: inajjar@dm.net.lb

FRANCE
142, rue de la Pompe, 75116 **Paris**
Tel: +33 1 47 04 82 81 **Fax:** +33 1 47 04 82 21
Email: inajjar@dm.net.lb

N

For other recommended firms see pages 1485-1520

NAUTADUTILH

HEAD OFFICE

Prinses Irenestraat 59, 1077 WV Amsterdam, PO 7113
1007 JC Amsterdam, The Netherlands
Tel: +31 20 541 46 46 **Fax:** +31 20 661 28 27
Website: www.nautadutilh.com

FIRM OVERVIEW

Management board chairman: Joan Van Marwijk Kooy
Number of partners worldwide: 120
Number of other lawyers worldwide: 306

AREAS OF PRACTICE:

Corporate and commercial 35%
Banking and finance 10%
Intellectual property 10%
Construction and commercial property 9%
Tax 9%
Employment 7%
Insurance and liability 5%
Litigation and arbitration 5%
Regulatory 5%
Transportation 5%

N

FIRM OVERVIEW: NautaDutilh is one of Europe's leading fully-independent law firms. With more than 400 attorneys, civil law notaries and tax advisers, the firm operates from three main offices in Amsterdam, Brussels and Rotterdam and from branch offices in London, Madrid, New York and Paris. NautaDutilh is the largest law firm in The Netherlands, with a very substantial foreign client base.

INTERNATIONAL EXPERIENCE: The firm handles many large deals in the corporate and commercial sectors. NautaDutilh is actively involved in major national and international industrial, telecom and utilities projects. The firm act as legal adviser to contractors and sponsors and is involved in a growing number of industrial projects abroad.

INTERNATIONAL CLIENTS: NautaDutilh's client-base includes banks, insurance companies, institutional and other investors, developers and municipalities.

MAIN INTERNATIONAL AREAS OF PRACTICE:

Corporate and commercial: With more than 120 lawyers this is the largest practice group within NautaDutilh. It offers advice and a wide range of services on many large, high profile transactions with a strong international component.
Banking and finance: The firm's banking and finance group acts for banks and other financial institutions, and for other organisations in the domestic and international markets.
Construction and commercial property: The firm offers an integrated approach to matters involving construction and commercial property.
Intellectual property and IT: The firm offers advice in traditional areas such as patent law, brand names, copyright and designs. NuataDutilh's intellectual property and IT group is influenced by new technologies and has developed a number of new areas of expertise with a focus on telecommunications and e-commerce.
Employment: The firm's practice group is actively involved in a wide range of issues associated with employment law.
Regulatory: The regulatory practice group represents clients in administrative and judicial review proceedings and advises on matters such as environmental law, permits, zoning laws, grants and subsidies.
Insurance and liability: The firm advises and litigates on all aspects of liability including professional, medical, environmental and product liability, and a wide range of additional forms of legal and contractual liability.
Transportation: The transportation practice group handles all aspects of shipping, transport and insurance law on both a national and international level.
Private client: The firm handles a wide range of family law matters, such as prenuptial agreements, matrimonial property law, estate planning, wills and estates and divorce law.
Tax: The tax practice group is active in all areas of taxation, with a strong emphasis on international taxation.
Litigation: The litigation department handles a wide range of civil and criminal actions before courts of first instance and appellate courts. The firm handles cases ranging from breach of contract and tort claims to criminal offences in the fields of finance, tax and environment.
Asset-based finance: The finance department has extensive experience in cross-border leasing transactions.
E-commerce: The firm's lawyers continually monitor and regularly participate in new ventures in the e-environment.
EC and competition law: The firm advises clients on a wide range of issues relating to competition and regulatory affairs in the EU, The Netherlands and Belgium.
Energy and utilities: At a national and European level, this practice group has established a leading position in representing major energy and oil companies, electricity generators and utility companies, public authorities and major purchasers of energy.
Public/private projects: The firm advises on all matters such as construction and property, procurement, project and asset finance, corporate, regulatory and taxation.
Telecom and media: The firm advises clients in the national and international telecommunications and media industry.

LANGUAGES: Dutch, English, French, German, Spanish

WORLDWIDE OFFICE CONTACTS

BELGIUM
Chausée de la Hulpe, 177/6, 1170 **Brussels**
Tel: +32 2 673 00 07 **Fax:** +32 2 672 28 54
Email: ndbru@nautadutilh.com

FRANCE
50, Avenue Victor Hugo, 75116 **Paris**
Tel: +33 1 53 64 66 60 **Fax:** +33 1 53 64 66 61
Email: nautaparis@aol.com

SPAIN
Plaza Marqués de Salamanca 3 y 4, 28006 **Madrid**
Tel: +34 91 426 48 40 **Fax:** +34 91 435 98 15
Email: emensing@nautadutilh.ddnet.es

NETHERLANDS
Weena 750, 3014 DA Rotterdam, PO Box 1110, 3000 BC **Rotterdam**
Tel: +31 10 224 00 00 **Fax:** +31 10 414 84 44

UNITED KINGDOM
Bowman House, 29 Wilson Street, **London** EC2M 2SJ
Tel: +44 207 786 9100 **Fax:** +44 207 588 6888
Email: ndlondon@nautadutilh.com

USA
One Rockefeller Plaza, **New York** 10020
Tel: +1 212 218 2990 **Fax:** +1 212 218 2999
Email: nautadutilh@nauta-ny.com

For other recommended firms see pages 1485-1520

NCTM STUDIO LEGALE ASSOCIATO

HEAD OFFICE

Via Monte Napoleone 12,
20121 Milan, Italy
Tel: +39 02 541 641 **Fax:** +39 02 541 64501-2

Email: info@nctm.it
Website: www.nctm.it

FIRM OVERVIEW

Senior partner: Gianfranco Negri-Clementi

Number of partners worldwide: 20
Number of other lawyers worldwide: 93

AREAS OF PRACTICE:

Antitrust law .... *%
Banking and finance .... *%
Bankruptcy .... *%
Corporate .... *%
Labour, employment law and administrative law .... *%
Litigation and arbitration .... *%
Mergers and acquisitions .... *%
* Workload % not disclosed

FIRM OVERVIEW: NCTM is the result of a merger between Negri-Clementi, Montironi & Soci and Toffoletto e Associati, both of which have traditionally occupied a prominent position in the Italian legal market. Negri-Clementi, Montironi & Soci, established in Milan by Gianfranco Negri-Clementi in 1955, has always focused on civil and commercial law with particular strength in litigation and arbitration. In the last ten years, the significant development of company law in Italy and the EU has led to the firm's rapid growth, and it has gained experience in providing specialist advice to large industrial groups, banks and insurance houses on corporate finance and M&A. Toffoletto & Associati was established in 1925, also in Milan, by Angelo Toffoletto. It has always been strong in employment and social security, as well as commercial distribution contracts. In recent years, the range of services offered has widened with the creation of specialist departments in anti-trust, M&A and company law. NCTM's widespread presence in Italy and at an international level enables it to advise clients such as multinational groups and large Italian companies. In all fields, NCTM has expertise in contentious and non-contentious matters. The firm provides specialist advice in all of its practice areas for both judicial and arbitration cases, as well as advising on alternative dispute resolution mechanisms and out-of-court proceedings in international contractual transactions.

INTERNATIONAL EXPERIENCE: The firm has acted for Credito Italiano on the privatisation of Bank Pekao in Holland; ILVA (Italy's main steel producer) on the sale of Erisider and on the privatisation of Corporate Siderurgica Integral in Spain; RAS on the reorganisation of its European joint ventures with Allianz and AGF; Cagiva Group on the sale of Ducati Motor Holding to Texas Pacific Group and others; Telecom Italia in the merger with Deutsche Telekom both on the contract law and anti-trust law aspects.

INTERNATIONAL CLIENTS: The firm's clientele includes major banks, merchant banks, insurance, trade and industrial, advertising, computer and internet companies.

WORLDWIDE OFFICE CONTACTS

ITALY
Via Monte Di Pietà,24, 20121 **Milan**
Tel: +39 02 725 511 **Fax:** +39 02 725 51333

Via Eugenio Chiesa, 4, 20122 **Milan**
Tel: +39 02 541 641 **Fax:** +39 02 541 64500

Via Monte Napoleone 12, 20121 **Milan**
Tel: +39 02 541 641 **Fax:** +39 02 541 64501-2

Via S Maria in Via, 12, 00187 **Rome**
Tel: +39 02 541641 **Fax:** +39 02 5416406
Email: info@NCTM.IT

NCTM e Caponi - Bulgarelli Studio Legale Associato, Contrà Porti, 15, 36100 **Vicenza**
Email: info@NCTM.IT

ASSOCIATED OFFICES

ITALY
Studio Legale Caponi - Bulgarelli e Associati, via Quattro Spade, 12, 37100 **Verona**
Tel: +39 04 5803 6111 **Fax:** +39 04 597367

MAIN INTERNATIONAL AREAS OF PRACTICE:

Banking and finance: The firm gives general advice on all regulatory aspects of banking activity, as well as on the structuring of banking operations, including major finance transactions (secured and syndicated loans and corporate finance amongst others).
Corporate: The firm gives general advice on all aspects of corporate law, with particular emphasis on major corporate operations such as mergers, demergers and flotations.
M&A: The firm's transactions range from small private acquisitions to cross-border takeovers of companies, also listed on their national stock exchange.
Litigation and arbitration: The firm deals with commercial and employment litigation at all court levels including the Supreme Court, as well as national and international arbitration, including ICC arbitration.
Bankruptcy: The firm advises on all aspects of Italian bankruptcy law, and was appointed by the Court of Milan as solicitor of Receivers.
Anti-trust law: The firm offers a wide range of services related to the application of both Italian and European antitrust law procedures before the Italian and European authorities, as well as in relation to judicial action before Civil Courts.
Employment and administrative law: There is a long-standing tradition in assisting clients with the drafting of employment contracts, restructuring process, collective labour agreements, coordination and localisation of the standard contracts used by the multinational companies, expatriates and stock option plans.

LANGUAGES: English, French, German, Italian, Russian, Spanish

NESTOR NESTOR & KINGSTON PETERSEN

HEAD OFFICE

Str. Aviator Mircea Zorileanu nr.39, Sector 1,
71334 Bucharest, Romania
Tel: +40 1 224 0890 **Fax:** +40 1 224 0891

Email: ion.nestor@nnkp.ro
Website: www.nnkp.com

WORLDWIDE OFFICE CONTACTS

ROMANIA
Str. Aviator Mircea Zorileanu nr.39, Sector 1, 71334 **Bucharest**
Tel: +40 1 224 0890 **Fax:** +40 1 224 0891
Email: ion.nestor@nnkp.ro

FIRM OVERVIEW

Managing partner: Manuela Nestor
Senior partner: Ion Nestor

Number of partners worldwide: 5
Number of other lawyers worldwide: 26

AREAS OF PRACTICE:
M&A (including privatisation) 35%
Project, corporate and trade finance 35%
Regulatory (including telecommunications/IT, competition, media, energy and public utilities, litigation and arbitration, real estate, intellectual property) 30%

N

FIRM OVERVIEW: Nestor Nestor & Kingston Petersen is a professional partnership providing a full range of legal and foreign investment advisory services to companies conducting business in Romania. The partnership, founded in 1995, assists multinational corporations, local and regional businesses and individual entrepreneurs with a broad range of legal and business matters. Nestor Nestor SCPA, founded in 1992, was among the first law practices established in Romania after 1990. With its 31 lawyers the firm is one of the largest law firms in Romania. Nestor Nestor & Kingston Petersen is the Romanian member of Lex Mundi, the world's leading association of independent law firms.

INTERNATIONAL EXPERIENCE: The firm advises foreign companies in connection with their investments in Romania. It specialises in structuring various corporate and financial transactions, and preparing and negotiating international contracts as well as loan and financing agreements.

INTERNATIONAL CLIENTS: The firm's clients include Allianz AG, AlliedSignal Corporation, Cargill plc, CPC Europe Foods Ltd., Electrolux AB, Eli Lilly (Suisse) AG, Estee Lauder International Inc., General Electric Corporation, General Motors Corporation, IBM Central Europe & Russia Inc., Kodak Ltd., Kraft Jacobs Suchard AG, Lafarge SA, Marriott International Inc., Metromidia International Telecommunications Inc., Microsoft Corporation, Motorola GmbH, Nokya OY, Philip Morris Group, Procter & Gamble Eastern Europe, Textil Finanz-Radici Group, Trinity Industries Inc., United Distillers & Vintners Ltd., William Wrigley Jr. Corporation. Clients from the financial sector include ABN AMRO Bank (Romania) S.A., BNP Paribas, The Chase Manhattan Bank N.A., Citibank Romania S.A., Credit Suisse/First Boston, European Bank for Reconstruction and Development (EBRD), HSBC Investment Bank plc; Merrill Lynch International, Nomura International plc, Romanian-American Enterprise Fund, Svenska Handelsbanken AB, Union Bank of Switzerland.

MAIN INTERNATIONAL AREAS OF PRACTICE:
Privatisation, mergers and acquisitions, direct investment: Nestor Nestor & Kingston Petersen is the acknowledged leader in Romanian acquisitions and privatisations. It handled the initial groundbreaking privatisations and represented either the seller or buyer in many significant transactions. The firm has also advised numerous clients on direct and greenfield investments in Romania.
Projects/corporate finance and banking: The firm has extensive experience acting as counsel to both lenders and borrowers in connection with a wide range of important project finance transactions. In particular, the firm's lawyers are widely recognised for their expertise in secured transactions. The firm assists a large number of foreign and local banks with commercial lending, regulatory and corporate activities.
Intellectual property: The firm has a dedicated practice group specialising in intellectual property matters, including patent, trademark, and licensing agreements. This practice group is also recognised within the international legal community as the leading expert on the development and harmonisation of Romanian legislation regarding e-commerce and the Internet.
Media, telecommunications and IT: Nestor Nestor & Kingston Petersen regularly advises clients in virtually every field of telecommunications activity on licensing and regulatory issues, privatisations, private acquisitions and mergers and project finance.
Competition and regulatory: The firm advises on compliance issues within Romania's corporate and regulatory framework.
Energy and public utilities: The firm assists clients in all areas of the energy and public utilities sectors, including obtaining exploration and concession rights, construction of energy facilities, privatisation and acquisition of public utilities, and regulatory compliance.
Labour and employment: The firm assists clients in the structuring and drafting of labour and employment relations, including collective bargaining agreements. The firm also has a specialised labour litigation group to assist clients involved in labour disputes.
Securities and financial markets: The firm is a recognised leader in the new and fast-changing field of Romanian securities legislation.

LANGUAGES: English, French, Romanian

For other recommended firms see pages 1485-1520

NICO HALLE LAW FIRM

HEAD OFFICE

8 Avenue Douala Manga Bell, PO Box 4876,
Douala, Cameroon
Tel: +237 42 6479 **Fax:** +237 43 2634

Email: hallelaw@aol.com

FIRM OVERVIEW

Partners: Nico Halle, Carlton Akkum

Number of partners worldwide: 2
Number of other lawyers worldwide: 6

AREAS OF PRACTICE:

Intellectual property	40%
Corporate	15%
Banking	10%
Civil aviation	10%
Maritime	10%
National resources litigation	10%
Arbitration	3%
Other	2%

FIRM OVERVIEW: Established in 1985, Nico Halle Law Firm is the largest law firm in Cameroon with three partners and six associates. It offers a full range of legal services to both national and international corporate and private clients. The firm has specialised in corporate and commercial transactions, and has a reputation for providing an efficient and bilingual service. Members of the firm have written for a number of international legal publications and the firm itself is a member of a number of associations including Terralex International, Commercial Law Affiliates, The American Bar Association, American Bank Attorneys and the International Association of Young Lawyers. It is also a member of the London Court of International Arbitration. An Associated lawyer, Bokwe G. Mofor, is located in Washington DC.

INTERNATIONAL EXPERIENCE: The firm has handled work for international clients with business in Cameroon. It acted for Unilever on the restructuring of its subsidiary Pamol and it advised in the privatisation of CAC Bananas and subsequent acquisition by Delmonte.

INTERNATIONAL CLIENTS: The firm advises a range of investors in Cameroon, notably on mergers, leases, and natural resource investment. Its client base also includes large multinational companies, banks, insurance companies, public and para-public companies. Amongst the most well known of the firm's clients are Delmonte, Unilever, TMOA, GEMSTAR, Iridium, American Express, Publex Co. and Cameroon Pipeline.

WORLDWIDE OFFICE CONTACTS

CAMEROON
8 Avenue Douala Manga Bell, PO Box 4876, **Douala**
Tel: +237 42 6479 **Fax:** +237 43 2634
Email: hallelaw@aol.com

MAIN INTERNATIONAL AREAS OF PRACTICE:

Intellectual property: This is a large and successful area of work for the firm, accounting for around 40% of the firm's business. Trademark and patent instructions come from around the world. Recently the firm was instructed by the Trade Mark Owners Association in London. It represents many trade mark attorneys at the African Intellectual Property Organisation.
Corporate: The firm offers advice to foreign investors in Cameroon and has particular experience in privatisations, mergers, leasing, natural resource investment and joint ventures.
Banking: The firm acts for a number of banks and financial institutions, handling their business in the Cameroon.
Other: Other international areas of practice include national resources litigation, civil aviation, maritime and arbitration.

LANGUAGES: English, French

For other recommended firms see pages 1485-1520

NIEDERER KRAFT & FREY

HEAD OFFICE

Bahnhofstrasse 13,
8001 Zurich, Switzerland
Tel: +41 1 217 10 00 **Fax:** +41 1 217 14 00

Email: nkf@nkf.ch
Website: www.nkf.ch

WORLDWIDE OFFICE CONTACTS

SWITZERLAND
Bahnhofstrasse 13, 8001 **Zurich**
Tel: +41 1 217 10 00 **Fax:** +41 1 217 14 00
Email: nkf@nkf.ch

FIRM OVERVIEW

Number of partners worldwide: 17
Number of fee-earners worldwide: 60

AREAS OF PRACTICE:

Banking, capital markets (incl. derivatives)	20%
Company, securities and commercial law	15%
M&A	15%
Arbitration, litigation and judicial assistance	10%
Competition, anti-trust and intellectual property	10%
IT and telecommunications	10%
Tax	10%
Wills, trusts and estate planning	10%

N

FIRM OVERVIEW: Niederer Kraft & Frey, established in 1936, is one Switzerland's largest law firms, currently comprising 60 lawyers. The firm has traditionally focused on banking, capital markets and company commercial work, including mergers and acquisitions and financings. Most of the firm's lawyers are fluent in several languages and have earned additional law degrees abroad, for the most part in the United States or England. Niederer Kraft & Frey has a strong and long-standing international network of contacts with law firms worldwide.

INTERNATIONAL CLIENTS: The firm's clients include banks, investment banks, clearing and settlement institutions, brokers, broker-dealers, other financial intermediaries, derivatives houses, mutual funds, private equity investors, insurance companies, IT and telecommunication providers, other corporate clients and private clients.

MAIN INTERNATIONAL AREAS OF PRACTICE:

Arbitration, litigation and judicial assistance: The firm handles corporate, commercial and contractual disputes, and has extensive experience in international arbitration. Firm members frequently represent banks, bank customers and other clients in judicial assistance proceedings.

Banking, capital markets, derivatives: The firm has long-standing experience in advising Swiss and foreign banks, and has expertise in both the traditional and recently-developed areas of debt financings.

Company, securities and commercial: The firm's expertise lies in corporate work, such as incorporation, IPOs, corporate transactions and reorganisations. It advises on all aspects relating to the Swiss Exchange and its regulations.

Competition, anti-trust and intellectual property: The firm advises on Swiss and European regulations. One of its counsels formerly chaired the Swiss Cartel Commission. The IP department is experienced in all fields.

Environmental and healthcare: The department advises on environmental clean-up, liability and compliance issues. It also assesses environmental legal issues in connection with acquisitions and other transactions.

EU and private international law: The firm advises on commercial and competition-related issues, and has substantial experience in corporate and commercial transactions involving private international law, including, inter alia, cross-border transactions and product liability.

Insurance and reinsurance: Lawyers have comprehensive experience of advising insurance clients on establishing and operating offices in Switzerland.

IT and telecommunications: The firm assists some of the market leaders in the telecommunications industries as well as other clients in the IT market.

Mergers and acquisitions: The firm has extensive experience in complex national and international business transactions, involving publicly and privately owned corporations and other entities.

Project finance, insolvency, restructurings: The firm handles a broad range of structured financing transactions, including lease finance transactions for transportation equipment, power plants and office buildings. It has played an active and innovative role in aircraft financing, privatisations, asset-backed securities and in other asset and financial instrument securitisations as well as regarding insolvencies and restructurings.

Sports: The firm advises and represents domestic and foreign sports clients on all forms of contracts, including international agreements for governing bodies, agreements on international events and competitions, international rights sales and promotion.

Tax: The firm advises on the fiscal and financial structuring of domestic and international transactions, property tax issues and international tax planning for both corporate and private clients. It also represents clients in appeals.

Wills, trusts and estate planning: The firm offers the full range of wealth preservation and transfer services.

LANGUAGES: Dutch, English, French, German, Italian, Spanish

For other recommended firms see pages 1485-1520

NIXON PEABODY LLP

HEAD OFFICES

See worldwide office contacts

Website: www.nixonpeabody.com

FIRM OVERVIEW

Co-managing partners: Nestor M Nicholas, Harry P Trueheart, III

Number of lawyers worldwide: 485

AREAS OF PRACTICE:

Litigation	33%
Business and corporate finance	23%
Real estate	11%
Employment	8%
Syndication	6%
Environmental	5%
Intellectual property	4%
Health care	3%
Project finance	3%

WORLDWIDE OFFICE CONTACTS

USA

437 Madison Avenue, **New York,** NY 10022
Tel: +1 212 940 3000 **Fax:** +1 212 940 3111
Email: nixonpeabody@nixonpeabody.com

Suite 900, 401 9th Street, N.W **Washington,** DC 20004
Tel: +1 202 585 8000 **Fax:** +1 202 585 8080
Email: nixonpeabody@nixonpeabody.com

FIRM OVERVIEW: Nixon Peabody has 485 lawyers who practise in virtually all business areas. The firm offers comprehensive legal services on local, state, national and international levels for major US and international companies, as well as individuals, private and publicly-owned businesses and many other types of organisations. The firm's practice areas include corporate finance, project finance, technology and intellectual property, litigation, environmental, health care, real estate, syndication, and labour. It is also experienced in the energy, media, telecommunications, internet, new media, information technology, biomedical, and optics industries.

INTERNATIONAL EXPERIENCE: The firm has handled many major international deals and transactions. These include the representation of AIG-GE Capital Latin America Infrastructure Fund LP, a private equity fund (in connection with its acquisition of an indirect equity interest in a US$1 billion ammonia/urea project in Venezuela, including advice regarding the financing of the project); Bausch & Lomb Incorporated (in connection with the US$640 million sale of its international sunglasses division, including the Ray Bans brand, to Luxottica Group Spa, Italy); and Canandaigua Brands Inc, now Constellation Brands Inc (in connection with its acquisition of Simi Winery Inc from LVMH, France; with its $185m acquisition of Black Velvet and other Canadian whiskey brands from Diageo plc, UK; its US$350 million acquisition of Matthew Clark plc, UK and the purchase of Franciscan Vineyards, including wineries and vineyards in Chile and California).
The firm has also acted on behalf of Coflexip SA, a French manufacturer of flexible pipes for the oil drilling industry; Crown Packaging Enterprises Ltd; Enterprises Development Ltd; the Ogden Corporation (and the Ogden Power Corporation); PSI Net Inc; and the Yemen Ministry of Oil & Mineral Resources in a joint venture with affiliates of Exxon Corporation, Hunt Oil, Total SA and Yukong (now SK).

INTERNATIONAL CLIENTS: The firm's clients include international banks and multinational and foreign-based corporations in a wide range of industries. It acts as general counsel not only to large industrial corporations and banks but also to media companies, developers, leasing companies and a number of public utilities as well as rendering advice to governments, developers, contractors, lenders, equity investors and investment bankers.

MAIN INTERNATIONAL AREAS OF PRACTICE:
Corporate finance: Services include securities offerings, corporate mergers, acquisitions, dispositions, strategic alliances and joint ventures, technology licensing and transfers, contracting, investing, international tax and tax treaties, and the establishment of foreign subsidiaries, sales and distribution relationships.
Project finance: The firm's global project finance practice focuses on the structuring, developing and financing of energy, infrastructure and privatisation projects throughout the USA, Latin America, Eastern Europe, Asia and the Far East.
Litigation: International dispute services range from drafting and negotiating arbitration and other dispute resolution mechanisms to representing clients in international arbitrations and mediations. Clients are represented in arbitrations administered by, among others, the International Chamber of Commerce, London Court of International Associations, the Netherlands Institute of Arbitration and the American Arbitration Association, as well as in ad hoc arbitrations.
Real estate: The firm represents real estate clients in commercial leasing, construction law, hotels and hospitality facilities, development, zoning and land use, acquisition and disposition of individual properties and portfolios, real estate investment trusts, tax abatements and tax assessment reductions.
Employment: The firm represents employers in the whole spectrum of issues that can arise, involving employment and personnel. It undertakes litigation work in local, state, national and international courts and before administrative and regulatory agencies.
Intellectual property: The firm helps clients identify, protect and commercially exploit their intellectual property interests, including patents, trademarks, copyrights and trade secrets.
Environmental: The practice encompasses all aspects of environmental law, with an emphasis on air, water and solid or hazardous waste matters. It handles international environmental work virtually worldwide, including Canada, the Caribbean, the Far East, Europe, Mexico and South America.

LANGUAGES: Afrikaans, Chinese, Danish, Dutch, French, German, Italian, Norwegian, Portuguese, Russian, Spanish, Swedish

N

NOLST TRENITÉ

HEAD OFFICE

Weena 666, 3012 CN, P.O. Box 190
NL-3000 AD Rotterdam, Netherlands
Tel: +31 10 404 2111 **Fax:** +31 10 404 2333

Email: rotterdam@nolsttrenite.com

FIRM OVERVIEW

Managing partners: Gerard Bruyninckx, Jan van Zuuren, Gerhard Gispen

Number of partners worldwide: 26
Number of other lawyers worldwide: 92

AREAS OF PRACTICE:

Corporate	70%
Logistics, customs and trade	10%
EU and competition	7%
Employment and benefits	5%
Property and environment	5%
Fraud and white collar crime	3%

WORLDWIDE OFFICE CONTACTS

BELGIUM
Avenue de Port 16, B-1080 **Brussels**
Tel: +32 2 421 50 75 **Fax:** +32 2 420 14 06
Email: brussel@nolsttrenite.com

NETHERLANDS
Weena 666, 3012 CN, P.O. Box 190, NL-3000 AD **Rotterdam**
Tel: +31 10 404 2111 **Fax:** +31 10 404 2333
Email: rotterdam@nolsttrenite.com

FIRM OVERVIEW: The firm is one of the longest established international law firms in the Netherlands, with roots going back to the 1880s. It has offices in Rotterdam and Brussels. The firm offers a full range of legal services, with a significant commercial and corporate practice and also has an experienced litigation practice which handles both civil and administrative proceedings. Lawyers work in specialised groups, co-operating across disciplines. The firm is a founding member of the Lex Mundi international legal network.

INTERNATIONAL EXPERIENCE: The firm focuses on Dutch, European and competition law, and has a commercial practice which provides a strategic advantage in bridging the legal complexities of European, transatlantic and other international projects and/or transactions. From the Brussels office, the firm's lawyers monitor and anticipate European developments. On this basis they are able to provide an extensive range of legal services to international companies and organisations. The international corporate finance practice has been expanding rapidly.

INTERNATIONAL EXPERIENCE: Members of the firm have advised internationally oriented companies in various transactions including on the merger of the automotive division of HIM Furness with the Koops Group; the publicly listed HIM Furness on successful court proceedings against VEB (Vereniging van EffectBezitters); Thai Airways on the asset based Eximbank/ECGD supported finance of one Boeing 747 and four Boeing 777 aircraft; Repsol International Finance B.V. and Repsol YPF, S.A. on various issues of bonds, notes, commercial paper and other capital market intstruments; a private property investment company in connection with a £51.5 million syndicated loan facility in connection with the disposal of a large portfolio of retail investments; lead counsel in merger between seven energy distribution companies constituting the third largest Dutch energy distribution company, ENECO Holding N.V.; co-counsel in take-over by Gas de France International S.A. from Transcanada Pipelines Limited of two of its subsidiaries holding (indirect) exploration and production rights on parts of the Dutch Continental Shelf; AVR, one of the largest waste managers in the Netherlands, on the acquisition of AVIRA from 18 Dutch municipalities. The firm also carried out a number of Article 81 and merger notifications. These notifications included the merger between Boskalis and HBG (which was cancelled after approval from the Commission was obtained) in 2000; assisting a foreign bidder in the auction of the VOPAK Botlek Tank Terminal; assisting bidder Greif Bros Corp. in the multi million dollar acquisition of the Industrial Van Leer Packaging Division from Huhtamäki.

INTERNATIONAL CLIENTS: The firm advises international corporations and financial institutions, including a large number of US and UK clients. It also advises foreign governments worldwide.

MAIN INTERNATIONAL AREAS OF PRACTICE:
Corporate: Work handled includes commercial contracting; corporate notarial book 2 and corporate governance; corporate and commercial litigation; corporate and financial restructurings; finance and capital markets; mergers and acquisitions; public bids, IPO's and venture capital.
Tax: The practice advises on varied tax issues, with an emphasis on corporate advice including international take-overs, mergers, reorganisations and financing, and privatisation, as well as tax planning for managing directors and majority shareholders.
EU: The firm advises companies on the EU dimension of their operations, including issues such as the environment, government tenders and subsidies, impediments to trade or establishment and concessions.
Logistics customs and trade: Nolst Trenité is the only Dutch law firm with a dedicated team of customs and international trade specialists. It is involved in several of the largest Dutch customs investigations into smuggling and duty avoidance on products such as tobacco, alcoholic beverages, meat, metals and dairy. Particular emphasis is placed on civil, tax and criminal litigation involving amounts between DFL1million to DFL20 million in alleged avoided duty.

LANGUAGES: Dutch, English, German, French, Spanish

 For other recommended firms see pages 1485-1520

NOMOS

HEAD OFFICE

13 rue Alphonse de Neuville,
75017 Paris, France
Tel: +33 1 4318 55 00 **Fax:** +33 1 4318 55 55

Email: nomos@nomosparis.com
Website: www.nomosparis.com

FIRM OVERVIEW

Contact partners: Eric Lauvaux, Christophe Pecnard, Monique Sentilles-Dupont

Number of partners worldwide: 11
Number of other lawyers worldwide: 30

AREAS OF PRACTICE:
Media/communications 20%
Private equity 20%
Consumer products 20%
Distribution 15%
Telecommunications and new technologies 15%
Outsourcing and business support services 5%
Pharmaceutical industry 5%

FIRM PROFILE: Established in 1998 by nine partners, Nomos provides legal services to French and international clients, including multinationals and dynamic small to medium-sized businesses. The firm assists clients in their day-to-day operations, as well as in their more unusual transactions and in litigation. Since it was formed the firm has expanded rapidly and now has more than 40 lawyers and 11 partners.

INTERNATIONAL EXPERIENCE: The firm's practice groups are well accustomed to international negotiations and include lawyers who are members of bar associations in other major jurisdictions. In addition, the firm's large network of correspondents allows it to support its clients' needs outside mainland France.

INTERNATIONAL CLIENTS: The firm's client's include subsidiaries of foreign groups, belonging to the world's leading companies in sectors such as agro-foods, media and entertainment, capital development, business support services and Internet directory.

MAIN INTERNATIONAL AREAS OF PRACTICE:
Corporate: Corporate restructuring and IPOs, lobbying with market authorities and handling securities issues, corporate reorganisations and shareholding structures. The firm also handles incorporating companies as well as advising on day-to-day management.
Contracts and competition: Recognising that contractual techniques differ from industry to industry the firm assesses its clients' risks and objectives in order to provide them with viable solutions.
Tax: Working both nationally and internationally the firm's experienced team advises on corporate restructuring operations, acquisitions, tax audits, tax authority rulings and asset taxation. It also advises on tax matters relating to charities and non-profit making associations.
Employment: Nomos advise on matters relating to individual personnel or broader industrial relations issues such as works committees or unions. Nomos experience also covers requirements regarding welfare protection, working hours management and remuneration structures.
Intellectual property: The firm offers advice on analysing a company's products and services, protecting against infringement and unfair competition, drawing up contracts for assignments, licences and filings.

LANGUAGES: French, English, German, Spanish

WORLDWIDE OFFICE CONTACTS

FRANCE
13 rue Alphonse de Neuville, 75017 **Paris**
Tel: +33 1 4318 55 00 **Fax:** +33 1 4318 55 55
Email: nomos@nomosparis.com

NORONHA ADVOGADOS

HEAD OFFICE

Av. Brig. Faria Lima, 1355, 3rd floor
01452-919 São Paulo, Brazil
Tel: +55 11 3038 8090 **Fax:** +55 11 3812 2495
Email: noadsao@noronhaadvogados.com.br
Website: www.noronhaadvogados.com.br

FIRM OVERVIEW

Senior partner: Durval de Noronha Goyos Jr.

Number of partners worldwide: 26
Number of other lawyers worldwide: 109

AREAS OF PRACTICE:

Banking and finance (including securities) 19%
Corporate 18%
M&A 18%
Tax 11%
Social security and commercial litigation 10%
Insurance 7%
Environment, energy and mining 5%
Intellectual property 4%
IT 4%
Real estate 3%
Employment 1%

FIRM OVERVIEW: Established in1978, Noronha Advogados is an international law firm. Based in São Paulo, Rio de Janeiro, Brasília, Curitiba, Salvador and Manaus, the firm also has a unique network of its own international offices including London, Lisbon, Buenos Aires, Los Angeles and Miami. The firm's international presence means it can offer a wide variety of legal services in the industrial, financial, commercial and service areas to a diversified clientele.

INTERNATIONAL EXPERIENCE: Noronha Advogados' international experience has strengthened over the years. The firm's foreign offices have become an important and integral part of its organisation, working in close cooperation with the firm's national offices.

INTERNATIONAL CLIENTS: Noronha Advogados has been involved in a number of international transactions. Its clients include a wide range of multinational organisations, and encompass a range of industry sectors ranging from primary industries like agriculture, mining, energy, to secondary industries like manufacturing, transport, banking, telecommunications and information technology.

MAIN INTERNATIONAL AREAS OF PRACTICE:

International banking and insurance: The firm advises foreign banks and financial institutions on project and trade finance and sovereign debt. The firm has recently been involved in structuring the securitisation of Brazilian receivables, as well as international funds trading on Brazilian and international stock exchanges. Since the insurance market has opened up the firm has advised a number of international insurance companies on establishing in Brazil and on cross-border supply of insurance and reinsurance.
International trade: The firm handles all aspects of Brazilian foreign commerce including export financing, taxation and government procurement. It also represents companies and governments before the World Trade Organisation and in all aspects relating to questions of regional integration agreements such as Mercosul, NAFTA, or the Free Trade Agreement for the Americas.

WORLDWIDE OFFICE CONTACTS

ARGENTINA
Carlos Pellegrini, 1069, Piso 11, 1009 **Buenos Aires**
Tel: +54 11 4328 6221 **Fax:** +54 11 4322 6222
Email: est_dedeu_ferrario@ciudad.com.ar

BRAZIL
SCN, Quadra 1, Bloco E, Ed. Central Park, conjunto 1802, 70711-903 DF **Brasília**
Tel: +55 61 327 1877 **Fax:** +55 61 327 1877
Email: noadbsb@noronhaadvogados.com.br

Av. Batel, 1230, Batel Trade Center, Bloco 2, 5th floor, conjunto 502, 80420-090 PR **Curitiba**
Tel: +55 41 343 2909 **Fax:** +55 41 343 5178
Email: noadctb@noronhaadvogados.com.br

Av. Nilo Peçanha, 50, Grupo 1718, 20044-900 RJ **Rio de Janeiro**
Tel: +55 21 3084 9080 **Fax:** +55 21 3084 4363
Email: noadrio@noronhaadvogados.com.br

Av. ACM, 3213, Ed. Golden Plaza, Sl 1301, 40275-000 BA **Salvador**
Tel: +55 71 351 9233 **Fax:** +55 71 351 9233
Email: noadne@noronhaadvogados.com.br

Av. Brig. Faria Lima, 1355, 3rd floor, 01452-919 **São Paulo**
Tel: +55 113038 8090 **Fax:** +55 11 212 2495
Email: noadsao@noronhaadvogados.com.br

PORTUGAL
Praça Marquês de Pombal, 16A, 5° Piso, 1250 **Lisbon**
Tel: +351 21 350 4005 **Fax:** +351 21 350 4030
Email: noadlis@noronhaadvogados.com.br

UNITED KINGDOM
4th Floor, 193-195 Brompton Road, **London** SW3 1NE
Tel: +44 20 7581 5040 **Fax:** +44 20 7581 8002
Email: noadlon@noronhaadvogados.com.br

USA
1801 Avenue of the Stars, 1200, **Los Angeles** CA 90067
Tel: +1 310 788 0294 **Fax:** +1 310 788 0225
Email: noadlax@noronhaadvogados.com.br

1221 Brickell Avenue, 9th floor, **Miami** FL 33131
Tel: +1 305 372 0844 **Fax:** +1 305 372 1792
Email: noadmia@noronadvogados.com.br

Tax: The firm advises on the structure of international tax planning in relation to international trade and investment activities in various countries for reducing tax burdens. Advice is given on the optimum usage of international tax treaties in the context of applicable tax legislation, as well as the efficient transfer of dividends, royalties, interest, resulting from transnational activities.
Corporate: The firm has handled a significant number of majority/minority shareholders conflicts involving local companies. Noronha Advogados also advises international companies establishing offices in Brazil.
Contracts and competition: The firm is involved in a wide range of commercial contracts including supply, franchise and distribution agreements, service agreements, contracts of guarantee, intellectual property and real estate contracts.
M&A: Noronha Advogados has one of the most active M&A departments in Latin America. The department structures leverage financial operations, take-overs and joint ventures. It has handled a number of successful leverage buy-outs and management buy-outs cases.

LANGUAGES: Afrikaans, English, French, German, Italian, Japanese, Korean, Mandarin, Portuguese, Russian, Spanish

N

For other recommended firms see pages 1485-1520

NORTON ROSE

HEAD OFFICE

Kempson House, Camomile Street,
London EC3A 7AN, United Kingdom
Tel: +44 20 7283 6000 **Fax:** +44 20 7283 6500

Website: www.nortonrose.com

FIRM OVERVIEW

Managing partner: Roger Birkby
Senior partner: David Lewis

Number of partners worldwide: 152
Number of other lawyers worldwide: 650

AREAS OF PRACTICE:

Banking and asset finance	27%
Corporate finance	27%
Litigation	24%
Other	12%
Property, planning and environmental	9%

FIRM OVERVIEW: Founded in London in 1794, Norton Rose now has over 600 lawyers worldwide. It has overseas and associated offices in Europe, the Middle East and Asia and is committed to international expansion. The firm focuses above all on finance and business, specialising in corporate finance, asset finance, project finance, acquisition finance and 'big ticket' litigation. It provides expert services in a select number of international industry and market sectors, including banking, insurance, transportation and infrastructure. The firm aims to maintain an in-depth understanding of industrial issues and to develop new techniques to accelerate clients' commercial advantage.

INTERNATIONAL EXPERIENCE: In addition to its international network of offices, Norton Rose has significant experience in advising clients in Western Europe, the emerging markets of Central and Southern Europe, the Middle East, Sub-Saharan Africa and the Indian subcontinent. The firm also acts for a number of US firms investing in Europe and elsewhere. In April 1999 Norton Rose's London office was awarded the Queen's Award for Export Achievement in recognition of the work done for its international clients. Norton Rose has been active in Russia, Central and Southern Europe since the early 1970s, and has recently been particularly busy in Romania, Bulgaria and the CIS. On the Indian sub-continent, the firm has been involved in major energy and utility projects, and is also very active in Indian shipping finance and port development. The firm has many years' experience in a large number of African countries, and has recently been particularly active in the African mining sector, where clients include Ashanti and Randgold. The firm has increased its activities in the Indonesian market in recent years, and is also active in Thailand and Malaysia. In South America, the firm is particularly experienced in Argentina, Colombia and Venezuela, where it has acted for a group of oil companies in the SINCOR Orinoco oil basin project. The firm's commercial litigation teams undertake a high proportion of multi-jurisdictional and international disputes.

INTERNATIONAL CLIENTS: The firm's international clients include banks, financial institutions and funds, multinational corporate businesses, major public and private companies, government departments and agencies, statutory undertakings and sovereign states. Some of the firm's better-known clients are AIG, AXA BMW, Carlsberg, Chase, HSBC, Bosch, Cable & Wireless, Cathay Pacific, Chase Manhattan Corp, DaimlerChrysler, De Beers, Emerson Electric, Enron, ENI, the EBRD, HSBC Holdings, Lukoil, Mobil Corporation, Nestle, Siemens, Texas Utilities, Total and US Exim Bank.

LANGUAGES: Afrikaans, Arabic, Bahasa Malay, Cantonese, Czech, Danish, Dutch, French, German, Greek, Hebrew, Hindi, Italian, Japanese, Maltese, Norwegian, Russian, Shona, Spanish, Swahili, Swedish

WORLDWIDE OFFICE CONTACTS

BAHRAIN
Unitag House, Government Avenue, PO Box 20437, **Manama**
Tel: +973 226 424 **Fax:** +973 229 810

BELGIUM
Rue Montoyer 40, B-1000 **Brussels**
Tel: +32 22 37 6111 **Fax:** +32 22 37 6136

FRANCE
Washington Plaza, 42 rue Washington, Cedex 08, 75408 **Paris**
Tel: +33 1 53 89 56 00 **Fax:** +33 1 53 89 56 56

ITALY
Via Visconti di Modrone, 21, 20122 **Milan**
Tel: +39 02 799 144 **Fax:** +39 02 7733 1538

POLAND
Norton Rose Piotrstrawa & Partners, Ul. Królewska 14, 00-065 **Warsaw**
Tel: +48 22 581 4900 **Fax:** +48 22 581 4950

RUSSIA
Bolshoi Sukharevsky Pereulok 26, 103051 **Moscow**
Tel: +7 095 244 3639 **Fax:** +7 095 244 3968

SINGAPORE
5 Shenton Way, #33-08, UIC Building, **Singapore** 068808
Tel: +65 223 7311 **Fax:** +65 224 5758

THAILAND
Norton Rose (Thailand) Limited, Sindhorn Building, Tower 2, Floor 14, 130-132 Wireless Road, **Bangkok** 10330
Tel: +662 263 2811 **Fax:** +662 256 6703/5

UNITED KINGDOM
Kempson House, Camomile Street, **London** EC3A 7AN
Tel: +44 20 7283 6000 **Fax:** +44 20 7283 6500

ASSOCIATED OFFICES

CZECH REPUBLIC
Balcar Polanský Norton Rose (BPNR), Elisky Peskove 15, CZ-151 31 **Prague**
Tel: +42 02 5731 0325 **Fax:** +42 02 5731 0327

GREECE
Law Firm Howard in association with Norton Rose, 21 Karneadou Street, 106 75 Kolonaki, **Athens**
Tel: +30 1 721 7111 **Fax:** +30 1 724 8775

INDONESIA
Lubis Ganie Surowidjojo, Menara Imperium, 30th Floor, Jalan H Rangkayo Rasuna Said, Kav. 1, Kuningan, **Jakarta** 12980
Tel: +62 21 831 5005 **Fax:** +62 21 831 5015

N

For other recommended firms see pages 1485-1520

BUFETE ODIO & RAVEN

HEAD OFFICE

Calle 31, Avenidas 7-9, Barrio Escalante, P.O. Box 5069-1000
San José Costa Rica
Tel: +50 6 234 9710 **Fax:** +50 6 253 1735

Email: info@odioraven.com
Website: www.odioraven.com

FIRM OVERVIEW

Managing partner: Claudio Donato
Senior partner: Alberto Raven
Manager: Gloriana Lara

AREAS OF PRACTICE:

Corporate and M&A	25%
Foreign investment, international trade and export regimes	25%
Government procurement/infrastructure projects	20%
Litigation and arbitration	10%
Tourism	7%
Banking, finance and stock exchange	5%
Energy and telecommunications	5%
Intellectual property	3%

FIRM OVERVIEW: Founded in 1960, Odio & Raven has an established reputation for quality service, and is one of the fastest growing firms in San José. Unlike most law offices in Central America, Odio & Raven operates as an integrated team of lawyers and a corporate firm. Since its creation, the firm's wide general practice has been centred in commercial and corporate law and has always kept a particular strength in economic regulation. The development of the firm's practice has been the result of a conscious effort to satisfy the needs of its clients, and to develop the related areas of international trade, taxation, real estate, investment and financial law, intellectual property, government procurement, immigration and administrative law. In the past decade, the development of modern legislation and the desire to provide adequate service resulted in the development of a series of specialised sub-areas of practice, such as public works concessions, telecommunications and energy regulations, tourism, export-oriented regulations and procedures, anti-trust and competition regulations, and securities trade regulations. Within all the areas of practice of the firm, its staff offers a full range of legal services, corporate assistance, and all sorts of administrative claims and judicial litigation. Odio & Raven has maintained strong professional and civic ties to key national institutions. The firm has had a distinguished role in major regulatory advances and in specific projects of national and regional importance.

INTERNATIONAL EXPERIENCE: The firm has handled a range of international work in international investment, international trade and expropriation issues. International involvement has often been the consequence of the participation of the firm cases in which international investment or trade conflicts are resolved through international diplomacy, arbitration and other conflict resolution means. Odio & Raven has often co-ordinated M&A transactions and corporate restructuring across the seven jurisdictions of Central America and Panama.

INTERNATIONAL CLIENTS: The firm typically represents medium or large international corporations and has distinguished itself by maintaining long-lasting relationships with such clients. It has enjoyed a long-standing relationship with prestigious names in a wide diversity of economic activities, such as electric and electronic equipment, petroleum, medical supplies, pharmaceutical products, and consumer products.

WORLDWIDE OFFICE CONTACTS

COSTA RICA
Calle 31, Avenidas 7-9, Barrio Escalante, P.O. Box 5069-1000, **San José**
Tel: +50 6 234 9710 **Fax:** +50 6 253 1735
Email: info@odioraven.com

MAIN INTERNATIONAL AREAS OF PRACTICE:

M&A: In the last two years, Odio & Raven has handled over 15 M&A transactions, worth in total over US$100 million. The firm's practice has developed rapidly, not only regarding operations that involve Costa Rican companies and assets, but also regional operations that involve multi-jurisdictional supervision of the legal aspects of complex mergers and acquisitions. Specifically in relation to acquisitions, the practice has had to deal with difficulties and issues that are particular to the regional conformation and to the adaptation to the local practices of every country in Central America.

Foreign investment: Odio & Raven specialises in foreign direct investment. The firm advises on import-export incentives and benefits, foreign investment benefits, and transfer of technology. The firm represents an important portfolio of foreign and domestic investors heavily involved in international trade (both import and export). The firm also handles a range of work in the pharmaceuticals, medical products, textiles, computer software, and citric products industries.

International trade: The firm specialises in international commerce. It handles complex and highly technical issues such as safeguard measures, anti-dumping measures, compensatory duties, management and distribution of export and import quotas, import-export processes, import tariffs, non-tariff barriers, customs, and unfair trade regulations. Odio & Raven also advises domestic and international companies in administrative and judicial procedures before the Costa Rican government and before other governments in Central America.

Tourism: In recent years, the tourism industry has become extremely important to the Costa Rican economy. The firm has responded to this and now assists local and foreign tourism oriented enterprises, such as hotel corporations and real estate developers, in all of their business dealings in Costa Rica. Odio & Raven advises on the elaboration of contracts, franchising, fiscal benefits, and legal issues involved with these corporations' daily administration and operation.

Regional infrastructure projects: The deficit in infrastructure and public services has been recognised by the Central American governments as one of the most important problems facing the region and a major issue to be included in common economic policies. Odio & Raven has taken part in the formation and implementation of this Central American strategy and has gained significant experience in this emerging area of practice. The firm advises on large infrastructure projects with the participation of private capital, and has achieved some notable results under adverse bureaucratic and regulatory circumstances.

Energy and telecommunications: Odio & Raven has handled a range of energy and telecommunications related work. The firm has advised a number of well-known multinational corporations on petroleum production, refining and commercialisation, and development and production of equipment for telecommunications and the transmission and generation of electric energy. More recently the firm has advised on the sale of equipment and international services in data transmission, the privately owned 'co-generation' of electricity (both hydroelectric and wind-powered), and the polemic operation of a privately owned cellular telephone system.

LANGUAGES: English, Spanish

OGIER & LE MASURIER

HEAD OFFICE

PO Box 404, Whiteley Chambers, Don Street,
St. Helier JE4 9WG, Jersey
Tel: +44 1534 504000 **Fax:** +44 1534 735328

Email: legal@ogier.com
Website: www.ogier.com

FIRM OVERVIEW

Managing partner: Sarah Fitz

Number of partners worldwide: 18
Number of other lawyers worldwide: 50

WORLDWIDE OFFICE CONTACTS

GUERNSEY
Coutts House, Le Truchot, **St Peter Port** GY1 1WD
Tel: +44 1481 721 672 **Fax:** +44 1481 721 575
Email: legal@ogier.com

JERSEY
PO Box 404, Whiteley Chambers, Don Street, **St. Helier** JE4 9WG
Tel: +44 1534 504000 **Fax:** +44 1534 735328
Email: legal@ogier.com

AREAS OF PRACTICE:

Banking	20%
Litigation	20%
Structured finance	20%
Investment funds	15%
Trusts	15%
Property	10%

FIRM OVERVIEW: Ogier & Le Masurier is one of the largest legal practices in the Channel Islands and is unique in having the first presence in both jurisdictions of Jersey and Guernsey, through associated offices. Ogier & Le Masurier traces its roots back to 1867 and has grown in parallel with the development of the Channel Islands as an international finance centre. The firm now has more than 50 lawyers and over 175 professional and support staff. It provides a specialised range of legal services to financial institutions and business clients with banking and finance work, securitisations, investment funds and commercial litigation forming the core of the practice. All the work handled by the firm is undertaken by teams of specialists, led by a partner, selected to achieve the commercial objectives of the client. A large number of the firm's lawyers have worked in major financial centres outside Jersey and bring to the firm the international experience and commercial awareness sought by its clients. The firm places a great importance on the referral of work to them by professional advisers in other jurisdictions.

INTERNATIONAL EXPERIENCE: The firm acts for banks from all over the world, as well as for private clients who use Jersey structures to preserve and manage their wealth and trust companies providing trustee services.

INTERNATIONAL CLIENTS: Clients for whom the firm acts on a regular basis include Abbey National, ANZ, Bank of America, Bank of Scotland, Barclays Private Bank, BNP, Cazenove, Chase Manhattan, Citibank, Deutsche Bank, Dresdner, Flemings, SG Hambros, Hill Samuel, HSBC, ING, Lloyds/TSB, Lazards, Merrill Lynch, Morgan Guaranty, Royal Bank of Canada, Schroders, UBS and Zurich Financial Services. The firm's clients also include a number of private clients worldwide who use Jersey structures to preserve and manage their wealth and trust companies providing trustee services.

MAIN INTERNATIONAL AREAS OF PRACTICE:
Banking: Ogier & Le Masurier is one of Jersey's leading banking and finance firms. It specialises in all aspects of banking, security, banking regulation and the establishment of banks.
Securitisation: The firm specialises in the securitisation of assets. During 1999 the firm acted on securitisation and capital markets issues exceeding US$100 billion in aggregate principal amount. With particular expertise in asset-backed securities, collateralised bond offerings and structured debt instruments, the firm is able to add value to the structuring process.
Investment funds: The firm advises on the establishment and structuring of funds, as well as on regulatory and compliance aspects. The firm also advises on listings on the Channel Islands Stock Exchange.
Trusts: Work is undertaken for private clients as well as corporate and institutional clients. Trusts are of increasing importance in the commercial field, particularly in structured financing and the employee benefits sphere.
Litigation: The firm's litigation group is particularly strong. It specialises in trust disputes, shareholder remedies and asset tracing and freezing.

LANGUAGES: English, French, German, Portuguese, Spanish

WORLDWIDE OFFICES

GUERNSEY

Coutts House, Le Truchot, St Peter Port GY1 1WD

Sole principal: Roger Le Tissier

Number of lawyers: 5
Number of dual qualified lawyers: 2
Number of locally qualified lawyers: 1

Office profile: The firm's associated office in Guernsey advises financial institutions, business and private clients on all aspects of commercial business, especially banking and finance, securitisations, investment funds, trusts and insurance. In the field of investment business the firm advises on the establishment and structuring of products, as well as on the regulatory and compliance aspects. The firm also advises in connection with listings on the Channel Islands Stock Exchange for funds, debt issues, and trading companies. The principal, Roger Le Tissier, was for a number of years the compliance officer, company secretary and head of the legal department of Guernsey's largest fund administrator, and also worked at the Guernsey Financial Services Commission, the local financial regulator.

OGIER & Le MASURIER

O

OGILVY RENAULT

HEAD OFFICE

1981 McGill College Avenue, Suite 1100,
Montreal QC H3A 3C1, Canada
Tel: +1 514 847 4747 **Fax:** +1 514 286 5474

Email: info@ogilvyrenault.com
Website: www.ogilvyrenault.com

FIRM OVERVIEW

Chairman: L. Yves Fortier, CC, QC
Managing partner: Raymond Crevier, QC

Number of partners worldwide: 161
Number of other lawyers worldwide: 133

AREAS OF PRACTICE:

Banking and finance	*%
Competition/anti-trust and trade law	*%
Corporate and commercial	*%
Intellectual property and technology	*%
Labour and employment	*%
Litigation, arbitration and ADR	*%
Mergers and acquisitions	*%
Securities	*%
Tax	*%

* Workload % not disclosed

WORLDWIDE OFFICE CONTACTS

CANADA
1981 McGill College Avenue, Suite 1100, **Montreal** QC H3A 3C1
Tel: +1 514 847 4747 **Fax:** +1 514 286 5474
Email: info@ogilvyrenault.com

Suite 1600, 45 O'Connor Street, **Ottawa** ON K1P 1A4
Tel: +1 613 780 8661 **Fax:** +1 613 230 5459
Email: ottawa@ogilvyrenault.com

Suite 520, 500 Grande Allée est, **Quebec City** QC G1R 2J7
Tel: +1 418 640 5000 **Fax:** +1 418 640 1500
Email: quebec@ogilvyrenault.com

Suite 2100, PO Box 141, Royal Trust Tower, TD Centre, **Toronto** ON M5K 1H1
Tel: +1 416 216 4000 **Fax:** +1 416 216 3930
Email: toronto@ogilvyrenault.com

800 Park Place, 666 Burrard Street, **Vancouver** BC V6C 3P3
Tel: +1 604 806 0922 **Fax:** +1 604 806 0933
Email: info@ogilvyrenault.com

UNITED KINGDOM
38 Charterhouse Square, **London** EC1M 6EQ
Tel: +44 20 7600 9005 **Fax:** +44 20 7600 9006
Email: info@ogilvyrenault.com

FIRM OVERVIEW: Founded in Montreal in 1879, Ogilvy Renault is one of Canada's oldest, largest and most distinguished law firms. Former members of the firm have served as Governor-General of Canada, Lieutenant-Governor of Quebec and Premier of Quebec. Current members of the firm include a former Prime Minister of Canada (1984-1993) and a former Ambassador of Canada to the United Nations (1988-1992). With close to 300 lawyers in strategically located offices in five of Canada's most important financial, corporate and government centers - Montreal, Ottawa, Quebec, Toronto and Vancouver, and in London, England - Ogilvy Renault provides a comprehensive range of legal services to many of Canada's largest privately-held or public corporations and financial institutions and government or quasi-government organisations. The firm plays an influential role in many of the most important national and international financings, mergers and acquisitions, reorganisations and restructurings.

INTERNATIONAL EXPERIENCE: Ogilvy Renault's English and French bilingual character and proficiency in both the civil and common law systems have naturally led to a strong national and international practice. The representation of foreign and multinational corporations, financial institutions and other organisations with respect to their interests not only in Canada but throughout Europe, the United States, Latin America and Asia constitutes a significant part of the firm's practice. The office in London, England facilitates this vital aspect of the firm's practice and enables it to assist Canadian clients in their European operations.

INTERNATIONAL CLIENTS: Clients include many of Canada's largest privately held or public corporations, and financial institutions, government or quasi-government organisations, foreign and multinational corporations, and other organisations.

MAIN INTERNATIONAL AREAS OF PRACTICE:
Banking law: The firm has expertise in all aspects of banking law, business reorganisations and bankruptcy, movable and immovable security, national and international banking transactions, commercial financing, cross-border financing and project finance.
M&A, anti-trust and trade: The firm advises international corporations and governments on a wide range of issues in the areas of mergers and acquisitions, trade practices, competition bureau inquiries and trade law, including interpretation of multilateral and bilateral international trade agreements. Lawyers advise businesses at the earliest stages and on their subsequent development, including acquisitions or mergers and design of the most tax-efficient structure.
Alternative dispute resolution: The firm is actively involved in ADR, acting as advisor, mediator and arbitrator. It has represented parties in arbitration proceedings, both domestic and international, conducted under the rules of most major arbitration institutions.
Intellectual property: Services are offered in all traditional areas of intellectual property law pertaining to trade-marks, patents, industrial design, copyright and unfair competition.
Technology: The firm's lawyers are active in computer and information technology, communications, biotechnology, multimedia and other high technology sectors. Ogilvy Renault works closely with the trademark and patent agents of Swabey Ogilvy Renault, all of whom have a strong technical background.

LANGUAGES: Lawyers provide services in English and French and communicate in several other languages including German, Italian and Spanish.

For other recommended firms see pages 1485-1520

ESTUDIO OLAECHEA

HEAD OFFICE

Bernardo Monteagudo 201, San Isidro,
Lima 27 Peru
Tel: +51 1 264 4040 **Fax:** +51 1 264 4050

Email: mpoac@esola.com.pe
Website: www.esola.com.pe

WORLDWIDE OFFICE CONTACTS

PERU
Bernardo Monteagudo 201, San Isidro, **Lima** 27
Tel: +51 1 264 4040/3620/3611 **Fax:** +51 1 264 4050/3080
Email: mpoac@esola.com.pe

FIRM OVERVIEW

Managing partner: José Antonio Olaechea
Senior partner: Manuel Pablo Olaechea
Number of partners worldwide: 3
Number of other lawyers worldwide: 14

FIRM PROFILE: Estudio Olaechea is the oldest firm in Peru and one of the oldest law firms in North and South America. It was founded in 1878 by Manuel Pablo Olaechea. In 1947, the firm was the first to become a Professional Corporation with lawyers specialised in the principal fields of law. The firm is an independent full service law firm, dedicated to providing legal services to companies, financial institutions and individuals seeking expertise in Peru.

INTERNATIONAL EXPERIENCE: Olaechea law firm is a full service firm specialising in foreign investment and international law. The firm has longstanding and valued professional relationships with banks, financial institutions and industries representing customers from all around the world. The firm has assisted many important transnational companies in establishing their business in Peru. Olaechea law firm has established close working relationships with a network of law firms throughout Latin America, North America, Europe and Asia. The firm has an independent correspondent relationship as the Peruvian member of the Club de Abogados and Lex Mundi, two global associations of independent law firms of the highest level.

MAIN INTERNATIONAL AREAS OF PRACTICE:
Banking and financing: The firm advises on all types of banking and insurance operations, such as the establishment of these institutions and their subsidiaries and representation offices, legal auditing, issuance and marketing of debt, secured and unsecured liabilities.
Capital markets: Securities practice involves representing operating companies, financial institutions, underwriters and sponsors of investment companies in a wide variety of capital market transaction, including public offerings and private placements of equity and debt securities in the domestic and international markets.
Commercial law: The firm advises on the incorporation of companies, their by-laws, public offering of shares, quotation on the stock exchange, financing programmes, joint venture agreements, shareholders' agreements, establishment of branches and subsidiaries.
Competition law: The firm advises domestic and foreign companies on subjects such as anti-monopoly laws, dumping, unfair competition, publicity, smuggling and consumer protection.
Construction: The firm advises on construction projects in the mining, energy, highway and building areas as well as advising on the ownership of property.
Environmental law: The firm provides assistance on the adaptation to environmental rules in force for domestic and foreign companies.
Energy law: The firm advises on regulation regarding different forms of generation, transmission and distribution of energy and acts related to its use.
Intellectual property: The firm advises on copyrights, patents, utility models, industrial designs, industrial secrets, trademarks, commercial names and slogans and denominations of origin.
International law: The firm counsels clients in selecting the most advantageous applicable law and jurisdiction, foreign investment regime and law stability agreements.
Labour and immigration: The firm handles all matters concerning foreign personnel hired by domestic and international companies. It defends clients against labour law claims.
Litigation: The firm handles the defence and execution of resolutions before government authorities and courts, gives advice on arbitration agreements, restructuring and brankruptcies of companies and individuals.
M&A: The firm assists companies and individuals interested in privatisations, mergers and acquisitions, including due diligences and legal auditing procedures, corporate restructuring and bankruptcy.
Mining law: The firm advises on processing mining claims up to their registration and on mining procedures to avoid overlaps. It also provides counseling in the incorporation of mining companies and negotiation of the different contracts in this area.
Taxation: The firm provides counseling regarding contentious and and non-contentious tax procedures before the Peruvian Government Authorities. It also gives assistance on tax stability agreements for several economic activities.
Transportation and communications: The firm advises on procedures to obtain operating licenses, frequencies, special flight permits, shared codes, contracts for the establishment of pools, maritime conferences, freight bookings as well as financial leasing, charter contracts and others.

LANGUAGES: English, French, Italian, Portuguese, Spanish

OLANIWUN AJAYI & CO

HEAD OFFICE

UBA House (Floor 4) 57 Marina
Lagos Nigeria
Tel: +234 1 264 2551 **Fax:** +234 1 264 2553

Email: lawyers@olaniwunajayi.com

WORLDWIDE OFFICE CONTACTS

NIGERIA
UBA House (Floor 4) 57 Marina, 57 Marina, **Lagos**
Tel: +234 1 264 2551 **Fax:** +234 1 264 2553
Email: lawyers@olaniwunajayi.com

FIRM OVERVIEW

Managing partner: Olukonyinsola Ajayi

Number of partners worldwide: 3
Number of other lawyers worldwide: 15

AREAS OF PRACTICE:

Admiralty and shipping .... *%
Banking and finance .... *%
Capital markets .... *%
Corporate and commercial .... *%
Energy and natural resources .... *%
Intellectual property .... *%
Litigation and arbitration .... *%
M&A .... *%
* Workload % not disclosed

O

FIRM OVERVIEW: Founded in 1962, Olaniwun Ajayi & Co comprises barristers, solicitors, arbitrators, chartered secretaries and trademark agents. A full service law firm, it specialises in corporate and commercial law, and has been involved in some of the largest and most complex transactions in the Nigerian energy and finance sectors. In addition to its in-house expertise, the firm has consultants versed in legal and business matters. These include a group of jurists and retired company directors. Olaniwun Ajayi & Co is represented in both the International Bar Association and the Association of Commercial Lawyers (ACL) based in the UK.

INTERNATIONAL EXPERIENCE: Olaniwun Ajayi & Co has been involved in a number of major international transactions including the Nigerian LNG US$4.5 billion project, a US$350 million international take-over in the downstream oil sector, the US$4.1 billion Nigerian International Debt Fund; the £15 million Guinness convertible loan stock; the N10 billion Nigeria Energy Sector Fund; the Nigerian Smart Card Project by a consortium of leading banks.

INTERNATIONAL CLIENTS: The firm advises medium and large-scale clients. Its client base includes international oil companies, banks and other multinationals.

MAIN INTERNATIONAL AREAS OF PRACTICE:

Banking and finance: The firm is at the forefront of the developments in both domestic and international banking law. It handles issues relating to project and joint venture finance, corporate finance and securities. It also advises on the regulation of banks and other financial institutions. The firm places a strong emphasis on innovative legal solutions and the observance of a high degree of confidentiality.

Energy and natural resources: The firm has advised local and international companies engaged in upstream and downstream petroleum activities in Nigeria. Olaniwun Ajayi & Co is experienced at dealing within the confines of the oil and gas laws. The firm also researches the growing area of environmental law, and advises on the settlement of environmental claims.

Company and commercial: The firm provides a full range of company secretarial services as well as legal advice on day-to-day business matters.

Arbitration and litigation: The firm advises on, and conducts, international arbitration under various internationally recognised arbitration bodies.

Admiralty and shipping: International trade, shipping and admiralty issues assume an important role in the firm's scope of services. It advises ship owners, managers, charterers, cargo interests, insurers and financiers. Olaniwun Ajayi & Co's activities in this field extend as far as trade within the transportation industry. The firm also handles a range of aviation issues including domestic and international compliance and regulatory issues.

LANGUAGES: English, French, Italian

For other recommended firms see pages 1485-1520

OLES & RODZYNKIEWICZ

HEAD OFFICE

ul.Retoryka 5/2,
31 -108 Cracow, Poland
Tel: +48 12 428 06 30 **Fax:** +48 12 422 67 85

Email: kancelaria@oles.com.pl
Website: www.oles.com.pl

WORLDWIDE OFFICE CONTACTS

POLAND
ul.Retoryka 5/2, 31 -108 **Cracow**
Tel: +48 12 428 06 30 **Fax:** +48 12 422 67 85
Email: kancelaria@oles.com.pl

FIRM OVERVIEW

Managing partners: Wieslaw Oles, Mateusz Rodzynkiewicz

Number of partners worldwide: 2
Number of other lawyers worldwide: 10

AREAS OF PRACTICE:

M&A	30%
IPO	20%
Corporate	15%
Bonds and securitisations	10%
Private equity and venture capital	10%
Litigation	5%
Privatisation	5%
Tax and accounting law	5%

O

FIRM OVERVIEW: The firm was founded in 1996 as a Cracow-Warsaw Legal Corporation Ltd. As a result of a change in legal regulations in Poland, the partners transformed the legal structure from a limited company into a partnership, establishing Oles & Rodzynkiewicz law practice. Based in Cracow, the practice offers services to various clients throughout Poland and co-operates with international law firms who have established offices in Warsaw. The partners lecture at international training institutions, take part in conferences related to the various legal aspects of capital markets and act as consultants to the Parliament in legislature proceedings in relation to legal regulations on capital markets. Oles & Rodzynkiewicz act as partner firm of Warsaw Stock Exchange within the scope of innovation technology sector (SiTech).

INTERNATIONAL EXPERIENCE: The practice mainly advises national clients on international transactions. It handles mergers and aquisitions in particular, advising international clients who are seeking to establish and reorganise commercial enterprises in Poland. Recent work includes representing HOCHTIEF AG in the concentration process of its polish enterprises, the preparation of a polish bank for Deutsche Bank AG investment, and the preparation of ELECTRABEL investments in the Polish energy sector. The firm offers permanent legal services to the PIONEER international investment fund whose activity is concentrated on venture capital transactions in Poland.

INTERNATIONAL CLIENTS: Oles & Rodzynkiewicz focuses mainly on co-operation with large and medium size private enterprises, state-owned and municipal enterprises, banks, brokerage houses and publicly-traded companies.

MAIN AREAS OF PRACTICE:

Mergers and acquisitions: The practice has advised on several M&A transactions including the first polish market merger of the publicly-traded companies, the first Polish market merger of banks and first Polish market merger of the investment fund societies.
IPO: Oles & Rodzynkiewicz has prepared over 20 issuance prospectuses, creating the rules and the structure of the public offers. The firm handles the issue of shares and specialises in managers programmes and convertible bonds.
Corporate: The firm advises on all aspects of corporate law and specialises in capital restructure of enterprises. Oles & Rodzynkiewicz has been involved in creating one of the largest Polish restructuring programmes - concentration of Polish coal mining sector and establishing South Energy Holding, which is considered to be the greatest producer of energy in Poland.
Bonds and securitisation: The firm handles the issuing of bonds and other securities such as revenue bonds. Members of the firm advised on the first market issue of communal bonds in Poland. Oles & Rodzynkiewicz specialises in securitisation issues and prepares financial programmes for financial institutions' projects regarding capital investments.
Private equity and venture capital: Oles & Rodzynkiewicz is experienced in all aspects of corporate finance and represents issuers, purchasers and underwriters of securities in private capital markets, particularly venture capital investments. Transactions handled include IPO, private placements, convertible debt, equity securities, venture capital and start-up financing.
Privatisation: The firm, in co-operation with Polish branch offices and associated companies of international law practices, takes part in preparation of due diligence reports of state-owned companies acquired in the privatisation process by strategic investors. Within the privatisation sector the firm is experienced in the energy field.
Tax and accounting law: The firm advises on tax and accounting law in relation to M&A, public issuance of shares and acquirement of capital in the private sector.
Litigation: The firm acts for clients in civil and commercial proceedings, as well as in administrative proceedings in relation to tax and commercial law.

LANGUAGES: English, Polish

Oles & Rodzynkiewicz

Radcowie Prawni

OLSENS

HEAD OFFICE

47 Esplanade,
St Helier JE1 0BD, Jersey
Tel: +44 1534 888 900 **Fax:** +44 1534 887 744

Email: enquiry@olsenslaw.com
Website: www.olsensgroup.com

WORLDWIDE OFFICE CONTACTS

GUERNSEY
PO Box 212, Hadsley House, Lefebvre Street, **St Peter Port** GY1 4JE
Tel: +44 1481 712277 **Fax:** +44 1481 710900
Email: enquiry@ofmlaw.com

JERSEY
47 Esplanade, **St Helier** JE1 0BD
Tel: +44 1534 888 900 **Fax:** +44 1534 887 744
Email: enquiry@olsenslaw.com

FIRM OVERVIEW

Chairman: Anthony Olsen

Number of partners worldwide: 13
Number of other lawyers worldwide: 44

AREAS OF PRACTICE:
Commercial dispute resolution, mediation and asset recovery . .20%
Banking and finance 15%
Capital markets and securitisation 15%
Investment funds and custody 15%
Corporate and fiduciary 10%
Regulation and compliance 8%
Captive insurance 5%
Commercial property 5%
Private client, wills and probate 5%
Pension and employee benefits 2%

O

FIRM OVERVIEW: Olsens' offices in Jersey and Guernsey provide legal services to both Channel Islands. The Jersey and Guernsey offices aim to provide quality service in both jurisdictions, based on practice teams whose personnel are drawn from both offices. A single client contact partner allows client instructions to be delivered to a single point of contact in either the Jersey or Guernsey offices. The total number of partners, fee earners and support personnel of nearly 150, places Olsens among the largest law firms in the Channel Islands.

INTERNATIONAL EXPERIENCE: A large proportion of the work carried out by Olsens has an international dimension, and the Channel Island offices act for many global corporations, banks and financial institutions. Olsens' partners and other lawyers have gained their academic and practical expertise in a wide variety of backgrounds, drawing on experience gained outside of the Channel Islands, in a variety of jurisdictions.

INTERNATIONAL CLIENTS: Clients include many leading international corporations and institutions. These include ABN Amro Bank, BNP Paribas, The Chase Manhattan Bank, Citibank, Credit Suisse First Boston, Dresdner, Kleinwort Benson, JP Morgan, Merrill Lynch, Morgan Stanley Dean Witter, Nomura International plc, N M Rothschilds, Royal Bank of Scotland International and Royal Bank of Scotland plc, and Sanwa International plc.

MAIN INTERNATIONAL AREAS OF PRACTICE:
Capital markets and securitisation: The capital markets and securitisation team regularly acts for issuers and leading global underwriters and promoters on ABS, repackaging and debt issues. Recent securitisation transactions have been undertaken for Marne et Champagne, Sainsburys, and Le SBAB.
Banking and finance: The banking and finance team has acted on a significant number of bank start-ups, mergers and reorganisations affecting group operations in the Channel Islands. It handles a wide range of work for international banks and financial institutions in support of lending, the taking and perfection of security and in customer relationship and product-related documentation.
Investment funds: Olsens advises on the establishment, promotion and operation of a range of investment funds, both in an institutional and retail context, and based in the Islands and in other jurisdictions. Olsens also advises managers, custodians and other investment fund functionaries in relation to their appointment and duties, and provides a comprehensive global custody and investment business service.
Corporate: The corporate and trust team is experienced in mergers and acquisitions and advises major foreign corporate and individual clients on all areas of the Islands' company and trust law. The team provides a company and trust formation service to private and institutional clients.
Regulation and compliance: The regulation and compliance team advises on complex issues arising from statutory and other regulation and enforcement powers already existing, or soon to be in place, in the Channel Islands. The team includes a former senior regulator and, in addition, an advisor on policy and technical issues who has acted for governments and regulatory authorities in many jurisdictions.
Pensions and employee benefits: The pensions and employee benefits team has considerable experience in setting up and acting for private and public sector pension and employee benefit schemes, domiciled and administered in the Islands.
Insurance: The captive insurance team advises on the set-up and conduct of captive insurance operations in the Channel Islands.
Dispute resolution: The dispute resolution group is made up of the commercial and trusts litigation, personal injury and insurance teams. It handles all areas of commercial and private client dispute resolution, including insurance and related claims, trust protection, asset recovery and tracing litigation. The firm's lawyers have conducted major cases for leading international law firms, government bodies, Heads of State and global corporate entities.

LANGUAGES: English, French, German, Italian, Spanish

For other recommended firms see pages 1485-1520

O'MELVENY & MYERS LLP

HEAD OFFICE

400 South Hope Street,
Los Angeles CA 90071-2899, USA
Tel: +1 213 430 6000 **Fax:** +1 213 430 6407

Email: omminfo@omm.com
Website: www.omm.com

FIRM OVERVIEW

Chairman: Arthur B. Culvahouse (Washington, DC)
Senior partner: Warren Christopher

Number of partners worldwide: 240
Number of other lawyers worlwide: 509

AREAS OF PRACTICE:

Litigation 40%
Corporate/commercial/finance/restructurings and insolvency ... 33%
Labour 9%
Property 9%
Tax 6%
Entertainment 3%

FIRM OVERVIEW: Founded in 1885, O'Melveny & Myers has approximately 700 lawyers. The firm operates in eight US locations and has offices in London, Tokyo, Hong Kong and Shanghai. Its lawyers include veteran US Executive Branch and Capitol Hill policymakers (including former cabinet ministers and highly experienced litigators and transactional lawyers).

INTERNATIONAL EXPERIENCE: O'Melveny has a strong international practice, regularly representing companies and financial institutions in Europe, the Pacific Rim and Latin America. The firm is active internationally in providing advice on multi-jurisdictional acquisitions, project and other financings, mergers and acquisitions, telecommunications matters, securities matters and insolvencies and restructurings. The firm also represents various governmental entities in such transactions. In the area of infrastructure finance, the firm's lawyers have worked on over 300 large and complex project financings in over 40 countries, including some of the more significant transactions in the field. These projects include power plants, toll roads, port facilities, rail corridors, airport terminals, telecommunications facilities, sports arenas, silicon wafer fabrication facilities, drilling rigs, petrochemical refineries and water and waste facilities. O'Melveny also provides strategic counseling and advice on US regulations for transactions inbound to the US, as well as representing US companies in their dealings with various foreign governments. Some of the firm's attorneys have foreign language proficiency that may be useful to its clients.

WORLDWIDE OFFICE CONTACTS

CHINA
20/F Kerry Centre, 1515 Nanjing Road West, **Shanghai** 200040
Tel: + 86 21 5298 5600 **Fax:** + 86 21 5298 5500

HONG KONG
O'Melveny & Myers
Suite 1905, Tower Two, Lippo Centre, 89 Queensway, Central, **Hong Kong**
Tel: + 852 2523 8266 **Fax:** + 852 2522 1760

JAPAN
Akasaka Twin Tower, East 14-F, 2-17-23 Akasaka, Minato-Ku, **Tokyo** 107-0052
Tel: + 81 3 5562 2800 **Fax:** + 81 3 5575 3840

UNITED KINGDOM
O'Melveny & Myers
3 Finsbury Square, **London** EC2A 1LA
Tel: + 44 20 7256 8451 **Fax:** + 44 20 7638 8205

USA
114 Pacifica, Suite 100, **Irvine** CA 92618-3318
Tel: + 1 949 737 2900 **Fax:** + 1 949 737 2300

1999 Avenue of the Stars, **Los Angeles** CA 90067-6035
Tel: + 1 310 553 6700 **Fax:** + 1 310 246 6779

400 South Hope Street, **Los Angeles** CA 90071-2899
Tel: +1 213 430 6000 **Fax:** +1 213 430 6407

1650 Tysons Boulevard, **McLean** VA 22102
Tel: + 1 703 883 2400 **Fax:** + 1 703 883 2404

Citigroup Center, 153 East 53rd Street, **New York** NY 10022-4611
Tel: + 1 212 326 2000 **Fax:** + 1 212 326 2061

610 Newport Center Drive, **Newport Beach** CA 92660-6429
Tel: + 1 949 760 9600 **Fax:** + 1 949 823 6994

Embarcadero Center West, 275 Battery Street, **San Francisco** CA 94111-3305
Tel: + 1 415 984 8700 **Fax:** + 1 415 984 8701

555 13th Street, NW, **Washington DC** 20004-1109
Tel: + 1 202 383 5300 **Fax:** + 1 202 383 5414

O'MELVENY & MYERS

For other recommended firms see pages 1485-1520

OPPENLÄNDER RECHTSANWÄLTE

HEAD OFFICE

Altenbergstrasse 3,
D-70180 Stuttgart, Germany
Tel: +49 711 601 870 **Fax:** +49 711 601 87222

Email: info@oppenlaender.de
Website: www.oppenlaender.de

WORLDWIDE OFFICE CONTACTS

GERMANY
Altenbergstrasse 3, D-70180 **Stuttgart**
Tel: +49 711 601 870 **Fax:** +49 711 601 87222
Email: info@oppenlaender.de

FIRM OVERVIEW

Number of partners worldwide: 9
Number of other lawyers worldwide: 1

AREAS OF PRACTICE:

Administrative .... *%
Anti-trust .... *%
Company .... *%
Employment .... *%
Intellectual property .... *%
M&A .... *%
Pharmaceuticals .... *%
* Workload % not disclosed

O

FIRM OVERVIEW: The firm was founded in 1998 by the corporate and commercial-oriented partners from Oppenländer Dolde Oesterle & Partners. Oppenländer Rechtsanwälte is a Stuttgart based boutique practice offering personal and specialised advice to corporate clients. The firm focuses on several areas of particular expertise including M&A, IP, anti-trust, pharmaceutical and administrative law. All the firm's partners have a strong academic background. Oppenländer Rechtsanwälte does not participate in any formal alliances.

INTERNATIONAL EXPERIENCE: While the majority of the firm's work is based in Germany, some practice areas, namely IP and antitrust, involve considerable international work. The firm advises Europe's leading pharmaceutical wholesaler on its European activities and a major French company on its German activities.

INTERNATIONAL CLIENTS: The firm acts for a number of international clients, including large corporations.

MAIN INTERNATIONAL AREAS OF PRACTICE:

M&A: The firm's transactions range from small private acquisitions to take-overs.
Intellectual property: The firm specialises on protection and enforcement of intellectual property rights including patents, trademarks, IT issues, multimedia, internet and unfair competition. Important clients come from cosmetics and healthcare sectors.
Corporate: The firm advises a substantial number of medium sized companies. Specialist advice is offered on corporate restructuring.
Anti-trust: The firm advises on EC and German anti-trust matters including merger control, structuring of transactions and distribution.
Pharmaceutical: Oppenländer Rechtsanwälte is one of the few German firms offering specialist advice on pharmaceutical law. It advises manufacturers of original preparations and generic products, and act for contract manufacturers, pharmaceutical wholesalers and pharmacists.
Administrative: The firm advises on all major aspects of administrative law including environmental issues and project development.

LANGUAGES: English, French, German

OPPENLÄNDER
RECHTSANWÄLTE

ORRICK, HERRINGTON & SUTCLIFFE

HEAD OFFICE

Old Federal Reserve Bank Building, 400 Sansome Street,
San Francisco CA 94111-3143, USA
Tel: +1 415 392 1122 **Fax:** +1 415 773 5759

Email: RalphBaxter@orrick.com
Website: www.orrick.com

FIRM OVERVIEW

Chairman and chief executive officer: Ralph H Baxter, Jr
Chief operating officer: Bruce A Boulware
Executive committee: Ralph H Baxter, Jr, Alan G Benjamin, Peter Coll, Mark R Levie and Carl F Lyon, Jr.

Number of partners worldwide: 194
Number of other lawyers worldwide: 365

AREAS OF PRACTICE:

Litigation	18%
Corporate and technology practice	17%
Structured finance	12%
Public finance	10%
Intellectual property	9%
Employment	7%
Global infrastructure	7%
Private banking	7%
Real estate	6%
Tax	5%
Compensation and benefits	2%

FIRM OVERVIEW: Orrick, Herrington & Sutcliffe LLP, founded in 1863, is a full-service law firm internationally recognized for its finance and technology practices, specialising in securitisation and structured finance, project finance, public finance, IPOs, intellectual property (corporate transactions and litigation) and commercial litigation. The firm has more than 570 attorneys practising both US and English law in offices in the US, Europe and Asia. The firm was selected by the Attorney General of Singapore as one of the international firms permitted to enter into a joint venture with a top Singaporean firm. The firm's Orrick Helen Yeo Pte Ltd joint law venture will expand the firm's Asian practice.

WORLDWIDE OFFICE CONTACTS

JAPAN
12th Floor, Main Tower, Akasaka Twin Towers, 17-22 Akasaka 2-Chome, Minato-ku, **Tokyo** 107-0052
Tel: +813 3224 2900 **Fax:** + 813 3224 2901
Email: mbacon@orrick.com

SINGAPORE
Orrick Helen Yeo Pte Ltd Joint Law Venture, 10 Collyer Quay, 23-08 Ocean Building, **Singapore** 049315
Tel: +65 538 6116 **Fax:** + 65 538 0606
Email: wcampbell@orrick.com

UNITED KINGDOM
5th Floor, Exchange House, Primrose Street, **London** EC2A 2HS
Tel: +44 207 562 5000 **Fax:** + 44 207 628 0078
Email: IanJohnson@orrick.com

USA
777 South Figueroa Street, Suite 3200, **Los Angeles** CA 90017
Tel: +1 213 629 2020 **Fax:** + 1 213 612 2499
Email: Isobel@orrick.com

666 Fifth Avenue, **New York** NY 10103
Tel: +1 212 506 5000 **Fax:** + 1 212 506 5151
Email: lfisher@orrick.com

400 Capitol Mall, Suite 3000, **Sacramento** CA 95814
Tel: +1 916 447 9200 **Fax:** + 1 916 329 4900
Email: clarsen@orrick.com

Old Federal Reserve Bank Building, 400 Sansome Street, **San Francisco** CA 94111-3143
Tel: +1 415 392 1122 **Fax:** +1 415 773 5759
Email: RalphBaxter@orrick.com

999 Third Ave, Suite 3800, **Seattle** WA 98104
Tel: +1 206 224 5690 **Fax:** + 1 206 224 6207
Email: bdoyle@orrick.com

1020 Marsh Road, Menlo Park, **Silicon Valley** CA 94025
Tel: +1 650 614 7400 **Fax:** +1 650 614 7401
Email: gweiss@orrick.com

Washington Harbour, 3050 K Street NW, **Washington DC** 20007
Tel: +1 202 339 8400 **Fax:** + 1 202 339 8500
Email: clcowan@orrick.com

O

INTERNATIONAL EXPERIENCE: The firm is one of the world's leading securitisation and structured finance firms. Its securitisation group has been active in Japan, Korea, Hong Kong, Indonesia, Malaysia and Thailand. The firm's project finance and infrastructure work is extensive and the firm is very active in infrastructure and other projects throughout Latin America, Asia and Europe. The firm has one of the leading emerging market financial sector reform and corporate debt restructuring practices and is currently increasing its high profile work in the IT and telecommunications sectors.

INTERNATIONAL CLIENTS: The firm's international clientele includes major industrial and financial corporations, commercial and investment banks, developers, high-technology companies, universities and governmental entities.

MAIN INTERNATIONAL AREAS OF PRACTICE: The firm practises several strategic areas of law: securitisation and structured finance, project finance (the Global Energy, Communications and Infrastructure Group), mergers and acquisitions, emerging market restructuring and privatiation, and banking and commercial finance.

Structured finance: The firm is a leading international securitisation and structured finance firm. Its lawyers have served as counsel to issuers, underwriters, credit enhancers, sellers, servicers, institutional purchasers and trustees in connection with the securitisation of a variety of assets, including mortgage loans, automobile loans, credit card, auto and trade receivables, instalment sales contracts, franchisee loans, sovereign debt, utility receivables, equipment leases, bank and corporate loans, insurance policy loans and high-yield bonds.

Project and infrastructure finance: The firm acts on behalf of developers, vendors, lenders and investors drawing upon the expertise of members of the firm's Public Finance Department and Structured Finance Group. It is actively involved in a number of projects concerned with utilising asset securitisation techniques and combining public and private financing components. It handles all phases of major infrastructure projects globally, including development, construction, financing and operation of power stations, telecommunications facilities, pipelines, roadways, petrochemical facilities, airports and other major public facilities.

Mergers and acquisitions: The firm's practice includes all types of M&A transactions, such as negotiated acquisitions, mergers, leveraged buyouts, private transactions, purchases and sales of divisions and subsidiaries, spin-offs, reorganisations and recapitalisations.

Emerging market restructuring and privatisation: In the climate of deregulation and financial turmoil in Asia, the firm's lawyers have assisted clients in a variety of acquisitions of stock and/or corporate assets within different industries. The firm is one of the leading international law firms in debt restructuring and privatisation in emerging markets with significant restructuring engagements in Indonesia, Japan, Korea, Malaysia, the Phillipines and Thailand. Its attorneys have provided specialised advice to governments and government agencies, banks and other financial institutions and corporate clients in connection with the debt restructuring process.

Banking and commercial finance: The firm maintains a strong international banking and commercial finance practice. Attorneys represent major finance institutions including banks, insurance companies, finance and leasing companies and institutional investors in a broad array of financing transactions. The firm's experience includes loan syndications, private placement debt and convertible debt issuances, assignments, participations and other secondary market transactions, tax-driven standby letter of credit and guarantee facilities, trade finance, aircraft finance, letters of credit, acquisition financings, swaps and other hedging mechanisms.

O

WORLDWIDE OFFICES

JAPAN

12th Floor, Main Tower, Akasaka Twin Towers, 17-22 Akasaka 2-Chome, Minato-ku, Tokyo 107-0052

Partner-in-charge: R Michael Bacon

Number of lawyers: 11
Number of dual qualified lawyers: 1

Main areas of work: Debt restructuring, project finance, commercial lending, structured finance and securitisation, intellectual property, emerging companies, real estate, corporate and securities law.

Highlight deals: Purchase of distressed loan portfolios, various power projects, M&A or European subsidiaries, overseas asset sales.

Languages: English, French, German, Japanese, Mandarin (and dialects), Portuguese, Vietnamese.

Office profile: Opened in 1997, the Tokyo office comprises 11 lawyers. It provides a full range of legal services including those pertaining to distressed asset transactions, cross-border real estate, restructuring, M&A and project finance. The firm is active in handling restructurings which resulted from Japan's deregulation. Project finance is a major area of work. The office has worked on a broad range of infrastructure projects (representing sponsors, developers, investors, suppliers and customers) in India, Indonesia, China, the Philippines, Singapore, Sri Lanka and Thailand.

SINGAPORE

Orrick Helen Yeo Pte Ltd Joint Law Venture, 10 Collyer Quay, 23-08 Ocean Building, Singapore 049315

Partner-in-charge: William B Campbell
Number of lawyers: 11
Number of dual qualified lawyers: 2
Number of locally qualified lawyers: 2

Main areas of work: Restructuring, privatisation, structured finance, securitisation. corporate and securities law, intellectual property, real estate, project finance.

Languages: Chinese dialects, English, French, Mandarin, Bahasa Malaysian.

Office profile: The newly created Orrick Helen Yeo Pte Ltd comprises more than 60 lawyers qualified to practice under US, English and Singaporean law. The office serves as the base for the firm's practice in Southeast Asia. Lawyers in the Singapore office advise clients on a broad range of transactions, especially debt restructuring, securitisation and structured finance, capital markets, project finance and commercial finance. The office represents a wide range of clients in their projects and financings both in Asia and in the US. It continues to advise government agencies, banks and other financial institutions as well as corporate clients in connection with the debt restructuring process now underway across Asia.

UNITED KINGDOM

5th Floor, Exchange House, Primrose Street, London EC2A 2HS

Partner-in-charge: Ian Johnson
Number of lawyers: 12
Number of dual qualified lawyers: 8
Number of locally qualified lawyers: 10

Main areas of work: Structured finance, mortgages, securitisation and project finance.

Top clients: Businesses in the securities industry, financial services industry and oil and gas industries.

Languages: English, French, German, Italian, Spanish.

Office profile: Opened in 1998 with six lawyers, the London office is part of the firms growing trans-Atlantic finance practice. It focuses on serving the financial services industry and on structured and project finance. The firm's Primrose Street outpost is led by former Ashurst Morris Crisp partner, Ian Johnson.

For other recommended firms see pages 1485-1520

OSBORNE CLARKE OWA

HEAD OFFICE

50 Queen Charlotte Street
Bristol BS1 4HE, United Kingdom
Tel: +44 117 917 3000 **Fax:** +44 117 917 3005
Email: info@osborneclarke.com
Website: www.osborneclarke.com

FIRM OVERVIEW

Managing partner: Leslie Perrin
Senior partner: Chris Curling
Chief executive of Osborne Westphalen Alliance: Adrian Taylor
Number of partners worldwide: 77
Number of other lawyers worldwide: 270

AREAS OF PRACTICE:

Corporate finance 32%
Litigation 17%
Employment and pensions 16%
Commerical property 15%
IT and telecoms 15%
Tax and trusts 5%

FIRM OVERVIEW: Osborne Clarke OWA is an English law firm with one US office, one Frankfurt office and a strong European alliance (Osborne Westphalen Alliance). It has 77 partners and over 270 other lawyers in the UK - and over 300 further lawyers in 18 cities throughout Europe. In the UK, Osborne Clarke OWA competes with the largest City and national firms in its chosen international practice areas, including corporate finance, private equity, IT, telecoms, media and employment. Increasingly international in focus, the firm also advises a growing number of clients from Europe and the US, and has an active London-based Anglo-Danish practice. The firm opened its Californian office in October 2000, providing pan-European legal advice on the ground to US clients.

INTERNATIONAL EXPERIENCE: Work includes representing StepStone ASA on its listing on the London and Oslo Stock Exchanges and on a £120 million institutional placing and retail offer; representing Riverwood International in obtaining clearance from the European Commission under Article 85(3) in relation to a strategic alliance; acting for Granville Baird Private Equity on a development capital investment in European Technology Consultants; advising the Deloro Stellite Group Ltd in the acquisitions of Teknecomp Industrie (Italy) and ATS (France) for lire 35.5 billion; advising the former NatWest Equity Partners on an OBO to acquire a 65% stake in IT consultancy Autinform Gmbh for DM 40.5 million; acting for Clondalkin Group plc in one of the most significant recent public to private take-overs by Edgemead Ltd for Euro 385 million and acting for Yardbrace Group Limited on the acquisition of the bulk transportation business of Rentokil Initial. The firm's Danish team advised Nordic TV Business News Luxembourg SA on all aspects of a joint venture with CNBC Europe; acted for Tektronix Inc on the Danish disposal as part of the worldwide sale of their printing and colour imaging division to Xerox Corp; acted for Danish institutional vendors in a cross-border disposal to Pangolin International Ltd of a majority shareholding in Infosport A/S; and obtained clearance from the EC Commission for a strategic alliance in the packaging industry. Further experience includes advising US resident holders of significant interests in Cable TV operations in Europe on corporate structures for the estalishment of a European holding company in the context of a proposed IPO on a US capital market; working with Investia (an e-commerce technology company) in a US$20 million joint venture with international merchant bank, Chase Manhattan; and advising Netscape on the structure and form of its European operations.

WORLDWIDE OFFICE CONTACTS

GERMANY
Eschersheimer Landstrasse 25-27, 60322 **Frankfurt am Main**
Tel: + 49 69 95 95 7241 **Fax:** + 49 69 95 95 7244
Email: adrian.taylor@osborneclarke.com

UNITED KINGDOM
50 Queen Charlotte Street **Bristol** BS1 4HE
Tel: +44 117 917 3000 **Fax:** +44 117 917 3005
Email: info@osborneclarke.com

Hillgate House, 26 Old Bailey, **London** EC4M 7HW
Tel: + 44 20 7809 1000 **Fax:** +44 20 7809 1005
Email: info@osborneclarke.com

Apex Plaza, Forbury Road, **Reading** RG1 1AX
Tel: +44 118 925 2000 **Fax:** +44 925 2005
Email: info@osborneclarke.com

USA
Osborne Westphalen, 303 Twin Dolphin Drive, Suite 600,
Redwood City CA 94065
Tel: +1 650 632 4660 **Fax:** +1 650 632 4605
Email: angus.finnegan@osborneclarke.com

ASSOCIATED OFFICES

BELGIUM
De Wolf & Partners OWA, Elite House, Square du Bastion 1/A, Porte de Namur, 1050 **Brussels**
Tel: +32 2 289 64 64 **Fax:** +32 2 503 48 58
Email: patrick.de.wolf@dewolf-law.be

DENMARK
Pedersen & Jantzen OWA, Nyropsgade 45, DK-1602 **Copenhagen** V
Tel: +45 33 12 95 12 **Fax:** +45 33 12 95 15
Email: amh@pedersen-jantzen.dk

FINLAND
Hedman Osborne Westphalen Alliance, Luotsikatu 7 A, FIN 00160 **Helsinki**
Tel: +358 9 177 060 **Fax:** +358 9 629 759
Email: hedman@hedman-attorneys.com

FRANCE
Stehlin & Associés OWA, 48 Avenue Victor Hugo, 75116 **Paris**
Tel: +33 1 44 17 07 70 **Fax:** +33 1 44 17 07 77
Email: mp.stehlin@stehlin-legal.com

GERMANY
Graf von Westphalen Fritze & Modest OWA, Postrasse 9a, D-20354 **Hamburg**
Tel: +49 40 35 92 20 **Fax:** + 49 40 35 92 21 23
Email: landry@wfm.de

NETHERLANDS
Ploum Lodder Princen OWA, Blaak 28, 3011 TA **Rotterdam**
Tel: +31 10 440 64 40 **Fax:** + 31 10 436 44 00
Email: dlodder@plp.nl

SPAIN
Osborne Clarke Europe OWA, Avda Diagonal 477, Torre de Barcelona 20th floor, 08036 **Barcelona**
Tel: +34 93 419 1818 **Fax:** + 34 93 410 2513
Email: osbornebcn@oceds.org

O

For other recommended firms see pages 1485-1520

OSLER, HOSKIN & HARCOURT LLP

HEAD OFFICE

PO Box 50, 1 First Canadian Place,
Toronto ON M5X 1B8, Canada
Tel: +1 416 362 2111 **Fax:** +1 416 862 6666
Email: counsel@osler.com
Website: www.osler.com

FIRM OVERVIEW

Managing partners Terrence Burgoyne, Dale Ponder
Chair J Timothy Kennish
Vice chair John F Petch
Number of partners worldwide: 156
Number of other lawyers worldwide: 162

WORLDWIDE OFFICE CONTACTS

CANADA

Suite 1900, Toronto Dominion Square, 333-7th Avenue SW, **Calgary**, AL T2P 2Z1
Tel: + 1 403 260 7000 **Fax:** + 1 403 260 7024

Suite 1500, 50 O'Connor Street, **Ottawa**, ON K1P 6L2
Tel: + 1 613 235 7234 **Fax:** + 1 613 235 2867

PO Box 50, 1 First Canadian Place, **Toronto** ON M5X 1B8
Tel: +1 416 362 2111 **Fax:** +1 416 862 6666
Email: counsel@osler.com

USA

280 Park Avenue - 30 W, **New York** NY 10017
Tel: + 1 212 867 5800 **Fax:** + 1 212 867 5802

AREAS OF PRACTICE:

Competition and trade .... *%
Corporate finance .... *%
Insolvency and restructuring .... *%
Litigation .... *%
M&A .... *%
Tax .... *%
* Work % not disclosed

FIRM OVERVIEW: Founded in 1862, Osler, Hoskin & Harcourt LLP has over 300 lawyers in Toronto, Ottawa, Calgary and New York. Oslers advises many of Canada's corporate leaders as well as US and international parties with extensive interests in Canada.

INTERNATIONAL EXPERIENCE: Oslers provides a broad range of legal services to a highly diverse international clientele. The firm advises international investors on the acquisition of Canadian assets and enterprises; international banks and financial institutions on financing Canadian projects and undertakings; international brokerage houses on placing stock issues in Canada; and foreign governments on the privatisation of national enterprises. It offers clients specialised expertise in areas such as telecommunications, intellectual property, employment and labour, pension and benefits, environmental and other specialised practices.

REPRESENTATIVE INTERNATIONAL CLIENTS: AT&T/Metronet, Allusuisse Lonza Group AG, American Express, Avis Car Inc, Bay Networks, Black & Decker, Blockbuster Video, British Gas, Cadbury Schweppes, Campbell Soup Company, Eastman Kodak, Eli Lilly, General Electric, General Motors, Goldman Sachs & Co, IBM, Illinois Central Corporation, Imperial Tobacco Limited, Magna International, Merrill Lynch & Co, Mobil Oil, Nova Gas International, Revlon Inc, PricewaterhouseCoopers, Sears, Roebuck & Co, The Procter & Gamble Company, Time Warner Inc and Viacom Inc.

MAIN INTERNATIONAL AREAS OF PRACTICE:

M&A: The firm is actively involved in both Canadian and multi-jurisdictional M&A transactions through the Canadian and New York offices. The firm is currently advising Imasco Limited in its announced transaction proposed with British American Tobacco Plc for a minimum of Canadian $10.3 billion. Completion of this transaction would represent the largest ever cash acquisition of a Canadian company. The firm is also advising Allusuisse Lonza Group AG in its proposed merger with Alcan Aluminium Limited of Canada and Pechiney of France, an international merger which will create the world's second largest aluminium company. The firm has provided inventive solutions to complex business transactions such as the first use of exchangeable shares to facilitate a cross-border acquisition transaction and the first simultaneous take-over bid and plan of arrangement to ensure the acquisition of all outstanding shares of a target corporation. Contact, Clay Horner, Chair of Oslers Business Law Group, tel: +1 416 862 5690.

Corporate finance: Lawyers in this group have experience in corporate debt securities, corporate equity offerings (including initial public offerings), hybrid instruments including preferred shares, private placements, international public and private issues of equity and debt, asset securitisations, derivative instruments, structured financings, project finance and venture capital.

Litigation: The firm conducts litigation in Ontario, throughout Canada and in international courts and tribunals. In addition to the commercial litigation practice, it has specialists in the areas of corporate governance/shareholder disputes; product liability/class action; environmental law; intellectual property; tax; securities law; pensions; employment law; insolvency/restructurings and competition/antitrust matters. Contact, John Roland, Chair of Oslers Litigation Group, tel: +1 416 862 6470.

Tax: The group is actively involved in M&A and Canadian and international joint ventures. It facilitates access to capital markets and corporate finance and the implementation of inbound and outbound cross-border transactions. The group advises on dispute resolution and tax litigation. Osler has provided tax advice for international transactions in the US, the UK, Mexico, the People's Republic of China, Australia, New Zealand and several South American countries. Contact, Norman Loveland, Chair of Oslers Tax Group, tel: +1 416 862 6463.

Competition and trade: Oslers assists US and international clients in structuring the Canadian components of their merger, acquisition and joint venture transactions in order to minimize antitrust and foreign investment costs and risks. The firm also works on clients' behalf with the Competition Bureau, Department of Foreign Affairs and International Trade, Revenue Canada, Industry Canada, the Canadian International Trade Tribunal and the North American Free Trade Agreement (NAFTA) Secretariat.

Insolvency and restructuring: Oslers' lawyers are among Canada's leaders on multi-jurisdictional bankruptcy and insolvency issues, with extensive experience in international proceedings and transactions involving foreign assets and foreign courts, including Chapters 7 and 11 of the US Bankruptcy Code. The group's chair is a past president of INSOL International, the leading global association for insolvency professionals.

LANGUAGES: Arabic, Cantonese, Czech, Dutch, English, Estonian, Filipino, French, German, Greek, Hebrew, Hindi, Hungarian, Italian, Japanese, Korean, Mandarin, Polish, Portuguese, Russian, Serbian, Slovak, Spanish, Swahili, Ukrainian

For other recommended firms see pages 1485-1520

PALACIOS ORTEGA Y ASOCIADOS

HEAD OFFICE

Av. Venezuela, Torre Clement, Piso 3, Ofic. B. El Rosal
Caracas 1010-A, Venezuela
Tel: +58 2 951 3333 **Fax:** +58 2 951 2851

Email: catilin@cantv.net

WORLDWIDE OFFICE CONTACTS

VENEZUELA
Av. Venezuela, Torre Clement, Piso 3, Ofic. B. El Rosal, **Caracas** 1010-A
Tel: +58 2 951 3333 **Fax:** +58 2 951 2851
Email: catilin@cantv.net

FIRM OVERVIEW

Senior partners: Luis Esteban Palacios, José Manuel Ortega P, Arturo H. Banegas Masiá

Number of partners worldwide: 3
Number of other lawyers worldwide: 7

AREAS OF PRACTICE:

Area	%
Corporate	25%
Employment	15%
M&A	15%
Banking and finance	10%
Capital markets	10%
Tax	10%
Telecommunications and IT	10%
Litigation and arbitration	3%
Industrial property	2%

FIRM OVERVIEW: Founded in 1999, the firm was established by two lawyers previously at Mendoza, Placios, Acedo, Borjas, Páez Pumar y Cia. As a general practice firm, the firm's members have handled a variety of transactions, both domestic and international, involving all types of business entities. It advises on banking law, capital markets, financing (institutional, equity and debt), general corporate law and corporate restructuring, IT, employment, tax, telecommunications, and litigation. A number of the firm's attorneys have been involved in the settlement of business disputes by amicable arrangements. The firm does not participate in formal alliances or networks, preferring to maintain contacts with various firms worldwide and to choose the firms with which it works on individual international transactions.

INTERNATIONAL EXPERIENCE: During 2000, Palacios, Ortega y Asociados advised on a range of major transaction in Venezuela, including bank mergers, takeovers, acquisitions, and tax planning, as well as the incorporation of several dot.com businesses. The firm was involved in the merger of two important Venezuelan banks, and designing anti-takeover protections on clients' bylaws.

INTERNATIONAL CLIENTS: The firm's client base includes large companies, banks, and public or supranational institutions conducting cross-border business.

MAIN INTERNATIONAL AREAS OF PRACTICE:

Corporate: Palacios, Ortega y Asociados' corporate law practice handles the drafting and negotiation of corporate charters and by-laws, joint venture agreements, investment agreements, voting trust, shareholders agreements, and due diligence. The firm also handles the preparation and filing of shareholder meetings, and issues relating to the structure of corporate by-laws for the management of a company. The firm advises medium-to-large corporate clients, individuals, and family groups.

M&A: The firm's transactions range from small private acquisitions to cross-border takeovers of listed companies.

Employment: The firm advises on personnel policies, grievance and litigation avoidance, and provides representation in labour-management relations. The firm handles employment contract negotiations and collective bargaining agreements, employment litigation before administrative agencies and employment courts, management-labour disputes, and employment aspects of mergers and acquisitions. It also handles a range of other corporate transactions, compensation issues for board members and management, compliance regulation regarding working conditions, worker safety issues, and severance payments.

Banking and finance: Palacios, Ortega y Asociados handles all aspects of banking and finance, including secured and syndicated loan transactions and guarantees, structured finance, project finance, leasing, and tax-based finance.

Telecommunications and IT: The firm's experience and understanding of the industry enables it to effectively guide its clients through complex deals and negotiations. The firm's clients include telecommunication companies, e-commerce and website operators, computer hardware vendors, and software developers.

Capital markets: The firm advises on securities offerings and transactions, and structured financing (institutional, equity and debt) in general. It handles the preparation of prospectus and registration forms, obtaining necessary approvals for ADR programs, preparation of the necessary documentation for a primary placement, including placement agreements, trust indentures and others, and structuring of international financing instruments.

Tax: The firm advises on all aspects of national, state and local taxation. Work handled includes business and personal tax issues including estate planning, trust and estate advice, tax-exempt entities and charitable institutions, mergers and acquisitions, tax audits, and national, state and local tax trials in all courts and administrative instances. Its international tax practice advises on both inbound and outbound matters.

LANGUAGES: English, Spanish

Escritorio
PALACIOS ORTEGA
Asociados

P

For other recommended firms see pages 1485-1520

ADVOCACIA PEDRO DUTRA

HEAD OFFICE

Rua Padre João Manuel, 923, 13th/14th floors,
SP-CEP 01411-001 São Paulo, Brazil
Tel: +55 11 3085 9033 **Fax:** +55 11 3064 7487

Email: pdutra@pedrodutra.com.br

FIRM OVERVIEW

Managing partner: Pedro Dutra
Senior partner: Pedro Dutra

AREAS OF PRACTICE:

Competition 55%
Regulatory law 45%

FIRM OVERVIEW: The firm was founded in 1988 in Rio de Janeiro and moved to São Paulo in 1992. With the liberalisation of the Brazilian economy the firm has handled regulatory, competition, anti-dumping and consumer law. The firm advises clients and other law firms on competition and regulatory law matters.

P

INTERNATIONAL EXPERIENCE: Advocacia Pedro Dutra advises a range of international clients, primarily multinational corporations, on competition and regulatory matters in Brazil. The firm has a close working relationship with a number of foreign law firms.

INTERNATIONAL CLIENTS: The firm advises domestic and international clients including IBM, Renault, TotalFinaElf, Pepsico, Telemar, TRW, Internet Group (iG), Aventis Animal Nutrition, Novo Nordisk, Brahma and Odebrecht Petrochemical.

WORLDWIDE OFFICE CONTACTS

BRAZIL
Rua Padre João Manuel, 923, 13th/14th floors, SP-CEP 01411-001
São Paulo
Tel: +55 11 3085 9033 **Fax:** +55 11 3064 7487
Email: pdutra@pedrodutra.com.br

MAIN INTERNATIONAL AREAS OF PRACTICE:
Competition: The firm advises on a range of business transactions and is active in competition litigation, representing national and international firms.
Regulatory law: Advocacia Pedro Dutra is a leading firm in the area of regulatory law, representing domestic and international clients before regulatory authorities in the sectors of Electric Power (ANEEL), Telecommunications (ANATEL), Oil and Gas (ANP), Pharmaceutics (ANVS) and Transport.

LANGUAGES: English, Portuguese

 For other recommended firms see pages 1485-1520

PENA, MACHETE, BOTELHO MONIZ, NOBRE GUEDES, RUIZ & ASSOCIADOS

HEAD OFFICE

Av Conselheiro Fernando de Sousa,
Nº 19, 18º, 1070-072 Lisbon, Portugal
Tel: +351 21 384 6300 **Fax:** +351 21 387 0167

Email: pmbgr@pmbgr.pt
Website: www.pmbgr.pt

WORLDWIDE OFFICE CONTACTS

PORTUGAL
Av Conselheiro Fernando de Sousa, Nº 19, 18º
1070-072 **Lisbon**
Tel: +351 21 384 6300 **Fax:** +351 21 387 0167
Email: pmbgr@pmbgr.pt

FIRM OVERVIEW

Partners: Rui Pena, Rui Machete, Nuno Ruiz, Botelho Moniz

Number of partners worldwide: 21
Number of other lawyers worldwide: 17

AREAS OF PRACTICE:

Area	%
Banking and finance	15%
Corporate	15%
Litigation and arbitration	15%
Public and administration	15%
European	10%
Insurance and reinsurance	10%
Intellectual property	10%
M&A	5%
Telecommunications	5%

FIRM OVERVIEW: Pena, Machete, Botelho Moniz, Nobre Guedes, Ruiz & Associados, Sociedade de Advogados, is a leading Portuguese law firm for domestic and international clients. The firm was created in 1999 and results from the merger of five existing law firms: Pena, Machete & Associados; Botelho Moniz, Ruiz & Associados; Nobre Guedes, Leónidas Rocha & Maleitas Corrêa; Perry da Câmara & Resina da Silva and Moreiro Rato, Durães Rocha & Associados; each specialising in various areas of law. At the time of incorporation the firm was composed of 41 lawyers and 23 trainees.

INTERNATIONAL EXPERIENCE: Pena, Machete, Botelho Moniz, Nobre Guedes, Ruiz & Associates are legal advisors to the underwriters of the fourth stage of the privatisation of Portugal Telecom (sale of existing shares and rights issue under a combined international offering with SEC registration). Other significant work includes advising the underwriters of the IPO of PT Multimedia (cable and multimedia subsidiary of Portugal Telecom Group) with a USA 144A offering, and advising PT Multimedia in the purchase of "SAPO," the leading Internet portal in Portugal.

INTERNATIONAL CLIENTS: The firm's clients include large private companies, banks, natural gas and oil companies, insurance and telecom companies, as well as public and supranational institutions.

MAIN INTERNATIONAL AREAS OF PRACTICE:

Banking, finance and insurance: Pena, Machete, Botelho Moniz, Nobre Guedes, Ruiz & Associados' involvement in these areas includes security and syndicated law, transaction and guarantees and project finance.
Corporate and tax: The firm advises in all matters relating to the drafting of national and international contracts as well as the setting up of new corporations, mergers and acquisitions and privatisations.
Competition: The firm deals with all aspects related to national, EC antitrust and competition cases.
Intellectual property: The firm is specialised in intellectual property law whether advising in all aspects of intellectual property or in litigation.
Litigation and arbitration: The firm deals with commercial litigation and national and international arbitration.
Public and administration: The firm is playing an active role in the development of public contracts as well as in energy and public utilities matters. It is also involved in all matters relating to state and municipal activities.
European: The firm advises government authorities and companies.
Telecommunications: The firm advises in all aspects of telecommunications law.

LANGUAGES: English, French, German, Portuguese, Spanish

P

For other recommended firms see pages 1485-1520

A. M. PEREIRA, S. LEAL, O. MARTINS, JÚDICE & ASSOC.

HEAD OFFICE

Edificio Eurolex, Avenida da Liberdade 224,
Lisbon 1250-148, Portugal
Tel: +351 21 319 7300 **Fax:** +351 21 319 7400

Email: plmjlaw@mail.telepac.pt

FIRM OVERVIEW

Managing partner: Luis Sáragga Leal

Number of partners worldwide: 58
Number of other lawyers worldwide: 43

AREAS OF PRACTICE:

Construction and tourism .... *%
Corporate/M&A .... *%
EU law and competition .... *%
Financial and capital markets .... *%
Foreign investment and international contracts .... *%
Intellectual property .... *%
Litigation and arbitration .... *%
Tax .... *%
Media .... *%
Energy and natural resources .... *%
Zoning and town planning .... *%
* Workload % not disclosed

WORLDWIDE OFFICE CONTACTS

PORTUGAL
Edificio Eurolex, Avenida da Liberdade 224, 1250-148, **Lisbon**
Tel: +351 21 319 7300 **Fax:** +351 21 319 7400
Email: plmjlaw@mail.telepac.pt.

Largo Pé da Cruz 26, 26 -1° Esq°, 8000-154, **Faro**
Tel: +351 289 804 137 **Fax:** +351 289 803 588

ASSOCIATED OFFICES

PORTUGAL
Carlos Osório de Castro, Eduardo Verde Pinho, JJ Vieira Peres Sociedade de Advogados, Av da Boavista, No 3265, 5°, 4100-137, **Porto**
Tel: +351 22 616 38 10 **Fax:** +351 22 616 69 50
Email: fbw2@plmj.pt

P

FIRM OVERVIEW: Established in the 1960s, A M Pereira, Sáragga Leal, Oliveira Martins, Júdice & Associados is the largest Portuguese law firm with experience in all areas of law. The firm comprises 27 senior partners and 31 junior partners and a total of more than 100 lawyers. The firm's internal departments specialise in intellectual property; employment; tax; EU and competition; corporate, mergers and acquisitions; real estate, construction and tourism; finance law; litigation and arbitration; energy law; telecommunications; transport and maritime; environment; administrative; criminal and pharmaceutical, media, energy and natural resources, zoning, and town planning.

INTERNATIONAL EXPERIENCE: The firm has developed a network of correspondents, both with domestic and foreign law firms. These connections allow the firm, where appropriate, to provide services in co-operation with other experts and consultants, as well as with banking and financial institutions.

INTERNATIONAL CLIENTS: The firm's client base includes large companies, banks, insurance companies, and public or supranational institutions conducting cross-border business.

MAIN INTERNATIONAL AREAS OF PRACTICE:
Corporate: PLMJ has served in-house and foreign clients globally in connection with all legal aspects of investment and business matters. The firm provides advice to foreign companies and assists foreign companies in the establishment of foreign investment enterprises (equity and contractual joint ventures, wholly foreign-owned enterprises and holding companies). Contact, Dr Luís Saragga Leal.
M&A: Over the last few years, PLMJ has built a team of lawyers specialised in M&A. Contact, Dr. Dulce Franco, Vitor Réfega Fernandes and Gabriela Rodrigues Martins.
EU and competition: The firm handles a wide range of matters in this area. Contact, Dr Jose Luís Cruz Villaça, assisted by Dr Luis Pais Antunes.
Financial and capital markets: The firm provides regular banking advice to a considerable number of banks and financial institutions, both in Portugal and abroad. Work includes initial public offerings, take-overs, mergers, and several recent Portuguese privatisations. Contact, Dr Fernando Campos Ferreira.
Intellectual property: PLMJ has specialised in this area since its foundation. The department deals with brand protection, trademark litigation, unfair competition and anti-counterfeiting, among others. Contact, Dr A M Pereira and Dr Luís Pais Antunes.
Real estate, construction and tourism: The firm advises domestic and international corporations and consortia in major infrastructure projects, as well as construction and engineering contracts. It is experienced in all areas of real estate, including construction, property, zoning, building and commercial leases. Contact, Dr Pedro Sáragga Leal.
Tax: The practice covers all areas of taxation. Contact, Prof Diogo Leite de Campos.
Litigation/arbitration: PLMJ provides litigation services whenever required, while its arbitration expertise covers proceedings under local and international rules (i.e. ICC), conducted both in Portugal and abroad. Contact, Dr José Miguel Júdice and Dr Nuno Libano Monteiro

LANGUAGES: English, French, German, Spanish

For other recommended firms see pages 1485-1520

PÉREZ ALATI, GRONDONA, BENITES, ARNTSEN & MARTÍNEZ DE HOZ

HEAD OFFICE

Suipacha 1111, Piso 18,
C1008AAW Buenos Aires, Argentina
Tel: +54 11 4114 3000 **Fax:** +54 11 4114 3001

Email: pagbam@pagbam.com.ar
Website: www.pagbam.com.ar

WORLDWIDE OFFICE CONTACTS

ARGENTINA
Suipacha 1111, Piso 18, C1008AAW **Buenos Aires**
Tel: +54 11 4114 3000 **Fax:** +54 11 4114 3001
Email: pagbam@pagbam.com.ar

USA
110 East 55th Street, 10th Floor, **New York,** NY 10002
Tel: +1 212 784 8800 **Fax:** +1 212 758 1028
Email: jpa@cgmp-law.com

FIRM OVERVIEW

Managing partner: Jorge Luis Pérez Alati

Senior partners: Mariano Florencio Grondona
Manuel María Benites
Alan Arntsen
José Alfredo Martínez de Hoz Jr.

Number of partners worldwide: 12
Number of other lawyers worldwide: 79

AREAS OF PRACTICE:

Banking and finance	*%
Corporate finance and securities	*%
Employment	*%
Litigation	*%
Oil and gas	*%
Privatisations	*%
Real estate	*%
Tax	*%
Telecommunications	*%

* Workload % not disclosed

FIRM OVERVIEW: Founded by Jorge Luis Pérez Alati, Mariano Florencio Grondona, Manuel María Benites, Alan Arntsen and José Alfredo Martínez de Hoz Jr., the firm advises on, and has experience in, a range of Argentine and foreign legal issues. Many of the firm's lawyers have post-graduate degrees from universities in the US and Europe and have worked for major law firms in the US. The firm maintains close links with firms in the US, Europe, Australia, Africa, Latin America, and Asia.

INTERNATIONAL EXPERIENCE: The firm has acted in a number of large transactions in Argentina involving local parties, foreign corporations and international institutions.

MAIN INTERNATIONAL AREAS OF PRACTICE:

Oil and gas: Pérez Alati, Grondona, Benites, Arntsen & Martínez de Hoz advises on all aspects of prospecting, exploration and the production of hydrocarbons. It handles the renegotiation of exploration and production contracts (on-shore and off-shore); joint ventures and joint operating agreements; submission of bids for exploration and production blocks; long and short term crude oil sales and purchase agreements; crude oil swapping agreements; gas transportation agreements; gas exchange and displacement agreements, swaps and forward contracts; regulatory and environmental matters. The firm also acts as counsel to the two chambers of the oil industry in Argentina.

Tax: The firm advises on all aspects of corporate tax planning, reorganisations, acquisitions, mergers, capital market transactions, international financing, foreign investments and offshore investment funds. The firm has experience in all aspects of tax and tax related litigation including federal and state taxes, income tax, stamp tax, excise taxes, oil and gas taxes, VAT, transfer of tax losses and credits, and protection of losses. Pérez Alati, Grondona, Benites, Arntsen & Martínez de Hoz also represents clients before the tax authorities and the judiciary in matters related to tax procedure and litigation.

Corporate finance and securities: The firm advises on equity, public debt offerings, private placements and underwriting. Work undertaken includes advising on the public offerings of the shares of two privatised telephone companies, a large gas distribution company, and the largest private bank in Argentina. The firm has been retained by prominent international underwriters and Argentine issuers in connection with equity and debt offerings in the domestic and international capital markets. It has also advised the Argentine government in connection with the public offering of the governments holding in the two privatised telephone companies and in a gas transmission company.

Banking and finance: The firm has advised a number of local and international banks and financial institutions on their activities in Argentina. The firm handles the establishment and transfer of banking businesses in Argentina and the creation of different types of guarantees and security interests. These include mortgages, chattel mortgages, ship mortgages, fiduciary assignments of rights, bonds, notes, and stand-by letters of credit. It also advises on project financings, leasing, hire, purchase, instalments, credit and deferred purchase facilities, trade and export financing, real estate financing, takeover financing, sovereign and corporate lending, general banking operations, and issues relating to the regulation and supervision of banks and financial institutions.

Privatisations: The firm has advised on the successful privatisations of cellular phone systems, the oil and gas main producing areas, railroads, the national and provincial water and effluent services, the energy distribution services and major hydroelectric facilities.

Telecommunications: The firm has advised the government on drafting the present regulations in the Argentinean telecommunications industry, and advised on the contracts with privatised companies involved.

Employment: The firm advises on all aspects of employment law and social security regulations including labour disputes (at individual and collective levels), claims made by trade unions and by the social security agencies, administrative proceedings relating to labour law regulations, disciplinary measures and dismissals, negotiation and execution of collective bargaining agreements, planning and implementation of incentive schemes, execution of workers' trade union privileges and conflicts under general bargaining agreements.

Litigation: The firm handles a range of litigation work.

LANGUAGES: English, French, German, Italian, Portuguese, Spanish

P

PESTALOZZI GMUER & PATRY

GENEVA OFFICE

15 Boulevard des Philosophes,
1205 Geneva, Switzerland
Tel: +41 22 809 4500 **Fax:** +41 22 809 45 01

ZURICH OFFICE

Löwenstrasse 1,
8001 Zurich, Switzerland
Tel: +41 1 217 91 11 **Fax:** +41 1 217 92 17

Website: www.pgp.ch

WORLDWIDE OFFICE CONTACTS

SWITZERLAND
15 Boulevard des Philosophes, 1205 **Geneva**
Tel: +41 22 809 4500 **Fax:** +41 22 809 45 01
Email: gva@pgp.ch

Löwenstrasse 1, 8001 **Zurich**
Tel: +41 1 217 91 11 **Fax:** +41 1 217 92 17
Email: zrh@pgp.ch

BELGIUM
165 Avenue Louise, B-1050 **Brussels**
Tel: +32 2 646 60 10 **Fax:** +32 2 646 75 34
Email: bru@pgp.ch

FIRM OVERVIEW

Managing partner: Dr Urs Jordi (Zurich) Guy-Philippe Rubeli (Geneva)
Senior partner: Dr. Rudolf Heiz (Zurich) Jean Patry (Geneva)

Number of partners worldwide: 23
Number of other lawyers worldwide: 38

AREAS OF PRACTICE:

Corporate	40%
Litigation	15%
Tax	15%
Arbitration	10%
Banking	10%

P

FIRM OVERVIEW: Pestalozzi, Gmuer & Patry is an independent multicultural and multilingual Swiss law firm dating from 1911, with a practice focusing on Swiss commercial law and international work. It is one of the country's largest law firms, with 23 partners and 38 other lawyers in Zurich, Geneva and Brussels, and an associated office in Bangkok. The firm is also part of the Lex Mundi and Unilaw international networks. Its lawyers are capable of leading complex transactions and are team players within interdisciplinary project groups.

INTERNATIONAL EXPERIENCE: Approximately half the firm's clients are international, coming mostly from the US, Europe, South America and Asia. The firm's Asian Practice Group provides a full range of services with a specific focus on cross-cultural communication and negotiation. It has strong relationships with corresponding law firms throughout Asia.

INTERNATIONAL CLIENTS: The firm's international clients are frequently traditional top-ranking enterprises, but may also be smaller or medium-sized businesses. They come from a broad range of sectors, including financial services (commercial and investment banks and financial intermediaries) industry (pharmaceuticals, chemicals and biotechnology, electronics, automobiles, mechanical engineering, food and beverages, tobacco, graphic products, textiles, watches and publishing), trading and retail, telecommunications, shipping, aviation and the travel and entertainment industries.

MAIN INTERNATIONAL AREAS OF PRACTICE:
Corporate: The firm advises Swiss and foreign clients on mergers, takeovers, joint ventures, spin-offs and other transactions.
Banking and capital markets: Work includes banking and securities regulatory matters, contracts and guarantees, secrecy obligations, securities trading and securitisation.
Commercial: The firm handles all types of commercial agreement.
Intellectual property: The practice has particular expertise in litigation and licensing. It handles computer, Internet, technology, telecommunications, advertising and media work.
Competition and trade: The practice advises on Swiss, EU and WTO law. Work includes the coordination of multi-jurisdictional transactions.
Employment: Work includes employer/employee representation, mass dismissals, contracts, residence and work permits.
Environmental: The firm advises on all aspects, especially water and air pollution, noise control, environmental audits, site contamination (including settlements with the authorities), zoning law and construction permits.
Construction/real estate: The firm handles real estate transactions with multifunctional legal aspects and construction site opposition
Social security/pensions: Work includes the divestiture of pension fund and the pension fund aspects of due diligence reports.
Commercial criminal law: The firm provides international judicial assistance in criminal matters, and represents the victims of white-collar crime.
Tax: The department advises international groups, corporations and individuals on Swiss and international tax planning and undertakes litigation.
Litigation and arbitration: The firm can undertake all types of dispute resolution in all its practice areas. It has particular expertise in arbitration, and can provide services in English, French, German, Italian and Thai anywhere in the world.

LANGUAGES: Dutch, English, French, German, Italian, Spanish, Swedish, Thai

For other recommended firms see pages 1485-1520

PF KOEP & CO

HEAD OFFICE

First Floor Acme Corner, Kasino Street, PO Box 3516,
Windhoek, Namibia
Tel: +264 61 224 591 **Fax:** +264 61 233 555

Email: pfk@koep.com.na

WORLDWIDE OFFICE CONTACTS

NAMIBIA
First Floor Acme Corner, Kasino Street, PO Box 3516, **Windhoek**
Tel: +264 61 224 591 **Fax:** +264 61 233 555
Email: pfk@koep.com.na

FIRM OVERVIEW

Managing and senior partner: Peter Frank Koep

Number of partners worldwide: 4
Number of other lawyers worldwide: 2

AREAS OF PRACTICE:

Corporate	30%
Litigation	20%
Property law	20%
Banking and finance	10%
Employment	10%
Mining and fishing	10%

FIRM PROFILE: PF Koep & Co was established in 1982 by Peter Frank Koep. The firm has no formal alliances but maintains links with various firms worldwide, specifically in the Republic of South Africa, Germany, the UK and the US. The firm offers a comprehensive legal service to clients with business interests in southern Africa and focuses on corporate and property work.

INTERNATIONAL EXPERIENCE: The firm has advised international clients on mergers and takeovers and continues to be involved in international litigation on behalf of clients in Namibia.

INTERNATIONAL CLIENTS: The firm's client base includes some of the largest companies and corporations in Namibia including major banks, insurance companies, large fishing and mining houses and construction companies.

MAIN INTERNATIONAL AREAS OF PRACTICE:

M&A: The firm handles work ranging from small private acquisitions to advising on company take-overs for Namibian firms based in South Africa.
Banking and finance: The firm advises two of the largest banks in Namibia and has also represented the Namibian Bankers Association. It also advises financial institutions on their loan transactions and mortgage policy. Members of the firm attend seminars on an annual basis in order to keep abreast of national and international developments.
Insurance: The firm advises the largest insurance company in Namibia on contracts and general insurance issues. It litigates for and on behalf of insurance companies in Namibia and South Africa.
Intellectual property: The firm specialises in trademarks, patents and copyright.
Litigation and arbitration: The firm specialises in commercial litigation and advises on national arbitrations and ADR. Its lawyers are frequently involved in cases before the High and Supreme Courts of Namibia.
Energy: The firm advises a major corporate client involved in the oil and gas industry.
Corporate: The firm advises on all aspects of general corporate law, including the drafting of contracts for Namibian and South African clients.
Property: The firm specialises in property law, transfer of properties and sectional titles and registration of mortgage bonds.
Employment: The firm specialises in Namibian employment law.
Mining and fishing: The firm's senior partner is a director of one of the major fishing companies and the firm represents this and other fishing companies. It advises clients on litigation, the drawing up of agreements, joint venture contracts and Government fishing policy. The firm is actively involved in the mining industry advising existent and incumbent mining companies, and has extensive knowledge of offshore diamond mining.
Administrative law: The firm is involved in a number of review applications to the High Court of Namibia, largely challenging actions taken by Ministers and other officials.

LANGUAGES: Afrikaans, English, German

P

For other recommended firms see pages 1485-1520

PIERGROSSI VILLA MANCA GRAZIADEI

HEAD OFFICE

Via Festa del Perdono, 10
20122 Milan, Italy
Tel: + 39 02 5830 3657 **Fax:** + 39 02 5830 3818

Email: pvmgmi@pvmg.com

FIRM OVERVIEW

Managing partner: Franco P Villa
Senior partner: Alberto Piergrossi

Number of partners worldwide: 17
Number of other lawyers worldwide: 18

AREAS OF PRACTICE:

M&A 30%
Corporate and commercial 25%
Litigation and arbitration 25%
Banking, finance and securities 20%

WORLDWIDE OFFICE CONTACTS

ITALY
Via Festa del Perdono 10, 20122 **Milan**
Tel: + 39 02 5830 3657 **Fax:** + 39 02 5830 3818
Email: pvmgmi@pvmg.com

Via Lombardia 23, 00187 **Rome**
Tel: + 39 06 427 44646 **Fax:** + 39 06 42741605
Email: pvmgrm@pvmg.com

UNITED KINGDOM
15 Great Stuart Street, **Edinburgh** EH3 7TS
Tel: +44 131 226 7722 **Fax:** +44 131 226 7887
Email: pvmged@dial.pipex.com

P

FIRM OVERVIEW: Piergrossi Villa Manca Graziadei was established in 1975 and has offices in Milan, Rome and Edinburgh. In 1996, the firm merged with Studio Legale di Palma e Pignatti. The firm comprises 17 partners, two permanent consultants and an equivalent number of associates and paralegals. In total, the firm comprises more than 30 lawyers, all conversant in the English language.

INTERNATIONAL EXPERIENCE: The firm provides an extensive range of services, including general corporate advice; assisting in the negotiation and drafting of commercial contracts and agreements; carrying out legal audits and due diligence reviews; drafting constituent documents and handling the process of setting up corporate entities. The firm also advises domestic and foreign clients on preparing, submitting and following up bids in a number of major tendering procedures.

INTERNATIONAL CLIENTS: The firm's clients include major local, foreign and multi-national corporations, as well as small and medium-sized businesses, predominantly from Italy, English-speaking countries, France, Germany, Spain and the Far East.

MAIN INTERNATIONAL AREAS OF PRACTICE:

Mergers and acquisitions: The firm assists a number of international clients with the sale and purchase of companies and businesses, the formation of joint ventures and consortia, mergers and de-mergers.

Corporate and commercial: The firm advises on a large number of matters, including the setting up and structuring of corporate entities, corporate reorganisations, intellectual property matters and commercial transactions in general, including the tax aspects.

Banking, finance and securities: The firm advises banks and borrowers in various financing transactions, including single bank and syndicated loan facilities, asset-based financing and debt restructuring. Acting for issuers, underwriters and advisors, the firm has developed a practice in the area of securities, including initial public offerings, issues of shares and debentures. Another important practice has been developed in the area of securitisation, where the firm has provided advice on Italian law to underwriters, issuers and originators in respect of asset-backed transactions originated in Italy.

Litigation and arbitration: The firm has an established litigation practice in the areas of civil, commercial, labour, environmental, intellectual property, insurance and tax laws. A large part of litigation work is characterised by international elements, as the firm both represents European, US and Far Eastern clients in procedures pending before Italian courts, and co-ordinates and instructs foreign solicitors on behalf of Italian clients in respect of litigation before other jurisdictions. The firm's lawyers have also acted as arbitrators in a variety of large domestic and international arbitrations.

EU and competition: The firm advises on the competition and regulatory aspects of acquisitions, mergers, joint ventures and consortia, distribution, licensing and supply agreements both at the EU and the domestic levels.

Environment: The environmental practice covers all aspects of environmental law arising in commercial transactions on which the firm is advising.

LANGUAGES: English, French, German, Italian, Portuguese, Spanish

For other recommended firms see pages 1485-1520

PIERRE TWEH & ASSOCIATES

HEAD OFFICE

Palm Hotel Building, Broad & Randall Streets, P. O. Box 10-2536
Monrovia 10 1000, Liberia
Tel: +231 226 577 **Fax:** +231 226 607

Email: pta@liberia.net

WORLDWIDE OFFICE CONTACTS

LIBERIA
Palm Hotel Building, Broad & Randall Streets, P. O. Box 10-2536,
Monrovia 10 1000
Tel: +231 226 577 **Fax:** +231 226 607
Email: pta@liberia.net

FIRM OVERVIEW

Managing partner: N. Oswald Tweh
Senior partner: James E. Pierre

Number of partners worldwide: 2
Number of other lawyers worldwide: 4

AREAS OF PRACTICE:

Corporate and commercial	35%
Incorporation and registered agent services	15%
Banking and finance	10%
Litigation and arbitration	10%
Natural resources	10%
Employment	5%
Intellectual property	5%
Maritime	5%
Real estate	5%

FIRM OVERVIEW: Pierre Tweh & Associates was formed in 1999. It comprises lawyers of diversified academic and professional backgrounds whose experience ensures that the firm provides high quality legal advice. The firm specialise in corporate, commercial, banking and finance, litigation and arbitration.

INTERNATIONAL EXPERIENCE: Pierre Tweh & Associates have advised foreign firms and individuals in the US, Canada, Europe and Asia on corporate and commercial transactions, intellectual property registration, banking and finance transactions, and maritime issues. They have also handled work relating to Liberia's liberal corporate laws, registered agent services for domestic Liberian corporations and obtained authorisations for foreign corporations operating in Liberia.

MAIN INTERNATIONAL AREAS OF PRACTICE:
Incorporation and registered agent services: The firm advises on incorporating companies, preparing organisational minutes, bylaws and share certificates. Its lawyers also act as directors and corporate secretaries.
Corporate and commercial: Work handled includes formation of companies, corporations, partnerships and joint ventures; asset purchases, sales, leases, agency work, distributorship and other contract related issues. It also negotiates for, and represents, clients before government agencies and advises foreign firms with subsidiaries in Liberia.
Litigation and arbitration: The firm specialises in informal dispute resolution and out of court settlements. It also advises on all aspects of international arbitration.
Maritime: Work undertaken includes the registration of vessels and other watercraft of all classes under the Liberian ship registry; negotiating and drafting agreements for the sale and purchase of ships and vessels of all classes; negotiating and drafting contracts for the carriage of goods and passengers by vessels and other watercraft; conducting title searches to identify and confirm the ownership and registered agents of vessels and other watercrafts; advising on the Liberian Maritime law and policies.
Banking and finance: The firm advises on the establishment of financial institutions (incorporating and securing licenses from the Central Bank of Liberia), loan negotiations and documentation (short, long term and revolving credits, secured and unsecured), asset based finance, construction finance, lease transaction, project financing, debt rescheduling and financing.
Intellectual property: Pierre Tweh & Associates advises on registration, protection, use and enforcement of trademarks, copyright, patents, design and trade secrets, licensing, technology transfer, media law, packaging, labelling, manufacture and distribution agreements.

LANGUAGES: English

For other recommended firms see pages 1485-1520

PINHEIRO GUIMARÃES - ADVOGADOS

HEAD OFFICE

Avenida Rio Branco 181, 27° andar,
Rio de Janeiro RJ 20040-007, Brazil
Tel: +55 21 533 3006 **Fax:** +55 21 532 7333

Email: pgarj@unisys.com.br
Website: www.pinheiroguimaraes.com.br

WORLDWIDE OFFICE CONTACTS

BRAZIL
Avenida Rio Branco 181, 27° andar,
RJ 20040-007, **Rio de Janeiro**
Tel: +55 21 533 3006 **Fax:** +55 21 532 7333
Email: pgarj@unisys.com.br

Av. Paulista 1842, 13° andar, 01310-200, **São Paulo** SP
Tel: +55 11 283 5811 **Fax:** +55 11 251 0627
Email: pgasp@uninet.com.br

FIRM OVERVIEW

Senior partner: Francisco Pinheiro Guimarães N

Number of partners worldwide: 9
Number of other lawyers worldwide: 28

AREAS OF PRACTICE:
Bank finance/project loans .... *%
Capital markets/corporate finance .... *%
Litigation .... *%
Mergers and acquisition .... *%
Taxes .... *%
Telecommunications law .... *%
* Workload % not disclosed

FIRM OVERVIEW: Pinheiro Guimarães - Advogados was established in 1922, when Plinio Pinheiro Guimarães joined the law offices of José de Miranda Valverde, already in existence for several decades. With offices in Rio de Janeiro and São Paulo, it represents a wide range of clients in Brazil and abroad. The firm's staff of qualified and experienced attorneys is fluent in several foreign languages. Four partners are qualified to practice both in Brazil and New York.

INTERNATIONAL EXPERIENCE: Pinheiro Guimarães has extensive international experience being, one of the leading Brazilian firms in connection with international debt and equity issuances, syndicated loans, trade finance, mergers and acquisitions, cross-border lease transactions, structured finance, project finance, private equity, securitisations of exports and other receivables, litigation and tax.

MAIN AREAS OF INTERNATIONAL PRACTICE:
Banking/capital markets: The firm has extensive experience in negotiating traditional credit facilities, recourse and non-recourse loan agreements, together with the collateral and guarantee packages inherent to such arrangements. Additionally, Pinheiro Guimarães has also been actively involved in alternative funding structures using both syndicated loans and issuances of debt, convertible securities and warrants. The firm also assists clients in the structuring, negotiation and establishment of American Depositary Receipts (ADRs) and Brazilian Depositary Receipts (BDRs) programmes. In the area of trade finance-related transactions the firm has been involved in export pre-payment and exports securitisations. Pinheiro Guimarães is also very active in aircraft leasing transactions having represented international leasing companies from the United States, Europe and Asia in transactions with Brazilian aviation companies. From 1983 to 1994, the firm represented the bank advisory committee for the restructuring of the Brazilian external debt, and was actively involved in the negotiations that resulted in the issuance of the 'Brazil Brady Bonds'. Pinheiro Guimarães represents foreign institutional investors in their transactions in Brazil, including investments in the fixed income and stock markets and derivative transactions, as well as investments in domestic investment funds. The firm advises foreign financial institutions and other institutional investors in connection with derivative transactions entered into outside Brazil with Brazilian counterparts, for hedging purposes or otherwise.
Corporate/mergers and acquisitions: On corporate matters, the firm assists its foreign clients in connection with the setting up of subsidiaries in Brazil, corporate restructurings and reorganisations, mergers and acquisitions and joint ventures.
Privatisation: Upon the privatisation of the telecommunications, mining and power sectors, the firm represented several major operators in structuring and negotiating investment alternatives through the use of different investment vehicles and investment funds. Pinheiro Guimarães also assists the corporate and regulatory day-to-day businesses of companies that won licenses for the rendering of telecommunications, mining, and electric power services in several states of Brazil.
Private equity/e-business: The firm advises financial institutions, venture capitalists and local entrepreneurs in connection with the structuring, negotiation and establishment of private equity funds and private equity investments, including start-up Internet companies.
Project finance: The firm has represented several bank syndicates in the negotiations of the financings for the construction of large nuclear and hydroelectric power plants in South America as well as other infrastructure projects. Pinheiro Guimarães has also participated in the structuring of transactions for the financing of several recently privatised telecommunications and electric power companies. In the area of infrastructure projects, the firm has worked in green field infrastructure EPC projects in Brazil involving the construction and operation of hydroelectric and thermoelectric power plants.
Litigation: The firm has vast experience in litigation involving contracts, torts, corporate and commercial matters, and bankruptcy. The firm has represented financial institutions and corporations in administrative proceedings involving foreign exchange, banking and corporate law initiated by the Central Bank of Brazil and the Comissão de Valores Mobiliários - CVM.
Tax: Pinheiro Guimarães advises international clients in the development of tax strategies with respect to their activities in connection with capital markets, mergers and acquisitions and e-business.

LANGUAGES: English, French, German and Portuguese

PINHEIRO GUIMARÃES - ADVOGADOS

For other recommended firms see pages 1485-1520

PINTÓ RUIZ & DEL VALLE SL

HEAD OFFICE

C/Velázquez, 146 - 1a planta,
28002 Madrid, Spain
Tel: + 34 91 563 8678 **Fax:** + 34 91 563 3229

Email: mad@pintoruizdelvalle.com
Website: www.pintoruizdelvalle.com

FIRM OVERVIEW

Managing partners: Salvador Ferrandis, Jóse Juan Pintó Sala
Senior partners: Jóse Juan Pintó Ruiz, Javier del Valle

Number of partners worldwide: 15
Number of other lawyers worldwide: 44

AREAS OF PRACTICE:

Area	%
Intellectual property	30%
Corporate and business law	15%
Tax	15%
Employment	10%
Litigation and arbitration	10%
Mergers and acquisitions	10%
Banking and finance	5%
Communications and computer law	5%

WORLDWIDE OFFICE CONTACTS

SPAIN

C/César Elguezábal, 39, ppl. Dcha., 03001 **Alicante**
Tel: +34 96 514 5914 **Fax:** +34 96 514 5353

C/Beethoven, 13 - 7a planta, 08021 **Barcelona**
Tel: + 34 93 414 5885 **Fax:** + 34 93 414 3885
Email: bcn@pintoruizdelvalle.com

C/Velázquez, 146 - 1a planta, 28002 **Madrid**
Tel: + 34 91 563 8678 **Fax:** + 34 91 563 3229
Email: mad@pintoruizdelvalle.com

FIRM OVERVIEW: Pintó Ruiz & Del Valle SL was formed in 1999 by the merger of two of the oldest law firms in Spain, Bufete Pintó Ruiz and Del Valle Abogados, founded in 1889 and 1910 respectively. Its staff comprises economists and the firm has over 60 lawyers who specialise in the fields of intellectual property and mercantile law. It advises Spanish and foreign clients on all aspects relating to business and investment in Spain and to the defence of their rights. Matters handled include mergers, mercantile contracts, patents and trademarks, banking operations, accounting and audits. Pintó Ruiz & Del Valle belongs to the Pannone Law Group which has law firms in many European countries and, since 1995, in North America, having joined with an associate law firm in Canada.

INTERNATIONAL EXPERIENCE: The firm has considerable background experience in international transactions. It acted as consultant in several IP related matters, due diligence, M&A, and has a litigation department representing foreign companies. The firm focuses particularly on banking and finance.

INTERNATIONAL CLIENTS: The firm represents leading foreign companies in Spain in various fields, such as sports, luxury goods and watches, and the spirits industry.

MAIN INTERNATIONAL AREAS OF PRACTICE:

Intellectual property: The firm advises on all aspects of intellectual property and represents clients in both contentious and non-contentious matters. It advises on licence agreements and infringements of IP rights. The firm is a member of the International Trademark Association, AIPPI, APRAM, Licence Executive Society, Pharmaceutical Trade Mark Group and the European Communities Trademark Association (ECTA).
Tax: The firm advises domestic and international clients on all aspects of tax. Its lawyers are experienced in international tax, audit and finance planning.
Corporate: Pintó Ruiz & Del Valle advises companies on all legal and accounting matters including the preparation of book-keeping, review of accounts books, accounting costs and on insolvency proceedings such as payment suspensions and bankruptcy.
Litigation and arbitration: The firm has considerable experience in litigation and arbitration, both on a national and international level.
Employment: The firm is experienced in all areas of employment law, particularly negotiation, collective conventions, conflicts, contracts and dismissals and advises on human resources, prevention of risk at work, and social security.
Banking and finance: The firm advises on all areas relating to banking and finance, focusing on syndication, transactions, project finance and taxation. The firm provides long-term investment strategies designed to fit the investment objectives of each client. The firm specialises in comprehensive financial plans including cash flow analysis, risk management considerations and projection for retierment planning. It also provides recommendations for home refinancing, retirement and pension distribution.
M&A: The firm advises on national and international mergers and acquisitions.
Communications and computer law: The firm advises companies on their day-to-day operations, and on acquisitions and transactions.
Internet: The firm has a highly specialised department in this emerging area, and advises on Turnkey projects B2B, B2C, C2C and C2B, contracts on the Internet, tax on the Internet, data protection and intellectual property rights protection.

LANGUAGES: English, French, German, Italian, Spanish

PINTÓ RUIZ & DEL VALLE
Abogados & Economistas

PIPER MARBURY RUDNICK & WOLFE LLP

HEAD OFFICE

see Worldwide Office Contacts

Email: info@piperrudnick.com
Website: www.piperrudnick.com

FIRM OVERVIEW

Managing partners: Francis B Burch Jr, Lee I Miller
Chief operating officer: Jeffrey F Liss
Number of partners worldwide: 344
Number of other lawyers worldwide: 503

AREAS OF PRACTICE:

Litigation	26%
Real estate	16%
Corporate and securities	12%
Banking, finance and business reorganisation	8%
Intellectual property, IT, e-commerce and privacy	8%
Venture capital	6%
Franchise and distribution	5%
Environmental	3%

FIRM OVERVIEW:

Piper Marbury Rudnick & Wolfe LLP operates out of offices nationwide. The firm's practice is focused on corporate IPOs, mergers and acquisitions, and other major transactions for companies of all sizes including those in the emerging company and technology sectors; real estate transactions finance and securities; litigation, including a white collar group led by a former Watergate prosecutor; national products liability; securities litigation practices; and government regulatory practices.

INTERNATIONAL EXPERIENCE: The firm has handled a wide range of work throughout the US and abroad. It represents businesses that cross international borders. The firm's experience includes deal structuring, negotiating agreements, contract performance or breach, product quality, letter-of-credit compliance, insurance coverage and losses, emergency injunctions, asset seizures to secure claims, and regulatory matters. The firm's international practice also includes seasoned litigators who frequently appear before trial and appellate courts and arbitration panels in a broad array of commercial matters.

MAIN INTERNATIONAL AREAS OF PRACTICE

Litigation: The litigation group includes eight members of the American College of Trial Lawyers, including the current President. For international clients in the US, the firm has litigated and arbitrated in matters including commercial litigation, product liability, intellectual property, securities class actions, white-collar crime, and tax issues.
Corporate, securities, and M&A: The firm has a specialist corporate and financial practice. It handles public and private debt and equity security, and mergers and acquisitions. The firm's representation of foreign companies in the US has focused on corporate structure, transfer pricing, trade issues, acquisitions, dispositions, joint ventures, financings, project finance, and other commercial relationships. Piper Marbury Rudnick & Wolfe LLP handles tax planning for cross-border acquisitions; advice on international tax issues related to the establishment of US business operations and the acquisition of US real estate by foreign investors; intercompany pricing rules in connection with commodities transactions; and tax matters related to transnational employees and employee benefit plans.
Real estate: The firm has handled the acquisition, construction, development, and workout of all types of properties, including regional shopping centres and power centres, urban and suburban office buildings, high-rise, mixed-use projects, industrial buildings, hotels, multifamily rental dwellings, condominiums, manufacturing and warehouse facilities. It has particular experience in the lodging and timeshare industry, as well as incorporating the usual aspects of a sophisticated, complex real estate practice, from eminent domain and environmental issues to foreclosures, securitised loans, and zoning disputes.
Intellectual property: The firm is responsible for over 25,000 active patents and trademarks in more than 150 countries. Clients range from small entrepreneurial companies and partnerships to Fortune 500 companies in diverse technological and service industries. In the patent area, the firm has 18 lawyers who are admitted to practice before the United States Patent and Trademark Office (PTO) with backgrounds in biotech, mechanical, chemical, electrical, metallurgical and nuclear engineering and computer science, as well as substantial trial experience.
E-commerce and privacy: The firm's e-commerce practice represents entities ranging from large, international corporations to start-up ventures in a wide variety of transactions ranging from complex e-commerce development initiatives to routine matters, including Web hosting and development agreements, and Web linking and partnering agreements. It also advises on intellectual property liability and protection, domain name registration, disputes and transfers, hacking and unsolicited commercial e-mail.
Franchise and distribution: The firm has represented more than 160 companies in international franchising and distribution matters. A substantial number are headquartered in Europe, Canada, Latin America, the Middle East and Japan, and represent a wide variety of industries.
Project finance: The project finance practice includes a strong outbound international component, with experience in projects in more than 30 countries, in Europe, Central and South America, the Middle East and Africa, and Asia. Projects have included power plants, transmission facilities, cross border and conduit leasing, mining tolling transactions, gas pipelines, municipal sewage facilities, telephone privatizations, and airport financings.

WORLDWIDE OFFICE CONTACTS

USA
6225 Smith Avenue, **Baltimore** MD 21209-3600
Tel: +1 410 580 3000 **Fax:** +1 410 580 3001

Piper Marbury Rudnick & Wolfe, an Illinois General Partnership, 203 North LaSalle Street, Suite 1800, **Chicago** IL 60601-1293
Tel: +1 312 368 4000 **Fax:** +1 312 236 7516

1717 Main Street, Suite 4600, **Dallas** TX 75201-4605
Tel: +1 214 743 4500 **Fax:** +1 214 743 4545

1251 Avenue of the Americas, **New York** NY 10020-1104
Tel: + 1 212 835 6000 **Fax:** + 1 212 835 6001

3400 Two Logan Square, 18th and Arch Streets,
Philadelphia PA 19103-2762
Tel: + 1 215 656 3300 **Fax:** + 1 215 656 3301

Commerce Executive Park III, Suite 610, 1850 Centennial Park Drive,
Reston VA 20191-1517
Tel: + 1 703 391 7100 **Fax:** + 1 703 309 5299

101 East Kennedy Boulevard, Suite 2000, **Tampa** FL
Tel: +1 813 229 2111 **Fax:** +1 813 229 1447

1200 Nineteenth Street, NW, **Washington DC** 20036-2412
Tel: + 1 202 861 3900 **Fax:** + 1 202 223 2085

PLATON MARTINEZ FLORES SAN PEDRO & LEAÑO

HEAD OFFICE

6th & 7th Floors, Tuscan Building, 114 Herrera Street, Legaspi Village
Makati City, The Philippines
Tel: +63 2 867 4696 **Fax:** +63 2 867 1304

Email: lawfirm@i-next.net
Website: www.platonmartinez.com

WORLDWIDE OFFICE CONTACTS

PHILIPPINES
6th & 7th Floors, Tuscan Building, 114 Herrera Street, Legaspi Village,
Makati City
Tel: +63 2 867 4696 **Fax:** +63 2 867 1304
Email: lawfirm@i-next.net

FIRM OVERVIEW

Senior Partners: Carlos G Platon, Hector A Martinez, Jose Pacis Flores, Augusto San Pedro and Saklolo A Leaño

Number of partners worldwide: 8
Number of other lawyers worldwide: 14

AREAS OF PRACTICE:

Corporate law and foreign investments	35%
Litigation	20%
Other	15%
Intellectual property	10%
Employment	10%
Tax	10%

FIRM OVERVIEW: The firm was established on September 1, 1996 by the founding partners, five of whom were, until then, senior partners and heads of their respective departments in one of the country's oldest law offices. Each of the five name partners has more than thirty years of extensive experience and exposure in various fields of law practice - specifically in corporate and investments law, general litigation, taxation, intellectual property, labour law, mining, commercial law, banking, immigration and insurance. The firm now has 22 lawyers, 3 paralegals and a support staff of 19 personnel.

INTERNATIONAL EXPERIENCE: The firm is currently assisting Freshfields of London in the recovery of assets located in the State of Brunei Darrusalam and the Brunei Investment Agency. The Philippines assets are the subject of initial adverse proceedings instituted by the firm worth an estimated US$100 million.The firm is also actively assisting the law firm of Liskow & Lewis of New Orleans and Fulbright and Jaworski of Houston in connection with a class suit instituted in Louisiana against Caltex Philippines and other Caltex Corporations in the U.S. on behalf of more than 3,800 Filipino plaintiffs who are the survivors or heirs of more than 4,000 passengers who died in the Philippines in 1989 in what is deemed to be the worst accident in maritime history. The cases for damages filed in the Philippines handled by our firm have been won for Caltex with the Supreme Court declaring in a precedent-setting final decision released late last year that Caltex, as the charterer of the oil tanker that was involved in the collision, could not be held liable.The firm, as the Philippine counsel for Agribands International, a corporation based in the U.S., is handling the negotiation for the acquisition of Metrovet, Inc, a wholly owned subsidiary of Metro Pacific Corporation. It is also acting as counsel for a major international telecommunications company which is establishing a joint venture with a large established Philippine company that will engage in a number of Internet related businesses. It also acts as counsel for Philip Morris in connection with current and potential tobacco-related claims for damages.

INTERNATIONAL CLIENTS: Include ABN-AMRO Bank, Air France/UTA, Beaumont & Son, Bristol-Myers Squibb, Cable & Wireless HKT Limited, California Clothing Inc, Cathay Pacific Airways, Caltex Petroleum, Coca-Cola Phils,Dole, Dow Chemical, Eveready, General Electric/RCA, HSBC Securities, KLM Royal Dutch Airlines, McDonald's Corporation, Maruboni Corporation, Motorola, Fuji Xerox Corp, Kawasaki Group, Philip Morris, San Miguel Corporation, Thai Airways International Ltd, Yokohama Tires Phils Inc,Union Carbide and Zurich Insurance Company.

MAIN INTERNATIONAL AREAS OF PRACTICE: The firm provides a full range of legal services for a complete and multi-disciplinary solution to the legal problems and needs of its clients. These services include:
Corporate law and foreign investments: The firm handles all aspects of corporate and securities work, including corporate mergers and acquisitions, joint ventures, special projects, franchising, registration with the Board of Investments and special economic zones, foreign investments, divestitures, spin-offs, liquidations, contracts, proxy disputes, and initial public offerings (IPOs). The firm secures working visas and alien employment permits for the expatriate employees of its corporate clients.
Litigation: The firm handles all types of civil, commercial, admiralty and administrative cases, including intra-corporate and stockholders' derivative suits, both at the trial and appellate levels. The firm has extensive litigation experience in aviation cases.
Intellectual and industrial property rights law: The firm is rated by all major law firm directories as one of the leading Philippine law firms in this area.
Employment: The firm's labor law specialists have extensive experience in collective bargaining negotiations, labor arbitration (voluntary and compulsory), certification and jurisdiction cases, lockouts, strikes and other forms of work stoppages and employee concerted actions, employee termination, contract hires, and all other disputes and problems arising from or related to employer-employee relations.
Tax, banking and insurance: The tax specialists of the firm have done extensive work in taxation, specifically income, business, estate and transfer taxes, including the handling of contested assessments and appeals to the Court of Tax Appeals. The firm handles substantial banking and insurance work, including the giving of advice on all laws and regulations administered by the Bangko Sentral ng Pilipinas and the Insurance Commission.

LANGUAGES: English, Tagalog

PLESNER SVANE GRØNBORG

HEAD OFFICE

Esplanaden 34,
DK-1263 Copenhagen, Denmark
Tel: +45 33 12 11 33 **Fax:** +45 33 12 00 14

Email: psg@psglaw.dk
Website: www.psglaw.dk

FIRM OVERVIEW

Head of Managing Committee: Peter-Ulrik Plesner

Number of partners worldwide: 36
Number of other lawyers worldwide: 80

AREAS OF PRACTICE:

Aviation and aircraft financing	*%
Banking and finance	*%
Competition and EU law	*%
Company and commercial	*%
Construction and real property	*%
Corporate finance	*%
Environmental	*%
Insolvency and reconstruction	*%
Insurance	*%
Intellectual property	*%
M&A	*%
Tax	*%

* Workload % not disclosed

WORLDWIDE OFFICE CONTACTS

DENMARK
Esplanaden 34, DK-1263 **Copenhagen**
Tel: +45 33 12 11 33 **Fax:** +45 33 12 00 14
Email: psg@psglaw.dk

Trondhjems Plads 3, DK-2100 **Copenhagen**
Tel: +45 33 12 11 33 **Fax:** +45 33 12 00 14
Email: psg@psglaw.dk

P

FIRM OVERVIEW: Plesner Svane Grønborg was created through a merger in September 2000 between the Copenhagen based law firms Plesner & Grønborg and O. Bondo Svane. With 115 lawyers and a total staff of 230, Plesner Svane Grønborg is one of Denmark's largest full service law firms with expertise within all areas of commercial and public law. The firm has long-standing non-exclusive relations with prominent law firms throughout the world.

INTERNATIONAL EXPERIENCE: The firm represents foreign and Danish corporations, organisations, financial institutions, public authorites and funds and foundations engaged in cross-border activities. At an international level the firm has extensive experience in M&A, IPOs, tax law, EU and competition law, construction law and IT and IP law.

MAIN INTERNATIONAL AREAS OF PRACTICE:

Corporate finance: The firm acts as adviser to investment banks, underwriters, equity and venture capital funds. The firm's corporate finance department often participates at an early stage in the planning and structuring of transactions such as IPOs, private offerings, MBOs and acquisition financing.

Banking and finance: Plesner Svane Grønborg advises on all aspects of financial law, including secured and unsecured lending, syndicated facilities, bond issues, derivatives and administration and transfers of loan portfolios. The firm acts on behalf of lenders, borrowers and other participants in connection with asset based financing with particular focus on aircraft and ship financing.

Insolvency and reconstruction: The firm has one of the largest insolvency practices in the country and has been engaged in most of the large insolvency and reconstruction cases in Denmark for over 20 years.

IP and IT law: Intellectual property has been one of the cornerstones of the firm's expertise for many years and it is widely regarded as the leading Danish practice in this area. Throughout the years the firm's lawyers have not only been engaged in the traditional aspects of IP protection, but have also explored new aspects of IP rights, including European Community Law, and of IT law, where the client list includes many dot.com companies. The firm represents Danish and international clients in IP cases before the full spectrum of Danish courts, the European Court of Justice, the Danish Patent and Trademark Office and Board of Appeals, OHIM (the European Community Trademark (CTM) Office), the OHIM Boards of Appeal, and the Danish Domain Name of Appeal.

Tax: The firm's tax department, for many years Denmark's largest, advises on all aspects of tax law and is experienced in issues connected with cross-border transactions. The firm was lead counsel on the US$3.6 billion demerger of Sophus Berendsen A/S, the first ever split of a Danish listed company.

LANGUAGES: English, French, German, Icelandic, Italian, Polish, Portuguese, Scandinavian, Spanish

 For other recommended firms see pages 1485-1520

P+P PÖLLATH + PARTNERS

HEAD OFFICE

Kardinal-Faulhaber-Strasse 10,
D-80333 Munich, Germany
Tel: +49 89 24 24 00 **Fax:** +49 89 24 24 09 99

Email: muc@pplaw.de
Website: www.pplaw.de

FIRM OVERVIEW

Number of partners worldwide: 10
Number of other lawyers worldwide: 21

AREAS OF PRACTICE:
Capital markets .... *%
Corporate restructuring .... *%
M&A .... *%
Private equity funds .... *%
Real estate .... *%
Tax .... *%
* Workload % not disclosed

WORLDWIDE OFFICE CONTACTS

GERMANY
Friedrichstrasse 200, 10117 **Berlin**
Tel: +49 30 2233 2233 **Fax:** +49 30 2233 2200
Email: ber@pplaw.de

Liebigstrasse 19, D-60323 **Frankfurt am Main**
Tel: +49 69 247 0470 **Fax:** +49 69 247 047 30
Email: fra@pplaw.de

Kardinal Faulhaber Strasse 10, D-80332 **Munich**
Tel: +49 89 24 24 00 **Fax:** +49 89 24 24 09 99
Email: muc@pplaw.de

FIRM OVERVIEW: P+P was founded in 1997. It is a 'boutique' firm specialising in two areas of legal and tax advice. These are transactions, (mainly M&A, private equity, real estate) and asset management, (mainly investments, financial products, successions). P+P is not affiliated with any other firm or group, but freely cooperates with leading experts at other firms as well as with local practitioners.

INTERNATIONAL EXPERIENCE: P+P has extensive experience in cross-border transactional and tax work and structuring of international private equity funds.

INTERNATIONAL CLIENTS: P+P's clients include major international private equity funds, investment banks and corporates.

MAIN AREAS OF PRACTICE:
M&A: P+P regularly advises major funds, institutions and private companies and gives specialist advice to one-time sellers or buyers. P+P is well known for its tax-structuring expertise. The firm assists sellers in structuring asset management prior and subsequent to a sale or succession of a private company.
Private equity: In addition to their M&A deal work, P+P partners have assisted in structuring many private equity transactions since these were introduced in Germany. P+P regularly obtains tax rulings for funds. The private equity practice is strengthened by P+P's established practice for private companies, institutional investors and banks.
Tax: P+P partners have an established reputation and are known to tax authorities nationwide at all levels. They offer reliable, high-quality services in tax planning, tax rulings and negotiated audit settlements to corporate and private clients. Second opinions and tax litigation are also undertaken.
Real estate: P+P has an established real estate practice for commercial and private investors as well as in East German restitution cases. Two P+P partners have previously held senior management positions in major real estate companies.

LANGUAGES: English, French, German

For other recommended firms see pages 1485-1520

PONCET TURRETTINI AMAUDRUZ NEYROUD & PARTNERS

HEAD OFFICE

8-10, Rue de Hesse, PO Box 5715,
CH-1211 Geneva 11, Switzerland
Tel: +41 22 319 1111 **Fax:** +41 22 312 1431

Website: www.ptan.ch

WORLDWIDE OFFICE CONTACTS

SWITZERLAND
8-10, Rue de Hesse, PO Box 5715, CH-1211 **Geneva** 11
Tel: + 41 22 319 1111 **Fax:** + 41 22 312 1431
Email: name.surname@ptan.ch

FIRM OVERVIEW

Number of partners worldwide: 13
Number of other lawyers worldwide: 16

AREAS OF PRACTICE:

Litigation and arbitration	20%
General corporate and contracts	15%
Banking, financial services, securities and capital markets	15%
Crime	10%
International judicial assistance in criminal and civil matters	10%
Others	30%

FIRM OVERVIEW: Founded in 1921, the firm is one of Switzerland's oldest law firms. It has a broad practice including banking, commercial, real estate and insurance, as well as international litigation and arbitration. Many of the firm's lawyers have attended universities abroad (mainly in the US), or have trained in foreign law firms. Several have also worked in the legal departments of major private firms.

INTERNATIONAL EXPERIENCE: The firm advises international clients, both corporate and individual, on a regular basis. It is involved in international cases pending before the local courts or before arbitral tribunals (ad hoc, ICC, Geneva Chamber of Commerce, Zurich Chamber of Commerce etc), with firm members acting as chairman, party-appointed arbitrator, sole arbitrator or counsel. The firm also has wide experience in international judicial assistance in criminal matters.

INTERNATIONAL CLIENTS: The firm's client base includes both corporate clients, such as banks, insurance companies and multinationals, and private individuals.

MAIN INTERNATIONAL AREAS OF PRACTICE:

General corporate and contracts: The firm advises on the negotiation and drafting of contracts, such as international sales, agency or distribution agreements, and services, as well as other general commercial documents. It also advises on all aspects of Swiss company law.

Banking, financial services, securities and capital markets: The firm has acquired wide experience in all aspects of banking and financial law, including advice to Swiss and foreign financial institutions, incorporation and licensing of banks, mergers or takeovers, as well as disputes between banks or asset managers and their clients.

M&A: Firm members are able to advise on all aspects, such as due diligence, drafting of contracts and the administrative aspects and so on of such transactions, both for small private acquisitions or major cross-border transactions.

Litigation and arbitration: One of the firm's main activities is representing clients before Swiss courts and before arbitral tribunals. Special emphasis is put on training all members of the firm and keeping their litigation skills up to date, in particular with regard to international litigation. Senior partners also act on a regular basis as members of arbitral tribunals or as sole arbitrators.

Private international law and comparative law: Due to its international orientation, members of the firm are well equipped to handle matters of private international law. Many of them have acquired experience in foreign law or in European Community law, and have become fully conversant with the technicalities of common law.

International judicial assistance in criminal and civil matters: The firm has a strong practice, representing foreign individuals, local banks and other entities as well as some foreign states in cases of international judicial assistance in criminal matters.

Crime: This has been a specialisation since the firm's foundation. More recently the firm has developed special expertise in the areas of international business crime, law enforcement issues and advice on anti-money-laundering legislation.

Insolvency and bankruptcy: The firm regularly acts for clients in attachment, insolvency and bankruptcy proceedings.

Telecommunications and computer law: The firm's specialists in this area advise clients on all related matters and represent them before the relevant administrative authorities.

Insurance: The firm advises on insurance law, social insurance and pensions funds, representing inter alia many Swiss and foreign insurance companies.

Employment and immigration: Services include the drafting of contracts and company regulations, securing work permits, tax arrangements, negotiating immigration packages with federal and local authorities and advising foreigners on the acquisition of real estate.

Estate planning, inheritance and family: The firm has long-standing experience in assisting private clients in estate planning, including settlement of trusts or foundations, drafting wills, pre- and post-nuptial agreements as well as financial settlements in divorce proceedings.

LANGUAGES: English, French, German, Italian, Spanish

P

For other recommended firms see pages 1485-1520

POROBIJA & POROBIJA

HEAD OFFICE

A. Brescenskog 4/I, PO Box 92,
HR-10000 Zagreb, Croatia
Tel: +385 1 4551 325 **Fax:** +385 1 4551 846
Email: p-p@ci.tel.hr

WORLDWIDE OFFICE CONTACTS

CROATIA
A. Brescenskog 4/I, PO Box 92, HR-10000 **Zagreb**
Tel: +385 1 4551 325 **Fax:** +385 1 4551 846
Email: p-p@ci.tel.hr

FIRM OVERVIEW

Senior partners: Boris Porobija, Sanja Porobija

Number of partners worldwide: 3
Number of other lawyers worldwide: 9

AREAS OF PRACTICE:

Banking and finance .... *%
Bankruptcy and restructuring .... *%
Corporate and commercial .... *%
Litigation and arbitration .... *%
Privatisations and M&A .... *%
Project finance .... *%
Telecommunications .... *%
* Workload % not disclosed

FIRM OVERVIEW: Porobija & Porobija was established in 1991. They advise on commercial, business, corporate and civil law. Most of the firm's work is related to cross-border or international transactions.
The firm is not part of formal associations, but maintains links with several leading international law firms in the EU and the US.

INTERNATIONAL EXPERIENCE: The firm has advised international clients on various privatisation and M&A projects, infrastructure and public utilities projects, on joint-ventures and commercial contracts with Croatian parties, as well as on commercial and sovereign borrowing. The firm also provides legal assistance to a number of foreign companies and their subsidiaries established in Croatia.

INTERNATIONAL CLIENTS: The firm's clients include leading international industrial and service corporations in a broad spectrum of businesses, major investment and commercial banks, international financial institutions and export agencies.

MAIN INTERNATIONAL AREAS OF PRACTICE:

Privatisations and M&A: The firm advises on all aspects of privatisation and mergers and acquisitions in various business sectors, notably banking. The firm handles different types of privatisation and M&A transactions such as negotiated acquisitions, privatisation transactions, mandatory public offers and asset deals.

Project finance: The firm has advised on the development, construction, financing and operation of several major infrastructure projects in Croatia (motorways, energy sector, public utilities). It acts for sponsors, project companies and lenders.

Banking and finance: The firm advises borrowers, international banks and financial institutions on Croatian legal aspects of loan documentation, security package, sovereign borrowing and state guarantees.

Telecommunications and IT: The firm advises on regulatory issues in telecommunications and e-commerce.

Corporate and commercial: The firm advises on investment and joint-venture structuring, the incorporation of various types of commercial companies, and company and securities matters. They also advise on commercial contracts, property law, employment law, as well as on immigration and other matters relevant for foreign businesses established in Croatia.

Litigation and arbitration: The firm represents clients in commercial, construction and civil law disputes before Croatian courts and arbitrations. The firm also acts as Croatian legal adviser in commercial litigations before foreign courts and arbitrations.

Bankruptcy and restructuring: The firm advises on bankruptcy proceedings including bankruptcy restructuring.

LANGUAGES: English, German, Hungarian, Italian

For other recommended firms see pages 1485-1520

POSSE, HERRERA & RUIZ

HEAD OFFICE

Carrera 7 A # 69-67, Ps. 1-4,
Bogotá, Colombia
Tel: +571 312 3157 **Fax:** +571 313 0259

Email: phr@posseherreraruiz.com
Website: www.posseherreraruiz.com

WORLDWIDE OFFICE CONTACTS

COLOMBIA
Carrera 7 A # 69-67, Ps. 1-4, **Bogotá**
Tel: +57 1 312 3157 **Fax:** +57 1 313 0259
Email: phr@posseherreraruiz.com

FIRM OVERVIEW

Managing partner: Jaime Herrera
Number of partners worldwide: 5
Number of other lawyers worldwide: 15

AREAS OF PRACTICE:

Financing and project financing	25%
Corporate and M&A	20%
Tax	20%
Energy, utilities and telecommunications	15%
Litigation	15%
Exchange control	5%

P

FIRM OVERVIEW: Posse, Herrera & Ruiz is a full service firm specialising in litigation and arbitration, banking, securities and capital markets, foreign investment, corporate law including corporate restructuring, reorganisation and liquidation proceedings, mergers and acquisitions, taxes and tax planning, utilities law, oil, gas and mining, telecommunications and employment law. It is committed to providing a personalised legal service to the international and Colombian business community, but is also expanding in order to meet its ever increasing client needs.

INTERNATIONAL EXPERIENCE: The firm specialises in advising multinational companies doing business in Colombia or with Colombian entities, as well as Colombian companies carrying out commercial and financial activities in the international marketplace. Currently more than 60% of the firm's turnover is derived from representing multinational companies doing business in Colombia.

INTERNATIONAL CLIENTS: The firm represents a wide variety of clients from North, Central and South America, Western Europe and Asia. Amongst the firm's international clients are American International Group, The Chase Manhattan Bank, InteGen, Diveo Broadband, Skytel, PSEG Americas, SAS Institute, Bankvision Software (US), Rail India (India), Diageo Plc (UK), Aldeasa (Spain) Lysa, Atofina, (France), Westfalia Separator (Germany), Santos (Australia), and Banmedica (Chile).

MAIN INTERNATIONAL AREAS OF PRACTICE:
General corporate: Posse, Herrera & Ruiz acts as regular outside counsel for a number of industries in Colombia including the manufacturing, construction, engineering, chemical, financial, consumer products and health industries. It advises clients on a wide range of corporate, contract and tax matters.
Employment: The firm advises on all aspects of employment law including the preparation and implementation of all necessary labour related documentation such as employment contracts, internal employment rulings, employment health programs and risk management manuals. The Firm has rendered legal advice to its clients in the implementation of employment benefit plans (including stock purchase options for executives) and its attorneys have been able to implement successful retirement plans. The Firm has also been active in the evaluation of employment risks in connection with acquisitions and privatisations.
Bankruptcy, workouts, arrangements and reorganisations: The firm represents creditors, financial advisers, and major domestic and foreign financial institutions in some of Colombia's largest rehabilitation proceedings, workouts, debt rescheduling, refinancing and bankruptcies.
M&A: The firm handles the structuring, negotiation and implementation of integration transactions and has participated in some of the largest acquisitions and privatisations in Colombia. The firm has a strong antitrust practice.
Foreign investment: The firm has experience advising foreign clients in connection with the establishment of business in Colombia, including the incorporation of subsidiaries and branches of foreign enterprises. The firm specialises in foreign investment in public utilities, particularly in the telecommunications and energy sectors.
Exchange control: Posse, Herrera & Ruiz advises on the Colombian foreign exchange control regime, in relation to foreign investment, foreign credits and debt, foreign capital market transactions, derivatives, technology transfers, and import and export operations.
Financing: Posse, Herrera & Ruiz has handled a large number of Colombia's major corporate financial transactions, acting on behalf of leading international banks and financial institutions. The firm specialises in a full range of international financing operations. It also advises on litigation related to banking transactions, public offerings, equity offerings, debt offerings, and securitisation. The firm has advised investors on the privatisation of Colombian state controlled entities.
Litigation: The firm represents a number of Colombian commercial banks, insurers, savings and loan institutions, investment banks, manufacturing, distribution and service companies in a broad range of litigation matters.
Real estate: The firm advises Colombian construction and engineering companies on all aspects of construction, development and financing of real estate projects, including contract drafting.
Tax: The firm provides a comprehensive range of tax services, including tax planning for ongoing and new projects, tax litigation and the design of specific tax structures. The firm also reviews and advises on specific issues regarding income tax returns, VAT, industry and commerce tax, stamp tax, remittance tax, and assessment of tax contingencies.
Oil and mining: The firm advises oil and mining companies on their Colombian ventures. The firm's lawyers advised the Ministry of Mines and Energy in the drafting of the recently enacted Mining Code paper and study in congress of other related statutes.
Telecommunications: The firm represents clients in the telecommunication sector in connection with a variety of related activities including the fulfilment of regulatory requirements.

LANGUAGES: English, French, German, Spanish

For other recommended firms see pages 1485-1520

PRESLMAYR & PARTNERS

HEAD OFFICE

Dr Karl Lueger-Ring 12,
A-1010 Vienna, Austria
Tel: + 43 1 533 16 95 **Fax:** + 43 1 535 56 86

Email: office@preslmayr.at
Website: www.preslmayr.at

FIRM OVERVIEW

Senior partner: Dr Karl Preslmayr
Senior partner: Dr Florian Gehmacher

Number of partners worldwide: 7
Number of other lawyers worldwide: 12

AREAS OF PRACTICE:

Banking	20%
Contract	10%
Corporate (incl corporate reorganisation)	15%
EU	10%
Insolvency	15%
M&A	15%
Anti-trust, competition	10%
Others	5%

FIRM OVERVIEW: With 19 lawyers, Preslmayr & Partners is one of the larger Austrian firms. It was founded in 1987 by Dr Karl Preslmayr and Dr Florian Gehmacher. The firm is a commercial law practice with particular expertise in M&A, project finance, due diligence, European law, advertising and intellectual property, public procurement, product liability, telecommunications, banking, corporate reorganisation and insolvency. Firm members are well-versed in economic reality and frequently cooperate with non-legal experts from other disciplines.

INTERNATIONAL EXPERIENCE: European law is one of the firm's areas of expertise, and it has been advising clients on Austria's integration into the EU from the beginning. During the early 1990s the firm advised investors establishing joint ventures and subsidiaries in the Czech Republic, Slovakia and Hungary, and is now active in many East-European jurisdictions, cooperating with leading law firms of the respective countries. The firm cooperates closely with law firms abroad, particularly in Germany, France, the UK, Scandinavia and the US.

INTERNATIONAL CLIENTS: The firm's worldwide clients are based in Europe and the US. They are primarily large to medium-sized international companies in banking, manufacturing, trade, investment, food and drugs, oil, microelectronics, software development, advertising, pharmaceuticals, tourism and institutional investing.

WORLDWIDE OFFICE CONTACTS

AUSTRIA
Dr Karl Lueger-Ring 12, A-1010 **Vienna**
Tel: + 43 1 533 16 95 **Fax:** + 43 1 535 56 86
Email: office@preslmayr.at

MAIN INTERNATIONAL AREAS OF PRACTICE:
M&A, including due diligences: The firm provides a comprehensive service covering all aspects of both national and cross-border mergers and acquisitions, public take-overs, international equity offerings and management buy-outs.
Finance, including project finance: The firm has a strong (project) finance practice advising all parties on major national and international projects. The firm acts for a wide range of banks, investment banks and corporations.
Banking: The firm has one of the leading banking practices in Austria acting for major national and international banks and financial institutions and borrowers on all types of national and international transactions.
Insolvency: The firm has a strong insolvency department acting on all aspects of domestic and international corporate insolvency and corporate reconstruction, emphasising advice on insolvency aspects of structures, finance, securitisation, security enforcements and asset realisation. The firm has acted in many major Austrian insolvency cases.
Foreign investment in Austria: The firm also publishes a guide *Investing in Austria.* For further information, visit the website at www.preslmayr.at

LANGUAGES: Chinese, English, French, German, Italian, Spanish

P

PRIETO GUTIERREZ CARRIZOSA & ASOCIADOS

HEAD OFFICE

Carrera 9 No. 74-08 Office 305, PO Box 7600,
Bogotá D.C. Colombia
Tel: +571 326 8600/3220000 **Fax:** +571 326 8610/3220010

Email: pgclaw@cable.net.co
Website: www.pgclaw.com

WORLDWIDE OFFICE CONTACTS

COLOMBIA
Carrera 9 No. 74-08 Oficina 305, PO Box 7600, **Bogotá**
Tel: +571 326 8600 **Fax:** +571 326 8610
Email: pgclaw@cable.net.co

FIRM OVERVIEW

Managing partners: Juan Manuel Prieto, Martin Carrizosa
Senior partner: Juan Manuel Prieto

Number of partners worldwide: 6
Number of other lawyers worldwide: 18

AREAS OF PRACTICE:

Corporate	20%
M&A	14%
International investments	12%
Intellectual property	10%
Privatisation and project finance	10%
Tax	7%
Banking, finance and capital markets	6%
Telecommunications and energy	5%
Anti-trust and competition	4%
Estate planning	3%
Litigation and arbitration	3%
Administrative	2%
Employment	2%
Environmental	1%
Maritime and aviation	1%

FIRM OVERVIEW: Prieto Gutierrez Carrizosa & Asociados was established in 1994 after the merger of Prieto Montoya, Estrada & Asociados and Gutierrez, Carrizosa & Asociados. The firm offers a full range of legal services including corporate, international investments, privatisation, international economic law, M&A, project finance, intellectual property, estate planning, and environmental law.

INTERNATIONAL EXPERIENCE: In recent years, Prieto, Gutierrez, Carrizosa & Asociados has been involved in several major transactions in Colombia. The firm advised on the restructuring and capitalisation of Bogotá's power supply company, worth US$2.3 million. It has been involved in some of the most important project finance ventures including the Termobarranquilla energy supply project; the Termovalle I project; and the Termopaipa IV project; and advised foreign investors during the concession scheme of the mobile telephone bidding process. The firm has advised clients in the privatisation of 14 energy distribution companies, and the structuring of the concession scheme for the administration and exploitation of the Airport of Cali. The firm has acted in more than 20 M&A transactions totaling more than US$3 billion, including the first international merger performed in Colombia.

INTERNATIONAL CLIENTS: The firm's client base includes major multinational companies and large local enterprises ranging from service providers, major manufacturers and distributors of commodities, investment banks, public entities and the main Colombian economic organisations.

MAIN INTERNATIONAL AREAS OF PRACTICE:

Banking and finance: The firm specialises in commercial banking, investment banking and financial services and also in the negotiation and preparation of contracts regarding international loans, trusts and financial leasing.

Capital markets: The firm advises on the issuance of securities in national and international markets (MTN programs, bonds, ADRs, GDRs) and the issuance and negotiation of derivative products (swaps, options and futures).

Corporate: The firm advises on all aspects of general corporate law including the drafting and execution of by-laws, the issuance of bonds and stock, the implementation of corporate transformations, mergers, spin-offs and reorganisations, and the creation and design of joint ventures. They also act on behalf of debtors and creditors in the restructuring of liabilities.

Estate planning: The firm advises on the full application and enforceability of testamentary dispositions, conflicts of law, immovable property regulations, the formal validity of marriage, the drafting of wills, and the establishment of trusts and international foundations.

Intellectual property: The firm advises through its specialised IP branch Prieto Gutierrez Carrizosa & Patiño on all aspects of intellectual property, patents, trademarks, industrial designs, utility models, litigation, unfair competition, pharmaceutical licensing and health registrations.

International investments: The firm handles a range of issues on international transactions, especially for firms in the energy sector (electricity and oil), telecommunications and international engineering firms. Work handled includes state concessions, financing of infrastructure projects, privatisation of state-owned companies, international tenders and bids, liquidation of large projects, and negotiation of concessions and reversions with the state. The firm also advises on direct and indirect foreign investment and Colombian investments abroad, including the preparation of contracts and related documents required for acquisitions.

Privatisations: The firm has advised the Colombian government on several important privatisations in the energy, telecommunications and airport industries. It has also advised private investors in bidding processes and in the subsequent international financing of projects.

Tax: The firm represents Colombian and foreign taxpayers and advises foreign investors on Colombian tax laws. They also advise national and international companies on the structuring of acquisitions, partnerships and business assets.

LANGUAGES: English, French, Spanish

 For other recommended firms see pages 1485-1520

QUEVEDO & PONCE

HEAD OFFICE

Av. 12 de Octubre y Lincoln, 16th Floor, Torre 1492, P.O. Box 17-01-600
Quito Ecuador
Tel: +593 2 986 570 **Fax:** +593 2 986 579

Email: quepon1@ecnet.ec
Website: www.quepon.com.ec

FIRM OVERVIEW

Number of partners worldwide: 18
Number of other lawyers worldwide: 0

AREAS OF PRACTICE:

Intellectual property 35%
Litigation and arbitration 22%
Corporate 18%
Contracts 8%
Oil and power 8%
Tax 5%
Insurance, reinsurance and banking 4%

FIRM OVERVIEW: Quevedo & Ponce was founded in 1940 by Dr Antonio Quevedo (1900-1987). Comprising 18 partners and 8 paralegal assistants the firm offers a full range of legal services, advising local and foreign corporations on domestic ventures, international transactions and projects. They also advise on administrative and government regulations and appear in administrative and tax courts, civil, employment and criminal courts and the Constitutional Court.

INTERNATIONAL EXERIENCE: The firm has represented clients including Procter & Gamble and Pfizer in proceedings before the Andean Community Secretariat in Lima Perú and have participated as 'foreign law experts' in proceedings in the United States. The firm has also been invited to participate in leagl strategy meetings by clients outside Ecuador.

INTERNATIONAL CLIENTS: The firm's clients include major national and multinational corporations operating in a range of industries. Many of the firm's clients are US or European companies including AGA SA, Alcon International, Cargil Incorporated, Cincinnati Milacron Marketing Co, Dow Chemical International Ltd, Eli Lilly & Co, F. Hoffman La Roche AG, Federal Mogul Corporation, Ferro Corporation, GFW Ingredients Limited, Gobal Silverhawk Inc, Herbalife, Intergel Limited, Johnson & Johnson Corp, Merck, Sharp & Dome (IA) Corp, Microsoft, Novartis PH Farma AG, Phillip Morris Management Corp, Procter & Gamble Co, The Sidney Ross Co, Visa International.

WORLDWIDE OFFICE CONTACTS

ECUADOR
Florencia Astudillo y Alfonso Cordero, Ed.Cárnara de Industriales, of. 701, **Cuenca**
Tel: +593 7 882 660 **Fax:**

Velez 220, Of.803, Ed Valco, **Guayaqui**
Tel: +593 4 523 410 **Fax:** +593 4 534 888

Av. 12 de Octubre y Lincoln, 16th Floor, Torre 1492,
P.O. Box 17-01-600, **Quito**
Tel: +593 2 986 570 **Fax:** +593 2 986 579

MAIN INTERNATIONAL AREAS OF PRACTICE:

Intellectual property: Quevedo & Ponce handles all aspects of intellectual property including litigation.
Insurance and reinsurance: Quevedo & Ponce advises on all aspects of insurance and reinsurance. The firm represents Colonial and Confianza insurance companies in Ecuador and has acted on behalf of Reinsurance Group of America Inc.
Corporate: The firm advises worldwide companies including Procter and Gamble, Pfizer, Texaco and Del Monte. It is actively involved in the incorporation of subsidiaries and registration of companies in Ecuador.
Oil and energy: The firm have advised major oil companies such as Amoco and Texaco.
Tax: The firm handles all aspects of tax law in an advisory capacity and in litigation before the Tax Court.

LANGUAGES: English, French, German, Portuguese, Spanish

For other recommended firms see pages 1485-1520

RAIDLA & PARTNERS LAW OFFICE

HEAD OFFICE

Roosikrantsi 2, 6th floor,
10119 Tallinn, Estonia
Tel: +372 640 7170 **Fax:** +372 640 7171
Email: email@raidla.ee
Website: www.raidla.ee

FIRM OVERVIEW

Managing partner: Jüri Raidla
Partners: Sven Papp, Raino Paron
Number of partners worldwide: 3
Number of other lawyers worldwide: 17

AREAS OF PRACTICE:

Banking, finance and securities	20%
Corporate	20%
M&A	20%
Other	20%
Litigation and arbitration	10%
Privatisation	10%

R

FIRM PROFILE: Raidla & Partners is a full-service law firm focusing on corporate law, banking and finance, M&A, privatisation and litigation. The firm was established in 1993 and was one of the first 'western-style' law firms established in Estonia after the country regained its independence. Raidla & Partners is one of the two largest Estonian law firms. Since its establishment, it has had an association with the French law firm Moquet, Borde & Associés. The firm is part of BBLP, a trans-continental partnership between the German law firm Beiten Burkhardt Mittl & Wegener, Italy's Pavia e Ansaldo, the Swiss firm Meyer Lustenberger and France's Moquet Borde & Associés. The firm also has good working relationships with leading law firms in the UK, the US and the Nordic countries.

INTERNATIONAL EXPERIENCE: Raidla & Partners has extensive experience advising international clients on their transactions in Estonia, as well as Estonian clients on their transactions abroad. The firm practises a policy of hiring lawyers who have been trained abroad after graduating from Estonian law school and as a result has one of the highest numbers of foreign-trained lawyers among the Estonian law firms.

INTERNATIONAL CLIENTS: International clients include large multinational corporations, banks, investment banks, investment funds and insurance companies, international organisations and development banks, foreign governments and embassies of foreign countries.

MAIN INTERNATIONAL AREAS OF PRACTICE:

Mergers and acquisitions: Transactions range from small private acquisitions to cross-border takeovers of listed companies.
Banking, finance and securities: The firm covers all areas of banking and finance, including IPOs and listings, secured and syndicated loan transactions and guarantees, structured finance, securitisations, project finance and leasing. The firm has been involved in the drafting of numerous laws and of the Rules of the Tallinn Stock Exchange. One of the partners is the Chairman of the Council of the Arbitration Court of the Tallinn Stock Exchange.
Corporate: Raidla & Partners advises domestic and foreign companies on general corporate matters including the establishment of subsidiaries and branches in Estonia. Such advice also includes contact with the relevant authorities and attention to all necessary formalities. The firm also provides a full range of corporate secretarial services including the drafting of minutes, commercial registry formalities for approval of accounts, and operations on capital.

WORLDWIDE OFFICE CONTACTS

ESTONIA
Roosikrantsi 2, 6th floor, 10119 **Tallinn**
Tel: +372 640 7170 **Fax:** +372 640 7171
Email: email@raidla.ee

ASSOCIATED OFFICES

FRANCE
BBLP Moquet, Borde & Associés, 30, Avenue de messine, 75008 **Paris**
Tel: +33 1 42 99 04 50 **Fax:** +33 1 45 6 3 91 49
Email: moquet_borde_paris@compuserve.com

GERMANY
BBLP Beiten Burkhardt Mittl & Wegener, Leopoldstrasse 236, 80807 **Munich**
Tel: +49 89 3 506500 **Fax:** +49 89 3 5065123
Email: bbmw.muenchen@bbmw.de

ITALY
BBLP Pavia e Ansaldo, Via dell'annunciata 7, 20121 **Milan**
Tel: +39 02 63381 **Fax:** +39 02 6554 055/ 65 70203
Email: pa_lawfirm@pavia-ansaldo.it

SWITZERLAND
BBLP Meyer Lustenberger, Forchstrasse 452, Postfach 832, 8029 **Zurich**
Tel: +41 1 396 9191 **Fax:** +41 1 396 9192
Email: mlp@bluewin.ch

Litigation and arbitration: Raidla & Partners has handled the most complex legal disputes before Estonian courts including the Estonian Supreme Court, and arbitration tribunals in Estonia and abroad.The firm act as representatives and arbitrators in various commercial disputes.
Privatisation: The firm's transactions in this area range from small privatisations to some of the largest Estonian privatisation deals. For example, in 1999 the firm advised on the privatisation, restructuring and IPO of AS Eesti Telekom, the Estonian telecommunications company.
Competition law: The firm's lawyers advise clients in competition and marketing-related cases involving companies in the Estonian market.
Telecommunications: The firm has acquired prominence in this area with the deregulation of the Estonian telecommunications market to be implemented in 2001. The firm has played an active role in this sector being one of the authors of the recent law on telecommunications.
Energy and public utilities: Raidla & Partners plays an active role in the public utilities sector where a number of service providers have recently been privatised. The firm is actively involved in the preparation for the restructuring and privatisation of the Estonian energy sector.
Intellectual property: The firm advises on issues related to intellectual property. In 2000, the firm advised the Estonian Central Bank in their acquisition of software for the Estonian inter-bank payment system.
E-commerce: Raidla & Partners often advises on legal issues related to e-commerce and IT matters. The firm was selected as the legal advisor to the first Estonian venture capital fund for investment in companies engaged in e-commerce.
Medical law: Raidla & Partners has gained a reputation as an expert in government entitlement programmes and medical law. The firm served as an advisor for the restructuring of the Estonian Social Security System and is currently participating in the government led project for the introduction of the Estonian gene database.
Employment: The firm handles all matters relating to Estonian employment law.

LANGUAGES: English, Estonian, German, Russian

For other recommended firms see pages 1485-1520

RAJAB BAKHNUG ATTORNEY AT LAW

HEAD OFFICE

Flat 5, Haddad Building, Omer Moktar Street, PO Box 646
Tripoli Libya
Tel: +218 21 444 0886 **Fax:** +218 21 444 1597

FIRM OVERVIEW

Managing partner: Rajab Bakhnug
Senior partner: Rajab Bakhnug

Number of partners worldwide: 4

AREAS OF PRACTICE:

Corporate	50%
Litigation and arbitration	30%
Other	20%

FIRM OVERVIEW: The firm was established in 1988. It has no formal alliances but prefers to maintain contacts with a number of firms worldwide. The firm specialises in contract and business law but also offers comprehensive legal advice to clients with international business interests.

INTERNATIONAL EXPERIENCE: Since 1988 the firm has acted for South Korean, Japanese and British companies operating in Libya. It has also advised on several major construction projects.

INTERNATIONAL CLIENTS: The majority of the firm's clients are large international companies in the construction, trading, communication, insurance and oil industries.

MAIN INTERNATIONAL AREAS OF PRACTICE:
Construction, communications and energy: The firm advises a range of clients from large multinationals to local enterprises. It advises foreign contractors currently involved in development and infrastructure projects in Libya in the areas of construction, oil and industry. The firm also acts for European companies in the oil industry.

General corporate: The firm advises on all aspects of general corporate law including the drafting of Libyan and international contracts.
Employment: The firm handles all matters relating to Libyan employment laws.
Litigation: The firm deals with employment and commercial litigation and national and international arbitration. The firm frequently advises in cases before the Libyan courts including the Supreme Court.

LANGUAGES: Arabic, English

WORLDWIDE OFFICE CONTACTS

LIBYA
Flat 5, Haddad Building, Omer Moktar Street, PO Box 646, **Tripoli**
Tel: +218 21 444 0886 **Fax:** +218 21 444 1597
Email:

RAJAH & TANN

A MEMBER OF ANDERSEN LEGAL

HEAD OFFICE

4 Battery Road, # 26-01 Bank of China Building,
Singapore 049908, Singapore
Tel: +65 535 3600 **Fax:** +65 538 8598

Email: legal@sg.rajahtann.com
Webite: www.rajahtann.com

FIRM OVERVIEW

Managing partner: V K Rajah

Number of partners worldwide: 47
Number of other lawyers worldwide: 106

AREAS OF PRACTICE:

Admiralty and shipping	22%
Banking	17%
Business restructuring and insolvency	11%
Projects and infrastructure	11%
Corporate and capital markets	10%
Dispute resolution, commercial litigation and arbitration	9%
IT	8%
Property	5%
China practice	1%

FIRM OVERVIEW: Established in 1953, Rajah & Tann is now the second largest law firm in Singapore with over 150 lawyers, two of which are Senior Counsels. In 1998, the firm joined the Andersen Worldwide International network of law firms (spanning 34 countries), and most recently entered into a strategic alliance with a leading international law firm, headquartered in New York, Weil Gotshal & Manges. The firm advises in all areas, including admiralty and maritime law, litigation, insolvency, banking and finance, projects and infrastructure, corporate, capital markets, finance and securities. The firm's practice extends beyond the shores of Singapore, with its lawyers being involved in a number of regional and international transactions.

INTERNATIONAL EXPERIENCE: The firm advises international companies in Singapore particularly in the corporate, construction, technology and shipping sectors as well as Singapore companies expanding internationally. Notable work includes advising government inspectors after the collapse of Barings and subsequently advising the judicial managers in the liquidation process. The firm continues to be active in most of Singapore's significant corporate insolvencies, including the liquidation of Amcol Holdings. The firm's projects and finance practice group has been involved in numerous major projects in various Asian countries including Thailand, Nepal, Malaysia, Vietnam, Hong Kong, Taiwan and Sri Lanka. The firm's Corporate and Regional Desks Practice Groups are frequently involved in cross-border joint ventures, investments and other international transactions.

INTERNATIONAL CLIENTS: These include large corporations, banks, insurance companies, construction and shipping companies, public institutions and government-linked corporations.

MAIN INTERNATIONAL AREAS OF PRACTICE:

Admiralty and shipping: The practice, one of Singapore's largest, includes a naval reserve officer, a former marine engineer, an in-house master mariner and a former academic who has written the only book on admiralty law and practice in Singapore. It handles collisions, explosions, fires, shipbuilding and ship repair disputes, marine insurance, cargo claims, towage disputes, bunker disputes, ship financing and other related issues.
Banking and financial services: Work includes dispute resolution, debt restructuring and recovery, corporate banking and finance, securitisation, project finance, compliance and documentation services. The practice group includes an Emeritus Professor.
Business restructuring and insolvency: The team has expertise in corporate rescue, business restructuring, debt restructuring, judicial management, investigation of inquiries, winding-up and receivership. Clients include financial institutions, banks, judicial managers and liquidators of publicly-listed companies.
China practice: This is a full-service team advising on investments in and out of the PRC, the acquisition of PRC industrial and infrastructure assets, banking and finance, corporate restructuring, dispute resolution relating to PRC matters, and the listing of PRC companies in Singapore. All of the group's lawyers are able to read, write, draft and negotiate in Chinese.
Projects and infrastructure: One of Singapore's largest construction practices, the team handles contract negotiation and drafting, claims, project financing, administration and dispute resolution for projects including hospitals, airports, power projects, offices, commercial developments, roads, quarries, ports and terminals both in Singapore and elsewhere in Asia.
Corporate and capital markets: The firm provides a full range of corporate services, with work including M&A, joint ventures, investments and cross-border transactions, as well as all aspects of corporate finance work.
Dispute resolution, commercial litigation and arbitration: The firm provides a wide range of expertise in corporate and commercial litigation, including matters relating to stockbroking. The group also undertakes both local and international arbitration, mediations and appeals to statutory or regulatory authorities.
Derivatives: The Derivatives Practice Group provides advice and a full range of services relating to banking, securities and derivative transactions including treasury and risk management transactions, and evolving derivative products from vanilla swaps to complex credit derivations and financial overlay products. The group regularly provides advice to financial institutions and corporate clients on product structuring, licensing applications, counter-party capacities and cross-border product documentation in banking, securities and derivative transactions.
Information technology: Work includes advising and structuring all forms of e-business models. The team also undertakes litigation and advises on the nascent Singapore laws governing the Internet, including Internet defamation, Internet mailbombing and electronic commerce. The team is also substantially involved in regular intellectual property and telecommunications matters.
Property: Work covers the whole spectrum of property law, including conveyancing services and development work.
Other areas of practice: Additional work handled includes enviromental law, administrative law, family, personal injury, tax, estates and wills.

LANGUAGES: Chinese (Cantonese, Hokkien, Mandarin, Teochew), English, French, German, Hebrew, Hindi, Japanese, Malay, Tamil

WORLDWIDE OFFICE CONTACTS

SINGAPORE
4 Battery Road, # 26-01 Bank of China Building, 049908, **Singapore**
Tel: +65 535 3600 **Fax:** +65 538 8598
Email: legal@sg.rajahtann.com

R

For other recommended firms see pages 1485-1520

RAMBAUD MARTEL

HEAD OFFICE

25 Boulevard de L'Amiral Bruix,
75782 Paris Cedex 16, France
Tel: +33 1 40 67 17 00 **Fax:** +33 1 40 67 28 80

Email: rm@rambaud-martel.com
Website: www.rambaud-martel.com

FIRM OVERVIEW

Senior partner: J-P Martel
Managing partner: J-M Lepretre
Partner in charge of communication: Delphine Deschamps

Number of partners worldwide: 28
Number of other lawyers worldwide: 50

AREAS OF PRACTICE:

Banking and finance	*%
Commercial litigation and arbitrartion	*%
Corporate/company/securities	*%
Employment	*%
Environmental/regulatory	*%
EU and competition	*%
Industrial and commercial contracts	*%
Intellectual property	*%
M&A/public offerings	*%
Media and advertising	*%
Product and industrial liability	*%
Property and construction	*%
Public law	*%
Sports and entertainment	*%
White collar crime	*%

*Workload % not disclosed

FIRM PROFILE: Rambaud Martel has developed a strong reputation and identity since it was founded in 1925. The firm's services are of the highest quality and combine adherence to strict professional rules with the most modern legal practices. The firm is considered by some to be the best possible match of a highly competent litigation practice and a high quality and vast advisory practice. This multifaceted law firm advises a broad range of clients and foreign law firms on a large number of business areas including industrial and service orientated companies, banking and financial institutions as well as multinational and small to medium sized businesses. Rambaud Martel's lawyers collaborate in flexible and highly responsive teams and are drawn from different areas of practice. The firm consists of 28 partners and 50 associates, with a total staff of over 130. The firm's business is equally balanced between litigation or dispute resolution and non contentious advice. Most partners have acquired wide experience in general legal work before developing their specific areas of expertise. All lawyers work in a close relationship with clients and their technical skills and knowledge of the client's activities and business allow them to provide sharply focused advice.

INTERNATIONAL EXPERIENCE: Most of Rambaud Martel's clients are international and multinational corporations. The firm advises on a large number of cross-border and multi-jurisdictional corporate transactions and has an active international and arbitration practice. It remains, however, independent from law firm network organisations, which would require the firm to work with designated firms or offices outside France.

WORLDWIDE OFFICE CONTACTS

FRANCE
25 Boulevard de L'Amiral Bruix, 75782 **Paris** Cedex 16
Tel: +33 1 40 67 17 00 **Fax:** +33 1 40 67 28 80
Email: rm@rambaud-martel.com

INTERNATIONAL CLIENTS: Clients include multinational corporations and international private companies in various areas of business which include banking and finance; major industrial areas and distribution indistries in the EU; real estate development and construction; local and national government agencies; heavy industry; computer and software; telecommunications; technology; medical and chemical companies and airline companies.

MAIN INTERNATIONAL AREAS OF PRACTICE:

Litigation and arbitration: The firm is an instrumental player in corporate and commercial litigation in both the national and international arenas. It handles matters concerning major corporate litigation with an emphasis on stock exchange related matters and international investment disputes.

Corporate: The firm counsels on restructuring groups, shareholders' agreements, joint ventures and strategic alliances in addition to leveraged and management buy-outs for public and private companies.

M&A: The firm is involved in transactions ranging from small private acquisitions to complex cross-border acquisitions and take-overs. It has specialised skills in public company acquisitions, stock exchange regulations, securities and capital markets.

Property and construction: The firm advises on cases involving construction and real estate property for multinationals.

EU and competition: The firm provides counsel and litigation on merger and anti-trust regulations and handle appeals to the European Commission in the interests of its international clients.

Product and industrial liability: The firm advises foreign and domestic companies on matters involving product and industrial liability, and has specialised skills in asbestos litigation.

Employment: The firm advises multinationals concerning French European labour litigation.

Sports and entertainment: Clients include international sports promoters and sponsors. The firm advises the Defi Français competitor regarding all the juridical aspects of its 2002-2003 America's Cup participation.

LANGUAGES: English, German, Spanish

RAMBAUD MARTEL

SOCIÉTÉ D'AVOCATS À LA COUR DE PARIS

For other recommended firms see pages 1485-1520

RAMÓN & CAJAL ABOGADOS

HEAD OFFICE

Velázquez 20, 1a,
28001 Madrid, Spain
Tel: +34 91 576 1900 **Fax:** +34 91 575 8678

Email: ramoncajal@ramoncajal.com

WORLDWIDE OFFICE CONTACTS

SPAIN
Velázquez 20, 1a, 28001 **Madrid**
Tel: +34 91 576 1900 **Fax:** +34 91 575 8678
Email: ramoncajal@ramoncajal.com

FIRM OVERVIEW

Senior partners: Sebastian Albella, Francisco Palá, José Manuel Villar, Pedro Ramón y Cajal

Number of partners worldwide: 13
Number of other lawyers worldwide: 24

AREAS OF PRACTICE:

Area	%
Finance and securities	30%
Litigation	22%
Telecommunications and IT	18%
Commercial	15%
Tax	7%
Project finance	5%
Property	2%

R

FIRM OVERVIEW: Ramón & Cajal was established in 1994 as a result of the merger between two firms, one headed by Pedro Ramón y Cajal and Rafael Mateu de Ros and the other headed by Sebastian Albella. Comprising 13 partners and 24 associates, it specialises in finance and securities markets, litigation, and general commercial work. In recent years the firm has handled an increasing volume of corporate finance, administrative, telecommunications, IT and competition related work.

INTERNATIONAL EXPERIENCE: In the last two years the firm has advised 15 of the 35 companies involved in the IBEX-35 (the Spanish securities market index). During 2000, the firm handled important capital market transactions, including various takeover bids, global offerings of shares and the merger of two major Spanish companies.

INTERNATIONAL CLIENTS: The firm's client base includes major Spanish companies, international corporations, banks, investment firms, fund managers, and major Spanish non-financial companies.

MAIN INTERNATIONAL AREAS OF PRACTICE:
Finance and securities: Ramón & Cajal advises on take-over bids, Eurobond issues and preference share issues. It also advises on Comisión Nacional del Mercado de Valores (Spanish securities and exchange commission) regulations and handles work relating to the authorisation, creation and establishment of finance companies and investment funds. The firm acts on behalf of banks (including one international bank), saving banks, investment services companies, mutual fund managers, management corporations of pension funds and venture capital companies, and insurance companies.
Corporate and commercial: The firm advises on general corporate and commercial law, mergers and acquisitions, contracts, intellectual and industrial property, and competition.
Litigation: Ramón & Cajal specialises in all aspects of litigation including quantity claims, claims against insurance companies, social agreement contestations, unfair competition trials, disputes related to audio-visual rights, criminal trials (in particular economic crimes), administrative and administrative appeals, civil law, and insolvency proceedings.
Telecommunications and IT: Ramón & Cajal's telecommunications and IT practice has expanded significantly in recent years. It advises on telecommunication law, e-commerce and Internet related matters.
Project finance: The firm advises on the financing of alternative energy, renewable energy, transportation, and telecommunications projects.
Property: The firm advises major companies on property transactions and town planning.
Tax: The firm specialises in income tax, corporate tax, and financial transactions.

LANGUAGES: English, French, German, Italian, Spanish

 For other recommended firms see pages 1485-1520

RAPHAËL & ASSOCIÉS FORMERLY RAPHAËL ZIADÉ ABIRACHED RIFAAT ET ASSOCIÉS

HEAD OFFICE

Almabani-Murr Tower, Dbayeh, PO Box 70-868 Antelias
Beirut Lebanon
Tel: +961 440 5401 **Fax:** +961 440 3735
Email: rzar@intracom.net.lb

WORLDWIDE OFFICE CONTACTS

LEBANON
Almabani-Murr Tower, Dbayeh, PO Box 70-868 Antelias, **Beirut**
Tel: +961 440 5401 **Fax:** +961 440 3735
Email: rzar@intracom.net.lb

ASSOCIATED OFFICES

FRANCE
HSD Ernst & Young, Tour Ernst & Young, Faubourg de L'Arche, 92037 **Paris** La Defense Cedex
Tel: +33 1 46 93 70 00 **Fax:** +33 1 58 47 48 00

SAUDI ARABIA
Hussein Shoucry Law Office, PO Box 2781, **Jeddah** 21461
Tel: +9662 651 3412 **Fax:** +9662 651 3412

FIRM OVERVIEW

Managing partner: Moussa Raphaël

Number of partners worldwide: 6
Number of other lawyers worldwide: 16

AREAS OF PRACTICE:

Banking and finance .... *%
Commercial and contract/international transactions .... *%
Corporate .... *%
Insurance .... *%
Intellectual property .... *%
Litigation and arbitration .... *%
M&A .... *%
Security and financial markets .... *%
Telecommunications and computer law .... *%
* Workload % not disclosed

FIRM OVERVIEW: Raphaël & Associés is one of the leading law firms in Lebanon. The firm is affiliated with Ernst & Young Law Practice and has a permanent office in Saudi Arabia. In addition it has co-operation agreements with law firms in other Arab countries. Raphaël & Associés consists of 22 lawyers, each with different academic and professional backgrounds.

INTERNATIONAL EXPERIENCE: Raphaël & Associés offers legal services in international business, corporate and banking transactions as well as litigation and arbitration. Matters previously handled by the firm include corporate organisation, issuance of financial instruments, drafting and negotiation of international contracts, construction set-ups, distribution, franchising and agency contracts, joint-venture contracts, project finance, insurance and restructuring of public entities.

INTERNATIONAL CLIENTS: Raphaël & Associés offers legal services to major Lebanese corporations or financial institutions involved in international transactions as well as to European, U.S or Asian entities doing business in the Arab world. Raphaël & Associés' client base includes banks, financial institutions, insurance companies, multinational construction companies, information technology start-ups, telecommunication companies and more generally, foreign and domestic clients conducting cross-border transactions and joint venture arrangements.

MAIN INTERNATIONAL AREAS OF PRACTICE:

Banking and finance: The firm covers all areas of banking and finance, including representing banks in their issuance of financial instruments.
Commercial and contract/international transactions: Raphaël & Associés' lawyers are specialised in the drafting and negotiation of commercial agreements on behalf of important international entities in the fields of distributorship, licensing, sale and purchase of aircraft and boats, joint ventures and other types of co-operation agreements (numerous areas including large construction projects, cellular telephone operation, cement companies and the tourism and leisure industry).
Corporate: The firm advises foreign companies with respect to their presence in Lebanon and the Middle East. The firm also advises companies on day-to-day business issues including corporate record keeping (preparation of minutes of annual board of directors' and shareholders' meetings) and employment issues (drafting employment agreements).
Insurance: The firm advises clients on Lebanese law pertaining to insurance and reinsurance. It represents one of the largest insurance companies before Lebanese Courts.
Intellectual property: Working with clients ranging from large multinationals to local enterprises, the firm has extensive experience in all matters related to trademarks, patents and copyrights. The firm's lawyers participate in the negotiation of license agreements and advise on infringement disputes and other aspects of IP law.
Litigation and arbitration: The firm has a broad-based litigation practice, representing both plaintiffs and defendants in litigation before trial court, court of appeal, the Supreme Court as well as the administrative court (Conseil d'Etat). In addition the firm has vast experience in alternative dispute resolution, international and domestic arbitration as well as mediation.
M&A: The firm has offered advice on due diligence with respect to Initial Public Offerings (IPO's) and company acquisitions. Raphaël & Associés also assists clients in post merger restructuring.
Telecommunications and IT law: The firm represents a Middle Eastern telecommunications operator in all aspects of its development, including bid for tender, negotiation of BOT contracts, creation of local operating companies and negotiation of telecommunications licenses. The firm also represents information technology start-up ventures in all aspects of their development including system purchase agreements, licensing and distribution.
Security and financial markets: The firm assists Lebanese and European banks and corporations in their issuance of financial instruments (funds, securities and derivatives). The firm also provides legal assistance to financial advisors, financial intermediaries and other providers of financial services.

LANGUAGES: Arabic, English, French, Greek, Italian, Portuguese,Spanish

For other recommended firms see pages 1483-1520

RASHID & LEE

HEAD OFFICE

Level 12, Menara Milenium, 8 Jalan Damalela, Damansara Heights
50490 Kuala Lumpur, Malaysia
Tel: +60 3 2710 5555 **Fax:** +60 3 2710 3104

Email: rnl@rashidnlee.com.my

WORLDWIDE OFFICE CONTACTS

MALAYSIA
Level 12, Menara Milenium, 8 Jalan Damalela, Damansara Heights, 50490
Kuala Lumpur
Tel: +60 3 2710 5555 **Fax:** +60 3 2710 3104
Email: rnl@rashidnlee.com.my

1st Floor, Wisma SP Setia, No. 1 Jalan Indah 15/1, Bukit India, 81200
Johor Bahru
Tel: +60 7 241 2084 **Fax:** +60 7 241 4089
Email: rljblaw@tm.net.my

FIRM OVERVIEW

Senior partners: Abdul Rashid Abdul Manaff, Peter Lee Siew Choong

Number of partners worldwide: 13
Number of other lawyers worldwide: 31

AREAS OF PRACTICE:
Banking and corporate banking ....*%
Capital markets and securities ....*%
Commercial litigation ....*%
Corporate and commercial ....*%
Corporate finance ....*%
Due diligence ....*%
Energy ....*%
M&A ....*%
Privatisation and projects ....*%
Technology and intellectual property ....*%
Telecommunications and infrastructure ....*%
Workload % not disclosed

FIRM OVERVIEW: The firm was established in 1964 and assumed its present name in 1984. It offers a wide spectrum of services with an experienced team of lawyers. The firm represents international and domestic clients in a range of corporate and commercial transactions, intellectual property, litigation and other areas of law.

INTERNATIONAL EXPERIENCE: The firm has acted on oil and gas projects in Uzbekistan, highway projects in India, hotels and infrastructure projects in South Africa and advisory work relating to investments in the US, UK, Philippines, Myanmar, Cambodia, China, Australia and New Zealand.

INTERNATIONAL CLIENTS: The firm's clients include large financial institutions, Malaysian multinationals and foreign companies.

MAIN INTERNATIONAL AREAS OF PRACTICE:
Corporate and commercial: The firm has advised clients on all aspects of corporate and commercial law including investments, projects and privatisations, initial public offerings and restructurings. The firm has expertise in telecommunications, oil and gas, power, infrastructure, manufacturing, industrial and residential property development, tax and regulatory and public policy issues.
M&A: The firm has acted in numerous M&A transactions, the latest involving the merger of Malaysia's largest bank. The firm has expertise in acquisition and has worked closely with various merchant banks.
Capital markets: Rashid & Lee handles all forms of securities issues and has advised extensively on the issue of all types of private debt securities including bonds, notes, loan certificates and various commercial papers. The firm was involved in establishing the Kuala Lumpur Options & Financial Futures Exchange (KLOFFE).
Intellectual property: The firm has developed a large domestic and regional trademark, patent and design registration practice. The firm comprises registered patent, industrial designs and trademark agents and is licensed to directly initiate and prosecute applications for registration in respect of trade marks, designs and patents.

LANGUAGES: Bahasa Malaysia, Chinese (various dialects), English, Tamil

For other recommended firms see pages 1485-1520

RASLAN LOONG

HEAD OFFICE

SERLAH level 3A, Menara John Hancock, 6 Jalan Gelenggang, 50490,
Kuala Lumpur, Malaysia
Tel: +60 3 253 3939 **Fax:** +60 3 253 4848

Email: rloong@po.jaring.my

WORLDWIDE OFFICE CONTACTS

MALAYSIA
SERLAH level 3A, Menara John Hancock, 6 Jalan Gelenggang, 50490,
Kuala Lumpur, Malaysia
Tel: +60 3 253 3939 **Fax**: +60 3 253 4848
Email: rloong@po.jaring.my

SOUTH AFRICA
2nd Floor, 38 Church Square, **Pretoria** 0001
Tel: +27 12 323 0500 **Fax:** +27 12 323 0746
Email: geldenhuys@vanzylrh.co.za

FIRM OVERVIEW

Senior partners: Loong Caesar and Karim Raslan

Number of partners worldwide: 5
Number of other lawyers worldwide: 23

AREAS OF PRACTICE:

Banking and corporate banking .... *%
Capital markets and securities .... *%
Commercial litigation .... *%
Corporate and commercial .... *%
Corporate finance .... *%
Due diligence .... *%
M&A .... *%
Power and electricity .... *%
Privatisation and projects .... *%
Technology and intellectual property .... *%
Telecommunications .... *%
*Workload % not disclosed

FIRM OVERVIEW: The firm was set up by senior corporate and finance lawyers, as a niche corporate pratice to provide legal services with an international outlook. Since then it has become one of the fastest growing law firms in the country with a cross-disciplinary professional team of lawyers, financial advisers, accountants and taxation experts.

INTERNATIONAL EXPERIENCE: The firm has advised and continues to advise on major cross-border and international transactions primarily in the capital markets and cross-border investments. The firm has acted for Malaysian multinationals as well as foreign companies in connection with the offering of Malaysian securities overseas. The firm maintains an office in South Africa, where it has been the principal legal adviser to Malaysian investors in that country.

INTERNATIONAL CLIENTS: Large financial institutions, Malaysian multinationals and foreign companies including, AGFA, Andersen Consulting, Citibank, CSFB, Ernst & Young, Euromoney, IKEA, Jardine Fleming, London Forfaiting, McKinsey & Co, Nomura Advisory Services, OCBC, PWC, Salomon Smith Barney and Sun Microsystems.

MAIN INTERNATIONAL AREAS OF PRACTICE:
Corporate and commercial: The firm has issued numerous confirmatory opinions for foreign companies investing in Malaysia or who have entered into agreements with Malaysian parties overseas.
M&A: Malaysian companies investing directly overseas have used the firm. The firm also conducts due diligence exercises for Malaysian companies overseas.
Capital markets and securities: This is the principal area of involvement by the firm in international legal practice, which entails advising Malaysian as well and foreign clients on securities offered by Malaysian companies in the international capital markets.
Joint ventures: The firm has established a number of foreign joint ventures between Malaysians and foreign companies, primarily in South Africa, the Philippines, Thailand and Indochina.

LANGUAGES: Afrikaans, Arabic, Bahasa Malaysia, Chinese (including dialects), English, Mandarin

R

RICHARDS BUTLER

HEAD OFFICE

Beaufort House, 15 St. Botolph Street,
London EC3A 7EE, United Kingdom
Tel: +44 20 7247 6555 **Fax:** +44 20 7247 5091
Email: law@richardsbutler.com
Website: www.richardsbutler.com

FIRM OVERVIEW

Chief Executive: Roger Parker
Chairman: Andrew Taylor
Number of partners worldwide: 105
Number of other lawyers worldwide: 264

AREAS OF PRACTICE:

Corporate, commercial, banking and finance 31%
Shipping, commodities and insurance 29%
Dispute management and commercial litigation 24%
Property (commercial) 16%

R

FIRM OVERVIEW: The firm was founded in 1920, specialising in marine law. Since then it has established overseas offices worldwide and has one of the largest international presences in the Asia Pacific region, as well as significant presence in the Middle East.

INTERNATIONAL EXPERIENCE: The majority of the firm's work has an international dimension. The firm acts for clients who are frequently involved in either cross-border transactions or disputes.

INTERNATIONAL CLIENTS: The firm's international clients operate in sectors such as banking and financial institutions; shipping; insurance; commodities; energy; media; entertainment and leisure; IT and telecommunications; property. The firm's clientele includes many inter-national merchant and investment banks, as well as many of the major corporations in each region.

MAIN INTERNATIONAL AREAS OF PRACTICE:

Corporate, commercial, banking and finance: The firm advises clients on domestic and cross-border mergers, acquisitions and disposals, corporate restructurings, joint ventures, licensing and inward investment; EU and competition law; intellectual property and information technology; insurance company regulatory requirements; international tax issues; all aspects of international finance and banking including syndicated lending, international capital markets, IPOs, export credit finance, investment and securities transactions; financial services and other regulatory requirements; fraud and money laundering deterrence; project finance including asset-based financing and cross-border leasing and aviation finance, e-commerce and electronic markets; media and entertainment law, both regulatory and transactional; film financing; anti-piracy and copyright protection; corporate recovery and insolvency including cross-border matters; employment and industrial relations; pensions and unit trust issues and advice on contracts in all areas of energy law.

Commercial dispute management: Advising on all matters of dispute resolution, including litigation at all Court levels. With litigation practices in the UK, France and Hong Kong, the firm has experience in all the major litigation areas.

Shipping, commodities and insurance: The firm advises on all aspects of international shipping, including: charterparty disputes; bill of lading claims; ship sale and purchase; the drafting of shipbuilding contracts and disputes concerning them; marine insurance and reinsurance; drafting and litigation concerning mutual insurance (such as P&I and Defence Clubs); salvage, collision and major casualties (the firm has a 24-hour casualty response line); all aspects of ship finance, acting both for banks and borrowers; trade and commodities, including the buying and selling of hard and soft commodities and trade finance.

WORLDWIDE OFFICE CONTACTS

BELGIUM
Avenue Louise 149, Bte 40, 1050 **Brussels**
Tel: + 32 2 535 7474 **Fax:** + 32 2 535 7475
Email: law@richardsbutler.com

BRAZIL
Advocacia Rodrigues Do Amaral (affiliated with Richards Butler), Faria Lima Business Centre, Av. Brigadeiro Faria Lima1309, 10° andar, CEP 01452-000 **São Paulo**
Tel: + 55 11 3039 7070 **Fax:** + 55 11 3039 7100
Email: aamaral@ibm.net

CHINA
Room 703B, Hua Pu International Plaza, 19 Chao Wai Avenue, Chao Yang District, **Beijing** 100020
Tel: + 86 10 6599 2690 **Fax:** + 86 10 6599 2701
Email: rb@ht.rol.cn.net

FRANCE
19 Avenue George V, 75008 **Paris**
Tel: + 33 1 53 57 30 30 **Fax:** + 33 1 47 20 49 89
Email: lawfr@richardsbutler.com

GREECE
Richards Butler Consultants OE, 17-19 Akti Miaouli, 185 35 **Piraeus**
Tel: + 301 41 19 490 **Fax:** + 301 41 19 497
Email: lawgr@richardsbutler.com

HONG KONG
20th Floor, Alexandra House, 16-20 Chater Road, Central, **Hong Kong**
Tel: + 852 2810 8008 **Fax:** + 852 2810 0664
Email: law@richards.butler.com.hk

POLAND
Richards Butler Sp. z.o.o., Nowy Swiat 53, 00-042 **Warsaw**
Tel: + 48 22 828 2277 **Fax:** + 48 22 828 2278
Email: lawpl@richardsbutler.com

UNITED ARAB EMIRATES
Al Sayegh Richards Butler, PO Box 46904, Falcon Tower, Al Nasr Street, **Abu Dhabi**
Tel: + 971 2 313 010 **Fax:** + 971 2 312 155
Email: abu-dhabi@richardsbutler.com

UNITED KINGDOM
Beaufort House, 15 St. Botolph Street, **London** EC3A 7EE
Tel: +44 20 7247 6555 **Fax:** +44 20 7247 5091
Email: law@richardsbutler.com

ASSOCIATED OFFICES

OMAN
Said Al-Shahry Law Office in association with Richards Butler, PO Box 1288, 112 Ruwi, **Muscat**
Tel: + 968 790 577 **Fax:** + 968 701 700
Email: legal1@omantel.net.om

QATAR
Law Offices of Dr. Najeeb bin Mohammed Al-Nauimi in association with Richards Butler, Gridco Building, C Ring Road, PO Box 9952, **Doha**
Tel: + 974 4311 124 **Fax:** + 974 4310 314
Email: nmrblaw@qatar.net.qa

 For other recommended firms see pages 1485-1520

RITCH, HEATHER Y MUELLER, S.C.

HEAD OFFICE

Amberes 5, P.H, Col. Juarez,
06600 Mexico City, Mexico
Tel: +52 5 207 6533 **Fax:** +52 5 207 5569

Email: rhm@rhm.com.mx

WORLDWIDE OFFICE CONTACTS

MEXICO
Amberes 5, P.H, Col. Juarez, 06600 **Mexico City**
Tel: +52 5 207 6533 **Fax:** +52 5 207 5569
Email: rhm@rhm.com.mx

FIRM OVERVIEW

Managing partner: Luis Nicolau
Senior partner: James E. Ritch, Jr.

Number of partners worldwide: 9
Number of other lawyers worldwide: 25

AREAS OF PRACTICE:

Banking and finance	40%
Privatisations, M&A and project finance	37%
Aircraft finance	10%
Telecommunications	8%
Dispute resolution	5%

FIRM OVERVIEW: Ritch, Heather y Mueller, S.C. was established in 1975 in Mexico City. It concentrates on providing legal advice and transaction support to international clients doing business in Mexico.

INTERNATIONAL EXPERIENCE: Ritch, Heather y Mueller, S.C. has advised clients in some of the most important acquisition and finance transactions in Mexico.

INTERNATIONAL CLIENTS: The firm's client base includes foreign financial institutions and international consortia specialising in infrastructure such as electricity and gas projects.

MAIN INTERNATIONAL AREAS OF PRACTICE:
Privatisations, M&A: The firm has advised on the privatisations of major Mexican public sector companies in areas including tourism, airlines, manufacturing, mining, banking, insurance, retirement fund management, bonded warehouses, airports and ports acting as legal adviser to bidders, purchasers and entities financing such acquisitions. It has also advised private sector companies on acquisitions, mergers and corporate restructuring and has handled M&A transactions in Mexico's financial sector.
Finance and banking. The firm advises commercial and investment banks, insurance companies and other financial institutions operating in Mexico. It advises on secured and unsecured credit facilities, leveraged leases in respect of ships and drilling platforms, synthetic leases, securitisations and other financing transactions.
Telecommunications: The firm has represented companies that hold concessions or permits for local, long-distance telephone and wireless telephone networks. It has also represented lenders, underwriters and minority partners of the Mexican companies involved. The firm has acted in the negotiation and execution of satellite launch service agreements and other complex agreements relating to telecommunications.
Foreign investment and corporate law: The firm has advised on a wide range of transactions involving corporate, commercial and foreign investment law. It has extensive experience in the formation and operation of corporations and other legal entities, joint venture agreements, distributorships, engineering and construction contracts and government contracts. The firm has participated in the structuring and operation of resort projects.
Securities: The firm has an extensive securities law practice and has represented a wide range of underwriters and Mexican issuers in respect of public and private equity and debt offerings. This practice has included simultaneous debt and equity offerings in the international and Mexican markets. The firm has also been involved in the development of innovative debt and equity instruments including convertible debentures and securitisation transactions. It has expertise in the Mexican legal issues that arise in connection with financial derivatives and has served as local counsel in the launching and operation of several registered and private debt and equity investment funds.
Project finance: The firm has acted in the structuring and financing of Mexico's principal toll-road projects, water-treatment plants, electricity generation and gas projects.
Aircraft finance: The firm has the leading Mexican practice in aircraft finance, representing foreign lessors and secured lenders.
Dispute resolution: Members of the firm have acted as panel members in international arbitrations and have acted as mediators in investor disputes. The firm acted successfully in the largest arbitration case involving a Mexican entity to date.
Anti-trust: The firm handles matters relating to the Federal Law of Economic Competition and has participated in multi-national transactions coordinating anti-trust matters.
NAFTA: The firm advised the Mexican private sector advisory board (COECE) during the negotiations of the North American Free Trade Agreement (Financial Services Chapter) and has advised clients on the formation of financial groups and financial services subsidiaries, including commercial banks, broker-dealers and insurance companies.
Tax: The firm advises on international transactions and acts for non-residents with dealings in Mexico.

LANGUAGES: English, French, German, Spanish

RIZVI, ISA & CO

HEAD OFFICE

517-519, Clifton Centre, DC-1, Block 5, Clifton,
Karachi 75600, Pakistan
Tel: +92 21 587 2879 **Fax:** +92 21 587 0014
Email: info@ric.com.pk
Website: www.ric.com.pk

FIRM OVERVIEW

Senior partner: Ahsan Zahir Rizvi
Number of partners worldwide: 3
Number of other lawyers worldwide: 10

AREAS OF PRACTICE:

M&A	20%
Oil and gas	15%
Telecommunications and IT	15%
Banking and finance	10%
Corporate	10%
Energy and power	10%
Litigation and arbitration	10%
Privatisation	10%

FIRM OVERVIEW: Rizvi, Isa & Co was formed in 1990. The firm currently comprises three partners and ten associates along with a team of trained support staff with correspondents around the world. Rizvi, Isa & Co has an international outlook and a flexible, client oriented approach which allows it to provide innovative legal solutions.

INTERNATIONAL EXPERIENCE: The firm has worked with foreign law firms and advised international clients on a variety of issues relating to project finance, privatisations, cross-border transactions, M&A, enterprise restructuring, banking, mark-up financing, syndications, security documentation, non-rupee advances and facilities to Pakistani entities by offshore lenders, taxation and fiscal efficiency, non-banking financial institutions rules and regulations, energy and power projects, petroleum, oil and gas, refineries, pipelines, distribution, exploration and mining projects and concessions, joint ventures, franchising, telecommunication and information technology projects, and general corporate advisory work.

INTERNATIONAL CLIENTS: Rizvi, Isa & Co has an extensive international client base, which includes major foreign financial institutions, multinational companies and corporate groups.

MAIN INTERNATIONAL AREAS OF PRACTICE:

M&A: The firm advises on issues ranging from cross-border takeovers of listed companies involving complex legal and fiscal issues to small private acquisitions by foreign companies and individuals of Pakistani entities. Recent transactions include acting as the legal counsel in the merger of Pfizer and Parke-Davis entities in Pakistan and in the acquisition of Phillips Projects business in Pakistan by Tyco Fire & Security.

Telecommunications and IT: The firm advises the Pakistan Telecommunication Company Limited and has advised PTCL on the expansion of its network and has negotiated all financial arrangements with foreign and local currency lenders. The firm drafted the regulatory framework for privatisation of the telecommunication sector of Pakistan and assisted Denton Hall in the drafting of the Pakistan Telecommunication (re-organisation) Ordinance 1995. The firm has acted on the acquisition of Cable & Wireless shares in Paktel Limited and is currently acting as the local counsel for the privatisation of PTCL. The firm also advises various international corporate groups on investments in the information technology, media and e-commerce sector in Pakistan. Rizvi, Isa & Co also advised on the formulation of the National IT Policy and drafted the IT Ordinance 2000 with ancillary regulations.

Oil and gas: The firm has negotiated and drafted various joint venture agreements, farm-in agreements, assignments, gas supply agreements, and gas equipment contracts. It has also advised on dispute resolutions, participated in dealings with the Ministry of Petroleum and OGDCL. Rizvi, Isa & Co handles all local law issues relating to Pakistani concessions including Securities & Exchange Commission of Pakistan, State Bank of Pakistan, income tax, employment and Ministry of Petroleum. The firm is the legal counsel for the privatisation of Sui Southern Gas Company Limited, Sui Northern Gas Pipelines Limited and the LPG business of SSGCL and advises Premier Oil plc (including the Premier-Shell joint venture in Pakistan) and Union Texas Pakistan.

Energy and power: The firm advises on implementation agreements, power purchase agreements, gas/fuel supply agreements, construction contracts, EPC contracts, O&M contracts, financing agreements, security documentation, and other material contracts. It also handles issues relating to land acquisition, local law disputes, tax matters and has obtained all consents, permissions and clarifications from various regulatory authorities. The firm is currently acting for Hubco, Uch, Tapal and Saba on non-conflicting matters.

Privatisation: The firm has acted as counsel for the government and as part of the bidding consortium on the privatisation of various entities in Pakistan. It has drafted regulatory frameworks for the privatisation of utilities and has undertaken detailed due diligence covering all legal aspects.

Corporate: The firm handles all corporate law matters including incorporation of companies, listing on stock exchanges, obtaining all requisite consents/approvals, tax authority registrations and returns and filing all statutory returns, obtaining work permits and registrations for expatriates. The firm has extensive experience in drafting and negotiating various types of contracts relating to international cross-border finance, project finance, export credit finance, supplier credit facility, buyer credit facility, employee's stock option schemes, share sale and purchase, joint venture arrangements, franchising, intellectual property licencing and software development agreements.

Banking and finance: The firm advises banks, various modarabas, and leasing, securities, brokerage and asset management companies. Rizvi, Isa & Co advises on new products, corporate financial transactions, corporate debt issues, local currency and foreign currency financing transactions, and general banking matters. It has conducted detailed legal due diligence exercises.

Litigation and arbitration: The firm handles international arbitration work in Pakistan, London, Brussels and Singapore under the ICC Arbitration and Reconciliation Rules. The firm undertakes litigation in Karachi, Lahore, Quetta and Islamabad in the Supreme Court, High Court, District Courts and before Civil Judges. It also appears before customs, excise duty and income tax authorities.

LANGUAGES: English, Urdu

WORLDWIDE OFFICE CONTACTS

PAKISTAN
517-519, Clifton Centre, DC-1, Block 5, Clifton, **Karachi** 75600
Tel: +92 21 586 5198 **Fax:** +92 21 586 5107
Email: info@ric.com.pk

8-9, 1st Floor, 73 Shadman Business Centre, Shadman Market, **Lahore**
Tel: + 92 42 756 6047 **Fax:** + 92 42 756 3990
Email: ric@nexlinx.net.pk

R

For other recommended firms see pages 1485-1520

RODRÍGUEZ & MENDOZA

HEAD OFFICE

Edf. Parque Cristal, Torre Este, Piso 11, Avenida Francisco De Miranda,
Los Palos Grandes
Caracas 1062, Venezuela
Tel: +582 285 4944 **Fax:** +582 285 1379

Email: romen@romen

WORLDWIDE OFFICE CONTACTS

VENEZUELA
Edf. Parque Cristal, Torre Este, Piso 11, Avenida Francisco De Miranda,
Los Palos Grandes, **Caracas** 1062
Tel: +582 285 4944 **Fax:** +582 285 1379
Email: romen@romen

FIRM OVERVIEW

Managing Partner: Luis Ignacio Mendoza

Number of partners worldwide: 9
Number of other lawyers worldwide: 27

AREAS OF PRACTICE:

Anti-trust	*%
Banking and finance	*%
Insurance and reinsurance	*%
Intellectual property	*%
Labour	*%
Litigation and arbitration	*%
M&A	*%
Oil and gas	*%
Privatisation	*%
Project finance, capital markets and financing agreements	*%
Taxation	*%
Telecommunications and computer law	*%

* Workload % not disclosed

FIRM PROFILE: The firm, founded in 1910, has grown to become one of the leading law fims in Venezuela. It maintains excellent relations with firms in Latin America as well as with leading US and UK firms.

INTERNATIONAL EXPERIENCE: The firm regards the practice of law in international matters as important as in national matters and its largest clients are corporations listed in the Fortune 500 list. The firm advised the Venezuelan Republic in the issue of registered bonds in New York and London and in many other issues of agencies of the Venezuelan Government. The firm also advised bankers in the largest placement of bonds by Venezuela corporations.

INTERNATIONAL CLIENTS: The firm's client base includes several of the largest banks, oil and industrial corporations in the world.

MAIN INTERNATIONAL AREAS OF PRACTICE:

Oil and gas: Rodríguez & Mendoza has extensive experience in advising international oil companies on their activities in Venezuela. It advises the three largest oil companies in the world and is involved in the joint ventures between Petroleos de Venezuela, S.A. (PDVSA), and private petroleum companies.

Mergers and acquisitions: Rodríguez & Mendoza has been involved in numerous joint ventures, analysing complex financial, tax, labour and anti-trust implications. It has performed several due diligence studies and has a permanent division dedicated to this activity.

Banking and finance: The firm represents a significant number of clients in major project transactions, acting for syndicates of lenders and investment bankers, and borrowers.

Privatisation: Rodríguez & Mendoza has been actively involved in the privatisation of banks, sugar mills, an aviation company, a steel mill, telephone company and hotels.

Project finance, capital markets and financing agreements: In the field of financing and capital markets, the firm has participated in the most important transactions that have taken place in recent years. The firm has provided assistance in the form of ADR to Venezuelan corporations in the New York Stock Exchange.

Taxation: The firm's tax department handles all aspects related to the law, its regulation and its jurisprudence. It is also involved in the filing of administrative tax claims and in fiscal litigation.

Labour law and industrial relations: This area of law has grown since the 1936 Labour Law. The firm has a team dedicated to protect and advise clients on this particularly sensitive area.

Anti-trust: In this relative new area of Venezuelan law, the firm has been actively involved with specialist lawyers and the firm has acted on behalf on an international client in a case which has had international repercussions.

Litigation and arbitration: The firm has a group of lawyers dedicated to arbitration and litigation, two of which have been appointed as permanent members of the Venezuelan American Chamber of Commerce, Arbitration Committee.

Corporate: The firm advises its clients on day to day corporate matters and compliance with regulations.

Insurance and reinsurance: The firm advises insurance companies in Venezuela and has acted as defence for a number of insurance companies.

Intellectual property: The firm has a team dedicated exclusively to this areas, which handles all patents, copyright and trademarks requirements of its clients, as well as litigations on matters related to intellectual property.

Telecommunications and computer law: The firm has acted for several clients in connection with transactions, including association of Internet portals to be placed in the international capital markets; setting up IP services, b2b, b2c, c2c and services application sites; establishing 'WAP' and other wireless technology communication applications.

LANGUAGES: English, French, Spanish

ROMULO MABANTA BUENAVENTURA SAYOC & DE LOS ANGELES

HEAD OFFICE

30th Floor, Citibank Tower, 8741 Paseo de Roxas, Makati City, Philippines
Tel: +63 2 848 0114 **Fax:** +63 2 815 3172

Email: rmbsa@rmbsa.com
Website: www.rmbsa.net

WORLDWIDE OFFICE CONTACTS

HONG KONG
4206 Far East Finance Centre, 16 Harcourt Road, **Hong Kong**
Tel: +852 2866 2292 **Fax:** +852 2866 1601
Email: romulohk@ibm.net

PHILIPPINES
30th Floor, Citibank Tower, 8741 Paseo de Roxas, **Makati City**
Tel: +63 2 848 0114 **Fax:** +63 2 815 3172
Email: rmbsa@rmbsa.com

FIRM OVERVIEW

Number of partners worldwide: 25
Number of other lawyers worldwide: 44

AREAS OF PRACTICE:

Area	%
Energy and infrastructure	15%
General corporate and foreign investments	15%
Intellectual property	15%
Litigation	12%
Banking and finance	10%
Securities	10%
Tax	10%
Employment	5%
Real estate	5%
Immigration	2%
Admiralty	1%

R

FIRM OVERVIEW: Romulo Mabanta Buenaventura Sayoc & De Los Angeles was established in 1957. It comprises 69 lawyers, the majority of whom have studied and worked abroad. The firm advises international investors on Philippine law and Philippine companies on international transactions. It has close links with foreign law firms and is the sole Philippine member of Lex Mundi, a worldwide network of approximately 151 independent firms. The firm is the only Philippine law firm to have an office in Hong Kong.

INTERNATIONAL EXPERIENCE: The firm is a member of the American Bar Association (ABA), Asian Law Association, Asia-Pacific Law Association, Asian Patent Attorneys Association (APAA), International Bar Association (IBA), International Trademark Association (INTA), Inter Pacific Bar Association (IPBA) and Law Asia: Lex Mundi.

INTERNATIONAL CLIENTS: Clients include Avon, British Gas, Casino Guichard-Perrachon, Cemex, SA de C.V., Chase Manhattan Bank N.A., Citibank N.A., Coca-Cola, Deutsche Bank, Ford Motors, Goldman Sachs, IBM, ING Bank N.V., Johnson & Johnson, Lufthansa, Nestlé, NTT of Japan, Pfizer, Philip Morris, Royal Dutch Shell, Southern Energy, and Sun Life of Canada.

MAIN INTERNATIONAL AREAS OF PRACTICE:

Admiralty and shipping: The firm advises on all admiralty and shipping matters including the mortgage and financing of ships and aircraft.
Dispute resolution: Work handled includes local and international arbitration.
Banking and finance: The firm advises on trusts, foreign exchange, private and corporate banking and loan syndications. It also advises on corporate finance, structured financing, trade financing and dealings with export credit agencies and multilateral and bilateral financial institutions.
Corporate and commercial: Romulo Mabanta Buenaventura Sayoc & De Los Angeles handles work relating to incorporations, joint ventures, reorganisations, mergers and acquisitions, and bankruptcy.
Energy and infrastructure: The firm advises on a range of energy projects including oil and gas, mining, power and water. It also handles a large amount of infrastructure related work including telecommunications, railways, airports, ports, industrial estates, project financing and structuring, build-operate-transfer (BOT) arrangements and privatisations.
Environmental: The firm advises on environmental impact studies and claims.
Foreign investment: Romulo Mabanta Buenaventura Sayoc & De Los Angeles handles investments in export and economic zones, securing grant incentives, and establishment of regional branches for multinational companies.
Immigration: The firm handles visa applications and alien legalisation.
Intellectual property: The firm advises on patents, trademarks, copyrights, and technology transfers.
Litigation: The firm represents clients in civil, commercial, administrative and criminal cases. It also advises on securities, public offerings of debt and equity issues, asset securitisation, derivatives, private placements, mutual funds, privatisation of government owned corporations and capital market developments.
Securities: The firm advises on securities, public offerings of debt and equity issues, asset securitisation, derivatives, private placements, mutual funds, privatisation of government owned corporations and capital market developments.
Tax: The firm advises on tax compliance audits, local and international tax and estate planning.

LANGUAGES: Chinese, English, Japanese, Spanish, Tagalog

ROMULO MABANTA BUENAVENTURA SAYOC & DE LOS ANGELES

For other recommended firms see pages 1485-1520

ROSCHIER-HOLMBERG & WASELIUS

HEAD OFFICE

Keskuskatu 7 A,
00100 Helsinki, Finland
Tel: + 358 9 228 551 **Fax:** + 358 9 664 303
Email: firstname.surname@rhw.fi
Website: www.rhw.fi

FIRM OVERVIEW

Managing partner: Tomas Lindholm

Number of partners worldwide: 18
Number of other lawyers worldwide: 58

AREAS OF PRACTICE:

Transactions	40%
Corporate	15%
Dispute resolution	15%
EU and competition	10%
General commercial	10%
Intellectual property and IT	10%

WORLDWIDE OFFICE CONTACTS

FINLAND
Keskuskatu 7 A, 00100 **Helsinki**
Tel: + 358 9 228 551 **Fax:** + 358 9 664 303
Email: firstname.surname@rhw.fi

Elektroniikkatie 8, 90570 **Oulu**
Tel: + 358 8 551 3300 **Fax:** + 358 8 551 3320
Email: firstname.surname@rhw.fi

Hermiankatu 8D, 33720 **Tampere**
Tel: + 358 3 316 7444 **Fax:** + 358 3 316 7445
Email: firstname.surname@rhw.fi

Alatori 3 A, 65100 **Vaasa**
Tel: + 358 6 320 0111 **Fax:** + 358 6 320 0114
Email: firstname.surname@rhw.fi

UNITED KINGDOM
36/38 Cornhill, **London** EC3V 3NG
Tel: + 44 20 7929 0966 **Fax:** + 44 20 7929 0933
Email: firstname.surname@rhw.fi

FIRM OVERVIEW: Roschier-Holmberg & Waselius is Finland's largest law firm, and has specialised in commercial law since its foundation in 1936. It has a national and international practice, providing a full range of legal services in all fields of corporate and business law. During the past decade the firm has continued to assist Finnish companies abroad. The firm maintains close ties to leading law firms in virtually all jurisdictions which have trade relations with Finland. It is also a member of Lex Mundi, a global association of 158 independent firms. The firm has grown rapidly during the last few years, mainly through internal growth, and it is expected that its legal staff will continue to grow to meet the increasing demand for legal services within Finland.

INTERNATIONAL CLIENTS: The firm regularly advises foreign and international businesses, investment banks and other financial institutions, equity investors as well as international organisations. Domestically, the firm advises major Finnish public and private corporations with international operations, including financial institutions.

MAIN INTERNATIONAL AREAS OF PRACTICE

Corporate M&A: The firm advises on most of the major transactions involving Finnish commerce and industry, including the privatisation process. Ad hoc transactional teams for each client are assembled from the group's 15 lawyers and from the specialist teams (see below) The firm also offers post-acquisition services and advises on project exports, joint ventures and construction and plant delivery projects.
New economy transactions (NET): The practice group specialises in venture capital and other private equity transactions in the New Economy. NET's 15 lawyers advise both investors, such as incubators, venture capitalists and private equity investors, as well as target companies such as start-ups, high tech and other companies. The firm provides services both through NET and through a close and seamless interchange between the NET and the other practice groups, offering the clients a tailored service concept.
Capital markets: The group numbers about 20 lawyers. It provides advice on all aspects of international finance, including IPOs, privatisations, public offerings, private placements, buy-backs, take-over bids, securitisation, asset and project finance and related issues, as well as shipping and aviation finance. It has advised the Finnish government throughout the post-war era.
Dispute resolution: The group's 10 lawyers participate mainly in international arbitrations as counsel or arbitrators, but also handle domestic work. In addition to Finnish and the Scandinavian languages they arbitrate in English and French. The firm specialises in intellectual property, transport and maritime litigation, having litigated landmark lawsuits in these areas, as well as in banking and securities.
Intellectual property, IT, EU and competition: The group has grown rapidly and now numbers around 20 lawyers. It advises and represents clients in copyright, patents, trademarks, design, technology transfers, licensing, computer law, telecommunications, media law, competition law proceedings and notifications, merger control filings and EU law. Group members are continuously involved in a large number of intellectual property rights infringement cases.
Other specialisations: The firm also has specialist teams for corporate, telecommunications, transport, tax, employment, real estate and environmental law, financial regulatory, marketing and consumer law and insolvency.

LANGUAGES: English, French, Finnish, German, Greek, Swedish and other Scandinavian languages.

WORLDWIDE OFFICES

UNITED KINGDOM

36/38 Cornhill, London EC3V 3NG
Tel: + 44 20 7929 0966 **Fax:** + 44 20 7929 0933
Email: firstname.surname@rhw.fi

Managing partner: Lauri Peltola
Number of lawyers: 3

Office profile: The London office was opened in 1993 in response to Finnish and international clients' needs, particularly in the fields of banking, finance and corporate law, and has been largely retained to assist companies in IPOs and in obtaining other means of equity financing. It has one partner and two associate lawyers.

RUCELLAI & RAFFAELLI

HEAD OFFICE

Via Monte Napoleone 18,
20121 Milan, Italy
Tel: +39 02 783 341 **Fax:** +39 02 783 524

Email: rucrafmi@tin.it

WORLDWIDE OFFICE CONTACTS

ITALY
Via Monte Napoleone 18, 20121 **Milan**
Tel: +39 02 783 341 **Fax:** +39 02 783 524
Email: rucrafmi@tin.it

Via Gregoriana, 5, 00187 **Rome**
Tel: +39 06 678 4778 **Fax:** +39 06 678 3915
Email: rucrafro@tin.it

FIRM OVERVIEW

Senior partners: Cosimo Rucellai, Enrico Adriano Raffaelli
Managing partner: Andrea Vischi

AREAS OF PRACTICE:

Banking, securities, finance and insurance .... *%
Competition and anti-trust .... *%
Corporate and commercial .... *%
Employment .... *%
Information technology .... *%
Intellectual property .... *%
* Workload % not disclosed

FIRM OVERVIEW: Rucellai & Raffaelli's head office is based in Milan with a branch office in Rome. Currently, with 35 lawyers, the firm focuses on corporate, anti-trust and competition, banking and finance, intellectual property, international and general civil practice, and employment. It provides legal consulting services for contractual, financial, compliance and/or decision making purposes, but is also traditionally very strong in the field of litigation, with special reference to IPRs and general commercial litigation.

INTERNATIONAL EXPERIENCE: The firm advises both national and international clients. It has established a large network of correspondent law fims covering Italy, all EU member states, North and South America and the Middle and Far East.

INTERNATIONAL CLIENTS: The firm's client base includes multinational companies (and their Italian subsidiaries) as well as large Italian corporations that operate internationally. Its clients are involved in various industries including information technology, manufacturing, chemicals, pharmaceutical, insurance, financial services and trade.

MAIN INTERNATIONAL AREAS OF PRACTICE:

Corporate and commercial: The firm advises on all general corporate matters. The firm handles joint ventures, mergers and de-mergers, corporate restructuring and corporate governance. Its M&A activity focuses on contract drafting and negotiation, including preparatory due diligence advice on specifically customised transactions. The firm handles the drafting of general and tailored commercial contracts, including agency, franchising, distribution and supply agreements

Competition and anti-trust law: The firm advises on anti-trust proceedings before both national and EU authorities, notification of mergers and agreements, organisation of anti-trust compliance programmes (including special education programmes) and anti-trust due diligence.

Banking, securities, finance and insurance: The firm specialises in business law, banking, financial and insurance law. Work handled includes advising on issuing shares and bonds, admission to the stock exchange, securitisation, leasing, factoring, trusts, investment trusts and pension funds and asset segregations. Rucellai & Rffaelli also advises banking and financial intermediaries in general and provides assistance on Bank of Italy regulations and other regulatory bodies.

Intellectual property: The firm advises on patents, trademarks, know-how and trade secrets and copyright (particularly IP licensing and litigation related matters). Rucellai & Raffaelli also specialises in advertisement law.

Information technology: The firm advises on software protection issues, e-commerce and Internet related matters.

Litigation and arbitration: The firm has a broad experience in litigation matters. The firm provides advice on national and international arbitration proceedings, including ICC and other international bodies.

Employment: The firm advises on labour and employment law, labour litigation and the drafting of labour contracts. It also advises on administrative law, especially public tenders and related matters.

LANGUAGES: English, French, German, Italian, Spanish

 For other recommended firms see pages 1485-1520

RYDIN & CARLSTEN ADVOKATBYRA AB

HEAD OFFICE

Norrmalmstorg 1, PO Box 1766,
S-111 87 Stockholm, Sweden
Tel: +46 8 679 51 70 **Fax:** +46 8 611 48 50

Email: all@rydinlaw.se
Website: www.rydinlaw.se

WORLDWIDE OFFICE CONTACTS

SWEDEN
Norrmalmstorg 1, PO Box 1766, S-111 87 **Stockholm**
Tel: +46 8 679 51 70 **Fax:** +46 8 611 48 50
Email: all@rydinlaw.se

FIRM OVERVIEW

Managing partner: Anders Rydin
Chairman of the board: Ulf Dahlgren

Number of partners worldwide: 10
Number of other lawyers worldwide: 7

AREAS OF PRACTICE:

Area	%
Corporate/M&A	40%
Intellectual property	30%
Litigation and arbitration	15%
Finance and stock exchange	10%
IT and telecommunications	5%

FIRM OVERVIEW: Rydin & Carlsten Advokatbyra AB, established in 1983, is a medium-sized firm. Its practice is focused on corporate law and M&A work, finance law, intellectual property and commercial litigation.

INTERNATIONAL EXPERIENCE: The firm has a tradition of advising US, Japanese and European corporate clients on all aspects relevant to their investments in Sweden.

INTERNATIONAL CLIENTS: Clients are drawn from a broad spectrum of industry and commerce, industry manufacturing, finance, trading, pharmaceutical, biotech and IT. The firm represents a significant number of major transnational corporations.

MAIN INTERNATIONAL AREAS OF PRACTICE:
Corporate and M&A: Rydin & Carlsten advises clients on cross-border transactions with a Swedish connection. In recent years, the firm has represented major international corporations with respect to their acquisitions of Swedish assets.
Intellectual property: The firm provides specialist advice on patents, trademarks, copyright and registered designs to Swedish and foreign clients. The firm also offers advice on licensing issues, technology transfers and protection of rights.
Litigation and arbitration: Rydin & Carlsten assists clients in commercial law disputes before courts or arbitral tribunals. The firm has considerable experience in international arbitration matters under the Rules of The Arbitration Institute of the Stockholm Chamber of Commerce.
Finance law: Rydin and Carlsten advises on regulatory aspects of finance law and the Stockholm Stock Exchange Regulations.
IT and telecommunications: The firm represents clients in these areas of law and offers advice on regulatory aspects and contract issues as well as internet-related matters.
Marketing and competition: The firm advises clients on their marketing projects and review contracts and provides general advice on competition law matters.

LANGUAGES: English, German, Russian, Swedish

RYDIN & CARLSTEN ADVOKATBYRÅ AB

SANTAMARINA Y STETA, SC

HEAD OFFICE

Edificio Omega, Campos Eliseos 345, 1er piso, Chapultepec Polanco
11560 Mexico, DF Mexico
Tel: +52 5 279 5400 **Fax:** +52 5 280 3214

Email: infomex@s-s.com.mx
Website: www.s-s.com.mx

FIRM OVERVIEW

Managing partner: Agustín Gutiérrez

Number of partners worldwide: 19
Number of other lawyers worldwide: 43

FIRM OVERVIEW: Since 1947, Santamarina y Steta has established its reputation as a pre-eminent, full-service law firm. With more than sixty-five lawyers, Santamarina y Steta is one of the largest Mexican firms. The firm provides legal representation and business advice to many of the most important companies operating in Mexico. Santamarina y Steta assists its clients with both complex and routine matters, from preparing corporate documents and filing trademark applications to structuring mergers and acquisitions, and planning and negotiating transnational business ventures. In the firm, each of the lawyers is a graduate of a Mexican university and admitted to practice in Mexico. In complement to their studies and practice in Mexico, many of the lawyers have spent time abroad to enhance their foreign language abilities and broaden their exposure to the international legal system. Many of the lawyers have trained in law firms in the United States or Europe. Several have done postgraduate studies at foreign universities.

WORLDWIDE OFFICE CONTACTS

MEXICO
Edificio Omega, Campos Eliseos 345, 1er piso, Chapultepec Polanco
11560 **Mexico City**
Tel: +525 279 5400 **Fax:** +52 5 280 3214

Torre Comercial América, Batallón de San Patricio No. 111-1102, Valle Oriente, 66269 Garza García, **Monterrey**
Tel: +52 8 368 0110 **Fax:** +52 8 368 0111
Email: infomty@s-s.com.mx

MAIN INTERNATIONAL AREAS OF PRACTICE: Santamarina y Steta provides full legal services to Mexican and international clients, including private and public entities, as well as government agencies, with particular emphasis on banking and securities, project financing, mergers and acquisitions, international trade, energy, antitrust, real estate, business, government procurement, tax, aviation, environment, intellectual property, labour, litigation, immigration and telecommunications.

LANGUAGES: In addition to Spanish, most of the firm's lawyers are fluent in English. Some are also fluent in French and German.

S

 For other recommended firms see pages 1485-1520

SARANTITIS & PARTNERS

HEAD OFFICE

9 Anagnostopoulou Street,
GR 106 73 Athens, Greece
Tel: +30 1 367 0400 **Fax:** +30 1 362 1595

Email: athens@sarantitis.com
Website: www.sarantitis.com

WORLDWIDE OFFICE CONTACTS

GREECE
9 Anagnostopoulou Street, GR 106 73 **Athens**
Tel: +30 1 367 0400 **Fax:** +30 1 362 1595
Email: athens@sarantitis.com

GREECE
91 Akti Miaouli, GR 185 38 **Piraeus**
Tel: + 30 1 429 0780 **Fax:** + 30 1 429 0791
Email: piraeus@sarantitis.com

FIRM OVERVIEW

Contact partners: Yiannis Sarantitis, Dorotheos Samoladas

Number of partners worldwide: 10
Number of other lawyers worldwide: 22

AREAS OF PRACTICE:

Area	%
Banking and finance	20%
Corporate and commercial	18%
Media, telecommunications and IT	18%
Investments/privatisations	10%
Maritime/transport law	10%
Administration and taxation	7%
Arbitration and litigation	7%
Employment	4%
EU Law	3%
Real estate	3%

FIRM OVERVIEW: Originally established in 1965, Sarantitis & Partners has expanded its activities to become one of Greece's leading law firms. The firm represents some of the largest and most well known Greek and foreign companies, as well as major banks. The firm's head office in Athens is particularly active in corporate, banking and finance and commercial and civil law, while the firm's Piraeus office concentrates on maritime law, banking and ship finance. Both offices are experienced in arbitration and litigation. In order to serve their clients more effectively, the firm have developed close links with prominent legal firms on an international basis. The firm's local network of correspondents covers the whole of Greece and Cyprus, especially in business centres and commercial ports.

INTERNATIONAL EXPERIENCE: The firm has handled various types of foreign investment transactions in Greece, as well as the restructuring of companies and corporate groups.

INTERNATIONAL CLIENTS: The firm's clientele includes multinational companies, major banks, governments and other organisations.

MAIN INTERNATIONAL AREAS OF PRACTICE:
Corporate, commercial: The firm has a diverse corporate and commercial practice representing a range of institutional and entrepreneurial clients in Greece and abroad. It brings experience, technical capabilities and creativity to each client project. These qualities enhance the firm's reputation as lawyers who assist clients to identify and to successfully pursue commercial opportunities.
M&A: The firm has been involved in the acquisition of interests in both state-owned and private corporations, as well as in corporate take-overs and mergers.
Banking: The firm represents domestic and foreign banks and other financial institutions throughout the region in a broad range of credit activities, general operational issues, lending, loan restructuring, insolvency litigation and regulatory compliance.
Media, telecommunications and IT: The practice represents clients who manufacture, use and distribute technology. Matters handled include licensing, acquisition and transfer agreements, supply agreements, research alliances and distribution agreements.
Maritime and transport: The firm is experienced in numerous aspects of admiralty and shipping law. Lawyers handle both litigation and non-contentious matters of concern to maritime industries.
Administrative and tax: Advice is provided on a broad range of tax issues. The firm has significant experience in tax litigation, representing major corporations before the Greek Administrative Courts. The firm also advises individual clients.
Public procurement: Sarantitis & Partners acts in this area as legal consultants and litigators for major contractors in both the private and public sector.
Stock exchange and securities: The firm has extensive experience of government securities laws and regulations and of the Athens Stock Exchange. Advice is provided to clients seeking additional capital through stock offerings, debentures, limited partnership interests or other securities or in offerings to the public at large.
Construction, engineering and energy: The firm's construction and engineering law practice covers a wide range of building and development work. It represents owners, tenants, lenders, contractors and design and engineering professionals in all aspects of the construction process.
EU law: Sarantitis &Partners offer advice to their clients in various aspects of EU law, taking actions before the competent community institutions and bringing cases before the E.C.J.
White collar crime: The firm has successfully protected clients involved in white collar crime cases.

LANGUAGES: English, French, German, Greek, Italian, Spanish

S

SARAVIA Y MUÑOZ

HEAD OFFICE

14 Calle 4-32, Zona 10, Cuarto Nivel,
Guatemala City 01010, Guatemala
Tel: +502 3 33 6576 **Fax:** +502 3 33 4925

Email: saraviamunoz@guate.net
Website: www.infovia.com.gt/saravia-munoz

FIRM OVERVIEW

Managing partner: Gisela Castillo
Senior partner: Salvador A Saravia

Number of partners worldwide: 4
Number of other lawyers worldwide: 4

AREAS OF PRACTICE:

Corporate	30%
Banking and finance	20%
Intellectual property	20%
Litigation and arbitration	10%
Telecommunications and computer law	10%
Insurance and reinsurance	5%
M&A	5%

FIRM OVERVIEW: Saravia y Muñoz offers a comprehensive legal service to clients with international business interests, focusing on intellectual property, banking and finance, M&A, and insurance and reinsurance. The firm does not belong to any alliances or networks. Instead, it maintains contact with various firms worldwide and works with them on individual international matters.

INTERNATIONAL EXPERIENCE: Over the last 40 years, Saravia y Muñoz has advised on international transactions, aiding the establishment of US and other foreign companies in Guatemala. The firm has handled the issuance of several local bonds and stocks at domestic and foreign exchanges.

INTERNATIONAL CLIENTS: The firm's client base includes large companies, banks, insurance companies and public or supranational institutions conducting cross-border business.

MAIN INTERNATIONAL AREAS OF PRACTICE:

Mergers and acquisitions: The firm's transactions in this area range from small private acquisitions to company take-overs.
Banking and finance: Saravia y Muñoz covers all areas of banking and finance at domestic and international levels.
Intellectual property: The firm specialises in trademarks, patents and copyrights. Its lawyers participate in the negotiation of license agreements, franchises and advise on infringement disputes.
Marketing law: Working with clients ranging from large multinationals to local enterprises, the firm has substantial experience in dealing with marketing guidelines, consumer disputes, regulatory issues and producer liability matters.
Litigation and arbitration: Saravia y Muñoz deals with commercial and civil litigation, as well as national and international arbitration. Its lawyers are frequently involved in cases before the Guatemalan courts, including the Supreme Court, and have participated in numerous matters under the rules of the local arbitration court of the Chamber of Commerce. The firm undertakes commercial and civil litigation as well as litigation in matters of unfair competition and industrial property.
Corporate: The firm advises on all aspects of general corporate law, including the drafting of local and international contracts as well as taxation.
Securities and financial markets: Saravia y Muñoz has handled the issuance of local bonds, securities and stocks at domestic and international exchanges.

LANGUAGES: English, French, German, Spanish

WORLDWIDE OFFICE CONTACTS

GUATEMALA
14 Calle 4-32, Zona 10, Cuarto Nivel, **Guatemala City** 01010
Tel: +502 3 33 6576 **Fax:** +502 3 33 4925
Email: samu@infovia.com.gt

S

For other recommended firms see pages 1485-1520

SCHELLENBERG WITTMER

HEAD OFFICE

Löwenstrasse 19, PO Box 6333,
CH-8023 Zurich, Switzerland
Tel: +41 1 215 52 52 **Fax:** +41 1 215 52 00

Email: zurich@swlegal.ch
Website: www.swlegal.ch

WORLDWIDE OFFICE CONTACTS

SWITZERLAND
10, cours de Rive, PO Box 3054, CH-1211 **Geneva** 3
Tel: + 41 22 707 8000 **Fax:** + 41 22 707 8001
Email: geneva@swlegal.ch

Neugasse 1, PO Box 1333, CH-6301, **Zug**
Tel: + 41 41 726 8050 **Fax:** + 41 41 726 8051
Email: zug@swlegal.ch

FIRM OVERVIEW

Managing partner: Martin Bernet

Number of partners worldwide: 25
Number of other lawyers worldwide: 47

AREAS OF PRACTICE:

Area	%
Corporate, takeovers and restructuring	25%
Litigation and arbitration	25%
Banking/finance/capital markets	10%
Estate planning/wills and trusts	10%
Intellectual property and competition	5%
Property and environment	5%
Taxation	5%
Telecommunications and IT	5%
Other	10%

FIRM OVERVIEW: Schellenberg Wittmer was founded on 1 May 2000 through the merger of Schellenberg & Haissly and Brunschwig Wittmer, two prominent Swiss law firms. With more than 70 lawyers, Schellenberg Wittmer is one of the largest business law firms in Switzerland. It is a truly multilingual and multicultural law firm with both Swiss and foreign qualified lawyers. The key specialisations are litigation, corporations including M&A, banking and finance including capital markets, taxation, intellectual property, information technology and private clients. The firm has developed a worldwide network of foreign correspondents and has considerable experience working as part of teams with firms in other countries.

INTERNATIONAL EXPERIENCE: The firm has long-standing international experience in all of the practice areas. The firm advises on large-scale global corporate and banking transactions and handles international litigations and arbitrations. It has recently advised international clients on several structured finance projects, on establishing internationally active investment funds and in corporate relocations. The firm also enforces foreign rulings which might affect Swiss companies. The firm's corporate and commercial practice is particularly active in Western Europe, the US and Asia, and its private client work is also focused on the Arabian Gulf and South America.

INTERNATIONAL CLIENTS: These come from the banking, finance and trade sectors, and more recently from aviation and new technologies such as telecoms, computing and the Internet.

MAIN INTERNATIONAL AREAS OF PRACTICE:

Litigation and arbitration: The firm has considerable experience in coordinating national and international commercial litigation through a network of correspondents. It conducts litigation and arbitration in all its practice areas. Firm members have particular expertise in tracing and recovering assets. Its international arbitration specialists act as both counsel and arbitrators, as well as in alternative dispute resolution.
Banking and finance: The firm handles compliance and regulatory work for financial institutions in both Swiss and foreign markets. It also advises them and their clients on all types of banking transactions, including asset, trade and project finance, guarantee and hedging transactions, capital markets legislation and securities law, derivatives and other financial products, securitisation, private asset management and mutual funds.
Corporate, takeovers and restructuring: The firm is experienced in advising Swiss and foreign companies on establishment in or relocation to Switzerland and representing them before the authorities. It handles M&A, joint ventures, participations, tender offers, MBOs, restructuring, public securities offerings (including IPOs) and listings on the Swiss stock exchange.
Tax: The firm handles all aspects of Swiss corporate and individual taxation, including indirect taxes. It advises on international corporate structures and tax planning, as well as assisting in contacts with the tax authorities (e.g., in obtaining rulings) and tax litigation.
Estate planning, wills and trust: The international private client team is composed of lawyers from both Anglo-Saxon and civil jurisdictions, familiar with the full range of international estate planning procedures involving trusts, foundations and companies around the world.
Business reorganisation and insolvency: The firm advises on all aspects of national and cross-border insolvency and reorganisation procedures and has experience of obtaining enforcement and recognition of foreign bankruptcy proceedings.
Property and environment: Work for both Swiss and foreign clients includes real estate contracts, zoning laws, rent controls, authorisation requirements and procedures, environmental regulations, warranties and mortgages.
Insurance and liability: The firm advises on insurance and reinsurance contracts and insurance compliance law, represents clients in insurance, reinsurance and liability matters and has experience in the establishment of new insurance companies.
Telecommunications and IT: The firm advises on product and service contracts, licence agreements, cooperation agreements, outsourcing projects and Internet transactions.
Transport and international trade: Expertise covers all aspects of trade and commerce law, maritime, shipping and aviation law.
Intellectual property and competition: The firm's expertise includes trademarks, patents, copyrights and licences, as well as national and international competition and anti-trust law.
Mutual assistance and white-collar crime: The firm has developed extensive know-how in locating and securing assets in complex cross-border frauds, as well as in coordinating international legal action. It deals with money-laundering cases investigated in Switzerland, requests for mutual assistance by foreign authorities and the protection of third-party interests.

LANGUAGES: English, French, German, Italian, Japanese, Spanish

ADVOKATFIRMAET SCHJØDT AS

HEAD OFFICE

Dr Mauds Gt 11, PO Box 2444 Solli,
N-0201 Oslo, Norway
Tel: +47 22 01 88 00 **Fax:** +47 22 83 17 12
Email: schjodt.osl@schjodt.no
Website: www.schjodt.no

FIRM OVERVIEW

Managing partner: Peter A. Hiorth
Senior partner: A.C. Høeg Rasmussen
Number of partners worldwide: 44
Number of other lawyers worldwide: 74

AREAS OF PRACTICE:

Corporate/M&A	20%
Securities, stock exchange and venture capital	15%
Construction	15%
Arbitration and litigation	10%
Banking	5%
Employment	5%
EU and competition	5%
Intellectuel property	5%
Media	5%
Oil and energy	5%
Tax	5%
Telecommunications and IT	5%

S

FIRM OVERVIEW: One of Norway's largest law firms, Schjødt has offices in each of the country's four major cities (Oslo, Trondheim, Stavanger and Bergen) and a new office (established 2000) in Alesund, the centre of the increasingly important fishing and aquaculture industries in Norway. The firm traces its origins back to the beginning of the century, when it was already actively involved with major foreign industrial corporations establishing businesses in Norway. Its litigation practice has acted in a large number of cases in the Supreme Court. The firm has followed Norway's development as an oil-producing nation and advises several of the international oil companies active in Norway. The firm also focuses on construction work, both on and offshore, fish farming, M&A, venture capital and telecommunications and IT.

INTERNATIONAL EXPERIENCE: The firm is regularly involved in international deals and transactions for both listed and non-listed companies, including traditional M&A work, more sophisticated capital markets and securities transactions, tender offers and stock exchange-related work. In the past year it has represented inter alia ICA/Canica in the cross border merger with Ahold(NV); PhotoCure ASA in the OSE listing; StepStone ASA in the dual listing on both OSE and LSE; ABB in the asset transaction to acquire the oil and energy division of UMOE ASA; and the spin-off of ACTA from Sundal Collier & Co ASA and the establishment of ACTA Bank, the new Nordic internet bank.

INTERNATIONAL CLIENTS: The firm has large and medium sized international clients in most industry sectors. They include some of the larger companies in their respective fields, and many have established their own presence in Norway through subsidiary companies for which the firm acts on an on-going basis. Industry sectors include banking and finance, venture capital, oil and energy, construction, pharmaceutical, IT and telecommunications, newspapers and other media, as well as other traditional industries and trading sectors.

WORLDWIDE OFFICE CONTACTS

NORWAY

Kongensgt 23, PO Box 996 Sentrum, N-6001 **Alesund**
Tel: +47 70 10 77 00 **Fax:** +47 70 10 77 01
Email: schjodt.aal@schjodt.no

Slottsgaten 3, PO Box 4104 Dreggen, N-5835 **Bergen**
Tel: +47 55 55 35 00 **Fax:** +47 55 55 35 01
Email: schjodt.ber@schjodt.no

Kongsgårdbakken 3, PO Box 440, N-4002 **Stavanger**
Tel: +47 51 91 88 00 **Fax:** +47 51 91 88 01
Email: schjodt.sta@schjodt.no

Munkegata 30, PO Box 132, N-7400 **Trondheim**
Tel: +47 73 87 12 00 **Fax:** +47 73 87 12 32
Email: schjodt.tro@schjodt.no

MAIN INTERNATIONAL AREAS OF PRACTICE:

M&A and corporate: The firm advises a large number of international clients on an ongoing basis in connection with their business activities in Norway. It conducts an increasing amount of ad hoc transactional work, in which it frequently acts for investment banks in the UK and US, and venture capital investors.

Banking, finance and capital markets: The firm acts on behalf of both domestic and international banks, for both regulatory work and traditional banking and finance. The firm undertakes a substantial amount of capital markets work.

National and international arbitration and litigation: The practice focuses primarily on commercial disputes, and the firm is extensively engaged in litigation work, both before arbitration tribunals and the ordinary courts, including the Supreme Court of Norway.

Tax: The firm's tax department primarily specialises in business and corporation tax matters, with accounting law and corporation law being adjacent areas of expertise.

Intellectual property: The firm is instructed by inventors, corporations and patent bureaus in disputes concerning intellectual property, and it assists with the protection of technical know-how and the drafting of licensing agreements, both for domestic and international corporations.

Telecommunications and IT: The firm's work covers the regulatory as well as the contractual and commercial aspects of this market. In addition, the firm has long-standing experience with telecommunications projects in the international arena, representing large telecom and media companies. It is also experienced in technology licensing and protection as well as regulatory matters.

EU and competition: Domestic competition law as well as the EU regulations are increasingly relevant to the firm's corporate practice, particularly in mergers and acquisitions. The firm advises on domestic and EU competition law matters applicable in Norway.

Construction: The firm has considerable experience in construction law, both on and offshore. The firm normally represents contractors, but also receives instructions from developers. It advises in connection with contract negotiations and disputes, and handles a large number of cases before arbitration courts and the ordinary courts.

Oil and energy: Major international oil companies have been among the firm's clients for many years. Work handled includes regulatory, exploration and transportation issues as well as construction disputes.

Media: The firm has amongst its clients a large number of prominent publishers, newspapers and other media.

LANGUAGES: Danish, English, French, German, Norwegian, Spanish, Swedish

For other recommended firms see pages 1485-1520

SCHNEIDER & SCHIFFER

HEAD OFFICE

Bavariaring 27,
80336 Munich, Germany
Tel: +49 89 5434 9100 **Fax:** +49 89 5434 9200

Email: schneider_schiffer@compuserve.com

WORLDWIDE OFFICE CONTACTS

GERMANY
Bavariaring 27, 80336 **Munich**
Tel: +49 89 5434 9100 **Fax:** +49 89 5434 9200
Email: schneider_schiffer@compuserve.com

Südliche Hauptstrasse 33, 83700 **Rottach-Egern**
Tel: +49 8022 27 67 87 **Fax:** +49 8022 27 67 07

FIRM OVERVIEW

Number of partners worldwide: 10
Number of other lawyers worldwide: 1

AREAS OF PRACTICE:

IT GROUP

Software contracts and projects	30%
Intellectual property	15%
Corporate and employment law in IT	15%
Data protection	10%
Outsourcing contracts	10%
Provider contracts	10%
Other IT related contracts	10%

FIRM OVERVIEW: Schneider & Schiffer was founded in 1998 as a result of the merger between the law firms Antoine & Schneider and Schiffer & Partner. Antoine & Schneider had specialised in information technology law since 1986. Based in Munich, and comprising eleven attorneys and four tax consultants, Schneider & Schiffer specialises in information technology and business law. It has a specialist IT group that handles all IT related transactions. The aim of the IT group is to consult IT companies, as well as commercial users, with regard to their market presentation and to lead them safely through projects and negotiations. Therefore, the IT group consults its clients on specific projects, if this is possible, and has extensive contact with its clients negotiating partners. The firm's IT group comprises five lawyers, who are supported by assistants. The group consists of Prof. Dr. Schneider, Mr. Ludwig Antoine, Ms. Anja Münz, Maîtrise en Droit de Affaires, Mr. Frieder Backu and Ms. Michaela Witzel, LL.M. The firm is part of an informal network of law firms in Europe and the US.

MAIN INTERNATIONAL AREAS OF PRACTICE:

IT GROUP

Software contracts and projects: The firm's IT group advises on EDP and IT contract law, especially software law, which also comprises consulting and negotiating of software project contracts.

Provider contracts and outsourcing: The firm advises on a range of issues from the outsourcing of computer centres, to the structuring of provider contracts and electronic media. It also handles contract disputes, as well as the registration of domains and disputes arising out of such registration.

Intellectual property and data protection: Schneider & Schiffer advises on data protection law and intellectual property law, specialising in copyright issues.

Corporate and employment: The firm handles all employment and corporate aspects of information technology law.

Litigation and ADR: Although litigation is often appropriate, especially regarding software distribution and use of domains, research and developing contracts, members of the IT group try to use mediation wherever possible (often in cooperation with technical experts). Escrow: Another specialist area of the IT group is escrow (source code deposit), an issue which is related to intellectual property law as well as to contract and bankruptcy law.

LANGUAGES: English, French, German

S

For other recommended firms see pages 1485-1520

SCHÖNHERR BARFUSS TORGGLER & PARTNERS

HEAD OFFICE

Tuchlauben 13, (Kleeblattgasse 4),
A-1014 Vienna, Austria
Tel: +43 1 534 37 0 **Fax:** +43 1 533 25 21

Email: schoenherr@schoenherr.at / ch.herbst@schoenherr.at
Website: www.schoenherr.at

FIRM OVERVIEW

Senior partner: Walter Barfuss
Senior Partner Hellwig Torggler

Number of partners: 20
Number of other lawyers: 37

AREAS OF PRACTICE:

Corporate/M&A	45%
IP/media/telecoms	20%
Banking and finance	12%
Public law	10%
Litigation and arbitration	8%
EU/competition	5%

WORLDWIDE OFFICE CONTACTS

AUSTRIA
Tuchlauben 13, (Kleeblattgasse 4), A-1014 **Vienna**
Tel: +43 1 534 37 0 **Fax:** +43 1 533 25 21
Email: schoenherr@schoenherr.at / ch.herbst@schoenherr.at

BELGIUM
Avenue de Cortenberg 52, B-1000 **Brussels**
Tel: + 32 2 743 4040 **Fax:** + 32 2 743 4049
Email: schoenherr@schoenherr.at

ROMANIA
Strada SF Spiridon 12/A/III/8, 70231 **Bucharest**
Tel: +40 1 310 15 33 **Fax:** +40 1 211 10 27
Email: schoenherr@schoenherr.at

S

FIRM OVERVIEW: Founded in 1950, the firm has almost 60 lawyers. It is a full-service commercial law firm covering all areas of corporate, civil and commercial law. In addition to its Vienna and Graz offices the firm has branches in Brussels (opened in 1995) and Bucharest (1998).

INTERNATIONAL EXPERIENCE: The firm has considerable experience in international transactions and cross-border M&A. In its transactional work, the firm advises on medium to large scale M&A transactions including takeovers of listed companies. The firm advises on highly publicised privatisations in the banking, telecoms and energy sectors. The firm has advised on the restructuring of the Austrian energy sector, large scale privatisations, IPOs with dual listings, cross-border leases, ABS, structured finance and numerous M&A transactions.

INTERNATIONAL CLIENTS: Clients come from the financial, industrial and services sectors including banking, insurance, information technology, media, food, pharmaceuticals, energy, construction, automotive and paper and packaging.

MAIN INTERNATIONAL AREAS OF PRACTICE:

Corporate: The firm is involved in setting up companies, corporations and partnerships, and group restructurings (mergers, de-mergers, spin-offs).
M&A: The firm handles private and public mergers and acquisitions, including auction sales, strategic alliances and joint ventures, takeovers of listed companies.
Banking and finance: The firm advises on general banking, including investment fund matters; and project, asset and structured finance including cross-border (equipment and facility) leases.
Capital markets: The firm has an IPO practice and advises on cross-border equity and debt offerings, advising issuers, underwriters and transaction counsel.
Privatisations: The firm advises divesting entities and acquirers in the privatisation and reorganisation of banks and industrial conglomerates, including in the telecoms and energy sectors.
Intellectual property and IT: The firm handles trademarks, patents and copyrights including litigation and in particular unfair competition matters. The firm has a broad IT practice advising on matters such as on computer law, internet and new media.
Public law: The firm's regulatory practice advises on plant licensing, environmental matters, data protection, telecoms and energy law.
Telecoms: The firm handles all aspects of telecoms including transactional and regulatory compliance, representing investors in JV projects and licence tenders.
EU and competition: The firm is involved in competition and regulatory law at both EC and national levels including compliance, merger control, assisting corporations in cartel, state aid investigations and proceedings.
Pharmaceuticals, food and drugs: The firm advises on all aspects of this sector including regulatory matters, licensing and litigation.
Property: The firm handles all types of commercial property transactions, in particular development projects.
Insolvency: The firm is involved in corporate and business rescues and reconstructions, receiverships and administration.
Litigation and arbitration: The firm has a broad practice and advises on large scale corporate and business litigation and arbitration under ICC, UNCITRAL and Vienna rules.

LANGUAGES: English, French, German, Italian, Romanian

For other recommended firms see pages 1485-1520

SEBALU & LULE ADVOCATES AND LEGAL CONSULTANTS

HEAD OFFICE

EADB Building, 4 Nile Avenue, Mezzanine Floor, PO Box 2255
Kampala Uganda
Tel: +256 41 232 604 **Fax:** +256 41 230 521

Email: seblul@imul.com

WORLDWIDE OFFICE CONTACTS

UGANDA
EADB Building, 4 Nile Avenue, Mezzanine Floor, PO Box 2255, **Kampala**
Tel: +256 41 232 604 **Fax:** +256 41 230 521
Email: seblul@imul.com

FIRM OVERVIEW

Managing partner: Paulo Sebalu
Senior partner: Godfrey Serunkuma Lule

Number of partners worldwide: 4
Number of other lawyers worldwide: 6

AREAS OF PRACTICE:

Acquisitions .... *%
Arbitration .... *%
Banking and finance .... *%
Corporate .... *%
Insurance .... *%
Intellectual property .... *%
Litigation (civil) .... *%
Telecommunications .... *%
* Workload % not disclosed

FIRM OVERVIEW: Sebalu & Lule Advocates comprises four partners, five associate lawyers and one legal assistant. The firm handles a range of corporate, intellectual property, telecommunications, and banking and finance transactions.

INTERNATIONAL EXPERIENCE: The firm has advised on a range of transactions including private power projects, Ugandan banking, privatisation of state owned companies, and telecommunication projects.

INTERNATIONAL CLIENTS: The firm's clients include Clifford Chance, Meryll Lynch, Ansett Worldwide, Private Sector Foundation, Overseas Private Investment Corporation, International Finance Corporation, Lonrho Africa, Concern Worldwide, Standard Chartered Bank Uganda Ltd, and Crown Beverages.

MAIN INTERNATIONAL AREAS OF PRACTICE:

Banking and finance: The firm advises on a range of banking and finance issues. Recent work includes conducting a legal audit on Greenland Bank Ltd while it was under the statutory management of the Central Bank. The firm is currently acting as consultant to the Ugandan Bankers Institute on the proposed Financial Institutions Statute that is being implemented to strengthen the regulatory regime of the banking sector in Uganda.

Corporate: The firm has a general corporate practice. It has advised on a range of privatisations, joint ventures, and power projects. The firm worked with Deloitte & Touché on the compilation of a legal review of the 70 state owned enterprises slated for privatisation. It has recently handled a number of transactions in the electricity sub sector. The firm was involved in the proposed joint venture to establish Pakwach hydroelectric power station. This was the first private power project to be considered in Uganda. The firm also represented IFC in conducting due diligence into the construction of a US$450 million hydro electric power station at Kalagala on the River Nile. This transaction involved advising on all aspects of BOOT contracts, repatriation of profits, investment, employment and tax issues.

Telecommunications: The firm advised the Privatisation Unit on the privatisation of the Ugandan Posts and Telecommunications Corporation, and handled the drafting of the Ugandan Communications Bill, which liberalised the communications sector and established a regulatory framework for the industry. This provided the basis for the granting of the Second National Operator's (SNO) license and the splitting of former Uganda Posts and Telecommunications Corporation into Uganda Post Limited, Uganda Telecom Ltd and Uganda Telecommunications Commission (the regulator).

Other: Other work handled includes insurance, intellectual property, litigation (civil), arbitration and acquisitions

LANGUAGES: English

S

For other recommended firms see pages 1485-1520

SEIM-HAUGEN, STEENSTRUP & CO

HEAD OFFICE

Fridtjof Nansens pl 5, PO Box 1348 Vika,
N-0113 Osló, Norway
Tel: + 47 22 40 56 00 **Fax:** + 47 22 40 56 10

Website: www.seim-haugen.no

WORLDWIDE OFFICE CONTACTS

NORWAY
Fridtjof Nansens pl 5, PO Box 1348 Vika, N-0113 **Oslo**
Tel: + 47 22 40 56 00 **Fax:** + 47 22 40 56 10
Email: h.c.steenstrup@seim-haugen.no

FIRM OVERVIEW

Contact partner Hans Chr Steenstrup

Number of partners worldwide: 11

AREAS OF PRACTICE:

Area	%
Company/commercial	40%
Insurance/injury	15%
Real estate	15%
Employment	10%
Family/inheritance	10%
Litigation	10%

S

FIRM OVERVIEW: The firm was founded in 1995 as a direct successor of the two law firms Engelshløn & Co DA and Bøhn, Seim-Haugen, Hartsang and Roshauw. The former started its practice in 1968 and the latter has its origin in the 1920s. As a medium-sized Norwegian law firm, the firm advises on most civil law fields. The firm's 11 partners have broad experience in the various fields that the firm covers.

INTERNATIONAL EXPERIENCE: The firm has been engaged in several transactions during the last three years, mostly for smaller and medium-sized clients and foreign law firms, including M&A transactions, distributorship agreements, intellectual property questions and other related work. The firm participates in the Euro-American Lawyers Group, which provides instant access to expert advice throughout Europe and America.

INTERNATIONAL CLIENTS: The firm's client base includes foreign banks, industrial and trade entities, research institutions, foreign law firms and individuals.

MAIN INTERNATIONAL AREAS OF PRACTICE:
Company and commercial: Includes mergers and acquisitions, establishing affiliated companies, distributor and agency agreements and general commercial, contract and corporate law.
Employment: The firm represents both employers and employees in various kinds of employment relations, including questions related to trade unions.
Litigation: The firm has an extensive litigation practice and is admitted to all Norwegian courts. The firm also assists in arbitration and mediation.
Insurance/injury: The firm's personal injury practice represents both individuals and insurance companies.
Real estate: The firm is involved in matters concerning both commercial and private property.
Private individuals: The firm's network of international contacts permits an active international practice in cross-border family and inheritance matters.
Tax: The firm assists both companies and private persons on national and international tax questions.

LANGUAGES: Danish, English, Norwegian, Swedish

 For other recommended firms see pages 1485-1520

SHEARMAN & STERLING

HEAD OFFICE

599 Lexington Avenue,
New York, NY 10022-6069, USA
Tel: +1 212 848 4000 **Fax:** +1 212 848 7179
Website: www.shearman.com

FIRM OVERVIEW

Managing partner: Whitney D. Pidot
Senior partner: Stephen R. Volk
Number of partners worldwide: 197
Number of other lawyers worldwide: 738

AREAS OF PRACTICE:

Capital markets/corporate finance 29%
Bank finance, bankruptcy, projects and leasing 21%
M&A 17%
Other 17%
International arbitration and litigation 15%

FIRM OVERVIEW: Shearman & Sterling, founded in New York in 1873, has over 900 lawyers and 16 offices in the major financial and commercial centres of the world. The firm's practice comprises major areas of corporate, commercial and business law, with particular strengths in M&A, debt and equity capital markets and private finance. The firm has established several industry-specific multidisciplinary teams, including global technology and oil and gas. The firm is one of the few genuinely integrated global firms, and practises English, French, German and US law.

INTERNATIONAL EXPERIENCE: Long a global firm, Shearman & Sterling has an integrated network of 16 offices in major financial centres in North America, Europe and Asia, each of which has an extensive portfolio of international representations.

MAIN INTERNATIONAL AREAS OF PRACTICE:

M&A: The firm is representing General Electric Company in its acquisition of Honeywell International Inc. and represented British Telecommunications plc in its acquisition of Esat Telecom Group plc; France Télécom in its purchase of Orange plc from Vodafone; and SmithKline Beecham in its merger with Glaxo Wellcome to form Glaxo SmithKline plc.
Global capital markets: The firm represented the underwriters in the privatisation of Telekom Austria AG and the partial privatisation of ENEL. The firm was involved in many significant European IPOs, including those of Wanadoo, Software AG and Freeserve plc, and represented a number of Asian and Latin American companies in global offerings including China Mobile, PetroChina, Votorantim Celulose e Papel S.A. and Embraer-Empresa Brasileira de Aeronautica S.A.
Project finance: The firm represented the project companies in the Adapazari, Gebze and Izmir gas-fired power projects in Turkey and KEPCO in connection with the Ilijan gas-fired power project in the Philippines.
International litigation and arbitration: The firm represents clients before US and European courts. The firm's lawyers also appear before the Commission des Operations de Bourse in France and the Securities and Exchange Commission and Federal Trade Commission in the US.
Restructuring and bankruptcy: The firm represented ICO Global Communications, a development stage satellite telecommunications company, in Chapter 11 proceedings; the Provincial Government of Guandong Province, in connection with the restructuring of its subsidiaries and affiliates; Salomon Smith Barney and Credit Suisse First Boston in the financial bailout of Long-Term Capital Management; and international lenders in connection with the rescheduling of Korean and Russian bank credits.

WORLDWIDE OFFICE CONTACTS

CANADA
Commerce Court West, Suite 4405, P.O. Box 247, **Toronto,** M5L 1E8
Tel: +1 416 360 8484 **Fax:** +1 416 360 2958
Email: bvoran@shearman.com

CHINA
Suite 2318, China World Tower II, 1 Jianguomenwai Dajie,
Chaoyang District, 100004 **Beijing**
Tel: +86 10 6505 3399 **Fax:** +86 10 6505 1818
Email: eturner@shearman.com

FRANCE
114, avenue des Champs-Elysées, **Paris** 75008
Tel: +33 1 53 89 7000 **Fax:** +33 1 53 89 7070
Email: egaillard@shearman.com

GERMANY
Breite Strasse 69, 40213 **Düsseldorf**
Tel: +49 211 178 88 0 **Fax:** +49 211 178 88 88
Email: hmeyer-lindermann@shearman.com

Mainzer Landstrasse 16, 60325 **Frankfurt am Main**
Tel: +49 69 9711 1000 **Fax:** +49 69 9711 1100
Email: shutter@shearman.com

Otto-Beck Strasse 42, 68165 **Mannheim**
Tel: +49 621 4257 0 **Fax:** +49 621 4257 280
Email: jreichert@shearman.com

HONG KONG
12/F, Gloucester Tower, The Landmark, 11 Pedder Street,
Central, **Hong Kong**
Tel: +852 2978 8000 **Fax:** +852 2978 8099
Email: eturner@shearman.com

JAPAN
Fukoku Seimei Building, 5th Floor, 2-2-2, Uchisaiwaicho, Chiyoda-ku,
Tokyo 100-0011
Tel: +81 3 5251 1601 **Fax:** +81 3 5251 1602
Email: ddeck@shearman.com

SINGAPORE
6 Battery Road, #25-03, **Singapore** 049909
Tel: +65 230 3800 **Fax:** +65 230 3899
Email: cmiller@shearman.com

UNITED ARAB EMIRATES
Butti Al Otaiba Building, 13th Floor, Suite #1302, Sheikh Khalifa Street,
P.O. Box 2948, **Abu Dhabi**
Tel: +971 2 627 44 77 **Fax:** +971 2 626 8933
Email: pdundas@shearman.com

UNITED KINGDOM
Broadgate West, 9 Appold Street, **London** EC2A 2AP
Tel: +44 20 7655 5000 **Fax:** +44 20 7655 5500
Email: pgibson@shearman.com

USA
1550 El Camino Real, **Menlo Park,** CA 94025-4100
Tel: +1 650 330 2200 **Fax:** +1 650 330 2299
Email: plyons@shearman.com/bczachor@shearman.com

599 Lexington Avenue, **New York,** NY 10022-6069
Tel: +1 212 848 4000 **Fax:** +1 212 848 7179
Email: wpidot@shearman.com

555 California Street, Suite 2000, **San Francisco,** CA 94104-1522
Tel: +1 415 616 1100 **Fax:** +1 415 616 1199
Email: plyons@shearman.com

INTERNATIONAL CLIENTS: DaimlerChrysler AG, Morgan Stanley, Citigroup, Viacom Inc., France Télécom, Salomon Smith Barney, Merrill Lynch & Co., Lazard Frères, CSFB, DeBeers, Toyota, ABN AMRO, Goldman Sachs, British Telecom, JP Morgan, China Mobile, Elf Aquitaine, Deutsche Bank, DLJ, Rhône-Poulenc, TrizecHahn, Doris Duke Charitable Foundation, SmithKline Beecham, Corning, Barclays Bank, Bayerische Vereinsbank, Hoechst, Chase Securities, Warburg Dillon Read, Hellenic Telecom, Mitsubishi Corp., Telstra, Volvo, Anglo-American, Novartis, Nokia Corp., Waste Management Services and Deutsche Telekom.

LANGUAGES: More than 13 including Arabic, English, French, German, Hungarian, Italian, Japanese, Korean, Mandarin and Spanish.

HEAD OFFICE

Number of lawyers: 506

Main areas of work: M&A, capital markets, project development and finance, bank finance, privatisations, restructuring and bankruptcy, lease financing, executive compensation and employee benefits, litigation and arbitration, property, anti-trust, intellectual property, tax, international trade regulation, general corporate and securities law.
Top clients: Leading corporations, investment and merchant banks, commercial banks, governments and state-owned enterprises.
Highlight deals: Representing Viacom in its merger with CBS; Bell Canada International and other shareholders in the sale of their interest in Hansol M.com Co., Ltd to Korea Telecom; Fiat S.p.A in its strategic cooperation agreement with General Motors Corp.; Toyota Motor Corporation in listing its shares on the New York and London stock exchanges; the Fairness Committee of the NASD in the restructuring of the NASD (an owner of NASDAQ); Merrill Lynch in the development of the 'HOLDRs' investment product; Compañía de Nitrógeno de Cantarell in the US$1 billion development and financing of the world's largest nitrogen generation plant, located in Mexico.
Office profile: One of the few genuinely integrated global firms with 16 offices in nine countries.

WORLDWIDE OFFICES

CANADA

Commerce Court West, Suite 4405, P.O. Box 247, Toronto, M5L 1E8

Managing partner: Brice T. Voran
Number of lawyers: 14
Main areas of work: Capital markets, mergers and acquisitions.
Top clients: Goldman Sachs, Morgan Stanley, Merrill Lynch, Petro-Canada, Barrick Gold Corp., EdperBrascan Group and the Province of Ontario.
Highlight deals: Representing Fairfax Financial Holdings in its acquisition of TIG Holdings; public offerings for Nova Chemicals, Petro-Canada, Suncor and Agrium; GT Group Telecom in its IPO and related transactions.
Languages: English
Office profile: Specialists in complex cross-border and international transactions with government entities, financial institutions and corporations.

FRANCE

114, avenue des Champs-Elysées, 75008, Paris

Managing partner: Emmanuel Gaillard
Number of lawyers: 75
Main areas of work: Capital markets, M&A, finance, project development and finance, banking, international arbitration and litigation.
Top clients: Air France, Alcatel, Aventis, Crédit Lyonnais, France Télécom, General Electric, Hochtief, Pechlney, Rhodia, Société Générale, STMicroelectronics, Thomson multimedia, Total Fina Elf, Usinor.
Highlight deals: Recent M&A deals include representing France Télécom

USA
801 Pennsylvania Avenue, N.W., **Washington, DC** 20004-2604
Tel: +1 202 508 8000 **Fax:** +1 202 508 8100
Email: tmartin@shearman.com

in its acquisition of Orange plc and Alcatel in its acquisition of Genesys Telecommunications Laboratories. Recent Capital Markets deals include representing France Télécom and Orange in the IPO of Orange, France Télécom and Wanadoo in the IPO of Wanadoo, Alcatel in its issuance of Tracking Stock, and Thomson multimedia in the two rounds of its privatisation in 1999 and 2000. Recent Arbitration and Litigation cases include representing the Slovak Republic in a US$1 billion ICSID arbitration against a Czech state entity, and many other large construction, energy and investments arbitration and litigations.
Languages: Arabic, English, French, German, Hungarian, Italian, Spanish, Polish, Portuguese
Office profile: The office is actively involved in the French privatisations and M&A and is the base of the firm's arbitration group.

GERMANY

Breite Strasse 69, 40213 Düsseldorf

Otto-Beck Strasse 42, 68165 Mannheim

Mainzer Landstrasse 16, 60325 Frankfurt am Main

Managing partner: Georg F. Thoma
Number of lawyers: 67
Main areas of work: Mergers and acquisitions, capital markets, finance, project development and finance, banking, corporate reorganisation, anti-trust, tax, labour law and private clients.
Top clients: German and Continental European companies, such as Aventis, DaimlerChrysler, E.ON, Allianz, Kamps and SGL Carbon, as well as investment, merchant and commercial banks, such as Goldman Sachs, Merrill Lynch, Dresdner Bank and Bank Vontobel.
Highlight deals: The privatisation of Telekom Austria; SIEMENS AG in its acquisition of Atecs and Bank Austria in its merger with HypoVereinsbank; Lehman Brothers as lead underwriters for Software AG in its IPO; and Pixelpark AG on its global share offering.
Office profiles: The offices in Düsseldorf, Frankfurt and Mannheim have been involved in most major cross-border M&A transactions by German and international companies as well as many of the most significant equity offerings by German, Austrian and Swiss companies during the past few years. The offices have full German and US law capability.

CHINA/HONG KONG

12/F, Gloucester Tower, The Landmark, 11 Pedder Street, Central, Hong Kong

Suite 2318, China World Tower II, 1 Jianguomenwai Dajie, Chaoyang District, 100004 Beijing

Managing partner: Edward L. Turner III
Number of lawyers: 8 (Beijing); 24 (Hong Kong)
Main areas of work: Capital markets, mergers and acquisitions, project development and finance and restructuring.
Top clients: Chinese, Taiwanese, Hong Kong and Korean companies and government entities, and US investment and commercial banks.
Highlight deals: Representing China Mobile in a follow-on US$6.9 billion equity and convertible notes offering; PetroChina in its global IPO and dual listing on the NYSE and the Hong Kong Stock Exchanges; Hutchison on its US$3 billion issuance of notes exchangeable in shares of Vodafone; and InterGen in the development of the Meizhou Wan Power Project in Fujian, China.
Languages: Chinese, English, Korean

S

For other recommended firms see pages 1485-1520

Office profiles: The Hong Kong and Beijing offices include specialists with diverse skillls and languages, including attorneys qualified as lawyers in the People's Republic of China.

JAPAN

Fukoku Seimei Building, 5th Floor, 2-2-2, Uchisaiwaicho, Chiyoda-ku, Tokyo 100-0011

Managing partner: David D. Deck
Number of lawyers: 7
Main areas of work: Capital markets, mergers and acquisitions, securitization, leasing, finance, project development and finance, banking, property and international trade regulation.
Top clients: Toyota, Furukawa Electric, Advantest, eAccess, Shop Japan, Merrill Lynch, Goldman Sachs, Morgan Stanley, Sanwa, Citigroup, Dresdner Kleinwort Wasserstein, ING Barings, Fuji, Mitsubishi, Kyushu Electric, and IBJ.
Highlight deals: Representing Dresdner Kleinwort Wasserstein, HSBC and China.com Studios in their investment in Dai-job.com; MAN Roland Drucksmachinen in its joint venture with Dai Nippon Ink and Chemicals; Merrill Lynch in its real estate conduit loan program; ING Barings in its investment in and warehouse facility to Nice Co.
Languages: English, Japanese
Office profile: The office has lawyers with specialisation in mergers and acquisitions, international securities offerings and private finance.

SINGAPORE

6 Battery Road, #25-03, Singapore 049909

Managing partner: Calvert Miller
Number of lawyers: 16
Main areas of work: Capital markets, project development and finance, banking, restructuring and mergers and acquisitions.
Top clients: ABN AMRO, Citibank, Kreditanstalt fur Wiederaufbau, Bank of Thailand, Credit Suisse First Boston, Merrill Lynch, Morgan Stanley, Salomon Smith Barney, British Gas and Bank of Tokyo Mitsubishi.
Highlight deals: Representing the lenders in the 500MW San Lorenzo Philippines Power Project; Wireless Communications Services (owned by Orange PLC and the Charoen Pokphand Group in Thailand) in the development and financing of a mobile telecoms system in Thailand; advising the creditors in the $2.2 billion restructuring of the debt of Thaioil; the underwriters in connection with the US$335 million initial public offering and NYSE listing by ICICI Limited; representing the underwriters in the US$10 billion partial privatisation of Telstra.
Languages: English, Mandarin
Office profile: Responsible for work in Malaysia, Indonesia, Thailand, India, Australia, New Zealand, the Philippines and Vietnam.

UNITED ARAB EMIRATES

Butti Al Otaiba Building, 13th Floor, Suite #1302, Sheikh Khalifa Street, P.O. Box 2948, Abu Dhabi

Managing partner: Philip B. Dundas Jr
Number of lawyers: 2
Main areas of work: Oil and gas, mergers and acquisitions, project development and finance, banking, capital markets and shipping matters.
Top clients: Multinational companies, banks, investment agencies, government oil/gas ministries and state owned entities in the Middle East.
Highlight deals: Representing International Petroleum Investment Company in the acquisition of a substantial interest in Hyundai OIl Refinery Co., Barclays in the financing of A1 Taweelah A2 power privatisation and Abu Dhabi National Oil Company in a number of joint ventures.
Languages: Arabic, English, French, German, Italian
Office profile: Represents clients in the Middle East and internationally.

UNITED KINGDOM

Broadgate West, 9 Appold Street, London EC2A 2AP

Managing partner: Pamela M. Gibson
Number of lawyers: 115
Main areas of work: Capital markets, mergers and acquisitions, project development and finance, banking and leveraged finance, tax, international arbitration and litigation.
Top clients: UK and Continental European companies, investment and merchant banks, commercial banks and European governments. Clients include BG, BT, The BOC Group, Barclays, Corus, Cinven, Citigroup, Deutsche Bank, Edison Mission Energy, LM Ericsson, Goldman Sachs, InterGen, Investcorp, Merrill Lynch, Morgan Stanley, Nokia, Novartis, Orange, PowerGen and Volvo.
Highlight deals: Representing British Telecommunications plc, as US and English counsel, in its US$2.5 billion recommended 'white knight' offer for Esat Telecom Group plc; Paribas, Société Générale, ABN Amro and Dresdner Kleinwort Benson as arrangers and lenders in the US$700 million financing of Sidi Krir Power Project; Deutsche Bank, DLJ, Chase as senior debt underwriters of the €1.03 billion financing in connection with the leverage buy-out of United Biscuits; Freeserve plc, the UK's largest Internet company, in its IPO; and served as the global coordinators of the US$7.6 billion government sale of the last tranche of Endesa, Spain's national electric company.
Languages: English
Office profile: The firm has maintained an office in London since 1972.

USA - WEST COAST

555 California Street, Suite 2000, San Francisco, CA 94104-1522

1550 El Camino Real, Menlo Park, CA 94025-4100

Managing partner: Peter D. Lyons
Number of lawyers: 42
Main areas of work: Mergers and acquisitions, emerging growth companies, capital markets, intellectual property, anti-trust, tax, executive compensation and employee benefits and litigation.
Top clients: US and non-US companies, investment and merchant banks, particularly those active in technology including hardware, software, Internet/e-commerce, wireless and business solutions services.
Highlight deals: Representing Nokia in its acquisition of Ramp Networks, Inc.; Intershop Communications in its US$107 million IPO; and the underwriters to Blue Martini Software in its US$150 million IPO.
Languages: English
Office profile: The San Francisco and Menlo Park offices are cornerstones of the firm's internationally recognised global technology practice.

USA - EAST COAST

801 Pennsylvania Avenue, N.W., Washington, DC 20004-2604

Managing partner: Thomas S. Martin
Number of lawyers: 58
Main areas of work: Litigation, international trade and government relations, anti-trust, tax, corporate securities and investment management regulation.
Top clients: Include national and international clients in their dealings with the political, judicial and regulatory authority of the US government.
Highlight deals: Represented Rhône-Poulenc before the US competition authorities in connection with the merger of equals with Hoechst AG to form Aventis.
Languages: English
Office profile: Many lawyers previously held high-level government positions in the US Dept of Justice and the Securities and Exchange Commission. Specialises in regulatory and other US goverment-related work.

For other recommended firms see pages 1485-1520

LAW OFFICES OF SHEIKH TARIQ ABDULLAH

HEAD OFFICE

Sabeel Street, PO Box 148, Crater, Aden Yemen
Tel: +967 2 255 305 **Fax:** +967 2 251 638

Email: relevant@y.net.ye

FIRM OVERVIEW

Managing partner: Tariq Abdullah
Senior partner: Khalid Abdullah

Number of partners worldwide: 3
Number of other lawyers worldwide: 12

AREAS OF PRACTICE:
Banking and insurance ....*%
Corporate and commercial ....*%
Litigation ....*%
Oil, gas, minerals and energy ....*%
Shipping ....*%
* Workload % not disclosed

WORLDWIDE OFFICE CONTACTS

YEMEN
Sabeel Street, PO Box 148, Crater, **Aden**
Tel: +967 2 255 305 **Fax:** +967 2 25 1 638
Email: relevant@y.net.ye

PO Box 12480, **Sanaa**
Tel: +967 1241805 **Fax:** +967 7912 798

The firm has an associate office in Karachi

S

FIRM OVERVIEW: The firm's origins date back to 1927 when Mohmmad Abdullah founded a legal practice in the British colony of Aden. It is the oldest office on the Arabian Sub Peninsula. The firm provides a range of services to international clients, and is supported by its close links with major law firms around the world. Much of the work handled by the firm is channelled through a number of leading international law firms in London and their Middle East offices including Allen & Overy, Clifford Chance, Linklaters, Denton Wilde Sapte, Clyde & Co, and Richards Butler.

INTERNATIONAL EXPERIENCE: The firm handles both local and international transactions.

INTERNATIONAL CLIENTS: The firm's client base includes large international and multinational companies including Canadian Oxidental, Port of Singapore Authority, McDonalds International, Coca-Cola Middle East and North Africa, Cadbury Schweppes International Beverages, Merrill Lynch, Credit Agricole Indosuez, Smithkline Beecham Plc, British North of England P&I clubs, the British Embassy, and the US Embassy.

MAIN INTERNATIONAL AREAS OF PRACTICE:
Corporate: The firm handles the negotiation and drafting of international agreements. Work undertaken includes concessions and production sharing agreements for oil companies, franchise agreements for international beverage companies, and distribution agreements for international pharmaceutical, food, and automobile companies. The firm also handles the negotiation and drafting of joint venture agreements between local and foreign partners, the drafting of memorandums and articles of association for foreign companies under the investment law and Aden Free Zone, registration of branches and representative offices of foreign companies.
Shipping: The firm specialises in all aspects of shipping law. It advises ship owners, P&I clubs and charterers on a range of shipping related issues.
Litigation: When dispute resolution fails the firm is able to handle all aspects of litigation. Every member of the firm is involved in litigation work.

LANGUAGES: Arabic, English

For other recommended firms see pages 1485-1520

SHIN & KIM

HEAD OFFICE

4th Floor, Samdo Building, 1-170 Soonhwa-dong, Chung Ku
Seoul 100-130, South Korea
Tel: +82 2 316 4114 **Fax:** +82 2 756 6226

Email: ymshin@shinkim.com
Website: www.shinkim.com

WORLDWIDE OFFICE CONTACTS

SOUTH KOREA
4th Floor, Samdo Building, 1-170 Soonhwa-dong, Chung Ku,
Seoul 100-130
Tel: +82 2 316 4114 **Fax:** +82 2 756 6226
Email: ymshin@shinkim.com

FIRM OVERVIEW

Managing partner: Young-Moo Shin

Number of partners worldwide: 16
Number of other lawyers worldwide: 44

AREAS OF PRACTICE:

M&A	40%
Corporate	25%
Litigation and arbitration	20%
Banking and finance	15%

FIRM OVERVIEW: Founded in 1981, Shin & Kim has grown steadily over the past two decades. The firm comprises Korean lawyers, foreign legal consultants, and certified public accountants. Many of the firm's Korean lawyers have studied abroad and are licensed in foreign jurisdictions including the State of New York. Shin & Kim offer comprehensive advice in all areas of commercial and business law and litigation. The firm has long-standing links with law firms worldwide, including the exchange of personnel.

INTERNATIONAL EXPERIENCE: Shin & Kim advises leading multinational corporations and prominent law firms on Korean law.
The firm advised Scudder Stevens & Clark (now Scudder Kemper Investments Inc) on the establishment of the Korea Fund, the first foreign mutual fund licensed to trade in Korean securities.

INTERNATIONAL CLIENTS: The firm's client base includes large companies, banks, insurance companies, and institutions conducting cross-border transactions or operations in Korea.

MAIN INTERNATIONAL AREAS OF PRACTICE:
M&A: The firm's M&A transactions range from small private acquisitions to cross-border takeovers of listed companies. During 1999 and 2000, Shin & Kim advised on over 100 M&A transactions, valued at approximately US$4 billion. Notable transactions include advising IPIC, an UAE investor, in its US$500 million acquisition of an oil refinery, and assisting a consortium led by AIG and WL Ross & Co. to invest US$1 billion in and assume control of Hyundai Securities.
Banking and finance: Shin & Kim advise on all areas of banking and finance, and counts most of the leading foreign banks and financial companies in Korea among its clients. The firm's practice areas include secured and syndicated loan transactions and guarantees, structured finance, project finance, leasing, and tax-based finance.
Corporate: The firm advise on all aspects of general corporate law and operations in Korea including the drafting and negotiation of contracts in English and Korean for international and domestic use.
Insurance and reinsurance: In recent years Shin & Kim's insurance practice has shifted focus from operational issues to advising foreign clients interested in M&A transactions with Korean insurance companies.
Intellectual property: Shin & Kim's lawyers act in the negotiation of licence agreements and disputes over intellectual property matters. The firm specialise in trademarks, patents, and copyrights, and has an integrated team of more than 12 professionals handling IP matters, including two Korean lawyers and ten patent attorneys. They are supported by a para-professional staff of more than 30.
Employment: The firm advises multinational and domestic corporations on compliance with labour regulations and employer obligations. They also advise on Korean labour law in relation to M & A transactions.
Litigation and arbitration: Shin & Kim has a major litigation practice that comprises retired senior judges and a former Justice of the Supreme Court of Korea. The firm has represented the state-owned Korea National Tobacco & Ginseng Corporation in tobacco-related litigation and also handles International Chamber of Commerce and Korean Commercial Arbitration Board arbitrations.
Private equity: Shin & Kim have assisted in the development of Korea's private equity markets, having established the first domestic private equity fund.
Securities and financial markets: The firm specialises in Korean law relating to funds, securities, and derivatives. In addition to advising foreign and domestic securities companies the firm has advised the Ministry of Finance and Economy, the Financial Supervisory Commission and Financial Supervisory Service, the Securities and Futures Board, the Korea Stock Exchange, and other institutions on the development of Korean securities laws.
Tax: The firm's three tax lawyers and four certified public accountants advise multinational and domestic clients, including structuring M&A transactions to reducing tax burdens.

LANGUAGES: Chinese, English, Japanese, Korean

SHONUBI, MUSOKE & CO

HEAD OFFICE

SM Chambers, Plot 36 Nile Avenue, PO Box 3213
Kampala, Uganda
Tel: +256 41 230 384 **Fax:** +256 41 230 388

Email: shonubi@starcom.co.ug
Website: www.shonubimusoke.co.ug

FIRM OVERVIEW

Senior partner: Alan Shonubi

Number of partners worldwide: 3
Number of other lawyers worldwide: 9

AREAS OF PRACTICE:

Corporate	30%
Banking and finance	20%
Telecommunications	15%
Litigation and arbitration	10%
Privatisation and deregulation	8%
General	7%
Intellectual property	5%
Transport	5%

WORLDWIDE OFFICE CONTACTS

UGANDA
SM Chambers, Plot 36 Nile Avenue, PO Box 3213, **Kampala**
Tel: +256 41 230 384 **Fax:** +256 41 230 388
Email: shonubi@starcom.co.ug

S

FIRM OVERVIEW: Shonubi, Musoke & Co Advocates was founded in 1987. The firm has steadily grown into one of the largest law firms in Uganda and has established a reputation as one of the leading law firms in the country.

INTERNATIONAL EXPERIENCE: The firm handles a large volume of international work mainly in the areas of commercial arbitration, civil litigation, intellectual property, mergers and acquisitions, privatisation, project finance, secured lending and telecommunications law.

INTERNATIONAL CLIENTS: The firm's client base includes international law firms, international lenders, banking and financial institutions, development agencies, foreign government departments, individuals, insurance companies, major airlines, multinational agencies and corporations, and non-governmental organisations.

MAIN INTERNATIONAL AREAS OF PRACTICE:

Banking and finance: Shonubi, Musoke & Co. advises on all areas of banking and finance law including complex banking issues, documentary credits, electronic banking, innovative finance structuring, project and asset finance, regulatory advice, secured and unsecured lending, securitisation and syndicated loans.

Transport: The firm advises on all aspects of maritime, aviation and general transport law. It regularly advises on diverse issues including breaches of contracts of carriage, customary terms of carriage, fatal accidents, loss and/or damage of cargo and the application of international conventions (including the Hague, Hamburg and Warsaw conventions).

Corporate: The firm offers a full range of corporate law services. It advises on company law, corporate governance, joint ventures, insolvency, and mergers and acquisitions. Shonubi, Musoke & Co also advises on structuring and incorporation of corporate entities and offers company secretarial services.

Intellectual property: The firm handles all aspects of intellectual property. Work undertaken includes advising on applications for intellectual property rights, dealings in intellectual property rights and intellectual property litigation.

Litigation and arbitration: The firm has advised several multinational corporations on commercial litigation issues. The firm also handles international commercial arbitration including arbitration before International Chamber of Commerce tribunals.

Privatisation and deregulation: The firm advises foreign and local investors and the Government of Uganda on all aspects of privatisation.

Telecommunications: Shonubi, Musoke & Co advises various international lenders involved in financing telecommunications companies. It also advises multinational corporations investing in telecommunications and has handled various acquisitions in the telecommunications industry.

General: The firm regularly advises international clients on local law matters encompassing a broad range of issues. It frequently advises on financing transactions and has also been requested to give evidence relating to Uganda law before international tribunals.

For other recommended firms see pages 1485-1520

SHOOK LIN & BOK

In joint venture with Allen & Overy, in Allen & Overy, Shook Lin & Bok Joint Law Venture, Singapore

HEAD OFFICE

1 Robinson Road, #18-00 AIA Tower,
Singapore 048542, Singapore
Tel: +65 535 1944 **Fax:** +65 535 8577

Email: slb@shooklin.com.sg

FIRM OVERVIEW

Senior partner: Philip N Pillai

Number of partners worldwide: 20
Number of other lawyers worldwide: 28

AREAS OF PRACTICE:

Banking and corporate banking .... *%
Banking and finance litigation .... *%
China practice .... *%
Corporate and commercial .... *%
Corporate finance and international finance .... *%
Regional practice .... *%
* Workload % not disclosed

FIRM OVERVIEW: Founded in Malaysia in 1918 and established in Singapore in 1964, Shook Lin & Bok currently employs 20 partners and 28 associates. It is a full service commercial law firm, acting for clients in Singapore and the Asia Pacific region. In September 2000, Allen & Overy Shook Lin & Bok Joint Law Venture (JLV) was established in Singapore. The JLV practice areas are banking, capital markets, derivatives, international arbitration, securitisation, project finance, and corporate.

INTERNATIONAL EXPERIENCE: The firm has handled listings on the Singapore Exchange of companies from the People's Republic of China, Taiwan and Hong Kong. It has also acted for financial institutions and corporate borrowers in the financing of major commercial and residential projects in Vietnam and Malaysia.

INTERNATIONAL CLIENTS: The firm's clients are based in Brunei, Indonesia, Laos, Malaysia, Myanmar, the People's Republic of China, the Philippines, Taiwan, Thailand, Vietnam, India and Cambodia.

MAIN INTERNATIONAL AREAS OF PRACTICE:

China practice: Activities include direct investment and financing of projects in China.
Regional practice: The firm acts for banks, listed companies and funds in their financing and investments in Southeast Asia, particularly Indonesia, Thailand, Malaysia, Vietnam and Cambodia.
Banking and corporate banking: The firm provides services relating to regulation and supervision of fully licensed, restricted and off-shore banks, merchant banks, finance companies and non-bank financial institutions in Singapore. It negotiates and drafts documents for domestic and cross border credit facilities. It also advises on Internet banking and Internet-only banking.
Corporate finance and international finance: The firm advises on and prepares documentation required for domestic and foreign listings and issues of equity, debt and hybrid instruments on the Singapore Exchange, derivatives, mergers and acquisitions of listed and non-listed companies, corporate restructuring and schemes of arrangement, fund management and venture capital investments including domestic and international unit trusts, investment companies and funds.

WORLDWIDE OFFICE CONTACTS

SINGAPORE
1 Robinson Road, #18-00 AIA Tower, **Singapore** 048542
Tel: +65 535 1944 **Fax:** +65 535 8577
Email: slb@shooklin.com.sg

ASSOCIATED OFFICES

MALAYSIA
Shook Lin & Bok, 20th floor Arab-Malaysian Building,
55 Jalan Raja Chulan, 50200 **Kuala Lumpur**
Tel: +60 3 2011788 **Fax:** +60 3 2011775
Email: shooklin@tm.net.my

Corporate and commercial: The firm provides comprehensive services relating to the setting up of businesses in Singapore. It advises on the structuring, negotiation and documentation of joint ventures, as well as business and asset acquisitions in Singapore and the Asian region. The firm also provides advice and documentation services in relation to general commercial matters.
Banking and finance litigation: The firm handles a broad range of both domestic and international litigation that involves banking and documentary credits, guarantees and other forms of security and debt recovery.
Corporate, insurance and commercial litigation: The firm deals with monetary and contractual claims, property litigation, construction disputes, securities. It also handles commodities and futures disputes, insurance, employment and matrimonial matters, as well as handling the enforcement of foreign judgements and arbitral awards.
Insolvency: The firm provides advisory and enforcement services in bankruptcies, liquidations and receiverships, judicial management, reconstructions, restructuring of companies and rescue operations.
Arbitration and alternative dispute resolution: The firm acts both as counsel and arbitrator in arbitrations, as well as providing advisory, negotiation and enforcement services in alternative methods of dispute resolution.
E-commerce: The firm advises on the establishment and initial development of Internet start-up companies including venture capital funding, IPOs, online financial services and products, joint ventures, B2B and B2C services.
Intellectual property and technology: The firm provides advisory, documentation, protection and enforcement services in copyright, designs, patents, trademarks, trade secrets and confidential information. The firm also advises on complex acquisitions, joint ventures and technology transfer matters involving transnational and multi-jurisdictional clients.
Telecommunications and broadcasting: The firm advises on communications law and regulation including the form and structure of regulatory frameworks, financing cross-border telecommunications network services, joint ventures, tenders, mergers and acquisitions and structuring and listings of IT/telecommunications companies on the NASDAQ/Singapore Exchange.

LANGUAGES: Bahasa Indonesia, Bahasa Malaysia, English, Mandarin

ShookLin & Bok

S

For other recommended firms see pages 1485-1520

S HOROWITZ & CO

HEAD OFFICE

31 Ahad Ha'am Street,
Tel-Aviv 65202, Israel
Tel: +972 3 567 0666 **Fax:** +972 3 566 0974
Email: Talb@s-horowitz.co.il

FIRM OVERVIEW

Managing partner: Tal Band

Number of partners worldwide: 15
Number of other lawyers worldwide: 41

AREAS OF PRACTICE:

Banking .... *%
Company and commercial .... *%
Intellectual property .... *%
Labour law .... *%
Litigation and arbitration .... *%
Pharmaceuticals .... *%
Property .... *%
Securities .... *%
Tax .... *%
Telecommunications .... *%
Transportation .... *%
* Workload % not disclosed

FIRM OVERVIEW: S Horowitz & Co was established in 1921 in Tel Aviv, Israel. The firm consists of approximately 60 lawyers and is the largest commercial law firm in Tel Aviv. It represents international and domestic clients in a range of commercial transactions, litigation, intellectual property and other areas of law. The firm is the member for Israel of Lex Mundi - an international network of law firms based in 76 countries world-wide.

INTERNATIONAL EXPERIENCE: S Horowitz & Co specialises in international corporate transactions, commercial litigation, intellectual property, banking, and company and commercial on an international scale. The firm specialises in international mergers and acquisitions, joint ventures and corporate finance. The firm has dealt with the ownership of foreign assets, companies, patents and real estate. It has represented companies and financial institutions in multi-million dollar transactions and has acted in M&A transactions involving the acquisition by major multinationals of Israeli companies and in the establishment of subsidiaries and branches in Israel.

INTERNATIONAL CLIENTS: S Horowitz & Co represents major Israeli and international companies, banks, insurance companies and public institutions in cross-border transactions, litigation and arbitration and other areas of practice. Chase Manhattan, ICI, Heinz, Alcatel, Starbucks, British Airways, Hilton Hotels, Bear Stearns, Hewlett Packard, PepsiCo, Bristol-Myers-Squibb, Glaxo Wellcome, Pfizer and BellSouth are just a sample of the multinationals represented by the firm. The firm's client base also includes major utility companies.

MAIN INTERNATIONAL AREAS OF PRACTICE:

Company and commercial: The firm has extensive experience in all company and commercial areas, including mergers and acquisitions, joint ventures, international contracts and all aspects of general company law. It represents two of Israel's largest accounting firms which are associates of the "Big Five" accounting firms.
Commercial litigation: S Horowitz & Co deals with commercial litigation and national and international arbitrations. The firm's lawyers frequently appear in the Supreme Court. Matters dealt with also include criminal and civil antitrust matters and corporate and agency issues. The firm deals with class actions, tenders and public/administrative law issues.
Banking: S Horowitz has wide experience in the field of multicurrency syndicated loan transactions. It has acted during the past year on virtually all the major syndicated lendings in Israel. The firm also has experience of international banking insurance claims and advises European and American banks on issues such as banking law, documentary credits and the establishment of offices in Israel. The firm acted for HSBC in the setting up of its branch office in Israel.
Project finance: The firm has advised on project financing in various sectors including electricity, roads, tunnels, construction, telecommunications and infrastructure. It acted for the bidder, the consortium member or the bank in most of Israel's major projects.
Securities: The firm acts in transactions relating to the issuance of debt securities and other instruments, international equity and equity-linked offerings, securitisations and derivatives. S Horowitz & Co is experienced in acting in relation to offerings in Israel and in the entering into of derivative transactions with Israeli counterparties. The firm also acts for foreign underwriters in relation to IPOs which require legal due diligence to be performed in relation to Israeli companies and Israeli law.
Intellectual property: With one of the largest intellectual property departments in Israel, the firm advises on all contentious and non-contentious aspects of intellectual property and information technology, including patents, trademarks, copyright, designs, trade secrets, anti-counterfeiting, marketing law and information technology, including technology transfer agreements and collaboration research agreements. The firm also provides a full patent and trademarks filing, prosecution and portfolio management service. Members of the firm sat on the relevant parliamentary committees which enacted TRIPS into Israel law and are regular contributors to practitioner books on intellectual property.
Pharmaceuticals: The firm advises clients in this field in general commercial matters and litigation as well as on issues particular to this industry. Major international companies have been represented with respect to issues from R&D agreements to the establishment of an Israeli presence, including Bristol-Myers Squibb, Glaxo Wellcome and Pfizer.
Telecommunications: S Horowitz represents a large number of international telecommunications companies including BellSouth and Motorola.
Tax: The firm's tax practice offers broad expertise in all aspects of business taxation, including mergers, acquisition, corporate restructurings, joint ventures, capital markets, international tax planning, property taxation, developments, value-added tax and customs duties. S. Horowitz & Co handles negotiations and, where necessary, contentious dealings with the Israeli tax authorities on behalf of its clients.
Commercial property: The firm deals with all types of commercial property transactions and is also involved in the construction and development aspects of law on behalf of both commercial and agricultural concerns.
Transportation: Flag carriers and major international airlines constitute some of the firm's client base in this field. The firm has also dealt with international freight issues.
Labour law: Representation in the labour courts is available in addition to the full range of advice.

LANGUAGES: English, German, Hebrew

OFFICE CONTACTS

ISRAEL
31 Ahad Ha'am Street, **Tel-Aviv** 65202
Tel: +972 3 567 0666 **Fax:** +972 3 566 0974
Email: Talb@s-horowitz.co.il

For other recommended firms see pages 1485-1520

SIDLEY & AUSTIN

HEAD OFFICE

Bank One Plaza, 10 South Dearborn Street,
Chicago Illinois 60603, USA
Tel: +1 312 853 7000 **Fax:** +1 312 853 7036
Website: www.sidley.com

FIRM OVERVIEW

Chairman of the management committee: Charles W Douglas
Chairman of the executive committee: Thomas A Cole

Number of partners worldwide: 385
Number of other lawyers worldwide: 546

AREAS OF PRACTICE:

Antitrust	*%
Appellate	*%
Banking and financial transactions	*%
Corporate	*%
Corporate reorganisation and bankruptcy	*%
Employment and labour	*%
Environmental	*%
Estate planning	*%
Government contracts	*%
Health care	*%
Immigration	*%
Insurance and financial services	*%
Intellectual property	*%
Investment products and derivatives	*%
Litigation	*%
Real estate	*%
Securitisation and structured finance	*%
Tax	*%
Technology and e-commerce	*%
Telecommunications	*%

* Workload % not disclosed

FIRM OVERVIEW: With lawyers on three continents, the firm has the resources to serve clients worldwide. The firm's lawyers take a problem-solving approach and offer clients practical advice and creative solutions to their business concerns. Sidley & Austin's aim is to create and build long-term value-added relationships.

INTERNATIONAL CLIENTS: The firm's clients include individuals, entrepreneurs and executives; industrial and service corporations; venture capital/private equity firms; partnerships; investment banks; commercial banks; public utilities; non-profit organisations; mutual funds; insurance and other financial services companies; government agencies.

MAIN INTERNATIONAL AREAS OF PRACTICE: Sidley & Austin has a major corporate and financial transactions practice with significant activity in all areas, including mergers and acquisitions, spin-offs, divestitures and joint ventures as well as all types of financings, including public offerings, project financings, asset securitisations and bank lending transactions.

LANGUAGES: Arabic, Bahasa (Indonesia), Chinese (Mandarin, Shanhainese, Cantonese, Hokkien, Fuchow), Danish, Efik (African), Finnish, French, Gaelic, German, Greek, Hebrew, Hindi, Hungarian, Italian, Japanese, Korean, Latin, Latvian, Lithuanian, Malay, Norwegian, Polish, Portuguese, Russian, Sanskrit, Spanish, Swahili (African), Swedish, Tagalog, Taiwanese, Tamil, Telugu, Welsh, Yoruba (African)

WORLDWIDE OFFICE CONTACTS

CHINA
Shui On Plaza, 333 Middle Huai Hai Road, **Shanghai** 200021
Tel: +86 21 5306 2866 **Fax:** +86 21 5306 8966

HONG KONG
Two Exchange Square, Suites 3403-5, Central **Hong Kong**
Tel: +852 2901 3800 **Fax:** +852 2901 3850

JAPAN
Taisho Seimei Hibiya Building, 7th Floor, 9-1, Yurakucho 1-Chome, Chiyoda-ku, **Tokyo** 100-0006
Tel: +81 3 3218 5900 **Fax:** +81 3 3218 5922

SINGAPORE
6 Battery Road, Suite 40-01, **Singapore** 049909
Tel: +65 230 3900 **Fax:** +65 230 3939

UNITED KINGDOM
One Threadneedle Street, **London** EC2R 8AW
Tel: +44 20 7360 3600 **Fax:** +44 20 7626 7937

USA
Bank One Plaza, 10 South Dearborn Street, **Chicago** Illinois 60603
Tel: +1 312 853 7000 **Fax:** +1 312 853 7036

717 N Harwood, Suite 3400, **Dallas** TX 75201
Tel: +1 214 981 3300 **Fax:** +1 214 981 3400

555 West Fifth Street, **Los Angeles** California 90013
Tel: +1 213 896 6000 **Fax:** +1 213 896 6600

875 Third Avenue, **New York** NY 10022
Tel: +1 212 906 2000 **Fax:** +1 212 906 2021

One Union Square, 600 University Street, Suite 1601, **Seattle** WA 98101
Tel: +1 206 224 4222 **Fax:** +1 206 224 4299

1722 Eye Street N.W., **Washington DC** 20006
Tel: +1 202 736 8000 **Fax:** +1 202 736 8711

HEAD OFFICE:

Bank One Plaza, 10 South Dearborn Street, Chicago IL 60603
Number of lawyers: 428
Office profile: The firm's largest office opened in 1866. Today, approximately 428 lawyers work in the Chicago office, representing a broad range of clients including major manufacturing, service, utility, communications, financial services and transportation businesses, in a broad range of transactional, litigation and regulatory matters.

WORLDWIDE OFFICES

CHINA

Shui On Plaza, 333 Middle Huai Hai Road, Shanghai 200021, P.R.C.
Number of lawyers: 4
Main areas of work: Corporate and commercial, private equity and venture capital, internet and e-commerce, banking, project finance, regulatory, intellectual property and tax.
Office Profile: This office was opened in April, 1999. Together with the Hong Kong office, it houses the firm's China Practice Group. Some of the recent matters involving this group include regulatory compliance and approvals, establishment and restructuring of enterprises, mergers and acquisitions, real property transactions and tax compliance.

S

HONG KONG

Two Exchange Square, Suites 3403-5, Central

Number of lawyers: 11

Main areas of work: Project finance transactions, investments in China, securitisations, private equity, venture capital, mergers and acquisitions, e-commerce, corporate finance, structured finance and other Hong Kong and cross-border corporate and securities matters.

Office Profile: Opened in 1999, the Hong Kong office is with the Shanghai office the newest of Sidley & Austin's international offices. In addition to practising the name of Sidley & Austin, the firm can also provide Hong Kong law capabilities through locally qualified lawyers practising under the name of Eric Ho & Co. The Hong Kong office works closely with the Shaghai office on projects involving investments in Chinese companies and financings from Chinese companies.

JAPAN

Taisho Seimei Hibiya Building, 7th Floor, 9-1, Yurakucho 1-Chome, Chiyoda-ku, Tokyo 100-0006

Number of lawyers: 3

Main areas of work: Acquisitions and joint ventures, project financing and secured financing, corporate restructurings, securitisations, license transactions and immigration.

Office Profile: Sidley & Austin was established in Tokyo in 1990. The office represents major Japanese trading companies, financial institutions, manufacturers and telecommunication companies in connection with their investments in the US, SE Asia and Latin America, and also represents US clients in connection with their investments in Japan. The office also assists Japanese clients with respect to litigation matters in the US.

SINGAPORE

6 Battery Road, Suite 40-01, Singapore 049909

Number of lawyers: 11

Main areas of work: Acquisitions, divestitures and joint ventures, corporate restructurings, securitisations, initial public offerings, privatisations, U.S. securities transactions, and project financings.

Office Profile: Sidley & Austin first established a presence in Singapore in 1982. The Singapore office has been involved in transactions in many Asian countries, including Indonesia, Malaysia, Thailand, The Philippines, China, Hong Kong, Pakistan and Sri Lanka.

UNITED KINGDOM

One Threadneedle Street, London EC2R 8AW

Number of lawyers: 50

Office profile: The firm opened its office in the City of London in 1974 and in 1994 it established a multinational partnership. The London office advises clients on both English and American law focusing on banking and structured finance, corporate commercial, tax and property. The London office now has approximately 50 solicitors. Many of the lawyers in the office have extensive European practice experience and can assist clients with matters within the European Union.

USA

717 N Harwood, Suite 3400, Dallas, TX 75201

Number of lawyers: 31

Office profile: With approximately 31 lawyers, the Dallas office focuses exclusively on patent, trademark, copyright and unfair competition law, and is the centre of the firmwide intellectual property practice. The lawyers in the office have backgrounds in technical disciplines including electrical, mechanical and chemical engineering as well as chemistry, biotechnology and computer-related technology, and the licensing of intellectual property are other services offered by the office.

555 West Fifth Street, Los Angeles, CA 90013

Number of lawyers: 118

Office profile: The firm has had a presence in Los Angeles since 1980, with approximately 118 lawyers. The California practice includes banking and corporate law, bankruptcy and corporate reorganisation, tax, environmental law, health care, labor and employment matters, general and appellate litigation, media and First Amendment matters, real estate law, corporate criminal defense and internal investigations, and intellectual property and technology.

875 Third Avenue, New York, NY 10022

Number of lawyers: 119

Office profile: The New York office, which opened in 1982, comprises approximately 119 lawyers. It represents international clients in corporate, securities and banking and commercial matters, as well as tax, trusts and estates, and real estate matters. The office handles a wide range of litigation, bankruptcies and corporate reorganisations, and environmental advice and litigation. Also experienced in domestic and cross-border transactions, including mergers and acquisitions, public offerings and private placements, structured finance transactions, secured lending, project finance and leasing transactions, commodities matters and international privatisation. Litigators in the office handle antitrust, commercial, financial, intellectual property, product liability, securities and tort disputes in state and federal coutrts.

One Union Square, 600 University Street, Suite 1601, Seattle, WA 98101

Number of lawyers: 5

Office profile: The firm's newest US office, opened in 1998. The lawyers in the Seattle office focus their corporate, commercial and finance practices on technology, telecommunications and commercial aviation and aerospace matters. It works closely with the Los Angeles office, as well as other firm offices, in advising the West Coast technology community.

1722 Eye Street N.W., Washington, DC 20006

Number of lawyers: 151

Office profile: Approximately 151 lawyers practise in this office, which opened in 1963. The office represents local, national and international business firms, as well as various governmental entities. Its lawyers handle antitrust, bank and other financial regulation, governmental contracts, health care, trade regulation, communications, food and drug, transportation, export controls, tax, energy, environmental and other legislative and regulatory issues. It represents clients in constitutional, appellate, commercial and corporate criminal litigation, and maintains a practice before the US Supreme Court.

SIDLEY & AUSTIN

For other recommended firms see pages 1485-1520

SIGUION REYNA MONTECILLO & ONGSIAKO

HEAD OFFICE

4th and 6th Floors, Citibank Centre, Paseo de Roxas Ave,
Makati City 1200, The Philippines
Tel: +63 2 810 0281 **Fax:** +63 2 8191 498

Email: srmo@i-next.net
Website: www.srmo-law.com

WORLDWIDE OFFICE CONTACTS

PHILIPPINES
4th and 6th Floors, Citibank Centre, Paseo de Roxas Ave, **Makati City** 1200
Tel: +63 2 810 0281 **Fax:** +63 2 8191 498
Email: srmo@i-next.net

FIRM OVERVIEW

Chairman: Leonardo T. Siguion Reyna
Vice-chairman: Manuel G. Montecillo
Managing partner: Victor N. Alimurung

Number of partners worldwide: 22
Number of other lawyers worldwide: 22

AREAS OF PRACTICE:

Employment and immigration 30%
Corporate/securities/banking and insurance 20%
Litigation/arbitration/aviation and maritime/product liability ...20%
Intellectual property 10%
Mergers and acquisitions 10%
Real estate transactions/tax and estate planning 8%
Computer and internet 2%

FIRM OVERVIEW: Established in 1901, Siguion Reyna Montecillo & Ongsiako is the oldest law firm in the Philippines. Comprising 22 partners and 22 associates, the firm handles a wide range of legal issues including corporate and commercial law, employment, litigation, banking and finance, intellectual property, tax, product liability, commercial real estate transactions, IT, aviation and maritime law.

INTERNATIONAL EXPERIENCE: The firm advises a number of multinational corporations (including Philippine subsidiaries) and have advised many foreign clients on a number of notable transactions. In recent years they have advised Unilever on its purchase of Selecta's ice cream business; Chempill, Albright and Wilson on the divestment of its surfactant business; HSBC's takeover of Republic National Bank of New York's Philippine branch operations; the merger of Siemens Nixdorf Information systems Philippines Inc with Siemens; Datastream International Limited in its purchase of FT Information from Pearson NV; Asea Brown Boveri on the sale of ABB Koppel to Fedders International.

INTERNATIONAL CLIENTS: The firm's clients include Fortune 500 companies from the US, Canada, Europe, Japan, South East Asia, and many of the Philippines' top 200 companies. Other clients include Cathay Pacific, Saudi Arabian Airlines, Malaysia Airlines, Eva Air, HSBC, Citibank, ABN-AMRO, Dao Heng Bank, Unilever, Coca-Cola, Autoliv AB, Swedish Match, Asea Brown Boveri, Siemens, Ericsson, ABB Alstom Power, Rolls Royce, and Adtranz Daimler.

MAIN INTERNATIONAL AREAS OF PRACTICE:

Employment: The firm is experienced in all aspects of Philippine employment law and is regarded as having one of the Philippines' leading employment practices. It handles collective bargaining negotiations, strike contingency and strike handling, labour litigation arising from termination, wage claims, unfair labour practice acts and other employment disputes. The firm advises its corporate clients on labour standards, occupational health and safety, and labour relation issues.

Corporate: The firm handles corporate and joint venture formation, corporate housekeeping (corporate secretary work), capital restructuring and quasi-reorganisations, application for incentives (under special laws and with specialised agencies such as the Philippines Export Zone authority and the Board of Investments). In conjunction with its corporate litigation and securities practice group, the firm also advises on corporate finance, securities regulation, bankruptcy and liquidation, Insurance Commission and Bangko Sentral ng Pilipinas (the Philippine Central Bank) proceedings.

Litigation and arbitration: The firm handles civil, criminal and administrative litigation and represents Philippine and foreign clients before municipal trial courts, regional trial courts, the Sandiganbayan (a special Philippine court with jurisdiction over matters involving public officers), the Court of Tax Appeals, the Court of Appeals, the Supreme Court, and almost all the quasi-judicial bodies.

M&A: The firm handles a wide range of commercial transactions including divestments, mergers and acquisitions, spin-offs and hive-downs.

Intellectual property: Siguion Reyna Montecillo & Ongsiako handles all types of intellectual property registrations and applications including patents, trademarks, trade name, service marks and copyright. It also handles the preparation of patent claims and application documents. The firm advises on the protection and enforcement of intellectual property rights including opposition and cancellation of registration, interference actions, suits for infringement and unfair competition. It also handles the preparation and review of technology transfer agreements, as well as other forms of licensing and assignments of intellectual property rights. Siguion Reyna Montecillo & Ongsiako's IP department has close links with several hundred patent attorneys around the world, as well as with the patent departments of major international corporations.

LANGUAGES: English, Filipino, Mandarin, Spanish

S

SILVA & PIÑEROS

HEAD OFFICE

Carrera 9 No. 74-08 Of. 210
Bogota, Colombia
Tel: +57 1 345 5066 **Fax:** +57 1 211 9068

Email: info@silvaypineros.com.co
Website: www.silvapineros.com

WORLDWIDE OFFICE CONTACTS

COLOMBIA
Carrera 9 No. 74-08 Of. 210, **Bogota**
Tel: +57 1 345 5066 **Fax:** +57 1 211 9068
Email: info@silvaypineros.com.co

FIRM OVERVIEW

Managing partner: Alejandro Silva

Number of partners worldwide: 3
Number of other lawyers worldwide: 5

AREAS OF PRACTICE:

Banking and finance	25%
Corporate	20%
M&A	20%
Telecommunications	15%
Internet and e-commerce	10%
Tax	10%

S

FIRM OVERVIEW: Established in 1997, Silva & Piñeros Abogados is one of Colombia's leading law firms. It has experience in local and international financing transactions, mergers and acquisitions, and privatisations. The firm also advises on administrative law matters and contracts, and its telecommunications and internet/e-commerce practice has grown steadily. Silva & Piñeros Abogados also handles corporate, tax, foreign exchange, and foreign investment matters.

INTERNATIONAL EXPERIENCE: Silva & Piñeros Abogados has represented multilateral lenders in infrastructure project finance transactions in Jamaica, Ecuador, and other countries in Latin America. The firm has acted as local counsel for major international clients in their transactions and businesses in Colombia, particularly in connection with privatisations, M&A, project finance, and general corporate matters.

INTERNATIONAL CLIENTS: The firm's international clients include International Finance Corporation, Citibank N.A., Inter-American Development Bank, ABN Amro Bank, Corporacion Andina de Fomento, Telefonica S.A., Cinemark, Terra Lycos Inc, Young & Rubicam, Dell Computer Inc., Televisa S.A. and MCI International Inc. The firm has also represented leading equity investment funds such as Newbridge Andean Partners, Scudder Latin America Power Investment Fund, Darby Latin American Mezzanine Holdings, and AIG-GE Capital Latin American Infrastructure Fund L.P.

MAIN INTERNATIONAL AREAS OF PRACTICE:

M&A: The firm's transactions range from small private acquisitions to multi-million dollar privatisations. The firm has represented buyers in M&A and privatisation transactions in the retail, telecommunications, consumer products, mining and power generation and distribution industries. It has represented one of only two international bidders in the privatisation of ETB, the largest telecom utility in Colombia, in a US$ 1.4 billion privatisation.

Banking and finance: Silva & Piñeros handles all aspects of banking and finance, including secured and syndicated loan transactions and guarantees, structured finance, project finance and leasing-based finance. The firm's partners have handled many of the major project finance transactions in Colombia, as well as participating in financings in Philippines, Indonesia, Honduras, Argentina, Jamaica, Dominican Republic, and Ecuador. The firm has advised on projects in power generation and transmission, toll roads, airports, telecom infrastructure, and potable and waste water treatment.

Internet/e-commerce: Silva & Piñeros represents a wide range of internet clients, including internationally affiliated local portals, an e-recruitment firm, a real estate e-commerce venture, and the first Colombian internet book retailer. The firm has assisted these clients in preparing their sites' legal support documents, acquiring infrastructure, securing domain names internationally, negotiating intellectual property agreements, and in general corporate matters.

Corporate and commercial: The firm advises on the establishment and management of companies, branches of foreign companies, spin-offs, shareholder agreements, joint ventures, security agreements, leasing agreements, lease, supply, rendering of services, purchases and sales, issuance of bonds and commercial papers, securitisations, and general commercial transactions.

Telecommunications: The firm advises local and international clients on regulatory and transactional matters in connection with data transmission, TV-cable operations, value-added services, LMDS, submarine cables, and private television channels.

Tax: The firm's practice focuses primarily on tax planning for businesses and individuals. It has been instrumental in structuring the complex project finance and M&A transactions in which it is involved.

Administrative and regulatory: The firm assists its clients in public bids and contracts as well as in their dealings with governmental entities. It has handled matters before the Ministry of Communications, Ministry of Finance, Superintendency of Companies, Superintendency of Securities, Telecommunications Regulatory Commission, National Television Commission, Banking Superintendency, and other agencies.

LANGUAGES: English, Spanish

SILVA & PIÑEROS
Abogados

For other recommended firms see pages 1485-1520

SIMÉON & ASSOCIÉS

HEAD OFFICE

5, avenue Percier,
75008 Paris, France
Tel: +33 1 40 75 08 08 **Fax:** +33 1 40 75 04 50

Email: simeon_paris@compuserve.com
Website: www.lswh.com

WORLDWIDE OFFICE CONTACTS

BELGIUM
Liedekerke Siméon Wessing Houthoff (LSWH), Boulevard de l'Empereur 3, 1000 **Brussels**
Tel: +32 2 551 1616 **Fax:** +32 2 551 1403
Email: E.Morgan_de_Rivery@lswh.be

FRANCE
5, avenue Percier, 75008 **Paris**
Tel: +33 1 40 75 08 08 **Fax:** +33 1 40 75 04 50
Email: simeon_paris@compuserve.com

FIRM OVERVIEW

Managing partner: Alexis Terray

Number of partners worldwide: 12
Number of other lawyers worldwide: 50

AREAS OF PRACTICE:

Corporate/M&A	50%
Litigation/arbitration	18%
Employment	10%
EU and competition	10%
IT/intellectual property	6%
Tax	6%

FIRM OVERVIEW: Established in 1974, Siméon & Associés is a medium-sized firm practising corporate and financial law with a focus on corporate M&A. The competition practice, divided between Paris and Brussels, forms another large department. The firm has expertise in advising clients from the aeronautics and telecommunications sectors.

INTERNATIONAL EXPERIENCE: Approximately half of Siméon & Associés' client base is foreign, and most of the firm's French clients have interests abroad or carry out cross-border activities. The firm is a founding member of the Conference of European Lawyers, which links the firm to over six hundred lawyers practising in key European jurisdictions. The firm has developed working relationships with law firms all over the world, particularly in Great Britain, the Scandinavian countries, Italy, Spain and Latin America. Siméon & Associés maintains an extensive network of contacts throughout the world.

INTERNATIONAL CLIENTS: The firm's clients cover a wide variety of sectors including telecommunications, pharmaceuticals, food, beverages and tobacco, automobiles and aviation, and postal services.

MAIN INTERNATIONAL AREAS OF PRACTICE:

Company law and M&A: The firm advises on all kinds of cross-border transactions, mergers and reorganisations.
EU and competition: The firm covers all types of filings with the EU Commission, relating to restrictive agreements and mergers; and with French anti-trust authorities for merger cases. It handles litigation before the French Competition Council and judicial courts and before Luxembourg EU courts.
Litigation and arbitration: The firm acts as counsel and arbitrator in a variety of international commercial arbitration proceedings. It handles a broad range of company law related litigation, and commercial and bankruptcy proceedings.
Employment and social litigation: The firm advises on collective and individual labour law issues and related litigation. Contact, Christian Belloin.
Tax: The firm advises on all tax matters relating to M&A as well as litigation.
Telecommunications: The firm offers regulatory and transaction advice to major operators and service providers seeking to enter the French market.
Advertising: The firm provides advice and litigation relating to French restrictive legislation on the advertising of alcohol and tobacco; and misleading advertising.

LANGUAGES: English, French, German

WORLDWIDE OFFICES

BELGIUM

Liedekerke Siméon Wessing Houthoff (LSWH), Boulevard de l'Empereur 3, 1000 Brussels

Number of lawyers: 30
Number of dual qualified lawyers: 10
Number of locally qualified lawyers: 20

Office profile: In 1996, Siméon & Associés opened a Brussels office in partnership with Belgian firm Liedekerke Wolters Waelbroeck & Kirkpatrick, German firm Wessing & Berenberg-Gossler and Dutch firm Houthoff-Buruma. The firm, known as Liedekerke Siméon Wessing Houthoff (LSWH), has over 30 lawyers who concentrate solely on European law, especially European competition, merger control, trade, subsidies and market regulations. The four firms have also formed the Conference of European Lawyers, a European Economic Interest Grouping (EEIG), offering clients a full range of legal services from the partners' home countries.

SIMMONS & SIMMONS

HEAD OFFICE

CityPoint, One Ropemaker Street
London EC2Y 9SS, United Kingdom
Tel: +44 20 7628 2020 **Fax:** +44 20 7628 2070
Email: enquiries@simmons-simmons.com
Website: www.simmons-simmons.com

FIRM OVERVIEW

Managing partner: David Dickinson
Senior partner: Bill Knight
Number of partners worldwide: 145
Number of other lawyers worldwide: 395

AREAS OF PRACTICE:

Corporate/corporate finance/M&A	41%
Commercial/IP/EU	14%
Property	13%
Litigation	12%
Banking and capital markets	10%
Tax	6%
Employment	3%
Environmental	1%

FIRM OVERVIEW: Simmons &Simmons is a leading international law firm. The firm in 1896 and since that time its growth has been continuous. Based in the City of London, the firm has 146 partners, with 39 partners overseas and a total staff worldwide of over 1,400. Since the early 1960s, the firm has been committed to developing an international practice. Offices were opened in 1962 in Brussels, in 1979 in Hong Kong, in 1988 in Paris, in 1990 in New York, in 1992 in Lisbon, in 1993 in Milan, in 1994 in Abu Dhabi, in 1995 in Shanghai, in 1997 in Rome and in 1999 in Madrid. The firm also has strong international practices serviced from its overseas offices and through its alliances advising clients in, for example, Japan, Australia, India, Thailand, Korea, Taiwan, Sweden, Germany, Spain, Poland and Brazil.

INTERNATIONAL EXPERIENCE: The firm has advised on a number of major international deals, including recently acting for Pacific Century Cyberworks Limited on its US$35.9bn offer for Cable and Wireless HKT Limited, one of Asia's biggest ever corporate takeovers; the United Arab Emirates Offsets Group on Project Dolphin (US$10bn), one of the world's largest integrated energy initiatives; One2One on winning a Third Generation Licence (£4003.6m), the world's first 3G spectrum auction; SEPI on the IPO of Iberia; Dresdner Kleinwort Benson on the listing of Zhejiang Expressway Co Ltd to the Official List of the UK Listing Authority, the first overseas listing application approved by the new UK Listing Authority; Global TeleSystems Group, Inc's on its acqisition of Netcom Internet Limited (US$91.5m); and Bank of Latvia on the rehabilitation of Rigas Komercbanka PLC (approx US$100m).

INTERNATIONAL CLIENTS: Through its network of offices, associations and alliances, the firm acts for a range of clients worldwide in all sectors of industry, commerce and government, including major international financial institutions and corporates, investment banks and foreign government departments.

MAIN INTERNATIONAL AREAS OF PRACTICE: Simmons & Simmons provides a comprehensive range of legal services to businesses and individuals worldwide. The firm's size enables it to specialise and to provide expert advice on all areas of commercial law. It has particular expertise in mergers and acquisitions, privatisations, venture capital, international securities, corporate finance, major projects, PFI and PPP, financial services, capital markets products, repackagings, securitisations, corporate treasury and bank lending. It is also able to provide advice in general commercial law, EU and competition, intellectual property, communications and media law, development and construction work, property and planning, environmental law, energy, biotechnology, railways, all forms of dispute resolution, employment and pensions advice, and taxation. Other areas of expertise include corporate recovery, structured finance, unit trusts, insurance, commodities, asset finance and aviation, entertainment, sports, shipping, and advice on private capital to individuals.

LANGUAGES: Afrikaans, Arabic, Cantonese, Czech, Dutch, English, French, German, Greek, Hindi, Hungarian, Italian, Japanese, Latvian, Mandarin, Polish, Portuguese, Russian, Slovakian, Spanish, Swedish, Vietnamese

WORLDWIDE OFFICE CONTACTS

UNITED KINGDOM
CityPoint, One Ropemaker Street, **London** EC2Y 9SS
Tel: +44 20 7628 2020 **Fax:** +44 20 7628 2070

BELGIUM
Avenue Louise 149b 16, B-1050, **Brussels**
Tel: +32 2 542 0960 **Fax:** +32 2 542 0961

CHINA
3rd Floor, Shanghai Dynasty Business Centre, 457 Wu Lu Mu Qi Bei Lu, 200040, **Shanghai**
Tel: +86 21 6249 0700 **Fax:** +86 21 6249 0706

FRANCE
68 rue du Faubourg Saint Honoré, 75008, **Paris**
Tel: +33 1 53 05 31 31 **Fax:** + 33 1 53 05 31 32

HONG KONG
35th Floor, Cheung Kong Center, 2 Queen's Road, Central, **Hong Kong**
Tel: +852 2868 1131 **Fax:** +852 2810 5040

ITALY
Corso Vittorio Emanuele, 1, 20122, **Milan**
Tel: +39 02 7250 51 **Fax:** +39 02 7250 5505

Via Barnaba Oriani, 85, 00197, **Rome**
Tel: +39 06 80955 1 **Fax:** +39 06 80955 955

PORTUGAL
Grupo Legal Português, in association with F Castelo Branco, P Rebelo de Sousa & Associados, Rua Castilho, no 32-9, 1250, **Lisbon**
Tel: +351 21 313 1500 **Fax:** +351 21 313 1501

SPAIN
Pases de la Castellana 93, 4 o Piso, 28046, **Madrid**
Tel: +34 91 418 5030 **Fax:** +34 91 418 5042

UNITED ARAB EMIRATES
The ADNIC Building, Khalifa Street, PO Box 5931, **Abu Dhabi**
Tel: +971 2 6275 568 **Fax:** +971 2 6275 223

USA
570 Lexington Avenue, 28th Floor, NY 10022, **New York**
Tel: +1 212 688 6620 **Fax:** +1 212 688 3237

S

For other recommended firms see pages 1485-1520

SIMONSEN MUSÆUS

HEAD OFFICE

Grev Wedels Plass 9, PO Box 727 Sentrum,
N-0105 Oslo, Norway
Tel: +47 22 93 65 00 **Fax:** +47 22 93 65 50

Email: simonsen.musaeus@simu.no
Website: www.simu.no

WORLDWIDE OFFICE CONTACTS

NORWAY
Grev Wedels Plass 9, PO Box 727 Sentrum, N-0105 **Oslo**
Tel: +47 22 93 65 00 **Fax:** +47 22 93 65 50
Email: simonsen.musaeus@simu.no

FIRM OVERVIEW

Managing director: Elisabeth Forsvåg Holthe
Chairman: Per Kyllingstad

Number of partners worldwide: 17
Number of other lawyers worldwide: 21

AREAS OF PRACTICE:

Banking and finance	*%
Company and commercial law including M&A	*%
EU and competition	*%
Information and communications technology (ICT)	*%
Insolvency	*%
Litigation and arbitration	*%
Offshore, shipping, oil and gas	*%
Real estate	*%
Sports and entertainment	*%
Tax	*%

* Workload % not disclosed

FIRM PROFILE: Established in Oslo in 1948, Simonsen Musæus is an international business law firm. The firm consists of 53 staff, 38 of which are lawyers. The client base ranges from small to large companies, banks and insurance companies to public and supranational institutions. The firm provides both general corporate advice on a regular basis and specialist advice in connection with business transactions or litigation matters. The firm has an international network of correspondant law firms that provide legal assistance in other jurisdictions. Simonsen Musæus is a member of Advocatia - Norwegian Law Alliance - a national network of eight independent law firms, with a total of 90 lawyers.

INTERNATIONAL EXPERIENCE: The firm has substantial experience in advising on the international implications of business law issues. It advises Norwegian firms on M&A transactions internationally as well as in the establishment of foreign companies in Norway. Maritime law and other assistance to the offshore, oil and shipping industries are traditional practice areas for Simonsen Musæus. The firm is well known for its ship and aviation financing practice.

INTERNATIONAL CLIENTS: The firm's clients include large and medium-sized companies, the financial sector and foreign law firms. The firm represents both Norwegian banks such as Christiania Bank and Nordlandsbanken, in their international banking activities, as well as foreign banks such as Landesbank Schleswig-Holstein, De Nationale Investeringsbank, Hamburgische Landesbank, Bank of Novia Scotia and SE Banken.

MAIN INTERNATIONAL AREAS OF PRACTICE:
Company and commercial law including M&A: The firm assists on all aspects of general company and commercial law, including drafting of Norwegian and international contracts. M&A and due diligence work represents an increasing part of the firms' activity.
Banking and finance: The firm covers all areas of banking and finance, including secured and syndicated loan transactions and guarantees, structured finance, project finance, leasing and tax-based finance.
Shipping: Simonsen Musæus acts for national and international shipowners, operators, brokers, charterers, underwriters and banks on all matters of maritime law, chartering, arrest of vessels, sale and purchase, new buildings, pollution and marine insurance.
Information and communications technology: Repesenting some of the leading players in the Norwegian market, the firm is actively involved in the regulatory framework for the ICT-industry and is working with the legal issues in connection with the integration (convergence) between Internet, telecommunication and computer industries. The firm assist sclients in restructuring processes in relation to changed market conditions, handling contract negotiations, mergers and acquituisions and regulatory issues. It also advises in developing and establishing e-commerce, m-commerce and auctions on the Internet.
EU/EEA and competition law: The firm's lawyers are experienced in the institutional and public law aspects of the EU/EEA-law and in all aspects of competition law.
Intellectual property: The firm advises on patents, trademarks, copyrights, licensing and franchising.
Litigation and arbitration: The firm's practice covers all forms of court and arbitral proceedings. Lawyers frequently act for clients before local Norwegian Courts and the Norwegian Supreme Court.
Tax law: The firm handles matters for both the private sector and public entities, both as advisers and litigators. The niche practice focuses on international taxation of sports athletes.

LANGUAGES: Danish, English, French, German, Italian, Norwegian, Swedish

SIMONSEN | MUSÆUS

SIMPSON THACHER & BARTLETT

HEAD OFFICE

425 Lexington Avenue,
New York NY 10017, USA
Tel: +1 212 455 2000 **Fax:** +1 212 455 2502
Website: www.simpsonthacher.com

FIRM OVERVIEW

Managing partner: Richard I Beattie
Number of partners worldwide: 138
Number of other lawyers worldwide: 452

AREAS OF PRACTICE:

Capital markets/banking ....*%
Litigation and international arbitration ....*%
M&A ....*%
Project finance ....*%
* Workload % not disclosed

FIRM OVERVIEW: Simpson Thacher & Bartlett was established in 1884 and currently has approximately 590 lawyers, including 138 partners. Through its New York City headquarters and its London, Hong Kong, Tokyo and Singapore offices, the firm provides coordinated legal advice and transactional capability in the world's principal international financial centres. The firm also maintains offices in Los Angeles and Palo Alto, California, and Columbus, Ohio.

S

INTERNATIONAL EXPERIENCE: International finance and capital markets, mergers and acquisitions, banking and bank regulation, sovereign finance and privatisation, asset-based and specialised financing, tax, employee benefits, litigation and arbitration, restructuring, bankruptcy and creditors' rights, real estate, insurance, environmental law and personal planning are important aspects of the firm's international practice.

INTERNATIONAL CLIENTS: The firm's clients include AIG, America Online, American Home Produscts, Accenture, The Blackstone Group, British American Tobacco, Covad, Credit Suisse First Boston, Deutsche Bank, GE Capital, Global Crossing Limited, Goldman Sachs, Industrial Bank of Korea, J.P. Morgan Chase & Co and its affiliates, Kohlberg Kravis Roberts & Co, Lehman Brothers, Northwest Airlines, Pohang Iron & Steel, Silver Lake Partners, Telefonica, SA, Telex Chile, SA, Toronto-Dominion Bank, Universal Polygram/Seagram, Virgin Atlantic Airways, and Willis Corroon, WorldCom Inc.

MAIN INTERNATIONAL AREAS OF PRACTICE:

M&A: The firm acts for purchasers, sellers, lenders and financial advisors and is experienced in leveraged buyouts, stock and asset purchases, restructurings, spinoffs and joint ventures, as well as contested transactions. Notable work includes representing AOL in its merger with Time Warner, representing Seagram in its merger with Vivendi, representing Chase in its recent merger with J. P. Morgan and its earlier acquisition of Robert Fleming, and advising Japan Telecom Co in its US$1.9 Billion sale of a 30% stake to AT&T. It has also represented companies in many of the major takeover litigations.

Banking: The practice has particular experience in syndicated lending and acquisition finance, with Chase Manhattan and its affiliates being among its principal clients. The practice is increasingly representing borrowers throughout Europe, Latin America and Asia. The firm is actively involved in financial institution mergers and acquisitions, as well as in the interpretation and application of laws and regulations governing consolidation and convergence in the financial sector.

WORLDWIDE OFFICES CONTACTS

HONG KONG
Asia Pacific Finance Tower, 7th Floor, 3 Garden Road, Central,
Hong Kong
Tel: +852 2514 7600 **Fax:** +852 2869 7694

JAPAN
Ark Mori Building, 30th Floor, 12-32 Akasaka 1-Chome, Minato-Ku,
Tokyo 107
Tel: +81 3 5562 8601 **Fax:** +81 3 5562 8606

SINGAPORE
Suntec Tower One, 33rd Floor, 7 Temasek Boulevard, **Singapore** 038987
Tel: +65 430 5100 **Fax:** +65 430 5151

UNITED KINGDOM
Citypoint, Ropemaker Street, **London** EC2Y 9HU
Tel: +44 20 7275 6500 **Fax:** +44 20 7275 6502

USA
10 Universal City Plaza, Suite 1850, **Los Angeles** CA 91608
Tel: +1 818 755 7000 **Fax:** +1 818 755 7009

425 Lexington Avenue, **New York** NY 10017
Tel: +1 212 455 2000 **Fax:** +1 212 455 2502

3330 Hillview Avenue, **Palo Alto** CA 94304-1204
Tel: +1 650 251 5000 **Fax:** +1 650 251 5002

Capital markets and securities: The firm advises both issuers and underwriters, with particular expertise in offerings by foreign issuers, IPOs, high-yield debt offerings and derivative and complex instruments. Recent European work includes IPOs, high-yield bond offerings or equity offerings by Versatel in the Netherlands, Baltimore Technologies in the UK, Enitel in Norway, Linde in Germany and Infovista in France. The firm recently represented Goldman Sachs in Abbey National's US$1 billion offering of preferred securities. In Asia, the firm recently handled IPOs for the Japanese subsidiaries of Oracle and Toys 'R' Us and for GigaMedia Ltd in Taiwan and Wherever.net Holdings in Korea. The firm also works on a number of Latin American transactions.

Project finance: The firm has represented parties on all sides of major project finance transactions, including power plants, fibre optic cable networks, satellite and other telecommunications systems, toll roads, water treatment plants, airports and manufacturing facilities. Recent work includes PG&E Generating's Lake Road merchant power plant (advising lenders including Citibank), the Global Crossing fibre optic cable system (advising Global Crossing) and the Atlantic Crossing fibre optic cable system (advising the sponsors headed by Pacific Capital Group).

Lease finance: The firm works chiefly in the transport, communications and utilities sectors, acting for lessees, equity investors, lenders and underwriters. It advised on the first 'double-dip' transactions in a number of jurisdictions, and has represented lessees in more than 50 international lease transactions in the last three years including the City of Zurich, Hypo Vereinsbank and Austrian Airlines.

Litigation and arbitration: The department represents clients in a broad range of commercial litigation and arbitration cases. International litigation cases have included representing Matsushita and MCA in 'Epstein v. MCA' and Virgin Atlantic Airways in 'Virgin v. British Airways'. International arbitration work has included representing clients such as Ford Motor Company, Andersen Consulting, DHL International, Travelers and CNA in arbitrations under UNCITRAL, ICC, AAA and ad hoc arbitrations.

 For other recommended firms see pages 1485-1520

SINGHANIA & CO

HEAD OFFICE

G-107, Himalaya House, Kasturba Gandhi Marg,
New Delhi 110 001, India
Tel: + 91 11 373 1400 **Fax:** + 91 11 331 4413

Email: new-delhi@singhania.com
Website: www.singhania.com

FIRM OVERVIEW

Senior partner: DC Singhania

Number of partners worldwide: 8
Number of other lawyers worldwide: 80

AREAS OF PRACTICE:

Corporate and commercial	50%
Arbitration	20%
Litigation (domestic and international)	20%
Intellectual property	5%
Conveyancing	3%
Miscellaneous	2%

FIRM OVERVIEW: The firm was founded by DC Singhania and is now supported by senior members of academic institutions in India and abroad, former members of the judiciary and high ranking government officials. With over 80 fee earners including senior consultants and Of-Counsel and other associates, the firm provides comprehensive legal services primarily in corporate and business law practice. Singhania & Co has its head office in New Delhi, and branches in Bangalore, Calcutta, Chandigarh, Chennai, Hyderabad and Mumbai in India and representative offices in London and in New York. The firm currently has more than 80 legal professionals. Their consultants and Of-Counsel have long-standing experience in the judiciary and with the State and Central Government.

INTERNATIONAL EXPERIENCE:

The firm has extensive experience in cross-border transactions involving corporate restructuring, acquisitions and mergers and international joint ventures. In addition to the corporate experience, the firm is involved with several international litigation and arbitration matters.

INTERNATIONAL CLIENTS: The firm represents clients in the IT, pharmaceutical, engineering, insurance, automotive and manufacturing sectors in over 50 countries from the Americas, Canada, Europe, Asia, Australia and Africa.

LANGUAGES: Bengali, English, French, German, Gujarati, Hindi, Marathi, Punjabi, Tamil, Urdu

WORLDWIDE OFFICE CONTACTS

INDIA
204-A Mittal Towers, 6, M.G. Road, **Bangalore** 560001
Tel: + 91 80 558 8763 **Fax:** + 91 80 558 4593
Email: bangalore@singhania.com

1st Floor Suite E-1, 75C Park Street, **Calcutta** 700016
Tel: + 91 33 249 2759 **Fax:** + 91 33 249 2751
Email: calcutta@singhania.com

38 Sector 9-A, **Chandigarh** 160017
Tel: + 91 172 742 059 **Fax:** + 91 172 742 060
Email: chandigarh@singhania.com

No.1 Rayala Towers, 781-785 Anna Salai, **Chennai** 600 002
Tel: + 91 44 852 1626 **Fax:** + 91 44 852 0280
Email: chennai@singhania.com

6th Floor Suite 164, Babu Khan Estate, **Hyderabad** 500 029
Tel: + 91 40 323 6219 **Fax:** + 91 40 324 1779
Email: hyderabad@singhania.com

83 C Mittal Towers, Nariman Point, **Mumbai** 400021
Tel: + 91 22 285 1011 **Fax:** + 91 22 204 5960
Email: singhania@bom3.vsnl.net.in

G-107 Himalaya House, Kasturba Gandhi Marg, **New Delhi** 110 001
Tel: + 91 11 373 1400 **Fax:** + 91 11 331 4413
Email: new-delhi@singhania.com

UNITED KINGDOM
24 Buckingham Gate, **London** SW1E 6LB
Tel: + 44 20 7233 5511 **Fax:** + 44 20 7233 5522
Email: london@singhania.com

USA
375 Park Avenue, Suite 1606, **New York,** NY 10118
Tel: + 1 212 563 1222 **Fax:** + 1 212 563 1444
Email: new-york@singhania.com

For other recommended firms see pages 1485-1520

SKADDEN, ARPS, SLATE, MEAGHER & FLOM LLP

HEAD OFFICE

Four Times Square, New York, NY 10036, USA
Tel: + 1 212 735 3000 **Fax:** + 1 212 735 2000/1

Website www.skadden.com

FIRM OVERVIEW

Executive partner: Robert C. Sheehan
Senior partner: Joseph H. Flom

Number of partners worldwide: 320
Number of other lawyers worldwide: 1247

AREAS OF PRACTICE:

Corporate .... *%
Energy/project finance .... *%
Finance .... *%
Industry-related practices .... *%
International .... *%
Litigation .... *%
Privatisations .... *%
Regulatory/legislative .... *%
Restructuring and bankruptcy reorganisation .... *%
*Workload % not disclosed

FIRM OVERVIEW: With over 1,500 attorneys in 22 offices, Skadden, Arps, Slate, Meagher & Flom LLP and its affiliates (collectively referred to as 'Skadden, Arps' or the 'firm') is one of the largest law firms in the world. The firm provides a wide array of legal services domestically and internationally to the corporate, financial, industrial and governmental communities.

INTERNATIONAL EXPERIENCE: Since its first non-US office opened in 1987, Skadden, Arps has expanded into major financial centres, and emerging market economies, around the globe. The firm has a total of 11 offices in Asia, Australia, Canada and Europe, as well as 11 US offices, and substantial practices in Israel and Latin America.

INTERNATIONAL CLIENTS: The firm represents a broad spectrum of clients, from small high-technology start-up companies to nearly one half of the Fortune 250 industrial and service corporations, in addition to many financial and governmental entities.

WORLDWIDE OFFICE CONTACTS

AUSTRALIA
Level 13, 131 Macquarie Street, **Sydney,** NSW 2000
Tel: + 61 2 9253 6000 **Fax:** + 61 2 9253 6044

BELGIUM
523 avenue Louise, Box 30, 1050 **Brussels**
Tel: + 32 2 639 0300 **Fax:** + 32 2 639 0339

CANADA
Suite 1820, North Tower, PO Box 189, Royal Bank Plaza,
Toronto, Ontario M5J 2J4
Tel: + 1 416 777 4700 **Fax:** + 1 416 777 4747

CHINA (PEOPLE'S REPUBLIC OF)
East Wing Office, Level 4, China World Trade Center, No. 1 Jian Guo Men Wai Avenue, **Beijing** 100004
Tel: + 86 10 6505 5511 **Fax:** + 86 10 6505 5522

FRANCE
68 rue du Faubourg Saint-Honoré, 75008 **Paris**
Tel: + 33 1 55 27 11 00 **Fax:** + 33 1 55 27 11 99

GERMANY
MesseTurm, 27th Floor, 60308 **Frankfurt am Main**
Tel: + 49 69 742 200 **Fax:** + 49 69 742 203 00

HONG KONG
30/F Tower Two, Lippo Centre, 89 Queensway, Central, **Hong Kong**
Tel: + 852 2820 0700 **Fax:** + 852 2820 0727

JAPAN
ATT Main Tower 12F, 2-17-22, Akasaka, Minato-ku, **Tokyo** 107-0052
Tel: + 813 3568 2600 **Fax:** + 813 3568 2626

RUSSIA
Degtyarniy Pereulok 4, Building 1, **Moscow** 103009
Tel: + 7 501 797 4600 **Fax:** + 7 501 797 4601

SINGAPORE
9 Temasek Boulevard, Suite 29-01, Suntec Tower Two,
Singapore 038989
Tel: + 65 434 2900 **Fax:** + 65 434 2988

UNITED KINGDOM
One Canada Square, Canary Wharf, **London** E14 5DS
Tel: + 44 20 7519 7000 **Fax:** + 44 20 7519 7070

USA
Four Times Square, **New York,** NY 10036
Tel: + 1 212 735 3000 **Fax:** + 1 212 735 2000/1

Additional US offices: Boston, Chicago, Houston, Los Angeles, Newark, Palo Alto, Reston, San Francisco, Washington DC, and Wilmington.

MAIN INTERNATIONAL AREAS OF PRACTICE:

Corporate: Represents US and non-US clients in many of the largest M&As to date as well as for middle-market and emerging technology companies. Also advises on federal securities laws, including matters involving the Securities and Exchange Commission.
Litigation: Skadden, Arps represents clients in federal and state trial and appellate courts and before administrative tribunals. The firm also helps clients to resolve disputes without litigation by using various alternative dispute resolution procedures.
Finance: Advises underwriters, issuers and purchasers in public and private financings via all types of debt and equity instruments; structured finance; lease and project financing; public finance; commodities, futures and derivative products; investment companies, advisors and broker-dealers; and private investment funds. It also has a strong privatisation practice.
Corporate restructuring: Skadden, Arps represents debtors, creditors, acquirors, investors and others in Chapter 11 reorganisation cases, Chapter 11 filings, and other debtor/creditor matters.
Regulatory/legislative: Advises US and non-US clients in international trade cases and market access especially for finance institutions. Also strong on lobbying for legislative developments.
Industry-related practices: The firm has a number of industry-specific practice areas - communications, energy, environmental, health care, information technology, insurance, real estate and utilities.

For other recommended firms see pages 1485-1520

SLAUGHTER AND MAY

HEAD OFFICE

35 Basinghall Street,
London EC2V 5DB, United Kingdom
Tel: +44 20 7600 1200 **Fax:** +44 20 7600 0289
Email: mail@slaughterandmay.com
Website: www.slaughterandmay.com

FIRM OVERVIEW

Senior partner: Giles Henderson CBE
Number of partners worldwide: 119
Number of other lawyers worldwide: 392

AREAS OF PRACTICE:

Area	%
Commercial, corporate and financial	67%
Litigation and arbitration	10%
Property	6%
Tax	6%
Competition	4%
Pensions and employment	4%
Intellectual property and IT	3%

FIRM OVERVIEW: Slaughter and May is a leading firm comprising over 500 partners and assistants worldwide. The firm has an extensive international practice that covers a wide range of corporate, commercial and financial work. Its lawyers handle a broad range of work in each of the firm's main practice areas. The firm encourages its lawyers to develop all-round business knowledge as well as technical legal ability.

WORLDWIDE OFFICE CONTACTS

BELGIUM
Avenue de Cortenberg 118, B-1000 **Brussels**
Tel: +32 2 737 94 00 **Fax:** +32 2 737 94 01
Email: william.sibree@slaughterandmay.com

FRANCE
112 Avenue Kléber, 75784 **Paris**
Tel: +33 1 44 05 60 00 **Fax:** +33 1 44 05 60 60
Email: peter.kett@slaughterandmay.com

HONG KONG
27th Floor, Two Exchange Square, **Hong Kong**
Tel: +852 2521 0551 **Fax:** +852 2845 2125
Email: richard.thornhill@slaughterandmay.com

SINGAPORE
80 Raffles Place, #14-04, UOB Plaza 1, **Singapore** 048624
Tel: +65 532 1200 **Fax:** +65 536 2001
Email: simon.hall@slaughterandmay.com

UNITED KINGDOM
35 Basinghall Street, **London** EC2V 5DB
Tel: +44 20 7600 1200 **Fax:** +44 20 7600 0289
Email: mail@slaughterandmay.com

USA
126 East 56th Street, 16th Floor, **New York** NY 10022-3613
Tel: +1 212 888 1112 **Fax:** +1 212 888 1170
Email: mark.cardale@slaughterandmay.com

INTERNATIONAL EXPERIENCE: International work is an essential part of the firm's practice and it has broad experience in multi-national and cross-border corporate, commercial and finance matters. These include M&A, debt finance and securities offerings, tax, competition, litigation and arbitration. Slaughter and May works with leading independent firms in other jurisdictions to provide an integrated international service. Recent international transactions include acting for Corus on its proposed merger of its Swedish subsidiary, Avesta Sheffield AB, with Outokumpu Steel to form the world's second largest stainless steel company with an estimated market capitalisation of €1.3 billion; acting for Cap Gemini SA in connection with the UK aspects of its acquisition of the Ernst & Young world-wide consulting business for an overall consideration of approximately US$7 billion; acting for QXL.com plc on its all-share merger with ricardo.de AG; acting for Telecom Italia on a €17.3 billion facility to back a tender offer for the shares which it did not already own in SEAT Pagine Gialle S.p.A.; acting for Huntsman Corporation in the leveraged financing for a new joint venture, Huntsman ICI, involving US dollar and euro denominated loans of over US$2 billion arranged by Bankers Trust; advising Deutsche Bank (jointly with Hengeler Mueller Weitzel Wirtz) on the start up financing for broadband service providers, FirstMark Communications Deutschland GmbH.

INTERNATIONAL CLIENTS: Include industrial and commercial companies from all business sectors; banks, financial institutions and professional firms; and governments, public bodies and other organisations.

HEAD OFFICE:

Number of lawyers: 434

Highlight deals: Acting for British Airways on the proposed sale of its subsidiary, Go; acting for LASMO in connection with the recommended share offer by Amerada Hess Corporation; acting for Carlton Communications plc in connection with the proposed acquisitition of HTV from Granada Media plc; acting for Thames Water in connection with the cash offer by RWE AG; acting for Glaxo Wellcome on the propsed merger with SmithKline Beecham; acting for Blue Circle on the succesful defence of the hostile bid by Lafarge SA; acting for Norwich Union on its merger with CGU; acting for Prudential Corporation and egg in connection with the flotation of its internet banking subsidiary, egg; acting for Psion in connection with Psion and United News and Media joint venture company, Trivanti, to develop and market wireless internet sevices for B2B and B2C communities; advising Schroder Ventures in relation to the £400 million senior, mezzanine and subordinated debt financing for the acquisition of Hogg Robinson by a consortium including Schroder Ventures; acting for Chase Manhattan Bank as lead arranger of the debt financing for the £660 million project to construct the new English National Stadium at Wembley.

Languages: Bengali, Cantonese, English, French, German, Gujarathi, Hindi, Italian, Japanese, Mandarin, Malay, Punjabi, Russian, Spanish, Swedish

Office profile: The office advises on a broad range of domestic and international issues. Its corporate and financial practice advises on mergers and acquisitions and other corporate and commercial transactions, flotations, domestic and international debt and equity issues, derivatives, international and domestic lending, structured finance and project and asset finance, insolvency, corporate recovery and asset tracing and financial regulation. It handles a wide range of commercial litigation and arbitration proceedings, and advises on all aspects of IT and intellectual property, technology, media and telecoms, commercial property, environmental matters, corporate tax, EC and competition questions and pensions and employment.

For other recommended firms see pages 1485-1520

WORLDWIDE OFFICES

BELGIUM

Avenue de Cortenberg 118, B-1000 Brussels

Number of lawyers: 6

Highlight deals: Acting for BOC in connection with the Commission's Phase II conditional clearance of the proposed Air Liquide/BOC merger; acting for Corus on the Commission's investigation of the merger of its stainless steel interest with Outokumpu; acting for Unilever on the monopoly inquiry into impulse ice-cream in the UK.
Languages: English, French, German
Office Profile: Established in 1990, the Brussels office is an integral part of the firm's Competition group which operates out of both London and Brussels. It advises on all aspects of EU law (including competition law). The office has close contacts with the Competition Directorate-General, in particular in the context of merger control work and other competition and state aid issues. It also undertakes litigation work in the Community courts.

FRANCE

112 Avenue Kléber, 75784 Paris

Number of lawyers: 30
Number of dual qualified lawyers: 7
Number of locally qualified lawyers: 30

Highlight deals: Acting on the Reuters acquisition of ORT; acting for Onditro on the reorganisation of E-Trades' European licensing rights; acting for BAe Systems on the Airbus restructuring; substantial acquisitions for the Williams Group; acting for the Post Office on its French acquisitions; acting for Worms & Cie in the friendly takeover of Arjo Wiggins Plc; and acting for the financing of sundry telecommunication and satellite projects for the Alcatel Group.
Languages: English, French, German, Spanish
Office Profile: Opened in 1974, the firm's Paris office practises French and English law. Nearly all of the lawyers are bilingual in French and English and many of the English lawyers are also qualified to practise French law. The office advises on general corporate matters including M&A and corporate finance, as well as on banking, capital markets transactions, tax, commercial property, litigation and arbitration.

HONG KONG

27th Floor, Two Exchange Square, Hong Kong

Number of lawyers: 26
Number of dual qualified lawyers: 12
Number of locally qualified lawyers: 15

Highlight deals: Acting for MTR Corporation Limited in connection with its listing on the Hong Kong Stock Exchange and the sale of shares by the Hong Kong Government in the first Hong Kong privatisation; acting for the independent board in connection with the merger of Cable & Wireless HKT Limited and Pacific Century CyberWorks Limited; acting for Standard Chartered Bank on their acquisition of the Chase Manhattan consumer banking business, including credit cards, in Hong Kong; acting for the underwriters led by Morgan Stanley Dean Witter Asia Limited and China International Capital Corporation Limited in the two largest PRC initial public offerings – China Unicom Limited and China Petroleum & Chemical Corporation (Sinopec). The China Unicom offering raised an aggregate of US$5.6 billion, and involved a dual Hong Kong and New York listing. Sinopec is the first PRC company to be simultaneously listed on three stock exchanges (Hong Kong, New York and London), raising approximately US$3.4. billion.
Languages: Cantonese, English, Mandarin
Office Profile: The Hong Kong office opened in 1974. It has a large local and regional practice, advising clients on Hong Kong, English and international aspects of a wide range of coporate finance, company, finance, banking and capital markets matters. It also has active property and litigation pactices. The office serves domestic and overseas clients with business interests in Hong Kong, the rest of China and other countries in the region.

SINGAPORE

80 Raffles Place, #14-04, UOB Plaza 1, Singapore 048624

Number of lawyers: 4
Number of dual qualified lawyers: 1

Highlight deals: Acting on the project financing for the Express Rail Link project in Malaysia with a contract value in excess of US$500 million for the leading sponsor of the project, which is also part of the contracting consortium; advising on a US$600 million acquisition financing for ABN AMRO supporting the hostile bid by Star Cruises of Malaysia for the Oslo Stock Exchange listed in NCL Holding ASA; advising the bidders on the privatisation of the generation assests of Tenaga Nasional Berbad (the Malaysian Electricity Utility); advising the sponsor on the BAPCO refinery upgrade and expansion project in Bahrain.
Languages: English, Mandarin
Office Profile: Opened in 1995, the Singapore office handles corporate, commercial and financial matters involving English law. It focuses on providing advice on transactions in South East Asia and the Indian sub-continent. Among the kinds of transactions undertaken by the office are debt and equity restructurings, asset sales, e-commerce and project finance.

USA

126 East 56th Street, 16th Floor, New York NY 10022-3613

Number of lawyers: 1

Highlight deals: The firm's New York office, established in 1984, advises corporate clients and other firms in North and South America. The office works closely with the London and other offices. It advises on the English law aspects of banking and financial securities, and other general corporate and commercial matters including M&A.
Languages: English

SLAUGHTER AND MAY

For other recommended firms see pages 1485-1520

SMITH LYONS

HEAD OFFICE

Suite 5800, Scotia Plaza, 40 King St West,
Toronto, Ontario M5H 3Z7, Canada
Tel: +1 416 369 7200 **Fax:** +1 416 369 7250

Email: DMiles@SmithLyons.ca
Website: www.SmithLyons.ca

WORLDWIDE OFFICE CONTACTS

CANADA
Suite 2300, 150 Metcalfe Street, Ontario K2P 1P1, **Ottawa,**
Tel: +1 613 230 3988 **Fax:** +1 613 230 7085
Email: PAMagnus@SmithLyons.ca

Suite 5800, Scotia Plaza, 40 King St West, M5H 3Z7, **Toronto,** Ontario
Tel: +1 416 369 7200 **Fax:** +1 416 369 7250
Email: DMiles@SmithLyons.ca

UKRAINE
Suite 507, 26 Lesia Ukrainka Blvd, 01133, **Kiev**
Tel: +380 44 573 8858 **Fax:** +380 44 295 5240
Email: PAMagnus@SmithLyons.ca

FIRM OVERVIEW

Managing partner: John R Finley

Number of partners worldwide: 77
Number of other lawyers worldwide: 51

AREAS OF PRACTICE:

Area	%
General practice	22%
Banking	15%
Litigation	15%
Corporate/commercial	15%
M&A	10%
Real estate	10%
Financial services	5%
IP/IT	5%
Energy	3%

FIRM OVERVIEW: Smith Lyons is a Canadian firm with 128 lawyers and a support staff of 300. Established on January 1, 1962, the firm has considerable experience acting for both Canadian and international clients on a large variety of matters. The firm's practice encompasses all major areas of law and is organised into three main groups: corporate/commercial, litigation and real estate.

INTERNATIONAL CLIENTS: In banking and secured transactions, the firm represents lenders and borrowers including banks, trust companies, insurance companies, pension plans, venture capital and others. Its corporate and commercial practice group acts for public and private corporations across industrial and financial sectors. The firm's M&A practice represents acquirers, sellers, banks, financial advisers and intermediaries, boards, directors and independent board committees. Real estate and development clients include developers, industrial and commercial corporations, banks, trust companies, insurers and other major lending institutions.

MAIN INTERNATIONAL AREAS OF PRACTICE:

Banking and secured transactions: The firm represents both lenders and borrowers in domestic and international financing transactions. It is active in all aspects of debt financing, subordinated and mezzanine debt, and venture capital. Also handles project finance and financings for co-generation, mine and real estate development.

Corporate and commercial: Work includes company formations; shareholder agreements; partnerships; joint ventures; distribution, licensing, and agency agreements; domestic and international commercial transactions; M&A; financed buy-outs; corporate governance and general regulatory compliance.

Energy: Experience includes advising on energy projects ranging from the development of hydro and fossil-fuel projects to the management and retrofitting of existing power facilities. The Smith Lyons energy group is positioned to provide unique advice on the many challenges and opportunities of a changing marketplace. Members of the group have acted in some of the most significant energy industry transactions and litigation to date.

Financial services: The firm's lawyers are experienced with regulations governing the conduct of financial institutions and the relationships between them, and have made many representations to Canada's federal financial regulator.

Intellectual property and IT: Handles full range of IP and IT work for a wide range of clients. The group specialises in the protection of computer software, databases and the technology used to deliver it.

Litigation: The Smith Lyons litigation group provides a wide range of litigation services to its clients across a broad spectrum of industries. Lawyers at Smith Lyons provide advice on the latest legal developments and their potential impact on internal procedures, risk assessment and future liabilities. They have also appeared before all levels of court in Canada as well as before boards, commissions and tribunals. Smith Lyons has the experience to handle cases ranging in size from small court disputes to multimillion dollar class action litigation.

M&A: The firm is active in all aspects of private and public M&A. Lawyers provide advice to clients involved in take-over bids, mergers or other restructuring of public and private company transactions.

Real estate and development: The firm's lawyers handle commercial real estate work including the planning, development and financing of office, retail, industrial and residential projects, not only throughout Canada but also internationally. Many of their lawyers are also directors of real estate entities or industry organisations. The firm advises real estate investors in the US, Hong Kong, the UK, Germany, Switzerland and elsewhere in Europe.

LANGUAGES: English, French, German, Italian, Spanish, Ukrainian

S

SOEWITO, SUHARDIMAN, EDDYMURTHY & KARDONO

HEAD OFFICE

Wisma Bank Dharmala,, 14th Floor, Jl. Jend. Sudirman Kav.28
Jakarta 12920, Indonesia
Tel: +62 21 521 2038 **Fax:** +62 21 521 2039

Email: ssek@ssek.com
Website: www.ssek.com

FIRM OVERVIEW

Managing partner: Dyah Soewito
Senior foreign legal adviser: Darrell R. Johnson

Number of partners worldwide: 4
Number of other lawyers worldwide: 41

AREAS OF PRACTICE:
Banking, finance and securities ....*%
Capital markets and securities ....*%
Direct and indirect investment ....*%
Employment ....*%
Energy and mining ....*%
Intellectual property ....*%
M&A ....*%
Project finance ....*%
Real estate ....*%
Tax ....*%
Tourism ....*%
* Workload % not disclosed

FIRM OVERVIEW: Founded in 1992, SSEK is one of the largest law firms in Indonesia. Comprising 45 attorneys, the firm is dedicated to providing quality legal work at an international standard while maintaining responsiveness to client needs. The firm engages in all aspects of commercial and corporate law practice.

INTERNATIONAL CLIENTS: Soewito, Suhardiman, Eddymurthy & Kardono has a diverse range of clients including local and multinational corporations, private and publicly listed companies, offshore and local banks, financial institutions and insurance companies, manufacturers, mining, oil and gas companies, traders, real estate developers, engineering and construction companies, and shipping companies.

MAIN INTERNATIONAL AREAS OF PRACTICE: Work undertaken includes direct and indirect investment; M&A; banking, finance and securities; capital markets and securities; energy and mining; project finance; employment; tax; intellectual property; real estate; and tourism.

LANGUAGES: English, French, Indonesian

WORLDWIDE OFFICE CONTACTS

INDONESIA
Wisma Bank Dharmala,, 14th Floor, Jl. Jend. Sudirman Kav.28, **Jakarta** 12920
Tel: +62 21 521 2038 **Fax:** +62 21 521 2039
Email: ssek@ssek.com

Soewito, Suhardiman, Eddymurthy & Kardono

For other recommended firms see pages 1485-1520

CABINET SOUNA & COULIBALY

HEAD OFFICE

BP 10269 Niamey,
Niamey BP 10269, Niger
Tel: +227 74 02 07 **Fax:** +227 74 14 88

Email: souna@intnet.ne

WORLDWIDE OFFICE CONTACTS

NIGER
BP 10269 Niamey, **Niamey** BP 10269
Tel: +227 74 02 07 **Fax:** +227 74 14 88
Email: souna@intnet.ne

FIRM OVERVIEW

Senior partners: Issaka Souna, Moussa Coulibaly

Number of partners worldwide: 2

AREAS OF PRACTICE:

Litigation and arbitration	40%
Employment	20%
Real property and construction	17%
Corporate recovery/insolvency	10%
Company and commercial	7%
Communications and media	2%
Matrimonial and family	2%
Privatisation	1%
Telecommunications	1%

FIRM OVERVIEW: The firm was founded in 1990 and comprises two qualified lawyers and two trainees.

INTERNATIONAL EXPERIENCE: The firm acts for multinational corporations such as Elf and Rothmans. It also works in partnership with international law firms and undertakes work in the privatisation of public companies such as that of the telecommunications sector, advising on the regulation of satellites and establishing international contacts. The firm also advises on Human Rights matters.

INTERNATIONAL CLIENTS: The firm acts for embassies, consulates, NGOs and multinational corporations.

MAIN INTERNATIONAL AREAS OF PRACTICE:

Litigation and arbitration: The firm handles a range of contentious matters representing clients before tribunals, the Court of Appeal and the Supreme Court. The firm also undertakes arbitration work.

Company and commercial: The firm handles a wide range of commercial work. It drafts contracts, handles various transactions and gives legal advice on a broad range of commercial matters.

Corporate recovery and insolvency: The firm handles prosecution and defence work for private individuals and financial institutions.

Real property and construction: This is one of the firm's core areas of expertise, handling the sale and transfer of commercial property. The firm also advises on construction law.

Employment: This is undoubtedly one of the firm's most notable areas of expertise. It acts for employers often advising on contentious matters and interpretation.

Matrimonial and family: The firm handles divorce, child protection and maintenance awards.

Telecommunications: The firm acts for national and international clients wishing to invest in this newly privatised sector. It advises on cellular telephony and the regulation of satellites.

Communication and media: The firm advises members of the local and international press on freedom of speech issues.

Privatisation: The firm has worked with foreign law firms on the privatisation of various public sector industries in Niger.

LANGUAGES: English, French

S

SQUIRE, SANDERS & DEMPSEY LLP

HEAD OFFICE

4900 Key Tower, 127 Public Square,
Cleveland OH 44114 -1304, USA
Tel: +1 216 479 8500 **Fax:** +1 216 479 8780
Email: ssdinfo@ssd.com
Website: www.ssd.com

FIRM OVERVIEW

Chairman: R. Thomas Stanton
Number of partners worldwide: 267
Number of other lawyers worldwide: 423

AREAS OF PRACTICE:

Corporate/finance 60%
Information technology 20%
Telecommunications 20%

FIRM OVERVIEW: Founded in 1890, Squire, Sanders & Dempsey has nearly 700 lawyers who act for local, national and multinational clients. It has expertise in cross-border mergers and acquisitions, joint ventures, EU regulatory law, utilities, energy, banking, infrastructure and corporate/project finance. It has also handled major telecommunications transactions and legislative and regulatory initiatives assembling teams for individual clients using the best qualified people regardless of their location. The firm has 25 offices in the major cities of the US, Europe and Asia, and also a 'renaissance network' of offices in China. It was the first US-based law firm to establish a permanent presence in the Eastern bloc, and its European offices have seen considerable growth over the last five years.

INTERNATIONAL EXPERIENCE: Major international deals or transactions handled over the past two years include representing a consortium of investors in structuring a multi-billion Euro joint venture with Europe's largest telecommunications company. The consortium of investors was formed for the purpose of owning and operating a broadband communications business in Germany. (2000); representing a consortium of international investors in a joint venture with Philippine investors to develop, own and operate the first broadband fixed wireless business in the Philippines (2000); advising a global producer of specialty materials and chemicals for manufacturers in its US$130 million acquisition of a polymer modifiers business (2000); representing a New York based investment boutique in forming a global private equity fund formed to invest in excess of US$500 million in forest plantations throughout the world (2000); representing one of the largest general trading companies in Korea in the acquisition and financing of a Ukrainian telecommunications company; representing a US based, worldwide supplier to the aerospace industry in its merger with a North American manufacturer of highly engineered products for the aerospace industry. The transaction, valued at more than US$2 billion, required securities and antitrust clearances, as well as meeting challenges from competitors and other potential bidders (1999); advising a US software and services company in a US$100 million share swap with a software and consulting company with operating entities in seven jurisdictions; representing a US manufacturer in connection with the establishment of a German joint venture (1999); advising the leading Spanish cable operator in its alliance with a French telecommunications carrier in its successful bid for an investment project exceeding US$700 million.

INTERNATIONAL CLIENTS: The firm's 30,000 private and public sector clients cover a wide range of industry sectors. Clients include some of the largest operators in the global telecommunications market, major producers of oil and gas, and include companies in the pharmaceuticals, energy, information technology, financial services, health care, real estate and manufacturing sectors.

WORLDWIDE OFFICE CONTACTS

USA
4900 Key Tower, 127 Public Square, **Cleveland** OH 44114-1304
Tel: +1 216 479 8500 **Fax:** +1 216 479 8780
Email: ssdinfo@ssd.com

The firm has offices in Almaty, Beijing, Bratislava, Brussels, Budapest, Cincinnati, Columbus, Hong Kong, Houston, Jacksonville, Kiev, London, Los Angeles, Madrid, Miami, Moscow, New York, Palo Alto, Phoenix, Prague, San Francisco, Taipei, Tokyo, and Washington DC. It also has associated offices in Dublin and Milan.

MAIN INTERNATIONAL AREAS OF PRACTICE:

Competition: The competition law group advises clients on both their rights and obligations arising from European competition law and the laws of the major EU member states.
Energy: The firm provides legal and business advice on virtually every aspect of the energy business including regulatory, corporate, antitrust/competition, transactional, finance, environmental, tax and litigation issues.
Information technology: The firm's IT practice represents sophisticated global vendors and purchasers of hardware, software, systems integration services, network configuration and management, outsourcing and other IT services of all kinds.
Litigation: The firm's litigation practice advises manufacturing and natural resources companies, utilities, health care entities, media and communications concerns, real estate and construction-related companies, banks and financial services providers, local, state, US and non-US governments and agencies, transportation companies and various other services and distribution businesses.
M&A: The firm's transactional lawyers advise on the process and strategies of entering into joint ventures and buying and selling multinational companies, with support from lawyers in related areas such as antitrust, litigation, environmental, labour and employment, tax, intellectual property and regulatory law.
Project finance: The firm has represented both public and private sector clients in negotiating and financing infrastructure projects, with extensive experience in water, highways, schools, hospitals and energy sources.
Tax: The tax practice advises large public and private companies, as well as emerging companies both in the US and abroad from the manufacturing, services, utilities, natural resources and other sectors. It also advises banks, investment banks and trade associations.
Telecommunications: The firm advises on regulatory and transactional matters to clients worldwide, including incumbent telephone companies, cable television and cable telephony companies, satellite service providers, GSM and other wireless operators, data service and network companies, Internet service providers, investors and investment banks, government agencies and multinational development organisations.
Real estate: The real estate practice deals with the full spectrum of issues and structures including construction, as well as interim and permanent loan financing transactions.

Languages: Arabic, Catalan, Chinese (Cantonese and Mandarin), Czech, Danish, Dutch, Estonian, Filipino, French, German, Greek, Hebrew, Hungarian, Italian, Japanese, Kazakh, Korean, Lebanese, Lithuanian, Polish, Portuguese, Russian, Slovak, Spanish, Taiwanese, Turkish, Tagalog, Ukrainian, Vietnamese, Visayan/Filipino, Yoruba

 For other recommended firms see pages 1485-1520

STANBROOK & HOOPER

HEAD OFFICE

Rue du Taciturne 42,
B-1000 Brussels, Belgium
Tel: +32 2 230 50 59 **Fax:** +32 2 230 57 13

Email: stanbrook.hooper@stanbrook.com
Website: www.stanbrook.com

WORLDWIDE OFFICE CONTACTS

BELGIUM
Rue du Taciturne 42, B-1000 **Brussels**
Tel: +32 2 230 50 59 **Fax:** +32 2 230 57 13
Email: stanbrook.hooper@stanbrook.com

SPAIN
Gran Via, 6, E-28013 **Madrid**
Tel: +34 91 531 48 00 **Fax:** +34 91 522 01 56
Email: guardia@teleline.es

FIRM OVERVIEW

Senior partner: Clive Stanbrook QC
Practice manager: Jean-Pol Warkin

Number of partners worldwide: 10
Number of other lawyers worldwide: 14

AREAS OF PRACTICE:

Area	%
Anti-dumping and anti-subsidy	20%
Commercial and corporate	20%
Competition and merger control	20%
Telecommunications and new technology	20%
Employment	10%
Arbitration	5%
Environment/food law	5%

FIRM OVERVIEW: Established in 1978, Stanbrook & Hooper is one of the longest-standing regulatory law firms in Brussels. A multinational and multi-jurisdictional office, it has lawyers qualified in most member states as well as in the US, India and China. It has recently expanded the scope of its practice to include Belgian law and now has strong corporate, commercial and employment law capability.

INTERNATIONAL EXPERIENCE: A significant amount of the firm's work is international, arising from issues of international trade and investment. The firm advises on anti-trust compliance, trade regulation, customs and regulatory standards. During the last 18 years, the firm has defended international clients in leading trade cases involving commodity and speciality chemicals, electronic office equipment, and fashion products. The firm has also successfully defended multinational companies in the major EU cartel cases of Woodpulp and LDPE.

INTERNATIONAL CLIENTS: The vast majority of the firm's clients are based in North and South America and the Far East and trade in the EU or have sales or production subsidiaries there. Due to the specialist nature of the firm's practice, work is regularly referred to it by other law firms from foreign jurisdictions. In recent years the firm has also advised governments in Eastern Europe and in Caribbean and European island economies and has also advised private clients with investments or business activities in Belgium.

MAIN INTERNATIONAL AREAS OF PRACTICE:

Competition and merger control: Stanbrook & Hooper has represented clients in leading EU cartel cases as well as advised on general competition matters. The firm has extensive experience of merger control filings, and has been involved over the past two years in the major second-phase MCR filings before the Commission of MCI/BT, MCI/WorldCom, Boeing/McDonnell Douglas and KPMG/Ernst & Young. For mergers that do not hit the EU thresholds, the firm organises and co-ordinates consistent and effective filings in multiple jurisdictions.

Telecommunications and new technologies: The firm has advised a wide range of companies on most aspects of EU telecom regulatory work, and has advised the Commission on a number of aspects of its telecommunications programme, including legal and institutional issues relating to full liberalisation, licensing and declaration procedures for mobile communications. The firm also has a growing practice in respect of new technologies, e-commerce and data protection. In particular the firm has advised firms on various aspects of internet law including issues relating to domain names as well as data protection provisions in the express package delivery service sector and the banking sector.

Anti-dumping and anti-subsidy: The firm is currently representing Indian and Chinese exporters of granite stones and Turkish exporters of colour televisions film in anti-dumping proceedings. The firm is also currently representing an EC producer of electronic equipment in court proceedings arising out of the EU Council's refusal to impose anti-dumping duties.

Commercial, corporate and employment: Stanbrook & Hooper has a well established team of Belgian qualified lawyers with extensive experience advising companies established or doing business in Belgium.

Arbitration: The firm has a growing international arbitration practice having recently represented a US oil and gas company in a Stockholm arbitration arising out of a contractual dispute and competition law issues and a US producer of polyurethane systems in a London arbitration arising out of an intellectual property dispute and share ownership rights.

Environment and food law: The firm advises international clients on an on-going basis in relation to EU environmental developments which have an impact on the pulp and paper sector, the chemicals sector, on the photocopying sector and on office machinery, particularly in relation to the Eco-label and the disposal and recycling of used equipment. The environmental dimension of the firm spreads over into veterinary and agricultural products. It has successfully represented a multinational client in litigation against the European Commission over minimum residue levels and has recently advised a North American producer of animal semen on marketing and distribution within Europe. In the food sector the firm has long been the adviser to Leatherhead, a food research association, and has recently advised a producer of genetically modified organisms in litigation before the French Conseil d'Etat in which a preliminary question of interpretation of Directive 90/220/EEC was referred to the European Court of Justice.

LANGUAGES: Dutch, English, French, German, Hindi, Italian, Mandarin, Spanish, Tamil

ADVOKATFIRMAET STEENSTRUP STORDRANGE DA

HEAD OFFICE

Fr Nansens Plass 4, PO Box 1829 Vika,
0123 Oslo, Norway
Tel: +47 2281 4500 **Fax:** +47 2281 4501

Email: lawyers@steenstrup.no
Website: www.steenstrup.no

FIRM OVERVIEW

Chairman of the board: Ove-Marthin Granlund

Number of partners worldwide: 15
Number of other lawyers worldwide: 37

AREAS OF PRACTICE:

M&A/corporate finance	15%
Telecom and information technology	12%
Contracts	10%
Litigation and arbitration	10%
Torts and compensation	10%
Banking and finance	5%
Bankruptcy and insolvency	5%
Commercial property/real estate	5%
Construction	5%
EU and competition	5%
Intellectual property, media and entertainment	5%
Labour	5%
Tax	5%
Maritime and shipping	2%
Consultations with government authorities	1%

WORLDWIDE OFFICE CONTACTS

NORWAY
Fr Nansens Plass 4, PO Box 1829 Vika, 0123 **Oslo**
Tel: +47 2281 4500 **Fax:** +47 2281 4501
Email: lawyers@steenstrup.no

Olav Tryggvasons gate 12, P.O. Box 692-Sentrum, 7407 **Trondheim**
Tel: +47 7351 5051 **Fax:** +47 7351 5017

S

FIRM OVERVIEW: Founded in 1989, this Norwegian firm has become one of the ten largest law firms in Oslo. New partners are recruited continuously, each of them working with two or three lawyers and associates. The partners are young and ambitious, and have a strong professional background. The firm is part of two international alliances, Interlex and State Capital Law Firm Group. Steenstrup Stordrange offers a large range of legal services to clients both in Norway and abroad, focusing heavily on corporate law, contracts, telecommunications and information technology.

INTERNATIONAL EXPERIENCE: The firm has an extensive EU and competition practice, both at national and EU/EFTA levels. The firm represented the Norwegian part of Acomarit during the Sea Empress catastrophe off the coast of Wales.

INTERNATIONAL CLIENTS: Advokatfirmaet Steenstrup Stordrange DA represents international companies' activities in Norway. Clients include PremiAir, BP Amoco, Daimler Chrysler, Ernst & Young, Adecco, KNPQwest, Time Warner, Nutricia, UPC, Getronics, Fabricom and Stolt Sea Farm. In addition the firm's client base includes crew development corporations, brewers, wine producers and various international banks.

MAIN INTERNATIONAL AREAS OF PRACTICE:
Merger and acquisitions: The firm's transactions in this area include private acquisition and cross-border take overs.
Corporate law: Steenstrup Stordrange advises on all aspects of general corporate law, including the drafting of contracts according to Norwegian law.
Stock exchange regulations: The firm handles matters for listed companies via the stock market and the Oslo Stock Exchange.
Telecommunications and computer law: The firm is very active in this sector. Steenstrup Stordrange advises on contracts, marketing law, intellectual property and employment matters, including CRM-related issues.
Litigation and arbitration: Steenstrup Stordrange deals with commercial litigation, national and international arbitration and regularly handles cases before the City Courts, the Courts of Appeal and the Supreme Court in Norway. The firm also represents international clients in criminal cases, specialising in white collar crime.
Employment: The firm handles all matters relating to Norwegian employment law.

LANGUAGES: English, French, German, Russian and the Scandinavian languages.

For other recommended firms see pages 1485-1520

STEPHENSON HARWOOD

HEAD OFFICE

One, St Paul's Churchyard,
London EC4M 8SH, United Kingdom
Tel: +44 20 7329 4422 **Fax:** +44 20 7606 0822

Email: info@shlegal.com
Website: www.shlegal.com

FIRM OVERVIEW

Number of partners worldwide: 77
Number of other lawyers worldwide: 195

AREAS OF PRACTICE:

Corporate 31%
Litigation 25%
Shipping 24%
Property 14%
Private capital 6%

FIRM OVERVIEW: Stephenson Harwood is an international law firm, with an established position in chosen sectors of the international financial markets. Worldwide revenue is over £50m and it has some 77 partners and a total of more than 500 staff. The firm practises through five principal legal disciplines: corporate law, commercial litigation, shipping, property and private capital and has a particular focus on the financial industry, maritime services and the property market, together with opportunities arising from today's information and technology driven economy.

MAIN INTERNATIONAL AREAS OF PRACTICE:

Corporate: The firm has a well-established corporate practice advising a broad cross section of clients including multi-national corporations, international financial institutions and banks, public and private sector companies both in the UK and overseas. The firm provides a full range of corporate finance advice as well as fund management, e-commerce, IT, IP, employment and pensions and tax.

Litigation: The firm handles an extensive range of commercial disputes including fraud, asset tracing, money laundering, professional indemnity and insurance cases. It also deals with regulation and corporate investigation work and alternative dispute resolution. A sizeable proportion of the firm's work is international and multi-jurisdictional.

Property: The firm handles all aspects of commercial property, property investment, planning, property finance, development, landlord and tenant, environmental law and private finance initiative transactions. Clients include property companies, institutional investors, banks, and professional service companies as well as local authorities, hotel groups and public bodies. Property investment clients include both international and domestic investors.

Private capital: Practical advice on trusts and trust litigation, tax, probate and administration of estates, heritage property and residential conveyancing. The firm advises charities, ranging from national institutions to small grant-making trusts, on a full range of issues arising from financing, tax and internal management to relations with regulators and other parties.

Shipping: The firm has a full service practice with a comprehensive range of specialist maritime lawyers . The firm advises on contentious and noncontentious aspects of the financing, ownership, trading, insurance and reinsurance of ships and cargoes.

LANGUAGES: Cantonese, Croatian, English, French, German, Greek, Mandarin, Russian, Spanish

WORLDWIDE OFFICE CONTACTS

BELGIUM

Stephenson Barbé, avenue du Diamant 139, 1030 **Brussels**
Tel: +32 2 735 3520 **Fax:** +32 2 732 2237
Email: antony.mair@shlegal.com

CHINA

Stephenson Harwood & Lo, 2809, Peace World Plaza, 28th Floor, 362-366 Huanshi Road East, Dongshan District, **Guangzhou** 510060
Tel: +86 20 8388 0590 **Fax:** +86 20 8386 3119
Email: gzo@shl.com.hk

GREECE

Stephenson Harwood Consultants OE, Pal Trapezis 10 & Sachtouri Street, 185 36 **Piraeus**
Tel: +30 1 429 5160 **Fax:** +30 1 429 5166
Email: nigel.bowen-morris@shlegal.com

HONG KONG

Stephenson Harwood & Lo, 18th Floor, Edinburgh Tower, The Landmark, 15 Queen's Road Central **Hong Kong**
Tel: +852 2868 0789 **Fax:** +852 2868 1504
Email: mhh@shl.com.hk

SINGAPORE

1 Shenton Way, #18-07 Robina House, **Singapore** 068803
Tel: +65 226 1600 **Fax:** +65 226 1661
Email: martin.green@shsing.com.sg

SPAIN

Fernando El Santo 15-3, 28010 **Madrid**
Tel: +34 91 319 1212 **Fax:** +34 91 319 1940
Email: kenneth.bonavia@shlegal.com

UNITED KINGDOM

One, St Paul's Churchyard, **London** EC4M 8SH
Tel: +44 20 7329 4422 **Fax:** +44 20 7606 0822
Email: info@shlegal.com

ASSOCIATED OFFICES

CROATIA

Zuric i Partneri, Gunduliceva 63, 10000 **Zagreb**
Tel: +385 1 488 1300/1311 **Fax:** +385 1 485 6704/3
Email: zuric-i-partneri@zg.tel.hr

FRANCE

Barbé Carpentier Thibault Groener, 14 Avenue Gourgaud, 75017 **Paris**
Tel: +33 1 44 15 61 00 **Fax:** +33 1 44 15 91 81
Email: jp.thibault@bctg-associes.com

GREECE

Elias SP Paraskevas, 7 Asklepiou Street, 106 79 **Athens**
Tel: +30 1 361 0333 **Fax:** +30 1 364 5329
Email: paraskev@hol.gr.dot

KUWAIT

Al Sarraf & Al Ruwayeh, Salhlya Complex, Gate 1, 3rd Floor, PO Box 1448, **Safat** 13015
Tel: +965 240 0061/2/3 **Fax:** +965 240 0064
Email: asar@asarlegal.com

SOUTH AFRICA

Routledge-Modise, 3rd Floor Office Tower, Sandton City, Riviona Road, Sandton, PO Box 78333, **Sandton** 2196
Tel: +27 11 286 6900 **Fax:** +27 11 286 6901
Email: info@routledges.co.za

STEPTOE & JOHNSON LLP

HEAD OFFICE

1330 Connecticut Avenue NW,
Washington DC 20036-1795, USA
Tel: +1 202 429 3000 **Fax:** +1 202 429 3902

Email: lcamalier@steptoe.com
Website: www.steptoe.com

FIRM OVERVIEW

Chairman of the executive committee: J.A. Bouknight, Jr.

Number of partners worldwide: 114
Number of other lawyers worldwide: 176

WORLDWIDE OFFICE CONTACTS

USA

Steptoe & Johnson LLP, 633 West 5th Street Suite 700, **Los Angeles** CA 90071
Tel: +1 213 439 9400 **Fax:** +1 213 439 9599

Steptoe & Johnson LLP, Two Renaissance Square, 24th Fl, 40 North Central Avenue, **Phoenix** AZ 85004
Tel: +1 602 257 5200 **Fax:** +1 602 257 5299

1330 Connecticut Avenue NW, **Washington** DC 20036-1795
Tel: +1 202 429 3000 **Fax:** +1 202 429 3902
Email: lcamalier@steptoe.com

AREAS OF PRACTICE:

Litigation	35%
Corporate	32%
Energy and natural resources	17%
International	8%
Technology	8%

FIRM OVERVIEW: Steptoe & Johnson LLP is a leading US law firm with more than 300 attorneys in Washington DC, Phoenix and Los Angeles. The firm practices in five core areas: business solutions, energy and natural resources, international, litigation, and technology.

INTERNATIONAL EXPERIENCE: Steptoe & Johnson LLP offers comprehensive and experienced international law and trade advice. It has represented foreign and domestic clients in all major forms of litigation and administrative proceedings. The firm also handles international business transactions, public international law issues, and has an active international aviation practice. Steptoe & Johnson's attorneys have held senior-level government positions in the State, Commerce, Justice, Treasury and Defence Departments, Office of the United States Trade Representative, and congressional committees. The firm has also been selected as the sole Washington, DC member of the prestigious Lex Mundi international legal network.

INTERNATIONAL CLIENTS: The firm's clients include transportation, manufacturing, technology, financial, utility and basic industries' companies doing business in the international arena.

MAIN INTERNATIONAL AREAS OF PRACTICE:

Trade litigation: Steptoe & Johnson LLP has a large international trade practice consisting of 30 lawyers. The firm represents both domestic and foreign clients in all major forms of trade litigation and administrative investigations. The firm has represented foreign and domestic clients in over 100 anti-dumping and countervailing duty cases. It has advised on nearly half of the Section 201 cases filed with the International Trade Commission and has also represented clients in Section 337 and Section 301 cases. Steptoe & Johnson LLP represents clients before the Customs Service in a wide variety of issues including classification, country of origin, duty preference programs and Section 592 penalty investigations. It also advises on the approval of imports for duty-free treatment. The firm regularly represents clients in anti-dumping and countervailing duty cases before the US Court of International Trade and Federal Circuit Court of Appeals. It also represents clients in both civil and criminal investigations of alleged import price-fixing.

Trade policy: Steptoe & Johnson LLP advises on market access efforts in the US and abroad and has expertise in commodity oversupply situations; customs issues; foreign subsidy practices; trade with non-market economies; agricultural trade; government procurement standards; technical telecommunications; and strategic counselling. The firm acts on behalf of its clients in advising US government officials involved in negotiations and dispute proceedings, both bilateral and multilateral, under NAFTA, the World Trade Organization (WTO) and other multinational bodies. It also has formal and informal links with foreign government decision makers.

International transactions: The firm's international corporate and finance practice focuses on emerging economies, infrastructure projects, and public finance transactions. It handles a large number of international contractual, licensing, joint venture, corporate acquisition, stock/asset purchases, and registration projects for US and foreign clients. The firm is involved in overseas markets in international telecommunication, electric power, transportation infrastructure, hydro-electric projects, and intellectual property protection. Steptoe & Johnson also advises on international lending, insurance, and participation from the major public finance institutions, such as the World Bank, Ex-Im Bank, European Bank Corporation and Overseas Private Investment Corporation. It also advises on privatisation projects.

Business regulation: Steptoe & Johnson's international practice includes advice and representation on business regulation. The firm focuses on export controls, economic sanctions, the Foreign Corrupt Practices Act, anti-boycott compliance, customs, investment reviews, and immigration.

Public international law: Steptoe & Johnson LLP is counsel to the Rule of Law Committee, a group made up of senior legal representatives of large US multinational corporations with a common interest in monitoring, responding to, and shaping critical issues in public international law. The firm advises on expropriation and international boundary disputes. It also represents clients before governmental agencies on broad public law issues affecting competitiveness in the global market.

Aviation: The firm advises on all aspects of US law and regulation including airline cooperative agreements, computer reservation systems, safety and security issues, liability concerns, facilitation issues, taxes and user fees, and a variety of commercial matters.

LANGUAGES: Arabic, Belarusan, Bengali, Cantonese, Chinese (Cantonese, Mandarin), Danish, English, French, German, Hebrew, Italian, Japanese, Malaysian, Norwegian, Papago, Portuguese, Spanish, Taiwanese, Tagalog, Ukranian, Vietnamese

For other recommended firms see pages 1485-1520

STIBBE

HEAD OFFICE

See worldwide office contacts

Website: www.stibbe.com

FIRM OVERVIEW

Managing partner: Allard Metzelaar (Amsterdam)
Chairman of the Board: Alain Georges (Paris)
Number of partners worldwide: 110
Number of other lawyers worldwide: 337

AREAS OF PRACTICE:

Administrative law	*%
Corporate	*%
EU and competition law	*%
Intellectual property	*%
Employment	*%
Litigation and arbitration	*%
New technology	*%
Real estate	*%
Tax	*%

* Workload % not disclosed

WORLDWIDE OFFICE CONTACTS

BELGIUM
Rue Henri Wafelaertsstraat 47-51, B-1060 **Brussels**
Tel: +32 2 533 5211 **Fax:** +32 2 533 52 12
Email: info@stibbe.be

FRANCE
154 rue de l'Université, 75007 **Paris**
Tel: +33 1 40 62 20 00 **Fax:** +33 1 40 62 20 62
Email: info@stibbe.fr

NETHERLANDS
Strawinskylaan 2001, 1077 ZZ **Amsterdam**
Tel: +31 20 546 06 06 **Fax:** +31 20 546 01 23
Email: info@stibbe.nl

UNITED KINGDOM
66 Gresham St, LONDON EC2V 7NH
Tel: +44 20 7600 4400 **Fax:** +44 20 7600 4411
Email: info@stibbe.co.uk

USA
350 Park Avenue, NEW YORK NY 10022
Tel: +1 212 972 4000 **Fax:** +1 212 972 4929
Email: info@stibbeus.com

S

FIRM OVERVIEW: Stibbe is an international law firm with main offices in Amsterdam, Brussels and Paris and branch offices in London and New York. The firm's present form is the result of three mergers.

INTERNATIONAL EXPERIENCE: With 450 lawyers based in Amsterdam, Brussels, Paris, London and New York, Stibbe is a full service law firm with an internationally oriented general commercial practice and special emphasis on mergers and acquisitions, banking, securities, tax, corporate and structured finance, project finance, real estate, telecommunications, intellectual property law, new technology law, labour law, litigation and arbitration, competition law, European law, WTO law, administrative law, energy and environmental law.

INTERNATIONAL CLIENTS: Ranging from multinational corporations to private companies, state organisations and other public authorities, the firm's clients represent a broad spectrum of activity in such areas as finance (bank, VC), industry (food, automobile, energy, chemical, electronics, high technology), retail, trade and distribution, real estate, information, technology and telecommunications. Among the firm's international clients are some of the world foremost companies. Many of the firm's clients are listed on one or more stock exchanges in continental Europe, London and New York.

MAIN INTERNATIONAL EXPERIENCE:

Administrative law: The firm advises on administrative spatial planning, environmental law, economic law and regulations, health, telecommunications, public/private ventures and administrative procedural law.
Competition law: The firm is involved in setting-up joint ventures, organisations and running distribution networks; transferring or exchanging technology; intellectual property rights; co-operating within economic interest groupings and trade associations; pricing policy; and commercial policy.
Employment: The firm covers a wide range of matters concerned with labour law and employment.
European community/world trade organisation law: The firm advises on rights and obligations under European Community law and international trade law; anti-trust provisions of EC law, agreements to the European Commission; impact of European antidumping law; antidumping proceedings before the European Commission; and interpretation and national implementation of EC rules.
Financial and stock exchange law: Work includes purchase tender offers and exchange tender offers for equity services; IPOs on European regulated markets and on foreign markets (NYSE, NASDAQ, EASDAQ); privatisation programmes; issuance and offering of stock or equity-linked securities; issuances of bonds; international loan or credit agreements; project financing; asset financing; securitisation; senior and intermediate financing in connection with company buyouts; laws and regulations relating to banking; and stock exchange and financial services.
Information and communication technologies: The firm offers advice on online networks and services, intellectual property, encryption, broadcasting and privacy, and on licences and approvals related to websites, electronic commerce and digital-video-on-demand systems. The firm is actively involved in the conception, creation, protection, marketing and maintenance of software, CD ROMs, databases and computer equipment.
Intellectual property: The firm handles matters such as industrial property, copyright, press law, advertising and regulatory aspects of products, presentation and packaging.
International litigation and arbitration: The firm is actively involved in all aspects of international litigation and arbitration.
M&A: The firm handles acquisitions and sales of companies, tender offers, acquisition or sale of shares, and mergers of listed and unlisted companies.
Real estate: The firm is involved in project development, building and construction, public procurement, real estate sales, purchases, leasing and financing.
Tax: The firm advises on tax planning; specific transactions for national and international companies; financing; complex financial products; litigation involving tax authorities; and the negotiation of rulings with the tax authorities.

LANGUAGES: Dutch, English, French, German, Italian, Spanish, Russian

For other recommended firms see pages 1485-1520

STRACHAN PARTNERS

HEAD OFFICE

5th Floor, Akuro House, 24 Campbell Street,
Lagos Nigeria
Tel: +234 1 263 4919 **Fax:** +234 1 263 7277

Email: strachan@infoweb.abs.net
Website: www.strachanpartners.com

WORLDWIDE OFFICE CONTACTS

NIGERIA
5th Floor, Akuro House, 24 Campbell Street, **Lagos**
Tel: +234 1 263 4919 **Fax:** +234 1 263 7277
Email: strachan@infoweb.abs.net

FIRM OVERVIEW

Managing partner: Charles A Candide-Johnson
Associate partners: Ugoji C Abagwe, Victor Udo, Mena Ajakpori

Number of partners worldwide: 4
Number of other lawyears worldwide: 8

AREAS OF PRACTICE:

Litigation and arbitration	35%
Corporate	15%
Intellectual property	10%
Telecommunications and computer law	10%
Shipping and admiralty	10%
Banking and finance	8%
M&A	8%

FIRM OVERVIEW: Strachan Partners was founded in Lagos, Nigeria in 1991 as an autonomous office of J.B. Majiyagbe & Co., a law firm established in 1971 in Kano, Nigeria. It has grown to be one of the leading litigation firms with a strong non-contentious practice. In July 1994, it became entirely independent and took the name Strachan Partners.

INTERNATIONAL EXPERIENCE: In 2000, Strachan Partners advised and provided services for international clients from Africa, Europe and America in such areas as banking, mergers and acquisitions, intellectual property, telecommunications and IT law as well as foreign investment and establishment of business in Nigeria.

INTERNATIONAL CLIENTS: Strachan Partners' client base includes banks, trading and manufacturing companies as well as high net-worth individuals doing international business.

MAIN INTERNATIONAL AREAS OF PRACTICE:
Intellectual property: The firm has extensive experience in trademarks, patents and designs. Lawyers within the firm have taken part in negotiating and drafting licensing agreements, and have advised and represented clients on infringement disputes.
Telecommunications and IT law: The firm's managing partner advises the Nigerian Government on telecommunications and regulatory reform. He has also written on this subject. Strachan Partners represents clients which are shaping telecommunications and IT law in Nigeria.
Litigation: A major area of concentration in the firm, international clients have been represented in a wide range of disputes covering shipping and admiralty, banking and insurance.
Corporate: Strachan Partners specialises in advising foreign clients who wish to invest in Nigeria either by setting up on their own or by investing in an already existing business. The firm regularly assists foreigners to set up business in Nigeria.
M&A: The firm advises on mergers and acquisitions in Nigeria. In 2000, the firm advised three foreign banks on a proposed merger with a Nigerian bank.

LANGUAGES: English, Hausa, Igbo, Yoruba

For other recommended firms see pages 1485-1520

STROOCK & STROOCK & LAVAN LLP

HEAD OFFICE

180 Maiden Lane,
New York, NY 10038-4982, USA
Tel: +1 212 806 5400 **Fax:** +1 212 806 6006

Email: info@stroock.com
Website: www.stroock.com

FIRM OVERVIEW

Managing partner: Thomas E. Heftler

Number of partners worldwide: 88
Number of other lawyers worldwide: 221

AREAS OF PRACTICE:

Corporate and structured finance	31%
Litigation	26%
Real estate	15%
Insolvency	8%
Intellectual property	7%
Taxation and ERISA	6%
Trusts and estates	4%
Insurance	3%

FIRM PROFILE: Stroock & Stroock & Lavan is a full-service, multidisciplinary law firm, providing counsel to financial, business and technology clients worldwide on a complete range of commercial matters. Stroock has offices in New York, Los Angeles, Miami, and Washington, D.C.

INTERNATIONAL EXPERIENCE: Stroock has represented governmental entities, consortia and private parties in connection with several precedent-setting infrastructure projects in Central/Eastern Europe and the Middle East, including the largest privately-financed power plant project completed to date, a ten-year highway privatisation project in Hungary, and the construction of the Carmel Tunnel in Israel. The firm represented the dealers in the US$25 billion Euro Medium-Term Note Program for Bank of America Corporation and Bank of America, N.A., facilitating the issuance of debt instruments in eighteen currencies that were listed on several foreign exchanges. Stroock represented the Foreign Exchange Committee (independent of, but sponsored by, the Federal Reserve Bank of NY), the British Bankers' Association, the Federation of Bankers Associations of Japan, and the Canadian Foreign Exchange Committee in connection with standard agreements governing foreign exchange trading and other issues related to Y2K and the introduction of the Euro. In a high-profile 1999 patent infringement suit, Stroock attorneys appeared before the International Trade Commission on behalf of a leading Japanese film manufacturer. In the resulting decision the ITC barred twenty-six respondents from importing or transferring previously imported one-time-use cameras in violation of the client's patent rights. Working on behalf of a cabinet-level department of the British Government, in its capacity as receiver of an insolvent company under the Companies Act, Stroock attorneys recovered millions of dollars in funds hidden in the US through a European-based fraudulent investment scheme. The firm is US counsel to Bank Austria/Creditanstalt.

INTERNATIONAL CLIENTS: Clients of the firm include large multinational corporations, entrprenerurial companies, financial instituations, major underwriters and issuers of securities, domestic and offshore private investment funds, venture capital firms, investors, and foreign governments.

WORLDWIDE OFFICE CONTACTS

USA

180 Maiden Lane, **New York**, NY 10038-4982
Tel: +1 212 806 5400 **Fax:** +1 212 806 6006

Additional offices in Los Angeles, Miami and Washington DC.

MAIN INTERNATIONAL AREAS OF PRACTICE:

Corporate and structured finance: Stroock attorneys have negotiated billions of dollars in financings on behalf of major international investment banking firms and syndicates. The firm has assisted in structuring numerous Euro loans, refinancings, equity participations, workouts, debt restructurings, and project financings in Latin America and Europe. Stroock is a longtime adviser to domestic and foreign companies on transnational acquisitions and divestitures, corporate operations, and regulatory matters.

Commodities and derivatives trading: Stroock attorneys handle matters involving forward and futures markets, interest rate swaps, equity and credit derivatives, commodity financing (particularly precious metals and financial commodities), foreign exchange trading, and hedging of physical, spot or forward positions. They are frequently involved in trade finance and merchant banking transactions supporting the production, refinement and/or recovery of a commodity, including mine development projects and the financing of LDC debt repayments.

Energy and project finance: Stroock played a leading role in the development of infrastructure and new business ventures in Hungary, and continues to be an active participant in power plant development in the Middle East. Stroock has significant experience in major US power plants acquisition and disposition. Stroock attorneys have extensive experience with the privatisation of state-owned entities, particularly in the communications industry.

Insolvency: Stroock represents foreign financial institutions and liquidators seeking ancillary support for foreign litigation and arbitration. The firm's expertise in asset recovery and effecting turnovers of property is invaluable to the administration of insolvent estates and payment of creditors. Stroock has represented the liquidators of several major overseas banks.

Insurance: Stroock attorneys negotiate regulatory approvals of mergers and acquisitions, holding company transactions, loss portfolio transfers, and other financial arrangements such as the formation of offshore captive insurers. The firm is actively involved in the emerging areas of non-traditional reinsurance, insurance risk securitisation and derivatives, 'insuritisation' of financial risks, and integrated risk solutions.

Intellectual property: With experience in a number of technical fields, Stroock attorneys provide counsel on patents, trademarks, copyrights, unfair competition, trade secrets, licensing, anti-trust, and technology transfer. They advise clients on the proper valuation of intellectual property assets in the context of strategic alliances, corporate reorganisations, and research and development.

Litigation: Stroock represents foreign financial institutions, governments and court-appointed representatives in matters ranging from fraud recovery to insolvencies. The firm has decades of experience in international litigation, alternative dispute resolution, and the coordination of provisional remedies across jurisdictions in order to halt and prevent secretion of assets.

LANGUAGES: Arabic, French, German, Greek, Hebrew, Hindi, Hungarian, Italian, Japanese, Polish, Portuguese, Russian, Spanish, Urdu

SULLIVAN & CROMWELL

HEAD OFFICE

125 Broad Street,
New York NY 10004-2498, USA
Tel: +1 212 558 4000 **Fax:** +1 212 558 3588
Email: osbornc@sullcrom.com
Website: www.sullcrom.com

FIRM OVERVIEW

Chairman: H. Rodgin Cohen
Number of partners worldwide: 138
Number of other lawyers worldwide: 460

AREAS OF PRACTICE:

Corporate and financial (including securities and privatisations) . . *%
E-Business and technology . . . . *%
Estates and personal . . . . *%
Financial institutions . . . . *%
Litigation (including antitrust and EC competition law) . . . . *%
M&A . . . . *%
Project finance . . . . *%
Real estate . . . . *%
Tax . . . . *%
* Workload % not disclosed

FIRM OVERVIEW: Founded in 1879, Sullivan & Cromwell comprises approximately 600 lawyers conducting a global practice through a network of 12 offices on four continents. The firm's organisation as a single, unified partnership worldwide, combined with its reliance primarily on internally generated growth, has contributed to its reputation for providing consistently high quality legal services.

INTERNATIONAL EXPERIENCE: Sullivan & Cromwell has played a leading role in recent global economic changes including successive waves of privatisation; the expansion of international access to US capital markets; cross-border mergers that are redefining the telecommunications, oil and gas, pharmaceutical and other sectors worldwide; the integration of financial services; the rapid evolution of e-business and technology companies; and the growth of international project finance.

INTERNATIONAL CLIENTS: Foreign enterprises comprise more than half of Sullivan & Cromwell's clients. Its lawyers provide legal advice and services to leading international industrial and commercial companies, financial enterprises as well as governments and governmental bodies.

WORLDWIDE OFFICE CONTACTS

AUSTRALIA
101 Collins Street, **Melbourne** 3000
Tel: +61 3 9635 1500 **Fax:** +61 3 9654 2422
Email: brownej@sullcrom.com

CHINA
Suite 501, China World Trade Center Tower 1, No. 1, Jianguo Menwai Avenue, **Beijing** 100004
Tel: +86 10 6505 6120 **Fax:** +86 10 6505 6136
Email: weic@sullcrom.com

FRANCE
8, place Vendôme, 75001 **Paris**
Tel: +33 1 4450 6000 **Fax:** +33 1 4450 6060
Email: asthalterr@sullcrom.com

GERMANY
Neue Mainzer Strasse 52, 60311 **Frankfurt am Main**
Tel: +49 69 7191 260 **Fax:** +49 69 7191 2610
Email: morrisond@sullcrom.com

HONG KONG
28th Floor, Nine Queens Rd, Central, **Hong Kong**
Tel: +852 2826 8688 **Fax:** +852 2522 2280
Email: delamaterr@sullcrom.com

JAPAN
Otemachi First Square East Tower 16F, 5-1, Otemachi 1-chome, Chiyoda-ku, **Tokyo** 100-0004
Tel: +81 3 3213 6140 **Fax:** +81 3 3213 6470
Email: akaii@sullcrom.com

UNITED KINGDOM
St. Olave's House, 9a Ironmonger Lane, **London** EC2V 8EY
Tel: +44 20 7710 6500 **Fax:** +44 20 7710 6565
Email: plapingerw@sullcrom.com

USA
1888 Century Park East, **Los Angeles** CA 90067-1725
Tel: +1 310 712 6600 **Fax:** +1 310 712 8800
Email: sacksr@sullcrom.com

1870 Embarcadero Road, **Palo Alto** CA 94303-3308
Tel: +1 650 461 5600 **Fax:** +1 650 461 5700
Email: millersc@sullcrom.com

1701 Pennsylvania Avenue, NW, **Washington DC** 20006-5805
Tel: +1 202 956 7500 **Fax:** +1 202 293 6330
Email: craftr@sullcrom.com

MAIN INTERNATIONAL AREAS OF PRACTICE:

Capital markets: The firm is the leader in US securities offerings by non-US issuers as well as a leading legal adviser in privatisations by international offering worldwide. The firm regularly advises on the largest and most complex international offerings.

Litigation: Sullivan & Cromwell's litigation group regularly represents leading international industrial corporations, financial institutions and individual clients before state and federal courts throughout the US. Anti-trust, EC competition and international commercial arbitration matters comprise a significant component of the overall litigation practice.

M&A: Sullivan & Cromwell has advised on some of the largest transactions in the telecommunications, financial institutions, pharmaceutical, and oil and gas industries worldwide.

Financial institutions: The firm's financial institutions practice encompasses M&A, the development of new products and services, regulatory matters, credit activities and litigation and enforcement matters for international banks, insurance companies and investment management firms.

E-business and technology: Sullivan & Cromwell has established itself as a major player in advising e-business and technology enterprises, at all stages of their development and growth. Its e-business and technology group focuses on the strategic opportunities and issues that challenge clients in this rapidly evolving sector.

Real estate: The firm advises on the purchase, sale, construction, financing, and securitisation of real estate assets worldwide. Clients include investors, developers, lenders and investment bankers.

Project finance: Sullivan & Cromwell is counsel to sponsors of, and lenders to, world-class projects in developed and emerging markets. The practice is well diversified by industry, including mining, natural resources, infrastructure development, telecommunications and power.

Tax: The firm's tax group plays a leading role in structuring new, tax-advantaged financial instruments and complex M&A transactions, and represents prominent industrial and commercial enterprises worldwide in both US and cross-border tax matters.

For other recommended firms see pages 1485-1520

SUMMIT LAW OFFICE

HEAD OFFICE

Suite 2010, Tower A, Vantone New World Plaza,
2 Fuchengmenwai Street, Xicheng District
Beijing 100037, China
Tel: +86 10 6804 6255 **Fax:** +8610 6804 6259

Email: summitlaw@bj.col.com.cn

FIRM OVERVIEW

Managing partner: Ji Jianfeng
Senior partners: Ji Jianfeng, Zhu Min

Number of partners worldwide: 3
Number of other lawyers worldwide: 3

AREAS OF PRACTICE:

Foreign investment	34%
Banking and finance	20%
Company and commercial	17%
M&A	15%
Litigation and arbitration	8%
Intellectual property	6%

FIRM OVERVIEW: Founded in 1995, Summit Law Office is a Beijing-based independent law partnership approved to practise Chinese law. Comprising Chinese qualified lawyers who have a firm commitment to its clients, the aim of the firm is to identify clients' needs and to meet those needs quickly, efficiently and effectively. The firm has handled a wide range of legal matters relating to corporate and commercial affairs, banking and finance, foreign investment, intellectual property, real estate, construction and project work, taxation, international trade and dispute resolution. Such experience is combined with professional knowledge and sensitivity to the myriad of requirements and disciplines in different parts of China. The experience, accumulated skills and resources of the firm enable it to handle both everyday matters and the largest and most complex transactions.

INTERNATIONAL EXPERIENCE: During the past five years, Summit Law Office has advised on over 50 large scale infrastructure projects involving foreign investment (including roads, bridges, tunnels, power plants, water treatment projects and waste water treatment projects), as well as in the establishment of Chinese-foreign equity joint ventures, Chinese-foreign co-operative joint ventures and wholly foreign-owned enterprises in China.

INTERNATIONAL CLIENTS: The firm's client base includes multinational corporations, banks and non-banking financial institutions and foreign companies investing and doing business in China.

WORLDWIDE OFFICE CONTACTS

CHINA
Suite 2010, Tower A, Vantone New World Plaza, 2 Fuchengmenwai Street, Xicheng District, **Beijing** 100037
Tel: +86 10 6804 6255 **Fax:** +8610 6804 6259
Email: summitlaw@bj.col.com.cn

MAIN INTERNATIONAL AREAS OF PRACTICE:

Banking and finance: Summit Law Office handles all aspects of banking and finance, including bank security and collateral, loans, loan syndications and other financings, project financing, structured financings, asset and lease financings and securitisations, commercial paper, certificates of deposit and other debt issues, equipment leasing and hire purchase, aircraft and ship financings, debt restructuring and rescheduling.

Company and commercial: The firm has extensive experience in project and commercial developments, project management, technical consultancies, partnerships, incorporations, joint ventures, licensing, agencies and distribution, taxation, labour management, bankruptcy, liquidation, company secretarial and administration services.

M&A: The firm's transactions in this area range from management buyouts, restructurings, reorganisations and schemes of arrangement to cross-border mergers, acquisitions and take-overs of companies of different scales.

Foreign investment: The firm has represented a number of multinational corporations in their investment in China, including identifying potential Chinese partners, assisting in the preparation of project feasibility study reports, conducting due diligence, drafting and negotiating project agreements and contracts and assisting in obtaining government approvals, consents, permits and licenses and effecting registrations and filings with the relevant governmental authorities.

Intellectual property: The firm has played an active role in intellectual property rights, including drafting and negotiating license agreements and advising on infringement disputes and other aspects of IP law.

Litigation and arbitration: The firm handles the mediation and reconciliation of commercial disputes, commercial litigation, national and international arbitration, as well as enforcement of foreign awards and judgements.

LANGUAGES: Chinese, English

S

For other recommended firms see pages 1485-1520

SURRIDGE & BEECHENO

HEAD OFFICE

Finlay House, I.I. Chundrigar Road,
Karachi 74000 Pakistan
Tel: +92 21 242 7292 **Fax:** +92 21 241 6830

Email: sbecheno@khi.comsats.net.pk
Website: www.surridgeandbeecheno.com

WORLDWIDE OFFICE CONTACTS

PAKISTAN

Finlay House, I.I. Chundrigar Road, **Karachi** 74000
Tel: +92 21 242 7292 **Fax:** +92 21 241 6830
Email: sbecheno@khi.comsats.net.pk

Ghulam Rasool Building, 60 Shahrah-e-Quaid-e-Azam, **Lahore**
Tel: +92 42 630 5178 **Fax:** +92 42 636 7390
Email: surridg@beechno.lcci.org.ok

FIRM OVERVIEW

Senior partners: Aftab Ahmed Khan (Lahore), A. A. Shareef (Karachi)
Other partners: Mohammad Naeem (Karachi), Kahlid A. Rehman (Karachi)

AREAS OF PRACTICE:

Area	%
Corporate/M&A	15%
Admirality and shipping	12%
Aviation	12%
Foreign investment and joint ventures	12%
Industrial relations and employment	8%
Banking and finance	7%
Trademarks and patents	7%
Satellite communication and broadcasting	5%
Securities and exchange regulations	5%
Insurance	4%
Arbitration	4%
Family	2%
Construction and engineering	2%

FIRM OVERVIEW: Surridge and Beecheno was founded in 1948 in Karachi by two British barristers and has a branch office in Lahore. The firm has three partners and eighteen associates in Karachi and one partner and five associates in Lahore. There are two senior active partners of the firm, one stationed in Karachi and the other in Lahore.

INTERNATIONAL CLIENTS: Clients include Abbott Laboratories; ABN Amro Bank; Al-Ghurair; ANZ Group; Asian Development Bank; Babcock & Wilcox; Bank of America; Bass International Holding NV; British Airways; The Burmah Oil Group; Ciba Geigy (Novartis); Cisco Systems Inc.; Cotecna; Corn Products (CPC Group); Daewoo Corporation; Deutsche Bank; GEC Finance; General Electric; Glaxo Wellcome; International Finance Corporation; Johnon & Johnson; KLM Royal Dutch Airline; London Protection & Indemnity Club; Mitsubishi; Pakistan State Oil Co; Pepsi Co Inc; Philip Morris; Shell; Standard Chartered Bank; Standard Chartered Grindlays Bank Ltd; and Bank of Tokyo.

MAIN INTERNATIONAL AREAS OF PRACTICE:
Foreign investment and joint ventures: The firm advises private power producing companies, financial institutions, sovereign governments, major international donors, and other multinational companies active in the technology, energy, telecommunications and insurance sectors on foreign investment in Pakistan and the laws governing this area. The firm also handles joint ventures betweeen local and foreign firms and companiesis.
Corporate/M&A/securities: The firm has expertise in corporate matters and advises local and international corporations on the incorporation and management of companies. It has been active in the successful negotiation and conclusion of several M&A projects. The firm specialises in securites and exchange laws of Pakistan advising clients on constantly changing rules and regulations of the State Bank of Pakistan.
Insurance: Surridge and Beecheno is widely experienced in advising local and international insurance companies on the detailed and complex rules and regulations that govern this area of law.
Arbitration: The firm is experienced in alternative dispute resolution methods, including mediation, conciliation, fact finding, mediation-arbitration, early neutral evaluation and multi-door courthouses. Many members and associates of the firm are members of international and local arbitration associations.
Banking and finance: Clients include leading local and international banks and financial institutions functioning or having dealings in Pakistan. The firm offers advice on banking and financial regulations in Pakistan and advises foreign institutions on entering the Pakistani financial market.
Admirality and shipping: The firm represents P&I clubs and shipping lines of the world, advising on matters concerning shipping, admirality and marine laws.
Aviation: The firm acts on behalf of airlines operating in Pakistan, and several local and international aviation authorities. It advises on all areas of aviation law, including matters of passenger and baggage handling, denied boarding carriers' liability, inter-line agreements and jurisdiction issues.
Construction and engineering: The firm is actively involved in assisting major lenders and construction firms with all types of building and engineering projects. The firm offers a one-stop strategy for foreign construction firms venturing into the Pakistan market.
Trademarks and patents: The firm has a specialised IP department which handles matters relating to trade mark, patents, copyright and other IP licensing issues.
Industrial relations and employment: The firm has an independent, highly specialised labour department that advises clients on legal requirements in the industrial, labour and services sectors.
Satellite communication and broadcasting: Since the recent deregulation in Pakistan, the firm has acted for major telecommunication companies in obtaining the necessary licences, setting up of the infrastructure, and post set-up matters such as repatriation of profits.The firm advises on all aspects of family law including divorce, child custody, marrriages, domestic violence, maintenance issues, succession, inheritance and administration.
Other: The firm also handles matters involving customs and excise law; transfer of property, including BOT projects; conveyancing; constitutional matters; transfer of technology; and rent laws.

LANGUAGES: English, Urdu

For other recommended firms see pages 1485-1520

STUDIO LEGALE SUTTI

HEAD OFFICE

Via Montenapoleone, 8,
20121 Milan, Italy
Tel: + 39 02 7620 41 **Fax:** + 39 02 7620 4805

Email: maildesk@sutti.com
Website: www.sutti.com

FIRM OVERVIEW

Managing partner: Stefano Sutti
Senior partner: Marco Monti

Number of partners worldwide: 10
Number of other lawyers worldwide: 31

AREAS OF PRACTICE:
Company/commercial 45%
Intellectual property and competition 35%
Employment law and related matters 20%

WORLDWIDE OFFICE CONTACTS

JAPAN
2-17-13 Asagaya-Kita, Suginami-Ku, **Tokyo** 166-0001
Tel: + 81 3 331 00693 **Fax:** + 81 3 331 00740
Email: maildesk@sutti.com

UNITED KINGDOM
19 Princes Street, **London** W1B 2LW
Tel: + 44 20 7409 1384 **Fax:** + 44 20 7409 1384
Email: maildesk@sutti.com

OTHER OFFICES IN ITALY
Rome, Abbiategrasso, Trescore Balneario

FIRM OVERVIEW: Established in 1952, Studio Legale Sutti is one of Italy's largest law firms, with ten partners and 31 other lawyers based in offices in Italy, London and Tokyo. Since its foundation, the firm has concentrated on company/commercial intellectual property and competition law. In the late 1970s it established an employment law department with its own premises, thereby restructuring the firm into three departments. In 1993, the firm merged with Monti & Partners, another Milan-based law firm established in 1927 which specialised in international investments, trade, banking and financial law. In 2000 the firm merged with Studio Legale Pennisi, based in Genoa and a specialist in maritime and real estate law. Studio Legale Sutti deals with its domestic clients' problems worldwide, instructing foreign advisers on their behalf. Via its overseas offices, the firm provides foreign firms with advice on Italian law, as well as representation in Italian courts.

INTERNATIONAL EXPERIENCE: The firm's international practice focuses in particular on legal and patent services to foreign firms, patent agencies and in-house legal departments. This is strengthened by its direct presence in London and Tokyo, as well as by the firm having a number of foreign lawyers and other professionals who facilitate contact with clients from different legal systems and cultures.

INTERNATIONAL CLIENTS: The firm's international client base includes individual entrepreneurs, medium-sized and large corporations and financial institutions, operating in over forty countries worldwide.

MAIN INTERNATIONAL AREAS OF PRACTICE:
Company/commercial: The firm's activities include commercial contracts, M&A, finance and banking, construction law, engineering contracts and industrial joint ventures, debt collection and insolvency, agency, distributorship and franchising law, international trade, administrative law, environmental law and white collar crime.
Intellectual property and competition: Includes trade marks, trade names and merchandising, unfair competition and anti-trust, patents, technology transfer and licence agreements, advertising and media law, pharmaceuticals, litigation and criminal prosecution, as well as patent and trademark agency services.
Employment law and related matters: Includes directors' service contracts, social security and pension law, industrial relations and trade union law and corporate immigration.

LANGUAGES: Italian, English, French, German, Japanese, Romanian, Spanish

WORLDWIDE OFFICES

JAPAN
2-17-13 Asagaya-Kita, Suginami-Ku, Tokyo 166-0001

Contact: Masako Nishina

Office profile: Opened in 1992, Studio Legale Sutti's Tokyo office provides advice on Italian and EU law, including assistance in negotiations, litigation and arbitration and criminal defence. The Japanese operation is not registered with the Japanese bar and does not conduct legal work on-site. Instead, it acts as intermediary between local firms and clients, as well as providing occasional assistance to Italian clients in Japan and the region. The office works in English, French, German, Italian and Japanese.

UNITED KINGDOM
19 Princes Street, London W1B 2LW

Contact: Livia Oglio

Office profile: Opened in 1993, Studio Legale Sutti's London office offers a complete range of on-site legal services regarding Italian law. The office provides counsel to British law firms and corporate clients. It specialises in servicing law firms, patent and trade mark agents and in-house lawyers, and advises them on everything pertaining to the Italian system of law including litigation in Italian civil, criminal and administrative courts.

S

SYCIP SALAZAR HERNANDEZ & GATMAITAN

HEAD OFFICE

SyCip Law, All Asia Center, 105 Paseo de Roxas,
Makati City 1226, The Philippines
Tel: +63 2 817 9811/2001 **Fax:** +63 2 817 3567/818 7562

Email: syciplaw@globe.com.ph
Website: www.syciplaw.com

WORLDWIDE OFFICE CONTACTS

PHILIPPINES
4th Floor, Keppel Center, Cardinal Rosales Avenue cor. Samar Loop St., Cebu Business Park, **Cebu City** 6000
Tel: +032 233 1211~13 **Fax:** +032 233 1682
Email: sycipceb@gisilink.com

Second Floor, Anthony Building J. P, Laurel Avenue, Bajada, 8000, **Davao City**
Tel: +082 221 3917/244 2742 **Fax:** +082 224 2743
Email: syciplaw@mozcom.com

SyCip Law, All Asia Center, 105 Paseo de Roxas, **Makati City** 1226
Tel: +63 2 817 9811/2001 **Fax:** +63 2 817 3567/818 7562
Email: syciplaw@globe.com.ph

FIRM OVERVIEW

Managing partner: Andres Gatmaitan

Number of partners worldwide: 41
Number of other lawyers worldwide: 86

AREAS OF PRACTICE:

Banking .... *%
Corporate services .... *%
Finance and securities .... *%
Human resources .... *%
Intellectual property .... *%
Litigation .... *%
Special projects .... *%
Tax .... *%
*Workload % not disclosed

S

FIRM OVERVIEW: Sycip Salazar Hernandez & Gatmaitan is the largest law firm in the Philippines, with its principal office in Makati City, the financial and business center of Metropolitan Manila. It has branch offices in Cebu City and Davao City.
Founded in 1945, the firm has grown to over 250 lawyers and staff, including 41 partners, three of-counsel and more than 80 associates. The firm's practice is diversified, as reflected in its seven principal departments. These are banking, finance and securities, corporate services, intellectual property, human resources, litigation, special projects and tax. Within this structure, some of the firm's lawyers are involved in further fields of specialisation, such as shipping and maritime law. Although the firm's practice centres on business activities, it has, since its foundation, offered a broad and integrated range of legal services that cover such areas as family relations, constitutional issues, and other matters of law unrelated to commerce.

INTERNATIONAL CLIENTS: The firm maintains links with established and leading firms in major cities throughout Asia, Europe, North, Central and South America and Australasia.

MAIN INTERNATIONAL AREAS OF PRACTICE:

Banking and finance: The firm provides advice on regulatory matters affecting banking institutions and on domestic and international financing transactions, including project financing, export credits and guarantees, debt-equity swaps, documentary credits, and non-traditional financial services. The firm has considerable experience in the acquisition of banking interests and the regularisation of international banking organisations and their affiliates in the Philippines.
Intellectual property: The firm's lawyers' involvement in the enactment of legislation and administrative regulation has positioned it to effectively advise and assist clients. The firm's practice in this field encompasses intellectual property registration, assignment, licensing, protection, and enforcement.
Human resources: The firm represents clients in compulsory and voluntary arbitration as well as in adversarial and non-adversarial labour proceedings, including strike disputes, mass action controversies, unfair labour practice cases, terminations of employment (both as part of the employee disciplinary process and as a direct result of corporate dissolutions and plant closures), labour standard complaints, employee money claims, and other conflicts between labour and management.
Litigation: The firm's litigation practice in courts and administrative agencies covers all types of commercial disputes, including disputes in specialised business areas, such as banking, securities law, insurance, transportation, construction, intellectual property, energy and natural resources, and asset recovery. The firm's litigation practice also covers civil law disputes, such as family and matrimonial relations, conjugal property regimes, testate and intestate succession, and torts.
Tax: The firm's tax practice covers all areas of planning, tax advising, and litigation. The firm has substantial expertise in providing specialised tax advice on all commercial transactions, including banking and financial transactions, project financing, construction contracts, corporate acquisitions, mergers and reorganisations, debt restructuring, workouts and bankruptcies, securities issues and public offerings, and real estate and stock transactions. The firm has specialists in international taxation in connection with in-bound investments by foreign investors and tax treaties between the Philippines and other tax treaty countries.

LANGUAGES: Chinese, English, Filipino, Japanese, Spanish

For other recommended firms see pages 1485-1520

TABOADA & ASOCIADOS

HEAD OFFICE

Del Hospital Militar, 1cuadro al Lago, Avenue Bolivar #1947
Managua PO Box 2382, Nicaragua
Tel: +505 268 3839 **Fax:** +505 266 8088

Email: taboada@taboada.com.ni
Website: www.taboada.com.ni

WORLDWIDE OFFICE CONTACTS

NICARAGUA
Del Hospital Militar, 1cuadro al Lago, Avenue Bolivar #1947, **Managua**
PO Box 2382
Tel: +505 268 3839 **Fax:** +505 266 8088
Email: taboada@taboada.com.ni

FIRM OVERVIEW

Senior partner: José Evenor Taboada

Number of partners worldwide: 3
Number of other lawyers worldwide: 14

AREAS OF PRACTICE:
Corporate 22%
Litigation and arbitration 21%
Banking and finance 20%
Telecommunications and computer law 13%
Natural resources 12%
Intellectual property 10%
Insurance and reinsurance 2%

FIRM OVERVIEW: Taboada & Associados, founded in 1969, is the largest and most well known firm in Nicaragua. The firm's lawyers have broad experience and excellent academic backgrounds having obtained their degrees at prestigious universities in Latin America with additional education in the United States and Europe. The firm provides excellent and timely services to a wide range of clients. Taboada & Asociados is a full service firm advising major private corporations, multilateral institutions, public institutions and foreign companies. Some members of the firm belong to professional organisations such as the American and the International Bar Associations. The firm has a long-standing relationship with major law firms worldwide allowing it to provide services to clients conducting business in Nicaragua and abroad.

INTERNATIONAL EXPERIENCE: The firm advises on all areas of law, including local and cross-border issues. It has been involved in project financing of major hydroelectric projects and other large projects; international lending; and M&A. The firm has been involved in the recapitalisation of the state bank in the telecommunications and energy sectors; has participated in several large international commercial litigations; and has acted as legal representative in Nicaragua for several large corporations, some of them locally.

INTERNATIONAL CLIENTS: The firm's clients include the Commonwealth Development Corporation (CDC), the International Finance Corporation (IFC), Philip Morris, Sony, the British Embassy, Hamilton Bank, Caterpillar, Iberdrola, Hydro Quebec and Unión Fenosa.

MAIN INTERNATIONAL AREAS OF PRACTICE:
International lending: The firm has participated in the structuring of all types of international lending, supplier credit, project financing; as well as restructuring agreements. The firm has been involved in lending from multinational institutions, such as IFC; from official institutions, such as CDC; and commercial Banks, including Credit Agricole, Hamilton Bank, and Banco Aliado.
Privatisation: The firm has handled the privatisation of industries such as Plywood of Nicaragua; Empresa Bananera; it has represented foreign companies bidding in the privatisation of ENITEL (telecommunication) and ENEL (energy); and has been involved in the capitalisation of BANIC, a state owned Bank that became majority owned by the private sector.
Litigation: Civil, commercial, criminal and labour litigations, both domestic and international.
Natural resources: The firm advises on negotiations of concessions; licenses and permits to fish; land use; exploration and exploitation in the mining sector; and geothermic resources.
Multilateral financial institutions: IFC; BID; BCIE

LANGUAGES: English, French, Spanish

T

LAW OFFICE TARK & CO

HEAD OFFICE

Roosikrantsi 2,
10119 Tallinn, Estonia
Tel: +372 611 0900 **Fax:** +372 611 0911

Email: tarkco@tarkco.ee
Website: www.tarkco.com

FIRM OVERVIEW

Senior partner: Aare Tark

Number of partners worldwide: 4
Number of other lawyers worldwide: 13

AREAS OF PRACTICE:

Banking and finance	20%
Corporate and contracts	20%
M&A	20%
Project finance	10%
Telecommunications, energy and technology	10%
Litigation and arbitration	8%
Employment	5%
Bankruptcy, reorganisation	2%
Intellectual property	2%
Maritime law	2%
Legislative	1%

T

FIRM OVERVIEW: Founded in 1991, Law Office Tark & Co is one of the first private law firms in Estonia. Since its foundation the firm has primarily specialised in corporate and commercial areas of law, offering comprehensive legal services to corporate clients. Law Office Tark & Co has a total of 17 lawyers, and is one of the largest law firms in Estonia.

INTERNATIONAL EXPERIENCE: More than half of the firm's clients are foreign and multinational companies. Several of the firm's lawyers have LL.M. degrees from foreign universities, including the University of Cambridge (UK), Georgetown University, College of William & Mary and the University of Connecticut (US). This enables better understanding of and service to foreign clients.
Among international projects, Law Office Tark & Co has advised foreign investors in several acquisition projects of major Estonian companies. The firm has advised foreign financial institutions on loan projects as well as on financing of major construction projects. Law Office Tark & Co has been actively involved in a number of privatisations of Estonian companies, including the privatisation of Estonian Telecom, Estonian Railways, Narva Power Plants, Tallinn Water Company and the Estonian Broadcasting Centre. Law Office Tark & Co has close contacts with law firms in the UK, Scandinavia, the Baltic countries and Russia, enabling the firm to offer combined services to its clients in international projects.

INTERNATIONAL CLIENTS: International clients include several major financial institutions, including Nomura International, Swedbank, Bankers Trust, Sampo, Lehman Brothers, Dresdner Bank, Chase Manhattan, Bankgesellschaft Berlin, Credit Suisse First Boston, Landesbank Schleswig-Holstein Girozentrale, Skandinaviska Enskilda Banken, Nordic Investment Bank and Société Générale. Among other clients Law Office Tark & Co has advised Autoliv AB and Falck on the acquisition of Estonian companies. In addition, the firm serves as counsel to Estonian subsidiaries of several foreign and multinational corporations.

WORLDWIDE OFFICE CONTACTS

ESTONIA
Roosikrantsi 2, 10119 **Tallinn**
Tel: +372 611 0900 **Fax:** +372 611 0911
Email: tarkco@tarkco.ee

MAIN INTERNATIONAL AREAS OF PRACTICE:
Corporate and contracts: The firm handles the establishment of subsidiaries belonging to foreign and multinational corporations, advising them on a day-to-day basis. The firm's lawyers are also involved in drafting major international contracts.
M&A: The firm handles due diligence in target companies, drafting transaction documents and assisting in closing and post-closing matters. Several listed companies are among the targeted companies.
Project financing: The firm advises on the financing of major hotel and office building constructions as well as production facilities in maritime ports, the latter being one of the biggest direct foreign investments made in Estonia.
Banking and finance: The firm handles loan projects, including subordinated and syndicated loans, advising clients on public issues of shares and debt instruments.

LANGUAGES: English, Estonian, Finnish, French, German, Russian, Swedish

ADVOKAADIBÜROO TARK & CO
LAW OFFICE TARK & CO

 For other recommended firms see pages 1485-1520

TAYLOR JOYNSON GARRETT

HEAD OFFICE

Carmelite, 50 Victoria Embankment, Blackfriars,
London EC4Y 0DX, United Kingdom
Tel: +44 20 7300 7000 **Fax:** +44 20 7300 7100

Email: enquiries@tjg.co.uk
Website: www.tjg.co.uk

FIRM OVERVIEW

Managing partner: Declan Tarpey
Senior partner: Richard Marsh

Number of partners worldwide: 87
Number of other lawyers worldwide: 203

AREAS OF PRACTICE:

Corporate	27%
Intellectual property	19%
Litigation	19%
Commercial property	14%
Private client	8%
Employment	7%
Banking	6%

FIRM OVERVIEW: Taylor Joynson Garrett is a leading, full service, City of London firm with a long established corporate, finance and commercial practice. It has long been a market leader in advising UK and international clients in protecting their intellectual property and exploiting their assets in today's knowledge driven economy. The firm, which comprises 87 partners, has, over the years, developed close relationships with practices in the major financial centres throughout the world. TJG has offices in Brussels and Bucharest and is also a member of Interlex.

INTERNATIONAL EXPERIENCE: A substantial amount of the firm's corporate and intellectual property work is international. TJG acts for a large number of leading international companies in relation to M&A matters, joint ventures and investments both outside and into the UK. Recent highlights include advising Ask Jeeves Inc on its joint venture with Carlton Communications and Granada; advising PETsMART, Inc on the sale of Pet City Holdings; advising Qualceram plc on its acquisition of the Shires Group in a £34 million Anglo-Irish deal; advising Sun Microsystems, Inc on its acquisition of Trustbase Limited.

INTERNATIONAL CLIENTS: Ask Jeeves Inc, Omnicom, TBWA, Amgen, Incyte Pharmaceuticals, Eli Lilly, ADTranz, Razorfish Inc, Eidos, Visa International, Qualceram plc, Landis Group N.V., PETsMART, Inc and Sun Microsystems, Inc amongst many others.

MAIN INTERNATIONAL AREAS OF PRACTICE:

Corporate and banking: The group has particular expertise in corporate and project finance, tax, M&A, energy, PFI and European law issues. It acts for public and private companies, banks and other financial institutions (including Eastern European banks), management teams and venture capitalists. The firm's Projects Group advises leading sponsors and finance providers on project and structured finance in a wide range of sectors.

Intellectual property: The firm's intellectual property department is one of the largest in Europe and handles contentious and non-contentious work in all aspects of intellectual property including patent litigation, trade marks, industrial design, passing-off and trade libel. An experienced and respected sector-focused group, forged from the firm's IP and corporate departments deals with the advances in digital media, e-commerce, internet, IT and telecoms issues, advising and protecting inventors, manufacturers, suppliers and users.

Commercial property: Services incorporate specialist planning, property management and environmental work, while clients include trading companies, developers, financial institutions and national and international investors. The firm's dedicated rail practice group adopts a multi-disciplinary approach to meet the needs of businesses active in the rail industry, including development companies.

Litigation: The firm's litigation department handles a wide variety of commercial litigation and arbitration matters and has particular experience in construction, banking, property and insurance.

Employment: The firm's specialist employment department handles a wide variety of employment related matters including pensions and employee benefits together with increasingly complex legal relationships both domestically and internationally.

LANGUAGES: Arabic, French, German, Hebrew, Italian, Mandarin, Persian, Romanian, Russian, Spanish

WORLDWIDE OFFICE CONTACTS

BELGIUM
14 Rue Montoyer, 1000 **Brussels**
Tel: +32 2 514 04 02 **Fax:** +32 2 514 00 88
Email: enquiries@tjg.co.uk

ROMANIA
Str. Popa Savu Nr.5, Sector 1, **Bucharest**
Tel: +40 1 222 1313 **Fax:** +40 1 222 2626
Email: tjg@tjg.ro

WORLDWIDE OFFICES

BELGIUM

14 Rue Montoyer, 1000 Brussels

Contacts: Martin Baker and Jane Golding

Number of lawyers: 3

Office profile: Advising and assisting clients on all EU related matters including, competition law, trade law, regulatory control and public procurement.

Languages: Dutch, English, French, German, Italian

ROMANIA

Str. Popa Savu Nr.5, Sector 1, Bucharest

Contact partner: Simon Dayes

Number of lawyers: 8

Office profile: Established in 1993, the Bucharest office is active in corporate, commercial, foreign investment, privatisation, M&A, banking, project finance, venture capital and securities.

Languages: English, French, German, Italian, Romanian, Russian

T

THANG & ASSOCIATES

HEAD OFFICE

Central Plaza Building, Unit 803, 17 Le Duan Boulevard
Ho Chi Minh City Vietnam
Tel: +848 825 0084 **Fax:** +848 825 0085

Email: thang.lawfirm@hcm.vnn.vn

FIRM OVERVIEW

Principal: Tran Quyet Thang
Senior lawyers: Tran Nhat Vinh, Le Cong Dinh

Number of partners worldwide: 1
Number of other lawyers worldwide: 9

AREAS OF PRACTICE:

Banking and finance ....*%
Corporate ....*%
Employment ....*%
Intellectual property ....*%
Litigation and arbitration ....*%
M&A ....*%
Real estate ....*%
Taxation ....*%
* Workload % not disclosed

FIRM OVERVIEW: Founded in 1997, Thang & Associates is a leading Vietnamese law firm that specialises in consulting services and dispute resolution. The firm has an experienced team of ten lawyers who trained at top law schools in the UK, US, France, Germany, Russia and Vietnam. The firm's lawyers have gained multi-jurisdictional experience with leading international law and accounting firms.

INTERNATIONAL EXPERIENCE: The firm works nationally and internationally, providing legal services to large international and national companies, commercial banks, and non-governmental institutions. It has recently advised an overseas investor on a US $100m BOT project and acted for a multi-national group of hotel and resort developers in a US $10m commercial dispute. The firm has recently been selected by four large multi-national companies as their local counsel, and appointed by a US $400m joint venture as its sole litigation counsel. Thang & Associates also has close working relationships with major international law firms. The firm is co-author of the Vietnam chapter in *The Herbert Smith Guide to Dispute Resolution in Asia* published in 2000.

INTERNATIONAL CLIENTS: The firm's client base is large and varied with the majority coming from the UK, US, France, Japan, Southeast Asia and Vietnam.

MAIN INTERNATIONAL AREAS OF PRACTICE:

Banking and finance: The practice focuses on domestic transactions and includes commercial lending and structured and project finance. The firm handles compliance and regulatory work for financial institutions in Vietnam. Thang & Associates also acts as a consultant to UNDP.
Corporate: The firm advises clients on company law, corporate formation and restructuring, and investment regulations. The work undertaken also includes advising on corporate governance agreements such as shareholders' agreements, and assisting shareholders with the protection of their rights.
M&A: Transactions include private and public acquisitions, and foreign investors acquisition of local corporations shares. The firm was selected as World Bank's consultant on the privatisation of local state-owned corporations.
Tax: The firm handles national tax issues, including corporate income tax, VAT, sales tax and import duties.
Employment: The firm focuses on employment disputes and issues relating to individual employees, trade unions and day-to-day employment matters. The firm also advises on employment contracts, collective labour agreements and companies' internal regulations.
Real estate: The firm advises on all matters relating to real estate law, including land lease for foreign investment projects, and the sale, purchase, auction, development, ownership and management of real estate.
Intellectual property: Thang & Associates handles copyright issues, patent law, trademarks and unfair competition. The firm acted for a large multinational television company in the first countrywide action against the violation of copyright in Vietnam.
Litigation and arbitration: The firm handles civil and commercial litigation before courts and tribunals in Vietnam. It also acts in arbitration procedures under VIAC rules.

LANGUAGES: English, French, German, Vietnamese

WORLDWIDE OFFICE CONTACTS

VIETNAM
Central Plaza Building, Unit 803, 17 Le Duan Boulevard, **Ho Chi Minh City**
Tel: +848 825 0084 **Fax:** +848 825 0085
Email: thang.lawfirm@hcm.vnn.vn

T

For other recommended firms see pages 1485-1520

THEO V. SIOUFAS, LAW OFFICES

HEAD OFFICE

Alassia Building, Defteras Merarchias 13,
GR 185 35 185 35 Piraeus, Greece
Tel: +30 1 422 12 10 **Fax:** +30 1 422 50 90

Email: info@sioufas.com
Website: www.sioufas.com

WORLDWIDE OFFICE CONTACTS

GREECE
Alassia Building, Defteras Merarchias 13, GR 185 35 185 35 **Piraeus**
Tel: +30 1 422 12 10 **Fax:** +30 1 422 50 96

Skoufa Street, Kolonaki, **Athens** GR 106.73
Tel: +301 3644 100 **Fax:** +301 3604 954

FIRM OVERVIEW

Senior partner: Theo V. Sioufas

Number of partners worldwide: 6
Number of other lawyers worldwide: 13

AREAS OF PRACTICE:

Banking and finance 30%
Civil and commercial litigation 18%
Corporate, privatisation and stock exchange 17%
Shipping and admiralty 17%
Employment 6%
Government and taxation 4%
Commercial arbitration 2%
Other 5%

FIRM OVERVIEW: Founded in 1971, Theo V. Sioufas Laws Offices has offices in Piraeus and Athens. Comprising 19 attorneys, it is one of Greece's largest international law firms. The firm engages in a broad range of international practice and has become increasingly diverse. The firm handles transactions involving international clients, and a number of Greek clients have retained the firm to handle the legal aspects of their worldwide operations. The firm has established an international network of correspondent relationships with local law offices.

INTERNATIONAL CLIENTS: The firm's clients include Greek companies (and individuals) doing business in Greece and abroad; non-Greek companies doing business internationally; and international banks involved in shipping, corporate, structure, and other types of financing and private banking.

MAIN INTERNATIONAL AREASOF PRACTICE:

Banking and finance: The firm advises a number of local banks on banking and financial law, as well as on banking litigation, regulatory matters, and specific transactions. The firm advises a number of foreign banks on lending and securities (mortgages on land/buildings, factories, ships, aircraft, guarantees, pledges and security assignments). It also handles work relating to trading and commercial enterprises, forms of finance, international trade contracts, letters of credit, letters of guarantee, mutual funds, leasing, stock exchange matters, foreign exchange contracts, monetary matters and related European law. It also advises on local and international financings.

Commercial arbitration: The firm acts as counsel in a range of international commercial arbitrations including sale and purchase of ships, owners- charterers disputes, admiralty cases, commodities trading, and industrial equipment. The firm also has experience in ad hoc arbitrations and a member of the firm has sat as arbitrator on arbitral tribunals.

Employment: The firm advises corporate clients on Greek labour law and on the highly regulated area of employer-employee relations. The firm also undertakes relevant litigation. Theo V. Sioufas Laws Offices specialises in disputes between seamen, ship-owners, and their insurers.

Shipping and admiralty: The firm handles shipping and admiralty matters including the establishment of shipping companies in Greece and abroad, registration of ships and mortgages, chartering, and sale and purchase. It also handles matters relating to the financing of shipping operations and the banking side of the business. Theo V. Sioufas Laws Offices also advises on the management of ships.

Corporate, privatisation and stock exchange: Theo V. Sioufas Laws Offices advises Greek and foreign companies on structuring and establishing branches. It handles internal corporation issues (interna corporis) and is involved in relevant litigation. Theo V. Sioufas Laws Offices also advises clients on criminal and tax laws. The firm is regularly involved in negotiating international contracts including sales contracts and joint ventures. It also advises Liberian, Cypriot, Swiss, Luxembourg, Maltese, Marshall Islands, Panamanian and other off-shore companies on incorporation issues. It advises national and international clients on acquisitions, mergers and spin-offs, leveraged buy-outs and stock exchange matters. The firm also advises on investment and exchange control regulations, obtains authorisations, and handles the participation of foreign technical corporations in related businesses in Greece.

Government and taxation: The firm advises local and foreign clients on a range of state regulations and tax matters, both corporate and individual. It also handles related litigation before the relevant courts and tribunals.

Civil and commercial litigation: The firm handles a range of civil and commercial litigation transactions involving corporate and shipping matters.

LANGUAGES: English, French, German, Greek, Italian, Spanish

T

ETUDE THIAM & THIAM

HEAD OFFICE

68 rue Wagane Diouf, Dakar Senegal
Tel: +221 823 1674 **Fax:** +221 823 41 91

Email: thiam@telecomplus.sn

FIRM OVERVIEW

Partner: Thiam Yerim

Number of partners worldwide: 1
Number of other lawyers worldwide: 2

AREAS OF PRACTICE:
Banking and finance .... *%
Corporate .... *%
Criminal .... *%
Employment .... *%
Family .... *%
Insurance .... *%
Intellectual property .... *%
Litigationa and arbitration .... *%
M&A .... *%
Maritime .... *%
* Workload % not disclosed

WORLDWIDE OFFICE CONTACTS

SENEGAL
68 rue Wagane Diouf, **Dakar**
Tel: +221 823 1674 **Fax:** +221 823 41 91
Email: thiam@telecomplus.sn

FIRM OVERVIEW: Founded in 1951 by Mr Doudou Thiam, Etude Thiam & Thiam comprises one partner and two other lawyers. It maintains contacts with a number of firms worldwide and offers comprehensive legal advice to clients with international business interests.

INTERNATIONAL EXPERIENCE: The firm has handled a range of international disputes, notably the demarcation of the maritime border between Senegal and Guinea Bissau. It also acted in the first case examined by the International Tribunal for the Law of the Sea in Hamburg.

INTERNATIONAL CLIENTS: The firm's client base includes large companies, banks and insurance companies conducting cross-border business.

MAIN INTERNATIONAL AREAS OF PRACTICE: The firm specialises in M&A, banking and finance, transactions and guarantees, intellectual property, marketing law, OHADA, and litigation and arbitration. Other work handled includes corporate, criminal, employment, family, insurance, and maritime.

LANGUAGES: English, French

T

For other recommended firms see pages 1485-1520

THOMANN FISCHER

HEAD OFFICE

Elisabethenstrasse 30, PO Box 632
CH-4010 Basel, Switzerland
Tel: +41 61 226 2424 **Fax:** +41 61 226 2425

Email: info@thomannfischerlaw.ch

WORLDWIDE OFFICE CONTACTS

SWITZERLAND
Elisabethenstrasse 30, PO Box 632, CH-4010 **Basel**
Tel: +41 61 226 2424 **Fax:** +41 61 226 2425
Email: info@thomannfischerlaw.ch

FIRM OVERVIEW

Senior partner: Felix H. Thomann

Number of partners worldwide: 5
Number of other lawyers worldwide: 3

AREAS OF PRACTICE:

Corporate and commercial	32%
M&A	15%
Intellectual property and competition	10%
Banking and capital markets	8%
Inheritance law	8%
Tax	8%
IT	7%
Asset management	6%
Media and telecommunications	6%

FIRM OVERVIEW: Thomann Fischer was founded in 1999 by partners from two well renowned firms. The firm's partners have a wealth of professional experience and comprehensive knowledge in their areas of practice. The firm offers services in all areas of business law and also provides full notarial services where such services are required. Thomann Fischer also advises on the implications of EU law for Swiss companies and for foreign enterprises with activities in Switzerland.

MAIN INTERNATIONAL AREAS OF PRACTICE:

Corporate and commercial: The firm handles the incorporation and restructuring of companies, mergers, acquisition and sale of companies, and corporate succession planning.
M&A: The firm handles both domestic and cross-border M&A work.
Intellectual property and competition: The firm advises on counseling, contracts and litigation in patent (particularly in the chemical/pharmaceutical field), design and model, trademark, copyright, competition and cartels law cases.
Banking and capital markets: The firm is involved in the organisation and proceedings regarding regulatory supervision of banks, capital market transactions, initial public offerings (IPOs), stock exchange and securities law, and employee stock participation plans.
Tax: The firm handles international and domestic tax planning. It advises companies and individuals.
Inheritance law: Thomann Fischer handles estate-planning, advice, drawing up wills and inheritance contracts, execution of wills, estate administration, and distribution.
IT: The firm is involved in counselling, contracts, project management and litigation in all IT fields.
Media and telecommunications: Work undertaken includes counselling, contracts and litigation in all fields, including data protection.
Asset management: The firm advises on portfolio management, including legal and investment advice.
Litigation: Work undertaken includes representation in all commercial and civil litigation, including intellectual property, software protection, online, media and telecommunications law.
Arbitration and mediation: The firm's lawyers act as arbitrators, mediators and party representatives in arbitration and mediation proceedings.

LANGUAGES: English, French, German, Italian, Spanish

T

THOMMESSEN KREFTING GREVE LUND

HEAD OFFICE

Haakon VII's Gate 10, PO Box 1484 Vika,
N-0116 Oslo, Norway
Tel: + 47 23 11 11 11 **Fax:** + 47 23 11 10 10

Email: firmapost@tkgl.no
Website: www.tkgl.no

FIRM OVERVIEW

Managing partner: Kim Dobrowen
Chairman: Pål W. Lorentzen

Number of partners worldwide: 40
Number of other lawyers worldwide: 82

AREAS OF PRACTICE:

Banking and finance	40%
Mergers and acquisitions	30%
Telecommunications and computer law	20%
Corporate	15%
Litigation and arbitration	15%
Other	20%

T

FIRM OVERVIEW: Thommessen Krefting Greve Lund was established in 1856 and is now one of the largest law firms in Norway, with over 100 lawyers. It practises in all areas of business law and in an international environment. The firm has offices in London and Brussels, and associate offices in Moscow, Hong Kong and Paris. Together with the Swedish firm Vinge and the Danish firm Kromann Reumert it is a member of the Scandinavian law alliance Vinge Kromann Thommessen, which has a total of 500 lawyers. The firm also belongs to the Lex Mundi network.

INTERNATIONAL EXPERIENCE: Thommessen Krefting Greve Lund has broad experience in advising foreign clients on tax, corporate law including takeovers, mergers and acquisitions, engineering contracts, property, contract, EU, competition, IT, telecommunications, media, intellectual property, environmental and employment law, securities trading, energy, oil and shipping, bankruptcy and debt negotiation. It advises major Norwegian companies on cross-border mergers and acquisitions and other international transactions. The firm also undertakes international litigation and arbitration. One of the partners is qualified both as a Norwegian Advokat and as a solicitor of the Supreme Court of England and Wales. One of the associates has been admitted to the New York Bar.

INTERNATIONAL CLIENTS: The firm's foreign clients include a number of major multinational corporations, foreign law firms and other consultancy firms.

LANGUAGES: Danish, Dutch, English, French, German, Italian, Norwegian, Spanish, Swedish

WORLDWIDE OFFICE CONTACTS

BELGIUM
rue du Luxembourg 3, B-1000 **Brussels**
Tel: +32 2 501 07 00 **Fax:** +32 2 501 07 01
Email: firmapost@tkgl.no

NORWAY
Strandgt. 209, PO Box 1970, Nordnes, 5817 **Bergen**
Tel: +47 55 30 6100 **Fax:** +47 55 30 6101
Email: firmapost@tkgl.no

UNITED KINGDOM
42 New Broad Street, **London** EC2M 1JD
Tel: +44 20 7920 3000 **Fax:** +44 20 7920 3099
Email: firmapost@tkgl.no

WORLDWIDE OFFICES

BELGIUM

rue du Luxembourg 3, B-1000 Brussels

Number of lawyers: 1

Office profile: The Brussels office, which opened in 1992, is part of the firm's EC/EEA and Competition law group and the firm's IT/Telecom/Media group. The principal areas of practice are general EC/EEA law, competition law, state aid, public procurement and IT related law. Lawyers in this office speak Danish, English, French, Norwegian and Swedish.

UNITED KINGDOM

42 New Broad Street, London EC2M 1JD

Number of lawyers: 1

Office profile: The London office, which opened in 1984, assists Scandinavian clients with their businesses abroad and non-Scandinavian clients with their businesses in Scandinavia. The principal areas of practice are international finance, banking, mergers and acquisitions, property, commercial and corporate, joint ventures, shipping and aviation, oil and gas, domestic and international tax, cross-border contracts, listing of companies, reorganisations, competition, intellectual property, litigation and arbitration. Lawyers in this office speak Danish, English, French, Norwegian and Swedish.

For other recommended firms see pages 1485-1520

THORSTEINSSONS

HEAD OFFICE

PO Box 611, BCE Place, 36th Floor, 161 Bay Street
Toronto ON M5J 2S1, Canada
Tel: +1 416 864 0829 **Fax:** +1 416 864 1106

Email: thor@thor.ca
Website: www.thor.ca

FIRM OVERVIEW

Managing partner: Douglas H. Mathew

Number of partners worldwide: 22
Number of other lawyers worldwide: 12

AREAS OF PRACTICE:
Tax 100%

FIRM OVERVIEW: Thorsteinssons is the largest law firm in Canada practising exclusively in the area of taxation. Since its establishment in 1964, the firm has come to occupy a leading position in the profession.Taxation is a legal area of great complexity. By restricting their practice to taxation matters, Thorsteinssons believes that they are better able to provide the level of competence demanded. Thorsteinssons also believes their practice should complement, not compete with, other professional advisors representing the same clients, and have intentionally remained independent rather than associate with firms practising in other areas of law.
Firm members regularly advise on new Canadian tax legislation and have published numerous articles, books and training materials on Canadian tax law. Many of the firm's members also teach at Canadian law schools and other institutions.
The firm is not part of an international network, but maintains close working relationships with several international law firms, as well as accountants and other professional advisors, to provide the best local advice and service to its clients.

INTERNATIONAL EXPERIENCE: Thorsteinssons has followed its Canadian client base around the world, assisting in the tax-effective structuring of business ventures in the United States, Latin America, Europe, Africa, Asia and Australia. In addition, Thorsteinssons advises non-Canadian individuals and corporations all over the world in the tax-effective structuring of their Canadian activities.

INTERNATIONAL CLIENTS: Thorsteinssons' internationally focussed clientele includes public multinationals in the mining, forestry, automotive, airline, financial services and e-commerce industries, as well as high net worth individuals and entrepreneurs with global financial and business interests.

WORLDWIDE OFFICE CONTACTS

CANADA

PO Box 611, BCE Place, 36th Floor, 161 Bay Street
Toronto ON, M5J 2S1
Tel: +1 416 864 0829 **Fax:** +1 416 864 1106
Email: thor@thor.ca

PO Box 49123, 3 Bentall Centre, 27th Floor, 595 Burrard Street,
Vancouver, BC, V7X 1J2
Tel: +1 604-689-1261 **Fax:** +1 604-688-4711
Email: thor@thor.ca

MAIN INTERNATIONAL AREAS OF PRACTICE:
Corporate: The firm advises on reorganisations, mergers and acquisitions, financing and structuring of foreign and Canadian operations and cross-border leasing.
Estate planning, wills and trusts: Thorsteinssons advises on cross-border estate planning to minimise the global incidence of estate and income taxes. Work undertaken also includes pre-immigration and pre-emigration tax planning for high net worth individuals and migrant executives.
Representation and litigation: The firm represents clients in all aspects of Canadian federal and provincial taxation, including income tax, goods and services tax, sales, excise, capital and resource taxes and customs matters.

LANGUAGES: English, French, German

TINOCO TRAVIESO PLANCHART & NÚÑEZ

HEAD OFFICE

Torre Country Club, Pisos 2 y 3, Av. Francisco de Miranda, Chacaíto
Caracas 1050, Venezuela
Tel: +582 952 9033 **Fax:** +582 953 1053

Email: ttpn@ttpn.com.ve

FIRM OVERVIEW

Managing partners: Carlos Lepervanche Michelena
Alfredo Travieso Passios

Number of partners worldwide: 11
Number of other lawyers worldwide: 15

WORLDWIDE OFFICE CONTACTS

USA
CCS 2165, PO Box 02-8537, **Miami**, Florida 33102

VENEZUELA
Torre Country Club, Pisos 2 y 3, Av. Francisco de Miranda, Chacaíto,
Caracas 1050
Tel: +58 2 952 9033 **Fax:** +582 953 1053
Email: ttpn@ttpn.com.ve

Centro Comercial Caroní Plaza, Mezz. 1-25, Alta Vista, Puerto Ordaz
Ciudad Guayana
Tel: +58 86 617984 **Fax:** +58 86 621135
Email: ttpn@ttpn.com.ve

AREAS OF PRACTICE:

Area	%
Banking and finance	25%
Civil and corporate	20%
Constitutional and administrative	20%
Taxation	15%
Litigation	10%
Intellectual property	5%
Labour	5%

T

FIRM OVERVIEW: Founded as a result of the merger between Tinoco, Travieso, Planchart, Erminy y Asociados (founded in 1914) and Núñez & Eiris (founded in 1971), two prestigious firms of long-standing reputation in Venezuela, the firm comprises 26 lawyers specialising in various areas of law. It provides high-quality legal services to Venezuelan and international clients in a wide range of areas, focusing on banking and finance, civil and corporate, constitutional and administrative, intellectual property, employment, litigation, and tax. In August 2000, Tinoco, Travieso, Planchart & Núñez entered into a strategic alliance agreement with Holland & Knight LLP, a prestigious US firm. The firm will be launching a joint effort to serve multinational clients doing business in the United States and in the commercial centers where Holland & Knight LLP is already established.

INTERNATIONAL EXPERIENCE: The firm has advised leading banks on international loans for the financing of industrial projects in Venezuela, refinancing of public debt, public bond issues, and secured transactions. Comprehensive legal advice is offered to multinational companies wishing to do business in Venezuela. The firm has undertaken litigation in competition matters involving multinational companies, and provides counsel to international telecommunications companies which are rapidly expanding their businesses in Venezuela.

INTERNATIONAL CLIENTS: The firm's client base includes large US and Venezuelan companies and banks.

MAIN INTERNATIONAL AREAS OF PRACTICE:

Banking and finance: Tinoco, Travieso, Planchart & Núñez has represented Venezuelan and foreign banks for many years, acting as counsel in numerous financing agreements, ranging from standard loans to more complex financing transactions, such as leasing, project finance and securities.

Civil and corporate: The firm handles a wide range of civil law matters. It also handles a wide range of corporate work, advising multinational companies on establishing branch offices in Venezuela.

Constitutional and administrative: The firm advises clients on their relations with government agencies. Work undertaken includes analysing the constitutional and legal aspects of actions taken by public entities, and representing clients in administrative and judicial proceedings, including actions seeking constitutional protection from governmental acts.

Intellectual property: The firm handles registration and protection of patents, trademarks and copyrights, as well as any transactions involving trademark rights. The firm undertakes litigation which may arise from the infringement of intellectual property rights.

Employment: Tinoco, Travieso, Planchart & Núñez handles all aspects of employment issues including human resource management, negotiating and drafting employment contracts and collective bargaining agreements. It is actively involved in the design and implementation of compensation, benefits and working conditions policies.

Litigation: The firm's attorneys have extensive experience in prosecution and other legal proceedings before the courts, including the Supreme Tribunal of Justice. They undertake alternative dispute resolution, drawing on their national and international arbitration experience.

Tax: The firm provides a full tax service advising on all tax related matters, such as compliance, tax benefits and benefits under double taxation treaties, as well as strategic tax planning, filing of income tax returns, and administrative and judicial solutions.

LANGUAGES: English, French, Italian, Spanish

For other recommended firms see pages 1485-1520

TIRARD NAUDIN

HEAD OFFICE

10 rue Clément Marot,
75008 Paris, France
Tel: +33 1 53 57 36 00 **Fax:** +33 1 47 23 63 31

Email: tirard.naudin@online.fr

FIRM OVERVIEW

Partners: Jean-Marc Tirard, Maryse Naudin

Number of partners worldwide: 2
Number of other lawyers worldwide: 2

AREAS OF PRACTICE:
Corporate tax planning 60%
Estate tax planning and trust work 15%
Transfer pricing 15%
Tax litigation 10%

FIRM OVERVIEW: Founded at the start of 1997, Tirard Naudin is a specialist tax boutique firm. The firm advises large French and foreign corporations seeking independent advice, as well as French medium sized corporations expanding overseas. The firm also acts for high net worth individuals. It handles a significant amount of work that is referred by other French and foreign law or accounting firms lacking international tax expertise. The firm remains independent and does not participate in formal alliances or networks, preferring to maintain contacts with various firms worldwide and to choose the firms it works with on individual international transactions.

INTERNATIONAL EXPERIENCE: A significant proportion of the firm's work is cross-border or international, advising international companies, primarily from the US, UK and Japan, seeking to invest in France, as well as working with French clients on projects which have an international element. Other law firms also frequently retain the firm when a specialist or second opinion is required.

INTERNATIONAL CLIENTS: The firm's client base includes large companies as well as wealthy individuals seeking expert tax planning and span a diverse range of industries including automotive, banks, e-commerce, engineering, entertainment, insurance companies, and pharmaceutical.

WORLDWIDE OFFICE CONTACTS

FRANCE
10 rue Clément Marot, 75008 **Paris**
Tel: +33 1 53 57 36 00 **Fax:** +33 1 47 23 63 31
Email: tirard.naudin@online.fr

MAIN INTERNATIONAL AREAS OF PRACTICE:
Corporate tax planning: Work undertaken includes tax planning for inbound investments into France (French acquisitions for foreign clients); outbound tax planning for French clients (Foreign acquisitions for French clients); cross-border mergers and restructuring; tax effective investments in French real estate; advance pricing agreements; taxation of executives including stock option plans; tax based structured financing and leasing; and transfer of technology tax issues.
Estate tax planning: The firm advises on a range of estate tax planning issues including use of common law trusts.
Tax litigation: The firm handles complex audit defence and litigation including transfer-pricing disputes.

LANGUAGES: English, French

TIRARD, NAUDIN

SOCIÉTÉ D'AVOCATS

For other recommended firms see pages 1485-1520

TITUS & CO

HEAD OFFICE

Titus House, R-4, Greater Kailash - 1,
New Delhi 110 048, India
Tel: +91 11 6470 700 **Fax:** +91 11 648 0300

Email: titus@nda.vsnl.net.in

FIRM OVERVIEW

Contacts: Diljeet Titus, Alfred Adebare, Rai S. Mittal, Seema Jhingan, Manisha More, Shkha Rana

Number of partners worldwide: 10
Number of other lawyers worldwide: 21

AREAS OF PRACTICE:

Aviation .... *%
Banking and finance .... *%
Capital markets .... *%
Commercial property .... *%
Corporate and commercial .... *%
Dispute resolution .... *%
Employment .... *%
Infrastructure projects .... *%
Intellectual property .... *%
Project finance .... *%
Tax .... *%
Telecommunication and IT .... *%
* Workload % not disclosed

WORLDWIDE OFFICE CONTACTS

INDIA
Suite 405, Regency Enclave, 4 Magrath Road, **Bangalore** 560 025
Tel: +80 559 9279 **Fax:** +80 532 0359
Email: titus@vsnl.net

Titus House, R-4,, Greater Kailash - 1, **New Delhi** 110 048
Tel: +91 11 6470 700 **Fax:** +91 11 648 0300
Email: titus@nda.vsnl.net.in

ASSOCIATED OFFICES

INDIA
The firm has associated offices in Calcutta, Chennai, Hyderabad, Jabalpur, Jalandhar, Mumbai

FIRM OVERVIEW: Comprising 10 partners and 21 other lawyers, Titus & Co advises on a range of legal issues. Operating from offices in New Delhi and Bangalore, the firm is part of the International Bar Association and the Asia Pacific Bar Association. It also has membership to the Supreme Court Bar Association, Delhi High Court Bar Association, Company Law Board Bar Association, India Israel Business Alliance, PHD, FICCI, CII, ASSOCHAM, and the Indian Council of Arbitration. Titus & Co is one of the founding members of the India Legal Group.

MAIN INTERNATIONAL AREAS OF PRACTICE:

Corporate and commercial: The firm advises on a diverse range of issues including M&A, cross-border transactions, inward and outward investment, joint ventures, technology transfers, regulatory, government approvals and relations, foreign exchange management, environmental issues, and anti-trust.
Project finance: The firm handles banking documents, debt documentation, inter-creditor and sponsor support issues, securing lender interests, debt refinancing and restructuring, and shareholder agreements.
Banking and finance: The firm handles cross border financing, loans, corporate finance, structured finance, asset finance, acquisition finance, lease finance, venture capital, and general and life insurance.
Capital markets: The firm advises on IPOs, securities, institutional investments, and mutual funds.
Tax: Titus & Co advises on direct and indirect tax, the structuring of sales tax, excise duty and customs duty, e-commerce taxation, tax rulings, expatriate taxation, and litigation.
Commercial property: Work undertaken includes due diligence, title investigation, contracts, construction, and mortgage advice.
Dispute resolution: The firm handles national and international arbitration, commercial litigation, and civil, criminal and constitutional litigation.
Infrastructure projects: The firm advises on various projects including power, oil and gas, telecommunications, railways, ports, roads, airports, and mining.
Telecommunication and IT: The firm handles all aspects of Internet infrastructure, e-commerce, IT related issues, cable, and broadcasting.
Intellectual property: Titus & Co advise on the registration, licensing and enforcement of all intellectual property rights.
Aviation: The firm advises on aircraft purchase, wet and dry aircraft leases, equipment purchases, repossession, aviation law, and accident enquiries.
Employment: Titus & Co advises on employment contracts, employee/staff manuals, industrial relations, conciliation, and litigation.

LANGUAGES: Bengali, English, French, German, Hindi, Gujarati, Kanadda, Marathi, Malayalam, Oriya, Punjabi, Rajasthani

For other recommended firms see pages 1485-1520

STUDIO LEGALE TONUCCI

HEAD OFFICE

Via Principessa Clotilde, 7,
00196 Rome, Italy
Tel: +39 06 362 271 **Fax:** +39 06 323 5161
Email: mail@tonucci.it
Website: www.tonucci.it

FIRM OVERVIEW

Managing partner: Mario Tonucci
Number of partners worldwide: 35
Number of other lawyers worldwide: 140

AREAS OF PRACTICE:

Mergers and acquisitions 25%
Banking, private finance and insurance 20%
Privatisation, corporate and commercial 15%
Litigation and arbitration 13%
Telecommunications, multimedia and IT 10%
Energy and environmental 7%
Employment 5%
EU regulation and anti-trust 5%

FIRM OVERVIEW: Studio Legale Tonucci is one of the largest independent Italian law firms with a significant background in international law. The firm has offices in Rome, Milan, Padua, Prato, New York, Paris, Tirana and Bucharest. It provides legal services in the major Italian financial and industrial centres and offers direct assistance to its clients in the US, EU and eastern European markets.

INTERNATIONAL EXPERIENCE: The firm's client base includes large Italian and international industrial multinationals and financial institutions. All the attorneys have a strong international background. The firm is appointed by the Italian Government, the EU, World Bank, IFC, EBRD and Eastern European institutions for domestic and international projects related to privatisation of state-owned assets and properties, alignment of national legislation to EU principles, preparation of legal feasibility study, and reform of economic and environmental regulation.

MAIN INTERNATIONAL AREAS OF PRACTICE:

Corporate and commercial: The firm has expertise in M&A of businesses via stock or asset transactions; performing the due diligence review of target operations and advising on the proper structuring of supporting financial arrangements; leveraged buyouts; spin-offs; IPOs and tender offers. Corporate transactional work includes setting up joint-ventures, drafting shareholders' agreements and other arrangements between business partners.
Banking, finance, insurance and project financing: The firm assists several major domestic and foreign banking and financial institutions and investment companies, with legislative and regulatory issues. It assists several financial institutions with national and international transactions including loans agreements, securitisations, project finance, issuing of bonds, derivates and other financial products including mutual funds and SICAVs.
Telecommunications, IT, Internet law: The firm assists top ranking telecom carriers, multimedia service providers and internet companies with starting process, the development and standardisation of commercial contracts, outsourcing agreements, licensing and regulatory issues.
Energy and environmental: The firm assists major operators in negotiating and drafting power generation and distribution agreements in the development and outgrowth of new electric generation plants and complexes. It is particularly involved with the enactment of new liberalisation principles and the application of state subsidies on tariffs and prices.
Intellectual property and data protection: The IP practice assists national and foreign clients with applications for trademark and patent protection both at national and international level, including European and Communitary procedures, and litigation.
Tax and anti-trust: The tax department provides a full range of consultancy services and assistance on domestic and international tax issues, involving corporate and commercial transactions, such as mergers and acquisitions; de-mergers; transformations; transfer of corporate assets; corporate restructuring and recapitalisations; tax planning; license and service agreements; inter-company agreements; financing; individuals' tax matters; trusts and estates.
Real estate and administrative law: The firm advises foreign companies and residents regarding properties and estates located in Italy or affected by Italian law. The firm advises the State and Social Security Agencies (including INPS, INAIL, INPDAP, INPDAI) on the sale of their assets worth over £70 million.
Employment and immigration: The firm has a strong general labour practice. Its attorneys assist several industrial and financial groups as well as medium sized businesses in all legal aspects relating to human resource management and other employment related matters. The firm has experience in advising leading US, French and UK companies with respect to the labour law implications of their start-up operations in Italy.

LANGUAGES: Albanian, English, French, German, Italian, Spanish, Romanian

WORLDWIDE OFFICE CONTACTS

ALBANIA
American Bank Building, Rruga Ismail Qemali, 27, **Tirana**
Tel: +355 42 507 11 **Fax:** +355 42 507 13
Email: tonucci-al@icc.al.eu.org

FRANCE
33 Rue de Lisbonne, 75008 **Paris**
Tel: +33 1 5393 93 00 **Fax:** +33 1 5393 93 19
Email: tonucci@wanadoo.fr

ITALY
Via dei Bossi, 4, 20121 **Milan**
Tel: +39 02 801 395 **Fax:** +39 02 860 468
Email: milano@tonucci.it

Piazzetta Gasparotto, 8, 35131 **Padua**
Tel: +39 049 658 655 **Fax:** +39 049 878 7993
Email: padova@tonucci.it

Via Giuseppe Valentini, 8/D, 59100 **Prato**
Tel: +39 0574 332 08 **Fax:** +39 0574 604 045
Email: prato@tonucci.it

Via Principessa Clotilde, 7, 00196 **Rome**
Tel: +39 06 362 271 **Fax:** +39 06 323 5161
Email: mail@tonucci.it

ROMANIA
Str, Spalaiul Unirii 10, B1.B5, Scara 1, Etaj. 6, Apartment 18, Sector 4, 75101 **Bucharest**
Tel: +40 1 33055 44 **Fax:** +40 1 3305 708
Email: bucharest@tonucci.it

USA
600 Madison Avenue, **New York** NY 10022
Tel: +1 212 980 3500 **Fax:** +1 212 980 3185
Email: tonucci@pavialaw.com

TORYS

HEAD OFFICE

Suite 3000, Maritime Life Tower, PO Box 270, Toronto Dominion Centre
Toronto M5K 1N2, Canada
Tel: +1 416 865 0040 **Fax:** +1 416 865 7380
Email: info@torys.com
Website: www.torys.com

WORLDWIDE OFFICE CONTACTS

CHINA

China Merchants Tower, Suite C, 29/F, 2 Dong Huan Nan Lu Jian Guo Men Wai, **Beijing**, Chaoyang District 100022
Tel: +86 10 6566- 9088 **Fax:** +86 10 6566 9096
Email: jwei@torys.com

USA

237 Park Avenue, New York, **New York** NY 10017-3142
Tel: +1 212 880 6000 **Fax:** +1 212 682 0200
Email: scurley@tory.com

FIRM OVERVIEW

Managing partner: Les Viner
Presiding partner: Stephen C. Curley
Number of partners worldwide: 120
Number of other lawyers worldwide: 155

AREAS OF PRACTICE:

Area	%
Corporate	75%
Litigation	15%
Insolvency	5%
Tax	3%
Environmental	2%

FIRM OVERVIEW: Torys is an international law firm with offices in New York, Toronto and Beijing. The firm's Toronto office has 150 lawyers in the corporate and commercial department and the office is involved in major transactional work. The Toronto office also has litigation and dispute resolution, tax, restructuring and insolvency and enviromental practices. The New York office acts for large and medium size industrial companies, service companies and financial institutions in US and cross-border corporate transactions and litigation.

INTERNATIONAL EXPERIENCE: The firm has extensive international experience in the fields of M&A, joint ventures and corporate finance and securities for major domestic and foreign clients, especially from the financial, telecommunications and energy sectors. Foreign clients come largely from Latin America, Cuba, the UK and China.The firm also undertakes a considerable amount of international work for Canadian and US companies, especially in Latin America and Asia. Joint ventures work includes acting for Rogers Cantel and Rogers Communications on their US$1.4 billion strategic partnership with AT&T, Rogers' joint venture with Microsoft to develop and deploy advanced broadband television services in Canada, Westcoast Energy as a member of a consortium awarded a US$1.4 billion contract to build a nitrogen facility in Mexico, Mitsubishi Corporation in a joint venture and US$1.3 billion financing for the Antamina Mine in Peru. International mergers and acquisitions work includes advising Janna Systems in its US$1.4 billion sale of US based Sibel Systems, Ontario Power Generation in the US$3.1 billion lease of its Bruce Nuclear facility to British Energy plc, The Thomson Corporation in the multi-billion sale of its newspaper assets in the US, Ernst & Young on the Canadian aspects of the US$16.2 billion merger of its consulting business with Cap Gemini SA in France, and Kohlberg Kravis Roberts in its US$2.5 billion purchase of Shoppers Drug Mart from British American Tobacco plc.

INTERNATIONAL CLIENTS: Include Thomson Corporation, Westcoast Energy, CanWest Global Communications, Heidelberger-Druckmaschinen AG, Mitsubishi Corporation, Sherritt International, Rogers Cantel and Rogers Communications, Hutchinson Telecommunications, Inmet Mining, Manulife Financial, Sunlife Financial.

MAIN INTERNATIONAL AREAS OF PRACTICE:

Corporate/commercial: Areas of expertise include asset/equipment financing and leasing, asset securitisation, banking and financial institutions, corporate finance and securities, public finance, corporate tax, derivatives, investment funds and asset management, mergers and acquisitions, mining and property development. In addition to M&A the firm handles corporate finance, corporate reorganisations, lending and other types of financing transactions - securitisations and leasing, joint ventures, technology, commercial real estate transactions, public/private partnerships and privatisations. There are specialist groups for outsourcing and entrepreneurial companies, particularly high-tech ones. Contact, Philip Symmonds.

Litigation: The firm's litigators act in a wide range of business disputes in the courts, both domestic and international, arising out of commercial transactions and relationships; securities laws; M&A; investor disputes; director and officer liability claims; business breakups; intellectual property and technology matters; anti-trust and competition laws; and insolvency and restructuring situations. Commercial litigation, securities and corporate litigation lie at the core of the firm's litigation and dispute resolution practice. The firm also has a leading class actions defence practice. Contact, Barry Leon.

Tax: The firm's tax practice includes domestic tax advice and planning in the United States and Canada, as well as international tax structuring. A significant part of the tax practice is cross-border between the US and Canada, and the firm has broad experience working on the multinational tax aspects of transactions in a variety of countries. Torys provides sophisticated tax planning in connection with M&A, divestitures, leveraged recapitalisations, leveraged buyouts, corporate finance transactions, and insolvency and restructuring matters. Contact, James Welkoff.

Environmental: Work includes the environmental aspects of commercial transactions, such as acquisitions and financings, as well as regulatory and litigation proceedings, environmental assessments and the defence of prosecutions. The firm helps companies to develop pro-active environmental management programmes and conducts compliance reviews. Contact, Robert Mansell.

Insolvency and financial restructuring: The firm has a large and highly-experienced group of lawyers dedicated to the practice of insolvency and financial restructuring. The firm has played a central role in most recent major Canadian corporate insolvencies, restructurings and work-outs, and has extensive experience in Canada/US cross-border and other international bankruptcies, creditor-protection applications and reorganisations.

LANGUAGES: English, French, German, Hebrew, Italian, Mandarin, Portuguese, Spanish

For other recommended firms see pages 1485-1520

TOZZINI FREIRE TEIXEIRA E SILVA

HEAD OFFICE

Rua Líbero Badaró, 293 - 21st Floor,
01095-900 São Paulo, SP, Brazil
Tel: +55 11 232 2100 **Fax:** +55 11 232 3100
Email: mail@tozzini.com.br
Website: www.tozzini.com.br

FIRM OVERVIEW

Main contacts: Syllas Tozzini, José Luis de Salles Freire
Number of partners worldwide: 51
Number of other lawyers worldwide: 184

AREAS OF PRACTICE:

Administrative law .... *%
Anti-trust .... *%
Banking, capital markets and corporate finance .... *%
Corporate and foreign investment .... *%
Energy .... *%
Environmental .... *%
Insurance .... *%
Intellectual property .... *%
International trade .... *%
IT and e-business .... *%
Labour and employment .... *%
Litigation and dispute resolution .... *%
M&A .... *%
Oil and gas .... *%
Project finance .... *%
Real estate .... *%
Tax .... *%
Telecommunications .... *%
* Workload % not disclosed

FIRM OVERVIEW: Established in 1976, Tozzini, Freire, Teixeira e Silva Advogados is a leading Brazilian law firm. Its commitment to creating opportunities for clients, in addition to anticipating and meeting their needs with efficiency and originality, has meant that the firm has grown to be one of the largest law firms in Latin America.

INTERNATIONAL EXPERIENCE: The firm has extensive experience in assisting international companies in setting up their companies or ventures in Brazil. Its areas of specialisation include corporate transactions, civil and commercial litigation, international and local contracts, corporate finance, project finance, banking, capital and financial market transactions, mergers and acquisitions, securities law, intellectual property (including franchising, software, entertainment and sports law) taxation, real estate and environmental law, labour relations, immigration, and the privatisation and concession of public services. The firm has formed industry focused groups with experience in various sectors, including oil and gas, power, telecommunications, water and sewage, toll roads, mining, insurance, financial institutions and information technology and e-business.

INTERNATIONAL CLIENTS: The firm's clients include industrial corporations, financial services companies, investment and commercial banks, governmental entities and multilateral institutions. Other clients come from the telecommunications, energy, oil and gas, chemical, automotive, media and technology industries.

MAIN INTERNATIONAL AREAS OF PRACTICE:

Corporate and foreign investment: Tozzini, Freire, Teixeira e Silva advises foreign investors in structuring and implementing multi-disciplinary and multi-jurisdictional business transactions. Tozzini, Freire, Teixeira e Silva also advises on investments, structuring and implementing IPOs, on investment alternatives, structuring of financing transactions and negotiations with venture capitalists, financial regulatory bodies, joint ventures, and other activities related to its mergers and acquisitions practice.
Banking and capital markets: Tozzini, Freire, Teixeira e Silva advises clients on the reorganisation of the financial industry in Brazil, and assists international banks in setting up their Brazilian operations, as well as local banks in their relationships with foreign partners. The firm also advises on compliance and has advised international financial institutions on loan agreements and other financial instruments, as well as in the structuring of complex corporate and project finance transactions. It also advises on structured trade finance transactions designed to finance imports or exports, such as pre-export financing and securitisation of receivables. The capital markets department handles the placement of securities in both the domestic and international markets, as well as eurobonds, commercial papers and DRs, acting either on behalf of the issuers or as an adviser to the underwriters or lead managers. The firm is also active in the organisation of offshore funds for investment in the Brazilian capital market, and works in partnership with financial institutions to develop new security instruments for the local market.
Telecommunications: Tozzini, Freire, Teixeira e Silva has experience in fixed and cellular telephone, paging, satellite, cable and satellite TV and restricted services transactions. The firm advises on the implementation of related infrastructure services and equipment, in corporate restructurings, general telecommunications licenses granted by the ANATEL, privatisations and M&A transactions.
Tax: The firm advises on tax planning structures. Its tax department handles complex cases tried at administrative level before government agencies or at the judicial level before courts of law.
M&A: The firm has handled some of the most significant transactions involving Brazilian companies in a wide range of industries, and has been involved in the largest Brazilian private acquisitions of recent years. The firm also handles a range of small and medium-sized acquisitions on a cost-efficient basis by reducing the scope of due diligence, where appropriate, and by custom-tailoring documentation and negotiation to the deal size.
Project finance: The project finance group is structured in a way that support the needs of a wide variety of clients, lenders and financiers and has assisted sponsors, including multinational agencies and investors.

LANGUAGES: English, French, German, Italian, Japanese, Korean, Portuguese, Spanish

WORLDWIDE OFFICE CONTACTS

BRAZIL
Setor Comercial Norte, Quadra 2, Bloco D, Torre A, Rooms 501 to 506, 70710-500 **Brasília**
Tel: +55 61 326 2100 **Fax:** +55 61 326 3100

R. Itaboraí, 123 - Petrópolis, 90670-030 **Porto Alegre**
Tel: +55 51 388 6244 **Fax:** +55 51 388 6344

Praça XV de Novembro, 34 - 9th Floor, 20010-010 **Rio de Janeiro**
Tel: +55 21 507 3565 **Fax:** +55 21 507 3803

USA
630 Fifth Avenue, Rockefeller Center 25th Floor, NEW YORK NY 10111
Tel: +1 212 698 1140 **Fax:** +1 212 698 1144

T

For other recommended firms see pages 1483-1520

TRAVERS SMITH BRAITHWAITE

HEAD OFFICE

10 Snow Hill,
London EC1A 2AL, United Kingdom
Tel: +44 20 7295 3000 **Fax:** +44 20 7295 3500

Email: Travers.Smith@TraversSmith.com
Website: www.TraversSmith.com

FIRM OVERVIEW

Managing partner: Christopher Carroll

AREAS OF PRACTICE:

Corporate	38%
Litigation	15%
Property	15%
Finance	14%
Tax	8%
Employment	5%
Pensions	5%

FIRM OVERVIEW: Travers Smith Braithwaite is a leading corporate, financial and commercial law firm with expertise and capability to advise on a wide range of business activities. Clients include regulatory, financial, trade and industrial organisations throughout the UK and worldwide. The firm provides a quality of work and has a range of clients normally associated with larger firms. Closely-knit and consistent teams of lawyers provide advice to clients, based on a thorough knowledge of their business and the firm's belief that the partners should be closely involved in most of the matters undertaken. The firm undertakes cross-border corporate finance and private equity transactions as well as such work in banking, employment and tax.

INTERNATIONAL EXPERIENCE: The firm has a close working relationship with foreign law firms in the main legal jurisdictions and is a member of a network of European law firms. This ensures that the firm has access to, and the ability to select, established overseas firms which have the necessary experience. This approach also allows the firm the flexibility to work with a client's existing advisers in different jurisdictions or to select alternative advisers where conflicts of interest arise.

INTERNATIONAL CLIENTS: In 2000, Travers Smith Braithwaite completed 12 major cross-border deals with European target companies having a total value in excess of US$15 billion, including the sale of TDL Infomedia (€ 501 million), the €1.2 billion investment by ntl in eKabel Hessen and the US$2.35 billion management buy-in of the Memec Division of E.On AG. The firm has close relationships with a number of leading firms in each European jurisdiction as well as with a number of US law firms.

MAIN INTERNATIONAL AREAS OF PRACTICE: Work handled includes corporate, litigation, finance and tax.

LANGUAGES: French, German, Italian, Spanish

WORLDWIDE OFFICE CONTACTS

FRANCE
21 Place de la Madeleine, 75008 **Paris**
Tel: +33 1 43 12 53 00 **Fax:** +33 1 43 12 53 09
Email: David.Patient@TraversSmith.com

UNITED KINGDOM
10 Snow Hill, **London** EC1A 2AL
Tel: +44 20 7295 3000 **Fax:** +44 20 7295 3500
Email: Travers.Smith@TraversSmith.com

WORLDWIDE OFFICES

FRANCE

21 Place de la Madeleine, 75008 Paris

Number of lawyers: 3

Office profile: Travers Smith Braithwaite opened its Paris liaison office in April 1999. The office sources and manages the provision of French legal services to the firm and its UK and overseas clients. In addition, the office acts as a liaison between French clients (including French law firms) and the London office.

For other recommended firms see pages 1485-1520

TRAVIESO EVANS HUGHES ARRIA RENGEL & PAZ

HEAD OFFICE

Torre La Castellana, 6th floor, Av. Principal, La Castellana,
Apartado de Correos 68278
Caracas 1062 A, Venezuela
Tel: +582 277 3333 **Fax:** +582 277 3334

Email: travieso@traviesoevans.com

FIRM OVERVIEW

Managing partner: Francisco Paz Parra

Number of partners worldwide: 15
Number of other lawyers worldwide: 24

AREAS OF PRACTICE:

Administrative and constitutional .... *%
Anti-trust .... *%
Banking and finance .... *%
Corporate .... *%
Employment .... *%
Energy .... *%
Environmental .... *%
Foreign investment .... *%
Insurance and reinsurance .... *%
Intellectual property .... *%
Litigation and arbitration .... *%
M&A .... *%
Privatisation .... *%
Tax .... *%
Telecommunications .... *%
* Workload % not disclosed

WORLDWIDE OFFICE CONTACTS

VENEZUELA
Torre La Castellana, 6th floor, Av. Principal, La Castellana, Apartado de Correos 68278, **Caracas** 1062 A
Tel: +582 277 3333 **Fax:** +582 277 3334
Email: travieso@traviesoevans.com

Edificio Paraguachi, 3rd Floor, Avenida Bicentenario, **Maturín**
Tel: +91 432333 **Fax:** +91 432333
Email: travieso@telcel.net.ve

Avenida Paseo Cabriales, Torre Movilnet, 7th Floor, ofc. n° 3, **Valencia**
Tel: +41 254793 **Fax:** +41 256456
Email: traviesoev@cantv.net

FIRM OVERVIEW: Travieso Evans Arria Rengel & Paz was founded in the 1920s as a result of the merger between Schuster & Feuille (later Schuster & Davenport) of New York City and the Travieso firm of Venezuela, originally specialising in mining and petroleum law until the nationalisation of the iron ore and oil industry at the end of 1974 and 1975 respectively. From then on the firm started to grow in other fields of law and at present it offers specialised advice in a range of areas of Venezuelan law. The firm delivers to its clients and other institutions a monthly newsletter called 'Venezuelan Legal and Economic Newsletter', which contains a summary of the most important legal and financial events that occur in the country.

INTERNATIONAL EXPERIENCE: During 2000, Travieso advised various foreign companies on joint ventures and major transactions in the energy, pharmaceutical and services industries. Travieso also advised new investors interested in the opening of the Venezuelan telecommunications industry.

INTERNATIONAL CLIENTS: Travieso's clients are mainly multinational companies engaged in a broad scope of activities ranging from large infrastructure, energy and industrial projects to service providers, telecom operators and equipment providers.

MAIN INTERNATIONAL AREAS OF PRACTICE:
Energy: The firm advises foreign energy companies doing business in Venezuela. Travieso specialises in advising foreign companies entering into joint ventures, exploration and profit sharing agreements and services agreements with Petróleos de Venezuela, S.A. and its affiliates.
Tax: The firm advises on all tax issues involving any type of transaction and provides tax planning services.
Litigation and arbitration: Travieso deals with commercial litigation and national and international arbitration. The firm had a major role in the creation of the Entrepreneurial Conciliation and Arbitration Center (Centro Empresarial de Conciliación y Arbitraje (CEDCA)) sponsored by the Venezuelan American Chamber of Commerce.
Telecommunications: The firm has advised telecom operators and equipment providers for approximately 9 years since the privatisation of CANTV. The firm advises clients on all regulatory issues and the preparation of applications for licenses to carry out telecom activities in Venezuela.
Employment: Travieso advises on all aspects of employment issues and litigation.
Banking and finance: The firm advises on all areas of banking and finance including secured loan transactions, project finance and guarantees.
Corporate: The firm advises on all aspects of corporate law including the drafting of all types of contracts, carrying of legal books and preparation of all company related legal obligations.
Intellectual property: The firm has an affiliate TEHAR that specialises in trademarks, patents and copyrights.

LANGUAGES: English, French, Portuguese, Spanish

T

TREVISAN & CUONZO

HEAD OFFICE

Via Brera 6,
20121 Milan, Italy
Tel: +39 02 8646 3313 **Fax:** +39 02 8646 3892

Email: trevisan.cuonzo@trevisan.inet.it
Website: www.trevisancuonzo.com

WORLDWIDE OFFICE CONTACTS

ITALY
Via Brera 6, 20121 **Milan**
Tel: +39 02 8646 3313 **Fax:** +39 02 8646 3892
Email: trevisan.cuonzo@trevisan.inet.it

FIRM OVERVIEW

Managing partner: Gabriel Cuonzo
Senior partner: Luca Trevisan

Number of partners worldwide: 7
Number of other lawyers worldwide: 12

AREAS OF PRACTICE:

Commercial contracts and litigation	*%
Corporate and commercial	*%
Intellectual property	*%
Internet and e-commerce	*%
IT	*%

* Workload % not disclosed

T

FIRM OVERVIEW: Trevisan & Cuonzo is one of the leading full service commercial law firms in Italy. Founded in 1993, the firm is located in the historic Palazzo Beccaria near La Scala and the Brera Art Gallery. The firm's strength lies in combining the highest professional standards in international practice with quality Italian advocacy. The practice, which includes a number of lawyers from other European jurisdictions, is multi-disciplinary and multi-lingual. It handles a comprehensive range of corporate, commercial and intellectual property transactions, and disputes both in Italy and internationally. The firm's services are structured to be flexible, affordable and responsive to client expectations and budget constraints. The firm represents a wide cross section of multi-national and national industry and commerce, trade associations, partnerships and individuals.

INTERNATIONAL EXPERIENCE: The firm is active in all aspects of industry and works with multi-national corporations, medium sized companies, non-profit organisations and private clients. A major part of the firm's work involves cross-border matters. The partnership is supported by Italian, German and UK admitted lawyers as well as external consultants. Many of its lawyers have experience in jurisdictions outside their own and are experienced in representing clients in multi-jurisdictional commercial transactions and disputes.

INTERNATIONAL CLIENTS: Trevisan & Cuonzo has a varied and international client base with a keen understanding of the approach and focus of US, European, Australian and Canadian businesses. Clients include ABB (Asea Brown Boveri), Aprilia, Apple Computer, Black & Decker, BSA (Business Software Alliance), DaimlerChrysler, Glaverbel, Harley-Davidson, IBM, Peg Perego, Poligrafici Editoriale, Philips, Reed Elsevier, Rieter, Saint-Gobain.

MAIN INTERNATIONAL AREAS OF PRACTICE:

Corporate and commercial: The firm advises on a broad range of general corporate issues including company formation, corporate regulations and compliance, joint ventures, start-ups and general commercial transactions. The corporate team conduct both domestic and cross-border mergers, acquisitions and disposals of private companies. The lawyers involved in this area of practice have a wide experience in preparing and negotiating the pertinent agreements and ancillary documents, including drafting company by-laws, shareholders' agreements, purchase-sale contracts. The corporate finance group deal with corporate reorganisation, financing and re-financing transactions, project finance transactions (particularly in the utility sector), corporate recovery and insolvency.

Commercial contracts and litigation: The firm assists corporate clients, ranging from large international organisations to medium sized businesses, with the negotiation and drafting of commercial contracts, advising on leasing agreements, agency and distribution agreements, supply, franchising, computer contracts and technology transfer. The commercial litigation team has a wide range of experience dealing with commercial disputes, employment disputes and negligence claims.

Intellectual property: The firm specialises in intellectual property including patents, utility models and industrial design, trade marks, domain name disputes, copyright, trade secrets and know-how, unfair competition and anti-trust, technology transfer and licence agreements, advertising and media law, pharmaceuticals, cross border IP civil litigation as well as criminal prosecutions.

IT: The IT team advises on all issues relating to information technology including software licensing agreements, IT procurement and maintenance contracts, outsourcing agreements, data protection compliance and IT litigation.

Internet and e-commerce: The Internet and e-commerce group combine the core skills of IP, IT and commercial law to provide a full range of services vital to clients in a digital environment.

LANGUAGES: English, French, German, Italian

 For other recommended firms see pages 1485-1520

TRONCOSO Y CACERES

HEAD OFFICE

Calle Socorro Sánchez No. 253, P.O. Box 1182,
Santo Domingo, Dominican Republic
Tel: +809 689 2158 **Fax:** +809 686 7212

Email: troncoso.caceres@codetel.net.do
Website: www.troncoso-caceres.com

FIRM OVERVIEW

Senior partner: Marcus Troncoso

Number of partners worldwide: 5
Number of other lawyers worldwide: 16

AREAS OF PRACTICE:

Banking 25%
General civil and commercial 25%
Intellectual property 20%
Tax 10%
Communication 5%
Free zone 5%
Mining 5%
Tourism 5%

FIRM OVERVIEW: The firm was established on March 2, 1915 by Manuel de Jesus Troncoso de la Concha under the name of Oficina Troncoso. Since then it has become one of the leading commercial and civil law firms in the Dominican Republic. The firm has had the largest and oldest intellectual property department in the country since 1917, and it presently maintains a successful leadership in that area, having formed strong relationships with other major intellectual property agencies throughout the world. The firm also specialises in banking, communication, mining, tourism, free zones, taxes and foreign investment legislation in the Dominican Republic. In 1983 it changed its name to Troncoso y Caceres. The firm currently comprises five partners and several other lawyers. The firm is a member of the International Trademark Association (INTA), TERRALEX and the Interamerican Association of Industrial Property.

WORLDWIDE OFFICE CONTACTS

DOMINICAN REPUBLIC
Calle Socorro Sánchez No. 253, P.O. Box 1182, **Santo Domingo**
Tel: +809 689 2158 **Fax:** +809 686 7212
Email: troncoso.caceres@codetel.net.do

MAIN INTERNATIONAL AREAS OF PRACTICE

General civil and commercial: General commercial and specific corporate transactional advice is given to international clients, a number of them from the US and Europe.
Intellectual property: The firm has one of the oldest IP practices in the Dominican Republic. Six of its lawyers specialise in the protection and exploitation of intellectual property rights, including trademarks and patents, copyright and designs.
Banking, finance and securities: Three of the firm's lawyers specialise in banking and finance work.
Tourism and Communications: The firm acts for clients in these growing areas of the country's economy.
Mining: The firm has practitioners who can advise clients in the mining sector and on issues pertaining to natural resources.
Tax: Two of the firm's lawyers are experts in fiscal law, providing assistance to commercial clients with tax-efficient structuring and planning. Tax advice is also given by the firm's consultant Luis Marrero De La Concha.

LANGUAGES: English, French, Italian, Spanish

For other recommended firms see pages 1485-1520

TROWERS & HAMLINS

HEAD OFFICE

Sceptre Court, 40 Tower Hill,
London EC3N 4DX, United Kingdom
Tel: +44 20 7423 8000 **Fax:** +44 20 7423 8001

Email: enquiries@trowers.com
Website: www.trowers.com

FIRM OVERVIEW

Managing partner: David Biggerstaff
Senior partner: Jonathan Adlington
Head of international practice: Martin Amison

Number of partners worldwide: 66
Number of other lawyers worldwide: 119

AREAS OF PRACTICE:

Property (housing, public sector, commercial property) 34%
Commercial (corporate, finance, construction, international) 32%
Litigation 26%
Private client 8%

T

FIRM OVERVIEW: Trowers & Hamlins is an international law firm with its head office in the City of London and offices in the UK and overseas. Over the last 40 years it has developed a substantial international practice, with five offices in the Middle East, in Abu Dhabi, Bahrain, Cairo, Dubai and Oman, as well as a number of active cooperation agreements with law firms in Yemen and Jordan. The firm has been working in the Middle East region since 1959 and currently has 25 lawyers (including nine partners) working in its five regional offices. It also has an associated office in Singapore, contacts in the USA and Europe and works with Ledingham Chalmers in Azerbaijan and Istanbul. The firm's head office in London acts as the nucleus for the network of international offices and for the international projects, public international and private finance practices.

WORLDWIDE OFFICE CONTACTS

BAHRAIN
9th Floor, The Tower, Sheraton Commercial Complex, PO Box 3012, **Manama**
Tel: +973 530 082 **Fax:** +973 535 616
Email: bahrain@trowers-hamlins.com

EGYPT
6th Floor, 6 El Koroum Street, Mohamdesseen, **Cairo**
Tel: +202 338 4410 **Fax:** +202 761 8773
Email: trowers@trowers.com.eg

OMAN
Al Mawarid House, PO Box 2991, Ruwi 112, **Muscat**
Tel: +968 771 5500 **Fax:** +968 771 5544
Email: trowers@omantel.net.om

UNITED ARAB EMIRATES
4th Floor, Butti Al Otaiba Building, Khalifa Street, PO Box 45628, **Abu Dhabi**
Tel: +971 2 626 7274 **Fax:** +971 2 626 7276
Email: abudhabi@trowers-hamlins.com

Rais Hassan Saadi Building, Mankhool Road, PO Box 23092, **Dubai**
Tel: +971 4 351 9201 **Fax:** +971 4 351 9205
Email: dubai@trowers-hamlins.com

UNITED KINGDOM
1st Floor, Portland House, Longbrook Street, **Exeter** EX4 6AB
Tel: +44 1392 217466 **Fax:** +44 1392 221047
Email: marketing@trowers.com

Sceptre Court, 40 Tower Hill, **London** EC3N 4DX
Tel: +44 20 7423 8000 **Fax:** +44 20 7423 8001
Email: enquiries@trowers.com

Heron House, Albert Square, **Manchester** M2 5HD
Tel: +44 161 211 0000 **Fax:** + 44 161 211 0001
Email: marketing@trowers.com

INTERNATIONAL EXPERIENCE: Trowers & Hamlins has been involved in a number of high-profile projects. The firm advised Salalah Port Services Company SAOG on the original concession agreement and related project documentation for a strategic container terminal development in the south of Oman. This initial private sector operated and financed project has been enhanced by a further 30 year concession agreement for the operation and management of the existing conventional port facilities. The company recently signed a memorandum of understanding to establish a free trade zone at the port on which the firm also advised. Following Financial Close being achieved in the Taweelah A2 power and water project in Abu Dhabi, the firm has maintained its involvement with the project (after initially advising the developers CMS energy on all aspects of this project from bid development through to Financial Close), and now advises on the new project, Emirates CMS Power Company, in connection with the construction and operation of the new facility. The firm also advised bidders on the Taweelah A1 independent power and water project in Abu Dhabi. The firm acts as lead counsel (international and local) for Borealis A/S in all aspects of the development and financing of this global-scale petrochemicals joint venture with ADNOC which is valued in excess of $1billion. As the plant nears commissioning, the firm continues to advise on the financing of the projects and on the arrangements for the completion of the construction phases. On Manah Independent Power Projects Phase II, Oman, the firm acted as project counsel advising on the development and negotiation of documentation to triple the capacity of the independent power generating station. Phase II, like Phase I (which in 1994/95 was the first BOT project in the region to reach Financial Close) was implemented on a BOT basis. The firm has acted as counsel to the project company, the United Power Company SAOG, since incorporation in 1994.

INTERNATIONAL CLIENTS: The firm advises multinationals, oil and gas companies, energy operators and distributors, financial institutions, trading houses, and governmental institutions. The firm also undertakes English legal work for overseas clients from yacht owners to foreign embassies and Middle Eastern merchants.

MAIN INTERNATIONAL AREAS OF PRACTICE:

Privatisation and projects: The firm undertakes project-related work (especially oil and gas) and project development work (particularly in energy and water projects). Project financing work includes BOOT/BOO/DBFO work, similar to UK PFI.
Corporate, commercial and corporate finance: Includes M&A, flotation and securities work, construction, industrial and retail projects, commercial agreements, joint ventures and franchises. The firm also advises international clients on corporate finance, banking, registration and compliance and tax law.
Public international: Work includes large-scale boundary disputes (highly sensitive and confidential).

LANGUAGES: Arabic, English, French, German, Italian, Russian

For other recommended firms see pages 1485-1520

TUMI AND ASSOCIATES

HEAD OFFICE

190 Khalid Ben El-Walid street, Dahra Area, PO Box 4444
Tripoli, Libya
Tel: +218 21 333 9024 **Fax:** +218 21 444 6097

Email: info@tumilawfirm.com
Website: www.tumilawfirm.com

WORLDWIDE OFFICE CONTACTS

LIBYA
190 Khalid Ben El-Walid street, Dahra Area, PO Box 4444, **Tripoli**
Tel: +218 21 333 9024 **Fax:** +218 21 444 6097
Email: info@tumilawfirm.com

FIRM OVERVIEW

Managing partner: Mohammed Tumi
Senior partner: Mohamed El-Naas

Number of partners worldwide: 2
Number of other lawyers worldwide: 5

AREAS OF PRACTICE:

Company formations	*%
Contracts	*%
Corporate	*%
Banking	*%
Arbitration	*%
Customs	*%
Immigration	*%
Labour Law	*%
Litigation	*%
Taxation	*%

* Workload % not disclosed

FIRM OVERVIEW: Tumi and Associates is one of the leading law firms in Libya and is very well known for its European corporate clients. A number of lawyers in the firm have full membership of the common law and civil code legal systems.

INTERNATIONAL EXPERIENCE: Tumi and Associates has been engaged in various arbitration cases before the ICC. The partners and associates participate in and attend different symposiums and seminars.

INTERNATIONAL CLIENTS: Tumi and Associate's clients include international construction companies; Bilfiger & Berger, Maltauro Group, Delma s.p.a., Del Favoro s.r.l., Foster Wheeler, Merloni Progetti, Polimex Cekop and ACS; international oil companies; Saipem (ENI GROUP), Enelpower, Ina Industrija Nafte, MAPEL (AMEC Group), Weatherford, SPIE, Computalog and Agip Oil Company; international airlines; Austrian Airlines, British Airways, P.I.A. (Pakistan International Airlines) and TAROM (Romanian Air Transport); insurance and manufacturing companies.

MAIN INTERNATIONAL AREAS OF PRACTICE:

Contracts: The firm advises on the drafting of various contracts including drilling, employment, shipping and sales contracts.
Banking: Tumi and Associates advises on L/C (Letters of Credits) and bank guarantees.
Arbitration: Tumi and Associates handles local and international arbitration.
Corporate: The firm has handled a number of company formations and advised foreign companies on the registration of branch offices in Libya. Clients include the Ministry of Economy, Chamber of Commerce, Ministry of Housing, Commercial Register Office and National Oil Corporation.
Employment: Tumi and Associates handles a wide range of employment related issues.
Tax: Tumi and Associates has represented a number of foreign companies before the tax department. It handles all issues relating to Libyan tax law.
Customs: The firm advises on customs laws and regulations (temporary and final import procedures). It has represented clients before the Customs Department.
Immigration: Tumi and Associates advises on entry and exit visas, residency permits and work permits. It has represented foreign companies before the Libyan immigration courts

LANGUAGES: Arabic, English, French

For other recommended firms see pages 1485-1520

UCHE NWOKEDI & CO

HEAD OFFICE

9 Military Street, Onikin,
Lagos Nigeria
Tel: +234 1 263 3728 **Fax:** +234 1 263 4726
Email: kedilaw@infoweb.abs.net

WORLDWIDE OFFICE CONTACTS

NIGERIA
9 Military Street, Onikin, **Lagos**
Tel: +234 1 263 3728 **Fax:** +234 1 263 4726
Email: kedilaw@infoweb.abs.net

FIRM OVERVIEW

Senior partner: Uche Nwokedi

AREAS OF PRACTICE:

Energy and natural resources ....*%
General orporate and commercial ....*%
Maritime ....*%
Solid minerals law ....*%
* Workload % not disclosed

FIRM OVERVIEW: Uche Nwokedi & Co specialises in commercial litigation, alternative dispute resolution, and representation at special and miscellaneous tribunals. The firm also offers legal advisory and consulting services, particularly in the areas of oil and gas law, shipping, foreign investment law, technical cooperation and collaboration agreements, and general commercial and corporate law.Approaching all work with a progressive yet traditional attitude, the firm's aim is to provide foreign clients with sound legal representation in order for them to successfully do business in Nigeria.

U

MAIN INTERNATIONAL AREAS OF PRACTICE:

Oil and gas: Uche Nwokedi & Co specialises in oil and gas law and has been actively involved in number of notable petroleum industry projects in Nigeria. It's clients include the Ministry of Petroleum and Mineral Resources; the Nigerian National Petroluem Corporation (NNPC); NAPIMS (a strategic business unit of NNPC). Some of the issues handled include the review of Nigeria's Production Sharing Contract model; NNPC's equity participation in some of the major oil service companies operating in Nigeria; advising and acting in arbitration in respect of the Strategic Storage Reserve Vessel Project; and acting for Amni International Petroleum Development Company Ltd, in respect of its joint-venture with Abacan Resources of Canada for the developmenet of OPL 469 and OPL 237. Other work handled in this area includes joint ventures, technical and managerial services arrangements, dispositions and acquisitions, farm-ins and farm-outs for indigenous and transnational corporations; oil industry service contracts, including transfer of technology arrangements, technical and engineering services and related collaberation arrangements; advising on petroleum products and oil trading arrangements, handling regulatory agency permits and approvals.
Solid minerals law: Uche Nwokedi & Co has played a leading role in the development of a legal framework for the exploitation of solid minerals in Nigeria. The firm's principal counsel currently serves on the Ministerial Committee of Legal Experts set up to review the enire minerals legislation of Nigeria for the Federal Government of Nigeria. In this respect, he advises the Ministry of Solid Development on related issues. The committee has been largely responsible for a new draft law which is to be passed this year.
Maritime: Uche Nwokedi & Co provides comprehensive legal services to clients in the shipping industry, on a multi-jurisdictional basis. Work handled includes FPSO and FSO and tanker storage vessels acquisition and financing including international charters and leases and structured financing; ship and vessel procurements, mortgages and lease financing including syndications, securitisation and asset sales; new building, including repair and conversion contracts and related documentation; registration of vessels within jurisdiction and flagging out in all jurisdictions; charter parties, contracts of affreightment, ship management, agency and crewing agreements; general maritime litigation and alternative dispute resolution.
General corporate and commercial: The firm advises on loan syndication, securitisation and escrow arrangement, mortgage debentures, liens, charges and related transactions, related litigation and representation at special tribunal. It advises on the review of contracts, briefs and business proposals. It also advises on the incorporation of comapnies, searches, investigations and general advice on trade practices and government regulations.
Litigation and arbitration: The firm handles litigation and arbitration pending in the UK and US involving Nigerian companies or individuals.

LANGUAGES: English

For other recommended firms see pages 1485-1520

UDO-UDOMA & BELO-OSAGIE

HEAD OFFICE

St Nicholas House (10th Floor), Catholic Mission Street,
Lagos, Nigeria
Tel: +234 1 263 4831 **Fax:** +234 1 263 4541

Email: uubo@infoweb.abs.net
Website: www.uubo.org

FIRM OVERVIEW

Senior partner: Udoma Udo Udoma
Managing partner: Myma Belo-Osagle

Number of partners worldwide: 6
Number of other lawyers worldwide: 11

AREAS OF PRACTICE:

Banking, finance and capital markets 20%
Power, energy and natural resources 20%
Civil, corporate and commercial litigation 15%
Commercial and property transactions 15%
Corporate restructuring, M&A 15%
Telecommunications 15%

WORLDWIDE OFFICE CONTACTS

NIGERIA
c/o Ferrostal A.G., Akwa Iborn State, **Ikot Abasi**

St Nicholas House (10th Floor), Catholic Mission Street, **Lagos**
Tel: +234 1 263 4831 **Fax:** +234 1 263 4541
Email: uubo@infoweb.abs.net

5 Igbokwe Street, D-Line, River State, **Port Harcourt**
Tel: +234 084 238049

ASSOCIATED OFFICES

GHANA
Bentsi-Enchill, Letsa & Mate, 1st Floor, East Bay Teachers, Hall Annex, Off Barnes Road, **Accra** PO Box 1632

U

FIRM OVERVIEW: Founded in 1983, Udo-Udoma & Belo-Osagie comprises six partners and eleven other lawyers. The firm has developed a broad based corporate and institutional commercial practice, and is one of the largest commercial law partnerships in Nigeria. It provides sophisticated legal advice in its core practice areas.

INTERNATIONAL EXPERIENCE: The firm has a wealth of experience in capital markets transactions affecting corporate restructurings, negotiating joint ventures, and other investment transactions in Nigeria and internationally. The firm handled the establishment of the Global Depository Receipt Programme; various syndicated loans; the review of agreements between Government and foreign investors; and advises local and international clients and legal colleagues on foreign investment in Nigeria. The firm maintains international affiliations through individual and firm memberships in several organisations including the International American and New York State Bar Association; the Bar of England and Wales; the Bar Association of Commerce, Finance and Industry; the International Tax Planning Association; the ICC Group of International Lawyers; the Nigerian Chapter of the Federation International De Abogadas; and the Law Association for Asia and the Pacific.

INTERNATIONAL CLIENTS: The firm's clients include multinational and domestic corporations, high net worth individuals, banks, insurance companies, embassies and state governments as well as the Federal Republic of Nigeria. It advises telecommunications companies, foreign and domestic commercial, merchant and investment banks, oil exploration companies, service and trade companies, consumer product companies, engineering and construction firms, manufacturing and trade companies, and pharmaceutical companies.

MAIN INTERNATIONAL AREAS OF PRACTICE:

Energy, power and natural resources: The firm's experience extends to upstream and downstream oil and gas projects as well as petrochemical and industry transactions. The firm also advises on the establishment of independent power projects.

Telecommunications: The firm has substantial experience in dealing with, and advising on, all aspects of telecommunication.

Banking, finance and capital markets: The firm advises on capital market transactions including corporate restructurings, negotiating joint ventures, secured and syndicated loan transactions and guarantees, project finance, equipment leasing and other areas of banking and finance. It also handles legal audit, training, and trusteeship services.

Corporate restructuring and M&A: The firm handles corporate restructuring and negotiates joint ventures and other investment transactions, both in Nigeria and internationally.

Foreign investment: The firm advises foreign clients investing in, or setting up in, Nigeria. It advises on Nigerian legislation regulating foreign investment including exchange control regulations.

Intellectual property: The firm handle registration of trademarks, patents, copyrights and trade names. It is also involved in drafting, reviewing and negotiating license agreements, and advising on infringement disputes and other aspects of ID law.

Real estate: The firm has a very active commercial property department that represents clients in various property transactions.

LANGUAGES: Akan, Andoni, Efik, English, French, Ga, Ibibio, Ibo, Itsekiri, Twi, Yoruba

UDO UDOMA & BELO-OSAGIE
BARRISTERS AND SOLICITORS

For other recommended firms see pages 1485-1520

STUDIO LEGALE UGHI e NUNZIANTE

HEAD OFFICE

Via Venti Settembre, 1,
00187 Rome, Italy
Tel: +39 06 474 831 **Fax:** +39 06 487 0397
Email: ughi.e.nunziante@unlaw.it

FIRM OVERVIEW

Management committee: Marcello Gioscia, Marco Brescia Rino Caiazzo

Number of partners worldwide: 12
Number of other lawyers worldwide: 49

AREAS OF PRACTICE:

Corporate and commercial	30%
EU, competition and real estate	25%
Telecommunications and e-commerce	20%
Administrative, litigation and arbitration	15%
Tax	10%

U

FIRM OVERVIEW: Founded in 1968, Studio Legale Ughi e Nunziante has domestic offices in Rome and Milan. Comprising 12 partners and 49 associates it specialises in corporate and commercial law, but also advises in a wide range of other areas.

INTERNATIONAL EXPERIENCE: All the firm's members hold degrees from foreign universities, and have worked abroad.

INTERNATIONAL CLIENTS: Many of the firm's international clients are either financial institutions or corporate entities from the EU or US.

MAIN INTERNATIONAL AREAS OF PRACTICE:

Corporate: The firm handles M&A and advises on corporate restructurings, demergers, regulatory compliance, corporate governance, and shareholder disputes.
Privatisations: The firm advises the Italian treasury, national and international financial institutions, government owned banks and companies on all aspects of privatisation.
Foreign investments and divestments: The firm advises foreign corporates in respect of productive investments carried out in Italy including joint ventures and subsidiaries.
Financial services: The firm handles loans, project finance, structured finance (including relevant tax advice), banking and investment services regulation, and derivatives.
Telecommunications and e-commerce: The firm provides a full range of services for major Italian and foreign companies operating in the TLC and e-commerce sectors. It advises on regulatory matters, anti-trust and judicial proceedings.
Aviation: Work handled includes leasing and financial issues.
Projects: The firm handles all aspects of projects concerning industrial investment in the depressed areas of Italy. It also advises on government contracts and public contributions at national, local and EU levels, and handles domestic and cross border project finance transactions.

WORLDWIDE OFFICE CONTACTS

ITALY

Via Sant' Andrea 19, 20121 **Milan**
Tel: +39 02 762 171 **Fax:** +39 02 784 140
Email: ughi.e.nunziante@unlaw.it

Via Venti Settembre, 1, 00187 **Rome**
Tel: +39 06 474 831 **Fax:** +39 06 487 0397
Email: ughi.e.nunziante@unlaw.it

Corporate finance: Work handled includes IPOs, listing and compliance, securitisation, recourse to capital markets through issuing of debt instruments, warrants and rights.
EU and competition: The firm handles all aspects of EU and competition law.
Adminstrative: The firm specialises in environmental and health and safety law. Its administrative law practice is very active in work relating to public works projects.
Litigation and arbitration: The firm handles domestic and cross-border litigation including disputes litigated before foreign courts. The firm has a strong presence in the domestic and international arbitration field.
Tax: The firm handles domestic and international tax issues.

LANGUAGES: English, French, German, Italian, Spanish

STUDIO LEGALE
UGHI E NUNZIANTE

For other recommended firms see pages 1485-1520

URÍA & MENÉNDEZ

HEAD OFFICE

Jorge Juan, 6, 28001 Madrid
Tel: +34 91 586 0400 **Fax:** +34 91 586 0403
Email: agg@uria.com
Website: www.uria.com

FIRM OVERVIEW

Senior partner: Rodrigo Uría Meruéndano
Number of partners worldwide: 49
Number of other lawyers worldwide: 165

AREAS OF PRACTICE:

Corporate and commercial/ M&A 40%
Litigation/arbitration/insolvency 17%
Financial law/capital markets 16%
Tax law 6%
Telecommunications/media and entertainment law 6%
Competition and intellectual property 5%
Administrative and constitutional/environmental/urban planning3%
Real estate/property 3%
Employment and pensions 2%
Maritime, transport and logistics 2%

FIRM OVERVIEW: Founded in the 1940s, Uría & Menéndez comprises 50 partners, 179 associates and over 50 trainee lawyers in 13 offices around the world. The firm focuses on banking and capital markets, company and commercial, environment, litigation and arbitration, project finance, telecommunications, EU and competition, intellectual property, labour, tax, maritime, transport and logistics.

INTERNATIONAL EXPERIENCE: Uría & Menéndez's London and New York offices provide advice to UK and US based clients who have interests in Spain, as well as Spanish companies established or wishing to become established in the UK or the US. From its Brussels office the firm provides advice covering all areas of EU law, particularly competition law and trade law. Uría and Menéndez has formed associations with several firms in Latin America and one in Portugal. In June 2000, the firm expanded its presence in Latin America

INTERNATIONAL CLIENTS: The firm's client base comprises mainly domestic and foreign companies in the banking and finance, real estate and construction, food and beverages, telecommunications, energy, steel and metal, insurance, IT, and motor industries.

MAIN INTERNATIONAL AREAS OF PRACTICE:

Corporate and commercial: Uría & Menéndez covers all areas of corporate and commercial including agency and distribution, commercial contracts, energy and utilities, food and beverages, insurance, mergers and acquisitions and real estate.
Financial: The firm handles all matters relating to banking, corporate finance, investment funds, project finance, securities and securitisation.
Competition and industrial property: Uría & Menéndez advises on all aspects of competition, European Union, intellectual property, copyright and data protection, pharmaceuticals, unfair competition, antidumping and WTO.
Telecommunications and media and entertainment: The firm has substantial experience in dealing with e-commerce and information technology, media and entertainment, sports and leisure, telecommunications and advertising.

LANGUAGES: Catalan, English, Finnish, French, German, Italian, Polish, Portuguese, Russian, Spanish

WORLDWIDE OFFICE CONTACTS

BELGIUM
Avenue Louise, 480, B-1050 **Brussels**
Tel: +32 2 639 64 64 **Fax:** +32 2 640 14 88
Email: env@uria.com

BRAZIL
Al Santos 2224, Conj 92, SP 014 18-200 **São Paulo**
Tel: +55 11 3898 1644 **Fax:** +55 11 3898 1645
Email: pge@uria.com.br

SPAIN
Diagonal, 514, 08006 **Barcelona**
Tel: +34 93 416 51 00 **Fax:** +34 93 416 51 11
Email: cvj@uria.com

Gran Vía, 39, 1-Dcha, 48009 **Bilbao**
Tel: +34 94 479 4920 **Fax:** +34 94 479 0761
Email: che@uria.com

Jorge Juan, 6, 28001 **Madrid**
Tel: +34 91 586 0400 **Fax:** +34 91 586 0403
Email: agg@uria.com

Colón, 28-4, 46004 **Valencia**
Tel: +34 96 352 91 91 **Fax:** +34 96 352 91 05
Email: jmm@uria.com

UNITED KINGDOM
Royex House, Aldermanbury Square, **London** EC2V 7NJ
Tel: +44 20 7367 0080 **Fax:** +44 20 7600 1718
Email: jgr@uria.com

USA
320 Park Avenue, 28th Floor, **New York** NY 10022
Tel: +1 212 593 1300 **Fax:** +1 212 593 7144
Email: egp@uria.com

ASSOCIATED OFFICES

ARGENTINA
In association with Marval, O'Farrell & Mairal, Av. Leandro N. Alem, 928, 1001 **Buenos Aires**
Tel: +54 11 43 10 01 00 **Fax:** +54 11 43 10 02 00
Email: rr@marval.com.ar

CHILE
In association with Philippi, Yrrázaval, Pulido & Brunner, Moneda 970-12°, **Santiago**
Tel: +562 364 3700 **Fax:** +562 364 3796
Email: vconde@philippi.cl

MEXICO
In collaboration with Franck, Galicia, Duclaud y Robles, S.C, Torre Óptima, Avda. Paseo de las Palmas 405, 3er piso, Col. Lomas de Chapultepec, 11000 **Mexico City**
Tel: +52 5 540 9200 **Fax:** +52 5 540 9202
Email: jvelayos@fgdr.com.mx

PERU
Estudio Uría, Abogados, Av. Victor Andrés Belaúnde 147, Edificio Real, 3 piso 12, San Isidro, **Lima** 27
Tel: +51 1 222 3202 **Fax:** +51 1 222 1573
Email: fmo@uria.com.pe

PORTUGAL
In association with Morais Leitão, J Galvão Teles & Associados, Rua Castilho, 75-1, 1250 **Lisbon**
Tel: +351 21 381 74 31 **Fax:** +351 21 381 74 96
Email: fav@uria.com

For other recommended firms see pages 1485-1520

VAN BAEL & BELLIS

HEAD OFFICE

Avenue Louise 165,
B-1050 Brussels, Belgium
Tel: +32 2 647 73 50 **Fax:** +32 2 640 64 99

Website: www.vanbaelbellis.com

FIRM OVERVIEW

Managing partner: Jean-François Bellis

Number of partners worldwide: 10
Number of other lawyers worldwide: 33

AREAS OF PRACTICE:
Competition, trade and other EU 70%
Belgian business law 30%

WORLDWIDE OFFICE CONTACTS

BELGIUM
Avenue Louise 165, B-1050 **Brussels**
Tel: +32 2 647 73 50 **Fax:** +32 2 640 64 99
Email: vbb@vanbaelbellis.com

SWITZERLAND
15, Boulevard des Philosophes, **Geneva**
Tel: +41 22 320 90 20 **Fax:** +41 22 320 94 20
Email: geneva@vanbaelbellis.com

V

FIRM OVERVIEW: Established in 1986, Van Bael & Bellis is a Brussels-based firm with a multinational team of lawyers who advise clients worldwide. In addition to its core EU practice the firm has established a substantial practice in Belgian business law. Its WTO trade law practice is also expanding, and the firm opened an office in Geneva in 1998. The firm's lawyers come from over 12 countries and have spoken and published widely on EU law and other areas. They also teach at leading academic institutions, including the College of Europe and the Universities of Brussels and Amsterdam.

INTERNATIONAL EXPERIENCE: The firm regularly advises on the EU aspects of major international transactions. Firm members have been involved in many landmark cases in EU competition law, including United Brands, IBM, Michelin, Boeing/McDonnell Douglas and Eco Swiss/Benetton. It has also advised East European countries including Russia, Poland and Slovakia on competition laws within the framework of the European Commission's Phare and Tacis programmes. The firm has handled over 200 anti-dumping and anti-subsidy cases. WTO work includes advising governments on their accession negotiations and the harmonisation of national trade legislation. The firm's Belgian business law practice advises a number of multinational clients, and the firm is frequently retained to advise clients on transactions in other parts of Europe and beyond, as well as on international tax planning.

INTERNATIONAL CLIENTS: The firm advises large multinational corporations, governments and international trade associations. Specific industry sectors include computing, consumer products, car manufacturers, aerospace, telecommunications, pharmaceuticals, air transport, energy and forest products. Clients come from all over the world, but in particular from North America, the Far East and Europe.

MAIN INTERNATIONAL AREAS OF PRACTICE:
Competition: The firm advises on all aspects of competition law, including merger control, Articles 81 and 82, states aid rules and compliance programmes at the EU and national level. It represents clients in competition cases before the European Commission, the European Court of Justice and the Court of First Instance, as well as before national courts, arbitral panels and competition authorities.
Trade, customs and WTO: The firm represents international clients in anti-dumping, anti-subsidy and related proceedings. It advises on trade relations with third world countries and on bilateral trade agreements. Customs law and WTO matters are also an important part of the firm's practice.
Other EU: Areas of practice include the free movement of goods, product regulation and market deregulation. The firm also monitors the activities of EU institutions and helps clients to devise lobbying strategies and gain access to key decision-makers.
Belgian business law: The firm advises on all aspects of doing business in Belgium including litigation, corporate transactions, trade practices, tax, employment and intellectual property.
Litigation and arbitration: The firm has extensive experience in litigating before the Belgian courts and the two EU courts. For its work in the Belgian courts the firm is known for combining arguments based on both EU and national law.

LANGUAGES: Dutch, English, French, German, Italian, Portuguese, Russian, Spanish, Swedish, Ukranian

VAN BAEL & BELLIS

For other recommended firms see pages 1485-1520

VAN DOORNE

HEAD OFFICE

De Lairessestraat 133, PO Box 75265,
1070 AG Amsterdam, Netherlands
Tel: +31 20 6789 123 **Fax:** +31 20 6789 589

Email: amsterdam@van-doorne.com
Website: www.van-doorne.com

FIRM OVERVIEW

Senior partner: Dries Fransen van de Putte
Managing partners: Albert van Marwijk Kooy, Gérard Moussault

Number of partners worldwide: 22
Number of other lawyers worldwide: 89

AREAS OF PRACTICE:

Corporate	25%
Finance	25%
Employment	15%
Litigation	15%
IP/IT	10%
Property	10%

FIRM OVERVIEW: The firm was formed following the breakup of Trenité Van Doorne on 1 January 2001. The firm can trace its history to the Amsterdam/Rotterdam firm Van Doorne & Sjollema. It has offices in Amsterdam and London and associated offices in Brussels and the Netherlands Antilles (Aruba and Curaçao). The firm offers a wide range of legal services with a strong focus on corporate and finance. In addition, it has a solid reputation in litigation, employment, property and IP/IT.

INTERNATIONAL EXPERIENCE: Corporate transactions include the acquisition of a Dutch aerospace company by a Swedish aircraft manufacturer and the acquisition of a Belgian/French multi-national sweets business by a Dutch food company. Lawyers have also advised on the establishment of a Dutch based internet investment vehicle by various large Swedish corporates and advised on a joint venture between a US telecommunications company and UK telecommunications company. Finance transactions include the structuring and creation of Dutch law security for international bank syndicates and advising on the taking of full asset security over substantial fibres and food businesses, both of which were subject to leveraged buy-outs. Lawyers have advised on and structured a proposed securitisation of the largest rental vehicle business in The Netherlands, advised a US investment bank on the securitisation of Dutch mortgage receivables and advised an international bank syndicate on a preferred share issue by a Mexican cement company. Capital markets work includes advising on the initial notes issue of a Polish commercial bank, a debt issuance programme for a UK tobacco company, the initial notes issue of an Italian fashion house, various notes issues of a Spanish oil company, a medium term note programme for a Mexican cement company, a high-yield notes issue for a Dutch packaging company, the update of a debt issuance programme for a UK commercial bank and various tranches under an asset backed note programme for a US car manufacturer. The firm has also advised on the restructuring of the public debt of a Russian commercial bank.

INTERNATIONAL CLIENTS: The firm's client base consists of multi-national and medium-sized companies in various industry sectors as well as governmental entities. Historically, the firm has served a large number of UK and US clients.

WORLDWIDE OFFICE CONTACTS

NETHERLANDS
De Lairessestraat 133, PO Box 75265, 1070 AG **Amsterdam**
Tel: +31 20 6789 123 **Fax:** +31 20 6789 589
Email: amsterdam@van-doorne.com

UNITED KINGDOM
1st Floor, 55 King William Street, **London** EC4R 9AD
Tel: +44 20 7648 0400 **Fax:** +44 20 7283 5001
Email: london@van-doorne.com

ASSOCIATED OFFICES

ANTILLES
Miramar Building, Suite 303, LG Smith Boulevard 62, Oranjestad, **Aruba**
Tel: +297 838 464 **Fax:** +297 838 442
Email: info@promes-vandoorne.aw

Promes Van Doorne, Julianaplein 22, PO Box 504, Willemstad, **Curaçao**
Tel: +599 94 61 34 00 **Fax:** +599 94 61 20 23
Email: info@promes-vandoorne.aw

BELGIUM
Van Doorne, Havenlaan 16, 1080 **Brussels**
Tel: +32 2 426 1414 **Fax:** +32 2 426 2030
Email: info@huysmans.com

V

MAIN INTERNATIONAL AREAS OF PRACTICE:
Corporate: The firm's corporate lawyers advise on cross-border M&A transactions, international private equity, multi-jurisdictional equity offerings and international public take-overs.
Finance: The lawyers in the finance practice group advise on lending and security in cross-border transactions, the structuring of investment funds, asset finance and leasing (in particular aircraft and ships), international capital markets and regulatory matters.
Litigation: The firm's litigators are involved in international litigation such as world-wide tobacco litigation and asbestos litigation, act in international arbitrations and advise on cross-border insolvencies.
IP/IT: The lawyers in the practice group advise on international licence, franchise, distribution and merchandise agreements, copyright, patent, design, trademark and name right infringements as well as misleading advertising.
Tax: The firm's tax lawyers are involved in the tax structuring of international transactions with a strong focus on structured finance, capital markets and M&A transactions including advice on tax treaties and EU legislation.
EU: Competition lawyers advise on Dutch and EU merger control, unfair competition, trade restrictions, procurement and government tenders, establishment conditions, subsidies and concessions.

LANGUAGES: Dutch, English, French, German, Italian, Spanish

VanDoorne Lawyers in Business 

VASCONCELOS, F Sá CARNEIRO, FONTES & ASSOCIADOS

HEAD OFFICE

Rua Castilho 20, 3rd floor,
1250 - 069 Lisbon, Portugal
Tel: +351 210 308 600 **Fax:** +351 210 308 601

Email: vscf@mail.telepac.pt

FIRM OVERVIEW

Senior partners: Duarte Vasconcelos
Francisco Sá Carneiro
Tito Arantes Fontes

Number of partners worldwide: 6
Number of other lawyers worldwide: 31

AREAS OF PRACTICE:

Banking and finance	20%
Corporate	20%
Litigation and arbitration	20%
Mergers and acquisitions	16%
Administrative, property and expropriations	8%
Employee and benefits	8%
Tax	8%

WORLDWIDE OFFICE CONTACTS

PORTUGAL

Rua Castilho 20, 3rd floor, 1250 - 069 **Lisbon**
Tel: +351 210 308 600 **Fax:** +351 210 308 601
Email: vscf@mail.telepac.pt

Rua Campo Alerge, 830, 3rd, sala 11 4150-171 **Porto**
Tel: +351 220 308 600 **Fax:** +351 220 308 601

V

FIRM OVERVIEW: The firm was founded in 1993, since when it has strengthened its initial practice areas and developed new ones. These include banking and finance, corporate, intellectual property, litigation and arbitration, M&A, telecommunications, employment and employee benefits, tax, property and expropriations, administrative and public law and crime. The firm will soon be opening a second office in Porto to meet client demand in the north of Portugal.

INTERNATIONAL EXPERIENCE: The firm has been actively involved in cross-border deals, especially M&A and banking. These have included advising one client on acquisitions and joint ventures in the UK, Poland and Germany. In 1998 and 1999 the firm acted as Portuguese legal counsel for banks involved in the Portuguese government's first road project. It also acted in the acquisition of a stake in a Portuguese telecommunications company by a leading foreign telecommunications company.

INTERNATIONAL CLIENTS: The firm's clients include listed and non-listed companies. They are large and medium-sized international clients from countries such as Belgium, Finland, France, Italy, Spain, the UK and the US, operating in a wide range of sectors such as banking, telecommunications, food processing and animal feed.

MAIN INTERNATIONAL AREAS OF PRACTICE:
Banking and finance: The firm covers all areas, including project finance, structured finance, acquisition finance, syndicated loan transactions, guarantees, securitisation and leasing.
Litigation and arbitration: The practice covers all forms of commercial and civil disputes, in employment, tax, insolvency and other areas, before the Portuguese courts and arbitration panels.
Corporate: A comprehensive service covering all aspects of company and commercial law including joint ventures, shareholders' agreements and corporate restructuring. The firm has been involved in both small private acquisitions and cross-border takeovers, for listed and non-listed companies, as well as in mergers of listed and non-listed companies.
Securities and financial markets: Work includes stock exchange flotations and listings, public offers of both equity and debt, as well as other instruments such as warrants and derivatives.
Tax: The firm provides a full range of tax services, including corporate and personal tax, tax planning (including off-shore and international), the taxation of employee benefits and share schemes, and VAT.

LANGUAGES: English, French, Italian, Portuguese, Spanish

For other recommended firms see pages 1485-1520

VASIL KISIL & PARTNERS

HEAD OFFICE

5/60 Zhylianska Street, Suite 1-2,
Kiev 01033, Ukraine
Tel: +380 44 220 5900 **Fax:** +380 44 220 4877

Email: vkp@vkp.kiev.ua

WORLDWIDE OFFICE CONTACTS

UKRAINE
5/60 Zhylianska Street, Suite 1-2, **Kiev** 01033
Tel: +380 44 220 5900 **Fax:** +380 44 220 4877
Email: vkp@vkp.kiev.ua

FIRM OVERVIEW

Managing partner: Oleg Y. Alyoshin
Senior partner: Vasil I Kisil

Number of partners worldwide: 7
Number of other lawyers worldwide: 22

AREAS OF PRACTICE:

Corporate	*%
Employment	*%
Foreign investments protection	*%
Intellectual property	*%
Litigation and arbitration	*%
Maritime	*%
Privatisation	*%
Real estate and construction	*%
Tax	*%

*Workload % not disclosed

FIRM OVERVIEW: The firm was founded in 1987, at the beginning of the democratic changes in the former USSR. All the partners have worked in Western law firms, and the firm was founded with the aim of emulating practice methods generally accepted in the West. It has a particular focus on work for international clients and inward and outward investment. The firm is a member of TERRALEX, a network of independent law firms.

INTERNATIONAL EXPERIENCE: Since its foundation the firm has been heavily involved in providing legal advice and support on various issues to international corporate clients and to the foreign law firms who act for them. As a local Ukrainian law firm it is permanent correspondent firm to a large number of international law firms, including ones with branch offices in Ukraine.

INTERNATIONAL CLIENTS: Include international companies and large Ukrainian enterprises, metallurgy, coal mining, heavy engineering, chemistry, high tech, agriculture, transport, general commodities trading companies, banks, religious and charitable organisations.

MAIN INTERNATIONAL AREAS OF PRACTICE:

Corporate: The firm specialises in corporate mergers, acquisitions, reorganisations and liquidations, the registration of foreign companies' representative offices, registration of affiliates and both joint ventures and 100 percent foreign-owned ventures in Ukraine.

Employment: Firm lawyers advise on all matters relating to Ukrainian employment law, including obtaining work permits for foreigners, registration with the immigration department, and employment, termination and trade union issues.

Foreign investments protection: Work covers all aspects of the registration and protection of foreign investments, including protection of investors' interests in court and arbitration.

Intellectual property: Together with licensed patent attorneys who specialise in the registration and protection of trade marks, patents and copyrights, the firm provides continuous support to its corporate clients in their day-to-day operations as well as when involved in litigation.

Ligitation: The firm handles domestic and international litigation and arbitration, including personal injury and consumer product liability cases in Ukraine and abroad.

Maritime: The firm advises clients and represents them in maritime cases in the Ukrainian courts.

Privatisation: The firm advises comprehensively on the privatisation of state-owned industrial and agricultural enterprises.

Real estate and construction: The firm provides advice on the acquisition of both commercial and residential property, throughout transactions. It helps clients obtain land land for perpetual and temporary use or in ownership, and also advises on all aspects of construction and development projects.

Tax: Clients range from large multinational companies to local enterprises and work covers all aspects of tax, including advice on joint ventures and other forms of cooperation.

LANGUAGES: English, French, German, Romanian, Russian, Ukrainian

V

VEIL ARMFELT JOURDE LA GARANDERIE

HEAD OFFICE

38 rue de Lisbonne,
75008 Paris, France
Tel: +33 1 56 69 56 62 **Fax:** +33 1 53 53 94 94

FIRM OVERVIEW

Partner: Henri Brandford Griffith

Number of partners worldwide: 15
Number of other lawyers worldwide: 25

AREAS OF PRACTICE:

Civil and commercial, litigation and arbitration	*%
Competition	*%
Employment	*%
Financial criminal litigation	*%
Intellectual property and new technologies	*%
M&A	*%
Tax	*%

* Workload % not disclosed

WORLDWIDE OFFICE CONTACTS

FRANCE
38 rue de Lisbonne, 75008 **Paris**
Tel: +33 1 56 69 56 62 **Fax:** +33 1 53 53 94 94

V

FIRM OVERVIEW: Veil Armfelt Jourde La Garanderie was established in 1990 through the merger of four separate practices. The firm is a partnership between French and English lawyers providing high quality services in the main areas of business law.

The firm comprises 40 lawyers, of which 15 are partners. Emphasis is placed on maintaining personal relationships with clients and working as a team. It is the firm's policy to adopt an informal yet professional interaction with clients and to promote personal case handling by the clients' preferred lawyers. It is the aim of the firm's lawyers to always dedicate the amount of time a client requires to any particular matter and to combine creativity with prudence, focusing on tailor-made solutions.

INTERNATIONAL EXPERIENCE: The firm's international experience derives mainly from significant cross-border mergers and acquisitions. The firm has also been actively involved in the restructuring of intergovernmental bodies.

INTERNATIONAL CLIENTS: The firm's international activity is based on strong relations developed with major global financial institutions and industrial companies.

MAIN INTERNATIONAL AREAS OF PRACTICE:

Corporate and M&A: The firm has experience of large deals including privatisation work, public offerings and corporate restructuring. Its lawyers are experienced in handling hostile takeovers. Major transactions have included the merger of Totalfina and Elf, for BNP in its hostile bids for Société Générale and Paribas, and for the French Treasury in the privatisation of Bull. It also acted in the restructuring of Publicis.

Tax: The firm has three dedicated tax partners and several other lawyers experienced in all aspects of tax advice, including issues arising out of corporate restructuring and international transactions.

Civil and commercial, litigation and arbitration: This is an area in which the firm has conducted several high profile cases in civil commercial matters. Financial litigation is a niche area and certain of the partners have specialised in arbitration, insolvency, or stock market disputes, for which the firm has a particular reputation.

Competition: Anti-trust lawyers assist the firm's major clients, appearing before both national and EU authorities and ensuring prompt compliance with merger control regulations.

Financial criminal litigation: This has developed as a specialist area for partner, Georges Jourde, who is well known for his advice and representation in proceedings of this nature.

Intellectual property and new technologies: The protection and exploitation of intellectual property rights (both trademarks and patents) and New Technologies are a growing area of expertise for the firm. A number of the partners are experienced in these areas of work.

Employment: Two of the partners, Marie-Alice Jourde and Dominique de La Garanderie specialise in Labour law, working with a team of dedicated associates.

LANGUAGES: English, French

For other recommended firms see pages 1485-1520

VELLANI & VELLANI

HEAD OFFICE

148, 18th East Street, Phase I, Defence Officers' Housing Authority
Karachi 75500, Pakistan
Tel: +92 21 580 1000 **Fax:** +92 21 580 2120
Email: email.khi@vellani.com

FIRM OVERVIEW

Managing partner: Fatehali W Vellani
Senior partner: B F Vellani

Number of partners worldwide: 2

AREAS OF PRACTICE:
Banking and finance .... *%
Corporate .... *%
Intellectual property .... *%
Tax .... *%
* Workload % not disclosed

FIRM OVERVIEW: Vellani & Vellani is a leading a law firm in Pakistan acting as legal consultants to a number of reputable clients in various fields, including beverages and foods, pharmaceuticals, petroleum, chemicals, cement, consumer durables, tobacco, edible oils, soaps and detergents, tea, vehicles, communications, banking and finance. Vellani & Vellani continues a practice first established in 1937 under the name of Wali Mohammad Vellani & Co and carried on under various names. It also incorporates the practice formerly known as Fatehali W. Vellani & Co.

INTERNATIONAL EXPERIENCE: Projects include petroleum projects such as petroleum concessions, exploration and production of oil and gas and the marketing of refined petroleum and the production and supply of natural gas and LPG; standardisation of the conditions of contract for the construction works of a major public sector manufacturing enterprise and its long term raw material purchase contracts; off-shore and on-shore syndicated loans and credit facilities; providing counsel on Pakistan Law issues and general legal assistance to domestic and foreign financial institutions providing finance to major projects, such as Power Generation and Port Infrastructure Projects, including the review of project documents, preparing Pakistan Law based finance and security documents, and reviewing off-shore finance documents; joint venture manufacturing and other projects in various industrial and commercial sectors, such as petroleum, pharmaceuticals, chemicals, food, engineering, vehicles, communications; corporate restructuring, mergers, acquisitions, divestments and tender offers; licensing of technology and trademarks and the grant of franchises; public flotation of shares.

INTERNATIONAL CLIENTS: Clients advised include those in the fields of banking, finance, shipping, pharmaceuticals, chemicals, pesticides, petroleum, cement, tobacco, beverages, edible oils, soaps and detergents, tea, vehicles, computers, communications, general services and other fields.

MAIN INTERNATIONAL AREAS OF PRACTICE: The firm provides legal services including consultancy services for corporate and other clients. The firm also provides intellectual property services. Additionally, the firm conducts cases and provides representation in courts and other tribunals and before arbitrators and experts.
General legal services: The firm specialises in commercial matters including the following: corporation work, anti-trust matters, finance and taxation, joint ventures, projects involving the grant and exploitation of government concessions, the setting up and operation of: manufacturing facilities, banking and financial institutions, trading and service companies, banking and financing transactions, syndicated loans, credit facilities, project financing, mergers, acquisitions and divestments, licensing and transfer of technology, the grant of franchises, agencies and distributorships, the incorporation of companies, private, public and listed, the public flotation and listing of securities and tender offers for listed securities
Intellectual property: The firm also specialises in intellectual property matters and provides services in the following fields and acts for a number of foreign corporations and associates in intellectual property matters: patents and designs, trade marks, copyright, internet domain names, unfair competition, licensing and franchising.
Patents: Patent services provided by the firm include searches with respect to new inventions, searches and opinions regarding the validity and scope of previously issued patents, and infringement investigations to determine if an article or process infringes a valid patent. The firm also offers comprehensive services in preparing, filing and prosecuting patent applications, oppositions and infringement litigation.
Trade marks: The firm serves its clients in every phase of the adoption and protection of trade marks and certification marks. This includes the carrying out of searches at the Trade Marks Registry for clearance and determining registrability of the mark, the preparation of trade mark applications and the representation of the client through every step of the process leading to the grant of registration.Following registration, the firm advises clients of the date of each renewal and being recorded at the Trade Marks Registry as the address for services for the client for the mark, the firm receives for and forwards to the client all communications received from the Trade Marks Registry. These communications include notices informing the client that its mark has been cited by the Trade Marks Registry in an application for the registration of another mark. Where required the firm also conducts a review of all marks which have been initially approved by the Trade Marks Registry in order to identify possible conflicts with the marks of its clients. These watch services afford an opportunity to oppose registration of conflicting marks which could damage a client's rights and also serve to detect possible infringements.The firm provides a full range of legal services in trade mark infringements, including litigation services.
Copyrights: Services offered to clients in the copyright field include infringement reviews, counselling and litigation, registration for all types of works. The firm represents both domestic and foreign copyright owners.
Licensing of Intellectual Property Rights and Transfers of Technology: Foreign and domestic licensing and assignment of various rights including patent, trade secret, trademark, copyright and 'know-how' constitute an important service to the firm's clients and are referred to generally as 'technology transfers'.

LANGUAGES: English, Urdu

WORLDWIDE OFFICE CONTACTS

PAKISTAN
148, 18th East Street, Phase I, Defence Officers' Housing Authority,
Karachi 75500
Tel: +92 21 580 1000 **Fax:** +92 21 580 2120
Email: email.khi@vellani.com

V

VIAL & PALMA

HEAD OFFICE

Isidora Goyenechea 3162, 7 Floor, Las Condes
Santiago 6760215, Chile
Tel: +56 2 240 6500 **Fax:** +56 2 240 6555

Email: vialpa@vialpa.cl
Website: www.vialpa.cl

WORLDWIDE OFFICE CONTACTS

CHILE
Isidora Goyenechea 3162, 7 Floor, Las Condes, **Santiago** 6760215
Tel: +56 2 240 6500 **Fax:** +56 2 240 6555
Email: vialpa@vialpa.cl

FIRM OVERVIEW

Senior partner: Juan Eduardo Palma Jara

Number of partners worldwide: 3
Number of other lawyers worldwide: 2

AREAS OF PRACTICE:

Corporate .... *%
E-commerce .... *%
Foreign investment .... *%
M&A and tax .... *%
Project finance .... *%
Telecommunications and media .... *%
* Workload % not disclosed

V

FIRM OVERVIEW: Founded in 1938, Vial y Palma is a full service corporate commercial law firm with a broad mix of local and international clients. It specialises in cross-border commercial transactions involving other Latin America countries including Panama, Peru, Ecuador, Colombia and Brazil. The firm is a member of the International Bar Association (IBA), the Union Internationale Des Avocats (UIA), and the Chilean, North American, Canadian and British Chambers of Commerce. Vial y Palma maintains strong links with several established law firms within the Latin American region, as well as with prominent North American and European law practices. In addition, Vial y Palma has a consultant member of the firm in the United Kingdom.

INTERNATIONAL EXPERIENCE: Recent transactions have included acting for British Petroleum (now British Petroleum Amoco or BP) in the incorporation in Chile of BP Chile Petrolera Limitada, a 100% subsidiary of British Petroleum Amoco; advising lenders and investors, project finance Nittetsu Mining Co Ltd in a joint venture for the construction and development of a copper concentrate flotation plant and a new copper mine in the North of Chile; acted for Inchcape Plc for its restructure in Latin America including the franchises of BMW, and New Holland; advising Canon Latin America Inc. the incorporation in Chile of Canon Chile S.A.; acted, as a member of the advising team, for the Luksic Group in the sale of Banco Santiago (Chile) to Banco Santander Central Hispano (España) as a result of the merger in Spain of Banco Santander and Banco Central Hispano; advised Compañía Cervecerías Unidas S.A. (CCU) (bottlers of Pepsi, Cadbury Schweppes and own products) on behalf of the Luksic Group in the purchase from Buenos Aires Embotelladora S.A. of its shareholding in Embotelladoras Chilenas Unidas S.A; Farmacias Ahumada S.A. in the purchase in Brazil of the Drogamed pharmaceutical chain and in the issue of new shares and their acquisition by Falabella (principal department store in Chile, with branches in Peru and Argentina) and The Latin Healthcare Fund, and in the development of a strategic alliance between the three companies.

INTERNATIONAL CLIENTS: The firm's client base includes Itochu Corporation, Lloyds TSB, Inchcape Plc, Canon Latin America, Inc., Toronto Dominion Bank, British Petroleum Amoco, Standard Wool (UK) Ltd., Nuskin International Inc., FCB Foot, Cone and Belding, Bozzel (True North Communications Inc.), Nittetsu Mining Co., Ltd., Solvay, Media Planning.

MAIN INTERNATIONAL AREAS OF PRACTICE:

Corporate: The firm advises on all matters arising out of the formation, financing and operation of business enterprises, in particular joint ventures and franchising operations entered into between foreign multinational and local enterprises, including intellectual property, tax and employment issues and expatriate visas.
E-commerce: The firm advises on a range of e-commerce and Internet law, including the current legal protection available to transactions and the procedures involved in the protection of websites and the protection of documents sent online.
Foreign investment: Working with clients ranging from large multinationals to local enterprises, the firm has substantial experience in the applicable laws and regulations and the practical steps that must be taken in their implementation, in connection with the entry into Chile of foreign investments of both debt and equity, giving clear guidance and step-by-step assistance at every stage.
M&A and tax: Recent transactions undertaken by the firm range from small private acquisitions to cross-border takeovers of listed companies. The firm's most recent cross-border experience has involved transactions in Chile, Peru and Brazil.
Project finance: The firm is active in project finance in the main sectors of the Chilean economy, in particular mining.
Telecommunications and media: The firm advises on the laws governing cable television, pay-per-view television, video-on-demand, Internet and other forms of digital media, including the contractual and commercial relationship between broadcasters, operators, suppliers and end-users of systems.

LANGUAGES: English, German, Spanish

For other recommended firms see pages 1485-1520

VICTOR CHU & CO

HEAD OFFICE

19th Floor, Tower II, The Gateway, 25 Canton Road, Kowloon
Hong Kong
Tel: +852 2956 1818 **Fax:** +852 2956 1161

Email: VC_CO@compuserve.com

FIRM OVERVIEW

Senior partner: Victor Chu

Number of partners worldwide: 5
Number of other lawyers worldwide: 20

AREAS OF PRACTICE:

Company and commercial 60%
Intellectual property 25%
Property 10%
Litigation 5%

FIRM OVERVIEW: Founded in 1985, Victor Chu & Co is a Hong Kong firm with 25 lawyers and 75 other staff. Principal areas of practice include corporate and commercial law, advising both domestic and overseas clients on public offerings, private debt and equity placements, mergers and acquisitions as well as setting up investment funds. The firm has an affiliated office in Beijing – a joint venture with China International Economic & Legal Consultants Corporation – which provides support for the firm's extensive involvement in transactions relating to China.

WORLDWIDE OFFICE CONTACTS

HONG KONG
19th Floor, Tower II, The Gateway, 25 Canton Road, Kowloon, **Hong Kong**
Tel: +852 2956 1818 **Fax:** +852 2956 1161
Email: VC_CO@compuserve.com

ASSOCIATED OFFICES

CHINA
First Eastern Hua Li International Investment Advisers Ltd., 11th floor, CNT Manhattan Building, 6 Chaoyangmen Beidajie, **Beijing** 100027
Tel: +86 10 8528 2505/2506 **Fax:** +86 10 8528 2508

First Eastern Hua Li International Investment Advisers Ltd, Room 709, Kerry Centre, 1515 Nanjing Road West, **Shanghai** 200040
Tel: +8621 5298 5788 **Fax:** +8621 5298 5792

THAILAND
Siam Premier International Law Office Ltd, 24-25th Floors, Thai Wah Tower II, No 21/147-150 South Sathorn Road, **Bangkok** 10120
Tel: +662 679 1333 **Fax:** +662 679 1314

V

INTERNATIONAL EXPERIENCE: The firm is involved in extensive China-related work. In corporate finance, the firm advises on investment, banking and trading activities, both to overseas companies with an interest in entering China and to Chinese entities wishing to operate in Hong Kong and elsewhere. Victor Chu & Co's litigation and real estate practices are becoming increasingly international, and are involved in transactions in Hong Kong, China and regionally.

INTERNATIONAL CLIENTS: The firm serves many listed companies in Hong Kong as well as international conglomerates from Asia, Australia, Europe and North America.

MAIN INTERNATIONAL AREAS OF PRACTICE:

Company and commercial: The company and commercial department covers all types of general corporate and commercial work. Work handled includes banking, investment funds, securities, listing, takeovers, mergers and China-related transactions. It also undertakes work in relation to listed and unlisted investment funds, both in relation to the Hong Kong stock exchange and to overseas exchanges.

Intellectual property: The firm handles all types of work relating to the registration and protection of intellectual property rights. This includes trademarks and service marks, copyright, industrial designs and patents worldwide and related litigation.

Property: The firm deals with tenancy agreements, mortgages, project finance, property development, and the sale and purchase of both commercial and residential properties.

Litigation: This department handles all aspects of commercial litigation and arbitration, including commercial crimes, disputes relating to sale of goods, building contracts and banking transactions. The firm is particularly active in resolution of disputes arising out of China-related matters.

LANGUAGES: Cantonese, English, French, Japanese, Mandarin and other dialects.

For other recommended firms see pages 1485-1520

VIEIRA DE ALMEIDA & ASSOCIADOS

HEAD OFFICE

Avenida Fontes Pereira de Melo, 3 - 11 th Floor,
1050-115 Lisbon, Portugal
Tel: +351 21 311 3400 **Fax:** +351 21 354 8939

Email: vieiradealmeida@vieiradealmeida.pt

FIRM OVERVIEW

Managing partner: João Vieira de Almeida
Senior partners: Vasco Vieira de Almeida, António Magalhães Cardoso

Number of lawyers worldwide: 47

AREAS OF PRACTICE:
Banking and finance ....*%
Corporate ....*%
EU and competition ....*%
Litigation and arbitration ....*%
M&A ....*%
Patents and trademarks ....*%
Pharmaceutical ....*%
Project finance ....*%
Telecommunications ....*%
* Workload % not disclosed

FIRM OVERVIEW: Founded in 1976, Vieira de Almeida & Associados' aim is to provide high quality, efficient and cost effective legal advice to large and small companies and projects. The firm's alliance with Gomez Acebo & Pombo, from Spain, Pinheiro Neto from Brazil, and Beccar Varela from Argentina consolidates the firm's presence of in the Latin American market.

INTERNATIONAL EXPERIENCE: The firm has been involved in the setting-up and restructuring of the activities of major international companies in Portugal as well as in the setting-up of Portuguese investments abroad. In the capital and securities market areas, the firm has acted as legal counsel for several transactions in the international markets both for Portuguese and foreign issuers/dealers including the setting up of Medium Term Notes and issues of notes there under, the issue of several equity and quasi equity instruments, as well as a variety of classical and innovative debt instruments. The firm has advised Portuguese banks in various debt placements abroad and advised international companies in transactions involving the purchase and sale of significant holdings in Lisbon-listed companies, including banks and other major Portuguese corporations. The firm has been strongly involved in the area of project finance, advising investors, lenders and public authorities. It has also provided legal counsel on European law matters, advising companies operating in different areas such as telecommunications, energy, transports, agriculture and banking.

WORLDWIDE OFFICE CONTACTS

PORTUGAL
Avenida Fontes Pereira de Melo, 3 - 11 th Floor, 1050-115 **Lisbon**
Tel: +351 21 311 3400 **Fax:** +351 21 354 8939
Email: vieiradealmeida@vieiradealmeida.pt

INTERNATIONAL CLIENTS: The firm's international clients operate in a range of sectors including financial, pharmaceutical, industry, transport, energy, entertainment, construction, and telecommunications.

MAIN INTERNATIONAL AREAS OF PRACTICE: Work undertaken includes corporate, M&A, project finance, telecoms, pharmaceutical, banking and finance, litigation and arbitration, EU and competition.

LANGUAGES: English, French, Portuguese, Spanish

For other recommended firms see pages 1485-1520

VIEIRA, REZENDE, BARBOSA E GUERREIRO

HEAD OFFICE

Av. Presidente Wilson, 231 - 27° andar,
Rio de Janeiro, RJ-Brazil 20030-021
Tel: +55 21 533 6240 **Fax:** +55 21 532 1946

Email: vrbg@vrbg.com.br
Website: www.vrbg.com.br

FIRM OVERVIEW

Managing Partners: Viviane Araújo Lima (Rio de Janeiro)
Luciane Cortez (São Paulo)
Senior Partners: Paulo Vieira, Cláudio Guerreiro

Number of partners worldwide: 8
Number of other lawyers worldwide: 20

AREAS OF PRACTICE:

Corporate	25%
Energy	15%
M&A	15%
Telecommunications and IT	15%
Anti-trust/competition	10%
Banking and finance	10%
Real estate	5%
Tax	5%

WORLDWIDE OFFICE CONTACTS

BRAZIL
Av. Presidente Wilson, 231 - 27° andar, **Rio de Janeiro,** 20030-021
Tel: +55 21 533 6240 **Fax:** +55 21 532 1946
Email: vrbg@vrbg.com.br

Rua Iguatemi, 192 - Cj. 122, **São Paulo,** 01451-010
Tel: +55 11 3040 3799 **Fax:** +55 11 3040 3770
Email: vrbgsp@vrbg.com.br

ASSOCIATED OFFICES

BRAZIL
Chaves & Chaves Advogados, SCS Setor Comercial Sul Quadra 1, Bloco G, Sala 606, **Brasília,** 70309-900
Tel: +55 61 321 0935 **Fax:** +55 61 322 6974
Email: chaves.chaves@zaz.com.br

V

FIRM OVERVIEW: The firm was established in 1995 and has a head office in Rio de Janeiro, a branch office in São Paulo and an associated office in Brasília. Members of Vieira, Rezende, Barbosa e Guerreiro come from a wide background and provide legal advice to a broad range of clients in every aspect of corporate law and matters concerning the investment of foreign capital. The firm's scope of activity encompasses areas as diverse as banking, project finance and infrastructure, insurance, mining and natural resources, privatisation, public utilities, real estate, tax, and transportation. It also has a significant antitrust/competition practice.

INTERNATIONAL EXPERIENCE: Since its foundation, Vieira, Rezende, Barbosa e Guerreiro has been involved in projects within the Brazilian privatisation programme, which resulted in a substantial increase in foreign investment in Brazil. Consequently, the firm has developed an international practice, and is strengthened by the fact that most members of the firm have worked with foreign clients and law firms or studied abroad.

INTERNATIONAL CLIENTS: The firm's clients include foreign companies, financial institutions and multilateral agencies conducting business in sectors such as banking and capital markets, insurance, power generation, transmission and distribution, oil and gas, mining, steel, telecommunications, information technology, real estate, railroads, ports, airports, logistics, water and sewage. Vieira, Rezende, Barbosa e Guerreiro Advogados has clients in Argentina, Australia, Canada, Chile, France, Germany, Holland, Italy, Japan, Norway, Portugal, South Africa, Spain, the UK, and the US.

MAIN INTERNATIONAL AREAS OF PRACTICE:

Anti-trust/competition: The firm has advised on a number of significant international transactions, with compliance to Brazilian anti-trust laws and regulations and representing clients before the anti-trust enforcement authorities.
Banking and finance: The firm covers a broad range of banking and financial activities, including international loan transactions, corporate and project finance, and leasing operations.
Energy and telecommunications: Work undertaken on infrastructure projects ranges from general corporate advice to counselling in specific regulatory matters.
Corporate and contracts: Vieira, Rezende, Barbosa e Guerreiro Advogados provide general corporate and commercial advice to a multitude of clients covering a wide range of sectors. The firm's experience encompasses corporate restructuring, formation and incorporation of new businesses and joint ventures, and assistance in shareholders' agreements, contracts, international trade, sales and marketing.
M&A: The firm has advised buyers and sellers, including the Federal Government in major and minor transactions, ranging from large M&A transactions, such as the privatisations of Vale do Rio Doce and TELEBRAS, to private acquisitions of small businesses.
Real estate: The firm has recently advised a major national telecoms company in the acquisition of property as part of its expansion into 27 Brazilian states.

LANGUAGES: English, French, German, Italian, Portuguese, Spanish

ADVOKATFIRMAN VINGE KB

HEAD OFFICE

Smålandsgatan 20, PO Box 1703,
SE-111 87 Stockholm, Sweden
Tel: + 46 8 614 30 00 **Fax:** + 46 8 614 31 90

Website: www.vinge.se

FIRM OVERVIEW

Managing partner: Michael Wigge

Number of partners worldwide: 84
Number of other lawyers worldwide: 161

AREAS OF PRACTICE:

Area	%
M&A	25%
Corporate	13%
Banking and finance	12%
Insolvency	8%
Tax	7%
Litigation and arbitration	6%
EU and competition	5%
Capital markets	5%
IT/media and intellectual property	4%
Insurance	4%
Employment	3%
Maritime and transport	1%
Environment	1%

V

FIRM OVERVIEW: Vinge was estabished through the merger of four Swedish law firms, and today is one of the largest commercial law firms in Scandinavia. It has a broad-based practice, offering a full range of legal services. In 1991 it formed the Scandinavian Law Alliance with the Danish firm Kromann Reumert and the Norwegian firm Thommessen Krefting Greve Lund. The firms share offices in London and Brussels.

INTERNATIONAL EXPERIENCE: Vinge has participated in most major mergers and acquisitions in Sweden in recent years, many of them cross-border transactions. The firm also has a large market share in debt and equity placements on the Euromarket and other non-Swedish securities markets. It has acted in a large number of domestic and cross-border lease financing transactions. It has helped several foreign financial institutions set up local subsidiaries or branches. The firm has helped to establish international telecommunications joint ventures in Europe and overseas, as well as helping introduce commercial television and radio in the Nordic and Baltic states. Vinge was one of the earliest Scandinavian law firms to develop an active EU competition practice, opening an office in Brussels in 1989. It is the only Scandinavian law firm active in China, through its offices in Hong Kong and Shanghai.

LANGUAGES: Dutch, English, French, German, Spanish, Swedish, Mandarin

WORLDWIDE OFFICE CONTACTS

BELGIUM
Rue du Luxembourg 3, BE-1000 **Brussels**
Tel: + 32 2 501 07 00 **Fax:** + 32 2 501 07 07

CHINA
Room2363, West Building, Jin Jiang Hotel, 59 Mao Ming Road South, **Shangai** 200020
Tel: + 86 21 6472 0732 **Fax:** + 86 21 6445 0150

FRANCE
21 Rue Jean Goujon, 75008 **Paris**
Tel: + 33 1 53 53 42 30 **Fax:** + 33 1 53 53 42 31

HONG KONG
2003 Hutchison House, 10 Harcourt Road, Central, **Hong Kong**
Tel: + 852 25 23 61 49 **Fax:** + 852 28 10 53 43

SWEDEN
Nils Ericsonsgatan 17, P O Box 11025, SE-404 21 **Gothenburg**
Tel: + 46 31 722 3500 **Fax:** + 46 31 722 37 00
Email: gbg@vinge.se

Rådhustorget b, PO Box 1064, SE- 251 10 **Helsingborg,**
Tel: + 46 42 24 80 80 **Fax:** + 46 42 24 80 85
Email: hbg@vinge.se

Östergatan 30, P O Box 4255, SE-203 13 **Malmö**
Tel: + 46 40 664 55 00 **Fax:** + 46 40 664 55 01
Email: malmo@vinge.se

UNITED KINGDOM
42 New Broad Street, **London** EC2M 2JD
Tel: + 44 20 7920 3000 **Fax:** + 44 20 7920 3099

For other recommended firms see pages 1485-1520

VINSON & ELKINS LLP

HEAD OFFICE

1001 Fannin, 2300 First City Tower,
Houston, TX 77002-6760, USA
Tel: +1 713 758 2222 **Fax:** +1 713 758 2346

Website: www.velaw.com

FIRM OVERVIEW

Managing partner: Harry M. Reasoner

Number of partners worldwide: 318
Number of other lawyers worldwide: 458

AREAS OF PRACTICE:

Litigation	30%
Corporate finance	9%
Property	6%
Banking	5%

FIRM OVERVIEW: Established in Houston in 1917, Vinson & Elkins has 776 lawyers, 393 of whom are based in its head office while the others are spread across its other US offices in Austin, Dallas, New York and Washington DC and its foreign offices in London, Moscow, Beijing and Singapore.

INTERNATIONAL EXPERIENCE: The firm's international practice has broad experience in energy, project finance and development, construction, M&A, privatisations, power, capital markets financings, insolvency/work-outs and litigation and arbitration. Notable transactions in which it has been involved include Sutton Bridge Project, a 790MW gas-fired combined -cycle power plant in England involving the offering and sale of £195 million and US150 million in bonds for the construction and term financing; Corridor Block Gas Project, a US$1.2 billion project in Indonesia, involving the development of gas reserves in South Sumatra, construction of a large gas-processing plant and related field pipelines, construction of a 541km pipeline, exchange of natural gas for crude oil and export of the crude oil; Aguaytia; an integrated gas/power project in Peru involving the development of a 300 BCF gas field, processing plant, 224km gas pipeline and a 105km liquids pipeline, a fractionation facility and a 398km transmission line across the Andes.

INTERNATIONAL CLIENTS: The firm represents clients around the world from the telecommunications, infrastructure, power, mining, oil and gas, refining, petrochemicals, power and other sectors as well as export credit agencies and other institutions.

LANGUAGES: Arabic, Cantonese, Chinese, Dutch, French, German, Greek, Gujarati, Hebrew, Hindi, Italian, Latin, Mandarin, Polish, Portuguese, Punjabi, Russian, Spanish, Taiwanese, Urdu

WORLDWIDE OFFICE CONTACTS

CHINA (PEOPLE'S REPUBLIC OF)
20/F Beijing Silver Tower, #2 Dong San Huan Bei Lu,
Chaoyang District, **Beijing** 100027
Tel: +8610 6410 6300 **Fax:** +8610 6410 6360
Email: hlee@velaw.com

RUSSIA
16 Ulitsa Spiridonovka, Second Floor, 103001 **Moscow**
Tel: +7 095 956 1995 **Fax:** + 7 095 956 1996 or
US satellite fax: +1 212 803 0142
Email: nmorozova@velaw.com

SINGAPORE
6 Battery Road, #39-01, **Singapore** 049909
Tel: + 65 536 8300 **Fax:** + 65 536 8311
Email: sdavis@velaw.com

UNITED KINGDOM
Regis House, 45 King William Street, **London** EC4R 9AN
Tel: +44 20 7618 6000 **Fax:** +44 20 7618 6001
Email: jlamaster@velaw.com

USA
One American Center, Suite 2700, 600 Congress Avenue,
Austin, Texas 78701-3200
Tel: + 1 512 495 8400 **Fax:** + 1 512 495 8612
Email: dwood@velaw.com

3700 Trammell Crow Center, 2001 Ross Avenue,
Dallas, Texas 75201-2975
Tel: + 1 214 220 7700 **Fax:** + 1 214 220 7716
Email: jchapman@velaw.com

666 Fifth Ave, 26th Floor, **New York**, NY 101031-0400
Tel: +1 917 206 8000 **Fax:** +1 917 206 8100
Email: pweller@velaw.com

The Willard Office Building, 1455 Pennsylvania Avenue,
NW **Washington, DC** 20004-1008
Tel: + 1 202 639 6500 **Fax:** + 1 202 639 6604
Email: jchapoton@velaw.com

WORLDWIDE OFFICES

UNITED KINGDOM

Regis House, 45 King William Street, London EC4R 9AN

Managing partner: John C LaMaster
Contact: John C LaMaster

Number of lawyers: 14

Office profile: The firm established its London office over 25 years ago, having been active in the US and the rest of Europe for many years. In 1994 it established a multi-national partnership (MNP) under the rules of the English Law Society to allow it to practise English as well as US law, and now employs English solicitors as well as US attorneys. The office acts as a coordinating centre in Europe, the Middle East, Africa, Russia and the former Soviet Union and advises clients operating out of the US, London and elsewhere in Europe. It has a broad-based UK and international commercial practice, with the core areas including project development and finance, energy and water infrastructure projects, corporate and securities advice and M&A.

VOGEL & VOGEL

HEAD OFFICE

30 avenue d'Iéna, 75 116 Paris,
France
Tel: + 33 1 53 67 76 20 **Fax:** + 33 1 53 67 76 25

Email: info@vogel-vogel.com
Website: www.vogel-vogel.com

WORLDWIDE OFFICE CONTACTS

BELGIUM
9, avenue des Gaulois, B-1040 **Brussels**
Tel: + 32 2 737 71 06 **Fax:** + 32 2 733 95 78

FRANCE
30 avenue d'Iéna, 75 116 **Paris**
Tel: + 33 1 53 67 76 20 **Fax:** + 33 1 53 67 76 25

GERMANY
Friedrich Ebert Anlage, 44, D-60325 **Frankfurt àm Main**
Tel: + 49 69 71 701 125 **Fax:** + 49 69 71 701 410

FIRM OVERVIEW

Managing partner: Louis Vogel
Senior partner: Joseph Vogel

Number of partners worldwide: 2
Number of other lawyers worldwide: 25

AREAS OF PRACTICE:
Competition and distribution law 80%
French, European and international business law 20%

V

FIRM OVERVIEW: Established in France in 1990, Vogel and Vogel currently employs 26 lawyers. It specialises in EU and French competition law, distribution law, product liability and automobile law, and is active in French, European and international business law. The firm works closely with economists.

INTERNATIONAL EXPERIENCE: The firm has considerable experience in European competition and business law, and is especially involved in business between France, Germany and Austria (the establishment of companies or branches, sales and distribution, dealer networks, product liability, debt collection); the US, the UK and France; Japan and Europe.

INTERNATIONAL CLIENTS: The firms clients include Colgate-Palmolive, Daewoo, Daimler Chrysler, Harley Davidson, Renault, Seat SA, Shiseido, Skoda and Volkswagen AG.

MAIN INTERNATIONAL AREAS OF PRACTICE:
European competition law: At European level, the firm advises on competition law, the validity of exclusive distribution contracts, selective distribution agreements, supply agreements, franchise and agency contracts, actions based on article 81 or 82 of the Treaty, merger notifications to the Merger Task Force, competition cases before the Commission, the Court of First Instance and the Court of Justice of the European Communities.
French competition law: The firm advises on matters such as dominant position or economic dependence, rules on buying power, mergers, general conditions of sale, restrictive agreements, competition cases before the French Competition Council and the Competition Chamber of the Court of Appeals of Paris. It has also developed special expertise in competition issues regarding telecoms, media and information technology.
Distribution law: Vogel & Vogel has broad experience in distribution law, particularly in exclusive distribution, exclusive supply, automobile distribution, franchising, selective distribution and agency agreements. The firm advises clients in all areas of distribution contracts such as negotiation, performance, assignment and termination of the contract. The firm also provides legal advice in actions arising out of distribution contracts (where the contract has been terminated or assigned, actions regarding the validity of the contract, labour law matters linked to the termination of the contract, debt collection and insolvency procedures).
Automobile distribution law: The firm has broad experience of all automobile distribution contracts (dealership, service agent, resale agent, sale contracts, financing agreements, leasing contract), guarantees in the automobile distribution business (sureties, securities, letters of intention, bank guarantees, liens, fixed or floating charges) and litigation regarding the cancellation of automobile distribution contracts, debt collection, bankruptcy, litigation linked to product liability for cars and consumer law.
General EU law: The firm advises clients in the fields of free circulation of goods, persons, services and capital, intellectual property rights and state aids.
French, European and international business law: The firm advises on unfair competition law, general conditions of sale, bankruptcy law, intellectual property, misleading advertising, product liability (defects or incorrect contractual information, hidden flaws, violation of security obligation) and criminal responsibility of directors.

LANGUAGES: English, French, German, Spanish

For other recommended firms see pages 1485-1520

VOISIN & CO

HEAD OFFICE

PO Box 31, Templar House, Don Road, St Helier,
Jersey JE4 8NU, Channel Islands
Tel: +44 1534 500 300 **Fax:** +44 1534 500 350

Email: enquiries@voisinlaw.com
Website: www.voisinlaw.com

WORLDWIDE OFFICE CONTACTS

CHANNEL ISLANDS
PO Box 31, Templar House, Don Road, St Helier,
Jersey JE4 8NU
Tel: +44 1534 500 300 **Fax:** +44 1534 500 350
Email: enquiries@voisinlaw.com

FIRM OVERVIEW

Managing partner: Ian W. S. Strang
Senior partner: Michael M. G. Voisin

Number of partners worldwide: 8
Number of other lawyers worldwide: 15

AREAS OF PRACTICE:

Area	%
International work	20%
Litigation	20%
Trusts	20%
Banking and finance	15%
Company law	15%
Probate law	10%

FIRM OVERVIEW: Established in 1963, Voisin & Co is one of Jersey's longest established law firms, with more than 60 staff based in Saint Helier. The firm offers advice on a wide range of legal and commercial matters to several international banks, fund managers and fiduciary service providers, as well as to a considerable number of international clients. The firm has strong connections within the City of London and the legal community in Paris. In addition, Jersey's position as a financial centre has allowed the firm to acquire expertise in numerous aspects of private international law.

INTERNATIONAL EXPERIENCE: Includes acting for several international banks in raising cost-effective regulatory capital; representing a number of UK plcs in establishing and administering ESOPs; advising on and establishing a number of offshore securitisation programmes, including the first Islamic Shariah compliant securitisation of US estate leases; acting for a leading French bank in relation to the creation and subsequent dismantling of several debt defeasance schemes; and acting for and advising a leading French financial institution in relation to the creation of an offshore fiduciary services company.

INTERNATIONAL CLIENTS: The firm's international clients include PricewaterhouseCoopers (France), BRED Banque Populaire, Bank of Ireland and Royal Bank of Scotland.

MAIN INTERNATIONAL AREAS OF PRACTICE:

Banking and finance: The firm is particularly experienced in lending and credit work and the preparation of security and guarantee documentation. It also handles the establishment of collective investment fund schemes through unit trusts, open-ended investment companies or limited partnerships.

Litigation: Most of the firm's litigation work consists of complex issues often involving cross-jurisdictional asset tracing or claims founded on breach of trust. The firm is also experienced in conducting commercial disputes and in asset recovery.

Probate law: The firm handles a considerable amount of probate work with an international dimension, and maintains an extremely efficient and motivated estate department.

International work: The firm works in close collaboration with associated trust company Volaw Trust & Corporate Services Limited and is able to provide professional corporate trustee services, company incorporation, secretarial and accounting facilities to clients wishing to conduct international business in an offshore context.

Company and trust law: The firm has wide experience of fiduciary services and in trust and company law (particularly in the areas of tax and succession planning).

LANGUAGES: French, Spanish

VON ROSPATT VON DER OSTEN PROSS

HEAD OFFICE

Kaiser-Friedrich-Ring 56, PO Box 11 09 35,
D-40547 Düsseldorf, Germany
Tel: +49 211 577 2450 **Fax:** +49 211 577 24555

Email: mail@rospatt.de
Website: www.rospatt.de

WORLDWIDE OFFICE CONTACTS

GERMANY
Kaiser-Friedrich-Ring 56, PO Box 11 09 35, D-40547 **Düsseldorf**
Tel: +49 211 577 2450 **Fax:** +49 211 577 24555
Email: mail@rospatt.de

Janderstraße 8, D-68199 **Mannheim**
Tel: +49 621 8455375 **Fax:** +49 621 8455376

FIRM OVERVIEW

Contact partners: Ulrich Pross
Bernward Zollner
Maximilian von Rospatt

Number of partners worldwide: 6
Number of other lawyers worldwide: 3

AREAS OF PRACTICE:
Copyrights .... *%
Design protection .... *%
Licensing .... *%
Litigation, arbitration, counselling on international property .... *%
Patents, utility models .... *%
Product liability .... *%
Trademarks .... *%
Unfair competition .... *%
* Workload % not disclosed

V

FIRM OVERVIEW: Founded in 1950, von Rospatt, von der Osten, Pross is a specialist intellectual property practice. It handles patent (all industrial sectors), trademark, copyright, design protection and unfair competition litigation before all German courts, especially the Duesseldorf District Court and the Duesseldorf Court of Appeal. The firm represents clients in trademark and design protection matters before the German Patent and Trademark Office, the German Federal Patent Court and Federal Supreme Court, WIPO, OHIM and the European Court of Justice. In 1998, the firm opened a second office in Mannheim. The firm is frequently co-operating with patent attorneys and law firms from all around the world.

INTERNATIONAL EXPERIENCE: The firm has played a prominent role in domestic and European IP litigation. It is a leading developer of strategies in cross border litigation. The firm handles major cases in all technical fields, especially in new technologies such as biotechnology and semi-conductors. It also handles leading trademark cases, e.g. first action on art. 63 CTMR against OHIM before the European Court of Justice

INTERNATIONAL CLIENTS: The firm's client base is European, North American and Far East. Major clients are companies in the fields of biotechnology, chemistry, electronics (semi-conductors and information technology), health care (pharmaceuticals and medicine technology), mechanical engineering, banking and insurance, furniture, fashion and jewellery.

MAIN INTERNATIONAL AREAS OF PRACTICE: Work handled includes litigation, arbitration, counselling on international property, patents, utility models, trademarks, design protection, copyrights, licensing, unfair competition, and product liability.

LANGUAGES: English

**VON ROSPATT
VON DER OSTEN
PROSS**

For other recommended firms see pages 1485-1520

VON WOBESER Y SIERRA S.C

HEAD OFFICE

G. González Camarena No. 1100, 7th Floor, Santa Fe Centro de Ciudad, Del. Alvaro Obregón, 01210 Mexico, D.F. Mexico City, Mexico
Tel: +525 258 1000 **Fax:** +525 258 1098

Email: vwyssc@infosel.net.mx
Website: www.vwys.com.mx

WORLDWIDE OFFICE CONTACTS

MEXICO
G. González Camarena No. 1100, 7th Floor, Santa Fe Centro de Ciudad, Del. Alvaro Obregón, 01210 Mexico, D.F. **Mexico City**, Mexico
Tel: +525 258 1000 **Fax:** +525 258 1098
Email: vwyssc@infosel.net.mx

FIRM OVERVIEW

Managing partner: Claus Von Wobeser
Senior partner: Claus Von Wobeser

Number of partners worldwide: 5
Number of other lawyers worldwide: 26

AREAS OF PRACTICE:

Corporate and commercial	40%
M&A	25%
Intellectual property	20%
Arbitration	10%
Tax	5%

FIRM OVERVIEW: Founded in 1986, Von Wobeser & Sierra provides legal services to national and foreign clients. The firm has established close links with law firms in Asia, Canada, Latin America, the EU, the US, and with other law firms in the major cities of Mexico. Comprising over 30 lawyers, including some North American and EU nationals, the firm is dedicated to providing a full range of legal advice. Many attorneys are graduates from some of the most reputable universities in Mexico, and have undertaken specific legal studies at other universities in the US, Canada and some EU countries. Members of the firm belong to the American Bar Association, the International Bar Association, the Mexican Bar Association, the Quebec Bar Association, the American Arbitration Association and the International Chamber of Commerce.

INTERNATIONAL EXPERIENCE: The firm has handled a range of international transactions including the drafting of international commercial contracts, the international registration of patents and trademarks, the application of international tax treaties, and due to the current wave of Mexican mergers and acquisitions, a significant number of concentration cases. The firm also has a large arbitration practice, which involves the firm's lawyers with parties and laws of other countries, as well as international arbitration agreements and institutions.

MAIN INTERNATIONAL AREAS OF PRACTICE:

Arbitration: The firm acts as arbitrators and as counsel for major multinational companies involved in international commercial disputes. Specific members of the firm have also participated in arbitration proceedings as witnesses in Mexican commercial law. Work undertaken includes advising on all commercial arbitration proceedings, including those conducted according to the Rules of the International Chamber of Commerce, the Inter-American Arbitration Commission, the UNCITRAL and in relation to NAFTA's Chapters 11 (investment) and 19 (review and dispute settlement in anti-dumping and countervailing duty matters).

Commercial: The firm handles the preparation and/or negotiation of commercial agreements such as distribution, supply, agency, purchase and sale of assets, and transportation.

Corporate: The firm handles a range of corporate work ranging from the planning of corporate structures to the incorporation of companies, including the preparation of shareholder agreements, joint ventures and other corporate arrangements. It has acted in a number of corporate restructurings, several of which involved the principal Mexican financial, industrial and commercial groups as well as important foreign companies, including some listed in the Fortune 500.Von Wobeser & Sierra advises on company legal audits and due diligence investigations for acquisitions, joint ventures or other transactions. It also handles the day to day corporate matters of many of its clients including acting as corporate secretaries, examiners (or board members) of a significant number of client companies, as well as attorneys-in-fact. Other corporate work undertaken includes the preparation of minutes of shareholders meetings, granting of powers of attorney, and transfer of shares together with all registrations required under Mexican law.

Intellectual Property: The firm advises on the protection or registration and maintenance of patents, utility models, industrial designs, integrated circuits, vegetal variations, industrial secrets, trademarks, slogans and copyrights, licensing, franchising and related agreements, transfer of technology, unfair competition, arbitration, and administrative litigation and litigation before district and circuit courts. In addition, it advises clients on industrial property mediation and/or arbitration, intellectual property due diligence, unfair competition, advertising and entertainment, as well as related anti-trust matters. The firm has been involved in landmark industrial property litigations in Mexico and has developed special programs for protection against various types of counterfeiting and infringement of intellectual property rights. Members of the firm have also acted as witnesses in Mexican industrial property law. Von Wobeser & Sierra works closely with the government where appropriate and is actively involved in promoting the development and revision of intellectual property laws in Mexico.

M&A: The firm provides a full range of services to clients desiring to merge with or to acquire other companies in Mexico. It advises both purchasers and sellers on domestic and international transactions including full-scale mergers, restructuring transactions, joint ventures, asset purchases, and spin-offs.

Tax: The firm provides advisory services and representation in administrative proceedings before the corresponding tax agencies as well as litigation in the Federal Tax Tribunal and other federal courts. The firm specialises in the taxation of foreign individuals and companies in Mexico, and double-taxation treaties to which Mexico is party.

LANGUAGES: English, French, German, Italian, Spanish

VOSSIUS & PARTNER

HEAD OFFICE

Siebertstrasse 4,
81675 Munich, Germany
Tel: +49 89 41 30 40˙ **Fax:** +49 89 41 30 4111

Email: info@vossiusandpartner.com
Website: www.vossiusandpartner.com

FIRM OVERVIEW

Senior partner: Paul Tauchner

Number of partners worldwide: 1
Number of other lawyers worldwide: 9

AREAS OF PRACTICE:

Trade marks, designs and unfair competition	20%
Chemistry and pharmacology	19%
Physics	18%
Mechanics	17%
Biotechnology	15%
IT	11%

FIRM OVERVIEW: Vossius & Partner was established in 1961. The firm specialises in intellectual property, including patents, utility models, trademarks, design patents, software protection, and related licensing and litigation matters. It currently comprises approximately 20 German and European Patent Attorneys and a number of Attorneys-at Law, as well as a trained staff of 20 further associates with postgraduate degrees in biotechnology, physics, mechanical engineering, and electrical engineering (IT specialists). The firm also has a Japanese patent specialist with an engineering degree. The firm's total staff comprises approximately 130 persons including paralegals and technical translators. The firm's Munich base gives it close proximity to the European Patent Office, the German Patent and Trademark Office, and the German Federal Patent Court. Vossius & Partner is also closely involved in patent litigation and invalidation matters before the competent courts in Germany as well as in trademark litigation and cancellation matters in Germany as well as before OHIM in Alicante. Patent litigation, including cross-border litigation, is done predominantly with renowned law firms who specialize in this field both within and outside Germany.

INTERNATIONAL EXPERIENCE: Vossius & Partner are amongst the most prolific of firms of patent attorneys in the field of patent registration, both nationally and in Europe. In 2000, for the third consecutive year it was voted No.1 among leading firms specialising in European patent applications in the annual World Intellectual Property Survey. Among the internationally litigated cases with which the firm has been involved are the terfenadine prodrug infringement case, the diltiazem manufacturing case, the colour capsule trademark infringement proceedings and the paclitaxel (Taxol) and Viagra patent opposition matters.

INTERNATIONAL CLIENTS: The firm represents major companies and academic and scientific institutions worldwide, with a particular emphasis on the US, Japan and Europe. Clients include 3M, NEC, Max Planck Society, HGS, NSC, Hoeclist Marion Roussel (Aventis Pharmaceuticals), Bristol-Myers, Squibb Company, SmithKline Beecham, Sumitomo Chemicals.

WORLDWIDE OFFICE CONTACTS

GERMANY
Siebertstrasse 4, 81675 **Munich**
Tel: +49 89 41 30 40 **Fax:** +49 89 41 30 4111
Email: info@vossiusandpartner.com

MAIN INTERNATIONAL AREAS OF PRACTICE:

Biotechnology: Presentation and prosecution of patents. The firm has worked on HSA, BGH, Insulin, Antibody technology (monoclonals, single chain and humanized etc), Erythropoietin, Ribozymes, recombinant viruses, transgenic plans and animals, Ti plasmid technology and other systems for the production of transgenic plants and animals.

Chemistry and pharmacology: All the attorneys in the department hold doctorates in chemistry as well as having additional experience in organic and inorganic chemistry, technical and pharmaceutical chemistry, pharmacology and biochemistry, polymer chemistry and other areas. The department handles the presentation and prosecution of patent applications and trademark protection for its clients.

Mechanics, Physics, Electronics and IT: The work of the department covers developments in high voltage and electrical power engineering, telecommunications, computer related technology, physics, nuclear technology, medical and other related fields.

Trademarks, designs, and unfair competition: The Trademark and Design group is located in its own headquarters in Munich's Bogenhausen district. It is staffed by Attorneys-at-Law who are admitted to various local and regional courts as well as the German Patent and Trademark Office, the European Patent office, the Federal Patent Court and the Office for Harmonization in the Internal Market in Alacante. The attorneys also specialise in unfair competition (passing off), licence agreements and common and commercial law.

LANGUAGES: English, German

 For other recommended firms see pages 1485-1520

WACHTELL, LIPTON, ROSEN & KATZ

HEAD OFFICE

51 West 52nd Street
New York, NY 10019, USA
Tel: +1 212 403 1000 **Fax:** +1 212 403 2000

Email: info@wlrk.com
Website: www.wlrk.com

WORLDWIDE OFFICE CONTACTS

USA
51 West 52nd Street, **New York,** NY 10019
Tel: +1 212 403 1000 **Fax:** +1 212 403 2000
Email: info@wlrk.com

FIRM OVERVIEW

Managing partner: Richard D. Katcher

Number of partners worldwide: 70
Number of other lawyers worldwide: 102

AREAS OF PRACTICE:

Anti-trust .... *%
Bankruptcy and creditors' rights .... *%
Corporate .... *%
Employment and benefits .... *%
Litigation .... *%
Real estate .... *%
* Workload % not disclosed

FIRM OVERVIEW: Founded in 1967, Wachtell, Lipton, Rosen & Katz is one of the most prominent business law firms in the United States. The firm specialises in large merger and acquisition transactions, sensitive litigation matters, corporate restructurings and refinancings. Comprising 172 lawyers, the firm handles demanding, high-profile transactions on a personalised basis. The relatively small nature of the practice, and the absence of repetitive, standardised transactions, means that the firm's lawyers each have a broad range of skills and experience. Clients include industrial firms, financial institutions, securities firms, healthcare providers, technology companies and news and information systems companies, including a number of Fortune 500 companies.

INTERNATIONAL EXPERIENCE: Corporate work handled in the last year includes representing Warner-Lambert Co. in its US$93.4 billion transaction with Pfizer Inc.; VoiceStream Wireless Corporation in its US$50.7 billion transaction with Deutsche Telecom; Vivendi in its US$52.0 billion acquisition of Seagram Company and Canal Plus S.A.; Monsanto Company in its US$26.5 billion transaction with Pharmacia & Upjohn Inc.; Motorola Inc. in its US$17 billion acquisition of General Instrument Corporation; Terra Networks S.A. in its US$12.5 billion acquisition of Lycos, Inc.; Philip Morris Companies, Inc. in its US$19.2 billion acquisition of Nabisco Holdings Corp.; Firstar Corporation in its US$21.2 billion merger with U.S. Bancorp; and Donaldson, Lufkin & Jenrette in its US$13.6 billion transaction with Credit Suisse First Boston. The firm also represents Pinault-Printemps-Redoute S.A. in its strategic investment in Gucci Group, as well as in a number of other group acquisitions; and AT&T Corp. in its acquisitions and pending restructuring. In addition, the firm represented Vivendi Environnement S.A. and Martha Stewart Living Omnimedia, Inc. in their initial public offerings.

MAIN INTERNATIONAL AREAS OF PRACTICE:

Corporate: The firm has handled some of the largest and most complex United States and international transactions. It advises on a range of corporate matters including mergers and acquisitions, public offerings, financial products and financing transactions. Wachtell, Lipton, Rosen & Katz also counsels companies, and their boards of directors, on difficult and sensitive corporate disclosure, governance and policy issues.

Litigation: The firm handles a wide variety of high profile, complex transactions for major corporations and leading financial institutions. Work undertaken includes precedent-setting securities and corporate governance litigation, and libel and First Amendment cases. The firm has been involved in landmark corporate governance litigation cases in Delaware including the Household, Revlon, Macmillan, Interco, Time Warner, and Paramount cases.

Bankruptcy and creditors' rights: The firm's bankruptcy and creditors' rights practice focuses on advising banks, insurance companies, investment funds and securities derivatives dealers as creditors in national and multinational bankruptcy cases and restructurings. Its lawyers work with the firm's corporate group in handling complicated acquisitions of businesses in bankruptcy or financial distress, highly leveraged transactions, and leading-edge transactions involving significant creditors' rights issues. Recent work includes representation of the official creditors' committees of Montgomery Ward Holding Corp., Vencor Inc. and United Companies Financial Corp., the senior lenders to BREED Technologies, Inc., Fruit of the Loom, Ltd., Paging Network, Inc., Bruno's Supermarkets, Inc. and the bondholders of Integrated Health Services, Inc.

Anti-trust: The firm's anti-trust practice focuses on mergers and acquisitions, government investigations, international anti-trust, and banking anti-trust issues. Wachtell, Lipton, Rosen & Katz analyses transactions to determine whether they raise anti-trust issues, develops strategies to address those issues, and represents clients before the United States Department of Justice, the United States Federal Trade Commission, the Board of Governors of the Federal Reserve System, state attorneys general, foreign anti-trust enforcement authorities, and in anti-trust litigation challenging transactions. Recent transactions handled by the firm that were subject to full investigations by and negotiation of consent decrees with the anti-trust authorities include AT&T Corp./MediaOne Group, Inc., Fort James Corp./Georgia-Pacific Corp., Alcoa, Inc./Reynolds Metals Company and British Petroleum Co. plc/Amoco Corp.

Tax: The firm's tax practice focuses on United States and international tax matters, primarily in connection with structuring complex mergers and acquisitions transactions, as well as divestitures, restructurings, and spin-offs. The firm's tax group also reviews the tax implications of structuring complicated financial instruments.

Employment and benefits: The firm's executive compensation and employee benefits practice focuses primarily on compensation and benefit issues in connection with mergers and acquisitions and other corporate transactions.

Real estate: The firm's real estate group focuses on mergers and acquisitions of REITs and other real estate companies and portfolios, strategic joint ventures, major development projects, structuring real estate opportunity funds, innovative capital markets transactions, and restructurings.

LANGUAGES: English

W

WALDER WYSS & PARTNERS

HEAD OFFICE

Münstergasse 2, PO Box 4081,
8022 Zurich, Switzerland
Tel: + 41 1 265 75 11 **Fax:** + 41 1 265 75 50
Email: reception@wwp.ch
Website: www.wwp.ch

FIRM OVERVIEW

Managing partner: Didier Sangiorgio
Number of partners worldwide: 14
Number of other lawyers worldwide: 26

AREAS OF PRACTICE:

Banking and finance	20%
M&A, restructuring, joint ventures, IPOs, privatisation	20%
IT, telecommunications and multimedia	15%
Litigation, arbitration and ADR	15%
Intellectual property	10%
Energy, utilities and public transport	5%
Insurance	5%
Technology transfer	5%
Venture capital and private equity	5%

W

FIRM OVERVIEW: WW&P is one of Switzerland's leading law firms, specialising in corporate and commercial law, banking and finance, intellectual property and competition law, and dispute resolution. WW&P seeks to establish a leading position in specific sectors and product areas. Its national and international network of correspondents and partners from a broad range of disciplines is selected according to the highest standards of professional competence.

INTERNATIONAL EXPERIENCE: WW&P handles a range of international transactions. The firm is regularly retained by large corporate clients and investment banks. Most of the firm's lawyers have gained international experience by obtaining postgraduate degrees from foreign universities and/or by working for law firms abroad.

INTERNATIONAL CLIENTS: WW&P's client base is diverse, but predominantly international, and includes multinational industrial companies, banks and financial institutions, investment banks and international organisations.

MAIN INTERNATIONAL AREAS OF PRACTICE:

Banking and finance: WW&P acts for Swiss banks, broker-dealers and insurance companies as well as for leading European and US commercial and investment banks. It handles domestic and international banking, securitisations, infrastructure and project finance, domestic and cross-border leasing, structured financial instruments as well as over-the-counter and exchange-traded derivatives. WW&P advises on all aspects of Swiss securities laws and regulations, including public equity and debt offerings, government finance, private placements and investment fund offerings.
Insurance: WW&P advises on insurance matters, including engagements regarding the establishment of agencies and branches, the formation of new insurance companies, cross-border provision of insurance services and contemplated acquisitions of, or joint ventures with, existing insurance companies. WW&P represents clients in major projects related to the insurance business including incorporation, demutualisation, structuring and financing of insurance companies as well as corporate and strategic planning. The firm is also involved in insurance and reinsurance contracts and claims-related matters.

WORLDWIDE OFFICE CONTACTS

SWITZERLAND
Münstergasse 2, PO Box 4081, 8022 **Zurich**
Tel: + 41 1 265 75 11 **Fax:** + 41 1 265 75 50

IT, telecommunications and multimedia: WW&P focuses on the interlinked and converging areas of information technology, Internet, multimedia, media and telecommunications law. It advise on software protection, licensing issues, systems integration contracts, data processing contracts, regulatory and other issues relating to the use of software by financial institutions, outsourcing contracts, distribution and supply agreements, on-line information systems, data protection, and electronic commerce. The firm's telecom practice covers the entire range of legal issues arising in this area such as corporate, contracts, intellectual property, application for and transfer of licenses, registrations, sharing/co-using of infrastructure, third party access, anti-trust, data protection, construction, and environmental.
Energy, utilities and public transport: WW&P advises on a range of legal issues including privatisation, deregulation, public procurement, market opening and market entry, including regulatory and contractual issues, antitrust topics, access to networks and infrastructure (essential facility), sharing and co-using of infrastructure and environmental issues. In particular, it deals with supply matters, rates and the regulation of public utilities and represents clients in dealing with rates and tariffs.
M&A, restructuring, joint ventures, IPOs, privatisation: WW&P handles the structuring and implementation of corporate mergers, acquisitions and divestitures, outsourcings, shareholder agreements, take-overs, de-mergers, capital restructurings, repurchases of shares, management buy-outs, joint ventures, re-organisations, cross-border business arrangements and other direct investment transactions. The firm's corporate finance work includes advice on domestic offerings on the Swiss Stock Exchange (SWX) and the SWX New Market, as well as double listings or cross-border offerings on many of the recognized exchanges.
Technology transfer: WW&P advises on the legal analysis of products and technology portfolios, intellectual property rights and human resources, development potential and market penetration strategies. The firm assists in finding the most adequate legal solution for the protection and transfer of rights in technology as well as the distribution of goods and the providing of services, in particular for the means of collaboration with business partners, such as strategic alliances, joint ventures, product development (R&D and specialisation agreements), patents, know how and trademark license agreements, franchising, manufacturing, sales, supply, purchase, lease, agency, and distribution arrangements.
Intellectual property: The firm has a wide range of experience in protecting intellectual property rights as well as exploiting such rights by way of licensing, franchising and merchandising. The firm's intellectual property lawyers assist in registration matters, negotiate acquisition of rights, and represent clients in infringement disputes.
Venture capital and private equity; The firm advises on seed, early stage and growth financings. It acts for a number of Swiss and foreign private investors, investment clubs, venture funds and private equity funds in relation to structuring and setting up the funds, preparing organisational and offering documents, fundraising, advising on legal tax and regulatory aspects of their investments, implementing the investment strategy and their exit from the target companies including IPOs.
Litigation, arbitration and ADR: The firm advises clients on choosing the most efficient way of dispute resolution, represents clients in court, arbitral and administrative proceedings, and offers alternative dispute resolution methods such as mediation or arbitration.

LANGUAGES: English, French, German, Italian, Spanish

For other recommended firms see pages 1485-1520

WALKERS

HEAD OFFICE

Walker House, P.O. Box 265, George Town
Grand Cayman, Cayman Islands
Tel: +1 345 949 0100 **Fax:** +1 345 949 7886

Email: walker@candw.com.ky
Website: www.walkers.com.ky

WORLDWIDE OFFICE CONTACTS

CAYMAN ISLANDS
Walker House, P.O. Box 265, **George Town,** Grand Cayman
Tel: +1 345 949 0100 **Fax:** +1 345 949 7886
Email: walker@candw.com.ky

UNITED KINGDOM
Blackwell House, Guildhall Yard, **London,** EC2V 5AE
Tel: +44 20 7830 9603 **Fax:** +44 20 7830 9604
Email: ancalon@walkerseurope.com

FIRM OVERVIEW

Senior partner: Grant J. R. Stein

Number of partners worldwide: 9
Number of other lawyers worldwide: 30

AREAS OF PRACTICE:

Banking and finance	*%
Capital markets/structured finance	*%
Corporate/commercial	*%
Investment funds	*%
Litigation	*%
Private client and international trust services	*%
Real estate	*%

*Workload % not disclosed

FIRM OVERVIEW: Walkers is one of the largest international law firms in the Cayman Islands where it has been practising law for more than 35 years. The firm now employs 120 staff worldwide including 40 lawyers drawn mainly from the top City of London law firms. The Cayman Islands is well known as one of the most sophisticated and successful offshore financial and business centres in the world. From offices in Grand Cayman and in London the firm provides a range of specialist services to corporate clients throughout the world.

INTERNATIONAL CLIENTS: The firm advises major corporations, banks, financial institutions, trust companies and insurance companies worldwide and in all time zones by way of a 24 hour service.

MAIN INTERNATIONAL AREAS OF PRACTICE:
Asset finance: The firm acts for the world's leading financial institutions, arrangers, airlines and shipping companies in relation to asset finance transactions, advising on both on and off-balance sheet vehicles utilising a Cayman Islands company, limited partnership or trust. These transactions include the sale and purchase of aircraft, ships, rolling stock, telecommunications systems and other 'big ticket' items. Contact, Ian Ashman and Wayne Panton.
Banking and international lending: The banking team advises international financial institutions on the establishment and licensing of banks and trust companies in the Cayman Islands and on all aspects of general banking business including international transactions involving Cayman Islands vehicles, secured and subordinated lending and security issues. It also advises many international banks in relation to ongoing commercial, operational and regulatory issues in liaison with the Cayman Islands Monetary Authority. Contact, Grant Stein and Angus Foster.
Capital markets and structured finance: The firm's capital markets and structured finance practice covers the full range of debt, equity, equity-linked and asset-backed securities, derivatives and structured products. The firm acts for the world's leading international financial institutions including lead managers, the trustees of securities issues and issuers established in the Cayman Islands. The firm's expertise covers securitisations, repackagings, collateralised bond and loan offerings, note programmes, preference share financings, commercial paper and depository receipt programmes and convertible debt and warrants. In addition to debt based capital markets/structured finance work, the firm also advises in relation to all types of equity-linked transactions. Contact, Ian Ashman and Wayne Panton.
Corporate: Cayman Islands' corporate vehicles are used increasingly in an extensive range of sophisticated transactions. The firm advises regularly on initial public offerings, mergers and acquisitions, disposals, reorganisations, joint ventures and a wide variety of project finance transactions which often involve infrastructure developments and the inward investment of capital into emerging and other markets. Contact, Ian Ashman, Mark Lewis, Wayne Panton and Jonathan Tonge.
Investment funds: The Cayman Islands is a leading centre for the establishment of investment funds and the firm has an international reputation for having the premier practice in this area, advising some of the best-known names in the investment world whether they be asset managers or institutional investors. The firm also has a significant hedge funds and private equity funds practice. Contact, Mark Lewis and Jonathan Tonge.
Insurance: The firm advises on the establishment of local insurers, captives, rent-a-captives and other insurance products and is also involved in the development of innovative financial products such as catastrophe bond issues and hybrid insurance/capital markets instruments. Contact, Grant Stein.
Litigation: The firm's litigation department is the largest in the Cayman Islands. It advises clients both onshore and offshore on all aspects of civil litigation with particular emphasis on commercial matters including asset recovery and economic fraud, insolvency, corporate recovery, banking disputes and trust litigation. The department also has experience in litigation involving investment funds and hedge funds. This includes shareholder, investor and partnership disputes, disputes concerning net asset values, redemption requests and general investor claims. Contact, Angus Foster, Diarmad Murray and Alan Turner.
Private client and international trust services: The firm has substantial experience in acting for high net worth individuals and their advisors worldwide in relation to all aspects of estate planning including the establishment of private purpose trusts and the structuring of private trust companies. Contact, Frank Banks and Grant Stein.

LANGUAGES: English, Spanish, French

For other recommended firms see pages 1485-1520

WANGER

HEAD OFFICE

Aeulestrasse 45,
9490 Vaduz, Liechtenstein
Tel: +423 237 52 52 **Fax:** +423 237 52 53

Email: wanger@wanger.net
Website: www.wanger.net

FIRM OVERVIEW

Senior partner: Markus Wanger FCIArb

Number of partners worldwide: 3
Number of other lawyers worldwide: 30
Number of lawyers in the Wanger Group: 200

AREAS OF PRACTICE:

Banking and finance	25%
Corporate finance	25%
Intellectual property	25%
IT and telecommunications	25%

W

FIRM OVERVIEW: The firm was founded in Liechtenstein in 1987 by Markus H. Wanger, and has grown internationally to include a Brussels office and representative offices in Switzerland, Austria, the Czech Republic, Slovakia, Brazil and China. The firm is a member of Wanger Group and is represented in Austria, Belgium, Brazil, China, Germany, Liechtenstein, Slovakia, Spain and Switzerland. The Wanger Group offers comprehensive advice to meet the needs of international clients.

INTERNATIONAL EXPERIENCE: More than 90% of the firm's work comes from international clients, covering the IP, IT, telecommunications/media and sports sectors as well as arbitration work. Most international work comes from Europe, North America and Asia.

WORLDWIDE OFFICE CONTACTS

LIECHTENSTEIN

Landstrasse 36, 9490 **Vaduz**
Tel: +423 237 52 52 **Fax:** +423 237 52 53
Email: wanger@wanger.net

ASSOCIATED OFFICES

AUSTRIA

Representative Office, Kirchgasse 2, A-6700 **Bludenz**
Tel: +43 5 552 33 901 **Fax:** +43 5 552 68 319
Email: wanger@wanger.net

Representative Office, Kärntner Strasse 49, Eingang Walfischgasse 1, A-1010 **Vienna**
Tel: +43 1 513 44 34 **Fax:** +43 1 513 38 38
Email: wanger@wanger.net

BELGIUM

EU Office, Avenue Louise 113, B-1050 **Brussels**
Tel: +32 2 541 03 36 **Fax:** +32 2 538 49 80
Email: wanger@wanger.net

SPAIN

HOIM Office, C. Raphael Altamier 2, E - 06002 **Alicante**
Tel: +34 96 520 05 00 **Fax:** +34 96 521 97 93
Email: wanger@wanger.net

SWITZERLAND

Representative Office, Rämistrasse 3, CH-8024 **Zurich**
Tel: +41 1 266 99 80 **Fax:** +41 1 266 99 81
Email: wanger@wanger.net

INTERNATIONAL CLIENTS: The firm acts for large Swiss, Austrian, German, UK and US companies. Work handled includes financial, IP/IT, telecommunications, and media-related matters.

MAIN INTERNATIONAL AREAS OF PRACTICE:

Intellectual property: Wanger Advokaturbüro provides all IP services such as patents, trademarks and licences and handles IP matters through PATAG, a licensed patent attorney agency of which Dr. Markus Wagner is managing director.
IT and telecommunications: Wanger Advokaturbüro represents international clients regarding matters relating to mobile phones and radio stations and provides legal opinions on data protection and cross border data flow.
Corporate finance, banking and finance: The firm advises mainly on art and media-related matters.
Sports and arbitration: Dr. Markus Wanger, as a member of CAS (Court of Arbitration for Sport), is strongly involved in sports and arbitration matters, and is also a member of the Chartered Institute of Arbitration, London.

LANGUAGES: English, French, German

For other recommended firms see pages 1485-1520

WATSON, FARLEY & WILLIAMS

HEAD OFFICE

15 Appold Street,
London EC2A 2HB, United Kingdom
Tel: +44 020 7814 8000 **Fax:** +44 020 7814 8141/2

Email: inquiries@wfw.com
Website: www.wfw.com

FIRM OVERVIEW

Chairman: Christopher Preston
Managing partner: David Warder
Chief executive: Michael Reid

Number of partners worldwide: 58
Number of other lawyers worldwide: 143

FIRM OVERVIEW: Established in 1982, Watson Farley & Williams is an international corporate and commercial law firm recognised for its excellence in the area of banking and asset financing, particularly ship and aircraft finance. The firm also advises in a number of specialist areas in corporate law, litigation and tax law. Through its international network the firm's lawyers are able to advise on English, French, Russian, New York and US Federal law. A key feature is the firm's division into four international practice groups: corporate, finance, litigation and tax. These groups are not divided by location but work together internationally, a structure of particular benefit to international clients.

INTERNATIONAL EXPERIENCE: The firm's international expertise has been acknowledged through a number of awards. Last year the firm was voted by the international shipping industry as the world's leading firm for ship finance, and throughout the year it has received international recognition for its asset finance, trade finance leasing and tax work, commercial litigation and corporate advice.

WORLDWIDE OFFICE CONTACTS

FRANCE
47 rue de Monceau, 75008 **Paris**
Tel: +33 1 53 83 12 12 **Fax:** +33 1 45 61 09 01
Email: ssalou@wfw.com

GREECE
5th Floor, Alassia Building, Defteras Merarchias 13, 185-35 **Piraeus**
Tel: +30 1 422 3660 **Fax:** +30 1 422 3664
Email: trice@wjw.com

RUSSIA
16/2 Tverskaya Ulitsa, Business Centre Building 3, The Actor Gallery, 103009 **Moscow**
Tel: +7 502 237 7770 **Fax:** +7 502 237 7771
Email: egiemulla@wfw.com

SINGAPORE
16 Collyer Quay, #12-02 Hitachi Tower, **Singapore** 049318
Tel: +65 532 5335 **Fax:** +65 532 5454
Email: nthomas@wfw.com

UNITED KINGDOM
15 Appold Street, **London** EC2A 2HB
Tel: +44 020 7814 8000 **Fax:** +44 020 7814 8141/2
Email: inquiries@wfw.com

USA
380 Madison Avenue, **New York** NY 10017
Tel: +1 212 922 2200 **Fax:** +1 212 922 1512
Email: josborne@wfw.com

INTERNATIONAL CLIENTS: The firm's client base is global, and includes international banks, financial institutions, quoted and private companies, in particular shipping, aviation, offshore oil and gas, power and energy, e-commerce and telecoms companies and governments and governmental agencies.

MAIN INTERNATIONAL AREAS OF PRACTICE:
International corporate group: The firm's public and private company clients have access to a wide range of domestic and international expertise covering all aspects of international corporate law, including acquisitions, disposals and mergers, public offerings of securities, management buy-outs and buy-ins, business and asset sales, debt structuring, equity financings, corporate restructurings, international privatisations, and a wide range of commercial agreements such as distributorship, outsourcing purchase and agency agreements, and joint ventures and partnerships. In addition, the group offers specialist advice on real property, intellectual property, employment, service agreements, share option and incentive schemes, executive immigration, and all aspects of European Union competition law. The group focuses particularly on the provision of advice to clients in the transportation, power, telecommunications and e-commerce sectors.
International finance group: The firm's lawyers advise all project participants, covering areas such as general banking finance, structured finance, securities and capital markets, derivatives, trade finance, asset finance, project finance, cross-border tax leverage lending and leasing, and work outs and insolvencies. The group has particular expertise and experience in a number of industry sectors heavily dependent on the financing of large capital assets.
International litigation group: Large scale litigation, arbitration and dispute resolution matters are handled by the group on a worldwide basis. The firm's lawyers have represented clients involved in international diputes in the areas of shipping (wet and dry), banking, offshore oil and gas, international trade, and aviation. The group also advises on the enforcement of security over vessels, marine pollution, marine insurance, shipbuilding, charterparties, and offshore oil and gas contracting. The firm has one of the largest litigation practices of the offshore firms in Singapore and in 2000 was expanded by the addition of a litigation practice in Piraeus.
International tax group: The firm's lawyers advise on domestic and cross-border tax leasing, non-asset based structured finance, international tax planning, investigations and litigation, and indirect tax. They also give advice generally on all types of transactions. The indirect tax team specialists have considerable VAT experience.

LANGUAGES: Cantonese, Dutch, English, French, Greek, Italian, Malay, Mandarin, Norwegian, Russian, Spanish, Swahili, Swedish

For other recommended firms see pages 1485-1520

WEDER KRUGER & HARTMANN

HEAD OFFICE

Ground Floor, Nimrod Building, Kasino Street
Windhoek PO Box 864, Namibia
Tel: +264 61 226551 **Fax:** +264 61 220533

Email: wkhlaw@iafrica.com.na

WORLDWIDE OFFICE CONTACTS

NAMIBIA
Ground Floor, Nimrod Building, Kasino Street, PO Box 864, **Windhoek**
Tel: +264 61 226551 **Fax:** +264 61 220533
Email: wkhlaw@iafrica.com.na

FIRM OVERVIEW

Managing partner: André Swanepoel
Senior partner: André Swanepoel

Number of partners worldwide: 7
Number of other lawyers worldwide: 2

AREAS OF PRACTICE:
Property 42%
Banking, finance and corporate 20%
Litigation and arbitration 20%
Criminal 5%
General commercial and employment 5%
Administration of estates 3%
Intellectual property 3%
Insurance 2%

W

FIRM OVERVIEW: Weder Kruger & Hartmann was founded in the mid 1930s by Dr Roseman and was later taken over by Dr W H Weder and his associates Kruger and Hartmann. The firm offers general and comprehensive legal advice on nearly all areas of legal practice in Namibia and Southern Africa but focuses on property, banking and finance and general legal services.

INTERNATIONAL EXPERIENCE: The firm acted in the negotiation and finalisation of the agreement entered into between the Agricultural Bank of Nambia and the African Development Bank relating to a development loan of $US10 million to provide financing for emerging communal and commercial farmers in Namibia. The firm acted for McDonald's Corporation relating to the possible establishment of their restaurant franchise in Namibia. The firm also offers advice to Coca-Cola Southern Africa on their legal interests relating to anti-trust legislation and competition law in Namibia.

INTERNATIONAL CLIENTS: The firm's client base includes large companies, banks, insurance companies and public or semi-state institutions in Namibia, Southern Africa and worldwide.

MAIN INTERNATIONAL AREAS OF PRACTICE:
Property: The firm advises on the acquisition and selling of property as well as other areas of property law.
Banking, finance and corporate: The firm advises on all aspects of banking, finance and general corporate law. It handles the drafting of Namibian, South African and international contracts.
Litigation and arbitration: The firm advises on commercial litigation and arbitration. Its lawyers are frequently involved in cases before the Namibian Courts including the Namibian Supreme Courts.
General commercial and employment: The firm handles all matters relating to general commercial work and Namibian employment law.
Intellectual property: The firm advises on all aspects of intellectual property law. It advises and acts as agents for South African firms operating in Namibia on patents, trademarks and copyright.
Insurance: The firm advises large insurance companies on all areas of insurance and related laws and transactions.
Criminal: The firm handles all areas of criminal law including the appearance and defence conducted in the lower and High Court of Namibia.
Administration of estates: The firm advises on all aspects of the administration of estates including the valuation of property.

LANGUAGES: Afrikaans, Dutch, English, German

For other recommended firms see pages 1485-1520

WEIL, GOTSHAL & MANGES

HEAD OFFICE

767 Fifth Avenue, New York NY 10153, USA
Tel: +1 212 310 8000 **Fax:** +1 212 310 8007
Email: postmaster@weil.com
Website: www.weil.com

FIRM OVERVIEW

Executive partner: Stephen Dannhauser

Number of partners worldwide: 230
Number of other lawyers worldwide: 696

AREAS OF PRACTICE:

Area	%
Corporate	20%
International finance	20%
Litigation	20%
Corporate restructuring and insolvency	10%
IP, technology and communications	6%
Real estate	6%
Telecommunications	6%
Corporate governance	5%
Taxation	5%
Trusts and estates	2%

FIRM OVERVIEW: Established in 1931 in New York, Weil, Gotshal & Manges' worldwide lawyers meet clients' needs by recognising the benefits of sectoral and regional experience. The lawyers in the firm's practice groups (which include anti-trust, bank lending, capital markets, corporate, corporate governance, corporate restructuring and insolvency, e-commerce, litigation, IP, IT, real estate, structured finance, tax, trade regulatory and trusts and estates) work together to provide full service legal advice to clients in sectors as diverse as energy, structured finance and the hi-tech industries.

INTERNATIONAL EXPERIENCE: The firm developed a network of offices across the United States in the 1960s and 70s to cater for the expansion of its client base. Weil was one of the first international law firms to establish a major presence in Central Europe. The firm now has established offices in Brussels, Budapest, Frankfurt, London, Prague and Warsaw. It also has a German desk in London which provides German corporate and finance law capability.

INTERNATIONAL CLIENTS: The firm advises a broad and diverse group of clients including many of the largest and most prominent corporations and government agencies around the globe and leading financial institutions.

MAIN INTERNATIONAL AREAS OF PRACTICE:

Corporate: The corporate department is the firm's largest, with lawyers in the US and across Europe. The department advises international financial institutions and corporate clients in complex public and private mergers and acquisitions, private equity deals, strategic alliances and other commercial transactions.

Finance: The firm advises on a wide range of financing activities and has particular interest and expertise in acquisition finance, asset based finance, debt restructuring and insolvency, debt and equity capital markets, derivatives, high yield debt, project finance, securitisation, structured finance and telecom and multi-media financing. In these areas, the firm is recognised as a market leader in the handling of complex and innovative finance transactions under both US and European law.

WORLDWIDE OFFICE CONTACTS

BELGIUM
Avenue Louise 81, PO Box 9-10, B-1050 **Brussels**
Tel: +32 2 543 7460 **Fax:** +32 2 543 7489

CZECH REPUBLIC
Charles Bridge Center, Krizovnicke Nam 1, 110 00 **Prague** 1
Tel: +420 2 2140 7300 **Fax:** +420 2140 7310

GERMANY
Maintower, Box 19, 31st Floor, Neue Mainzer Strasse 52-58, 60311 **Frankfurt**
Tel: +49 69 216 59 600 **Fax:** +49 69 216 59 699

HUNGARY
Bank Center, Granite Tower, H-1944 **Budapest**
Tel: +361 302 9100 **Fax:** +361 302 9110

POLAND
Warsaw Financial Center, ul Emilii Plater 53, 00-113 **Warsaw**
Tel: +48 22 520 4000 **Fax:** +48 22 520 4001

UNITED KINGDOM
Head Office - Europe, One South Place, **London** EC2M 2WG
Tel: +44 20 7903 1000 **Fax:** +44 20 7903 0990

USA
100 Crescent Court, Suite 1300, **Dallas** TX 75201-6950
Tel: +1 214 746 7700 **Fax:** +1 214 746 7777

700 Louisiana, Suite 1600, **Houston** TX 77002
Tel: +1 713 546 5000 **Fax:** +1 713 224 9511

701 Brickell Avenue, Suite 2100, **Miami** FL 33131
Tel: +1 305 577 3100 **Fax:** +1 305 374 7159

Head Office - USA, 767 Fifth Avenue, **New York** NY 10153
Tel: +1 212 310 8000 **Fax:** +1 212 310 8007

2882 Sand Hill Road, Suite 280, Menlo Park, **Silicon Valley** CA 94025
Tel: +1 650 926 6200 **Fax:** +1 650 854 3713

1615 L Street NW, Suite 700, **Washington** DC 20036
Tel: +1 202 682 7000 **Fax:** +1 202 857 0940

IP, technology and communications: The firm has a leading intellectual property and technology practice and advises a number of the world's major technology, media and telecommunications companies. It also acts for investors in technology, media and communications entities. The practice handles patent infringement, outsourcing transactions, strategic alliances, cross border mergers and acquisitions, investments and IPOs. The firm advises on the protection and exploitation of IP and on a wide range of e-commerce matters including data protection. It has expertise in regulatory telecoms matters.

Real estate: The firm's real estate practice handles complex real estate transactions (including finance, securitisations, development, leasing, sales, acquisitions and debt restructurings) across the US and Europe. It also advises clients on real estate M&A transactions and transactions involving real estate investment trusts.

Tax: The tax department provides advice on international and domestic taxation, covering many different economic sectors. The department works closely with the firm's other departments to find innovative solutions to problems that present various and competing multi-disciplinary considerations.

W

WEIL, GOTSHAL & MANGES cont'd

Corporate governance: The firm has been at the forefront of the field of corporate governance for more than two decades. The firm's corporate governance practice group draws from the expertise of virtually all the firm's specialities - including its corporate, finance, litigation, tax and restructuring practices.

Litigation: The firm's litigation practice advises international clients on all major areas of the law and has extensive experience in all aspects of dispute resolution. It advises clients in jury trials and appeals, as well as arbitration and alternative dispute forums.

Corporate restructuring and insolvency: The firm has one of the largest, most broadly based bankruptcy and business reorganisation practices in the US. It includes attorneys in New York, Houston, Dallas and Miami. The department has been involved in virtually all major chapter 11 reorganisation cases in the US and in major national and international out-of-court debt restructuring.

WORLDWIDE OFFICES

BELGIUM

Avenue Louise, 81, Box 9-10, B1050 Brussels

Number of lawyers: 12

Managing partner: David Cantor

Main areas of work: Competition, European Union and national regulatory law and policy, with a particular emphasis on the telecoms and new media sector, IP, technology and communictions.

W

CZECH REPUBLIC

Charles Bridge Center, Krizovnicke Nam 1, 110 00 Prague 1

Number of lawyers: 23

Managing partners: Ken Schiff, Karel Muzikar

Main areas of work: Capital markets, corporate, corporate restructuring and insolvency, finance and property finance, IP, technology and communications, litigation, telecoms.

GERMANY

Maintower, Box 19, 31st floor, Neue Mainzer Strasse 52-58, 60311 Frankfurt

Number of lawyers: 9

Managing Partner: Joe Tortorici

Main areas of work: Capital markets, corporate, finance, tax.

HUNGARY

Bank Center, Granite Tower, H-1944 Budapest

Number of lawyers: 10

Managing partner: David Dederick

Main areas of work: Corporate, finance, IP, technology and communications, real estate, telecoms.

POLAND

Warsaw Financial Center, ul Emilii Plater 53, 00-113, Warsaw

Number of lawyers: 45

Managing partner: Pawel Rymarz

Main areas of work: Capital markets, corporate, finance, IP, technology and communications, real estate, telecoms.

UNITED KINGDOM

Head Office - Europe, One South Place, London, EC2M 2 WG

Number of lawyers: 114

Head of office: Mike Francies

Main areas of work: Capital markets, corporate, finance, IP, technology and communications, litigation, real estate, telecoms, tax.

USA

100 Crescent Court, Suite 1300, Dallas, Texas 752501-6950

Number of lawyers: 64

Managing partner: Glenn West

Main areas of work: Corporate, corporate restructuring and insolvency, finance, litigation

700 Louisiana, Suite 1600, Houston, Texas 77002

Number of lawyers: 35

Managing partner: Scott Lassetter

Main areas of work: Corporate, corporate restructuring and insolvency, finance, litigation, tax.

701 Brickell Avenue, Suite 2100, Miami, Florida 33131

Number of lawyers: 24

Managing partner: Oscar Cantu

Main areas of work: Corporate, corporate restructuring and insolvency, finance, real estate, litigation.

767 Fifth Avenue, New York, NY 10153

Number of lawyers: 497

Executive partner: Stephen Dannhauser

Main areas of work: Corporate, corporate governance, corporate restructuring and insolvency, finance, litigation, real estate, tax, trade practices and regulatory law, trusts and estates.

2882 Sand Hill Road, Suite 280, Menlo Park, Silicon Valley, California 94025

Number of lawyers: 43

Managing partner: Matt Powers

Main areas of work: Corporate, finance, IP, technology and communications (litigation, transactions).

1615 L Street NW, Suite 700, Washington DC 20036

Number of lawyers: 50

Managing partner: David Berz

Main areas of work: Corporate, environmental law, finance, healthcare, international trade, litigation, public policy, real estate, taxation.

For other recommended firms see pages 1485-1520

WENGER PLATTNER

HEAD OFFICES

See worldwide office contacts

Website: www.wenger-plattner.ch

FIRM OVERVIEW

Senior partners: Dr Werner Wenger, Dr Jürg Plattner
Number of partners worldwide: 13
Number of other lawyers worldwide: 17

AREAS OF PRACTICE:

Corporate and contract: 25%
Arbitration and litigation: 15%
Debt collection, bankruptcy and restructuring: 12%
Intellectual property, competition and IT: 10%
Banking, finance and insurance: 8%
Civil law: 8%
Estate planning, tax and trusts: 8%
Pharmaceutical and biotechnology: 8%
Entertainment, new media and telecoms: 6%

OFFICE CONTACTS

SWITZERLAND
Aeschenvorstadt 55, CH-4010 **Basel**
Tel: + 41 61 279 7000 **Fax:** + 41 61 279 7001
Email: basel@wenger-plattner.ch

Seestrasse 39, CH-8700 **Küsnacht-Zürich**
Tel: + 41 1 914 2770 **Fax:** + 41 1 914 2788
Email: zuerich@wenger-plattner.ch

Jungfraustrasse 1, CH-3000 **Bern** 6
Tel: + 41 31 356 4943 **Fax:** + 41 31 351 2883
Email: bern@wenger-plattner.ch

FIRM OVERVIEW: Established in 1980 through the merger of two Basel law firms, with the Zurich office opening in 1993, Wenger Plattner now has 13 partners and 17 other lawyers. On January 1, 2000, Wenger Plattner opened a third office in Bern, the capital of Switzerland. Wenger Plattner has a broadly-based commercial practice with a strong emphasis on corporate and international work. The firm provides advice and representation primarily on matters of Swiss law. It also works with an extensive international network of foreign correspondents. Litigation represents a significant part of the firm's practice, with members leading or participating in litigation teams in large-scale international and domestic legal disputes. Some partners act as judges or teach at universities. Most have experience of acting in-house in industry or large accounting firms.

INTERNATIONAL EXPERIENCE: Wenger Plattner's international experience includes litigation in large-scale international disputes and international arbitration, in which firm members act as chairmen and party-appointed arbitrators. The firm advises foreign investment funds on entering the Swiss market and provides Swiss and international tax advice and representation. In the field of mergers and acquisitions it advises Swiss companies abroad and foreign companies in Switzerland. The firm also handles international trading and copyright work.

INTERNATIONAL CLIENTS: The firm's international clients come mainly from Germany, Britain, France, Italy and the US, and include pharmaceutical, telecommunications, biotechnology, shipping and transport companies and banks.

MAIN INTERNATIONAL AREAS OF PRACTICE:

Corporate and contract: The firm's activities cover corporate organisation, share issues and share redemptions, mergers and acquisitions, reorganisations, joint ventures, management buyouts, distribution agreements, loan and other agreements and outsourcing.

Arbitration and litigation: Members participate in international and domestic proceedings and also act as arbitrators under institutional arbitration rules and in non-administered arbitrations.The firm advises on alternative dispute resolution and participates in structured dispute resolution proceedings. In litigation the firm represents clients in all areas of civil and administrative law, and provides criminal litigation in selected areas such as tax, environmental and competition law.

Bankruptcy: The firm has particular expertise in the handling of complex liquidation, reorganisation and bankruptcy cases as well as financial restructurings.

Intellectual property and competition: The firm is thoroughly experienced in the area of intellectual property rights, and advises on patent, trademark, media and copyright and entertainment law, as well as on Swiss and EU competition law.

Biotechnology: The firm has actively participated in the evolution of Swiss biotechnology law and has advised leading companies in the industry. It also maintains relationships with key people in universities and government.

Banking, finance and insurance: The firm advises on banking contracts, takeovers and securities law. It also advises investment funds on how to adapt to the new Swiss regulatory environment. The firm helps clients develop an appropriate risk strategy, advises on insurance placement and contracts and handles insurance claims for both buyers and providers.

Estate planning, tax and trusts: The firm uses its established network of correspondents abroad to provide creative estate planning for both domestic and international clients. It provides tax planning for business and individuals, legal representation before tax agencies and courts, and complex tax returns for individuals.

Constitutional and administrative law: The firm has particular expertise in Swiss environmental law, bolstered by the industry experience of its partners. It both advises clients on to acquisitions and other ventures and represents them in court.

Information technology and communication law: The firm advises clients in the high-tech market on contract law and represents them before agencies and courts.

Notary public services: The notary public services are provided at the Basel office. The firm's notaries have particular experience in the notarisation of acquisitions, mergers, asset deals and other business transactions under German corporate and contract law.

LANGUAGES: English, French, German, Italian, Polish, Portuguese

WENGER PLATTNER
BASEL BERN ZÜRICH

W

WESSING

HEAD OFFICE

see Worldwide Office Contacts

FIRM OVERVIEW

Managing partner: Wolfgang von Meibom (Dusseldorf)

Number of partners worldwide: 124
Number of other lawyers worldwide: 245

AREAS OF PRACTICE:

Arbitration/mediation .... *%
Banking and finance .... *%
Civil and commercial .... *%
Communications and IP .... *%
Corporate/M&A .... *%
Energy .... *%
Insurance .... *%
IT, e-commerce and internet .... *%
Litigation .... *%
Maritime and transport .... *%
Medical/pharmaceutical law .... *%
Intellectual property .... *%
Public/environmental law .... *%
Regulatory .... *%
Sports .... *%
* Workload % not disclosed

W

FIRM OVERVIEW: Wessing, formerly Wessing & Berenberg-Gossler, is established as one of Germany's largest law firms. Together with its partners Liederke (Belgium), Simeon (France) and Houthoff (Netherlands), Wessing operates a joint multinational office in Brussels. Wessing is a member of The Conference of European Lawyers, The European Law Unit, Unilaw, Techlaw, World Law Group, State Capital Law Firm Group and European Environmental Network. The firm's Frankfurt office offers notary services.

MAIN INTERNATIONAL AREAS OF PRACTICE:

Corporate finance: Wessing provides transactional and regulatory advice. Specific legal services include IPOs, capital increases, equity carve-outs and spin offs.
Corporate: Wessing acts for conglomerates, large and medium sized companies, and high net worth individuals. The scope of the firm's work includes business formations, structuring and restructuring of businesses, joint venture formations and business succession.
EU and competition: The firm focuses on merger control and other aspects of EU competition law, particularly in distribution, licensing, research and development, 'know-how', franchising and joint ventures. The firm also provides specialist advice on public procurement, anti-dumping, and European trademark law.
Intellectual property, patents and trademarks: The firm advises on the selection, availability and proper usage requirements of trademarks and registered designs. It also advises on whether patents and utility models can be protected and assists with the negotiation, drafting and reviewing of patent licensing and 'know-how' agreements.
Other: In order to advise its clients most effectively, the firm has set up practice groups which target specific sectors.

LANGUAGES: Chinese, Danish, English, French, German, Italian, Portuguese, Russian, Spanish

WORLDWIDE OFFICE CONTACTS

BELGIUM
Boulevard de l'Empereur 3, B-1000 **Brussels**
Tel: +32 551 1632 **Fax:** +32 551 1643
Email: bruessels@wessing.com

CHINA
11th floor Shanghai Senmao, International Building, 101 Yin Cheng East Road, Pudong New Area, **Shanghai** 200120
Tel: +86 21 6841 5525 **Fax:** +86 21 6841 0066
Email: shanghai@wessing.com.cn

GERMANY
Kurfürstendamm 31, D-10719 **Berlin**
Tel: +49 88 3056 360 **Fax:** +49 30 8856 3646
Email: berlin@wessing.com

Königsallee 92 A, 40212 **Dusseldorf**
Tel: +49 211 83 870 **Fax:** +49 211 83 87 100
Email: dusseldorf@wessing.com

Senckenberganlage 20-22, D 60325 **Frankfurt am Main**
Tel: +49 69 97 1300 **Fax:** +49 69 97 130 100
Email: frankfurt@wessing.com

Neuer Wall 44, D-20354 **Hamburg**
Tel: +49 40 368 030 **Fax:** +49 40 368 03 280
Email: hamburg@wessing.com

Peterskirchhof 1-5, D-04109 **Leipzig**
Tel: +49 89 213 980 **Fax:** +49 341 213 98 300
Email: leipzig@wessing.com

Isartorplatz 8, D-80331 **Munich**
Tel: +49 89 210 380 **Fax:** +49 89 210 38300
Email: muenchen@wessing.com

Am Krausenbaum 42, D-41464 **Neuss**
Tel: +49 2131 740 300 **Fax:** +49 2131 740 3050
Email: neuss@wessing.com

SPAIN
Av. Maisonnave, 28 bis 2-8, E-03003 **Alicante**
Tel: +34 598 6230 **Fax:** +34 598 4004
Email: byl@arrakis.es

For other recommended firms see pages 1485-1520

WHITE & CASE LLP

HEAD OFFICE

1155 Avenue of the Americas,
New York NY 10036-2787, USA
Tel: +1 212 819 8200 **Fax:** +1 212 354 8113

Website: www.whitecase.com

FIRM OVERVIEW

Managing partner: Duane D. Wall

Number of partners worldwide: 284
Number of other lawyers worldwide: 975

AREAS OF PRACTICE:

General practice	21%
Banking	15%
Corporate, M&A, joint ventures	11%
Capital markets	9%
Intellectual property	9%
Project finance	9%
Dispute resolution	8%
Privatisation	6%
Antitrust	4%
Sovereign representation	4%
Tax	4%

FIRM OVERVIEW: Founded in New York in 1901, White & Case has over 1,300 lawyers in 40 offices in 28 countries across the US, Europe, Middle East, Asia, Africa and Latin America. The firm functions as a single partnership. Its practice encompasses the full range of international finance and corporate law disciplines.

INTERNATIONAL EXPERIENCE: White & Case lawyers act on major finance and corporate law transactions in the world's primary financial and commercial centres as well as in emerging market economies. The firm's lawyers advise under local, US and UK law on the full range of domestic and cross-border transactions.

INTERNATIONAL CLIENTS: Clients include public and private corporations and financial institutions, governments and state-owned entities.

MAIN INTERNATIONAL AREAS OF WORK: A large part of the firm's practice is transactional, involving mergers and acquisitions, divestitures, leveraged buy-outs, securities offerings, financings, joint ventures and restructurings. This often involves assets in multiple countries, and the firm is able to perform global due diligence, obtain regulatory approvals, structure financings and handle documentation in the law of more than one jurisdiction.
Capital markets: The firm advises issuers, underwriters, placement agents and other particpants in a wide range of debt, equity and derivatives offerings in world markets. It has particular experience of offerings with non-US issuers in the US and Euromarkets. The firm has also represented many governments in raising funds on the international capital markets and the restructuring of external debt, as well as in developing legislative and regulatory frameworks for securities programs in emerging market countries.
Project finance: The firm is acknowledged as one of the world's leading providers of project finance law advice. Lawyers from the region combine resources for its work across the US, Europe, the Middle East, Africa and Asia. A number of projects that the firm's lawyers have advised on have

WORLDWIDE OFFICE CONTACTS

BELGIUM
White & Case LLP incorporating Forrester Norall & Sutton, 1 Place Madou, Box 34, 1210 **Brussels**
Tel: +32 2 219 1620 **Fax:** +32 2 219 1626

BRAZIL
White & Case LLP, Alameda Santos, 1940 - 3° Andar, 01418 200 **São Paulo**
Tel: +55 11 3171 0011 **Fax:** +55 11 3171 0041

CHINA
White & Case LLP, 218 Shanghai Bund No12 Building, 12 Zhongshan Dong Yi Road, **Shanghai** 200002
Tel: +86 21 6321 2200 **Fax:** +86 21 6323 9252

CZECH REPUBLIC
White & Case, Feddersen, Advokátní Kancelár, Staroměstské náměstí 15, 110 00 **Prague**
Tel: +420 2 2481 1796 **Fax:** +420 2 2481 0252

FINLAND
Asianajotoimisto, White & Case Oy, Eteläranta 14, FIN-00130 **Helsinki**
Tel: +358 9 228 641 **Fax:** +358 9 228 64 228

FRANCE
White & Case LLP, 11, Boulevard de la Madeleine, 75001 **Paris**
Tel: +33 1 55 04 15 15 **Fax:** +33 1 55 04 15 16

GERMANY
White & Case, Feddersen, Kurfürstendamm 32, 10719 **Berlin**
Tel: +49 30 8 80 911 0 **Fax:** + 49 30 8 80 911 297

White & Case, Feddersen, Königstrasse 1, 01097 **Dresden**
Tel: +49 351 802 02 77 **Fax:** + 49 351 802 02 79

White & Case, Feddersen, Jägerhofstrasse 29, 40479 **Düsseldorf**
Tel: +49 211 491 95 0 **Fax:** +49 211 491 95 100

White & Case Feddersen, Bockenheimer Landstrasse, 51-53 60325 **Frankfurt am Main**
Tel: +49 69 713 770 **Fax:** +49 69 713 77 100

White & Case, Feddersen, Stiftstrasse 9-17, 60313 **Frankfurt am Main**
Tel: +49 69 2 99 94 0 Fax: +49 69 28 26 15

White & Case, Feddersen, Jungfernstieg 51, (Prien-Haus), 20354, **Hamburg**
Tel:+49 40 350 050 **Fax:** +49 40 350 05111

HONG KONG
White & Case, Solicitors, 9th Floor, Gloucester Tower, 11 Pedder Street, Central, **Hong Kong**
Tel: +852 2822 8700 **Fax:** +852 2845 9070

HUNGARY
Réczicza Law Firm White & Case LLP, Szalag utca 19, 1011 **Budapest**
Tel: +36 1 488 5200 **Fax:** +36 1 488 5299

INDIA
White & Case LLP, Nirmal Building, 1214, 12th Floor, Maker Chambers V, Nariman Point, **Bombay** 400 021
Tel: +91 22 282 6300 **Fax:** +91 22 282 6305

JAPAN
White & Case LLP, Kandabashi Law Offices, Kandabashi Park Building, 19-1, Kanda-nishikicho 1-chome, Chiyoda-ku, **Tokyo** 101-0054
Tel: +81 3 3259 0200 **Fax:** +81 3 3259 0150

KAZAKHSTAN
White & Case LLP, 64 Amangeldy Street, 480012 **Almaty**
Tel: +7 3272 50 74 91 / 2 **Fax:** +7 3272 50 74 93

WHITE & CASE LLP cont'd

gained recognition for their size and innovation.

Asset finance and leasing: The firm is one of the world's leading providers of US, UK and local asset finance law advice. Its lawyers have particular experience advising the aviation industry.

Bank finance: The firm represents leading financial institutions and corporations on the full range of financing transactions from complex acquisitions financings to straightforward syndications transactions. The firm has invested heavily in the build-out of its UK law capabilities over the past year.

Privatisation: The firm has considerable privatisation experience, having advised on over 100 privatisation transactions worldwide in industries including telecommunications, water, energy, mining and airlines. It has acted for governments, state-owned enterprises, multilateral institutions, international banks and strategic and financial investors on privatisations in Asia, Latin America, Eastern Europe, the Middle East and Africa.

Disputes: The firm handles a range of disputes arising from clients' banking and financial transactions, international trade matters, cross-border corporate transactions, construction contracts and alleged anti-competitive practices.

Commercial litigation: Work includes several high profile US government-initiated court cases and investigations, cases in the English High Court and Companies Court and in EU institutions such as the Court of First Instance and the European Court of Justice.

Arbitration: The firm has a number of arbitration specialists, with experience of acting in ICC arbitrations worldwide. Disputes have been successfully concluded in the International Centre for the Settlement of Investment Disputes in Washington, the London Court of International Arbitration, the Hong Kong International Arbitration Centre and the China International Economic and Trade Arbitration Commission. The firm also has extensive experience of arbitrations conducted under ad-hoc procedures in countries including Jordan, South Africa, Switzerland, the UK and the US.

Intellectual property: Work spans the identification and registration of intellectual property rights and their protection and enforcement (through litigation where necessary), and experience covers patent, trademark, licensing, copyright, computer, libel, advertising, multimedia, trade regulation, unfair competition and antitrust. The practice is also involved in the interpretation of new treaties and legislative initiatives worldwide. Clients come from diverse sectors including biogenetics, chemical engineering and satellite systems, and may be involved in the negotiation of joint ventures or marketing alliances.

Anti-trust: The antitrust group has advised on some of the largest recent worldwide corporate and banking mergers, and has assisted clients with antitrust and merger compliance in over 80 countries and jurisdictions. The firm has particular experience of co-ordinating US, European and other foreign antitrust clearances on complex cross-border deals. It has successfully defended mergers before the US Department of Justice, the Federal Trade Commission and the European Commission as well as various regulatory bodies.

Tax: The firm structures the tax aspects of a wide range of corporate and financial transactions, develops tax-advantaged financial products and investment vehicles and helps multinational clients achieve worldwide tax efficiency.

E-commerce, media and technology: The firm offers a full service to clients in the e-commerce, media and technology sectors. The firm provides sector specialists to advise on the full range of matters from venture capital funding to intellectual property issues.

W

MEXICO
White & Case SC, Paseo de las Palmas 405, 5° Piso, Col. Lomas de Chapultepec, 11000 **Mexico City**
Tel: +52 5 540 9600 **Fax:** +52 5 540 9699

POLAND
White & Case (Poland) SP. Zo.o., ul. Bagatela 12,, 00-585 **Warsaw**
Tel: +48 22 625 33 33 **Fax:** +48 22 628 22 28

RUSSIA
White & Case LLC, 4 Romanov Pereulok, 103009 **Moscow**
Tel: +7 095 787 3000 **Fax:** +7 095 787 3001

SINGAPORE
White & Case LLP, 50 Raffles Place #30-00, Singapore Land Tower, **Singapore** 048623
Tel: +65 225 6000 **Fax:** +65 225 6009

SLOVAKIA
White & Case, Feddersen, Hlavné Námestie 5, 81101 **Bratislava**
Tel: +421 7 5441 5100 **Fax:** +.421 7 5441 6100

SOUTH AFRICA
White & Case LLP, PO Box 784440, Sandton 2146, The Forum Building, 14th Floor, Maude & Fifth Streets, Sandton, **Johannesburg** 2196
Tel: +27 11 884 7689 **Fax:** +27 11 884 7229

SWEDEN
White & Case Advokat AB, Nybrogatan 3, PO Box 5573, S-114 85 **Stockholm**
Tel: +46 8 506 32 300 **Fax:** +46 8 611 21 22

THAILAND
White & Case (Thailand) Ltd,4th- 5th Floors, Gaysorn Plaza, 999 Ploenchit Road, Lumpini, Pathumwan, **Bangkok** 10330
Tel: +662 656 1721/32 **Fax:** +662 656 1733

TURKEY
White & Case Müsavirlik Ltd. Şti, Piyade Sokak No. 18, Portakal Çiçěği Apt. C Blok Kat 2, 06550 Çankaya, **Ankara**
Tel: +90 312 442 5680 **Fax:** +90 312 442 5691/4

White & Case Müsavirlik Ltd Şti, Maya Akar Center, Büyükdere Caddesi No 100, B Blok, Kat 12, 80280 Esentepe **Istanbul**
Tel: +90 212 275 7533 **Fax:** +90 212 275 7543

UNITED KINGDOM
White & Case, 7-11 Moorgate, **London** EC2R 6HH
Tel: +44 20 7600 7300 **Fax:** +44 20 7600 7030

USA
White & Case LLP, 633 West Fifth Street, Suite 1900, **Los Angeles** CA 90071-2007
Tel: +1 213 620 7700 **Fax:** +1 213 687 0758

White & Case LLP, First Union Financial Center, 200 South Biscayne Boulevard, **Miami** FL 33131-2352
Tel: +1 305 371 2700 **Fax:** +1 305 358 5744 / 5766

1155 Avenue of the Americas, **New York** NY 10036-2787
Tel: +1 212 819 8200 **Fax:** +1 212 354 8113

White & Case LLP, 3000 El Camino Real, 5 Palo Alto Square, 10th Floor, **Palo Alto** CA 94306
Tel: +1 650 213 0300 **Fax:** +1 650 213 8158

White & Case LLP, Two Emborcadero Center, Suite 650, **San Francisco** CA 94111-3162
Tel: +1 415 544 1100 **Fax:** +1 415 544 0202

White & Case LLP, 601 Thirteenth Street NW, Suite 600 South, **Washington** DC 20005-3807
Tel: +1 202 626 3600 **Fax:** +1 202 639 9355

For other recommended firms see pages 1485-1520

WHITE & CASE LLP cont'd

Corporate practice: There are more than 600 lawyers in the firm's corporate department who provide a wide range of corporate and business services to publicly held corporations and private businesses. White & Case has a full service international practice covering all aspects of major corporate transactions from taxation to financing.

M&A and joint ventures: The firm is one of the most active in the world in M&A transactions and has taken the lead in devising creative deal structures and acquisition programmes. Its lawyers plan and implement strategies for both acquirers and potential acquisition targets in domestic and cross-border transactions. White & Case has particularly strong experience in advising clients on structured transactions which often involve multiple jurisdisctions. Thanks to the firm's unrivalled international network, White & Case can rationalise the diverse legal regimes these major cross-border transactions engender.

Sovereign: White & Case has represented more countries in sovereign-related projects than any other law firm in the world. The firm has particular experience assisting governments in developing or emerging markets.

VIETNAM

White & Case LLP Hanoi,, 63 Ly Thai To Street, 2nd Floor, Hoan Kiem District, **Hanoi**
Tel: +84 4934 5355 **Fax:** +84 4 934 5356

White & Case LLP, The Metropolitan, Suite 405, 61 Nguyen Du Street, District 1, **Ho Chi Minh City**
Tel: +84 8 821 0888 **Fax:** +84 8 823 6902

ASSOCIATED OFFICES

BAHRAIN

White & Case LLP in association with Qays Zu'bi Al- Jasrah Tower, 12th Floor Building 95, Road 1702, Area 317, **Manama** Area 317 POBox 2397
Tel: +973 538 600 **Fax:** +973 532 342

INDONESIA

Associated Office, Ali Budiardjo, Nugroho, Reksodiputro Counsellors at Law, Graha Niaga, 24th Floor, Jalan Jenderal Sudirman Kav, 58, **Jakarta** 12190
Tel: +62 21 250 5125 **Fax:** +62 21 250 5646

SAUDI ARABIA

Law Office of Hassan Mahassni in association with White & Case LLP, Al-Nakheel Centre, 3rd Floor, Medina Road on Palestine Circle, PO Box 2256, **Jeddah** 21451
Tel: +966 2 665 4353 **Fax:** +966 2 669 2996

Law Office of Hassan Mahassni in association with White & Case LLP, The Saudi Ceramic Company Building, 5th Floor, King Fahd Highway, PO Box 17411, **Riyadh** 11484
Tel: +966 1 464 4006 **Fax:** +966 1 465 1348

W

WHITE & CASE LLP

WIERSHOLM, MELLBYE & BECH

HEAD OFFICE

Ruselokkveien 26, PO Box 1400 Vika,
N-0115 Oslo, Norway
Tel: +47 210 210 00 **Fax:** +47 210 210 01

Website: www.wiersholm.no

WORLDWIDE OFFICE CONTACTS

NORWAY
Ruselokkveien 26, PO Box 1400 Vika, N-0115 **Oslo**
Tel: +47 210 210 00 **Fax:** +47 210 210 01
Email: mail@wiersholm.no

FIRM OVERVIEW

Managing director: Torill L. Rambjor
Senior partner: Harold Schjoldager

Number of partners worldwide: 34
Number of other lawyers worldwide: 69

AREAS OF PRACTICE:

Mergers and acquisitions	35%
Tax law	13%
Banking and finance	10%
Construction	10%
EU and competition	10%
IT, Telecommunications and media	10%
Labour and employment	5%
Maritime and transportation	5%
Intellectual property, copyright	2%

W

FIRM OVERVIEW: Established in 1875, Wiersholm, Mellbye & Bech is one of Norway's largest firms, with 103 lawyers, 34 of whom are partners. The firm is first and foremost a commercial law practice, offering services across the entire range of commercial law. The firm acts for most sectors of commerce and industry and corporate structures. The firm's clients include individuals and governmental agencies, as well as Norwegian and international corporate clients. Indeed, as a considerable amount of the firm's work is of an international nature, the firm represents a growing number of foreign corporate clients with Norwegian operations, as well as Norwegian clients who market their expertise, services and products overseas. The firm has regular contact with external foreign lawyers and has established an extensive international network, to which its clients have worldwide access.

INTERNATIONAL EXPERIENCE: Over the past three years, Wiersholm, Mellbye & Bech has advised on more than 20 M&A transactions, as well as in the establishment of foreign companies in Norway.

INTERNATIONAL CLIENTS: The firm's clients are primarily from the Nordic countries, the UK and the US. They come from the following sectors: shipping, banking, M&A, EU and competition.

MAIN INTERNATIONAL AREAS OF PRACTICE:

Mergers and acquisitions: Wiersholm, Mellbye & Bech's transactions in this area range from small private acquisitions to cross-border takeovers of listed companies.
Banking and finance: The firm covers all areas of banking, finance and capital markets work, including secured and syndicated loan transactions and guarantees, structured finance and project finance.
Maritime and transportation: The firm's lawyers handle a variety of shipping related issues, including charter party compliance, insurance claims, ship finance and maritime regulation compliance, including oil pollution and safety at sea.
Intellectual property, copyright: The firm advises on all areas of IP law, with an emphasis on litigation, and is highly regarded for its patent and copyright work.
IT, telecommunications and media: The firm is active in all areas of this field, including broadcasting, internet and entertainment law.
Construction: Wiersholm, Mellbye & Bech is one of the leading developers' firms in Norway. It is involved in a number of infrastructure construction projects that include acting on behalf of a property developer for the ongoing new Oslo airport and for the offshore construction business, mainly in litigation matters.
EU and competition: This practice area has become increasingly important since Norway's membership of the EFA in January 1995, when national laws were brought into line with EU legislation. The firm's lawyers handle anti-trust, competition and marketing-related cases involving companies in the Norwegian market.
Tax law: The firm has experience in both national and international tax law, VAT law and customs law, with a particular emphasis on international tax and customs law.
Labour and employment: Wiersholm, Mellbye & Bech is one of the leading firms in Norway with regard to both employer and employees' work, and clients include a number of state-owned institutions and unions, as well as the private sector.

LANGUAGES: The Scandinavian languages, as well as English, French, German, Italian and Spanish.

For other recommended firms see pages 1485-1520

WIKBORG, REIN & CO

HEAD OFFICE

Kronprinsesse Märtha's Plass 1, PO Box 1513 Vika,
0117 Oslo, Norway
Tel: +47 22 82 75 00 **Fax:** +47 22 82 75 01

Website: www.wrco.no

FIRM OVERVIEW

Managing partner: Tom B. Knudsen
Senior partner: Erling C. Hjort

Number of partners worldwide: 41
Number of other lawyers worldwide: 82

AREAS OF PRACTICE:

Banking, securities, M&A, IPOs, company and commercial	20%
Shipping and marine insurance	15%
Energy	10%
Financing	10%
IT and telecommunications	10%
Litigation and arbitration	10%
Real estate	10%
Tax	10%
Insolvency	5%

FIRM OVERVIEW: The firm was founded in Oslo 1923 by Erling Wikborg, who was joined by shipping lawyer Alex Rein as a partner in 1945. The firm is large by Norwegian standards, with a total of approximately 120 lawyers. It has offices in Bergen, Norway's second-largest city, London, Singapore and Kobe. The practice is diversified, but specialises in shipping, energy, financing, tax, M&A, securities and banking regulations and IT and telecommunications. The firm is active in recruiting new law graduates, and has an exclusive sponsorship agreement with the Oslo law students' association.

INTERNATIONAL EXPERIENCE: The firm has a long history of international practice, reflecting Norway's international tradition as a shipping and trading nation. A considerable portion of the client base is non-Norwegian, coming mostly from Scandinavia, Western Europe, North and South America, Japan, Korea and Australia. More than any other Norwegian firm, Wikborg, Rein & Co has chosen to develop an international network of offices; in addition to its present ones it has in the past had offices in New York (1955-1980) and Rotterdam (1971-1987). Most of the firm's partners have practised abroad for several years. International work includes shipping (maritime casualties, ship purchase and sales, shipping finance, shipbuilding contracts), cross-border M&A, banking and finance (syndicated loans, asset finance and project finance) and energy (especially offshore drilling contracts and cross-border electricity transmission contracts).

INTERNATIONAL CLIENTS: The firm's international clients include companies involved in trade and industry, banking and finance, natural resources, technology, media and telecommunication transport, shipping and aviation.

LANGUAGES: English, French, German, Norwegian

WORLDWIDE OFFICE CONTACTS

JAPAN
J-1, 5-Chome Minarojima, Nakamachi Chuo-Ku, **Kobe** 650
Tel: +81 78 303 1772 **Fax:** +81 78 303 1781
Email: wikrein@gol.com

NORWAY
Olav Kyrresgt 11, PB 1233 Sentrum, 5811 **Bergen**
Tel: +47 55 21 52 00 **Fax:** +47 55 21 52 01
Email: bergen@wrco.no

Kronprinsesse Märtha's plass 1, PO Box 1513 Vika, 0117 **Oslo**
Tel: +47 55 21 52 00 **Fax:** +47 55 21 52 01

SINGAPORE
8 A Lorong Telok, PO Box 425 Chinatown Point, **Singapore** 910501
Tel: +65 438 4498 **Fax:** +65 438 4496
Email: wrco@wrco.com.sg

UNITED KINGDOM
One Knightrider Court, **London** EC4 5JP
Tel: +44 20 7236 4598 **Fax:** +44 20 7236 4599
Email: wrco@wrco.co.uk

W

WORLDWIDE OFFICES

JAPAN
J-1, 5-Chome Minarojima, Nakamachi Chuo-Ku, Kobe 650

Contact: Gaute Gjelsten

Number of lawyers: 1

SINGAPORE
8 A Lorong Telok, PO Box 425 Chinatown Point, Singapore 910501

Resident partner: Dag Rommen

Number of lawyers: 3

UNITED KINGDOM
One Knightrider Court, London EC4 5JP

Managing partner: Morten Lund Mathisen

Number of lawyers: 3

WILKINSON BARKER KNAUER, LLP

HEAD OFFICE

2300 N Street NW, Suite 700,
Washington DC 20037-1128, USA
Tel: +1 202 783 4141 **Fax:** +1 202 783 5851

Email: info@wbklaw.com
Website: www.wbklaw.com

FIRM OVERVIEW

Managing partner: Andrew L. Tollin
Senior partner: Leon T. Knauer

Number of partners worldwide: 22
Number of other lawyers worldwide: 31

AREAS OF PRACTICE:
Communication and technology 70%
Corporate finance 10%
M&A 10%
Intellectual property 5%
Litigation and arbitration 5%

WORLDWIDE OFFICE CONTACTS

GERMANY
Am Opernplatz 2, 60313 **Frankfurt am Main**
Tel: +49 69 20876 **Fax:** +49 69 297 8453

USA
2300 N Street NW, Suite 700, **Washington** DC 20037-1128
Tel: +1 202 783 4141 **Fax:** +1 202 783 5851
Email: info@wbklaw.com

VENEZUELA
Torre Banco Lara, Av. Principal con Primera Transversal, Urbanización La Castellana, **Caracas** 1060
Tel: +582 263 2624 **Fax:** +582 263 2743

W

FIRM OVERVIEW: Founded after World War II, Wilkinson Barker Knauer LLP initially handled the restitution claims of Indians. The firm now focuses on communication, technology and mass media law, and has one of the leading US practices in this area.

INTERNATIONAL EXPERIENCE: To compliment its Washington headquarters, the firm maintains offices in Frankfurt, Germany and Caracas, Venezuela. The firm's presence on three continents enhances its ability to structure international ventures, assist businesses in establishing a presence in the US, Europe and Latin America, and to advise on privatisation and trade matters.

INTERNATIONAL CLIENTS: The firm's clients range from Fortune 500 companies to small and medium sized companies including regional Bell operating companies, utilities, municipalities, independent providers of telecommunications and media services, communications equipment manufacturers, universities, trade associations, foreign governments and foundations.

MAIN INTERNATIONAL AREAS OF PRACTICE:
Communication and technology: A major focus of the telecom practice is wireless services. The firm has a broad base of experience in the commercial mobile radio services such as cellular and paging. The firm also advises on microwave and mobile satellite matters. In the mass media field, Wilkinson Barker Knauer advises a number of clients involved in analog and digital broadcasting and cable services. The firm also handles regulatory licensing and compliance issues and advises on all aspects of Internet law.
Corporate finance: The firm advises start-up companies on secured loan transactions and guarantees, project finance, leasing and tax based finance.
Intellectual property: The firm specialises in trademarks, patents, copyrights and domain name registrations. It handles the negotiation of licence agreements and advises on infringement disputes and other aspects of IP law.
Litigation and arbitration: The firm is primarily involved in all litigation and arbitration matters involving the telecommunications industry. Wilkinson Barker Knauer comprises practitioners admitted to all circuits of the US Supreme Court of Appeals, the US Supreme Court, the US Claims Court, and a number of US District Courts.
M&A: The firm's transactions range from small private acquisitions to cross-border takeovers of companies.

LANGUAGES: English, French, German, Spanish

WORLDWIDE OFFICES

GERMANY
Am Opernplatz 2, 60313 Frankfurt am Main

Managing partner: Richard J Leitermann

Number of lawyers: 6
Number of locally qualified lawyers: 6

Office profile: Established in 1993, the German office is the European presence of Wilkinson Barker Knauer. It specialises in telecommunications issues, particularly regulatory aspects. The firm also handles financing issues and advises start up companies.

VENEZUELA
Torre Banco Lara, Av. Principal con Primera Transversal, Urbanización La Castellana, Caracas 1060

Managing partner: Linda M. Wellstein

Number of lawyers: 3
Number of locally qualified lawyers: 3

Office profile: Established in 1999, the Caracas office is the Latin American office of Wilkinson Barker Knauer, specialising in telecommunications, privatisations and trade matters. In Latin America, Wilkinson Barker Knauer has advised several regional governments on telecommunications privatisations. This work has included the preparation of concession agreements and drafting the new telecommunications agreements with bidders.

For other recommended firms see pages 1485-1520

WILKINSON & GRIST

HEAD OFFICE

6th Floor, Prince's Building, 10 Chater Road,
Hong Kong
Tel: + 852 2524 6011 **Fax:** + 852 2520 2090

Email: partners@wilgrist.com
Website: www.wilgrist.com

WORLDWIDE OFFICE CONTACTS

CHINA

Suite 5, 10th Floor, Beijing Oriental Plaza, Office Tower W2, 1 East Chang An Ave., **Beijing,** People's Republic of China

HONG KONG

6th Floor, Prince's Building, 10 Charter Road, **Hong Kong**
Tel: + 852 2524 6011 **Fax:** + 852 2520 2090
Email: partners@wilgrist.com

9th Floor, Prestige Tower, 23-25 Nathan Road, **Kowloon**
Tel: + 852 2369 9236 **Fax:** + 852 2369 4577
Email: kwnoff@wilgrist.com

FIRM OVERVIEW

Managing partner: Michael Chan
Senior partner: Ella Cheong

Number of partners worldwide: 22
Number of other lawyers worldwide: 21

AREAS OF PRACTICE:

Intellectual property and IT	35%
Company and commercial	20%
Litigation, liquidation, bankruptcy and insolvency	20%
Conveyancing and real estate	15%
Trade with PRC	5%
Wills, tax and trusts	5%

FIRM OVERVIEW: The firm is one of Hong Kong's oldest, having been established in 1860. It undertakes a wide range of commercial work for international companies and financial institutions. While a major part of its practice consists of intellectual property and IT, the firm also has substantial experience in company, commercial, banking and litigation. Firm members sit on government or non-government advisory bodies and committees of Hong Kong Law Society and other international associations. The firm works closely with law firms in China and many other parts of the world.

INTERNATIONAL EXPERIENCE: The firm's international experience has developed on the basis of notable representations of infrastructure companies listed on Hong Kong Stock Exchange and multinational banks and corporations in the areas of infrastructure, property and hotel investments, cross-border financing and leasing, and intellectual property protection and enforcement in China, South East Asia and elsewhere.The firm's practice includes working with clients and their legal teams in the region outside Hong Kong on contract negotiation and drafting, risk assessment, financing and governmental approval for project investments, intellectual property protection and enforcement against infringement activities.The firm has extensive experience in representing bank creditors in cross-border litigation and insolvency, as well as in proceedings to trace, preserve and recover assets of defendants in the USA, UK, other EU countries and Asia.

INTERNATIONAL CLIENTS: A broad range of multinational banks, investment funds and corporations with headquarters in the USA, UK, other EU countries and Asia are currently the firm's clients. They come from a variety of industries, including finance, aviation, computer, tobacco, energy, telecommunications, chemical, pharmaceuticals, manufacturing, retail and distribution, food and beverages and others.

MAIN INTERNATIONAL AREAS OF PRACTICE:

Intellectual property and IT: Work involves advice on copyright, trademark and patent protection and enforcement in Hong Kong, China and elsewhere in Asia, as well as licensing and franchising work of a transactional nature. The IT partners advise on outsourcing, system integration and development, e-commerce, m-commerce, other ISP, ICP and fibre optic contracts and related privacy, internet and telecommunications issues. The IP partners are active in international IP organisations, the Hong Kong government and other committees.

Company and commercial: The firm advises on company and commercial matters including banking, corporate finance, project finance, M&A, construction and shipping. Services have included recent advice provided to a consortium of Hong Kong and foreign entertainment corporations on the establishment of a movie city in Hong Kong, a first major project of its kind in the movie industry in South East Asia in terms of its size and the sum invested.

Litigation, arbitration and insolvency: The firm handles all aspects of civil litigation, ADR and arbitration, including company, commercial, banking, construction disputes, public or tribunal inquiries, professional negligence, insurance, shipping, employment, contentious probate and trust. It also advises on the local and international aspects of insolvency, and the interaction of foreign and local insolvency administrations.

Conveyancing and real estate: Work includes the sale, purchase, letting and financing of properties; land purchase; real estate planning and development; sale of commercial and residential projects; and tenancy matters.

Trade with China: Services are provided on all aspects of commercial and conveyancing transactions in China. Typical transactions involve joint ventures, acquisitions and restructuring of infrastructural projects such as power plants, water treatment plants, toll roads and bridges, as well as hotel investments and cross-border leasing and financing.

Succession, tax and trusts: Work covers all aspects of taxation, trust and succession matters including corporate and personal tax, estate duty planning, wills, probate and estate or trust administration.

LANGUAGES: Cantonese, English, Putonghua

WILLIAM FRY

HEAD OFFICE

Fitzwilton House, Wilton Place,
Dublin 2, Ireland
Tel: +353 1 639 5000 **Fax:** +353 1 639 5333

Email: central.mail@williamfry.ie
Website: www.williamfry.ie

WORLDWIDE OFFICE CONTACTS

IRELAND
Fitzwilton House, Wilton Place, **Dublin** 2
Tel: +353 1 639 5000 **Fax:** +353 1 639 5333
Email: central.mail@williamfry.ie

FIRM OVERVIEW

Managing partner: Owen O'Connell
Senior partner: Houghton Fry

Number of partners worldwide: 30
Number of other lawyers worldwide: 105

AREAS OF PRACTICE:
Commercial/financial services/funds 60%
Litigation and insolvency 20%
Property and development 20%

W

FIRM OVERVIEW: Founded in 1847, William Fry is one of Ireland's largest law firms. The firm currently employs over 240 people and is situated adjacent to the offices of the Industrial Development Authority at Wilton Place in Dublin's City Centre. It is a full service law firm, specialising in corporate and commercial work with significant litigation and commercial property capabilities. The firm has particular experience in helping organisations establish operations in Ireland.

INTERNATIONAL EXPERIENCE: William Fry operates a large international practice and regularly acts in cases involving all major European jurisdictions and the USA. The firm has experience in take-over and cross border activity as well as major financing, reconstruction projects and workouts, provide the firm with a strong background in organisational liaison skills.

INTERNATIONAL CLIENTS: The firm has a number of multinational clients both Irish and non-Irish. These include banks, telecommunications and technology companies, manufacturing and pharmaceutical companies.

MAIN INTERNATIONAL AREAS OF PRACTICE:
Corporate finance: The firm provides specialist expertise on a range of areas such as M&A, flotations, management buy-outs, corporate restructurings, privatisations, International Financial Services Centre transactions, building societies and insurance industry.
Banking and financial services: The firm's lawyers are involved in all aspects of financial transactions for both Irish and international clients, including those based in Dublin's International Financial Services Centre (IFSC). Areas of expertise include acquisition finance, derivatives securitisations, bond issues, lease finance, and structured and finance transactions.
Investment funds: The firm is actively involved in assisting international companies to establish operations in the IFSC, including custodians, administrators and investment funds themselves. It also advises clients on the marketing and ongoing servicing of investment funds.
Technology/intellectual property: The firm handles all aspects of technology law and has experience in advising indigenous and international organisations, from start-up through to large multi-national companies. The firm also advises on intellectual property disputes conducted through traditional litigation, arbitration or alternative dispute resolution mechanisms.
EU/competition: The firm advises domestic and international clients on EU, competition, e-commerce regulatory and trade law matters
Corporate tax: William Fry Tax Advisers is the correspondent tax practice of William Fry Solicitors. It comprises a team of tax lawyers, accountants and consultants advising a broad range of international and domestic clients on all major business sectors including finance, technology, communications, construction, leisure and entertainment.
Employment/pensions: The firm provides employment and pensions advice to corporate clients and has particular skills in advising on corporate reorganisation, profit share plans, dismissals, redundancy arrangements, preparation and revision of employee handbooks, and health and safety.
Telecommunications: The firm advises corporate clients and state organisations specifically on liberalisation and regulations in relation to the telecommunications industry.
Insurance: The firm advises on both general and life assurances issues, and has acted for clients in take-overs, disposals, restructurings and privatisations.
Commercial property: The firm advises land owners, developers, investors and banks on matters such as commercial property purchase, sale and letting/leasing.
Construction law: The firm advises builders and developers on all aspects of contruction law.
Planning: The firm provides expert advice to corporate clients and state organisations on all aspects of planning law
Public private partnerships (PFI): The firm's property lawyers have been actively involved in this developing area, with one of its lawyers advising the government on the implementation of PPP/PFI projects.
Litigation and arbitration: The firm represents clients at every level in the Irish courts and before a wide range of tribunals. It covers all forms of commercial disputes including banking, crime, defamation, IT, licensing, professional negligence, intellectual property, and insurance.
Insolvency: The firm has extensive experience in advising financial institutions and companies on corporate recovery and protection of securities. It specialises in all forms of insolvency procedures including forensic investigations, corporate reorganisations, examinerships, creditor arrangements, receiverships and liquidations.

LANGUAGES: English, French, German

WILLIAM FRY
SOLICITORS

For other recommended firms see pages 1485-1520

WILLKIE FARR & GALLAGHER

HEAD OFFICE

787 Seventh Avenue,
New York NY 10019-6099, USA
Tel: +1 212 728 8000 **Fax:** +1 212 728 8111

Website: www.willkie.com

FIRM OVERVIEW

Chairman, executive committee Jack H Nusbaum

Number of partners worldwide: 121
Number of other lawyers worldwide: 354

AREAS OF PRACTICE:

Area	%
Litigation	24%
Other	18%
M&A	15%
Accessing of US capital markets	14%
Business and finance	14%
Real estate	7%
Bankruptcy and business reorganisation	6%
International trade	2%

FIRM OVERVIEW: Established in New York City in 1888, the firm comprises 121 partners and 354 other lawyers in offices in New York, Washington, D.C, Paris, London, Rome, Milan and Frankfurt. The firm's international practice has expanded and the firm's lawyers regularly handle international transactions. The firm represents financial buyers of businesses in New York requiring M&A, private equity and related advice on business operations in multiple juridictions throughout the world.

WORLDWIDE OFFICE CONTACTS

FRANCE
21-23 rue de la Ville l'Evêque, 75008 **Paris**
Tel: +33 1 53 43 45 00 **Fax:** +33 1 40 06 96 06

GERMANY
Frankfurter Welle, An der Welle 4, 60322 **Frankfurt am Main**
Tel: +49 69 79 30 20 **Fax:** +49 69 971 255 531

ITALY
Studio Legale, Delfino e Associati Willkie Farr & Gallagher, Via Michele Barozzi, 2, 20122 **Milan**
Tel: +39 02 76363 1 **Fax:** +39 02 76363 636

Studio Legale, Delfino e Associati Willkie Farr & Gallagher, Via di Ripetta, 142, 00186 **Rome**
Tel: +39 06 68636 1 **Fax:** +39 06 68636 363

UNITED KINGDOM
35 Wilson Street, **London** EC2M 2UA
Tel: +44 207 696 5454 **Fax:** +44 207 696 5455

USA
787 Seventh Avenue, **New York** NY 10019-6099
Tel: +1 212 728 8000 **Fax:** +1 212 728 8111

Three Lafayette Centre, 1155 21st Street, NW, **Washington DC** 20036-3384
Tel: +1 202 328 8000 **Fax:** +1 202 887 8979

W

INTERNATIONAL EXPERIENCE: Recent international transactions involving the firm include CVC Capital Partners' acquisition of Danone SA's BSN Emballage, SBS Broadcasting's acquisition of Central European Media Enterprises, Securitas AB's acquisition of Pinkerton's Inc, Swiss Reinsurance Company's acquisition of Fox Pitt Kelton, Olivetti & Mannesman's acquisition of Cellular Communications International Inc, La Salle Partners acquisition of Jones Lang Wootton and the merger of Zurich Group and financial service business of BAT.

INTERNATIONAL CLIENTS: Clients include Goldman Sachs International, Thompson CSF, Elf Acquitaine, France Telecom, Royal and Sun Alliance, the Zurich Group, Chanel, Fuji Photo Film Co.Ltd, TotalFina, Level 3 Communications GmbH, and Andersen Consulting.

MAIN INTERNATIONAL AREAS OF PRACTICE:

M&A: The firm buys and sells companies in cross-Atlantic and intra-European cross-border transactions. The firm represents a large number of issuers and underwriters in relation to debt and equity offerings in the United States.
International trade: The firm advises many foreign manufacturers and foreign governmental bodies on issues arising from regulations governing the importation of goods from the United States.
Business and finance: The firm handles matters such as corporate law, prvate equity, litigation, securitisations/structured finance, taxation, environmental and international trade.
Telecommunications and IT/Internet media: The firm has expertise in telecommunications, information technology and outsourcing, media and entertainment.

LANGUAGES: Dutch, English, French, German, Italian, Japanese, Spanish

WILLKIE FARR & GALLAGHER

WISTRAND ADVOKATBYRÅ

HEAD OFFICE

Klarabergsviadukten 70, PO Box 70393,
SE 107 24 Stockholm, Sweden
Tel: +46 8 50 72 00 00 **Fax:** +46 8 50 73 00 00

Email: sthlm@wistrand.net
Website: www.wistrand.net

WORLDWIDE OFFICE CONTACTS

SWEDEN
Lilla Bommen, SE 411 04 **Gothenburg**
Tel: +46 31 771 21 00 **Fax:** +46 31 771 21 50
Email: gbg@wistrand.net

Norra Vallgatan 64, SE 211 22 **Malmo**
Tel: +46 40 741 20 **Fax:** +46 40 611 91 19
Email: malmoe@wistrand.net

Klarabergsviadukten 70, PO Box 70393, SE 107 24 **Stockholm**
Tel: +46 8 50 72 00 00 **Fax:** +46 8 50 73 00 00
Email: sthlm@wistrand.net

FIRM OVERVIEW

Chairman: Peter Hedborg (Gothenburg)
Directors: Lennart Olsson (Malmo), Lars Hasp (Stockholm)

Number of partners worldwide: 35
Number of other lawyers worldwide: 35

AREAS OF PRACTICE:

Corporate and commercial	25%
M&A	15%
Banking and finance	10%
Insolvency	10%
Litigation and arbitration	10%
Telecommunications and IT	10%
Other	20%

W

FIRM OVERVIEW: The firm, originally founded in 19,15 is a full service firm specialising in corporate law, commercial law, litigation, banking and finance law and IT and telecommunications law. Wistrand is a member firm of Denton International, an alliance of European law firms that provides a fully co-ordinated legal service from over 1200 experienced lawyers. The network spans 23 jurisdictions around the globe, with a total of 35 offices covering Europe, the Middle East and Asia.

INTERNATIONAL EXPERIENCE: The firm provides legal advice and assistance to foreign legal entities, including multinational enterprises, international banks, financial institutions and foreign governments in all areas of business law. The firm has advised foreign and Swedish clients on acquisitions, joint ventures, technology transfers and financing facilities, with significant cross-border elements. The firm has acted on behalf of foreign companies and governments before the courts of Sweden and dispute resolution forums.

INTERNATIONAL CLIENTS: The firm's international clients include major business corporations and companies within the old and new economy, as well as banks and governmental entities.

MAIN INTERNATIONAL AREAS OF PRACTICE:

Company and commercial: The firm advises on all aspects of general corporate and commercial law, including corporate restructuring, corporate financing, stock market introduction, corporate governance, employee incentive programs and the drafting of Swedish and international contracts.

M&A: The firm represents Swedish clients in the acquisition and sale of foreign companies and foreign companies in the acquisition and sale of Swedish companies.

Litigation and arbitration: Headed by Stefan Lindskog, one of Sweden's most prominent legal practitioners, the firm advises Swedish governmental bodies, foreign governments, multinational corporations and major Swedish and foreign corporations on significant, complex and contentious matters.

Telecommunications and IT law: The firm advises on a wide range of matters such as regulatory issues, governmental licensing, IT acquisitions, technology transfer, internet law/e-commerce, outsourcing and project agreements. Clients include pan-European and US market leaders in the internet/digital media/e-commerce and fixed and mobile telecommunications sectors

Banking and finance: The firm assists Swedish and international banks and financial companies in all areas, including secured and syndicated loan transactions and guarantees, structured finance, lease finance, project finance and market flotation.

Tax: The firm's tax lawyers deal with national and international corporate tax issues arising in connection with commercial operations, acquisitions, restructurings and incentive programs.

Competition and EU: The firm advises on regulatory issues related to the utility, telecommunication and financial services industry and in relation to national and EU legislation related to acquisitions, vertical arrangements and freedom of movement.

Intellectual property: The firm provides legal assistance related to the prosecution of trademark, copyright and design right applications and the licensing, exploitation, maintenance and protection thereof. This area of practice is of increasing importance in relation to the firm's expanding IT/internet and telecommunications practice and media and entertainment practice.

Employment: The firm frequently advises major foreign corporations on the establishment of Swedish subsidiaries and branch offices and on labour and employee company policy.

Insurance and reinsurance: The firm was appointed receivers in two of the largest bankruptcy cases in Swedish history, Njord and Svenska Kredit. It has gained valuable experience and provides legal advice regarding restructuring, insurance contracts, insurance related litigation and claims related disputes.

Insolvency: The firm's specialists provide bankruptcy and insolvency counselling and act as court appointed receivers.

LANGUAGES: Czech, English, Finnish, French, German, Swedish

For other recommended firms see pages 1485-1520

WOLF THEISS & PARTNERS

HEAD OFFICE

Schubertring 6,
A-1010 Vienna, Austria
Tel: +43 1 515 10 **Fax:** +43 1 515 1025

Email: wtp@wtp.at

WORLDWIDE OFFICE CONTACTS

AUSTRIA
Schubertring 6, A-1010 **Vienna**
Tel: +43 1 515 10 **Fax:** +43 1 515 1025
Email: wtp@wtp.at

CZECH REPUBLIC
Klimentská 10, CZ-110 00 **Prague** 1
Tel: +420 2 510 186 11 **Fax:** +420 2 510 186 25
Email: wtp@wtp.at

FIRM OVERVIEW

Number of partners worldwide: 20
Number of other lawyers worldwide: 55

AREAS OF PRACTICE:

Arbitration and commercial litigation	*%
Banking	*%
Eastern Europe	*%
Finance and capital markets	*%
Insurance	*%
Intellectual property	*%
M&A and corporate	*%
Merger control and anti-trust	*%
Pharmaceuticals	*%
Project finance	*%
Property and leasing	*%
Public procurement	*%
Tax	*%
Telecommunications and media	*%

* Workload not disclosed

FIRM OVERVIEW: Wolf Theiss is a leading Austrian law firm. Since 1957 the firm has acted for national and international companies, banks and investors as well as for public institutions and has built an excellent reputation domestically and abroad. With approximately 75 lawyers, the firm ranks among the three largest firms in Austria. Over the years, Wolf Theiss has strengthened its international relations with clients and law firms abroad. Due to its increased work in Central and Eastern Europe, the firm opened an office in Prague in 1998.

INTERNATIONAL EXPERIENCE: The firm's client base spans the range of banking and finance, industry, energy and utilities, telecommunications, media, IT, pharmaceuticals, transportation and construction.

INTERNATIONAL CLIENTS: Clients are based predominantly in Europe, USA, Japan and South-East Asia.

MAIN INTERNATIONAL AREAS OF PRACTICE:

Banking and finance: Wolf Theiss acts for major Austrian banks as well as foreign international banks, financial institutions, funds and other businesses in the finance sector. Work handled includes the issue and listing of securities, derivatives, loan and finance facilities, regulatory and anti-trust matters. Particular emphasis is placed on corporate finance including structured and project finance.

Capital Markets: The firm has one of the leading capital markets departments in Austria. It has extensive experience in handling IPOs, secondary offerings and other capital markets transactions in Austria. The firm's work also extends to foreign jurisdictions.

M&A: The firm specialises in domestic and international mergers and acquisitions including joint ventures. Wolf Theiss advises national and international clients on acquisitions of companies and enterprises as well as the setting up of joint ventures in Austria and Eastern Europe. Work handled in particular includes due diligence investigations, tax and corporate structurings, contract drafting and negotiations, anti-trust and merger control.

Telecommunications and new media: Wolf Theiss advises a large number of private telecom operators in Austria in all fields relevant to their business. The firm's telecom lawyers have long-standing experience in drafting and negotiating interconnection, leases, lines and related agreements, and advising on regulatory matters. Media lawyers act for major media enterprises in Austria and advise on all media law matters including the provision of radio and television by private entities.

Property and infrastructure: The firm specialises in property and project development. It acts as permanent counsel to major developers and investors in Austria and the Czech Republic. The firm's work in project development and project finance has seen an increasing volume in infrastructure-related matters.

Tax restructuring: In conjunction with its work in M&A, refinancing and corporate restructuring, the firm offers highly specialised advice on tax structuring. The tax department acts in full integration with transactions lawyers. Most of the lawyers in the tax department are certified tax advisers.

EU law: The firm's practice encompasses EU law. It advises on the full scope of EU law and offers sophisticated EU litigation.

Employment and social security: Wolf Theiss offers a first-rate service, advising on personnel restructuring measures and projects, particularly in connection with acquisitions and transfers of business. Services offered include employment litigation; drafting of employment contracts and workshop agreements; devising pension plans; negotiation with work councils and union representatives and employment-related due diligence investigations.

Arbitration and commercial litigation: The firm advises on commercial disputes before all major international institutional arbitration tribunals and ad hoc tribunals. The firm also acts in major national commercial litigation cases before national courts.

LANGUAGES: Czech, English, German, French

WOLF THEISS & PARTNERS

W

WOMBLE CARLYLE SANDRIDGE & RICE PLLC

HEAD OFFICE

200 West Second Street, P.O. Drawer 84,
Winston-Salem NC 27102, USA
Tel: +1 336 721 3600 **Fax:** +1 336 721 3660
Email: info@wcsr.com
Website: www.wcsr.com

FIRM OVERVIEW

Firm managing member: John L.W. Garrou
Office managing member: Kenneth A. Moser

Number of members worldwide: 178
Number of other lawyers worldwide: 224

AREAS OF PRACTICE:

Antitrust, trade practices and commerce ....*%
Banking, finance and property ....*%
Bankruptcy ....*%
Corporate and securities ....*%
Employment ....*%
Health ....*%
Intellectual property ....*%
Life science ....*%
Litigation and arbitration ....*%
Tax ....*%
Technology and e-commerce ....*%
Trusts and estates ....*%
* Workload % not dislcosed

FIRM OVERVIEW: Womble Carlyle Sandridge & Rice, PLLC, traces its history back to 1876. The firm is comprised of over 400 lawyers operating from seven offices throughout the southeastern United States. It is a full service business law firm that provides innovative legal advice to a wide spectrum of regional, national and international business clients. Womble Carlyle's aim is to deliver a high quality, cost-effective and responsive service. The firm is a member of Lex Mundi, the world's leading association of independent law firms (158 member firms with 12,000 lawyers in over 100 jurisdictions worldwide).

INTERNATIONAL EXPERIENCE: The firm's lawyers advise on business acquisitions, joint ventures, the protection and licensing of intellectual property, commercial leasing, sales and distribution arrangements, US export controls, customs and immigration in the context of inbound and outbound international transactions and operations. The firm defends the interests of its clients, including patent and trademark rights, in dispute resolution involving litigation, mediation and international arbitration throughtout the world.

INTERNATIONAL CLIENTS: Womble Carlyle represents businesses in sectors that include manufacturing, transportation and energy, financial services, insurance, health care, education and technology. Clients include Ætna Life & Casualty; American International Group Inc; Armstrong World Industries Inc; Bayer Corporation; Branch Banking & Trust Company; Ciba Specialty Chemicals Corp; Clarus Corporation; Collins & Aikman Floorcoverings Inc; DB Alex Brown LLC; Debiopharm SA; Flextronics International; Glaxo Wellcome Inc; Innogenetics NV; IntelliNet Corporation; International Business Machines Corporation; JA Jones Construction Company; LastMinuteTravel.com, Inc; Medigital Inc; Novartis Pharmaceuticals Corporation; Pillowtex; RF Micro Devices Inc; RJ Reynolds Tobacco Company; Remington Arms Corporation Inc; Technology Ventures LLC; Thomas Built Buses Inc; Thomasville Furniture Industries Inc; Unicomp Inc; Universal Tax Systems Inc; UnumProvident Corporation; Wachovia Bank, NA.

WORLDWIDE OFFICE CONTACTS

USA
One Atlantic Center, Suite 3500, West Peachtree Street, **Atlanta** GA 30309
Tel: +1 404 872 7000 **Fax:** +1 404 888 7490

3300 One First Union Center, 301 South College Street, **Charlotte** NC 28202-6025
Tel: +1 704 331 4900 **Fax:** +1 704 331 4955

Suite 400, 2530 Meridian Parkway, Research Triangle Park, PO Box 13069, NC 27713, **Durham**
Tel: +1 919 484 2300 **Fax:** +1 919 484 2340

700 Poinsett Plaza, 104 South Main Street, PO Box 10208, **Greenville** SC 29603-0208
Tel: +1 864 255 5400 **Fax:** +1 864 255 5440

Suite 2100, 150 Fayetteville Street Mall, PO Box 831, **Raleigh** NC 27602
Tel: +1 919 755 2100 **Fax:** +1 919 755 2150

1120 19th Street, NW, 8th Floor, **Washington DC** 20036
Tel: +1 202 857 4400 **Fax:** +1 202 467 6910

MAIN AREAS OF INTERNATIONAL PRACTICE:

Antitrust, trade practices and commerce: The firm advises on a wide variety of issues involving business and trade regulation, including sales and distribution arrangements, advertising, compliance issues relating to export controls, import restrictions, the Foreign Corrupt Practices Act and anti-boycott laws.
M&A and joint venture: The firm advises clients with respect to business acquisitions, joint ventures, strategic partnerships, corporate structure and reorganisations, enforceability of international agreements, as well as general corporate matters.
Intellectual property: The firm's representation includes all aspects of domestic and foreign intellectual property law, including patent investigations and analyses, procurement of US and foreign patents and general client counseling regarding license agreements, corporate-sponsered research contracts, development agreements, technology transfer agreements and software protection.
Banking, finance and property: The firm advises financial institutions and other capital providers, commercial finance and real estate finance institutions and to commercial real estate developers and corporations regarding the acquisition, financing and development of real property and commercial leasing.
Litigation and arbitration: The firm defends the interests of its clients, including patent and trademark rights, in dispute resolution involving litigation, mediation and international arbitration. Lawyers with the firm have served as lead counsel, co-counsel and supervising counsel in matters before tribunals in a number of countries outside the US.
Tax: The firm provides creative tax planning and advice on mergers and acquisitions, corporate reorganisations, real estate development; tax controversies before the Internal Revenue Service and state taxing authorities; and tax-sensitive and tax-enhanced financings, to clients conducting business internationally.

LANGUAGES: Arabic, Dutch, English, French, German, Greek, Hebrew, Hungarian, Italian, Japanese, Mandarin, Persian, Portuguese, Russian, Spanish, Turkish

 For other recommended firms see pages 1485-1520

WONG PARTNERSHIP

HEAD OFFICE

80 Raffles Place, #58-01 UOB Plaza 1,
Singapore 048624
Tel: + 65 532 7488 **Fax:** + 65 532 5711

Email: wonglaw@singnet.com.sg

FIRM OVERVIEW

Managing partner: Mr Wong Meng Meng, Senior Counsel

Number of partners worldwide: 23
Number of other lawyers worldwide: 43

AREAS OF PRACTICE:

Alternative dispute resolution and litigation: 35%
Banking, finance and corporate: 35%
Building and construction: 20%
Conveyancing and real estate: 8%
Intellectual property and technology: 2%

FIRM OVERVIEW: Established in 1992, Wong Partnership has 23 partners and 43 other lawyers in its two Singapore offices. It has a broad-based commercial law practice with five main practice groups.

INTERNATIONAL EXPERIENCE: The ADR and litigation group has extensive experience of representing clients in multi-jurisdictional disputes; recent cases have involved the coordination of litigation in several jurisdictions including the USA, Russia, the Netherlands, Britain and Mauritius. It acted for the auditors of Baring Futures (Singapore) Pte Ltd in relation to the collapse of the Barings Group, and for an international grouping of airlines in a shareholder and confidentiality dispute. The banking, finance and corporate group has advised financial institutions and multinational corporations on transactions in Singapore and the region. Significant corporate transactions in which the firm has been involved include: representing a consortium of 11 Asian airlines and Abacus Distribution Systems Pte Ltd. in its $757million merger with the Asia-Pacific operations of the Sabre Group Inc; representing the Development Bank of Singapore in its acquisition of the Bank of South East Asia Inc. in the Philippines; acting for Neptune Orient Lines in its international share placement for new ordinary shares and the offering of a non-voting redeemable non-convertible preference shares; acting for Natsteel Electronics Ltd in a US$300 million 1.5% convertible bonds issue lead managed by Merrill Lynch (Singapore) and sold in the US, Europe and Asia; representing Morgan Stanley Dean Witter and The Development Bank of Singapore Ltd as lead managers of the US$1billion exchangeable bond issue by Fullerton Global Corporation; acting for two Singapore Airline subsidaries (SIA Engineering and Singapore Terminal Services) in connection with their international offering of shares; representing SPH Asia One in the first initial public offering in Singapore with a separate tranche offered through the Internet; acting for United Overseas Bank in its acquisition of Westmont Bank in the Philippines.

INTERNATIONAL CLIENTS: The firm's clients include multinational corporations in banking, securities and finance, insurance, property development and construction, the hotel and leisure industry, telecommunications, manufacturing and trading and the petroleum and chemicals industry. Other clients are foreign governments, quasi-governmental organisations and state-owned corporations, as well as international professional firms.

WORLDWIDE OFFICE CONTACTS

SINGAPORE
80 Raffles Place, #58-01 UOB Plaza 1, **Singapore** 048624
Tel: + 65 532 7488 **Fax:** + 65 532 5711
Email: wonglaw@singnet.com.sg

298 Tiong Bahru Road, #18-01/06, Central Plaza,
Singapore 168730
Tel: + 65 222 2000 **Fax:** + 65 277 1800
Email: wonglaw@singnet.com.sg

MAIN INTERNATIONAL AREAS OF PRACTICE:
Intellectual property: The firm has global experience in a wide range of legal issues in trade marks, patents, designs, information, technology transfers, franchise agreements and business goodwill in a variety of contexts, and advises on international protection strategies.
General corporate and commercial transactions: The team helps clients set up businesses in Singapore and the Asia Pacific region, and advises on joint ventures and shareholding agreements, distributorship and agency agreements, employment and immigration law, asset and business acquisitions, corporate secretarial services, tax planning and trusts and stamp duty savings schemes. It also acts for Singaporean companies acquiring foreign businesses or assets.
Securities and financial markets: The firm advises on corporate restructuring, including privatisation and schemes of arrangements, takeovers, M&A, private placements and public offerings of shares, bonds and other securities, securities listings on the Singapore Exchange Securities Trading Limited and other securities exchanges, fund management including unit trusts and other collective investment schemes, legal and regulatory issues concerning securities, futures and commodities, venture capital and direct investments. In line with the growth of its regional practice, the firm has developed specific experience in securities offerings for foreign companies in Singapore, including PRC-based ones.

LANGUAGES: Bahasa Indonesia, Bahasa Melayu, Chinese (Mandarin and dialects), English, French, Hindi, Tamil

W

For other recommended firms see pages 1485-1520

WONG TAN & MOLLY LIM

HEAD OFFICE

80 Robinson Road #17-02,
Singapore 068898, Singapore
Tel: +65 222 8008 **Fax:** +65 222 8001

Email: office@wtl.com.sg
Website: http://homel.pacific.net.sg/~wtl

WORLDWIDE OFFICE CONTACTS

SINGAPORE
80 Robinson Road #17-02, **Singapore** 068898
Tel: +65 222 8008 **Fax:** +65 222 8001
Email: office@wtl.com.sg

FIRM OVERVIEW

Managing partner: Sunny Wong
Senior partner: Molly Lim, Senior Counsel

Number of partners worldwide: 7
Number of other lawyers worldwide: 8

AREAS OF PRACTICE:

Area	Workload
Banking and finance	*%
Corporate	*%
Employment	*%
Litigation and arbitration, mediation	*%
Mergers and acquisitions	*%
Property	*%
Securities and financial markets	*%

* Workload % not disclosed

W

FIRM OVERVIEW: Wong Tan & Molly Lim was established by a group of lawyers who, up to December 1986, were senior associates with a major international law firm. The firm works frequently with lawyers from different jurisdictions, but has chosen not to participate in formal alliances or networks, preferring to remain independent and to maintain contacts with various firms worldwide and to choose the firms it works with on individual international transactions. The firm offers a comprehensive legal service to clients with international business interests, but focuses on banking and finance, mergers and acquisitions, corporate finance and general commercial and corporate law.

INTERNATIONAL EXPERIENCE: The firm works frequently on referrals from international law firms as well as directly with multinational corporations and Fortune 500 companies, particularly on international transactions with an Asian involvement. The firm has established working relationships with a network of lawyers across Asia with whom it has worked on many cross-border and international M&A and financing transactions.

INTERNATIONAL CLIENTS: The firm's client base includes major local corporations, local statutory boards, multinational companies, international and foreign law firms and accounting firms, international banks and public or supranational institutions conducting cross-border business.

MAIN INTERNATIONAL AREAS OF PRACTICE:

Mergers and acquisitions: The firm's transactions in this area range from small private acquisitions to cross-border takeovers of listed companies.
Banking and finance: The firm covers all areas of banking and finance, including secured and syndicated loan transactions and guarantees, structured finance and project finance. It has acted for many international banks in drafting and advising on standard form documentation for general banking transactions.
Corporate: The firm advises on all aspects of general corporate law, including the drafting of contracts, the provision of corporate secretarial services and provides local representation services for many foreign and multinational companies.
Employment: The firm handles all matters relating to employment law, and has advised on, and structured, many Employee Share Option Schemes.
Securities and financial markets: The firm advises clients on regulatory and other legal issues pertaining to fund management, securities and derivatives. It also assists investment firms to structure and license their operations.
Litigation and arbitration, mediation: The litigation department, headed by Molly Lim, Senior Counsel, deals with commercial litigation, national and international arbitration, and ADR. Its lawyers are frequently involved in cases before the Singapore Courts, including the Supreme Court.
Property: The firm advises clients on all aspects of property law including those relating to purchase, lease and development of residential and commercial properties.

LANGUAGES: Chinese, English, Malay

For other recommended firms see pages 1485-1520

WOO, KWAN, LEE & LO

HEAD OFFICE

see Worldwide Office Contacts

FIRM OVERVIEW

Contact partners: Angelina PL Lee, Edward WY Cheung

Number of partners worldwide: 21
Number of other lawyers worldwide: 45

AREAS OF PRACTICE:

Conveyancing .... *%
Corporate and commercial .... *%
Litigation .... *%
Others .... *%
*Workload % not disclosed

FIRM OVERVIEW: Established in 1973 as a result of the merger between Woo & Kwan and Charles Lee & Stephen Lo. Woo, Kwan, Lee & Lo is one of the largest law firms in Hong Kong, with 21 partners and a total staff of more than 250 located in offices in Hong Kong and Beijing. The conveyancing practice is one of Hong Kong's largest and handles a variety of large property development projects. The firm is also experienced in corporate and commercial law.

INTERNATIONAL CLIENTS: The firm's clients include local blue chip companies, as well as red-chip corporations. It also advises major developers, banks and financial institutions, private companies and individuals.

MAIN INTERNATIONAL AREAS OF PRACTICE:

Conveyancing: The firm's conveyancing department deals mainly with development and leasing projects and sale and purchase of properties (residential, commercial and industrial). Work includes agreements for sale and purchase, sub-sales, assignments, mortgages, tenancies, licences, application for modification of land grant conditions, assessment of premium and rates and government rent. Contact, Ivy SC Chan.

Corporate and commercial: The firm deals with corporate finance transactions such as initial public offerings (including H-shares and B-shares of PRC companies), issue of shares, debt, derivatives and other securities, mergers and acquisitions, reorganisations, ongoing compliance by public listed companies; general corporate and commercial transactions such as purchase and sale of companies and joint ventures; financing and banking transactions such as secured loans, syndicated loans and other capital market transactions; taxation matters such as taxplanning, tax appeals, trusts and estate duty planning; general advice in relation to the legal requirements of doing business in Hong Kong. Contact, Angelina PL Lee.

PRC related matters: The firm's PRC division which forms part of the Corporate and Commercial department, handles joint venture agreements (especially in property development and infrastructure work), fund raising for PRC enterprises in Hong Kong through the issue of H-shares and B-shares, sale of properties in the PRC and investment in Hong Kong and overseas by PRC enterprises. Contact, Edward WY Cheung.

WORLDWIDE OFFICE CONTACTS

CHINA
Room 611, 6th Floor, Beijing Tower, 10 Dong Chang An Jie, **Beijing** 100006
Tel: + 86 10 6522 6950 **Fax:** + 86 10 6522 6995

HONG KONG
26th Floor, Jardine House, 1 Connaught Place, Central, **Hong Kong**
Tel: + 852 2847 7888 **Fax:** + 852 2845 0239

27th Floor, Jardine House, 1 Connaught Place, Central, **Hong Kong**
Tel: + 852 2847 7999 **Fax:** + 852 2845 9225

Room 2801, Sun Hung Kai Centre, 30 Harbour Road, **Hong Kong**
Tel: + 852 2586 9898 **Fax:** + 852 2827 6046

ASSOCIATED OFFICES

THAILAND
Siam Premier International Law Office Ltd, 24th-25th Floor,
Thai Wah Tower II, No. 21/147-150 South Sathorn Road, **Bangkok** 10120
Tel: + 66 2 679 1333 **Fax:** + 66 2 679 1314
Email: siamlaw@loxinfo.co.th

Litigation: The firm's litigation department deals mainly with dispute resolution in all areas of civil law including pre-litigation advice, legal proceedings in courts of all levels in Hong Kong, proceedings before various statutory boards and tribunals such as the Inland Revenue Board of Review and Town Planning Appeal Board, co-ordination of litigation processes in other jurisdictions, domestic and international arbitration and enforcement of judgements and awards both in Hong Kong and other jurisdictions, as well as settlement negotiation. The firm also acts for clients in statutory inquiries such as those conducted by the Financial Secretary under the Companies Ordinance, securities laws and regulations of the Securities and Futures Commission and The Stock Exchange of Hong Kong Limited, including at the Insider Dealing Tribunal. It has also defended clients in complicated matters such as cases brought by the Commercial Crime Bureau and the Independent Commission Against Corruption. Contact, Cheung Wai Hing.

Others: The firm also provides full services in the areas of probate and intellectual property.

LANGUAGES: Chinese (Cantonese, Putonghua and other dialects), English

WOO, YUN, KANG, JEONG & HAN

HEAD OFFICE

Textile Center, 12F, 944-31 Daechi-dong, Kangnam-ku
Seoul 135-713, South Korea
Tel: +82 2 528 5200 **Fax:** +82 2 528 5300

Email: mail@wooyun.co.kr
Website: www.wooyun.co.kr

WORLDWIDE OFFICE CONTACTS

SOUTH KOREA
Textile Center, 12F, 944-31 Daechi-dong, Kangnam-ku, **Seoul** 135-713
Tel: +82 2 528 5200 **Fax:** +82 2 528 5300
Email: mail@wooyun.co.kr

FIRM OVERVIEW

Managing partner: Chang Rok Woo

Number of partners worldwide: 14
Number of other lawyers worldwide: 35

AREAS OF PRACTICE:

Anti-trust and fair trade	*%
Banking and finance	*%
General corporate	*%
Intellectual property	*%
International investments	*%
International trade	*%
Litigation and arbitration	*%
Real estate	*%
Tax	*%

* Workload % not disclosed

FIRM OVERVIEW: Established in 1997, Woo,Yun, Kang, Jeong & Han is a leading Korean law firm. The firm is currently comprised of 14 partners, 25 associates, 10 foreign legal consultants and 3 accountants. In addition, a former Chief Justice of the Constitutional Court of Korea is a full-time counsel of the firm. Many of the partners have international experience either through education abroad and/or training at leading international law firms. Some of the firm's partners and associates also have extensive experience as former judges or prosecutors.

INTERNATIONAL EXPERIENCE: The firm advises international corporations and businesses on cross border and local issues in areas including M&A, capital markets transactions, asset-backed securitisation, corporate restructurings, corporate governance, company establishment, anti-trust and fair trade, domestic and international tax, joint ventures, franchising, technology transfers, licensing, distributorships, agencies, employment, and immigration.

INTERNATIONAL CLIENTS: The firm represents international clients of all sizes and from all sectors of industry, including automotive, manufacturing, electronics, high technology, financial institutions, telecommunications, energy, and pharmaceuticals.

MAIN INTERNATIONAL AREAS OF PRACTICE:
General corporate: The firm handles domestic and cross-border mergers, acquisitions, and other forms of consolidation and divestiture. It also advises on securities, labour and employment, bankruptcy and reorganisations, telecommunications and e-commerce business, and privatisation.
International trade: Woo, Yun, Kang, Jeong & Han advises on import/export agreements, distributorship agreements, customs and foreign exchange regulation, anti-dumping, and countervailing duty investigations.
International investments: The firm advises on direct investments or establishment of joint ventures, subsidiaries, branches, and liaison offices in Korea, and private equity investment.
Anti-trust and fair trade: The firm handles issues related to unfair trade practices, anti-competitive aspects of mergers and acquisitions, and various other transactions (domestically and internationally).
Banking and finance: The firm advises on domestic and international finance and banking matters, including securities issue, mergers and acquisitions, investment trusts, asset-backed securitisation, offshore financing, project financing, financial derivatives, and dispute resolution.
Tax: The firm advises on complex international and domestic tax planning, compliance, and dispute resolution. It also advises on obtaining official advisories, opinions, and rulings from tax authorities with respect to corporate, individual income, value-added, real property, and other taxes and customs duties.
Litigation and arbitration: The firm has a full-service litigation and arbitration team composed of trial lawyers with extensive experience as judges. Work handled includes advising, assisting, representing and advocating international and Korean clients with respect to all legal disputes or potential disputes.
Intellectual property: The firm advises on the protection of patents, know-how, trade secrets, trademarks, service marks, trade names, computer programs, and copyrights of software, literary works, music, audio and video recordings, and movies.
Real estate: The firm advises on a range of issues including real property sale and purchase, lease, construction, and environmental.

LANGUAGES: English, German, Japanese, Korean

WOO, YUN, KANG, JEONG & HAN

 For other recommended firms see pages 1485-1520

XAVIER, BERNARDES, BRAGANÇA

HEAD OFFICE

Av. Brasil 1008,
01430 000 São Paulo, Brazil
Tel: +55 11 3069 4300 **Fax:** +55 11 3069 4301

Email: xbblawsaopaulo@xbb.com.br
Website: www.xbb.com.br

FIRM OVERVIEW

Senior partners: Alberto Xavier, Horácio Bernardes Neto, Alberto de Orleans e Bragança

Number of partners worldwide: 7
Number of other lawyers worldwide: 45

AREAS OF PRACTICE:

Commercial and corporate	20%
Tax	20%
Aviation	10%
Foreign investment	10%
Infrastructure	10%
International commerce	10%
Litigation and arbitration	10%
Administrative	5%
Banking and capital markets	5%

WORLDWIDE OFFICE CONTACTS

BRAZIL
Rua Dona Francisca, 260-1409, 89201-250 **Joinville**
Tel: + 55 47 422 7955 **Fax:** + 55 47 422 7956
Email: xbblawjoinville@xbb.com.br

Av. Rio Branco 1-14A, 20090-003, **Rio de Janeiro**
Tel: +55 21 272 9200 **Fax:** +55 21 283 0023
Email: xbblawriodejaneiro@xbb.com.br

PORTUGAL
Av. da Liberdade, 144-7E, 7th Floor E, 1250-146 **Lisbon**
Tel: +351 21 321 9470 **Fax:** +351 21 347 1455
Email: xbblawlisboa@xbb.pt

Rua João Tavira, 22-2o F, 9000 Funchal, **Madeira**
Tel: +351 291 23 78 47 **Fax:** +351 291 23 86 49
Email: xbblawlisboa@xbb.pt

FIRM OVERVIEW: XBB was founded in 1995 by a group of partners from well-established and prestigious law firms. With offices in São Paulo, Rio de Janeiro, Joinville, Lisbon and Funchal (Madeira), Xavier, Bernardes, Bragança comprises highly qualified and experienced lawyers. The firm offers a full range of legal services and has been at the forefront of some of the most prestigious financial and commercial transactions in Brazil.

INTERNATIONAL EXPERIENCE: The firm has advised international companies investing in Brazil, either by acquiring operative Brazilian companies or by forming Brazilian subsidiaries. XBB has also advised foreign investors involved in the privatisation of Brazilian companies in the energy, telecommunications, sanitation and gas industries.

INTERNATIONAL CLIENTS: Clients include Booz Allen & Hamilton Inc.; Thyssen Krupp Stahl; Amanco Holding Inc; IFX Corporation; Credit Agriole Indosuez; Lloyds Bank; Southwestern Bell Corporation; Hypo-Vereinsbank; Warburg Pincus Ventures L.P.; Sampoerna Latin America Ltd.; Bombardier Capital Inc.; Pegasus Capital Corporation; Aircraft Inventory Corporation; The Willis Group; The Cit Group Equipment Financing Inc.; Debis Financial Services Inc.; Colliers Macaulay Nicholls Inc.; Giesecke & Devrient MGBH; Smithline Beecham Plc.; Daimler Chrysler Systems N.V/S.A; Petroleo Brasil S/A; Grupo Monteriro Aranha; Banco Bradesco S/A; Bradespar S/A; Bradesco Administradora de Cartoes de Credito Ltd.; Brasil Telecom; Paging Network of Brasil Ltd.; Ericsson Telecomunications; Alcatel Telecommunications; General Motors of Brasil.

MAIN INTERNATIONAL AREAS OF PRACTICE

Commercial and corporate: The firm handles corporate reorganisations, restructuring, mergers and acquisitions, due diligence, shareholder agreements, joint ventures, insurance matters, and commercial contracts.

Banking and capital markets: The firm advises on all aspects of banking and capital markets including international financial operations, listed company regulation (securities and exchange commission), securitisation, futures and derivatives markets, project and equipment financing, domestic and cross-border leasing, as well as regulations governing financial markets. It also handles administrative litigation relating to Central Bank and Securities and Exchange Commission investment funds.

Tax: Xavier, Bernardes, Bragança specialises in all aspects of tax law. It advises on domestic and international tax planning and treaties for avoidance of double taxation.

Foreign investment: The firm advises on a broad range of foreign investment issues including direct investments, foreign loans, technology transfer, exchange operations, and Brazilian investments abroad.

Administrative: The firm's administrative practice handles a wide range of work including privatisations, out-sourcing, public service concessions, public works, administrative litigation, and foreign investments in telecommunications and satellites. It also advises on electricity regulations, gas and petroleum projects, water and sanitation, transport law, and environmental law.

Aviation: The firm has a very active practice in cross border aircraft financing, both in the importation of foreign aircraft to Brazil, under operating and finance leases, as well as in the exportation of Brazilian manufactured aircraft.

LANGUAGES: English, French, German, Italian, Portuguese, Spanish

For other recommended firms see pages 1485-1520

YC LEE & COMPANY

HEAD OFFICE

Suites 507-510, 5th Floor, Kompleks Jalan Sultan,
Bandar Seri Begawan BSB B58811, Brunei
Tel: +673 2 228 725 **Fax:** +673 2 240 786

Email: ycleelaw@brunet.bn.

FIRM OVERVIEW

Managing partner: Yew Choh Lee

Number of partners worldwide: 3
Number of other lawyers worldwide: 2

AREAS OF PRACTICE:
Litigation and arbitration 40%
Corporate and commercial 20%
Insurance and banking 20%
Intellectual property 20%

WORLDWIDE OFFICE CONTACTS

BRUNEI
Suites 507-510, 5th Floor, Kompleks Jalan Sultan, **Bandar Seri Begawan** BSB B58811
Tel: +673 2 228 725 **Fax:** +673 2 240 786
Email: ycleelaw@brunet.bn.

No.82, 2nd Floor, Jalan Bunga Tanjong, **Kuala Belait** KA 1131
Tel: +673 3 342583 **Fax:** +673 3 331116

Y

FIRM OVERVIEW: YC Lee & Company was founded in 1992. Comprising five lawyers, the firm handles general corporate work and specialises in litigation and intellectual property. The firm has offices in the capital city Bandar Seri Begawan and Kuala Belait.

INTERNATIONAL EXPERIENCE: The firm's client base includes local and foreign banks. YC Lee & Company advises the British High Commission, the German Embassy and the French Embassy. The firm maintains contact with regional and international law firms and is a member of the State Capital Law Firm Group and the ICC Counterfeiting Intelligence Bureau.

INTERNATIONAL CLIENTS: Clients include Lucent Technologies (USA); Goldman Sachs (Hong Kong); Kumagai Gumi Co Ltd (Japan); Cable & Wireless HKT (Hong Kong); Canon Kabushiki Kaisha (Japan); SmithKline Beecham (UK); and Royal Brunei Airlines (Brunei).

MAIN INTERNATIONAL AREAS OF PRACTICE:
Corporate: The firm advises on all aspects of general corporate law including restriction of offshore funds and securities, and drafting and setting up joint venture vehicles. It handles due diligence issues relating to the private acquisition of Brunei companies.
Litigation and arbitration: The firm has a very strong litigation practice. It advises on all aspects of litigation and arbitration and represents clients before the Brunei High Court.
Intellectual property: The firm advises on all aspects of intellectual property including infringement disputes and registration services.
Trust, securities and financial markets: The firm's subsidiary company, Serangan Star Trust Corporation (SSTC), provides international trusteeship advice in accordance with Brunei's new International Trusts Order (2000). SSTC are able to establish a broad range of secure corporate and personal trust structures, and advises on the licensing and structure of investment firms.

LANGUAGES: English, Malay, Mandarin

YC Lee & Company

For other recommended firms see pages 1485-1520

YIGAL ARNON & CO

HEAD OFFICE

1 Azrieli Center,
Tel Aviv 67021, Israel
Tel: +972 3 608 7777 **Fax:** +972 3 608 7724

FIRM OVERVIEW

Founding partner: Yigal Arnon
Chairman - International Department: Paul H Baris

Number of partners worldwide: 21
Number of other lawyers worldwide: 65

AREAS OF PRACTICE:

Banking and project finance	*%
Corporate	*%
High tech	*%
Litigation	*%
Property	*%

* Workload % not disclosed

WORLDWIDE OFFICE CONTACTS

ISRAEL
1 Azrieli Center, **Tel Aviv** 67021
Tel: +972 3 608 7777 **Fax:** +972 3 608 7724
Email: [name of lawyer]@arnon.co.il

FIRM OVERVIEW: Founded by Yigal Arnon in the 1950s, the firm has over 60 lawyers located in Tel Aviv and Jerusalem, and represents the full gamut of industry and business, including private and public investments, mergers, acquisitions, venture capital funds, litigation, property, banking and project finance. The firm has developed a distinguished international and local client base, making it one of the most prominent and largest law firms in Israel.

INTERNATIONAL CLIENTS: Clients range from global companies to private companies and individuals involved in strategic alliances, mergers and acquisitions, joint ventures, public and private financings, distributorships, franchises, property transactions and others.

INTERNATIONAL EXPERIENCE: A substantial part of the firm's practice is international. The firm is particulaly active in the US and Europe but is advising clients in their business activities throughout the world, including China, Japan, Australia, South Africa and South America. Members of the firm have brought to the practice a combined wealth of expertise from the United States, England, South Africa, Australia and Israel, providing a full-service presence and bringing together a unique cultural and intellectual appreciation of the requirements of its clients.

MAIN INTERNATIONAL AREAS OF PRACTICE:

Corporate: The firm has represented clients in many of the leading transactions which have taken place in Israel over recent years and has an outstanding M&A practice. It has considerable expertise in obtaining approvals for transactions from government agencies such as the Controller of Restrictive Trade Practices, the Office of the Chief Scientist and the Investment Centre.

High-Tech: Yigal Annon & Co is a leader in this field, representing several of the leading Israeli venture capital funds and numerous US and European funds as well as a whole gamut of high-tech and 'start-up' companies in their varying stages of development.

Property: The property department represents some of the leading property companies in Israel and abroad and is involved in a large number of major property development projects (both commercial and residential) and acquisitions.

Banking and project finance: The firm represents Israeli, US and European banks in all manner of services including the provision of legal opinions to foreign counsel. Yigal Arnon & Co has represented a number of major international consortia tendering for national infrastructure and complex project finance undertakings on BOT and other bases.

Securities: Yigal Arnon & Co has a dominant position in representing companies and underwriters in IPO's in New York, the European stock markets and Tel Aviv.

Litigation and arbitration: The firm represents domestic and international clients in a wide range of cases, including arbitration, commercial litigation and high profile civil and criminal matters and has an active appeals practice before the Supreme Court. The firm's litigation practice is one of the largest in Israel.

Telecommunications: The firm represents a number of major international and domestic telecommunication companies and has frequent dealings with the Ministry of Communications.

Employment: The department advises international and domestic clients in all areas of Israeli employment law.

LANGUAGES: English, Hebrew and various European languages.

Y

YRARRÁZAVAL, RUIZ TAGLE, LAGOS & SILVA

HEAD OFFICE

Hendaya 60, Suite 202, Las Condes,
Santiago Chile
Tel: +56 2 750 0200 **Fax:** +56 2 750 0201
Email: yrls@yrls.cl

FIRM OVERVIEW

Managing partner: Luis Fernando Silva
Senior partners: Arturo Yrarrázaval, Francisco Ruiz-Tagle, Juan Ignacio Lagos

Number of partners worldwide: 4
Number of other lawyers worldwide: 8

AREAS OF PRACTICE:

Area	%
Company, commercial and M&A	40%
Banking, finance and project financing	20%
Litigation and arbitration	15%
Competition and anti-trust	10%
Insurance and social security	5%
Property	5%
Tax	5%

FIRM OVERVIEW: Yrarrázaval, Ruiz Tagle, Lagos & Silva was founded in 2000 as a result of the break up of Philippi, Yrarrázaval, Pulido & Brunner. Globalisation, innovation and technology are among the driving forces that inspired the creation of the firm, and its aim is to provide quality legal advice to both international and domestic corporations. Members of the firm all have strong academic backgrounds.

INTERNATIONAL EXPERIENCE: During 2000 the firm has acted in important international acquisitions of companies, especially in Chile. It has also acted in the restructuring of international corporations. One of the partners of the firm was appointed by the International Chamber of Commerce in an important international arbitration proceeding and members of the firm have defended foreign investors in local arbitration proceedings. The firm has also acted in large international financial transactions.

INTERNATIONAL CLIENTS: The firm's clients include Aetna, ABN AMRO Bank, Arcor, Banco Santander, Basic, BOC, Borland, Bourjois, Brandes, Bristol Myers-Squibb, Cemex, Centennial, Ciba Especialidades Químicas, Chiquita, Clariant, Compaq, Continental Airlines, Credit Swiss, Dailey, Dart, Donaldson Luftkin & Jeanrett, Dow Jones, Dun&Bradstreet, Dyno Nobel, EMC, Estee Lauder, Everest, Federal-Mogul, Femsa, Five Arrow Fund, Freddo, Fuller, Generali, Harnischfeger, Hilti, Home Depot, Industria Azucarera Nacional, Intel, JDA Software, Kal-Tire, Latinoshopping, Leo Burnett, Levi Strauss, Leviton, M&M Mars, Macquarie Bank, Mayo Foundation, McDonald's, Mitsubishi, Morris, NewBasis, Nielsen, Nissho Iwai, Norhtrup Grumman, Northwestern Airlines, Novell, NutraSweet, Ocasa Courier, Paccar, Packard Bell, Pearson, Perkin Elmer / EG&G, Polaroid, Procter & Gamble, Prudential, Riggs, Salomon Smith Barney, Samsung, Simons, Summit, Swiss American Securities, Toronto Dominion, Tyco Electronics, Union Bank of Switzerland, US Filter, United Utilities, Warner Brothers, Waste, Whirlpool, Wolverine.

WORLDWIDE OFFICE CONTACTS

CHILE
Hendaya 60, Suite 202, Las Condes, **Santiago**
Tel: +56 2 750 0200 **Fax:** +56 2 750 0201
Email: yrls@yrls.cl

MAIN INTERNATIONAL AREAS OF PRACTICE:

M&A: The firm's transactions in this area range from private acquisitions to cross-border takeovers of listed companies.

Banking and finance: The firm handles all aspects of international banking and finance, including secured and syndicated loan transactions and guarantees, structured finance and project finance.

Insurance and reinsurance: The firm has advised insurance companies and reinsurers operating in Chile.

Private social security system: The firm has acted as consultant to private social security companies.

Litigation and arbitration: The firm handles commercial litigation, national and international arbitration. Its lawyers handle cases before the Chilean Courts, including the Chilean Supreme Court and have participated as arbitrators in cases before the International Chamber of Commerce.

Competition: The firm has handled several cases before the Chilean Antitrust Commissions.

Foreign investment: The firm has substantial experience, advising international clients.

LANGUAGES: English, Spanish

For other recommended firms see pages 1485-1520

ZAKI HASHEM & PARTNERS

HEAD OFFICE

23 Kasr El Nil Street, Cairo 11211, Egypt
Tel: +20 2 393 3766 **Fax:** +20 2 393 3585

Email: law@hashemlaw.com
Website: www.hashemlaw.com

WORLDWIDE OFFICE CONTACTS

EGYPT
23 Kasr El Nil Street, **Cairo** 11211
Tel: +20 2 393 3766 **Fax:** +20 2 393 3585
Email: law@hashemlaw.com

FIRM OVERVIEW

Managing partner: Yasser Hashem
Senior partners: Zaki Hashem, Mohamed Mahmoud Ibrahim

Number of partners worldwide: 8
Number of other lawyers worldwide: 36

AREAS OF PRACTICE:
Banking and finance .... *%
Energy .... *%
M&A .... *%
Securities .... *%
Telecommunications .... *%
* Workload % not disclosed

FIRM OVERVIEW: Zaki Hashem & Partners was established in Cairo in 1953. Traditionally focusing on corporate law and international business transactions related to the oil and gas industries, the firm has expanded into a full service commercial firm, particularly successful in the international corporate sector. It now offers legal services in areas such as litigation and arbitration, banking and finance, M&A and privatisation, taxation, telecommunications, venture capital, intellectual property, energy and real estate.

INTERNATIONAL EXPERIENCE: From its earliest days, international work has been central to the firm's activities. In 1956 the firm advised in the incorporation of Pfizer Egypt - the first foreign company to be authorised by the national legislation. In 1963 it secured the first Petroleum Concession Agreement granted to a US company. Since the liberalisation of foreign investment rules in the 1970s, Zaki Hashem & Partners has acquired a growing reputation acting for both government authorities and private investors.

INTERNATIONAL CLIENTS: Zaki Hashem & Partners represents numerous major international companies, the majority being of US, British, Italian, German, French, Japanese, Swiss and Swedish origins.

MAIN INTERNATIONAL AREAS OF PRACTICE:
Banking and finance: The firm has advised multinational companies on project finance matters and sizeable banking projects in Egypt. Clients include Arab Bank Ltd, Banca Commerciale Italiana, Bank of Tokyo-Mitsubishi, Deutsche Bank, EFG-Hermes, Export Credit Guarantee Dept (UK), Monte dei Pascheidi Siena Banking Group, Overseas Economic Cooperation Fund of Japan.
Telecommunications: The firm advises on mobile phone licenses, the Internet and new media and value added services. Clients include France Telecom, Alcatel and Vodafone Airtouch.
Corporate and M&A: The firm handles a large amount of M&A work and advises companies seeking to streamline and increase productivity and profits. Clients include many in manufacturing industries, such as Pepsi-Cola, General Electric, Rothmans, Heinz, Colgate-Palmolive, Fiat, BASF and Thompson. In Hotels and Tourism, clients include Sheraton Corporation, Thomas Cook, American Express and Club Mediterranee. The firm is also instructed by some of the largest international names in pharmaceuticals and chemicals.
Energy: The firm has advised clients in the petroleum industry on drafting and negotiating concession agreements and deeds of assignment. It also advises on natural gas, notably on the export of hydrocarbons and liquefied gas. Clients include Apache, British Gas, ENI, Edison Gas and Edison International SpA, Global Natural Resources, IEOC, Phillips Petrolium Co, Phoenix Resources, Seagull Energy Corporation, Tullow Oil plc, SK Corporation, Baroid Ltd, Dresser Security, McDermott International, Pyramid Drilling, Saipem, Santa Fe International, Snamprogetti and Sperry Sun International.
Securities: The firm advises several pioneering companies in the Egyptian securities sector.

LANGUAGES: Arabic, English, French, German

ZHENG LIU YUAN & ZHOU LAW OFFICE

HEAD OFFICE

Suite 818, Tower 2, Bright China Chang An Building, 7 Jianguomennei Dajie
Beijing 100005, China

Tel: +86 10 6510 1250 **Fax:** +8610 6510 1253

Email: sjzheng@junyilaw.com.cn

WORLDWIDE OFFICE CONTACTS

CHINA
Suite 818, Tower 2, Bright China Chang An Building, 7 Jianguomennei Dajie, **Beijing** 100005
Tel: +86 10 6510 1250 **Fax:** +8610 6510 1253
Email: sjzheng@junyilaw.com.cn

FIRM OVERVIEW

Managing partner: Yi Liu
Senior partner: Zheng Shujun

Number of partners worldwide: 5
Number of other lawyers worldwide: 6

AREAS OF PRACTICE:
Infrastructure and project finance 30%
Corporate and M&A 25%
Banking and finance 12%
Foreign direct investment 10%
IT and telecommunications 10%
Real estate 7%
Aviation 3%
Litigation and arbitration 3%

Z

FIRM OVERVIEW: Founded in 1995, this Beijing based law firm was established by a group of lawyers who have advised on international business activities in China since the beginning of China's opening up in the early 1980s. Many of the firm's lawyers have been educated and trained in Germany, the UK, Canada and the US in addition to their legal education and training in China. The firm offers comprehensive and sophisticated legal advice to both Chinese and international clients.

INTERNATIONAL EXPERIENCE: Zheng, Liu, Yuan & Zhou Law Office has acted as the PRC counsel in numerous high profile foreign-invested infrastructure and project finance projects and aircraft leasing transactions in China. It has advised many internationally renowned companies and banks on commercial transactions and investments in relation to China and has served as the general retainer PRC counsel for some of them.

INTERNATIONAL CLIENTS: The firm's client base includes various US, European and Asian companies, investors, financial institutions, and international organisations, and covers various industries such as automobile, aviation, banking, computer, chemical, electronics, food and beverage, gas, oil, power, water and other infrastructure industries, IT and telecommunication, and real estate.

MAIN INTERNATIONAL AREAS OF PRACTICE:
Aviation: The firm specialises in advising on all types of aircraft leasing transactions, whether finance lease or operating lease, aircraft mortgages and liens, establishment of air transport enterprises, as well as claims relating to air transportation.
Foreign direct investment: The firm offers a full range of services to international investors in their direct investment in China including the establishment of companies and other forms of presence, PRC governmental approval issues, operational and commercial issues, restructuring, M&A, liquidation and bankruptcy.
Banking and finance: The firm has advised international banks and other financial institutions on various operational issues. It advises on secured loans, syndicated loans, guarantees, financial leasing, trade finance, project finance, derivatives transactions, and securitisation.
IT and telecommunication: In recent years, the firm has been very active in advising on telecommunication and IT projects in China and has represented foreign investors participating in the financing of construction and operation of telecommunication businesses, purchasing and launching of telecommunication satellites, establishment of data networks, as well as providing regulatory advice on the control of the Internet in China.
Infrastructure: As the firm's traditional practice, its infrastructure lawyers handle projects by project finance or corporate finance for power stations (thermal, hydro and nuclear), water plants, and coalmines.
Real estate: The firm has represented overseas developers in the setting up of real estate developments in China. It has advised and served overseas developers and purchasers regarding the PRC approval issues, construction, sales, mortgage filing, perfection and release, and title transfer.
Litigation and arbitration: The firm has acted in numerous arbitration cases in the most established arbitration institution in China, the China International Economic and Trade Arbitration Commission, and has represented many international clients in their commercial litigation cases in various PRC courts.

LANGUAGES: Chinese, English

For other recommended firms see pages 1485-1520

ZÜRCHER, MONTOYA & ZÜRCHER

HEAD OFFICE

1st. Street, 11th Avenue, #959,
San José, Costa Rica
Tel: +506 222 6633 **Fax:** +506 221 9127

Email: zmzlaw@racsa.co.cr
Website: www.zurcherlawyers.com

WORLDWIDE OFFICE CONTACTS

COSTA RICA
1st. Street, 11th Avenue, #959, **San José**
Tel: +506 222 6633 **Fax:** +506 221 9127
Email: zmzlaw@racsa.co.cr

FIRM OVERVIEW

Managing partner: Edgar A. Zürcher
Senior partners: Harry A. Zürcher, Harry J. Zürcher, Erick Montoya, Edgar A. Zürcher, Mario Pacheco

Number of partners worldwide: 9
Number of other lawyers worldwide: 7

AREAS OF PRACTICE:

Corporate	20%
Intellectual property	20%
Banking and finance	15%
Foreign investment	15%
M&A	15%
Energy and public utilities	5%
Litigation and arbitration	5%
Other	5%

FIRM OVERVIEW: Founded in 1936, Zürcher, Montoya & Zürcher comprises professional and competitive attorneys practising in general corporate law and other related areas. The firm offers comprehensive legal advice to clients with international business interests.

INTERNATIONAL EXPERIENCE: Zürcher, Montoya & Zürcher has advised major multinational corporations on investment projects in Costa Rica. Many of the projects involved mergers and acquisitions that required counseling in other related areas of law. The firm advised Procter & Gamble and Gerber Products on two of the largest foreign investment projects during 1999 and 2000.

INTERNATIONAL CLIENTS: The firm's client base includes large companies, mostly multinationals, in various sectors of the economy including banks and financial institutions, international airlines, retail chains, and manufacturers.

MAIN INTERNATIONAL AREAS OF PRACTICE:

Corporate: The firm handles a range of issues including incorporation, bylaws and internal corporate regulations, contract law, and counseling on day to day business issues.
M&A: The firm's transactions range from small private acquisitions to cross-border transactions. The firm has acted in a significant number of M&A transactions.
Banking and finance: The firm advises local and foreign banks and financial institutions as well as counseling clients on project finance and all aspects of loan agreements.
Intellectual property: The firm specialises in trademarks, patents and copyrights. Its intellectual property team works with corporate attorneys in negotiating licensing agreements and disputes.
Foreign investment: The firm advises on a range of issues relating to the Costa Rican Free Zone Regime.
Litigation and arbitration: The firm deals with civil and commercial litigation, usually protecting the interests of foreign corporations. It has also participated in large ad hoc arbitration proceedings and appeared before the local Chamber of Commerce.
Competition and consumer protection: Zürcher, Montoya & Zürcher has taken part in a range of proceedings before the competition and consumer protection authorities. Although competition and consumer protection law is relatively new to Costa Rica, the firm has made significant efforts to contribute to its development and implementation.
Energy and public utilities: Despite heavy government regulation in these sectors, the firm has advised on major energy and public utility projects.
Insolvency proceedings: The firm advises on bankruptcy law and different insolvency proceedings.
Aviation: The firm advises various international airlines on general corporate and contract law, and on government regulation.
Public contract: The firm counsels clients participating in public bids issued by the government for ordinary supply, construction, and service agreements. More recently, it has handled BOT and BOO projects.
Employment and immigration: The firm handles all matters relating to Costa Rican employment and immigration law.
Tax: Although this has been an area usually covered by corporate law, in recent years new legislation has made this a more specialised practice area.

LANGUAGES: English, Spanish

Z

OTHER FIRMS RECOMMENDED

AAB GEYE - SOLE PRACTITIONER (The Gambia)
78 Leberation Avenue, Banjul **Tel:** +220 229 941 **Fax:** +220 229 347 **Contact:** Mr AAB Geye

DR ABDULLA MAKTARI - SOLE PRACTITIONER (Yemen)
PO Box 111, Sana'a **Tel:** +967 1 248 018 **Fax:** +967 1 265 320 **Contact:** Dr Abdulla Maktari

ABELEDO GOTTHEIL ABOGADOS (Argentina)
Avenida Madero 1020, Piso 5, C1106 ACX Buenos Aires **Tel:** +54 11 4315 4721 **Fax:** +54 11 4311 3560 **Contact:** Mr Pablo Pinnel

ABOUHAMAD, MERHEB, NOHRA, CHAMOUN, CHEDID (Lebanon)
22 Shebaro Street, PO Box 165126, Beirut **Tel:** +961 1331 737 **Fax:** +961 1200 179 **Contact:** Mr Antoine Merheb

ABOUSLEIMAN & PARTNERS (Lebanon)
11 Place del'Etoile, 4th Floor, Riad El-Solh Sector, Beirut **Tel:** +961 1 987733 **Fax:** +961 1 987734

ABRAHAMS, DAVIDSON & CO (Brunei Darussalam)
1st & 2nd Floor, Units 1&2, Block B, Bangunan Begawan Pehin Dato Haji Md Yusof, Kampong Kiulap, Bandar Seri Begawan BE1518 **Tel:** +673 2 242 819 **Fax:** +673 2 242 836 **Contact:** Mr WSW Davidson

ABREU & MARQUES (Portugal)
Rua Filipe Folque, No. 2, 4th Floor, PO Box 1069-121, Lisbon **Tel:** +351 21 330 7100 **Fax:** +351 21 314 7491 **Contact:** Dr Jorge de Abreu

ADACHI HENDERSON MIYATAKE & FUJITA (Japan)
Inoue Akasaka Building, 5th Floor, 6-8, Akasaka 1-chome, Minato-ku, Tokyo 107-0052 **Tel:** +81 3 5562 0910 **Fax:** +81 3 5562 0916 **Contact:** Mr Toshio Miyatake

ADLY BELLAGHA & ASSOCIÉS (Tunisia)
126 rue de Yougoslavie, Tunis 1000 **Tel:** +216 1 327 122/329117/328625 **Fax:** +216 1 323 746 **Contact:** Mr Adly Bellagha

ADNAN, SUNDRA & LOW (Malaysia)
Level 11, Menara Olympia No 8, Jalan Raja Chulan, 50200 Kuala Lumpur **Tel:** +603 230 0466 **Fax:** +603 230 7945 / 238 3382

ADONNINO ASCOLI & CAVASOLA SCAMONI (Italy)
Via Principessa Clotilde 7, 00196 Rome **Tel:** +39 06 322 0662 **Fax:** +39 06 321 9128 **Contact:** Mr Pietro Adonnino

AF & R SHEHADEH LAW OFFICE (Palestinian Territories)
26 Main Street, PO Box 20007, Ramallah **Tel:** +972 2 295 6441 **Fax:** +972 2 295 3471

ÉTUDE AGBOYIBO (Togo)
64 Avenue du 24 Janvier, BP 06, Lomé **Tel:** +228 21 27 64 **Fax:** +228 21 62 54 **Contact:** M Agboyibo

BUFETE AGUIRRE (Bolivia)
Av. Arce 2071, Piso 1, PO Box 994, La Paz **Tel:** +591 2 440937 **Fax:** +591 2 440065 **Contact:** Mr Fernando Aguirre

AIDOUD LAW FIRM (Algeria)
83 Rue Didouche Mourad, Algiers 16005 **Tel:** +213 21 719655/+213 21 719736 **Fax:** +213 21 360 326

AJAY BAHL & CO ADVOCATES & SOLICITORS (India)
F-40 NDSE Part-1, New Delhi 110049 **Tel:** +91 11 461 7697 **Fax:** +91 11 462 5302 **Contact:** Mr Ajay Bahl

AKIN, GUMP, STRAUSS, HAUER & FELD LLP (USA)
1333 New Hampshire Avenue, N.W., Washington DC 20036 **Tel:** +1 202 887 4000 **Fax:** +1 202 887 4288 **Contact:** Mr R. Bruce McLean

LAW OFFICE OF AL-ESSA, AL-BADER & PARTNERS (Kuwait)
Al-Nafisi & Al-Khatrash Building, 3rd & 4th Floor, Jaber Al-Mubarak Street, Sharq, PO Box 4207, Safat, Kuwait 13043 **Tel:** +965 243 8020/1/2 **Fax:** +965 243 2272 **Contact:** Mr Hamad Yousuf Al-Essa

AL-MAHMOOD & ZU'BI (Bahrain)
Suite No. 1, 3rd Floor, Bab El Bahrain Building, Government Road, PO Box 502, Manama **Tel:** +973 225 151 **Fax:** +973 224 744 **Contact:** Mr Hatim Zubi

ALAIN BENSOUSSAN (France)
29 Rue du Colonel Pierre Avia, 75508 Paris **Tel:** +33 1 4133 3535 **Fax:** +33 1 4133 3536

AL ALAWI, MANSOOR JAMAL & CO (Oman)
PO Box 686, Ruwi 112 **Tel:** +968 707 162 **Fax:** +968 704 579

ALBUQUERQUE & ASSOCIADOS (Portugal)
Rua Victor Cordon 21, 1200 Lisbon **Tel:** +351 21 343 15 70 **Fax:** +351 21 343 15 68 **Contact:** Prof Martim de Albuquerque

ALEMÁN, CORDERO, GALINDO & LEE (Panama)
Swiss Bank Corporation Buildling, 2nd Floor, 53 Street East, Urbanización, Marbella, PO Box 6-1014, El Dorado, Panama City **Tel:** +50 7 269 2620 **Fax:** +50 7 263 5895

ALEXANDRA CARVALHO - SOLE PRACTITIONER (Mozambique)
Rua Pereira do Lago No 56, Maputo **Tel:** +258 82 310 900 **Fax:** +258 1 493 694

If you can't find a firm here, see full profiles (pages 957-1481)

ETUDE ALEXIS VINCENT GOMES (Congo)
BP 542, Pointe-Noire **Tel:** +242 942 104/944 550 **Fax:** +242 942 972

ALI BUDIARDJO, NUGROHO, REKSODIPUTRO (Indonesia)
Graha Niaga (24th Floor), Jalan Jenderal Sudirman Kav 58, Jakarta 12190 **Tel:** +62 21 250 5125 **Fax:** +62 21 250 5392
Contact: Mr T M Zahirsjah

ALI SHARIF ZU'BI & SHARIF ALI ZU'BI LAW OFFICE (Jordan)
Astra Building, Jebel Amman, PO Box 35267, Amman 11180
Tel: +962 6464 2908 **Fax:** +962 6463 4277
Contact: Mr Sharif Ali Zu'bi

ESTUDIO JURÍDICO ALMAGRO (Spain)
Consuegra n 3, 28036 Madrid **Tel:** +34 91 383 0192
Fax: +34 91 767 2561 **Contact:** Mr Jose Antonio

AL-SARRAF & AL-RUWAYEH (IN ASSOCIATION WITH STEPHENSON HARWOOD) (Kuwait)
Salhiya Complex Gate 1, 3rd Floor, PO Box 1448, Safat 13015
Tel: +965 240 0061/2/3 **Fax:** +965 240 0064
Contact: Mr Hameed Al-Sarraf

AL TAMIMI & CO (United Arab Emirates)
18th Floor, Dubai World Trade Centre, PO Box 9275, Dubai
Tel: +971 4 331 7090 **Fax:** +971 4 331 3177
Contact: Mr Essam Al Tamimi

ALTMARK & BRENNA (Argentina)
Junin 1054, 7 Piso, A, C1113AAF Buenos Aires
Tel: +54 11 4826 2628 **Fax:** +54 11 4821 2682

ALVARADO Y ASOCIADOS (Nicaragua)
Reparto Colonial Los Robles, VI Etrapa Rel Restaurante Lacmiel 5 Cuadras Arriva, 300 Metros A La Derecha, Casa #75, Managua PO Box 5983 **Tel:** +505 277 4028/278 7708 **Fax:** +505 278 7491
Contact: Dr Gloria Maria de Alvarado

ALVAREZ PRADO, CABANELLAS & KELLY ABOGADOS (Argentina)
San Martin 323, 18th Floor, C1004AAG Buenos Aires **Tel:** +54 11 4324 7600 **Fax:** +54 11 4324 7601 **Contact:** Mrs Patricia O'Connor

AMIE N.D. BENSOUDA - SOLE PRACTITIONER (The Gambia)
78 Hagan Street, Banjul **Tel:** +220 223 256 **Fax:** +220 223 257
Contact: Mrs Amie Bensouda

AMIN HAJJI LAW OFFICE (Morocco)
31 rue Ahmed Touki (ex. Labas), Casablanca 20000
Tel: +212 2 248 7474 **Fax:** +212 2 248 7475 **Contact:** Mr Amin Hajji

AM PRAXIS (Iceland)
Sigtun 42, PO Box 5189, Reykjavik 125 **Tel:** +354 533 3333
Fax: +354 533 2333 **Contact:** Mr Hroejartur Janotansson

AMRO & ASSOCIATES LAW OFFICES (Palestinian Territories)
Ramallah Commercial Centre, 5th Floor Office, 501 Jaffa Street, Ramallah PO Box 1903 **Tel:** +970 or +972 2 298 0128
Fax: +970 or +972 2 298 7678 **Contact:** Mr Thaer Yaser Amro

ANDERSON MORI (Japan)
AIG Building, 1-3 Marunouchi 1-chome, Chiyoda-ku, Tokyo 100-0005
Tel: +81 3 3214 1371 **Fax:** +81 3 3201 7334
Contact: Mr Tsuyoshi Nagahama

ANDREAS REINER - SOLE PRACTITIONER (Austria)
Freyung 6/12, A-1010 Vienna **Tel:** +43 1 532 23 32 0
Fax: +43 1 532 23 32 10 **Contact:** Mr Andreas Reiner

ANDREZANI ADVOCACIA IMPRESAREIAL (Brazil)
Rua Campos Bicudo, 98, 14th Floor, SP04536010 São Paulo
Tel: +55 11 3078 5344 **Fax:** +55 11 3079 2069
Contact: Mr Luis Carlos Andrezani

ATTORNEYS' HOUSE ANPR LTD (Finland)
Stenbackinkatu 26, FIN-00250 Helsinki **Tel:** +358 9 474 21
Fax: +358 9 474 2222 **Contact:** Mr Jorgen Hammarstrom

ANTIS TRIANTAFYLLIDES & SONS (Cyprus)
Triantafyllides Building, Capital Centre, 9th Floor, PO Box 21255, Nicosia Cyprus **Tel:** +357 267 8888 **Fax:** +357 267 0670
Contact: Mr Stelios Triantafyllides

ANUP & ASSOCIATES (Nepal)
Ramamshah Tath, Kathmandu
Tel: +977 1258 445 **Fax:** +977 1 228 497 **Contact:** Mr A. R Sharma

AOKI & PARTNERS (Japan)
Suite 521 Fuji Building, 3-2-3 Marunouchi 3-Chome, Chiyoda-ku, CPO Box, Tokyo 100-0005
Tel: +81 3 3211 8871 **Fax:** +81 3 3213 2365 **Contact:** Mr Sumiya

APICES JURIS (Belarus)
Flat 225, 9 Golubeva, Minsk **Tel:** +375 29 276 6226 / 17 271 0639
Fax: +375 17 220 1710 **Contact:** Mr Dimitry Hadas

APPLEBY SPURLING & KEMPE (Hong Kong)
5511 The Center, 99 Queen's Road Central, Central, Hong Kong
Tel: +852 2523 8123 **Fax:** +852 2 524 5548 **Contact:** Ms Frances Woo

AQUEREBURU & PARTNERS (Togo)
23, Rue Bis Kokéti, BP 8989, Lomé
Tel: +228 21 05 05/21 49 01 **Fax:** +228 220 158

If you can't find a firm here, see full profiles (pages 957-1481)

ARAOZ Y RUEDA (Spain)
Castellana 15, 28046 Madrid
Tel: +34 91 319 0233 **Fax:** +34 91 319 1350

ARAQUE REYNA SOSA VISO & PITTIER (Venezuela)
Centro Lido, Torre C, Piso 5 y Piso 8, Avenida Francisco De Miranda, El Rosal, Apartado 50925, Sabana Grande, Caracas 1060
Tel: +582 953 9244/8411 **Fax:** +582 953 7777/7666

ARENDT & MEDERNACH (Luxembourg)
8-10, Rue Mathias Hardt, PO Box 39, L-2010 Luxembourg
Tel: +352 40 78 78 **Fax:** +352 40 78 04 **Contact:** Mr Guy Harles

ARFAT SELVAM & GUNASINGHAM (Singapore)
30 Raffles Place, Harfax Building, Singapore 048622
Tel: +65 538 5138 **Fax:** +65 538 4757

ARIAS, FÁBREGA & FÁBREGA (Panama)
16th Floor, Plaza Bancomer Building, 50th Street, PO Box 6307, Panama City 5 **Tel:** +50 7 263 9200 **Fax:** +50 7 263 8919
Contact: Mr Roy Durling

ARMSTRONGS (Botswana)
5th Floor Barclays House, Khama Crescent, PO Box 1368, Gabarone
Tel: +267 353 481 **Fax:** +267 352 757
Contact: Mr Neill William Armstrong

ARNANDER IRVINE & ZIETMAN (FORMERLY LLEWELYN ZIETMAN) (United Kingdom)
Temple Bar House, 23-28 Fleet Street, London EC4Y 1AA **Tel:** +44 20 7842 5400 **Fax:** +44 20 7842 5444 **Contact:** Mr John Bramhall

ARNOLD BLOCH LEIBLER (Australia)
Level 21, 333 Collins Street, Melbourne, Victoria 3000 **Tel:** +61 3 9229 9999 **Fax:** +61 3 9229 9900 **Contact:** Mr Mark Leibler

AROSEMENA NORIEGA & CONTRERAS (Panama)
Calle Elvira Menvez, Edificio Interseco, Piso2, 5246, Panama City 5
Tel: +507 265 3411 **Fax:** +507 264 4569
Contact: Mr Carlos Arosemena

ASAHI (Japan)
New ATT Building, 7th & 8th Floors, 11-7, Akasaka 2-Chome, Minato-Ku, Tokyo 107-8485 **Tel:** +81 3 35 050 003
Fax: +81 3 35 051 333 **Contact:** Mr Takashiejir

CABINET ASTÈRE BAPFUNYA (Burundi)
BP 2274, Bujumbura **Tel:** +257 222 475 **Fax:** +257 213 368
Contact: M Astère Bapfunya

ASTIGARRAGA DAVIS (USA)
Miami Center, 201 South Biscayne Boulevard, 20th Floor, Miami FL 33131 **Tel:** +1 305 372 8282 **Fax:** +1 305 372 8202
Contact: Mr Jose Astigarraga

ATHERSTONE & COOK (Zimbabwe)
PO Box 2625, Seventh Floor, Mercury House, 24 George Silundika Ave., Harare **Tel:** +263 4 704 244 **Fax:** +263 4 705180 / 794 998
Contact: Mr Lindsay Hugh Cook

ATSUMI & USUI (Japan)
614 Shuwa Kioicho TBR Building, 5-7 Kojimachi, Chiyoda-ku, Tokyo 102-0083 **Tel:** +81 3 5276 6131 **Fax:** +81 3 5276 6292
Contact: Mr Hirooatsumi

AUGUST & DEBOUZY (France)
6-8 Avenue de Messine, 75008 Paris **Tel:** +33 1 45 61 51 80
Fax: +33 1 45 61 51 99 **Contact:** Ms Emmanuelle Barbara

CABINET AUGUSTIN MABUSHI (Burundi)
BP 1972, Bujumbura **Tel:** +257 217 475 **Fax:** +257 217 476
Contact: Maître Augustin Mabushi

ESTUDIO AURELIO GARCIA SAYAN (Peru)
Av El Rosario No 380, San Isidro, Lima 27 **Tel:** +51 1 440 7341
Fax: +51 1 440 5218 **Contact:** Mr Francisco Garcia Sayan

AVITAL DROMI & CO (Israel)
4 Taas Street, Tel Aviv 52512
Tel: +972 3 575 5755 **Fax:** +972 3 575 5777
Contact: Mr Gideon Avital

CABINET BAADHIO (Burkina Faso)
01 BP 2100, Ouagadougou 01 **Tel:** +226 312 101 **Fax:** +226 312 100
Contact: Maître Seydou Baadhio

BABBE LE PELLEY TOSTEVIN (Guernsey)
PO Box 69, 18-20 Smith Street, St Peter Port GY1 4BL
Tel: +44 1481 713 371 **Fax:** +44 1481 711 607
Contact: Mr Richard Babbe

BADO KUSTER ZERBINO & RACHETTI (Uruguay)
Paysandú 935, Piso 3°, Montevideo 11.100 **Tel:** +598 2 902 0395
Fax: +598 2 902 5950 **Contact:** Mr Fernando Rachetti Olaso

BADRI ET SALIM EL MEOUCHI (Lebanon)
Khater Building, PO Box 56, Mansourieh, Metn
Tel: +961 4 530263 / 409 493 **Fax:** +961 4 409 673
Contact: Mr Salim El Moeuchi

BAE, KIM & LEE (South Korea)
Hankook Tire Building, Floors 5-12, 647-15 Yoksam-Dong, Kangnam-ku, Seoul 135-723 **Tel:** +82 2 3404 0000 **Fax:** +82 2 3404 0001

BAIER BÖHM ORATOR & PARTNERS (Austria)
Rotenturmstrasse 12, 1010 Vienna **Tel:** +43 1 516 20
Fax: +43 1 512 46 55

ETUDE BAL AHMEDOU TIDJANE (Mauritania)
PO Box 122, Avenue Kennedy, Nouakchott **Tel:** +222 252 133 **Fax:** +222 252 133 **Contact:** Mr Bal Ahmedou Tidjane

BALLEM MACINNES LLP (Canada)
1800-350 7th Avenue South West, Calgary Alberta T2P 3N9 **Tel:** +1 403 292 9800 **Fax:** +1 403 292 9880 **Contact:** Mr John B. Ballem

BALSANYDA & ASOCIADOS (Cuba)
20 Street No. 515, 2nd Floor, Miramar, Playa, Havana **Tel:** +537 240672/245944/245945 **Fax:** +537 242 278 **Contact:** Mr Ydael Leon Montesino

BÁN, S. SZABÓ & PARTNERS IN CO-OPERATION WITH ALTHEIMER & GRAY (Hungary)
Szerb utca 17-19, 1056 Budapest **Tel:** +36 1 266 3522 **Fax:** +36 1 266 3523 **Contact:** Dr Peter S Szabo

BARENTS & KRANS (Netherlands)
Parkstraat 107, 2514jh, Postbox 30457,2500 GL The Hague **Tel:** +31 70 376 06 06 **Fax:** +31 70 365 1856 **Contact:** Mrs Irene Nabben

BARROW & CO (Belize)
23 Regent Street, PO Box 63, Belize City BE **Tel:** +501 277 410 **Fax:** +501 278 460 **Contact:** Mr Andrew Marshalleck

BARROW & WILLIAMS (Belize)
99 Albert Street, PO Box 617, Belize City **Tel:** +501 275 280 **Fax:** +501 275 278 **Contact:** Mr Rodwell Williams

BASANGSANG CHAMBERS (The Gambia)
18-19 Liberation Avenue, Banjul **Tel:** +220 227 442 **Fax:** +220 460 951 **Contact:** Mr ANMO Dabo

BASMA & MACAULAY (Sierra Leone)
19 Siaka Stevens Street, Freetown PO Box 83 **Tel:** +232 22 22 2798 **Fax:** +232 2222 4248 **Contact:** Mr Macaulay Jr

BATLINER & PARTNERS (Liechtenstein)
Aeulestrasse 74, PO Box 86, 9490 Vaduz **Tel:** +423 236 0404 **Fax:** +423 236 0405 **Contact:** The Managing Partner

BATRES Y ASOCIADOS (Honduras)
Colonia Palmira, Sendero Guyana, Avendia Juan Lindo Casa 24-29, Tegucigalpa **Tel:** +504 236 9200 **Fax:** +504 236 6872 **Contact:** Mr Carlos Batres

CABINET BATWARE ET NKURUNZIZA (Rwanda)
BP 127, Kigali **Tel:** +250 73432 **Fax:** +250 73432 **Contact:** Mr Jean-Claude Batware

BAZAN CAMBRÉ & ORTS (Argentina)
Edificio Canada Florida 234, Piso 4, C1005 AAF Buenos Aires **Tel:** +54 11 4326 7777 **Fax:** +54 11 4325 3564 **Contact:** Mr Mario Orts

BBLP BEITEN BURKHARDT MITTL & WEGENER (Germany)
Leopoldstrasse 236, D-80807 Munich **Tel:** +49 89 3 50 65 00 **Fax:** +49 89 3 50 65 123 **Contact:** Dr. Jürgen Burkhardt

BBLP PAVIA E ANSALDO (Italy)
Via Dell' Annunciata, 7, 20121 Milan **Tel:** +39 02 63381 **Fax:** +39 02 655 4055 / 657 0203 **Contact:** Mr Marcello Agnoli

BEATA GESSEL & PARTNERS (Poland)
8 Widok Street, 00-023 Warsaw **Tel:** +48 22 690 6901 **Fax:** +48 22 690 6931 **Contact:** Ms Beata Gessel-Kalinowska vel Kalisz

BEGIASHVILI & CO LIMITED (Georgia)
Suite 42, 39 Gamsakhurdia Ave, Tbisili 380060 **Tel:** +995 32 251 454 **Fax:** +995 32 934 906 **Contact:** Mr Giorgi Begiashvili

INTERNATIONAL LAW OFFICE DR BEHROOZ AKHLAGHI & ASSOCIATES (Iran)
No. 17 Fourth St, Ahmad Ghassir Ave. (Bukharest Ave.), PO Box 15745/759, Tehran 15146 **Tel:** +98 21 873 2138 **Fax:** +98 21 874 4129

BELL DEWAR & HALL (South Africa)
Landwell Place, 37 West Street, Houghton, Johannesburg 2041 **Tel:** +27 11 710 6000 **Fax:** +27 11 710 6115 **Contact:** Mr Duncan Sinclair

CABINET BENOÎT JOSEPH SAWADOGO (Burkina Faso)
994 Rue Agostino Neto 01, BP.827, Ouagadougou 01 **Tel:** +226 306 975 **Fax:** +226 310 012 **Contact:** Maître Benoît Sawadogo

BENSON, PEREZ MATOS, ANTAKLY & WATTS (Venezuela)
8th Floor, Edificio Centro Altamira, Avenida San Juan Bosco - Urb. Altamira, Apartado Postal 69056, Caracas 1062-A **Tel:** +582 266 8292 **Fax:** +582 261 2493 **Contact:** Mr Farid Antakly

ESTUDIO JURÍDICO BERCOVITZ-CARVAJAL SOCIEDAD CIVIL (Spain)
C/ Santa Engracia, 15 - 4º Dcha., Madrid **Tel:** +34 91 445 2161 **Fax:** +34 91 446 0826

BERRYMANS LACE MAWER (United Kingdom)
Salisbury House, London Wall, London EC2M 5QN **Tel:** +44 20 7638 2811 **Fax:** +44 20 7920 0361 **Contact:** Mr Damian Greiff

ETUDE BETTAH & SALAH (Mauritania)
Immeuble BMCI 3ieme etage BP 883, Nouakchott **Tel:** +222 251 540 **Fax:** +222 290 172 **Contact:** Maître Salah

If you can't find a firm here, see full profiles (pages 957-1481)

BINDER, GRÖSSWANG & PARTNER (Austria)
Sterngasse 13, A-1010 Vienna **Tel:** +43 1 534 800 **Fax:** +43 1 534 808
Contact: Dr Michael Binder

BIRSEL LAW OFFICES (Turkey)
Cunhuriyet Bulvari, 140/1 8th floor, Alsancak-Izmir
Tel: +90 232 489 0519 **Fax:** +90 232 483 2387

STUDIO BISCOZZI NOBILI (Italy)
Via Cino del Duca, 8, 20122 Milan **Tel:** +39 02 76 36931
Fax: +39 02 78 01 46 **Contact:** Mr Luigi Biscozzi

BLUEGER & PLAUDE (Latvia)
Wielandes St 12, LV-10 Riga **Tel:** +371 722 5231 **Fax:** +371 782 0612
Contact: Mr Valentin Blueger

BLUKIS, ELKSNE & ROZENFELDS (Latvia)
Brivibas Street 40-24, LV-1050 Riga **Tel:** +371 782 1563
Fax: +371 724 2208 **Contact:** Mr Raimonds Blukis

BOEHMERT & BOEHMERT (Germany)
Franz-Joseph-Strasse 38, D-80801 München
Tel: +49 89 384 07 20 **Fax:** +49 89 34 70 10

BOGA & ASSOCIATES (Albania)
Alitalia Building, Ismail Qemali Street, Tirana Mail to: PO Box 8264, Tirana
Tel: +355 42 51050 **Fax:** +355 42 51055 **Contact:** Mr Genc Boga

BOGDANOVIC & DOLICKI (Croatia)
A. von Humboldta 4b, 10000 Zagreb **Tel:** +385 1 615 9595
Fax: +385 1 615 7733 **Contact:** Mr Din Tindolcki

BOIES, SCHILLER & FLEXNER (USA)
80 Business Park Drive, Armonk, New York NY 10504-1710 **Tel:** +1 914 273 9800 **Fax:** +1 914 273 9810 **Contact:** Mr Phil Korlogos

BONELLI-EREDE-PAPPALARDO (Italy)
Via Barozzi 1, 20122 Milan **Tel:** +39 02 771 131
Fax: +39 02 7711 3260 **Contact:** Mr Alberto Saravalle

BORISLAV BOYANOV & CO (Bulgaria)
24 Patriarch Evtimii Blvd, Sofia 1000 **Tel:** +359 2 981 30 07/+359 29813103 **Fax:** +359 2 981 77 33 **Contact:** Mr Borislav T Boyanov

BOROVTSOV & SALEI (Belarus)
21 Chicherin Street, Minsk 220029 **Tel:** +375 17 239 44 18
Fax: +375 17 239 44 22 **Contact:** Mr Vassili Salei

BRACEWELL & PATTERSON LLP (USA)
South Tower Pennzoil Place, 711 Louisiana Street, Suite 2900, Houston TX-77002-2781 **Tel:** +1 713 223 2900 **Fax:** +1 713 221 1212
Contact: Mr Kelly Frels

ETUDE BRAHIM OULD EBETY (Mauritania)
PO Box 2570, Nouakchott **Tel:** +222 251 607 **Fax:** +222 253 687
Contact: Mme Tahirou Moussa

BRAND FARRAR BUXBAUM LLP (Mongolia)
MCS Plaza, 3rd Floor, Ulaanbaatar 44 **Tel:** +976 11 31 0711/32 9170
Fax: +976 1 32 5102 **Contact:** Mr David Buxbaum

BRAYKOV'S LEGAL OFFICE (Bulgaria)
Bl.15 Dimiter Manov Street, Apt.43, Sofia 1408 **Tel:** +359 2 951 6040
Fax: +359 2 954 9325

BRIGARD & URRUTIA (Colombia)
Calle 70 No 4-60, PO Box 3692, Santa Fe de Bogota, DC
Tel: +57 1 346 2011 **Fax:** +57 1 310 0609
Contact: Mr Carlos Urrutia-Valenzuela

BRINK COHEN LE ROUX & ROODT INC (South Africa)
19 West Street, Houghton 2198, PO Box 2404, Houghton 2041
Tel: +27 11 242 8000 **Fax:** +27 11 242 8001

BRISTOWS (United Kingdom)
3 Lincoln's Inn Fields, London WC2A 3AA **Tel:** +44 20 7400 8000
Fax: +44 20 7400 8050 **Contact:** Mr Edward Nodder

BROBECK PHLEGER & HARRISON (USA)
One Market Plaza, Spear Street Tower, San Francisco CA 94105
Tel: +1 415 442 0900 **Fax:** +1 415 442 1010
Contact: Mrs Karen Johnson-McKewan

BROSIO, CASATI E ASSOCIATI (IN ASSOCIATION WITH ALLEN & OVERY) (Italy)
Corso Vittorio Emanuele II 284, I-00186 Rome **Tel:** +39 06 684271
Fax: +39 06 68427333 **Contact:** Mr G.M. Danusso

BROWN RAYSMAN AND MILLSTEIN FELDER & STEINER LLP (USA)
120 West 45th Street, 21st Floor, New York 10036
Tel: +1 212 944 1515 **Fax:** +1 212 840 2429

BRUDER GENTILE & MARCOUX LLP (USA)
1100 New York Avenue, NW, Suite 510 East, Washington DC DC 20005-3934 **Tel:** +1 202 783 1350 **Fax:** +1 202 737 9117
Contact: Mr Carmen Gentile

ESTUDIO BRUZZON & ASOCIADOS (Argentina)
Reconquista 458, Piso 14, AC1003ABJ Buenos Aires **Tel:** +54 11 4325 5500 **Fax:** +54 11 4325 3032 **Contact:** Mr Pablo Javier Alliani

BRYAN CAVE LLP (USA)
One Metropolitan Square, 211 North Broadway, Suite 3600, St Louis MO 63102-2750 **Tel:** +1 314 259 2000 **Fax:** +1 314 259 2020
Contact: Mr Walter L. Metcalfe, Jr.

If you can't find a firm here, see full profiles (pages 957-1481)

BUDDLE FINDLAY (New Zealand)
BNZ Centre, 1 Willis Street, PO Box 2694, Wellington **Tel:** +64 4 499 4242 **Fax:** +64 4 499 4141 **Contact:** Ms Helen Hines- Randall

BULHÕES PEDREIRA, BULHÕES CARVALHO & ADVOGADOS ASSOCIADOS (Brazil)
Rua Assemblea 10-38, Centro Rio de Janeiro, 20119 Rio de Janeiro **Tel:** +55 21 531 2414 **Fax:** +55 21 531 2674

BURKE & PARSONS (USA)
1114 Avenue of Americas, 34th Floor, New York NY 10036-7743 **Tel:** +1 212 354 3800 **Fax:** +1 212 221 1432 **Contact:** The Managing Partner

BURLINGHAM UNDERWOOD LLP (USA)
One Battery Park Plaza, 24th Floor, New York NY 10004-1484 **Tel:** +1 212 422 7585 **Fax:** +1 212 425 4107

BURNET DUCKWORTH & PALMER LLP (Canada)
Suite 1400, 350-7th Avenue SW, Calgary Alberta T2P 3N9 **Tel:** +1 403 260 0100 **Fax:** +1 403 260 0332 **Contact:** Mr Harry S Campbell

BUSINESSCONSULT (Belarus)
Office 203, Mogilevskaya str. 39, Minsk 220007 **Tel:** +375 17 229 1633/1695/206 6304 **Fax:** +375 17 229 1630 **Contact:** Mr Igor Verkhovodko

BUSINESS STRATEGIES INTERNATIONAL INC (Cuba)
Ciudad de la Habana, Havana **Tel:** +537 80 5780 **Fax:** +537 24 2278

CADWALADER, WICKERSHAM & TAFT (USA)
100 Maiden Lane, New York NY 10038 **Tel:** +1 212 504 6000 **Fax:** +1 212 504 6666 **Contact:** Mr Robert O Link Jr

CAHILL GORDON & REINDEL (USA)
80 Pine Street, New York NY 10005-1702 **Tel:** +1 212 701 3900 **Fax:** +1 212 269 5420 **Contact:** Mr Roger Meltzer

CAINS (Isle of Man)
15-19 Athol Street, Douglas IM1 1LB **Tel:** +44 1624 638 300 **Fax:** +44 1624 638 333 **Contact:** Mr A.J Corlett

ÇAKMAK ORTAK AVUKAT BÜROSU (Turkey)
Piyade Sokak No 18, Portakal Cicegi Apt. C Blok Kat 3, Cankaya, 06550 Ankara **Tel:** +90 312 442 4680 **Fax:** +90 312 442 4690 **Contact:** Mr Mesut Cakmak

CAMERON & SHEPHERD (Guyana)
2 Avenue of the Republic, PO Box 10109, Georgetown **Tel:** +592 22 62671/2/3 **Fax:** +592 22 67809 **Contact:** Mr Joseph Arthur King

CAMILLERI PREZIOSI (Malta)
Level 2, Valetta Buildings, South St, Valetta VLT 11 **Tel:** +356 238 989 **Fax:** +356 223 048

CAPLIN & DRYSDALE (USA)
One Thomas Circle NW, Suite 1100, Washington DC DC 20005-5802 **Tel:** +1 202 862 5000 **Fax:** +1 202 429 3301 **Contact:** Mr H David Rosenbloom

CARDENAS & CARDENAS (Colombia)
Carrera 7 No. 71-52,, Torre B, Piso 9, Bogota Columbia **Tel:** +57 1 312 3600/2369 **Fax:** +57 1 312 2420/2410 **Contact:** Ms Claudia Caballero

CARLOS GERKE MENDIETA ESTUDIO JURÍDICO (Bolivia)
Avenida Arce N° 2132, Edificio Illampu Piso 1°, PO Box 14606, La Paz **Tel:** +591 2 441351/441456 **Fax:** +591 2 441891 **Contact:** Mr Carlos Gerke Mendieta

CARRILLO Y ASOCIADOS (Guatemala)
1 Avenida 8-24 Zona 10, Guatemala City 01010 **Tel:** +50 2 331 5441 **Fax:** +502 339 0307 **Contact:** Ms Maria Isabel Frech

CARTER, LEDYARD & MILBURN (USA)
2 Wall Street, New York NY 10005 **Tel:** +1 212 732 3200 **Fax:** +1 212 732 3232 **Contact:** Mr Jerome Caulfield

CARVALHO DE FREITAS E FERREIRA ADVOGADOS ASSOCIADOS (Brazil)
Av. 9 de Julho n° 5593, 9º andar, CEP 01407-200 São Paulo **Tel:** +55 11 3066 5999 **Fax:** +55 11 3167 4735 **Contact:** Mr Theodor Carvalho de Freitas/ Mr Ricardo Barretto Ferreira da Silva

CARVALHOSA EIZIRIK & MOTTA VEIGA (Brazil)
Rua Araujo Porto Alegre, 70 gr. 1101, 20030-010 Rio de Janiero **Tel:** +55 21 240 4724 **Fax:** +55 21 262 7784 **Contact:** Mr Modesto Carvalhosa

CASPI & CO (Israel)
33 Yavetz Street, Tel Aviv 65258 **Tel:** +972 3 796 1000 **Fax:** +972 3 796 1001 **Contact:** Mr Ram Caspi

CASTILLO LAMAN TAN PANTALEON & SAN JOSE (Philippines)
2nd, 3rd & 4th Floors, The Valero Towers, 122 Valero Street, Salcedo Village, Makati City 1227 **Tel:** +63 2 817 6791 **Fax:** +63 2 819 2724/25

CB & M LAW OFFICES (Latvia)
4 Terbatas Street, Second Floor, LV-1050 Riga **Tel:** +371 782 8181 **Fax:** +371 782 8171 **Contact:** Mr Ziedonis Udris

If you can't find a firm here, see full profiles (pages 957-1481)

C & C LAW FIRM (Macau)
Av. Praia Grande, 759, 3/F, Macau **Tel:** +853 372 623 / 642 **Fax:** +853 553 098 **Contact:** Mr Rui José Cunha

CCW PARTNERSHIP (Brunei Darussalam)
Units 9 & 10, 2nd Floor, Block C, Kiarong Complex, Lebuhraya Sultan Hassanal Bolkiah, Bandar Seri Begawan BE1318 **Tel:** +673 2 451 606 **Fax:** +673 2 451 611 **Contact:** Mr Andrew Ong

CHADBOURNE & PARKE LLP (USA)
30 Rockefeller Plaza, New York NY 10112-0127 **Tel:** +1 212 408 5100 **Fax:** +1 212 541 5369 **Contact:** Mr Aniello Bianco

CHAPMAN AND CUTLER (USA)
111 West Monroe Street, Chicago IL 60603-4080 **Tel:** +1 312 845 3000 **Fax:** +1 312 701 2361 **Contact:** Mr John M. Dixon

CABINET CHAUVEAU (Cote D'Ivoire)
29 Boulevard Clozel, Abidjan 01 BP 3586 **Tel:** +225 20 212852 **Fax:** +225 20 22 37 14 **Contact:** M Jean-Francois Chauveau

CHEANG & ARIFF (Malaysia)
39 Court, 39 Jalan Yap Kwan Seng, Kuala Lumpur 50450 **Tel:** +60 3 2161 0803 **Fax:** +60 3 2161 4475 **Contact:** Mr Loh Siew Cheang

CHERNEV, KOMITOVA & PARTNERS (Bulgaria)
2nd Floor, 51 Parensov str., Sofia 1000 **Tel:** +359 2980 2733 **Fax:** +359 2980 2733 **Contact:** Dr Silvy Vasilev Chernev

CHIMA & IBRAHIM (Pakistan)
32K-B/1, Gulberg II, Lahore **Tel:** +92 42 575 5233 / 575 7373 **Fax:** +92 42 576 3233 **Contact:** Mr Khalid S Ibrahim

CHOOI & CO (Malaysia)
Penthouse PH-01, Bangunan Ming, Jalan Bukit Nanas, Kuala Lumpur 50250 **Tel:** +60 3 2055 3888 **Fax:** +60 3 2055 3880

CHRISTOPHER, RUSSELL COOK & COMPANY (Zambia)
PO Box 34091, Lusaka **Tel:** +260 1 229 366 **Fax:** +260 1 225 713 **Contact:** Mr Kanti Patel

CHRYSSES DEMETRIADES & CO (Cyprus)
Fortuna Court, Block B, 284 Arch. Makarios III Ave, Limassol 3601 PO Box 50132 **Tel:** +357 5 582424 **Fax:** +357 5 588055 / 587191 **Contact:** Mr John Agapiou

CICHANOWICZ, CALLAN, KEANE, VENGROW & TEXTOR (USA)
61 Broadway, 30th Floor, Suite 3000, New York NY 10006-2802 **Tel:** +1 212 344 7042 **Fax:** +1 212 344 7285 **Contact:** Mr Stephen Vengrow

CLARICH, LIBERTINI, MACALUSO & VALLI (Italy)
Via Del Quirinale, 26, I-00138 Rome **Tel:** +39 06 4782 3746 **Fax:** +39 06 4741 353 **Contact:** Mr Fabio Macaluso

CLARK, ATCHESON & REISERT (USA)
535 Fifth Avenue, New York NY 10017 **Tel:** +1 212 297 0257 **Fax:** +1 212 297 0316 **Contact:** Mr Frank Atcheson

CLARKE & CO (Barbados)
Parker House, Wildey Business Park, Wildey Road, St Michael **Tel:** +1 246 436 6287 **Fax:** +1 246 436 9812 **Contact:** Mr Alfred H Clarke

CLEMENS WALLÉN ÖSTLUND (Sweden)
Grev Turegatan 9a, 114 46 Stockholm **Tel:** +46 8 678 4000 **Fax:** +46 8 678 3500

CMS VON ERLACH KLAINGUTI STETTLER WILLE (Switzerland)
Dreikönigstrasse 7, PO Box 4088, CH-8022 Zurich **Tel:** +41 1 285 1111 **Fax:** +41 1 285 1122 **Contact:** Dr Rudolf von Erlach

COGHLAN WELSH & GUEST (Zimbabwe)
Executive Chambers, 14-16 George Silundika Ave, PO Box 53 and PO Box 2093, Harare **Tel:** +263 4 758472 **Fax:** +263 4 756 268 **Contact:** Mr David John Lewis

COLIN NG & PARTNERS (Singapore)
14 Robinson Road #03-01, Far East Finance Building, Singapore 048545 **Tel:** +65 323 8383 **Fax:** +65 323 8282 **Contact:** Mr Tan Chong Huat

DR COLIN ONG LEGAL SERVICES (Brunei Darussalam)
Suites 3-5, 2nd Floor Gadong Properties Centre, Km 3-6, Jalan Gadong, Bandar Seri Begawan BA 1511 **Tel:** +673 2 420 913 **Fax:** +673 2 420 911 **Contact:** Mr Colin Ong

COLLAS DAY (Guernsey)
Manor Place, PO Box 140, St Peter Port GY1 4EW **Tel:** +44 1481 723191 **Fax:** +44 1481 711880 **Contact:** Mr Peter JG Atkinson

COLLIER SHANNON SCOTT (USA)
3050 K Street, N.W., Suite 400, Washington DC 20007 **Tel:** +1 202 342 8400 **Fax:** +1 202 342 8451 **Contact:** Mr Paul Rosenthal

COLLINS NEWMAN & CO (Botswana)
Dintala Court, Plot 4863, PO Box 882, Gaborone **Tel:** +267 352 702 **Fax:** +267 314 230 **Contact:** Mr David Newman

COMMERCE & FINANCE LAW OFFICES (China)
714 Huapu International Plaza, 19 Chaowai Avenue, Beijing **Tel:** +86 10 6599 2255 **Fax:** +8610 6599 2678/79/2203 **Contact:** Mr Liu Gang

If you can't find a firm here, see full profiles (pages 957-1481)

COOLEY GODWARD LLP (USA)
5 Palo Alto Square, 3000 El Camino Real, Palo Alto CA 94306-2155
Tel: +1 650 843 5000 **Fax:** +1 650 857 0663
Contact: Mr Lee F. Benton

CORNELIUS, LANE & MUFTI (Pakistan)
Nawa-i-Waqt House, 4 Shahrah-e-Fatima Jinnah, Lahore 52000
Tel: +92 42 636 0824 / 630 6301 **Fax:** +92 42 630 2965
Contact: Mr Afzal H Mufti

CORONEL Y PEREZ (Ecuador)
Edificio La Previsora Av. 9 de Octubre 100 y Malecon, 24th Floor, Offices # 2401 and 2402, PO Box 09016086, Guayaquil
Tel: +59 34 519 900 **Fax:** +59 34 320 657 **Contact:** Dr Cesare Coronel

CORPUS GLOBE (Zambia)
The Globe Building, Plot 2386, Longolongo Road, Lusaka PO Box 32115 **Tel:** +260 1 235 479 / 235 481 **Fax:** +260 1 238 657

CORRS CHAMBERS WESTGARTH (Australia)
Level 32, Governor Phillip Tower, 1 Farrer Place, Sydney NSW 2000
Tel: +61 2 9210 6500 **Fax:** +61 2 9210 6611
Contact: Ms Meredith Hellicar

COSTER ADVOCATEN (Surinam)
No 7 Costerstraat-Paramaribo **Tel:** +597 473 358 **Fax:** +597 477 035

COUTRELIS & ASSOCIÉS (France)
55 Avenue Marceau, 75116 Paris **Tel:** +33 1 53 57 47 95
Fax: +33 1 53 57 47 97 **Contact:** Mr André Coutrelis

COX HANSON O'REILLY MATHESON (Canada)
1100 Purdy's Wharf Tower One, 1959 Upper Water Street, PO Box 2380 Stn. Central RPO, Halifax NS B3J 3E5 **Tel:** +1 902 421 6262
Fax: +1 902 421 3130 **Contact:** Mr Peter Gurnham QC

CRAVATH, SWAINE & MOORE (USA)
Worldwide Plaza, 825 Eighth Avenue, New York NY 10019-7475
Tel: +1 212 474 1000 **Fax:** +1 212 474 3700
Contact: Mr C Allen Parker

CR & F ROJAS ABOGADOS (Bolivia)
c/ Federico Zuazo, Edificio Park Inn, Piso 11, La Paz **Tel:** +591 2 313 737 **Fax:** +591 2 376 380 **Contact:** Mr Fernando Rojas

CROWELL & MORING LLP (USA)
1001 Pennsylvania Avenue NW, Suite 1100, Washington DC 20004-2595 **Tel:** +1 202 624 2500 **Fax:** +1 202 628 5116
Contact: Mr Herbert J Martin

CRUMP & CO (Hong Kong)
9th Floor, Asian House, 1 Hennessy Road, Wanchai, Hong Kong
Tel: +852 2537 7000 **Fax:** +852 2804 6615

CSEKES, VILÁGI, DRGONEC & PARTNERS (Slovakia)
Sasinkova 12, 811 08 Bratislava
Tel: +421 7 52 731 419 **Fax:** +421 7 52 932 461

CUATRECASAS (Spain)
Paseo de Gracia 111, 08008 Barcelona **Tel:** +34 93 290 5500
Fax: +34 93 290 5567 **Contact:** Mr Enric Picanyol

CURTIS, MALLET-PREVOST, COLT & MOSLE LLP (USA)
101 Park Avenue, 35th Floor, New York NY 10178-0061 **Tel:** +1 212 696 6000 **Fax:** +1 212 697 1559 **Contact:** Mr George Cahale

DAG WERSÉN - SOLE PRACTITIONER (Sweden)
Jakobsbergsgatan 6, PO Box 7758, 103 96 Stockholm
Tel: +46 8 663 77 22 **Fax:** +46 8 679 84 98

DALLAL & ASSOCIATES (Jordan)
Citibank Building, 3rd Circle, PO Box 741, Jebel, Amman 11118
Tel: +962 6464 2468 **Fax:** +962 6464 2468

DALLA VEDOVA (Italy)
12 Via Bachelet, 00185 Rome
Tel: +39 06 444 0821 **Fax:** +39 06 446 2165

DALLMANN & PARTNERS (Austria)
Gusshausstr. 2, 1040 Vienna
Tel: +43 1 504 4142 **Fax:** +43 1 504 414243
Contact: Mr Armin Dallmann

DANIEL DA SILVA - SOLE PRACTITIONER (Mozambique)
PO Box 4517, Maputo **Tel:** +258 1 780 225 **Fax:** +258 1 780 614

DANZIGER, KLAGSBALD, ROSEN & CO (Israel)
Gibor Sport Building, 24th Floor, 28 Bezalel Street, Ramat Gran 52521
Tel: +972 3 611 0700 **Fax:** +972 3 611 0707
Contact: Dr Yoram Danziger

DARRYL DAWSON - SOLE PRACTITIONER (Australia)
The Institute of Arbitrators and Mediators Australia, Level 1, 22 William Street, Melbourne Victoria 3000
Tel: +61 3 9629 6799 **Fax:** +61 3 9629 5250

THE DAVID AB JALLAH LAW FIRM (Liberia)
Johnson & Broad Streets, PO Box 4069, Monrovia
Tel: +231 226285 **Fax:** +231 44 271 **Contact:** Mr David AB Jallah

DAVID KING & CO (Barbados)
First Floor, Trident House, Broad Street, Bridgetown
Tel: +1 246 427 3174 **Fax:** +1 246 436 9541
Contact: Mr David N King

If you can't find a firm here, see full profiles (pages 957-1481)

DAVIS & CO (Canada)
2800 Park Place, 666 Burrard Street, Vancouver BC V6C 2Z7
Tel: +1 604 687 9444 **Fax:** +1 604 687 1612 **Contact:** Mr Paul Albi

DAVIS POLK & WARDWELL (USA)
450 Lexington Avenue, New York NY 10017 **Tel:** +1 212 450 4000
Fax: +1 212 450 3800 **Contact:** Mr John R Ettinger

CABINET D'AVOCATS BARTHÉLÉMY KERÉ (Burkina Faso)
01 BP 2173, Ouagadougou 01 **Tel:** +226 31 08 60 **Fax:** +226 31 52 12
Contact: Maître Barthélémy Keré

DAY CASEBEER MADRID & BATCHELDER LLP (USA)
20400 Stevens Creek Boulevard, Suite 750, Cupertino CA 95014
Tel: +1 408 255 3255 **Fax:** +1 408 255 3254
Contact: Mr Josh Rosenfeld

DEACONS (Hong Kong)
3rd - 7th & 18th Floor, Alexandra House, 16-20 Chater Road, Central Hong Kong 2825 9211 **Tel:** +852 2825 9211 **Fax:** +852 2810 0431
Contact: Mr Mark Roberts

DEBEVOISE & PLIMPTON (USA)
875 Third Avenue, New York NY 10022 **Tel:** +1 212 909 6000
Fax: +1 212 909 6836 **Contact:** Mr Martin Frederic Evans

DE CAIRES, FITZPATRICK & KARRAN (Guyana)
80 Cowan Street, Kingston, Georgetown **Tel:** +592 261 126
Fax: +592 262 522 **Contact:** Mr Miles Fitzpatrick

DECHERT (USA)
4000 Bell Atlantic Tower, 1717 Arch Street, Philadelphia PA 19103-2793 **Tel:** +1 215 994 4000 **Fax:** +1 215 994 2222
Contact: Mr Bart Winokur

DE COMARMOND & KOENIG (Mauritius)
5th Floor, Chancery House, Lislet Geoffrey Street, Port Louis **Tel:** +230 212 2215 **Fax:** +230 208 2986 **Contact:** Mr Thierry Koenig

DELVOLVÉ ROUCHE (France)
5 rue Margueritte, 75017 Paris **Tel:** +33 1 42 27 70 68
Fax: +33 1 43 80 27 89 **Contact:** Mr Jean-Louis Delvolvé

D'EMPAIRE REYNA BERMUDEZ & ASOCIADOS (Venezuela)
Edificio Bancaracas P H, Plaza La Castellana, Caracas 1160 **Tel:** +58 2 264 62 44 **Fax:** +58 2 264 75 43 **Contact:** Mr Gustavo J Reyna

DENEYS REITZ INC (South Africa)
PO Box 784903, Sandton 2146 **Tel:** +27 11 685 8500
Fax: +27 11 883 4000 **Contact:** Mr Michael Hart

DE NOBRIGA, INNISS & CO (Trinidad & Tobago)
PO Box 1165, 5-7 Sweet Briar Road, St Clair, Port of Spain **Tel:** +1 868 628 9255 **Fax:** +1 868 628 6714 **Contact:** Mr Andrew C Johnson

DENTON SALÈS VINCENT & THOMAS (France)
43 Rue du Faubourg St-Honoré, 75008 Paris **Tel:** +33 1 5305 1600
Fax: +33 1 5305 9727 **Contact:** M Jacques Salès

DERAINS & ASSOCIÉS (France)
167 Bis Avenue Victor Hugo, 75116 Paris **Tel:** +33 1 45 533 838
Fax: +33 1 45 536 348

DERMAN ORTAK AVUKAT BUROSU (Turkey)
Maya Akar Center Buyukdere Caddesi 100/17, Esentepe, 80280 Istanbul **Tel:** +90 212 275 7155 **Fax:** +90 212 275 7156
Contact: Mr Emre Derman

DESAI & DIWANJI (India)
Lentin Chambers, Dalal, Fort Street, Bombay 400 023 **Tel:** +91 22 2651 682 **Fax:** +91 22 2658 245 **Contact:** Mr Vishwang Desai

DESJARDINS DUCHARME STEIN MONAST (Canada)
600 rue de La Gauchetière West, Bureau 2400, Montréal Québec H3B 4L8 **Tel:** +1 514 878 5526 **Fax:** +1 514 878 9092
Contact: Mr Gerard Coulomb

DEUCALION REDIADIS & SONS (Greece)
rd - 7th & 18th Floors, Chater Road, 185-35 Piraeus **Tel:** +30 1 429 4900 **Fax:** +30 1 429 4941 **Contact:** Mr Deucalion Rediadis

DF ABANG ZEN (Brunei Darussalam)
4th Floor Wisma Hajjah Fatimah, 22/23 Jalan Sultan Bandar Seri Begawan BS8811, PO Box 2822, Bandar Seri Begawan BS8675 **Tel:** +673 2 22 1877/236681/236680 **Fax:** +673 2 224 351
Contact: Dyang Hajah Feridahanam Abang HJ Zen

DH KEMP & CO (Zambia)
6941 Suez Road, Off Church Road near Holiday Inn Garden Court, Lusaka **Tel:** +260 1 252 381 **Fax:** +260 1 255 225
Contact: Mr Newton K Mubonda

DIAS DE SOUZA ADVOGADOS ASSOCIADOS SC (Brazil)
Av. Brasil 1575, Jardim América, 01431 001 São Paulo **Tel:** +55 11 3083 4277 **Fax:** +55 11 3082 6255
Contact: Mr Hamilton Dias de Souza

DICKINSON CRUICKSHANK & CO (Isle of Man)
33-37 Athol Street, Douglas IM3 1LB **Tel:** +44 1624 647 647
Fax: +44 1624 620 992 **Contact:** Mr Martin Moore

DICKSON MINTO WS (United Kingdom)
Royal London House, 22-25 Finsbury Square, London EC2A 1DS
Tel: +44 20 7628 4455 **Fax:** +44 20 7628 0027
Contact: Mr Bruce W. Minto

DICKSTEIN SHAPIRO MORIN & OSHINSKY LLP (USA)
2101 L Street NW, Washington DC DC 20037-1526 **Tel:** +1 202 785 9700 **Fax:** +1 202 887 0689 **Contact:** Mr Angelo V Arcadipane

DIEUX GEENS CORNELIS (Belgium)
Rue de la Bonté 5-7, 1000 Brussels **Tel:** +32 2 538 68 69
Fax: +32 2 538 68 67 **Contact:** Mr Jean-Quenten De Cypiu

DILLON EUSTACE (Ireland)
Grand Canal House, 1 Upper Grand Canal Street, Dublin 4
Tel: +353 1 66 700 22 **Fax:** +353 1 66 700 42
Contact: Mr David Dillon

DIRKSEN FLIPSE DORAN & LÊ (Cambodia)
#45, Preah Suramarit Boulevard, PO Box 7, Phnom Penh
Tel: +855 23 428 726 / 360 545 **Fax:** +855 23 428 227
Contact: Mr David Doran

DI TANNO E ASSOCIATI (Italy)
Via G. Paisiello, 33, 00198 Rome
Tel: +39 06 845 661 **Fax:** +39 06 841 9500

DITTMAR & INDRENIUS (Finland)
Pohjoisplanadi 25 A, FIN-00100 Helsinki **Tel:** +358 9 681 700
Fax: +358 9 652 406 **Contact:** Mr Markus Troberg

DOGRU LAW OFFICE (Turkey)
Tevfik Erdonmez Sokak Yayla Palas Apt. No. 22/4, Esentepe, 80280 Istanbul **Tel:** +90 212 212 8882 **Fax:** +90 212 212 8805
Contact: Mr Halil Dogru

CABINET DONGAR ET MODIBO KONE (Mali)
BP 841, Bamako **Tel:** +223 225 240 **Fax:** +223 225 240

DORALT SEIST & CSOKLICH (Austria)
Waehringrstrasse 2-4, A-1090 Vienna
Tel: +43 1 319 45 20 **Fax:** +43 1 319 83 22 **Contact:** Dr Paul Doralt

DORDA BRUGGER & JORDIS (Austria)
Dr Karl Lueger - Ring 12, A-1010 Vienna
Tel: +43 1 533 47 95-0 **Fax:** +43 1 533 47 97
Contact: Dr Christian Dorda

DOUGHERTY & ASSOCIATES (Isle of Man)
Ground Floor, Atlantic House, 4-8 Circular Road, Douglas IM1 1AG
Tel: +44 1624 671 155 **Fax:** +44 1624 610 414
Contact: Mr Paul Dougherty

DRYLLERAKIS & ASSOCIATES (Greece)
25 Voukourestiou Str., 106 71 Athens
Tel: +30 1 362 8159 **Fax:** +30 1 364 4218
Contact: Mr Emmanuel Dryllerakis

DS AVOCATS (France)
46 Rue de Bassano, 75008 Paris
Tel: +33 1 5367 5000 **Fax:** +33 1 5367 5001
Contact: M Thierry Carliur

DUA ASSOCIATES (India)
202-206, Tolstoy House, 15 Tolstoy Marg, New Delhi 110001
Tel: +91 11 371 4408 **Fax:** +91 11 331 7746/335 7097
Contact: Mr C.R. Dua

DUANE, MORRIS & HECKSCHER LLP (USA)
One Liberty Place, 1650 Market Street, Philadelphia PA 19103-7396
Tel: +1 215 979 1000 **Fax:** +1 215 979 1020
Contact: Mr Sheldon M. Bonovitz

DUNBAR & DUNBAR LAW OFFICES (Liberia)
Suite 203, KLM Building, 56 Broad Street, PO Box 474, Monrovia
Tel: +231 227 746 / 226 112 **Fax:** +231 226 112
Contact: Mr Stephen Dunbar, Jnr

DUNN, COX, ORRETT & ASHENHEIM (Jamaica)
48 Duke Street, PO Box 365, Kingston **Tel:** +1 876 922 1500
Fax: +1 876 922 9002 **Contact:** Mr Christohper Bovell

DUYGEN YARSUVAT & ÖMÜR YARSUVAT (Turkey)
Haci Adil Sok 44 2. Levent, 80620 Istanbul **Tel:** +90 212 283 9226
Fax: +90 212 282 7910 **Contact:** Mr Omur Yarsuvat

EAST ASSOCIATES (China)
19/F, Tower 2, Landmark Towers, 8 North Dongsanhuan Road, Chaoyang District, Beijing 100004 **Tel:** +86 10 6590 6639 ext. 255
Fax: +86 10 6590 6650 **Contact:** Mr Wei Zhao

EISENFÜHR, SPEISER & PARTNER (Germany)
Arnulfstr. 25, D-80335 München **Tel:** +49 89 54 90 75 0
Fax: +49 89 55 02 75 55 **Contact:** Dieter Speiser

ELISHA & ASSOCIÉS (Cote D'Ivoire)
Immeuble Eden 10th Floor, 44 Avenue Lamblin, Abidjan BP 1687 Abidjan 04 **Tel:** +225 20 211880/321880
Fax: +225 20 211870/331870 **Contact:** M Jean-Pierre Elisha

ELLIS & CO (Zambia)
Phillip Ellis House, 8 Tito Road, Rhodes Park, PO Box 31902, Lusaka
Tel: +260 1 252 709 / 809 / 738 **Fax:** +260 1 250 802 / 251 982

ELVINGER, HOSS & PRUSSEN (Luxembourg)
2 Place Winston Churchill, BP 425, L-2014 Luxembourg
Tel: +352 44 66 440 **Fax:** +352 44 22 55

ELZABURU (Spain)
Miguel Angel, 21, Madrid **Tel:** +34 91 700 9400
Fax: +34 91 319 3810 **Contact:** Mr Alberto de Elzaburu

If you can't find a firm here, see full profiles (pages 957-1481)

ENGLING, STRITTER & PARTNERS (Namibia)
PO Box 43, Windhoek **Tel:** +264 61 235031 **Fax:** +264 61 233672
Contact: Mr Hans-Bruno Geroes

ERNST & YOUNG ABOGADOS (Spain)
Torre Picasso 3-5, Plaza Pablo Ruiz Picasso, s/n, 28020 Madrid
Tel: +34 91 572 7200 **Fax:** +34 91 572 7427

ESSED & SOHANSINGH ADVOCATEN (Surinam)
Prinshendrikstraat 76, PO Box 620, Paramaribo Surinam
Tel: +597 424 231 **Fax:** +597 420 944 **Contact:** Ms Rani Sohansingh

EUGENE F COLLINS (Ireland)
Temple Chambers, 3 Burlington Road, Dublin 4 **Tel:** +353 1 202 6400
Fax: +353 1 667 5200 **Contact:** Mr David Cantrell

FACIO & CAÑAS (Costa Rica)
Barrio Tournon, PO Box 5173, San José 1000 **Tel:** +506 256 5555
Fax: +50 6 255 2510 **Contact:** Mr Gonzalo J Facio

FAEGRE & BENSON LLP (USA)
2200 Wells Fargo Center, 90 South Seventh Street, Minneapolis MN 55402-3901 **Tel:** +1 612 336 3000 **Fax:** +1 612 336 3026
Contact: Mr Philip S Garon

FANTOZZI E ASSOCIATI (Italy)
Via Sicilia 66, Rome **Tel:** +39 06 4200 611 **Fax:** +39 06 4201 1976

FARARA GEORGE-CREQUE & KERINS (British Virgin Islands)
125 Main Street, PO Box 144, Road Town, Tortola
Tel: +1 284 494 2717/ 494 2068 **Fax:** +1 284 494 4834
Contact: Mr Gerald Farrara

FASKEN MARTINEAU DUMOULIN (FORMERLY FASKEN CAMPBELL GODFREY) (Canada)
Toronto-Dominion Bank Tower, PO Box 20, Toronto Dominion Centre, Toronto M5K 1N6
Tel: +1 416 366 8381 **Fax:** +1 416 364 7813

FDKA (Cote D'Ivoire)
Residence "Les Harmonies" rue du Dr Jamot, Abidjan 01
Tel: +225 20 212031 **Fax:** +225 20 212843 **Contact:** Mr Karim Fadika

FELESKY FLYNN (Canada)
350 7th Ave SW, Suite 3400, Calgary AB T2P 3N9
Tel: +1 403 260 3301 **Fax:** +1 403 263 9649
Contact: Mr Brian Felesky

FENWICK & WEST (USA)
Two Palo Alto Square, Palo Alto CA 94306 **Tel:** +1 650 494 0600
Fax: +1 650 494 1417 **Contact:** Mr Gordon K. Davidson

FERDINAND HERMANNS - SOLE PRACTITIONER (Germany)
Hildegundis Allee 44, D-40667 Meerbusch **Tel:** +49 2132 5835
Fax: +49 2132 5450 **Contact:** Ferdinand Hermanns

CABINET D'AVOCATS FERNAND CARLE (Congo)
B.P. 607, Pointe-Noire **Tel:** +242 940 293/940 195 **Fax:** +242 942 745
Contact: Mr Fernand Carle

FERNANDO DOS SANTOS - SOLE PRACTITIONER (Angola)
Rua Rainha Ginga, 186 - 4ʃ DTʃ, PO Box 1361, Luanda
Tel: +244 2 332 2944 **Fax:** +244 2 335895

FESSEHAYE HABTE - SOLE PRACTITIONER (Eritrea)
P.O. Box 5530, Asmara **Tel:** +291 1 24444 **Fax:** +291 1 120646

FFA ERNST & YOUNG (Gabon)
Immeuble Sonagar, Avenue du Colonel Parant, BP 2278, Libreville
Tel: +241 742 168 **Fax:** +241 726 494 **Contact:** M Claude Henry Jour

STUDIO LEGALE TRIBUTARIO F GALLO E ASSOCIATI (Italy)
Viale Mazzini 11, 00195 Rome **Tel:** +39 063 600 1069
Fax: +39 063 223 294 **Contact:** Mr Franco Gallo

FIDAFRICA (Gabon)
Rue Alfred Marche, BP 2164, Libreville **Tel:** +241 762 508
Fax: +241 765 953 **Contact:** M Christophe Relongoue

FINNEGAN HENDERSON FARABOW GARRETT & DUNNER LLP (USA)
Suite 700, 1300 I Street, Washington DC DC 20005-3315 **Tel:** +1 202 408 4000 **Fax:** +1 202 408 4400 **Contact:** Mr Thomas H. Jenkins

FIOCCO POSMAN & KUA (Papua New Guinea)
Level 1 Mogoru Moto Building, Champion Parade. Mail to: PO Box 228, Port Moresby **Tel:** +675 320 0127 **Fax:** +675 320 0361
Contact: Mr Rio Fiocco

FIORIO, CARDOZO & ALVARADO (Paraguay)
Avda. Perú no. 708, Tte. Ruiz, Asuncion
Tel: +595 2161 0229 **Fax:** +595 2161 0240

FISCHER, BEHAR, CHEN & CO (Israel)
3 Daniel Frisch Street, Tel Aviv 64731 **Tel:** +972 3 694 4111
Fax: +972 3 609 1116 **Contact:** Mr Amir Chen

FISCHER & FORSTER ADVOGADOS (Brazil)
Avenida Cidade Jardim, 377-Sobreloja, 01453-900 São Paulo
Tel: +55 11 3168 1799 **Fax:** +55 11 3167 6629 **Contact:** Mr Georges Charles Fischer

FISH & RICHARDSON (USA)
45 Rockefeller Plaza, Suite 2800, New York NY 10111
Tel: +1 212 765 5070 **Fax:** +1 212 258 2291 **Contact:** Mr Fred Rabin

FISH & NEAVE (USA)
1251 Avenue of the Americas, New York NY 10020
Tel: +1 212 596 9000 **Fax:** +1 212 596 9090
Contact: Mr Jesse J Jenner

FITZPATRICK, CELLA, HARPER & SCINTO (USA)
30 Rockefeller Plaza, New York NY 10012 **Tel:** +1 212 218 2100
Fax: +1 212 218 2200 **Contact:** Mr Bruce Haas

FITZWILLIAM, STONE, FURNESS-SMITH & MORGAN (Trinidad & Tobago)
36 Pembroke Street, PO Box 75, Port of Spain **Tel:** +1 868 623 1618
Fax: +1 868 623 0605 **Contact:** Mr Winston Thompson

FJ & G DE SARAM (Sri Lanka)
31 -2/1 Mudaliga Mawatha, Colombo 1 **Tel:** +94 1 347 729
Fax: +94 1 449 482 **Contact:** Mr Gsherat Gunaratne

FLUXMAN RABINOWITZ - RAPHAELY WEINER (South Africa)
4th Floor, Allianz House, 33 Baker Street, Rosebank
Tel: +27 11 328 1700 **Fax:** +27 11 880 2261
Contact: Mr Phillip Vallet

FOLEY & LARDNER (USA)
Firstar Center, 777 East Wisconsin Avenue, Milwaukee WI 53202-5367
Tel: +1 414 271 2400 **Fax:** +1 414 297 4900
Contact: Mr Stanley S. Jaspan

FORESTA BUSINESS LAW GROUP (Lithuania)
22 Kudirkos Street, LT-2001 Vilnius **Tel:** +370 2 224 564
Fax: +370 2 223 749 **Contact:** Ms Virginija Smilgeviciene

FOURGOUX ET ASSOCIÉS (France)
111 Boulevard Pereire, Paris **Tel:** +33 1 5565 1665
Fax: +33 14754 9190 **Contact:** M Fourgoux

FORMOSA TRANSNATIONAL (Taiwan)
15th Floor, Lotus Building, 136 Jen-Ai Road, Section 3, Taipei 106 **Tel:** +886 2 2755 7366 **Fax:** +886 2 2755 6486 **Contact:** Mr John C Chen

FRANCESCHINI E MIRANDA - ADVOGADOS (Brazil)
Av. Brig. Faria Lima, 1461, 13° andar-Torre Sul, 01480-900 São Paulo
Tel: +55 11 3814 2566 **Fax:** +55 11 3813 9693
Contact: Mr José Inácio Gonzaga Fraceschini

BUREAU FRANCIS LEFÈBVRE (France)
1/3 Villa Emile Bergerat, 92522 Neuilly-sur-Seine Cedex **Tel:** +33 1 47 38 55 00 **Fax:** +33 1 47 38 55 55 **Contact:** M Robert Baconnier

FRANCK, GALICIA, DUCLAUD Y ROBLES, S.C. (Mexico)
Torre Optima, Av Paseo de las Palmas No 405 - 3rd Floor, Lomas de Chapultepec, 11000 Mexico City **Tel:** +525 540 9200
Fax: +525 540 9202 **Contact:** Mr Antonio Franck C

FRANÇOIS SARR & ASSOCIATES (Senegal)
33 Av L.S. Senghor BP-160, Dakar
Tel: +221 822 2722/+221 821 4528 **Fax:** +221 821 6659

FREEHILL HOGAN & MAHAR LLP (USA)
80 Pine Street, New York NY 10005 **Tel:** +1 212 425 1900
Fax: +1 212 425 1901 **Contact:** Mr William Juska, Jr

FRIGNANI E ASSOCIATI (Italy)
Via Argonne, 1, I-10133 Turin **Tel:** +39 0116 604 257
Fax: +39 0116 601 884 **Contact:** Mr Aldo Frignani

FRISHBERG & PARTNERS (Ukraine)
10 Gorky Street, Suite 8, 01004 Kiev **Tel:** +380 44 224 8314
Fax: +380 44 220 1406

G.J. TIMAGENIS LAW OFFICE (Greece)
57 Notara Street, 18535 Piraeus **Tel:** +30 1 422 0001
Fax: +30 1 422 1388 **Contact:** Mr G.J. Timagenis

GABRIELA MARSIGLIA - SOLE PRACTITIONER (Argentina)
Avenida Santa Fe, 995, Piso 6, 1059 Buenos Aires **Tel:** +54 11 4325 5050 **Fax:** +54 11 4393 2420 **Contact:** Mrs Gabriela Marsiglia

GADENS (Papua New Guinea)
Pacific Place, 12th Floor,, Corner Musgrave Street and Champion Parade, Port Moresby PO Box 1042 **Tel:** +675 321 1033
Fax: +675 321 1885

GAEDERTZ RECHTSANWÄLTE (Germany)
Fasanenstrasse 33, D-10719 Berlin **Tel:** +49 30 88 02 50
Fax: +49 30 88 02 52 00 **Contact:** Karlheinz Quack

GAGRAT & CO (India)
Alli Chambers, Nagindas Master Road, Fort, Mumbai 400 001
Tel: +91 22 265 0057 / 0084 **Fax:** +91 22 265 7876 / 9803 **Contact:** Mr JR Gagrat

GALINDO, ARIAS & LOPEZ (Panama)
Scotia Plaza, Floors 9,10,11,18 Federico Boyd Avenue, PO Box 8629, Panama City 5 **Tel:** +507 263 5633 **Fax:** +507 263 5335
Contact: Ms Namette Svenson

GALLANT Y.T. HO & CO (Hong Kong)
4th Floor, Jardine House, 1 Connaught Place, Hong Kong **Tel:** +852 2526 3336 **Fax:** +852 2845 9294 **Contact:** Mr Vincent WS Lo

If you can't find a firm here, see full profiles (pages 957-1481)

GANDRA MARTINS LAW FIRM (Brazil)
Alamada Jau 1742, 14th Floor, SP01420002 São Paulo
Tel: +55 11 3085 4544 **Fax:** +55 11 3083 7932
Contact: Mr Ives Gandra Martins

GARDERE WYNNE SEWELL LLP (USA)
3000 Thanksgiving Tower, 1601 Elm Street, Dallas TX 75201 **Tel:** +1 214 999 3000 **Fax:** +1 214 999 4667 **Contact:** Mr Larry L. Schoenbrun

GÁRDOS, BENKE, MOSONYI, TOMORI (Hungary)
Havas u.6, H-1056 Budapest **Tel:** +36 1 235 7460 **Fax:** +36 1 235 7461
Contact: Mr István Gárdos

GARRETTS, MEMBER FIRM OF ANDERSON LEGAL WCB (United Kingdom)
180 Strand, London WC2R 2NN **Tel:** +44 20 7344 0344
Fax: +44 20 7438 2518 **Contact:** Mr Peter Ridley

GARRY DOWNES QC - SOLE PRACTITIONER (Australia)
Seven Wentworth Chambers, 180 Phillip Street, Sydney NSW 2000
Tel: +61 2 8224 3004 **Fax:** +61 2 9233 1849

G. BREUER (Argentina)
25 de Mayo 460, 1 Floor, PO Box 1287, 1002 Buenos Aires
Tel: +54 11 4312 5678 **Fax:** +54 11 4311 4199

LAW OFFICES OF GEBRAN MAJDALANY (Qatar)
PO Box 4004, Doha **Tel:** +974 442 8899 **Fax:** +974 441 7817
Contact: Mr Gebran Majdalany

GEORGES ROBERT - SOLE PRACTITIONER (Mauritius)
8, Georges Guibert Street, Port Louis **Tel:** +230 212 0862
Fax: +230 212 3147 **Contact:** Mr Georges Robert

GEORGIAN CONSULTING GROUP (Georgia)
GCG Law Office, 24 Rustaveli Avenue, Tbilisi 380008 **Tel:** +995 32 936422/996006/920777 **Fax:** +995 32 932752
Contact: Mr Constantine Rizhinashvili

GILBERT PARLEANI (France)
18 Avenue Victoria, 75001 Paris **Tel:** +33 1 4476 8378
Fax: +33 1 40 41 94 21 **Contact:** M Gilbert Parleani

GILIBERTI & ASSOCIATI (Italy)
Via Visconti di Modrone, 21, 20122 Milan **Tel:** +39 02 7600 1585
Fax: +39 02 780 858 **Contact:** Mr Enrico Giliberti

GILL, GODLONTON & GERRANS (Zimbabwe)
Beverley Court, 100 Nelson Mandela Avenue, PO Box 8, Harare
Tel: +263 4 707 023 **Fax:** +263 4 707 380 / 707 388
Contact: Mr J H P Back

GILMARTIN, POSTER & SHAFTO (USA)
One William Street, New York NY 10004
Tel: +1 212 425 3220 **Fax:** +1 212 425 3130

GINESTIÉ PALEY-VINCENT & ASSOCIÉS (France)
10 Place des Etats-Unis, 75116 Paris
Tel: +33 1 5323 4000 **Fax:** +33 1 5323 9700

GLOOR & SIEGER (Switzerland)
Utoquai 37, PO Box 581, 8024 Zürich
Tel: +41 1 254 6161 **Fax:** +41 1 254 6171 **Contact:** Dr Sieger

GOLDFARB, LEVY, ERAN & CO (Israel)
Eliahu House, 2 Ibn Gvirol Street, Tel Aviv 64077
Tel: +972 3 608 9999 **Fax:** +972 3 608 9909
Contact: Mr. Yehuda M Levy

GOODRICH, RIQUELME Y ASOCIADOS (Mexico)
Paseo de la Reforma 265, PO Box 93 -Bis, 06500 Mexico, DF
Tel: +525 533 0040 **Fax:** +525 525 1227
Contact: Mr Alvaro Gonzáles-Ocampo

GORRISSEN FEDERSPIEL KIERKEGAARD (Denmark)
H C Andersens Boulevard 12, DK-1553 Copenhagen K **Tel:** +45 33 41 41 41 **Fax:** +45 33 41 41 33 **Contact:** Mr Thomas Federspiel

ESCRITORIO DE ADVOCACIA GOUVEA VIEIRA (Brazil)
Av. Rio Branco 85, 13° andar, 20040-004 Rio de Janeiro RJ
Tel: +55 21 276 4000 **Fax:** +55 21 263 2088
Contact: Mr Joao Pedro Gouvea Vieira

GRAF VON WESTPHALEN FRITZE & MODEST (Germany)
Eschersheimer Landstrasse 25-27, D-60322 Frankfurt
Tel: +49 69 959 570 **Fax:** +49 69 959 57166 **Contact:** Ulrich Fritze

GRAHAM THOMPSON & CO (Bahamas)
Sassoon House, Shirley St & Victoria Av, PO Box N272, Nassau **Tel:** +1 242 322 4130 **Fax:** +1 242 328 1069 **Contact:** Ms Judith A Whitehead

GRANDE STEVENS & PEDERSOLI (Italy)
Via Gesu, 2/A, I-20121 Milan
Tel: +39 02 76 03 31 **Fax:** +39 02 760 33 400

ESTUDIO GRAU (Peru)
Santa Maria No. 110-140, Miraflores, Lima 18 **Tel:** +51 1 422 0830
Fax: +51 1 440 6158 **Contact:** Mr Miguel Grau M

GREENBERG TRAURIG (USA)
1221 Brickell Avenue, Miami FL 33131
Tel: +1 305 579 0500 **Fax:** +1 305 579 0717
Contact: Mr Cesar L. Alvarez

GRISCHENKO & PARTNERS (Ukraine)
20 Mechnikova Street, 252021 Kiev **Tel:** +380 44 290 0458
Fax: +380 44 290 9529 **Contact:** Mr Dmitri Grischenko

ESTUDIO JURÍDICO GROSS BROWN (Paraguay)
1st Floor, Benjamin Constant 624, PO Box 730, Asuncion
Tel: +595 2149 4644 **Fax:** +595 2149 8169
Contact: Mr Jorge Gross Brown

GRÜNECKER, KINKELDEY, STOCKMAIER & SCHWANHÄUSER (Germany)
Maximilianstr. 58, D-80538 München **Tel:** +49 89 212 350
Fax: +49 89 220 287 **Contact:** Hermann Kinkeldey

GRUNTE & CERS, LAW OFFICE (Latvia)
40 Brivibas Street,, Office 31, 2nd Floor, LV-1050 Riga
Tel: +371 782 1315 **Fax:** +371 782 1231 **Contact:** Mr Ivars Grunte

GRUPO LEGAL PORTUGUÊS (Portugal)
Rua Castilho No. 32-9, 1250-070 Lisbon **Tel:** +351 2 1 313 1500
Fax: +351 2 1 313 1501 **Contact:** Mr Pedro R de Sousa

GUANDIQUE SEGOVIA QUINTANILLA (El Salvador)
Pasaje Senda Florida Norte No 124, Colonia Escalon, San Salavador
Tel: +503 245 3444 **Fax:** +503 298 6613

ETUDE GUEDEL NDIAYE & ASSOCIÉS (Senegal)
73, bis Rue A Assane Ndoye Dakar, Assane, Ndoye, Dakar BP2656
Tel: +221 8215858/+221 822 1075 **Fax:** +221 821 86 51
Contact: Maître Guedel Ndiaye

GUERRERO, OLIVOS, NOVOA Y ERRAZURIZ (Chile)
Abogados, Miraflores 178, 12th Floor, Santiago
Tel: +56 2 639 0169 **Fax:** +56 2 639 0170

GUNDERSON DETTMER STOUGH VILLENEUVE FRANKLIN & HACHIGIAN (USA)
155 Constitution Drive, Menlo Park CA 94025
Tel: +1 650 321 2400 **Fax:** +1 650 321 2800
Contact: Ms Sandrine Ghosh

BUFETE GUTIERREZ FALLA (Honduras)
PO Box 3175, Tegucigalpa **Tel:** +504 236 5455 **Fax:** +504 236 6149
Contact: Dr Laureano F Gutierrez Falla

GUYER & REGULES (Uruguay)
Plaza Independencia 811, P.B., Montevideo 11100
Tel: +598 2902 1515 **Fax:** +598 2902 5454

H2O (HENRY HEPWORTH ORGANISATION) (United Kingdom)
5 John Street, London WC1N 2HH **Tel:** +44 20 7539 7200
Fax: +44 20 7539 7201 **Contact:** Ms Catrin Turner

ADVOKATFIRMAET HAAVIND VISLIE DA (Norway)
Raadhuist 27, PO Box 359, Sentrum, N-0101 Oslo
Tel: +47 22 40 21 00 **Fax:** +47 22 40 21 01

HADEF AL DHAHIRI & ASSOCIATES (United Arab Emirates)
12th floor, Blue Tower, Khalifa Street, PO Box 3727, Abu Dhabi **Tel:** +9712 6276 622 **Fax:** +971 2 627 6556 **Contact:** Dr Faraj A Ahnish

HAKIM LAW FIRM (Syria)
Victoria Bridge, Mardam Building, PO Box 5788, Damascus
Tel: +963 11 22 23 577 **Fax:** +963 11 22 44 370
Contact: Mr Jacques El Hakim

HALE AND DORR (USA)
60 State Street, Boston MA 02109-1803
Tel: +1 617 526 6000 **Fax:** +1 617 526 5000 **Contact:** Mr Bill Lee

HAMADA & MATSUMOTO (Japan)
Kasumigaseki Building, 25th Floor, 2-5, Kasumigaseki 3-chome, Chiyoda-ku, Tokyo 100-6025 **Tel:** +81 3 3580 3377
Fax: +81 3 3581 4713 **Contact:** Mr Kunio Hamada

HAMILTON HARRISON & MATTHEWS (Kenya)
I.C.E.A. Building, 4th Floor, Kenyatta Avenue, PO Box 30333, Nairobi
Tel: +254 2 330870 **Fax:** +254 2 222 318 **Contact:** Mr Peter Le Pelley

HANG LE COMPANY LTD (Vietnam)
34 Quang Trung Street, Hanoi, Hanoi
Tel: +84 4 822 3986 **Fax:** +84 4 942 2063

HANS HELLMANN - SOLE PRACTITIONER (Germany)
Am Morsdorfer Hof 16, 50933 Cologne **Tel:** +49 221 494 058
Fax: +49 221 494 040 **Contact:** Hans Hellmann

HANZEKOVIC & RADAKOVIC (Croatia)
Radnicka cesta 22, 10000 Zagreb
Tel: +385 1 618 4611 **Fax:** +385 1 618 4816

HARBOTTLE & LEWIS (United Kingdom)
Hanover House, 14 Hanover Square, London W1R 0BE
Tel: +44 20 7667 5000 **Fax:** +44 20 7667 5100
Contact: Ms Samantha Phillips

HARFOUCHE, GRANEROS & ASOCIADOS (Argentina)
Laballe 1312, Piso 5, Departmento A, 1048 Buenos Aires
Tel: +54 11 4371 0012 **Fax:** +54 11 4371 6890

HARIDASS HO & PARTNERS (Singapore)
24 Raffles Place, #18-00 Clifford Centre, Singapore 048621
Tel: +65 533 2323 **Fax:** +65 533 7029 **Contact:** Mr Ho Wah Onn

If you can't find a firm here, see full profiles (pages 957-1481)

HARLEY & MORRIS (Lesotho)
3rd Floor, Christie House, PO Box 7755, Masem
Tel: +266 313 840 **Fax:** +266 310 076
Contact: Mr Seymour Harley

HARMSEN & UTESCHER (Germany)
Alter Wall 55, D-20457 Hamburg **Tel:** +49 40 376 909 0
Fax: +49 40 376 909 99 **Contact:** Dr Michael Schaeffer

HARNEY WESTWOOD & RIEGELS (British Virgin Islands)
Craigmuir Chambers, PO Box 71, Road Town, Tortola
Tel: +1 284 494 2233 **Fax:** +1 284 494 3547/4885
Contact: Mr Richard A Peters

HARRIS, WILTSHIRE & GRANNIS LLP (USA)
1200 Eighteenth Street NW, Suite 1200, Washington DC 20036-2560
Tel: +1 202 730 1300 **Fax:** +1 202 730 1301 **Contact:** Mr Scott Harris

HART MUIRHEAD FATTA (Jamaica)
2 St Lucia Ave, 3rd Floor, Kingston 5 **Tel:** +1 876 929 9677
Fax: +1 876 929 5755 **Contact:** Mr Hugh C Hart, Esq

HASHIDATE LAW OFFICE (Japan)
7th Floor, Imperial Tower, 1-1, Uchisaiwai-cho, 1-Chome, Chiyoda-Ku, Tokyo 100-0011 **Tel:** +81 3 3504 3800 / 1007 **Fax:** +81 3 3504 1009
Contact: Mr Kenji Hashidate

HASSAN & HASSAN (Pakistan)
Paaf Building, 7D Kashmir Egerton Road, Lahore
Tel: +92 42 636 0800 03 **Fax:** +92 42 636 0811-12

HASSAN AL-KHATER LAW OFFICES (Qatar)
PO Box 1737, Doha **Tel:** +974 443 7770 **Fax:** +974 443 7772
Contact: Mr Hassan A-Alkhater

LAW OFFICE OF HASSAN MAHASSNI (IN ASSOC. WITH WHITE & CASE) (Saudi Arabia)
Al Nakheel Ceter, 3rd Floor, Medina Road on Palestine Circle, PO Box 2256, Jeddah 21451 **Tel:** +966 2 665 4353 **Fax:** +966 2 669 2996
Contact: Mr. Hassan MS Mahassni

HASSAN RADHI & ASSOCIATES (Bahrain)
Suite 605, Diplomat Tower, Diplomatic Area, PO Box 5366, Manama
Tel: +973 535 252 **Fax:** +973 533 358 **Contact:** Mr Hassan Ali Radhi

HAUSMANINGER HERBST WIETRZYK (Austria)
Franz Josefs-Kai 3, A-1010 Vienna
Tel: +43 1 513 9540 **Fax:** +43 1 513 9540 12
Contact: Dr Christian Hausmaninger

HAYNES AND BOONE LLP (USA)
1000 Louisiana Street Suite 4300, Houston TX 77002-5012
Tel: +1 713 547 2000 **Fax:** +1 713 547 2600

HEADRICK RIZIK ALVAREZ & FERNANDEZ (Dominican Republic)
Elvira de Mendoza No. 51, PO Box 524121, Santo Domingo
Tel: +1 809 685 4137/686 0404 **Fax:** +1 809 685 2936
Contact: Mr William Headrick

HEALY & BAILLIE LLP (USA)
29 Broadway, New York NY 10004 **Tel:** +1 212 943 3980
Fax: +1 212 425 0131 **Contact:** Mr John D Kimball

ESTUDIO HECTOR A VIANA (Uruguay)
Juan Carlos Gómez 1251, Montevideo CP 11 000 **Tel:** +598 2 916 1460
Fax: +598 2 916 2199 **Contact:** Mr Hector A Viana

HEENAN BLAIKIE (Canada)
1250 René-Lévesque Blvd West, Suite 2500, Montréal H3B 4Y1
Tel: +1 514 846 1212 **Fax:** +1 514 846 3427
Contact: Ms Lyne Beauregard

HELEN YEO & PARTNERS (Singapore)
80 Raffles Place, #33-00, UOB Plaza 1, Singapore 048624
Tel: +65 225 1400 **Fax:** +65 225 0020 **Contact:** Mrs Helen Yeo

HENRI JOB LAW FIRM (Cameroon)
Groundfloor Stamatiades Building, 1059 Boulevard de la Republique, PO Box 5482, Douala **Tel:** +237 424 802 **Fax:** +237 420 549
Contact: Mr Henri Job

ADVOKATFIRMA HENRIK HEY (Greenland)
PO Box 510, Nuuk DK-3900 **Tel:** +299 321 252 **Fax:** +299 325 877
Contact: Mr Henrik Hey

HERGÜNER, BILGEN & ÖZEKE (Turkey)
Süleyman Seba Caddesi No. 95, Akaretler - Besiktas, 80680 Istanbul
Tel: +90 212 236 57 07 **Fax:** +90 212 236 57 06
Contact: Ümit Hergüner

HERZFELD & RUBIN (USA)
40 Wall Street, New York NY 10005
Tel: +1 212 344 5500 **Fax:** +1 212 344 3333 **Contact:** Mr Ian Ceresney

HETA LAW OFFICES (Estonia)
Rutli str. 4, 10130 Tallinn **Tel:** +372 6 996 611 **Fax:** +372 6 442 889
Contact: Mr Kaido Pihlakas

HIBIYA PARK LAW OFFICES (Japan)
5th Floor, Asahi Feimei Hibiya Building, 1-5-1 Yurakucho, Chiyoda-ku, Tokyo **Tel:** +81 3 5532 8888 **Fax:** +81 3 5532 8800

HIGGS & JOHNSON (Bahamas)
83 Shirley Street, Sandringham House, PO Box N-3247, Nassau
Tel: +1 242 322 8571 **Fax:** +1 242 328 7727
Contact: Mr Philip Dunkly

If you can't find a firm here, see full profiles (pages 957-1481)

HILL RIVKINS & HAYDEN LLP (USA)
90 West Street, New York NY 10006 **Tel:** +1 212 669 0600
Fax: +1 212 669 0698 **Contact:** Mr Raymond P. Hayden

HILL TAYLOR DICKINSON (United Kingdom)
Irongate House, Duke's Place, London EC3A 7HX
Tel: +44 20 7283 9033 **Fax:** +44 20 7283 1144 **Contact:** Mr Rhys Clift

HJEJLE GERSTED & MORGENSEN (Denmark)
24 Amagertorv, DK-1553 Copenhagen
Tel: +45 33 13 4262 **Fax:** +45 33 111 250 **Contact:** Mr Olaf Egell

HOET PELAEZ CASTILLO & DUQUE (Venezuela)
Centro San Ignacio, Torre Kepler, Avenue Blandin, La Castellana, Caracas 1060 **Tel:** +582 263 6644 **Fax:** +582 263 7744
Contact: Mr Francisco Castillo

HOFFMANN EITLE (Germany)
Arabellastrasse 4, D-81925 München
Tel: +49 89 92 40 90 **Fax:** +49 89 91 83 56 **Contact:** Werner Eitle

HOFMEYR HERBSTEIN GIHWALA INC (South Africa)
6 Sandown Valley Crescent, Sandown, Sandton, Johannesburg 2196
Tel: +27 11 286 1100 **Fax:** +27 11 286 1264
Contact: Mr Dines Gihwala (Chairman)

HOGAN & HARTSON LLP (USA)
Columbia Square, 555 Thirteenth Street NW, Washington DC 20004-1109 **Tel:** +1 202 637 5600 **Fax:** +1 202 637 5910
Contact: Mr Bob Glen Odle

HOLLIS & CO (Bermuda)
PO Box 463, Hamilton HM BX **Tel:** +1 441 295 2208
Fax: +1 441 295 3404 **Contact:** Mr Wendell M Hollis, JP

HONEY & BLANCKENBERG (Zimbabwe)
Throgmorton House, 51 Samora Machel Avenue, PO Box 85, Harare
Tel: +263 4 75 02 95/775573/751887 **Fax:** +263 4 75 22 83/775578
Contact: Mr A M Rosettenstein

LAW FIRM HOOPLOT (Surinam)
36 Watermolen Straat, PO Box 1466, Paramaribo
Tel: +597 476 406 **Fax:** +597 476 829

HORI & ASSOCIATES (Japan)
35th Floor Kasumigaseki Building, 3-2-5 Kasumigaseki, Chiyoda-Ku, Tokyo 100-6035 **Tel:** +81 3 5512 7377 **Fax:** +81 3 5512 7385

CABINET HUDICOURT-WOOLLEY (Haiti)
27 Avenue Marie Jeanne, Port-au-Prince
Tel: +509 223 9555 / +509 223 9666 **Fax:** +509 223 9444

HUGHES, FIELDS & STOBY (Guyana)
62 Hadfield & Cross Streets, Werk-en-rust, Georgetown
Tel: +592 2 58914 **Fax:** +592 2 57996 **Contact:** Mr Clarence Hughes

HUGHES & HUGHES (Uruguay)
25 de Mayo 455, 4th Floor, Montevideo 11000
Tel: +598 2 916 0988 **Fax:** +598 2 916 1003
Contact: Mr Conrado Hughes Delgado

HUGHES & LUCE LLP (USA)
1717 Main Street, Suite 2800, Dallas TX 75201 **Tel:** +1 214 939 5500
Fax: +1 214 939 6100 **Contact:** Mr William A. McCormack

HUNTER & GREIG (FORMERLY KATEERA & KAGAMIRE) (Uganda)
Stanbic Bank Chambers, PO Box 7026, Kampala
Tel: +256 41 234 483/4/5 **Fax:** +256 41 234 486
Contact: Mr Yusufu Kagumire

HUNTER & HUNTER (Cayman Islands)
Huntlaw Building, PO Box 190 GT, Grand Cayman
Tel: +1 345 949 4900 **Fax:** +1 345 949 4901
Contact: Mr Andrew Bolton

HUNTON & WILLIAMS (USA)
Riverfront Plaza, East Tower, 951 East Byrd Street, Richmond VA 23219-4074 **Tel:** +1 804 788 8200 **Fax:** +1 804 788 8218
Contact: Mr Thurston R. Moore

HUQ & CO (Bangladesh)
47-1 Purana Paldan, Dhaka 1000 **Tel:** +880 2 955 2196/ 955 5953
Fax: +880 2 956 2434 **Contact:** Mr Rafique-ul Huq

HUTCHINS, WHEELER & DITTMAR (USA)
101 Federal Street, Boston MA 02110
Tel: +1 617 951 6600 **Fax:** +1 617 951 1295

BUTTIGIEG & REFALO ADVOCATES (Malta)
54 St Christopher Street, Valleta VLT08 **Tel:** +356 223515/ 32479
Fax: +356 241170 **Contact:** Prof Ian Refalo

ICAZA, GONZALEZ-RUIZ & ALEMÁN (Panama)
Calle Aquilino de la Guardia No 8, PO Box 87-1371, Panama City 7
Tel: +507 263 5555 **Fax:** +507 269 4891 **Contact:** Dr Roberto R Aléman

IDA DRAMEH, LEGAL PRACTITIONER (The Gambia)
13A Marine Parade, Banjul **Tel:** +220 228 882 **Fax:** +220 228 248
Contact: Ms Ida Drameh

I GORNITZKY & CO (Israel)
Rothschild Boulevard 45, Tel Aviv 65784 **Tel:** +972 3 710 9191
Fax: +972 3 560 6555 **Contact:** Mr Pinhas Rubin

If you can't find a firm here, see full profiles (pages 957-1481)

INDACOCHEA & ASOCIADOS (Bolivia)
Av. Pirai No.2115, Esquina Baracea, Urbari, Santa Cruz
Tel: +591 353 5355/6 **Fax:** +591 358 1200
Contact: Mr Ricardo Indacochea San Martin

INTERNATIONAL LEGAL COUNSELLORS THAILAND (Thailand)
18th Floor, Sathorn City Tower, 175 South Sathorn Road 18th Floor, Tungmahamek, Sathorn, Bangkok 10120 **Tel:** +662 679 6005
Fax: +662 679 6041 **Contact:** Mr Jayavadh Bunnag

INVEST CONSULT (Vietnam)
260 Ba Trieu St, PO Box 615 Bo Ho, Hanoi 10000
Tel: +84 4 826 9223 **Fax:** +84 4 825 2282

IRELL & MANELLA (USA)
1800 Avenue of the Stars, Suite 900, Los Angeles CA 90067-4276
Tel: +1 310 277 1010 **Fax:** +1 310 203 7199
Contact: Mr Morgan Chu

ISHENGOMA, MASHA, MUJULIZI & MAGAI ADVOCATES (Tanzania)
11th Floor, PPF Tower, 20/21 Garden Av/Ohio St, PO Box 72484, Dar Es Salaam **Tel:** +255 22 212 0469/0406/0483/ **Fax:** +255 22 211 1621/212 0401 **Contact:** Mr Protase Rwezahura G Ishengoma

ISOLA & ISOLA (Gibraltar)
Portland House, Glacis Road, PO Box 204, Gibraltar **Tel:** +350 78363
Fax: +350 78990 **Contact:** Hon Peter J Isola, OBE MA (Oxon)

IU, LAI & LI (Hong Kong)
9th & 15th Floors, The Bank of East Asia Building, 10 Des Voeux Road, Central, Hong Kong **Tel:** +852 2810 8082 **Fax:** +852 2845 9103

IVINS, PHILLIPS & BARKER (USA)
1700 Pennsylvania Ave NW, Suite 600, Washington DC 20006
Tel: +1 202 393 7600 **Fax:** +1 202 393 7601 **Contact:** Mr Eric Fox

IVOR FITZPATRICK & CO (Ireland)
44-45 St Stephen's Green, Dublin 2 **Tel:** +353 1 6787000
Fax: +353 1 6787004 **Contact:** Mr Ivor Fitzpatrick

JADEK & PENSA (Slovenia)
6 Tavcarjeva, Ljubljana 1000
Tel: +386 1 234 2520 **Fax:** +386 1 234 2532

JAMES BERRY & ASSOCIATES (United Arab Emirates)
ABN Amro Bank Building, Khalid Bin Walid Street, PO Box 52294, Dubai **Tel:** +971 4351 1020 **Fax:** +971 4351 3799

JAN RAMBERG - SOLE PRACTITIONER (Sweden)
Vretvägen 13, S-183 63 Täby
Tel: +46 8 756 6225 **Fax:** +46 8 756 2460

JARDIM, SAMPAIO, CALDAS E ASSOCIADOS VIEGA GOMES, MARQUES DA CRUZ, COLMONERO (Portugal)
Av. Duque D'Avila, 66, 5th Floor, 1069-075 Lisbon
Tel: +351 21 356 4300 **Fax:** +351 21 356 4350
Contact: Mr M Magalhaes Silva

J.B. DADACHANJI & CO (India)
Jeevan Vihar, 3 Parliament Street, New Delhi 110 001
Tel: +91 11 334 2628 **Fax:** +91 11 373 2505 **Contact:** Mr Rajan Narin

JD SELLIER & CO (Trinidad & Tobago)
129-131 Abercromby Street, PO Box 116, Port of Spain **Tel:** +1 868 623 4283 **Fax:** +1 868 623 4281 **Contact:** Mr David Boucaud

JEAN-FRANÇOIS POUDRET - SOLE PRACTITIONER (Switzerland)
29 Route du Port, 1009 Pulli **Tel:** +41 21 728 1077
Fax: +41 21 729 0546 **Contact:** Dr Jean-Francois Poudret

JENKENS & GILCHRIST (USA)
1445 Ross Avenue, Suite 3200, Dallas TX 75202-2799
Tel: +1 214 855 4500 **Fax:** +1 214 855 4300
Contact: Mr David M. Laney

JIMÉNEZ DE ARÉCHAGA & BRAUSE (Uruguay)
Cerrido 415, 6th Floor, Montevideo 11000 **Tel:** +598 2 915 3188
Fax: +598 2 916 3931 **Contact:** Mr Fernando Jiménez de Aréchaga

JM GANADO & ASSOCIATES (Malta)
171 Old Bakery Street, Valletta VLT09
Tel: +356 235 406 **Fax:** +356 225 908

JOHNSON STOKES & MASTER (Hong Kong)
16-19th Floors, Prince's Building, 10 Chater Road, Central, Hong Kong
Tel: +852 2843 2211 **Fax:** +852 2845 9121
Contact: Mrs Wendy Mahbubani

JOHNSTON & BUCHAN (Canada)
275 Slater Street, Suite 1700, Ottawa K1P 5H9 **Tel:** +1 613 236 3882
Fax: +1 613 230 6423 **Contact:** Mr Stephen Whitehead

JOHN WILSON PARTNERS (Sri Lanka)
365 Dam Street, Colombo, Colombo 12
Tel: +94 1 324579/448931/321652 **Fax:** +94 1 446954/699165
Contact: Mr John Wilson

JONAS BRUUN (Denmark)
Bredgade 38, DK-1260 Copenhagen K
Tel: +45 33 47 88 00 **Fax:** +45 33 47 88 88 **Contact:** Mr Per Magid

JONSSON & HALL (Iceland)
Morkin 1, Reykjavik 108 **Tel:** +354 581 2122 **Fax:** +354 581 2150

If you can't find a firm here, see full profiles (pages 957-1481)

JOWELL GLYN & MARAIS INC (South Africa)
PO Box 652361, Benmore 2010 **Tel:** +27 11 784 4200
Fax: +27 11 784 4215 **Contact:** Mr Donn Edward Jowell

JULIUS & CREASY (Sri Lanka)
41 Janadhipathi Mawatha, PO Box 154, Colombo 1
Tel: +94 1 422 601 **Fax:** +94 1 446663 / 435451

JUN HE LAW OFFICES (China)
China Resources Building, 20th Floor, 8 Jianguomenbei Avenue, Beijing 100005 **Tel:** +86 10 8519 1300 **Fax:** +86 10 8519 1350

JURGENS BEZUIDENHOUT ATTORNEYS (South Africa)
Harrow Court 3, Isle of Houghton, Boundary Road, Parktown 2193
Tel: +27 11 645 6040 **Fax:** +27 11 484 1165
Contact: Mr Jurgens Bezuidenhout

JURISTCONSULT CHAMBERS (Mauritius)
Cathedral Square, Port Louis **Tel:** +230 208 5526
Fax: +230 208 5586 **Contact:** Mr R M Marc Hein

JYOTI SAGAR & ASSOCIATES (India)
84-E, C-6 Lane, (Off Central Avenue), Sainik Farms, New Delhi 110062 **Tel:** +91 11 651 8714 **Fax:** +91 11 651 8717
Contact: Mr J Sagar

KADIR, ANDRI AIDHAM & PARTNERS (Malaysia)
8th Floor, Menara Safuan, 80 Jalan Ampang, 50450 Kuala Lumpur
Tel: +60 3 238 2888 **Fax:** +60 3 238 8431 **Contact:** Mr Kadir Kassim

KAHN ASSOCIÉS (France)
51, Rue Dumont D'Urville, 75116 Paris
Tel: +33 1 4501 4501 **Fax:** +33 1 4501 4500

KALO & ASSOCIATES (Albania)
Brigada VIII Street, Green Building, Canadian Embassy Location, Suite 3-4, PO Box 235, Tirana **Tel:** +355 42 335 32 **Fax:** +355 42 247 27
Contact: Mr Përparim Kalo

DR KAMAL HOSSAIN & ASSOCIATES (Bangladesh)
Chambers Building, 2nd Floor, 122-124 Motijheel CA, Dhaka 1000
Tel: +880 2 956 0655 **Fax:** +880 2 956 4953

KAMEL LAW OFFICE (Egypt)
4 El Shaheed Ahmed Yehia Ibrahim Street, Mohandesseen 12411, Giza, Cairo **Tel:** +202 347 4102/9453 OR 303 6404
Fax: +202 345 2009/302 3649 **Contact:** Dr Mohamed Kamel

KANTOR & IMMERMAN (Zimbabwe)
MacDonald House, Selous, 2nd Street, PO Box 19, Harare
Tel: +263 4 700 454 **Fax:** +263 4 704 436 **Contact:** Mr ABC Chinake

KANTOR, ELHANANI, TAL & CO (Israel)
Mozes House, 74-76 Rothschild Blvd, Tel Aviv 65785
Tel: +972 3 714 0400 **Fax:** +972 3 714 0401
Contact: Mr Israel Kantor

KAPLAN & STRATTON (Kenya)
Queensway House, Kaunda Street, PO Box 40111, Nairobi
Tel: +254 2 335 333 **Fax:** +254 2 242 245 **Contact:** Mr Zul Alibhai

LAW FIRM KARATZAS & PARTNERS (Greece)
6 Omirou Street, 10564 Athens
Tel: +30 1 371 3600 **Fax:** +30 1 3234 363

CABINET KAZUNGU (Rwanda)
BP 3371, Kigali **Tel:** +250 0830 0827 **Fax:** +250 717 67
Contact: M Kazungu

MR KEBREAB HABTE MICHAEL - SOLE PRACTITIONER (Eritrea)
University of Asmara, PO Box 1220, Asmara
Tel: +291 1 616 1935 **Fax:** +291 1 162236

KEESAL, YOUNG & LOGAN LLP (Hong Kong)
1603 The Centre Mark, 287 Queen's Road, Central Hong Kong
Tel: +852 2854 1718 **Fax:** +852 2541 6189 **Contact:** Mr Skip Keesal

KELLEY DRYE & WARREN (USA)
101 Park Avenue, New York NY 10178 **Tel:** +1 212 808 7800
Fax: +1 212 808 7898 **Contact:** Mr Merill Stone

KELLOGG, HUBER, HANSEN, TODD & EVANS PLLC (USA)
1615 M Street NW, Suite 400, Washington DC 20036
Tel: +1 202 326 7900 **Fax:** +1 202 326 7999
Contact: Mr Michael Kellogg

KEMP & CO (United Kingdom)
Saddlers House, Gutter Lane, London EC2V 6BR
Tel: +44 20 7600 8080 **Fax:** +44 20 7600 7878
Contact: Mr Richard Kemp

KENNEDY VAN DER LAAN (Netherlands)
Keizersgracht 555, PO Box 15744, 1017 DR Amsterdam
Tel: +31 20 550 6666 **Fax:** +31 20 550 6777

KENYON & KENYON (USA)
1500 K Street, NW, Suite 700, Washington DC 20005 -1257 **Tel:** +1 202 220 4200 **Fax:** +1 202 220 4201 **Contact:** Mr John Altmiller

KETTANI LAW FIRM (Morocco)
23 rue El Amraoui Brahim, Casablanca 20000 **Tel:** +212 2 220 1898
Fax: +212 2 220 5925 **Contact:** Mr Azzedine Kettani

If you can't find a firm here, see full profiles (pages 957-1481)

KEVIN KILMARTIN - SOLE PRACTITIONER (Falkland Islands)
John Street Chambers, PO Box 802, Stanley
Tel: +500 22765 **Fax:** +500 22766

KEY & DIXON (United Arab Emirates)
PO Box 33675, Standard Chartered Bank Building, Al Mankhool Road, Dubai **Tel:** +97 1 4359 0096 **Fax:** +97 1 4359 0029
Contact: Ms Nicolette Fleming

KHAITAN & CO (India)
Khaitan House, B-1 Defence Colony, New Delhi 110024 **Tel:** +91 11 464 6516 - 18 **Fax:** +91 11 464 6958 **Contact:** Mr Gutan Khaitan

KHATTAR ASSOCIATES (Lebanon)
669 Corniche du Fleuve, Place du Musee, PO Box 116-2211, Beirut
Tel: +961 1 614969/70/424898 **Fax:** +9611 614969
Contact: Mr Naou M Khattar

KHATTAR WONG & PARTNERS (Singapore)
80 Raffles Place #25-01, UOB Plaza 1, Singapore 048624
Tel: +65 535 6844 **Fax:** +65 534 4892 **Contact:** Mr Rajan Menon

KIERAN B. SHAH (Seychelles)
State House Avenue, Victoria Mahe, PO Box 297, Victoria
Tel: +248 322 608 **Fax:** +248 324 176 **Contact:** Mr Kieran Shah

KING & WOOD (China)
Level 30, North Office Tower, Beijing Kerry Centre, 1 Guanghua Road, Chaoyang District, Beijing 100020 **Tel:** +86 10 65612299
Fax: +86 10 65610830 / 0830 **Contact:** Mr Wang Junfeng

KIRKLAND & ELLIS (USA)
Aon Centre, 200 East Randolph Drive, Chicago IL 60601
Tel: +1 312 861 2000 **Fax:** +1 312 861 2200

KIRKPATRICK & LOCKHART LLP (USA)
535 Smithfield St, Pittsburgh PA 15222-2312 **Tel:** +1 412 355 6500
Fax: +1 412 355 6501 **Contact:** Mr Peter J. Kalis

CABINET KISIMBA-NGOY (Democratic Republic of Congo)
Galeries Pacha Immeuble BYBLOS 2eme etage, Kinshasa Gombe
Tel: +243 12 41869/+243 12 25586 **Fax:** +243 882 0972
Contact: M Honorius Kisimba-Ngoy

KLAKA RECHTSANWÄLTE (Germany)
Delpstrasse 4, 81679 Munich
Tel: +49 89 99 89 190 **Fax:** +49 89 98 00 36

KLEGAL (United Kingdom)
1-2 Dorset Rise, London EC4Y 8AE **Tel:** +44 20 7694 2500
Fax: +44 20 7694 2501 **Contact:** Mr Nick Holt

KNOEPFLER GABUS GEHRIG (Switzerland)
4 Rue de La Serre, 2001, Neuchatel **Tel:** +41 32 724 3522
Fax: +41 32 725 01 29 **Contact:** Mr Francois Knoepfler

KOCIAN SOLC BALASTÍK (Czech Republic)
Jindrisska 34, 110 00 Prague 1 **Tel:** +420 2 2410 3316
Fax: +420 2 2410 3234 **Contact:** Mr Jiri Balastik

CABINET KONJBETO (Central African Republic)
BP 510, Rue de l'Industrie, Bangui **Tel:** +236 611 762
Fax: +236 613 217 **Contact:** M Konjbeto

KPMG ABOGADOS (Spain)
Paseo de la Castellana, 95, Edificio Torre Europa planta 24, 28046 Madrid **Tel:** +34 91 456 3481 **Fax:** +34 91 555 0132
Contact: Ms Mercedes de Rojas

KPMG FIDAL (France)
2 Bis Rue De Villiers, 92200 Neuilly-sur-Seine
Tel: +33 1 46 39 46 39 **Fax:** +33 1 47 58 8121

KRIEGER GENTZ MES & GRAF VON DER GROEBEN (Germany)
Georg-Glock-Str. 3, D-40474 Düsseldorf **Tel:** +49 211 450711
Fax: +49 211 4370707 **Contact:** Mr Ulrich Krieger

KROMANN REUMERT (Denmark)
Rådhuspladsen 14, DK-1550 Copenhagen V **Tel:** +45 33 11 1110
Fax: +45 70 121311 **Contact:** Mr Henrik Stenbjerre

KURI BREÑA, SÁNCHEZ UGARTE, CORCUERA Y AZNAR (Mexico)
Bosque de Ciruelos 168 6 Piso, Bosques de las Lomas, 11700 Mexico City **Tel:** +525 251 7220 **Fax:** +525 251 2031
Contact: Mr Sanpiago Corcuera

KUSUM LAW FIRM (Nepal)
2-Chha-110, Lazimpat Kathmandu, PO Box 2384, Kathmandu
Tel: +977 1 417236 **Fax:** +977 1 423353 **Contact:** Kusum Shrestha

KVALE & CO (Norway)
Fridtjof Nansens Plass 4, PO Box 1752 Vika, 0122 Oslo
Tel: +47 22 47 97 00 **Fax:** +47 22 47 97 01 **Contact:** Mr Amders Kvale

KWOK & YIH (Hong Kong)
37th Floor, Gloucester Tower, The Landmark, Central, Hong Kong
Tel: +852 2523 1000 **Fax:** +852 2530 4300
Contact: Mr Larry L K Kwok

KYRIAKIDES - GEORGOPOULOS LAW FIRM (Greece)
268 Kifissias Ave, Halandri 152 32, Athens **Tel:** +30 1 683 7520
Fax: +30 1 685 6658 **Contact:** Mr Costas K. Kyriakides

If you can't find a firm here, see full profiles (pages 957-1481)

LACAZ MARTINS, HALEMBECK, PEREIRA NETO, GUREVICH & SCHOUERI (Brazil)
Rua Padre Joao Manvel n° 923, 7° andar, SP 01411-001 São Paulo
Tel: +55 11 3068 8373 **Fax:** +55 11 3068 8379
Contact: Mr Christiano Diogo de Faria

LALIVE & PARTNERS (Switzerland)
6, Rue de l' Athenee, PO Box 393, 1211 12 Geneva
Tel: +41 22 319 8700 **Fax:** +41 22 319 87 60 **Contact:** Mr Vueillety

LANDWELL ABOGADOS Y ASESORES FISCALES (PRICEWATERHOUSECOOPERS) (Spain)
Paseo de la Castellana 53, 28046 Madrid
Tel: +34 91 568 4000 **Fax:** +34 91 308 3566

LANG MICHENER (Canada)
181 Bay Street, Suite 2500, PO Box 747, Toronto ON M5J 2T7
Tel: +1 416 360 8600 **Fax:** +1 416 365 1719

LARA LOPEZ MATAMOROS RODRIGUEZ & TINOCO (Costa Rica)
P.O. Box 4612-1000, San José **Tel:** +506 223 1628 **Fax:** +506 222 9936
Contact: Mr Arnoldo Lopez

LARRAIN Y ASOCIADOS (Chile)
Ave. El Bosque Sur130, Piso 12, Santiago **Tel:** +56 2 203 1241
Fax: +56 2 203 1246/47 **Contact:** Mr Carlos Larrain

CABINET LAURELLI (Gabon)
BP 3927, Libreville **Tel:** +241 7721 42/43 **Fax:** +241 774 077
Contact: M Laurelli

SIR LAURENCE STREET - COMMERCIAL MEDIATOR (Australia)
121 Macquarie Street, Sydney NSW 2000
Tel: +61 2 9258 0801 **Fax:** +61 2 9258 0833

THE LAW ASSOCIATES (Bangladesh)
203 Concord Tower, 2nd Floor, 113 Kazi Nazrul Islam Avenue, Dhaka 1000 **Tel:** +880 2 933 0877/3253 **Fax:** +880 2 933 7746

LAWRENCE GRAHAM (United Kingdom)
190 Strand, London WC2R 1JN **Tel:** +44 20 7379 0000
Fax: +44 20 7379 6854 **Contact:** Mr Bill Richards

CABINET D'AVOCATS LAZAREFF & ASSOCIÉS (France)
24 rue de Prony, 75809 Paris
Tel: +33 1 44 29 32 53 **Fax:** +33 1 44 29 32 60 **Contact:** M Lazareff

LEDINGHAM CHALMERS (United Kingdom)
5 Melville Crescent, Edinburgh EH3 7JA **Tel:** +44 131 200 1000
Fax: +44 131 200 1080 **Contact:** Mr David K Laing

LEE AND LI (Taiwan)
7th Floor Formosa Plastics Building, 201 Tun Hua North Road, PO Box 118-619, Taipei 105 **Tel:** +886 2 2715 3300 **Fax:** +886 2 2713 3966

LEE HISHAMMUDDIN (Malaysia)
16th Floor, Menara Phileo, 189, Jalan Tun Razak, Kuala Lumpur 50400
Tel: +60 3 2161 2330 **Fax:** +60 3 2161 3933
Contact: Mr Thomas ML Lee

LEE & LEE (Singapore)
5 Shenton Way, UIC Building, Singapore 068808
Tel: +65 220 0666 **Fax:** +65 225 0438 **Contact:** Mr Andrew Ang

LEGACOM ANTOV & PARTNERS (Bulgaria)
45-47 Burel Street, Sofia 1408
Tel: +359 2 950 1030 **Fax:** +359 2 950 1070

LEGEXP (Kyrgyz Republic)
Apartments 4, 5, 8, Kievskaya 131, Bishkek **Tel:** +996 312 21 3278
Fax: +996 312 61 04 02 **Contact:** Mr Tony Shea

LEMA (Spain)
Calle Velayos No 4, 2º D, Distrito 28035, Madrid
Tel: +34 91 316 4828 **Fax:** +34 91 373 8686

LEONEL ALVES (Macau)
Avenida da Praia Grande, No 517, 20th Floor, Macau
Tel: +853 378 579 **Fax:** +853 305 197 **Contact:** Mr Leonel Alves

LAW OFFICE OF LEPIK & LUHAÄÄR (Estonia)
Dunkri Street 7, 10123 Tallinn
Tel: +372 6 306 460 **Fax:** +372 6 306 463 **Contact:** Mr Peeter Lepik

LEVINE, BLASZAK, BLOCK & BOOTHBY LLP (USA)
2001 L Street NW, Suite 900, Washington DC 20036 **Tel:** +1 202 857 2550 **Fax:** +1 202223 0833 **Contact:** Ms Colleen Boothby

LEVY & SALOMÃO ADVOGADOS (Brazil)
Av. Brigadeiro Faria Lima, 2.601 11th Floor, 01473-900 São Paulo
Tel: +55 11 3030 0500 **Fax:** +55 11 3812 6232

STUDIO LEGALE LIBONATI JAEGER (Italy)
Via San Damiano 4, 20122 Milan **Tel:** +39 02 762 3271
Fax: +39 02 762 32751 **Contact:** Prof Jaeger Pier Giusto

LIDEIKA, PETRAUSKAS, VALIÛNAS & PARTNERS (Lithuania)
Labdariu 5, LT-2001 Vilnius **Tel:** +370 2 681 888 **Fax:** +370 2 225 591
Contact: Mr Rolandas Valiunas

LIEDEKERKE SIMÉON WESSING HOUTHOFF (Belgium)
3, Bd de l'Empereur, BE-1000 Brussels **Tel:** +32 2 551 16 15
Fax: +32 2 551 16 03 **Contact:** Mr Alexandre Van Dan Casteele

If you can't find a firm here, see full profiles (pages 957-1481)

LIM A PO (Surinam)
No1 Lim A Po Straat, PO Box 92, Paramaribo Surinam
Tel: +597 473514 **Fax:** +597 475394 **Contact:** Mr Ban Halfhide

LIND & CADOVIUS (Denmark)
Ostergade 38, Postboks 2256, DK-1019 Copenhagen K
Tel: +45 33 338100 **Fax:** +45 33 338101

LINDH STABELL HORTEN (Sweden)
Regeringsgatan 38, PO Box 7315, SE-103 90 Stockholm
Tel: +46 8 701 78 00 **Fax:** +46 8 796 82 23
Contact: Ms Annica Woxback

LIVINGSTON, ALEXANDER & LEVY (Jamaica)
72 Harbour Street, PO Box 142, Kingston **Tel:** +1 876 922 6310
Fax: +1 876 922 0713 **Contact:** Mrs Angela Fowler

ESTUDIO LLONA & BUSTAMANTE (Peru)
Edificio "La Positiva", Av. Javier Prado (Este) y Francisco Masias, n°370, 7° Piso, Lima 27 **Tel:** +511 221 2634 **Fax:** +511 442 7697
Contact: Mr Juan Prado Bustamante

LOBO & IBEAS LAWYERS (Brazil)
Avenida Rio Branco 125, 10th/11th/12th Floor, 20040-006 Rio de Janeiro **Tel:** +55 21 509 4818/ 517 6300
Fax: +55 21 221 5070/ 507 0798 **Contact:** Mr Luis Carlos Nunes

LOCKE LIDDELL & SAPP LLP (USA)
2200 Ross Avenue, Suite 2200, Dallas TX 75201-6776 **Tel:** +1 214 740 8000 **Fax:** +1 214 740 8800 **Contact:** Mr R. Bruce La Boon

LOGOS (Iceland)
Borgartun 24, Reykjavik 105 **Tel:** +354 540 0300 **Fax:** +354 540 0301
Contact: Mr Johannes Sigurdsson

LOIS YOUNG BARROW & CO (Belize)
120A New Road, Belize City **Tel:** +501 235 924 **Fax:** +501 231 123
Contact: Miss Lois Young Barrow

LOLOÇI & ASSOCIATES (Albania)
Blv. Zhan D'Ark, Kulla Nr. 2, Ap. 1, Tirana
Tel: +355 4 250 736 **Fax:** +355 4 250 735

LORENTZ & BONE (Namibia)
12th & 13th Floors, Franz Indongo Gardens, 19 Bülow Street, PO Box 85, Windhoek **Tel:** +264 61 273600 **Fax:** +264 61 224529
Contact: Mr Claus Jürgen Hinrichsen

LORENZ SEIDLER GOSSEL (Germany)
Widenmayerstr. 23, 80538 Munich
Tel: +49 89 290 100 **Fax:** +49 89 290 101 00 **Contact:** Hans Gossel

LOUIS W TRIAY & PARTNERS (Gibraltar)
Suite 2C, 2nd Floor, Regal House, Queensway, PO Box 147, Gibraltar
Tel: +350 79423 **Fax:** +350 71405

LOYENS & LOEFF (Netherlands)
PO Box 2888, 3000 CW Rotterdam **Tel:** +31 10 224 6224
Fax: +31 10 412 5839 **Contact:** Mr Bert Westendorp

LUBIS GANIE SUROWIDJOJO (Indonesia)
Menara Imperium, 30th Floor, JL H Rangkayo Rasuna Said, Kav 1, Kuningan, Jakarta 12980
Tel: +62 21 831 5005 **Fax:** +62 21 831 5015 **Contact:** Dr Idwan Ganie

LUCKHOO & LUCKHOO (Guyana)
Whitehall, 1 Croal Street, PO Box 10294, Georgetown
Tel: +592 259 232 **Fax:** +592 256 301 **Contact:** Mr Edward Luckhoo

LUCY WAYNE & ASSOCIATES (Vietnam)
8th Floor, Central Plaza Office Building, 17 Le Duan Boulevard, District 1, Ho Chi Minh City **Tel:** +84 8 8244 395 **Fax:** +84 8 8 244 396
Contact: Ms Lucy Wayne

ESTUDIO LUIS ECHECOPAR GARCIA (Peru)
Av. De la Floresta 497, 5th Floor, San Borja, Lima
Tel: +511 372 7373 **Fax:** +511 372 7374

LUTHRA & LUTHRA LAW OFFICES (India)
103 Ashoka Estate, 24 Brakhamba Road, New Delhi 110001
Tel: +91 11 335 0633 **Fax:** +91 11 372 3909
Contact: Mr Rajiv K. Luthra

LWA CONSULTANTS LIMITED (Myanmar)
The Strand, 92 Strand Road, Kyauktada Township, Yangon
Tel: +95 1 254 816 / 54817 **Fax:** +95 1 254 818
Contact: Mr Alec Christie

LYNCH, IDESH & MAHONEY (Mongolia)
International Trade Centre, Suite 500, Baga Toiruu 37B, Central PO Box 348, Ulaanbaatar 13 **Tel:** +976 11 325344 **Fax:** +976 1 325358
Contact: Mr Maurice M Lynch

MAAJAR, RWECHUNGURA, KAMEJA & NGULUMA (Tanzania)
3rd Floor, 50 Mirambo Street, PO Box 7495, Dar Es Salaam
Tel: +255 22 211 4291/899/213 7191 **Fax:** +255 22 211 2830/211 9474
Contact: Mrs Mwanaidi Sinare Maajar

MACHADO, MEYER, SENDACZ E OPICE (Brazil)
Rua da Consolacao 247, 4th, 5th, 6th and 8th Floors, SP 01301-903 São Paulo **Tel:** +55 11 3150 7000 **Fax:** +55 11 3150 7071
Contact: Mr Pedro Helfenstein Prado Filho

MADAGASCAR CONSEIL INTERNATIONAL (Madagascar)
Route des Hydrocarbures, Village des Jeux de la Francophonie, Bât G5 Ankorondrano, Antananarivo
Tel: +261 2 0222 9525 **Fax:** +261 2 0226 1907
Contact: Mr Raphaël Jakoba

MAGALHÃES, FERRAZ, PRADO, LINO E BRUNA (Brazil)
Rua Armando Penteado, 304 Pacaembu, SP01242-010 São Paulo
Tel: +55 11 3826 4411 **Fax:** +55 11 3825 8695
Contact: Mr Carlos Francisco de Magalhãesa

CHAMBERS OF SIR HAMID MOOLLAN (Mauritius)
PCL Building, 6th Floor, 43 Sir William Newton Street, Port Louis
Tel: +230 212 6913 **Fax:** +230 208 8351 **Contact:** Sir Hamid Moollan

MAITLAND & CO (United Kingdom)
5th Floor, 44-48 Dover Street, London W1S 4NX
Tel: +44 20 7344 7500 **Fax:** +44 20 7344 7555 **Contact:** Mr Eric Pfaff

MAÎTRE EMMANUEL EKOBO - SOLE PRACTITIONER (Cameroon)
PO Box 241, Douala
Tel: +237 422 053 **Fax:** +237 422 053 **Contact:** Mr Pierre Ebosse

MAKARIM & TAIRA S (Indonesia)
Summitmas 1, 17th Floor, JL Jenderal Sudirman Kav 61-62, Jakarta 12069 **Tel:** +62 21 252 1272 / 520 0001 **Fax:** +62 21 252 2750 / 2751
Contact: Mrs Galinar Adiwoso

MAME ADAMA GUEYE & ASSOCIÉS (Senegal)
107-109 Rues Moussé Diop x Amadou Assane Ndoye, BP 11443 Dakar
Tel: +221 849 28 00 **Fax:** +221 822 3972
Contact: Mr Mame Adama Gueye

MAMO TCV - ADVOCATES (Malta)
52 Old Theatre Street, Valletta VLT 08
Tel: +356 232 271 **Fax:** +356 244 291 **Contact:** Dr David Tonna

MANDVIWALLA & ZAFAR (Pakistan)
Mandviwalla Chambers, Old Queens Road, Karachi
Tel: +92 21 241 4746 **Fax:** +92 21 241 4815
Contact: Mehmood Mandviwalla

MAPONYA INCORPORATED (South Africa)
Sanlam Centre Middestad, 2nd Floor, 252 Andries Street, Pretoria 0002
PO Box 13659, The Tramshed, 0126
Tel: +27 12 3322 4221 **Fax:** +27 12 3322 4231

CABINET MARCAULT-DEROUARD (French Guiana)
26 Avenue de la Liberté, Cayenne 97300
Tel: +594 255 100 **Fax:** +59 431 4071
Contact: Maître Marcault-Derouard

CABINET MARIE-ANDRÉE NGWE (Cameroon)
517, Rue Clemenceau (Bonanjo) BP 4870 Douala, Douala BP 4870
Tel: +237 425 362 **Fax:** +237 432 153
Contact: Ms Marie-Andrée Ngwe

MARIZ DE OLIVEIRA, SIQUEIRA CAMPOS E BIANCO ADVOGADOS SC (Brazil)
Avenida Ipiranga n. 324, Bloco C, 9º andar, 01046-922 São Paulo
Tel: +55 11 257 7600 **Fax:** +55 11 256 2008
Contact: Mr Ricardo Mariz de Oliveira

MARKOVIC & PLISO (Croatia)
Smeceklasova 21, 10000 Zagreb
Tel: +385 1 455 3221 **Fax:** +385 1 455 3710 **Contact:** Mr Markovic

ETUDE MAROUFA DIABIRA (Mauritania)
BP 522, Nouakchott **Tel:** +222 251 502 / 222 252 894
Fax: +222 251 502 / 222 252 894 **Contact:** Mr Maroufa Diabira

MARRACHE & CO (Gibraltar)
5 Cannon Lane, PO Box 85, Gibraltar **Tel:** +350 79918
Fax: +350 73315 **Contact:** Mr Isaac S. Marrache

MARTELLI ABOGADOS (Argentina)
San Martin 323, Piso 13, C1004AAG Buenos Aires **Tel:** +54 11 4328 7337 **Fax:** +54 11 4328 7557 **Contact:** Mr Hugo Martelli

MARTINET & MARTINET (Djibouti)
Le Heron, B.P. 169, Djibouti **Tel:** +253 35 28 79 **Fax:** +253 35 25 43

MARTINEZ, ALGABA, ESTRELLA, DE HARO Y GALVAN DUQUE (Mexico)
Edificio Bosques Corporativo, 400 Paseo de los Tamarindos Floor 20, Cologna Bosques de las Lomas, 05120 Mexico City **Tel:** +525 258 0202 **Fax:** +525 25 80 188 **Contact:** Mr Agustin Barranco

MARTINEZ LAGE & ASOCIADOS (Spain)
Serrano 25, 2º, izda., 28001 Madrid **Tel:** +34 91 426 4470
Fax: +34 91 577 3774 **Contact:** Mr Santiago Martinez Lage

MARXER & PARTNERS (Liechtenstein)
Heiligkreuz 6, PO Box 484, 9490 Vaduz
Tel: +423 235 8181 **Fax:** +423 235 8282 **Contact:** Mr Peter Marxer

MASSIAS & PARTNERS (Gibraltar)
117 Main Street, PO Box 213, Gibraltar
Tel: +350 40888 **Fax:** +350 40999 **Contact:** Mr Isaac C Massias

MATSUO & KOSUGI (Japan)
7-14-16 Ginza-Taiyo Ginza Building, 7 chome-, 2 Chuo-ku, Tokyo 104-0061 **Tel:** +81 3 3542 9141 **Fax:** +81 3 3542 9699
Contact: Mr Takeo Kosugi

MATTOS FILHO, VEIGA FILHO, MARREY JR, MOHERDAUI E QUIROGA (Brazil)
Avenida Paulista 1499, 20 andar, 01311-928 SP São Paulo
Tel: +55 11 3170 7600 **Fax:** +55 11 3147 7770
Contact: Mr Celidonio Neto

If you can't find a firm here, see full profiles (pages 957-1481)

MAUNG MAUNG GYI (Myanmar)
39A Golden Valley, Bahab Township, Yangon **Tel:** +95 1 533 720
Fax: +95 1 525 940 **Contact:** Mr Maung Maung Gyi

MAYARD-PAUL LAW FIRM (Haiti)
Rue Pavae, Port-au-Prince BP 1745 **Tel:** +509 222 2343/2238288
Fax: +509 223 8288 **Contact:** M Gregory Mayard-Paul

MCKEE NELSON ERNST & YOUNG (USA)
1150 18 Street NW, Suite 500, Washington DC DC 20036
Tel: +1 202 775 1880 **Fax:** +1 202 775 8586 **Contact:** Mr Will Nelson

MCKINNEY, BANCROFT & HUGHES (Bahamas)
4 George Street, Mareva House, PO Box N-3937, Nassau
Tel: +1 242 322 4195/96/98 **Fax:** +1 242 328 2520
Contact: Mr Brian M Moree

MCMILLAN BINCH (Canada)
Suite 3800, South Tower, Royal Bank Plaza, Toronto ON M5J 2J7 **Tel:** +1 416 865 7000 **Fax:** +1 416 865 7048 **Contact:** Mr Graham Scott

MCNEIVE SOLICITORS (United Kingdom)
26 Cowper Street, London EC2A 4AP **Tel:** +44 20 7253 0535
Fax: +44 20 7253 0537 **Contact:** Mr Liam McNeive

MEHMET GÜN & CO (Turkey)
Zincirlikuyu Koresehitleri Cad, No: 30, Kat 4, Daire: 13, 80300 Istanbul
Tel: +90 212 275 90 03 **Fax:** +90 212 272 50 78
Contact: Mr Mehmet Gün

MEISSNER, BOLTE & PARTNER (Germany)
Hollerallee 73, D-28209 Bremen
Tel: +49 421 34 87 40 **Fax:** +49 421 34 22 96 **Contact:** Eugen Popp

MEITAR, LIQUORNIK, GEVA & CO (Israel)
16 Abba Hillel Silver St., 12th floor, Ramat Gan
Tel: +972 3 610 3100 **Fax:** +972 3 610 3111

ESTUDIO MERSAN (Paraguay)
F.R. Moreno 509, PO Box 693, Asuncion **Tel:** +595 2144 7739
Fax: +595 2149 6039 **Contact:** Dr Hugo Mersan

MESNY ET ASSOCIÉS (France)
50 Boulevard de Courcelles, 75017 Paris
Tel: +33 1 4380 7194 **Fax:** +33 1 4380 0815

LAW OFFICES OF M FADULLAH CERRAHOGLU (Turkey)
Gullu Sok. No. 1,3. Levent, Istanbul **Tel:** +90 212 270 7014
Fax: +90 212 269 8910 **Contact:** M. Fadullah Cerrahoglu

M FETHI PEKIN & SEFIKA PEKIN LAW FIRM (Turkey)
Meydan Sok., N 28, Beybi Giz Plaza 14th Floor - Maslak, 80670 Istanbul
Tel: +90 212 290 2363 **Fax:** +90 212 290 2377/8
Contact: Ms Sefika Pekin

MGA (MONTEIRO, GRAÇA & ASSOCIADOS) (Mozambique)
Avenue 25. Septembre 1230, 4th Floor, Block 5, Maputo
Tel: +258 1 302 336 **Fax:** +258 1 302 341

M HAMEL-SMITH & CO (Trinidad & Tobago)
19 St. Vincent Street, Port of Spain **Tel:** +1 868 623 4237
Fax: +1 868 627 8564 **Contact:** Mr Philip Hamel-Smith

ETUDE MHAYIMANA ISAÏE (Rwanda)
BP 731 Kigali, Rwanda, Kigali **Tel:** +250 72564/+250 083 00698
Fax: +250 823 82 **Contact:** Maître Mhayimana Isaïe

MIDDLETONS MOORE & BEVINS (Australia)
Level 6, 7 Macquarie Place, Sydney New South Wales 2000 **Tel:** +61 2 9390 8100 **Fax:** +61 2 9247 2866 **Contact:** Mr Theo Casimatis

MIGUEL GALVÃO TELES, JOÃO SOARES DA SILVA & ASSOCIADOS (Portugal)
Rua Castilho, 75-6.E., 1250-068 Lisbon **Tel:** +351 2 1382 6600
Fax: +3512 1382 6628 **Contact:** Mr Miguel Galvão Teles

MIJARES, ANGOITIA, CORTÉS Y FUENTES, S.C. (Mexico)
Montes Urales No. 505 - Piso 3, Col. Lomas de Chapultepec, 11000 Mexico, D.F. **Tel:** +525 201 7400 **Fax:** +525 520 1065/75
Contact: Mr Juan G. Mijares

ESTUDIO MILLÉ (Argentina)
Mitre 226, Piso 5, C1036 AAD Buenos Aires **Tel:** +54 11 4331 8191
Fax: +54 11 4334 0203 **Contact:** Mr Antonio Mill Snr

MILLER BAYLIS & O'NEILL (USA)
1140 Nineteenth Street NW, Suite 700, Washington DC DC 20036
Tel: +1 202 296 2960 **Fax:** +1 202 296 0166 **Contact:** Mr John Gregg

MILLER & CHEVALIER (USA)
655 Fifteenth Street NW, Suite 900, Washington DC 20005-5701
Tel: +1 202 626 5800 **Fax:** +1 202 628 0858

MILLIN & CURRIE INCORPORATING RD FRIEDLANDER & CO (Swaziland)
Development House, 1st Floor,, PO Box A240, Swazi Plaza, Mbabane H101 **Tel:** +268 404 2936 **Fax:** +268 404 0357
Contact: Mr David Millin

MINCHIN & KELLY (Botswana)
Plot 688 Khwai Road, PO Box 1339, Gabarone
Tel: +267 312 734 **Fax:** +267 308 500 **Contact:** Mr Dave Williams

ETUDE MINE OULD ABDOULLAH (Mauritania)
Immeuble BMCI 2eme etage, Avenue Gemal Abdel Nasser BP 3807, Nouakchott **Tel:** +222 255 954 **Fax:** +222 255 955
Contact: Maître Djindo

If you can't find a firm here, see full profiles (pages 957-1481)

MINTZ LEVIN COHN FERRIS GLOVSKY AND POPEO PC (USA)
One Financial Center, Boston MA 02111 **Tel:** +1 617 542 6000
Fax: +1 617 542 2241 **Contact:** Mr Irwin M Heller

MIRANDA GUTIERREZ & GUEVARA SERVICIOS LEGALES (Bolivia)
Servicios Legales SC, Calle Socabaya No 240, Edificio Hawdal, La Paz Oficina 1103 **Tel:** +591 231 6868 **Fax:** +591 239 1205
Contact: Mr Ramiro Guevara Rodriguez

LAW OFFICES OF MISHARE M AL-GHAZALI & PARTNERS (Kuwait)
1st Floor, Chamber of Commerce Building, Al-shuhada Street, PO Box 26161, Safat 13122 **Tel:** +965 243 9690/1 **Fax:** +965 242 2895
Contact: Mr Mishare M Al-Ghazali

MITSUI YASUDA WANI & MAEDA (Japan)
Akasaka 2.14 Plaza Building, 14-32, Akasaka 2-chome, Minato-ku, Tokyo 107-0052 **Tel:** +81 3 3224 0020 **Fax:** +81 3 3224 0030
Contact: Mr Akihiro Wani

M & M BOMCHIL (Argentina)
Suipacha 268, 12th Floor, 5411 Buenos Aires **Tel:** +54 11 4321 7500
Fax: +54 11 4321 7555 **Contact:** Mr Maximo Montil

MOGHAIZEL LAW OFFICES (Lebanon)
145 Gebran Tuéni Square, PO Box 16-6742, Ashrafieh, Beirut 1100 2150 **Tel:** +961 1333 753 **Fax:** +961 1201 354
Contact: Mr Fadi Moghaizel

MOHAMMED ZAHIR - SOLE PRACTITIONER (Bangladesh)
50, Dahanmandi Residential Area, Road 11A, Dhaka, Dhaka
Tel: +880 2 911 4850 **Fax:** +880 2 811 3183
Contact: Dr Mohammed Zahir

MOHSIN TAYEBALY & CO (Pakistan)
2nd Floor Dime Centre, BC-4 Block 9 KDA Scheme 5, Clifton, Karachi
Tel: +92 21 587 2690/586 6354 **Fax:** +92 21 587 0240
Contact: Mr Irfan Mohsin Tayebaly

MOREAU-BERNARD-AMIGUES ET DARMON (France)
3 Rue de la Boetié, 75008 Paris
Tel: +33 1 42 66 10 11 **Fax:** +33 1 42 66 33 33

MORENO RUFFINELLI & ASOCIADOS (Paraguay)
Avenida Perú 1044, PO Box 2437, Asunción
Tel: +595 21 214 688 **Fax:** +595 21 215 134

ADVOKATFIRMAN MORSSING & NYCANDER (Sweden)
Sveavägen 31, PO Box 3299, SE-103 66 Stockholm
Tel: +46 8 587 05100 **Fax:** +46 8 587 05120 **Contact:** Mr Lars Boman

MOSSACK FONSECA & CO (Panama)
Arango-Orillac Building, 54 Avenue Marbella, 1 Floor, PO Box 8320, Panama City 7 **Tel:** +507 263 8899 **Fax:** +507 263 9218

MOTTA FERNANDES ROCHA ADVOGADOS (Brazil)
Av. Almirante Barroso n° 52, 5° andar, 20031-000 Rio de Janeiro
Tel: +55 21 533 2200 **Fax:** +55 212 622 459
Contact: Mr Luiz Leonardo Cantidiano

LAW OFFICES OF DR MOUSTAFA AL-SAYED (Syria)
23 Bahsa Street, PO Box 11317, Damascus **Tel:** +963 11 231 9177
Fax: +963 11 231 1251 **Contact:** Dr Moiustafa Al-Sayed

M & P BERNITSAS LAW OFFICES (Greece)
5 Lykavittou Street, GR-10672 Athens **Tel:** +30 1 361 5395
Fax: +30 1 364 0805 **Contact:** Mr Panayotis M Bernitsas

MTL LAW OFFICE (Libya)
Mohamed Mashi Street, PO Box 82680, Tripoli **Tel:** +218 21 4440571 / 3331079 **Fax:** +218 21 4443554 **Contact:** Mr Salah Marghani

LAW OFFICE OF DR MUJAHID M AL-SAWWAF (Saudi Arabia)
PO Box 5840, Jeddah 21432 **Tel:** +966 2 669 0751
Fax: +966 2 665 5052 **Contact:** Dr Mujahid Sawwaf

BUFETE MULLERAT (Spain)
Av. Diagonal 640, 4th, 08017 Barcelona
Tel: +34 93 405 93 00 **Fax:** +34 93 405 91 76 **Contact:** Mr Carles Prat

MUNGUIA VIDAURRE CHAVEZ (Nicaragua)
2do Piso, Edificio Malaga, Plaza España, PO Box 3960, Managua
Tel: +505 266 7102 **Fax:** +505 266 4156
Contact: Dr Juan Alvaro Munguia

MUÑOZ DE TORO & MUÑOZ DE TORO (Argentina)
Alicia Moreau de Justo 740, Loft 212, C1107 AAP Puerto Madero Buenos Aires **Tel:** +54 11 43 43 34 88 **Fax:** +54 11 43 43 86 63

MUÑOZ TAMAYO & ASOCIADOS (Colombia)
Carrera 11A No 94A-23, Oficina 209, Bogota Columbia
Tel: +57 1 621 2855 **Fax:** +57 1 621 3058
Contact: Mr Diego Muñoz Tamayo

MUSA DUDHIA & CO (Zambia)
Permanent House, Cairo Road, PO Box 31198, Lusaka 10101
Tel: +260 1 228 426 or 30 **Fax:** +260 1 227 188

If you can't find a firm here, see full profiles (pages 957-1481)

MUSSA & VALDERAMOS (Belize)
91 North Front Street, PO Box 571, Belize City
Tel: +501 232 940 **Fax:** +501 231 149 **Contact:** Mr Edwin Flowers

MUSTAPHA HAMDANE (Algeria)
3 Place Port Saïd, Algiers 16000 **Tel:** +213 21 714803
Fax: +213 21 713325 **Contact:** Mr Mustapha Hamdane

M VEGA PENICHET (Spain)
C/. Alcalá 115, 28009 Madrid
Tel: +34 91 431 5500 **Fax:** +34 91 431 5938 / 576 0434

MYANMAR LEGAL SERVICES LIMITED (Myanmar)
International Business Center, Suite 106, 88 Pyay Road 6.5 Miles, Hlaing Township, Yangon **Tel:** +95 1 650 740 **Fax:** +95 1 650 466
Contact: Miss Khin Chokyi

MYA THEIN & ASSOCIATES (Myanmar)
52 Mahabandoola Garden Street, Kyauktada Township, Yangon
Tel: +95 1 245 968 **Fax:** +95 1 285 882

MYERS, FLETCHER & GORDON (Jamaica)
Park Place, 21 East Street, Kingston
Tel: +1 876 922 5860 **Fax:** +1 876 922 4811 **Contact:** Mr Barry Curtis

NABARRO NATHANSON (United Kingdom)
Lacon House, 84 Theobald's Road, London WC1X 8RW **Tel:** +44 20 7524 6000 **Fax:** +44 20 7524 6524 **Contact:** Ms Nicole Paradise

NABIL ABDEL-MALEK LAW OFFICES (Lebanon)
Pasteur St, Pasteur 40 Bldg, 8th Floor, Medawar, Achrafieh, Beirut
Tel: +961 1564 105 **Fax:** +961 1564 104
Contact: Mr Nabil Abdel-Malek

NABULSI & ASSOCIATES (Jordan)
Riyadh Center, 3rd Circle, PO Box 35116, Amman 11181 **Tel:** +962 6465 4411 **Fax:** +962 6465 7555 **Contact:** Mr Omar N Nabulsi

NAGASHIMA, OHNO & TSUNEMATSU (Japan)
Kioicho Building, 3-12 Kioicho, Chiyoda-ku, Tokyo 102-0094 **Tel:** +81 3 3288 7000 **Fax:** +81 3 5213 7800 **Contact:** Mr Hisashi Hara

NAGY ÉS TRÓCSÁNYI (Hungary)
H-1126, Ugocsa u. 4/B, 1012 Budapest **Tel:** +36 1 487 8700
Fax: +36 1 487 8701 **Contact:** Dr Ildikó Varga

NAHLAWI LAW OFFICE (Syria)
Sabbagh Building, 55 Port Said Street, PO Box 2491, Damascus **Tel:** +963 11 221 0027 **Fax:** +963 11 221 2952 **Contact:** Mr Mizar Nahlawi

NASCHITZ, BRANDES & CO (Israel)
5 Tuval Street, Tel Aviv 67897 **Tel:** +972 3 623 5000
Fax: +972 3 623 5005 **Contact:** Mr Peter Gad Naschitz

NEAL GERBER & EISENBERG (USA)
Two North La Salle Street, Suite 2200, Chicago IL 60602
Tel: +1 312 269 8000 **Fax:** +1 312 269 1747
Contact: Mr Jerry H Biederman

NEGRI TEIJEIRO & INCERA (Argentina)
Av. Corrientes 316, Piso 4, C1043AAQ Buenos Aires
Tel: +54 11 4328 8008 / 1273 / 6746 **Fax:** +54 11 4328 5628 / 0664
Contact: Mr Juan Javier Negri

NELLIGAN O'BRIEN PAYNE (Canada)
Suite 1900, 66 Slater Street, Ottawa ON K1P 5H1
Tel: +1 613 238 8080 **Fax:** +1 613 238 2098

NETO VALENTE (Macau)
Avenida da Torre Mario Soales, 2nd Floor,, Apartment 25, Macau
Tel: +853 382 222 **Fax:** +853 712 633

N'GOAN ASMAN & ASSOCIÉS (Cote D'Ivoire)
37 rue de la canebière, Cocody 01 BP 3361, Abidjan
Tel: +225 22 404700/22 404701 **Fax:** +225 22 404719
Contact: Mr Georges N'Goan

LAW OFFICES N GOYIOS - A NASSIKAS (Greece)
8th Floor, Livanos Building, Akti Miaouli 47/49, GRY 18536 Piraeus
Tel: +30 1 429 2904 **Fax:** +30 1 429 3129 **Contact:** Mr N.C. Goyios

CABINET NICOLAS TIANGAYE (Central African Republic)
BP 2094, Bangui **Tel:** +236 612 571 **Fax:** +236 612 210
Contact: M Nicolas Tiangaye

NICHOLSON GRAHAM & JONES (United Kingdom)
110 Cannon Street, London EC4N 6AR **Tel:** +44 20 7648 9000
Fax: +44 20 7648 9001 **Contact:** Mr Michael Johns

NIELSEN & NØRAGER (Denmark)
Metropol House, 16 Frederiksberggade, DK-1459 Copenhagen K
Tel: +45 33 11 4545 **Fax:** +45 33 11 80 81

NILS SETTERWALLS ADVOKATBYRÅ AB (Sweden)
Arsenalsgatan 6, S-111 47 Stockholm **Tel:** +46 8 598 890 00
Fax: +46 8 598 890 90 **Contact:** Ms Owe Hjelmqvist

NISHIMURA & PARTNERS (Japan)
29th Floor, ARK Mori Building, 12-32 Akasaka 1-chome, Minato-ku, Tokyo 107-6029 **Tel:** +81 3 5562 8500 **Fax:** +81 3 5561 9711
Contact: Mr Akira Kosugi

NISHITH DESAI ASSOCIATES (India)
93-B Mittal Court, Nariman Point, Mumbai 400 021
Tel: +91 22 282 0609/204 0068 **Fax:** +91 22 287 5792
Contact: Mr Nishith Desai

NÖRR STIEFENHOFER LUTZ (Germany)
Brienner Strasse 28, 80333 Munich
Tel: +49 89 28 6280 **Fax:** +49 89 28 01 10 **Contact:** Dr Rudolf Nörr

NOURSE & BOWLES LLP (USA)
One Exchange Plaza at 55 Broadway, New York NY 10006
Tel: +1 212 952 6200 **Fax:** +1 212 952 0345
Contact: Mr John P Vayda

NUNA ADVOKATER I/S (Greenland)
Fjeldvej 16, PO Box 59, Nuuk DK-3900
Tel: +299 321 370 **Fax:** +299 324 117 **Contact:** Mr Peter Schiuer

NUNES, SCHOLEFIELD, DELEON & CO (Jamaica)
6a Holborn Road, Kingston 10 **Tel:** +1 876 960 8995
Fax: +1 876 968 9692 **Contact:** Mr Anthony Jenkinson

O'DONNELL SWEENEY (Ireland)
Earlsfort centre , Earlsfort Terrace, Dublin 2 **Tel:** +353 1 662 5222
Fax: +353 1 6644300 **Contact:** Mr David Obiarne

ODVETNISKA, DRUZBA, COLJA, ROJS & PARTNERS (Slovenia)
Prazakova 8, Ljubljana 1000 **Tel:** +386 1 4315207/4316297
Fax: +386 1 4325123 **Contact:** Mr Marjan Colja

ESTUDIO O'FARRELL (Argentina)
Avenida de Mayo 645, Piso 1, 1084 Buenos Aires
Tel: +54 11 4346 1000 **Fax:** +54 11 4331 1659
Contact: Mr Ariel F O'Farrell

OKRUASHVILI & PARTNERS LP (Georgia)
3 Lesia Ukrainka St. 4, Tbilisi 380008
Tel: +995 32 921537/921506 **Fax:** +995 32 921496

OLIVERA & DELPIAZZO (Uruguay)
Misiones 1424, Piso 2, Montevideo 11000 **Tel:** +598 2 916 5859
Fax: +598 2 916 5863 **Contact:** Mr Ricardo Olivera Garcia

OLSWANG (United Kingdom)
90 Long Acre, London WC2E 9TT **Tel:** +44 20 7208 8888
Fax: +44 20 7208 8800 **Contact:** Mr Kevin Munslow

O'NEAL WEBSTER O'NEAL MYERS FLETCHER & GORDON (British Virgin Islands)
Simmonds Building, 30 DeCastro Street, P.O. Box 961, Road Town, Tortola **Tel:** +1 284 494 5808/5908 **Fax:** +1 284 494 5811/7843
Contact: Miss Barbara O'Neal

ORR, DIGNAM & CO (Pakistan)
Building 1-B, State Life Square, I.I. Chundrigar Road, Karachi 74000
Tel: +92 21 2413422/6003 **Fax:** +92 21 2416571
Contact: Mr Mahomed J. Jaffer

ORTNER PÖCH FORAMITTI (Austria)
Strauchgasse 1-3, A-1010 Vienna **Tel:** +43 1 535 3721
Fax: +43 1 533 1555 **Contact:** Dr Louis Foramitti and Dr Peter Pöch

OSTERLING ARIAS-SCHREIBER VEGA ORBEGOSO & ASOCIADOS (Peru)
Avenida Pardo y Aliaga 640, Piso 8, San Isidro, Lima 27
Tel: +51 1 442 0770 **Fax:** +51 1 442 0770 **Contact:** Mr Jorge Vega

BUFETE OTERO LASTRES (Spain)
Avenida de Alberto Alcozen, 8-2ºA, Madrid **Tel:** +34 91 458 2356
Fax: +34 91 458 2865 **Contact:** Mr J.M. Otero Lastres

OYHANARTE & FARGOSI (Argentina)
Av. Alvear 1580, 1st Floor, 1014 Capital Federal Buenos Aires **Tel:** +54 11 4815 7650 **Fax:** +54 11 4815 1084 **Contact:** Miss Eugerina Vareas

OZANNES (Guernsey)
PO Box 186, 1 Le Marchant Street, St Peter Port GY1 4HP **Tel:** +44 1481 723466 **Fax:** +44 1481 714653 **Contact:** Mr Peter Harwood

PACHECO COTO (Costa Rica)
PO Box 6610, 517 Eleventh Avenue, San José 1000 **Tel:** +506 258 1619
Fax: +506 255 2783 **Contact:** Mr Humberto Pacheco A

PAISNER & CO (United Kingdom)
Bouverie House, 154 Fleet Street, London EC4A 2JD **Tel:** +44 20 7353 0299 **Fax:** +44 20 7583 8621 **Contact:** Mr Stephen Rosefield

PAKSOY & CO (Turkey)
Attorneys at Law, Beybi Giz Plaza, Meydan Sk. No.28 Kat 10 Maslak, 80670 Istanbul **Tel:** +90 212 290 2350 **Fax:** +90 212 290 2355

PARDIWALLA TWOMEY LABLACHE (Seychelles)
Premier Building, Rm 109, Victoria Mahe
Tel: +248 321 071 **Fax:** +248 324 100 **Contact:** Mr Pesi Pardiwalla

PARRA RODRIGUEZ & CAVELIER (Colombia)
Edificio Profinanzas, Carrera 9 No. 74-08 Of. 504, Bogota D.C.
Tel: +57 1 376 4200 **Fax:** +57 1 376 1707
Contact: Mr Ernesto Cavelier-Franco

PASQUET & GOUSSE ET ASSOCIÉS (Haiti)
5 Avenue Marie Jeanne, Port-au-Prince **Tel:** +503 2 22 56 21
Fax: +509 222 6090 **Contact:** M Gerds Pasquet

PATHAK & ASSOCIATES (India)
13th Floor, Dr. Gopal Das Bhavan, 28 Barakhamba Road, New Delhi 110-001 **Tel:** +91 11 373 8793 **Fax:** +91 11 335 3761

PATTON, MORENO & ASVAT (Panama)
Samuel Lewis Av. Hong Kong Bank Building, 6th Floor , El Dorado, PO Box 6-4298, Panama **Tel:** +507 264 8044 **Fax:** +507 263 7887
Contact: Mr Brett R Patton

If you can't find a firm here, see full profiles (pages 957-1481)

PAUL RATNAYEKE ASSOCIATES (Sri Lanka)
59 Gregorys Road, Colombo 7 **Tel:** +94 1 697 893/697 894
Fax: +94 1 688 410 **Contact:** Mr JHP Ratnayeke

PAUL, WEISS, RIFKIND, WHARTON & GARRISON (USA)
1285 Avenue of the Americas, New York NY 10019-6064
Tel: +1 212 373 3000 **Fax:** +1 212 757 3990
Contact: Mr Neale M. Albert

PEKIN & PEKIN (Turkey)
Lamartine Caddesi 10, Taksim 80090, Istanbul **Tel:** +90 212 253 3710
Fax: +90 212 250 3147 **Contact:** Mr Ahmed Pekin

PELLERANO & HERRERA (Dominican Republic)
Ave. John F. Kennedy #10, EPA A-303, PO Box 52-4121, Miami, Fla 33152, Santo Domingo **Tel:** +1 809 541 5200 **Fax:** +1 809 567 0773

PENGIRAN IZAD & LEE (Brunei Darussalam)
6th Floor, Bangunan Hj Ahmad Laksamana Othman, 38-39 Jalan Sultan, Bandar Seri Begawan BS8811 **Tel:** +673 2 232 945
Fax: +673 2 232 949 **Contact:** Dr Ronnie Lee

PENNIE & EDMONDS LLP (USA)
1155 Avenue of the Americas, New York NY 10036-2711
Tel: +1 212 790 9090 **Fax:** +1 212 869 8864
Contact: Mr Stephen J. Harbulak

PEREZ BUSTAMANTE & PONCE (Ecuador)
Avenida Patria No. 640, 8vo. Piso, PO Box 17-01-3188, Quito
Tel: +593 2 561 710 **Fax:** +593 2 561 798 **Contact:** Mr Edgar Espinoza

PÉREZ DEL CASTILLO-NAVARRO-INCIARTE-GARI (Uruguay)
Juncal 1355, Piso 10, Montevideo 11000 **Tel:** +598 2 915 0742/43/47
Fax: +598 2 915 0762 **Contact:** Mr Santiago Pérez del Castillo

PEREZ LUNA ALVINS PAOLI & ASOCIADOS (Venezuela)
Torre La Primera, Piso 5, Officina 5-D, Avenida Francisco de Miranda, Campo Alegre, Caracas 1060 **Tel:** +582 953 0857 **Fax:** +582 953 3077
Contact: Mr Jose Domingo Paoli Carias

PERKINS & COIE LLP (USA)
1201 Third Avenue, Seattle WA 98101-3099
Tel: +1 206 583 8888 **Fax:** +1 206 583 8500

PERONI, SOSA, TELLECHEA, BURT & NARVAJA (Paraguay)
J.Eulogio Estigarribia No 4846 esq Monseñor Bogarin, Villa Morra, Casilla de Correo 114, Asuncion
Tel: +595 21 663 536 **Fax:** +595 21 600 448
Contact: Mr Guillermo F Peroni

PHILIPPE BOULLÉ - SOLE PRACTITIONER (Seychelles)
314 Victoria House, PO Box 673, Victoria
Tel: +248 225 633 **Fax:** +248 225 626

PHILIPPI, YRARRAZAVAL, PULIDO & BRUNNER (Chile)
Moneda 970, Piso 12, Santiago CP 6500710
Tel: +56 2 364 3700 **Fax:** +56 2 364 3796/97/98

PHILLIPS FOX (Australia)
255 Elizabeth Street, Sydney NSW 2000 **Tel:** +61 2 9286 8000
Fax: +61 2 9283 4144 **Contact:** Mr Tony Crawford

PICAZO BUYCO TAN FIDER & SANTOS (Philippines)
8th Floor, Singapore Airlines Building, 138 H.V. de la Costa Street, Salcedo Village, Makati City **Tel:** +63 2 810 4766 **Fax:** +63 2 810 4768

PIEPENBROCK & SCHUSTER (Germany)
Achenbachstr 73, 40237 Düsseldorf **Tel:** +49 211 6878 880
Fax: +49 211 6878 8868 **Contact:** Hermann-Josef Piepenbrock

PIERRE MAYER - SOLE PRACTITIONER (France)
14 Rue d'Alger, 75001 Paris **Tel:** +33 1 4020 9622
Fax: +33 1 4260 6048 **Contact:** M Pierre Mayer

PIERRE TERCIER - SOLE PRACTITIONER (Switzerland)
5 Chenin Ritter, CH 2700 Fribourg **Tel:** +41 26 425 4848
Fax: +41 26 425 4849 **Contact:** Prof Pierre Tercier

PILLSBURY WINTHROP (USA)
One Battery Park Plaza, New York NY 10004-1490
Tel: +1 212 858 1000 **Fax:** +1 212 858 1500
Contact: Mr John F. Pritchard

PINSENT CURTIS (United Kingdom)
Dashwood House, 69 Old Broad St, London EC2M 1NR
Tel: +44 20 7418 7000 **Fax:** +44 20 7418 7050
Contact: Ms Clare Turnbull

PINTÓ RUIZ & DEL VALLE (Spain)
Velázquez, 146, 28002 Madrid **Tel:** +34 91 563 86 78
Fax: +34 91 563 32 29 **Contact:** Mr José Juan Pintó Ruiz

PIONEER LAW (Nepal)
Anamnagar, PO Box 4865, Kathmandu **Tel:** +977 1 221 340 / 261 000
Fax: +977 1 226 770 **Contact:** Mr Bharat Raj Upreti

PIQUET CARNEIRO & ASSOCIADOS (Brazil)
SCS Q1 Bl.k, Edificio Denasa 12 Andar, DF 70398-900 Brasilia
Tel: +55 61 2232 402/236 349 **Fax:** +55 612 240 906
Contact: Mr Joao Geraldo Piquet Carneiro

If you can't find a firm here, see full profiles (pages 957-1481)

POLLONAIS, BLANC, DE LA BASTIDE & JACELON (Trinidad & Tobago)
17-19 Pembroke Street, PO Box 350, Port of Spain
Tel: +1 868 623 5461 **Fax:** +1 868 624 5644/625 8415
Contact: Mr Edward Collier

PORTO & SUNDFELD ADVOGADOS (Brazil)
Av. 9 de Julho, 5109, 3°, SP01407-200 São Paulo
Tel: +55 11 3079 4244 **Fax:** +55 11 3079 2257
Contact: Mr Pedro Paulo/ Carlos Ari de Rezende Porto

POSADAS, POSADAS & VECINO (Uruguay)
Juncal 1305, Piso 21, Montevideo 11000 **Tel:** +598 2916 2202
Fax: +598 2916 2429 **Contact:** Dr Ijnacio de Posadas

PRAGER DREIFUSS (Switzerland)
Mühlebachstrasse 6, 8008 Zurich **Tel:** +41 1 254 5555
Fax: +41 1 254 5599 **Contact:** Ms Bak-Haeng Ung

PRESTON GATES & ELLIS LLP (USA)
701 Fifth Avenue, Suite 5000, Seattle WA 98104-7078 **Tel:** +1 206 623 7580 **Fax:** +1 206 623 7022 **Contact:** Mr Gerald Johnson

CABINET PREVOT (French Guiana)
PK2 Route de Baduel, No. 794, Cayenne 97300 **Tel:** +59 428 2121
Fax: +59 431 2542 **Contact:** Mme Thérèse-Murielle Prevot

PRICEWATERHOUSECOOPERS VELTINS (Germany)
Berliner Allee 15, Schadow-Arkaden, 40212 Düsseldorf
Tel: +49 211 8289 380 **Fax:** +49 211 8289 3810
Contact: Michael Veltins

PRIETO Y CIA (Chile)
Huerfanos 835, Piso 18, PO Box 3269, Santiago
Tel: +56 2 280 5000 **Fax:** +562 280 5001/2
Contact: Mr Patrico Prieto

PROCHÁZKA RANDL KUBR (Czech Republic)
Jáchymova 2, 110 00 Prague 1 **Tel:** +420 2 2143 0111
Fax: +420 2 2423 5450 **Contact:** Mr Marek Procházka

PROSKAUER ROSE LLP (USA)
1585 Broadway, New York NY 10036-8299 **Tel:** +1 212 969 3000
Fax: +1 212 969 2900 **Contact:** Mr Stanley Komaroff

PROXEN (Ukraine)
12-A Kibalchicha Street, U2139 Kiev **Tel:** +380 44 512 7000
Fax: +380 44 514 3305 **Contact:** Mr Andriy Zadorozhny

PYTHON SCHIFFERLI PETER & PARTNER (Switzerland)
3, rue Bellot, CH-1206 Geneva **Tel:** +41 22 347 46 45
Fax: +41 22 347 80 54 **Contact:** Mr Pyphon

QUATTRINI, LAPRIDA & ASOCIADOS (Argentina)
Av. del Liberdator 602 -, 4th Floor, 1001 Buenos Aires
Tel: +54 11 4814 1190 **Fax:** +54 11 4814 1091
Contact: Mr Federico Laprido

QUINTANILLA & SORIA (Bolivia)
Calle Loayza N° 250,, Edificio Castilla 7° Piso, PO Box 3143, La Paz
Tel: +591 2 201 015 **Fax:** +591 811 3470
Contact: Mr Eduardo R Quintanilla B

QUISUMBING TORRES (Philippines)
11th Floor, Makati Avenue, Makati City **Tel:** +632 817 3016
Fax: +632 811 5460 **Contact:** Mr Juan G Collas

CABINET RADILOFE (Madagascar)
Rue Vittori François, Ambanidia - Ampasanimalo Rue Vittori François Rue Vittori François Rue Vittori François Rue Vittori François, 101 - Antananarivo
Tel: +2612 0222 1228 **Fax:** +261 2 0223 1019
Contact: M Justin Radilofe

RADO & ASOCIADOS (Cuba)
Calle de Los Oficios No. 152, Habana Vieja, Código Postal 10100, Havana **Tel:** +537 338 186 **Fax:** +537 338 185
Contact: Mr Leonardo Dodico

RAGNAR ADALSTEINSSON - SOLE PRACTITIONER (Iceland)
Klapparstegur 25-27, Reykjavik 101 **Tel:** +354 511 1206
Fax: +354 511 1207 **Contact:** Mr Ragnar Adalsteinsson

RAISBECK LARA RODRIGUEZ & RUEDA (BAKER & MCKENZIE) (Colombia)
Calle 35 No 7/25, 4th Floor, Apartado Aéreo No.3746, Bogota Columbia **Tel:** +57 1 332 2600/5700010/2851400
Fax: +57 1 285 6908/232 4983 **Contact:** Mr Alvaro O Correa

RAJAI KW DAJANI & ASSOCIATES (Jordan)
Astra Building, First Circle, Jabal Amman, PO Box 5590, Amman 11183 **Tel:** +962 6461 7417 **Fax:** +962 6461 7418
Contact: Mr Rajai KW Dajani

RAJINDER NARAIN & CO (India)
Shivam House, 14-F Connaught House, New Delhi 110 001
Tel: +91 11 331 3232 /335 2831 **Fax:** +91 11 332 8319/371 2386
Contact: Mr Ravi Nath

CABINET RAKOTOARIVONY (Madagascar)
34 Avenue Andrianampoinimerina 101, BP199 Antananarivo, Antananarivo **Tel:** +2612 0223 3360 **Fax:** +261 2 0226 2382
Contact: M Rakotoarivony

If you can't find a firm here, see full profiles (pages 957-1481)

ESTUDIO RAMOS MEJÍA (Argentina)
Tucumán 1438, Piso 6, oficina 602, 1050 Buenos Aires
Tel: +54 11 4371 9851 **Fax:** +54 11 43 74 3445
Contact: Mr Fernando Goldaracena

RAUPACH & WOLLERT-ELMENDORFF (Germany)
Thomas-Wimmer-Ring 3, 80539 Munich **Tel:** +49 89 29 03 69 01
Fax: +49 89 29 03 69 11 **Contact:** Arndt Raupach

REBOUL, MACMURRAY, HEWITT, MAYNARD & KRISTOL (USA)
45 Rockefeller Plaza, New York NY 10020-10111 **Tel:** +1 212 841 5700
Fax: +1 212 841 5725 **Contact:** Ms Nicolie Christin

REDEKER SELLNER DAHS & WIDMAIER (Germany)
Mozartstrasse 4-10, 53115 Bonn **Tel:** +49 228 726 250
Fax: +49 228 650 479 **Contact:** Konrad Redeker

REISOGLU ENSARI BUDAK LAW FIRM (Turkey)
Sehit Ersan Cad. 4/3, Çankaya, 06680 Ankara **Tel:** +90 312 467 9103
Fax: +90 312 467 4692 **Contact:** Prof Dr Seza Reisoglu

RENNER-THOMAS & CO (Sierra Leone)
Africanus House, 13A Howe Street, Freetown PO Box 303
Tel: +232 22 22 5143 **Fax:** +232 2222 4256

REX MCKAY & PARTNERS (Guyana)
1 Croal Street, Stabroek, PO Box 10745, Georgetown **Tel:** +592 22 72317/ 57457 **Fax:** +592 22 5718 **Contact:** Mr Fitz Leroy Peters

REYMOND, BONNARD, MAIRE, FREYMOND, TSCHUMY (Switzerland)
5, rue du Grand-Chêne, PO Box 3633, 1002 Lausanne **Tel:** +41 21 320 68 51 **Fax:** +41 21 320 82 49 **Contact:** Mr Alexandre Bonnard

RICHARD WHISH - SOLE PRACTITIONER (United Kingdom)
School of Law, King's College, The Strand, London WC2R 2LS **Tel:** +44 20 7848 2237 **Fax:** +44 20 7848 2211 **Contact:** Mr Richard Whish

ROBINSON BERTRAM (Swaziland)
3rd Floor, Sokhamlilo Building, Cnr Johnstone & Walker Streets, Mbabane PO Box 24 **Tel:** +268 4042826 **Fax:** +268 4046454
Contact: Mr Knox Mshumayeli Nxumalo

RODNER MARTÍNEZ & ASOCIADOS (Venezuela)
Avenida Venezuela, El Rosal, Edificio Torre Clement, Piso 2, Caracas 1060 **Tel:** +58 2 951 3811 **Fax:** +58 2 951 7707
Contact: Mr Jaime Martínez-Estévez

RODRIGO ELIAS Y MEDRANO (Peru)
Avenida San Felipe 758, Lima 11 **Tel:** +51 1 219 1900
Fax: +51 1 463 7300 **Contact:** Mr Enrique Elías

ROITER ZUCKER (United Kingdom)
5-7 Broadhurst Gardens, Swiss Cottage, London NW6 3RZ
Tel: +44 20 7328 9111 **Fax:** +44 20 7644 8953
Contact: Ms Anna McKay

ROKANUDDIN MAHMUD & ASSOCIATES (Bangladesh)
Walsow Tower (First Floor), 21-23 Kazi Nazrul Islam Avenue, Dhaka 1000 **Tel:** +880 2 862 0078/ 862 5350 **Fax:** +880 2 966 9122
Contact: Mr Rokanuddin Mahmud

ROLF SCHULZ-SÜCHTIG - SOLE PRACTITIONER (Germany)
Ballindamm 9, 20095 Hamburg **Tel:** +49 40 309 6760
Fax: +49 40 309 67 666 **Contact:** Rolf Schulz-Süchtig

CHIEF ROTIMI WILLIAMS' CHAMBERS (Nigeria)
Palm Grove House, 1, Shagamu Avenue, Ilupeju, PO Box 3426, Lagos
Tel: +234 1 496 1916 **Fax:** +234 1 496 1652
Contact: Chief FRA Williams

ROUSE & CO INTERNATIONAL IN ASSOCIATION WITH WILLOUGHBY & PARTNERS (United Kingdom)
The Isis Building, Thames Quay, 193 Marsh Wall, London E14 9SG
Tel: +44 20 7345 8888 **Fax:** +44 20 7345 4555
Contact: Mrs Sharon Amiralai

ROWE & MAW (United Kingdom)
20 Black Friars Lane, London EC4V 6HD **Tel:** +44 20 7248 4282
Fax: +44 20 7248 2009 **Contact:** Mr Stuart James

ESTUDIO RUBIO LEGUIA NORMAND & ASOCIADOS (Peru)
Avenida Dos de Mayo #1321, Lima 27 **Tel:** +51 1 442 4900
Fax: +51 1 442 3511 **Contact:** Dr Enrique Normand Sparks

RUDD WATTS & STONE (New Zealand)
BNZ Tower, 125 Queen Street, PO Box 3798, Auckland
Tel: +64 9 353 9700 **Fax:** +64 9 353 9701 **Contact:** Mr Peter Rowe

RUI BARREIRA, MAGALHAES CORREIA, TERESA CARREGUEIRO E GORJAO HENRIQUES (Portugal)
Rua Fialho de Almeida, n 32 - 1 Esq, 1070 Lisbon
Tel: +351 21 387 5167 **Fax:** +351 21 387 8440
Contact: Mr Duarte Henriques

RUSSELL MCVEAGH (New Zealand)
Royal & SunAlliance Centre, 48 Shortland Street, PO Box 8, Auckland
Tel: +64 9 367 8000 **Fax:** +64 9 367 8163 **Contact:** Mr John Lusk

RUSSIN & VECCHI LTD (Myanmar)
22 Wingaba Road, Bahan Township, Mail to: Box No. 729, GPO, Yangon
Tel: +95 1 541 794 / 540 995 **Fax:** +95 1 548 835
Contact: Mr James Finch

If you can't find a firm here, see full profiles (pages 957-1481)

SACRANIE, GOW & CO (Malawi)
PO Box 5133, Limbe **Tel:** +265 640 311 **Fax:** +265 640 750
Contact: Mr Shabir Latif

THE LAW FIRM OF SALAH AL-HEJAILAN (Saudi Arabia)
Al-Dahna Center, 54 Al-Ahsaa Street, PO Box 1454, Riyadh 11431
Tel: +966 1 479 2200 **Fax:** +966 1 479 1717
Contact: Sheikh Salah Ibrahim Al-Hejailan

SALAHEDDINE CAID ESSEBSI & ASSOCIÉS (Tunisia)
14 Avenue Alain Savary, Tunis 1002 **Tel:** +216 1 785 611
Fax: +216 1 783 913 **Contact:** Mr Salaheddine Caïd Essebsi

SALANS HERTZFELD & HEILBRONN (France)
9 Rue Boissy D'Anglas, 75008 Paris **Tel:** +33 1 42 68 48 00
Fax: +33 1 42 68 15 45/6

CABINET SALES (Haiti)
16 Rue Eden, PO Box 211, Port-au-Prince HT 6110
Tel: +509 510 3991 **Fax:** +509 223 0994
Contact: Mr Jean Frederic Sales

SANCHEZ ELIA, PINEDO, DIAZ BOBILLO & RICHARD (Argentina)
Leandro, Alem 884, 5th Floor, 1001 Buenos Aires
Tel: +54 11 4312 4991 **Fax:** +54 11 4314 8889

CABINET SATOR (Algeria)
22 rue Abane Ramdane, Algiers 16000
Tel: +213 21 73 5659 / 7482 **Fax:** +213 21 73 8468

SAVJANI & CO (Malawi)
PO Box 2790, Blantyre **Tel:** +265 624 555 **Fax:** +265 621 064
Contact: Mr Krishna Savjani SC

S B S JANNEH, BARRISTER AT LAW (The Gambia)
15 Hagan Street, Banjul **Tel:** +220 228 174 **Fax:** +220 497 367

SCANLEN & HOLDERNESS (Zimbabwe)
13th Floor, CABS Centre, 74 Jason Moyo Avenue, PO Box 188, Harare
Tel: +263 4 702 561 **Fax:** +263 4 702569
Contact: Mr William Homan Turpin

SCHIFF HARDIN & WAITE (USA)
6600 Sears Tower, 233 S.Wacker Drive, Chicago Il 60606-6473 **Tel:** +1 312 258 5500 **Fax:** +1 312 258 5600/5700 **Contact:** Mr Peter V Fazio, Jr

SCORINIS LAW OFFICES (Greece)
67 Iroon Polytechniou Ave, 185 36 Piraeus **Tel:** +30 1 418 1818
Fax: +30 1 418 1822 **Contact:** Mr N Scorinis

SCPA KONATE, MOISE-BAZIE & KOYO (Cote D'Ivoire)
30 Boulevard Carde RÈsidence les Harmonies, BP 3926, Abidjan 01
Tel: +225 20 22 7753 **Fax:** +225 20 21 3202

SEELIG & PREU, BOHLIG (Germany)
Seestr. 13, 80802 Munich **Tel:** +49 89 3838 700 **Fax:** +49 89 392 522
Contact: Matthias Brandi-Dohrn

SELIH, REMEC & JANEZIC (Slovenia)
Resljeva 24, Ljubljana 1000 **Tel:** +386 1 300 7650/7660
Fax: +386 1 433 7098

ADVOKATFIRMAET SELMER DA (Norway)
Mail to: PO Box 1324 Vika, 0112 Oslo. Visiting address: Støperigaten 2, Aker Brygge, 0112 Oslo **Tel:** +47 23 11 65 00 **Fax:** +47 23 11 65 01
Contact: Mr Thomas Michelet

SERGIY KOZIAKOV & PARTNERS (Ukraine)
Gorkogo 102, Street, 03150 Kyiv **Tel:** +380 44 251 1011
Fax: +380 44 230 2663 **Contact:** Mr Sergiy Koziakov

SERRA MICHAUD & ASSOCIÉS (France)
2 Rue de la Baume, 75008 Paris **Tel:** +33 1 44 21 97 97
Fax: +33 1 42 89 57 90 **Contact:** Mr Patrick Michaud

SÉRVULO CORREIA & ASSOCIADOS (Portugal)
Rua Artilharia Um 79, 5, P 1250-038 Lisbon **Tel:** +351 21 383 69 00
Fax: +351 21 383 69 01 **Contact:** Prof Sérvulo Correia

SEWARD & KISSEL (USA)
One Battery Park Plaza, New York NY 10004 **Tel:** +1 212 574 1200
Fax: +1 212 480 8421

SEY & CO (Ghana)
PO Box 9918, Airport Accra, Accra **Tel:** +233 21 220 624 / 225 778
Fax: +233 21 224 694 **Contact:** Mr K K Sey

SHALAKANY LAW OFFICE (Egypt)
12 Marashly Street, Zamalek, Cairo **Tel:** +202 735 3331
Fax: +202 737 0661 **Contact:** Mr Ali El Shalakany

SHARHABEEL AL ZAEEM & ASSOCIATES (Palestinian Territories)
PO Box 1153, Gaza City, Gaza Strip, Gaza
Tel: +972 7 282 0445 **Fax:** +972 7 282 0598 **Contact:** Mr A Sharhabeel

SHAW PITTMAN (USA)
2300 N Street N.W., Washington DC 20037 **Tel:** +1 202 663 8000
Fax: +1 202 663 8007 **Contact:** Mr Paul F. Mickey, Jr.

SHEARN DELAMORE & CO (Malaysia)
7th Floor, Wisma Hamzah-Kwong Hing, No 1 Leboh Ampang, Kuala Lumpur 50100 **Tel:** +60 3 230 0644 **Fax:** +60 3 238 2376
Contact: Mr Dato V L Kandan

If you can't find a firm here, see full profiles (pages 957-1481)

SHERMAN & SHERMAN INC (Liberia)
Ashmun & Meclin Streets, PO Box 10-3218, Monrovia 1000
Tel: +231 226 927 **Fax:** +231 226 523

SHIBOLETH, YISRAELI, ROBERTS, ZISMAN & CO (Israel)
46 Montifiore Street, Tel Aviv 65201 **Tel:** +972 3 710 3311
Fax: +972 3 710 3322 **Contact:** Mr Richard M. Roberts

DR SHLOMO COHEN & CO LAW OFFICE (Israel)
Century Tower, 124 IBN Gvirol, Tel Aviv 62 038 **Tel:** +972 3 527 1919
Fax: +972 3 527 2666 **Contact:** Dr Shlomo Cohen

SIAM PREMIER INTERNATIONAL LAW OFFICE LTD (Thailand)
24th & 26h Floor Thai Wah Tower II, 21/147-150 South Sathorn Road, Bangkok 10120 **Tel:** +66 2 679 1333 **Fax:** +66 2 679 1314

SIMPSON GRIERSON (New Zealand)
Simpson Grierson Building, 92-96 Albert Street, Auckland
Tel: +64 9 358 2222 **Fax:** +64 9 307 0331 **Contact:** Mr Peter Hinton

SINARE, SHIYO & MWANDAMBO ADVOCATES (Tanzania)
Fifth Floor, Sukari House, Sokoine Drive/Ohio Street, PO Box 13179, Dar es Salaam **Tel:** +255 22 211 3203/211 4676
Fax: +225 22 211 3200 **Contact:** Dr Hawa Sinare

SINCLAIR ROCHE & TEMPERLEY (United Kingdom)
5 Aldermanbury Square, London EC2V 7LE **Tel:** +44 20 7452 4000
Fax: +44 20 7452 4001 **Contact:** Mr Jeff Morgan

SINGLETONS (United Kingdom)
The Ridge, South View Road, Pinner HA5 3YD **Tel:** +44 20 8866 1934
Fax: +44 20 8429 9212 **Contact:** Mrs E. Susan Singleton

SKRINE & CO (Malaysia)
8th Floor, Wisma Uoa Damansara, 50 Jalan Dungun, Damansara Heights, Kuala Lumpur 50490
Tel: +60 3 254 8111 **Fax:** +60 3 254 3211

SMITH-HUGHES, RAWORTH & MCKENZIE (British Virgin Islands)
Sea Meadow House, PO Box 173, Road Town, Tortola **Tel:** +1 284 494 3384/5 **Fax:** +1 284 494 4643/2914 **Contact:** Mr Chris McKenzie

BUFETE SOCORÓ & GRAU (Spain)
Muntaner, 452-454, 1º 2º, 08006 Barcelona **Tel:** +34 93 209 07 65
Fax: +34 93 414 44 50 **Contact:** Mr Jorge Grau Mora

ADVOKATFIRMAN SÖDERMARK (Sweden)
Strandvagen 1, PO Box 14055, SE-104 40 Stockholm **Tel:** +46 8 670 57 50 **Fax:** +46 8 663 67 20 **Contact:** Mr Bertil Sodermark

SOEBAGJO ROOSDIONO JATIM & DJAROT (Indonesia)
17th Floor, Plaza Mashill, Jalan Jenderal Sudirman Kav 25, Jakarta 12910 **Tel:** +62 21 522 9765 **Fax:** +62 21 522 9752/53
Contact: Mr Soebagjo

SOEMADIPRADJA & TAHER (Indonesia)
Wisma GKB1, Suite 905, Jl. Jenderal Sudirman No 28, Jakarta Pusat 10220 **Tel:** +62 21 574 0088 **Fax:** +62 21 574 0068
Contact: Mr Soemadipradja

SOLOMON HARRIS (Cayman Islands)
Barclays House, PO Box 1990, Georgetown, Grand Cayman
Tel: +1 345 949 0488 **Fax:** +1 345 949 0364
Contact: Ms Sophia Harris

SOLTYSIŃSKI KAWECKI & SZLÊZAK LEGAL ADVISORS (Poland)
ul. Wawelska 15 B, 02-034 Warsaw **Tel:** +48 22 608 7000
Fax: +48 22 608 7070 **Contact:** Mr Stanislaw Soltysinski

SOMAY HUKUK BÜROSU (Turkey)
Buyukdere Caddesi, No: 118/10, Esentepe, 80280 Istanbul
Tel: +90 212 216 7562 **Fax:** +90 212 288 3748
Contact: Mr Metin Somay

SONNENBERG HOFFMANN & GALOMBIK (South Africa)
PO Box 2293, Cape Town 8000
Tel: +27 21 410 2500 **Fax:** +27 21 410 2555 **Contact:** Mr Piet Faber

SONNENSCHEIN (USA)
8000 Sears Tower, 233 South Wacker Drive, Chicago IL 60606-6404
Tel: +1 312 876 8000 **Fax:** +1 312 876 7934
Contact: Mr Errol L. Stone

STAMFORD LLC (Singapore)
6 Battery Road, #25-01, Singapore 049909
Tel: +65 532 0409 **Fax:** +65 534 3632 **Contact:** Ms Suet-Fern Lee

STANISLAW PIATEK - PROFESSOR AT WARSAW UNIVERSITY (Poland)
Michalów Grabina, ul Bukowa 3, PL 05-126 Niporet
Tel: +48 22 676 9836 **Fax:** +48 22 676 9586

STEEL HECTOR & DAVIS (USA)
200 South Biscayne Boulevard, SUITE 4000, Miami FL 33131-2398
Tel: +1 305 577 7000 **Fax:** +1 305 577 7001
Contact: Mr Joseph.P Klock, Jr.

STIKEMAN ELLIOTT (Canada)
Suite 3603, 1155 René-Lévesque Blvd. West, Montréal Québec H3B 3V2
Tel: +1 514 397 3000 **Fax:** +1 514 397 3222 **Contact:** Mr Ed Waitzer

STOICA & ASSOCIATES (Romania)
Splaiul Independentei Nr 17, Bloc 101, Sc 2, Et 4, Apartment 30,Sector 5, 70501 Bucharest **Tel:** +40 1 336 70 10/00 **Fax:** +40 1 336 71 30
Contact: Mrs Cristiana Stoica

STRECK MACK SCHWEDHELM (Germany)
Hans-Willy-Mertens Str 6, D-50855 Köln **Tel:** +49 2234 94 6660
Fax: +49 2234 946 659 **Contact:** Dr Michael Streck

STRINGER SAUL (United Kingdom)
17 Hanover Square, London W1S 1HU **Tel:** +44 20 7917 8500
Fax: +44 20 7917 8555 **Contact:** Mr Nigel Gordon

LAW FIRM STRUIKEN (Surinam)
Wagenwegstraat 41, Paramaribo
Tel: +597 474 024 **Fax:** +597 475 063 **Contact:** H.E. Struiken

STUDIO TRIBUTARIO E SOCIETARIO (Italy)
Corso Venezia 61, 20121 Milan **Tel:** +39 02 2951 0809
Fax: +39 02 2951 8036 **Contact:** Mr Claudio Zulli

STUDNICKI PLESZKA CWIAKALSKI GØRSKI (Poland)
Kraszewhkigo 14, 30-110 Krakow **Tel:** +48 12 427 2424
Fax: +48 12 427 2323 **Contact:** Mr Tomas Studnicki

STUMBLES & ROWE (Zimbabwe)
Fourth Floor, Takura House, 67-69 Union Avenue, PO Box 495, Harare
Tel: +263 4 738903 **Fax:** +263 4 738909
Contact: Mr John Bourchier Meyburgh

SURANA & SURANA INTERNATIONAL ATTORNEYS (India)
National Insurance Building, 224, NSC Bose Road, Chennai 600 001
Tel: +91 44 539 0121/2 **Fax:** +91 44 538 3339
Contact: Mr Vinod Surana

SWIDLER BERLIN SHEREFF FRIEDMAN LLP (USA)
3000 K Street N.W., Suite 300, Washington DC 20007-5116 **Tel:** +1 202 424 7500 **Fax:** +1 202 424 7643 **Contact:** Mr Roger Frankel

SYED ISHTIAQ AHMED & ASSOCIATES (Bangladesh)
1st Floor, Walsow Tower, 21-23 Kazi Nazrul Islam Avenue, Dhaka
Tel: +880 2 966 5355 **Fax:** +880 2 966 5354
Contact: Mr Syed Ishtiaq Ahmed

CABINET SYLVESTRE BANZUBAZE (Burundi)
BP 3031, Bujumbura **Tel:** +257 226 427 **Fax:** +257 229 711
Contact: Mr Sylvestre Banzubaze

SYRIAN ARAB CONSULTANTS LAW OFFICE (Syria)
PO Box 254, Port Said Street, Nahas Building, 5th Floor, Damascus
Tel: +963 11 231 7577 **Fax:** +963 11 441 2848
Contact: Mr Antoine Goubran

TANAKA & TAKAHASHI (Japan)
New Aoyama Building W-1352, 1-1 Minami Aoyama 1-chome, Minato-ku, Tokyo 107-0062 **Tel:** +81 3 3475 1631 **Fax:** +81 3 3403 8820
Contact: Mr Isao Takahashi

TARLO LYONS (United Kingdom)
Watchmaker Court, 33 St. John's Lane, London EC1M 4DB **Tel:** +44 20 7405 2000 **Fax:** +44 20 7814 9421 **Contact:** Ms Alison Boling

TAVAKOLI & SHAHABI (Iran)
PO Box 19395-3448, Tehran
Tel: +98 21 26 86 65 **Fax:** +98 21 26 86 22 **Contact:** Mr Shahabi

TAVERNIER TSCHANZ (Switzerland)
11-bis Rue Toepffer, CH-1206 Geneva **Tel:** +41 22 704 3700
Fax: +41 22 704 3777 **Contact:** Mr Pierre-Yves Tschanz

TEFERI BERHANE - SOLE PRACTITIONER (Eritrea)
PO Box 1518, Asmara **Tel:** +291 1 123 337 **Fax:** +291 1 123 644
Contact: Mr Teferi Berhane

TESHOME GABRE-MARIAM BOKAN LAW OFFICE (Ethiopia)
PO Box 101485, Addis Ababa **Tel:** +251 1 518 484
Fax: +251 1 158 020 **Contact:** Mr Teshome Gabre-Mariam

TESTA, HURWITZ & THIBEAULT LLP (USA)
High Street Tower, 125 High Street, Boston MA 02110
Tel: +1 617 248 7000 **Fax:** +1 617 248 7100
Contact: Mr Richard J. Testa

TETTEH & CO (Ghana)
Suite 305-306, 3rd Floor, Kingsway Building, 45 Kwame Nkrumah Ave, P O Box 14764, Accra, Ghana **Tel:** +233 21 221433
Fax: +233 21 662 117 **Contact:** Mr Solomon Kwami Tetteh

THACHER PROFFITT & WOOD (USA)
Two World Trade Center, 38th - 40th Floors, New York NY 10048
Tel: +1 212 912 7400 **Fax:** +1 212 912 7751
Contact: Mr Omer S.J. Williams

CABINET THARCISSE NTAKIYICA (Burundi)
BP 582, Bujumbura **Tel:** +257 223 871 **Fax:** +257 215 232
Contact: Maître Tharcisse Ntakiyica

THELEN REID & PRIEST LLP (USA)
101 Second Street, Suite 1800, San Francisco CA 94105-3601
Tel: +1 415 371 1200 **Fax:** +1 415 371 1211
Contact: Ms Michelle Johnson

THEODORE GODDARD (United Kingdom)
150 Aldersgate Street, London EC1A 4EJ **Tel:** +44 20 7606 8855
Fax: +44 20 7606 4390 **Contact:** Mr Peter Cooke

If you can't find a firm here, see full profiles (pages 957-1481)

THIO SU MIEN & PARTNERS (Singapore)
6 Battery Road, #33-01, Singapore 049909
Tel: +65 534 4877 **Fax:** +65 534 4822 **Contact:** Dr Thio Su Mien

THOMAS COOPER & STIBBARD (United Kingdom)
Ibex House, 42-47 Minories, London EC3N 1HA **Tel:** +44 20 7481 8851 **Fax:** +44 20 7480 6097 **Contact:** Mr T.J.R. Goode

CABINET THOMAS DINGAMGOTO (Chad)
314 Avenue Charles De Gaulle, N'Djamena BP 1003 **Tel:** +235 515 588 **Fax:** +235 515 080 **Contact:** M Thomas Dingamgoto

THOMPSON HINE & FLORY LLP (USA)
3900 Key Centre, 127 Public Square, Cleveland OH 44114-1216
Tel: +1 216 566 5500 **Fax:** +1 216 566 5800
Contact: Mr David J Hooker

TILLEKE & GIBBINS AND ASSOCIATES (Cambodia)
No. 56, Regents Park Hotel, Samdech Sothearos Boulevard, Khan Daun Penh, Phnom Penh **Tel:** +855 23 362 670
Fax: +855 23 362 671 **Contact:** Mr Bdrep Poomscirioni

TILMAN SCHILLING - SOLE PRACTITIONER (Germany)
Otto-Beck-Strasse 38, 68165 Mannheim **Tel:** +49 621 32 85 631
Fax: +49 621 32 85 641 **Contact:** Tilman Schilling

TIRUCHELVAM ASSOCIATES (Sri Lanka)
8 Kynsey Terrace, Colombo 8 **Tel:** +94 1 694664/698110
Fax: +94 1 696618 **Contact:** Ms Sithie Tiruchelvam

LAW OFFICE TJ KOUTALIDIS (Greece)
4 Valaoritou Street, GR-10671 Athens **Tel:** +30 1 360 7811
Fax: +30 1 360 0069 **Contact:** Mr Nicolas C Koritsas

TMI ASSOCIATES (Japan)
Suiite 803, 37 Mori Building, 5-1 Toranomon 3-chome, Minato-ku, Tokyo 105-0001 **Tel:** +81 3 5472 8511
Fax: +81 3 5472 0866 **Contact:** Mr Katsuro Tanaka

TOMOTSUNE KIMURA & MITOMI (Japan)
Sanno Grand Building, 14-2 Nagatacho, 2 Chome, Chiyoda-Ku, Tokyo 100-0014 **Tel:** +81 3 3580 0800 **Fax:** +81 3 3593 3336
Contact: Mr Tstumo Miyano

CABINET TORDJMAN & ASSOCIÉS (France)
217 rue du Faubourg St Honore, 75008 Paris **Tel:** +33 1 5836 2020
Fax: +33 1 5836 2021 **Contact:** Mr Olivier Tordjman

TOROSSIAN, AVANESSIAN & ASSOCIATES (Iran)
No. 26, Magnolia, Golriz Street, G Farahani Avenue, Tehran 15886
Tel: +98 21 884 3139 **Fax:** +98 21 884 1725
Contact: Mr. Vrej Torossian

TORRES PLAZ & ARAUJO (Venezuela)
Apartado Postal 61.106, Caracas 1060 **Tel:** +58 2 709 53 11
Fax: +58 2 709 53 00 **Contact:** Mr Manuel Torres

TOUREH ET ASSOCIÉS (Mali)
BP 19923, Bamako **Tel:** +223 214 578 **Fax:** +223 210 886
Contact: Mr Moctah Mariko

TOWNSEND AND TOWNSEND AND CREW LLP (USA)
Two Embarcadero Center, Eighth Floor, San Francisco CA 94111-3834
Tel: +1 415 576 0200 **Fax:** +1 415 576 0300 **Contact:** Mr David Slone

STUDIO TREMONTI (Italy)
Via Croce Fisso, 12, 20122 Milan **Tel:** +39 02 5831 3707/8
Fax: +39 02 5831 3714 **Contact:** Mr Enrico Vitalli

TRIAY & TRIAY (Gibraltar)
28 Irish Town, PO Box 15, Gibraltar **Tel:** +350 72020
Fax: +350 72270 **Contact:** Mr RA Triay

TRUST (Belarus)
21-614 Chicherina St, Minsk 220029 **Tel:** +375 1 7239 4708
Fax: +375 17 210 1169 **Contact:** Mr Eugenie Lazarenkou

TSAR & TSAI (Taiwan)
8th Floor, 245 Tun Hwa S Road, Sec 1, Taipei 106
Tel: +886 2 2781 4111 **Fax:** +886 2 2721 3834

TUMBUAN PANE COUNSELLORS AT LAW (Indonesia)
JL Gandaria Tengah III/8, Kebayoran Baru, Jakarta 12130
Tel: +62 21 720 8172 / 720 2516 **Fax:** +62 21 724 4579 / 739 9017
Contact: Mr Fred B.G. Tumbuan

TURCAN & TURCAN (Moldova)
67 Bucuresti St, Chisinau MD 2012 **Tel:** +373 221 2031
Fax: +373 222 3806 **Contact:** Mr Alexander Turcan

TURLOT & ASSOCIATES (Democratic Republic of Congo)
Mail to: c/o EAC - Brucargo 740, Zaventum, B-1931 Belgium.
Residence: Mercure, 37 Avenue Kalemie, PO Box 12709, Kinshasa-Gombe **Tel:** +243 884 4578 **Fax:** +243 880 4685

CABINET TUROT (France)
3 Rue Saint Dominique, 75007 Paris **Tel:** +33 1 4548 5596
Fax: +33 1 4548 5597 **Contact:** M Jérome Turot

TYAN & ASSOCIÉS (Lebanon)
22, Rue La Sagesse, Rmeil, PO Box 175563, Beirut 11 04 20 50
Tel: +961 1 561 673 **Fax:** +961 1 561 435 **Contact:** Ms Yara Maroun

STUDIO UCKMAR MAGNANI MARONGIU (Italy)
Via Bacigalupo, 4/15, 16149 Genoa **Tel:** +39 010 831 8871
Fax: +39 010 812 656 **Contact:** Prof Victor Uckmar

UDWADIA UDESHI & BERJIS (India)
2nd & 3rd Floors, Thomas Cook Building, 324 DN Road, Fort, Mumbai 400 001 **Tel:** +91 22 288 3341 **Fax:** +91 22 287 1437

UEXKÜLL & STOLBERG (Germany)
Beselerstr. 4, 22607 Hamburg
Tel: +49 40 899 6540 **Fax:** +49 40 899 654 88

ULHÔA CANTO, REZENDE E GUERRA ADVOGADOS (Brazil)
Av. Presidente Antonio Carlos, 51, 12th Floor, RJ 20020-010 Rio de Janeiro **Tel:** +55 21 824 3265 **Fax:** +55 21 240 7360/ 3824 3333
Contact: Mr Condorcet Rezende

URENDA RENCORET ORREGO & DÖRR (Chile)
Torre de la Costanera, Avda. Andres Bello 2711, piso 16, Santiago
Tel: +56 2 655 9090 **Fax:** +56 2 655 9148/49
Contact: Mr Juan Carlos Dorr Z

URÍA ABOGADOS (Peru)
Av. Víctor Andrés Belaúnde 147, Vía Principal 155, Torre Real Tres - Piso 12, Lima 27 **Tel:** +51 1 222 3202 **Fax:** +51 1 222 1573
Contact: Mr Jose A Payet

VANI & ASSOCIATES (Albania)
Ismail Qemail 27, Noli, suite1, Tirana **Tel:** +355 4250 719
Fax: +355 4250 718 **Contact:** Mr George Vani

VARGAS JIMENEZ & PERALTA (Costa Rica)
Apartado 2727, San José **Tel:** +506 222 8622 **Fax:** +506 255 2174
Contact: Mr Ferman Vargas

VASHKEVICH SAPEGO & KAZNACHEEV (Belarus)
Kalvariyskaya St 1-603, Minsk 220004
Tel: +375 17 222 4433 **Fax:** +375 17 226 5190

VEDDER, PRICE, KAUFMAN & KAMMHOLZ (USA)
222 North LaSalle Street, Suite 2600, Chicago IL 60601-1003
Tel: +1 312 609 7500 **Fax:** +1 312 609 5005

VEIRANO ADVOGADOS ASSOCIADOS (Brazil)
Av. Presidente Wilson 231, 23rd Floor, PO Box 2748, Edificio Palacio Austregesilo de Athayde, RJ 20030-021 Rio de Janeiro
Tel: +55 21 824 4747/ 282 1232 **Fax:** +55 21 262 4247
Contact: Mr Ronaldo Carcamargo Veirano

VENTURE LAW GROUP (USA)
2800 Sand Hill Road, Menlo Park CA 94025 **Tel:** +1 650 854 4488
Fax: +1 650 233 8386 **Contact:** Mr Craig Johnson

VGENOPOULOS & PARTNERS (Greece)
15 Kolonaki Square, 10673 Athens **Tel:** +30 1 7220 150
Fax: +30 1 7231 462 **Contact:** Mr John Papapetros

VIETBID LAW FIRM (Vietnam)
Suite 436, 27 Ly Thai To Str., Hanoi
Tel: +84 4 934 4226 **Fax:** +84 4 934 4225

VISCHER (Switzerland)
Arterstrasse 24, 8032 Zurich **Tel:** +41 1 254 3400
Fax: +41 1 254 3410 **Contact:** Mr Marcus Gugglenbuhl

VISION & ASSOCIATES (Vietnam)
17 Ngo Quyen St, Unit 02, First Floor, International Centre, Hanoi
Tel: +84 4 934 0629 **Fax:** +84 4 934 0631
Contact: Mr Pham Nghiem Xuan Bac

VITERI & VITERI (Guatemala)
6a Calle 5-47, Zona 9, Edificio Vasil, 4th Level, Guatemala City
Tel: +50 2 331 1707 **Fax:** +50 2 331 1768

V KAASIK & CO (Estonia)
Jõe 3, 10151 Tallinn **Tel:** +372 6 106 000
Fax: +372 6 106 011 **Contact:** Mr Viktor Kaasik

VLASOVA & PARTNERS (Belarus)
Parnikovaya St, 57-2,, Minsk 220114 **Tel:** +375 17 211 8142
Fax: +375 17 211 8142 **Contact:** Mrs Lilia Vlasova

VON KREISLER SELTING WERNER (Germany)
Deichmannhaus am Dom, D-50667 Cologne
Tel: +49 221 91 65 20 **Fax:** +49 221 13 42 97

VOUGA & OLMEDO (Paraguay)
España Avenue and Perú Avenue, PO Box 1374, Asuncion 1407
Tel: +595 21 213598 / 230100 **Fax:** +595 21 214556
Contact: Mr Rodolfo Vouga

VUKIC, JELUSIC, SULINA & STANKOVIC (Croatia)
Nikole Teslse 9/VI, 51000 Rijeka
Tel: +385 51 211 600 **Fax:** +385 51 336 884 **Contact:** Mr Vukic

VUKMIR LAW OFFICE (Croatia)
Pantovcak 35, HR-10000 Zagreb **Tel:** +385 1 376 0511
Fax: +385 1 376 0555 **Contact:** Mr Mladen Vukmir

CABINET WABAT DAOUD (Djibouti)
PO Box 3294, Rue Bourhan Bey, Djibouti
Tel: +253 35 47 02 **Fax:** +253 35 23 18 **Contact:** M Wabat Daoud

 If you can't find a firm here, see full profiles (pages 957-1481)

WAKEFIELD QUIN (Bermuda)
Bermuda Commercial Bank Building, 44 Church St, Hamilton HM 12
Tel: +1 441 292 7070 **Fax:** +1 441 292 8899

WALCH & SCHURTI (Liechtenstein)
Zollstrasse 9, PO Box 1611, FL-9490 Vaduz
Tel: +423 237 2000 **Fax:** +423 237 2100 **Contact:** Dr Andreas Schurti

WALD E ASSOCIADOS ADVOGADOS (Brazil)
Av. Juscelino Kubitschek, 50/12th Floor, SP04543-000 São Paulo
Tel: +55 11 3048 0600 **Fax:** +55 11 3048 0648
Contact: Mr Arnoldo Wald

WARDYNSKI & PARTNERS (Poland)
Al Ujazdowskie 12, 00-478 Warsaw **Tel:** +48 22 622 0400
Fax: +48 22 628 9040 **Contact:** Mr Tomasz Wardynski

WARNER SHAND (Papua New Guinea)
2nd Floor Brian Bell Plaza, Turumu Street, PO Box 1817, Boroko
Tel: +675 325 4422 **Fax:** +675 325 0682 **Contact:** Mr Michael Wilson

WEBBER NEWDIGATE (Lesotho)
PO Box 1176, 2nd Floor Metropolitan Life Building, Kingsway, Maseru 100 **Tel:** +266 315 811 **Fax:** +266 310 066 / 324 048
Contact: Mr Michael Krohn

WEBBER WENTZEL BOWENS (South Africa)
60 Main St, Johannesberg 2001, PO Box 61771, Johannesburg 2107
Tel: +27 11 240 5000 **Fax:** +27 11 240 5111
Contact: Mr Murray Thompson

WENGER VIELI BELSER (Switzerland)
Dufourstrasse 56, Postfach 8034, CH-8008 Zürich **Tel:** +41 156 333 33
Fax: +41 156 333 66 **Contact:** Mr Jean-Claude Wenger

WERKSMANS (South Africa)
PO Box 927, Johannesburg 2000 **Tel:** +27 11 488 0000
Fax: +27 11 484 3100/3200 **Contact:** Mr Tony Behrmann

WH COURTENAY & CO (Belize)
37 Regent St, PO Box 214, Belize City **Tel:** +501 2 72037
Fax: +501 2 74645 **Contact:** Mr Eamon H Courtenay

WIEDERKEHR FORSTER RECHTSANWÄLTE (Switzerland)
Bahnhofstrasse 44, Postfach 6040, CH-8023 Zürich **Tel:** +41 1 215 12 12 **Fax:** +41 1 215 12 00 **Contact:** Dr Martin Forster

WIERZBOWSKI & SZUBIELSKA (MEMBER OF LANDWELL, CORRESPONDENT LAW FIRMS OF PRICEWATERHOUSECOOPERS) (Poland)
ul Nowogrodzka 68, 02-014 Warsaw **Tel:** +48 22 523 4111
Fax: +48 22 523 4755 **Contact:** Mr Krzysztof Wierzbowski

WILDANGER & KEHRWALD (Germany)
Freiligrathstr. 13, 40479 Düsseldorf **Tel:** +49 211 498 2911
Fax: +49 211 493 0265 **Contact:** Günther Wildanger

WILEY REIN & FIELDING (USA)
1776 K Street N. W., Washington DC 20006 **Tel:** +1 202 719 7010
Fax: +1 202 719 7049 **Contact:** Mr Richard E. Wiley

ADVOKATFIRMA WILHELM MALLING & CO (Greenland)
PO Box 1046, Nuuk DK-3900 **Tel:** +299 323 400 **Fax:** +299 323 868
Contact: Mr Wilhelm Malling

WILLIAM W. PARK - SOLE PRACTITIONER (USA)
Professor of Law, Boston University Law School, 765 Commonwealth Ave, Boston MA-02215 **Tel:** +1 617 353 3149 **Fax:** +1 617 353 3077
Contact: Mr William Park

WILMER, CUTLER & PICKERING (USA)
2445 M Street NW, Washington DC 20037-1420 **Tel:** +1 202 663 6000
Fax: +1 202 663 6363 **Contact:** Mrs Mary-Ann Henle

WILSON & MORGAN (Malawi)
P O Box 527, Whitehall, Victoria Avenue, Blantyre **Tel:** +265 620 988
Fax: +265 6 229 93 **Contact:** Mr D A Raval

WILSON, SONSINI, GOODRICH & ROSATI (USA)
650 Page Mill Road, Palo Alto CA 94304-1050 **Tel:** +1 650 493 9300
Fax: +1 650 493 6811 **Contact:** Mr Larry Sonsini

WINSTON & STRAWN (USA)
35 West Wacker Drive, Chicago IL 60601-9703 **Tel:** +1 312 558 5600
Fax: +1 312 558 5700 **Contact:** Mr James M Neis

WINTERTONS (Zimbabwe)
11 Selous Avenue, Corner third Steet, PO Box 452, Harare
Tel: +263 4 250113 - 250129 **Fax:** +263 4 727353/733270
Contact: Mr Alwyn Pichanick

WIRIADINATA & WIDYAWAN (Indonesia)
Niaga Tower, 26th Floor, Jalan Jend Sudirman Kav.28, Jakarta 12190
Tel: +62 21 250 5175 **Fax:** +62 21 250 5185
Contact: Mr Hoesien Wiriadinata

PROFESSOR WITOLD MODZELEWSKI - SOLE PRACTITIONER (Poland)
Instytut Studiów Podatkowych Modzelewski i Wspólnicy, Ul. Korytnicka 28, 04-085 Warsaw **Tel:** +48 22 810 8780
Fax: +48 22 870 4178 **Contact:** Prof W Modzelewski

WONG & PARTNERS (Malaysia)
Level 41 Suite A, Menara Maxis, Kuala Lumpur City Centre, Kuala Lumpur 50088 **Tel:** +60 3 2055 1888 **Fax:** +60 3 2161 2919
Contact: Ms Kate Stonestreet

WRAGGE & CO (United Kingdom)
55 Colmore Row, Birmingham B3 2AS **Tel:** +44 870 903 1000
Fax: +44 870 904 1099 **Contact:** Ms Alisa Stevens

WRIGHT & CO (Sierra Leone)
Barristers-at-Law & Solicitors of the High Court of Sierra Leone, 32 Bathurst Street, 3rd Floor, Freetown
Tel: +232 22 227376 **Fax:** +232 22 224 439

YKVN LTD (Vietnam)
Suite 402, 61 Nguyen Du Street, District 1, Ho Chi Minh City
Tel: +84 8 823 6880 **Fax:** +84 8 823 6975

YOHANNES BERHANE - SOLE PRACTITIONER (Eritrea)
PO Box 1144, Asmara **Tel:** +291 114 306 **Fax:** +291 122 718

YOON & PARTNERS (South Korea)
Suite 831, KCCI Building, 45 Namdaemoonro-4-ka, Chung-ku, Seoul 100-743 **Tel:** +82 2 773 0161 **Fax:** +82 2 773 4947

YOUNG'S LAW FIRM (Belize)
28 Regent Street, Belize City PO Box 111 **Tel:** +501 277 406
Fax: +501 275 157 **Contact:** Mr Michael Young

ZAID IBRAHIM & CO (Malaysia)
Level 19 Menara Millennium, Jalan Damanlela, Pusat Bandar Damansara, Kuala Lumpur 50490
Tel: +60 3 257 9999 **Fax:** +60 3 254 4888

ZAIN & CO (Malaysia)
6th & 7th Floors, Dato Zainal Building, 23 Melaka Street, 50100 Kuala Lumpur **Tel:** +60 3 2698 6255 **Fax:** +60 3 2698 6969
Contact: Mr Zain Azlan

ZAMFIRESCU & PARTNERS (Romania)
Mircea Voba Boulevard, 35, Block M 27, Et4, Sector 3, Bucharest
Tel: +40 1 327 4788 **Fax:** +40 1 327 4789 **Contact:** Mr K Zamfirescu

CABINET ZARAMBAUD ASSINGAMBI (Central African Republic)
BP 64, Avenue Mobuto, Bangui
Tel: +236 612 416 **Fax:** +236 617 773

ZELLERMAYER, PELOSSOF & CO (Israel)
The Rubenstein House, Main Entrance - Floor 12, 20 Lincoln Street, Tel Aviv 67134 **Tel:** +972 3 625 5555 **Fax:** +972 3 625 5500
Contact: Mr Michael Zellermayer

ZEPOS & ZEPOS (Greece)
120 Vas Sophias Ave, GR-11526 Athens **Tel:** +30 1 775 3341
Fax: +30 1 770 2825 **Contact:** Mr Dimitris J Zepos

CHAMBERS OF ZIA MODY, ADVOCATE (India)
16 Alli Chambers, N. Master Road, Fort, Mumbai 400 001
Tel: +91 22 265 4340 **Fax:** +91 22 267 1656 **Contact:** Ms Zia Mody

ZULETA GARRIDO ARAQUE & JARAMILLO (Colombia)
Carrera 9 No. 73-24, 5th Floor, Bogota D.C.
Tel: +57 1 3106614 **Fax:** +57 1 3106286 **Contact:** Mr Eduardo Zuleta

ZUL RAFIQUE & PARTNERS (Malaysia)
Suite 17.01, 17th Floor Menara PanGlobal, No. 8 Lorong P. Ramlee, 50250 Kuala Lumpur **Tel:** +603 238 8228
Fax: +603 230 0193 **Contact:** Mr Dato' Zulkifly Rafique

ŽURIĆ i PARTNERI (Croatia)
Gundulićeva 63, 10000 Zagreb **Tel:** +385 1 48 81 333
Fax: +385 1 48 45 704 **Contact:** Mr Ratko Žurić

ZÜRCHER BLICKENSTORFER & WIDMER (Switzerland)
Löwenstrasse 61, CH-8023 Zürich
Tel: +41 1 224 66 00 **Fax:** +41 1 224 66 24

If you can't find a firm here, see full profiles (pages 957-1481)

INDEXES

INDEX TO THE FIRMS

A

Firm Index

B

Profile: Contact details in the 'directory' section of the Guide. Table: Refers to the specialist lists in which the firm appears

C

Profile: Contact details in the 'directory' section of the Guide. **Table:** Refers to the specialist lists in which the firm appears

Firm Index

E

F

G

Firm Index

H

Profile: Contact details in the 'directory' section of the Guide. **Table:** Refers to the specialist lists in which the firm appears

I

J

K

Firm Index

L

M

Profile: Contact details in the 'directory' section of the Guide. **Table:** Refers to the specialist lists in which the firm appears

O

Profile: Contact details in the 'directory' section of the Guide. **Table:** Refers to the specialist lists in which the firm appears

Q

R

S

Firm Index

Profile: Contact details in the 'directory' section of the Guide. **Table:** Refers to the specialist lists in which the firm appears

Profile: Contact details in the 'directory' section of the Guide. **Table:** Refers to the specialist lists in which the firm appears

Profile: Contact details in the 'directory' section of the Guide. **Table:** Refers to the specialist lists in which the firm appears

CHAMBERS 4000 LEADING LAWYERS

A

A'Court, Alan S.J. (New Zealand)
Profile: p. 509
Banking & Finance ★★★★
Table: p. 507

Aalto, Johan (Finland)
Profile: p. 257
Corporate/M&A ★★★
Table: p. 257

Aalto-Setälä, Ilkka (Finland)
Profile: p. 257
Competition/Anti-trust ★★
Table: p. 256

Aaron, Max D. (Italy)
Profile: p. 423
Banking & Finance ★
Table: p. 414

Aaron, Roger S. (USA)
Profile: p. 848
Corporate/M&A ★★★★
Table: p. 820

Aasmul-Olsen, Henning (Denmark)
Profile: p. 240
Corporate/M&A ★★
Table: p. 239

Abang Zen, Dayang Feridahanam (Brunei Darussalam)
Profile: p. 163
Corporate/Commercial ★★★★
Table: p. 162

Abbé Yao, Vincent (Cote D'Ivoire)
Profile: p. 227
Corporate/Commercial ★★★★
Table: p. 227

Abdelly, Samir (Tunisia)
Profile: p. 678
Corporate/Commercial ★★★
Table: p. 678

Abdullah, Sheikh Khalid T (Yemen)
Profile: p. 917
Corporate/Commercial ★★★★
Table: p. 917

Abels, Michael (Germany)
Profile: p. 320
Communications: IT ★★★
Table: p. 307

Abreu, Miguel Teixeira de (Portugal)
Profile: p. 562
Corporate/M&A ★
Table: p. 560
Tax ★★★
Table: p. 562

Abugov, Lorne (Canada)
Profile: p. 183
Communications ★★★★
Table: p. 173

Abuhoff, Dan (USA)
Profile: p. 848
Competition/Anti-trust ★
Table: p. 808

Acard, Claire (France)
Profile: p. 282
Tax ★★★
Table: p. 281

Acedo, Carlos Eduardo (Venezuela)
Profile: p. 912
Corporate/M&A ★
Table: p. 909

Acker, Lawrence G. (USA)
Profile: p. 848
Energy & Natural Resources ★★★
Table: p. 827

Adalsteinsson, Jónas A. (Iceland)
Profile: p. 379
Corporate/Commercial ★★★
Table: p. 378

Adalsteinsson, Ragnar (Iceland)
Profile: p. 379
Corporate/Commercial ★★★
Table: p. 378

Adams, Simon (United Arab Emirates)
Profile: p. 692
Corporate/M&A ★★
Table: p. 690

Addis, Rosemary (Australia)
Profile: p. 82
Intellectual Property **U**
Table: p. 77

Adepetun, Sola (Nigeria)
Profile: p. 514
Energy & Natural Resources ★★★★
Table: p. 513

Adonnino, Pietro (Italy)
Profile: p. 423
Tax ★★★
Table: p. 422

Aeschimann, Jean-Paul (Switzerland)
Profile: p. 658
Banking & Finance ★★★★
Table: p. 654

af Petersens, Carl Johan (Sweden)
Profile: p. 646
Communications: Telecoms ★★★
Table: p. 642

Affleck, Donald S. (Canada)
Profile: p. 183
Competition/Anti-trust ★★★
Table: p. 175

Afridi, Ali (United Arab Emirates)
Profile: p. 692
Banking & Finance ★★
Table: p. 688

Agbor, Dan (Nigeria)
Profile: p. 514
Corporate/Commercial ★★
Table: p. 512

Agboyibo, Yawovi (Togo)
Profile: p. 675
Corporate/Commercial ★★★★
Table: p. 675

Agnoli, Marcello (Italy)
Profile: p. 423
Corporate/M&A ★★
Table: p. 419

Ago, Francesco (Italy)
Profile: p. 423
Banking & Finance ★★★★
Table: p. 414
Corporate/M&A ★★
Table: p. 419

Aguiar, Carlos (Portugal)
Profile: p. 562
Corporate/M&A ★
Table: p. 560

Aguirre, Fernando (Bolivia)
Profile: p. 139
Corporate/Commercial ★★★★
Table: p. 138

Aguirre, Ignacio (Bolivia)
Profile: p. 139
Corporate/Commercial ★★★
Table: p. 138

Agulhon, Vincent (France)
Profile: p. 282
Tax ★★
Table: p. 281

Ahern, Chris (Australia)
Profile: p. 82
Communications: IT ★★
Table: p. 69

Ahmad, Raufiud (Pakistan)
Profile: p. 531
Corporate/Commercial ★★★
Table: p. 529

Ahmed, Firoz (Canada)
Profile: p. 183
Tax ★★
Table: p. 182

Ahmed, Syed Ishtiaq (Bangladesh)
Profile: p. 112
Corporate/Commercial ★★★★
Table: p. 112

Aidoud, Mamoun (Algeria)
Profile: p. 51
Corporate/Commercial ★★★
Table: p. 51

Ainley, William M. (Canada)
Profile: p. 183
Corporate/M&A ★★★★
Table: p. 177

Ainsworth, Lesley (United Kingdom)
Profile: p. 741
Competition/Anti-trust ★
Table: p. 714

Airs, Graham (United Kingdom)
Profile: p. 741
Tax ★★★
Table: p. 739

Aitman, David (United Kingdom)
Profile: p. 741
Competition/Anti-trust ✪
Table: p. 714

Aizenstein, Neal (USA)
Profile: p. 848
Corporate/M&A **U**
Table: p. 813

Ajaib, Haridass (Singapore)
Profile: p. 597
Shipping ★★
Table: p. 595

Ajayi, Koyinsola (Nigeria)
Profile: p. 514
Corporate/Commercial ★★★★
Table: p. 512
Energy & Natural Resources ★★★
Table: p. 513

Ajumogobia, Odein (Nigeria)
Profile: p. 514
Corporate/Commercial ★★
Table: p. 512

Akai, Izumi (Japan)
Profile: p. 443
Banking & Finance: Japan Foreign ★★★
Table: p. 435
Capital Markets: Japan Foreign ★★★★
Table: p. 437

Akhlaghi, Behrooz (Iran)
Profile: p. 393
Corporate/Commercial ★★★★
Table: p. 393

Akinrele, Ade Dolapo (Nigeria)
Profile: p. 514
Corporate/Commercial ★★
Table: p. 512
Energy & Natural Resources ★★★
Table: p. 513

Aksen, Gerald (USA)
Profile: p. 848
Arbitration (International) ✪
Table: p. 785

Al Tamimi, Essam (United Arab Emirates)
Profile: p. 692
Corporate/M&A ★★★
Table: p. 690

Al Zaeem, Sharhabeel (Palestinian Territories)
Profile: p. 532
Corporate/Commercial ★★★★
Table: p. 532

Al-Khater, Hassan (Qatar)
Profile: p. 569
Corporate/Commercial ★★
Table: p. 568

Al-Nauimi, Najeeb (Qatar)
Profile: p. 569
Corporate/Commercial ★★
Table: p. 568

Al-Sayed, Moustafa (Syria)
Profile: p. 665
Corporate/Commercial ★★★★
Table: p. 665

Al-Shahry, Said Bin Saad (Oman)
Profile: p. 528
Corporate/M&A ★★★
Table: p. 527
Project Finance ★★★★
Table: p. 527

Albella, Sebastian (Spain)
Profile: p. 629
Banking & Finance ★★★
Table: p. 619

Albiñana Cilveti, César (Spain)
Profile: p. 629
Banking & Finance ★★
Table: p. 619
Corporate/M&A ★★★
Table: p. 624

Albrecht, Thomas (USA)
Profile: p. 848
Banking & Finance ★★★
Table: p. 787

Albuquerque, Rui (Portugal)
Profile: p. 562
Corporate/M&A ★
Table: p. 560

Aldashev, Niyaz (Kyrgyz Republic)
Profile: p. 455
Corporate/Commercial ★★★
Table: p. 455

Alder, Ashley (Hong Kong)
Profile: p. 362
Corporate/M&A ★★
Table: p. 357

Alegria, Hector (Argentina)
Profile: p. 60
Corporate/M&A ★★★
Table: p. 57

Aleksandrowicz, Mariusz (Poland)
Profile: p. 552
Tax ★★
Table: p. 551

Alemán, Alvaro (Panama)
Profile: p. 534
Corporate/Commercial ★★★
Table: p. 533

Alemán, Jaime (Panama)
Profile: p. 534
Corporate/Commercial ★★★★
Table: p. 533

Alemán, Roberto (Panama)
Profile: p. 534
Corporate/Commercial ★★★★
Table: p. 533

Alexander, Deborah M. (Canada)
Profile: p. 184
Corporate/M&A ★★★
Table: p. 177

Alexander, Graeme (Papua New Guinea)
Profile: p. 535
Corporate/Commercial ★★★
Table: p. 535

Alexander, Guy David (Papua New Guinea)
Profile: p. 535
Corporate/Commercial ★★★★
Table: p. 535

Alexander, Troy (USA)
Profile: p. 848
Project Finance ★★
Table: p. 837

Alexiadis, Peter (Belgium)
Profile: p. 127
Communications ★★★★
Table: p. 118

Alibhai, Zul (Kenya)
Profile: p. 453
Corporate/Commercial ★★★
Table: p. 453

Allan, Bill (United Kingdom)
Profile: p. 741
Competition/Anti-trust ★★★★
Table: p. 714

Allchurch, Matthew (Australia)
Profile: p. 82
Capital Markets ★★★
Table: p. 67

Allen, Francis (Canada)
Profile: p. 184
Corporate/M&A ★★
Table: p. 177

Allen, Maurice (United Kingdom)
Profile: p. 741
Banking & Finance ★★★
Table: p. 699

Allen-Jones, Charles (United Kingdom)
Profile: p. 741
Corporate/M&A ★★
Table: p. 717

KEY TO RANKINGS: ✪ = Star Individual ★★★★ = Top Band ★★★ = Second Band ★★ = Third Band ★ = Fourth Band **U** = Up and coming

Allendesalazar Corcho, Rafael (Spain)
Profile: p. 629
Competition/Anti-trust ★★★
Table: p. 622

Alonso, Felipe (Spain)
Profile: p. 629
Tax ★★★
Table: p. 628

Alvarado, Marcelo (Paraguay)
Profile: p. 537
Corporate/M&A ★★★★
Table: p. 537

Alvarez, José Julián (Puerto Rico)
Profile: p. 567
Corporate/Commercial ★★★★
Table: p. 567

Alves, Leonel (Macau)
Profile: p. 467
Corporate/Commercial ★★★★
Table: p. 467

Alves Pereira, José (Portugal)
Profile: p. 562
Corporate/M&A ★
Table: p. 560

Amado, Jose Daniel (Peru)
Profile: p. 541
Corporate/M&A ★★★
Table: p. 540

Amdur, Martin (USA)
Profile: p. 848
Tax ★
Table: p. 845

Amin, Pratap (United Kingdom)
Profile: p. 387
Corporate/M&A: India Foreign ★★★★
Table: p. 383
Project Finance: India Foreign ★★★★
Table: p. 386

Amory, Bernard E. (Belgium)
Profile: p. 127
Communications ✪
Table: p. 118

Andersen, Richard E. (USA)
Profile: p. 848
Tax ★★
Table: p. 845

Anderson, Jean E. (Canada)
Profile: p. 184
Banking & Finance ★
Table: p. 171

Anderson, Neil T. (United Kingdom)
Profile: p. 741
Corporate/M&A ★★
Table: p. 717

Anderson, Robert (United Kingdom)
Profile: p. 741
Intellectual Property ★★★★
Table: p. 729

Andersson, André (Sweden)
Profile: p. 646
Banking & Finance ★★★★
Table: p. 641

Andrezani, Luis Carlos (Brazil)
Profile: p. 152
Tax ★★
Table: p. 150

Andriani, Bertrand (France)
Profile: p. 282
Banking & Finance ★★★
Table: p. 265
Capital Markets ★★★
Table: p. 268
Project Finance ★★★★
Table: p. 277
Project Finance: Francophone Africa ★★★★
Table: p. 278

Andrieux, Jean-Pierre (France)
Profile: p. 282
Project Finance: Francophone Africa ★★★★
Table: p. 278
Tax ★★★
Table: p. 281

Andril, David (USA)
Profile: p. 849
Energy & Natural Resources ★
Table: p. 827

Ang, Andrew (Singapore)
Profile: p. 597
Banking & Finance ★★★★
Table: p. 586
Corporate/M&A ★★★
Table: p. 590

Ang, David (Singapore)
Profile: p. 597
Banking & Finance ★★
Table: p. 586

Ang, Vivian (Singapore)
Profile: p. 597
Shipping ★★★
Table: p. 595

Ang-Fong, Belinda (Singapore)
Profile: p. 597
Shipping ★★★★
Table: p. 595

Angle, Sean (Oman)
Profile: p. 528
Banking & Finance ★★★
Table: p. 526
Corporate/M&A ★★★★
Table: p. 527
Project Finance ★★★★
Table: p. 527

Angulo, Alejandro (Spain)
Profile: p. 629
Intellectual Property ★★★
Table: p. 626

Angus, John (Australia)
Profile: p. 82
Banking & Finance ★★★
Table: p. 65

Anjarwalla, Atiq (Kenya)
Profile: p. 453
Corporate/Commercial ★★★
Table: p. 453

Antakly, Farid (Venezuela)
Profile: p. 912
Corporate/M&A ★
Table: p. 909

Anwer, Khalid (Pakistan)
Profile: p. 531
Corporate/Commercial ★★
Table: p. 529

Anzola, J Eloy (Venezuela)
Profile: p. 912
Corporate/M&A ★★★
Table: p. 909
Energy & Natural Resources ★★★
Table: p. 911

Anzola, Oswaldo (Venezuela)
Profile: p. 912
Corporate/M&A ★★★★
Table: p. 909
Energy & Natural Resources ★★★★
Table: p. 911

Aoki, Kunio (Japan)
Profile: p. 443
Capital Markets ★★★
Table: p. 436

Ap Simon, Charles (United Kingdom)
Profile: p. 741
Corporate/M&A ★★
Table: p. 717

Apocalypse, Sidney (Brazil)
Profile: p. 152
Tax ★★★
Table: p. 150

Aquereburu, Coffi Alexis (Togo)
Profile: p. 675
Corporate/Commercial ★★★★
Table: p. 675

Aquila, Francis J. (USA)
Profile: p. 849
Corporate/M&A ★★
Table: p. 820

Aragão, Paulo Cezar (Brazil)
Profile: p. 152
Banking & Finance ★★★
Table: p. 142
Corporate/M&A ✪
Table: p. 147
Project Finance ★★
Table: p. 149

Arango, Ricardo Manuel (Panama)
Profile: p. 534
Corporate/Commercial ★★★
Table: p. 533

Aranovich, Fernando (Argentina)
Profile: p. 60
Competition/Anti-trust ★★★★
Table: p. 56

Arantes Pedroso, Filipa (Portugal)
Profile: p. 563
Competition/Anti-trust ★
Table: p. 559

Araujo, Federico (Venezuela)
Profile: p. 912
Corporate/M&A ★★★
Table: p. 909
Energy & Natural Resources ★★★
Table: p. 911

Araujo, Marcos (Spain)
Profile: p. 629
Competition/Anti-trust ★★★★
Table: p. 622

Archer, Quentin (United Kingdom)
Profile: p. 742
Communications: IT ★★
Table: p. 709

Argy, Philip (Australia)
Profile: p. 82
Communications: IT ★★
Table: p. 69
Intellectual Property ★★★
Table: p. 77

Arias, Francisco Armando (El Salvador)
Profile: p. 249
Corporate/Commercial ★★★★
Table: p. 249

Armitage, Charles (Australia)
Profile: p. 82
Tax ★★
Table: p. 81

Armitage, Peter (Australia)
Profile: p. 82
Communications: IT **U**
Table: p. 69

Armstrong, Fergus (Ireland)
Profile: p. 399
Corporate/M&A ★★
Table: p. 397

Armstrong, Neill (Botswana)
Profile: p. 140
Corporate/Commercial ★★★★
Table: p. 140

Arnaboldi, Luca (Italy)
Profile: p. 423
Corporate/M&A ★
Table: p. 419

Árnason, Hákon (Iceland)
Profile: p. 379
Corporate/Commercial ★★★★
Table: p. 378

Arnon, Yigal (Israel)
Profile: p. 410
Corporate/M&A ★★★★
Table: p. 409

Arocena, Juan Martín (Argentina)
Profile: p. 60
Communications ★★★
Table: p. 54

Arosemena, Carlos (Panama)
Profile: p. 534
Corporate/Commercial ★★★★
Table: p. 533

Arossa, Fabrizio (Italy)
Profile: p. 423
Competition/Anti-trust ★
Table: p. 417

Arpón de Mendívil, Almudena (Spain)
Profile: p. 629
Communications ★★★★
Table: p. 620
Competition/Anti-trust ★★★
Table: p. 622

Arquit, Kevin J. (USA)
Profile: p. 849
Competition/Anti-trust ★★★★
Table: p. 808

Art, Jean-Yves (Belgium)
Profile: p. 127
Competition/Anti-trust **U**
Table: p. 122

Arthur, John (Australia)
Profile: p. 82
Communications: IT ★★★★
Table: p. 69

Aschenbrenner, Martin (Czech Republic)
Profile: p. 235
Banking & Finance ★★★
Table: p. 232

Ashall, Pauline (Hong Kong)
Profile: p. 362
Capital Markets: Derivatives ★★★★
Table: p. 355

Ashman, Ian (Cayman Islands)
Profile: p. 203
Corporate/Commercial ★★★
Table: p. 203

Ashworth, Chris (United Kingdom)
Profile: p. 742
Corporate/M&A ★★★
Table: p. 717

Asmus, David (USA)
Profile: p. 849
Energy & Natural Resources ★★★★
Table: p. 829

Aspelin, Mikael (Finland)
Profile: p. 258
Corporate/M&A ★★
Table: p. 257

Astigarraga, José I. (USA)
Profile: p. 849
Arbitration (International) ★
Table: p. 785

Atanaskovic, John (Australia)
Profile: p. 82
Corporate/M&A ★★★★
Table: p. 73

Atkin, John (Australia)
Profile: p. 82
Corporate/M&A ★★
Table: p. 73

Atkins, Peter Allan (USA)
Profile: p. 849
Corporate/M&A ★★★★
Table: p. 820

Atkinson, Joe (United Kingdom)
Profile: p. 742
Shipping ★★
Table: p. 737

Atsumi, Hiroo (Japan)
Profile: p. 443
Banking & Finance ★★★★
Table: p. 433
Capital Markets ★★★
Table: p. 436

Auerbach, Reed (USA)
Profile: p. 849
Capital Markets: Securitisation ★★★
Table: p. 795

auf der Maur, Rolf (Switzerland)
Profile: p. 658
Communications ★★★
Table: p. 655

August, Gilles (France)
Profile: p. 282
Corporate/M&A ★
Table: p. 275

Austmann, Andreas (Germany)
Profile: p. 320
Corporate/M&A ★★
Table: p. 311

Avital, Gideon (Israel)
Profile: p. 410
Communications ★★★
Table: p. 407

Awoonor, Ekow (Ghana)
Profile: p. 336
Corporate/Commercial ★★
Table: p. 336

Azevedo Sette, Ordelio (Brazil)
Profile: p. 152
Corporate/M&A ★★★
Table: p. 147

B

Baadhio, Issous (Burkina Faso)
Profile: p. 166
Corporate/Commercial ★★★★
Table: p. 166

Bac, Pham Nghiem Xuan (Vietnam)
Profile: p. 916
Corporate/Commercial ★★★★
Table: p. 915

KEY TO RANKINGS: ✪ = Star Individual ★★★★ = Top Band ★★★ = Second Band ★★ = Third Band ★ = Fourth Band **U** = Up and coming

Bach, Albrecht (Germany)
Profile: p. 320
Competition/Anti-trust ★
Table: p. 309

Back, James (Zimbabwe)
Profile: p. 920
Corporate/Commercial ★★★★
Table: p. 919

Backman, Philip (Canada)
Profile: p. 184
Banking & Finance ★
Table: p. 171

Baecher, John (USA)
Profile: p. 849
Project Finance ★★★
Table: p. 837

Baechtold, Robert (USA)
Profile: p. 849
Intellectual Property ★★
Table: p. 831

Baer, William (USA)
Profile: p. 849
Competition/Anti-trust ★★★
Table: p. 811

Bagnall, James (Cayman Islands)
Profile: p. 204
Corporate/Commercial ★★★★
Table: p. 203

Bahl, Ajay (India)
Profile: p. 387
Corporate/M&A ★★
Table: p. 381

Baibarza, Volodymyr (Ukraine)
Profile: p. 687
Corporate/Commercial ★★
Table: p. 686

Baier, Anton (Austria)
Profile: p. 105
Arbitration (International) ★★★
Table: p. 102

Baillie, Brigitte (South Africa)
Profile: p. 612
Banking & Finance **U**
Table: p. 610

Baillie Q.C., James C. (Canada)
Profile: p. 184
Banking & Finance ★★★★
Table: p. 171
Corporate/M&A ✪
Table: p. 177

Baird, James (United Kingdom)
Profile: p. 742
Private Equity: Buyouts ★★★★
Table: p. 731

Baird, Jim (Hong Kong)
Profile: p. 362
Capital Markets: Debt & Equity ★★★
Table: p. 353
Corporate/M&A ★★★★
Table: p. 357

Baker, David (Greece)
Profile: p. 342
Shipping: Foreign Firms ★★
Table: p. 341

Baker Jr, William (USA)
Profile: p. 850
Energy & Natural Resources ★★★
Table: p. 827

Bakhnug, Rajab (Libya)
Profile: p. 461
Corporate/Commercial ★★★★
Table: p. 461

Balastík, Jirí (Czech Republic)
Profile: p. 235
Communications ★★★★
Table: p. 233

Baldissoni, Mauro (Albania)
Profile: p. 50
Corporate/Commercial: Albania Foreign ★★★★
Table: p. 49

Baldock, Anne (United Kingdom)
Profile: p. 742
PFI ✪
Table: p. 733

Baldwin, Mark (United Kingdom)
Profile: p. 742
Tax ★★
Table: p. 739

Balfour, Andrew (United Kingdom)
Profile: p. 742
Banking & Finance ★★★
Table: p. 699

Ballard, Richard (United Kingdom)
Profile: p. 742
Tax ★★★★
Table: p. 739

Balois, Edgardo (Philippines)
Profile: p. 543
Corporate/Commercial ★
Table: p. 542

Balsdon, John (Russia)
Profile: p. 577
Corporate/M&A ★★
Table: p. 574

Bancroft, Anthony (Australia)
Profile: p. 82
Corporate/M&A ★★★★
Table: p. 73

Banes, John (Germany)
Profile: p. 320
Capital Markets: Equity ★★
Table: p. 304

Banoff, Sheldon (USA)
Profile: p. 850
Tax ★
Table: p. 843

Bányaiová, Alena (Czech Republic)
Profile: p. 235
Corporate/M&A ★★
Table: p. 234

Banzubaze, Sylvestre (Burundi)
Profile: p. 167
Corporate/Commercial ★★★★
Table: p. 167

Bapfunya, Astère (Burundi)
Profile: p. 167
Corporate/Commercial ★★★
Table: p. 167

Baptista, Robert C., Jr (USA)
Profile: p. 850
Banking & Finance ★★★★
Table: p. 787

Barakonyi, Zoltán (Hungary)
Profile: p. 376
Corporate/M&A ★★
Table: p. 375

Barale, Lucille (Hong Kong)
Profile: p. 216
Corporate/M&A: China Foreign ★★★
Table: p. 213
Project Finance: China Foreign ★★★
Table: p. 215

Barbas, Constant (Netherlands)
Profile: p. 501
Corporate/M&A ★★★
Table: p. 496

Barbosa, Plinio (Brazil)
Profile: p. 152
Banking & Finance ★
Table: p. 142
Project Finance ★★
Table: p. 149

Bardet, Henri (France)
Profile: p. 282
Tax ★★★★
Table: p. 281

Baris, Paul (Israel)
Profile: p. 410
Corporate/M&A ★★
Table: p. 409

Barker, Bruce (Canada)
Profile: p. 184
Banking & Finance ★
Table: p. 171

Barnard, Stephen (United Kingdom)
Profile: p. 742
Corporate/M&A ★
Table: p. 717

Barnes, Jeffery A. (Canada)
Profile: p. 184
Corporate/M&A ★★★
Table: p. 177

Barr, Mike (USA)
Profile: p. 850
Energy & Natural Resources ★
Table: p. 827

Barratt, Jeffery (United Kingdom)
Profile: p. 742
Projects ★★★★
Table: p. 733

Barreira, Rui (Portugal)
Profile: p. 563
Tax ★★★
Table: p. 562

Barreto, Robson (Brazil)
Profile: p. 152
Corporate/M&A ★★
Table: p. 147

Barrett, Reg (Australia)
Profile: p. 82
Capital Markets ★★★★
Table: p. 67
Corporate/M&A ★★★
Table: p. 73

Barrett, Roderick (Canada)
Profile: p. 184
Banking & Finance ★★★
Table: p. 171

Barretto, Ricardo (Brazil)
Profile: p. 152
Communications ★★★
Table: p. 143

Barrilero, Eduardo (Spain)
Profile: p. 629
Tax ★★★
Table: p. 628

Barrocas, Manuel P. (Portugal)
Profile: p. 563
Corporate/M&A ★
Table: p. 560

Barron, Bill (Hong Kong)
Profile: p. 362
Capital Markets: Debt & Equity ★★★
Table: p. 353

Barros, Cristián (Chile)
Profile: p. 209
Banking & Finance ★★
Table: p. 206

Barros, Fernando (Chile)
Profile: p. 209
Corporate/M&A ★★
Table: p. 208

Barrow, Dean (Belize)
Profile: p. 134
Corporate/Commercial ★★★
Table: p. 134

Barrow, Denys (Belize)
Profile: p. 134
Corporate/Commercial ★★★★
Table: p. 134

Barrow, Peter (USA)
Profile: p. 850
Banking & Finance ★
Table: p. 787

Barry, Robert (United Kingdom)
Profile: p. 742
Intellectual Property ★
Table: p. 729

Barrymore, Stuart (Australia)
Profile: p. 83
Energy & Natural Resources ★★★
Table: p. 75

Bartel, Paul (USA)
Profile: p. 850
Competition/Anti-trust ★
Table: p. 808

Barter, Charles (United Kingdom)
Profile: p. 742
Private Equity: Buyouts ★★★
Table: p. 731

Bartlett, Sara (USA)
Profile: p. 850
Banking & Finance ★★★
Table: p. 787

Bartsch, Andreas (Germany)
Profile: p. 320
Capital Markets: Securitisation ★★
Table: p. 304

Barutciski, Milos (Canada)
Profile: p. 184
Competition/Anti-trust ★
Table: p. 175

Basdevant, Dominique (France)
Profile: p. 282
Project Finance ★★
Table: p. 277

Basgoz, Asli (Turkey)
Profile: p. 683
Banking & Finance: Turkey Foreign ★★★★
Table: p. 680
Project Finance: Turkey Foreign ★★★★
Table: p. 682

Bason Jnr, George (USA)
Profile: p. 850
Corporate/M&A ★★
Table: p. 820
Private Equity: Buyouts ★★★
Table: p. 834

Basso, Maristela (Brazil)
Profile: p. 152
Communications ★★
Table: p. 143

Bastianini, Marino (Italy)
Profile: p. 423
Corporate/M&A ★★
Table: p. 419

Bastianini, Nicolo (Italy)
Profile: p. 423
Corporate/M&A ★
Table: p. 419

Bastuck, Burkhard (Germany)
Profile: p. 320
Corporate/M&A ★
Table: p. 311

Bath, Vivienne (China)
Profile: p. 216
Corporate/M&A: China Foreign ★★
Table: p. 213

Batievsky, Jack (Peru)
Profile: p. 541
Banking & Finance ★★★★
Table: p. 538
Corporate/M&A ★★★
Table: p. 540

Batiuc, Olegh (Ukraine)
Profile: p. 687
Corporate/Commercial ★
Table: p. 686

Batliner, Herbert (Liechtenstein)
Profile: p. 462
Corporate/Commercial ★★★★
Table: p. 462

Batres, Cesar A. (Honduras)
Profile: p. 350
Corporate/Commercial ★★★★
Table: p. 350

Batware, Jean-Claude (Rwanda)
Profile: p. 579
Corporate/Commercial ★★★★
Table: p. 579

Baudon, Jacky (Russia)
Profile: p. 577
Corporate/M&A ★★★★
Table: p. 574
Energy & Natural Resources ★★★★
Table: p. 576

Baum, Axel H. (France)
Profile: p. 282
Arbitration (International) ★★
Table: p. 262

Bautista, Fernando (Spain)
Profile: p. 629
Banking & Finance ★★★★
Table: p. 619

Baxt, Robert (Australia)
Profile: p. 83
Competition/Anti-trust ★★★★
Table: p. 71

Baxter, Elena (France)
Profile: p. 282
Corporate/M&A ★★★
Table: p. 275

Baxter, Simon (Belgium)
Profile: p. 127
Competition/Anti-trust ★
Table: p. 122

Baylis, Stanley (USA)
Profile: p. 850
Energy & Natural Resources ★★★
Table: p. 827

Bean, Bruce W. (Russia)
Profile: p. 577
Corporate/M&A ★★
Table: p. 574
Energy & Natural Resources ★★★★
Table: p. 576

Beare, Tony (United Kingdom)
Profile: p. 742
Tax ★★
Table: p. 739

Beattie, David (Ireland)
Profile: p. 399
Corporate/M&A ★★
Table: p. 397

Beattie, Richard (USA)
Profile: p. 850
Corporate/M&A ★★★★
Table: p. 820
Private Equity: Buyouts ★★★★
Table: p. 834

Beaumont, Rupert (United Kingdom)
Profile: p. 743
Capital Markets: Securitisation ★
Table: p. 704

KEY TO RANKINGS: ✪ = Star Individual ★★★★ = Top Band ★★★ = Second Band ★★ = Third Band ★ = Fourth Band **U** = Up and coming

Beauvais, Richard (France)
Profile: p. 282
Tax ★★★
Table: p. 281

Beauvisage, Patrick (France)
Profile: p. 283
Corporate/M&A ★
Table: p. 275

Beccar Varela, Damian (Argentina)
Profile: p. 60
Corporate/M&A ★★
Table: p. 57

Becerra, Javier (Mexico)
Profile: p. 481
Corporate/M&A ★★★
Table: p. 480

Bechtold, Rainer (Germany)
Profile: p. 320
Competition/Anti-trust ✪
Table: p. 309

Becker, Ricardo (Brazil)
Profile: p. 152
Banking & Finance ★
Table: p. 142

Beddow, Simon (United Kingdom)
Profile: p. 743
Private Equity: Buyouts ★★
Table: p. 731

Bedford, Paul (United Kingdom)
Profile: p. 743
Capital Markets: Securitisation ★★★
Table: p. 704

Bednall, Timothy (Australia)
Profile: p. 83
Competition/Anti-trust ★★★
Table: p. 71
Corporate/M&A ★★
Table: p. 73
Energy & Natural Resources ★★
Table: p. 75

Bedrick, Mel (USA)
Profile: p. 850
Corporate/M&A ★
Table: p. 820

Beechey, John (United Kingdom)
Profile: p. 743
Arbitration (International) ★★★★
Table: p. 696

Beesley, Clive (Hong Kong)
Profile: p. 362
Shipping ★★★★
Table: p. 361

Behar, Reuven (Israel)
Profile: p. 410
Communications ★★★
Table: p. 407
Corporate/M&A ★★
Table: p. 409

Beharrell, Steven (United Kingdom)
Profile: p. 743
Energy: Oil and Gas ★★★
Table: p. 723

Behrmann, Tony (South Africa)
Profile: p. 612
Corporate/M&A ★★★★
Table: p. 611

Bell, Alan (Canada)
Profile: p. 185
Corporate/M&A ★★★
Table: p. 177

Bell, Thomas (USA)
Profile: p. 850
Private Equity: Fund Formation ★★★★
Table: p. 835

Bellagha, Adly (Tunisia)
Profile: p. 678
Corporate/Commercial ★★★★
Table: p. 678

Beller, Alan (USA)
Profile: p. 850
Capital Markets: Debt & Equity ★★★
Table: p. 793
Capital Markets: Derivatives ★★★
Table: p. 798

Bellhouse, John (United Kingdom)
Profile: p. 743
Projects ★★
Table: p. 733

Bellis, Jean-François (Belgium)
Profile: p. 127
Competition/Anti-trust ★
Table: p. 122

Bellis, Tim (United Kingdom)
Profile: p. 743
Corporate/M&A **U**
Table: p. 717

Belo-Osagie, Myma (Nigeria)
Profile: p. 514
Corporate/Commercial ★★
Table: p. 512

Beltramo, Susanna (Italy)
Profile: p. 423
Banking & Finance ★★
Table: p. 414

Ben Salah, Kamel (France)
Profile: p. 283
Banking & Finance ★★
Table: p. 265

Beneyto, José María (Spain)
Profile: p. 629
Competition/Anti-trust ★★
Table: p. 622

Benitez, Carlos (Spain)
Profile: p. 630
Tax ★
Table: p. 628

Benkert, Manfred (Germany)
Profile: p. 320
Tax ★
Table: p. 319

Bennett, Jeremy (Hong Kong)
Profile: p. 362
Shipping ★★
Table: p. 361

Bennett, Mary (USA)
Profile: p. 851
Tax ★
Table: p. 847

Benny, Jude (Singapore)
Profile: p. 598
Shipping ★★★
Table: p. 595

Bensouda, Amie (The Gambia)
Profile: p. 298
Corporate/Commercial ★★★★
Table: p. 298

Bensoussan, Alain (France)
Profile: p. 283
Communications: IT ★★★
Table: p. 271

Benton, David (United Kingdom)
Profile: p. 743
Capital Markets: Derivatives ★★★
Table: p. 706

Bentsi-Enchill, Kojo (Ghana)
Profile: p. 336
Corporate/Commercial ★★★
Table: p. 336

Bercovitz Rodriguez-Cano, Rodrigo (Spain)
Profile: p. 630
Intellectual Property ★★★
Table: p. 626

Berecz, Csaba (Hungary)
Profile: p. 376
Banking & Finance ★★★★
Table: p. 372

Berg, Eric L. (USA)
Profile: p. 851
Banking & Finance ★★★
Table: p. 791

Bergenstråhle, Erik (Sweden)
Profile: p. 646
Communications: Telecoms ★★★★
Table: p. 642

Berger, Julian (United Kingdom)
Profile: p. 424
Corporate/M&A ★
Table: p. 419

Berglöf, Per (Sweden)
Profile: p. 646
Corporate/M&A ★★
Table: p. 645

Berhane, Teferi (Eritrea)
Profile: p. 250
Corporate/Commercial ★★★★
Table: p. 250

Berhane, Yohannes (Eritrea)
Profile: p. 250
Corporate/Commercial ★★★★
Table: p. 250

Bériault, Yves (Canada)
Profile: p. 185
Competition/Anti-trust ★★★★
Table: p. 175

Beringer, Guy (United Kingdom)
Profile: p. 743
Corporate/M&A ★
Table: p. 717

Berkemeyer Jr, Hugo (Paraguay)
Profile: p. 537
Corporate/M&A ★★★★
Table: p. 537

Berlin, Edward (USA)
Profile: p. 851
Energy & Natural Resources ★★★
Table: p. 827

Berlin, Emily (USA)
Profile: p. 851
Banking & Finance ★
Table: p. 791

Bernardes-Neto, Horacio (Brazil)
Profile: p. 152
Corporate/M&A ★★
Table: p. 147

Bernardi, Maurizio (Italy)
Profile: p. 424
Corporate/M&A ★
Table: p. 419

Bernasconi, Michele (Switzerland)
Profile: p. 658
Communications ★★
Table: p. 655

Berner, Frederic G., JR. (USA)
Profile: p. 851
Energy & Natural Resources ★★
Table: p. 827

Bernhard, Stefan (Sweden)
Profile: p. 646
Communications: IT ★★★★
Table: p. 642

Bernitsas, Panayotis M (Greece)
Profile: p. 342
Corporate/M&A ★★★★
Table: p. 339

Bernotas, Egidijus (Lithuania)
Profile: p. 464
Corporate/Commercial ★★★
Table: p. 463

Bernstein, Bruce H. (USA)
Profile: p. 851
Banking & Finance ✪
Table: p. 787

Bersani, Matthew D. (China/Hong Kong)
Profile: p. 216, 363
Capital Markets: Debt & Equity ★★★★
Table: p. 353
Corporate/M&A: China Foreign ★★★
Table: p. 213

Bertelsen, Erik (Denmark)
Profile: p. 240
Competition/Anti-trust **U**
Table: p. 238

Bertelsen, Mark (USA)
Profile: p. 851
Communications: IT ★
Table: p. 805

Bertin-Mourot, Olivier (France)
Profile: p. 283
Banking & Finance ★★★
Table: p. 265
Capital Markets ★★★
Table: p. 268

Bertoldi, Alexandre (Brazil)
Profile: p. 152
Banking & Finance ★★
Table: p. 142
Corporate/M&A ★★★
Table: p. 147

Besa, Eugenio (Chile)
Profile: p. 209
Banking & Finance ★★
Table: p. 206

Besse, Antonin (France)
Profile: p. 283
Capital Markets ★★★
Table: p. 268

Besse, Eryl (France)
Profile: p. 283
Banking & Finance ★
Table: p. 265

Besson, Garry (Australia)
Profile: p. 83
Corporate/M&A ★
Table: p. 73

Bettah, Mahfoud Ould (Mauritania)
Profile: p. 477
Corporate/Commercial ★★★★
Table: p. 477

Beurier, Philippe (France)
Profile: p. 283
Corporate/M&A ★
Table: p. 275

Bezuidenhout, Jurgens (South Africa)
Profile: p. 612
Banking & Finance ★★★★
Table: p. 610

Bhakta, M.L. (India)
Profile: p. 387
Corporate/M&A ★★★★
Table: p. 381
Project Finance ★★
Table: p. 384

Bharucha, M.P. (India)
Profile: p. 387
Corporate/M&A ★
Table: p. 381

Biagosch, Patrick (Germany)
Profile: p. 320
Banking & Finance ★★
Table: p. 301

Bialik, Wojciech (Poland)
Profile: p. 552
Communications ★★★
Table: p. 547

Bialkin, Kenneth J. (USA)
Profile: p. 851
Corporate/M&A ★★
Table: p. 820

Bianchi, Daniel (Argentina)
Profile: p. 60
Energy & Natural Resources ★★
Table: p. 59

Bianchi, François M. (Switzerland)
Profile: p. 658
Banking & Finance ★★
Table: p. 654

Bibbings, Jennifer (United Arab Emirates)
Profile: p. 692
Corporate/M&A ★★
Table: p. 690

Bich, Nguyen Ngoc (Vietnam)
Profile: p. 916
Corporate/Commercial ★★★★
Table: p. 915

Bick, John (USA)
Profile: p. 851
Private Equity: Buyouts ★
Table: p. 834

Bickerstaff, Roger (United Kingdom)
Profile: p. 743
Communications: IT ★★
Table: p. 709

Bickerton, David (United Kingdom)
Profile: p. 743
Capital Markets: Debt & Equity ★
Table: p. 702
Projects ★
Table: p. 733

Bienenstock, Peter (Belgium)
Profile: p. 127
Banking & Finance ★★★
Table: p. 117
Corporate/M&A ★★★★
Table: p. 125

Bier, Jacob (Denmark)
Profile: p. 240
Banking & Finance ★★★★
Table: p. 237

Bieronski, Jaroslaw (Poland)
Profile: p. 552
Tax ★★
Table: p. 551

Bies, Bill (Canada)
Profile: p. 185
Tax ★
Table: p. 182

Biesheuvel, Mark (Netherlands)
Profile: p. 501
Competition/Anti-trust ★★★★
Table: p. 494

Bilger, Bruce (USA)
Profile: p. 851
Energy & Natural Resources ★★★★
Table: p. 829

Billot, Philippe (France)
Profile: p. 283
Banking & Finance ★★★
Table: p. 265
Capital Markets ★★★
Table: p. 268

Binder, Michael (Austria)
Profile: p. 105
Banking & Finance ★★★
Table: p. 103

Bird, Alistair (United Kingdom)
Profile: p. 743
Corporate/M&A ★
Table: p. 717

Birsel, Mahmut (Turkey)
Profile: p. 683
Banking & Finance ★★★★
Table: p. 679
Corporate/M&A ★★★
Table: p. 681

Biscozzi, Luigi (Italy)
Profile: p. 424
Tax ★★★
Table: p. 422

Bishop, Archie (United Kingdom)
Profile: p. 743
Shipping ✪
Table: p. 737

Bisnaire, J-P (Canada)
Profile: p. 185
Corporate/M&A ✪
Table: p. 177

Bjørnstad, Finn (Norway)
Profile: p. 521
Banking & Finance ★★★★
Table: p. 517

Black, Alan (United Kingdom)
Profile: p. 744
Projects ★★★★
Table: p. 733

Blackaby, Nigel (United Kingdom)
Profile: p. 744
Arbitration (International) ★★
Table: p. 696

Blackburn, Thomas (USA)
Profile: p. 851
Energy & Natural Resources ★
Table: p. 827

Blaikie, Allan (Australia)
Profile: p. 83
Tax ★★★★
Table: p. 81

Blake, Jonathan D. (USA)
Profile: p. 851
Communications: Regulatory ★★★★
Table: p. 803

Blake, Peter M.W. (United Kingdom)
Profile: p. 744
Energy: Electricity ★★★
Table: p. 725
Projects ★★★
Table: p. 733

Blakemore, Haywood (Singapore)
Profile: p. 598
Project Finance ★★
Table: p. 594

Blanch, Juliet (United Kingdom)
Profile: p. 744
Shipping ★★
Table: p. 737

Blanco, José-Luis (Spain)
Profile: p. 630
Corporate/M&A ★★★
Table: p. 624

Blanluet, Gauthier (France)
Profile: p. 283
Tax ★★
Table: p. 281

Blassberg, Franci (USA)
Profile: p. 851
Private Equity: Buyouts ★★★★
Table: p. 834

Bleck, Jorge Maria (Portugal)
Profile: p. 563
Corporate/M&A ★★★
Table: p. 560

Blessing, Mark (Switzerland)
Profile: p. 658
Arbitration (International) ★★★★
Table: p. 653

Blessing, Peter H. (USA)
Profile: p. 851
Tax ★★
Table: p. 845

Bliss, Nick (United Kingdom)
Profile: p. 744
PFI ✪
Table: p. 733

Bloch, François (France)
Profile: p. 283
Communications: Telecoms ★★
Table: p. 271

Block, Dennis (USA)
Profile: p. 852
Corporate/M&A ★★★
Table: p. 820

Blom, Marc (Netherlands)
Profile: p. 501
Banking & Finance ★★★
Table: p. 491

Blum, Oliver (Switzerland)
Profile: p. 658
Communications ★★★
Table: p. 655

Blumberg, Jean-Pierre (Belgium)
Profile: p. 127
Corporate/M&A ★★★
Table: p. 125

Blumers, Wolfgang (Germany)
Profile: p. 320
Corporate/M&A ★★
Table: p. 311

Blumkin, Linda R. (USA)
Profile: p. 852
Competition/Anti-trust ★★
Table: p. 808

Blunt, Gaire (Australia)
Profile: p. 83
Competition/Anti-trust ★★★★
Table: p. 71

Boardman, Nigel (United Kingdom)
Profile: p. 744
Corporate/M&A ✪
Table: p. 717

Bodrug, John D. (Canada)
Profile: p. 185
Competition/Anti-trust ★
Table: p. 175

Boe, Jørgen (Denmark)
Profile: p. 240
Corporate/M&A ★★
Table: p. 239

Boehrer, Charles (USA)
Profile: p. 852
Banking & Finance ★★
Table: p. 787

Boele, Bas (Netherlands)
Profile: p. 501
Banking & Finance ★★
Table: p. 491

Boga, Genc (Albania)
Profile: p. 50
Corporate/Commercial ★★★★
Table: p. 49

Bogdanovic, Mirko (Croatia)
Profile: p. 229
Corporate/Commercial ★★★★
Table: p. 228

Bogdanow, Alan (USA)
Profile: p. 852
Corporate/M&A ★★
Table: p. 824

Bogen, Andy (USA)
Profile: p. 852
Corporate/M&A ★★★★
Table: p. 825

Bohm, Rick (USA)
Profile: p. 852
Private Equity: Buyouts ★★
Table: p. 834

Boidman, Nathan (Canada)
Profile: p. 185
Tax ★★★
Table: p. 182

Boies, David (USA)
Profile: p. 852
Competition/Anti-trust ★★★★
Table: p. 808

Boivin, Charles J. (Canada)
Profile: p. 185
Banking & Finance ★★
Table: p. 171

Bokan, Teshome Gabre-Mariam (Ethiopia)
Profile: p. 253
Corporate/Commercial ★★★★
Table: p. 253

Bolger, Ciarán (Ireland)
Profile: p. 399
Corporate/M&A ★★
Table: p. 397

Bollmann, Hans (Switzerland)
Profile: p. 658
Corporate/M&A ★★
Table: p. 657

Boman, Lars (Sweden)
Profile: p. 646
Arbitration (International) ★★★
Table: p. 640

Bomchil, Maximo (Argentina)
Profile: p. 61
Corporate/M&A ★★
Table: p. 57
Energy & Natural Resources ★★★
Table: p. 59

Bompoint, Dominique (France)
Profile: p. 283
Corporate/M&A ★
Table: p. 275

Bond, Richard (United Kingdom)
Profile: p. 744
Corporate/M&A ★★★
Table: p. 717
Energy: Oil and Gas ★★★★
Table: p. 723

Bond, Stephen (France)
Profile: p. 283
Arbitration (International) ★★★
Table: p. 262

Bonelli, Franco (Italy)
Profile: p. 424
Corporate/M&A ★★★
Table: p. 419

Bonetti, Luis (Dominican Republic)
Profile: p. 243
Corporate/Commercial ★★★★
Table: p. 243

Bonifant, Sam (Singapore)
Profile: p. 598
Banking & Finance: Singapore Foreign ★★★★
Table: p. 588
Project Finance ★★★★
Table: p. 594

Bonilla, Guillermo (Guatemala)
Profile: p. 345
Corporate/Commercial ★★
Table: p. 345

Bonnasse, Antoine (France)
Profile: p. 284
Corporate/M&A ★
Table: p. 275

Bonvarlet, Patrick (France)
Profile: p. 284
Banking & Finance ★★
Table: p. 265
Capital Markets ★★★
Table: p. 268
Corporate/M&A ★★★
Table: p. 275
Project Finance ★★★
Table: p. 277

Bookbinder, Jeffrey (Botswana)
Profile: p. 140
Corporate/Commercial **U**
Table: p. 140

Boone, Michael (USA)
Profile: p. 852
Corporate/M&A ★★
Table: p. 824

Booth, Robert (Canada)
Profile: p. 186
Energy & Natural Resources ★★★★
Table: p. 180

Borde, Dominique (France)
Profile: p. 284
Corporate/M&A ★★
Table: p. 275

Bordeaux-Grouelt, Robert (France)
Profile: p. 284
Corporate/M&A ★
Table: p. 275

Borders, Thomas (USA)
Profile: p. 852
Tax ★
Table: p. 843

Borgese, Anthony (Australia)
Profile: p. 83
Communications: IT ★★★
Table: p. 69
Intellectual Property ★★
Table: p. 77

Borjas, Arminio F (Venezuela)
Profile: p. 912
Corporate/M&A ★★
Table: p. 909

Born, Gary (United Kingdom)
Profile: p. 744
Arbitration (International) ★★★
Table: p. 696

Börresen, Martin (Sweden)
Profile: p. 646
Corporate/M&A ★★★
Table: p. 645

Borthwick, Trevor (United Kingdom)
Profile: p. 744
Banking & Finance **U**
Table: p. 699

Bortoluzzi, Dominic (Australia)
Profile: p. 83
Energy & Natural Resources **U**
Table: p. 75

Boruc, Slawomir (Poland)
Profile: p. 552
Tax ★★
Table: p. 551

Bos, Jos A.M. (Netherlands)
Profile: p. 501
Energy & Natural Resources ★★
Table: p. 498

Bösch, René (Switzerland)
Profile: p. 658
Banking & Finance ★★★
Table: p. 654

Bosch, Wolfgang (Germany)
Profile: p. 320
Competition/Anti-trust ★
Table: p. 309

Boscoli, Altamiro (Brazil)
Profile: p. 153
Corporate/M&A ★★★★
Table: p. 147

Bossau, Hanno (Namibia)
Profile: p. 488
Corporate/Commercial ★★★★
Table: p. 488

Botelho Moniz, Carlos (Portugal)
Profile: p. 564
Competition/Anti-trust ★★★
Table: p. 559

Bouchard, Jean-Claude (France)
Profile: p. 284
Tax ★★★
Table: p. 281

Bouknight Jr, Lon (USA)
Profile: p. 853
Energy & Natural Resources ★★★★
Table: p. 827

Boullé, Philippe (Seychelles)
Profile: p. 584
Corporate/Commercial ★★★★
Table: p. 665

Bourtourault, Pierre-Yves (France)
Profile: p. 284
Tax ★★
Table: p. 281

Bovell, Christopher (Jamaica)
Profile: p. 432
Corporate/Commercial ★★★
Table: p. 431

Bowe, James F. (USA)
Profile: p. 853
Energy & Natural Resources ★★
Table: p. 827

Bowen, Stephen S. (USA)
Profile: p. 853
Tax ★★★★
Table: p. 843

Bowie, Scott (USA)
Profile: p. 853
Private Equity: Fund Formation ★★
Table: p. 835

Bowman, Marcus (United Kingdom)
Profile: p. 744
Shipping ★★
Table: p. 737

Bown, Christopher (United Kingdom)
Profile: p. 745
Private Equity: Buyouts ★★
Table: p. 731

Boxall, Andrew (Australia)
Profile: p. 83
Tax: Goods & Services Tax ★★★
Table: p. 81

Boyanov, Borislav (Bulgaria)
Profile: p. 165
Corporate/Commercial ★★★★
Table: p. 164

Boyce, John (Belgium)
Profile: p. 127
Competition/Anti-trust ★★★
Table: p. 122

Brabant, Stéphane (France)
Profile: p. 284
Project Finance: Francophone Africa ★★★★
Table: p. 278

KEY TO RANKINGS: ✪ = Star Individual ★★★★ = Top Band ★★★ = Second Band ★★ = Third Band ★ = Fourth Band **U** = Up and coming

Brach, Richard (USA)
Profile: p. 853
Project Finance ★★
Table: p. 837

Bradley, Edward (United Kingdom)
Profile: p. 387
Corporate/M&A: India Foreign ★★★
Table: p. 383

Braham, Edward (United Kingdom)
Profile: p. 745
Corporate/M&A ★★
Table: p. 717

Braithwaite, William J. (Canada)
Profile: p. 186
Corporate/M&A ★★★★
Table: p. 177

Branco, Luis (Portugal)
Profile: p. 564
Banking & Finance ★★★★
Table: p. 558

Brandenburger, Rachel (Belgium)
Profile: p. 127
Communications ★★★
Table: p. 118
Competition/Anti-trust ★★★
Table: p. 122

Brandes, Hanina (Israel)
Profile: p. 410
Communications ★★★
Table: p. 407
Corporate/M&A ★★
Table: p. 409

Brandford Griffith, Henri (France)
Profile: p. 284
Corporate/M&A ★★★
Table: p. 275

Brandi-Dohrn, Matthias (Germany)
Profile: p. 321
Intellectual Property: General ★★★
Table: p. 314

Brandow, John (USA)
Profile: p. 853
Capital Markets: Derivatives ★★★
Table: p. 798

Brands, Andrew D. (Canada)
Profile: p. 186
Banking & Finance ★★★
Table: p. 171

Brannan, Guy C.H. (United Kingdom)
Profile: p. 745
Tax ★★
Table: p. 739

Brannan, John (USA)
Profile: p. 853
Energy & Natural Resources ★★
Table: p. 829

Brausch, Freddie (Luxembourg)
Profile: p. 466
Corporate/Commercial ★★★
Table: p. 465

Bräutigam, Peter (Germany)
Profile: p. 321
Communications: IT ★
Table: p. 307

Bray, Michael (United Kingdom)
Profile: p. 745
Banking & Finance ★★★★
Table: p. 699

Braykov, Valentin (Bulgaria)
Profile: p. 165
Corporate/Commercial ★★★★
Table: p. 164

Breban, Yann (France)
Profile: p. 284
Communications: Telecoms ★★★
Table: p. 271

Brechan, Peter (Norway)
Profile: p. 521
Banking & Finance ★★
Table: p. 517

Breheny, Mark (Australia)
Profile: p. 83
Capital Markets ★
Table: p. 67

Brembati, Fabio (Italy)
Profile: p. 424
Communications ★★
Table: p. 415
Corporate/M&A ★
Table: p. 419

Brenner, Alan Gordon (Singapore)
Profile: p. 598
Project Finance ★
Table: p. 594

Brescia, Marco (Italy)
Profile: p. 424
Corporate/M&A ★★
Table: p. 419

Bresslaw, James (United Kingdom)
Profile: p. 745
Capital Markets: Securitisation ★
Table: p. 704

Bretton, Linda (United Kingdom)
Profile: p. 745
Energy: Oil and Gas ★
Table: p. 723

Breuninger, Gottfried (Germany)
Profile: p. 321
Tax ★★★★
Table: p. 319

Brewster, David (Australia)
Profile: p. 84
Competition/Anti-trust **U**
Table: p. 71

Brien, Peter (Hong Kong)
Profile: p. 363
Capital Markets: Debt & Equity ★★★
Table: p. 353

Bright, Christopher (United Kingdom)
Profile: p. 745
Competition/Anti-trust ✪
Table: p. 714

Brimson, Neil (France)
Profile: p. 284
Project Finance ★★★
Table: p. 277

Briner, Robert (Switzerland)
Profile: p. 658
Arbitration (International) ★★★★
Table: p. 653

Briner, Robert (Switzerland)
Profile: p. 658
Communications ★★
Table: p. 655

Brink, Johan (South Africa)
Profile: p. 612
Banking & Finance ★★★
Table: p. 610
Corporate/M&A ★★★
Table: p. 611

Briones Fernandez, Luis (Spain)
Profile: p. 630
Tax ★★★★
Table: p. 628

Briscoe, Simon N. (Singapore)
Profile: p. 598
Banking & Finance: Singapore Foreign ★★
Table: p. 588

Brito Pereira, Jorge (Portugal)
Profile: p. 564
Banking & Finance ★★
Table: p. 558

Brocas, Thierry (France)
Profile: p. 284
Corporate/M&A ★★
Table: p. 275

Brochier, Emmanuel (France)
Profile: p. 284
Corporate/M&A ★
Table: p. 275

Brodersen, Christian (Germany)
Profile: p. 321
Private Equity ★★★★
Table: p. 316

Brodey, Martin (Austria)
Profile: p. 105
Corporate/M&A **U**
Table: p. 104

Bromfield, Nick (Belgium)
Profile: p. 127
Competition/Anti-trust ★★
Table: p. 122

Bronfman, Jimena (Chile)
Profile: p. 209
Banking & Finance ★★★
Table: p. 206

Brooks, Tim (Australia)
Profile: p. 84
Communications: IT ★★
Table: p. 69

Brouwer, Onno (Netherlands)
Profile: p. 501
Competition/Anti-trust ★★★★
Table: p. 494

Brown, Barry J. (New Zealand)
Profile: p. 509
Corporate/M&A ★★★
Table: p. 508

Brown, Claude (United Kingdom)
Profile: p. 745
Capital Markets: Derivatives ★★★
Table: p. 706

Brown, David (United Kingdom)
Profile: p. 745
Intellectual Property ★★★★
Table: p. 729

Brown, Dickson (USA)
Profile: p. 853
Tax: Financial Products ★★★
Table: p. 845

Brown, Jane (United Kingdom)
Profile: p. 745
Capital Markets: Debt & Equity ★★
Table: p. 702

Brown, Jeremy (United Kingdom)
Profile: p. 745
Intellectual Property ★★★★
Table: p. 729

Brown, Leigh (Australia)
Profile: p. 84
Capital Markets ★★
Table: p. 67
Corporate/M&A ★★
Table: p. 73

Brown, Meredith (USA)
Profile: p. 853
Corporate/M&A ★★
Table: p. 820

Browne, Benjamin (United Kingdom)
Profile: p. 745
Shipping ★★
Table: p. 737

Brownlow, Jeremy (United Kingdom)
Profile: p. 745
Corporate/M&A ★★★
Table: p. 717

Brownstein, Andy (USA)
Profile: p. 853
Corporate/M&A ★
Table: p. 820

Bruchou, Enrique (Argentina)
Profile: p. 61
Banking & Finance ★★★
Table: p. 53
Corporate/M&A ★
Table: p. 57

Brun, Alexandra (Haiti)
Profile: p. 349
Corporate/Commercial ★★★★
Table: p. 349

Brun-Lie, Nicolas (Norway)
Profile: p. 521
Banking & Finance ★★
Table: p. 517

Bruna, Sergio (Brazil)
Profile: p. 153
Competition/Anti-trust **U**
Table: p. 145

Brundtland, Knut (Norway)
Profile: p. 521
Corporate/M&A ★★★★
Table: p. 519

Bruneau, Pierre-Pascal (France)
Profile: p. 284
Tax ★★
Table: p. 281

Brunet, François (France)
Profile: p. 284
Competition/Anti-trust ★
Table: p. 272

Bruse, Matthias (Germany)
Profile: p. 321
Corporate/M&A ★★
Table: p. 311
Private Equity ★★★
Table: p. 316

Bruski, Johannes (Germany)
Profile: p. 321
Banking & Finance ★★★
Table: p. 301

Bruusgaard, Christian (Norway)
Profile: p. 521
Energy & Natural Resources ★★★
Table: p. 520

Bruyneel, André (Belgium)
Profile: p. 127
Banking & Finance ★★★
Table: p. 117
Corporate/M&A ★★★
Table: p. 125

Brynmor Thomas, David (United Kingdom)
Profile: p. 745
Arbitration (International) ★★
Table: p. 696

Bryson, William E. (Taiwan)
Profile: p. 667
Corporate/Commercial ★★★
Table: p. 666

Bubenzer, Peter (Bermuda)
Profile: p. 136
Corporate/Commercial ★★★
Table: p. 136

Buchan, Robert (Canada)
Profile: p. 186
Communications ★★★
Table: p. 173

Buckworth, Nicolas (United Kingdom)
Profile: p. 746
Projects ★★
Table: p. 733

Buey Fernandez, Pablo Andres (Argentina)
Profile: p. 61
Corporate/M&A ★
Table: p. 57

Buhart, Jacques (France)
Profile: p. 284
Corporate/M&A ★
Table: p. 275

Buhl, Thomas (Germany)
Profile: p. 321
Corporate/M&A ★
Table: p. 311

Bühler, Michael (France)
Profile: p. 284
Arbitration (International) ★
Table: p. 262

Bukhamana, Thinawat (Thailand)
Profile: p. 673
Banking & Finance ★★
Table: p. 670

Bulhões Pedreira, José Luiz (Brazil)
Profile: p. 153
Corporate/M&A ★★★★
Table: p. 147
Tax ✪
Table: p. 150

Bunnag, Jayavadh (Thailand)
Profile: p. 673
Corporate/M&A ★★★★
Table: p. 672

Burgess, John (USA)
Profile: p. 853
Communications: Transactional (IT) ★★
Table: p. 801

Burggraaf, Jan Louis (Netherlands)
Profile: p. 501
Corporate/M&A ★★
Table: p. 496

Burke, Arthur (USA)
Profile: p. 853
Competition/Anti-trust ★
Table: p. 808

Burke, Frederick (Vietnam)
Profile: p. 916
Corporate/Commercial: Vietnam Foreign ★★★
Table: p. 916

Burke, Ray (USA)
Profile: p. 853
Shipping: Litigation ★★
Table: p. 841

Burke, Ted (USA)
Profile: p. 853
Project Finance ★★★
Table: p. 837

Burkill, Steven (Singapore)
Profile: p. 598
Shipping: Foreign Firms ★★
Table: p. 596

Burley, Rob (Japan)
Profile: p. 444
Banking & Finance: Japan Foreign ★★★★
Table: p. 435
Capital Markets: Japan Foreign ★★
Table: p. 437
Corporate/M&A: Japan Foreign ★★★
Table: p. 441
Project Finance ★★
Table: p. 442

 KEY TO RANKINGS: ✪ = Star Individual ★★★★ = Top Band ★★★ = Second Band ★★ = Third Band ★ = Fourth Band **U** = Up and coming

C

KEY TO RANKINGS: ✪ = Star Individual ★★★★ = Top Band ★★★ = Second Band ★★ = Third Band ★ = Fourth Band **U** = Up and coming

Caspi, Ram (Israel)
Profile: p. 410
Corporate/M&A ★★
Table: p. 409

Cass-Gottlieb, Gina (Australia)
Profile: p. 84
Communications: Telecoms ★★★
Table: p. 69
Competition/Anti-trust ★★★
Table: p. 71

Cassagne, Juan Carlos (Argentina)
Profile: p. 61
Corporate/M&A ★★★
Table: p. 57
Energy & Natural Resources ★★
Table: p. 59

Cassiano Santos, Pedro (Portugal)
Profile: p. 564
Banking & Finance ★★
Table: p. 558

Cassin, Jr., Vernon (Saudi Arabia)
Profile: p. 581
Banking & Finance ★★★
Table: p. 580
Corporate/M&A ★★★★
Table: p. 581

Cassingham, Paul (Taiwan)
Profile: p. 667
Corporate/Commercial ★★
Table: p. 666

Castan, Antonio (Spain)
Profile: p. 630
Intellectual Property ★★★
Table: p. 626

Castellani, Enrico (Italy)
Profile: p. 424
Banking & Finance ★★★★
Table: p. 414

Castelo Branco, Manuel (Portugal)
Profile: p. 564
Corporate/M&A ★★★
Table: p. 560

Castiel, Michael (Gibraltar)
Profile: p. 337
Corporate/Commercial ★★★★
Table: p. 337

Castillo, Francisco (Venezuela)
Profile: p. 913
Banking & Finance ★★★
Table: p. 908

Castle, Louise (Australia)
Profile: p. 84
Competition/Anti-trust ★★★
Table: p. 71

Castle, Peter R. (New Zealand)
Profile: p. 509
Corporate/M&A ★★★
Table: p. 508

Castro, Javier (Peru)
Profile: p. 541
Banking & Finance ★★★
Table: p. 538

Cave-Browne-Cave, Myles (United Kingdom)
Profile: p. 746
Energy: Oil and Gas ★★★★
Table: p. 723

Cavelier, Ernesto (Colombia)
Profile: p. 222
Corporate/M&A ★★
Table: p. 221

Cavelier, Germán (Colombia)
Profile: p. 222
Corporate/M&A ★★
Table: p. 221

Caxton-Martins, Afolabi (Nigeria)
Profile: p. 515
Corporate/Commercial ★★★
Table: p. 512

Celedonio, Lauro (Brazil)
Profile: p. 153
Competition/Anti-trust ★★
Table: p. 145

Celli, Riccardo (Belgium)
Profile: p. 128
Competition/Anti-trust ★
Table: p. 122

Celli Jr, Umberto (Brazil)
Profile: p. 153
Communications ★★★
Table: p. 143

Cera, Roberto (Italy)
Profile: p. 424
Banking & Finance ★★★
Table: p. 414
Corporate/M&A ★
Table: p. 419

Cerabino, Thomas M. (USA)
Profile: p. 854
Corporate/M&A ★
Table: p. 820

Cernejová, Alena (Slovakia)
Profile: p. 608
Corporate/Commercial ★★★★
Table: p. 607

Cerrahoglu, M Fadullah (Turkey)
Profile: p. 683
Corporate/M&A ★★★★
Table: p. 681

Cerrisola, Andres (Uruguay)
Profile: p. 906
Corporate/M&A ★★★
Table: p. 905

Cers, Gundars (Latvia)
Profile: p. 457
Corporate/Commercial ★★★★
Table: p. 456

Cervelló, José María (Spain)
Profile: p. 630
Tax ★
Table: p. 628

Cescon Avedissian, Maria Cristina (Brazil)
Profile: p. 153
Corporate/M&A ★★★
Table: p. 147

Cestr, Ivan (Czech Republic)
Profile: p. 235
Banking & Finance ★★★
Table: p. 232

Chabert, Pierre-Yves (France)
Profile: p. 285
Capital Markets ★★★★
Table: p. 268
Corporate/M&A ★★★
Table: p. 275

Chacon, Francisco (Costa Rica)
Profile: p. 226
Corporate/Commercial ★★★★
Table: p. 225

Chadwick, Roger (Zimbabwe)
Profile: p. 920
Corporate/Commercial ★★★
Table: p. 919

Chajec, Andrzej (Poland)
Profile: p. 552
Corporate/M&A ★★
Table: p. 548

Chan, Jeanette K. (China)
Profile: p. 216
Corporate/M&A: China Foreign ★★
Table: p. 213

Chan, Kenneth D.C. (China)
Profile: p. 216
Corporate/M&A: China Foreign ★★
Table: p. 213

Chandler, Albert (Thailand)
Profile: p. 673
Banking & Finance ★★★★
Table: p. 670

Chang, Ernest (Australia)
Profile: p. 84
Tax **U**
Table: p. 81

Chang, See Hiang (Singapore)
Profile: p. 598
Corporate/M&A ★★★★
Table: p. 590

Chao, Chukin (Cuba)
Profile: p. 230
Corporate/Commercial ★★★★
Table: p. 230

Chao, Howard (China)
Profile: p. 216
Corporate/M&A: China Foreign ★★★
Table: p. 213

Chao, Tien-yo (Hong Kong)
Profile: p. 363
Corporate/M&A ★★
Table: p. 357

Chaplin, Clive (Jersey)
Profile: p. 448
Corporate/Commercial ★★★
Table: p. 448

Chapman, Ian (Hong Kong)
Profile: p. 363
Banking & Finance ★★★★
Table: p. 352

Chappatte, Philippe (United Kingdom)
Profile: p. 746
Competition/Anti-trust ★★
Table: p. 714

Chareyre, Jacques (Gabon)
Profile: p. 297
Corporate/Commercial ★★★★
Table: p. 297

Charnley, William (United Kingdom)
Profile: p. 747
Corporate/M&A ★
Table: p. 717

Charpentier, Catherine (France)
Profile: p. 285
Tax ★
Table: p. 281

Chatzinoff, Howard (USA)
Profile: p. 854
Communications: Transactional (Telecoms) ★★★
Table: p. 801

Chauveau, Jean-François (Cote D'Ivoire)
Profile: p. 227
Corporate/Commercial ★★★
Table: p. 227

Chavez Escotto, Luis (Nicaragua)
Profile: p. 511
Corporate/Commercial ★★★★
Table: p. 510

Chedid, Nassib (Lebanon)
Profile: p. 459
Corporate/Commercial ★★★★
Table: p. 458

Chen, Ji Yuan (China)
Profile: p. 217
Project Finance ★★★★
Table: p. 214

Chen, John (Taiwan)
Profile: p. 667
Corporate/Commercial ★★
Table: p. 666

Chen, Kah Leng (Malaysia)
Profile: p. 472
Corporate/M&A ★★
Table: p. 471

Cheong, Kee Fong (Malaysia)
Profile: p. 472
Banking & Finance ★★★★
Table: p. 470
Corporate/M&A ★★★★
Table: p. 471

Cherry, James (Australia)
Profile: p. 84
Intellectual Property ★★
Table: p. 77

Chesler, Evan (USA)
Profile: p. 854
Competition/Anti-trust ★★
Table: p. 808

Chessa, Luigi (Italy)
Profile: p. 424
Banking & Finance ★★★
Table: p. 414
Corporate/M&A ★
Table: p. 419

Cheung, Yuk Tong (Hong Kong)
Profile: p. 363
Corporate/M&A ★★
Table: p. 357

Chew, Seng Kok (Malaysia)
Profile: p. 472
Corporate/M&A ★★★
Table: p. 471

Cheyne, David (United Kingdom)
Profile: p. 747
Corporate/M&A ✪
Table: p. 717

Chia, Cerintha (Singapore)
Profile: p. 598
Banking & Finance ★★
Table: p. 586

Chiam, Louis (Australia)
Profile: p. 84
Energy & Natural Resources **U**
Table: p. 75

Chibesakunda, Mwelwa (Zambia)
Profile: p. 918
Corporate/Commercial ★★
Table: p. 918

Chiew, James (Brunei Darussalam)
Profile: p. 163
Corporate/Commercial ★★★★
Table: p. 162

Chihambakwe, Simplicius (Zimbabwe)
Profile: p. 920
Corporate/Commercial ★★★
Table: p. 919

Childs, David (United Kingdom)
Profile: p. 747
Corporate/M&A ★★
Table: p. 717

Chima, Salman (Pakistan)
Profile: p. 531
Corporate/Commercial ★★★
Table: p. 529

Chimuka, Constantine (Zambia)
Profile: p. 918
Corporate/Commercial ★★★★
Table: p. 918

Chinn, Adam (USA)
Profile: p. 854
Tax ★★
Table: p. 845

Chinsangaram, Chinnavat (Thailand)
Profile: p. 673
Banking & Finance ★★★
Table: p. 670

Chipimo, Elias (Zambia)
Profile: p. 918
Corporate/Commercial ★★★
Table: p. 918

Chissick, Michael (United Kingdom)
Profile: p. 747
Communications: E-commerce ★★★
Table: p. 711
Communications: IT ★★
Table: p. 709

Chittmittrapap, Weerawong (Thailand)
Profile: p. 673
Corporate/M&A ★★★★
Table: p. 672

Cho, Yuen-Yee (Australia)
Profile: p. 84
Project Finance **U**
Table: p. 79

Choi, Dong Shik (South Korea)
Profile: p. 616
Corporate/Commercial ★★
Table: p. 614

Choi, Dyoung Seon (South Korea)
Profile: p. 616
Corporate/Commercial ★★
Table: p. 614

Choi, Paul L. (USA)
Profile: p. 854
Corporate/M&A ★
Table: p. 813

Chong, Steven (Singapore)
Profile: p. 599
Shipping ★★★★
Table: p. 595

Chow, Walter (Puerto Rico)
Profile: p. 567
Corporate/Commercial ★★★★
Table: p. 567

Christensen, Jan Schans (Denmark)
Profile: p. 240
Corporate/M&A ★★★★
Table: p. 239

Christiansen, Erling (Norway)
Profile: p. 521
Corporate/M&A ★★★
Table: p. 519

Christie, Alec (Myanmar)
Profile: p. 487
Corporate/Commercial: Myanmar Foreign ★★★★
Table: p. 487

Christie, James (Canada)
Profile: p. 186
Banking & Finance ★★★★
Table: p. 171

Christner, Anders (Sweden)
Profile: p. 647
Communications: IT ★★★★
Table: p. 642

Christopher, Steven (Hong Kong)
Profile: p. 363
Banking & Finance ★★★
Table: p. 352

Chrocziel, Peter (Germany)
Profile: p. 321
Communications: IT ✪
Table: p. 307
Intellectual Property: General ★★★
Table: p. 314

KEY TO RANKINGS: ✪ = Star Individual ★★★★ = Top Band ★★★ = Second Band ★★ = Third Band ★ = Fourth Band **U** = Up and coming

Chu, Morgan (USA)
Profile: p. 854
Intellectual Property ✪
Table: p. 833

Chu Hyun, Hong (South Korea)
Profile: p. 516
Corporate/Commercial: North Korea Foreign ★★★★
Table: p. 516

Chua, Danny (Singapore)
Profile: p. 599
Shipping ★
Table: p. 595

Chung, Julian (Hong Kong)
Profile: p. 363
Corporate/M&A ★
Table: p. 357

Churchill, Greg (Indonesia)
Profile: p. 392
Corporate/Commercial ★★★
Table: p. 391

Cigna, GianPiero (Albania)
Profile: p. 50
Corporate/Commercial: Albania Foreign ★★★
Table: p. 49

Citroen, René (Netherlands)
Profile: p. 501
Banking & Finance ★★
Table: p. 491

Citron, Diane (USA)
Profile: p. 854
Capital Markets: Securitisation ★★
Table: p. 795

Clagett, Brice (USA)
Profile: p. 854
Arbitration (International) ★
Table: p. 785

Clark, Adrian (United Kingdom)
Profile: p. 747
Corporate/M&A ★★
Table: p. 717

Clark, Charles (United Kingdom)
Profile: p. 747
Capital Markets: Debt & Equity ★
Table: p. 702

Clark, James E. (USA)
Profile: p. 855
Banking & Finance ★★★★
Table: p. 787

Clark, Jeff (Australia)
Profile: p. 85
Project Finance ★★★
Table: p. 79

Clark, Jim (USA)
Profile: p. 855
Capital Markets: Debt & Equity ★
Table: p. 793

Clark, Peter (USA)
Profile: p. 855
Shipping: Litigation ★★
Table: p. 841

Clark, Tim (United Kingdom)
Profile: p. 747
Corporate/M&A ★★
Table: p. 717

Clarke, Gillian (Barbados)
Profile: p. 113
Corporate/Commercial ★★★
Table: p. 113

Clarke, Julia (United Kingdom)
Profile: p. 747
Private Equity: Buyouts ★★★
Table: p. 731

Clarke, Simon (Australia)
Profile: p. 85
Tax: Goods & Services Tax ★★★
Table: p. 81

Clarke, Tim (United Kingdom)
Profile: p. 747
Corporate/M&A ★★
Table: p. 717

Cleary, Peter (Hong Kong)
Profile: p. 363
Project Finance ★★★★
Table: p. 359

Clemens, Mikael (Sweden)
Profile: p. 647
Communications: IT ★★★★
Table: p. 642

Clements, Andrew (Australia)
Profile: p. 85
Tax ★★★
Table: p. 81

Clifford, John Frederick (Canada)
Profile: p. 187
Competition/Anti-trust ★
Table: p. 175

Climan, Richard (USA)
Profile: p. 855
Communications: IT ★★★
Table: p. 805

Cloete, Robert (Swaziland)
Profile: p. 639
Corporate/Commercial ★★★★
Table: p. 639

Clough, Adrian (United Kingdom)
Profile: p. 747
Energy: Electricity ★★★
Table: p. 725

Clough, Michael (Australia)
Profile: p. 85
Tax ★★★
Table: p. 81

Clough QC, Mark (Belgium)
Profile: p. 128
Competition/Anti-trust ★
Table: p. 122

Coben, Jerry (USA)
Profile: p. 855
Corporate/M&A ★★
Table: p. 825

Coelho, Ricardo (Brazil)
Profile: p. 153
Banking & Finance ★
Table: p. 142

Coelho, Tulio (Brazil)
Profile: p. 153
Competition/Anti-trust ★★★
Table: p. 145

Cogan, John P. (USA)
Profile: p. 855
Energy & Natural Resources ★★★
Table: p. 829

Cogut, Charles (USA)
Profile: p. 855
Communications: Transactional (Telecoms) ★★★★
Table: p. 801
Corporate/M&A ★★★★
Table: p. 820
Private Equity: Buyouts ★★★
Table: p. 834

Cohen, Ben (USA)
Profile: p. 855
Tax ★★
Table: p. 845

Cohen, Evan (Hong Kong)
Profile: p. 363
Project Finance ★★★
Table: p. 359

Cohen, H. Rodgin (USA)
Profile: p. 855
Corporate/M&A ★★★★
Table: p. 820

Cohen, Laurence J. (United Kingdom)
Profile: p. 748
Intellectual Property ★★★
Table: p. 729

Cohen, Michael Marks (USA)
Profile: p. 855
Shipping: Litigation ★★★
Table: p. 841

Cohen, Ralph (United Kingdom)
Profile: p. 748
Competition/Anti-trust ★
Table: p. 714

Cohen, Shlomo (Israel)
Profile: p. 410
Communications ★★★★
Table: p. 407

Cohen-Tanugi, Laurent (France)
Profile: p. 285
Competition/Anti-trust ★
Table: p. 272

Colbridge, Christopher (United Kingdom)
Profile: p. 748
Arbitration (International) ★★
Table: p. 696

Cole, Thomas A. (USA)
Profile: p. 855
Corporate/M&A ✪
Table: p. 813

Coleman, Lynn R. (USA)
Profile: p. 855
Energy & Natural Resources ★★★★
Table: p. 827

Colja, Marjan (Slovenia)
Profile: p. 608
Corporate/Commercial ★★★★
Table: p. 608

Coll, Gerard (Ireland)
Profile: p. 399
Corporate/M&A ★
Table: p. 397

Collier, Edward (Trinidad & Tobago)
Profile: p. 677
Corporate/Commercial ★★★★
Table: p. 676

Collins, Anthony E. (Ireland)
Profile: p. 400
Corporate/M&A ★
Table: p. 397

Collins, Damian (Belgium)
Profile: p. 400
Competition/Anti-trust ★★★★
Table: p. 396

Collins, E. Michael (USA)
Profile: p. 855
Private Equity: Fund Formation ★★
Table: p. 835

Collins, John (Australia)
Profile: p. 85
Intellectual Property ★
Table: p. 77

Collins, Joseph P. (USA)
Profile: p. 855
Capital Markets: Derivatives ★★
Table: p. 798

Collins, Paul (Canada)
Profile: p. 187
Competition/Anti-trust ★
Table: p. 175

Collins, Philip (Belgium)
Profile: p. 128
Competition/Anti-trust ★★★★
Table: p. 122

Collins, Wayne Dale (USA)
Profile: p. 856
Competition/Anti-trust ★★
Table: p. 808

Collis, John C.R. (Bermuda)
Profile: p. 136
Corporate/Commercial ★★★★
Table: p. 136

Colonna d'Istria, Antoine (France)
Profile: p. 285
Tax ★★
Table: p. 281

Cominos, David (Australia)
Profile: p. 85
Tax ★★★★
Table: p. 81

Compagnoni, Marco (United Kingdom)
Profile: p. 748
Private Equity: Buyouts ★★★
Table: p. 731

Comtois, Yves (Canada)
Profile: p. 187
Competition/Anti-trust **U**
Table: p. 175

Concha, Carlos (Chile)
Profile: p. 209
Corporate/M&A ★★
Table: p. 208

Condon, Creighton (USA)
Profile: p. 856
Communications: Transactional (Telecoms) ★★★★
Table: p. 801
Corporate/M&A ★★
Table: p. 820

Condon, Wayne (Australia)
Profile: p. 85
Intellectual Property ★★★
Table: p. 77

Conley, William (Australia)
Profile: p. 85
Corporate/M&A ★
Table: p. 73

Conlon, Michael (USA)
Profile: p. 856
Corporate/M&A ★★
Table: p. 824

Conrad Jr, Winthrop (USA)
Profile: p. 856
Capital Markets: Debt & Equity ★
Table: p. 793

Consentino, Arion (Brazil)
Profile: p. 153
Tax ★★
Table: p. 150

Contratto, Dana (USA)
Profile: p. 856
Energy & Natural Resources ★★
Table: p. 827

Coogans, David (Hong Kong)
Profile: p. 363
Shipping ★
Table: p. 361

Cook, John (United Kingdom)
Profile: p. 748
Competition/Anti-trust ★
Table: p. 714

Cook, Lindsay (Zimbabwe)
Profile: p. 920
Corporate/Commercial ★★★★
Table: p. 919

Cook, Trevor (United Kingdom)
Profile: p. 748
Intellectual Property ✪
Table: p. 729

Cooke, Adam (United Kingdom)
Profile: p. 748
Intellectual Property ★★★
Table: p. 729

Cooke, David W.P. (Bermuda)
Profile: p. 137
Corporate/Commercial ★★★
Table: p. 136

Cooke, Stephen (United Kingdom)
Profile: p. 748
Corporate/M&A ★★★
Table: p. 717

Cooper, Bruce (Singapore)
Profile: p. 599
Banking & Finance: Singapore Foreign ★★★
Table: p. 588
Project Finance ★★★
Table: p. 594

Cooper, Jim (USA)
Profile: p. 856
Banking & Finance ★★★
Table: p. 791

Cooper, Stephen H. (USA)
Profile: p. 856
Capital Markets: Debt & Equity ★
Table: p. 793

Cooperstein, Gary P. (USA)
Profile: p. 856
Corporate/M&A ★
Table: p. 820

Coppin, Jonathan (United Kingdom)
Profile: p. 749
Corporate/M&A **U**
Table: p. 717

Cordero, Carlos (Panama)
Profile: p. 534
Corporate/Commercial ★★★
Table: p. 533

Cork, Rod (France)
Profile: p. 285
Banking & Finance ★★
Table: p. 265

Corlett, Andrew (Isle of Man)
Profile: p. 405
Corporate/Commercial ★★★★
Table: p. 405

Cornelis, Ludo (Belgium)
Profile: p. 128
Corporate/M&A ★★★
Table: p. 125

Cornish, Robert (Australia)
Profile: p. 86
Project Finance ★★★
Table: p. 79

Cornwell, Phillip (Australia)
Profile: p. 86
Banking & Finance ★★★★
Table: p. 65
Project Finance ★★★★
Table: p. 79

Coronel, César (Ecuador)
Profile: p. 245
Corporate/Commercial ★★★★
Table: p. 244

Corrigan, Michael (Australia)
Profile: p. 86
Competition/Anti-trust ★★
Table: p. 71

Cortes-Rocha, Jaime (Mexico)
Profile: p. 481
Corporate/M&A ★★★
Table: p. 480

Cot, Jean-Mathieu (France)
Profile: p. 285
Competition/Anti-trust ★★★
Table: p. 272

Cotait, Elinor (Brazil)
Profile: p. 153
Communications ★★★
Table: p. 143

Cotoni, Jean-Claude (France)
Profile: p. 285

Corporate/M&A ★
Table: p. 275

Cottis, Matthew (United Kingdom)
Profile: p. 749
Banking & Finance ★
Table: p. 699

Coudin, Pascal (France)
Profile: p. 285
Tax ★★★
Table: p. 281

Coulombe, Gérard (Canada)
Profile: p. 187
Tax ★★
Table: p. 182

Coulter, David (United Kingdom)
Profile: p. 749
PFI ★★★
Table: p. 733

Courtenay, Derek (Belize)
Profile: p. 134
Corporate/Commercial ★★★★
Table: p. 134

Cousi, Olivier (France)
Profile: p. 285
Communications: Telecoms ★★★
Table: p. 271

Couto, Margarida (Portugal)
Profile: p. 564
Banking & Finance ★
Table: p. 558

Coutrelis, André (France)
Profile: p. 285
Competition/Anti-trust ★
Table: p. 272

Cowan, Cameron (USA)
Profile: p. 856
Capital Markets: Securitisation ★★★
Table: p. 795

Cowan, Matthew (United Kingdom)
Profile: p. 749
Communications: E-commerce ★★
Table: p. 711

Coyet, Johan (Sweden)
Profile: p. 647
Competition/Anti-trust ★★★★
Table: p. 644

Craig, William Laurence (France)
Profile: p. 285
Arbitration (International) ★★★
Table: p. 262

Crampton, Paul S. (Canada)
Profile: p. 187
Competition/Anti-trust ★★★
Table: p. 175

Crane, David (United Kingdom)
Profile: p. 749
Projects ★
Table: p. 733

Cranfield, Richard (United Kingdom)
Profile: p. 749
Corporate/M&A ★★
Table: p. 717

Craven, Clive (Australia)
Profile: p. 86
Project Finance ★★
Table: p. 79

Craven, George (USA)
Profile: p. 857
Tax ★★★
Table: p. 843

Crawford, Sue (United Kingdom)
Profile: p. 749
Tax ★★
Table: p. 739

Crean, Mark (Australia)
Profile: p. 86
Communications: Telecoms ★★★
Table: p. 69

Creed, Adrian (United Arab Emirates)
Profile: p. 692
Project Finance ★★★★
Table: p. 691

Creed, Nicholas (Australia)
Profile: p. 86
Project Finance **U**
Table: p. 79

Cremades, Javier (Spain)
Profile: p. 630
Communications ★★★
Table: p. 620

Cresswell, Corinna (Hong Kong)
Profile: p. 364
Shipping ★★★
Table: p. 361

Creus, Antonio (Spain)
Profile: p. 630
Competition/Anti-trust ★★★
Table: p. 622

Croall, Philip (United Kingdom)
Profile: p. 749
Arbitration (International) ★★
Table: p. 696

Croff, Carlo (Italy)
Profile: p. 424
Corporate/M&A ★★
Table: p. 419

Cron, Kevin (South Africa)
Profile: p. 612
Banking & Finance ★★★★
Table: p. 610
Corporate/M&A ★★★★
Table: p. 611

Cron, Thomas (Germany)
Profile: p. 321
Capital Markets: Debt ★★
Table: p. 303

Crook, Vivien (Hong Kong)
Profile: p. 364
Communications ★★★★
Table: p. 356

Crothers, John (France)
Profile: p. 286
Project Finance ★★
Table: p. 277

Crozer, George K. (Hong Kong)
Profile: p. 217, 364
Project Finance ★★★★
Table: p. 359
Project Finance: China Foreign ★★★
Table: p. 215

Crumbaugh, David G. (USA)
Profile: p. 857
Banking & Finance ★★★★
Table: p. 787

Crump, Richard (United Kingdom)
Profile: p. 749
Shipping ★★★★
Table: p. 737

Cruz Amoros, Miguel (Spain)
Profile: p. 630
Tax ★★★★
Table: p. 628

Csekes, Erika (Slovakia)
Profile: p. 608
Corporate/Commercial ★★★
Table: p. 607

Cuatrecasas, Emilio (Spain)
Profile: p. 630
Corporate/M&A ★★★
Table: p. 624

Cugia di Sant'Orsola, Fabrizio (Italy)
Profile: p. 424
Communications ★
Table: p. 415

Cullen, Gary (USA)
Profile: p. 857
Corporate/M&A ★
Table: p. 813

Cullinane, Lee (United Kingdom)
Profile: p. 749
Banking & Finance ★
Table: p. 699

Culotta, Ken (USA)
Profile: p. 857
Energy & Natural Resources ★★
Table: p. 829

Cunha, Rui (Macau)
Profile: p. 467
Corporate/Commercial ★★★★
Table: p. 467

Cunningham, Dan (USA)
Profile: p. 857
Capital Markets: Derivatives ★★★★
Table: p. 798
Corporate/M&A ★
Table: p. 820

Curran, John (Canada)
Profile: p. 187
Energy & Natural Resources ★★★
Table: p. 180

Currie, Gordon (Canada)
Profile: p. 187
Corporate/M&A ★
Table: p. 177

Curtis, John (Australia)
Profile: p. 86
Project Finance ★★★
Table: p. 79

Curtis, Susan M. (USA)
Profile: p. 857
Capital Markets: Securitisation ★★★
Table: p. 795

Cuthbert, Michael (United Kingdom)
Profile: p. 749
Energy: Mining ★★★
Table: p. 725

Cuthbertson, John (Canada)
Profile: p. 187
Energy & Natural Resources ★★
Table: p. 180

Cutler, Andrew (Hong Kong)
Profile: p. 364
Shipping ★
Table: p. 361

Cutting, Michael (United Kingdom)
Profile: p. 749
Competition/Anti-trust **U**
Table: p. 714

Czabanski, Jacek (Poland)
Profile: p. 552
Banking & Finance ★★
Table: p. 545

D

D'Alberti, Silvia (Italy)
Profile: p. 424
Competition/Anti-trust ★★
Table: p. 417

D'Alimonte, John S. (USA)
Profile: p. 857
Communications: Transactional (Telecoms) ★★★★
Table: p. 801

d'Angelo, Davide (Italy)
Profile: p. 424
Communications ★★★
Table: p. 415

d'Hérouville, Jean-Guillaume (France)
Profile: p. 286
Capital Markets ★
Table: p. 268

d'Ormesson, Olivier (France)
Profile: p. 286
Competition/Anti-trust ★★★
Table: p. 272

da Cruz Vilaça, José Luís (Portugal)
Profile: p. 564
Competition/Anti-trust ★★★
Table: p. 559

da Silva, Daniel (Mozambique)
Profile: p. 486
Corporate/Commercial ★★★★
Table: p. 486

da Silveira Lobo, Carlos Alberto (Brazil)
Profile: p. 153
Corporate/M&A ★★
Table: p. 147

Dabo, Ousainou (The Gambia)
Profile: p. 298
Corporate/Commercial ★★★★
Table: p. 298

Dadachanji, J.B. (India)
Profile: p. 387
Corporate/M&A ★
Table: p. 381

Daeniker, Daniel (Switzerland)
Profile: p. 659
Banking & Finance ★★
Table: p. 654

Dalfen, Charles (Canada)
Profile: p. 187
Communications ★★★
Table: p. 173

Dalla Vedova, Marco (Italy)
Profile: p. 424
Communications ★★★
Table: p. 415

Dallal, Mubadda (Jordan)
Profile: p. 450
Corporate/Commercial ★★★
Table: p. 450

Dallas, James (United Kingdom)
Profile: p. 749
Energy: Oil and Gas ★★★★
Table: p. 723

Dallmann, Armin (Austria)
Profile: p. 105
Banking & Finance ★★★
Table: p. 103

Damm, Wilhelm (Norway)
Profile: p. 521
Banking & Finance ★★★
Table: p. 517

Dang, Nguyen Thi (Vietnam)
Profile: p. 917
Corporate/Commercial ★★★
Table: p. 915

Danielsson, Karl-Erik (Sweden)
Profile: p. 647
Banking & Finance ★★★
Table: p. 641

Danilowicz, Witold (Poland)
Profile: p. 552
Corporate/M&A ★★★
Table: p. 548

Dankó, Péter (Hungary)
Profile: p. 376
Banking & Finance ★★★★
Table: p. 372

Danos, Trevor (Australia)
Profile: p. 86
Banking & Finance ★
Table: p. 65

Danusso, Massimiliano (Italy)
Profile: p. 424
Banking & Finance ★★
Table: p. 414
Corporate/M&A ★★
Table: p. 419
Tax ★
Table: p. 422

Dany, Mireille (France)
Profile: p. 286
Competition/Anti-trust ★
Table: p. 272

Danziger, Yoram (Israel)
Profile: p. 410
Corporate/M&A ★
Table: p. 409

Daoud, Wabat (Djibouti)
Profile: p. 242
Corporate/Commercial ★★★
Table: p. 242

Darrois, Jean-Michel (France)
Profile: p. 286
Corporate/M&A ★★★★
Table: p. 275

Darton, Robin (Hong Kong)
Profile: p. 364
Shipping ★
Table: p. 361

Dass, George Anthony David (Malaysia)
Profile: p. 472
Corporate/M&A ★★
Table: p. 471

Davenport, Kirk A. (USA)
Profile: p. 857
Capital Markets: Debt & Equity ★★★
Table: p. 793

Davey, Henry (United Kingdom)
Profile: p. 749
Energy: Electricity ★★
Table: p. 725
Energy: Oil and Gas ★★
Table: p. 723

David, Martin (Singapore)
Profile: p. 599
Project Finance ★★
Table: p. 594

David, Patricia (Malaysia)
Profile: p. 472
Banking & Finance ★★★★
Table: p. 470

Davidge, Marlene (Canada)
Profile: p. 187
Corporate/M&A ★
Table: p. 177

Davidson, Gordon (USA)
Profile: p. 857
Communications: IT ★★★★
Table: p. 805

Davidson, John (United Kingdom)
Profile: p. 750
Corporate/M&A ★
Table: p. 717

Davies, Don (Canada)
Profile: p. 187
Energy & Natural Resources ★★★
Table: p. 180

Davies, Isabel (United Kingdom)
Profile: p. 750
Intellectual Property ★★★★
Table: p. 729

KEY TO RANKINGS: ✪ = Star Individual ★★★★ = Top Band ★★★ = Second Band ★★ = Third Band ★ = Fourth Band **U** = Up and coming

Davies, John (Belgium)
Profile: p. 128
Competition/Anti-trust ★★★★
Table: p. 122

Davies, Michael (Poland)
Profile: p. 552
Corporate/M&A ★★
Table: p. 548
Energy & Natural Resources ★★★★
Table: p. 550

Davies, Roger (United Kingdom)
Profile: p. 750
Energy: Oil and Gas ★★★
Table: p. 723

Davis, James (United Kingdom)
Profile: p. 750
Corporate/M&A ★
Table: p. 717

Davis, Jim (USA)
Profile: p. 858
Intellectual Property ★
Table: p. 831

Davis, Platt (USA)
Profile: p. 858
Energy & Natural Resources ★★
Table: p. 829

Davis, Scott (USA)
Profile: p. 858
Corporate/M&A ★★★
Table: p. 813

Davis, Steven (United Kingdom)
Profile: p. 750
Private Equity: Buyouts ★★
Table: p. 731

Davoudet, Eric (France)
Profile: p. 286
Tax ★★
Table: p. 281

Dawson, Darryl (Australia)
Profile: p. 86
Arbitration (International) ★★★
Table: p. 64

Day, Lloyd (Rusty) (USA)
Profile: p. 858
Intellectual Property ★★★★
Table: p. 833

Dayes, Simon (Romania)
Profile: p. 572
Banking & Finance ★★★★
Table: p. 570
Corporate/M&A ★★★
Table: p. 571

de Abreu, Jorge (Portugal)
Profile: p. 564
Corporate/M&A ★★
Table: p. 560

de Almeida Prado, Fernando (Brazil)
Profile: p. 153
Banking & Finance ★
Table: p. 142

de Alvarado, Gloria Maria (Nicaragua)
Profile: p. 511
Corporate/Commercial ★★★★
Table: p. 510

de Andrade, Mario Cezar (Brazil)
Profile: p. 154
Banking & Finance ★
Table: p. 142

de Araujo Cintra, Antonio Felix (Brazil)
Profile: p. 154
Banking & Finance ★★
Table: p. 142
Project Finance ★★
Table: p. 149

De Beaufort, Hector (Netherlands)
Profile: p. 501
Corporate/M&A ★★★
Table: p. 496

de Belder, Richard T. (United Arab Emirates)
Profile: p. 693
Banking & Finance ★★★
Table: p. 688

de Boisséson, Matthieu (France)
Profile: p. 286
Arbitration (International) ★
Table: p. 262

De Bouter, Eduard C. (Netherlands)
Profile: p. 501
Banking & Finance ★
Table: p. 491

de Brosses, Arnaud (France)
Profile: p. 286
Tax ★
Table: p. 281

de Cárdenas, Carlos (Spain)
Profile: p. 630
Banking & Finance ★★
Table: p. 619

de Carlos Bertrán, Luis (Spain)
Profile: p. 630
Banking & Finance ★★★★
Table: p. 619

De Cort, André (Russia)
Profile: p. 577
Corporate/M&A ★★
Table: p. 574

de Coulon, Philippe (Switzerland)
Profile: p. 659
Arbitration (International) ★★
Table: p. 653

de Cunto, Rafael (Brazil)
Profile: p. 154
Communications ★★
Table: p. 143

de Feydeau, Henri (France)
Profile: p. 286
Tax ★
Table: p. 281

de Francisco, José Antonio (Spain)
Profile: p. 630
Tax ★
Table: p. 628

de Gabriele, Louis (Malta)
Profile: p. 475
Corporate/Commercial ★★★
Table: p. 475

De Geer, Carl Gustaf (Sweden)
Profile: p. 647
Banking & Finance ★★★
Table: p. 641
Corporate/M&A ★★★★
Table: p. 645

de Geer, Stefan (Sweden)
Profile: p. 647
Banking & Finance ★★★
Table: p. 641
Communications: Telecoms ★★★★
Table: p. 642
Corporate/M&A ★★★
Table: p. 645

de Givré, Yann (France)
Profile: p. 286
Tax ★★
Table: p. 281

de Hevesy, Stefan (Sweden)
Profile: p. 647
Banking & Finance ★★★★
Table: p. 641

De Hosson, Fred (Netherlands)
Profile: p. 501
Tax ★★★
Table: p. 500

de Juvigny, Olivier (France)
Profile: p. 286
Competition/Anti-trust ★
Table: p. 272

De Keijzer, Jaap (Netherlands)
Profile: p. 501
Energy & Natural Resources ★★★★
Table: p. 498

de Kergommeaux, Xavier (France)
Profile: p. 286
Capital Markets ★★★★
Table: p. 268

de Kergos, Yann (France)
Profile: p. 287
Tax ★
Table: p. 281

de la Guardia, Juan Raul (Panama)
Profile: p. 534
Corporate/Commercial ★★★
Table: p. 533

de la Laurencie, Jean-Patrice (France)
Profile: p. 287
Competition/Anti-trust ★★★★
Table: p. 272

de la Rue, Colin (United Kingdom)
Profile: p. 750
Shipping ★★
Table: p. 737

de la Taille, Benoît (France)
Profile: p. 287
Communications: IT ★★
Table: p. 271
Communications: Telecoms ★★
Table: p. 271

de las Cuevas, Fernando (Spain)
Profile: p. 630
Banking & Finance ★★
Table: p. 619
Corporate/M&A ★★
Table: p. 624

De Los Angeles, Eduardo (Philippines)
Profile: p. 544
Corporate/Commercial ★★★
Table: p. 542

de Lousanoff, Oleg (Germany)
Profile: p. 321
Corporate/M&A ★★
Table: p. 311

De Moüy, Diane (France)
Profile: p. 287
Banking & Finance ★
Table: p. 265

De Orchis, Vincent M. (USA)
Profile: p. 858
Shipping: Litigation ★★
Table: p. 841

De Pardieu, Charles-Henri (France)
Profile: p. 287
Corporate/M&A ★★
Table: p. 275

de Posadas, Ignacio (Uruguay)
Profile: p. 906
Corporate/M&A ★★★★
Table: p. 905

de Rojas, Mercedes (Spain)
Profile: p. 630
Tax ★
Table: p. 628

de Roux, Xavier (France)
Profile: p. 287
Competition/Anti-trust ★
Table: p. 272

de Salles Freire, Jose Luis (Brazil)
Profile: p. 154
Banking & Finance ★★
Table: p. 142
Corporate/M&A ★★★
Table: p. 147

de San Roman, Jaime (Spain)
Profile: p. 630
Banking & Finance ★★★★
Table: p. 619
Corporate/M&A ★
Table: p. 624

De Sear, Edward (USA)
Profile: p. 858
Capital Markets: Securitisation ★★★★
Table: p. 795

De Serière, Victor (Netherlands)
Profile: p. 502
Banking & Finance ★★
Table: p. 491

de Sousa, Luis Antonio (Brazil)
Profile: p. 154
Project Finance ★★★★
Table: p. 149

de Sousa da Câmara, Francisco (Portugal)
Profile: p. 564
Tax ★★★
Table: p. 562

de Ulloa, Gonzalo (Spain)
Profile: p. 630
Intellectual Property ★★★★
Table: p. 626

De Varax, Matthieu (France)
Profile: p. 287
Banking & Finance ★
Table: p. 265

De Vos, Frank (Netherlands)
Profile: p. 502
Tax ★★★★
Table: p. 500

de Waal, Allard (France)
Profile: p. 287
Tax ★★★
Table: p. 281

De Waard, Tom (Netherlands)
Profile: p. 502
Corporate/M&A ★★
Table: p. 496
Energy & Natural Resources ★★★
Table: p. 498

Deane, Simon (Hong Kong)
Profile: p. 364
Banking & Finance ★
Table: p. 352

Debouzy, Olivier (France)
Profile: p. 287
Communications: Telecoms ★★
Table: p. 271

Debroux, Michel (France)
Profile: p. 287
Competition/Anti-trust ★
Table: p. 272

Deck, David D. (Japan)
Profile: p. 444
Capital Markets: Japan Foreign ★★
Table: p. 437

Dederick, David (Hungary)
Profile: p. 376
Corporate/M&A ★★
Table: p. 375

Deering, Bob (United Kingdom)
Profile: p. 750
Shipping ★★★★
Table: p. 737

Dejean, Neils (France)
Profile: p. 287
Tax ★★
Table: p. 281

del Calvo, Jorge (USA)
Profile: p. 858
Communications: IT ★★★
Table: p. 805

Del Chiaro, José (Brazil)
Profile: p. 154
Competition/Anti-trust ★★★
Table: p. 145

del Piano, Jorge (Chile)
Profile: p. 209
Banking & Finance ★★
Table: p. 206

del Saz Cordero, Isidro (Spain)
Profile: p. 631
Tax ★★★
Table: p. 628

del Valle, Javier (Spain)
Profile: p. 631
Intellectual Property ★★★
Table: p. 626

DeLaMater, Robert G. (Hong Kong)
Profile: p. 364
Capital Markets: Debt & Equity ★★★★
Table: p. 353

Delaney, John (Bahamas)
Profile: p. 109
Corporate/Commercial ★★★★
Table: p. 109

Delattre, Olivier (France)
Profile: p. 287
Tax ★★
Table: p. 281

Delgado, Abelardo (Spain)
Profile: p. 631
Tax ★★★
Table: p. 628

Delgado, Alejandro (Mexico)
Profile: p. 481
Corporate/M&A ★★
Table: p. 480

Dell'Oro Maini, Atilio (Argentina)
Profile: p. 61
Banking & Finance ★★
Table: p. 53

Delvolvé, Jean-Louis (France)
Profile: p. 287
Arbitration (International) ★
Table: p. 262

Demers, Jacques (Canada)
Profile: p. 188
Banking & Finance ★★★★
Table: p. 171
Corporate/M&A ★★
Table: p. 177

Denger, Michael (USA)
Profile: p. 858
Competition/Anti-trust ★
Table: p. 811

Dennis, Graeme (Australia)
Profile: p. 86
Energy & Natural Resources ★★★
Table: p. 75

Denny, Roger (Hong Kong)
Profile: p. 364
Capital Markets: Debt & Equity ★★
Table: p. 353
Corporate/M&A ★★★
Table: p. 357

KEY TO RANKINGS: ✪ = Star Individual ★★★★ = Top Band ★★★ = Second Band ★★ = Third Band ★ = Fourth Band **U** = Up and coming

Duncan, Michael G. (United Kingdom)
Profile: p. 751
Banking & Finance ★★
Table: p. 699

Dundas, Philip (United Arab Emirates)
Profile: p. 693
Project Finance ★★★★
Table: p. 691

Dunlop, Stuart (United Kingdom)
Profile: p. 751
Capital Markets: Debt & Equity ★
Table: p. 702

Dunn, Charles (Thailand)
Profile: p. 673
Banking & Finance ★★★
Table: p. 670

Dunn, Douglas (USA)
Profile: p. 859
Corporate/M&A ★
Table: p. 820

Dunne, Ambrose (Australia)
Profile: p. 87
Banking & Finance ★
Table: p. 65
Project Finance ★★
Table: p. 79

Dunner, Donald (USA)
Profile: p. 860
Intellectual Property ✪
Table: p. 831

Dunnigan, David (United Kingdom)
Profile: p. 751
Capital Markets: Debt & Equity ★★★
Table: p. 702

Dunstan, Jim (Australia)
Profile: p. 87
Banking & Finance ★★
Table: p. 65

Dupuis-Toubol, Frédérique (France)
Profile: p. 288
Communications: IT ★★★★
Table: p. 271
Communications: Telecoms ★★★★
Table: p. 271

Durand, Ronald (Canada)
Profile: p. 188
Tax ★★★
Table: p. 182

Dutra, Pedro (Brazil)
Profile: p. 154
Competition/Anti-trust ★★★★
Table: p. 145

Duvernoy, Christian (Belgium)
Profile: p. 129
Communications ★★
Table: p. 118

Dwyer, Jim (Australia)
Profile: p. 87
Intellectual Property ★★★★
Table: p. 77

Dyekjær-Hansen, Karen (Denmark)
Profile: p. 240
Competition/Anti-trust ★★★★
Table: p. 238

Dyer, Roger (Singapore)
Profile: p. 599
Banking & Finance: Singapore Foreign ★
Table: p. 588

E

Earley, William (Ireland)
Profile: p. 400
Corporate/M&A ★★★
Table: p. 397

East, John (Hong Kong)
Profile: p. 365
Project Finance ★★★
Table: p. 359

East, Lindsay (United Kingdom)
Profile: p. 751
Shipping ★★★
Table: p. 737

Eastment, Thomas James (USA)
Profile: p. 860
Energy & Natural Resources ★★★
Table: p. 827

Eastwell, Nicholas W. (United Kingdom)
Profile: p. 751
Capital Markets: Debt & Equity ★★★★
Table: p. 702

Easun, William (Monaco)
Profile: p. 483
Corporate/Commercial ★★★★
Table: p. 483

Ebeling, Mogens (Denmark)
Profile: p. 240
Corporate/M&A ★★
Table: p. 239

Ebety, Brahim Ould (Mauritania)
Profile: p. 477
Corporate/Commercial ★★★
Table: p. 477

Edge, Steve (United Kingdom)
Profile: p. 751
Tax ✪
Table: p. 739

Edlmann, Stephen R.R. (United Kingdom)
Profile: p. 751
Capital Markets: Debt & Equity ★★★
Table: p. 702

Edwards, Alina (Cuba)
Profile: p. 230
Corporate/Commercial ★★★★
Table: p. 230

Edwards, Gareth (United Kingdom)
Profile: p. 751
Communications: E-commerce ★★
Table: p. 711

Egan, James (USA)
Profile: p. 860
Competition/Anti-trust ★
Table: p. 811

Egan, Paul (Ireland)
Profile: p. 401
Corporate/M&A ★★★★
Table: p. 397

Ehrat, Felix (Switzerland)
Profile: p. 659
Corporate/M&A ★★
Table: p. 657

Eijsvoogel, Peter (Netherlands)
Profile: p. 502
Communications ★★★★
Table: p. 492

Eilers, Stephan (Germany)
Profile: p. 321
Tax ★★
Table: p. 319

Einem, Christoph von (Germany)
Profile: p. 321
Private Equity ★
Table: p. 316

Einhorn, David (USA)
Profile: p. 860
Tax ★★★
Table: p. 845

Eisenberg, David (USA)
Profile: p. 860
Capital Markets: Securitisation ★★
Table: p. 795

Eisma, Sjoerd (Netherlands)
Profile: p. 502
Corporate/M&A ★★★
Table: p. 496

Eitan, Tally (Israel)
Profile: p. 410
Communications ★★★★
Table: p. 407
Corporate/M&A ★
Table: p. 409

Eizirik, Nelson (Brazil)
Profile: p. 154
Corporate/M&A ★★★
Table: p. 147

Ejiri, Takashi (Japan)
Profile: p. 444
Corporate/M&A ★★
Table: p. 439

Ekbom, Per Gustaf (Sweden)
Profile: p. 647
Banking & Finance ★★
Table: p. 641

Ekobo, Emmanuel (Cameroon)
Profile: p. 169
Corporate/Commercial ★★★
Table: p. 169

el Tahir, Kamal (Sudan)
Profile: p. 638
Corporate/Commercial ★★★★
Table: p. 638

El-Hakim, Jacques (Syria)
Profile: p. 665
Corporate/Commercial ★★★★
Table: p. 665

Elder, Ian (United Kingdom)
Profile: p. 751
Energy: Electricity ★★★
Table: p. 725

Elias, Enrique (Peru)
Profile: p. 541
Corporate/M&A ★★★★
Table: p. 540

Eliathamby, Sreesanthan (Malaysia)
Profile: p. 472
Corporate/M&A ★
Table: p. 471

Elisha, Jean Pierre (Cote D'Ivoire)
Profile: p. 227
Corporate/Commercial ★★★
Table: p. 227

Eljuri, Elizabeth (Venezuela)
Profile: p. 913
Energy & Natural Resources ★★★
Table: p. 911

Elland-Goldsmith, Michael (France)
Profile: p. 288
Project Finance ★★★★
Table: p. 277

Ellard, John (United Kingdom)
Profile: p. 751
Corporate/M&A ★
Table: p. 717

Elliott, John (Australia)
Profile: p. 87
Corporate/M&A **U**
Table: p. 73

Elliott, Peter (United Kingdom)
Profile: p. 751
Tax ★★
Table: p. 739

Elliott, Robert (United Kingdom)
Profile: p. 752
Banking & Finance ★
Table: p. 699

Ellison, Julian (Belgium)
Profile: p. 129
Competition/Anti-trust ★
Table: p. 122

Elman, Jonathan (United Kingdom)
Profile: p. 752
Tax ★★★
Table: p. 739

Elsey, Mark (United Kingdom)
Profile: p. 752
PFI ★★★
Table: p. 733
Projects ★★
Table: p. 733

Elvey, Jonathan (Greece)
Profile: p. 342
Shipping: Foreign Firms ★★★★
Table: p. 341

Elvinger, André (Luxembourg)
Profile: p. 466
Corporate/Commercial ★★★★
Table: p. 465

Embree, Kirsten (Canada)
Profile: p. 188
Communications ★
Table: p. 173

Emde, Thomas (Germany)
Profile: p. 322
Banking & Finance ★★★
Table: p. 301
Capital Markets: Equity ★★★
Table: p. 304

Emerson, Carter (USA)
Profile: p. 860
Corporate/M&A ★★★
Table: p. 813

Emmerich, Adam (USA)
Profile: p. 860
Corporate/M&A ★★
Table: p. 820

Emmerson, Tim (United Kingdom)
Profile: p. 752
Corporate/M&A ★★★
Table: p. 717

Endréo, Gilles (France)
Profile: p. 288
Capital Markets ★★★★
Table: p. 268

Endresen, Clement (Norway)
Profile: p. 522
Corporate/M&A ★★
Table: p. 519

Engell, Oluf (Denmark)
Profile: p. 240
Corporate/M&A ★★★
Table: p. 239

Eno, Stephen (Hong Kong)
Profile: p. 365
Banking & Finance ★★★
Table: p. 352

Enser, John (United Kingdom)
Profile: p. 752
Communications: E-commerce ★★★★
Table: p. 711

Entraygues, Gilles (France)
Profile: p. 288
Tax ★★★★
Table: p. 281

Epe, Axel (Germany)
Profile: p. 322
Corporate/M&A ★★
Table: p. 311

Epstein, Gary (USA)
Profile: p. 860
Communications: Regulatory ★★★★
Table: p. 803

Epstein, Jacques Henri (France)
Profile: p. 288
Corporate/M&A ★
Table: p. 275

Epstein, Michael (USA)
Profile: p. 860
Communications: Transactional (IT) ★★
Table: p. 801

Eran, Oded (Israel)
Profile: p. 410
Corporate/M&A ★★★★
Table: p. 409

Erch, Andrei N. (Belarus)
Profile: p. 115
Corporate/Commercial ★★★
Table: p. 114

Erede, Sergio (Italy)
Profile: p. 425
Corporate/M&A ✪
Table: p. 419

Ereira, David (United Kingdom)
Profile: p. 752
Banking & Finance ★★★★
Table: p. 699

Ericsson, Eric (Sweden)
Profile: p. 647
Competition/Anti-trust ★★★
Table: p. 644

Erize, Luis Alberto (Argentina)
Profile: p. 62
Energy & Natural Resources ★★
Table: p. 59

Ernst, Reinhold (Germany)
Profile: p. 322
Private Equity ★
Table: p. 316

Erös, Ákos (Hungary)
Profile: p. 376
Corporate/M&A ★★
Table: p. 375

Errazuriz, José Thomas (Chile)
Profile: p. 209
Corporate/M&A ★★★
Table: p. 208

Errecondo, Javier (Argentina)
Profile: p. 62
Banking & Finance ★★
Table: p. 53

Escoda, Alex (Spain)
Profile: p. 631
Tax ★★
Table: p. 628

Escudero, Antonio (Puerto Rico)
Profile: p. 567
Corporate/Commercial ★★★★
Table: p. 567

Esposito, Paolo (Italy)
Profile: p. 425
Project Finance ★★
Table: p. 421

KEY TO RANKINGS: ✪ = Star Individual ★★★★ = Top Band ★★★ = Second Band ★★ = Third Band ★ = Fourth Band **U** = Up and coming

Esser-Wellié, Michael (Germany)
Profile: p. 322
Communications: Regulatory ★★★
Table: p. 306
Competition/Anti-trust ★★★
Table: p. 309

Esteve, Bernard (Gabon)
Profile: p. 297
Corporate/Commercial ★★★★
Table: p. 297

Etah, Akoh (Cameroon)
Profile: p. 169
Corporate/Commercial ★★★★
Table: p. 169

Ettinger, John (USA)
Profile: p. 860
Private Equity: Buyouts ★
Table: p. 834

Evanich, Kevin (USA)
Profile: p. 860
Corporate/M&A ★★★
Table: p. 813

Evans, Bernard (Australia)
Profile: p. 87
Energy & Natural Resources ★★
Table: p. 75

Evans, Edward (United Kingdom)
Profile: p. 752
Banking & Finance ★★
Table: p. 699

Evans, John (United Kingdom)
Profile: p. 752
Shipping ★★★
Table: p. 737

Evans, Linda (Australia)
Profile: p. 87
Competition/Anti-trust ★★
Table: p. 71

Evans, Martin Frederick (USA)
Profile: p. 860
Competition/Anti-trust ★★
Table: p. 808

Evans, Robert III (USA)
Profile: p. 860
Capital Markets: Debt & Equity ★
Table: p. 793

Evans, Stuart (United Kingdom)
Profile: p. 752
Corporate/M&A ★★
Table: p. 717

Everett, Kathryn (Australia)
Profile: p. 87
Intellectual Property U
Table: p. 77

Ewens QC, Douglas S. (Canada)
Profile: p. 188
Tax ★★
Table: p. 182

Ewing, Chris (South Africa)
Profile: p. 612
Corporate/M&A ★★★
Table: p. 611

Eyzaguirre, Cristián (Chile)
Profile: p. 209
Corporate/M&A ★★★★
Table: p. 208

Eyzaguirre Jnr, José María (Chile)
Profile: p. 210
Banking & Finance ★★★★
Table: p. 206
Corporate/M&A ✪
Table: p. 208

Eyzaguirre Snr, José María (Chile)
Profile: p. 210
Corporate/M&A ★★
Table: p. 208

F

Fabritius, Andreas (Germany)
Profile: p. 322
Corporate/M&A ★★★
Table: p. 311

Fachler, Freddy (Costa Rica)
Profile: p. 226
Corporate/Commercial ★★★
Table: p. 225

Fadika, Karim (Cote D'Ivoire)
Profile: p. 227
Corporate/Commercial ★★★★
Table: p. 227

Fairbairn, Mark (Hong Kong)
Profile: p. 365
Banking & Finance ★★
Table: p. 352

Falconer, Ian (United Kingdom)
Profile: p. 752
Capital Markets: Securitisation ★★★★
Table: p. 704

Falk, Sarah (United Kingdom)
Profile: p. 752
Tax ★★★
Table: p. 739

Familton, Keith R. (New Zealand)
Profile: p. 509
Corporate/M&A ★★★★
Table: p. 508

Fantozzi, Augusto (Italy)
Profile: p. 425
Tax ★★★
Table: p. 422

Farabow, Ford (USA)
Profile: p. 861
Intellectual Property ★★
Table: p. 831

Fargosi, Alejandro (Argentina)
Profile: p. 62
Communications ★★★★
Table: p. 54

Farley, Alastair (United Kingdom)
Profile: p. 752
Shipping: Finance ★★★
Table: p. 737

Farmer, Scott (USA)
Profile: p. 861
Tax ★
Table: p. 847

Farquharson, Melanie (United Kingdom)
Profile: p. 752
Competition/Anti-trust U
Table: p. 714

Farrell, Kathleen (Australia)
Profile: p. 87
Capital Markets ★
Table: p. 67

Farroco Jr, Antonio Carlos (Brazil)
Profile: p. 154
Tax ★
Table: p. 150

Fastow, Jay N. (USA)
Profile: p. 861
Competition/Anti-trust ★
Table: p. 808

Faugérolas, Laurent (France)
Profile: p. 288
Capital Markets ★★
Table: p. 268
Corporate/M&A ★★★
Table: p. 275

Faurès, André (Belgium)
Profile: p. 129
Arbitration (International) ★★★★
Table: p. 116

Featherston, Roger (Australia)
Profile: p. 88
Communications: Telecoms ★★★
Table: p. 69
Competition/Anti-trust ★★★★
Table: p. 71

Federspiel, Herman (Denmark)
Profile: p. 240
Banking & Finance ★★★★
Table: p. 237

Feenstra, Jaap (Netherlands)
Profile: p. 502
Competition/Anti-trust ★★★
Table: p. 494

Feetham, Nigel (Gibraltar)
Profile: p. 338
Corporate/Commercial ★★
Table: p. 337

Feick, Carl-Peter (Germany)
Profile: p. 322
Banking & Finance ★★★
Table: p. 301

Feick, Hans-Georg (Germany)
Profile: p. 322
Banking & Finance ★★
Table: p. 301

Feider, Marc (Luxembourg)
Profile: p. 466
Corporate/Commercial ★★★★
Table: p. 465

Feinstein, Deborah (USA)
Profile: p. 861
Competition/Anti-trust ★
Table: p. 811

Felesky, Brian Q.C. (Canada)
Profile: p. 188
Tax ★★
Table: p. 182

Felig, Clifford (Israel)
Profile: p. 410
Communications ★★★★
Table: p. 407
Corporate/M&A ★★★
Table: p. 409

Fenech, Tonio (Malta)
Profile: p. 476
Corporate/Commercial ★★
Table: p. 475

Féral-Schuhl, Christiane (France)
Profile: p. 288
Communications: IT ★★★
Table: p. 271

Ferchiou, Noureddine (Tunisia)
Profile: p. 678
Corporate/Commercial ★★★★
Table: p. 678

Ferguson, Hugh (Falkland Islands)
Profile: p. 254
Corporate/Commercial ★★★★
Table: p. 254

Ferguson, M. Carr (USA)
Profile: p. 861
Tax ★★
Table: p. 845

Fernandes Ferreira, Rogerio Manuel (Portugal)
Profile: p. 564
Tax ★★★
Table: p. 562

Fernández, Cani (Belgium)
Profile: p. 631
Competition/Anti-trust ★
Table: p. 622

Fernández de Araoz, Alejandro (Spain)
Profile: p. 631
Competition/Anti-trust ★★★
Table: p. 622
Corporate/M&A ★
Table: p. 624

Fernandez-Novoa, Luis (Spain)
Profile: p. 631
Intellectual Property ★★★
Table: p. 626

Ferraro, Michael (Australia)
Profile: p. 88
Communications: Telecoms ★
Table: p. 69

Ferraz, Helena (Brazil)
Profile: p. 155
Competition/Anti-trust U
Table: p. 145

Ferraz Jr, Tercio Sampaio (Brazil)
Profile: p. 155
Competition/Anti-trust ★★
Table: p. 145

Ferrer, Eduardo (Panama)
Profile: p. 534
Corporate/Commercial ★★★
Table: p. 533

Ferrere, Daniel (Uruguay)
Profile: p. 906
Banking & Finance ★★★
Table: p. 904
Corporate/M&A ★★★★
Table: p. 905

Ferris, Charles D. (USA)
Profile: p. 861
Communications: Regulatory ★★★★
Table: p. 803

Feuring, Wolfgang (Germany)
Profile: p. 322
Banking & Finance ★★
Table: p. 301
Capital Markets: Equity ★★★★
Table: p. 304

Fey, Albert E. (USA)
Profile: p. 861
Intellectual Property ★★★★
Table: p. 831

Field, John (Australia)
Profile: p. 88
Banking & Finance ★★★★
Table: p. 65
Project Finance ★★
Table: p. 79

Field, Sally (United Kingdom)
Profile: p. 752
Intellectual Property ✪
Table: p. 729

Fields, Richard (Guyana)
Profile: p. 348
Corporate/Commercial ★★★
Table: p. 348

Figari, Alberta (Italy)
Profile: p. 425
Banking & Finance ★
Table: p. 414

Finbow, Roger (United Kingdom)
Profile: p. 752
Competition/Anti-trust ★★
Table: p. 714

Finch, James (Myanmar)
Profile: p. 487
Corporate/Commercial: Myanmar Foreign ★★★★
Table: p. 487

Fingerhut, Martin (Canada)
Profile: p. 189
Banking & Finance ★★★
Table: p. 171

Finkelson, Allen (USA)
Profile: p. 861
Communications: Transactional (Telecoms) ★★★★
Table: p. 801
Corporate/M&A ★★★★
Table: p. 820

Finkelstein, Neil (Canada)
Profile: p. 189
Competition/Anti-trust ★★
Table: p. 175

Finlay, Peter (United Kingdom)
Profile: p. 753
Projects ★★
Table: p. 733

Finley, John (USA)
Profile: p. 861
Corporate/M&A ★
Table: p. 820
Private Equity: Buyouts ★
Table: p. 834

Finnerty, Patrick (Canada)
Profile: p. 189
Corporate/M&A ★
Table: p. 177

Fiocco, Rio George (Papua New Guinea)
Profile: p. 535
Corporate/Commercial ★★★
Table: p. 535

Fiorio, Juan (Paraguay)
Profile: p. 537
Banking & Finance ★★★★
Table: p. 536
Corporate/M&A ★★★★
Table: p. 537

Firth, Simon (United Kingdom)
Profile: p. 753
Capital Markets: Derivatives ★★★
Table: p. 706

Fischer, George Charles (Brazil)
Profile: p. 155
Communications ★★★
Table: p. 143
Corporate/M&A ★★
Table: p. 147

Fiszer, Janusz (Poland)
Profile: p. 552
Tax ★★★★
Table: p. 551

Fitzgerald, Eithne (Ireland)
Profile: p. 401
Corporate/M&A U
Table: p. 397

FitzGerald, Fiona (Singapore)
Profile: p. 599
Banking & Finance: Singapore Foreign ★★
Table: p. 588
Project Finance ★★
Table: p. 594

Fitzgerald, Gerald (Ireland)
Profile: p. 401
Competition/Anti-trust ★★★★
Table: p. 396

Fitzgerald, Peter (USA)
Profile: p. 861
Project Finance ★
Table: p. 837

 KEY TO RANKINGS: ✪ = Star Individual ★★★★ = Top Band ★★★ = Second Band ★★ = Third Band ★ = Fourth Band U = Up and coming

Fitzpatrick, Miles (Guyana)
Profile: p. 348
Corporate/Commercial ★★★★
Table: p. 348

FitzSimons, James (Australia)
Profile: p. 88
Communications: Telecoms ★
Table: p. 69

Fitzwilliam, Daniel John (Trinidad & Tobago)
Profile: p. 677
Corporate/Commercial ★★★★
Table: p. 676

Flacks, Prue (New Zealand)
Profile: p. 509
Banking & Finance ★★
Table: p. 507

Flaherty, St John (Hong Kong)
Profile: p. 365
Banking & Finance ★★
Table: p. 352
Capital Markets: Debt & Equity ★★
Table: p. 353
Corporate/M&A ★★★
Table: p. 357
Project Finance ★★★
Table: p. 359

Flaum, Keith (USA)
Profile: p. 861
Communications: IT **U**
Table: p. 805

Fleck, Richard (United Kingdom)
Profile: p. 753
Competition/Anti-trust ★
Table: p. 714

Fleischer Jr., Arthur (USA)
Profile: p. 861
Corporate/M&A ★★★★
Table: p. 820

Flesch, Cristiane (Brazil)
Profile: p. 155
Project Finance ★★
Table: p. 149

Fletcher, Nicholas (Poland)
Profile: p. 553
Corporate/M&A ★
Table: p. 548

Fletcher, Philip (United Kingdom)
Profile: p. 753
Projects ★★
Table: p. 733

Fletcher, Simon (United Kingdom)
Profile: p. 753
Shipping ★★★
Table: p. 737

Fleury, Joachim (Netherlands)
Profile: p. 502
Communications ★★★★
Table: p. 492
Corporate/M&A ★★★★
Table: p. 496

Flexner, Don (USA)
Profile: p. 862
Competition/Anti-trust ★★
Table: p. 808

Flipse, Mary (Laos)
Profile: p. 455
Corporate/Commercial ★★★★
Table: p. 455

Flom, Joseph H. (USA)
Profile: p. 862
Corporate/M&A ★★★★
Table: p. 820

Florack, James A. (USA)
Profile: p. 862
Banking & Finance ★★
Table: p. 791

Flynn, Steve (New Zealand)
Profile: p. 509
Banking & Finance ★★★
Table: p. 507

Fogelman, Lejb (Poland)
Profile: p. 553
Corporate/M&A ★★★★
Table: p. 548

Fogg, Blaine V. (USA)
Profile: p. 862
Corporate/M&A ★★
Table: p. 820

Foley, Anthony (Australia)
Profile: p. 88
Communications: IT ★★★
Table: p. 69
Intellectual Property ★
Table: p. 77

Folguera Crespo, Jaime (Spain)
Profile: p. 631
Competition/Anti-trust ★★★★
Table: p. 622

Follie, Robert (France)
Profile: p. 288
Corporate/M&A ★
Table: p. 275

Fontaine, Emmanuel (France)
Profile: p. 288
Project Finance ★★★★
Table: p. 277

Fontaine, Patrick B. (Hong Kong)
Profile: p. 365
Banking & Finance ★★
Table: p. 352

Fontana, Rafael (Spain)
Profile: p. 631
Tax ★★
Table: p. 628

Fonteijn, Chris (Netherlands)
Profile: p. 502
Energy & Natural Resources ★★★★
Table: p. 498

Foramitti, Louis (Austria)
Profile: p. 105
Banking & Finance ★★★★
Table: p. 103

Ford, Paul (USA)
Profile: p. 862
Capital Markets: Debt & Equity ★★
Table: p. 793

Foriers, Paul Alain (Belgium)
Profile: p. 129
Banking & Finance ★★★
Table: p. 117

Forrester, Ian S. (Belgium)
Profile: p. 129
Competition/Anti-trust ★★★★
Table: p. 122

Forrester, Paul J. (USA)
Profile: p. 862
Banking & Finance ★★★
Table: p. 787

Forryan, Andrew (United Kingdom)
Profile: p. 753
Capital Markets: Securitisation ★★
Table: p. 704

Forschbach, Thomas (France)
Profile: p. 288
Corporate/M&A ★★
Table: p. 275

Forsyth, Albert (Peru)
Profile: p. 541
Banking & Finance ★★★
Table: p. 538

Corporate/M&A ★★★
Table: p. 540

Fortunati, Roberto (Argentina)
Profile: p. 62
Banking & Finance ★★★
Table: p. 53
Energy & Natural Resources ★★★
Table: p. 59

Foster, Tony (Vietnam)
Profile: p. 917
Corporate/Commercial: Vietnam Foreign ★★★★
Table: p. 916

Foulkes, Hilary (Germany)
Profile: p. 322
Communications: Transactional ★★★
Table: p. 306

Fourgoux, Jean-Louis (France)
Profile: p. 288
Competition/Anti-trust ★
Table: p. 272

Fowler, Oliver (Kenya)
Profile: p. 454
Corporate/Commercial ★★★★
Table: p. 453

Fox, Jason (United Kingdom)
Profile: p. 753
PFI ★★★
Table: p. 733
Projects ★★
Table: p. 733

Fox, Michael (Israel)
Profile: p. 410
Banking & Finance ★★
Table: p. 406
Corporate/M&A ★
Table: p. 409

Fox, Ruth (United Kingdom)
Profile: p. 753
Banking & Finance ★
Table: p. 699

Fraidin, Stephen (USA)
Profile: p. 862
Corporate/M&A ★
Table: p. 820
Private Equity: Buyouts ★★★
Table: p. 834

Franceschini, José Inácio (Brazil)
Profile: p. 155
Competition/Anti-trust ★★★★
Table: p. 145

Francies, Mike (United Kingdom)
Profile: p. 753
Corporate/M&A ★★★
Table: p. 717

Franck, Antonio (Mexico)
Profile: p. 481
Banking & Finance ★★★
Table: p. 479

Franco, Carlos (Argentina)
Profile: p. 62
Competition/Anti-trust ★★
Table: p. 56

Frank, David (United Kingdom)
Profile: p. 753
Capital Markets: Debt & Equity ★★★
Table: p. 702

Frankle, Diane (USA)
Profile: p. 862
Communications: IT ★★
Table: p. 805

Franklyn, Peter (Canada)
Profile: p. 189
Competition/Anti-trust ★★
Table: p. 175

Franson, Marc P. (USA)
Profile: p. 862
Banking & Finance ★
Table: p. 787

Fraser, David (United Kingdom)
Profile: p. 754
Arbitration (International) **U**
Table: p. 696

Fraser, Jean (Canada)
Profile: p. 189
Corporate/M&A ★★
Table: p. 177

Fraser, Ross (United Kingdom)
Profile: p. 754
Tax ★★★
Table: p. 739

Frecker, David (Australia)
Profile: p. 88
Energy & Natural Resources ★★
Table: p. 75

Freehill, George (USA)
Profile: p. 863
Shipping: Litigation ★★
Table: p. 841

Freeland, Rowan (United Kingdom)
Profile: p. 754
Intellectual Property ★★★★
Table: p. 729

Freeman, Louis (USA)
Profile: p. 863
Tax ★★★★
Table: p. 843

Freeman, Mark W. (New Zealand)
Profile: p. 509
Corporate/M&A ★★★
Table: p. 508

Freeman, Peter (United Kingdom)
Profile: p. 754
Competition/Anti-trust ★★★
Table: p. 714

Freget, Olivier (France)
Profile: p. 288
Communications: IT ★★
Table: p. 271

Fremuth, Michael (USA)
Profile: p. 863
Energy & Natural Resources ★★★
Table: p. 827

French, Douglas (United Kingdom)
Profile: p. 754
Tax ★★★★
Table: p. 739

Frenkel, Alain (France)
Profile: p. 288
Tax ★★
Table: p. 281

Frey, Martin (Switzerland)
Profile: p. 659
Corporate/M&A ★★★
Table: p. 657

Freyer, Dana (USA)
Profile: p. 863
Arbitration (International) ★
Table: p. 785

Friedland, Paul (USA)
Profile: p. 863
Arbitration (International) ★★
Table: p. 785

Friedli, Helen (USA)
Profile: p. 863
Corporate/M&A ★
Table: p. 813

Friedman, Gary (USA)
Profile: p. 863
Tax ★
Table: p. 845

Friend, Mark (United Kingdom)
Profile: p. 754
Competition/Anti-trust ★★★
Table: p. 714

Frignani, Aldo (Italy)
Profile: p. 425
Competition/Anti-trust ★★
Table: p. 417

Fritzemeyer, Wolfgang (Germany)
Profile: p. 322
Communications: IT ★★
Table: p. 307

Frotz, Stephan (Austria)
Profile: p. 105
Corporate/M&A **U**
Table: p. 104

Froy, Michael M. (USA)
Profile: p. 863
Corporate/M&A ★
Table: p. 813

Frutuoso de Melo, Antonio (Portugal)
Profile: p. 564
Banking & Finance ★★
Table: p. 558
Corporate/M&A ★★
Table: p. 560

Fry, Houghton (Ireland)
Profile: p. 401
Corporate/M&A ★★★
Table: p. 397

Fuentes, Sandro (Peru)
Profile: p. 541
Banking & Finance ★★★
Table: p. 538

Fugar, William (Ghana)
Profile: p. 336
Corporate/Commercial ★★★★
Table: p. 336

Fujieda, Atsushi (Japan)
Profile: p. 444
Corporate/M&A ★★
Table: p. 439

Fujinawa, Kenichi (Japan)
Profile: p. 444
Corporate/M&A ★★★★
Table: p. 439

Fuller, Geoff (United Kingdom)
Profile: p. 754
Capital Markets: Securitisation ★★★
Table: p. 704

Fuller, Jeff (Australia)
Profile: p. 88
Tax ★
Table: p. 81

Fuller, Stuart (Australia)
Profile: p. 88
Capital Markets ★★★★
Table: p. 67

Furphy, Baden (Australia)
Profile: p. 88
Energy & Natural Resources **U**
Table: p. 75

Furter, Robert (Switzerland)
Profile: p. 659
Banking & Finance ★★★★
Table: p. 654

Fuster, Rafael (Spain)
Profile: p. 631
Tax ★★
Table: p. 628

Fuzi, Grant (Australia)
Profile: p. 88
Banking & Finance ★
Table: p. 65
Project Finance ★★★
Table: p. 79

KEY TO RANKINGS: ✪ = Star Individual ★★★★ = Top Band ★★★ = Second Band ★★ = Third Band ★ = Fourth Band **U** = Up and coming

G

Gaffney, John (USA)
Profile: p. 863
Communications: Transactional (Telecoms) ★★
Table: p. 801

Gaillard, Emmanuel (France)
Profile: p. 288
Arbitration (International) ★★★★
Table: p. 262

Galavazi, Hans (Netherlands)
Profile: p. 502
Tax ★★★★
Table: p. 500

Galbraith, Colin (Australia)
Profile: p. 88
Corporate/M&A ★
Table: p. 73

Galbraith, Steven (Singapore)
Profile: p. 599
Banking & Finance: Singapore Foreign ★★
Table: p. 588
Corporate/M&A: Singapore Foreig ★★
Table: p. 592
Project Finance ★★★
Table: p. 594

Gale, John (Hong Kong)
Profile: p. 365
Corporate/M&A ★
Table: p. 357

Galhardo, Luciana Rosanova (Brazil)
Profile: p. 155
Tax ★
Table: p. 150

Galicia, Manuel (Mexico)
Profile: p. 481
Corporate/M&A ★★★★
Table: p. 480

Galindo, Anibal (Panama)
Profile: p. 534
Corporate/Commercial ★★★
Table: p. 533

Galindo, Mario (Panama)
Profile: p. 534
Corporate/Commercial ★★★
Table: p. 533

Galledari, Arman (Singapore)
Profile: p. 599
Banking & Finance: Singapore Foreign ★★
Table: p. 588

Gallo, Francesco (Italy)
Profile: p. 425
Tax ★★
Table: p. 422

Gallo, Greg (USA)
Profile: p. 863
Communications: IT ★★★★
Table: p. 805

Gallo, Juan Antonio (Argentina)
Profile: p. 62
Banking & Finance ★★★
Table: p. 53

Galvan, Carlos (Mexico)
Profile: p. 481
Banking & Finance ★★★
Table: p. 479

Galvão Teles, Miguel (Portugal)
Profile: p. 564
Banking & Finance ★★★
Table: p. 558
Corporate/M&A ★★
Table: p. 560

Galvão Teles, Nuño (Portugal)
Profile: p. 564
Corporate/M&A ★
Table: p. 560

Galvis, Sergio J. (USA)
Profile: p. 864
Project Finance ★★
Table: p. 837

Ganado, Max (Malta)
Profile: p. 476
Corporate/Commercial ★★★★
Table: p. 475

Gandra Martins, Ives (Brazil)
Profile: p. 155
Tax ★★★
Table: p. 150

Gangemi, Bruno (Italy)
Profile: p. 425
Tax ★★★★
Table: p. 422

Gannon, Lawrence J. (USA)
Profile: p. 864
Project Finance ★
Table: p. 837

Gao, Peiji (China)
Profile: p. 217
Corporate/M&A: China Foreign ★★★★
Table: p. 213
Project Finance: China Foreign ★★★
Table: p. 215

García Llaneza, Rafael (Spain)
Profile: p. 631
Tax ★★
Table: p. 628

Garcia Sayan, Francisco Moreyra (Peru)
Profile: p. 541
Banking & Finance ★★★
Table: p. 538
Corporate/M&A ★★★★
Table: p. 540

García-Cuéllar, Samuel (Mexico)
Profile: p. 481
Corporate/M&A ★★★★
Table: p. 480

García-Pita, Daniel (Spain)
Profile: p. 631
Corporate/M&A ★★★★
Table: p. 624

Gardeta, Eduardo (Spain)
Profile: p. 632
Tax ★
Table: p. 628

Gardner, Nick (United Kingdom)
Profile: p. 754
Communications: IT ★★
Table: p. 709

Gárdos, Istvan (Hungary)
Profile: p. 376
Banking & Finance ★★★
Table: p. 372

Garfinkel, Barry (USA)
Profile: p. 864
Arbitration (International) ★★
Table: p. 785

Garita, Victor (Costa Rica)
Profile: p. 226
Corporate/Commercial ★★★
Table: p. 225

Garrido, Gustavo (Argentina)
Profile: p. 62
Communications ★★★
Table: p. 54

Garrido, Gustavo Enrique (Argentina)
Profile: p. 62
Communications ★★
Table: p. 54

Garrin, Duarte (Portugal)
Profile: p. 565
Corporate/M&A ★
Table: p. 560

Gascon, Denis (Canada)
Profile: p. 189
Competition/Anti-trust ★
Table: p. 175

Gasteyer, Thomas (Germany)
Profile: p. 322
Corporate/M&A ★
Table: p. 311

Gately, Denis (Australia)
Profile: p. 88
Energy & Natural Resources ★
Table: p. 75

Gates, Stephen (Australia)
Profile: p. 88
Tax ★
Table: p. 81

Gatmaitan, Andres (Philippines)
Profile: p. 544
Corporate/Commercial ★★
Table: p. 542

Gaythwaite, Miles (United Kingdom)
Profile: p. 754
Intellectual Property ★★
Table: p. 729

Gdanski, Martin (France)
Profile: p. 289
Banking & Finance ★★
Table: p. 265

Geary, Sean (USA)
Profile: p. 864
Banking & Finance ★★★
Table: p. 791

Geens, Koen (Belgium)
Profile: p. 129
Corporate/M&A ★★★
Table: p. 125

Geffen, Charles (United Kingdom)
Profile: p. 754
Private Equity: Buyouts ✪
Table: p. 731

Geissler, Bernhard (Germany)
Profile: p. 322
Intellectual Property: Patent ★★★
Table: p. 313

Gelfand, David (USA)
Profile: p. 864
Competition/Anti-trust ★★
Table: p. 811

Gelston, Philip (USA)
Profile: p. 864
Corporate/M&A ★★★
Table: p. 820

Gentile, Carmen (USA)
Profile: p. 864
Energy & Natural Resources ★★
Table: p. 827

Georges, Alain (France)
Profile: p. 289
Competition/Anti-trust ★★★
Table: p. 272

Georges, Martine (France)
Profile: p. 289
Communications: Telecoms ★★
Table: p. 271

Georgopoulos, Leonidas (Greece)
Profile: p. 342
Corporate/M&A ★★★★
Table: p. 339

Gerdes, Hans-Bruno (Namibia)
Profile: p. 488
Corporate/Commercial ★★★★
Table: p. 488

Gerke Mendieta, Carlos (Bolivia)
Profile: p. 139
Corporate/Commercial ★★★★
Table: p. 138

Gerstein, Mark D. (USA)
Profile: p. 864
Corporate/M&A ★
Table: p. 813

Gerstell, Glenn (USA)
Profile: p. 864
Communications: Transactional (Telecoms) ★★★
Table: p. 801

Gerwat, Richard (Jersey)
Profile: p. 449
Corporate/Commercial **U**
Table: p. 448

Gessel, Beata (Poland)
Profile: p. 553
Corporate/M&A ★★
Table: p. 548

Geus, Marjolein (Netherlands)
Profile: p. 502
Communications ★★★★
Table: p. 492

Geva, Dan (Israel)
Profile: p. 411
Communications ★★★
Table: p. 407

Geye, Antouman (The Gambia)
Profile: p. 299
Corporate/Commercial ★★★★
Table: p. 298

Ghio, Roberto (Italy)
Profile: p. 425
Banking & Finance ★
Table: p. 414

Ghirardani, Paolo (United Kingdom)
Profile: p. 754
Shipping ★★★
Table: p. 737

Giampieri, Alberto (Italy)
Profile: p. 425
Banking & Finance ★★
Table: p. 414
Corporate/M&A ★
Table: p. 419

Gianni, Francesco (Italy)
Profile: p. 425
Banking & Finance ★★★
Table: p. 414
Corporate/M&A ★★★★
Table: p. 419

Giarda, Raffaele (Italy)
Profile: p. 425
Communications ★★★★
Table: p. 415

Gibb, Jeremy S.P. (United Kingdom)
Profile: p. 755
Shipping: Finance ★★
Table: p. 737

Gibbins, David (United Kingdom)
Profile: p. 755
Intellectual Property ★★
Table: p. 729

Giebe, Olaf (Germany)
Profile: p. 322
Intellectual Property: General ★★★
Table: p. 314

Gilberg, David J. (USA)
Profile: p. 864
Capital Markets: Derivatives ★★
Table: p. 798

Gilbert, Victoria (USA)
Profile: p. 865
Banking & Finance ★
Table: p. 787

Giles, Paul A. (Singapore)
Profile: p. 599
Banking & Finance: Singapore Foreign ★★★
Table: p. 588

Giliberti, Enrico (Italy)
Profile: p. 426
Corporate/M&A ★★
Table: p. 419

Gill, Judith (United Kingdom)
Profile: p. 755
Arbitration (International) ★★★
Table: p. 696

Gillespie, Stephen (United Kingdom)
Profile: p. 755
Banking & Finance ★★
Table: p. 699
Projects ★★
Table: p. 733

Ginestié, Philippe (France)
Profile: p. 289
Tax ★
Table: p. 281

Gioscia, Marcello (Italy)
Profile: p. 426
Banking & Finance ★★★
Table: p. 414
Corporate/M&A ★★
Table: p. 419

Giovannini, Teresa (Switzerland)
Profile: p. 659
Arbitration (International) ★★
Table: p. 653

Girvan, Garth M. (Canada)
Profile: p. 189
Corporate/M&A ★★★★
Table: p. 177

Gissinger, Pierre (France)
Profile: p. 289
Capital Markets ★★★★
Table: p. 268

Gisvold, Marius Moursund (Norway)
Profile: p. 522
Corporate/M&A ★★★
Table: p. 519

Gittes, Franklin M. (USA)
Profile: p. 865
Corporate/M&A ★
Table: p. 820

Giustini, Anthony (France)
Profile: p. 289
Project Finance ★★★★
Table: p. 277
Project Finance: Francophone Africa ★★★★
Table: p. 278

Givant, Norman (China)
Profile: p. 217
Corporate/M&A: China Foreign ★★★★
Table: p. 213
Project Finance: China Foreign ★★
Table: p. 215

Glanz, Steven (Australia)
Profile: p. 89
Corporate/M&A ★
Table: p. 73

Glas, Geert (Belgium)
Profile: p. 129
Communications ★★★★
Table: p. 118

Glass, Adam W. (USA)
Profile: p. 865
Capital Markets: Securitisation ★★
Table: p. 795

 KEY TO RANKINGS: ✪ = Star Individual ★★★★ = Top Band ★★★ = Second Band ★★ = Third Band ★ = Fourth Band **U** = Up and coming

Glazener, Paul (Netherlands)
Profile: p. 502
Competition/Anti-trust ★★★★
Table: p. 494
Energy & Natural Resources ★★★
Table: p. 498

Glick, Anna (USA)
Profile: p. 865
Capital Markets: Securitisation ★
Table: p. 795

Gluhovskaya, Valentina (Russia)
Profile: p. 577
Corporate/M&A ★★
Table: p. 574

Glyn, Richard (South Africa)
Profile: p. 612
Banking & Finance ★★★★
Table: p. 610

Gmaj, Marcin (Poland)
Profile: p. 553
Corporate/M&A **U**
Table: p. 548

Goddar, Heinz (Germany)
Profile: p. 322
Intellectual Property: Patent ★★★★
Table: p. 313

Godden, Richard (United Kingdom)
Profile: p. 755
Corporate/M&A ★★★★
Table: p. 717

Godet, Dominique (France)
Profile: p. 289
Tax ★★
Table: p. 281

Godfrey, Keith (United Kingdom)
Profile: p. 755
Corporate/M&A ★
Table: p. 717

Goenechea, Juan Miguel (Spain)
Profile: p. 632
Corporate/M&A ★★★★
Table: p. 624

Goin, Thomas (Indonesia)
Profile: p. 392
Corporate/Commercial ★★
Table: p. 391

Gold, Michael (USA)
Profile: p. 865
Banking & Finance ★
Table: p. 787

Gold, Stuart (USA)
Profile: p. 865
Competition/Anti-trust ★
Table: p. 808

Goldaracena, Fernando (Argentina)
Profile: p. 62
Competition/Anti-trust ★★★
Table: p. 56

Goldberg, Fred (USA)
Profile: p. 865
Tax ★★★
Table: p. 847

Goldberg, Louis (USA)
Profile: p. 865
Private Equity: Buyouts ★★
Table: p. 834

Golden, Arthur (USA)
Profile: p. 865
Competition/Anti-trust ★★
Table: p. 808

Golden, Jeffrey (United Kingdom)
Profile: p. 755
Capital Markets: Derivatives ★★★★
Table: p. 706

Goldenberg, Amnon (Israel)
Profile: p. 411
Corporate/M&A ★★
Table: p. 409

Golder, Tim (Australia)
Profile: p. 89
Intellectual Property ★
Table: p. 77

Goldfein, Shepard (USA)
Profile: p. 865
Competition/Anti-trust ★★
Table: p. 808

Golding, Greg (Australia)
Profile: p. 89
Capital Markets ★★★
Table: p. 67
Corporate/M&A ★★★★
Table: p. 73

Goldman, Calvin S. (Canada)
Profile: p. 190
Competition/Anti-trust ★★★★
Table: p. 175

Goldman, Mike (USA)
Profile: p. 865
Banking & Finance ★
Table: p. 791

Goldschmidt, David (USA)
Profile: p. 866
Capital Markets: Debt & Equity ★
Table: p. 793

Goldson, Peter (Jamaica)
Profile: p. 432
Corporate/Commercial ★★★
Table: p. 431

Goldstein, Marc (USA)
Profile: p. 866
Arbitration (International) ★
Table: p. 785

Goldstein, Marvin (USA)
Profile: p. 866
Capital Markets: Derivatives ★
Table: p. 798

Gomes, Vincent (Congo)
Profile: p. 223
Corporate/Commercial ★★★★
Table: p. 223

Gomes de Souza, Renato (Brazil)
Profile: p. 155
Banking & Finance ★
Table: p. 142

Gómez, Ricardo (Spain)
Profile: p. 632
Tax ★★
Table: p. 628

Gómez-Acebo, Javier (Spain)
Profile: p. 632
Banking & Finance ★★★
Table: p. 619

Gómez-Acebo, Juan (Spain)
Profile: p. 632
Corporate/M&A ★★★
Table: p. 624

Gomez-Jordana, Iñigo (Spain)
Profile: p. 632
Banking & Finance ★★★
Table: p. 619
Corporate/M&A ★★
Table: p. 624

Gonçalves Pereira, André (Portugal)
Profile: p. 565
Corporate/M&A ★★
Table: p. 560

Gonsalves, Maurice (Australia)
Profile: p. 89
Communications: IT ★★
Table: p. 69
Intellectual Property ★★
Table: p. 77

González-Deleito, Nicolás (Spain)
Profile: p. 632
Communications ★★
Table: p. 620

Goodall, Caroline (United Kingdom)
Profile: p. 755
Corporate/M&A ★
Table: p. 717

Goodman, Stuart (USA)
Profile: p. 866
Corporate/M&A ★★
Table: p. 813

Goodwillie, Eugene (USA)
Profile: p. 388, 866
Project Finance ★★★
Table: p. 837
Project Finance: India Foreign ★★★
Table: p. 386

Goodwin, Lee (USA)
Profile: p. 866
Energy & Natural Resources ★
Table: p. 827

Goolsby, George (USA)
Profile: p. 866
Energy & Natural Resources ★★★★
Table: p. 829

Gordon, David A. (USA)
Profile: p. 866
Project Finance ★★★★
Table: p. 837

Gordon, Steve (USA)
Profile: p. 866
Tax ★★
Table: p. 845

Gorrie, Euan (United Kingdom)
Profile: p. 755
Banking & Finance **U**
Table: p. 699

Gosling, James (United Kingdom)
Profile: p. 755
Shipping ★★★★
Table: p. 737

Gossling, Margaret (United Kingdom)
Profile: p. 755
Projects ★★
Table: p. 733

Goto, Izuru (Japan)
Profile: p. 444
Banking & Finance ★★★
Table: p. 433

Gottdiener, Scott (USA)
Profile: p. 866
Communications: Transactional (Telecoms) ★★
Table: p. 801

Gough, Richard (Australia)
Profile: p. 89
Intellectual Property ★★
Table: p. 77

Goulart Penteado, João Caio (Brazil)
Profile: p. 155
Corporate/M&A ★★★★
Table: p. 147

Gouthière, Bruno (France)
Profile: p. 289
Tax ★★★
Table: p. 281

Gow, Graham P. C. (Canada)
Profile: p. 190
Corporate/M&A ★
Table: p. 177

Goyios, Nicholas (Greece)
Profile: p. 342
Shipping ★★
Table: p. 340

Graaf, Frank (Netherlands)
Profile: p. 502
Banking & Finance ★★★★
Table: p. 491

Graça, Georges (Mozambique)
Profile: p. 486
Corporate/Commercial ★★★★
Table: p. 486

Graham, Bruce M. (Canada)
Profile: p. 190
Competition/Anti-trust ★★★
Table: p. 175

Graham, Rory (United Kingdom)
Profile: p. 755
Communications: IT ★★
Table: p. 709

Grambas, Nicholas (Australia)
Profile: p. 89
Project Finance ★★★★
Table: p. 79

Grande Stevens, Franzo (Italy)
Profile: p. 426
Corporate/M&A ★★
Table: p. 419

Grandi, Giorgio (Italy)
Profile: p. 426
Corporate/M&A ★
Table: p. 419

Granich, Jorge (Chile)
Profile: p. 210
Banking & Finance ★★
Table: p. 206

Grant, Gregor (United Kingdom)
Profile: p. 755
Intellectual Property ✪
Table: p. 729

Grant, Peter S. (Canada)
Profile: p. 190
Communications ★
Table: p. 173

Grassani, Stefano (Italy)
Profile: p. 426
Competition/Anti-trust ★
Table: p. 417

Grau, Jorge (Spain)
Profile: p. 632
Intellectual Property ★★★★
Table: p. 626

Gray, John (Australia)
Profile: p. 89
Communications: IT **U**
Table: p. 69

Gray, Julian (Singapore)
Profile: p. 599
Shipping: Foreign Firms ★★★
Table: p. 596

Gray, Michael (Australia)
Profile: p. 89
Competition/Anti-trust ★
Table: p. 71

Gray, Richard (Australia)
Profile: p. 89
Capital Markets ★★
Table: p. 67

Greco, Marco Aurelio (Brazil)
Profile: p. 155
Tax ★★
Table: p. 150

Green, Douglas (USA)
Profile: p. 866
Energy & Natural Resources ★★
Table: p. 827

Green, Frederick (USA)
Profile: p. 866
Communications: Transactional (Telecoms) ★★
Table: p. 801

Green, Geoffrey (United Kingdom)
Profile: p. 756
Private Equity: Buyouts ★★★
Table: p. 731

Green, Jonathan (USA)
Profile: p. 867
Project Finance ★★
Table: p. 837

Green, Josh (USA)
Profile: p. 867
Communications: IT ★★★
Table: p. 805

Green, Martin (Singapore)
Profile: p. 600
Shipping: Foreign Firms ★★
Table: p. 596

Green, Peter (Australia)
Profile: p. 89
Tax ★★★
Table: p. 81

Greenbank, Ashley (United Kingdom)
Profile: p. 756
Tax ★★
Table: p. 739

Greig, John (Australia)
Profile: p. 90
Energy & Natural Resources ★
Table: p. 75

Gremillion, Tod (USA)
Profile: p. 867
Energy & Natural Resources ★
Table: p. 829

Greve, Einar J. (Norway)
Profile: p. 522
Corporate/M&A ★★
Table: p. 519

Griffin, Paul (United Kingdom)
Profile: p. 756
Energy: Oil and Gas ★★★★
Table: p. 723

Griffiths, David (United Kingdom)
Profile: p. 756
Communications: IT ★★
Table: p. 709

Grimaldi, Vittorio (Italy)
Profile: p. 426
Banking & Finance ★★★
Table: p. 414
Corporate/M&A ★★★
Table: p. 419

Grippo, Eugenio (Italy)
Profile: p. 426
Corporate/M&A ★★
Table: p. 419

Groll, William A. (USA)
Profile: p. 867
Communications: Transactional (Telecoms) ★★★
Table: p. 801
Corporate/M&A ★
Table: p. 820

Grondine, Robert (Japan)
Profile: p. 444
Corporate/M&A: Japan Foreign ★★★★
Table: p. 441
Project Finance ★★★
Table: p. 442

Grondona, Mariano (Argentina)
Profile: p. 62
Banking & Finance ★★
Table: p. 53

Gross, Joseph (Israel)
Profile: p. 411
Corporate/M&A ★★★
Table: p. 409

Gross Brown, Jorge (Paraguay)
Profile: p. 537

Corporate/M&A ★★★★
Table: p. 508

Harms, David B. (USA)
Profile: p. 867
Capital Markets: Debt & Equity ★★
Table: p. 793

Harper, Conrad K. (USA)
Profile: p. 867
Arbitration (International) ★★
Table: p. 785

Harpole, Sally A. (China)
Profile: p. 217
Corporate/M&A: China Foreign ★★★★
Table: p. 213

Harrell, Michael P. (USA)
Profile: p. 868
Private Equity: Fund Formation ★★★★
Table: p. 835

Harrer, Herbert (Germany)
Profile: p. 323
Capital Markets: Equity ★★★
Table: p. 304

Harrington, Michael (USA)
Profile: p. 868
Corporate/M&A ★★
Table: p. 824

Harris, Douglas (USA)
Profile: p. 868
Project Finance ★
Table: p. 837

Harris, Graham D. (United Kingdom)
Profile: p. 757
Shipping ★★
Table: p. 737

Harris, Neil (Canada)
Profile: p. 190
Tax ★★★
Table: p. 182

Harris, Paul (United Kingdom)
Profile: p. 757
Intellectual Property ★★
Table: p. 729

Harris, Scott (USA)
Profile: p. 868
Communications: Regulatory ★★
Table: p. 803

Harrison, Brian (United Kingdom)
Profile: p. 757
Projects ★★
Table: p. 733

Harrison, David (Belgium)
Profile: p. 129
Competition/Anti-trust ★★
Table: p. 122

Harrison, Kate (Australia)
Profile: p. 90
Intellectual Property ★★
Table: p. 77

Harrison, Vaughn (South Africa)
Profile: p. 612
Corporate/M&A ★★★
Table: p. 611

Harriss, David (United Kingdom)
Profile: p. 757
Intellectual Property ★★★★
Table: p. 729

Harry, John (Australia)
Profile: p. 90
Corporate/M&A ★★
Table: p. 73

Hart, Hugh (Jamaica)
Profile: p. 432
Corporate/Commercial ★★★★
Table: p. 431

Hart, Michael (United Kingdom)
Profile: p. 757
Intellectual Property ★★
Table: p. 729

Harte-Bavendamm, Henning (Germany)
Profile: p. 323
Communications: IT ★
Table: p. 307
Intellectual Property: General ★★★
Table: p. 314

Hartley, Simon (United Kingdom)
Profile: p. 757
Shipping: Finance **U**
Table: p. 737

Hartnell, Anthony (Australia)
Profile: p. 90
Corporate/M&A ★★★
Table: p. 73

Hartnett, Bill (USA)
Profile: p. 868
Capital Markets: Debt & Equity ★★★
Table: p. 793

Harty, Ronan (USA)
Profile: p. 868
Competition/Anti-trust ★★★
Table: p. 808

Harvey, Richard (United Kingdom)
Profile: p. 757
Shipping ★★★
Table: p. 737

Harvey-Samuel, Ian (Singapore)
Profile: p. 600
Banking & Finance: Singapore Foreign ★★★
Table: p. 588

Harwood, Peter (Guernsey)
Profile: p. 346
Corporate/Commercial ★★★★
Table: p. 346

Hashem, Yasser (Egypt)
Profile: p. 248
Corporate/M&A ★★★★
Table: p. 247
Project Finance ★★★
Table: p. 247

Hashidate, Kenji (Japan)
Profile: p. 444
Corporate/M&A ★
Table: p. 439

Haslam, Peter (Singapore)
Profile: p. 600
Project Finance ★
Table: p. 594

Hassan, Parvez (Pakistan)
Profile: p. 531
Corporate/Commercial ★★
Table: p. 529

Hatchard, Michael (United Kingdom)
Profile: p. 757
Corporate/M&A ★★
Table: p. 717

Hattrell, Martin (United Kingdom)
Profile: p. 757
Corporate/M&A ★★★
Table: p. 717

Hatzer, Paul (Hong Kong)
Profile: p. 365
Shipping ★★★★
Table: p. 361

Haughey, Stephen (Ireland)
Profile: p. 401
Banking & Finance ★★★★
Table: p. 394

Haukali, Bernhard (Norway)
Profile: p. 522
Banking & Finance ★★★★
Table: p. 517

Hausman, James (Canada)
Profile: p. 190
Tax ★★
Table: p. 182

Hausmaninger, Christian (Austria)
Profile: p. 105
Arbitration (International) ★★★
Table: p. 102
Banking & Finance ★★★
Table: p. 103

Haussila, Petri Y J (Finland)
Profile: p. 258
Corporate/M&A ★★★★
Table: p. 257

Hawes, Douglas (USA)
Profile: p. 868
Energy & Natural Resources ★★★
Table: p. 827

Hawk, Barry (USA)
Profile: p. 868
Competition/Anti-trust ★★★★
Table: p. 808

Hawkins, Patrick (Greece)
Profile: p. 342
Shipping: Foreign Firms ★★
Table: p. 341

Hay, Peter (Australia)
Profile: p. 90
Corporate/M&A ★★★
Table: p. 73
Energy & Natural Resources ★★★
Table: p. 75

Hayden, Raymond P. (USA)
Profile: p. 868
Shipping: Litigation ★★★★
Table: p. 841

Hayes, David (USA)
Profile: p. 868
Intellectual Property ★★★
Table: p. 833

Hazelwood, Steven (Singapore)
Profile: p. 600
Shipping: Foreign Firms ★★★
Table: p. 596

He, Fei (China)
Profile: p. 217
Corporate/M&A ★★★★
Table: p. 211

Headrick, William (Dominican Republic)
Profile: p. 243
Corporate/Commercial ★★★★
Table: p. 243

Healy, Nathaniel (Ireland)
Profile: p. 402
Banking & Finance ★★★★
Table: p. 394

Heath, Martin (Hong Kong)
Profile: p. 365
Shipping ★★★★
Table: p. 361

Heather, Thomas (Mexico)
Profile: p. 481
Banking & Finance ★★★★
Table: p. 479

Heemann, Manfred (Germany)
Profile: p. 323
Banking & Finance ★★★★
Table: p. 301

Heering, Niels (Denmark)
Profile: p. 240
Corporate/M&A ★★★
Table: p. 239

Heftler, Thomas (USA)
Profile: p. 868
Capital Markets: Derivatives ★★★
Table: p. 798

Hegedûs, Éva (Hungary)
Profile: p. 376
Banking & Finance ★★
Table: p. 372
Corporate/M&A ★★
Table: p. 375

Heidinger, Markus (Austria)
Profile: p. 105
Banking & Finance ★★★
Table: p. 103

Hein, Peter E. (Germany)
Profile: p. 324
Banking & Finance ★★★★
Table: p. 301

Heinzelman, Kris (USA)
Profile: p. 868
Capital Markets: Debt & Equity ★★
Table: p. 793

Heitner, Kenneth H. (USA)
Profile: p. 868
Tax ★★★
Table: p. 845

Heleniak, David W. (USA)
Profile: p. 868
Corporate/M&A ★★★
Table: p. 820

Heller, Kurt (Austria)
Profile: p. 106
Arbitration (International) ★★★★
Table: p. 102

Hellmann, Hans (Germany)
Profile: p. 324
Competition/Anti-trust ★★
Table: p. 309

Hellmund, Reinaldo (Venezuela)
Profile: p. 913
Energy & Natural Resources ★★★
Table: p. 911

Helman, Robert A. (USA)
Profile: p. 869
Corporate/M&A ★★★★
Table: p. 813

Helmy, Taher (Egypt)
Profile: p. 248
Banking & Finance ★★★
Table: p. 246
Corporate/M&A ★★★
Table: p. 247
Project Finance ★★★
Table: p. 247

Hempel, Karl (Austria)
Profile: p. 106
Arbitration (International) ★★★★
Table: p. 102
Banking & Finance ★★
Table: p. 103
Corporate/M&A ★★
Table: p. 104

Henderson, Angus (Australia)
Profile: p. 90
Communications: Telecoms ★
Table: p. 69

Henderson CBE, Giles (United Kingdom)
Profile: p. 758
Corporate/M&A ★★
Table: p. 717

Henderson, Schuyler (United Kingdom)
Profile: p. 757
Capital Markets: Derivatives ★★★★
Table: p. 706

Heneghan, Brendan (Ireland)
Profile: p. 402
Corporate/M&A ★★
Table: p. 397

Hengen, Nancy (USA)
Profile: p. 869
Shipping: Finance ★★★
Table: p. 841

Henle, Walter (Germany)
Profile: p. 324
Private Equity ★★★★
Table: p. 316

Hennessy, Grainne (Ireland)
Profile: p. 402
Banking & Finance ★★★★
Table: p. 394

Henriques, R.N.A. (Jamaica)
Profile: p. 432
Corporate/Commercial ★★★★
Table: p. 431

Henry, Michael (United Kingdom)
Profile: p. 758
Communications: E-commerce ★★
Table: p. 711

Hentzen, Matthias (Germany)
Profile: p. 324
Communications: Transactional ★★★
Table: p. 306

Hepkema, Sietze (Netherlands)
Profile: p. 502
Corporate/M&A ★★
Table: p. 496

Herbelin, Philippe (France)
Profile: p. 289
Capital Markets **U**
Table: p. 268

Herbert, Tim (Jersey)
Profile: p. 449
Corporate/Commercial ★★★
Table: p. 448

Herbst, Christian (Austria)
Profile: p. 106
Corporate/M&A ★★★★
Table: p. 104

Hergüner, Ümit (Turkey)
Profile: p. 683
Corporate/M&A ★★★★
Table: p. 681
Project Finance ★★★★
Table: p. 682

Herinckx, Yves (Belgium)
Profile: p. 129
Banking & Finance ★★★★
Table: p. 117

Herlihy, Ed (USA)
Profile: p. 869
Corporate/M&A ★★★★
Table: p. 820

Hermanns, Ferdinand (Germany)
Profile: p. 324
Competition/Anti-trust ★★
Table: p. 309

Hernandez-Breton, Eugenio (Venezuela)
Profile: p. 913
Corporate/M&A ★★
Table: p. 909

Herrera, Jaime (Colombia)
Profile: p. 222
Corporate/M&A ★★
Table: p. 221

Herrera, Luis Oscar (Chile)
Profile: p. 210
Corporate/M&A ★★★
Table: p. 208

KEY TO RANKINGS: ✪ = Star Individual ★★★★ = Top Band ★★★ = Second Band ★★ = Third Band ★ = Fourth Band **U** = Up and coming

Herrera, Nicolás (Uruguay)
Profile: p. 906
Banking & Finance ★★★★
Table: p. 904
Corporate/M&A ★★★★
Table: p. 905

Herring, Michael (Australia)
Profile: p. 90
Communications: Telecoms ★★
Table: p. 69

Herring, Paul (United Kingdom)
Profile: p. 758
Shipping ★★★★
Table: p. 737

Herron, Louise (Australia)
Profile: p. 90
Communications: IT ★★
Table: p. 69

Hersch, Dennis (USA)
Profile: p. 869
Corporate/M&A ★★★★
Table: p. 820

Hertman, Alex (Israel)
Profile: p. 411
Banking & Finance ★★
Table: p. 406

Hervada, Joaquín (Spain)
Profile: p. 632
Corporate/M&A ★★★
Table: p. 624

Heun, Sven-Erik (Germany)
Profile: p. 324
Communications: Regulatory ★★★
Table: p. 306

Heussen, Benno (Germany)
Profile: p. 324
Communications: IT ★★★★
Table: p. 307

Hewitt, William J. (USA)
Profile: p. 869
Private Equity: Fund Formation ★★★★
Table: p. 835

Hewko, John (Czech Republic)
Profile: p. 236
Corporate/M&A ★★
Table: p. 234

Hey, Christian (Germany)
Profile: p. 324
Communications: Transactional ★★
Table: p. 306

Hey, Henrik (Greenland)
Profile: p. 344
Corporate/Commercial ★★★★
Table: p. 344

Heyes, Philip (Russia)
Profile: p. 577
Corporate/M&A ★★
Table: p. 574

Heymann, Thomas (Germany)
Profile: p. 324
Communications: IT ✪
Table: p. 307

Hickson, Chris (United Kingdom)
Profile: p. 758
Intellectual Property ★★★
Table: p. 729

Hiester, Elizabeth (United Kingdom)
Profile: p. 758
Communications: Telecoms ★★★★
Table: p. 707

Higginson, Tony J. (United Kingdom)
Profile: p. 758
Energy: Oil and Gas ★★
Table: p. 723

Hilton, Michael (Jamaica)
Profile: p. 432
Corporate/Commercial ★★★★
Table: p. 431

Hiltunen, Sari (Finland)
Profile: p. 258
Competition/Anti-trust **U**
Table: p. 256

Hines, Jonathan H. (Russia)
Profile: p. 577
Energy & Natural Resources ★★★★
Table: p. 576

Hirakawa, Osamu (Japan)
Profile: p. 444
Corporate/M&A ★★
Table: p. 439

Hirschberg, William E. (Bill) (USA)
Profile: p. 869
Banking & Finance ★★★★
Table: p. 791

Hirst, Tom (Canada)
Profile: p. 190
Energy & Natural Resources ★★★
Table: p. 180

Hitchings, Paul (Spain)
Profile: p. 632
Communications ★★
Table: p. 620

Hlawati, Edith (Austria)
Profile: p. 106
Banking & Finance ★★★★
Table: p. 103
Corporate/M&A ★★★★
Table: p. 104

Hobbelen, Hein (Netherlands)
Profile: p. 502
Communications ★★
Table: p. 492

Hobbs, Christopher (United Kingdom)
Profile: p. 758
Shipping ★★★
Table: p. 737

Hodgson, Derek (United Kingdom)
Profile: p. 758
Shipping ★★★★
Table: p. 737

Hodgson, Mark (United Kingdom)
Profile: p. 758
Intellectual Property ✪
Table: p. 729

Hodgson, Stephen (Germany)
Profile: p. 324
Project Finance ★★★
Table: p. 317

Høeg Rasmussen, Annikken (Norway)
Profile: p. 522
Energy & Natural Resources ★
Table: p. 520

Hoene, Thomas (Germany)
Profile: p. 324
Communications: IT ★★
Table: p. 307

Hoenike, Mark (Germany)
Profile: p. 325
Communications: Regulatory ★★
Table: p. 306

Hoffet, Franz (Switzerland)
Profile: p. 659
Communications ★
Table: p. 655

Hoffmann-Becking, Michael (Germany)
Profile: p. 325
Corporate/M&A ✪
Table: p. 311

Hofland, Dick (Netherlands)
Profile: p. 502
Tax ★★★★
Table: p. 500

Högström, Peter (Sweden)
Profile: p. 648
Banking & Finance ★★★
Table: p. 641

Höhn, Jakob (Switzerland)
Profile: p. 659
Corporate/M&A ★★★
Table: p. 657

Holgate, David (Canada)
Profile: p. 191
Energy & Natural Resources ★★★
Table: p. 180

Holland, Peter Rodney James (United Kingdom)
Profile: p. 758
Corporate/M&A ★
Table: p. 717

Holland, Tony (Australia)
Profile: p. 90
Project Finance ★★★
Table: p. 79

Hollis, Wendell (Bermuda)
Profile: p. 137
Corporate/Commercial ★★★
Table: p. 136

Holm, Christer A. (Sweden)
Profile: p. 648
Competition/Anti-trust ★★
Table: p. 644

Holm, Sverre André (Norway)
Profile: p. 522
Banking & Finance ★★
Table: p. 517

Holmes, Simon (United Kingdom)
Profile: p. 758
Competition/Anti-trust **U**
Table: p. 714

Holsten, R. Jay (Canada)
Profile: p. 191
Competition/Anti-trust ★
Table: p. 175

Holzapfel, Hans-Joachim (Germany)
Profile: p. 325
Private Equity ★★★
Table: p. 316

Honan III, William J (USA)
Profile: p. 869
Shipping: Litigation ★★★★
Table: p. 841

Hönig, Klaus (Germany)
Profile: p. 325
Corporate/M&A ★
Table: p. 311

Hooghoudt, Hein (Netherlands)
Profile: p. 503
Corporate/M&A ★★★★
Table: p. 496

Hooper, Chester (USA)
Profile: p. 869
Shipping: Litigation ★★★
Table: p. 841

Hooplot, Edward (Surinam)
Profile: p. 639
Corporate/Commercial ★★★★
Table: p. 638

Hope, Adrian (Argentina)
Profile: p. 62
Banking & Finance ★★★
Table: p. 53
Corporate/M&A ★★★
Table: p. 57

Hopkinson, R. Ronald (USA)
Profile: p. 869
Private Equity: Buyouts **U**
Table: p. 834

Horáková, Karolina (Czech Republic)
Profile: p. 236
Banking & Finance ★★★★
Table: p. 232

Horner, Clay (Canada)
Profile: p. 191
Corporate/M&A ★★★
Table: p. 177

Hornick, Robert (USA)
Profile: p. 869
Arbitration (International) ★
Table: p. 785

Horsfall Turner, Jonathan (United Kingdom)
Profile: p. 758
Banking & Finance ★★
Table: p. 699
Projects ★★★
Table: p. 733

Horsfall Turner, Richard (Qatar)
Profile: p. 569
Corporate/Commercial ★★★★
Table: p. 568

Horvath, Günther (Austria)
Profile: p. 106
Arbitration (International) ★★★
Table: p. 102
Corporate/M&A ★★
Table: p. 104

Hoss, Philippe (Luxembourg)
Profile: p. 466
Corporate/Commercial ★★★★
Table: p. 465

Hossain, Kamal (Bangladesh)
Profile: p. 112
Corporate/Commercial ★★★★
Table: p. 112

Hounnou, Severin (Benin)
Profile: p. 135
Corporate/Commercial ★★★★
Table: p. 135

Houston, Donald B. (Canada)
Profile: p. 191
Competition/Anti-trust ★★
Table: p. 175

Howard, Simon (Jersey)
Profile: p. 449
Corporate/Commercial ★★★★
Table: p. 448

Howard, Tim (Greece)
Profile: p. 342
Shipping: Foreign Firms ★★★
Table: p. 341

Howitt, Simon (Guernsey)
Profile: p. 346
Corporate/Commercial ★★★
Table: p. 346

Howse, Chris (Hong Kong)
Profile: p. 366
Shipping ★★★
Table: p. 361

Howson, Nicholas C. (China)
Profile: p. 217
Corporate/M&A: China Foreign ★★
Table: p. 213

Hsu, Paul (Taiwan)
Profile: p. 667
Corporate/Commercial ★★★★
Table: p. 666

Htoon, Ye (Myanmar)
Profile: p. 487
Corporate/Commercial ★★★★
Table: p. 487

Huang, Jack J.T. (Taiwan)
Profile: p. 667
Corporate/Commercial ★★★
Table: p. 666

Huang, Remington (Taiwan)
Profile: p. 667
Corporate/Commercial ★★★★
Table: p. 666

Huber, Peter (Austria)
Profile: p. 106
Banking & Finance ★★
Table: p. 103

Huck, L. Francis (USA)
Profile: p. 869
Banking & Finance ★★★★
Table: p. 791

Hudd, David G.T. (United Kingdom)
Profile: p. 759
Capital Markets: Securitisation ★
Table: p. 704

Hudicourt Ewald, Chantal (Haiti)
Profile: p. 349
Corporate/Commercial ★★★★
Table: p. 349

Hudspeth, Mark (Singapore)
Profile: p. 600
Banking & Finance ★★
Table: p. 586

Huenerwadel, Patrick (Switzerland)
Profile: p. 660
Banking & Finance **U**
Table: p. 654

Hügel, Hanns F. (Austria)
Profile: p. 106
Corporate/M&A ★★★
Table: p. 104

Hughes, Clarence (Guyana)
Profile: p. 348
Corporate/Commercial ★★★
Table: p. 348

Hughes, Conrado (Uruguay)
Profile: p. 906
Corporate/M&A ★★★★
Table: p. 905

Hughes, Geraint (Singapore)
Profile: p. 600
Project Finance ★
Table: p. 594

Hughes, Gordon (Australia)
Profile: p. 91
Communications: IT ★★★★
Table: p. 69

Hughes, Paul (Australia)
Profile: p. 91
Competition/Anti-trust ★
Table: p. 71

Hughes, Randal T. (Canada)
Profile: p. 191
Competition/Anti-trust ★★★
Table: p. 175

Hughes, Richard (United Kingdom)
Profile: p. 759
Capital Markets: Securitisation ★★
Table: p. 704

Hultqvist, Svante (Sweden)
Profile: p. 648
Banking & Finance ★★★
Table: p. 641

Humphrey, Anthony R. (United Kingdom)
Profile: p. 759
Banking & Finance ★★★
Table: p. 699
Projects ★★
Table: p. 733

Hunsaker, Mark (Japan)
Profile: p. 444
Capital Markets: Japan Foreign **U**
Table: p. 437

KEY TO RANKINGS: ✪ = Star Individual ★★★★ = Top Band ★★★ = Second Band ★★ = Third Band ★ = Fourth Band **U** = Up and coming

Hunt, Hilary (New Zealand)
Profile: p. 509
Banking & Finance ★★
Table: p. 507

Hunter, Lawson (Canada)
Profile: p. 191
Competition/Anti-trust ★★★★
Table: p. 175

Huq, Rafique-ul (Bangladesh)
Profile: p. 112
Corporate/Commercial ★★★
Table: p. 112

Hurst, Philip (United Kingdom)
Profile: p. 759
Energy: Mining ★★★★
Table: p. 725

Hurstel, Daniel (France)
Profile: p. 289
Corporate/M&A ★★
Table: p. 275

Huse, Joseph (France)
Profile: p. 289
Project Finance ★★
Table: p. 277

Huser, Henry L. (Belgium)
Profile: p. 129
Competition/Anti-trust ★★
Table: p. 122

Husted, Catherine (Hong Kong)
Profile: p. 366
Capital Markets: Derivatives ★★★
Table: p. 355

Hutter, Stephan (Germany)
Profile: p. 325
Capital Markets: Equity ★★★★
Table: p. 304
Project Finance ★★
Table: p. 317

Huyghé De Mahenge, Yves (France)
Profile: p. 289
Corporate/M&A ★
Table: p. 275

Hylton, Hartwell (USA)
Profile: p. 870
Banking & Finance ★★
Table: p. 791

Hyman, Neil (United Kingdom)
Profile: p. 759
Corporate/M&A ★
Table: p. 717

I

Iatridis, George (Greece)
Profile: p. 342
Shipping ★★
Table: p. 340

Ibrahim, Khalid (Pakistan)
Profile: p. 531
Corporate/Commercial ★★★
Table: p. 529

Igartua, Fernando (Spain)
Profile: p. 632
Banking & Finance ★★
Table: p. 619

Igartua, Íñigo (Spain)
Profile: p. 632
Competition/Anti-trust ★
Table: p. 622

Ighodalo, Asue (Nigeria)
Profile: p. 515
Corporate/Commercial ★★★
Table: p. 512
Energy & Natural Resources ★★★★
Table: p. 513

Iglesias Prada, Juan Luis (Spain)
Profile: p. 632
Corporate/M&A ★★
Table: p. 624

Ihrig, Hans-Christoph (Germany)
Profile: p. 325
Capital Markets: Equity ★
Table: p. 304

Illanes, Francisco Javier (Chile)
Profile: p. 210
Banking & Finance ★★★
Table: p. 206

Ilundain, Santiago (Spain)
Profile: p. 633
Tax ★★★★
Table: p. 628

Imperio, Angelito (Philippines)
Profile: p. 544
Corporate/Commercial ★★
Table: p. 542

In de Braekt, Martin (Netherlands)
Profile: p. 503
Energy & Natural Resources ★★★★
Table: p. 498

Indacochea, Ricardo (Bolivia)
Profile: p. 139
Corporate/Commercial ★★★
Table: p. 138

Indoe, William F. (USA)
Profile: p. 870
Tax ★★
Table: p. 845

Ingerl, Reinhard (Germany)
Profile: p. 325
Intellectual Property: General ★★
Table: p. 314

Inglis, Alan (United Kingdom)
Profile: p. 759
Banking & Finance ★
Table: p. 699

Inglis, Andrew (United Kingdom)
Profile: p. 759
Intellectual Property ★★★
Table: p. 729

Inglis, John (Bahrain)
Profile: p. 111
Banking & Finance ★★★★
Table: p. 110
Corporate/M&A ★★★★
Table: p. 111
Project Finance ★★★★
Table: p. 111

Ingram, Kevin (United Kingdom)
Profile: p. 759
Capital Markets: Securitisation ★★★
Table: p. 704

Inman, Jonathan (Japan)
Profile: p. 388, 444
Project Finance ★★★
Table: p. 442
Project Finance: India Foreign ★★★
Table: p. 386

Inoue, Satoshi (Japan)
Profile: p. 444
Banking & Finance ★★
Table: p. 433

Instance, Mark (Italy)
Profile: p. 426
Project Finance ★★
Table: p. 421

Intven, Hank (Canada)
Profile: p. 191
Communications ★★★★
Table: p. 173

Irgens, Einar (Norway)
Profile: p. 522
Banking & Finance ★★★
Table: p. 517

Irvine, James (United Kingdom)
Profile: p. 759
Intellectual Property ★★
Table: p. 729

Irving, Robert (Hungary)
Profile: p. 376
Banking & Finance ★★
Table: p. 372
Corporate/M&A ★★★
Table: p. 375

Isaacson, Laurence B. (USA)
Profile: p. 870
Capital Markets: Securitisation ★★
Table: p. 795

Ishengoma, Protase Rwenzahura (Tanzania)
Profile: p. 669
Corporate/Commercial ★★★
Table: p. 668

Ishiguro, Toru (Japan)
Profile: p. 444
Banking & Finance ★★★
Table: p. 433
Capital Markets ✪
Table: p. 436

Iskandar, Ratna (Indonesia)
Profile: p. 392
Corporate/Commercial ★★
Table: p. 391

Isler, Peter R (Switzerland)
Profile: p. 660
Banking & Finance ★★★★
Table: p. 654
Corporate/M&A ★★★★
Table: p. 657

Isola Sr, Peter (Gibraltar)
Profile: p. 338
Corporate/Commercial ★★
Table: p. 337

Italiani, Fulvio (Venezuela)
Profile: p. 913
Corporate/M&A ★★
Table: p. 909

J

Jaakke, John C. (Netherlands)
Profile: p. 503
Corporate/M&A ★★
Table: p. 496

Jaatinen, Pekka (Finland)
Profile: p. 258
Corporate/M&A ★★
Table: p. 257

Jäckle, Christof (Germany)
Profile: p. 325
Communications: Transactional ★★★
Table: p. 306

Jackson, Ian (Germany)
Profile: p. 325
Capital Markets: Debt ★★★
Table: p. 303

Jackson, J. David A. (Canada)
Profile: p. 191
Corporate/M&A ✪
Table: p. 177

Jacob, Friedhelm (Germany)
Profile: p. 325
Tax ★
Table: p. 319

Jacobs, Lawrence (United Kingdom)
Profile: p. 759
Communications: IT ★★
Table: p. 709

Jacobs, Micheal A. (USA)
Profile: p. 870
Intellectual Property ★★
Table: p. 833

Jacobs, Robert A. (USA)
Profile: p. 870
Tax ★★
Table: p. 845

Jacobs, Stephen (USA)
Profile: p. 870
Corporate/M&A ★★
Table: p. 820
Private Equity: Buyouts ★★
Table: p. 834

Jacobsen, Ulrik (Denmark)
Profile: p. 241
Banking & Finance ★★★
Table: p. 237

Jacobson, Martin (USA)
Profile: p. 870
Project Finance ★★
Table: p. 837

Jacobson, Ronald H. (USA)
Profile: p. 870
Banking & Finance ★★
Table: p. 787

Jadek, Srecko (Slovenia)
Profile: p. 608
Corporate/Commercial ★★★★
Table: p. 608

Jaenichen, Hans-Rainer (Germany)
Profile: p. 325
Intellectual Property: Patent ★★
Table: p. 313

Jaffar, Mohammed (Pakistan)
Profile: p. 531
Corporate/Commercial ★★
Table: p. 529

Jaffe, Helene D. (USA)
Profile: p. 871
Competition/Anti-trust ★★★
Table: p. 808

Jakoba, Raphaël (Madagascar)
Profile: p. 468
Corporate/Commercial ★★★★
Table: p. 468

Jakutis, Remigijus (Lithuania)
Profile: p. 464
Corporate/Commercial ★★★
Table: p. 463

Jaletzke, Matthias (Germany)
Profile: p. 326
Private Equity ★★
Table: p. 316

Jallah, David A.B. (Liberia)
Profile: p. 461
Corporate/Commercial ★★★★
Table: p. 460

Jalles, Isabel (Portugal)
Profile: p. 565
Competition/Anti-trust ★★
Table: p. 559

James, Glen William (United Kingdom)
Profile: p. 759
Corporate/M&A ★★
Table: p. 717

James, Ian (Jersey)
Profile: p. 449
Corporate/Commercial ★★★★
Table: p. 448

James, Martin (Australia)
Profile: p. 91
Energy & Natural Resources ★★
Table: p. 75

Jamieson, William (Singapore)
Profile: p. 600
Corporate/M&A: Singapore Foreign ★★★★
Table: p. 592

Jansen, Jan (Norway)
Profile: p. 523
Corporate/M&A ★★
Table: p. 519
Energy & Natural Resources ★
Table: p. 520

Jarvin, Sigvard (France)
Profile: p. 289
Arbitration (International) ★★
Table: p. 262

Jason, John (Canada)
Profile: p. 192
Banking & Finance ★
Table: p. 171

Jauffret, Olivier (France)
Profile: p. 290
Banking & Finance **U**
Table: p. 265

Jáuregui-Rojas, Miguel (Mexico)
Profile: p. 481
Corporate/M&A ★★★★
Table: p. 480

Javaras, George (USA)
Profile: p. 871
Tax ★★★★
Table: p. 843

Jedrzejewski, Slawomir (Poland)
Profile: p. 553
Tax ★★
Table: p. 551

Jeffares, Tim (Thailand)
Profile: p. 673
Banking & Finance ★★★
Table: p. 670

Jeffrey, John Alasdair (Oman)
Profile: p. 528
Corporate/M&A ★★★★
Table: p. 527

Jenkins, Huw (China/Hong Kong)
Profile: p. 217, 366
Banking & Finance ★★★
Table: p. 352
Project Finance ★★★★
Table: p. 359
Project Finance: China Foreign ★★★★
Table: p. 215

Jenkinson, Tony (Jamaica)
Profile: p. 432
Corporate/Commercial ★★★
Table: p. 431

Jenner, Jesse (USA)
Profile: p. 871
Intellectual Property ★★
Table: p. 831

Jennings, Charles (Cayman Islands)
Profile: p. 204
Corporate/Commercial ★★★
Table: p. 203

Jensen, Jørgen Reimer (Denmark)
Profile: p. 241
Banking & Finance ★★★
Table: p. 237

Jestaedt, Thomas (Germany)
Profile: p. 326
Competition/Anti-trust ★
Table: p. 309

Jetter, Yorck (Russia)
Profile: p. 578

KEY TO RANKINGS: ✪ = Star Individual ★★★★ = Top Band ★★★ = Second Band ★★ = Third Band ★ = Fourth Band **U** = Up and coming

Corporate/M&A ★★★
Table: p. 574

Jetzer, Rolf (Switzerland)
Profile: p. 660
Communications ★★★
Table: p. 655

Jewell, Robert V. (USA)
Profile: p. 871
Corporate/M&A ★★★★
Table: p. 824

Jewett, Peter E. S. (Canada)
Profile: p. 192
Corporate/M&A ★★★★
Table: p. 177

Ji, Jianfeng (China)
Profile: p. 217
Corporate/M&A ★★★★
Table: p. 211
Project Finance ★★★★
Table: p. 214

Jijon, Rodrigo (Ecuador)
Profile: p. 245
Corporate/Commercial ★★★★
Table: p. 244

Jiménez, Ernesto (Spain)
Profile: p. 633
Tax ★★
Table: p. 628

Jiménez Blanco, José Ignacio (Spain)
Profile: p. 633
Tax ★★★
Table: p. 628

Jiménez de Arechaga, Fernando (Uruguay)
Profile: p. 906
Banking & Finance ★★★
Table: p. 904
Corporate/M&A ★★★
Table: p. 905

Jiménez-Laiglesia, José M. (Spain)
Profile: p. 633
Competition/Anti-trust ★★
Table: p. 622

Jiménez-Laiglesia, Juan (Spain)
Profile: p. 633
Competition/Anti-trust ★★
Table: p. 622

Jing, Paul T. (Cameroon)
Profile: p. 169
Corporate/Commercial ★★★
Table: p. 169

Jinks, Andrew (Australia)
Profile: p. 91
Capital Markets ★★★★
Table: p. 67

Job, Henri Pierre (Cameroon)
Profile: p. 169
Corporate/Commercial ★★★★
Table: p. 169

Joffe, Bob (USA)
Profile: p. 871
Competition/Anti-trust ★★★★
Table: p. 808

Johnson, Andrew (United Kingdom)
Profile: p. 759
Shipping ★★★
Table: p. 737

Johnson, Claes (Sweden)
Profile: p. 648
Corporate/M&A ★★
Table: p. 645

Johnson, Clayton (Hong Kong)
Profile: p. 366
Capital Markets: Debt & Equity ★★★
Table: p. 353

Johnson, Clifford D. (Canada)
Profile: p. 192
Energy & Natural Resources ★★
Table: p. 180

Johnson, Craig (USA)
Profile: p. 871
Communications: IT ★★★★
Table: p. 805

Johnson, Darrell (Indonesia)
Profile: p. 392
Corporate/Commercial ★★
Table: p. 391

Johnson, Ian (United Kingdom)
Profile: p. 759
Tax ★★
Table: p. 739

Johnson, James (United Kingdom)
Profile: p. 759
Banking & Finance ★★★
Table: p. 699

Johnson, Jaroslawa Zelinsky (Ukraine)
Profile: p. 687
Corporate/Commercial ★★★
Table: p. 686

Johnson, Nick (Czech Republic)
Profile: p. 236
Corporate/M&A ★★
Table: p. 234

Johnston, Bruce (United Kingdom)
Profile: p. 759
PFI ★★★
Table: p. 733

Johnston, Campbell (Australia)
Profile: p. 91
Project Finance ★★★
Table: p. 79

Johnston, Chris (Canada)
Profile: p. 192
Communications ★★★
Table: p. 173

Johnston, Graeme (Singapore)
Profile: p. 600
Banking & Finance: Singapore Foreign ★
Table: p. 588

Johnston, M. Elaine (USA)
Profile: p. 871
Competition/Anti-trust ★
Table: p. 808

Johnston, Nic (Hong Kong)
Profile: p. 366
Banking & Finance ★★★
Table: p. 352
Project Finance ★★
Table: p. 359

Johnston, William (Ireland)
Profile: p. 402
Banking & Finance ★★★★
Table: p. 394

Jolley, Braddon (Australia)
Profile: p. 91
Corporate/M&A ★★★
Table: p. 73

Jonak, Jacek (Poland)
Profile: p. 553
Banking & Finance ★★
Table: p. 545

Jonas, Kay-Uwe (Germany)
Profile: p. 326
Intellectual Property: General ★
Table: p. 314

Jonas, Michael D. (New Zealand)
Profile: p. 509
Banking & Finance ★★★★
Table: p. 507

Jonatansson, Hrobjartur (Iceland)
Profile: p. 379
Corporate/Commercial ★★★
Table: p. 378

Jones, Angus (Australia)
Profile: p. 91
Energy & Natural Resources U
Table: p. 75

Jones, Arfon (United Kingdom)
Profile: p. 759
Corporate/M&A ★
Table: p. 717

Jones, Gareth (United Kingdom)
Profile: p. 759
Energy: Oil and Gas ★★
Table: p. 723

Jones, Jeffrey (South Korea)
Profile: p. 516
Corporate/Commercial: North Korea Foreign ★★★★
Table: p. 516

Jones, Nigel (United Kingdom)
Profile: p. 760
Intellectual Property ★★
Table: p. 729

Jones, Stephen (United Kingdom)
Profile: p. 760
Intellectual Property ★★★
Table: p. 729

Jones, Thomas (Hong Kong)
Profile: p. 217
Corporate/M&A: China Foreign ★★★★
Table: p. 213
Project Finance: China Foreign ★★★
Table: p. 215

Jonsson, Gestur (Iceland)
Profile: p. 379
Corporate/Commercial ★★★★
Table: p. 378

Jonsson, Gunnar (Iceland)
Profile: p. 379
Corporate/Commercial ★★★★
Table: p. 378

Jordis, Teresa (Austria)
Profile: p. 106
Corporate/M&A ★★
Table: p. 104

Joris, Jean-Louis (Belgium)
Profile: p. 129
Corporate/M&A ★★
Table: p. 125

Josephus Jitta, Marius W. (Netherlands)
Profile: p. 503
Corporate/M&A ★★
Table: p. 496

Joyce, Tom (United Kingdom)
Profile: p. 760
Corporate/M&A ★
Table: p. 717

Judge, Ian (United Kingdom)
Profile: p. 760
Intellectual Property ✪
Table: p. 729

Júdice, José Miguel (Portugal)
Profile: p. 565
Corporate/M&A ★★
Table: p. 560

Jung, Harald (Germany)
Profile: p. 326
Corporate/M&A ★
Table: p. 311

Jung, Kyung Taek (South Korea)
Profile: p. 616
Corporate/Commercial ★★★★
Table: p. 614

Jurecewicz, Witold (Poland)
Profile: p. 553
Corporate/M&A ★★★
Table: p. 548
Energy & Natural Resources ★★★
Table: p. 550

Jury, Caroline (Germany)
Profile: p. 326
Banking & Finance ★★★★
Table: p. 301

K

Kaasik, Viktor (Estonia)
Profile: p. 252
Corporate/Commercial ★★★★
Table: p. 251

Kabraji, Kairas N (Pakistan)
Profile: p. 531
Corporate/Commercial ★★★★
Table: p. 529

Kacymirow, Tomasz (Poland)
Profile: p. 553
Tax ★★★★
Table: p. 551

Kaden, Lewis (USA)
Profile: p. 871
Corporate/M&A ★
Table: p. 820

Kadlick, Richard (USA)
Profile: p. 871
Capital Markets: Securitisation ★★
Table: p. 795

Kadurugamuwa, Udaya (Sri Lanka)
Profile: p. 637
Corporate/Commercial ★★★★
Table: p. 637

Kahn, Daniel (France)
Profile: p. 290
Communications: IT ★★
Table: p. 271

Kail, Michael (USA)
Profile: p. 871
Energy & Natural Resources ★
Table: p. 827

Kaiser, Bernhard (Germany)
Profile: p. 326
Capital Markets: Securitisation ★★
Table: p. 304

Kakuyama, Kazutoshi (Japan)
Profile: p. 444
Corporate/M&A ★
Table: p. 439

Kalikova, Gulnara (Kyrgyz Republic)
Profile: p. 455
Corporate/Commercial ★★★
Table: p. 455

Kalo, Perparim (Albania)
Profile: p. 50
Corporate/Commercial ★★★★
Table: p. 49

Kamstra, Gerry (United Kingdom)
Profile: p. 760
Intellectual Property ★★
Table: p. 729

Kane, Gregory T. (Canada)
Profile: p. 192
Communications ★★★
Table: p. 173

Kang, Hee Chul (South Korea)
Profile: p. 616
Corporate/Commercial ★★
Table: p. 614

Kang, Hyo Young (Hong Kong)
Profile: p. 616
Corporate/Commercial: South Korea Foreign ★★★
Table: p. 615

Kanter, Lennart (Sweden)
Profile: p. 648
Corporate/M&A ★★★
Table: p. 645

Kantor, Israel (Israel)
Profile: p. 411
Corporate/M&A ★
Table: p. 409

Kapinga, Wilbert (Tanzania)
Profile: p. 669
Corporate/Commercial ★★★★
Table: p. 668

Kaplan, Cathy (USA)
Profile: p. 871
Capital Markets: Securitisation ★★★
Table: p. 795

Kaplan, Charles (France)
Profile: p. 290
Arbitration (International) ★
Table: p. 262

Karatzas, Katarina (Greece)
Profile: p. 342
Corporate/M&A ★★★★
Table: p. 339

Kärde, Bengt (Sweden)
Profile: p. 649
Banking & Finance ★★★★
Table: p. 641

Karet, Ian (United Kingdom)
Profile: p. 760
Intellectual Property ★★★
Table: p. 729

Karlsson, Johan (Sweden)
Profile: p. 649
Competition/Anti-trust ★★
Table: p. 644

Karrer, Pierre A. (Switzerland)
Profile: p. 660
Arbitration (International) ★★★★
Table: p. 653

Karugaba, Phillip (Uganda)
Profile: p. 685
Corporate/Commercial ★★
Table: p. 684

Kassim, Kadir (Malaysia)
Profile: p. 472
Banking & Finance ★★★★
Table: p. 470

Katayama, Tatsu (Japan)
Profile: p. 445
Banking & Finance ★★★
Table: p. 433
Capital Markets ★★
Table: p. 436

Katcher, Richard (USA)
Profile: p. 871
Corporate/M&A ★★★
Table: p. 820

Katende, John W. (Uganda)
Profile: p. 685
Corporate/Commercial ★★★
Table: p. 684

Katsh, Salem M. (USA)
Profile: p. 871
Intellectual Property ★
Table: p. 831

Kattan, Joseph (USA)
Profile: p. 871
Competition/Anti-trust ★
Table: p. 811

KEY TO RANKINGS: ✪ = Star Individual ★★★★ = Top Band ★★★ = Second Band ★★ = Third Band ★ = Fourth Band **U** = Up and coming

Katz, David (USA)
Profile: p. 872
Corporate/M&A ★★
Table: p. 820

Kaufman, Christopher ("Kit") (USA)
Profile: p. 872
Communications: IT ★★★
Table: p. 805
Corporate/M&A ★★★★
Table: p. 825

Kaufmann-Kohler, Gabrielle (Switzerland)
Profile: p. 660
Arbitration (International) ★★★
Table: p. 653

Kawamura, Akira (Japan)
Profile: p. 445
Corporate/M&A ★★★
Table: p. 439

Kawata, Yukako (USA)
Profile: p. 872
Private Equity: Fund Formation ★★★★
Table: p. 835

Kawecki, W. Andrzej (Poland)
Profile: p. 553
Corporate/M&A ★★★
Table: p. 548

Kay, David Ben (China)
Profile: p. 217
Corporate/M&A: China Foreign ★★★
Table: p. 213

Kaye, Laurence (United Kingdom)
Profile: p. 760
Communications: E-commerce ★★
Table: p. 711

Kazanjian, John (Canada)
Profile: p. 192
Corporate/M&A ★
Table: p. 177

Kazungu, Jean-Bosco (Rwanda)
Profile: p. 579
Corporate/Commercial ★★★★
Table: p. 579

Keal, Anthony C. (United Kingdom)
Profile: p. 760
Banking & Finance ★★★
Table: p. 699

Keane, Paul (USA)
Profile: p. 872
Shipping: Litigation ★★
Table: p. 841

Kee, David (Canada)
Profile: p. 192
Banking & Finance ★★★
Table: p. 171

Keefe, Blair (Canada)
Profile: p. 192
Banking & Finance ★
Table: p. 171

Keefe, Charles (Russia)
Profile: p. 578
Corporate/M&A ★★
Table: p. 574

Keeler, Mark (Japan)
Profile: p. 445
Capital Markets: Japan Foreign ★★★
Table: p. 437
Project Finance ★★
Table: p. 442

Keenleyside, Anthony H.A. (Canada)
Profile: p. 192
Communications ★★★
Table: p. 173

Keith, Hamish (Kenya)
Profile: p. 454
Corporate/Commercial ★★★★
Table: p. 453

Keller, Don (USA)
Profile: p. 872
Communications: IT ★★★
Table: p. 805

Kellerman, Joanne (Netherlands)
Profile: p. 503
Banking & Finance ★★
Table: p. 491

Kellet, Christopher (Germany)
Profile: p. 326
Corporate/M&A ★★
Table: p. 311
Private Equity ★★★
Table: p. 316

Kelley, Jay (USA)
Profile: p. 872
Energy & Natural Resources ★★
Table: p. 829

Kellogg, Michael (USA)
Profile: p. 872
Communications: Regulatory ★★
Table: p. 803

Kellough, Howard J. (Canada)
Profile: p. 193
Tax ★★
Table: p. 182

Kelly, Christopher (United Kingdom)
Profile: p. 760
Energy: Mining **U**
Table: p. 725

Kelly, Jacky (United Kingdom)
Profile: p. 760
Capital Markets: Securitisation ★★★
Table: p. 704

Kelly, John (Australia)
Profile: p. 91
Energy & Natural Resources ★★★★
Table: p. 75

Kelly, Mark (USA)
Profile: p. 872
Corporate/M&A ★★★★
Table: p. 824

Kelly, Mary (Canada)
Profile: p. 193
Banking & Finance **U**
Table: p. 171

Kelly, Peter (Australia)
Profile: p. 91
Competition/Anti-trust ★★★
Table: p. 71

Kemp, Richard (United Kingdom)
Profile: p. 760
Communications: E-commerce ★★★
Table: p. 711
Communications: IT ★★★★
Table: p. 709

Kenadjian, Patrick S. (Germany)
Profile: p. 326
Capital Markets: Equity ✪
Table: p. 304

Kench, John (Australia)
Profile: p. 91
Competition/Anti-trust ★★★★
Table: p. 71

Kenjebayeva, Aigoul (Kazakhstan)
Profile: p. 452
Energy & Natural Resources ★★★★
Table: p. 451

Kennedy, Donald J. (USA)
Profile: p. 872
Shipping: Litigation ★★★
Table: p. 841

Kennedy, Mike (USA)
Profile: p. 872
Communications: IT ★★
Table: p. 805

Kennedy, Rowan (Australia)
Profile: p. 91
Energy & Natural Resources ★★★
Table: p. 75

Kennedy, Tom (USA)
Profile: p. 872
Communications: Transactional (IT) ★★★★
Table: p. 801
Corporate/M&A ★
Table: p. 820

Kennish, Tim (Canada)
Profile: p. 193
Competition/Anti-trust ★★★★
Table: p. 175

Kent, Andrew J. F. (Canada)
Profile: p. 193
Banking & Finance ★★★
Table: p. 171

Keough, Loyola (Canada)
Profile: p. 193
Energy & Natural Resources ★★
Table: p. 180

Keré, Barthélémy (Burkina Faso)
Profile: p. 166
Corporate/Commercial ★★★★
Table: p. 166

Kerins, Charles (British Virgin Islands)
Profile: p. 161
Corporate/Commercial ★★★
Table: p. 160

Kerr, David (United Kingdom)
Profile: p. 761
Communications: Telecoms ★★★★
Table: p. 707

Kerr, Edward (Australia)
Profile: p. 92
Capital Markets ★★
Table: p. 67

Kerr, John (USA)
Profile: p. 872
Arbitration (International) ★★★
Table: p. 785

Kerr, Philip (Australia)
Profile: p. 92
Intellectual Property ★★★
Table: p. 77

Kershaw, Nick (Jersey)
Profile: p. 449
Corporate/Commercial ★★★
Table: p. 448

Kessel, Mark (USA)
Profile: p. 872
Capital Markets: Debt & Equity ★
Table: p. 793

Ketelsen, Peter (Denmark)
Profile: p. 241
Corporate/M&A **U**
Table: p. 239

Kett, Peter (France)
Profile: p. 290
Banking & Finance ★★
Table: p. 265

Kettani, Azzedine (Morocco)
Profile: p. 485
Corporate/Commercial ★★★★
Table: p. 485

Kettani, Nadia (Morocco)
Profile: p. 485
Corporate/Commercial **U**
Table: p. 485

Key, Jeremy (United Arab Emirates)
Profile: p. 693
Project Finance ★★★
Table: p. 691

Kezsbom, Allen (USA)
Profile: p. 873
Competition/Anti-trust ★
Table: p. 808

Khaitan, O.P. (India)
Profile: p. 388
Corporate/M&A ★★
Table: p. 381

Khalilieh, Yousef S (Jordan)
Profile: p. 450
Corporate/Commercial ★★★
Table: p. 450

Khan, Aftab Ahmad (Pakistan)
Profile: p. 531
Corporate/Commercial ★
Table: p. 529

Khan, Maudood (Pakistan)
Profile: p. 531
Corporate/Commercial ★★
Table: p. 529

Khan, Rafique (United Kingdom)
Profile: p. 761
Energy: Oil and Gas ★★
Table: p. 723

Khodadad, Nabil (Uzbekistan)
Profile: p. 907
Corporate/Commercial ★★★★
Table: p. 907

Kidd, John (USA)
Profile: p. 873
Intellectual Property ★★
Table: p. 831

Kiely, Bruce F. (USA)
Profile: p. 873
Energy & Natural Resources ★★
Table: p. 827

Kiessling, Rob (USA)
Profile: p. 873
Banking & Finance ★★★★
Table: p. 791

Kilmartin, Kevin (Falkland Islands)
Profile: p. 254
Corporate/Commercial ★★★★
Table: p. 254

Kim, Doo Sik (South Korea)
Profile: p. 616
Corporate/Commercial ★★★
Table: p. 614

Kim, John (Cuba)
Profile: p. 230
Corporate/Commercial ★★★★
Table: p. 230

Kim, Soo Chang (South Korea)
Profile: p. 616
Corporate/Commercial ★★★
Table: p. 614

Kim, Young Joon (Japan)
Profile: p. 445, 617
Corporate/Commercial: South Korea Foreign ★★★★
Table: p. 615
Project Finance ★★
Table: p. 442

Kimball, John (USA)
Profile: p. 873
Shipping: Litigation ★★★★
Table: p. 841

Kimmel, Roger H. (USA)
Profile: p. 873
Private Equity: Buyouts ★★
Table: p. 834

Kimura, Akiko (Japan)
Profile: p. 445
Capital Markets ✪
Table: p. 436

Kinami, Naoki (Japan)
Profile: p. 445
Banking & Finance ★★★
Table: p. 433
Capital Markets ★
Table: p. 436

Kines, Stephen (Czech Republic)
Profile: p. 236
Communications ★★★★
Table: p. 233

King, Christopher (Thailand)
Profile: p. 673
Corporate/M&A ★★★★
Table: p. 672

King, David (Barbados)
Profile: p. 113
Corporate/Commercial ★★★
Table: p. 113

King, John (Australia)
Profile: p. 92
Tax ★
Table: p. 81

King, John C. (New Zealand)
Profile: p. 509
Corporate/M&A ★★★★
Table: p. 508

King, Ken (USA)
Profile: p. 873
Communications: IT ★★
Table: p. 805

King, Peter (United Kingdom)
Profile: p. 761
Corporate/M&A ★
Table: p. 717

Kinsella, Stephen (Belgium)
Profile: p. 129
Competition/Anti-trust ★★
Table: p. 122

Kirk, Ian (Guernsey)
Profile: p. 347
Corporate/Commercial ★★★
Table: p. 346

Kirkland, David (USA)
Profile: p. 873
Corporate/M&A ★★★
Table: p. 824

Kirry, Antoine (France)
Profile: p. 290
Arbitration (International) ★
Table: p. 262

Kirsch, Bill (USA)
Profile: p. 874
Corporate/M&A ★★★
Table: p. 813

Kisil, Vasil (Ukraine)
Profile: p. 687
Corporate/Commercial ★★★★
Table: p. 686

Kisimba-Ngoy, Honorius (Democratic Republic of Congo)
Profile: p. 224
Corporate/Commercial ★★★★
Table: p. 224

Kitanosono, Masayuki (Japan)
Profile: p. 445
Capital Markets ★
Table: p. 436

Kitazawa, Masaakira (Japan)
Profile: p. 445
Banking & Finance ★★
Table: p. 433
Capital Markets ★★★
Table: p. 436

Kitchin, Alan (Japan)
Profile: p. 445
Corporate/M&A: Japan Foreign ★★★
Table: p. 441
Project Finance ★★★★
Table: p. 442

Kjølbye, Christian Th. (Denmark)
Profile: p. 241
Corporate/M&A ★★
Table: p. 239

Kjørnæs, Arne Didrik (Norway)
Profile: p. 523
Corporate/M&A ★★★★
Table: p. 519

Klavins, Filip (Latvia)
Profile: p. 457
Corporate/Commercial ★★★★
Table: p. 456

Klein, Guillermo Walter (Argentina)
Profile: p. 62
Corporate/M&A ★★★
Table: p. 57

Klein, Linda B. (USA)
Profile: p. 874
Capital Markets: Derivatives ★
Table: p. 798

Kleinbard, Edward (USA)
Profile: p. 874
Tax: Financial Products ★★★★
Table: p. 845

Klepper, Martin (USA)
Profile: p. 388, 874
Energy & Natural Resources ★★★★
Table: p. 827
Project Finance ★★★
Table: p. 837
Project Finance: India Foreign ★★★
Table: p. 386

Klingenberg, Miguel (Spain)
Profile: p. 633
Tax ★★
Table: p. 628

Klusmann, Martin (Germany)
Profile: p. 326
Competition/Anti-trust ★★★
Table: p. 309

Knapp, Vanessa (United Kingdom)
Profile: p. 761
Corporate/M&A ★
Table: p. 717

Knibbeler, Winfred (Netherlands)
Profile: p. 503
Competition/Anti-trust ★★★★
Table: p. 494

Knight, Adrian (United Kingdom)
Profile: p. 761
Corporate/M&A ★★
Table: p. 717

Knight, James T. (USA)
Profile: p. 874
Banking & Finance ★
Table: p. 791

Knight, Peter (Australia)
Profile: p. 92
Communications: IT ★★
Table: p. 69
Intellectual Property ★
Table: p. 77

Knight, William (United Kingdom)
Profile: p. 761
Corporate/M&A ★★
Table: p. 717

Knoepfler, François (Switzerland)
Profile: p. 660
Arbitration (International) ★★
Table: p. 653

Knudsen, Gudmund (Norway)
Profile: p. 523
Corporate/M&A ★★
Table: p. 519

Knutson, Robert (United Kingdom)
Profile: p. 761
Arbitration (International) ★★
Table: p. 696

Ko, Teresa (Hong Kong)
Profile: p. 366
Capital Markets: Debt & Equity ★★★★
Table: p. 353
Corporate/M&A ★★★★
Table: p. 357

Koch, Michael Steven (Canada)
Profile: p. 193
Communications ★★
Table: p. 173

Kocharyan, Levon (Russia)
Profile: p. 578
Energy & Natural Resources ★★★★
Table: p. 576

Köck, Stefan (Austria)
Profile: p. 106
Corporate/M&A **U**
Table: p. 104

Koeck, William (Australia)
Profile: p. 92
Corporate/M&A ★
Table: p. 73

Koenig, Thierry (Mauritius)
Profile: p. 478
Corporate/Commercial ★★★★
Table: p. 478

Koep, Peter (Namibia)
Profile: p. 488
Corporate/Commercial ★★★★
Table: p. 488

Koerfer, Hans Rolf (Germany)
Profile: p. 326
Corporate/M&A ★★★
Table: p. 311

Kofmann, Morten (Belgium)
Profile: p. 241
Competition/Anti-trust ★★★★
Table: p. 238

Koh, Ian (Singapore)
Profile: p. 601
Shipping ★★
Table: p. 595

Kohn, Richard (USA)
Profile: p. 874
Banking & Finance ★★★★
Table: p. 787

Kok, Che Kheong (Malaysia)
Profile: p. 473
Banking & Finance ★★
Table: p. 470
Corporate/M&A ★
Table: p. 471

Kolasky, William J. (USA)
Profile: p. 874
Competition/Anti-trust ★★★
Table: p. 811

Kon, Stephen (United Kingdom)
Profile: p. 761
Competition/Anti-trust ✪
Table: p. 714

Kone, Modibo (Mali)
Profile: p. 474
Corporate/Commercial ★★★★
Table: p. 474

König, Andreas (Germany)
Profile: p. 327
Capital Markets: Debt ★★★★
Table: p. 303
Capital Markets: Equity ★★★
Table: p. 304

König, Stephan (Germany)
Profile: p. 327
Corporate/M&A ★★
Table: p. 311

Konii, Junri (Hong Kong)
Profile: p. 366
Capital Markets: Securitisation ★★
Table: p. 354

Konjbeto, Martin (Central African Republic)
Profile: p. 205
Corporate/Commercial ★★★
Table: p. 205

Koo, Donald (Hong Kong)
Profile: p. 366
Banking & Finance ★
Table: p. 352

Koob, Charles E. (USA)
Profile: p. 874
Competition/Anti-trust ★★
Table: p. 808

Korff, Phyllis (USA)
Profile: p. 874
Capital Markets: Debt & Equity ★
Table: p. 793

Koritsas, Nikos (Greece)
Profile: p. 342
Corporate/M&A **U**
Table: p. 339

Korman, Marti (USA)
Profile: p. 874
Communications: IT ★
Table: p. 805

Korpiola, Eki (Finland)
Profile: p. 258
Communications **U**
Table: p. 255

Koshland, Jim (USA)
Profile: p. 874
Communications: IT **U**
Table: p. 805

Koster, Weero (Netherlands)
Profile: p. 503
Energy & Natural Resources ★★★
Table: p. 498

Kostka, Carlo (Italy)
Profile: p. 426
Banking & Finance ★
Table: p. 414

Kosugi, Akira (Japan)
Profile: p. 445
Banking & Finance ★★★
Table: p. 433

Kosugi, Takeo (Japan)
Profile: p. 445
Capital Markets ★★
Table: p. 436

Kotáb, Petr (Czech Republic)
Profile: p. 236
Corporate/M&A ★★
Table: p. 234

Kothe, Tineke (Netherlands)
Profile: p. 503
Banking & Finance ★
Table: p. 491

Kouaovi, Bernard-Olivier (Niger)
Profile: p. 511
Corporate/Commercial ★★★★
Table: p. 511

Koutalidis, Tryfon (Greece)
Profile: p. 342
Corporate/M&A ★★★★
Table: p. 339

Kovács, Zsuzsanna (Hungary)
Profile: p. 376
Corporate/M&A ★★
Table: p. 375

Kovari, Istvan (Hungary)
Profile: p. 376
Corporate/M&A ★★
Table: p. 375

Köves, Péter (Hungary)
Profile: p. 376
Banking & Finance ★★★★
Table: p. 372

Koziakov, Sergiy Y. (Ukraine)
Profile: p. 687
Corporate/Commercial ★★
Table: p. 686

Krämer, Lutz (Germany)
Profile: p. 327
Capital Markets: Equity ★★
Table: p. 304

Kramer, Morris (USA)
Profile: p. 874
Corporate/M&A ★★
Table: p. 820

Krasnodêbski, Arek (Poland)
Profile: p. 554
Energy & Natural Resources ★★★★
Table: p. 550

Krasnodebski, Robert (Poland)
Profile: p. 554
Tax ★★★
Table: p. 551

Kraus, Bruce R. (USA)
Profile: p. 875
Communications: Transactional (Telecoms) ★★★
Table: p. 801

Krauss, Stefan (Germany)
Profile: p. 327
Capital Markets: Derivatives ★★★★
Table: p. 304
Capital Markets: Securitisation ★★★★
Table: p. 304

Kravitt, Jason H.P. (USA)
Profile: p. 875
Banking & Finance ★★★
Table: p. 787

Krefting, Carl-Erik (Norway)
Profile: p. 523
Corporate/M&A ★★★
Table: p. 519

Kremer, Christian (Luxembourg)
Profile: p. 466
Corporate/Commercial ★★★
Table: p. 465

Krieger, Sanford (USA)
Profile: p. 875
Corporate/M&A ★
Table: p. 820

Krischer, David S. (United Kingdom)
Profile: p. 761
Capital Markets: Securitisation ★★★★
Table: p. 704

Krogstrup, Sven (Denmark)
Profile: p. 241
Corporate/M&A ★★
Table: p. 239

Kroll, Markus J. (Switzerland)
Profile: p. 660
Banking & Finance ★★★
Table: p. 654

Krotoff, François (France)
Profile: p. 290
Project Finance: Francophone Africa ★★★★
Table: p. 278

Krouse Jr., George R. (USA)
Profile: p. 875
Capital Markets: Debt & Equity ★★
Table: p. 793

Kruger, Paul (Hong Kong)
Profile: p. 366
Capital Markets: Securitisation ★★★★
Table: p. 354

Kruisland, Freddy (Surinam)
Profile: p. 639
Corporate/Commercial ★★★★
Table: p. 638

Krupka, Bob (USA)
Profile: p. 875
Intellectual Property ★★
Table: p. 833

Kryshtalowych, Helen Z (Ukraine)
Profile: p. 687
Corporate/Commercial ★★
Table: p. 686

Krzywkowski, John (Greece)
Profile: p. 342
Shipping: Foreign Firms ★★★
Table: p. 341

Kubek, Gary (USA)
Profile: p. 875
Competition/Anti-trust ★
Table: p. 808

Kucera, Francis (Czech Republic)
Profile: p. 236
Banking & Finance ★★★
Table: p. 232

Kudenholdt, Stephen S. (USA)
Profile: p. 875
Capital Markets: Securitisation ★
Table: p. 795

Kudjawu, Norbert (Ghana)
Profile: p. 336
Corporate/Commercial ★★★★
Table: p. 336

Kuek, Richard (Singapore)
Profile: p. 601
Shipping ★★★
Table: p. 595

Kulkarni, Ravindra (India)
Profile: p. 388
Corporate/M&A ★★★★
Table: p. 381
Project Finance ★★★★
Table: p. 384

Kull, Ulf-Henrik (Finland)
Profile: p. 258
Corporate/M&A ★★★
Table: p. 257

Kullmann, Walburga (Germany)
Profile: p. 327
Banking & Finance ★
Table: p. 301

Kunkel, William (USA)
Profile: p. 875
Corporate/M&A ★★★
Table: p. 813

Kunz, C. Thomas (USA)
Profile: p. 875
Capital Markets: Securitisation ★★★★
Table: p. 795

Kurer, Peter (Switzerland)
Profile: p. 660
Corporate/M&A ★★★★
Table: p. 657

KEY TO RANKINGS: ✪ = Star Individual ★★★★ = Top Band ★★★ = Second Band ★★ = Third Band ★ = Fourth Band **U** = Up and coming

KEY TO RANKINGS: ✪ = Star Individual ★★★★ = Top Band ★★★ = Second Band ★★ = Third Band ★ = Fourth Band U = Up and coming

Lefosse Jr., Geraldo Roberto (Brazil)
Profile: p. 155
Corporate/M&A ★★★
Table: p. 147

Lega, Giovanni (Italy)
Profile: p. 426
Corporate/M&A ★
Table: p. 419

Lehr, Gernot (Germany)
Profile: p. 327
Communications: IT ★
Table: p. 307

Lehtinen, Pekka (Finland)
Profile: p. 258
Corporate/M&A ★★
Table: p. 257

Leibler, Mark (Australia)
Profile: p. 92
Tax ★★★
Table: p. 81

Leigh, Guy (United Kingdom)
Profile: p. 762
Competition/Anti-trust ★★
Table: p. 714

Leijonhielm, Thorsten (Sweden)
Profile: p. 649
Arbitration (International) ★★★
Table: p. 640

Leijten, Alfons (Netherlands)
Profile: p. 503
Corporate/M&A ★★★★
Table: p. 496
Energy & Natural Resources ★★★
Table: p. 498

Leitão, João Morais (Portugal)
Profile: p. 565
Corporate/M&A ★★★★
Table: p. 560

Leitermann, Richard (Germany)
Profile: p. 327
Communications: Regulatory ★★
Table: p. 306

Leivo, Kirsi (Finland)
Profile: p. 258
Competition/Anti-trust ★★★
Table: p. 256

Lejins, Girts (Latvia)
Profile: p. 457
Corporate/Commercial ★★★★
Table: p. 456

Lema Devesa, Carlos (Spain)
Profile: p. 633
Intellectual Property ★★★
Table: p. 626

Lemein, Gregg D. (USA)
Profile: p. 876
Tax ★★
Table: p. 843

Leon Sanchez, Enrique (Spain)
Profile: p. 633
Tax ★★
Table: p. 628

Leonard, Peter (Australia)
Profile: p. 93
Communications: Telecoms ★★★★
Table: p. 69

Lepik, Peeter (Estonia)
Profile: p. 252
Corporate/Commercial ★★★★
Table: p. 251

Lepretre, Jean-Michel (France)
Profile: p. 291
Corporate/M&A ★
Table: p. 275

Lernø, Finn J. (Denmark)
Profile: p. 241
Corporate/M&A ★★
Table: p. 239

Lessa, Rogerio (Brazil)
Profile: p. 155
Corporate/M&A ★★
Table: p. 147

Lesser, Henry (USA)
Profile: p. 877
Communications: IT ★
Table: p. 805

Letréguilly, Hervé (France)
Profile: p. 291
Capital Markets ★
Table: p. 268

Letzler, Kenneth (USA)
Profile: p. 877
Competition/Anti-trust ★★
Table: p. 811

Leung, Cheuk Yan (Hong Kong)
Profile: p. 367
Capital Markets: Debt & Equity ★★★
Table: p. 353

Levenfeld, Barry (Israel)
Profile: p. 411
Communications ★★★
Table: p. 407
Corporate/M&A ★★
Table: p. 409

Levet, Aaron (Mexico)
Profile: p. 481
Corporate/M&A ★★
Table: p. 480

Levi, Stuart (USA)
Profile: p. 877
Communications: Transactional (IT) ★★
Table: p. 801

Levin, Charles E. (USA)
Profile: p. 877
Banking & Finance ★
Table: p. 787

Levin, Jack (USA)
Profile: p. 877
Corporate/M&A ★★★★
Table: p. 813
Tax ★★★★
Table: p. 843

Levin, Jonathan A. (Canada)
Profile: p. 194
Banking & Finance ★★★★
Table: p. 171
Corporate/M&A ★★★★
Table: p. 177

Levin, Juan Guillermo (Chile)
Profile: p. 210
Banking & Finance ★★★★
Table: p. 206

Levin, Peter (USA)
Profile: p. 877
Banking & Finance ★★
Table: p. 791

Levine, Hank (USA)
Profile: p. 877
Communications: Transactional (Telecoms) ★★
Table: p. 801

Levine, Iona (United Kingdom)
Profile: p. 762
Capital Markets: Derivatives ★★
Table: p. 706

Levine, Marshall (United Kingdom)
Profile: p. 762
Projects ★
Table: p. 733

Levine, Robert (Japan)
Profile: p. 445
Corporate/M&A: Japan Foreign ★★
Table: p. 441

Levy, James (Gibraltar)
Profile: p. 338
Corporate/Commercial ★★★★
Table: p. 337

Levy, Nicholas (Belgium)
Profile: p. 130
Competition/Anti-trust ★★★★
Table: p. 122

Levy, Noel (Jamaica)
Profile: p. 432
Corporate/Commercial ★★★★
Table: p. 431

Levy, Yehuda (Israel)
Profile: p. 411
Corporate/M&A ★★★
Table: p. 409

Lévy, Laurent (Switzerland)
Profile: p. 661
Arbitration (International) ★
Table: p. 653

Lew, Julian (United Kingdom)
Profile: p. 762
Arbitration (International) ★★★★
Table: p. 696

Lewi, Rupert (Japan)
Profile: p. 445
Project Finance ★★
Table: p. 442

Lewis, Christopher (Japan)
Profile: p. 445
Capital Markets: Japan Foreign ★★
Table: p. 437

Lewis, David (United Kingdom)
Profile: p. 763
Corporate/M&A ★★★
Table: p. 717

Lewis, David (United Kingdom)
Profile: p. 763
Tax ★★★★
Table: p. 739

Lewis, Jonathan (France)
Profile: p. 291
Capital Markets **U**
Table: p. 268

Lewis, Mark Phillip (Cayman Islands)
Profile: p. 204
Corporate/Commercial ★★★★
Table: p. 203

Lewis, Rhys (United Arab Emirates)
Profile: p. 693
Corporate/M&A ★★
Table: p. 690

Lewis, Steve (Japan)
Profile: p. 445
Corporate/M&A: Japan Foreign ★★
Table: p. 441

Lewkow, Victor (USA)
Profile: p. 877
Communications: Transactional (Telecoms) ★★★★
Table: p. 801
Corporate/M&A ★★★
Table: p. 820

Leyendecker, Ludwig (Germany)
Profile: p. 327
Communications: Transactional ★★★★
Table: p. 306

Leygonie, Jean (France)
Profile: p. 291
Corporate/M&A ★★
Table: p. 275

Libertini, Mario (Italy)
Profile: p. 426
Competition/Anti-trust ★★
Table: p. 417

Libin, Jerome (USA)
Profile: p. 877
Tax ★★
Table: p. 847

Lie, Sue (Hong Kong)
Profile: p. 367
Corporate/M&A ★★
Table: p. 357

Liebscher, Christoph (Austria)
Profile: p. 106
Arbitration (International) ★★★
Table: p. 102

Liew, Chin-Chong (Hong Kong)
Profile: p. 367
Capital Markets: Derivatives ★★
Table: p. 355

Lim, Cheng (Australia)
Profile: p. 93
Communications: IT **U**
Table: p. 69
Intellectual Property ★★★
Table: p. 77

Lim, Michael (Malaysia)
Profile: p. 473
Corporate/M&A ★★
Table: p. 471

Lim, Teong Sit (Malaysia)
Profile: p. 473
Banking & Finance ★★★★
Table: p. 470

Limbers, Peter (Australia)
Profile: p. 93
Energy & Natural Resources ★★
Table: p. 75

Linares-Cantillo, Alejandro (Colombia)
Profile: p. 222
Banking & Finance ★★
Table: p. 219
Corporate/M&A ★★★
Table: p. 221

Lind, Erling (Norway)
Profile: p. 523
Banking & Finance ★★★
Table: p. 517

Lind, Henrik (Denmark)
Profile: p. 241
Banking & Finance ★★★
Table: p. 237
Corporate/M&A ★★★★
Table: p. 239

Lindauer, Erik D. (USA)
Profile: p. 877
Banking & Finance ★★★
Table: p. 791

Lindberg, Agne (Sweden)
Profile: p. 649
Communications: IT ★★★★
Table: p. 642

Lindholm, Tomas (Finland)
Profile: p. 259
Corporate/M&A ✪
Table: p. 257

Lindsey, David (USA)
Profile: p. 877
Arbitration (International) **U**
Table: p. 785

Lindskog, Stefan (Sweden)
Profile: p. 649
Arbitration (International) ★★★
Table: p. 640

Lines, David (Bermuda)
Profile: p. 137
Corporate/Commercial ★★★
Table: p. 136

Lines, Patrick (Hong Kong)
Profile: p. 367
Capital Markets: Derivatives ★★★
Table: p. 355

Ling, Timothy (United Kingdom)
Profile: p. 763
Tax ★★
Table: p. 739

Lipman, Andy (USA)
Profile: p. 877
Communications: Regulatory ★★★★
Table: p. 803

Lipsey, Charles (USA)
Profile: p. 877
Intellectual Property ★
Table: p. 831

Lipton, Martin (USA)
Profile: p. 878
Corporate/M&A ✪
Table: p. 820

Lipton, Richard (USA)
Profile: p. 878
Tax ★★★
Table: p. 843

Lishman, Michael (Australia)
Profile: p. 93
Corporate/M&A ★★
Table: p. 73

Lisson, James (Canada)
Profile: p. 194
Banking & Finance ★★★
Table: p. 171

Liston, Stephanie (United Kingdom)
Profile: p. 763
Communications: Telecoms ★★★
Table: p. 707

Litwin, Stuart M. (USA)
Profile: p. 878
Corporate/M&A **U**
Table: p. 813

Liu, David Dali (China)
Profile: p. 217
Corporate/M&A ★★
Table: p. 211

Liu, Gang (China)
Profile: p. 217
Corporate/M&A ★★★
Table: p. 211

Liu, Lawrence (Taiwan)
Profile: p. 667
Corporate/Commercial ★★★★
Table: p. 666

Liu, Linfei (China)
Profile: p. 217
Corporate/M&A ★★
Table: p. 211

Liu, Michael S.L. (Hong Kong)
Profile: p. 368
Capital Markets: Debt & Equity ★★★
Table: p. 353
Corporate/M&A ★★★
Table: p. 357

Livingston, Dorothy (United Kingdom)
Profile: p. 763
Competition/Anti-trust ★★★★
Table: p. 714

Livingstone, Hugh (United Kingdom)
Profile: p. 763
Shipping ★★★
Table: p. 737

Llewelyn, David (United Kingdom)
Profile: p. 763
Intellectual Property ★★★
Table: p. 729

 KEY TO RANKINGS: ✪ = Star Individual ★★★★ = Top Band ★★★ = Second Band ★★ = Third Band ★ = Fourth Band **U** = Up and coming

Llona, Alvaro (Peru)
Profile: p. 541
Corporate/M&A ★★★
Table: p. 540

Lloreda, Jose Antonio (Colombia)
Profile: p. 222
Corporate/M&A ★★★
Table: p. 221

Lloreda Camacho, Jose (Colombia)
Profile: p. 222
Corporate/M&A ★★
Table: p. 221

Lo, Siew Cheang (Malaysia)
Profile: p. 473
Corporate/M&A ★★★
Table: p. 471

Löber, Heinz (Austria)
Profile: p. 106
Corporate/M&A ★★★
Table: p. 104

Lobo-Xavier, Antonio (Portugal)
Profile: p. 565
Tax ★★★★
Table: p. 562

Lock, Richard (Hungary)
Profile: p. 376
Corporate/M&A ★★★★
Table: p. 375

Lockhart, Andrew (Hong Kong)
Profile: p. 368
Capital Markets: Derivatives ★★
Table: p. 355

Lodigiani, Francesca (Italy)
Profile: p. 426
Communications ★★★
Table: p. 415

Loesch, Tom (Luxembourg)
Profile: p. 466
Corporate/Commercial ★★★★
Table: p. 465

Loftis, Jim (USA)
Profile: p. 878
Competition/Anti-trust ★★★
Table: p. 811

Logan, Kenneth (USA)
Profile: p. 878
Competition/Anti-trust ★★★
Table: p. 808

Loloçi, Krenar (Albania)
Profile: p. 50
Corporate/Commercial ★★★
Table: p. 49

Lombardi, Michael (Jersey)
Profile: p. 449
Corporate/Commercial ★★★★
Table: p. 448

Lombardo, Nino (Antonio) (Italy)
Profile: p. 426
Communications ★★★
Table: p. 415

Long, Colin (United Kingdom)
Profile: p. 763
Communications: Telecoms ★★★★
Table: p. 707

Long, Julian (United Kingdom)
Profile: p. 763
Corporate/M&A ★★
Table: p. 717

Loo, Dip Seng (Singapore)
Profile: p. 601
Shipping ★
Table: p. 595

Looman, James (USA)
Profile: p. 878
Banking & Finance ★
Table: p. 787

Loong, Caesar (Malaysia)
Profile: p. 473
Corporate/M&A ★★
Table: p. 471

Lopez, Arnoldo (Costa Rica)
Profile: p. 226
Corporate/Commercial ★★★
Table: p. 225

Lopez Aufranc, Patricia (Argentina)
Profile: p. 62
Banking & Finance ★★
Table: p. 53

Lopez Chicheri, Jaime (Spain)
Profile: p. 633
Tax ★★★
Table: p. 628

López Rodezno, René (Honduras)
Profile: p. 350
Corporate/Commercial ★★★★
Table: p. 350

López Tello, Jesús (Spain)
Profile: p. 633
Tax ★★★
Table: p. 628

Loring, Carlos (Spain)
Profile: p. 633
Banking & Finance ★★★★
Table: p. 619
Corporate/M&A ★★★
Table: p. 624

Louveaux, Bertrand (United Kingdom)
Profile: p. 764
Competition/Anti-trust **U**
Table: p. 714

Loveland, Norman (Canada)
Profile: p. 194
Tax ★★★
Table: p. 182

Lovell, Richard (Singapore)
Profile: p. 601
Shipping: Foreign Firms ★★★★
Table: p. 596

Low, Chee Choon (Malaysia)
Profile: p. 473
Banking & Finance ★★★
Table: p. 470

Lowe, Charles (Greece)
Profile: p. 342
Shipping: Foreign Firms ★★
Table: p. 341

Lowe, John (Canada)
Profile: p. 194
Communications ★★
Table: p. 173

Lowe, Steven (United Kingdom)
Profile: p. 764
Shipping ★★
Table: p. 737

Lowinger, Frederick C. (USA)
Profile: p. 878
Corporate/M&A ★★★★
Table: p. 813

Lowther, Frederick (USA)
Profile: p. 878
Energy & Natural Resources ★
Table: p. 827

Lowy, George (USA)
Profile: p. 878
Corporate/M&A ★
Table: p. 820

Loxton, Diccon (Australia)
Profile: p. 93
Banking & Finance ★★★★
Table: p. 65
Project Finance ★★★★
Table: p. 79

Loze, Janis (Latvia)
Profile: p. 457
Corporate/Commercial ★★★
Table: p. 456

Lubin, Don (USA)
Profile: p. 878
Corporate/M&A ★★★
Table: p. 813

Lucas de Leyssac, Claude (France)
Profile: p. 291
Competition/Anti-trust ★★★
Table: p. 272

Lucero, Luis E (Argentina)
Profile: p. 62
Corporate/M&A **U**
Table: p. 57

Luckhoo, Edward (Guyana)
Profile: p. 348
Corporate/Commercial ★★★
Table: p. 348

Lüdicke, Jochen (Germany)
Profile: p. 327
Banking & Finance ★★★
Table: p. 301
Tax ★★
Table: p. 319

Luhaäär, Toomas (Estonia)
Profile: p. 252
Corporate/Commercial ★★★★
Table: p. 251

Lule, Godfrey S (Uganda)
Profile: p. 685
Corporate/Commercial ★★
Table: p. 684

Lumor, Fred (Belize)
Profile: p. 134
Corporate/Commercial ★★★
Table: p. 134

Lundblad, Claes (Sweden)
Profile: p. 649
Arbitration (International) ★★★
Table: p. 640

Lundin, Anders (Sweden)
Profile: p. 649
Corporate/M&A ★★★
Table: p. 645

Lundqvist, Dick (Sweden)
Profile: p. 649
Banking & Finance ★★★★
Table: p. 641

Lüning, Wilhelm (Sweden)
Profile: p. 650
Corporate/M&A ★★★
Table: p. 645

Luscombe, George A. (USA)
Profile: p. 879
Tax ★
Table: p. 843

Lusk, John O. (New Zealand)
Profile: p. 509
Banking & Finance ★★★
Table: p. 507

Luthra, Rajiv (India)
Profile: p. 388
Project Finance ★★
Table: p. 384

Lux, Jonathan (United Kingdom)
Profile: p. 764
Shipping ★★★
Table: p. 737

Lynch, Alex (USA)
Profile: p. 879
Communications: Transactional (IT) ★★
Table: p. 801

Lynch, John (USA)
Profile: p. 879
Intellectual Property ★★
Table: p. 831

Lynch, Maurice M. (Mongolia)
Profile: p. 484
Corporate/Commercial ★★★★
Table: p. 484

Lynch, Simon (Australia)
Profile: p. 93
Banking & Finance ★★
Table: p. 65

M

Maajar, Mwanaidi (Tanzania)
Profile: p. 669
Corporate/Commercial ★★★
Table: p. 668

Mabeka, Nicholas (Democratic Republic of Congo)
Profile: p. 224
Corporate/Commercial ★★★
Table: p. 224

Mabushi, Augustin (Burundi)
Profile: p. 167
Corporate/Commercial ★★★★
Table: p. 167

Macaluso, Fabio (Italy)
Profile: p. 426
Communications ★★
Table: p. 415

Macaraig, Mel A (Philippines)
Profile: p. 544
Corporate/Commercial ★
Table: p. 542

Macaulay, Anthony (United Kingdom)
Profile: p. 764
Corporate/M&A ★★★★
Table: p. 717

Macaulay, Berthan (Sierra Leone)
Profile: p. 585
Corporate/Commercial ★★★★
Table: p. 585

Macchi di Cellere, Luigi (Italy)
Profile: p. 426
Corporate/M&A ★★
Table: p. 419

Macchi di Cellere, Stefano (Italy)
Profile: p. 426
Communications ★
Table: p. 415

MacDonald, Ken (Australia)
Profile: p. 93
Corporate/M&A ★
Table: p. 73

MacDonald, Morag (United Kingdom)
Profile: p. 764
Intellectual Property ★★★★
Table: p. 729

MacDonald-Brown, Charters (United Kingdom)
Profile: p. 764
Intellectual Property ★★
Table: p. 729

Macfarlane, David (United Kingdom)
Profile: p. 764
Corporate/M&A ★
Table: p. 717

MacFarlane, Nicholas (United Kingdom)
Profile: p. 764
Intellectual Property ★★★★
Table: p. 729

Machin, Peter (Australia)
Profile: p. 93
Project Finance ★
Table: p. 79

Machlin, Barry N. (USA)
Profile: p. 879
Project Finance ★
Table: p. 837

Mackenzie, Marcus (United Kingdom)
Profile: p. 764
Capital Markets: Securitisation ★★
Table: p. 704

MacKinnon, Robert (Hong Kong)
Profile: p. 368
Banking & Finance ★★
Table: p. 352

Maclean, Alan (Australia)
Profile: p. 94
Project Finance ★
Table: p. 79

MacLeod, William (USA)
Profile: p. 879
Competition/Anti-trust ★
Table: p. 811

MacMurray, John C. (USA)
Profile: p. 879
Private Equity: Fund Formation ★★★
Table: p. 835

Macnab, Duncan (United Arab Emirates)
Profile: p. 693
Corporate/M&A ★★
Table: p. 690
Project Finance ★★★
Table: p. 691

MacRitchie, Kenneth (United Kingdom)
Profile: p. 764
Projects ★★★
Table: p. 733

Madden, John (USA)
Profile: p. 879
Communications: Transactional (Telecoms) ★★★
Table: p. 801
Corporate/M&A ★
Table: p. 820

Madero, Jaime (Argentina)
Profile: p. 63
Banking & Finance ★★
Table: p. 53

Madsen, Jørgen Kjegaard (Denmark)
Profile: p. 241
Banking & Finance ★★★★
Table: p. 237

Maeda, Hiroshi (Japan)
Profile: p. 445
Banking & Finance ★★★
Table: p. 433

Maeda, Toshihiro (Japan)
Profile: p. 445
Capital Markets ★
Table: p. 436

Maes, Ignace (Belgium)
Profile: p. 130
Banking & Finance ★★★
Table: p. 117

Maffei, Antoine (France)
Profile: p. 291
Banking & Finance ★★★
Table: p. 265
Capital Markets ★★★
Table: p. 268

Magalhães, Carlos (Brazil)
Profile: p. 155
Competition/Anti-trust ★★★
Table: p. 145

Magalhães Cardoso, Antonio (Portugal)
Profile: p. 565
Competition/Anti-trust ★
Table: p. 559

Magennis, Bill (Vietnam)
Profile: p. 917
Corporate/Commercial: Vietnam Foreign ★★★★
Table: p. 916

Magid, Larry (Australia)
Profile: p. 94
Tax ★★★★
Table: p. 81

Magold, Rainer (Germany)
Profile: p. 327
Banking & Finance ★★★★
Table: p. 301
Capital Markets: Derivatives ★★★★
Table: p. 304
Project Finance ★★
Table: p. 317

Maguire, Gary (Australia)
Profile: p. 94
Energy & Natural Resources ★★★
Table: p. 75

Mahmud, Rokanuddin (Bangladesh)
Profile: p. 112
Corporate/Commercial ★★★
Table: p. 112

Mahony, Michael (United Kingdom)
Profile: p. 764
Communications: IT ★★
Table: p. 709

Maier-Reimer, Georg (Germany)
Profile: p. 327
Corporate/M&A ★★★
Table: p. 311

Maillot, Alain (France)
Profile: p. 291
Corporate/M&A ★★★
Table: p. 275

Mairal, Héctor A. (Argentina)
Profile: p. 63
Corporate/M&A ★★★★
Table: p. 57
Energy & Natural Resources ★★
Table: p. 59

Maisto, Guglielmo (Italy)
Profile: p. 427
Tax ★★★★
Table: p. 422

Maître-Devallon, Claudine (France)
Profile: p. 291
Competition/Anti-trust ★★
Table: p. 272

Majdalany, Gebran (Qatar)
Profile: p. 569
Corporate/Commercial ★★★
Table: p. 568

Majerholc, Norbert (France)
Profile: p. 291
Tax ★
Table: p. 281

Makes, Yozua (Indonesia)
Profile: p. 392
Corporate/Commercial ★
Table: p. 391

Mäkinen, Juhani (Finland)
Profile: p. 259
Corporate/M&A ★★★★
Table: p. 257

Makinson, Simon (Thailand)
Profile: p. 673
Corporate/M&A ★★★
Table: p. 672

Maktari, Abdulla (Yemen)
Profile: p. 917
Corporate/Commercial ★★★★
Table: p. 917

Malcolm, Andrew (Hong Kong)
Profile: p. 368
Capital Markets: Debt & Equity ★★★
Table: p. 353

Malik, Mansoor (Oman)
Profile: p. 528
Banking & Finance ★★★
Table: p. 526
Corporate/M&A ★★★
Table: p. 527

Mallard, Nicholas H. (Hong Kong)
Profile: p. 368
Shipping ★★
Table: p. 361

Malling, Wilhelm (Greenland)
Profile: p. 344
Corporate/Commercial ★★★★
Table: p. 344

Mallow, Matthew (USA)
Profile: p. 879
Capital Markets: Debt & Equity ★★★★
Table: p. 793

Maloney, David (Australia)
Profile: p. 94
Energy & Natural Resources ★
Table: p. 75

Malt, Brad (USA)
Profile: p. 879
Private Equity: Fund Formation ★
Table: p. 835

Maltsev, Yuriy (Kazakhstan)
Profile: p. 452
Energy & Natural Resources ★★★
Table: p. 451

Manalastas, Jesus M. (Philippines)
Profile: p. 544
Corporate/Commercial ★
Table: p. 542

Manara, Francesco (Italy)
Profile: p. 427
Banking & Finance ★★
Table: p. 414

Mandal, Som (India)
Profile: p. 388
Corporate/M&A ★
Table: p. 381
Project Finance ★★★
Table: p. 384

Manganelli, Andrea (Italy)
Profile: p. 427
Tax ★★
Table: p. 422

Manikai, Edwin (Zimbabwe)
Profile: p. 920
Corporate/Commercial ★★★
Table: p. 919

Mann, Christopher L. (USA)
Profile: p. 879
Project Finance **U**
Table: p. 837

Mann, Geoff (Australia)
Profile: p. 94
Tax ★
Table: p. 81

Mannsfeldt, Ulrich (Germany)
Profile: p. 327
Project Finance ★★★★
Table: p. 317

Manring, Tim (Indonesia)
Profile: p. 392
Corporate/Commercial ★★★
Table: p. 391

Manzitti, Andrea (Italy)
Profile: p. 427
Tax ★★
Table: p. 422

Mao, Baigen (China)
Profile: p. 217
Corporate/M&A ★★
Table: p. 211

Marcault-Derouard, Jean (French Guiana)
Profile: p. 296
Corporate/Commercial ★★★★
Table: p. 296

Marghani, Salah (Libya)
Profile: p. 461
Corporate/Commercial ★★★★
Table: p. 461

Maricoto Monteiro, João Filipe (Portugal)
Profile: p. 565
Tax ★★
Table: p. 562

Marisin, Ivan (Russia)
Profile: p. 578
Corporate/M&A ★★
Table: p. 574

Mariz Oliveira, Ricardo (Brazil)
Profile: p. 155
Tax ★★★★
Table: p. 150

Marques, Paulo (Portugal)
Profile: p. 565
Corporate/M&A ★
Table: p. 560

Marques Mendes, Mario (Portugal)
Profile: p. 565
Competition/Anti-trust ★★
Table: p. 559

Marques Pinto, João (Portugal)
Profile: p. 565
Tax ★★
Table: p. 562

Marrache, Benjamin John Samuel (Gibraltar)
Profile: p. 338
Corporate/Commercial ★★
Table: p. 337

Marrache, Isaac Samuel (Gibraltar)
Profile: p. 338
Corporate/Commercial ★★
Table: p. 337

Marrey Jr, Pedro Luciano (Brazil)
Profile: p. 155
Tax ★★★
Table: p. 150

Marriott QC, Arthur (United Kingdom)
Profile: p. 765
Arbitration (International) ★★★★
Table: p. 696

Marseille, Hans (Netherlands)
Profile: p. 503
Tax ★★★
Table: p. 500

Marshall, James (United Kingdom)
Profile: p. 765
Intellectual Property ★★
Table: p. 729

Marshall, Richard (Australia)
Profile: p. 94
Energy & Natural Resources ★
Table: p. 75

Marsiglia, Gabriela (Argentina)
Profile: p. 63
Communications ★★★★
Table: p. 54

Marsland, Vanessa (United Kingdom)
Profile: p. 765
Intellectual Property ★★★★
Table: p. 729

Marston, Edgar (USA)
Profile: p. 880
Corporate/M&A ★★
Table: p. 824

Martel, Jean-Pierre (France)
Profile: p. 291
Corporate/M&A ★★★★
Table: p. 275

Martelli, Hugo (Argentina)
Profile: p. 63
Energy & Natural Resources ★★★
Table: p. 59

Martin, Andrew (Australia)
Profile: p. 94
Energy & Natural Resources ★★
Table: p. 75

Martin, Charles (United Kingdom)
Profile: p. 765
Private Equity: Buyouts ★★
Table: p. 731

Martin, David (United Kingdom)
Profile: p. 765
Tax ★★★★
Table: p. 739

Martin, Didier (France)
Profile: p. 292
Corporate/M&A ★★★★
Table: p. 275

Martin, Eckhard (Germany)
Profile: p. 327
Capital Markets: Equity ★
Table: p. 304

Martin, Peter (Bermuda)
Profile: p. 137
Corporate/Commercial ★★★★
Table: p. 136

Martin, Renwick (USA)
Profile: p. 880
Capital Markets: Securitisation ★★★★
Table: p. 795

Martin Alegi, Lynda (United Kingdom)
Profile: p. 765
Competition/Anti-trust ★★
Table: p. 714

Martindale, Avril (United Kingdom)
Profile: p. 765
Intellectual Property ★★
Table: p. 729

Martinet, Alain (Djibouti)
Profile: p. 242
Corporate/Commercial ★★★★
Table: p. 242

Martinet, Marie-Paule (Djibouti)
Profile: p. 242
Corporate/Commercial ★★★
Table: p. 242

Martínez, Jaime (Chile)
Profile: p. 210
Banking & Finance ★★★
Table: p. 206
Corporate/M&A ★★
Table: p. 208

Martinez de Hoz, José (Argentina)
Profile: p. 63
Energy & Natural Resources ★★★★
Table: p. 59

Martinez Lage, Santiago (Spain)
Profile: p. 633
Competition/Anti-trust ★★★★
Table: p. 622

Martis, Xeno C. (Canada)
Profile: p. 195
Banking & Finance ★★
Table: p. 171

Marxer, Peter (Liechtenstein)
Profile: p. 462
Corporate/Commercial ★★★★
Table: p. 462

Marzo, Javier (Spain)
Profile: p. 633
Communications ★★
Table: p. 620

Marzulli, John A. Jr. (USA)
Profile: p. 880
Communications: Transactional (Telecoms) ★★
Table: p. 801

Masembe Kanyerezi, Timothy (Uganda)
Profile: p. 685
Corporate/Commercial ★★★
Table: p. 684

Mashlenko, Irina (Russia)
Profile: p. 578
Corporate/M&A ★★
Table: p. 574

Mason, David (USA)
Profile: p. 880
Banking & Finance **U**
Table: p. 787

Massad, Stephen A. (USA)
Profile: p. 880
Corporate/M&A ★★★
Table: p. 824

Massaguer, José (Spain)
Profile: p. 634
Intellectual Property ★★★★
Table: p. 626

Massias, Isaac (Gibraltar)
Profile: p. 338
Corporate/Commercial ★★★
Table: p. 337

Masterson, Alex (Zimbabwe)
Profile: p. 920
Corporate/Commercial ★★★★
Table: p. 919

Masur, Daniel (USA)
Profile: p. 880
Communications: Transactional (IT) ★★★
Table: p. 801

Matadiwamba, Tharcisse (Democratic Republic of Congo)
Profile: p. 224
Corporate/Commercial ★★★
Table: p. 224

Matarasso, Gabriel (Argentina)
Profile: p. 63
Communications ★★★
Table: p. 54

Matejcek, Jan (Czech Republic)
Profile: p. 236
Banking & Finance ★★★
Table: p. 232
Corporate/M&A ★★★
Table: p. 234

Matheou, Michael (United Kingdom)
Profile: p. 765
PFI ★★★★
Table: p. 733

Matheson, Glenn (France)
Profile: p. 292
Banking & Finance ★
Table: p. 265

KEY TO RANKINGS: ✪ = Star Individual ★★★★ = Top Band ★★★ = Second Band ★★ = Third Band ★ = Fourth Band **U** = Up and coming

Mattos, Ubiratan (Brazil)
Profile: p. 155
Competition/Anti-trust ★★★
Table: p. 145

Mattos Filho, Ary Oswaldo (Brazil)
Profile: p. 155
Banking & Finance ★
Table: p. 142
Corporate/M&A ★★
Table: p. 147

Maughan, Alistair (United Kingdom)
Profile: p. 765
Communications: IT ★★
Table: p. 709

Maung Maung Gyi, Henry (Myanmar)
Profile: p. 487
Corporate/Commercial ★★★★
Table: p. 487

Max, Dietrich (Germany)
Profile: p. 327
Corporate/M&A ★
Table: p. 311

Maxton, Alan (Australia)
Profile: p. 94
Banking & Finance ★★
Table: p. 65

May, Gregory (USA)
Profile: p. 880
Tax ★
Table: p. 847

May, Henry (USA)
Profile: p. 880
Energy & Natural Resources ★
Table: p. 829

Mayard-Paul, Constantin (Haiti)
Profile: p. 349
Corporate/Commercial ★★★★
Table: p. 349

Mayen, Thomas (Germany)
Profile: p. 327
Communications: Regulatory ★★★★
Table: p. 306

Mayer, Pierre (France)
Profile: p. 292
Arbitration (International) ★★★
Table: p. 262

Mayne, Eric (Australia)
Profile: p. 94
Tax: Goods & Services Tax ★★★★
Table: p. 81

Mayor, Pablo (Spain)
Profile: p. 634
Communications ★★★
Table: p. 620

Mayora Alvarado, Eduardo (Guatemala)
Profile: p. 345
Corporate/Commercial ★★★★
Table: p. 345

Mayora Dawe, Eduardo (Guatemala)
Profile: p. 345
Corporate/Commercial ★★★
Table: p. 345

Mazet, Gérard (France)
Profile: p. 292
Corporate/M&A ★★
Table: p. 275

Mazzochi, Richard (Australia)
Profile: p. 94
Capital Markets ★★
Table: p. 67

Mboza, Gaëtan (Gabon)
Profile: p. 297
Corporate/Commercial ★★★★
Table: p. 297

McAlpine, Stuart (Singapore)
Profile: p. 601
Shipping: Foreign Firms ★★
Table: p. 596

Mccague, Eugene (Ireland)
Profile: p. 402
Corporate/M&A ★★★
Table: p. 397

McCallough, Robert (United Kingdom)
Profile: p. 765
Communications: IT ★★★
Table: p. 709

McCann, Kevin (Australia)
Profile: p. 94
Energy & Natural Resources ★★
Table: p. 75

McCarthy, Alan (Ireland)
Profile: p. 402
Competition/Anti-trust **U**
Table: p. 396

McCarthy, Jack (United Kingdom)
Profile: p. 765
Corporate/M&A ★★
Table: p. 717

McClenahan, John H. (Japan)
Profile: p. 445
Project Finance ★★★
Table: p. 442

McCormack, Howard (USA)
Profile: p. 880
Shipping: Litigation ★★★
Table: p. 841

McCormack, William F. (USA)
Profile: p. 880
Private Equity: Fund Formation ★★
Table: p. 835

McCormick, Bill (USA)
Profile: p. 881
Corporate/M&A ★★
Table: p. 824

McCormick, Roger (United Kingdom)
Profile: p. 765
Projects ★
Table: p. 733

McDaid, Ray (Czech Republic)
Profile: p. 236
Corporate/M&A ★★★
Table: p. 234

McDavid, Janet L. (USA)
Profile: p. 881
Competition/Anti-trust ★★★
Table: p. 811

McDermott, Robert K. (Canada)
Profile: p. 195
Corporate/M&A ★
Table: p. 177

McDonald, Thomas J. (France)
Profile: p. 292
Banking & Finance ★
Table: p. 265

McEvoy, Bernard (Ireland)
Profile: p. 402
Corporate/M&A ★
Table: p. 397

McFadden, Laurie (Italy)
Profile: p. 427
Corporate/M&A ★
Table: p. 419

McGehee, Jeffrey A (Czech Republic)
Profile: p. 236
Communications ★★★★
Table: p. 233
Corporate/M&A ★★
Table: p. 234

McGill, Ian (Australia)
Profile: p. 95
Communications: Telecoms ★★
Table: p. 69

McGovern, Patricia (Ireland)
Profile: p. 402
Corporate/M&A ★
Table: p. 397

McGraw-Weiss, Donna (USA)
Profile: p. 881
Project Finance **U**
Table: p. 837

McGregor, Sheila (Australia)
Profile: p. 95
Communications: Telecoms ★★★
Table: p. 69

McGuinness, John D. (Hong Kong)
Profile: p. 368
Banking & Finance ★★★
Table: p. 352

McGuire, Keith (Singapore)
Profile: p. 601
Corporate/M&A: Singapore Foreign ★★★
Table: p. 592

McIntyre, Rob (British Virgin Islands)
Profile: p. 161
Corporate/Commercial ★★★
Table: p. 160

McKay, Rex (Guyana)
Profile: p. 348
Corporate/Commercial ★★★★
Table: p. 348

McKee, Bill (USA)
Profile: p. 881
Tax ★★★★
Table: p. 847

McKenna, Justin (Ireland)
Profile: p. 402
Corporate/M&A ★
Table: p. 397

McKenzie, Christopher (British Virgin Islands)
Profile: p. 161
Corporate/Commercial ★★★
Table: p. 160

McKnight, Elizabeth (United Kingdom)
Profile: p. 765
Competition/Anti-trust ★★★★
Table: p. 714

McLarty, Allan Lawrence (Canada)
Profile: p. 195
Energy & Natural Resources ★★
Table: p. 180

McMahon, Terry (USA)
Profile: p. 881
Intellectual Property ★★
Table: p. 833

McMenamin, J. Robert (USA)
Profile: p. 881
Banking & Finance ★★★
Table: p. 787

McNair, Alastair J. (United Arab Emirates)
Profile: p. 693
Project Finance ★★★★
Table: p. 691

McNeill, Michael (Singapore)
Profile: p. 601
Project Finance ★
Table: p. 594

McNeive, Liam (United Kingdom)
Profile: p. 765
Communications: E-commerce ★★★★
Table: p. 711

McQuail, Tom (Belgium)
Profile: p. 130
Competition/Anti-trust **U**
Table: p. 122

McQuater, Gavin J. (United Kingdom)
Profile: p. 765
Projects ★
Table: p. 733

McReynolds, Shawn (Canada)
Profile: p. 195
Corporate/M&A ★
Table: p. 177

McWeeney, Sean (Bahamas)
Profile: p. 109
Corporate/Commercial ★★★★
Table: p. 109

Mead, Stephen (Australia)
Profile: p. 95
Communications: Telecoms ★★★
Table: p. 69

Meade, John (Ireland)
Profile: p. 402
Competition/Anti-trust ★★★★
Table: p. 396

Meadows, Stanley (USA)
Profile: p. 881
Corporate/M&A ★★★
Table: p. 813

Mears, Patrick M. (United Kingdom)
Profile: p. 765
Tax ★★★★
Table: p. 739

Medrano, Humberto (Peru)
Profile: p. 541
Corporate/M&A ★★
Table: p. 540

Meerburg, Dirk C. (Netherlands)
Profile: p. 503
Banking & Finance ★★★★
Table: p. 491

Meesters, Bart J.M.A. (Netherlands)
Profile: p. 503
Banking & Finance ★★★
Table: p. 491

Meeus, Dirk (Belgium)
Profile: p. 130
Corporate/M&A ★★
Table: p. 125

Meghen, Michael (Ireland)
Profile: p. 402
Corporate/M&A ★★★
Table: p. 397

Mehigan, Bertie M. (Singapore)
Profile: p. 602
Banking & Finance: Singapore Foreign ★★★
Table: p. 588

Mehta, Dara (India)
Profile: p. 389
Corporate/M&A ★★★
Table: p. 381

Mehta, Nikhil (United Kingdom)
Profile: p. 389, 766
Corporate/M&A: India Foreign ★★★
Table: p. 383
Tax ★★
Table: p. 739

Meiklejohn, D. Stuart (USA)
Profile: p. 881
Competition/Anti-trust ★
Table: p. 808

Meirelles de Miranda, Aloysio (Brazil)
Profile: p. 155
Corporate/M&A ★★
Table: p. 147
Tax ★
Table: p. 150

Meisling, Soren (Denmark)
Profile: p. 241
Corporate/M&A ★★★
Table: p. 239

Meister, Burkhardt (Germany)
Profile: p. 328
Corporate/M&A ★★
Table: p. 311

Meister, Norbert (Germany)
Profile: p. 328
Corporate/M&A ★★
Table: p. 311

Melis, Werner (Austria)
Profile: p. 107
Arbitration (International) ★★★★
Table: p. 102

Mellbye, Andreas (Norway)
Profile: p. 523
Corporate/M&A ★★
Table: p. 519

Melling, Paul (Russia)
Profile: p. 578
Corporate/M&A ★★★
Table: p. 574

Meltzer, Stephen (South Africa)
Profile: p. 613
Banking & Finance ★★★
Table: p. 610

Mendelson, Alan C. (USA)
Profile: p. 881
Communications: IT ★★★★
Table: p. 805

Mendes, Antonio (Brazil)
Profile: p. 155
Banking & Finance ✪
Table: p. 142
Corporate/M&A ★★★★
Table: p. 147

Mendieta, Gonzalo (Bolivia)
Profile: p. 139
Corporate/Commercial ★★★
Table: p. 138

Mendoza, Luis Ignacio (Venezuela)
Profile: p. 913
Corporate/M&A ★★
Table: p. 909

Mentula, Arttu (Finland)
Profile: p. 259
Competition/Anti-trust **U**
Table: p. 256

Mercer, Edward (United Kingdom)
Profile: p. 766
Communications: Telecoms ★★★
Table: p. 707

Merchant, Kalpana (India)
Profile: p. 389
Corporate/M&A ★
Table: p. 381
Project Finance ★★★
Table: p. 384

Merilampi, Pekka (Finland)
Profile: p. 259
Corporate/M&A ★★★
Table: p. 257

Merola, Massimo (Italy)
Profile: p. 427
Competition/Anti-trust ★
Table: p. 417

Mersan, Carlos (Paraguay)
Profile: p. 537
Corporate/M&A ★★★★
Table: p. 537

Mersing, Erik Mohr (Denmark)
Profile: p. 241
Competition/Anti-trust ★★★★
Table: p. 238

Mes, Peter (Germany)
Profile: p. 328
Intellectual Property: General ★★★★
Table: p. 314

Mesny, Jean-Paul (France)
Profile: p. 292
Tax ★★★
Table: p. 281

Mestres Jr., Ricardo A. (USA)
Profile: p. 882
Capital Markets: Debt & Equity ★★
Table: p. 793

Metallinos, Alexander (Greece)
Profile: p. 342
Corporate/M&A **U**
Table: p. 339

Metaxas, George (Belgium)
Profile: p. 130
Communications ★★★★
Table: p. 118

Meyer, Antonio (Brazil)
Profile: p. 155
Corporate/M&A ★★★★
Table: p. 147
Project Finance ★★★
Table: p. 149
Tax ★
Table: p. 150

Meyers, Jan (Belgium)
Profile: p. 130
Corporate/M&A ★★★
Table: p. 125

Meyers, Michael (USA)
Profile: p. 882
Project Finance ★
Table: p. 837

Mhayimana, Isaïe (Rwanda)
Profile: p. 579
Corporate/Commercial ★★★★
Table: p. 579

Michael, Kebreab Habte (Eritrea)
Profile: p. 250
Corporate/Commercial ★★★★
Table: p. 250

Michalski, Jacek (Poland)
Profile: p. 554
Corporate/M&A ★★
Table: p. 548

Michaud, Jean-Luc (France)
Profile: p. 292
Banking & Finance ★★
Table: p. 265
Capital Markets ★
Table: p. 268

Michelet, Christian Fredrik (Norway)
Profile: p. 524
Energy & Natural Resources ★★★★
Table: p. 520

Michelmore, Peter (United Arab Emirates)
Profile: p. 693
Corporate/M&A ★★
Table: p. 690
Project Finance ★★★
Table: p. 691

Michelsen, Sergio (Colombia)
Profile: p. 222
Banking & Finance ★★
Table: p. 219
Corporate/M&A ★★★
Table: p. 221

Michelutti, Riccardo (Italy)
Profile: p. 427
Tax ★
Table: p. 422

Middleditch, Matthew (United Kingdom)
Profile: p. 766
Corporate/M&A ★★★
Table: p. 717

Mihara, Hidetaka (Japan)
Profile: p. 445
Banking & Finance ★★★★
Table: p. 433
Capital Markets ★★★★
Table: p. 436

Mijares Davalos, Juan G (Mexico)
Profile: p. 481
Corporate/M&A ★★★★
Table: p. 480

Millar, Timothy G. (Canada)
Profile: p. 195
Energy & Natural Resources ★★★
Table: p. 180

Millard, Christopher (United Kingdom)
Profile: p. 766
Communications: E-commerce ★★★★
Table: p. 711
Communications: IT ★★★★
Table: p. 709

Millard, John A. (USA)
Profile: p. 882
Banking & Finance ★★
Table: p. 791

Millé, Antonio (Argentina)
Profile: p. 63
Communications ★★
Table: p. 54

Miller, Axel (Belgium)
Profile: p. 130
Corporate/M&A ★★★★
Table: p. 125

Miller, Brian M. (Singapore)
Profile: p. 602
Project Finance ★★★
Table: p. 594

Miller, Calvert (Singapore)
Profile: p. 602
Project Finance ★★★
Table: p. 594

Miller, Stephen (United Kingdom)
Profile: p. 766
Capital Markets: Debt & Equity ★★
Table: p. 702

Miller, Stephen (Thailand)
Profile: p. 673
Banking & Finance ★★★★
Table: p. 670

Miller, Thomas (Thailand)
Profile: p. 673
Corporate/M&A ★★★
Table: p. 672

Milliner, Robert (Australia)
Profile: p. 95
Energy & Natural Resources ★★★★
Table: p. 75
Project Finance ★
Table: p. 79

Mills, Philip (USA)
Profile: p. 882
Corporate/M&A ★
Table: p. 820

Millstein, Julian (USA)
Profile: p. 882
Communications: Transactional (IT) ★★
Table: p. 801

Mine, Abdoullah Ould (Mauritania)
Profile: p. 477
Corporate/Commercial ★★★★
Table: p. 477

Mínguez Prieto, Rafael (Spain)
Profile: p. 634
Banking & Finance ★★
Table: p. 619

Minns, Stephen (Australia)
Profile: p. 95
Corporate/M&A ★★★
Table: p. 73

Minor, Pierre (France)
Profile: p. 292
Capital Markets ★
Table: p. 268

Mioduski, Dariusz (Poland)
Profile: p. 554
Energy & Natural Resources ★★★★
Table: p. 550

Misrock, Leslie (USA)
Profile: p. 882
Intellectual Property ★★★
Table: p. 831

Mitchard, Paul (United Kingdom)
Profile: p. 766
Arbitration (International) ★★
Table: p. 696

Mitchell, David (USA)
Profile: p. 882
Capital Markets: Derivatives ★★★
Table: p. 798

Mitchell, Warren J. A., Q.C. (Canada)
Profile: p. 195
Tax ★★
Table: p. 182

Mitomi, Fuyuo (Japan)
Profile: p. 445
Capital Markets ★★★★
Table: p. 436

Mitsui, Takuhide (Japan)
Profile: p. 445
Capital Markets ★
Table: p. 436
Corporate/M&A ★★★
Table: p. 439

Mizzi, Henri (Malta)
Profile: p. 476
Corporate/Commercial ★★★
Table: p. 475

Mkono, Nimrod Elireheemah (Tanzania)
Profile: p. 669
Corporate/Commercial ★★★
Table: p. 668

Mlodzianowska, Justyna (Poland)
Profile: p. 554
Banking & Finance ★★
Table: p. 545

Mo, Philip (Hong Kong)
Profile: p. 368
Shipping ★
Table: p. 361

Mody, Zia (India)
Profile: p. 389
Corporate/M&A ★★★
Table: p. 381

Modzelewski, Witold (Poland)
Profile: p. 554
Tax ★★★
Table: p. 551

Møgelmose, Henrik (Denmark)
Profile: p. 241
Corporate/M&A ★★
Table: p. 239

Mogg, Jason (Slovakia)
Profile: p. 608
Corporate/Commercial ★★★★
Table: p. 607

Moghaizel, Fadi (Lebanon)
Profile: p. 459
Corporate/Commercial ★★★★
Table: p. 458

Mohamed Salah, Mohamed Mahmoud Ould (Mauritania)
Profile: p. 477
Corporate/Commercial ★★★★
Table: p. 477

Mohan, S. (Singapore)
Profile: p. 602
Shipping ★
Table: p. 595

Mokhzani, Charon Wardini bin (Malaysia)
Profile: p. 473
Corporate/M&A ★
Table: p. 471

Möller, Jakob R. (Iceland)
Profile: p. 379
Corporate/Commercial ★★★★
Table: p. 378

Molony, Ronan (Ireland)
Profile: p. 403
Banking & Finance ★★★★
Table: p. 394

Monaghan, K. A. Siobhan (Canada)
Profile: p. 195
Tax **U**
Table: p. 182

Monnou, Edgar (Benin)
Profile: p. 135
Corporate/Commercial ★★★★
Table: p. 135

Montag, Frank (Belgium)
Profile: p. 130
Competition/Anti-trust ★★★★
Table: p. 122

Montañá Mora, Miquel (Spain)
Profile: p. 634
Intellectual Property ★★★
Table: p. 626

Montironi, Paolo (Italy)
Profile: p. 427
Corporate/M&A ★★
Table: p. 419

Moodie, Bill (United Kingdom)
Profile: p. 766
Intellectual Property ★★
Table: p. 729

Moollan, Hamid (Mauritius)
Profile: p. 478
Corporate/Commercial ★★★★
Table: p. 478

Mooney, Kevin (United Kingdom)
Profile: p. 766
Intellectual Property ✪
Table: p. 729

Moore, Charles (USA)
Profile: p. 882
Energy & Natural Resources ★★
Table: p. 829

Moore, Chris (Singapore)
Profile: p. 602
Corporate/M&A: Singapore Foreign ★★★
Table: p. 592

Moore, Harold (USA)
Profile: p. 882
Project Finance ★★★★
Table: p. 837

Moore, Robert (USA)
Profile: p. 882
Tax ★★★
Table: p. 847

Moosecker, Karlheinz (Germany)
Profile: p. 328
Competition/Anti-trust ★★★★
Table: p. 309

Morales, Guillermo (Chile)
Profile: p. 210
Corporate/M&A ★★★★
Table: p. 208

Moreau, Bertrand (France)
Profile: p. 292
Arbitration (International) ★
Table: p. 262

Morgan, Charles (USA)
Profile: p. 882
Tax: Financial Products ★★★
Table: p. 845

Morgan, David (Zimbabwe)
Profile: p. 920
Corporate/Commercial ★★★★
Table: p. 919

Morgan, Frank (Indonesia)
Profile: p. 392
Corporate/Commercial ★★★
Table: p. 391

Morgan, Juan David (Panama)
Profile: p. 534
Corporate/Commercial ★★★★
Table: p. 533

Morgan, Leslie (Canada)
Profile: p. 195
Tax ★
Table: p. 182

Morgan, Simon (United Kingdom)
Profile: p. 766
Arbitration (International) **U**
Table: p. 696

Morgan de Rivery, Eric (France)
Profile: p. 292
Competition/Anti-trust ★★★
Table: p. 272

Morgan Sr, Eduardo (Panama)
Profile: p. 534
Corporate/Commercial ★★★★
Table: p. 533

Morishita, Kunihiko (Japan)
Profile: p. 445
Banking & Finance ★★★★
Table: p. 433

Morison, Frank (USA)
Profile: p. 882
Capital Markets: Debt & Equity ★★★
Table: p. 793

Moritz, Hans-Werner (Germany)
Profile: p. 328
Communications: IT ★★★
Table: p. 307

Morley, David (United Kingdom)
Profile: p. 766
Banking & Finance ✪
Table: p. 699

Moroney, David (United Kingdom)
Profile: p. 766
Energy: Electricity ★★★
Table: p. 725

Morphy, James C. (USA)
Profile: p. 882
Corporate/M&A ★
Table: p. 820

KEY TO RANKINGS: ✪ = Star Individual ★★★★ = Top Band ★★★ = Second Band ★★ = Third Band ★ = Fourth Band **U** = Up and coming

Morrison, David F. (France)
Profile: p. 328
Capital Markets: Debt ★★★★
Table: p. 303
Capital Markets: Equity ★★★★
Table: p. 304

Morrison, Ernest (Bermuda)
Profile: p. 137
Corporate/Commercial ★★★
Table: p. 136

Morrissey, Daniel (Ireland)
Profile: p. 403
Banking & Finance ★★★
Table: p. 394

Mortimer, Peter (USA)
Profile: p. 883
Banking & Finance ★★
Table: p. 791

Moser, Michael (Hong Kong)
Profile: p. 217
Corporate/M&A: China Foreign ★★★★
Table: p. 213

Moss, Gary (United Kingdom)
Profile: p. 766
Intellectual Property ★★★★
Table: p. 729

Mostafavi, Siamak (France)
Profile: p. 292
Tax ★★★
Table: p. 281

Motani, Habib (United Kingdom)
Profile: p. 766
Capital Markets: Derivatives ★★★★
Table: p. 706

Moult, Jonathan (Hong Kong)
Profile: p. 368
Banking & Finance ★★★
Table: p. 352

Moura Rocha, Bolivar (Brazil)
Profile: p. 156
Competition/Anti-trust ★★
Table: p. 145

Mousel, Paul (Luxembourg)
Profile: p. 466
Corporate/Commercial ★★★★
Table: p. 465

Mrowiec, Zbigniew (Poland)
Profile: p. 554
Banking & Finance ★★
Table: p. 545

Mrozek, Therese (USA)
Profile: p. 883
Communications: IT ★★
Table: p. 805

Mubaydeen, Ibrahim (United Arab Emirates)
Profile: p. 693
Banking & Finance ★★
Table: p. 688
Corporate/M&A ★★★★
Table: p. 690

Mubirigi, Gédéon (Burundi)
Profile: p. 167
Corporate/Commercial ★★★
Table: p. 167

Mubonda, Newton (Zambia)
Profile: p. 918
Corporate/Commercial ★★★
Table: p. 918

Muci Abraham, José (Venezuela)
Profile: p. 913
Corporate/M&A ★★★
Table: p. 909

Mueller, Thomas (Belgium)
Profile: p. 130
Competition/Anti-trust **U**
Table: p. 122

Mueller-Gastell, Thomas (Mexico)
Profile: p. 481
Banking & Finance ★★★
Table: p. 479

Mühlmann, Johann Georg (Germany)
Profile: p. 328
Capital Markets: Debt ★★★
Table: p. 303
Capital Markets: Equity ★★★
Table: p. 304

Mulaney, Charles (USA)
Profile: p. 883
Corporate/M&A ★★★★
Table: p. 813

Muljadi, Kartini (Indonesia)
Profile: p. 392
Corporate/Commercial ★★★★
Table: p. 391

Muller, Maarten (Netherlands)
Profile: p. 503
Corporate/M&A ★★
Table: p. 496

Müller, Welf (Germany)
Profile: p. 328
Tax ★
Table: p. 319

Mullins, Bruce (Oman)
Profile: p. 528
Project Finance ★★★
Table: p. 527

Mummery, Dan (USA)
Profile: p. 883
Communications: Transactional (IT) ★★★★
Table: p. 801

Mun Sou, Chooi (Malaysia)
Profile: p. 473
Banking & Finance ★★★
Table: p. 470

Mundie, Kevin Louis (Brazil)
Profile: p. 156
Communications ★★★★
Table: p. 143

Munguia Alvarez, Juan Alvaro (Nicaragua)
Profile: p. 511
Corporate/Commercial ★★★
Table: p. 510

Muñiz, Jorge (Peru)
Profile: p. 541
Corporate/M&A ★★
Table: p. 540

Muñoz-Delgado, Jesús (Spain)
Profile: p. 634
Intellectual Property ★★★★
Table: p. 626

Muñoz de Toro, Fernando (Argentina)
Profile: p. 63
Corporate/M&A ★
Table: p. 57

Muñoz Tamayo, Diego (Colombia)
Profile: p. 223
Corporate/M&A ★★
Table: p. 221

Muratore, Tony (Australia)
Profile: p. 95
Intellectual Property ★★★★
Table: p. 77

Murphy, Frances (United Kingdom)
Profile: p. 766
Corporate/M&A ★
Table: p. 717

Murphy, Peter Eugene (Canada)
Profile: p. 195
Banking & Finance ★★★
Table: p. 171

Murray, Alan (Australia)
Profile: p. 95
Energy & Natural Resources ★★
Table: p. 75

Murray, Gregory (USA)
Profile: p. 883
Banking & Finance ★★★★
Table: p. 787

Murray, Stephen (Singapore)
Profile: p. 602
Project Finance ★
Table: p. 594

Musat, Gheorghe (Romania)
Profile: p. 572
Corporate/M&A ★★★
Table: p. 571

Muscat, Andrew (Malta)
Profile: p. 476
Corporate/Commercial ★★★★
Table: p. 475

Musgrove, James (Canada)
Profile: p. 196
Competition/Anti-trust ★★
Table: p. 175

Müssnich, Francisco (Brazil)
Profile: p. 156
Banking & Finance ★★★
Table: p. 142
Corporate/M&A ★★★
Table: p. 147

Muszynski, Igor (Poland)
Profile: p. 554
Energy & Natural Resources ★★★★
Table: p. 550

Mycyk, Adam M (Ukraine)
Profile: p. 687
Corporate/Commercial ★★
Table: p. 686

Myhre, Finn (Norway)
Profile: p. 524
Banking & Finance ★★★★
Table: p. 517

Myska, Jan (Czech Republic)
Profile: p. 236
Corporate/M&A ★★
Table: p. 234

N

Nabarro, Jonathan (France)
Profile: p. 292
Banking & Finance ★★
Table: p. 265

Nabulsi, Omar (Jordan)
Profile: p. 450
Corporate/Commercial ★★★
Table: p. 450

Naciri, Hicham (Morocco)
Profile: p. 485
Corporate/Commercial **U**
Table: p. 485

Naciri, Mohamed (Morocco)
Profile: p. 485
Corporate/Commercial ★★★
Table: p. 485

Nader, Michell (Mexico)
Profile: p. 481
Corporate/M&A ★★★
Table: p. 480

Naeve, Clifford (USA)
Profile: p. 883
Energy & Natural Resources ★★★★
Table: p. 827

Nagahama, Tsuyoshi (Japan)
Profile: p. 446
Banking & Finance ★★
Table: p. 433
Corporate/M&A ★★★
Table: p. 439

Nagashima, Yasuharu (Japan)
Profile: p. 446
Corporate/M&A ★★★
Table: p. 439

Nairn, Karyl (United Kingdom)
Profile: p. 767
Arbitration (International) ★★
Table: p. 696

Nakajima, Tohru (Japan)
Profile: p. 446
Corporate/M&A ★★
Table: p. 439

Namekata, Kunio (Japan)
Profile: p. 446
Corporate/M&A ★
Table: p. 439

Namiotkiewicz, Grzegorz (Poland)
Profile: p. 554
Banking & Finance ★★★★
Table: p. 545

Nassikas, Andreas (Greece)
Profile: p. 342
Shipping ★★
Table: p. 340

Nath, Ravindra (India)
Profile: p. 389
Corporate/M&A ★★
Table: p. 381
Project Finance ★★★★
Table: p. 384

Ndiaye, Guedel (Senegal)
Profile: p. 583
Corporate/Commercial ★★★
Table: p. 583

Neale, Alastair (Oman)
Profile: p. 528
Banking & Finance ★★★★
Table: p. 526

Neckles, Peter (USA)
Profile: p. 883
Banking & Finance ★
Table: p. 791

Nee, Owen (China)
Profile: p. 218
Corporate/M&A: China Foreign ★★★
Table: p. 213
Project Finance: China Foreign ★★
Table: p. 215

Neelakandan, Kandhia (Sri Lanka)
Profile: p. 637
Corporate/Commercial ★★★
Table: p. 637

Neeman, Yaakov (Israel)
Profile: p. 411
Banking & Finance ★★★
Table: p. 406
Corporate/M&A ★★★★
Table: p. 409

Negri, Juan Javier (Argentina)
Profile: p. 63
Corporate/M&A ★★
Table: p. 57

Negri-Clementi, Gianfranco (Italy)
Profile: p. 428
Corporate/M&A ★★
Table: p. 419

Neish QC, James (Gibraltar)
Profile: p. 338
Corporate/Commercial ★★★
Table: p. 337

Nelissen Grade, Jean-Marie (Belgium)
Profile: p. 130
Banking & Finance ★★★
Table: p. 117
Corporate/M&A ★★
Table: p. 125

Nelson, Stephen (Hong Kong)
Profile: p. 218
Corporate/M&A: China Foreign ★★★
Table: p. 213
Project Finance: China Foreign ★★★
Table: p. 215

Nelson, William (USA)
Profile: p. 883
Tax ★★
Table: p. 847

Nestor, Ion I. (Romania)
Profile: p. 572
Banking & Finance ★★★★
Table: p. 570
Corporate/M&A ★★★★
Table: p. 571

Neuenschwander, Peter (Switzerland)
Profile: p. 661
Communications ★★★★
Table: p. 655

Neuhaus, Joseph (USA)
Profile: p. 883
Arbitration (International) ★★★
Table: p. 785

Neuner, Robert (USA)
Profile: p. 883
Intellectual Property ★
Table: p. 831

Neuville, David E. (Hong Kong)
Profile: p. 368
Capital Markets: Debt & Equity ★★
Table: p. 353

Newbery, Mark (Singapore)
Profile: p. 389, 602
Corporate/M&A: Singapore Foreign ★
Table: p. 592
Project Finance ★
Table: p. 594
Project Finance: India Foreign ★★
Table: p. 386

Newborn, Steve A. (USA)
Profile: p. 883
Competition/Anti-trust ★★
Table: p. 811

Newhouse, Anthony J.R. (United Kingdom)
Profile: p. 767
Corporate/M&A ★
Table: p. 717

Newman, Helen (United Kingdom)
Profile: p. 767
Intellectual Property ★★★★
Table: p. 729

Newman, Lawrence W. (USA)
Profile: p. 883
Arbitration (International) ★★★
Table: p. 785

Newton, Alan (Italy)
Profile: p. 428
Banking & Finance ★★
Table: p. 414

Ng, Wai King (Singapore)
Profile: p. 602
Corporate/M&A ★★
Table: p. 590

Ngwe, Marie-Andrée (Cameroon)
Profile: p. 169
Corporate/Commercial ★★★★
Table: p. 169

Nicholls, Dale (Australia)
Profile: p. 95
Energy & Natural Resources ★★★
Table: p. 75

Nicholls, Philip (Barbados)
Profile: p. 113
Corporate/Commercial ★★★
Table: p. 113

Nicholson, Kim (United Kingdom)
Profile: p. 767
Communications: E-commerce ★★
Table: p. 711
Communications: IT ★★
Table: p. 709

Nicholson, Malcolm (United Kingdom)
Profile: p. 767
Competition/Anti-trust ✪
Table: p. 714

Nicholson, Robert (Australia)
Profile: p. 95
Corporate/M&A ★★
Table: p. 73
Energy & Natural Resources ★★★★
Table: p. 75

Nicholson, Robin (Hong Kong)
Profile: p. 368
Capital Markets: Debt & Equity ★★
Table: p. 353
Corporate/M&A ★★★★
Table: p. 357

Nicodano, Umberto (Italy)
Profile: p. 428
Corporate/M&A ★★★
Table: p. 419

Nicolau, Luis (Mexico)
Profile: p. 481
Banking & Finance ★★★★
Table: p. 479

Nicoletti, Hélio (Brazil)
Profile: p. 156
Corporate/M&A ★★
Table: p. 147

Nicotra, Aldo (Australia)
Profile: p. 95
Competition/Anti-trust ★★
Table: p. 71

Nieder, Michael (Germany)
Profile: p. 328
Intellectual Property: General ★★★★
Table: p. 314

Niederer, Hans (Switzerland)
Profile: p. 661
Banking & Finance ★★★★
Table: p. 654

Nielsen, Niels Erik (Denmark)
Profile: p. 241
Corporate/M&A ★★★★
Table: p. 239

Nieuwdorp, Roel (Belgium)
Profile: p. 130
Corporate/M&A ★★
Table: p. 125

Nilsson, Bo (Sweden)
Profile: p. 650
Arbitration (International) ★★★
Table: p. 640

Nishimura, Toshiro (Japan)
Profile: p. 446
Corporate/M&A ★★★
Table: p. 439

Nishizawa Takano, Santiago (Bolivia)
Profile: p. 139
Corporate/Commercial ★★★★
Table: p. 138

Nixon, Christopher (Canada)
Profile: p. 196
Corporate/M&A ★
Table: p. 177

Nkambo-Mugerwa, P J (Uganda)
Profile: p. 685
Corporate/Commercial ★★
Table: p. 684

Nobili, Rafaele (Italy)
Profile: p. 428
Corporate/M&A ★
Table: p. 419

Noble, Nicholas (United Kingdom)
Profile: p. 767
Tax ★★★
Table: p. 739

Noble, Perry (United Kingdom)
Profile: p. 767
PFI ★★★★
Table: p. 733

Nocco, Frank (USA)
Profile: p. 884
Capital Markets: Securitisation ★
Table: p. 795

Nodder, Edward (United Kingdom)
Profile: p. 767
Intellectual Property ★★★★
Table: p. 729

Nogueira, Mario (Brazil)
Profile: p. 156
Competition/Anti-trust ★★
Table: p. 145

Nolte, Norbert (Germany)
Profile: p. 328
Communications: Regulatory ★★★★
Table: p. 306

Norall, Christopher (Belgium)
Profile: p. 130
Competition/Anti-trust ★
Table: p. 122

Nordhues, Hans-Günther (Germany)
Profile: p. 328
Banking & Finance ★★★★
Table: p. 301

Norfolk, Edward Christopher Dominic (United Kingdom)
Profile: p. 767
Tax ★★★★
Table: p. 739

Norman, David (Hong Kong)
Profile: p. 369
Capital Markets: Debt & Equity ★★
Table: p. 353
Corporate/M&A ★★★★
Table: p. 357

Norman, Guy (United Kingdom)
Profile: p. 767
Corporate/M&A **U**
Table: p. 717

Norman, Justo (Argentina)
Profile: p. 63
Energy & Natural Resources ★★★★
Table: p. 59

Normand, Enrique (Peru)
Profile: p. 541
Banking & Finance ★★★
Table: p. 538
Corporate/M&A ★★★★
Table: p. 540

Norris, Brian (Australia)
Profile: p. 95
Tax ★
Table: p. 81

Norris, Nicholas (Hong Kong)
Profile: p. 369
Corporate/M&A ★★
Table: p. 357

Norton, Floyd (USA)
Profile: p. 884
Energy & Natural Resources ★
Table: p. 827

Nourse, David A. (USA)
Profile: p. 884
Shipping: Litigation ★★★★
Table: p. 841

Novais, Raquel (Brazil)
Profile: p. 156
Tax ★
Table: p. 150

Novelli, Francesco (Italy)
Profile: p. 428
Banking & Finance ★
Table: p. 414
Project Finance ★★★★
Table: p. 421

Novo, Massimo (Italy)
Profile: p. 428
Project Finance ★★
Table: p. 421

Nowlan, Howard (United Kingdom)
Profile: p. 767
Tax ★★★★
Table: p. 739

Noya de la Piedra, Ismael (Peru)
Profile: p. 541
Banking & Finance ★★★★
Table: p. 538

Ntakiyica, Tharcisse (Burundi)
Profile: p. 167
Corporate/Commercial ★★★★
Table: p. 167

Nunes, Esther (Brazil)
Profile: p. 156
Communications ★★★★
Table: p. 143
Corporate/M&A ★★
Table: p. 147

Nunes Pinto, José Emilio (Brazil)
Profile: p. 156
Banking & Finance ★★
Table: p. 142
Project Finance ✪
Table: p. 149

Nunziante, Gianni (Italy)
Profile: p. 428
Corporate/M&A ★★
Table: p. 419

Nurmamsyah, Emir (Indonesia)
Profile: p. 392
Corporate/Commercial **U**
Table: p. 391

Nusbaum, Jack (USA)
Profile: p. 884
Corporate/M&A ★★
Table: p. 820
Private Equity: Buyouts ★★★
Table: p. 834

Nussbaum, Andrew (USA)
Profile: p. 884
Corporate/M&A **U**
Table: p. 820

Nussbaum, Peter (Germany)
Profile: p. 328
Private Equity ★★
Table: p. 316

O

O'Beirne, David (Ireland)
Profile: p. 403
Corporate/M&A ★★
Table: p. 397

O'Brien, Barry (United Kingdom)
Profile: p. 767
Corporate/M&A ★★★★
Table: p. 717

O'Brien, Judith (USA)
Profile: p. 884
Communications: IT ★
Table: p. 805

O'Brien, Patrick (Ireland)
Profile: p. 403
Competition/Anti-trust ★★★
Table: p. 396

O'Brien, Timothy (Hong Kong)
Profile: p. 516, 617
Corporate/Commercial: North Korea Foreign ★★★★
Table: p. 516
Corporate/Commercial: South Korea Foreign ★★★
Table: p. 615

O'Bryan, Michael (Australia)
Profile: p. 95
Competition/Anti-trust ★★
Table: p. 71

O'Connell, Owen (Ireland)
Profile: p. 403
Corporate/M&A ★★★★
Table: p. 397

O'Connor, Patrick (Hong Kong)
Profile: p. 369
Banking & Finance ★★
Table: p. 352

O'Conor, John (United Kingdom)
Profile: p. 768
Arbitration (International) **U**
Table: p. 696

O'Dwyer, James (Ireland)
Profile: p. 403
Corporate/M&A ★★★★
Table: p. 397

O'Farrell, Alfredo Miguel (Argentina)
Profile: p. 63
Corporate/M&A ★
Table: p. 57

O'Farrell, Jack (Ireland)
Profile: p. 403
Corporate/M&A ★★★★
Table: p. 397

O'Farrell, Juan Patricio (Argentina)
Profile: p. 63
Corporate/M&A ★★★
Table: p. 57

O'Farrell, Uriel (Argentina)
Profile: p. 63
Energy & Natural Resources ★★
Table: p. 59

O'Hare, Caroline (United Arab Emirates)
Profile: p. 693
Banking & Finance ★★★★
Table: p. 688

O'Keefe, Michael J., Q.C. (Canada)
Profile: p. 196
Tax ★★★
Table: p. 182

O'Leary, Michael (USA)
Profile: p. 884
Corporate/M&A ★★★★
Table: p. 824

O'Neill, Brian (USA)
Profile: p. 884
Energy & Natural Resources ★★★
Table: p. 827

O'Riordan, Frank (Ireland)
Profile: p. 403
Corporate/M&A ★★★
Table: p. 397

O'Rourke, Kieron J. (British Virgin Islands)
Profile: p. 161
Corporate/Commercial ★★★
Table: p. 160

O'Sullivan, John (Australia)
Profile: p. 95
Capital Markets ★★★★
Table: p. 67
Corporate/M&A ★★★★
Table: p. 73

O'Sullivan, John (USA)
Profile: p. 884
Energy & Natural Resources ★★
Table: p. 827

O'Toole, Niall (United Arab Emirates)
Profile: p. 693
Corporate/M&A ★★
Table: p. 690

Oakley, Chris (United Kingdom)
Profile: p. 768
Capital Markets: Securitisation ★★
Table: p. 704

Obach, Sebastian (Chile)
Profile: p. 210
Banking & Finance ★★
Table: p. 206
Corporate/M&A ★★
Table: p. 208

Oddie, Carolyn (Australia)
Profile: p. 96
Intellectual Property ★★
Table: p. 77

Odriozola, Miguel (Spain)
Profile: p. 634
Competition/Anti-trust ★★
Table: p. 622

Oertle, Matthias (Switzerland)
Profile: p. 661
Corporate/M&A ★★★
Table: p. 657

Ogg, Terry (Singapore)
Profile: p. 603
Shipping: Foreign Firms ★
Table: p. 596

Oh, Yong Suk (Y.S.) (South Korea)
Profile: p. 617
Corporate/Commercial ★★
Table: p. 614

Ohlsson, Alex (Jersey)
Profile: p. 449
Corporate/Commercial **U**
Table: p. 448

Ojanguren, Ignacio (Spain)
Profile: p. 634
Corporate/M&A ★
Table: p. 624

Okanurak, Wilailuk (Thailand)
Profile: p. 674
Banking & Finance ★★★
Table: p. 670

Okeke, Chris (Nigeria)
Profile: p. 515
Corporate/Commercial ★★★★
Table: p. 512

Olasker, Patricia L. (Canada)
Profile: p. 196
Corporate/M&A ★★
Table: p. 177

KEY TO RANKINGS: ✪ = Star Individual ★★★★ = Top Band ★★★ = Second Band ★★ = Third Band ★ = Fourth Band **U** = Up and coming

Olden, John (Ireland)
Profile: p. 403
Corporate/M&A ★
Table: p. 397

Oldfield, John Paul H. (New Zealand)
Profile: p. 509
Corporate/M&A ★★★★
Table: p. 508

Oles, Wieslaw (Poland)
Profile: p. 554
Corporate/M&A ★
Table: p. 548

Olivera, Ricardo (Uruguay)
Profile: p. 906
Banking & Finance ★★★
Table: p. 904

Olivier, Jeanne C. (USA)
Profile: p. 884
Project Finance ★★
Table: p. 837

Olivos, Carlos (Chile)
Profile: p. 210
Banking & Finance ★★★
Table: p. 206

Olmedo, Gustavo (Paraguay)
Profile: p. 537
Banking & Finance ★★★★
Table: p. 536
Corporate/M&A ★★★
Table: p. 537

Olofsson, Rolf (Sweden)
Profile: p. 650
Communications: Telecoms ★★★
Table: p. 642

Olson, Gary (USA)
Profile: p. 885
Corporate/M&A ★★★
Table: p. 825

Olsson, David (Australia)
Profile: p. 96
Capital Markets ★★
Table: p. 67
Project Finance ★
Table: p. 79

Ong, Andrew (Brunei Darussalam)
Profile: p. 163
Corporate/Commercial ★★★★
Table: p. 162

Ong, Andrew (Singapore)
Profile: p. 603
Shipping ★
Table: p. 595

Ong, Christina (Singapore)
Profile: p. 603
Banking & Finance ★★
Table: p. 586

Ong, Colin (Brunei Darussalam)
Profile: p. 163
Corporate/Commercial ★★★★
Table: p. 162

Ono, Masaru (Japan)
Profile: p. 446
Capital Markets ★★★★
Table: p. 436

Ooi, Eugene (Singapore)
Profile: p. 603
Banking & Finance ★★★
Table: p. 586

Oosterhuis, Paul (USA)
Profile: p. 885
Tax ★★★
Table: p. 847

Opice, José Roberto (Brazil)
Profile: p. 157
Banking & Finance ✪
Table: p. 142
Corporate/M&A ★★★★
Table: p. 147

Project Finance ★★★
Table: p. 149

Opitz, Peter (Germany)
Profile: p. 328
Banking & Finance ★★
Table: p. 301

Oppenhoff, Michael (Germany)
Profile: p. 328
Corporate/M&A ★★
Table: p. 311

Oreamuno, Rodrigo (Costa Rica)
Profile: p. 226
Corporate/Commercial ★★★★
Table: p. 225

Oreggia, Juan Carlos (Uruguay)
Profile: p. 906
Corporate/M&A ★★★
Table: p. 905

Oren, Ruth (Israel)
Profile: p. 411
Corporate/M&A ★★★
Table: p. 409

Ormai, Gabriella (Hungary)
Profile: p. 376
Banking & Finance ★★★
Table: p. 372
Corporate/M&A ★★★
Table: p. 375

Orrego, Alberto (Chile)
Profile: p. 210
Banking & Finance ★★★
Table: p. 206
Corporate/M&A ★★
Table: p. 208

Ortigão Ramos, Diogo (Portugal)
Profile: p. 565
Tax ★★
Table: p. 562

Ortiz Blanco, Luis (Spain)
Profile: p. 634
Competition/Anti-trust ★
Table: p. 622

Orts, Mario Jorge (Argentina)
Profile: p. 63
Energy & Natural Resources ★★★★
Table: p. 59

Osborn, John (USA)
Profile: p. 885
Capital Markets: Derivatives ★★★
Table: p. 798

Osborne, John (USA)
Profile: p. 885
Shipping: Finance ★★★★
Table: p. 841

Osborne, John (United Kingdom)
Profile: p. 768
Competition/Anti-trust ★
Table: p. 714

Osborne, Robert Stephen (USA)
Profile: p. 885
Corporate/M&A ★★
Table: p. 813

Osório de Castro, Carlos (Portugal)
Profile: p. 566
Banking & Finance ★
Table: p. 558
Corporate/M&A ★★
Table: p. 560

Osterling, Felipe (Peru)
Profile: p. 541
Corporate/M&A ★★
Table: p. 540

Osti, Cristoforo (Italy)
Profile: p. 428
Communications ★
Table: p. 415
Competition/Anti-trust ★★★
Table: p. 417

Otamendi, Jorge (Argentina)
Profile: p. 63
Competition/Anti-trust ★★★
Table: p. 56

Otero Lastres, José Manuel (Spain)
Profile: p. 634
Intellectual Property ★★★
Table: p. 626

Ottervanger, Tom (Belgium)
Profile: p. 130
Competition/Anti-trust ★
Table: p. 122

Ottervanger, Tom R. (Netherlands)
Profile: p. 503
Competition/Anti-trust ★★★★
Table: p. 494
Energy & Natural Resources ★★★
Table: p. 498

Ottow, Annetje (Netherlands)
Profile: p. 503
Communications ★★★★
Table: p. 492
Competition/Anti-trust ★★
Table: p. 494

Overlack, Arndt (Germany)
Profile: p. 328
Corporate/M&A ★
Table: p. 311

Owen, Gail (Australia)
Profile: p. 96
Energy & Natural Resources ★★
Table: p. 75

Oxford, Patrick (USA)
Profile: p. 885
Corporate/M&A ★★
Table: p. 824

Oyebode, Gbenga (Nigeria)
Profile: p. 515
Corporate/Commercial ★★★
Table: p. 512
Energy & Natural Resources ★★★★
Table: p. 513

Özeke, Ender (Turkey)
Profile: p. 683
Project Finance ★★★★
Table: p. 682

Özel, Haluk Can (Turkey)
Profile: p. 683
Corporate/M&A ★★★★
Table: p. 681

P

Pacheco, Humberto (Costa Rica)
Profile: p. 226
Corporate/Commercial ★★★
Table: p. 225

Pacheco, Mario (Costa Rica)
Profile: p. 226
Corporate/Commercial ★★★
Table: p. 225

Padovani, Stefano (Italy)
Profile: p. 428
Banking & Finance ★
Table: p. 414

Pagenberg, Jochen (Germany)
Profile: p. 328
Intellectual Property: General ★
Table: p. 314

Painter, Robin (USA)
Profile: p. 885
Private Equity: Fund Formation ★★★
Table: p. 835

Pais Antunes, Luis (Portugal)
Profile: p. 566
Competition/Anti-trust ★★★
Table: p. 559

Paksoy, Serdar (Turkey)
Profile: p. 683
Banking & Finance ★★★
Table: p. 679

Palacios, José (Spain)
Profile: p. 634
Tax ★★
Table: p. 628

Palacios, Luis Esteban (Venezuela)
Profile: p. 913
Corporate/M&A ★★
Table: p. 909

Palenberg, John (Germany)
Profile: p. 329
Capital Markets: Equity ★★★
Table: p. 304

Pálka, Igor (Slovakia)
Profile: p. 608
Corporate/Commercial ★★★★
Table: p. 607

Palma, Juan Eduardo (Chile)
Profile: p. 210
Corporate/M&A ★★
Table: p. 208

Palma, Laura (USA)
Profile: p. 885
Capital Markets: Securitisation ★★★
Table: p. 795

Palmer, James (United Kingdom)
Profile: p. 768
Corporate/M&A ★★★
Table: p. 717

Pande, Raj (Singapore)
Profile: p. 389, 603
Corporate/M&A: India Foreign ★★
Table: p. 383
Project Finance ★★
Table: p. 594
Project Finance: India Foreign ★★
Table: p. 386

Pantaleon, Polo S (Philippines)
Profile: p. 544
Corporate/Commercial ★
Table: p. 542

Papangelis, Miltos (Greece)
Profile: p. 343
Shipping ★★★
Table: p. 340

Papirnik, Vladimira N (Czech Republic)
Profile: p. 236
Corporate/M&A ★★
Table: p. 234

Papp, Sven (Estonia)
Profile: p. 252
Corporate/Commercial ★★★★
Table: p. 251

Pappalardo, Aurelio (Italy)
Profile: p. 428
Competition/Anti-trust ★★★★
Table: p. 417

Pappalettera, Carlo (Italy)
Profile: p. 428
Corporate/M&A ★★
Table: p. 419

Paradise, Theodore (Japan)
Profile: p. 446
Banking & Finance: Japan Foreign ★★★
Table: p. 435
Capital Markets: Japan Foreign ★★★
Table: p. 437

Pardiwalla, Pesi (Seychelles)
Profile: p. 584
Corporate/Commercial ★★★★
Table: p. 584

Paré, Jay (USA)
Profile: p. 885
Shipping: Litigation **U**
Table: p. 841

Park, Jay (Canada)
Profile: p. 196
Energy & Natural Resources ★★★★
Table: p. 180

Park, Jin Hyuk (Hong Kong)
Profile: p. 617
Corporate/Commercial: South Korea Foreign **U**
Table: p. 615

Park, Joon (South Korea)
Profile: p. 617
Corporate/Commercial ★★★
Table: p. 614

Park, Sang Il (South Korea)
Profile: p. 617
Corporate/Commercial ★★★
Table: p. 614

Park, William W. (USA)
Profile: p. 885
Arbitration (International) ★★★
Table: p. 785

Parker, Allen (USA)
Profile: p. 885
Banking & Finance ★★★★
Table: p. 791

Parleani, Gilbert (France)
Profile: p. 292
Competition/Anti-trust ★
Table: p. 272

Parolai, Richard (France)
Profile: p. 292
Capital Markets ★★
Table: p. 268

Parr, Nigel (United Kingdom)
Profile: p. 768
Competition/Anti-trust ★★★
Table: p. 714

Parsons, Chris (United Kingdom)
Profile: p. 768
Corporate/M&A ★★
Table: p. 717

Parsons, Richard (British Virgin Islands)
Profile: p. 161
Corporate/Commercial ★★★★
Table: p. 160

Pascarl, Ian (Australia)
Profile: p. 96
Intellectual Property ★
Table: p. 77

Pasqualin, Roberto (Brazil)
Profile: p. 157
Tax ★★
Table: p. 150

Pasquet, Gerds (Haiti)
Profile: p. 349
Corporate/Commercial ★★★★
Table: p. 349

Pasztory, Blaise G A (Hungary)
Profile: p. 377
Corporate/M&A ★★
Table: p. 375

Patel, Kanti (Zambia)
Profile: p. 918
Corporate/Commercial ★★★★
Table: p. 918

Paternollo, Renato (Italy)
Profile: p. 428
Tax ★★
Table: p. 422

Pathak, Jai (India)
Profile: p. 389
Corporate/M&A ★★
Table: p. 381
Project Finance ★★
Table: p. 384

Patocchi, Paolo Michele (Switzerland)
Profile: p. 661
Arbitration (International) ★★
Table: p. 653

Patterson, Donna (USA)
Profile: p. 885
Competition/Anti-trust ★
Table: p. 811

Pattison, Michael (Australia)
Profile: p. 96
Communications: IT ★★★
Table: p. 69

Paul, Alan D. (United Kingdom)
Profile: p. 768
Corporate/M&A ★★★★
Table: p. 717
Private Equity: Buyouts ★★★
Table: p. 731

Paulsson, Jan (France)
Profile: p. 292
Arbitration (International) ✪
Table: p. 262

Pavesio, Carlo (Italy)
Profile: p. 428
Competition/Anti-trust ★
Table: p. 417

Payan, Daniel (France)
Profile: p. 292
Banking & Finance ★★
Table: p. 265
Corporate/M&A ★★★
Table: p. 275

Payet, Jose Antonio (Peru)
Profile: p. 541
Banking & Finance ★★★★
Table: p. 538
Corporate/M&A ★★★★
Table: p. 540

Paz Parra, Francisco (Venezuela)
Profile: p. 913
Corporate/M&A ★
Table: p. 909

Pazos, Carlos (Spain)
Profile: p. 634
Communications ★★
Table: p. 620

Pearlstein, Debra J. (USA)
Profile: p. 886
Competition/Anti-trust ★
Table: p. 808

Pearson, Chris (United Kingdom)
Profile: p. 768
Corporate/M&A ★★
Table: p. 717

Pearson, David (United Kingdom)
Profile: p. 768
Corporate/M&A ★
Table: p. 717

Pearson, Hilary (United Kingdom)
Profile: p. 768
Communications: IT ★★
Table: p. 709

Peaslee, James (USA)
Profile: p. 886
Tax: Financial Products ★★★★
Table: p. 845

Peck, Andrew (United Kingdom)
Profile: p. 768
Corporate/M&A ★★
Table: p. 717

Pedersen, Jonathan (Hong Kong)
Profile: p. 369
Capital Markets: Debt & Equity ★★★
Table: p. 353

Pedersoli, Alessandro (Italy)
Profile: p. 428
Corporate/M&A ★★
Table: p. 419

Pêdzich, Arkadiusz (Poland)
Profile: p. 554
Banking & Finance ★★★
Table: p. 545

Peeters, Ivan (Belgium)
Profile: p. 130
Banking & Finance ★★★★
Table: p. 117

Peeters, Jan (Belgium)
Profile: p. 131
Corporate/M&A ★★★
Table: p. 125

Pegg, Garry (United Kingdom)
Profile: p. 768
Energy: Oil and Gas ★
Table: p. 723

Peigney, Gilles (France)
Profile: p. 292
Banking & Finance ★★★★
Table: p. 265

Pekin, Ahmed (Turkey)
Profile: p. 683
Banking & Finance ★★★★
Table: p. 679

Pell, Marian (United Kingdom)
Profile: p. 769
Corporate/M&A ★
Table: p. 717

Pellerano, Juan Manuel (Dominican Republic)
Profile: p. 243
Corporate/Commercial ★★★★
Table: p. 243

Pemberton, Stephen (Australia)
Profile: p. 96
Banking & Finance ★
Table: p. 65
Project Finance ★★
Table: p. 79

Peña, Francisco (Spain)
Profile: p. 634
Corporate/M&A ★★★
Table: p. 624

Pena, Rui (Portugal)
Profile: p. 566
Corporate/M&A ★
Table: p. 560

Penkov, Vladimir (Bulgaria)
Profile: p. 165
Corporate/Commercial ★★★
Table: p. 164

Penn, Graham (United Kingdom)
Profile: p. 769
Capital Markets: Securitisation ★★
Table: p. 704

Pennycook, Carol D. (Canada)
Profile: p. 196
Banking & Finance ★★
Table: p. 171

Penzer, Michele (USA)
Profile: p. 886
Project Finance **U**
Table: p. 837

Peralta, Diego (Chile)
Profile: p. 210
Banking & Finance ★★★★
Table: p. 206

Pereira Coutinho, Frederico (Portugal)
Profile: p. 566
Competition/Anti-trust ★
Table: p. 559

Perez, José Maria (Ecuador)
Profile: p. 245
Corporate/Commercial ★★★★
Table: p. 244

Perez Alati, Jorge Luis (Argentina)
Profile: p. 63
Corporate/M&A ★★
Table: p. 57

Pérez Ardá, Javier (Spain)
Profile: p. 634
Communications ★★★
Table: p. 620

Pérez de la Sota, Fernando (Spain)
Profile: p. 634
Communications ★★★
Table: p. 620

Pérez Santos, José (Spain)
Profile: p. 634
Communications ★★★★
Table: p. 620
Competition/Anti-trust ★★★
Table: p. 622

Perhard, Lars (Sweden)
Profile: p. 650
Communications: IT ★★★
Table: p. 642

Perkins, David (United Kingdom)
Profile: p. 769
Intellectual Property ★★★★
Table: p. 729

Permin, Jørgen (Denmark)
Profile: p. 241
Banking & Finance ★★★★
Table: p. 237

Perrick, Steven (Netherlands)
Profile: p. 503
Energy & Natural Resources ★★★
Table: p. 498

Pescod, Michael (United Kingdom)
Profile: p. 769
Corporate/M&A ★★★★
Table: p. 717

Petch, Jack (Canada)
Profile: p. 196
Corporate/M&A ★
Table: p. 177

Peter, Wendy (Australia)
Profile: p. 96
Competition/Anti-trust ★★
Table: p. 71

Peter, Wolfgang (Switzerland)
Profile: p. 661
Arbitration (International) ★★★★
Table: p. 653

Peters, Richard A. (British Virgin Islands)
Profile: p. 161
Corporate/Commercial ★★★
Table: p. 160

Petilon, Jean-Claude (France)
Profile: p. 292
Project Finance: Francophone Africa ★★★★
Table: p. 278

Petrus, Vladimir (Czech Republic)
Profile: p. 236
Banking & Finance ★★★★
Table: p. 232

Pettersson, Tommy (Sweden)
Profile: p. 650
Competition/Anti-trust ★★★
Table: p. 644

Peytz, Henrik (Denmark)
Profile: p. 242
Competition/Anti-trust ★★★
Table: p. 238

Pfeiffer, Steven (USA)
Profile: p. 886
Energy & Natural Resources ★★
Table: p. 827

Pfenninger, Markus D. (Switzerland)
Profile: p. 661
Banking & Finance ★
Table: p. 654

Pfüller, Markus (Germany)
Profile: p. 329
Capital Markets: Equity ★★★
Table: p. 304

Pheasant, John (United Kingdom)
Profile: p. 769
Competition/Anti-trust ★★★
Table: p. 714

Philip, Marianne (Denmark)
Profile: p. 242
Corporate/M&A ★★★
Table: p. 239

Phillips, Barnet (USA)
Profile: p. 886
Tax ★
Table: p. 845

Phillips, Craig (Australia)
Profile: p. 96
Competition/Anti-trust ★★
Table: p. 71

Phillips, Mark (United Kingdom)
Profile: p. 769
Communications: E-commerce ★★
Table: p. 711

Phillips, Robert (United Kingdom)
Profile: p. 769
Projects ★
Table: p. 733

Piatek, Stanislaw (Poland)
Profile: p. 554
Communications ★★★★
Table: p. 547

Piatek, Tadeusz (Poland)
Profile: p. 554
Communications ★★★
Table: p. 547

Picazo, Antonio (Philippines)
Profile: p. 544
Corporate/Commercial ★★★
Table: p. 542

Piccardi, Lorenzo (Italy)
Profile: p. 428
Tax ★★
Table: p. 422

Pichanick, Alan (Zimbabwe)
Profile: p. 920
Corporate/Commercial ★★★★
Table: p. 919

Pickens, Scott (USA)
Profile: p. 886
Banking & Finance ★★★
Table: p. 787

Picón, Juan (Spain)
Profile: p. 635
Communications ★★★★
Table: p. 620

Picot, Gerhard (Germany)
Profile: p. 329
Corporate/M&A ★★★★
Table: p. 311

Picton-Turbervill, Geoffrey (United Kingdom)
Profile: p. 769
Energy: Electricity ★★★
Table: p. 725
Energy: Oil and Gas ★★★
Table: p. 723

Piepenbrock, Hermann-Josef (Germany)
Profile: p. 329
Communications: Regulatory ★★
Table: p. 306

Pierce, Morton A. (USA)
Profile: p. 886
Corporate/M&A ★
Table: p. 820

Pierce, Sean (United Kingdom)
Profile: p. 769
Banking & Finance ★★
Table: p. 699

Pijnacker Hordijk, Erik (Netherlands)
Profile: p. 503
Competition/Anti-trust ★★★★
Table: p. 494

Pillai, Philip (Singapore)
Profile: p. 603
Corporate/M&A ★★★★
Table: p. 590

Piltz, Detlev (Germany)
Profile: p. 329
Tax ★★★★
Table: p. 319

Pinder, Hartis (Bahamas)
Profile: p. 109
Corporate/Commercial ★★★★
Table: p. 109

Pinedo, Federico (Argentina)
Profile: p. 63
Communications ★★★★
Table: p. 54

Pineros, Mauricio (Colombia)
Profile: p. 223
Corporate/M&A ★★★
Table: p. 221

Pingue, Filippo (Italy)
Profile: p. 428
Banking & Finance ★★
Table: p. 414

Pinheiro Guimaraes, Francisco (Brazil)
Profile: p. 157
Banking & Finance ★★★
Table: p. 142

Pinheiro Guimaraes, Plinio (Brazil)
Profile: p. 157
Banking & Finance ★★
Table: p. 142

Pinsler, Leena (Singapore)
Profile: p. 604
Corporate/M&A ★★★
Table: p. 590

Pinto Correia, Carlos (Portugal)
Profile: p. 566
Competition/Anti-trust ★★
Table: p. 559

Piquet Carneiro, João Geraldo (Brazil)
Profile: p. 157

KEY TO RANKINGS: ✪ = Star Individual ★★★★ = Top Band ★★★ = Second Band ★★ = Third Band ★ = Fourth Band **U** = Up and coming

Competition/Anti-trust ★★
Table: p. 145

Pisani, José Roberto (Brazil)
Profile: p. 157
Tax ★★
Table: p. 150

Pisano, Vince (USA)
Profile: p. 886
Capital Markets: Debt & Equity ★★
Table: p. 793

Pitkin, Jeremy (United Kingdom)
Profile: p. 769
Capital Markets: Debt & Equity ★★
Table: p. 702

Pitlarge, David (Greece)
Profile: p. 343
Shipping: Foreign Firms ★★
Table: p. 341

Planchart Manrique, Gustavo (Venezuela)
Profile: p. 914
Corporate/M&A ★★
Table: p. 909

Platt, David (Hong Kong)
Profile: p. 218, 369
Project Finance ★★★
Table: p. 359
Project Finance: China Foreign ★★★★
Table: p. 215

Plaz, Rodolfo (Venezuela)
Profile: p. 914
Corporate/M&A ★
Table: p. 909

Plesser, Willibald (Austria)
Profile: p. 107
Corporate/M&A ★
Table: p. 104

Plum, Jens Munk (Denmark)
Profile: p. 242
Competition/Anti-trust ★★
Table: p. 238

Poddar, Dave (Australia)
Profile: p. 96
Competition/Anti-trust **U**
Table: p. 71

Podolsky, Andrea (USA)
Profile: p. 886
Capital Markets: Securitisation ★
Table: p. 795

Pokela, Hannu (Finland)
Profile: p. 259
Competition/Anti-trust ★★★★
Table: p. 256

Polglase, Timothy (United Kingdom)
Profile: p. 769
Banking & Finance ★
Table: p. 699

Polito, Simon (United Kingdom)
Profile: p. 769
Competition/Anti-trust ★★★★
Table: p. 714

Pollack, Martin (USA)
Profile: p. 886
Tax ★★
Table: p. 845

Pöllath, Reinhard (Germany)
Profile: p. 329
Corporate/M&A ★★★
Table: p. 311
Private Equity ★★★
Table: p. 316
Tax ★★★★
Table: p. 319

Pombo, Fernando (Spain)
Profile: p. 635
Corporate/M&A ★★★
Table: p. 624

Ponce, Alejandro (Ecuador)
Profile: p. 245
Corporate/Commercial ★★★★
Table: p. 244

Poonsombudlert, Ratana (Thailand)
Profile: p. 674
Corporate/M&A ★★
Table: p. 672

Poonsuwan, Wirot (Thailand)
Profile: p. 674
Corporate/M&A ★★★
Table: p. 672

Pope, Gus (Cayman Islands)
Profile: p. 204
Corporate/Commercial ★★★★
Table: p. 203

Popham, Stuart (United Kingdom)
Profile: p. 770
Banking & Finance ★★★★
Table: p. 699

Popp, Eugen (Germany)
Profile: p. 329
Intellectual Property: Patent ★★
Table: p. 313

Porobija, Boris (Croatia)
Profile: p. 229
Corporate/Commercial ★★★★
Table: p. 228

Portella, Roberto (Brazil)
Profile: p. 157
Banking & Finance ★★★
Table: p. 142

Porteous, Jonathan (Hungary)
Profile: p. 377
Corporate/M&A ★★★
Table: p. 375

Porter, Susan (United Kingdom)
Profile: p. 770
Tax ★★★
Table: p. 739

Portier, Philippe (France)
Profile: p. 293
Capital Markets ★
Table: p. 268

Portner, Christopher (Canada)
Profile: p. 196
Corporate/M&A ★★★
Table: p. 177

Pose, Kevin (Australia)
Profile: p. 96
Tax ★★
Table: p. 81

Poster, Bob (USA)
Profile: p. 886
Shipping: Finance ★★★
Table: p. 841

Potts, Chris (Hong Kong)
Profile: p. 369
Shipping ★
Table: p. 361

Poudelet, François (France)
Profile: p. 293
Capital Markets ★★★
Table: p. 268

Poudret, Jean-François (Switzerland)
Profile: p. 662
Arbitration (International) ★★★★
Table: p. 653

Powell, Mark (Belgium)
Profile: p. 131
Communications ★★
Table: p. 118

Power, Vincent (Ireland)
Profile: p. 403
Competition/Anti-trust ★★★★
Table: p. 396

Powers, Matthew D. (USA)
Profile: p. 886
Intellectual Property ✪
Table: p. 833

Prado, Claudia (Brazil)
Profile: p. 157
Corporate/M&A ★★
Table: p. 147

Prat, Jean-François (France)
Profile: p. 293
Corporate/M&A ★★★★
Table: p. 275

Prat, Sebastien (France)
Profile: p. 293
Corporate/M&A ★★
Table: p. 275

Preece, Andrew (United Kingdom)
Profile: p. 770
Projects ★
Table: p. 733

Prentice, William (Ireland)
Profile: p. 404
Banking & Finance ★★★
Table: p. 394

Preslmayr, Karl (Austria)
Profile: p. 107
Banking & Finance ★★
Table: p. 103

Preslmayr, Martin (Austria)
Profile: p. 107
Corporate/M&A ★
Table: p. 104

Prevot, Thérèse-Murielle (French Guiana)
Profile: p. 296
Corporate/Commercial ★★★★
Table: p. 296

Price, Alvin (Ireland)
Profile: p. 404
Corporate/M&A ★★
Table: p. 397

Price, Harvey (Thailand)
Profile: p. 674
Corporate/M&A ★★
Table: p. 672

Price, Richard (United Kingdom)
Profile: p. 770
Intellectual Property ★★★
Table: p. 729

Prieto, Juan Manuel (Colombia)
Profile: p. 223
Corporate/M&A ★★★★
Table: p. 221

Prieto, Patricio (Chile)
Profile: p. 210
Corporate/M&A ★★★
Table: p. 208

Prince, Kenneth S. (USA)
Profile: p. 887
Competition/Anti-trust ★
Table: p. 808

Proger, Phillip A. (USA)
Profile: p. 887
Competition/Anti-trust ★★
Table: p. 811

Pross, Ulrich (Germany)
Profile: p. 329
Intellectual Property: General ★★★★
Table: p. 314

Protasio, Manuel (Portugal)
Profile: p. 566
Banking & Finance ★★
Table: p. 558

Provasoli, Anthony (Gibraltar)
Profile: p. 338
Corporate/Commercial ★★★
Table: p. 337

Pryke, Gary (Singapore)
Profile: p. 604
Corporate/M&A ★★
Table: p. 590

Pryles AM, Michael (Australia)
Profile: p. 96
Arbitration (International) ★★★★
Table: p. 64

Psillaki, Efti (Cyprus)
Profile: p. 231
Corporate/Commercial ★★★★
Table: p. 231

Pucci, Fred (Australia)
Profile: p. 97
Capital Markets ★
Table: p. 67

Puleo, Frank (USA)
Profile: p. 887
Banking & Finance ★★★
Table: p. 791

Puleston Jones, Haydn (United Kingdom)
Profile: p. 770
Banking & Finance ★★★★
Table: p. 699

Pulido Snr, Alberto (Chile)
Profile: p. 210
Banking & Finance ★★★★
Table: p. 206

Pulver, Urs (Switzerland)
Profile: p. 662
Corporate/M&A ★★★
Table: p. 657

Putterill, Bruce (Cayman Islands)
Profile: p. 204
Corporate/Commercial ★★★★
Table: p. 203

Q

Qasim, Imad I. (USA)
Profile: p. 887
Corporate/M&A ★★
Table: p. 813

Quack, Karlheinz (Germany)
Profile: p. 329
Competition/Anti-trust ★★
Table: p. 309

Quale, John (USA)
Profile: p. 887
Communications: Regulatory ★★
Table: p. 803

Quattrini, Sergio (Argentina)
Profile: p. 63
Corporate/M&A ★★★
Table: p. 57

Queen, Eric (USA)
Profile: p. 887
Competition/Anti-trust ★
Table: p. 808

Quéré, Michel (France)
Profile: p. 293
Banking & Finance ★★★
Table: p. 265

Quigley, Michael G. (Canada)
Profile: p. 196
Tax ★
Table: p. 182

Quin, Max (Bermuda)
Profile: p. 137
Corporate/Commercial ★★★
Table: p. 136

Quinn, John Joseph (Canada)
Profile: p. 196
Competition/Anti-trust ★★
Table: p. 175

Quinn, Linda C. (USA)
Profile: p. 887
Capital Markets: Debt & Equity ★★★★
Table: p. 793

Quintanilla Ballivián, Eduardo (Bolivia)
Profile: p. 139
Corporate/Commercial ★★★★
Table: p. 138

Quiroga Mosquera, Roberto (Brazil)
Profile: p. 157
Tax ★★★
Table: p. 150

R

Radhi, Hassan (Bahrain)
Profile: p. 111
Banking & Finance ★★★
Table: p. 110
Corporate/M&A ★★★
Table: p. 111

Radicati di Brozolo, Luca (Italy)
Profile: p. 429
Communications ★★★
Table: p. 415
Competition/Anti-trust ★★★
Table: p. 417

Radilofe, José (Madagascar)
Profile: p. 468
Corporate/Commercial ★★★
Table: p. 468

Radke, Kirk (USA)
Profile: p. 887
Private Equity: Buyouts ★★
Table: p. 834
Private Equity: Fund Formation ★★★
Table: p. 835

Radmilovic, Ines (Hungary)
Profile: p. 377
Corporate/M&A ★★★
Table: p. 375

Rae Smith, Alan (Hong Kong)
Profile: p. 369
Banking & Finance ★★★★
Table: p. 352
Project Finance ★★★★
Table: p. 359

Raffaelli, Enrico Adriano (Italy)
Profile: p. 429
Competition/Anti-trust ★★
Table: p. 417

Raffin, Marie-Hélène (France)
Profile: p. 293
Tax ★
Table: p. 281

Raidla, Juri (Estonia)
Profile: p. 252
Corporate/Commercial ★★★★
Table: p. 251

Raimundo, Antonio (Portugal)
Profile: p. 566
Corporate/M&A ★
Table: p. 560

Raines, Marke (United Kingdom)
Profile: p. 770
Capital Markets: Securitisation ★★★
Table: p. 704

Rainey, Paul (Australia)
Profile: p. 97
Energy & Natural Resources ★
Table: p. 75

KEY TO RANKINGS: ✪ = Star Individual ★★★★ = Top Band ★★★ = Second Band ★★ = Third Band ★ = Fourth Band **U** = Up and coming

Raisler, Kenneth M. (USA)
Profile: p. 887
Capital Markets: Derivatives ★★★★
Table: p. 798

Raizenne, Robert (Canada)
Profile: p. 197
Tax ★★★
Table: p. 182

Rajah, R. Senathi (Sri Lanka)
Profile: p. 637
Corporate/Commercial ★★★★
Table: p. 637

Rakotoarivony, Hary Ratsimba (Madagascar)
Profile: p. 468
Corporate/Commercial ★★★
Table: p. 468

Ramberg, Göran (Sweden)
Profile: p. 650
Arbitration (International) ★★★
Table: p. 640

Ramberg, Jan (Sweden)
Profile: p. 650
Arbitration (International) ★★★★
Table: p. 640

Ramírez, Eduardo (Spain)
Profile: p. 635
Tax ★★★
Table: p. 628

Ramkarran, Hari (Guyana)
Profile: p. 348
Corporate/Commercial ★★★
Table: p. 348

Ramm, Erik (Norway)
Profile: p. 524
Banking & Finance ★★★★
Table: p. 517

Ramon Ramos, Juan (Spain)
Profile: p. 635
Tax ★
Table: p. 628

Ramón y Cajal, Pedro (Spain)
Profile: p. 635
Corporate/M&A ★★
Table: p. 624

Ramsey, Thomas J (Belgium)
Profile: p. 131
Communications ★★
Table: p. 118

Randell, Charles (United Kingdom)
Profile: p. 770
Corporate/M&A ★★
Table: p. 717

Rank, Pim (Netherlands)
Profile: p. 504
Banking & Finance ★
Table: p. 491

Ransome, Clive (United Kingdom)
Profile: p. 770
Projects ★★
Table: p. 733

Raphael, Moussa (Lebanon)
Profile: p. 459
Corporate/Commercial ★★★★
Table: p. 458

Rapp, Lucien (France)
Profile: p. 293
Communications: Telecoms ★★★
Table: p. 271

Ratliff, John (Belgium)
Profile: p. 131
Competition/Anti-trust ★★
Table: p. 122

Rauber, Georg (Switzerland)
Profile: p. 662
Communications ★★★★
Table: p. 655

Raupach, Arndt (Germany)
Profile: p. 329
Tax ★★★
Table: p. 319

Rausch, János (Hungary)
Profile: p. 377
Communications **U**
Table: p. 373

Raustøl, Per (Norway)
Profile: p. 524
Corporate/M&A ★★
Table: p. 519

Raval, Dinker (Malawi)
Profile: p. 469
Corporate/Commercial ★★★
Table: p. 469

Raven-Odio, Alberto (Costa Rica)
Profile: p. 226
Corporate/Commercial ★★
Table: p. 225

Raven-Ramirez, Alberto (Costa Rica)
Profile: p. 226
Corporate/Commercial ★★★
Table: p. 225

Rawding, Nigel (United Kingdom)
Profile: p. 770
Arbitration (International) ★★★
Table: p. 696

Rawlinson, Mark (United Kingdom)
Profile: p. 770
Corporate/M&A ★★★★
Table: p. 717

Rawlinson, Paul (United Kingdom)
Profile: p. 770
Intellectual Property ★
Table: p. 729

Ray, Jon (Singapore)
Profile: p. 604
Shipping: Foreign Firms ★
Table: p. 596

Raymond, Pierre A. (Canada)
Profile: p. 197
Corporate/M&A ★
Table: p. 177

Raynaud, Daniele (Italy)
Profile: p. 429
Banking & Finance ★★
Table: p. 414

Raz-Guzmán, José (Mexico)
Profile: p. 482
Banking & Finance ★★★
Table: p. 479

Read, Nigel (United Kingdom)
Profile: p. 771
Corporate/M&A ★
Table: p. 717

Rebaza, Alberto (Peru)
Profile: p. 541
Banking & Finance ★★★
Table: p. 538

Rebelo de Sousa, Pedro (Portugal)
Profile: p. 566
Banking & Finance ★
Table: p. 558
Corporate/M&A ★
Table: p. 560

Réczicza, István (Hungary)
Profile: p. 377
Communications ★★★★
Table: p. 373
Corporate/M&A ★★★★
Table: p. 375

Rediadis, Deucalion (Greece)
Profile: p. 343
Shipping ★★
Table: p. 340

Reding, Jacques (Belgium)
Profile: p. 131
Corporate/M&A ★★
Table: p. 125

Reece, John (Greece)
Profile: p. 343
Shipping: Foreign Firms ★★
Table: p. 341

Reed, Bjørn Gabriel (Norway)
Profile: p. 524
Corporate/M&A ★★★
Table: p. 519

Reed, Lucy (USA)
Profile: p. 887
Arbitration (International) ★★
Table: p. 785

Reede, Michael (Hong Kong)
Profile: p. 369
Communications ★★★★
Table: p. 356

Reeder, Robert W. (USA)
Profile: p. 888
Capital Markets: Derivatives ★
Table: p. 798

Rees, Christopher (United Kingdom)
Profile: p. 771
Communications: IT ★★★
Table: p. 709

Rees, Jonathan (United Kingdom)
Profile: p. 771
Energy: Oil and Gas ★★
Table: p. 723

Rees, Nick (Hong Kong)
Profile: p. 369
Corporate/M&A ★★★
Table: p. 357

Rees Smith, Peter (Hong Kong)
Profile: p. 369
Shipping ★★★★
Table: p. 361

Reese, P. Mark (New Zealand)
Profile: p. 509
Banking & Finance ★★★
Table: p. 507

Refalo, Iain (Malta)
Profile: p. 476
Corporate/Commercial ★★★★
Table: p. 475

Réfega Fernandes, Victor (Portugal)
Profile: p. 566
Corporate/M&A ★
Table: p. 560

Regala, Teodoro (Philippines)
Profile: p. 544
Corporate/Commercial ★★★★
Table: p. 542

Regazzini, José Augusto (Brazil)
Profile: p. 157
Competition/Anti-trust ★★
Table: p. 145

Reich-Rohrwig, Johannes (Austria)
Profile: p. 107
Corporate/M&A ★★★
Table: p. 104

Reimann, Thomas (Germany)
Profile: p. 329
Intellectual Property: General ★★
Table: p. 314

Rein, John (Norway)
Profile: p. 524
Energy & Natural Resources ★
Table: p. 520

Rein, Ulrike (Hungary)
Profile: p. 377
Corporate/M&A ★★
Table: p. 375

Reiner, Andreas (Austria)
Profile: p. 107
Arbitration (International) ★★★
Table: p. 102

Reinhardt, Christoph (Switzerland)
Profile: p. 662
Corporate/M&A ★★★
Table: p. 657

Reinhold, Richard L. (USA)
Profile: p. 888
Tax ★
Table: p. 845

Reisoglu, Seza (Turkey)
Profile: p. 683
Banking & Finance ★★★
Table: p. 679

Rekola, Kimmo (Finland)
Profile: p. 259
Communications ★★★★
Table: p. 255

Relongoue, Christophe (Gabon)
Profile: p. 297
Corporate/Commercial ★★★★
Table: p. 297

Remón Peñalver, Jesús (Spain)
Profile: p. 635
Communications ★★★
Table: p. 620

Renard, Ian (Australia)
Profile: p. 97
Capital Markets ★
Table: p. 67
Corporate/M&A ★
Table: p. 73

Renaud, Madeleine (Canada)
Profile: p. 197
Competition/Anti-trust ★
Table: p. 175

Rendell, Simon (United Kingdom)
Profile: p. 771
Communications: IT ★★★
Table: p. 709

Rengel Jr, Pedro (Venezuela)
Profile: p. 914
Corporate/M&A ★
Table: p. 909

Renner-Thomas, Ade (Sierra Leone)
Profile: p. 585
Corporate/Commercial ★★★★
Table: p. 585

Rentmeesters, Luc (France)
Profile: p. 293
Banking & Finance ★
Table: p. 265

Reudelhuber, Eva (Germany)
Profile: p. 329
Banking & Finance ★
Table: p. 301
Project Finance ★★
Table: p. 317

Reymond, Claude (Switzerland)
Profile: p. 662
Arbitration (International) ★★★★
Table: p. 653

Reyna, Gustavo (Venezuela)
Profile: p. 914
Banking & Finance ★★★
Table: p. 908
Corporate/M&A ★★
Table: p. 909

Reynolds, Michael (Belgium)
Profile: p. 131
Competition/Anti-trust ★★★★
Table: p. 122

Rezende, Condorcet (Brazil)
Profile: p. 157
Tax ★
Table: p. 150

Rezende, Fabio de (Brazil)
Profile: p. 157
Corporate/M&A ★★
Table: p. 147

Riaz, Zahir (Pakistan)
Profile: p. 531
Corporate/Commercial ★★
Table: p. 529

Ribeiro, João Ricardo de Azevedo (Brazil)
Profile: p. 157
Corporate/M&A ★★★
Table: p. 147
Project Finance ★★
Table: p. 149

Rice, Jim (United Kingdom)
Profile: p. 771
Capital Markets: Securitisation ★
Table: p. 704

Rice, Tony (Greece)
Profile: p. 343
Shipping: Foreign Firms ★★★
Table: p. 341

Rich, Andrew (United Kingdom)
Profile: p. 771
Intellectual Property ★★
Table: p. 729

Rich, Frederic C. (USA)
Profile: p. 888
Project Finance ★★★
Table: p. 837

Rich, R. Bruce (USA)
Profile: p. 888
Competition/Anti-trust ★
Table: p. 808

Richards, Gabrielle M.R. (Canada)
Profile: p. 197
Tax ★
Table: p. 182

Richards, Philip (United Kingdom)
Profile: p. 771
Corporate/M&A ★★★
Table: p. 717

Richardson, Elinore (Canada)
Profile: p. 197
Tax ★★
Table: p. 182

Richardson, Stephen R. (Canada)
Profile: p. 197
Tax ★★★★
Table: p. 182

Richomme, Jacqueline (Jersey)
Profile: p. 449
Corporate/Commercial ★★★★
Table: p. 448

Ricou, Maria João (Portugal)
Profile: p. 566
Banking & Finance ★
Table: p. 558

Rider, Cameron (Australia)
Profile: p. 97
Tax ★
Table: p. 81

KEY TO RANKINGS: ✪ = Star Individual ★★★★ = Top Band ★★★ = Second Band ★★ = Third Band ★ = Fourth Band **U** = Up and coming

Riedy, James (USA)
Profile: p. 888
Tax ★
Table: p. 847

Riehmer, Klaus (Germany)
Profile: p. 329
Communications: Transactional ★★
Table: p. 306

Riese, Biörn (Sweden)
Profile: p. 650
Communications: Telecoms ★★★★
Table: p. 642

Riesz, Tamás (Hungary)
Profile: p. 377
Communications ★★★
Table: p. 373

Riggs, John (France)
Profile: p. 293
Project Finance ★★★
Table: p. 277

Rigotti, Mark (Australia)
Profile: p. 97
Capital Markets ★★
Table: p. 67

Riley, James A. (Canada)
Profile: p. 197
Banking & Finance ★★★★
Table: p. 171
Corporate/M&A ★★★★
Table: p. 177

Rill, James F. (USA)
Profile: p. 888
Competition/Anti-trust ★★★★
Table: p. 811

Rimmer, John (Isle of Man)
Profile: p. 405
Corporate/Commercial **U**
Table: p. 405

Rinaldi, Joseph (USA)
Profile: p. 889
Corporate/M&A ★
Table: p. 820

Ringdal, Rolf Johan (Norway)
Profile: p. 524
Banking & Finance ★★★
Table: p. 517

Ritson, Lisa (Australia)
Profile: p. 97
Communications: IT ★★
Table: p. 69
Intellectual Property ★★★
Table: p. 77

Rittatore Vonwiller, Andrea (Italy)
Profile: p. 429
Tax ★
Table: p. 422

Rivkin, David (USA)
Profile: p. 889
Arbitration (International) ★★★★
Table: p. 785

Rizhinashvili, Constantin (Georgia)
Profile: p. 299
Corporate/Commercial ★★★★
Table: p. 299

Rizvi, Ahsan (Pakistan)
Profile: p. 531
Corporate/Commercial ★★★★
Table: p. 529

Robb, Philip (Singapore)
Profile: p. 604
Project Finance ★
Table: p. 594

Robert, Gavin (United Kingdom)
Profile: p. 771
Competition/Anti-trust ★
Table: p. 714

Robert, Georges (Mauritius)
Profile: p. 478
Corporate/Commercial ★★★★
Table: p. 478

Roberts, Andrew (Singapore)
Profile: p. 604
Banking & Finance: Singapore Foreign ★
Table: p. 588

Roberts, Martin (United Kingdom)
Profile: p. 771
Energy: Oil and Gas ★★★
Table: p. 723

Roberts, Swain (Singapore)
Profile: p. 604
Banking & Finance: Singapore Foreign ★★★
Table: p. 588
Corporate/M&A: Singapore Foreign ★★★★
Table: p. 592

Roberts, Thomas A. (USA)
Profile: p. 889
Private Equity: Buyouts ★★
Table: p. 834

Robertson, Don (Australia)
Profile: p. 97
Competition/Anti-trust ★★
Table: p. 71

Robertson, Holly (Canada)
Profile: p. 197
Banking & Finance **U**
Table: p. 171

Robins, Charles W. (USA)
Profile: p. 889
Private Equity: Fund Formation ★
Table: p. 835

Robinson, Kathryn (Canada)
Profile: p. 197
Communications ★★★
Table: p. 173

Robinson, Trevor (Australia)
Profile: p. 97
Banking & Finance ★★
Table: p. 65

Robles, Rafael (Mexico)
Profile: p. 482
Corporate/M&A ★★★★
Table: p. 480

Robottom, David T. (Canada)
Profile: p. 198
Corporate/M&A ★
Table: p. 177

Rocap, Don (USA)
Profile: p. 889
Tax ★★★
Table: p. 843

Rocha, Juan Carlos (Colombia)
Profile: p. 223
Banking & Finance ★★
Table: p. 219

Roche, Donal (Ireland)
Profile: p. 404
Corporate/M&A ★
Table: p. 397

Rod, Jonathan (USA)
Profile: p. 889
Project Finance ★
Table: p. 837

Roderick, Simon (United Arab Emirates)
Profile: p. 694
Banking & Finance ★★★★
Table: p. 688
Corporate/M&A ★★★★
Table: p. 690

Rodin, Andreas (Germany)
Profile: p. 330
Private Equity ★★★★
Table: p. 316
Tax ★★★
Table: p. 319

Rodner, James (Venezuela)
Profile: p. 914
Banking & Finance ★★★★
Table: p. 908
Corporate/M&A ★
Table: p. 909

Rodrigues Martins, Gabriela (Portugal)
Profile: p. 566
Corporate/M&A ★
Table: p. 560

Rodriguez, Bernardo (Colombia)
Profile: p. 223
Banking & Finance ★★
Table: p. 219
Corporate/M&A ★★
Table: p. 221

Rogers, Phil (Canada)
Profile: p. 198
Communications ★★★
Table: p. 173

Rogers, William (USA)
Profile: p. 889
Capital Markets: Debt & Equity ★
Table: p. 793

Rogers QC, Andrew (Australia)
Profile: p. 97
Arbitration (International) ★★★★
Table: p. 64

Röhling, Andreas (Germany)
Profile: p. 330
Competition/Anti-trust ★★
Table: p. 309

Rohrbach, Peter (USA)
Profile: p. 889
Communications: Regulatory ★★★
Table: p. 803

Rojahn, Sabine (Germany)
Profile: p. 330
Intellectual Property: General ★★
Table: p. 314

Rojas, Fernando (Bolivia)
Profile: p. 139
Corporate/Commercial ★★★★
Table: p. 138

Rojas, Héctor (Mexico)
Profile: p. 482
Corporate/M&A ★★
Table: p. 480

Rokosz, Ronald (USA)
Profile: p. 889
Banking & Finance ★★★
Table: p. 787

Rolfe, Ron (USA)
Profile: p. 889
Competition/Anti-trust ★★
Table: p. 808

Romagnoli, Dario (Italy)
Profile: p. 429
Tax ★
Table: p. 422

Romander, Claes (Sweden)
Profile: p. 651
Banking & Finance ★★
Table: p. 641

Romaneli, Mario Antonio (Brazil)
Profile: p. 157
Tax ★
Table: p. 150

Romano, Simon A. (Canada)
Profile: p. 198
Corporate/M&A ★
Table: p. 177

Romlov, Robert (Sweden)
Profile: p. 651
Arbitration (International) ★★★★
Table: p. 640

Romulo, Ricardo (Philippines)
Profile: p. 544
Corporate/Commercial ★★★
Table: p. 542

Ronca, Marc (Switzerland)
Profile: p. 662
Arbitration (International) ★★
Table: p. 653

Roodt, Johan (South Africa)
Profile: p. 613
Corporate/M&A ★★★
Table: p. 611

Rook, John (Canada)
Profile: p. 198
Competition/Anti-trust ★★★
Table: p. 175

Root, Anthony (Hong Kong)
Profile: p. 369
Capital Markets: Debt & Equity ★★★
Table: p. 353

Rooth, Tony (United Kingdom)
Profile: p. 771
Shipping ★★★★
Table: p. 737

Rosati, Mario (USA)
Profile: p. 889
Communications: IT ★
Table: p. 805

Rosefield, Stephen (United Kingdom)
Profile: p. 771
Communications: E-commerce ★★
Table: p. 711

Rosen, Burt (USA)
Profile: p. 889
Tax ★
Table: p. 845

Rosen, Edward (USA)
Profile: p. 889
Capital Markets: Derivatives ★★★★
Table: p. 798

Rosen, Matthew A. (USA)
Profile: p. 889
Tax ★★★★
Table: p. 845

Rosen, Ori (Israel)
Profile: p. 411
Communications ★★★★
Table: p. 407

Rosen, Richard L. (USA)
Profile: p. 889
Competition/Anti-trust ★★★
Table: p. 811

Rosenberg, Marc S. (USA)
Profile: p. 890
Capital Markets: Debt & Equity ★
Table: p. 793

Rosenbloom, David (USA)
Profile: p. 890
Tax ★★★★
Table: p. 847

Rosenblum, Steve (USA)
Profile: p. 890
Communications: Transactional (Telecoms) ★★
Table: p. 801

Rosenstein, Mace J. (USA)
Profile: p. 890
Communications: Regulatory ★★
Table: p. 803

Rosensweig, Joshua (Israel)
Profile: p. 411
Corporate/M&A ★
Table: p. 409

Rosettenstein, Albert (Zimbabwe)
Profile: p. 920
Corporate/Commercial ★★★★
Table: p. 919

Ross, Dermot (New Zealand)
Profile: p. 509
Banking & Finance ★★★★
Table: p. 507

Ross, Donald (Canada)
Profile: p. 198
Corporate/M&A ★★
Table: p. 177

Ross, Howard (United Kingdom)
Profile: p. 771
Tax ★★
Table: p. 739

Rossi, Carlos Alberto de Souza (Brazil)
Profile: p. 158
Corporate/M&A ★★
Table: p. 147

Rossi, Guido (Italy)
Profile: p. 429
Competition/Anti-trust ★★
Table: p. 417
Corporate/M&A ★★★
Table: p. 419

Rossi, Mariza (Brazil)
Profile: p. 158
Communications ★★★
Table: p. 143

Rossman, Vladimir R. (USA)
Profile: p. 890
Banking & Finance ★★★
Table: p. 791

Rostron, Jonathan E.S. (Hong Kong)
Profile: p. 369
Shipping ★
Table: p. 361

Rothermel, Sarah (USA)
Profile: p. 890
Private Equity: Fund Formation ★
Table: p. 835

Rough, Clive (Hong Kong)
Profile: p. 370
Capital Markets: Securitisation ★★★
Table: p. 354

Rovine, Arthur (USA)
Profile: p. 890
Arbitration (International) ★★
Table: p. 785

Rovira, Alfredo (Argentina)
Profile: p. 63
Corporate/M&A ★★
Table: p. 57

Rowe, Heather (United Kingdom)
Profile: p. 771
Communications: IT ★★
Table: p. 709

Rowe, Larry (USA)
Profile: p. 890
Private Equity: Fund Formation ★
Table: p. 835

Rowe, Michael (United Kingdom)
Profile: p. 772
Competition/Anti-trust ★
Table: p. 714

Rowe, Peter J. (New Zealand)
Profile: p. 510
Corporate/M&A ★★★
Table: p. 508

Rowey, Kent (United Kingdom)
Profile: p. 772
Energy: Electricity ★★
Table: p. 725
Projects ★★
Table: p. 733

Rowley QC, J. William F. (Canada)
Profile: p. 198
Competition/Anti-trust ★★★
Table: p. 175

Rozzell, Scott (USA)
Profile: p. 890
Energy & Natural Resources ★★★
Table: p. 829

Rubin, Pinhas (Israel)
Profile: p. 411
Corporate/M&A ★★★
Table: p. 409

Ruby, Stephen (Canada)
Profile: p. 198
Tax ★★★★
Table: p. 182

Rudder, Richard D. (USA)
Profile: p. 890
Capital Markets: Securitisation ★
Table: p. 795

Rudin, Simeon (United Kingdom)
Profile: p. 772
Capital Markets: Derivatives ★★
Table: p. 706

Rueda, Pedro A. (Spain)
Profile: p. 635
Corporate/M&A ★★★
Table: p. 624

Ruegger, Philip (Pete) (USA)
Profile: p. 890
Corporate/M&A ★
Table: p. 820
Private Equity: Buyouts ★★
Table: p. 834

Ruiz, Nuno (Portugal)
Profile: p. 566
Competition/Anti-trust ★★★★
Table: p. 559

Rule, Charles F. (Rick) (USA)
Profile: p. 890
Competition/Anti-trust ★★★★
Table: p. 811

Rumanzo-Arcos, José (Ecuador)
Profile: p. 245
Corporate/Commercial ★★★★
Table: p. 244

Ruoti, Nora (Paraguay)
Profile: p. 537
Corporate/M&A ★★★
Table: p. 537

Rupal, Yash (United Kingdom)
Profile: p. 772
Tax ★★★
Table: p. 739

Rushton, Chris (Singapore)
Profile: p. 389, 604
Banking & Finance: Singapore Foreign ★★★
Table: p. 588
Project Finance ★★★★
Table: p. 594
Project Finance: India Foreign ★★
Table: p. 386

Russell, John (United Kingdom)
Profile: p. 772
Capital Markets: Securitisation ★★
Table: p. 704

Russell, Mark A. (United Kingdom)
Profile: p. 772
Shipping: Finance ★★
Table: p. 737

Russell, Nigel (Vietnam)
Profile: p. 917
Corporate/Commercial: Vietnam Foreign ★★★
Table: p. 916

Russell, Rowan (Australia)
Profile: p. 97
Banking & Finance ★★
Table: p. 65

Rutkowski, Larry (USA)
Profile: p. 891
Shipping: Finance ★★★★
Table: p. 841

Ruys, Willem (Netherlands)
Profile: p. 504
Banking & Finance ★★
Table: p. 491

Ryan, Barry J. (Canada)
Profile: p. 198
Banking & Finance ★★
Table: p. 171

Ryan, Patrick (Australia)
Profile: p. 98
Competition/Anti-trust ★★★
Table: p. 71

Rydbeck, Otto (Sweden)
Profile: p. 651
Corporate/M&A ★★★
Table: p. 645

Ryde, Andy (United Kingdom)
Profile: p. 772
Corporate/M&A **U**
Table: p. 717

Rymarz, Pawel (Poland)
Profile: p. 554
Corporate/M&A ★★★★
Table: p. 548

S

Sá Carneiro, Francisco (Portugal)
Profile: p. 566
Banking & Finance ★★★
Table: p. 558
Corporate/M&A ★★
Table: p. 560

Saccab Zarzur, Cristianne (Brazil)
Profile: p. 158
Competition/Anti-trust **U**
Table: p. 145

Sachi, Kayal (Singapore)
Profile: p. 604
Project Finance **U**
Table: p. 594

Sachs, John (USA)
Profile: p. 891
Energy & Natural Resources ★
Table: p. 827

Sachs, Mark (Singapore)
Profile: p. 604
Shipping: Foreign Firms ★★★
Table: p. 596

Sachse, Hans (Netherlands)
Profile: p. 504
Banking & Finance ★★
Table: p. 491

Sackman, Simon (United Kingdom)
Profile: p. 772
Corporate/M&A ★★
Table: p. 717

Sacks, Alan (Israel)
Profile: p. 412
Corporate/M&A ★★★
Table: p. 409

Sacks, Ira (USA)
Profile: p. 891
Competition/Anti-trust ★
Table: p. 808

Saeed, Faiza (USA)
Profile: p. 891
Corporate/M&A **U**
Table: p. 820

Safwat, Mahmoud (Egypt)
Profile: p. 248
Banking & Finance ★★★
Table: p. 246

Sagar, Jyoti (India)
Profile: p. 389
Corporate/M&A ★
Table: p. 381

Saggese, Nicholas P. (USA)
Profile: p. 891
Corporate/M&A ★★
Table: p. 825

Sahachaiyunta, Pradit (Thailand)
Profile: p. 674
Corporate/M&A ★★
Table: p. 672

Saibil, Norman (Canada)
Profile: p. 198
Banking & Finance ★★★
Table: p. 171

Saint-Esteben, Robert (France)
Profile: p. 293
Competition/Anti-trust ✪
Table: p. 272

Sainty, Katherine (Australia)
Profile: p. 98
Communications: IT ★★★
Table: p. 69

Sáinz, Álvaro (Spain)
Profile: p. 635
Corporate/M&A ★★★
Table: p. 624

Salas, Julio (Peru)
Profile: p. 541
Corporate/M&A ★★
Table: p. 540

Salbaing, Christian (France)
Profile: p. 293
Project Finance ★★
Table: p. 277

Salei, Vassili (Belarus)
Profile: p. 115
Corporate/Commercial ★★★
Table: p. 114

Salès, Jacques (France)
Profile: p. 293
Corporate/M&A ★
Table: p. 275

Salles, Ricardo (Brazil)
Profile: p. 158
Banking & Finance ★
Table: p. 142

Sallustio, Riccardo (Albania)
Profile: p. 50
Corporate/Commercial: Albania Foreign ★★★
Table: p. 49

Salomão, Eduardo (Brazil)
Profile: p. 158
Banking & Finance ★★★
Table: p. 142

Salomão Filho, Calixto (Brazil)
Profile: p. 158
Competition/Anti-trust ★★
Table: p. 145

Salt, Stuart (United Kingdom)
Profile: p. 772
Energy: Electricity ★★★★
Table: p. 725
Energy: Oil and Gas ★★★★
Table: p. 723
Projects ★★★★
Table: p. 733

Salter, Brian (Australia)
Profile: p. 98
Capital Markets ★★★★
Table: p. 67

Salz, Anthony (United Kingdom)
Profile: p. 772
Corporate/M&A ★★★★
Table: p. 717

Salzman, Lorne P. (Canada)
Profile: p. 198
Communications ★★
Table: p. 173

Salzmann, Joëlle (France)
Profile: p. 293
Competition/Anti-trust ★★
Table: p. 272

Samuels, Leslie (USA)
Profile: p. 891
Tax ★
Table: p. 845

Samuelsen, Erik (Norway)
Profile: p. 524
Energy & Natural Resources ★★★
Table: p. 520

San Jose, Roberto (Philippines)
Profile: p. 544
Corporate/Commercial ★
Table: p. 542

Sanchez de Movellan, Manuel (Spain)
Profile: p. 635
Banking & Finance ★★
Table: p. 619

Sanchez Elia, José (Argentina)
Profile: p. 63
Communications ★★★★
Table: p. 54

Sánchez-Pedreño, Antonio (Spain)
Profile: p. 635
Communications ★★
Table: p. 620

Sánchez-Terán, Salvador (Spain)
Profile: p. 635
Banking & Finance ★★
Table: p. 619
Corporate/M&A ★★★★
Table: p. 624

Sanders, Maarten (Netherlands)
Profile: p. 504
Communications ★★
Table: p. 492

Sandison, Francis (United Kingdom)
Profile: p. 772
Tax ★★★
Table: p. 739

Sandison, Hamish (United Kingdom)
Profile: p. 772
Communications: IT ★★★★
Table: p. 709

Sandler, Richard (USA)
Profile: p. 891
Capital Markets: Debt & Equity ★★★
Table: p. 793

Sanfelt, Trond (Norway)
Profile: p. 524
Corporate/M&A ★★
Table: p. 519

Sanfrutos, Eduardo (Spain)
Profile: p. 635
Tax ★★
Table: p. 628

SanGiorgio, Didier (Switzerland)
Profile: p. 662
Communications ★★
Table: p. 655

Santamarina, Augustin (Mexico)
Profile: p. 482
Corporate/M&A ★★★★
Table: p. 480

Santoni, George (Dominican Republic)
Profile: p. 243
Corporate/Commercial ★★★★
Table: p. 243

Santos, Gemma (Philippines)
Profile: p. 544
Corporate/Commercial ★
Table: p. 542

Santos, Javier (Spain)
Profile: p. 635
Banking & Finance ★★
Table: p. 619

Sanz, Enrique (Spain)
Profile: p. 635
Communications ★★
Table: p. 620

Saper, Jeff (USA)
Profile: p. 891
Communications: IT ★★★
Table: p. 805

Sáragga Leal, Luís (Portugal)
Profile: p. 566
Banking & Finance ★★
Table: p. 558
Corporate/M&A ★★★★
Table: p. 560

Sarantitis, Vassilis (Greece)
Profile: p. 343
Shipping ★★★
Table: p. 340

Saravalle, Alberto (Italy)
Profile: p. 429
Banking & Finance ★★
Table: p. 414
Corporate/M&A ★
Table: p. 419

Saravia Castillo, Salvador (Guatemala)
Profile: p. 345
Corporate/Commercial ★★★★
Table: p. 345

Sarr, François (Senegal)
Profile: p. 583
Corporate/Commercial ★★★★
Table: p. 583

Sarrailhé, Philippe (France)
Profile: p. 293
Corporate/M&A ★
Table: p. 275

Sato, Masanori (Japan)
Profile: p. 446
Capital Markets ✪
Table: p. 436

Sator, Mohamed (Algeria)
Profile: p. 51
Corporate/Commercial ★★★★
Table: p. 51

Satty, Andrea (USA)
Profile: p. 891
Project Finance ★
Table: p. 837

Satzky, Horst (Germany)
Profile: p. 309
Competition/Anti-trust ★★
Table: p. 309

Saunders, Mark (United Kingdom)
Profile: p. 773
Energy: Oil and Gas ★★
Table: p. 723

KEY TO RANKINGS: ✪ = Star Individual ★★★★ = Top Band ★★★ = Second Band ★★ = Third Band ★ = Fourth Band **U** = Up and coming

Saville, Francis M. Q.C. (Canada)
Profile: p. 198
Energy & Natural Resources ★★★
Table: p. 180

Savjani, Krishna (Malawi)
Profile: p. 469
Corporate/Commercial ★★★★
Table: p. 469

Sawadogo, Benoît (Burkina Faso)
Profile: p. 166
Corporate/Commercial ★★★★
Table: p. 166

Sayen, George (Saudi Arabia)
Profile: p. 581
Corporate/M&A ★★★★
Table: p. 581

Sayer, Richard (United Kingdom)
Profile: p. 773
Shipping ✪
Table: p. 737

Scanlon, Tim (Ireland)
Profile: p. 404
Corporate/M&A ★★★
Table: p. 397

Scarlett, James (Canada)
Profile: p. 198
Corporate/M&A ★★★
Table: p. 177

Scassellati-Sforzolini, Giuseppe (Italy)
Profile: p. 429
Banking & Finance ★
Table: p. 414

Scavone, Arthur (USA)
Profile: p. 891
Project Finance ★★★★
Table: p. 837

Schaar, Bodo (Germany)
Profile: p. 330
Capital Markets: Derivatives ★★
Table: p. 304
Capital Markets: Securitisation ★★
Table: p. 304

Schaeffer, Michael (Germany)
Profile: p. 330
Intellectual Property: General ★
Table: p. 314

Schäfer, Helge (Germany)
Profile: p. 330
Communications: Transactional ★★
Table: p. 306
Private Equity ★★
Table: p. 316

Schapiro, David H. (Israel)
Profile: p. 412
Corporate/M&A ★
Table: p. 409

Schärer, Heinz (Switzerland)
Profile: p. 662
Corporate/M&A ★★★
Table: p. 657

Scharfstein, Joel (USA)
Profile: p. 891
Tax ★★
Table: p. 845

Schaumburg, Harald (Germany)
Profile: p. 330
Tax ★★★★
Table: p. 319

Scheja, Katharina (Germany)
Profile: p. 330
Communications: IT ★
Table: p. 307

Schell, Michael (USA)
Profile: p. 891
Corporate/M&A ★
Table: p. 820

Schenker, Urs (Switzerland)
Profile: p. 662
Corporate/M&A ★★★★
Table: p. 657

Scherer, Joachim (Germany)
Profile: p. 330
Communications: Regulatory ★★★★
Table: p. 306

Scherer, Peter (Germany)
Profile: p. 330
Capital Markets: Derivatives ★★★
Table: p. 304

Scherman, William S. (USA)
Profile: p. 891
Energy & Natural Resources ★★★★
Table: p. 827

Schetman, Richard (USA)
Profile: p. 891
Capital Markets: Securitisation ★★★
Table: p. 795

Schiessl, Maximilian (Germany)
Profile: p. 331
Corporate/M&A ★★★★
Table: p. 311
Private Equity ★★★
Table: p. 316

Schiff, Kenneth E. (Czech Republic)
Profile: p. 236
Corporate/M&A ★★★
Table: p. 234

Schiller, Jonathan (USA)
Profile: p. 892
Arbitration (International) ★
Table: p. 785

Schilling, Tilman (Germany)
Profile: p. 331
Intellectual Property: General ★★
Table: p. 314

Schler, Michael (USA)
Profile: p. 892
Tax ★★★★
Table: p. 845

Schlingmann, Francine (Netherlands)
Profile: p. 504
Banking & Finance ★
Table: p. 491

Schlitt, Michael (Germany)
Profile: p. 331
Capital Markets: Equity ★
Table: p. 304

Schlosberg, Jonathan (South Africa)
Profile: p. 613
Banking & Finance ★★★
Table: p. 610
Corporate/M&A ★★★
Table: p. 611

Schmalenbach, Dirk (Germany)
Profile: p. 331
Banking & Finance ★★★★
Table: p. 301

Schmeding, Jörg (Germany)
Profile: p. 331
Corporate/M&A ★
Table: p. 311

Schmidt, Gerhard (Germany)
Profile: p. 331
Corporate/M&A ★
Table: p. 311

Schmittmann, Michael (Germany)
Profile: p. 331
Communications: Regulatory ★★★
Table: p. 306

Schnabl, Marco (USA)
Profile: p. 892
Arbitration (International) ★
Table: p. 785

Schneider, Hannes (Germany)
Profile: p. 331
Banking & Finance ★★★★
Table: p. 301
Capital Markets: Debt ★★★★
Table: p. 303
Capital Markets: Derivatives ★★★★
Table: p. 304

Schneider, Jochen (Germany)
Profile: p. 331
Communications: IT ✪
Table: p. 307

Schneider, Leslie (USA)
Profile: p. 892
Tax ★★
Table: p. 847

Schneider, Michael (Switzerland)
Profile: p. 662
Arbitration (International) ★★★
Table: p. 653

Schödermeier, Martin (Germany)
Profile: p. 331
Banking & Finance ★★★★
Table: p. 301

Schoen, Thierry (France)
Profile: p. 293
Corporate/M&A ★★
Table: p. 275

Schoenbrun, Larry (USA)
Profile: p. 892
Corporate/M&A ★★
Table: p. 824

Schoueri, Luis Eduardo (Brazil)
Profile: p. 158
Tax ★★★
Table: p. 150

Schrey, Joachim (Germany)
Profile: p. 332
Communications: IT ★★
Table: p. 307

Schroeder, Dirk (Germany)
Profile: p. 332
Competition/Anti-trust ★★★
Table: p. 309

Schroeder, Piet (Netherlands)
Profile: p. 504
Banking & Finance ★
Table: p. 491

Schücking, Christoph (Germany)
Profile: p. 332
Private Equity ★★★
Table: p. 316

Schuit, Steven (Netherlands)
Profile: p. 504
Corporate/M&A ★★★★
Table: p. 496
Energy & Natural Resources ★★★
Table: p. 498

Schulruff, Stuart (USA)
Profile: p. 892
Banking & Finance ★
Table: p. 787

Schulz, Peter F. (United Kingdom)
Profile: p. 773
Banking & Finance ★
Table: p. 699

Schulz-Süchtig, Rolf (Germany)
Profile: p. 332
Intellectual Property: General ★★
Table: p. 314

Schuppert, Stefan (Germany)
Profile: p. 332
Communications: IT **U**
Table: p. 307

Schurti, Andreas (Liechtenstein)
Profile: p. 462
Corporate/Commercial ★★★★
Table: p. 462

Schuster, Thomas (Germany)
Profile: p. 332
Intellectual Property: Patent ★★
Table: p. 313

Schütte, Michael (Belgium)
Profile: p. 131
Competition/Anti-trust ★
Table: p. 122

Schütz, Raimund (Germany)
Profile: p. 332
Communications: Regulatory ★★
Table: p. 306

Schütze, Joachim (Germany)
Profile: p. 332
Competition/Anti-trust ★
Table: p. 309

Schwartz, Donald (USA)
Profile: p. 892
Banking & Finance ★★★
Table: p. 787

Schwartz, Eric (France)
Profile: p. 293
Arbitration (International) ★★★
Table: p. 262

Schwartz, Herb (USA)
Profile: p. 892
Intellectual Property ★★★★
Table: p. 831

Schwartz, Jodi (USA)
Profile: p. 892
Tax ★★★
Table: p. 845

Schwarz, Tim (United Kingdom)
Profile: p. 773
Communications: Telecoms ★★★
Table: p. 707

Schwed, Robert A. (USA)
Profile: p. 892
Private Equity: Fund Formation ★
Table: p. 835

Sciaroni, Bretton (Cambodia)
Profile: p. 168
Corporate/Commercial ★★★
Table: p. 168

Scorinis, Nicholas (Greece)
Profile: p. 343
Shipping ★★★
Table: p. 340

Scott, David (Ukraine)
Profile: p. 687
Corporate/Commercial ★★
Table: p. 686

Scott, Jonathan (United Kingdom)
Profile: p. 773
Competition/Anti-trust ★★★
Table: p. 714

Scott, Thomas A. (United Kingdom)
Profile: p. 773
Tax ★★
Table: p. 739

Scrivener, Paul (Cayman Islands)
Profile: p. 204
Corporate/Commercial ★★★
Table: p. 203

Seah, Collin (Singapore)
Profile: p. 605
Shipping ★
Table: p. 595

Sebastián, Rafael (Spain)
Profile: p. 635
Banking & Finance ★★★
Table: p. 619

Sedemund, Jochim (Germany)
Profile: p. 332
Competition/Anti-trust ★★★★
Table: p. 309

Sederowsky, Peter (Sweden)
Profile: p. 651
Banking & Finance ★★
Table: p. 641

Sedgley, David (United Kingdom)
Profile: p. 773
Projects ★★★
Table: p. 733

Seferovich, Pat (Russia)
Profile: p. 578
Energy & Natural Resources ★★★★
Table: p. 576

Segni, Antonio (Italy)
Profile: p. 429
Banking & Finance ★★
Table: p. 414

Sekine, Osamu (Japan)
Profile: p. 446
Capital Markets ★
Table: p. 436

Selih, Rudi (Slovenia)
Profile: p. 608
Corporate/Commercial ★★★★
Table: p. 608

Selting, Günther (Germany)
Profile: p. 332
Intellectual Property: Patent ★★★
Table: p. 313

Selvam, Arfat (Singapore)
Profile: p. 605
Banking & Finance ★★★
Table: p. 586
Corporate/M&A ★★★★
Table: p. 590

Semega-Janneh, Surahata (The Gambia)
Profile: p. 299
Corporate/Commercial ★★★★
Table: p. 298

Sendacz, Moshe (Brazil)
Profile: p. 158
Communications ★★★
Table: p. 143

Sengoku, Katsu (Japan)
Profile: p. 446
Banking & Finance ★★★★
Table: p. 433

Seppala, Christopher (France)
Profile: p. 293
Arbitration (International) ★★
Table: p. 262

Sepúlveda Cosío, Alberto (Mexico)
Profile: p. 482
Banking & Finance ★★★
Table: p. 479
Corporate/M&A ★★
Table: p. 480

KEY TO RANKINGS: ✪ = Star Individual ★★★★ = Top Band ★★★ = Second Band ★★ = Third Band ★ = Fourth Band **U** = Up and coming

Serfaty QC, Abraham (Gibraltar)
Profile: p. 338
Corporate/Commercial ★★
Table: p. 337

Serra, Claude (France)
Profile: p. 293
Communications: Telecoms ★★
Table: p. 271

Serrano, Diego (Argentina)
Profile: p. 63
Banking & Finance ★★
Table: p. 53

Servan-Schreiber, Pierre (France)
Profile: p. 293
Corporate/M&A ★★★
Table: p. 275

Sethsathira, Pises (Thailand)
Profile: p. 674
Banking & Finance ★★★
Table: p. 670

Sethsathira, Sawanee (Thailand)
Profile: p. 674
Banking & Finance ★★★
Table: p. 670

Sey, Kweku (Ghana)
Profile: p. 336
Corporate/Commercial ★★
Table: p. 336

Shachar, Avishai (USA)
Profile: p. 892
Tax ★★
Table: p. 845

Shackleton, Stewart (United Kingdom)
Profile: p. 773
Arbitration (International) U
Table: p. 696

Shah, Kieran (Seychelles)
Profile: p. 584
Corporate/Commercial ★★★★
Table: p. 665

Shah, Rajendra (India)
Profile: p. 389
Corporate/M&A ★★★★
Table: p. 381

Shao, Zili (China)
Profile: p. 218
Project Finance: China Foreign ★★
Table: p. 215

Shapiro, Robert (USA)
Profile: p. 892
Energy & Natural Resources ★★
Table: p. 827

Sharma, Anup Raj (Nepal)
Profile: p. 489
Corporate/Commercial ★★★★
Table: p. 489

Sharp, Jeff (Australia)
Profile: p. 98
Tax ★
Table: p. 81

Shaw, Gregory (USA)
Profile: p. 892
Capital Markets: Securitisation ★★★★
Table: p. 795

Shea, Tony (Kyrgyz Republic)
Profile: p. 455
Corporate/Commercial ★★★★
Table: p. 455

Sheach, Andrew (United Kingdom)
Profile: p. 773
Private Equity: Buyouts ★★
Table: p. 731

Sheffield, Jeffrey (USA)
Profile: p. 892
Tax ★★★
Table: p. 843

Sheldon, Jeremy N. (United Kingdom)
Profile: p. 774
Private Equity: Buyouts ★★
Table: p. 731

Shelford, Peter (Hong Kong)
Profile: p. 370
Shipping ★★★★
Table: p. 361

Shelton, John H. (United Kingdom)
Profile: p. 774
Shipping: Finance ★★★★
Table: p. 737

Shepherd, Geoff (Papua New Guinea)
Profile: p. 535
Corporate/Commercial ★★★
Table: p. 535

Sheppard, Audley (United Kingdom)
Profile: p. 774
Arbitration (International) ★★
Table: p. 696

Shepro, Richard Warren (USA)
Profile: p. 892
Corporate/M&A ★★
Table: p. 813

Sherck, Timothy (USA)
Profile: p. 893
Tax ★★★★
Table: p. 843

Sheridan, Jane (Australia)
Profile: p. 98
Corporate/M&A ★
Table: p. 73

Sherlock, David (Isle of Man)
Profile: p. 405
Corporate/Commercial U
Table: p. 405

Sherman, H. Vaney G. (Liberia)
Profile: p. 461
Corporate/Commercial ★★★★
Table: p. 460

Shields, Laurence K. (Ireland)
Profile: p. 404
Corporate/M&A ★★★
Table: p. 397

Shillito, Mark (United Kingdom)
Profile: p. 774
Intellectual Property ★★
Table: p. 729

Shin, Hi Taek (South Korea)
Profile: p. 617
Corporate/Commercial ★★★★
Table: p. 614

Shindo, Isao (Japan)
Profile: p. 446
Capital Markets ★★★
Table: p. 436

Shine, Christopher (Australia)
Profile: p. 98
Communications: Telecoms ★★★
Table: p. 69

Shirbin, John (Australia)
Profile: p. 98
Project Finance ★★
Table: p. 79

Shonubi, Alan (Uganda)
Profile: p. 685
Corporate/Commercial ★★★
Table: p. 684

Shore, Larry (United Kingdom)
Profile: p. 774
Arbitration (International) U
Table: p. 696

Showering, Adrienne (Australia)
Profile: p. 98
Capital Markets ★★★
Table: p. 67

Shrestha, Kusum (Nepal)
Profile: p. 489
Corporate/Commercial ★★★★
Table: p. 489

Shroff, Cyril (India)
Profile: p. 389
Corporate/M&A ★★★★
Table: p. 381
Project Finance ✪
Table: p. 384

Shroff, Shardul (India)
Profile: p. 389
Corporate/M&A ★★★★
Table: p. 381
Project Finance ★★★★
Table: p. 384

Shuke, Enyal (Albania)
Profile: p. 50
Corporate/Commercial: Albania Foreign ★★★
Table: p. 49

Shurman, Daniel (United Kingdom)
Profile: p. 774
Capital Markets: Debt & Equity ★
Table: p. 702

Shutran, Richard (USA)
Profile: p. 893
Project Finance ★★★★
Table: p. 837

Sibree, William (Belgium)
Profile: p. 131
Competition/Anti-trust ★★
Table: p. 122

Siddell, Ian (Saudi Arabia)
Profile: p. 581
Banking & Finance ★★★★
Table: p. 580

Siegler, Konrád (Hungary)
Profile: p. 377
Banking & Finance ★★★★
Table: p. 372

Siemiatkowski, Andrzej (Poland)
Profile: p. 554
Corporate/M&A ★★★
Table: p. 548

Signy, Adam (United Kingdom)
Profile: p. 774
Corporate/M&A ★★★
Table: p. 717

Sigurdsson, Jóhannes (Iceland)
Profile: p. 379
Corporate/Commercial ★★★
Table: p. 378

Silk, Mitchell (China)
Profile: p. 218
Corporate/M&A: China Foreign ★★
Table: p. 213
Project Finance: China Foreign ★★★
Table: p. 215

Silva, Alejandro (Colombia)
Profile: p. 223
Banking & Finance ★★★
Table: p. 219
Corporate/M&A ★★★
Table: p. 221

Silva, Eugenio (Brazil)
Profile: p. 158
Competition/Anti-trust ★★
Table: p. 145

Silva, Roberto (Argentina)
Profile: p. 63
Banking & Finance ★★
Table: p. 53
Corporate/M&A ★★★
Table: p. 57

Silver, David (Qatar)
Profile: p. 569
Corporate/Commercial ★★★
Table: p. 568

Silver, Jonathan (United Arab Emirates)
Profile: p. 694
Banking & Finance ★★
Table: p. 688
Corporate/M&A ★★
Table: p. 690

Silverman, Eric (USA)
Profile: p. 893
Project Finance ★★★★
Table: p. 837

Silverman, Mark (USA)
Profile: p. 893
Tax ★★
Table: p. 847

Simmat, Udo (Germany)
Profile: p. 332
Private Equity ★
Table: p. 316

Simms, Marsha E. (USA)
Profile: p. 893
Banking & Finance ★
Table: p. 791

Simonis, Paul (Netherlands)
Profile: p. 504
Tax ★★★★
Table: p. 500

Simons, Laird (USA)
Profile: p. 893
Communications: IT ★
Table: p. 805

Simonsen, Lennart (Finland)
Profile: p. 259
Corporate/M&A ★★★★
Table: p. 257

Simont, Lucien (Belgium)
Profile: p. 131
Arbitration (International) ★★★★
Table: p. 116

Simpson, Paul (United Kingdom)
Profile: p. 774
Energy: Electricity ★★
Table: p. 725

Simpson, Robert (Australia)
Profile: p. 99
Communications: Telecoms ★★★
Table: p. 69

Simpson, William (Guernsey)
Profile: p. 347
Corporate/Commercial ★★★★
Table: p. 346

Simpson Sr., Scott V. (United Kingdom)
Profile: p. 774
Corporate/M&A ★
Table: p. 717

Sims, Joseph (USA)
Profile: p. 893
Competition/Anti-trust ★★★★
Table: p. 811

Sinare, Hawa (Tanzania)
Profile: p. 669
Corporate/Commercial ★★
Table: p. 668

Singer, Andrew (USA)
Profile: p. 893
Project Finance ★
Table: p. 837

Singh OBE, Arun (United Kingdom)
Profile: p. 389
Corporate/M&A: India Foreign ★★
Table: p. 383

Singleton, Susan (United Kingdom)
Profile: p. 774
Communications: IT ★★
Table: p. 709

Sioufas, Theo V (Greece)
Profile: p. 343
Shipping ★★★★
Table: p. 340

Sippens Groenewegen, Piet (Netherlands)
Profile: p. 504
Communications ★★★
Table: p. 492

Siragusa, Mario (Italy)
Profile: p. 429
Competition/Anti-trust ★★★★
Table: p. 417

Skadhauge, Jeppe (Denmark)
Profile: p. 242
Competition/Anti-trust ★★
Table: p. 238

Skinner, Stephen (Vietnam)
Profile: p. 917
Corporate/Commercial: Vietnam Foreign ★★★
Table: p. 916

Skipper-Pedersen, Mogens (Denmark)
Profile: p. 242
Corporate/M&A ★★★
Table: p. 239

Slach, Petr (Czech Republic)
Profile: p. 236
Communications U
Table: p. 233

Slade, David (Greece)
Profile: p. 343
Shipping: Foreign Firms ★★
Table: p. 341

Slaidins, Raymond (Latvia)
Profile: p. 457
Corporate/Commercial ★★★
Table: p. 456

Slater, Richard (United Kingdom)
Profile: p. 774
Banking & Finance ★★★
Table: p. 699

Slattery, John (Australia)
Profile: p. 99
Corporate/M&A ★
Table: p. 73

Sledzinski, Janusz (Poland)
Profile: p. 554
Banking & Finance ★★
Table: p. 545

Slotboom, Marco Marinus (Netherlands)
Profile: p. 504
Competition/Anti-trust ★★★
Table: p. 494

Small, Harry (United Kingdom)
Profile: p. 774
Communications: E-commerce ★★★
Table: p. 711
Communications: IT ★★★
Table: p. 709

Small, Jeff (USA)
Profile: p. 894
Capital Markets: Debt & Equity ★★
Table: p. 793

Smit, Robert (USA)
Profile: p. 894
Arbitration (International) ★★★
Table: p. 785

KEY TO RANKINGS: ✪ = Star Individual ★★★★ = Top Band ★★★ = Second Band ★★ = Third Band ★ = Fourth Band U = Up and coming

KEY TO RANKINGS: ✪ = Star Individual ★★★★ = Top Band ★★★ = Second Band ★★ = Third Band ★ = Fourth Band **U** = Up and coming

Table: p. 787

Stern, Martin L. (USA)
Profile: p. 896
Communications: Regulatory ★★
Table: p. 803

Stern, Robert (United Kingdom)
Profile: p. 776
Corporate/M&A ★
Table: p. 717

Sterzinger, Richard (Germany)
Profile: p. 333
Corporate/M&A ★
Table: p. 311

Stevens, Charles (Japan)
Profile: p. 446
Corporate/M&A: Japan Foreign ★★★
Table: p. 441

Stewart, Mark (United Kingdom)
Profile: p. 776
Banking & Finance ★★★
Table: p. 699

Stickland, Kenneth (Canada)
Profile: p. 199
Energy & Natural Resources ★★★★
Table: p. 180

Still, Charles (USA)
Profile: p. 896
Corporate/M&A ★★★
Table: p. 824

Stiller, Dietrich (Germany)
Profile: p. 333
Project Finance ★★★★
Table: p. 317

Stinessen, Stein Erik (Norway)
Profile: p. 525
Energy & Natural Resources ★
Table: p. 520

Stoby, Robin (Guyana)
Profile: p. 348
Corporate/Commercial ★★★
Table: p. 348

Stockdale, Peter (Australia)
Profile: p. 99
Arbitration (International) ★★★★
Table: p. 64

Stoica, Cristiana (Romania)
Profile: p. 572
Corporate/M&A ★★★
Table: p. 571

Stokes, Hugh (Bahrain)
Profile: p. 111
Banking & Finance ★★★
Table: p. 110
Corporate/M&A ★★★
Table: p. 111

Stokholm, Jon (Denmark)
Profile: p. 242
Corporate/M&A ★★
Table: p. 239

Stoll, Neal R. (USA)
Profile: p. 896
Competition/Anti-trust ★★
Table: p. 808

Stone, Phillipa (Australia)
Profile: p. 99
Capital Markets ★★
Table: p. 67

Storey, John (Australia)
Profile: p. 99
Corporate/M&A ★
Table: p. 73

Storr, David (Australia)
Profile: p. 99
Project Finance ★
Table: p. 79

Stransman, John M. (Canada)
Profile: p. 199
Corporate/M&A ✪
Table: p. 177

Stratmann, Günther (Germany)
Profile: p. 333
Corporate/M&A ★★
Table: p. 311

Strauss, Bob (USA)
Profile: p. 896
Energy & Natural Resources ★★★
Table: p. 829

Streck, Michael (Germany)
Profile: p. 333
Tax ★
Table: p. 319

Street, Laurence (Australia)
Profile: p. 100
Arbitration (International) ★★★
Table: p. 64

Streichenberger, Renaud (France)
Profile: p. 293
Tax ★★★★
Table: p. 281

Strekaf, Jo'Anne (Canada)
Profile: p. 199
Competition/Anti-trust ★★
Table: p. 175

Strelow, Markus (Germany)
Profile: p. 333
Private Equity ★
Table: p. 316

Strivens, Peter (United Kingdom)
Profile: p. 776
Communications: Telecoms ★★★
Table: p. 707

Stromfeld, Lary (USA)
Profile: p. 896
Capital Markets: Derivatives ★
Table: p. 798

Strong, Malcolm (United Kingdom)
Profile: p. 776
Shipping ★★★
Table: p. 737

Strowger, W. John (New Zealand)
Profile: p. 510
Corporate/M&A ★★★
Table: p. 508

Struiken, Henk (Surinam)
Profile: p. 639
Corporate/Commercial ★★★★
Table: p. 638

Stuber, Walter Douglas (Brazil)
Profile: p. 158
Corporate/M&A ★★
Table: p. 147

Studnicki, Tomasz (Poland)
Profile: p. 555
Corporate/M&A ★★★
Table: p. 548

Stumbles, John (Australia)
Profile: p. 100
Banking & Finance ★★★★
Table: p. 65

Stumbles, Robert Atherstone (Zimbabwe)
Profile: p. 920
Corporate/Commercial ★★★
Table: p. 919

Style, Christopher (United Kingdom)
Profile: p. 776
Arbitration (International) ★★
Table: p. 696

Suárez de Lezo, Rafael (Spain)
Profile: p. 635
Banking & Finance ★★
Table: p. 619
Corporate/M&A ★
Table: p. 624

Subiotto, Romano (Belgium)
Profile: p. 131
Competition/Anti-trust ★★★
Table: p. 122

Subpaisarn, Dumnern (Thailand)
Profile: p. 674
Corporate/M&A ★★
Table: p. 672

Sueiro, Miguel (Spain)
Profile: p. 635
Banking & Finance ★★
Table: p. 619

Sugimoto, Fumihide (Japan)
Profile: p. 446
Banking & Finance ★★★
Table: p. 433
Capital Markets ★★
Table: p. 436

Sugiyama, Constance L. (Canada)
Profile: p. 200
Corporate/M&A ★
Table: p. 177

Sullivan, Michael (United Kingdom)
Profile: p. 776
Corporate/M&A ★
Table: p. 717

Summerfield, Spencer (United Kingdom)
Profile: p. 776
Communications: E-commerce ★★★
Table: p. 711

Sundfeld, Carlos (Brazil)
Profile: p. 158
Communications ★★★
Table: p. 143

Sunshine, Steven C. (USA)
Profile: p. 897
Competition/Anti-trust ★★★
Table: p. 811

Sunt, Chris (Belgium)
Profile: p. 131
Banking & Finance ★★★★
Table: p. 117
Corporate/M&A ★★★★
Table: p. 125

Sureau, François (France)
Profile: p. 293
Corporate/M&A ★
Table: p. 275

Surowidjojo, Arief (Indonesia)
Profile: p. 392
Corporate/Commercial ★★★
Table: p. 391

Sutkiene, Eugenija (Lithuania)
Profile: p. 464
Corporate/Commercial ★★★★
Table: p. 463

Sutton, David (United Kingdom)
Profile: p. 776
Arbitration (International) ★★★
Table: p. 696

Svanholm, Michael (Denmark)
Profile: p. 242
Corporate/M&A ★★
Table: p. 239

Svensson, Jan-Erik (Denmark)
Profile: p. 242
Competition/Anti-trust ★★★★
Table: p. 238

Svoren, Rune (Norway)
Profile: p. 525
Energy & Natural Resources ★★★
Table: p. 520

Swaak, Christof (Netherlands)
Profile: p. 504
Competition/Anti-trust ★★★
Table: p. 494

Swanson, Joel (USA)
Profile: p. 897
Corporate/M&A ★★★
Table: p. 824

Swartz, Jay A. (Canada)
Profile: p. 200
Banking & Finance ★★★★
Table: p. 171
Corporate/M&A ★
Table: p. 177

Sweeney, Joseph (Ireland)
Profile: p. 404
Corporate/M&A ★
Table: p. 397

Sweeting, Malcom (United Kingdom)
Profile: p. 776
Banking & Finance ★★★
Table: p. 699

Swiecicki, Piotr (Poland)
Profile: p. 555
Banking & Finance ★★★
Table: p. 545

Swift, Robert (United Kingdom)
Profile: p. 776
Intellectual Property ★★★
Table: p. 729

Swycher, Nigel (United Kingdom)
Profile: p. 777
Communications: IT ★★
Table: p. 709
Intellectual Property ★★★
Table: p. 729

Syed, David (France)
Profile: p. 293
Banking & Finance ★★
Table: p. 265

Symes, Nicholas (Greenland)
Profile: p. 344
Corporate/Commercial ★★★★
Table: p. 344

Symons, Howard J. (USA)
Profile: p. 897
Communications: Regulatory ★★★★
Table: p. 803

Sysuev, Timur (Belarus)
Profile: p. 115
Corporate/Commercial ★★★★
Table: p. 114

Szasz, Ivan (Hungary)
Profile: p. 377
Corporate/M&A ★★★★
Table: p. 375

Sze, Beryl (Hong Kong)
Profile: p. 370
Capital Markets: Debt & Equity ★★
Table: p. 353

Szecskay, András (Hungary)
Profile: p. 377
Corporate/M&A ★★★★
Table: p. 375

Szlezak, S. Andrzej (Poland)
Profile: p. 555
Corporate/M&A ★
Table: p. 548

Szubielska, Dorota (Poland)
Profile: p. 555
Tax ★★★★
Table: p. 551

T

Tabak, Jeffrey E. (USA)
Profile: p. 897
Private Equity: Fund Formation ★★
Table: p. 835

Taboada, Jose Evenor (Nicaragua)
Profile: p. 511
Corporate/Commercial ★★★★
Table: p. 510

Tacit, Christian (Canada)
Profile: p. 200
Communications ★
Table: p. 173

Tähtinen, Jyrki (Finland)
Profile: p. 259
Corporate/M&A ★★
Table: p. 257

Takki, Pekka (Finland)
Profile: p. 260
Communications ★★★★
Table: p. 255

Tal, Dalia (Israel)
Profile: p. 412
Banking & Finance ★★★★
Table: p. 406
Corporate/M&A ★★
Table: p. 409

Talibuddin, Salman (Pakistan)
Profile: p. 531
Corporate/Commercial ★★
Table: p. 529

Talmácsi, Éva (Hungary)
Profile: p. 377
Corporate/M&A ★★★
Table: p. 375

Talviste, Üllar (Estonia)
Profile: p. 252
Corporate/Commercial ★★★★
Table: p. 251

Talwar, Suresh (India)
Profile: p. 390
Corporate/M&A ★★★
Table: p. 381

Tamaki, Paul (Canada)
Profile: p. 200
Tax ★
Table: p. 182

Tamayo, Gustavo (Colombia)
Profile: p. 223
Corporate/M&A ★★
Table: p. 221

Tan, Poh Lee (Hong Kong)
Profile: p. 370
Communications ★★★★
Table: p. 356

Tanaka, Hideaki (Japan)
Profile: p. 446
Corporate/M&A ★
Table: p. 439

Tang, Michael (Malaysia)
Profile: p. 473
Corporate/M&A **U**
Table: p. 471

Tanner, Douglas (Hong Kong)
Profile: p. 370
Capital Markets: Debt & Equity ★★★
Table: p. 353

Tanoury, Mark (USA)
Profile: p. 897
Communications: IT ★★
Table: p. 805

KEY TO RANKINGS: ✪ = Star Individual ★★★★ = Top Band ★★★ = Second Band ★★ = Third Band ★ = Fourth Band **U** = Up and coming

KEY TO RANKINGS: ✪ = Star Individual ★★★★ = Top Band ★★★ = Second Band ★★ = Third Band ★ = Fourth Band **U** = Up and coming

Trahair, Andrew (Australia)
Profile: p. 100
Project Finance ★
Table: p. 79

Trapp, Deirdre (United Kingdom)
Profile: p. 778
Competition/Anti-trust ★★★★
Table: p. 714

Travieso, Eduardo (Venezuela)
Profile: p. 914
Corporate/M&A ★★★
Table: p. 909
Energy & Natural Resources ★★★
Table: p. 911

Treacy, Peter (Hong Kong)
Profile: p. 370
Project Finance ★★★
Table: p. 359

Tregubenko, Yevgeniy (Mongolia)
Profile: p. 484
Corporate/Commercial **U**
Table: p. 484

Tremblay, Richard (Canada)
Profile: p. 201
Tax ★★★★
Table: p. 182

Tremonti, Giulio (Italy)
Profile: p. 430
Tax ★★★★
Table: p. 422

Treuhold, Robert C. (France)
Profile: p. 294
Capital Markets ★★★★
Table: p. 268
Corporate/M&A ★
Table: p. 275

Trew OBE, Anthony (United Arab Emirates)
Profile: p. 694
Corporate/M&A ★★★
Table: p. 690

Triantafyllides, George (Cyprus)
Profile: p. 231
Corporate/Commercial ★★★
Table: p. 231

Triantafyllides, Stelios (Cyprus)
Profile: p. 231
Corporate/Commercial ★★★★
Table: p. 231

Triay QC, Joseph Emanuel (Gibraltar)
Profile: p. 338
Corporate/Commercial ★★★★
Table: p. 337

Triay QC, Louis W. (Gibraltar)
Profile: p. 338
Corporate/Commercial ★★★
Table: p. 337

Trier, Dana (USA)
Profile: p. 898
Tax ★★★
Table: p. 845

Tringali, Joseph (USA)
Profile: p. 898
Competition/Anti-trust ★
Table: p. 808

Triscornia, Alessandro (Italy)
Profile: p. 430
Corporate/M&A ★★
Table: p. 419

Troberg, Markus (Finland)
Profile: p. 260
Corporate/M&A ★★★★
Table: p. 257

Tron, Jean-Michel (France)
Profile: p. 294
Corporate/M&A ★★★
Table: p. 275
Tax ★★
Table: p. 281

Troncoso, Marcos (Dominican Republic)
Profile: p. 243
Corporate/Commercial ★★★★
Table: p. 243

Trott, David (United Kingdom)
Profile: p. 778
Capital Markets: Securitisation ★★★
Table: p. 704

Trower, Christopher (Bahrain)
Profile: p. 111
Banking & Finance ★★★★
Table: p. 110
Corporate/M&A ★★★★
Table: p. 111
Project Finance ★★★
Table: p. 111

Tsai, Paul (Taiwan)
Profile: p. 667
Corporate/Commercial ★★★
Table: p. 666

Tschäni, Rudolf (Switzerland)
Profile: p. 663
Corporate/M&A ★★★★
Table: p. 657

Tschanz, Pierre-Yves (Switzerland)
Profile: p. 663
Arbitration (International) ★★
Table: p. 653

Tschentscher, Thomas (Germany)
Profile: p. 333
Communications: Regulatory ★★★★
Table: p. 306

Tse, Joseph L.B. (Hong Kong)
Profile: p. 370
Banking & Finance ★★★
Table: p. 352

Tsunematsu, Ken (Japan)
Profile: p. 446
Capital Markets ★★★★
Table: p. 436

Tucker, John C. (United Kingdom)
Profile: p. 778
Banking & Finance ★
Table: p. 699

Tucker, Julian (United Kingdom)
Profile: p. 778
Capital Markets: Securitisation ★
Table: p. 704

Tudway, Robert (United Kingdom)
Profile: p. 778
Energy: Electricity ★★
Table: p. 725

Tuffnell, Kevin (United Kingdom)
Profile: p. 778
Private Equity: Buyouts ★★★
Table: p. 731

Tumbuan, Fred B G (Indonesia)
Profile: p. 392
Corporate/Commercial ★★★★
Table: p. 391

Tumi, Mohamed (Libya)
Profile: p. 461
Corporate/Commercial ★★★★
Table: p. 461

Turcan, Alexander (Moldova)
Profile: p. 483
Corporate/Commercial ★★★★
Table: p. 483

Turlot, Jean-Michel (Democratic Republic of Congo)
Profile: p. 224
Corporate/Commercial ★★★★
Table: p. 224

Turner, Edward L. (Hong Kong)
Profile: p. 617
Corporate/Commercial: South Korea Foreign ★★★
Table: p. 615

Turner, Malcolm (Japan)
Profile: p. 446
Banking & Finance: Japan Foreign ★★★
Table: p. 435
Project Finance ★★★
Table: p. 442

Turner, Mark (United Kingdom)
Profile: p. 778
Communications: E-commerce ★★
Table: p. 711

Turner, Paul (United Kingdom)
Profile: p. 778
Shipping: Finance ★
Table: p. 737

Turot, Jérôme (France)
Profile: p. 294
Tax ★★★★
Table: p. 281

Turpin, Dick (Zimbabwe)
Profile: p. 920
Corporate/Commercial ★★★★
Table: p. 919

Tweh, Oswald (Liberia)
Profile: p. 461
Corporate/Commercial ★★★★
Table: p. 460

Twentyman, Jeff (United Kingdom)
Profile: p. 778
Corporate/M&A **U**
Table: p. 717

Tyan, Nady (Lebanon)
Profile: p. 459
Corporate/Commercial ★★★★
Table: p. 458

Tyne, Sally M. (United Kingdom)
Profile: p. 778
Energy: Oil and Gas ★★
Table: p. 723

Tysland, Sverre (Norway)
Profile: p. 525
Corporate/M&A ★★
Table: p. 519

U

Uchida, Harumichi (Japan)
Profile: p. 446
Corporate/M&A ★
Table: p. 439

Uckmar, Victor (Italy)
Profile: p. 430
Tax ★★★
Table: p. 422

Udwadia, Darius (India)
Profile: p. 390
Project Finance ★★★★
Table: p. 384

Ul-Islam, Amir (Bangladesh)
Profile: p. 112
Corporate/Commercial ★★★
Table: p. 112

Ulhôa Canto, Carlos Alberto (Brazil)
Profile: p. 158
Banking & Finance ★
Table: p. 142
Corporate/M&A ★★
Table: p. 147
Tax ★
Table: p. 150

Ullmann, Pierre (France)
Profile: p. 294
Tax ★★★★
Table: p. 281

Ulmer, John M. (Canada)
Profile: p. 201
Tax ★★★
Table: p. 182

Umana, Carlos (Colombia)
Profile: p. 223
Corporate/M&A ★★★
Table: p. 221

Umaña, Felipe Francisco (El Salvador)
Profile: p. 249
Corporate/Commercial ★★★★
Table: p. 249

Underhill, William (United Kingdom)
Profile: p. 778
Corporate/M&A ★★★★
Table: p. 717

Undurraga, Claudio (Chile)
Profile: p. 210
Corporate/M&A ★★★
Table: p. 208

Unger, Timothy (USA)
Profile: p. 899
Energy & Natural Resources ★★★
Table: p. 829

Upfold, Robert (Australia)
Profile: p. 100
Tax ★★★
Table: p. 81

Upreti, Bharat Raj (Nepal)
Profile: p. 489
Corporate/Commercial ★★★★
Table: p. 489

Urapeepatanapong, Kitipong (Thailand)
Profile: p. 674
Corporate/M&A ★★★★
Table: p. 672

Urda Kassis, Cynthia (USA)
Profile: p. 899
Banking & Finance ★
Table: p. 791
Project Finance ★
Table: p. 837

Uría Meruéndano, Rodrigo (Spain)
Profile: p. 636
Corporate/M&A ★★★
Table: p. 624

Urrutia-Valenzuela, Carlos (Colombia)
Profile: p. 223
Banking & Finance ★★★★
Table: p. 219
Corporate/M&A ★★★★
Table: p. 221

V

Vajasit, Surasak (Thailand)
Profile: p. 674
Banking & Finance ★★★★
Table: p. 670

Valdez, Marla (Kazakhstan)
Profile: p. 452
Energy & Natural Resources ★★★★
Table: p. 451

Valente, Neto (Macau)
Profile: p. 467
Corporate/Commercial ★★★★
Table: p. 467

Valentine, Stuart (China)
Profile: p. 218
Corporate/M&A: China Foreign ★★★
Table: p. 213

Valiente-Noailles, Carlos (Argentina)
Profile: p. 63
Energy & Natural Resources ★★
Table: p. 59

Valiunas, Rolandas (Lithuania)
Profile: p. 464
Corporate/Commercial ★★★★
Table: p. 463

Valkin, Charles (South Africa)
Profile: p. 613
Corporate/M&A ★★★★
Table: p. 611

Valle, Regina (Brazil)
Profile: p. 158
Communications ★★★★
Table: p. 143

Valls, Carlos (Spain)
Profile: p. 636
Intellectual Property ★★★★
Table: p. 626

Valverde, Antoni (Spain)
Profile: p. 636
Corporate/M&A ★
Table: p. 624

Van Bael, Ivo (Belgium)
Profile: p. 132
Competition/Anti-trust ★★
Table: p. 122

Van De Vijver, Niels (Netherlands)
Profile: p. 505
Banking & Finance ★
Table: p. 491

van de Walle de Ghelcke, Bernard (Belgium)
Profile: p. 132
Competition/Anti-trust ★★
Table: p. 122

van der Haegen, Marc (Belgium)
Profile: p. 132
Banking & Finance ★★★★
Table: p. 117
Corporate/M&A ★★★★
Table: p. 125

Van der Klis, Geert (Netherlands)
Profile: p. 505
Communications ★★★
Table: p. 492
Competition/Anti-trust ★★
Table: p. 494

Van Der Lande, Maarten (Netherlands)
Profile: p. 505
Tax ★★★
Table: p. 500

Van Der Staay, Jan Willem (Netherlands)
Profile: p. 505
Corporate/M&A ★★
Table: p. 496

Van Der Wal, Gerard (Netherlands)
Profile: p. 505
Competition/Anti-trust ★★
Table: p. 494

KEY TO RANKINGS: ✪ = Star Individual ★★★★ = Top Band ★★★ = Second Band ★★ = Third Band ★ = Fourth Band **U** = Up and coming

van der Weijden, Maarten (Netherlands)
Profile: p. 505
Tax ★★★
Table: p. 500

Van Der Woude, Marc (Netherlands)
Profile: p. 505
Competition/Anti-trust ★★★
Table: p. 494

van Empel, Martijn (Netherlands)
Profile: p. 505
Competition/Anti-trust ★★★
Table: p. 494

Van Everdingen, Huib (Netherlands)
Profile: p. 505
Banking & Finance ★★
Table: p. 491

van Gerven, Gerwin (Belgium)
Profile: p. 132
Competition/Anti-trust ★★★
Table: p. 122

van Hooghten, Paul (Belgium)
Profile: p. 132
Corporate/M&A ★★
Table: p. 125

van Houtte, Hans (Belgium)
Profile: p. 133
Arbitration (International) ★★★★
Table: p. 116

van Kempen, Jan (Netherlands)
Profile: p. 505
Tax ★★★★
Table: p. 500

Van Kerckhove, Marleen (Belgium)
Profile: p. 133
Competition/Anti-trust **U**
Table: p. 122

van Leeuwe, Jean-Pierre (Netherlands)
Profile: p. 505
Corporate/M&A ★★
Table: p. 496

Van Leeuwen, Gijs CL (Netherlands)
Profile: p. 505
Banking & Finance ★
Table: p. 491

Van Liedekerke, Dirk (Belgium)
Profile: p. 133
Communications ★★★★
Table: p. 118

Van Marwijk Kooy, Johan (Netherlands)
Profile: p. 506
Corporate/M&A ★★
Table: p. 496

Van Sasse Van Ysselt, Charles (Netherlands)
Profile: p. 506
Competition/Anti-trust ★★★
Table: p. 494

van Verschuer, Philip (Netherlands)
Profile: p. 506
Corporate/M&A ★★
Table: p. 496

van Weeghel, Stef (Netherlands)
Profile: p. 506
Tax ★★★★
Table: p. 500

Vandencasteele, Alexandre (Belgium)
Profile: p. 133
Competition/Anti-trust ★
Table: p. 122

Vanderplank, Richard (Isle of Man)
Profile: p. 405
Corporate/Commercial ★★★★
Table: p. 405

Vanezis, Riko (Germany)
Profile: p. 333
Banking & Finance ★★
Table: p. 301
Project Finance ★★
Table: p. 317

Vanhaerents, Koen (Belgium)
Profile: p. 133
Corporate/M&A ★★★
Table: p. 125

Vani, Gjergji (Albania)
Profile: p. 50
Corporate/Commercial ★★
Table: p. 49

Varanese, James (Kazakhstan)
Profile: p. 452
Energy & Natural Resources ★★★★
Table: p. 451

Vardell, James (USA)
Profile: p. 899
Banking & Finance ★★
Table: p. 791

Varela Varas, Angel (Spain)
Profile: p. 636
Banking & Finance ★★
Table: p. 619

Varga, Ildiko (Hungary)
Profile: p. 377
Corporate/M&A ★★
Table: p. 375

Vargas, Fernan (Costa Rica)
Profile: p. 226
Corporate/Commercial ★★
Table: p. 225

Vargas, Fernando (Costa Rica)
Profile: p. 226
Corporate/Commercial ★★
Table: p. 225

Vashkevich, Andrei (Belarus)
Profile: p. 115
Corporate/Commercial ★★★
Table: p. 114

Vassogne, Thierry (France)
Profile: p. 294
Corporate/M&A ★★★★
Table: p. 275

Vasu, Kirti (Germany)
Profile: p. 333
Capital Markets: Securitisation ★★★
Table: p. 304

Vaudoyer, James (France)
Profile: p. 295
Tax ★
Table: p. 281

Vaupel, Christoph (Germany)
Profile: p. 333
Capital Markets: Equity ★★
Table: p. 304

Vazquez, Robert (Gibraltar)
Profile: p. 338
Corporate/Commercial ★★★
Table: p. 337

Vázquez, Renato (Peru)
Profile: p. 541
Corporate/M&A ★★★
Table: p. 540

Vecchi, Sesto E. (Vietnam)
Profile: p. 917
Corporate/Commercial: Vietnam Foreign ★★★
Table: p. 916

Vecchio, Cesare (Italy)
Profile: p. 430
Tax ★
Table: p. 422

Vega Penichet, Luis (Spain)
Profile: p. 636
Competition/Anti-trust ★★
Table: p. 622

Veil, Jean (France)
Profile: p. 295
Corporate/M&A ★★
Table: p. 275

Veirano, Ricardo (Brazil)
Profile: p. 158
Corporate/M&A ★★
Table: p. 147

Veirano, Ronaldo (Brazil)
Profile: p. 158
Corporate/M&A ★★★
Table: p. 147

Vellani, Badaruddin (Pakistan)
Profile: p. 531
Corporate/Commercial ★★★★
Table: p. 529

Vellani, Fatehali (Pakistan)
Profile: p. 532
Corporate/Commercial ★★★
Table: p. 529

Venit, James S. (Belgium)
Profile: p. 133
Communications ★★
Table: p. 118
Competition/Anti-trust ★★★★
Table: p. 122

Vento, Cesare (Italy)
Profile: p. 430
Communications ★
Table: p. 415

Verbeke, Louis (Belgium)
Profile: p. 133
Corporate/M&A ★★★★
Table: p. 125

Verheyden, Alexandre (Belgium)
Profile: p. 133
Communications ★★
Table: p. 118

Verkhovodko, Igor (Belarus)
Profile: p. 115
Corporate/Commercial ★★★★
Table: p. 114

Verkhovskoy, Pierre (France)
Profile: p. 295
Corporate/M&A ★
Table: p. 275

Verloren Van Themaat, Weyer (Netherlands)
Profile: p. 506
Competition/Anti-trust ★★★
Table: p. 494

Verrier, Hugh (Russia)
Profile: p. 578
Corporate/M&A ★★
Table: p. 574

Verrill, John (United Kingdom)
Profile: p. 778
Energy: Oil and Gas ★★
Table: p. 723

Verveer, Philip L. (USA)
Profile: p. 899
Communications: Regulatory ★★★★
Table: p. 803

Vetter, Jeff (USA)
Profile: p. 899
Communications: IT **U**
Table: p. 805

Vickers, Mark (United Kingdom)
Profile: p. 778
Banking & Finance ★
Table: p. 699

Victor, A. Paul (USA)
Profile: p. 899
Competition/Anti-trust ★★
Table: p. 808

Viegas, Juliana (Brazil)
Profile: p. 158
Communications ★★★★
Table: p. 143
Corporate/M&A ★★
Table: p. 147

Vieira, Paulo (Brazil)
Profile: p. 159
Corporate/M&A ★★★
Table: p. 147

Vieira, Pedro Siza (Portugal)
Profile: p. 566
Banking & Finance ★
Table: p. 558

Vieira Coelho, Ricardo E. (Brazil)
Profile: p. 159
Project Finance ★★★
Table: p. 149

Vieira de Almeida, João (Portugal)
Profile: p. 566
Banking & Finance ★★
Table: p. 558
Corporate/M&A ★
Table: p. 560

Vieira de Almeida, Vasco (Portugal)
Profile: p. 566
Banking & Finance ★★★
Table: p. 558
Corporate/M&A ★★
Table: p. 560

Vigliano, Franco (Italy)
Profile: p. 430
Project Finance ★★★★
Table: p. 421

Vignaud, Jean-Pierre (France)
Profile: p. 295
Project Finance: Francophone Africa ★★★★
Table: p. 278

Vilanova, Richard (France)
Profile: p. 295
Banking & Finance ★★★
Table: p. 265
Project Finance ★★★
Table: p. 277

Vilhjálmsson, Árni (Iceland)
Profile: p. 379
Corporate/Commercial ★★★★
Table: p. 378

Villey, Philippe (France)
Profile: p. 295
Corporate/M&A ★★
Table: p. 275

Vine, Stephen (USA)
Profile: p. 899
Private Equity: Fund Formation ★
Table: p. 835

Vinter, Graham (United Kingdom)
Profile: p. 390, 779
Project Finance: India Foreign ★★★★
Table: p. 386
Projects ★★★★
Table: p. 733

Vischer, Bernard (Switzerland)
Profile: p. 663
Corporate/M&A ★
Table: p. 657

Vischer, Markus (Switzerland)
Profile: p. 663
Corporate/M&A ★★
Table: p. 657

Visco, Claudio (Italy)
Profile: p. 430
Banking & Finance ★★
Table: p. 414
Project Finance ★★★
Table: p. 421

Viswanathan, L (India)
Profile: p. 390
Project Finance ★★
Table: p. 384

Vitali, Enrico (Italy)
Profile: p. 430
Tax ★★
Table: p. 422

Viteri Arriola, Ernesto Jose (Guatemala)
Profile: p. 345
Corporate/Commercial ★★★★
Table: p. 345

Viteri Echeverria, Ernesto Ricardo (Guatemala)
Profile: p. 345
Corporate/Commercial ★★★
Table: p. 345

Vives, Fernando (Spain)
Profile: p. 636
Banking & Finance ★★
Table: p. 619

Vlahakis, Patricia (USA)
Profile: p. 899
Corporate/M&A ★
Table: p. 820

Vlasova, Lilia (Belarus)
Profile: p. 115
Corporate/Commercial ★★★
Table: p. 114

Vlasto, Tony (United Kingdom)
Profile: p. 779
Shipping ✪
Table: p. 737

Vletter, Bas (Netherlands)
Profile: p. 506
Corporate/M&A ★★
Table: p. 496

Voge, William (USA)
Profile: p. 899
Project Finance ★★★★
Table: p. 837

Vogel, Joseph (France)
Profile: p. 295
Competition/Anti-trust ★★
Table: p. 272

Vogel, Louis (France)
Profile: p. 295
Competition/Anti-trust ★★★★
Table: p. 272

Vogt, Nedim Peter (Switzerland)
Profile: p. 663
Corporate/M&A ★
Table: p. 657

Voisey, Peter G. (United Kingdom)
Profile: p. 779
Capital Markets: Securitisation ★★
Table: p. 704

Voisin, Michael (United Kingdom)
Profile: p. 779
Capital Markets: Securitisation ★★
Table: p. 704

Volk, Stephen R. (USA)
Profile: p. 899
Corporate/M&A ★★★★
Table: p. 820

Vollmer, Andrew N. (USA)
Profile: p. 899
Arbitration (International) ★★
Table: p. 785

von Bismarck, Nilufer (United Kingdom)
Profile: p. 779
Corporate/M&A U
Table: p. 717

Von Bülow, Christoph (Germany)
Profile: p. 334
Corporate/M&A ★
Table: p. 311

Von Dryander, Christof (Germany)
Profile: p. 334
Banking & Finance ★★
Table: p. 301
Capital Markets: Debt ★★★★
Table: p. 303
Capital Markets: Equity ★★★★
Table: p. 304

Von Meibom, Wolfgang (Germany)
Profile: p. 334
Intellectual Property: General ★
Table: p. 314

Von Mettenheim, Heinrich (Germany)
Profile: p. 334
Private Equity ★
Table: p. 316

von Planta, Andreas (Switzerland)
Profile: p. 663
Banking & Finance ★★
Table: p. 654

Von Schenck, Kersten (Germany)
Profile: p. 334
Corporate/M&A ★
Table: p. 311

von Schlabrendorff, Fabian (Germany)
Profile: p. 334
Project Finance ★★
Table: p. 317

von Wallis, Georg (Germany)
Profile: p. 334
Tax U
Table: p. 319

Von Werder, Andreas (Germany)
Profile: p. 334
Corporate/M&A ★
Table: p. 311

Von Wobeser, Claus (Mexico)
Profile: p. 482
Corporate/M&A ★★★★
Table: p. 480

Vonsovics, Romualds (Latvia)
Profile: p. 457
Corporate/Commercial ★★★
Table: p. 456

Voss, Harald (Germany)
Profile: p. 334
Corporate/M&A ✪
Table: p. 311

Vouga, Rodolfo (Paraguay)
Profile: p. 537
Corporate/M&A ★★★
Table: p. 537

Vouterakos, Costas (Greece)
Profile: p. 343
Corporate/M&A U
Table: p. 339

Vukmir, Mladen (Croatia)
Profile: p. 229
Corporate/Commercial ★★★★
Table: p. 228

W

Wachsberger, Chaim (USA)
Profile: p. 899
Project Finance ★★★★
Table: p. 837

Wadia, Dina (India)
Profile: p. 390
Corporate/M&A ★
Table: p. 381

Wadlow, R. Clark (USA)
Profile: p. 899
Communications: Regulatory ★★
Table: p. 803

Wadolowski, Wojciech (Poland)
Profile: p. 555
Banking & Finance ★★★
Table: p. 545

Waelbroeck, Denis (Belgium)
Profile: p. 133
Competition/Anti-trust ★★
Table: p. 122

Waimon, David (USA)
Profile: p. 899
Tax U
Table: p. 843

Wakkie, Peter (Netherlands)
Profile: p. 506
Corporate/M&A ★★★★
Table: p. 496

Wald, Alexandre (Brazil)
Profile: p. 159
Banking & Finance ★
Table: p. 142

Wald, Arnoldo (Brazil)
Profile: p. 159
Banking & Finance ★★★
Table: p. 142

Wald, Douglas (USA)
Profile: p. 900
Competition/Anti-trust ★
Table: p. 811

Walford, Peter (Monaco)
Profile: p. 483
Corporate/Commercial ★★★★
Table: p. 483

Walker, James (Hong Kong)
Profile: p. 617
Corporate/Commercial: South Korea Foreign ★★★
Table: p. 615

Walker, Ross (Canada)
Profile: p. 201
Banking & Finance ★
Table: p. 171

Wall, Robert (USA)
Profile: p. 900
Corporate/M&A ★★★★
Table: p. 813

Wallace, Ian (Australia)
Profile: p. 100
Banking & Finance ★★★
Table: p. 65

Wallace, Patrick (United Kingdom)
Profile: p. 779
Energy: Electricity ★★
Table: p. 725

Wallgren, Carita (Finland)
Profile: p. 260
Corporate/M&A ★★★
Table: p. 257

Wallin, Carl-Henrik (Finland)
Profile: p. 260
Competition/Anti-trust ★★★★
Table: p. 256

Wallis, Robert (United Kingdom)
Profile: p. 779
Shipping ★★★★
Table: p. 737

Walsh, Jonathan (United Kingdom)
Profile: p. 779
Capital Markets: Securitisation ★★
Table: p. 704

Walsh, Paul (United Kingdom)
Profile: p. 779
Intellectual Property ★★★★
Table: p. 729

Walter, Jeremy (Hong Kong)
Profile: p. 370
Capital Markets: Derivatives ★★★★
Table: p. 355

Walton, Miles (United Kingdom)
Profile: p. 779
Tax ★★★
Table: p. 739

Wander, Herb (USA)
Profile: p. 900
Corporate/M&A ★★★★
Table: p. 813

Wang, Ling (China)
Profile: p. 218
Corporate/M&A ★★★
Table: p. 211
Project Finance ★★★
Table: p. 214

Wanger, Markus (Liechtenstein)
Profile: p. 462
Corporate/Commercial ★★★★
Table: p. 462

Wani, Akihiro (Japan)
Profile: p. 447
Banking & Finance ★★★★
Table: p. 433
Capital Markets ★★★★
Table: p. 436

Ward, Andrew (United Arab Emirates)
Profile: p. 694
Corporate/M&A ★★
Table: p. 690

Ward, Conor (United Kingdom)
Profile: p. 779
Communications: IT ★★
Table: p. 709

Ward, David A. (Canada)
Profile: p. 201
Tax ★
Table: p. 182

Ward, Erica A. (USA)
Profile: p. 900
Project Finance ★★★
Table: p. 837

Ward, Penny (Australia)
Profile: p. 100
Communications: Telecoms ★
Table: p. 69

Warden, John L. (USA)
Profile: p. 900
Competition/Anti-trust ★★★
Table: p. 808

Warder, David (United Kingdom)
Profile: p. 779
Shipping: Finance ★★
Table: p. 737

Wardynski, Tomasz (Poland)
Profile: p. 555
Corporate/M&A ★★
Table: p. 548

Warna-Kula-Suriya, Sanjev (United Kingdom)
Profile: p. 779
Capital Markets: Derivatives ★★
Table: p. 706

Warner Jr, Waide (USA)
Profile: p. 900
Project Finance ★★★
Table: p. 837

Wassaf, Anthony (Australia)
Profile: p. 100
Energy & Natural Resources ★★★★
Table: p. 75

Wasserman, Craig (USA)
Profile: p. 900
Corporate/M&A ★★
Table: p. 820

Waters, Jennifer (USA)
Profile: p. 900
Energy & Natural Resources ★
Table: p. 827

Waters, Peter (Australia)
Profile: p. 100
Communications: Telecoms ★★★★
Table: p. 69

Watson, Chris (United Kingdom)
Profile: p. 779
Communications: Telecoms ★★★
Table: p. 707

Watson, Jeremy (Greece)
Profile: p. 343
Shipping: Foreign Firms ★★★
Table: p. 341

Watson, John G. (United Kingdom)
Profile: p. 779
Tax ★★★
Table: p. 739

Watson, Martin A. (United Kingdom)
Profile: p. 779
Shipping: Finance ★★★★
Table: p. 737

Watson, Sean (United Kingdom)
Profile: p. 780
Corporate/M&A ★
Table: p. 717

Watter, Rolf (Switzerland)
Profile: p. 663
Banking & Finance ★★★★
Table: p. 654
Corporate/M&A ★★★★
Table: p. 657

Wayaiki, Peter (Kenya)
Profile: p. 454
Corporate/Commercial ★★★
Table: p. 453

Wayland, Joseph F. (USA)
Profile: p. 900
Competition/Anti-trust ★
Table: p. 808

Wayne, Lucy (Vietnam)
Profile: p. 917
Corporate/Commercial: Vietnam Foreign ★★★★
Table: p. 916

Wayte, Peter B. (United Kingdom)
Profile: p. 780
Private Equity: Buyouts ★★
Table: p. 731

Weber, David (United Kingdom)
Profile: p. 780
Projects ★★
Table: p. 733

Weber, Rolf (Switzerland)
Profile: p. 663
Communications ★★★★
Table: p. 655

Weber-Rey, Daniela (Germany)
Profile: p. 334
Corporate/M&A ★
Table: p. 311
Private Equity ★
Table: p. 316

Webster, Jon (Australia)
Profile: p. 101
Corporate/M&A U
Table: p. 73

Webster, Michael (United Kingdom)
Profile: p. 780
Communications: IT ★★
Table: p. 709

Webster, Paul (British Virgin Islands)
Profile: p. 161
Corporate/Commercial ★★★
Table: p. 160

Wedderburn-Day, Roger (United Kingdom)
Profile: p. 780
Capital Markets: Debt & Equity ★
Table: p. 702

Wegen, Gerhard (Germany)
Profile: p. 334
Corporate/M&A ★★★
Table: p. 311

Wehrli, Daniel (Switzerland)
Profile: p. 663
Arbitration (International) ★
Table: p. 653

Wehrli, Yves (France)
Profile: p. 295
Corporate/M&A ★
Table: p. 275

Weir, Michael W. (USA)
Profile: p. 900
Banking & Finance ★★
Table: p. 791

Weisburg, Henry (USA)
Profile: p. 900
Arbitration (International) ★★
Table: p. 785

Weiss, Gregory A. (USA)
Profile: p. 900
Banking & Finance ★★
Table: p. 791

Weitzman, Polly (United Kingdom)
Profile: p. 780
Competition/Anti-trust U
Table: p. 714

Welke, William R (USA)
Profile: p. 901
Tax ★★★
Table: p. 843

Welkoff, Jim (Canada)
Profile: p. 201
Tax ★
Table: p. 182

Wellen, Robert (USA)
Profile: p. 901
Tax ★★
Table: p. 847

Welling, Mark (Germany)
Profile: p. 334
Capital Markets: Debt ★★
Table: p. 303

Wells, Boyan S. (United Kingdom)
Profile: p. 780
Capital Markets: Debt & Equity ★★★★
Table: p. 702

Wells, Russell (United Kingdom)
Profile: p. 390
Project Finance: India Foreign ★★★
Table: p. 386

KEY TO RANKINGS: ✪ = Star Individual ★★★★ = Top Band ★★★ = Second Band ★★ = Third Band ★ = Fourth Band U = Up and coming

 KEY TO RANKINGS: ✪ = Star Individual ★★★★ = Top Band ★★★ = Second Band ★★ = Third Band ★ = Fourth Band **U** = Up and coming